What You Should Know About Private Education

Contents

Contents

A Note from the Peterson's Editors

Peterson's Private Secondary Schools 2011–12 is the authoritative source of information for parents and students who are exploring the alternative of privately provided education. In this edition, you will find information for more than 1,600 schools worldwide. The data published in this guide are obtained directly from the schools themselves to help you make a fully informed decision.

If you've decided to look into private schooling for your son or daughter but aren't sure how to begin, relax. You won't have to go it alone. **What You Should Know About Private Education** can help you plan your search and demystify the admission process. In the articles that follow, you'll find valuable advice from admission experts about applying to private secondary schools and choosing the school that's right for your child.

In "Why Choose an Independent School?" Patrick F. Bassett, President of the National Association of Independent Schools (NAIS), describes the reasons why an increasing number of families are considering private schooling.

If you want a private education for your child but are hesitant about sending him or her away to a boarding school, read "Another Option: Independent Day Schools" where Lila Lohr, former Head of School at Princeton Day School in Princeton, New Jersey, discusses the benefits of day schools.

From Howard and Matthew Greenes' "The Contemporary Boarding School: Change and Adaptability" to The Association of Boarding Schools' (TABS) "Study Confirms Benefits of Boarding School"—if you are having doubts about boarding schools, you'll want to check out these articles!

Mark Braun, Head of School at the Outdoor Academy, offers "Semester Schools: Great

> *Schools will be pleased to know that Peterson's helped you in your private secondary school selection.*

Opportunities," which explores various options for students to spend an exciting semester in a new "school-away-from-school."

If you are considering a special needs or therapeutic school for your child, you will want to read "Why a Therapeutic or Special Needs School?" by Diederik van Renesse, an educational consultant who specializes in this area.

To help you compare private schools and make the best choice for your child, check out "Finding the Perfect Match" by Helene Reynolds, a former educational planning and placement counselor.

"Plan a Successful School Search" gives you an overview of the admission process.

If the admission application forms have you baffled and confused, read "Understanding the Admission Application Form," by Gregg W. M. Maloberti, Dean of Admission at The Lawrenceville School.

For the lowdown on standardized testing, Heather Hoerle, Vice President of Member Relations at NAIS, describes the two tests most often required by private schools and the role that tests play in admission decisions in "About Standardized Tests."

In "Paying for a Private Education," Mark Mitchell, Vice President, School Information Services at NAIS, shares some thoughts on financing options.

Finally, "How to Use This Guide" gives you all the information you need on how to make *Peterson's Private Secondary Schools 2011–12* work for you!

Next up, the **Quick-Reference Chart**, "Private Secondary Schools At-a-Glance," lists schools by state, U.S. territory, or country and provides essential information about a school's students, range of grade levels, enrollment figures, faculty, and special offerings.

A Note from the Peterson's Editors

The **School Profiles** follow, and it's here you can learn more about particular schools. *Peterson's Private Secondary Schools 2011–12* contains three **School Profiles** sections—one for traditional college-preparatory and general academic schools, one for special needs schools that serve students with a variety of special learning and social needs, and one for junior boarding schools that serve students in middle school grades. Many schools have chosen to submit a display ad, which appears near their profile and offers specific information the school wants you to know.

Close-Ups follow each **School Profiles** section and feature expanded two-page school descriptions written exclusively for this guide. There is a reference at the end of a profile directing you to that school's **Close-Up.**

The **Specialized Directories** are generated from responses to Peterson's annual school survey. These directories group schools by the categories considered most important when choosing a private school, including type, entrance requirements, curricula, financial aid data, and special programs.

Finally, in the **Index** you'll find the "Alphabetical Listing of Schools" for the page references of schools that have already piqued your interest.

Peterson's publishes a full line of resources to help guide you and your family through the private secondary school admission process. Peterson's publications can be found at your local bookstore and library and your school guidance office, and you can access us online at www.petersonspublishing.com. Peterson's books are now also available as eBooks.

Join Peterson's Private Schools conversation at www.facebook.com/sec.schools and www.twitter.com/sec_schools. The resources of Peterson's Publishing are available to help you with your private school search.

We welcome any comments or suggestions you may have about this publication. Write to us at:

Publishing Department
Peterson's, a Nelnet company
2000 Lenox Drive
Lawrenceville, NJ 08648

Your feedback will help us make your educational dreams possible.

Schools will be pleased to know that Peterson's helped you in your private secondary school selection. Admission staff members are more than happy to answer questions, address specific problems, and help in any way they can. The editors at Peterson's wish you great success in your search!

Why Choose an Independent School?

Patrick F. Bassett
President of the National Association of Independent Schools (NAIS)

Why do families choose independent private schools for their children? Many cite the intimate school size and setting, individualized attention, and high academic standards.

Recent research highlights the success of independent school graduates, who outperform graduates from all other types of schools in a whole host of categories, reflecting exceptional preparation for academic and civic life.

Although nearly all independent school graduates go on to attend college, *The Freshman Survey Trends Report*, a study conducted by the Higher Education Research Institute, found that 85 percent of students who attended independent schools that belong to the National Association of Independent Schools (NAIS) went on to attend "very high" or "highly selective" colleges and universities. This "persistence factor" is largely attributable to attending a school with high expectations for all students and a culture that reinforces achievement. The ethos of independent schools contributes to this equation, since everybody is expected to work hard and succeed academically.

NAIS school graduates were also more engaged with their communities than students from other types of schools. Forty-one percent of NAIS graduates said they expected to participate in volunteer or community activities in college, compared to just 24 percent of the whole group. NAIS graduates were also far more inclined to consider "keeping up-to-date with political affairs" essential (46 percent NAIS, 31 percent all).

Another study, the *National Educational Longitudinal Study* (conducted by the U.S. Department of Education) tracked students from public schools, parochial schools, NAIS independent schools, and other private schools from the time they were eighth graders in 1988 until the year 2000. Nearly all of the NAIS students in the NELS study had pursued postsecondary education by their mid-20s. More than three quarters had graduated from a college or university, including 8 percent who completed master's degrees, and 1.5 percent who achieved a Ph.D. or professional degree (e.g., M.D. or LL.B.) by their mid-20s.

Perhaps the most significant factor that distinguished NAIS graduates from graduates of other types of schools was the strength of their commitment to community service and active civic participation. While slightly more than 1 out of 5 survey participants reported volunteering for civic events, nearly one third of NAIS school graduates said that they regularly participated in voluntary activities in their communities. NAIS students were also nearly twice as likely to volunteer to work for political campaigns and political causes. And NAIS students were committed to exercising their civic duty as voters. Whereas slightly more than half of all NELS participants voted in the presidential election before the study, more than 75 percent of NAIS school graduates registered their voices.

Another factor that contributes to the success of students in independent schools is the partnership with families. This coalescing of parental and school voices helps children prosper because the key adults in their lives reinforce a common set of values and speak with a common voice. Indeed, the great achievement of American education is that it offers families many choices of schooling so that they can find a school with a voice and vision to match their own.

Each independent school has a unique mission, culture, and personality. There are day schools, boarding schools, and combination day-boarding

> *With independent schools, you have the opportunity to choose a school with a philosophy, values, and approach to teaching that is the right fit for your child.*

schools. Some independent schools have a few dozen students; others have several thousand. Some are coed; others are single-sex. Some independent schools have a religious affiliation; some are nonsectarian. Most serve students of average to exceptional academic ability, but some serve exclusively those with learning differences, and others serve highly gifted students. The vast majority of independent schools are college-prep.

With independent schools, you have the opportunity to choose a school with a philosophy, values, and approach to teaching that is the right fit for your child.

Make the choice of a lifetime. Choose an independent school.

Another Option: Independent Day Schools

Lila Lohr

For those of us who are fortunate enough to be able to send our children to an independent day school, it seems to offer the best of both worlds. Our children are able to reap the enormous benefits of an independent school education and we, as parents, are able to continue to play a vital, daily role in the education of our children. Parents enjoy being seen as partners with day schools in educating their children.

As more and more independent day schools have sprung up in communities across the country, more and more parents are choosing to send their children to them, even when it might involve a lengthy daily commute. Contrary to some old stereotypes, parents of independent school students are not all cut from the same mold, living in the same neighborhood with identical dreams and aspirations for their children. Independent school parents represent a wide range of interests, attitudes, and parenting styles.

They also have several things in common. Most parents send their children to independent day schools because they think their children will get a better education in a safe, value-laden environment. Many parents are willing to pay substantial annual tuition because they believe their children will be held to certain standards, challenged academically, and thoroughly prepared for college.

This willingness to make what are, for many, substantial financial sacrifices reflects the recognition that much of one's character is formed in school. Concerned parents want their children to go to schools where values are discussed and reinforced. They seek schools that have clear expectations and limits. The

Most independent schools welcome and encourage parental involvement and support.

nonpublic status allows independent schools to establish specific standards of behavior and performance and to suspend or expel students who don't conform to those expectations.

Understanding the power of adolescent peer pressure, parents are eager to have their children go to school with other teens who are academically ambitious and required to behave. They seek an environment where it is "cool" to be smart, to work hard, and to be involved in the school community. In independent day schools, students spend their evenings doing homework, expect to be called on in class, and participate in sports or clubs.

Successful independent schools, whether elementary or high school, large or small, single-sex or coed, recognize the importance of a school-parent partnership in educating each child. Experienced faculty members and administrators readily acknowledge that, while they are experts on education, parents are the experts on their own children. Gone are the days when parents simply dropped their children off in the morning, picked them up at the end of the day, and assumed the school would do the educating. Clearly, children benefit enormously when their parents and teachers work together, sharing their observations and concerns openly and frequently.

Independent schools encourage this two-way give-and-take and are committed to taking it well beyond the public school model. Annual back-to-school nights are attended by more than 90 percent of parents. Teacher-parent and student-teacher-parent conferences, extensive written comments as part of the report cards, and adviser systems that encourage close faculty-student relationships are all structures that facilitate this parent-school partnership. Although more and more independent school parents work full-time, they make time for these critical opportunities to sit down and discuss their children's progress.

Most independent schools welcome and encourage parental involvement and support. Although the individual structures vary from school to school, most include opportunities beyond making cookies and chaperoning dances. Many parents enjoy being involved in community service projects, working on school fund raisers, participating in admission activities, sharing their expertise in appropriate academic classes, and even offering student internships. Most schools have made a concerted effort to structure specific opportunities for working parents to participate in the life of the school.

Independent day schools recognize the benefits of parent volunteers and of extending themselves so that parents feel that they are an important part of the school family. Buddy systems that pair new parents with families who have been at the school for several years help ease the transition for families who are new to the independent school sector.

Independent schools have also responded to increased parental interest in programs focusing on parenting skills. Recognizing the inherent difficulties of raising children, independent day schools have provided forums for discussing and learning about drugs, depression, stress management, peer pressure, and the like. Book groups, panel discussions, and workshops provide important opportunities for parents to share their concerns and to get to know the parents of their children's classmates. Schools recognize that this parent-to-parent communication and networking strengthens the entire school community.

Many current day school parents would contend that when you choose an independent day school for your child you are really choosing a school for the entire family. The students become so involved in their academic and extracurricular activities and the parents spend so much time at school supporting those activities that it does become the entire family's school.

Lila Lohr is a former Head of School at Princeton Day School in Princeton, New Jersey, and the Friends School of Baltimore in Baltimore, Maryland. She has been a teacher and an administrator in independent day schools for more than thirty years and is the mother of 3 independent day school graduates.

The Contemporary Boarding School: Change and Adaptability

Howard Greene
Matthew Greene

One of the most telling characteristics of the independent schools since their inception has been their ability to adapt to the significant social, political, and economic movements that have defined the evolutionary unfolding of an extraordinary nation. Those boarding schools that have survived and flourished over time have done so by adapting their curricula, the composition of their student bodies, and their facilities and resources to continue their role in training future leaders, regardless of their social, religious, and economic backgrounds.

How does this continuous state of adaptation and development translate to contemporary boarding school programs and populations? What do these schools stand for? How do they accomplish their primary goals? Here are the key features you should take note of as you consider this unique form of education.

Diversity

The American boarding school is viewed worldwide as an outstanding venue for students to obtain a first-rate education while they interact with a broad mix of other people. The resources and facilities are unmatched in any other country. Currently, more than 11,000 of the enrolled students in NAIS boarding schools are foreign nationals. Some of the larger, internationally recognized American schools enroll a large number of geographically diverse students.

The modern boarding school is, in fact, far more diverse than the local public schools that the majority of American students attend. Significant socioeconomic and continuing racial and ethnic segregation has resulted in homogeneous student bodies in many public school districts across the country. By contrast, boarding schools have a commitment to enroll outstanding students of all economic and social circumstances.

A Sense of Community

School leaders, when asked what defines their particular school, often refer to the power of community that envelops students, teachers, deans and administrators, coaches, and staff members. How valuable this is to all parties, especially to young men and women caught up in today's frenzied, competitive, and disjointed culture where it is easy to feel overwhelmed and uncertain. The desire to be in an environment where peers and adults are engaged with one another in a caring and supportive culture is a driving force for many who feel disconnected from, or simply not fully engaged with, the people and programs in their current school.

A Beacon of Educational Standards

Boarding schools have always set their own standards of educational attainment and pedagogy. Since they are not regulated by state educational bodies or influenced by the agendas of individual or party politics, the school professionals can design an academic and nonacademic curriculum that reflects the standards and goals they have set for their students.

Building Character

While all boarding schools have as their historic mission preparing students for university entrance and a successful academic experience, most have loftier goals in mind. Character is as important as acquired information and credits. Schools emphasize the development of critical thinking and analytical skills, an open mind to new and different ideas and opinions, excellent writing and oral skills, and an ability to think in mathematical and scientific terms. Most boarding schools look beyond these critical intellectual skills to the emotional, social, moral, and intellectual components of the education of the students in their charge. The residential community becomes a vital and active force in developing and honing these crucial skills. Every day, an individual might be called upon to make a decision in the classroom, on the playing field, or in the dormitory or dining hall that can have either a negative or positive impact on another student or the larger community.

The ultimate goal of the boarding school is not to create privileged adolescents who think and act alike but rather to consider the whole child at a critical stage in his or her moral and social development. There is a powerful force of stated ideals in the community at large that can be drawn on to help guide a young woman or man who has to decide how to behave in social situations, the classroom, the playing field, the dormitory, or even at home.

Boarding Schools as a Partnership

The Board of Trustees' Role

The members of the Board of Trustees are committed volunteers who have been elected to work as a cohesive group in overseeing the well-being of the school. The board is a legal entity charged with the responsibility of making certain the school is in sound fiscal and administrative condition and is fulfilling its stated mission. The board oversees the work of the head of school in the broadest sense and determines if he or she is responsibly managing the school. Typically, board members are recent and older graduates, parents of past and current students, or professional experts, all of whom work together to ensure that the school functions soundly on both an educational and financial basis. Boards generally choose their own members on the basis of a commitment to that institution's mission and purposes.

An independent school that is functioning well is, in large measure, the result of a healthy working relationship between the board and the senior management of the school. Together they review the annual operating budget, consider current and long-term strategic planning, and oversee fund-raising—in particular, capital campaigns to enlarge the school's endowment and physical facilities.

A number of schools include students in board meetings and specific committees. Typically, this includes the president of the student council who attends the general board meetings and student leaders who are active members of the student life committee. Their voices play a helpful role in determining school policies, rules, activities, and programs. In addition to

the value added to the school community, these students gain a significant learning experience from such a deliberative process.

The School Head's Role

The head of school, reporting to the Board of Trustees, is the chief executive officer and is responsible for the operation of the school. It is his or her responsibility to execute the broad range of academic and noncurricular programs with the assistance of the faculty and other senior administrators, to hire and fire, to lead the faculty, to maintain a sound fiscal operation, to raise money from outside sources, and to serve as the educational visionary for the institution. A successfully run boarding school is a reflection of the mutual respect and effective working relationship between the head and the trustees.

In reviewing the merits of any boarding school for your child, be certain to learn about the relationship between the school head and the board, as well as the composition of the board. The days of a head staying at a school for twenty or thirty years are long gone, though some sitting heads have been in their position for close to that length of time. The norm these days is closer to the decade mark for a successful head running a well-managed school. A long-established or new head is not necessarily a sign either of school strength or weakness. Look beyond a head's tenure to seek out his or her experience level, accomplishments, energy, philosophy, and personal impact on a school.

The Faculty's Role

The opportunity to teach, counsel, and coach students in an intimate setting is what attracts most teachers to boarding schools. It is common practice for a faculty member in her role as dormitory parent, adviser, classroom teacher, coach, or administrator to seek out students whom she identifies as needing her help through the daily interaction that is part and parcel of the boarding life.

Boarding school teachers play an active and respected role in the affairs of their school. They serve on committees that set academic programs, grading standards, requirements for graduation, and standards of behavior. Faculty members work through academic departments to be certain that students are gaining a comprehensive and coherent education.

It is not happenstance that the great majority of boarding school teachers are graduates of strong liberal arts colleges and, most frequently, have graduate degrees in their particular discipline. A great many also played a sport at the intercollegiate level or were actively engaged in campus governance or the arts. The boarding school offers the teacher who loves her academic subject and has other talents the opportunity to share her enthusiasm with her students. The independent status of the school encourages the dedicated teacher to create and deliver a stimulating, effective curriculum that is usually free of topics, content, or lesson plans mandated by outside sources and without an end goal of preparation for standardized testing.

The Students' Role

Despite its traditions and culture, a school can, and often in large part does, reinvent itself every four years as new classes of students enter the school, gradually assume leadership responsibilities, and graduate, making room for new students to take their places. What an individual school "is" represents a shifting target because of the constant influx and egress of students. For prospective students, who those students are when they arrive constitutes one of the most significant influences on the boarding school experience and whether or not it is a good one.

Students in boarding schools today sit in on board meetings, judge fellow students on disciplinary committees, edit papers and yearbooks, serve as proctors or resident advisers in dormitories, and captain sports teams. They also conduct independent study projects, work with faculty as teaching assistants, guide tours on campus, talk with accreditation committees, and babysit faculty members' children. Students are active in community service projects on campus, in town, and around the world. They start new clubs, raise money for capital campaigns, and publish scientific research. They protest, vote, and serve as peer mediators and advisers. They sit around seminar tables discussing advanced literature and historical topics. They speak their minds, challenging faculty and administrators to improve courses, revise standards, and maintain their composure. Students at boarding schools are clearly not passive recipients; rather they are active participants in all aspects of school and community life.

The Parents' Role

One of the major changes in the boarding school partnership in recent years is the more active role that

One of the major changes in the boarding school partnership in recent years is the more active role that parents play.

parents play. In past generations when the schools were more homogeneous in their student composition, parents were basically expected to leave the care and education of their children to the school's head and faculty. They were reassured that the moral, spiritual, and intellectual training of their offspring would be seen to. This is a far cry from the relationship contemporary parents, school administrators, and teachers understand as a partnership. Parents expect regular communications from their child's teachers and house advisers regarding student progress or any personal or academic difficulties. Heads of school and deans acknowledge that there is a regular flow of telephone calls and e-mails from the concerned parent. There is greater communication with parents regarding campus events and specific information about their child's engagement and performance.

Parenting a boarding school student involves a balancing act between being overly involved and too distant. Parents should neither assume that boarding schools will take over all parental and educational responsibilities for their children nor seek to insinuate themselves into every aspect of a student's school life. Parents should be watchful, involved, supportive, and attuned to the messages both the school and student are sending regarding the most appropriate and desirable level of engagement.

Schools also acknowledge that past and current parents are a major source of the financial support that enables them to carry on their stated purposes at the highest level of quality. Parents play a significant role in supporting fund-raising efforts and sponsoring events for current and prospective students and their parents. Most boarding schools have established parent committees that help to keep an open line of communication with the school's administrative leaders regarding parental concerns and recommendations for effective support of the students.

The Student Experience

Rather than interpreting discipline strictly as a punitive concept, schools use discipline as a teaching and learning tool. The community of faculty, deans, and students works together to establish agreeable rules of behavior. Each student must abide by this community ethos and, in the process of doing so, learns much about the interests and needs of others, the responsibility of an individual toward the common good, and the self-discipline and restraint that make this possible. The rewards are ample: a sense of responsibility and empowerment and the freedom to carry on one's daily life of activities and studies and time for friends. Those who break the rules find there is a response from the community and that appropriate action is taken.

Students play a major role in the smooth running of their school. Any school head will quickly confirm that his or her students are never shy or reluctant to make their voices heard on issues that affect their lives. Boarding students take it as fact that articulating their opinions to their teachers and administrators is a fundamental right.

Howard R. Greene, M.A., M.Ed., and Matthew W. Greene, Ph.D., have been providing personalized admissions counseling to guide students to the right secondary school, college, or graduate school for more than 35 years. They are the hosts of two PBS specials on college admission and have written numerous books, including the **Greenes' Guides to Educational Planning Series.**

Originally published in a slightly different form in **The Greenes' Guide to Boarding Schools** *(Princeton: Peterson's, 2006), 9-19. Reprinted by permission of the authors.*

Study Confirms Benefits of Boarding School

Many people have long sung the praises of the boarding school experience. The high-level academics, the friendships, and the life lessons learned are without rival at private day or public schools, they say.

Now, a study released by The Association of Boarding Schools (TABS), a nonprofit organization of independent, college-preparatory schools, validates these claims. Not only do boarding school students spend more time studying (and less time watching TV), they are also better prepared for college and progress more quickly in their careers than their counterparts who attended private day or public schools.

The survey, which was conducted by the Baltimore-based research firm the Art & Science Group, involved interviews with 1,000 students and alumni from boarding schools, 1,100 from public schools, and 600 from private day schools (including independent day and parochial schools).

The results not only affirm the benefits enjoyed by boarding school graduates but those bestowed upon current boarding school students as well. "The study helps us better understand how the opportunities for interaction and learning beyond the classroom found at boarding schools impact a student's life at school and into adulthood," explained Steve Ruzicka, former TABS executive director. Ruzicka said the survey also provides boarding school alumni with empirical data to help when considering their children's educational options.

Rigorous Academics Prevail

Why do students apply to boarding schools? The TABS study found that the primary motivation for both applicants and their parents is the promise of a better education. And, happily, the vast majority of current and past students surveyed reported that their schools deliver on this promise. Current students indicated significantly higher levels of satisfaction with their academic experience at boarding schools than their peers at public and private day schools by more than ten percentage points (54 percent of boarding students versus 42 percent of private day students and 40 percent of public school students). Boarders reported in greater relative percentages that they find their schools academically challenging, that their peers are more motivated, and the quality of teaching is very high.

But the boarding environment is valued just as much for the opportunities for interaction and learning beyond the classroom. Interactions in the dining room, the dormitory, and on the playing field both complement and supplement academics, exposing students to a broad geographic and socioeconomic spectrum, challenging their boundaries, and broadening their vision of the world.

The Boarding School Boost

The 24/7 life at boarding schools also gives students a significant leg up when they attend college, the survey documents.

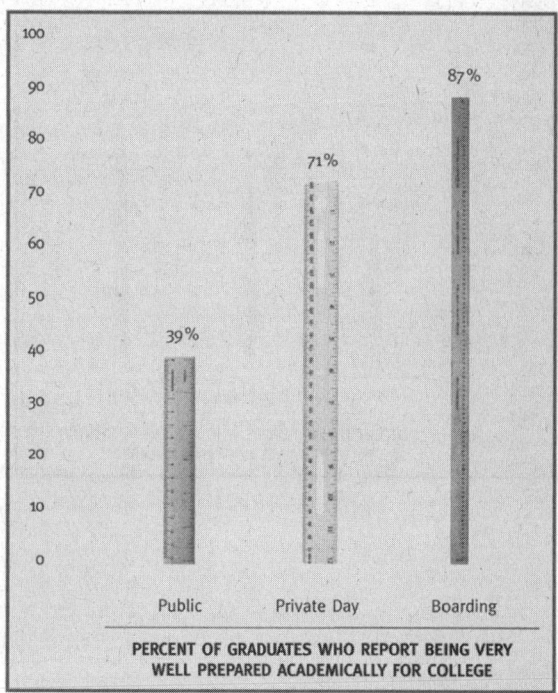

PERCENT OF GRADUATES WHO REPORT BEING VERY
WELL PREPARED ACADEMICALLY FOR COLLEGE

Some 87 percent of boarding school graduates said they were very well prepared academically for college, with only 71 percent of private day and just 39 percent of public school alumni saying the same. And 78 percent of boarders reported that their schools also helped better prepare them to face the nonacademic aspects of college life, such as independence, social life,

Study Confirms Benefits of Boarding School

and time management. Only 36 percent of private day graduates and 23 percent of public school graduates said the same. The TABS survey also documented that a larger percentage of boarding school graduates go on to earn advanced degrees once they finish college: 50 percent, versus 36 percent of private day and 21 percent of public school alumni.

Beyond college, boarding school graduates also reap greater benefits from their on-campus experiences, advancing faster and further in their careers comparatively. The study scrutinized former boarders versus private day and public school graduates in terms of achieving positions in top management and found that by midcareer, 44 percent of boarding school graduates had reached positions in top management versus 33 percent of private day school graduates and 27 percent of public school graduates.

By late in their careers, more than half of the surveyed boarding school sample, 52 percent, held positions in top management as opposed to 39 percent of private day and 27 percent of public school graduates.

But perhaps the most compelling statistic that the study produced is the extremely high percentage—some 90 percent—of boarding school alumni who say they would, if given the opportunity, repeat their boarding school experience. This alone is a strong argument that validates the enduring value of the boarding school model. It is hoped that the study will help dispel many of the myths and stereotypes that have dogged the image of boarding schools over the last century and spread the good news that boarding schools today are diverse, exciting places for bright, well-adjusted students who are looking for success in their academic lives—and beyond.

For more information on TABS visit the Web site at www.schools.com.

Used by permission of The Association of Boarding Schools.

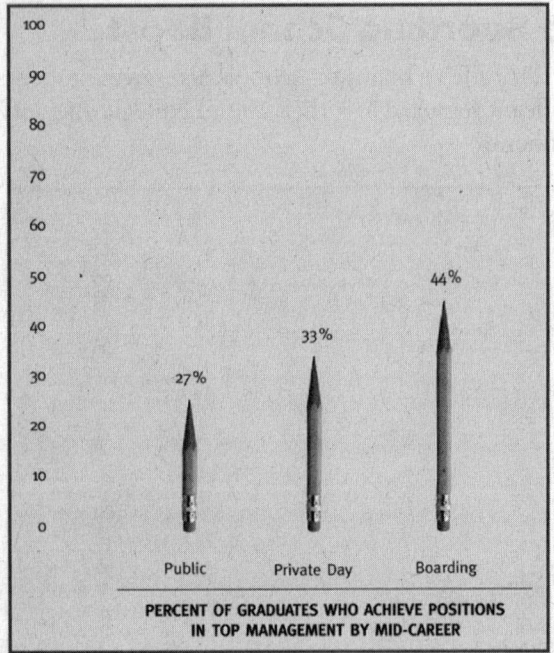

PERCENT OF GRADUATES WHO ACHIEVE POSITIONS IN TOP MANAGEMENT BY MID-CAREER

Semester Schools: Great Opportunities

Mark Braun
Head of School
The Outdoor Academy

Over the last twenty years, there has been tremendous growth in the range of educational opportunities available to young Americans. The advent of semester schools has played no small part in this trend. Similar in many ways to semester-abroad programs, semester schools provide secondary school students the opportunity to leave their home school for half an academic year to have a very different kind of experience—the experience of living and learning within a small community, among diverse students, and in a new and different place. The curricula of such schools tend to be thematic, interdisciplinary, rigorous, and experiential.

What Are the Benefits?

As a starting point for their programs, semester schools have embraced many of the qualities typical of independent schools. In fact, a number of semester schools were developed as extension programs by existing independent schools, providing unusual opportunities to their own students and those from other schools. Other semester schools have grown from independent educational organizations or foundations that bring their own educational interests and expertise to their semester programs. In both cases, semester schools provide the kind of challenging environment for which independent schools are known.

Across the board, semester school programs provide students with exceptional opportunities for contact with their teachers. Individual instruction and intimate classes are common, as is contact with teachers outside the classroom. At semester schools, students have a full-immersion experience in a tightly knit learning community. In such a setting, teachers are able to challenge each student in his or her own area of need, mentoring students to both academic and personal fulfillment.

Semester schools have developed around specialized curricular interests, often involving unique offerings or nontraditional subjects. In almost every case, these specialized curricula are related to the school's location. Indeed, place-based learning is a common thread in semester school education. Whether in New York City or the Appalachian Mountains, semester schools enable students to cultivate a sense of place and develop greater sensitivity to their surroundings. This is often accomplished through a combination of experiential education and traditional instruction. Students develop academic knowledge and practical skills in tandem through active participation in intellectual discourse, creative projects, hands-on exercises, and service learning opportunities. Throughout, emphasis is placed on the importance of combining intellectual exploration with thoughtful self-reflection, often facilitated by journaling exercises or group processing activities.

At semester schools, students have a full-immersion experience in a tightly knit learning community.

At semester schools, students inevitably learn their most important lessons through their membership in the school community. Living closely with peers and teachers and working together for the benefit of the group enables students to develop extraordinary communication skills and high levels of interpersonal accountability. Through this experience, students gain invaluable leadership and cooperation skills.

Ultimately, semester schools seek to impart translatable skills to their students. The common goal is for students to return to their schools and families with greater motivation, empathy, self-knowledge, and self determination. These skills help to prepare students for the college experience and beyond. In addition, semester school participants report that their experiences helped to distinguish them in the college application process. Semester school programs are certainly not for everybody, but they serve an important role for students who are seeking something beyond the ordinary—

students who wish to know themselves and the world in a profound way. All of the following semester school programs manifest these same values in their own distinctive way.

CITYterm

CITYterm, founded in 1996, is an interdisciplinary, experience-based program that takes 30 juniors and seniors from across the country and engages them in a semester-long study of New York City. CITYterm students typically spend three days a week in the classroom, reading, writing, and thinking about New York City, and three days a week in the city working on projects, studying diverse neighborhoods, or meeting with politicians, urban historians, authors, artists, actors, and various city experts. Much of the excitement of CITYterm comes from experiencing firsthand in the city what has been studied in the classroom. Many of the projects are done in collaborative teams where the groups engage not only in formal academic research at the city's libraries but also use the resources of New York City's residents and institutions to gather the information necessary for presentations. Students come to see themselves as the active creators of their own learning both in the classroom and in the world. Learn more about CITYterm by visiting www.cityterm.org.

Conserve School

Conserve School is a semester school for high school juniors that is focused on the theme of environmental stewardship. Attending Conserve School gives high school students a one-semester opportunity to step out of their regular school and into a unique educational setting, while still continuing their required academic studies. Conserve School's challenging, college-preparatory curriculum immerses high school juniors in environmental history, nature literature, and the science of conservation. Because Conserve School is located on a 1,200-acre wilderness campus, a significant portion of the curriculum is delivered via outdoors, hands-on, active learning. Conserve School is located just west of Land O' Lakes, Wisconsin, near the border of Michigan's Upper Peninsula. Learn more about Conserve School at www.conserveschool.org/Home.aspx.

The Island School

The Island School, founded in 1999 by The Lawrenceville School, is an independent academic program in the Bahamas for high school sophomores or juniors. The fourteen-week academic course of study includes honors classes in science, field research

(a laboratory science), history, math, art, English literature, and physical/outdoor education and a weekly community service component. All courses are place-based and explicitly linked, taking advantage of the school's surroundings to both deepen understandings of complex academic and social issues and to make those understandings lasting by connecting course content with experience. Students apply their investigative, interpretive, and problem-solving skills during four- and eight-day kayaking expeditions, SCUBA diving opportunities, teaching environmental issues to local students, and in daily life at the school. In addition to traditional classroom assessments, students conduct research on mangrove communities, coastal management, artificial reefs, permaculture, and marine protected areas. These projects support national research and are conducted under the auspices of the Bahamian government. At the conclusion of the semester, students present their work to a panel of visiting scientists and educators, including local and national government officials from the Bahamas. The opportunity to interact with the local community through research, outreach, and the rigorous physical and academic schedule creates a transformative experience for students. The admissions process is competitive, and selected students demonstrate solid academic performance, leadership potential, and a high degree of self-motivation. Contact The Island School for more information at www.islandschool.org.

The Maine Coast Semester

The Maine Coast Semester (MCS) offers a small group of eleventh-grade students the chance to live and work on a 400-acre saltwater peninsula with the goal of exploring the natural world through courses in natural science, environmental issues, literature and writing, art, history, mathematics, and foreign language. Since 1988, MCS has welcomed nearly

1,300 students from more than 230 public and private schools across the country and in Canada. The MCS community is small—39 students and 20 faculty members—and the application process is competitive. In addition to their studies, students work for several hours each afternoon on an organic farm, in a wood lot, or on maintenance and construction projects. Students who attend MCS are highly motivated, capable, and willing to take the risk of leaving friends and family for a portion of their high school career. They enjoy hard work, both intellectual and physical, and they demonstrate a tangible desire to contribute to the world. MCS students return to their schools with self-confidence, an appreciation for the struggles and rewards of community living, and an increased sense of ownership of their education. For information on The Maine Coast Semester, go to www.chewonki.org.

The Mountain School

The Mountain School of Milton Academy, founded in 1984, hosts 45 high school juniors from private and public schools throughout the United States who have chosen to spend four months on a working organic farm in Vermont. Courses provide a demanding and integrated learning experience, taking full advantage of the school's small size and mountain campus. Students and adults develop a social contract of mutual trust that expects individual and communal responsibility, models the values of simplicity and sustainability, and challenges teenagers to engage in meaningful work. Students live with teachers in small houses and help make important decisions concerning how to live together and manage the farm. Courses offered include English, environmental science, U.S. history, and all levels of math, physics, chemistry, Spanish, French, Latin, studio art, and humanities. To learn more about The Mountain School, please visit the Web site at www.mountainschool.org.

The Outdoor Academy of the Southern Appalachians

The Outdoor Academy offers tenth-grade and select eleventh-grade students from across the country a semester away in the mountains of North Carolina. Arising from more than eighty years of experiential education at Eagle's Nest Foundation, this school-away-from-school provides a college-preparatory curriculum along with special offerings in environmental education, outdoor leadership, the arts, and community service. Each semester, up to 35 students embrace the Southern Appalachians as a unique ecological, historical, and cultural American region. In this setting,

students and teachers live as a close-knit community, and lessons of cooperation and responsibility abound. Students develop a healthy work ethic as course work and projects are pursued both in and out of the classroom. Courses in English, mathematics, science, history, foreign language, visual and performing arts, and music emphasize hands-on and cooperative learning. Classes often meet outside on the 180-acre wooded campus or in nearby national wilderness areas, where the natural world enhances intellectual pursuits. On weekends and extended trips, the outdoor leadership program teaches hiking, backpacking, caving, canoeing, and rock-climbing skills. The Outdoor Academy is open to students from both public and private secondary schools and is accredited by the Southern Association of Colleges and Schools. Learn more about The Outdoor Academy at www.enf.org/outdoor_academy/academic_program.

The Oxbow School

The Oxbow School in Napa, California, is a one-semester visual arts program for high school juniors and seniors from public and private schools nationwide. Oxbow offers students a unique educational experience focused on in-depth study in sculpture, printmaking, drawing and painting, and photography and digital media, including animation. The interdisciplinary, project-based curriculum emphasizes experiential learning, critical thinking, and the development of research skills as a means of focused artistic inquiry. Each semester, 2 Visiting Artists are invited to work collaboratively with students and teachers. By engaging students in the creative process, Oxbow fosters a deep appreciation for creativity in all areas of life beyond the classroom. Since its founding in 1998, students who have spent a semester at The Oxbow School have matriculated to leading universities, colleges, and independent colleges of art and design around the country. Learn more at www.oxbowschool.org.

The Rocky Mountain Semester

The Rocky Mountain Semester (RMS) at the High Mountain Institute is an opportunity for high school juniors and seniors to examine the human relationship to the natural world through a combination of rigorous academics and extended wilderness expeditions. During the 110-day program, up to 38 students spend five weeks backpacking, skiing, and studying throughout the wilderness of Colorado and Utah. The remainder of the semester is spent on campus near Leadville, Colorado, where students pursue a rigorous course of study and learn how to live successfully in a small community environment. While at the RMS, most students take five or six classes—the only required elective is Practices and Principles: Ethics of the Natural World. It is in this class that students are taught the theoretical foundations for all that is done in the field, examine the human relationship to the natural world, and learn the skills necessary to travel safely and comfortably in remote settings. Students may also take literature of the natural world, natural science, U.S. history or AP U.S. history, Spanish or French, and mathematics. Interested parties can learn more about The Rocky Mountain Semester at www.hminet.org/RockyMountainSemester.

The Woolman Semester

The Woolman Semester is a community-based, sixteen-week, interdisciplinary program for high school juniors and seniors and first-year postgraduates. The mission of the school is to weave together peace, sustainability, and social action into an intensely rigorous academic experience. The school is located at the Sierra Friends Center in Nevada City, California, on a 230-acre campus complete with forests, fields, gardens, and livestock to use as a living laboratory, as well as for the wood chopping and lettuce harvesting of daily life! Classes generally meet in the morning, while labs, study groups, and farm work take place in the afternoon. Students and faculty members also participate in a two-week service project and a one-week wilderness trip. Get all the information on The Woolman Semester program at www.woolman.org.

The author wishes to acknowledge and thank all the semester school programs for contributing their school profiles and collaborating in order to spread the word about semester school education.

Why a Therapeutic or Special Needs School?

Diederik van Renesse

Families contact me when a son or daughter is experiencing increased difficulties in school or has shown a real change in attitude at home. Upon further discussion, parents often share the fact that they have spoken with their child's teachers and have held meetings to establish support systems in the school and at home. Evaluations, medications, therapists, and motivational counseling are but a few of the multiple approaches that parents and educators take—yet in some cases, the downward spiral continues. Anxiety builds in the student and family members; school avoidance and increased family turmoil reach a point where the situation is intolerable, and alternatives must be explored—be it a special needs school, a therapeutic school, or a combination of both.

But should that school be a day or residential school, and how do parents decide which will best meet their child's needs? Resources such as *Peterson's Private Secondary Schools*, the Internet, guidance/school counselors, and therapists are valuable; however, the subtle nuances involved in determining the environment that will best serve the child are difficult to ascertain. Some families seek the help of an independent education consultant to identify the most appropriate setting. Many independent education consultants specialize in working with children who have special needs such as learning differences, anxiety disorders, emotional issues, ADHD, opposition, defiance, school phobia, drug or alcohol abuse, Asperger Syndrome, autism, and more. Consultants

Some families seek the help of an independent education consultant to identify the most appropriate setting.

have frequent contact with the schools, and they work closely with parents during the enrollment process.

Given the broad spectrum of needs presented by individual students, many parents question whether there is indeed a day school that can meet the needs of their child. The answer often depends on location, space availability, willingness to relocate, and appropriateness of the options. While there are many day school options throughout the United States, there are even more residential or boarding options. Clearly the decision to have your child attend a residential school is not made easily. As a family you may feel as though you do not have a choice—but you should undertake a thorough assessment of all the day options and how they might meet the majority of your child's needs.

When the primary concerns are learning differences, many local options (though often small and issue-specific) are available to families. Local counselors are often valuable resources as are local chapters of national LD organizations. If you come up with a variety of options, carefully compare them by visiting the schools and meeting with the specialists at each school—those individuals who will work directly with your child.

With the day options, it is important to keep the following factors in mind: program and staff credentials, transportation time to and from the school, availability of additional resources (support services) in or outside the school setting, sports and extracurricular offerings, facilities and accessibility, and your child's potential peer group. You will also need to assess many of these factors when considering residential schools, although most residential schools are more self-contained than day schools. Also significant is whether the school has been approved by and accepts funding from its state and/or school district.

For families who cannot avail themselves of local day options or whose child is best served in a residential setting, an even greater spectrum of options is available. These range from traditional boarding schools with built-in academic support services to therapeutic boarding schools, wilderness or outdoor therapeutic programs, emotional growth or behavior modification schools, transitional or independent living programs, and even residential treatment centers, hospitals, or other health facilities.

Given the breadth of the residential schools or programs, most families are best served by a team that includes not only the parents (and at times the student), but also the professionals who have taught, counseled, and worked closely with the child. Together, the team can identify the specific needs, deficits, or behavioral issues that must be addressed, and they can work together to match those with the appropriate schools. As with day schools, you should arrange to visit the facilities so that you are well-informed about each option and will be comfortable with your final decision. These visits are not only opportunities for you to meet the staff and students, but also for you and your child to begin a relationship that will continue when your child is enrolled.

There is no question that seeking alternative options, whether they are special needs or therapeutic, is a daunting task. However, with the help of expert resources and reliable professionals, the right school can make a significant and lasting impact on your child's health and well-being.

_____

Diederik van Renesse is a Senior Partner at Steinbrecher & Partners Educational Consulting Services in Westport, Connecticut. A former teacher, admission director, and private school counselor, he now specializes in helping families throughout the United States and abroad with youngsters who require special needs or alternative schools or who need interventions and therapeutic settings.

Finding the Perfect Match

Helene Reynolds

One of the real benefits of independent education is that it allows you to deliberately seek out and choose a school community for your child. If you are like most parents, you want your child's school years to reflect an appropriate balance of academic challenge, social development, and exploration into athletics and the arts. You hope that through exposure to new ideas and sound mentoring your child will develop an awareness of individual social responsibility, as well as the study skills and work ethic to make a contribution to his or her world. It is every parent's fondest wish to have the school experience spark those areas of competence that can be pursued toward excellence and distinction.

An increasing number of parents realize that this ideal education is found outside their public school system, that shrinking budgets, divisive school boards, and overcrowded classrooms have resulted in schools where other agendas vie with education for attention and money. In this environment there is less time and energy for teachers to focus on individual needs.

The decision to choose a private school can be made for as many different reasons as there are families making the choice. Perhaps your child would benefit from smaller classes or accelerated instruction. Perhaps your child has needs or abilities that can be more appropriately addressed in a specialized environment. Perhaps you are concerned about the academic quality of your local public school and the impact it may have on your child's academic future. Or perhaps you feel that a private school education is a gift you can give your child to guide him or her toward a more successful future.

Every child is an individual, and this makes school choice a process unique to each family. The fact that your father attended a top-flight Eastern boarding school to prepare for the Ivy League does not necessarily make this educational course suitable for all of his grandchildren. In addition to determining the school's overall quality, you must explore the appropriateness of philosophy, curriculum, level of academic difficulty, and style before making your selection. The right school is the school where your child will thrive, and a famous name and a hallowed reputation are not necessarily the factors that define the right environment. The challenge is in discovering what the factors are that make the match between your child and his or her school the right one.

No matter how good its quality and reputation, a single school is unlikely to be able to meet the needs of all children. The question remains: How do families begin their search with confidence so they will find what they are looking for? How do they make the right connection?

As a parent, there are a number of steps you can follow to establish a reasoned and objective course of information gathering that will lead to a subjective discussion of this information and the way it applies to the student in question. This can only occur if the first step is done thoroughly and in an orderly manner. Ultimately, targeting a small group of schools, any of which could be an excellent choice, is only possible after information gathering and discussion have taken place. With work and a little luck, the result of this process is a school with an academically sound and challenging program based on an educational philosophy that is an extension of the family's views and which will provide an emotionally and socially supportive milieu for the child.

Step 1: Identify Student Needs

Often the decision to change schools seems to come out of the blue, but, in retrospect, it can be seen as a decision the family has been leading up to for some time. I would urge parents to decide on their own goals for the search first and to make sure, if possible, that they can work in concert toward meeting these goals before introducing the idea to their child. These goals are as different as the parents who hold them. For one parent, finding a school with a state-of-the-art computer program is a high priority. For another, finding a school with a full dance and music program is important. Others will be most concerned about finding a school that has the best record of college acceptances and highest SAT or ACT scores.

Once you have decided your own goals for the search, bring the child into the discussion. I often say to parents that the decision to explore is *not* the decision to change schools but only the decision to gather information and consider options. It is important to be aware that everyone has an individual style of decision making and that the decision to make a change is loaded with concerns, many of which will not be discovered until the process has begun.

If you have already made the decision to change your child's school, it is important to let your child know that this aspect of the decision is open to discussion but not to negotiation. It is equally important that you let your child know that he or she will have responsibility in choosing the specific school. Without that knowledge, your son or daughter may feel that he or she has no control over the course of his or her own life.

Some students are responsible enough to take the lead in the exploration; some are too young to do so. But in all cases, children need reassurance about their future and clarity about the reasons for considering other school settings. Sometimes the situation is fraught with disparate opinions that can turn school choice into a family battleground, one in which the child is the ultimate casualty. It is always important to keep in mind that the welfare of the child is the primary goal.

The knowledge that each individual has his or her own agenda and way of making decisions should be warning enough to pursue some preliminary discussion so that you, as parents, can avoid the pitfall of conflicting goals and maintain a united front and a reasonably directed course of action. The family discussion should be energetic, and differences of opinion should be encouraged as healthy and necessary and expressed in a climate of trust and respect.

There are many reasons why you may, at this point, decide to involve a professional educational consultant. Often this choice is made to provide a neutral ground where you and your child can both

If you have already made the decision to change your child's school, it is important to let your child know that this aspect of the decision is open to discussion but not to negotiation.

speak and be heard. Another reason is to make sure that you have established a sound course of exploration that takes both your own and your child's needs into consideration. Consultants who are up-to-date on school information, who have visited each campus, and who are familiar with the situations of their clients can add immeasurably to the process. They can provide a reality check, reinforcement of personal impressions, and experience-based information support for people who are doing a search of this type for the first time. All the research in the world cannot replace the experience and industry knowledge of a seasoned professional. In addition, if the specific circumstances of the placement are delicate, the educational consultant is in a position to advocate for your child during the placement process. There are also situations in which a family in crisis doesn't have the time or the ability to approach school choice in a deliberate and objective manner.

These are some of the many reasons to engage the services of a consultant, but it is the family guidance aspect that most families overlook at the start of the process and value most highly after they have completed it. A good consultant provides neutral ground and information backup that are invaluable.

Step 2: Evaluate Your Child's Academic Profile

If your child's academic profile raises questions about his or her ability, learning style, or emotional profile, get a professional evaluation to make sure that your expectations for your child are congruent with the child's actual abilities and needs.

Start gathering information about your child from the current school. Ask guidance counselors and teachers for their observations, and request a formal meeting to review the standardized testing that virtually every school administers. Question their views of your child's behavior, attentiveness, and areas of strength and weakness. Make sure you fully understand the reasons behind their recommendations. Do not feel shy about calling back to ask questions at a later date, after you have had time to think and consider this important information. Your child's future may depend on the decisions you are making; don't hesitate to keep asking until you have the information you need.

If a picture of concern emerges, ask the guidance counselor, other parents, or your pediatrician for suggestions regarding learning specialists or psychologists in the community who work with children and can provide an evaluation of their academic ability, academic achievement, and learning style. The evaluation should be reviewed in-depth with the specialist, who should be asked about specific recommendations for changes in the youngster's schooling.

Remember, as the parent, it is ultimately your responsibility to weigh the ideas of others and to decide if the difficulty lies with your child or the environment, either of which could indicate a need for a change of school.

Step 3: Review the Goals of Placement

Discuss your differences of opinion about making a change. Identify a list of schools that creates a ballpark of educational possibilities. (An educational consultant can also be helpful at this stage.)

It is important that both you and your child take the time to consider what characteristics, large and small, you would like in the new school and which you would like to avoid. As you each make lists of priorities and discuss them, the process of school choice enters the subjective arena. The impersonal descriptions of school environments transform into very personal visualizations of the ways you and your child view the child in a new setting.

A chance to play ice hockey, a series of courses in Mandarin Chinese, the opportunity to take private flute lessons, or a desire to meet others from all over the world may sound like a bizarre mix of criteria, but the desire to explore and find all of these options in a single environment expresses the expansiveness of the student's mind and the areas he or she wants to perfect, try out, or explore. Don't expect perfectly logical thinking from your child as he or she considers options; don't take everything he or she says literally or too seriously. Open and respectful discussion will allow a child to embrace a new possibility one day and reject it the next—this is part of the process of decision making and affirmation and part of the fun of exploration.

Step 4: Set an Itinerary

Set an itinerary for visits and interviews so that you and your child can compare campuses and test your preconceived ideas of the schools you have researched against the reality of the campus community; forward standardized testing scores and transcripts to the schools prior to visits so that the admission office has pertinent information in advance of your meeting.

In order to allow your child the freedom to form opinions about the schools you visit, you may want to keep these pointers in mind:

- Parents should allow their child to be front and center during the visits and interviews—allow your child to answer questions, even if they leave out details you think are important.
- Parents should stay in the background and have confidence that the admission officers know how to engage kids in conversation.
- This may be the first time your child has been treated by a school as an individual and responsible person—enjoy watching him or her adjust to this as an observer, not as a protector or participant.
- Don't let your own anxiety ruin your child's experience.
- Discuss dress in advance so it doesn't become the issue and focus of the trip.

Keep your ideas and impressions to yourself and allow your child first shot at verbalizing opinions. Remember that immediate reactions are not final decisions; often the first response is only an attempt to process the experience.

Step 5: Use the Application Process for Personal Guidance

Make sure your child uses the application process not only to satisfy the school's need for information but also to continue the personal guidance process of working through and truly understanding his or her goals and expectations.

Application questions demand your child's personal insight and exploration. Addressing questions about significant experiences, people who have influenced his or her life, or selecting four words that best describe him or her are ways of coming to grips with who your child is and what he or she wants to accomplish both at the new school and in life. Although parents want their children to complete seamless and perfect applications, it is important to remember that the application must be the work of the child and that the parent has an excellent opportunity to discuss the questions and answers to help guide the student in a positive and objective self-review.

It is more important that the application essays accurately reflect the personality and values of the student than that they be technically flawless. Since the school is basing part of its acceptance decision on the contents of the application, the school needs to meet the real student in the application. The child's own determination of what it is important for the school to know about them is crucial to this process. That being said, parents can play an important role in helping the child understand the difference between unnecessarily brutal honesty and putting his or her best foot forward.

Step 6: Trust Your Observations

Although the process of school exploration depends on objectivity, it is rare that a family will embrace a school solely because of its computer labs, endowment, library, SAT or ACT scores, or football team. These objective criteria frame the search, but it tends to be the intangibles that determine the decision. It is the subjective—instinctive responses to events on campus, people met, quality of interview, unfathomable vibes—that makes the match.

It is important to review what aspects of the school environment made you feel at home. These questions apply equally to parent and child. Did you like the people you met on campus? Was the tour informational but informal, with students stopping to greet you or the tour guide? Was the tone of the campus (austere or homey, modern or traditional) consistent with the kind of educational atmosphere you are looking for? Are the sports facilities beyond your wildest expectation? Does the college-sending record give you confidence that your child will find an intellectually comfortable peer group? How long do the teachers tend to stay with the school, and do they send their own children there? If it is a boarding school, do teachers live on campus? How homey is the dorm setup?

The most fundamental questions are: Do people in the school community like where they are, trust each other, have respect for each other, and feel comfortable there? Is it a family you would care to join? These subjective responses will help you recognize which schools will make your child feel he or she is part of the community, where he or she will fit in and be respected for who he or she is and wants to become.

Helene Reynolds is a former educational consultant from Princeton, New Jersey.

Plan a Successful School Search

Application deadlines, entrance exams, interviews, and acceptance or rejection letters—these are some of the challenges you can expect to encounter when applying to private schools. The school search may seem daunting, but it doesn't have to be. Here are some tips to help get you on your way.

The first step is to gather information, preferably in the spring before you plan on applying. *Peterson's Private Secondary Schools*, with vital statistics on more than 1,400 leading private schools in the United States and abroad, can help you evaluate schools, clarify your choices, and hone your search.

If you're considering boarding schools, you may also want to obtain a free copy of the *Boarding Schools Directory* from The Association of Boarding Schools (TABS) by calling 828-258-5354 or visiting TABS's Web site (www.boardingschools.com).

Visiting Schools

The next step is to start a list of schools that pique your or your child's interest. You'll want to call, fax, e-mail, or write to admission offices for catalogs and applications. At this stage, don't let cost rule out choices. You'll learn more about the school later—the financing resources it makes available to students and its policies of awarding aid.

With school brochures and catalogs in hand, start planning fall visits and interviews. Review your school calendar, noting Saturdays, holidays, and vacations. Try to plan interviews for these days off. Each interview could last about 3 hours, as campus tours and other activities are often included.

Once you have determined which schools you want to see, where they are, and in what order you want to see them, call each school to set the interview date and time.

Keep in mind that there is no "magic number" of schools to see. Some students interview at and apply to

only one school, feeling that if they are not accepted, they will stay at their current school. Some students interview at many, thinking that considering a large number and a variety of schools will help them focus on real needs and desires.

After you've made an appointment to visit the school, reread the school's catalog and, if possible, its description in this guide, and check out its Web site so that facts about the school will be fresh in your mind when you visit.

The Application Process

Once the fact-finding is completed, your child will need to work on applications. Most schools have January or February deadlines, so it pays to begin filling out forms in November.

Applications may ask for all or some of the following: school records, references from teachers, a student statement, a writing sample or essay, an application fee, and medical history form.

If you are working with a hard-copy form, make photocopies of all application pages before your child begins to complete them. That way, he or she will have at least one copy for use as a rough draft. Also make copies of each completed application for your records.

References are usually written on specific school forms and are considered confidential. To ensure confidentiality, people providing references mail their comments directly to the school. A school may require four or five references—three academic references, usually from an English teacher, a math teacher, and one other teacher, and one or two references from other evaluators who know your child's strengths in areas other than academics. Ask these people in advance if they will write on your child's behalf. Give reference-writers appropriate forms with any special instructions and stamped envelopes addressed to the school; be sure to provide as much lead time before the deadline as possible.

The student application is completed on a special form and consists of factual family

Most schools have January or February deadlines, so it pays to begin filling out forms in November.

information, as well as some long or short essay questions. As tempting as it may be to help, let your child do the writing. The schools need to see the student's style, mechanical skills, and the way he or she looks at life and education. Some schools require a corrected writing sample from an English assignment. In this case, have your child ask his or her English teacher to help choose his or her best work.

For additional information on applications, including the common application forms, check out "Understanding the Admission Application Form" on page 25.

Once the applications are mailed or submitted online, the hard part is done. Ask admission officers when you can expect to hear their decisions. Most schools will let you know in early March. While you wait, you may want to remind your son or daughter that being turned down by a school is not a statement about his or her worth. Schools have many different objectives in putting a class together. And that's a lesson that will come in handy when you face the college application process.

Understanding the Admission Application Form

Gregg W. M. Maloberti
Dean of Admission
The Lawrenceville School
Lawrenceville, New Jersey

Students applying to independent schools are presented with a myriad of options when it comes time to choose the method of completing the application process. Where once each school issued and required its own paper application, many schools now accept common applications such as the Secondary Schools Application from SSAT (Secondary School Admission Test), the Admission Application Form from TABS (The Association of Boarding Schools), or various other online application forms sponsored by individual schools and placement programs. With so many options, many applicants and parents are perplexed as to which method to employ, and others worry that the choice of one method over another may have a negative effect on their chances of admission. Understanding more about why these changes came about and how they save applicants and schools time and money may help applicants and their parents make an informed choice about which method to use.

The recent developments and innovations in independent school applications mirror the changes that have occurred at the college level. The College Board's Common Application is accepted at over 300 colleges and is available online. The Internet has accelerated the interest in online applications. At the same time, students are much more accustomed to writing on a computer than they once were with pen and paper. Concerns about the financial and environmental costs of a paper-based application that travels from the printer to the school, to the candidate, to the candidate's school, and back to the admission office by mail or courier contribute to the idea that the time of an online commonly accepted application has come.

The current version of the Secondary Schools Application is available on the SSAT Web site at http://www.ssat.org/publicsite.nsf/ssat/info/Application+Service. The Boarding Schools Admission Application Form is available in the TABS Boarding Schools Directory and in electronic form from the TABS Web site: http://www.boardingschools.com/how-to-apply/application.aspx.

There are a few schools that accept only the recommendation forms from the Admission Application Form. It's best to check with each school to find out which forms are preferred. The list of schools accepting the Secondary Schools Application from SSAT is available at this SSAT Web site: http://www.ssat.org/publicsite.nsf/ssat/info/Application+Service.

Common Applications Make Sense

Anxious parents' lingering doubts about the use of one of the common application forms are hard to ignore: Will the substitution of the common application for the individual school's application cause the admission committee to be offended and compromise my child's chances for admission? Parents should rest assured that schools agreeing to accept the common application forms believe that a fair and effective admission decision can be made on the basis of the common form and that its use in no way erodes the quality of their selection process.

How Does the Common Application Differ?

All applications begin with a biographical sketch of the candidate: name, address, birth date, mailing address, parents' names, and schools attended. Information regarding sibling or legacy relationships, interest in financial aid, citizenship, language spoken, and even racial and ethnic diversity is collected as well. Except for the order in which these questions appear, there is little variation in these question types from one school's application to another. The common application forms certainly relieve candidates of the burden of providing the very same biographical information over and over again.

The second section of an application generally reveals a candidate's accomplishments and ambitions. Often, the applicants are asked to catalog their interests and activities in list or narrative form. Schools want to know what the candidate has done, for how long, with whom, and to what distinction, if any. In a few cases, some schools ask for a series of short answers to a combination of questions or look for the applicant to complete a sentence. There are generally no "right" answers to these questions—but honest answers can help the school begin to characterize the applicant's curiosity, maturity, ambition, and self-esteem. Here again, great similarity exists in the manner and style with which this information is gathered. While the common application forms ask these question types in a more direct manner, they are no less effective than the individual school's application, and their use affords a candidate a genuine measure of efficiency without compromising individuality.

Schools that advocate the use of their own applications over that of the common application forms often bitterly defend the third and final portion of their applications since it generally includes essay questions. With few exceptions, these questions, while occasionally posed in a unique or original manner, seek to probe much the same territory covered by the three choices listed in the essay section of the common application forms:

1. Describe a person you admire or who has influenced you a great deal.
2. What makes you the interesting person that you are?
3. Explain the impact of an event or activity that has created a change in your life or in your way of thinking.

Many schools that use the common applications require a supplement that affords an opportunity for candidates to provide information that is not requested by the common applications.

While the candidate's ability to write well is certainly under review in the essay question, the exercise investigates a candidate's values and explores the individual experiences that have shaped his or her character. These questions give candidates a chance to reveal such qualities as independence, self-reliance, creativity, originality, humility, generosity, curiosity, and genius. Viewed in this light, answering these questions becomes a tall order. The best advice may be to just answer them. In addition, candidates should recognize that although the content of their essays is always of interest, grammar, spelling, punctuation, organization, and the inclusion of evidence or examples are of equal importance.

Using a common application makes the process of applying to multiple schools a much more manageable endeavor.

Candidates who come from disadvantaged backgrounds often find this section of the application the most challenging and occasionally exclusionary. Some schools assume that all applicants have access to opportunities such as summer camps, music instruction, and periodicals and newspapers. Whatever the case, the common application forms attempt to be more inclusive of a broader set of experiences. In fact, many outreach agencies who seek to identify and place disadvantaged students in independent schools have either used one of the existing common application forms or have developed their own applications in lieu of individual school application forms.

If a student fears that using one of the common applications will somehow fail to convey a unique aspect of his or her individuality or that the essay question answers will not speak to the unique qualities of why a particular school might be a good match, he or she may want to think about including an extra essay. Just because a candidate uses a common application does not mean that he or she must use a common approach to completing it. Imagine how welcome a splash of creativity might be to an individual reader or committee of admission officers who may read hundreds or even thousands of applications each admission season. An application that parrots the list of school courses, sports, and activities offers little insight into the candidate. A well-written application will be as unique as the individual who wrote it.

Applicants and their parents are not the only winners when a common application form is used. The teachers who dutifully complete countless recommendation forms enjoy the convenience of having to complete only one form for each of their students applying to independent schools. Practically speaking, if there is ever a time that a student wants to be in good favor with his or her teacher, it is the moment at which a reference is being given. Using a common application makes the process of applying to multiple schools a much more manageable endeavor. When there is only one form to complete, most teachers will provide longer and more informative answers that are far more helpful to admission officers. Common applications are a great remedy for the fatigue and frustration endured by teachers who have been overwhelmed by a barrage of recommendation forms. Currently, there are even more schools accepting common recommendation forms than there are schools accepting the entire Secondary School Application or the Admission Application Form. Before discounting the benefits of a common application, be sure to consider at least the use of the recommendation forms.

Counselors and Consultants Speak Out

Lee Cary, Director of Admissions, Shore Country Day School in Beverly, Massachusetts, has been advising eighth-graders for many years and finds the workload associated with the application process unreasonable for most of her students. "It is inconceivable to expect a 14-year-old student to write upwards of eight individual essays, all of top quality. From taking time for school visits, making up missed schoolwork, organizing forms, completing paperwork, and polishing writing, the act of applying to secondary schools becomes a whole second job for eighth-and ninth-grade students." Considering that the average application includes up to ten documents, some of which must pass between the applicant, the sending school, and back to the applicant or the receiving school, an eighth grader and his or her parents are now looking at completing more than eighty documents! On top of the testing process and applying for financial aid, this amounts to an enormous administrative challenge.

Karl Koenigsbauer, Director of Secondary School Placement, Eaglebrook School in Deerfield, Massachusetts, agrees that the common application forms make the process more efficient, but he worries about how they might erode the process as well. "My goal is to help students find the school that will be the best match for their abilities and interests. The essay questions from some schools really help the candidate to understand more about what qualities of mind and spirit a school values. When a candidate comes to me and says a particular question is too difficult, too simplistic, or just plain confusing, it gives me an opportunity to help him or her see how that question represents the identity of that particular school and why it may or may not be a good match. I worry that the common application forms will homogenize the application process to the point where I lose this opportunity to fine-tune the placement process."

Faith Howland, an independent educational consultant in Boston, Massachusetts, and a member of the Independent Educational Consultants Association (IECA), works with families to find the right school and is also often contacted for help when a student's

first round of applications has not been successful. "The application process can be near overwhelming for 13- and 14-year-olds. To write as many as eight different applications, each with different essays, just when you are expected to get great grades and continue your sports commitments and other extracurricular activities—not to mention working to prepare for entrance tests. This is high stress! Use of a common application form would be supportive to students and would be extremely helpful in streamlining the teacher recommendations. For those kids who need to submit a second round of applications, the common application forms could be invaluable. These youngsters are coping with disappointment while needing to research new possibilities. If schools were willing to share the common application forms, it's conceivable that many more students who might simply give up if not successful on their first applications could be placed."

Many Schools, One Application

Increased acceptance of the Secondary Schools Application and the Admission Application Form could lead to a marked increase in applications. Common applications are especially helpful to the candidate who fails to earn any acceptance letters at the end of the application process. Traditionally, if a candidate wants to apply to a new list of schools, he or she must start from scratch and complete a new set of forms. Common applications certainly speed up this process, and in the case of the Secondary School Application from SSAT, sending an application to an additional school is as easy as sending the test scores. Candidates simply sign in to their accounts and select another school.

More than half of the candidates who apply to independent schools come from public schools and may not enjoy the benefit of placement counselors at their schools nor do they seek the advice of independent counselors. Regardless, most candidates are well served in using one of the common application forms when applying to multiple schools. One strategy may be to complete a few individual applications and then submit one of the common application forms to a few other schools—identifying some additional options and increasing the likelihood of having meaningful choices after the decision letters are mailed. Many candidates find it much easier to figure out which school they want once they know which school wants them.

Few schools realize how difficult the application process can be for families who are applying to more than one school. Common application forms make the process of applying to multiple schools a much more manageable endeavor. The use of a common application form affords families much more time and energy to devote to other aspects of the application and interview process. By reducing the duplicated paperwork of recommendations and the need to complete so many essays, applicants and their parents are granted a greater opportunity to discuss the real issues surrounding school selection, such as the compatibility of curriculum, style of teaching, and program offerings. Rather than creating folders for each school and chasing down multiple letters of recommendation, applicants and their parents can focus on just a few essays and remove the stress associated with sorting and tracking multiple documents.

Candidates and their families can be assured of the professionalism of admission officers and feel free to use one of the common applications. The Secondary School Application and the Admission Application Form represent the efforts of the very best admission officers who have put the interests of the applicant at the fore— shifting the focus away from the school and back to the candidate. Candidates can be confident that either common application form will more than adequately allow them to make a strong case for their own admission at any school accepting the form.

About Standardized Tests

Heather Hoerle
Vice President, Member Relations
National Association of Independent Schools
(NAIS)

Mention the word "testing" to even the most capable student and he or she is likely to freeze in fear. It's no wonder, then, that standardized testing in the independent school admission process causes nail-biting among students and parents alike.

You may be wondering why private schools test prospective students in the first place. In most cases, standardized testing is used to evaluate a student's ability to perform outside of the classroom. Often, testing helps schools to understand whether they have an appropriate program for applicants. In some cases, private schools find they are best equipped to serve students with test results that fit within a specific range or percentile. Note that standardized testing is also used to place accepted students into appropriate classes in their new school.

Years ago, I took the Secondary School Admission Test (SSAT) as part of the admission process to a boarding school. After my scores came back, my grim-faced mother called the boarding school's admission director to discuss the results. Much to her relief and surprise, I was accepted by the school in spite of mediocre quantitative testing. Indeed, the strength of my application assured school officials that I was ready for their academic challenge, despite the "average" test results. The SSAT, while an important part of my application, did not tell admission officials about my motivation, nor did it yield any information about my academic and creative achievements.

While it is true that some schools assign a great deal of importance to standardized testing, it is just as true that many schools regard testing as only one part of the application process. Many private schools place equal value on the applicant's campus interview, the student's record of achievement, teacher recommendations, and student/parent written statements. In short, test scores cannot tell an individual's full story, and admission officials recognize this limitation, even as they require standardized testing.

Often, testing helps schools to understand whether they have an appropriate program for applicants.

The tests that are most frequently used by private secondary schools are the Secondary School Admission Test Board's SSAT and the Educational Records Bureau's Independent School Entrance Exam (ISEE).

Taking the SSAT

The SSAT, which is used to evaluate applicants for admission to grades 5–11, is a multiple-choice test that measures students' abilities in math and verbal areas and enables counselors to compare students' scores with those of private school applicants and the national school population. The SSAT takes more than 2 hours to complete. Two levels are administered. The lower level exam is taken by students in grades 5–7. The upper level is administered to students in grades 8–11. Students' scores are compared only to students in the same grade. The exam contains multiple-choice questions and a writing sample.

The SSAT is given nationally at more than 600 test sites in all fifty states on selected Saturdays during the school year (in October, November, December, January, February, March, April, and June). It is also given internationally in November, December, January, March, and April.

Applicants can arrange to have SSAT scores sent to several different schools. Registration forms and details about specific test sites, dates, and fees are available at www.ssat.org or by calling 609-683-4440. You can download a free copy of the *SSAT Student Guide* from the Web site. The Secondary School Admission Test Board also sells *Preparing and Applying for Independent School Admission and the SSAT*, a sample test booklet that contains an actual test form for student practice, for a small fee.

Taking the ISEE

The ISEE is used to assess the math and verbal abilities and achievement of students entering grades 5 through 12. The test is administered at three levels: a lower level for students applying to grades 5 and 6; a middle level for those students applying to grades 7 and 8; and an upper level for students applying to grades 9 through 12. Students' scores are compared only to students in the same grade.

The test, which takes about 3 hours to complete, has two components—a multiple-choice segment and a 30-minute essay. The essay, although not scored, gives schools a chance to see a student's writing on an informal topic. The turnaround time for score reporting is seven to ten business days.

The ISEE is administered at sites across the United States and abroad on dates chosen by the schools. Families can obtain test dates and locations by requesting a free student guide from the Educational Records Bureau online at http://erblearn.org. The Educational Records Bureau also publishes *What to Expect on the ISEE*, a sample test booklet that contains half-length practice tests.

How Important Are the Tests?

Parents may want to assure their child that his or her fate does not rely solely on test performance. According to admission counselors, test results are only one part of the admission process. Test scores may not directly relate to the grades a student is capable of achieving in school, and tests cannot measure motivation. Because admission representatives know that a student can contribute to the life of the school community in many different ways, they are careful to keep all of an applicant's talents, abilities, and achievements in mind when evaluating his or her potential for success.

Attention Students: Worried About Taking the SSAT or ISEE?

Here are a few tips to help ban the testing blues.

- Get plenty of rest the day before the test. You will need all of your concentration on the test date, and fatigue can wreak havoc on your ability to focus.
- Eat a meal before you take the test. Your brain needs the energy that food provides!
- Carefully read the materials provided by the sponsoring test group several days before testing is scheduled. Often a "practice test" is included in your registration materials and can be helpful in preparing you for the upcoming test.
- Be well prepared. Advance registration materials offer plenty of guidance on what you will need to bring to the test, such as your registration ticket and No. 2 pencils.
- Allow plenty of time to get to your test site. Be sure that you have directions to the test center, and arrive ahead of the test administration time in order to register on-site, find a bathroom, and get acclimated to the setting.
- As you are taking the test, do not get hung up on hard questions. Skip them and move on. If you have time at the end of each test section, return to unanswered questions and try again.
- Don't forget personal "comfort" items. If you have a cold, be sure to bring tissues and cough drops along. Have extra money on hand, since you may want something to drink during the break. Wear layers, just in case you get too hot or too cold while taking the test.
- Finally, relax! While it is important to do your best work on standardized tests, your future does not depend solely on your test results.

Paying for a Private Education

Mark J. Mitchell
Vice President, School Information Services
National Association of Independent Schools (NAIS)

Imagine asking a car dealer to sell you a $15,000 sedan for $5000 because that is all you can afford. When you buy a car, you know that you will be paying more than it cost to design, build, ship, and sell the car. The sales staff will not offer you a price based on your income. At best, you may receive discounts, rebates, or other incentives that allow you to pay the lowest price the dealer is willing to accept. As a buyer, you even accept the notion that the car's value will depreciate as soon as you drive it off the lot. No matter how you look at it, you pay more than the car cost to make and ultimately more than it's worth.

Tuition at many private schools can easily approach the cost of a new car; however, paying for a private school education is not the same as buying a car. One difference is the availability of financial aid at thousands of schools in the United States and abroad to help offset the tuition. Imagine asking a school to accept $5000 for a $15,000 tuition because that is all you can afford to pay. That is exactly what private schools that provide need-based financial aid programs accomplish. Learning about the financing options and procedures available at private schools can make this imagined scenario a reality for many families.

Need-Based Financial Aid

Many private schools offer assistance to families who demonstrate financial need. In fact, for academic year 2007–08, schools that belong to the National Association of Independent Schools (NAIS) provided more than $1 trillion in need-based financial aid to nearly 18 percent of their students. The average grant for boarding school students was $20,818 and the average grant for day school students was $10,436. These need-based grants do not need to be repaid and are used to offset the school's tuition. Schools make this

substantial commitment as one way of ensuring a socioeconomically diverse student body and to help ensure that every student qualified for admission has the best chance to enroll, regardless of his or her financial circumstances.

How Financial Need Is Determined

Many schools use a process of determining financial need that requires the completion of applications and the submission of tax forms and other documentation to help them decide how much help each family needs. Currently, more than 2,400 schools nationwide ask families to complete The School and Student Service (SSS) Parents' Financial Statement (PFS) online at www.nais.org to determine eligibility for aid. The PFS gathers information about family size, income and expenses, parents' assets and indebtedness, and the child's assets. From this and other information, schools are provided with an estimate of the amount of discretionary income (after several allowances are made for basic necessities) available for education costs. Schools review each case individually and use this estimate, along with such supporting documentation as most recent income tax forms, to make a final decision on your need for a financial aid grant. For more information, please visit www.nais.org/go/parents.

The amount of a need-based financial aid award varies from person to person and school to school. Just as individuals have different financial resources and obligations that dictate their need for assistance, schools have different resources and policies that dictate their ability to meet your financial need. Tuition costs, endowment incomes, and the school's philosophy about financial aid are a few of the things that can affect how much aid a school can offer. If your decision to send your child to a private school depends heavily on getting financial help, you would benefit from applying for aid at more than one school.

Merit-Based Awards

While the majority of aid offered is based on a family's financial situation, not everyone who receives financial assistance must demonstrate financial need. Private schools offer millions of dollars in merit-based scholarships to thousands of students. In the 2007–08 academic year, 299 NAIS-member schools awarded an average annual merit award worth $4151 to students, totaling more than $32.3 million. Even with this level of commitment, such awards are rare (just 5.2 percent of all enrolled students receive this type of aid) and, therefore, highly competitive. They may serve to reward demonstrated talents or achievements in areas ranging from academics to athletics to the arts.

Some additional resources may be available from organizations and agencies in your community. Civic and religious groups, foundations, and even your employer may sponsor scholarships for students at private schools. Unfortunately, these options tend to be few and far between, limited in number and size of award. Be sure to ask a financial aid officer at the school(s) in which you are interested if he or she is aware of such organizations and opportunities.

Whether it is offered by the school or a local organization, be sure to understand the requirements or conditions on which a merit-based scholarship is based. Ask if the award is renewable and, if so, under what conditions. Often, certain criteria must be met (such as minimum GPA, community service, or participation in activities) to ensure renewal of the award in subsequent years. (Some merit awards are available for just one year.)

Tuition Financing Options

Whether or not you qualify for grants or scholarships, another way to get financial help involves finding ways to make tuition payments easier on your family's monthly budget. One common option is the tuition payment plan. These plans allow you to spread tuition payments (less any forms of financial aid you receive) over a period of eight to ten months. In most cases, payments start before the school year begins, but this method can be more feasible than coming up with one or two lump sum payments before the beginning of the school year. Payment plans may be administered by the schools themselves or by a private company approved by the school. They do not normally require credit checks or charge interest; however, they typically charge an application or service fee, which may include tuition insurance.

The financial aid officer at the school is the best source of information about your options.

Since a high-quality education is one of the best investments they can make in their child's future, many parents finance the cost just as they would any other important expense. A number of schools, banks, and other agencies offer tuition loan programs specifically for elementary and secondary school expenses. While such loans are subject to credit checks and must be repaid with interest, they tend to offer rates and terms that are more favorable than those of other consumer loans. It pays to compare the details of more than one type of loan program to find the best one for your needs. Although they should always be regarded as an option of last resort, tuition loan programs can be helpful. Of course, every family must consider both the short- and long-term costs of borrowing and make its decision part of a larger plan for education financing.

A Final Word

Although the primary responsibility to pay for school costs rests with the family, there are options available if you need help. As you can see, financing a private school education can result in a partnership between the family, the school, and sometimes outside agencies or companies, with each making an effort to provide ways to meet the costs. The financial aid officer at the school is the best source of information about your options and is willing to help you in every way he or she can. Always go to the financial aid officer at a school in which you are interested whenever you have any questions or concerns about programs or the application process. Understanding your responsibilities, meeting deadlines, and learning about the full range of options is your best strategy for obtaining assistance. Although there are no guarantees, with proper planning and by asking the right questions, your family just might get the high-quality private education for less.

How to Use This Guide

Quick-Reference Chart

"Private Secondary Schools At-a-Glance" presents data listed in alphabetical order by state and U.S. territories; schools in Canada and other countries follow state listings. If your search is limited to a specific state, turn to the appropriate section and scan the chart for quick information about each school in that state: Are students boarding, day, or both? Is it coeducational? What grade levels are offered? How many students are enrolled? What is the student/faculty ratio? How many sports are offered? Does the school offer Advanced Placement test preparation?

School Profiles and Displays

The **School Profiles** and **Displays** contain basic information about the schools and are listed alphabetically in each section. An outline of a **School Profile** follows. The items of information found under each section heading are defined and displayed. Any item discussed below that is omitted from a **School Profile** either does not apply to that particular school or is one for which no information was supplied.

Heading Name and address of school, along with the name of the Head of School.

General Information Type (boys', girls', coeducational, boarding/day, distance learning) and academic emphasis, religious affiliation, grades, founding date, campus setting, nearest major city, housing, campus size, total number of buildings, accreditation and memberships, languages of instruction, endowment, enrollment, upper school average class size, upper school faculty-student ratio, number of required school days per year (Upper School), number of days per week Upper School students typically attend, and length of the average school day.

Upper School Student Profile Breakdown by grade, gender, boarding/day, geography, and religion.

Faculty Total number; breakdown by gender, number with advanced degrees, and number who reside on campus.

Subjects Offered Academic and general subjects.

Graduation Requirements Subjects and other requirements, including community service.

Special Academic Programs Honors and Advanced Placement courses, accelerated programs, study at local college for college credit, study abroad, independent study, ESL programs, programs for gifted/remedial students and students with learning disabilities.

College Admission Counseling Number of recent graduates, representative list of colleges attended. May include mean or median SAT/ACT scores and percentage of students scoring over 600 on each section of the SAT, over 1800 on the combined SAT, or over 26 on the composite ACT.

Student Life Dress code, student council, discipline, and religious service attendance requirements.

Summer Programs Programs offered and focus; location; open to boys, girls, or both and availability to students from other schools; usual enrollment; program dates and application deadlines.

Tuition and Aid Costs, available financial aid.

Admissions New-student figures, admissions requirements, application deadlines, fees.

Athletics Sports, levels, and gender; number of PE instructors, coaches, and athletic trainers.

Computers List of classes that use computers, campus technology, and availability of student e-mail accounts, online student grades, and a published electronic and media policy.

Contact Person to whom inquiries should be addressed.

Displays, provided by school administrators, present information designed to complement the data already appearing in the **School Profile.**

Close-Ups

Close-Ups, written expressly for Peterson's by school administrators, provide in-depth information about the schools that have chosen to submit them. These descriptions are all in the same format to provide maximum comparability. **Close-Ups** follow each **School Profile** section; there is a page reference at the end of a **School Profile** directing you to that school's **Close-Up.** Schools are listed alphabetically in each section.

Special Needs Schools

One of the great strengths of private schools is their variety. This section is dedicated to the belief that there is an appropriate school setting for every child, one in which he or she will thrive academically, socially, and emotionally. The task for parents, counselors, and educators is to know the child's needs and the schools' resources well enough to make the right match.

Schools in this section serve those students who may have special challenges, including learning differences, dyslexia, language delay, attention deficit disorders, social maladjustment to family and surroundings, or emotional disturbances; these students may need individual attention or are underachieving for some other reason. Parents of children who lag significantly behind their grade level in basic academic skills or who have little or no motivation for schoolwork will also want to consult this section. (For easy reference, schools that offer extra help for students are identified in two directories: "Schools Reporting Programs for Students with Special Needs" and "Schools Reporting That They Accommodate Underachievers.") The schools included here chose to be in this section because they consider special needs education to be their primary focus. It is the mission of these schools, whose curricula and methodologies vary widely, to uncover a student's strengths and, with appropriate academic, social, and psychological counseling, enable him or her to succeed.

Junior Boarding Schools

As parents know, the early adolescent years are ones of tremendous physical and emotional change. Junior boarding schools specialize in this crucial period by taking advantage of children's natural curiosity, zest for learning, and growing self-awareness. While junior boarding schools enroll students with a wide range of academic abilities and levels of emotional self-assurance, their goal is to meet each youngster's individual needs within a supportive community. They accomplish this through low student-teacher ratios and enrollment numbers deliberately kept low.

The boarding schools featured in this section serve students in the middle school grades (6–9); some offer primary programs as well. For more information about junior boarding schools, visit the Junior Boarding Schools Association Web site at www. jbsa.org.

Specialized Directories

These directories are compiled from the information gathered in *Peterson's Annual Survey of Private Secondary Schools*. The schools that did not return a survey or provided incomplete data are not fully represented in these directories. For ease of reference, the directories are grouped by category: type, curricula, financial data, special programs, and special needs.

Index

The "Alphabetical Listing of Schools" shows page numbers for School Profiles in regular type, page numbers for Displays in italics, and page numbers for Close-Ups in boldface type.

Data Collection Procedures

The data contained in *Peterson's Private Secondary Schools 2011–12* **School Profiles, Quick-Reference Chart, Specialized Directories,** and **Index** were collected through *Peterson's Annual Survey of Private Secondary Schools* during fall 2010. Also included were schools that submitted information for the 2009–10 data collection effort but did not submit updates in the fall of 2010. Questionnaires were posted online. With minor exceptions, data for those schools that responded to the questionnaire were submitted by officials at the schools themselves. All usable information received in time for publication has been included. The omission of a particular item from a **School Profile** means that it is either not applicable to that school or not available or usable. Because of Peterson's extensive system of checking data, we believe that the information presented in this guide is accurate. However, errors and omissions are possible in a data collection and processing endeavor of this scope. Therefore, students and parents should check with a specific school at the time of application to verify all pertinent information.

Criteria for Inclusion in This Book

Most schools in this book have curricula that are primarily college preparatory. If a school is accredited or is a candidate for accreditation by a regional accrediting group, including the European Council of International Schools, and/or is approved by a state Department of Education, and/or is a member of the National Association of Independent Schools or the European Council of International Schools, then such accreditation, approval, or membership is stated. Schools appearing in the **Special Needs Schools** section may not have such accreditation or approval.

Quick-Reference Chart

Private Secondary Schools At-a-Glance

| | STUDENTS ACCEPTED | | | | GRADES | | | STUDENT/FACULTY | | | SCHOOL OFFERINGS | |
| | Boarding | | Day | | | | | | | | | |
	Boys	Girls	Boys	Girls	Lower	Middle	Upper	Total	Upper	Student/Faculty Ratio	Advanced Placement Preparation	Sports
UNITED STATES												
Alabama												
Bayside Academy, Daphne			X	X	PK–6	7–8	9–12	753	250	7:1	X	28
Briarwood Christian High School, Birmingham			X	X	K–6	7–8	9–12	1,956	576	23:1	X	18
Edgewood Academy, Elmore					K–5	6–8	9–12	243	85	11:1	X	11
Lyman Ward Military Academy, Camp Hill	X				6–8		9–12	115	70	15:1	X	34
Madison Academy, Madison			X	X	PS–6		7–12	860	420	15:1		7
Marion Academy, Marion			X	X	K–3	4–6	7–12	83	46	8:1		7
Mars Hill Bible School, Florence			X	X	K–4	5–8	9–12	600	237	14:1	X	11
McGill-Toolen Catholic High School, Mobile			X	X			9–12	1,078	1,078	14:1	X	18
Pickens Academy, Carrollton			X	X	K4–6		7–12	309	147	20:1		12
Randolph School, Huntsville			X	X	K–4	5–8	9–12	939	293	10:1	X	18
St. Paul's Episcopal School, Mobile			X	X	PK–4	5–8	9–12	1,405	495	12:1	X	18
Shades Mountain Christian School, Hoover			X	X	K–6	7–8	9–12	408	119	10:1	X	16
Tuscaloosa Academy, Tuscaloosa			X	X	PK–4	5–8	9–12	366	117	15:1	X	14
Westminster Christian Academy, Huntsville			X	X	K–5	6–8	9–12	675	229	16:1	X	16
Arizona												
Blueprint Education, Glendale												
Bourgade Catholic High School, Phoenix			X	X			9–12	406	406	13:1	X	16
Copper Canyon Academy, Rimrock		X					9–12	95	95	10:1		19
The Orme School, Mayer	X	X	X	X	1–5	6–8	9–PG	124	114	6:1	X	41
Phoenix Christian Unified Schools, Phoenix			X	X	PS–5	6–8	9–12	476	220	20:1	X	17
Phoenix Country Day School, Paradise Valley			X	X	PK–4	5–8	9–12	681	239	9:1	X	22
St. Gregory College Preparatory School, Tucson			X	X		6–8	9–PG	290	167	9:1	X	23
Saint Mary's High School, Phoenix			X	X			9–12	601	601	17:1	X	18
Scottsdale Christian Academy, Phoenix			X	X	PK–5	6–8	9–12	934	341	25:1	X	15
Seton Catholic High School, Chandler			X	X			9–12	541	541	13:1	X	18
Southwestern Academy, Rimrock	X	X	X	X			9–PG	32	32	3:1	X	37
Valley Lutheran High School, Phoenix			X	X			9–12	190	190	12:1	X	17
Arkansas												
Episcopal Collegiate School, Little Rock			X	X	PK–5	6–8	9–12	676	212	10:1	X	16
West Memphis Christian High School, West Memphis			X	X	K–6	7–9	10–12	208	66	12:1		
California												
Academy of Our Lady of Peace, San Diego				X			9–12	733	733	14:1	X	6
Alma Heights Christian High School, Pacifica			X	X	K–4	5–8	9–12	324	144	10:1	X	9
Archbishop Mitty High School, San Jose			X	X			9–12	1,640	1,640	17:1	X	27
The Archer School for Girls, Los Angeles				X		6–8	9–12	440	257	8:1	X	9
Armona Union Academy, Armona			X	X	K–4	5–8	9–12	112	44	10:1		11
Army and Navy Academy, Carlsbad	X		X		7–9		10–12	292	214	15:1	X	30
The Athenian School, Danville	X	X	X	X		6–8	9–12	463	299	10:1	X	15
Bellarmine College Preparatory, San Jose			X				9–12	1,600	1,600	18:1	X	22
Bellarmine-Jefferson High School, Burbank			X	X							X	3
Bishop Conaty-Our Lady of Loretto High School, Los Angeles				X			9–12	313	313	15:1	X	5
Bishop Montgomery High School, Torrance			X	X			9–12	1,072	1,072	19:1	X	16
Bishop O'Dowd High School, Oakland			X	X			9–12	1,125	1,125	15:1	X	32
Brentwood School, Los Angeles			X	X	K–6	7–8	9–12	990	460	7:1	X	41
Bridges Academy, Studio City			X	X		5–8	9–12	130	76	8:1		3
The Buckley School, Sherman Oaks			X	X	K–5	6–8	9–12	770	302	8:1	X	9
Calvary Chapel High School, Downey			X	X	K–5	6–8	9–12	725	331	20:1	X	17
Calvin Christian High School, Escondido			X	X	PK–5	6–8	9–12	442	133	15:1	X	11
Campbell Hall (Episcopal), North Hollywood			X	X	K–6	7–8	9–12	1,085	533	8:1	X	20
Capistrano Valley Christian Schools, San Juan Capistrano			X	X	JK–6	7–8	9–12	404	174	13:1	X	14
Castilleja School, Palo Alto				X		6–8	9–12	415	235	6:1	X	14
Central Catholic High School, Modesto			X	X			9–12	435	435	15:1	X	15
Chaminade College Preparatory, West Hills			X	X			9–12	1,288	1,288	15:1	X	25
Chinese Christian Schools, San Leandro			X	X	K–5	6–8	9–12	776	213	8:1	X	15
Crespi Carmelite High School, Encino			X				9–12	585	585	23:1	X	17
Crystal Springs Uplands School, Hillsborough			X	X		6–8	9–12	358	250	9:1	X	15
Damien High School, La Verne			X				9–12	980	980	22:1	X	24
De La Salle High School, Concord			X				9–12	1,042	1,042	28:1	X	19
Faith Christian High School, Yuba City			X	X			9–12	99	99	12:1	X	7
Fresno Adventist Academy, Fresno			X	X	K–5	6–8	9–12	193	65	19:1	X	5
Fresno Christian Schools, Fresno			X	X	K–6	7–8	9–12	612	218	10:1	X	17
The Frostig School, Pasadena			X	X	1–5	6–8	9–12	114	60	6:1		4
Garces Memorial High School, Bakersfield			X	X			9–12	627	627	28:1	X	17
The Grauer School, Encinitas			X	X		6–8	9–12	150	75	7:1	X	44
The Harker School, San Jose			X	X	K–5	6–8	9–12	1,750	682	16:1	X	21
Harvard-Westlake School, North Hollywood			X	X		7–9	10–12	1,609	875	8:1	X	21
Head-Royce School, Oakland			X	X	K–5	6–8	9–12	815	339	9:1	X	20

Private Secondary Schools At-a-Glance

	STUDENTS ACCEPTED				GRADES			STUDENT/FACULTY			SCHOOL OFFERINGS	
	Boarding		Day									
	Boys	Girls	Boys	Girls	Lower	Middle	Upper	Total	Upper	Student/Faculty Ratio	Advanced Placement Preparation	Sports
Highland Hall Waldorf School, Northridge			X	X	N–6	7–8	9–12	360	89	6:1		6
Idyllwild Arts Academy, Idyllwild	X	X	X	X			9–PG	278	278	12:1	X	38
International High School, San Francisco			X	X	PK–5	6–8	9–12	1,003	341	10:1		24
Junipero Serra High School, Gardena			X	X			9–12	686	68	25:1	X	13
Kings Christian School, Lemoore			X	X	PK–6	7–8	9–12	283	98	11:1	X	17
La Jolla Country Day School, La Jolla			X	X	N–4	5–8	9–12	1,136	471	15:1	X	29
La Salle High School, Pasadena			X	X			9–12	740	740	11:1	X	20
Laurel Springs School, Ojai					1–5	6–8	9–12	2,369	1,449	1:1		
Le Lycee Francais de Los Angeles, Los Angeles			X	X	PS–5	6–8	9–12	732	129	15:1		9
Liberty Christian School, Huntington Beach			X	X	K–6	7–8	9–12	348	91	7:1	X	6
Lick-Wilmerding High School, San Francisco			X	X			9–12	440	440	9:1	X	18
Linfield Christian School, Temecula			X	X	K–5	6–8	9–12	750	365	14:1	X	12
Lodi Academy, Lodi			X	X			9–12	101	101	11:1		5
Los Angeles Baptist Middle School/High School, North Hills			X	X		6–8	9–12	829	541	22:1	X	11
Louisville High School, Woodland Hills				X			9–12	439	439	25:1	X	14
Lutheran High School, La Verne			X	X				130	130	9:1	X	16
Lutheran High School of San Diego, Chula Vista			X	X			9–12	78	78	12:1	X	6
Marin Academy, San Rafael			X	X			9–12	406	406	9:1	X	34
The Marin School, Sausalito			X	X			9–12	100	100	7:1		5
Marlborough School, Los Angeles				X		7–9	10–12	530		8:1	X	12
Marymount High School, Los Angeles				X			9–12	366	366	7:1	X	20
Mary Star of the Sea High School, San Pedro			X	X			9–12	519	519	17:1	X	11
Menlo School, Atherton			X	X		6–8	9–12	810	580	10:1	X	16
Mercy High School College Preparatory, San Francisco				X			9–12	486	486	15:1	X	11
Montclair College Preparatory School, Van Nuys	X	X	X	X		7–8	9–12	254	208	15:1	X	21
Monterey Bay Academy, La Selva Beach	X	X	X				9–12	211	211	13:1	X	4
Monte Vista Christian School, Watsonville	X	X	X	X		6–8	9–12	808	598	9:1	X	20
Moreau Catholic High School, Hayward			X	X			9–12	930	930	18:1	X	21
Notre Dame Academy, Los Angeles				X			9–12	400	400	14:1	X	8
Notre Dame High School, San Jose				X			9–12	620	620	13:1	X	11
Oak Grove School, Ojai	X	X	X	X	PK–6	7–8	9–12	180	36	7:1	X	15
Ojai Valley School, Ojai	X	X	X	X	PK–5	6–8	9–12	287	103	6:1	X	31
Orinda Academy, Orinda			X	X		7–8	9–12	69	64	9:1	X	4
Paradise Adventist Academy, Paradise			X	X	K–4	5–8	9–12	191	84	8:1		4
Polytechnic School, Pasadena			X	X	K–5	6–8	9–12	860	374	17:1	X	25
Providence High School, Burbank			X	X			9–12	375	375	12:1	X	15
Redwood Adventist Academy, Santa Rosa			X	X	K–4	5–8	9–12	107	39	5.5:1		6
Redwood Christian Schools, Castro Valley			X	X	K–5	6–8	9–12	593	217	15:1	X	8
Rio Hondo Preparatory School, Arcadia			X	X		6–8	9–12	187	96	4:1	X	6
Rolling Hills Preparatory School, San Pedro			X	X		6–8	9–12	235	135	9:1	X	19
Saddleback Valley Christian School, San Juan Capistrano			X	X	JK–6	7–8	9–12	816	302	12:1	X	14
Sage Hill School, Newport Coast			X	X			9–12	429	429	9:1	X	14
St. Bernard's Catholic School, Eureka	X	X	X	X	K–8		9–12	300	150	12:1	X	11
St. Catherine's Academy, Anaheim	X		X		K–6	7–8		154	83	8:1		24
Saint Elizabeth High School, Oakland			X	X			9–12	165	165	15:1	X	7
Saint Francis Girls High School, Sacramento				X			9–12	1,139	1,139	15:1	X	12
Saint Francis High School, La Canada Flintridge			X				9–12	671	671	15:1	X	9
St. Joseph High School, Santa Maria			X	X			9–12	561	561	19:1		16
Saint Lucy's Priory High School, Glendora				X			9–12	696	696	20:1	X	15
St. Margaret's Episcopal School, San Juan Capistrano			X	X	PS–5	6–8	9–12	1,228	431	7:1	X	14
Saint Mary's College High School, Berkeley			X	X			9–12	625	625	16:1	X	11
St. Michael's Preparatory School of the Norbertine Fathers, Silverado	X						9–12	64	64	3:1	X	11
Saint Patrick—Saint Vincent High School, Vallejo			X	X			9–12	558	558	30:1	X	15
Salesian High School, Richmond			X	X			9–12	524	524	22:1	X	15
Santa Catalina School, Monterey		X		X			9–12	252	252	8:1	X	32
Sonoma Academy, Santa Rosa			X	X			9–12	231		12:1	X	25
Southwestern Academy, San Marino	X	X	X	X		6–8	9–PG	139	122	6:1	X	22
Squaw Valley Academy, Olympic Valley	X	X	X	X			8–12	74	74	7:1	X	68
Sterne School, San Francisco			X	X		6–8	9–12	43	23	8:1		11
Stevenson School, Pebble Beach	X	X	X	X	K–5	6–8	9–12	730	531	10:1	X	34
Summerfield Waldorf School, Santa Rosa			X	X	K–6	7–8	9–12	390	95	7:1		5
The Thacher School, Ojai	X	X	X				9–12	249	249	5:1		40
Ursuline High School, Santa Rosa				X			9–12	281	281	18:1	X	12
Village Christian Schools, Sun Valley			X	X	JK–5	6–8	9–12	1,091	483	25:1	X	15
Western Christian Schools, Upland			X	X		6–8	9–12	475	375	17:1	X	10
Westmark School, Encino			X	X	3–5	6–8	9–12			12:1		11
Westridge School, Pasadena				X	4–6	7–8	9–12	495	282	6:1	X	19
West Valley Christian Church Schools, West Hills			X	X	K–5	6–8	9–12	204	63	15:1	X	9
Windward School, Los Angeles			X	X		7–8	9–12	525	363	7:1	X	5
York School, Monterey			X	X			8–12	230	230	9:1	X	19

Private Secondary Schools At-a-Glance

| | STUDENTS ACCEPTED | | | | GRADES | | | STUDENT/FACULTY | | | SCHOOL OFFERINGS | |
| | Boarding | | Day | | | | | | | | | |
	Boys	Girls	Boys	Girls	Lower	Middle	Upper	Total	Upper	Student/Faculty Ratio	Advanced Placement Preparation	Sports
Colorado												
Alexander Dawson School, Lafayette			X	X	K–4	5–8	9–12	453	183	7:1	X	43
Bridge School, Boulder			X	X		6–8	9–12	22	13	4:1		4
The Colorado Rocky Mountain School, Carbondale	X	X	X	X			9–12	145	145	5:1	X	30
The Colorado Springs School, Colorado Springs			X	X	PK–5	6–8	9–12	305	113	6:1	X	18
Denver Lutheran High School, Denver			X	X			9–12	182	182	17:1	X	13
Fountain Valley School of Colorado, Colorado Springs	X	X	X	X			9–12	251	251	6:1	X	42
Humanex Academy, Englewood			X	X		7–8	9–12	63	56	7:1		16
J. K. Mullen High School, Denver			X	X			9–12	1,010	1,010	17:1		21
Telluride Mountain School, Telluride			X	X	PK–4	5–8	9–12	102	12			24
Vail Mountain School, Vail			X	X	K–5	6–8	9–12	349	106	8:1	X	46
Connecticut												
Academy of Our Lady of Mercy, Milford				X			9–12	437	437	12:1		18
Brunswick School, Greenwich			X		PK–4	5–8	9–12	940	356	5:1	X	20
Choate Rosemary Hall, Wallingford	X	X	X	X			9–12	850	850	6:1	X	41
Convent of the Sacred Heart, Greenwich				X	PS–4	5–8	9–12	777	290	7:1	X	23
Eagle Hill-Southport, Southport			X					112	24	4:1		9
The Ethel Walker School, Simsbury		X		X		6–8	9–12	253	214	9:1	X	41
Franklin Academy, East Haddam	X	X	X	X			9–PG	92	92	3:1		35
The Glenholme School, a Devereux Center, Washington	X	X	X	X	5–6	7–8	9–PG	88	75	10:1		45
Greenwich Academy, Greenwich				X	PK–4	5–8	9–12	802	339	6:1	X	34
Hamden Hall Country Day School, Hamden			X	X	PS–6	7–8	9–12	563	267	8:1	X	18
Holy Cross High School, Waterbury			X	X			9–12	730	730	15:1	X	22
Hopkins School, New Haven			X	X		7–8	9–12	681	526	6:1	X	43
The Hotchkiss School, Lakeville	X	X	X	X			9–PG	598	598	6:1	X	46
Kent School, Kent	X	X	X	X			9–PG	560	560	7.7:1	X	43
King Low Heywood Thomas, Stamford			X	X	PK–5	6–8	9–12	685	308	7:1	X	24
Kingswood-Oxford School, West Hartford			X	X		6–8	9–12	508	364	8:1	X	20
Mercy High School, Middletown				X			9–12	683	683	13:1	X	16
Miss Porter's School, Farmington		X		X			9–12	322	322	8:1	X	40
Northwest Catholic High School, West Hartford			X	X			9–12	623	623	12:1	X	33
The Norwich Free Academy, Norwich			X	X						22:1	X	33
The Oxford Academy, Westbrook	X						9–PG	38	38	1:1	X	13
The Rectory School, Pomfret	X	X	X	X	1–4	5–9		244	169	4:1		36
South Kent School, South Kent	X		X				9–PG	163	163	5:1		24
The Stanwich School, Greenwich			X	X	PK–6		7–12	407	109	10:1	X	13
Suffield Academy, Suffield	X	X	X	X			9–PG	412	412	5:1	X	31
Watkinson School, Hartford			X	X		6–8	9–PG	245	162	6:1		30
Wellspring Foundation, Bethlehem	X	X	X	X				52				
Westover School, Middlebury		X		X			9–12	210	210	8:1	X	47
The Williams School, New London			X	X		7–8	9–12	271	223	6:1	X	19
The Woodhall School, Bethlehem	X		X				9–PG	38	38	4:1	X	34
Delaware												
St. Andrew's School, Middletown	X	X					9–12	290	290	5:1		34
Salesianum School, Wilmington			X				9–12	1,027	1,027	12:1	X	22
Sanford School, Hockessin			X	X	PK–4	5–8	9–12	572	221	10:1	X	13
Tower Hill School, Wilmington			X	X	PS–4	5–8	9–12	756	222	8:1	X	21
District of Columbia												
Edmund Burke School, Washington			X	X		6–8	9–12	275	207	7:1	X	17
Georgetown Visitation Preparatory School, Washington				X			9–12	484	484	10:1	X	18
Gonzaga College High School, Washington			X				9–12	957	957	15:1	X	33
Kirov Academy of Ballet of Washington, D.C., Washington	X	X				6–8	9–12	63	54	8:1		2
Maret School, Washington			X	X	K–4	5–8	9–12	636	309	7:1	X	25
St. Albans School, Washington	X		X		4–8		9–12	583	324	7:1	X	34
Florida												
Academy at the Lakes, Land O'Lakes			X	X	PK–4	5–8	9–12	380	112	5:1	X	18
Academy of the Holy Names, Tampa			X	X	PK–4	5–8	9–12	801	339	15:1	X	19
Admiral Farragut Academy, St. Petersburg	X	X	X	X	P4–5	6–8	9–12	358	221	8:1	X	41
Allison Academy, North Miami Beach			X	X		6–8	9–12	93	74	10:1	X	17
American Academy, Plantation			X	X	1–6	7–8	9–12	319	159	12:1		21
American Heritage School, Delray Beach			X	X	PK–8		9–12				X	17
American Heritage School, Plantation			X	X	PK–6		7–12	2,202	1,424	14:1	X	19
Berkeley Preparatory School, Tampa			X	X	PK–5	6–8	9–12	1,200	500	8:1	X	28
Bishop Kenny High School, Jacksonville			X	X			9–12	1,274	1,274	15:1	X	18
The Bolles School, Jacksonville	X	X	X	X	PK–5	6–8	9–12	1,651	767	10:1	X	18
Canterbury School, Fort Myers			X	X	PK–6	7–8	9–12	600	193	10:1	X	13
The Canterbury School of Florida, St. Petersburg			X	X	PK–4	5–8	9–12	402	153	4:1	X	30
Cardinal Mooney Catholic High School, Sarasota			X	X			9–12	467	467	13:1	X	18

Private Secondary Schools At-a-Glance

	Boarding Boys	Boarding Girls	Day Boys	Day Girls	Lower	Middle	Upper	Total	Upper	Student/Faculty Ratio	Advanced Placement Preparation	Sports
Cardinal Newman High School, West Palm Beach....			X	X			9–12	642	642	25:1	X	18
Carrollton School of the Sacred Heart, Miami......				X	PK–3	4–6	7–12	775	423	9:1	X	14
Chaminade-Madonna College Preparatory, Hollywood.			X	X			9–12	594	594	19:1	X	19
Christian Home and Bible School, Mount Dora.....			X	X	K–5	6–8	9–12	533	207	15:1	X	15
Christopher Columbus High School, Miami			X				9–12	1,380	1,380	17:1	X	18
Clearwater Central Catholic High School, Clearwater.			X	X						16:1	X	20
The Community School of Naples, Naples.........			X	X	PK–5	6–8	9–12	720	270	7:1	X	19
Episcopal High School of Jacksonville, Jacksonville ...			X	X		6–8	9–12	857	566	10:1	X	22
Father Lopez High School, Daytona Beach			X	X			9–12	297	297	20:1	X	16
The First Academy, Orlando			X	X	K4–5	6–8	9–12	975	342	10:1	X	22
Florida Air Academy, Melbourne	X	X	X	X		7–8	9–12	237	212	11:1	X	57
Forest Lake Academy, Apopka................	X	X	X	X			9–12	426	426	15:1		10
Fort Lauderdale Preparatory School, Fort Lauderdale .			X	X	PK–6		7–12	202	107	8:1		
Foundation Academy, Winter Garden			X	X	K–5	6–8	9–12	539	109	16:1	X	12
The Geneva School, Winter Park..............			X	X	K4–6	7–8	9–12	474	88	9:1	X	9
Glades Day School, Belle Glade			X	X	PK–6	7–8	9–12	395	190	15:1	X	12
Gulliver Preparatory School, Miami.............			X	X	PK–4	5–8	9–12	1,834	754	8:1	X	38
Immaculata-La Salle High School, Miami			X	X			9–12	751	751	15:1	X	23
Jesuit High School of Tampa, Tampa			X				9–12	709	709	13:1	X	18
John Paul II Catholic High School, Tallahassee			X	X			9–12	119	119	8:1	X	9
Kaplan College Preparatory School, Hollywood.....	X	X				6–8	9–12	256	225		X	
Lake Mary Preparatory School, Lake Mary	X	X	X	X	PK–5	6–8	9–12	644	250	22:1	X	31
Orangewood Christian School, Maitland			X	X	K–6	7–8	9–12	711	273	11:1	X	22
Out-Of-Door-Academy, Sarasota..............			X	X	PK–6	7–8	9–12	580	219	8:1	X	19
Pensacola Catholic High School, Pensacola........			X	X			9–12	571	571	18:1	X	9
Pine Crest School, Fort Lauderdale.............			X	X	PK–5	6–8	9–12	1,691	795	10:1	X	21
Ransom Everglades School, Miami			X	X		6–8	9–12	1,069	602	10:1	X	22
Saddlebrook Preparatory School, Wesley Chapel	X	X	X	X	3–5	6–8	9–12	89	68	11:1	X	1
St. Brendan High School, Miami			X	X			9–12	1,181	1,181	15:1	X	11
Saint Edward's School, Vero Beach			X	X	PK–5	6–8	9–12	541	228	8:1	X	20
St. Joseph Academy, St. Augustine............			X	X			9–12	270	270	13:1	X	17
Saint Stephen's Episcopal School, Bradenton			X	X	PK–6	7–8	9–12	646	261	10:1	X	32
Trinity Preparatory School, Winter Park			X	X			9–12	834	492	12:1	X	22
University School of Nova Southeastern University, Fort Lauderdale			X	X	PK–5	6–8	9–12	1,902	680	11:1	X	20
The Vanguard School, Lake Wales.............	X	X	X	X		5–8	9–PG	109	99	7:1		25
Windermere Preparatory School, Windermere	X		X	X	PK–5	6–8	9–12	969	275	11:1	X	23

Georgia

	Boarding Boys	Boarding Girls	Day Boys	Day Girls	Lower	Middle	Upper	Total	Upper	Student/Faculty Ratio	Advanced Placement Preparation	Sports
Augusta Christian School (I), Martinez			X	X	K–5	6–8	9–12	481	219	14:1		13
Augusta Preparatory Day School, Martinez			X	X	PS–4	5–8	9–12	548	206	9:1		8
Ben Franklin Academy, Atlanta			X	X			9–12	130	130	4:1	X	6
Blessed Trinity High School, Roswell............			X	X			9–12	935	935	13:1	X	17
Brookstone School, Columbus.................			X	X	PK–5	6–8	9–12	788	269	10:1	X	12
Chatham Academy, Savannah			X	X	1–5	6–8	9–12	99	35	10:1		18
Deerfield-Windsor School, Albany.............			X	X	PK–5	6–8	9–12	864	245	18:1	X	15
First Presbyterian Day School, Macon			X	X	PK–5	6–8	9–12	976	353	12:1	X	17
Flint River Academy, Woodbury			X	X		6–8	9–12	340	98	14:1		15
Frederica Academy, St. Simons Island			X	X	PK–5	6–8	9–12	357	112	9:1	X	13
George Walton Academy, Monroe			X	X	K4–5	6–8	9–12	945	340	12:1	X	19
Greater Atlanta Christian Schools, Norcross.......			X	X	P4–5	6–8	9–12	1,850	719	13:1	X	25
The Heritage School, Newnan			X	X	PK–4	5–8	9–12	424	144	7:1	X	28
Holy Innocents' Episcopal School, Atlanta.........			X	X	PS–5	6–8	9–12	1,330	430	10:1	X	19
The Howard School, Atlanta.................			X	X	PK–5	6–8	9–12	232	76	8:1		7
King's Ridge Christian School, Alpharetta			X	X	K–5	6–8	9–12	650	110	8:1	X	17
The Lovett School, Atlanta			X	X	K–5	6–8	9–12	1,587	599	15:1	X	45
Marist School, Atlanta....................			X	X			7–12	1,079	1,079	12:1	X	19
Mt. De Sales Academy, Macon			X	X		6–8	9–12	656	445	10:1	X	14
National High School, Atlanta................							9–12	396	396	10:1	X	
North Cobb Christian School, Kennesaw			X	X	PK–5	6–8	9–12	780	249	10:1	X	22
Oak Mountain Academy, Carrollton			X	X	K4–5	6–8	9–12	191	69	5:1	X	12
The Paideia School, Atlanta			X	X	PK–6	7–8	9–12	972	408	9:1	X	21
Piedmont Academy, Monticello			X	X	PK–5	6–8	9–12	314	95	13:1	X	16
Pinecrest Academy, Cumming			X	X	PK–5	6–8	9–12	892	228	8:1	X	11
St. Pius X Catholic High School, Atlanta			X	X			9–12	1,075	1,075	12:1	X	23
Stratford Academy, Macon..................						6–8	9–12	948	288	13:1	X	16
The Walker School, Marietta.................			X	X	PK–5	6–8	9–12	1,039	349	14:1	X	30
Woodward Academy, College Park.............			X	X	PK–6	7–8	9–12	2,729	1,038		X	20

Hawaii

	Boarding Boys	Boarding Girls	Day Boys	Day Girls	Lower	Middle	Upper	Total	Upper	Student/Faculty Ratio	Advanced Placement Preparation	Sports
ASSETS School, Honolulu...................			X	X	K–8		9–12	359	116	8:1		30
Damien Memorial School, Honolulu.............			X			7–8	9–12	407	363	10:1		16
Hanalani Schools, Mililani..................			X	X	PK–6		7–12	769	342	16:1	X	25
Hawaiian Mission Academy, Honolulu...........	X	X	X	X			9–12	110	110	15:1		3
Hawaii Baptist Academy, Honolulu			X	X	K–6	7–8	9–12	1,099	470	12:1	X	22
Iolani School, Honolulu			X	X	K–6	7–12		1,867	1,326	12:1	X	27
Island School, Lihue.....................			X	X	PK–5	6–8	9–12	362	125	11:1		26

Private Secondary Schools At-a-Glance

| | STUDENTS ACCEPTED | | | | GRADES | | | STUDENT/FACULTY | | | SCHOOL OFFERINGS | |
| | Boarding | | Day | | | | | | | | | |
	Boys	Girls	Boys	Girls	Lower	Middle	Upper	Total	Upper	Student/Faculty Ratio	Advanced Placement Preparation	Sports
Kauai Christian Academy, Kilauea			X	X	PS–3	4–6	7–12	80	28	11:1	X	
Lutheran High School of Hawaii, Honolulu			X	X			9–12	98	98	7:1	X	23
Maryknoll School, Honolulu			X	X	PK–5	6–8	9–12	1,465	608	11:1	X	32
Maui Preparatory Academy, Lahaina			X	X							X	
Mid-Pacific Institute, Honolulu			X	X	K–5	6–8	9–12	1,525	846	20:1	X	31
St. Andrew's Priory School, Honolulu				X	K–5	6–8	9–12	401	113	8:1	X	36
St. Anthony's Junior-Senior High School, Wailuku			X	X		7–8	9–12	153	114	10:1	X	29
Saint Francis School, Honolulu			X	X	K–6	7–8	9–12	412	250	20:1	X	25
Saint Joseph Junior-Senior High School, Hilo			X	X		7–8	9–12	193	143	12:1	X	11
Seabury Hall, Makawao			X	X		6–8	9–12	449	315	11:1	X	15
Idaho												
Bishop Kelly High School, Boise			X	X			9–12	626	626	18:1	X	18
Gem State Adventist Academy, Caldwell	X	X	X	X			9–12	104	104	9:1	X	7
Riverstone International School, Boise			X	X	PS–5	6–8	9–12	314	107	6:1		25
Sheridan Academy, Boise			X	X	1–5	6–8	9–12	19	10	10:1		14
Turning Winds Academic Institute, Bonners Ferry										2:1		
Illinois												
Boylan Central Catholic High School, Rockford			X	X			9–12	1,187	1,187	13:1	X	30
Brother Rice High School, Chicago			X				9–12	900	900	15:1	X	19
Carmel High School, Mundelein			X				9–12	1,370	1,370	16:1	X	18
The Chicago Academy for the Arts, Chicago			X	X			9–12	140	140	12:1	X	
Chicago Waldorf School, Chicago			X	X	1–5	6–8	9–12	277	67			6
Elgin Academy, Elgin			X	X	PS–4	5–8	9–12	424	135	5:1	X	13
Fenwick High School, Oak Park			X	X			9–12	1,196	1,196	16:1	X	35
The Governor French Academy, Belleville	X	X	X	X	1–8		9–12	182	54	6:1	X	6
Holy Trinity High School, Chicago			X	X			9–12	300	300	11:1	X	11
Immaculate Conception School, Elmhurst			X	X			9–12	344	344	14:1	X	18
Keith Country Day School, Rockford			X	X	PK–5	6–8	9–12	307	113	6:1	X	9
Lake Forest Academy, Lake Forest	X	X	X	X			9–12	391	391	7:1	X	27
The Latin School of Chicago, Chicago			X	X	JK–5	6–8	9–12	1,107	435	8:1	X	25
Leo Catholic High School, Chicago							9–12	141	141	12:1		12
Loyola Academy, Wilmette			X	X			9–12	2,000	2,000	17:1	X	55
Luther High School North, Chicago			X	X			9–12	180	180	16:1	X	10
Marian Central Catholic High School, Woodstock			X	X			9–12	717	717	16:1	X	17
Marmion Academy, Aurora			X				9–12	499	499	11:1	X	22
Mother McAuley High School, Chicago				X			9–12	1,362	1,362	17:1	X	17
Mount Carmel High School, Chicago			X				9–12	790	790	19:1	X	19
Nazareth Academy, LaGrange Park			X	X			9–12	824	824	17:1	X	16
North Shore Country Day School, Winnetka			X	X	PK–5	6–8	9–12	500	200	8:1	X	15
Notre Dame College Prep, Niles			X				9–12	831	831	17:1	X	27
Roycemore School, Evanston			X	X	PK–4	5–8	9–12	262	93	5:1	X	7
Saint Anthony High School, Effingham			X	X			9–12	190	190	10:1	X	12
Saint Joseph High School, Westchester			X	X			9–12	671	671	17:1	X	18
Saint Patrick High School, Chicago			X				9–12	844	844	17:1	X	16
Saint Viator High School, Arlington Heights			X	X			9–12	1,041	1,041	18:1		18
Timothy Christian High School, Elmhurst			X	X	K–6	7–8	9–12	1,074	395	13:1	X	12
University of Chicago Laboratory Schools, Chicago			X	X	N–4	5–8	9–12	1,801	499	10:1	X	16
Wheaton Academy, West Chicago			X	X			9–12	645	645	15:1	X	33
Indiana												
Bishop Luers High School, Fort Wayne			X	X			9–12	545	545	17:1	X	21
Concordia Lutheran High School, Fort Wayne			X	X			9–12	645	645	16:1	X	19
The Culver Academies, Culver	X	X	X	X			9–PG	792	792	9:1	X	86
The Howe School, Howe	X	X	X	X	5–8		9–12	114	89	9:1	X	16
La Lumiere School, La Porte	X	X	X	X			9–PG	209	209	8:1	X	46
Lutheran High School, Indianapolis			X	X			9–12	246	246	15:1	X	16
Marian High School, Mishawaka			X	X			9–12	676	676	22:1	X	30
Oldenburg Academy, Oldenburg			X	X			9–12	209	209	12:1	X	6
Reitz Memorial High School, Evansville			X	X			9–12	790	790	16:1	X	21
Shawe Memorial Junior/Senior High School, Madison			X	X	K–6	7–8	9–12	408	112	10:1	X	12
Trinity School at Greenlawn, South Bend			X	X		7–8				7:1		4
Iowa												
Alpha Omega Academy, Rock Rapids			X	X	K–5	6–8	9–12	2,268	1,441	32:1		
Des Moines Christian School, Urbandale			X	X	PK–6	7–8	9–12	744	226	18:1	X	11
Dowling Catholic High School, West Des Moines			X	X			9–12	1,372	1,372	17:1	X	21
Maharishi School of the Age of Enlightenment, Fairfield			X	X	PS–6	7–9	10–12	198	52			20
Rivermont Collegiate, Bettendorf			X	X	PS–5	6–8	9–12	194	35	4:1	X	12
Kansas												
Hyman Brand Hebrew Academy of Greater Kansas City, Overland Park			X	X	K–5	6–8	9–12	233	50	5:1	X	4
Maur Hill-Mount Academy, Atchison	X	X	X	X			9–12	198	198	9:1		35
Saint Thomas Aquinas High School, Overland Park			X	X			9–12	1,001	1,001	15:1	X	18

Private Secondary Schools At-a-Glance

	Boarding Boys	Boarding Girls	Day Boys	Day Girls	Lower	Middle	Upper	Total	Upper	Student/Faculty Ratio	Advanced Placement Preparation	Sports
Kentucky												
Calvary Christian School, Covington			X	X	K4–6	7–8	9–12	388	100	10:1	X	19
Community Christian Academy, Independence			X	X	PS–6	7–8	9–12	219	54	15:1		5
Covington Catholic High School, Park Hills			X				9–12	499	499	14:1	X	12
Kentucky Country Day School, Louisville			X	X	JK–4	5–8	9–12	921	299	7:1	X	20
Landmark Christian Academy, Louisville			X	X	K4–6	7–8	9–12	121	23	11:1		4
Louisville Collegiate School, Louisville			X	X	JK–5	6–8	9–12	650		8:1	X	15
Oneida Baptist Institute, Oneida	X	X	X	X		6–8	9–12	300	225	11:1	X	10
Sacred Heart Academy, Louisville				X						15:1	X	11
Sayre School, Lexington			X	X	PK–5	6–8	9–12	563	222	9:1	X	13
Trinity High School, Louisville			X				9–12	1,333	1,333	13:1	X	48
Whitefield Academy, Louisville			X	X	PS–5	6–8	9–12	726	213	20:1	X	16
Louisiana												
Academy of the Sacred Heart, New Orleans				X	1–4	5–8	9–12	645	209	16:1	X	21
Archbishop Rummel High School, Metairie			X			8–12		1,150	1,000	13:1	X	21
Hanson Memorial High School, Franklin			X	X		6–8	9–12	275	165	13:1		12
Holy Savior Menard Catholic High School, Alexandria			X	X		7–8	9–12	465	307	14:1	X	14
Isidore Newman School, New Orleans			X	X	PK–5	6–8	9–12	921	309	17:1	X	15
Jesuit High School of New Orleans, New Orleans			X			8	9–12	1,346	1,087	12:1	X	25
Riverfield Academy, Rayville					K–5	6–8	9–12	280	100	10:1		4
St. Joseph's Academy, Baton Rouge				X			9–12	952	952	13:1	X	23
St. Martin's Episcopal School, Metairie			X	X	PK–5	6–8	9–12	510	221	8:1	X	15
Saint Thomas More Catholic High School, Lafayette			X	X			9–12	1,029	1,029	25:1	X	26
Teurlings Catholic High School, Lafayette			X	X			9–12	658	658	21:1		23
University Christian Preparatory School, Shreveport			X	X	K–5	6–8	9–12	59	19	14:1		2
Westminster Christian Academy, Opelousas			X	X	PK–6	7–8	9–12	1,042	226	13:1	X	12
Maine												
Berwick Academy, South Berwick			X	X	K–4	5–8	9–12	567	275	12:1	X	16
Cheverus High School, Portland			X	X			9–12	497	497	12:1	X	23
Elan School, Poland	X	X					9–12	35	35	6:1		37
George Stevens Academy, Blue Hill	X	X	X	X			9–12	299	299	10:1	X	41
Gould Academy, Bethel	X	X	X	X			9–PG	249	249	6:1	X	12
Hyde School, Bath	X	X	X	X			9–12	143	143	6:1		31
Lincoln Academy, Newcastle			X	X			9–12	547	547	8:1	X	17
Maine Central Institute, Pittsfield	X	X	X	X			9–PG	462	462	14:1	X	26
Saint Dominic Academy, Auburn			X	X	PK–6	7–8	9–12	598	242	12:1	X	15
Waynflete School, Portland			X	X	PK–5	6–8	9–12	553	240	12:1		23
Maryland												
Academy of the Holy Cross, Kensington				X			9–12	581	581	14:1	X	19
Archbishop Curley High School, Baltimore			X				9–12	570	570	14:1	X	18
The Baltimore Actors' Theatre Conservatory, Baltimore			X	X	3–5	7–8	9–12	24	11	3:1	X	
Baltimore Lutheran Middle and Upper School, Towson			X	X		6–8	9–12	330	231	12:1	X	15
Barrie School, Silver Spring			X	X	N–5	6–8	9–12	299	70	5:1	X	13
Bishop Walsh Middle High School, Cumberland			X	X	PK–5	6–8	9–12	428	198	15:1	X	13
The Bryn Mawr School for Girls, Baltimore			X	X	K–5	6–8	9–12	717	304	6:1	X	41
Calvert Hall College High School, Baltimore			X				9–12	1,226	1,226	12:1	X	27
The Calverton School, Huntingtown			X	X	PS–5	6–8	9–12	405	157	7:1	X	7
The Catholic High School of Baltimore, Baltimore				X			9–12	314	314	12:1	X	17
DeMatha Catholic High School, Hyattsville			X				9–12	954	954	13:1	X	23
Elizabeth Seton High School, Bladensburg				X			9–12	654	654	13:1		38
Garrison Forest School, Owings Mills		X	X	X	N–5	6–8	9–12	671	289	7:1	X	26
Georgetown Preparatory School, North Bethesda	X		X				9–12	484	484	8:1	X	51
Gilman School, Baltimore			X		K–5	6–8	9–12	1,012	454	8:1	X	26
Glenelg Country School, Ellicott City			X	X	PK–5	6–8	9–12	797	296	6:1	X	26
Griggs International Academy, Silver Spring			X	X	PK–6	7–8	9–12	728	434			
Gunston Day School, Centreville			X	X			9–12	147	147	6:1	X	15
Institute of Notre Dame, Baltimore				X			9–12	318	318	12:1	X	32
Landon School, Bethesda			X		3–5	6–8	9–12	685	337	8:1	X	28
Maryvale Preparatory School, Brooklandville				X		6–8	9–12	362	280	8:1	X	14
McDonogh School, Owings Mills	X	X	X	X	K–4	5–8	9–12	1,297	585	9:1	X	26
The Nora School, Silver Spring			X	X			9–12	60	60	5:1		24
The Park School of Baltimore, Brooklandville			X	X	PK–5	6–8	9–12	879	330	7:1	X	17
Queen Anne School, Upper Marlboro			X	X		6–12		92	92	7:1	X	9
Roland Park Country School, Baltimore				X	K–5	6–8	9–12	675	289	7:1	X	25
Saint Mary's High School, Annapolis			X	X			9–12	490	490	15:1	X	20
Saints Peter and Paul High School, Easton			X	X			9–12	206	206	9:1	X	11
St. Timothy's School, Stevenson		X		X			9–12	150	150	5:1		24
St. Vincent Pallotti High School, Laurel			X	X			9–12	500	500	18:1	X	19
Sandy Spring Friends School, Sandy Spring	X	X	X	X	PK–5	6–8	9–12	571	265	8:1	X	22

Private Secondary Schools At-a-Glance	Boarding Boys	Boarding Girls	Day Boys	Day Girls	Lower	Middle	Upper	Total	Upper	Student/Faculty Ratio	Advanced Placement Preparation	Sports
Severn School, Severna Park			X	X		6–8	9–12	582	397	8:1	X	23
Worcester Preparatory School, Berlin			X	X	PK–5	6–8	9–12	548	203	9:1	X	12
Massachusetts												
The Academy at Charlemont, Charlemont			X	X		7–8	9–PG	114	75	7:1		22
The Bement School, Deerfield	X	X	X	X	K–5		6–9	246	126	6:1		33
Bishop Connolly High School, Fall River			X	X			9–12	300	300	16:1	X	17
Bishop Stang High School, North Dartmouth			X	X			9–12	750	750	13:1	X	39
Boston College High School, Boston			X			7–8	9–12	1,591	1,261	13:1	X	21
Brooks School, North Andover	X	X	X	X			9–12	365	365	5:1	X	17
Buxton School, Williamstown	X	X	X	X			9–12	90	90	5:1		21
Central Catholic High School, Lawrence			X				9–12	1,342	1,342	24:1	X	31
Chapel Hill–Chauncy Hall School, Waltham	X	X	X	X			9–12	165	165	5:1	X	22
Commonwealth School, Boston			X	X			9–12	149	149	5:1	X	16
Concord Academy, Concord	X	X	X	X			9–12	365	365	6:1		35
Cushing Academy, Ashburnham	X	X	X	X			9–PG	445	445	8:1	X	38
Deerfield Academy, Deerfield	X	X	X	X			9–PG	630	630	6:1	X	41
Dexter School, Brookline			X			7–8	9–12	444	155	7:1	X	14
Eaglebrook School, Deerfield	X		X			6–9		265	246	4:1		64
Falmouth Academy, Falmouth			X	X		7–8	9–12	188	123	4:1	X	3
Fay School, Southborough	X	X	X	X	PK–5		6–9	459	249	7:1		38
Gann Academy (The New Jewish High School of Greater Boston), Waltham			X	X			9–12	323	323	5:1	X	14
The Governor's Academy (formerly Governor Dummer Academy), Byfield	X	X	X	X			9–12	395	395	5:1	X	22
Groton School, Groton	X	X	X	X		8	9–12	372	345	6:1	X	38
Holyoke Catholic High School, Chicopee			X	X						12:1	X	23
The John Dewey Academy, Great Barrington	X	X					10–PG	20	20	3:1		3
The Judge Rotenberg Educational Center, Canton	X	X							130			
Landmark School, Prides Crossing	X	X	X	X	1–5	6–7	8–12	449	305	3:1		16
Matignon High School, Cambridge			X	X			9–12	418	418	15:1	X	25
Middlesex School, Concord	X	X	X	X			9–12	374	374	6:1	X	22
Milton Academy, Milton	X	X	X	X	K–5	6–8	9–12	980	675	5:1	X	28
Phillips Academy (Andover), Andover	X	X	X	X			9–PG	1,109	1,109	5:1	X	48
Pioneer Valley Christian School, Springfield			X	X	PS–5	6–8	9–12	263	87	5:1	X	11
The Rivers School, Weston			X	X		6–8	9–12	457	343	6:1	X	18
The Roxbury Latin School, West Roxbury			X				7–12	296	296	8:1	X	10
St. John's Preparatory School, Danvers			X				9–12	1,248	1,248	11:1	X	47
Saint Mark's School, Southborough	X	X	X	X			9–12	340	340	5:1	X	24
St. Sebastian's School, Needham			X			7–8	9–12	355	257	7:1	X	18
Stoneleigh–Burnham School, Greenfield		X				7–8	9–PG	140	108	6:1		21
The Sudbury Valley School, Framingham			X	X				160		16:1		
Tabor Academy, Marion	X	X	X	X			9–12	500	500	6:1	X	27
Ursuline Academy, Dedham		X				7–8	9–12	397	278	9:1	X	17
Valley View School, North Brookfield	X					5–8	9–12	56	30	6:1		43
Waldorf High School of Massachusetts Bay, Belmont			X	X			9–12	50	50	4:1		3
Waring School, Beverly			X	X		6–8	9–12	150	96	8:1	X	10
The Williston Northampton School, Easthampton	X	X	X	X		7–8	9–PG	529	441	7:1	X	37
The Winsor School, Boston				X		5–8	9–12	436	237	5:1	X	13
Worcester Academy, Worcester	X	X	X	X		6–8	9–PG	651	491	8:1	X	20
Michigan												
Academy of the Sacred Heart, Bloomfield Hills			X	X	N–4	5–8	9–12	493	129	7:1	X	11
Brother Rice High School, Bloomfield Hills			X				9–12	688	688	13:1	X	26
Cardinal Mooney Catholic College Preparatory High School, Marine City			X	X			9–12	180	180	10:1	X	12
Greenhills School, Ann Arbor			X	X		6–8	9–12	538	317	7:1	X	15
Interlochen Arts Academy, Interlochen	X	X	X	X			9–PG	455	455	6:1	X	42
Kalamazoo Christian High School, Kalamazoo			X	X	K–5	6–8	9–12	811	270	11:1	X	17
Ladywood High School, Livonia				X			9–12	347	347	12:1	X	25
Lutheran High School Northwest, Rochester Hills			X	X			9–12	284	284	16:1	X	18
Powers Catholic High School, Flint			X	X			9–12	539	539	19:1	X	30
The Roeper School, Bloomfield Hills			X	X	PK–5	6–8	9–12	625	192	6:1	X	10
St. Mary's Preparatory School, Orchard Lake	X		X				9–12	480	480	10:1	X	43
Southfield Christian High School, Southfield			X	X	PK–5	6–8	9–12	489	178	20:1	X	19
University of Detroit Jesuit High School and Academy, Detroit			X			7–8	9–12	858	745	14:1	X	18
West Catholic High School, Grand Rapids			X	X			9–12	544	544	25:1	X	22
Minnesota												
Breck School, Minneapolis			X	X	PK–4	5–8	9–12	1,131	400	11:1	X	19
Cotter Schools, Winona	X	X	X	X		7–8	9–12	380	298	11:1		24
St. Croix Schools, West St. Paul	X	X	X	X		6–8	9–12	460	420	15:1	X	34
St. Paul Academy and Summit School, St. Paul			X	X	K–5	6–8	9–12	855	360	7:1		25
Saint Thomas Academy, Mendota Heights			X			7–8	9–12	669	534	10:1	X	30
Shattuck-St. Mary's School, Faribault	X	X	X	X		6–8	9–PG	438	398	9:1	X	29

Private Secondary Schools At-a-Glance

| | STUDENTS ACCEPTED | | | | GRADES | | | STUDENT/FACULTY | | | SCHOOL OFFERINGS | |
| | Boarding | | Day | | | | | | | | | |
	Boys	Girls	Boys	Girls	Lower	Middle	Upper	Total	Upper	Student/Faculty Ratio	Advanced Placement Preparation	Sports
Mississippi												
Canton Academy, Canton			X	X			7–12	323	183	17:1		19
Chamberlain-Hunt Academy, Port Gibson	X		X	X		7–9	10–12	90	51	5:1		42
Hillcrest Christian School, Jackson			X	X	K–6		7–12	595	267	11:1	X	14
Jackson Preparatory School, Jackson			X	X		6–9	10–12	801	390	13:1	X	15
Lee Academy, Clarksdale					1–5	6–8	9–12	386	174	20:1		7
Madison-Ridgeland Academy, Madison			X	X	K–5	6–8	9–12	926	146	13:1	X	13
St. Patrick Catholic High School, Biloxi			X	X			7–12	491	491	15:1	X	18
St. Stanislaus College, Bay St. Louis	X		X			7–8	9–PG	381	269	23:1	X	34
Vicksburg Catholic School, Vicksburg			X	X	PK–6		7–12	577	257	11:1	X	14
Missouri												
Chaminade College Preparatory School, St. Louis	X		X			6–8	9–12	770	495	10:1	X	21
Crossroads College Preparatory School, St. Louis			X	X		7–8	9–12	215	152	9:1	X	22
John Burroughs School, St. Louis			X	X		7–8	9–12	600	410	7:1	X	27
Lutheran High School, Kansas City			X	X			9–12	120	120	12:1		19
Lutheran High School North, St. Louis			X	X			9–12	341	341	10:1	X	13
Lutheran High School South, St. Louis			X	X			9–12	544	544	14:1	X	19
MU High School, Columbia			X	X							X	
Nerinx Hall, Webster Groves				X			9–12	631	631	10:1		13
New Covenant Academy, Springfield			X	X	JK–6	7–8	9–12	337	110	10:1		6
Thomas Jefferson School, St. Louis	X	X	X	X		7–8	9–PG	89	72	6:1	X	9
Valle Catholic High School, Ste. Genevieve			X	X			9–12	132	132	9:1	X	14
Vianney High School, St. Louis			X				9–12	622	622	12:1	X	22
Villa Duchesne and Oak Hill School, St. Louis			X	X	JK–6	7–8	9–12	710	333	9:1	X	13
Visitation Academy of St. Louis County, St. Louis			X	X	PK–6		7–12	633	468	9:1	X	14
Montana												
Manhattan Christian High School, Manhattan			X	X	PK–5	6–8	9–12	268	94	10:1	X	7
Nebraska												
Central Catholic Mid-High School, Grand Island			X	X		6–8	9–12	340	185	15:1	X	16
Duchesne Academy of the Sacred Heart, Omaha				X			9–12	303	303	9:1	X	16
Mercy High School, Omaha				X			9–12	360	360	12:1	X	25
Mount Michael Benedictine School, Elkhorn	X		X				9–12	206	206	7:1	X	21
Nebraska Christian Schools, Central City	X	X	X	X	K–6	7–8	9–12	215	116	10:1		6
Saint Cecilia High School, Hastings			X	X		6–8	9–12	262	162	5:1	X	23
Scotus Central Catholic High School, Columbus			X	X		7–8	9–12	369	241	12:1	X	13
Nevada												
Faith Lutheran High School, Las Vegas			X	X		6–8	9–12	1,318	716	17:1	X	23
The Meadows School, Las Vegas			X	X	PK–5	6–8	9–12	897	267	11:1	X	16
Sage Ridge School, Reno			X	X		5–8	9–12	227	91	8:1	X	15
New Hampshire												
Bishop Brady High School, Concord			X	X			9–12	365	365	15:1	X	29
Bishop Guertin High School, Nashua			X	X			9–12	900	900		X	35
Brewster Academy, Wolfeboro	X	X	X	X			9–PG	365	365	6:1	X	32
Cardigan Mountain School, Canaan	X		X			6–9		195	177	4:1		41
The Derryfield School, Manchester			X	X		6–8	9–12	381	248	8:1	X	20
Dublin School, Dublin	X	X	X	X			9–12	127	127	4:1	X	60
Hampshire Country School, Rindge	X		X		3–6		7–12	20	12	2:1		23
Kimball Union Academy, Meriden	X	X	X	X			9–PG	317	317	9:1	X	36
Portsmouth Christian Academy, Dover			X	X	PK–5	6–8	9–12	617	181	13:1	X	14
St. Thomas Aquinas High School, Dover			X	X			9–12	664	664	14:1	X	18
Trinity High School, Manchester			X	X			9–12	428	428	14:1	X	22
The White Mountain School, Bethlehem	X	X	X	X			9–PG	99	99	5:1	X	45
New Jersey												
Academy of Saint Elizabeth, Convent Station				X			9–12	245	245	9:1	X	12
The American Boychoir School, Princeton	X		X		4–5	6–8		48	27	6:1		21
Bishop Eustace Preparatory School, Pennsauken			X	X			9–12	767	767	13:1	X	20
Blair Academy, Blairstown	X	X	X	X			9–PG	454	454	7:1	X	40
Christian Brothers Academy, Lincroft			X				9–12	973	973	16:1	X	15
Community High School, Teaneck			X	X				184	184			7
DePaul Catholic High School, Wayne			X	X						19:1	X	35
Eastern Christian High School, North Haledon			X	X	PK–4	5–8	9–12	757	327	10:1	X	30
Gill St. Bernard's School, Gladstone			X	X	PK–4	5–8	9–12	703	308	7:1	X	23
Hawthorne Christian Academy, Hawthorne			X	X	PS–5	6–8	9–12	456	143	7:1		10
The Hun School of Princeton, Princeton	X	X	X	X		6–8	9–PG	597	502	8:1	X	35
Immaculate Conception High School, Lodi				X			9–12	167	167	10:1	X	14
The Lawrenceville School, Lawrenceville	X	X	X	X			9–PG	810	810	8:1		51
Marylawn of the Oranges, South Orange				X		7–8	9–12	143	127	15:1	X	11
Monsignor Donovan High School, Toms River			X	X			9–12	836	836	15:1	X	21
Montclair Kimberley Academy, Montclair			X	X	PK–3	4–8	9–12	997	435	6:1	X	22
Moorestown Friends School, Moorestown			X	X	PS–4	5–8	9–12	708	289	9:1	X	17
Morristown-Beard School, Morristown			X	X		6–8	9–12	548	397	7:1	X	23

Private Secondary Schools At-a-Glance

| | STUDENTS ACCEPTED | | | | GRADES | | | STUDENT/FACULTY | | | SCHOOL OFFERINGS | |
| | Boarding | | Day | | | | | | | | | |
	Boys	Girls	Boys	Girls	Lower	Middle	Upper	Total	Upper	Student/Faculty Ratio	Advanced Placement Preparation	Sports
Mt. Saint Dominic Academy, Caldwell				X			9–12	315	315	12:1	X	21
Newark Academy, Livingston			X	X		6–8	9–12	557	396	12:1	X	32
Notre Dame High School, Lawrenceville			X	X			9–12	1,266	1,266	23:1	X	30
Oak Knoll School of the Holy Child, Summit				X	K–6		7–12	544	314	8:1	X	17
Our Lady of Mercy Academy, Newfield				X			9–12	177	177	11:1		22
Peddie School, Hightstown	X	X	X	X			9–PG	550	550	6:1	X	24
The Pingry School, Martinsville			X	X	K–5	6–8	9–12	1,065	538	8:1	X	25
Pope John XXIII Regional High School, Sparta			X	X			8–12	961	961	13:1		19
Queen of Peace High School, North Arlington			X	X			9–12	525	525	15:1	X	29
Ranney School, Tinton Falls			X	X	N–5	6–8	9–12	807	231	9:1	X	17
Saint Augustine Preparatory School, Richland			X				9–12	681	681	13:1	X	23
St. Benedict's Preparatory School, Newark			X		7–8		9–12	561	475	11:1		21
Saint Joseph High School, Hammonton			X	X			9–12	520	520	17:1		27
Saint Joseph's High School, Metuchen			X				9–12	810	810	16:1	X	24
St. Peter's Preparatory School, Jersey City			X				9–12	905	905	12:1	X	31
Villa Walsh Academy, Morristown				X		7–8	9–12	254	224	8:1	X	11
New Mexico												
Menaul School, Albuquerque	X	X	X	X		6–8	9–12	175	104	9:1	X	10
Navajo Preparatory School, Inc., Farmington	X	X	X	X					183	15:1		8
Sandia Preparatory School, Albuquerque			X	X		6–8	9–12	659	327	10:1		32
Santa Fe Preparatory School, Santa Fe			X	X		7–8	9–12	323	208	10:1	X	16
The United World College—USA, Montezuma	X	X					11–12	206	206	8:1		50
New York												
Allendale Columbia School, Rochester			X	X	N–5	6–8	9–12	344	114	4:1	X	12
All Hallows High School, Bronx			X				9–12	640	640	15:1		18
The Beekman School, New York			X	X			9–PG	80	80	8:1	X	
The Birch Wathen Lenox School, New York			X	X	K–5	6–8	9–12	550	170	15:1		23
The Calhoun School, New York			X	X	N–4	5–8	9–12	724	184	6:1		16
Cathedral High School, New York				X			9–12	600	600	17:1		5
Christian Brothers Academy, Albany			X			6–8	9–12	360	279	17:1	X	25
Christian Brothers Academy, Syracuse			X				7–12	750	750		X	18
Christian Central Academy, Williamsville			X	X	K–5	6–8	9–12	423	124	10:1	X	9
Collegiate School, New York			X		K–4	5–8	9–12	642	225	4:1	X	14
Convent of the Sacred Heart, New York				X	PK–4	5–8	9–12	691	200	16:1	X	23
The Dalton School, New York			X	X	K–3	4–8	9–12	1,306	461	7:1	X	16
Doane Stuart School, Rensselaer			X	X	N–4	5–8	9–12	284	119	7:1	X	23
The Dominican Academy of the City of New York, New York				X			9–12	231	231	9:1	X	9
Emma Willard School, Troy		X		X			9–PG	319	319	5:1	X	37
The Family Foundation School, Hancock	X	X					9–12	125	125	4:1		28
Fontbonne Hall Academy, Brooklyn				X			9–12	521	521	14:1	X	17
Fordham Preparatory School, Bronx			X				9–12	974	974	11:1	X	22
French-American School of New York, Mamaroneck			X	X	N–5	6–8	9–12	825	162	7:1	X	8
Friends Academy, Locust Valley			X	X	N–5	6–8	9–12	751	374	6:1	X	17
Hackley School, Tarrytown	X	X	X	X	K–4	5–8	9–12	841	384	6:1	X	34
The Harley School, Rochester			X	X	N–4	5–8	9–12	492	160	7:1	X	15
Harmony Heights Residential and Day School, Oyster Bay		X		X			9–12	70	70	12:1		
The Harvey School, Katonah	X	X	X	X		6–8	9–12	330	250	7:1		21
Hebrew Academy-the Five Towns, Cedarhurst			X	X			9–12	488	488		X	7
The Hewitt School, New York				X	K–3	4–7	8–12	498	115	7:1	X	10
Hoosac School, Hoosick	X	X	X	X			8–PG	125	125	5:1	X	22
Houghton Academy, Houghton	X	X	X	X		6–8	9–PG	142	117	8:1	X	15
Iona Preparatory School, New Rochelle			X				9–12	741	741	13:1	X	36
The Karafin School, Mount Kisco			X	X			9–12	75	75	6:1	X	36
The Kew-Forest School, Forest Hills			X	X	PK–6	7–8	9–12	237	99	6:1	X	6
Kildonan School, Amenia	X	X	X	X	2–6	7–8	9–PG	91	50	2:1		39
Long Island Lutheran Middle and High School, Brookville			X	X		6–8	9–12	600	420	9:1	X	23
Loyola School, New York			X	X			9–12	202	202	9:1	X	16
Manlius Pebble Hill School, DeWitt			X	X	PK–5	6–8	9–12	588	250	6:1	X	25
Maplebrook School, Amenia	X	X	X	X				70	60	8:1		41
Martin Luther High School, Maspeth			X	X			9–12	211	211	12:1		19
The Masters School, Dobbs Ferry	X	X	X	X		5–8	9–12	580	415	6:1	X	30
Millbrook School, Millbrook	X	X	X	X			9–12	260	260	5:1	X	28
Mount Mercy Academy, Buffalo				X			9–12	273	273	20:1	X	13
The Nichols School, Buffalo			X	X		5–8	9–12	556	376	8:1	X	20
North Country School, Lake Placid	X	X	X	X			4–9	88	66	3:1		39
Northwood School, Lake Placid	X	X	X	X			9–12	181	181	6:1	X	49
Our Lady of Mercy High School, Rochester				X		7–8	9–12	707	557	12:1	X	17
The Park School of Buffalo, Snyder			X	X	N–4	5–8	9–12	242	106	8:1	X	36
Poughkeepsie Day School, Poughkeepsie			X	X	PK–5	6–8	9–12	290	9	7:1	X	27
Professional Children's School, New York			X	X		6–8	9–12	183	152	8:1		
Regis High School, New York			X				9–12	535	535	15:1	X	5
Riverdale Country School, Bronx			X	X	PK–5	6–8	9–12	1,127	493	8:1		22

Private Secondary Schools At-a-Glance

	Boarding		Day		GRADES			STUDENT/FACULTY			SCHOOL OFFERINGS	
	Boys	Girls	Boys	Girls	Lower	Middle	Upper	Total	Upper	Student/Faculty Ratio	Advanced Placement Preparation	Sports
Robert Louis Stevenson School, New York			X	X			7–PG	65	65	5:1		27
Rockland Country Day School, Congers			X	X	PK–5	6–8	9–12	130	61	8:1	X	9
Ross School, East Hampton	X	X	X	X	N–4	5–8	9–12	476	226	7:1	X	20
Rye Country Day School, Rye			X	X	PK–4	5–8	9–12	876	385	7:1	X	27
School of the Holy Child, Rye				X		5–8	9–12	345	250	7:1	X	20
Seton Catholic Central High School, Binghamton			X	X			9–12	330	330	23:1	X	20
Smith School, New York			X	X		7–8	9–12	54	42	4:1		7
Soundview Preparatory School, Yorktown Heights			X	X		6–8	9–12	75	64	5:1	X	8
The Spence School, New York				X	K–4	5–8	9–12	690	220	10:1	X	13
Trinity-Pawling School, Pawling	X		X			7–8	9–PG	300	280	8:1	X	39
Trinity School, New York			X	X	K–4	5–8	9–12	990	440	7:1	X	15
United Nations International School, New York			X	X	K–4	5–8	9–12	1,542	468	3:1		46
The Windsor School, Flushing			X	X		6–8	9–13	160	148	14:1	X	11
Winston Preparatory School, New York			X	X		6–8	9–12	203	167	3:1		15
York Preparatory School, New York			X	X		6–8	9–12	351	245	6:1	X	29
North Carolina												
Arendell Parrott Academy, Kinston			X	X	PK–5	6–8	9–12	741	236		X	19
Arthur Morgan School, Burnsville	X	X	X	X		7–9		22	22	2:1		26
Auldern Academy, Siler City		X				8–8	9–12	60	54	10:1	X	32
Bishop McGuinness Catholic High School, Kernersville			X	X			9–12	549	549	14:1	X	15
Cape Fear Academy, Wilmington			X	X	PK–5	6–8	9–12	628	238	7:1	X	11
Cary Academy, Cary			X	X		6–8	9–12	710	408	14:1	X	49
Charlotte Christian School, Charlotte			X	X	JK–5	6–8	9–12	989	360	11:1	X	22
Charlotte Country Day School, Charlotte			X	X	PK–4	5–8	9–12	1,602	480	12:1		21
Charlotte Latin School, Charlotte			X	X	K–5	6–8	9–12	1,383	475	7:1	X	20
Durham Academy, Durham			X	X	PK–4	5–8	9–12	1,135	384	12:1	X	24
Fayetteville Academy, Fayetteville			X	X	PK–5	6–8	9–12	403	143	14:1	X	12
Forsyth Country Day School, Lewisville			X	X	PK–4	5–8	9–12	909	386	12:1	X	17
Gaston Day School, Gastonia			X	X	PS–4	5–8	9–12	480	140	6:1	X	24
Greenfield School, Wilson			X	X	PS–4	5–8	9–12	298	74	3:1	X	7
Greensboro Day School, Greensboro			X	X	K–5	6–8	9–12	904	357	13:1	X	18
Harrells Christian Academy, Harrells			X	X	K–5	6–8	9–12	452	146	9:1	X	10
The Hill Center, Durham Academy, Durham			X	X	K–5	6–8	9–12	120	46	4:1		
Kerr-Vance Academy, Henderson			X	X	PK–6	7–8	9–12	472	132	10:1	X	14
Noble Academy, Greensboro			X	X	K–5	6–8	9–12	143	50	8:1		8
Oak Ridge Military Academy, Oak Ridge	X	X	X	X		7–8	9–12	65	50	11:1		25
The O'Neal School, Southern Pines			X	X	PK–4	5–8	9–12	410	149	12:1	X	11
Providence Day School, Charlotte			X	X	PK–5	6–8	9–12	1,501	534	12:1	X	23
St. David's School, Raleigh			X	X	K–4	5–8	9–12	611	195	7:1	X	16
Saint Mary's School, Raleigh		X		X			9–12	274	274	8:1	X	15
Salem Baptist Christian School, Winston-Salem			X	X	P3–4	5–8	9–12	391	132	10:1	X	8
Stone Mountain School, Black Mountain	X					6–8	9–12	58	39	4:1		39
Westchester Country Day School, High Point			X	X	K–5	6–8	9–12	419	160	7:1	X	15
Ohio												
Archbishop Alter High School, Kettering			X	X			9–12	650	650	15:1	X	20
Archbishop Hoban High School, Akron			X	X			9–12	857	857	15:1	X	23
Archbishop McNicholas High School, Cincinnati			X	X			9–12	677	677	14:1	X	18
Beaumont School, Cleveland Heights				X				442	442	12:1	X	10
Benedictine High School, Cleveland			X				9–12	352	352	11:1	X	22
Bishop Fenwick High School, Franklin			X	X			9–12	558	558	15:1	X	23
Central Catholic High School, Canton			X	X			9–12	444	444	16:1	X	13
Central Catholic High School, Toledo			X	X				1,070		17:1	X	
Cincinnati Country Day School, Cincinnati			X	X	PK–5	6–8	9–12	775	250	9:1	X	15
The Columbus Academy, Gahanna			X	X	PK–4	5–8	9–12	1,072	352	8:1	X	15
Columbus School for Girls, Columbus				X	PK–5	6–8	9–12	615	222	9:1	X	52
Gilmour Academy, Gates Mills	X	X	X	X	PK–6	7–8	9–12	713	428	10:1	X	37
Hawken School, Gates Mills			X	X	PS–5	6–8	9–12	942	425	9:1	X	16
Lake Ridge Academy, North Ridgeville			X	X	K–5	6–8	9–12	339	159	8:1	X	23
Lawrence School, Sagamore Hills			X	X	1–6	7–8	9–12	281	140	11:1		11
Lehman High School, Sidney			X	X			9–12	230	230	16:1	X	17
Lima Central Catholic High School, Lima			X	X			9–12	350	350	13:1	X	13
Magnificat High School, Rocky River				X			9–12	800	800	12:1	X	14
The Miami Valley School, Dayton			X	X	PK–5	6–8	9–12	439	188	9:1	X	18
Padua Franciscan High School, Parma			X	X			9–12	833	833	19:1	X	40
St. Francis de Sales High School, Toledo			X				9–12	604	604	14:1	X	17
Saint Joseph Academy High School, Cleveland				X			9–12	650	650	12:1	X	16
Saint Ursula Academy, Toledo				X			9–12	511	511	16:1	X	30
The Seven Hills School, Cincinnati			X	X	PK–5	6–8	9–12	966	266	9:1	X	13
Stephen T. Badin High School, Hamilton			X	X			9–12	449	449	17:1	X	16
The Wellington School, Columbus			X	X	PK–4	5–8	9–12	621	198	12:1	X	15
Western Reserve Academy, Hudson	X	X	X	X			9–PG	389	389	6:1	X	43

Private Secondary Schools At-a-Glance

| | STUDENTS ACCEPTED | | | | GRADES | | | STUDENT/FACULTY | | | SCHOOL OFFERINGS | |
| | Boarding | | Day | | | | | | | | | |
	Boys	Girls	Boys	Girls	Lower	Middle	Upper	Total	Upper	Student/Faculty Ratio	Advanced Placement Preparation	Sports
Oklahoma												
Bishop McGuinness Catholic High School, Oklahoma City			X	X	9–10		11–12	714	360	14:1	X	18
Cascia Hall Preparatory School, Tulsa			X	X		6–8	9–12	574	397	12:1	X	18
Rejoice Christian Schools, Owasso			X	X	P3–5	6–8	9–12	713	84	12:1		19
Oregon												
Blanchet School, Salem			X	X		6–8	9–12	396	270	18:1	X	15
Canyonville Christian Academy, Canyonville	X	X	X	X						15:1	X	11
Cascades Academy of Central Oregon, Bend					K–5	6–8	9–12	109	12	6:1		
The Catlin Gabel School, Portland			X	X	PS–5	6–8	9–12	728	287	8:1		48
Lifegate School, Eugene	X	X	X	X		6–8	9–12	44	30	10:1	X	5
Oak Hill School, Eugene			X	X	K–5	6–8	9–12	115	32	8:1	X	10
Oregon Episcopal School, Portland	X	X	X	X	PK–5	6–8	9–12	849	314	7:1	X	22
Pacific Crest Community School, Portland			X	X		7–8	9–12	85	70	9:1		12
St. Mary's School, Medford	X	X	X	X		6–8	9–12	448	311	11:1	X	26
Salem Academy, Salem			X	X	K–5	6–8	9–12	608	225	9:1	X	11
Wellsprings Friends School, Eugene			X	X			9–12	60	60	8:1		9
Western Mennonite School, Salem	X	X	X	X		6–8	9–12	251	159	14:1		6
Pennsylvania												
Academy of Notre Dame de Namur, Villanova				X		6–8	9–12	513	389	8:1		17
Academy of the New Church Boys' School, Bryn Athyn	X		X				9–12	124	124	8:1	X	6
Academy of the New Church Girls' School, Bryn Athyn		X		X				108	108	8:1	X	8
The Baldwin School, Bryn Mawr				X	PK–5	6–8	9–12	560	193	7:1	X	19
Blue Mountain Academy, Hamburg	X	X	X	X			9–12	216	216	12:1		6
Camphill Special School, Glenmore	X	X	X	X	K–5	6–8	9–13	105	63	5:1		
Cardinal O'Hara High School, Springfield												
Central Catholic High School, Pittsburgh			X				9–12	835	835	16:1	X	22
CFS, The School at Church Farm, Exton	X		X			7–8	9–12	183	149	7:1	X	17
Christopher Dock Mennonite High School, Lansdale			X	X			9–12	385	385	12:1	X	12
The Concept School, Westtown			X	X		6–8	9–12	33	24	8:1		11
Country Day School of the Sacred Heart, Bryn Mawr				X	PK–4	5–8	9–12	325	180	8:1	X	11
Delaware Valley Friends School, Paoli			X	X		6–8	9–12	187	148	5:1		15
Devon Preparatory School, Devon			X			6–8	9–12	275	197	10:1		11
The Episcopal Academy, Newtown Square			X	X	PK–5	6–8	9–12	1,223	509	7:1	X	30
Friends' Central School, Wynnewood			X	X	N–4	5–8	9–12	955	394	9:1		12
Friends Select School, Philadelphia			X	X	PK–5	6–8	9–12	536	165	15:1		10
George School, Newtown	X	X	X	X			9–12	539	539	7:1	X	21
Germantown Friends School, Philadelphia			X	X	K–5	6–8	9–12	861	346	9:1		16
Girard College, Philadelphia	X	X			1–6		7–12	530	348	16:1	X	32
Gwynedd Mercy Academy, Gwynedd Valley				X			9–12	387	387	11:1	X	14
The Haverford School, Haverford			X		PK–5	6–8	9–12	981	398	7:1		24
The Hill Top Preparatory School, Rosemont			X	X		5–9	9–12	75	45	4:1		34
Holy Ghost Preparatory School, Bensalem			X				9–12	502	502	11:1	X	18
Holy Name High School, Reading			X	X			9–12	461	461	13:1	X	15
Lancaster Mennonite High School, Lancaster	X	X	X	X	PK–5	6–8	9–12	1,481	640	15:1	X	11
Lehigh Valley Christian High School, Catasauqua			X	X			9–12	143	143	12:1	X	7
Mercy Vocational High School, Philadelphia			X	X					382	16:1		10
Merion Mercy Academy, Merion Station				X			9–12	484	484	9:1	X	15
MMI Preparatory School, Freeland			X	X		6–8	9–12	250	160	12:1	X	12
Moravian Academy, Bethlehem			X	X	PK–5	6–8	9–12	764	287	7:1	X	13
Mount Saint Joseph Academy, Flourtown				X			9–12	568	568	10:1	X	15
Notre Dame Junior/Senior High School, East Stroudsburg			X	X			7–12	258	258	15:1	X	14
The Oakland School, Pittsburgh			X	X			8–12	53	53	6:1		32
The Pathway School, Norristown			X	X				115	60	6:1		5
The Phelps School, Malvern	X		X				7–PG	138	138	5:1	X	31
Saint Basil Academy, Jenkintown				X			9–12	365	365	12:1	X	12
St. Joseph's Preparatory School, Philadelphia			X				9–12	987	987	16:1	X	27
Sewickley Academy, Sewickley			X	X	PK–5	6–8	9–12	733	294	8:1	X	16
Shady Side Academy, Pittsburgh	X	X	X	X	PK–5	6–8	9–12	931	486	8:1	X	24
The Shipley School, Bryn Mawr			X		PK–5	6–8	9–12	835	330	7:1	X	25
Springside School, Philadelphia				X	PK–4	5–8	9–12	655	239	7:1	X	33
Villa Joseph Marie High School, Holland				X			9–12	381	381	14:1	X	13
Villa Maria Academy, Erie			X	X			9–12	303	303	12:1	X	13
Winchester Thurston School, Pittsburgh			X	X	PK–5	6–8	9–12	642	242	8:1	X	25
Woodlynde School, Strafford			X	X	1–5	6–8	9–12	262	100	5:1		7
Wyoming Seminary, Kingston	X	X	X	X	PK–8		9–PG	771	427	10:1	X	38
York Catholic High School, York			X	X		7–8	9–12	656	465			20
York Country Day School, York			X	X	PS–5	6–8	9–12	206	57	4:1	X	13
Puerto Rico												
Colegio San Jose, San Juan			X			7–9	10–12	491	239		X	13

Private Secondary Schools At-a-Glance

	STUDENTS ACCEPTED				GRADES			STUDENT/FACULTY			SCHOOL OFFERINGS	
	Boarding		Day									
	Boys	Girls	Boys	Girls	Lower	Middle	Upper	Total	Upper	Student/Faculty Ratio	Advanced Placement Preparation	Sports
Commonwealth Parkville School, San Juan			X	X	PS–6	7–8	9–12	669	178	7:1	X	26
Fowlers Academy, Guaynabo			X	X		7–8	9–12	64	52	15:1		7
Wesleyan Academy, Guaynabo			X	X	PK–6	7–8	9–12	922	332	23:1	X	9
Rhode Island												
Mount Saint Charles Academy, Woonsocket			X	X			7–12	993	993	18:1	X	27
Portsmouth Abbey School, Portsmouth	X	X	X	X			9–12	373	373	8:1	X	22
The Prout School, Wakefield			X	X			9–12	640	640	18:1	X	27
Providence Country Day School, East Providence			X	X		6–8	9–12	233	183	7:1	X	19
St. Andrew's School, Barrington	X	X	X	X	3–5	6–8	9–12	213	162	4:1	X	30
St. George's School, Middletown	X	X	X	X			9–12	367	367	6:1	X	21
The Wheeler School, Providence			X	X	N–5	6–8	9–12	787	322	9:1	X	15
South Carolina												
The Byrnes Schools, Florence			X	X	PK–5	6–8	9–12	238	73	9:1	X	14
Christ Church Episcopal School, Greenville			X	X	K–4	5–8	9–12	990	323	10:1		17
Hank Haney International Junior Golf Academy, Hilton Head Island .	X	X	X	X			5–PG	140	140	10:1		1
Hilton Head Preparatory School, Hilton Head Island .			X	X	K–5	6–8	9–12	439	180	12:1	X	17
Porter-Gaud School, Charleston			X	X	1–5	6–8	9–12	896	354	15:1	X	21
St. Joseph's Catholic School, Greenville			X	X		6–8	9–12	594	347	12:1	X	16
Shannon Forest Christian School, Greenville			X	X	PK–5		6–12	445	217	17:1	X	11
Spartanburg Day School, Spartanburg			X	X	PK–4	5–8	9–12	487	141	9:1	X	16
Wilson Hall, Sumter			X	X	PS–5	6–8	9–12	837	250	13:1	X	33
South Dakota												
Dakota Christian High School, Corsica			X	X	PK–6	7–8	9–12	126	49	8:1		15
Freeman Academy, Freeman	X	X	X	X	5–8		9–12	70	46	5:1		7
Tennessee												
Baylor School, Chattanooga	X	X	X	X		6–8	9–12	1,053	732	8:1	X	50
Briarcrest Christian High School, Eads			X	X	PK–5	6–8	9–12	1,590	574	14:1	X	17
Chattanooga Christian School, Chattanooga			X	X	K–5	6–8	9–12	1,118	452	17:1	X	49
Collegedale Academy, Collegedale			X	X				363		17:1	X	11
Columbia Academy, Columbia			X	X	K–6		7–12	594	265	11:1	X	15
Currey Ingram Academy, Brentwood			X	X	K–4	5–8	9–12	280	67	4:1		9
David Lipscomb High School, Nashville			X	X	PK–4	5–8	9–12	1,386	538	15:1	X	13
Davidson Academy, Nashville			X	X	PK–6	7–8	9–12			10:1	X	15
Donelson Christian Academy, Nashville			X	X	K4–5	6–8	9–12	754	279	16:1	X	17
Father Ryan High School, Nashville			X	X			9–12	920	920	12:1	X	30
Franklin Road Academy, Nashville			X	X	PK–4	5–8	9–12	816	240	8:1	X	24
Friendship Christian School, Lebanon			X	X	PK–4	5–8	9–12	627	203	15:1	X	8
Girls Preparatory School, Chattanooga				X		6–8	9–12	607	376	8:1	X	45
Grace Baptist Academy, Chattanooga			X	X	K4–5	6–8	9–12	704	189	20:1		16
Harding Academy, Memphis			X	X	PS–6		7–12	1,276	528	13:1	X	13
Harding Academy, Nashville			X	X	K–5	6–8		480	100			23
Jackson Christian School, Jackson			X	X	JK–5	6–8	9–12	857	286	19:1		10
The King's Academy, Seymour	X	X	X	X	K4–5	6–8	9–12	402	143	14:1	X	22
Memphis University School, Memphis			X		7–8		9–12	658	432	8:1	X	13
Nashville Christian School, Nashville			X	X	K4–4	5–8	9–12	483	175	18:1	X	20
Notre Dame High School, Chattanooga			X	X			9–12	413	413	10:1	X	42
St. Benedict at Auburndale, Cordova			X	X			9–12	982	982	15:1	X	23
St. Cecilia Academy, Nashville				X			9–12	257	257	9:1	X	23
St. George's Independent School, Collierville			X	X	PK–5	6–8	9–12	1,189	367	7:1	X	15
St. Mary's Episcopal School, Memphis				X	PK–4	5–8	9–12	858	252	13:1	X	12
Trinity Christian Academy, Jackson			X	X	K4–5	6–8	9–12	752	249	9:1		11
University School of Jackson, Jackson			X	X	PK–5	6–8	9–12	1,232	348	13:1	X	16
The Webb School, Bell Buckle	X	X	X	X		6–8	9–PG	310	229	7:1	X	40
Webb School of Knoxville, Knoxville			X	X	K–5	6–8	9–12	1,040	464	10:1		19
Texas												
The Awty International School, Houston			X	X	PK–5	6–8	9–12	1,230	357	18:1		15
Central Catholic High School, San Antonio			X				9–12	535	535	12:1	X	20
Cistercian Preparatory School, Irving			X			5–8	9–12	356	178	7:1	X	14
Dallas Christian School, Mesquite			X		PK–5	6–8	9–12	595	226	12:1		12
Duchesne Academy of the Sacred Heart, Houston				X	PK–4	5–8	9–12	675	240	7:1	X	14
Episcopal High School, Bellaire			X	X			9–12	664	664	9:1	X	21
Fairhill School, Dallas			X	X	1–5	6–8	9–12	219	66	12:1		8
First Baptist Academy, Dallas			X	X	K–5	6–8	9–12	366	143	8:1	X	14
Gateway School, Arlington			X	X						8:1		6
Greenhill School, Addison			X	X	PK–4	5–8	9–12	1,273	453	18:1	X	32
Happy Hill Farm Academy, Granbury	X	X	X	X	K–6	7–8	9–12	125	45	7:1		17
Hillcrest School, Midland			X	X	1–5	6–8	9–12	34	23	10:1		14
Hill School of Fort Worth, Fort Worth			X	X								
Huntington-Surrey School, Austin			X	X			9–12	46	46	4:1		
Incarnate Word Academy, Houston				X			9–12	272	272	13:1	X	13
Jesuit College Preparatory School, Dallas			X				9–12	1,064	1,064	11:1	X	28

Private Secondary Schools At-a-Glance

	STUDENTS ACCEPTED				GRADES			STUDENT/FACULTY			SCHOOL OFFERINGS	
	Boarding		Day									
	Boys	Girls	Boys	Girls	Lower	Middle	Upper	Total	Upper	Student/Faculty Ratio	Advanced Placement Preparation	Sports
The John Cooper School, The Woodlands			X	X	PK–5	6–8	9–12	985	339	12:1	X	10
Key School, Fort Worth			X	X	K–3	4–8	9–12	76	23	4:1		
Lakehill Preparatory School, Dallas			X	X	K–4	5–8	9–12	400	110	10:1	X	14
Loretto Academy, El Paso			X	X	PK–5	6–8	9–12	659	348	13:1	X	13
Lydia Patterson Institute, El Paso			X	X			9–12	399	231	20:1	X	9
Marine Military Academy, Harlingen	X						8–12	402	402	12:1	X	27
Memorial Hall School, Houston			X	X	4–5	6–8	9–12	80	70	14:1		10
The Oakridge School, Arlington			X	X	PS–4	5–8	9–12	870	306	10:1	X	28
Presbyterian Pan American School, Kingsville	X	X	X	X			9–12	130	130	9:1		13
Prestonwood Christian Academy, Plano			X	X	PK–4	5–8	9–12	1,410	480	18:1	X	13
Providence Catholic School, The College Preparatory School for Girls Grades 6-12, San Antonio				X		6–8	9–12	346	206	11:1	X	21
St. Agnes Academy, Houston				X			9–12	864	864	15:1	X	18
St. Anthony Catholic High School, San Antonio	X	X	X	X			9–12	453	453	22:1	X	16
St. Mark's School of Texas, Dallas			X		1–4	5–8	9–12	854	367	8:1	X	41
Saint Mary's Hall, San Antonio			X	X	PK–5	6–8	9–PG	988	367	6:1	X	19
St. Pius X High School, Houston			X	X			9–12	689	689	12:1	X	15
St. Stephen's Episcopal School, Austin	X	X	X	X		6–8	9–12	668	460	8:1	X	34
St. Thomas High School, Houston			X				9–12	709	709	14:1	X	11
San Marcos Baptist Academy, San Marcos	X	X	X	X		7–8	9–12	271	219	5:1	X	26
Second Baptist School, Houston			X	X	PK–4	5–8	9–12				X	9
Shelton School and Evaluation Center, Dallas			X	X	PS–4	5–8	9–12	855	242	8:1		9
Southwest Christian School, Inc., Fort Worth			X	X	PK–6	7–8	9–12	929	315	11:1	X	21
Strake Jesuit College Preparatory, Houston			X				9–12	895	895	11:1	X	13
The Tenney School, Houston			X	X		6–8	9–12	65	54	2:1	X	
TMI—The Episcopal School of Texas, San Antonio	X	X	X	X		6–8	9–12	428	280	15:1	X	21
Trinity School of Texas, Longview			X	X	PK–5	6–8	9–12	326	64	8:1	X	12
Tyler Street Christian Academy, Dallas			X	X	P3–6	7–8	9–12	198	47	8:1	X	8
The Ursuline Academy of Dallas, Dallas				X			9–12	800	800	10:1	X	14
Westbury Christian School, Houston			X	X	PK–6	7–8	9–12	518	229	10:1	X	14
The Winston School San Antonio, San Antonio			X	X	K–6	7–8	9–12	189	85	8:1		14
Utah												
Aspen Ranch, Loa	X	X				7–8	9–12	72	66	8:1		29
Cedar Ridge Academy, Roosevelt	X	X	X	X			9–12	50	50	15:1		9
Cross Creek Programs, LaVerkin	X	X				7–8	9–12	86	66	15:1		22
Rowland Hall, Salt Lake City			X	X	PK–5	6–8	9–12	985	286	8:1	X	29
Salt Lake Lutheran High School, Salt Lake City			X	X			9–12	58	58	7:1		14
Sunhawk Adolescent Recovery Center, St. George	X	X					8–12	52	52	7:1		14
Wasatch Academy, Mt. Pleasant	X	X					8–12	250	250	10:1	X	69
The Waterford School, Sandy			X	X	PK–5	6–8	9–12	900	232	5:1	X	25
Vermont												
Burr and Burton Academy, Manchester	X	X	X	X			9–12	692	692	12:1	X	21
The Greenwood School, Putney	X							50		2:1		27
King George School, Sutton	X	X					9–12	60		3:1		40
Rock Point School, Burlington	X	X	X	X			9–12	29	29	5:1		34
Stratton Mountain School, Stratton Mountain	X	X	X	X		7–8	9–PG	120	92	6:1		15
Virgin Islands												
Kingshill School, St. Croix			X	X		7–8	9–PG	33	25	5:1		25
St. Croix Country Day School, Kingshill			X	X	N–6	7–8	9–12	460	166	12:1	X	12
Virginia												
Benedictine High School, Richmond			X				9–12	278	278	9:1	X	26
Bishop Denis J. O'Connell High School, Arlington			X	X				1,219	1,219	12:1	X	21
Bishop Ireton High School, Alexandria			X	X				822	822	14:1	X	25
The Blue Ridge School, St. George	X						9–12	195	195	5:1		48
Cape Henry Collegiate School, Virginia Beach			X	X	PK–5	6–8	9–12	924	369	10:1	X	45
Christchurch School, Christchurch	X		X	X	1–4	5–8	9–PG	204	204	7:1	X	32
The Collegiate School, Richmond			X	X	K–4	5–8	9–12	1,578	496	15:1	X	24
Episcopal High School, Alexandria	X	X					9–12	435	435	6:1	X	44
Fishburne Military School, Waynesboro	X		X			7–8	9–12	170	155	9:1		10
Flint Hill School, Oakton			X	X	JK–4	5–8	9–12	1,110	485	8:1	X	35
Foxcroft School, Middleburg		X		X			9–12	157	157	7:1		27
Fuqua School, Farmville			X	X	PK–5	6–8	9–12	431	145	16:1	X	12
Hampton Roads Academy, Newport News			X	X	PK–5	6–8	9–12	585	281	10:1	X	24
Hargrave Military Academy, Chatham	X		X			7–9	10–PG	310	260	12:1	X	48
Little Keswick School, Keswick	X							34		4:1		17
Norfolk Academy, Norfolk			X	X	1–6	7–9	10–12	1,230	347	10:1	X	26
Oakcrest School, McLean				X		6–8	9–12	187	120			
Oak Hill Academy, Mouth of Wilson	X	X	X	X			8–12	142	142	10:1		34
Oakland School, Keswick	X	X	X	X						5:1		35
Peninsula Catholic High School, Newport News			X	X			8–12	305	305	16:1		12
The Potomac School, McLean			X	X	K–3	4–8	9–12	1,005	407	6:1	X	26
Randolph-Macon Academy, Front Royal	X	X	X	X		6–8	9–PG	358	286	9:1	X	27
St. Catherine's School, Richmond				X	JK–4	5–8	9–12	909	278		X	36

Private Secondary Schools At-a-Glance

	Boarding Boys	Boarding Girls	Day Boys	Day Girls	Lower	Middle	Upper	Total	Upper	Student/Faculty Ratio	Advanced Placement Preparation	Sports
St. Christopher's School, Richmond			X		JK–5	6–8	9–12	952	281	6:1	X	26
St. Margaret's School, Tappahannock		X					8–12	123	123	6:1	X	26
St. Stephen's & St. Agnes School, Alexandria			X	X	JK–5	6–8	9–12	1,123	451	9:1	X	28
Tandem Friends School, Charlottesville			X	X		5–8	9–12	205	123	6:1	X	10
Tidewater Academy, Wakefield			X	X	PK–5	6–8	9–12	198	74	15:1	X	7
Washington												
Bishop Blanchet High School, Seattle			X	X			9–12	1,036	1,036	13:1	X	23
Cascade Christian Academy, Wenatchee			X	X	K–5	6–8	9–12	146	38	5:1		12
Charles Wright Academy, Tacoma			X	X	PK–5	6–8	9–12	668	274	8:1	X	23
Chrysalis School, Woodinville			X	X	K–6	7–8	9–12	257	198	5:1		
Crosspoint Academy, Bremerton			X	X	K–6		7–12	242	141	8:1		8
Eastside Catholic School, Sammamish			X	X		6–8	9–12	808		14:1	X	19
Explorations Academy, Bellingham			X	X				26	24	7:1	X	
Lakeside School, Seattle			X	X		5–8	9–12	793	534	9:1		19
The Northwest School, Seattle	X	X	X	X		6–8	9–12	462	326	9:1		14
Northwest Yeshiva High School, Mercer Island			X	X			9–12	79	79	4:1		5
The Overlake School, Redmond			X	X		5–8	9–12	531	294	9:1	X	36
Seattle Academy of Arts and Sciences, Seattle			X	X		6–8	9–12	619	374	9:1		23
Seattle Christian Schools, Seattle			X	X	K–6	7–8	9–12	567	219	12:1	X	19
Shoreline Christian, Shoreline			X	X	PS–6	7–8	9–12	222	76	7:1		8
University Prep, Seattle			X	X		6–8	9–12	501	289	9:1	X	32
West Sound Academy, Poulsbo	X	X	X	X		6–8	9–12	96	58	7:1	X	5
West Virginia												
The Linsly School, Wheeling	X	X	X	X	5–8		9–12	444	284	9:1	X	47
Wisconsin												
Catholic Central High School, Burlington			X	X			9–12	141	141	8:1	X	23
Fox Valley Lutheran High School, Appleton			X	X			9–12	563	563	14:1		13
Marquette University High School, Milwaukee			X				9–12	1,067	1,067	13:1	X	29
St. John's Northwestern Military Academy, Delafield	X		X			7–8	9–PG	300	225	12:1		14
Saint Joseph High School, Kenosha			X	X	K–5	6–8	9–12	654	304	20:1	X	15
University School of Milwaukee, Milwaukee			X	X	PK–4	5–8	9–12	1,058	357	9:1	X	16
Wyoming												
The Journeys School of Teton Science School, Jackson			X	X								
CANADA												
The Academy for Gifted Children (PACE), Richmond Hill, ON			X	X	1–3	4–7	8–12	295	119	15:1	X	43
Académie Ste Cécile International School, Windsor, ON	X	X	X	X	JK–8		9–12	236	113	15:1		25
Arrowsmith School, Toronto, ON			X	X	1–5	6–9	10–12	75	20	10:1		
Balmoral Hall School, Winnipeg, MB		X		X	N–5	6–8	9–12	414	190	7:1	X	67
Bishop's College School, Sherbrooke, QC	X	X	X	X		7–9	10–12	236	169	12:1	X	46
Branksome Hall, Toronto, ON		X		X	JK–6	7–8	9–12	870	445	18:1		40
Brentwood College School, Mill Bay, BC	X	X	X	X			9–12	435	435	9:1	X	43
Columbia International College of Canada, Hamilton, ON	X	X	X	X		7–9	10–12	1,400	1,216	20:1	X	44
Community Hebrew Academy, Toronto, ON			X	X			9–12	1,400	1,400	8:1		17
Concordia High School, Edmonton, AB	X	X	X	X				137		10:1		14
The Country Day School, King City, ON			X	X	JK–6	7–8	9–12	720	320	10:1	X	25
Covenant Canadian Reformed School, Neerlandia, AB			X	X	K–6	7–9	10–12	177	26	10:1		17
Crawford Adventist Academy, Willowdale, ON			X	X	JK–6	7–8	9–12	189	189	16:1	X	13
Eastside Christian Academy, Calgary, AB			X	X	K–6	7–9	10–12	97	26	25:1		6
Foothills Academy, Calgary, AB			X	X	1–6	7–8	9–12	200	102	12:1		43
Fraser Academy, Vancouver, BC			X	X	1–7		8–12	191	116	3:1		25
Glen Eden School, Vancouver, BC			X	X						5:1		
Glenlyon Norfolk School, Victoria, BC			X	X	JK–5	6–8	9–12	673	246	8:1		27
Grace Christian School, Charlottetown, PE			X	X	JK–6	7–9	10–12	124	23	10:1		5
Hamilton District Christian High, Ancaster, ON			X	X			9–12	480	480	19:1	X	25
Hawthorn School for Girls, North York, ON				X				145				
Heritage Christian Academy, Calgary, AB			X	X	K–5	6–9	10–12	568	97	9:1		17
Heritage Christian School, Jordan, ON			X	X	K–8		9–12	571	171	15:1		5
Immanuel Christian High School, Lethbridge, AB			X	X		7–9	10–12	228	116	19:1		9
King's-Edgehill School, Windsor, NS	X	X	X	X		6–9	10–12	290	200	10:1		33
Kingsway College, Oshawa, ON	X	X	X	X			9–12	185	185	11:1		18
Lakefield College School, Lakefield, ON	X	X	X	X			7–12	371	371	7:1	X	31
The Laureate Academy, Winnipeg, MB			X	X	1–5	6–8	9–12	95	45	6:1		36
Lighthouse Christian School, Sylvan Lake, AB			X	X	PK–5	6–9	10–12	84	22	15:1		
Luther College High School, Regina, SK	X	X	X	X			9–12	370	370	16:1		21

Quick-Reference Chart
CANADA

Private Secondary Schools At-a-Glance

| | STUDENTS ACCEPTED | | | | GRADES | | | STUDENT/FACULTY | | | SCHOOL OFFERINGS | |
| | Boarding | | Day | | | | | | | | | |
	Boys	Girls	Boys	Girls	Lower	Middle	Upper	Total	Upper	Student/Faculty Ratio	Advanced Placement Preparation	Sports
MacLachlan College, Oakville, ON			X	X	PK–8		9–12	344	133	10:1	X	39
Meadowridge School, Maple Ridge, BC			X	X	JK–5		6–12	511	196	9:1		12
Miss Edgar's and Miss Cramp's School, Montreal, QC				X	K–5	6–8	9–11	335	115	9:1	X	26
MPS Etobicoke, Toronto, ON			X	X	JK–6	7–8	9–12	318	135	14:1		27
Niagara Christian Community of Schools, Fort Erie, ON	X	X	X	X	JK–6	7–8	9–12	266	191	17:1		17
Pickering College, Newmarket, ON	X	X	X	X	JK–8		9–12	400	230	9:1		35
Pic River Private High School, Heron Bay, ON			X	X						10:1		
Pinehurst School, St. Catharines, ON	X	X			7–8	9–10	11–12	26	13	10:1		68
Providence Christian School, Monarch, AB			X	X	K–6	7–9	10–12	134	29	11:1		
Quinte Christian High School, Belleville, ON			X	X			9–12	161	161	15:1		8
Ridley College, St. Catharines, ON	X	X	X	X	JK–8		9–PG	591	416	8:1	X	77
Rocklyn Academy, Meaford, ON		X					9–12	27	27	3:1		25
Ron Pettigrew Christian School, Dawson Creek, BC			X	X	JK–6	7–8	9–12	88	25	5:1		
Rosseau Lake College, Rosseau, ON	X	X	X	X		7–8	9–12	105	86	6:1		82
Rothesay Netherwood School, Rothesay, NB	X	X	X	X		6–8	9–12	244	187	8:1		48
Royal Canadian College, Vancouver, BC			X	X		9–10	11–12	54	41	15:1		5
Rundle College, Calgary, AB			X	X	PK–6	7–9	10–12	783	245	14:1		23
Sacred Heart School of Halifax, Halifax, NS			X	X	K–6		7–12	485	285	15:1	X	17
St. Andrew's College, Aurora, ON	X		X			6–8	9–12	580	444	9:1	X	62
St. Andrew's Regional High School, Victoria, BC			X	X		8–9	10–12			14:1	X	13
St. Ann's Academy, Kamloops, BC			X	X	K–6	7–9	10–12	528	166	24:1		14
St. Clement School, Ottawa, ON			X	X		7–8	9–12	37	25	3:1		11
St. Clement's School, Toronto, ON				X	1–6	7–9	10–12	455	180	7:1	X	37
St. George's School, Vancouver, BC	X		X		1–7		8–12	1,157	761	10:1	X	33
St. George's School of Montreal, Montreal, QC			X	X	K–6		7–11	445	255	17:1	X	44
St. John's-Ravenscourt School, Winnipeg, MB	X	X	X	X	K–5	6–8	9–12	836	373	9:1	X	31
St. Jude's School, Kitchener, ON			X	X	1–6	7–9	10–12	30	10	6:1		13
St. Michael's College School, Toronto, ON			X			7–8	9–12	1,072	861	16:1	X	23
St. Michaels University School, Victoria, BC	X	X	X	X	K–5	6–8	9–12	934	570	10:1	X	56
St. Patrick's Regional Secondary, Vancouver, BC			X	X				500			X	6
St. Paul's High School, Winnipeg, MB			X				9–12	585	585	14:1	X	21
Scarborough Christian School, North York, ON			X	X	JK–8			78	29	7:1		8
Scholar's Hall Preparatory School, Kitchener, ON			X	X	JK–3	4–8	9–12	105	35	10:1		23
Selwyn House School, Westmount, QC			X		K–6	7–8	9–11	546	184	8:1	X	19
Shoore Centre for Learning, Toronto, ON			X	X		6–8	9–12	30	22	6:1		
Solomon College, Edmonton, AB			X	X				15	15	10:1		
Southern Ontario College, Hamilton, ON			X	X						15:1		
Toronto District Christian High School, Woodbridge, ON			X	X			9–12	430	421	14:1		10
Town Centre Private High School, Markham, ON			X	X	PK–8		9–12	192	192	15:1	X	21
Trafalgar Castle School, Whitby, ON		X		X		5–8	9–12	189	114	9:1	X	28
Trinity College School, Port Hope, ON	X	X	X	X		5–8	9–12	590	475	8:1	X	41
Venta Preparatory School, Ottawa, ON	X	X	X	X	1–7		8–10	96	37	6:1		8
West Island College, Calgary, AB			X	X		7–9	10–12	464	207	17:1	X	35
Willow Wood School, Don Mills, ON			X	X	1–6	7–8	9–12	191	105	7:1		34

INTERNATIONAL

Australia

SCECGS Redlands, Cremorne			X	X	PK–5	6–8	9–12	1,500				19

Bangladesh

American International School, Dhaka, Dhaka			X	X	PK–5	6–8	9–12	753	208	15:1		7

Bermuda

Saltus Grammar School, Hamilton			X	X	K–5	6–8	9–12	1,015	238	13:1	X	22

Colombia

Colegio Nueva Granada, Bogota			X	X	PK–5	6–8	9–12	1,801	527	22:1	X	8

Costa Rica

American International School of Costa Rica, San Jose			X	X	PK–6	7–8	9–12	199	47	10:1	X	7

Ecuador

Alliance Academy, Quito	X	X	X	X	PK–6	7–8	9–12	531	167	6:1		23

France

The Lycee International, American Section, Saint-Germain-en-Laye Cedex			X	X	PK–5	6–9	10–12	705	200	18:1	X	13

Germany

Bavarian International School, Haimhausen			X	X	PK–5	6–9	10–12	854	243	7:1		41
Berlin International School, Berlin					1–5	6–8	9–12	820	240	11:1		15

www.facebook.com/sec.schools

Private Secondary Schools At-a-Glance

	Boarding Boys	Boarding Girls	Day Boys	Day Girls	Lower	Middle	Upper	Total	Upper	Student/Faculty Ratio	Advanced Placement Preparation	Sports
International School Hamburg, Hamburg			X	X	PK–5	6–8	9–12	669	195	8:1		19
Munich International School, Starnberg			X	X	PK–4	5–8	9–12	1,215	416	6:1		25
Greece												
American Community Schools of Athens, Athens			X	X	JK–5	6–8	9–12	859	342	17:1	X	11
International School of Athens, Kifissia—Athens			X	X	PK–6	7–9	10–12	358	123	9:1		9
India												
American School of Bombay, Mumbai	X	X	X	X	PK–5	6–8	9–12	700	181	5:1		13
Woodstock School, Uttarakhand	X	X	X	X	N–6		7–12	522	417	17:1	X	29
Italy												
American School of Milan, Noverasco di Opera, Milan			X	X	N–5	6–8	9–12	658	180	9:1		14
Marymount International School, Rome			X	X	PK–5	6–8	9–12	637	201	15:1		7
Japan												
Canadian Academy, Kobe	X	X	X	X	PK–5	6–8	9–13	690	223	10:1	X	9
Saint Maur International School, Yokohama			X	X	PK–5	6–8	9–12	434	122	5:1	X	7
Seisen International School, Tokyo			X	X	K–6	7–8	9–12	680	162	3:1		12
Yokohama International School, Yokohama			X	X	N–5	6–8	9–12	670	238	8:1		22
Kuwait												
New English School, Hawalli			X	X	K–2	4–6	7–13	2,249	1,161	12:1		16
New English School, Kuwait			X	X	K–2	4–6	7–13	2,249	1,161	12:1		16
Malaysia												
The International School of Kuala Lumpur, Ampang, Selangor			X	X	PK–5	6–8	9–13	1,588	604	9:1	X	42
Malta												
Verdala International School, Pembroke	X	X	X	X	PK–5	6–8	9–12	310	109	7:1		6
Netherlands												
American School of The Hague, Wassenaar			X	X	PS–4	5–8	9–12	1,035	363	7:1	X	11
International School of Amsterdam, Amstelveen			X	X	PS–5	6–8	9–12	895	218	6:1		6
Rotterdam International Secondary School, Wolfert van Borselen, Rotterdam			X	X	6–8	9–10	11–12	193	76	10:1		8
Peru												
Colegio Franklin D. Roosevelt, Lima 12			X	X	N–5	6–8	9–12	1,452	388	11:1		16
Philippines												
International School Manila, 1634 Taguig City			X	X	PK–4	5–8	9–12	1,966	722	9:1	X	19
Portugal												
Carlucci American International School of Lisbon, Linhó, Sintra.			X	X	PK–5	6–8	9–12	523	158	8:1		6
Puerto Rico												
Robinson School, San Juan	X	X	X	X	PK–6	7–8	9–12	604	211	18:1	X	27
Republic of Korea												
Seoul Foreign School, Seoul			X	X	PK–5	6–8	9–12	1,414	433	10:1	X	12
Spain												
The American School of Madrid, Madrid			X	X	PK–5	6–8	9–12	868	284	8:1		8
International College Spain, Madrid			X	X	PK–5	6–8	9–12	709	222	9:1		25
Switzerland												
Ecole d'Humanité, CH 6085 Hasliberg Goldern	X	X	X	X					110	5:1	X	40
International School of Berne, Guemligen 3073			X	X	PK–5		6–12	246	152	5:1		13
International School of Zug and Luzern (ISZL), Baar .			X	X	1–5	6–8	9–12	1,189	269	6:1	X	36
TASIS, The American School in Switzerland, Montagnola-Lugano	X	X	X	X	1–6	7–8	9–PG	599	339	5:1	X	35
Taiwan												
Taipei American School, Taipei			X	X	PK–5	6–8	9–12	2,163	867	11:1	X	11
Thailand												
International School Bangkok, Pakkret			X	X	PK–5	6–8	9–12	1,818	705	10:1	X	15
United Kingdom												
The American School in London, London			X	X	PK–4	5–8	9–12	1,346	464	10:1	X	17
Harrow School, Middlesex	X				9–9	10–11	12–13	820	330	8:1	X	57
The International School of London, London			X	X	K–6	7–10	11–13	340	60	8:1		7
Marymount International School, Surrey		X		X		6–8	9–12	212	169	7:1		17
Merchiston Castle School, Edinburgh	X		X						196	9:1		26

Traditional Day and
Boarding Schools

ABUNDANT LIFE ACADEMY

220 West 300 North
Kanab, Utah 84741
Head of School: Mr. Rod Quarnberg

General Information Coeducational boarding and day college-preparatory, general academic, vocational, and religious studies school, affiliated with Christian faith; primarily serves underachievers, individuals with Attention Deficit Disorder, and individuals with emotional and behavioral problems. Boarding grades 7–12, day grades 9–12. Founded: 2000. Setting: rural. Nearest major city is St George. Students are housed in single-sex dormitories. 1-acre campus. 2 buildings on campus. Approved or accredited by Association of Christian Schools International, Northwest Accreditation Commission, and Utah Department of Education. Total enrollment: 58. Upper school average class size: 5. Upper school faculty-student ratio: 1:8.

Upper School Student Profile Grade 8: 2 students (1 boy, 1 girl); Grade 9: 9 students (5 boys, 4 girls); Grade 10: 22 students (12 boys, 10 girls); Grade 11: 20 students (10 boys, 10 girls); Grade 12: 5 students (2 boys, 3 girls). 100% of students are boarding students. 1% are state residents. 26 states are represented in upper school student body. 3% are international students. International students from Canada and Cayman Islands. 100% of students are Christian.

Faculty School total: 7. In upper school: 4 men, 2 women; 3 have advanced degrees.

Subjects Offered 1½ elective credits, 20th century American writers, 20th century history, 20th century physics, 20th century world history, algebra, American government, American history, American history-AP, American literature, American literature-AP, anatomy, animal behavior, animal husbandry, athletic training, athletics, auto mechanics, band, baseball, basketball, Bible, Bible studies, biology, biology-AP, British literature, British literature-AP, calculus, calculus-AP, cheerleading, chemistry, chemistry-AP, Christian scripture, Christian studies, Christianity, constitutional history of U.S., English, English composition, English literature, English literature and composition-AP, English literature-AP, English-AP, English/composition-AP, equestrian sports, equine management, general math, general science, geography, geometry, guitar, health, health and safety, health and wellness, health education, history, history-AP, math applications, New Testament, science, scripture, Spanish, Spanish language-AP, student government.

Graduation Requirements We individualize the student requirements by the state in which they reside.

Special Academic Programs Honors section; accelerated programs.

College Admission Counseling 9 students graduated in 2009; 8 went to college. Other: 1 went to work.

Student Life Upper grades have uniform requirement, student council, honor system. Discipline rests equally with students and faculty. Attendance at religious services is required.

Tuition and Aid 7-day tuition and room/board: $1063. Guaranteed tuition plan. Tuition installment plan (monthly payment plans, individually arranged payment plans). Tuition reduction for siblings available. In 2009–10, 15% of upper-school students received aid. Total amount of financial aid awarded in 2009–10: $250,000.

Admissions Deadline for receipt of application materials: none. Application fee required: $2430. Interview required.

Athletics Interscholastic: baseball (boys), basketball (b,g), cheering (g), fitness (b,g), football (b), horseback riding (b,g), softball (g), table tennis (b), volleyball (g), weight lifting (b), weight training (b,g), wrestling (b); intramural: dance team (g), equestrian sports (g). 2 coaches, 2 athletic trainers.

Computers Computers are regularly used in all classes. The school has a published electronic and media policy.

Contact Mr. Ron Tuit, Admissions Director. 505-506-8703. Fax: 435-644-8293. E-mail: ron@abundantlifeacademy.com. Web site: www.abundantlifeacademy.com.

ACADEMIA BRITANICA CUSCATLECA

Apartado Postal 121
Santa Tecla, El Salvador
Head of School: Mr. J. George Hobson

General Information Coeducational day college-preparatory school. Grades PK–12. Founded: 1971. Setting: suburban. Nearest major city is San Salvador, El Salvador. 12.5-acre campus. 10 buildings on campus. Approved or accredited by European Council of International Schools, Headmasters' Conference, and International Baccalaureate Organization. Languages of instruction: English and Spanish. Total enrollment: 1,414. Upper school average class size: 16. Upper school faculty-student ratio: 1:9. There are 182 required school days per year for Upper School students. Upper School students typically attend 5 days per week. The average school day consists of 5 hours and 15 minutes.

Faculty School total: 128. In upper school: 30 men, 20 women; 8 have advanced degrees.

Graduation Requirements International Baccalaureate Diploma courses.

Special Academic Programs International Baccalaureate program.

College Admission Counseling 68 students graduated in 2009; all went to college.

Student Life Upper grades have uniform requirement, student council, honor system. Discipline rests equally with students and faculty.

Tuition and Aid Day student tuition: $5481. Tuition installment plan (monthly payment plans). Tuition reduction for siblings, merit scholarship grants, merit-based scholarship for those entering 11th and 12th grade available. In 2009–10, 2% of

upper-school students received aid; total upper-school merit-scholarship money awarded: $2500. Total amount of financial aid awarded in 2009–10: $25,000.

Admissions Traditional secondary-level entrance grade is 9. For fall 2009, 36 students applied for upper-level admission, 10 were accepted, 10 enrolled. Admissions testing required. Deadline for receipt of application materials: none. Application fee required: $40. Interview required.

Athletics Interscholastic: ballet (girls), basketball (b,g), soccer (b,g), swimming and diving (b,g), track and field (b,g), volleyball (b,g); intramural: basketball (b,g), hockey (b,g), in-line hockey (b), running (b,g), soccer (b,g), street hockey (b), swimming and diving (b,g), track and field (b,g), volleyball (b,g); coed interscholastic: archery, cricket, outdoor education, outdoor skills, soccer, swimming and diving, table tennis, track and field, volleyball; coed intramural: archery, badminton, cricket, deck hockey, field hockey, floor hockey, in-line hockey, indoor hockey, indoor soccer, physical fitness, running, sailing, soccer, swimming and diving, table tennis, tennis, volleyball. 8 PE instructors, 15 coaches.

Computers Computers are regularly used in all academic classes. Computer network features include on-campus library services, online commercial services, Internet access, wireless campus network, Internet filtering or blocking technology. Campus intranet, student e-mail accounts, and computer access in designated common areas are available to students. The school has a published electronic and media policy.

Contact Ms. Estefania Chacon, Admissions Assistant. 503-22414413. Fax: 503-22282956. E-mail: estefaniachacon@abc-net.edu.sv. Web site: www.abc.edu.sv.

THE ACADEMY AT CHARLEMONT

1359 Route 2
The Mohawk Trail
Charlemont, Massachusetts 01339
Head of School: Mr. Todd A. Sumner

General Information Coeducational day college-preparatory and arts school. Grades 7–PG. Founded: 1981. Setting: rural. Nearest major city is Springfield. 52-acre campus. 3 buildings on campus. Approved or accredited by New England Association of Schools and Colleges and Massachusetts Department of Education. Member of National Association of Independent Schools. Endowment: $307,000. Total enrollment: 114. Upper school average class size: 17. Upper school faculty-student ratio: 1:7. There are 166 required school days per year for Upper School students. Upper School students typically attend 5 days per week. The average school day consists of 7 hours.

Upper School Student Profile Grade 9: 20 students (12 boys, 8 girls); Grade 10: 20 students (12 boys, 8 girls); Grade 11: 19 students (10 boys, 9 girls); Grade 12: 16 students (7 boys, 9 girls).

Faculty School total: 18. In upper school: 9 men, 9 women; 6 have advanced degrees.

Subjects Offered Algebra, American legal systems, American literature, art, art history, biology, calculus, chemistry, computer science, creative writing, drama, earth science, ecology, English, English literature, environmental science, ethics, European history, expository writing, fine arts, French, geography, geometry, government/civics, grammar, health, history, Latin, mathematics, music, philosophy, photography, physical education, physics, religion, Russian, science, social studies, Spanish, speech, theater, trigonometry, world history, world literature, zoology.

Graduation Requirements Algebra, American government, American literature, American studies, arts and fine arts (art, music, dance, drama), biology, calculus, chemistry, civics, computer literacy, English, foreign language, four units of summer reading, geography, geometry, Latin, mathematics, physics, pre-calculus, science, senior project, social studies (includes history), Year-long senior project equal to one full course, requiring outside evaluation and a presentation.

Special Academic Programs Independent study; study abroad.

College Admission Counseling 15 students graduated in 2010; all went to college, including Berklee College of Music; Guilford College; Middlebury College; Skidmore College; University of Vermont; Williams College. Mean SAT critical reading: 657, mean SAT math: 591, mean SAT writing: 634, mean combined SAT: 1881, mean composite ACT: 27.

Student Life Upper grades have specified standards of dress, student council, honor system. Discipline rests primarily with faculty.

Summer Programs Sports, art/fine arts programs offered; session focuses on drama, music, soccer, recording; held on campus; accepts boys and girls; open to students from other schools. 2011 schedule: June 28 to August 6. Application deadline: June 15.

Tuition and Aid Day student tuition: $22,600. Tuition installment plan (monthly payment plans, individually arranged payment plans). Need-based scholarship grants available. In 2010–11, 70% of upper-school students received aid. Total amount of financial aid awarded in 2010–11: $1,000,000.

Admissions Traditional secondary-level entrance grade is 9. For fall 2010, 40 students applied for upper-level admission, 38 were accepted, 28 enrolled. School's own test and writing sample required. Deadline for receipt of application materials: February 15. Application fee required: $30. On-campus interview required.

Athletics Interscholastic: alpine skiing (boys, girls), basketball (b,g), cross-country running (b,g), lacrosse (b,g), skiing (downhill) (b,g), soccer (b,g), ultimate Frisbee (b,g); intramural: indoor soccer (b,g); coed interscholastic: basketball; coed intramural: aerobics/dance, alpine skiing, basketball, bicycling, bocce, canoeing/kayaking, cooperative games, croquet, hiking/backpacking, kayaking, outdoor activities, outdoor recreation, rafting, skiing (cross-country), skiing (downhill), soccer, tennis, ultimate Frisbee, yoga. 7 coaches.

Computers Computers are regularly used in all classes. Computer network features include on-campus library services, Internet access, wireless campus network, Internet filtering or blocking technology, school Website for schedules and other administrative information. Student e-mail accounts and computer access in designated common areas are available to students. Students grades are available online. The school has a published electronic and media policy.

Contact Sandy Warren, Director of Admissions. 413-339-4912. Fax: 413-339-4324. E-mail: swarren@charlemont.org. Web site: www.charlemont.org.

ACADEMY AT SWIFT RIVER
Cummington, Massachusetts
See Special Needs Schools section.

ACADEMY AT THE LAKES
2331 Collier Parkway
Land O'Lakes, Florida 34639
Head of School: Mr. Mark Heller
General Information Coeducational day college-preparatory and arts school. Grades PK–12. Founded: 1992. Setting: suburban. Nearest major city is Tampa. 9-acre campus. 9 buildings on campus. Approved or accredited by Florida Council of Independent Schools, Southern Association of Colleges and Schools, and Florida Department of Education. Total enrollment: 380. Upper school average class size: 14. Upper school faculty-student ratio: 1:5. There are 176 required school days per year for Upper School students. Upper School students typically attend 5 days per week. The average school day consists of 7 hours and 15 minutes.
Upper School Student Profile Grade 9: 28 students (13 boys, 15 girls); Grade 10: 31 students (10 boys, 21 girls); Grade 11: 23 students (12 boys, 11 girls); Grade 12: 30 students (10 boys, 20 girls).
Faculty School total: 55. In upper school: 13 men, 10 women; 13 have advanced degrees.
Graduation Requirements Standard curriculum.
Special Academic Programs 8 Advanced Placement exams for which test preparation is offered; honors section.
College Admission Counseling 29 students graduated in 2010; all went to college, including Rollins College; The Johns Hopkins University; The University of Tampa; University of South Florida; Yale University.
Student Life Upper grades have specified standards of dress, student council, honor system. Discipline rests primarily with faculty.
Tuition and Aid Day student tuition: $16,680. Tuition installment plan (monthly payment plans). Merit scholarship grants, need-based scholarship grants available. In 2010–11, 24% of upper-school students received aid.
Admissions Traditional secondary-level entrance grade is 9. For fall 2010, 189 students applied for upper-level admission, 150 were accepted, 106 enrolled. SSAT required. Deadline for receipt of application materials: none. Application fee required: $50. Interview required.
Athletics Interscholastic: baseball (boys), basketball (b,g), cheering (g), cross-country running (b,g), football (b), golf (b,g), physical fitness (b,g), physical training (b,g), soccer (b,g), softball (g), strength & conditioning (b,g), swimming and diving (b,g), tennis (b,g), touch football (b), track and field (b,g), volleyball (g), weight training (b,g), winter soccer (b,g); coed interscholastic: physical fitness, physical training, soccer, strength & conditioning, weight training. 3 PE instructors, 11 coaches, 1 athletic trainer.
Computers Computer network features include on-campus library services, Internet access, wireless campus network, Internet filtering or blocking technology. Students grades are available online. The school has a published electronic and media policy.
Contact Mrs. Melissa Starkey, Associate Director of Admissions. 813-909-7919. Fax: 813-949-0563. E-mail: mstarkey@academyatthelakes.org. Web site: http://www.academyatthelakes.org/.

THE ACADEMY FOR GIFTED CHILDREN (PACE)
12 Bond Crescent
Richmond Hill, Ontario L4E 3K2, Canada
Head of School: Barbara Rosenberg
General Information Coeducational day college-preparatory and intellectually gifted school. Grades 1–12. Founded: 1993. Setting: suburban. Nearest major city is Toronto, Canada. 3-acre campus. 1 building on campus. Approved or accredited by Ontario Ministry of Education and Ontario Department of Education. Language of instruction: English. Total enrollment: 295. Upper school average class size: 17. Upper school faculty-student ratio: 1:15. There are 187 required school days per year for Upper School students. Upper School students typically attend 5 days per week. The average school day consists of 6 hours.
Upper School Student Profile Grade 6: 32 students (17 boys, 15 girls); Grade 7: 26 students (14 boys, 12 girls); Grade 8: 36 students (24 boys, 12 girls); Grade 9: 17

students (10 boys, 7 girls); Grade 10: 20 students (10 boys, 10 girls); Grade 11: 24 students (17 boys, 7 girls); Grade 12: 22 students (14 boys, 8 girls).
Faculty School total: 27. In upper school: 5 men, 6 women; 3 have advanced degrees.
Subjects Offered 20th century world history, Advanced Placement courses, algebra, analytic geometry, biology, calculus, calculus-AP, Canadian geography, Canadian history, Canadian law, career education, chemistry, chemistry-AP, civics, computer programming, computer science, computer science-AP, computer studies, dramatic arts, English, finite math, French, French as a second language, geometry, health education, language, law, literature, mathematics, modern Western civilization, music, philosophy, physical education, physics, science, sociology, visual arts, world civilizations, writing.
Graduation Requirements Advanced chemistry, advanced math, algebra, analytic geometry, biology, calculus, Canadian geography, Canadian history, Canadian literature, career education, chemistry, civics, drawing, English literature, French as a second language, healthful living, law, music, philosophy, pre-algebra, pre-calculus, science, senior humanities, social sciences, sociology, theater arts, visual arts, minimum of 40 hours of community service, OSSLT.
Special Academic Programs 5 Advanced Placement exams for which test preparation is offered; honors section; academic accommodation for the gifted.
College Admission Counseling 20 students graduated in 2010; all went to college, including Harvard University; McMaster University; Queen's University at Kingston; The University of Western Ontario; University of Toronto. Median SAT critical reading: 780, median SAT math: 800, median SAT writing: 780, median combined SAT: 2360. 100% scored over 600 on SAT critical reading, 100% scored over 600 on SAT math, 100% scored over 600 on SAT writing, 100% scored over 1800 on combined SAT.
Student Life Upper grades have student council. Discipline rests primarily with faculty.
Tuition and Aid Day student tuition: CAN$11,000. Tuition installment plan (monthly payment plans).
Admissions Traditional secondary-level entrance grade is 8. For fall 2010, 25 students applied for upper-level admission, 8 were accepted, 8 enrolled. Psychoeducational evaluation, Wechsler Individual Achievement Test and WISC III or other aptitude measures; standardized achievement test required. Deadline for receipt of application materials: none. No application fee required. On-campus interview required.
Athletics Interscholastic: badminton (boys, girls), ball hockey (b), baseball (b,g), basketball (b,g), flag football (b), floor hockey (b), golf (b,g), independent competitive sports (b,g), indoor soccer (b,g), soccer (b,g), softball (b,g), track and field (b,g), volleyball (b,g), winter soccer (b,g); intramural: badminton (b,g), basketball (b,g), soccer (b,g), softball (b,g); coed interscholastic: badminton, baseball, bowling, cross-country running, flag football, Frisbee, indoor soccer, ultimate Frisbee; coed intramural: alpine skiing, badminton, ball hockey, basketball, blading, climbing, cooperative games, cross-country running, curling, dance, diving, floor hockey, handball, ice skating, indoor soccer, jogging, jump rope, life saving, martial arts, outdoor activities, outdoor education, outdoor skills, physical fitness, rock climbing, ropes courses, scuba diving, skiing (downhill), snowboarding, snowshoeing, ultimate Frisbee, volleyball, wall climbing, yoga. 2 PE instructors, 10 coaches.
Computers Computers are regularly used in career exploration, desktop publishing, digital applications, English, information technology, keyboarding, news writing, newspaper, photography, programming, science, technology, theater, writing, yearbook classes. Computer network features include Internet access, wireless campus network. Computer access in designated common areas is available to students. The school has a published electronic and media policy.
Contact Barbara Rosenberg, Director. 905-773-3997. Fax: 905-773-4722. Web site: www.pace.on.ca.

ACADEMY FOR GLOBAL EXPLORATION
PO Box 712
Ashland, Oregon 97520
Head of School: Mr. Greg Guevara
General Information Coeducational boarding college-preparatory, cultural studies, and outdoor education school. Grades 9–12. Founded: 2002. Setting: small town. Nearest major city is Portland. Students are housed in coed dormitories. 81-acre campus. 1 building on campus. Approved or accredited by Northwest Accreditation Commission and Oregon Department of Education. Total enrollment: 8. Upper school average class size: 4. Upper school faculty-student ratio: 1:3.
Upper School Student Profile Grade 10: 2 students (2 boys); Grade 11: 3 students (3 girls); Grade 12: 3 students (2 boys, 1 girl); Postgraduate: 2 students (2 boys). 100% of students are boarding students. 10% are state residents. 7 states are represented in upper school student body.
Faculty School total: 6. In upper school: 2 men, 2 women; 2 have advanced degrees; 4 reside on campus.
Subjects Offered Algebra, biology, chemistry, computer skills, cultural geography, earth science, English, environmental studies, foreign language, geometry, health, mathematics, photography, physical education, science, social studies, space and physical sciences, U.S. history, world history.
Graduation Requirements Cultural geography, electives, English, foreign language, mathematics, outdoor education, physical education (includes health), science, social studies (includes history), cultural studies, outdoor adventure.

Academy for Global Exploration

Special Academic Programs Honors section; accelerated programs; independent study; study abroad; academic accommodation for the gifted; remedial reading and/or remedial writing; remedial math.

College Admission Counseling 2 students graduated in 2009.

Student Life Upper grades have student council, honor system. Discipline rests primarily with faculty.

Tuition and Aid 7-day tuition and room/board: $27,540. Guaranteed tuition plan. Tuition installment plan (monthly payment plans, individually arranged payment plans, semester payment plan). Tuition reduction for siblings, merit scholarship grants, need-based scholarship grants available.

Admissions Traditional secondary-level entrance grade is 11. Deadline for receipt of application materials: none. Application fee required: $125. Interview required.

Athletics Coed Intramural: alpine skiing, backpacking, bicycling, canoeing/kayaking, climbing, combined training, cross-country running, fishing, fitness, fitness walking, fly fishing, Frisbee, hiking/backpacking, independent competitive sports, indoor soccer, jogging, kayaking, life saving, mountain biking, mountaineering, nordic skiing, outdoor activities, outdoor adventure, outdoor education, paddling, physical fitness, physical training, project adventure, rafting, rappelling, rock climbing, running, scuba diving, skateboarding, skiing (cross-country), skiing (downhill), skydiving, snowboarding, snowshoeing, soccer, speleology, surfing, telemark skiing, ultimate Frisbee, wall climbing, wilderness, wilderness survival, wildernessways, windsurfing, winter walking. 3 PE instructors.

Computers Computers are regularly used in all classes. Computer resources include Internet access, wireless campus network. Student e-mail accounts are available to students.

Contact Mr. Greg Guevara, Head of School. 541-913-0660. E-mail: admissions@agexplore.org. Web site: www.AGExplore.org.

ACADEMY FOR INDIVIDUAL EXCELLENCE

3101 Bluebird Lane
Louisville, Kentucky 40299
Head of School: Mr. John Savage

General Information Coeducational day college-preparatory and general academic school. Grades K–12. Founded: 1984. Setting: suburban. 9-acre campus. 1 building on campus. Total enrollment: 359. Upper school average class size: 16. Upper school faculty-student ratio: 1:9. There are 174 required school days per year for Upper School students. Upper School students typically attend 5 days per week. The average school day consists of 6 hours and 10 minutes.

Upper School Student Profile Grade 9: 45 students (32 boys, 13 girls); Grade 10: 44 students (29 boys, 15 girls); Grade 11: 37 students (27 boys, 10 girls); Grade 12: 35 students (22 boys, 13 girls).

Faculty School total: 46. In upper school: 8 men, 10 women; 12 have advanced degrees.

Subjects Offered Algebra, American government, American history, American literature, American sign language, art, art appreciation, biology, business mathematics, calculus, chemistry, composition, computer applications, creative writing, critical thinking, drama, English, English literature, foreign language, general math, general science, geography, geometry, government, health, music appreciation, personal finance, physical education, psychology, world history.

College Admission Counseling 47 students graduated in 2009; 28 went to college, including Lipscomb University; University of Louisville; Western Kentucky University. Other: 11 went to work, 4 entered a postgraduate year, 3 had other specific plans.

Student Life Upper grades have specified standards of dress. Discipline rests primarily with faculty.

Tuition and Aid Day student tuition: $7182. Tuition installment plan (monthly payment plans). Tuition reduction for siblings, need-based scholarship grants available. In 2009–10, 7% of upper-school students received aid.

Admissions Traditional secondary-level entrance grade is 9. Deadline for receipt of application materials: none. No application fee required. On-campus interview required.

Athletics Interscholastic: basketball (boys, girls), volleyball (g); coed interscholastic: archery, soccer; coed intramural: bowling, cross-country running, golf. 1 PE instructor.

Computers Computers are regularly used in computer applications classes. Computer resources include Internet filtering or blocking technology. Computer access in designated common areas is available to students.

Contact 502-267-6187. Fax: 502-261-9687. Web site: www.aiexcellence.com.

ACADEMY OF MOUNT SAINT URSULA

330 Bedford Park Boulevard
Bronx, New York 10458-2493
Head of School: Ms. Lisa Harrison

General Information Girls' day college-preparatory, arts, business, religious studies, and technology school, affiliated with Roman Catholic Church. Grades 9–12. Founded: 1855. Setting: urban. Nearest major city is New York. 10-acre campus. 1 building on campus. Approved or accredited by Middle States Association of Colleges and Schools, National Catholic Education Association, and New York State Board of Regents. Total enrollment: 343. Upper school average class size: 27. There are 180

required school days per year for Upper School students. Upper School students typically attend 5 days per week. The average school day consists of 6 hours and 15 minutes.

Upper School Student Profile Grade 9: 84 students (84 girls); Grade 10: 99 students (99 girls); Grade 11: 77 students (77 girls); Grade 12: 83 students (83 girls). 66% of students are Roman Catholic.

Faculty School total: 25. In upper school: 8 men, 17 women.

Subjects Offered Accounting, algebra, American history, American literature, anatomy, anthropology, art, Bible studies, biology, biology-AP, business law, calculus-AP, chemistry, community service, composition, computer math, computer programming, computer science, creative writing, driver education, earth science, economics, English, English literature, English-AP, European history, fine arts, French, general science, geometry, government/civics, health, history, history-AP, Italian, Latin, mathematics, music, physical education, physics, pre-calculus, religion, science, Shakespeare, social studies, sociology, Spanish, Spanish language-AP, Spanish literature-AP, speech, trigonometry, women's literature, word processing, world history, world literature, writing.

Graduation Requirements Arts and fine arts (art, music, dance, drama), business skills (includes word processing), computer science, English, foreign language, mathematics, physical education (includes health), religion (includes Bible studies and theology), science, social studies (includes history). Community service is required.

Special Academic Programs 6 Advanced Placement exams for which test preparation is offered; honors section; study at local college for college credit; academic accommodation for the musically talented and the artistically talented; remedial reading and/or remedial writing; remedial math.

College Admission Counseling 101 students graduated in 2009; 100 went to college, including City College of the City University of New York; Fordham University; Hunter College of the City University of New York; Manhattanville College; New York Institute of Technology; New York University. Other: 1 went to work.

Student Life Upper grades have uniform requirement, student council, honor system. Discipline rests primarily with faculty. Attendance at religious services is required.

Tuition and Aid Day student tuition: $6600. Tuition installment plan (monthly payment plans, semester payment plan, prepayment discount plan). Merit scholarship grants, need-based scholarship grants, archdiocese program available. In 2009–10, 40% of upper-school students received aid; total upper-school merit-scholarship money awarded: $165,500. Total amount of financial aid awarded in 2009–10: $249,220.

Admissions Traditional secondary-level entrance grade is 9. For fall 2009, 535 students applied for upper-level admission, 350 were accepted, 116 enrolled. New York Archdiocesan Cooperative Entrance Examination required. Deadline for receipt of application materials: none. Application fee required: $100.

Athletics Interscholastic: basketball, cheering, soccer, softball, swimming and diving, volleyball; intramural: basketball, dance, swimming and diving. 2 PE instructors, 3 coaches.

Computers Computers are regularly used in accounting, English, foreign language, mathematics, science, social studies classes. Computer network features include on-campus library services, Internet access, wireless campus network, Internet filtering or blocking technology, science labs. Campus intranet, student e-mail accounts, and computer access in designated common areas are available to students. The school has a published electronic and media policy.

Contact Ms. Kate Ostrander, Director of Admissions and Recruitment. 718-364-5353 Ext. 231. Fax: 718-364-2354. E-mail: admissions@amsu.org. Web site: www.amsu.org.

ACADEMY OF NOTRE DAME DE NAMUR

560 Sproul Road
Villanova, Pennsylvania 19085-1220
Head of School: Mrs. Veronica Collins Harrington

General Information Girls' day college-preparatory school, affiliated with Roman Catholic Church. Grades 6–12. Founded: 1856. Setting: suburban. Nearest major city is Philadelphia. 38-acre campus. 9 buildings on campus. Approved or accredited by Middle States Association of Colleges and Schools, National Catholic Education Association, and Pennsylvania Department of Education. Member of National Association of Independent Schools. Endowment: $4 million. Total enrollment: 513. Upper school average class size: 15. Upper school faculty-student ratio: 1:8. There are 170 required school days per year for Upper School students. Upper School students typically attend 5 days per week. The average school day consists of 6 hours and 45 minutes.

Upper School Student Profile Grade 9: 88 students (88 girls); Grade 10: 107 students (107 girls); Grade 11: 100 students (100 girls); Grade 12: 94 students (94 girls). 88% of students are Roman Catholic.

Faculty School total: 59. In upper school: 8 men, 45 women; 39 have advanced degrees.

Subjects Offered Advanced biology, American history-AP, Bible, biology, biology-AP, calculus, calculus-AP, ceramics, chemistry, chemistry-AP, choral music, Christian and Hebrew scripture, Christian ethics, comparative government and politics-AP, computer skills, computer-aided design, contemporary history, dance, economics, English, English literature, English literature and composition-AP, environmental science, French, French language-AP, geometry, government and politics-AP, health, health education, Hebrew scripture, instrumental music, journalism, Latin, Latin-AP, literature, literature and composition-AP, mathematics, multimedia design, music, music performance, music theory, music theory-AP, music-AP, physical education, physics-AP, pre-algebra, pre-calculus, SAT/ACT preparation, Spanish, Spanish language-AP, Spanish-AP, studio art-AP, U.S. government and politics-AP, U.S. history-AP, United States government-AP, video film production, visual and performing arts, vocal music, world cultures.

Graduation Requirements Art, dance, English, foreign language, guidance, mathematics, music, physical education (includes health), religion (includes Bible studies and theology), science, social studies (includes history), trigonometry, 40 hours of social service.

Special Academic Programs Honors section; independent study; study at local college for college credit; study abroad.

College Admission Counseling 96 students graduated in 2010; all went to college, including Penn State University Park; Saint Joseph's University; University of Delaware; University of Pittsburgh; Villanova University. Median SAT critical reading: 580, median SAT math: 600, median SAT writing: 620, median combined SAT: 1780, median composite ACT: 25. 50% scored over 600 on SAT critical reading, 44% scored over 600 on SAT math, 57% scored over 600 on SAT writing, 50% scored over 1800 on combined SAT, 40% scored over 26 on composite ACT.

Student Life Upper grades have uniform requirement, student council, honor system. Discipline rests primarily with faculty. Attendance at religious services is required.

Summer Programs Enrichment, advancement, sports, art/fine arts, computer instruction programs offered; session focuses on academic enrichment; held on campus; accepts boys and girls; open to students from other schools. 100 students usually enrolled. 2011 schedule: June 13 to July 22.

Tuition and Aid Day student tuition: $17,500–$18,700. Tuition installment plan (monthly payment plans, quarterly and semi-annual payment plans). Merit scholarship grants, need-based scholarship grants available. In 2010–11, 32% of upper-school students received aid; total upper-school merit-scholarship money awarded: $370,500. Total amount of financial aid awarded in 2010–11: $449,500.

Admissions Traditional secondary-level entrance grade is 9. For fall 2010, 210 students applied for upper-level admission, 168 were accepted, 48 enrolled. High School Placement Test required. Deadline for receipt of application materials: December 17. Application fee required: $40. Interview recommended.

Athletics Interscholastic: basketball, crew, cross-country running, diving, field hockey, golf, lacrosse, soccer, softball, swimming and diving, tennis, track and field, volleyball, winter (indoor) track; intramural: dance, kickball, modern dance. 3 PE instructors, 31 coaches, 1 athletic trainer.

Computers Computers are regularly used in all classes. Computer network features include on-campus library services, online commercial services, Internet access, Internet filtering or blocking technology, Smart Boards in classrooms. Student e-mail accounts are available to students. Students grades are available online. The school has a published electronic and media policy.

Contact Mrs. Diane Sander, Director of Admissions. 610-971-0498. Fax: 610-687-1912. E-mail: dsander@ndapa.org. Web site: www.ndapa.org.

ACADEMY OF OUR LADY OF MERCY

200 High Street
Milford, Connecticut 06460

Head of School: Dr. Antoinette Iadarola

General Information Girls' day college-preparatory, arts, religious studies, and technology school, affiliated with Roman Catholic Church. Grades 9–12. Founded: 1905. Setting: suburban. Nearest major city is New Haven. 30-acre campus. 5 buildings on campus. Approved or accredited by Connecticut Association of Independent Schools, Mercy Secondary Education Association, New England Association of Schools and Colleges, and Connecticut Department of Education. Total enrollment: 437. Upper school average class size: 18. Upper school faculty-student ratio: 1:12. There are 165 required school days per year for Upper School students. Upper School students typically attend 5 days per week. The average school day consists of 6 hours and 15 minutes.

Upper School Student Profile Grade 9: 124 students (124 girls); Grade 10: 113 students (113 girls); Grade 11: 111 students (111 girls); Grade 12: 89 students (89 girls). 77% of students are Roman Catholic.

Faculty School total: 38. In upper school: 2 men, 35 women; 29 have advanced degrees.

Subjects Offered Algebra, American history, American literature, anatomy, art, biology, business, calculus, chemistry, computer math, computer programming, English, English literature, environmental science, European history, fine arts, French, geometry, government/civics, health, history, journalism, Latin, mathematics, music, physical education, physics, physiology, religion, science, social studies, Spanish, trigonometry, world history, writing.

Graduation Requirements Arts and fine arts (art, music, dance, drama), English, foreign language, mathematics, physical education (includes health), religion (includes Bible studies and theology), science, social studies (includes history). Community service is required.

Special Academic Programs Honors section; study at local college for college credit.

Connecticut's oldest Catholic college preparatory school for girls.

ACADEMY OF OUR LADY OF MERCY
Lauralton Hall

200 High Street | Milford, CT 06460 | tel: 203.877.2786
www.lauraltonhall.org

College Admission Counseling 104 students graduated in 2010; all went to college, including Boston College; College of the Holy Cross; Fairfield University; Loyola University Maryland; Quinnipiac University; University of Connecticut. Mean SAT critical reading: 536, mean SAT math: 537, mean SAT writing: 555.

Student Life Upper grades have uniform requirement, student council, honor system. Discipline rests primarily with faculty. Attendance at religious services is required.

Tuition and Aid Day student tuition: $14,250. Tuition installment plan (FACTS Tuition Payment Plan, 1- and 2-payment plans). Tuition reduction for siblings, merit scholarship grants, need-based scholarship grants available. In 2010–11, 28% of upper-school students received aid; total upper-school merit-scholarship money awarded: $125,000. Total amount of financial aid awarded in 2010–11: $300,000.

Admissions Traditional secondary-level entrance grade is 9. For fall 2010, 323 students applied for upper-level admission, 247 were accepted, 124 enrolled. High School Placement Test required. Deadline for receipt of application materials: none. Application fee required: $60.

Athletics Interscholastic: basketball, cheering, cross-country running, diving, field hockey, golf, gymnastics, ice hockey, indoor track, lacrosse, running, skiing (downhill), soccer, softball, swimming and diving, tennis, track and field, volleyball; intramural: basketball. 1 PE instructor, 27 coaches, 1 athletic trainer.

Computers Computers are regularly used in mathematics classes. Computer network features include on-campus library services, online commercial services, Internet access, wireless campus network, Internet filtering or blocking technology. Campus intranet, student e-mail accounts, and computer access in designated common areas are available to students. The school has a published electronic and media policy.

Contact Mrs. Kathleen O. Shine, Director of Admissions and Financial Aid. 203-877-2786 Ext. 125. Fax: 203-876-9760. E-mail: kshine@lauraltonhall.org. Web site: www.lauraltonhall.org.

See Display on page 57 and Close-Up on page 726.

ACADEMY OF OUR LADY OF PEACE

4860 Oregon Street
San Diego, California 92116-1393
Head of School: Sr. Dolores Anchondo

General Information Girls' day college-preparatory, arts, and religious studies school, affiliated with Roman Catholic Church. Grades 9–12. Founded: 1882. Setting: urban. 20-acre campus. 7 buildings on campus. Approved or accredited by Western Association of Schools and Colleges, Western Catholic Education Association, and California Department of Education. Endowment: $250,000. Total enrollment: 733. Upper school average class size: 28. Upper school faculty-student ratio: 1:14. There are 280 required school days per year for Upper School students. Upper School students typically attend 5 days per week. The average school day consists of 6 hours and 30 minutes.

Upper School Student Profile Grade 9: 199 students (199 girls); Grade 10: 201 students (201 girls); Grade 11: 168 students (168 girls); Grade 12: 158 students (158 girls). 91% of students are Roman Catholic.

Faculty School total: 52. In upper school: 11 men, 41 women; 34 have advanced degrees.

Subjects Offered Algebra, American literature, art, astronomy, Bible studies, biology, biology-AP, British literature, calculus, ceramics, chemistry, chemistry-AP, creative writing, dance, drama, economics, English, English-AP, ethics, fitness, French, French-AP, genetics, geometry, government, graphic arts, health, integrated science, marine biology, mathematics-AP, music appreciation, music theory-AP, oceanography, painting, physical education, physics, pre-calculus, psychology, Spanish, Spanish-AP, speech, studio art-AP, study skills, trigonometry, U.S. government and politics-AP, U.S. history, U.S. history-AP, Western civilization, yearbook, yoga.

Graduation Requirements Arts and fine arts (art, music, dance, drama), English, foreign language, mathematics, physical education (includes health), religion (includes Bible studies and theology), science, social sciences, social studies (includes history), speech, 75 hours of community service, 9-11 reflection paper required for seniors.

Special Academic Programs 33 Advanced Placement exams for which test preparation is offered; honors section.

College Admission Counseling 174 students graduated in 2010; 170 went to college, including Gonzaga University; San Diego State University; San Francisco State University; Sonoma State University; University of California, Berkeley; University of San Francisco. Other: 4 went to work. Median SAT critical reading: 570, median SAT math: 560, median SAT writing: 590, median combined SAT: 1720. 35% scored over 600 on SAT critical reading, 30% scored over 600 on SAT math, 42% scored over 600 on SAT writing, 32% scored over 1800 on combined SAT, 34% scored over 26 on composite ACT.

Student Life Upper grades have uniform requirement, student council, honor system. Discipline rests equally with students and faculty. Attendance at religious services is required.

Tuition and Aid Day student tuition: $11,760. Tuition installment plan (FACTS Tuition Payment Plan). Need-based scholarship grants available. In 2010–11, 38% of upper-school students received aid. Total amount of financial aid awarded in 2010–11: $1,500,000.

Admissions Traditional secondary-level entrance grade is 9. For fall 2010, 248 students applied for upper-level admission, 223 were accepted, 210 enrolled. High School Placement Test required. Deadline for receipt of application materials: none. Application fee required: $50. On-campus interview required.

Athletics Interscholastic: basketball, cheering, cross-country running, golf, gymnastics, independent competitive sports. 4 PE instructors, 16 coaches.

Computers Computers are regularly used in computer applications, music, music technology, Web site design, word processing classes. Computer network features include on-campus library services, online commercial services, Internet access, wireless campus network, Internet filtering or blocking technology. Campus intranet, student e-mail accounts, and computer access in designated common areas are available to students. Students grades are available online. The school has a published electronic and media policy.

Contact Mrs. Sue De Winter, Administrative Assistant/Registrar. 619-725-9118. Fax: 619-297-2473. E-mail: admissions@aolp.org. Web site: www.aolp.org.

ACADEMY OF SAINT ELIZABETH

Box 297
Convent Station, New Jersey 07961-0297
Head of School: Sr. Patricia Costello, OP

General Information Girls' day college-preparatory, arts, religious studies, and technology school, affiliated with Roman Catholic Church. Grades 9–12. Founded: 1860. Setting: suburban. Nearest major city is Morristown. 200-acre campus. 2 buildings on campus. Approved or accredited by Middle States Association of Colleges and Schools, National Catholic Education Association, and New Jersey Association of Independent Schools. Total enrollment: 245. Upper school average class size: 15. Upper school faculty-student ratio: 1:9.

Upper School Student Profile Grade 9: 75 students (75 girls); Grade 10: 67 students (67 girls); Grade 11: 49 students (49 girls); Grade 12: 54 students (54 girls). 90% of students are Roman Catholic.

Faculty School total: 30. In upper school: 6 men, 22 women; 12 have advanced degrees.

Subjects Offered 20th century American writers, algebra, American history, American literature, art, Bible studies, biology, calculus, ceramics, chemistry, dance, drama, driver education, ecology, English, English literature, environmental science, European history, expository writing, fine arts, French, geometry, grammar, health, history, journalism, Latin, mathematics, music, photography, physical education, physics, psychology, religion, science, social sciences, social studies, sociology, Spanish, theater, theology, trigonometry, word processing, world history, world literature.

Graduation Requirements Arts and fine arts (art, music, dance, drama), computer education, English, foreign language, mathematics, physical education (includes health), religion (includes Bible studies and theology), science, social sciences, social studies (includes history), senior independent study.

Special Academic Programs Advanced Placement exam preparation; honors section; independent study; study at local college for college credit.

College Admission Counseling 57 students graduated in 2010; all went to college, including American University; Boston College; College of the Holy Cross; Seton Hall University; University of Notre Dame; Villanova University.

Student Life Upper grades have uniform requirement, student council, honor system. Discipline rests primarily with faculty. Attendance at religious services is required.

Tuition and Aid Day student tuition: $11,000. Tuition installment plan (monthly payment plans, individually arranged payment plans). Merit scholarship grants, need-based scholarship grants available. In 2010–11, 35% of upper-school students received aid.

Admissions Traditional secondary-level entrance grade is 9. For fall 2010, 150 students applied for upper-level admission, 115 were accepted, 75 enrolled. School's own exam required. Deadline for receipt of application materials: January 15. Application fee required: $100. On-campus interview recommended.

Athletics Interscholastic: aquatics, basketball, cross-country running, field hockey, lacrosse; intramural: aerobics, aerobics/dance, alpine skiing, dance, equestrian sports, horseback riding, independent competitive sports. 1 PE instructor, 9 coaches.

Computers Computers are regularly used in English, foreign language, history, mathematics, science, study skills classes. Computer network features include on-campus library services, online commercial services, Internet access. The school has a published electronic and media policy.

Contact Sr. Patricia Costello, OP, Principal. 973-290-5200. Fax: 973-290-5232. Web site: academyofsaintelizabeth.org.

ACADEMY OF THE HOLY CROSS

4920 Strathmore Avenue
Kensington, Maryland 20895-1299
Head of School: Dr. Claire M. Helm, PhD

General Information Girls' day college-preparatory, arts, and religious studies school, affiliated with Roman Catholic Church. Grades 9–12. Founded: 1868. Setting: suburban. Nearest major city is Rockville. 28-acre campus. 2 buildings on campus. Approved or accredited by Association of Independent Schools of Greater Washington, International Baccalaureate Organization, Middle States Association of

Colleges and Schools, National Catholic Education Association, and Maryland Department of Education. Upper school average class size: 20. Upper school faculty-student ratio: 1:14. There are 176 required school days per year for Upper School students. Upper School students typically attend 5 days per week. The average school day consists of 7 hours and 10 minutes.

Upper School Student Profile Grade 9: 175 students (175 girls); Grade 10: 125 students (125 girls); Grade 11: 144 students (144 girls); Grade 12: 137 students (137 girls). 87% of students are Roman Catholic.

Faculty School total: 53. In upper school: 16 men, 37 women.

Subjects Offered Acting, Advanced Placement courses, African studies, algebra, American history, American literature, Arabic, art, art history-AP, Asian studies, biology, biology-AP, calculus, calculus-AP, ceramics, chemistry, chemistry-AP, Christian scripture, computer science, concert choir, creative writing, design, drama, drawing, earth science, economics, English, English language and composition-AP, English literature, English literature and composition-AP, environmental science, ethnic studies, expository writing, fine arts, forensics, French, genetics, geography, geometry, government/civics, grammar, health, Hebrew scripture, history, history of the Catholic Church, honors English, honors geometry, humanities, instrumental music, jazz dance, Latin, Latin American studies, madrigals, mathematics, moral theology, music, music appreciation, musical theater, musical theater dance, painting, peace studies, personal finance, photography, physical education, physical science, physics, physiology, pre-calculus, psychology, public speaking, religion, religious studies, science, sculpture, Shakespeare, social sciences, social studies, Spanish, sports medicine, statistics, studio art, studio art-AP, tap dance, technology, theater, theater design and production, theology, trigonometry, U.S. government, U.S. government and politics-AP, U.S. history, U.S. history-AP, Web site design, world history, world studies.

Graduation Requirements Art, electives, English, foreign language, mathematics, performing arts, physical education (includes health), science, senior project, social sciences, social studies (includes history), theology, Christian service commitment, Senior Project Internship.

Special Academic Programs International Baccalaureate program; Advanced Placement exam preparation; honors section; independent study; academic accommodation for the gifted and the artistically talented.

College Admission Counseling 131 students graduated in 2010; 129 went to college, including Clemson University; High Point University; Saint Joseph's University; The Catholic University of America; University of Maryland, College Park; University of South Carolina. Other: 2 had other specific plans. Mean SAT critical reading: 576, mean SAT math: 557, mean SAT writing: 578, mean combined SAT: 1711, mean composite ACT: 26.

Student Life Upper grades have uniform requirement, student council, honor system. Discipline rests equally with students and faculty. Attendance at religious services is required.

Summer Programs Enrichment, advancement, sports, art/fine arts, computer instruction programs offered; session focuses on enrichment and athletic skill-building; held on campus; accepts girls; open to students from other schools. 200 students usually enrolled. 2011 schedule: June 20 to July 15. Application deadline: May 31.

Tuition and Aid Day student tuition: $16,800. Tuition installment plan (individually arranged payment plans). Tuition reduction for siblings, merit scholarship grants, need-based scholarship grants, alumnae stipends available. In 2010–11, 54% of upper-school students received aid; total upper-school merit-scholarship money awarded: $851,450. Total amount of financial aid awarded in 2010–11: $1,974,821.

Admissions Traditional secondary-level entrance grade is 9. High School Placement Test required. Deadline for receipt of application materials: December 15. Application fee required: $50. On-campus interview required.

Athletics Interscholastic: archery, basketball, crew, cross-country running, diving, equestrian sports, field hockey, golf, lacrosse, soccer, softball, swimming and diving, tennis, track and field, volleyball; intramural: basketball, cheering, dance, dance team, kayaking, lacrosse, soccer. 2 PE instructors, 35 coaches, 1 athletic trainer.

Computers Computers are regularly used in art, foreign language, mathematics, science, social sciences classes. Computer network features include on-campus library services, online commercial services, Internet access, wireless campus network, Internet filtering or blocking technology. Students grades are available online. The school has a published electronic and media policy.

Contact Mrs. Louise Hendon, Director of Admissions. 301-929-6442. Fax: 301-929-6440. E-mail: admissions@ahctartans.org. Web site: www.ahctartans.org.

ACADEMY OF THE HOLY NAMES

3319 Bayshore Boulevard
Tampa, Florida 33629-8899
Head of School: Dr. Harry Purpur

General Information Coeducational day college-preparatory, arts, religious studies, and technology school, affiliated with Roman Catholic Church. Boys grades PK–8, girls grades PK–12. Founded: 1881. Setting: urban. 19-acre campus. 6 buildings on campus. Approved or accredited by Florida Council of Independent Schools, National Catholic Education Association, Southern Association of Colleges and Schools, and Florida Department of Education. Endowment: $4 million. Total enrollment: 801.

Upper school average class size: 18. Upper school faculty-student ratio: 1:15. Upper School students typically attend 5 days per week. The average school day consists of 7 hours and 25 minutes.

Upper School Student Profile Grade 6: 41 students (13 boys, 28 girls); Grade 7: 54 students (22 boys, 32 girls); Grade 8: 70 students (24 boys, 46 girls); Grade 9: 108 students (108 girls); Grade 10: 76 students (76 girls); Grade 11: 78 students (78 girls); Grade 12: 77 students (77 girls). 70% of students are Roman Catholic.

Faculty School total: 95. In upper school: 3 men, 36 women; 24 have advanced degrees.

Subjects Offered 20th century history, accounting, algebra, American history, American history-AP, anatomy and physiology, art history-AP, biology, biology-AP, calculus, calculus-AP, ceramics, chemistry, chemistry-AP, Christian and Hebrew scripture, communications, computer applications, computer science, contemporary history, economics, English, English literature and composition-AP, environmental science-AP, ethics, French, French-AP, geometry, government, government-AP, honors algebra, honors English, honors geometry, honors U.S. history, honors world history, journalism, Latin, Latin-AP, law studies, marine biology, marketing, media, music, physical education, physics, physics-AP, psychology, religious education, social justice, Spanish, Spanish-AP, speech, statistics, studio art-AP, U.S. government and politics-AP, world history, world religions.

Graduation Requirements 100 community service hours.

Special Academic Programs 16 Advanced Placement exams for which test preparation is offered; honors section.

College Admission Counseling 76 students graduated in 2010; all went to college, including Boston College; College of Charleston; Florida State University; University of Florida; University of South Florida; Vanderbilt University. Mean SAT critical reading: 567, mean SAT math: 558, mean SAT writing: 579, mean composite ACT: 25.

Student Life Upper grades have uniform requirement, student council, honor system. Discipline rests primarily with faculty. Attendance at religious services is required.

Summer Programs Sports, art/fine arts programs offered; session focuses on enrichment; held on campus; accepts boys and girls; open to students from other schools. 2011 schedule: June to August.

Tuition and Aid Day student tuition: $14,980. Tuition installment plan (monthly payment plans). Merit scholarship grants, need-based scholarship grants, paying campus jobs available. In 2010–11, 29% of upper-school students received aid; total upper-school merit-scholarship money awarded: $40,320. Total amount of financial aid awarded in 2010–11: $515,525.

Admissions Traditional secondary-level entrance grade is 9. For fall 2010, 140 students applied for upper-level admission, 110 were accepted, 74 enrolled. High School Placement Test (closed version) from Scholastic Testing Service or Stanford Achievement Test required. Deadline for receipt of application materials: December 10. Application fee required: $50. On-campus interview required.

Athletics Interscholastic: aerobics/dance (girls), aquatics (g), basketball (g), cheering (g), crew (g), cross-country running (g), dance (g), dance squad (g), dance team (g), diving (g), golf (g), physical fitness (g), softball (g), swimming and diving (g), tennis (g), track and field (g), volleyball (g), winter soccer (g); coed interscholastic: soccer. 3 PE instructors, 10 coaches, 1 athletic trainer.

Computers Computers are regularly used in all academic classes. Computer network features include on-campus library services, Internet access, Internet filtering or blocking technology. Students grades are available online. The school has a published electronic and media policy.

Contact Mrs. Pam Doherty, Enrollment Assistant. 813-839-5371 Ext. 307. Fax: 813-839-1486. E-mail: pdoherty@holynamestpa.org. Web site: www.holynamestpa.org.

ACADEMY OF THE NEW CHURCH BOYS' SCHOOL

2815 Benade Circle
Box 707
Bryn Athyn, Pennsylvania 19009
Head of School: Mr. Jeremy T. Irwin

General Information Boys' boarding and day college-preparatory, arts, and religious studies school, affiliated with Church of the New Jerusalem. Grades 9–12. Founded: 1887. Setting: suburban. Nearest major city is Philadelphia. Students are housed in single-sex dormitories. 200-acre campus. 8 buildings on campus. Approved or accredited by Middle States Association of Colleges and Schools and Pennsylvania Department of Education. Endowment: $200 million. Total enrollment: 124. Upper school average class size: 15. Upper school faculty-student ratio: 1:8. There are 175 required school days per year for Upper School students. Upper School students typically attend 5 days per week. The average school day consists of 7 hours and 15 minutes.

Upper School Student Profile Grade 9: 28 students (28 boys); Grade 10: 26 students (26 boys); Grade 11: 36 students (36 boys); Grade 12: 34 students (34 boys). 35% of students are boarding students. 75% are state residents. 18 states are represented in upper school student body. 3% are international students. International students from China and Republic of Korea; 2 other countries represented in student body. 85% of students are Church of the New Jerusalem.

Faculty School total: 40. In upper school: 20 men, 20 women; 35 have advanced degrees; 10 reside on campus.

Academy of the New Church Boys' School

Subjects Offered Advanced chemistry, Advanced Placement courses, African-American literature, algebra, American history, American history-AP, American literature, American literature-AP, anatomy, anatomy and physiology, ancient world history, art, art history, Bible studies, biology, British literature, calculus, calculus-AP, ceramics, chemistry, civics, computer programming, computer science, creative writing, dance, drama, ecology, English, English literature, English literature-AP, environmental science, European history, expository writing, fine arts, French, geometry, German, government/civics, grammar, health, history, honors U.S. history, industrial arts, journalism, Latin, mathematics, music, music theater, musical theater, philosophy, photography, physical education, physical science, physics, physiology, portfolio art, pre-calculus, printmaking, probability and statistics, religion, religious education, religious studies, science, sculpture, senior project, social sciences, social studies, sociology, Spanish, speech, statistics, studio art, theater, theater arts, theater design and production, theater production, theology, trigonometry, U.S. history-AP, vocal ensemble, vocal music, women in literature, world history, world literature.

Graduation Requirements Arts and fine arts (art, music, dance, drama), English, foreign language, mathematics, physical education (includes health), religion (includes Bible studies and theology), science, social sciences, social studies (includes history).

Special Academic Programs Advanced Placement exam preparation; honors section; independent study; study at local college for college credit; academic accommodation for the gifted, the musically talented, and the artistically talented; remedial reading and/or remedial writing; remedial math; programs in English, mathematics, general development for dyslexic students; ESL (6 students enrolled).

College Admission Counseling 31 students graduated in 2010; 30 went to college, including Bryn Athyn College of the New Church; Gettysburg College; Penn State University Park; University of Pennsylvania; Virginia Polytechnic Institute and State University; West Chester University of Pennsylvania. Other: 1 entered military service. Median SAT critical reading: 540, median SAT math: 560, median SAT writing: 530, median combined SAT: 1630. 28% scored over 600 on SAT critical reading, 33% scored over 600 on SAT math, 31% scored over 600 on SAT writing, 31% scored over 1800 on combined SAT.

Student Life Upper grades have specified standards of dress, student council. Discipline rests primarily with faculty. Attendance at religious services is required.

Summer Programs Enrichment, advancement, sports, art/fine arts, computer instruction programs offered; session focuses on enrichment; held on campus; accepts boys and girls; open to students from other schools. 110 students usually enrolled. 2011 schedule: July 11 to August 1. Application deadline: June 1.

Tuition and Aid Day student tuition: $11,901; 7-day tuition and room/board: $17,055. Tuition installment plan (monthly payment plans, individually arranged payment plans, term payment plan). Need-based scholarship grants, middle-income loans available. In 2010–11, 60% of upper-school students received aid. Total amount of financial aid awarded in 2010–11: $510,000.

Admissions Traditional secondary-level entrance grade is 9. For fall 2010, 110 students applied for upper-level admission, 40 were accepted, 12 enrolled. Iowa Subtests, PSAT, SAT or SSAT required. Deadline for receipt of application materials: none. Application fee required: $50. Interview required.

Athletics Interscholastic: baseball, basketball, football, ice hockey, lacrosse, wrestling. 1 PE instructor, 6 coaches, 1 athletic trainer.

Computers Computers are regularly used in English, foreign language, history, mathematics, science classes. Computer network features include on-campus library services, online commercial services, Internet access, wireless campus network, Internet filtering or blocking technology. Campus intranet and student e-mail accounts are available to students.

Contact Denise DiFiglia, Director of Admissions. 267-502-4855. Web site: www.ancss.org.

ACADEMY OF THE NEW CHURCH GIRLS' SCHOOL

2815 Benade Circle

Box 707

Bryn Athyn, Pennsylvania 19009

Head of School: Susan O. Odhner

General Information Girls' boarding and day college-preparatory, general academic, arts, and religious studies school, affiliated with Church of the New Jerusalem, Christian faith. Grades 9–12. Founded: 1884. Setting: suburban. Nearest major city is Philadelphia. Students are housed in single-sex dormitories. 200-acre campus. 8 buildings on campus. Approved or accredited by Middle States Association of Colleges and Schools and Pennsylvania Department of Education. Endowment: $200 million. Total enrollment: 108. Upper school average class size: 15. Upper school faculty-student ratio: 1:8. There are 175 required school days per year for Upper School students. Upper School students typically attend 5 days per week. The average school day consists of 7 hours and 15 minutes.

Upper School Student Profile Grade 9: 17 students (17 girls); Grade 10: 19 students (19 girls); Grade 11: 25 students (25 girls); Grade 12: 38 students (38 girls). 33% of students are boarding students. 70% are state residents. 13 states are represented in upper school student body. 9% are international students. International students from Canada, China, and Republic of Korea. 85% of students are Church of the New Jerusalem, Christian.

Faculty School total: 40. In upper school: 20 men, 20 women; 35 have advanced degrees; 10 reside on campus.

Subjects Offered Advanced chemistry, Advanced Placement courses, African-American literature, algebra, American history, American history-AP, American literature, anatomy, ancient history, ancient world history, art, art history, Bible studies, biology, British literature, calculus, calculus-AP, chemistry, civics, computer science, creative writing, drafting, drama, dramatic arts, drawing, ecology, ecology, environmental systems, economics, English, English literature, English literature-AP, English-AP, European history, expository writing, film studies, fine arts, French, geometry, government/civics, grammar, health, history, honors algebra, honors English, honors geometry, honors U.S. history, human anatomy, Latin, mathematics, medieval history, music, painting, philosophy, photography, physical education, physical science, physics, physiology, pre-calculus, printmaking, religion, science, sculpture, senior project, social sciences, social studies, Spanish, speech, stained glass, statistics-AP, theater, theology, trigonometry, women in literature, world history, world literature.

Graduation Requirements Arts and fine arts (art, music, dance, drama), English, foreign language, mathematics, physical education (includes health), religion (includes Bible studies and theology), science, social sciences, social studies (includes history).

Special Academic Programs Advanced Placement exam preparation; honors section; independent study; study at local college for college credit; academic accommodation for the gifted, the musically talented, and the artistically talented; remedial reading and/or remedial writing; remedial math; special instructional classes for students with Attention Deficit Disorder and learning-disabled children; ESL (6 students enrolled).

College Admission Counseling 38 students graduated in 2010; 37 went to college, including Bryn Athyn College of the New Church; Gettysburg College; Penn State University Park; University of Pennsylvania; Virginia Polytechnic Institute and State University; West Chester University of Pennsylvania. Other: 1 went to work. Median SAT critical reading: 540, median SAT math: 560, median SAT writing: 530, median combined SAT: 1630. 28% scored over 600 on SAT critical reading, 33% scored over 600 on SAT math, 31% scored over 600 on SAT writing, 31% scored over 1800 on combined SAT.

Student Life Upper grades have uniform requirement, student council. Discipline rests primarily with faculty. Attendance at religious services is required.

Summer Programs Enrichment, advancement, art/fine arts, computer instruction programs offered; session focuses on enrichment; held on campus; accepts boys and girls; open to students from other schools. 130 students usually enrolled. 2011 schedule: July 11 to August 1. Application deadline: June 1.

Tuition and Aid Day student tuition: $11,901; 7-day tuition and room/board: $17,055. Tuition installment plan (monthly payment plans, individually arranged payment plans, term payment plan). Need-based scholarship grants, need-based loans, middle-income loans available. In 2010–11, 53% of upper-school students received aid. Total amount of financial aid awarded in 2010–11: $400,000.

Admissions Traditional secondary-level entrance grade is 9. For fall 2010, 106 students applied for upper-level admission, 40 were accepted, 12 enrolled. Iowa Subtests, PSAT, SAT or SSAT required. Deadline for receipt of application materials: none. Application fee required: $50. Interview required.

Athletics Interscholastic: basketball, dance team, field hockey, lacrosse, soccer, softball, tennis, volleyball. 1 PE instructor, 6 coaches, 1 athletic trainer.

Computers Computers are regularly used in English, foreign language, history, mathematics, science classes. Computer network features include on-campus library services, online commercial services, Internet access, wireless campus network, Internet filtering or blocking technology. Campus intranet and student e-mail accounts are available to students.

Contact Denise DiFiglia, Director of Admissions. 267-502-4855. Fax: 267-502-2617. Web site: www.ancss.org.

ACADEMY OF THE SACRED HEART

1821 Academy Road

Grand Coteau, Louisiana 70541

Head of School: Sr. Lynne Lieux, RSCJ

General Information Girls' boarding and day college-preparatory, arts, religious studies, bilingual studies, technology, and liberal arts and sciences school, affiliated with Roman Catholic Church. Boarding grades 7–12, day grades PK–12. Founded: 1821. Setting: small town. Nearest major city is Lafayette. Students are housed in single-sex dormitories. 250-acre campus. 9 buildings on campus. Approved or accredited by Independent Schools Association of the Southwest and Louisiana Department of Education. Endowment: $8 million. Total enrollment: 389. Upper school average class size: 18. Upper school faculty-student ratio: 1:8.

Upper School Student Profile Grade 9: 26 students (26 girls); Grade 10: 29 students (29 girls); Grade 11: 33 students (33 girls); Grade 12: 31 students (31 girls). 6% of students are boarding students. 80% are state residents. 6 states are represented in upper school student body. 5% are international students. International students from Germany, Mexico, and Taiwan; 2 other countries represented in student body. 77% of students are Roman Catholic.

Faculty School total: 50. In upper school: 2 men, 19 women; 6 have advanced degrees; 3 reside on campus.

Subjects Offered Advanced math, Advanced Placement courses, algebra, American literature, art appreciation, biology, biology-AP, British literature, British literature (honors), calculus, calculus-AP, chemistry, chorus, creative dance, creative writing, dance, drama, English, English literature-AP, environmental science, equestrian sports, equine science, ESL, ethical decision making, fine arts, French, French language-AP, French-AP, geometry, government-AP, government/civics, health, independent study, mathematics, moral reasoning, music theater, photography, physical education, physics, play production, pottery, pre-algebra, religion and culture, scripture, social justice, social sciences, Spanish, Spanish language-AP, Spanish-AP, studio art, theater, U.S. government, U.S. government and politics-AP, U.S. history, U.S. history-AP, women's studies, world history, world history-AP, yearbook.

Graduation Requirements Arts and fine arts (art, music, dance, drama), English, foreign language, mathematics, physical education (includes health), religion (includes Bible studies and theology), science, social sciences, social studies (includes history), May project. Community service is required.

Special Academic Programs International Baccalaureate program; Advanced Placement exam preparation; honors section; independent study; term-away projects; study at local college for college credit; domestic exchange program; study abroad; academic accommodation for the gifted, the musically talented, and the artistically talented; ESL (13 students enrolled).

College Admission Counseling 29 students graduated in 2009; all went to college, including Baylor University; Louisiana State University and Agricultural and Mechanical College; Loyola University New Orleans; Tulane University; University of Louisiana at Lafayette. Mean composite ACT: 25.

Student Life Upper grades have uniform requirement, student council, honor system. Discipline rests equally with students and faculty. Attendance at religious services is required.

Tuition and Aid Day student tuition: $4460–$11,800; 5-day tuition and room/board: $22,290; 7-day tuition and room/board: $23,390. Tuition installment plan (monthly payment plans, 2-payment plan, 3-payment plan, monthly payment plan for day students). Tuition reduction for siblings, merit scholarship grants, need-based scholarship grants available. In 2009–10, 16% of upper-school students received aid; total upper-school merit-scholarship money awarded: $7500.

Admissions Traditional secondary-level entrance grade is 9. For fall 2009, 26 students applied for upper-level admission, 22 were accepted, 20 enrolled. Metropolitan Achievement Short Form and Stanford Achievement Test required. Deadline for receipt of application materials: none. Application fee required: $100. Interview required.

Athletics Interscholastic: aquatics, basketball, cheering, cross-country running, dance, dance team, dressage, equestrian sports, horseback riding, soccer, softball, swimming and diving, tennis, track and field, volleyball. 2 PE instructors, 3 coaches.

Computers Computers are regularly used in all academic, English, history, mathematics, science classes. Computer network features include on-campus library services, Internet access.

Contact D'Lane Wimberley Thomas, Director of Admission. 337-662-5275 Ext. 3036. Fax: 337-662-3011. E-mail: admission@sshcoteau.org. Web site: www.sshcoteau.org.

ACADEMY OF THE SACRED HEART

4521 St. Charles Avenue
New Orleans, Louisiana 70115-4831

Head of School: Dr. Timothy Matthew Burns, PhD

General Information Girls' day college-preparatory, arts, religious studies, bilingual studies, and technology school, affiliated with Roman Catholic Church. Grades 1–12. Founded: 1887. Setting: urban. 7-acre campus. 2 buildings on campus. Approved or accredited by Independent Schools Association of the Southwest, National Catholic Education Association, Network of Sacred Heart Schools, Southern Association of Colleges and Schools, and Louisiana Department of Education. Endowment: $8.3 million. Total enrollment: 645. Upper school average class size: 18. Upper school faculty-student ratio: 1:16. There are 180 required school days per year for Upper School students. Upper School students typically attend 5 days per week. The average school day consists of 6 hours and 15 minutes.

Upper School Student Profile Grade 9: 55 students (55 girls); Grade 10: 45 students (45 girls); Grade 11: 43 students (43 girls); Grade 12: 66 students (66 girls). 88% of students are Roman Catholic.

Faculty School total: 104. In upper school: 7 men, 23 women; 19 have advanced degrees.

Subjects Offered Advanced chemistry, algebra, American government, American history, American history-AP, American literature, American literature-AP, anatomy and physiology, art, astronomy, athletics, basketball, biology, biology-AP, calculus, calculus-AP, campus ministry, Catholic belief and practice, ceramics, cheerleading, chemistry, chemistry-AP, clayworking, college admission preparation, college awareness, college counseling, college planning, computer applications, computer education, computer processing, computer resources, computer science, computer skills, computer studies, creative writing, drawing, electives, English, English literature, English literature-AP, English-AP, foreign language, French, French-AP, geometry, government, government-AP, guidance, history of the Catholic Church, honors algebra, honors English, honors geometry, honors U.S. history, honors world history, painting, peer counseling, pre-calculus, religion, robotics, social justice,

Spanish, Spanish-AP, U.S. government, U.S. government and politics-AP, U.S. history, U.S. history-AP, video communication, Web site design, world history, world history-AP, world religions, zoology.

Graduation Requirements Advanced Placement courses, algebra, American government, American literature, arts and fine arts (art, music, dance, drama), athletics, Basic programming, British literature, calculus, career/college preparation, computer applications, computer literacy, electives, English, foreign language, geometry, guidance, moral theology, peer counseling, physical education (includes health), physics, religion (includes Bible studies and theology), robotics, science, scripture, social justice, social studies (includes history), U.S. government, yearbook, senior speech, 50 hours of required community service.

Special Academic Programs Advanced Placement exam preparation; honors section; study at local college for college credit; domestic exchange program (with Network of Sacred Heart Schools).

College Admission Counseling 58 students graduated in 2010; all went to college, including Louisiana State University and Agricultural and Mechanical College; Loyola University New Orleans; Rhodes College; Tulane University; University of Georgia; University of Mississippi.

Student Life Upper grades have uniform requirement, student council, honor system. Discipline rests equally with students and faculty. Attendance at religious services is required.

Summer Programs Sports programs offered; session focuses on strength and conditioning; held both on and off campus; held at area tracks; accepts girls; not open to students from other schools. 12 students usually enrolled. 2011 schedule: June to August.

Tuition and Aid Day student tuition: $13,400. Tuition installment plan (The Tuition Plan, individually arranged payment plans, bank loan). Merit scholarship grants, need-based scholarship grants available. In 2010–11, 24% of upper-school students received aid; total upper-school merit-scholarship money awarded: $10,700. Total amount of financial aid awarded in 2010–11: $241,400.

Admissions Traditional secondary-level entrance grade is 9. For fall 2010, 20 students applied for upper-level admission, 18 were accepted, 9 enrolled. Achievement tests, admissions testing, ERB, OLSAT/Stanford or PSAT or SAT for applicants to grade 11 and 12 required. Deadline for receipt of application materials: none. Application fee required: $50. Interview required.

Athletics Interscholastic: aerobics, baseball, basketball, cheering, cross-country running, fitness, golf, indoor track & field, physical fitness, sailing, soccer, softball, strength & conditioning, swimming and diving, tennis, track and field, volleyball; intramural: aerobics, cooperative games, fitness, jogging, outdoor activities, outdoor recreation, physical fitness. 5 PE instructors, 14 coaches, 1 athletic trainer.

Computers Computers are regularly used in all classes. Computer network features include on-campus library services, online commercial services, Internet access, wireless campus network, Internet filtering or blocking technology. Campus intranet, student e-mail accounts, and computer access in designated common areas are available to students. Students grades are available online. The school has a published electronic and media policy.

Contact Ms. Christy Sevante, Admission Director. 504-269-1214. Fax: 504-896-7880. E-mail: csevante@ashrosary.org. Web site: www.ashrosary.org.

ACADEMY OF THE SACRED HEART

1250 Kensington Road
Bloomfield Hills, Michigan 48304-3029

Head of School: Bridget Bearss, RSCJ

General Information Coeducational day college-preparatory, arts, religious studies, technology, experiential learning, and community service school, affiliated with Roman Catholic Church. Boys grades N–8, girls grades N–12. Founded: 1851. Setting: suburban. Nearest major city is Detroit. 45-acre campus. 1 building on campus. Approved or accredited by Independent Schools Association of the Central States, Network of Sacred Heart Schools, and Michigan Department of Education. Endowment: $3.4 million. Total enrollment: 493. Upper school average class size: 12. Upper school faculty-student ratio: 1:7. There are 180 required school days per year for Upper School students. Upper School students typically attend 5 days per week. The average school day consists of 7 hours.

Upper School Student Profile Grade 9: 27 students (27 girls); Grade 10: 29 students (29 girls); Grade 11: 33 students (33 girls); Grade 12: 40 students (40 girls). 69% of students are Roman Catholic.

Faculty School total: 79. In upper school: 11 men, 13 women; 16 have advanced degrees.

Subjects Offered 20th century history, Advanced Placement courses, algebra, American literature, art, art history, biology, calculus, calculus-AP, chemistry, child development, clayworking, community service, computer applications, computer graphics, concert band, concert choir, crafts, creative writing, earth science, economics, English literature, English literature-AP, English-AP, environmental science, European history, European history-AP, forensics, French, genetics, geometry, global studies, government/civics, health, health and wellness, honors algebra, honors geometry, interior design, jewelry making, Latin, literature, mathematics, photography, physical education, physical science, physics, pre-calculus, psychology, publications, social studies, sociology, Spanish, theater, theology, U.S. history, U.S. history-AP, video, Web site design, world history, world literature.

Graduation Requirements Arts and fine arts (art, music, dance, drama), computer applications, foreign language, government, health and wellness, literature, mathematics, physical education (includes health), science, social studies (includes history), theology, U.S. government, U.S. history, world history, world literature, Project Term, First Year Experience (arts lab). Community service is required.

Special Academic Programs 3 Advanced Placement exams for which test preparation is offered; honors section; independent study; term-away projects; domestic exchange program (with Network of Sacred Heart Schools); academic accommodation for the gifted, the musically talented, and the artistically talented.

College Admission Counseling 34 students graduated in 2010; all went to college, including Brown University; Denison University; Michigan State University; Oakland University; University of Michigan; University of Notre Dame. Mean SAT critical reading: 550, mean SAT math: 531, mean SAT writing: 540, mean composite ACT: 24.

Student Life Upper grades have uniform requirement, student council, honor system. Discipline rests primarily with faculty. Attendance at religious services is required.

Summer Programs Enrichment, sports, art/fine arts, computer instruction programs offered; session focuses on enrichment/day camp; held on campus; accepts boys and girls; open to students from other schools. 195 students usually enrolled. 2011 schedule: June 20 to July 29. Application deadline: none.

Tuition and Aid Day student tuition: $19,900. Tuition installment plan (FAST). Merit scholarship grants, need-based scholarship grants available. In 2010–11, 51% of upper-school students received aid; total upper-school merit-scholarship money awarded: $8000. Total amount of financial aid awarded in 2010–11: $834,755.

Admissions Traditional secondary-level entrance grade is 9. For fall 2010, 26 students applied for upper-level admission, 22 were accepted, 12 enrolled. Scholastic Testing Service High School Placement Test or Stanford Achievement Test required. Deadline for receipt of application materials: none. Application fee required: $50. On-campus interview required.

Athletics Interscholastic: basketball, dance team, equestrian sports, field hockey, figure skating, golf, lacrosse, skiing (downhill), softball, tennis, volleyball. 1 PE instructor, 13 coaches.

Computers Computers are regularly used in all academic classes. Computer network features include on-campus library services, online commercial services, Internet access, wireless campus network, Internet filtering or blocking technology, tablet PC program with wireless network and print services, classroom multimedia services, computer in each classroom. Campus intranet, student e-mail accounts, and computer access in designated common areas are available to students. Students grades are available online. The school has a published electronic and media policy.

Contact Barbara Lopiccolo, Director of Admissions. 248-646-8900 Ext. 129. Fax: 248-646-4143. E-mail: blopiccolo@ashmi.org. Web site: www.ashmi.org.

ACADÉMIE STE CÉCILE INTERNATIONAL SCHOOL

925 Cousineau Road
Windsor, Ontario N9G 1V8, Canada
Head of School: Mlle. Thérèse H. Gadoury

General Information Coeducational boarding and day college-preparatory, arts, and bilingual studies school, affiliated with Roman Catholic Church. Boarding grades 6–12, day grades JK–12. Founded: 1993. Setting: suburban. Nearest major city is Toronto, Canada. Students are housed in single-sex by floor dormitories. 33-acre campus. 2 buildings on campus. Approved or accredited by International Baccalaureate Organization, Ontario Ministry of Education, The Association of Boarding Schools, and Ontario Department of Education. Languages of instruction: English and French. Total enrollment: 236. Upper school average class size: 15. Upper school faculty-student ratio: 1:15. There are 180 required school days per year for Upper School students. Upper School students typically attend 5 days per week. The average school day consists of 6 hours and 15 minutes.

Upper School Student Profile Grade 9: 18 students (6 boys, 12 girls); Grade 10: 22 students (16 boys, 6 girls); Grade 11: 27 students (13 boys, 14 girls); Grade 12: 36 students (17 boys, 19 girls). 98% of students are boarding students. 2% are province residents. 2 provinces are represented in upper school student body. 50% are international students. International students from Bermuda, Hong Kong, Mexico, Nigeria, Republic of Korea, and Taiwan; 3 other countries represented in student body. 70% of students are Roman Catholic.

Faculty School total: 50. In upper school: 13 men, 11 women; 10 have advanced degrees; 4 reside on campus.

Subjects Offered Accounting, advanced chemistry, advanced computer applications, advanced math, algebra, art, art education, art history, audio visual/media, ballet, basketball, biology, business technology, calculus, campus ministry, career education, careers, Catholic belief and practice, chemistry, choir, choral music, civics, classical music, computer information systems, computer programming, computer science, concert band, concert bell choir, concert choir, creative dance, creative drama, creative thinking, creative writing, critical thinking, critical writing, dance, dance performance, decision making skills, desktop publishing, desktop publishing, ESL, discrete mathematics, drama performance, drama workshop, dramatic arts, drawing, drawing and design, driver education, earth science, economics, English, English literature, environmental studies, ethics, expository writing, family living, French, French studies, geography, geometry, German, golf, handbells, health and wellness, health education, history, history of dance, history of music, history of religion, history of the Catholic Church, honors algebra, honors English, honors geometry, honors world

history, instrumental music, International Baccalaureate courses, Internet, Internet research, intro to computers, Italian, jazz band, jazz dance, journalism, keyboarding, Latin, leadership, library skills, Life of Christ, literature, literature and composition-AP, mathematics, media studies, music, music appreciation, music composition, music history, music performance, music theory, organ, painting, philosophy, photography, physical education, physics, piano, poetry, prayer/spirituality, pre-algebra, pre-calculus, probability and statistics, public speaking, reading, reading/study skills, religion, research skills, SAT preparation, science, sculpture, Shakespeare, social studies, softball, Spanish, stage and body movement, stained glass, strings, student government, swimming, tennis, TOEFL preparation, track and field, values and decisions, visual arts, vocal ensemble, voice, volleyball, wind ensemble, wind instruments, world religions, writing, yearbook.

Graduation Requirements Ontario Ministry of Education requirements.

Special Academic Programs International Baccalaureate program; Advanced Placement exam preparation; honors section; accelerated programs; academic accommodation for the gifted, the musically talented, and the artistically talented; remedial reading and/or remedial writing; remedial math; ESL (60 students enrolled).

College Admission Counseling 36 students graduated in 2010; they went to McMaster University; The University of British Columbia; The University of Western Ontario; University of Toronto; University of Waterloo; University of Windsor. Other: 35 entered a postgraduate year, 1 had other specific plans. Mean SAT critical reading: 593, mean SAT math: 655, mean SAT writing: 615. 67% scored over 600 on SAT critical reading, 83% scored over 600 on SAT math, 67% scored over 600 on SAT writing.

Student Life Upper grades have uniform requirement, student council, honor system. Discipline rests primarily with faculty.

Summer Programs Remediation, enrichment, advancement, ESL, art/fine arts programs offered; session focuses on ESL; held on campus; accepts boys and girls; open to students from other schools. 25 students usually enrolled. 2011 schedule: July 4 to September 2. Application deadline: May 31.

Tuition and Aid Day student tuition: CAN$13,850; 7-day tuition and room/board: CAN$38,000. Tuition installment plan (Insured Tuition Payment Plan). Tuition reduction for siblings, merit scholarship grants available. In 2010–11, 5% of upper-school students received aid; total upper-school merit-scholarship money awarded: CAN$4500. Total amount of financial aid awarded in 2010–11: CAN$15,000.

Admissions Traditional secondary-level entrance grade is 9. For fall 2010, 30 students applied for upper-level admission, 29 were accepted, 27 enrolled. Deadline for receipt of application materials: none. Application fee required: CAN$300. Interview recommended.

Athletics Interscholastic: aquatics (boys, girls), badminton (b,g), basketball (b,g), equestrian sports (b,g), golf (b,g), horseback riding (b,g), ice hockey (g), independent competitive sports (b,g), modern dance (b,g), physical fitness (b,g), soccer (b,g), softball (b,g), swimming and diving (b,g), tennis (b,g), volleyball (b,g); intramural: aquatics (b,g), badminton (b,g), ballet (g), basketball (b,g), bowling (b,g), cross-country running (b,g), dance (b,g), dressage (b,g), equestrian sports (b,g), golf (b,g), horseback riding (b,g), paddle tennis (b,g), soccer (b,g), softball (b,g), swimming and diving (b,g), table tennis (b,g), tennis (b,g), volleyball (b,g); coed interscholastic: aquatics, badminton, basketball, dressage, equestrian sports, fitness, golf, horseback riding, indoor track & field, modern dance, physical fitness, soccer, softball, swimming and diving, tennis, volleyball; coed intramural: aquatics, badminton, basketball, bowling, cross-country running, dance, dressage, equestrian sports, floor hockey, golf, horseback riding, modern dance, soccer, softball, swimming and diving, tennis, volleyball. 2 PE instructors, 8 coaches.

Computers Computers are regularly used in accounting, business, desktop publishing, ESL, information technology, mathematics classes. Computer network features include Internet access, wireless campus network.

Contact Ms. Gwen A. Gatt, Admissions Clerk. 519-969-1291. Fax: 519-969-7953. E-mail: info@stececile.ca. Web site: www.stececile.ca.

ACCELERATED SCHOOLS

2160 South Cook Street
Denver, Colorado 80210
Head of School: John Klieforth

General Information Coeducational boarding and day college-preparatory, bilingual studies, and technology school; primarily serves underachievers, students with learning disabilities, individuals with Attention Deficit Disorder, individuals with emotional and behavioral problems, dyslexic students, and bipolar disorders. Boarding boys grades 7–12, boarding girls grades 8–12, day boys grades K–12, day girls grades K–12. Founded: 1920. Setting: urban. Students are housed in host family homes. 3.5-acre campus. 3 buildings on campus. Approved or accredited by North Central Association of Colleges and Schools and Colorado Department of Education. Languages of instruction: English, Spanish, and French. Total enrollment: 29. Upper school average class size: 7. Upper school faculty-student ratio: 1:7. There are 180 required school days per year for Upper School students. The average school day consists of 6 hours.

Upper School Student Profile 15% of students are boarding students. 85% are state residents. 3 states are represented in upper school student body. 8% are international students. International students from Japan, Republic of Korea, and Spain; 1 other country represented in student body.

Faculty School total: 10. In upper school: 2 men, 3 women; 1 has an advanced degree.

Subjects Offered ACT preparation, algebra, American history, American literature, art, art history, biology, business, business skills, calculus, chemistry, computer math, computer science, creative writing, earth science, economics, English, English literature, French, geography, geology, geometry, government/civics, grammar, history, human biology, mathematics, philosophy, photography, physical education, physics, psychology, reading, science, social studies, sociology, Spanish, TOEFL preparation, trigonometry, world history, zoology.

Graduation Requirements Business skills (includes word processing), computer science, English, foreign language, mathematics, physical education (includes health), science, social studies (includes history).

Special Academic Programs Honors section; accelerated programs; study at local college for college credit; academic accommodation for the gifted; remedial reading and/or remedial writing; remedial math; programs in English, mathematics, general development for dyslexic students; special instructional classes for students with Attention Deficit Disorder, learning disabilities, and dyslexia; ESL (5 students enrolled).

College Admission Counseling Colleges students went to include Arapahoe Community College; Colorado State University; Metropolitan State College of Denver; University of Denver; University of Northern Colorado.

Student Life Upper grades have specified standards of dress. Discipline rests primarily with faculty.

Tuition and Aid Day student tuition: $20,750; 7-day tuition and room/board: $27,950. Guaranteed tuition plan. Tuition installment plan (Key Tuition Payment Plan, monthly payment plans, individually arranged payment plans, Sallie Mae, Wells Fargo plan). Tuition reduction for siblings, need-based scholarship grants available. In 2009–10, 10% of upper-school students received aid. Total amount of financial aid awarded in 2009–10: $50,000.

Admissions Traditional secondary-level entrance grade is 10. For fall 2009, 60 students applied for upper-level admission, 40 were accepted, 29 enrolled. CTBS or ERB, Iowa Test of Educational Development or Iowa Tests of Basic Skills required. Deadline for receipt of application materials: none. No application fee required. Interview recommended.

Athletics Intramural: bowling (boys, girls); coed intramural: aerobics, aerobics/dance, alpine skiing, aquatics, archery, backpacking, badminton, baseball, basketball, bicycling, billiards, bowling, croquet, dance, fishing, flag football, Frisbee, golf, hiking/backpacking, horseback riding, ice skating, jogging.

Computers Computers are regularly used in English, mathematics classes. Computer resources include Internet access, wireless campus network. Computer access in designated common areas is available to students.

Contact Jane T. Queen, Executive Director. 303-758-2003. Fax: 303-757-4336. E-mail: queenjbqueen@aol.com. Web site: www.acceleratedschools.org.

ACS COBHAM INTERNATIONAL SCHOOL

Heywood, Portsmouth Road
Cobham, Surrey KT11 1BL, United Kingdom
Head of School: Tom Lehman

General Information Coeducational boarding and day college-preparatory, International Baccalaureate, and Advanced Placement school. Boarding grades 7–12, day grades N–12. Founded: 1967. Setting: suburban. Nearest major city is London, United Kingdom. Students are housed in single-sex dormitories. 128-acre campus. 4 buildings on campus. Approved or accredited by Independent Schools Council (UK), International Baccalaureate Organization, and New England Association of Schools and Colleges. Member of European Council of International Schools. Language of instruction: English. Total enrollment: 1,338. Upper school average class size: 18. Upper school faculty-student ratio: 1:9.

Faculty School total: 140. In upper school: 19 men, 26 women; 20 have advanced degrees; 16 reside on campus.

Subjects Offered Algebra, American history, American literature, art, art history, biology, calculus, ceramics, chemistry, computer programming, computer science, drama, Dutch, economics, English, ESL, European history, fine arts, French, geometry, German, Japanese, journalism, mathematics, music, Norwegian, photography, physical education, physics, psychology, science, social studies, Spanish, speech, Swedish, theater, theory of knowledge, trigonometry, typing, world history, world literature, writing.

Graduation Requirements Arts and fine arts (art, music, dance, drama), English, foreign language, mathematics, physical education (includes health), science, social studies (includes history).

Special Academic Programs International Baccalaureate program; Advanced Placement exam preparation; honors section; academic accommodation for the gifted; ESL (25 students enrolled).

College Admission Counseling 125 students graduated in 2009; they went to Harvard University; New York University; Northwestern University; The University of Texas at Austin; University of Florida; Yale University.

Student Life Upper grades have specified standards of dress, student council, honor system. Discipline rests primarily with faculty.

Tuition and Aid Day student tuition: £18,650; 5-day tuition and room/board: £29,100; 7-day tuition and room/board: £32,960. Tuition installment plan (quarterly installment plan). Bursaries available.

Admissions Traditional secondary-level entrance grade is 9. English for Non-native Speakers required. Deadline for receipt of application materials: none. Application fee required: £125. Interview recommended.

Athletics Interscholastic: baseball (boys), basketball (b,g), cheering (g), cross-country running (b,g), dance team (g), rugby (b), soccer (b,g), softball (g), tennis (b,g), track and field (b,g), volleyball (b,g); intramural: soccer (b,g), water polo (b); coed interscholastic: golf; coed intramural: horseback riding, weight training. 2 PE instructors.

Computers Computers are regularly used in all academic classes. Computer network features include on-campus library services, online commercial services, Internet access. The school has a published electronic and media policy.

Contact Heidi Ayoub, Dean of Admissions. 44-01932-867-251. Fax: 44-01932 869 789. E-mail: hayoub@acs-england.co.uk. Web site: www.acs-england.co.uk.

ACS EGHAM INTERNATIONAL SCHOOL

Woodlee, London Road (A30)
Surrey TW20 0HS, United Kingdom
Head of School: Mr. Peter Hosier

General Information Coeducational day college-preparatory and International Baccalaureate school. Grades N–12. Founded: 1967. Setting: suburban. Nearest major city is London, United Kingdom. 20-acre campus. 5 buildings on campus. Approved or accredited by Independent Schools Council (UK), International Baccalaureate Organization, and New England Association of Schools and Colleges. Member of European Council of International Schools. Language of instruction: English. Total enrollment: 562. Upper school average class size: 15. Upper school faculty-student ratio: 1:9.

Faculty School total: 68. In upper school: 9 men, 12 women; 10 have advanced degrees.

Subjects Offered Algebra, art, band, biology, chemistry, choir, college counseling, computer science, computer skills, drama, Dutch, economics, English, environmental systems, European history, forensics, French, geometry, German, history, information technology, integrated mathematics, International Baccalaureate courses, Korean, mathematics, model United Nations, music, philosophy, physical education, physics, Polish, Portuguese, psychology, Russian, Spanish, Swedish, theater arts, theory of knowledge, visual arts, world studies.

Graduation Requirements Arts and fine arts (art, music, dance, drama), English, foreign language, mathematics, physical education (includes health), science, social studies (includes history).

Special Academic Programs International Baccalaureate program; academic accommodation for the gifted; ESL (55 students enrolled).

College Admission Counseling 26 students graduated in 2009; they went to Boston University; James Madison University; Lewis & Clark College; The George Washington University; University of Vermont; Washington and Lee University. Mean SAT critical reading: 580, mean SAT math: 573, mean SAT writing: 562, mean combined SAT: 1715.

Student Life Upper grades have specified standards of dress, student council, honor system. Discipline rests primarily with faculty.

Tuition and Aid Day student tuition: £18,350–£18,410. Tuition installment plan (quarterly payment plan). Bursaries available. In 2009–10, 3% of upper-school students received aid.

Admissions Traditional secondary-level entrance grade is 9. English for Non-native Speakers required. Deadline for receipt of application materials: none. Application fee required: £125. Interview recommended.

Athletics Interscholastic: baseball (boys), cheering (g), rugby (b), softball (g), track and field (b,g), volleyball (g); intramural: dance (g); coed interscholastic: basketball, cross-country running, indoor track & field, soccer, tennis; coed intramural: fencing, golf, soccer. 4 PE instructors, 4 coaches.

Computers Computers are regularly used in all classes. Computer network features include on-campus library services, online commercial services, Internet access, wireless campus network, Internet filtering or blocking technology. Student e-mail accounts are available to students.

Contact Ms. Julia Love, Dean of Admissions. 44-01784-430611. Fax: 44-01784-430626. E-mail: eghamadmission@acs-england.co.uk. Web site: www.acs-england.co.uk/schools/egham/index.htm.

ACS HILLINGDON INTERNATIONAL SCHOOL

Hillingdon Court
108 Vine Lane
Hillingdon, Middlesex UB10 0BE, United Kingdom
Head of School: Mrs. Ginger G. Apple

General Information Coeducational day college-preparatory, International Baccalaureate, and Advanced Placement school. Grades PK–12. Founded: 1967. Setting: suburban. Nearest major city is London, United Kingdom. 11-acre campus. 1 building on campus. Approved or accredited by Independent Schools Council (UK), International Baccalaureate Organization, New England Association of Schools and Colleges, and The College Board. Member of European Council of International Schools. Language of instruction: English. Total enrollment: 511. Upper school average class

size: 15. Upper school faculty-student ratio: 1:9. Upper School students typically attend 5 days per week. The average school day consists of 6 hours and 40 minutes.
Faculty School total: 70. In upper school: 11 men, 15 women; 12 have advanced degrees.
Subjects Offered Advanced Placement courses, algebra, art, art-AP, biology, calculus, chemistry, chemistry-AP, computer graphics, computer science, Dutch, economics, English, English language-AP, English literature and composition-AP, English literature-AP, environmental science, ESL, French, geography, geometry, German, health, information technology, integrated science, Japanese, macro/microeconomics-AP, math methods, music theory-AP, physical education, physics, physics-AP, psychology, psychology-AP, Spanish, theory of knowledge, U.S. history-AP, Web site design, world history.
Graduation Requirements Arts and fine arts (art, music, dance, drama), English, foreign language, mathematics, physical education (includes health), science, social studies (includes history).
Special Academic Programs International Baccalaureate program; Advanced Placement exam preparation; honors section; academic accommodation for the gifted; ESL.
College Admission Counseling 47 students graduated in 2009; they went to Baylor University; Bowdoin College; Furman University; The University of Kansas; University of Chicago; Wheaton College. Mean SAT critical reading: 531, mean SAT math: 571, mean combined SAT: 1102, mean composite ACT: 24.
Student Life Upper grades have specified standards of dress, student council, honor system. Discipline rests primarily with faculty.
Tuition and Aid Day student tuition: £8850–£17,760. Tuition installment plan (quarterly installment plan). Bursaries available.
Admissions Traditional secondary-level entrance grade is 9. English for Non-native Speakers required. Deadline for receipt of application materials: none. Application fee required: £125. Interview recommended.
Athletics Interscholastic: baseball (boys), basketball (b,g), cross-country running (b,g), rugby (b), soccer (b,g), softball (g), swimming and diving (b,g), tennis (b,g), track and field (b,g), volleyball (b,g). 4 PE instructors, 20 coaches.
Computers Computers are regularly used in all academic classes. Computer network features include on-campus library services, Internet access, Internet filtering or blocking technology. The school has a published electronic and media policy.
Contact Ms. Rudianne Soltis, Dean of Admissions. 44-01895-818402. Fax: 44-01895-818404. E-mail: rsoltis@acs-england.co.uk. Web site: www.acs-england.co.uk.

ADELPHI ACADEMY
8515 Ridge Boulevard
Brooklyn, New York 11209
Head of School: Dr. Roy J. Blash
General Information Coeducational day college-preparatory, arts, technology, and writing school; primarily serves students with learning disabilities, individuals with Attention Deficit Disorder, individuals with emotional and behavioral problems, and dyslexic students. Grades PK–12. Founded: 1863. Setting: urban. Nearest major city is New York. 1-acre campus. 3 buildings on campus. Approved or accredited by New York Department of Education. Candidate for accreditation by Middle States Association of Colleges and Schools. Endowment: $2.6 million. Total enrollment: 110. Upper school average class size: 14. Upper school faculty-student ratio: 1:6. There are 153 required school days per year for Upper School students. Upper School students typically attend 5 days per week. The average school day consists of 7 hours.
Upper School Student Profile Grade 9: 8 students (5 boys, 3 girls); Grade 10: 7 students (6 boys, 1 girl); Grade 11: 14 students (6 boys, 8 girls); Grade 12: 22 students (12 boys, 10 girls).
Faculty School total: 18. In upper school: 6 men, 1 woman; 6 have advanced degrees.
Subjects Offered Acting, algebra, American history, American literature, art, art history, athletics, biology, business, calculus, chemistry, choir, chorus, college counseling, college placement, communication arts, community service, computer applications, computer education, computer math, computer science, computer skills, computer studies, computers, creative writing, dance, digital photography, drama, drama performance, drawing, driver education, earth science, English, English composition, English literature, environmental science, European history, film, fine arts, fitness, foreign language, general science, geography, geometry, government, government/civics, grammar, guidance, health, health and wellness, health education, health science, history, history of the Americas, independent study, Internet, Internet research, intro to computers, keyboarding, lab science, language arts, languages, leadership, library, library research, library skills, literature, math analysis, math applications, math methods, mathematics, modern history, music, music appreciation, newspaper, nutrition, photography, physical education, physics, public speaking, publications, publishing, SAT preparation, science, senior seminar, Spanish, speech, strategies for success, student teaching, studio art, study skills, technology, The 20th Century, theater, theater arts, trigonometry, U.S. government, U.S. literature, visual arts, voice, volleyball, Web site design, weight fitness, Western literature, word processing, world civilizations, world cultures, world history, writing, writing.
Graduation Requirements 20th century American writers, advanced biology, advanced math, African-American literature, American literature, 50 hours of community/school service, extracurricular participation.

Special Academic Programs Honors section; independent study; study at local college for college credit; academic accommodation for the gifted, the musically talented, and the artistically talented; remedial reading and/or remedial writing; remedial math; special instructional classes for students with mild learning disabilities and/or Attention Deficit Disorder issues.
College Admission Counseling 13 students graduated in 2009; all went to college, including Adelphi University; Bucknell University; Harvard University; St. John's University; Syracuse University. 50% scored over 600 on SAT critical reading, 50% scored over 600 on SAT math.
Student Life Upper grades have uniform requirement, student council, honor system. Discipline rests primarily with faculty.
Tuition and Aid Day student tuition: $17,500. Tuition installment plan (individually arranged payment plans). Tuition reduction for siblings, merit scholarship grants, need-based scholarship grants, paying campus jobs available. In 2009–10, 25% of upper-school students received aid; total upper-school merit-scholarship money awarded: $35,000. Total amount of financial aid awarded in 2009–10: $125,000.
Admissions Traditional secondary-level entrance grade is 9. For fall 2009, 125 students applied for upper-level admission, 65 were accepted, 50 enrolled. Stanford Diagnostic Test required. Deadline for receipt of application materials: none. Application fee required: $100. On-campus interview required.
Athletics Interscholastic: aerobics/dance (girls), baseball (b), basketball (b,g), cheering (g), dance (g), dance squad (g), dance team (g), danceline (g), jogging (b,g), soccer (b), softball (b,g); coed interscholastic: bowling, cross-country running, fitness, golf, indoor hockey, martial arts, physical fitness, self defense, tennis, weight lifting, weight training; coed intramural: bowling, Cosom hockey, cross-country running, gymnastics, juggling. 3 PE instructors, 4 coaches, 4 athletic trainers.
Computers Computers are regularly used in all classes. Computer network features include on-campus library services, online commercial services, Internet access. The school has a published electronic and media policy.
Contact Mr. Iphigenia Romanos, Coordinator of Lower and Middle Schools. 718-238-3308 Ext. 312. Fax: 718-238-2894. E-mail: romanosi@adelphiacademy.org. Web site: www.adelphiacademy.org.

ADMIRAL FARRAGUT ACADEMY
501 Park Street North
St. Petersburg, Florida 33710
Head of School: Capt. Robert J. Fine Jr.
General Information Coeducational boarding and day college-preparatory, Naval Junior ROTC, aviation, and military school. Boarding grades 6–12, day grades P3–12. Founded: 1933. Setting: suburban. Students are housed in single-sex by floor dormitories. 35-acre campus. 20 buildings on campus. Approved or accredited by Florida Council of Independent Schools, Southern Association of Colleges and Schools, The Association of Boarding Schools, and Florida Department of Education. Member of National Association of Independent Schools and Secondary School Admission Test Board. Endowment: $2 million. Total enrollment: 358. Upper school average class size: 16. Upper school faculty-student ratio: 1:8. There are 189 required school days per year for Upper School students. Upper School students typically attend 5 days per week. The average school day consists of 7 hours.
Upper School Student Profile Grade 9: 40 students (27 boys, 13 girls); Grade 10: 51 students (39 boys, 12 girls); Grade 11: 63 students (51 boys, 12 girls); Grade 12: 67 students (51 boys, 16 girls). 50% of students are boarding students. 73% are state residents. 14 states are represented in upper school student body. 30% are international students. International students from China, Colombia, Japan, Republic of Korea, Russian Federation, and Spain; 14 other countries represented in student body.
Faculty School total: 63. In upper school: 20 men, 14 women; 20 have advanced degrees; 20 reside on campus.
Subjects Offered ACT preparation, advanced math, algebra, American history, American literature, analytic geometry, anatomy and physiology, art, art history, aviation, band, biology, boating, British literature, business communications, calculus, calculus-AP, chemistry, Chinese, chorus, community service, computer programming, computer science, computer science-AP, creative writing, drama, driver education, earth science, economics, English, English composition, English language-AP, English literature, environmental science, ESL, ethics and responsibility, fine arts, French, geography, geometry, government/civics, grammar, health, history, journalism, keyboarding, Latin, library assistant, marching band, marine biology, mathematics, meteorology, military science, music, music history, navigation, NJROTC, oceanography, physical education, physics, pre-algebra, science, sign language, social studies, sociology, Spanish, Spanish language-AP, speech, statistics, swimming test, trigonometry, world history, world literature, yearbook.
Graduation Requirements Arts and fine arts (art, music, dance, drama), economics, English, ethics, foreign language, government, health education, mathematics, NJROTC, physical education (includes health), science, social studies (includes history), U.S. history, world history, Qualified Boat Handler (QBH) test, 80 hours of community service.
Special Academic Programs Advanced Placement exam preparation; honors section; study at local college for college credit; academic accommodation for the gifted; remedial reading and/or remedial writing; remedial math; ESL (10 students enrolled).
College Admission Counseling 53 students graduated in 2010; 52 went to college, including Florida State University; Georgia Institute of Technology; Syracuse

University; United States Naval Academy; University of Florida; University of South Florida. Other: 1 entered military service. Mean SAT critical reading: 488, mean SAT math: 520, mean SAT writing: 478, mean composite ACT: 20. 10% scored over 600 on SAT critical reading, 20% scored over 600 on SAT math, 3% scored over 600 on SAT writing, 15% scored over 26 on composite ACT.

Student Life Upper grades have uniform requirement, student council. Discipline rests equally with students and faculty.

Tuition and Aid Day student tuition: $17,070; 5-day tuition and room/board: $29,610; 7-day tuition and room/board: $35,400. Tuition installment plan (monthly payment plans, individually arranged payment plans, AFA Payment Plan). Tuition reduction for siblings, need-based scholarship grants, tuition reduction for children of faculty available. In 2010–11, 22% of upper-school students received aid. Total amount of financial aid awarded in 2010–11: $500,000.

Admissions Traditional secondary-level entrance grade is 10. For fall 2010, 200 students applied for upper-level admission, 122 were accepted, 106 enrolled. Any standardized test required. Deadline for receipt of application materials: none. Application fee required: $100. Interview required.

Athletics Interscholastic: aquatics (boys, girls), baseball (b), basketball (b,g), cross-country running (b,g), diving (b,g), drill team (b,g), football (b,g), golf (b,g), riflery (b,g), soccer (b,g), softball (g), swimming and diving (b,g), tennis (b,g), track and field (b,g), volleyball (g), wrestling (b); intramural: badminton (b,g), fishing (b,g), fitness walking (b,g), jogging (b,g), kayaking (b,g), riflery (b,g), running (b,g), wall climbing (b,g), weight training (b,g); coed interscholastic: aquatics, bowling, cheering, drill team, football, golf, JROTC drill, marksmanship, riflery; coed intramural: badminton, basketball, bicycling, billiards, canoeing/kayaking, fitness, flag football, Frisbee, martial arts, paint ball, physical training, sailing, scuba diving, strength & conditioning, table tennis, volleyball. 4 PE instructors, 3 coaches, 1 athletic trainer.

Computers Computers are regularly used in aviation, computer applications, English, foreign language, history, keyboarding, NJROTC, programming, science, writing, yearbook classes. Computer network features include on-campus library services, online commercial services, Internet access, wireless campus network, Internet filtering or blocking technology, faculty Web pages, Cisco Networking Academy. Students grades are available online. The school has a published electronic and media policy.

Contact Cmdr. Gretchen Herbst, Director of Admissions. 727-384-5500 Ext. 220. Fax: 727-347-5160. E-mail: gherbst@farragut.org. Web site: www.farragut.org.

ADVANCED ACADEMY OF GEORGIA

Honors House
University of West Georgia
Carrollton, Georgia 30118

Head of School: Dr. Michael Hester

General Information Coeducational boarding college-preparatory, arts, business, bilingual studies, technology, and mathematics, science, and humanities school. Grades 10–12. Founded: 1995. Setting: small town. Nearest major city is Atlanta. Students are housed in coed dormitories. 394-acre campus. 89 buildings on campus. Approved or accredited by Southern Association of Colleges and Schools and Georgia Department of Education. Total enrollment: 83. Upper school average class size: 14. Upper school faculty-student ratio: 1:14.

Upper School Student Profile 100% of students are boarding students. 86% are state residents. 4 states are represented in upper school student body. 8% are international students. International students from Republic of Korea and Spain.

Faculty School total: 270. In upper school: 149 men, 121 women; all have advanced degrees.

Subjects Offered 20th century American writers, 20th century history, 20th century physics, 20th century world history, accounting, acting, advanced chemistry, advanced computer applications, advanced math, advanced studio art-AP, African American history, African American studies, African-American literature, algebra, American biography, American Civil War, American culture, American democracy, American foreign policy, American government, American history, American legal systems, American literature, American sign language, analysis, analysis and differential calculus, analysis of data, analytic geometry, anatomy, ancient world history, ancient/medieval philosophy, animal behavior, anthropology, archaeology, art, art and culture, art appreciation, art education, art history, Asian history, Asian literature, Asian studies, astronomy, astrophysics, athletics, band, banking, Bible as literature, biochemistry, bioethics, DNA and culture, biology, biotechnology, Black history, British history, British literature, British literature (honors), British National Curriculum, business applications, business communications, business education, business law, business mathematics, business skills, business studies, business technology, calculus, cell biology, chemistry, child development, Chinese, Chinese history, Chinese literature, Chinese studies, choir, cinematography, civics/free enterprise, civil rights, Civil War, civil war history, classical civilization, classical Greek literature, classical language, classical music, classical studies, communications, comparative government and politics, comparative politics, computer animation, computer applications, computer art, computer education, computer graphics, computer information systems, computer math, computer multimedia, computer music, computer processing, computer programming, computer science, computer technologies, constitutional history of U.S., constitutional law, consumer economics, critical thinking, critical writing, data analysis, debate, democracy in America, desktop publishing, discrete mathematics, DNA, DNA research, DNA science lab, drama, drawing, drawing and design, early childhood, earth and space science, earth science, earth systems analysis, East Asian history, East European studies, Eastern religion and philosophy, Eastern world civilizations, ecology, economics, economics and history, education, English, English composition, English literature, ensembles, entrepreneurship, environmental geography, environmental science, environmental systems, ethics, ethnic literature, ethnic studies, European civilization, European history, film appreciation, film studies, first aid, fitness, forensics, French, gender issues, genetics, geography, geology, geometry, German, German literature, global issues, global science, global studies, golf, government/civics, graphic arts, graphic design, graphics, Greek, Greek culture, Holocaust and other genocides, Holocaust legacy, Holocaust seminar, Holocaust studies, honors algebra, honors English, honors geometry, honors U.S. history, honors world history, human anatomy, human sexuality, intro to computers, Japanese, jazz, jazz band, Jewish history, Jewish studies, language arts, Latin, law, law and the legal system, law studies, library, library research, life saving, linear algebra, literature by women, literature seminar, logic, logic, rhetoric, and debate, management information systems, marching band, marine biology, marketing, math analysis, math applications, mathematical modeling, media communications, methods of research, microbiology, microeconomics, Middle East, military history, minority studies, model United Nations, modeling, modern Chinese history, modern civilization, modern European history, modern political theory, modern politics, modern problems, modern Western civilization, modern world history, money management, music, music appreciation, music composition, Native American history, Native American studies, natural history, newspaper, North American literature, oceanography, organic chemistry, painting, parent/child development, performing arts, personal and social education, personal development, personal finance, personal fitness, philosophy, philosophy of government, photography, photojournalism, physical education, physical fitness, physical science, physics, physiology, piano, political economy, political science, political systems, political thought, post-calculus, pre-calculus, printmaking, probability, probability and statistics, psychology, public policy, public speaking, publications, publishing, radio broadcasting, religion and culture, religious education, religious studies, Roman civilization, Roman culture, ROTC, Russian, Russian history, Russian literature, Russian studies, science and technology, science fiction, Shakespeare, Shakespearean histories, social education, social justice, social psychology, social sciences, social studies, society, society and culture, society challenge and change, society, politics and law, sociology, South African history, Southern literature, Spanish, Spanish literature, speech and debate, speech and oral interpretations, speech communications, sports medicine, sports nutrition, state government, state history, statistics, stock market, student teaching, studio art, technical arts, technical drawing, technical education, technical skills, technical studies, technical theater, technical writing, technology, telecommunications, telecommunications and the Internet, television, The 20th Century, the Presidency, the Sixties, traditional camping, U.S. constitutional history, U.S. government, U.S. government and politics, U.S. history, U.S. literature, U.S. Presidents, United Nations and international issues, Vietnam War, visual and performing arts, visual arts, visual literacy, visual reality, water color painting, weight training, Western civilization, Western literature, Western philosophy, Western religions, women in literature, women in society, women in the classical world, women in world history, women spirituality and faith, women's health, women's literature, women's studies, world civilizations, world cultures, world geography, world governments, world history, world issues, world literature, world religions, world studies, World War I, World War II, World-Wide-Web publishing, writing.

Graduation Requirements Students must complete Georgia high school requirements which are satisfied through equivalent college courses offered by the university.

Special Academic Programs Honors section; independent study; study at local college for college credit; study abroad; academic accommodation for the gifted, the musically talented, and the artistically talented.

College Admission Counseling 32 students graduated in 2009; all went to college, including Agnes Scott College; Brown University; Georgia Institute of Technology; Georgia State University; Savannah College of Art and Design; University of Georgia. Mean SAT critical reading: 648, mean SAT math: 645. 79% scored over 600 on SAT critical reading, 75% scored over 600 on SAT math.

Student Life Upper grades have student council, honor system. Discipline rests equally with students and faculty.

Tuition and Aid 5-day tuition and room/board: $5600; 7-day tuition and room/board: $5600. Merit scholarship grants, need-based scholarship grants, need-based loans, middle-income loans, paying campus jobs available. In 2009–10, 65% of upper-school students received aid; total upper-school merit-scholarship money awarded: $56,000. Total amount of financial aid awarded in 2009–10: $109,000.

Admissions Traditional secondary-level entrance grade is 11. ACT or SAT required. Deadline for receipt of application materials: June 1. Application fee required: $30. Interview required.

Athletics Coed Intramural: aerobics, basketball, flag football, Frisbee, paint ball, soccer, softball, ultimate Frisbee.

Computers Computers are regularly used in all classes. Computer network features include on-campus library services, online commercial services, Internet access, wireless campus network, Internet filtering or blocking technology. Student e-mail accounts are available to students. Students grades are available online. The school has a published electronic and media policy.

Contact Ms. Anneliesa Finch, Program Specialist. 678-839-6249. Fax: 678-839-0636. E-mail: afinch@westga.edu. Web site: www.advancedacademy.org.

AIRDRIE KOINONIA CHRISTIAN SCHOOL

2104 Yankee Valley Blvd.
Airdrie, Alberta T4B 2A3, Canada
Head of School: Mr. Earl Driedger

General Information Coeducational day and distance learning college-preparatory, general academic, and religious studies school, affiliated with Christian faith, Evangelical/Fundamental faith. Grades K–12. Distance learning grades 10–12. Founded: 1987. Setting: suburban. Nearest major city is Calgary, Canada. 5-acre campus. 1 building on campus. Approved or accredited by Association of Christian Schools International, Association of Independent Schools and Colleges of Alberta, and Alberta Department of Education. Language of instruction: English. Total enrollment: 264. Upper school average class size: 15. Upper school faculty-student ratio: 1:14. There are 182 required school days per year for Upper School students. Upper School students typically attend 5 days per week. The average school day consists of 6 hours.

Upper School Student Profile Grade 7: 21 students (14 boys, 7 girls); Grade 8: 25 students (13 boys, 12 girls); Grade 9: 19 students (7 boys, 12 girls); Grade 10: 16 students (5 boys, 11 girls); Grade 11: 13 students (8 boys, 5 girls); Grade 12: 22 students (11 boys, 11 girls). 100% of students are Christian faith, Evangelical/Fundamental faith.

Faculty School total: 16. In upper school: 3 men, 2 women; 2 have advanced degrees.

Subjects Offered Art, biology, career and personal planning, chemistry, Christian doctrine, Christian ethics, Christian scripture, computer information systems, computer processing, drama, English, ethics, family living, French, general math, health education, keyboarding, law studies, mathematics, physics, pre-algebra, science, world religions.

Graduation Requirements Career planning, career technology, Christian studies, English, science, social studies (includes history), 75 hours of community service.

Special Academic Programs Independent study; academic accommodation for the gifted; remedial math; special instructional classes for students with learning disabilities and Attention Deficit Disorder.

College Admission Counseling 22 students graduated in 2009; 8 went to college, including University of Calgary. Other: 14 went to work.

Student Life Upper grades have specified standards of dress, student council, honor system. Discipline rests primarily with faculty. Attendance at religious services is required.

Tuition and Aid Day student tuition: CAN$4368. Tuition installment plan (monthly payment plans, individually arranged payment plans). Tuition reduction for siblings, need-based scholarship grants available. In 2009–10, 1% of upper-school students received aid. Total amount of financial aid awarded in 2009–10: CAN$4300.

Admissions For fall 2009, 5 students applied for upper-level admission, 5 were accepted, 5 enrolled. Deadline for receipt of application materials: none. Application fee required: CAN$25. On-campus interview required.

Athletics Interscholastic: badminton (boys, girls), basketball (b,g), cross-country running (b,g), track and field (b,g), volleyball (b,g); coed interscholastic: badminton, physical fitness, soccer; coed intramural: floor hockey, mountain biking, outdoor adventure, outdoor education, rock climbing, skiing (downhill), snowboarding, soccer, softball. 1 PE instructor.

Computers Computer network features include on-campus library services, Internet access, Internet filtering or blocking technology. Computer access in designated common areas is available to students. Students grades are available online.

Contact Mrs. Mardelle Zieman, Office Manager. 403-948-5100. Fax: 403-948-5563. E-mail: officemanager@akcs.com. Web site: www.akcs.com.

ALABAMA CHRISTIAN ACADEMY

4700 Wares Ferry Road
Montgomery, Alabama 36109
Head of School: Mr. Ronnie C. Sewell

General Information Coeducational day college-preparatory, general academic, arts, religious studies, bilingual studies, and technology school, affiliated with Church of Christ. Grades K4–12. Founded: 1942. Setting: urban. 23-acre campus. 3 buildings on campus. Approved or accredited by Southern Association of Colleges and Schools and Alabama Department of Education. Total enrollment: 1,014. Upper school average class size: 21. Upper school faculty-student ratio: 1:22. There are 180 required school days per year for Upper School students. Upper School students typically attend 5 days per week. The average school day consists of 8 hours.

Upper School Student Profile 46% of students are members of Church of Christ.

Faculty School total: 64. In upper school: 15 men, 26 women; 10 have advanced degrees.

Subjects Offered Algebra, American government, American literature, Bible, biology, British literature, business mathematics, calculus, chemistry, composition, computer applications, English, finite math, geography, geometry, grammar, health, honors English, physical education, physical science, physics, physiology, pre-algebra, pre-calculus, Spanish, trigonometry, U.S. history, world history.

Graduation Requirements American government, Bible, computer applications, economics, English, geography, mathematics, physical education (includes health), science, U.S. history, world history.

Special Academic Programs Advanced Placement exam preparation; honors section.

College Admission Counseling 81 students graduated in 2009; 78 went to college, including Auburn University; Auburn University Montgomery; Freed-Hardeman University; Harding University; Lipscomb University; The University of Alabama. Other: 2 went to work, 1 entered military service.

Student Life Upper grades have uniform requirement, student council, honor system. Discipline rests primarily with faculty.

Tuition and Aid Day student tuition: $5526. Guaranteed tuition plan. Tuition installment plan (monthly payment plans). Tuition reduction for siblings, contact school for financial aid available. In 2009–10, 7% of upper-school students received aid. Total amount of financial aid awarded in 2009–10: $82,000.

Admissions Traditional secondary-level entrance grade is 9. Any standardized test required. Deadline for receipt of application materials: none. Application fee required: $240. On-campus interview required.

Athletics Interscholastic: baseball (boys), basketball (b,g), cheering (g), cross-country running (b,g), football (b), golf (b), physical training (b,g), running (b,g), soccer (b), softball (g), strength & conditioning (b,g), track and field (b,g), volleyball (g), weight training (b,g); coed interscholastic: jump rope, track and field. 2 PE instructors.

Computers Computers are regularly used in basic skills, business applications, career technology, reading, technology classes. Computer network features include on-campus library services, Internet access. The school has a published electronic and media policy.

Contact Mrs. Harriett Parker, Admissions. 334-277-1985 Ext. 227. Fax: 334-279-0604. E-mail: hparker@alabamachristian.com. Web site: www.alabamachristian.com.

ALBERT COLLEGE

160 Dundas Street West
Belleville, Ontario K8P 1A6, Canada
Head of School: Mr. Keith Stansfield

General Information Coeducational boarding and day college-preparatory, arts, and technology school, affiliated with United Church of Canada. Boarding grades 7–PG, day grades JK–PG. Founded: 1857. Setting: small town. Nearest major city is Toronto, Canada. Students are housed in single-sex dormitories. 25-acre campus. 7 buildings on campus. Approved or accredited by Conference of Independent Schools of Ontario, Ontario Ministry of Education, and Standards in Excellence And Learning (SEAL). Affiliate member of National Association of Independent Schools; member of Secondary School Admission Test Board. Language of instruction: English. Endowment: CAN$1.4 million. Total enrollment: 293. Upper school average class size: 14. Upper school faculty-student ratio: 1:8.

Upper School Student Profile Grade 9: 19 students (13 boys, 6 girls); Grade 10: 24 students (10 boys, 14 girls); Grade 11: 38 students (22 boys, 16 girls); Grade 12: 49 students (28 boys, 21 girls); Postgraduate: 10 students (4 boys, 6 girls). 63% of students are boarding students. 65% are province residents. 6 provinces are represented in upper school student body. 34% are international students. International students from Barbados, Bermuda, Hong Kong, Mexico, Republic of Korea, and Spain; 22 other countries represented in student body.

Faculty School total: 34. In upper school: 15 men, 14 women; 4 have advanced degrees; 14 reside on campus.

Subjects Offered Algebra, ancient history, art, art history, biology, business, calculus, Canadian geography, Canadian history, chemistry, computer science, drama, economics, English, English literature, English-AP, environmental science, ESL, European history, family studies, fine arts, finite math, French, geography, history, law, mathematics, music, physical education, physics, science, social sciences, social studies, society challenge and change, world history.

Graduation Requirements Arts and fine arts (art, music, dance, drama), business skills (includes word processing), English, foreign language, mathematics, physical education (includes health), science, social sciences, social studies (includes history).

Special Academic Programs Advanced Placement exam preparation; accelerated programs; independent study; academic accommodation for the gifted, the musically talented, and the artistically talented; ESL (22 students enrolled).

College Admission Counseling 54 students graduated in 2009; all went to college, including Carleton University; McGill University; Queen's University at Kingston; The University of Western Ontario; University of Ottawa.

Student Life Upper grades have uniform requirement, student council, honor system. Discipline rests equally with students and faculty. Attendance at religious services is required.

Tuition and Aid Day student tuition: CAN$15,000–CAN$19,800; 5-day tuition and room/board: CAN$31,800; 7-day tuition and room/board: CAN$37,000–CAN$43,000. Tuition installment plan (Insured Tuition Payment Plan, monthly payment plans, individually arranged payment plans, 3-payment plan). Tuition reduction for siblings, bursaries, merit scholarship grants, need-based scholarship grants available. In 2009–10, 35% of upper-school students received aid; total upper-school merit-scholarship money awarded: CAN$185,200. Total amount of financial aid awarded in 2009–10: CAN$282,000.

Admissions Traditional secondary-level entrance grade is 9. For fall 2009, 81 students applied for upper-level admission, 66 were accepted, 38 enrolled. Gates MacGinite Reading Tests, Nelson-Denny Reading Test or SSAT required. Deadline for receipt of application materials: none. Application fee required: CAN$100. Interview required.

Athletics Interscholastic: alpine skiing (boys, girls), aquatics (b,g), badminton (b,g), basketball (b,g), cross-country running (b,g), field hockey (g), golf (b,g), ice hockey (b), lacrosse (g), rugby (b), running (b,g), skiing (cross-country) (b,g), skiing (downhill) (b,g), soccer (b,g), squash (b,g), tennis (b,g), track and field (b,g), volleyball (b,g); intramural: aerobics (g), aerobics/Nautilus (b,g), ball hockey (b), basketball (b,g), cross-country running (b,g), field hockey (g), floor hockey (b,g), golf (b), hockey (b), ice skating (b), indoor soccer (b,g), kayaking (b,g), lacrosse (g), rowing (b,g), rugby (b), running (b,g), soccer (b,g), tennis (b,g), track and field (b,g), volleyball (b,g), weight training (b); coed interscholastic: aquatics, nordic skiing, sailing, swimming and diving, tennis; coed intramural: aerobics, aerobics/dance, alpine skiing, aquatics, backpacking, bicycling, canoeing/kayaking, climbing, dance, fitness, flag football, Frisbee, gymnastics, hiking/backpacking, jogging, modern dance, mountain biking, nordic skiing, outdoor activities, outdoor recreation, outdoors, paddle tennis, paint ball, physical fitness, physical training, rafting, rappelling, rock climbing, roller blading, ropes courses, sailing, skateboarding, skiing (cross-country), skiing (downhill), snowboarding, squash, swimming and diving, table tennis, triathlon, ultimate Frisbee, wall climbing, wilderness, winter soccer, yoga. 4 PE instructors, 2 coaches.

Computers Computers are regularly used in English, mathematics, science classes. Computer network features include on-campus library services, Internet access, wireless campus network, Internet filtering or blocking technology. Campus intranet and student e-mail accounts are available to students. The school has a published electronic and media policy.

Contact Mrs. Heather Kidd, Director of Admission. 800-952-5237 Ext. 2204. Fax: 613-968-9651. E-mail: hkidd@albertc.on.ca. Web site: www.albertc.on.ca.

ALBUQUERQUE ACADEMY
6400 Wyoming Boulevard NE
Albuquerque, New Mexico 87109
Head of School: Andrew Watson

General Information Coeducational day college-preparatory, arts, technology, Experiential education, and global languages school. Grades 6–12. Founded: 1955. Setting: suburban. 312-acre campus. 10 buildings on campus. Approved or accredited by Independent Schools Association of the Southwest and New Mexico Department of Education. Member of National Association of Independent Schools and Secondary School Admission Test Board. Endowment: $18 million. Total enrollment: 1,096. Upper school average class size: 15. Upper school faculty-student ratio: 1:9. There are 171 required school days per year for Upper School students. Upper School students typically attend 5 days per week. The average school day consists of 7 hours and 30 minutes.

Upper School Student Profile Grade 9: 172 students (83 boys, 89 girls); Grade 10: 165 students (84 boys, 81 girls); Grade 11: 155 students (78 boys, 77 girls); Grade 12: 158 students (79 boys, 79 girls).

Faculty School total: 180. In upper school: 66 men, 61 women; 100 have advanced degrees.

Subjects Offered Advanced Placement courses, algebra, American history, anatomy, Arabic, art, art history, astronomy, band, biochemistry, biology, calculus, chemistry, chemistry-AP, computer science, creative writing, dance, drama, drawing, earth science, economics, electronics, English, English-AP, European history, fine arts, French, French language-AP, genetics, geometry, German, government/civics, Hindi, history, history-AP, horticulture, Japanese, jazz, Latin American history, law, library studies, Mandarin, mathematics, media, music, outdoor education, painting, philosophy, photography, physical education, physics, physiology, printmaking, psychology, religion, robotics, Russian, science, social studies, Spanish, speech, swimming, theater, trigonometry, weight training, women's studies, world history, writing.

Graduation Requirements English, experiential education, foreign language, mathematics, physical education (includes health), science, social studies (includes history), experiential education (environmental and outdoor activities).

Special Academic Programs 18 Advanced Placement exams for which test preparation is offered; independent study; term-away projects; study abroad.

College Admission Counseling 164 students graduated in 2009; all went to college, including Stanford University; The University of Texas at Austin; Trinity University; University of New Mexico; University of Notre Dame. Mean SAT critical reading: 665, mean SAT math: 655, mean SAT writing: 646, mean combined SAT: 1808, mean composite ACT: 30. 88% scored over 600 on SAT critical reading, 81% scored over 600 on SAT math, 79% scored over 600 on SAT writing, 92% scored over 1800 on combined SAT, 92% scored over 26 on composite ACT.

Student Life Upper grades have specified standards of dress, student council, honor system. Discipline rests primarily with faculty.

Tuition and Aid Day student tuition: $16,189. Tuition installment plan (FACTS Tuition Payment Plan, monthly payment plans, individually arranged payment plans, 1- and 2-payment plans). Need-based scholarship grants available. In 2009–10, 30% of upper-school students received aid. Total amount of financial aid awarded in 2009–10: $2,472,786.

Admissions Traditional secondary-level entrance grade is 9. For fall 2009, 150 students applied for upper-level admission, 62 were accepted, 44 enrolled. ISEE, school's own exam or SSAT required. Deadline for receipt of application materials: February 15. Application fee required: $50. On-campus interview required.

Athletics Interscholastic: baseball (boys), basketball (b,g), bowling (b,g), cross-country running (b,g), dance (b,g), diving (b,g), football (b), golf (b,g), hiking/backpacking (b,g), life saving (b,g), modern dance (b,g), outdoor education (b,g), outdoor skills (b,g), physical training (b,g), rafting (b,g), rappelling (b,g), rock climbing (b,g), soccer (b,g), softball (g), swimming and diving (b,g), tennis (b,g), track and field (b,g), volleyball (g), wrestling (b,g); coed intramural: ballet, basketball, canoeing/kayaking, wilderness, wilderness survival. 9 PE instructors, 84 coaches, 3 athletic trainers.

Computers Computers are regularly used in foreign language, history, library science, mathematics classes. Computer network features include on-campus library services, online commercial services, Internet access, wireless campus network, Internet filtering or blocking technology. Campus intranet and student e-mail accounts are available to students. The school has a published electronic and media policy.

Contact Judy Hudenko, Director of Admission. 505-828-3208. Fax: 505-828-3128. E-mail: hudenko@aa.edu. Web site: www.aa.edu.

ALEXANDER DAWSON SCHOOL
10455 Dawson Drive
Lafayette, Colorado 80026
Head of School: Mr. Brian Johnson

General Information Coeducational day college-preparatory, arts, technology, and engineering school. Grades K–12. Founded: 1970. Setting: rural. Nearest major city is Boulder. 113-acre campus. 11 buildings on campus. Approved or accredited by Association of Colorado Independent Schools and Colorado Department of Education. Member of National Association of Independent Schools and Secondary School Admission Test Board. Total enrollment: 453. Upper school average class size: 15. Upper school faculty-student ratio: 1:7. There are 172 required school days per year for Upper School students. Upper School students typically attend 5 days per week. The average school day consists of 9 hours and 30 minutes.

Upper School Student Profile Grade 9: 62 students (27 boys, 35 girls); Grade 10: 43 students (23 boys, 20 girls); Grade 11: 44 students (25 boys, 19 girls); Grade 12: 44 students (17 boys, 27 girls).

Faculty School total: 53. In upper school: 17 men, 10 women; 23 have advanced degrees.

Subjects Offered Algebra, American history, American literature, art, art history, biology, calculus, ceramics, chemistry, Chinese, computer math, computer multimedia, computer programming, computer science, creative writing, dance, drafting, drama, earth science, economics, English, English literature, European history, expository writing, fine arts, French, geography, geometry, government-AP, government/civics, grammar, health, history, industrial arts, journalism, Latin, mathematics, mechanical drawing, music, photography, physical education, physics, science, social sciences, social studies, Spanish, speech, theater, trigonometry, world history, world literature, writing.

Graduation Requirements Arts and fine arts (art, music, dance, drama), computer science, English, foreign language, history, mathematics, science, sports.

Special Academic Programs 15 Advanced Placement exams for which test preparation is offered; honors section; independent study; term-away projects; study at local college for college credit; study abroad; academic accommodation for the gifted, the musically talented, and the artistically talented; remedial reading and/or remedial writing; remedial math; special instructional classes for deaf students.

College Admission Counseling 27 students graduated in 2010; all went to college, including Middlebury College; Pomona College; University of Denver; Wellesley College. Mean SAT critical reading: 616, mean SAT math: 620, mean composite ACT: 27.

Student Life Upper grades have specified standards of dress, student council, honor system. Discipline rests equally with students and faculty.

Tuition and Aid Day student tuition: $19,200. Tuition installment plan (Insured Tuition Payment Plan, monthly payment plans, individually arranged payment plans). Need-based scholarship grants, need-based loans available. In 2010–11, 13% of upper-school students received aid. Total amount of financial aid awarded in 2010–11: $905,000.

Admissions Traditional secondary-level entrance grade is 9. For fall 2010, 45 students applied for upper-level admission, 31 were accepted, 24 enrolled. Deadline for receipt of application materials: none. Application fee required: $100. Interview required.

Athletics Interscholastic: baseball (boys), basketball (b,g), lacrosse (b), soccer (b,g), swimming and diving (b,g), synchronized swimming (g), tennis (b,g), track and field (b,g), volleyball (g); intramural: lacrosse (b); coed interscholastic: bicycling, canoeing/kayaking, cross-country running, equestrian sports, golf, kayaking, martial arts, paddling, skiing (downhill), Special Olympics; coed intramural: aerobics, aerobics/dance, backpacking, Circus, climbing, dance, equestrian sports, fitness, flag football, football, Frisbee, golf, hiking/backpacking, indoor soccer, martial arts, modern dance, outdoor activities, outdoor education, outdoor recreation, outdoor skills, physical fitness, rafting, rock climbing, ropes courses, running, strength & conditioning, weight lifting. 3 PE instructors, 22 coaches, 1 athletic trainer.

Computers Computers are regularly used in art, engineering, mathematics, science classes. Computer network features include on-campus library services, online commercial services, Internet access, wireless campus network, Internet filtering or blocking technology. Student e-mail accounts and computer access in designated

common areas are available to students. Students grades are available online. The school has a published electronic and media policy.
Contact Ms. Denise LaRusch, Assistant to the Director of Admissions. 303-665-6679. Fax: 303-381-0415. E-mail: dlarusch@dawsonschool.org. Web site: www.dawsonschool.org.

THE ALEXANDER SCHOOL
409 International Parkway
Richardson, Texas 75081
Head of School: Mr. David B. Bowlin

General Information Coeducational day college-preparatory, arts, and technology school. Grades 8–12. Founded: 1975. Setting: suburban. Nearest major city is Dallas. 2-acre campus. 1 building on campus. Approved or accredited by Southern Association of Colleges and Schools, Texas Education Agency, and The College Board. Languages of instruction: English and Spanish. Endowment: $1 million. Total enrollment: 32. Upper school average class size: 5. Upper school faculty-student ratio: 1:5. There are 180 required school days per year for Upper School students. Upper School students typically attend 5 days per week. The average school day consists of 6 hours and 15 minutes.
Upper School Student Profile Grade 8: 3 students (3 boys); Grade 9: 6 students (3 boys, 3 girls); Grade 10: 6 students (3 boys, 3 girls); Grade 11: 9 students (5 boys, 4 girls); Grade 12: 8 students (4 boys, 4 girls).
Faculty School total: 8. In upper school: 3 men, 3 women; 4 have advanced degrees.
Subjects Offered 20th century physics, advanced chemistry, advanced math, African American history, algebra, alternative physical education, American Civil War, American history-AP, analysis and differential calculus, anatomy and physiology, ancient history, ancient world history, art, biology, biology-AP, British literature, British literature (honors), British literature-AP, business applications, calculus, calculus-AP, chemistry, chemistry-AP, civics/free enterprise, Civil War, composition, computer applications, computer literacy, consumer mathematics, critical studies in film, ecology, environmental systems, economics, English composition, English language and composition-AP, English literature, English literature and composition-AP, environmental science, ethics, European history-AP, general business, geography, geometry, government, grammar, health, history, honors algebra, honors English, honors geometry, honors U.S. history, honors world history, human anatomy, Japanese, keyboarding, Latin, martial arts, math review, mathematical modeling, music appreciation, music theory, personal fitness, philosophy, photography, photojournalism, physical education, physics, physics-AP, pre-algebra, pre-calculus, psychology, public speaking, science fiction, Shakespeare, Spanish, Spanish language-AP, U.S. government, U.S. history, U.S. history-AP, U.S. literature, weight training, yearbook.
Graduation Requirements Algebra, American government, American history, American literature, arts and fine arts (art, music, dance, drama), biology, British literature, chemistry, computer literacy, economics, electives, English, foreign language, geometry, health, physical fitness, physics, public speaking, world geography, world history.
Special Academic Programs Advanced Placement exam preparation; honors section; accelerated programs; independent study; study at local college for college credit; academic accommodation for the gifted.
College Admission Counseling 14 students graduated in 2009; all went to college, including Texas Christian University; The University of Texas at Austin. Median SAT critical reading: 615, median SAT math: 540, median SAT writing: 620, median combined SAT: 1155, median composite ACT: 21. 75% scored over 600 on SAT critical reading, 25% scored over 600 on SAT math, 75% scored over 600 on SAT writing, 50% scored over 1800 on combined SAT.
Student Life Upper grades have specified standards of dress, student council, honor system. Discipline rests primarily with faculty.
Tuition and Aid Day student tuition: $20,000. Tuition installment plan (Key Tuition Payment Plan, SMART Tuition Payment Plan, monthly payment plans). Tuition reduction for siblings, need-based scholarship grants, paying campus jobs available. In 2009–10, 10% of upper-school students received aid. Total amount of financial aid awarded in 2009–10: $50,000.
Admissions Traditional secondary-level entrance grade is 10. For fall 2009, 30 students applied for upper-level admission, 15 were accepted, 15 enrolled. California Achievement Test required. Deadline for receipt of application materials: none. No application fee required. On-campus interview required.
Athletics Interscholastic: cross-country running (boys, girls), golf (b,g), independent competitive sports (b,g), tennis (b,g), track and field (b,g); intramural: basketball (b,g), flag football (b), martial arts (b,g), weight training (b,g); coed interscholastic: physical fitness; coed intramural: basketball, strength & conditioning, weight training. 1 PE instructor.
Computers Computers are regularly used in English, geography, history, keyboarding, photography, photojournalism, yearbook classes. Computer network features include Internet access, wireless campus network, Internet filtering or blocking technology. Students grades are available online.
Contact Ms. Kimberly V. Walker, Administration. 972-690-9210. Fax: 972-690-9284. E-mail: kim@alexanderschool.com. Web site: www.alexanderschool.com.

ALLEN ACADEMY
3201 Boonville Road
Bryan, Texas 77802
Head of School: Mr. John Rouse

General Information Coeducational day college-preparatory and ESL school. Grades PK–12. Founded: 1886. Setting: small town. Nearest major city is Houston. 40-acre campus. 4 buildings on campus. Approved or accredited by Southern Association of Colleges and Schools, Texas Education Agency, and The College Board. Total enrollment: 284. Upper school average class size: 18. Upper school faculty-student ratio: 1:10. There are 171 required school days per year for Upper School students. Upper School students typically attend 5 days per week. The average school day consists of 7 hours and 30 minutes.
Upper School Student Profile Grade 9: 19 students (11 boys, 8 girls); Grade 10: 15 students (9 boys, 6 girls); Grade 11: 18 students (12 boys, 6 girls); Grade 12: 26 students (13 boys, 13 girls).
Faculty School total: 45. In upper school: 8 men, 8 women; 6 have advanced degrees.
Subjects Offered Algebra, American history, American history-AP, American literature, art, band, biology, biology-AP, calculus, calculus-AP, chemistry, choir, drama, drawing, English language-AP, English literature, English literature and composition-AP, English literature-AP, ESL, European history, European history-AP, French, French-AP, geometry, honors English, keyboarding, multimedia, painting, physical education, physics-AP, pre-calculus, Spanish, Spanish-AP, world history, yearbook.
Graduation Requirements Algebra, American history, American literature, arts and fine arts (art, music, dance, drama), biology, chemistry, English composition, English literature, European history, geometry, physics, pre-calculus, world history, 40 hours of community service.
Special Academic Programs Advanced Placement exam preparation; honors section; study at local college for college credit; ESL (34 students enrolled).
College Admission Counseling 14 students graduated in 2009; all went to college, including Baylor University; Carnegie Mellon University; Sam Houston State University; Texas A&M University; The University of Texas at Austin; Trinity University.
Student Life Upper grades have uniform requirement, student council, honor system. Discipline rests equally with students and faculty.
Tuition and Aid Day student tuition: $5030–$10,475. Tuition installment plan (FACTS Tuition Payment Plan, semester payment plan). Need-based scholarship grants available. In 2009–10, 15% of upper-school students received aid. Total amount of financial aid awarded in 2009–10: $100,000.
Admissions Traditional secondary-level entrance grade is 9. Any standardized test, ERB CTP IV, ISEE, PSAT, PSAT, SAT, or ACT for applicants to grade 11 and 12 or writing sample required. Deadline for receipt of application materials: none. Application fee required: $200. Interview recommended.
Athletics Interscholastic: baseball (boys), basketball (b,g), cheering (g), cross-country running (b,g), football (b), golf (b,g), softball (g), strength & conditioning (b), tennis (b,g), track and field (b,g), volleyball (g), winter soccer (b); coed intramural: basketball, combined training, weight training. 2 PE instructors, 4 coaches.
Computers Computers are regularly used in keyboarding, multimedia classes. Computer network features include Internet access, wireless campus network, Internet filtering or blocking technology. The school has a published electronic and media policy.
Contact Mrs. Kathy Duewall. 979-776-0731. E-mail: kduewall@allenacademy.org. Web site: www.allenacademy.org.

ALLENDALE COLUMBIA SCHOOL
519 Allens Creek Road
Rochester, New York 14618-3405
Head of School: David Blanchard

General Information Coeducational day college-preparatory school. Grades N–12. Founded: 1890. Setting: suburban. 33-acre campus. 5 buildings on campus. Approved or accredited by New York State Association of Independent Schools. Member of National Association of Independent Schools. Endowment: $15 million. Total enrollment: 344. Upper school average class size: 7. Upper school faculty-student ratio: 1:4. There are 165 required school days per year for Upper School students. Upper School students typically attend 5 days per week. The average school day consists of 6 hours and 30 minutes.
Upper School Student Profile Grade 9: 24 students (16 boys, 8 girls); Grade 10: 22 students (11 boys, 11 girls); Grade 11: 32 students (16 boys, 16 girls); Grade 12: 37 students (21 boys, 16 girls).
Faculty School total: 59. In upper school: 10 men, 17 women; 25 have advanced degrees.
Subjects Offered Advanced Placement courses, advanced studio art-AP, algebra, American history, American history-AP, American literature, American literature-AP, art, art-AP, bioethics, biology, biology-AP, calculus, calculus-AP, chemistry, chemistry-AP, composition-AP, computer science, earth science, English, English language and composition-AP, English literature, environmental science, environmental science-AP, European history, European history-AP, expository writing, French, French-AP, geology, geometry, government/civics, grammar, health, history, jazz ensemble, Latin, Latin-AP, mathematics, mathematics-AP, music, photography,

physical education, physics, pre-calculus, science, social studies, Spanish, Spanish-AP, U.S. history, U.S. history-AP, world history, writing.

Graduation Requirements Art, arts, computer science, English, foreign language, history, mathematics, physical education (includes health), science, participation in at least one team sport in both 9th and 10th grade.

Special Academic Programs 17 Advanced Placement exams for which test preparation is offered; independent study.

College Admission Counseling 48 students graduated in 2010; all went to college, including Cornell University; Massachusetts Institute of Technology; New York University; Rhode Island School of Design; Rochester Institute of Technology; The Johns Hopkins University. Mean SAT critical reading: 592, mean SAT math: 616, mean SAT writing: 603. 46% scored over 600 on SAT critical reading, 59% scored over 600 on SAT math, 54% scored over 600 on SAT writing.

Student Life Upper grades have specified standards of dress, student council. Discipline rests primarily with faculty.

Summer Programs Enrichment, sports, art/fine arts programs offered; session focuses on athletics and arts; held on campus; accepts boys and girls; open to students from other schools. 600 students usually enrolled. 2011 schedule: June 14 to August 1. Application deadline: none.

Tuition and Aid Day student tuition: $6510–$18,600. Tuition installment plan (FACTS Tuition Payment Plan). Need-based scholarship grants available. In 2010–11, 46% of upper-school students received aid. Total amount of financial aid awarded in 2010–11: $648,364.

Admissions Traditional secondary-level entrance grade is 9. For fall 2010, 30 students applied for upper-level admission, 14 were accepted, 11 enrolled. ERB—verbal abilities, reading comprehension, quantitative abilities (level F, form 1), ERB Reading and Math, essay, math and English placement tests, school's own exam or writing sample required. Deadline for receipt of application materials: none. Application fee required: $50. Interview required.

Athletics Interscholastic: baseball (boys), basketball (b,g), cross-country running (b,g), soccer (b,g), softball (g), tennis (b,g), track and field (b,g), volleyball (g); coed interscholastic: bowling, golf, running, swimming and diving. 4 PE instructors.

Computers Computers are regularly used in all academic classes. Computer network features include on-campus library services, Internet access, wireless campus network, Internet filtering or blocking technology, county-wide library services. Computer access in designated common areas is available to students. The school has a published electronic and media policy.

Contact Sara Scharr, Director of Admissions. 585-381-4560. Fax: 585-383-1191. E-mail: sscharr@allendalecolumbia.org. Web site: www.allendalecolumbia.org.

ALL HALLOWS HIGH SCHOOL

111 East 164th Street
Bronx, New York 10452-9402
Head of School: Mr. Paul P. Krebbs

General Information Boys' day college-preparatory, general academic, business, and religious studies school, affiliated with Roman Catholic Church. Grades 9–12. Founded: 1909. Setting: urban. 1 building on campus. Approved or accredited by Christian Brothers Association, Middle States Association of Colleges and Schools, and New York Department of Education. Total enrollment: 640. Upper school average class size: 27. Upper school faculty-student ratio: 1:15. There are 180 required school days per year for Upper School students. The average school day consists of 6 hours and 8 minutes.

Upper School Student Profile 85% of students are Roman Catholic.

Faculty School total: 42. In upper school: 37 men, 5 women; 33 have advanced degrees.

Subjects Offered Algebra, American history, art, Bible studies, biology, calculus, chemistry, computer science, economics, English, English literature, environmental science, geometry, government/civics, grammar, history, humanities, Latin, mathematics, media studies, physical education, physics, political science, religion, science, social studies, Spanish, speech, trigonometry.

Graduation Requirements Arts and fine arts (art, music, dance, drama), business skills (includes word processing), computer science, English, foreign language, mathematics, physical education (includes health), religion (includes Bible studies and theology), science, social sciences, social studies (includes history). Community service is required.

Special Academic Programs Remedial reading and/or remedial writing; remedial math.

College Admission Counseling 154 students graduated in 2010; all went to college.

Student Life Upper grades have specified standards of dress, student council, honor system. Discipline rests primarily with faculty. Attendance at religious services is required.

Admissions Cooperative Entrance Exam (McGraw-Hill) and school's own exam required. Deadline for receipt of application materials: none. No application fee required. On-campus interview required.

Athletics Interscholastic: baseball, basketball, bowling, cross-country running, dance, fencing, golf, handball, indoor track, indoor track & field, martial arts, soccer, swimming and diving, track and field; intramural: field hockey, indoor soccer, lacrosse, tennis. 1 PE instructor, 3 athletic trainers.

Computers Computers are regularly used in English, history, mathematics, media studies, science classes. Computer resources include on-campus library services, Internet access.

Contact Sean Sullivan, Principal. 718-293-4545. Fax: 718-293-8634. E-mail: alhallow@aol.com. Web site: www.allhallows.org.

ALLIANCE ACADEMY

Casilla 17-11-06186
Quito, Ecuador
Head of School: Dr. David Wells

General Information Coeducational boarding and day and distance learning college-preparatory, arts, and religious studies school, affiliated with Christian faith. Boarding grades 7–12, day grades PK–12. Distance learning grades 10–12. Founded: 1929. Setting: urban. Students are housed in single-sex by floor dormitories and mission agency dormitories. 8-acre campus. 6 buildings on campus. Approved or accredited by Association of American Schools in South America, Association of Christian Schools International, and Southern Association of Colleges and Schools. Language of instruction: English. Total enrollment: 531. Upper school average class size: 20. Upper school faculty-student ratio: 1:6. There are 190 required school days per year for Upper School students. Upper School students typically attend 5 days per week. The average school day consists of 6 hours and 30 minutes.

Upper School Student Profile Grade 7: 37 students (19 boys, 18 girls); Grade 8: 45 students (25 boys, 20 girls); Grade 9: 48 students (21 boys, 27 girls); Grade 10: 35 students (11 boys, 24 girls); Grade 11: 45 students (24 boys, 21 girls); Grade 12: 39 students (20 boys, 19 girls). 1% of students are boarding students. 34% are international students. International students from Canada, China, Japan, Republic of Korea, Taiwan, and United States; 9 other countries represented in student body. 50% of students are Christian faith.

Faculty School total: 57. In upper school: 19 men, 22 women; 14 have advanced degrees.

Subjects Offered Algebra, American history, American history-AP, American literature, art, auto mechanics, band, Bible, Bible as literature, Bible studies, biology, biology-AP, business, calculus, calculus-AP, chemistry, choir, Christian doctrine, Christian ethics, Christian studies, church history, computer applications, computer art, computer math, computer programming, computer science, computer science-AP, concert band, creative writing, debate, desktop publishing, drama, earth science, economics, English, English as a foreign language, English language-AP, English literature, English literature-AP, ESL, family and consumer science, fine arts, French, French as a second language, geography, geometry, government/civics, grammar, health, health education, history, home economics, industrial arts, jazz band, journalism, keyboarding, Life of Christ, marching band, mathematics, music, novels, photography, physical education, physics, piano, pre-algebra, pre-calculus, public speaking, religion, religion and culture, science, senior seminar, small engine repair, social sciences, social studies, Spanish, Spanish literature, Spanish literature-AP, speech, speech and debate, theater, trigonometry, U.S. history-AP, video communication, vocal ensemble, woodworking, world geography, world history, world religions, writing, yearbook.

Graduation Requirements 1½ elective credits, algebra, arts and fine arts (art, music, dance, drama), comparative government and politics, computer applications, English, foreign language, health education, mathematics, physical education (includes health), religion (includes Bible studies and theology), science, social sciences, social studies (includes history), U.S. government and politics, U.S. history.

Special Academic Programs 12 Advanced Placement exams for which test preparation is offered; independent study; academic accommodation for the gifted and the artistically talented; remedial reading and/or remedial writing; remedial math; programs in English, mathematics, general development for dyslexic students; special instructional classes for students with developmental and/or learning disabilities; ESL (26 students enrolled).

College Admission Counseling 45 students graduated in 2010; 35 went to college, including Azusa Pacific University; Calvin College; John Brown University; Simpson University; Worcester Polytechnic Institute. Other: 3 went to work, 2 entered military service, 5 had other specific plans. Median SAT critical reading: 535, median SAT math: 490, median SAT writing: 520, median combined SAT: 1545, median composite ACT: 23. 36% scored over 600 on SAT critical reading, 29% scored over 600 on SAT math, 30% scored over 600 on SAT writing, 32% scored over 1800 on combined SAT, 26% scored over 26 on composite ACT.

Student Life Upper grades have specified standards of dress, student council, honor system. Discipline rests primarily with faculty. Attendance at religious services is required.

Summer Programs Remediation, ESL, sports programs offered; session focuses on ESL; held on campus; accepts boys and girls; not open to students from other schools. 12 students usually enrolled. 2011 schedule: July 6 to July 31. Application deadline: June 12.

Tuition and Aid Day student tuition: $8900. Tuition installment plan (monthly payment plans, individually arranged payment plans). Tuition reduction for siblings, need-based scholarship grants, paying campus jobs, tuition reduction for children of missionaries, two full scholarships for children of Ecuadorian military personnel available. In 2010–11, 30% of upper-school students received aid. Total amount of financial aid awarded in 2010–11: $800,000.

Alliance Academy

Admissions Traditional secondary-level entrance grade is 9. For fall 2010, 65 students applied for upper-level admission, 45 were accepted, 43 enrolled. English entrance exam, English proficiency, WRAT or writing sample required. Deadline for receipt of application materials: none. Application fee required: $100. On-campus interview required.

Athletics Interscholastic: basketball (boys, girls), soccer (b,g), volleyball (b,g); intramural: badminton (b,g), ball hockey (b), horseshoes (b), in-line hockey (b), modern dance (g), table tennis (b,g); coed intramural: backpacking, basketball, bocce, climbing, flag football, football, hiking/backpacking, indoor soccer, martial arts, outdoor adventure, paddle tennis, running, soccer, softball, strength & conditioning, table tennis, volleyball, wall climbing. 2 PE instructors, 1 coach.

Computers Computers are regularly used in basic skills, business education, career exploration, college planning, computer applications, design, desktop publishing, desktop publishing, ESL, digital applications, graphic design, independent study, information technology, introduction to technology, keyboarding, lab/keyboard, language development, media arts, media production, media services, photography, photojournalism, programming, publications, technology, video film production, word processing, writing, yearbook classes. Computer network features include on-campus library services, online commercial services, Internet access, Internet filtering or blocking technology. Campus intranet is available to students. The school has a published electronic and media policy.

Contact Mrs. Alexandra Chavez, Director of Admissions. 593-2-226-6985. Fax: 593-2-226-4350. E-mail: achavez@alliance.k12.ec. Web site: www.alliance.k12.ec.

ALLISON ACADEMY
1881 Northeast 164th Street
North Miami Beach, Florida 33162
Head of School: Dr. Sarah F. Allison

General Information Coeducational day college-preparatory, general academic, arts, business, and English for Speakers of Other Languages school. Grades 6–12. Founded: 1983. Setting: urban. Nearest major city is Miami. 1-acre campus. 2 buildings on campus. Approved or accredited by Association of Independent Schools of Florida, National Council for Private School Accreditation, Southern Association of Colleges and Schools, and Florida Department of Education. Total enrollment: 93. Upper school average class size: 15. Upper school faculty-student ratio: 1:10. There are 180 required school days per year for Upper School students. Upper School students typically attend 5 days per week. The average school day consists of 5 hours and 50 minutes.

Upper School Student Profile Grade 6: 3 students (3 boys); Grade 7: 8 students (6 boys, 2 girls); Grade 8: 8 students (7 boys, 1 girl); Grade 9: 15 students (11 boys, 4 girls); Grade 10: 19 students (12 boys, 7 girls); Grade 11: 20 students (11 boys, 9 girls); Grade 12: 24 students (13 boys, 11 girls).

Faculty School total: 11. In upper school: 6 men, 5 women; 6 have advanced degrees.

Subjects Offered Advanced Placement courses, algebra, American government, American history, anatomy, art history, arts, biology, chemistry, chorus, computer science, consumer mathematics, creative drama, drama, drawing, ecology, environmental systems, economics, economics and history, English, English language and composition-AP, English literature, environmental science, ESL, film studies, fine arts, French, French language-AP, general math, geography, geometry, health education, history, humanities, life management skills, life skills, mathematics, painting, peer counseling, photography, physical education, physical science, physics, pre-calculus, psychology, reading, reading/study skills, SAT/ACT preparation, science, social sciences, social studies, Spanish, sports, trigonometry, world cultures, writing, yearbook.

Graduation Requirements Algebra, American government, arts and fine arts (art, music, dance, drama), business skills (includes word processing), chemistry, computer applications, computer science, creative writing, current events, drama, earth and space science, economics, English, English literature, environmental education, foreign language, health education, life management skills, mathematics, physical education (includes health), psychology, SAT/ACT preparation, science, social sciences, social studies (includes history), Spanish, U.S. history, world history, 75 hours of community service.

Special Academic Programs 1 Advanced Placement exam for which test preparation is offered; honors section; accelerated programs; study at local college for college credit; academic accommodation for the gifted, the musically talented, and the artistically talented; remedial reading and/or remedial writing; remedial math; programs in English, mathematics, general development for dyslexic students; special instructional classes for students with learning disabilities, dyslexia, and Attention Deficit Disorder; ESL (3 students enrolled).

College Admission Counseling 22 students graduated in 2010; 15 went to college, including Barry University; Broward College; Drexel University; Florida International University; Florida State University; Miami Dade College. Other: 3 went to work, 4 had other specific plans. Median SAT critical reading: 500, median SAT math: 510, median composite ACT: 19. 20% scored over 600 on SAT critical reading, 10% scored over 600 on SAT math, 8% scored over 26 on composite ACT.

Student Life Upper grades have uniform requirement, student council. Discipline rests primarily with faculty.

Summer Programs Remediation, enrichment, advancement, ESL programs offered; session focuses on Academics for credit courses, remedial reading, and ESL; held on campus; accepts boys and girls; open to students from other schools. 2011 schedule: June 20 to July 28. Application deadline: June 17.

Tuition and Aid Day student tuition: $14,000. Tuition installment plan (monthly payment plans, individually arranged payment plans). Tuition reduction for siblings, merit scholarship grants, need-based scholarship grants available. In 2010–11, 24% of upper-school students received aid; total upper-school merit-scholarship money awarded: $25,000. Total amount of financial aid awarded in 2010–11: $97,000.

Admissions Traditional secondary-level entrance grade is 9. For fall 2010, 42 students applied for upper-level admission, 34 were accepted, 32 enrolled. Admissions testing, CAT, CTBS (or similar from their school), Woodcock-Johnson or Woodcock-Johnson Revised Achievement Test required. Deadline for receipt of application materials: none. Application fee required: $450. Interview required.

Athletics Interscholastic: basketball (boys), cheering (g), swimming and diving (b), tennis (b,g), walking (g), weight training (b); intramural: basketball (b,g), cheering (g), golf (b), martial arts (b,g), soccer (b,g), softball (b,g), swimming and diving (b,g), table tennis (b,g), tennis (b,g), walking (g); coed interscholastic: bowling, flag football, kickball, physical fitness, tennis; coed intramural: badminton, martial arts, physical fitness, soccer, softball, swimming and diving, table tennis, tennis, volleyball. 2 PE instructors, 2 coaches.

Computers Computers are regularly used in art, business applications, computer applications, current events, drawing and design, English, foreign language, geography, health, history, keyboarding, life skills, mathematics, psychology, reading, SAT preparation, science, Spanish, video film production, word processing classes. Computer resources include on-campus library services, online commercial services, Internet access, wireless campus network. Computer access in designated common areas is available to students. Students grades are available online. The school has a published electronic and media policy.

Contact Margaret Sheriff, Administrator. 305-940-3922. Fax: 305-940-1820. E-mail: margaretsheriff@bellsouth.net. Web site: www.allisonacademy.com.

ALL SAINTS' EPISCOPAL SCHOOL OF FORT WORTH
9700 Saints Circle
Fort Worth, Texas 76108
Head of School: Dr. Thaddeus B. Bird

General Information Coeducational day college-preparatory, arts, and religious studies school, affiliated with Episcopal Church. Grades K–12. Founded: 1951. Setting: suburban. 103-acre campus. 4 buildings on campus. Approved or accredited by Independent Schools Association of the Southwest, National Association of Episcopal Schools, Southwest Association of Episcopal Schools, and Texas Department of Education. Member of National Association of Independent Schools. Endowment: $5 million. Total enrollment: 801. Upper school average class size: 12. Upper school faculty-student ratio: 1:9.

Upper School Student Profile Grade 9: 70 students (36 boys, 34 girls); Grade 10: 67 students (43 boys, 24 girls); Grade 11: 68 students (33 boys, 35 girls); Grade 12: 63 students (40 boys, 23 girls). 21% of students are members of Episcopal Church.

Faculty School total: 83. In upper school: 15 men, 21 women; 17 have advanced degrees.

Subjects Offered Advanced math, algebra, anatomy and physiology, art, ballet, Bible studies, biology, biology-AP, calculus-AP, chemistry, chemistry-AP, choral music, classical civilization, classical studies, classics, college admission preparation, college planning, college writing, computer science-AP, computers, dance, digital photography, drama, ecology, environmental systems, economics, English, English language and composition-AP, English literature and composition-AP, environmental science, environmental studies, ethics, forensics, geometry, honors algebra, honors English, honors geometry, honors U.S. history, honors world history, Latin, Latin-AP, musical productions, physics, physics-AP, pre-calculus, publications, Spanish, Spanish language-AP, Spanish-AP, speech, studio art-AP, U.S. government and politics-AP, U.S. history, U.S. history-AP, Western civilization, writing.

Graduation Requirements Arts and fine arts (art, music, dance, drama), computer science, English, foreign language, mathematics, religion (includes Bible studies and theology), science, social studies (includes history), speech. Community service is required.

Special Academic Programs Advanced Placement exam preparation; honors section.

College Admission Counseling 63 students graduated in 2009; all went to college, including Baylor University; Texas A&M University; Texas Christian University; Texas Tech University; The University of Texas at Austin; University of Mississippi. Mean SAT critical reading: 564, mean SAT math: 550, mean SAT writing: 570, mean combined SAT: 1684.

Student Life Upper grades have uniform requirement, student council, honor system. Discipline rests equally with students and faculty. Attendance at religious services is required.

Tuition and Aid Day student tuition: $14,500. Tuition installment plan (Insured Tuition Payment Plan, monthly payment plans). Merit scholarship grants, need-based scholarship grants available. In 2009–10, 20% of upper-school students received aid; total upper-school merit-scholarship money awarded: $78,710. Total amount of financial aid awarded in 2009–10: $260,930.

Admissions Traditional secondary-level entrance grade is 9. For fall 2009, 50 students applied for upper-level admission, 30 were accepted, 22 enrolled. ERB or ISEE required. Deadline for receipt of application materials: none. Application fee required: $75. Interview required.

Athletics Interscholastic: ballet (boys, girls), baseball (b), basketball (b,g), cheering (g), combined training (b,g), cross-country running (b,g), dance team (g), field hockey (g), football (b), golf (b,g), rodeo (b,g), soccer (b,g), softball (g), swimming and diving (b,g), tennis (b,g), track and field (b,g), volleyball (g), winter soccer (b,g), wrestling (g); intramural: outdoor adventure (b,g), physical training (b,g), weight lifting (b,g), weight training (b,g); coed intramural: cooperative games, strength & conditioning. 10 PE instructors, 15 coaches, 1 athletic trainer.

Computers Computers are regularly used in college planning, data processing, drawing and design, foreign language, library, newspaper, science, yearbook classes. Computer network features include on-campus library services, online commercial services, Internet access, wireless campus network, Internet filtering or blocking technology. Computer access in designated common areas is available to students. The school has a published electronic and media policy.

Contact Robyn Rutkowski, Admissions Assistant. 817-560-5746 Ext. 330. Fax: 817-560-5720. E-mail: robynrutkowski@aseschool.org. Web site: www.asesftw.org.

ALMA HEIGHTS CHRISTIAN HIGH SCHOOL

1030 Linda Mar Boulevard
Pacifica, California 94044
Head of School: David Gross

General Information Coeducational day college-preparatory, general academic, arts, religious studies, and technology school, affiliated with Christian faith. Grades K–12. Founded: 1955. Setting: suburban. Nearest major city is San Francisco. 40-acre campus. 5 buildings on campus. Approved or accredited by Association of Christian Schools International, Western Association of Schools and Colleges, and California Department of Education. Upper school average class size: 22. Upper school faculty-student ratio: 1:10. There are 176 required school days per year for Upper School students. Upper School students typically attend 5 days per week. The average school day consists of 7 hours and 45 minutes.

Upper School Student Profile Grade 9: 30 students (17 boys, 13 girls); Grade 10: 38 students (18 boys, 20 girls); Grade 11: 31 students (13 boys, 18 girls); Grade 12: 29 students (17 boys, 12 girls). 80% of students are Christian.

Faculty School total: 17. In upper school: 10 men, 7 women; 4 have advanced degrees.

Special Academic Programs International Baccalaureate program; 6 Advanced Placement exams for which test preparation is offered; honors section; accelerated programs; special instructional classes for students with ADD and dyslexia.

College Admission Counseling 34 students graduated in 2010; 32 went to college, including Biola University; Skyline College; University of California, Berkeley; University of California, Davis; University of California, Irvine; Whitworth University. Other: 2 went to work. Mean SAT critical reading: 574, mean SAT math: 559, mean SAT writing: 585.

Student Life Upper grades have uniform requirement, student council, honor system. Discipline rests primarily with faculty. Attendance at religious services is required.

Summer Programs Enrichment, sports, art/fine arts, rigorous outdoor training, computer instruction programs offered; held both on and off campus; held at Highlands Christian Schools; accepts boys and girls; open to students from other schools.

Tuition and Aid Day student tuition: $9400. Tuition installment plan (monthly payment plans, individually arranged payment plans). Tuition reduction for siblings, merit scholarship grants, need-based scholarship grants, paying campus jobs available. In 2010–11, 5% of upper-school students received aid.

Admissions Placement test required. Deadline for receipt of application materials: none. Application fee required: $75. Interview required.

Athletics Interscholastic: baseball (boys), basketball (b,g), football (b), soccer (b), softball (g), volleyball (b,g); intramural: flag football (b), indoor soccer (b); coed interscholastic: cross-country running, soccer. 3 PE instructors, 6 coaches.

Computers Computer resources include on-campus library services, online commercial services, Internet access, wireless campus network, Internet filtering or blocking technology. Campus intranet, student e-mail accounts, and computer access in designated common areas are available to students. Students grades are available online. The school has a published electronic and media policy.

Contact 650-355-1935. Fax: 650-355-3488. Web site: www.almaheights.org.

ALPHA OMEGA ACADEMY

804 North Second Avenue East
Rock Rapids, Iowa 51246
Head of School: Mr. Gary O'Neill

General Information Coeducational day and distance learning college-preparatory, general academic, and distance learning school, affiliated with Christian faith. Grades K–12. Distance learning grades K–12. Founded: 1992. Setting: small town. Approved or accredited by Association of Christian Schools International, CITA (Commission on International and Trans-Regional Accreditation), and North Central Association of

Colleges and Schools. Total enrollment: 2,268. Upper school faculty-student ratio: 1:32. Upper School students typically attend 5 days per week.

Faculty School total: 58. In upper school: 23 men, 35 women; 10 have advanced degrees.

Subjects Offered Accounting, algebra, American government, American history, American literature, art, Bible, biology, British literature, calculus, career planning, chemistry, civics, consumer mathematics, earth science, English, English composition, English literature, general math, general science, geography, geometry, health, history, home economics, language arts, mathematics, physical fitness, science, Spanish, state history, world geography, world history.

Graduation Requirements Algebra, biology, chemistry, language arts, mathematics, physical education (includes health), science, social studies (includes history), One credit of Bible.

Special Academic Programs Accelerated programs; independent study.

College Admission Counseling 120 students graduated in 2010; 78 went to college. Mean SAT critical reading: 542, mean SAT math: 510, mean SAT writing: 511, mean composite ACT: 23.

Student Life Discipline rests equally with students and faculty.

Tuition and Aid Day student tuition: $600–$1100. Tuition installment plan (The Tuition Plan). Tuition reduction for siblings available.

Admissions Traditional secondary-level entrance grade is 9. Placement test required. Deadline for receipt of application materials: none. Application fee required: $100. Interview required.

Computers Computers are regularly used in Bible studies, college planning, English, foreign language, geography, health, history, mathematics, science, social sciences, social studies, Spanish classes. The school has a published electronic and media policy.

Contact Mrs. Kelli Hoogers, Academy Services Department Head. 800-682-7396 Ext. 1736. Fax: 712-472-6830. E-mail: khoogers@aoacademy.com. Web site: www.aoacademy.com.

THE ALTAMONT SCHOOL

4801 Altamont Road South
Birmingham, Alabama 35222
Head of School: Mrs. Sarah W. Whiteside

General Information Coeducational day college-preparatory, arts, and technology school. Grades 5–12. Founded: 1922. Setting: urban. 40-acre campus. 4 buildings on campus. Approved or accredited by National Independent Private Schools Association, Southern Association of Colleges and Schools, Southern Association of Independent Schools, The College Board, and Alabama Department of Education. Member of National Association of Independent Schools. Endowment: $5 million. Total enrollment: 340. Upper school average class size: 15. Upper school faculty-student ratio: 1:5. The average school day consists of 6 hours and 30 minutes.

Upper School Student Profile Grade 9: 60 students (30 boys, 30 girls); Grade 10: 59 students (33 boys, 26 girls); Grade 11: 40 students (25 boys, 15 girls); Grade 12: 56 students (31 boys, 25 girls).

Faculty School total: 56. In upper school: 19 men, 24 women; 32 have advanced degrees.

Subjects Offered 20th century American writers, acting, advanced chemistry, advanced computer applications, algebra, American history, American literature, anatomy and physiology, art, art history, astronomy, biology, calculus, chemistry, Chinese, Chinese history, Chinese literature, Chinese studies, computer programming, computer science, concert choir, creative drama, creative writing, earth science, ecology, economics and history, English, English literature, European history, film and new technologies, finite math, French, geography, geometry, government/civics, Greek, health, history, independent study, instruments, Internet research, jazz band, journalism, keyboarding, Latin, mathematics, music, orchestra, photography, physical education, physics, pre-calculus, science, social studies, Spanish, speech, speech and debate, statistics, theater, theater arts, track and field, travel, trigonometry, U.S. government, U.S. history, video film production, visual and performing arts, vocal music, weight training, world history, world literature, writing.

Graduation Requirements American history, English, foreign language, health and wellness, history, lab science, mathematics, physical education (includes health), science, speech.

Special Academic Programs Advanced Placement exam preparation; honors section; independent study; study abroad.

College Admission Counseling 54 students graduated in 2009; 53 went to college, including Birmingham-Southern College; Sewanee: The University of the South; The University of Alabama; Vanderbilt University; Wake Forest University. Other: 1 had other specific plans. Median SAT critical reading: 610, median SAT math: 625, median SAT writing: 625, median combined SAT: 1870, median composite ACT: 29.

Student Life Upper grades have specified standards of dress, student council, honor system. Discipline rests primarily with faculty.

Tuition and Aid Day student tuition: $12,348–$16,176. Tuition installment plan (FACTS Tuition Payment Plan). Tuition reduction for siblings, merit scholarship grants, need-based scholarship grants available. Total amount of financial aid awarded in 2009–10: $740,000.

Admissions Traditional secondary-level entrance grade is 9. For fall 2009, 33 students applied for upper-level admission, 27 were accepted, 20 enrolled. ISEE required. Deadline for receipt of application materials: none. Application fee required: $50. On-campus interview required.

Athletics Interscholastic: baseball (boys), basketball (b,g), combined training (b,g), cross-country running (b,g), indoor track & field (b,g), physical training (b,g), running (b,g), soccer (b,g), softball (g), strength & conditioning (b,g), swimming and diving (b,g), tennis (b,g), track and field (b,g), volleyball (g), weight training (b,g), winter (indoor) track (b,g); coed interscholastic: golf, running; coed intramural: ultimate Frisbee. 4 PE instructors, 6 coaches, 1 athletic trainer.

Computers Computers are regularly used in all academic, basic skills, multimedia classes. Computer network features include on-campus library services, online commercial services, Internet access, wireless campus network, Internet filtering or blocking technology. Computer access in designated common areas is available to students. Students grades are available online. The school has a published electronic and media policy.

Contact Mr. James M. Wiygul, Director of Admissions. 205-445-1232. Fax: 205-871-5666. E-mail: admissions@altamontschool.org. Web site: www.altamontschool.org.

AMERICAN ACADEMY
Plantation, Florida
See Special Needs Schools section.

THE AMERICAN BOYCHOIR SCHOOL
Princeton, New Jersey
See Junior Boarding Schools section.

AMERICAN CHRISTIAN ACADEMY
2300 Veterans Memorial Parkway
Tuscaloosa, Alabama 35404
Head of School: Dr. Dan Carden

General Information Coeducational day college-preparatory, religious studies, and technology school, affiliated with Christian faith; primarily serves individuals with Attention Deficit Disorder. Grades K–12. Founded: 1979. Setting: small town. 20-acre campus. 6 buildings on campus. Approved or accredited by Association of Christian Schools International and Southern Association of Colleges and Schools. Endowment: $200,000. Total enrollment: 882. Upper school average class size: 20. Upper school faculty-student ratio: 1:12. There are 180 required school days per year for Upper School students. Upper School students typically attend 5 days per week. The average school day consists of 7 hours and 40 minutes.

Upper School Student Profile Grade 6: 62 students (32 boys, 30 girls); Grade 7: 71 students (35 boys, 36 girls); Grade 8: 72 students (41 boys, 31 girls); Grade 9: 60 students (28 boys, 32 girls); Grade 10: 74 students (32 boys, 42 girls); Grade 11: 65 students (37 boys, 28 girls); Grade 12: 55 students (29 boys, 26 girls). 75% of students are Christian.

Faculty School total: 55. In upper school: 21 men, 32 women; 19 have advanced degrees.

Subjects Offered Algebra, anatomy, Bible, biology, calculus, chemistry, computers, earth science, economics, English, English-AP, fine arts, geography, geology, government, health, history, life science, marine biology, mathematics, physical education, physics, reading, science, Southern literature, Spanish, typing, world history.

Graduation Requirements Arts and fine arts (art, music, dance, drama), business skills (includes word processing), computer science, English, foreign language, mathematics, physical education (includes health), religion (includes Bible studies and theology), science, social sciences, social studies (includes history), accelerated reading is required in all grades, religion classes required in all grades. Community service is required.

Special Academic Programs Advanced Placement exam preparation; honors section; accelerated programs; independent study; study at local college for college credit; study abroad; special instructional classes for deaf students.

College Admission Counseling 38 students graduated in 2009; 37 went to college, including Auburn University; Birmingham-Southern College; Samford University; Shelton State Community College; The University of Alabama; University of South Alabama. Other: 1 went to work. Median composite ACT: 24. 38% scored over 26 on composite ACT.

Student Life Upper grades have specified standards of dress, student council, honor system. Discipline rests primarily with faculty. Attendance at religious services is required.

Tuition and Aid Day student tuition: $4800. Tuition installment plan (monthly payment plans, individually arranged payment plans). Tuition reduction for siblings, need-based scholarship grants, paying campus jobs available. In 2009–10, 12% of upper-school students received aid. Total amount of financial aid awarded in 2009–10: $65,000.

Admissions For fall 2009, 91 students applied for upper-level admission, 56 were accepted, 52 enrolled. Scholastic Achievement Test required. Deadline for receipt of application materials: none. Application fee required: $125. Interview required.

Athletics Interscholastic: baseball (boys), basketball (b,g), cheering (g), cross-country running (b,g), dance squad (g), dance team (g), danceline (g), flag football (b), football (b), golf (b,g), indoor track (b,g), indoor track & field (b,g), power lifting (b), soccer (b,g), softball (g), strength & conditioning (b,g), swimming and diving (b,g), tennis (b,g), track and field (b,g), volleyball (g), weight lifting (g), weight training (b,g), wrestling (b); intramural: aerobics (g), aerobics/dance (g), basketball (b,g), cheering (g), dance squad (g), dance team (g), danceline (g), flagball (b,g), gymnastics (g), in-line skating (b,g), outdoor activities (b,g), paint ball (b), physical training (b,g), roller blading (b,g), softball (g), strength & conditioning (b,g), swimming and diving (b,g), touch football (b,g); coed intramural: flagball, outdoor activities, physical fitness, running. 3 PE instructors, 12 coaches, 1 athletic trainer.

Computers Computers are regularly used in computer applications, foreign language, mathematics, typing, video film production classes. Computer network features include on-campus library services, Internet access, wireless campus network, Internet filtering or blocking technology. Campus intranet, student e-mail accounts, and computer access in designated common areas are available to students. Students grades are available online.

Contact Nancy Hastings, Director of Admissions. 205-553-5963 Ext. 12. Fax: 205-553-5942. E-mail: nhastings@acacademy.com. Web site: www.acacademy.com.

AMERICAN COMMUNITY SCHOOLS OF ATHENS
129 Aghias Paraskevis Street
Halandri
Athens 152 34, Greece
Head of School: Dr. Stefanos Gialamas

General Information Coeducational day college-preparatory, arts, and technology school. Grades JK–12. Founded: 1945. Setting: suburban. 3-hectare campus. 4 buildings on campus. Approved or accredited by CITA (Commission on International and Trans-Regional Accreditation), European Council of International Schools, and Middle States Association of Colleges and Schools. Language of instruction: English. Total enrollment: 859. Upper school average class size: 17. Upper school faculty-student ratio: 1:17. There are 180 required school days per year for Upper School students. Upper School students typically attend 5 days per week. The average school day consists of 6 hours and 30 minutes.

Upper School Student Profile Grade 9: 77 students (35 boys, 42 girls); Grade 10: 87 students (43 boys, 44 girls); Grade 11: 96 students (41 boys, 55 girls); Grade 12: 82 students (43 boys, 39 girls).

Faculty School total: 95. In upper school: 15 men, 37 women; 40 have advanced degrees.

Subjects Offered Algebra, American history, American literature, analysis, Arabic, art, art history, band, biology, business skills, calculus, chemistry, Chinese, computer programming, computer science, dance, drama, earth science, economics, English, English literature, environmental science, ESL, European history, expository writing, fine arts, French, geometry, German, government/civics, grammar, Greek, history, humanities, information technology, journalism, mathematics, music, peer counseling, photography, physical education, physical science, physics, psychology, science, social sciences, social studies, sociology, Spanish, speech, statistics, theater, theory of knowledge, trigonometry, writing.

Graduation Requirements Arts and fine arts (art, music, dance, drama), computer science, English, foreign language, mathematics, physical education (includes health), science, social sciences, social studies (includes history).

Special Academic Programs International Baccalaureate program; 4 Advanced Placement exams for which test preparation is offered; honors section; accelerated programs; independent study; study at local college for college credit; academic accommodation for the gifted; remedial reading and/or remedial writing; remedial math; programs in English, mathematics, general development for dyslexic students; special instructional classes for deaf students, blind students, mild learning disabilities; ESL (17 students enrolled).

College Admission Counseling 97 students graduated in 2010; 96 went to college, including Boston College; Boston University; Columbia University; Georgetown University; New York University; Tufts University. Other: 1 had other specific plans. Mean SAT critical reading: 543, mean SAT math: 550, mean SAT writing: 579. 27% scored over 600 on SAT critical reading, 25% scored over 600 on SAT math, 26% scored over 600 on SAT writing.

Student Life Upper grades have specified standards of dress, student council. Discipline rests primarily with faculty.

Summer Programs Enrichment, advancement, ESL, sports, art/fine arts, computer instruction programs offered; session focuses on recreational and international leadership, creative thinking through mathematical thinking; held both on and off campus; held at various museums and historical sites (for the leadership program); accepts boys and girls; open to students from other schools. 150 students usually enrolled. 2011 schedule: June 20 to July 8. Application deadline: April 15.

Tuition and Aid Day student tuition: €11,758. Tuition installment plan (individually arranged payment plans, semester and quarterly payment plans). Tuition reduction for siblings, need-based scholarship grants available. In 2010–11, 1% of upper-school students received aid. Total amount of financial aid awarded in 2010–11: €60,000.

Admissions Traditional secondary-level entrance grade is 9. For fall 2010, 340 students applied for upper-level admission, 307 were accepted, 219 enrolled. English for Non-native Speakers or math and English placement tests required. Deadline for receipt of application materials: none. No application fee required. Interview required.

Athletics Interscholastic: basketball (boys, girls), cross-country running (b,g), soccer (b,g), softball (b,g), swimming and diving (b,g), tennis (b,g), track and field (b,g), volleyball (b,g), wrestling (b); coed interscholastic: gymnastics; coed intramural: martial arts. 2 PE instructors, 3 coaches.

Computers Computers are regularly used in all academic classes. Computer network features include on-campus library services, Internet access. Campus intranet, student e-mail accounts, and computer access in designated common areas are available to students. Students grades are available online.

Contact John G. Papadakis, Director of Enrollment, Communications and Technology. 30-210-639-3200. Fax: 30-210-639-0051. E-mail: papadakisj@acs.gr. Web site: www.acs.gr.

AMERICAN HERITAGE SCHOOL

6200 Linton Boulevard
Delray Beach, Florida 33484
Head of School: Robert Stone

General Information Coeducational day college-preparatory, arts, and pre-medical, pre-law, pre-engineering school. Grades PK–12. Founded: 1994. Setting: suburban. Nearest major city is Fort Lauderdale. 40-acre campus. Approved or accredited by Association of Independent Schools of Florida, CITA (Commission on International and Trans-Regional Accreditation), Southern Association of Colleges and Schools, and Florida Department of Education. Upper school average class size: 17.

Subjects Offered Acting, algebra, American government, American history, American history-AP, American legal systems, American literature, American literature-AP, anatomy and physiology, architectural drawing, art, art history-AP, band, biology, biology-AP, calculus-AP, ceramics, chemistry, chemistry-AP, Chinese, chorus, community service, computer graphics, computer science, computer science-AP, constitutional law, costumes and make-up, creative writing, dance, drama, drawing, economics, economics-AP, engineering, English, English language and composition-AP, English literature, English literature and composition-AP, environmental science, environmental science-AP, ESL, European history-AP, film and literature, fine arts, forensics, French, French-AP, geometry, graphic design, guitar, honors algebra, honors English, honors geometry, honors U.S. history, honors world history, journalism, law studies, mathematics, music theory, music theory-AP, oceanography, orchestra, painting, photography, physical education, physics, physics-AP, portfolio art, pre-algebra, pre-calculus, probability and statistics, psychology, psychology-AP, public policy, research skills, SAT/ACT preparation, science, sculpture, set design, sociology, Spanish, Spanish-AP, speech and debate, sports medicine, stagecraft, statistics-AP, studio art, theater, U.S. government and politics-AP, vocal music, Web site design, weight training, word processing, world history, world history-AP, world literature, world religions, writing, writing, yearbook.

Graduation Requirements Arts and fine arts (art, music, dance, drama), English, foreign language, mathematics, physical education (includes health), science, social studies (includes history), acceptance to a 4-year college. Community service is required.

Special Academic Programs Advanced Placement exam preparation; honors section; academic accommodation for the gifted, the musically talented, and the artistically talented; ESL.

College Admission Counseling Median SAT critical reading: 570, median SAT math: 590, median SAT writing: 560. 36% scored over 600 on SAT critical reading, 36% scored over 600 on SAT math, 33% scored over 600 on SAT writing.

Student Life Upper grades have uniform requirement, student council. Discipline rests primarily with faculty.

Summer Programs Remediation, enrichment, advancement, ESL, art/fine arts, computer instruction programs offered; session focuses on academics; held on campus; accepts boys and girls; open to students from other schools. 550 students usually enrolled. 2011 schedule: June 13 to August 12. Application deadline: none.

Tuition and Aid Tuition installment plan (monthly payment plans, semester payment plan, yearly). Tuition reduction for siblings, merit scholarship grants, need-based scholarship grants available.

Admissions Traditional secondary-level entrance grade is 9. Slossen Intelligence and Stanford Achievement Test required. Deadline for receipt of application materials: none. Application fee required: $100. On-campus interview required.

Athletics Interscholastic: baseball (boys), basketball (b,g), cross-country running (b,g), diving (b,g), football (b), golf (b,g), soccer (b,g), softball (g), swimming and diving (b,g), tennis (b,g), track and field (b,g), volleyball (g), weight training (b,g), winter soccer (b,g), wrestling (b); coed interscholastic: cheering, physical fitness.

Computers Computers are regularly used in computer applications, desktop publishing, digital applications, drafting, drawing and design, economics, engineering, English, ESL, French, geography, graphic design, history, keyboarding, library, literary magazine, mathematics, media arts, media production, multimedia, music, music technology, newspaper, photography, programming, psychology, reading, SAT preparation, social sciences, Spanish, speech, Web site design, writing, yearbook classes. Computer network features include on-campus library services, online commercial services, Internet access, wireless campus network, Internet filtering or blocking technology, Questia. Computer access in designated common areas is available to students. Students grades are available online. The school has a published electronic and media policy.

Contact Web site: http://www.ahschool.com/BocaDelraynew/ahhome/ahhomepage.html.

See Display below and Close-Up on page 728.

American Heritage School

Boca Delray Campus

Plantation Campus

- College Preparatory Program for PK3-Grade 12 • Accredited by SACS & AISF
- College Counseling from Junior High Through High School
- Low Student/Teacher Ratios • College Prep, Honors & AP Level Courses
- Pre-Med, Pre-Law & Pre-Engineering Programs
- High-Tech Computer Labs/Media Centers

- Athletic Teams for all Major Sports (with a "no-cut" policy)
- Award-Winning Fine Arts Program • $25 million Center for the Arts
- Graduates Admitted to the Nation's Finest Colleges and Universities
- 40 Acre Campus • Gymnasium • Olympic-size Pool • Tennis Courts
- Financial Aid Available • Extended Care & Bus Transportation Available

12200 W. Broward Blvd. • Plantation, FL • 954-472-0022
6200 Linton Blvd. • Delray Beach • 561-495-7272
Visit our website at www.ahschool.com

AMERICAN HERITAGE SCHOOL

12200 West Broward Boulevard
Plantation, Florida 33325
Head of School: William R. Laurie
General Information Coeducational day college-preparatory, arts, and pre-medical, pre-law, pre-engineering school. Grades PK–12. Founded: 1969. Setting: suburban. Nearest major city is Fort Lauderdale. 40-acre campus. 5 buildings on campus. Approved or accredited by Association of Independent Schools of Florida, CITA (Commission on International and Trans-Regional Accreditation), Southern Association of Colleges and Schools, and Florida Department of Education. Total enrollment: 2,202. Upper school average class size: 17. Upper school faculty-student ratio: 1:14. There are 175 required school days per year for Upper School students. Upper School students typically attend 5 days per week. The average school day consists of 7 hours and 15 minutes.
Upper School Student Profile Grade 7: 165 students (86 boys, 79 girls); Grade 8: 160 students (92 boys, 68 girls); Grade 9: 310 students (144 boys, 166 girls); Grade 10: 276 students (129 boys, 147 girls); Grade 11: 266 students (132 boys, 134 girls); Grade 12: 247 students (130 boys, 117 girls).
Faculty School total: 166. In upper school: 35 men, 69 women; 65 have advanced degrees.
Subjects Offered Acting, algebra, American government, American history, American history-AP, American legal systems, American literature, American literature-AP, anatomy and physiology, architectural drawing, architecture, art, art history-AP, band, biology, biology-AP, business law, calculus-AP, ceramics, chemistry, chemistry-AP, Chinese, chorus, community service, computer graphics, computer science, computer science-AP, constitutional law, costumes and make-up, creative writing, dance, drama, drawing, economics, economics-AP, engineering, English, English language and composition-AP, English literature, English literature and composition-AP, environmental science, environmental science-AP, ESL, European history-AP, film and literature, fine arts, forensics, French, French language-AP, French-AP, geometry, government-AP, graphic design, guitar, honors algebra, honors English, honors geometry, honors U.S. history, honors world history, human geography—AP, journalism, law studies, literary magazine, mathematics, music theory, music theory-AP, oceanography, orchestra, organic chemistry, painting, photography, physical education, physics, physics-AP, portfolio art, pre-algebra, pre-calculus, probability and statistics, psychology, psychology-AP, public policy, public speaking, research, research skills, SAT preparation, SAT/ACT preparation, science, sculpture, set design, sociology, Spanish, Spanish-AP, speech and debate, sports medicine, stage design, stagecraft, statistics-AP, studio art, technical theater, theater, U.S. government and politics-AP, video film production, visual arts, vocal music, Web site design, weight training, word processing, world history, world history-AP, world literature, world religions, writing, writing, yearbook.
Graduation Requirements Arts and fine arts (art, music, dance, drama), English, foreign language, mathematics, physical education (includes health), science, social studies (includes history), acceptance to a 4-year college. Community service is required.
Special Academic Programs Advanced Placement exam preparation; honors section; academic accommodation for the gifted, the musically talented, and the artistically talented; ESL (33 students enrolled).
College Admission Counseling 242 students graduated in 2010; all went to college, including Florida Atlantic University; Florida State University; Nova Southeastern University; University of Central Florida; University of Florida; University of Miami. Median SAT critical reading: 580, median SAT math: 569, median SAT writing: 578. 46% scored over 600 on SAT critical reading, 50% scored over 600 on SAT math, 42% scored over 600 on SAT writing.
Student Life Upper grades have uniform requirement, student council. Discipline rests primarily with faculty.
Summer Programs Remediation, enrichment, advancement, ESL, art/fine arts, computer instruction programs offered; session focuses on academics; held on campus; accepts boys and girls; open to students from other schools. 550 students usually enrolled. 2011 schedule: June 13 to August 12. Application deadline: none.
Tuition and Aid Day student tuition: $19,570–$21,121. Tuition installment plan (monthly payment plans, Semester payment plan, yearly). Tuition reduction for siblings, merit scholarship grants, need-based scholarship grants available. In 2010–11, 22% of upper-school students received aid; total upper-school merit-scholarship money awarded: $3,163,147. Total amount of financial aid awarded in 2010–11: $4,050,006.
Admissions Traditional secondary-level entrance grade is 9. Slossen Intelligence and Stanford Achievement Test required. Deadline for receipt of application materials: none. Application fee required: $100. On-campus interview required.
Athletics Interscholastic: baseball (boys), basketball (b,g), cross-country running (b,g), diving (b,g), football (b), golf (b,g), lacrosse (b,g), soccer (b,g), softball (g), swimming and diving (b,g), tennis (b,g), track and field (b,g), volleyball (b,g), weight training (b,g), winter soccer (b,g), wrestling (b); coed interscholastic: cheering, physical fitness, physical training. 4 PE instructors, 4 coaches.
Computers Computers are regularly used in all academic, computer applications, desktop publishing, digital applications, drafting, drawing and design, economics, engineering, English, ESL, French, geography, graphic design, history, keyboarding, library, literary magazine, mathematics, media arts, media production, multimedia, music, music technology, newspaper, photography, programming, psychology,

reading, SAT preparation, social sciences, Spanish, speech, Web site design, writing, yearbook classes. Computer network features include on-campus library services, online commercial services, Internet access, wireless campus network, Internet filtering or blocking technology, Questia. Campus intranet, student e-mail accounts, and computer access in designated common areas are available to students. Students grades are available online. The school has a published electronic and media policy.
Contact William R. Laurie, President. 954-472-0022 Ext. 3062. Fax: 954-472-3088. E-mail: admissions.pl@ahschool.com. Web site: www.ahschool.com.

See Display on page 73 and Close-Up on page 728.

THE AMERICAN INTERNATIONAL SCHOOL

Salmannsdorfer Strasse 47
Vienna A-1190, Austria
Head of School: Dr. Sheila Breen
General Information Coeducational day college-preparatory, International Baccalaureate, and US High School Diploma school. Grades PK–12. Founded: 1959. Setting: suburban. 15-acre campus. 1 building on campus. Approved or accredited by Middle States Association of Colleges and Schools. Affiliate member of National Association of Independent Schools; member of European Council of International Schools. Language of instruction: English. Total enrollment: 787. Upper school average class size: 20. Upper school faculty-student ratio: 1:6. There are 180 required school days per year for Upper School students. Upper School students typically attend 5 days per week. The average school day consists of 7 hours.
Upper School Student Profile Grade 9: 70 students (32 boys, 38 girls); Grade 10: 55 students (25 boys, 30 girls); Grade 11: 65 students (35 boys, 30 girls); Grade 12: 63 students (29 boys, 34 girls); Postgraduate: 2 students (1 boy, 1 girl).
Faculty School total: 94. In upper school: 19 men, 18 women; 22 have advanced degrees.
Subjects Offered Algebra, American history, American literature, band, biology, ceramics, chemistry, computer science, computers, drama, economics, English, English literature, European history, fine arts, French, geometry, German, health, history, mathematics, music, physical education, physical science, physics, programming, psychology, science, social sciences, social studies, Spanish, statistics, strings, studio art, theory of knowledge, visual arts, world history, yearbook.
Graduation Requirements Arts and fine arts (art, music, dance, drama), English, foreign language, mathematics, physical education (includes health), science, social studies (includes history).
Special Academic Programs International Baccalaureate program; independent study; ESL.
College Admission Counseling 54 students graduated in 2009; 52 went to college, including Brown University; Columbia University; McGill University; Ohio Wesleyan University; Stanford University; University of Pennsylvania. Other: 1 entered military service, 1 had other specific plans.
Student Life Upper grades have student council, honor system. Discipline rests equally with students and faculty.
Tuition and Aid Day student tuition: €16,850–€17,100. Tuition installment plan (individually arranged payment plans). Need-based scholarship grants available.
Admissions Deadline for receipt of application materials: none. Application fee required: €165. On-campus interview recommended.
Athletics Interscholastic: baseball (boys), basketball (b,g), cross-country running (b,g), soccer (b,g), softball (g), swimming and diving (b,g), tennis (b,g), track and field (b,g), volleyball (b,g); intramural: ballet (g), weight lifting (b,g); coed interscholastic: aquatics; coed intramural: aerobics/dance, badminton, basketball, dance, golf, gymnastics, martial arts, soccer, softball. 2 PE instructors, 19 coaches.
Computers Computers are regularly used in English, ESL, French, mathematics, science, Spanish, yearbook classes. Computer network features include on-campus library services, Internet access, wireless campus network, Internet filtering or blocking technology. Campus intranet, student e-mail accounts, and computer access in designated common areas are available to students. Students grades are available online. The school has a published electronic and media policy.
Contact Jennifer Wallner, Director of Admissions. 43-1-40132 Ext. 218. Fax: 43-1-40132-5. E-mail: J.Wallner@ais.at. Web site: www.ais.at.

AMERICAN INTERNATIONAL SCHOOL, DHAKA

PO Box 6106
Gulshan
Dhaka, Bangladesh
Head of School: Mr. Richard E. Boerner
General Information Coeducational day college-preparatory school. Grades PK–12. Founded: 1972. Setting: suburban. 4-acre campus. 1 building on campus. Approved or accredited by European Council of International Schools and New England Association of Schools and Colleges. Language of instruction: English. Total enrollment: 753. Upper school average class size: 18. Upper school faculty-student ratio: 1:15. There are 180 required school days per year for Upper School students. Upper School students typically attend 5 days per week. The average school day consists of 6 hours and 42 minutes.

Upper School Student Profile Grade 9: 53 students (34 boys, 19 girls); Grade 10: 56 students (27 boys, 29 girls); Grade 11: 41 students (18 boys, 23 girls); Grade 12: 58 students (30 boys, 28 girls).
Faculty School total: 102. In upper school. 29 men, 17 women; 38 have advanced degrees.
Subjects Offered Algebra, American literature, art, biology, chemistry, choir, choral music, computer science, concert band, creative writing, critical writing, digital photography, drawing, economics, electives, English, English literature, environmental science, ESL, fine arts, fitness, French, geography, geometry, language arts, mathematics, media arts, model United Nations, modern languages, modern world history, music, music theory, painting, physical education, physics, printmaking, psychology, science, sculpture, senior project, social studies, Spanish, speech, sports, study skills, symphonic band, theater arts, theory of knowledge, trigonometry, visual arts, women in literature, yearbook.
Special Academic Programs International Baccalaureate program; ESL.
College Admission Counseling 53 students graduated in 2010; all went to college, including Franklin & Marshall College; McGill University; The George Washington University; University of Toronto; Wellesley College. Mean SAT critical reading: 519, mean SAT math: 573, mean SAT writing: 516, mean combined SAT: 1608, mean composite ACT: 22. 27% scored over 600 on SAT critical reading, 42% scored over 600 on SAT math, 19% scored over 600 on SAT writing, 19% scored over 1800 on combined SAT, 18% scored over 26 on composite ACT.
Student Life Upper grades have student council, honor system. Discipline rests primarily with faculty.
Tuition and Aid Day student tuition: $18,820.
Admissions For fall 2010, 69 students applied for upper-level admission, 57 were accepted, 57 enrolled. School's own test required. Deadline for receipt of application materials: none. Application fee required: $50. On-campus interview required.
Athletics Interscholastic: basketball (boys, girls), cricket (b), soccer (b,g), swimming and diving (b,g), tennis (b,g), track and field (b,g), volleyball (b,g); intramural: basketball (b,g), soccer (b,g), swimming and diving (b,g), volleyball (b,g).
Computers Computers are regularly used in all academic classes. Computer network features include on-campus library services, online commercial services, Internet access, wireless campus network. Student e-mail accounts are available to students. Students grades are available online. The school has a published electronic and media policy.
Contact Mrs. Kanwal Bhagat, Registrar. 880-2 882 2452 Ext. 139. Fax: 880-2 882 3175. E-mail: aisdadmissions@ais-dhaka.net. Web site: www.ais-dhaka.net.

AMERICAN INTERNATIONAL SCHOOL IN CYPRUS

11 Kassos Street
Nicosia 1086, Cyprus
Head of School: Ms. Michelle Kleiss
General Information Coeducational day college-preparatory, arts, and technology school. Grades K–12. Founded: 1987. Setting: small town. 1 building on campus. Approved or accredited by Middle States Association of Colleges and Schools. Member of European Council of International Schools. Language of instruction: English. Total enrollment: 281. Upper school average class size: 15. Upper school faculty-student ratio: 1:15. The average school day consists of 7 hours.
Upper School Student Profile Grade 9: 20 students (10 boys, 10 girls); Grade 10: 29 students (11 boys, 18 girls); Grade 11: 19 students (7 boys, 12 girls); Grade 12: 20 students (11 boys, 9 girls).
Faculty School total: 45. In upper school: 6 men, 14 women; 17 have advanced degrees.
Subjects Offered Algebra, American history, art, biology, calculus, chemistry, drama, English, ESL, French, geometry, information technology, International Baccalaureate courses, journalism, mathematics, music, physical education, physical science, physics, pre-calculus, science, social studies, Spanish, Western civilization, yearbook.
Graduation Requirements Arts and fine arts (art, music, dance, drama), computer science, English, foreign language, junior and senior seminars, mathematics, physical education (includes health), science, senior project, senior seminar, social studies (includes history). Community service is required.
Special Academic Programs International Baccalaureate program; academic accommodation for the gifted; programs in general development for dyslexic students; special instructional classes for students with mild learning disabilities; ESL (45 students enrolled).
College Admission Counseling 20 students graduated in 2009; 18 went to college. Other: 2 entered military service. Mean SAT critical reading: 526, mean SAT math: 512, mean SAT writing: 524, mean combined SAT: 1562.
Student Life Upper grades have uniform requirement, student council, honor system. Discipline rests primarily with faculty.
Tuition and Aid Day student tuition: €9980.
Admissions Traditional secondary-level entrance grade is 9. For fall 2009, 3 students applied for upper-level admission, 3 were accepted, 3 enrolled. ESL, Math Placement Exam or school's own exam required. Deadline for receipt of application materials: none. Application fee required: €350. Interview required.
Athletics Interscholastic: basketball (boys, girls), field hockey (b,g), running (b,g), soccer (b,g), swimming and diving (b,g), tennis (b,g), track and field (b,g), volleyball (b,g); intramural: aerobics/dance (g), weight training (b,g); coed interscholastic:

aquatics; coed intramural: aquatics, archery, basketball, cross-country running, field hockey, flag football, jogging, tennis, weight training. 2 PE instructors, 2 coaches.
Computers Computers are regularly used in computer applications, English, foreign language, history, journalism, mathematics, science, technology classes. Computer network features include on-campus library services, Internet access. Student e-mail accounts are available to students.
Contact Mrs. Helen Sphikas, Director's Secretary. 357-22316345. Fax: 357-22316549. E-mail: hsphikas@aisc.ac.cy. Web site: www.aisc.ac.cy/.

AMERICAN INTERNATIONAL SCHOOL OF BUCHAREST

Sos. Pipera-Tunari 196
Commune Voluntari-Pipera
Bucharest, Romania
Head of School: Dr. David Ottaviano
General Information Coeducational day college-preparatory and International Baccalaureate school. Grades PK–12. Founded: 1962. Setting: suburban. 10-hectare campus. 4 buildings on campus. Approved or accredited by European Council of International Schools, International Baccalaureate Organization, and New England Association of Schools and Colleges. Language of instruction: English. Total enrollment: 707. Upper school average class size: 17. Upper school faculty-student ratio: 1:9. There are 180 required school days per year for Upper School students. Upper School students typically attend 5 days per week. The average school day consists of 7 hours.
Upper School Student Profile Grade 6: 56 students (32 boys, 24 girls); Grade 7: 48 students (22 boys, 26 girls); Grade 8: 50 students (24 boys, 26 girls); Grade 9: 61 students (27 boys, 34 girls); Grade 10: 46 students (26 boys, 20 girls); Grade 11: 37 students (20 boys, 17 girls); Grade 12: 42 students (19 boys, 23 girls).
Faculty School total: 93. In upper school: 18 men, 30 women; 28 have advanced degrees.
Subjects Offered Advanced math, art, arts, athletics, band, biology, chemistry, choir, chorus, computer graphics, computers, design, desktop publishing, drama, economics, English, ESL, filmmaking, French, global issues, history, integrated mathematics, language, literature, mathematics, music, physical education, physics, Spanish, technology, theory of knowledge, world cultures.
Graduation Requirements Art, biology, chemistry, computer literacy, economics and history, English, foreign language, history, International Baccalaureate courses, life skills, mathematics, physical education (includes health), 25 hours of community service each year of high school.
Special Academic Programs International Baccalaureate program; independent study; ESL (175 students enrolled).
College Admission Counseling 40 students graduated in 2009; 37 went to college, including Bates College; Columbia College; Pomona College; University of Chicago; University of Pennsylvania; Vassar College. Other: 2 entered military service, 1 had other specific plans.
Student Life Upper grades have specified standards of dress, student council. Discipline rests primarily with faculty.
Tuition and Aid Day student tuition: €18,605. Tuition installment plan (individually arranged payment plans, 2-payment installment plan). Need-based scholarship grants available. In 2009–10, 2% of upper-school students received aid. Total amount of financial aid awarded in 2009–10: €5000.
Admissions Traditional secondary-level entrance grade is 9. For fall 2009, 32 students applied for upper-level admission, 27 were accepted, 27 enrolled. English entrance exam, Math Placement Exam, Secondary Level English Proficiency or writing sample required. Deadline for receipt of application materials: May 1. Application fee required: €200. On-campus interview recommended.
Athletics Interscholastic: basketball (boys, girls), cross-country running (b,g), soccer (b,g), softball (b,g), swimming and diving (b,g), tennis (b,g), volleyball (b,g); intramural: basketball (b,g), indoor hockey (b,g), indoor soccer (b,g); coed intramural: outdoor adventure, outdoor education, physical fitness, sailing, soccer, softball. 5 PE instructors, 4 coaches, 1 athletic trainer.
Computers Computers are regularly used in desktop publishing, graphics, information technology, video film production, yearbook classes. Computer network features include on-campus library services, online commercial services, Internet access, wireless campus network, Internet filtering or blocking technology. Campus intranet, student e-mail accounts, and computer access in designated common areas are available to students. Students grades are available online. The school has a published electronic and media policy.
Contact Mrs. Catalina Pieptea, Admission Officer. 40-21-204-4300 Ext. 368. Fax: 40-21-204-4384. E-mail: cpieptea@aisb.ro. Web site: www.aisb.ro.

AMERICAN INTERNATIONAL SCHOOL OF COSTA RICA

Apartado Postal 4941-1000
Cariari
San Jose, Costa Rica
Head of School: Mr. Charles Ernest Prince
General Information Coeducational day college-preparatory, general academic, arts, technology, Spanish as a Second language, and English as a Second language school. Grades PK–12. Founded: 1970. Setting: suburban. 6-acre campus. 5 buildings on campus. Approved or accredited by Southern Association of Colleges and Schools, The College Board, and US Department of State. Languages of instruction: English and Spanish. Total enrollment: 199. Upper school average class size: 25. Upper school faculty-student ratio: 1:10. There are 184 required school days per year for Upper School students. Upper School students typically attend 5 days per week. The average school day consists of 6 hours.
Upper School Student Profile Grade 7: 15 students (7 boys, 8 girls); Grade 8: 13 students (5 boys, 8 girls); Grade 9: 13 students (8 boys, 5 girls); Grade 10: 14 students (7 boys, 7 girls); Grade 11: 9 students (5 boys, 4 girls); Grade 12: 11 students (8 boys, 3 girls).
Faculty School total: 32. In upper school: 10 men, 4 women; 6 have advanced degrees.
Subjects Offered Algebra, American literature, art, biology, biology-AP, chemistry, civics, college counseling, computer applications, computer skills, earth science, economics, English, English composition, environmental science, ESL, geometry, government/civics, health, history, language arts, mathematics, physical education, pre-calculus, science, social studies, Spanish, Spanish language-AP, Spanish-AP, technology, U.S. government, U.S. history, world history, yearbook.
Graduation Requirements American government, British literature, foreign language, music, physical education (includes health).
Special Academic Programs 5 Advanced Placement exams for which test preparation is offered; accelerated programs; independent study; remedial reading and/or remedial writing; remedial math; programs in English, mathematics, general development for dyslexic students; ESL (12 students enrolled).
College Admission Counseling 15 students graduated in 2010; 13 went to college, including University of Victoria. Other: 2 had other specific plans. Mean SAT critical reading: 460, mean SAT math: 600, mean SAT writing: 520, mean combined SAT: 1580. 5% scored over 600 on SAT critical reading, 10% scored over 600 on SAT math.
Student Life Upper grades have uniform requirement, student council, honor system. Discipline rests primarily with faculty.
Tuition and Aid Day student tuition: $6910. Tuition installment plan (monthly payment plans, annual payments with 10% discount, Semester payment with 5% discount). Tuition reduction for siblings available.
Admissions For fall 2010, 17 students applied for upper-level admission, 13 were accepted, 13 enrolled. School placement exam required. Deadline for receipt of application materials: none. No application fee required. On-campus interview required.
Athletics Interscholastic: basketball (boys, girls), football (b,g), gymnastics (g), outdoor activities (b,g), physical training (b,g), soccer (b,g), volleyball (b,g); intramural: basketball (b,g), football (b,g), soccer (b,g), volleyball (b,g). 1 PE instructor, 1 coach.
Computers Computers are regularly used in English, ESL, history, mathematics, science, Spanish, word processing, writing, yearbook classes. Computer network features include on-campus library services, Internet access, wireless campus network, Internet filtering or blocking technology, equipment support and software. Campus intranet and computer access in designated common areas are available to students. Students grades are available online. The school has a published electronic and media policy.
Contact Mrs. Ivania Quesada, Counselor. 011-506-2293-2567. Fax: 011-506-2239-0625. E-mail: counselor@aiscr.com. Web site: www.aiscr.com.

THE AMERICAN SCHOOL FOUNDATION

Bondojito 215
Colonia Las Americas
Mexico City, D.F. 01120, Mexico
Head of School: Mr. Paul Williams
General Information Coeducational day college-preparatory, arts, bilingual studies, and technology school. Grades PK–12. Founded: 1888. Setting: urban. 17-acre campus. 4 buildings on campus. Approved or accredited by International Baccalaureate Organization and Southern Association of Colleges and Schools. Affiliate member of National Association of Independent Schools. Languages of instruction: English and Spanish. Endowment: 36 million Mexican pesos. Total enrollment: 2,565. Upper school average class size: 18. Upper school faculty-student ratio: 1:10.
Upper School Student Profile Grade 9: 182 students (98 boys, 84 girls); Grade 10: 172 students (90 boys, 82 girls); Grade 11: 185 students (94 boys, 91 girls); Grade 12: 157 students (79 boys, 78 girls).
Faculty School total: 252. In upper school: 27 men, 39 women; 37 have advanced degrees.

Subjects Offered Advanced Placement courses, algebra, American history, American literature, anatomy, anthropology, art, art history, biology, business skills, calculus, ceramics, chemistry, community service, computer programming, computer science, drafting, drama, driver education, earth science, ecology, economics, English, English literature, European history, expository writing, film, fine arts, French, geography, geometry, government/civics, grammar, health, history, humanities, Italian, journalism, mathematics, mechanical drawing, Mexican history, music, personal development, philosophy, photography, physical education, physics, physiology, psychology, religion, science, social sciences, social studies, Spanish, speech, statistics, theater, trigonometry, typing, world history, world literature, writing, zoology.
Graduation Requirements Arts and fine arts (art, music, dance, drama), computer science, English, foreign language, foreign policy, mathematics, physical education (includes health), science, social sciences, social studies (includes history). Community service is required.
Special Academic Programs International Baccalaureate program; 15 Advanced Placement exams for which test preparation is offered; honors section; remedial reading and/or remedial writing; remedial math; programs in English, mathematics, general development for dyslexic students; special instructional classes for students with learning disabilities (through the Learning Skills Center), Attention Deficit Disorder, and dyslexia; ESL (20 students enrolled).
College Admission Counseling 152 students graduated in 2009; 140 went to college, including American University; Babson College; Boston University; Bryn Mawr College; New York University; University of Pennsylvania. Other: 12 had other specific plans. Median SAT critical reading: 553, median SAT math: 560, median SAT writing: 550, median composite ACT: 26.
Student Life Upper grades have specified standards of dress, student council. Discipline rests primarily with faculty.
Tuition and Aid Day student tuition: 13,600 Mexican pesos. Merit scholarship grants, need-based scholarship grants available. In 2009–10, 13% of upper-school students received aid; total upper-school merit-scholarship money awarded: 750,000 Mexican pesos. Total amount of financial aid awarded in 2009–10: 4,500,000 Mexican pesos.
Admissions Traditional secondary-level entrance grade is 10. For fall 2009, 121 students applied for upper-level admission, 104 were accepted, 100 enrolled. Gates MacGinite Reading Tests required. Deadline for receipt of application materials: none. Application fee required: 700 Mexican pesos. On-campus interview required.
Athletics Interscholastic: basketball (boys, girls), football (b), soccer (b,g), swimming and diving (b,g), touch football (b), volleyball (b,g); intramural: basketball (b,g), football (b), soccer (b); coed interscholastic: gymnastics, tennis, track and field; coed intramural: swimming and diving, tennis, track and field, volleyball. 8 PE instructors, 24 coaches.
Computers Computers are regularly used in all academic classes. Computer network features include on-campus library services, online commercial services, Internet access, wireless campus network, Internet filtering or blocking technology. Student e-mail accounts and computer access in designated common areas are available to students. Students grades are available online. The school has a published electronic and media policy.
Contact Julie Hellmund, Director of Admission. 52-555-227-4900. Fax: 52-55273-4357. E-mail: hellmundj@asf.edu.mx. Web site: www.asf.edu.mx.

THE AMERICAN SCHOOL IN LONDON

One Waverley Place
London NW8 0NP, United Kingdom
Head of School: Coreen R. Hester
General Information Coeducational day college-preparatory school. Grades PK–12. Founded: 1951. Setting: urban. 3-acre campus. 1 building on campus. Approved or accredited by European Council of International Schools and Middle States Association of Colleges and Schools. Affiliate member of National Association of Independent Schools; member of Secondary School Admission Test Board. Language of instruction: English. Endowment: £10 million. Total enrollment: 1,346. Upper school average class size: 15. Upper school faculty-student ratio: 1:10. There are 175 required school days per year for Upper School students. Upper School students typically attend 5 days per week. The average school day consists of 5 hours and 50 minutes.
Upper School Student Profile Grade 9: 118 students (66 boys, 52 girls); Grade 10: 122 students (68 boys, 54 girls); Grade 11: 104 students (58 boys, 46 girls); Grade 12: 120 students (50 boys, 70 girls).
Faculty School total: 180. In upper school: 28 men, 39 women; 55 have advanced degrees.
Subjects Offered Acting, African studies, algebra, American literature, anatomy and physiology, Arabic, architectural drawing, art, art history-AP, astronomy, biology, biology-AP, British literature, calculus, calculus-AP, chemistry, chemistry-AP, Chinese, Chinese studies, comparative cultures, computer applications, computer science-AP, concert band, concert choir, dance, digital art, digital imaging, digital music, digital photography, drawing, ecology, economics, English language and composition-AP, English literature and composition-AP, environmental science, environmental studies, European history, European history-AP, European literature, film, French, French language-AP, French literature-AP, genetics, geometry, German, German-AP, health, human geography—AP, independent study, Japanese, jazz band,

journalism, Latin, macro/microeconomics-AP, Middle East, modern European history-AP, music theory-AP, mythology, orchestra, painting, photography, physical education, physics-AP, play production, poetry, pre-calculus, psychology, psychology-AP, Russian, Russian literature, Russian studies, Shakespeare, Spanish, Spanish language-AP, Spanish literature-AP, statistics-AP, studio art-AP, trigonometry, U.S. history, U.S. history-AP, video and animation, video film production, Web site design, Western civilization, world geography, writing, yearbook.

Graduation Requirements Arts and fine arts (art, music, dance, drama), computer science, English, foreign language, mathematics, physical education (includes health), science, social studies (includes history).

Special Academic Programs Advanced Placement exam preparation; independent study; programs in general development for dyslexic students; ESL (49 students enrolled).

College Admission Counseling 111 students graduated in 2010; all went to college, including Boston University; Duke University; Georgetown University; Princeton University; The George Washington University; University of Southern California. Mean SAT critical reading: 640, mean SAT math: 643, mean SAT writing: 644.

Student Life Upper grades have student council, honor system. Discipline rests primarily with faculty.

Tuition and Aid Day student tuition: £21,700. Tuition installment plan (monthly payment plans, individually arranged payment plans). Need-based scholarship grants available. In 2010–11, 6% of upper-school students received aid. Total amount of financial aid awarded in 2010–11: £411,150.

Admissions Any standardized test, ERB or ISEE required. Deadline for receipt of application materials: none. Application fee required: £100.

Athletics Interscholastic: baseball (boys); basketball (b,g); cheering (g); crew (b,g); cross-country running (b,g); dance (g); field hockey (g); rugby (b); soccer (b,g); softball (g); swimming and diving (b,g); tennis (b,g); track and field (b,g); volleyball (b,g); coed interscholastic: golf; coed intramural: badminton, kickball, soccer, swimming and diving, tennis. 3 PE instructors, 52 coaches.

Computers Computers are regularly used in animation, English, foreign language, journalism, mathematics, media arts, media production, science, social studies, video film production, Web site design, yearbook classes. Computer network features include on-campus library services, Internet access, wireless campus network. Student e-mail accounts are available to students. Students grades are available online.

Contact Jodi Coats, Dean of Admissions. 44-20-7449-1221. Fax: 44-20-7449-1350. E-mail: admissions@asl.org. Web site: www.asl.org.

AMERICAN SCHOOL OF BOMBAY

SF2, G Block
Bandra Kurla Complex Road
Mumbai 400 098, India
Head of School: Mr. Craig Johnson

General Information Coeducational day college-preparatory school. Grades PK–12. Founded: 1981. Setting: urban. 2-acre campus. 1 building on campus. Approved or accredited by Middle States Association of Colleges and Schools and National Independent Private Schools Association. Member of European Council of International Schools. Language of instruction: English. Total enrollment: 700. Upper school average class size: 18. Upper school faculty-student ratio: 1:5. There are 183 required school days per year for Upper School students. Upper School students typically attend 5 days per week. The average school day consists of 5 hours and 40 minutes.

Upper School Student Profile Grade 6: 41 students (23 boys, 18 girls); Grade 7: 51 students (30 boys, 21 girls); Grade 8: 60 students (31 boys, 29 girls); Grade 9: 51 students (26 boys, 25 girls); Grade 10: 42 students (12 boys, 30 girls); Grade 11: 44 students (18 boys, 26 girls); Grade 12: 43 students (19 boys, 24 girls).

Faculty School total: 100. In upper school: 18 men, 23 women; 35 have advanced degrees.

Special Academic Programs International Baccalaureate program; ESL (16 students enrolled).

College Admission Counseling 30 students graduated in 2010; 29 went to college. Other: 1 had other specific plans. Median SAT critical reading: 600, median SAT math: 600, median SAT writing: 635, median combined SAT: 1845.

Student Life Upper grades have specified standards of dress, student council, honor system. Discipline rests primarily with faculty.

Admissions For fall 2010, 43 students applied for upper-level admission, 29 were accepted, 25 enrolled. Deadline for receipt of application materials: none. Application fee required: $250.

Athletics Interscholastic: aquatics (boys, girls), badminton (b,g), basketball (b,g), soccer (b,g), tennis (b,g), track and field (b,g), volleyball (b,g); coed intramural: cricket, floor hockey, Frisbee, indoor track, juggling, life saving. 4 PE instructors, 20 coaches.

Computers Computer resources include on-campus library services, online commercial services, Internet access, wireless campus network, Internet filtering or blocking technology, 1-1 laptop program. Campus intranet and student e-mail accounts are available to students. Students grades are available online. The school has a published electronic and media policy.

Contact Ms. Vanita Barrett, Admissions Assistant. 91-22-6772-7272 Ext. 322. Fax: 91-22-2652-6666. E-mail: admissionassistant@asbindia.org. Web site: www.asbindia.org.

THE AMERICAN SCHOOL OF EL SALVADOR

Apartado Postal 01-35
San Salvador, El Salvador
Head of School: Mr. Ken Templeton

General Information Coeducational day college-preparatory school. Grades PK–12. Founded: 1946. Setting: suburban. 43-acre campus. 6 buildings on campus. Approved or accredited by Southern Association of Colleges and Schools. Affiliate member of National Association of Independent Schools. Languages of instruction: English and Spanish. Endowment: $3 million. Total enrollment: 1,731. Upper school average class size: 18. Upper school faculty-student ratio: 1:20. Upper School students typically attend 5 days per week. The average school day consists of 5 hours and 50 minutes.

Upper School Student Profile Grade 9: 118 students (58 boys, 60 girls); Grade 10: 108 students (53 boys, 55 girls); Grade 11: 119 students (62 boys, 57 girls); Grade 12: 116 students (54 boys, 62 girls).

Faculty School total: 221. In upper school: 25 men, 32 women; 36 have advanced degrees.

Subjects Offered Algebra, American history, American literature, art, art history, biology, calculus, chemistry, computer science, creative writing, earth science, economics, electronics, English, English literature, English-AP, environmental science, French, geography, geometry, government/civics, health, history, history-AP, mathematics, mathematics-AP, music, philosophy, photography, physical education, physics, psychology, social sciences, social studies, sociology, Spanish, Spanish-AP, statistics, trigonometry, world history.

Graduation Requirements 1½ elective credits, English, foreign language, mathematics, physical education (includes health), social sciences, written competency examination.

Special Academic Programs Advanced Placement exam preparation; honors section; remedial reading and/or remedial writing; remedial math; programs in general development for dyslexic students.

College Admission Counseling 110 students graduated in 2009; 109 went to college, including Loyola University New Orleans; Penn State University Park; Texas A&M University; University of Notre Dame. Other: 1 had other specific plans.

Student Life Upper grades have uniform requirement, student council, honor system. Discipline rests primarily with faculty.

Tuition and Aid Day student tuition: $7400. Guaranteed tuition plan. Tuition installment plan (individually arranged payment plans). Merit scholarship grants, need-based scholarship grants available. In 2009–10, 20% of upper-school students received aid; total upper-school merit-scholarship money awarded: $88,400.

Admissions Traditional secondary-level entrance grade is 10. For fall 2009, 17 students applied for upper-level admission, 11 were accepted, 11 enrolled. Admissions testing and Iowa Tests of Basic Skills required. Deadline for receipt of application materials: none. Application fee required: $40. On-campus interview required.

Athletics Interscholastic: baseball (boys, girls), basketball (b,g), soccer (b,g), softball (b,g), swimming and diving (b,g), tennis (b,g), track and field (b,g), volleyball (b,g); intramural: basketball (b,g), equestrian sports (b,g), golf (b,g), soccer (b,g), track and field (b,g), volleyball (b,g), weight lifting (b,g). 2 PE instructors, 11 coaches.

Computers Computer network features include Internet access, Internet filtering or blocking technology. Student e-mail accounts and computer access in designated common areas are available to students. Students grades are available online.

Contact Mrs. Yolanda Lopez, Admission Director. 503-2528-8220. Fax: 503-2528-8222. E-mail: lopez.yolanda@amschool.edu.sv. Web site: www.amschool.edu.sv.

THE AMERICAN SCHOOL OF MADRID

Apartado 80
Madrid 28080, Spain
Head of School: Mr. William D. O'Hale

General Information Coeducational day college-preparatory, arts, and technology school. Grades PK–12. Founded: 1961. Setting: suburban. 4-hectare campus. 2 buildings on campus. Approved or accredited by International Baccalaureate Organization and Middle States Association of Colleges and Schools. Affiliate member of National Association of Independent Schools; member of European Council of International Schools. Language of instruction: English. Total enrollment: 868. Upper school average class size: 20. Upper school faculty-student ratio: 1:8. There are 175 required school days per year for Upper School students. Upper School students typically attend 5 days per week. The average school day consists of 6 hours and 45 minutes.

Upper School Student Profile Grade 9: 67 students (37 boys, 30 girls); Grade 10: 72 students (38 boys, 34 girls); Grade 11: 73 students (38 boys, 35 girls); Grade 12: 72 students (31 boys, 41 girls).

Faculty School total: 103. In upper school: 20 men, 15 women; 30 have advanced degrees.

Subjects Offered 3-dimensional art, algebra, American history, American literature, art, biology, business studies, calculus, chemistry, choir, computer math, computer

The American School of Madrid

science, computer skills, computer-aided design, creative writing, debate, earth science, English, English literature, environmental science, European history, expository writing, French, geography, geometry, government/civics, health, history, instrumental music, jazz band, journalism, mathematics, music, orchestra, philosophy, physical education, physics, psychology, science, social studies, Spanish, speech, U.S. history, world history, world literature, world wide web design, yearbook.

Graduation Requirements Electives, English, foreign language, information technology, mathematics, physical education (includes health), science, social studies (includes history).

Special Academic Programs International Baccalaureate program; independent study; ESL (50 students enrolled).

College Admission Counseling 65 students graduated in 2010; 63 went to college, including Georgetown University; New York University; Saint Louis University; Suffolk University; The University of Tampa. Other: 2 entered military service. Mean SAT critical reading: 551, mean SAT math: 566, mean SAT writing: 558.

Student Life Upper grades have specified standards of dress, student council, honor system. Discipline rests equally with students and faculty.

Summer Programs ESL, sports, art/fine arts, computer instruction programs offered; session focuses on ESL, soccer; held on campus; accepts boys and girls; open to students from other schools. 275 students usually enrolled. 2011 schedule: July 1 to July 31. Application deadline: June.

Tuition and Aid Day student tuition: €17,415. Tuition installment plan (monthly payment plans, individually arranged payment plans, semester payment plan). Tuition reduction for siblings, need-based scholarship grants, scholarships for children of employees available. In 2010–11, 5% of upper-school students received aid.

Admissions Traditional secondary-level entrance grade is 11. For fall 2010, 83 students applied for upper-level admission, 50 were accepted, 50 enrolled. Achievement/Aptitude/Writing, Comprehensive Test of Basic Skills, ERB, independent norms, Iowa Tests of Basic Skills, PSAT or TAP required. Deadline for receipt of application materials: none. Application fee required: €140. On-campus interview required.

Athletics Interscholastic: basketball (boys, girls), soccer (b,g), volleyball (b,g); coed interscholastic: golf, gymnastics, martial arts, tennis; coed intramural: weight lifting. 2 PE instructors, 7 coaches.

Computers Computers are regularly used in all classes. Computer network features include on-campus library services, Internet access, wireless campus network, Internet filtering or blocking technology. Campus intranet is available to students. The school has a published electronic and media policy.

Contact Ms. Sholeh Farpour, Admissions Head. 34-91 740 1904. Fax: 34-91 357 2678. E-mail: admissions@asmadrid.org. Web site: www.asmadrid.org.

AMERICAN SCHOOL OF MILAN

Via K. Marx 14
Noverasco di Opera, Milan 20090, Italy
Head of School: Dr. Alan Austen

General Information Coeducational day college-preparatory, bilingual studies, and International Baccalaureate school. Grades N–12. Founded: 1962. Setting: suburban. Nearest major city is Milan, Italy. 9-acre campus. 1 building on campus. Approved or accredited by Department of Defense Dependents Schools, International Baccalaureate Organization, Middle States Association of Colleges and Schools, and US Department of State. Affiliate member of National Association of Independent Schools; member of European Council of International Schools. Language of instruction: English. Total enrollment: 658. Upper school average class size: 20. Upper school faculty-student ratio: 1:9. Upper School students typically attend 5 days per week.

Faculty School total: 74. In upper school: 7 men, 18 women; 19 have advanced degrees.

Subjects Offered Algebra, art, biology, business studies, calculus, chemistry, community service, computer programming, computer science, creative writing, ecology, economics, English, English literature, ESL, European history, expository writing, fine arts, French, geology, geometry, grammar, history, Italian, mathematics, music, physical education, physics, psychology, science, social sciences, social studies, theory of knowledge, trigonometry, world history, world literature, writing.

Graduation Requirements Arts and fine arts (art, music, dance, drama), computer science, English, foreign language, mathematics, physical education (includes health), science, social sciences, social studies (includes history), 100 hours of CAS (Creativity, Action, Service) each year.

Special Academic Programs International Baccalaureate program; independent study; remedial reading and/or remedial writing; remedial math; ESL (14 students enrolled).

College Admission Counseling 49 students graduated in 2010; 47 went to college. Other: 2 had other specific plans.

Student Life Upper grades have specified standards of dress, student council, honor system. Discipline rests primarily with faculty.

Tuition and Aid Day student tuition: €8290–€17,150. Tuition installment plan (individually arranged payment plans).

Admissions Traditional secondary-level entrance grade is 9. For fall 2010, 229 students applied for upper-level admission, 183 were accepted, 178 enrolled. Admissions testing, English for Non-native Speakers, English proficiency and

mathematics proficiency exam required. Deadline for receipt of application materials: none. Application fee required: €250. On-campus interview recommended.

Athletics Interscholastic: basketball (boys, girls), cross-country running (b,g), dance team (g), soccer (b,g), tennis (b,g), track and field (b,g), volleyball (b,g); intramural: golf (b,g); coed interscholastic: aerobics/dance; coed intramural: aerobics/dance, ballet, basketball, martial arts, soccer, softball, swimming and diving, table tennis, tennis, volleyball. 3 PE instructors, 4 coaches.

Computers Computers are regularly used in college planning, desktop publishing, ESL, English, ESL, history, humanities, journalism, library, library skills, literary magazine, mathematics, media arts, research skills, science, technology, writing, yearbook classes. Computer network features include on-campus library services, online commercial services, Internet access, wireless campus network, Internet filtering or blocking technology. Student e-mail accounts and computer access in designated common areas are available to students. Students grades are available online. The school has a published electronic and media policy.

Contact Ms. Neda Buncic, Admissions Assistant. 39-02-53000015. Fax: 39-02-93660932. E-mail: admissions@asmilan.org. Web site: www.asmilan.org.

THE AMERICAN SCHOOL OF PUERTO VALLARTA

Albatros # 129
Marina Vallarta
Puerto Vallarta, Jalisco 48354, Mexico
Head of School: Mr. Gerald Selitzer

General Information Coeducational day college-preparatory, arts, bilingual studies, and technology school. Grades N–12. Founded: 1986. Setting: small town. Nearest major city is Puerto Vallarta, Mexico. 7-acre campus. 3 buildings on campus. Approved or accredited by Association of Independent Schools of Florida, Southern Association of Colleges and Schools, US Department of State, and state department of education. Languages of instruction: English and Spanish. Endowment: 2 million Mexican pesos. Total enrollment: 343. Upper school average class size: 25. Upper school faculty-student ratio: 1:7. There are 200 required school days per year for Upper School students. Upper School students typically attend 5 days per week. The average school day consists of 5 hours and 40 minutes.

Upper School Student Profile Grade 10: 23 students (15 boys, 8 girls); Grade 11: 21 students (6 boys, 15 girls); Grade 12: 23 students (10 boys, 13 girls).

Faculty School total: 42. In upper school: 8 men, 12 women; 8 have advanced degrees.

Subjects Offered Advanced Placement courses, algebra, American literature, art, biology, British literature, calculus, chemistry, chorus, civics, comparative government and politics-AP, computer science, computers, conceptual physics, earth science, economics-AP, English, English literature, English literature and composition-AP, etymology, geography, journalism, law, life science, literature, literature and composition-AP, mathematics, Mexican history, Mexican literature, philosophy, physical science, physics, pre-algebra, pre-calculus, robotics, Spanish, Spanish language-AP, Spanish literature, Spanish literature-AP, statistics-AP, studio art-AP, trigonometry, U.S. history, U.S. history-AP, world history.

Graduation Requirements American literature, art, art education, biology, British literature, calculus, chemistry, computer education, conceptual physics, economics, English literature, mathematics, Mexican history, Mexican literature, physical education (includes health), pre-calculus, Spanish, Spanish literature, U.S. history.

Special Academic Programs Advanced Placement exam preparation; independent study; remedial reading and/or remedial writing; remedial math; ESL (4 students enrolled).

College Admission Counseling 29 students graduated in 2009; 24 went to college, including Austin College; Boston University; Clark University; Colgate University; Cornell University; The University of British Columbia. Other: 2 went to work, 3 had other specific plans.

Student Life Upper grades have uniform requirement, student council, honor system. Discipline rests primarily with faculty.

Tuition and Aid Day student tuition: $6404–$7076. Tuition installment plan (monthly payment plans, individually arranged payment plans). Tuition reduction for siblings available. In 2009–10, 10% of upper-school students received aid.

Admissions Traditional secondary-level entrance grade is 10. For fall 2009, 19 students applied for upper-level admission, 8 were accepted, 4 enrolled. Achievement tests, admissions testing, English language, math and English placement tests, Math Placement Exam and math, reading, and mental ability tests required. Deadline for receipt of application materials: none. No application fee required. Interview required.

Athletics Interscholastic: basketball (boys, girls), golf (b,g), soccer (b,g), tennis (b,g); intramural: baseball (b), basketball (b,g), dance (g), jump rope (g), modern dance (g), soccer (b,g), swimming and diving (b,g), tennis (b,g). 3 PE instructors, 4 coaches, 3 athletic trainers.

Computers Computers are regularly used in computer applications, history, keyboarding, lab/keyboard, music, science, social studies, Spanish, technology, yearbook classes. Computer network features include on-campus library services, Internet access, wireless campus network, Internet filtering or blocking technology. Campus intranet and computer access in designated common areas are available to students. Students grades are available online. The school has a published electronic and media policy.

Contact Ms. Elise Langley, Director of Admissions and College Guidance. 52-322 226 7672. Fax: 52-322 226 7677. E-mail: llangley@aspv.edu.mx. Web site: www.aspv.edu.mx.

AMERICAN SCHOOL OF THE HAGUE
Rijksstraatweg 200
Wassenaar 2241 BX, Netherlands
Head of School: Richard Spradling

General Information Coeducational day college-preparatory, arts, technology, and applied and performing arts school. Grades PS–12. Founded: 1953. Setting: suburban. Nearest major city is The Hague, Netherlands. 11-acre campus. 1 building on campus. Approved or accredited by European Council of International Schools, International Baccalaureate Organization, Middle States Association of Colleges and Schools, The College Board, and US Department of State. Language of instruction: English. Total enrollment: 1,035. Upper school average class size: 18. Upper school faculty-student ratio: 1:7. There are 183 required school days per year for Upper School students. Upper School students typically attend 5 days per week. The average school day consists of 6 hours.

Upper School Student Profile Grade 9: 77 students (35 boys, 42 girls); Grade 10: 86 students (48 boys, 38 girls); Grade 11: 104 students (51 boys, 53 girls); Grade 12: 96 students (58 boys, 38 girls).

Faculty School total: 144. In upper school: 24 men, 29 women; 42 have advanced degrees.

Subjects Offered Advanced chemistry, advertising design, algebra, American literature, art history, art-AP, band, biology, biology-AP, calculus, calculus-AP, chemistry, chemistry-AP, choir, comparative government and politics, computer applications, computer multimedia, computer music, computer science, computer-aided design, creative writing, current events, dance, debate, dramatic arts, Dutch, economics, economics-AP, English, English literature, English-AP, environmental systems, ESL, European history, French, French-AP, geometry, German, German-AP, global studies, guidance, health and wellness, honors algebra, honors geometry, human geography—AP, information technology, instrumental music, international affairs, International Baccalaureate courses, jazz band, math analysis, math methods, mathematics-AP, multimedia, music composition, music technology, music theory-AP, music-AP, orchestra, peer counseling, photography, physical education, physics, physics-AP, pre-calculus, programming, psychology, public speaking, senior composition, sociology, Spanish, Spanish-AP, speech and debate, stagecraft, student publications, studio art, theater arts, theater design and production, theory of knowledge, trigonometry, U.S. history, U.S. history-AP, video film production, Web site design, Western civilization, world history, writing, yearbook.

Graduation Requirements Arts, computer information systems, electives, English, health and wellness, human issues, lab science, mathematics, modern languages, physical education (includes health), science, service learning/internship, social studies (includes history), technology.

Special Academic Programs International Baccalaureate program; Advanced Placement exam preparation; honors section; independent study; academic accommodation for the gifted, the musically talented, and the artistically talented; remedial reading and/or remedial writing.

College Admission Counseling 89 students graduated in 2010; 87 went to college, including Massachusetts Institute of Technology; Parsons The New School for Design; Queen's University at Kingston; United States Air Force Academy; Vassar College; Virginia Polytechnic Institute and State University. Other: 1 entered military service, 1 had other specific plans. Mean SAT critical reading: 570, mean SAT math: 597, mean SAT writing: 560, mean combined SAT: 1727.

Student Life Upper grades have specified standards of dress, student council, honor system. Discipline rests primarily with faculty.

Tuition and Aid Day student tuition: €17,320. Tuition installment plan (individually arranged payment plans).

Admissions For fall 2010, 84 students applied for upper-level admission, 78 were accepted, 65 enrolled. Deadline for receipt of application materials: none. No application fee required. Interview recommended.

Athletics Interscholastic: baseball (boys), basketball (b,g), cross-country running (b,g), soccer (b,g), softball (g), swimming and diving (b,g), tennis (b,g), track and field (b,g), volleyball (b,g); intramural: baseball (b), basketball (b,g), cheering (g), cross-country running (b,g), dance team (g), soccer (b,g), softball (g), volleyball (b,g); coed intramural: cheering. 2 PE instructors, 9 coaches.

Computers Computers are regularly used in all classes. Computer network features include on-campus library services, online commercial services, Internet access, wireless campus network, Internet filtering or blocking technology. Campus intranet, student e-mail accounts, and computer access in designated common areas are available to students. Students grades are available online. The school has a published electronic and media policy.

Contact Admissions Office. 31-70-512-1080. Fax: 31-70-512-1076. E-mail: admissions@ash.nl. Web site: www.ash.nl.

ANACAPA SCHOOL
814 Santa Barbara Street
Santa Barbara, California 93101
Head of School: Mr. Gordon Sichi

General Information Coeducational day college-preparatory and arts school. Grades 7–12. Founded: 1981. Setting: urban. 2 buildings on campus. Approved or accredited by Western Association of Schools and Colleges and California Department of Education. Total enrollment: 56. Upper school average class size: 12. Upper school faculty-student ratio: 1:10. Upper School students typically attend 5 days per week. The average school day consists of 6 hours and 25 minutes.

Upper School Student Profile Grade 9: 9 students (7 boys, 2 girls); Grade 10: 13 students (6 boys, 7 girls); Grade 11: 11 students (4 boys, 7 girls); Grade 12: 7 students (2 boys, 5 girls).

Faculty School total: 12. In upper school: 6 men, 6 women; 4 have advanced degrees.

Special Academic Programs Advanced Placement exam preparation.

College Admission Counseling 7 students graduated in 2009; all went to college, including De Anza College; Santa Barbara City College; University of California, Santa Barbara.

Student Life Upper grades have specified standards of dress, student council, honor system. Discipline rests primarily with faculty.

Tuition and Aid Day student tuition: $21,500. Tuition installment plan (individually arranged payment plans). Need-based scholarship grants, paying campus jobs available. In 2009–10, 49% of upper-school students received aid.

Admissions Traditional secondary-level entrance grade is 9. For fall 2009, 4 students applied for upper-level admission, 4 were accepted, 3 enrolled. Deadline for receipt of application materials: none. Application fee required: $100. On-campus interview required.

Athletics Coed Intramural: aquatics, backpacking, basketball, canoeing/kayaking, dance, fitness, flag football, golf, hiking/backpacking, kayaking, martial arts, outdoor activities, outdoor adventure, sailing, scuba diving, skiing (downhill), snowboarding, soccer, softball, squash, surfing, swimming and diving, table tennis, volleyball, yoga.

Computers Computer resources include Internet access, wireless campus network, Internet filtering or blocking technology. Computer access in designated common areas is available to students.

Contact Ms. Sheryn Sears, Executive Administrator. 805-965-0228. Fax: 805-899-2758. E-mail: anacapa@anacapaschool.org. Web site: www.anacapaschool.org.

ANDREWS ACADEMY
8833 Garland Avenue
Berrien Springs, Michigan 49104-0560
Head of School: Mr. Cleon E. White

General Information Coeducational day college-preparatory, arts, business, vocational, religious studies, and technology school, affiliated with Seventh-day Adventists. Grades 9–12. Founded: 1874. Setting: small town. Nearest major city is South Bend, IN. 20-acre campus. 1 building on campus. Approved or accredited by National Council for Private School Accreditation, North Central Association of Colleges and Schools, and Michigan Department of Education. Endowment: $500,000. Total enrollment: 270. Upper school average class size: 20. Upper school faculty-student ratio: 1:15.

Upper School Student Profile 90% of students are Seventh-day Adventists.

Faculty School total: 18. In upper school: 11 men, 7 women; 13 have advanced degrees.

Subjects Offered 20th century history, accounting, advanced math, aerobics, algebra, American Civil War, American democracy, American government, American history, American literature, ancient world history, art, art appreciation, auto mechanics, backpacking, band, basketball, bell choir, Bible, Bible studies, biology, British literature, business applications, career and personal planning, career exploration, chemistry, child development, choir, choral music, Christian ethics, Christian studies, church history, civil war history, classics, clayworking, composition, computer education, computer literacy, concert band, concert bell choir, creative drama, desktop publishing, drawing, driver education, early childhood, earth science, English composition, English literature, European history, family living, foods, foreign language, general math, geography, government, health education, instrumental music, international foods, keyboarding, lab science, leadership, mathematics, media production, painting, participation in sports, photography, physical fitness, physics, play production, pre-algebra, pre-calculus, reading, reading/study skills, religion, science, softball, Spanish, speech, state government, state history, swimming, tennis, U.S. government, U.S. history, voice, volleyball, weight training, woodworking, world geography, World-Wide-Web publishing, writing, yearbook.

Graduation Requirements American literature, British literature, civil war history, computer literacy, creation science, keyboarding, mathematics, speech, world history, senior portfolio, work experience.

Special Academic Programs Independent study; term-away projects; study at local college for college credit; study abroad; academic accommodation for the gifted, the musically talented, and the artistically talented; remedial reading and/or remedial writing; remedial math.

College Admission Counseling 61 students graduated in 2009; 59 went to college, including Andrews University; Southern Adventist University; Southwestern Adventist University; University of Michigan. Other: 2 went to work. Mean composite ACT: 23.

Student Life Upper grades have specified standards of dress, student council, honor system. Discipline rests primarily with faculty. Attendance at religious services is required.

Tuition and Aid Day student tuition: $7500. Tuition installment plan (monthly payment plans, individually arranged payment plans). Tuition reduction for siblings, need-based scholarship grants, paying campus jobs available. In 2009–10, 33% of upper-school students received aid. Total amount of financial aid awarded in 2009–10: $150,000.

Admissions Achievement tests, Iowa Tests of Basic Skills or Math Placement Exam required. Deadline for receipt of application materials: none. Application fee required: $10. Interview recommended.

Athletics Coed Intramural: aerobics, backpacking, badminton, baseball, basketball, bicycling, Cosom hockey, fitness, flag football, floor hockey, golf, hiking/ backpacking, in-line hockey, mountain biking, outdoor education, physical fitness, skateboarding, soccer, softball, strength & conditioning, swimming and diving, tennis, volleyball, weight training. 3 PE instructors.

Computers Computers are regularly used in accounting, business applications, career education, keyboarding, news writing, word processing, yearbook classes. Computer network features include on-campus library services, Internet access, wireless campus network, Internet filtering or blocking technology. Campus intranet, student e-mail accounts, and computer access in designated common areas are available to students. Students grades are available online. The school has a published electronic and media policy.

Contact Mr. Cleon E. White, Vice Principal. 269-471-3138 Ext. 6234. Fax: 269-471-6368. E-mail: whitec@andrews.edu. Web site: www.andrews.edu/AA/.

ANNIE WRIGHT SCHOOL
827 North Tacoma Avenue
Tacoma, Washington 98403
Head of School: Rick Clarke

General Information Girls' boarding and coeducational day college-preparatory, arts, technology, and mathematics, science and music school, affiliated with Episcopal Church. Boarding girls grades 9–12, day boys grades PS–8, day girls grades PS–12. Founded: 1884. Setting: suburban. Nearest major city is Seattle. Students are housed in single-sex dormitories. 10-acre campus. 2 buildings on campus. Approved or accredited by National Association of Episcopal Schools, National Independent Private Schools Association, Northwest Association of Schools and Colleges, Pacific Northwest Association of Independent Schools, The Association of Boarding Schools, and Washington Department of Education. Member of National Association of Independent Schools and Secondary School Admission Test Board. Endowment: $13 million. Total enrollment: 479. Upper school average class size: 11. Upper school faculty-student ratio: 1:7.

Upper School Student Profile Grade 9: 30 students (30 girls); Grade 10: 31 students (31 girls); Grade 11: 40 students (40 girls); Grade 12: 38 students (38 girls). 51% of students are boarding students. 64% are state residents. 7 states are represented in upper school student body. 31% are international students. International students from Bermuda, China, Republic of Korea, Taiwan, United Republic of Tanzania, and Venezuela; 7 other countries represented in student body. 10% of students are members of Episcopal Church.

Faculty School total: 52. In upper school: 12 men, 17 women; 15 have advanced degrees; 6 reside on campus.

Subjects Offered Algebra, American history, American literature, anatomy, art, art history, biology, calculus, ceramics, chemistry, computer programming, computer science, creative writing, dance, drama, earth science, economics, English, English literature, ESL, fine arts, French, geometry, government/civics, health, history, Japanese, mathematics, music, music history, physical education, physics, religion, science, social studies, Spanish, theater, world history, world literature.

Graduation Requirements Arts and fine arts (art, music, dance, drama), computer science, English, foreign language, mathematics, physical education (includes health), religion (includes Bible studies and theology), science, social studies (includes history), swim safety test.

Special Academic Programs International Baccalaureate program; independent study; term-away projects; study abroad; ESL.

College Admission Counseling 16 students graduated in 2009; 15 went to college, including Brown University; Cornell University; Macalester College; Rhode Island School of Design; Rice University; University of Michigan–Dearborn. Other: 1 had other specific plans.

Student Life Upper grades have uniform requirement, student council, honor system. Discipline rests equally with students and faculty.

Tuition and Aid Day student tuition: $19,700; 7-day tuition and room/board: $34,000. Tuition installment plan (monthly payment plans, individually arranged payment plans). Merit scholarship grants, need-based scholarship grants available. In 2009–10, 43% of upper-school students received aid; total upper-school merit-scholarship money awarded: $300,000. Total amount of financial aid awarded in 2009–10: $300,000.

Admissions Traditional secondary-level entrance grade is 9. ISEE, SSAT and TOEFL required. Deadline for receipt of application materials: February 16. Application fee required: $100. Interview required.

Athletics Interscholastic: basketball, crew, cross-country running, golf, soccer. 5 PE instructors, 10 coaches, 1 athletic trainer.

Computers Computers are regularly used in all classes.

Contact Jesse W. Fortney, Director of Admissions and Financial Aid. 253-284-8601. Fax: 253-572-3616. E-mail: admission@aw.org. Web site: www.aw.org.

ANTELOPE VALLEY CHRISTIAN SCHOOL
3700 West Avenue L
Lancaster, California 93536
Head of School: Mr. Douglas McKenzie

General Information Coeducational boarding and day college-preparatory school, affiliated with Assemblies of God, Christian faith. Boarding grades 6–12, day grades K–12. Founded: 1987. Setting: suburban. Nearest major city is Los Angeles. Students are housed in single-sex by floor dormitories. 35-acre campus. 8 buildings on campus. Approved or accredited by Association of Christian Schools International, Western Association of Schools and Colleges, and California Department of Education. Total enrollment: 257. Upper school average class size: 24. Upper school faculty-student ratio: 1:15. There are 180 required school days per year for Upper School students. Upper School students typically attend 5 days per week. The average school day consists of 6 hours and 15 minutes.

Upper School Student Profile Grade 6: 10 students (5 boys, 5 girls); Grade 7: 16 students (12 boys, 4 girls); Grade 8: 14 students (6 boys, 8 girls); Grade 9: 10 students (6 boys, 4 girls); Grade 10: 19 students (10 boys, 9 girls); Grade 11: 28 students (18 boys, 10 girls); Grade 12: 14 students (7 boys, 7 girls). 40% of students are boarding students. 60% are state residents. 1 state is represented in upper school student body. 40% are international students. International students from Cambodia, China, Hong Kong, and Republic of Korea. 65% of students are Assemblies of God, Christian faith.

Faculty School total: 26. In upper school: 5 men, 6 women; 3 have advanced degrees; 4 reside on campus.

Subjects Offered Acting, advanced math, advanced TOEFL/grammar, American history-AP, American literature, American literature-AP, analytic geometry, athletics, Bible, biology-AP, business, calculus, cheerleading, chemistry, computer programming, computers, consumer economics, consumer mathematics, design, drama, drawing, earth science, economics, electives, English, English as a foreign language, English language and composition-AP, English language-AP, English literature and composition-AP, English-AP, fine arts, foreign language, geography, geometry, government, government/civics, health, health education, history, history-AP, journalism, leadership and service, mathematics, music, newspaper, physical education, physics, SAT preparation, science, TOEFL preparation, trigonometry, typing, U.S. government, U.S. government and politics-AP, U.S. history, weight training, weight-lifting, world geography, world history, world literature, writing, yearbook.

Graduation Requirements All academic.

Special Academic Programs 4 Advanced Placement exams for which test preparation is offered; ESL (20 students enrolled).

College Admission Counseling 18 students graduated in 2009; 16 went to college. Other: 1 went to work, 1 had other specific plans.

Student Life Upper grades have specified standards of dress, student council, honor system. Discipline rests primarily with faculty.

Tuition and Aid Tuition reduction for siblings, need-based scholarship grants available. In 2009–10, 2% of upper-school students received aid.

Admissions Traditional secondary-level entrance grade is 9. TOEFL or SLEP required. Deadline for receipt of application materials: none. Application fee required: $100. Interview recommended.

Athletics Interscholastic: baseball (boys), basketball (b,g), cheering (g), flag football (b,g), football (b), physical fitness (b,g), physical training (b), softball (g), volleyball (g), weight training (b); coed interscholastic: physical fitness, soccer, volleyball. 2 PE instructors, 5 coaches.

Computers Computers are regularly used in college planning, computer applications, creative writing, keyboarding, lab/keyboard, mathematics, news writing, speech, typing, yearbook classes. Computer network features include Internet access, wireless campus network, Internet filtering or blocking technology. Student e-mail accounts are available to students. Students grades are available online. The school has a published electronic and media policy.

Contact Mrs. Christina M. Clark, International Programs/Students Director. 661-943-0044 Ext. 122. Fax: 661-943-6774. E-mail: cclark@avcs.edu. Web site: www.avcs.edu.

ARCHBISHOP ALTER HIGH SCHOOL
940 East David Road
Kettering, Ohio 45429-5512
Head of School: Mrs. Nicole Brainard

General Information Coeducational day college-preparatory, general academic, and arts school, affiliated with Roman Catholic Church. Grades 9–12. Founded: 1962. Setting: suburban. Nearest major city is Dayton. 3 buildings on campus. Approved or accredited by North Central Association of Colleges and Schools, Ohio Catholic

Schools Accreditation Association (OCSAA), and Ohio Department of Education. Total enrollment: 650. Upper school average class size: 25. Upper school faculty-student ratio: 1:15. There are 185 required school days per year for Upper School students.

Upper School Student Profile Grade 9: 164 students (92 boys, 72 girls); Grade 10: 170 students (84 boys, 86 girls); Grade 11: 170 students (90 boys, 80 girls); Grade 12: 146 students (69 boys, 77 girls). 90% of students are Roman Catholic.

Faculty School total: 62. In upper school: 19 men, 30 women; 38 have advanced degrees.

Subjects Offered Accounting, advanced chemistry, advanced math, Advanced Placement courses, algebra, American Civil War, American government, American history, American history-AP, American literature, American literature-AP, analysis and differential calculus, analytic geometry, anatomy and physiology, band, Basic programming, biology-AP, British literature, business, business law, calculus, calculus-AP, Catholic belief and practice, chemistry, chemistry-AP, choir, choral music, Christian and Hebrew scripture, church history, Civil War, civil war history, costumes and make-up, ecology, environmental systems, economics, English, English literature, French, health, history, history of the Catholic Church, honors algebra, honors English, honors geometry, honors U.S. history, integrated mathematics, introduction to theater, keyboarding, Latin, marching band, mechanical drawing, music appreciation, personal finance, physical fitness, physics, physics-AP, pre-calculus, public speaking, reading/study skills, Spanish, speech, theater arts, U.S. government and politics-AP, U.S. history, U.S. history-AP.

Graduation Requirements Arts and fine arts (art, music, dance, drama), English, health, keyboarding, mathematics, physical education (includes health), science, social studies (includes history), speech, theology, word processing, Additional requirements for students enrolled in the Alter Scholars Program or Conservatory for the Arts.

Special Academic Programs Advanced Placement exam preparation; honors section; study at local college for college credit.

College Admission Counseling 156 students graduated in 2010; 153 went to college, including Miami University; Ohio University; The Ohio State University; University of Cincinnati; University of Dayton; Wright State University. Other: 2 went to work, 1 had other specific plans. Mean SAT critical reading: 580, mean SAT math: 600, mean SAT writing: 560, mean combined SAT: 1180, mean composite ACT: 25.

Student Life Upper grades have uniform requirement, student council, honor system. Discipline rests equally with students and faculty. Attendance at religious services is required.

Summer Programs Remediation, sports programs offered; held both on and off campus; held at Local YMCA and other venues; accepts boys and girls; open to students from other schools. 75 students usually enrolled.

Tuition and Aid Day student tuition: $5750–$8095. Tuition installment plan (FACTS Tuition Payment Plan). Tuition reduction for siblings, merit scholarship grants, need-based scholarship grants available. In 2010–11, 15% of upper-school students received aid; total upper-school merit-scholarship money awarded: $32,000. Total amount of financial aid awarded in 2010–11: $150,000.

Admissions Traditional secondary-level entrance grade is 9. For fall 2010, 190 students applied for upper-level admission, 185 were accepted, 170 enrolled. Scholastic Testing Service High School Placement Test (open version) or STS required. Deadline for receipt of application materials: none. Application fee required: $100.

Athletics Interscholastic: baseball (boys), basketball (b,g), bowling (b,g), cheering (g), cross-country running (b,g), dance team (g), diving (b,g), football (b), golf (b,g), gymnastics (g), ice hockey (b,g), lacrosse (b), soccer (b,g), softball (g), strength & conditioning (b,g), swimming and diving (b,g), tennis (b,g), track and field (b,g), volleyball (b,g), wrestling (b). 2 PE instructors, 3 coaches, 1 athletic trainer.

Computers Computer network features include Internet access, wireless campus network, Internet filtering or blocking technology. Campus intranet and student e-mail accounts are available to students. Students grades are available online. The school has a published electronic and media policy.

Contact Mrs. Mary Ruth Shearer, Director of Enrollment Management and Marketing. 937-428-5394. Fax: 937-434-0507. E-mail: mshearer@alterhighschool.org. Web site: www.alterhighschool.org.

ARCHBISHOP CURLEY HIGH SCHOOL

3701 Sinclair Lane
Baltimore, Maryland 21213
Head of School: Fr. Joseph Benicewicz

General Information Boys' day college-preparatory school, affiliated with Roman Catholic Church. Grades 9–12. Founded: 1961. Setting: urban. 33-acre campus. 2 buildings on campus. Approved or accredited by Middle States Association of Colleges and Schools and Maryland Department of Education. Endowment: $3.2 million. Total enrollment: 570. Upper school average class size: 22. Upper school faculty-student ratio: 1:14. Upper School students typically attend 5 days per week. The average school day consists of 6 hours and 30 minutes.

Upper School Student Profile Grade 9: 156 students (156 boys); Grade 10: 147 students (147 boys); Grade 11: 127 students (127 boys); Grade 12: 143 students (143 boys). 70% of students are Roman Catholic.

Faculty School total: 52. In upper school: 41 men, 11 women; 24 have advanced degrees.

Subjects Offered 20th century world history, 3-dimensional design, accounting, advanced chemistry, advanced computer applications, advanced math, algebra, American government, American history, American history-AP, American literature, analytic geometry, art, art appreciation, astronomy, band, Basic programming, biology, biology-AP, British literature, British literature (honors), business law, business mathematics, calculus, calculus-AP, campus ministry, Catholic belief and practice, chemistry, chemistry-AP, choral music, Christian and Hebrew scripture, Christian doctrine, Christian ethics, computer applications, computer studies, concert band, consumer law, consumer mathematics, earth science, English, English literature and composition-AP, environmental science, ethical decision making, European history, fine arts, French, freshman seminar, geography, geometry, government, government-AP, health, history of the Catholic Church, HTML design, instrumental music, jazz band, journalism, keyboarding, Latin, Life of Christ, music theory, photography, physical science, physics, physics-AP, pre-algebra, pre-calculus, probability and statistics, psychology, psychology-AP, reading/study skills, SAT/ACT preparation, Spanish, Spanish language-AP, U.S. government and politics-AP.

Graduation Requirements Algebra, American government, American history, art appreciation, biology, British literature, chemistry, church history, computer applications, English, foreign language, geometry, keyboarding, Life of Christ, physical fitness, physics, world history, world religions, 30 hours of community service with a written paper.

Special Academic Programs Advanced Placement exam preparation; honors section; independent study; study at local college for college credit; remedial reading and/or remedial writing; remedial math; programs in English, mathematics for dyslexic students.

College Admission Counseling 143 students graduated in 2010; they went to Frostburg State University; Loyola University Maryland; Mount St. Mary's University; Stevenson University; Towson University; York College of Pennsylvania.

Student Life Upper grades have specified standards of dress, student council, honor system. Discipline rests primarily with faculty. Attendance at religious services is required.

Summer Programs Remediation, enrichment, advancement, sports, art/fine arts, computer instruction programs offered; held on campus; accepts boys and girls; open to students from other schools. 2011 schedule: June 15 to August 20. Application deadline: June 15.

Tuition and Aid Day student tuition: $10,800. Tuition installment plan (Academic Management Services Plan, monthly payment plans, individually arranged payment plans). Tuition reduction for siblings, merit scholarship grants, need-based scholarship grants, paying campus jobs available.

Admissions Traditional secondary-level entrance grade is 9. For fall 2010, 304 students applied for upper-level admission, 156 enrolled. High School Placement Test (closed version) from Scholastic Testing Service required. Deadline for receipt of application materials: December 31. Application fee required: $10. Interview required.

Athletics Interscholastic: baseball, basketball, cross-country running, football, golf, indoor track & field, lacrosse, soccer, tennis, track and field, volleyball, wrestling; intramural: basketball, bowling, golf, martial arts, tennis, touch football, volleyball, weight lifting, weight training, whiffle ball, wrestling. 2 PE instructors, 32 coaches, 1 athletic trainer.

Computers Computers are regularly used in English, graphic arts, journalism, library, photography, SAT preparation, science, technology classes. Computer network features include on-campus library services, Internet access.

Contact Mr. John Tucker, Admissions Director. 410-485-5000 Ext. 289. Fax: 410-485-1090. E-mail: jtucker@archbishopcurley.org. Web site: www.archbishopcurley.org.

ARCHBISHOP EDWARD A. MCCARTHY HIGH SCHOOL

5451 South Flamingo Road
SW Ranches, Florida 33330
Head of School: Dr. Richard Perhla

General Information Coeducational day college-preparatory, arts, business, religious studies, bilingual studies, and technology school, affiliated with Roman Catholic Church. Grades 9–12. Founded: 1998. Setting: suburban. Nearest major city is Fort Lauderdale. 11 buildings on campus. Approved or accredited by National Catholic Education Association, Southern Association of Colleges and Schools, and Florida Department of Education. Total enrollment: 1,400. Upper school average class size: 25. Upper school faculty-student ratio: 1:25. There are 181 required school days per year for Upper School students. Upper School students typically attend 5 days per week. The average school day consists of 6 hours and 30 minutes.

Subjects Offered Aerospace education, aerospace science, agroecology, Alabama history and geography, aquatics, Arabic, Arabic studies, arts and crafts, ASB Leadership, astrophysics, atomic theory, auto mechanics, aviation, backpacking, bacteriology, batik, bell choir, bivouac, boat building, boating, Bolivian history, Bolivian social studies, bookbinding, bookkeeping, bookmaking, bowling, Brazilian history, Brazilian social studies, Brazilian studies, cabinet making, California writers, Canadian geography, Canadian history, Canadian law, Canadian literature, Cantonese, celestial navigation, ceremonies of life, chamber groups, chaplaincy, Cherokee, Chesapeake Bay studies, Cheyenne history, Cheyenne language, circus acts, Colorado ecology.

Special Academic Programs Advanced Placement exam preparation; honors section; study at local college for college credit; academic accommodation for the gifted, the musically talented, and the artistically talented; remedial reading and/or remedial writing; remedial math.

Student Life Upper grades have uniform requirement, student council, honor system. Discipline rests primarily with faculty. Attendance at religious services is required.

Tuition and Aid Tuition installment plan (FACTS Tuition Payment Plan). Tuition reduction for siblings, paying campus jobs available.

Admissions High School Placement Test or High School Placement Test (closed version) from Scholastic Testing Service required. Deadline for receipt of application materials: January 27. Application fee required: $50.

Computers Computer network features include on-campus library services, online commercial services, Internet access, Internet filtering or blocking technology. Students grades are available online.

Contact Ms. Kathy Manning, Director of Admissions. 954-434-8820. Fax: 954-680-4835. E-mail: kmanning@mccarthyhigh.org.

ARCHBISHOP HOBAN HIGH SCHOOL

1 Holy Cross Boulevard
Akron, Ohio 44306

Head of School: Br. Kenneth Haders, CSC

General Information Coeducational day college-preparatory, arts, business, religious studies, technology, and family and consumer sciences school, affiliated with Roman Catholic Church. Grades 9–12. Founded: 1953. Setting: urban. 75-acre campus. 3 buildings on campus. Approved or accredited by National Catholic Education Association, North Central Association of Colleges and Schools, Ohio Catholic Schools Accreditation Association (OCSAA), and Ohio Department of Education. Endowment: $6 million. Total enrollment: 857. Upper school average class size: 23. Upper school faculty-student ratio: 1:15. There are 178 required school days per year for Upper School students. Upper School students typically attend 5 days per week. The average school day consists of 6 hours and 55 minutes.

Upper School Student Profile Grade 9: 230 students (125 boys, 105 girls); Grade 10: 210 students (101 boys, 109 girls); Grade 11: 219 students (95 boys, 124 girls); Grade 12: 198 students (100 boys, 98 girls). 82% of students are Roman Catholic.

Faculty School total: 58. In upper school: 28 men, 30 women; 45 have advanced degrees.

Subjects Offered Advanced Placement courses, advanced studio art-AP, algebra, American literature, anatomy and physiology, art, astronomy, biology, biology-AP, British literature, calculus-AP, Catholic belief and practice, ceramics, chemistry, chemistry-AP, child development, Chinese, choir, Christian and Hebrew scripture, church history, computer applications, computer graphics, conceptual physics, concert choir, desktop publishing, digital imaging, digital music, drawing, earth science, economics, electronic music, engineering, English, English literature and composition-AP, ensembles, environmental science, European history-AP, fine arts, food and nutrition, French, geometry, guitar, health education, history of the Catholic Church, honors algebra, honors English, honors geometry, honors world history, human anatomy, Italian, Latin, learning strategies, moral and social development, newspaper, orchestra, painting, philosophy, physical education, physics, physics-AP, pre-algebra, pre-calculus, printmaking, social justice, Spanish, statistics-AP, studio art, television, trigonometry, U.S. government, U.S. history, U.S. history-AP, values and decisions, Web site design, world cultures, world literature, yearbook.

Graduation Requirements Algebra, arts and fine arts (art, music, dance, drama), biology, economics, electives, English, health education, mathematics, physical education (includes health), religious studies, science, social studies (includes history), U.S. government, Christian service totaling 75 hours over four years.

Special Academic Programs 9 Advanced Placement exams for which test preparation is offered; honors section; academic accommodation for the gifted; remedial reading and/or remedial writing; remedial math.

College Admission Counseling 227 students graduated in 2010; 224 went to college, including Kent State University; Ohio University; The Ohio State University; The University of Akron; The University of Toledo; University of Dayton. Other: 2 entered military service, 1 had other specific plans. Median SAT critical reading: 570, median SAT math: 570, median SAT writing: 560, median combined SAT: 1720, median composite ACT: 24. 44% scored over 600 on SAT critical reading, 46% scored over 600 on SAT math, 39% scored over 600 on SAT writing, 39% scored over 1800 on combined SAT, 40% scored over 26 on composite ACT.

Student Life Upper grades have specified standards of dress, student council, honor system. Discipline rests primarily with faculty. Attendance at religious services is required.

Tuition and Aid Day student tuition: $8350. Tuition installment plan (FACTS Tuition Payment Plan, individually arranged payment plans, Semester Payment Plan, Quarterly Payment Plan). Tuition reduction for siblings, merit scholarship grants, need-based scholarship grants, paying campus jobs available. In 2010–11, 37% of upper-school students received aid; total upper-school merit-scholarship money awarded: $247,840. Total amount of financial aid awarded in 2010–11: $1,722,500.

Admissions Traditional secondary-level entrance grade is 9. For fall 2010, 305 students applied for upper-level admission, 250 were accepted, 240 enrolled. High School Placement Test required. Deadline for receipt of application materials: none. No application fee required. Interview recommended.

Athletics Interscholastic: baseball (boys), basketball (b,g), bowling (b,g), cross-country running (b,g), dance team (g), football (b), golf (b,g), gymnastics (g), ice hockey (b), indoor track & field (b), lacrosse (b), soccer (b,g), softball (g), swimming and diving (b,g), tennis (b,g), track and field (b,g), volleyball (b,g), wrestling (b); intramural: flag football (g); coed interscholastic: cheering; coed intramural: basketball, strength & conditioning, ultimate Frisbee, weight training. 1 PE instructor, 1 athletic trainer.

Computers Computers are regularly used in desktop publishing, graphic design, newspaper, science, video film production, Web site design, yearbook classes. Computer network features include on-campus library services, Internet access, wireless campus network, Internet filtering or blocking technology. Campus intranet, student e-mail accounts, and computer access in designated common areas are available to students. Students grades are available online. The school has a published electronic and media policy.

Contact Mrs. Katy Karg, Admissions Counselor. 330-773-6658 Ext. 258. Fax: 330-773-9100. E-mail: kargk@hoban.org. Web site: www.hoban.org.

ARCHBISHOP MCNICHOLAS HIGH SCHOOL

6536 Beechmont Avenue
Cincinnati, Ohio 45230-2098

Head of School: Mr. Gregory R. Saelens

General Information Coeducational day college-preparatory, general academic, arts, business, technology, and services for the Learning Disabled school, affiliated with Roman Catholic Church. Grades 9–12. Founded: 1951. Setting: suburban. 48-acre campus. 3 buildings on campus. Approved or accredited by North Central Association of Colleges and Schools, Ohio Catholic Schools Accreditation Association (OCSAA), and Ohio Department of Education. Total enrollment: 677. Upper school average class size: 19. Upper school faculty-student ratio: 1:14. There are 180 required school days per year for Upper School students. Upper School students typically attend 5 days per week. The average school day consists of 7 hours.

Upper School Student Profile Grade 9: 171 students (79 boys, 92 girls); Grade 10: 177 students (90 boys, 87 girls); Grade 11: 156 students (80 boys, 76 girls); Grade 12: 173 students (84 boys, 89 girls). 92% of students are Roman Catholic.

Faculty School total: 51. In upper school: 19 men, 32 women; 24 have advanced degrees.

Subjects Offered Accounting, advanced computer applications, advanced math, Advanced Placement courses, advanced studio art-AP, algebra, American history, American history-AP, American legal systems, American literature, anatomy and physiology, architectural drawing, band, Basic programming, biology, biology-AP, British literature, business applications, calculus-AP, Catholic belief and practice, ceramics, chemistry, choir, church history, civics, communication skills, computer art, computer processing, computer programming, computer programming-AP, computer technologies, computer-aided design, concert band, concert choir, creative writing, design, developmental math, digital photography, directing, drama, drawing and design, English, English literature and composition-AP, European history-AP, French, government and politics-AP, guitar, health, honors algebra, honors English, honors geometry, integrated science, intro to computers, journalism, Latin, Latin-AP, Life of Christ, marching band, moral theology, music appreciation, music theory-AP, Native American studies, photography, physical education, physical science, physics, physics-AP, portfolio art, pottery, pre-algebra, pre-calculus, reading, reading/study skills, skills for success, Spanish, Spanish language-AP, Spanish literature-AP, speech and debate, street law, studio art, studio art-AP, theater, U.S. government and politics-AP, video film production, Web site design, world history, world religions, writing.

Graduation Requirements Algebra, American government, American history, American literature, arts and fine arts (art, music, dance, drama), biology, British literature, Catholic belief and practice, civics, communication skills, computer applications, English, foreign language, geometry, mathematics, religion (includes Bible studies and theology), science, social justice, world history, senior-year retreat, a minimum of 40 hours of community service.

Special Academic Programs Advanced Placement exam preparation; honors section; academic accommodation for the gifted, the musically talented, and the artistically talented; remedial reading and/or remedial writing; remedial math; programs in English, mathematics, general development for dyslexic students.

College Admission Counseling 183 students graduated in 2010; 181 went to college, including Miami University; Northern Kentucky University; Ohio University; University of Cincinnati; University of Dayton; Xavier University. Other: 2 went to work. Median SAT critical reading: 549, median SAT math: 549, median combined SAT: 1090. 24% scored over 26 on composite ACT.

Student Life Upper grades have uniform requirement, student council. Discipline rests primarily with faculty. Attendance at religious services is required.

Summer Programs Remediation programs offered; session focuses on remediation of failed courses or new PE credit; held on campus; accepts boys and girls; not open to students from other schools. 40 students usually enrolled. 2011 schedule: June 15 to July 19. Application deadline: June 9.

Tuition and Aid Day student tuition: $8375. Tuition installment plan (FACTS Tuition Payment Plan). Tuition reduction for siblings, merit scholarship grants, need-based scholarship grants available. In 2010–11, 14% of upper-school students received aid;

total upper-school merit-scholarship money awarded: $330,000. Total amount of financial aid awarded in 2010–11: $480,000.

Admissions Traditional secondary-level entrance grade is 9. High School Placement Test (closed version) from Scholastic Testing Service required. Deadline for receipt of application materials: December 10. No application fee required.

Athletics Interscholastic: baseball (boys), basketball (b,g), bowling (b,g), cheering (g), dance team (g), football (b), golf (b,g), soccer (b,g), softball (g), track and field (b,g), volleyball (b,g), wrestling (b); coed interscholastic: cross-country running, swimming and diving, track and field; coed intramural: bicycling, flag football, skiing (downhill), snowboarding. 44 coaches, 3 athletic trainers.

Computers Computers are regularly used in computer applications, data processing, English, foreign language, French, graphic design, history, journalism, mathematics, multimedia, photography, programming, publications, reading, religion, science, Spanish, video film production, Web site design, writing classes. Computer network features include on-campus library services, Internet access, Internet filtering or blocking technology, student files, Edline. Campus intranet and student e-mail accounts are available to students. Students grades are available online. The school has a published electronic and media policy.

Contact Mrs. Catherine H. Sherrick, Director of Admissions. 513-231-3500 Ext. 5817. Fax: 513-231-1351. E-mail: csherrick@mcnhs.org. Web site: www.mcnhs.org.

ARCHBISHOP MITTY HIGH SCHOOL
5000 Mitty Avenue
San Jose, California 95129
Head of School: Mr. Tim Brosnan

General Information Coeducational day college-preparatory, arts, religious studies, and technology school, affiliated with Roman Catholic Church. Grades 9–12. Founded: 1964. Setting: suburban. 24-acre campus. 11 buildings on campus. Approved or accredited by Western Association of Schools and Colleges, Western Catholic Education Association, and California Department of Education. Endowment: $8 million. Total enrollment: 1,640. Upper school average class size: 27. Upper school faculty-student ratio: 1:17. There are 180 required school days per year for Upper School students. Upper School students typically attend 5 days per week. The average school day consists of 6 hours and 45 minutes.

Upper School Student Profile Grade 9: 421 students (202 boys, 219 girls); Grade 10: 417 students (198 boys, 219 girls); Grade 11: 400 students (177 boys, 223 girls); Grade 12: 401 students (183 boys, 218 girls). 75% of students are Roman Catholic.

Faculty School total: 110. In upper school: 55 men, 55 women; 70 have advanced degrees.

Subjects Offered 3-dimensional art, acting, American history-AP, American literature-AP, ancient world history, art, biology, biology-AP, British literature, calculus, calculus-AP, Catholic belief and practice, chemistry, chemistry-AP, choral music, chorus, church history, college placement, college writing, community service, computer graphics, computer multimedia, concert band, concert choir, drawing, economics and history, English, English language and composition-AP, English literature, English literature-AP, French, French language-AP, French literature-AP, French studies, French-AP, geometry, history-AP, honors algebra, honors English, honors geometry, honors U.S. history, honors world history, music, music appreciation, music theory-AP, philosophy, physics, physics-AP, political science, religion, social sciences, Spanish, Spanish language-AP, Spanish literature, Spanish literature-AP, student government, theater arts, U.S. government and politics, U.S. government and politics-AP, U.S. history, U.S. history-AP, U.S. literature, visual and performing arts, visual arts, world history.

Graduation Requirements Art, English, foreign language, mathematics, philosophy, physical education (includes health), religious studies, science, social sciences, 100 hours of Christian service.

Special Academic Programs 17 Advanced Placement exams for which test preparation is offered; honors section; study at local college for college credit; academic accommodation for the gifted, the musically talented, and the artistically talented.

College Admission Counseling 410 students graduated in 2010; all went to college, including Georgetown University; Harvard University; New York University; Santa Clara University; Stanford University; University of Notre Dame. Mean SAT critical reading: 650, mean SAT math: 680, mean SAT writing: 670.

Student Life Upper grades have specified standards of dress, student council, honor system. Discipline rests primarily with faculty. Attendance at religious services is required.

Summer Programs Remediation, enrichment, advancement, sports, art/fine arts, computer instruction programs offered; session focuses on academics and athletics; held on campus; accepts boys and girls; open to students from other schools. 500 students usually enrolled. 2011 schedule: June 14 to July 23. Application deadline: May 31.

Tuition and Aid Day student tuition: $14,250. Tuition installment plan (SMART Tuition Payment Plan). Need-based scholarship grants, middle-income loans, paying campus jobs available. In 2010–11, 20% of upper-school students received aid. Total amount of financial aid awarded in 2010–11: $2,300,000.

Admissions Traditional secondary-level entrance grade is 9. For fall 2010, 1,300 students applied for upper-level admission, 420 were accepted, 420 enrolled. High School Placement Test required. Deadline for receipt of application materials: December 17. Application fee required: $75.

Athletics Interscholastic: aquatics (boys, girls), badminton (b,g), baseball (b), basketball (b,g), cross-country running (b,g), dance team (g), diving (b,g), field hockey (g), football (b), golf (b,g), lacrosse (b), soccer (b,g), softball (g), swimming and diving (b,g), tennis (b,g), track and field (b,g), volleyball (b,g), water polo (b,g), weight training (b,g), winter soccer (b,g); intramural: roller hockey (b,g); coed interscholastic: physical fitness, strength & conditioning, wrestling; coed intramural: basketball, ice hockey, in-line hockey, table tennis. 4 PE instructors, 110 coaches, 2 athletic trainers.

Computers Computers are regularly used in computer applications, design, desktop publishing, drawing and design, photography, yearbook classes. Computer network features include on-campus library services, online commercial services, Internet access, wireless campus network, Internet filtering or blocking technology. Campus intranet, student e-mail accounts, and computer access in designated common areas are available to students. Students grades are available online. The school has a published electronic and media policy.

Contact Mrs. Lori Robowski, Assistant for Admissions. 408-342-4300. Fax: 408-342-4308. E-mail: admissions@mitty.com. Web site: www.mitty.com/.

ARCHBISHOP RIORDAN HIGH SCHOOL
175 Phelan Avenue
San Francisco, California 94112
Head of School: Mr. Kevin R. Asbra

General Information Boys' day college-preparatory school, affiliated with Roman Catholic Church; primarily serves students with learning disabilities. Grades 9–12. Founded: 1949. Setting: urban. 10-acre campus. 4 buildings on campus. Approved or accredited by National Catholic Education Association, Western Association of Schools and Colleges, and California Department of Education. Endowment: $3 million. Total enrollment: 566. Upper school average class size: 26. Upper school faculty-student ratio: 1:14. There are 260 required school days per year for Upper School students. Upper School students typically attend 5 days per week. The average school day consists of 7 hours.

Upper School Student Profile Grade 9: 147 students (147 boys); Grade 10: 155 students (155 boys); Grade 11: 117 students (117 boys); Grade 12: 147 students (147 boys). 81% of students are Roman Catholic.

Faculty School total: 59. In upper school: 39 men, 20 women; 35 have advanced degrees.

Subjects Offered 20th century American writers, algebra, American history, American literature, anatomy, art, art appreciation, biology, broadcasting, business, calculus, chemistry, community service, computer science, creative writing, drama, earth science, economics, English, English literature, ethics, European history, expository writing, fine arts, geography, geometry, government/civics, grammar, health, history, mathematics, music, physical education, physics, physiology, religion, science, social studies, Spanish, statistics, theater, theology, trigonometry, world history, world literature, writing.

Graduation Requirements Arts and fine arts (art, music, dance, drama), computer science, English, foreign language, mathematics, physical education (includes health), religion (includes Bible studies and theology), science, social sciences, social studies (includes history). Community service is required.

Special Academic Programs Advanced Placement exam preparation; honors section; study at local college for college credit; programs in English, mathematics, general development for dyslexic students.

College Admission Counseling 160 students graduated in 2009; all went to college, including City College of San Francisco; San Francisco State University; San Jose State University; Santa Clara University; University of California, Berkeley.

Student Life Upper grades have specified standards of dress, student council, honor system. Discipline rests primarily with faculty. Attendance at religious services is required.

Tuition and Aid Day student tuition: $13,610. Tuition installment plan (monthly payment plans). Need-based scholarship grants available. In 2009–10, 20% of upper-school students received aid. Total amount of financial aid awarded in 2009–10: $750,000.

Admissions Traditional secondary-level entrance grade is 9. For fall 2009, 380 students applied for upper-level admission, 330 were accepted, 147 enrolled. High School Placement Test required. Deadline for receipt of application materials: December 12. Application fee required: $100.

Athletics Interscholastic: baseball, basketball, cross-country running, football, golf, soccer, tennis, track and field, wrestling; intramural: basketball, bowling, cheering, physical fitness, physical training, soccer, speedball, strength & conditioning, table tennis, volleyball, weight lifting. 4 coaches, 1 athletic trainer.

Computers Computers are regularly used in computer applications, desktop publishing, English, foreign language, humanities, journalism, mathematics, newspaper, religion, science, social studies, Web site design, word processing, writing, yearbook classes. Computer network features include on-campus library services, online commercial services, Internet access, wireless campus network, Internet filtering or blocking technology. Students grades are available online.

Contact Ms. Rose Aragon, Admission Secretary. 415-586-1256. Fax: 415-587-1310. E-mail: raragon@riordanhs.org. Web site: www.riordanhs.org.

ARCHBISHOP RUMMEL HIGH SCHOOL
1901 Severn Avenue
Metairie, Louisiana 70001-2893
Head of School: Mr. Michael J. Begg
General Information Boys' day college-preparatory, arts, religious studies, and technology school, affiliated with Roman Catholic Church. Grades 8–12. Founded: 1962. Setting: suburban. Nearest major city is New Orleans. 20-acre campus. 10 buildings on campus. Approved or accredited by Association for Experiential Education, National Catholic Education Association, Southern Association of Colleges and Schools, and Louisiana Department of Education. Total enrollment: 1,150. Upper school average class size: 27. Upper school faculty-student ratio: 1:13. Upper School students typically attend 5 days per week. The average school day consists of 5 hours and 30 minutes.
Upper School Student Profile Grade 8: 131 students (131 boys); Grade 9: 168 students (168 boys); Grade 10: 176 students (176 boys); Grade 11: 196 students (196 boys); Grade 12: 219 students (219 boys). 90% of students are Roman Catholic.
Faculty School total: 75. In upper school: 50 men, 25 women; 45 have advanced degrees.
Subjects Offered ACT preparation, advanced biology, advanced chemistry, advanced computer applications, advanced math, advanced studio art-AP, algebra, American government, American history, American history-AP, American literature, American literature-AP, anatomy, anatomy and physiology, ancient world history, art, art appreciation, art-AP, band, biology, British literature, British literature (honors), British literature-AP, calculus, calculus-AP, campus ministry, Catholic belief and practice, ceramics, chemistry, chemistry-AP, civics, computer applications, computer literacy, computer science, creative writing, economics, English, English language and composition-AP, English literature, English literature and composition-AP, environmental science, European history, European literature, fine arts, French, geography, geometry, government-AP, health education, history of the Catholic Church, honors algebra, honors English, honors geometry, honors U.S. history, honors world history, human anatomy, instrumental music, language arts, Latin, moral theology, physics, psychology, reading, sociology, Spanish, Spanish literature, speech, statistics-AP, street law, studio art, studio art-AP, U.S. government and politics-AP, U.S. history, U.S. history-AP, U.S. literature, United States government-AP, Web site design, Western civilization, world geography.
Graduation Requirements ACT preparation, advanced math, American history, art appreciation, biology, Catholic belief and practice, chemistry, civics, computer applications, computer literacy, computer science, English, environmental science, foreign language, geography, health education, history of the Catholic Church, physical education (includes health), physical science, physics, reading, U.S. history, Western civilization, world geography.
Special Academic Programs Advanced Placement exam preparation; honors section; programs in general development for dyslexic students.
College Admission Counseling 210 students graduated in 2010; 200 went to college, including Louisiana State University with Agricultural and Mechanical College; Loyola University New Orleans; Nicholls State University; University of New Orleans. Other: 10 went to work.
Student Life Upper grades have uniform requirement, student council, honor system. Discipline rests primarily with faculty. Attendance at religious services is required.
Summer Programs Remediation, enrichment, advancement, sports, art/fine arts, rigorous outdoor training, computer instruction programs offered; session focuses on student involvement and fun; held on campus; accepts boys and girls; open to students from other schools. 200 students usually enrolled. 2011 schedule: June 2 to July 18.
Tuition and Aid Day student tuition: $7150. Tuition installment plan (monthly payment plans). Merit scholarship grants, need-based scholarship grants, paying campus jobs available. In 2010–11, 20% of upper-school students received aid.
Admissions Traditional secondary-level entrance grade is 8. High School Placement Test required. Deadline for receipt of application materials: January 8. Application fee required: $20. Interview required.
Athletics Interscholastic: baseball, basketball, bowling, cheering, cross-country running, field hockey, football, Frisbee, golf, hockey, in-line hockey, jogging, rugby, soccer, strength & conditioning, swimming and diving, tennis, track and field, whiffle ball, wrestling; intramural: flag football. 10 PE instructors, 25 coaches, 2 athletic trainers.
Computers Computers are regularly used in computer applications, creative writing, English, multimedia, programming, reading, science classes. Computer resources include on-campus library services, Internet access, Internet filtering or blocking technology. Students grades are available online. The school has a published electronic and media policy.
Contact Joseph A. Serio, Director of Communications. 504-834-5592 Ext. 263. Fax: 504-833-2232. E-mail: jserio@rummelraiders.com. Web site: www.rummelraiders.com.

ARCHBISHOP SPALDING HIGH SCHOOL
8080 New Cut Road
Severn, Maryland 21144
Head of School: Mrs. Kathleen Mahar
General Information Coeducational day college-preparatory, arts, business, religious studies, and technology school, affiliated with Roman Catholic Church. Grades 9–12. Founded: 1966. Setting: suburban. Nearest major city is Annapolis. 52-acre campus. 3 buildings on campus. Approved or accredited by Association of Independent Maryland Schools, Middle States Association of Colleges and Schools, National Catholic Education Association, and Maryland Department of Education. Endowment: $1 million. Total enrollment: 1,180. Upper school average class size: 23. Upper school faculty-student ratio: 1:15. The average school day consists of 6 hours and 45 minutes.
Upper School Student Profile Grade 9: 304 students (150 boys, 154 girls); Grade 10: 295 students (145 boys, 150 girls); Grade 11: 312 students (149 boys, 163 girls); Grade 12: 269 students (130 boys, 139 girls). 79.5% of students are Roman Catholic.
Faculty School total: 81. In upper school: 24 men, 57 women; 48 have advanced degrees.
Subjects Offered 20th century American writers, 20th century history, 3-dimensional art, accounting, advanced biology, advanced chemistry, advanced computer applications, advanced math, Advanced Placement courses, advanced studio art-AP, advertising design, aerobics, algebra, American government, American history, American literature, American literature-AP, anatomy, anatomy and physiology, applied arts, applied music, art, art history, astronomy, band, Basic programming, biology, botany, business, business law, calculus, calculus-AP, campus ministry, Catholic belief and practice, ceramics, chemistry, chemistry-AP, chorus, Christian and Hebrew scripture, college counseling, college placement, college writing, communication skills, community service, comparative religion, computer animation, computer applications, computer art, computer education, computer graphics, computer information systems, computer literacy, computer multimedia, computer processing, computer programming, computer programming-AP, computer resources, computer science, computer science-AP, computer skills, computer studies, computer technologies, computer technology certification, computer tools, computer-aided design, computers, conceptual physics, CPR, creative writing, drama, drawing and design, earth science, ecology, environmental systems, economics, English, English language and composition-AP, English literature, English literature and composition-AP, ethics, European history, European history-AP, film, film and new technologies, film appreciation, film history, film series, film studies, filmmaking, fine arts, French, geology, geometry, grammar, guitar, health education, honors algebra, honors English, honors geometry, honors U.S. history, honors world history, jazz band, keyboarding, Latin, Latin-AP, law, literary magazine, marine biology, music, music theory, painting, photography, physical education, physics, pre-calculus, psychology, religion, science, social studies, sociology, Spanish, Spanish-AP, sports medicine, statistics-AP, strings, student government, student publications, studio art-AP, symphonic band, theater, theology, trigonometry, U.S. government and politics-AP, U.S. history, U.S. history-AP, visual and performing arts, visual arts, vocal ensemble, vocal jazz, vocal music, voice, Web site design, weight fitness, weight training, weightlifting, Western civilization, wind ensemble, work-study, world history, world literature, world religions, writing, yearbook, zoology.
Graduation Requirements Arts and fine arts (art, music, dance, drama), computer science, CPR, English, foreign language, health and wellness, mathematics, physical education (includes health), religion (includes Bible studies and theology), science, social sciences, 3 day retreat in senior year, CPR Certification. Community service is required.
Special Academic Programs Advanced Placement exam preparation; honors section; accelerated programs; independent study; study at local college for college credit; academic accommodation for the gifted, the musically talented, and the artistically talented; programs in English, mathematics for dyslexic students; special instructional classes for students with mild language-based learning differences (additional cost).
College Admission Counseling 239 students graduated in 2009; 237 went to college, including Penn State University Park; Salisbury University; Towson University; University of Maryland, Baltimore County; University of Maryland, College Park; Virginia Polytechnic Institute and State University. Other: 2 entered military service. Mean SAT critical reading: 551, mean SAT math: 558, mean SAT writing: 554.
Student Life Upper grades have uniform requirement, student council, honor system. Discipline rests primarily with faculty. Attendance at religious services is required.
Tuition and Aid Day student tuition: $11,295. Tuition installment plan (The Tuition Plan, monthly payment plans, one-time, semiannual, quarterly payment plans, monthly with Tuition Management). Merit scholarship grants, need-based scholarship grants, paying campus jobs, music scholarships (vocal, instrumental, strings, piano), leadership scholarships, academic scholarships available. In 2009–10, 30% of upper-school students received aid; total upper-school merit-scholarship money awarded: $96,115. Total amount of financial aid awarded in 2009–10: $900,000.
Admissions Traditional secondary-level entrance grade is 9. For fall 2009, 587 students applied for upper-level admission, 340 were accepted, 303 enrolled. High School Placement Test (closed version) from Scholastic Testing Service or Scholastic Testing Service High School Placement Test required. Deadline for receipt of application materials: January 6. Application fee required: $100. On-campus interview recommended.
Athletics Interscholastic: aerobics/dance (girls), baseball (b), basketball (b,g), cheering (b,g), cross-country running (b,g), dance team (g), field hockey (g), football (b), hockey (b,g), ice hockey (b,g), indoor track & field (b,g), lacrosse (b,g), rugby (b), soccer (b,g), softball (g), swimming and diving (b,g), tennis (b,g), track and field (b,g), volleyball (b,g), winter (indoor) track (b,g), wrestling (b); intramural: flag football (g), triathlon (b); coed interscholastic: golf; coed intramural: backpacking, bicycling, canoeing/kayaking, climbing, combined training, equestrian sports, hiking/

backpacking, horseback riding, kayaking, outdoor adventure, outdoor skills, sailboarding, sailing, skiing (downhill), snowboarding, strength & conditioning, ultimate Frisbee, weight training, yoga. 5 PE instructors, 82 coaches, 2 athletic trainers.
Computers Computers are regularly used in accounting, art, business, career exploration, computer applications, economics, English, foreign language, graphic design, keyboarding, literary magazine, mathematics, music, newspaper, programming, religion, religious studies, science, social studies, study skills, technology, Web site design, word processing, writing, yearbook classes. Computer network features include on-campus library services, online commercial services, Internet access, wireless campus network, Internet filtering or blocking technology. Computer access in designated common areas is available to students. Students grades are available online. The school has a published electronic and media policy.
Contact Mr. Thomas Miller, Director of Admissions. 410-969-9105 Ext. 232. Fax: 410-969-1026. E-mail: millert@archbishopspalding.org. Web site: www.archbishopspalding.org.

THE ARCHER SCHOOL FOR GIRLS

11725 Sunset Boulevard
Los Angeles, California 90049
Head of School: Elizabeth English
General Information Girls' day college-preparatory school. Grades 6–12. Founded: 1995. Setting: suburban. 6-acre campus. 1 building on campus. Approved or accredited by California Association of Independent Schools, The College Board, Western Association of Schools and Colleges, and California Department of Education. Endowment: $2.6 million. Total enrollment: 440. Upper school average class size: 16. Upper school faculty-student ratio: 1:8. The average school day consists of 5 hours and 45 minutes.
Faculty School total: 60. In upper school: 15 men, 45 women; 40 have advanced degrees.
Subjects Offered 20th century history, acting, advanced chemistry, advanced math, algebra, American literature, ancient history, archaeology, architectural drawing, art, art appreciation, art history, art history-AP, biology, biology-AP, calculus, calculus-AP, career/college preparation, ceramics, chemistry, chemistry-AP, Chinese, choir, classical studies, college admission preparation, college counseling, community service, computer applications, computer graphics, computer literacy, critical studies in film, dance, debate, digital imaging, drama, drawing and design, earth and space science, English, English composition, English language-AP, English literature, English literature-AP, environmental science-AP, experiential education, film appreciation, fitness, French, French language-AP, geometry, history, honors U.S. history, human development, human geography—AP, independent study, intro to computers, journalism, Latin, law studies, literary magazine, marine biology, marine ecology, media literacy, modern world history, music, orchestra, painting, performing arts, photography, physics, portfolio art, pre-algebra, pre-calculus, psychology, robotics, Roman civilization, self-defense, senior seminar, Spanish, Spanish language-AP, speech and debate, statistics-AP, student government, student publications, studio art, theater, theater arts, U.S. history, U.S. history-AP, wilderness experience, yearbook.
Graduation Requirements Arts and fine arts (art, music, dance, drama), English, fitness, foreign language, history, human development, mathematics, performing arts, science, annual participation in Arrow Week (experiential education program). Community service is required.
Special Academic Programs 14 Advanced Placement exams for which test preparation is offered; honors section.
College Admission Counseling 65 students graduated in 2010; all went to college, including Barnard College; University of California, Berkeley; University of Southern California; Wesleyan University; Yale University. Median SAT critical reading: 600, median SAT math: 575, median SAT writing: 645, median combined SAT: 1820.
Student Life Upper grades have uniform requirement, student council, honor system. Discipline rests primarily with faculty.
Tuition and Aid Day student tuition: $28,750. Tuition installment plan (FACTS Tuition Payment Plan). Need-based scholarship grants available. In 2010–11, 24% of upper-school students received aid. Total amount of financial aid awarded in 2010–11: $2,500,000.
Admissions Traditional secondary-level entrance grade is 9. ISEE required. Deadline for receipt of application materials: December 10. Application fee required: $115. On-campus interview required.
Athletics Interscholastic: basketball, cross-country running, equestrian sports, soccer, softball, swimming and diving, tennis, track and field, volleyball. 5 PE instructors, 16 coaches.
Computers Computers are regularly used in all academic classes. Computer network features include on-campus library services, online commercial services, Internet access, wireless campus network, 1 to 1 laptop program for grades 6 and 9. Student e-mail accounts are available to students. The school has a published electronic and media policy.
Contact Beth Kemp, Director of Admissions. 310-873-7037. Fax: 310-873-7052. E-mail: bkemp@archer.org. Web site: www.archer.org/.

See Display on this page.

ARENDELL PARROTT ACADEMY

PO Box 1297
Kinston, North Carolina 28503-1297

General Information Coeducational day college-preparatory school. Grades PK–12. Founded: 1964. Setting: small town. 80-acre campus. 6 buildings on campus. Approved or accredited by Southern Association of Colleges and Schools and North Carolina Department of Education. Total enrollment: 741. Upper school average class size: 18. There are 180 required school days per year for Upper School students. Upper School students typically attend 5 days per week. The average school day consists of 6 hours and 20 minutes.

Faculty School total: 60. In upper school: 9 men, 21 women; 16 have advanced degrees.

Special Academic Programs Advanced Placement exam preparation; honors section; study at local college for college credit.

College Admission Counseling 53 students graduated in 2010; all went to college. Mean SAT critical reading: 600, mean SAT math: 600, mean SAT writing: 589, mean combined SAT: 1789.

Student Life Upper grades have specified standards of dress, student council, honor system. Discipline rests primarily with faculty.

Tuition and Aid Day student tuition: $9200. Tuition installment plan (monthly payment plans, individually arranged payment plans). Need-based scholarship grants available. In 2010–11, 23% of upper-school students received aid. Total amount of financial aid awarded in 2010–11: $290,000.

Admissions Traditional secondary-level entrance grade is 9. Deadline for receipt of application materials: none. Application fee required: $550. Interview required.

Athletics Interscholastic: baseball (boys), basketball (b,g), canoeing/kayaking (g), cross-country running (b,g), dance squad (g), field hockey (g), football (b), lacrosse (b), soccer (b,g), softball (g), swimming and diving (b,g), tennis (b,g), volleyball (g); coed interscholastic: dance, fitness, golf, physical fitness, physical training, strength & conditioning.

Computers Computer network features include on-campus library services, Internet access, wireless campus network, Internet filtering or blocking technology. Computer access in designated common areas is available to students. Students grades are available online. The school has a published electronic and media policy.

Contact Julie Rogers, Director of Admissions. 252-522-0410 Ext. 202. Fax: 919-522-0672. E-mail: jrogers@parrottacademy.org. Web site: www.parrottacademy.org.

ARMBRAE ACADEMY

1400 Oxford Street
Halifax, Nova Scotia B3H 3Y8, Canada
Head of School: Gary D. O'Meara

General Information Coeducational day college-preparatory school. Grades K–12. Founded: 1887. Setting: urban. 2-acre campus. 3 buildings on campus. Approved or accredited by Standards in Excellence And Learning (SEAL) and Nova Scotia Department of Education. Language of instruction: English. Endowment: CAN$1 million. Total enrollment: 228. Upper school average class size: 18. Upper school faculty-student ratio: 1:9. There are 185 required school days per year for Upper School students. Upper School students typically attend 5 days per week. The average school day consists of 5 hours.

Faculty School total: 26. In upper school: 5 men, 8 women; 3 have advanced degrees.

Subjects Offered Algebra, American history, art, biology, calculus, chemistry, computer science, earth science, economics, English, English literature, European history, French, geography, geology, geometry, government/civics, grammar, health, history, keyboarding, mathematics, music, physical education, physics, science, social studies, study skills, trigonometry, word processing, world literature, writing.

Graduation Requirements Computer science, English, foreign language, mathematics, physical education (includes health), science, social studies (includes history), 6 courses each in grades 11 and 12.

Special Academic Programs Advanced Placement exam preparation; accelerated programs; study at local college for college credit; academic accommodation for the artistically talented.

College Admission Counseling 16 students graduated in 2009; all went to college, including Acadia University; Carleton University; Dalhousie University; McGill University; Saint Mary's University; St. Francis Xavier University.

Student Life Upper grades have uniform requirement, student council. Discipline rests equally with students and faculty.

Tuition and Aid Day student tuition: CAN$7950. Tuition installment plan (monthly payment plans, term payment plan). Tuition reduction for siblings, bursaries available. In 2009–10, 4% of upper-school students received aid. Total amount of financial aid awarded in 2009–10: CAN$30,000.

Admissions Traditional secondary-level entrance grade is 10. For fall 2009, 25 students applied for upper-level admission, 22 were accepted, 15 enrolled. CTBS (or similar from their school) required. Deadline for receipt of application materials: none. Application fee required: CAN$150. On-campus interview required.

Athletics Interscholastic: badminton (boys, girls), basketball (b,g), cross-country running (b,g), field hockey (g), ice hockey (b), soccer (b,g), swimming and diving (b,g), tennis (b,g), track and field (b,g), volleyball (b,g); intramural: badminton (b,g), cross-country running (b,g), coed interscholastic: curling, ice hockey; coed intramural: ice hockey. 2 PE instructors, 4 coaches.

Computers Computers are regularly used in all classes. Computer network features include Internet access. The school has a published electronic and media policy.

Contact Gary D. O'Meara, Headmaster. 902-423-7920. Fax: 902-423-9731. E-mail: head@armbrae.ns.ca. Web site: www.armbrae.ns.ca.

ARMONA UNION ACADEMY

14435 Locust Street
PO Box 397
Armona, California 93202
Head of School: Mr. Erik Borges

General Information Coeducational day college-preparatory, general academic, and religious studies school, affiliated with Seventh-day Adventists. Grades K–12. Founded: 1904. Setting: small town. Nearest major city is Fresno. 20-acre campus. 5 buildings on campus. Approved or accredited by Western Association of Schools and Colleges and California Department of Education. Member of Secondary School Admission Test Board. Endowment: $98,000. Total enrollment: 112. Upper school average class size: 15. Upper school faculty-student ratio: 1:10. There are 180 required school days per year for Upper School students. Upper School students typically attend 5 days per week. The average school day consists of 7 hours and 45 minutes.

Upper School Student Profile Grade 9: 10 students (8 boys, 2 girls); Grade 10: 7 students (4 boys, 3 girls); Grade 11: 15 students (9 boys, 6 girls); Grade 12: 12 students (5 boys, 7 girls). 85% of students are Seventh-day Adventists.

Faculty School total: 13. In upper school: 5 men, 1 woman; 3 have advanced degrees.

Subjects Offered Algebra, American history, American literature, art, Bible studies, biology, chemistry, choir, community service, computer science, economics, English, English literature, geometry, government, mathematics, physical education, physical science, physics, religion, science, Spanish, world history, world literature, yearbook.

Graduation Requirements Arts and fine arts (art, music, dance, drama), business skills (includes word processing), computer science, English, foreign language, mathematics, physical education (includes health), religion (includes Bible studies and theology), science, social sciences, social studies (includes history). Community service is required.

Special Academic Programs Study at local college for college credit.

College Admission Counseling 11 students graduated in 2010; 9 went to college, including La Sierra University; Southern Adventist University; University of California, Irvine; West Hills Community College. Other: 1 went to work, 1 entered military service.

Student Life Upper grades have specified standards of dress, student council. Discipline rests primarily with faculty. Attendance at religious services is required.

Tuition and Aid Day student tuition: $5140. Guaranteed tuition plan. Tuition installment plan (monthly payment plans, individually arranged payment plans). Tuition reduction for siblings, need-based scholarship grants available. In 2010–11, 60% of upper-school students received aid. Total amount of financial aid awarded in 2010–11: $50,000.

Admissions Traditional secondary-level entrance grade is 9. For fall 2010, 11 students applied for upper-level admission, 7 were accepted, 7 enrolled. Deadline for receipt of application materials: August 15. Application fee required: $75. Interview required.

Athletics Interscholastic: basketball (boys, girls), flag football (b,g), football (b,g), volleyball (b,g); intramural: basketball (b,g), flag football (b,g); coed interscholastic: baseball, outdoor education, soccer, softball, track and field; coed intramural: baseball, outdoor education, paddle tennis, soccer, softball, table tennis, track and field, volleyball.

Computers Computers are regularly used in English, history, mathematics, science, yearbook classes. Computer network features include on-campus library services, online commercial services, Internet access, wireless campus network, Internet filtering or blocking technology. Students grades are available online. The school has a published electronic and media policy.

Contact Mrs. Aniesha Kleinhammer, Registrar. 559-582-4468 Ext. 10. Fax: 559-582-6609. E-mail: auaregistrar@gmail.com. Web site: www.auaweb.com.

ARMY AND NAVY ACADEMY

2605 Carlsbad Boulevard
PO Box 3000
Carlsbad, California 92018-3000
Head of School: Brig. Gen. Stephen M. Bliss, Retd.

General Information Boys' boarding and day college-preparatory, Junior ROTC, and military school. Grades 7–12. Founded: 1910. Setting: small town. Nearest major city is San Diego. Students are housed in single-sex dormitories. 16-acre campus. 34 buildings on campus. Approved or accredited by California Association of Independent Schools and Western Association of Schools and Colleges. Member of National Association of Independent Schools and Secondary School Admission Test Board. Endowment: $420,615. Total enrollment: 292. Upper school average class size: 15. Upper school faculty-student ratio: 1:15. There are 180 required school days per year for Upper School students. Upper School students typically attend 5 days per week. The average school day consists of 6 hours and 30 minutes.

Upper School Student Profile Grade 10: 73 students (73 boys); Grade 11: 73 students (73 boys); Grade 12: 68 students (68 boys). 92% of students are boarding students. 70% are state residents. 9 states are represented in upper school student body. 20% are international students. International students from China, Mexico, Republic of Korea, Russian Federation, Taiwan, and Viet Nam; 5 other countries represented in student body.

Faculty School total: 28. In upper school: 17 men, 11 women; 13 have advanced degrees; 5 reside on campus.

Subjects Offered Algebra, art, biology, biology-AP, calculus-AP, chemistry, drama, economics, English, English-AP, ESL, French, geography, geometry, guitar, marching band, music appreciation, music technology, photography, physical education, physics, physics-AP, pre-calculus, psychology-AP, Spanish, Spanish-AP, study skills, U.S. government, U.S. history, U.S. history-AP, world history, yearbook.

Graduation Requirements Arts and fine arts (art, music, dance, drama), electives, English, foreign language, lab science, leadership education training, mathematics, physical education (includes health), SAT preparation, social studies (includes history).

Special Academic Programs 8 Advanced Placement exams for which test preparation is offered; honors section; special instructional classes for students with Attention Deficit Disorder and learning disabilities; ESL.

College Admission Counseling 59 students graduated in 2010; 57 went to college, including Arizona State University; The University of Arizona; United States Military Academy; University of California, Riverside; University of California, Santa Barbara; University of Oregon. Other: 2 went to work. Mean SAT critical reading: 496, mean SAT math: 546, mean SAT writing: 478.

Student Life Upper grades have uniform requirement, student council, honor system. Discipline rests primarily with faculty.

Summer Programs Remediation, enrichment, ESL, sports, art/fine arts, rigorous outdoor training, computer instruction programs offered; session focuses on Academic, JROTC Leadership, and recreation; held on campus; accepts boys and girls; open to students from other schools. 200 students usually enrolled. 2011 schedule: June 30 to August 2. Application deadline: none.

Tuition and Aid Day student tuition: $18,950; 7-day tuition and room/board: $31,950. Tuition installment plan (individually arranged payment plans). Tuition reduction for siblings, need-based scholarship grants, Military Discount available. In 2010–11, 20% of upper-school students received aid. Total amount of financial aid awarded in 2010–11: $458,200.

Admissions Traditional secondary-level entrance grade is 10. For fall 2010, 127 students applied for upper-level admission, 73 were accepted, 70 enrolled. Otis-Lennon School Ability Test required. Deadline for receipt of application materials: none. Application fee required: $100. On-campus interview required.

Athletics Interscholastic: aquatics, baseball, basketball, cross-country running, drill team, football, golf, in-line hockey, marksmanship, riflery, roller hockey, ropes courses, soccer, surfing, swimming and diving, tennis, track and field, water polo, weight lifting, wrestling; intramural: aquatics, combined training, fitness, hockey, independent competitive sports, JROTC drill, outdoor activities, outdoor recreation, physical fitness, physical training, roller hockey, strength & conditioning, surfing. 15 coaches, 1 athletic trainer.

Computers Computers are regularly used in music technology, yearbook classes. Computer network features include on-campus library services, Internet access, wireless campus network, Internet filtering or blocking technology. Student e-mail accounts and computer access in designated common areas are available to students. Students grades are available online. The school has a published electronic and media policy.

Contact Candice Heidenrich, Director of Admissions. 888-762-2338. Fax: 760-434-5948. E-mail: admissions@armyandnavyacademy.org. Web site: www.armyandnavyacademy.org.

ARROWHEAD CHRISTIAN ACADEMY

105 Tennessee Street
Redlands, California 92373
Head of School: Mr. Nick Sweeney

General Information Coeducational day college-preparatory, arts, religious studies, and technology school, affiliated with Christian faith. Grades 7–12. Founded: 1979. Setting: suburban. Nearest major city is San Bernardino. 24-acre campus. 3 buildings on campus. Approved or accredited by Association of Christian Schools International, Western Association of Schools and Colleges, and California Department of Education. Total enrollment: 442. Upper school average class size: 20. Upper school faculty-student ratio: 1:17. There are 180 required school days per year for Upper School students. Upper School students typically attend 5 days per week. The average school day consists of 6 hours and 50 minutes.

Upper School Student Profile Grade 9: 82 students (40 boys, 42 girls); Grade 10: 85 students (40 boys, 45 girls); Grade 11: 84 students (47 boys, 37 girls); Grade 12: 87 students (35 boys, 52 girls). 100% of students are Christian faith.

Faculty School total: 29. In upper school: 14 men, 12 women; 9 have advanced degrees.

Subjects Offered Advanced math, algebra, American government, American history, American history-AP, American literature, anatomy, art, ASB Leadership, athletic training, athletics, baseball, basketball, Bible, Bible studies, biology, British literature, British literature (honors), calculus, calculus-AP, cheerleading, chemistry, choir, choral music, chorus, Christian doctrine, Christian education, Christian ethics, Christian scripture, Christian studies, Christianity, church history, college admission preparation, college awareness, college counseling, college placement, college planning, community service, computer graphics, computer technologies, concert choir, drama, economics, English, English composition, English literature, English literature and composition-AP, ESL, forensics, geometry, graphic design, guitar, honors English, honors geometry, honors world history, instrumental music, international studies, internship, jazz band, journalism, Korean, Korean culture, library, Life of Christ, participation in sports, physical education, physical science, physics, pre-algebra, pre-calculus, psychology, SAT preparation, SAT/ACT preparation, softball, Spanish, sports medicine, student government, theater arts, track and field, U.S. government and politics-AP, U.S. history-AP, visual and performing arts, volleyball, world history, world literature, yearbook.

Graduation Requirements Arts and fine arts (art, music, dance, drama), English, foreign language, mathematics, physical education (includes health), religion (includes Bible studies and theology), science, social studies (includes history). Community service is required.

Special Academic Programs Advanced Placement exam preparation; honors section; study at local college for college credit; remedial reading and/or remedial writing; remedial math; programs in general development for dyslexic students; ESL (25 students enrolled).

College Admission Counseling 107 students graduated in 2009; 103 went to college, including Azusa Pacific University; Biola University; California State University, San Bernardino; Point Loma Nazarene University; University of California, Los Angeles; University of California, Riverside. Other: 4 went to work. Mean SAT critical reading: 518, mean SAT math: 527, mean SAT writing: 519, mean combined SAT: 1564, mean composite ACT: 23. 22% scored over 600 on SAT critical reading, 25% scored over 600 on SAT math, 21% scored over 600 on SAT writing, 19% scored over 1800 on combined SAT, 45% scored over 26 on composite ACT.

Student Life Upper grades have specified standards of dress, student council, honor system. Discipline rests primarily with faculty. Attendance at religious services is required.

Tuition and Aid Day student tuition: $7663. Tuition installment plan (monthly payment plans). Need-based scholarship grants, faculty/staff discounts, graduates from other Christian elementary/middle schools available. In 2009–10, 19% of upper-school students received aid. Total amount of financial aid awarded in 2009–10: $179,800.

Admissions Traditional secondary-level entrance grade is 9. For fall 2009, 83 students applied for upper-level admission, 76 were accepted, 66 enrolled. Admissions testing required. Deadline for receipt of application materials: none. Application fee required: $125. Interview required.

Athletics Interscholastic: baseball (boys), basketball (b,g), cheering (g), football (b), soccer (b,g), softball (g), tennis (b,g), track and field (b,g), volleyball (b,g); coed interscholastic: cross-country running, golf; coed intramural: archery, broomball. 3 PE instructors, 28 coaches, 1 athletic trainer.

Computers Computers are regularly used in all academic, yearbook classes. Computer network features include on-campus library services, online commercial services, Internet access, Internet filtering or blocking technology. Students grades are available online. The school has a published electronic and media policy.

Contact Mrs. Fritzetta Lawton, Admissions Assistant. 909-793-0601 Ext. 162. Fax: 909-792-5691. E-mail: flawton@arrowheadchristian.com. Web site: www.arrowheadchristian.org.

ARROWSMITH SCHOOL

Toronto, Ontario, Canada
See Special Needs Schools section.

ARTHUR MORGAN SCHOOL

Burnsville, North Carolina
See Junior Boarding Schools section.

ASHBURY COLLEGE

362 Mariposa Avenue
Ottawa, Ontario K1M 0T3, Canada
Head of School: Mr. Tam Matthews

General Information Coeducational boarding and day college-preparatory, bilingual studies, and International Baccalaureate school. Boarding grades 9–12, day grades 4–12. Founded: 1891. Setting: urban. Students are housed in single-sex dormitories. 13-acre campus. 3 buildings on campus. Approved or accredited by Conference of Independent Schools of Ontario, International Baccalaureate Organization, Ontario Ministry of Education, Standards in Excellence And Learning (SEAL), and The Association of Boarding Schools. Affiliate member of National Association of Independent Schools. Languages of instruction: English and French. Endowment: CAN$6.5 million. Total enrollment: 690. Upper school average class size: 16. Upper school faculty-student ratio: 1:9. There are 180 required school days per year for Upper

Ashbury College

School students. Upper School students typically attend 5 days per week. The average school day consists of 6 hours and 5 minutes.

Upper School Student Profile Grade 6: 35 students (35 boys); Grade 7: 50 students (50 boys); Grade 8: 50 students (50 boys); Grade 9: 118 students (68 boys, 50 girls); Grade 10: 125 students (61 boys, 64 girls); Grade 11: 141 students (71 boys, 70 girls); Grade 12: 141 students (81 boys, 60 girls). 20% of students are boarding students. 75% are province residents. 7 provinces are represented in upper school student body. 15% are international students. International students from Germany, Hong Kong, Japan, Mexico, Republic of Korea, and United States; 24 other countries represented in student body.

Faculty School total: 60. In upper school: 30 men, 30 women; 45 have advanced degrees; 15 reside on campus.

Subjects Offered Accounting, advanced chemistry, advanced math, algebra, American history, art, art history, biology, business, business skills, calculus, Canadian geography, Canadian history, chemistry, computer applications, computer programming, computer science, creative writing, drama, driver education, economics, English, English literature, environmental science, ESL, European history, fine arts, French, geography, geometry, health, history, mathematics, music, physical education, physics, science, social studies, sociology, Spanish, theater, theory of knowledge, world history, world literature.

Graduation Requirements English, mathematics, science. Community service is required.

Special Academic Programs International Baccalaureate program; independent study; term-away projects; study abroad; ESL (22 students enrolled).

College Admission Counseling 141 students graduated in 2009; all went to college, including Dalhousie University; McGill University; Queen's University at Kingston; The University of Western Ontario; University of Ottawa; University of Toronto. Mean SAT critical reading: 600, mean SAT math: 644, mean SAT writing: 591.

Student Life Upper grades have uniform requirement, student council, honor system. Discipline rests primarily with faculty.

Tuition and Aid Day student tuition: CAN$18,250; 7-day tuition and room/board: CAN$40,250. Tuition installment plan (monthly payment plans, individually arranged payment plans). Tuition reduction for siblings, bursaries, merit scholarship grants available. In 2009–10, 20% of upper-school students received aid; total upper-school merit-scholarship money awarded: CAN$9000. Total amount of financial aid awarded in 2009–10: CAN$470,000.

Admissions Traditional secondary-level entrance grade is 9. For fall 2009, 350 students applied for upper-level admission, 266 were accepted, 123 enrolled. Canadian Standardized Test, SLEP or TOEFL required. Deadline for receipt of application materials: none. Application fee required: CAN$100. Interview required.

Athletics Interscholastic: alpine skiing (boys, girls), badminton (b,g), basketball (b,g), cross-country running (b,g), field hockey (g), football (b), golf (b,g), hockey (b), ice hockey (b), independent competitive sports (b,g), rowing (b,g), rugby (b,g), skiing (downhill) (b,g), soccer (b,g), tennis (b,g), track and field (b,g), volleyball (b,g); intramural: badminton (b,g), ball hockey (b,g), basketball (b,g), ice hockey (b), modern dance (b), outdoor education (b,g), rugby (b,g); coed interscholastic: baseball, running; coed intramural: alpine skiing, basketball, canoeing/kayaking, climbing, cooperative games, fitness, flag football, Frisbee, hiking/backpacking, indoor soccer, life saving, martial arts, Nautilus, nordic skiing, outdoor activities, physical fitness, physical training, skiing (cross-country), skiing (downhill), snowboarding, soccer, softball, strength & conditioning, tennis, track and field, ultimate Frisbee, volleyball, weight training, yoga. 5 PE instructors, 10 coaches.

Computers Computers are regularly used in art, business applications, business education, data processing, economics, geography, graphic arts, humanities, information technology, mathematics, music, science, yearbook classes. Computer network features include on-campus library services, Internet access, wireless campus network, Internet filtering or blocking technology. Campus intranet, student e-mail accounts, and computer access in designated common areas are available to students. Students grades are available online. The school has a published electronic and media policy.

Contact Mrs. Padme Raina, Manager of International Admissions. 613-749-5954 Ext. 368. Fax: 613-749-9724. E-mail: praina@ashbury.ca. Web site: www.ashbury.ca.

ASHEVILLE SCHOOL
360 Asheville School Road
Asheville, North Carolina 28806
Head of School: Archibald R. Montgomery, IV

General Information Coeducational boarding and day college-preparatory, arts, and technology school, affiliated with Christian faith. Grades 9–12. Founded: 1900. Setting: suburban. Students are housed in single-sex by floor dormitories. 300-acre campus. 19 buildings on campus. Approved or accredited by North Carolina Association of Independent Schools, Southern Association of Colleges and Schools, Southern Association of Independent Schools, The Association of Boarding Schools, and North Carolina Department of Education. Member of National Association of Independent Schools and Secondary School Admission Test Board. Endowment: $30 million. Total enrollment: 260. Upper school average class size: 13. Upper school faculty-student ratio: 1:7. The average school day consists of 6 hours.

Upper School Student Profile Grade 9: 41 students (25 boys, 16 girls); Grade 10: 77 students (33 boys, 44 girls); Grade 11: 83 students (37 boys, 46 girls); Grade 12: 59 students (29 boys, 30 girls). 75% of students are boarding students. 50% are state residents. 22 states are represented in upper school student body. 14% are international

students. International students from Bahamas, China, Republic of Korea, Saudi Arabia, Taiwan, and Thailand; 6 other countries represented in student body. 75% of students are Christian faith.

Faculty School total: 36. In upper school: 21 men, 15 women; 25 have advanced degrees; 28 reside on campus.

Subjects Offered Algebra, American history, American literature, ancient history, art, biology, calculus, chemistry, Chinese, creative writing, English, English literature, European history, finite math, French, geometry, grammar, humanities, Latin, literature, mathematics, medieval/Renaissance history, music, physics, pre-calculus, science, social studies, Spanish, studio art, Western civilization, world history, world literature, writing.

Graduation Requirements Arts and fine arts (art, music, dance, drama), English, foreign language, history, mathematics, music, science, senior demonstration (series of research papers and oral defense of work), three-day camping trip, senior chapel talk (public speaking).

Special Academic Programs 17 Advanced Placement exams for which test preparation is offered; honors section; academic accommodation for the gifted.

College Admission Counseling 60 students graduated in 2009; 59 went to college, including Cornell University; Harvard University; New York University; Sewanee: The University of the South; The University of North Carolina at Chapel Hill. Other: 1 had other specific plans.

Student Life Upper grades have specified standards of dress, student council, honor system. Discipline rests equally with students and faculty. Attendance at religious services is required.

Tuition and Aid Day student tuition: $22,420; 7-day tuition and room/board: $38,720. Tuition installment plan (monthly payment plans, individually arranged payment plans). Need-based scholarship grants, tuition remission for children of faculty available. In 2009–10, 25% of upper-school students received aid. Total amount of financial aid awarded in 2009–10: $1,803,000.

Admissions Traditional secondary-level entrance grade is 9. For fall 2009, 300 students applied for upper-level admission, 150 were accepted, 80 enrolled. ISEE, PSAT or SAT for applicants to grade 11 and 12, SSAT or TOEFL required. Deadline for receipt of application materials: February 1. Application fee required: $50. On-campus interview required.

Athletics Interscholastic: baseball (boys), basketball (b,g), cross-country running (b,g), field hockey (g), football (b), running (b,g), soccer (b,g), swimming and diving (b,g), tennis (b,g), track and field (b,g), volleyball (g), wrestling (b); intramural: alpine skiing (b,g), dance (g), lacrosse (b); coed interscholastic: equestrian sports, horseback riding; coed intramural: backpacking, canoeing/kayaking, climbing, dance, equestrian sports, fitness, fly fishing, Frisbee, hiking/backpacking, horseback riding, kayaking, life saving, modern dance, mountain biking, mountaineering, Nautilus, outdoor activities, physical fitness, rock climbing, ropes courses, skateboarding, skiing (downhill), snowboarding, strength & conditioning, table tennis, wall climbing, weight lifting, wilderness, yoga. 3 coaches, 1 athletic trainer.

Computers Computers are regularly used in French, humanities, Latin, mathematics, science, Spanish classes. Computer network features include on-campus library services, online commercial services, Internet access, Internet filtering or blocking technology. Campus intranet, student e-mail accounts, and computer access in designated common areas are available to students. Students grades are available online. The school has a published electronic and media policy.

Contact Cyndi Madden, Admission Coordinator. 828-254-6345 Ext. 4022. Fax: 828-210-6109. E-mail: admission@ashevilleschool.org. Web site: www.ashevilleschool.org.

ASPEN RANCH
Loa, Utah
See Special Needs Schools section.

ASSETS SCHOOL
Honolulu, Hawaii
See Special Needs Schools section.

ASSUMPTION HIGH SCHOOL
2170 Tyler Lane
Louisville, Kentucky 40205
Head of School: Mrs. Elaine Salvo

General Information Girls' day college-preparatory, arts, business, religious studies, and technology school, affiliated with Roman Catholic Church. Grades 9–12. Founded: 1955. Setting: suburban. 5-acre campus. 3 buildings on campus. Approved or accredited by National Catholic Education Association, Southern Association of Colleges and Schools, and Kentucky Department of Education. Endowment: $672,000. Total enrollment: 930. Upper school average class size: 18. Upper school faculty-student ratio: 1:10. Upper School students typically attend 5 days per week. The average school day consists of 7 hours and 5 minutes.

Upper School Student Profile Grade 9: 219 students (219 girls); Grade 10: 217 students (217 girls); Grade 11: 207 students (207 girls); Grade 12: 287 students (287 girls). 86% of students are Roman Catholic.

Faculty School total: 91. In upper school: 14 men, 77 women; 82 have advanced degrees.

Subjects Offered 3-dimensional art, accounting, acting, advanced chemistry, advanced math, Advanced Placement courses, algebra, American history, American history-AP, American literature, anatomy, art, art history-AP, astronomy, biology, biology-AP, broadcast journalism, business, business law, calculus, calculus-AP, ceramics, chemistry, chemistry-AP, child development, choral music, chorus, community service, computer applications, computer graphics, computer information systems, computer programming, computer science, crafts, creative writing, death and loss, drama, economics, English, English literature, English literature and composition-AP, environmental science, European history, family living, fine arts, finite math, fitness, forensics, French, French language-AP, geography, geometry, government/civics, health, health education, history, home economics, humanities, Internet, journalism, leadership, marine biology, mathematics, music, personal development, physical education, physical science, physics, physiology, pre-calculus, psychology, psychology-AP, public speaking, religion, SAT/ACT preparation, science, social studies, sociology, Spanish, Spanish language-AP, speech, studio art-AP, theater, theology, U.S. government and politics-AP, word processing, world history, world literature.

Graduation Requirements Arts and fine arts (art, music, dance, drama), English, foreign language, health, humanities, mathematics, personal development, physical education (includes health), public speaking, religion (includes Bible studies and theology), science, social studies (includes history). Community service is required.

Special Academic Programs 20 Advanced Placement exams for which test preparation is offered; honors section; study at local college for college credit; academic accommodation for the gifted; programs in English, mathematics, general development for dyslexic students; special instructional classes for deaf students, learning difference students.

College Admission Counseling 240 students graduated in 2009; 238 went to college, including Bellarmine University; Jefferson Community and Technical College; Morehead State University; University of Kentucky; University of Louisville; Western Kentucky University. Other: 2 went to work. Mean SAT critical reading: 572, mean SAT math: 564, mean SAT writing: 588, mean combined SAT: 1724, mean composite ACT: 23.

Student Life Upper grades have uniform requirement, student council, honor system. Discipline rests primarily with faculty. Attendance at religious services is required.

Tuition and Aid Day student tuition: $9375. Tuition installment plan (FACTS Tuition Payment Plan). Merit scholarship grants, need-based scholarship grants available. In 2009–10, 17% of upper-school students received aid; total upper-school merit-scholarship money awarded: $21,950. Total amount of financial aid awarded in 2009–10: $386,900.

Admissions Traditional secondary-level entrance grade is 9. For fall 2009, 276 students applied for upper-level admission, 276 were accepted, 219 enrolled. Scholastic Testing Service and STS required. Deadline for receipt of application materials: none. Application fee required: $200. On-campus interview required.

Athletics Interscholastic: basketball, cheering, cross-country running, dance team, field hockey, golf, ice hockey, lacrosse, rowing, soccer, softball, swimming and diving, tennis, track and field, volleyball; intramural: basketball, hiking/backpacking, kickball, table tennis, volleyball, walking. 2 PE instructors, 33 coaches.

Computers Computers are regularly used in all academic classes. Computer network features include on-campus library services, online commercial services, Internet access, wireless campus network, Internet filtering or blocking technology. Campus intranet, student e-mail accounts, and computer access in designated common areas are available to students. Students grades are available online. The school has a published electronic and media policy.

Contact Mrs. Becky Henle, Principal. 502-458-9551. Fax: 502-454-8411. E-mail: becky.henle@ahsrockets.org. Web site: www.ahsrockets.org.

THE ATHENIAN SCHOOL
2100 Mount Diablo Scenic Boulevard
Danville, California 94506
Head of School: Eric Feron Niles

General Information Coeducational boarding and day college-preparatory school. Boarding grades 9–12, day grades 6–12. Founded: 1965. Setting: suburban. Nearest major city is San Francisco. Students are housed in single-sex dormitories. 75-acre campus. 25 buildings on campus. Approved or accredited by California Association of Independent Schools, The Association of Boarding Schools, The College Board, Western Association of Schools and Colleges, and California Department of Education. Member of National Association of Independent Schools and Secondary School Admission Test Board. Endowment: $550,000. Total enrollment: 463. Upper school average class size: 15. Upper school faculty-student ratio: 1:10. Upper School students typically attend 5 days per week. The average school day consists of 5 hours and 35 minutes.

Upper School Student Profile Grade 9: 72 students (39 boys, 33 girls); Grade 10: 75 students (34 boys, 41 girls); Grade 11: 74 students (31 boys, 43 girls); Grade 12: 78 students (40 boys, 38 girls). 14% of students are boarding students. 90% are state residents. 1 state is represented in upper school student body. 10% are international students. International students from China, Republic of Korea, Russian Federation, Taiwan, Thailand, and Viet Nam; 5 other countries represented in student body.

Faculty School total: 53. In upper school: 20 men, 23 women; 31 have advanced degrees; 25 reside on campus.

Subjects Offered African-American studies, algebra, American history, American literature, American literature-AP, anatomy, art, art history, Asian history, Asian literature, biology, calculus-AP, ceramics, chemistry, classical studies, college writing, community service, comparative cultures, comparative religion, computer programming, computer science, computer skills, contemporary history, creative writing, dance, dance performance, debate, drama, drama performance, drama workshop, drawing, earth science, ecology, economics, economics and history, English, English as a foreign language, English literature, English-AP, environmental studies, ESL, ethics, European history, European history-AP, expository writing, fencing, fine arts, French, French-AP, geography, geology, geometry, government/civics, graphic design, health, history, humanities, introduction to technology, jazz band, jewelry making, literary magazine, literature seminar, literature-AP, mathematics, modern European history-AP, music, music history, music performance, musical theater, painting, philosophy, photography, physical education, physics, science, science project, sculpture, sociology, Spanish, Spanish literature-AP, Spanish-AP, stained glass, statistics, statistics-AP, theater, theater design and production, trigonometry, U.S. history-AP, wilderness experience, world cultures, world history, world literature, writing, yearbook, yoga.

Graduation Requirements American history, arts and fine arts (art, music, dance, drama), English, foreign language, history, literature, mathematics, physical education (includes health), science, wilderness experience, world history. Community service is required.

Special Academic Programs Advanced Placement exam preparation; honors section; independent study; term-away projects; study at local college for college credit; domestic exchange program; study abroad; ESL (8 students enrolled).

College Admission Counseling 71 students graduated in 2010; all went to college, including California Polytechnic State University, San Luis Obispo; University of California, Berkeley; University of California, Davis; University of California, Santa Barbara; University of California, Santa Cruz; University of Washington. Median SAT critical reading: 630, median SAT math: 660, median SAT writing: 640, median combined SAT: 1900. 62% scored over 600 on SAT critical reading, 71% scored over 600 on SAT math, 73% scored over 600 on SAT writing, 70% scored over 1800 on combined SAT.

Student Life Upper grades have specified standards of dress, student council. Discipline rests equally with students and faculty.

Summer Programs Enrichment, advancement, ESL, sports, art/fine arts, computer instruction programs offered; session focuses on academic enrichment, sports, and ESL; held on campus; accepts boys and girls; open to students from other schools. 200 students usually enrolled. 2011 schedule: June 14 to August 4. Application deadline: none.

Tuition and Aid Day student tuition: $29,736; 5-day tuition and room/board: $46,414; 7-day tuition and room/board: $46,414. Tuition installment plan (Insured Tuition Payment Plan, monthly payment plans). Need-based scholarship grants available. In 2010–11, 22% of upper-school students received aid. Total amount of financial aid awarded in 2010–11: $1,900,000.

Admissions Traditional secondary-level entrance grade is 9. For fall 2010, 399 students applied for upper-level admission, 105 were accepted, 45 enrolled. International English Language Test, ISEE, SSAT or TOEFL required. Deadline for receipt of application materials: January 13. Application fee required: $75. Interview required.

Athletics Interscholastic: baseball (boys), basketball (b,g), cross-country running (b,g), golf (b), soccer (b,g), softball (g), swimming and diving (b,g), tennis (b,g); coed interscholastic: volleyball, wrestling; coed intramural: basketball, climbing, cross-country running, dance, fencing, weight training, yoga. 12 coaches.

Computers Computers are regularly used in English, foreign language, graphic design, history, humanities, information technology, library science, literary magazine, mathematics, publications, science, yearbook classes. Computer network features include on-campus library services, online commercial services, Internet access, wireless campus network, Internet filtering or blocking technology. Student e-mail accounts and computer access in designated common areas are available to students. Students grades are available online. The school has a published electronic and media policy.

Contact Beverly Gomer, Associate Director of Admission. 925-362-7223. Fax: 925-362-7228. E-mail: bgomer@athenian.org. Web site: www.athenian.org.

ATHENS ACADEMY
1281 Spartan Lane
PO Box 6548
Athens, Georgia 30604
Head of School: J. Robert Chambers Jr.

General Information Coeducational day college-preparatory and technology school. Grades N–12. Founded: 1967. Setting: suburban. Nearest major city is Atlanta. 105-acre campus. 11 buildings on campus. Approved or accredited by Georgia Independent School Association, Southern Association of Colleges and Schools, Southern Association of Independent Schools, and Georgia Department of Education.

Member of National Association of Independent Schools. Endowment: $4.9 million. Total enrollment: 917. Upper school average class size: 18. Upper school faculty-student ratio: 1:8.

Upper School Student Profile Grade 9: 83 students (49 boys, 34 girls); Grade 10: 79 students (39 boys, 40 girls); Grade 11: 85 students (41 boys, 44 girls); Grade 12: 65 students (30 boys, 35 girls).

Faculty School total: 102. In upper school: 22 men, 20 women; 31 have advanced degrees.

Subjects Offered Algebra, American history, American literature, anatomy, art, art history, biology, calculus, chemistry, chemistry-AP, computer math, creative writing, drama, ecology, economics, English, English literature, European history, expository writing, fine arts, French, geography, geometry, government/civics, grammar, health, history, Latin, mathematics, music, photography, physical education, physical science, physics, physiology, science, social studies, Spanish, statistics, theater, trigonometry, world history, world literature.

Graduation Requirements Arts and fine arts (art, music, dance, drama), English, foreign language, mathematics, physical education (includes health), science, social studies (includes history).

Special Academic Programs 13 Advanced Placement exams for which test preparation is offered; honors section.

College Admission Counseling 65 students graduated in 2009; all went to college, including Georgia Institute of Technology; University of Georgia. Median SAT critical reading: 623, median SAT math: 629, median SAT writing: 606, median combined SAT: 1858, median composite ACT: 27.

Student Life Upper grades have specified standards of dress, student council, honor system. Discipline rests primarily with faculty.

Tuition and Aid Day student tuition: $13,200. Tuition installment plan (Insured Tuition Payment Plan, monthly payment plans). Tuition reduction for siblings, need-based scholarship grants available. In 2009–10, 20% of upper-school students received aid. Total amount of financial aid awarded in 2009–10: $400,000.

Admissions Traditional secondary-level entrance grade is 9. For fall 2009, 48 students applied for upper-level admission, 31 enrolled. CTP III and Otis-Lennon School Ability Test, ERB CPT III required. Deadline for receipt of application materials: February 12. Application fee required: $85. On-campus interview required.

Athletics Interscholastic: baseball (boys), basketball (b,g), cheering (g), cross-country running (b,g), football (b), soccer (b,g), swimming and diving (b,g), tennis (b,g), track and field (b,g), volleyball (g); coed interscholastic: cross-country running, golf, swimming and diving, tennis, track and field. 6 PE instructors, 5 coaches.

Computers Computers are regularly used in English, French, history, Latin, mathematics, science, Spanish classes. Computer network features include on-campus library services, online commercial services, Internet access, wireless campus network. Student e-mail accounts are available to students. The school has a published electronic and media policy.

Contact Stuart A. Todd, Director of Admissions. 706-549-9225. Fax: 706-354-3775. E-mail: stodd@athensacademy.org. Web site: www.athensacademy.org.

AUGUSTA CHRISTIAN SCHOOL (I)

313 Baston Road
Martinez, Georgia 30907
Head of School: Dr. David M. Piccolo

General Information Coeducational day college-preparatory, arts, religious studies, and technology school. Grades K–12. Founded: 1958. Setting: suburban. Nearest major city is Augusta. 26-acre campus. 10 buildings on campus. Approved or accredited by Association of Christian Schools International, South Carolina Independent School Association, Southern Association of Colleges and Schools, and Georgia Department of Education. Total enrollment: 481. Upper school average class size: 18. Upper school faculty-student ratio: 1:14. There are 180 required school days per year for Upper School students. Upper School students typically attend 5 days per week. The average school day consists of 7 hours and 5 minutes.

Upper School Student Profile Grade 6: 34 students (21 boys, 13 girls); Grade 7: 37 students (16 boys, 21 girls); Grade 8: 46 students (27 boys, 19 girls); Grade 9: 47 students (27 boys, 20 girls); Grade 10: 57 students (32 boys, 25 girls); Grade 11: 62 students (38 boys, 24 girls); Grade 12: 53 students (22 boys, 31 girls).

Faculty School total: 54. In upper school: 10 men, 13 women; 3 have advanced degrees.

Subjects Offered Advanced chemistry, advanced computer applications, advanced math, Advanced Placement courses, algebra, American government, American history, American history-AP, American literature, anatomy and physiology, art, athletic training, athletics, band, baseball, basketball, Bible, Bible studies, biology, biology-AP, British literature, British literature-AP, calculus-AP, ceramics, cheerleading, chemistry, choir, choral music, chorus, Christian education, Christian studies, college counseling, comparative religion, computer education, computer skills, drama, drama performance, earth science, ecology, economics and history, electives, English, English composition, English literature, English literature-AP, English-AP, European history, French, general science, geography, geometry, government, grammar, health, history, instrumental music, keyboarding, life skills, mathematics, mathematics-AP, music appreciation, musical productions, New Testament, physics, piano, pre-algebra, pre-calculus, public speaking, reading, remedial/makeup course work, SAT preparation, science, social studies, Spanish, speech, sports, state history, student gov-

ernment, swimming, U.S. government, U.S. history, U.S. history-AP, U.S. literature, volleyball, weight training, weightlifting, world history, wrestling, yearbook.

Graduation Requirements Bible, computers, electives, English, foreign language, health, mathematics, physical education (includes health), science, social studies (includes history), speech.

Special Academic Programs Advanced Placement exam preparation; honors section; programs in English, mathematics for dyslexic students.

College Admission Counseling 65 students graduated in 2010; 63 went to college, including Augusta State University; Georgia Institute of Technology; Georgia Southern University; University of Georgia. Other: 2 went to work.

Student Life Upper grades have specified standards of dress, student council. Discipline rests primarily with faculty. Attendance at religious services is required.

Summer Programs Remediation programs offered; session focuses on academics; held on campus; accepts boys and girls; open to students from other schools.

Tuition and Aid Day student tuition: $6004–$8416. Tuition installment plan (Insured Tuition Payment Plan, monthly payment plans, individually arranged payment plans). Tuition reduction for siblings, need-based scholarship grants available.

Admissions Traditional secondary-level entrance grade is 9. Stanford Achievement Test required. Deadline for receipt of application materials: none. Application fee required: $600. Interview required.

Athletics Interscholastic: baseball (boys), basketball (b,g), cheering (g), cross-country running (b,g), football (b), golf (b), soccer (b,g), softball (g), swimming and diving (b,g), tennis (b,g), track and field (b,g), volleyball (g), wrestling (b). 4 PE instructors.

Computers Computers are regularly used in computer applications, keyboarding, yearbook classes. Computer network features include on-campus library services, Internet access, Internet filtering or blocking technology. Campus intranet is available to students. Students grades are available online. The school has a published electronic and media policy.

Contact Mrs. Lauren Banks, Director of Admissions. 706-863-2905 Ext. 144. Fax: 706-860-6618. E-mail: laurenbanks@augustachristian.org.

AUGUSTA PREPARATORY DAY SCHOOL

285 Flowing Wells Road
Martinez, Georgia 30907
Head of School: Jack R. Hall

General Information Coeducational day college-preparatory school. Grades PS–12. Founded: 1960. Setting: suburban. Nearest major city is Augusta. 52-acre campus. 6 buildings on campus. Approved or accredited by Georgia Independent School Association, Southern Association of Colleges and Schools, and Southern Association of Independent Schools. Member of National Association of Independent Schools and Secondary School Admission Test Board. Endowment: $2.4 million. Total enrollment: 548. Upper school average class size: 11. Upper school faculty-student ratio: 1:9. There are 180 required school days per year for Upper School students. Upper School students typically attend 5 days per week. The average school day consists of 7 hours and 15 minutes.

Upper School Student Profile Grade 9: 49 students (27 boys, 22 girls); Grade 10: 48 students (18 boys, 30 girls); Grade 11: 53 students (25 boys, 28 girls); Grade 12: 56 students (28 boys, 28 girls).

Faculty School total: 65. In upper school: 15 men, 10 women; 18 have advanced degrees.

Subjects Offered 20th century world history, Advanced Placement courses, advanced studio art-AP, algebra, American history, American literature, art, biology, biology-AP, calculus, calculus-AP, chemistry, chemistry-AP, computer programming, debate, drama, ecology, economics, English, English literature, English literature-AP, European history-AP, French, French-AP, geometry, government, government/civics, grammar, Latin, Latin-AP, marine science, physics, pre-calculus, senior project, Spanish, Spanish-AP, statistics-AP, studio art-AP, theater design and production, U.S. history-AP, world history, zoology.

Graduation Requirements American government, American history, arts and fine arts (art, music, dance, drama), English, foreign language, mathematics, science, social studies (includes history), senior speech, senior project.

Special Academic Programs Honors section; independent study; term-away projects; academic accommodation for the gifted.

College Admission Counseling 48 students graduated in 2010; 47 went to college, including Augusta State University; College of Charleston; Furman University; Georgia Institute of Technology; Mercer University; University of Georgia. Other: 1 had other specific plans.

Student Life Upper grades have specified standards of dress, student council, honor system. Discipline rests equally with students and faculty.

Tuition and Aid Day student tuition: $12,335. Tuition installment plan (monthly payment plans). Tuition reduction for siblings, merit scholarship grants, need-based scholarship grants, Community Enrichment Scholarship Program, merit and need-based, Malone Foundation Scholarship, Goizueta Foundation Scholarship available. In 2010–11, 20% of upper-school students received aid; total upper-school merit-scholarship money awarded: $24,700. Total amount of financial aid awarded in 2010–11: $426,016.

Admissions Traditional secondary-level entrance grade is 9. For fall 2010, 30 students applied for upper-level admission, 28 were accepted, 18 enrolled. ERB CTP

III required. Deadline for receipt of application materials: none. Application fee required: $75. On-campus interview required.

Athletics Interscholastic: baseball (boys), basketball (b,g), cheering (g), cross-country running (b,g), fitness (b,g), football (b), golf (b), physical training (b,g). 3 PE instructors, 1 athletic trainer.

Computers Computers are regularly used in all classes. Computer network features include on-campus library services, online commercial services, Internet access, wireless campus network, Internet filtering or blocking technology. Campus intranet and computer access in designated common areas are available to students. Students grades are available online. The school has a published electronic and media policy.

Contact Rosie Herrmann, Director of Admission. 706-863-1906 Ext. 201. Fax: 706-863-6198. E-mail: admissions@augustaprep.org. Web site: www.augustaprep.org.

AULDERN ACADEMY
990 Glovers Grove Church Road
Siler City, North Carolina 27344
Head of School: Ms. Jane Samuel

General Information Girls' boarding college-preparatory and arts school; primarily serves underachievers. Grades 8–12. Founded: 2001. Setting: rural. Nearest major city is Chapel Hill. Students are housed in single-sex dormitories. 86-acre campus. 4 buildings on campus. Approved or accredited by National Independent Private Schools Association, Southern Association of Colleges and Schools, and North Carolina Department of Education. Total enrollment: 60. Upper school average class size: 10. Upper school faculty-student ratio: 1:10. There are 225 required school days per year for Upper School students. Upper School students typically attend 5 days per week. The average school day consists of 6 hours.

Upper School Student Profile Grade 9: 6 students (6 girls); Grade 10: 12 students (12 girls); Grade 11: 16 students (16 girls); Grade 12: 20 students (20 girls). 100% of students are boarding students. 10% are state residents. 18 states are represented in upper school student body. 3% are international students. International students from Bahamas.

Faculty School total: 7. In upper school: 5 men, 2 women; 1 has an advanced degree.

Subjects Offered Advanced math, Advanced Placement courses, algebra, American literature, art, arts and crafts, biology, biology-AP, British literature, ceramics, chemistry, choir, clayworking, college planning, dance, discrete mathematics, drawing, earth science, economics, English, English composition, English language and composition-AP, environmental science, environmental science-AP, equestrian sports, geometry, health, health education, honors algebra, honors English, honors geometry, honors U.S. history, honors world history, jewelry making, library assistant, life skills, nutrition, oil painting, painting, photography, physical education, physical fitness, pottery, pre-algebra, pre-calculus, printmaking, SAT preparation, science, sex education, sociology, Spanish, study skills, U.S. government, U.S. history, U.S. history-AP, world history.

Graduation Requirements Electives, English, foreign language, mathematics, physical education (includes health), science, social studies (includes history), 30 hours of community service.

Special Academic Programs Advanced Placement exam preparation; honors section; accelerated programs; independent study; academic accommodation for the gifted; remedial reading and/or remedial writing; remedial math; programs in English, mathematics for dyslexic students; special instructional classes for students with mild learning disabilities, mild Attention Deficit Disorder, mild behavioral and/or emotional problems (anxiety, depression).

College Admission Counseling 15 students graduated in 2010; 13 went to college, including Brevard College; Georgia Southern University; Ithaca College; Meredith College; Pratt Institute; The University of North Carolina at Greensboro. Other: 2 went to work. Mean SAT critical reading: 580, mean SAT math: 550.

Student Life Upper grades have specified standards of dress, student council, honor system. Discipline rests primarily with faculty.

Summer Programs Remediation, enrichment, advancement, art/fine arts, computer instruction programs offered; session focuses on academics; held on campus; accepts girls; not open to students from other schools. 39 students usually enrolled. 2011 schedule: June 13 to August 12.

Tuition and Aid 7-day tuition and room/board: $69,000. Guaranteed tuition plan. Tuition installment plan (monthly payment plans, individually arranged payment plans, Clark Educational Loans, Serenity Loans). Need-based scholarship grants available.

Admissions Battery of testing done through outside agency, comprehensive educational evaluation, psychoeducational evaluation, Stanford Achievement Test and WISC-III and Woodcock-Johnson required. Deadline for receipt of application materials: none. Application fee required: $1500. Interview recommended.

Athletics Intramural: ballet, basketball, bicycling, billiards, combined training, cooperative games, croquet, dance, fishing, fitness, fitness walking, flag football, horseback riding, indoor soccer, jogging, kickball, outdoor activities, outdoor adventure, outdoor education, outdoor recreation, physical fitness, roller skating, running, soccer, softball, strength & conditioning, table tennis, tennis, volleyball, walking, weight training, yoga.

Computers Computer resources include on-campus library services, Internet access, Internet filtering or blocking technology. Campus intranet, student e-mail accounts, and computer access in designated common areas are available to students.

Contact Ms. Joyce Latimer, Director of Business Development and Admission. 919-837-2336 Ext. 200. Fax: 919-837-5284. E-mail: joyce.latimer@sequeltsi.com. Web site: www.auldern.com.

AURORA CENTRAL HIGH SCHOOL
1255 North Edgelawn Drive
Aurora, Illinois 60506-1673
Head of School: Rev. F. William Etheredge

General Information Coeducational day college-preparatory, arts, religious studies, bilingual studies, and technology school, affiliated with Roman Catholic Church. Grades 9–12. Founded: 1968. Setting: urban. 35-acre campus. 1 building on campus. Approved or accredited by National Catholic Education Association, North Central Association of Colleges and Schools, and Illinois Department of Education. Endowment: $8.1 million. Total enrollment: 525. Upper school average class size: 25. Upper school faculty-student ratio: 1:16. There are 180 required school days per year for Upper School students. Upper School students typically attend 5 days per week. The average school day consists of 6 hours and 50 minutes.

Upper School Student Profile Grade 11: 110 students (52 boys, 58 girls); Grade 12: 135 students (61 boys, 74 girls). 87% of students are Roman Catholic.

Faculty School total: 40. In upper school: 18 men, 17 women; 31 have advanced degrees.

Subjects Offered American history, American literature-AP, art, athletics, band, Bible, biology, biology-AP, calculus-AP, campus ministry, chemistry, chemistry-AP, civil war history, comparative religion, computer skills, constitutional history of U.S., consumer economics, contemporary history, CPR, creative writing, earth science, ecology, environmental systems, electives, engineering, English, English composition, English literature, English literature-AP, environmental science, ethics, fine arts, foreign language, French, French-AP, geometry, health, history, home economics, honors algebra, honors English, honors geometry, honors U.S. history, honors world history, instrumental music, Internet, journalism, keyboarding, Latin, math applications, mathematics, medieval history, moral theology, music, newspaper, oral communications, physical education, political science, pre-algebra, pre-calculus, psychology, reading/study skills, science, Shakespeare, social justice, Spanish, Spanish-AP, theology, U.S. government and politics, U.S. government and politics-AP, U.S. history-AP, Western civilization, world history, World War II, yearbook.

Graduation Requirements Algebra, biology, Catholic belief and practice, Christian and Hebrew scripture, constitutional history of U.S., consumer economics, English, English literature, geometry, history, keyboarding, language and composition, moral theology, physical education (includes health), religion (includes Bible studies and theology), science, scripture, U.S. government, U.S. history, retreat programs. Community service is required.

Special Academic Programs 6 Advanced Placement exams for which test preparation is offered; honors section; independent study; study at local college for college credit; academic accommodation for the gifted; remedial reading and/or remedial writing; remedial math.

College Admission Counseling 93 students graduated in 2009; 90 went to college, including Benedictine University; Illinois State University; Loyola University Chicago; Marquette University; Northern Illinois University; University of Illinois at Urbana–Champaign. Other: 1 went to work, 2 entered military service. Median composite ACT: 19.

Student Life Upper grades have uniform requirement, student council, honor system. Discipline rests primarily with faculty. Attendance at religious services is required.

Tuition and Aid Day student tuition: $4200. Tuition installment plan (monthly payment plans). Tuition reduction for siblings, merit scholarship grants, need-based scholarship grants, need-based loans available. In 2009–10, 15% of upper-school students received aid; total upper-school merit-scholarship money awarded: $20,000. Total amount of financial aid awarded in 2009–10: $100,000.

Admissions Traditional secondary-level entrance grade is 9. For fall 2009, 283 students applied for upper-level admission, 283 were accepted, 283 enrolled. High School Placement Test required. Deadline for receipt of application materials: none. Application fee required: $50. Interview recommended.

Athletics Interscholastic: aerobics/dance (girls), baseball (b,g), basketball (b,g), cheering (g), cross-country running (b,g), dance (g), dance squad (g), dance team (g), football (b), golf (b,g), indoor track (b,g), indoor track & field (b,g), pom squad (g), soccer (b,g), softball (g), tennis (b,g), volleyball (g), wrestling (b); intramural: aerobics/dance (b,g), baseball (b,g), basketball (b,g), flag football (b), floor hockey (g), football (b), indoor track (b,g), indoor track & field (b,g), jogging (b,g), physical fitness (b,g), physical training (b,g), power lifting (b,g), soccer (b,g), softball (b,g), volleyball (b,g), weight lifting (b,g), weight training (b,g), winter (indoor) track (b,g), wrestling (b); coed intramural: modern dance, physical fitness, physical training, power lifting, soccer, swimming and diving, volleyball, weight lifting, weight training, winter (indoor) track. 2 PE instructors, 18 coaches, 2 athletic trainers.

Computers Computers are regularly used in drafting, engineering, English, French, history, Spanish, technology classes. Computer network features include on-campus library services, online commercial services, Internet access, Internet filtering or blocking technology. The school has a published electronic and media policy.

Contact Mr. Brian Casey, Assistant AD and Assistant Development. 630-907-0095 Ext. 109. Fax: 630-907-1076. E-mail: bcasey@auroracentral.com. Web site: www.auroracentral.com.

AUSTIN PREPARATORY SCHOOL

101 Willow Street
Reading, Massachusetts 01867
Head of School: Mr. Paul J. Moran

General Information Coeducational day college-preparatory and religious studies school, affiliated with Roman Catholic Church. Grades 6–12. Founded: 1961. Setting: suburban. Nearest major city is Boston. 42-acre campus. 2 buildings on campus. Approved or accredited by New England Association of Schools and Colleges and Massachusetts Department of Education. Member of National Association of Independent Schools. Upper school average class size: 15. Upper school faculty-student ratio: 1:15. There are 168 required school days per year for Upper School students. Upper School students typically attend 5 days per week. The average school day consists of 6 hours.

Upper School Student Profile Grade 9: 128 students (59 boys, 69 girls); Grade 10: 117 students (56 boys, 61 girls); Grade 11: 125 students (64 boys, 61 girls); Grade 12: 144 students (60 boys, 84 girls). 85% of students are Roman Catholic.

Faculty School total: 64. In upper school: 25 men, 15 women.

Subjects Offered Algebra, American history, American literature, anatomy, Bible studies, biology, botany, business, calculus, chemistry, computer math, computer programming, computer science, creative writing, earth science, economics, English, English literature, environmental science, French, geography, geology, geometry, government/civics, grammar, history, Latin, marine biology, mathematics, oceanography, physics, physiology, religion, Russian, science, social studies, sociology, Spanish, statistics, trigonometry, writing.

Graduation Requirements English, foreign language, mathematics, religion (includes Bible studies and theology), science, social studies (includes history).

Special Academic Programs Advanced Placement exam preparation; honors section; study at local college for college credit.

College Admission Counseling 109 students graduated in 2009; all went to college, including Assumption College; Boston College; Boston University; Merrimack College; Northeastern University; University of Massachusetts Lowell. 30% scored over 600 on SAT critical reading, 30% scored over 600 on SAT math.

Student Life Upper grades have uniform requirement, student council. Discipline rests primarily with faculty.

Tuition and Aid Day student tuition: $13,700. Tuition installment plan (Academic Management Services Plan, monthly payment plans, see school Website for full description). Tuition reduction for siblings, merit scholarship grants, need-based scholarship grants available.

Admissions Traditional secondary-level entrance grade is 9. Archdiocese of Boston or STS required. Deadline for receipt of application materials: December 31. No application fee required. Interview recommended.

Athletics Interscholastic: baseball (boys), basketball (b,g), cross-country running (b,g), football (b), golf (b,g), ice hockey (b), lacrosse (b), skiing (downhill) (b,g), soccer (b,g), softball (g), swimming and diving (b,g), tennis (b,g), track and field (b,g); intramural: basketball (b,g), skiing (downhill) (b,g), softball (b,g); coed interscholastic: golf, skiing (downhill), swimming and diving; coed intramural: basketball, skiing (downhill), softball. 52 coaches, 1 athletic trainer.

Computers Computers are regularly used in English, foreign language, mathematics, science classes. Computer network features include on-campus library services, Internet access.

Contact Mr. Kevin J. Driscoll, Director of Admissions and Financial Aid. 781-944-4900 Ext. 835. Fax: 781-942-4593. E-mail: Kdriscoll@austinprepschool.org. Web site: www.austinprepschool.org.

THE AWTY INTERNATIONAL SCHOOL

7455 Awty School Lane
Houston, Texas 77055
Head of School: Mr. Peter Cooper

General Information Coeducational day college-preparatory and bilingual studies school. Grades PK–12. Founded: 1956. Setting: urban. 25-acre campus. 15 buildings on campus. Approved or accredited by French Ministry of Education, Independent Schools Association of the Southwest, International Baccalaureate Organization, and Texas Department of Education. Member of National Association of Independent Schools, Secondary School Admission Test Board, and European Council of International Schools. Languages of instruction: English, Spanish, and French. Endowment: $2.8 million. Total enrollment: 1,230. Upper school average class size: 18. Upper school faculty-student ratio: 1:18.

Upper School Student Profile Grade 9: 92 students (46 boys, 46 girls); Grade 10: 86 students (34 boys, 52 girls); Grade 11: 93 students (41 boys, 52 girls); Grade 12: 86 students (32 boys, 54 girls).

Faculty School total: 145. In upper school: 31 men, 52 women; 39 have advanced degrees.

Subjects Offered Algebra, American history, Arabic, art, biology, calculus, chemistry, community service, computer programming, computer science, computer studies, drama, Dutch, English, ESL, fine arts, French, geography, geometry, German, grammar, history, Italian, Mandarin, mathematics, music, Norwegian, philosophy, physical education, physics, science, social sciences, social studies, Spanish, theater, theory of knowledge, trigonometry, world history, world literature, writing.

Graduation Requirements Arts and fine arts (art, music, dance, drama), computer science, English, foreign language, mathematics, physical education (includes health), science, social science, social studies (includes history), 4000-word extended essay. Community service is required.

Special Academic Programs International Baccalaureate program; ESL (20 students enrolled).

College Admission Counseling 84 students graduated in 2010; 82 went to college, including Boston University; Carnegie Mellon University; Duke University; McGill University; Rice University; University of Houston.

Student Life Upper grades have uniform requirement, student council, honor system. Discipline rests primarily with faculty.

Tuition and Aid Day student tuition: $18,927. Tuition installment plan (monthly payment plans, semiannual payment plan, Dewar Tuition Refund Plan). Need-based financial aid available. In 2010–11, 7% of upper-school students received aid. Total amount of financial aid awarded in 2010–11: $287,033.

Admissions Traditional secondary-level entrance grade is 9. For fall 2010, 170 students applied for upper-level admission, 76 were accepted, 46 enrolled. ISEE, OLSAT, ERB and writing sample required. Deadline for receipt of application materials: none. Application fee required: $100. On-campus interview required.

Athletics Interscholastic: basketball (boys, girls), cheering (g), cross-country running (b,g), soccer (b,g), tennis (b,g), track and field (b,g), volleyball (g), winter soccer (g); intramural: dance (g), dance squad (g), dance team (g), flag football (b); coed interscholastic: golf, swimming and diving; coed intramural: badminton. 5 PE instructors, 20 coaches.

Computers Computers are regularly used in foreign language, science classes. Computer network features include on-campus library services, Internet access. The school has a published electronic and media policy.

Contact Mrs. Erika Benavente, Director of Admissions. 713-686-4850. Fax: 713-579-0003. E-mail: ebenavente@awty.org. Web site: www.awty.org.

BAKERSFIELD CHRISTIAN HIGH SCHOOL

12775 Stockdale Highway
Bakersfield, California 93314
Head of School: Mr. Daniel H. Cole

General Information Coeducational day college-preparatory and religious studies school, affiliated with Christian faith. Grades 9–12. Founded: 1979. Setting: suburban. 47-acre campus. 9 buildings on campus. Approved or accredited by Association of Christian Schools International, Western Association of Schools and Colleges, and California Department of Education. Endowment: $500,000. Total enrollment: 506. Upper school average class size: 22. Upper school faculty-student ratio: 1:17.

Faculty School total: 44. In upper school: 21 men, 23 women; 7 have advanced degrees.

Subjects Offered Advanced Placement courses, advanced studio art-AP, agriculture, American literature, American literature-AP, Bible, biology, biology-AP, British literature, British literature-AP, calculus, calculus-AP, chemistry, chemistry-AP, choir, Christian ethics, comparative religion, computer animation, contemporary issues, digital photography, drama, economics, economics-AP, English, English literature, English literature-AP, English-AP, European history, European history-AP, foreign language, forensics, French, history-AP, human anatomy, introduction to literature, jazz band, performing arts, photography, physical science, physics, physics-AP, pre-calculus, Spanish, Spanish-AP, statistics, statistics-AP, studio art, studio art-AP, U.S. history, U.S. history-AP, video and animation, world history, world literature.

Graduation Requirements 40 hours community service.

Special Academic Programs Advanced Placement exam preparation; independent study.

Student Life Upper grades have specified standards of dress, student council, honor system. Discipline rests primarily with faculty. Attendance at religious services is required.

Tuition and Aid Day student tuition: $8025. Tuition installment plan (FACTS Tuition Payment Plan, monthly payment plans, individually arranged payment plans). Tuition reduction for siblings, need-based financial aid available. In 2009–10, 26% of upper-school students received aid.

Admissions Traditional secondary-level entrance grade is 9. Application fee required: $50. On-campus interview required.

Athletics Interscholastic: baseball (boys), basketball (b,g), cheering (g), football (b), golf (b,g), soccer (b,g), softball (g), tennis (b,g), volleyball (g), weight lifting (b), wrestling (b); coed interscholastic: cross-country running, swimming and diving, track and field. 10 coaches, 1 athletic trainer.

Computers Computer network features include on-campus library services, Internet access, Internet filtering or blocking technology. Computer access in designated common areas is available to students. Students grades are available online. The school has a published electronic and media policy.

Contact Mrs. Debbie Camp, Director of Admissions. 661-410-7000. Fax: 661-410-7007. E-mail: dcamp@bakersfieldchristian.com. Web site: www.bakersfieldchristian.com.

THE BALDWIN SCHOOL

701 West Montgomery Avenue
Bryn Mawr, Pennsylvania 19010
Head of School: Mrs. Sally M. Powell

General Information Girls' day college-preparatory, arts, technology, and athletics school. Grades PK–12. Founded: 1888. Setting: suburban. Nearest major city is Philadelphia. 25-acre campus. 5 buildings on campus. Approved or accredited by Middle States Association of Colleges and Schools and Pennsylvania Association of Independent Schools. Member of National Association of Independent Schools and Secondary School Admission Test Board. Endowment: $7 million. Total enrollment: 560. Upper school average class size: 14. Upper school faculty-student ratio: 1:7. There are 171 required school days per year for Upper School students. Upper School students typically attend 5 days per week. The average school day consists of 7 hours.

Upper School Student Profile Grade 9: 54 students (54 girls); Grade 10: 44 students (44 girls); Grade 11: 37 students (37 girls); Grade 12: 58 students (58 girls).

Faculty School total: 90. In upper school: 9 men, 31 women; 34 have advanced degrees.

Subjects Offered Advanced Placement courses, algebra, American history, American history-AP, American literature, anthropology, architecture, art, art history, art history-AP, athletics, basketball, bell choir, biology, biology-AP, calculus, calculus-AP, ceramics, chemistry, chemistry-AP, chorus, classical Greek literature, college admission preparation, college counseling, community service, computer resources, computer science, computer studies, contemporary issues, creative writing, current history, dance, digital photography, drama, drama performance, dramatic arts, earth and space science, earth science, English, English literature, environmental studies, ethics, European history, fine arts, French, French literature-AP, geometry, golf, handbells, health, health education, history, history-AP, honors algebra, human development, Latin, library skills, life science, Mandarin, mathematics, mentorship program, model United Nations, music, peer counseling, performing arts, photography, photojournalism, physical education, physics, physics-AP, play production, playwriting, public speaking, SAT preparation, science, senior internship, social studies, softball, Spanish, speech, squash, swimming, swimming competency, tennis, theater, trigonometry, U.S. history, U.S. history-AP, vocal ensemble, volleyball, world history, world literature.

Graduation Requirements Arts, English, foreign language, history, life skills, mathematics, physical education (includes health), science, U.S. history.

Special Academic Programs Advanced Placement exam preparation; honors section; independent study; academic accommodation for the gifted, the musically talented, and the artistically talented.

College Admission Counseling 49 students graduated in 2010; all went to college, including Cornell University; Franklin & Marshall College; New York University; Princeton University; The Johns Hopkins University; University of Pennsylvania. Mean SAT critical reading: 660, mean SAT math: 660, mean SAT writing: 682. 100% scored over 600 on SAT critical reading, 100% scored over 600 on SAT math, 100% scored over 600 on SAT writing.

Student Life Upper grades have uniform requirement, student council, honor system. Discipline rests equally with students and faculty.

Summer Programs Enrichment, art/fine arts, computer instruction programs offered; session focuses on Academic programs with Baldwin faculty; held on campus; accepts boys and girls; open to students from other schools. 2011 schedule: June 10 to August 20. Application deadline: April 2.

Tuition and Aid Day student tuition: $28,000. Tuition installment plan (monthly payment plans, individually arranged payment plans). Need-based scholarship grants available. In 2010–11, 35% of upper-school students received aid. Total amount of financial aid awarded in 2010–11: $1,700,000.

Admissions Traditional secondary-level entrance grade is 9. For fall 2010, 60 students applied for upper-level admission, 34 were accepted, 12 enrolled. ISEE, SSAT, Wechsler Intelligence Scale for Children or writing sample required. Deadline for receipt of application materials: February 1. Application fee required: $50. On-campus interview required.

Athletics Interscholastic: aquatics, basketball, crew, cross-country running, dance, field hockey, golf, independent competitive sports, indoor track, lacrosse, rowing, running, soccer, softball, squash, swimming and diving, tennis, volleyball, winter (indoor) track. 7 PE instructors, 40 coaches, 1 athletic trainer.

Computers Computers are regularly used in all academic classes. Computer network features include on-campus library services, Internet access, wireless campus network. Campus intranet, student e-mail accounts, and computer access in designated common areas are available to students. The school has a published electronic and media policy.

Contact Sarah J. Goebel, Director of Admissions and Financial Aid. 610-525-2700 Ext. 251. Fax: 610-581-7231. E-mail: sgoebel@baldwinschool.org. Web site: www.baldwinschool.org.

See Display below and Close-Up on page 730.

BALDWIN SCHOOL OF PUERTO RICO, INC.

PO Box 1827

Bayamón, Puerto Rico 00960-1827

Head of School: Mr. Albert R. Cauz

General Information Coeducational day college-preparatory school. Grades PK–12. Founded: 1968. Setting: suburban. Nearest major city is San Juan. 23-acre campus. 6 buildings on campus. Approved or accredited by Middle States Association of Colleges and Schools and Puerto Rico Department of Education. Member of National Association of Independent Schools. Languages of instruction: English and Spanish. Total enrollment: 777. Upper school average class size: 20. Upper school faculty-student ratio: 1:8.

Upper School Student Profile Grade 9: 44 students (9 boys, 35 girls); Grade 10: 55 students (30 boys, 25 girls); Grade 11: 42 students (24 boys, 18 girls); Grade 12: 55 students (31 boys, 24 girls).

Faculty School total: 76. In upper school: 6 men, 24 women; 20 have advanced degrees.

Subjects Offered Algebra, American history, American literature, art, biology, biology-AP, British literature, calculus, calculus-AP, chemistry, chemistry-AP, computer information systems, computer literacy, computer programming, computer science, computers, English, English literature, English literature-AP, environmental science, ESL, European history-AP, fine arts, French, French-AP, geography, geometry, grammar, history, mathematics, music, physical education, physics, pre-calculus, psychology, Puerto Rican history, science, social studies, Spanish, Spanish language-AP, Spanish literature-AP, study skills, visual arts, vocal music, world literature, writing.

Graduation Requirements Algebra, American history, American literature, arts and fine arts (art, music, dance, drama), biology, British literature, chemistry, computer science, English, English literature, geometry, mathematics, physical education (includes health), Puerto Rican history, science, social studies (includes history), Spanish, U.S. history, Western civilization.

Special Academic Programs Advanced Placement exam preparation; honors section.

College Admission Counseling 43 students graduated in 2009; all went to college, including Boston College; Boston University; Purdue University; The George Washington University; Tufts University; University of Puerto Rico, Río Piedras. Median SAT critical reading: 606, median SAT math: 628, median SAT writing: 622.

Student Life Upper grades have uniform requirement, student council, honor system. Discipline rests equally with students and faculty.

Tuition and Aid Day student tuition: $10,395–$10,995. Guaranteed tuition plan. Tuition installment plan (biannual payment plan). Tuition reduction for siblings, need-based scholarship grants, tuition reduction for children of staff, full scholarship program for eligible students available. In 2009–10, 1% of upper-school students received aid. Total amount of financial aid awarded in 2009–10: $28,000.

Admissions Traditional secondary-level entrance grade is 9. For fall 2009, 25 students applied for upper-level admission, 12 were accepted, 12 enrolled. Stanford Achievement Test, Otis-Lennon required. Deadline for receipt of application materials: none. Application fee required: $150. On-campus interview required.

Athletics Interscholastic: baseball (boys), basketball (b,g), cheering (g), indoor soccer (b,g), soccer (b,g), swimming and diving (b,g), tennis (b,g), volleyball (b,g); intramural: flag football (b,g), touch football (b,g); coed interscholastic: golf, physical fitness. 6 PE instructors, 17 coaches, 1 athletic trainer.

Computers Computers are regularly used in English, history, mathematics, science, Spanish, technology classes. Computer network features include on-campus library services, Internet access, wireless campus network, Internet filtering or blocking technology. Computer access in designated common areas is available to students. Students grades are available online.

Contact Mrs. Ely Mejías, Director of Admissions. 787-720-2421 Ext. 239. Fax: 787-790-0619. E-mail: emejias@baldwin-school.org. Web site: www.baldwin-school.org.

BALMORAL HALL SCHOOL

630 Westminster Avenue

Winnipeg, Manitoba R3C 3S1, Canada

Head of School: Mrs. Joanne Kamins

General Information Girls' boarding and day college-preparatory, arts, technology, and athletics/prep hockey school. Boarding grades 6–12, day grades N–12. Founded: 1901. Setting: urban. Students are housed in apartment-style residence. 12-acre campus. 2 buildings on campus. Approved or accredited by Canadian Association of Independent Schools, Canadian Educational Standards Institute, International Baccalaureate Organization, The Association of Boarding Schools, and Manitoba Department of Education. Affiliate member of National Association of Independent Schools; member of Secondary School Admission Test Board. Language of instruction: English. Endowment: CAN$550,000. Total enrollment: 414. Upper school average class size: 18. Upper school faculty-student ratio: 1:7. There are 185 required school days per year for Upper School students. Upper School students typically attend 5 days per week. The average school day consists of 6 hours and 30 minutes.

Upper School Student Profile Grade 9: 46 students (46 girls); Grade 10: 27 students (27 girls); Grade 11: 49 students (49 girls); Grade 12: 68 students (68 girls). 21% of

students are boarding students. 10% are province residents. 3 provinces are represented in upper school student body. 85% are international students. International students from China, Hong Kong, Mexico, Republic of Korea, Taiwan, and United States.

Faculty School total: 69. In upper school: 10 men, 16 women; 7 have advanced degrees; 5 reside on campus.

Subjects Offered Acting, advanced math, Advanced Placement courses, advanced studio art-AP, advanced TOEFL/grammar, aerobics, art, art-AP, biology, biology-AP, business, calculus, calculus-AP, career and personal planning, career/college preparation, chemistry, chemistry-AP, choir, college planning, communications, community service, computer science, computer science-AP, consumer mathematics, dance performance, debate, desktop publishing, digital art, digital photography, drama, driver education, English, English language and composition-AP, English literature, English literature and composition-AP, English literature-AP, English/composition-AP, ESL, ethics, European history, French, French language-AP, French literature-AP, general science, geography, health, history, history-AP, jazz ensemble, journalism, mathematics, mathematics-AP, media arts, modern Western civilization, multimedia, music, musical theater, performing arts, personal development, physical education, physics, physics-AP, pre-calculus, psychology-AP, SAT/ACT preparation, science, social studies, Spanish, Spanish-AP, studio art-AP, technology, vocal ensemble, world affairs, world history.

Graduation Requirements Minimum of 10 hours per year of Service Learning participation in grades 9 through 12.

Special Academic Programs Advanced Placement exam preparation; honors section; accelerated programs; study at local college for college credit; academic accommodation for the gifted; ESL (15 students enrolled).

College Admission Counseling 47 students graduated in 2010; all went to college, including McGill University; Queen's University at Kingston; The University of Western Ontario; The University of Winnipeg; University of Manitoba; University of Toronto.

Student Life Upper grades have uniform requirement, student council, honor system. Discipline rests primarily with faculty.

Tuition and Aid 7-day tuition and room/board: CAN$39,836. Tuition installment plan (The Tuition Plan, international students must pay in full prior to official letter of acceptance). Tuition reduction for siblings, merit scholarship grants available. In 2010–11, 45% of upper-school students received aid. Total amount of financial aid awarded in 2010–11: CAN$300,000.

Admissions Traditional secondary-level entrance grade is 9. School's own exam required. Deadline for receipt of application materials: none. Application fee required: CAN$150. Interview recommended.

Athletics Interscholastic: badminton, basketball, cross-country running, curling, Frisbee, golf, ice hockey, indoor track & field, outdoor skills, running, soccer, speedskating, track and field, ultimate Frisbee, volleyball; intramural: aerobics, aerobics/dance, aerobics/Nautilus, alpine skiing, backpacking, badminton, ballet, baseball, basketball, bicycling, bowling, broomball, cooperative games, Cosom hockey, cross-country running, curling, dance, dance team, fencing, field hockey, figure skating, fitness, fitness walking, flag football, floor hockey, Frisbee, golf, gymnastics, handball, hiking/backpacking, hockey, ice hockey, ice skating, in-line skating, indoor hockey, indoor track & field, jogging, jump rope, modern dance, netball, outdoor activities, outdoor education, outdoor skills, physical fitness, physical training, roller blading, rowing, rugby, running, skiing (cross-country), skiing (downhill), snowboarding, snowshoeing, soccer, softball, speedskating, strength & conditioning, swimming and diving, table tennis, tennis, track and field, ultimate Frisbee, volleyball, walking, wall climbing, weight training, yoga. 2 PE instructors, 4 coaches.

Computers Computers are regularly used in all classes. Computer network features include on-campus library services, Internet access, wireless campus network, Internet filtering or blocking technology. Campus intranet, student e-mail accounts, and computer access in designated common areas are available to students. Students grades are available online. The school has a published electronic and media policy.

Contact Ms. Pamela K. McGhie, Director of Admissions. 204-784-1600 Ext. 621. Fax: 204-774-5534. E-mail: pmcghie@balmoralhall.com. Web site: www.balmoralhall.com.

THE BALTIMORE ACTORS' THEATRE CONSERVATORY

The Dumbarton House

300 Dumbarton Road

Baltimore, Maryland 21212-1532

Head of School: Walter E. Anderson

General Information Coeducational day and distance learning college-preparatory and arts school. Grades K–12. Distance learning grades 9–12. Founded: 1979. Setting: suburban. 35-acre campus. 3 buildings on campus. Approved or accredited by Association of Independent Maryland Schools, Middle States Association of Colleges and Schools, and Maryland Department of Education. Endowment: $200,000. Total enrollment: 24. Upper school average class size: 6. Upper school faculty-student ratio:

1:3. There are 175 required school days per year for Upper School students. Upper School students typically attend 5 days per week. The average school day consists of 7 hours and 30 minutes.

Upper School Student Profile Grade 9: 4 students (2 boys, 2 girls); Grade 10: 4 students (2 boys, 2 girls); Grade 11: 2 students (2 girls); Grade 12: 1 student (1 girl).

Faculty School total: 12. In upper school: 2 men, 8 women; 9 have advanced degrees.

Subjects Offered Acting, algebra, American history-AP, ballet, biology-AP, British literature, chemistry, English language-AP, French, geometry, health science, music history, music theory-AP, novels, physics, pre-calculus, psychology, sociology, theater history, trigonometry, world history, world history-AP.

Graduation Requirements Algebra, American history, ballet, chemistry, English, French, geometry, modern dance, music history, music theory, physical science, psychology, sociology, theater history, world history, students are required to complete graduation requirements in the three performing arts areas of music, drama, and dance.

Special Academic Programs Advanced Placement exam preparation; honors section; accelerated programs; independent study; study at local college for college credit; academic accommodation for the gifted, the musically talented, and the artistically talented.

College Admission Counseling 2 students graduated in 2010; all went to college. Median SAT critical reading: 600, median SAT math: 570, median composite ACT: 26.

Student Life Upper grades have uniform requirement, student council, honor system. Discipline rests primarily with faculty.

Summer Programs Remediation, art/fine arts programs offered; session focuses on music, drama, dance, and art; held off campus; held at theatre in Oregon Ridge Park, Hunt Valley, Maryland; accepts boys and girls; open to students from other schools. 30 students usually enrolled. 2011 schedule: July 24 to August 8. Application deadline: none.

Tuition and Aid Day student tuition: $10,000. Tuition installment plan (SMART Tuition Payment Plan, FACTS Tuition Payment Plan, individually arranged payment plans). Need-based scholarship grants available. In 2010–11, 10% of upper-school students received aid. Total amount of financial aid awarded in 2010–11: $12,000.

Admissions Traditional secondary-level entrance grade is 9. For fall 2010, 50 students applied for upper-level admission, 15 were accepted, 7 enrolled. Any standardized test, English, French, and math proficiency and writing sample required. Deadline for receipt of application materials: April 3. Application fee required: $50. On-campus interview required.

Computers Computers are regularly used in college planning, creative writing, dance, desktop publishing, English, historical foundations for arts, history, independent study, introduction to technology, keyboarding, music, music technology, psychology, senior seminar, theater, theater arts, word processing, writing classes. Computer network features include Internet access, wireless campus network, Internet filtering or blocking technology. Student e-mail accounts are available to students. The school has a published electronic and media policy.

Contact Mr. Walter E. Anderson, Headmaster. 410-337-8519. Fax: 410-337-8582. E-mail: batpro@baltimoreactorstheatre.org. Web site: www.baltimoreactorstheatre.org.

BALTIMORE LUTHERAN MIDDLE AND UPPER SCHOOL

1145 Concordia Drive
Towson, Maryland 21286-1796
Head of School: Mr. Alan Freeman

General Information Coeducational day and distance learning college-preparatory, arts, religious studies, and technology school, affiliated with Lutheran Church–Missouri Synod. Grades 6–12. Distance learning grades 9–12. Founded: 1965. Setting: suburban. Nearest major city is Baltimore. 25-acre campus. 4 buildings on campus. Approved or accredited by Association of Independent Maryland Schools, Middle States Association of Colleges and Schools, and Maryland Department of Education. Endowment: $1.3 million. Total enrollment: 330. Upper school average class size: 16. Upper school faculty-student ratio: 1:12. There are 174 required school days per year for Upper School students. Upper School students typically attend 5 days per week. The average school day consists of 6 hours and 45 minutes.

Upper School Student Profile 30% of students are Lutheran Church–Missouri Synod.

Faculty School total: 36. In upper school: 14 men, 15 women; 16 have advanced degrees.

Subjects Offered 20th century history, 3-dimensional art, acting, advanced biology, Advanced Placement courses, algebra, American government, American history, American literature, analytic geometry, anatomy, art, Bible studies, biology, biology-AP, brass choir, British literature, British literature (honors), calculus, chemistry, Chesapeake Bay studies, Christian doctrine, Christian scripture, church history, college counseling, college planning, computer education, computer graphics, computer programming, computers, concert band, concert choir, creative writing, drama, drama performance, dramatic arts, drawing, drawing and design, earth science,

ecology, economics, economics and history, English, English literature, English literature-AP, expository writing, French, geometry, German, government/civics, grammar, graphic arts, graphic design, health, honors English, independent study, intro to computers, jazz band, journalism, keyboarding, Latin, law, mathematics, music, painting, photography, physical education, physics, pre-algebra, psychology, religion, SAT/ACT preparation, science, social studies, Spanish, Spanish-AP, speech, studio art, theater, theology, trigonometry, Web site design, word processing, world history, world literature, writing, yearbook.

Graduation Requirements Arts and fine arts (art, music, dance, drama), English, foreign language, mathematics, physical education (includes health), religion (includes Bible studies and theology), science, social studies (includes history), technology.

Special Academic Programs 4 Advanced Placement exams for which test preparation is offered; honors section; independent study; study at local college for college credit; academic accommodation for the gifted; programs in English, mathematics for dyslexic students.

College Admission Counseling 76 students graduated in 2010; 72 went to college, including Loyola University Maryland; Rutgers, The State University of New Jersey, Newark; Stevenson University; Towson University; University of Maryland, Baltimore County; University of Maryland, College Park. Other: 1 went to work. Mean SAT critical reading: 539, mean SAT math: 522, mean SAT writing: 545.

Student Life Upper grades have uniform requirement, student council, honor system. Discipline rests primarily with faculty. Attendance at religious services is required.

Summer Programs Remediation, sports programs offered; session focuses on general activities; held on campus; accepts boys and girls; open to students from other schools. 2011 schedule: June 12 to August 11.

Tuition and Aid Day student tuition: $10,521. Tuition installment plan (FACTS Tuition Payment Plan). Tuition reduction for siblings, need-based scholarship grants available. In 2010–11, 22% of upper-school students received aid. Total amount of financial aid awarded in 2010–11: $82,000.

Admissions Traditional secondary-level entrance grade is 9. For fall 2010, 95 students applied for upper-level admission, 80 were accepted, 60 enrolled. School placement exam, SLEP for foreign students, Terra Nova-CTB and writing sample required. Deadline for receipt of application materials: none. Application fee required: $150. On-campus interview required.

Athletics Interscholastic: baseball (boys), basketball (b,g), cheering (g), cross-country running (b,g), field hockey (g), football (b), golf (b), indoor soccer (g), lacrosse (b,g), soccer (b,g), softball (g), tennis (b,g), track and field (b,g), volleyball (g), wrestling (b). 2 PE instructors, 5 coaches, 1 athletic trainer.

Computers Computers are regularly used in English, graphic design, history, independent study, journalism, library, mathematics, newspaper, photography, SAT preparation, social sciences, writing, yearbook classes. Computer network features include on-campus library services, Internet access, wireless campus network, Internet filtering or blocking technology. The school has a published electronic and media policy.

Contact Mrs. Ruth A. Heilman, Director of Admissions. 410-825-2323 Ext. 272. Fax: 410-825-2506. E-mail: rheilman@baltimorelutheran.org. Web site: www.baltimorelutheran.org.

BANCROFT SCHOOL

110 Shore Drive
Worcester, Massachusetts 01605
Head of School: Mr. Scott R. Reisinger

General Information Coeducational day college-preparatory school. Grades K–12. Founded: 1900. Setting: suburban. Nearest major city is Boston. 30-acre campus. 7 buildings on campus. Approved or accredited by Association of Independent Schools in New England, New England Association of Schools and Colleges, and Massachusetts Department of Education. Member of National Association of Independent Schools and Secondary School Admission Test Board. Endowment: $20 million. Total enrollment: 558. Upper school average class size: 12. Upper school faculty-student ratio: 1:8.

Upper School Student Profile Grade 6: 44 students (21 boys, 23 girls); Grade 7: 54 students (22 boys, 32 girls); Grade 8: 58 students (23 boys, 35 girls); Grade 9: 60 students (26 boys, 34 girls); Grade 10: 64 students (28 boys, 36 girls); Grade 11: 53 students (22 boys, 31 girls); Grade 12: 60 students (19 boys, 41 girls).

Faculty School total: 75. In upper school: 20 men, 15 women; 28 have advanced degrees.

Subjects Offered Acting, Advanced Placement courses, advanced studio art-AP, algebra, American history, American history-AP, American literature, art, art history, art history-AP, biology, biology-AP, biotechnology, calculus, calculus-AP, ceramics, chamber groups, chemistry, chemistry-AP, chorus, community service, computer graphics, computer science, DNA, drama, dramatic arts, English, English language and composition-AP, English literature, English literature and composition-AP, ethics, European history, European history-AP, French, French-AP, geometry, health, history, jazz band, Latin, Latin-AP, literature by women, marine biology, music, music appreciation, photography, physical education, physics, pre-calculus, psychology, science, senior project, Shakespeare, Spanish, Spanish-AP, theater, theater production, trigonometry, U.S. history-AP, women in world history, world history.

Graduation Requirements Arts and fine arts (art, music, dance, drama), English, foreign language, mathematics, physical education (includes health), science, senior project, social studies (includes history), senior thesis and spring senior project. Community service is required.

Special Academic Programs Advanced Placement exam preparation; honors section; independent study; study at local college for college credit; study abroad.

College Admission Counseling 56 students graduated in 2009; all went to college, including Connecticut College; Harvard University; Rensselaer Polytechnic Institute; The George Washington University; Tufts University; University of Pennsylvania. Median SAT critical reading: 650, median SAT math: 650.

Student Life Upper grades have specified standards of dress, student council, honor system. Discipline rests primarily with faculty.

Tuition and Aid Day student tuition: $22,900. Tuition installment plan (Insured Tuition Payment Plan, individually arranged payment plans, 10-month school payment plan). Need-based scholarship grants, scholarship for Worcester residents available. In 2009–10, 30% of upper-school students received aid. Total amount of financial aid awarded in 2009–10: $340,000.

Admissions Traditional secondary-level entrance grade is 9. For fall 2009, 49 students applied for upper-level admission, 37 were accepted, 24 enrolled. ISEE, SSAT or Wechsler Intelligence Scale for Children required. Deadline for receipt of application materials: February 1. Application fee required: $50. On-campus interview required.

Athletics Interscholastic: alpine skiing (boys, girls), baseball (b), basketball (b,g), crew (b,g), cross-country running (b,g), field hockey (g), lacrosse (b,g), soccer (b,g), softball (g), tennis (b,g), volleyball (g), wrestling (b); coed interscholastic: golf, skiing (downhill); coed intramural: dance, track and field. 5 PE instructors, 9 coaches, 1 athletic trainer.

Computers Computers are regularly used in all classes. Computer network features include on-campus library services, online commercial services, Internet access, wireless campus network, Internet filtering or blocking technology. Student e-mail accounts and computer access in designated common areas are available to students. Students grades are available online. The school has a published electronic and media policy.

Contact Mrs. Debbie Lamir, Admission Office Assistant. 508-853-2640 Ext. 206. Fax: 508-853-7824. E-mail: dlamir@bancroftschool.org. Web site: www.bancroftschool.org.

BANGOR CHRISTIAN SCHOOL

1476 Broadway
Bangor, Maine 04401
Head of School: Mr. James Frost

General Information Coeducational day college-preparatory, arts, business, vocational, religious studies, bilingual studies, and technology school, affiliated with Baptist Church. Grades K4–12. Founded: 1970. Setting: suburban. 35-acre campus. 3 buildings on campus. Approved or accredited by New England Association of Schools and Colleges and Maine Department of Education. Total enrollment: 294. Upper school average class size: 20. Upper school faculty-student ratio: 1:10.

Upper School Student Profile Grade 9: 24 students (11 boys, 13 girls); Grade 10: 23 students (9 boys, 14 girls); Grade 11: 32 students (16 boys, 16 girls); Grade 12: 25 students (11 boys, 14 girls). 55% of students are Baptist.

Faculty School total: 23. In upper school: 3 men, 8 women; 2 have advanced degrees.

Special Academic Programs Advanced Placement exam preparation; honors section; accelerated programs; independent study; study at local college for college credit.

College Admission Counseling 20 students graduated in 2009; 16 went to college, including University of Maine. Other: 1 went to work, 2 entered military service, 1 had other specific plans.

Student Life Upper grades have specified standards of dress, student council, honor system. Discipline rests primarily with faculty. Attendance at religious services is required.

Tuition and Aid Day student tuition: $4000. Guaranteed tuition plan. Tuition installment plan (monthly payment plans). Tuition reduction for siblings, need-based scholarship grants available.

Admissions Traditional secondary-level entrance grade is 9. Deadline for receipt of application materials: none. Application fee required: $100. Interview required.

Athletics Interscholastic: baseball (boys), basketball (b,g), cheering (b,g), cross-country running (b,g), indoor track & field (b,g), soccer (b,g), softball (g), swimming and diving (b,g), track and field (b,g), wrestling (b); intramural: basketball (b,g), cheering (b,g), soccer (b,g), wrestling (b); coed interscholastic: cheering; coed intramural: bowling. 2 PE instructors, 12 coaches.

Computers Computer network features include on-campus library services, Internet access, wireless campus network, Internet filtering or blocking technology. Student e-mail accounts are available to students. Students grades are available online.

Contact Mrs. Terri L. Conley, Main Office Secretary. 207-947-7356 Ext. 1. Fax: 207-262-9528. E-mail: tconley@bangorchristian.org. Web site: www.bangorchristian.org.

BARRIE SCHOOL

13500 Layhill Road
Silver Spring, Maryland 20906
Head of School: Mr. Charles Abelmann

General Information Coeducational day college-preparatory school. Grades N–12. Founded: 1932. Setting: suburban. Nearest major city is Washington, DC. 45-acre campus. 8 buildings on campus. Approved or accredited by Middle States Association of Colleges and Schools and Maryland Department of Education. Member of National Association of Independent Schools. Endowment: $1 million. Total enrollment: 299. Upper school average class size: 15. Upper school faculty-student ratio: 1:5. There are 174 required school days per year for Upper School students. Upper School students typically attend 5 days per week. The average school day consists of 7 hours.

Upper School Student Profile Grade 9: 22 students (8 boys, 14 girls); Grade 10: 15 students (8 boys, 7 girls); Grade 11: 12 students (8 boys, 4 girls); Grade 12: 22 students (8 boys, 14 girls).

Faculty School total: 30. In upper school: 12 men, 8 women; 12 have advanced degrees.

Subjects Offered Algebra, animation, art, biology, calculus, calculus-AP, chemistry, chemistry-AP, chorus, crafts, drama, drawing, English literature and composition-AP, environmental science-AP, film studies, finance, fitness, forensics, French, French-AP, geometry, health, health and wellness, history, humanities, illustration, instrumental music, journalism, media arts, media studies, music, mythology, painting, physics, physics-AP, pre-algebra, pre-calculus, reading, science, sculpture, sociology, Spanish, Spanish-AP, statistics-AP, studio art, study skills, textiles, world history, writing.

Graduation Requirements Algebra, art, biology, chemistry, English, foreign language, health, history, humanities, mathematics, physics, pre-algebra, science, sports, U.S. history, 96 hours of community service.

Special Academic Programs 11 Advanced Placement exams for which test preparation is offered.

College Admission Counseling 22 students graduated in 2010; 21 went to college, including California Institute of Technology; Earlham College; Princeton University; Rhode Island School of Design; St. Mary's College of Maryland; University of Maryland, Baltimore County. Other: 1 went to work. Mean SAT critical reading: 588, mean SAT math: 560, mean SAT writing: 593, mean combined SAT: 1741, mean composite ACT: 24.

Student Life Upper grades have student council. Discipline rests primarily with faculty.

Summer Programs Advancement programs offered; session focuses on Day Camp; held on campus; accepts boys and girls; open to students from other schools. 700 students usually enrolled. 2011 schedule: June 20 to August 12. Application deadline: none.

Tuition and Aid Day student tuition: $24,565. Tuition installment plan (Key Tuition Payment Plan, FACTS Tuition Payment Plan, monthly payment plans, The Tuition Refund Plan). Need-based scholarship grants, need-based financial aid grants available. In 2010–11, 45% of upper-school students received aid. Total amount of financial aid awarded in 2010–11: $814,427.

Admissions Traditional secondary-level entrance grade is 9. For fall 2010, 28 students applied for upper-level admission, 9 were accepted, 7 enrolled. ISEE, SSAT, Wechsler Intelligence Scale for Children III or WISC-R required. Deadline for receipt of application materials: January 14. Application fee required: $100. Interview required.

Athletics Interscholastic: baseball (boys), basketball (b,g), lacrosse (g), soccer (b,g), volleyball (g); coed interscholastic: cross-country running, equestrian sports, golf, outdoor activities, physical fitness, running, tennis, track and field. 1 PE instructor, 6 coaches, 1 athletic trainer.

Computers Computer network features include Internet access, wireless campus network, Internet filtering or blocking technology. Campus intranet and student e-mail accounts are available to students. The school has a published electronic and media policy.

Contact Ms. Diane Clem, Admission Officer. 301-576-2823. Fax: 301-576-2803. E-mail: dclem@barrie.org. Web site: www.barrie.org.

See Display on next page and Close-Up on page 732.

THE BARSTOW SCHOOL

11511 State Line Road
Kansas City, Missouri 64114
Head of School: Mr. Shane A. Foster

General Information Coeducational day college-preparatory school. Grades PS–12. Founded: 1884. Setting: suburban. 40-acre campus. 1 building on campus. Approved or accredited by Independent Schools Association of the Central States and Missouri Independent School Association. Member of National Association of Independent Schools. Endowment: $7.9 million. Total enrollment: 649. Upper school average class size: 15. Upper school faculty-student ratio: 1:8.

Upper School Student Profile Grade 9: 46 students (25 boys, 21 girls); Grade 10: 62 students (28 boys, 34 girls); Grade 11: 48 students (26 boys, 22 girls); Grade 12: 38 students (23 boys, 15 girls).

Faculty School total: 70. In upper school: 14 men, 11 women; 20 have advanced degrees.

Subjects Offered Acting, advanced chemistry, advanced math, Advanced Placement courses, algebra, American history, American literature, ancient history, art, art history, Asian history, astronomy, biology, biology-AP, calculus, calculus-AP, ceramics, chemistry, chemistry-AP, Chinese, choir, community service, computer programming, computer science, computer science-AP, creative writing, debate, drawing, English, English language-AP, English literature, English literature-AP, ethics, European history, European history-AP, fine arts, French, French language-AP, French literature-AP, geography, geology, geometry, Japanese, journalism, mathematics, music, photography, physical education, physics, science, social studies, Spanish, Spanish language-AP, speech, statistics, statistics-AP, trigonometry, U.S. government, U.S. history-AP, world history, writing.

Graduation Requirements Arts and fine arts (art, music, dance, drama), computer literacy, English, foreign language, mathematics, physical education (includes health), science, social studies (includes history), service hour requirement. Community service is required.

Special Academic Programs Advanced Placement exam preparation; honors section; independent study; study at local college for college credit.

College Admission Counseling 48 students graduated in 2009; all went to college, including Brown University; Chapman University; Southern Methodist University; The University of Kansas; University of Missouri; Washington University in St. Louis. Mean SAT critical reading: 582, mean SAT math: 602, mean composite ACT: 28. 65% scored over 600 on SAT critical reading, 50% scored over 600 on SAT math.

Student Life Upper grades have specified standards of dress, student council, honor system. Discipline rests equally with students and faculty.

Tuition and Aid Day student tuition: $11,125–$16,480. Tuition installment plan (SMART Tuition Payment Plan). Merit scholarship grants, need-based scholarship grants, need-based loans available. In 2009–10, 17% of upper-school students received aid; total upper-school merit-scholarship money awarded: $40,500. Total amount of financial aid awarded in 2009–10: $349,386.

Admissions Traditional secondary-level entrance grade is 9. For fall 2009, 210 students applied for upper-level admission, 162 were accepted, 119 enrolled. ERB, Otis-Lennon Mental Ability Test and writing sample required. Deadline for receipt of application materials: none. Application fee required: $45. On-campus interview recommended.

Athletics Interscholastic: aquatics (boys, girls), baseball (b), basketball (b,g), cheering (g), cross-country running (b,g), dance team (g), golf (b,g), soccer (b,g), softball (g), tennis (b,g), track and field (b,g), volleyball (g). 3 PE instructors, 15 coaches.

Computers Computers are regularly used in all academic classes. Computer network features include on-campus library services, online commercial services, Internet access, wireless campus network, Internet filtering or blocking technology. Campus intranet and student e-mail accounts are available to students. Students grades are available online. The school has a published electronic and media policy.

Contact Mrs. Barb Enyeart, Admissions Coordinator. 816-942-3255. Fax: 816-942-3227. E-mail: benyeart@barstowschool.org. Web site: www.barstowschool.org.

BASS MEMORIAL ACADEMY
6433 US Highway 11
Lumberton, Mississippi 39455
Head of School: Elder Gary Dwain Wilson

General Information Coeducational boarding and day college-preparatory, general academic, and religious studies school, affiliated with Seventh-day Adventists. Grades 9–12. Founded: 1961. Setting: rural. Nearest major city is Hattiesburg. Students are housed in single-sex dormitories. 350-acre campus. 10 buildings on campus. Approved or accredited by National Council for Private School Accreditation and Southern Association of Colleges and Schools. Upper school average class size: 28. Upper school faculty-student ratio: 1:12. There are 180 required school days per year for Upper School students. Upper School students typically attend 5 days per week. The average school day consists of 6 hours.

Upper School Student Profile Grade 9: 28 students (12 boys, 16 girls); Grade 10: 27 students (12 boys, 15 girls); Grade 11: 18 students (12 boys, 6 girls); Grade 12: 28 students (12 boys, 16 girls). 93% of students are boarding students. 46% are state residents. 7 states are represented in upper school student body. International students from Canada and Mexico; 1 other country represented in student body. 95% of students are Seventh-day Adventists.

Faculty School total: 12. In upper school: 6 men, 5 women; 6 have advanced degrees; 9 reside on campus.

Subjects Offered Advanced math, algebra, anatomy, biology, chemistry, community service, computer science, concert band, economics, English, English literature, fine arts, geometry, government/civics, grammar, health, history, journalism, mathematics, music, physical education, physics, religion, Spanish, world history, writing.

Graduation Requirements Arts and fine arts (art, music, dance, drama), business skills (includes word processing), computer science, English, foreign language, mathematics, physical education (includes health), religion (includes Bible studies and theology), science, social studies (includes history). Community service is required.

Special Academic Programs Accelerated programs; independent study; study at local college for college credit; academic accommodation for the gifted and the musically talented; remedial reading and/or remedial writing; remedial math.

College Admission Counseling 20 students graduated in 2009; 15 went to college, including Florida Hospital College of Health Sciences; Southern Adventist University; Southwestern Adventist University. Other: 5 went to work.

Student Life Upper grades have specified standards of dress, student council. Discipline rests equally with students and faculty. Attendance at religious services is required.

Tuition and Aid Day student tuition: $7500; 7-day tuition and room/board: $13,000. Tuition installment plan (individually arranged payment plans). Tuition reduction for siblings, merit scholarship grants, need-based scholarship grants, paying campus jobs, matching scholarships paid by donors, alumni, and churches available. In 2009–10, 75% of upper-school students received aid.

Admissions Traditional secondary-level entrance grade is 9. Deadline for receipt of application materials: none. Application fee required. Interview recommended.

Athletics Interscholastic: basketball (boys, girls); intramural: basketball (b,g), flag football (b,g), floor hockey (b,g), football (b,g), soccer (b,g), softball (b,g); coed intramural: gymnastics, tennis, volleyball. 1 PE instructor, 1 coach.

Computers Computers are regularly used in foreign language, history, mathematics, science, yearbook classes. Computer network features include on-campus library services, Internet access, Internet filtering or blocking technology. Campus intranet, student e-mail accounts, and computer access in designated common areas are available to students. Students grades are available online. The school has a published electronic and media policy.

Contact Cathy Barker, Registrar. 601-794-8561. Fax: 601-794-8881. E-mail: cbark123@aol.com.

BAVARIAN INTERNATIONAL SCHOOL

Schloss Haimhausen
Hauptstrasse 1
Haimhausen D-85778, Germany
Head of School: Bryan Nixon

General Information Coeducational day college-preparatory, general academic, arts, business, bilingual studies, technology, and physical education school. Grades PK–12. Founded: 1991. Setting: small town. Nearest major city is Munich, Germany. 10-acre campus. 5 buildings on campus. Approved or accredited by European Council of International Schools, International Baccalaureate Organization, and New England Association of Schools and Colleges. Language of instruction: English. Total enrollment: 854. Upper school average class size: 19. Upper school faculty-student ratio: 1:7. There are 190 required school days per year for Upper School students. Upper School students typically attend 5 days per week. The average school day consists of 7 hours.

Upper School Student Profile Grade 9: 57 students (28 boys, 29 girls); Grade 10: 68 students (35 boys, 33 girls); Grade 11: 63 students (34 boys, 29 girls); Grade 12: 54 students (28 boys, 26 girls).

Faculty School total: 110. In upper school: 9 men, 26 women; 24 have advanced degrees.

Subjects Offered Art, chemistry, community service, computer science, English, fine arts, French, French language-AP, geography, German, history, Japanese, mathematics, music, physical education, physics, science, social studies, theater.

Graduation Requirements Youth culture.

Special Academic Programs International Baccalaureate program; independent study; remedial reading and/or remedial writing; remedial math; programs in English, mathematics, general development for dyslexic students; special instructional classes for students with learning disabilities and dyslexia; ESL (40 students enrolled).

Student Life Upper grades have specified standards of dress, student council, honor system. Discipline rests primarily with faculty.

Summer Programs Enrichment, ESL, sports, art/fine arts, computer instruction programs offered; session focuses on English as an additional language; held on campus; accepts boys and girls; open to students from other schools. 2011 schedule: July 1 to July 31. Application deadline: none.

Tuition and Aid Day student tuition: €13,900–€14,100. Tuition installment plan (yearly payment plan, 2-payment plan). Tuition reduction for siblings available.

Admissions English proficiency or mathematics proficiency exam required. Deadline for receipt of application materials: none. No application fee required. On-campus interview required.

Athletics Interscholastic: cheering (girls); coed interscholastic: aerobics, aerobics/dance, alpine skiing, badminton, ball hockey, ballet, baseball, basketball, climbing, combined training, cooperative games, cricket, cross-country running, dance, field

hockey, football, golf, gymnastics, handball, indoor hockey, indoor soccer, indoor track & field, jogging, judo, netball, outdoor activities, outdoors, physical training, rock climbing, rugby, running, skiing (downhill), snowboarding, soccer, softball, swimming and diving, tennis, track and field, volleyball, winter soccer. 3 PE instructors, 6 coaches.

Computers Computers are regularly used in art, business, English, ESL, information technology, photography, science, typing, video film production, writing, yearbook classes. Computer network features include on-campus library services, online commercial services, Internet access, wireless campus network, Internet filtering or blocking technology. Campus intranet, student e-mail accounts, and computer access in designated common areas are available to students. The school has a published electronic and media policy.

Contact Katharina Lippacher, Registrar. 49-8133-917 Ext. 121. Fax: 49-8133-917 Ext. 182. E-mail: k.lippacher@bis-school.com. Web site: www.bis-school.com.

BAYLOR SCHOOL

171 Baylor School Road
Chattanooga, Tennessee 37405
Head of School: Mr. Scott Wilson

General Information Coeducational boarding and day college-preparatory and arts school. Boarding grades 9–12, day grades 6–12. Founded: 1893. Setting: suburban. Nearest major city is Atlanta, GA. Students are housed in single-sex dormitories. 670-acre campus. 30 buildings on campus. Approved or accredited by Southern Association of Colleges and Schools, Southern Association of Independent Schools, Tennessee Association of Independent Schools, The Association of Boarding Schools, and Tennessee Department of Education. Member of National Association of Independent Schools and Secondary School Admission Test Board. Endowment: $80 million. Total enrollment: 1,053. Upper school average class size: 14. Upper school faculty-student ratio: 1:8. There are 180 required school days per year for Upper School students. Upper School students typically attend 5 days per week. The average school day consists of 7 hours and 30 minutes.

Upper School Student Profile Grade 9: 174 students (85 boys, 89 girls); Grade 10: 193 students (98 boys, 95 girls); Grade 11: 198 students (104 boys, 94 girls); Grade 12: 167 students (90 boys, 77 girls). 30% of students are boarding students. 74% are state residents. 21 states are represented in upper school student body. 10% are international students. International students from Bermuda, China, Germany, Mexico, Republic of Korea, and Taiwan; 13 other countries represented in student body.

Faculty School total: 144. In upper school: 77 men, 67 women; 91 have advanced degrees; 45 reside on campus.

Subjects Offered Algebra, American history, American literature, anthropology, art, art history, art history-AP, art-AP, astronomy, biology, biology-AP, calculus-AP, ceramics, chemistry, chemistry-AP, computer math, computer science, computer science-AP, creative writing, dance, drama, driver education, economics, English, English language-AP, English literature, English literature-AP, environmental science, environmental science-AP, ethics, European history, European history-AP, film, fine arts, finite math, forensics, French, French-AP, genetics, geography, geometry, German, German-AP, government/civics, history, human geography—AP, Latin, Latin-AP, mathematics, music, photography, physical education, physics, physics-AP, religion, science, social studies, Spanish, Spanish-AP, speech, statistics, statistics-AP, theater, trigonometry, U.S. history-AP, video, world history, world literature.

Graduation Requirements Arts and fine arts (art, music, dance, drama), English, foreign language, mathematics, physical education (includes health), science, social studies (includes history), Leadership Baylor, summer reading.

Special Academic Programs 22 Advanced Placement exams for which test preparation is offered; honors section; study abroad; academic accommodation for the gifted, the musically talented, and the artistically talented; special instructional classes for deaf students.

College Admission Counseling 175 students graduated in 2010; all went to college, including Georgia Institute of Technology; Sewanee: The University of the South; The University of Alabama; The University of Tennessee; University of Georgia; University of Illinois at Urbana–Champaign.

Student Life Upper grades have specified standards of dress, student council, honor system. Discipline rests primarily with faculty.

Summer Programs Enrichment, sports, art/fine arts, rigorous outdoor training, computer instruction programs offered; session focuses on sports, arts, wilderness activities; held both on and off campus; held at locations near Chattanooga and various locations throughout the U.S.; accepts boys and girls; open to students from other schools. 500 students usually enrolled. 2011 schedule: June 6 to July 29. Application deadline: none.

Tuition and Aid Day student tuition: $19,536; 7-day tuition and room/board: $39,790. Tuition installment plan (The Tuition Plan, Insured Tuition Payment Plan, Key Tuition Payment Plan, FACTS Tuition Payment Plan, monthly payment plans, individually arranged payment plans). Merit scholarship grants, need-based scholarship grants available. In 2010–11, 35% of upper-school students received aid; total upper-school merit-scholarship money awarded: $350,000. Total amount of financial aid awarded in 2010–11: $2,500,000.

Admissions Traditional secondary-level entrance grade is 9. For fall 2010, 301 students applied for upper-level admission, 183 were accepted, 118 enrolled. ISEE, SSAT or TOEFL required. Deadline for receipt of application materials: none. Application fee required: $75. Interview required.

Athletics Interscholastic: aquatics (boys, girls), baseball (b), basketball (b,g), bowling (b,g), cheering (g), crew (b,g), cross-country running (b,g), dance (g), dance team (g), diving (b,g), fencing (b,g), football (b), golf (b,g), lacrosse (b,g), modern dance (g), soccer (b,g), softball (g), swimming and diving (b,g), tennis (b,g), track and field (b,g), volleyball (g), wrestling (b); intramural: ballet (g), dance (g), weight lifting (b,g); coed interscholastic: aerobics/dance, rowing, running, strength & conditioning; coed intramural: backpacking, bicycling, canoeing/kayaking, climbing, fitness, fly fishing, Frisbee, hiking/backpacking, kayaking, mountain biking, mountaineering, ocean paddling, outdoor activities, outdoor adventure, outdoor education, physical fitness, rafting, rock climbing, scuba diving, ultimate Frisbee, wall climbing, wilderness survival. 4 PE instructors, 10 coaches, 2 athletic trainers.

Computers Computers are regularly used in art, English, history, mathematics, photography, publications, science, Spanish, technology, theater arts, writing, yearbook classes. Computer network features include on-campus library services, online commercial services, Internet access, wireless campus network, Internet filtering or blocking technology. Student e-mail accounts and computer access in designated common areas are available to students. Students grades are available online. The school has a published electronic and media policy.

Contact Mr. Jon Bloom, Associate Director of Admission. 423-267-8505 Ext. 804. Fax: 423-757-2525. E-mail: jbloom@baylorschool.org. Web site: www.baylorschool.org.

See Display below and Close-Up on page 734.

BAYSIDE ACADEMY

303 Dryer Avenue
Daphne, Alabama 36526
Head of School: Mr. Thomas F. Johnson

General Information Coeducational day college-preparatory, arts, and technology school. Grades PK–12. Founded: 1970. Setting: small town. Nearest major city is Mobile. 44-acre campus. 9 buildings on campus. Approved or accredited by Southern Association of Colleges and Schools, Southern Association of Independent Schools, and Alabama Department of Education. Endowment: $1.4 million. Total enrollment: 753. Upper school average class size: 18. Upper school faculty-student ratio: 1:7. There are 178 required school days per year for Upper School students. The average school day consists of 7 hours.

Faculty School total: 108. In upper school: 18 men, 22 women; 32 have advanced degrees.

Subjects Offered Advanced Placement courses, algebra, American history, American literature, art, art history, biology, biology-AP, calculus, chemistry, chemistry-AP, computer programming, computer science, creative writing, drama, economics, English, English literature, environmental science, ethics, European history, film, fine arts, French, genetics, geography, geometry, government/civics, grammar, histology, history, Latin, marine biology, mathematics, multimedia, music, oceanography, photography, physical education, physics, science, social studies, Spanish, speech, theater, trigonometry, world history, world literature, writing.

Graduation Requirements Arts and fine arts (art, music, dance, drama), computer science, English, foreign language, mathematics, physical education (includes health), science, social studies (includes history).

Special Academic Programs Advanced Placement exam preparation; honors section; independent study; study abroad; programs in English, mathematics, general development for dyslexic students.

College Admission Counseling 67 students graduated in 2010; all went to college, including Auburn University; Birmingham-Southern College; College of Charleston; The University of Alabama; Tulane University; Vanderbilt University. 60% scored over 600 on SAT critical reading, 60% scored over 600 on SAT math, 70% scored over 26 on composite ACT.

Student Life Upper grades have uniform requirement, student council, honor system. Discipline rests primarily with faculty.

Tuition and Aid Day student tuition: $9500. Tuition installment plan (monthly payment plans, individually arranged payment plans). Need-based scholarship grants available. In 2010–11, 15% of upper-school students received aid.

Admissions Traditional secondary-level entrance grade is 9. For fall 2010, 36 students applied for upper-level admission, 25 were accepted, 20 enrolled. Otis-Lennon School Ability Test, Stanford Achievement Test and Stanford Achievement Test, Otis-Lennon School Ability Test required. Deadline for receipt of application materials: none. Application fee required: $100. On-campus interview required.

Athletics Interscholastic: aerobics/dance (girls), aquatics (b,g), baseball (b), basketball (b,g), cheering (g), cross-country running (b,g), dance (g), dance squad (g), dance team (g), football (b), golf (b,g), indoor track (b,g), soccer (b,g), softball (g), swimming and diving (b,g), tennis (b,g), track and field (b,g), volleyball (g);

intramural: ballet (g), dance (g), dance team (g), football (b), soccer (b,g); coed intramural: ballet, basketball, bicycling, canoeing/kayaking, dance, equestrian sports, physical training, sailing, scuba diving, soccer, strength & conditioning, track and field, weight training, yoga. 6 PE instructors, 26 coaches, 1 athletic trainer.

Computers Computer network features include on-campus library services, online commercial services, Internet access, wireless campus network, Internet filtering or blocking technology. Campus intranet is available to students. Students grades are available online.

Contact Alan M. Foster, Director of Admissions. 251-338-6415. Fax: 251-338-6310. E-mail: afoster@baysideacademy.org. Web site: www.baysideacademy.org.

BEACON HIGH SCHOOL

Brookline, Massachusetts
See Special Needs Schools section.

BEAUMONT SCHOOL

3301 North Park Boulevard
Cleveland Heights, Ohio 44118
Head of School: Mrs. Mary Whelan

General Information Girls' day college-preparatory, arts, and religious studies school, affiliated with Roman Catholic Church. Grades 9–12. Founded: 1850. Setting: suburban. Nearest major city is Cleveland. 21-acre campus. 2 buildings on campus. Approved or accredited by North Central Association of Colleges and Schools, Ohio Catholic Schools Accreditation Association (OCSAA), and Ohio Department of Education. Endowment: $7.5 million. Total enrollment: 442. Upper school average class size: 20. Upper school faculty-student ratio: 1:12. There are 180 required school days per year for Upper School students. Upper School students typically attend 5 days per week. The average school day consists of 6 hours and 30 minutes.

Upper School Student Profile Grade 9: 107 students (107 girls); Grade 10: 107 students (107 girls); Grade 11: 115 students (115 girls); Grade 12: 113 students (113 girls). 80% of students are Roman Catholic.

Faculty School total: 52. In upper school: 4 men, 42 women; 40 have advanced degrees.

Subjects Offered Algebra, American history, American history-AP, American literature, analysis, anatomy, applied arts, art, art appreciation, art history, astronomy, biology, biology-AP, British literature, British literature (honors), business skills, calculus, calculus-AP, campus ministry, Catholic belief and practice, ceramics, chemistry, chemistry-AP, choir, Christian and Hebrew scripture, Christian testament, church history, college counseling, college planning, community service, comparative government and politics, comparative politics, comparative religion, competitive science projects, computer applications, computer art, computer education, computer graphics, computer multimedia, computer programming, computer science, creative writing, critical thinking, critical writing, culinary arts, desktop publishing, drama, dramatic arts, drawing and design, economics, economics and history, electives, English, English literature, English literature-AP, English-AP, ethics, fashion, film history, fine arts, foreign language, French, French language-AP, French-AP, genetics, geology, geometry, government, government and politics-AP, government-AP, guidance, health, health education, Hebrew scripture, history, history-AP, honors algebra, honors English, honors geometry, honors U.S. history, honors world history, human relations, instrumental music, integrated science, journalism, keyboarding, lab science, language arts, Latin, Latin-AP, leadership and service, Life of Christ, mathematics, mathematics-AP, media production, media studies, music, music appreciation, music history, music theater, music theory, mythology, New Testament, peace and justice, peer ministry, performing arts, personal development, photo shop, photography, physical education, physical fitness, physical science, physics, piano, play production, pottery, prayer/spirituality, pre-calculus, probability and statistics, psychology, public speaking, reading/study skills, religion, religious studies, SAT preparation, SAT/ACT preparation, science, senior project, service learning/internship, social sciences, social studies, sociology, Spanish, Spanish language-AP, Spanish literature-AP, speech, speech and debate, speech and oral interpretations, stagecraft, student government, studio art, study skills, theater history, theater production, theology, trigonometry, U.S. history-AP, voice, voice ensemble, Web site design, world affairs, world geography, world history, world literature, world studies, writing, writing, yearbook.

Graduation Requirements Arts and fine arts (art, music, dance, drama), computer science, English, foreign language, health, mathematics, physical education (includes health), religion (includes Bible studies and theology), science, social sciences, social studies (includes history), Senior Project R.E.A.L, junior career shadowing day. Community service is required.

Special Academic Programs Advanced Placement exam preparation; honors section; independent study; study at local college for college credit; academic accommodation for the gifted, the musically talented, and the artistically talented.

College Admission Counseling 120 students graduated in 2010; all went to college, including Cleveland State University; John Carroll University; Miami University; Ohio University; The Ohio State University; University of Dayton. Mean SAT critical reading: 559, mean SAT math: 548, mean composite ACT: 23. 25% scored over 600 on SAT critical reading, 25% scored over 600 on SAT math, 36% scored over 26 on composite ACT.

Student Life Upper grades have uniform requirement, student council, honor system. Discipline rests primarily with faculty. Attendance at religious services is required.

Summer Programs Enrichment, sports, art/fine arts, computer instruction programs offered; session focuses on enrichment and credit courses; held on campus; accepts girls; not open to students from other schools. 175 students usually enrolled. 2011 schedule: June to July.

Tuition and Aid Day student tuition: $10,700. Tuition installment plan (monthly payment plans, individually arranged payment plans, Quarterly). Tuition reduction for siblings, merit scholarship grants, need-based scholarship grants, paying campus jobs available. In 2010–11, 41% of upper-school students received aid. Total amount of financial aid awarded in 2010–11: $1,200,000.

Admissions Traditional secondary-level entrance grade is 9. For fall 2010, 188 students applied for upper-level admission, 175 were accepted, 137 enrolled. High School Placement Test required. Deadline for receipt of application materials: none. No application fee required. On-campus interview required.

Athletics Interscholastic: basketball, cross-country running, diving, lacrosse, softball, swimming and diving, tennis, track and field, volleyball, winter (indoor) track. 1 PE instructor, 11 coaches, 1 athletic trainer.

Computers Computers are regularly used in English, foreign language, keyboarding, media, publications, science, social studies, yearbook classes. Computer network features include on-campus library services, Internet access, wireless campus network, Internet filtering or blocking technology. Student e-mail accounts are available to students. Students grades are available online. The school has a published electronic and media policy.

Contact Ms. Kaitlin Daly, Recruitment and Admission Associate. 216-325-7336. Fax: 216-325-1688. E-mail: kdaly@beaumontschool.org. Web site: www.beaumontschool.org.

THE BEEKMAN SCHOOL

220 East 50th Street
New York, New York 10022
Head of School: George Higgins

General Information Coeducational day college-preparatory, general academic, arts, and technology school. Grades 9–PG. Founded: 1925. Setting: urban. 1 building on campus. Approved or accredited by New York State Board of Regents. Total enrollment: 80. Upper school average class size: 8. Upper school faculty-student ratio: 1:8. There are 165 required school days per year for Upper School students. Upper School students typically attend 5 days per week. The average school day consists of 6 hours and 15 minutes.

Upper School Student Profile Grade 9: 15 students (8 boys, 7 girls); Grade 10: 19 students (11 boys, 8 girls); Grade 11: 21 students (12 boys, 9 girls); Grade 12: 25 students (13 boys, 12 girls); Postgraduate: 2 students (1 boy, 1 girl).

Faculty School total: 13. In upper school: 4 men, 9 women; 11 have advanced degrees.

Subjects Offered Advanced Placement courses, algebra, American history, ancient world history, art, astronomy, bioethics, biology, business mathematics, calculus, calculus-AP, chemistry, computer animation, computer art, computer science, conceptual physics, creative writing, drama, drawing, Eastern religion and philosophy, ecology, economics, electronics, English, environmental science, ESL, European history, film, French, geometry, government, health, modern politics, modern world history, photography, physical education, physical science, physics, poetry, pre-calculus, psychology, SAT preparation, sculpture, Spanish, TOEFL preparation, trigonometry, U.S. history, video film production, Web site design, Western philosophy.

Graduation Requirements Art, computer technologies, electives, English, foreign language, health education, mathematics, physical education (includes health), science, social studies (includes history).

Special Academic Programs Advanced Placement exam preparation; honors section; accelerated programs; independent study; academic accommodation for the gifted, the musically talented, and the artistically talented; remedial reading and/or remedial writing; remedial math; programs in English, mathematics, general development for dyslexic students; ESL (4 students enrolled).

College Admission Counseling 28 students graduated in 2010; 27 went to college, including Arizona State University; Boston University; Fordham University; New York University; Sarah Lawrence College; University of Vermont. Other: 1 had other specific plans. Mean SAT critical reading: 556, mean SAT math: 519, mean SAT writing: 543. 33% scored over 600 on SAT critical reading, 27% scored over 600 on SAT math, 30% scored over 600 on SAT writing.

Student Life Upper grades have honor system. Discipline rests primarily with faculty.

Summer Programs Remediation, enrichment, advancement, ESL programs offered; session focuses on academics; held on campus; accepts boys and girls; open to students from other schools. 35 students usually enrolled. 2011 schedule: July 5 to August 15. Application deadline: July 1.

Tuition and Aid Day student tuition: $30,000. Tuition installment plan (monthly payment plans, individually arranged payment plans).

Admissions Traditional secondary-level entrance grade is 9. For fall 2010, 39 students applied for upper-level admission, 38 were accepted, 33 enrolled. Deadline for receipt of application materials: none. No application fee required. On-campus interview required.
Athletics 1 PE instructor.
Computers Computer resources include online commercial services, Internet access.
Contact George Higgins, Headmaster. 212-755-6666. Fax: 212-888-6085. E-mail: georgeh@beekmanschool.org. Web site: www.BeekmanSchool.org.

See Close-Up on page 736.

BELEN JESUIT PREPARATORY SCHOOL

500 Southwest 127th Avenue
Miami, Florida 33184
Head of School: Fr. Pedro A. Suarez, SJ
General Information Boys' day college-preparatory and religious studies school, affiliated with Roman Catholic Church. Grades 6–12. Founded: 1854. Setting: urban. 28-acre campus. 3 buildings on campus. Approved or accredited by CITA (Commission on International and Trans-Regional Accreditation), European Council of International Schools, Jesuit Secondary Education Association, National Catholic Education Association, Southern Association of Colleges and Schools, and Florida Department of Education. Endowment: $4 million. Total enrollment: 1,500. Upper school average class size: 27. Upper school faculty-student ratio: 1:13. Upper School students typically attend 5 days per week.
Upper School Student Profile Grade 9: 228 students (228 boys); Grade 10: 237 students (237 boys); Grade 11: 232 students (232 boys); Grade 12: 189 students (189 boys). 98% of students are Roman Catholic.
Faculty School total: 90. In upper school: 35 men, 19 women; 46 have advanced degrees.
Subjects Offered Art, art history, biology, chemistry, composition, computers, English, English literature, French, history, mathematics, music, philosophy, physical education, physics, religion, science, social studies, Spanish.
Graduation Requirements Arts and fine arts (art, music, dance, drama), English, foreign language, mathematics, philosophy, physical education (includes health), religion (includes Bible studies and theology), science, social sciences, social studies (includes history). Community service is required.
Special Academic Programs Advanced Placement exam preparation; honors section; study at local college for college credit.
College Admission Counseling 215 students graduated in 2009; all went to college, including Florida International University; Florida State University; Georgetown University; Loyola University New Orleans; University of Florida; University of Miami. Median SAT critical reading: 560, median SAT math: 570. Mean composite ACT: 24. 27% scored over 600 on SAT critical reading, 26% scored over 600 on SAT math.
Student Life Upper grades have uniform requirement, student council. Discipline rests primarily with faculty.
Tuition and Aid Day student tuition: $12,200. Need-based scholarship grants available. In 2009–10, 35% of upper-school students received aid. Total amount of financial aid awarded in 2009–10: $400,000.
Admissions Traditional secondary-level entrance grade is 9. For fall 2009, 122 students applied for upper-level admission, 92 were accepted, 67 enrolled. School's own exam required. Deadline for receipt of application materials: none. Application fee required: $50.
Athletics Interscholastic: baseball, basketball, cross-country running, football, golf, rowing, soccer, swimming and diving, tennis, track and field, volleyball, water polo, weight lifting, wrestling; intramural: bowling, fishing, in-line hockey, weight training. 5 PE instructors, 22 coaches, 1 athletic trainer.
Computers Computers are regularly used in art, English, foreign language, history, mathematics, music, science classes. Computer network features include on-campus library services, online commercial services, Internet access, Internet filtering or blocking technology. Students grades are available online. The school has a published electronic and media policy.
Contact Mrs. Chris Besil, Admissions Secretary. 786-621-4032. Fax: 305-227-2565. E-mail: admissions@belenjesuit.org. Web site: belenjesuit.org.

BELLARMINE COLLEGE PREPARATORY

960 West Hedding Street
San Jose, California 95126
Head of School: Mr. Chris Meyercord
General Information Boys' day college-preparatory, arts, religious studies, and technology school, affiliated with Roman Catholic Church. Grades 9–12. Founded: 1851. Setting: suburban. 21-acre campus. 14 buildings on campus. Approved or accredited by National Catholic Education Association and Western Association of Schools and Colleges. Endowment: $50 million. Total enrollment: 1,600. Upper school average class size: 25. Upper school faculty-student ratio: 1:18. There are 170 required school days per year for Upper School students. Upper School students typically attend 5 days per week. The average school day consists of 6 hours and 25 minutes.

Upper School Student Profile Grade 9: 415 students (415 boys); Grade 10: 410 students (410 boys); Grade 11: 390 students (390 boys); Grade 12: 385 students (385 boys). 75% of students are Roman Catholic.
Faculty School total: 90. In upper school: 60 men, 30 women; 65 have advanced degrees.
Subjects Offered Algebra, American history, American literature, anatomy, art, arts, biology, calculus, ceramics, chemistry, community service, computer science, drama, English, English literature, ethics, European history, expository writing, fine arts, French, geography, geometry, government/civics, history, international relations, Latin, Mandarin, mathematics, music, physical education, physics, psychology, religion, science, social sciences, social studies, Spanish, speech, theater, theology, trigonometry, world history, world literature, writing.
Graduation Requirements Arts and fine arts (art, music, dance, drama), English, foreign language, mathematics, physical education (includes health), religion (includes Bible studies and theology), science, social sciences, social studies (includes history), 75 hours of Christian service.
Special Academic Programs Advanced Placement exam preparation; honors section; independent study; study at local college for college credit; special instructional classes for students with learning disabilities and Attention Deficit Disorder.
College Admission Counseling 392 students graduated in 2010; 390 went to college, including California Polytechnic State University, San Luis Obispo; San Jose State University; Santa Clara University; University of California, Berkeley; University of California, Davis; University of Southern California. Other: 1 entered a postgraduate year, 1 had other specific plans. Mean combined SAT: 1884, mean composite ACT: 27.
Student Life Upper grades have specified standards of dress, student council, honor system. Discipline rests primarily with faculty. Attendance at religious services is required.
Summer Programs Remediation, enrichment, advancement, sports, art/fine arts, computer instruction programs offered; session focuses on enrichment; held on campus; accepts boys and girls; open to students from other schools. 1,320 students usually enrolled. 2011 schedule: June 14 to July 21. Application deadline: June 14.
Tuition and Aid Day student tuition: $15,250. Tuition installment plan (FACTS Tuition Payment Plan, semester payment plan, 10-installment plan). Need-based scholarship grants available. In 2010–11, 23% of upper-school students received aid. Total amount of financial aid awarded in 2010–11: $3,200,000.
Admissions Traditional secondary-level entrance grade is 9. For fall 2010, 950 students applied for upper-level admission, 500 were accepted, 415 enrolled. High School Placement Test required. Deadline for receipt of application materials: December 15. Application fee required: $70.
Athletics Interscholastic: aquatics, baseball, basketball, cross-country running, diving, football, golf, ice hockey, in-line hockey, indoor hockey, lacrosse, soccer, swimming and diving, tennis, track and field, volleyball, water polo, wrestling; intramural: basketball, flag football, in-line hockey, soccer, softball, tai chi, yoga. 4 PE instructors, 15 coaches, 2 athletic trainers.
Computers Computers are regularly used in art, English, foreign language, mathematics, music, science classes. Computer network features include on-campus library services, online commercial services, Internet access, wireless campus network. Student e-mail accounts are available to students. Students grades are available online. The school has a published electronic and media policy.
Contact Terry Council, Admissions Assistant. 408-294-9224. Fax: 408-294-1894. E-mail: admissions@bcp.org. Web site: www.bcp.org.

BELLARMINE-JEFFERSON HIGH SCHOOL

465 East Olive Avenue
Burbank, California 91501-2176
Head of School: Sr. Cheryl Milner
General Information Coeducational day college-preparatory, arts, business, religious studies, and technology school, affiliated with Roman Catholic Church. Grades 9–12. Founded: 1940. Setting: urban. 4 buildings on campus. Approved or accredited by Western Association of Schools and Colleges and California Department of Education. Upper school average class size: 20.
Faculty In upper school: 30 have advanced degrees.
Special Academic Programs International Baccalaureate program; Advanced Placement exam preparation; honors section.
College Admission Counseling 91 students graduated in 2010; they went to California State University, Fullerton; California State University, Long Beach; California State University, Los Angeles; California State University, Monterey Bay; California State University, Northridge; California State University, Sacramento.
Student Life Upper grades have uniform requirement, student council, honor system. Discipline rests primarily with faculty. Attendance at religious services is required.
Tuition and Aid Tuition installment plan (The Tuition Plan). Tuition reduction for siblings, merit scholarship grants, need-based scholarship grants available.
Admissions High School Placement Test required. Deadline for receipt of application materials: January 16. Application fee required: $50. Interview required.
Athletics Interscholastic: aerobics (girls), baseball (b); coed interscholastic: basketball.

Computers The school has a published electronic and media policy.
Contact 818-972-1400. Web site: www.bell-jeff.net.

BELLEVUE CHRISTIAN SCHOOL
1601 98th Avenue NE
Clyde Hill, Washington 98004-3400
Head of School: Ron Taylor
General Information Coeducational day college-preparatory, general academic, arts, business, vocational, religious studies, and technology school, affiliated with Christian faith. Grades PK–12. Founded: 1950. Setting: suburban. Nearest major city is Bellevue. 10-acre campus. 5 buildings on campus. Approved or accredited by Christian Schools International, Northwest Accreditation Commission, and Washington Department of Education. Endowment: $1 million. Total enrollment: 1,160. Upper school average class size: 20. Upper school faculty-student ratio: 1:21. There are 180 required school days per year for Upper School students. Upper School students typically attend 5 days per week. The average school day consists of 6 hours and 30 minutes.
Upper School Student Profile Grade 7: 74 students (38 boys, 36 girls); Grade 8: 71 students (43 boys, 28 girls); Grade 9: 90 students (51 boys, 39 girls); Grade 10: 86 students (49 boys, 37 girls); Grade 11: 83 students (39 boys, 44 girls); Grade 12: 80 students (41 boys, 39 girls). 95% of students are Christian faith.
Faculty School total: 39. In upper school: 19 men, 20 women.
Subjects Offered 20th century world history, advanced chemistry, advanced computer applications, Advanced Placement courses, advanced studio art-AP, algebra, American history-AP, American literature-AP, architectural drawing, art, athletics, band, Basic programming, Bible, biology, calculus, calculus-AP, choral music, church history, community service, computer applications, computer multimedia, computer programming, creative writing, culinary arts, digital photography, drama, English, English-AP, environmental science, ESL, ethics, fine arts, foods, foreign language, geometry, German, government, health, human relations, integrated mathematics, interior design, jazz band, jazz ensemble, library assistant, math analysis, mathematics, media communications, photography, physical education, physical science, physics, physics-AP, religion, social sciences, social studies, Spanish, Spanish language-AP, studio art, technical drawing, trigonometry, U.S. history-AP, vocal ensemble, wind ensemble, woodworking, work experience, world history, yearbook.
Graduation Requirements Algebra, art, arts and fine arts (art, music, dance, drama), band, baseball, basketball, Bible, calculus-AP, computer technologies, concert choir, English, English-AP, ethics, geometry, German, golf, health, international foods, jazz band, marine biology, mathematics, photography, physical education (includes health), physical fitness, physics-AP, religion (includes Bible studies and theology), science, social sciences, social studies (includes history), softball, Spanish-AP, speech, technology, theater arts, track and field, U.S. history-AP, video film production, visual and performing arts, vocal ensemble, volleyball, woodworking, wrestling. Community service is required.
Special Academic Programs 7 Advanced Placement exams for which test preparation is offered; honors section; study at local college for college credit; academic accommodation for the gifted, the musically talented, and the artistically talented; remedial math; programs in English, mathematics, general development for dyslexic students; special instructional classes for student academic support; ESL (18 students enrolled).
College Admission Counseling 89 students graduated in 2009; 81 went to college, including Bellevue College; Gonzaga University; Pepperdine University; Seattle Pacific University; University of Washington; Washington State University. Other: 1 entered military service, 7 had other specific plans. Median SAT critical reading: 550, median SAT math: 510, median SAT writing: 550, median combined SAT: 1690, median composite ACT: 24. 19% scored over 600 on SAT critical reading, 37% scored over 600 on SAT math, 19% scored over 600 on SAT writing, 31% scored over 1800 on combined SAT, 27% scored over 26 on composite ACT.
Student Life Upper grades have specified standards of dress, student council, honor system. Discipline rests primarily with faculty.
Tuition and Aid Day student tuition: $10,650. Tuition installment plan (monthly payment plans). Tuition reduction for siblings, need-based scholarship grants, financial aid awarded on basis of report and ability to pay available. In 2009–10, 15% of upper-school students received aid. Total amount of financial aid awarded in 2009–10: $900,000.
Admissions Deadline for receipt of application materials: none. Application fee required: $75. Interview required.
Athletics Interscholastic: baseball (boys), basketball (b,g), cheering (g), combined training (b,g), cooperative games (b,g), cross-country running (b,g), fitness (b,g), golf (b,g), outdoor activities (b,g), outdoor education (b,g), physical fitness (b,g), physical training (b,g), running (b,g), soccer (b,g), softball (g), strength & conditioning (b,g), track and field (b,g), volleyball (g), weight lifting (b,g), weight training (b,g), wrestling (b).
Computers Computers are regularly used in art, Bible studies, computer applications, creative writing, desktop publishing, drawing and design, English, ESL, foreign language, health, keyboarding, library, mathematics, media production, newspaper, photography, religious studies, science, social studies, technical drawing, technology, video film production, Web site design, writing, yearbook classes. Computer network features include on-campus library services, Internet access, wireless campus network, Internet filtering or blocking technology. Student e-mail accounts are available to students. Students grades are available online. The school has a published electronic and media policy.
Contact Jaime Heise, Admissions Coordinator. 425-454-4402 Ext. 215. Fax: 425-454-4418. E-mail: jheise@bellevuechristian.org. Web site: www. bellevuechristian.org.

BELMONT HILL SCHOOL
350 Prospect Street
Belmont, Massachusetts 02478-2662
Head of School: Dr. Richard I. Melvoin
General Information Boys' boarding and day college-preparatory, arts, and technology school. Boarding grades 9–12, day grades 7–12. Founded: 1923. Setting: suburban. Nearest major city is Boston. Students are housed in single-sex dormitories. 34-acre campus. 14 buildings on campus. Approved or accredited by Association of Independent Schools in New England, Massachusetts Department of Education, and New England Association of Schools and Colleges. Member of National Association of Independent Schools and Secondary School Admission Test Board. Endowment: $61 million. Total enrollment: 452. Upper school average class size: 12. Upper school faculty-student ratio: 1:6.
Upper School Student Profile Grade 7: 51 students (51 boys); Grade 8: 63 students (63 boys); Grade 9: 95 students (95 boys); Grade 10: 81 students (81 boys); Grade 11: 82 students (82 boys); Grade 12: 80 students (80 boys). 1% of students are boarding students. 100% are state residents.
Faculty School total: 68. In upper school: 54 men, 14 women; 67 have advanced degrees; 6 reside on campus.
Subjects Offered Algebra, American history, American literature, architecture, art, art history, astronomy, biology, calculus, ceramics, chemistry, Chinese, computer math, computer programming, computer science, creative writing, drafting, drama, earth science, economics, engineering, English, English literature, ethics, European history, expository writing, fine arts, French, geography, geology, geometry, German, government/civics, grammar, health, history, industrial arts, journalism, Latin, mathematics, mechanical drawing, music, philosophy, photography, physical education, physics, psychology, science, social studies, Spanish, speech, statistics, theater, trigonometry, woodworking, world history, writing.
Graduation Requirements Arts and fine arts (art, music, dance, drama), computer science, English, foreign language, mathematics, physical education (includes health), science, social studies (includes history), senior wooden panel carving (a tradition since 1923).
Special Academic Programs Advanced Placement exam preparation; honors section; independent study; term-away projects; study at local college for college credit; study abroad.
College Admission Counseling 73 students graduated in 2009; all went to college, including Boston College; Brown University; Georgetown University; Harvard University; Trinity College; Tufts University. Mean SAT critical reading: 650, mean SAT math: 682, mean SAT writing: 660.
Student Life Upper grades have specified standards of dress, student council, honor system. Discipline rests equally with students and faculty.
Tuition and Aid Day student tuition: $32,700; 5-day tuition and room/board: $3885. Tuition installment plan (Key Tuition Payment Plan, FACTS Tuition Payment Plan, monthly payment plans, individually arranged payment plans). Need-based scholarship grants, need-based loans, middle-income loans available. In 2009–10, 29% of upper-school students received aid. Total amount of financial aid awarded in 2009–10: $2,900,000.
Admissions Traditional secondary-level entrance grade is 10. For fall 2009, 385 students applied for upper-level admission, 131 were accepted, 89 enrolled. ISEE and SSAT required. Deadline for receipt of application materials: February 1. Application fee required: $40. On-campus interview required.
Athletics Interscholastic: alpine skiing, baseball, basketball, crew, cross-country running, football, golf, ice hockey, lacrosse, sailing, skiing (cross-country), skiing (downhill), soccer, squash, tennis, track and field, wrestling; intramural: basketball, bicycling, crew, cross-country running, football, ice hockey, skiing (cross-country), squash, strength & conditioning, tennis, touch football, weight lifting. 2 athletic trainers.
Computers Computers are regularly used in economics, foreign language, mathematics, science classes. Computer network features include on-campus library services, online commercial services, Internet access.
Contact Mr. Michael R. Grant, Director of Admission. 617-993-5257. Fax: 617-484-4829. E-mail: grant@belmonthill.org. Web site: www.belmonthill.org.

THE BEMENT SCHOOL

Deerfield, Massachusetts
See Junior Boarding Schools section.

BENEDICTINE HIGH SCHOOL

2900 Martin Luther King, Jr. Drive
Cleveland, Ohio 44104

Head of School: Mr. Joseph Gressock

General Information Boys' day college-preparatory and religious studies school, affiliated with Roman Catholic Church. Grades 9–12. Founded: 1927. Setting: urban. 13-acre campus. 3 buildings on campus. Approved or accredited by North Central Association of Colleges and Schools, Ohio Catholic Schools Accreditation Association (OCSAA), and Ohio Department of Education. Total enrollment: 352. Upper school average class size: 15. Upper school faculty-student ratio: 1:11. There are 180 required school days per year for Upper School students. Upper School students typically attend 5 days per week. The average school day consists of 6 hours and 30 minutes.

Upper School Student Profile Grade 9: 110 students (110 boys); Grade 10: 68 students (68 boys); Grade 11: 90 students (90 boys); Grade 12: 82 students (82 boys). 85% of students are Roman Catholic.

Faculty School total: 37. In upper school: 32 men, 5 women; 31 have advanced degrees.

Subjects Offered Advanced chemistry, advanced math, Advanced Placement courses, aesthetics, algebra, American literature, American literature-AP, analysis and differential calculus, analytic geometry, Ancient Greek, ancient history, ancient world history, art, athletic training, band, Basic programming, Bible studies, biology, biology-AP, British literature-AP, business education, business law, calculus, calculus-AP, Catholic belief and practice, Central and Eastern European history, ceramics, chemistry, choir, chorus, church history, Civil War, civil war history, classical Greek literature, classical language, computer education, computer graphics, computer information systems, computer literacy, computer programming, computer skills, computer-aided design, concert band, concert choir, current events, drawing, drawing and design, economics, electives, English, English literature and composition-AP, European history-AP, film studies, foreign language, French, geometry, German, government, government-AP, government/civics, government/civics-AP, graphic design, health, honors algebra, honors English, honors geometry, honors U.S. history, honors world history, human geography—AP, jazz band, journalism, keyboarding, lab science, Latin, Latin-AP, Life of Christ, marching band, marketing, moral theology, music, music appreciation, New Testament, painting, physical education, pre-calculus, probability and statistics, psychology, Russian, Shakespeare.

Graduation Requirements 1½ elective credits, 20th century American writers, 20th century history, 20th century world history, algebra, American government, American history, American literature, ancient history, ancient world history, art, biology, British literature, chemistry, church history, computer applications, English, foreign language, geometry, physical education (includes health), physics, senior project, theology, U.S. history, world history, community service hours.

Special Academic Programs 8 Advanced Placement exams for which test preparation is offered; honors section; independent study; study at local college for college credit; study abroad; remedial reading and/or remedial writing; remedial math.

College Admission Counseling 79 students graduated in 2010; 77 went to college, including Bowling Green State University; Case Western Reserve University; Cleveland State University; Kent State University; The University of Akron; University of Dayton. Other: 2 went to work. Mean SAT critical reading: 554, mean SAT math: 526, mean SAT writing: 542, mean combined SAT: 1622, mean composite ACT: 22.

Student Life Upper grades have specified standards of dress, student council, honor system. Discipline rests primarily with faculty. Attendance at religious services is required.

Summer Programs Enrichment, sports, computer instruction programs offered; held on campus; accepts boys and girls; open to students from other schools. 150 students usually enrolled. 2011 schedule: June 8 to July 24. Application deadline: June 1.

Tuition and Aid Day student tuition: $8200. Tuition installment plan (monthly payment plans, individually arranged payment plans). Tuition reduction for siblings, merit scholarship grants, need-based scholarship grants, paying campus jobs available. In 2010–11, 73% of upper-school students received aid.

Admissions Traditional secondary-level entrance grade is 9. For fall 2010, 250 students applied for upper-level admission, 175 were accepted, 132 enrolled. High School Placement Test required. Deadline for receipt of application materials: none. Application fee required: $150. Interview recommended.

Athletics Interscholastic: baseball, basketball, bowling, cross-country running, football, golf, hockey, ice hockey, lacrosse, soccer, swimming and diving, track and field, wrestling; intramural: baseball, basketball, flag football, football, physical fitness, physical training, skiing (downhill), snowboarding, strength & conditioning, volleyball, weight lifting, weight training. 10 coaches, 2 athletic trainers.

Computers Computers are regularly used in computer applications, creative writing, current events, data processing, design, English, graphic design, history, independent study, information technology, library, mathematics, newspaper, technical drawing, yearbook classes. Computer network features include on-campus library services, online commercial services, Internet access, wireless campus network, Internet filtering or blocking technology. Student e-mail accounts are available to students. Students grades are available online. The school has a published electronic and media policy.

Contact Mr. Kieran Patton, Director of Admissions. 216-421-2080 Ext. 356. Fax: 216-421-1100. E-mail: kpatton@cbhs.net. Web site: www.cbhs.net.

BENEDICTINE HIGH SCHOOL

304 North Sheppard Street
Richmond, Virginia 23221

Head of School: Mr. Jesse Grapes

General Information Boys' day college-preparatory, arts, religious studies, Junior ROTC, and military school, affiliated with Roman Catholic Church. Grades 9–12. Founded: 1911. Setting: urban. 28-acre campus. 4 buildings on campus. Approved or accredited by National Catholic Education Association, Southern Association of Colleges and Schools, Virginia Association of Independent Schools, and Virginia Department of Education. Member of National Association of Independent Schools. Endowment: $1.5 million. Total enrollment: 278. Upper school average class size: 15. Upper school faculty-student ratio: 1:9. There are 180 required school days per year for Upper School students. Upper School students typically attend 5 days per week. The average school day consists of 7 hours and 30 minutes.

Upper School Student Profile Grade 9: 63 students (63 boys); Grade 10: 65 students (65 boys); Grade 11: 79 students (79 boys); Grade 12: 71 students (71 boys). 65% of students are Roman Catholic.

Faculty School total: 40. In upper school: 28 men, 12 women; 20 have advanced degrees.

Subjects Offered 3-dimensional art, advanced studio art-AP, algebra, American literature, anatomy and physiology, art, art-AP, band, biology, biology-AP, calculus, calculus-AP, Catholic belief and practice, chemistry, communication arts, computer applications, computer programming, creative writing, discrete mathematics, economics, engineering, English, English literature, English literature and composition-AP, geography, geometry, graphic arts, journalism, JROTC, Latin, Latin-AP, physical education, physical science, physics, pre-calculus, psychology, religion, robotics, Spanish, sports team management, statistics, U.S. and Virginia government, U.S. government, U.S. government and politics, U.S. government and politics-AP, U.S. history, U.S. history-AP, United States government-AP, world history, world literature, yearbook.

Graduation Requirements Arts and fine arts (art, music, dance, drama), electives, English, JROTC, lab science, language, mathematics, physical education (includes health), religion (includes Bible studies and theology), social studies (includes history), Community Service Requrement.

Special Academic Programs Advanced Placement exam preparation; honors section; independent study; academic accommodation for the gifted and the artistically talented; remedial math.

College Admission Counseling 57 students graduated in 2010; 52 went to college, including The College of William and Mary; University of Notre Dame; University of Virginia; Virginia Polytechnic Institute and State University. Other: 1 went to work, 1 entered military service, 3 had other specific plans. Mean combined SAT: 1580, mean composite ACT: 22.

Student Life Upper grades have uniform requirement, student council, honor system. Discipline rests equally with students and faculty. Attendance at religious services is required.

Summer Programs Remediation programs offered; session focuses on remediation for incoming freshmen, upper classmen; held on campus; accepts boys; not open to students from other schools. 12 students usually enrolled. 2011 schedule: June 20 to July 21.

Tuition and Aid Day student tuition: $14,500. Tuition installment plan (FACTS Tuition Payment Plan). Merit scholarship grants, need-based scholarship grants available. In 2010–11, 35% of upper-school students received aid; total upper-school merit-scholarship money awarded: $50,000. Total amount of financial aid awarded in 2010–11: $500,000.

Admissions Traditional secondary-level entrance grade is 9. For fall 2010, 138 students applied for upper-level admission, 115 were accepted, 92 enrolled. SSAT required. Deadline for receipt of application materials: none. Application fee required: $50. Interview required.

Athletics Interscholastic: baseball, basketball, cross-country running, football, golf, indoor track & field, JROTC drill, lacrosse, marksmanship, outdoor skills, riflery, soccer, swimming and diving, tennis, track and field, winter (indoor) track, wrestling; intramural: Frisbee, outdoor adventure, outdoor education, strength & conditioning, volleyball, weight lifting, weight training, wilderness survival, wildernessways. 1 PE instructor, 30 coaches, 1 athletic trainer.

Computers Computers are regularly used in graphic arts, journalism, photojournalism, programming, yearbook classes. Computer resources include on-campus library services, Internet access. Student e-mail accounts are available to students. The school has a published electronic and media policy.

Contact Mrs. Sandy M. Carli, Associate Director of Admission. 804-342-1314. Fax: 804-342-1349. E-mail: scarli@bhsrva.org. Web site: www.benedictinehighschool.org.

BENEDICTINE MILITARY SCHOOL

6502 Seawright Drive
Savannah, Georgia 31406
Head of School: Ms. Deborah Antosca, EdD

General Information Boys' day college-preparatory, arts, religious studies, technology, and military school, affiliated with Roman Catholic Church. Grades 9–12. Founded: 1902. Setting: suburban. 100-acre campus. 4 buildings on campus. Approved or accredited by Southern Association of Colleges and Schools and Georgia Department of Education. Endowment: $2.1 million. Total enrollment: 309. Upper school average class size: 15. Upper school faculty-student ratio: 1:11. There are 180 required school days per year for Upper School students. Upper School students typically attend 5 days per week. The average school day consists of 5 hours and 45 minutes.

Upper School Student Profile Grade 9: 88 students (88 boys); Grade 10: 80 students (80 boys); Grade 11: 70 students (70 boys); Grade 12: 71 students (71 boys). 70% of students are Roman Catholic.

Faculty School total: 33. In upper school: 22 men, 10 women; 20 have advanced degrees.

Subjects Offered Algebra, American history, American literature, band, biology, calculus, calculus-AP, chemistry, chorus, Christian and Hebrew scripture, communications, comparative religion, computer programming, economics, English, English language and composition-AP, English literature, English literature and composition-AP, English-AP, environmental science-AP, European history-AP, French, geography, geometry, health, Hebrew scripture, honors English, honors geometry, JROTC, Latin, photography, physical education, physics, religion, robotics, Spanish, studio art, trigonometry, U.S. government, U.S. history, U.S. history-AP, weight training, world history, world wide web design.

Graduation Requirements English, foreign language, mathematics, physical education (includes health), religion (includes Bible studies and theology), science, social sciences, social studies (includes history), JROTC for students entering as freshmen and sophomores, 70 hour minimum community service.

Special Academic Programs 6 Advanced Placement exams for which test preparation is offered; honors section; independent study; academic accommodation for the gifted.

College Admission Counseling 91 students graduated in 2009; 87 went to college, including Armstrong Atlantic State University; Georgia Institute of Technology; Georgia Southern University; Kennesaw State University; University of Georgia. Other: 3 went to work, 1 entered military service. Mean SAT critical reading: 529, mean SAT math: 523, mean SAT writing: 498, mean combined SAT: 1550. 25% scored over 600 on SAT critical reading, 25% scored over 600 on SAT math, 25% scored over 600 on SAT writing, 25% scored over 1800 on combined SAT.

Student Life Upper grades have uniform requirement, student council, honor system. Discipline rests primarily with faculty. Attendance at religious services is required.

Tuition and Aid Day student tuition: $9200. Tuition installment plan (FACTS Tuition Payment Plan, monthly payment plans). Need-based scholarship grants, discount for children of employees (50%) available. In 2009–10, 34% of upper-school students received aid. Total amount of financial aid awarded in 2009–10: $380,000.

Admissions Traditional secondary-level entrance grade is 9. For fall 2009, 109 students applied for upper-level admission, 98 were accepted, 88 enrolled. Explore required. Deadline for receipt of application materials: none. Application fee required: $50. Interview required.

Athletics Interscholastic: baseball, basketball, cross-country running, drill team, football, golf, in-line hockey, JROTC drill, physical fitness, physical training, riflery, sailing, soccer, swimming and diving, tennis, track and field, weight lifting, wrestling; intramural: physical fitness, racquetball, strength & conditioning, weight training. 3 PE instructors, 14 coaches, 1 athletic trainer.

Computers Computers are regularly used in English, programming, SAT preparation, Web site design classes. Computer network features include on-campus library services, Internet access. Students grades are available online.

Contact Mr. Will Fleming, Director of Admissions. 912-644-7007. Fax: 912-356-3527. E-mail: will.fleming@bcsav.net. Web site: www.bcsav.net.

BEN FRANKLIN ACADEMY

1585 Clifton Road
Atlanta, Georgia 30329
Head of School: Dr. Wood Smethurst

General Information Coeducational day college-preparatory school. Grades 9–12. Founded: 1987. Setting: urban. 3-acre campus. 2 buildings on campus. Approved or accredited by Georgia Independent School Association, Southern Association of Colleges and Schools, and Georgia Department of Education. Total enrollment: 130. Upper school average class size: 1. Upper school faculty-student ratio: 1:4.

Faculty School total: 29. In upper school: 12 men, 17 women; 15 have advanced degrees.

Subjects Offered 1½ elective credits.

Graduation Requirements We have a work-study component in addition to the academic requirements.

Special Academic Programs Advanced Placement exam preparation; honors section; accelerated programs; academic accommodation for the gifted.

College Admission Counseling 40 students graduated in 2010; all went to college.

Student Life Upper grades have specified standards of dress. Discipline rests primarily with faculty.

Tuition and Aid Tuition reduction for siblings, need-based scholarship grants available.

Admissions Traditional secondary-level entrance grade is 10. Deadline for receipt of application materials: none. No application fee required. On-campus interview required.

Athletics Coed Interscholastic: basketball, cross-country running, Frisbee, golf, tennis, ultimate Frisbee.

Computers Computer resources include on-campus library services, Internet access, Internet filtering or blocking technology. Campus intranet and student e-mail accounts are available to students. The school has a published electronic and media policy.

Contact Dr. Martha B. Burdette, Dean of Studies. 404-633-7404. Fax: 404-321-0610. E-mail: bfa@benfranklinacademy.org. Web site: www.benfranklinacademy.org.

THE BENJAMIN SCHOOL

11000 Ellison Wilson Road
North Palm Beach, Florida 33408
Head of School: Mr. Robert S. Goldberg

General Information Coeducational day college-preparatory and arts school. Grades PK–12. Founded: 1960. Setting: suburban. Nearest major city is West Palm Beach. 50-acre campus. 5 buildings on campus. Approved or accredited by Florida Council of Independent Schools, Southern Association of Colleges and Schools, and Florida Department of Education. Member of National Association of Independent Schools and Secondary School Admission Test Board. Endowment: $3.2 million. Total enrollment: 1,190. Upper school average class size: 16. Upper school faculty-student ratio: 1:8. There are 175 required school days per year for Upper School students. Upper School students typically attend 5 days per week. The average school day consists of 5 hours and 30 minutes.

Upper School Student Profile Grade 9: 117 students (61 boys, 56 girls); Grade 10: 116 students (59 boys, 57 girls); Grade 11: 110 students (40 boys, 70 girls); Grade 12: 92 students (47 boys, 45 girls).

Faculty School total: 154. In upper school: 18 men, 26 women; 35 have advanced degrees.

Subjects Offered 3-dimensional art, acting, African studies, algebra, American history, anatomy and physiology, art, art history, Asian studies, band, Basic programming, biology, biology-AP, calculus, calculus-AP, Caribbean history, cartooning/animation, ceramics, chemistry, chemistry-AP, choral music, chorus, comparative government and politics-AP, comparative religion, composition-AP, computer animation, computer programming, computer science, computer science-AP, current events, dance, debate, drama, earth science, ecology, economics, economics-AP, English, English language and composition-AP, English literature, English literature and composition-AP, environmental science, European history, expository writing, film studies, French, French language-AP, genetics, geometry, government-AP, government/civics, grammar, honors English, honors geometry, literature and composition-AP, marine biology, modern European history-AP, mythology, physical education, physics, piano, pre-calculus, psychology, SAT preparation, Spanish, Spanish language-AP, Spanish literature-AP, speech, statistics-AP, theater, trigonometry, U.S. government, U.S. government and politics-AP, U.S. history-AP, video film production, world history.

Graduation Requirements Arts and fine arts (art, music, dance, drama), computer science, English, foreign language, mathematics, physical education (includes health), science, social sciences, social studies (includes history), work program for seniors.

Special Academic Programs 18 Advanced Placement exams for which test preparation is offered; honors section; academic accommodation for the gifted, the musically talented, and the artistically talented.

College Admission Counseling 100 students graduated in 2009; all went to college, including Boston University; Florida State University; The University of Alabama; University of Central Florida; University of Florida; University of Notre Dame. Mean SAT critical reading: 580, mean SAT math: 587, mean SAT writing: 590, mean composite ACT: 26.

Student Life Upper grades have uniform requirement, student council, honor system. Discipline rests primarily with faculty.

Tuition and Aid Day student tuition: $21,525. Tuition installment plan (monthly payment plans, The Tuition Solution). Merit scholarship grants, need-based scholarship grants, need-based loans available. In 2009–10, 17% of upper-school students received aid; total upper-school merit-scholarship money awarded: $21,525. Total amount of financial aid awarded in 2009–10: $750,000.

Admissions Traditional secondary-level entrance grade is 9. For fall 2009, 93 students applied for upper-level admission, 86 were accepted, 49 enrolled. ERB or SSAT required. Deadline for receipt of application materials: February 1. Application fee required: $100. On-campus interview required.

Athletics Interscholastic: baseball (boys), basketball (b,g), bowling (b,g), cross-country running (b,g), dance (g), dance team (g), football (b), golf (b,g), lacrosse (b,g), modern dance (g), soccer (b,g), softball (g), tennis (b,g), volleyball (g), wrestling (b); coed interscholastic: aerobics/dance, cheering, diving, swimming and diving, track and field; coed intramural: sailing. 2 PE instructors, 1 coach, 1 athletic trainer.

Computers Computers are regularly used in art, English, foreign language, history, mathematics, science classes. Computer network features include on-campus library services, Internet access, wireless campus network, Internet filtering or blocking technology, tablet laptop program for grades 9 to 12. Student e-mail accounts are available to students. The school has a published electronic and media policy.

Contact Mrs. Mary Lou Primm, Director of Admission. 561-472-3451. Fax: 561-472-3410. E-mail: mprimm@thebenjaminschool.org. Web site: www.thebenjaminschool.org.

BERKELEY CARROLL SCHOOL

181 Lincoln Place
Brooklyn, New York 11217
Head of School: Mr. Robert D. Vitalo

General Information Coeducational day college-preparatory school. Grades N–12. Founded: 1886. Setting: urban. Nearest major city is New York. 3 buildings on campus. Approved or accredited by New York State Association of Independent Schools and New York Department of Education. Member of National Association of Independent Schools. Endowment: $2.5 million. Total enrollment: 785. Upper school average class size: 15. Upper school faculty-student ratio: 1:8.

Upper School Student Profile Grade 9: 54 students (30 boys, 24 girls); Grade 10: 51 students (27 boys, 24 girls); Grade 11: 50 students (23 boys, 27 girls); Grade 12: 60 students (32 boys, 28 girls).

Faculty School total: 132. In upper school: 28 men, 27 women; 47 have advanced degrees.

Subjects Offered Algebra, American history, American literature, art, art history, astronomy, biology, calculus, ceramics, chemistry, community service, computer applications, computer programming, conceptual physics, creative writing, dance, democracy in America, drama, driver education, economics, engineering, English, English literature, environmental science, European history, expository writing, fine arts, fractal geometry, French, geometry, government/civics, health, history, humanities, Japanese studies, journalism, Latin, marine biology, music, photography, physical education, physics, science, Shakespeare, Spanish, statistics, theater, trigonometry, video and animation, world history, World-Wide-Web publishing, writing.

Graduation Requirements Arts and fine arts (art, music, dance, drama), computer science, English, foreign language, mathematics, physical education (includes health), science, social sciences, 6-week senior year internship. Community service is required.

Special Academic Programs Advanced Placement exam preparation; independent study; study abroad; academic accommodation for the gifted, the musically talented, and the artistically talented.

College Admission Counseling 50 students graduated in 2009; all went to college, including Brown University; Columbia College; Oberlin College; Tufts University.

Student Life Upper grades have student council, honor system. Discipline rests equally with students and faculty.

Tuition and Aid Tuition installment plan (Insured Tuition Payment Plan, Academic Management Services Plan, Key Tuition Payment Plan, monthly payment plans, individually arranged payment plans). Need-based scholarship grants available.

Admissions Traditional secondary-level entrance grade is 9. For fall 2009, 110 students applied for upper-level admission, 40 were accepted, 15 enrolled. Deadline for receipt of application materials: December 15. Application fee required: $50. On-campus interview required.

Athletics Interscholastic: baseball (boys), basketball (b,g), cross-country running (b,g), indoor track & field (b,g), soccer (b,g), track and field (b,g), volleyball (b,g); intramural: fencing (b,g), yoga (b,g); coed interscholastic: aquatics, dance, judo, swimming and diving, tennis; coed intramural: aquatics, fitness, swimming and diving. 2 PE instructors, 10 coaches.

Computers Computers are regularly used in art, English, foreign language, history, mathematics, music, science classes. Computer network features include on-campus library services, online commercial services, Internet access, Internet filtering or blocking technology. The school has a published electronic and media policy.

Contact Ms. Vanessa Prescott, Director of Admissions. 718-789-6060 Ext. 6527. Fax: 718-398-3640. E-mail: vprescott@berkeleycarroll.org. Web site: www.berkeleycarroll.org.

BERKELEY PREPARATORY SCHOOL

4811 Kelly Road
Tampa, Florida 33615
Head of School: Joseph A. Merluzzi

General Information Coeducational day college-preparatory, arts, religious studies, bilingual studies, and technology school, affiliated with Episcopal Church. Grades PK–12. Founded: 1960. Setting: suburban. 80-acre campus. 8 buildings on campus.

Berkeley Preparatory School

Approved or accredited by Florida Council of Independent Schools, National Association of Episcopal Schools, Southern Association of Colleges and Schools, Southern Association of Independent Schools, The College Board, and Florida Department of Education. Member of National Association of Independent Schools and Secondary School Admission Test Board. Total enrollment: 1,200. Upper school average class size: 18. Upper school faculty-student ratio: 1:8. The average school day consists of 7 hours.

Faculty School total: 175.

Subjects Offered African history, algebra, American government, American history, American literature, art, art history, biology, biology-AP, calculus, calculus-AP, ceramics, chemistry, chemistry-AP, China/Japan history, community service, computer math, computer programming, computer science, creative writing, dance, drama, drama performance, drama workshop, early childhood, economics, English, English literature, English-AP, environmental science-AP, etymology, European history, expository writing, fine arts, French, French-AP, freshman seminar, geography, geometry, government/civics, grammar, guitar, health, history, history of China and Japan, honors algebra, honors English, honors geometry, instruments, Latin, Latin American history, Latin-AP, logic, Mandarin, math analysis, mathematics, media arts, microbiology, modern European history, modern European history-AP, music, performing arts, philosophy, physical education, physics, physics-AP, pre-calculus, psychology, religious studies, SAT preparation, science, social studies, Spanish, Spanish-AP, speech, stage design, statistics, statistics-AP, technical theater, television, theater, theater production, U.S. history, U.S. history-AP, video, video film production, Western civilization, world history, world literature, writing.

Graduation Requirements Arts and fine arts (art, music, dance, drama), computer science, English, foreign language, mathematics, physical education (includes health), religious studies, science, social studies (includes history). Community service is required.

Special Academic Programs Advanced Placement exam preparation; honors section; independent study; study abroad.

College Admission Counseling 128 students graduated in 2010; all went to college, including Cornell University; Florida State University; Harvard University; New York University; University of Florida; University of Miami. Mean SAT critical reading: 612, mean SAT math: 631, mean SAT writing: 622, mean combined SAT: 1865, mean composite ACT: 27.

Student Life Upper grades have specified standards of dress, student council, honor system. Discipline rests equally with students and faculty.

Summer Programs Remediation, enrichment, advancement, sports, art/fine arts, computer instruction programs offered; session focuses on setting a fun pace for excellence; held on campus; accepts boys and girls; open to students from other schools. 2,000 students usually enrolled. 2011 schedule: June 6 to August 1. Application deadline: none.

Tuition and Aid Day student tuition: $18,940. Tuition installment plan (8-installment plan). Need-based scholarship grants available.

Admissions Traditional secondary-level entrance grade is 9. Otis-Lennon Mental Ability Test and SSAT required. Deadline for receipt of application materials: January 30. Application fee required: $50. On-campus interview required.

Athletics Interscholastic: baseball (boys), basketball (b,g), cheering (g), crew (b,g), cross-country running (b,g), dance squad (g), dance team (g), diving (b,g), football (b), golf (b,g), lacrosse (b), rowing (b,g), soccer (b,g), softball (g), swimming and diving (b,g), tennis (b,g), track and field (b,g), volleyball (b,g); coed interscholastic: ice hockey, weight lifting, wrestling; coed intramural: physical fitness, physical training, power lifting, project adventure, strength & conditioning, wall climbing, weight training. 14 PE instructors, 74 coaches, 2 athletic trainers.

Computers Computers are regularly used in art, English, foreign language, history, mathematics, music, science classes. Computer network features include on-campus library services, online commercial services, Internet access, wireless campus network, Internet filtering or blocking technology. Student e-mail accounts are available to students. Students grades are available online. The school has a published electronic and media policy.

Contact Janie McIlvaine, Director of Admissions. 813-885-1673. Fax: 813-886-6933. E-mail: mcilvjan@berkeleyprep.org. Web site: www.berkeleyprep.org.

See Display on page 105 and Close-Up on page 738.

BERKSHIRE SCHOOL
245 North Undermountain Road
Sheffield, Massachusetts 01257

General Information Coeducational boarding and day college-preparatory, arts, and technology school. Grades 9–PG. Founded: 1907. Setting: rural. Nearest major city is Hartford, CT. Students are housed in single-sex dormitories. 550-acre campus. 36 buildings on campus. Approved or accredited by Association of Independent Schools in New England, New England Association of Schools and Colleges, and The Association of Boarding Schools. Member of National Association of Independent

Schools and Secondary School Admission Test Board. Endowment: $83.5 million. Total enrollment: 371. Upper school average class size: 12. Upper school faculty-student ratio: 1:6.

See Display on page 106 and Close-Up on page 740.

BERLIN INTERNATIONAL SCHOOL

Lentzeallee 8—14
Berlin 14195, Germany
Head of School: Mr. Hubert Keulers

General Information college-preparatory, general academic, arts, business, and bilingual studies school. Founded: 1998. Setting: suburban. 3 buildings on campus. Approved or accredited by European Council of International Schools, International Baccalaureate Organization, and New England Association of Schools and Colleges. Languages of instruction: English and German. Total enrollment: 820. Upper school average class size: 22. Upper school faculty-student ratio: 1:11. There are 180 required school days per year for Upper School students. Upper School students typically attend 5 days per week. The average school day consists of 8 hours and 45 minutes.

Faculty School total: 75. In upper school: 15 men, 28 women; 35 have advanced degrees.

Subjects Offered Advanced biology, advanced chemistry, advanced math, advanced studio art-AP, art, art history, art-AP, biology, biology-AP, British literature-AP, business studies, chemistry, chemistry-AP, computer studies, drama, economics, economics-AP, English, English as a foreign language, English language-AP, English literature-AP, ESL, foreign language, French, French language-AP, geography, German, German-AP, history, history-AP, International Baccalaureate courses, mathematics-AP, music, music-AP, physical education, physics, physics-AP, SAT preparation, SAT/ACT preparation, senior thesis, service learning/internship, Spanish, Spanish-AP, student government, student publications, theory of knowledge, visual arts.

Special Academic Programs International Baccalaureate program; academic accommodation for the gifted; remedial reading and/or remedial writing; remedial math; ESL (80 students enrolled).

College Admission Counseling 30 students graduated in 2010; 27 went to college. Other: 3 had other specific plans.

Student Life Upper grades have student council, honor system. Discipline rests primarily with faculty.

Tuition and Aid Day student tuition: €10,000. Tuition installment plan (monthly payment plans, individually arranged payment plans, Scholarship programme for academically, artistically highly able and/or gifted students.). Tuition reduction for siblings, merit scholarship grants, need-based scholarship grants available. In 2010–11, 10% of upper-school students received aid.

Admissions Traditional secondary-level entrance grade is 11. For fall 2010, 65 students applied for upper-level admission, 33 were accepted, 33 enrolled. Admissions testing required. Deadline for receipt of application materials: none. Application fee required: €800. Interview recommended.

Athletics Interscholastic: badminton (boys, girls), basketball (b,g), cross-country running (b,g), field hockey (b,g), football (b,g), soccer (b,g), swimming and diving (b,g), tennis (b,g), track and field (b,g); intramural: handball (b,g), hockey (b,g), indoor hockey (b,g), indoor soccer (b,g), soccer (b,g), team handball (b,g), track and field (b,g), volleyball (b,g); coed interscholastic: basketball, cross-country running, field hockey, football, soccer, swimming and diving, tennis, track and field; coed intramural: handball, hockey, indoor hockey, indoor soccer, soccer, team handball, track and field, volleyball. 2 PE instructors.

Computers Computers are regularly used in all academic classes. Computer network features include on-campus library services, Internet access, wireless campus network, Internet filtering or blocking technology. Student e-mail accounts and computer access in designated common areas are available to students.

Contact Ms. Ute Harris. +49-30820077780. Fax: +49-30820077789. E-mail: admissions@berlin-international-school.de. Web site: www.berlin-international-school.de.

BERWICK ACADEMY

31 Academy Street
South Berwick, Maine 03908
Head of School: Gregory J. Schneider

General Information Coeducational day college-preparatory and arts school. Grades K–PG. Founded: 1791. Setting: small town. Nearest major city is Portsmouth, NH. 72-acre campus. 11 buildings on campus. Approved or accredited by New England Association of Schools and Colleges and Maine Department of Education. Member of National Association of Independent Schools and Secondary School Admission Test Board. Endowment: $21 million. Total enrollment: 567. Upper school average class size: 14. Upper school faculty-student ratio: 1:12. There are 169 required school days per year for Upper School students.

Upper School Student Profile Grade 9: 77 students (37 boys, 40 girls); Grade 10: 70 students (32 boys, 38 girls); Grade 11: 62 students (38 boys, 24 girls); Grade 12: 63 students (29 boys, 34 girls); Postgraduate: 3 students (2 boys, 1 girl).

Faculty School total: 89. In upper school: 13 men, 18 women; 16 have advanced degrees.

Subjects Offered Algebra, American history, American literature, art, art history, biology, calculus, chemistry, computer math, computer programming, computer science, dance, English, ethics, European history, fine arts, French, geometry, government/civics, health, history, journalism, Latin, mathematics, metalworking, music, physical education, physics, science, social studies, Spanish, statistics, theater arts, trigonometry, world history.

Graduation Requirements Algebra, analysis, arts and fine arts (art, music, dance, drama), biology, chemistry, computer science, English, English literature, European civilization, foreign language, languages, mathematics, physical education (includes health), physics, science, social studies (includes history).

Special Academic Programs Advanced Placement exam preparation; honors section; independent study; term-away projects; study abroad; academic accommodation for the gifted, the musically talented, and the artistically talented.

College Admission Counseling 63 students graduated in 2010; 59 went to college, including Connecticut College; Middlebury College; Rensselaer Polytechnic Institute; University of New Hampshire; University of Vermont; Worcester Polytechnic Institute. Other: 2 entered a postgraduate year, 2 had other specific plans. Mean SAT critical reading: 611, mean SAT math: 613, mean SAT writing: 627.

Student Life Upper grades have specified standards of dress, student council, honor system. Discipline rests equally with students and faculty.

Summer Programs Enrichment, sports programs offered; session focuses on study skills; held on campus; accepts boys and girls; open to students from other schools. 48 students usually enrolled. 2011 schedule: August 1 to August 15. Application deadline: June 30.

Tuition and Aid Day student tuition: $23,250. Tuition installment plan (FACTS Tuition Payment Plan). Need-based scholarship grants, need-based loans available. In 2010–11, 33% of upper-school students received aid. Total amount of financial aid awarded in 2010–11: $2,200,000.

Admissions Traditional secondary-level entrance grade is 9. For fall 2010, 159 students applied for upper-level admission, 103 were accepted, 51 enrolled. ERB or SSAT or WISC III required. Deadline for receipt of application materials: January 31. Application fee required: $50. Interview required.

Athletics Interscholastic: alpine skiing (boys, girls), baseball (b), basketball (b,g), cross-country running (b,g), dance (b,g), field hockey (g), golf (b,g), hockey (b,g), ice hockey (b,g), lacrosse (b,g), modern dance (b,g), skiing (downhill) (b,g), soccer (b,g), softball (g), wilderness (b,g); intramural: wilderness (g); coed intramural: bicycling, wilderness. 3 PE instructors, 4 coaches, 2 athletic trainers.

Computers Computers are regularly used in art, dance, English, foreign language, graphic design, history, humanities, independent study, library, mathematics, SAT preparation, science, social studies, theater arts, writing, yearbook classes. Computer network features include on-campus library services, Internet access, wireless campus network, Internet filtering or blocking technology. Student e-mail accounts are available to students. The school has a published electronic and media policy.

Contact Diane M. Field, Director of Admission and Financial Aid. 207-384-2164 Ext. 2301. Fax: 207-384-3332. E-mail: dfield@berwickacademy.org. Web site: www.berwickacademy.org.

BESANT HILL SCHOOL

8585 Ojai Santa Paula Road
PO Box 850
Ojai, California 93023
Head of School: Mr. Paul Amadio

General Information Coeducational boarding and day college-preparatory and arts school; primarily serves students with learning disabilities, individuals with Attention Deficit Disorder, and dyslexic students. Grades 9–12. Founded: 1946. Setting: small town. Nearest major city is Los Angeles. Students are housed in single-sex dormitories. 500-acre campus. 14 buildings on campus. Approved or accredited by California Association of Independent Schools, The Association of Boarding Schools, Western Association of Schools and Colleges, and California Department of Education. Member of National Association of Independent Schools and Secondary School Admission Test Board. Languages of instruction: English, Spanish, and French. Endowment: $1 million. Total enrollment: 100. Upper school average class size: 10. Upper school faculty-student ratio: 1:4. The average school day consists of 8 hours and 15 minutes.

Upper School Student Profile Grade 9: 20 students (10 boys, 10 girls); Grade 10: 24 students (12 boys, 12 girls); Grade 11: 26 students (13 boys, 13 girls); Grade 12: 28 students (14 boys, 14 girls); Postgraduate: 2 students (1 boy, 1 girl). 80% of students are boarding students. 50% are state residents. 17 states are represented in upper school student body. 25% are international students. International students from Cameroon, Canada, China, Germany, Japan, and Taiwan; 5 other countries represented in student body.

Faculty School total: 25. In upper school: 12 men, 13 women; 13 have advanced degrees; 22 reside on campus.

Subjects Offered Acting, adolescent issues, algebra, American history, art, art history, astronomy, biology, calculus, calculus-AP, ceramics, chemistry, computer science, digital art, drama, driver education, English, English as a foreign language, English language and composition-AP, English literature, English-AP, environmental science, ESL, ethics, expository writing, film, fine arts, geography, geometry, government/civics, history, mathematics, music, music history, music theory, music theory-AP, philosophy, photography, physical education, physics, psychology, scene study, science, social sciences, social studies, Spanish, theater, world history.

Graduation Requirements Arts and fine arts (art, music, dance, drama), English, foreign language, mathematics, physical education (includes health), science, social sciences, social studies (includes history).

Special Academic Programs Advanced Placement exam preparation; honors section; independent study; study at local college for college credit; academic accommodation for the musically talented and the artistically talented; programs in English, mathematics, general development for dyslexic students; ESL (10 students enrolled).

College Admission Counseling 27 students graduated in 2009; all went to college, including Pitzer College; Sarah Lawrence College; The Evergreen State College; University of California, Santa Barbara; University of California, Santa Cruz; University of Puget Sound. Median SAT critical reading: 580, median SAT math: 550, median SAT writing: 500. 18% scored over 600 on SAT critical reading, 10% scored over 600 on SAT math, 15% scored over 600 on SAT writing.

Student Life Upper grades have student council, honor system. Discipline rests equally with students and faculty.

Tuition and Aid Day student tuition: $19,900; 7-day tuition and room/board: $39,990. Tuition installment plan (Academic Management Services Plan, Key Tuition Payment Plan). Tuition reduction for siblings, need-based scholarship grants, paying campus jobs available. In 2009–10, 22% of upper-school students received aid. Total amount of financial aid awarded in 2009–10: $325,000.

Admissions Traditional secondary-level entrance grade is 9. For fall 2009, 245 students applied for upper-level admission, 118 were accepted, 47 enrolled. Deadline for receipt of application materials: February 19. Application fee required: $75. Interview required.

Athletics Interscholastic: basketball (boys); intramural: baseball (b), basketball (b), soccer (b,g), softball (b), volleyball (g), wrestling (b); coed interscholastic: aerobics, aerobics/dance, backpacking, cross-country running, dance, fitness, fitness walking, Frisbee, golf, hiking/backpacking, mountain biking, outdoor activities, outdoor education, outdoor skills, paddle tennis, physical training, ropes courses, skeet shooting, surfing, ultimate Frisbee, walking, yoga; coed intramural: bicycling, billiards, climbing, running, skiing (downhill), swimming and diving, table tennis, tennis, track and field, wall climbing, weight lifting. 2 coaches.

Computers Computers are regularly used in desktop publishing, graphic arts, graphic design, mathematics, media arts, publications, video film production classes.

Computer network features include on-campus library services, online commercial services, Internet access, wireless campus network, Internet filtering or blocking technology. Student e-mail accounts are available to students.

Contact Terra Furguiel, Associate Director of Admissions. 805-646-4343 Ext. 111. Fax: 805-258-5101. E-mail: tfurguiel@besanthill.org. Web site: www.besanthill.org.

See Display below and Close-Up on page 742.

BETH HAVEN CHRISTIAN SCHOOL

5515 Johnsontown Road
Louisville, Kentucky 40272
Head of School: Mr. Joseph Bailey

General Information Coeducational day college-preparatory and religious studies school, affiliated with Baptist Church. Grades K4–12. Founded: 1971. Setting: suburban. 2-acre campus. 1 building on campus. Approved or accredited by Association of Christian Schools International and Kentucky Department of Education. Total enrollment: 216. Upper school average class size: 18. Upper school faculty-student ratio: 1:8. There are 177 required school days per year for Upper School students. Upper School students typically attend 5 days per week. The average school day consists of 7 hours and 5 minutes.

Upper School Student Profile Grade 9: 22 students (13 boys, 9 girls); Grade 10: 23 students (13 boys, 10 girls); Grade 11: 26 students (13 boys, 13 girls); Grade 12: 20 students (14 boys, 6 girls). 65% of students are Baptist.

Faculty School total: 18. In upper school: 5 men, 7 women; 4 have advanced degrees.

Subjects Offered ACT preparation, Advanced Placement courses, algebra, American history, American literature, analytic geometry, art appreciation, Bible studies, biology, British literature (honors), business mathematics, calculus-AP, chemistry, computer applications, drama, dramatic arts, earth science, economics, English, English composition, English language and composition-AP, health, honors algebra, honors English, honors geometry, honors U.S. history, honors world history, independent study, journalism, keyboarding, lab science, psychology, psychology-AP, senior seminar, Spanish, speech, trigonometry, U.S. government and politics-AP, world geography, world history, yearbook.

Graduation Requirements ACT preparation, algebra, American government, American history, American literature, analytic geometry, arts appreciation, Bible,

biology, British literature, chemistry, earth science, economics, English, language, physical education (includes health), world geography, world history.

Special Academic Programs Advanced Placement exam preparation; honors section; independent study; study at local college for college credit.

College Admission Counseling 26 students graduated in 2009; 24 went to college, including Bellarmine University; Indiana University Bloomington; Jefferson Community and Technical College; Liberty University; University of Louisville. Other: 2 went to work. Median composite ACT: 22. 5% scored over 26 on composite ACT.

Student Life Upper grades have uniform requirement, honor system. Discipline rests primarily with faculty.

Tuition and Aid Day student tuition: $3900. Tuition installment plan (FACTS Tuition Payment Plan). Tuition reduction for siblings, need-based scholarship grants, two full-tuition memorial scholarships are awarded each year based on a combination of merit and need available. In 2009–10, 2% of upper-school students received aid. Total amount of financial aid awarded in 2009–10: $7700.

Admissions Traditional secondary-level entrance grade is 9. For fall 2009, 17 students applied for upper-level admission, 15 were accepted, 14 enrolled. Stanford Test of Academic Skills required. Deadline for receipt of application materials: none. Application fee required: $250. Interview required.

Athletics Interscholastic: baseball (boys), basketball (b,g), cheering (g), football (b), softball (g), volleyball (g); coed interscholastic: cross-country running. 1 PE instructor.

Computers Computers are regularly used in business applications, computer applications, English, journalism, yearbook classes. Computer network features include Internet access, Internet filtering or blocking technology. Computer access in designated common areas is available to students. Students grades are available online. The school has a published electronic and media policy.

Contact Ms. Lisa Vincent, Registrar. 502-937-3516. Fax: 502-937-3364. E-mail: lvincent@bethhaven.com.

THE BIRCH WATHEN LENOX SCHOOL

210 East 77th Street
New York, New York 10075
Head of School: Mr. Frank J. Carnabuci III

General Information Coeducational day college-preparatory school. Grades K–12. Founded: 1916. Setting: urban. 1 building on campus. Approved or accredited by New York State Association of Independent Schools and New York Department of Education. Member of National Association of Independent Schools. Endowment: $7.4 million. Total enrollment: 550. Upper school average class size: 15. Upper school faculty-student ratio: 1:15. Upper School students typically attend 5 days per week. The average school day consists of 7 hours.

Upper School Student Profile Grade 9: 46 students (24 boys, 22 girls); Grade 10: 45 students (25 boys, 20 girls); Grade 11: 46 students (23 boys, 23 girls); Grade 12: 48 students (22 boys, 26 girls).

Faculty School total: 120. In upper school: 30 men, 85 women; 115 have advanced degrees.

Subjects Offered Algebra, American history, American history-AP, American literature, American literature-AP, art, art history, biology, calculus, ceramics, chemistry, community service, computer math, computer science, creative writing, dance, drama, driver education, economics, English, English literature, environmental science, European history, expository writing, fine arts, French, geography, geology, geometry, government/civics, grammar, industrial arts, Japanese, journalism, mathematics, music, philosophy, photography, physical education, physics, science, Shakespeare, social studies, Spanish, speech, swimming, theater, trigonometry, typing, world history, writing.

Graduation Requirements 20th century world history, arts and fine arts (art, music, dance, drama), computer science, English, foreign language, mathematics, physical education (includes health), science, social studies (includes history). Community service is required.

Special Academic Programs Advanced Placement exam preparation; honors section; independent study; study abroad; academic accommodation for the gifted, the musically talented, and the artistically talented.

College Admission Counseling 44 students graduated in 2010; all went to college, including Columbia University; Princeton University; Stanford University; University of Pennsylvania; Vanderbilt University; Williams College. Mean SAT critical reading: 670, mean SAT math: 650, mean SAT writing: 700.

Student Life Upper grades have uniform requirement, student council, honor system. Discipline rests equally with students and faculty.

Tuition and Aid Day student tuition: $32,615. Tuition installment plan (Key Tuition Payment Plan, monthly payment plans, individually arranged payment plans). Merit scholarship grants, need-based scholarship grants available. In 2010–11, 17% of upper-school students received aid; total upper-school merit-scholarship money awarded: $100,000. Total amount of financial aid awarded in 2010–11: $1,200,000.

Admissions Traditional secondary-level entrance grade is 9. For fall 2010, 100 students applied for upper-level admission, 30 were accepted, 20 enrolled. ERB, ISEE, Math Placement Exam or writing sample required. Deadline for receipt of application materials: none. Application fee required: $50. On-campus interview required.

Athletics Interscholastic: baseball (boys), basketball (b,g), cross-country running (b,g), field hockey (g), hockey (b), ice hockey (b), soccer (b,g), softball (g), swimming and diving (b,g), tennis (b,g), track and field (b,g), volleyball (b,g); intramural: aerobics (b,g), baseball (b), basketball (b,g), dance (b), ice hockey (b), indoor soccer

(b), running (b,g), skiing (downhill) (b,g), soccer (b,g), softball (g), swimming and diving (b,g), tennis (b,g), track and field (b,g), volleyball (b,g); coed interscholastic: cross-country running, golf, indoor track & field, lacrosse; coed intramural: bicycling, dance, golf, gymnastics, indoor track & field, skiing (cross-country), skiing (downhill). 5 PE instructors, 8 coaches.

Computers Computers are regularly used in all academic classes. Computer network features include on-campus library services, Internet access, wireless campus network, MOBY, Smartboard. Student e-mail accounts are available to students.

Contact Billie Williams, Admissions Coordinator. 212-861-0404. Fax: 212-879-3388. E-mail: bwilliams@bwl.org. Web site: www.bwl.org.

BISHOP ALEMANY HIGH SCHOOL

11111 North Alemany Drive
Mission Hills, California 91345
Head of School: Mr. Frank Ferry

General Information Coeducational day college-preparatory and religious studies school, affiliated with Roman Catholic Church. Grades 9–12. Founded: 1956. Setting: suburban. Nearest major city is Los Angeles. 22-acre campus. 5 buildings on campus. Approved or accredited by National Lutheran School Accreditation and Western Association of Schools and Colleges. Total enrollment: 1,624. Upper school average class size: 22. Upper school faculty-student ratio: 1:19.

Upper School Student Profile Grade 9: 411 students (230 boys, 181 girls); Grade 10: 469 students (245 boys, 224 girls); Grade 11: 388 students (199 boys, 189 girls); Grade 12: 356 students (166 boys, 190 girls). 88% of students are Roman Catholic.

Faculty School total: 85. In upper school: 41 men, 44 women; 51 have advanced degrees.

Subjects Offered Algebra, American history, American history-AP, American literature, anatomy, architecture, art, art history, athletics, Bible studies, biology, biology-AP, business, calculus, calculus-AP, ceramics, chemistry, chemistry-AP, computer programming, computer science, drafting, drama, earth science, economics, economics-AP, engineering, English, English literature, English-AP, ethics, European history, European history-AP, fine arts, French, geography, geometry, government-AP, government/civics, grammar, health, history, journalism, mathematics, music, philosophy, physical education, physics, physics-AP, physiology, psychology, religion, science, social studies, Spanish, Spanish language-AP, Spanish literature-AP, speech, theater, theology, trigonometry, typing, world history, world literature, writing.

Graduation Requirements Arts and fine arts (art, music, dance, drama), computer science, English, foreign language, mathematics, physical education (includes health), religion (includes Bible studies and theology), science, social studies (includes history).

Special Academic Programs Advanced Placement exam preparation; honors section; remedial reading and/or remedial writing; remedial math.

College Admission Counseling 317 students graduated in 2009; 305 went to college, including California State University, Northridge; Loyola Marymount University; University of California, Los Angeles; University of California, Santa Barbara. Other: 3 went to work, 3 entered military service, 6 had other specific plans.

Student Life Upper grades have uniform requirement, student council, honor system. Discipline rests primarily with faculty. Attendance at religious services is required.

Tuition and Aid Day student tuition: $7205. Tuition installment plan (FACTS Tuition Payment Plan). Tuition reduction for siblings, financial aid for Catholic students available. Total amount of financial aid awarded in 2009–10: $210,000.

Admissions Traditional secondary-level entrance grade is 9. For fall 2009, 600 students applied for upper-level admission, 505 were accepted, 500 enrolled. SAS, STS-HSPT required. Deadline for receipt of application materials: none. Application fee required: $60. Interview required.

Athletics Interscholastic: aquatics (boys, girls), baseball (b), basketball (b,g), cheering (b,g), cross-country running (b,g), drill team (g), football (b), golf (b,g), soccer (b,g), softball (g), swimming and diving (b,g), tennis (g), track and field (b,g), volleyball (b,g), water polo (b,g), wrestling (b); coed interscholastic: wrestling. 12 coaches, 1 athletic trainer.

Computers Computers are regularly used in newspaper, yearbook classes. Computer network features include on-campus library services, Internet access. Student e-mail accounts are available to students. Students grades are available online. The school has a published electronic and media policy.

Contact Mr. Bill Oates, Director, Community Outreach. 818-365-3925 Ext. 5222. Fax: 818-837-5390. Web site: www.alemany.org.

BISHOP BLANCHET HIGH SCHOOL

8200 Wallingford Avenue North
Seattle, Washington 98103-4599
Head of School: Kristine Ann Brynildsen-Smith, EdD

General Information Coeducational day college-preparatory, arts, religious studies, and technology school, affiliated with Roman Catholic Church. Grades 9–12. Founded: 1954. Setting: urban. 9-acre campus. 1 building on campus. Approved or accredited by National Catholic Education Association, Northwest Association of Schools and Colleges, and Washington Department of Education. Endowment: $5.5 million. Total enrollment: 1,036. Upper school average class size: 21. Upper school faculty-student ratio: 1:13. There are 180 required school days per year for Upper

Bishop Blanchet High School

School students. Upper School students typically attend 5 days per week. The average school day consists of 6 hours and 30 minutes.

Upper School Student Profile Grade 9: 276 students (153 boys, 123 girls); Grade 10: 241 students (128 boys, 113 girls); Grade 11: 252 students (136 boys, 116 girls); Grade 12: 225 students (130 boys, 95 girls). 82% of students are Roman Catholic.

Faculty School total: 78. In upper school: 33 men, 45 women; 45 have advanced degrees.

Subjects Offered 20th century American writers, 20th century world history, 3-dimensional design, American foreign policy, American history-AP, American literature, anatomy and physiology, applied arts, art, arts and crafts, ASB Leadership, band, biology, business applications, calculus, calculus-AP, Catholic belief and practice, ceramics, chamber groups, chemistry, chemistry-AP, choral music, comparative religion, contemporary history, desktop publishing, discrete mathematics, drama, drama performance, economics, English composition, English literature, ethics, ethnic literature, ethnic studies, European history, family living, French, German, government, guitar, health, history of rock and roll, history of the Catholic Church, instrumental music, Japanese, jazz band, language arts, Life of Christ, literature, marching band, math analysis, musical productions, performing arts, personal finance, philosophy, photography, physical education, physics, psychology, religion, scripture, set design, Spanish, U.S. history, vocal ensemble.

Graduation Requirements Art, business education, English, lab science, mathematics, physical education (includes health), religion (includes Bible studies and theology), social studies (includes history).

Special Academic Programs Advanced Placement exam preparation; honors section; study at local college for college credit; programs in general development for dyslexic students.

College Admission Counseling 259 students graduated in 2010; 256 went to college, including Gonzaga University; Seattle University; University of Portland; University of Washington; Washington State University; Western Washington University. Other: 3 went to work.

Student Life Upper grades have specified standards of dress, student council. Discipline rests primarily with faculty. Attendance at religious services is required.

Summer Programs Remediation programs offered; session focuses on students with learning needs; held on campus; accepts boys and girls; not open to students from other schools. 20 students usually enrolled. 2011 schedule: June 20 to July 22. Application deadline: May 6.

Tuition and Aid Day student tuition: $10,020. Tuition installment plan (monthly payment plans, individually arranged payment plans). Tuition reduction for siblings, merit scholarship grants, need-based scholarship grants, paying campus jobs available. In 2010–11, 50% of upper-school students received aid; total upper-school merit-scholarship money awarded: $50,000. Total amount of financial aid awarded in 2010–11: $1,500,000.

Admissions Traditional secondary-level entrance grade is 9. For fall 2010, 600 students applied for upper-level admission, 400 were accepted, 276 enrolled. ISEE required. Deadline for receipt of application materials: January 13. Application fee required: $25.

Athletics Interscholastic: baseball (boys), basketball (b,g), cheering (g), cross-country running (b,g), football (b), golf (b,g), lacrosse (b), soccer (b,g), softball (g), volleyball (g), wrestling (b); coed interscholastic: swimming and diving, tennis, track and field; coed intramural: alpine skiing, basketball, bowling, dance team, golf, hiking/backpacking, skiing (downhill), snowboarding, soccer, softball, strength & conditioning, table tennis, tennis, volleyball, weight lifting. 6 PE instructors, 1 athletic trainer.

Computers Computers are regularly used in accounting, business applications, business education, career exploration, college planning, computer applications, desktop publishing, foreign language, journalism, keyboarding, library skills, mathematics, newspaper, photography, science, video film production, word processing, yearbook classes. Computer network features include on-campus library services, online commercial services, Internet access, wireless campus network, Internet filtering or blocking technology. Campus intranet, student e-mail accounts, and computer access in designated common areas are available to students. Students grades are available online. The school has a published electronic and media policy.

Contact Ann Alokolaro, Director of Admissions. 206-527-7741. Fax: 206-527-7712. E-mail: aalokola@bishopblanchet.org. Web site: www.bishopblanchet.org.

BISHOP BRADY HIGH SCHOOL

25 Columbus Avenue
Concord, New Hampshire 03301
Head of School: Mr. Trevor Bonat

General Information Coeducational day college-preparatory school, affiliated with Roman Catholic Church. Grades 9–12. Founded: 1963. Setting: suburban. 8-acre campus. 1 building on campus. Approved or accredited by National Catholic Education Association, New England Association of Schools and Colleges, and New Hampshire Department of Education. Total enrollment: 365. Upper school average class size: 17. Upper school faculty-student ratio: 1:15. There are 180 required school days per year for Upper School students. Upper School students typically attend 5 days per week. The average school day consists of 6 hours and 30 minutes.

Upper School Student Profile Grade 9: 93 students (45 boys, 48 girls); Grade 10: 84 students (43 boys, 41 girls); Grade 11: 93 students (43 boys, 50 girls); Grade 12: 95 students (47 boys, 48 girls). 70% of students are Roman Catholic.

Faculty School total: 34. In upper school: 14 men, 20 women; 25 have advanced degrees.

Subjects Offered Advanced chemistry, advanced math, algebra, anatomy and physiology, art appreciation, arts, biology, biology-AP, calculus-AP, career/college preparation, chemistry, chemistry-AP, Christian scripture, civics, college awareness, college counseling, computer education, conceptual physics, drama, English, English literature-AP, English-AP, film studies, French-AP, freshman seminar, geometry, guidance, health education, history, history-AP, honors English, Latin, moral theology, music appreciation, musical theater, physical education, physics-AP, pre-calculus, probability and statistics, psychology, religious studies, research and reference, SAT preparation, social justice, Spanish-AP, theology, trigonometry, U.S. history-AP, world religions, writing.

Graduation Requirements Algebra, American literature, arts and fine arts (art, music, dance, drama), biology, chemistry, computer education, English, geometry, languages, physical education (includes health), science, social studies (includes history), theology, 90 hours of community service.

Special Academic Programs 8 Advanced Placement exams for which test preparation is offered; honors section; independent study; study at local college for college credit; academic accommodation for the gifted; ESL (21 students enrolled).

College Admission Counseling 90 students graduated in 2010; 87 went to college, including Boston College; McGill University; Providence College; Saint Anselm College; University of New Hampshire. Other: 2 went to work, 1 entered military service. Mean SAT critical reading: 556, mean SAT math: 544, mean SAT writing: 552, mean composite ACT: 25. 30% scored over 600 on SAT critical reading, 30% scored over 600 on SAT math.

Student Life Upper grades have specified standards of dress, student council, honor system. Discipline rests primarily with faculty. Attendance at religious services is required.

Summer Programs Remediation, sports programs offered; session focuses on football and conditioning, mathematics, study skills; held on campus; accepts boys and girls; open to students from other schools. 60 students usually enrolled. 2011 schedule: June 20 to August 15.

Tuition and Aid Day student tuition: $8600. Tuition installment plan (Insured Tuition Payment Plan, monthly payment plans, individually arranged payment plans). Tuition reduction for siblings, merit scholarship grants, need-based scholarship grants available. In 2010–11, 25% of upper-school students received aid.

Admissions Traditional secondary-level entrance grade is 9. For fall 2010, 135 students applied for upper-level admission, 130 were accepted, 93 enrolled. ACT-Explore and SSAT required. Deadline for receipt of application materials: June 15. Application fee required: $25. Interview required.

Athletics Interscholastic: alpine skiing (boys, girls), baseball (b), basketball (b,g), cheering (g), cross-country running (b,g), field hockey (g), football (b), golf (b,g), hockey (b), ice hockey (b), indoor track (b,g), lacrosse (b,g), skiing (downhill) (b,g), soccer (b,g), softball (g), tennis (b,g), track and field (b,g); intramural: basketball (b,g); coed interscholastic: equestrian sports, juggling, outdoor activities, outdoor adventure; coed intramural: basketball, indoor track, outdoor activities, outdoor adventure, rock climbing, skiing (cross-country), skiing (downhill), snowboarding, strength & conditioning, table tennis, volleyball, weight lifting, weight training. 1 PE instructor.

Computers Computers are regularly used in business applications, college planning, journalism, literary magazine, newspaper classes. Computer network features include on-campus library services, online commercial services, Internet access, wireless campus network, Internet filtering or blocking technology. Student e-mail accounts and computer access in designated common areas are available to students. Students grades are available online. The school has a published electronic and media policy.

Contact Mrs. Lonna J. Abbott, Director of Admissions and Enrollment. 603-224-7419. Fax: 603-228-6664. E-mail: labbott@bishopbrady.edu. Web site: www.bishopbrady.edu.

BISHOP CONATY-OUR LADY OF LORETTO HIGH SCHOOL

2900 West Pico Boulevard
Los Angeles, California 90006
Head of School: Mr. Richard A. Spicer

General Information Girls' day college-preparatory, general academic, arts, religious studies, and technology school, affiliated with Roman Catholic Church. Grades 9–12. Founded: 1923. Setting: urban. 3-acre campus. 2 buildings on campus. Approved or accredited by National Catholic Education Association, The College Board, Western Catholic Education Association, and California Department of Education. Candidate for accreditation by Western Association of Schools and Colleges. Endowment: $707,799. Total enrollment: 313. Upper school average class size: 21. Upper school faculty-student ratio: 1:15. There are 182 required school days per year for Upper School students. Upper School students typically attend 5 days per week. The average school day consists of 4 hours and 30 minutes.

Upper School Student Profile Grade 9: 86 students (86 girls); Grade 10: 88 students (88 girls); Grade 11: 71 students (71 girls); Grade 12: 68 students (68 girls). 91% of students are Roman Catholic.

Faculty School total: 21. In upper school: 8 men, 13 women; 18 have advanced degrees.

Subjects Offered Aerobics, algebra, American literature, anatomy and physiology, athletics, biology, British literature, Catholic belief and practice, ceramics, chemistry, Christian and Hebrew scripture, computer literacy, dance performance, drama, drawing, drawing and design, economics, English, French, geometry, government, government-AP, health, honors algebra, honors English, honors geometry, honors U.S. history, honors world history, integrated science, moral reasoning, music, painting, physical education, physics, pre-calculus, religion, social justice, Spanish, Spanish language-AP, Spanish literature-AP, trigonometry, U.S. history, video film production, visual arts, Web site design, world history, world religions, world religions, yearbook.

Graduation Requirements Arts and fine arts (art, music, dance, drama), computer science, English, foreign language, health education, mathematics, physical education (includes health), religion (includes Bible studies and theology), science, social studies (includes history), 100 hours of community service, senior project.

Special Academic Programs 4 Advanced Placement exams for which test preparation is offered; honors section; remedial reading and/or remedial writing; remedial math.

College Admission Counseling 73 students graduated in 2010; 67 went to college, including California State University, Los Angeles; California State University, Northridge; El Camino College; Mt. San Antonio College; Santa Monica College; University of La Verne. Other: 1 went to work, 5 had other specific plans. Median SAT critical reading: 430, median SAT math: 410, median SAT writing: 450, median combined SAT: 1300, median composite ACT: 21. 3% scored over 600 on SAT math.

Student Life Upper grades have uniform requirement, student council, honor system. Discipline rests primarily with faculty. Attendance at religious services is required.

Summer Programs Remediation, enrichment, advancement, art/fine arts, computer instruction programs offered; session focuses on make-up courses and strengthening incoming freshmen skills; held on campus; accepts boys and girls; open to students from other schools. 195 students usually enrolled. 2011 schedule: June 20 to July 22. Application deadline: June 15.

Tuition and Aid Day student tuition: $5995–$6450. Tuition installment plan (monthly payment plans, individually arranged payment plans). Tuition reduction for siblings, need-based scholarship grants, paying campus jobs available. In 2010–11, 86% of upper-school students received aid. Total amount of financial aid awarded in 2010–11: $616,223.

Admissions Traditional secondary-level entrance grade is 9. For fall 2010, 115 students applied for upper-level admission, 109 were accepted, 86 enrolled. High School Placement Test required. Deadline for receipt of application materials: August 15. Application fee required: $25. On-campus interview required.

Athletics Interscholastic: basketball, cross-country running, soccer, softball, volleyball. 6 coaches.

Computers Computers are regularly used in computer applications, video film production, Web site design, yearbook classes. Computer network features include on-campus library services, Internet access, Internet filtering or blocking technology. Students grades are available online. The school has a published electronic and media policy.

Contact Sr. Harriet Stellern, Director of Admissions. 323-737-0012 Ext. 103. Fax: 323-737-1749. E-mail: hstellern@bishopconatyloretto.org. Web site: www.bishopconatyloretto.org.

BISHOP CONNOLLY HIGH SCHOOL

373 Elsbree Street
Fall River, Massachusetts 02720
Head of School: Mr. Christopher Myron

General Information Coeducational day college-preparatory and religious studies school, affiliated with Roman Catholic Church. Grades 9–12. Founded: 1966. Setting: suburban. Nearest major city is Providence, RI. 72-acre campus. 1 building on campus. Approved or accredited by New England Association of Schools and Colleges and Massachusetts Department of Education. Total enrollment: 300. Upper school average class size: 18. Upper school faculty-student ratio: 1:16. There are 185 required school days per year for Upper School students. Upper School students typically attend 5 days per week. The average school day consists of 6 hours and 30 minutes.

Upper School Student Profile 90% of students are Roman Catholic.

Faculty School total: 30. In upper school: 18 men, 12 women; 22 have advanced degrees.

Subjects Offered Advanced Placement courses, algebra, American literature, American studies, anatomy and physiology, art, art history, Bible studies, biology, biology-AP, British literature, British literature (honors), calculus, calculus-AP, campus ministry, chemistry, chemistry-AP, choir, chorus, community service, computer programming, creative writing, desktop publishing, drama, English, English literature, English-AP, environmental science, European history-AP, French, French-AP, geometry, health, history, honors algebra, honors English, honors geometry, honors U.S. history, honors world history, human biology, instrumental music, keyboarding, math analysis, mathematics, music, music history, music theory, physical education, physics, Portuguese, psychology, religion, science, social studies, Spanish, theology, trigonometry, U.S. history-AP, world history, world literature.

Graduation Requirements English, foreign language, mathematics, religion (includes Bible studies and theology), science, social studies (includes history). Community service is required.

Special Academic Programs Advanced Placement exam preparation; honors section; independent study; study at local college for college credit.

College Admission Counseling 108 students graduated in 2010; they went to Bridgewater State University; Northeastern University; Providence College; Quinnipiac University; University of Massachusetts Dartmouth; University of Rhode Island. Mean SAT critical reading: 525, mean SAT math: 471. 13% scored over 600 on SAT critical reading, 11% scored over 600 on SAT math.

Student Life Upper grades have uniform requirement, student council. Discipline rests primarily with faculty. Attendance at religious services is required.

Tuition and Aid Day student tuition: $7600. Tuition installment plan (FACTS Tuition Payment Plan, monthly payment plans). Merit scholarship grants, need-based scholarship grants available. In 2010–11, 33% of upper-school students received aid.

Admissions Traditional secondary-level entrance grade is 9. High School Placement Test required. Deadline for receipt of application materials: none. No application fee required. Interview recommended.

Athletics Interscholastic: baseball (boys), basketball (b,g), cheering (b,g), cross-country running (b,g), football (b), ice hockey (b), lacrosse (b), soccer (b,g), softball (g), tennis (b,g), track and field (b,g), volleyball (g), winter (indoor) track (b,g); intramural: field hockey (g); coed interscholastic: golf, indoor soccer, indoor track & field. 2 PE instructors, 32 coaches, 1 athletic trainer.

Computers Computers are regularly used in all classes. Computer network features include online commercial services, Internet access, wireless campus network, Internet filtering or blocking technology. Computer access in designated common areas is available to students. The school has a published electronic and media policy.

Contact Mr. Anthony C. Ciampanelli, Director of Admissions/Alumni. 508-676-1071 Ext. 333. Fax: 508-676-8594. E-mail: aciampanelli@bishopconnolly.com. Web site: www.bishopconnolly.com.

BISHOP DENIS J. O'CONNELL HIGH SCHOOL

6600 Little Falls Road
Arlington, Virginia 22213
Head of School: Mrs. Katy Prebble

General Information Coeducational day college-preparatory, arts, business, religious studies, bilingual studies, and technology school, affiliated with Roman Catholic Church. Grades 9–12. Founded: 1957. Setting: suburban. Nearest major city is Washington, DC. 28-acre campus. 1 building on campus. Approved or accredited by National Catholic Education Association, Southern Association of Colleges and Schools, Southern Association of Independent Schools, Virginia Association of Independent Schools, and Virginia Department of Education. Member of Secondary School Admission Test Board. Total enrollment: 1,219. Upper school average class size: 21. Upper school faculty-student ratio: 1:12. Upper School students typically attend 5 days per week. The average school day consists of 6 hours and 50 minutes.

Upper School Student Profile Grade 9: 293 students (150 boys, 143 girls); Grade 10: 308 students (160 boys, 148 girls); Grade 11: 283 students (140 boys, 143 girls); Grade 12: 335 students (148 boys, 187 girls). 90% of students are Roman Catholic.

Faculty School total: 105.

Subjects Offered Accounting, algebra, American history, American literature, analysis, art, art history, athletic training, Basic programming, Bible studies, biology, biology-AP, business, calculus, calculus-AP, chemistry, chemistry-AP, choir, choral music, chorus, comparative government and politics-AP, computer graphics, computer multimedia, computer programming, computer science, computer science-AP, computer skills, creative writing, digital art, dramatic arts, driver education, earth science, East Asian history, economics, English, English language-AP, English literature, English literature-AP, environmental science-AP, European history, European history-AP, fine arts, forensics, French, French language-AP, geography, geometry, German, German-AP, government-AP, government/civics, guitar, health, history, honors English, honors geometry, honors U.S. history, honors world history, introduction to theater, Italian, jazz band, journalism, Latin, macroeconomics-AP, marketing, mathematics, media arts, microeconomics-AP, modern European history-AP, music, music theory-AP, New Testament, physical education, physics, physics-AP, piano, psychology-AP, public speaking, religion, remedial study skills, science, social sciences, social studies, sociology, Spanish, Spanish language-AP, Spanish literature-AP, speech, sports conditioning, statistics-AP, studio art-AP, theology, trigonometry, U.S. and Virginia history, U.S. government, U.S. history, U.S. history-AP, United States government-AP, voice ensemble, Web site design, world history, world literature.

Graduation Requirements Arts and fine arts (art, music, dance, drama), computer science, English, foreign language, mathematics, physical education (includes health), religion (includes Bible studies and theology), science, social sciences, social studies (includes history), community service program incorporated into graduation requirements.

Special Academic Programs Advanced Placement exam preparation; honors section; study at local college for college credit; academic accommodation for the gifted; remedial math; programs in general development for dyslexic students.

College Admission Counseling 330 students graduated in 2010; 327 went to college, including George Mason University; James Madison University; The College of William and Mary; University of Mary Washington; University of Virginia; Virginia

Bishop Denis J. O'Connell High School

Polytechnic Institute and State University. Other: 1 went to work, 1 entered military service, 1 entered a postgraduate year. Median SAT critical reading: 565, median SAT math: 551, median SAT writing: 559.

Student Life Upper grades have uniform requirement, student council, honor system. Discipline rests equally with students and faculty. Attendance at religious services is required.

Summer Programs Remediation, enrichment, advancement, sports, art/fine arts, computer instruction programs offered; held on campus; accepts boys and girls; open to students from other schools. 220 students usually enrolled. 2011 schedule: June 15 to August 15. Application deadline: none.

Tuition and Aid Day student tuition: $9995–$14,665. Tuition installment plan (FACTS Tuition Payment Plan). Tuition reduction for siblings, merit scholarship grants, need-based scholarship grants, scholarship competition only for eighth graders currently enrolled in a Diocese of Arlington Catholic school available. In 2010–11, 20% of upper-school students received aid; total upper-school merit-scholarship money awarded: $30,000. Total amount of financial aid awarded in 2010–11: $1,400,000.

Admissions High School Placement Test required. Deadline for receipt of application materials: January 24. Application fee required: $50.

Athletics Interscholastic: baseball (boys), basketball (b,g), crew (b,g), cross-country running (b,g), dance team (g), diving (b,g), football (b), ice hockey (b), lacrosse (b,g), soccer (b,g), softball (g), swimming and diving (b,g), tennis (b,g), track and field (b,g), volleyball (g), wrestling (b); intramural: basketball (b,g), weight lifting (b,g); coed interscholastic: golf, sailing; coed intramural: crew, flag football, softball, ultimate Frisbee, volleyball. 7 PE instructors, 7 coaches, 1 athletic trainer.

Computers Computers are regularly used in art, business, computer applications, English, foreign language, health, history, mathematics, science, social sciences classes. Computer network features include on-campus library services, online commercial services, Internet access, Internet filtering or blocking technology. Computer access in designated common areas is available to students. Students grades are available online. The school has a published electronic and media policy.

Contact Mrs. Mary McAlevy, Director of Admissions. 703-237-1433. Fax: 703-241-9066. E-mail: mmcalevy@bishopoconnell.org. Web site: www.bishopoconnell.org.

BISHOP DUNNE HIGH SCHOOL
3900 Rugged Drive
Dallas, Texas 75224
Head of School: Kate C. Dailey

General Information Coeducational day college-preparatory, arts, religious studies, technology, and writing school, affiliated with Roman Catholic Church. Grades 6–12. Founded: 1961. Setting: urban. 21-acre campus. 5 buildings on campus. Approved or accredited by Independent Schools Association of the Southwest, Texas Catholic Conference, and Texas Department of Education. Endowment: $100,000. Total enrollment: 613. Upper school average class size: 22. Upper school faculty-student ratio: 1:13. There are 190 required school days per year for Upper School students. Upper School students typically attend 5 days per week. The average school day consists of 6 hours and 30 minutes.

Upper School Student Profile Grade 9: 122 students (66 boys, 56 girls); Grade 10: 114 students (55 boys, 59 girls); Grade 11: 106 students (63 boys, 43 girls); Grade 12: 104 students (53 boys, 51 girls). 70% of students are Roman Catholic.

Faculty School total: 67. In upper school: 33 men, 34 women; 15 have advanced degrees.

Subjects Offered ACT preparation, Advanced Placement courses, algebra, American history, American literature, anatomy, art, art history, band, biology, broadcast journalism, calculus, calculus-AP, ceramics, chemistry, chemistry-AP, community service, computer programming, computer science, drama, economics, English, English language and composition-AP, English literature, English literature and composition-AP, environmental science, European history, European history-AP, film, fine arts, French, French language-AP, geography, geometry, government-AP, government/civics, grammar, graphics, health, history, history-AP, journalism, Latin, Latin-AP, mathematics, microeconomics-AP, music, physical education, physics, psychology, SAT preparation, science, social sciences, social studies, Spanish, Spanish language-AP, Spanish literature-AP, speech, sports, statistics-AP, studio art-AP, theater arts, theology, U.S. history-AP, world history, world literature, writing, yearbook.

Graduation Requirements Arts and fine arts (art, music, dance, drama), economics, English, foreign language, mathematics, physical education (includes health), religion (includes Bible studies and theology), science, social studies (includes history), speech, technology, U.S. government, U.S. history. Community service is required.

Special Academic Programs 19 Advanced Placement exams for which test preparation is offered; honors section; study at local college for college credit; programs in English, mathematics for dyslexic students.

College Admission Counseling 104 students graduated in 2009; 100 went to college, including Baylor University; St. Edward's University; Texas A&M University; Texas State University–San Marcos; University of Dallas; University of North Texas. Mean SAT critical reading: 513, mean SAT math: 482, mean composite ACT: 21. 16% scored over 600 on SAT critical reading, 12% scored over 600 on SAT math, 15% scored over 26 on composite ACT.

Student Life Upper grades have uniform requirement, student council, honor system. Discipline rests primarily with faculty. Attendance at religious services is required.

Tuition and Aid Day student tuition: $9500. Tuition installment plan (monthly payment plans, individually arranged payment plans, Texas Catholic Credit Union). Tuition reduction for siblings, merit scholarship grants, need-based scholarship grants available. In 2009–10, 60% of upper-school students received aid; total upper-school merit-scholarship money awarded: $31,900. Total amount of financial aid awarded in 2009–10: $800,000.

Admissions Traditional secondary-level entrance grade is 9. For fall 2009, 193 students applied for upper-level admission, 144 were accepted, 109 enrolled. ISEE required. Deadline for receipt of application materials: January 31. Application fee required: $125. On-campus interview required.

Athletics Interscholastic: baseball (boys), basketball (b,g), cross-country running (b,g), dance team (g), drill team (g), football (b), golf (b,g), rugby (b), soccer (b,g), softball (g), swimming and diving (b,g), tennis (b,g), track and field (b,g), volleyball (g), wrestling (b,g); coed interscholastic: cheering; coed intramural: strength & conditioning, weight lifting, yoga. 4 PE instructors, 8 coaches, 1 athletic trainer.

Computers Computers are regularly used in desktop publishing, economics, English, foreign language, geography, history, Latin, mathematics, multimedia, newspaper, religion, science, social sciences, social studies, Spanish, theology, yearbook classes. Computer network features include on-campus library services, online commercial services, Internet access, wireless campus network, Internet filtering or blocking technology. Student e-mail accounts are available to students. Students grades are available online. The school has a published electronic and media policy.

Contact Mr. Richard Mullin, Director of Admission. 214-339-6561 Ext. 230. Fax: 214-339-1438. E-mail: rmullin@bdhs.org. Web site: www.bdhs.org.

BISHOP EUSTACE PREPARATORY SCHOOL
5552 Route 70
Pennsauken, New Jersey 08109-4798
Head of School: Br. James Beamesderfer, SAC

General Information Coeducational day college-preparatory, arts, religious studies, and technology school, affiliated with Roman Catholic Church. Grades 9–12. Founded: 1954. Setting: suburban. Nearest major city is Philadelphia, PA. 32-acre campus. 7 buildings on campus. Approved or accredited by Middle States Association of Colleges and Schools and New Jersey Department of Education. Endowment: $3.3 million. Total enrollment: 767. Upper school average class size: 21. Upper school faculty-student ratio: 1:13. There are 169 required school days per year for Upper School students. Upper School students typically attend 5 days per week. The average school day consists of 6 hours and 20 minutes.

Upper School Student Profile 88% of students are Roman Catholic.

Faculty School total: 60. In upper school: 28 men, 32 women; 44 have advanced degrees.

Subjects Offered Advanced chemistry, advanced computer applications, Advanced Placement courses, algebra, American history, American history-AP, American literature, anatomy, anatomy and physiology, applied music, art and culture, art history, band, Bible studies, biology, biology-AP, British literature, British literature (honors), calculus, calculus-AP, campus ministry, career education, career exploration, career/college preparation, chemistry, chemistry-AP, choir, Christian doctrine, Christian education, Christian ethics, Christian scripture, clinical chemistry, college counseling, college placement, college planning, comparative religion, computer education, computer science, creative writing, driver education, economics and history, electives, English, English literature, English literature and composition-AP, environmental science, environmental science-AP, ethics, European history-AP, film, film and literature, fine arts, French, French as a second language, gender issues, genetics, geometry, German, government and politics-AP, government/civics, grammar, health, history, honors algebra, honors English, honors geometry, honors U.S. history, honors world history, instrumental music, journalism, Latin, law, law studies, macroeconomics-AP, mathematics, mathematics-AP, music, music composition, music history, music theory, music theory-AP, physical education, physical science, physics, physics-AP, physiology, pre-calculus, psychology, psychology-AP, science, sex education, social studies, sociology, Spanish, Spanish-AP, statistics-AP, theology, trigonometry, U.S. government and politics-AP, U.S. history, U.S. history-AP, vocal music, women's studies, world affairs, world history, world religions.

Graduation Requirements Arts and fine arts (art, music, dance, drama), career exploration, computer science, English, foreign language, mathematics, physical education (includes health), religion (includes Bible studies and theology), science, social studies (includes history). Community service is required.

Special Academic Programs 15 Advanced Placement exams for which test preparation is offered; honors section; independent study; study at local college for college credit; academic accommodation for the gifted and the musically talented.

College Admission Counseling 185 students graduated in 2010; 183 went to college, including Drexel University; La Salle University; Northeastern University; Saint Joseph's University; The Catholic University of America; University of Delaware. Other: 2 had other specific plans. 40% scored over 600 on SAT critical reading, 37% scored over 600 on SAT math, 36% scored over 600 on SAT writing.

Student Life Upper grades have uniform requirement, student council, honor system. Discipline rests primarily with faculty. Attendance at religious services is required.

Summer Programs Enrichment, advancement, sports programs offered; session focuses on student recruitment and enrichment; held on campus; accepts boys and girls; open to students from other schools. 150 students usually enrolled. 2011 schedule: June 20 to August 4. Application deadline: June 15.

Tuition and Aid Day student tuition: $14,500. Tuition installment plan (FACTS Tuition Payment Plan). Merit scholarship grants, need-based scholarship grants available. In 2010–11, 35% of upper-school students received aid; total upper-school merit-scholarship money awarded: $261,000. Total amount of financial aid awarded in 2010–11: $550,000.

Admissions Traditional secondary-level entrance grade is 9. Common entrance examinations, math and English placement tests or placement test required. Deadline for receipt of application materials: none. Application fee required: $60.

Athletics Interscholastic: baseball (boys), basketball (b,g), bowling (b,g), cheering (g), crew (b,g), cross-country running (b,g), field hockey (g), football (b), ice hockey (b), indoor track & field (b,g), lacrosse (b,g), running (b,g), soccer (b,g), softball (g), swimming and diving (b,g), tennis (b,g), track and field (b,g); coed interscholastic: aquatics, diving, golf. 3 PE instructors, 61 coaches, 1 athletic trainer.

Computers Computers are regularly used in all academic classes. Computer network features include on-campus library services, online commercial services, Internet access, wireless campus network, Internet filtering or blocking technology. Campus intranet and computer access in designated common areas are available to students. Students grades are available online. The school has a published electronic and media policy.

Contact Mr. Nicholas Italiano, Director of Institutional Advancement. 856-662-2160 Ext. 252. Fax: 856-665-2184. E-mail: nitaliano@eustace.org. Web site: www.eustace.org.

BISHOP FEEHAN HIGH SCHOOL
70 Holcott Drive
Attleboro, Massachusetts 02703
Head of School: Mr. Christopher E. Servant

General Information Coeducational day college-preparatory, arts, and religious studies school, affiliated with Roman Catholic Church. Grades 9–12. Founded: 1961. Setting: suburban. Nearest major city is Providence, RI. 25-acre campus. 4 buildings on campus. Approved or accredited by National Catholic Education Association, New England Association of Schools and Colleges, and Massachusetts Department of Education. Total enrollment: 1,050. Upper school average class size: 17. Upper school faculty-student ratio: 1:13.

Upper School Student Profile Grade 9: 286 students (120 boys, 166 girls); Grade 10: 278 students (132 boys, 146 girls); Grade 11: 239 students (114 boys, 125 girls); Grade 12: 245 students (99 boys, 146 girls). 90% of students are Roman Catholic.

Faculty School total: 95. In upper school: 35 men, 60 women; 52 have advanced degrees.

Subjects Offered Advanced chemistry, algebra, American literature, analytic geometry, anatomy and physiology, Arabic, art, art history, Bible studies, bioethics, biology, biology-AP, British literature, British literature (honors), business applications, business law, calculus, calculus-AP, campus ministry, Catholic belief and practice, chemistry, chemistry-AP, choir, choral music, chorus, Christian and Hebrew scripture, Christian doctrine, Christian education, Christian ethics, Christian studies, Christian testament, Christianity, college counseling, college planning, composition, computer animation, computer applications, computer graphics, computer programming, conceptual physics, concert band, concert choir, dance, drama, drama workshop, drawing, driver education, earth science, ecology, environmental systems, economics, English, English composition, English language and composition-AP, English literature and composition-AP, environmental science, European history, French, genetics, geometry, government and politics-AP, guidance, health and wellness, history of the Catholic Church, honors algebra, honors English, honors geometry, honors U.S. history, honors world history, integrated mathematics, jazz ensemble, keyboarding, lab science, Latin, Mandarin, music theory, mythology, oral communications, physical education, physics, pre-calculus, probability and statistics, psychology, psychology-AP, SAT preparation, Shakespeare, sign language, sociology, Spanish, Spanish language-AP, statistics, statistics-AP, studio art-AP, theater arts, theology, U.S. history, U.S. history-AP, Web site design, word processing, world religions.

Graduation Requirements Biology, career education, chemistry, electives, English, foreign language, mathematics, physics, research skills, SAT preparation, science, study skills, theology, U.S. history, word processing, world history.

Special Academic Programs Advanced Placement exam preparation; honors section.

College Admission Counseling 252 students graduated in 2009; 251 went to college, including Assumption College; Merrimack College; Providence College; Stonehill College; University of Massachusetts Amherst; University of Rhode Island. Other: 1 went to work. Mean SAT critical reading: 570, mean SAT math: 571, mean SAT writing: 573, mean composite ACT: 24.

Student Life Upper grades have uniform requirement, student council. Discipline rests primarily with faculty. Attendance at religious services is required.

Tuition and Aid Day student tuition: $8150. Tuition installment plan (FACTS Tuition Payment Plan). Merit scholarship grants, need-based scholarship grants available. In 2009–10, 20% of upper-school students received aid; total upper-school merit-scholarship money awarded: $10,000. Total amount of financial aid awarded in 2009–10: $400,000.

Admissions Traditional secondary-level entrance grade is 10. For fall 2009, 535 students applied for upper-level admission, 300 were accepted, 280 enrolled.

Scholastic Testing Service High School Placement Test required. Deadline for receipt of application materials: December 17. No application fee required. Interview required.

Athletics Interscholastic: baseball (boys), basketball (b,g), cheering (g), diving (b,g), football (b), indoor track & field (b,g), lacrosse (b,g), soccer (b,g), softball (g), swimming and diving (b,g), tennis (b,g), track and field (b,g), volleyball (g); intramural: ice skating (g); coed interscholastic: cross-country running, dance, dance squad, fencing, golf, ice hockey; coed intramural: fencing. 2 PE instructors, 30 coaches, 1 athletic trainer.

Computers Computers are regularly used in all classes. Computer network features include on-campus library services, Internet access, wireless campus network, Internet filtering or blocking technology. Campus intranet and computer access in designated common areas are available to students. Students grades are available online. The school has a published electronic and media policy.

Contact Lynn Gale, Admissions Assistant. 508-226-6223 Ext. 119. Fax: 508-226-7696. E-mail: lgale@bishopfeehan.com. Web site: www.bishopfeehan.com.

BISHOP FENWICK HIGH SCHOOL
4855 State Route 122
Franklin, Ohio 45005
Head of School: Mr. Michael Miller

General Information Coeducational day college-preparatory, arts, and religious studies school, affiliated with Roman Catholic Church. Grades 9–12. Founded: 1952. Setting: small town. Nearest major city is Cincinnati. 66-acre campus. 1 building on campus. Approved or accredited by National Catholic Education Association, North Central Association of Colleges and Schools, Ohio Catholic Schools Accreditation Association (OCSAA), and Ohio Department of Education. Upper school average class size: 24. Upper school faculty-student ratio: 1:15. There are 184 required school days per year for Upper School students. Upper School students typically attend 5 days per week. The average school day consists of 6 hours and 35 minutes.

Upper School Student Profile Grade 9: 163 students (95 boys, 68 girls); Grade 10: 127 students (62 boys, 65 girls); Grade 11: 129 students (61 boys, 68 girls); Grade 12: 139 students (84 boys, 55 girls). 85% of students are Roman Catholic.

Faculty School total: 38. In upper school: 20 men, 18 women; 21 have advanced degrees.

Subjects Offered Accounting, ACT preparation, algebra, American democracy, art, art-AP, athletic training, biology, botany, calculus-AP, cell biology, chemistry, computer graphics, computer programming, concert band, creative writing, economics, English, English-AP, ensembles, fine arts, French, functions, general business, geometry, government, government/civics-AP, health, honors algebra, honors English, honors geometry, integrated mathematics, jazz band, Latin, Latin-AP, leadership, marching band, mathematics, multimedia, music appreciation, mythology, physical education, physical science, physics, physiology, portfolio art, pre-algebra, psychology, publications, religion, science, social studies, Spanish, statistics, study skills, technology, theater, theater arts, trigonometry, U.S. history, U.S. history-AP, Web site design, world geography, world history, writing, yearbook, zoology.

Graduation Requirements Arts and fine arts (art, music, dance, drama), English, foreign language, mathematics, religion (includes Bible studies and theology), science, social studies (includes history), community service, retreats, pass the Ohio Graduation Test.

Special Academic Programs Advanced Placement exam preparation; honors section; study at local college for college credit; special instructional classes for deaf students.

College Admission Counseling 130 students graduated in 2010; 125 went to college, including Miami University; Ohio University; The Ohio State University; University of Cincinnati; University of Dayton; Xavier University. Other: 5 went to work. Median SAT critical reading: 560, median SAT math: 560, median SAT writing: 540, median combined SAT: 1680. Mean composite ACT: 25. 38.5% scored over 600 on SAT critical reading, 32.8% scored over 600 on SAT math, 30% scored over 600 on SAT writing, 28.5% scored over 1800 on combined SAT, 34% scored over 26 on composite ACT.

Student Life Upper grades have uniform requirement, student council, honor system. Discipline rests primarily with faculty. Attendance at religious services is required.

Tuition and Aid Day student tuition: $7400. Tuition installment plan (TMS). Tuition reduction for siblings, merit scholarship grants, need-based scholarship grants available. In 2010–11, 11% of upper-school students received aid.

Admissions Traditional secondary-level entrance grade is 9. High School Placement Test required. Deadline for receipt of application materials: none. Application fee required: $400.

Athletics Interscholastic: baseball (boys), basketball (b,g), cheering (g), cross-country running (b,g), dance team (g), football (b), golf (b,g), lacrosse (b,g), soccer (b,g), softball (g), tennis (b,g), volleyball (b,g), weight training (b,g), wrestling (b); intramural: basketball (b), weight training (b,g); coed interscholastic: bowling, in-line hockey, roller hockey, swimming and diving, track and field; coed intramural: freestyle skiing, paint ball, skiing (downhill), snowboarding. 52 coaches.

Computers Computers are regularly used in graphic arts, graphic design, introduction to technology, multimedia, photography, publications, technology, video film production, Web site design, yearbook classes. Computer network features include on-campus library services, Internet access, wireless campus network, Internet

filtering or blocking technology. Campus intranet, student e-mail accounts, and computer access in designated common areas are available to students. Students grades are available online. The school has a published electronic and media policy.
Contact Mrs. Betty Turvy, Director of Admissions. 513-428-0525. Fax: 513-727-1501. E-mail: bturvy@fenwickfalcons.org. Web site: www.fenwickfalcons.org.

BISHOP GARCIA DIEGO HIGH SCHOOL

4000 La Colina Road
Santa Barbara, California 93110-1496
Head of School: Rev. Fr. Thomas J. Elewaut

General Information Coeducational day and distance learning college-preparatory, arts, religious studies, and technology school, affiliated with Roman Catholic Church; primarily serves students with learning disabilities, individuals with Attention Deficit Disorder, and dyslexic students. Grades 9–12. Distance learning grades 9–12. Founded: 1959. Setting: small town. Nearest major city is Los Angeles. 16-acre campus. 10 buildings on campus. Approved or accredited by California Association of Independent Schools, National Catholic Education Association, Western Association of Schools and Colleges, Western Catholic Education Association, and California Department of Education. Endowment: $250,000. Total enrollment: 307. Upper school average class size: 18. Upper school faculty-student ratio: 1:12.
Upper School Student Profile Grade 9: 77 students (38 boys, 39 girls); Grade 10: 85 students (44 boys, 41 girls); Grade 11: 73 students (38 boys, 35 girls); Grade 12: 65 students (30 boys, 35 girls). 80% of students are Roman Catholic.
Faculty School total: 31. In upper school: 15 men, 16 women; 21 have advanced degrees.
Subjects Offered Algebra, American history-AP, American literature, anatomy, arts, band, biology, calculus, calculus-AP, ceramics, chemistry, chemistry-AP, chorus, community service, composition, computer science, dance, economics, English, English literature, English-AP, fine arts, fitness, French, French-AP, geometry, government-AP, history-AP, humanities, mathematics, music, physical education, physical science, physics, physics-AP, psychology, religion, science, Shakespeare, social sciences, social studies, Spanish, Spanish-AP, speech, statistics-AP, U.S. government and politics-AP, weight training, world history, world literature, yearbook.
Graduation Requirements Arts and fine arts (art, music, dance, drama), computer science, English, foreign language, mathematics, physical education (includes health), religion (includes Bible studies and theology), science, social sciences, social studies (includes history), CAP portfolio. Community service is required.
Special Academic Programs Advanced Placement exam preparation; honors section; independent study; study at local college for college credit; remedial reading and/or remedial writing; remedial math; programs in English, mathematics, general development for dyslexic students.
College Admission Counseling 63 students graduated in 2009; all went to college, including Loyola Marymount University; Santa Barbara City College; University of California, Santa Barbara; University of San Diego. 31% scored over 600 on SAT critical reading, 37% scored over 600 on SAT math, 28% scored over 600 on SAT writing, 36% scored over 26 on composite ACT.
Student Life Upper grades have specified standards of dress, student council. Discipline rests primarily with faculty. Attendance at religious services is required.
Tuition and Aid Day student tuition: $12,200. Guaranteed tuition plan. Tuition installment plan (FACTS Tuition Payment Plan, annual and semiannual payment plan). Need-based scholarship grants, paying campus jobs available. In 2009–10, 60% of upper-school students received aid. Total amount of financial aid awarded in 2009–10: $940,000.
Admissions Traditional secondary-level entrance grade is 9. For fall 2009, 131 students applied for upper-level admission, 105 were accepted, 77 enrolled. High School Placement Test or High School Placement Test (closed version) from Scholastic Testing Service required. Deadline for receipt of application materials: none. Application fee required: $50. On-campus interview recommended.
Athletics Interscholastic: baseball (boys), basketball (b,g), cheering (g), cross-country running (b,g), football (b), golf (b,g), soccer (b,g), softball (g), tennis (b,g), track and field (b,g), volleyball (b,g), wrestling (b); intramural: physical fitness (b,g), physical training (b,g), power lifting (b,g), weight lifting (b,g), weight training (b,g); coed intramural: bicycling, crew, martial arts, mountain biking, physical fitness, physical training, power lifting, ropes courses, weight lifting, weight training. 2 PE instructors, 25 coaches, 1 athletic trainer.
Computers Computers are regularly used in business applications, college planning, desktop publishing, ESL, graphic design, information technology, introduction to technology, keyboarding, library science, mathematics, media, media production, photography, programming, publications, science, technology, yearbook classes. Computer network features include on-campus library services, online commercial services, Internet access. The school has a published electronic and media policy.

Contact Mrs. Debbie Herrrera, Director of Admissions and Public Relations. 805-967-1266 Ext. 118. Fax: 805-964-3178. E-mail: dherrera@bishopdiego.org. Web site: www.bishopdiego.org.

BISHOP GORMAN HIGH SCHOOL

5959 South Hualapai Way
Las Vegas, Nevada 89148
Head of School: Mrs. Aggie Evert

General Information Coeducational day college-preparatory and religious studies school, affiliated with Roman Catholic Church. Grades 9–12. Founded: 1954. Setting: urban. 36-acre campus. 10 buildings on campus. Approved or accredited by Northwest Accreditation Commission, Northwest Association of Schools and Colleges, and Nevada Department of Education. Total enrollment: 1,170. Upper school average class size: 25. Upper school faculty-student ratio: 1:25. There are 181 required school days per year for Upper School students. Upper School students typically attend 5 days per week. The average school day consists of 6 hours and 15 minutes.
Upper School Student Profile Grade 9: 327 students (163 boys, 164 girls); Grade 10: 327 students (176 boys, 151 girls); Grade 11: 270 students (142 boys, 128 girls); Grade 12: 246 students (130 boys, 116 girls). 77% of students are Roman Catholic.
Faculty School total: 65. In upper school: 29 men, 36 women; 50 have advanced degrees.
Subjects Offered Accounting, Advanced Placement courses, algebra, anatomy and physiology, art, band, biology, biology-AP, calculus, campus ministry, chemistry, choral music, chorus, church history, college counseling, composition, computer applications, criminal justice, drama, driver education, economics, economics-AP, English language and composition-AP, English literature-AP, ethics, French, geometry, government-AP, government/civics, health education, honors algebra, honors English, honors geometry, honors U.S. history, honors world history, human anatomy, journalism, literature and composition-AP, literature-AP, macro/microeconomics-AP, marine biology, microeconomics-AP, music, New Testament, performing arts, photography, physical education, physics, physiology, pottery, pre-calculus, probability and statistics, psychology, publications, religion, SAT/ACT preparation, sociology, Spanish, Spanish language-AP, Spanish-AP, speech, statistics-AP, student publications, theater, theater arts, theater design and production, theology, trigonometry, U.S. constitutional history, U.S. government, U.S. government and politics-AP, U.S. history, U.S. history-AP, United States government-AP, world cultures, world geography, world history, world history-AP, world religions, world religions, writing workshop, yearbook.
Graduation Requirements American government, arts and fine arts (art, music, dance, drama), computer science, English, foreign language, lab science, mathematics, physical education (includes health), science, social studies (includes history), theology. Community service is required.
Special Academic Programs Advanced Placement exam preparation; honors section.
College Admission Counseling 229 students graduated in 2009; 217 went to college, including Loyola Marymount University; Northern Arizona University; Santa Clara University; University of Nevada, Las Vegas; University of Nevada, Reno; University of San Diego. Other: 5 went to work, 5 entered military service, 2 had other specific plans. Median SAT critical reading: 542, median SAT math: 535, median SAT writing: 536, median combined SAT: 1610, median composite ACT: 23.
Student Life Upper grades have uniform requirement, student council, honor system. Discipline rests primarily with faculty. Attendance at religious services is required.
Tuition and Aid Day student tuition: $10,100–$11,500. Tuition installment plan (monthly payment plans). Merit scholarship grants, need-based scholarship grants available. In 2009–10, 40% of upper-school students received aid; total upper-school merit-scholarship money awarded: $278,200. Total amount of financial aid awarded in 2009–10: $1,000,000.
Admissions Traditional secondary-level entrance grade is 9. High School Placement Test required. Deadline for receipt of application materials: none. Application fee required: $50. Interview recommended.
Athletics Interscholastic: baseball (boys), basketball (b,g), bowling (b,g), cheering (g), cross-country running (b,g), diving (b,g), football (b), golf (b,g), lacrosse (b,g), soccer (b,g), softball (g), swimming and diving (b,g), tennis (b,g), volleyball (b,g), winter soccer (b,g), wrestling (b); coed interscholastic: strength & conditioning, track and field, weight lifting; coed intramural: equestrian sports, horseback riding. 1 PE instructor, 50 coaches, 1 athletic trainer.
Computers Computers are regularly used in English, French, geography, journalism, library, mathematics, newspaper, photography, religion, science, yearbook classes. Computer network features include on-campus library services, Internet access, wireless campus network, Internet filtering or blocking technology. Students grades are available online. The school has a published electronic and media policy.

Contact Mr. Tracy Goode, Assistant Principal of Admissions. 702-732-1945 Ext. 4011. Fax: 702-732-2856. E-mail: admissions@bishopgorman.org. Web site: www. bishopgorman.org.

BISHOP GUERTIN HIGH SCHOOL

194 Lund Road
Nashua, New Hampshire 03060-4398
Head of School: Br. Mark Hilton, SC

General Information Coeducational day college-preparatory and religious studies school, affiliated with Roman Catholic Church. Grades 9–12. Founded: 1963. Setting: suburban. Nearest major city is Boston, MA. 1 building on campus. Approved or accredited by New England Association of Schools and Colleges and New Hampshire Department of Education. Total enrollment: 900. Upper school average class size: 20.
Upper School Student Profile 80% of students are Roman Catholic.
Faculty In upper school: 35 men, 30 women.
Subjects Offered 20th century history, acting, advanced chemistry, advanced computer applications, advanced math, algebra, American literature-AP, analysis and differential calculus, anatomy and physiology, art appreciation, art history, band, Bible studies, biology, biology-AP, British history, British literature, British literature (honors), business law, calculus, calculus-AP, campus ministry, career/college preparation, chemistry, chemistry-AP, chorus, Christian and Hebrew scripture, Christian doctrine, Christian education, Christian ethics, Christianity, church history, civics, college admission preparation, college counseling, college writing, community service, comparative government and politics, comparative government and politics-AP, comparative religion, computer applications, computer art, computer education, computer literacy, computer multimedia, computer processing, computer programming, computer programming-AP, computer science, computer technologies, computer-aided design, constitutional history of U.S., consumer economics, contemporary history, CPR, creative writing, death and loss, debate, desktop publishing, digital photography, discrete mathematics, dramatic arts, drawing, driver education, economics, emergency medicine, English, English composition, English literature, English literature and composition-AP, English-AP, environmental science, ethics, European history, fine arts, foreign language, French, geography, geometry, government/civics, grammar, health, health and wellness, health education, history, honors geometry, honors U.S. history, honors world history, human anatomy, human biology, human sexuality, instrumental music, journalism, Latin, Latin-AP, law, literary magazine, marching band, mechanics of writing, moral reasoning, moral theology, music, philosophy, physical education, physics, pre-calculus, psychology, religion, religious studies, science, senior seminar, Shakespeare, social studies, Spanish, statistics, studio art, studio art-AP, The 20th Century, theater, trigonometry, U.S. government and politics, U.S. government and politics-AP, U.S. history, U.S. history-AP, U.S. literature, world history, world literature.
Graduation Requirements Arts and fine arts (art, music, dance, drama), computer science, physical education (includes health), religion (includes Bible studies and theology). Community service is required.
Special Academic Programs 13 Advanced Placement exams for which test preparation is offered; honors section; study at local college for college credit; academic accommodation for the gifted.
College Admission Counseling 211 students graduated in 2010; 208 went to college. Other: 2 entered military service, 1 entered a postgraduate year.
Student Life Upper grades have specified standards of dress, student council, honor system. Discipline rests primarily with faculty. Attendance at religious services is required.
Summer Programs Held on campus; accepts boys and girls; not open to students from other schools. 40 students usually enrolled. 2011 schedule: July 1 to July 31. Application deadline: May 1.
Tuition and Aid Tuition installment plan (FACTS Tuition Payment Plan, individually arranged payment plans). Merit scholarship grants, need-based scholarship grants available. In 2010–11, 10% of upper-school students received aid.
Admissions Traditional secondary-level entrance grade is 9. Catholic High School Entrance Examination required. Deadline for receipt of application materials: January 7. Application fee required: $35.
Athletics Interscholastic: baseball (boys), basketball (b,g), cheering (b,g), cross-country running (b,g), field hockey (g), football (b), gymnastics (g), hockey (b,g), ice hockey (b,g), lacrosse (b), skiing (downhill) (b,g), soccer (b,g), softball (g), swimming and diving (b,g), tennis (b,g), track and field (b,g), volleyball (g), wrestling (b); intramural: crew (b,g); coed interscholastic: aquatics, cheering, golf, ice hockey, indoor track, nordic skiing, paint ball, skiing (downhill); coed intramural: aerobics/dance, basketball, bowling, crew, dance, fishing, freestyle skiing, golf, mountain biking, outdoor education, strength & conditioning, swimming and diving, table tennis, tennis, volleyball, weight lifting, weight training. 4 PE instructors, 55 coaches, 2 athletic trainers.
Computers Computers are regularly used in career education, career exploration, career technology, college planning, data processing, desktop publishing, independent study, information technology, introduction to technology, library, library science, library skills, literary magazine, multimedia, music, news writing, newspaper,

programming, publications, publishing, research skills, stock market, technology, Web site design, word processing, yearbook classes. Computer network features include on-campus library services, online commercial services, Internet access, wireless campus network, Internet filtering or blocking technology. The school has a published electronic and media policy.
Contact Ms. Jamie Gregoire, Director of Admissions. 603-889-4107 Ext. 4304. Fax: 603-889-0701. E-mail: admit@bghs.org. Web site: www.bghs.org.

BISHOP HENDRICKEN HIGH SCHOOL

2615 Warwick Avenue
Warwick, Rhode Island 02889
Head of School: Br. Thomas R. Leto

General Information Boys' day college-preparatory, arts, business, religious studies, and technology school, affiliated with Roman Catholic Church. Grades 9–12. Founded: 1959. Setting: suburban. Nearest major city is Providence. 34-acre campus. 1 building on campus. Approved or accredited by New England Association of Schools and Colleges and Rhode Island Department of Education. Total enrollment: 955. Upper school average class size: 22. Upper school faculty-student ratio: 1:14. There are 180 required school days per year for Upper School students. Upper School students typically attend 5 days per week. The average school day consists of 6 hours.
Upper School Student Profile Grade 9: 244 students (244 boys); Grade 10: 252 students (252 boys); Grade 11: 242 students (242 boys); Grade 12: 233 students (233 boys). 85% of students are Roman Catholic.
Faculty School total: 75. In upper school: 53 men, 22 women; 45 have advanced degrees.
Special Academic Programs 10 Advanced Placement exams for which test preparation is offered; honors section.
College Admission Counseling 245 students graduated in 2009; 241 went to college. Other: 2 entered a postgraduate year. Mean SAT critical reading: 532, mean SAT math: 543, mean SAT writing: 537.
Student Life Upper grades have specified standards of dress, student council, honor system. Discipline rests primarily with faculty. Attendance at religious services is required.
Tuition and Aid Day student tuition: $11,050. Tuition installment plan (FACTS Tuition Payment Plan, individually arranged payment plans). Merit scholarship grants, need-based scholarship grants available. In 2009–10, 33% of upper-school students received aid; total upper-school merit-scholarship money awarded: $160,000. Total amount of financial aid awarded in 2009–10: $500,000.
Admissions Traditional secondary-level entrance grade is 9. Catholic High School Entrance Examination required. Deadline for receipt of application materials: December 15. Application fee required: $25.
Athletics Interscholastic: baseball, basketball, cross-country running, diving, football, golf, ice hockey, indoor track, indoor track & field, lacrosse, rugby, sailing, soccer, swimming and diving, tennis, track and field, volleyball, winter (indoor) track, wrestling; intramural: archery, badminton, billiards, bocce, bowling, flag football, golf, handball, rugby, whiffle ball. 4 PE instructors, 1 athletic trainer.
Computers Computer resources include Internet access, wireless campus network, Internet filtering or blocking technology. Students grades are available online. The school has a published electronic and media policy.
Contact Mrs. Dianne M. O'Reilly, Director of Admissions. 401-739-3450 Ext. 163. Fax: 401-732-8261. E-mail: doreilly@hendricken.com. Web site: www.hendricken.com.

BISHOP IRETON HIGH SCHOOL

201 Cambridge Road
Alexandria, Virginia 22314-4899
Head of School: Mr. Timothy Hamer

General Information Coeducational day college-preparatory, arts, religious studies, and technology school, affiliated with Roman Catholic Church. Grades 9–12. Founded: 1964. Setting: suburban. 12-acre campus. 1 building on campus. Approved or accredited by National Catholic Education Association and Southern Association of Colleges and Schools. Endowment: $1 million. Total enrollment: 822. Upper school average class size: 24. Upper school faculty-student ratio: 1:14. There are 180 required school days per year for Upper School students. Upper School students typically attend 5 days per week. The average school day consists of 7 hours.
Upper School Student Profile Grade 9: 220 students (95 boys, 125 girls); Grade 10: 202 students (100 boys, 102 girls); Grade 11: 206 students (90 boys, 116 girls); Grade 12: 199 students (93 boys, 106 girls). 89% of students are Roman Catholic.
Faculty School total: 64. In upper school: 28 men, 35 women; 46 have advanced degrees.
Subjects Offered Advanced Placement courses, Catholic belief and practice, computer science, driver education, English, film, fine arts, foreign language, health, mathematics, physical education, religion, science, social studies.

Bishop Ireton High School

Graduation Requirements Arts and fine arts (art, music, dance, drama), computer science, English, foreign language, mathematics, physical education (includes health), religion (includes Bible studies and theology), science, social studies (includes history), 60 hours of community service.

Special Academic Programs Advanced Placement exam preparation; honors section; academic accommodation for the musically talented; special instructional classes for students with Attention Deficit Disorder.

College Admission Counseling 199 students graduated in 2010; 198 went to college, including George Mason University; James Madison University; Old Dominion University; University of Virginia; Virginia Commonwealth University; Virginia Polytechnic Institute and State University. Other: 1 had other specific plans. Mean SAT critical reading: 581, mean SAT math: 563, mean SAT writing: 585, mean combined SAT: 1729.

Student Life Upper grades have uniform requirement, honor system. Discipline rests primarily with faculty. Attendance at religious services is required.

Summer Programs Remediation, enrichment, art/fine arts, computer instruction programs offered; session focuses on remediation; held on campus; accepts boys and girls; open to students from other schools. 50 students usually enrolled. 2011 schedule: June to July.

Tuition and Aid Day student tuition: $11,360–$15,300. Tuition installment plan (FACTS Tuition Payment Plan, monthly payment plans). Tuition reduction for siblings, merit scholarship grants, need-based scholarship grants available. In 2010–11, 15% of upper-school students received aid; total upper-school merit-scholarship money awarded: $100,000. Total amount of financial aid awarded in 2010–11: $575,000.

Admissions Traditional secondary-level entrance grade is 9. For fall 2010, 400 students applied for upper-level admission, 353 were accepted, 214 enrolled. High School Placement Test (closed version) from Scholastic Testing Service required. Deadline for receipt of application materials: January 24. Application fee required: $50.

Athletics Interscholastic: baseball (boys), basketball (b,g), football (b), lacrosse (b,g), soccer (b,g), softball (g), swimming and diving (b,g), tennis (b,g), track and field (b,g), volleyball (g), water polo (b), winter (indoor) track (b,g), wrestling (b); intramural: weight training (b,g); coed interscholastic: cheering, crew, cross-country running, diving, golf, ice hockey, indoor track, water polo, weight training; coed intramural: dance team, freestyle skiing, skiing (downhill), table tennis. 4 PE instructors, 3 coaches, 1 athletic trainer.

Computers Computers are regularly used in all academic classes. Computer network features include on-campus library services, online commercial services, Internet access, Internet filtering or blocking technology. Student e-mail accounts and computer access in designated common areas are available to students. The school has a published electronic and media policy.

Contact Mr. Peter J. Hamer, Director of Admissions. 703-212-5190. Fax: 703-212-8173. E-mail: hamerp@bishopireton.org. Web site: www.bishopireton.org.

BISHOP KELLY HIGH SCHOOL

7009 Franklin Road
Boise, Idaho 83709-0922
Head of School: Mr. Robert R. Wehde

General Information Coeducational day college-preparatory and religious studies school, affiliated with Roman Catholic Church. Grades 9–12. Founded: 1964. Setting: urban. 68-acre campus. 2 buildings on campus. Approved or accredited by National Catholic Education Association, Northwest Accreditation Commission, Western Catholic Education Association, and Idaho Department of Education. Endowment: $6.2 million. Total enrollment: 626. Upper school average class size: 21. Upper school faculty-student ratio: 1:18. There are 175 required school days per year for Upper School students. Upper School students typically attend 5 days per week. The average school day consists of 7 hours.

Upper School Student Profile Grade 9: 163 students (84 boys, 79 girls); Grade 10: 144 students (74 boys, 70 girls); Grade 11: 156 students (85 boys, 71 girls); Grade 12: 155 students (91 boys, 64 girls); Grade 13: 8 students (8 girls). 84% of students are Roman Catholic.

Faculty School total: 42. In upper school: 21 men, 21 women; 22 have advanced degrees.

Subjects Offered Advanced Placement courses, algebra, American government, American history-AP, art, art-AP, band, biology, biology-AP, calculus, calculus-AP, campus ministry, Catholic belief and practice, chemistry, chemistry-AP, choir, Christianity, comparative religion, computer applications, computer programming, computer programming-AP, conceptual physics, creative writing, drawing, earth science, ecology, economics, engineering, English, English-AP, fitness, French, geology, geometry, health, history of the Catholic Church, horticulture, instrumental music, journalism, literature, moral reasoning, painting, physical education, physical science, physics, physics-AP, pottery, pre-algebra, pre-calculus, psychology, reading/study skills, religious education, religious studies, senior seminar, service learning/internship, social justice, Spanish, Spanish-AP, speech, speech and debate, sports medicine, statistics-AP, theater, theater arts, theology, U.S. government, U.S. history, video film production, weight training, Western civilization, world history, yearbook.

Graduation Requirements Computer science, English, foreign language, mathematics, physical education (includes health), religion (includes Bible studies and theology), science, social studies (includes history), 30 hours of community service.

Special Academic Programs Advanced Placement exam preparation; honors section; independent study; study at local college for college credit.

College Admission Counseling 155 students graduated in 2010; 147 went to college, including Boise State University; Chapman University; The College of Idaho; University of Idaho; University of Portland; University of Utah. Mean SAT critical reading: 581, mean SAT math: 585, mean SAT writing: 559, mean combined SAT: 1725.

Student Life Upper grades have specified standards of dress, student council, honor system. Discipline rests primarily with faculty. Attendance at religious services is required.

Tuition and Aid Day student tuition: $6890. Tuition installment plan (The Tuition Plan, monthly payment plans, individually arranged payment plans). Need-based scholarship grants available. In 2010–11, 81% of upper-school students received aid. Total amount of financial aid awarded in 2010–11: $956,972.

Admissions Traditional secondary-level entrance grade is 9. Deadline for receipt of application materials: none. Application fee required: $205.

Athletics Interscholastic: baseball (boys), basketball (b,g), cheering (g), cross-country running (b,g), football (b), golf (b,g), ice hockey (b), lacrosse (b,g), skiing (downhill) (b,g), snowboarding (b,g), soccer (b,g), softball (g), swimming and diving (b,g), tennis (b,g), track and field (b,g), volleyball (g), weight lifting (b,g), wrestling (b). 2 PE instructors, 10 coaches, 1 athletic trainer.

Computers Computers are regularly used in art, economics, English, foreign language, history, journalism, mathematics, science classes. Computer network features include on-campus library services, Internet access, Internet filtering or blocking technology, Blackboard. Student e-mail accounts and computer access in designated common areas are available to students. Students grades are available online. The school has a published electronic and media policy.

Contact Mrs. Kelly Shockey, Director of Admissions. 208-375-6010. Fax: 208-375-3626. E-mail: kshockey@bk.org. Web site: www.bk.org.

BISHOP KENNY HIGH SCHOOL

1055 Kingman Avenue
Jacksonville, Florida 32207
Head of School: Rev. Michael R. Houle

General Information Coeducational day college-preparatory school, affiliated with Roman Catholic Church. Grades 9–12. Founded: 1952. Setting: urban. 55-acre campus. 10 buildings on campus. Approved or accredited by Southern Association of Colleges and Schools. Total enrollment: 1,274. Upper school average class size: 22. Upper school faculty-student ratio: 1:15. There are 76 required school days per year for Upper School students. Upper School students typically attend 5 days per week. The average school day consists of 6 hours and 30 minutes.

Upper School Student Profile Grade 9: 285 students (128 boys, 157 girls); Grade 10: 339 students (169 boys, 170 girls); Grade 11: 337 students (170 boys, 167 girls); Grade 12: 313 students (155 boys, 158 girls). 85% of students are Roman Catholic.

Faculty In upper school: 28 men, 48 women; 36 have advanced degrees.

Subjects Offered Accounting, desktop publishing, technology, word processing.

Graduation Requirements Electives, English, foreign language, health, mathematics, performing arts, personal fitness, practical arts, religion (includes Bible studies and theology), science, social studies (includes history), service hour requirements.

Special Academic Programs Advanced Placement exam preparation; honors section.

College Admission Counseling 334 students graduated in 2010; 332 went to college, including Florida State University; University of Central Florida; University of Florida. Other: 2 went to work. Mean SAT critical reading: 526, mean SAT math: 517, mean SAT writing: 510, mean combined SAT: 1553, mean composite ACT: 23. 22% scored over 600 on SAT critical reading, 20% scored over 600 on SAT math, 18% scored over 600 on SAT writing.

Student Life Upper grades have uniform requirement, student council, honor system. Discipline rests primarily with faculty. Attendance at religious services is required.

Summer Programs Remediation, enrichment, sports programs offered; session focuses on enrichment/remediation; held on campus; accepts boys and girls; not open to students from other schools. 300 students usually enrolled. 2011 schedule: June 15 to July 14.

Tuition and Aid Day student tuition: $6200. Tuition installment plan (FACTS Tuition Payment Plan, individually arranged payment plans). Tuition reduction for siblings, need-based scholarship grants available. In 2010–11, 20% of upper-school students received aid.

Admissions Traditional secondary-level entrance grade is 9. ACT-Explore or Explore required. Deadline for receipt of application materials: none. Application fee required. On-campus interview required.

Athletics Interscholastic: baseball (boys), basketball (b,g), cheering (g), cross-country running (b,g), diving (b,g), drill team (g), football (b), golf (b,g), JROTC drill (b,g), riflery (b,g), soccer (b,g), softball (g), swimming and diving (b,g), tennis (b,g), track and field (b,g), volleyball (g), weight lifting (b), wrestling (b).

Computers Computers are regularly used in computer applications, journalism, keyboarding, newspaper, yearbook classes. Computer resources include on-campus library services, Internet access, Internet filtering or blocking technology, design software for Journalism and MultiMedia, CS4 Suite, 5 computer labs. The school has a published electronic and media policy.

Contact Mrs. Sheila W. Marovich, Director of Admissions. 904-398-7545. Fax: 904-398-5728. E-mail: development@bishopkenny.org. Web site: www. bishopkenny.org.

BISHOP LUERS HIGH SCHOOL

333 East Paulding Road
Fort Wayne, Indiana 46816
Head of School: Mrs. Mary T. Keefer
General Information Coeducational day college-preparatory and religious studies school, affiliated with Roman Catholic Church. Grades 9–12. Founded: 1958. Setting: urban. 5-acre campus. 1 building on campus. Approved or accredited by National Catholic Education Association, North Central Association of Colleges and Schools, and Indiana Department of Education. Total enrollment: 545. Upper school average class size: 25. Upper school faculty-student ratio: 1:17. There are 180 required school days per year for Upper School students. Upper School students typically attend 5 days per week. The average school day consists of 6 hours and 35 minutes.
Upper School Student Profile Grade 9: 135 students (70 boys, 65 girls); Grade 10: 150 students (80 boys, 70 girls); Grade 11: 127 students (52 boys, 75 girls); Grade 12: 133 students (63 boys, 70 girls). 89% of students are Roman Catholic.
Faculty School total: 31. In upper school: 10 men, 21 women; 18 have advanced degrees.
Subjects Offered 3-dimensional art, accounting, algebra, Bible, biology, biology-AP, business, business law, calculus-AP, chamber groups, chemistry, chemistry-AP, chorus, church history, computer applications, computer programming, concert band, creative writing, drawing, economics, English, French, geometry, government, health education, honors algebra, honors English, honors geometry, honors U.S. history, honors world history, Latin, music appreciation, music theory, painting, physical education, physics, physiology, pre-calculus, probability and statistics, psychology, sculpture, sociology, Spanish, speech communications, student government, student publications, study skills, theater arts, theater production, theology, trigonometry, U.S. history, world civilizations, world geography, world history.
Graduation Requirements Computers, English, mathematics, physical education (includes health), religion (includes Bible studies and theology), science, social studies (includes history).
Special Academic Programs Advanced Placement exam preparation; honors section; study at local college for college credit; academic accommodation for the gifted and the musically talented; remedial reading and/or remedial writing; remedial math.
College Admission Counseling Colleges students went to include Indiana University–Purdue University Fort Wayne; Purdue University. Mean SAT critical reading: 513, mean SAT math: 507, mean SAT writing: 495.
Student Life Upper grades have specified standards of dress, student council. Discipline rests equally with students and faculty. Attendance at religious services is required.
Summer Programs Remediation, sports programs offered; session focuses on camps and enrichment; held on campus; accepts boys and girls; open to students from other schools. 250 students usually enrolled. 2011 schedule: June 15 to August 10. Application deadline: May 30.
Tuition and Aid Day student tuition: $3875. Tuition installment plan (FACTS Tuition Payment Plan). Tuition reduction for siblings, merit scholarship grants, need-based scholarship grants, paying campus jobs available. In 2010–11, 61% of upper-school students received aid.
Admissions Deadline for receipt of application materials: none. Application fee required: $120.
Athletics Interscholastic: baseball (boys), basketball (b,g), bowling (b,g), cheering (g), cross-country running (b,g), dance (g), dance team (g), diving (b,g), football (b), golf (b,g), lacrosse (b), riflery (b,g), running (b,g), soccer (b,g), softball (g), swimming and diving (b,g), tennis (b,g), track and field (b,g), volleyball (g), wrestling (g); intramural: lacrosse (b,g); coed intramural: lacrosse, riflery, weight training. 2 PE instructors, 25 coaches, 2 athletic trainers.
Computers Computers are regularly used in all academic, business, yearbook classes. Computer network features include on-campus library services, Internet access, Internet filtering or blocking technology. Students grades are available online. The school has a published electronic and media policy.
Contact Mrs. Jennifer Andorfer, Co-Director of Admissions and Public Relations. 260-456-1261 Ext. 3141. Fax: 260-456-1262. E-mail: jandorfer@bishopluers.org. Web site: www.bishopluers.org/.

BISHOP MANOGUE HIGH SCHOOL

110 Bishop Manogue Drive
Reno, Nevada 89511
Head of School: Mr. Tim Jaureguito
General Information Coeducational day college-preparatory, arts, religious studies, and technology school, affiliated with Roman Catholic Church. Grades 9–12. Founded: 1948. Setting: urban. 52-acre campus. 1 building on campus. Approved or accredited by Northwest Accreditation Commission, Northwest Association of Schools and Colleges, and Nevada Department of Education. Endowment: $650,000.

Total enrollment: 609. Upper school average class size: 20. Upper school faculty-student ratio: 1:17. There are 180 required school days per year for Upper School students. Upper School students typically attend 5 days per week. The average school day consists of 6 hours and 35 minutes.
Upper School Student Profile Grade 9: 150 students (81 boys, 69 girls); Grade 10: 145 students (80 boys, 65 girls); Grade 11: 155 students (83 boys, 72 girls); Grade 12: 159 students (85 boys, 74 girls). 68% of students are Roman Catholic.
Faculty School total: 48. In upper school: 23 men, 25 women; 28 have advanced degrees.
Subjects Offered Algebra, anatomy and physiology, art, biology, biology-AP, calculus-AP, chemistry, chemistry-AP, choir, communications, community service, computer applications, computer graphics, creative writing, drama, drawing, English, English language and composition-AP, English literature and composition-AP, French, French language-AP, geography, geometry, health, history, history-AP, honors algebra, honors English, honors geometry, honors U.S. history, honors world history, journalism, Latin, microbiology, peer ministry, personal finance, physical education, physical science, physics, physics-AP, portfolio art, pre-algebra, pre-calculus, reading/study skills, religion, religious studies, remedial study skills, sculpture, senior internship, Spanish, Spanish language-AP, speech and debate, sports medicine, statistics-AP, street law, strings, student government, studio art-AP, trigonometry, U.S. government and politics, U.S. government and politics-AP, U.S. history, U.S. history-AP, world history, yearbook.
Graduation Requirements English, mathematics, physical education (includes health), religion (includes Bible studies and theology), science, social studies (includes history), passing grade on the Reading, Writing, Science, and Mathematics Proficiency Exams. Community service is required.
Special Academic Programs Honors section; remedial reading and/or remedial writing; remedial math.
College Admission Counseling 127 students graduated in 2009; 126 went to college, including Saint Mary's College of California; Santa Clara University; University of Nevada, Las Vegas; University of Nevada, Reno; University of San Diego. Other: 1 entered military service. Median SAT critical reading: 550, median SAT math: 510, median SAT writing: 520, median combined SAT: 1600, median composite ACT: 25. 30% scored over 600 on SAT critical reading, 38% scored over 600 on SAT math, 24% scored over 600 on SAT writing, 25% scored over 1800 on combined SAT, 46% scored over 26 on composite ACT.
Student Life Upper grades have uniform requirement, student council, honor system. Discipline rests primarily with faculty. Attendance at religious services is required.
Tuition and Aid Day student tuition: $8500. Tuition installment plan (FACTS Tuition Payment Plan). Tuition reduction for siblings, merit scholarship grants, need-based scholarship grants available. In 2009–10, 25% of upper-school students received aid; total upper-school merit-scholarship money awarded: $1000. Total amount of financial aid awarded in 2009–10: $664,330.
Admissions Traditional secondary-level entrance grade is 9. STS required. Deadline for receipt of application materials: none. Application fee required: $75.
Athletics Interscholastic: baseball (boys), basketball (b,g), cheering (g), cross-country running (b,g), football (b), golf (b,g), skiing (downhill) (b,g), soccer (b,g), softball (g), swimming and diving (b,g), tennis (b,g), track and field (b,g), volleyball (g), wrestling (b); coed interscholastic: bowling. 3 PE instructors, 45 coaches, 1 athletic trainer.
Computers Computers are regularly used in English, history, mathematics, science classes. Computer resources include on-campus library services, online commercial services, Internet access, wireless campus network, Internet filtering or blocking technology. Student e-mail accounts are available to students. Students grades are available online. The school has a published electronic and media policy.
Contact Mr. Bruce J. Stewart, Assistant Principal. 775-336-6000. Fax: 775-336-6015. E-mail: bruce.stewart@bishopmanogue.org. Web site: www.bishopmanogue.org.

BISHOP MCGUINNESS CATHOLIC HIGH SCHOOL

1725 NC Highway 66 South
Kernersville, North Carolina 27284
Head of School: Mr. George L. Repass
General Information Coeducational day college-preparatory, arts, and religious studies school, affiliated with Roman Catholic Church. Grades 9–12. Founded: 1959. Setting: suburban. Nearest major city is Winston-Salem. 42-acre campus. 2 buildings on campus. Approved or accredited by National Catholic Education Association, Southern Association of Colleges and Schools, The College Board, and North Carolina Department of Education. Endowment: $100,000. Total enrollment: 549. Upper school average class size: 18. Upper school faculty-student ratio: 1:14. There are 180 required school days per year for Upper School students. Upper School students typically attend 5 days per week. The average school day consists of 6 hours and 50 minutes.
Upper School Student Profile Grade 9: 156 students (86 boys, 70 girls); Grade 10: 122 students (75 boys, 47 girls); Grade 11: 151 students (80 boys, 71 girls); Grade 12: 120 students (66 boys, 54 girls). 75% of students are Roman Catholic.
Faculty School total: 39. In upper school: 20 men, 19 women; 31 have advanced degrees.

Bishop McGuinness Catholic High School

Subjects Offered Algebra, American history, anatomy, art history, arts, biology, biology-AP, calculus, calculus-AP, chemistry, chemistry-AP, community service, computer science, computer science-AP, creative writing, earth science, English, English language-AP, English literature and composition-AP, environmental science, European history-AP, fine arts, French, French language-AP, French-AP, geometry, health, Latin, Latin-AP, mathematics, music, music theory-AP, photography, physical education, physical science, physics, political science, religion, science, social studies, Spanish, Spanish-AP, statistics-AP, trigonometry, U.S. history-AP, world history.

Graduation Requirements Arts and fine arts (art, music, dance, drama), English, foreign language, health, mathematics, physical education (includes health), religion (includes Bible studies and theology), science, social studies (includes history), All students must attend the retreat for their grade level; all seniors must complete the senior career project. Community service is required.

Special Academic Programs 14 Advanced Placement exams for which test preparation is offered; honors section; independent study; term-away projects; study at local college for college credit.

College Admission Counseling 134 students graduated in 2010; 131 went to college, including Appalachian State University; North Carolina State University; The University of North Carolina at Asheville; The University of North Carolina at Chapel Hill; The University of North Carolina at Charlotte; The University of North Carolina Wilmington. Other: 3 had other specific plans. Mean SAT critical reading: 553, mean SAT math: 539, mean SAT writing: 534, mean combined SAT: 1626, mean composite ACT: 24. 30% scored over 600 on SAT critical reading, 29% scored over 600 on SAT math, 20% scored over 600 on SAT writing, 27% scored over 1800 on combined SAT, 29% scored over 26 on composite ACT.

Student Life Upper grades have specified standards of dress, student council, honor system. Discipline rests primarily with faculty. Attendance at religious services is required.

Tuition and Aid Day student tuition: $6900–$9700. Tuition installment plan (monthly payment plans, yearly, semester, and quarterly payment plans). Tuition reduction for siblings, need-based scholarship grants available. In 2010–11, 18% of upper-school students received aid. Total amount of financial aid awarded in 2010–11: $304,000.

Admissions Traditional secondary-level entrance grade is 9. For fall 2010, 195 students applied for upper-level admission, 182 were accepted, 168 enrolled. Achievement/Aptitude/Writing or High School Placement Test required. Deadline for receipt of application materials: none. Application fee required: $75. On-campus interview required.

Athletics Interscholastic: baseball (boys), basketball (b,g), cheering (g), football (b), lacrosse (b), soccer (b,g), softball (g), tennis (b,g), volleyball (g), wrestling (b); coed interscholastic: cross-country running, golf, swimming and diving, track and field, weight training. 3 PE instructors, 40 coaches, 2 athletic trainers.

Computers Computer resources include on-campus library services, Internet access, Internet filtering or blocking technology. Student e-mail accounts and computer access in designated common areas are available to students. Students grades are available online.

Contact Mr. Robert Belcher, Admissions Director. 336-564-1011. Fax: 336-564-1060. E-mail: rb@bmhs.us. Web site: www.bmhs.us.

BISHOP MCGUINNESS CATHOLIC HIGH SCHOOL
801 Northwest 50th Street
Oklahoma City, Oklahoma 73118-6001
Head of School: Mr. David L. Morton

General Information Coeducational day college-preparatory, arts, business, religious studies, bilingual studies, and technology school, affiliated with Roman Catholic Church. Grades 9–12. Founded: 1950. Setting: urban. 20-acre campus. 4 buildings on campus. Approved or accredited by North Central Association of Colleges and Schools and Oklahoma Department of Education. Endowment: $1.2 million. Total enrollment: 714. Upper school average class size: 14. Upper school faculty-student ratio: 1:14. There are 177 required school days per year for Upper School students. Upper School students typically attend 5 days per week. The average school day consists of 6 hours and 10 minutes.

Upper School Student Profile Grade 11: 183 students (98 boys, 85 girls); Grade 12: 177 students (82 boys, 95 girls). 78% of students are Roman Catholic.

Faculty School total: 55. In upper school: 12 men, 14 women; 12 have advanced degrees.

Subjects Offered Algebra, American literature, American literature-AP, art, band, Bible studies, biology, biology-AP, business, calculus-AP, Catholic belief and practice, ceramics, chemistry, chorus, church history, computer technologies, creative writing, culinary arts, current events, dance, debate, design, drama, drawing, economics, electives, English, English literature, English literature-AP, ethics, French, geography, geometry, German, government, government-AP, health and wellness, history of the Catholic Church, honors algebra, honors English, honors geometry, HTML design, introduction to theater, Latin, leadership, learning lab, newspaper, orchestra, painting, personal finance, photography, physical education, physical science, physics, physics-AP, physiology, play production, practical arts, prayer/spirituality, pre-calculus, psychology, scripture, sociology, Spanish, speech, stagecraft, theater, U.S. history, U.S. history-AP, weight training, world history, world history-AP, world religions, writing workshop, yearbook.

Graduation Requirements Arts and fine arts (art, music, dance, drama), electives, English, foreign language, mathematics, physical education (includes health), practical arts, science, social studies (includes history), theology, 90 hours of Christian service.

Special Academic Programs 9 Advanced Placement exams for which test preparation is offered; honors section; academic accommodation for the gifted and the artistically talented; programs in English, mathematics for dyslexic students; special instructional classes for students with learning differences.

College Admission Counseling 158 students graduated in 2010; 155 went to college, including Oklahoma City University; Oklahoma State University; Texas Christian University; University of Arkansas; University of Oklahoma. Other: 1 went to work, 1 entered military service, 1 had other specific plans. Median SAT critical reading: 590, median SAT math: 570, median SAT writing: 580. Mean composite ACT: 25. 42% scored over 600 on SAT critical reading, 45% scored over 600 on SAT math, 48% scored over 600 on SAT writing, 46% scored over 1800 on combined SAT, 38% scored over 26 on composite ACT.

Student Life Upper grades have uniform requirement, student council, honor system. Discipline rests primarily with faculty. Attendance at religious services is required.

Tuition and Aid Day student tuition: $7500. Tuition installment plan (FACTS Tuition Payment Plan). Need-based scholarship grants, paying campus jobs available. In 2010–11, 24% of upper-school students received aid. Total amount of financial aid awarded in 2010–11: $206,620.

Admissions Traditional secondary-level entrance grade is 11. For fall 2010, 7 students applied for upper-level admission, 7 were accepted, 7 enrolled. School placement exam, STS or writing sample required. Deadline for receipt of application materials: May 1. Application fee required: $350. On-campus interview required.

Athletics Interscholastic: baseball (boys), basketball (b,g), bowling (b,g), cheering (g), cross-country running (b,g), dance team (b,g), football (b), golf (b,g), soccer (b,g), softball (g), swimming and diving (b,g), tennis (b,g), track and field (b,g), volleyball (g), weight training (b,g), winter (indoor) track (b,g), wrestling (b); coed interscholastic: bowling, physical fitness. 1 PE instructor.

Computers Computers are regularly used in all academic classes. Computer network features include on-campus library services, online commercial services, Internet access, wireless campus network, Internet filtering or blocking technology, laptop classroom computers, wireless printing, eBooks, and My Road. Student e-mail accounts and computer access in designated common areas are available to students. Students grades are available online. The school has a published electronic and media policy.

Contact Ms. Amy Hanson, 9th Grade Counselor. 405-842-6638 Ext. 225. Fax: 405-858-9550. E-mail: ahanson@bmchs.org. Web site: www.bmchs.org.

BISHOP MONTGOMERY HIGH SCHOOL
5430 Torrance Boulevard
Torrance, California 90503
Head of School: Ms. Rosemary Distaso-Libbon

General Information Coeducational day college-preparatory, arts, religious studies, and technology school, affiliated with Roman Catholic Church. Grades 9–12. Founded: 1957. Setting: suburban. Nearest major city is Los Angeles. 27-acre campus. 8 buildings on campus. Approved or accredited by National Catholic Education Association, Western Association of Schools and Colleges, Western Catholic Education Association, and California Department of Education. Total enrollment: 1,072. Upper school average class size: 19. Upper school faculty-student ratio: 1:19. There are 180 required school days per year for Upper School students. Upper School students typically attend 5 days per week. The average school day consists of 6 hours and 10 minutes.

Upper School Student Profile Grade 9: 253 students (112 boys, 141 girls); Grade 10: 260 students (115 boys, 145 girls); Grade 11: 289 students (131 boys, 158 girls); Grade 12: 270 students (130 boys, 140 girls). 75% of students are Roman Catholic.

Faculty School total: 60. In upper school: 27 men, 33 women; 20 have advanced degrees.

Subjects Offered Advanced Placement courses, algebra, American history, American history-AP, American literature, anatomy, art, Bible studies, biology, calculus, chemistry, chorus, composition, computer science, drama, economics, English, English literature, English literature-AP, fine arts, French, geometry, government/civics, health, history, languages, life science, literature, mathematics, physical education, physics, physics-AP, physiology, religion, science, social studies, Spanish, statistics, theater, trigonometry, weight training, world history, yearbook.

Graduation Requirements Arts and fine arts (art, music, dance, drama), business skills (includes word processing), computer science, English, mathematics, physical education (includes health), religion (includes Bible studies and theology), science, social studies (includes history).

Special Academic Programs Advanced Placement exam preparation; honors section.

College Admission Counseling 282 students graduated in 2010; all went to college, including California State University, Dominguez Hills; California State University, Long Beach; El Camino College; Loyola Marymount University; University of California, Irvine; University of California, Riverside. Mean SAT critical reading: 528, mean SAT math: 525, mean SAT writing: 527.

Student Life Upper grades have uniform requirement, student council. Discipline rests primarily with faculty. Attendance at religious services is required.

Summer Programs Remediation, enrichment, advancement, sports, art/fine arts, computer instruction programs offered; session focuses on academic enrichment/remediation and athletic conditioning; held on campus; accepts boys and girls; open to students from other schools. 900 students usually enrolled. 2011 schedule: June 20 to July 22. Application deadline: May 3.

Tuition and Aid Day student tuition: $7100. Tuition installment plan (monthly payment plans). Tuition reduction for siblings, financial need available. In 2010–11, 3% of upper-school students received aid. Total amount of financial aid awarded in 2010–11: $30,000.

Admissions Traditional secondary-level entrance grade is 9. High School Placement Test, Iowa Tests of Basic Skills and Stanford 9 required. Deadline for receipt of application materials: January 13. Application fee required: $75.

Athletics Interscholastic: baseball (boys), basketball (b,g), cross-country running (b,g), dance (g), dance team (g), football (b), golf (b,g), soccer (b,g), softball (g), strength & conditioning (b,g), tennis (b,g), volleyball (b,g); coed interscholastic: aerobics, surfing, swimming and diving, track and field. 3 PE instructors, 32 coaches, 2 athletic trainers.

Computers Computers are regularly used in library, newspaper, programming, publications, technology, Web site design classes. Computer network features include on-campus library services, Internet access, wireless campus network. Students grades are available online. The school has a published electronic and media policy.

Contact Mrs. Casey Dunn, Director of Admissions. 310-540-2021 Ext. 227. Fax: 310-543-5102. E-mail: cdunn@bmhs-la.org. Web site: www.bmhs-la.org.

BISHOP O'DOWD HIGH SCHOOL
9500 Stearns Avenue
Oakland, California 94605-4799
Head of School: Dr. Stephen Phelps, EdD

General Information Coeducational day college-preparatory, arts, religious studies, and technology school, affiliated with Roman Catholic Church. Grades 9–12. Founded: 1951. Setting: urban. 8-acre campus. 12 buildings on campus. Approved or accredited by Western Association of Schools and Colleges, Western Catholic Education Association, and California Department of Education. Endowment: $1 million. Total enrollment: 1,125. Upper school average class size: 26. Upper school faculty-student ratio: 1:15. Upper School students typically attend 5 days per week. The average school day consists of 6 hours and 30 minutes.

Upper School Student Profile Grade 9: 257 students (118 boys, 139 girls); Grade 10: 282 students (151 boys, 131 girls); Grade 11: 314 students (153 boys, 161 girls); Grade 12: 276 students (127 boys, 149 girls). 55% of students are Roman Catholic.

Faculty School total: 78. In upper school: 41 men, 37 women; 55 have advanced degrees.

Subjects Offered Art, computer science, English, fine arts, foreign language, mathematics, physical education, religion, science, social studies.

Graduation Requirements Arts and fine arts (art, music, dance, drama), English, foreign language, mathematics, physical education (includes health), religion (includes Bible studies and theology), religious studies, science, social studies (includes history), 100 hour service learning project to be completed over all four years.

Special Academic Programs Advanced Placement exam preparation; honors section; academic accommodation for the gifted, the musically talented, and the artistically talented; remedial reading and/or remedial writing; remedial math; special instructional classes for students with ADD and dyslexia.

College Admission Counseling 296 students graduated in 2010; 294 went to college, including California Polytechnic State University, San Luis Obispo; San Francisco State University; University of California, Berkeley; University of California, Davis; University of California, Santa Cruz; University of Oregon. Other: 2 had other specific plans. Mean SAT critical reading: 561, mean SAT math: 566, mean SAT writing: 576.

Student Life Upper grades have specified standards of dress, student council. Discipline rests equally with students and faculty.

Summer Programs Remediation, computer instruction programs offered; session focuses on review; held on campus; accepts boys and girls; open to students from other schools. 120 students usually enrolled. 2011 schedule: June 13 to July 20. Application deadline: June 1.

Tuition and Aid Day student tuition: $13,840. Tuition installment plan (monthly payment plans, individually arranged payment plans). Tuition reduction for siblings, merit scholarship grants, need-based scholarship grants available. In 2010–11, 30% of upper-school students received aid; total upper-school merit-scholarship money awarded: $15,000. Total amount of financial aid awarded in 2010–11: $2,100,000.

Admissions Traditional secondary-level entrance grade is 9. For fall 2010, 550 students applied for upper-level admission, 430 were accepted, 265 enrolled. High School Placement Test and High School Placement Test (closed version) from Scholastic Testing Service required. Deadline for receipt of application materials: none. Application fee required: $90.

Athletics Interscholastic: aquatics (boys, girls), baseball (b), basketball (b,g), cheering (g), cross-country running (b,g), diving (b,g), football (b), golf (b,g), lacrosse (b,g), rugby (b,g), soccer (b,g), softball (g), swimming and diving (b,g), tennis (b,g),

track and field (b,g), volleyball (g), water polo (b,g); intramural: basketball (b,g), dance squad (g), physical training (b,g), soccer (b,g), weight training (b,g); coed interscholastic: cross-country running; coed intramural: aerobics, aerobics/dance, alpine skiing, backpacking, bicycling, combined training, flag football, Frisbee, hiking/backpacking, mountain biking, skiing (downhill), snowboarding, weight training. 5 PE instructors, 36 coaches, 1 athletic trainer.

Computers Computers are regularly used in all academic, career exploration, library, library skills, mathematics, media arts, media production, newspaper, programming, research skills, science, video film production, yearbook classes. Computer network features include on-campus library services, online commercial services, Internet access, wireless campus network, Internet filtering or blocking technology, one to one laptop program: every student has a laptop on campus. Student e-mail accounts are available to students. Students grades are available online. The school has a published electronic and media policy.

Contact Tyler Kreitz, Director of Admissions. 510-577-9100. Fax: 510-638-3259. E-mail: tkreitz@bishopodowd.org. Web site: www.bishopodowd.org.

BISHOP'S COLLEGE SCHOOL
80 Moulton Hill Road
PO Box 5001, Succ. Lennoxville
Sherbrooke, Quebec J1M 1Z8, Canada
Head of School: Mr. Ian Watt

General Information Coeducational boarding and day college-preparatory, arts, and bilingual studies school. Grades 7–12. Founded: 1836. Setting: rural. Nearest major city is Montreal, Canada. Students are housed in single-sex dormitories. 350-acre campus. 30 buildings on campus. Approved or accredited by Canadian Association of Independent Schools, Canadian Educational Standards Institute, Quebec Association of Independent Schools, The Association of Boarding Schools, and Quebec Department of Education. Affiliate member of National Association of Independent Schools. Languages of instruction: English and French. Total enrollment: 236. Upper school average class size: 12. Upper school faculty-student ratio: 1:12.

Upper School Student Profile Grade 10: 63 students (38 boys, 25 girls); Grade 11: 61 students (41 boys, 20 girls); Grade 12: 45 students (27 boys, 18 girls). 78% of students are boarding students. 45% are province residents. 9 provinces are represented in upper school student body. 46% are international students. International students from Bermuda, Germany, Mexico, Saudi Arabia, Taiwan, and United States; 20 other countries represented in student body.

Faculty School total: 33. In upper school: 17 men, 13 women.

Subjects Offered Algebra, art, biology, calculus, chemistry, computer science, creative writing, drama, economics, English, environmental science, ESL, ethics, European history, finite math, French, French as a second language, geography, geometry, history, mathematics, music, philosophy, physical education, physical science, physics, political science, religion, science, sociology, study skills, technology, theater, trigonometry, world history.

Special Academic Programs Advanced Placement exam preparation; term-away projects; study at local college for college credit; study abroad; academic accommodation for the gifted, the musically talented, and the artistically talented; remedial math; ESL.

College Admission Counseling Colleges students went to include Dalhousie University.

Student Life Upper grades have uniform requirement, student council, honor system. Discipline rests equally with students and faculty.

Summer Programs Remediation, enrichment, advancement, ESL, sports, art/fine arts, rigorous outdoor training, computer instruction programs offered; session focuses on English or French as a Second Language; held on campus; accepts boys and girls; open to students from other schools. 150 students usually enrolled. 2011 schedule: July 3 to July 30. Application deadline: none.

Tuition and Aid Day student tuition: CAN$17,200; 5-day tuition and room/board: CAN$44,500; 7-day tuition and room/board: CAN$44,500. Tuition installment plan (monthly payment plans, individually arranged payment plans, single payment plan). Tuition reduction for siblings, bursaries, merit scholarship grants, need-based scholarship grants, need-based loans available.

Admissions Admissions testing required. Deadline for receipt of application materials: none. Application fee required: CAN$100. Interview required.

Athletics Interscholastic: baseball (boys), football (b,g), gymnastics (g), hockey (b), ice hockey (b), softball (g); coed interscholastic: alpine skiing, aquatics, basketball, bicycling, climbing, cross-country running, equestrian sports, golf, horseback riding, independent competitive sports, nordic skiing, outdoor adventure, rugby, skiing (cross-country), skiing (downhill), soccer, swimming and diving, track and field; coed intramural: aerobics, alpine skiing, backpacking, badminton, basketball, climbing, Cosom hockey, curling, figure skating, fitness, fitness walking, floor hockey, hiking/backpacking, hockey, horseback riding, ice hockey, ice skating, indoor hockey, jogging, mountain biking, outdoor activities, outdoor education, physical fitness, rock climbing, snowshoeing, squash, strength & conditioning, yoga. 1 PE instructor, 10 coaches, 1 athletic trainer.

Computers Computers are regularly used in all classes. Computer network features include on-campus library services, Internet access, wireless campus network, Internet

filtering or blocking technology, school wide laptop initiative (included in tuition), fiber optic network. Student e-mail accounts are available to students. Students grades are available online. The school has a published electronic and media policy.

Contact Valerie Scullion, Director of Admissions and Marketing. 819-566-0227 Ext. 248. Fax: 819-566-8123. E-mail: vscullion@bishopscollegeschool.com. Web site: www.bishopscollegeschool.com.

THE BISHOP'S SCHOOL

7607 La Jolla Boulevard
La Jolla, California 92037
Head of School: Aimeclaire Roche

General Information Coeducational day college-preparatory, arts, religious studies, and technology school, affiliated with Episcopal Church. Grades 6–12. Founded: 1909. Setting: suburban. Nearest major city is San Diego. 11-acre campus. 7 buildings on campus. Approved or accredited by Western Association of Schools and Colleges and California Department of Education. Member of National Association of Independent Schools. Endowment: $22.8 million. Total enrollment: 780. Upper school average class size: 15. Upper school faculty-student ratio: 1:9. Upper School students typically attend 5 days per week. The average school day consists of 7 hours.

Upper School Student Profile Grade 6: 32 students (17 boys, 15 girls); Grade 7: 94 students (47 boys, 47 girls); Grade 8: 104 students (60 boys, 44 girls); Grade 9: 136 students (71 boys, 65 girls); Grade 10: 142 students (68 boys, 74 girls); Grade 11: 145 students (69 boys, 76 girls); Grade 12: 131 students (50 boys, 81 girls).

Faculty School total: 86. In upper school: 39 men, 41 women; 65 have advanced degrees.

Subjects Offered Acting, Advanced Placement courses, advanced studio art-AP, algebra, American history, American literature, art history, art history-AP, arts, ASB Leadership, biology, biology-AP, calculus, calculus-AP, ceramics, chemistry, chemistry-AP, Chinese, Chinese studies, chorus, community service, comparative government and politics-AP, comparative religion, computer programming, computer science, creative writing, dance, discrete mathematics, drama, drawing, earth science, ecology, economics, economics and history, economics-AP, English, English literature, environmental science, ethics, European history, European history-AP, forensics, French, French language-AP, French literature-AP, genetics, geography, geometry, government/civics, health, history, human anatomy, humanities, integrated mathematics, Internet, jazz band, journalism, Latin, Latin American studies, Latin-AP, literature and composition-AP, literature-AP, macro/microeconomics-AP, marine biology, mathematics, music, painting, philosophy, photography, physical education, physical science, physics, physics-AP, physiology, pre-algebra, pre-calculus, probability, programming, religious studies, Shakespeare, social studies, Spanish, Spanish language-AP, Spanish literature-AP, speech, speech and debate, stained glass, statistics, statistics-AP, studio art-AP, tap dance, theater, theater design and production, typing, U.S. government and politics-AP, U.S. history, U.S. history-AP, visual reality, world history, yearbook.

Graduation Requirements Arts and fine arts (art, music, dance, drama), computer science, English, foreign language, mathematics, physical education (includes health), religion (includes Bible studies and theology), science, social sciences, social studies (includes history), swimming test, computer proficiency. Community service is required.

Special Academic Programs Advanced Placement exam preparation; honors section; independent study.

College Admission Counseling 138 students graduated in 2009; 136 went to college, including Princeton University; Stanford University; University of California, Berkeley; University of California, Los Angeles; University of California, Santa Barbara; University of Southern California. Other: 2 had other specific plans. Mean SAT critical reading: 649, mean SAT math: 663, mean SAT writing: 663.

Student Life Upper grades have uniform requirement, student council, honor system. Discipline rests equally with students and faculty. Attendance at religious services is required.

Tuition and Aid Day student tuition: $26,500. Tuition installment plan (FACTS Tuition Payment Plan, semester payment plans, Key Resources Achiever Loan). Need-based scholarship grants available. In 2009–10, 20% of upper-school students received aid. Total amount of financial aid awarded in 2009–10: $290,000.

Admissions Traditional secondary-level entrance grade is 9. For fall 2009, 155 students applied for upper-level admission, 125 were accepted, 101 enrolled. Admissions testing, ISEE and Otis-Lennon School Ability Test required. Deadline for receipt of application materials: February 1. Application fee required: $100. On-campus interview required.

Athletics Interscholastic: baseball (boys), basketball (b,g), cross-country running (b,g), equestrian sports (b,g), field hockey (g), football (b), golf (b,g), gymnastics (g), lacrosse (b,g), soccer (b,g), softball (g), swimming and diving (b,g), tennis (b,g), track and field (b,g), volleyball (b,g), water polo (b,g); intramural: weight training (b,g); coed interscholastic: sailing. 5 PE instructors, 38 coaches, 1 athletic trainer.

Computers Computers are regularly used in English, foreign language, history, journalism, library, music, science, yearbook classes. Computer network features include on-campus library services, online commercial services, Internet access.

Contact Josie R. Alvarez, Director of Admissions. 858-459-4021 Ext. 255. Fax: 858-459-3914. E-mail: alvarezj@bishops.com. Web site: www.bishops.com.

BISHOP STANG HIGH SCHOOL

500 Slocum Road
North Dartmouth, Massachusetts 02747-2999
Head of School: Mrs. Theresa E. Dougall

General Information Coeducational day college-preparatory, arts, business, religious studies, technology, science, and arts school, affiliated with Roman Catholic Church. Grades 9–12. Founded: 1959. Setting: suburban. Nearest major city is New Bedford. 8-acre campus. 1 building on campus. Approved or accredited by New England Association of Schools and Colleges and Massachusetts Department of Education. Endowment: $2 million. Total enrollment: 750. Upper school average class size: 20. Upper school faculty-student ratio: 1:13. There are 180 required school days per year for Upper School students. Upper School students typically attend 5 days per week. The average school day consists of 6 hours and 30 minutes.

Upper School Student Profile Grade 9: 185 students (83 boys, 102 girls); Grade 10: 174 students (82 boys, 92 girls); Grade 11: 200 students (92 boys, 108 girls); Grade 12: 191 students (102 boys, 89 girls). 85% of students are Roman Catholic.

Faculty School total: 61. In upper school: 23 men, 38 women; 29 have advanced degrees.

Subjects Offered 3-dimensional design, advanced biology, algebra, American history, American literature, anatomy and physiology, art, biochemistry, bioethics, biology, biology-AP, calculus, calculus-AP, campus ministry, Catholic belief and practice, chemistry, chemistry-AP, chorus, church history, communications, community service, computer science, concert band, criminal justice, criminology, death and loss, driver education, ecology, English, English literature, English-AP, environmental science, fine arts, French, geometry, government/civics, health, history, history of the Catholic Church, instrumental music, introduction to theater, Latin, Life of Christ, marine biology, marketing, mathematics, mechanical drawing, media production, modern European history-AP, moral theology, music, oceanography, photography, physical education, physics, physics-AP, physiology, Portuguese, prayer/spirituality, psychology, psychology-AP, religion, religious studies, science, social sciences, social studies, sociology, Spanish, study skills, technical drawing, theater arts, trigonometry, Web authoring, world history, world literature, writing, yearbook.

Graduation Requirements Arts and fine arts (art, music, dance, drama), business skills (includes word processing), computer science, English, foreign language, mathematics, physical education (includes health), religion (includes Bible studies and theology), science, social sciences, social studies (includes history), service project. Community service is required.

Special Academic Programs 7 Advanced Placement exams for which test preparation is offered; honors section; remedial reading and/or remedial writing; remedial math; programs in English, mathematics, general development for dyslexic students.

College Admission Counseling 190 students graduated in 2010; 186 went to college, including Providence College; Quinnipiac University; Salve Regina University; University of Massachusetts Amherst; University of Massachusetts Dartmouth; Worcester Polytechnic Institute. Other: 4 went to work. Mean SAT critical reading: 553, mean SAT math: 535, mean SAT writing: 540, mean combined SAT: 1629.

Student Life Upper grades have uniform requirement, student council, honor system. Discipline rests primarily with faculty. Attendance at religious services is required.

Summer Programs Enrichment, computer instruction programs offered; session focuses on computer and math enrichment; held on campus; accepts boys and girls; not open to students from other schools. 15 students usually enrolled. 2011 schedule: July to July.

Tuition and Aid Day student tuition: $7600. Tuition installment plan (FACTS Tuition Payment Plan, monthly payment plans). Merit scholarship grants, need-based scholarship grants available. In 2010–11, 27% of upper-school students received aid; total upper-school merit-scholarship money awarded: $12,500. Total amount of financial aid awarded in 2010–11: $500,000.

Admissions Traditional secondary-level entrance grade is 9. For fall 2010, 275 students applied for upper-level admission, 261 were accepted, 185 enrolled. Scholastic Testing Service High School Placement Test required. Deadline for receipt of application materials: none. No application fee required. On-campus interview recommended.

Athletics Interscholastic: aquatics (boys, girls), baseball (b), basketball (b,g), cheering (g), cross-country running (b,g), diving (b,g), field hockey (g), football (b), golf (b,g), ice hockey (b), lacrosse (b,g), soccer (b,g), softball (g), swimming and diving (b,g), tennis (b,g), track and field (b,g), volleyball (g), winter (indoor) track (b,g); intramural: fitness (b,g); coed interscholastic: indoor track & field, sailing; coed intramural: backpacking, bicycling, canoeing/kayaking, climbing, crew, hiking/backpacking, kayaking, outdoor activities, outdoor adventure, physical training, rock climbing, sailing, skiing (downhill), snowboarding, strength & conditioning, ultimate Frisbee, wall climbing, weight lifting, weight training. 10 coaches, 1 athletic trainer.

Computers Computers are regularly used in all classes. Computer network features include on-campus library services, online commercial services, Internet access, wireless campus network, Internet filtering or blocking technology. Campus intranet and computer access in designated common areas are available to students. The school has a published electronic and media policy.

Contact Mrs. Christine Payette, Admissions Director. 508-996-5602 Ext. 424. Fax: 508-994-6756. E-mail: admits@bishopstang.com Web site: www.bishopstang.com.

BISHOP VEROT HIGH SCHOOL
5598 Sunrise Drive
Fort Myers, Florida 33919-1799
Head of School: Fr. J. Christian Beretta, OSFS

General Information Coeducational day college-preparatory, arts, religious studies, technology, honors, and Advanced Placement school, affiliated with Roman Catholic Church. Grades 9–12. Founded: 1962. Setting: suburban. Nearest major city is Tampa. 20-acre campus. 8 buildings on campus. Approved or accredited by Southern Association of Colleges and Schools and Florida Department of Education. Endowment: $800,000. Total enrollment: 708. Upper school average class size: 26. Upper school faculty-student ratio: 1:18. There are 180 required school days per year for Upper School students. Upper School students typically attend 5 days per week. The average school day consists of 7 hours.

Upper School Student Profile Grade 9: 168 students (79 boys, 89 girls); Grade 10: 190 students (88 boys, 102 girls); Grade 11: 167 students (95 boys, 72 girls); Grade 12: 183 students (94 boys, 89 girls). 65% of students are Roman Catholic.

Faculty School total: 46. In upper school: 18 men, 27 women; 32 have advanced degrees.

Subjects Offered Acting, Advanced Placement courses, algebra, American government, American history, American history-AP, American literature, American sign language, art, athletic training, band, Bible studies, biology, biology-AP, British literature, British literature (honors), broadcast journalism, business, calculus-AP, ceramics, chemistry, chemistry-AP, choir, church history, comparative government and politics-AP, computer studies, creative writing, drafting, drama, drawing, driver education, economics, electives, English, English literature and composition-AP, English literature-AP, environmental science, European history-AP, fine arts, foreign language, French, geometry, government, government-AP, health education, history, history of the Catholic Church, history-AP, honors algebra, honors English, honors geometry, honors U.S. history, honors world history, industrial arts, integrated mathematics, journalism, law studies, marine biology, mathematics, newspaper, painting, personal fitness, photography, physical education, physics, physics-AP, pottery, practical arts, pre-algebra, pre-calculus, probability and statistics, psychology, SAT preparation, Spanish, Spanish language-AP, speech, studio art, television, theater, U.S. government and politics-AP, U.S. history, U.S. history-AP, Web site design, weightlifting, world history, world history-AP, writing, yearbook.

Graduation Requirements Algebra, American government, arts and fine arts (art, music, dance, drama), biology, British literature, chemistry, economics, electives, English, English composition, foreign language, geometry, government, health education, mathematics, moral theology, personal fitness, physics, practical arts, psychology, religion (includes Bible studies and theology), science, U.S. history, world history, world literature.

Special Academic Programs Advanced Placement exam preparation; honors section; study at local college for college credit; remedial math.

College Admission Counseling 165 students graduated in 2009; 161 went to college, including Florida Gulf Coast University; Florida State University; University of Central Florida; University of Florida; University of Miami; University of Notre Dame. Other: 1 went to work, 2 entered military service, 1 entered a postgraduate year. Mean SAT critical reading: 529, mean SAT math: 535, mean SAT writing: 511, mean combined SAT: 1575, mean composite ACT: 23. 21% scored over 600 on SAT critical reading, 26% scored over 600 on SAT math, 17% scored over 600 on SAT writing, 21% scored over 26 on composite ACT.

Student Life Upper grades have specified standards of dress, student council, honor system. Discipline rests primarily with faculty. Attendance at religious services is required.

Tuition and Aid Day student tuition: $9625. Tuition installment plan (FACTS Tuition Payment Plan, monthly payment plans, individually arranged payment plans, quarterly payment plan). Merit scholarship grants, need-based scholarship grants, tuition reduction for contributing Catholic families available. In 2009–10, 40% of upper-school students received aid; total upper-school merit-scholarship money awarded: $100,000. Total amount of financial aid awarded in 2009–10: $1,057,000.

Admissions Traditional secondary-level entrance grade is 9. High School Placement Test required. Deadline for receipt of application materials: none. Application fee required: $50.

Athletics Interscholastic: baseball (boys), basketball (b,g), cheering (g), cross-country running (b,g), diving (b,g), football (b), golf (b,g), soccer (b,g), softball (g), swimming and diving (b,g), tennis (b,g), track and field (b,g), volleyball (g), weight lifting (b,g); intramural: ice hockey (b), weight training (b,g); coed interscholastic: lacrosse, strength & conditioning; coed intramural: lacrosse. 2 PE instructors, 20 coaches, 1 athletic trainer.

Computers Computers are regularly used in career exploration, college planning, drafting, information technology, library, media production, newspaper, photography, publications, SAT preparation, technology, vocational-technical courses, Web site design, yearbook classes. Computer network features include on-campus library

services, Internet access, Internet filtering or blocking technology. Students grades are available online. The school has a published electronic and media policy.

Contact Ms. Deanna Custer, Director of Admission. 239-274-6760. Fax: 239-274-6795. E-mail: deanna.custer@bvhs.org. Web site: www.bvhs.org.

BISHOP WALSH MIDDLE HIGH SCHOOL
700 Bishop Walsh Road
Cumberland, Maryland 21502
Head of School: Sr. Phyllis McNally

General Information Coeducational day college-preparatory school, affiliated with Roman Catholic Church. Grades PK–12. Founded: 1966. Setting: small town. 10-acre campus. 1 building on campus. Approved or accredited by National Catholic Education Association and Maryland Department of Education. Total enrollment: 428. Upper school average class size: 20. Upper school faculty-student ratio: 1:15.

Upper School Student Profile Grade 9: 46 students (13 boys, 33 girls); Grade 10: 58 students (28 boys, 30 girls); Grade 11: 47 students (25 boys, 22 girls); Grade 12: 47 students (25 boys, 22 girls). 70% of students are Roman Catholic.

Faculty School total: 45. In upper school: 8 men, 12 women; 15 have advanced degrees.

Subjects Offered Western civilization.

Special Academic Programs Advanced Placement exam preparation; honors section; remedial reading and/or remedial writing; programs in English, general development for dyslexic students; ESL (6 students enrolled).

College Admission Counseling 54 students graduated in 2010; 52 went to college, including Frostburg State University; West Virginia University. Other: 2 entered military service. Median SAT critical reading: 505, median SAT math: 504, median SAT writing: 500, median combined SAT: 1509, median composite ACT: 25.

Student Life Upper grades have uniform requirement, student council. Discipline rests primarily with faculty. Attendance at religious services is required.

Summer Programs Enrichment, advancement programs offered; session focuses on European history, Spanish, and math; held on campus; accepts boys and girls; not open to students from other schools. 40 students usually enrolled. 2011 schedule: June 15 to July 15. Application deadline: May 29.

Tuition and Aid Day student tuition: $4900. Tuition installment plan (FACTS Tuition Payment Plan, monthly payment plans). Need-based scholarship grants available. In 2010–11, 50% of upper-school students received aid. Total amount of financial aid awarded in 2010–11: $30,000.

Admissions Traditional secondary-level entrance grade is 9. For fall 2010, 20 students applied for upper-level admission, 19 were accepted, 19 enrolled. Deadline for receipt of application materials: August 31. Application fee required: $30. Interview required.

Athletics Interscholastic: baseball (boys), basketball (b,g), bowling (b,g), cheering (g), football (b), golf (b), soccer (b,g), softball (g), tennis (b,g), volleyball (g), weight training (b,g); coed interscholastic: cross-country running, track and field. 2 PE instructors, 8 coaches, 1 athletic trainer.

Computers Computers are regularly used in all classes. Computer network features include Internet access. Students grades are available online. The school has a published electronic and media policy.

Contact Mrs. Erin Dale, Administrative Assistant. 301-724-5360 Ext. 104. Fax: 301-722-0555. E-mail: edale@bishopwalsh.org. Web site: www.bishopwalsh.org.

BISHOP WARD HIGH SCHOOL
708 North 18 Street
Kansas City, Kansas 66102
Head of School: Fr. Michael Hermes

General Information Coeducational day college-preparatory, general academic, religious studies, and technology school, affiliated with Roman Catholic Church. Grades 9–12. Founded: 1908. Setting: urban. 5-acre campus. 1 building on campus. Approved or accredited by North Central Association of Colleges and Schools and Kansas Department of Education. Endowment: $1 million. Total enrollment: 305. Upper school average class size: 20. Upper school faculty-student ratio: 1:18. There are 186 required school days per year for Upper School students. Upper School students typically attend 5 days per week. The average school day consists of 7 hours and 30 minutes.

Upper School Student Profile Grade 9: 95 students (38 boys, 57 girls); Grade 10: 83 students (38 boys, 45 girls); Grade 11: 68 students (36 boys, 32 girls); Grade 12: 59 students (30 boys, 29 girls). 90% of students are Roman Catholic.

Faculty School total: 30. In upper school: 10 men, 15 women; 15 have advanced degrees.

Subjects Offered Accounting, advanced math, algebra, American government, American history, American history-AP, anatomy and physiology, biology, calculus, calculus-AP, chemistry, composition, computer-aided design, current events, drafting, economics, English, English literature and composition-AP, environmental science, geometry, physical science, physics, psychology, Spanish, world civilizations, world geography.

Bishop Ward High School

Graduation Requirements Arts and fine arts (art, music, dance, drama), computer technologies, electives, English, foreign language, mathematics, physical education (includes health), practical arts, science, social studies (includes history), speech, theology. Community service is required.

Special Academic Programs Study at local college for college credit; remedial reading and/or remedial writing; remedial math.

College Admission Counseling 72 students graduated in 2009; 68 went to college, including Avila University; Benedictine College; Johnson County Community College; Kansas City Kansas Community College; Kansas State University; The University of Kansas. Other: 4 went to work. Median composite ACT: 20. 20% scored over 26 on composite ACT.

Student Life Upper grades have uniform requirement, student council, honor system. Discipline rests primarily with faculty. Attendance at religious services is required.

Tuition and Aid Day student tuition: $6350. Tuition installment plan (monthly payment plans). Tuition reduction for siblings, merit scholarship grants, need-based scholarship grants available. In 2009–10, 65% of upper-school students received aid; total upper-school merit-scholarship money awarded: $3000. Total amount of financial aid awarded in 2009–10: $80,000.

Admissions Traditional secondary-level entrance grade is 9. Scholastic Testing Service required. Deadline for receipt of application materials: March 7. Application fee required: $150. Interview required.

Athletics Interscholastic: baseball (boys), basketball (b,g), dance team (g), football (b), soccer (b,g), softball (g), volleyball (g); coed interscholastic: aquatics, bowling, cheering, cross-country running, golf, swimming and diving, track and field, wrestling. 2 PE instructors, 8 coaches.

Computers Computer network features include on-campus library services.

Contact Mr. Dennis Dorr, Principal. 913-371-1201. Fax: 913-371-2145. E-mail: ddorr@wardhigh.org. Web site: www.wardhigh.org.

BLAIR ACADEMY
2 Park Street
Blairstown, New Jersey 07825
Head of School: T. Chandler Hardwick III

General Information Coeducational boarding and day college-preparatory and arts school, affiliated with Presbyterian Church. Boarding grades 9–PG, day grades 9–12. Founded: 1848. Setting: rural. Nearest major city is New York, NY. Students are housed in single-sex dormitories. 423-acre campus. 42 buildings on campus.

Approved or accredited by Middle States Association of Colleges and Schools, New Jersey Association of Independent Schools, The Association of Boarding Schools, and New Jersey Department of Education. Member of National Association of Independent Schools and Secondary School Admission Test Board. Endowment: $57 million. Total enrollment: 454. Upper school average class size: 11. Upper school faculty-student ratio: 1:7. Upper School students typically attend 6 days per week. The average school day consists of 7 hours.

Upper School Student Profile Grade 9: 73 students (41 boys, 32 girls); Grade 10: 119 students (69 boys, 50 girls); Grade 11: 123 students (67 boys, 56 girls); Grade 12: 128 students (71 boys, 57 girls); Postgraduate: 11 students (9 boys, 2 girls). 78% of students are boarding students. 44% are state residents. 22 states are represented in upper school student body. 15% are international students. International students from China, Hong Kong, Republic of Korea, Spain, Thailand, and United Kingdom; 15 other countries represented in student body.

Faculty School total: 86. In upper school: 45 men, 34 women; 45 have advanced degrees; 74 reside on campus.

Subjects Offered 3-dimensional art, 3-dimensional design, advanced math, Advanced Placement courses, advanced studio art-AP, African history, algebra, American government, American history, American history-AP, American literature, anatomy, architectural drawing, architecture, art, art history-AP, art-AP, Asian studies, biochemistry, biology, biology-AP, biotechnology, calculus, calculus-AP, ceramics, chemistry, chemistry-AP, Chinese, comparative government and politics-AP, computer programming, computer science, computer science-AP, creative writing, dance, drafting, drama, drawing, drawing and design, driver education, economics, economics and history, economics-AP, English, English language-AP, English literature, English literature-AP, environmental science, environmental science-AP, ethics, European history, European history-AP, filmmaking, fine arts, French, French language-AP, geometry, government/civics, health, history, Japanese history, jazz band, Latin, marine biology, marine science, mathematics, mechanical drawing, music, music theory-AP, painting, philosophy, photography, physics, pre-calculus, psychology, religion, science, social studies, Spanish, Spanish language-AP, statistics-AP, theater, theology, world history, world literature, writing.

Graduation Requirements Arts and fine arts (art, music, dance, drama), biology, English, foreign language, mathematics, religion (includes Bible studies and theology), science, social studies (includes history), U.S. history, athletic requirement.

Special Academic Programs 22 Advanced Placement exams for which test preparation is offered; honors section; independent study; study abroad.

College Admission Counseling 140 students graduated in 2010; all went to college, including Boston College; Boston University; Cornell University; Lehigh University; New York University; The George Washington University. Mean SAT critical reading: 610, mean SAT math: 620, mean SAT writing: 630.

Student Life Upper grades have specified standards of dress, student council, honor system. Discipline rests equally with students and faculty.

Tuition and Aid Day student tuition: $32,500; 7-day tuition and room/board: $45,700. Tuition installment plan (Key Tuition Payment Plan, monthly payment plans). Need-based scholarship grants, need-based loans available. In 2010–11, 32% of upper-school students received aid. Total amount of financial aid awarded in 2010–11: $4,000,000.

Admissions Traditional secondary-level entrance grade is 9. For fall 2010, 716 students applied for upper-level admission, 249 were accepted, 150 enrolled. SSAT or TOEFL required. Deadline for receipt of application materials: February 1. Application fee required: $50. On-campus interview required.

Athletics Interscholastic: alpine skiing (boys, girls), baseball (b), basketball (b,g), crew (b,g), cross-country running (b,g), field hockey (g), football (b), golf (b,g), ice hockey (b), indoor track (b,g), lacrosse (b,g), rowing (b,g), running (b,g), skiing (downhill) (b,g), soccer (b,g), softball (g), squash (b,g), swimming and diving (b,g), tennis (b,g), track and field (b,g), winter (indoor) track (b,g), wrestling (b); intramural: basketball (b,g), crew (b,g), ice hockey (g), rowing (b,g), volleyball (g); coed intramural: alpine skiing, bicycling, canoeing/kayaking, dance, equestrian sports, fitness, flag football, golf, horseback riding, kayaking, life saving, modern dance, mountain biking, outdoor skills, physical fitness, skiing (downhill), snowboarding, squash, swimming and diving, tennis, weight lifting, weight training, wrestling, yoga. 3 athletic trainers.

Computers Computers are regularly used in architecture, drawing and design, English, foreign language, graphic arts, graphic design, history, information technology, mathematics, media production, science, video film production, writing classes. Computer network features include on-campus library services, online commercial services, Internet access, Internet filtering or blocking technology. Campus intranet, student e-mail accounts, and computer access in designated common areas are available to students. The school has a published electronic and media policy.

Contact Nancy Klein, Administrative. 800-462-5247. Fax: 908-362-7975. E-mail: admissions@blair.edu. Web site: www.blair.edu.

See Display on page 122 and Close-Up on page 744.

THE BLAKE SCHOOL

110 Blake Road South
Hopkins, Minnesota 55343

Head of School: John C. Gulla

General Information Coeducational day college-preparatory school. Grades PK–12. Founded: 1900. Setting: urban. Nearest major city is Minneapolis. 5-acre campus. 1 building on campus. Approved or accredited by Independent Schools Association of the Central States. Member of National Association of Independent Schools. Endowment: $40 million. Total enrollment: 1,386. Upper school average class size: 16. Upper school faculty-student ratio: 1:8.

Upper School Student Profile Grade 9: 133 students (67 boys, 66 girls); Grade 10: 123 students (62 boys, 61 girls); Grade 11: 135 students (61 boys, 74 girls); Grade 12: 126 students (67 boys, 59 girls).

Faculty School total: 136. In upper school: 26 men, 30 women; 36 have advanced degrees.

Subjects Offered Advanced chemistry, African-American literature, algebra, American history, American literature, art, Asian studies, astronomy, band, biology, biology-AP, calculus, calculus-AP, ceramics, chemistry, chemistry-AP, Chinese, choir, chorus, communication arts, communications, computer math, creative writing, debate, design, drama, drawing, economics, English, English literature, English-AP, ethics, European history, European history-AP, fine arts, French, French language-AP, French literature-AP, geology, geometry, German-AP, government/civics, history, instrumental music, jazz ensemble, journalism, Latin, mathematics, multicultural studies, music, painting, performing arts, photography, physical education, physics, physics-AP, policy and value, political science, printmaking, psychology, religion, science, sculpture, senior project, social psychology, social studies, Spanish, Spanish language-AP, speech, statistics, statistics-AP, studio art, studio art-AP, theater, theater arts, trigonometry, visual and performing arts, vocal ensemble, women's studies, world cultures, world history, world literature, writing.

Graduation Requirements Arts and fine arts (art, music, dance, drama), communications, English, foreign language, mathematics, physical education (includes health), science, social studies (includes history), assembly speech.

Special Academic Programs 14 Advanced Placement exams for which test preparation is offered; term-away projects; study at local college for college credit; study abroad.

College Admission Counseling 125 students graduated in 2009; all went to college, including Colgate University; Columbia College; Georgetown University; Harvard University; Northwestern University. Median SAT critical reading: 650, median SAT math: 650, median SAT writing: 650, median combined SAT: 1950, median composite ACT: 29. 68% scored over 600 on SAT critical reading, 64% scored over 600 on SAT math, 69% scored over 600 on SAT writing, 75% scored over 26 on composite ACT.

Student Life Upper grades have specified standards of dress, student council, honor system. Discipline rests primarily with faculty.

Tuition and Aid Day student tuition: $21,600. Tuition installment plan (local bank-arranged plan). Need-based scholarship grants, need-based loans, academic year low-interest loans, tuition remission for children of faculty available. In 2009–10, 23% of upper-school students received aid. Total amount of financial aid awarded in 2009–10: $1,981,190.

Admissions Traditional secondary-level entrance grade is 9. For fall 2009, 89 students applied for upper-level admission, 53 were accepted, 32 enrolled. ERB or WISC/Woodcock-Johnson required. Deadline for receipt of application materials: January 31. Application fee required: $100. On-campus interview required.

Athletics Interscholastic: alpine skiing (boys, girls), baseball (b), basketball (b,g), cross-country running (b,g), diving (b,g), football (b), golf (b,g), ice hockey (b,g), lacrosse (b,g), skiing (cross-country) (b,g), skiing (downhill) (b,g), soccer (b,g), softball (g), swimming and diving (b,g); coed interscholastic: fencing. 1 PE instructor, 45 coaches, 1 athletic trainer.

Computers Computers are regularly used in all classes. Computer network features include on-campus library services, online commercial services, Internet access, wireless campus network, Internet filtering or blocking technology, laptops. Campus intranet, student e-mail accounts, and computer access in designated common areas are available to students. Students grades are available online. The school has a published electronic and media policy.

Contact Adaline Shinkle, Director of Admissions. 952-988-3420. Fax: 952-988-3455. E-mail: ashinkle@blakeschool.org. Web site: www.blakeschool.org.

BLANCHET SCHOOL

4373 Market Street NE
Salem, Oregon 97305

Head of School: Mr. Anthony Guevara

General Information Coeducational day college-preparatory, arts, and religious studies school, affiliated with Roman Catholic Church. Grades 6–12. Founded: 1995. Setting: suburban. 22-acre campus. 2 buildings on campus. Approved or accredited by National Catholic Education Association, Northwest Association of Schools and Colleges, and Oregon Department of Education. Endowment: $120,000. Total enrollment: 396. Upper school average class size: 18. Upper school faculty-student ratio: 1:18. There are 175 required school days per year for Upper School students. Upper School students typically attend 5 days per week. The average school day consists of 7 hours.

Upper School Student Profile Grade 6: 14 students (6 boys, 8 girls); Grade 7: 56 students (29 boys, 27 girls); Grade 8: 56 students (31 boys, 25 girls); Grade 9: 54 students (29 boys, 25 girls); Grade 10: 80 students (36 boys, 44 girls); Grade 11: 70 students (31 boys, 39 girls); Grade 12: 66 students (34 boys, 32 girls). 70% of students are Roman Catholic.

Faculty School total: 31. In upper school: 13 men, 18 women; 21 have advanced degrees.

Subjects Offered Advanced Placement courses, algebra, American government, American history-AP, American literature, anatomy, anatomy and physiology, art, art education, band, Bible studies, biology, British literature, calculus, campus ministry, career and personal planning, Catholic belief and practice, chemistry, choir, civics, college counseling, college placement, comparative religion, composition, computer programming, critical thinking, critical writing, debate, digital photography, drama, economics, economics and history, English literature, English literature and composition-AP, first aid, fitness, French, geometry, global studies, government, great books, health, health and safety, health and wellness, health education, history of the Catholic Church, history-AP, lab science, literature and composition-AP, mathematics, media production, music, personal finance, photography, physical education, physical fitness, physical science, physics, pre-algebra, pre-calculus, psychology, publications, religion, religion and culture, SAT/ACT preparation, sociology, Spanish, speech and debate, U.S. government, U.S. history, U.S. history-AP, urban design, weight training, world history, world religions, World War II, yearbook.

Graduation Requirements Applied arts, arts and fine arts (art, music, dance, drama), electives, English, foreign language, mathematics, physical education (includes health), religion (includes Bible studies and theology), science, social studies (includes history), 20 hours of community service for each year in attendance.

Special Academic Programs 2 Advanced Placement exams for which test preparation is offered; honors section; study at local college for college credit; special instructional classes for deaf students; ESL (6 students enrolled).

College Admission Counseling 56 students graduated in 2010; 55 went to college, including Chemeketa Community College; Gonzaga University; Oregon State University; University of Oregon; University of Portland; Willamette University. Other: 1 went to work. Median SAT critical reading: 583, median SAT math: 586, median SAT writing: 564, median composite ACT: 26.

Student Life Upper grades have specified standards of dress, student council. Discipline rests equally with students and faculty. Attendance at religious services is required.

Summer Programs Remediation, enrichment, sports programs offered; session focuses on preparation for the next academic year, athletic training; held on campus;

accepts boys and girls; open to students from other schools. 75 students usually enrolled. 2011 schedule: June 13 to August 17.

Tuition and Aid Day student tuition: $6890. Tuition installment plan (FACTS Tuition Payment Plan). Tuition reduction for siblings, merit scholarship grants, need-based scholarship grants available. In 2010–11, 40% of upper-school students received aid; total upper-school merit-scholarship money awarded: $8500. Total amount of financial aid awarded in 2010–11: $240,000.

Admissions Deadline for receipt of application materials: none. Application fee required: $100. Interview recommended.

Athletics Interscholastic: baseball (boys), basketball (b,g), cheering (g), cross-country running (b,g), fencing (b,g), football (b), golf (b,g), physical fitness (b,g), soccer (b,g), softball (g), swimming and diving (b,g), tennis (b,g), track and field (b,g), volleyball (g), weight training (b,g); intramural: weight training (b,g). 4 PE instructors, 60 coaches.

Computers Computer resources include on-campus library services, online commercial services, Internet access, wireless campus network, Internet filtering or blocking technology. Students grades are available online. The school has a published electronic and media policy.

Contact Mrs. Cathy McClaughry, Admissions Office. 503-485-4491. Fax: 503-399-1259. E-mail: cathy@blanchetcatholicschool.com. Web site: www.blanchetcatholicschool.com.

BLESSED TRINITY HIGH SCHOOL

11320 Woodstock Road
Roswell, Georgia 30075
Head of School: Mr. Frank Moore

General Information Coeducational day college-preparatory and religious studies school, affiliated with Roman Catholic Church. Grades 9–12. Founded: 2000. Setting: suburban. Nearest major city is Atlanta. 68-acre campus. 2 buildings on campus. Approved or accredited by Georgia Independent School Association, Southern Association of Colleges and Schools, and Georgia Department of Education. Upper school average class size: 20. Upper school faculty-student ratio: 1:13.

Upper School Student Profile 87% of students are Roman Catholic.

Faculty School total: 71. In upper school: 32 men, 39 women; 36 have advanced degrees.

Graduation Requirements American government, American history, American literature, ancient world history.

Special Academic Programs 22 Advanced Placement exams for which test preparation is offered.

College Admission Counseling 199 students graduated in 2010; all went to college, including Auburn University; Georgia College & State University; Georgia Institute of Technology; Georgia Southern University; The University of Alabama; University of Georgia.

Student Life Upper grades have uniform requirement, student council. Discipline rests primarily with faculty. Attendance at religious services is required.

Tuition and Aid Tuition installment plan (FACTS Tuition Payment Plan). Need-based scholarship grants available. In 2010–11, 18% of upper-school students received aid.

Admissions Traditional secondary-level entrance grade is 9. SSAT required. Deadline for receipt of application materials: February 1. Application fee required: $100.

Athletics Interscholastic: baseball (boys), basketball (b,g), cheering (g), cross-country running (b,g), dance (b,g), dance team (g), football (b), golf (b,g), lacrosse (b,g), soccer (b,g), softball (g), strength & conditioning (b,g), swimming and diving (b,g), tennis (b,g), track and field (b,g), volleyball (g), wrestling (b). 4 PE instructors, 1 athletic trainer.

Contact Mr. Brian Marks, Director of Admissions. 678-277-0983 Ext. 502. Fax: 678-277-9756. E-mail: bmarks@btcatholic.org. Web site: www.btcatholic.org.

BLUE MOUNTAIN ACADEMY

2363 Mountain Road
Hamburg, Pennsylvania 19526
Head of School: Mr. W. Craig Ziesmer

General Information Coeducational boarding and day college-preparatory, religious studies, leadership, and aviation school, affiliated with Seventh-day Adventists. Grades 9–12. Founded: 1955. Setting: rural. Students are housed in single-sex dormitories. 735-acre campus. 6 buildings on campus. Approved or accredited by Board of Regents, General Conference of Seventh-day Adventists and Middle States Association of Colleges and Schools. Total enrollment: 216. Upper school average class size: 22. Upper school faculty-student ratio: 1:12. There are 180 required school days per year for Upper School students. Upper School students typically attend 5 days per week. The average school day consists of 6 hours and 30 minutes.

Upper School Student Profile Grade 9: 35 students (12 boys, 23 girls); Grade 10: 29 students (15 boys, 14 girls); Grade 11: 56 students (29 boys, 27 girls); Grade 12: 66 students (23 boys, 43 girls). 81% of students are boarding students. 47% are state residents. 16 states are represented in upper school student body. 4% are international students. International students from Bermuda, Canada, Malaysia, Mexico, Republic of Korea, and Saudi Arabia. 95% of students are Seventh-day Adventists.

Faculty School total: 18. In upper school: 12 men, 6 women; 14 have advanced degrees; 16 reside on campus.

Subjects Offered Accounting, Advanced Placement courses, algebra, anatomy and physiology, art, auto mechanics, band, bell choir, Bible, biology, business mathematics, chemistry, chemistry-AP, choir, computer applications, desktop publishing, digital photography, English, English literature and composition-AP, fiber arts, flight instruction, food and nutrition, French, geometry, golf, gymnastics, health, home economics, honors English, honors world history, leadership, life science, music appreciation, music theory, organ, physical education, physics, piano, pre-algebra, pre-calculus, psychology, sewing, Spanish, U.S. government, U.S. history, U.S. history-AP, weightlifting, Western civilization, world history.

Graduation Requirements Algebra, arts, Bible, biology, computer applications, electives, English, foreign language, mathematics, physical education (includes health), science, social sciences, U.S. government, U.S. history, work-study, work study credit per semester enrolled.

Special Academic Programs 3 Advanced Placement exams for which test preparation is offered; honors section; accelerated programs; study at local college for college credit; academic accommodation for the musically talented; remedial reading and/or remedial writing; remedial math; programs in English, mathematics, general development for dyslexic students.

College Admission Counseling 69 students graduated in 2010; 60 went to college, including Andrews University; La Sierra University; Pacific Union College; Southern Adventist University; Washington Adventist University.

Student Life Upper grades have specified standards of dress, student council, honor system. Discipline rests primarily with faculty. Attendance at religious services is required.

Tuition and Aid Day student tuition: $10,390; 7-day tuition and room/board: $16,600. Tuition reduction for siblings, need-based scholarship grants, paying campus jobs available. In 2010–11, 45% of upper-school students received aid. Total amount of financial aid awarded in 2010–11: $265,000.

Admissions Traditional secondary-level entrance grade is 9. Math Placement Exam required. Deadline for receipt of application materials: none. Application fee required: $15. Interview recommended.

Athletics Intramural: basketball (boys, girls), flag football (b,g), soccer (b,g), softball (b,g), volleyball (b,g); coed intramural: basketball, flag football, gymnastics, soccer, softball, volleyball. 1 PE instructor.

Computers Computers are regularly used in accounting, desktop publishing, history, keyboarding, mathematics, photography, psychology, religion, science, yearbook classes. Computer network features include on-campus library services, Internet access. Student e-mail accounts and computer access in designated common areas are available to students. Students grades are available online. The school has a published electronic and media policy.

Contact Mrs. Diana Engen, Registrar. 610-562-2291. Fax: 610-562-8050. E-mail: dianae@bma.us. Web site: www.bma.us.

BLUEPRINT EDUCATION

5651 West Talavi Boulevard
Suite 170
Glendale, Arizona 85306
Head of School: Beth Collins

General Information Distance learning only college-preparatory, general academic, technology, and distance learning school. Distance learning grades 7–12. Founded: 1969. Approved or accredited by Arizona Association of Independent Schools, CITA (Commission on International and Trans-Regional Accreditation), North Central Association of Colleges and Schools, and Arizona Department of Education.

Faculty School total: 6. In upper school: 2 men, 4 women; all have advanced degrees.

Subjects Offered Algebra, American government, American history, art, art history, auto mechanics, biology, British literature, calculus, career experience, career exploration, career planning, careers, chemistry, child development, communications, computer applications, computer education, driver education, earth science, economics, English, English composition, entrepreneurship, foreign language, geometry, government, health and wellness, health education, independent study, interpersonal skills, mathematics, parenting, personal development, physical education, physical fitness, physics, pre-algebra, psychology, psychology-AP, reading, remedial/makeup course work, single survival, sociology, Spanish, speech, speech communications, statistics, travel, trigonometry, U.S. government, wellness, wilderness education, work experience, world geography, world history.

Graduation Requirements Arts and fine arts (art, music, dance, drama), computers, English, foreign language, geography, mathematics, science, social studies (includes history), speech.

Special Academic Programs Accelerated programs; independent study; academic accommodation for the musically talented and the artistically talented; remedial reading and/or remedial writing; remedial math.

College Admission Counseling Colleges students went to include Arizona State University; Northern Arizona University; Pima Community College; The University of Arizona; The University of North Carolina at Chapel Hill.

Summer Programs Remediation, advancement programs offered; session focuses on remediation and advancement; held off campus; held at various locations for independent study; accepts boys and girls; open to students from other schools.

Admissions Deadline for receipt of application materials: none. Application fee required: $39.
Computers Computers are regularly used in all academic classes. Computer resources include Internet access. Students grades are available online. The school has a published electronic and media policy.
Contact Jennifer Blackstone, Assistant Superintendent for Distance Learning. 800-426-4952 Ext. 4820. Fax: 602-943-9700. E-mail: jenniferb@blueprinteducation.org. Web site: www.blueprinteducation.org.

THE BLUE RIDGE SCHOOL
273 Mayo Drive
St. George, Virginia 22935
Head of School: Dr. John R. O'Reilly
General Information Boys' boarding college-preparatory, general academic, arts, business, and technology school, affiliated with Episcopal Church; primarily serves underachievers. Grades 9–12. Founded: 1909. Setting: rural. Nearest major city is Charlottesville. Students are housed in single-sex dormitories. 750-acre campus. 11 buildings on campus. Approved or accredited by National Association of Episcopal Schools, Southern Association of Colleges and Schools, The Association of Boarding Schools, Virginia Association of Independent Schools, and Virginia Department of Education. Member of National Association of Independent Schools and Secondary School Admission Test Board. Endowment: $12 million. Total enrollment: 195. Upper school average class size: 8. Upper school faculty-student ratio: 1:5. There are 180 required school days per year for Upper School students. Upper School students typically attend 6 days per week. The average school day consists of 6 hours.
Upper School Student Profile Grade 9: 30 students (30 boys); Grade 10: 47 students (47 boys); Grade 11: 58 students (58 boys); Grade 12: 60 students (60 boys). 100% of students are boarding students. 25% are state residents. 27 states are represented in upper school student body. 32% are international students. International students from Canada, China, Ghana, Nigeria, Republic of Korea, and Taiwan; 16 other countries represented in student body.
Faculty School total: 35. In upper school: 25 men, 7 women; 18 have advanced degrees; 27 reside on campus.
Subjects Offered Algebra, American history, American literature, anatomy, anatomy and physiology, art, astronomy, biology, calculus, chemistry, choir, decision making skills, discrete mathematics, drama, economics, English, environmental science, ESL, European history, French, geometry, guitar, health, honors English, honors geometry, honors U.S. history, integrated science, keyboarding, leadership, marketing, mathematics, music, music history, outdoor education, physics, pre-algebra, pre-calculus, Spanish, trigonometry, U.S. history, world history, world literature, writing, yearbook.
Graduation Requirements Algebra, American history, American literature, biology, decision making skills, English, foreign language, geometry, leadership, mathematics, physical education (includes health), science, social studies (includes history), three years of a single foreign language.
Special Academic Programs Honors section; independent study; study at local college for college credit; remedial reading and/or remedial writing; remedial math; programs in English, general development for dyslexic students; ESL (20 students enrolled).
College Admission Counseling 46 students graduated in 2010; 44 went to college, including Emory University; Franklin & Marshall College; Hampden-Sydney College; Kenyon College; The Johns Hopkins University; University of California, Berkeley. Other: 1 entered military service, 1 had other specific plans.
Student Life Upper grades have specified standards of dress, student council, honor system. Discipline rests primarily with faculty. Attendance at religious services is required.
Tuition and Aid 7-day tuition and room/board: $37,500. Guaranteed tuition plan. Tuition installment plan (monthly payment plans). Merit scholarship grants, need-based scholarship grants, paying campus jobs available. In 2010–11, 40% of upper-school students received aid; total upper-school merit-scholarship money awarded: $85,000. Total amount of financial aid awarded in 2010–11: $1,700,000.
Admissions For fall 2010, 290 students applied for upper-level admission, 133 were accepted, 93 enrolled. Deadline for receipt of application materials: none. Application fee required: $50. Interview required.
Athletics Interscholastic: baseball, basketball, cross-country running, football, golf, indoor soccer, lacrosse, mountain biking, soccer, tennis, track and field, volleyball, wrestling; intramural: alpine skiing, aquatics, backpacking, bicycling, canoeing/kayaking, climbing, cooperative games, fishing, fitness, Frisbee, hiking/backpacking, kayaking, mountain biking, mountaineering, outdoor activities, outdoor adventure, outdoor education, outdoor recreation, outdoor skills, outdoors, paint ball, physical fitness, physical training, rafting, rappelling, rock climbing, ropes courses, skiing (downhill), snowboarding, soccer, strength & conditioning, tennis, ultimate Frisbee, wall climbing, weight lifting, weight training, wilderness, wilderness survival. 2 coaches, 2 athletic trainers.
Computers Computers are regularly used in business studies, English, ESL, foreign language, mathematics, science, study skills, word processing, writing, yearbook classes. Computer network features include on-campus library services, online commercial services, Internet access, wireless campus network, Internet filtering or blocking technology. Campus intranet, student e-mail accounts, and computer access in designated common areas are available to students. The school has a published electronic and media policy.

Contact Mr. James H. Miller III, Director of Financial Aid. 434-985-2811 Ext. 143. Fax: 434-992-0536. E-mail: jmiller@blueridgeschool.com. Web site: www.blueridgeschool.com.

BODWELL HIGH SCHOOL
955 Harbourside Drive
North Vancouver, British Columbia V7P 3S4, Canada
Head of School: Mr. Stephen Smith
General Information Coeducational boarding and day college-preparatory, arts, business, and technology school. Grades 8–12. Founded: 1991. Setting: suburban. Students are housed in single-sex by floor dormitories. 2-acre campus. 2 buildings on campus. Approved or accredited by British Columbia Department of Education. Language of instruction: English. Total enrollment: 372. Upper school average class size: 20. Upper school faculty-student ratio: 1:15. Upper School students typically attend 5 days per week. The average school day consists of 5 hours and 50 minutes.
Upper School Student Profile 35% of students are boarding students. 25% are province residents. 8 provinces are represented in upper school student body. 75% are international students. International students from China, Hong Kong, Japan, Mexico, Republic of Korea, and Taiwan; 30 other countries represented in student body.
Faculty School total: 30. In upper school: 17 men, 13 women; 12 have advanced degrees; 2 reside on campus.
Subjects Offered 3-dimensional art, art, art-AP, band, biology, calculus, chemistry, choral music, communications, composition, computer applications, drama, economics, English, entrepreneurship, French as a second language, geography, global studies, health and wellness, history, information technology, Japanese, Mandarin, mathematics, physical education, physics, psychology, science, social studies, Spanish, sports, studio art.
Graduation Requirements British Columbia Ministry of Education requirements.
Special Academic Programs Advanced Placement exam preparation; accelerated programs; academic accommodation for the gifted; ESL (90 students enrolled).
College Admission Counseling 130 students graduated in 2009; 100 went to college, including Simon Fraser University; The University of British Columbia; University of Alberta; University of Calgary; University of Toronto. Other: 20 had other specific plans.
Student Life Upper grades have uniform requirement, student council, honor system. Discipline rests primarily with faculty.
Tuition and Aid Day student tuition: CAN$12,400; 7-day tuition and room/board: CAN$28,000. Guaranteed tuition plan. Tuition installment plan (individually arranged payment plans). Merit scholarship grants available. In 2009–10, 2% of upper-school students received aid; total upper-school merit-scholarship money awarded: CAN$50,000.
Admissions Traditional secondary-level entrance grade is 10. For fall 2009, 220 students applied for upper-level admission, 145 were accepted, 140 enrolled. Deadline for receipt of application materials: none. Application fee required: CAN$200. Interview recommended.
Athletics Interscholastic: aquatics (boys, girls), baseball (b), basketball (b,g), cross-country running (b,g), soccer (b), swimming and diving (b,g), volleyball (g); intramural: aquatics (b,g), badminton (b,g), baseball (b,g), basketball (b,g), cheering (g), fitness (b,g), floor hockey (b,g), hiking/backpacking (b,g), ice skating (b,g), indoor soccer (b), kayaking (b), martial arts (b), mountain biking (b,g), outdoor activities (b,g), outdoor education (b,g), running (b,g), skateboarding (b,g), skiing (downhill) (b,g), snowboarding (b,g), snowshoeing (b,g), soccer (b), swimming and diving (b,g), table tennis (b,g), tennis (b,g), track and field (b,g), triathlon (b), volleyball (b,g), wilderness (b,g); coed interscholastic: aerobics/dance, aquatics, backpacking, badminton, ball hockey, bicycling, blading, bowling, canoeing/kayaking, fitness, floor hockey, swimming and diving; coed intramural: aquatics, badminton, bicycling, bowling, canoeing/kayaking, climbing, cross-country running, dance, fishing, fitness, floor hockey, fly fishing, golf, hiking/backpacking, ice skating, indoor soccer, kayaking, martial arts, mountain biking, outdoor activities, outdoor education, physical fitness, rock climbing, roller blading, running, skateboarding, skiing (downhill), snowboarding, snowshoeing, swimming and diving, table tennis, tennis, track and field, volleyball, wilderness. 3 PE instructors, 5 coaches.
Computers Computers are regularly used in all academic classes. Computer network features include on-campus library services, Internet access, wireless campus network, Internet filtering or blocking technology. Student e-mail accounts are available to students. The school has a published electronic and media policy.
Contact Ms. Jennifer Chen, Admissions Officer. 604-924-5066 Ext. 118. Fax: 604-924-5058. E-mail: office@bodwell.edu. Web site: www.bodwell.edu.

THE BOLLES SCHOOL
7400 San Jose Boulevard
Jacksonville, Florida 32217-3499
Head of School: John E. Trainer, Jr., PhD
General Information Coeducational boarding and day college-preparatory and arts school. Boarding grades 7–PG, day grades PK–PG. Founded: 1933. Setting: suburban. Students are housed in single-sex dormitories. 52-acre campus. 8 buildings on campus. Approved or accredited by Florida Council of Independent Schools, Southern Association of Colleges and Schools, Southern Association of Independent Schools,

The Bolles School

The Association of Boarding Schools, and Florida Department of Education. Member of National Association of Independent Schools and Secondary School Admission Test Board. Endowment: $10.7 million. Total enrollment: 1,651. Upper school average class size: 17. Upper school faculty-student ratio: 1:10. There are 175 required school days per year for Upper School students. Upper School students typically attend 5 days per week. The average school day consists of 6 hours.

Upper School Student Profile Grade 9: 183 students (100 boys, 83 girls); Grade 10: 196 students (113 boys, 83 girls); Grade 11: 195 students (101 boys, 94 girls); Grade 12: 193 students (112 boys, 81 girls). 10% of students are boarding students. 92% are state residents. 8 states are represented in upper school student body. 8% are international students. International students from Brazil, China, Colombia, Democratic People's Republic of Korea, Germany, and Mexico; 13 other countries represented in student body.

Faculty School total: 169. In upper school: 40 men, 51 women; 55 have advanced degrees; 9 reside on campus.

Subjects Offered Acting, algebra, American Civil War, American government, American history, American literature, anatomy, art, art history, art history-AP, art-AP, band, biology, biology-AP, British literature, calculus, calculus-AP, ceramics, chemistry, chemistry-AP, Chinese, chorus, comparative government and politics-AP, composition, computer applications, computer science, computer science-AP, contemporary history, creative writing, dance, data analysis, design, directing, drama, drawing, driver education, earth science, ecology, economics, English, English literature-AP, environmental science, ESL, European history, fine arts, fitness, French, French-AP, geography, geometry, German, government/civics, health, history, history-AP, humanities, Japanese, journalism, Latin, Latin-AP, life management skills, life skills, literature, marine science, mathematics, Middle Eastern history, modern European history-AP, multimedia, music, mythology, neurobiology, painting, performing arts, photography, physical education, physics, physics-AP, portfolio art, pre-algebra, pre-calculus, programming, psychology, public speaking, publications, science, sculpture, social sciences, social studies, Spanish, Spanish-AP, statistics, statistics-AP, studio art, theater, U.S. government and politics-AP, visual arts, Web site design, weight training, world cultures, world history.

Graduation Requirements Arts and fine arts (art, music, dance, drama), English, foreign language, mathematics, physical education (includes health), science, social studies (includes history).

Special Academic Programs Advanced Placement exam preparation; honors section; independent study; term-away projects; study at local college for college credit; ESL (45 students enrolled).

College Admission Counseling 200 students graduated in 2010; 192 went to college, including Florida State University; Tallahassee Community College; The University of Alabama; University of Central Florida; University of Florida; University of North Florida. Other: 2 entered a postgraduate year, 6 had other specific plans. 50% scored over 600 on SAT critical reading, 50% scored over 600 on SAT math, 49% scored over 600 on SAT writing, 47% scored over 1800 on combined SAT, 50% scored over 26 on composite ACT.

Student Life Upper grades have specified standards of dress, student council, honor system. Discipline rests primarily with faculty.

Summer Programs Enrichment, ESL, art/fine arts, computer instruction programs offered; held on campus; accepts boys and girls; open to students from other schools. 150 students usually enrolled. 2011 schedule: June 6 to July 22.

Tuition and Aid Day student tuition: $18,750; 7-day tuition and room/board: $38,950. Tuition installment plan (major increment payment plan, 10-month plan, June payment plan). Need-based scholarship grants, faculty tuition remission available. In 2010–11, 18% of upper-school students received aid. Total amount of financial aid awarded in 2010–11: $1,772,385.

Admissions Traditional secondary-level entrance grade is 9. For fall 2010, 266 students applied for upper-level admission, 137 were accepted, 77 enrolled. ISEE required. Deadline for receipt of application materials: none. Application fee required: $45. Interview required.

Athletics Interscholastic: baseball (boys), basketball (b,g), cheering (g), crew (b,g), cross-country running (b,g), dance (b,g), diving (b,g), football (b), golf (b,g), lacrosse (b), soccer (b,g), softball (g), swimming and diving (b,g), tennis (b,g), track and field (b,g), volleyball (g), weight lifting (b), wrestling (b). 2 PE instructors, 5 coaches, 1 athletic trainer.

Computers Computers are regularly used in all academic classes. Computer network features include on-campus library services, online commercial services, Internet access, wireless campus network, Internet filtering or blocking technology. Computer access in designated common areas is available to students. Students grades are available online. The school has a published electronic and media policy.

Contact Mark I. Frampton, Director of Upper School and Boarding Admission. 904-256-5032. Fax: 904-739-9929. E-mail: framptonm@bolles.org. Web site: www.bolles.org.

BOSTON COLLEGE HIGH SCHOOL

150 Morrissey Boulevard
Boston, Massachusetts 02125
Head of School: Mr. William Kemeza

General Information Boys' day college-preparatory, arts, and religious studies school, affiliated with Roman Catholic Church. Grades 7–12. Founded: 1863. Setting: urban. 40-acre campus. 5 buildings on campus. Approved or accredited by Association of Independent Schools in New England, Jesuit Secondary Education Association, National Catholic Education Association, New England Association of Schools and Colleges, and Massachusetts Department of Education. Member of Secondary School Admission Test Board. Endowment: $40 million. Total enrollment: 1,591. Upper school average class size: 23. Upper school faculty-student ratio: 1:13. Upper School students typically attend 5 days per week. The average school day consists of 6 hours.

Upper School Student Profile Grade 9: 331 students (331 boys); Grade 10: 365 students (365 boys); Grade 11: 397 students (397 boys); Grade 12: 268 students (268 boys). 85% of students are Roman Catholic.

Faculty School total: 143. In upper school: 69 men, 50 women; 87 have advanced degrees.

Subjects Offered Acting, Advanced Placement courses, algebra, American history, American history-AP, American literature, anatomy and physiology, Ancient Greek, art, art history, astronomy, band, Bible studies, biology, biology-AP, British literature, British literature (honors), calculus, calculus-AP, calligraphy, chemistry, chemistry-AP, Chinese, choir, Christian doctrine, composition-AP, computer math, computer programming, computer science, computer science-AP, creative writing, digital photography, drafting, drama, dramatic arts, driver education, ecology, economics, economics-AP, electronics, English, English language and composition-AP, English literature, English literature and composition-AP, environmental science, environmental science-AP, environmental studies, ethics, European history, European history-AP, film, fine arts, forensics, French, French language-AP, French literature-AP, geometry, German, government and politics-AP, government/civics, grammar, graphic design, Greek, guitar, health, health and wellness, history, Homeric Greek, integrated science, Japanese, Latin, Latin-AP, marine biology, mathematics, modern world history, music, music theory-AP, physics, physics-AP, pre-calculus, printmaking, probability and statistics, psychology, religion, science, social justice, social studies, Spanish, Spanish language-AP, Spanish literature-AP, statistics-AP, trigonometry, U.S. government and politics-AP, U.S. history-AP, world history, world literature.

Graduation Requirements Arts and fine arts (art, music, dance, drama), English, foreign language, mathematics, religion (includes Bible studies and theology), science, social studies (includes history), 150+ hours of community service over 4 years.

Special Academic Programs 24 Advanced Placement exams for which test preparation is offered; honors section; independent study; term-away projects; study abroad; academic accommodation for the gifted; special instructional classes for blind students; ESL (10 students enrolled).

College Admission Counseling 283 students graduated in 2010; 278 went to college, including Boston College; Boston University; Fordham University; Loyola University Maryland; Northeastern University; University of Massachusetts Amherst. Other: 3 went to work, 1 entered military service, 1 entered a postgraduate year. Mean SAT critical reading: 598, mean SAT math: 611, mean SAT writing: 598, mean combined SAT: 1808.

Student Life Upper grades have specified standards of dress, student council. Discipline rests primarily with faculty.

Summer Programs Remediation, enrichment, advancement, sports, art/fine arts, computer instruction programs offered; session focuses on enrichment/advancement in academics and athletics; held on campus; accepts boys and girls; open to students from other schools. 100 students usually enrolled. 2011 schedule: June 28 to July 30. Application deadline: none.

Tuition and Aid Day student tuition: $15,900. Tuition installment plan (monthly payment plans). Merit scholarship grants, need-based scholarship grants, need-based loans, paying campus jobs available. In 2010–11, 35% of upper-school students received aid; total upper-school merit-scholarship money awarded: $140,000. Total amount of financial aid awarded in 2010–11: $4,300,000.

Admissions Traditional secondary-level entrance grade is 9. For fall 2010, 700 students applied for upper-level admission, 350 were accepted, 200 enrolled. Catholic High School Entrance Examination, High School Placement Test or SSAT required. Deadline for receipt of application materials: December 31. No application fee required.

Athletics Interscholastic: baseball, basketball, cross-country running, football, golf, ice hockey, lacrosse, rugby, sailing, skiing (downhill), soccer, swimming and diving, tennis, track and field, volleyball, winter (indoor) track; intramural: basketball, bicycling, crew, flag football, Frisbee, hiking/backpacking, tennis. 42 coaches, 1 athletic trainer.

Computers Computers are regularly used in English, foreign language, mathematics, religious studies, science, social sciences classes. Computer network features include on-campus library services, online commercial services, Internet access, wireless campus network, Internet filtering or blocking technology. Student e-mail accounts and computer access in designated common areas are available to students. Students grades are available online.

Contact Mr. Michael Brennan, Director of Admissions. 617-474-5010. Fax: 617-474-5015. E-mail: brennan@bchigh.edu. Web site: www.bchigh.edu/.

BOSTON TRINITY ACADEMY

17 Hale Street
Boston, Massachusetts 02136
Head of School: Dr. Timothy P. Wiens
General Information Coeducational day college-preparatory school, affiliated with Christian faith. Grades 6–12. Founded: 2002. Setting: urban. 5-acre campus. 1 building on campus. Approved or accredited by Association of Independent Schools in New England, New England Association of Schools and Colleges, and Massachusetts Department of Education. Total enrollment: 213. Upper school average class size: 16. Upper school faculty-student ratio: 1:9. There are 173 required school days per year for Upper School students. Upper School students typically attend 5 days per week. The average school day consists of 7 hours.
Upper School Student Profile Grade 6: 10 students (5 boys, 5 girls); Grade 7: 24 students (15 boys, 9 girls); Grade 8: 27 students (14 boys, 13 girls); Grade 9: 33 students (15 boys, 18 girls); Grade 10: 39 students (19 boys, 20 girls); Grade 11: 46 students (27 boys, 19 girls); Grade 12: 34 students (14 boys, 20 girls). 70% of students are Christian faith.
Faculty School total: 30. In upper school: 15 men, 15 women; 17 have advanced degrees.
Subjects Offered 20th century history, 20th century physics, 20th century world history, advanced biology, advanced math, African American studies, algebra, American history-AP, American literature-AP, anatomy and physiology, ancient history, art, art history, basketball, Bible, biology-AP, British literature-AP, calculus-AP, chemistry, choir, civil rights, drama performance, English, English language and composition-AP, European history-AP, French, geometry, New Testament, participation in sports, performing arts, physics, pre-algebra, pre-calculus, Spanish, transition mathematics, U.S. history-AP.
Graduation Requirements All students must take four advanced placement courses to graduate, seniors write a thesis for Senior Synthesis (Christianity and Culture) that they defend in front of a panel of college professors.
Special Academic Programs Study at local college for college credit; ESL (6 students enrolled).
College Admission Counseling 34 students graduated in 2009; all went to college, including Dartmouth College; Gordon College; McGill University; University of Virginia.
Student Life Upper grades have uniform requirement, student council, honor system. Discipline rests primarily with faculty. Attendance at religious services is required.
Tuition and Aid Day student tuition: $12,900. Tuition installment plan (FACTS Tuition Payment Plan). Need-based scholarship grants available. In 2009–10, 60% of upper-school students received aid. Total amount of financial aid awarded in 2009–10: $900,000.
Admissions Traditional secondary-level entrance grade is 9. For fall 2009, 241 students applied for upper-level admission, 108 were accepted, 59 enrolled. ISEE or SSAT required. Deadline for receipt of application materials: February 15. Application fee required: $50. Interview required.
Athletics Interscholastic: basketball (boys, girls); cross-country running (b), lacrosse (b,g), soccer (b,g), tennis (g), ultimate Frisbee (b,g), wrestling (b). 1 coach.
Computers Computer network features include on-campus library services, Internet access, wireless campus network, Internet filtering or blocking technology. Campus intranet, student e-mail accounts, and computer access in designated common areas are available to students. Students grades are available online. The school has a published electronic and media policy.
Contact Mrs. Susan Yem, Assistant Director of Admission. 617-364-3700 Ext. 219. Fax: 617-364-3800. E-mail: syem@bostontrinity.org. Web site: www.bostontrinity.org.

BOSTON UNIVERSITY ACADEMY

One University Road
Boston, Massachusetts 02215
Head of School: Mr. James Berkman
General Information Coeducational day college-preparatory and arts school. Grades 9–12. Founded: 1993. Setting: urban. 132-acre campus. 1 building on campus. Approved or accredited by Association of Independent Schools in New England, New England Association of Schools and Colleges, and Massachusetts Department of Education. Member of National Association of Independent Schools and Secondary School Admission Test Board. Total enrollment: 154. Upper school average class size: 13. Upper school faculty-student ratio: 1:7.
Upper School Student Profile Grade 9: 42 students (23 boys, 19 girls); Grade 10: 42 students (24 boys, 18 girls); Grade 11: 36 students (20 boys, 16 girls); Grade 12: 34 students (21 boys, 13 girls).
Faculty School total: 21. In upper school: 13 men, 8 women; 15 have advanced degrees.
Subjects Offered Advanced math, African American studies, algebra, American history, American literature, ancient history, anthropology, Arabic, archaeology, art, art history, astronomy, biochemistry, biology, calculus, chemistry, Chinese, classical studies, college counseling, community service, computer programming, drama,

English, English literature, European history, French, geometry, German, Greek, Hebrew, history, Italian, Japanese, Latin, music, physical education, physics, robotics, Russian, sculpture, senior project, Spanish, statistics, theater, trigonometry, women's studies, writing.
Graduation Requirements Arts and fine arts (art, music, dance, drama), chemistry, English, Greek, history, Latin, mathematics, physical education (includes health), physics, two-semester senior thesis project, coursework at Boston University. Community service is required.
Special Academic Programs Honors section; accelerated programs; independent study; study at local college for college credit; academic accommodation for the gifted.
College Admission Counseling 39 students graduated in 2009; 38 went to college, including Boston University; Brandeis University; Brown University; Harvard University; Macalester College; Massachusetts Institute of Technology. Other: 1 had other specific plans. Mean SAT critical reading: 722, mean SAT math: 694, mean SAT writing: 713, mean combined SAT: 2129. 92% scored over 600 on SAT critical reading, 90% scored over 600 on SAT math, 92% scored over 600 on SAT writing, 92% scored over 1800 on combined SAT.
Student Life Upper grades have student council, honor system. Discipline rests equally with students and faculty.
Tuition and Aid Day student tuition: $30,123. Tuition installment plan (Insured Tuition Payment Plan, Academic Management Services Plan, monthly payment plans). Merit scholarship grants, need-based scholarship grants available. In 2009–10, 32% of upper-school students received aid; total upper-school merit-scholarship money awarded: $3000. Total amount of financial aid awarded in 2009–10: $916,794.
Admissions Traditional secondary-level entrance grade is 9. For fall 2009, 169 students applied for upper-level admission, 90 were accepted, 50 enrolled. SSAT required. Deadline for receipt of application materials: January 31. Application fee required: $45. On-campus interview required.
Athletics Interscholastic: baseball (boys), basketball (b,g), crew (b,g); coed interscholastic: cross-country running, fencing, sailing, soccer, tennis, ultimate Frisbee; coed intramural: climbing, dance, fitness, hiking/backpacking, softball. 10 PE instructors, 7 coaches.
Computers Computers are regularly used in art, English, foreign language, history, mathematics, science classes. Computer network features include on-campus library services, online commercial services, Internet access, Internet filtering or blocking technology, internal electronic bulletin board system. Student e-mail accounts are available to students. Students grades are available online. The school has a published electronic and media policy.
Contact Ms. Nicole White, Admission Coordinator. 617-358-2493. Fax: 617-353-8999. E-mail: nicole_white@buacademy.org. Web site: www.buacademy.org.

BOURGADE CATHOLIC HIGH SCHOOL

4602 North 31st Avenue
Phoenix, Arizona 85017
Head of School: Sr. Mary McGreevy, SSND
General Information Coeducational day college-preparatory, general academic, arts, and religious studies school, affiliated with Roman Catholic Church. Grades 9–12. Founded: 1962. Setting: urban. 27-acre campus. 6 buildings on campus. Approved or accredited by North Central Association of Colleges and Schools, Western Catholic Education Association, and Arizona Department of Education. Total enrollment: 406. Upper school average class size: 25. Upper school faculty-student ratio: 1:13. There are 184 required school days per year for Upper School students. Upper School students typically attend 5 days per week. The average school day consists of 6 hours.
Upper School Student Profile Grade 9: 130 students (65 boys, 65 girls); Grade 10: 90 students (38 boys, 52 girls); Grade 11: 96 students (56 boys, 46 girls); Grade 12: 90 students (41 boys, 49 girls). 94% of students are Roman Catholic.
Faculty School total: 33. In upper school: 18 men, 15 women; 22 have advanced degrees.
Subjects Offered Acting, advanced biology, advanced chemistry, algebra, American government, American history, American history-AP, American sign language, ancient world history, art, band, bell choir, biology, broadcasting, calculus, calculus-AP, Catholic belief and practice, chemistry, chemistry-AP, choir, Christian and Hebrew scripture, Christian doctrine, Christian ethics, church history, college admission preparation, comparative religion, computer graphics, constitutional history of U.S., creative dance, dance, desktop publishing, digital photography, drama performance, earth science, economics, English, English composition, foreign language, general science, geography, government, graphic design, health education, Hebrew scripture, honors algebra, honors English, honors geometry, honors U.S. history, honors world history, keyboarding, leadership and service, modern dance, New Testament, newspaper, photography, pre-algebra, psychology, reading, sexuality, social justice, Spanish, Spanish-AP, speech, study skills, theater arts, U.S. government, U.S. history, U.S. history-AP, video communication, world religions, yearbook, yoga.
Graduation Requirements Advanced Placement courses, arts and fine arts (art, music, dance, drama), English, foreign language, mathematics, physical education (includes health), religion (includes Bible studies and theology), science.

Special Academic Programs Advanced Placement exam preparation; honors section.

College Admission Counseling 86 students graduated in 2010; 82 went to college, including Arizona State University; Embry-Riddle Aeronautical University; Grand Canyon University; Northern Arizona University; The University of Arizona. Other: 2 went to work, 2 entered military service.

Student Life Upper grades have uniform requirement, student council, honor system. Discipline rests primarily with faculty. Attendance at religious services is required.

Tuition and Aid Day student tuition: $8320–$10,450. Tuition installment plan (monthly payment plans). Tuition reduction for siblings, need-based scholarship grants, Catholic Tuition Organization Diocese of Phoenix (CTODP) available. In 2010–11, 80% of upper-school students received aid. Total amount of financial aid awarded in 2010–11: $800,000.

Admissions Traditional secondary-level entrance grade is 9. For fall 2010, 484 students applied for upper-level admission, 430 were accepted, 406 enrolled. ETS high school placement exam or Stanford 9 required. Deadline for receipt of application materials: February 10. Application fee required: $10,450. Interview required.

Athletics Interscholastic: baseball (boys), basketball (b,g), cheering (g), dance (g), dance squad (g), dance team (g), danceline (g), football (b), golf (b), soccer (b), softball (g), tennis (b,g), track and field (b,g), volleyball (g), wrestling (b); intramural: weight training (b,g). 2 PE instructors, 2 coaches, 1 athletic trainer.

Computers Computers are regularly used in all academic classes. Computer resources include Internet access.

Contact Mrs. Vicki Kilgarriff, Assistant Principal/Academic Director. 602-973-4000 Ext. 112. Fax: 602-973-5854. E-mail: vkilgarriff@bourgade.org. Web site: www.bourgadecatholic.org.

BOYLAN CENTRAL CATHOLIC HIGH SCHOOL

4000 Saint Francis Drive
Rockford, Illinois 61103-1699
Head of School: Rev. Paul Lipinski

General Information Coeducational day and distance learning college-preparatory, general academic, arts, business, vocational, religious studies, bilingual studies, and technology school, affiliated with Roman Catholic Church. Grades 9–12. Distance learning grades 9–12. Founded: 1960. Setting: urban. Nearest major city is Chicago. 60-acre campus. 3 buildings on campus. Approved or accredited by National Catholic Education Association, North Central Association of Colleges and Schools, and Illinois Department of Education. Endowment: $3 million. Total enrollment: 1,187. Upper school average class size: 24. Upper school faculty-student ratio: 1:13. There are 176 required school days per year for Upper School students. Upper School students typically attend 5 days per week. The average school day consists of 7 hours.

Upper School Student Profile Grade 9: 293 students (145 boys, 148 girls); Grade 10: 274 students (144 boys, 130 girls); Grade 11: 322 students (152 boys, 170 girls); Grade 12: 297 students (151 boys, 146 girls). 87% of students are Roman Catholic.

Faculty School total: 89. In upper school: 34 men, 52 women; 62 have advanced degrees.

Subjects Offered 20th century history, 3-dimensional art, accounting, ACT preparation, acting, advanced computer applications, Advanced Placement courses, advanced studio art-AP, algebra, American history, American history-AP, American literature-AP, analysis and differential calculus, analytic geometry, anatomy and physiology, architectural drawing, architecture, art, art history, art history-AP, art-AP, athletics, auto mechanics, band, biology, bookkeeping, botany, British literature, British literature (honors), broadcast journalism, broadcasting, business, business education, business law, calculus, calculus-AP, career education, career exploration, career planning, Catholic belief and practice, cheerleading, chemistry, chemistry-AP, choir, chorus, Christian and Hebrew scripture, Christian doctrine, Christian ethics, church history, college counseling, communications, comparative religion, composition-AP, computer multimedia, computer-aided design, concert band, concert choir, consumer economics, consumer education, consumer law, consumer mathematics, contemporary history, contemporary issues, contemporary studies, creative writing, critical thinking, culinary arts, debate, desktop publishing, drafting, drama, dramatic arts, earth science, English, English language-AP, English literature-AP, English/composition-AP, environmental science, European history, European history-AP, family and consumer science, family living, fashion, fiction, finite math, foods, French, French as a second language, French literature-AP, French-AP, freshman foundations, general math, geography, geometry, German, government, graphics, guitar, health, health education, history of music, illustration, industrial technology, information processing, integrated science, jazz band, keyboarding, library assistant, marketing, music appreciation, music composition, music theory, physical science, physics, physics-AP, pre-algebra, pre-calculus, psychology, psychology-AP, religion, senior composition, Spanish, statistics, strings, studio art, swimming, technological applications, technology/design, trigonometry, U.S. history, Web authoring, Web site design, wood lab, woodworking, world geography, world history, world literature, writing, yearbook, zoology.

Graduation Requirements Consumer education, English, mathematics, physical education (includes health), religious studies, science, social studies (includes history), fine and applied arts, community service.

Special Academic Programs 12 Advanced Placement exams for which test preparation is offered; honors section; independent study; academic accommodation for the gifted, the musically talented, and the artistically talented; remedial reading and/or remedial writing; remedial math; programs in general development for dyslexic students; special instructional classes for deaf students, blind students.

College Admission Counseling 262 students graduated in 2010; 255 went to college, including Illinois State University; Loyola University Chicago; Marquette University; Northern Illinois University; The University of Iowa; University of Illinois at Urbana–Champaign. Other: 4 went to work, 3 entered military service.

Student Life Upper grades have uniform requirement, student council. Discipline rests primarily with faculty. Attendance at religious services is required.

Summer Programs Enrichment, sports, art/fine arts, rigorous outdoor training programs offered; session focuses on enrichment; held on campus; accepts boys and girls; open to students from other schools. 150 students usually enrolled. 2011 schedule: June 5 to July 30.

Tuition and Aid Day student tuition: $5100. Tuition installment plan (monthly payment plans, individually arranged payment plans, full-year or semester payment plan). Tuition reduction for siblings, need-based scholarship grants, paying campus jobs available. In 2010–11, 100% of upper-school students received aid. Total amount of financial aid awarded in 2010–11: $390,750.

Admissions Traditional secondary-level entrance grade is 9. For fall 2010, 310 students applied for upper-level admission, 310 were accepted, 292 enrolled. ETS HSPT (closed) required. Deadline for receipt of application materials: none. Application fee required: $75. Interview required.

Athletics Interscholastic: aerobics/dance (girls), baseball (b), basketball (b,g), bowling (b,g), cheering (g), cross-country running (b,g), dance team (g), diving (b,g), fishing (b,g), football (b), golf (b,g), ice hockey (b,g), soccer (b,g), softball (g), swimming and diving (b,g), tennis (b,g), track and field (b,g), volleyball (g), wrestling (b); intramural: aerobics (g), archery (b,g), fitness (b,g), golf (b,g), outdoor education (b,g), physical fitness (b,g), physical training (b,g), rowing (b,g), running (b,g), strength & conditioning (b,g), track and field (b,g), volleyball (b,g), weight training (b,g); coed intramural: dance. 6 PE instructors, 1 coach, 2 athletic trainers.

Computers Computers are regularly used in all academic, architecture, business applications, computer applications, desktop publishing, drawing and design, keyboarding, photography, publications, technical drawing, technology, video film production, Web site design, word processing, yearbook classes. Computer network features include on-campus library services, online commercial services, Internet access, Internet filtering or blocking technology. Campus intranet, student e-mail accounts, and computer access in designated common areas are available to students. Students grades are available online. The school has a published electronic and media policy.

Contact Mr. Dennis Hiemenz, Assistant Principal. 815-877-0531 Ext. 227. Fax: 815-877-2544. E-mail: dhiemenz@boylan.org. Web site: www.boylan.org.

THE BOYS' LATIN SCHOOL OF MARYLAND

822 West Lake Avenue
Baltimore, Maryland 21210
Head of School: Mr. Christopher J. Post

General Information Boys' day college-preparatory, arts, and technology school. Grades K–12. Founded: 1844. Setting: suburban. 32.6-acre campus. 4 buildings on campus. Approved or accredited by Association of Independent Maryland Schools and Maryland Department of Education. Member of National Association of Independent Schools. Endowment: $26 million. Total enrollment: 624. Upper school average class size: 15. Upper school faculty-student ratio: 1:8. There are 173 required school days per year for Upper School students. Upper School students typically attend 5 days per week. The average school day consists of 6 hours and 30 minutes.

Upper School Student Profile Grade 9: 75 students (75 boys); Grade 10: 60 students (60 boys); Grade 11: 71 students (71 boys); Grade 12: 80 students (80 boys).

Faculty School total: 95. In upper school: 27 men, 12 women; 20 have advanced degrees.

Subjects Offered Advanced Placement courses, African-American history, algebra, American history, American literature, art, biology, calculus, calculus-AP, chemistry, chemistry-AP, drama, dramatic arts, economics, English, English language-AP, English literature, English literature-AP, environmental science, European history, European history-AP, expository writing, film, fine arts, French, geometry, government, Greek culture, health education, history-AP, honors algebra, honors English, honors geometry, honors U.S. history, honors world history, journalism, Latin, mathematics, military history, music, music appreciation, physical education, physics, psychology, Spanish, technology, theater, trigonometry, world history.

Graduation Requirements Arts and fine arts (art, music, dance, drama), English, foreign language, mathematics, physical education (includes health), science, social studies (includes history). Community service is required.

Special Academic Programs Honors section; term-away projects.

College Admission Counseling 67 students graduated in 2009; 64 went to college, including Case Western Reserve University; Cornell University; Dartmouth College; Duke University; University of Maryland, College Park; Washington College. Other: 3 entered a postgraduate year. Median SAT critical reading: 550, median SAT math: 570, median SAT writing: 550, median combined SAT: 1660, median composite ACT: 22. 24% scored over 600 on SAT critical reading, 42% scored over 600 on SAT math, 31% scored over 600 on SAT writing, 31% scored over 1800 on combined SAT, 24% scored over 26 on composite ACT.

Student Life Upper grades have specified standards of dress, student council, honor system. Discipline rests primarily with faculty.

Tuition and Aid Day student tuition: $20,920. Tuition installment plan (monthly payment plans, individually arranged payment plans, TuitionPay). Need-based scholarship grants available. In 2009–10, 35% of upper-school students received aid. Total amount of financial aid awarded in 2009–10: $991,200.

Admissions Traditional secondary-level entrance grade is 9. ERB, ISEE or Otis-Lennon School Ability Test required. Deadline for receipt of application materials: January 15. Application fee required: $50. On-campus interview required.

Athletics Interscholastic: baseball (boys), basketball (b), cross-country running (b), football (b), golf (b), ice hockey (b), lacrosse (b), outdoor adventure (b), outdoor education (b), physical fitness (b), physical training (b), soccer (b), squash (b), strength & conditioning (b), tennis (b), volleyball (b), wrestling (b); intramural: hiking/backpacking (b). 5 coaches, 1 athletic trainer.

Computers Computers are regularly used in all academic classes. Computer network features include on-campus library services, online commercial services, Internet access, wireless campus network, Internet filtering or blocking technology, Intranet combining technology, curricular, and research capabilities. Campus intranet, student e-mail accounts, and computer access in designated common areas are available to students. Students grades are available online. The school has a published electronic and media policy.

Contact Mr. James W. Currie Jr., Director of Middle and Upper School Admissions. 410-377-5192 Ext. 1139. Fax: 410-433-2571. E-mail: jcurrie@boyslatinmd.com. Web site: www.boyslatinmd.com.

BRADENTON CHRISTIAN SCHOOL

3304 43rd Street West
Bradenton, Florida 34209
Head of School: Mr. Dan van der Kooy

General Information Coeducational day college-preparatory, arts, business, religious studies, and technology school, affiliated with Christian Reformed Church, Baptist Church. Grades PK–12. Founded: 1960. Setting: suburban. Nearest major city is Tampa. 24-acre campus. 5 buildings on campus. Approved or accredited by Christian Schools International, Christian Schools of Florida, Southern Association of Colleges and Schools, and Florida Department of Education. Total enrollment: 563. Upper school average class size: 18. Upper school faculty-student ratio: 1:14. Upper School students typically attend 5 days per week. The average school day consists of 6 hours.

Upper School Student Profile 45% of students are members of Christian Reformed Church, Baptist.

Faculty School total: 51. In upper school: 13 men, 9 women; 12 have advanced degrees.

Graduation Requirements 3½ credits of Bible.

Special Academic Programs Honors section; study at local college for college credit.

College Admission Counseling 43 students graduated in 2009; 42 went to college. Other: 1 went to work. Mean SAT critical reading: 565, mean SAT math: 545, mean composite ACT: 25. 43% scored over 600 on SAT critical reading, 25% scored over 600 on SAT math.

Student Life Upper grades have specified standards of dress, student council. Discipline rests primarily with faculty. Attendance at religious services is required.

Tuition and Aid Day student tuition: $9460. Tuition installment plan (monthly payment plans, individually arranged payment plans). Tuition reduction for siblings, need-based scholarship grants available. In 2009–10, 23% of upper-school students received aid. Total amount of financial aid awarded in 2009–10: $47,000.

Admissions Traditional secondary-level entrance grade is 9. Academic Profile Tests or audition required. Deadline for receipt of application materials: none. Application fee required: $100. On-campus interview required.

Athletics Interscholastic: baseball (boys), basketball (b,g), cheering (b,g), football (b), golf (b), soccer (b,g), softball (g), swimming and diving (g), tennis (b,g), track and field (b,g), volleyball (g); intramural: flag football (b), touch football (b); coed interscholastic: physical fitness. 2 PE instructors, 25 coaches.

Computers Computers are regularly used in art, Bible studies, business, business applications, business skills, career exploration, Christian doctrine, creative writing, design, desktop publishing, ESL, drawing and design, economics, English, ethics, foreign language classes. Computer network features include on-campus library services, Internet access, Internet filtering or blocking technology. Student e-mail accounts and computer access in designated common areas are available to students. Students grades are available online. The school has a published electronic and media policy.

Contact Jannon Pierce, Director of Admissions. 941-792-5454 Ext. 117. Fax: 941-795-7190. E-mail: jannonpierce@bcspanthers.org. Web site: www.bcspanthers.org.

BRANDON HALL SCHOOL

Atlanta, Georgia
See Special Needs Schools section.

BRANKSOME HALL

10 Elm Avenue
Toronto, Ontario M4W 1N4, Canada
Head of School: Karen Murton

General Information Girls' boarding and day college-preparatory and arts school. Boarding grades 8–12, day grades JK–12. Founded: 1903. Setting: urban. Students are housed in single-sex dormitories. 13-acre campus. 6 buildings on campus. Approved or accredited by Canadian Association of Independent Schools, Canadian Educational Standards Institute, International Baccalaureate Organization, Ontario Ministry of Education, The Association of Boarding Schools, and Ontario Department of Education. Affiliate member of National Association of Independent Schools; member of Secondary School Admission Test Board. Language of instruction: English. Endowment: CAN$1 million. Total enrollment: 870. Upper school average class size: 18. Upper school faculty-student ratio: 1:18. There are 180 required school days per year for Upper School students. Upper School students typically attend 5 days per week. The average school day consists of 8 hours.

Upper School Student Profile Grade 6: 44 students (44 girls); Grade 7: 76 students (76 girls); Grade 8: 89 students (89 girls); Grade 9: 106 students (106 girls); Grade 10: 115 students (115 girls); Grade 11: 122 students (122 girls); Grade 12: 113 students (113 girls). 15% of students are boarding students. 1% are province residents. 5 provinces are represented in upper school student body. 94% are international students. International students from China, Democratic People's Republic of Korea, Germany, Kenya, Saint Kitts and Nevis, and Taiwan; 8 other countries represented in student body.

Faculty School total: 115. In upper school: 15 men, 70 women; 40 have advanced degrees; 3 reside on campus.

Subjects Offered Accounting, acting, advanced math, algebra, all academic, American history, American literature, ancient history, ancient world history, Arabic, art, art and culture, art history, arts, athletics, band, biology, British history, British literature, business, calculus, Canadian geography, Canadian history, Canadian law, Canadian literature, Cantonese, career and personal planning, career exploration, career/college preparation, chemistry, Chinese, Chinese studies, classical civilization, classical Greek literature, computer multimedia, computer programming, computer science, critical thinking, critical writing, drama, drawing, economics, economics and history, English, English literature, environmental science, environmental systems, ethics, European history, European literature, expository writing, film studies, fine arts, food science, French, French studies, geography, geometry, German, government/civics, health, history, home economics, independent study, interdisciplinary studies, Latin, mathematics, music, physical education, physics, science, social sciences, social studies, Spanish, theater, theory of knowledge, trigonometry, typing, vocal ensemble, vocal music, world affairs, world arts, world civilizations, world cultures, world geography, world governments, world history, world issues, world literature, world religions, world studies, writing, writing workshop, yearbook.

Graduation Requirements Arts and fine arts (art, music, dance, drama), business skills (includes word processing), English, International Baccalaureate courses, mathematics, physical education (includes health), science, social sciences, social studies (includes history), IB Diploma or certificate requirements.

Special Academic Programs International Baccalaureate program; honors section; academic accommodation for the gifted, the musically talented, and the artistically talented; ESL (12 students enrolled).

College Admission Counseling 113 students graduated in 2010; 112 went to college, including McGill University; Parsons The New School for Design; Queen's University at Kingston; The University of British Columbia; The University of Western Ontario; University of Toronto. Other: 1 had other specific plans.

Student Life Upper grades have uniform requirement, student council, honor system. Discipline rests primarily with faculty.

Tuition and Aid Day student tuition: CAN$25,450; 7-day tuition and room/board: CAN$47,480. Tuition installment plan (monthly payment plans, tri-annual payment, early payment option ($500 savings)). Bursaries, merit scholarship grants available. In 2010–11, 10% of upper-school students received aid; total upper-school merit-scholarship money awarded: CAN$12,500. Total amount of financial aid awarded in 2010–11: CAN$650,000.

Admissions Traditional secondary-level entrance grade is 9. For fall 2010, 325 students applied for upper-level admission, 225 were accepted, 170 enrolled. SSAT required. Deadline for receipt of application materials: December 10. Application fee required: CAN$200. Interview required.

Athletics Interscholastic: alpine skiing, aquatics, badminton, baseball, basketball, crew, cross-country running, field hockey, golf, hockey, ice hockey, indoor track, indoor track & field, rowing, rugby, skiing (downhill), soccer, softball, swimming and diving, synchronized swimming, tennis, track and field, volleyball; intramural: aerobics, aerobics/dance, aquatics, badminton, ball hockey, ballet, baseball, basketball, cheering, climbing, cooperative games, cross-country running, dance, field hockey, fitness, gymnastics, outdoor activities, paddle tennis, physical fitness, rugby, soccer, softball, squash, strength & conditioning, swimming and diving, table tennis, tennis, track and field, volleyball, yoga. 6 PE instructors, 2 coaches, 1 athletic trainer.

Computers Computers are regularly used in art, mathematics, music, science classes. Computer network features include on-campus library services, Internet access, wireless campus network, Internet filtering or blocking technology. Campus intranet and student e-mail accounts are available to students. The school has a published electronic and media policy.

Contact Karrie Weinstock, Head of Senior/Middle School and Admissions. 416-920-9741. Fax: 416-920-5390. E-mail: kweinstock@branksome.on.ca. Web site: www.branksome.on.ca.

THE BRANSON SCHOOL
39 Fernhill Avenue
PO Box 887
Ross, California 94957
Head of School: Mr. Thomas Woody Price, EdD

General Information Coeducational day college-preparatory and arts school. Grades 9–12. Founded: 1916. Setting: suburban. Nearest major city is San Francisco. 18-acre campus. 12 buildings on campus. Approved or accredited by California Association of Independent Schools and Western Association of Schools and Colleges. Member of National Association of Independent Schools and Secondary School Admission Test Board. Endowment: $14 million. Total enrollment: 320. Upper school average class size: 13. Upper school faculty-student ratio: 1:8. There are 173 required school days per year for Upper School students. Upper School students typically attend 5 days per week. The average school day consists of 5 hours.

Upper School Student Profile Grade 9: 89 students (43 boys, 46 girls); Grade 10: 75 students (40 boys, 35 girls); Grade 11: 75 students (31 boys, 44 girls); Grade 12: 81 students (38 boys, 43 girls).

Faculty School total: 51. In upper school: 27 men, 24 women; 29 have advanced degrees.

Subjects Offered African-American literature, algebra, American history, American literature, art, art history, biology, calculus, ceramics, chemistry, community service, creative writing, dance, digital applications, drama, earth science, economics, English, English literature, English-AP, environmental science, European history, fine arts, geometry, government/civics, history, Latin, mathematics, mathematics-AP, music, outdoor education, philosophy, photography, physical education, physics, poetry, science, social sciences, social studies, Spanish, statistics, theater, trigonometry, world history, world literature.

Graduation Requirements Arts and fine arts (art, music, dance, drama), English, foreign language, mathematics, physical education (includes health), science, social sciences, social studies (includes history). Community service is required.

Special Academic Programs Advanced Placement exam preparation; honors section; independent study; study abroad.

College Admission Counseling 79 students graduated in 2009; 77 went to college, including Princeton University; Stanford University; University of California, Berkeley; University of Pennsylvania. Other: 2 entered a postgraduate year. Mean SAT critical reading: 646, mean SAT math: 664, mean SAT writing: 671, mean combined SAT: 1981, mean composite ACT: 27.

Student Life Upper grades have student council, honor system. Discipline rests equally with students and faculty.

Tuition and Aid Day student tuition: $32,275. Tuition installment plan (FACTS Tuition Payment Plan, individually arranged payment plans). Need-based scholarship grants available. In 2009–10, 20% of upper-school students received aid. Total amount of financial aid awarded in 2009–10: $1,400,000.

Admissions Traditional secondary-level entrance grade is 9. For fall 2009, 333 students applied for upper-level admission, 147 were accepted, 91 enrolled. ERB, ISEE, SSAT or Star-9 required. Deadline for receipt of application materials: January 15. Application fee required: $100. Interview required.

Athletics Interscholastic: baseball (boys), basketball (b,g), cross-country running (b,g), diving (b,g), equestrian sports (g), fencing (b,g), golf (b,g), lacrosse (b), mountain biking (b,g), sailing (b,g), soccer (b,g), softball (g), swimming and diving (b,g), tennis (b,g); coed interscholastic: crew. 3 PE instructors, 3 coaches.

Computers Computers are regularly used in English, foreign language, mathematics, music, science classes. Computer network features include on-campus library services, online commercial services, Internet access, wireless campus network. Campus intranet and student e-mail accounts are available to students. The school has a published electronic and media policy.

Contact Andrea Molina, Senior Admission Assistant. 415-454-3612 Ext. 207. Fax: 415-454-4669. E-mail: andrea_molina@branson.org. Web site: www.branson.org.

THE BREARLEY SCHOOL
610 East 83rd Street
New York, New York 10028
Head of School: Dr. Stephanie J. Hull

General Information Girls' day college-preparatory school. Grades K–12. Founded: 1884. Setting: urban. 2 buildings on campus. Approved or accredited by New York State Association of Independent Schools. Member of National Association of Independent Schools. Endowment: $101 million. Total enrollment: 692. Upper school average class size: 12. Upper school faculty-student ratio: 1:6.

Upper School Student Profile Grade 9: 52 students (52 girls); Grade 10: 61 students (61 girls); Grade 11: 51 students (51 girls); Grade 12: 51 students (51 girls).

Faculty School total: 134. In upper school: 21 men, 53 women; 56 have advanced degrees.

Subjects Offered 20th century world history, advanced biology, advanced chemistry, African history, African literature, algebra, American history, American literature, applied music, art, art history, astronomy, biology, calculus, calculus-AP, chamber groups, chemistry, computer science, contemporary women writers, critical writing, drama, drama performance, drawing, English, English literature, environmental science, equality and freedom, expository writing, fiction, finite math, French, French language-AP, French literature-AP, geometry, history, history of China and Japan, Homeric Greek, independent study, Latin, Mandarin, mathematics, modern European history, multimedia design, music, music history, oil painting, painting, physics, political thought, pre-calculus, senior project, Shakespeare, Spanish, Spanish literature, statistics, trigonometry, vocal music, water color painting, Web site design, world history.

Graduation Requirements Arts and fine arts (art, music, dance, drama), English, foreign language, history, mathematics, physical education (includes health), science.

Special Academic Programs 12 Advanced Placement exams for which test preparation is offered; independent study; term-away projects; study abroad.

College Admission Counseling 46 students graduated in 2009; all went to college, including Barnard College; Columbia University; Cornell University; Dartmouth College; Harvard University; The Johns Hopkins University. Median SAT critical reading: 730, median SAT math: 690. 99% scored over 600 on SAT critical reading, 92% scored over 600 on SAT math.

Student Life Upper grades have specified standards of dress, student council. Discipline rests equally with students and faculty.

Tuition and Aid Day student tuition: $34,350. Tuition installment plan (Key Tuition Payment Plan, individually arranged payment plans). Need-based scholarship grants, need-based loans available. In 2009–10, 20% of upper-school students received aid. Total amount of financial aid awarded in 2009–10: $3,487,470.

Admissions For fall 2009, 121 students applied for upper-level admission, 21 were accepted, 6 enrolled. ISEE and school's own exam required. Deadline for receipt of application materials: December 1. Application fee required: $60. On-campus interview required.

Athletics Interscholastic: aquatics, badminton, basketball, cross-country running, field hockey, gymnastics, lacrosse, soccer, softball, squash, swimming and diving, tennis, track and field, volleyball; intramural: aquatics, badminton, basketball, cooperative games, cricket, dance, dance team, field hockey, fitness, gymnastics, jogging, lacrosse, modern dance, physical fitness, soccer, softball, strength & conditioning, swimming and diving, tai chi, team handball, track and field, volleyball, yoga. 12 PE instructors, 3 coaches, 2 athletic trainers.

Computers Computers are regularly used in classics, computer applications, English, foreign language, history, mathematics, multimedia, music, photography, science, theater arts, Web site design classes. Computer network features include on-campus library services, Internet access, wireless campus network, Britannica Online, EBSCO, SIRS Researcher, ProQuest, JSTOR, ArtStor, AtomicLearning.com (software tutorials), a file server. Student e-mail accounts and computer access in designated common areas are available to students. The school has a published electronic and media policy.

Contact Ms. Joan Kaplan, Director of Middle and Upper School Admission. 212-744-8582. Fax: 212-472-8020. E-mail: admission@brearley.org. Web site: www.brearley.org.

BRECK SCHOOL
123 Ottawa Avenue North
Minneapolis, Minnesota 55422
Head of School: Edward Kim

General Information Coeducational day college-preparatory, arts, and religious studies school, affiliated with Episcopal Church. Grades PK–12. Founded: 1886. Setting: suburban. 53-acre campus. 1 building on campus. Approved or accredited by Independent Schools Association of the Central States. Member of National Association of Independent Schools and Secondary School Admission Test Board. Endowment: $43.2 million. Total enrollment: 1,131. Upper school average class size: 17. Upper school faculty-student ratio: 1:11.

Upper School Student Profile Grade 9: 99 students (42 boys, 57 girls); Grade 10: 92 students (44 boys, 48 girls); Grade 11: 101 students (47 boys, 54 girls); Grade 12: 108 students (55 boys, 53 girls). 10% of students are members of Episcopal Church.

Faculty School total: 145. In upper school: 12 men, 17 women; 22 have advanced degrees.

Subjects Offered Algebra, American history, American literature, art, astronomy, biology, calculus, ceramics, chemistry, Chinese, chorus, community service, computer math, computer programming, creative writing, dance, drama, ecology, economics, English, English literature, environmental science, ethics, European history, expository writing, fine arts, French, geometry, health, history, mathematics, music, orchestra, physical education, physics, religion, science, social studies, Spanish, statistics, theater, theology, trigonometry, world history, world literature, writing.

Graduation Requirements Arts and fine arts (art, music, dance, drama), English, foreign language, mathematics, physical education (includes health), religion (includes Bible studies and theology), science, social studies (includes history), senior speech, May Program. Community service is required.

Special Academic Programs Advanced Placement exam preparation; honors section; independent study; term-away projects; academic accommodation for the gifted, the musically talented, and the artistically talented.

College Admission Counseling 94 students graduated in 2010; all went to college, including Amherst College; Boston University; Bowdoin College; Pitzer College; St. Olaf College; The Colorado College. Mean SAT critical reading: 609, mean SAT math: 594, mean SAT writing: 617. 47% scored over 600 on SAT critical reading, 68% scored over 600 on SAT math, 58% scored over 600 on SAT writing.

Student Life Upper grades have specified standards of dress, student council, honor system. Discipline rests equally with students and faculty. Attendance at religious services is required.

Tuition and Aid Day student tuition: $23,525. Tuition installment plan (Key Tuition Payment Plan). Need-based scholarship grants available. In 2010–11, 14% of upper-school students received aid. Total amount of financial aid awarded in 2010–11: $1,170,570.

Admissions Traditional secondary-level entrance grade is 9. For fall 2010, 75 students applied for upper-level admission, 48 were accepted, 24 enrolled. CTP III required. Deadline for receipt of application materials: February 1. Application fee required: $75. On-campus interview required.

Athletics Interscholastic: alpine skiing (boys, girls), baseball (b), basketball (b,g), cross-country running (b,g), diving (b,g), football (b), golf (b,g), gymnastics (g), ice hockey (b,g), lacrosse (b,g), nordic skiing (b,g), skiing (cross-country) (b,g), skiing (downhill) (b,g), soccer (b,g), softball (g), swimming and diving (b,g), tennis (b,g), track and field (b,g), volleyball (g). 6 PE instructors, 82 coaches, 1 athletic trainer.

Computers Computers are regularly used in all classes. Computer network features include on-campus library services, online commercial services, Internet access, wireless campus network, Internet filtering or blocking technology, multimedia imaging, video presentation, student laptop program. Campus intranet and student e-mail accounts are available to students. The school has a published electronic and media policy.

Contact Scott D. Wade, Director of Admissions. 763-381-8200. Fax: 763-381-8288. E-mail: scott.wade@breckschool.org. Web site: www.breckschool.org.

BREHM PREPARATORY SCHOOL

Carbondale, Illinois
See Special Needs Schools section.

BRENTWOOD COLLEGE SCHOOL

2735 Mount Baker Road
Mill Bay, British Columbia V0R 2P1, Canada
Head of School: Mrs. Andrea M. Pennells

General Information Coeducational boarding and day college-preparatory, arts, and athletics, leadership, and citizenship school school. Grades 9–12. Founded: 1923. Setting: rural. Nearest major city is Victoria, Canada. Students are housed in single-sex dormitories. 47-acre campus. 15 buildings on campus. Approved or accredited by British Columbia Independent Schools Association, Canadian Association of Independent Schools, The Association of Boarding Schools, Western Boarding Schools Association, and British Columbia Department of Education. Affiliate member of National Association of Independent Schools. Language of instruction: English. Total enrollment: 435. Upper school average class size: 16. Upper school faculty-student ratio: 1:9.

Upper School Student Profile Grade 9: 83 students (53 boys, 30 girls); Grade 10: 115 students (61 boys, 54 girls); Grade 11: 124 students (62 boys, 62 girls); Grade 12: 113 students (62 boys, 51 girls). 81% of students are boarding students. 58% are province residents. 20 provinces are represented in upper school student body. 27% are international students. International students from Germany, Hong Kong, Mexico, Republic of Korea, Saudi Arabia, and United States; 12 other countries represented in student body.

Faculty School total: 50. In upper school: 24 men, 17 women; 13 have advanced degrees; 30 reside on campus.

Subjects Offered Advanced Placement courses, algebra, art history-AP, athletics, audio visual/media, band, basketball, biology, biology-AP, business, calculus, calculus-AP, Canadian geography, Canadian history, Canadian law, career and personal planning, ceramics, chemistry, chemistry-AP, choir, choreography, computer graphics, computer science, dance, dance performance, debate, design, drafting, drama, dramatic arts, drawing, economics, economics-AP, English, English literature, English literature-AP, French, French language-AP, geography, geometry, golf, government and politics-AP, health and wellness, history, human geography—AP, information technology, instrumental music, international studies, jazz band, jazz ensemble, marketing, mathematics, musical productions, musical theater, orchestra, outdoor education, painting, photography, physics, physics-AP, pottery, psychology, psychology-AP, public speaking, science, sculpture, sex education, social studies,

Spanish, Spanish-AP, stagecraft, technical theater, tennis, theater design and production, video film production, visual and performing arts, vocal jazz, volleyball, yearbook.

Graduation Requirements Arts and fine arts (art, music, dance, drama), career and personal planning, English, foreign language, mathematics, physical education (includes health), science, social studies (includes history).

Special Academic Programs Advanced Placement exam preparation.

College Admission Counseling 112 students graduated in 2010; all went to college, including Duke University; McGill University; Queen's University at Kingston; The University of British Columbia; University of California, Berkeley; University of California, Los Angeles.

Student Life Upper grades have uniform requirement, student council, honor system. Discipline rests primarily with faculty.

Tuition and Aid Day student tuition: CAN$18,300; 7-day tuition and room/board: CAN$36,000–CAN$46,500. Tuition reduction for siblings available.

Admissions Traditional secondary-level entrance grade is 9. Henmon-Nelson or SSAT required. Deadline for receipt of application materials: none. Application fee required: CAN$2500. Interview required.

Athletics Interscholastic: basketball (boys, girls), crew (b,g), cross-country running (b,g), field hockey (g), hockey (g), rowing (b,g), rugby (b,g), running (b,g), soccer (b,g), squash (b,g), tennis (b,g), volleyball (g); intramural: crew (b,g), cross-country running (b,g), field hockey (g), indoor hockey (g), soccer (b,g), squash (b,g), tennis (b,g), track and field (b,g), volleyball (g), weight training (g); coed interscholastic: badminton, ballet, canoeing/kayaking, fitness, golf, ice hockey, judo, kayaking, modern dance, ocean paddling, outdoor activities, rock climbing, sailing; coed intramural: aerobics, aerobics/dance, badminton, canoeing/kayaking, cooperative games, dance, fitness, floor hockey, hiking/backpacking, indoor soccer, kayaking, outdoor activities, physical fitness, physical training, rowing, rugby, running, skiing (downhill), snowboarding, strength & conditioning, table tennis, touch football, weight lifting, weight training. 6 PE instructors, 36 coaches.

Computers Computers are regularly used in photojournalism, video film production classes. Computer network features include on-campus library services, Internet access, wireless campus network, Internet filtering or blocking technology. Campus intranet and student e-mail accounts are available to students. The school has a published electronic and media policy.

Contact Mr. Clayton Johnston, Director of Admissions. 250-743-5521. Fax: 250-743-2911. E-mail: admissions@brentwood.bc.ca. Web site: www.brentwood.bc.ca.

See Display on next page and Close-Up on page 746.

BRENTWOOD SCHOOL

100 South Barrington Place
Los Angeles, California 90049
Head of School: Dr. Michael Pratt

General Information Coeducational day college-preparatory school. Grades K–12. Founded: 1972. Setting: suburban. 30-acre campus. 12 buildings on campus. Approved or accredited by California Association of Independent Schools and Western Association of Schools and Colleges. Member of National Association of Independent Schools and Secondary School Admission Test Board. Endowment: $7 million. Total enrollment: 990. Upper school average class size: 17. Upper school faculty-student ratio: 1:7. Upper School students typically attend 5 days per week. The average school day consists of 8 hours.

Upper School Student Profile Grade 9: 121 students (60 boys, 61 girls); Grade 10: 123 students (62 boys, 61 girls); Grade 11: 111 students (61 boys, 50 girls); Grade 12: 108 students (56 boys, 52 girls).

Faculty School total: 125. In upper school: 45 men, 49 women; 70 have advanced degrees.

Subjects Offered Acting, Advanced Placement courses, advanced studio art-AP, algebra, American history, American literature, Ancient Greek, anthropology, art, art history, art history-AP, art-AP, astronomy, biology, biology-AP, calculus, calculus-AP, ceramics, chemistry, chemistry-AP, Chinese, choir, choral music, chorus, community service, comparative government and politics-AP, computer programming, computer programming-AP, computer science, computer science-AP, concert choir, creative writing, dance, digital photography, directing, drama, drawing, ecology, economics, economics-AP, English, English literature, environmental science-AP, European history, filmmaking, fine arts, French, French-AP, geometry, global studies, government and politics-AP, government-AP, history, honors algebra, honors English, honors geometry, human development, human geography—AP, Japanese, jazz band, jazz dance, journalism, language-AP, Latin, Latin-AP, literature-AP, math analysis, mathematics, music, music theater, music theory-AP, orchestra, organic chemistry, philosophy, photography, physical education, physics, physics-AP, probability and statistics, robotics, science, senior seminar, senior thesis, social sciences, social studies, Spanish, Spanish-AP, speech, speech and debate, stagecraft, stained glass, statistics-AP, studio art-AP, theater, U.S. government and politics-AP, U.S. history-AP, video, word processing, world history, world literature.

Graduation Requirements Arts and fine arts (art, music, dance, drama), English, foreign language, mathematics, physical education (includes health), science, senior seminar, senior thesis, social sciences, social studies (includes history). Community service is required.

Special Academic Programs 26 Advanced Placement exams for which test preparation is offered; honors section; independent study; study at local college for college credit; academic accommodation for the gifted and the artistically talented.

College Admission Counseling 115 students graduated in 2010; 114 went to college, including Brown University; Cornell University; Stanford University; University of Pennsylvania; University of Southern California. Other: 1 entered a postgraduate year. Mean SAT critical reading: 660, mean SAT math: 670, mean SAT writing: 680, mean combined SAT: 2010.

Student Life Upper grades have specified standards of dress, student council, honor system. Discipline rests primarily with faculty.

Summer Programs Remediation, enrichment, advancement, sports, art/fine arts, computer instruction programs offered; session focuses on academic enrichment and sports; held on campus; accepts boys and girls; open to students from other schools. 350 students usually enrolled. 2011 schedule: June 13 to July 29. Application deadline: none.

Tuition and Aid Day student tuition: $29,650. Tuition installment plan (Insured Tuition Payment Plan, monthly payment plans, individually arranged payment plans). Need-based scholarship grants available. In 2010–11, 16% of upper-school students received aid. Total amount of financial aid awarded in 2010–11: $3,500,000.

Admissions Traditional secondary-level entrance grade is 9. For fall 2010, 165 students applied for upper-level admission, 27 were accepted, 21 enrolled. ISEE required. Deadline for receipt of application materials: January 14. Application fee required: $100. On-campus interview required.

Athletics Interscholastic: baseball (boys), basketball (b,g), cheering (g), cross-country running (b,g), dance squad (g), dance team (g), football (b), independent competitive sports (b,g), lacrosse (b,g), soccer (b,g), softball (g), swimming and diving (b,g), tennis (b,g), track and field (b,g), volleyball (b,g), water polo (b), wrestling (b); intramural: modern dance (g), ultimate Frisbee (b); coed interscholastic: dance, diving, drill team, equestrian sports, fencing, football, golf, swimming and diving, water polo; coed intramural: bicycling, fitness, Frisbee, jogging, mountain biking, outdoor activities, physical fitness, physical training, running, sailing, surfing, table tennis, ultimate Frisbee, weight lifting, weight training, wilderness, yoga. 6 PE instructors, 40 coaches, 2 athletic trainers.

Computers Computers are regularly used in college planning, computer applications, desktop publishing, digital applications, foreign language, graphic design, introduction to technology, journalism, literary magazine, mathematics, media arts, media production, photojournalism, programming, publications, research skills, science, technical drawing, technology, video film production, Web site design classes. Computer network features include on-campus library services, online commercial services, Internet access, wireless campus network, Internet filtering or blocking technology, Moodle. Campus intranet, student e-mail accounts, and computer access in designated common areas are available to students. Students grades are available online. The school has a published electronic and media policy.

Contact Ms. Colleen Ward, Admissions Assistant. 310-889-2657. Fax: 310-476-4087. E-mail: cward@bwscampus.com. Web site: www.bwscampus.com.

BRENTWOOD SCHOOL

PO Box 955
725 Linton Road
Sandersville, Georgia 31082
Head of School: Mrs. Jackie W. Holton

General Information Coeducational day college-preparatory school. Grades PK–12. Founded: 1969. Setting: rural. Nearest major city is Macon. 20-acre campus. 2 buildings on campus. Approved or accredited by Georgia Accrediting Commission, Southern Association of Colleges and Schools, and Southern Association of Independent Schools. Endowment: $3 million. Total enrollment: 386. Upper school average class size: 16. Upper school faculty-student ratio: 1:11. There are 180 required school days per year for Upper School students. Upper School students typically attend 5 days per week. The average school day consists of 6 hours.

Upper School Student Profile Grade 6: 30 students (12 boys, 18 girls); Grade 7: 32 students (18 boys, 14 girls); Grade 8: 43 students (27 boys, 16 girls); Grade 9: 33 students (18 boys, 15 girls); Grade 10: 26 students (13 boys, 13 girls); Grade 11: 20 students (10 boys, 10 girls); Grade 12: 35 students (19 boys, 16 girls).

Faculty School total: 33. In upper school: 3 men, 11 women; 9 have advanced degrees.

Subjects Offered Advanced Placement courses, algebra, American history, American literature, art, art history, biology, calculus, chemistry, computer science, earth science, economics, English, English literature, environmental science, French, geography, geometry, government/civics, grammar, history, mathematics, music appreciation, physical education, physics, psychology, science, social studies, statistics, trigonometry, world history, world literature.

Graduation Requirements Algebra, American government, American history, American literature, biology, British literature, chemistry, composition, computer applications, economics, electives, English, English composition, environmental science, foreign language, French, geography, geometry, mathematics, physical education (includes health), physical science, science, social studies (includes history), world history.

Special Academic Programs 4 Advanced Placement exams for which test preparation is offered.

College Admission Counseling 30 students graduated in 2009; all went to college, including Georgia College & State University; Georgia Southern University; Middle Georgia College; University of Georgia; Valdosta State University. Median SAT critical reading: 530, median SAT math: 530, median SAT writing: 580, median combined SAT: 1650. 17% scored over 600 on SAT critical reading, 14% scored over 600 on SAT math, 38% scored over 600 on SAT writing, 28% scored over 1800 on combined SAT.

Student Life Upper grades have specified standards of dress, student council, honor system. Discipline rests primarily with faculty.

Tuition and Aid Day student tuition: $5975. Tuition installment plan (monthly payment plans). Tuition reduction for siblings, need-based scholarship grants available.

Admissions Traditional secondary-level entrance grade is 9. For fall 2009, 5 students applied for upper-level admission, 5 were accepted, 5 enrolled. Admissions testing required. Deadline for receipt of application materials: none. No application fee required. On-campus interview required.

Athletics Interscholastic: baseball (boys), basketball (b,g), cheering (g), cross-country running (b,g), dance team (g), football (b), golf (b,g), softball (g), tennis (b,g), track and field (b,g); coed interscholastic: cross-country running. 4 PE instructors, 4 coaches, 1 athletic trainer.

Computers Computers are regularly used in computer applications classes. Computer network features include on-campus library services, Internet access, Internet filtering or blocking technology. Campus intranet and computer access in designated common areas are available to students. The school has a published electronic and media policy.

Contact Mrs. Jackie W. Holton, Head of School. 478-552-5136. Fax: 478-552-2947. E-mail: jackie.holton@brentwoodschool.org. Web site: www.brentwoodschool.org.

BREWSTER ACADEMY

80 Academy Drive
Wolfeboro, New Hampshire 03894
Head of School: Dr. Michael E. Cooper

General Information Coeducational boarding and day college-preparatory, arts, and technology school. Grades 9–PG. Founded: 1820. Setting: small town. Nearest major city is Boston, MA. Students are housed in single-sex dormitories. 91-acre campus. 39 buildings on campus. Approved or accredited by Independent Schools of Northern New England, New England Association of Schools and Colleges, and The Association of Boarding Schools. Member of National Association of Independent Schools and Secondary School Admission Test Board. Endowment: $9.8 million. Total enrollment: 365. Upper school average class size: 12. Upper school faculty-student ratio: 1:6. There are 165 required school days per year for Upper School students. Upper School students typically attend 6 days per week. The average school day consists of 6 hours.

Upper School Student Profile Grade 9: 52 students (33 boys, 19 girls); Grade 10: 93 students (58 boys, 35 girls); Grade 11: 104 students (55 boys, 49 girls); Grade 12: 104 students (55 boys, 49 girls); Postgraduate: 13 students (13 boys). 80% of students are boarding students. 27% are state residents. 31 states are represented in upper school student body. 18% are international students. International students from Bermuda, Canada, China, Japan, Republic of Korea, and Taiwan; 13 other countries represented in student body.

Faculty School total: 69. In upper school: 39 men, 30 women; 31 have advanced degrees; 67 reside on campus.

Subjects Offered 3-dimensional design, acting, algebra, art, art history, astronomy, biology, biology-AP, calculus, calculus-AP, chemistry, chorus, community service, computer graphics, creative writing, dance, dance performance, digital photography, drama, driver education, ecology, environmental systems, economics, English, English language and composition-AP, English literature, English literature-AP, environmental science, ESL, European history-AP, filmmaking, French, geometry, jazz band, journalism, macroeconomics-AP, mathematics, media arts, music, music history, music technology, music theory, orchestra, physics, physics-AP, pottery, science, Spanish, studio art, theater, U.S. history, U.S. history-AP, Web authoring, Web site design, wind ensemble, world history, writing.

Graduation Requirements English, foreign language, mathematics, science, social studies (includes history).

Special Academic Programs 9 Advanced Placement exams for which test preparation is offered; honors section; study abroad; programs in English, mathematics, general development for dyslexic students; ESL (21 students enrolled).

College Admission Counseling 114 students graduated in 2010; 113 went to college, including Boston University; Hobart and William Smith Colleges; Saint Michael's College; Syracuse University; University of New Hampshire; University of Vermont.

Other: 1 entered a postgraduate year. Median SAT critical reading: 500, median SAT math: 530, median SAT writing: 500, median combined SAT: 1560, median composite ACT: 22. 19% scored over 600 on SAT critical reading, 29% scored over 600 on SAT math, 15% scored over 600 on SAT writing, 17% scored over 1800 on combined SAT, 21% scored over 26 on composite ACT.

Student Life Upper grades have specified standards of dress, student council, honor system. Discipline rests primarily with faculty.

Summer Programs Enrichment, advancement, ESL, sports, art/fine arts, computer instruction programs offered; session focuses on humanities and math, study skills, technology in academics and the arts, outdoor adventure education; held on campus; accepts boys and girls; open to students from other schools. 60 students usually enrolled. 2011 schedule: June 23 to August 4. Application deadline: May 15.

Tuition and Aid Day student tuition: $26,685; 7-day tuition and room/board: $43,370. Tuition installment plan (monthly payment plans). Need-based scholarship grants, Sallie Mae loans available. In 2010–11, 28% of upper-school students received aid. Total amount of financial aid awarded in 2010–11: $2,400,000.

Admissions Traditional secondary-level entrance grade is 9. For fall 2010, 502 students applied for upper-level admission, 308 were accepted, 135 enrolled. SSAT required. Deadline for receipt of application materials: February 1. Application fee required: $50. On-campus interview required.

Athletics Interscholastic: alpine skiing (boys, girls), baseball (b), basketball (b,g), crew (b,g), cross-country running (b,g), field hockey (g), ice hockey (b,g), lacrosse (b,g), running (b,g), skiing (downhill) (b,g), soccer (b,g), softball (g), tennis (b,g); coed interscholastic: golf, sailing, snowboarding; coed intramural: aerobics, alpine skiing, climbing, croquet, dance, equestrian sports, fitness, indoor soccer, outdoor skills, rock climbing, sailing, skiing (downhill), snowboarding, strength & conditioning, table tennis, tennis, touch football, ultimate Frisbee, wall climbing, weight training, yoga. 2 athletic trainers.

Computers Computers are regularly used in all classes. Computer network features include on-campus library services, online commercial services, Internet access, Internet filtering or blocking technology. Campus intranet, student e-mail accounts, and computer access in designated common areas are available to students. Students grades are available online. The school has a published electronic and media policy.

Contact Mary Roetger, Admission Coordinator. 603-569-7200. Fax: 603-569-7272. E-mail: mary_roetger@brewsteracademy.org. Web site: www.brewsteracademy.org.

BRIARCREST CHRISTIAN HIGH SCHOOL

76 S. Houston Levee Road
Eads, Tennessee 38028
Head of School: Mr. Eric Sullivan

General Information Coeducational day college-preparatory, arts, religious studies, and technology school, affiliated with Christian faith. Grades 9–12. Founded: 1973. Setting: suburban. Nearest major city is Memphis. 100-acre campus. 1 building on campus. Approved or accredited by Southern Association of Colleges and Schools, Southern Association of Independent Schools, and Tennessee Department of Education. Total enrollment: 1,590. Upper school average class size: 18. Upper school faculty-student ratio: 1:14. There are 176 required school days per year for Upper School students. Upper School students typically attend 5 days per week. The average school day consists of 7 hours.

Upper School Student Profile Grade 9: 145 students (69 boys, 76 girls); Grade 10: 164 students (81 boys, 83 girls); Grade 11: 136 students (71 boys, 65 girls); Grade 12: 146 students (78 boys, 68 girls). 94% of students are Christian.

Faculty School total: 42. In upper school: 17 men, 25 women; 26 have advanced degrees.

Subjects Offered Algebra, American history, American literature, anatomy, art, Bible studies, biology, business, calculus, chemistry, computer math, computer programming, computer science, creative writing, drama, driver education, English, English literature, environmental science, European history, expository writing, French, geography, geometry, government/civics, grammar, health, history, Latin, mathematics, music, physical education, physics, physiology, psychology, religion, science, social sciences, social studies, sociology, Spanish, speech, theater, trigonometry, typing, world history, writing.

Graduation Requirements Arts and fine arts (art, music, dance, drama), business skills (includes word processing), English, foreign language, mathematics, physical education (includes health), religion (includes Bible studies and theology), science, social sciences, social studies (includes history).

Special Academic Programs Advanced Placement exam preparation; honors section; term-away projects; study at local college for college credit; academic accommodation for the gifted, the musically talented, and the artistically talented; programs in English, mathematics, general development for dyslexic students.

College Admission Counseling 146 students graduated in 2010; 144 went to college, including Auburn University; Mississippi State University; The University of Alabama; The University of Tennessee; University of Memphis; University of Mississippi. Other: 1 went to work, 1 had other specific plans. Median SAT critical reading: 610, median SAT math: 625, median SAT writing: 600, median combined

Briarcrest Christian High School

SAT: 1830, median composite ACT: 24. 83% scored over 600 on SAT critical reading, 50% scored over 600 on SAT math, 50% scored over 600 on SAT writing, 67% scored over 1800 on combined SAT, 33% scored over 26 on composite ACT.

Student Life Upper grades have uniform requirement, student council, honor system. Discipline rests primarily with faculty. Attendance at religious services is required.

Tuition and Aid Day student tuition: $11,895. Tuition installment plan (Insured Tuition Payment Plan, monthly payment plans, individually arranged payment plans, 2-payment plan). Tuition reduction for siblings, need-based tuition assistance available. In 2010–11, 12% of upper-school students received aid.

Admissions Traditional secondary-level entrance grade is 9. For fall 2010, 110 students applied for upper-level admission, 100 were accepted, 56 enrolled. ISEE required. Deadline for receipt of application materials: none. Application fee required: $50. On-campus interview required.

Athletics Interscholastic: baseball (boys), basketball (b,g), cheering (g), cross-country running (b,g), drill team (g), football (b), golf (b,g), lacrosse (b), soccer (b,g), softball (g), swimming and diving (b,g), tennis (b,g), track and field (b,g), volleyball (g), weight lifting (b), wrestling (b); coed interscholastic: bowling, cross-country running, swimming and diving. 2 PE instructors.

Computers Computers are regularly used in accounting, art, English, history, journalism, keyboarding, lab/keyboard, language development, mathematics, newspaper, science, social sciences, social studies, Spanish, speech, yearbook classes. Computer network features include on-campus library services, Internet access, wireless campus network, Internet filtering or blocking technology. Campus intranet, student e-mail accounts, and computer access in designated common areas are available to students. Students grades are available online. The school has a published electronic and media policy.

Contact Mrs. Claire Foster, Admissions Coordinator. 901-765-4605. Fax: 901-765-4614. E-mail: cofoster@briarcrest.com. Web site: www.briarcrest.com.

BRIARWOOD CHRISTIAN HIGH SCHOOL

6255 Cahaba Valley Road
Birmingham, Alabama 35242
Head of School: Dr. Barrett Mosbacker

General Information Coeducational day college-preparatory, arts, and religious studies school, affiliated with Presbyterian Church in America. Grades K4–12. Founded: 1964. Setting: suburban. 85-acre campus. 5 buildings on campus. Approved or accredited by Association of Christian Schools International, Southern Association of Colleges and Schools, and Alabama Department of Education. Endowment: $500,000. Total enrollment: 1,956. Upper school average class size: 23. Upper school faculty-student ratio: 1:23. There are 177 required school days per year for Upper School students. Upper School students typically attend 5 days per week. The average school day consists of 6 hours and 10 minutes.

Upper School Student Profile Grade 9: 144 students (74 boys, 70 girls); Grade 10: 146 students (75 boys, 71 girls); Grade 11: 148 students (78 boys, 70 girls); Grade 12: 133 students (68 boys, 65 girls). 30% of students are Presbyterian Church in America.

Faculty School total: 122. In upper school: 30 men, 25 women; 35 have advanced degrees.

Subjects Offered Accounting, algebra, American history, American literature, art, band, Bible studies, biology, calculus, chemistry, community service, computer science, creative writing, debate, drama, driver education, economics, English, English literature, ethics, European history, French, geometry, government, grammar, health, history, home economics, mathematics, music, philosophy, photo shop, physical education, physics, psychology, religion, science, social sciences, social studies, Spanish, speech, trigonometry, world history, world literature.

Graduation Requirements 20th century history, business skills (includes word processing), computer science, English, foreign language, mathematics, physical education (includes health), religion (includes Bible studies and theology), science, social sciences, social studies (includes history). Community service is required.

Special Academic Programs Advanced Placement exam preparation; honors section; academic accommodation for the gifted; special instructional classes for students with learning disabilities, Attention Deficit Disorder.

College Admission Counseling 133 students graduated in 2010; 132 went to college, including Auburn University; Birmingham-Southern College; Samford University; The University of Alabama; Troy University; University of Mississippi. Other: 1 had other specific plans. Mean combined SAT: 1250, mean composite ACT: 26.

Student Life Upper grades have specified standards of dress, student council. Discipline rests primarily with faculty. Attendance at religious services is required.

Summer Programs Remediation, advancement programs offered; session focuses on social studies and mathematics; held on campus; accepts boys and girls; not open to students from other schools. 50 students usually enrolled. 2011 schedule: June to July.

Tuition and Aid Day student tuition: $6375. Tuition installment plan (monthly payment plans). Tuition reduction for siblings available. In 2010–11, 3% of upper-school students received aid. Total amount of financial aid awarded in 2010–11: $5000.

Admissions Traditional secondary-level entrance grade is 9. For fall 2010, 83 students applied for upper-level admission, 42 were accepted, 41 enrolled. SSAT required. Deadline for receipt of application materials: none. Application fee required: $75. On-campus interview required.

Athletics Interscholastic: baseball (boys), basketball (b,g), cheering (g), cross-country running (b,g), dance team (g), football (b), golf (b,g), indoor track (b,g), indoor track & field (b,g), outdoor activities (b,g), physical fitness (b,g), soccer (b,g), softball (g), strength & conditioning (b), swimming and diving (b,g), tennis (b,g), track and field (b,g), volleyball (g). 5 PE instructors, 15 coaches, 1 athletic trainer.

Computers Computers are regularly used in computer applications classes. Computer network features include on-campus library services, online commercial services, Internet access. Students grades are available online.

Contact Mrs. Kelly McCarthy Mooney, Director of Admissions. 205-776-5812. Fax: 205-776-5816. E-mail: kmooney@bcsk12.org. Web site: www.bcsk12.org.

THE BRIARWOOD SCHOOL

Houston, Texas
See Special Needs Schools section.

BRIDGEMONT HIGH SCHOOL

444 East Market Street
Daly City, California 94014
Head of School: Mr. Peter Tropper

General Information Coeducational day college-preparatory, arts, religious studies, and technology school, affiliated with Christian faith. Grades 9–12. Founded: 1975. Setting: urban. Nearest major city is San Francisco. 1-acre campus. 4 buildings on campus. Approved or accredited by Association of Christian Schools International, CITA (Commission on International and Trans-Regional Accreditation), and Western Association of Schools and Colleges. Total enrollment: 35. Upper school average class size: 10. Upper school faculty-student ratio: 1:4. There are 176 required school days per year for Upper School students. Upper School students typically attend 5 days per week. The average school day consists of 6 hours and 25 minutes.

Upper School Student Profile Grade 9: 7 students (3 boys, 4 girls); Grade 10: 10 students (4 boys, 6 girls); Grade 11: 11 students (4 boys, 7 girls); Grade 12: 7 students (3 boys, 4 girls). 50% of students are Christian faith.

Faculty School total: 10. In upper school: 4 men, 6 women; 3 have advanced degrees.

Subjects Offered Advanced math, algebra, American history, American literature, art, arts, Bible studies, biology, calculus, chemistry, creative writing, drama, earth science, economics, English, English literature, European history, expository writing, fine arts, French, French as a second language, geography, geometry, government/civics, grammar, health, history, mathematics, music, physical education, physics, religion, science, social sciences, social studies, Spanish, study skills, theater, trigonometry, U.S. history, world history, world literature, writing, yearbook.

Graduation Requirements Arts and fine arts (art, music, dance, drama), English, foreign language, mathematics, physical education (includes health), religion (includes Bible studies and theology), science, social sciences, social studies (includes history), field studies.

Special Academic Programs Independent study.

College Admission Counseling 12 students graduated in 2009; all went to college, including California State University, Los Angeles; City College of San Francisco; San Francisco State University; San Jose State University; University of California, Davis; University of California, Irvine.

Student Life Upper grades have specified standards of dress, student council, honor system. Discipline rests primarily with faculty. Attendance at religious services is required.

Tuition and Aid Day student tuition: $9950. Tuition installment plan (FACTS Tuition Payment Plan, monthly payment plans, Tuition Management Systems Plan). Tuition reduction for siblings, need-based scholarship grants available. In 2009–10, 62% of upper-school students received aid. Total amount of financial aid awarded in 2009–10: $108,660.

Admissions Traditional secondary-level entrance grade is 9. For fall 2009, 6 students applied for upper-level admission, 6 were accepted, 5 enrolled. Essay, math and English placement tests and writing sample required. Deadline for receipt of application materials: none. Application fee required: $60. On-campus interview required.

Athletics Interscholastic: baseball (boys, girls), basketball (b,g), flag football (b), soccer (b), softball (g), volleyball (g); intramural: basketball (b,g), flag football (b,g), weight lifting (b); coed intramural: flag football, floor hockey, football, judo, jump rope, physical training, volleyball. 1 PE instructor, 4 coaches.

Computers Computers are regularly used in yearbook classes. Computer resources include Internet access, wireless campus network, Internet filtering or blocking technology, independent study courses through Acellus and NovelStar. Computer access in designated common areas is available to students. Students grades are available online.

Contact Mr. Paul S. Choy, Director of Student Development. 650-746-2522. Fax: 650-746-2529. E-mail: admissions@bridgemont.org. Web site: www.bridgemont.org.

BRIDGES ACADEMY

Studio City, California
See Special Needs Schools section.

BRIDGE SCHOOL

6717 South Boulder Road
Boulder, Colorado 80303-4319
Head of School: Mr. David Hazen

General Information Coeducational day college-preparatory, arts, and technology school. Grades 6–12. Founded: 1994. Setting: suburban. 5-acre campus. 1 building on campus. Approved or accredited by North Central Association of Colleges and Schools, The College Board, and Colorado Department of Education. Endowment: $20,000. Total enrollment: 22. Upper school average class size: 6. Upper school faculty-student ratio: 1:4. There are 178 required school days per year for Upper School students. Upper School students typically attend 5 days per week. The average school day consists of 6 hours and 50 minutes.

Upper School Student Profile Grade 7: 1 student (1 girl); Grade 8: 6 students (5 boys, 1 girl); Grade 9: 4 students (2 boys, 2 girls); Grade 10: 4 students (4 boys); Grade 11: 1 student (1 girl); Grade 12: 4 students (4 boys).

Faculty School total: 9. In upper school: 3 men, 5 women; 5 have advanced degrees.

Subjects Offered Algebra, American culture, American democracy, American literature, ancient world history, art, basketball, biology, calculus, chemistry, computers, digital art, drama, English composition, ESL, European civilization, European history, foreign language, geometry, geometry with art applications, history, human development, life science, mathematics, physics, pre-algebra, pre-calculus, public speaking, senior project, U.S. government, volleyball, world governments.

Graduation Requirements Art, arts and fine arts (art, music, dance, drama), computer literacy, English, foreign language, mathematics, public service, public speaking, science, senior project, social studies (includes history), May Term participation each year of attendance.

Special Academic Programs Honors section; accelerated programs; independent study; term-away projects; study at local college for college credit; academic accommodation for the gifted.

College Admission Counseling 14 students graduated in 2010; 13 went to college, including Colorado State University; Cornell College; University of Colorado at Boulder; University of San Diego. Other: 1 had other specific plans.

Student Life Upper grades have specified standards of dress, student council, honor system. Discipline rests equally with students and faculty.

Tuition and Aid Day student tuition: $15,200. Tuition installment plan (individually arranged payment plans). Need-based scholarship grants available. In 2010–11, 35% of upper-school students received aid. Total amount of financial aid awarded in 2010–11: $60,000.

Admissions Traditional secondary-level entrance grade is 9. For fall 2010, 15 students applied for upper-level admission, 10 were accepted, 10 enrolled. Achievement tests, school's own test and writing sample required. Deadline for receipt of application materials: none. Application fee required: $100. Interview required.

Athletics Coed Interscholastic: ultimate Frisbee; coed intramural: basketball, soccer, ultimate Frisbee, volleyball. 1 PE instructor, 2 coaches.

Computers Computers are regularly used in independent study, journalism, science, video film production, writing, yearbook classes. Computer network features include Internet access, wireless campus network. Campus intranet and computer access in designated common areas are available to students. The school has a published electronic and media policy.

Contact Mrs. Debby Wislon, Director of Admissions and Marketing. 303-494-7551. Fax: 303-494-7558. E-mail: info@bridgeschoolboulder.org. Web site: www.bridgeschoolboulder.org.

BRIMMER AND MAY SCHOOL

69 Middlesex Road
Chestnut Hill, Massachusetts 02467
Head of School: Anne Reenstierna

General Information Coeducational day college-preparatory, arts, technology, and student-centered learning school. Grades PK–12. Founded: 1880. Setting: suburban. Nearest major city is Boston. 7-acre campus. 7 buildings on campus. Approved or accredited by Association of Independent Schools in New England, Department of Education of Bern, New England Association of Schools and Colleges, and Massachusetts Department of Education. Member of National Association of Independent Schools and Secondary School Admission Test Board. Endowment: $5.2 million. Total enrollment: 400. Upper school average class size: 12. Upper school faculty-student ratio: 1:7. There are 180 required school days per year for Upper School students. Upper School students typically attend 5 days per week. The average school day consists of 7 hours and 10 minutes.

Upper School Student Profile Grade 9: 28 students (13 boys, 15 girls); Grade 10: 33 students (12 boys, 21 girls); Grade 11: 32 students (16 boys, 16 girls); Grade 12: 43 students (20 boys, 23 girls).

Faculty School total: 70. In upper school: 15 men, 19 women; 24 have advanced degrees.

Subjects Offered Acting, adolescent issues, Advanced Placement courses, advanced studio art-AP, algebra, American history, American literature, art, biology, biology-AP, calculus, ceramics, chamber groups, chemistry, chorus, college counseling, community service, computer education, computer programming, creative arts, creative writing, desktop publishing, drama, earth science, economics, economics-AP, elec-

tronic music, English, English as a foreign language, English literature, English literature-AP, ESL, European history, expository writing, fine arts, foreign policy, French, geometry, grammar, health, health education, history, Holocaust and other genocides, humanities, Internet research, life management skills, mathematics, music, music theory, newspaper, participation in sports, performing arts, photography, physical education, physical science, physics, psychology, social studies, Spanish, theater, trigonometry, typing, U.S. history, video film production, world history, world literature, writing, yearbook.

Graduation Requirements Computer science, creative arts, English, foreign language, history, mathematics, physical education (includes health), science, senior independent project, Creative Art Diploma Program (optional). Community service is required.

Special Academic Programs 11 Advanced Placement exams for which test preparation is offered; honors section; independent study; study at local college for college credit; ESL (9 students enrolled).

College Admission Counseling 32 students graduated in 2009; all went to college, including Boston College; Harvard University; University of Vermont; Vanderbilt University; Wheaton College.

Student Life Upper grades have specified standards of dress, student council, honor system. Discipline rests equally with students and faculty.

Tuition and Aid Day student tuition: $33,200. Tuition installment plan (The Tuition Plan, Academic Management Services Plan, monthly payment plans). Need-based scholarship grants available. In 2009–10, 43% of upper-school students received aid. Total amount of financial aid awarded in 2009–10: $1,353,690.

Admissions Traditional secondary-level entrance grade is 9. For fall 2009, 109 students applied for upper-level admission, 70 were accepted, 23 enrolled. ISEE, SSAT or TOEFL or SLEP required. Deadline for receipt of application materials: January 15. Application fee required: $50. On-campus interview required.

Athletics Interscholastic: baseball (boys), basketball (b,g), field hockey (g), lacrosse (b,g), soccer (b,g), softball (g), tennis (b,g); intramural: dance team (g); coed interscholastic: cross-country running, golf; coed intramural: alpine skiing, fitness, outdoor education, physical fitness, skiing (downhill), snowboarding, strength & conditioning, tennis, weight training. 5 PE instructors, 3 coaches, 2 athletic trainers.

Computers Computers are regularly used in desktop publishing, foreign language, graphic design, humanities, journalism, media production, technology, typing, video film production, Web site design, yearbook classes. Computer network features include on-campus library services, online commercial services, Internet access, wireless campus network, Internet filtering or blocking technology. Campus intranet, student e-mail accounts, and computer access in designated common areas are available to students. Students grades are available online. The school has a published electronic and media policy.

Contact Myra Korin, Admissions Coordinator. 617-738-8695. Fax: 617-734-5147. E-mail: admissions@brimmer.org. Web site: www.brimmerandmay.org.

BROMLEY BROOK SCHOOL

Manchester Center, Vermont
See Special Needs Schools section.

BROOKHAVEN ACADEMY

943 Brookway Boulevard Extension
Brookhaven, Mississippi 39601
Head of School: Mr. Herbert Davis

General Information Coeducational day college-preparatory and general academic school, affiliated with Christian faith. Grades PK–12. Founded: 1970. Setting: small town. Nearest major city is Jackson. 25-acre campus. 1 building on campus. Approved or accredited by Mississippi Private School Association, Southern Association of Colleges and Schools, and Mississippi Department of Education. Total enrollment: 481. Upper school average class size: 22. Upper school faculty-student ratio: 1:20.

Upper School Student Profile Grade 7: 38 students (24 boys, 14 girls); Grade 8: 42 students (27 boys, 15 girls); Grade 9: 36 students (20 boys, 16 girls); Grade 10: 30 students (19 boys, 11 girls); Grade 11: 43 students (18 boys, 25 girls); Grade 12: 38 students (21 boys, 17 girls). 100% of students are Christian faith.

Faculty School total: 20. In upper school: 4 men, 14 women; 9 have advanced degrees.

Subjects Offered Accounting, algebra, American history, anatomy, Bible studies, biology, business law, calculus, chemistry, composition, economics, English, geography, geometry, government, health, physics, physiology, reading, Spanish, speech, speech communications, state history, world history.

Graduation Requirements Advanced math, business skills (includes word processing), computer science, English, foreign language, mathematics, science, social studies (includes history).

Special Academic Programs Honors section; study at local college for college credit.

College Admission Counseling 38 students graduated in 2009; 37 went to college, including Millsaps College; Mississippi College; Mississippi State University; University of Mississippi; University of Southern Mississippi. Other: 1 entered military service. Median composite ACT: 22. 10% scored over 26 on composite ACT.

Student Life Upper grades have specified standards of dress, student council, honor system. Discipline rests primarily with faculty.

Tuition and Aid Day student tuition: $2916. Tuition installment plan (monthly payment plans, individually arranged payment plans). Tuition reduction for siblings available.

Admissions Traditional secondary-level entrance grade is 9. For fall 2009, 15 students applied for upper-level admission, 15 were accepted, 15 enrolled. Admissions testing required. Deadline for receipt of application materials: none. No application fee required. On-campus interview required.

Athletics Interscholastic: baseball (boys), basketball (b,g), cheering (g), cross-country running (b,g), dance team (g), football (b), golf (b), soccer (b,g), softball (g), tennis (b,g), track and field (b,g). 1 PE instructor, 1 coach.

Computers Computers are regularly used in yearbook classes. Computer network features include on-campus library services, Internet access. Campus intranet is available to students. Students grades are available online.

Contact Teresa Reed, Counselor. 601-833-4041. Fax: 601-833-1846. E-mail: bacounselor@cableone.net. Web site: www.brookhavenacademy.org.

THE BROOK HILL SCHOOL
PO Box 668
Bullard, Texas 75757
Head of School: Rod Fletcher

General Information Coeducational boarding and day college-preparatory and arts school, affiliated with Christian faith. Boarding grades 8–12, day grades PK–12. Founded: 1997. Setting: small town. Nearest major city is Tyler. Students are housed in single-sex houses for 16 to 20 students. 200-acre campus. 8 buildings on campus. Approved or accredited by Association of Christian Schools International, Southern Association of Colleges and Schools, The Association of Boarding Schools, and The College Board. Endowment: $1 million. Total enrollment: 502. Upper school average class size: 18. Upper school faculty-student ratio: 1:9. There are 176 required school days per year for Upper School students. Upper School students typically attend 5 days per week. The average school day consists of 6 hours and 30 minutes.

Upper School Student Profile Grade 9: 40 students (16 boys, 24 girls); Grade 10: 50 students (18 boys, 32 girls); Grade 11: 44 students (22 boys, 22 girls); Grade 12: 50 students (27 boys, 23 girls). 21% of students are boarding students. 84% are state residents. 2 states are represented in upper school student body. 15% are international students. International students from China, Ghana, Japan, Nigeria, Republic of Korea, and Turks and Caicos Islands; 1 other country represented in student body. 70% of students are Christian faith.

Faculty School total: 44. In upper school: 14 men, 17 women; 19 have advanced degrees; 3 reside on campus.

Subjects Offered ACT preparation, advanced chemistry, advanced math, Advanced Placement courses, algebra, American government, American history-AP, American literature-AP, analysis and differential calculus, anatomy and physiology, ancient history, ancient world history, art, athletics, baseball, basketball, Bible as literature, Bible studies, biology, British literature, British literature-AP, calculus, calculus-AP, career/college preparation, chemistry, chemistry-AP, choir, choral music, Christian ethics, Christian studies, civics/free enterprise, classics, college admission preparation, college awareness, college writing, communication skills, community service, comparative religion, composition, composition-AP, computer applications, computer education, conceptual physics, concert choir, creation science, drama, drama performance, dramatic arts, drawing, economics, economics-AP, English, English composition, English language and composition-AP, English language-AP, English literature, English literature and composition-AP, English literature-AP, English/composition-AP, ensembles, environmental science, epic literature, ESL, European history, European history-AP, European literature, fine arts, foreign language, four units of summer reading, French, French as a second language, geometry, government, government and politics-AP, government-AP, great books, health, history-AP, honors algebra, honors English, honors geometry, human biology, lab science, Latin, leadership and service, literary genres, literature and composition-AP, logic, logic, rhetoric, and debate, mathematics-AP, modern European history-AP, modern languages, orchestra, painting, physical education, physics, pre-calculus, public speaking, rhetoric, SAT preparation, SAT/ACT preparation, senior project, Spanish, speech communications, stagecraft, strings, student government, student publications, theater arts, TOEFL preparation, U.S. government and politics, U.S. government and politics-AP, U.S. history, U.S. history-AP, volleyball, yearbook.

Graduation Requirements Arts and fine arts (art, music, dance, drama), Bible, college admission preparation, economics, electives, English, foreign language, government, history, lab science, leadership, mathematics, physical education (includes health). Community service is required.

Special Academic Programs 12 Advanced Placement exams for which test preparation is offered; honors section; study at local college for college credit; ESL (3 students enrolled).

College Admission Counseling 33 students graduated in 2009; 32 went to college, including Baylor University; Penn State University Park; Texas A&M University; Texas Tech University; The University of Texas at Austin; University of Michigan–Dearborn. Other: 1 entered military service. Mean SAT critical reading: 549, mean SAT math: 547, mean SAT writing: 529, mean composite ACT: 24.

Student Life Upper grades have uniform requirement, student council, honor system. Discipline rests primarily with faculty. Attendance at religious services is required.

Tuition and Aid Day student tuition: $8510; 7-day tuition and room/board: $29,950. Tuition installment plan (FACTS Tuition Payment Plan, individually arranged payment plans). Tuition reduction for siblings, need-based scholarship grants available. In 2009–10, 50% of upper-school students received aid. Total amount of financial aid awarded in 2009–10: $750,000.

Admissions Traditional secondary-level entrance grade is 10. For fall 2009, 50 students applied for upper-level admission, 40 were accepted, 25 enrolled. Iowa Test, CTBS, or TAP, Iowa Tests of Basic Skills, SLEP for foreign students, SSAT, Stanford Achievement Test, Otis-Lennon School Ability Test, TOEFL or TOEFL or SLEP required. Deadline for receipt of application materials: none. Application fee required: $50. Interview recommended.

Athletics Interscholastic: baseball (boys, girls), basketball (b,g), cheering (g), cross-country running (b,g), football (b,g), golf (b,g), independent competitive sports (b,g), physical fitness (b,g), physical training (b,g), soccer (b), softball (g), strength & conditioning (b,g), tennis (b,g), track and field (b,g), volleyball (g), weight training (b,g); intramural: baseball (b,g), basketball (b,g), flag football (b,g); coed interscholastic: cheering, soccer, tennis; coed intramural: flag football. 1 PE instructor, 2 coaches, 1 athletic trainer.

Computers Computers are regularly used in all classes. Computer network features include on-campus library services, Internet access, wireless campus network, Internet filtering or blocking technology. Computer access in designated common areas is available to students. Students grades are available online. The school has a published electronic and media policy.

Contact Mrs. Shelly Lebo, Admissions Associate. 903-894-5000 Ext. 1011. Fax: 903-894-6332. E-mail: slebo@brookhill.org. Web site: www.brookhill.org/.

BROOKS SCHOOL
1160 Great Pond Road
North Andover, Massachusetts 01845-1298
Head of School: Mr. John R. Packard

General Information Coeducational boarding and day college-preparatory school, affiliated with Episcopal Church. Grades 9–12. Founded: 1926. Setting: suburban. Nearest major city is Boston. Students are housed in single-sex dormitories. 251-acre campus. 39 buildings on campus. Approved or accredited by Association of Independent Schools in New England, National Association of Episcopal Schools, New England Association of Schools and Colleges, The Association of Boarding Schools, and Massachusetts Department of Education. Member of National Association of Independent Schools and Secondary School Admission Test Board. Endowment: $58.7 million. Total enrollment: 365. Upper school average class size: 12. Upper school faculty-student ratio: 1:5. There are 180 required school days per year for Upper School students. Upper School students typically attend 5 days per week. The average school day consists of 7 hours.

Upper School Student Profile Grade 9: 80 students (36 boys, 44 girls); Grade 10: 100 students (56 boys, 44 girls); Grade 11: 96 students (51 boys, 45 girls); Grade 12: 95 students (56 boys, 39 girls). 70% of students are boarding students. 60% are state residents. 26 states are represented in upper school student body. 13% are international students. International students from Canada, China, Hong Kong, Nigeria, Republic of Korea, and Thailand; 9 other countries represented in student body.

Faculty School total: 77. In upper school: 42 men, 35 women; 61 have advanced degrees; 47 reside on campus.

Subjects Offered Algebra, American history, American history-AP, American literature, art history, art history-AP, astronomy, Bible studies, biology, biology-AP, calculus, calculus-AP, ceramics, chemistry, chemistry-AP, Chinese, chorus, computer math, creative writing, drama, driver education, earth science, English, English literature, English-AP, environmental science-AP, ethics, European history, European history-AP, expository writing, film, fine arts, French, French language-AP, French literature-AP, French-AP, geometry, government and politics-AP, grammar, Greek, health, history, history-AP, honors algebra, honors geometry, honors world history, integrated arts, journalism, Latin, Latin-AP, life skills, Mandarin, mathematics, Middle East, music, music theory, painting, photography, physics, physics-AP, playwriting, poetry, psychology, public speaking, religion, rhetoric, robotics, senior project, senior seminar, Southern literature, Spanish, Spanish language-AP, Spanish literature, Spanish literature-AP, Spanish-AP, statistics, studio art, theater, theater design and production, theology, trigonometry, U.S. government and politics-AP, visual arts, world history, world history-AP, world literature, writing.

Graduation Requirements Arts and fine arts (art, music, dance, drama), English, foreign language, health, history, mathematics, religion (includes Bible studies and theology), science. Community service is required.

Special Academic Programs 14 Advanced Placement exams for which test preparation is offered; honors section; independent study; term-away projects; study abroad.

College Admission Counseling 109 students graduated in 2010; all went to college, including Bowdoin College; Brown University; Connecticut College; Hamilton College; Trinity College; University of Vermont.

Student Life Upper grades have specified standards of dress, student council. Discipline rests primarily with faculty. Attendance at religious services is required.

Summer Programs Enrichment, advancement, sports, computer instruction programs offered; session focuses on English, mathematics, and SAT preparation; held on campus; accepts boys and girls; open to students from other schools. 70 students usually enrolled. 2011 schedule: June 28 to August 20. Application deadline: none.

Tuition and Aid Day student tuition: $34,973; 7-day tuition and room/board: $44,935. Tuition installment plan (Academic Management Services Plan, individually arranged payment plans). Need-based scholarship grants available. In 2010–11, 22% of upper-school students received aid. Total amount of financial aid awarded in 2010–11: $2,600,000.

Admissions Traditional secondary-level entrance grade is 9. For fall 2010, 883 students applied for upper-level admission, 282 were accepted, 109 enrolled. ISEE, SSAT, ERB, PSAT, SAT, PLAN or ACT or TOEFL required. Deadline for receipt of application materials: February 1. Application fee required: $50. Interview required.

Athletics Interscholastic: baseball (boys), basketball (b,g), crew (b,g), cross-country running (b,g), field hockey (g), football (b), ice hockey (b,g), lacrosse (b,g), soccer (b,g), softball (g), squash (b,g), tennis (b,g), wrestling (b); intramural: ice hockey (b); coed intramural: fitness, golf, sailing, skiing (downhill). 1 athletic trainer.

Computers Computers are regularly used in all academic classes. Computer network features include on-campus library services, online commercial services, Internet access, wireless campus network, Internet filtering or blocking technology. Campus intranet, student e-mail accounts, and computer access in designated common areas are available to students. The school has a published electronic and media policy.

Contact Director of Admission. 978-725-6272. Fax: 978-725-6298. E-mail: admission@brooksschool.org. Web site: www.brooksschool.org.

BROOKSTONE SCHOOL
440 Bradley Park Drive
Columbus, Georgia 31904
Head of School: Brian D. Kennerly

General Information Coeducational day college-preparatory school. Grades PK–12. Founded: 1951. Setting: suburban. Nearest major city is Atlanta. 112-acre campus. 11 buildings on campus. Approved or accredited by Georgia Independent School Association, Southern Association of Colleges and Schools, Southern Association of Independent Schools, and Georgia Department of Education. Member of National Association of Independent Schools. Endowment: $18 million. Total enrollment: 788. Upper school average class size: 14. Upper school faculty-student ratio: 1:10. There are 180 required school days per year for Upper School students. Upper School students typically attend 5 days per week. The average school day consists of 5 hours and 50 minutes.

Upper School Student Profile Grade 9: 80 students (42 boys, 38 girls); Grade 10: 65 students (33 boys, 32 girls); Grade 11: 51 students (25 boys, 26 girls); Grade 12: 73 students (48 boys, 25 girls).

Faculty School total: 75. In upper school: 17 men, 15 women; 24 have advanced degrees.

Subjects Offered Advanced computer applications, Advanced Placement courses, algebra, American Civil War, American government, American history, American history-AP, American literature, anatomy and physiology, art, art-AP, band, biology, biology-AP, calculus, calculus-AP, chemistry, chemistry-AP, choral music, chorus, Civil War, communications, comparative government and politics-AP, comparative religion, computer applications, computer multimedia, computer programming, computer science, computer science-AP, computers, concert band, concert choir, constitutional law, creative writing, drama, ecology, economics, economics-AP, English, English composition, English literature, English literature and composition-AP, European history, European history-AP, fine arts, French, French language-AP, French-AP, geometry, government and politics-AP, graphic design, health, history-AP, honors algebra, honors English, honors geometry, human geography—AP, humanities, Latin, Latin-AP, law, literature and composition-AP, literature-AP, macro/microeconomics-AP, marine biology, mathematics, mythology, neuroanatomy, ornithology, physical education, physics, pre-calculus, psychology, science, social sciences, social studies, Southern literature, Spanish, Spanish language-AP, Spanish-AP, statistics, statistics-AP, studio art-AP, theater, trigonometry, U.S. government, U.S. government and politics-AP, U.S. history, U.S. history-AP, weight training, world history, yearbook, zoology.

Graduation Requirements 3-dimensional design, algebra, American government, American history, arts and fine arts (art, music, dance, drama), biology, chemistry, computer science, economics, electives, English, foreign language, geometry, mathematics, physical education (includes health), science, social sciences, social studies (includes history), speech, world history, senior year speech.

Special Academic Programs 14 Advanced Placement exams for which test preparation is offered; honors section.

College Admission Counseling 79 students graduated in 2010; all went to college, including Auburn University; Columbus State University; Georgia Institute of Technology; Mercer University; The University of Alabama; University of Georgia. Median SAT critical reading: 560, median SAT math: 570, median SAT writing: 580, median combined SAT: 1720. 37% scored over 600 on SAT critical reading, 45% scored over 600 on SAT math, 43% scored over 600 on SAT writing, 66% scored over 1800 on combined SAT.

Student Life Upper grades have specified standards of dress, student council, honor system. Discipline rests equally with students and faculty.

Tuition and Aid Day student tuition: $13,350. Tuition installment plan (monthly payment plans, individually arranged payment plans, 3 payments in months July, November, and February (no interest)). Tuition reduction for siblings, merit scholarship grants, need-based scholarship grants, need-based loans, middle-income loans available. In 2010–11, 18% of upper-school students received aid; total upper-school merit-scholarship money awarded: $356,380. Total amount of financial aid awarded in 2010–11: $360,550.

Admissions Traditional secondary-level entrance grade is 9. For fall 2010, 63 students applied for upper-level admission, 50 were accepted, 30 enrolled. Otis-Lennon IQ Test or SSAT, ERB, PSAT, SAT, PLAN or ACT required. Deadline for receipt of application materials: none. Application fee required: $50. On-campus interview required.

Athletics Interscholastic: baseball (boys), basketball (b,g), cheering (g), cross-country running (b,g), football (b), golf (b,g), soccer (b,g), softball (g), tennis (b,g), track and field (b,g), volleyball (g), wrestling (b); intramural: basketball (b,g). 6 PE instructors.

Computers Computers are regularly used in college planning, computer applications, creative writing, English, foreign language, French, graphic arts, history, information technology, mathematics, media production, Spanish, video film production, yearbook classes. Computer network features include on-campus library services, online commercial services, Internet access, wireless campus network, Internet filtering or blocking technology. Campus intranet and student e-mail accounts are available to students. Students grades are available online. The school has a published electronic and media policy.

Contact Mary S. Snyder, Enrollment Director. 706-324-1392. Fax: 706-571-0178. E-mail: msnyder@brookstoneschool.org. Web site: www.brookstoneschool.org.

BROOKWOOD SCHOOL
301 Cardinal Ridge Road
Thomasville, Georgia 31792
Head of School: Mr. Notaro Mike

General Information Coeducational day college-preparatory and arts school. Grades PK–12. Founded: 1970. Setting: small town. Nearest major city is Tallahassee, FL. 40-acre campus. 10 buildings on campus. Approved or accredited by Georgia Accrediting Commission, Georgia Independent School Association, Southern Association of Colleges and Schools, and Georgia Department of Education. Member of National Association of Independent Schools. Endowment: $11 million. Total enrollment: 436. Upper school average class size: 11. Upper school faculty-student ratio: 1:10.

Upper School Student Profile Grade 9: 32 students (17 boys, 15 girls); Grade 10: 24 students (11 boys, 13 girls); Grade 11: 36 students (13 boys, 23 girls); Grade 12: 27 students (15 boys, 12 girls).

Faculty School total: 57. In upper school: 6 men, 8 women; 8 have advanced degrees.

Subjects Offered Algebra, American history, American literature, art, art history, art-AP, biology, biology-AP, business, calculus, calculus-AP, cheerleading, chemistry, college counseling, computer science, computers, drama performance, economics, English, English literature, English-AP, ethics, ethics and responsibility, European history, European history-AP, French, geometry, government/civics, health, history, journalism, learning lab, mathematics, music, physical education, physics, psychology, science, social studies, Spanish, student government, study skills, trigonometry, typing, U.S. history, U.S. history-AP, world history, writing.

Special Academic Programs Advanced Placement exam preparation; independent study; academic accommodation for the gifted.

College Admission Counseling 31 students graduated in 2009; all went to college, including Auburn University; Furman University; Georgia Institute of Technology; University of Georgia; Valdosta State University. Median SAT critical reading: 540, median SAT math: 530.

Student Life Upper grades have specified standards of dress, student council, honor system. Discipline rests primarily with faculty.

Tuition and Aid Day student tuition: $5800. Tuition installment plan (monthly payment plans). Merit scholarship grants, need-based scholarship grants available. In 2009–10, 17% of upper-school students received aid; total upper-school merit-scholarship money awarded: $6000. Total amount of financial aid awarded in 2009–10: $40,000.

Admissions Traditional secondary-level entrance grade is 9. For fall 2009, 20 students applied for upper-level admission, 15 were accepted, 12 enrolled. Achievement tests required. Deadline for receipt of application materials: none. Application fee required: $50. On-campus interview required.

Athletics Interscholastic: aquatics (boys, girls), baseball (b), basketball (b,g), cross-country running (b,g), football (b), soccer (b,g), softball (g), swimming and diving (b,g), tennis (b,g), track and field (b,g); intramural: cheering (g), power lifting (b,g), surfing (b,g); coed interscholastic: golf. 2 PE instructors, 6 coaches, 1 athletic trainer.

Computers Computers are regularly used in accounting, English, history classes. Computer network features include on-campus library services, Internet access.

Contact Mr. David L. Grooms Jr., Assistant Headmaster/Principal. 229-226-8070 Ext. 42. Fax: 229-227-0326. E-mail: dgrooms@brookwoodschool.org. Web site: www.brookwoodschool.org/.

BROPHY COLLEGE PREPARATORY

4701 North Central Avenue
Phoenix, Arizona 85012-1797
Head of School: Mr. Robert E. Ryan III

General Information Boys' day college-preparatory, arts, religious studies, and technology school, affiliated with Roman Catholic Church (Jesuit order). Grades 9–12. Founded: 1928. Setting: urban. 38-acre campus. 8 buildings on campus. Approved or accredited by Jesuit Secondary Education Association, National Catholic Education Association, North Central Association of Colleges and Schools, and Western Catholic Education Association. Endowment: $19 million. Total enrollment: 1,270. Upper school average class size: 24. Upper school faculty-student ratio: 1:15. There are 178 required school days per year for Upper School students. Upper School students typically attend 5 days per week. The average school day consists of 6 hours and 40 minutes.

Upper School Student Profile Grade 9: 340 students (340 boys); Grade 10: 329 students (329 boys); Grade 11: 291 students (291 boys); Grade 12: 310 students (310 boys). 64% of students are Roman Catholic Church (Jesuit order).

Faculty School total: 91. In upper school: 66 men, 22 women; 76 have advanced degrees.

Subjects Offered Advanced Placement courses, advanced studio art-AP, algebra, American history, American literature, anatomy, art, Bible studies, biology, business, calculus, chemistry, community service, computer math, computer programming, computer science, creative writing, drama, earth science, economics, engineering, English, English literature, ethics, European history, expository writing, fine arts, French, geography, geometry, government/civics, health, history, Latin, mathematics, mechanical drawing, music, physical education, physics, probability and statistics, psychology, religion, science, social sciences, social studies, sociology, Spanish, speech, theater, theology, trigonometry, video film production, world history, world literature.

Graduation Requirements Arts and fine arts (art, music, dance, drama), English, foreign language, mathematics, physical education (includes health), religion (includes Bible studies and theology), science, social studies (includes history). Community service is required.

Special Academic Programs Advanced Placement exam preparation; honors section; study at local college for college credit; study abroad.

College Admission Counseling 276 students graduated in 2009; all went to college, including Arizona State University; Boston College; Loyola Marymount University; Northern Arizona University; Santa Clara University; The University of Arizona. Median SAT critical reading: 585, median SAT math: 606, median SAT writing: 576, median combined SAT: 1767, median composite ACT: 26.

Student Life Upper grades have specified standards of dress, student council, honor system. Discipline rests primarily with faculty. Attendance at religious services is required.

Tuition and Aid Day student tuition: $12,000. Tuition installment plan (The Tuition Plan, monthly payment plans, individually arranged payment plans). Need-based scholarship grants, paying campus jobs available. In 2009–10, 29% of upper-school students received aid. Total amount of financial aid awarded in 2009–10: $2,241,937.

Admissions Traditional secondary-level entrance grade is 9. For fall 2009, 630 students applied for upper-level admission, 382 were accepted, 343 enrolled. STS required. Deadline for receipt of application materials: January 29. Application fee required: $50. On-campus interview required.

Athletics Interscholastic: aquatics, baseball, basketball, cross-country running, diving, flagball, football, golf, ice hockey, lacrosse, soccer, swimming and diving, tennis, track and field, volleyball, wrestling; intramural: aquatics, badminton, baseball, basketball, bicycling, bowling, cheering, climbing, crew, cricket, fishing, fitness, flag football, Frisbee, golf, handball, hockey, ice hockey, lacrosse, mountain biking, outdoor activities, physical fitness, physical training, rock climbing, skiing (downhill), softball, strength & conditioning, table tennis, touch football, ultimate Frisbee, volleyball, wall climbing, water polo, weight lifting, weight training. 2 PE instructors, 15 coaches, 2 athletic trainers.

Computers Computers are regularly used in all academic classes. Computer network features include on-campus library services, online commercial services, Internet access, wireless campus network, Blackboard, computer tablets. Student e-mail accounts are available to students. Students grades are available online. The school has a published electronic and media policy.

Contact Ms. Alana Dorsey, Assistant to Director of Admissions. 602-264-5291 Ext. 6233. Fax: 602-234-1669. E-mail: adorsey@brophyprep.org. Web site: www.brophyprep.org/.

BROTHER RICE HIGH SCHOOL

10001 South Pulaski Road
Chicago, Illinois 60655
Head of School: Mr. James P. Antos

General Information Boys' day college-preparatory school, affiliated with Roman Catholic Church. Grades 9–12. Founded: 1956. Setting: urban. 23-acre campus. 1 building on campus. Approved or accredited by European Council of International Schools, North Central Association of Colleges and Schools, and Illinois Department of Education. Total enrollment: 900. Upper school average class size: 30. Upper school faculty-student ratio: 1:15. There are 183 required school days per year for Upper School students. Upper School students typically attend 5 days per week. The average school day consists of 6 hours and 45 minutes.

Upper School Student Profile Grade 9: 245 students (245 boys); Grade 10: 231 students (231 boys); Grade 11: 225 students (225 boys); Grade 12: 200 students (200 boys). 75% of students are Roman Catholic.

Faculty School total: 75. In upper school: 35 men, 40 women; 40 have advanced degrees.

Subjects Offered 20th century history, 20th century physics, 20th century world history, accounting, ACT preparation, acting, advanced biology, advanced chemistry, advanced computer applications, advanced math, Advanced Placement courses, algebra, American Civil War, American democracy, American government, American history, American history-AP, American literature, American literature-AP, American studies, analytic geometry, anatomy and physiology, ancient history, ancient world history, art, astronomy, athletics, band, baseball, Basic programming, basic skills, basketball, Bible studies, biology, biology-AP, bowling, business law, calculus, calculus-AP, campus ministry, career and personal planning, career exploration, career planning, career/college preparation, careers, Catholic belief and practice, cell biology, chemistry, chemistry-AP, Christian education, civil war history, classical civilization, college admission preparation, college awareness, college counseling, college placement, college planning, college writing, community service, comparative government and politics, comparative government and politics-AP, comparative political systems-AP, composition, composition-AP, computer education, computer information systems, computer skills, concert band, constitutional history of U.S., developmental math, drama, drawing and design, driver education, economics, electives, English, English composition, English language and composition-AP, English language-AP, English literature, English literature and composition-AP, English literature-AP, English-AP, English/composition-AP, equality and freedom, fine arts, foreign language, French, general math, general science, geography, geometry, German, government, guidance, health education, history-AP, honors algebra, honors English, honors geometry, honors U.S. history, honors world history, journalism, language, language and composition, language arts, language-AP, languages, library, library assistant, library research, literature and composition-AP, logic, macro/microeconomics-AP, macroeconomics-AP, marching band, math analysis, math applications, math methods, math review, mathematics, mathematics-AP, Microsoft, participation in sports, performing arts, photography, physical education, physics, physics-AP, pre-algebra, pre-calculus, pre-college orientation, psychology, public service, publications, reading/study skills, religion, religious education, religious studies, remedial/makeup course work, science, social studies, Spanish, Spanish language-AP, Spanish-AP, student government, student publications, student teaching, swimming, swimming competency, swimming test, tennis, theater arts, track and field, trigonometry, U.S. government, U.S. government and politics, U.S. government and politics-AP, U.S. history, U.S. history-AP, Vietnam, Vietnam history, Vietnam War, volleyball, water polo, Western civilization, world civilizations, world cultures, world geography, world governments, world history, world history-AP, World War II, wrestling, yearbook.

Graduation Requirements 1½ elective credits, 20th century history, algebra, American government, American history, ancient world history, biology, chemistry, Christian studies, civil war history, classical civilization, composition, computer literacy, constitutional history of U.S., electives, English, English composition, English literature, foreign language, general science, geometry, government, health education, history, intro to computers, language arts, mathematics, physical education (includes health), physical science, religious education, U.S. constitutional history, U.S. history, Western civilization, service hours required for all students.

Special Academic Programs 10 Advanced Placement exams for which test preparation is offered; honors section; study at local college for college credit;

academic accommodation for the gifted; remedial reading and/or remedial writing; remedial math; programs in English, mathematics, general development for dyslexic students.

College Admission Counseling 278 students graduated in 2010; 256 went to college, including Eastern Illinois University; Illinois State University; Saint Xavier University; University of Illinois at Chicago; University of Illinois at Urbana–Champaign; Western Illinois University. Other: 10 went to work, 2 entered military service, 10 had other specific plans.

Student Life Upper grades have specified standards of dress, student council, honor system. Discipline rests primarily with faculty. Attendance at religious services is required.

Summer Programs Remediation, sports programs offered; held on campus; accepts boys; not open to students from other schools. 2011 schedule: June 16 to July 22.

Tuition and Aid Day student tuition: $9000. Tuition installment plan (monthly payment plans). Merit scholarship grants, need-based scholarship grants, need-based loans available. In 2010–11, 11% of upper-school students received aid; total upper-school merit-scholarship money awarded: $18,000. Total amount of financial aid awarded in 2010–11: $782,000.

Admissions Traditional secondary-level entrance grade is 9. For fall 2010, 1,000 students applied for upper-level admission, 900 were accepted, 900 enrolled. High School Placement Test (closed version) from Scholastic Testing Service required. Deadline for receipt of application materials: none. Application fee required: $200.

Athletics Interscholastic: baseball, basketball, bowling, cross-country running, fishing, football, golf, hockey, ice hockey, indoor track & field, lacrosse, rugby, soccer, swimming and diving, tennis, track and field, volleyball, water polo, wrestling. 3 PE instructors, 50 coaches, 1 athletic trainer.

Computers Computers are regularly used in all academic classes. Computer network features include on-campus library services, online commercial services, Internet access, Internet filtering or blocking technology. Campus intranet and student e-mail accounts are available to students. Students grades are available online. The school has a published electronic and media policy.

Contact Mr. Tim O'Connell, Recruitment Director. 773-429-4312. Fax: 773-779-5239. E-mail: tlyons@brrice.org. Web site: www.brrice.org.

BROTHER RICE HIGH SCHOOL

7101 Lahser Road
Bloomfield Hills, Michigan 48301
Head of School: Mr. John Birney

General Information Boys' day college-preparatory, arts, business, religious studies, and technology school, affiliated with Roman Catholic Church. Grades 9–12. Founded: 1960. Setting: suburban. Nearest major city is Detroit. 20-acre campus. 1 building on campus. Approved or accredited by North Central Association of Colleges and Schools and Michigan Department of Education. Total enrollment: 688. Upper school average class size: 22. Upper school faculty-student ratio: 1:13. Upper School students typically attend 5 days per week. The average school day consists of 6 hours and 51 minutes.

Upper School Student Profile Grade 9: 180 students (180 boys); Grade 10: 180 students (180 boys); Grade 11: 154 students (154 boys); Grade 12: 174 students (174 boys). 75% of students are Roman Catholic.

Faculty School total: 60. In upper school: 32 men, 10 women; 36 have advanced degrees.

Subjects Offered 20th century world history, accounting, algebra, American government, anatomy, anthropology, architectural drawing, art, band, biology, biology-AP, business law, calculus, calculus-AP, chemistry, choir, church history, computer science, computer science-AP, computers, concert band, creative writing, death and loss, debate, drama, earth science, economics, electronics, engineering, English, English composition, English language-AP, ensembles, European history, family living, forensics, French, French-AP, geometry, German, global science, health, jazz band, Latin, library science, literature, mathematics, mechanical drawing, music, music history, music theory, organic chemistry, photography, photojournalism, physical education, physics, physiology, pre-calculus, probability and statistics, psychology, social justice, Spanish, Spanish-AP, speech, studio art-AP, theology, trigonometry, U.S. government and politics-AP, U.S. history, U.S. history-AP, Western civilization, world geography, world religions.

Graduation Requirements Computer science, electives, English, foreign language, mathematics, physical education (includes health), science, social studies (includes history), speech, theology.

Special Academic Programs Advanced Placement exam preparation; honors section; remedial reading and/or remedial writing; remedial math.

College Admission Counseling 171 students graduated in 2010; all went to college, including Central Michigan University; Michigan State University; University of Michigan. Median combined SAT: 1793, median composite ACT: 26.

Student Life Upper grades have specified standards of dress, student council, honor system. Discipline rests primarily with faculty. Attendance at religious services is required.

Summer Programs Remediation, enrichment, art/fine arts programs offered; session focuses on camps and enrichment; held on campus; accepts boys and girls; open to students from other schools. 400 students usually enrolled. 2011 schedule: June to August.

Tuition and Aid Day student tuition: $10,100. Tuition installment plan (The Tuition Plan, monthly payment plans, individually arranged payment plans). Tuition reduction for siblings, merit scholarship grants, need-based scholarship grants available. In 2010–11, 15% of upper-school students received aid; total upper-school merit-scholarship money awarded: $150,000. Total amount of financial aid awarded in 2010–11: $300,000.

Admissions Traditional secondary-level entrance grade is 9. For fall 2010, 441 students applied for upper-level admission, 265 were accepted, 180 enrolled. SAS, STS-HSPT required. Deadline for receipt of application materials: none. No application fee required. Interview required.

Athletics Interscholastic: alpine skiing, baseball, basketball, bowling, cross-country running, diving, football, golf, hockey, ice hockey, lacrosse, skiing (downhill), soccer, swimming and diving, tennis, track and field, wrestling; intramural: basketball, bowling, drill team, fitness, football, golf, ice hockey, paint ball, rugby, skiing (downhill), snowboarding, strength & conditioning, touch football, ultimate Frisbee, winter (indoor) track. 50 coaches, 1 athletic trainer.

Computers Computer resources include online commercial services, Internet access. The school has a published electronic and media policy.

Contact Mr. David D. Sofran, Director of Admissions. 248-647-2526 Ext. 123. Fax: 248-647-2532. E-mail: sofran@brrice.edu.

BRUNSWICK SCHOOL

100 Maher Avenue
Greenwich, Connecticut 06830
Head of School: Thomas W. Philip

General Information Boys' day college-preparatory school. Grades PK–12. Founded: 1902. Setting: suburban. Nearest major city is New York, NY. 118-acre campus. 4 buildings on campus. Approved or accredited by Connecticut Association of Independent Schools, New England Association of Schools and Colleges, and Connecticut Department of Education. Member of National Association of Independent Schools. Endowment: $75 million. Total enrollment: 940. Upper school average class size: 15. Upper school faculty-student ratio: 1:5.

Upper School Student Profile Grade 9: 88 students (88 boys); Grade 10: 90 students (90 boys); Grade 11: 94 students (94 boys); Grade 12: 84 students (84 boys).

Faculty School total: 162. In upper school: 42 men, 14 women; 46 have advanced degrees.

Subjects Offered 20th century history, 3-dimensional design, acting, advanced chemistry, African-American literature, algebra, American history, American history-AP, American literature, anthropology, Arabic, architecture, art, art history, art history-AP, astronomy, biology, biology-AP, calculus, calculus-AP, ceramics, chemistry, chemistry-AP, Chinese, choir, community service, computer graphics, computer programming, computer programming-AP, creative writing, digital art, digital music, drama, earth science, economics, economics-AP, English, environmental science-AP, ethics, European history, European history-AP, film and literature, fine arts, French, French language-AP, French literature-AP, geometry, government-AP, Greek, Greek culture, health, history, honors algebra, honors geometry, human geography—AP, Italian, Japanese history, jazz, jazz band, jazz ensemble, Latin, Latin American literature, Latin-AP, mathematics, media studies, microeconomics, military history, music, oceanography, philosophy, photography, physical education, physics, physics-AP, poetry, pre-calculus, psychology, psychology-AP, science, senior seminar, Shakespeare, short story, social studies, Spanish, Spanish language-AP, Spanish literature-AP, speech and debate, statistics-AP, studio art, studio art-AP, theater, trigonometry, U.S. government and politics-AP, U.S. history-AP, world cultures, world history-AP, writing.

Graduation Requirements Arts and fine arts (art, music, dance, drama), English, foreign language, mathematics, physical education (includes health), science, social studies (includes history). Community service is required.

Special Academic Programs Advanced Placement exam preparation; honors section; independent study; term-away projects; academic accommodation for the gifted, the musically talented, and the artistically talented.

College Admission Counseling 82 students graduated in 2010; all went to college, including Dartmouth College; Duke University; Georgetown University; Wake Forest University; Yale University. Mean SAT critical reading: 660, mean SAT math: 668, mean SAT writing: 666, mean combined SAT: 1994. 75% scored over 600 on SAT critical reading, 83% scored over 600 on SAT math, 85% scored over 600 on SAT writing, 85% scored over 1800 on combined SAT.

Student Life Upper grades have specified standards of dress, student council, honor system. Discipline rests equally with students and faculty.

Summer Programs Enrichment programs offered; session focuses on academic enrichment; held on campus; accepts boys and girls; open to students from other schools. 2011 schedule: June 13 to July 8. Application deadline: April 1.

Tuition and Aid Day student tuition: $33,300. Tuition installment plan (Key Tuition Payment Plan, monthly payment plans). Need-based scholarship grants available. In 2010–11, 6% of upper-school students received aid. Total amount of financial aid awarded in 2010–11: $1,700,000.

Admissions Traditional secondary-level entrance grade is 9. For fall 2010, 115 students applied for upper-level admission, 37 were accepted, 30 enrolled. ISEE, PSAT or SSAT required. Deadline for receipt of application materials: December 15. Application fee required: $75. On-campus interview required.

Athletics Interscholastic: baseball, basketball, crew, cross-country running, fencing, fitness, football, golf, ice hockey, lacrosse, sailing, soccer, squash, tennis, track and field, water polo, wrestling; intramural: basketball, softball, squash, touch football, ultimate Frisbee. 4 PE instructors, 2 athletic trainers.

Computers Computers are regularly used in all classes. Computer network features include online commercial services, Internet access, wireless campus network, Internet filtering or blocking technology. Campus intranet and student e-mail accounts are available to students. The school has a published electronic and media policy.

Contact Stephen Garnett, Director, Upper School Admission. 203-625-5842. Fax: 203-625-5863. E-mail: Stephen_Garnett@brunswickschool.org. Web site: www.brunswickschool.org.

THE BRYN MAWR SCHOOL FOR GIRLS

109 West Melrose Avenue
Baltimore, Maryland 21210
Head of School: Maureen E. Walsh

General Information Coeducational day (boys' only in lower grades) college-preparatory and arts school. Boys grade PK, girls grades PK–12. Founded: 1885. Setting: suburban. 26-acre campus. 9 buildings on campus. Approved or accredited by Association of Independent Maryland Schools and Maryland Department of Education. Member of National Association of Independent Schools. Endowment: $22.2 million. Total enrollment: 717. Upper school average class size: 13. Upper school faculty-student ratio: 1:6. There are 172 required school days per year for Upper School students. Upper School students typically attend 5 days per week. The average school day consists of 7 hours.

Upper School Student Profile Grade 9: 77 students (77 girls); Grade 10: 75 students (75 girls); Grade 11: 75 students (75 girls); Grade 12: 77 students (77 girls).

Faculty School total: 141. In upper school: 15 men, 39 women; 23 have advanced degrees.

Subjects Offered Accounting, acting, African studies, African-American history, African-American literature, algebra, American history, American literature, anatomy, anatomy and physiology, Arabic, architectural drawing, art, art history, art history-AP, astronomy, biology, biology-AP, British literature, calculus, ceramics, chemistry, chemistry-AP, Chinese, comparative religion, computer programming, computer science, computer science-AP, creative writing, dance, design, digital art, digital photography, drama, drawing, ecology, economics, emerging technology, English, English literature, English-AP, environmental science-AP, ethics, European history, fine arts, forensics, French, French literature-AP, genetics, geography, geology, geometry, German, grammar, Greek, health, Holocaust studies, Irish literature, Latin, Latin American history, mathematics, mechanical drawing, moral theology, music, music theory, mythology, Native American studies, orchestra, painting, personal finance, photography, physical education, physics, physics-AP, poetry, pre-calculus, public speaking, rite of passage, Russian, science, Shakespearean histories, short story, social studies, Spanish, statistics, strings, technology, theater, trigonometry, U.S. government and politics-AP, U.S. history, U.S. history-AP, urban studies, Vietnam War, world history, world history-AP, world literature, World War I, World War II, writing.

Graduation Requirements Arts and fine arts (art, music, dance, drama), emerging technology, English, foreign language, history, mathematics, physical education (includes health), public speaking, science, 50 hours of community service, convocation speech.

Special Academic Programs Advanced Placement exam preparation; honors section; independent study; term-away projects; study abroad; academic accommodation for the gifted, the musically talented, and the artistically talented.

College Admission Counseling 72 students graduated in 2010; all went to college, including Cornell University; Dartmouth College; Georgetown University; Tulane University; University of Maryland, College Park; Wellesley College. Median SAT critical reading: 640, median SAT math: 640, median SAT writing: 680, median combined SAT: 1960, median composite ACT: 28. 69.6% scored over 600 on SAT critical reading, 66.7% scored over 600 on SAT math, 81.1% scored over 600 on SAT writing, 78.3% scored over 1800 on combined SAT, 59.4% scored over 26 on composite ACT.

Student Life Upper grades have uniform requirement, student council, honor system. Discipline rests equally with students and faculty.

Summer Programs Enrichment, sports, art/fine arts programs offered; session focuses on arts, crafts, language, culture, and sports; held on campus; accepts boys and girls; open to students from other schools. 725 students usually enrolled. 2011 schedule: June 20 to August 19. Application deadline: none.

Tuition and Aid Day student tuition: $23,800. Tuition installment plan (FACTS Tuition Payment Plan, individually arranged payment plans, Tuition Management Services, Bi-weekly Payroll Deduction (for employees only)). Need-based scholarship grants, need-based loans, middle-income loans available. In 2010–11, 28% of upper-school students received aid. Total amount of financial aid awarded in 2010–11: $1,222,050.

Admissions Traditional secondary-level entrance grade is 9. For fall 2010, 87 students applied for upper-level admission, 57 were accepted, 31 enrolled. ISEE required. Deadline for receipt of application materials: January 3. Application fee required: $60. On-campus interview required.

Athletics Interscholastic: badminton, ballet, basketball, crew, cross-country running, dance, field hockey, hockey, indoor soccer, indoor track & field, lacrosse, rowing, running, soccer, softball, squash, tennis, track and field, volleyball, winter (indoor) track, winter soccer; intramural: aerobics, aerobics/dance, aerobics/Nautilus, archery, badminton, ball hockey, basketball, bowling, cooperative games, croquet, cross-country running, dance, fitness, flag football, floor hockey, ice hockey, jogging, outdoor activities, physical training, pillo polo, ropes courses, running, strength & conditioning, tennis, touch football, weight training. 5 PE instructors, 45 coaches, 1 athletic trainer.

Computers Computers are regularly used in all academic, animation, art, computer applications, Web site design classes. Computer network features include on-campus library services, online commercial services, Internet access, off-campus e-mail. Campus intranet and student e-mail accounts are available to students. Students grades are available online. The school has a published electronic and media policy.

Contact Talia Titus, Director of Admission and Financial Aid. 410-323-8800 Ext. 1237. Fax: 410-435-4678. E-mail: titust@brynmawrschool.org. Web site: www.brynmawrschool.org.

THE BUCKLEY SCHOOL

3900 Stansbury Avenue
Sherman Oaks, California 91423
Head of School: Larry W. Dougherty, EdD

General Information Coeducational day college-preparatory, arts, and technology school. Grades K–12. Founded: 1933. Setting: suburban. Nearest major city is Los Angeles. 20-acre campus. 8 buildings on campus. Approved or accredited by California Association of Independent Schools, Western Association of Schools and Colleges, and California Department of Education. Member of National Association of Independent Schools. Endowment: $2.7 million. Total enrollment: 770. Upper school average class size: 14. Upper school faculty-student ratio: 1:8. There are 180 required school days per year for Upper School students. Upper School students typically attend 5 days per week. The average school day consists of 6 hours and 15 minutes.

Upper School Student Profile Grade 9: 73 students (47 boys, 26 girls); Grade 10: 76 students (43 boys, 33 girls); Grade 11: 70 students (40 boys, 30 girls); Grade 12: 70 students (35 boys, 35 girls).

Faculty School total: 100. In upper school: 28 men, 27 women; 31 have advanced degrees.

Subjects Offered Algebra, American history, American literature, art history, biology, calculus, ceramics, chemistry, chorus, computer graphics, computer science, creative writing, dance, drama, ecology, English, English literature, fine arts, French, geology, geometry, government/civics, humanities, journalism, Latin, mathematics, music, music theory, orchestra, photography, physical education, physics, science, social sciences, Spanish, theater, trigonometry, world history, world literature, yoga.

Graduation Requirements Arts and fine arts (art, music, dance, drama), computer science, English, foreign language, humanities, mathematics, performing arts, physical education (includes health), science, social sciences. Community service is required.

Special Academic Programs Advanced Placement exam preparation; honors section; study abroad.

College Admission Counseling 74 students graduated in 2010; all went to college, including New York University; Stanford University; University of California, Berkeley; University of California, Los Angeles; University of Southern California.

Student Life Upper grades have uniform requirement, student council, honor system. Discipline rests primarily with faculty.

Summer Programs Advancement, art/fine arts, computer instruction programs offered; session focuses on college preparatory courses and enrichment; held on campus; accepts boys and girls; open to students from other schools. 100 students usually enrolled. 2011 schedule: June to July.

Tuition and Aid Day student tuition: $30,025. Tuition installment plan (Key Tuition Payment Plan, individually arranged payment plans, For families that qualify for Financial Aid). Need-based scholarship grants available. In 2010–11, 14% of upper-school students received aid. Total amount of financial aid awarded in 2010–11: $421,225.

Admissions Traditional secondary-level entrance grade is 9. ISEE required. Deadline for receipt of application materials: January 10. Application fee required: $100. On-campus interview required.

Athletics Interscholastic: baseball (boys), softball (g), volleyball (g); coed interscholastic: basketball, cross-country running, equestrian sports, soccer, swimming and diving, tennis. 12 PE instructors, 11 coaches, 2 athletic trainers.

Computers Computers are regularly used in art, English, graphic design, music, science, video film production classes. Computer network features include on-campus library services, online commercial services, Internet access, wireless campus network, Internet filtering or blocking technology, Web page design, online syllabi. Student e-mail accounts are available to students. The school has a published electronic and media policy.

Contact Carinne M. Barker, Director of Admission and Financial Aid. 818-783-1610 Ext. 709. Fax: 818-461-6714. E-mail: admissions@buckley.org. Web site: www.buckley.org.

BULLOCH ACADEMY
873 Westside Road
Statesboro, Georgia 30458
Head of School: Mr. Roy Alexander

General Information Coeducational day college-preparatory and technology school, affiliated with Christian faith, Baptist Church. Grades PK–12. Founded: 1971. Setting: small town. Nearest major city is Savannah. 35-acre campus. 4 buildings on campus. Approved or accredited by Georgia Accrediting Commission, Georgia Independent School Association, Southern Association of Colleges and Schools, and Southern Association of Independent Schools. Total enrollment: 454. Upper school average class size: 17. Upper school faculty-student ratio: 1:17. There are 180 required school days per year for Upper School students. Upper School students typically attend 5 days per week. The average school day consists of 8 hours.

Upper School Student Profile Grade 9: 36 students (16 boys, 20 girls); Grade 10: 21 students (13 boys, 8 girls); Grade 11: 29 students (20 boys, 9 girls); Grade 12: 27 students (8 boys, 19 girls). 98% of students are Christian, Baptist.

Faculty School total: 14. In upper school: 5 men, 9 women; 3 have advanced degrees.

Subjects Offered Advanced Placement courses, American government, American history, anatomy and physiology, art, art education, biology, calculus, chemistry, computer applications, computer science, earth science, economics, economics and history, English, ethics, geometry, government, government-AP, government/civics, health education, journalism, language and composition, language arts, literature-AP, mathematics-AP, music, performing arts, physical education, physics, pre-algebra, pre-calculus, research skills, science, social sciences, Spanish, speech and debate, technology, U.S. government and politics-AP, U.S. history, Web site design, world geography, world history.

Graduation Requirements Computer science, English, foreign language, mathematics, physical education (includes health), science, social sciences, social studies (includes history).

Special Academic Programs 6 Advanced Placement exams for which test preparation is offered; honors section; independent study; study at local college for college credit; academic accommodation for the gifted, the musically talented, and the artistically talented.

College Admission Counseling 27 students graduated in 2009; all went to college, including Georgia College & State University; Georgia Southern University; Mercer University; University of Georgia. Median SAT critical reading: 584, median SAT math: 583, median SAT writing: 571, median combined SAT: 1738.

Student Life Upper grades have specified standards of dress, student council, honor system. Discipline rests primarily with faculty.

Tuition and Aid Day student tuition: $6082. Tuition installment plan (monthly payment plans, individually arranged payment plans). Tuition reduction for siblings, need-based scholarship grants, tuition assistance available. In 2009–10, 10% of upper-school students received aid. Total amount of financial aid awarded in 2009–10: $10,000.

Admissions Traditional secondary-level entrance grade is 9. For fall 2009, 8 students applied for upper-level admission, 8 were accepted, 8 enrolled. Any standardized test required. Deadline for receipt of application materials: none. Application fee required: $350. Interview recommended.

Athletics Interscholastic: baseball (boys), basketball (b,g), cheering (g), cross-country running (b,g), dance team (g), football (b), golf (b,g), physical fitness (b,g), running (b,g), soccer (b,g), softball (g), strength & conditioning (b,g), tennis (b,g), track and field (b,g), weight lifting (b,g), weight training (b,g), wrestling (b); intramural: cheering (g), cross-country running (b,g), football (b), physical fitness (b,g); coed interscholastic: physical fitness; coed intramural: basketball, football, physical fitness. 3 PE instructors, 7 coaches, 2 athletic trainers.

Computers Computers are regularly used in art, career education, career exploration, computer applications, creative writing, desktop publishing, economics, geography, history, independent study, keyboarding, technology classes. Computer network features include on-campus library services, Internet access, Internet filtering or blocking technology. Student e-mail accounts are available to students. Students grades are available online. The school has a published electronic and media policy.

Contact Mr. Roy Alexander, Head of School. 912-764-6297. Fax: 912-764-3165. E-mail: ralexander@bullochacademy.com. Web site: www.bullochacademy.com.

BURKE MOUNTAIN ACADEMY
PO Box 78
East Burke, Vermont 05832
Head of School: Kirk Dwyer

General Information Coeducational boarding and day college-preparatory school. Grades 7–PG. Founded: 1970. Setting: rural. Nearest major city is St. Johnsbury. Students are housed in coed dormitories. 33-acre campus. 9 buildings on campus. Approved or accredited by New England Association of Schools and Colleges and Vermont Department of Education. Member of National Association of Independent Schools. Total enrollment: 68. Upper school average class size: 15. Upper school faculty-student ratio: 1:7. There are 180 required school days per year for Upper School students. Upper School students typically attend 5 days per week. The average school day consists of 6 hours and 30 minutes.

Upper School Student Profile Grade 7: 2 students (2 girls); Grade 8: 6 students (3 boys, 3 girls); Grade 9: 12 students (9 boys, 3 girls); Grade 10: 12 students (6 boys, 6 girls); Grade 11: 13 students (7 boys, 6 girls); Grade 12: 13 students (7 boys, 6 girls); Postgraduate: 9 students (7 boys, 2 girls). 95% of students are boarding students. 23% are state residents. 17 states are represented in upper school student body. 5% are international students. International students from Australia and Canada.

Faculty School total: 9. In upper school: 4 men, 5 women; 6 have advanced degrees; 3 reside on campus.

Subjects Offered Algebra, American history, American literature, art, biology, calculus, chemistry, creative writing, current events, English, English literature, European history, fine arts, French, geometry, history, mathematics, physical education, physics, science, social studies, world history, world literature, writing.

Graduation Requirements Arts and fine arts (art, music, dance, drama), English, foreign language, mathematics, physical education (includes health), science, social studies (includes history).

Special Academic Programs Advanced Placement exam preparation; independent study; term-away projects; study at local college for college credit; study abroad.

College Admission Counseling 15 students graduated in 2009; 10 went to college, including Middlebury College; St. Lawrence University; University of Vermont; Williams College. Other: 5 entered a postgraduate year.

Student Life Upper grades have honor system. Discipline rests equally with students and faculty.

Tuition and Aid Day student tuition: $27,720; 7-day tuition and room/board: $39,320. Tuition installment plan (monthly payment plans, individually arranged payment plans). Need-based scholarship grants available.

Admissions SSAT required. Deadline for receipt of application materials: none. Application fee required: $100. Interview recommended.

Athletics Interscholastic: alpine skiing (boys, girls), golf (b,g), nordic skiing (b,g), skiing (cross-country) (b,g), skiing (downhill) (b,g), soccer (b,g); intramural: alpine skiing (b,g), nordic skiing (b,g), soccer (b,g); coed interscholastic: cross-country running. 6 coaches, 1 athletic trainer.

Computers Computers are regularly used in English, foreign language, mathematics, science classes. Computer resources include Internet access, wireless campus network. Computer access in designated common areas is available to students.

Contact Marcia Berry, Office Manager. 802-626-5607. Fax: 802-626-3784. E-mail: mberry@burkemtnacademy.org. Web site: www.burkemtnacademy.org.

BURR AND BURTON ACADEMY
57 Seminary Avenue
Manchester, Vermont 05254
Head of School: Mr. Mark Tashjian

General Information Coeducational boarding and day college-preparatory, general academic, arts, and technology school. Grades 9–12. Founded: 1829. Setting: small town. Nearest major city is Albany, NY. Students are housed in single-sex dormitories and homes of host families. 29-acre campus. 7 buildings on campus. Approved or accredited by New England Association of Schools and Colleges and Vermont Department of Education. Member of National Association of Independent Schools. Total enrollment: 692. Upper school average class size: 19. Upper school faculty-student ratio: 1:12. There are 175 required school days per year for Upper School students. Upper School students typically attend 5 days per week. The average school day consists of 6 hours and 40 minutes.

Upper School Student Profile Grade 9: 144 students (71 boys, 73 girls); Grade 10: 150 students (79 boys, 71 girls); Grade 11: 183 students (102 boys, 81 girls); Grade 12: 164 students (70 boys, 94 girls). 1% are international students.

Faculty School total: 60. In upper school: 35 men, 25 women; 30 have advanced degrees.

Subjects Offered Algebra, American history, American literature, anatomy, art, art history, biology, business, calculus, chemistry, computer math, computer programming, computer science, drafting, drama, driver education, earth science, ecology, English, English literature, environmental science, expository writing, French, geometry, German, government/civics, health, history, industrial arts, mathematics, music, photography, physical education, physics, psychology, science, social studies, Spanish, theater, trigonometry, typing, world history, world literature.

Graduation Requirements Arts, computer literacy, English, mathematics, physical education (includes health), science, social studies (includes history), U.S. history. Community service is required.

Special Academic Programs 10 Advanced Placement exams for which test preparation is offered; honors section; independent study; term-away projects; study abroad; remedial reading and/or remedial writing; remedial math; programs in English, mathematics, general development for dyslexic students; special instructional classes for deaf students, blind students; ESL (12 students enrolled).

College Admission Counseling 198 students graduated in 2010; 158 went to college, including High Point University; Montana State University; St. Lawrence University; University of Utah; University of Vermont. Other: 20 went to work, 2 entered military service, 18 had other specific plans.

Student Life Upper grades have specified standards of dress, student council. Discipline rests primarily with faculty.

Tuition and Aid Day student tuition: $14,900; 7-day tuition and room/board: $36,600. Tuition installment plan (individually arranged payment plans). Financial aid available to upper-school students. In 2010–11, 2% of upper-school students received aid.

Admissions Traditional secondary-level entrance grade is 9. School's own test and SLEP for foreign students required. Deadline for receipt of application materials: none. No application fee required. Interview recommended.

Athletics Interscholastic: alpine skiing (boys, girls), baseball (b), basketball (b,g), cross-country running (b,g), dance team (g), football (b), golf (b,g), ice hockey (b,g), lacrosse (b,g), nordic skiing (b,g), skiing (cross-country) (b,g), skiing (downhill) (b,g), soccer (b,g), softball (g), tennis (b,g), track and field (b,g); coed intramural: field hockey, floor hockey, outdoor adventure, outdoor education, volleyball. 3 PE instructors.

Computers Computers are regularly used in drafting, drawing and design, English, foreign language, graphic design, history, information technology, mathematics, science, video film production, Web site design, yearbook classes. Computer network features include on-campus library services, online commercial services, Internet access, Internet filtering or blocking technology.

Contact Mr. Philip G. Anton, Director of Admission and School Counseling. 802-362-1775 Ext. 125. Fax: 802-362-0574. E-mail: panton@burrburton.org. Web site: www.burrburton.org.

THE BUSH SCHOOL
3400 East Harrison Street
Seattle, Washington 98112
Head of School: Mr. Frank Magusin
General Information Coeducational day college-preparatory and experiential learning school. Grades K–12. Founded: 1924. Setting: urban. 6-acre campus. 2 buildings on campus. Approved or accredited by Northwest Accreditation Commission, Northwest Association of Schools and Colleges, Pacific Northwest Association of Independent Schools, and Washington Department of Education. Member of National Association of Independent Schools. Endowment: $10 million. Total enrollment: 577. Upper school average class size: 13. Upper school faculty-student ratio: 1:6.

Upper School Student Profile Grade 9: 54 students (34 boys, 20 girls); Grade 10: 58 students (23 boys, 35 girls); Grade 11: 65 students (29 boys, 36 girls); Grade 12: 56 students (32 boys, 24 girls).

Faculty School total: 80. In upper school: 18 men, 19 women; 28 have advanced degrees.

Subjects Offered Acting, advanced chemistry, advanced math, African American history, African American studies, algebra, American literature, anatomy and physiology, animal behavior, animal science, anthropology, art, art history, astronomy, Bible as literature, biology, biotechnology, calculus, career experience, cartooning/animation, ceramics, chemistry, civics, community service, comparative religion, composition, computer art, computer graphics, computer math, computer multimedia, computer programming, computer science, creative writing, critical writing, dance, digital art, directing, diversity studies, drama, drama workshop, drawing, drawing and design, earth science, ecology, English, English composition, English literature, ensembles, environmental science, environmental studies, ethics, ethics and responsibility, European civilization, European history, experiential education, expository writing, fiber arts, filmmaking, fine arts, fitness, foreign policy, French, genetics, geography, geology, geometry, glassblowing, golf, government/civics, health education, history, history of China and Japan, history of religion, human anatomy, improvisation, Indian studies, instrumental music, internship, Latin American literature, literary magazine, literature, literature by women, logic, marine science, mathematics, metalworking, microbiology, Middle East, music, music composition, music performance, music theater, music theory, musical productions, musical theater, newspaper, nuclear science, oceanography, oil painting, opera, outdoor education, painting, photography, physical education, physics, play production, playwriting and directing, poetry, pre-calculus, printmaking, probability and statistics, programming, psychology, public policy issues and action, religion and culture, Romantic period literature, Russia and contemporary Europe, Russian studies, science, sculpture, senior career experience, senior internship, senior project, service learning/internship, sewing, Shakespeare, short story, social studies, South African history, Spanish, Spanish literature, statistics, student publications, tennis, Thailand and Southeast Asia, theater, theater production, track and field, trigonometry, U.S. history, vocal ensemble, voice ensemble, volleyball, Western civilization, Western philosophy, wilderness education, wilderness experience, women's literature, women's studies, woodworking, work experience, world cultures, world history, world literature, world religions, writing workshop, yearbook.

Graduation Requirements Arts and fine arts (art, music, dance, drama), computer science, English, foreign language, mathematics, physical education (includes health), physiology, science, social studies (includes history), experiential learning course every trimester. Community service is required.

Special Academic Programs Advanced Placement exam preparation; independent study; domestic exchange program (with The Network Program Schools); study abroad; academic accommodation for the gifted.

College Admission Counseling 51 students graduated in 2009; all went to college, including Lewis & Clark College; Mount Holyoke College; New York University; Pitzer College; The Colorado College; University of Washington.

Student Life Upper grades have student council, honor system. Discipline rests primarily with faculty.

Tuition and Aid Day student tuition: $24,530. Tuition installment plan (Insured Tuition Payment Plan, monthly payment plans, individually arranged payment plans, Dewar Tuition Refund Plan). Need-based scholarship grants available. In 2009–10, 15% of upper-school students received aid. Total amount of financial aid awarded in 2009–10: $495,178.

Admissions Traditional secondary-level entrance grade is 9. ISEE required. Deadline for receipt of application materials: January 14. Application fee required: $60. Interview required.

Athletics Interscholastic: baseball (boys), basketball (b,g), cross-country running (b,g), golf (b,g), running (b,g), skiing (cross-country) (b,g), soccer (b,g), tennis (b,g), track and field (b,g), ultimate Frisbee (b,g), volleyball (g); intramural: lacrosse (g); coed interscholastic: nordic skiing, skiing (cross-country), ultimate Frisbee; coed intramural: backpacking, climbing, curling, fencing, Frisbee, hiking/backpacking, outdoor activities, outdoor adventure, outdoor education, outdoor skills, rafting, rock climbing, skiing (downhill), ultimate Frisbee, weight training, wilderness. 3 PE instructors, 3 coaches.

Computers Computers are regularly used in art, English, foreign language, mathematics, multimedia, music, science, yearbook classes. Computer network features include on-campus library services, online commercial services, Internet access, wireless campus network, access to wide range of subscription databases with school password. Student e-mail accounts and computer access in designated common areas are available to students. The school has a published electronic and media policy.

Contact Ms. Elizabeth Atcheson, Director of Admissions and Financial Aid. 206-326-7735. E-mail: elizabeth.atcheson@bush.edu. Web site: www.bush.edu.

BUXTON SCHOOL
291 South Street
Williamstown, Massachusetts 01267
Head of School: C. William Bennett and Peter Smith
General Information Coeducational boarding and day college-preparatory and arts school. Grades 9–12. Founded: 1928. Setting: small town. Nearest major city is Boston. Students are housed in single-sex dormitories. 150-acre campus. 17 buildings on campus. Approved or accredited by Association of Independent Schools in New England, New England Association of Schools and Colleges, The Association of Boarding Schools, and Massachusetts Department of Education. Member of National Association of Independent Schools and Secondary School Admission Test Board. Endowment: $1.7 million. Total enrollment: 90. Upper school average class size: 9. Upper school faculty-student ratio: 1:5. There are 224 required school days per year for Upper School students. The average school day consists of 5 hours and 45 minutes.

Upper School Student Profile Grade 9: 10 students (7 boys, 3 girls); Grade 10: 23 students (9 boys, 14 girls); Grade 11: 25 students (13 boys, 12 girls); Grade 12: 32 students (19 boys, 13 girls). 86% of students are boarding students. 13% are state residents. 12 states are represented in upper school student body. 13% are international students. International students from Bermuda, China, Ecuador, Mexico, Rwanda, and Switzerland; 2 other countries represented in student body.

Faculty School total: 21. In upper school: 12 men, 9 women; 4 have advanced degrees; 13 reside on campus.

Subjects Offered 20th century history, advanced math, African dance, African drumming, African studies, algebra, American history, American literature, American minority experience, anatomy and physiology, anthropology, astronomy, biology, calculus, cell biology, ceramics, chemistry, costumes and make-up, creative writing, critical writing, dance performance, drama, drama performance, drawing, English, English literature, ensembles, environmental studies, ESL, European history, expository writing, fiction, film history, French, geology, geometry, global issues, grammar, improvisation, independent study, Indonesian, instruments, lab science, Latin American literature, linear algebra, literary genres, literature, marine biology, media literacy, multicultural studies, music, music composition, music performance, music theory, oceanography, painting, performing arts, philosophy, photography, physics, poetry, pre-calculus, printmaking, set design, social sciences, Spanish, studio art, technical theater, TOEFL preparation, trigonometry, video film production, voice, writing workshop.

Graduation Requirements American history, English, foreign language, lab science, mathematics, social sciences.

Special Academic Programs Honors section; academic accommodation for the gifted, the musically talented, and the artistically talented; ESL (6 students enrolled).

College Admission Counseling 24 students graduated in 2010; 22 went to college, including Bard College; Goucher College; Middlebury College; Reed College; Smith College; Swarthmore College. Other: 2 had other specific plans.

Student Life Discipline rests primarily with faculty.

Tuition and Aid Day student tuition: $27,500; 7-day tuition and room/board: $43,500. Tuition installment plan (Academic Management Services Plan, Key Tuition Payment Plan, individually arranged payment plans). Need-based scholarship grants, need-based loans with limited in-house financing available. In 2010–11, 47% of upper-school students received aid. Total amount of financial aid awarded in 2010–11: $1,200,000.

Admissions Traditional secondary-level entrance grade is 9. SSAT or TOEFL required. Deadline for receipt of application materials: February 1. Application fee required: $50. On-campus interview required.

Athletics Interscholastic: soccer (boys, girls); intramural: soccer (b,g); coed inter-scholastic: basketball, ultimate Frisbee; coed intramural: bicycling, dance, fitness, hiking/backpacking, horseback riding, indoor soccer, jogging, martial arts, mountain biking, outdoor activities, physical training, running, skiing (downhill), snow-boarding, soccer, table tennis, tennis, ultimate Frisbee, weight lifting, yoga.

Computers Computers are regularly used in history, mathematics, media, media production, multimedia, music, photography, science, Spanish, video film production classes. Computer network features include Internet access, wireless campus network, Internet filtering or blocking technology. Campus intranet and computer access in designated common areas are available to students. The school has a published electronic and media policy.

Contact Admissions Office. 413-458-3919. Fax: 413-458-9428. E-mail: Admissions@BuxtonSchool.org. Web site: www.BuxtonSchool.org.

See Display below and Close-Up on page 748.

THE BYRNES SCHOOLS
1201 East Ashby Road
Florence, South Carolina 29506
Head of School: Mr. John W. Colby Jr.

General Information Coeducational day college-preparatory school. Grades PK–12. Founded: 1966. Setting: small town. 16-acre campus. 3 buildings on campus. Approved or accredited by South Carolina Independent School Association and Southern Association of Independent Schools. Candidate for accreditation by Southern Association of Colleges and Schools. Endowment: $25,000. Total enrollment: 238. Upper school average class size: 13. Upper school faculty-student ratio: 1:9. There are 175 required school days per year for Upper School students. Upper School students typically attend 5 days per week. The average school day consists of 6 hours and 50 minutes.

Upper School Student Profile Grade 9: 21 students (12 boys, 9 girls); Grade 10: 18 students (9 boys, 9 girls); Grade 11: 20 students (9 boys, 11 girls); Grade 12: 14 students (10 boys, 4 girls).

Faculty School total: 28. In upper school: 6 men, 6 women; 5 have advanced degrees.

Subjects Offered Advanced Placement courses, algebra, American history, biology, biology-AP, calculus-AP, chemistry, chemistry-AP, computer science, earth science, economics, English, English-AP, environmental science, geography, geometry, government/civics, history-AP, mathematics, physical education, physics, science, social studies, Spanish, Spanish-AP, world history.

Graduation Requirements English, foreign language, mathematics, physical education (includes health), science, social studies (includes history).

Special Academic Programs Advanced Placement exam preparation; honors section; academic accommodation for the gifted.

College Admission Counseling 23 students graduated in 2010; all went to college, including Clemson University; Francis Marion University; Furman University; The Citadel, The Military College of South Carolina; University of South Carolina.

Student Life Upper grades have specified standards of dress, student council, honor system. Discipline rests primarily with faculty.

Summer Programs Remediation, advancement programs offered; session focuses on college prep; held on campus; accepts boys and girls; open to students from other schools. 10 students usually enrolled.

Tuition and Aid Day student tuition: $6750. Tuition installment plan (Insured Tuition Payment Plan, monthly payment plans). Need-based scholarship grants available. In 2010–11, 15% of upper-school students received aid. Total amount of financial aid awarded in 2010–11: $25,000.

Admissions Traditional secondary-level entrance grade is 9. For fall 2010, 12 students applied for upper-level admission, 12 were accepted, 12 enrolled. Metro-politan Achievement Test or Stanford Achievement Test required. Deadline for receipt of application materials: none. Application fee required: $50. On-campus interview required.

Athletics Interscholastic: baseball (boys), basketball (b,g), cheering (g), football (b), golf (b,g), soccer (b,g), softball (g), volleyball (g); intramural: aerobics/dance (g), strength & conditioning (b,g), weight lifting (b,g), weight training (b,g); coed interscholastic: cross-country running; coed intramural: tennis. 1 PE instructor, 1 athletic trainer.

Computers Computers are regularly used in mathematics, yearbook classes. Computer network features include Internet access. Students grades are available online. The school has a published electronic and media policy.

Contact Mr. John W. Colby Jr., Headmaster. 843-622-0131 Ext. 153. Fax: 843-669-2466. E-mail: JColby@byrnesschools.org. Web site: www. byrnesschools.org.

CALGARY ACADEMY
9400 17 Avenue SW
Calgary, Alberta T3H 4A6, Canada
Head of School: Mr. Barry Russell

General Information Coeducational day college-preparatory, arts, and technology school; primarily serves underachievers, students with learning disabilities, individuals with Attention Deficit Disorder, and dyslexic students. Grades 2–12. Founded: 1981. Setting: suburban. 17-acre campus. 3 buildings on campus. Approved or

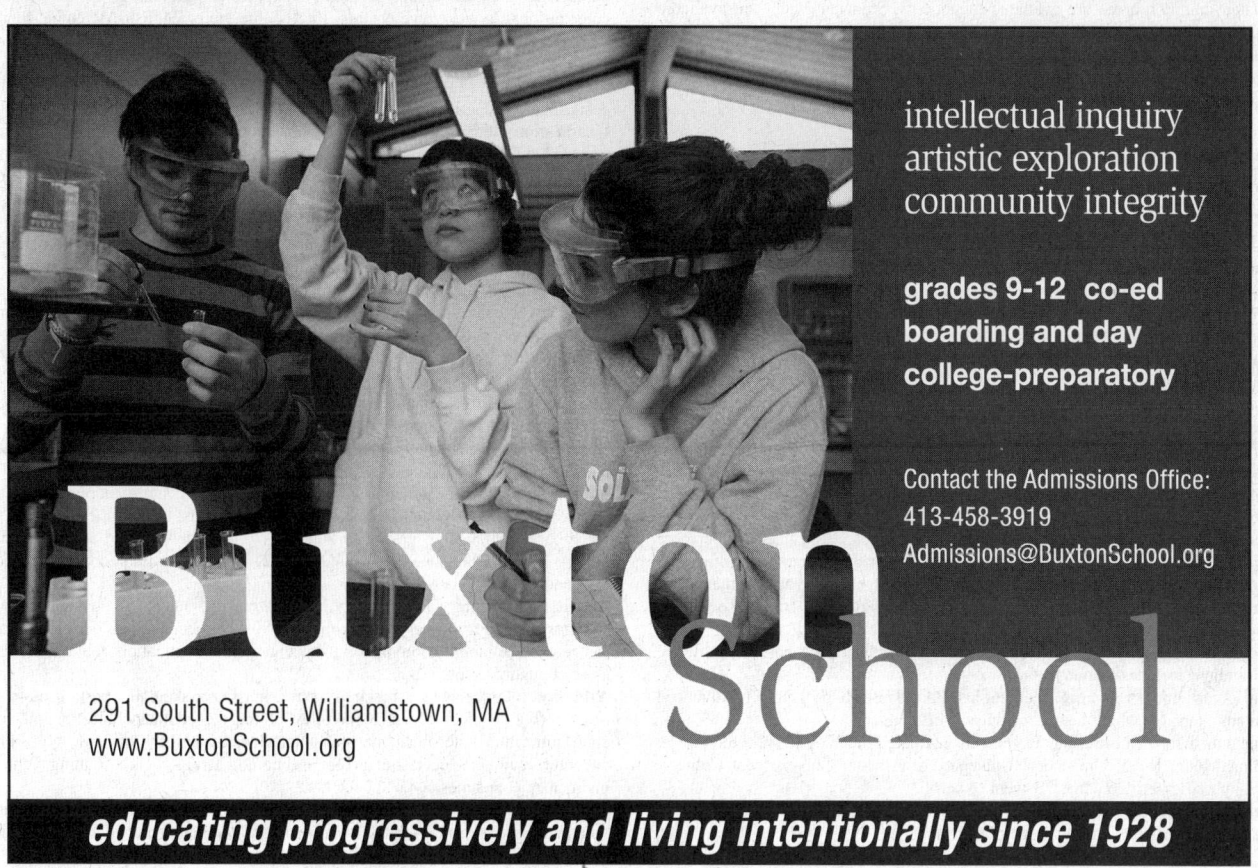

intellectual inquiry
artistic exploration
community integrity

grades 9-12   co-ed
boarding and day
college-preparatory

Contact the Admissions Office:
413-458-3919
Admissions@BuxtonSchool.org

291 South Street, Williamstown, MA
www.BuxtonSchool.org

educating progressively and living intentionally since 1928 accredited by Association of Independent Schools and Colleges of Alberta and Alberta Department of Education. Language of instruction: English. Endowment: CAN$3 million. Total enrollment: 370. Upper school average class size: 16. Upper school faculty-student ratio: 1:8. There are 188 required school days per year for Upper School students. Upper School students typically attend 5 days per week. The average school day consists of 6 hours and 10 minutes.

Upper School Student Profile Grade 10: 41 students (21 boys, 20 girls); Grade 11: 49 students (29 boys, 20 girls); Grade 12: 50 students (32 boys, 18 girls).

Faculty School total: 25. In upper school: 10 men, 15 women; 10 have advanced degrees.

Subjects Offered Art history, athletics, band, biology, calculus, career and personal planning, character education, chemistry, computer animation, computer multimedia, creative drama, drama, English composition, English literature, general science, grammar, language arts, mathematics, outdoor education, physical education, physics, psychology, reading/study skills, remedial study skills, sociology, Spanish, study skills.

Graduation Requirements Biology, chemistry, English, mathematics, physics, science, social studies (includes history).

Special Academic Programs Remedial reading and/or remedial writing; remedial math; programs in English, mathematics for dyslexic students.

College Admission Counseling 64 students graduated in 2009; 55 went to college, including Mount Royal University; University of Alberta; University of Calgary; University of Lethbridge. Other: 5 went to work, 4 had other specific plans.

Student Life Upper grades have specified standards of dress, student council, honor system. Discipline rests primarily with faculty.

Tuition and Aid Day student tuition: CAN$15,000. Tuition installment plan (monthly payment plans, individually arranged payment plans). Bursaries available. In 2009–10, 5% of upper-school students received aid. Total amount of financial aid awarded in 2009–10: CAN$300,000.

Admissions Traditional secondary-level entrance grade is 10. For fall 2009, 100 students applied for upper-level admission, 30 were accepted, 25 enrolled. Achievement tests, Wechsler Individual Achievement Test and Wechsler Intelligence Scale for Children III required. Deadline for receipt of application materials: none. Application fee required: CAN$950. On-campus interview required.

Athletics Interscholastic: badminton (boys, girls), ball hockey (b), basketball (b,g), cross-country running (b,g), golf (b,g), handball (b,g), track and field (b,g), volleyball (b,g), wrestling (b,g); intramural: ice hockey (b,g); coed interscholastic: curling, soccer; coed intramural: outdoor recreation, triathlon. 6 PE instructors.

Computers Computers are regularly used in all academic classes. Computer network features include on-campus library services, Internet access, wireless campus network, Internet filtering or blocking technology. Campus intranet and computer access in designated common areas are available to students. Students grades are available online. The school has a published electronic and media policy.

Contact Ms. Joanne Endacott, Director of Admissions. 403-686-6444 Ext. 236. Fax: 403-240-3427. E-mail: jendacott@calgaryacademy.com. Web site: www.calgaryacademy.com.

CALGARY ACADEMY COLLEGIATE

9400 17 Avenue SW
Calgary, Alberta T3H 4A6, Canada
Head of School: Mr. Barry Russell

General Information Coeducational day college-preparatory, arts, and technology school. Grades 4–12. Founded: 1995. Setting: suburban. 17-acre campus. 3 buildings on campus. Approved or accredited by Association of Independent Schools and Colleges of Alberta and Alberta Department of Education. Language of instruction: English. Endowment: CAN$3 million. Total enrollment: 225. Upper school average class size: 17. Upper school faculty-student ratio: 1:8. There are 188 required school days per year for Upper School students. Upper School students typically attend 5 days per week. The average school day consists of 6 hours and 10 minutes.

Upper School Student Profile Grade 10: 30 students (20 boys, 10 girls); Grade 11: 30 students (19 boys, 11 girls); Grade 12: 35 students (21 boys, 14 girls).

Faculty School total: 25. In upper school: 10 men, 15 women; 10 have advanced degrees.

Subjects Offered Art history, athletics, band, biology, calculus, career and personal planning, character education, chemistry, computer animation, computer multimedia, drama, English composition, English literature, grammar, language arts, mathematics, outdoor education, physical education, physics, psychology, social studies, sociology, Spanish, study skills.

Graduation Requirements Biology, chemistry, English, mathematics, physics, social studies (includes history).

Special Academic Programs International Baccalaureate program; 1 Advanced Placement exam for which test preparation is offered.

College Admission Counseling 39 students graduated in 2009; 36 went to college, including Mount Royal University; University of Alberta; University of Calgary; University of Lethbridge. Other: 3 went to work.

Student Life Upper grades have specified standards of dress, student council, honor system. Discipline rests primarily with faculty.

Tuition and Aid Day student tuition: CAN$8600. Tuition installment plan (monthly payment plans, individually arranged payment plans). Bursaries available. In 2009–10, 5% of upper-school students received aid. Total amount of financial aid awarded in 2009–10: CAN$300,000.

Admissions Traditional secondary-level entrance grade is 10. For fall 2009, 50 students applied for upper-level admission, 30 were accepted, 20 enrolled. Achievement tests, Wechsler Individual Achievement Test or Wechsler Intelligence Scale for Children III required. Deadline for receipt of application materials: none. Application fee required: CAN$950. On-campus interview required.

Athletics Interscholastic: badminton (boys, girls), ball hockey (b), basketball (b,g), cross-country running (b,g), golf (b,g), handball (b,g), track and field (b,g), volleyball (b,g), wrestling (b,g); intramural: ice hockey (b,g); coed interscholastic: badminton, curling, soccer; coed intramural: outdoor recreation, triathlon. 6 PE instructors.

Computers Computers are regularly used in all academic classes. Computer network features include on-campus library services, Internet access, wireless campus network, Internet filtering or blocking technology. Computer access in designated common areas is available to students. Students grades are available online. The school has a published electronic and media policy.

Contact Ms. Joanne Endacott, Director of Admissions. 403-686-6444 Ext. 236. Fax: 403-686-3427. E-mail: jendacott@calgaryacademy.com.

THE CALHOUN SCHOOL

433 West End Avenue
New York, New York 10024
Head of School: Steven J. Nelson

General Information Coeducational day college-preparatory and arts school. Grades N–12. Founded: 1896. Setting: urban. 2 buildings on campus. Approved or accredited by New York State Association of Independent Schools and New York Department of Education. Member of National Association of Independent Schools. Endowment: $2.5 million. Total enrollment: 724. Upper school average class size: 15. Upper school faculty-student ratio: 1:6.

Upper School Student Profile Grade 9: 50 students (21 boys, 29 girls); Grade 10: 41 students (23 boys, 18 girls); Grade 11: 51 students (25 boys, 26 girls); Grade 12: 41 students (16 boys, 25 girls).

Faculty School total: 122. In upper school: 18 men, 18 women; 28 have advanced degrees.

Subjects Offered Acting, advanced biology, advanced chemistry, advanced computer applications, African-American literature, algebra, American history, American literature, anthropology, arts, biology, calculus, chemistry, child development, chorus, community service, computer math, computer programming, computer science, constitutional law, creative writing, English literature, English-AP, ethnic literature, French, geometry, healthful living, human sexuality, independent study, instrumental music, music history, peer counseling, photography, physical education, physics, pre-calculus, psychology, Shakespeare, Spanish, speech, studio art, theater, theater design and production, Web site design, world history, world literature.

Graduation Requirements Arts and fine arts (art, music, dance, drama), English, foreign language, mathematics, physical education (includes health), science, social studies (includes history), 9th grade Life Skills with peer leaders. Community service is required.

Special Academic Programs Independent study; domestic exchange program (with The Network Program Schools); academic accommodation for the gifted.

College Admission Counseling 48 students graduated in 2010; all went to college, including American University; Bard College; Bates College; Goucher College; New York University; Syracuse University. Mean SAT critical reading: 610, mean SAT math: 578, mean SAT writing: 608, mean combined SAT: 1796.

Student Life Upper grades have student council. Discipline rests primarily with faculty.

Summer Programs Art/fine arts programs offered; session focuses on Shakespeare production; held on campus; accepts boys and girls; open to students from other schools. 16 students usually enrolled. 2011 schedule: June 17 to July 26. Application deadline: March 1.

Tuition and Aid Day student tuition: $35,900. Tuition installment plan (Key Tuition Payment Plan, individually arranged payment plans, 60%/40% payment plan). Need-based scholarship grants, tuition reduction for faculty and staff available. In 2010–11, 35% of upper-school students received aid. Total amount of financial aid awarded in 2010–11: $1,800,000.

Admissions Traditional secondary-level entrance grade is 9. For fall 2010, 240 students applied for upper-level admission, 80 were accepted, 23 enrolled. Deadline for receipt of application materials: January 15. Application fee required: $65. On-campus interview required.

Athletics Interscholastic: baseball (boys, girls), basketball (b,g), cross-country running (b,g), track and field (b,g), volleyball (b,g); coed interscholastic: golf, soccer; coed intramural: aerobics, aerobics/Nautilus, basketball, fitness, golf, project adventure, sailing, soccer, strength & conditioning, tennis, weight training, yoga. 5 PE instructors, 2 coaches.

Computers Computers are regularly used in basic skills, mathematics, programming, video film production, Web site design classes. Computer network features include

Internet access, MS Office, PowerPoint, Basic, Dreameaver, and Flash Software. Student e-mail accounts are available to students. The school has a published electronic and media policy.

Contact Jenny Eugenio, Director of Admissions, Upper School. 212-497-6510. Fax: 212-497-6531. E-mail: jenny.eugenio@calhoun.org. Web site: www.calhoun.org.

CALVARY CHAPEL HIGH SCHOOL

12808 Woodruff Avenue
Downey, California 90242
Head of School: Pastor Yuri Escandon

General Information Coeducational day college-preparatory, arts, business, religious studies, and technology school, affiliated with Christian faith. Grades K–12. Founded: 1978. Setting: suburban. Nearest major city is Los Angeles. 16-acre campus. 1 building on campus. Approved or accredited by Western Association of Schools and Colleges and California Department of Education. Total enrollment: 725. Upper school average class size: 19. Upper school faculty-student ratio: 1:20. There are 173 required school days per year for Upper School students. Upper School students typically attend 5 days per week. The average school day consists of 6 hours and 6 minutes.

Faculty School total: 52. In upper school: 13 men, 13 women; 3 have advanced degrees.

Subjects Offered Algebra, American history-AP, anatomy, art, arts, band, Bible studies, biology, business mathematics, calculus-AP, chemistry, choir, community service, computer science, creative writing, current events, drama, earth science, ecology, economics, English, ethics, fine arts, geometry, government, health, humanities, mathematics, media, music appreciation, physical education, physical science, physics, physiology, pre-calculus, religion, science, social studies, sociology, Spanish, speech, U.S. history, world history.

Graduation Requirements Computers.

Special Academic Programs Advanced Placement exam preparation; honors section; independent study; study at local college for college credit.

College Admission Counseling 101 students graduated in 2010; 93 went to college, including Azusa Pacific University; Biola University; California State University, Fullerton; California State University, Long Beach; Chapman University; Vanguard University of Southern California. Other: 1 entered military service. Mean SAT critical reading: 491, mean SAT math: 444, mean SAT writing: 484.

Student Life Upper grades have specified standards of dress, honor system. Discipline rests primarily with faculty. Attendance at religious services is required.

Summer Programs Remediation, advancement, sports programs offered; held on campus; accepts boys and girls; not open to students from other schools. 60 students usually enrolled. 2011 schedule: June 27 to August 17. Application deadline: April 10.

Tuition and Aid Day student tuition: $7810. Guaranteed tuition plan. Tuition installment plan (monthly payment plans). Tuition reduction for siblings, need-based scholarship grants available.

Admissions Traditional secondary-level entrance grade is 9. Admissions testing required. Deadline for receipt of application materials: none. Application fee required: $125. Interview required.

Athletics Interscholastic: aquatics (boys, girls), baseball (b), basketball (b,g), cheering (g), cross-country running (b,g), football (b), outdoor activities (b,g), physical fitness (b,g), soccer (b,g), softball (g), strength & conditioning (b,g), swimming and diving (b,g), track and field (b,g), volleyball (b,g), water polo (b,g), weight training (b,g), wrestling (b); coed interscholastic: aquatics, swimming and diving, water polo. 4 PE instructors, 25 coaches, 1 athletic trainer.

Computers Computers are regularly used in all academic classes. Computer resources include on-campus library services, Internet access, Internet filtering or blocking technology. Students grades are available online. The school has a published electronic and media policy.

Contact Diane Kirkhuff, Office/Admissions. 562-803-4076 Ext. 302. Fax: 562-803-1292. E-mail: dkirkhuff@calvarydowney.org. Web site: cccsdowney.org.

CALVARY CHRISTIAN SCHOOL

5955 Taylor Mill Road
Covington, Kentucky 41015
Head of School: Mr. Ed Ryan

General Information Coeducational day college-preparatory, arts, religious studies, and technology school, affiliated with Baptist Church. Grades K4–12. Founded: 1974. Setting: suburban. Nearest major city is Cincinnati, OH. 72-acre campus. 1 building on campus. Approved or accredited by Association of Christian Schools International, CITA (Commission on International and Trans-Regional Accreditation), Southern Association of Colleges and Schools, and Kentucky Department of Education. Total enrollment: 388. Upper school average class size: 17. Upper school faculty-student ratio: 1:10. There are 178 required school days per year for Upper School students. Upper School students typically attend 5 days per week. The average school day consists of 7 hours.

Upper School Student Profile Grade 9: 26 students (10 boys, 16 girls); Grade 10: 24 students (10 boys, 14 girls); Grade 11: 28 students (15 boys, 13 girls); Grade 12: 23 students (10 boys, 13 girls). 30% of students are Baptist.

Faculty School total: 30. In upper school: 10 men, 8 women; 15 have advanced degrees.

Subjects Offered Advanced math, algebra, American literature-AP, ancient history, art, art appreciation, Bible, biology, calculus, chemistry, chemistry-AP, choir, chorus, Christian doctrine, Christian ethics, communication arts, computer applications, computer multimedia, computer science, concert band, concert choir, consumer mathematics, creative writing, cultural geography, drama, drama performance, earth science, economics, English, English composition, English language and composition-AP, English language-AP, English literature, English literature and composition-AP, English literature-AP, English-AP, ethics, European history-AP, fitness, food and nutrition, general math, general science, geography, geometry, government-AP, grammar, health education, home economics, honors algebra, independent study, journalism, Kentucky history, keyboarding, lab science, language arts, library assistant, literature-AP, logic, music theory, newspaper, physical education, physical science, physics-AP, pre-algebra, pre-calculus, rhetoric, Spanish, Spanish-AP, speech and debate, state history, student government, student publications, student teaching, U.S. government, U.S. government and politics-AP, U.S. history, U.S. history-AP, world governments, world history, yearbook.

Graduation Requirements Algebra, art appreciation, Bible, biology, chemistry, Christian doctrine, church history, civics, economics, English, English composition, English literature, European history, foreign language, geometry, health, physical science, U.S. government, U.S. history, world history, 4 years of HS Bible required for graduation.

Special Academic Programs Advanced Placement exam preparation; honors section; independent study; study at local college for college credit.

College Admission Counseling 38 students graduated in 2010; 35 went to college, including Eastern Kentucky University; Northern Kentucky University; University of Cincinnati; University of Kentucky; University of Louisville. Other: 1 went to work, 2 entered military service. Median composite ACT: 26. 25% scored over 26 on composite ACT.

Student Life Upper grades have uniform requirement, student council. Discipline rests primarily with faculty. Attendance at religious services is required.

Tuition and Aid Day student tuition: $5800. Tuition installment plan (FACTS Tuition Payment Plan, monthly payment plans, individually arranged payment plans). Tuition reduction for siblings, need-based scholarship grants, paying campus jobs available. In 2010–11, 9% of upper-school students received aid. Total amount of financial aid awarded in 2010–11: $25,000.

Admissions Traditional secondary-level entrance grade is 9. For fall 2010, 14 students applied for upper-level admission, 14 were accepted, 14 enrolled. Stanford Achievement Test required. Deadline for receipt of application materials: none. Application fee required: $285. Interview required.

Athletics Interscholastic: baseball (boys), basketball (b,g), bowling (b,g), cheering (g), cross-country running (b,g), diving (b,g), golf (b), horseback riding (b,g), physical fitness (b,g), soccer (b,g), softball (g), swimming and diving (b,g), volleyball (g), weight lifting (b), weight training (b); intramural: indoor soccer (b,g), strength & conditioning (b,g), weight training (b); coed intramural: bowling, gymnastics, physical fitness, running. 2 PE instructors, 15 coaches.

Computers Computers are regularly used in architecture, art, computer applications, design, desktop publishing, drafting, graphics, information technology, journalism, keyboarding, lab/keyboard, library, photography, photojournalism, science, Spanish, technical drawing, Web site design, yearbook classes. Computer network features include on-campus library services, Internet access, wireless campus network, Internet filtering or blocking technology. Campus intranet is available to students. Students grades are available online. The school has a published electronic and media policy.

Contact Mrs. Laurie Switzer, Registrar. 859-356-9201. Fax: 859-359-8962. E-mail: laurie.switzer@calvarychristianky.org. Web site: www.calvarychristianky.org.

CALVERT HALL COLLEGE HIGH SCHOOL

8102 LaSalle Road
Baltimore, Maryland 21286
Head of School: Br. Thomas Zoppo, FSC

General Information Boys' day college-preparatory, arts, business, religious studies, and technology school, affiliated with Roman Catholic Church. Grades 9–12. Founded: 1845. Setting: suburban. 32-acre campus. 6 buildings on campus. Approved or accredited by Christian Brothers Association, Middle States Association of Colleges and Schools, National Catholic Education Association, and Maryland Department of Education. Endowment: $4.3 million. Total enrollment: 1,226. Upper school average class size: 21. Upper school faculty-student ratio: 1:12. There are 174 required school days per year for Upper School students. Upper School students typically attend 5 days per week. The average school day consists of 6 hours and 20 minutes.

Upper School Student Profile Grade 9: 304 students (304 boys); Grade 10: 308 students (308 boys); Grade 11: 310 students (310 boys); Grade 12: 304 students (304 boys). 71% of students are Roman Catholic.

Faculty School total: 101. In upper school: 73 men, 28 women; 65 have advanced degrees.

Subjects Offered Algebra, American history, American literature, art, art history, band, Bible studies, biology, business, business skills, calculus, chemistry, chorus, computer programming, computer science, creative writing, drama, earth science,

Calvert Hall College High School

economics, engineering, English, English literature, ethics, European history, fine arts, French, geography, geometry, German, government/civics, graphic arts, history, journalism, Latin, leadership, mathematics, music, painting, philosophy, physical education, physics, psychology, religion, science, sculpture, social sciences, social studies, Spanish, speech, statistics, theater, theology, typing, world history, world literature, writing.

Graduation Requirements Arts and fine arts (art, music, dance, drama), English, foreign language, mathematics, physical education (includes health), religion (includes Bible studies and theology), science, social sciences, social studies (includes history).

Special Academic Programs 21 Advanced Placement exams for which test preparation is offered; honors section; academic accommodation for the gifted, the musically talented, and the artistically talented; programs in English, mathematics, general development for dyslexic students.

College Admission Counseling 267 students graduated in 2010; 260 went to college, including Loyola University Maryland; Salisbury University; Stevenson University; Towson University; University of Maryland, College Park. Other: 2 went to work, 2 entered military service, 3 entered a postgraduate year.

Student Life Upper grades have specified standards of dress, student council, honor system. Discipline rests primarily with faculty. Attendance at religious services is required.

Summer Programs Remediation, enrichment, sports, art/fine arts, computer instruction programs offered; session focuses on remediation and make-up courses; held on campus; accepts boys and girls; open to students from other schools. 250 students usually enrolled. 2011 schedule: June 25 to July 27. Application deadline: June 15.

Tuition and Aid Day student tuition: $11,300. Tuition installment plan (monthly payment plans, individually arranged payment plans). Merit scholarship grants, need-based scholarship grants available. In 2010–11, 40% of upper-school students received aid; total upper-school merit-scholarship money awarded: $428,000. Total amount of financial aid awarded in 2010–11: $1,142,000.

Admissions Traditional secondary-level entrance grade is 9. For fall 2010, 649 students applied for upper-level admission, 544 were accepted, 304 enrolled. High School Placement Test (closed version) from Scholastic Testing Service required. Deadline for receipt of application materials: none. Application fee required: $20.

Athletics Interscholastic: aquatics, baseball, basketball, cross-country running, diving, football, golf, ice hockey, indoor track & field, lacrosse, rugby, soccer, swimming and diving, tennis, track and field, volleyball, water polo, winter (indoor) track, wrestling; intramural: basketball, billiards, bocce, bowling, fitness, flag football, freestyle skiing, rugby, table tennis, weight lifting. 2 PE instructors, 12 coaches.

Computers Computers are regularly used in accounting, business, college planning, computer applications, digital applications, economics, English, foreign language, graphic design, history, independent study, journalism, keyboarding, library, literary magazine, mathematics, music, programming, religion, SAT preparation, science, social sciences, stock market, video film production, writing, yearbook classes. Computer network features include on-campus library services, Internet access, wireless campus network, Internet filtering or blocking technology. Campus intranet, student e-mail accounts, and computer access in designated common areas are available to students. Students grades are available online. The school has a published electronic and media policy.

Contact Chris Bengel, Director of Admissions. 410-825-4266 Ext. 126. Fax: 410-825-6826. E-mail: bengelc@calverthall.com. Web site: www.calverthall.com.

THE CALVERTON SCHOOL

300 Calverton School Road
Huntingtown, Maryland 20639
Head of School: Mr. Daniel Hildebrand

General Information Coeducational day college-preparatory, arts, and technology school. Grades PS–12. Founded: 1967. Setting: rural. Nearest major city is Annapolis. 159-acre campus. 3 buildings on campus. Approved or accredited by Association of Independent Maryland Schools, The College Board, and Maryland Department of Education. Member of National Association of Independent Schools. Total enrollment: 405. Upper school average class size: 18. The average school day consists of 7 hours and 20 minutes.

Faculty School total: 49.

Subjects Offered Advanced Placement courses, algebra, American history, American literature, art, art history, biology, calculus, chemistry, Chesapeake Bay studies, chorus, creative writing, drama, economics, English, English literature, environmental science, European civilization, fine arts, French, French-AP, geometry, government/civics, health, humanities, journalism, literature, mathematics, physical education, physics, pre-calculus, public speaking, publications, SAT/ACT preparation, science, social studies, Spanish, Spanish-AP, studio art-AP, theater, trigonometry, U.S. history, U.S. history-AP, visual and performing arts, world civilizations, world history, world literature, yearbook.

Graduation Requirements Algebra, arts and fine arts (art, music, dance, drama), biology, chemistry, English, English composition, English literature, foreign language, geometry, mathematics, physical education (includes health), physics, science, social studies (includes history), trigonometry, U.S. history, world history.

Special Academic Programs Advanced Placement exam preparation; honors section; independent study.

College Admission Counseling 34 students graduated in 2010; all went to college. Median SAT critical reading: 562, median SAT math: 570, median SAT writing: 475, median combined SAT: 1600, median composite ACT: 25. 29% scored over 600 on SAT critical reading, 29% scored over 600 on SAT math, 22% scored over 600 on SAT writing, 14% scored over 1800 on combined SAT, 40% scored over 26 on composite ACT.

Student Life Upper grades have specified standards of dress, student council, honor system. Discipline rests equally with students and faculty.

Summer Programs Enrichment, advancement, sports, art/fine arts, computer instruction programs offered; session focuses on enrichment; held both on and off campus; held at various sites; accepts boys and girls; open to students from other schools. 125 students usually enrolled. 2011 schedule: June to August. Application deadline: none.

Tuition and Aid Day student tuition: $17,358. Tuition installment plan (Insured Tuition Payment Plan, FACTS Tuition Payment Plan, monthly payment plans, individually arranged payment plans). Need-based scholarship grants available.

Admissions Traditional secondary-level entrance grade is 9. Admissions testing required. Deadline for receipt of application materials: none. Application fee required: $100. On-campus interview required.

Athletics Interscholastic: basketball (boys, girls), cross-country running (b,g), lacrosse (b,g); coed interscholastic: field hockey, golf, soccer, tennis; coed intramural: basketball. 3 PE instructors, 10 coaches.

Computers Computers are regularly used in all academic classes. Computer network features include on-campus library services, online commercial services, Internet access, Internet filtering or blocking technology, research services and encyclopedia research programs. Student e-mail accounts are available to students.

Contact Mrs. Julie M. Simpson, Director of Admission. 888-678-0216 Ext. 108. Fax: 410-535-6169. E-mail: jsimpson@CalvertonSchool.org. Web site: www.CalvertonSchool.org.

CALVIN CHRISTIAN HIGH SCHOOL

2000 North Broadway
Escondido, California 92026
Head of School: Mr. Terry D. Kok

General Information Coeducational day college-preparatory, arts, and religious studies school, affiliated with Reformed Church, Presbyterian Church. Grades PK–12. Founded: 1980. Setting: suburban. Nearest major city is San Diego. 15-acre campus. 2 buildings on campus. Approved or accredited by Christian Schools International, Western Association of Schools and Colleges, and California Department of Education. Endowment: $960,000. Total enrollment: 442. Upper school average class size: 18. Upper school faculty-student ratio: 1:15. There are 176 required school days per year for Upper School students. Upper School students typically attend 5 days per week. The average school day consists of 5 hours and 35 minutes.

Upper School Student Profile Grade 9: 39 students (22 boys, 17 girls); Grade 10: 26 students (11 boys, 15 girls); Grade 11: 36 students (20 boys, 16 girls); Grade 12: 32 students (16 boys, 16 girls). 35% of students are Reformed, Presbyterian.

Faculty School total: 15. In upper school: 9 men, 6 women; 8 have advanced degrees.

Subjects Offered Algebra, American government, anatomy and physiology, art, band, Bible, biology, biology-AP, business mathematics, calculus-AP, chemistry, choir, Christian doctrine, Christian ethics, Christian studies, Civil War, computer applications, computers, creative writing, current events, drama, dramatic arts, earth science, economics, electives, English, English literature-AP, geometry, grammar, health, instrumental music, intro to computers, journalism, novels, photography, physical education, physical science, physics, pre-calculus, psychology, sociology, Spanish, Spanish-AP, speech, U.S. history, U.S. history-AP, world history, yearbook.

Graduation Requirements Arts and fine arts (art, music, dance, drama), English, foreign language, mathematics, media, physical education (includes health), religion (includes Bible studies and theology), science, social studies (includes history), technology.

Special Academic Programs 5 Advanced Placement exams for which test preparation is offered; remedial reading and/or remedial writing.

College Admission Counseling 42 students graduated in 2010; 41 went to college, including California State University, San Marcos; Calvin College; Dordt College; Palomar College; Point Loma Nazarene University; University of California, San Diego. Other: 1 went to work. Mean SAT critical reading: 561, mean SAT math: 547, mean SAT writing: 552, mean composite ACT: 24.

Student Life Upper grades have specified standards of dress, student council, honor system. Discipline rests primarily with faculty. Attendance at religious services is required.

Summer Programs Sports programs offered; session focuses on Bible courses; held on campus; accepts boys and girls; open to students from other schools. 60 students usually enrolled. 2011 schedule: June 7 to July 23. Application deadline: May 30.

Tuition and Aid Day student tuition: $8148. Tuition installment plan (monthly payment plans, individually arranged payment plans). Need-based scholarship grants, need-based loans available. In 2010–11, 20% of upper-school students received aid. Total amount of financial aid awarded in 2010–11: $225,000.

Admissions Traditional secondary-level entrance grade is 9. For fall 2010, 16 students applied for upper-level admission, 15 were accepted, 14 enrolled. Deadline for receipt of application materials: none. Application fee required: $100. Interview required.

Athletics Interscholastic: baseball (boys), basketball (b,g), cross-country running (b,g), football (b), soccer (b,g), softball (g), track and field (b,g), volleyball (g); coed interscholastic: golf, in-line hockey; coed intramural: weight training. 2 PE instructors, 16 coaches.

Computers Computers are regularly used in computer applications, drafting, introduction to technology, keyboarding, photography, science, yearbook classes. Computer network features include on-campus library services, Internet access, Internet filtering or blocking technology. Students grades are available online. The school has a published electronic and media policy.

Contact Mr. Frank Steidl, Principal. 760-489-6430. Fax: 760-489-7055. E-mail: franksteidl@calvinchristianescondido.org. Web site: www.calvinchristianescondido.org.

CAMDEN MILITARY ACADEMY

520 Highway 1 North
Camden, South Carolina 29020
Head of School: Col. Eric Boland

General Information Boys' boarding college-preparatory and military school; primarily serves students with learning disabilities, individuals with Attention Deficit Disorder, individuals with emotional and behavioral problems, and dyslexic students. Grades 7–PG. Founded: 1892. Setting: small town. Nearest major city is Columbia. Students are housed in single-sex dormitories. 50-acre campus. 15 buildings on campus. Approved or accredited by South Carolina Independent School Association and Southern Association of Colleges and Schools. Member of National Association of Independent Schools. Total enrollment: 305. Upper school average class size: 15. Upper school faculty-student ratio: 1:12.

Upper School Student Profile Grade 9: 54 students (54 boys); Grade 10: 58 students (58 boys); Grade 11: 60 students (60 boys); Grade 12: 64 students (64 boys). 100% of students are boarding students. 39% are state residents. 23 states are represented in upper school student body. International students from Bermuda, Cayman Islands, Ghana, Mexico, and Trinidad and Tobago.

Faculty School total: 49. In upper school: 35 men, 3 women; 23 have advanced degrees; 9 reside on campus.

Subjects Offered Algebra, American government, anatomy and physiology, band, biology, calculus, chemistry, computer applications, computer literacy, driver education, economics, English, French, geometry, humanities, physical science, physics, pre-calculus, psychology, sociology, Spanish, U.S. history, world geography, world history.

Graduation Requirements Computer literacy, English, foreign language, history, JROTC, mathematics, science.

Special Academic Programs Advanced Placement exam preparation; honors section; study at local college for college credit; remedial reading and/or remedial writing.

College Admission Counseling Colleges students went to include University of South Carolina.

Student Life Upper grades have uniform requirement, student council, honor system. Discipline rests primarily with faculty.

Tuition and Aid 7-day tuition and room/board: $17,595. Tuition installment plan (monthly payment plans, individually arranged payment plans). Tuition reduction for siblings, need-based scholarship grants available. In 2009–10, 20% of upper-school students received aid.

Admissions Traditional secondary-level entrance grade is 9. Deadline for receipt of application materials: none. Application fee required: $100. Interview required.

Athletics Interscholastic: baseball, basketball, cross-country running, football, golf; intramural: aerobics, aquatics. 2 PE instructors, 15 coaches, 1 athletic trainer.

Computers Computers are regularly used in all academic classes. Computer resources include on-campus library services, Internet access. Student e-mail accounts are available to students.

Contact Mr. Casey Robinson, Director of Admissions. 803-432-6001. Fax: 803-425-1020. E-mail: admissions@camdenmilitary.com. Web site: www.camdenmilitary.com.

CAMELOT ACADEMY

809 Proctor Street
Durham, North Carolina 27707
Head of School: Thelma DeCarlo Glynn

General Information Coeducational day college-preparatory school. Grades K–12. Founded: 1982. Setting: small town. Nearest major city is Raleigh. 3-acre campus. 1 building on campus. Approved or accredited by National Independent Private Schools Association and North Carolina Department of Education. Total enrollment: 98. Upper school average class size: 10. Upper school faculty-student ratio: 1:10. There are 170 required school days per year for Upper School students. Upper School students typically attend 5 days per week. The average school day consists of 6 hours and 45 minutes.

Faculty School total: 13. In upper school: 3 men, 4 women; 6 have advanced degrees.

Graduation Requirements Electives, foreign language, language arts, mathematics, physical education (includes health), science, social studies (includes history).

Special Academic Programs Advanced Placement exam preparation; honors section; accelerated programs; independent study; study at local college for college credit; academic accommodation for the gifted; remedial reading and/or remedial writing; remedial math; ESL (1 student enrolled).

College Admission Counseling 2 students graduated in 2009; all went to college, including New York University; The University of North Carolina at Chapel Hill. Median SAT critical reading: 625, median SAT math: 645, median SAT writing: 595, median combined SAT: 1865. Mean composite ACT: 30. 75% scored over 600 on SAT critical reading, 75% scored over 600 on SAT math, 75% scored over 600 on SAT writing, 75% scored over 1800 on combined SAT, 100% scored over 26 on composite ACT.

Student Life Upper grades have specified standards of dress, honor system. Discipline rests primarily with faculty.

Tuition and Aid Day student tuition: $10,450. Tuition installment plan (monthly payment plan through YourTuitionSolution.com, early re-enrollment plan (which freezes tuition at initial enrollment rate)). Tuition reduction for siblings, merit scholarship grants, need-based scholarship grants available. In 2009–10, 55% of upper-school students received aid; total upper-school merit-scholarship money awarded: $77,000. Total amount of financial aid awarded in 2009–10: $85,000.

Admissions Traditional secondary-level entrance grade is 9. ERB required. Deadline for receipt of application materials: none. Application fee required: $50. Interview required.

Athletics Interscholastic: basketball (boys); intramural: volleyball (g); coed interscholastic: soccer; coed intramural: aerobics, dance team, fitness. 1 PE instructor, 1 coach.

Computers Computer network features include Internet access. Computer access in designated common areas is available to students. The school has a published electronic and media policy.

Contact Ms. Wendy Morris, Office Manager. 919-688-3040. Fax: 919-682-4320. E-mail: wendy@camelotacademy.org. Web site: www.camelotacademy.org/.

CAMPBELL HALL (EPISCOPAL)

4533 Laurel Canyon Boulevard
North Hollywood, California 91607
Head of School: Rev. Julian Bull

General Information Coeducational day college-preparatory, arts, and technology school, affiliated with Episcopal Church. Grades K–12. Founded: 1944. Setting: suburban. Nearest major city is Los Angeles. 15-acre campus. 12 buildings on campus. Approved or accredited by California Association of Independent Schools, The College Board, Western Association of Schools and Colleges, and California Department of Education. Member of National Association of Independent Schools. Endowment: $5 million. Total enrollment: 1,085. Upper school average class size: 15. Upper school faculty-student ratio: 1:8. There are 140 required school days per year for Upper School students. Upper School students typically attend 5 days per week. The average school day consists of 7 hours and 15 minutes.

Upper School Student Profile Grade 7: 121 students (67 boys, 54 girls); Grade 8: 105 students (55 boys, 50 girls); Grade 9: 134 students (62 boys, 72 girls); Grade 10: 136 students (58 boys, 78 girls); Grade 11: 135 students (67 boys, 68 girls); Grade 12: 128 students (55 boys, 73 girls). 7% of students are members of Episcopal Church.

Faculty School total: 110. In upper school: 23 men, 32 women; 30 have advanced degrees.

Subjects Offered Algebra, American history, American literature, American studies, ancient history, art, art history, astronomy, band, biology, calculus, ceramics, chemistry, community service, computer programming, computer science, creative writing, dance, drama, drawing, earth science, ecology, economics, English, English literature, environmental science, ethics, European history, filmmaking, fine arts, French, geography, geometry, government/civics, history, human development, humanities, instrumental music, Japanese, law, mathematics, music, orchestra, painting, philosophy, photography, physical education, physics, physiology, pre-calculus, printmaking, psychology, science, sculpture, senior seminar, social studies, sociology, Spanish, speech, statistics, theater, theater arts, trigonometry, voice, yearbook.

Graduation Requirements Arts and fine arts (art, music, dance, drama), computer science, English, foreign language, mathematics, physical education (includes health), science, social studies (includes history). Community service is required.

Special Academic Programs Advanced Placement exam preparation; honors section; independent study; study at local college for college credit.

College Admission Counseling 139 students graduated in 2010; all went to college, including Boston University; New York University; Syracuse University; University of California, Berkeley; University of California, Los Angeles; University of Southern California.

Student Life Upper grades have uniform requirement, student council, honor system. Discipline rests equally with students and faculty. Attendance at religious services is required.

Summer Programs Enrichment, advancement, sports, art/fine arts, computer instruction programs offered; session focuses on creative arts and sports; held on campus; accepts boys and girls; open to students from other schools. 200 students usually enrolled. 2011 schedule: June 13 to July 29. Application deadline: June 1.

Campbell Hall (Episcopal)

Tuition and Aid Day student tuition: $27,220. Tuition installment plan (Insured Tuition Payment Plan, monthly payment plans, individually arranged payment plans). Need-based scholarship grants, Episcopal Credit Union tuition loans available. In 2010–11, 25% of upper-school students received aid. Total amount of financial aid awarded in 2010–11: $3,500,000.

Admissions Traditional secondary-level entrance grade is 9. ISEE required. Deadline for receipt of application materials: January 28. Application fee required: $100. Interview required.

Athletics Interscholastic: aerobics/dance (boys, girls), ballet (b,g), baseball (b), basketball (b,g), cheering (b,g), cross-country running (b,g), dance (b,g), dance squad (b,g), equestrian sports (b,g), flag football (b,g), football (b), golf (b,g), horseback riding (b,g), modern dance (b,g), soccer (b,g), softball (g), tennis (b,g), track and field (b,g), volleyball (b,g); intramural: weight lifting (b,g); coed interscholastic: aerobics/dance, ballet, cheering, cross-country running, dance, dance squad, golf, horseback riding, modern dance, track and field. 5 PE instructors, 13 coaches, 2 athletic trainers.

Computers Computers are regularly used in art, English, foreign language, history, humanities, mathematics, science, theater arts classes. Computer network features include on-campus library services, online commercial services, Internet access, wireless campus network, Internet filtering or blocking technology. Campus intranet, student e-mail accounts, and computer access in designated common areas are available to students. The school has a published electronic and media policy.

Contact Ms. Alice Fleming, Director of Admissions. 818-980-7280. Fax: 818-762-3269. Web site: www.campbellhall.org.

See Display below and Close-Up on page 750.

CAMPHILL SPECIAL SCHOOL
Glenmoore, Pennsylvania
See Special Needs Schools section.

CANADIAN ACADEMY
4-1 Koyo-cho Naka
Higashinada-ku
Kobe 658-0032, Japan
Head of School: Mr. Frederic Wesson

General Information Coeducational boarding and day college-preparatory school. Boarding grades 9–13, day grades PK–13. Founded: 1913. Setting: urban. Nearest major city is Osaka, Japan. Students are housed in single-sex dormitories. 3-hectare campus. 2 buildings on campus. Approved or accredited by Council of International Schools, European Council of International Schools, International Baccalaureate Organization, Ministry of Education, Japan, The College Board, and Western Association of Schools and Colleges. Language of instruction: English. Total enrollment: 690. Upper school average class size: 15. Upper school faculty-student ratio: 1:10. There are 180 required school days per year for Upper School students. The average school day consists of 6 hours and 55 minutes.

Upper School Student Profile Grade 9: 58 students (31 boys, 27 girls); Grade 10: 58 students (29 boys, 29 girls); Grade 11: 48 students (28 boys, 20 girls); Grade 12: 58 students (23 boys, 35 girls); Grade 13: 1 student (1 girl).

Faculty School total: 87. In upper school: 20 men, 14 women; 20 have advanced degrees; 19 reside on campus.

Subjects Offered Algebra, art, biology, calculus, chemistry, choir, college writing, concert band, drama, economics, English, ESL, French, geometry, health, integrated mathematics, introduction to literature, Japanese, Japanese history, jazz band, music, orchestra, peer counseling, physical education, physics, publications, social studies, Spanish, theater arts, theory of knowledge, U.S. history, world literature.

Graduation Requirements Electives, English, health, mathematics, modern languages, performing arts, physical education (includes health), science, social studies (includes history), senior project.

Special Academic Programs International Baccalaureate program; Advanced Placement exam preparation; independent study; ESL (11 students enrolled).

College Admission Counseling 53 students graduated in 2010; 43 went to college, including Boston University; Cornell University; Northeastern University; Rhode Island School of Design; The University of British Columbia. Other: 1 had other specific plans. Mean SAT critical reading: 543, mean SAT math: 610, mean SAT writing: 572. 27% scored over 600 on SAT critical reading, 62% scored over 600 on SAT math, 49% scored over 600 on SAT writing.

Student Life Upper grades have specified standards of dress, student council, honor system. Discipline rests primarily with faculty.

Summer Programs Enrichment, sports, computer instruction programs offered; session focuses on SAT preparation; held on campus; accepts boys and girls; open to students from other schools. 2011 schedule: June 13 to July 15. Application deadline: May 27.

Tuition and Aid Day student tuition: ¥1,962,000; 7-day tuition and room/board: ¥3,000,000. Tuition installment plan (semester payment plan). Need-based scholarship grants available. In 2010–11, 20% of upper-school students received aid. Total amount of financial aid awarded in 2010–11: ¥575,000.

Admissions Traditional secondary-level entrance grade is 9. For fall 2010, 27 students applied for upper-level admission, 20 were accepted, 19 enrolled. English for Non-native Speakers, essay, Measurements of Academic Progress, math and English placement tests or SLEP for foreign students required. Deadline for receipt of application materials: none. Application fee required: ¥61,000. On-campus interview required.

Athletics Interscholastic: baseball (boys), basketball (b,g), soccer (b,g), softball (g), tennis (b,g), volleyball (b,g); intramural: baseball (b), basketball (b,g), soccer (b,g), softball (g), table tennis (b,g), volleyball (b,g), weight training (b,g); coed interscholastic: dance, tennis. 4 PE instructors.

Computers Computers are regularly used in all classes. Computer network features include on-campus library services, online commercial services, Internet access, wireless campus network, Internet filtering or blocking technology. Campus intranet and student e-mail accounts are available to students. Students grades are available online. The school has a published electronic and media policy.

Contact Ms. Sandra Ota, Director of Admissions. 81-78-857-0100. Fax: 81-78-857-4095. E-mail: sandyo@canacad.ac.jp. Web site: www.canacad.ac.jp.

CANNON SCHOOL

5801 Poplar Tent Road
Concord, North Carolina 28027
Head of School: Mr. Matthew Gossage

General Information Coeducational day college-preparatory school. Grades PK–12. Founded: 1969. Setting: suburban. Nearest major city is Charlotte. 65-acre campus. 3 buildings on campus. Approved or accredited by Southern Association of Colleges and Schools and North Carolina Department of Education. Endowment: $2.8 million. Total enrollment: 825. Upper school average class size: 17. Upper school faculty-student ratio: 1:9.

Faculty School total: 97. In upper school: 18 men, 28 women; 27 have advanced degrees.

Subjects Offered Acting, advanced math, algebra, American history, American history-AP, American literature, anatomy and physiology, biology, biology-AP, British literature, calculus-AP, character education, chemistry, chemistry-AP, Chinese, chorus, college counseling, computer programming-AP, creative writing, dance, directing, discrete mathematics, drawing, English, English language-AP, English literature-AP, environmental science-AP, ethics, film and literature, film history, finance, French, French-AP, functions, geometry, jazz band, law and the legal system, marine science, mathematical modeling, painting, physics, physics-AP, playwriting, poetry, pre-calculus, psychology-AP, publications, sculpture, senior project, Spanish, Spanish language-AP, statistics-AP, strings, studio art-AP, theater design and production, trigonometry, U.S. government and politics-AP, visual arts, weight training, wind ensemble, world history, world literature, world religions, yearbook.

Graduation Requirements Arts and fine arts (art, music, dance, drama), biology, chemistry, computer literacy, English, foreign language, history, mathematics, physical education (includes health), science, senior project, trigonometry, U.S. history. Community service is required.

Special Academic Programs Advanced Placement exam preparation; honors section; independent study.

College Admission Counseling 87 students graduated in 2009; all went to college, including Appalachian State University; Clemson University; Emory University; Furman University; North Carolina State University; The University of North Carolina at Chapel Hill. Mean SAT critical reading: 610, mean SAT math: 624, mean SAT writing: 623, mean combined SAT: 1857, mean composite ACT: 27.

Student Life Upper grades have specified standards of dress, student council, honor system. Discipline rests primarily with faculty.

Tuition and Aid Day student tuition: $16,100. Tuition installment plan (Insured Tuition Payment Plan, monthly payment plans). Need-based scholarship grants available. In 2009–10, 10% of upper-school students received aid. Total amount of financial aid awarded in 2009–10: $310,000.

Admissions Traditional secondary-level entrance grade is 9. For fall 2009, 79 students applied for upper-level admission, 33 were accepted, 24 enrolled. Admissions testing and ISEE required. Deadline for receipt of application materials: none. Application fee required: $90. On-campus interview required.

Athletics Interscholastic: baseball (boys), basketball (b,g), cheering (g), cross-country running (b,g), dance (g), dance team (g), football (b), indoor track (b,g), lacrosse (b), soccer (b,g), softball (g), swimming and diving (b,g), tennis (b,g), track and field (b,g), volleyball (g); intramural: ballet (g); coed interscholastic: golf, indoor track, weight training; coed intramural: blading, cheering, croquet, dance, Frisbee, independent competitive sports, jump rope, kickball, Newcombe ball, track and field, weight training, whiffle ball, yoga. 6 PE instructors, 28 coaches, 1 athletic trainer.

Computers Computers are regularly used in all academic, art, music classes. Computer network features include on-campus library services, online commercial services, Internet access, wireless campus network, Internet filtering or blocking technology, productivity software. Campus intranet, student e-mail accounts, and computer access in designated common areas are available to students. Students grades are available online. The school has a published electronic and media policy.

Contact Mr. William D. Diskin, Director of Admission. 704-721-7164. Fax: 704-788-7779. E-mail: wdiskin@cannonschool.org. Web site: www.cannonschool.org.

CANTERBURY SCHOOL

101 Aspetuck Avenue
New Milford, Connecticut 06776
Head of School: Thomas J. Sheehey III

General Information Coeducational boarding and day college-preparatory, arts, business, religious studies, bilingual studies, and technology school, affiliated with Roman Catholic Church. Grades 9–PG. Founded: 1915. Setting: small town. Nearest major city is Hartford. Students are housed in single-sex dormitories. 150-acre campus. 20 buildings on campus. Approved or accredited by New England Association of Schools and Colleges, The Association of Boarding Schools, and Connecticut Department of Education. Member of National Association of Independent Schools and Secondary School Admission Test Board. Endowment: $25 million. Total enrollment: 350. Upper school average class size: 11. Upper school faculty-student ratio: 1:6.

Upper School Student Profile Grade 9: 50 students (30 boys, 20 girls); Grade 10: 82 students (39 boys, 43 girls); Grade 11: 108 students (63 boys, 45 girls); Grade 12: 107 students (62 boys, 45 girls); Postgraduate: 21 students (19 boys, 2 girls). 70% of students are boarding students. 50% are state residents. 18 states are represented in upper school student body. 17% are international students. International students from Australia, China, Germany, Republic of Korea, Spain, and Taiwan; 12 other countries represented in student body. 65% of students are Roman Catholic.

Faculty School total: 76. In upper school: 40 men, 36 women; 45 have advanced degrees; 56 reside on campus.

Subjects Offered 1½ elective credits, adolescent issues, algebra, American history, American literature, anthropology, art, art history, astronomy, biochemistry, biology, calculus, ceramics, chemistry, civil rights, computer programming, computer science, creative writing, dance, drama, driver education, earth science, economics, English, English literature, environmental science, ethics, European history, expository writing, fine arts, French, geography, geology, geometry, grammar, history, Irish studies, Latin, marine biology, mathematics, microbiology, music, oceanography, philosophy, photography, physics, physiology, religion, science, social studies, Spanish, Spanish literature, speech, statistics, theater, theology, trigonometry, women's studies, world history, world literature, writing.

Graduation Requirements Arts and fine arts (art, music, dance, drama), computer science, English, foreign language, mathematics, New Testament, religion (includes Bible studies and theology), science, social studies (includes history).

Special Academic Programs Advanced Placement exam preparation; honors section; independent study; ESL (15 students enrolled).

College Admission Counseling 108 students graduated in 2009; all went to college, including Boston University; Hobart and William Smith Colleges; Sacred Heart University; University of Connecticut. 25% scored over 600 on SAT critical reading, 35% scored over 600 on SAT math.

Student Life Upper grades have specified standards of dress, student council, honor system. Discipline rests primarily with faculty. Attendance at religious services is required.

Tuition and Aid Day student tuition: $33,000; 7-day tuition and room/board: $42,500. Tuition installment plan (Academic Management Services Plan, Key Tuition Payment Plan). Need-based scholarship grants, need-based loans, middle-income loans available. In 2009–10, 36% of upper-school students received aid. Total amount of financial aid awarded in 2009–10: $3,500,000.

Admissions Traditional secondary-level entrance grade is 9. For fall 2009, 700 students applied for upper-level admission, 250 were accepted, 125 enrolled. SLEP, SSAT, TOEFL and writing sample required. Deadline for receipt of application materials: January 31. Application fee required: $50. Interview required.

Athletics Interscholastic: baseball (boys), basketball (b,g), cross-country running (b,g), diving (b,g), field hockey (g), football (b), ice hockey (b,g), lacrosse (b,g), soccer (b,g), softball (g), squash (b,g), swimming and diving (b,g), tennis (b,g), track and field (b,g), volleyball (g); intramural: dance (g), equestrian sports (g), hockey (b,g), horseback riding (b,g); coed interscholastic: crew, golf, water polo, wrestling; coed intramural: fitness, softball, Special Olympics, strength & conditioning, weight lifting, weight training. 40 coaches, 2 athletic trainers.

Computers Computers are regularly used in accounting, English, mathematics, multimedia, science classes. Computer network features include on-campus library services, Internet access, wireless campus network, Internet filtering or blocking technology. Student e-mail accounts and computer access in designated common areas are available to students. Students grades are available online. The school has a published electronic and media policy.

Contact Keith R. Holton, Director of Admission. 860-210-3832. Fax: 860-350-1120. E-mail: admissions@cbury.org. Web site: www.cbury.org.

CANTERBURY SCHOOL

8141 College Parkway
Fort Myers, Florida 33919
Head of School: Mr. John Anthony (Tony) Paulus II

General Information Coeducational day college-preparatory and liberal arts school. Grades PK–12. Founded: 1964. Setting: suburban. Nearest major city is Fort Myers-Sarasota. 33-acre campus. 7 buildings on campus. Approved or accredited by Council of Accreditation and School Improvement, Florida Council of Independent Schools, Southern Association of Colleges and Schools, Southern Association of Independent Schools, The College Board, and Florida Department of Education. Member of National Association of Independent Schools and Secondary School Admission Test Board. Endowment: $7.5 million. Total enrollment: 600. Upper school average class size: 18. Upper school faculty-student ratio: 1:10. There are 181 required school days per year for Upper School students. Upper School students typically attend 5 days per week. The average school day consists of 7 hours and 10 minutes.

Upper School Student Profile Grade 9: 55 students (23 boys, 32 girls); Grade 10: 50 students (22 boys, 28 girls); Grade 11: 40 students (19 boys, 21 girls); Grade 12: 48 students (23 boys, 25 girls).

Faculty School total: 95. In upper school: 21 men, 19 women; 22 have advanced degrees.

Subjects Offered Advanced Placement courses, algebra, American history, American history-AP, American literature, anatomy, art, art history, biology, biology-AP, British literature, calculus, calculus-AP, ceramics, chemistry, chemistry-AP, comparative government and politics-AP, computer programming, constitutional law, creative writing, critical writing, drama, earth science, ecology, economics, English, English literature, English literature-AP, environmental science-AP, European history, fine arts, French, French language-AP, geography, geometry, government-AP, government/civics, grammar, health, history, Latin, leadership, macroeconomics-AP, marine biology, mathematics, music, nationalism and ethnic conflict, photography, physical education, physics, physics-AP, physiology, SAT preparation, science, social studies, sociology, Spanish, Spanish language-AP, speech, statistics, theater, U.S. government and politics-AP, U.S. history, United Nations and international issues, world history, world literature, writing, yearbook.

Graduation Requirements Arts and fine arts (art, music, dance, drama), English, foreign language, mathematics, physical education (includes health), science, social studies (includes history), speech. Community service is required.

Special Academic Programs 15 Advanced Placement exams for which test preparation is offered; independent study; study at local college for college credit.

College Admission Counseling 56 students graduated in 2010; all went to college, including Boston College; Carnegie Mellon University; Northwestern University; Notre Dame de Namur University; University of Florida; University of Miami. Median SAT critical reading: 590, median SAT math: 600, median SAT writing: 590, median combined SAT: 1780, median composite ACT: 26.

Student Life Upper grades have specified standards of dress, student council, honor system. Discipline rests primarily with faculty.

Summer Programs Remediation, enrichment, advancement, sports, art/fine arts programs offered; session focuses on academic enrichment; held on campus; accepts boys and girls; open to students from other schools. 125 students usually enrolled. 2011 schedule: June 14 to July 30. Application deadline: none.

Tuition and Aid Day student tuition: $17,760. Tuition installment plan (Insured Tuition Payment Plan, monthly payment plans, quarterly payment plan). Merit scholarship grants, need-based scholarship grants available. In 2010–11, 46% of upper-school students received aid; total upper-school merit-scholarship money awarded: $259,320. Total amount of financial aid awarded in 2010–11: $599,605.

Admissions Traditional secondary-level entrance grade is 9. For fall 2010, 24 students applied for upper-level admission, 16 were accepted, 12 enrolled. ERB CTP IV or SSAT required. Deadline for receipt of application materials: none. Application fee required: $75. Interview required.

Athletics Interscholastic: baseball (boys), basketball (b,g), cheering (g), cross-country running (b,g), football (b), lacrosse (b,g), soccer (b,g), volleyball (g), winter soccer (b,g); intramural: basketball (b,g), cross-country running (b,g), soccer (b,g), volleyball (b,g), winter soccer (b,g); coed interscholastic: golf, swimming and diving, tennis, track and field; coed intramural: swimming and diving. 2 PE instructors, 2 coaches, 1 athletic trainer.

Computers Computers are regularly used in art, college planning, English, foreign language, French, history, independent study, journalism, Latin, library, mathematics, science, social sciences, Spanish, speech, theater arts, yearbook classes. Computer network features include on-campus library services, Internet access, wireless campus network, Internet filtering or blocking technology. Campus intranet, student e-mail accounts, and computer access in designated common areas are available to students. Students grades are available online. The school has a published electronic and media policy.

Contact Ms. Julie A. Peters, Director of Admission. 239-415-8945. Fax: 239-481-8339. E-mail: jpeters@canterburyfortmyers.org. Web site: www.canterburyfortmyers.org.

See Display on page 150 and Close-Up on page 752.

THE CANTERBURY SCHOOL OF FLORIDA

990 62nd Avenue NE
St. Petersburg, Florida 33702
Head of School: Mr. Mac H. Hall

General Information Coeducational day college-preparatory, arts, and marine studies, international program school, affiliated with Episcopal Church. Grades PK–12. Founded: 1968. Setting: suburban. Nearest major city is Tampa. 20-acre campus. 5 buildings on campus. Approved or accredited by Florida Council of Independent Schools, National Association of Episcopal Schools, National Independent Private Schools Association, The College Board, and Florida Department of Education. Endowment: $115,000. Total enrollment: 402. Upper school average class size: 13. Upper school faculty-student ratio: 1:4.

Upper School Student Profile Grade 9: 49 students (24 boys, 25 girls); Grade 10: 38 students (12 boys, 26 girls); Grade 11: 33 students (13 boys, 20 girls); Grade 12: 33 students (14 boys, 19 girls). 5% of students are members of Episcopal Church.

Faculty School total: 60. In upper school: 12 men, 15 women; 18 have advanced degrees.

Subjects Offered 20th century world history, advanced computer applications, Advanced Placement courses, advanced studio art-AP, algebra, American government, American literature, anatomy, Ancient Greek, ancient world history, art, art history, art history-AP, astronomy, athletics, band, Basic programming, biology, biology-AP, British literature, British literature (honors), calculus, calculus-AP, career exploration, ceramics, character education, chemistry, chemistry-AP, choral music, chorus, classical language, classical studies, college counseling, college placement, community service, competitive science projects, computer multimedia, computer science, computer science-AP, computer skills, contemporary issues, creative writing, dance, dance performance, digital imaging, earth science, economics, English, English composition, English literature, English literature-AP, environmental science, environmental science-AP, environmental studies, ethics, European history, expository writing, film studies, fine arts, finite math, foreign language, French, French-AP, freshman seminar, geography, geometry, government/civics, grammar, Greek culture, guitar, health, history, history of music, history-AP, honors algebra, honors geometry, human geography—AP, independent living, interdisciplinary studies, journalism, keyboarding, Latin, Latin-AP, leadership, leadership and service, library skills, life science, life skills, macroeconomics-AP, marine biology, marine ecology, marine science, marine studies, mathematics, mathematics-AP, mechanical drawing, mentorship program, modern world history, multimedia, music, musical productions, musical theater, oceanography, outdoor education, personal and social education, personal fitness, photojournalism, physical education, physical science, physics, physics-AP, play production, portfolio art, pottery, prayer/spirituality, pre-algebra, pre-calculus, pre-college orientation, psychology, psychology-AP, reading/study skills, robotics, SAT preparation, SAT/ACT preparation, science, senior composition, senior seminar, senior thesis, Shakespeare, social sciences, social studies, Spanish, Spanish language-AP, Spanish literature-AP, Spanish-AP, speech, speech and debate, sports conditioning, stagecraft, statistics-AP, student government, student publications, student teaching, studio art-AP, technical theater, theater arts, theater design and production, theater history, U.S. history, U.S. history-AP, values and decisions, visual and performing arts, weight fitness, weight training, Western philosophy, world history, world literature, world religions, yearbook.

Graduation Requirements Arts and fine arts (art, music, dance, drama), career/college preparation, electives, English, ethics, foreign language, history, mathematics, physical education (includes health), research, science, senior seminar, writing, research and writing, miniterms, ethics and world religions. Community service is required.

Special Academic Programs Advanced Placement exam preparation; honors section; independent study; term-away projects; study at local college for college credit; study abroad.

College Admission Counseling 27 students graduated in 2010; all went to college.

Student Life Upper grades have specified standards of dress, student council, honor system. Discipline rests equally with students and faculty. Attendance at religious services is required.

Summer Programs Remediation, enrichment, sports, art/fine arts, computer instruction programs offered; session focuses on multi-discipline skills and abilities; held on campus; accepts boys and girls; open to students from other schools. 50 students usually enrolled. 2011 schedule: June 8 to August 7. Application deadline: March 15.

Tuition and Aid Day student tuition: $15,100–$16,100. Tuition installment plan (Insured Tuition Payment Plan, monthly payment plans, individually arranged payment plans). Tuition reduction for siblings, need-based scholarship grants available. In 2010–11, 20% of upper-school students received aid. Total amount of financial aid awarded in 2010–11: $575,000.

Admissions Traditional secondary-level entrance grade is 9. For fall 2010, 35 students applied for upper-level admission, 30 were accepted, 28 enrolled. 3-R Achievement Test, any standardized test, ERB, SSAT or TOEFL required. Deadline for receipt of application materials: none. Application fee required: $75. On-campus interview required.

Athletics Interscholastic: baseball (boys), basketball (b,g), cross-country running (b,g), diving (g), football (b), golf (b), soccer (b,g), softball (g), swimming and diving (b,g), tennis (b,g), track and field (b,g), volleyball (g); intramural: strength & conditioning (b); coed interscholastic: cheering, cross-country running, golf, soccer; coed intramural: canoeing/kayaking, dance, fitness, flag football, floor hockey, hiking/backpacking, indoor hockey, kayaking, modern dance, outdoor activities, outdoor education, paddle tennis, physical fitness, ropes courses, ultimate Frisbee, weight training. 4 PE instructors, 21 coaches, 1 athletic trainer.

Computers Computers are regularly used in all academic classes. Computer network features include on-campus library services, online commercial services, Internet access, wireless campus network, Internet filtering or blocking technology, remote access to second campus. Computer access in designated common areas is available to students. Students grades are available online. The school has a published electronic and media policy.

Contact Dr. Ashley L. Gairing, Director of Advancement/Admission/Alumni. 727-521-5903. Fax: 727-521-5991. E-mail: agairing@canterbury-fl.org. Web site: www.canterbury-fl.org.

CANTON ACADEMY

Post Office Box 116
One Nancy Drive
Canton, Mississippi 39046
Head of School: Mr. Curt McCain

General Information Coeducational day college-preparatory school. Grades 6–12. Founded: 1965. Setting: small town. Nearest major city is Jackson. Students are housed in day school. 1 building on campus. Approved or accredited by Mississippi Private School Association, Southern Association of Independent Schools, and Mississippi Department of Education. Total enrollment: 323. Upper school average class size: 17. Upper school faculty-student ratio: 1:17. There are 175 required school days per year for Upper School students. Upper School students typically attend 5 days per week. The average school day consists of 7 hours and 20 minutes.

Upper School Student Profile Grade 6: 20 students (9 boys, 11 girls); Grade 7: 21 students (8 boys, 13 girls); Grade 8: 23 students (13 boys, 10 girls); Grade 9: 39 students (24 boys, 15 girls); Grade 10: 32 students (17 boys, 15 girls); Grade 11: 27 students (15 boys, 12 girls); Grade 12: 44 students (27 boys, 17 girls).

Faculty School total: 50. In upper school: 6 men, 7 women.

Graduation Requirements Accounting, Community Service Hours.

College Admission Counseling 32 students graduated in 2010; all went to college, including Delta State University; Millsaps College; Mississippi College; Mississippi State University; University of Mississippi; University of Southern Mississippi.

Student Life Upper grades have specified standards of dress, student council, honor system. Discipline rests primarily with faculty.

Summer Programs Remediation programs offered; session focuses on remediation make-up, advancement; held on campus; accepts boys and girls; open to students from other schools. 25 students usually enrolled. 2011 schedule: May 25 to July 31. Application deadline: May.

Tuition and Aid Tuition installment plan (monthly payment plans, individually arranged payment plans). Tuition reduction for siblings, need-based scholarship grants, paying campus jobs available. In 2010–11, 11% of upper-school students received aid. Total amount of financial aid awarded in 2010–11: $50,000.

Admissions Traditional secondary-level entrance grade is 10. Comprehensive Test of Basic Skills required. Deadline for receipt of application materials: January 26. Application fee required: $35. Interview recommended.

Athletics Interscholastic: aerobics/dance (girls), baseball (b,g), basketball (b,g), cheering (g), cross-country running (b,g), dance team (g), equestrian sports (b,g), football (b), golf (b), horseback riding (b,g), jogging (b,g), power lifting (b), running (b,g), soccer (b,g), softball (g), swimming and diving (b,g), tennis (b,g), weight training (b,g), yoga (g).

Contact 601-859-5231. Fax: 601-859-5232. Web site: www.cantonacademy.org.

CANYONVILLE CHRISTIAN ACADEMY

PO Box 1100
Canyonville, Oregon 97417-1100
Head of School: Mr. Noel Schaak

General Information Coeducational boarding and day college-preparatory, religious studies, and English for Speakers of Other Languages school, affiliated with Christian faith. Grades 9–12. Founded: 1924. Setting: rural. Nearest major city is Medford. Students are housed in single-sex dormitories. 10-acre campus. 11 buildings on campus. Approved or accredited by Association of Christian Schools International, Northwest Association of Schools and Colleges, The Association of Boarding Schools, and Oregon Department of Education. Upper school average class size: 20. Upper school faculty-student ratio: 1:15. There are 180 required school days per year for Upper School students. Upper School students typically attend 5 days per week. The average school day consists of 7 hours.

Upper School Student Profile 90% of students are boarding students. 5% are state residents. 10 states are represented in upper school student body. 85% are international students. International students from China, Hong Kong, Republic of Korea, and Taiwan; 10 other countries represented in student body. 70% of students are Christian faith.

Faculty School total: 20. In upper school: 5 men, 7 women; 5 have advanced degrees; 14 reside on campus.

Subjects Offered Advanced Placement courses, aerobics, algebra, American culture, American history, art, Bible, biology, calculus, calculus-AP, career/college preparation, chemistry, choir, Christian doctrine, composition, computer education, computer technologies, computers, consumer economics, culinary arts, desktop publishing, economics, English, English literature, ESL, foreign language, French as a second language, general science, government, grammar, health, integrative seminar, keyboarding, language and composition, library assistant, Life of Christ, mathematics, New Testament, orchestra, physical education, physical science, physics, pre-calculus, religious education, Spanish, speech and debate, theology, U.S. government, U.S. history, United States government-AP, world history.

Graduation Requirements 1½ elective credits, algebra, arts and fine arts (art, music, dance, drama), Bible, biology, economics, English, foreign language, government, health and wellness, mathematics, physical education (includes health), physical science, speech and debate, U.S. history, world history.

Special Academic Programs Advanced Placement exam preparation; honors section; accelerated programs; independent study; study at local college for college credit; remedial math; ESL (50 students enrolled).

College Admission Counseling 60 students graduated in 2010; 55 went to college, including Oregon State University; Penn State University Park; Rutgers, The State University of New Jersey, Newark; University of Oregon; University of Washington; Washington State University. Other: 3 went to work. Mean SAT critical reading: 462, mean SAT math: 519, mean SAT writing: 453, mean combined SAT: 1434.

Student Life Upper grades have specified standards of dress, student council, honor system. Discipline rests primarily with faculty. Attendance at religious services is required.

Tuition and Aid Day student tuition: $4600; 7-day tuition and room/board: $23,000. Tuition installment plan (monthly payment plans, individually arranged payment plans). Tuition reduction for siblings, merit scholarship grants, need-based scholarship grants, paying campus jobs available. In 2010–11, 10% of upper-school students received aid; total upper-school merit-scholarship money awarded: $30,000. Total amount of financial aid awarded in 2010–11: $147,900.

Admissions Traditional secondary-level entrance grade is 9. TOEFL or SLEP required. Deadline for receipt of application materials: none. Application fee required: $100. Interview recommended.

Athletics Interscholastic: basketball (boys, girls), cheering (g), cross-country running (b,g), soccer (b), tennis (b,g), track and field (b,g), volleyball (g); intramural: aerobics (g), soccer (b); coed interscholastic: soccer, tennis; coed intramural: badminton, basketball, billiards, table tennis, tennis, volleyball. 3 PE instructors, 9 coaches.

Computers Computers are regularly used in business applications, technology, yearbook classes. Computer network features include Internet access, wireless campus network, Internet filtering or blocking technology. Student e-mail accounts and computer access in designated common areas are available to students. Students grades are available online.

Contact Mr. Ed Lovato, Director of Admissions. 541-839-4401. Fax: 541-839-6228. E-mail: cca@canyonville.net. Web site: www.canyonville.net.

CAPE COD ACADEMY

50 Osterville–West Barnstable Road
Osterville, Massachusetts 02655
Head of School: Clark J. Daggett

General Information Coeducational day college-preparatory, arts, and technology school. Grades K–12. Founded: 1976. Setting: small town. Nearest major city is

Boston. 47-acre campus. 5 buildings on campus. Approved or accredited by Association of Independent Schools in New England and New England Association of Schools and Colleges. Member of National Association of Independent Schools and Secondary School Admission Test Board. Endowment: $2.2 million. Total enrollment: 334. Upper school average class size: 13. Upper school faculty-student ratio: 1:4. There are 172 required school days per year for Upper School students. Upper School students typically attend 5 days per week. The average school day consists of 6 hours and 30 minutes.

Upper School Student Profile Grade 9: 33 students (17 boys, 16 girls); Grade 10: 31 students (17 boys, 14 girls); Grade 11: 44 students (20 boys, 24 girls); Grade 12: 44 students (29 boys, 15 girls).

Faculty School total: 54. In upper school: 19 men, 20 women; 28 have advanced degrees.

Subjects Offered Advanced biology, advanced chemistry, advanced math, Advanced Placement courses, advanced studio art-AP, algebra, American history, American literature, art, art history, art history-AP, art-AP, biology, calculus, calculus-AP, ceramics, chemistry, chemistry-AP, community service, computer math, computer programming, computer science, digital photography, drama, earth science, English, English literature, English-AP, environmental science, ethics, European history, expository writing, fine arts, French, French-AP, geography, geometry, health, history, history-AP, honors algebra, honors geometry, Latin, mathematics, music, music composition, music history, music theory, philosophy, photography, physical education, physics, SAT preparation, science, senior internship, social sciences, social studies, Spanish, Spanish-AP, statistics-AP, studio art-AP, theater, trigonometry, world history, world literature.

Graduation Requirements Arts and fine arts (art, music, dance, drama), computer science, English, foreign language, history, independent study, mathematics, physical education (includes health), science. Community service is required.

Special Academic Programs 10 Advanced Placement exams for which test preparation is offered; honors section; independent study; term-away projects; study abroad.

College Admission Counseling 39 students graduated in 2009; all went to college, including Boston College; Boston University; Providence College; Tufts University; University of Massachusetts Amherst; University of Pennsylvania. Mean SAT critical reading: 595, mean SAT math: 624.

Student Life Upper grades have specified standards of dress, student council, honor system. Discipline rests primarily with faculty.

Tuition and Aid Day student tuition: $18,470–$22,270. Tuition installment plan (Academic Management Services Plan, monthly payment plans). Need-based scholarship grants available. In 2009–10, 35% of upper-school students received aid. Total amount of financial aid awarded in 2009–10: $1,115,000.

Admissions Traditional secondary-level entrance grade is 9. For fall 2009, 31 students applied for upper-level admission, 29 were accepted, 13 enrolled. ISEE, Otis-Lennon School Ability Test or SSAT required. Deadline for receipt of application materials: February 1. Application fee required: $95. On-campus interview required.

Athletics Interscholastic: baseball (boys), basketball (b,g), lacrosse (b,g), soccer (b,g), tennis (b,g); coed interscholastic: cross-country running, golf; coed intramural: aerobics, aerobics/Nautilus, archery, basketball, combined training, fitness, floor hockey, physical training, sailing, soccer, strength & conditioning, weight training. 1 PE instructor, 11 coaches, 1 athletic trainer.

Computers Computers are regularly used in all classes. Computer network features include on-campus library services, online commercial services, Internet access, wireless campus network, Internet filtering or blocking technology. Campus intranet, student e-mail accounts, and computer access in designated common areas are available to students. Students grades are available online. The school has a published electronic and media policy.

Contact Laurie A. Wyndham, Director of Admissions. 508-428-5400 Ext. 226. Fax: 508-428-0701. E-mail: Lwyndham@capecodacademy.org. Web site: www.capecodacademy.org.

CAPE FEAR ACADEMY

3900 South College Road
Wilmington, North Carolina 28412
Head of School: Mr. John B. Meehl

General Information Coeducational day college-preparatory and arts school. Grades PK–12. Founded: 1967. Setting: suburban. 27-acre campus. 3 buildings on campus. Approved or accredited by Southern Association of Colleges and Schools, Southern Association of Independent Schools, and North Carolina Department of Education. Member of National Association of Independent Schools. Endowment: $562,250. Total enrollment: 628. Upper school average class size: 17. Upper school faculty-student ratio: 1:7. There are 177 required school days per year for Upper School students. Upper School students typically attend 5 days per week. The average school day consists of 7 hours and 20 minutes.

Upper School Student Profile Grade 9: 56 students (23 boys, 33 girls); Grade 10: 74 students (35 boys, 39 girls); Grade 11: 52 students (22 boys, 30 girls); Grade 12: 56 students (30 boys, 26 girls).

Faculty School total: 76. In upper school: 15 men, 18 women; 16 have advanced degrees.

Subjects Offered 3-dimensional art, Advanced Placement courses, algebra, American history, American history-AP, American literature, analysis, art, art history, band, biology, biology-AP, British literature, calculus-AP, chemistry, choral music, comparative government and politics-AP, computer science, conceptual physics, critical studies in film, discrete mathematics, drama, earth and space science, English, English language-AP, English literature, English literature-AP, environmental science, environmental science-AP, European history, European history-AP, film studies, finance, fine arts, fitness, geometry, global studies, government and politics-AP, government-AP, history, honors geometry, human anatomy, independent study, journalism, language, literature, marine science, mathematics, music, music theory-AP, musical theater, newspaper, organizational studies, photography, physical education, physics, pre-calculus, psychology, publications, religion, SAT preparation, science, sculpture, social studies, Spanish, student publications, theater, video film production, vocal ensemble, weight training, world history.

Graduation Requirements Arts and fine arts (art, music, dance, drama), biology, English, foreign language, mathematics, physical education (includes health), science, social studies (includes history), U.S. government, U.S. history. Community service is required.

Special Academic Programs 11 Advanced Placement exams for which test preparation is offered; honors section; independent study; study at local college for college credit.

College Admission Counseling 56 students graduated in 2010; all went to college, including Davidson College; East Carolina University; Elon University; High Point University; North Carolina State University; The University of North Carolina at Chapel Hill. Mean SAT critical reading: 591, mean SAT math: 586.

Student Life Upper grades have specified standards of dress, student council, honor system. Discipline rests primarily with faculty.

Summer Programs Enrichment, sports, art/fine arts programs offered; session focuses on enrichment and sports; held on campus; accepts boys and girls; open to students from other schools. 250 students usually enrolled. 2011 schedule: June 11 to August 10. Application deadline: none.

Tuition and Aid Day student tuition: $12,345. Tuition installment plan (Insured Tuition Payment Plan, FACTS Tuition Payment Plan, monthly payment plans). Merit scholarship grants, need-based scholarship grants available. In 2010–11, 17% of upper-school students received aid; total upper-school merit-scholarship money awarded: $9500. Total amount of financial aid awarded in 2010–11: $241,773.

Admissions Traditional secondary-level entrance grade is 9. For fall 2010, 52 students applied for upper-level admission, 36 were accepted, 28 enrolled. ERB, ISEE, PSAT or SAT or SSAT required. Deadline for receipt of application materials: none. Application fee required: $75. On-campus interview recommended.

Athletics Interscholastic: basketball (boys, girls), field hockey (g), lacrosse (b,g), soccer (b,g), tennis (b,g), volleyball (g); coed interscholastic: cheering, cross-country running, golf, surfing, swimming and diving. 2 PE instructors, 11 coaches, 1 athletic trainer.

Computers Computers are regularly used in all academic classes. Computer network features include on-campus library services, online commercial services, Internet access, wireless campus network, Internet filtering or blocking technology. Campus intranet, student e-mail accounts, and computer access in designated common areas are available to students. Students grades are available online. The school has a published electronic and media policy.

Contact Mrs. Susan Mixon Harrell, Director of Admission. 910-791-0287 Ext. 1015. Fax: 910-791-0290. E-mail: sharrell@capefearacademy.org. Web site: www.capefearacademy.org.

CAPE HENRY COLLEGIATE SCHOOL

1320 Mill Dam Road
Virginia Beach, Virginia 23454-2306
Head of School: Dr. John P. Lewis

General Information Coeducational day college-preparatory, arts, technology, and global education school. Grades PK–12. Founded: 1924. Setting: suburban. 30-acre campus. 9 buildings on campus. Approved or accredited by Virginia Association of Independent Schools. Member of National Association of Independent Schools. Endowment: $6 million. Total enrollment: 924. Upper school average class size: 14. Upper school faculty-student ratio: 1:10.

Upper School Student Profile Grade 9: 108 students (62 boys, 46 girls); Grade 10: 89 students (42 boys, 47 girls); Grade 11: 93 students (57 boys, 36 girls); Grade 12: 77 students (42 boys, 35 girls).

Faculty School total: 135. In upper school: 21 men, 39 women; 34 have advanced degrees.

Subjects Offered Algebra, American history, American literature, art, art history, biology, botany, business skills, calculus, ceramics, chemistry, community service, computer programming, computer science, creative writing, drama, driver education, earth science, ecology, economics, English, English literature, environmental science, European history, expository writing, fine arts, French, geography, geology, geometry, government/civics, health, history, journalism, Latin, law, marine biology, mathematics, music, oceanography, photography, physical education, physics, science, social sciences, social studies, sociology, Spanish, speech, statistics, theater, trigonometry, world history, world literature, writing.

Graduation Requirements Arts and fine arts (art, music, dance, drama), computer science, English, foreign language, mathematics, physical education (includes health), science, social sciences, social studies (includes history). Community service is required.

Special Academic Programs Advanced Placement exam preparation; honors section; independent study; academic accommodation for the gifted, the musically talented, and the artistically talented; ESL (25 students enrolled).

College Admission Counseling 84 students graduated in 2010; all went to college, including Hampden-Sydney College; James Madison University; The College of William and Mary; University of Virginia; Virginia Polytechnic Institute and State University; Washington and Lee University.

Student Life Upper grades have specified standards of dress, student council, honor system. Discipline rests equally with students and faculty.

Summer Programs Enrichment, advancement, ESL, sports, art/fine arts, computer instruction programs offered; session focuses on academics and enrichment; held on campus; accepts boys and girls; open to students from other schools. 1,200 students usually enrolled. 2011 schedule: June 8 to August 14. Application deadline: none.

Tuition and Aid Day student tuition: $16,350. Tuition installment plan (The Tuition Plan, Insured Tuition Payment Plan, monthly payment plans, individually arranged payment plans, 3-payment plan). Merit scholarship grants, need-based scholarship grants available. In 2010–11, 20% of upper-school students received aid; total upper-school merit-scholarship money awarded: $16,350.

Admissions Traditional secondary-level entrance grade is 9. For fall 2010, 74 students applied for upper-level admission, 69 were accepted, 50 enrolled. ERB CTP, ISEE or writing sample required. Deadline for receipt of application materials: February 15. Application fee required: $50. On-campus interview required.

Athletics Interscholastic: baseball (boys), basketball (b,g), crew (b,g), cross-country running (b,g), field hockey (g), golf (b,g), lacrosse (b,g), soccer (b,g), softball (g), tennis (b,g), volleyball (b,g), wrestling (b); intramural: baseball (b), basketball (b,g), crew (b,g), cross-country running (b,g), field hockey (g), floor hockey (b,g), wrestling (b); coed interscholastic: cheering, swimming and diving, track and field; coed intramural: aerobics, aerobics/dance, aerobics/Nautilus, archery, backpacking, badminton, ballet, cheering, dance, fishing, fitness, fitness walking, golf, hiking/backpacking, jogging, kayaking, lacrosse, modern dance, ocean paddling, outdoor activities, outdoor adventure, physical fitness, physical training, skiing (downhill), snowboarding, soccer, strength & conditioning, surfing, swimming and diving, table tennis, tennis, volleyball, weight lifting, weight training, wilderness, yoga. 5 PE instructors, 16 coaches, 1 athletic trainer.

Computers Computers are regularly used in computer applications, desktop publishing, graphic arts, information technology, literary magazine, newspaper, publications, technology, video film production, Web site design, word processing, yearbook classes. Computer network features include on-campus library services, online commercial services, Internet access, wireless campus network, Internet filtering or blocking technology. Student e-mail accounts and computer access in designated common areas are available to students. Students grades are available online. The school has a published electronic and media policy.

Contact Mrs. Angie Finley, Admissions Associate. 757-963-8234. E-mail: angiefinley@capehenry.org. Web site: www.capehenrycollegiate.org.

CAPISTRANO VALLEY CHRISTIAN SCHOOLS

32032 Del Obispo Street
San Juan Capistrano, California 92675
Head of School: Dr. Ron Sipus

General Information Coeducational day college-preparatory, arts, religious studies, bilingual studies, and technology school, affiliated with Christian faith. Grades JK–12. Founded: 1972. Setting: suburban. 8-acre campus. 2 buildings on campus. Approved or accredited by Association of Christian Schools International, Department of Education of Bern, Western Association of Schools and Colleges, and California Department of Education. Total enrollment: 404. Upper school average class size: 18. Upper school faculty-student ratio: 1:13. There are 180 required school days per year for Upper School students. Upper School students typically attend 5 days per week. The average school day consists of 6 hours.

Upper School Student Profile Grade 9: 41 students (19 boys, 22 girls); Grade 10: 40 students (19 boys, 21 girls); Grade 11: 36 students (15 boys, 21 girls); Grade 12: 60 students (39 boys, 21 girls). 80% of students are Christian faith.

Faculty School total: 42. In upper school: 8 men, 12 women; 9 have advanced degrees.

Subjects Offered ACT preparation, advanced biology, advanced chemistry, advanced computer applications, advanced math, Advanced Placement courses, advanced TOEFL/grammar, algebra, American government, American history, American history-AP, American literature, American literature-AP, anatomy, art, ASB Leadership, athletic training, athletics, Bible studies, biology, biology-AP, calculus-AP, career planning, chemistry, choir, college counseling, college placement, composition, composition-AP, computer animation, computer applications, computer education, computer information systems, computer literacy, computer multimedia, computer skills, computer technologies, desktop publishing, drama performance, ecology, economics, English, English literature-AP, English-AP, ESL, European history, freshman foundations, geometry, government, health, history, honors algebra, honors English, independent study, Internet, intro to computers, journalism, keyboarding, lab science, leadership, physical education, physical science, physics, public speaking, research skills, Spanish, Spanish-AP, student government, U.S. government and politics-AP, U.S. history-AP, Web site design, world cultures, yearbook.

Graduation Requirements Algebra, American government, American history, American literature, arts and fine arts (art, music, dance, drama), Bible, biology, composition, computer skills, economics, electives, English, European history, foreign language, freshman foundations, geometry, physical education (includes health), research skills, speech, our grad requirements meet UC and CSU entrance requirements.

Special Academic Programs Advanced Placement exam preparation; honors section; independent study; ESL (30 students enrolled).

College Admission Counseling 56 students graduated in 2010; 55 went to college, including Azusa Pacific University; Biola University; California State University, Long Beach; Point Loma Nazarene University; University of California, Berkeley; University of California, Irvine. Other: 1 went to work. Median SAT critical reading: 549, median SAT math: 581, median SAT writing: 561, median combined SAT: 1691.

Student Life Upper grades have uniform requirement, student council, honor system. Discipline rests primarily with faculty.

Summer Programs Remediation, advancement, sports programs offered; held on campus; accepts boys and girls; open to students from other schools. 35 students usually enrolled. 2011 schedule: July 11 to August 5. Application deadline: May 1.

Tuition and Aid Day student tuition: $10,790. Tuition installment plan (FACTS Tuition Payment Plan). Tuition reduction for siblings, need-based scholarship grants available. In 2010–11, 40% of upper-school students received aid. Total amount of financial aid awarded in 2010–11: $225,000.

Admissions Traditional secondary-level entrance grade is 9. For fall 2010, 38 students applied for upper-level admission, 38 were accepted, 38 enrolled. ESOL English Proficiency Test, High School Placement Test, Stanford Test of Academic Skills or TOEFL required. Deadline for receipt of application materials: none. Application fee required: $100. On-campus interview required.

Athletics Interscholastic: baseball (boys), basketball (b,g), cheering (g), cross-country running (b,g), football (b), softball (g), tennis (b,g), volleyball (b,g), weight lifting (b); coed interscholastic: equestrian sports, golf, physical training, soccer, strength & conditioning. 2 PE instructors, 53 coaches, 1 athletic trainer.

Computers Computers are regularly used in all academic, Bible studies, journalism, yearbook classes. Computer network features include on-campus library services, Internet access, wireless campus network, Internet filtering or blocking technology, 1 to 1 Tablet PC program. Campus intranet, student e-mail accounts, and computer access in designated common areas are available to students. Students grades are available online. The school has a published electronic and media policy.

Contact Jo Beveridge, Director of Admissions/Development. 949-493-5683 Ext. 109. Fax: 949-493-6057. E-mail: jbeveridge@cvcs.org. Web site: www.cvcs.org.

CARDIGAN MOUNTAIN SCHOOL

Canaan, New Hampshire
See Junior Boarding Schools section.

CARDINAL GIBBONS HIGH SCHOOL

1401 Edwards Mill Road
Raleigh, North Carolina 27607
Head of School: Mr. Jason Curtis
General Information Coeducational day college-preparatory, arts, business, religious studies, and technology school, affiliated with Roman Catholic Church. Grades 9–12. Founded: 1909. Setting: suburban. 36-acre campus. 1 building on campus. Approved or accredited by Southern Association of Colleges and Schools and Southern Association of Independent Schools. Endowment: $750,000. Total enrollment: 1,192. Upper school average class size: 14. Upper school faculty-student ratio: 1:14. Upper School students typically attend 5 days per week. The average school day consists of 7 hours.

Upper School Student Profile Grade 9: 317 students (175 boys, 142 girls); Grade 10: 300 students (153 boys, 147 girls); Grade 11: 300 students (152 boys, 148 girls); Grade 12: 268 students (148 boys, 120 girls). 86% of students are Roman Catholic.

Faculty School total: 95. In upper school: 40 men, 55 women; 60 have advanced degrees.

Special Academic Programs Advanced Placement exam preparation; honors section; accelerated programs; independent study.

College Admission Counseling 286 students graduated in 2009; 285 went to college, including Appalachian State University; University of Notre Dame. Other: 1 had other specific plans.

Student Life Upper grades have uniform requirement, student council. Discipline rests primarily with faculty. Attendance at religious services is required.

Tuition and Aid Day student tuition: $8345–$11,785. Tuition installment plan (FACTS Tuition Payment Plan). Need-based scholarship grants available.

Admissions Traditional secondary-level entrance grade is 9. Application fee required: $75. On-campus interview required.

Athletics Interscholastic: aerobics/dance (boys, girls), baseball (b,g), basketball (b,g), cheering (g), cross-country running (b,g), dance (g), dance squad (g), dance team (g), football (b), golf (b,g), lacrosse (b,g), outdoor education (b,g), roller hockey (b), soccer (b,g), softball (g), swimming and diving (b,g), tennis (b,g), track and field (b,g), volleyball (g), weight lifting (b,g), weight training (g), wrestling (b).

Computers Computer network features include Internet access, wireless campus network, Internet filtering or blocking technology. Campus intranet, student e-mail accounts, and computer access in designated common areas are available to students.

Contact Mrs. Marianne McCarty, Admissions Director. 919-834-1625 Ext. 209. Fax: 919-834-9771. E-mail: mmccarty@cghsnc.org. Web site: www.cghsnc.org.

CARDINAL MOONEY CATHOLIC COLLEGE PREPARATORY HIGH SCHOOL

660 South Water Street
Marine City, Michigan 48039
Head of School: Sr. Karen Lietz, OP
General Information Coeducational day college-preparatory school, affiliated with Roman Catholic Church. Grades 9–12. Founded: 1977. Setting: small town. Nearest major city is Mount Clemens. 1-acre campus. 1 building on campus. Approved or accredited by Michigan Association of Non-Public Schools, North Central Association of Colleges and Schools, and Michigan Department of Education. Total enrollment: 180. Upper school average class size: 22. Upper school faculty-student ratio: 1:10. There are 186 required school days per year for Upper School students. Upper School students typically attend 5 days per week. The average school day consists of 6 hours and 25 minutes.

Upper School Student Profile Grade 9: 44 students (19 boys, 25 girls); Grade 10: 46 students (23 boys, 23 girls); Grade 11: 47 students (23 boys, 24 girls); Grade 12: 43 students (19 boys, 24 girls). 90% of students are Roman Catholic.

Faculty School total: 20. In upper school: 4 men, 16 women; 10 have advanced degrees.

Subjects Offered Advanced Placement courses, algebra, American literature, anatomy, art, biology, calculus, Catholic belief and practice, chemistry, choir, computer applications, computer skills, drama, economics, English, fiction, French, French language-AP, geography, geometry, government, government-AP, health, humanities, Italian, library science, moral and social development, mythology, physical education, physical science, physics, poetry, pre-calculus, Spanish, Spanish language-AP, statistics, study skills, U.S. history, U.S. history-AP, world history, world literature, yearbook.

Special Academic Programs Advanced Placement exam preparation; honors section.

College Admission Counseling 49 students graduated in 2010; 47 went to college, including Central Michigan University; Grand Valley State University; Michigan State University; Oakland University; University of Detroit Mercy; University of Michigan. Other: 2 entered military service.

Student Life Upper grades have uniform requirement, student council, honor system. Discipline rests primarily with faculty. Attendance at religious services is required.

Tuition and Aid Tuition installment plan (monthly payment plans). Tuition reduction for siblings available.

Admissions Traditional secondary-level entrance grade is 9. For fall 2010, 44 students applied for upper-level admission, 44 were accepted, 44 enrolled. High School Placement Test required. Deadline for receipt of application materials: none. Application fee required: $250. Interview required.

Athletics Interscholastic: baseball (boys), basketball (b,g), bowling (b,g), cheering (g), cross-country running (b,g), equestrian sports (b,g), football (b), golf (b), soccer (b,g), softball (g), volleyball (g); coed interscholastic: cross-country running, track and field. 2 PE instructors, 6 coaches.

Computers Computers are regularly used in computer applications, data processing, desktop publishing, graphic design, library science, word processing, yearbook classes. Computer network features include on-campus library services, Internet access, Internet filtering or blocking technology. Computer access in designated common areas is available to students. Students grades are available online. The school has a published electronic and media policy.

Contact Sr. Karen Lietz, OP, Principal. 810-765-8825 Ext. 14. Fax: 810-765-7164. E-mail: principal@cardinalmooneycatholic.com.

CARDINAL MOONEY CATHOLIC HIGH SCHOOL

4171 Fruitville Road
Sarasota, Florida 34232
Head of School: Mr. Stephen J. Christie
General Information Coeducational day college-preparatory, arts, and religious studies school, affiliated with Roman Catholic Church. Grades 9–12. Founded: 1959. Setting: suburban. Nearest major city is Tampa. 36-acre campus. 7 buildings on campus. Approved or accredited by Southern Association of Colleges and Schools. Endowment: $1.8 million. Total enrollment: 467. Upper school average class size: 18. Upper school faculty-student ratio: 1:13. There are 180 required school days per year for Upper School students. Upper School students typically attend 5 days per week. The average school day consists of 6 hours and 35 minutes.

Upper School Student Profile Grade 9: 91 students (46 boys, 45 girls); Grade 10: 132 students (57 boys, 75 girls); Grade 11: 119 students (72 boys, 47 girls); Grade 12: 125 students (74 boys, 51 girls). 80% of students are Roman Catholic.

Faculty School total: 45. In upper school: 20 men, 25 women; 25 have advanced degrees.

Subjects Offered Algebra, American government, American history, anatomy, art, biology, business, calculus, ceramics, chemistry, chorus, Christian and Hebrew scripture, community service, computer applications, computer graphics, contemporary history, creative writing, drama, earth science, economics, economics and history, English, English literature, environmental science, fine arts, French, geometry, guitar, health, history, instrumental music, integrated mathematics, journalism, keyboarding, learning strategies, marine biology, mathematics, music, physical education, physics, psychology, science, social justice, social studies, sociology, Spanish, speech, theology, trigonometry, U.S. government and politics-AP, world history, world literature, world religions.

Graduation Requirements Arts and fine arts (art, music, dance, drama), electives, English, foreign language, mathematics, musical theater, physical education (includes health), religion (includes Bible studies and theology), science, social sciences, social studies (includes history), 100 hours of community service.

Special Academic Programs 8 Advanced Placement exams for which test preparation is offered; honors section; academic accommodation for the musically talented and the artistically talented.

College Admission Counseling 147 students graduated in 2010; all went to college, including Florida Gulf Coast University; Florida State University; University of Central Florida; University of Florida; University of North Florida; University of South Florida. Median SAT critical reading: 510, median SAT math: 520, median SAT writing: 518, median composite ACT: 22. 31% scored over 600 on SAT critical reading, 41% scored over 600 on SAT math, 35% scored over 600 on SAT writing, 38% scored over 26 on composite ACT.

Student Life Upper grades have specified standards of dress, student council. Discipline rests primarily with faculty. Attendance at religious services is required.

Summer Programs Advancement, sports programs offered; session focuses on math advancement/athletic camps; held on campus; accepts boys and girls; open to students from other schools. 250 students usually enrolled. 2011 schedule: June 10 to June 30. Application deadline: June 1.

Tuition and Aid Day student tuition: $7875–$10,300. Tuition installment plan (monthly payment plans, semester payment plan). Tuition reduction for siblings, merit scholarship grants, need-based scholarship grants, paying campus jobs available. In 2010–11, 15% of upper-school students received aid; total upper-school merit-scholarship money awarded: $12,250. Total amount of financial aid awarded in 2010–11: $200,000.

Admissions Traditional secondary-level entrance grade is 9. For fall 2010, 180 students applied for upper-level admission, 180 were accepted, 133 enrolled. Placement test or STS required. Deadline for receipt of application materials: none. No application fee required. On-campus interview required.

Athletics Interscholastic: baseball (boys), basketball (b,g), cheering (g), cross-country running (b,g), dance team (g), diving (b,g), football (b), golf (b,g), lacrosse (b,g), modern dance (g), soccer (b,g), softball (g), strength & conditioning (b,g), swimming and diving (b,g), track and field (b,g), volleyball (g), weight lifting (b,g), weight training (b,g); intramural: basketball (b,g), volleyball (b,g); coed intramural: volleyball. 4 PE instructors, 66 coaches, 1 athletic trainer.

Computers Computers are regularly used in art, computer applications, English, mathematics, science classes. Computer network features include on-campus library services, online commercial services, Internet access, wireless campus network. Students grades are available online. The school has a published electronic and media policy.

Contact Mrs. Joanne Mades, Registrar. 941-371-4917. Fax: 941-371-6924. E-mail: jmades@cmhs-sarasota.org. Web site: www.cmhs-sarasota.org.

CARDINAL NEWMAN HIGH SCHOOL

50 Ursuline Road
Santa Rosa, California 95403
Head of School: Mr. Mike Truesdell
General Information Boys' day college-preparatory and religious studies school, affiliated with Roman Catholic Church. Grades 9–12. Founded: 1964. Setting: suburban. Nearest major city is San Francisco. 40-acre campus. 16 buildings on campus. Approved or accredited by Western Association of Schools and Colleges, Western Catholic Education Association, and California Department of Education. Endowment: $4.3 million. Total enrollment: 447. Upper school average class size: 22. Upper school faculty-student ratio: 1:18. There are 181 required school days per year for Upper School students. Upper School students typically attend 5 days per week. The average school day consists of 6 hours and 30 minutes.

Upper School Student Profile Grade 9: 131 students (131 boys); Grade 10: 114 students (114 boys); Grade 11: 119 students (119 boys); Grade 12: 83 students (83 boys). 66% of students are Roman Catholic.

Faculty School total: 34. In upper school: 23 men, 10 women; 20 have advanced degrees.

Subjects Offered Algebra, art appreciation, biology, calculus-AP, campus ministry, chemistry, chemistry-AP, computer science, creative writing, design, desktop publishing, drama, drawing, driver education, economics, English, English-AP, environmental science, ethics, fine arts, French, geometry, health, journalism, Latin, Latin-AP, performing arts, photography, physics-AP, psychology, social justice, Spanish, Spanish-AP, theology, trigonometry, U.S. government, U.S. history, U.S. history-AP, world history, yearbook.

Graduation Requirements Arts and fine arts (art, music, dance, drama), computer science, English, foreign language, mathematics, physical education (includes health), religion (includes Bible studies and theology), science, social studies (includes history), senior service project, 20 hours of community service work per year.

Special Academic Programs 13 Advanced Placement exams for which test preparation is offered; honors section; study at local college for college credit.

College Admission Counseling 99 students graduated in 2009; all went to college, including California Polytechnic State University, San Luis Obispo; California State University; California State University, Chico; Santa Clara University; University of California, Davis; University of California, Santa Barbara. Mean SAT critical reading: 550, mean SAT math: 580, mean composite ACT: 24.

Student Life Upper grades have specified standards of dress, student council, honor system. Discipline rests equally with students and faculty. Attendance at religious services is required.

Tuition and Aid Day student tuition: $10,980. Tuition installment plan (monthly payment plans, individually arranged payment plans, monthly, quarterly, semester, and annual payment plans). Merit scholarship grants, need-based scholarship grants available. In 2009–10, 21% of upper-school students received aid. Total amount of financial aid awarded in 2009–10: $285,000.

Admissions For fall 2009, 160 students applied for upper-level admission, 140 were accepted, 133 enrolled. Scholastic Testing Service High School Placement Test and STS required. Deadline for receipt of application materials: January 13. Application fee required: $120. On-campus interview required.

Athletics Interscholastic: aquatics, baseball, basketball, cheering (g), cross-country running, diving, football, golf, ice hockey, independent competitive sports, lacrosse, rugby, soccer, swimming and diving, tennis, track and field, water polo, weight training, wrestling; intramural: baseball, basketball, fencing, soccer, table tennis, touch football, ultimate Frisbee, volleyball; coed interscholastic: cross-country running. 3 PE instructors, 21 coaches, 2 athletic trainers.

Computers Computers are regularly used in art, Bible studies, college planning, desktop publishing, economics, English, French as a second language, geography, health, history, humanities, Latin, mathematics, music, photography, religious studies, SAT preparation, science, senior seminar, social sciences, social studies, Spanish, speech, theater arts, theology, video film production, writing, yearbook classes. Computer network features include on-campus library services, online commercial services, Internet access, Internet filtering or blocking technology. Computer access in designated common areas is available to students. Students grades are available online. The school has a published electronic and media policy.

Contact Mr. Pat Piehl, Director of Enrollment. 707-546-6470 Ext. 220. Fax: 707-544-8502. E-mail: piehl@cardinalnewman.org. Web site: www.cardinalnewman.org.

CARDINAL NEWMAN HIGH SCHOOL

512 Spencer Drive
West Palm Beach, Florida 33409-3699
Head of School: Fr. David W. Carr
General Information Coeducational day college-preparatory and IB diploma school, affiliated with Roman Catholic Church. Grades 9–12. Founded: 1961. Setting: suburban. Nearest major city is Miami. 50-acre campus. 5 buildings on campus. Approved or accredited by National Catholic Education Association, Southern Association of Colleges and Schools, and Florida Department of Education. Total enrollment: 642. Upper school average class size: 25. Upper school faculty-student ratio: 1:25. There are 180 required school days per year for Upper School students. Upper School students typically attend 5 days per week. The average school day consists of 6 hours and 40 minutes.

Upper School Student Profile Grade 9: 160 students (78 boys, 82 girls); Grade 10: 144 students (64 boys, 80 girls); Grade 11: 153 students (70 boys, 83 girls); Grade 12: 185 students (95 boys, 90 girls). 80% of students are Roman Catholic.

Faculty School total: 49. In upper school: 13 men, 36 women; 39 have advanced degrees.

Subjects Offered Algebra, American government, American history, American literature, anatomy and physiology, art, band, Bible studies, biology, biology-AP, calculus, calculus-AP, chemistry, chorus, church history, college writing, computer applications, computer science, creative writing, desktop publishing, drama, economics, English, English literature, English-AP, ethics, European history, fine arts, French, French-AP, geometry, government/civics, health, history, honors algebra, honors English, honors geometry, integrated science, International Baccalaureate courses, journalism, leadership, marine biology, mathematics, music appreciation, newspaper, physical education, physics, political science, pre-calculus, probability and statistics, religion, social justice, social studies, Spanish, speech, world history, world literature, writing, yearbook.

Graduation Requirements Arts and fine arts (art, music, dance, drama), English, foreign language, mathematics, physical education (includes health), religion (includes Bible studies and theology), science, social studies (includes history), 100-hour community service requirement.

Special Academic Programs International Baccalaureate program; Advanced Placement exam preparation; honors section; study at local college for college credit; academic accommodation for the gifted; remedial reading and/or remedial writing; remedial math.

College Admission Counseling 174 students graduated in 2010; all went to college, including Florida Atlantic University; Florida State University; Palm Beach State College; University of Central Florida; University of Florida; University of North Florida.

Cardinal Newman High School

Student Life Upper grades have uniform requirement, student council, honor system. Discipline rests primarily with faculty. Attendance at religious services is required.
Summer Programs Remediation, enrichment, sports programs offered; session focuses on freshman preparation; held on campus; accepts boys and girls; not open to students from other schools. 75 students usually enrolled. 2011 schedule: June 15 to June 30.
Tuition and Aid Day student tuition: $8950–$9950. Tuition installment plan (FACTS Tuition Payment Plan). Need-based scholarship grants available. In 2010–11, 18% of upper-school students received aid.
Admissions Traditional secondary-level entrance grade is 9. STS required. Deadline for receipt of application materials: none. Application fee required: $50. On-campus interview recommended.
Athletics Interscholastic: baseball (boys), basketball (b,g), bowling (b,g), cheering (g), cross-country running (b,g), dance team (g), diving (b,g), football (b), golf (b,g), lacrosse (b,g), physical fitness (b,g), soccer (b,g), softball (g), swimming and diving (b,g), tennis (b,g), track and field (b,g), volleyball (g), wrestling (b). 2 PE instructors, 1 athletic trainer.
Computers Computers are regularly used in all academic, Bible studies, yearbook classes. Computer resources include on-campus library services, online commercial services, Internet access, Internet filtering or blocking technology. Students grades are available online. The school has a published electronic and media policy.
Contact Mrs. Jan Joy, Admissions Coordinator. 561-242-2268. Fax: 561-683-7307. E-mail: jjoy@cardinalnewman.com. Web site: www.cardinalnewman.com.

CARDINAL O'HARA HIGH SCHOOL

1701 South Sproul Road
Springfield, Pennsylvania 19064-1199
Head of School: Mrs. Marie Rogai
General Information college-preparatory school, affiliated with Roman Catholic Church. Approved or accredited by Pennsylvania Department of Education.
Admissions No application fee required.
Contact Mrs. Patti Arnold, Admissions Director. 610-544-3800 Ext. 70. Fax: 610-544-1189. E-mail: pattiarnold@cohs.com. Web site: www.cohs.com.

THE CARIBBEAN SCHOOL

1689 Calle Navarra
Urb. La Rambla
Ponce, Puerto Rico 00730-4043
Head of School: Mr. James E. DiSebastian
General Information Coeducational day college-preparatory school. Grades PK–12. Founded: 1954. Setting: suburban. 10-acre campus. 3 buildings on campus. Approved or accredited by Middle States Association of Colleges and Schools, The College Board, US Department of State, and Puerto Rico Department of Education. Member of European Council of International Schools. Total enrollment: 570. Upper school average class size: 20. Upper school faculty-student ratio: 1:7.
Faculty School total: 75. In upper school: 4 have advanced degrees.
Special Academic Programs Advanced Placement exam preparation; honors section; independent study.
College Admission Counseling 19 students graduated in 2009; all went to college.
Student Life Upper grades have uniform requirement, student council. Discipline rests primarily with faculty.
Admissions Application fee required: $25. Interview required.
Athletics 3 PE instructors.
Computers Computer resources include Internet access, Internet filtering or blocking technology. The school has a published electronic and media policy.
Contact Mrs. Mayra Bonilla, Administrative Manager. 787-843-2048 Ext. 2. Fax: 787-844-5626. E-mail: discovercs@gmail.com. Web site: www.caribbeanschool.org.

CARLISLE SCHOOL

300 Carlisle Road
Axton, Virginia 24054
Head of School: Mr. Simon A. Owen-Williams
General Information Coeducational boarding and day college-preparatory, International Baccalaureate (IB), and IB Middle Years Program school. Boarding grades 9–12, day grades PK–12. Founded: 1968. Setting: rural. Nearest major city is Danville. Students are housed in single-sex dormitories. 50-acre campus. 5 buildings on campus. Approved or accredited by International Baccalaureate Organization, Southern Association of Colleges and Schools, Virginia Association of Independent Schools, and Virginia Department of Education. Member of National Association of Independent Schools. Endowment: $1.5 million. Total enrollment: 484. Upper school average class size: 16. Upper school faculty-student ratio: 1:10.
Upper School Student Profile Grade 9: 31 students (21 boys, 10 girls); Grade 10: 34 students (20 boys, 14 girls); Grade 11: 49 students (26 boys, 23 girls); Grade 12: 41 students (24 boys, 17 girls). 5% of students are boarding students. 70% are state residents. 2 states are represented in upper school student body. 19% are international students. International students from China, Nigeria, Republic of Korea, Taiwan, and Viet Nam.

Faculty School total: 59. In upper school: 1 man, 20 women; 9 have advanced degrees; 1 resides on campus.
Subjects Offered Advanced computer applications, advanced math, Advanced Placement courses, algebra, American government, American history, American history-AP, American literature, art, art history, arts, band, biology, biology-AP, calculus, calculus-AP, chemistry, chemistry-AP, choir, composition-AP, computer information systems, computer programming, computer science, computer science-AP, concert band, creative dance, creative drama, creative writing, dance, drama, earth science, economics, economics-AP, English, English language and composition-AP, English literature, English literature and composition-AP, English literature-AP, fine arts, geography, geometry, government, government/civics, grammar, health, health and wellness, history, history of the Americas, honors algebra, honors English, honors geometry, independent study, International Baccalaureate courses, intro to computers, jazz band, jazz ensemble, journalism, lab science, madrigals, mathematics, mathematics-AP, Microsoft, music, physical education, physics, physics-AP, play production, pre-algebra, pre-calculus, psychology, psychology-AP, publications, science, senior project, sex education, social studies, Spanish, Spanish literature, Spanish-AP, speech, statistics, statistics-AP, studio art, theater, theory of knowledge, U.S. government and politics-AP, U.S. history-AP, wind ensemble, world civilizations, world history, world history-AP, World War I, World War II, world wide web design, yearbook.
Graduation Requirements Advanced math, algebra, arts and fine arts (art, music, dance, drama), computer science, electives, English, foreign language, mathematics, physical education (includes health), science, social studies (includes history), U.S. and Virginia history, U.S. government, community and service, senior project.
Special Academic Programs International Baccalaureate program; Advanced Placement exam preparation; honors section; independent study; term-away projects; study at local college for college credit; ESL (17 students enrolled).
College Admission Counseling 30 students graduated in 2009; all went to college, including Hampden-Sydney College; Penn State Erie, The Behrend College; The College of William and Mary; University of Virginia; Virginia Polytechnic Institute and State University; Wake Forest University. Median SAT critical reading: 546, median SAT math: 540, median SAT writing: 526. 33% scored over 600 on SAT critical reading, 37% scored over 600 on SAT math, 33% scored over 600 on SAT writing.
Student Life Upper grades have specified standards of dress, student council, honor system. Discipline rests equally with students and faculty.
Tuition and Aid Day student tuition: $8950. Tuition installment plan (Insured Tuition Payment Plan, FACTS Tuition Payment Plan). Need-based scholarship grants available. In 2009–10, 50% of upper-school students received aid. Total amount of financial aid awarded in 2009–10: $112,000.
Admissions Traditional secondary-level entrance grade is 9. For fall 2009, 145 students applied for upper-level admission, 111 were accepted, 98 enrolled. Nelson-Denny Reading Test, Woodcock-Johnson or writing sample required. Deadline for receipt of application materials: none. Application fee required: $50. On-campus interview required.
Athletics Interscholastic: basketball (boys, girls), cheering (g), field hockey (g), football (b), soccer (b,g), softball (g), tennis (b,g), volleyball (g); intramural: basketball (b,g), cheering (g), softball (g); coed interscholastic: baseball, cross-country running, dance, fencing, golf; coed intramural: aerobics/Nautilus, basketball, Frisbee, weight lifting. 2 PE instructors, 12 coaches.
Computers Computers are regularly used in all academic classes. Computer network features include on-campus library services, online commercial services, Internet access, wireless campus network, Internet filtering or blocking technology. Campus intranet is available to students. The school has a published electronic and media policy.
Contact Mrs. Celeste Graves, Admissions Assistant. 276-632-7288 Ext. 221. Fax: 276-632-9545. E-mail: cgraves@carlisleschool.org. Web site: www.carlisleschool.org.

CARLUCCI AMERICAN INTERNATIONAL SCHOOL OF LISBON

Rua António dos Reis, 95
Linhó, Sintra 2710-301, Portugal
Head of School: Ms. Blannie M. Curtis
General Information Coeducational day college-preparatory and Portuguese Equivalência Program school. Grades PK–12. Founded: 1956. Setting: small town. Nearest major city is Lisbon, Portugal. 4-hectare campus. 4 buildings on campus. Approved or accredited by European Council of International Schools, International Baccalaureate Organization, New England Association of Schools and Colleges, US Department of State, and state department of education. Language of instruction: English. Total enrollment: 523. Upper school average class size: 15. Upper school faculty-student ratio: 1:8. There are 180 required school days per year for Upper School students. Upper School students typically attend 5 days per week. The average school day consists of 5 hours and 30 minutes.
Upper School Student Profile Grade 9: 47 students (22 boys, 25 girls); Grade 10: 39 students (20 boys, 19 girls); Grade 11: 31 students (17 boys, 14 girls); Grade 12: 45 students (30 boys, 15 girls).

Faculty School total: 64. In upper school: 19 men, 16 women; 11 have advanced degrees.

Subjects Offered Algebra, art, biology, business studies, chemistry, choir, computer applications, computer art, economics, English, European history, French, geography, geometry, International Baccalaureate courses, journalism, model United Nations, modern civilization, music, physical education, physics, Portuguese, Portuguese literature, SAT preparation, Spanish, theory of knowledge, U.S. history, U.S. literature, writing workshop, yearbook.

Graduation Requirements Arts and fine arts (art, music, dance, drama), computer science, electives, English, foreign language, mathematics, physical education (includes health), science, social studies (includes history), International Baccalaureate diploma candidates have to complete 150 Community Action Service hours, plus Theory of Knowledge and Extended Essay.

Special Academic Programs International Baccalaureate program; honors section; independent study; academic accommodation for the gifted; remedial reading and/or remedial writing; remedial math; programs in general development for dyslexic students; ESL (57 students enrolled).

College Admission Counseling 27 students graduated in 2010; 26 went to college, including Amherst College; Boston University; California State University, Fullerton; Rensselaer Polytechnic Institute; Rollins College; Suffolk University. Other: 1 had other specific plans. Median SAT critical reading: 580, median SAT math: 565, median SAT writing: 600, median combined SAT: 1785.

Student Life Upper grades have specified standards of dress, student council. Discipline rests equally with students and faculty.

Tuition and Aid Day student tuition: €7064–€16,480. Tuition installment plan (monthly payment plans, individually arranged payment plans, early payment discount, quarterly payment plan). Tuition reduction for siblings, merit scholarship grants, need-based scholarship grants, merit-based scholarships are available to student residents in Sintra, Portugal only available. In 2010–11, 7% of upper-school students received aid; total upper-school merit-scholarship money awarded: €115,072.

Admissions English for Non-native Speakers or Math Placement Exam required. Deadline for receipt of application materials: none. No application fee required. Interview recommended.

Athletics Interscholastic: basketball (boys, girls), cross-country running (b,g), soccer (b,g), track and field (b,g), volleyball (b,g); intramural: basketball (b,g), soccer (b,g); coed intramural: golf, volleyball. 4 PE instructors, 12 coaches.

Computers Computers are regularly used in computer applications, digital applications, graphic design classes. Computer resources include on-campus library services, Internet access, wireless campus network, Internet filtering or blocking technology. Campus intranet and computer access in designated common areas are available to students. Students grades are available online. The school has a published electronic and media policy.

Contact Ms. Cynthia Ferrell, Enrollment Coordinator. 351-21-923-9800. Fax: 351-21-923-9809. E-mail: admissions@caislisbon.org. Web site: www.caislisbon.org.

CARMEL HIGH SCHOOL

One Carmel Parkway
Mundelein, Illinois 60060-2499
Head of School: Judith Mucheck, PhD

General Information Coeducational day college-preparatory, arts, business, religious studies, and technology school, affiliated with Roman Catholic Church. Grades 9–12. Founded: 1962. Setting: suburban. Nearest major city is Libertyville. 45-acre campus. 1 building on campus. Approved or accredited by National Catholic Education Association, North Central Association of Colleges and Schools, and Illinois Department of Education. Total enrollment: 1,370. Upper school average class size: 25. Upper school faculty-student ratio: 1:16.

Upper School Student Profile 90% of students are Roman Catholic.

Faculty School total: 90. In upper school: 33 men, 57 women; 63 have advanced degrees.

Subjects Offered 20th century world history, accounting, advanced chemistry, advanced math, Advanced Placement courses, advanced studio art-AP, algebra, American government, American history, American literature, American literature-AP, anatomy and physiology, art, athletic training, band, biology, biology-AP, biotechnology, botany, British literature, British literature (honors), business, calculus, calculus-AP, chemistry, chemistry-AP, choir, choral music, chorus, community service, computer applications, computer programming, computer programming-AP, concert band, drama, drama performance, drawing, economics, English, English composition, English language and composition-AP, English literature, English literature-AP, European history-AP, French, French language-AP, French-AP, geography, geometry, government, government-AP, history of religion, honors algebra, honors English, honors geometry, honors U.S. history, honors world history, instrumental music, Internet research, intro to computers, jazz band, journalism, Latin, Latin-AP, marching band, music, music composition, music theory-AP, orchestra, performing arts, physical education, physical science, physics, physics-AP, pre-algebra, pre-calculus, probability and statistics, psychology, reading/study skills, religion, religious education, scripture, sociology, Spanish, strings, student government, student publications, student teaching, studio art, studio art-AP, theater arts, trigonometry, U.S. government and politics-AP, U.S. history, U.S.

history-AP, Web site design, wind ensemble, women spirituality and faith, world history, world history-AP, world literature, yearbook, zoology.

Graduation Requirements Ministry requirement, 20 hours of ministry service per semester.

Special Academic Programs Honors section; special instructional classes for deaf students, blind students.

College Admission Counseling 320 students graduated in 2010; 316 went to college, including Marquette University; Purdue University; The University of Iowa; University of Illinois at Urbana–Champaign. Other: 1 went to work, 3 entered military service. Mean composite ACT: 25.

Student Life Upper grades have specified standards of dress, student council. Discipline rests primarily with faculty. Attendance at religious services is required.

Summer Programs Enrichment, advancement, sports, art/fine arts, computer instruction programs offered; session focuses on courses for enrolled students; held on campus; accepts boys and girls; not open to students from other schools. 200 students usually enrolled. 2011 schedule: June 9 to July 2. Application deadline: May 8.

Tuition and Aid Day student tuition: $8460. Tuition installment plan (FACTS Tuition Payment Plan). Merit scholarship grants, need-based scholarship grants available. In 2010–11, 10% of upper-school students received aid; total upper-school merit-scholarship money awarded: $16,000. Total amount of financial aid awarded in 2010–11: $82,000.

Admissions Traditional secondary-level entrance grade is 9. Explore required. Deadline for receipt of application materials: January 29. Application fee required: $350.

Athletics Interscholastic: baseball (boys), basketball (b,g), cheering (g), cross-country running (b,g), football (b), golf (b,g), gymnastics (g), ice hockey (b), pom squad (g), soccer (b,g), softball (g), tennis (b,g), track and field (b,g), volleyball (b,g), wrestling (b); intramural: basketball (b,g); coed intramural: Frisbee, volleyball, winter soccer, yoga.

Computers Computers are regularly used in all classes. Computer resources include on-campus library services, Internet access. Students grades are available online. The school has a published electronic and media policy.

Contact Mr. Brian Stith, Director of Admissions. 847-388-3320. Fax: 847-566-8465. E-mail: bstith@carmelhs.org. Web site: www.carmelhs.org.

CAROLINA DAY SCHOOL

1345 Hendersonville Road
Asheville, North Carolina 28803
Head of School: Beverly H. Sgro, PhD

General Information Coeducational day college-preparatory school. Grades PK–12. Founded: 1987. Setting: suburban. 60-acre campus. 9 buildings on campus. Approved or accredited by North Carolina Association of Independent Schools, Southern Association of Colleges and Schools, Southern Association of Independent Schools, and North Carolina Department of Education. Member of National Association of Independent Schools. Endowment: $2.7 million. Total enrollment: 662. Upper school average class size: 17. There are 180 required school days per year for Upper School students. Upper School students typically attend 5 days per week.

Upper School Student Profile Grade 9: 49 students (22 boys, 27 girls); Grade 10: 55 students (26 boys, 29 girls); Grade 11: 36 students (13 boys, 23 girls); Grade 12: 43 students (20 boys, 23 girls).

Faculty In upper school: 10 men, 19 women; 18 have advanced degrees.

Subjects Offered Acting, advanced chemistry, advanced studio art-AP, algebra, American literature, art history, art history-AP, biology, biology-AP, calculus, calculus-AP, ceramics, chemistry, chemistry-AP, chorus, CPR, creative writing, debate, ecology, English, English language and composition-AP, English literature, environmental science-AP, European history-AP, fiction, French, French-AP, functions, geometry, global studies, history, jewelry making, language and composition, linear algebra, linguistics, literature, literature and composition-AP, Mandarin, martial arts, music theory, music theory-AP, philosophy, photography, physical education, physics, physics-AP, pre-calculus, psychology-AP, reading/study skills, research, science, Shakespeare, Spanish, Spanish-AP, speech, statistics-AP, studio art, theater, U.S. government and politics-AP, U.S. history, U.S. history-AP, world literature.

Graduation Requirements Algebra, arts and fine arts (art, music, dance, drama), biology, chemistry, electives, English, geometry, global studies, history, modern languages, physical education (includes health), public speaking, social studies (includes history), U.S. history, CPR/First Aid (non-credit class).

Special Academic Programs 17 Advanced Placement exams for which test preparation is offered; honors section; independent study.

College Admission Counseling 39 students graduated in 2009; 38 went to college, including Appalachian State University; East Carolina University; North Carolina State University; The University of North Carolina at Chapel Hill; Yale University. Other: 1 had other specific plans. Median SAT critical reading: 630, median SAT math: 620, median SAT writing: 625, median combined SAT: 1800. 68% scored over 600 on SAT critical reading, 58% scored over 600 on SAT math, 58% scored over 600 on SAT writing, 58% scored over 1800 on combined SAT.

Student Life Upper grades have specified standards of dress, student council, honor system. Discipline rests equally with students and faculty.

Tuition and Aid Day student tuition: $16,860–$18,140. Tuition installment plan (Insured Tuition Payment Plan, FACTS Tuition Payment Plan, monthly payment plans, individually arranged payment plans, 1-payment plan or 2-installments plan (August and January)). Merit scholarship grants, need-based scholarship grants available.

Admissions Traditional secondary-level entrance grade is 9. ERB, ISEE, PSAT or SAT or SSAT required. Deadline for receipt of application materials: none. Application fee required: $100. On-campus interview required.

Athletics Interscholastic: baseball (boys), basketball (b,g), cross-country running (b,g), field hockey (g), martial arts (b,g), soccer (b,g), swimming and diving (b,g), tennis (b,g), track and field (b,g), volleyball (g); coed interscholastic: golf; coed intramural: basketball, kickball, soccer, touch football, volleyball. 2 PE instructors, 23 coaches, 1 athletic trainer.

Computers Computers are regularly used in all academic classes. Computer network features include on-campus library services, online commercial services, Internet access, wireless campus network, Internet filtering or blocking technology. Student e-mail accounts and computer access in designated common areas are available to students.

Contact Robin Goertz, Director of Admissions. 828-274-0757. Fax: 828-274-0756. E-mail: admissions@cdschool.org. Web site: www.cdschool.org.

CARONDELET HIGH SCHOOL

1133 Winton Drive
Concord, California 94518
Head of School: Teresa Hurlbut, EdD

General Information Girls' day college-preparatory, arts, religious studies, and technology school, affiliated with Roman Catholic Church. Grades 9–12. Founded: 1965. Setting: suburban. Nearest major city is Oakland. 9-acre campus. 5 buildings on campus. Approved or accredited by Western Association of Schools and Colleges. Total enrollment: 800. Upper school average class size: 30. Upper school faculty-student ratio: 1:25.

Upper School Student Profile Grade 9: 200 students (200 girls); Grade 10: 200 students (200 girls); Grade 11: 200 students (200 girls); Grade 12: 200 students (200 girls). 90% of students are Roman Catholic.

Faculty School total: 61. In upper school: 13 men, 48 women; 30 have advanced degrees.

Subjects Offered Algebra, American studies, animation, architectural drawing, art, band, biology, calculus, calculus-AP, cartooning/animation, chemistry, chorus, church history, civics, community service, computer applications, concert band, concert choir, creative writing, criminal justice, dance, design, drafting, drawing, economics, English, English-AP, ethics, finite math, fitness, French, geometry, government-AP, health, honors algebra, honors English, honors geometry, Italian, jazz band, journalism, Latin, marching band, marine biology, music history, music theory, musical theater, orchestra, painting, physical education, physics, physics-AP, physiology, pre-algebra, pre-calculus, psychology, psychology-AP, relationships, sculpture, Spanish, Spanish-AP, sports medicine, statistics, studio art-AP, technical drawing, transition mathematics, U.S. history, U.S. history-AP, water color painting, Web site design, women's health, world arts, world civilizations, world religions, writing, yearbook.

Graduation Requirements Computer literacy, English, mathematics, modern languages, physical education (includes health), religious studies, science, social studies (includes history), visual and performing arts.

Special Academic Programs 12 Advanced Placement exams for which test preparation is offered; honors section; independent study; academic accommodation for the gifted.

College Admission Counseling 200 students graduated in 2009; 198 went to college, including California Polytechnic State University, San Luis Obispo; California State University, Chico; University of California, Berkeley. Other: 2 went to work. Mean SAT critical reading: 548, mean SAT math: 538, mean SAT writing: 556, mean composite ACT: 24.

Student Life Upper grades have uniform requirement, honor system. Discipline rests primarily with faculty. Attendance at religious services is required.

Tuition and Aid Day student tuition: $12,700. Tuition installment plan (monthly payment plans, prepayment plan, semester or quarterly payment plans). Need-based scholarship grants, paying campus jobs available. In 2009–10, 17% of upper-school students received aid.

Admissions Traditional secondary-level entrance grade is 9. For fall 2009, 380 students applied for upper-level admission, 240 were accepted, 220 enrolled. High School Placement Test required. Deadline for receipt of application materials: December 7. Application fee required: $75. On-campus interview recommended.

Athletics Interscholastic: aquatics, basketball, cheering, combined training, cross-country running, dance squad, dance team, diving, golf, lacrosse, soccer, softball, swimming and diving, tennis, volleyball, water polo; intramural: badminton, basketball, broomball, flag football, physical fitness, physical training, touch football, volleyball. 3 PE instructors, 40 coaches, 1 athletic trainer.

Computers Computers are regularly used in computer applications classes. Computer resources include on-campus library services, Internet access, wireless campus network, Internet filtering or blocking technology. Student e-mail accounts are available to students. Students grades are available online. The school has a published electronic and media policy.

Contact Ms. Kathy Harris, Director of Admissions. 925-686-5353 Ext. 161. Fax: 925-671-9429. E-mail: kharris@carondeleths.org. Web site: www.carondelet.pvt.k12.ca.us/.

CARROLLTON SCHOOL OF THE SACRED HEART

3747 Main Highway
Miami, Florida 33133
Head of School: Sr. Suzanne Cooke

General Information Girls' day college-preparatory, arts, religious studies, bilingual studies, and technology school, affiliated with Roman Catholic Church. Grades PK–12. Founded: 1961. Setting: urban. 17-acre campus. 5 buildings on campus. Approved or accredited by Florida Council of Independent Schools, Network of Sacred Heart Schools, and Southern Association of Colleges and Schools. Endowment: $2 million. Total enrollment: 775. Upper school average class size: 16. Upper school faculty-student ratio: 1:9.

Upper School Student Profile Grade 6: 48 students (48 girls); Grade 7: 45 students (45 girls); Grade 8: 48 students (48 girls); Grade 9: 64 students (64 girls); Grade 10: 64 students (64 girls); Grade 11: 80 students (80 girls); Grade 12: 73 students (73 girls). 87% of students are Roman Catholic.

Faculty School total: 74. In upper school: 9 men, 24 women; 20 have advanced degrees.

Subjects Offered Algebra, American history, American literature, anatomy and physiology, art, art history, Bible studies, biology, British literature, calculus, chemistry, computer science, debate, drama, earth systems analysis, economics, English, English literature, environmental science, ethics, expository writing, fine arts, French, general science, geometry, government/civics, grammar, health, history, humanities, journalism, mathematics, music, photography, physical education, physical science, physics, pre-calculus, psychology, religion, science, scripture, social sciences, social studies, Spanish, speech, theater, trigonometry, vocal ensemble, world history, world literature.

Graduation Requirements Arts and fine arts (art, music, dance, drama), computer science, English, foreign language, mathematics, physical education (includes health), religion (includes Bible studies and theology), science, social studies (includes history). Community service is required.

Special Academic Programs International Baccalaureate program; Advanced Placement exam preparation; honors section; independent study; study at local college for college credit; domestic exchange program; study abroad.

College Admission Counseling 66 students graduated in 2010; all went to college, including Boston College; Massachusetts Institute of Technology; Northwestern University; University of Miami; Vanderbilt University. Median SAT math: 590, median composite ACT: 24. Mean SAT critical reading: 590. 51% scored over 600 on SAT critical reading, 47% scored over 600 on SAT math, 30% scored over 26 on composite ACT.

Student Life Upper grades have uniform requirement, student council, honor system. Discipline rests primarily with faculty. Attendance at religious services is required.

Tuition and Aid Day student tuition: $23,150. Tuition installment plan (Insured Tuition Payment Plan, monthly payment plans). Merit scholarship grants, need-based scholarship grants available. In 2010–11, 25% of upper-school students received aid; total upper-school merit-scholarship money awarded: $45,000. Total amount of financial aid awarded in 2010–11: $920,000.

Admissions Traditional secondary-level entrance grade is 9. For fall 2010, 132 students applied for upper-level admission, 37 were accepted, 30 enrolled. Admissions testing or ISEE required. Deadline for receipt of application materials: February 1. Application fee required: $100. On-campus interview required.

Athletics Interscholastic: aquatics, basketball, crew, cross-country running, golf, sailing, soccer, softball, swimming and diving, tennis, track and field, volleyball, water polo, winter soccer. 4 PE instructors, 8 coaches.

Computers Computers are regularly used in all academic classes. Computer network features include on-campus library services, online commercial services, Internet access, laptop program. The school has a published electronic and media policy.

Contact Ms. Ana J. Roye, Director of Admission and Financial Aid. 305-446-5673 Ext. 1224. Fax: 305-446-4160. E-mail: aroye@carrollton.org. Web site: www.carrollton.org.

CARY ACADEMY

1500 North Harrison Avenue
Cary, North Carolina 27513
Head of School: Mr. Donald S. Berger

General Information Coeducational day college-preparatory, arts, and technology school. Grades 6–12. Founded: 1996. Setting: suburban. Nearest major city is Raleigh. 55-acre campus. 6 buildings on campus. Approved or accredited by North Carolina Association of Independent Schools, Southern Association of Colleges and Schools, Southern Association of Independent Schools, and North Carolina Department of Education. Total enrollment: 710. Upper school average class size: 14. Upper school faculty-student ratio: 1:14. Upper School students typically attend 5 days per week. The average school day consists of 7 hours and 10 minutes.

Upper School Student Profile Grade 9: 104 students (54 boys, 50 girls); Grade 10: 106 students (61 boys, 45 girls); Grade 11: 100 students (52 boys, 48 girls); Grade 12: 98 students (45 boys, 53 girls).

Faculty School total: 77. In upper school: 29 men, 19 women; 38 have advanced degrees.

Subjects Offered Advanced Placement courses, algebra, American history, American history-AP, American literature, American literature-AP, anatomy and physiology, biology, biology-AP, calculus, calculus-AP, ceramics, chamber groups, chemistry, chemistry-AP, Chinese, computer programming, computer programming-AP, concert choir, debate, digital photography, drawing, economics, economics-AP, environmental science, environmental science-AP, film studies, forensics, French language-AP, French literature-AP, French-AP, genetics, geometry, German, German literature, German-AP, health education, instruments, jazz band, journalism, modern European history-AP, multimedia design, music composition, music theory, music theory-AP, orchestra, painting, photography, physical education, physics, physics-AP, pre-calculus, probability and statistics, programming, Spanish language-AP, Spanish literature, Spanish literature-AP, Spanish-AP, statistics-AP, studio art, studio art-AP, technical theater, theater production, trigonometry, U.S. government and politics-AP, video, voice, Web site design, wind ensemble, world arts, world history, world literature, yearbook.

Graduation Requirements Algebra, American history, American literature, biology, chemistry, foreign language, physical education (includes health), physics, world history, world literature.

Special Academic Programs Advanced Placement exam preparation; honors section; independent study; academic accommodation for the gifted, the musically talented, and the artistically talented.

College Admission Counseling 99 students graduated in 2010; all went to college, including Duke University; North Carolina State University; Princeton University; The University of North Carolina at Chapel Hill; The University of North Carolina Wilmington; University of Maryland, College Park. Mean SAT critical reading: 646, mean SAT math: 647, mean SAT writing: 639, mean combined SAT: 1932.

Student Life Upper grades have specified standards of dress, student council, honor system. Discipline rests equally with students and faculty.

Admissions Traditional secondary-level entrance grade is 9. For fall 2010, 82 students applied for upper-level admission, 50 were accepted, 37 enrolled. Achievement/Aptitude/Writing, ERB CTP IV or ISEE required. Deadline for receipt of application materials: none. Application fee required: $110. Interview required.

Athletics Interscholastic: aquatics (boys, girls), baseball (b), basketball (b,g), cheering (b,g), cross-country running (b,g), field hockey (g), golf (b), lacrosse (b), soccer (b,g), softball (g), swimming and diving (b,g), tennis (b,g), track and field (b,g), volleyball (g), wrestling (g); intramural: baseball (b), basketball (b,g), cooperative games (b,g), dance (b,g), dance squad (g), fitness (b,g), fitness walking (b,g), Fives (b,g), floor hockey (b,g), indoor soccer (b,g), modern dance (g), soccer (b,g), softball (g), strength & conditioning (b,g), tennis (b,g), touch football (b,g), track and field (b,g), ultimate Frisbee (b,g), volleyball (b,g), walking (b,g), weight lifting (b,g); coed intramural: aerobics, aerobics/dance, aerobics/Nautilus, badminton, basketball, billiards, bowling, cooperative games, dance, fitness, fitness walking, Fives, floor hockey, Frisbee, golf, gymnastics, handball, indoor soccer, jogging, jump rope, kickball, martial arts, modern dance, Newcombe ball, physical fitness, running, soccer, strength & conditioning, table tennis, tai chi, tennis, touch football, track and field, ultimate Frisbee, volleyball, walking, weight lifting, weight training, winter walking. 4 PE instructors, 40 coaches, 1 athletic trainer.

Computers Computers are regularly used in all academic, animation, desktop publishing, drawing and design, independent study, media arts, media production, music, theater arts, video film production, yearbook classes. Computer network features include on-campus library services, online commercial services, Internet access, wireless campus network, Internet filtering or blocking technology, each student is issued a free laptop computer. Campus intranet, student e-mail accounts, and computer access in designated common areas are available to students. Students grades are available online. The school has a published electronic and media policy.

Contact Ms. Denise Goodman, Director of Admissions. 919-228-4550. Fax: 919-677-4002. E-mail: denise_goodman@caryacademy.org. Web site: www.caryacademy.org.

CASADY SCHOOL

9500 North Pennsylvania Avenue
PO Box 20390
Oklahoma City, Oklahoma 73120

Head of School: Mr. Chris C. Bright

General Information Coeducational day college-preparatory school, affiliated with Episcopal Church. Grades PK–12. Founded: 1947. Setting: suburban. 80-acre campus. 29 buildings on campus. Approved or accredited by Independent Schools Association of the Southwest, National Independent Private Schools Association, Southwest Association of Episcopal Schools, and The College Board. Member of National Association of Independent Schools and Secondary School Admission Test Board. Endowment: $16 million. Total enrollment: 871. Upper school average class size: 15. Upper school faculty-student ratio: 1:15.

Upper School Student Profile Grade 6: 68 students (37 boys, 31 girls); Grade 7: 47 students (32 boys, 15 girls); Grade 8: 50 students (27 boys, 23 girls); Grade 9: 67

students (37 boys, 30 girls); Grade 10: 79 students (33 boys, 46 girls); Grade 11: 79 students (31 boys, 48 girls); Grade 12: 75 students (44 boys, 31 girls). 30% of students are members of Episcopal Church.

Faculty School total: 115. In upper school: 32 men, 21 women; 35 have advanced degrees.

Subjects Offered African-American studies, algebra, American history, American literature, art, art history, Asian history, athletic training, band, Bible studies, biochemistry, biology, biology-AP, British literature, calculus, calculus-AP, ceramics, chemistry, chemistry-AP, Chinese, choir, choral music, college counseling, college placement, college planning, computer applications, computer programming, computer science, creative writing, data processing, digital imaging, drama, drama performance, drawing, driver education, earth science, economics, English, English language-AP, English literature, English literature-AP, environmental science, European history, expository writing, fine arts, French, French language-AP, French literature-AP, freshman seminar, functions, geology, geometry, German, government/civics, grammar, Greek, health, history, human anatomy, journalism, Latin, Latin-AP, mathematics, Middle Eastern history, modern languages, music, mythology, Native American history, painting, photography, physical education, physics, physiology, religion, Russian history, science, social studies, Spanish, Spanish language-AP, Spanish literature-AP, speech, statistics, theater, theology, trigonometry, U.S. history-AP, water color painting, weight training, word processing, world history, world literature, writing, yearbook.

Graduation Requirements Arts and fine arts (art, music, dance, drama), computer science, English, foreign language, mathematics, physical education (includes health), science, social studies (includes history), service learning.

Special Academic Programs Advanced Placement exam preparation; independent study; study abroad; academic accommodation for the gifted, the musically talented, and the artistically talented.

College Admission Counseling 83 students graduated in 2009; all went to college, including Brown University; Dartmouth College; Duke University; Oklahoma State University; University of Oklahoma; Vassar College. Median SAT critical reading: 625, median SAT math: 630, median SAT writing: 608, median combined SAT: 1255. 55% scored over 600 on SAT critical reading, 55% scored over 600 on SAT math.

Student Life Upper grades have specified standards of dress, student council, honor system. Discipline rests equally with students and faculty. Attendance at religious services is required.

Tuition and Aid Day student tuition: $6750–$14,850. Tuition installment plan (The Tuition Plan, Insured Tuition Payment Plan, FACTS Tuition Payment Plan, monthly payment plans, individually arranged payment plans, 2-installment plan). Merit scholarship grants, need-based scholarship grants available. In 2009–10, 11% of upper-school students received aid; total upper-school merit-scholarship money awarded: $4000. Total amount of financial aid awarded in 2009–10: $400,000.

Admissions Traditional secondary-level entrance grade is 9. For fall 2009, 60 students applied for upper-level admission, 45 were accepted, 27 enrolled. CTP and school's own exam required. Deadline for receipt of application materials: none. Application fee required: $50. On-campus interview required.

Athletics Interscholastic: baseball (boys), basketball (b,g), cheering (g), cross-country running (b,g), field hockey (g), football (b), golf (b,g), soccer (b,g), softball (g), swimming and diving (b,g), tennis (b,g), track and field (b,g), volleyball (b,g), wrestling (b); intramural: aerobics/dance (g), dance (g), martial arts (b,g), modern dance (g), physical fitness (b,g), physical training (b,g); coed intramural: aerobics, bowling, climbing, fencing, fitness walking, racquetball, sailing, weight lifting, yoga. 9 PE instructors, 23 coaches, 2 athletic trainers.

Computers Computers are regularly used in all academic classes. Computer resources include on-campus library services, Internet access.

Contact Mrs. Lori Collins, Admission Office Coordinator. 405-749-3185. Fax: 405-749-3223. E-mail: collinsl@casady.org. Web site: www.casady.org.

CASCADE CHRISTIAN ACADEMY

600 North Western Avenue
Wenatchee, Washington 98801

Head of School: Mr. Brian Harris

General Information Coeducational day college-preparatory, arts, business, vocational, religious studies, bilingual studies, and technology school, affiliated with Seventh-day Adventist Church. Grades K–12. Founded: 1905. Setting: small town. Nearest major city is Seattle. 15-acre campus. 1 building on campus. Approved or accredited by Northwest Association of Schools and Colleges and Washington Department of Education. Endowment: $25,000. Total enrollment: 146. Upper school average class size: 10. Upper school faculty-student ratio: 1:5. There are 180 required school days per year for Upper School students. Upper School students typically attend 5 days per week. The average school day consists of 7 hours and 10 minutes.

Upper School Student Profile Grade 6: 13 students (7 boys, 6 girls); Grade 7: 11 students (6 boys, 5 girls); Grade 8: 9 students (3 boys, 6 girls); Grade 9: 11 students (3 boys, 8 girls); Grade 10: 9 students (4 boys, 5 girls); Grade 11: 9 students (6 boys, 3 girls); Grade 12: 9 students (4 boys, 5 girls). 45% of students are Seventh-day Adventists.

Faculty School total: 9. In upper school: 4 men, 3 women; 5 have advanced degrees.

Subjects Offered Accounting, algebra, American history, anatomy and physiology, arts, band, Bible, biology, calculus, chemistry, choir, computer science, drama, earth science, English, fine arts, foreign language, geometry, history, marine biology, mathematics, physical education, physics, science, social studies, world history.

Graduation Requirements Arts and fine arts (art, music, dance, drama), Bible, computer science, English, foreign language, mathematics, physical education (includes health), science, social studies (includes history).

Special Academic Programs Accelerated programs; independent study; remedial reading and/or remedial writing; remedial math; programs in English, mathematics, general development for dyslexic students.

College Admission Counseling 15 students graduated in 2010; 13 went to college, including Walla Walla University. Other: 2 went to work. Median SAT critical reading: 515, median SAT math: 495, median composite ACT: 19. 11% scored over 600 on SAT critical reading, 11% scored over 600 on SAT math.

Student Life Upper grades have uniform requirement, student council, honor system. Discipline rests primarily with faculty. Attendance at religious services is required.

Tuition and Aid Day student tuition: $6942. Tuition installment plan (monthly payment plans, individually arranged payment plans). Tuition reduction for siblings, need-based scholarship grants, paying campus jobs, church subsidy available. Total amount of financial aid awarded in 2010–11: $119,000.

Admissions Traditional secondary-level entrance grade is 10. For fall 2010, 10 students applied for upper-level admission, 10 were accepted, 10 enrolled. Deadline for receipt of application materials: none. Application fee required: $50. Interview required.

Athletics Interscholastic: basketball (boys, girls), volleyball (g); coed interscholastic: flag football, soccer; coed intramural: fitness, flag football, floor hockey, ice hockey, ice skating, skiing (downhill), snowboarding, soccer, softball, volleyball, weight training. 1 PE instructor, 4 coaches.

Computers Computers are regularly used in accounting, career education, desktop publishing, English, mathematics, publications classes. Computer network features include online commercial services, Internet access.

Contact Mrs. Ayrin Harris, Administrative Assistant/Registrar. 509-662-2723 Ext. 10. Fax: 509-662-5892. E-mail: ayrin.harris@ccawenatchee.org. Web site: ccawenatchee.org.

CASCADES ACADEMY OF CENTRAL OREGON

2150 NE Studio Road
Suite 2
Bend, Oregon 97701
Head of School: Blair Jenkins

General Information Distance learning only college-preparatory and experiential education school. Distance learning grades K–12. Founded: 2003. Setting: suburban. 1 building on campus. Approved or accredited by Northwest Accreditation Commission and Oregon Department of Education. Total enrollment: 109. Upper school average class size: 6. Upper school faculty-student ratio: 1:6. There are 168 required school days per year for Upper School students. Upper School students typically attend 5 days per week. The average school day consists of 7 hours and 15 minutes.

Upper School Student Profile Grade 6: 9 students (6 boys, 3 girls); Grade 7: 15 students (5 boys, 10 girls); Grade 8: 7 students (4 boys, 3 girls); Grade 9: 5 students (5 boys); Grade 10: 1 student (1 girl); Grade 12: 6 students (1 boy, 5 girls).

Faculty School total: 21. In upper school: 3 men, 3 women; 3 have advanced degrees.

Graduation Requirements 3-dimensional art, Internship.

College Admission Counseling 3 students graduated in 2010; all went to college.

Student Life Upper grades have honor system. Discipline rests primarily with faculty.

Tuition and Aid Day student tuition: $10,875. Tuition installment plan (monthly payment plans). Need-based scholarship grants available.

Admissions Traditional secondary-level entrance grade is 9. For fall 2010, 54 students applied for upper-level admission, 48 were accepted, 37 enrolled. Deadline for receipt of application materials: none. Application fee required: $50. On-campus interview required.

Computers The school has a published electronic and media policy.

Contact 541-382-0699. Fax: 541-382-0225. Web site: http://www.cascadesacademy.org/.

CASCADILLA SCHOOL

116 Summit Street
Ithaca, New York 14850
Head of School: Patricia T. Kendall

General Information Coeducational boarding and day college-preparatory, arts, bilingual studies, and English/language arts (The Cascadilla Seminar/Cornell Univ.) school. Grades 9–PG. Founded: 1870. Setting: urban. Nearest major city is Syracuse. Students are housed in single-sex dormitories. 2-acre campus. 3 buildings on campus. Approved or accredited by New York State Board of Regents, New York State University, The College Board, and US Department of State. Endowment: $1.2 million. Total enrollment: 52. Upper school average class size: 7. Upper school faculty-student ratio: 1:6.

Upper School Student Profile Grade 9: 16 students (8 boys, 8 girls); Grade 10: 10 students (5 boys, 5 girls); Grade 11: 16 students (8 boys, 8 girls); Grade 12: 10 students (5 boys, 5 girls). 15% of students are boarding students. 80% are state residents. 6

states are represented in upper school student body. 15% are international students. International students from Angola, Austria, China, Colombia, Republic of Korea, and Taiwan; 4 other countries represented in student body.

Faculty School total: 14. In upper school: 7 men, 7 women; 12 have advanced degrees; 4 reside on campus.

Subjects Offered Advanced chemistry, Advanced Placement courses, advanced TOEFL/grammar, African literature, algebra, American history, American literature, anatomy and physiology, art, biochemistry, biology, biology-AP, calculus, calculus-AP, career/college preparation, chemistry, chemistry-AP, college admission preparation, college awareness, college counseling, college placement, college planning, college writing, computer programming, computer science, creative writing, decision making skills, drama performance, driver education, earth science, economics, English, English as a foreign language, English composition, English literature, English literature and composition-AP, English literature-AP, environmental education, environmental science, ESL, ethics, European history, expository writing, fabric arts, French, French as a second language, geometry, government/civics, health, health and wellness, health education, history, honors algebra, honors English, honors geometry, honors U.S. history, honors world history, lab science, leadership, mathematics, philosophy, photography, physical education, physics, psychology, public speaking, reading, reading/study skills, SAT preparation, SAT/ACT preparation, science, Shakespeare, social studies, Spanish, trigonometry, typing, video film production, world history, world history-AP, world literature, writing.

Graduation Requirements Arts and fine arts (art, music, dance, drama), computer science, current events, debate, economics, English, foreign language, international affairs, mathematics, physical education (includes health), political science, public speaking, research, research and reference, science, social studies (includes history), English V -The Cascadilla Seminar (for college research preparation). Community service is required.

Special Academic Programs Advanced Placement exam preparation; honors section; accelerated programs; independent study; study at local college for college credit; academic accommodation for the gifted and the artistically talented; remedial reading and/or remedial writing; remedial math; programs in English, mathematics for dyslexic students; special instructional classes for students with learning disabilities and Attention Deficit Disorder; ESL (17 students enrolled).

College Admission Counseling 18 students graduated in 2009; 17 went to college, including Cornell University; Emory University; Syracuse University; University of Colorado at Boulder; University of Michigan. Other: 1 had other specific plans. Median SAT critical reading: 600, median SAT math: 650, median SAT writing: 550. 50% scored over 600 on SAT critical reading, 50% scored over 600 on SAT math, 15% scored over 600 on SAT writing.

Student Life Upper grades have specified standards of dress, student council, honor system. Discipline rests equally with students and faculty.

Tuition and Aid Day student tuition: $10,000; 7-day tuition and room/board: $30,000. Tuition installment plan (monthly payment plans, individually arranged payment plans). Tuition reduction for siblings, merit scholarship grants, need-based scholarship grants available. In 2009–10, 40% of upper-school students received aid; total upper-school merit-scholarship money awarded: $50,000. Total amount of financial aid awarded in 2009–10: $60,000.

Admissions Traditional secondary-level entrance grade is 10. For fall 2009, 50 students applied for upper-level admission, 15 were accepted, 15 enrolled. English Composition Test for ESL students, English entrance exam, English for Non-native Speakers, English language, English proficiency, High School Placement Test, math and English placement tests, mathematics proficiency exam, non-standardized placement tests, Reading for Understanding, school's own exam, skills for ESL students or writing sample required. Deadline for receipt of application materials: none. Application fee required: $50. Interview recommended.

Athletics Interscholastic: crew (boys, girls); intramural: crew (b,g), fencing (b), independent competitive sports (b,g), rowing (b,g), sailing (b,g), skiing (cross-country) (b,g), skiing (downhill) (b,g), soccer (b,g); coed interscholastic: aerobics, aerobics/Nautilus, alpine skiing, aquatics, backpacking, badminton, basketball, billiards, blading, bowling, climbing, combined training, fitness, fitness walking, Frisbee, hiking/backpacking, jogging, kayaking, nordic skiing, physical fitness, physical training, swimming and diving, table tennis, weight lifting, yoga; coed intramural: aerobics, aerobics/dance, badminton, basketball, blading, bowling, horseback riding, independent competitive sports, jogging, Nautilus, nordic skiing, outdoor activities, outdoor adventure, physical fitness, physical training, pillo polo, racquetball, rowing, sailboarding, skiing (cross-country), skiing (downhill), snowboarding, strength & conditioning, volleyball, walking, wall climbing, windsurfing. 2 PE instructors.

Computers Computers are regularly used in career exploration, college planning, creative writing, desktop publishing, desktop publishing, ESL, literary magazine, mathematics, media arts, newspaper, photography, publishing, research skills, SAT preparation, senior seminar, Spanish, stock market, theater, theater arts, video film production, Web site design, word processing, writing, writing, yearbook classes. Computer network features include on-campus library services, online commercial services, Internet access, Internet filtering or blocking technology. Student e-mail accounts are available to students. Students grades are available online.

Contact Donna W. Collins, Administrative Assistant. 607-272-3110. Fax: 607-272-0747. E-mail: admissions@cascadillaschool.org. Web site: www.cascadillaschool.org.

CASCIA HALL PREPARATORY SCHOOL

2520 South Yorktown Avenue
Tulsa, Oklahoma 74114-2803

Head of School: Mr. Roger C. Carter

General Information Coeducational day college-preparatory and liberal arts school, affiliated with Roman Catholic Church. Grades 6–12. Founded: 1926. Setting: urban. 40-acre campus. 10 buildings on campus. Approved or accredited by North Central Association of Colleges and Schools and Oklahoma Department of Education. Endowment: $7 million. Total enrollment: 574. Upper school average class size: 18. Upper school faculty-student ratio: 1:12. There are 180 required school days per year for Upper School students. Upper School students typically attend 5 days per week. The average school day consists of 6 hours and 30 minutes.

Upper School Student Profile Grade 9: 98 students (50 boys, 48 girls); Grade 10: 108 students (57 boys, 51 girls); Grade 11: 94 students (52 boys, 42 girls); Grade 12: 97 students (54 boys, 43 girls). 45% of students are Roman Catholic.

Faculty School total: 48. In upper school: 19 men, 20 women; 32 have advanced degrees.

Subjects Offered 20th century physics, ACT preparation, Advanced Placement courses, algebra, American history-AP, American literature, anatomy and physiology, ancient world history, art, art-AP, Asian studies, astronomy, Basic programming, Bible studies, biology, business, calculus, calculus-AP, career experience, career exploration, Catholic belief and practice, Central and Eastern European history, chemistry, chemistry-AP, Chinese, Chinese studies, chorus, Christian ethics, church history, college admission preparation, composition, computer science, CPR, creative writing, digital photography, drama, drawing, driver education, English language and composition-AP, English literature and composition-AP, environmental studies, ethics, European history, European history-AP, French, geography, geometry, German, government-AP, grammar, health, history of the Catholic Church, Holocaust studies, independent study, Latin, literature, philosophy, photography, physical science, physics, physics-AP, pre-calculus, probability and statistics, psychology, Russian studies, SAT/ACT preparation, senior seminar, senior thesis, Shakespeare, Spanish, Spanish language-AP, speech, speech and debate, theater, theology, trigonometry, U.S. government and politics-AP, U.S. history, world history, yearbook.

Graduation Requirements Arts and fine arts (art, music, dance, drama), career exploration, college admission preparation, computer science, English, foreign language, mathematics, religion (includes Bible studies and theology), science, senior seminar, social sciences, social studies (includes history), community service.

Special Academic Programs 11 Advanced Placement exams for which test preparation is offered; honors section; independent study; study at local college for college credit; academic accommodation for the gifted.

College Admission Counseling 88 students graduated in 2010; all went to college, including Kansas State University; Oklahoma State University; Texas Christian University; University of Arkansas; University of Oklahoma; University of Tulsa. Median SAT critical reading: 611, median SAT math: 602, median SAT writing: 600, median composite ACT: 26. 56% scored over 600 on SAT critical reading, 56% scored over 600 on SAT math, 53% scored over 600 on SAT writing, 45% scored over 26 on composite ACT.

Student Life Upper grades have uniform requirement, student council. Discipline rests primarily with faculty. Attendance at religious services is required.

Summer Programs Enrichment, sports, art/fine arts programs offered; session focuses on sports camp, driver's education, and fine arts; held on campus; accepts boys and girls; open to students from other schools. 500 students usually enrolled. 2011 schedule: June to August. Application deadline: May.

Tuition and Aid Day student tuition: $11,425. Tuition installment plan (monthly payment plans). Tuition reduction for siblings, need-based scholarship grants available. In 2010–11, 20% of upper-school students received aid. Total amount of financial aid awarded in 2010–11: $450,000.

Admissions Traditional secondary-level entrance grade is 9. For fall 2010, 75 students applied for upper-level admission, 59 were accepted, 44 enrolled. STS—Educational Development Series required. Deadline for receipt of application materials: none. Application fee required: $25. On-campus interview required.

Athletics Interscholastic: baseball (boys), basketball (b,g), bowling (h,g), cheering (g), cross-country running (b,g), dance team (g), football (b), golf (b,g), power lifting (b,g), soccer (b,g), softball (g), strength & conditioning (b,g), tennis (b,g), track and field (b,g), volleyball (g), weight training (b,g), wrestling (b); coed intramural: ultimate Frisbee. 1 PE instructor, 17 coaches, 1 athletic trainer.

Computers Computer network features include on-campus library services, online commercial services, Internet access, wireless campus network, Internet filtering or blocking technology, InfoTrac Search Bank, Internet access to local and state university library catalogues. Campus intranet, student e-mail accounts, and computer access in designated common areas are available to students. Students grades are available online. The school has a published electronic and media policy.

Contact Carol A. Bradley, Coordinator of Admissions and Communications. 918-746-2604. Fax: 918-746-2640. E-mail: cbradley@casciahall.org. Web site: www.casciahall.org.

CASTILLEJA SCHOOL

1310 Bryant Street
Palo Alto, California 94301

Head of School: Nanci Z. Kauffman

General Information Girls' day college-preparatory, arts, and technology school. Grades 6–12. Founded: 1907. Setting: suburban. Nearest major city is San Francisco/San Jose. 5-acre campus. 7 buildings on campus. Approved or accredited by California Association of Independent Schools, National Council for Private School Accreditation, and Western Association of Schools and Colleges. Member of National Association of Independent Schools and Secondary School Admission Test Board. Endowment: $35 million. Total enrollment: 415. Upper school average class size: 14. Upper school faculty-student ratio: 1:6. Upper School students typically attend 5 days per week. The average school day consists of 7 hours.

Upper School Student Profile Grade 9: 61 students (61 girls); Grade 10: 58 students (58 girls); Grade 11: 55 students (55 girls); Grade 12: 61 students (61 girls).

Faculty School total: 75. In upper school: 12 men, 34 women; 40 have advanced degrees.

Subjects Offered Advanced Placement courses, African studies, algebra, American history, American literature, art, art history, biology, calculus, ceramics, chemistry, computer math, computer science, creative writing, drama, economics, English, English literature, environmental science, European history, expository writing, fine arts, French, geometry, global issues, government/civics, grammar, health, history, journalism, Latin, marine biology, mathematics, music, philosophy, physical education, physics, psychology, Russian history, science, social studies, Spanish, speech, statistics, theater, trigonometry, world history, writing.

Graduation Requirements Arts and fine arts (art, music, dance, drama), English, foreign language, health and wellness, mathematics, science, social studies (includes history).

Special Academic Programs 16 Advanced Placement exams for which test preparation is offered; honors section; independent study; academic accommodation for the gifted.

College Admission Counseling 60 students graduated in 2010; all went to college, including Harvard University; Santa Clara University; Scripps College; Stanford University; Tufts University; University of California, Berkeley. Mean SAT critical reading: 706, mean SAT math: 693, mean SAT writing: 731.

Student Life Upper grades have uniform requirement, student council, honor system. Discipline rests equally with students and faculty.

Tuition and Aid Day student tuition: $32,250. Tuition installment plan (monthly payment plans, individually arranged payment plans). Need-based scholarship grants available. In 2010–11, 19% of upper-school students received aid. Total amount of financial aid awarded in 2010–11: $1,800,000.

Admissions Traditional secondary-level entrance grade is 9. For fall 2010, 122 students applied for upper-level admission, 26 were accepted, 18 enrolled. ISEE, SSAT or TOEFL required. Deadline for receipt of application materials: January 14. Application fee required: $75. On-campus interview required.

Athletics Interscholastic: basketball, cross-country running, golf, lacrosse, soccer, softball, swimming and diving, tennis, track and field, volleyball, water polo; intramural: climbing, fitness, rock climbing. 6 PE instructors, 15 coaches, 1 athletic trainer.

Computers Computers are regularly used in art, English, foreign language, history, mathematics, science classes. Computer network features include on-campus library services, online commercial services, Internet access, wireless campus network, Internet filtering or blocking technology, one to one laptop program. Campus intranet and student e-mail accounts are available to students. Students grades are available online. The school has a published electronic and media policy.

Contact Jill V.W. Lee, Director of Admission. 650-470-7731. Fax: 650-326-8036. E-mail: jlee@castilleja.org. Web site: www.castilleja.org.

CATE SCHOOL

1960 Cate Mesa Road
Carpinteria, California 93013

Head of School: Benjamin D. Williams, IV

General Information Coeducational boarding and day college-preparatory school. Grades 9–12. Founded: 1910. Setting: small town. Nearest major city is Santa Barbara. Students are housed in single-sex dormitories. 150-acre campus. 18 buildings on campus. Approved or accredited by California Association of Independent Schools, The Association of Boarding Schools, and Western Association of Schools and Colleges. Member of National Association of Independent Schools and Secondary School Admission Test Board. Endowment: $60 million. Total enrollment: 265. Upper school average class size: 10. Upper school faculty-student ratio: 1:5. There are 184 required school days per year for Upper School students. Upper School students typically attend 6 days per week. The average school day consists of 6 hours and 45 minutes.

Upper School Student Profile Grade 9: 55 students (27 boys, 28 girls); Grade 10: 70 students (35 boys, 35 girls); Grade 11: 70 students (35 boys, 35 girls); Grade 12: 70 students (35 boys, 35 girls). 83% of students are state residents. 23 states are represented in upper school student body. 15% are international students. International students from Hong Kong, Japan, Republic of Korea, Saudi Arabia, Switzerland, and Thailand; 7 other countries represented in student body.

Faculty School total: 52. In upper school: 34 men, 18 women; 43 have advanced degrees; 51 reside on campus.

Subjects Offered Advanced studio art-AP, African American history, algebra, American history, American literature, anatomy and physiology, art, art history-AP, Asian history, astronomy, biology, biology-AP, calculus, California writers, ceramics, chemistry, chemistry-AP, Chinese, choir, computer programming, computer science, computer science-AP, creative writing, digital art, drama, drama performance, economics-AP, English, English literature, environmental science-AP, ethics, European history, finance, fine arts, French, French language-AP, French literature-AP, French-AP, freshman seminar, genetics, geometry, government-AP, human development, international relations, Japanese, marine biology, Middle Eastern history, multimedia, music, photography, photojournalism, physics, physics-AP, pre-calculus, psychology, research skills, Russian literature, Spanish, Spanish language-AP, Spanish literature-AP, Spanish-AP, statistics, statistics-AP, studio art-AP, the Sixties, theater, trigonometry, U.S. government and politics-AP, U.S. history-AP, world history, writing.

Graduation Requirements 1½ elective credits, arts and fine arts (art, music, dance, drama), English, foreign language, history, human development, mathematics, science, social sciences.

Special Academic Programs 19 Advanced Placement exams for which test preparation is offered; honors section; independent study; term-away projects; study abroad; academic accommodation for the gifted, the musically talented, and the artistically talented; special instructional classes for deaf students.

College Admission Counseling 70 students graduated in 2009; all went to college, including Columbia College; New York University; Stanford University; University of California, Berkeley; University of Pennsylvania; University of Southern California. Median SAT critical reading: 660, median SAT math: 660, median SAT writing: 680, median combined SAT: 1970. 81% scored over 600 on SAT critical reading, 81% scored over 600 on SAT math, 83% scored over 600 on SAT writing, 82% scored over 1800 on combined SAT.

Student Life Upper grades have specified standards of dress, student council, honor system. Discipline rests equally with students and faculty.

Tuition and Aid Day student tuition: $32,750; 7-day tuition and room/board: $41,600. Tuition installment plan (The Tuition Plan, Insured Tuition Payment Plan, Key Tuition Payment Plan, monthly payment plans). Need-based scholarship grants available. In 2009–10, 35% of upper-school students received aid. Total amount of financial aid awarded in 2009–10: $500,000.

Admissions Traditional secondary-level entrance grade is 9. For fall 2009, 500 students applied for upper-level admission, 125 were accepted, 76 enrolled. ISEE, PSAT and SAT for applicants to grade 11 and 12 or SSAT, ERB, PSAT, SAT, PLAN or ACT required. Deadline for receipt of application materials: January 15. Application fee required: $75. On-campus interview required.

Athletics Interscholastic: baseball (boys), basketball (b,g), cross-country running (b,g), football (b), lacrosse (b,g), soccer (b,g), softball (g), squash (b,g), tennis (b,g), track and field (b,g), volleyball (b,g), water polo (b,g); coed interscholastic: golf, swimming and diving; coed intramural: aerobics, aerobics/Nautilus, backpacking, ballet, bicycling, canoeing/kayaking, climbing, dance, fitness, Frisbee, hiking/backpacking, kayaking, martial arts, modern dance, mountain biking, ocean paddling, outdoor activities, outdoors, physical fitness, physical training, rock climbing, ropes courses, surfing, ultimate Frisbee, yoga. 3 coaches, 1 athletic trainer.

Computers Computers are regularly used in English, history, humanities, literary magazine, mathematics, media arts, media production, multimedia, music, newspaper, photography, science, yearbook classes. Computer network features include on-campus library services, online commercial services, Internet access, wireless campus network, Internet filtering or blocking technology. Campus intranet, student e-mail accounts, and computer access in designated common areas are available to students. The school has a published electronic and media policy.

Contact Charlotte Brownlee, Director of Admission. 805-684-8409 Ext. 216. Fax: 805-684-2279. E-mail: charlotte_brownlee@cate.org. Web site: www.cate.org.

CATHEDRAL HIGH SCHOOL

5225 East 56th Street
Indianapolis, Indiana 46226
Head of School: Mr. Stephen J. Helmich

General Information Coeducational day college-preparatory, arts, religious studies, technology, International Baccalaureate, and AP/honors school, affiliated with Roman Catholic Church; primarily serves students with learning disabilities and dyslexic students. Grades 9–12. Founded: 1918. Setting: urban. 40-acre campus. 5 buildings on campus. Approved or accredited by Independent Schools Association of the Central States, National Catholic Education Association, National Council for Private School Accreditation, North Central Association of Colleges and Schools, and Indiana Department of Education. Endowment: $30 million. Total enrollment: 1,254. Upper school average class size: 19. Upper school faculty-student ratio: 1:13. There are 185 required school days per year for Upper School students. Upper School students typically attend 5 days per week. The average school day consists of 7 hours and 40 minutes.

Upper School Student Profile 80% of students are Roman Catholic.

Faculty School total: 100. In upper school: 47 men, 53 women; 54 have advanced degrees.

Subjects Offered Advanced biology, advanced chemistry, advanced math, Advanced Placement courses, algebra, American history, American history-AP, American literature-AP, American studies, anatomy, anatomy and physiology, art and culture, art history, arts, Bible, Bible studies, biology, botany, business, business communications, business education, business law, calculus, calculus-AP, career and personal planning, Catholic belief and practice, ceramics, chemistry, chemistry-AP, choir, choral music, chorus, Christianity, civics, civil war history, college counseling, composition-AP, computer science, debate, drama, driver education, earth science, economics, economics-AP, English, English literature, English literature and composition-AP, English literature-AP, English-AP, English/composition-AP, environmental science, fine arts, French, French language-AP, geography, geology, geometry, German, German-AP, government and politics-AP, government-AP, history, history-AP, independent study, journalism, lab science, language development, Latin, life science, macro/microeconomics-AP, mathematics, mathematics-AP, microbiology, music, music appreciation, news writing, newspaper, organic chemistry, photography, photojournalism, physical education, physical fitness, physics, physiology, psychology, religion, SAT/ACT preparation, science, social sciences, social studies, sociology, Spanish, speech, textiles, theater, theater design and production, theater production, theory of knowledge, trigonometry, U.S. government and politics-AP, U.S. history, U.S. history-AP, vocal music, world history, world literature.

Graduation Requirements Arts and fine arts (art, music, dance, drama), biology, composition, economics, English, foreign language, government, mathematics, modern world history, physical education (includes health), religious studies, science, social studies (includes history), speech and debate, technology, U.S. history, 30 hours annually of community service.

Special Academic Programs International Baccalaureate program; Advanced Placement exam preparation; honors section; independent study; academic accommodation for the gifted, the musically talented, and the artistically talented; remedial reading and/or remedial writing; remedial math; programs in English, mathematics for dyslexic students; special instructional classes for deaf students, blind students, students with learning disabilities, Attention Deficit Disorder, and dyslexia.

College Admission Counseling 314 students graduated in 2009; 312 went to college, including Ball State University; Indiana University Bloomington; Loyola University Chicago; Purdue University; University of Dayton; Xavier University. Other: 2 entered military service. Median SAT critical reading: 562, median SAT math: 565, median SAT writing: 554, median combined SAT: 1681. Mean composite ACT: 25.

Student Life Upper grades have uniform requirement, student council, honor system. Discipline rests primarily with faculty. Attendance at religious services is required.

Tuition and Aid Day student tuition: $10,390. Tuition installment plan (Key Tuition Payment Plan, monthly payment plans). Merit scholarship grants, need-based scholarship grants, paying campus jobs available. In 2009–10, 35% of upper-school students received aid; total upper-school merit-scholarship money awarded: $300,000. Total amount of financial aid awarded in 2009–10: $2,300,000.

Admissions Traditional secondary-level entrance grade is 9. For fall 2009, 552 students applied for upper-level admission, 432 were accepted, 352 enrolled. High School Placement Test and High School Placement Test (closed version) from Scholastic Testing Service required. Deadline for receipt of application materials: none. No application fee required. On-campus interview required.

Athletics Interscholastic: baseball (boys), basketball (b,g), cheering (g), cross-country running (b,g), football (b), golf (b,g), soccer (b,g), softball (g), swimming and diving (b,g), tennis (b,g), track and field (b,g), volleyball (g), wrestling (b); intramural: dance squad (g), dance team (g), field hockey (g), kickball (g), lacrosse (b,g), rugby (b,g), volleyball (b), weight lifting (b,g); coed interscholastic: bowling, diving, ice hockey; coed intramural: badminton, bicycling, crew, fencing, Frisbee, martial arts, skiing (downhill), ultimate Frisbee. 6 PE instructors, 1 athletic trainer.

Computers Computers are regularly used in business, business skills, creative writing, desktop publishing, English, foreign language, history, information technology, journalism, mathematics, newspaper, photography, photojournalism, SAT preparation, science, writing, writing, yearbook classes. Computer network features include on-campus library services, online commercial services, Internet access, wireless campus network, Internet filtering or blocking technology. Student e-mail accounts are available to students. Students grades are available online. The school has a published electronic and media policy.

Contact Mr. Duane Emery, Vice President for Enrollment Management. 317-542-1481. Fax: 317-542-1484. E-mail: demery@cathedral-irish.org. Web site: www.cathedral-irish.org.

CATHEDRAL HIGH SCHOOL

350 East 56th Street
New York, New York 10022-4199
Head of School: Ms. Joan Close

General Information Girls' day college-preparatory, arts, business, religious studies, and technology school, affiliated with Roman Catholic Church. Grades 9–12. Founded: 1905. Setting: urban. 1 building on campus. Approved or accredited by Middle States Association of Colleges and Schools, National Catholic Education Association, New York Department of Education, New York State Board of Regents, The College Board, and New York Department of Education. Total enrollment: 600. Upper school average class size: 35. Upper school faculty-student ratio: 1:17. The average school day consists of 7 hours.

Upper School Student Profile 75% of students are Roman Catholic.

Subjects Offered Advanced Placement courses, algebra, art, band, biology, biology-AP, business law, business skills, business studies, calculus, calculus-AP, campus ministry, career education internship, career exploration, Catholic belief and practice, chemistry, chemistry-AP, choir, chorus, Christian doctrine, college admission preparation, college counseling, computer education, computer graphics, computers, constitutional history of U.S., crafts, drama, earth science, economics, electives, English composition, English literature, English-AP, English/composition-AP, fashion, fitness, foreign language, French, general math, geometry, government, guidance, health, health education, honors algebra, honors English, honors geometry, honors U.S. history, honors world history, HTML design, integrated mathematics, internship, lab science, law and the legal system, literature, mathematics-AP, physics, physics-AP, physiology, portfolio art, pre-algebra, pre-calculus, psychology, psychology-AP, religion, science, social education, sociology, Spanish literature, Spanish-AP, studio art, U.S. government, U.S. history, U.S. history-AP, world history, world wide web design.

Graduation Requirements Art, electives, English, foreign language, mathematics, music, physical education (includes health), religion (includes Bible studies and theology), science, social studies (includes history), New York State Regents.

Special Academic Programs 7 Advanced Placement exams for which test preparation is offered; honors section; remedial reading and/or remedial writing; remedial math.

Student Life Upper grades have uniform requirement, student council, honor system. Discipline rests primarily with faculty. Attendance at religious services is required.

Summer Programs Remediation programs offered; held on campus; accepts boys and girls; open to students from other schools. 2011 schedule: July to August. Application deadline: July.

Tuition and Aid Day student tuition: $6225. Tuition installment plan (monthly payment plans). Tuition reduction for siblings, merit scholarship grants, need-based scholarship grants available.

Admissions Traditional secondary-level entrance grade is 9. Catholic High School Entrance Examination required. Deadline for receipt of application materials: August. No application fee required.

Athletics Interscholastic: basketball, soccer, softball, volleyball; intramural: basketball, swimming and diving. 1 PE instructor, 4 coaches.

Computers Computers are regularly used in all academic classes. Computer network features include on-campus library services, Internet access, Internet filtering or blocking technology. Campus intranet, student e-mail accounts, and computer access in designated common areas are available to students. Students grades are available online.

Contact Mrs. Johanna Velez, Director of Recruitment. 212-688-1545 Ext. 224. Fax: 212-754-2024. E-mail: jcastex@cathedralhs.org. Web site: www.cathedralhs.org.

CATHEDRAL PREPARATORY SCHOOL
225 West Ninth Street
Erie, Pennsylvania 16501
Head of School: Rev. Scott William Jabo

General Information Boys' day college-preparatory, arts, religious studies, and technology school, affiliated with Roman Catholic Church. Grades 9–12. Founded: 1921. Setting: urban. 16-acre campus. 1 building on campus. Approved or accredited by Middle States Association of Colleges and Schools and Pennsylvania Department of Education. Endowment: $2.9 million. Total enrollment: 554. Upper school average class size: 22. Upper school faculty-student ratio: 1:14.

Upper School Student Profile Grade 9: 163 students (163 boys); Grade 10: 127 students (127 boys); Grade 11: 140 students (140 boys); Grade 12: 124 students (124 boys). 80% of students are Roman Catholic.

Faculty School total: 46. In upper school: 30 men, 16 women; 15 have advanced degrees.

Subjects Offered Aerospace science, algebra, American history, anatomy and physiology, aviation, Basic programming, biology, calculus, ceramics, chemistry, chemistry-AP, church history, computer literacy, computer programming, creative writing, critical thinking, death and loss, debate, desktop publishing, discrete mathematics, drawing, driver education, English, expository writing, finance, first aid, flight instruction, French, geometry, German, health, history of the Catholic Church, history-AP, human anatomy, integrated science, interpersonal skills, introduction to theater, jazz band, keyboarding, Latin, leadership, Mandarin, mechanical drawing, men's studies, Microsoft, moral theology, newspaper, physical education, physics, pre-calculus, probability and statistics, public speaking, reading, ROTC, sexuality, social justice, Spanish, studio art, theater, trigonometry, video communication, world geography, world history, writing, yearbook.

Graduation Requirements American government, biology, chemistry, economics, English, English composition, English literature, geography, government, language, mathematics, physical education (includes health), physics, psychology, social studies (includes history), theology, U.S. government.

Special Academic Programs Advanced Placement exam preparation; honors section; study at local college for college credit.

College Admission Counseling 158 students graduated in 2009; 153 went to college, including Edinboro University of Pennsylvania; Gannon University; John Carroll University; Penn State Erie, The Behrend College; Penn State University Park; University of Pittsburgh. Other: 3 went to work, 2 entered military service. 21% scored over 600 on SAT critical reading, 25% scored over 600 on SAT math.

Student Life Upper grades have uniform requirement, student council, honor system. Discipline rests equally with students and faculty. Attendance at religious services is required.

Tuition and Aid Day student tuition: $6230. Tuition installment plan (FACTS Tuition Payment Plan). Tuition reduction for siblings, merit scholarship grants, need-based scholarship grants available. In 2009–10, 53% of upper-school students received aid; total upper-school merit-scholarship money awarded: $2000. Total amount of financial aid awarded in 2009–10: $550,000.

Admissions Traditional secondary-level entrance grade is 9. For fall 2009, 212 students applied for upper-level admission, 195 were accepted, 163 enrolled. High School Placement Test required. Deadline for receipt of application materials: March 1. Application fee required: $10. Interview recommended.

Athletics Interscholastic: baseball, basketball, cross-country running, football, golf, hockey, independent competitive sports, JROTC drill, lacrosse, outdoor recreation, power lifting, skiing (cross-country), skiing (downhill), soccer, swimming and diving, tennis, track and field, water polo, weight lifting, weight training, wrestling; intramural: bowling, table tennis, weight lifting. 2 PE instructors, 1 athletic trainer.

Computers Computers are regularly used in all academic classes. Computer network features include on-campus library services, Internet access, wireless campus network, Internet filtering or blocking technology, all students receive a Tablet PC upon admission. Campus intranet and student e-mail accounts are available to students. Students grades are available online. The school has a published electronic and media policy.

Contact Mr. Timothy Dougherty, Director of Admissions. 814-453-7737 Ext. 242. Fax: 814-455-5462. E-mail: tdougherty@cathedral-prep.com. Web site: www.cathedral-prep.com.

CATHERINE MCAULEY HIGH SCHOOL
631 Stevens Avenue
Portland, Maine 04103
Head of School: Sr. Edward Mary Kelleher, RSM

General Information Girls' day college-preparatory, arts, and religious studies school, affiliated with Roman Catholic Church. Grades 9–12. Founded: 1969. Setting: suburban. 10-acre campus. 2 buildings on campus. Approved or accredited by National Catholic Education Association, New England Association of Schools and Colleges, and Maine Department of Education. Total enrollment: 210. Upper school average class size: 15. Upper school faculty-student ratio: 1:8. There are 175 required school days per year for Upper School students. The average school day consists of 6 hours and 15 minutes.

Upper School Student Profile Grade 9: 55 students (55 girls); Grade 10: 55 students (55 girls); Grade 11: 50 students (50 girls); Grade 12: 50 students (50 girls). 60% of students are Roman Catholic.

Faculty School total: 25. In upper school: 4 men, 21 women.

Subjects Offered Algebra, American history, American literature, anatomy, art, biology, chemistry, chorus, community service, creative writing, drama, ecology, economics, English, English literature, English literature and composition-AP, English literature-AP, ensembles, environmental science, ethics, fine arts, French, geography, geometry, grammar, health, history-AP, honors algebra, honors English, honors geometry, honors U.S. history, Latin, mathematics, physical education, physical science, physics, pre-calculus, psychology, religion, science, social studies, Spanish, trigonometry, women's studies, world history, world literature.

Graduation Requirements Arts and fine arts (art, music, dance, drama), English, foreign language, mathematics, physical education (includes health), religion (includes Bible studies and theology), science, social studies (includes history), Religious Studies I-IV. Community service is required.

Special Academic Programs Advanced Placement exam preparation; honors section; accelerated programs; independent study; term-away projects; study at local college for college credit; study abroad; academic accommodation for the gifted, the musically talented, and the artistically talented.

College Admission Counseling 54 students graduated in 2009; all went to college, including Bowdoin College; College of the Holy Cross; Dartmouth College; Davidson College; Fairfield University.

Student Life Upper grades have uniform requirement, student council, honor system. Discipline rests primarily with faculty.

Tuition and Aid Day student tuition: $11,900 Tuition installment plan (FACTS Tuition Payment Plan, monthly payment plans, individually arranged payment plans). Tuition reduction for siblings, merit scholarship grants, need-based scholarship grants, paying campus jobs available. In 2009–10, 40% of upper-school students received aid; total upper-school merit-scholarship money awarded: $5000. Total amount of financial aid awarded in 2009–10: $300,000.

Admissions Traditional secondary-level entrance grade is 9. High School Placement Test required. Deadline for receipt of application materials: none. Application fee required: $50. On-campus interview required.

Athletics Interscholastic: aquatics, basketball, cheering, cross-country running, diving, field hockey, indoor track, indoor track & field, lacrosse, soccer, softball, swimming and diving, tennis, track and field, winter (indoor) track; intramural: floor hockey, physical fitness, rock climbing, volleyball, winter soccer. 1 PE instructor, 20 coaches, 2 athletic trainers.

Computers Computers are regularly used in economics, English, foreign language, science classes. Computer network features include on-campus library services, online commercial services, Internet access, wireless campus network, Internet filtering or blocking technology, every student receives a laptop computer. Campus intranet and student e-mail accounts are available to students. Students grades are available online. The school has a published electronic and media policy.

Contact Mrs. Ericka P. Sanborn, Director of Admissions/Marketing. 207-797-3802 Ext. 2022. Fax: 207-797-3804. E-mail: esanborn@mcauleyhs.org. Web site: www.mcauleyhs.org.

CATHOLIC CENTRAL HIGH SCHOOL
625 Seventh Avenue
Troy, New York 12182-2595
Head of School: Mr. Christopher Bott

General Information Coeducational day college-preparatory, arts, business, and religious studies school, affiliated with Roman Catholic Church. Grades 7–12. Founded: 1924. Setting: suburban. 4-acre campus. 2 buildings on campus. Approved or accredited by National Catholic Education Association and New York State Board of Regents. Endowment: $500,000. Total enrollment: 520. Upper school average class size: 16. Upper school faculty-student ratio: 1:13. There are 168 required school days per year for Upper School students. Upper School students typically attend 5 days per week. The average school day consists of 6 hours and 21 minutes.

Upper School Student Profile Grade 7: 52 students (23 boys, 29 girls); Grade 8: 55 students (26 boys, 29 girls); Grade 9: 119 students (47 boys, 72 girls); Grade 10: 95 students (46 boys, 49 girls); Grade 11: 93 students (33 boys, 60 girls); Grade 12: 108 students (46 boys, 62 girls). 86% of students are Roman Catholic.

Faculty School total: 39. In upper school: 16 men, 23 women; 28 have advanced degrees.

Subjects Offered Accounting, algebra, anatomy and physiology, art, astronomy, band, biology, business communications, business law, calculus, Catholic belief and practice, chemistry, chorus, computer art, computer science, drama, drawing and design, driver education, earth science, economics, English, English language-AP, global studies, government, health, history, honors English, honors U.S. history, Internet, keyboarding, library skills, mathematics, physics, pre-calculus, printmaking, religion, social studies, Spanish, U.S. history.

Graduation Requirements Art, English, mathematics, physical education (includes health), science, social studies (includes history), theology.

Special Academic Programs Advanced Placement exam preparation; remedial reading and/or remedial writing; remedial math; ESL (9 students enrolled).

College Admission Counseling 110 students graduated in 2009; all went to college, including Rensselaer Polytechnic Institute; Siena College; State University of New York at New Paltz; State University of New York College at Geneseo; University at Albany, State University of New York.

Student Life Upper grades have uniform requirement, student council. Discipline rests primarily with faculty. Attendance at religious services is required.

Tuition and Aid Day student tuition: $5500. Tuition installment plan (FACTS Tuition Payment Plan). Need-based scholarship grants, paying campus jobs available. In 2009–10, 26% of upper-school students received aid. Total amount of financial aid awarded in 2009–10: $45,500.

Admissions Traditional secondary-level entrance grade is 9. Scholastic Testing Service High School Placement Test required. Deadline for receipt of application materials: none. Application fee required: $100. Interview recommended.

Athletics Interscholastic: baseball (boys), basketball (b,g), bowling (b,g), cross-country running (b,g), dance squad (g), football (b), golf (b), indoor track & field (b,g), soccer (b,g), softball (g), tennis (b,g), track and field (b,g), volleyball (g); intramural: figure skating (g); coed interscholastic: cheering. 2 PE instructors, 8 coaches, 1 athletic trainer.

Computers Computers are regularly used in accounting, art, business applications, graphic design, programming classes. Computer network features include on-campus library services, Internet access, Internet filtering or blocking technology.

Contact Mrs. Teresa Mainello, Publicity Director. 518-235-7100 Ext. 224. Fax: 518-237-1796. Web site: www.cchstroy.org.

CATHOLIC CENTRAL HIGH SCHOOL
148 McHenry Street
Burlington, Wisconsin 53105
Head of School: Mr. Gregory J. Groth

General Information Coeducational day college-preparatory, arts, business, religious studies, bilingual studies, and technology school, affiliated with Roman Catholic Church. Grades 9–12. Founded: 1920. Setting: small town. Nearest major city is Milwaukee. 25-acre campus. 2 buildings on campus. Approved or accredited by North Central Association of Colleges and Schools and Wisconsin Department of Education. Endowment: $1 million. Total enrollment: 141. Upper school average class size: 14. Upper school faculty-student ratio: 1:8. There are 180 required school days per year for Upper School students. Upper School students typically attend 5 days per week. The average school day consists of 7 hours.

Upper School Student Profile Grade 9: 40 students (26 boys, 14 girls); Grade 10: 39 students (24 boys, 15 girls); Grade 11: 30 students (17 boys, 13 girls); Grade 12: 32 students (20 boys, 12 girls); Postgraduate: 131 students (77 boys, 54 girls). 86% of students are Roman Catholic.

Faculty School total: 17. In upper school: 9 men, 8 women; 7 have advanced degrees.

Subjects Offered 20th century American writers, 3-dimensional art, 3-dimensional design, accounting, advanced biology, advanced chemistry, advanced computer applications, advanced math, Advanced Placement courses, algebra, American government, American history, American literature, American literature-AP, analytic geometry, anatomy, anatomy and physiology, Arabic, art, band, Bible, biology, botany, business, business education, calculus, calculus-AP, cartooning/animation, Catholic belief and practice, chemistry, Chinese, choir, college planning, composition, computer animation, computer graphics, computer skills, consumer education, digital photography, diversity studies, drawing, earth science, economics, English, environmental science, finance, forensics, French, geography, geometry, health, history of religion, history of the Catholic Church, human anatomy, human biology, integrated science, intro to computers, journalism, marketing, music theory, New Testament, painting, personal fitness, photography, physical fitness, physics, physiology, pre-calculus, probability and statistics, psychology, religion, religious studies, skills for success, social justice, Spanish, speech, theology, U.S. history, world religions, zoology.

Graduation Requirements Religious education.

Special Academic Programs International Baccalaureate program; Advanced Placement exam preparation; honors section; independent study; study at local college for college credit; study abroad; academic accommodation for the gifted.

College Admission Counseling 41 students graduated in 2010; all went to college, including Marquette University; University of Wisconsin–Eau Claire; University of Wisconsin–Madison; University of Wisconsin–Milwaukee; University of Wisconsin–Stevens Point; University of Wisconsin–Whitewater. Median composite ACT: 23. 21% scored over 26 on composite ACT.

Student Life Upper grades have specified standards of dress, student council, honor system. Discipline rests primarily with faculty. Attendance at religious services is required.

Summer Programs Sports programs offered; session focuses on basketball; held on campus; accepts boys and girls; open to students from other schools. 150 students usually enrolled. 2011 schedule: June 15 to July 31. Application deadline: June 15.

Tuition and Aid Day student tuition: $6950–$7600. Tuition installment plan (individually arranged payment plans). Tuition reduction for siblings, need-based scholarship grants, paying campus jobs available. In 2010–11, 75% of upper-school students received aid. Total amount of financial aid awarded in 2010–11: $113,000.

Admissions Traditional secondary-level entrance grade is 9. For fall 2010, 150 students applied for upper-level admission, 142 were accepted, 141 enrolled. ACT, ACT-Explore or PSAT required. Deadline for receipt of application materials: none. Application fee required: $80. On-campus interview required.

Athletics Interscholastic: baseball (boys), basketball (b,g), dance team (g), football (b), golf (b), softball (g), tennis (g), volleyball (g), wrestling (b); coed interscholastic: bowling, cheering, cross-country running, fitness, gymnastics, physical fitness, strength & conditioning, track and field; coed intramural: bicycling, dance, dance squad, table tennis, ultimate Frisbee, weight training. 1 PE instructor, 32 coaches, 1 athletic trainer.

Computers Computers are regularly used in accounting, business, economics, journalism, newspaper, typing, Web site design, writing classes. Computer network features include Internet access, Internet filtering or blocking technology. Student e-mail accounts and computer access in designated common areas are available to students. Students grades are available online. The school has a published electronic and media policy.

Contact Mrs. Joanne C. Kresken, Admissions Director. 262-763-1510 Ext. 225. Fax: 262-763-1509. E-mail: jkresken@cchsnet.org. Web site: www.cchsnet.org.

THE CATHOLIC HIGH SCHOOL OF BALTIMORE
2800 Edison Highway
Baltimore, Maryland 21213
Head of School: Dr. Barbara D. Nazelrod

General Information Girls' day and distance learning college-preparatory, general academic, arts, business, religious studies, and technology school, affiliated with Roman Catholic Church. Grades 9–12. Distance learning grades 9–12. Founded: 1939. Setting: urban. 6-acre campus. 1 building on campus. Approved or accredited by Association of Independent Maryland Schools, Middle States Association of Colleges and Schools, National Catholic Education Association, and Maryland Department of Education. Endowment: $2.9 million. Total enrollment: 314. Upper school average class size: 17. Upper school faculty-student ratio: 1:12. There are 175 required school days per year for Upper School students. Upper School students typically attend 5 days per week. The average school day consists of 6 hours and 45 minutes.

Upper School Student Profile Grade 9: 67 students (67 girls); Grade 10: 66 students (66 girls); Grade 11: 104 students (104 girls); Grade 12: 77 students (77 girls). 75% of students are Roman Catholic.

Faculty School total: 32. In upper school: 12 men, 15 women; 18 have advanced degrees.

Subjects Offered Algebra, American history, American literature, anatomy, art, band, biology, calculus, chemistry, community service, computer programming, computer science, creative writing, dance, drama, driver education, earth science, economics, English, English literature, expository writing, fine arts, French, geometry, government/civics, grammar, health, history, instrumental music, journalism, keyboarding, literature, mathematics, music, personal development, photography, physical education, physics, physiology, psychology, reading, religion, science, social studies, Spanish, speech, study skills, technology, theater, theology, world history, world literature.

Graduation Requirements Arts and fine arts (art, music, dance, drama), computer science, English, foreign language, mathematics, physical education (includes health), religion (includes Bible studies and theology), science, social studies (includes history). Community service is required.

Special Academic Programs Advanced Placement exam preparation; honors section; independent study; study at local college for college credit; remedial reading and/or remedial writing; remedial math; programs in English, mathematics, general development for dyslexic students.

College Admission Counseling 68 students graduated in 2010; 66 went to college, including Stevenson University; Towson University; University of Maryland, Baltimore County. Other: 2 went to work. Median SAT critical reading: 500, median SAT math: 460, median SAT writing: 510. 20% scored over 600 on SAT critical reading, 4% scored over 600 on SAT math, 18% scored over 600 on SAT writing.

Student Life Upper grades have uniform requirement, student council, honor system. Discipline rests primarily with faculty. Attendance at religious services is required.

Tuition and Aid Day student tuition: $9950. Tuition installment plan (Insured Tuition Payment Plan, FACTS Tuition Payment Plan, biannual payment plan, annual payment plan). Tuition reduction for siblings, merit scholarship grants, need-based scholarship grants available. In 2010–11, 62% of upper-school students received aid; total upper-school merit-scholarship money awarded: $237,625. Total amount of financial aid awarded in 2010–11: $388,132.

Admissions Traditional secondary-level entrance grade is 9. For fall 2010, 162 students applied for upper-level admission, 140 were accepted, 68 enrolled. High School Placement Test required. Deadline for receipt of application materials: none. Application fee required: $30. On-campus interview required.

Athletics Interscholastic: basketball, cheering, cross-country running, dance team, field hockey, golf, indoor track & field, lacrosse, soccer, softball, swimming and diving, tennis, track and field, volleyball; intramural: aerobics, aerobics/dance, cooperative games. 1 PE instructor, 22 coaches.

Computers Computers are regularly used in art, English, foreign language, history, mathematics, music, science, theology classes. Computer network features include on-campus library services, online commercial services, Internet access, wireless campus network, Internet filtering or blocking technology. Campus intranet and student e-mail accounts are available to students. Students grades are available online. The school has a published electronic and media policy.

Contact Mrs. Barbara Czawlytko, Administrative Assistant. 410-732-6200 Ext. 213. Fax: 410-732-7639. E-mail: bczawlytko@thecatholichighschool.org. Web site: www.thecatholichighschool.org.

CATHOLIC MEMORIAL
235 Baker Street
West Roxbury, Massachusetts 02132
Head of School: Mr. Paul E. Sheff '62

General Information Boys' day college-preparatory, arts, religious studies, and technology school, affiliated with Roman Catholic Church. Grades 7–12. Founded: 1957. Setting: suburban. Nearest major city is Boston. 15-acre campus. 3 buildings on campus. Approved or accredited by Association of Independent Schools in New England, National Catholic Education Association, New England Association of Schools and Colleges, and Massachusetts Department of Education. Endowment: $2.5 million. Total enrollment: 750. Upper school average class size: 21. Upper school faculty-student ratio: 1:12. The average school day consists of 7 hours.

Upper School Student Profile Grade 7: 70 students (70 boys); Grade 8: 85 students (85 boys); Grade 9: 150 students (150 boys); Grade 10: 155 students (155 boys); Grade 11: 145 students (145 boys); Grade 12: 145 students (145 boys). 80% of students are Roman Catholic.

Faculty School total: 66. In upper school: 50 men, 16 women; 50 have advanced degrees.

Subjects Offered Accounting, algebra, American history, American literature, anatomy, art, art history, Bible studies, biology, business skills, calculus, chemistry, Chinese, Chinese studies, computer math, computer programming, computer science, creative writing, driver education, earth science, economics, English, English literature, ethics, European history, expository writing, fine arts, French, geography, geometry, government/civics, grammar, health, history, Italian, journalism, Latin, Mandarin, mathematics, physical education, physics, physiology, psychology, public speaking, religion, science, social sciences, social studies, sociology, Spanish, trigonometry, typing, world geography, world history, world literature, writing.

Graduation Requirements Arts and fine arts (art, music, dance, drama), business skills (includes word processing), computer science, English, foreign language, mathematics, physical education (includes health), religion (includes Bible studies and theology), science, senior seminar, social sciences, social studies (includes history), senior service project.

Special Academic Programs 16 Advanced Placement exams for which test preparation is offered; honors section; independent study; academic accommodation for the musically talented and the artistically talented.

College Admission Counseling 150 students graduated in 2009; 143 went to college, including Boston College; Boston University; College of the Holy Cross; Northeastern University; Stonehill College; University of Massachusetts Amherst. Other: 1 went

to work, 3 entered military service, 3 entered a postgraduate year. Mean SAT critical reading: 564, mean SAT math: 571, mean SAT writing: 559, mean combined SAT: 1694.

Student Life Upper grades have uniform requirement, student council. Discipline rests primarily with faculty. Attendance at religious services is required.

Tuition and Aid Day student tuition: $12,825. Tuition installment plan (FACTS Tuition Payment Plan). Merit scholarship grants, need-based scholarship grants available. In 2009–10, 33% of upper-school students received aid; total upper-school merit-scholarship money awarded: $500,000. Total amount of financial aid awarded in 2009–10: $1,300,000.

Admissions Traditional secondary-level entrance grade is 9. For fall 2009, 270 students applied for upper-level admission, 180 were accepted, 100 enrolled. Archdiocese of Boston High School entrance exam provided by STS required. Deadline for receipt of application materials: December 20. No application fee required. Interview recommended.

Athletics Interscholastic: baseball, basketball, cross-country running, football, golf, ice hockey, lacrosse, rugby, soccer, swimming and diving, tennis, track and field, volleyball, weight lifting, winter (indoor) track, wrestling; intramural: baseball, basketball, bowling, football, skiing (downhill), snowboarding, softball, strength & conditioning, table tennis, touch football, volleyball, whiffle ball. 3 PE instructors, 32 coaches, 2 athletic trainers.

Computers Computers are regularly used in art, computer applications, graphic design, Web site design classes. Computer network features include on-campus library services, Internet access, wireless campus network, Internet filtering or blocking technology. Campus intranet is available to students. The school has a published electronic and media policy.

Contact Mr. John Mazza '98, Director of Admissions. 617-469-8034. Fax: 617-325-0888. Web site: www.catholicmemorial.org.

THE CATLIN GABEL SCHOOL
8825 SW Barnes Road
Portland, Oregon 97225
Head of School: Dr. Lark P. Palma

General Information Coeducational day college-preparatory, arts, technology, and sciences school. Grades PK–12. Founded: 1957. Setting: suburban. 54-acre campus. 13 buildings on campus. Approved or accredited by Northwest Association of Schools and Colleges and Pacific Northwest Association of Independent Schools. Member of National Association of Independent Schools and Secondary School Admission Test Board. Endowment: $19.5 million. Total enrollment: 728. Upper school average class size: 13. Upper school faculty-student ratio: 1:8. There are 169 required school days per year for Upper School students. Upper School students typically attend 5 days per week. The average school day consists of 7 hours and 10 minutes.

Upper School Student Profile Grade 9: 75 students (39 boys, 36 girls); Grade 10: 70 students (33 boys, 37 girls); Grade 11: 71 students (39 boys, 32 girls); Grade 12: 71 students (35 boys, 36 girls).

Faculty School total: 87. In upper school: 28 men, 22 women; 34 have advanced degrees.

Subjects Offered Acting, advanced chemistry, advanced computer applications, advanced math, algebra, American democracy, American history, American literature, ancient world history, applied music, art, art history, arts, astronomy, athletics, baseball, Basic programming, basketball, biology, bookmaking, bowling, calculus, ceramics, chemistry, Chinese, choir, college admission preparation, college counseling, comedy, computer art, computer graphics, computer programming, computer resources, computer science, computer skills, computer studies, concert choir, creative writing, critical studies in film, critical thinking, debate, digital imaging, digital photography, drama, drama performance, dramatic arts, drawing and design, driver education, ecology, economics, English, English literature, ensembles, ethics and responsibility, European history, expository writing, fiber arts, film studies, fine arts, foreign language, foreign policy, French, geometry, golf, government/civics, graphic arts, graphic design, health, history, human sexuality, Japanese, jazz band, mathematics, model United Nations, music, music theory, musical productions, ornithology, outdoor education, peer counseling, performing arts, photo shop, photography, physical education, physical fitness, physics, playwriting and directing, pre-calculus, probability and statistics, robotics, science, set design, Shakespeare, social studies, Spanish, Spanish literature, speech and debate, stage design, stagecraft, statistics, strings, studio art, study skills, technical theater, tennis, theater, theater arts, theater design and production, track and field, trigonometry, U.S. history, visual and performing arts, vocal ensemble, voice, voice ensemble, volleyball, weight fitness, weight training, woodworking, world affairs, world history, world literature, world wide web design, writing, writing workshop, yearbook.

Graduation Requirements Arts and fine arts (art, music, dance, drama), English, foreign language, mathematics, physical education (includes health), science, social studies (includes history). Community service is required.

Special Academic Programs Honors section; independent study; term-away projects; study at local college for college credit; study abroad; academic accommodation for the gifted, the musically talented, and the artistically talented.

College Admission Counseling 77 students graduated in 2010; 71 went to college, including Bard College; Boston College; Claremont McKenna College; Occidental College; Reed College; University of Oregon. Other: 6 had other specific plans. Mean SAT critical reading: 632, mean SAT math: 637, mean SAT writing: 627, mean

The Catlin Gabel School

combined SAT: 1896, mean composite ACT: 27. 89% scored over 600 on SAT critical reading, 87% scored over 600 on SAT math, 80% scored over 600 on SAT writing, 86% scored over 1800 on combined SAT, 96% scored over 26 on composite ACT. **Student Life** Upper grades have student council, honor system. Discipline rests equally with students and faculty.

Summer Programs Enrichment, art/fine arts, computer instruction programs offered; session focuses on arts and enrichment; held both on and off campus; held at various outdoor areas—hiking, climbing, etc.; accepts boys and girls; open to students from other schools. 85 students usually enrolled. 2011 schedule: June 27 to August 5.

Tuition and Aid Day student tuition: $22,700. Tuition installment plan (Insured Tuition Payment Plan, monthly payment plans, individually arranged payment plans). Need-based scholarship grants available. In 2010–11, 24% of upper-school students received aid. Total amount of financial aid awarded in 2010–11: $2,900,000.

Admissions Traditional secondary-level entrance grade is 9. For fall 2010, 64 students applied for upper-level admission, 50 were accepted, 29 enrolled. SSAT required. Deadline for receipt of application materials: February 7. Application fee required: $75. On-campus interview required.

Athletics Interscholastic: baseball (boys, girls), basketball (b,g), cross-country running (b,g), golf (b,g), racquetball (b,g), soccer (b,g), tennis (b,g), track and field (b,g), volleyball (g); coed interscholastic: racquetball; coed intramural: alpine skiing, backpacking, bicycling, bowling, canoeing/kayaking, climbing, fishing, fitness, Frisbee, hiking/backpacking, jogging, kayaking, mountain biking, mountaineering, nordic skiing, ocean paddling, outdoor activities, outdoor education, outdoor recreation, paddling, physical fitness, physical training, rafting, rock climbing, ropes courses, running, skiing (cross-country), skiing (downhill), snowshoeing, strength & conditioning, telemark skiing, ultimate Frisbee, walking, wall climbing, weight lifting, weight training, wilderness, wilderness survival, yoga. 6 PE instructors, 20 coaches.

Computers Computers are regularly used in animation, art, engineering, English, foreign language, graphic design, mathematics, science, theater, writing classes. Computer network features include on-campus library services, online commercial services, Internet access, wireless campus network, laptop requirement for all upper school students, videoconferencing, SmartBoards. Campus intranet and student e-mail accounts are available to students. The school has a published electronic and media policy.

Contact Ms. Marsha V. Trump, Assistant Director of Admission. 503-297-1894 Ext. 349. Fax: 503-297-0139. E-mail: trumpm@catlin.edu. Web site: www.catlin.edu.

CEDAR RIDGE ACADEMY

Roosevelt, Utah
See Special Needs Schools section.

CENTENNIAL ACADEMY

3641 Prud'homme Avenue
Montreal, Quebec H4A 3H6, Canada
Head of School: Mrs. Angela Burgos

General Information Coeducational day college-preparatory school; primarily serves students with learning disabilities, individuals with Attention Deficit Disorder, and dyslexic students. Grades 7–11. Founded: 1969. Setting: urban. 1 building on campus. Approved or accredited by Quebec Association of Independent Schools, Standards in Excellence And Learning (SEAL), and Quebec Department of Education. Language of instruction: English. Total enrollment: 222. Upper school average class size: 17. Upper school faculty-student ratio: 1:10.

Upper School Student Profile Grade 7: 31 students (24 boys, 7 girls); Grade 8: 38 students (31 boys, 7 girls); Grade 9: 60 students (52 boys, 8 girls); Grade 10: 60 students (45 boys, 15 girls); Grade 11: 71 students (51 boys, 20 girls).

Faculty School total: 30. In upper school: 12 men, 18 women; 18 have advanced degrees.

Subjects Offered Advanced chemistry, advanced math, art, art history, athletics, audio visual/media, band, basketball, biology, body human, bowling, Canadian geography, Canadian history, career and personal planning, career/college preparation, chemistry, competitive science projects, computer applications, computer multimedia, computer resources, computer science, creative writing, drama, economics, electives, English, fitness, French as a second language, general science, geography, golf, guidance, jazz band, lab science, language arts, leadership, library, mathematics, media studies, music, physical education, reading, science, sports, student government, swimming, tennis, volleyball, wrestling, yearbook.

Special Academic Programs International Baccalaureate program; honors section; independent study; remedial reading and/or remedial writing; remedial math; programs in English, mathematics, general development for dyslexic students.

College Admission Counseling 66 students graduated in 2009.

Student Life Upper grades have uniform requirement, honor system. Discipline rests primarily with faculty.

Tuition and Aid Day student tuition: CAN$15,560–CAN$15,750. Tuition installment plan (monthly payment plans, individually arranged payment plans). Bursaries, merit scholarship grants available. In 2009–10, 6% of upper-school students received aid. Total amount of financial aid awarded in 2009–10: CAN$80,000.

Admissions Traditional secondary-level entrance grade is 7. For fall 2009, 136 students applied for upper-level admission, 90 were accepted, 55 enrolled. Canadian Standardized Test, CTBS, OLSAT and Otis-Lennon School Ability Test required. Deadline for receipt of application materials: none. Application fee required: CAN$50. Interview required.

Athletics Interscholastic: basketball (boys, girls), lacrosse (b,g), rugby (b,g), soccer (b,g), touch football (g); coed interscholastic: cross-country running, curling, golf, indoor track, indoor track & field, running, track and field; coed intramural: badminton, ball hockey, basketball, bowling, broomball, Cosom hockey, cross-country running, fitness, floor hockey, handball, hockey, ice hockey, indoor track, indoor track & field, Newcombe ball, running, soccer, softball, tennis, track and field, volleyball. 2 PE instructors.

Computers Computers are regularly used in all academic classes. Computer network features include on-campus library services, Internet access, wireless campus network, Internet filtering or blocking technology. Campus intranet and student e-mail accounts are available to students. The school has a published electronic and media policy.

Contact Ms. Andrea Burdman, Administrative Assistant, Admissions. 514-486-5533 Ext. 236. Fax: 514-486-1401. E-mail: aburdman@centennial.qc.ca. Web site: www.centennial.qc.ca.

CENTRAL CATHOLIC HIGH SCHOOL

200 South Carpenter Road
Modesto, California 95351
Head of School: Jim Pecchenino

General Information Coeducational day college-preparatory, arts, religious studies, bilingual studies, and technology school, affiliated with Roman Catholic Church. Grades 9–12. Founded: 1966. Setting: urban. Nearest major city is Sacramento. 21-acre campus. 13 buildings on campus. Approved or accredited by Western Association of Schools and Colleges and Western Catholic Education Association. Endowment: $2.9 million. Total enrollment: 435. Upper school average class size: 24. Upper school faculty-student ratio: 1:15. There are 180 required school days per year for Upper School students. Upper School students typically attend 5 days per week. The average school day consists of 6 hours and 50 minutes.

Upper School Student Profile Grade 9: 109 students (57 boys, 52 girls); Grade 10: 105 students (56 boys, 49 girls); Grade 11: 117 students (64 boys, 53 girls); Grade 12: 113 students (64 boys, 49 girls). 83% of students are Roman Catholic.

Faculty School total: 29. In upper school: 8 men, 21 women; 14 have advanced degrees.

Subjects Offered Algebra, American history, American literature, art, Bible studies, biology, broadcast journalism, calculus, chemistry, choir, computer programming, computer science, creative writing, dance, drama, earth science, economics, English, English literature, environmental science, ethics, European history, expository writing, film appreciation, fine arts, geometry, government/civics, grammar, graphics, health, history, mathematics, music, music appreciation, philosophy, physical education, physical science, physics, pre-algebra, pre-calculus, psychology, psychology-AP, religion, science, social sciences, social studies, Spanish, speech, theater, theology, trigonometry, vocal ensemble, world history, world literature, writing, yearbook.

Graduation Requirements Arts and fine arts (art, music, dance, drama), computer science, English, mathematics, physical education (includes health), religion (includes Bible studies and theology), science, social sciences, social studies (includes history), speech, 80 Christian service hours. Community service is required.

Special Academic Programs Advanced Placement exam preparation; honors section; study at local college for college credit; academic accommodation for the gifted; remedial reading and/or remedial writing; remedial math; programs in English, mathematics, general development for dyslexic students.

College Admission Counseling 98 students graduated in 2010; 97 went to college, including California Polytechnic State University, San Luis Obispo; Modesto Junior College; Saint Mary's College of California; San Francisco State University; University of California, Berkeley; University of the Pacific. Other: 1 entered military service. Mean SAT critical reading: 534, mean SAT math: 524, mean SAT writing: 528, mean combined SAT: 1586, mean composite ACT: 23.

Student Life Upper grades have specified standards of dress, student council, honor system. Discipline rests primarily with faculty. Attendance at religious services is required.

Summer Programs Remediation programs offered; session focuses on remediation and SAT Prep; held on campus; accepts boys and girls; open to students from other schools. 109 students usually enrolled. 2011 schedule: June 3 to July 7. Application deadline: May 10.

Tuition and Aid Day student tuition: $8733–$9105. Guaranteed tuition plan. Tuition installment plan (monthly payment plans, individually arranged payment plans, Tuition Management Systems Plan, quarterly and semiannual payment plans). Tuition reduction for siblings, merit scholarship grants, need-based scholarship grants, paying campus jobs available. In 2010–11, 36% of upper-school students received aid; total upper-school merit-scholarship money awarded: $11,950. Total amount of financial aid awarded in 2010–11: $175,020.

Admissions Traditional secondary-level entrance grade is 9. For fall 2010, 134 students applied for upper-level admission, 109 were accepted, 109 enrolled. Cognitive Abilities Test, Iowa Test of Educational Development or USC/UC Math Diagnostic Test required. Deadline for receipt of application materials: none. Application fee required: $45. On-campus interview required.

Athletics Interscholastic: baseball (boys), basketball (b,g), cheering (g), cross-country running (b,g), football (b), golf (b,g), soccer (b,g), softball (g), tennis (b,g), track and field (b,g), volleyball (g), wrestling (b); coed interscholastic: dance, swimming and diving, water polo. 2 PE instructors, 72 coaches.

Computers Computers are regularly used in English, foreign language, graphic arts, literacy, mathematics, science, social studies, technology, Web site design, yearbook classes. Computer network features include on-campus library services, Internet access, Internet filtering or blocking technology. Student e-mail accounts and computer access in designated common areas are available to students. Students grades are available online. The school has a published electronic and media policy.

Contact Jodi Tybor, Admissions Coordinator/Registrar. 209-524-9611 Ext. 104. Fax: 209-524-4913. E-mail: tybor@cchsca.org. Web site: www.cchsca.org.

CENTRAL CATHOLIC HIGH SCHOOL

300 Hampshire Street
Lawrence, Massachusetts 01841
Head of School: Mrs. Doreen A. Keller

General Information Coeducational day college-preparatory, arts, business, religious studies, and technology school, affiliated with Roman Catholic Church. Grades 9–12. Founded: 1935. Setting: urban. Nearest major city is Boston. 1 building on campus. Approved or accredited by Commission on Independent Schools, New England Association of Schools and Colleges, and Massachusetts Department of Education. Total enrollment: 1,342. Upper school average class size: 25. Upper school faculty-student ratio: 1:24. There are 165 required school days per year for Upper School students. Upper School students typically attend 5 days per week. The average school day consists of 6 hours and 15 minutes.

Upper School Student Profile Grade 9: 341 students (169 boys, 172 girls); Grade 10: 328 students (170 boys, 158 girls); Grade 11: 349 students (166 boys, 183 girls); Grade 12: 324 students (147 boys, 177 girls). 80% of students are Roman Catholic.

Faculty School total: 93. In upper school: 50 men, 43 women; 72 have advanced degrees.

Subjects Offered Art, arts, computer science, English, fine arts, French, health, mathematics, physical education, religion, science, social studies, Spanish.

Graduation Requirements Arts and fine arts (art, music, dance, drama), computer science, English, foreign language, mathematics, religion (includes Bible studies and theology), science, social studies (includes history).

Special Academic Programs Advanced Placement exam preparation; honors section.

College Admission Counseling 323 students graduated in 2010; 322 went to college. Other: 1 went to work.

Student Life Upper grades have uniform requirement, student council, honor system. Discipline rests primarily with faculty. Attendance at religious services is required.

Tuition and Aid Day student tuition: $10,225. Tuition installment plan (FACTS Tuition Payment Plan, monthly payment plans). Merit scholarship grants, need-based scholarship grants available.

Admissions Traditional secondary-level entrance grade is 9. Archdiocese of Boston High School entrance exam provided by STS and High School Placement Test required. Deadline for receipt of application materials: none. No application fee required. Interview required.

Athletics Interscholastic: baseball (boys), basketball (b,g), bowling (b,g), cheering (g), cross-country running (b,g), dance squad (b,g), diving (b,g), equestrian sports (b,g), field hockey (g), figure skating (g), fishing (b,g), football (b), golf (b), gymnastics (g), hockey (b), ice hockey (b), ice skating (g), indoor hockey (g), indoor track (b,g), lacrosse (b,g), martial arts (b,g), modern dance (b,g), soccer (b,g), softball (g), swimming and diving (b,g), tennis (b,g), track and field (b,g), volleyball (b,g), wall climbing (b,g), winter (indoor) track (b,g), wrestling (b). 3 PE instructors, 1 athletic trainer.

Computers Computer network features include on-campus library services, Internet access, wireless campus network, Internet filtering or blocking technology. Campus intranet, student e-mail accounts, and computer access in designated common areas are available to students. The school has a published electronic and media policy.

Contact Mr. Christopher Merrill, Director of Admissions. 978-682-0260. Fax: 978-685-2707. E-mail: cmerrill@centralcatholic.net. Web site: www.centralcatholic.net.

CENTRAL CATHOLIC HIGH SCHOOL

4824 Tuscarawas Street West
Canton, Ohio 44708-5198
Head of School: Rev. Robert W. Kaylor

General Information Coeducational day college-preparatory school, affiliated with Roman Catholic Church. Grades 9–12. Founded: 1905. Setting: suburban. 65-acre campus. 1 building on campus. Approved or accredited by Ohio Catholic Schools Accreditation Association (OCSAA) and Ohio Department of Education. Total enrollment: 444. Upper school average class size: 25. Upper school faculty-student ratio: 1:16.

Upper School Student Profile Grade 9: 126 students (69 boys, 57 girls); Grade 10: 90 students (60 boys, 30 girls); Grade 11: 101 students (55 boys, 46 girls); Grade 12: 127 students (62 boys, 65 girls). 90% of students are Roman Catholic.

Faculty School total: 45. In upper school: 23 men, 22 women; 25 have advanced degrees.

Special Academic Programs Advanced Placement exam preparation.

College Admission Counseling 115 students graduated in 2010; 110 went to college, including Kent State University; Ohio University; The Ohio State University; The University of Akron. Other: 4 went to work, 1 entered military service. Mean SAT critical reading: 543, mean SAT math: 527, mean SAT writing: 527, mean composite ACT: 23.

Student Life Upper grades have specified standards of dress, student council, honor system. Discipline rests equally with students and faculty. Attendance at religious services is required.

Tuition and Aid Day student tuition: $5800–$6200. Tuition installment plan (FACTS Tuition Payment Plan, monthly payment plans, individually arranged payment plans). Tuition reduction for siblings, merit scholarship grants, need-based scholarship grants available. In 2010–11, 35% of upper-school students received aid; total upper-school merit-scholarship money awarded: $20,000. Total amount of financial aid awarded in 2010–11: $125,000.

Admissions Deadline for receipt of application materials: May 15. Application fee required: $15.

Athletics Interscholastic: baseball (boys), basketball (b,g), bowling (b,g), cheering (g), cross-country running (b,g), football (b), golf (b,g), soccer (b,g), softball (g), swimming and diving (b,g), tennis (b,g), volleyball (g), wrestling (b). 1 PE instructor.

Computers Computer resources include on-campus library services, Internet access. Campus intranet and student e-mail accounts are available to students. Students grades are available online. The school has a published electronic and media policy.

Contact 330-478-2131. Fax: 330-478-6086. Web site: www.cchsweb.com.

CENTRAL CATHOLIC HIGH SCHOOL

2550 Cherry Street
Toledo, Ohio 43608
Head of School: Rev. Dennis P. Hartigan

General Information Coeducational day college-preparatory, technology, and International Baccalaureate programme school, affiliated with Roman Catholic Church. Grades 9–12. Founded: 1920. Setting: urban. 25-acre campus. 3 buildings on campus. Approved or accredited by North Central Association of Colleges and Schools and Ohio Department of Education. Upper school average class size: 17. Upper school faculty-student ratio: 1:17. There are 181 required school days per year for Upper School students. Upper School students typically attend 5 days per week. The average school day consists of 7 hours.

Upper School Student Profile Grade 9: 250 students (130 boys, 120 girls); Grade 10: 264 students (135 boys, 129 girls); Grade 11: 260 students (116 boys, 144 girls); Grade 12: 296 students (157 boys, 139 girls). 75% of students are Roman Catholic.

Faculty School total: 74. In upper school: 31 men, 41 women; 24 have advanced degrees.

Special Academic Programs International Baccalaureate program; Advanced Placement exam preparation; honors section.

College Admission Counseling 222 students graduated in 2010; 210 went to college, including Bowling Green State University; Kent State University; Ohio University; The Ohio State University; The University of Toledo. Other: 1 went to work, 2 entered military service, 8 had other specific plans.

Student Life Upper grades have uniform requirement, student council, honor system. Discipline rests primarily with faculty. Attendance at religious services is required.

Summer Programs Remediation, enrichment, advancement, sports programs offered; session focuses on enrichment; held on campus; accepts boys and girls; open to students from other schools.

Tuition and Aid Day student tuition: $7400. Tuition installment plan (FACTS Tuition Payment Plan, monthly payment plans). Tuition reduction for siblings, merit scholarship grants, need-based scholarship grants, paying campus jobs available. In 2010–11, 80% of upper-school students received aid.

Admissions Traditional secondary-level entrance grade is 9. Catholic High School Entrance Examination required. Deadline for receipt of application materials: none. Application fee required. Interview required.

Computers Computer network features include on-campus library services, Internet access, wireless campus network, Internet filtering or blocking technology. Campus intranet and student e-mail accounts are available to students. Students grades are available online. The school has a published electronic and media policy.

Contact Mrs. Sandy Faunce, Registrar. 419-255-2280 Ext. 1107. Fax: 419-259-2848. E-mail: sfaunce@centralcatholic.org. Web site: www.centralcatholic.org.

CENTRAL CATHOLIC HIGH SCHOOL

4720 Fifth Avenue
Pittsburgh, Pennsylvania 15213
Head of School: Br. Richard F. Grzeskiewicz, FSC

General Information Boys' day college-preparatory, arts, business, and religious studies school, affiliated with Roman Catholic Church. Grades 9–12. Founded: 1927. Setting: urban. 2 buildings on campus. Approved or accredited by Middle States

Central Catholic High School

Association of Colleges and Schools and Pennsylvania Department of Education. Endowment: $6 million. Total enrollment: 835. Upper school average class size: 21. Upper school faculty-student ratio: 1:16.

Upper School Student Profile Grade 9: 192 students (192 boys); Grade 10: 226 students (226 boys); Grade 11: 225 students (225 boys); Grade 12: 223 students (223 boys). 83% of students are Roman Catholic.

Faculty School total: 54. In upper school: 44 men, 10 women; 23 have advanced degrees.

Subjects Offered 1968, accounting, algebra, American foreign policy, American literature, art, biology, biology-AP, British literature, British literature (honors), business, business mathematics, calculus, calculus-AP, chemistry, chemistry-AP, computer science, computers, consumer education, debate, economics-AP, electives, English, English-AP, environmental science, European history-AP, foreign language, French, geometry, German, health, history, honors algebra, honors English, honors geometry, instrumental music, Italian, Latin, law, marketing, math analysis, mathematics, music, music theory, physical education, physics, physics-AP, pre-calculus, probability and statistics, programming, psychology, religion, science, social studies, sociology, Spanish, Spanish-AP, studio art, theater arts, trigonometry, U.S. history, U.S. history-AP, vocal music, world history, world literature, writing.

Special Academic Programs Advanced Placement exam preparation; honors section; study at local college for college credit; academic accommodation for the gifted.

College Admission Counseling 191 students graduated in 2010; 187 went to college, including Carnegie Mellon University; Duquesne University; Miami University; Penn State University Park; University of Pittsburgh. Other: 3 went to work, 1 entered military service. Mean SAT critical reading: 549, mean SAT math: 563, mean SAT writing: 534, mean combined SAT: 1646. 35% scored over 600 on SAT critical reading, 35% scored over 600 on SAT math, 35% scored over 600 on SAT writing.

Student Life Upper grades have specified standards of dress, student council. Discipline rests primarily with faculty. Attendance at religious services is required.

Summer Programs Remediation programs offered; session focuses on make-up courses; held on campus; accepts boys and girls; open to students from other schools. 60 students usually enrolled. 2011 schedule: June to July.

Tuition and Aid Day student tuition: $7750. Tuition installment plan (SMART Tuition Payment Plan). Merit scholarship grants, need-based scholarship grants available. In 2010–11, 35% of upper-school students received aid; total upper-school merit-scholarship money awarded: $20,000. Total amount of financial aid awarded in 2010–11: $1,250,000.

Admissions Traditional secondary-level entrance grade is 9. For fall 2010, 300 students applied for upper-level admission, 240 were accepted, 192 enrolled. Scholastic Testing Service High School Placement Test or STS Examination required. Deadline for receipt of application materials: February 1. No application fee required. Interview recommended.

Athletics Interscholastic: baseball, basketball, bowling, crew, cross-country running, fencing, football, golf, hockey, ice hockey, in-line hockey, lacrosse, soccer, squash, swimming and diving, tennis, track and field, volleyball, wrestling; intramural: basketball, flag football, football, Frisbee, touch football. 2 PE instructors, 27 coaches, 2 athletic trainers.

Computers Computers are regularly used in business applications, college planning, data processing, library skills, mathematics, newspaper, yearbook classes. Computer network features include on-campus library services, online commercial services, Internet access, wireless campus network, Internet filtering or blocking technology. Campus intranet, student e-mail accounts, and computer access in designated common areas are available to students. Students grades are available online. The school has a published electronic and media policy.

Contact Mr. Brian Miller, Director of Admissions. 412-621-7505. Fax: 412-208-0555. E-mail: bmiller@centralcatholichs.com. Web site: www.centralcatholichs.com.

CENTRAL CATHOLIC HIGH SCHOOL

1403 North St. Mary's Street
San Antonio, Texas 78215-1785
Head of School: Br. Peter A. Pontolillo, S. M., PhD

General Information Boys' day college-preparatory school, affiliated with Roman Catholic Church. Grades 9–12. Founded: 1852. Setting: urban. 10-acre campus. 2 buildings on campus. Approved or accredited by National Catholic Education Association, Southern Association of Colleges and Schools, Texas Catholic Conference, and Texas Department of Education. Endowment: $1 million. Total enrollment: 535. Upper school average class size: 23. Upper school faculty-student ratio: 1:12. There are 180 required school days per year for Upper School students. Upper School students typically attend 5 days per week. The average school day consists of 6 hours and 30 minutes.

Upper School Student Profile Grade 9: 146 students (146 boys); Grade 10: 155 students (155 boys); Grade 11: 120 students (120 boys); Grade 12: 114 students (114 boys). 90% of students are Roman Catholic.

Faculty School total: 46. In upper school: 33 men, 13 women; 23 have advanced degrees.

Subjects Offered Algebra, American government, American history-AP, anatomy, art, biology, calculus-AP, ceramics, chemistry, chemistry-AP, chorus, Christian and Hebrew scripture, church history, community service, computer science, concert band, economics, English, English language and composition-AP, English language-AP, English literature and composition-AP, English literature-AP, environmental science, fine arts, geometry, health, honors algebra, honors English, honors geometry, honors world history, humanities, information technology, jazz band, journalism, JROTC, languages, Latin, marching band, physics, pre-calculus, probability and statistics, psychology, religion, science, social studies, Spanish, Spanish literature-AP, speech, theater, trigonometry, world geography, world history.

Graduation Requirements Algebra, American government, American history, arts and fine arts (art, music, dance, drama), biology, chemistry, Christian and Hebrew scripture, Christian doctrine, computer information systems, computer science, economics, English, foreign language, geometry, health, JROTC, moral reasoning, religion (includes Bible studies and theology), religious education, social justice, speech, trigonometry, world civilizations, world geography, world history, world religions, requirements for Marianist Honors Diploma differ. Community service is required.

Special Academic Programs 6 Advanced Placement exams for which test preparation is offered; honors section; independent study; study at local college for college credit; study abroad.

College Admission Counseling 114 students graduated in 2010; 113 went to college, including Saint Mary's University; Texas A&M University; Texas Tech University; The University of Texas at Austin; The University of Texas at San Antonio; University of the Incarnate Word. Other: 1 entered military service. Mean SAT critical reading: 534, mean SAT math: 532, mean SAT writing: 519, mean combined SAT: 1585, mean composite ACT: 24.

Student Life Upper grades have specified standards of dress, student council, honor system. Discipline rests primarily with faculty. Attendance at religious services is required.

Summer Programs Remediation, enrichment, advancement, sports, computer instruction programs offered; session focuses on enrichment and make-up courses, sports; held on campus; accepts boys and girls; open to students from other schools. 300 students usually enrolled. 2011 schedule: June 13 to July 22. Application deadline: none.

Tuition and Aid Day student tuition: $8995. Tuition installment plan (monthly payment plans, semester payment plan, Tuition Management Systems). Tuition reduction for siblings, merit scholarship grants, need-based scholarship grants, paying campus jobs available. In 2010–11, 45% of upper-school students received aid; total upper-school merit-scholarship money awarded: $54,000. Total amount of financial aid awarded in 2010–11: $584,420.

Admissions Traditional secondary-level entrance grade is 9. For fall 2010, 220 students applied for upper-level admission, 170 were accepted, 150 enrolled. Essay, Scholastic Testing Service High School Placement Test and writing sample required. Deadline for receipt of application materials: none. No application fee required. On-campus interview recommended.

Athletics Interscholastic: baseball, basketball, cheering (g), cross-country running, drill team, football, golf, JROTC drill, lacrosse, physical training, riflery, soccer, strength & conditioning, swimming and diving, tennis, track and field, weight training; intramural: basketball, bowling, football, softball, strength & conditioning, swimming and diving, volleyball. 1 PE instructor, 21 coaches, 1 athletic trainer.

Computers Computers are regularly used in college planning, drawing and design, information technology, journalism, newspaper, science, yearbook classes. Computer network features include on-campus library services, Internet access, Internet filtering or blocking technology, access to other libraries through Texas Library Connection. Students grades are available online. The school has a published electronic and media policy.

Contact Mrs. Belia Gonzalez McDonald, Director of Admissions and Tuition Assistance. 210-225-6794 Ext. 209. Fax: 210-227-9353. E-mail: admissions@cchs-satx.org. Web site: www.cchs-satx.org.

CENTRAL CATHOLIC MID-HIGH SCHOOL

1200 Ruby Avenue
Grand Island, Nebraska 68803-3799
Head of School: Mr. John Golka

General Information Coeducational day college-preparatory and religious studies school, affiliated with Roman Catholic Church. Grades 6–12. Founded: 1956. Setting: suburban. 1 building on campus. Approved or accredited by National Catholic Education Association, North Central Association of Colleges and Schools, The College Board, and Nebraska Department of Education. Total enrollment: 340. Upper school average class size: 17. Upper school faculty-student ratio: 1:15. There are 175 required school days per year for Upper School students. Upper School students typically attend 5 days per week. The average school day consists of 7 hours.

Upper School Student Profile Grade 9: 54 students (22 boys, 32 girls); Grade 10: 38 students (18 boys, 20 girls); Grade 11: 44 students (24 boys, 20 girls); Grade 12: 52 students (26 boys, 26 girls). 98% of students are Roman Catholic.

Faculty School total: 36. In upper school: 8 men, 28 women; 13 have advanced degrees.

Subjects Offered ACT preparation, advanced chemistry, Advanced Placement courses, algebra, American government, American history, art, audio visual/media, basketball, biology, calculus-AP, career education, careers, Catholic belief and practice, cheerleading, chemistry, college writing, commercial art, computer applications, concert band, concert choir, contemporary problems, CPR, desktop publishing, drama, driver education, economics, English, English composition, English/

composition-AP, environmental science, general science, golf, government, guidance, health, history, human biology, instrumental music, jazz band, journalism, marching band, mechanical drawing, music, music theory, newspaper, novels, physical education, physics, pre-algebra, pre-calculus, psychology, public speaking, religious studies, senior seminar, sociology, Spanish, speech, tennis, U.S. government, video film production, vocal music, volleyball, Web site design, weight training, world history, world history-AP, wrestling, yearbook.

Graduation Requirements American government, American history, American literature, biology, composition, computer applications, English, English composition, English literature, English literature and composition-AP, English/composition-AP, geography, government, history, mathematics, physical education (includes health), religion (includes Bible studies and theology), science, senior seminar, world history, world history-AP, community service.

Special Academic Programs Advanced Placement exam preparation; study at local college for college credit.

College Admission Counseling 38 students graduated in 2010; 36 went to college, including Creighton University; University of Nebraska–Lincoln; University of Nebraska at Kearney; University of Nebraska at Omaha. Other: 1 went to work, 1 entered military service. Median composite ACT: 24. 29% scored over 26 on composite ACT.

Student Life Upper grades have uniform requirement, student council. Discipline rests primarily with faculty. Attendance at religious services is required.

Summer Programs Remediation programs offered; session focuses on English and math; held on campus; accepts boys and girls; not open to students from other schools. 10 students usually enrolled. 2011 schedule: June to July. Application deadline: May.

Tuition and Aid Tuition installment plan (monthly payment plans). Tuition reduction for siblings, need-based scholarship grants, paying campus jobs available.

Admissions Traditional secondary-level entrance grade is 9. Deadline for receipt of application materials: none. Application fee required: $100. Interview recommended.

Athletics Interscholastic: baseball (boys), basketball (b,g), cheering (g), cross-country running (b,g), dance team (g), football (b), golf (b,g), physical fitness (b,g), soccer (b,g), tennis (b,g), track and field (b,g), volleyball (g), weight lifting (b,g), weight training (b,g), wrestling (b); coed interscholastic: power lifting; coed intramural: volleyball. 2 PE instructors.

Computers Computers are regularly used in computer applications, desktop publishing, drafting, English, journalism, keyboarding, Web site design, writing, yearbook classes. Computer network features include on-campus library services, Internet access, Internet filtering or blocking technology. Computer access in designated common areas is available to students. Students grades are available online. The school has a published electronic and media policy.

Contact Admissions. 308-384-2440. Fax: 308-389-3274. Web site: www.gicentralcatholic.org/.

CENTRAL CHRISTIAN HIGH SCHOOL

3970 Kidron Road
PO Box 9
Kidron, Ohio 44636
Head of School: Eugene Miller

General Information Coeducational day college-preparatory, general academic, arts, business, and religious studies school, affiliated with Mennonite Church. Grades K–12. Founded: 1962. Setting: rural. Nearest major city is Wooster. 60-acre campus. 1 building on campus. Approved or accredited by Mennonite Schools Council and Ohio Department of Education. Endowment: $500,000. Total enrollment: 286. Upper school average class size: 20. Upper school faculty-student ratio: 1:13.

Upper School Student Profile 61% of students are Mennonite.

Faculty School total: 31. In upper school: 8 men, 7 women; 4 have advanced degrees.

Subjects Offered Algebra, American government, American history, American literature, anatomy, art, Bible studies, biology, business, business skills, ceramics, chemistry, child development, community service, current events, ecology, English, English literature, environmental science, European history, fine arts, general science, geography, geometry, government/civics, grammar, health, history, home economics, human development, industrial arts, journalism, mathematics, music, photography, physical education, physics, pre-calculus, religion, Romantic period literature, science, sculpture, social sciences, social studies, sociology, Spanish, trigonometry, world history, world literature, writing.

Graduation Requirements Arts and fine arts (art, music, dance, drama), business skills (includes word processing), English, foreign language, mathematics, physical education (includes health), religion (includes Bible studies and theology), science, social sciences, social studies (includes history). Community service is required.

Special Academic Programs Advanced Placement exam preparation; honors section; independent study; term-away projects; study at local college for college credit; academic accommodation for the gifted and the musically talented; remedial reading and/or remedial writing; remedial math.

College Admission Counseling 35 students graduated in 2009; 21 went to college, including Eastern Mennonite University; Goshen College; Malone University; The University of Akron. Other: 5 went to work, 2 entered military service, 2 had other specific plans.

Student Life Upper grades have specified standards of dress, student council, honor system. Discipline rests primarily with faculty.

Tuition and Aid Day student tuition: $4999–$6499. Tuition installment plan (monthly payment plans, individually arranged payment plans). Need-based scholarship grants available. In 2009–10, 8% of upper-school students received aid.

Admissions Traditional secondary-level entrance grade is 9. Deadline for receipt of application materials: none. Application fee required: $295. Interview required.

Athletics Interscholastic: baseball (boys), basketball (b,g), cross-country running (b,g), golf (b), soccer (b), softball (g), tennis (b,g), volleyball (g); intramural: basketball (b,g), soccer (b,g), softball (b,g), tennis (b,g), volleyball (b,g), weight lifting (b,g); coed intramural: skiing (downhill), soccer, softball, table tennis, tennis, volleyball. 2 PE instructors.

Computers Computers are regularly used in desktop publishing, English, keyboarding, science classes. Computer network features include on-campus library services, Internet access, Internet filtering or blocking technology. The school has a published electronic and media policy.

Contact Doris Risser, Admissions Director. 330-857-7311 Ext. 206. Web site: www.ccscomets.org.

CENTRAL VALLEY CHRISTIAN ACADEMY

2020 Academy Place
Ceres, California 95071
Head of School: Wayne Dunbar

General Information Coeducational day college-preparatory, arts, vocational, religious studies, and technology school, affiliated with Seventh-day Adventist Church. Grades K–12. Founded: 1910. Setting: suburban. 10-acre campus. 3 buildings on campus. Approved or accredited by Board of Regents, General Conference of Seventh-day Adventists, Western Association of Schools and Colleges, and California Department of Education. Total enrollment: 219. Upper school average class size: 24. Upper school faculty-student ratio: 1:10. There are 180 required school days per year for Upper School students. Upper School students typically attend 5 days per week. The average school day consists of 7 hours and 20 minutes.

Upper School Student Profile Grade 9: 15 students (7 boys, 8 girls); Grade 10: 22 students (15 boys, 7 girls); Grade 11: 15 students (9 boys, 6 girls); Grade 12: 27 students (15 boys, 12 girls); Postgraduate: 79 students (46 boys, 33 girls). 85% of students are Seventh-day Adventists.

Faculty School total: 20. In upper school: 6 men, 2 women; 3 have advanced degrees.

Subjects Offered Algebra, art, audio visual/media, auto mechanics, band, biology, broadcasting, business mathematics, chemistry, choir, community service, computer resources, economics, English, geometry, gymnastics, health, home economics, keyboarding, music, physical education, physical science, physics, pre-algebra, religion, Spanish, U.S. government, U.S. history, world history.

Graduation Requirements Algebra, American government, American history, arts and fine arts (art, music, dance, drama), biology, career education, chemistry, computer literacy, earth science, electives, English, geometry, government/civics, keyboarding, physical education (includes health), physics, practical arts, religion (includes Bible studies and theology), science, Spanish, work experience. Community service is required.

Special Academic Programs Honors section; accelerated programs; independent study; study at local college for college credit.

College Admission Counseling 25 students graduated in 2009; 20 went to college, including Pacific Union College; Walla Walla University. Other: 2 went to work, 1 had other specific plans.

Student Life Upper grades have uniform requirement, student council, honor system. Discipline rests primarily with faculty. Attendance at religious services is required.

Tuition and Aid Day student tuition: $7200. Tuition installment plan (monthly payment plans, individually arranged payment plans). Tuition reduction for siblings, need-based scholarship grants, paying campus jobs available. In 2009–10, 30% of upper-school students received aid. Total amount of financial aid awarded in 2009–10: $75,000.

Admissions Traditional secondary-level entrance grade is 9. TOEFL required. Deadline for receipt of application materials: none. No application fee required. Interview required.

Athletics Interscholastic: basketball (boys, girls), fitness (b,g), flag football (b,g), independent competitive sports (b,g), indoor track & field (b,g), soccer (b,g), softball (b,g), volleyball (b,g); intramural: baseball (g), basketball (b,g), fitness (b,g), flag football (b,g), gymnastics (b,g), indoor track & field (b,g), physical fitness (b,g), soccer (b,g), softball (b,g), tennis (b,g), track and field (b,g), ultimate Frisbee (b,g), volleyball (b,g); coed interscholastic: basketball, fitness, flag football, independent competitive sports, indoor track & field, soccer, softball, volleyball; coed intramural: basketball, fitness, flag football, gymnastics, indoor track & field, physical fitness, soccer, softball, tennis, track and field, ultimate Frisbee, volleyball. 1 PE instructor, 1 coach.

Computers Computers are regularly used in independent study, journalism, keyboarding, mathematics, media production, science, Spanish, video film production, yearbook classes. Computer resources include Internet access, wireless campus network, Internet filtering or blocking technology. Students grades are available online. The school has a published electronic and media policy.

Contact Lisa Nuss, Registrar. 209-537-4521. Fax: 209-538-0706. E-mail: nussl@cvcaonline.net. Web site: cvcaonline.net.

CENTRAL VALLEY CHRISTIAN SCHOOL

5600 West Tulare Avenue
Visalia, California 93277
Head of School: Dr. John De Leeuw

General Information Coeducational boarding and day and distance learning college-preparatory school, affiliated with Christian Reformed Church, Protestant Church. Distance learning grade X. Founded: 1979. Setting: urban. 30-acre campus. 6 buildings on campus. Approved or accredited by Association of Independent Schools and Colleges of Alberta, Christian Schools International, European Council of International Schools, Western Association of Schools and Colleges, and California Department of Education. Total enrollment: 909. Upper school average class size: 22. Upper school faculty-student ratio: 1:16. There are 180 required school days per year for Upper School students. Upper School students typically attend 5 days per week. The average school day consists of 6 hours and 45 minutes.

Upper School Student Profile 50% of students are members of Christian Reformed Church, Protestant.

Faculty School total: 75. In upper school: 20 men, 10 women; 14 have advanced degrees.

Student Life Upper grades have honor system. Attendance at religious services is required.

Admissions Woodcock-Johnson required. Deadline for receipt of application materials: July 1. Application fee required: $100. Interview required.

Computers Students grades are available online. The school has a published electronic and media policy.

Contact Mrs. Bernita Vander Schaaf, Director of Admissions. 559-734-2684 Ext. 260. Fax: 559-734-2051. E-mail: admissions@cvc.org. Web site: www.cvc.org.

CENTURY HIGH SCHOOL

300-1788 West Broadway
Vancouver, British Columbia V6J 1Y1, Canada
Head of School: Dr. Godwin S. Choy

General Information Coeducational day college-preparatory school. Grades 8–12. Founded: 1997. Setting: urban. 1 building on campus. Approved or accredited by British Columbia Department of Education. Language of instruction: English. Total enrollment: 200. Upper school average class size: 20. Upper school faculty-student ratio: 1:22.

Faculty School total: 9. In upper school: 4 men, 2 women; 3 have advanced degrees.

Subjects Offered Accounting, biology, calculus, career and personal planning, chemistry, creative arts, English, geography, Japanese, language arts, Mandarin, mathematics, physics, science, social studies.

Special Academic Programs ESL (6 students enrolled).

College Admission Counseling 100 students graduated in 2009; 90 went to college, including Dalhousie University; Queen's University at Kingston; Simon Fraser University; The University of British Columbia; University of Toronto; University of Victoria. Other: 10 went to work.

Student Life Discipline rests primarily with faculty.

Tuition and Aid Day student tuition: CAN$13,200.

Admissions Traditional secondary-level entrance grade is 8. Deadline for receipt of application materials: none. Application fee required: CAN$200.

Computers Computers are regularly used in accounting classes. Computer resources include Internet access, wireless campus network, Internet filtering or blocking technology. Student e-mail accounts are available to students.

Contact Ms. Noel P. Lee, Director of Admissions. 604-730-8138 Ext. 106. Fax: 604-731-9542. E-mail: noellee@centuryhighschool.ca. Web site: www. centuryhighschool.ca.

CFS, THE SCHOOL AT CHURCH FARM

1001 East Lincoln Highway
Exton, Pennsylvania 19341
Head of School: Rev. Edmund K. Sherrill II

General Information Boys' boarding and day college-preparatory, arts, and technology school, affiliated with Episcopal Church. Grades 7–12. Founded: 1918. Setting: suburban. Nearest major city is Philadelphia. Students are housed in single-sex dormitories. 200-acre campus. 19 buildings on campus. Approved or accredited by Middle States Association of Colleges and Schools, National Association of Episcopal Schools, The Association of Boarding Schools, and Pennsylvania Department of Education. Member of National Association of Independent Schools and Secondary School Admission Test Board. Endowment: $125 million. Total enrollment: 183. Upper school average class size: 10. Upper school faculty-student ratio: 1:7. There are 180 required school days per year for Upper School students. Upper School students typically attend 5 days per week. The average school day consists of 7 hours and 30 minutes.

Upper School Student Profile Grade 9: 34 students (34 boys); Grade 10: 40 students (40 boys); Grade 11: 41 students (41 boys); Grade 12: 34 students (34 boys). 93% of students are boarding students. 52% are state residents. 11 states are represented in upper school student body. 19% are international students. International students from China, Czech Republic, Nigeria, Puerto Rico, Republic of Korea, and Thailand; 2 other countries represented in student body. 15% of students are members of Episcopal Church.

Faculty School total: 35. In upper school: 24 men, 11 women; 18 have advanced degrees; 26 reside on campus.

Subjects Offered 20th century history, 3-dimensional design, African-American history, algebra, American government, American history, American history-AP, American literature, American studies, anatomy and physiology, art, art history, biology, biology-AP, British literature, calculus-AP, ceramics, chemistry, chemistry-AP, choir, choral music, clayworking, college writing, composition, computer science, construction, creative writing, design, drama, driver education, earth science, ecology, economics, English, English-AP, environmental science, ethics, European history, expository writing, film and literature, fine arts, French, geometry, government/civics, grammar, health, history, history of jazz, industrial arts, instrumental music, journalism, leadership, mathematics, medieval history, music, music history, music technology, musicianship, mythology, photography, physical education, physics, physics-AP, poetry, pre-calculus, psychology, public speaking, Russian history, science, Shakespeare, Shakespearean histories, social studies, sociology, Spanish, speech, statistics, technology, theater, trigonometry, Vietnam history, Vietnam War, weaving, Web site design, woodworking, world history, world literature, world religions, World War II, writing.

Graduation Requirements Arts and fine arts (art, music, dance, drama), English, foreign language, mathematics, physical education (includes health), religion (includes Bible studies and theology), science, social studies (includes history), technology, Challenge of Required Experience (combination of community service and outdoor educational experience).

Special Academic Programs 5 Advanced Placement exams for which test preparation is offered; honors section; accelerated programs; independent study; study at local college for college credit; academic accommodation for the gifted, the musically talented, and the artistically talented.

College Admission Counseling 28 students graduated in 2010; 27 went to college, including American University; Northwestern University; Purdue University; University of Maryland, College Park; University of Pennsylvania; Washington University in St. Louis. Other: 1 entered a postgraduate year. Median SAT critical reading: 540, median SAT math: 580, median SAT writing: 500, median combined SAT: 1580. 24% scored over 600 on SAT critical reading, 35% scored over 600 on SAT math, 21% scored over 600 on SAT writing, 21% scored over 1800 on combined SAT.

Student Life Upper grades have specified standards of dress, student council. Discipline rests primarily with faculty. Attendance at religious services is required.

Tuition and Aid Day student tuition: $15,000; 5-day tuition and room/board: $25,000; 7-day tuition and room/board: $25,000. Tuition installment plan (monthly payment plans, individually arranged payment plans). Need-based scholarship grants, scholarships from third-party agencies with which the school has established relationships available. In 2010–11, 92% of upper-school students received aid. Total amount of financial aid awarded in 2010–11: $3,397,205.

Admissions Traditional secondary-level entrance grade is 9. For fall 2010, 226 students applied for upper-level admission, 85 were accepted, 62 enrolled. ISEE, SSAT or TOEFL required. Deadline for receipt of application materials: none. Application fee required: $25. Interview required.

Athletics Interscholastic: baseball, basketball, cross-country running, fencing, golf, indoor track, soccer, tennis, track and field, wrestling; intramural: fitness, floor hockey, indoor soccer, physical fitness, strength & conditioning, touch football, weight lifting. 10 coaches.

Computers Computers are regularly used in art, English, foreign language, history, mathematics, music, science, technology classes. Computer network features include on-campus library services, online commercial services, Internet access, wireless campus network, Internet filtering or blocking technology, each student receives a laptop computer. Campus intranet and student e-mail accounts are available to students. Students grades are available online. The school has a published electronic and media policy.

Contact Bart Bronk, Director of Admissions. 610-363-5346. Fax: 610-280-6746. E-mail: bbronk@gocfs.net. Web site: www.gocfs.net.

CHADWICK SCHOOL

26800 South Academy Drive
Palos Verdes Peninsula, California 90274
Head of School: Frederick T. Hill

General Information Coeducational day college-preparatory, arts, and technology school. Grades K–12. Founded: 1935. Setting: suburban. Nearest major city is Los Angeles. 45-acre campus. 5 buildings on campus. Approved or accredited by Association for Experiential Education, California Association of Independent Schools, The College Board, Western Association of Schools and Colleges, and California Department of Education. Member of National Association of Independent Schools. Endowment: $18 million. Total enrollment: 875. Upper school average class size: 16. Upper school faculty-student ratio: 1:6. Upper School students typically attend 5 days per week. The average school day consists of 6 hours and 15 minutes.

Upper School Student Profile Grade 9: 97 students (47 boys, 50 girls); Grade 10: 99 students (47 boys, 52 girls); Grade 11: 98 students (44 boys, 54 girls); Grade 12: 82 students (36 boys, 46 girls).

Faculty School total: 67. In upper school: 27 men, 36 women; 43 have advanced degrees.

Subjects Offered Advanced Placement courses, African history, algebra, American history, American literature, art, art history-AP, art-AP, Asian history, biology, calculus, calculus-AP, ceramics, chemistry, chemistry-AP, choral music, computer math, computer programming, computer science, creative writing, dance, drama, English, English literature, English literature-AP, European history; expository writing, fine arts, forensics, French, French-AP, geometry, grammar, health, history, history of science, honors algebra, honors geometry, instrumental music, integrated science, Latin, Latin American history, Latin American studies, life science, Mandarin, marine biology, mathematics, Middle East, Middle Eastern history, music, music theory-AP, outdoor education, photography, physical education, physics, pre-calculus, probability, robotics, science, social studies, South African history, Spanish, Spanish-AP, speech, statistics, theater, trigonometry, U.S. history-AP, wilderness education, world history, world literature, writing, yearbook.

Graduation Requirements Arts and fine arts (art, music, dance, drama), English, foreign language, history, mathematics, outdoor education, physical education (includes health), science.

Special Academic Programs Advanced Placement exam preparation; honors section; independent study; term-away projects; study abroad; academic accommodation for the gifted, the musically talented, and the artistically talented.

College Admission Counseling 78 students graduated in 2009; all went to college, including Dartmouth College; Loyola Marymount University; Stanford University; University of California, Berkeley; University of Southern California; Williams College. Mean SAT critical reading: 654, mean SAT math: 685, mean SAT writing: 702, mean combined SAT: 2041.

Student Life Upper grades have specified standards of dress, student council, honor system. Discipline rests equally with students and faculty.

Tuition and Aid Day student tuition: $25,100. Tuition installment plan (Key Tuition Payment Plan, individually arranged payment plans). Need-based scholarship grants, paying campus jobs, Malone Scholarships (need/merit-based), MacFarlane Scholarship (need/merit-based) available. In 2009–10, 22% of upper-school students received aid. Total amount of financial aid awarded in 2009–10: $1570.

Admissions Traditional secondary-level entrance grade is 9. ISEE required. Deadline for receipt of application materials: January 15. Application fee required: $125. On-campus interview required.

Athletics Interscholastic: baseball (boys), basketball (b,g), cheering (g), cross-country running (b,g), diving (b,g), football (b), golf (b,g), lacrosse (b,g), soccer (b,g), softball (g), swimming and diving (b,g), tennis (b,g), track and field (b,g), volleyball (b,g), water polo (b,g); intramural: aerobics/dance (g), dance (g), horseback riding (g); coed interscholastic: cheering, equestrian sports. 11 coaches, 1 athletic trainer.

Computers Computers are regularly used in art, computer applications, creative writing, drawing and design, English, foreign language, geography, graphic arts, health, history, humanities, mathematics, music, newspaper, photography, photojournalism, publications, science, social studies, Web site design, yearbook classes. Computer network features include on-campus library services, Internet access, wireless campus network, Internet filtering or blocking technology. Campus intranet, student e-mail accounts, and computer access in designated common areas are available to students. Students grades are available online. The school has a published electronic and media policy.

Contact Rita Mills, Admission Manager. 310-377-1543 Ext. 4025. Fax: 310-377-0380. E-mail: admissions@chadwickschool.org. Web site: www.chadwickschool.org.

CHAMBERLAIN-HUNT ACADEMY
124 McComb Avenue
Port Gibson, Mississippi 39150
Head of School: Col. Jack Gardner West

General Information Boys' boarding and coeducational day college-preparatory, arts, religious studies, music, and military school, affiliated with Presbyterian Church, Reformed Church. Boarding boys grades 7–12, day boys grades 7–12, day girls grades 7–12. Founded: 1879. Setting: small town. Nearest major city is Vicksburg. Students are housed in single-sex dormitories. 230-acre campus. 11 buildings on campus. Approved or accredited by Assocaition of Classical Christian Schools, Mississippi Private School Association, Southern Association of Colleges and Schools, and Mississippi Department of Education. Endowment: $29 million. Total enrollment: 90. Upper school average class size: 5. Upper school faculty-student ratio: 1:5. There are 180 required school days per year for Upper School students. Upper School students typically attend 5 days per week. The average school day consists of 7 hours and 45 minutes.

Upper School Student Profile Grade 7: 9 students (6 boys, 3 girls); Grade 8: 18 students (16 boys, 2 girls); Grade 9: 20 students (17 boys, 3 girls); Grade 10: 26 students (24 boys, 2 girls); Grade 11: 14 students (14 boys); Grade 12: 15 students (15 boys). 87% of students are boarding students. 27% are state residents. 20 states are represented in upper school student body. 4% are international students. International students from Australia and China. 12% of students are Presbyterian, Reformed.

Faculty School total: 23. In upper school: 14 men, 4 women; 12 have advanced degrees; 14 reside on campus.

Subjects Offered ACT preparation, advanced math, Advanced Placement courses, algebra, American Civil War, American government, American history, American

literature-AP, ancient history, art, Bible, biology, British literature, business, calculus, chemistry, choir, Christian doctrine, Christian ethics, church history, classical Greek literature, computer programming, computer skills, CPR, earth science, economics, English, English literature, English literature-AP, ethics, French, geometry, government, keyboarding, Latin, logic, men's studies, military history, physics, pre-algebra, rhetoric, Spanish, theology, U.S. government, U.S. history, vocal ensemble, wilderness experience, world history, world wide web design.

Graduation Requirements Algebra, American literature, anatomy and physiology, Bible, biology, British literature, chemistry, classical Greek literature, economics, electives, geometry, intro to computers, languages, medieval literature, rhetoric, state history, Talmud, U.S. government, U.S. history, world geography, world history, oral comprehensive exams, senior speech, worldview class.

Special Academic Programs International Baccalaureate program; honors section; accelerated programs; independent study; academic accommodation for the gifted, the musically talented, and the artistically talented; remedial reading and/or remedial writing; remedial math; special instructional classes for students with ADD and emotional/behavioral problems.

College Admission Counseling 14 students graduated in 2010; 9 went to college, including Harding University; Louisiana State University and Agricultural and Mechanical College; Mississippi College; Mississippi State University; Palm Beach Atlantic University; University of Mississippi. Other: 2 went to work, 3 entered military service. 50% scored over 26 on composite ACT.

Student Life Upper grades have uniform requirement, student council, honor system. Discipline rests primarily with faculty. Attendance at religious services is required.

Summer Programs Remediation, enrichment, advancement, sports, rigorous outdoor training programs offered; session focuses on remediation and advancement courses along with weekend activities such as rafting, paintball, and ropes course; held both on and off campus; held at professional sporting events; accepts boys; open to students from other schools. 55 students usually enrolled. 2011 schedule: June 6 to July 2. Application deadline: May 21.

Tuition and Aid Day student tuition: $8500; 7-day tuition and room/board: $19,000. Tuition installment plan (The Tuition Plan, monthly payment plans, individually arranged payment plans). Merit scholarship grants, need-based scholarship grants available. In 2010–11, 40% of upper-school students received aid; total upper-school merit-scholarship money awarded: $10,000. Total amount of financial aid awarded in 2010–11: $276,530.

Admissions Traditional secondary-level entrance grade is 10. For fall 2010, 117 students applied for upper-level admission, 100 were accepted, 76 enrolled. Math and English placement tests required. Deadline for receipt of application materials: none. Application fee required: $50. On-campus interview required.

Athletics Interscholastic: basketball (boys), soccer (b), track and field (b), winter soccer (b); intramural: baseball (b), basketball (b), canoeing/kayaking (b), climbing (b), cross-country running (b), fishing (b), fitness (b), flag football (b), hiking/backpacking (b), jogging (b), life saving (b), marksmanship (b), outdoor activities (b), outdoor adventure (b), outdoor education (b), outdoor recreation (b), outdoor skills (b), paint ball (b), physical fitness (b), physical training (b), rappelling (b), riflery (b), rock climbing (b), ropes courses (b), running (b), skeet shooting (b), soccer (b), softball (b), strength & conditioning (b), swimming and diving (b), table tennis (b), tennis (b), track and field (b,g), ultimate Frisbee (b), volleyball (b), wall climbing (b), weight lifting (b), weight training (b), wilderness (b), wilderness survival (b), wildernessways (b); coed interscholastic: cross-country running. 6 PE instructors, 4 coaches, 1 athletic trainer.

Computers Computers are regularly used in library skills, programming, typing, Web site design classes. Computer network features include on-campus library services, online commercial services, Internet access, wireless campus network, Internet filtering or blocking technology. Students grades are available online. The school has a published electronic and media policy.

Contact Mrs. Beth Cade, Director of Admissions. 601-437-8855 Ext. 239. Fax: 601-437-3212. E-mail: beth.cade@chamberlain-hunt.com. Web site: www.chamberlain-hunt.com/.

CHAMINADE COLLEGE PREPARATORY
7500 Chaminade Avenue
West Hills, California 91304
Head of School: Br. Thomas Fahy

General Information Coeducational day college-preparatory, arts, business, religious studies, and technology school, affiliated with Roman Catholic Church. Grades 9–12. Founded: 1952. Setting: suburban. Nearest major city is Los Angeles. 21-acre campus. 13 buildings on campus. Approved or accredited by Western Association of Schools and Colleges, Western Catholic Education Association, and California Department of Education. Endowment: $5 million. Total enrollment: 1,288. Upper school average class size: 26. Upper school faculty-student ratio: 1:15. There are 178 required school days per year for Upper School students. Upper School students typically attend 5 days per week. The average school day consists of 6 hours and 25 minutes.

Upper School Student Profile Grade 9: 331 students (176 boys, 155 girls); Grade 10: 284 students (153 boys, 131 girls); Grade 11: 319 students (166 boys, 153 girls); Grade 12: 354 students (191 boys, 163 girls). 52% of students are Roman Catholic.

Faculty School total: 86. In upper school: 36 men, 50 women; 60 have advanced degrees.

Chaminade College Preparatory

Subjects Offered Algebra, American history, American literature, anatomy, art, art history, athletic training, band, baseball, basketball, biology, biology-AP, British literature, British literature (honors), calculus, calculus-AP, chemistry, chemistry-AP, Chinese, Christian and Hebrew scripture, community service, comparative government and politics-AP, composition, computer programming, computer programming-AP, computer science, creative writing, dance, dance performance, debate, drama, drawing, driver education, economics, economics and history, English, English language-AP, English literature and composition-AP, environmental science-AP, ethics, European history, expository writing, film studies, finance, fine arts, finite math, French, French language-AP, French literature-AP, geography, geometry, government-AP, government/civics, guitar, jazz ensemble, journalism, Latin, Latin-AP, literature and composition-AP, macroeconomics-AP, marching band, mathematics, microeconomics-AP, modern European history-AP, music, music appreciation, music performance, physical education, physical science, physics, physics-AP, physiology, play/screen writing, probability and statistics, psychology, psychology-AP, religion, science, science fiction, scripture, Shakespeare, social studies, Spanish, Spanish language-AP, Spanish literature-AP, speech, speech and debate, sports medicine, statistics-AP, studio art, theater, trigonometry, U.S. government, U.S. history, U.S. history-AP, United States government-AP, visual and performing arts, visual arts, Western philosophy, Western religions, women's studies, world history, world history-AP, world literature, writing.

Graduation Requirements Arts and fine arts (art, music, dance, drama), college writing, computer science, English, foreign language, mathematics, physical education (includes health), religious studies, science, social studies (includes history), speech. Community service is required.

Special Academic Programs Advanced Placement exam preparation; honors section.

College Admission Counseling 278 students graduated in 2010; 266 went to college, including California State University, Northridge; Loyola Marymount University; University of California, Irvine; University of California, Los Angeles; University of Oregon; University of Southern California. Other: 1 went to work, 11 had other specific plans. Mean SAT critical reading: 581, mean SAT math: 582, mean SAT writing: 596, mean combined SAT: 1759, mean composite ACT: 26. 44% scored over 600 on SAT critical reading, 47% scored over 600 on SAT math, 54% scored over 600 on SAT writing, 48% scored over 1800 on combined SAT, 45% scored over 26 on composite ACT.

Student Life Upper grades have uniform requirement, student council, honor system. Discipline rests primarily with faculty. Attendance at religious services is required.

Summer Programs Remediation, enrichment, advancement, sports, computer instruction programs offered; session focuses on remediation; held on campus; accepts boys and girls; open to students from other schools. 600 students usually enrolled. 2011 schedule: June 20 to July 27. Application deadline: none.

Tuition and Aid Day student tuition: $11,650. Tuition installment plan (monthly payment plans, 2-payment plan, discounted one-payment plan). Merit scholarship grants, need-based scholarship grants available. In 2010–11, 22% of upper-school students received aid; total upper-school merit-scholarship money awarded: $13,500. Total amount of financial aid awarded in 2010–11: $1,856,378.

Admissions Traditional secondary-level entrance grade is 9. For fall 2010, 329 students applied for upper-level admission, 225 were accepted, 164 enrolled. Non-standardized placement tests required. Deadline for receipt of application materials: January 14. Application fee required: $100. On-campus interview required.

Athletics Interscholastic: aquatics (boys, girls), baseball (b), basketball (b,g), cross-country running (b,g), equestrian sports (b,g), fencing (b,g), field hockey (g), football (b), golf (b,g), lacrosse (b,g), soccer (b,g), softball (g), strength & conditioning (b,g), swimming and diving (b,g), tennis (b,g), track and field (b,g), volleyball (b,g), weight training (b,g), wrestling (b); coed interscholastic: cheering, dance, equestrian sports, physical fitness, strength & conditioning, weight training; coed intramural: dance team, hiking/backpacking, table tennis. 4 PE instructors, 85 coaches, 2 athletic trainers.

Computers Computers are regularly used in creative writing, data processing, information technology, introduction to technology, literary magazine, news writing, newspaper, photojournalism, writing, writing, yearbook classes. Computer network features include on-campus library services, online commercial services, Internet access, wireless campus network, Internet filtering or blocking technology, laptops are issued to students in grades 9-11, Blackboard online learning system. Student e-mail accounts are available to students. Students grades are available online. The school has a published electronic and media policy.

Contact Ms. Carrin Torres, Assistant to Admissions and Registrar. 818-347-8300 Ext. 355. Fax: 818-348-8374. E-mail: catorres@chaminade.org. Web site: www.chaminade.org.

CHAMINADE COLLEGE PREPARATORY SCHOOL

425 South Lindbergh Boulevard
St. Louis, Missouri 63131-2799

Head of School: Rev. Ralph A. Siefert, SM

General Information Boys' boarding and day college-preparatory, arts, business, religious studies, bilingual studies, and technology school, affiliated with Roman Catholic Church. Grades 6–12. Founded: 1910. Setting: suburban. Students are housed in single-sex dormitories. 55-acre campus. 12 buildings on campus. Approved or accredited by Independent Schools Association of the Central States, Midwest Association of Boarding Schools, National Catholic Education Association, North Central Association of Colleges and Schools, The Association of Boarding Schools, The College Board, and Missouri Department of Education. Member of National Association of Independent Schools and Secondary School Admission Test Board. Endowment: $6 million. Total enrollment: 770. Upper school average class size: 18. Upper school faculty-student ratio: 1:10. There are 174 required school days per year for Upper School students. Upper School students typically attend 5 days per week. The average school day consists of 7 hours.

Upper School Student Profile Grade 9: 124 students (124 boys); Grade 10: 123 students (123 boys); Grade 11: 123 students (123 boys); Grade 12: 125 students (125 boys). 6% of students are boarding students. 93% are state residents. 5 states are represented in upper school student body. 5% are international students. International students from China, Mexico, Republic of Korea, Rwanda, Taiwan, and Viet Nam; 2 other countries represented in student body. 83% of students are Roman Catholic.

Faculty School total: 88. In upper school: 66 men, 14 women; 61 have advanced degrees; 6 reside on campus.

Subjects Offered Accounting, algebra, American government, American history, American history-AP, American literature, architecture, art, art history, band, Bible studies, biology, biology-AP, botany, business, business law, business skills, calculus, calculus-AP, campus ministry, Catholic belief and practice, chemistry, chemistry-AP, Chinese, church history, civics, communication skills, communications, community service, comparative government and politics-AP, comparative political systems-AP, computer literacy, computer processing, computer programming, computer programming-AP, computer science, computer science-AP, concert band, creative writing, drama, dramatic arts, earth science, ecology, economics, economics-AP, engineering, English, English composition, English literature, English literature-AP, English/composition-AP, ESL, European history, European history-AP, expository writing, fine arts, French, French-AP, geography, geology, geometry, government/civics, grammar, health, history, industrial arts, keyboarding, Latin, Latin-AP, mathematics, music theory-AP, physical education, physics, physics-AP, psychology, psychology-AP, religion, science, social studies, sociology, Spanish, Spanish-AP, speech, statistics, statistics-AP, studio art-AP, theater, theology, trigonometry, weight training, world affairs, world history, world literature, writing.

Graduation Requirements Arts and fine arts (art, music, dance, drama), computer science, English, foreign language, mathematics, physical education (includes health), practical arts, religion (includes Bible studies and theology), science, social studies (includes history). Community service is required.

Special Academic Programs 21 Advanced Placement exams for which test preparation is offered; honors section; study at local college for college credit; academic accommodation for the gifted; ESL (22 students enrolled).

College Admission Counseling 130 students graduated in 2010; 129 went to college, including Purdue University; Saint Louis University; University of Dayton; University of Illinois at Urbana–Champaign; University of Missouri; Vanderbilt University. Other: 1 entered military service.

Student Life Upper grades have specified standards of dress, honor system. Discipline rests primarily with faculty. Attendance at religious services is required.

Summer Programs Enrichment, sports programs offered; held on campus; accepts boys; open to students from other schools. 500 students usually enrolled. 2011 schedule: June to July.

Tuition and Aid Day student tuition: $14,480; 5-day tuition and room/board: $29,330; 7-day tuition and room/board: $30,380. Tuition installment plan (FACTS Tuition Payment Plan). Merit scholarship grants, need-based scholarship grants, need-based loans, paying campus jobs available. In 2010–11, 27% of upper-school students received aid; total upper-school merit-scholarship money awarded: $50,000. Total amount of financial aid awarded in 2010–11: $1,600,000.

Admissions Traditional secondary-level entrance grade is 9. For fall 2010, 54 students applied for upper-level admission, 46 were accepted, 39 enrolled. SSAT required. Deadline for receipt of application materials: none. Application fee required: $50. Interview required.

Athletics Interscholastic: baseball, basketball, bowling, cross-country running, football, golf, ice hockey, lacrosse, racquetball, soccer, swimming and diving, tennis, track and field, volleyball, water polo, wrestling; intramural: in-line hockey, rugby, table tennis, ultimate Frisbee, weight training. 5 PE instructors, 30 coaches, 1 athletic trainer.

Computers Computers are regularly used in all academic classes. Computer network features include on-campus library services, online commercial services, Internet access, wireless campus network, Internet filtering or blocking technology. Campus intranet and student e-mail accounts are available to students. Students grades are available online. The school has a published electronic and media policy.

Contact Ms. Dianne Dunning-Gill, Associate Director of Admissions. 314-692-6640. Fax: 314-993-5732. E-mail: ddunning-gill@chaminade-stl.com. Web site: www.chaminade-stl.org.

CHAMINADE HIGH SCHOOL

340 Jackson Avenue
Mineola, New York 11501

Head of School: Br. Joseph D. Bellizzi, SM

General Information Boys' day college-preparatory school, affiliated with Roman Catholic Church. Grades 9–12. Founded: 1930. Setting: suburban. Nearest major city is New York. 11-acre campus. 1 building on campus. Approved or accredited by Middle States Association of Colleges and Schools and New York State Association of Independent Schools.

Upper School Student Profile 100% of students are Roman Catholic.

Faculty School total: 74. In upper school: 69 men, 5 women; 65 have advanced degrees.

Subjects Offered Algebra, American history, American literature, art, Bible studies, biology, calculus, chemistry, computer programming, computer science, creative writing, earth science, English, English literature, ethics, European history, expository writing, fine arts, French, geography, geometry, German, government/civics, grammar, health, history, Latin, mathematics, oceanography, philosophy, physical education, physics, religion, science, social sciences, social studies, Spanish, speech, theology, trigonometry, typing, world history.

Graduation Requirements Arts and fine arts (art, music, dance, drama), computer science, English, foreign language, mathematics, physical education (includes health), religion (includes Bible studies and theology), science, social sciences, social studies (includes history).

Special Academic Programs Study at local college for college credit.

College Admission Counseling 374 students graduated in 2009; all went to college, including College of the Holy Cross; Fordham University; Loyola University Maryland; St. John's University; University of Notre Dame; Villanova University. Mean SAT critical reading: 632, mean SAT math: 649.

Student Life Upper grades have specified standards of dress. Discipline rests primarily with faculty. Attendance at religious services is required.

Tuition and Aid Day student tuition: $7160. Tuition installment plan (3-installment plan). Merit scholarship grants, need-based scholarship grants available.

Admissions Catholic High School Entrance Examination required. Deadline for receipt of application materials: November 16. No application fee required.

Athletics Interscholastic: baseball, basketball, bowling, crew, cross-country running, diving, football, golf, ice hockey, lacrosse, riflery, soccer, swimming and diving, tennis, track and field, volleyball, wrestling; intramural: basketball, hiking/backpacking, martial arts, paddle tennis, roller hockey, soccer, swimming and diving, table tennis, ultimate Frisbee, volleyball, water polo, weight lifting, wrestling. 7 PE instructors, 15 coaches, 1 athletic trainer.

Computers Computers are regularly used in mathematics, science classes. Computer network features include on-campus library services, Internet access.

Contact Fr. James C. Williams, SM, President. 516-742-5555 Ext. 510. Fax: 516-742-1989. E-mail: frjames@chaminade-hs.org. Web site: www.chaminade-hs.org.

CHAMINADE-MADONNA COLLEGE PREPARATORY

500 Chaminade Drive
Hollywood, Florida 33021-5800
Head of School: Fr. Larry Doersching, SM

General Information Coeducational day college-preparatory, arts, business, and religious studies school, affiliated with Roman Catholic Church. Grades 9–12. Founded: 1960. Setting: suburban. Nearest major city is Fort Lauderdale. 13-acre campus. 10 buildings on campus. Approved or accredited by Southern Association of Colleges and Schools and Florida Department of Education. Total enrollment: 594. Upper school average class size: 26. Upper school faculty-student ratio: 1:19. There are 180 required school days per year for Upper School students. Upper School students typically attend 5 days per week. The average school day consists of 6 hours and 45 minutes.

Upper School Student Profile Grade 9: 147 students (92 boys, 55 girls); Grade 10: 154 students (83 boys, 71 girls); Grade 11: 143 students (94 boys, 49 girls); Grade 12: 150 students (85 boys, 65 girls). 70% of students are Roman Catholic.

Faculty School total: 48. In upper school: 23 men, 25 women.

Subjects Offered Advanced chemistry, advanced computer applications, advanced math, advanced studio art-AP, algebra, American history, American literature, anatomy, art, art history, band, biology, business skills, calculus, ceramics, chemistry, choir, community service, computer applications, creative writing, design, directing, drama, economics, English, fine arts, French, geography, geometry, government/civics, health, history, international relations, journalism, keyboarding, marine biology, mathematics, music, philosophy, physical education, physics, physiology, play production, practical arts, pre-calculus, psychology, reading, religion, science, Shakespeare, social studies, sociology, Spanish, speech, stagecraft, theater, trigonometry, word processing, world history, writing, yearbook.

Graduation Requirements Arts and fine arts (art, music, dance, drama), business skills (includes word processing), English, foreign language, mathematics, physical education (includes health), practical arts, religion (includes Bible studies and theology), science, social studies (includes history), 80 community service hours.

Special Academic Programs 10 Advanced Placement exams for which test preparation is offered; honors section; study at local college for college credit; academic accommodation for the gifted, the musically talented, and the artistically talented; remedial reading and/or remedial writing; remedial math; programs in general development for dyslexic students; special instructional classes for students with learning disabilities, Attention Deficit Disorder, and dyslexia.

College Admission Counseling 184 students graduated in 2010; 176 went to college, including Florida Atlantic University; Florida International University; Florida State University; University of Central Florida; University of Florida; University of Miami. Mean SAT critical reading: 512, mean SAT math: 504, mean composite ACT: 20.

Student Life Upper grades have uniform requirement, student council, honor system. Discipline rests primarily with faculty. Attendance at religious services is required.

Tuition and Aid Day student tuition: $9700. Tuition installment plan (FACTS Tuition Payment Plan). Tuition reduction for siblings, need-based scholarship grants available. In 2010–11, 33% of upper-school students received aid. Total amount of financial aid awarded in 2010–11: $400,000.

Admissions Traditional secondary-level entrance grade is 9. For fall 2010, 250 students applied for upper-level admission, 200 were accepted, 147 enrolled. High School Placement Test (closed version) from Scholastic Testing Service required. Deadline for receipt of application materials: January 20. Application fee required: $50. Interview required.

Athletics Interscholastic: baseball (boys), basketball (b,g), cheering (g), cross-country running (b,g), dance (g), dance team (g), flag football (g), football (b), golf (b,g), hockey (b,g), ice hockey (b,g), lacrosse (g), soccer (b,g), swimming and diving (b,g), track and field (b,g), volleyball (b,g), wrestling (b); intramural: aerobics/dance (g), danceline (g), football (b,g). 2 PE instructors, 1 athletic trainer.

Computers Computers are regularly used in English, mathematics, reading classes. Computer resources include on-campus library services, online commercial services, Internet access. The school has a published electronic and media policy.

Contact Mr. Tim Tyrrell, Director of Enrollment Management. 954-989-5150 Ext. 112. Fax: 954-983-4663. E-mail: ttyrrell@cmlions.org. Web site: www.cmlions.org.

CHAMISA MESA HIGH SCHOOL

PO Box 3560
Taos, New Mexico 87571
Head of School: Mr. Michael LaValley

General Information Coeducational day college-preparatory and arts school. Grades 9–12. Founded: 1990. Setting: small town. Nearest major city is Santa Fe. 2-acre campus. 4 buildings on campus. Approved or accredited by North Central Association of Colleges and Schools and New Mexico Department of Education. Total enrollment: 27. Upper school average class size: 10. Upper school faculty-student ratio: 1:5.

Upper School Student Profile Grade 9: 8 students (1 boy, 7 girls); Grade 10: 9 students (4 boys, 5 girls); Grade 11: 6 students (2 boys, 4 girls); Grade 12: 4 students (3 boys, 1 girl).

Faculty School total: 5. In upper school: 2 men, 3 women; 1 has an advanced degree.

Special Academic Programs Honors section.

College Admission Counseling 23 students graduated in 2009; 20 went to college, including Stanford University; University of New Mexico. Other: 2 went to work, 1 had other specific plans.

Student Life Upper grades have honor system. Discipline rests primarily with faculty.

Tuition and Aid Day student tuition: $6000. Tuition installment plan (monthly payment plans).

Admissions Traditional secondary-level entrance grade is 9. Deadline for receipt of application materials: none. No application fee required. Interview required.

Athletics Coed Interscholastic: judo. 1 PE instructor.

Computers Computers are regularly used in foreign language classes. Computer network features include Internet access.

Contact Admissions. 575-751-0943. Fax: 575-751-3715. E-mail: clavalley@chamisamesa.net. Web site: www.chamisamesa.net.

CHAPEL HILL–CHAUNCY HALL SCHOOL

785 Beaver Street
Waltham, Massachusetts 02452
Head of School: Mr. Lance Conrad

General Information Coeducational boarding and day college-preparatory and arts school. Grades 9–PG. Founded: 1828. Setting: suburban. Nearest major city is Boston. Students are housed in single-sex dormitories. 37-acre campus. 11 buildings on campus. Approved or accredited by New England Association of Schools and Colleges and Massachusetts Department of Education. Member of National Association of Independent Schools and Secondary School Admission Test Board. Endowment: $1.8 million. Total enrollment: 165. Upper school average class size: 12. Upper school faculty-student ratio: 1:5. The average school day consists of 7 hours.

Upper School Student Profile Grade 9: 35 students (16 boys, 19 girls); Grade 10: 42 students (25 boys, 17 girls); Grade 11: 47 students (24 boys, 23 girls); Grade 12: 41 students (25 boys, 16 girls). 45% of students are boarding students. 65% are state residents. 7 states are represented in upper school student body. 25% are international students. International students from China, Japan, Kazakhstan, Republic of Korea, Taiwan, and Viet Nam; 6 other countries represented in student body.

Faculty School total: 35. In upper school: 18 men, 17 women; 23 have advanced degrees; 20 reside on campus.

Subjects Offered 20th century history, 3-dimensional design, acting, adolescent issues, advanced biology, advanced chemistry, advanced studio art-AP, algebra,

American history, American literature, anatomy and physiology, art, biology, calculus, ceramics, chamber groups, chemistry, chorus, comparative religion, creative writing, drama, economics, English, English literature, English-AP, ESL, European history, fine arts, geography, geometry, government/civics, grammar, health, history, journalism, Mandarin, mathematics, music, music theory, photography, physical education, physics, psychology, science, social studies, Spanish, theater, world history, world literature, writing.

Graduation Requirements Arts and fine arts (art, music, dance, drama), English, foreign language, mathematics, physical education (includes health), science, social studies (includes history), senior presentations, earn Charger Points for service. Community service is required.

Special Academic Programs Advanced Placement exam preparation; independent study; programs in general development for dyslexic students; special instructional classes for students with mild to moderate learning disabilities; ESL (12 students enrolled).

College Admission Counseling 48 students graduated in 2010; all went to college, including Clark University; Curry College; Drew University; Roger Williams University; University of Illinois at Urbana–Champaign; Wheaton College. Mean SAT critical reading: 520, mean SAT math: 540, mean SAT writing: 530.

Student Life Upper grades have student council. Discipline rests equally with students and faculty.

Tuition and Aid Day student tuition: $32,900; 7-day tuition and room/board: $43,900. Tuition installment plan (Key Tuition Payment Plan, monthly payment plans, individually arranged payment plans). Need-based scholarship grants available. In 2010–11, 22% of upper-school students received aid. Total amount of financial aid awarded in 2010–11: $850,000.

Admissions Traditional secondary-level entrance grade is 9. For fall 2010, 221 students applied for upper-level admission, 121 were accepted, 56 enrolled. SSAT or WISC III, TOEFL or SLEP or WISC or WAIS required. Deadline for receipt of application materials: February 1. Application fee required: $50. Interview required.

Athletics Interscholastic: baseball (boys), basketball (b,g), lacrosse (b,g), soccer (b,g), softball (g), volleyball (g), wrestling (b); coed interscholastic: climbing, combined training, cross-country running, fitness, Frisbee, golf, rock climbing, ropes courses, ultimate Frisbee; coed intramural: aerobics/dance, cooperative games, fitness, physical fitness, racquetball, rock climbing, ropes courses, swimming and diving, yoga. 1 PE instructor, 1 athletic trainer.

Computers Computers are regularly used in art, English, history, mathematics, multimedia, newspaper, yearbook classes. Computer network features include on-campus library services, online commercial services, Internet access, wireless campus network, Internet filtering or blocking technology. Campus intranet, student e-mail accounts, and computer access in designated common areas are available to students. Students grades are available online. The school has a published electronic and media policy.

Contact Ms. Lauren Lewis, Admissions Administrative Assistant. 781-314-0800. Fax: 781-894-5205. E-mail: llewis@chch.org. Web site: www.chch.org.

THE CHAPIN SCHOOL

100 East End Avenue
New York, New York 10028
Head of School: Dr. Patricia T. Hayot

General Information Girls' day college-preparatory school. Grades K–12. Founded: 1901. Setting: urban. 1 building on campus. Approved or accredited by New York State Association of Independent Schools and New York Department of Education. Member of National Association of Independent Schools. Endowment: $90.1 million. Total enrollment: 694. Upper school average class size: 16. Upper school faculty-student ratio: 1:4. The average school day consists of 6 hours and 45 minutes.

Upper School Student Profile Grade 8: 61 students (61 girls); Grade 9: 44 students (44 girls); Grade 10: 57 students (57 girls); Grade 11: 42 students (42 girls); Grade 12: 46 students (46 girls).

Faculty School total: 118. In upper school: 16 men, 45 women; 50 have advanced degrees.

Subjects Offered Advanced Placement courses, African drumming, African history, African-American history, algebra, American history, American literature, art, art history, Asian history, astronomy, biology, calculus, ceramics, chemistry, Chinese, comparative religion, computer math, computer science, creative writing, dance, design, digital imaging, DNA, drama, drawing, electronics, English, English literature, European history, expository writing, fine arts, French, geography, geometry, government/civics, grammar, Greek, health, history, Latin, Latin American literature, life skills, mathematics, multimedia, music, painting, philosophy, photography, physical education, physics, poetry, psychology, public speaking, religion, Russian literature, science, sculpture, social studies, Spanish, statistics, theater, trigonometry, video, writing.

Graduation Requirements Arts and fine arts (art, music, dance, drama), computer science, English, English literature and composition-AP, foreign language, mathematics, physical education (includes health), science, social studies (includes history).

Special Academic Programs Advanced Placement exam preparation; honors section; term-away projects; study abroad; special instructional classes for deaf students.

College Admission Counseling 34 students graduated in 2009; all went to college, including Cornell College; Dartmouth College; Duke University; Georgetown University; Wesleyan University; Yale University.

Student Life Upper grades have uniform requirement, student council, honor system. Discipline rests primarily with faculty.

Tuition and Aid Day student tuition: $31,500. Need-based scholarship grants, Key Education Resources available. In 2009–10, 28% of upper-school students received aid. Total amount of financial aid awarded in 2009–10: $1,775,520.

Admissions Traditional secondary-level entrance grade is 9. For fall 2009, 78 students applied for upper-level admission, 34 were accepted, 14 enrolled. ISEE and math and English placement tests required. Deadline for receipt of application materials: December 15. Application fee required: $50. On-campus interview required.

Athletics Interscholastic: badminton, basketball, cross-country running, field hockey, gymnastics, independent competitive sports, lacrosse, soccer, softball, squash, swimming and diving, tennis, track and field, volleyball; intramural: aerobics, aerobics/dance, aerobics/Nautilus, aquatics, badminton, ball hockey, ballet, basketball, cooperative games, cross-country running, curling, dance, diving, fencing, field hockey, fitness, fitness walking, flag football, floor hockey, football, Frisbee, gymnastics, handball, indoor hockey, indoor soccer, indoor track & field, jogging, kickball, lacrosse, life saving, martial arts, modern dance, Nautilus, outdoor activities, physical fitness, physical training, project adventure, ropes courses, self defense, skiing (downhill), snowboarding, soccer, softball, squash, strength & conditioning, swimming and diving, tai chi, team handball, tennis, touch football, track and field, ultimate Frisbee, volleyball, walking, water polo, weight training, whiffle ball, yoga; coed interscholastic: fencing. 14 PE instructors, 6 coaches, 1 athletic trainer.

Computers Computers are regularly used in art, dance, English, foreign language, history, mathematics, music, science classes. Computer network features include on-campus library services, Internet access, wireless campus network, ProQuest, SIRS Knowledge Source. Campus intranet and student e-mail accounts are available to students. The school has a published electronic and media policy.

Contact Tina I. Herman, Director of Admissions. 212-744-2335. Fax: 212-628-2126. E-mail: admissions@chapin.edu. Web site: www.chapin.edu.

CHARLES WRIGHT ACADEMY

7723 Chambers Creek Road
Tacoma, Washington 98467-2099
Head of School: Mr. Robert Camner

General Information Coeducational day college-preparatory and arts school. Grades PK–12. Founded: 1957. Setting: suburban. Nearest major city is Seattle. 100-acre campus. 8 buildings on campus. Approved or accredited by Pacific Northwest Association of Independent Schools and Washington Department of Education. Member of National Association of Independent Schools. Endowment: $15 million. Total enrollment: 668. Upper school average class size: 14. Upper school faculty-student ratio: 1:8. There are 180 required school days per year for Upper School students. Upper School students typically attend 5 days per week. The average school day consists of 5 hours and 45 minutes.

Upper School Student Profile Grade 9: 62 students (43 boys, 19 girls); Grade 10: 65 students (43 boys, 22 girls); Grade 11: 77 students (43 boys, 34 girls); Grade 12: 70 students (35 boys, 35 girls).

Faculty School total: 77. In upper school: 25 men, 16 women; 26 have advanced degrees.

Subjects Offered Algebra, American history, American literature, art history, biology, calculus, ceramics, chemistry, choir, community service, computer programming, computer science, creative writing, criminology, drama, earth science, English, English literature, environmental science, European history, expository writing, French, geometry, government/civics, history, Japanese, journalism, mathematics, music, outdoor education, performing arts, photography, physical education, physics, science, social studies, Spanish, statistics, theater, trigonometry, visual arts, world history, world religions, yearbook.

Graduation Requirements 20th century history, arts and fine arts (art, music, dance, drama), English, foreign language, mathematics, outdoor education, performing arts, physical education (includes health), science, social studies (includes history), participation in Winterim courses, participation in outdoor education/experiences, participation in community service. Community service is required.

Special Academic Programs Advanced Placement exam preparation; honors section.

College Admission Counseling 76 students graduated in 2010; all went to college, including University of Oregon; University of Puget Sound; University of Washington; Western Washington University; Whitman College.

Student Life Upper grades have specified standards of dress, student council, honor system. Discipline rests equally with students and faculty.

Summer Programs Sports programs offered; session focuses on league play, team practices, weights and conditioning; held on campus; accepts boys and girls; not open to students from other schools. 150 students usually enrolled. 2011 schedule: June 15 to July 30.

Tuition and Aid Day student tuition: $20,900. Tuition installment plan (monthly payment plans). Need-based scholarship grants available. In 2010–11, 23% of upper-school students received aid. Total amount of financial aid awarded in 2010–11: $1,025,446.

Admissions Traditional secondary-level entrance grade is 9. For fall 2010, 67 students applied for upper-level admission, 38 were accepted, 28 enrolled. ISEE, SSAT, TOEFL or Woodcock-Johnson required. Deadline for receipt of application materials: none. Application fee required: $40. Interview required.

Athletics Interscholastic: baseball (boys), basketball (b,g), cross-country running (b,g), football (b), golf (b,g), soccer (b,g), tennis (b,g), track and field (b,g), volleyball (g); intramural: crew (b,g), strength & conditioning (b,g); coed intramural: backpacking, canoeing/kayaking, climbing, hiking/backpacking, kayaking, outdoor adventure, outdoor education, outdoors, physical fitness, strength & conditioning, ultimate Frisbee, weight training, yoga. 4 PE instructors, 7 coaches, 1 athletic trainer.

Computers Computer network features include on-campus library services, online commercial services, Internet access, wireless campus network, Internet filtering or blocking technology. Student e-mail accounts and computer access in designated common areas are available to students. Students grades are available online.

Contact Mrs. Sue Johnson, Admissions Secretary. 253-620-8373. Fax: 253-620-8357. E-mail: admissions@charleswright.org. Web site: www.charleswright.org.

CHARLOTTE CATHOLIC HIGH SCHOOL
7702 Pineville Matthews Road
Charlotte, North Carolina 28226
Head of School: Mr. Gerald S. Healy

General Information Coeducational day college-preparatory, arts, and religious studies school, affiliated with Roman Catholic Church. Grades 9–12. Founded: 1955. Setting: urban. 1 building on campus. Approved or accredited by National Catholic Education Association, North Carolina Association of Independent Schools, and Southern Association of Colleges and Schools. Total enrollment: 1,416. Upper school average class size: 20. There are 180 required school days per year for Upper School students. Upper School students typically attend 5 days per week. The average school day consists of 7 hours.

Upper School Student Profile 92% of students are Roman Catholic.

Faculty School total: 105. In upper school: 27 men, 56 women; 50 have advanced degrees.

Subjects Offered Accounting, algebra, American literature, American literature-AP, analysis, analysis and differential calculus, anatomy and physiology, applied arts, applied music, art, band, Basic programming, Bible studies, biology, biology-AP, British literature, British literature (honors), business, calculus, calculus-AP, campus ministry, Catholic belief and practice, chemistry, chemistry-AP, choir, chorus, Christian and Hebrew scripture, Christian ethics, Christian scripture, college counseling, college placement, computer applications, computer programming, computers, concert band, dance, dance performance, desktop publishing, drama, drama performance, earth science, economics, English, English language and composition-AP, English literature and composition-AP, environmental science, environmental science-AP, ethics and responsibility, European history, European history-AP, fitness, French, geography, German, government, government-AP, guidance, guitar, health, history of the Catholic Church, honors algebra, honors English, honors U.S. history, honors world history, jazz band, Latin, Latin-AP, library, library assistant, Life of Christ, marching band, math analysis, model United Nations, musical productions, musical theater, newspaper, oceanography, painting, performing arts, physical education, physics, physics-AP, piano, play production, politics, psychology, public speaking, religion, remedial study skills, SAT preparation, social justice, Spanish, Spanish language-AP, statistics-AP, student government, theater, track and field, trigonometry, U.S. government and politics-AP, U.S. history, U.S. history-AP, Web site design, word processing, world geography, world history, world religions, wrestling, yearbook.

Graduation Requirements Algebra, biology, British literature, chemistry, economics, English, geometry, public service, religion (includes Bible studies and theology), trigonometry, U.S. government, U.S. history, world history.

Special Academic Programs 15 Advanced Placement exams for which test preparation is offered; honors section.

College Admission Counseling 333 students graduated in 2009; 330 went to college, including Appalachian State University; East Carolina University; North Carolina State University; The University of North Carolina at Chapel Hill; The University of North Carolina at Charlotte; University of South Carolina. Other: 1 went to work, 2 entered military service. Mean composite ACT: 25.

Student Life Upper grades have specified standards of dress, student council, honor system. Discipline rests primarily with faculty. Attendance at religious services is required.

Tuition and Aid Day student tuition: $7500. Tuition installment plan (monthly payment plans). Need-based scholarship grants available.

Admissions Explore required. Deadline for receipt of application materials: none. Application fee required: $100. Interview required.

Athletics Interscholastic: baseball (boys), basketball (b,g), cheering (g), cross-country running (b,g), dance (g), dance team (g), diving (b,g), football (b), golf (b,g), lacrosse (b), running (b,g), soccer (b,g), softball (g), swimming and diving (b,g), tennis (b,g), volleyball (g), wrestling (b); intramural: dance (g), rugby (b); coed intramural: archery, backpacking, badminton, basketball, bowling, fitness, physical fitness, ultimate Frisbee. 4 PE instructors, 2 athletic trainers.

Computers Computers are regularly used in accounting, college planning, desktop publishing, yearbook classes. Computer network features include Internet access. The school has a published electronic and media policy.

Contact Mr. Steven H. Carpenter, Assistant Principal. 704-543-1127. Fax: 704-543-1217. E-mail: shcarpenter@charlottecatholic.com. Web site: www.gocougars.org.

CHARLOTTE CHRISTIAN SCHOOL
7301 Sardis Road
Charlotte, North Carolina 28270
Head of School: Mr. Barry Giller

General Information Coeducational day college-preparatory and arts school, affiliated with Christian faith. Grades JK–12. Founded: 1950. Setting: suburban. 55-acre campus. 4 buildings on campus. Approved or accredited by Association of Christian Schools International, North Carolina Association of Independent Schools, Southern Association of Colleges and Schools, Southern Association of Independent Schools, and North Carolina Department of Education. Total enrollment: 989. Upper school average class size: 20. Upper school faculty-student ratio: 1:11. There are 172 required school days per year for Upper School students. Upper School students typically attend 5 days per week. The average school day consists of 7 hours.

Upper School Student Profile Grade 9: 85 students (54 boys, 31 girls); Grade 10: 77 students (46 boys, 31 girls); Grade 11: 91 students (42 boys, 49 girls); Grade 12: 107 students (61 boys, 46 girls). 100% of students are Christian faith.

Faculty School total: 121. In upper school: 18 men, 18 women; 14 have advanced degrees.

Subjects Offered Accounting, acting, advanced studio art-AP, algebra, American culture, American government, American literature, anatomy and physiology, art, art history-AP, athletic training, band, biology, biology-AP, British literature, business, business law, calculus-AP, chamber groups, chemistry, choir, choreography, Christian doctrine, Christian education, Christian ethics, church history, civil war history, computer applications, computer science-AP, computer-aided design, economics, English literature, environmental science-AP, European history-AP, French, French-AP, geometry, German, graphic arts, graphic design, health and wellness, language-AP, Latin, leadership, learning strategies, Life of Christ, literature and composition-AP, marketing, math applications, music composition, music theory-AP, newspaper, painting, photography, physical education, physical science, physics, physics-AP, pre-calculus, psychology, public speaking, research skills, SAT preparation, sign language, Spanish, Spanish-AP, speech and debate, sports medicine, stage design, statistics-AP, studio art-AP, theater, theater design and production, trigonometry, U.S. government and politics-AP, U.S. history, U.S. history-AP, video film production, voice, voice and diction, Web site design, weight training, wind ensemble, world civilizations, world literature, World War II, yearbook.

Graduation Requirements Bible studies, English, foreign language, mathematics, physical education (includes health), SAT preparation, science, social studies (includes history), service hours, visual or performing arts.

Special Academic Programs Advanced Placement exam preparation; honors section; study at local college for college credit.

College Admission Counseling 93 students graduated in 2010; 92 went to college, including Appalachian State University; Clemson University; Furman University; North Carolina State University; The University of North Carolina at Chapel Hill; Wake Forest University. Other: 1 had other specific plans.

Student Life Upper grades have specified standards of dress, student council, honor system. Discipline rests primarily with faculty. Attendance at religious services is required.

Summer Programs Enrichment, advancement, sports, art/fine arts, rigorous outdoor training, computer instruction programs offered; session focuses on enrichment; held both on and off campus; held at area farms; accepts boys and girls; open to students from other schools. 300 students usually enrolled. 2011 schedule: June to August. Application deadline: none.

Tuition and Aid Day student tuition: $10,760–$15,360. Tuition installment plan (The Tuition Plan, Insured Tuition Payment Plan, monthly payment plans, individually arranged payment plans). Tuition reduction for siblings, need-based scholarship grants available. In 2010–11, 20% of upper-school students received aid. Total amount of financial aid awarded in 2010–11: $389,150.

Admissions Traditional secondary-level entrance grade is 9. Admissions testing, ISEE, TOEFL or SLEP, Wechsler Intelligence Scale for Children III or Woodcock-Johnson required. Deadline for receipt of application materials: none. Application fee required: $90. On-campus interview required.

Athletics Interscholastic: baseball (boys), basketball (b,g), cheering (g), cross-country running (b,g), dance (g), football (b), golf (b), indoor track (b,g), soccer (b,g), softball (g), swimming and diving (b,g), tennis (b,g), track and field (b,g), volleyball (g), wrestling (b); intramural: basketball (b,g), cheering (g), flag football (b), jogging (g); coed interscholastic: physical fitness, physical training, strength & conditioning, weight training; coed intramural: basketball, fencing, tennis, weight training. 2 PE instructors, 25 coaches, 1 athletic trainer.

Computers Computers are regularly used in all classes. Computer network features include on-campus library services, Internet access, wireless campus network, Internet filtering or blocking technology, NewsBank InfoWeb. Students grades are available online. The school has a published electronic and media policy.

Contact Mrs. Cathie Broocks, Director of Admissions. 704-366-5657. Fax: 704-366-5678. E-mail: cathie.broocks@charchrist.com. Web site: www.charlottechristian.com.

CHARLOTTE COUNTRY DAY SCHOOL

1440 Carmel Road
Charlotte, North Carolina 28226
Head of School: Mr. Mark Reed
General Information Coeducational day college-preparatory school. Grades JK–12. Founded: 1941. Setting: suburban. 60-acre campus. 10 buildings on campus. Approved or accredited by North Carolina Association of Independent Schools, Southern Association of Colleges and Schools, Southern Association of Independent Schools, and North Carolina Department of Education. Member of National Association of Independent Schools and Secondary School Admission Test Board. Endowment: $18.6 million. Total enrollment: 1,602. Upper school average class size: 15. Upper school faculty-student ratio: 1:12. There are 170 required school days per year for Upper School students. Upper School students typically attend 5 days per week. The average school day consists of 7 hours and 15 minutes.
Upper School Student Profile Grade 9: 124 students (68 boys, 56 girls); Grade 10: 117 students (68 boys, 49 girls); Grade 11: 117 students (70 boys, 47 girls); Grade 12: 122 students (53 boys, 69 girls).
Faculty School total: 218. In upper school: 36 men, 35 women; 51 have advanced degrees.
Subjects Offered Algebra, American history, American history-AP, anatomy, art, art history-AP, astronomy, biology, biology-AP, biotechnology, calculus-AP, ceramics, chemistry, chemistry-AP, Chinese, computer graphics, computer science, computer science-AP, creative writing, dance, debate, discrete mathematics, drama, ecology, economics, English, English literature, English-AP, environmental science-AP, ESL, European history, European history-AP, French, French-AP, geography, geometry, German, German-AP, Japanese, journalism, Latin, Latin-AP, library studies, music, non-Western societies, novels, photography, physical education, physics, physics-AP, physiology, poetry, political science, pre-calculus, probability and statistics, psychology-AP, sculpture, Shakespeare, short story, Spanish, Spanish-AP, studio art-AP, theater, theory of knowledge, trigonometry, typing, visual arts, yearbook.
Graduation Requirements Arts and fine arts (art, music, dance, drama), computer science, English, foreign language, mathematics, physical education (includes health), science, social sciences, social studies (includes history). Community service is required.
Special Academic Programs International Baccalaureate program; honors section; independent study; term-away projects; study abroad; academic accommodation for the gifted; ESL (11 students enrolled).
College Admission Counseling 108 students graduated in 2010; all went to college, including Clemson University; Davidson College; Furman University; The University of North Carolina at Chapel Hill; University of South Carolina; Washington and Lee University. Median SAT critical reading: 630, median SAT math: 650, median SAT writing: 630, median combined SAT: 1890, median composite ACT: 27. 58% scored over 600 on SAT critical reading, 74% scored over 600 on SAT math, 61% scored over 600 on SAT writing, 66% scored over 1800 on combined SAT, 54% scored over 26 on composite ACT.
Student Life Upper grades have specified standards of dress, student council, honor system. Discipline rests primarily with faculty.
Summer Programs Remediation, enrichment, advancement, ESL, sports, art/fine arts, computer instruction programs offered; session focuses on enrichment classes, academic courses, and sports camps; held on campus; accepts boys and girls; open to students from other schools. 200 students usually enrolled. 2011 schedule: June 13 to July 29. Application deadline: none.
Tuition and Aid Day student tuition: $20,505. Tuition installment plan (The Tuition Plan, Insured Tuition Payment Plan, monthly payment plans). Need-based scholarship grants available. In 2010–11, 20% of upper-school students received aid. Total amount of financial aid awarded in 2010–11: $1,391,307.
Admissions Traditional secondary-level entrance grade is 9. For fall 2010, 85 students applied for upper-level admission, 62 were accepted, 42 enrolled. CTP III, ERB or ISEE required. Deadline for receipt of application materials: January 15. Application fee required: $90. On-campus interview required.
Athletics Interscholastic: baseball (boys), basketball (b,g), cheering (g), crew (g), cross-country running (b,g), dance (g), dance team (g), field hockey (g), fitness (b,g), football (b), golf (b,g), lacrosse (b,g), soccer (b,g), softball (g), strength & conditioning (b,g), swimming and diving (b,g), tennis (b,g), track and field (b,g), volleyball (g), weight training (b,g), wrestling (b). 1 PE instructor, 38 coaches, 3 athletic trainers.
Computers Computers are regularly used in art, computer applications, English, foreign language, mathematics, photography, science, yearbook classes. Computer network features include on-campus library services, Internet access, wireless campus network, Internet filtering or blocking technology. Campus intranet and student e-mail accounts are available to students. Students grades are available online. The school has a published electronic and media policy.
Contact Nancy R. Ehringhaus, Director of Admissions. 704-943-4530 Ext. 4531. Fax: 704-943-4536. E-mail: nancy.ehringhaus@charlottecountryday.org. Web site: www.charlottecountryday.org.

CHARLOTTE LATIN SCHOOL

9502 Providence Road
Charlotte, North Carolina 28277-8695
Head of School: Mr. Arch N. McIntosh Jr.
General Information Coeducational day college-preparatory school. Grades K–12. Founded: 1970. Setting: suburban. 122-acre campus. 14 buildings on campus. Approved or accredited by North Carolina Association of Independent Schools, Southern Association of Colleges and Schools, Southern Association of Independent Schools, and North Carolina Department of Education. Member of National Association of Independent Schools and Secondary School Admission Test Board. Endowment: $22.5 million. Total enrollment: 1,383. Upper school average class size: 16. Upper school faculty-student ratio: 1:7. There are 173 required school days per year for Upper School students. Upper School students typically attend 5 days per week. The average school day consists of 7 hours and 5 minutes.
Upper School Student Profile Grade 9: 120 students (61 boys, 59 girls); Grade 10: 123 students (58 boys, 65 girls); Grade 11: 114 students (60 boys, 54 girls); Grade 12: 119 students (64 boys, 55 girls).
Faculty School total: 172. In upper school: 39 men, 32 women; 49 have advanced degrees.
Subjects Offered 20th century American writers, 20th century history, 20th century physics, 20th century world history, 3-dimensional art, acting, advanced chemistry, Advanced Placement courses, algebra, American culture, American government, American history, American history-AP, American literature, anatomy and physiology, art, biology, biology-AP, British literature, calculus, calculus-AP, ceramics, chemistry, chemistry-AP, college counseling, computer applications, computer math, computer programming, computer science, computer science-AP, conceptual physics, concert band, concert choir, creative writing, debate, discrete mathematics, drama, dramatic arts, earth science, ecology, economics, economics and history, engineering, English, English literature, English-AP, environmental science, European history, European history-AP, expository writing, finite math, French, French-AP, geography, geology, geometry, German, German-AP, government/civics, grammar, Greek, health, history, Holocaust and other genocides, honors algebra, honors English, honors geometry, human rights, international relations, international studies, journalism, Latin, Latin-AP, leadership and service, mathematics, media literacy, music, music theory, music theory-AP, physical education, physics, physics-AP, pre-calculus, programming, psychology, science, social studies, Southern literature, Spanish, Spanish language-AP, Spanish-AP, speech, sports medicine, statistics-AP, studio art, technical theater, theater, trigonometry, U.S. government and politics-AP, Web site design, world history, world literature, world religions, writing, yearbook.
Graduation Requirements Electives, English, foreign language, history, mathematics, physical education (includes health), science.
Special Academic Programs 16 Advanced Placement exams for which test preparation is offered; honors section; study abroad; academic accommodation for the gifted.
College Admission Counseling 121 students graduated in 2010; 118 went to college, including Elon University; North Carolina State University; The University of North Carolina at Chapel Hill; University of Georgia; University of South Carolina; Wake Forest University. Other: 1 went to work, 2 had other specific plans. Median SAT critical reading: 620, median SAT math: 650, median SAT writing: 640, median combined SAT: 1950, median composite ACT: 27. 59% scored over 600 on SAT critical reading, 73% scored over 600 on SAT math, 64% scored over 600 on SAT writing, 64% scored over 1800 on combined SAT, 62% scored over 26 on composite ACT.
Student Life Upper grades have specified standards of dress, student council, honor system. Discipline rests primarily with faculty.
Summer Programs Enrichment, sports, art/fine arts, computer instruction programs offered; session focuses on enrichment, sports camps; held both on and off campus; held at N.C. coast (offered for Charlotte Latin students only); accepts boys and girls; open to students from other schools. 850 students usually enrolled. 2011 schedule: June 8 to July 29. Application deadline: none.
Tuition and Aid Day student tuition: $18,700. Tuition installment plan (monthly payment plans, individually arranged payment plans). Merit scholarship grants, need-based scholarship grants available. In 2010–11, 14% of upper-school students received aid; total upper-school merit-scholarship money awarded: $169,325. Total amount of financial aid awarded in 2010–11: $745,700.
Admissions Traditional secondary-level entrance grade is 9. For fall 2010, 124 students applied for upper-level admission, 59 were accepted, 32 enrolled. ERB, ISEE, Wechsler Intelligence Scale for Children III or Woodcock-Johnson required. Deadline for receipt of application materials: none. Application fee required: $90. On-campus interview required.
Athletics Interscholastic: aquatics (boys, girls), baseball (b), basketball (b,g), cross-country running (b,g), dance team (g), field hockey (g), football (b), golf (b,g), independent competitive sports (b,g), indoor track (b,g), lacrosse (b,g), soccer (b,g), softball (g), swimming and diving (b,g), tennis (b,g), track and field (b,g), volleyball (g), wrestling (b); intramural: basketball (b,g), outdoor activities (b,g); coed interscholastic: ultimate Frisbee; coed intramural: outdoor activities. 3 PE instructors, 44 coaches, 3 athletic trainers.
Computers Computers are regularly used in all academic classes. Computer network features include on-campus library services, online commercial services, Internet

access, wireless campus network, Internet filtering or blocking technology. Computer access in designated common areas is available to students. The school has a published electronic and media policy.

Contact Ms. Kathryn B. Booe, Director of Admissions. 704-846-7207. Fax: 704-847-8776. E-mail: kbooe@charlottelatin.org. Web site: www.charlottelatin.org.

CHASE COLLEGIATE SCHOOL

565 Chase Parkway
Waterbury, Connecticut 06708-3394
Head of School: John D. Fixx

General Information Coeducational day college-preparatory and arts school. Grades PK–12. Founded: 1865. Setting: suburban. 47-acre campus. 8 buildings on campus. Approved or accredited by Connecticut Association of Independent Schools, New England Association of Schools and Colleges, and Connecticut Department of Education. Member of National Association of Independent Schools and Secondary School Admission Test Board. Endowment: $8.3 million. Total enrollment: 471. Upper school average class size: 11. Upper school faculty-student ratio: 1:6. There are 173 required school days per year for Upper School students. Upper School students typically attend 5 days per week. The average school day consists of 6 hours and 45 minutes.

Upper School Student Profile Grade 9: 54 students (27 boys, 27 girls); Grade 10: 51 students (27 boys, 24 girls); Grade 11: 36 students (20 boys, 16 girls); Grade 12: 42 students (19 boys, 23 girls).

Faculty School total: 67. In upper school: 18 men, 13 women; 25 have advanced degrees.

Subjects Offered 20th century American writers, 20th century history, 3-dimensional art, acting, Advanced Placement courses, African-American literature, algebra, American foreign policy, ancient world history, animation, archaeology, art, art history-AP, astronomy, band, biology, biology-AP, calculus, calculus-AP, ceramics, chamber groups, chemistry, chemistry-AP, China/Japan history, chorus, classical Greek literature, classical language, college writing, computer animation, computer graphics, computer programming, computer science-AP, concert band, concert bell choir, current events, digital photography, directing, drama, drawing, ecology, economics, economics-AP, English, English language-AP, English literature and composition-AP, environmental science, environmental science-AP, ethics, film studies, filmmaking, fine arts, foreign policy, French, French language-AP, French literature-AP, freshman seminar, geometry, Greek, handbells, health and wellness, history of China and Japan, honors algebra, honors geometry, humanities, independent study, introduction to theater, jazz band, jazz ensemble, journalism, Latin, Latin-AP, macro/microeconomics-AP, model United Nations, modern European history, music, music technology, natural history, oceanography, oil painting, photography, physics, physics-AP, play production, playwriting and directing, pre-calculus, probability and statistics, public speaking, sculpture, senior project, society and culture, socioeconomic problems, sociology, Spanish, Spanish literature-AP, Spanish-AP, statistics, technical theater, technology, theater, U.S. government and politics-AP, U.S. history, U.S. history-AP, visual arts, water color painting, Web site design, woodworking, world cultures, world history-AP, yearbook.

Graduation Requirements Arts and fine arts (art, music, dance, drama), athletics, computer literacy, electives, English, ethics, foreign language, history, lab science, mathematics, music appreciation, psychology, public speaking, science, technology, theater arts, senior speech.

Special Academic Programs 18 Advanced Placement exams for which test preparation is offered; honors section; accelerated programs; independent study; study abroad; academic accommodation for the gifted.

College Admission Counseling 53 students graduated in 2009; all went to college, including Bentley University; College of the Holy Cross; Connecticut College; Georgetown University; Northeastern University; Northwestern University. Mean SAT critical reading: 596, mean SAT math: 583, mean SAT writing: 589, mean combined SAT: 1768. 42% scored over 600 on SAT critical reading, 36.5% scored over 600 on SAT math, 48% scored over 600 on SAT writing, 53.8% scored over 1800 on combined SAT, 34% scored over 26 on composite ACT.

Student Life Upper grades have specified standards of dress, student council, honor system. Discipline rests equally with students and faculty.

Tuition and Aid Day student tuition: $28,790. Tuition installment plan (Key Tuition Payment Plan, monthly payment plans). Merit scholarship grants, need-based scholarship grants, Founders' Scholarships (for students entering 9th grade) available. In 2009–10, 40% of upper-school students received aid; total upper-school merit-scholarship money awarded: $394,585. Total amount of financial aid awarded in 2009–10: $2,680,000.

Admissions Traditional secondary-level entrance grade is 9. For fall 2009, 86 students applied for upper-level admission, 68 were accepted, 33 enrolled. SSAT required. Deadline for receipt of application materials: none. Application fee required: $60. On-campus interview required.

Athletics Interscholastic: baseball (boys), basketball (b,g), cross-country running (b,g), independent competitive sports (b,g), lacrosse (b,g), soccer (b,g), softball (g), tennis (b,g), volleyball (g), wrestling (b,g); intramural: ice hockey (b,g), strength & conditioning (b,g); coed interscholastic: crew, Frisbee, golf, independent competitive sports, swimming and diving, ultimate Frisbee, wrestling; coed intramural: aerobics/dance, aerobics/Nautilus, curling, dance, equestrian sports, figure skating, fitness, ice skating, modern dance, outdoor education, physical fitness, skiing (downhill), snowboarding, weight training. 4 PE instructors, 12 coaches, 1 athletic trainer.

Computers Computers are regularly used in art, creative writing, English, foreign language, history, humanities, library, literary magazine, mathematics, music, newspaper, photography, research skills, SAT preparation, science, social sciences, study skills, technology, yearbook classes. Computer network features include on-campus library services, online commercial services, Internet access, wireless campus network, Internet filtering or blocking technology. Campus intranet, student e-mail accounts, and computer access in designated common areas are available to students. Students grades are available online. The school has a published electronic and media policy.

Contact Margy Foulk, Director of Admission. 203-236-9560. Fax: 203-236-9503. E-mail: mfoulk@chasemail.org. Web site: www.chasemail.org.

CHATHAM ACADEMY

Savannah, Georgia
See Special Needs Schools section.

CHATHAM HALL

800 Chatham Hall Circle
Chatham, Virginia 24531
Head of School: Dr. Gary J. Fountain

General Information Girls' boarding and day college-preparatory and arts school, affiliated with Episcopal Church. Grades 9–12. Founded: 1894. Setting: small town. Nearest major city is Greensboro, NC. Students are housed in single-sex dormitories. 362-acre campus. 9 buildings on campus. Approved or accredited by National Association of Episcopal Schools, Southern Association of Colleges and Schools, The Association of Boarding Schools, and Virginia Association of Independent Schools. Member of Secondary School Admission Test Board. Endowment: $20 million. Total enrollment: 131. Upper school average class size: 8. Upper school faculty-student ratio: 1:7.

Upper School Student Profile 82% of students are boarding students. 34% are state residents. 20 states are represented in upper school student body. 14% are international students. International students from Bermuda, China, Costa Rica, Germany, Republic of Korea, and Taiwan; 12 other countries represented in student body. 20% of students are members of Episcopal Church.

Faculty School total: 34. In upper school: 11 men, 23 women; 19 have advanced degrees; 25 reside on campus.

Subjects Offered Algebra, American history-AP, American literature, art, art history, biology, biology-AP, calculus, calculus-AP, ceramics, chemistry, chemistry-AP, choir, college counseling, computer art, creative writing, dance, DNA science lab, drama, drama performance, earth science, economics, English, English language-AP, English literature, English-AP, ESL, ethics, European history, European history-AP, fine arts, French, French-AP, general science, geography, geometry, history, instrumental music, journalism, Latin, mathematics, medieval/Renaissance history, model United Nations, modern European history, modern European history-AP, music, music composition, music theory, music theory-AP, photography, physical education, physics, pre-calculus, psychology, religion, robotics, SAT/ACT preparation, science, service learning/internship, social studies, Spanish, Spanish-AP, studio art-AP, swimming, theater design and production, trigonometry, U.S. government and politics, U.S. history, veterinary science, Western civilization, world history, writing workshop, yearbook.

Graduation Requirements Arts and fine arts (art, music, dance, drama), English, ethics, foreign language, mathematics, physical education (includes health), religion (includes Bible studies and theology), science, social studies (includes history).

Special Academic Programs 13 Advanced Placement exams for which test preparation is offered; honors section; independent study; study abroad; academic accommodation for the gifted, the musically talented, and the artistically talented; ESL (3 students enrolled).

College Admission Counseling 38 students graduated in 2009; all went to college, including Cornell University; Dartmouth College; Duke University; Georgetown University; University of Virginia; Vanderbilt University. Median SAT critical reading: 605, median SAT math: 600. 61% scored over 600 on SAT critical reading, 55% scored over 600 on SAT math.

Student Life Upper grades have specified standards of dress, student council, honor system. Discipline rests equally with students and faculty. Attendance at religious services is required.

Tuition and Aid Day student tuition: $16,500; 7-day tuition and room/board: $38,000. Tuition installment plan (Key Tuition Payment Plan, increments of 45%, 30%, and 20% due July 1, September 1, and December 1 respectively). Merit scholarship grants, need-based scholarship grants available.

Admissions Traditional secondary-level entrance grade is 9. For fall 2009, 114 students applied for upper-level admission, 89 were accepted, 49 enrolled. ISEE, PSAT or SAT, SSAT or TOEFL required. Deadline for receipt of application materials: February 10. Application fee required: $50. Interview required.

Athletics Interscholastic: aquatics, basketball, cross-country running, diving, equestrian sports, field hockey, horseback riding, soccer, swimming and diving, tennis, volleyball; intramural: aerobics, aquatics, ballet, basketball, dance, diving, equestrian

sports, field hockey, horseback riding, lacrosse, modern dance, soccer, softball, swimming and diving, tennis, volleyball. 2 PE instructors, 3 coaches, 1 athletic trainer.
Computers Computers are regularly used in art, English, foreign language, graphic design, history, independent study, journalism, literary magazine, mathematics, music, newspaper, photography, science, yearbook classes. Computer network features include on-campus library services, online commercial services, Internet access, Internet filtering or blocking technology. Campus intranet, student e-mail accounts, and computer access in designated common areas are available to students. The school has a published electronic and media policy.
Contact Vicki Wright, Director of Admission and Financial Aid. 434-432-5613. E-mail: vwright@chathamhall.org. Web site: www.chathamhall.org.

See Display below and Close-Up on page 754.

CHATTANOOGA CHRISTIAN SCHOOL
3354 Charger Drive
Chattanooga, Tennessee 37409
Head of School: Mr. Chad Dirkse
General Information Coeducational day college-preparatory, arts, religious studies, technology, college-level (AP) courses, and dual enrollment courses school, affiliated with Christian faith. Grades K–12. Founded: 1970. Setting: urban. Nearest major city is Atlanta, GA. 40-acre campus. 6 buildings on campus. Approved or accredited by Christian Schools International, Southern Association of Colleges and Schools, and Tennessee Department of Education. Endowment: $10 million. Total enrollment: 1,118. Upper school average class size: 17. Upper school faculty-student ratio: 1:17. There are 175 required school days per year for Upper School students. Upper School students typically attend 5 days per week. The average school day consists of 7 hours.
Upper School Student Profile Grade 9: 108 students (43 boys, 65 girls); Grade 10: 116 students (53 boys, 63 girls); Grade 11: 122 students (71 boys, 51 girls); Grade 12: 106 students (49 boys, 57 girls). 100% of students are Christian faith.
Faculty School total: 104. In upper school: 27 men, 19 women; 19 have advanced degrees.
Subjects Offered African-American history, algebra, American government, American history, American literature, anatomy, art, art appreciation, art history, astronomy, Bible studies, biology, biology-AP, calculus, calculus-AP, character education, chemistry, choir, civil rights, community service, computer applications, computer programming, computer science, concert band, consumer economics, creative writing, dance, drama, Eastern world civilizations, economics, English,

English literature, entrepreneurship, environmental science, ethics, European history, European history-AP, fine arts, French, geology, geometry, German, grammar, health, industrial arts, Japanese studies, jazz band, journalism, keyboarding, kinesiology, Latin, leadership education training, mathematics, mechanical drawing, music, music appreciation, physical education, physical science, physics, physics-AP, physiology, psychology, religion, science, shop, Spanish, speech, statistics-AP, studio art-AP, theater, trigonometry, U.S. history-AP, Web site design, world literature, writing.
Graduation Requirements Arts and fine arts (art, music, dance, drama), computer science, English, foreign language, mathematics, physical education (includes health), religion (includes Bible studies and theology), science, social sciences, social studies (includes history). Community service is required.
Special Academic Programs Advanced Placement exam preparation; honors section; academic accommodation for the gifted, the musically talented, and the artistically talented; remedial reading and/or remedial writing; remedial math.
College Admission Counseling 98 students graduated in 2010; 96 went to college, including Chattanooga State Community College; Covenant College; Middle Tennessee State University; The University of Tennessee; The University of Tennessee at Chattanooga. Other: 2 had other specific plans. Mean SAT critical reading: 569, mean SAT math: 522, mean SAT writing: 554, mean composite ACT: 24. 46% scored over 600 on SAT critical reading, 30% scored over 600 on SAT math, 28% scored over 600 on SAT writing.
Student Life Upper grades have specified standards of dress, student council, honor system. Discipline rests primarily with faculty. Attendance at religious services is required.
Summer Programs Remediation, enrichment, sports, art/fine arts, computer instruction programs offered; session focuses on sports camps; held on campus; accepts boys and girls; open to students from other schools. 100 students usually enrolled. 2011 schedule: June 2 to June 27. Application deadline: May 30.
Tuition and Aid Day student tuition: $8409. Tuition installment plan (monthly payment plans, individually arranged payment plans). Tuition reduction for siblings, need-based scholarship grants, paying campus jobs available. In 2010–11, 15% of upper-school students received aid. Total amount of financial aid awarded in 2010–11: $250,000.
Admissions Traditional secondary-level entrance grade is 9. For fall 2010, 35 students applied for upper-level admission, 35 were accepted, 32 enrolled. Any standardized test required. Deadline for receipt of application materials: February 1. Application fee required: $75. Interview required.
Athletics Interscholastic: baseball (boys), basketball (b,g), bowling (b,g), cheering (g), cross-country running (b,g), football (b), golf (b,g), soccer (b,g), softball (g),

strength & conditioning (b,g), tennis (b,g), track and field (b,g), volleyball (g), weight lifting (b,g), weight training (b,g), wrestling (b); intramural: badminton (b,g), basketball (b,g), fencing (b,g), field hockey (g), flag football (b,g), indoor soccer (b,g), lacrosse (b,g), paddle tennis (b,g), soccer (b,g), softball (g), speedball (b,g), table tennis (b,g), tennis (b,g), touch football (b), track and field (b,g), volleyball (g), weight lifting (b,g), wrestling (b); coed intramural: aerobics/dance, bowling, cooperative games, dance, fitness, Frisbee, handball, hockey, independent competitive sports, jump rope, kickball, modern dance, outdoor activities, outdoor adventure, outdoor education, outdoor recreation, paddle tennis, physical fitness, physical training, running, street hockey, strength & conditioning, swimming and diving, table tennis, ultimate Frisbee, wall climbing, weight training, whiffle ball. 3 PE instructors, 15 coaches, 1 athletic trainer.
Computers Computers are regularly used in all academic, drawing and design, English, foreign language, lab/keyboard, library, mathematics, psychology, science, technology classes. Computer network features include on-campus library services, Internet access, wireless campus network, Internet filtering or blocking technology. Students grades are available online. The school has a published electronic and media policy.
Contact Mrs. Debbie Grisham, Admission Director. 423-265-6411 Ext. 209. Fax: 423-664-1245. E-mail: dgrisham@ccsk12.com. Web site: www.ccsk12.com.

CHELSEA SCHOOL
Silver Spring, Maryland
See Special Needs Schools section.

CHEROKEE CREEK BOYS SCHOOL
Westminster, South Carolina
See Special Needs Schools section.

CHERRY GULCH
Emmett, Idaho
See Special Needs Schools section.

CHESHIRE ACADEMY
10 Main Street
Cheshire, Connecticut 06410
Head of School: Douglas G. Rogers
General Information Coeducational boarding and day college-preparatory school. Boarding grades 9–PG, day grades 6–PG. Founded: 1794. Setting: small town. Nearest major city is New Haven. Students are housed in single-sex dormitories. 104-acre campus. 24 buildings on campus. Approved or accredited by Connecticut Association of Independent Schools, New England Association of Schools and Colleges, and The Association of Boarding Schools. Member of National Association of Independent Schools and Secondary School Admission Test Board. Endowment: $8 million. Total enrollment: 363. Upper school average class size: 12. Upper school faculty-student ratio: 1:7.
Upper School Student Profile Grade 6: 9 students (7 boys, 2 girls); Grade 7: 14 students (8 boys, 6 girls); Grade 8: 22 students (12 boys, 10 girls); Grade 9: 54 students (34 boys, 20 girls); Grade 10: 82 students (46 boys, 36 girls); Grade 11: 94 students (60 boys, 34 girls); Grade 12: 87 students (50 boys, 37 girls); Postgraduate: 7 students (6 boys, 1 girl). 62% of students are boarding students. 63% are state residents. 14 states are represented in upper school student body. 30% are international students. International students from China, Democratic People's Republic of Korea, Jamaica, and Taiwan; 15 other countries represented in student body.
Faculty School total: 82. In upper school: 36 men, 46 women; 55 have advanced degrees.
Subjects Offered Acting, Advanced Placement courses, algebra, American Civil War, American government, American history, American literature, anatomy, art, art history, Asian studies, biology, calculus, ceramics, chemistry, Chinese, community service, computer programming, computer science, creative writing, digital imaging, drama, earth science, ecology, economics, English, English literature, environmental science, ESL, European history, expository writing, fine arts, French, geography, geometry, government/civics, grammar, health, history, Latin American studies, mathematics, music, photography, physical education, physics, physiology, psychology, reading, science, social sciences, social studies, Spanish, speech, statistics, theater, Vietnam, world history, world literature, writing.
Graduation Requirements Arts and fine arts (art, music, dance, drama), computer science, electives, English, foreign language, history, mathematics, science, social sciences, social studies (includes history), senior speech, 10 hours of community service, Discover Week program.
Special Academic Programs Advanced Placement exam preparation; honors section; independent study; academic accommodation for the musically talented and the artistically talented; remedial reading and/or remedial writing; remedial math; programs in English, mathematics, general development for dyslexic students; ESL (30 students enrolled).

College Admission Counseling 95 students graduated in 2009; all went to college, including Carnegie Mellon University; Clark University, Fordham University, Ohio University; University of Michigan. Mean SAT critical reading: 523, mean SAT math: 618, mean SAT writing: 519, mean combined SAT: 1660, mean composite ACT: 23. 11% scored over 600 on SAT critical reading, 31% scored over 600 on SAT math, 13% scored over 600 on SAT writing, 19% scored over 1800 on combined SAT, 33% scored over 26 on composite ACT.
Student Life Upper grades have specified standards of dress, student council, honor system. Discipline rests primarily with faculty.
Tuition and Aid Day student tuition: $30,590; 7-day tuition and room/board: $42,575. Tuition installment plan (Key Tuition Payment Plan, monthly payment plans). Merit scholarship grants, need-based scholarship grants, need-based loans available. In 2009–10, 30% of upper-school students received aid; total upper-school merit-scholarship money awarded: $120,000. Total amount of financial aid awarded in 2009–10: $2,000,000.
Admissions Traditional secondary-level entrance grade is 9. ACT, ISEE, PSAT, SAT, SSAT or TOEFL required. Deadline for receipt of application materials: February 1. Application fee required: $50. Interview required.
Athletics Interscholastic: baseball (boys), basketball (b,g), cross-country running (b,g), fencing (b,g), field hockey (g), football (b), golf (b), lacrosse (b,g), soccer (b,g), softball (g), swimming and diving (b,g), tennis (b,g), track and field (b,g), volleyball (g); coed interscholastic: ultimate Frisbee, wrestling; coed intramural: fitness, freestyle skiing, physical training, ropes courses, skiing (downhill), snowboarding, weight training. 1 PE instructor, 30 coaches, 1 athletic trainer.
Computers Computers are regularly used in art, Christian doctrine, classics, college planning, computer applications, creative writing, design, English, foreign language, mathematics, science classes. Computer network features include on-campus library services, online commercial services, Internet access, wireless campus network, Internet filtering or blocking technology. Campus intranet, student e-mail accounts, and computer access in designated common areas are available to students. The school has a published electronic and media policy.
Contact Jane Hanrahan, Associate Director of Admission. 203-272-5396 Ext. 455. Fax: 203-250-7209. E-mail: jane.hanrahan@cheshireacademy.org. Web site: www.cheshireacademy.org.

CHEVERUS HIGH SCHOOL
267 Ocean Avenue
Portland, Maine 04103
Head of School: Mr. John H.R. Mullen
General Information Coeducational day college-preparatory, religious studies, technology, honors, and AP courses school, affiliated with Roman Catholic Church (Jesuit order). Grades 9–12. Founded: 1917. Setting: suburban. 32-acre campus. 2 buildings on campus. Approved or accredited by Association of Independent Schools in New England, Independent Schools of Northern New England, Jesuit Secondary Education Association, New England Association of Schools and Colleges, The College Board, and Maine Department of Education. Endowment: $3 million. Total enrollment: 497. Upper school average class size: 22. Upper school faculty-student ratio: 1:12. There are 175 required school days per year for Upper School students. Upper School students typically attend 5 days per week. The average school day consists of 6 hours and 30 minutes.
Upper School Student Profile Grade 9: 127 students (68 boys, 59 girls); Grade 10: 130 students (84 boys, 46 girls); Grade 11: 120 students (64 boys, 56 girls); Grade 12: 120 students (62 boys, 58 girls). 65% of students are Roman Catholic Church (Jesuit order).
Faculty School total: 44. In upper school: 23 men, 16 women; 26 have advanced degrees.
Subjects Offered Advanced Placement courses, algebra, American history, art, biology, calculus, chemistry, college counseling, community service, creative writing, economics, English, European history, fine arts, French, geography, geometry, government/civics, history, journalism, Latin, library skills, mathematics, music, physics, religion, science, social studies, Spanish, statistics, trigonometry, world history, yearbook.
Graduation Requirements Arts and fine arts (art, music, dance, drama), computer science, English, foreign language, health, mathematics, science, social studies (includes history), theology, all seniors are required to fill a community service requirement. Community service is required.
Special Academic Programs Advanced Placement exam preparation; honors section; study at local college for college credit; programs in general development for dyslexic students.
College Admission Counseling 135 students graduated in 2010; 129 went to college, including College of the Holy Cross; Loyola University Maryland; Saint Anselm College; Saint Mary's University; Southern Maine Community College; University of Maine. Other: 2 went to work, 2 entered military service, 1 entered a postgraduate year, 1 had other specific plans. Median SAT critical reading: 536, median SAT math: 535, median SAT writing: 537.
Student Life Upper grades have specified standards of dress, student council, honor system. Discipline rests primarily with faculty. Attendance at religious services is required.

Summer Programs Enrichment programs offered; session focuses on enrichment; held on campus; accepts boys and girls; open to students from other schools. 2011 schedule: June 21 to July 2. Application deadline: May 8.

Tuition and Aid Day student tuition: $14,605. Tuition installment plan (FACTS Tuition Payment Plan, monthly payment plans, individually arranged payment plans). Tuition reduction for siblings, merit scholarship grants, need-based scholarship grants, paying campus jobs available. In 2010–11, 64% of upper-school students received aid; total upper-school merit-scholarship money awarded: $12,500. Total amount of financial aid awarded in 2010–11: $1,932,399.

Admissions Traditional secondary-level entrance grade is 9. For fall 2010, 250 students applied for upper-level admission, 190 were accepted, 145 enrolled. English language and Math Placement Exam required. Deadline for receipt of application materials: none. Application fee required: $50. On-campus interview required.

Athletics Interscholastic: baseball (boys), basketball (b,g), cross-country running (b,g), diving (b,g), field hockey (g), football (b), golf (b,g), ice hockey (b,g), indoor track & field (b,g), lacrosse (b,g), sailing (b,g), skiing (downhill) (b,g), soccer (b,g), softball (g), swimming and diving (b,g), tennis (b,g), track and field (b,g); intramural: basketball (b,g), flag football (b,g); coed interscholastic: alpine skiing, outdoor adventure; coed intramural: basketball, bicycling, flag football, hiking/backpacking, volleyball. 82 coaches, 2 athletic trainers.

Computers Computers are regularly used in creative writing, economics, history, information technology, journalism, mathematics, SAT preparation, science, word processing, yearbook classes. Computer network features include on-campus library services, online commercial services, Internet access. Student e-mail accounts are available to students. Students grades are available online. The school has a published electronic and media policy.

Contact Ms. Kate Luke-Jenkins, Admissions Assisstant. 207-774-6238 Ext. 35. Fax: 207-321-0004. E-mail: luke-jenkins@cheverus.org. Web site: www.cheverus.org.

THE CHICAGO ACADEMY FOR THE ARTS

1010 West Chicago Avenue
Chicago, Illinois 60642
Head of School: Ms. Pamela Jordan

General Information Coeducational day college-preparatory and arts school. Grades 9–12. Founded: 1981. Setting: urban. 1-acre campus. 1 building on campus. Approved or accredited by Independent Schools Association of the Central States, North Central Association of Colleges and Schools, and Illinois Department of Education. Member of National Association of Independent Schools. Total enrollment: 140. Upper school average class size: 12. Upper school faculty-student ratio: 1:12. There are 163 required school days per year for Upper School students. Upper School students typically attend 5 days per week. The average school day consists of 8 hours.

Faculty School total: 42. In upper school: 21 men, 21 women; 19 have advanced degrees.

Subjects Offered Algebra, American history, anatomy, art history, arts, biology, calculus, chemistry, consumer law, creative writing, dance, drama, English, film, fine arts, French, geometry, historical foundations for arts, humanities, mathematics, music, physics, science, social sciences, Spanish, speech, theater.

Graduation Requirements Arts and fine arts (art, music, dance, drama), English, foreign language, mathematics, science, social sciences, U.S. history, Requirements vary according to arts discipline.

Special Academic Programs Advanced Placement exam preparation; honors section; academic accommodation for the musically talented and the artistically talented; programs in general development for dyslexic students.

College Admission Counseling 44 students graduated in 2010; 42 went to college, including New England Conservatory of Music; New York University; Rhode Island School of Design; School of the Art Institute of Chicago; The Juilliard School; University of Michigan. Other: 2 went to work. Median composite ACT: 24.

Student Life Upper grades have student council, honor system. Discipline rests equally with students and faculty.

Tuition and Aid Day student tuition: $19,675. Tuition installment plan (FACTS Tuition Payment Plan, monthly payment plans). Need-based scholarship grants available. In 2010–11, 48% of upper-school students received aid.

Admissions Traditional secondary-level entrance grade is 9. For fall 2010, 113 students applied for upper-level admission, 67 were accepted, 46 enrolled. ISEE required. Deadline for receipt of application materials: January 22. Application fee required: $60. On-campus interview required.

Computers Computers are regularly used in English, historical foundations for arts classes. Computer resources include online commercial services, Internet access, graphic design and production.

Contact Ms. Kaitlyn Myzwinski, Associate Director of Admissions. 312-421-0202 Ext. 21. Fax: 312-421-3816. E-mail: kmyzwinski@chicagoartsacademy.org. Web site: www.chicagoartsacademy.org.

CHICAGO WALDORF SCHOOL

1300 West Loyola Avenue
Chicago, Illinois 60626
Head of School: Mr. Leukos Goodwin

General Information Coeducational day college-preparatory, arts, vocational, service learning, and arts integrated into all core academic subjects school. Grades 1–12. Founded: 1974. Setting: urban. Students are housed in Day school. 2 buildings on campus. Approved or accredited by Independent Schools Association of the Central States and Illinois Department of Education. Total enrollment: 277. Upper school average class size: 25.

Upper School Student Profile Grade 6: 33 students (12 boys, 21 girls); Grade 7: 19 students (10 boys, 9 girls); Grade 8: 18 students (11 boys, 7 girls); Grade 9: 14 students (7 boys, 7 girls); Grade 10: 14 students (5 boys, 9 girls); Grade 11: 24 students (9 boys, 15 girls); Grade 12: 15 students (6 boys, 9 girls).

Subjects Offered All academic.

Special Academic Programs Independent study; study abroad.

College Admission Counseling 18 students graduated in 2010; all went to college, including DePaul University; Grinnell College; Knox College; Skidmore College; University of Illinois at Urbana–Champaign; Vassar College.

Student Life Upper grades have specified standards of dress, student council. Discipline rests primarily with faculty.

Tuition and Aid Day student tuition: $16,478. Tuition installment plan (monthly payment plans, individually arranged payment plans). Tuition reduction for siblings, need-based scholarship grants available. In 2010–11, 55% of upper-school students received aid. Total amount of financial aid awarded in 2010–11: $272,880.

Admissions Traditional secondary-level entrance grade is 9. For fall 2010, 18 students applied for upper-level admission, 13 were accepted, 9 enrolled. Deadline for receipt of application materials: none. Application fee required: $75. Interview required.

Athletics Interscholastic: basketball (boys, girls), soccer (g), volleyball (g); coed interscholastic: Circus, cross-country running, ultimate Frisbee. 1 PE instructor.

Computers Computers are regularly used in all academic classes. Computer network features include Internet access, wireless campus network. The school has a published electronic and media policy.

Contact Ms. Lisa Payton, Admissions Director. 773-465-2371. Fax: 773-465-6648. E-mail: lpayton@chicagowaldorf.org. Web site: http://www.chicagowaldorf.org/dir/highschool.aspx.

CHILDREN'S CREATIVE AND PERFORMING ARTS ACADEMY—CAPA DIVISION

3051 El Cajon Boulevard
San Diego, California 92104
Head of School: Janet M. Cherif

General Information Coeducational boarding and day college-preparatory and arts school. Boarding grades 6–12, day grades K–12. Founded: 1981. Setting: urban. Students are housed in homestay families. 1-acre campus. 1 building on campus. Approved or accredited by Western Association of Schools and Colleges and California Department of Education. Total enrollment: 265. Upper school average class size: 16. Upper school faculty-student ratio: 1:15. There are 186 required school days per year for Upper School students. Upper School students typically attend 5 days per week. The average school day consists of 7 hours and 30 minutes.

Upper School Student Profile Grade 6: 15 students (8 boys, 7 girls); Grade 7: 15 students (8 boys, 7 girls); Grade 8: 15 students (9 boys, 6 girls); Grade 9: 31 students (11 boys, 20 girls); Grade 10: 28 students (12 boys, 16 girls); Grade 11: 28 students (13 boys, 15 girls); Grade 12: 28 students (15 boys, 13 girls). 20% of students are boarding students. 80% are state residents. 1 state is represented in upper school student body. 20% are international students. International students from China, Mexico, Republic of Korea, Taiwan, Thailand, and Viet Nam; 3 other countries represented in student body.

Faculty School total: 30. In upper school: 3 men, 14 women; 10 have advanced degrees.

Subjects Offered 3-dimensional art, 3-dimensional design, accounting, algebra, American government, anatomy and physiology, art, art history, art history-AP, art-AP, audition methods, ballet, band, biology, business skills, calculus, calculus-AP, ceramics, chamber groups, cheerleading, chemistry, Chinese, choir, choreography, chorus, communications, community service, comparative government and politics-AP, computer applications, computer literacy, computer programming-AP, concert band, concert choir, creative writing, dance performance, digital photography, drama, drama performance, earth science, ecology, English, English literature-AP, English-AP, English/composition-AP, ensembles, environmental science-AP, ESL, European history-AP, film, fitness, French, French language-AP, French literature-AP, geometry, government and politics-AP, government/civics, government/civics-AP, graphic design, gymnastics, health, history of music, history-AP, honors algebra, honors English, honors geometry, honors U.S. history, honors world history, HTML design, human anatomy, humanities, instrumental music, Japanese, jazz band, jazz dance, jazz ensemble, journalism, Latin, library studies, mathematics, mathematics-AP, modern dance, music history, music performance, music theory-AP, orchestra, performing arts, physical education, physics, physics-AP, playwriting and directing, political science, portfolio art, pottery, pre-algebra, pre-calculus, psychology, reading/study skills, SAT preparation, SAT/ACT preparation, science, senior seminar, social sciences, social studies, Spanish, Spanish language-AP, Spanish literature-AP, speech, sports, stage design, statistics, studio art-AP, tap dance, tennis, theater design and production, TOEFL preparation, track and field, trigonometry, U.S. government and politics-AP, U.S. history, U.S. history-AP, vocal ensemble, vocal jazz, voice ensemble, volleyball, Web site design, Western civilization, world history, world history-AP, writing, writing workshop, yearbook.

Graduation Requirements Algebra, arts, biology, business skills (includes word processing), chemistry, choir, chorus, computer applications, computer skills, English, English composition, English literature, foreign language, government/civics, history, mathematics, modern world history, music, physical education (includes health), physics, science, social sciences, Spanish, sports, trigonometry, U.S. government, U.S. history, visual and performing arts, senior recital or project, 30 hours of community service per year of attendance. Community service is required.

Special Academic Programs 14 Advanced Placement exams for which test preparation is offered; honors section; accelerated programs; independent study; study at local college for college credit; academic accommodation for the gifted, the musically talented, and the artistically talented; remedial reading and/or remedial writing; remedial math; ESL (10 students enrolled).

College Admission Counseling 15 students graduated in 2009; all went to college, including San Diego State University; The George Washington University; The University of Texas at Austin; University of California, Berkeley; University of California, Davis; University of California, San Diego. Median SAT critical reading: 627, median SAT math: 677, median SAT writing: 590, median combined SAT: 1894. 50% scored over 600 on SAT critical reading, 50% scored over 600 on SAT math, 45% scored over 600 on SAT writing, 45% scored over 1800 on combined SAT.

Student Life Upper grades have uniform requirement, student council, honor system. Discipline rests primarily with faculty.

Tuition and Aid Day student tuition: $8650; 7-day tuition and room/board: $15,400. Tuition installment plan (monthly payment plans, individually arranged payment plans). Tuition reduction for siblings, merit scholarship grants, need-based scholarship grants, paying campus jobs available. In 2009–10, 20% of upper-school students received aid; total upper-school merit-scholarship money awarded: $10,000. Total amount of financial aid awarded in 2009–10: $25,000.

Admissions Traditional secondary-level entrance grade is 9. For fall 2009, 20 students applied for upper-level admission, 8 were accepted, 8 enrolled. Admissions testing, any standardized test, audition, math and English placement tests, Math Placement Exam or writing sample required. Deadline for receipt of application materials: none. Application fee required: $50. Interview recommended.

Athletics Interscholastic: artistic gym (girls), baseball (b,g), basketball (b,g), cross-country running (b,g), flag football (b), gymnastics (g), indoor soccer (b,g), soccer (b,g), softball (g), track and field (b,g), volleyball (b,g); intramural: aerobics/dance (b,g), artistic gym (g), backpacking (b,g), badminton (b,g), ballet (b,g), baseball (b,g), basketball (b,g), bowling (b,g), cheering (g), dance (b,g), dance squad (b,g), dance team (b,g), fitness (b,g), flag football (b,g), floor hockey (b,g), gymnastics (b,g), hiking/backpacking (b,g), horseback riding (b,g), indoor soccer (b,g), jump rope (b,g), modern dance (b,g), outdoor activities (b,g), outdoor education (b,g), physical fitness (b,g), soccer (b,g), softball (b,g), surfing (b,g), swimming and diving (b,g), table tennis (b,g), tennis (b,g), track and field (b,g), volleyball (b,g); coed interscholastic: indoor soccer; coed intramural: aerobics/dance, backpacking, badminton, ballet, baseball, bowling, dance, dance squad, dance team, fitness, flag football, floor hockey, hiking/backpacking, indoor soccer, jump rope, modern dance, outdoor activities, outdoor education, physical fitness, softball, surfing, swimming and diving, table tennis, track and field. 2 PE instructors, 2 coaches.

Computers Computers are regularly used in architecture, business skills, commercial art, creative writing, data processing, desktop publishing, drawing and design, journalism, keyboarding, media arts, music, programming, SAT preparation, typing, video film production, Web site design, word processing, yearbook classes. Computer network features include Internet access, college credit classes online.

Contact Karen Peterson, Admissions Department. 619-584-2454. Fax: 619-584-2422. E-mail: jmcherif@yahoo.com. Web site: www.ccpaasd.com.

CHINESE CHRISTIAN SCHOOLS

750 Fargo Avenue
San Leandro, California 94579
Head of School: Mr. Robin S. Hom

General Information Coeducational day college-preparatory and religious studies school, affiliated with Bible Fellowship Church, Evangelical/Fundamental faith. Grades K–12. Founded: 1979. Setting: suburban. Nearest major city is Oakland. 10-acre campus. 7 buildings on campus. Approved or accredited by Association of Christian Schools International, The College Board, Western Association of Schools and Colleges, and California Department of Education. Languages of instruction: English and Mandarin. Endowment: $14,000. Total enrollment: 776. Upper school average class size: 20. Upper school faculty-student ratio: 1:8. There are 173 required school days per year for Upper School students. Upper School students typically attend 5 days per week. The average school day consists of 6 hours and 50 minutes.

Upper School Student Profile Grade 9: 48 students (21 boys, 27 girls); Grade 10: 63 students (38 boys, 25 girls); Grade 11: 50 students (19 boys, 31 girls); Grade 12: 53 students (30 boys, 23 girls). 20% of students are Bible Fellowship Church, Evangelical/Fundamental faith.

Faculty School total: 40. In upper school: 15 men, 20 women; 12 have advanced degrees.

Subjects Offered Advanced computer applications, Advanced Placement courses, aerobics, algebra, American government, American history, American history-AP, American literature, American literature-AP, applied music, art, art-AP, audio visual/media, Basic programming, basketball, Bible, Bible studies, biology, biology-AP, British literature, calculus, calculus-AP, career/college preparation, chemistry, Chinese, Chinese studies, choir, choral music, Christian doctrine, Christian ethics, Christian studies, civics, civics/free enterprise, college counseling, college placement, college planning, communications, community service, comparative religion, computer applications, computer graphics, computer science, computer science-AP, CPR, debate, drama, driver education, economics, economics-AP, electives, English, English language-AP, English literature, English literature-AP, ESL, European history-AP, first aid, foreign language, general science, geometry, government, government and politics-AP, government-AP, graphic arts, honors English, intro to computers, language arts, leadership and service, learning strategies, library assistant, literature and composition-AP, literature-AP, macro/microeconomics-AP, Mandarin, marching band, marine science, martial arts, mathematics-AP, microeconomics, microeconomics-AP, music, newspaper, participation in sports, physical education, physics, physics-AP, pre-algebra, pre-calculus, probability and statistics, public speaking, religious education, religious studies, ROTC (for boys), SAT preparation, SAT/ACT preparation, science, science research, Spanish, speech, speech and debate, speech communications, sports, state history, statistics, student government, theater, theater arts, trigonometry, U.S. government, U.S. government and politics-AP, U.S. history, U.S. history-AP, visual and performing arts, volleyball, Web authoring, world history, world wide web design, yearbook.

Graduation Requirements Algebra, American government, American history, Bible, Chinese, CPR, driver education, economics, English, first aid, foreign language, geometry, history, lab science, Life of Christ, mathematics, physical education (includes health), physics, pre-algebra, science, visual and performing arts, world history, Mandarin I or Chinese Culture class.

Special Academic Programs 13 Advanced Placement exams for which test preparation is offered; honors section; term-away projects; study at local college for college credit; study abroad; academic accommodation for the gifted; remedial reading and/or remedial writing; ESL (15 students enrolled).

College Admission Counseling 59 students graduated in 2010; 58 went to college, including San Jose State University; University of California, Berkeley; University of California, Davis; University of California, Irvine; University of California, Riverside; University of California, San Diego. Other: 1 entered military service. Mean SAT critical reading: 563, mean SAT math: 622, mean SAT writing: 558, mean combined SAT: 1743. 43% scored over 600 on SAT critical reading, 59% scored over 600 on SAT math, 39% scored over 600 on SAT writing, 38% scored over 1800 on combined SAT.

Student Life Upper grades have uniform requirement, student council. Discipline rests primarily with faculty. Attendance at religious services is required.

Summer Programs Remediation, enrichment, advancement, ESL, sports programs offered; session focuses on academic enrichment or remediation; held on campus; accepts boys and girls; open to students from other schools. 270 students usually enrolled. 2011 schedule: June 22 to July 22. Application deadline: May 15.

Tuition and Aid Day student tuition: $6950–$8950. Tuition installment plan (monthly payment plans, individually arranged payment plans, eTuition automatic electronic deposit). Tuition reduction for siblings, merit scholarship grants, need-based scholarship grants, paying campus jobs; tuition reduction for staff children, tuition reduction for children of full-time Christian ministers of like faith available. In 2010–11, 10% of upper-school students received aid; total upper-school merit-scholarship money awarded: $10,000. Total amount of financial aid awarded in 2010–11: $160,000.

Admissions Traditional secondary-level entrance grade is 9. For fall 2010, 28 students applied for upper-level admission, 25 were accepted, 22 enrolled. Achievement/Aptitude/Writing, admissions testing, California Achievement Test, CTBS (or similar from their school), Math Placement Exam, Stanford Achievement Test or writing sample required. Deadline for receipt of application materials: none. No application fee required. Interview required.

Athletics Interscholastic: basketball (boys, girls), cross-country running (b,g), drill team (b), JROTC drill (b), soccer (b,g), tennis (b,g), track and field (b,g), volleyball (b,g); intramural: basketball (b,g), drill team (b), flag football (b), outdoor education (b,g), outdoor recreation (b,g), soccer (b,g), softball (b,g), street hockey (b,g), table tennis (b,g), volleyball (b,g); coed interscholastic: cross-country running, swimming and diving; coed intramural: outdoor education, outdoor recreation, softball, table tennis, volleyball. 2 PE instructors, 1 coach.

Computers Computers are regularly used in lab/keyboard, programming, science, senior seminar, Web site design classes. Computer network features include on-campus library services, Internet access, wireless campus network, Internet filtering or blocking technology. Student e-mail accounts are available to students. Students grades are available online. The school has a published electronic and media policy.

Contact Mrs. Cindy Loh, Admissions Director. 510-351-4957 Ext. 210. Fax: 510-351-1789. E-mail: CindyLoh@ccs-rams.org. Web site: www.ccs-rams.org.

CHOATE ROSEMARY HALL

333 Christian Street
Wallingford, Connecticut 06492-3800
Head of School: Edward J. Shanahan, PhD
General Information Coeducational boarding and day college-preparatory school. Grades 9–PG. Founded: 1890. Setting: small town. Nearest major city is New Haven. Students are housed in single-sex dormitories. 458-acre campus. 121 buildings on campus. Approved or accredited by Connecticut Association of Independent Schools, New England Association of Schools and Colleges, The Association of Boarding Schools, and Connecticut Department of Education. Member of National Association of Independent Schools and Secondary School Admission Test Board. Endowment: $240 million. Total enrollment: 850. Upper school average class size: 12. Upper school faculty-student ratio: 1:6. There are 166 required school days per year for Upper School students. Upper School students typically attend 5 days per week. The average school day consists of 5 hours.
Upper School Student Profile Grade 9: 148 students (72 boys, 76 girls); Grade 10: 217 students (115 boys, 102 girls); Grade 11: 228 students (111 boys, 117 girls); Grade 12: 235 students (112 boys, 123 girls); Postgraduate: 22 students (18 boys, 4 girls). 75% of students are boarding students. 47% are state residents. 40 states are represented in upper school student body. 12% are international students. International students from Canada, China, Hong Kong, Republic of Korea, Saudi Arabia, and Thailand; 39 other countries represented in student body.
Faculty School total: 130. In upper school: 67 men, 54 women; 89 have advanced degrees; 99 reside on campus.
Subjects Offered Algebra, American history, American literature, anatomy, Arabic, architecture, art, astronomy, biology, British history, calculus, calculus-AP, ceramics, chemistry, chemistry-AP, child development, Chinese, computer programming, computer science, computer science-AP, creative writing, dance, drama, ecology, economics, English, English literature, environmental science, environmental science-AP, European history-AP, fine arts, French, French language-AP, French studies, geometry, government and politics-AP, history, history-AP, Holocaust, interdisciplinary studies, international studies, Italian, language, Latin, Latin-AP, linear algebra, macroeconomics-AP, marine biology, mathematics, microbiology, microeconomics-AP, music, music composition, music history, music performance, music technology, music theater, music theory-AP, music-AP, musical productions, musical theater, musical theater dance, musicianship, philosophy, photography, physics, physics-AP, psychology, psychology-AP, public speaking, religion, Spanish, Spanish language-AP, Spanish literature, Spanish literature-AP, Spanish-AP, statistics, statistics-AP, studio art, theater, trigonometry, U.S. history, U.S. history-AP, visual arts, world history, world literature, world religions, world studies, wrestling, writing, writing, writing workshop.
Graduation Requirements Art, English, foreign language, global studies, history, mathematics, philosophy, physical education (includes health), science, 30 hours of community service.
Special Academic Programs 25 Advanced Placement exams for which test preparation is offered; honors section; independent study; term-away projects; study abroad; academic accommodation for the gifted, the musically talented, and the artistically talented.
College Admission Counseling 249 students graduated in 2010; 245 went to college, including Boston University; Cornell University; Georgetown University; New York University; Wesleyan University; Yale University. Other: 4 had other specific plans. Mean SAT critical reading: 668, mean SAT math: 678, mean SAT writing: 679, mean combined SAT: 2025, mean composite ACT: 29.
Student Life Upper grades have specified standards of dress, student council, honor system. Discipline rests primarily with faculty.
Summer Programs Enrichment, advancement, ESL, sports, art/fine arts programs offered; session focuses on academic growth and enrichment; held both on and off campus; held at China, France, and Spain; accepts boys and girls; open to students from other schools. 500 students usually enrolled. 2011 schedule: June 26 to July 29. Application deadline: May 1.
Tuition and Aid Day student tuition: $34,320; 7-day tuition and room/board: $45,070. Tuition installment plan (Insured Tuition Payment Plan, Key Tuition Payment Plan, monthly payment plans, individually arranged payment plans). Need-based scholarship grants, need-based loans available. In 2010–11, 33% of upper-school students received aid. Total amount of financial aid awarded in 2010–11: $8,500,000.
Admissions Traditional secondary-level entrance grade is 9. For fall 2010, 1,761 students applied for upper-level admission, 418 were accepted, 262 enrolled. ACT, ISEE, PSAT or SAT for applicants to grade 11 and 12, SSAT or TOEFL required. Deadline for receipt of application materials: January 10. Application fee required: $60. Interview required.
Athletics Interscholastic: baseball (boys), basketball (b,g), crew (b,g), cross-country running (b,g), diving (b,g), field hockey (g), football (b), golf (b,g), ice hockey (b,g), lacrosse (b,g), soccer (b,g), softball (g), squash (b,g), swimming and diving (b,g), tennis (b,g), track and field (b,g), volleyball (b,g), water polo (b,g), wrestling (b); intramural: crew (b,g), squash (b,g); coed interscholastic: archery; coed intramural: aerobics, aerobics/dance, aerobics/Nautilus, ballet, basketball, dance, dance squad, fitness, martial arts, modern dance, Nautilus, outdoor activities, physical fitness, physical training, rock climbing, running, soccer, softball, strength & conditioning, swimming and diving, tennis, ultimate Frisbee, volleyball, wall climbing, weight training, winter (indoor) track, yoga. 10 coaches, 3 athletic trainers.
Computers Computers are regularly used in all academic, art, college planning, computer applications, desktop publishing, drawing and design, graphic design, information technology, library skills, literary magazine, media production, music, newspaper, photography, programming, stock market, study skills, theater arts, video film production, word processing, yearbook classes. Computer network features include on-campus library services, online commercial services, Internet access, wireless campus network, Internet filtering or blocking technology. Campus intranet, student e-mail accounts, and computer access in designated common areas are available to students. Students grades are available online. The school has a published electronic and media policy.
Contact Raymond M. Diffley III, Director of Admission. 203-697-2239. Fax: 203-697-2629. E-mail: admission@choate.edu. Web site: www.choate.edu.

See Close-Up on page 756.

CHRISTA McAULIFFE ACADEMY SCHOOL OF ARTS AND SCIENCES

5200 SW Meadows Road, Suite 150
Lake Oswego, Oregon 97035
Head of School: Christopher M. Geis
General Information Coeducational day and distance learning college-preparatory, general academic, vocational, bilingual studies, technology, and advanced placement, honors, credit recovery school. Grades K–12. Distance learning grades K–12. Founded: 1985. Setting: small town. Nearest major city is Seattle, WA. 1 building on campus. Approved or accredited by CITA (Commission on International and Trans-Regional Accreditation), Northwest Association of Schools and Colleges, and Oregon Department of Education. Total enrollment: 154. Upper school average class size: 25. Upper school faculty-student ratio: 1:25.
Faculty School total: 15. In upper school: 7 women; 4 have advanced degrees.
Subjects Offered ACT preparation, American sign language, art, career education, electives, English, foreign language, health, mathematics, music, occupational education, physical education, science, social studies, standard curriculum, technology.
Graduation Requirements Art, career exploration, computer applications, English, mathematics, music, pre-vocational education, science, social studies (includes history).
Special Academic Programs Advanced Placement exam preparation; honors section; accelerated programs; independent study; academic accommodation for the gifted, the musically talented, and the artistically talented; remedial reading and/or remedial writing; remedial math; programs in general development for dyslexic students.
College Admission Counseling 15 students graduated in 2009; 12 went to college, including Florida State University; Massachusetts Institute of Technology; Penn State University Park; University of Illinois at Chicago; University of Washington; Washington State University.
Student Life Upper grades have student council, honor system. Discipline rests equally with students and faculty.
Tuition and Aid Day student tuition: $4797. Guaranteed tuition plan. Tuition installment plan (monthly payment plans, individually arranged payment plans). Tuition reduction for siblings available. In 2009–10, 10% of upper-school students received aid.
Admissions Traditional secondary-level entrance grade is 9. Achievement/Aptitude/Writing required. Deadline for receipt of application materials: none. Application fee required: $99. Interview recommended.
Computers Computers are regularly used in all academic classes. Computer network features include Internet access. The school has a published electronic and media policy.
Contact Christopher M. Geis, Director of Administrative Services. 509-388-0717. Fax: 866-920-1619. E-mail: christopher.geis@cmacademy.org. Web site: http://www.personalizededucation.org/schools/sas/index.html.

CHRIST CHURCH EPISCOPAL SCHOOL

245 Cavalier Drive
Greenville, South Carolina 29607
Head of School: Dr. Leonard Kupersmith
General Information Coeducational day college-preparatory, arts, religious studies, technology, and International Baccalaureate school, affiliated with Episcopal Church. Grades K–12. Founded: 1959. Setting: suburban. Nearest major city is Charlotte, NC. 72-acre campus. 7 buildings on campus. Approved or accredited by International Baccalaureate Organization, National Association of Episcopal Schools, Southern Association of Colleges and Schools, Southern Association of Independent Schools, and The College Board. Member of National Association of Independent Schools. Endowment: $6 million. Total enrollment: 990. Upper school average class size: 18. Upper school faculty-student ratio: 1:10. The average school day consists of 7 hours.

Upper School Student Profile Grade 9: 90 students (51 boys, 39 girls); Grade 10: 88 students (44 boys, 44 girls); Grade 11: 71 students (40 boys, 31 girls); Grade 12: 74 students (40 boys, 34 girls). 15% of students are members of Episcopal Church. **Faculty** School total: 121. In upper school: 16 men, 23 women; 30 have advanced degrees.

Subjects Offered 20th century history, algebra, American history, American literature, American literature-AP, Ancient Greek, art, biology, biology-AP, calculus, calculus-AP, chemistry, chemistry-AP, China/Japan history, Christian education, Christian ethics, Christian scripture, Christian studies, computer art, computer graphics, computer programming, computer programming-AP, computer science, creative writing, drama, earth science, economics, English, English literature, environmental science, ESL, ethics, ethics and responsibility, European history, European history-AP, expository writing, fine arts, French, French-AP, geometry, German, government and politics-AP, government/civics, grammar, graphic arts, history, history-AP, honors English, honors U.S. history, honors world history, humanities, International Baccalaureate courses, journalism, keyboarding, Latin, Latin-AP, marine biology, mathematics, music, music theory-AP, music-AP, physical education, physics, physics-AP, psychology, public speaking, religion, SAT/ACT preparation, science, social studies, Spanish, Spanish-AP, speech, statistics, statistics-AP, theater, theology, theory of knowledge, trigonometry, U.S. history-AP, Web site design, world history, world history-AP, world literature.

Graduation Requirements American history, arts and fine arts (art, music, dance, drama), British literature, electives, English, foreign language, mathematics, physical education (includes health), religion (includes Bible studies and theology), science, senior thesis, service learning/internship, technology, U.S. government, extended essay (for IB diploma candidates), sophomore project (all students).

Special Academic Programs International Baccalaureate program; honors section; independent study; ESL.

College Admission Counseling 69 students graduated in 2010; all went to college, including Clemson University; Emory University; The University of Alabama at Birmingham; University of Georgia; University of South Carolina; Wofford College. Mean SAT critical reading: 624, mean SAT math: 627, mean SAT writing: 624, mean combined SAT: 1876, mean composite ACT: 27. 58% scored over 600 on SAT critical reading, 69.5% scored over 600 on SAT math, 62% scored over 600 on SAT writing.

Student Life Upper grades have specified standards of dress, student council, honor system. Discipline rests equally with students and faculty. Attendance at religious services is required.

Summer Programs Remediation, enrichment, advancement, sports programs offered; session focuses on Enrichment, athletics, academics; held both on and off campus; held at Field trips to other locations; accepts boys and girls; open to students from other schools. 650 students usually enrolled. 2011 schedule: May 31 to August 12.

Tuition and Aid Day student tuition: $15,885. Tuition installment plan (Insured Tuition Payment Plan, FACTS Tuition Payment Plan, monthly payment plans). Tuition reduction for siblings, merit scholarship grants, need-based scholarship grants available. In 2010–11, 25% of upper-school students received aid; total upper-school merit-scholarship money awarded: $114,000. Total amount of financial aid awarded in 2010–11: $523,000.

Admissions Traditional secondary-level entrance grade is 9. For fall 2010, 41 students applied for upper-level admission, 33 were accepted, 30 enrolled. PSAT required. Deadline for receipt of application materials: December 1. Application fee required: $150. On-campus interview required.

Athletics Interscholastic: baseball (boys), basketball (b,g), cheering (g), cross-country running (b,g), dance team (g), field hockey (g), football (b), golf (b,g), soccer (b,g), softball (g), swimming and diving (b,g), tennis (b,g), track and field (b,g), volleyball (g), weight training (b,g), wrestling (b); intramural: dance team (g), fencing (b). 4 PE instructors, 45 coaches, 2 athletic trainers.

Computers Computers are regularly used in all classes. Computer network features include on-campus library services, online commercial services, Internet access, Internet filtering or blocking technology, classroom computers. Computer access in designated common areas is available to students. Students grades are available online. The school has a published electronic and media policy.

Contact Mrs. Kathy Jones, Director of Student Recruitment. 864-299-1522 Ext. 1208. Fax: 864-299-8861. E-mail: jonesk@cces.org. Web site: www.cces.org.

CHRISTCHURCH SCHOOL

49 Seahorse Lane
Christchurch, Virginia 23031
Head of School: Mr. John E. Byers

General Information Boys' boarding and coeducational day college-preparatory, marine and environmental sciences, and ESL school, affiliated with Episcopal Church. Boarding boys grades 9–PG, day boys grades 9–PG, day girls grades 9–PG. Founded: 1921. Setting: rural. Nearest major city is Richmond. Students are housed in single-sex dormitories. 125-acre campus. 14 buildings on campus. Approved or accredited by National Association of Episcopal Schools, The Association of Boarding Schools, The College Board, Virginia Association of Independent Schools, and Virginia Department of Education. Member of National Association of Independent Schools and Secondary School Admission Test Board. Endowment: $2 million. Total enrollment: 204. Upper school average class size: 12. Upper school faculty-student ratio: 1:7. There are 165

required school days per year for Upper School students. Upper School students typically attend 5 days per week. The average school day consists of 9 hours.

Upper School Student Profile Grade 9: 45 students (29 boys, 16 girls); Grade 10: 51 students (47 boys, 4 girls); Grade 11: 66 students (53 boys, 13 girls); Grade 12: 40 students (33 boys, 7 girls); Postgraduate: 2 students (2 boys). 54% of students are boarding students. 65% are state residents. 14 states are represented in upper school student body. 19% are international students. International students from Bermuda, China, Hong Kong, Republic of Korea, Taiwan, and Viet Nam; 2 other countries represented in student body. 17% of students are members of Episcopal Church.

Faculty School total: 32. In upper school: 20 men, 12 women; 14 have advanced degrees; 20 reside on campus.

Subjects Offered Advanced biology, advanced chemistry, algebra, American Civil War, ancient world history, art, biology, calculus, chemistry, Chesapeake Bay studies, Chinese, computer art, computer-aided design, conceptual physics, digital art, drawing and design, economics, English, English language and composition-AP, English literature and composition-AP, environmental science, environmental science-AP, ESL, fine arts, finite math, geography, geometry, health and wellness, honors U.S. history, honors world history, marine biology, modern world history, Native American history, physical education, physics, pre-calculus, probability and statistics, SAT/ACT preparation, Spanish, Spanish-AP, technology/design, theology, U.S. government, U.S. government and politics-AP, U.S. history, U.S. history-AP, world geography, world history.

Graduation Requirements Arts and fine arts (art, music, dance, drama), English, foreign language, health and wellness, mathematics, physical education (includes health), religion (includes Bible studies and theology), science, social studies (includes history).

Special Academic Programs 11 Advanced Placement exams for which test preparation is offered; honors section; independent study; academic accommodation for the gifted; ESL (18 students enrolled).

College Admission Counseling 62 students graduated in 2010; all went to college, including James Madison University; University of Mary Washington; Virginia Commonwealth University. Mean SAT critical reading: 521, mean SAT math: 554, mean SAT writing: 516, mean combined SAT: 1591. 25% scored over 600 on SAT critical reading, 25% scored over 600 on SAT math.

Student Life Upper grades have specified standards of dress, student council, honor system. Discipline rests equally with students and faculty. Attendance at religious services is required.

Summer Programs Enrichment, sports programs offered; session focuses on marine and environmental science, sailing, camping, fishing; held on campus; accepts boys and girls; open to students from other schools. 75 students usually enrolled. 2011 schedule: June 27 to July 17. Application deadline: none.

Tuition and Aid Day student tuition: $17,300; 7-day tuition and room/board: $40,850. Tuition installment plan (monthly payment plans, individually arranged payment plans, 10 month plan, 1st payment due 6/15, 4-payment plan, first payment due 6/15, 2-payment plan, first payment due 6/15). Need-based scholarship grants available. In 2010–11, 40% of upper-school students received aid. Total amount of financial aid awarded in 2010–11: $1,270,125.

Admissions Traditional secondary-level entrance grade is 9. For fall 2010, 194 students applied for upper-level admission, 136 were accepted, 93 enrolled. PSAT or SAT, SSAT, TOEFL or WISC/Woodcock-Johnson required. Deadline for receipt of application materials: none. Application fee required: $50. Interview required.

Athletics Interscholastic: baseball (boys), basketball (b,g), crew (b,g), field hockey (g), football (b), golf (b), lacrosse (b), sailing (b,g), soccer (b,g), volleyball (g); intramural: basketball (b), weight training (b,g); coed interscholastic: golf, sailing; coed intramural: canoeing/kayaking, fishing, fitness, fly fishing, Frisbee, hiking/backpacking, indoor soccer, kayaking, outdoor activities, outdoor adventure, outdoor education, outdoor recreation, outdoor skills, outdoors, paint ball, physical training, rock climbing, sailing, snowboarding, soccer, strength & conditioning, tennis, winter soccer. 1 athletic trainer.

Computers Computers are regularly used in all academic classes. Computer network features include on-campus library services, online commercial services, Internet access, wireless campus network, Internet filtering or blocking technology. Campus intranet, student e-mail accounts, and computer access in designated common areas are available to students. Students grades are available online. The school has a published electronic and media policy.

Contact Mr. Lawrence J. Jensen, Director of Admission. 804-758-2306. Fax: 804-758-0721. E-mail: admission@christchurchschool.org. Web site: www.christchurchschool.org.

CHRISTIAN BROTHERS ACADEMY

850 Newman Springs Road
Lincroft, New Jersey 07738
Head of School: Br. James Butler, FSC

General Information Boys' day college-preparatory school, affiliated with Roman Catholic Church. Grades 9–12. Founded: 1959. Setting: suburban. Nearest major city is New York, NY. 157-acre campus. 3 buildings on campus. Approved or accredited by Middle States Association of Colleges and Schools. Endowment: $9.7 million. Total enrollment: 973. Upper school average class size: 18. Upper school faculty-student ratio: 1:16.

Christian Brothers Academy

Upper School Student Profile Grade 9: 266 students (266 boys); Grade 10: 254 students (254 boys); Grade 11: 233 students (233 boys); Grade 12: 220 students (220 boys). 80% of students are Roman Catholic.

Faculty School total: 63. In upper school: 42 men, 17 women; 48 have advanced degrees.

Subjects Offered Algebra, American government, American history, anatomy and physiology, Bible studies, biology, business, business skills, calculus, chemistry, computer science, creative writing, driver education, economics, English, environmental science, European history, French, geometry, health, history, journalism, Latin, mathematics, physical education, physics, psychology, religion, science, social sciences, social studies, Spanish, theology, trigonometry, world history, world literature, writing.

Graduation Requirements Business skills (includes word processing), computer science, English, foreign language, mathematics, physical education (includes health), religion (includes Bible studies and theology), science, social sciences, social studies (includes history).

Special Academic Programs Advanced Placement exam preparation; honors section.

College Admission Counseling 226 students graduated in 2010; 220 went to college, including Fordham University; Manhattan College; Rutgers, The State University of New Jersey, New Brunswick; Stevens Institute of Technology; The University of Scranton; Villanova University. Median SAT critical reading: 580, median SAT math: 610, median SAT writing: 580, median combined SAT: 1770.

Student Life Upper grades have specified standards of dress, student council. Discipline rests primarily with faculty. Attendance at religious services is required.

Tuition and Aid Day student tuition: $12,500. Tuition installment plan (Academic Management Services Plan, individually arranged payment plans). Merit scholarship grants, need-based scholarship grants available. In 2010–11, 15% of upper-school students received aid; total upper-school merit-scholarship money awarded: $260,000. Total amount of financial aid awarded in 2010–11: $950,000.

Admissions For fall 2010, 479 students applied for upper-level admission, 335 were accepted, 266 enrolled. School's own test required. Deadline for receipt of application materials: none. Application fee required: $75.

Athletics Interscholastic: baseball, basketball, bowling, cross-country running, golf, ice hockey, lacrosse, soccer, swimming and diving, tennis, track and field, winter (indoor) track, wrestling; intramural: baseball, basketball, bowling, Frisbee, soccer, tennis, volleyball. 3 PE instructors, 21 coaches, 1 athletic trainer.

Computers Computers are regularly used in mathematics, science classes. Computer network features include on-campus library services, Internet access.

Contact Br. James Butler, FSC, Principal. 732-747-1959 Ext. 100. Fax: 732-747-1643. Web site: www.cbalincroftnj.org.

CHRISTIAN BROTHERS ACADEMY

12 Airline Drive
Albany, New York 12205
Head of School: Mr. James P. Schlegel

General Information Boys' day college-preparatory, business, religious studies, Junior ROTC, and military school, affiliated with Roman Catholic Church. Grades 6–12. Founded: 1859. Setting: suburban. 120-acre campus. 1 building on campus. Approved or accredited by Middle States Association of Colleges and Schools and New York Department of Education. Endowment: $2 million. Total enrollment: 360. Upper school average class size: 17. Upper school faculty-student ratio: 1:17. There are 180 required school days per year for Upper School students. Upper School students typically attend 5 days per week. The average school day consists of 6 hours and 36 minutes.

Upper School Student Profile Grade 9: 63 students (63 boys); Grade 10: 69 students (69 boys); Grade 11: 76 students (76 boys); Grade 12: 71 students (71 boys). 71% of students are Roman Catholic.

Faculty School total: 31. In upper school: 22 men, 5 women; 10 have advanced degrees.

Subjects Offered Accounting, advanced computer applications, algebra, American government, art, band, biology, biology-AP, business law, calculus-AP, chemistry, driver education, earth science, economics, English, English-AP, forensics, geometry, global studies, health, life science, math analysis, mathematics, mechanical drawing, military science, music, physical education, physical science, physics, physics-AP, psychology, religion, science, sociology, Spanish, Spanish-AP, trigonometry, U.S. history, U.S. history-AP, world history-AP.

Graduation Requirements Arts and fine arts (art, music, dance, drama), English, foreign language, health education, lab science, mathematics, military science, physical education (includes health), religion (includes Bible studies and theology), social studies (includes history), a service requirement.

Special Academic Programs 8 Advanced Placement exams for which test preparation is offered; honors section; study at local college for college credit.

College Admission Counseling 64 students graduated in 2010; 62 went to college, including Clarkson University; Le Moyne College; Manhattan College; Rensselaer Polytechnic Institute; Rochester Institute of Technology; Siena College. Other: 1 entered military service, 1 entered a postgraduate year. Mean SAT critical reading: 505, mean SAT math: 523, mean SAT writing: 501.

Student Life Upper grades have uniform requirement, student council, honor system. Discipline rests primarily with faculty. Attendance at religious services is required.

Summer Programs Sports programs offered; session focuses on youth basketball, youth lacrosse; held on campus; accepts boys and girls; open to students from other schools. 50 students usually enrolled. 2011 schedule: July 6 to July 24.

Tuition and Aid Day student tuition: $10,900. Tuition installment plan (monthly payment plans). Tuition reduction for siblings, merit scholarship grants, need-based scholarship grants available. In 2010–11, 65% of upper-school students received aid; total upper-school merit-scholarship money awarded: $223,650. Total amount of financial aid awarded in 2010–11: $739,500.

Admissions Traditional secondary-level entrance grade is 9. For fall 2010, 72 students applied for upper-level admission, 66 were accepted, 47 enrolled. Iowa Test of Educational Development required. Deadline for receipt of application materials: none. No application fee required.

Athletics Interscholastic: baseball, basketball, bowling, cross-country running, football, golf, ice hockey, indoor track, indoor track & field, JROTC drill, lacrosse, marksmanship, riflery, skiing (downhill), soccer, swimming and diving, tennis, track and field, weight lifting, wrestling; intramural: hiking/backpacking, outdoor activities, outdoor adventure, outdoor education, skiing (downhill), speleology, weight lifting. 3 PE instructors, 18 coaches, 1 athletic trainer.

Computers Computers are regularly used in all academic, career exploration, college planning, computer applications, JROTC, yearbook classes. Computer network features include on-campus library services, Internet access, wireless campus network, Internet filtering or blocking technology.

Contact Mr. Martin McGraw, AIA, Director of Admissions. 518-452-9809 Ext. 110. Fax: 518-452-9806. E-mail: mcgrawmp@aol.com. Web site: www.cbaalbany.org.

CHRISTIAN BROTHERS ACADEMY

6245 Randall Road
Syracuse, New York 13214
Head of School: Br. Joseph Jozwiak, FSC

General Information Coeducational day college-preparatory and religious studies school, affiliated with Roman Catholic Church. Grades 7–12. Founded: 1900. Setting: suburban. 40-acre campus. 1 building on campus. Approved or accredited by Christian Brothers Association, Middle States Association of Colleges and Schools, and New York State Board of Regents. Endowment: $800,000. Total enrollment: 750. Upper school average class size: 25.

Upper School Student Profile 85% of students are Roman Catholic.

Faculty School total: 62. In upper school: 32 men, 30 women; 58 have advanced degrees.

Subjects Offered Advanced Placement courses, American history, American literature, art, biology, business, calculus, chemistry, chemistry-AP, earth science, economics, English, English literature, European history, expository writing, fine arts, French, government/civics, grammar, health, history, mathematics, music, physical education, physics, pre-calculus, psychology, religion, science, social sciences, social studies, Spanish, theology, world history, world literature.

Graduation Requirements Arts and fine arts (art, music, dance, drama), English, foreign language, mathematics, physical education (includes health), religion (includes Bible studies and theology), science, social sciences, social studies (includes history), community service for seniors.

Special Academic Programs Advanced Placement exam preparation; honors section.

College Admission Counseling 113 students graduated in 2010; all went to college, including Le Moyne College; Loyola University Maryland; New York University; Saint Joseph's University; Syracuse University. Mean SAT critical reading: 579, mean SAT math: 581, mean composite ACT: 26.

Student Life Upper grades have specified standards of dress, student council. Discipline rests primarily with faculty. Attendance at religious services is required.

Tuition and Aid Day student tuition: $8650. Tuition installment plan (SMART Tuition Payment Plan, individually arranged payment plans). Merit scholarship grants, need-based scholarship grants available. In 2010–11, 95% of upper-school students received aid; total upper-school merit-scholarship money awarded: $650,000.

Admissions Traditional secondary-level entrance grade is 9. For fall 2010, 50 students applied for upper-level admission, 38 were accepted, 38 enrolled. Admissions testing required. Deadline for receipt of application materials: February 1. Application fee required: $40. Interview recommended.

Athletics Interscholastic: baseball (boys), basketball (b,g), cheering (g), cross-country running (b,g), diving (b,g), football (b), golf (b,g), gymnastics (b), ice hockey (b), lacrosse (b,g), soccer (b,g), softball (g), swimming and diving (b,g), tennis (b,g), track and field (b,g), volleyball (g), wrestling (b); coed interscholastic: bowling. 3 PE instructors, 1 athletic trainer.

Computers Computer network features include on-campus library services, Internet access, Internet filtering or blocking technology. Students grades are available online. The school has a published electronic and media policy.

Contact Mr. Mark Person, Assistant Principal for Student Affairs. 315-446-5960 Ext. 1227. Fax: 315-446-3393. E-mail: mperson@cbasyracuse.org. Web site: www. cbasyracuse.org.

CHRISTIAN CENTRAL ACADEMY

39 Academy Street
Williamsville, New York 14221
Head of School: Mrs. Nurline Lawrence
General Information Coeducational day college-preparatory, arts, and religious studies school, affiliated with Christian faith. Grades K–12. Founded: 1949. Setting: suburban. Nearest major city is Buffalo. 5-acre campus. 4 buildings on campus. Approved or accredited by Association of Christian Schools International, New York State Board of Regents, and New York Department of Education. Candidate for accreditation by Middle States Association of Colleges and Schools. Endowment: $55,000. Total enrollment: 423. Upper school average class size: 20. Upper school faculty-student ratio: 1:10. There are 180 required school days per year for Upper School students. Upper School students typically attend 5 days per week. The average school day consists of 6 hours and 30 minutes.
Upper School Student Profile Grade 6: 37 students (20 boys, 17 girls); Grade 7: 38 students (19 boys, 19 girls); Grade 8: 34 students (12 boys, 22 girls); Grade 9: 28 students (8 boys, 20 girls); Grade 10: 42 students (22 boys, 20 girls); Grade 11: 28 students (13 boys, 15 girls); Grade 12: 26 students (11 boys, 15 girls). 100% of students are Christian faith.
Faculty School total: 39. In upper school: 5 men, 13 women; 9 have advanced degrees.
Subjects Offered Advanced computer applications, advertising design, algebra, art, band, Bible, biology, biology-AP, calculus-AP, career/college preparation, chemistry, chorus, communications, computer skills, drawing, driver education, earth science, economics, English, English-AP, European history-AP, geometry, global studies, government, health, honors English, independent study, journalism, mathematics, music, music theory, orchestra, painting, physical education, physics, physics-AP, pre-calculus, Spanish, studio art, trigonometry, U.S. history, U.S. history-AP, yearbook.
Graduation Requirements Algebra, American government, American history, American literature, arts and fine arts (art, music, dance, drama), Bible, biology, chemistry, earth science, economics, English, geometry, global studies, health, keyboarding, physical education (includes health), physics, pre-calculus, Spanish, trigonometry, writing, community service hours for all four years, completion of standardized NYS Regents exams, honors and high honors diplomas have more rigorous requirements.
Special Academic Programs 6 Advanced Placement exams for which test preparation is offered; honors section; independent study.
College Admission Counseling 29 students graduated in 2010; 28 went to college, including Buffalo State College, State University of New York; Cedarville University; Grove City College; Houghton College; University at Buffalo, the State University of New York. Other: 1 had other specific plans. Median SAT critical reading: 560, median SAT math: 560, median SAT writing: 540, median combined SAT: 1600. 38% scored over 600 on SAT critical reading, 24% scored over 600 on SAT math, 39% scored over 600 on SAT writing, 34% scored over 1800 on combined SAT.
Student Life Upper grades have specified standards of dress, student council, honor system. Discipline rests primarily with faculty. Attendance at religious services is required.
Summer Programs Sports programs offered; session focuses on basketball camp, soccer camp; held on campus; accepts boys and girls; open to students from other schools. 45 students usually enrolled. 2011 schedule: July 12 to July 19. Application deadline: June 1.
Tuition and Aid Day student tuition: $7050. Tuition installment plan (FACTS Tuition Payment Plan, monthly payment plans, prepayment discount plans, multiple-student discounts, pastors/full-time Christian service discounts). Tuition reduction for siblings, merit scholarship grants, need-based scholarship grants available. In 2010–11, 23% of upper-school students received aid; total upper-school merit-scholarship money awarded: $12,000. Total amount of financial aid awarded in 2010–11: $58,420.
Admissions Traditional secondary-level entrance grade is 9. For fall 2010, 13 students applied for upper-level admission, 12 were accepted, 9 enrolled. Admissions testing, Brigance Test of Basic Skills, essay, Iowa Subtests, school's own test or writing sample required. Deadline for receipt of application materials: none. Application fee required: $50. Interview recommended.
Athletics Interscholastic: baseball (boys), basketball (b,g), cheering (g), cross-country running (b,g), flag football (b), soccer (b,g), softball (g); intramural: basketball (b,g), physical fitness (b,g), soccer (b,g); coed interscholastic: cross-country running, soccer; coed intramural: basketball, volleyball. 2 PE instructors, 17 coaches.
Computers Computers are regularly used in college planning, computer applications, desktop publishing, drawing and design, English, journalism, library skills, photojournalism, yearbook classes. Computer resources include on-campus library services, Internet access, Internet filtering or blocking technology, teacher-guided use of programs in various subject areas. Computer access in designated common areas is available to students. The school has a published electronic and media policy.
Contact Deborah L. White, Director of Admissions and Public Relations. 716-634-4821 Ext. 107. Fax: 716-634-5851. E-mail: dwhitecca@gmail.com. Web site: www.christianca.com.

CHRISTIAN HERITAGE SCHOOL

575 White Plains Road
Trumbull, Connecticut 06611-4898
Head of School: Barry Giller
General Information Coeducational day college-preparatory, religious studies, and technology school. Grades K–12. Founded: 1977. Setting: suburban. Nearest major city is Bridgeport. 5-acre campus. 3 buildings on campus. Approved or accredited by Association of Christian Schools International, New England Association of Schools and Colleges, The College Board, and Connecticut Department of Education. Member of European Council of International Schools. Endowment: $470,000. Total enrollment: 527. Upper school average class size: 19. Upper school faculty-student ratio: 1:9.
Upper School Student Profile Grade 9: 53 students (27 boys, 26 girls); Grade 10: 36 students (19 boys, 17 girls); Grade 11: 44 students (25 boys, 19 girls); Grade 12: 46 students (20 boys, 26 girls).
Faculty School total: 59. In upper school: 18 men, 13 women; 16 have advanced degrees.
Subjects Offered 20th century American writers, 20th century history, 20th century physics, 20th century world history, advanced chemistry, advanced math, Advanced Placement courses, algebra, American democracy, American foreign policy, American government, American history, American history-AP, American literature, applied music, art, athletics, band, Basic programming, Bible, Bible studies, biology, biology-AP, British literature, business, calculus, calculus-AP, career and personal planning, career exploration, career/college preparation, chamber groups, chemistry, choir, choral music, chorus, Christian and Hebrew scripture, Christian doctrine, Christian education, Christian ethics, Christian scripture, Christian studies, Christian testament, Christianity, church history, classical Greek literature, classics, college admission preparation, college awareness, college counseling, college placement, college planning, college writing, communication skills, comparative government and politics, computer education, computer processing, computer programming, computer programming-AP, computer science, computer skills, computer technologies, concert band, concert choir, constitutional history of U.S., consumer mathematics, contemporary history, contemporary issues, contemporary issues in science, creative arts, current events, current history, data processing, desktop publishing, drama performance, drawing, earth science, English, English composition, English language-AP, English literature, English literature-AP, ensembles, ethics, ethics and responsibility, expository writing, functions, general science, geography, geometry, government/civics, grammar, health and wellness, health education, history, history-AP, honors algebra, honors English, honors geometry, honors U.S. history, human anatomy, human biology, inorganic chemistry, instrumental music, instruments, intro to computers, journalism, keyboarding, language and composition, life issues, Life of Christ, life science, literature, mathematics, mathematics-AP, moral and social development, moral reasoning, moral theology, music, music theory, musical productions, newspaper, novels, oral communications, painting, philosophy, physical education, physical science, physics, poetry, prayer/spirituality, pre-algebra, pre-calculus, public speaking, publications, reading/study skills, religion, religious education, science, science project, Shakespeare, social studies, Spanish, Spanish-AP, speech, statistics, student government, student publications, U.S. government, U.S. history-AP, vocal ensemble, vocal music, volleyball, work experience, world affairs, world history, writing, yearbook.
Graduation Requirements Electives, English, foreign language, mathematics, physical education (includes health), religion (includes Bible studies and theology), science, social studies (includes history).
Special Academic Programs Advanced Placement exam preparation; honors section; independent study.
College Admission Counseling 44 students graduated in 2009; all went to college, including Eastern University; LeTourneau University; University of Connecticut; Wheaton College. Median SAT critical reading: 579, median SAT math: 597, median SAT writing: 538, median combined SAT: 1695, median composite ACT: 25. 9% scored over 600 on SAT critical reading, 9% scored over 600 on SAT math, 8% scored over 600 on SAT writing, 10% scored over 1800 on combined SAT.
Student Life Upper grades have specified standards of dress, student council. Discipline rests primarily with faculty. Attendance at religious services is required.
Tuition and Aid Day student tuition: $14,850. Tuition installment plan (monthly payment plans, individually arranged payment plans, Tuition Management Systems). Need-based scholarship grants available. In 2009–10, 46% of upper-school students received aid. Total amount of financial aid awarded in 2009–10: $500,000.
Admissions Traditional secondary-level entrance grade is 9. For fall 2009, 53 students applied for upper-level admission, 34 were accepted, 31 enrolled. Admissions testing, Otis-Lennon School Ability Test and Stanford Achievement Test required. Deadline for receipt of application materials: none. Application fee required: $50. On-campus interview required.
Athletics Interscholastic: baseball (boys), basketball (b,g), soccer (b,g), tennis (b,g), volleyball (g); intramural: baseball (b), soccer (b,g), softball (g), weight lifting (b), weight training (b); coed interscholastic: cross-country running, golf; coed intramural: basketball, Frisbee. 4 PE instructors, 31 coaches.
Computers Computers are regularly used in business education, college planning, data processing, desktop publishing, journalism, keyboarding, mathematics, newspaper, programming, word processing, yearbook classes. Computer network features include on-campus library services, online commercial services, Internet access,

Internet filtering or blocking technology. Campus intranet and student e-mail accounts are available to students. Students grades are available online. The school has a published electronic and media policy.
Contact Mrs. Martha Olson, Director of Admissions. 203-261-6230 Ext. 555. Fax: 203-268-1046. E-mail: molson@kingsmen.org. Web site: www.kingsmen.org.

CHRISTIAN HIGH SCHOOL

2300 Plymouth SE
Grand Rapids, Michigan 49506-5297
Head of School: Mr. James Primus

General Information Coeducational day college-preparatory, general academic, arts, business, and religious studies school, affiliated with Calvinist faith. Grades 9–12. Founded: 1921. Setting: suburban. 22-acre campus. 1 building on campus. Approved or accredited by Christian Schools International, North Central Association of Colleges and Schools, and Michigan Department of Education. Endowment: $5.5 million. Total enrollment: 955. Upper school average class size: 25. Upper school faculty-student ratio: 1:17. There are 180 required school days per year for Upper School students. Upper School students typically attend 5 days per week. The average school day consists of 6 hours and 45 minutes.
Upper School Student Profile Grade 9: 219 students (109 boys, 110 girls); Grade 10: 246 students (126 boys, 120 girls); Grade 11: 225 students (129 boys, 96 girls); Grade 12: 265 students (140 boys, 125 girls). 80% of students are Calvinist.
Faculty School total: 58. In upper school: 30 men, 28 women; 50 have advanced degrees.
Subjects Offered Advanced chemistry, algebra, American literature, analysis and differential calculus, art, band, Bible, biology, business, calculus-AP, chemistry, chemistry-AP, church history, composition, computer applications, computer literacy, concert band, concert choir, consumer economics, CPR, criminal justice, critical studies in film, debate, drafting, drama, drawing, economics, English, English composition, English literature, English literature and composition-AP, foods, forensics, French, German, global issues, government, honors algebra, honors English, honors geometry, honors U.S. history, human biology, jazz band, keyboarding, Latin, marketing, orchestra, physical science, physics, physiology, pre-algebra, pre-calculus, probability and statistics, religion, sociology, Spanish, speech, statistics-AP, U.S. government, U.S. history, U.S. literature, video, voice, Western civilization, world literature.
Graduation Requirements Algebra, American government, American history, American literature, biology, English, English literature, mathematics, physical science, religion (includes Bible studies and theology), U.S. history, Western civilization, world cultures.
Special Academic Programs Advanced Placement exam preparation; independent study; remedial reading and/or remedial writing; remedial math.
College Admission Counseling 256 students graduated in 2009; 245 went to college, including Calvin College; Grand Valley State University; Hope College; Michigan State University; University of Michigan; Western Michigan University. Other: 10 went to work, 1 entered military service. Mean composite ACT: 24. 35% scored over 26 on composite ACT.
Student Life Upper grades have specified standards of dress, student council. Discipline rests primarily with faculty. Attendance at religious services is required.
Tuition and Aid Day student tuition: $6218. Tuition installment plan (monthly payment plans, individually arranged payment plans). Need-based scholarship grants available. In 2009–10, 60% of upper-school students received aid.
Admissions Traditional secondary-level entrance grade is 9. Deadline for receipt of application materials: none. No application fee required. Interview recommended.
Athletics Interscholastic: baseball (boys), basketball (b,g), cheering (g), cross-country running (b,g), diving (b,g), equestrian sports (b,g), football (b), golf (b,g), hockey (b), ice hockey (b), running (b,g), soccer (b,g), softball (g), swimming and diving (b,g), tennis (b,g), track and field (b,g), volleyball (g); coed intramural: equestrian sports. 2 PE instructors.
Computers Computers are regularly used in accounting, business applications, drafting, economics, history, information technology, introduction to technology, mathematics, speech, writing, yearbook classes. Computer network features include on-campus library services, online commercial services, Internet access. The school has a published electronic and media policy.
Contact Mr. James Primus, Principal. 616-574-5506. Fax: 616-241-3141. E-mail: jstapert@grcs.org. Web site: www.grcs.org/grch/.

CHRISTIAN HOME AND BIBLE SCHOOL

301 West 13th Avenue
Mount Dora, Florida 32757
Head of School: Patrick Todd

General Information Coeducational day college-preparatory, general academic, arts, religious studies, and technology school, affiliated with Church of Christ. Grades PK–12. Founded: 1945. Setting: small town. Nearest major city is Orlando. 70-acre campus. 9 buildings on campus. Approved or accredited by National Christian School Association, Southern Association of Colleges and Schools, and Florida Department of Education. Total enrollment: 533. Upper school average class size: 21. Upper school faculty-student ratio: 1:15. There are 180 required school days per year for Upper

School students. Upper School students typically attend 5 days per week. The average school day consists of 6 hours and 30 minutes.
Upper School Student Profile Grade 9: 62 students (32 boys, 30 girls); Grade 10: 48 students (33 boys, 15 girls); Grade 11: 50 students (27 boys, 23 girls); Grade 12: 47 students (30 boys, 17 girls). 20% of students are members of Church of Christ.
Faculty School total: 46. In upper school: 12 men, 12 women; 10 have advanced degrees.
Subjects Offered Algebra, American government, American history, anatomy and physiology, art, band, Bible, biology, calculus-AP, ceramics, chemistry, computer applications, computer skills, consumer mathematics, drama, drawing, economics, English, English literature-AP, European history, geography, geometry, government, health, honors algebra, honors English, honors geometry, honors world history, intro to computers, jazz band, journalism, life management skills, life skills, math applications, Microsoft, painting, personal fitness, photography, physical education, physical science, physics, pre-algebra, pre-calculus, probability and statistics, psychology, sculpture, sign language, Spanish, speech, state history, student publications, technology/design, television, theater, theater production, trigonometry, video communication, video film production, visual and performing arts, Web site design, weight training, word processing, world history.
Graduation Requirements Advanced math, algebra, American government, American history, arts and fine arts (art, music, dance, drama), Bible, biology, chemistry, economics, electives, English, foreign language, keyboarding, lab science, life skills, physical education (includes health), physical science, world history, 80 hours of community service.
Special Academic Programs 4 Advanced Placement exams for which test preparation is offered; honors section; independent study; study at local college for college credit.
College Admission Counseling 43 students graduated in 2010; 41 went to college, including Florida State University; Harding University; University of Central Florida; University of Florida; University of Miami; University of South Florida. Other: 2 went to work. Mean SAT critical reading: 572, mean SAT math: 580, mean SAT writing: 535, mean combined SAT: 1686, mean composite ACT: 23.
Student Life Upper grades have specified standards of dress, student council. Discipline rests primarily with faculty. Attendance at religious services is required.
Summer Programs Remediation programs offered; session focuses on math; held on campus; accepts boys and girls; not open to students from other schools. 10 students usually enrolled. 2011 schedule: June 5 to June 20.
Tuition and Aid Day student tuition: $7518. Tuition installment plan (monthly payment plans). Tuition reduction for siblings, need-based scholarship grants, discount for members of the Churches of Christ available. In 2010–11, 15% of upper-school students received aid.
Admissions Traditional secondary-level entrance grade is 9. For fall 2010, 50 students applied for upper-level admission, 47 were accepted, 47 enrolled. Any standardized test required. Deadline for receipt of application materials: none. Application fee required: $100. On-campus interview required.
Athletics Interscholastic: baseball (boys), basketball (b,g), bowling (b,g), cheering (g), cross-country running (b,g), fitness (b,g), football (b), golf (b,g), physical fitness (b,g), physical training (b,g), softball (g), tennis (b,g), track and field (b,g), volleyball (g), weight training (b,g). 2 coaches.
Computers Computers are regularly used in independent study, journalism, library, mathematics, publications, reading, video film production, Web site design, yearbook classes. Computer network features include on-campus library services, Internet access, wireless campus network, Internet filtering or blocking technology, Net Classroom-communication for students and parents, Desk Top Monitoring and manage software, Accelerated Reader Access. Computer access in designated common areas is available to students. Students grades are available online. The school has a published electronic and media policy.
Contact Natalie Yawn, Admissions Director. 352-383-2155 Ext. 261. Fax: 352-383-0098. E-mail: natalie.yawn@chbs.org. Web site: www.chbs.org.

CHRISTOPHER COLUMBUS HIGH SCHOOL

3000 Southwest 87th Avenue
Miami, Florida 33165-3293
Head of School: Br. Michael Brady, FMS

General Information Boys' day college-preparatory school, affiliated with Roman Catholic Church. Grades 9–12. Founded: 1958. Setting: suburban. 19-acre campus. 10 buildings on campus. Approved or accredited by National Catholic Education Association, Southern Association of Colleges and Schools, and Florida Department of Education. Total enrollment: 1,380. Upper school average class size: 24. Upper school faculty-student ratio: 1:17. There are 180 required school days per year for Upper School students. Upper School students typically attend 5 days per week. The average school day consists of 6 hours and 25 minutes.
Upper School Student Profile Grade 9: 358 students (358 boys); Grade 10: 373 students (373 boys); Grade 11: 304 students (304 boys); Grade 12: 345 students (345 boys). 95% of students are Roman Catholic.
Faculty School total: 82. In upper school: 56 men, 26 women; 35 have advanced degrees.
Subjects Offered 3-dimensional art, accounting, acting, advanced biology, advanced chemistry, advanced computer applications, advanced math, Advanced Placement courses, algebra, American government, American history, American history-AP,

American literature, analysis, anatomy, ancient world history, architectural drawing, art, athletic training, athletics, band, Basic programming, Bible, biology, biology-AP, British literature (honors), business law, business skills, calculus, calculus-AP, campus ministry, Catholic belief and practice, chemistry, chemistry-AP, Christian and Hebrew scripture, Christian doctrine, Christian ethics, church history, college counseling, composition-AP, computer applications, computer information systems, computer programming, computer science, computer science-AP, computer-aided design, contemporary history, debate, drama, economics, economics-AP, English, English language and composition-AP, English literature, English literature-AP, English-AP, ethics, European history, European history-AP, French, French language-AP, French-AP, geometry, global studies, government, government and politics-AP, health, history of the Catholic Church, Holocaust studies, keyboarding, library assistant, marine biology, physical education, physical fitness, physics, physics-AP, pre-algebra, pre-calculus, psychology, Spanish, Spanish language-AP, Spanish literature, Spanish literature-AP, speech, U.S. government, U.S. government and politics, U.S. government and politics-AP, U.S. history, U.S. history-AP, Vietnam War, word processing, world governments, yearbook.

Graduation Requirements Algebra, arts and fine arts (art, music, dance, drama), computer applications, English, lab science, language, mathematics, personal fitness, physical education (includes health), practical arts, religion (includes Bible studies and theology), science, social studies (includes history), Students must earn a Florida scale GPA of 2.0, Students must complete 75 hours of community service during their four years of high school.

Special Academic Programs Advanced Placement exam preparation; honors section; study at local college for college credit; academic accommodation for the gifted; remedial reading and/or remedial writing.

College Admission Counseling 303 students graduated in 2010; 302 went to college, including Florida International University; The University of Alabama; University of Florida; University of Miami; University of Notre Dame; University of Pennsylvania. Other: 1 entered military service.

Student Life Upper grades have uniform requirement, student council, honor system. Discipline rests primarily with faculty. Attendance at religious services is required.

Summer Programs Remediation, enrichment programs offered; session focuses on enrichment, remediation and study skills; held on campus; accepts boys; not open to students from other schools. 154 students usually enrolled. 2011 schedule: June 10 to June 30.

Tuition and Aid Tuition installment plan (monthly payment plans, individually arranged payment plans). Bursaries available. In 2010–11, 22% of upper-school students received aid. Total amount of financial aid awarded in 2010–11: $800,000.

Admissions Traditional secondary-level entrance grade is 9. For fall 2010, 484 students applied for upper-level admission, 354 were accepted, 354 enrolled. High School Placement Test required. Deadline for receipt of application materials: none. Application fee required: $50. Interview required.

Athletics Interscholastic: baseball, basketball, bowling, cross-country running, football, golf, lacrosse, soccer, swimming and diving, tennis, track and field, volleyball, water polo, wrestling; intramural: basketball, flag football, power lifting, roller hockey, weight training. 2 PE instructors, 25 coaches, 2 athletic trainers.

Computers Computers are regularly used in architecture, computer applications, history, journalism, keyboarding, media production, science, yearbook classes. Computer network features include on-campus library services, online commercial services, Internet access, wireless campus network, Internet filtering or blocking technology. Campus intranet and computer access in designated common areas are available to students. Students grades are available online. The school has a published electronic and media policy.

Contact Mrs. Rebecca Rafuls, Registrar. 305-223-5650 Ext. 2239. Fax: 305-559-4306. E-mail: rrafuls@columbushs.com. Web site: www.columbushs.com.

CHRISTOPHER DOCK MENNONITE HIGH SCHOOL

1000 Forty Foot Road
Lansdale, Pennsylvania 19446
Head of School: Dr. Conrad Swartzentruber

General Information Coeducational day college-preparatory, general academic, arts, vocational, religious studies, and technology school, affiliated with Mennonite Church. Grades 9–12. Founded: 1954. Setting: suburban. Nearest major city is Philadelphia. 75-acre campus. 6 buildings on campus. Approved or accredited by Mennonite Education Agency, Mennonite Schools Council, Middle States Association of Colleges and Schools, and Pennsylvania Department of Education. Endowment: $1.1 million. Total enrollment: 385. Upper school average class size: 21. Upper school faculty-student ratio: 1:12. There are 182 required school days per year for Upper School students. Upper School students typically attend 5 days per week. The average school day consists of 6 hours and 55 minutes.

Upper School Student Profile Grade 9: 100 students (45 boys, 55 girls); Grade 10: 77 students (35 boys, 42 girls); Grade 11: 114 students (58 boys, 56 girls); Grade 12: 94 students (40 boys, 54 girls). 48% of students are Mennonite.

Faculty School total: 31. In upper school: 15 men, 16 women; 23 have advanced degrees.

Subjects Offered Accounting, advanced biology, advanced chemistry, advanced math, Advanced Placement courses, algebra, American government, American history, American literature, anatomy, anatomy and physiology, art, art history, arts, arts appreciation, athletic training, athletics, Basic programming, Bible, Bible studies,

biology, British literature, business, business mathematics, business skills, calculus, calculus-AP, career education internship, career technology, ceramics, chemistry, child development, choir, choral music, chorus, Christian and Hebrew scripture, Christian doctrine, Christian education, Christian ethics, Christian scripture, Christian studies, Christian testament, Christianity, church history, communication skills, communications, composition-AP, computer graphics, computer information systems, computer literacy, computer programming, computer science, computer skills, computer technologies, computers, concert choir, consumer economics, creative writing, design, drama, driver education, early childhood, earth science, ecology, environmental systems, economics, economics and history, English, English language and composition-AP, English literature, environmental science, European history, family and consumer science, family living, family studies, fine arts, food science, foreign language, genetics, geography, geology, geometry, global studies, government/civics, grammar, graphic design, guitar, health, health and wellness, health education, history, honors English, honors geometry, instrumental music, instruments, international foods, jazz band, journalism, keyboarding, language and composition, Life of Christ, life saving, life science, mathematics, mathematics-AP, music, New Testament, oral communications, parent/child development, peace and justice, peace education, peace studies, personal finance, photography, physical education, physics, religion, religion and culture, religious education, religious studies, research and reference, rhetoric, science, science research, scripture, sculpture, senior internship, service learning/internship, social sciences, social studies, Spanish, Spanish language-AP, Spanish literature-AP, Spanish-AP, speech, speech communications, sports team management, stage and body movement, statistics, student government, student publications, theater, trigonometry, U.S. government, U.S. history, U.S. literature, Vietnam, vocal ensemble, vocal music, vocational skills, vocational-technical courses, Web site design, word processing, work-study, world cultures, world history, world literature.

Graduation Requirements Arts and fine arts (art, music, dance, drama), business skills (includes word processing), computer science, English, family and consumer science, mathematics, physical education (includes health), religion (includes Bible studies and theology), science, social sciences, social studies (includes history), three-day urban experience, senior independent study/service experience (one week), Senior presentation.

Special Academic Programs Advanced Placement exam preparation; honors section; term-away projects; study at local college for college credit; remedial reading and/or remedial writing; programs in English for dyslexic students.

College Admission Counseling 95 students graduated in 2010; 89 went to college, including Eastern Mennonite University; Eastern University; Goshen College; Messiah College; Montgomery County Community College. Other: 2 went to work, 1 entered military service, 3 had other specific plans. Mean SAT critical reading: 525, mean SAT math: 555, mean SAT writing: 518, mean combined SAT: 1698. 20% scored over 600 on SAT critical reading, 34% scored over 600 on SAT math, 22% scored over 600 on SAT writing, 21% scored over 1800 on combined SAT, 50% scored over 26 on composite ACT.

Student Life Upper grades have specified standards of dress, student council, honor system. Discipline rests primarily with faculty. Attendance at religious services is required.

Tuition and Aid Day student tuition: $13,950. Tuition installment plan (monthly payment plans). Tuition reduction for siblings, need-based scholarship grants available. In 2010–11, 26% of upper-school students received aid. Total amount of financial aid awarded in 2010–11: $492,500.

Admissions Traditional secondary-level entrance grade is 9. For fall 2010, 148 students applied for upper-level admission, 144 were accepted, 122 enrolled. Deadline for receipt of application materials: none. Application fee required: $50. On-campus interview required.

Athletics Interscholastic: baseball (boys), basketball (b,g), bowling (b,g), cheering (g), cross-country running (b,g), field hockey (g), golf (b), soccer (b,g), softball (g), tennis (b,g), track and field (b,g), volleyball (b,g); coed interscholastic: bowling. 3 PE instructors, 32 coaches, 1 athletic trainer.

Computers Computers are regularly used in accounting, keyboarding, lab/keyboard, mathematics, music, programming, SAT preparation, science, Web site design, word processing, yearbook classes. Computer network features include on-campus library services, online commercial services, Internet access, wireless campus network, Internet filtering or blocking technology, PowerSchool, WinSNAP. Computer access in designated common areas is available to students. Students grades are available online. The school has a published electronic and media policy.

Contact Lois Boaman, Admissions Director. 215-362-2675. Fax: 215-362-2943. E-mail: laboaman@dockhs.org. Web site: www.dockhs.org.

CHRIST SCHOOL

500 Christ School Road
Asheville, North Carolina 28704
Head of School: Mr. Paul Krieger

General Information Boys' boarding and day college-preparatory, arts, religious studies, and technology school, affiliated with Episcopal Church. Grades 8–12. Founded: 1900. Setting: rural. Students are housed in single-sex dormitories. 500-acre campus. 15 buildings on campus. Approved or accredited by National Association of Episcopal Schools, North Carolina Association of Independent Schools, Southern Association of Colleges and Schools, Southern Association of Independent Schools, The Association of Boarding Schools, and North Carolina Department of Education.

Christ School

Member of National Association of Independent Schools and Secondary School Admission Test Board. Endowment: $10 million. Total enrollment: 227. Upper school average class size: 11. Upper school faculty-student ratio: 1:6.

Upper School Student Profile Grade 8: 18 students (18 boys); Grade 9: 44 students (44 boys); Grade 10: 56 students (56 boys); Grade 11: 58 students (58 boys); Grade 12: 51 students (51 boys). 75% of students are boarding students. 58% are state residents. 17 states are represented in upper school student body. 12% are international students. International students from Bahamas, China, Germany, Hong Kong, Republic of Korea, and Spain; 3 other countries represented in student body. 35% of students are members of Episcopal Church.

Faculty School total: 41. In upper school: 28 men, 9 women; 24 have advanced degrees; 30 reside on campus.

Subjects Offered Advanced Placement courses, African-American history, algebra, American history, American history-AP, American literature, anatomy and physiology, ancient history, art, art-AP, biology, calculus, calculus-AP, chemistry, computer programming, computer science-AP, drama, economics, English, English literature, English literature-AP, environmental science, ESL, European history, fine arts, French, geography, geometry, government, journalism, Latin, law, mathematics, medieval/Renaissance history, modern European history-AP, music, music theory, photography, physical science, physics, physics-AP, pre-calculus, religion, SAT/ACT preparation, science, social studies, Spanish, statistics, studio art, theater, TOEFL preparation, trigonometry, U.S. government, U.S. history, U.S. history-AP, Vietnam history, world geography, world history.

Graduation Requirements Arts and fine arts (art, music, dance, drama), computer literacy, English, foreign language, mathematics, physical education (includes health), religion (includes Bible studies and theology), science, social studies (includes history).

Special Academic Programs Advanced Placement exam preparation; honors section; independent study; academic accommodation for the gifted; ESL (13 students enrolled).

College Admission Counseling 52 students graduated in 2009; all went to college, including Duke University; Furman University; Hampden-Sydney College; The University of North Carolina at Chapel Hill; Wofford College.

Student Life Upper grades have specified standards of dress, student council, honor system. Discipline rests equally with students and faculty. Attendance at religious services is required.

Tuition and Aid Day student tuition: $19,200; 5-day tuition and room/board: $37,800; 7-day tuition and room/board: $37,800. Tuition installment plan (monthly payment plans, 2-payment plan). Merit scholarship grants, need-based scholarship grants available. In 2009–10, 43% of upper-school students received aid; total upper-school merit-scholarship money awarded: $250,000. Total amount of financial aid awarded in 2009–10: $1,250,000.

Admissions Traditional secondary-level entrance grade is 9. For fall 2009, 170 students applied for upper-level admission, 110 were accepted, 84 enrolled. ACT, ISEE, PSAT, SAT, SSAT or Wechsler Intelligence Scale for Children III required. Deadline for receipt of application materials: none. Application fee required: $50. On-campus interview required.

Athletics Interscholastic: baseball, basketball, cross-country running, football, golf, lacrosse, soccer, swimming and diving, tennis, track and field, wrestling; intramural: alpine skiing, backpacking, bicycling, billiards, bowling, canoeing/kayaking, climbing, fishing, flag football, Frisbee, hiking/backpacking, indoor soccer, kayaking, life saving, martial arts, mountain biking, mountaineering, outdoor activities, paint ball, racquetball, rappelling, rock climbing, running, skeet shooting, skiing (cross-country), skiing (downhill), strength & conditioning, table tennis, ultimate Frisbee, wallyball, weight lifting, weight training. 3 coaches, 1 athletic trainer.

Computers Computers are regularly used in all classes. Computer network features include on-campus library services, Internet access, wireless campus network, Internet filtering or blocking technology. Student e-mail accounts are available to students. Students grades are available online.

Contact Mr. Denis Stokes, Director of Admission. 828-684-6232 Ext. 118. Fax: 828-209-0003. E-mail: dstokes@christschool.org. Web site: www.christschool.org.

See Display below and Close-Up on page 758.

CHRYSALIS SCHOOL

14241 North East Woodinville-Duvall Road
PMB 243
Woodinville, Washington 98072
Head of School: Karen Fogle

General Information Coeducational day college-preparatory, general academic, arts, and technology school. Grades 1–12. Founded: 1983. Setting: suburban. Nearest major city is Seattle. 2 buildings on campus. Approved or accredited by Northwest Accreditation Commission, Northwest Association of Schools and Colleges, and Washington Department of Education. Total enrollment: 257. Upper school average class size: 8. Upper school faculty-student ratio: 1:5.

Upper School Student Profile Grade 9: 35 students (22 boys, 13 girls); Grade 10: 34 students (22 boys, 12 girls); Grade 11: 53 students (36 boys, 17 girls); Grade 12: 76 students (47 boys, 29 girls).

Faculty School total: 41. In upper school: 13 men, 20 women; 30 have advanced degrees.

Subjects Offered Advanced biology, advanced chemistry, advanced computer applications, advanced math, art, audio visual/media, career planning, college

an Episcopal school for
boys

E WORLD

Boarding and Day for Grades 8-12

Headmaster's Scholarships

College Preparatory

Individual College Counseling

Outdoor Program & Competitive Athletics

CHRIST SCHOOL

500 CHRIST SCHOOL ROAD, ARDEN, NC 28704
ADMISSION OFFICE 800-422-3212

www.christschool.org

www.facebook.com/sec.schools

counseling, computer technologies, drama, English, filmmaking, French, geography, German, graphics, history, Japanese, mathematics, physical education, SAT preparation, science, social sciences, Spanish.

Graduation Requirements Career and personal planning, computer literacy, English, foreign language, history, mathematics, physical education (includes health), science, portfolio.

Special Academic Programs Honors section; accelerated programs; study at local college for college credit; academic accommodation for the gifted; remedial reading and/or remedial writing; remedial math; programs in English, mathematics, general development for dyslexic students; special instructional classes for students with learning disabilities.

College Admission Counseling 73 students graduated in 2010; 65 went to college, including Bellevue College; Central Washington University; University of Washington; Washington State University; Western Washington University. Other: 2 went to work, 2 entered military service, 4 had other specific plans.

Student Life Upper grades have specified standards of dress, honor system. Discipline rests primarily with faculty.

Summer Programs Remediation, enrichment, advancement, computer instruction programs offered; session focuses on Enrichment; held on campus; accepts boys and girls; open to students from other schools. 35 students usually enrolled. 2011 schedule: July 12 to August 18. Application deadline: June 20.

Tuition and Aid Tuition installment plan (monthly payment plans).

Admissions Traditional secondary-level entrance grade is 9. For fall 2010, 100 students applied for upper-level admission, 90 were accepted, 80 enrolled. Deadline for receipt of application materials: none. Application fee required: $450. On-campus interview required.

Computers Computers are regularly used in computer applications, English, foreign language, graphic arts, history, information technology, introduction to technology, keyboarding, mathematics, media, science, video film production, Web site design, word processing, yearbook classes. Computer resources include on-campus library services, online commercial services, Internet access. Computer access in designated common areas is available to students.

Contact Wanda Metcalfe, Director of Student Services. 425-481-2228. Fax: 425-486-8107. E-mail: wanda@chrysalis-school.com. Web site: www.chrysalis-school.com.

CINCINNATI COUNTRY DAY SCHOOL

6905 Given Road
Cincinnati, Ohio 45243-2898

Head of School: Dr. Robert P. Macrae

General Information Coeducational day college-preparatory, arts, and technology school. Grades PK–12. Founded: 1926. Setting: suburban. 62-acre campus. 8 buildings on campus. Approved or accredited by Independent Schools Association of the Central States, Ohio Association of Independent Schools, and Ohio Department of Education. Member of National Association of Independent Schools and Secondary School Admission Test Board. Endowment: $13.5 million. Total enrollment: 775. Upper school average class size: 15. Upper school faculty-student ratio: 1:9. There are 170 required school days per year for Upper School students. Upper School students typically attend 5 days per week. The average school day consists of 7 hours.

Upper School Student Profile Grade 9: 73 students (33 boys, 40 girls); Grade 10: 54 students (22 boys, 32 girls); Grade 11: 71 students (41 boys, 30 girls); Grade 12: 52 students (25 boys, 27 girls).

Faculty School total: 110. In upper school: 24 men, 14 women; 32 have advanced degrees.

Subjects Offered Acting, algebra, American history, American history-AP, American literature, analysis, art, art history, biology, biology-AP, calculus, calculus-AP, ceramics, chemistry, chemistry-AP, choir, computer graphics, computer programming, computer science, CPR, creative writing, dance, drama, earth science, English, English literature, European history, fine arts, French, French language-AP, French literature-AP, genetics, geometry, health, humanities, music, photography, physical education, physics, psychology, public speaking, Spanish, Spanish language-AP, Spanish literature-AP, speech, statistics, theater, trigonometry, world history.

Graduation Requirements Arts and fine arts (art, music, dance, drama), computer science, English, foreign language, history, mathematics, physical education (includes health), science, senior project. Community service is required.

Special Academic Programs Advanced Placement exam preparation; honors section; independent study; study abroad.

College Admission Counseling 63 students graduated in 2010; all went to college, including Amherst College; Dartmouth College; Emory University; Wesleyan University; Yale University. Mean SAT critical reading: 620, mean SAT math: 630, mean SAT writing: 630, mean combined SAT: 1880.

Student Life Upper grades have specified standards of dress, student council, honor system. Discipline rests equally with students and faculty.

Summer Programs Remediation, enrichment, advancement, sports, art/fine arts, computer instruction programs offered; session focuses on camps and academic programs; held on campus; accepts boys and girls; open to students from other schools. 500 students usually enrolled. 2011 schedule: June 14 to August 7. Application deadline: May 31.

Tuition and Aid Day student tuition: $20,290. Tuition installment plan (Insured Tuition Payment Plan, FACTS Tuition Payment Plan, monthly payment plans, individually arranged payment plans). Merit scholarship grants, need-based scholarship grants, parent loans, Sallie Mae loans available. In 2010–11, 20% of upper-school students received aid; total upper-school merit-scholarship money awarded: $180,000. Total amount of financial aid awarded in 2010–11: $930,000.

Admissions Traditional secondary-level entrance grade is 9. For fall 2010, 65 students applied for upper-level admission, 40 were accepted, 25 enrolled. ISEE, Otis-Lennon Ability or Stanford Achievement Test or SSAT, ERB, PSAT, SAT, PLAN or ACT required. Deadline for receipt of application materials: March 15. Application fee required: $50. Interview recommended.

Athletics Interscholastic: baseball (boys), basketball (b,g), crew (b,g), cross-country running (b,g), football (b), golf (b,g), gymnastics (g), lacrosse (b,g), softball (g), swimming and diving (b,g), tennis (b,g), track and field (b,g); intramural: dance team (g); coed interscholastic: crew, dance, dance squad; coed intramural: dance. 5 PE instructors, 1 athletic trainer.

Computers Computers are regularly used in all academic classes. Computer network features include on-campus library services, online commercial services, Internet access, wireless campus network, Internet filtering or blocking technology. Campus intranet, student e-mail accounts, and computer access in designated common areas are available to students. Students grades are available online. The school has a published electronic and media policy.

Contact Aaron B. Kellenberger, Director of Admission. 513-979-0220. Fax: 513-527-7614. E-mail: kellenbea@countryday.net. Web site: www.countryday.net.

CISTERCIAN PREPARATORY SCHOOL

3660 Cistercian Road
Irving, Texas 75039

Head of School: Fr. Peter Verhalen

General Information Boys' day college-preparatory, arts, and religious studies school, affiliated with Roman Catholic Church. Grades 5–12. Founded: 1962. Setting: suburban. Nearest major city is Dallas. 80-acre campus. 7 buildings on campus. Approved or accredited by Independent Schools Association of the Southwest, Texas Catholic Conference, and Texas Department of Education. Member of National Association of Independent Schools. Endowment: $5 million. Total enrollment: 356. Upper school average class size: 22. Upper school faculty-student ratio: 1:7. There are 180 required school days per year for Upper School students. Upper School students typically attend 5 days per week. The average school day consists of 8 hours.

Upper School Student Profile Grade 9: 46 students (46 boys); Grade 10: 43 students (43 boys); Grade 11: 47 students (47 boys); Grade 12: 42 students (42 boys). 81% of students are Roman Catholic.

Faculty School total: 52. In upper school: 24 men, 7 women; 23 have advanced degrees.

Subjects Offered Advanced biology, advanced chemistry, algebra, American history, American literature, art, athletics, baseball, basketball, biology, calculus, chemistry, computer science, creative writing, digital applications, drama, earth science, ecology, economics, English, English composition, English literature, epic literature, ethics, European history, expository writing, fine arts, French, geometry, government/civics, grammar, health, history, history of the Catholic Church, Latin, modern world history, music, performing arts, photography, physical education, physics, pre-algebra, pre-calculus, religion, science, senior project, social studies, Spanish, speech, studio art, swimming, tennis, Texas history, theology, trigonometry, world history, world literature.

Graduation Requirements Arts and fine arts (art, music, dance, drama), electives, English, foreign language, mathematics, physical education (includes health), science, senior project, social studies (includes history), theology, completion of an independent senior project during fourth quarter of senior year.

Special Academic Programs 18 Advanced Placement exams for which test preparation is offered; independent study; study at local college for college credit.

College Admission Counseling 40 students graduated in 2010; all went to college, including Auburn University Montgomery; Southern Methodist University; Texas A&M University; Texas Christian University; The University of Texas at Austin; University of Oklahoma. Median SAT critical reading: 680, median SAT math: 700, median SAT writing: 690, median combined SAT: 2090, median composite ACT: 31. 92% scored over 600 on SAT critical reading, 100% scored over 600 on SAT math, 87% scored over 600 on SAT writing, 95% scored over 1800 on combined SAT, 86% scored over 26 on composite ACT.

Student Life Upper grades have uniform requirement, student council. Discipline rests primarily with faculty. Attendance at religious services is required.

Summer Programs Remediation, enrichment, sports, art/fine arts programs offered; session focuses on remediation and enrichment in mathematics and English, arts and fine arts, computers, and sports camp; held on campus; accepts boys; open to students from other schools. 125 students usually enrolled. 2011 schedule: June 7 to July 1. Application deadline: none.

Tuition and Aid Day student tuition: $15,400. Tuition installment plan (Tuition Management Systems Plan). Need-based scholarship grants available. In 2010–11, 26% of upper-school students received aid. Total amount of financial aid awarded in 2010–11: $383,350.

Admissions Traditional secondary-level entrance grade is 9. For fall 2010, 19 students applied for upper-level admission, 8 were accepted, 6 enrolled. English language, High School Placement Test, Iowa Tests of Basic Skills, ITBS achievement test, Kuhlmann-Anderson, mathematics proficiency exam or writing sample required. Deadline for receipt of application materials: January 28. Application fee required: $75.

Athletics Interscholastic: baseball, basketball, cross-country running, football, physical training, soccer, swimming and diving, tennis, track and field; intramural: basketball, physical training, soccer, strength & conditioning, ultimate Frisbee, volleyball, weight lifting, weight training. 2 coaches, 1 athletic trainer.

Computers Computers are regularly used in college planning, computer applications, digital applications, library, literary magazine, newspaper, photography, programming, publications, yearbook classes. Computer network features include on-campus library services, Internet access, online college applications, numerous online databases, reference sources, Moodle. Student e-mail accounts and computer access in designated common areas are available to students. The school has a published electronic and media policy.

Contact Mrs. Sally L. Cook, Registrar. 469-499-5402. Fax: 469-499-5440. E-mail: scook@cistercian.org. Web site: www.cistercian.org.

CLARKSVILLE ACADEMY

710 North Second Street
Clarksville, Tennessee 37040-2998
Head of School: Mrs. Kay D. Drew

General Information Coeducational day college-preparatory school. Grades PK–12. Founded: 1970. Setting: urban. 31-acre campus. 7 buildings on campus. Approved or accredited by Southern Association of Colleges and Schools and Tennessee Department of Education. Endowment: $1 million. Total enrollment: 487. Upper school average class size: 13. Upper school faculty-student ratio: 1:12. There are 175 required school days per year for Upper School students. Upper School students typically attend 5 days per week. The average school day consists of 7 hours.

Faculty School total: 36. In upper school: 5 men, 27 women; 30 have advanced degrees.

Subjects Offered Algebra, American history, art, biology, calculus, chemistry, chorus, computer science, driver education, economics, English, geography, geometry, German, graphic design, health, keyboarding, Latin, music, physical education, physics, physiology, political science, pre-calculus, psychology, Spanish, trigonometry, U.S. history, U.S. history-AP, world history, writing, youth culture.

Graduation Requirements 24 credit, 4 years of high school math required.

Special Academic Programs 6 Advanced Placement exams for which test preparation is offered; honors section; independent study; study at local college for college credit; academic accommodation for the gifted, the musically talented, and the artistically talented.

College Admission Counseling 42 students graduated in 2009; all went to college, including Austin Peay State University; Lipscomb University; Massachusetts Institute of Technology; The University of Tennessee; The University of Tennessee at Chattanooga; University of Memphis.

Student Life Upper grades have specified standards of dress, student council, honor system. Discipline rests primarily with faculty.

Tuition and Aid Day student tuition: $6100. Tuition installment plan (monthly payment plans). Tuition reduction for siblings, paying campus jobs available. In 2009–10, 5% of upper-school students received aid. Total amount of financial aid awarded in 2009–10: $25,000.

Admissions Otis-Lennon School Ability Test required. Deadline for receipt of application materials: none. Application fee required: $50. On-campus interview required.

Athletics Interscholastic: baseball (boys), basketball (b,g), cheering (g), dance team (g), football (b), soccer (b,g), softball (g), volleyball (g), wrestling (b); coed interscholastic: bowling, golf, tennis. 4 PE instructors.

Computers Computers are regularly used in all academic, art classes. Computer network features include Internet access, wireless campus network, Internet filtering or blocking technology. Computer access in designated common areas is available to students. Students grades are available online. The school has a published electronic and media policy.

Contact Mrs. Kay D. Drew, Head of School. 931-647-6311. Fax: 931-906-0610. E-mail: kdrew@clarksvilleacademy.com. Web site: www.clarksvilleacademy.com.

CLEARWATER CENTRAL CATHOLIC HIGH SCHOOL

2750 Haines Bayshore Road
Clearwater, Florida 33760
Head of School: Dr. John A. Venturella

General Information Coeducational day college-preparatory, arts, religious studies, technology, and International Baccalaureate diploma programme school, affiliated with Roman Catholic Church. Grades 9–12. Founded: 1962. Setting: suburban. Nearest major city is Tampa. 40-acre campus. 7 buildings on campus. Approved or accredited by International Baccalaureate Organization, National Catholic Education Association, Southern Association of Colleges and Schools, The College Board, and Florida Department of Education. Upper school average class size: 25. Upper school faculty-student ratio: 1:16. There are 190 required school days per year for Upper School students. Upper School students typically attend 5 days per week. The average school day consists of 6 hours and 13 minutes.

Upper School Student Profile 80% of students are Roman Catholic.

Faculty School total: 41. In upper school: 14 men, 27 women; 32 have advanced degrees.

Subjects Offered Acting, advanced chemistry, Advanced Placement courses, aerobics, algebra, American government, American history, American history-AP, American literature, American literature-AP, American sign language, anatomy, architecture, Bible studies, biology, biology-AP, British literature, British literature (honors), calculus, calculus-AP, campus ministry, chemistry, chemistry-AP, choral music, chorus, church history, composition, computer processing, creative writing, desktop publishing, discrete mathematics, drama, drawing, drawing and design, ecology, economics, English, English literature and composition-AP, foreign language, French, general science, geometry, health, honors algebra, honors English, honors geometry, honors U.S. history, honors world history, information technology, journalism, keyboarding, language arts, law, law studies, leadership, learning strategies, life management skills, marine biology, music appreciation, oral communications, painting, personal fitness, philosophy, physical education, physics, pre-algebra, probability and statistics, psychology, sociology, Spanish, Spanish language-AP, speech, speech and debate, theater, theology, trigonometry, U.S. government, U.S. government and politics-AP, U.S. history, U.S. history-AP, video, volleyball, Web site design, wellness, world history.

Graduation Requirements Algebra, biology, economics, English, general science, geometry, global studies, physical education (includes health), physical fitness, Spanish, theology, U.S. government, U.S. history, world history.

Special Academic Programs International Baccalaureate program; Advanced Placement exam preparation; honors section; study at local college for college credit; programs in English, mathematics, general development for dyslexic students.

College Admission Counseling 130 students graduated in 2010; all went to college, including Florida State University; University of Central Florida; University of Florida; University of South Florida.

Student Life Upper grades have uniform requirement, student council, honor system. Discipline rests primarily with faculty. Attendance at religious services is required.

Summer Programs Remediation, enrichment, advancement, sports, computer instruction programs offered; session focuses on work-ahead classes for credit; held on campus; accepts boys and girls; open to students from other schools. 225 students usually enrolled. 2011 schedule: June 9 to June 27. Application deadline: May 15.

Tuition and Aid Day student tuition: $8925–$11,775. Tuition installment plan (SMART Tuition Payment Plan). Tuition reduction for siblings, merit scholarship grants, need-based scholarship grants available. In 2010–11, 20% of upper-school students received aid.

Admissions Traditional secondary-level entrance grade is 9. For fall 2010, 230 students applied for upper-level admission, 200 were accepted, 170 enrolled. Explore required. Deadline for receipt of application materials: none. Application fee required: $100.

Athletics Interscholastic: aerobics (girls), baseball (b), basketball (b,g), cheering (g), cross-country running (b,g), diving (b,g), football (b), golf (b,g), physical fitness (b,g), running (b,g), soccer (b,g), softball (g), swimming and diving (b,g), tennis (b,g), track and field (b,g), volleyball (g), weight lifting (b,g), weight training (b,g), winter soccer (b,g), wrestling (b). 2 PE instructors, 43 coaches, 1 athletic trainer.

Computers Computer network features include on-campus library services, online commercial services, Internet access. The school has a published electronic and media policy.

Contact Mrs. Helen Lambert, Director of Admissions. 727-531-1449 Ext. 304. Fax: 727-451-0003. E-mail: hlambert@ccchs.org. Web site: www.ccchs.org.

COLEGIO BOLIVAR

Calle 5 # 122-21 Via a Pance
Cali, Colombia
Head of School: Dr. Joseph Nagy

General Information Coeducational day college-preparatory, bilingual studies, and technology school. Grades PK–12. Founded: 1947. Setting: suburban. 14-hectare campus. 7 buildings on campus. Approved or accredited by Association of American Schools in South America, Colombian Ministry of Education, and Southern Association of Colleges and Schools. Languages of instruction: English and Spanish. Total enrollment: 1,219. Upper school average class size: 18. Upper school faculty-student ratio: 1:9. There are 180 required school days per year for Upper School students. The average school day consists of 7 hours.

Upper School Student Profile Grade 9: 100 students (50 boys, 50 girls); Grade 10: 99 students (45 boys, 54 girls); Grade 11: 73 students (35 boys, 38 girls); Grade 12: 84 students (36 boys, 48 girls).

Faculty School total: 150. In upper school: 20 men, 16 women; 20 have advanced degrees.

Subjects Offered Advanced chemistry, Advanced Placement courses, algebra, American history, American literature, art, art history, biology, business, calculus, chemistry, computer science, dance, drama, English, English literature, environmental science, ESL, ethics, French, geology, government/civics, graphic design, history, journalism, mathematics, music, philosophy, photography, physical education, physics, programming, psychology, religion, robotics, social studies, Spanish, theater, trigonometry, world literature.

Graduation Requirements Algebra, American history, American literature, art, biology, calculus, chemistry, computer education, economics, electives, geography, geometry, history of the Americas, music, physical education (includes health), physics, political science, pre-calculus, senior project, Spanish, Spanish literature, trigonometry, world history, world literature, writing, social service hours.

Special Academic Programs Advanced Placement exam preparation; independent study; remedial reading and/or remedial writing; ESL.

College Admission Counseling 82 students graduated in 2009; 72 went to college, including Bentley University; DePaul University; Loras College; The University of Montana Western; University of Central Florida; University of Pittsburgh. Other: 10 had other specific plans. Median combined SAT: 1550. Mean SAT critical reading: 510, mean SAT math: 540, mean SAT writing: 510. 22% scored over 600 on SAT critical reading, 28% scored over 600 on SAT math, 18% scored over 600 on SAT writing, 15% scored over 1800 on combined SAT.

Student Life Upper grades have specified standards of dress, student council, honor system. Discipline rests equally with students and faculty.

Tuition and Aid Day student tuition: 17,830,452 Colombian pesos–19,194,803 Colombian pesos. Tuition installment plan (monthly payment plans, annual payment plan). Need-based scholarship grants available. In 2009–10, 6% of upper-school students received aid.

Admissions Traditional secondary-level entrance grade is 9. For fall 2009, 26 students applied for upper-level admission, 6 enrolled. School's own exam required. Deadline for receipt of application materials: none. Application fee required: 80,000 Colombian pesos. On-campus interview required.

Athletics Interscholastic: aerobics/dance (girls), baseball (b), basketball (b,g), dance (g), equestrian sports (b,g), gymnastics (b,g), horseback riding (b,g), running (b,g), soccer (b,g), swimming and diving (b,g), track and field (b,g), volleyball (b,g); intramural: gymnastics (b,g), soccer (b,g), softball (b), swimming and diving (b,g), track and field (b,g), volleyball (b,g). 9 PE instructors, 24 coaches.

Computers Computers are regularly used in graphic design, photography, Web site design, yearbook classes. Computer network features include Internet access, Internet filtering or blocking technology. The school has a published electronic and media policy.

Contact Mrs. Patricia Nasser, Admissions Assistant. 57-2-555-2039 Ext. 274. Fax: 57-2-555-2041. E-mail: pnasser@colegiobolivar.edu.co. Web site: www.colegiobolivar.edu.co.

COLEGIO FRANKLIN D. ROOSEVELT

Av. Las Palmeras 325, Urbanizacion Camacho La Molina
Lima 12, Peru
Head of School: Mr. Russel D. Junes

General Information Coeducational day college-preparatory, general academic, arts, and technology school. Grades N–12. Founded: 1946. Setting: suburban. Nearest major city is Lima, Peru. 23-acre campus. 5 buildings on campus. Approved or accredited by International Baccalaureate Organization and Southern Association of Colleges and Schools. Languages of instruction: English and Spanish. Total enrollment: 1,452. Upper school average class size: 20. Upper school faculty-student ratio: 1:11. There are 179 required school days per year for Upper School students. Upper School students typically attend 5 days per week. The average school day consists of 7 hours and 30 minutes.

Upper School Student Profile Grade 9: 109 students (57 boys, 52 girls); Grade 10: 89 students (51 boys, 38 girls); Grade 11: 97 students (56 boys, 41 girls); Grade 12: 93 students (47 boys, 46 girls).

Faculty School total: 182. In upper school: 20 men, 25 women; 26 have advanced degrees.

Subjects Offered Algebra, American history, American literature, art, biology, calculus, chemistry, computer programming, computer science, debate, digital photography, drama, drama performance, early childhood, earth science, economics, English, English literature, ESL, fine arts, French, geography, geometry, global issues, health, history, International Baccalaureate courses, mathematics, model United Nations, music, orchestra, photography, physical education, physical science, physics, psychology, science, social studies, Spanish, theater, theory of knowledge, trigonometry, U.S. history, world history, yearbook.

Graduation Requirements Arts and fine arts (art, music, dance, drama), English, foreign language, information technology, mathematics, physical education (includes health), science, social studies (includes history).

Special Academic Programs International Baccalaureate program; honors section; special instructional classes for students with mild learning disabilities; ESL (15 students enrolled).

College Admission Counseling 93 students graduated in 2010; 92 went to college, including Boston College; Michigan State University; Northwestern University; Purdue University; Texas A&M University; University of California, Berkeley. Other: 1 had other specific plans. Mean SAT critical reading: 548, mean SAT math: 576, mean SAT writing: 548, mean composite ACT: 23.

Student Life Upper grades have uniform requirement, student council, honor system. Discipline rests primarily with faculty.

Tuition and Aid Day student tuition: $9660–$10,980. Tuition installment plan (monthly payment plans). Need-based scholarship grants available. In 2010–11, 0% of upper-school students received aid. Total amount of financial aid awarded in 2010–11: $5490.

Admissions Traditional secondary-level entrance grade is 9. For fall 2010, 34 students applied for upper-level admission, 32 were accepted, 32 enrolled. ESL or math and English placement tests required. Deadline for receipt of application materials: none. Application fee required: $250. On-campus interview required.

Athletics Interscholastic: aquatics (boys, girls), basketball (b,g), field hockey (b), soccer (b,g), softball (b,g), swimming and diving (b,g), track and field (b,g), volleyball (b,g); intramural: aquatics (b,g), basketball (b,g), soccer (b,g), softball (b,g), swimming and diving (b,g), volleyball (b,g); coed interscholastic: aerobics, aquatics, dance, field hockey, fitness, floor hockey, martial arts, soccer, swimming and diving, track and field, volleyball, water polo; coed intramural: aerobics, aquatics, floor hockey, martial arts, outdoor adventure, soccer, swimming and diving, volleyball, wall climbing, water polo. 3 PE instructors, 18 coaches.

Computers Computers are regularly used in art, digital applications, English, history, mathematics, music, photography, science, technology classes. Computer network features include on-campus library services, online commercial services, Internet access, wireless campus network, Internet filtering or blocking technology. Campus intranet and student e-mail accounts are available to students. Students grades are available online. The school has a published electronic and media policy.

Contact Ms. Nora Marquez, Admissions Officer. 51-1-435-0890 Ext. 1004. Fax: 51-1-6199301. E-mail: nmarquez@amersol.edu.pe. Web site: www.amersol.edu.pe.

COLEGIO NUEVA GRANADA

Carrera 2E #70-20
Bogota, Colombia
Head of School: Dr. Eric H Habegger

General Information Coeducational day college-preparatory, Colombian Bachillerato, and Advanced Placement school. Grades PK–12. Founded: 1938. Setting: urban. 17-acre campus. 2 buildings on campus. Approved or accredited by Southern Association of Colleges and Schools. Languages of instruction: English and Spanish. Total enrollment: 1,801. Upper school average class size: 23. Upper school faculty-student ratio: 1:22. There are 183 required school days per year for Upper School students. Upper School students typically attend 5 days per week. The average school day consists of 7 hours.

Upper School Student Profile Grade 9: 160 students (77 boys, 83 girls); Grade 10: 127 students (58 boys, 69 girls); Grade 11: 119 students (61 boys, 58 girls); Grade 12: 121 students (64 boys, 57 girls).

Faculty School total: 233. In upper school: 28 men, 35 women; 27 have advanced degrees.

Subjects Offered Art, art history-AP, basketball, biology, biology-AP, calculus, chemistry, crafts, dance performance, drama, drawing, economics-AP, English, English-AP, ESL, ethics, European history-AP, French, graphic design, human geography—AP, macroeconomics-AP, Mandarin, mathematics, model United Nations, music, philosophy, photography, physical education, physics, pre-calculus, religion, science, sex education, social studies, Spanish, Spanish language-AP, studio art-AP, theater, U.S. history, U.S. history-AP, volleyball, weight training, world history, world history-AP.

Graduation Requirements Arts and fine arts (art, music, dance, drama), computer education, electives, English, foreign language, mathematics, physical education (includes health), science, social studies (includes history), senior independent project.

Special Academic Programs Advanced Placement exam preparation; honors section; independent study; academic accommodation for the gifted; programs in English, mathematics, general development for dyslexic students; special instructional classes for students with learning disabilities, students with emotional and behavioral problems, Attention Deficit Disorder; ESL (8 students enrolled).

College Admission Counseling 114 students graduated in 2010; 90 went to college, including Florida International University; Massachusetts Institute of Technology; Northeastern University; Penn State University Park; University of Miami; University of Pennsylvania. Other: 1 went to work, 23 had other specific plans. Median SAT critical reading: 470, median SAT math: 500, median SAT writing: 490, median combined SAT: 1470.

Student Life Upper grades have uniform requirement, student council, honor system. Discipline rests equally with students and faculty.

Tuition and Aid Tuition installment plan (5-installment plan). Need-based scholarship grants available.

Admissions For fall 2010, 50 students applied for upper-level admission, 38 were accepted, 38 enrolled. Academic Profile Tests, admissions testing and writing sample required. Deadline for receipt of application materials: none. Application fee required: $85. On-campus interview required.

Athletics Interscholastic: aerobics/dance (girls), baseball (b), basketball (b,g), gymnastics (b,g), soccer (b,g), table tennis (b,g), volleyball (b,g); intramural: basketball (b,g), soccer (b,g), table tennis (b,g), volleyball (b,g), weight training (b,g); coed interscholastic: gymnastics; coed intramural: basketball, soccer, table tennis, volleyball, weight training. 5 PE instructors, 11 coaches.

Computers Computers are regularly used in desktop publishing, ESL, introduction to technology, mathematics, science, technology, video film production, Web site design classes. Computer network features include on-campus library services, Internet access, wireless campus network, Internet filtering or blocking technology, Sharepoint, SDS. Campus intranet, student e-mail accounts, and computer access in designated common areas are available to students. Students grades are available online.

Colegio Nueva Granada

Contact Laura De Brigard, Director of Admissions. 57-1-359-9344. Fax: 57-1-211-3720. E-mail: lbrigard@cng.edu. Web site: www.cng.edu.

COLEGIO SAN JOSE

PO Box 21300
San Juan, Puerto Rico 00928-1300
Head of School: Br. Francisco T. Gonzalez, DMD

General Information Boys' day college-preparatory, arts, business, religious studies, bilingual studies, technology, science, anatomy and marine biology, and psychology, humanities, health school, affiliated with Roman Catholic Church. Grades 7–12. Founded: 1938. Setting: urban. 6-acre campus. 1 building on campus. Approved or accredited by European Council of International Schools, National Catholic Education Association, The College Board, and Puerto Rico Department of Education. Languages of instruction: English and Spanish. Endowment: $200,000. Total enrollment: 491. Upper school average class size: 22.

Upper School Student Profile Grade 10: 77 students (77 boys); Grade 11: 81 students (81 boys); Grade 12: 81 students (81 boys). 90% of students are Roman Catholic.

Faculty School total: 43. In upper school: 24 men, 19 women; 24 have advanced degrees.

Subjects Offered Accounting, algebra, American history, American literature, anatomy, art, art history, biology, biology-AP, broadcasting, business skills, calculus, chemistry, choir, Christian ethics, computer science, ecology, English, English literature, ethics, European history, French, French as a second language, geography, geometry, government/civics, grammar, health, history, instrumental music, keyboarding, marine biology, mathematics, music, physical education, physics, pre-calculus, psychology, religion, science, social studies, Spanish, world history.

Graduation Requirements Business skills (includes word processing), computer science, English, foreign language, mathematics, physical education (includes health), religion (includes Bible studies and theology), science, social studies (includes history), Spanish, 40 hours of Christian community service.

Special Academic Programs Advanced Placement exam preparation; honors section.

College Admission Counseling 84 students graduated in 2010; 83 went to college, including Boston College; University of Dayton; University of Puerto Rico, Mayagüez Campus; University of Puerto Rico, Río Piedras. Other: 1 entered military service.

Student Life Upper grades have uniform requirement, student council, honor system. Discipline rests equally with students and faculty. Attendance at religious services is required.

Summer Programs Remediation programs offered; session focuses on remediation/make-up; held on campus; accepts boys and girls; open to students from other schools. 150 students usually enrolled. 2011 schedule: June 1 to June 29. Application deadline: May 31.

Tuition and Aid Day student tuition: $6750. Tuition installment plan (The Tuition Plan, individually arranged payment plans). Need-based scholarship grants available. In 2010–11, 12% of upper-school students received aid. Total amount of financial aid awarded in 2010–11: $250,000.

Admissions Traditional secondary-level entrance grade is 10. Admissions testing and Catholic High School Entrance Examination required. Deadline for receipt of application materials: February 4. Application fee required: $10. On-campus interview required.

Athletics Interscholastic: baseball, basketball, bowling, cross-country running, fitness, golf, indoor soccer, physical fitness, soccer, swimming and diving, tennis, track and field, volleyball; intramural: cross-country running, indoor soccer, soccer, swimming and diving, tennis, track and field, volleyball. 3 PE instructors, 5 coaches, 1 athletic trainer.

Computers Computers are regularly used in accounting, art, data processing, English, foreign language, mathematics, music, psychology, science, Spanish, yearbook classes. Computer resources include on-campus library services, Internet access, wireless campus network, Internet filtering or blocking technology, Edline. Students grades are available online. The school has a published electronic and media policy.

Contact Mrs. María E. Guzmán, Guidance Advisor. 787-751-8177 Ext. 229. Fax: 866-955-7646. E-mail: mguzman@csj-rpi.org. Web site: www.csj-rpi.org.

COLE VALLEY CHRISTIAN HIGH SCHOOL

200 East Carlton Avenue
Meridian, Idaho 83642
Head of School: Mr. Bradley Carr

General Information Coeducational day college-preparatory, general academic, arts, religious studies, and bilingual studies school, affiliated with Christian faith. Grades K–12. Founded: 1990. Setting: suburban. Nearest major city is Boise. 5-acre campus. 2 buildings on campus. Approved or accredited by Association of Christian Schools International and Idaho Department of Education. Total enrollment: 689. Upper school average class size: 20. Upper school faculty-student ratio: 1:10. There are 180 required school days per year for Upper School students. Upper School students typically attend 5 days per week. The average school day consists of 5 hours and 50 minutes.

Upper School Student Profile 100% of students are Christian.

Faculty School total: 22. In upper school: 10 men, 12 women; 5 have advanced degrees.

Subjects Offered 20th century history, algebra, American government, American literature, art, Bible, biology, British literature, calculus-AP, chemistry, choral music, computer literacy, ecology, economics, English, English literature, French, geometry, honors English, Latin, physical education, physical science, physics, pre-algebra, pre-calculus, Spanish, speech, U.S. history, world history, yearbook.

Graduation Requirements 20th century history, American government, economics, English, mathematics, physical education (includes health), religion (includes Bible studies and theology), science, social studies (includes history), speech, Bible classes are required.

Special Academic Programs Advanced Placement exam preparation; honors section; independent study; study at local college for college credit.

College Admission Counseling 68 students graduated in 2009; 63 went to college, including Boise State University; Northwest Nazarene University; The College of Idaho. Other: 2 went to work, 1 entered military service.

Student Life Upper grades have specified standards of dress, student council, honor system. Discipline rests primarily with faculty. Attendance at religious services is required.

Tuition and Aid Day student tuition: $6000. Tuition installment plan (monthly payment plans, individually arranged payment plans). Tuition reduction for siblings, need-based scholarship grants available. In 2009–10, 20% of upper-school students received aid.

Admissions Traditional secondary-level entrance grade is 9. Deadline for receipt of application materials: none. Application fee required: $125. Interview required.

Athletics Interscholastic: basketball (boys, girls), cheering (g), cross-country running (b,g), football (b), track and field (b,g), volleyball (g), wrestling (b); intramural: skiing (cross-country) (b,g), skiing (downhill) (b,g), snowboarding (b,g). 3 PE instructors, 12 coaches.

Computers Computers are regularly used in all academic classes. Computer network features include on-campus library services, Internet access, Internet filtering or blocking technology. Student e-mail accounts are available to students. Students grades are available online.

Contact Mrs. Robin Didriksen, Administrative Assistant to the Guidance Counselor/Registrar. 208-898-9003. Fax: 208-898-9016. E-mail: rdidriksen@cvcsonline.org. Web site: colevalleychristian.org.

COLLEGEDALE ACADEMY

PO Box 628
4855 College Drive East
Collegedale, Tennessee 37315
Head of School: Mr. Murray J. Cooper

General Information Coeducational day college-preparatory and arts school, affiliated with Seventh-day Adventists. Grades 9–12. Founded: 1892. Setting: small town. Nearest major city is Chattanooga. 20-acre campus. 3 buildings on campus. Approved or accredited by Southern Association of Colleges and Schools and Tennessee Department of Education. Endowment: $496,487. Upper school average class size: 25. Upper school faculty-student ratio: 1:17. There are 180 required school days per year for Upper School students. Upper School students typically attend 5 days per week. The average school day consists of 7 hours.

Upper School Student Profile Grade 9: 98 students (47 boys, 51 girls); Grade 10: 86 students (39 boys, 47 girls); Grade 11: 90 students (51 boys, 39 girls); Grade 12: 89 students (48 boys, 41 girls). 98% of students are Seventh-day Adventists.

Faculty School total: 34. In upper school: 18 men, 13 women; 21 have advanced degrees.

Subjects Offered Algebra, American history, American literature, anatomy, art, art appreciation, Bible studies, biology, cabinet making, calculus-AP, chemistry, choir, composition, computer skills, concert band, digital imaging, drawing, earth science, economics, English, English literature, environmental science, fine arts, French, geometry, government/civics, gymnastics, health, health and wellness, history, home economics, jazz band, journalism, mathematics, music, music appreciation, personal fitness, physical education, physical science, physics, physiology, pre-calculus, religion, social studies, Spanish, woodworking, world history, yearbook.

Graduation Requirements Arts and fine arts (art, music, dance, drama), computer science, English, foreign language, mathematics, physical education (includes health), religion (includes Bible studies and theology), science, social studies (includes history).

Special Academic Programs 1 Advanced Placement exam for which test preparation is offered; accelerated programs; study at local college for college credit.

College Admission Counseling 102 students graduated in 2010; 97 went to college, including Chattanooga State Community College; Cleveland State University; Southern Adventist University; The University of Tennessee at Chattanooga. Other: 3 went to work, 1 entered military service, 1 had other specific plans. 24.5% scored over 26 on composite ACT.

Student Life Upper grades have uniform requirement, student council, honor system. Discipline rests equally with students and faculty. Attendance at religious services is required.

Summer Programs Advancement programs offered; session focuses on U.S. History; held on campus; accepts boys and girls; open to students from other schools. 20 students usually enrolled. 2011 schedule: May 24 to July 7. Application deadline: none.

Tuition and Aid Day student tuition: $8440. Tuition installment plan (monthly payment plans). Need-based scholarship grants available. In 2010–11, 15% of upper-school students received aid. Total amount of financial aid awarded in 2010–11: $51,000.

Admissions Traditional secondary-level entrance grade is 9. Mathematics proficiency exam required. Deadline for receipt of application materials: August 1. Application fee required: $50. On-campus interview required.

Athletics Interscholastic: cross-country running (boys, girls), golf (b), tennis (b,g); intramural: basketball (b,g), soccer (b,g), track and field (b,g), volleyball (b,g); coed intramural: flag football, gymnastics, hiking/backpacking, paddle tennis, volleyball. 1 PE instructor, 2 coaches.

Computers Computers are regularly used in business applications, computer applications, digital applications, English, library, publications, yearbook classes. Computer network features include on-campus library services, Internet access, wireless campus network, Internet filtering or blocking technology. Student e-mail accounts and computer access in designated common areas are available to students. Students grades are available online. The school has a published electronic and media policy.

Contact Miss Kerre Conerly, Vice Principal, Academic Services. 423-396-2124 Ext. 415. Fax: 423-396-3363. E-mail: kconerly@collegedaleacademy.com. Web site: www.collegedaleacademy.com.

THE COLLEGE PREPARATORY SCHOOL

6100 Broadway
Oakland, California 94618
Head of School: Murray Cohen

General Information Coeducational day college-preparatory school. Grades 9–12. Founded: 1960. Setting: urban. 6-acre campus. 14 buildings on campus. Approved or accredited by California Association of Independent Schools, Western Association of Schools and Colleges, and California Department of Education. Member of National Association of Independent Schools. Endowment: $9.5 million. Total enrollment: 355. Upper school average class size: 14. Upper school faculty-student ratio: 1:8. Upper School students typically attend 5 days per week.

Upper School Student Profile Grade 9: 88 students (49 boys, 39 girls); Grade 10: 92 students (52 boys, 40 girls); Grade 11: 90 students (49 boys, 41 girls); Grade 12: 85 students (43 boys, 42 girls).

Faculty School total: 52. In upper school: 19 men, 33 women; 43 have advanced degrees.

Subjects Offered 20th century American writers, 3-dimensional art, acting, advanced math, Advanced Placement courses, algebra, American government, American history, American literature, animal behavior, art, art-AP, astronomy, audio visual/media, biology, biology-AP, calculus, calculus-AP, chemistry, chemistry-AP, Chinese, Chinese literature, chorus, comparative religion, computer science, contemporary issues in science, creative writing, dance, dance performance, debate, digital applications, drama, drama performance, drawing and design, economics, English, English literature, environmental science-AP, European history, forensics, French, French literature-AP, French-AP, freshman foundations, genetics, geometry, health education, history, independent study, instruments, Japanese, jazz band, junior and senior seminars, language-AP, Latin, Latin American literature, Latin-AP, linguistics, mathematics, music, music theory-AP, orchestra, peer counseling, philosophy, photography, physical education, physical science, physics, physics-AP, poetry, psychology, science, Shakespeare, Spanish, Spanish-AP, stagecraft, statistics, statistics-AP, theater, theater design and production, U.S. government, vocal ensemble, Western civilization, women's studies, world civilizations, zoology.

Graduation Requirements Arts and fine arts (art, music, dance, drama), English, foreign language, freshman foundations, history, mathematics, physical education (includes health), science, sophomore health, Intraterm Program.

Special Academic Programs Advanced Placement exam preparation; honors section; independent study.

College Admission Counseling 81 students graduated in 2009; all went to college, including Columbia University; Dartmouth College; Harvard University; Stanford University; University of Pennsylvania. Mean SAT critical reading: 717, mean SAT math: 726, mean SAT writing: 726, mean composite ACT: 30.

Student Life Upper grades have student council. Discipline rests equally with students and faculty.

Tuition and Aid Day student tuition: $29,950. Tuition installment plan (FACTS Tuition Payment Plan, monthly payment plans). Need-based scholarship grants available. In 2009–10, 25% of upper-school students received aid. Total amount of financial aid awarded in 2009–10: $1,700,000.

Admissions Traditional secondary-level entrance grade is 9. For fall 2009, 302 students applied for upper-level admission, 146 were accepted, 88 enrolled. ISEE or SSAT required. Deadline for receipt of application materials: January 15. Application fee required: $75. On-campus interview required.

Athletics Interscholastic: baseball (boys), basketball (b,g), cross-country running (b,g), outdoor recreation (b,g), soccer (b,g), softball (g), swimming and diving (b,g), tennis (b,g), track and field (b,g), volleyball (b,g); intramural: dance (b,g); coed

interscholastic: golf; coed intramural: badminton, basketball, cross-country running, dance, golf, outdoor recreation, soccer, volleyball. 4 PE instructors, 21 coaches.

Computers Computers are regularly used in art, drawing and design, freshman foundations, mathematics, music, newspaper, science, theater arts, yearbook classes. Computer network features include on-campus library services, online commercial services, Internet access, wireless campus network, remote access to library services, Web publishing, remote file-server access, video recording and editing. Student e-mail accounts and computer access in designated common areas are available to students. The school has a published electronic and media policy.

Contact Jonathan Zucker, Director of Admission and Financial Aid. 510-652-4364. Fax: 510-652-7467. E-mail: jonathan@college-prep.org. Web site: www.college-prep.org.

COLLEGIATE SCHOOL

260 West 78th Street
New York, New York 10024
Head of School: Dr. Lee M. Levison

General Information Boys' day college-preparatory and arts school. Grades K–12. Founded: 1628. Setting: urban. 4 buildings on campus. Approved or accredited by New York State Association of Independent Schools. Member of National Association of Independent Schools. Endowment: $70 million. Total enrollment: 642. Upper school average class size: 14. Upper school faculty-student ratio: 1:4. There are 164 required school days per year for Upper School students. Upper School students typically attend 5 days per week. The average school day consists of 6 hours and 45 minutes.

Upper School Student Profile Grade 9: 60 students (60 boys); Grade 10: 56 students (56 boys); Grade 11: 54 students (54 boys); Grade 12: 55 students (55 boys).

Faculty School total: 111. In upper school: 39 men, 22 women; 56 have advanced degrees.

Subjects Offered African drumming, African history, algebra, American history, Ancient Greek, applied music, architecture, art, art appreciation, art history, Asian history, athletics, biology, calculus, ceramics, chemistry, Chinese, chorus, contemporary issues in science, digital photography, drama, dramatic arts, drawing, drawing and design, East Asian history, economics, English, environmental science, European history, film, film appreciation, film studies, foreign policy, French, geometry, health and wellness, history, Latin, Latin American history, linear algebra, literature, logic, Mandarin, mathematics, Middle Eastern history, music, music composition, music theory, orchestra, painting, philosophy, photography, physical education, physics, play production, poetry, pre-calculus, religion, sculpture, senior project, Shakespeare, social studies, Spanish, technical theater, theater, U.S. history, Web site design, world history, world literature, world religions.

Graduation Requirements Drama, English, foreign language, history, mathematics, music, physical education (includes health), religion (includes Bible studies and theology), science, visual arts. Community service is required.

Special Academic Programs 13 Advanced Placement exams for which test preparation is offered; honors section; independent study; term-away projects; study abroad.

College Admission Counseling 54 students graduated in 2010; all went to college, including Georgetown University; Harvard University; Pomona College; Princeton University; Tufts University; Yale University.

Student Life Upper grades have specified standards of dress, student council, honor system. Discipline rests equally with students and faculty.

Tuition and Aid Day student tuition: $35,700. Tuition installment plan (SMART Tuition Payment Plan). Need-based scholarship grants available. In 2010–11, 21% of upper-school students received aid. Total amount of financial aid awarded in 2010–11: $1,215,000.

Admissions Traditional secondary-level entrance grade is 9. ERB or ISEE required. Deadline for receipt of application materials: December 1. Application fee required: $50. On-campus interview required.

Athletics Interscholastic: baseball, basketball, cross-country running, fencing, indoor track & field, lacrosse, soccer, tennis, track and field, winter (indoor) track, wrestling; intramural: physical fitness, weight training, yoga. 3 PE instructors, 8 coaches, 2 athletic trainers.

Computers Computers are regularly used in all academic classes. Computer network features include on-campus library services, online commercial services, Internet access, wireless campus network, Internet filtering or blocking technology. Campus intranet, student e-mail accounts, and computer access in designated common areas are available to students. The school has a published electronic and media policy.

Contact Joanne P. Heyman, Director of Admissions and Financial Aid. 212-812-8552. Fax: 212-812-8547. E-mail: jheyman@collegiateschool.org. Web site: www.collegiateschool.org.

THE COLLEGIATE SCHOOL

North Mooreland Road
Richmond, Virginia 23229
Head of School: Keith A. Evans

General Information Coeducational day college-preparatory, arts, and technology school. Grades K–12. Founded: 1915. Setting: suburban. 211-acre campus. 13

buildings on campus. Approved or accredited by Southern Association of Colleges and Schools, Virginia Association of Independent Schools, and Virginia Department of Education. Member of National Association of Independent Schools and Secondary School Admission Test Board. Endowment: $34.4 million. Total enrollment: 1,578. Upper school average class size: 15. Upper school faculty-student ratio: 1:15. There are 175 required school days per year for Upper School students. Upper School students typically attend 5 days per week. The average school day consists of 7 hours.

Upper School Student Profile Grade 9: 123 students (62 boys, 61 girls); Grade 10: 127 students (63 boys, 64 girls); Grade 11: 126 students (57 boys, 69 girls); Grade 12: 119 students (52 boys, 67 girls).

Faculty School total: 188. In upper school: 29 men, 38 women; 52 have advanced degrees.

Subjects Offered 20th century history, acting, advanced chemistry, algebra, American Civil War, American history, American history-AP, American literature, art, Asian literature, Bible as literature, biology, biology-AP, calculus-AP, ceramics, chemistry, chemistry-AP, community service, computer applications, creative writing, drama, driver education, earth science, economics, economics-AP, English, English literature, ethics, European history, film and literature, fine arts, French, French-AP, geometry, government and politics-AP, government/civics, health, journalism, Latin, music, photography, physics, physics-AP, religion, robotics, Russian literature, senior seminar, Spanish, Spanish language-AP, statistics, theater, trigonometry, world history, World War II.

Graduation Requirements Arts and fine arts (art, music, dance, drama), English, ethics, foreign language, government, history, mathematics, physical education (includes health), religion (includes Bible studies and theology), science, sports, senior speech. Community service is required.

Special Academic Programs 12 Advanced Placement exams for which test preparation is offered; honors section; independent study; study at local college for college credit; programs in general development for dyslexic students.

College Admission Counseling 129 students graduated in 2010; all went to college, including Elon University; Hampden-Sydney College; James Madison University; The College of William and Mary; University of Virginia; Virginia Polytechnic Institute and State University.

Student Life Upper grades have specified standards of dress, student council, honor system. Discipline rests equally with students and faculty.

Summer Programs Remediation, enrichment, advancement, sports, art/fine arts, computer instruction programs offered; session focuses on advancement, remediation, sports; held both on and off campus; held at various locations in metro Richmond; accepts boys and girls; open to students from other schools. 1,426 students usually enrolled. 2011 schedule: June 13 to August 5. Application deadline: none.

Tuition and Aid Day student tuition: $19,800. Tuition installment plan (Insured Tuition Payment Plan, monthly payment plans). Need-based scholarship grants available. In 2010–11, 12% of upper-school students received aid. Total amount of financial aid awarded in 2010–11: $655,087.

Admissions Traditional secondary-level entrance grade is 9. For fall 2010, 82 students applied for upper-level admission, 43 were accepted, 25 enrolled. PSAT and SAT for applicants to grade 11 and 12 or SSAT required. Deadline for receipt of application materials: none. Application fee required: $50. Interview required.

Athletics Interscholastic: baseball (boys), basketball (b,g), cross-country running (b,g), diving (b,g), field hockey (g), football (b), indoor track & field (b,g), lacrosse (b,g), soccer (b,g), softball (g), swimming and diving (b,g), tennis (b,g), track and field (b,g), volleyball (g), winter (indoor) track (b,g), wrestling (b); coed interscholastic: golf, indoor soccer; coed intramural: combined training, dance, dance squad, dance team, fitness, modern dance. 3 PE instructors, 48 coaches, 2 athletic trainers.

Computers Computers are regularly used in all academic classes. Computer network features include on-campus library services, Internet access, wireless campus network, Internet filtering or blocking technology. Student e-mail accounts are available to students. The school has a published electronic and media policy.

Contact Amanda L. Surgner, Director of Admission. 804-741-9722. Fax: 804-741-5472. E-mail: asurgner@collegiate-va.org. Web site: www.collegiate-va.org/.

THE COLORADO ROCKY MOUNTAIN SCHOOL

1493 County Road 106
Carbondale, Colorado 81623
Head of School: Jeff Leahy

General Information Coeducational boarding and day college-preparatory and arts school. Grades 9–12. Founded: 1953. Setting: small town. Nearest major city is Denver. Students are housed in single-sex dormitories. 350-acre campus. 23 buildings on campus. Approved or accredited by Association for Experiential Education, Association of Colorado Independent Schools, The Association of Boarding Schools, and Colorado Department of Education. Member of National Association of Independent Schools and Secondary School Admission Test Board. Endowment: $13.8 million. Total enrollment: 145. Upper school average class size: 12. Upper school faculty-student ratio: 1:5. Upper School students typically attend 5 days per week. The average school day consists of 8 hours.

Upper School Student Profile Grade 9: 32 students (21 boys, 11 girls); Grade 10: 38 students (20 boys, 18 girls); Grade 11: 53 students (33 boys, 20 girls); Grade 12: 33 students (16 boys, 17 girls). 64% of students are boarding students. 56% are state residents. 19 states are represented in upper school student body. 22% are international

students. International students from China, Democratic People's Republic of Korea, Germany, Japan, Rwanda, and Venezuela; 7 other countries represented in student body.

Faculty School total: 42. In upper school: 21 men, 21 women; 21 have advanced degrees; 40 reside on campus.

Subjects Offered Advanced Placement courses, algebra, American literature, anthropology, art, art history, biology, botany, calculus, ceramics, chemistry, computer programming, computer science, creative writing, drama, earth science, ecology, English, English literature, environmental science, ESL, ethics, European history, expository writing, fine arts, French, gardening, geography, geology, geometry, geopolitics, government/civics, grammar, guitar, history, history of ideas, journalism, mathematics, music, philosophy, photography, physical education, physics, physiology, religion, science, Shakespeare, social studies, Spanish, theater, trigonometry, Western civilization, world history, world literature, writing.

Graduation Requirements Arts and fine arts (art, music, dance, drama), chemistry, English, foreign language, mathematics, science, senior project, social studies (includes history), participation in outdoor program. Community service is required.

Special Academic Programs Advanced Placement exam preparation; academic accommodation for the gifted, the musically talented, and the artistically talented; ESL (10 students enrolled).

College Admission Counseling 37 students graduated in 2010; all went to college, including Bates College; Lewis & Clark College; Middlebury College; The Colorado College; University of Pennsylvania; University of Vermont. Mean SAT critical reading: 576, mean SAT math: 582, mean SAT writing: 543, mean combined SAT: 1701, mean composite ACT: 24. 28% scored over 600 on SAT critical reading, 23% scored over 600 on SAT math, 25% scored over 600 on SAT writing, 25% scored over 1800 on combined SAT, 28% scored over 26 on composite ACT.

Student Life Upper grades have student council, honor system. Discipline rests equally with students and faculty.

Tuition and Aid Day student tuition: $23,375; 7-day tuition and room/board: $37,650. Tuition installment plan (monthly payment plans, individually arranged payment plans, 3rd party loan options). Merit scholarship grants, need-based scholarship grants, middle-income loans available. In 2010–11, 41% of upper-school students received aid; total upper-school merit-scholarship money awarded: $40,000. Total amount of financial aid awarded in 2010–11: $1,000,000.

Admissions Traditional secondary-level entrance grade is 9. For fall 2010, 143 students applied for upper-level admission, 108 were accepted, 66 enrolled. PSAT or SAT, SLEP, SSAT or TOEFL required. Deadline for receipt of application materials: February 15. Application fee required: $50. Interview required.

Athletics Intramural: aerobics/dance (girls), basketball (b,g), dance (b,g), fly fishing (b,g), freestyle skiing (b,g), kayaking (b,g); coed interscholastic: alpine skiing, bicycling, canoeing/kayaking, climbing, cross-country running, independent competitive sports, kayaking, nordic skiing; coed intramural: alpine skiing, backpacking, basketball, bicycling, canoeing/kayaking, climbing, cross-country running, dance, equestrian sports, fishing, fitness, floor hockey, fly fishing, freestyle skiing, Frisbee, hiking/backpacking, horseshoes, jogging, kayaking, martial arts, mountain biking, mountaineering, nordic skiing, outdoor adventure, outdoor education, outdoor recreation, outdoor skills, outdoors. 4 coaches.

Computers Computers are regularly used in art, college planning, ESL, mathematics, science classes. Computer network features include on-campus library services, online commercial services, Internet access, wireless campus network, Internet filtering or blocking technology. Students grades are available online. The school has a published electronic and media policy.

Contact Molly Dorais, Director of Admission and Financial Aid. 970-963-2562. Fax: 970-963-9865. E-mail: mdorais@crms.org. Web site: www.crms.org.

THE COLORADO SPRINGS SCHOOL

21 Broadmoor Avenue
Colorado Springs, Colorado 80906
Head of School: Mr. Kevin Reel

General Information Coeducational day college-preparatory, arts, and experiential learning school. Grades PK–12. Founded: 1962. Setting: suburban. 30-acre campus. 6 buildings on campus. Approved or accredited by Association of Colorado Independent Schools. Member of National Association of Independent Schools, Secondary School Admission Test Board, and National Association for College Admission Counseling. Endowment: $3.1 million. Total enrollment: 305. Upper school average class size: 16. Upper school faculty-student ratio: 1:6. There are 160 required school days per year for Upper School students. Upper School students typically attend 5 days per week. The average school day consists of 6 hours and 30 minutes.

Upper School Student Profile Grade 6: 26 students (13 boys, 13 girls); Grade 7: 22 students (9 boys, 13 girls); Grade 8: 32 students (10 boys, 22 girls); Grade 9: 23 students (15 boys, 8 girls); Grade 10: 29 students (10 boys, 19 girls); Grade 11: 30 students (15 boys, 15 girls); Grade 12: 31 students (13 boys, 18 girls).

Faculty School total: 46. In upper school: 11 men, 13 women; 18 have advanced degrees.

Subjects Offered 20th century history, acting, African history, African studies, algebra, American literature, anatomy and physiology, art history, band, biology, biology-AP, botany, calculus-AP, chemistry, choir, community service, composition, computer applications, directing, drama, drawing, economics, economics-AP,

English, English literature-AP, environmental science, environmental science-AP, ethics, European history-AP, European literature, filmmaking, French, French language-AP, French literature-AP, functions, geography, geology, geometry, glass-blowing, global studies, government and politics-AP, grammar, history, Latin American history, literature, macro/microeconomics-AP, microeconomics, music, music appreciation, painting, philosophy, photography, physical education, physics, playwriting, pottery, pre-calculus, printmaking, SAT/ACT preparation, sculpture, Spanish, Spanish literature, Spanish literature-AP, speech, statistics, statistics-AP, studio art-AP, textiles, theater, trigonometry, U.S. history, U.S. history-AP, Western civilization, world geography, world history, world literature, writing, writing workshop, yearbook.

Graduation Requirements Arts and fine arts (art, music, dance, drama), athletics, college admission preparation, computer science, English, experiential education, foreign language, history, mathematics, science, social studies (includes history), speech and oral interpretations, experience-centered seminar each year, college overview course, 24 hours of community service per each year of high school.

Special Academic Programs Advanced Placement exam preparation; honors section; independent study; term-away projects; academic accommodation for the gifted; programs in general development for dyslexic students; special instructional classes for deaf students.

College Admission Counseling 39 students graduated in 2010; 37 went to college, including Colorado State University; The Colorado College; University of Denver. Other: 2 entered a postgraduate year. Mean combined SAT: 1873, mean composite ACT: 28.

Student Life Upper grades have specified standards of dress, student council, honor system. Discipline rests equally with students and faculty.

Summer Programs Enrichment, advancement, sports, art/fine arts, computer instruction programs offered; held both on and off campus; held at various field trip locations; accepts boys and girls; open to students from other schools. 90 students usually enrolled. 2011 schedule: May 26 to August 19. Application deadline: none.

Tuition and Aid Day student tuition: $17,675; 7-day tuition and room/board: $26,675. Tuition installment plan (Insured Tuition Payment Plan, monthly payment plans). Merit scholarship grants, need-based scholarship grants available. In 2010–11, 44% of upper-school students received aid; total upper-school merit-scholarship money awarded: $92,675. Total amount of financial aid awarded in 2010–11: $352,334.

Admissions Traditional secondary-level entrance grade is 9. For fall 2010, 5 students applied for upper-level admission, 5 were accepted, 4 enrolled. Otis-Lennon School Ability Test or SLEP for foreign students required. Deadline for receipt of application materials: none. Application fee required: $50. Interview required.

Athletics Interscholastic: basketball (boys, girls), cross-country running (b,g), golf (b), lacrosse (b), soccer (b,g), tennis (b,g), volleyball (g); intramural: archery (b,g), physical fitness (b,g), physical training (b,g); coed intramural: fly fishing, golf, mountaineering, outdoor education, rock climbing, skiing (cross-country), skiing (downhill), wilderness, yoga. 2 PE instructors, 8 coaches.

Computers Computers are regularly used in all academic classes. Computer network features include on-campus library services, online commercial services, Internet access, wireless campus network, Internet filtering or blocking technology. Campus intranet, student e-mail accounts, and computer access in designated common areas are available to students. Students grades are available online. The school has a published electronic and media policy.

Contact Ms. Tiffany Williamson, Director of Admission and Financial Assistance. 719-475-9747 Ext. 524. Fax: 719-475-9864. E-mail: twilliamson@css.org. Web site: www.css.org.

COLUMBIA ACADEMY

1101 West 7th Street
Columbia, Tennessee 38401
Head of School: Dr. James Thomas

General Information Coeducational day college-preparatory, arts, business, religious studies, and technology school, affiliated with Church of Christ. Grades K–12. Founded: 1978. Setting: small town. Nearest major city is Nashville. 67-acre campus. 6 buildings on campus. Approved or accredited by National Christian School Association, Southern Association of Colleges and Schools, and Tennessee Department of Education. Endowment: $1.2 million. Total enrollment: 594. Upper school average class size: 18. Upper school faculty-student ratio: 1:11. There are 175 required school days per year for Upper School students. Upper School students typically attend 5 days per week. The average school day consists of 7 hours.

Upper School Student Profile Grade 7: 41 students (19 boys, 22 girls); Grade 8: 49 students (27 boys, 22 girls); Grade 9: 41 students (19 boys, 22 girls); Grade 10: 27 students (14 boys, 13 girls); Grade 11: 57 students (18 boys, 39 girls); Grade 12: 50 students (27 boys, 23 girls). 60% of students are members of Church of Christ.

Faculty School total: 56. In upper school: 16 men, 13 women; 14 have advanced degrees.

Subjects Offered Accounting, advanced math, algebra, American history, American literature, anatomy and physiology, art, band, Bible, biology, British literature, calculus, chemistry, chorus, computer science, concert band, economics, English, English literature and composition-AP, environmental science, fine arts, geography, geometry, government/civics, grammar, health, keyboarding, math review, music,

personal finance, physical education, physics, pre-calculus, psychology, religion, Spanish, speech, U.S. history-AP, world history.

Graduation Requirements Arts and fine arts (art, music, dance, drama), computer science, economics, electives, English, foreign language, mathematics, physical education (includes health), religion (includes Bible studies and theology), science, social sciences, social studies (includes history), speech, successfully pass the state Gateway Exams in Algebra I, English II and Biology (required for students who were freshmen before 2009), four hours of approved service required for each quarter enrolled.

Special Academic Programs Advanced Placement exam preparation; honors section; independent study; study at local college for college credit.

College Admission Counseling 34 students graduated in 2010; 32 went to college, including Columbia State Community College; Freed-Hardeman University; Harding University; Lipscomb University; Tennessee Technological University; Vanderbilt University. Other: 2 went to work. Median composite ACT: 22. 31% scored over 26 on composite ACT.

Student Life Upper grades have specified standards of dress, student council, honor system. Discipline rests primarily with faculty.

Tuition and Aid Day student tuition: $5950. Tuition installment plan (monthly payment plans, individually arranged payment plans). Tuition reduction for siblings, need-based scholarship grants, paying campus jobs available. In 2010–11, 6% of upper-school students received aid. Total amount of financial aid awarded in 2010–11: $21,500.

Admissions Traditional secondary-level entrance grade is 9. For fall 2010, 19 students applied for upper-level admission, 18 were accepted, 18 enrolled. Otis-Lennon School Ability Test required. Deadline for receipt of application materials: none. Application fee required: $50. On-campus interview recommended.

Athletics Interscholastic: baseball (boys), basketball (b,g), cheering (g), football (b), golf (b,g), soccer (b,g), softball (g), strength & conditioning (b), trap and skeet (b,g), volleyball (g); intramural: flag football (g); coed interscholastic: bowling, cross-country running, marksmanship, tennis. 1 PE instructor.

Computers Computers are regularly used in accounting, computer applications, keyboarding, library, yearbook classes. Computer network features include on-campus library services, Internet access. Students grades are available online. The school has a published electronic and media policy.

Contact Mrs. Benja White, Director of Admissions. 931-490-4302. Fax: 931-380-8506. E-mail: btwhite@colacademy.com. Web site: www.columbia-academy.net.

COLUMBIA INTERNATIONAL COLLEGE OF CANADA

1003 Main Street West
Hamilton, Ontario L8S 4P3, Canada
Head of School: Mr. Ron Rambarran

General Information Coeducational boarding and day college-preparatory, general academic, arts, business, technology, science, and mathematics school. Grades 7–12. Founded: 1979. Setting: urban. Nearest major city is Toronto, Canada. Students are housed in single-sex by floor dormitories and single-sex dormitories. 20-acre campus. 3 buildings on campus. Approved or accredited by Ontario Ministry of Education and Ontario Department of Education. Language of instruction: English. Endowment: CAN$1 million. Total enrollment: 1,400. Upper school average class size: 20. Upper school faculty-student ratio: 1:20. There are 208 required school days per year for Upper School students. Upper School students typically attend 5 days per week. The average school day consists of 7 hours and 15 minutes.

Upper School Student Profile Grade 7: 44 students (22 boys, 22 girls); Grade 8: 60 students (30 boys, 30 girls); Grade 9: 80 students (40 boys, 40 girls); Grade 10: 131 students (66 boys, 65 girls); Grade 11: 222 students (116 boys, 106 girls); Grade 12: 863 students (495 boys, 368 girls). 80% of students are boarding students. 5% are province residents. 5 provinces are represented in upper school student body. 95% are international students. International students from China, Indonesia, Mexico, Nigeria, Russian Federation, and Viet Nam; 60 other countries represented in student body.

Faculty School total: 75. In upper school: 22 men, 49 women; 30 have advanced degrees.

Subjects Offered 20th century world history, accounting, advanced TOEFL/grammar, algebra, analytic geometry, anthropology, art, biology, business, calculus, calculus-AP, Canadian geography, Canadian history, career education, chemistry, Chinese, civics, computer education, computer programming, computer science, computer technologies, discrete mathematics, dramatic arts, economics, English, English composition, English literature, ESL, family studies, food and nutrition, French, French as a second language, general business, general math, general science, geography, geometry, history, intro to computers, kinesiology, lab science, language arts, law, law and the legal system, leadership, life management skills, life skills, Mandarin, math applications, mathematics, mathematics-AP, music, outdoor education, physical education, physical fitness, physics, psychology, science, society challenge and change, sociology, Spanish, visual arts.

Graduation Requirements Arts, business, English, mathematics, science, social studies (includes history), community volunteer hours, Ontario Secondary School Literacy Test.

Columbia International College of Canada

Special Academic Programs 4 Advanced Placement exams for which test preparation is offered; accelerated programs; study at local college for college credit; academic accommodation for the gifted; ESL (250 students enrolled).

College Admission Counseling 536 students graduated in 2010; all went to college, including McMaster University; University of Alberta; University of Ottawa; University of Toronto; University of Waterloo; York University.

Student Life Upper grades have uniform requirement, student council. Discipline rests primarily with faculty.

Summer Programs Remediation, advancement, ESL, sports, art/fine arts, computer instruction programs offered; session focuses on Academics, ESL, and leadership education; held both on and off campus; held at Bark Lake Outdoor Education and Leadership Centre; accepts boys and girls; open to students from other schools. 700 students usually enrolled. 2011 schedule: June 27 to August 14. Application deadline: May 31.

Tuition and Aid Day student tuition: CAN$9510–CAN$22,520; 7-day tuition and room/board: CAN$17,391–CAN$30,031. Tuition reduction for siblings, merit scholarship grants, Tuition Reduction for Canadian Citizens and Permanent Residents available.

Admissions Traditional secondary-level entrance grade is 11. For fall 2010, 981 students applied for upper-level admission, 874 were accepted, 800 enrolled. Math and English placement tests required. Deadline for receipt of application materials: none. Application fee required: CAN$200. Interview recommended.

Athletics Interscholastic: badminton (boys, girls), basketball (b), indoor soccer (b), soccer (b); intramural: aerobics (g), aquatics (b,g), badminton (b,g), ball hockey (b,g), basketball (b,g), cheering (g), fishing (b), fitness (b,g), floor hockey (b), football (b), indoor soccer (b,g), martial arts (b), outdoor activities (b,g), soccer (b,g), squash (b), strength & conditioning (b), swimming and diving (b,g), table tennis (b,g), tennis (b,g), volleyball (b,g), wallyball (b,g), weight training (b,g); coed interscholastic: badminton, indoor track & field; coed intramural: aquatics, badminton, ball hockey, canoeing/kayaking, cooperative games, cross-country running, fishing, floor hockey, golf, hiking/backpacking, ice skating, in-line skating, indoor track & field, jogging, kayaking, martial arts, outdoor activities, physical fitness, physical training, roller blading, ropes courses, running, self defense, skiing (cross-country), snowshoeing, squash, strength & conditioning, swimming and diving, table tennis, volleyball, wallyball, weight training, wilderness, wilderness survival, winter walking, yoga. 3 PE instructors, 4 coaches.

Computers Computers are regularly used in accounting, business, business applications, career education, economics, English, ESL, geography, information technology, music, SAT preparation, science classes. Computer network features include Internet access, wireless campus network. Computer access in designated common areas is available to students. Students grades are available online.

Contact Ms. Marina Rosas, Admissions Officer. 905-572-7883 Ext. 2835. Fax: 905-572-9332. E-mail: admissions02@cic-totalcare.com. Web site: www.cic-TotalCare.com.

COLUMBIA INTERNATIONAL SCHOOL

153 Matsugo
Tokorozawa, Saitama 359-0027, Japan
Head of School: Mr. Barrie McCliggott

General Information Coeducational boarding and day college-preparatory, business, bilingual studies, and technology school. Boarding grades 7–12, day grades 1–12. Founded: 1988. Setting: suburban. Nearest major city is Tokyo, Japan. Students are housed in single-sex dormitories. 2-acre campus. 2 buildings on campus. Approved or accredited by Ontario Ministry of Education, Western Association of Schools and Colleges, and state department of education. Language of instruction: English. Endowment: ¥10 million. Total enrollment: 278. Upper school average class size: 14. Upper school faculty-student ratio: 1:12.

Upper School Student Profile Grade 10: 25 students (13 boys, 12 girls); Grade 11: 23 students (10 boys, 13 girls); Grade 12: 25 students (14 boys, 11 girls). 5% of students are boarding students. 10% are international students. International students from Canada, China, Philippines, Republic of Korea, United Kingdom, and United States; 10 other countries represented in student body.

Faculty School total: 32. In upper school: 18 men, 5 women; 7 have advanced degrees; 6 reside on campus.

Subjects Offered 1½ elective credits, 20th century world history, advanced TOEFL/grammar, algebra, ancient world history, art, Asian history, biology, business, calculus, Canadian geography, Canadian history, chemistry, communications, community service, computer science, computers, economics, English, ESL, foreign language, geography, geometry, global issues, history, Internet, keyboarding, literacy, mathematics, media studies, physical education, reading, TOEFL preparation, world issues, yearbook.

Graduation Requirements 20th century history, arts, Asian history, biology, chemistry, economics, English, geography, humanities, law, mathematics, physical education (includes health), science, social sciences, Ontario Literacy Test, 40 hours of community involvement activities.

Special Academic Programs Advanced Placement exam preparation; honors section; accelerated programs; independent study; study abroad; remedial reading and/or remedial writing; remedial math; ESL (70 students enrolled).

College Admission Counseling 21 students graduated in 2009; 19 went to college, including Queen's University at Kingston; Temple University; The University of

British Columbia; University of Saskatchewan; University of Victoria; Western Michigan University. Other: 2 had other specific plans.

Student Life Upper grades have uniform requirement, student council, honor system. Discipline rests primarily with faculty.

Tuition and Aid Day student tuition: ¥1,575,000; 7-day tuition and room/board: ¥2,805,000. Tuition installment plan (individually arranged payment plans, term payment plans). Tuition reduction for siblings, merit scholarship grants available. In 2009–10, 5% of upper-school students received aid; total upper-school merit-scholarship money awarded: ¥2,735,000. Total amount of financial aid awarded in 2009–10: ¥3,360,000.

Admissions Traditional secondary-level entrance grade is 10. For fall 2009, 53 students applied for upper-level admission, 30 were accepted, 26 enrolled. Any standardized test required. Deadline for receipt of application materials: none. Application fee required: ¥25,000. On-campus interview required.

Athletics Coed Intramural: aerobics, alpine skiing, artistic gym, badminton, ball hockey, baseball, basketball, bicycling, blading, bowling, climbing, cooperative games, dance, dance team, field hockey, floor hockey, football, freestyle skiing, Frisbee, hiking/backpacking, hockey, indoor hockey, indoor soccer, juggling, kickball, life saving, mountain biking, outdoor activities, physical fitness, power lifting, rock climbing, self defense, ski jumping, skiing (downhill), snowboarding, soccer, softball, table tennis, team handball, tennis, volleyball, wall climbing, weight lifting, weight training, yoga. 2 PE instructors.

Computers Computers are regularly used in wilderness education classes. Computer network features include Internet access, wireless campus network, Internet filtering or blocking technology, repair service. Campus intranet and student e-mail accounts are available to students. The school has a published electronic and media policy.

Contact Mr. Yoshitaka Matsumura, Administrator. 81-4-2946-1911. Fax: 81-4-2946-1955. E-mail: admissions@columbia-ca.co.jp. Web site: www.columbia-ca.co.jp.

THE COLUMBUS ACADEMY

4300 Cherry Bottom Road
Gahanna, Ohio 43230
Head of School: John M. Mackenzie

General Information Coeducational day college-preparatory school. Grades PK–12. Founded: 1911. Setting: suburban. Nearest major city is Columbus. 233-acre campus. 16 buildings on campus. Approved or accredited by Independent Schools Association of the Central States, Ohio Association of Independent Schools, and Ohio Department of Education. Member of National Association of Independent Schools and Secondary School Admission Test Board. Endowment: $23.5 million. Total enrollment: 1,072. Upper school average class size: 14. Upper school faculty-student ratio: 1:8. The average school day consists of 7 hours and 5 minutes.

Upper School Student Profile Grade 9: 97 students (54 boys, 43 girls); Grade 10: 81 students (42 boys, 39 girls); Grade 11: 91 students (45 boys, 46 girls); Grade 12: 83 students (47 boys, 36 girls).

Faculty School total: 135. In upper school: 27 men, 22 women; 37 have advanced degrees.

Subjects Offered Advanced chemistry, advanced computer applications, advanced math, Advanced Placement courses, advanced studio art-AP, algebra, American history, American history-AP, American literature, analysis and differential calculus, art history, biology, biology-AP, British literature, calculus, calculus-AP, career/college preparation, ceramics, chemistry, chemistry-AP, China/Japan history, Chinese, choir, choral music, chorus, college counseling, comparative government and politics-AP, comparative political systems-AP, computer applications, computer education, computer programming-AP, computer science, computer science-AP, concert band, concert choir, creative writing, drawing and design, economics, economics-AP, English, European history, European history-AP, fine arts, French, French-AP, geology, geometry, government and politics-AP, government-AP, health education, history of China and Japan, instrumental music, Latin, Latin-AP, military history, photography, physical education, physics, physics-AP, pre-calculus, senior career experience, South African history, Spanish, Spanish language-AP, Spanish literature-AP, speech, statistics-AP, strings, theater, trigonometry, U.S. government and politics-AP, U.S. history-AP, United States government-AP, weight training, world history, world religions.

Graduation Requirements Arts and fine arts (art, music, dance, drama), English, foreign language, mathematics, science, social studies (includes history), formal speech delivered to the students and faculty of the upper school during junior year, community service requirement.

Special Academic Programs 23 Advanced Placement exams for which test preparation is offered; honors section; independent study; academic accommodation for the gifted.

College Admission Counseling 93 students graduated in 2010; all went to college, including Kenyon College; Miami University; Southern Methodist University; The Ohio State University; University of Chicago; University of Richmond. Median SAT critical reading: 640, median SAT math: 670, median SAT writing: 650, median combined SAT: 1970, median composite ACT: 27. 74% scored over 600 on SAT critical reading, 78% scored over 600 on SAT math, 78% scored over 600 on SAT writing, 78% scored over 1800 on combined SAT, 74% scored over 26 on composite ACT.

Student Life Upper grades have specified standards of dress, student council. Discipline rests equally with students and faculty.

Summer Programs Remediation, enrichment, advancement, art/fine arts, computer instruction programs offered; session focuses on academic enrichment, fine arts, fun and games; held on campus; accepts boys and girls; open to students from other schools. 400 students usually enrolled. 2011 schedule: June 15 to August 22.

Tuition and Aid Day student tuition: $19,500. Tuition installment plan (The Tuition Plan, Academic Management Services Plan, Tuition Management Systems Plan). Merit scholarship grants, need-based scholarship grants available. In 2010–11, 18% of upper-school students received aid. Total amount of financial aid awarded in 2010–11: $792,750.

Admissions Traditional secondary-level entrance grade is 9. For fall 2010, 53 students applied for upper-level admission, 33 were accepted, 23 enrolled. ISEE or SSAT required. Deadline for receipt of application materials: February 10. Application fee required: $50. On-campus interview required.

Athletics Interscholastic: baseball (boys), basketball (b,g), bowling (b,g), cross-country running (b,g), diving (b,g), field hockey (g), football (b), lacrosse (b,g), soccer (b,g), swimming and diving (b,g), tennis (b,g), track and field (b,g), volleyball (g), wrestling (b); coed intramural: bicycling. 3 PE instructors, 2 athletic trainers.

Computers Computers are regularly used in college planning, current events, economics, English, foreign language, humanities, journalism, Latin, learning cognition, library skills, mathematics, media production, multimedia, music, photography, publications, reading, research skills, SAT preparation, science, technology, theater, writing classes. Computer network features include on-campus library services, online commercial services, Internet access, wireless campus network. Campus intranet, student e-mail accounts, and computer access in designated common areas are available to students. The school has a published electronic and media policy.

Contact John Wuorinen, Director of Admissions and Financial Aid. 614-509-2220. Fax: 614-475-0396. E-mail: admissions@columbusacademy.org. Web site: www.ColumbusAcademy.org.

COLUMBUS HIGH SCHOOL

710 South Columbus Avenue
Marshfield, Wisconsin 54449-3499
Head of School: Mr. David J. Eaton

General Information Coeducational day college-preparatory school, affiliated with Roman Catholic Church. Grades 9–12. Founded: 1952. Setting: small town. Nearest major city is Wausau. 20-acre campus. 1 building on campus. Approved or accredited by North Central Association of Colleges and Schools and Wisconsin Department of Education. Endowment: $3.5 million. Total enrollment: 517. Upper school average class size: 15. Upper school faculty-student ratio: 1:10. There are 180 required school days per year for Upper School students. Upper School students typically attend 5 days per week. The average school day consists of 7 hours.

Upper School Student Profile Grade 9: 21 students (13 boys, 8 girls); Grade 10: 41 students (16 boys, 25 girls); Grade 11: 39 students (22 boys, 17 girls); Grade 12: 35 students (17 boys, 18 girls). 90% of students are Roman Catholic.

Faculty School total: 21. In upper school: 8 men, 11 women; 9 have advanced degrees.

Subjects Offered Accounting, advanced biology, advanced chemistry, advanced math, Advanced Placement courses, algebra, American government, American history, American history-AP, American literature, American literature-AP, anatomy and physiology, art, athletics, auto mechanics, band, biology, biology-AP, calculus, calculus-AP, chemistry, chemistry-AP, choral music, computer skills, consumer economics, consumer mathematics, creative writing, current history, drama, early childhood, English, English language and composition-AP, English literature and composition-AP, fitness, general math, geometry, German, government, health, history, honors algebra, honors English, honors world history, independent study, jazz band, oceanography, parent/child development, physical education, physics, political science, pre-calculus, religion, social psychology.

Special Academic Programs Advanced Placement exam preparation.

College Admission Counseling 31 students graduated in 2009; all went to college, including University of Minnesota, Twin Cities Campus; University of Wisconsin–Eau Claire; University of Wisconsin–Green Bay; University of Wisconsin–Madison; University of Wisconsin–Stevens Point. Mean composite ACT: 23.

Student Life Upper grades have specified standards of dress, student council, honor system. Discipline rests primarily with faculty. Attendance at religious services is required.

Tuition and Aid Day student tuition: $3153. Tuition installment plan (monthly payment plans, individually arranged payment plans). Merit scholarship grants, need-based scholarship grants available. In 2009–10, 25% of upper-school students received aid; total upper-school merit-scholarship money awarded: $5000. Total amount of financial aid awarded in 2009–10: $75,000.

Admissions Traditional secondary-level entrance grade is 9. For fall 2009, 6 students applied for upper-level admission, 6 were accepted, 6 enrolled. Deadline for receipt of application materials: none. Application fee required: $75. Interview recommended.

Athletics Interscholastic: baseball (boys), basketball (b,g), cheering (g), dance squad (g), dance team (g), football (b), hockey (b), softball (g), tennis (b,g), volleyball (g);

coed interscholastic: cross-country running, golf, soccer, track and field; coed intramural: skiing (downhill), strength & conditioning, weight training. 2 PE instructors, 12 coaches, 1 athletic trainer.

Computers Computer network features include Internet access. Student e-mail accounts are available to students. Students grades are available online.

Contact Mrs. Mary S. Hartl, Coordinator of Recruitment, Retention, and Alumni Relations. 715-387-2444. Fax: 715-384-4535. E-mail: hartlmary@mfldacs.net. Web site: www.marshfieldareacatholicschools.org/.

COLUMBUS SCHOOL FOR GIRLS

56 South Columbia Avenue
Columbus, Ohio 43209
Head of School: Mrs. Elizabeth M. Lee

General Information Girls' day college-preparatory, arts, and technology school. Grades PK–12. Founded: 1898. Setting: urban. 78-acre campus. 1 building on campus. Approved or accredited by Independent Schools Association of the Central States and Ohio Association of Independent Schools. Member of National Association of Independent Schools. Endowment: $18.8 million. Total enrollment: 615. Upper school average class size: 15. Upper school faculty-student ratio: 1:9. There are 180 required school days per year for Upper School students. Upper School students typically attend 5 days per week. The average school day consists of 7 hours and 30 minutes.

Upper School Student Profile Grade 9: 53 students (53 girls); Grade 10: 59 students (59 girls); Grade 11: 48 students (48 girls); Grade 12: 63 students (63 girls).

Faculty School total: 77. In upper school: 9 men, 20 women; 23 have advanced degrees.

Subjects Offered Acting, Advanced Placement courses, algebra, American history, American literature, American literature-AP, Asian history, astronomy, band, biology, biology-AP, British literature, British literature-AP, calculus, calculus-AP, chemistry, chemistry-AP, civics, college admission preparation, comparative government and politics-AP, computer science, computer science-AP, concert choir, digital photography, discrete mathematics, economics, economics and history, English, English language and composition-AP, English literature, English literature and composition-AP, English literature-AP, European history-AP, filmmaking, geography, geometry, German, German-AP, health, international relations, lab science, Latin, Latin-AP, Mandarin, modern European history-AP, music theory-AP, newspaper, painting, photography, physical education, physics, physics-AP, pre-calculus, psychology-AP, public speaking, sculpture, senior seminar, Spanish, Spanish language-AP, Spanish-AP, statistics, strings, studio art-AP, theater, trigonometry, U.S. government and politics-AP, U.S. history, visual arts, vocal ensemble, wind ensemble, world history, world literature, yearbook.

Graduation Requirements Algebra, arts and fine arts (art, music, dance, drama), biology, civics, college planning, electives, English, foreign language, geometry, health, history, lab science, mathematics, physical education (includes health), public speaking, science, technology, U.S. history, world history, Senior May program, Service Hours, Self Defense / Water Safety.

Special Academic Programs Advanced Placement exam preparation; honors section; independent study; study at local college for college credit.

College Admission Counseling 58 students graduated in 2010; all went to college, including Kenyon College; Northeastern University; The Ohio State University; University of Miami; University of Virginia; Xavier University. Mean SAT critical reading: 620, mean SAT math: 621, mean SAT writing: 580, mean combined SAT: 1879, mean composite ACT: 28.

Student Life Upper grades have uniform requirement, student council, honor system. Discipline rests primarily with faculty.

Summer Programs Remediation, enrichment, advancement, sports, art/fine arts, rigorous outdoor training, computer instruction programs offered; session focuses on academic areas; held both on and off campus; held at various sites in community and CSG's Kirk Athletic Campus; accepts boys and girls; open to students from other schools. 600 students usually enrolled. 2011 schedule: June 20 to August 12. Application deadline: none.

Tuition and Aid Day student tuition: $19,000–$19,700. Tuition installment plan (Tuition Management Systems Plan). Tuition reduction for siblings, need-based scholarship grants, tuition reduction for three or more siblings available. In 2010–11, 30% of upper-school students received aid. Total amount of financial aid awarded in 2010–11: $720,655.

Admissions Traditional secondary-level entrance grade is 9. For fall 2010, 25 students applied for upper-level admission, 22 were accepted, 17 enrolled. CTP, ISEE or school's own test required. Deadline for receipt of application materials: February 11. Application fee required: $50. On-campus interview required.

Athletics Interscholastic: aquatics, basketball, cross-country running, diving, field hockey, golf, indoor track & field, lacrosse, running, soccer, swimming and diving, tennis, track and field, volleyball, winter (indoor) track; intramural: aerobics, aerobics/dance, aerobics/Nautilus, aquatics, archery, badminton, basketball, bocce, bowling, cooperative games, diving, field hockey, fitness, fitness walking, flag football, Frisbee, golf, indoor hockey, indoor soccer, jogging, jump rope, kickball, lacrosse, life saving, martial arts, outdoor activities, paddle tennis, physical fitness, physical training, racquetball, ropes courses, running, self defense, skiing (downhill), soccer, softball, strength & conditioning, swimming and diving, synchronized swimming, table tennis, team handball, tennis, track and field, ultimate Frisbee, volleyball, walking, water polo, weight training, yoga. 4 PE instructors, 20 coaches, 1 athletic trainer.

Computers Computers are regularly used in art, English, foreign language, freshman foundations, health, history, mathematics, music, publications, science, technology, theater, yearbook classes. Computer network features include on-campus library services, online commercial services, Internet access, wireless campus network, Internet filtering or blocking technology. Campus intranet, student e-mail accounts, and computer access in designated common areas are available to students. Students grades are available online. The school has a published electronic and media policy.

Contact Jodie Moriarty, Assistant Director of Admission and Financial Aid. 614-252-0781 Ext. 295. Fax: 614-252-0571. E-mail: jmoriarty@columbusschoolforgirls.org. Web site: www.columbusschoolforgirls.org.

See Display below and Close-Up on page 760.

COMMONWEALTH PARKVILLE SCHOOL

PO Box 70177

San Juan, Puerto Rico 00936-8177

Head of School: Mr. F. Richard Marracino

General Information Coeducational day college-preparatory, arts, and technology school. Grades PS–12. Founded: 1952. Setting: urban. 1-acre campus. 1 building on campus. Approved or accredited by Middle States Association of Colleges and Schools and Puerto Rico Department of Education. Endowment: $502,005. Total enrollment: 669. Upper school average class size: 13. Upper school faculty-student ratio: 1:7. There are 180 required school days per year for Upper School students. Upper School students typically attend 5 days per week. The average school day consists of 5 hours and 8 minutes.

Upper School Student Profile Grade 9: 39 students (19 boys, 20 girls); Grade 10: 54 students (36 boys, 18 girls); Grade 11: 46 students (26 boys, 20 girls); Grade 12: 39 students (26 boys, 13 girls).

Faculty School total: 30. In upper school: 12 men, 18 women; 13 have advanced degrees.

Subjects Offered Advanced Placement courses, algebra, American history, American literature, art, art history-AP, band, biology, business mathematics, calculus, ceramics, chemistry, chemistry-AP, civics, computer science, computer technologies,

creative writing, drama, drawing, ecology, English, English language and composition-AP, English literature, ethics, European history, forensics, French, geometry, health, journalism, mathematics, modern world history, music, music appreciation, music history, painting, physical education, physics, play production, pre-calculus, sculpture, Spanish, Spanish-AP, stained glass, theater, trigonometry, world history.

Graduation Requirements Art, computer science, English, ethics, health, mathematics, music, physical education (includes health), Puerto Rican history, science, social studies (includes history), Spanish, community service hours.

Special Academic Programs 8 Advanced Placement exams for which test preparation is offered; honors section; independent study; domestic exchange program (with The Network Program Schools); study abroad; programs in English, mathematics, general development for dyslexic students; special instructional classes for students with mild learning disabilities and Attention Deficit Disorder.

College Admission Counseling 33 students graduated in 2010; all went to college, including Bentley University; New York University; Swarthmore College; Syracuse University; University of Puerto Rico, Río Piedras; Williams College. Mean SAT critical reading: 560, mean SAT math: 570, mean SAT writing: 575.

Student Life Upper grades have uniform requirement, student council, honor system. Discipline rests primarily with faculty.

Summer Programs Remediation, enrichment, ESL, sports, art/fine arts, computer instruction programs offered; session focuses on improving grades on previously taken courses; held on campus; accepts boys and girls; open to students from other schools. 90 students usually enrolled. 2011 schedule: June 1 to June 30. Application deadline: June 1.

Tuition and Aid Day student tuition: $10,204–$12,080. Tuition installment plan (monthly payment plans, individually arranged payment plans, annual and semester payment plans). Tuition reduction for siblings, merit scholarship grants, need-based scholarship grants available. In 2010–11, 16% of upper-school students received aid; total upper-school merit-scholarship money awarded: $36,720. Total amount of financial aid awarded in 2010–11: $81,560.

Admissions Traditional secondary-level entrance grade is 9. For fall 2010, 34 students applied for upper-level admission, 32 were accepted, 26 enrolled. Math and English placement tests, Stanford Achievement Test and writing sample required. Deadline for receipt of application materials: none. Application fee required: $85. Interview required.

Athletics Interscholastic: baseball (boys), basketball (b,g), cross-country running (b,g), football (b), indoor soccer (b,g), soccer (b,g), softball (g), track and field (b,g), volleyball (b,g); intramural: soccer (b,g), softball (b,g), volleyball (b,g); coed interscholastic: swimming and diving; coed intramural: badminton, basketball, cooperative games, field hockey, fitness, flag football, Frisbee, indoor soccer, jogging, outdoor activities, outdoor education, outdoor recreation, physical fitness, physical training, soccer, softball, strength & conditioning, table tennis, tennis, track and field, volleyball, walking. 3 PE instructors, 9 coaches.

Computers Computers are regularly used in all academic, music, yearbook classes. Computer network features include on-campus library services, Internet access, wireless campus network, Internet filtering or blocking technology. Campus intranet, student e-mail accounts, and computer access in designated common areas are available to students. Students grades are available online. The school has a published electronic and media policy.

Contact Mrs. Jo-Ann Aranguren, Director of Admissions. 787-765-4411 Ext. 232. Fax: 787-764-3809. E-mail: jaranguren@cpspr.org. Web site: www.cpspr.org.

COMMONWEALTH SCHOOL
151 Commonwealth Avenue
Boston, Massachusetts 02116
Head of School: Mr. William D. Wharton

General Information Coeducational day college-preparatory school. Grades 9–12. Founded: 1957. Setting: urban. 1 building on campus. Approved or accredited by Association of Independent Schools in New England, New England Association of Schools and Colleges, and Massachusetts Department of Education. Member of National Association of Independent Schools and Secondary School Admission Test Board. Endowment: $12 million. Total enrollment: 149. Upper school average class size: 12. Upper school faculty-student ratio: 1:5. Upper School students typically attend 5 days per week. The average school day consists of 6 hours and 30 minutes.

Upper School Student Profile Grade 9: 39 students (18 boys, 21 girls); Grade 10: 36 students (15 boys, 21 girls); Grade 11: 37 students (23 boys, 14 girls); Grade 12: 37 students (19 boys, 18 girls).

Faculty School total: 33. In upper school: 14 men, 19 women; 30 have advanced degrees.

Subjects Offered 20th century American writers, 20th century history, acting, advanced biology, advanced chemistry, advanced computer applications, advanced math, Advanced Placement courses, African-American literature, algebra, American history, American history-AP, American literature, analysis and differential calculus, analysis of data, analytic geometry, ancient history, ancient world history, art, art history, biology, biology-AP, calculus, calculus-AP, ceramics, chamber groups, chemistry, chemistry-AP, choral music, chorus, classics, college counseling, community service, computer programming, computer science, constitutional law, creative writing, current events, dance, drama, drawing, economics, economics-AP, English, English literature, English-AP, environmental science, environmental studies, ethics, European history, European history-AP, expository writing, film series, film studies, fine arts, foreign language, French, French language-AP, French literature-AP, French studies, French-AP, geometry, Greek, health and safety, Hispanic literature, history of the Americas, history-AP, honors algebra, honors English, honors geometry, honors U.S. history, Japanese history, jazz, jazz band, jazz ensemble, jazz theory, Latin, Latin American history, Latin-AP, mathematics, mathematics-AP, medieval history, medieval/Renaissance history, modern European history-AP, music, music theory, music theory-AP, orchestra, organic chemistry, painting, performing arts, philosophy, photography, physical education, physics, physics-AP, poetry, pottery, pre-calculus, printmaking, probability and statistics, psychology, science, short story, society, politics and law, Spanish, Spanish language-AP, Spanish literature, Spanish literature-AP, Spanish-AP, studio art, tap dance, theater, U.S. history-AP, visual and performing arts, visual arts, vocal music, voice, voice ensemble, writing.

Graduation Requirements Algebra, ancient history, art, biology, calculus, chemistry, English, ethics, foreign language, geometry, medieval history, physical education (includes health), physics, U.S. history, City of Boston course, completion of a one- to three-week project each year, with report, Health and Community. Community service is required.

Special Academic Programs Advanced Placement exam preparation; honors section; independent study; study abroad; academic accommodation for the gifted, the musically talented, and the artistically talented.

College Admission Counseling 37 students graduated in 2010; 36 went to college, including Amherst College; Brown University; Haverford College; University of Chicago; Wesleyan University. Other: 1 had other specific plans. Median SAT critical reading: 760, median SAT math: 700, median SAT writing: 730.

Student Life Discipline rests primarily with faculty.

Tuition and Aid Day student tuition: $31,685. Tuition installment plan (Key Tuition Payment Plan). Need-based scholarship grants, need-based loans available. In 2010–11, 36% of upper-school students received aid. Total amount of financial aid awarded in 2010–11: $1,100,000.

Admissions Traditional secondary-level entrance grade is 9. For fall 2010, 184 students applied for upper-level admission, 77 were accepted, 42 enrolled. ISEE or SSAT required. Deadline for receipt of application materials: February 1. Application fee required: $50. On-campus interview required.

Athletics Interscholastic: basketball (boys, girls), independent competitive sports (b,g), soccer (b,g); coed interscholastic: baseball, fencing, squash, ultimate Frisbee;

coed intramural: aerobics/Nautilus, ballet, cross-country running, dance, fencing, fitness, martial arts, sailing, squash, tai chi, yoga. 12 coaches.

Computers Computers are regularly used in computer applications, photography, programming classes. Computer network features include on-campus library services, Internet access, wireless campus network, Internet filtering or blocking technology. Campus intranet, student e-mail accounts, and computer access in designated common areas are available to students. The school has a published electronic and media policy.

Contact Ms. Robyn Gibson, Assistant Director of Admissions. 617-266-7525. Fax: 617-266-5769. E-mail: admissions@commschool.org. Web site: www.commschool.org.

COMMUNITY CHRISTIAN ACADEMY
11875 Taylor Mill Road
Independence, Kentucky 41051
Head of School: Tara Montez Bates

General Information Coeducational day college-preparatory and religious studies school, affiliated with Pentecostal Church. Grades PS–12. Founded: 1983. Setting: rural. Nearest major city is Cincinnati, OH. 107-acre campus. 2 buildings on campus. Approved or accredited by International Christian Accrediting Association and Kentucky Department of Education. Total enrollment: 219. Upper school average class size: 15. Upper school faculty-student ratio: 1:15. There are 175 required school days per year for Upper School students. Upper School students typically attend 5 days per week. The average school day consists of 6 hours.

Upper School Student Profile Grade 9: 13 students (9 boys, 4 girls); Grade 10: 13 students (6 boys, 7 girls); Grade 11: 16 students (11 boys, 5 girls); Grade 12: 12 students (7 boys, 5 girls). 50% of students are Pentecostal.

Faculty School total: 14. In upper school: 1 man, 4 women; 2 have advanced degrees.

Subjects Offered Advanced math, algebra, American history, art appreciation, Bible, biology, business skills, calculus, chemistry, choral music, computer applications, cultural geography, English, geography, health, integrated science, life skills, literature, pre-algebra, pre-calculus, Spanish.

Graduation Requirements Bible, electives, English, foreign language, mathematics, physical education (includes health), science, social studies (includes history), statistics, visual and performing arts.

College Admission Counseling 10 students graduated in 2010; 7 went to college, including Cincinnati State Technical and Community College; Northern Kentucky University; University of Cincinnati. Other: 3 went to work. Mean composite ACT: 20.

Student Life Upper grades have uniform requirement, student council, honor system. Discipline rests primarily with faculty. Attendance at religious services is required.

Tuition and Aid Day student tuition: $3249. Guaranteed tuition plan. Tuition installment plan (The Tuition Plan, monthly payment plans). Financial aid available to upper-school students. In 2010–11, 5% of upper-school students received aid. Total amount of financial aid awarded in 2010–11: $9000.

Admissions Traditional secondary-level entrance grade is 9. For fall 2010, 14 students applied for upper-level admission, 12 were accepted, 12 enrolled. Admissions testing required. Deadline for receipt of application materials: none. Application fee required: $50. Interview required.

Athletics Interscholastic: basketball (boys, girls), cheering (g), golf (b), volleyball (g); coed interscholastic: archery. 1 PE instructor, 5 coaches.

Computers Computers are regularly used in foreign language classes. Computer network features include Internet access.

Contact Edie Carkeek, Secretary. 859-356-7990 Ext. 112. Fax: 859-356-7991. E-mail: edie.carkeek@ccaky.org. Web site: www.ccaky.org.

COMMUNITY HEBREW ACADEMY
200 Wilmington Avenue
Toronto, Ontario M3H 5J8, Canada
Head of School: Mr. Paul Shaviv

General Information Coeducational day college-preparatory, general academic, arts, religious studies, and technology school, affiliated with Jewish faith. Grades 9–12. Founded: 1964. Setting: urban. 6-acre campus. 2 buildings on campus. Approved or accredited by Ontario Department of Education. Language of instruction: English. Endowment: CAN$250,000. Total enrollment: 1,400. Upper school average class size: 22. Upper school faculty-student ratio: 1:8. There are 185 required school days per year for Upper School students. Upper School students typically attend 5 days per week. The average school day consists of 8 hours.

Upper School Student Profile 100% of students are Jewish.

Faculty School total: 195. In upper school: 85 men, 110 women; 40 have advanced degrees.

Subjects Offered Accounting, American history, art, athletics, biology, business, calculus, Canadian history, Canadian law, careers, chemistry, communications, computer information systems, computer technologies, creative writing, discrete mathematics, drama, economics, English, entrepreneurship, exercise science, first aid, French, general math, geography, health education, Hebrew, Hebrew scripture, Holocaust, information technology, interdisciplinary studies, Jewish history, math-

Community Hebrew Academy

ematics, media studies, modern Western civilization, peer counseling, personal fitness, physical education, physics, Rabbinic literature, remedial study skills, social studies, Spanish, Talmud.

Graduation Requirements English, 72 hours of community service over 4 years.

Special Academic Programs ESL (2 students enrolled).

College Admission Counseling 300 students graduated in 2010; 270 went to college, including McGill University; Queen's University at Kingston; The University of Western Ontario; University of Guelph; University of Toronto; York University. Other: 30 had other specific plans.

Student Life Upper grades have specified standards of dress, student council. Discipline rests primarily with faculty.

Tuition and Aid Day student tuition: CAN$20,100. Tuition installment plan (monthly payment plans, individually arranged payment plans, individual payment plans). Need-based scholarship grants, need-based loans available. In 2010–11, 25% of upper-school students received aid. Total amount of financial aid awarded in 2010–11: CAN$2,000,000.

Admissions Traditional secondary-level entrance grade is 9. For fall 2010, 400 students applied for upper-level admission, 357 enrolled. Math and English placement tests and writing sample required. Deadline for receipt of application materials: January 14. Application fee required: CAN$150. On-campus interview required.

Athletics Interscholastic: baseball (boys), basketball (b,g), field hockey (g), flag football (b), ice hockey (b,g), rugby (b), soccer (b,g), softball (b), tennis (b,g), volleyball (b,g); coed interscholastic: alpine skiing, cross-country running, curling, golf, skiing (cross-country), skiing (downhill), snowboarding. 10 PE instructors.

Computers Computers are regularly used in business applications, information technology, media classes. Computer resources include on-campus library services, Internet access. Computer access in designated common areas is available to students. Students grades are available online.

Contact Ms. Jill Garazi, Admissions Coordinator. 905-787-8772 Ext. 2509. Fax: 905-787-8773. E-mail: jgarazi@tanenbaumchat.org. Web site: www.tanenbaumchat.org.

COMMUNITY HIGH SCHOOL
Teaneck, New Jersey
See Special Needs Schools section.

THE COMMUNITY SCHOOL
PO Box 2118
Sun Valley, Idaho 83353
Head of School: Andy Jones-Wilkins

General Information Coeducational day college-preparatory, arts, and technology school. Grades K–12. Founded: 1973. Setting: small town. Nearest major city is Boise. 33-acre campus. 4 buildings on campus. Approved or accredited by Northwest Association of Schools and Colleges, Pacific Northwest Association of Independent Schools, and Idaho Department of Education. Member of National Association of Independent Schools, Secondary School Admission Test Board, and Council for the Advancement and Support of Education. Endowment: $3.1 million. Total enrollment: 287. Upper school average class size: 15. Upper school faculty-student ratio: 1:8. The average school day consists of 6 hours and 30 minutes.

Upper School Student Profile Grade 9: 26 students (13 boys, 13 girls); Grade 10: 26 students (12 boys, 14 girls); Grade 11: 25 students (11 boys, 14 girls); Grade 12: 25 students (11 boys, 14 girls).

Faculty School total: 46. In upper school: 11 men, 6 women; 13 have advanced degrees.

Subjects Offered Algebra, American history, American literature, art, biology, calculus, ceramics, chemistry, computer graphics, computer math, computer programming, computer science, constitutional law, creative writing, drama, earth science, ecology, economics, English, English literature, environmental science, ethics, European history, expository writing, fine arts, forensics, French, geography, geology, geometry, government/civics, history, human development, information technology, mathematics, music, musical productions, philosophy, photography, physical education, physics, science, social studies, Spanish, speech, statistics, theater, trigonometry, world history, world literature, writing.

Graduation Requirements Arts and fine arts (art, music, dance, drama), computer science, English, foreign language, mathematics, outdoor education, physical education (includes health), science, social studies (includes history), speech, senior project presentation, senior speech, outdoor program.

Special Academic Programs Advanced Placement exam preparation; honors section; independent study; term-away projects; academic accommodation for the gifted; programs in English, mathematics, general development for dyslexic students.

College Admission Counseling 27 students graduated in 2009; 26 went to college, including Dartmouth College; Middlebury College; The Colorado College; Tufts University; University of Colorado at Boulder. Other: 1 had other specific plans. Mean SAT critical reading: 580, mean SAT math: 568, mean SAT writing: 596.

Student Life Upper grades have specified standards of dress, student council, honor system. Discipline rests primarily with faculty.

Tuition and Aid Day student tuition: $22,890. Tuition installment plan (individually arranged payment plans). Merit scholarship grants, need-based scholarship grants

available. In 2009–10, 29% of upper-school students received aid; total upper-school merit-scholarship money awarded: $10,700. Total amount of financial aid awarded in 2009–10: $470,550.

Admissions Traditional secondary-level entrance grade is 9. For fall 2009, 14 students applied for upper-level admission, 11 were accepted, 9 enrolled. SSAT and writing sample required. Deadline for receipt of application materials: February 22. Application fee required: $35. Interview required.

Athletics Interscholastic: basketball (boys, girls), golf (b,g), ice hockey (b,g), ice skating (b,g), physical fitness (b,g), rock climbing (b,g), soccer (b,g), swimming and diving (g), tennis (b,g), volleyball (g); coed interscholastic: alpine skiing, backpacking, bicycling, canoeing/kayaking, climbing, cooperative games, cross-country running, equestrian sports, figure skating, fitness, flag football, freestyle skiing, hiking/backpacking, independent competitive sports, kayaking, mountain biking, mountaineering, nordic skiing, outdoor adventure, physical fitness, rafting, rock climbing, ropes courses, skiing (cross-country), skiing (downhill), snowboarding, snowshoeing, soccer, squash, telemark skiing, tennis. 2 PE instructors, 9 coaches.

Computers Computers are regularly used in English, foreign language, independent study, science, yearbook classes. Computer network features include on-campus library services, online commercial services, Internet access, wireless campus network. Student e-mail accounts and computer access in designated common areas are available to students. The school has a published electronic and media policy.

Contact Katie Robins, Director of Admission. 208-622-3960 Ext. 117. Fax: 208-622-3962. E-mail: krobins@communityschool.org. Web site: www.communityschool.org.

COMMUNITY SCHOOL
1164 Bunker Hilll Road
South Tamworth, New Hampshire 03883-4181
Head of School: Jenny Rowe

General Information Coeducational day college-preparatory, arts, and environmental studies school. Grades 7–12. Founded: 1988. Setting: rural. Nearest major city is Conway. 310-acre campus. 2 buildings on campus. Approved or accredited by Association of Independent Schools in New England, New England Association of Schools and Colleges, and New Hampshire Department of Education. Endowment: $60,000. Total enrollment: 26. Upper school average class size: 6. Upper school faculty-student ratio: 1:6. There are 180 required school days per year for Upper School students. Upper School students typically attend 5 days per week. The average school day consists of 7 hours.

Upper School Student Profile Grade 7: 3 students (3 boys); Grade 9: 4 students (2 boys, 2 girls); Grade 10: 4 students (1 boy, 3 girls); Grade 11: 7 students (4 boys, 3 girls); Grade 12: 5 students (2 boys, 3 girls).

Faculty School total: 10. In upper school: 2 men, 8 women; 7 have advanced degrees.

Subjects Offered 20th century history, 20th century world history, advanced math, agriculture, agroecology, algebra, American culture, American democracy, American studies, ancient world history, applied skills, art and culture, art appreciation, biology, botany, calculus, career/college preparation, cell biology, chemistry, civics, civil rights, college planning, college writing, community garden, community service, composition, computer literacy, conflict resolution, consumer mathematics, CPR, creative thinking, creative writing, critical thinking, decision making skills, drama performance, earth science, ecology, environmental systems, English composition, English literature, environmental studies, ethics and responsibility, field ecology, first aid, food and nutrition, forestry, French, gardening, geography, geometry, global issues, high adventure outdoor program, human anatomy, human biology, independent study, integrated science, interdisciplinary studies, Internet research, land management, language arts, leadership, literature, math applications, methods of research, modern European history, multicultural literature, music appreciation, natural resources management, navigation, novels, oceanography, organic gardening, philosophy, poetry, pre-algebra, pre-calculus, probability and statistics, reading/study skills, research skills, senior project, sex education, short story, social studies, Spanish, trigonometry, U.S. government, U.S. history, U.S. literature, wilderness education, wilderness experience, woodworking, world cultures, world geography, writing, writing workshop.

Graduation Requirements Art, computer education, English, foreign language, home economics, mathematics, physical education (includes health), science, senior project, social studies (includes history), technology, vocational arts, senior project, community service.

Special Academic Programs Independent study; term-away projects; study abroad; academic accommodation for the gifted and the artistically talented; remedial reading and/or remedial writing; remedial math.

College Admission Counseling 7 students graduated in 2009; 6 went to college, including Beloit College; University of Maine. Other: 1 went to work.

Student Life Upper grades have student council, honor system. Discipline rests equally with students and faculty.

Tuition and Aid Day student tuition: $12,900. Tuition installment plan (monthly payment plans, individually arranged payment plans). Tuition reduction for siblings, need-based scholarship grants, paying campus jobs available. In 2009–10, 65% of upper-school students received aid. Total amount of financial aid awarded in 2009–10: $108,000.

Admissions Traditional secondary-level entrance grade is 9. For fall 2009, 13 students applied for upper-level admission, 12 were accepted, 11 enrolled. Deadline for receipt of application materials: none. Application fee required: $25. Interview required.

Athletics Coed Interscholastic: aerobics, alpine skiing, aquatics, backpacking, cross-country running, fitness walking, hiking/backpacking, mountaineering, outdoor activities, outdoor education, outdoor skills, skiing (cross-country), skiing (downhill), snowboarding, snowshoeing, soccer, strength & conditioning, swimming and diving, tai chi, wilderness survival, winter walking.

Computers Computers are regularly used in accounting classes. Computer network features include on-campus library services, Internet access, wireless campus network. The school has a published electronic and media policy.

Contact Ms. Joan Hodges, Admissions. 603-323-7000. Fax: 603-323-8240. E-mail: admissions@communityschoolnh.org. Web site: www.communityschoolnh.org.

THE COMMUNITY SCHOOL OF NAPLES
13275 Livingston Road
Naples, Florida 34109
Head of School: Mr. John E. Zeller Jr.

General Information Coeducational day college-preparatory and arts school. Grades PK–12. Founded: 1982. Setting: suburban. Nearest major city is Miami. 110-acre campus. 3 buildings on campus. Approved or accredited by Florida Council of Independent Schools and Florida Department of Education. Member of National Association of Independent Schools and Secondary School Admission Test Board. Endowment: $9.8 million. Total enrollment: 720. Upper school average class size: 12. Upper school faculty-student ratio: 1:7. There are 172 required school days per year for Upper School students. Upper School students typically attend 5 days per week. The average school day consists of 5 hours and 20 minutes.

Upper School Student Profile Grade 9: 58 students (37 boys, 21 girls); Grade 10: 63 students (23 boys, 40 girls); Grade 11: 73 students (36 boys, 37 girls); Grade 12: 76 students (36 boys, 40 girls).

Faculty School total: 102. In upper school: 19 men, 29 women; 23 have advanced degrees.

Subjects Offered Algebra, American government, American history, American history-AP, American literature, American literature-AP, anatomy and physiology, art, band, biology, biology-AP, calculus, calculus-AP, chemistry, chemistry-AP, chorus, clayworking, comparative government and politics-AP, computer programming, computer science, computer science-AP, creative writing, digital photography, dramatic arts, drawing, economics, economics-AP, electives, English, English language and composition-AP, English language-AP, English literature and composition-AP, English literature-AP, English-AP, English/composition-AP, environmental science-AP, European history-AP, fine arts, French, French language-AP, French literature-AP, French-AP, geometry, government and politics-AP, government-AP, government/civics-AP, graphic design, health, history, history-AP, honors algebra, honors English, honors geometry, honors U.S. history, honors world history, Italian, jazz band, Latin, marine science, mathematics, mathematics-AP, music, music theory-AP, painting, performing arts, personal fitness, photography, physical education, physics, physics-AP, pre-calculus, psychology, science, Spanish, Spanish language-AP, Spanish literature-AP, Spanish-AP, statistics-AP, strings, studio art-AP, theater, U.S. government and politics-AP, U.S. history-AP, vocal music, Web site design, world history, world literature.

Graduation Requirements Arts and fine arts (art, music, dance, drama), computer science, electives, English, foreign language, history, mathematics, physical education (includes health), science, community service-20 per year.

Special Academic Programs 23 Advanced Placement exams for which test preparation is offered; honors section; independent study; study at local college for college credit; study abroad.

College Admission Counseling 54 students graduated in 2010; 53 went to college, including Florida Atlantic University; Florida State University; The University of Tampa; University of Florida; University of Miami; University of Pennsylvania. Other: 1 had other specific plans. Mean SAT critical reading: 587, mean SAT math: 632, mean SAT writing: 600, mean composite ACT: 27.

Student Life Upper grades have specified standards of dress, student council, honor system. Discipline rests equally with students and faculty.

Summer Programs Remediation, enrichment, ESL, sports, art/fine arts programs offered; session focuses on Mathematics, English, and SAT preparation. Sports; held on campus; accepts boys and girls; open to students from other schools. 150 students usually enrolled. 2011 schedule: June 13 to August 9. Application deadline: April 15.

Tuition and Aid Day student tuition: $21,700. Tuition installment plan (Insured Tuition Payment Plan, monthly payment plans, individually arranged payment plans). Merit scholarship grants, need-based scholarship grants available. In 2010–11, 20% of upper-school students received aid; total upper-school merit-scholarship money awarded: $50,000. Total amount of financial aid awarded in 2010–11: $755,900.

Admissions Traditional secondary-level entrance grade is 9. For fall 2010, 72 students applied for upper-level admission, 53 were accepted, 43 enrolled. School's own exam or SSAT required. Deadline for receipt of application materials: February 1. Application fee required: $100. On-campus interview required.

Athletics Interscholastic: baseball (boys), basketball (b,g), cheering (g), cross-country running (b,g), diving (b,g), football (b), golf (b,g), lacrosse (b), soccer (b,g), softball (g), swimming and diving (b,g), tennis (b,g), track and field (b,g), volleyball

(g), winter soccer (b,g); intramural: cheering (g), cross-country running (g), football (b), lacrosse (g); coed intramural: indoor soccer, rock climbing, sailing, weight training. 5 PE instructors, 42 coaches, 1 athletic trainer.

Computers Computers are regularly used in art, computer applications, creative writing, design, desktop publishing, digital applications, English, foreign language, history, mathematics, music, science, Web site design, writing, writing, yearbook classes. Computer network features include on-campus library services, Internet access, wireless campus network, Internet filtering or blocking technology. Campus intranet, student e-mail accounts, and computer access in designated common areas are available to students. The school has a published electronic and media policy.

Contact Mr. Scott Vasey, Director of Admissions. 239-597-7575 Ext. 205. Fax: 239-598-2973. E-mail: Svasey@communityschoolnaples.org. Web site: www.communityschoolnaples.org.

THE CONCEPT SCHOOL
1120 E. Street Rd
PO Box 54
Westtown, Pennsylvania 19395
Head of School: Mrs. Lauren Vangieri

General Information Coeducational day college-preparatory, general academic, arts, and technology school. Grades 6–12. Founded: 1972. Setting: suburban. Nearest major city is Philadelphia. 10-acre campus. 1 building on campus. Approved or accredited by Pennsylvania Department of Education. Endowment: $75,000. Total enrollment: 33. Upper school average class size: 8. Upper school faculty-student ratio: 1:8. There are 180 required school days per year for Upper School students. Upper School students typically attend 5 days per week. The average school day consists of 6 hours and 15 minutes.

Upper School Student Profile Grade 9: 7 students (6 boys, 1 girl); Grade 10: 5 students (5 boys); Grade 11: 3 students (3 boys); Grade 12: 10 students (4 boys, 6 girls).

Faculty School total: 14. In upper school: 4 men, 4 women; 6 have advanced degrees.

Subjects Offered 20th century world history, acting, advanced computer applications, algebra, American history, art, art history, biology, career and personal planning, chemistry, computer graphics, consumer mathematics, criminal justice, cultural arts, earth science, economics, English, environmental science, film, film appreciation, fine arts, foreign language, general science, geometry, government, government/civics, health, history, human development, independent study, keyboarding, lab science, language arts, Latin, mathematics, physical education, physics, physiology, pre-algebra, pre-calculus, psychology, science, Shakespeare, social sciences, social studies, trigonometry, U.S. government, visual arts.

Graduation Requirements Arts and fine arts (art, music, dance, drama), computer science, English, mathematics, physical education (includes health), science, social sciences, social studies (includes history).

Special Academic Programs Accelerated programs; independent study; study at local college for college credit; academic accommodation for the gifted and the artistically talented; remedial reading and/or remedial writing; remedial math; programs in English, mathematics, general development for dyslexic students; special instructional classes for deaf students, blind students, students with learning differences, Attention Deficit Disorder, Asperger's Syndrome, school phobia, dyslexia, Attention Deficit Hyperactivity Disorder, and Non-verbal Learning Disorder.

College Admission Counseling 10 students graduated in 2010; 9 went to college, including Albright College; Drexel University; Immaculata University; Neumann University; Pennsylvania State University System; West Chester University of Pennsylvania. Other: 1 went to work. Mean SAT critical reading: 575, mean SAT math: 580, mean SAT writing: 585.

Student Life Upper grades have specified standards of dress, honor system. Discipline rests primarily with faculty.

Tuition and Aid Day student tuition: $17,400. Tuition installment plan (monthly payment plans). Tuition reduction for siblings available.

Admissions Traditional secondary-level entrance grade is 9. For fall 2010, 15 students applied for upper-level admission, 6 were accepted, 6 enrolled. Math and English placement tests and WISC/Woodcock-Johnson required. Deadline for receipt of application materials: none. Application fee required: $50. On-campus interview required.

Athletics Coed Intramural: aerobics, basketball, bowling, ice skating, in-line skating, physical fitness, physical training, roller skating, skiing (downhill), snowboarding, yoga. 1 PE instructor.

Computers Computers are regularly used in all academic classes. Computer network features include on-campus library services, Internet access, wireless campus network, Internet filtering or blocking technology. Campus intranet is available to students. The school has a published electronic and media policy.

Contact Mrs. Carol McAdam, School Secretary. 610-399-1135. Fax: 610-399-0767. E-mail: cmcadam@theconceptschool.org. Web site: www.theconceptschool.org.

CONCORD ACADEMY

166 Main Street
Concord, Massachusetts 01742
Head of School: Rick Hardy

General Information Coeducational boarding and day college-preparatory and arts school. Grades 9–12. Founded: 1922. Setting: suburban. Nearest major city is Boston. Students are housed in single-sex dormitories. 39-acre campus. 29 buildings on campus. Approved or accredited by New England Association of Schools and Colleges, The Association of Boarding Schools, and Massachusetts Department of Education. Member of National Association of Independent Schools and Secondary School Admission Test Board. Endowment: $44.4 million. Total enrollment: 365. Upper school average class size: 12. Upper school faculty-student ratio: 1:6. Upper School students typically attend 5 days per week. The average school day consists of 6 hours and 30 minutes.

Upper School Student Profile Grade 9: 77 students (34 boys, 43 girls); Grade 10: 95 students (46 boys, 49 girls); Grade 11: 96 students (45 boys, 51 girls); Grade 12: 97 students (53 boys, 44 girls). 41% of students are boarding students. 74% are state residents. 20 states are represented in upper school student body. 9% are international students. International students from Canada, China, Indonesia, Republic of Korea, Taiwan, and Thailand; 3 other countries represented in student body.

Faculty School total: 63. In upper school: 29 men, 34 women; 43 have advanced degrees; 26 reside on campus.

Subjects Offered 20th century American writers, 3-dimensional art, advanced chemistry, advanced math, African history, African-American literature, algebra, American history, American literature, ancient history, ancient world history, anthropology, applied music, architecture, art, art history, Asian history, astronomy, astrophysics, batik, Bible as literature, biochemistry, biology, bookmaking, British literature, calculus, ceramics, chamber groups, chemistry, Chinese history, choreography, chorus, classical civilization, classical Greek literature, classical language, computer multimedia, computer programming, computer science, computer studies, creative writing, critical studies in film, dance, dance performance, digital imaging, directing, drama, drama performance, drawing, earth science, economics, English, English literature, environmental science, environmental studies, European history, experimental science, expository writing, fiber arts, fiction, film, film history, filmmaking, forensics, French, freshman seminar, geology, geometry, German, German literature, guitar, health and wellness, history, history of China and Japan, history of music, Holocaust, HTML design, improvisation, instruments, introduction to digital multitrack recording techniques, Irish literature, Islamic history, jazz ensemble, journalism, Latin, Latin American history, Latin American literature, life management skills, literature seminar, math analysis, mathematics, medieval/Renaissance history, Middle East, Middle Eastern history, model United Nations, modern dance, modern European history, modern languages, music, music composition, music history, music technology, music theory, musical productions, neuroscience, newspaper, novels, oceanography, orchestra, painting, performing arts, philosophy, photography, physical education, physics, piano, play/screen writing, poetry, post-calculus, pre-calculus, printmaking, probability and statistics, Roman civilization, science, science fiction, sculpture, senior project, sex education, Shakespeare, Spanish, Spanish literature, statistics, student publications, studio art, technical theater, theater, theater design and production, theater history, trigonometry, U.S. history, urban studies, visual arts, voice, Web site design, wind ensemble, writing.

Graduation Requirements Computer science, English, foreign language, history, mathematics, performing arts, physical education (includes health), science, visual arts.

Special Academic Programs Honors section; independent study; term-away projects; study abroad; academic accommodation for the gifted, the musically talented, and the artistically talented.

College Admission Counseling 85 students graduated in 2010; 80 went to college, including Brown University; Carleton College; Columbia College; New York University; The George Washington University; Tufts University. Mean SAT critical reading: 685, mean SAT math: 674, mean SAT writing: 697, mean combined SAT: 2057.

Student Life Upper grades have student council, honor system. Discipline rests equally with students and faculty.

Tuition and Aid Day student tuition: $37,350; 7-day tuition and room/board: $46,200. Guaranteed tuition plan. Tuition installment plan (Key Tuition Payment Plan, monthly payment plans). Need-based scholarship grants, need-based loans available. In 2010–11, 24% of upper-school students received aid. Total amount of financial aid awarded in 2010–11: $3,120,000.

Admissions Traditional secondary-level entrance grade is 9. For fall 2010, 707 students applied for upper-level admission, 216 were accepted, 89 enrolled. ISEE, SSAT or TOEFL required. Deadline for receipt of application materials: January 15. Application fee required: $45. Interview recommended.

Athletics Interscholastic: baseball (boys), basketball (b,g), cross-country running (b,g), field hockey (g), lacrosse (g), skiing (downhill) (b,g), soccer (b,g), squash (g), tennis (b,g), volleyball (g), wrestling (b); intramural: lacrosse (b), softball (g), squash (b); coed interscholastic: alpine skiing, golf, ultimate Frisbee; coed intramural: aerobics, aerobics/dance, ballet, canoeing/kayaking, combined training, cross-country running, dance, fencing, fitness, jogging, martial arts, modern dance, outdoor activities, physical fitness, physical training, sailing, self defense, skiing (downhill),

strength & conditioning, track and field, ultimate Frisbee, weight training, yoga. 8 PE instructors, 35 coaches, 2 athletic trainers.

Computers Computers are regularly used in English, foreign language, history, library skills, mathematics, music, newspaper, science, social studies, technology, video film production, Web site design, yearbook classes. Computer network features include on-campus library services, online commercial services, Internet access, wireless campus network, Internet filtering or blocking technology. Campus intranet and student e-mail accounts are available to students. The school has a published electronic and media policy.

Contact Marie D. Myers, Director of Admissions. 978-402-2250. Fax: 978-402-2345. E-mail: admissions@concordacademy.org. Web site: www.concordacademy.org.

CONCORDIA HIGH SCHOOL

7128 Ada Boulevard
Edmonton, Alberta T5B 4E4, Canada
Head of School: Mr. David Eifert

General Information Coeducational boarding and day college-preparatory, arts, and religious studies school, affiliated with Lutheran Church. Grades 9–12. Founded: 1921. Setting: urban. Students are housed in single-sex dormitories. 12-acre campus. 1 building on campus. Approved or accredited by Association of Independent Schools and Colleges of Alberta, Canadian Association of Independent Schools, and Alberta Department of Education. Languages of instruction: English and French. Total enrollment: 137. Upper school average class size: 16. Upper school faculty-student ratio: 1:10.

Upper School Student Profile 24% of students are boarding students. International students from Brazil, Hong Kong, Mexico, Republic of Korea, Thailand, and United States; 6 other countries represented in student body. 12% of students are Lutheran.

Faculty School total: 15. In upper school: 5 men, 10 women; 7 have advanced degrees.

Subjects Offered Art, athletics, biology, career and personal planning, chemistry, choir, Christian education, drama, drama performance, English, French, information processing, mathematics, media arts, physical education, physics, religious studies, service learning/internship, social studies.

Graduation Requirements Advanced chemistry, advanced math, arts and fine arts (art, music, dance, drama), Christian education, French, language, religious studies.

Special Academic Programs Study at local college for college credit.

College Admission Counseling 42 students graduated in 2010; 39 went to college. Other: 3 went to work.

Student Life Upper grades have uniform requirement, student council. Discipline rests primarily with faculty. Attendance at religious services is required.

Admissions TOEFL or SLEP required. Deadline for receipt of application materials: none. Application fee required: CAN$150. Interview required.

Athletics Interscholastic: basketball (boys, girls); intramural: basketball (b,g), soccer (b,g), volleyball (b,g); coed interscholastic: badminton, fitness, lacrosse; coed intramural: alpine skiing, canoeing/kayaking, cheering, cross-country running, curling, golf, outdoor activities, physical fitness.

Computers Computers are regularly used in media arts classes.

Contact Mr. Keith Kruse, Dean of Operations. 780-479-9392. Fax: 780-479-5050. E-mail: keith.kruse@concordia.ab.ca. Web site: www.concordiahighschool.com.

CONCORDIA LUTHERAN HIGH SCHOOL

1601 Saint Joe River Drive
Fort Wayne, Indiana 46805
Head of School: Mr. Terry Breininger

General Information Coeducational day college-preparatory and religious studies school, affiliated with Lutheran Church–Missouri Synod. Grades 9–12. Founded: 1935. Setting: urban. Nearest major city is Indianapolis. 3 buildings on campus. Approved or accredited by National Lutheran School Accreditation, North Central Association of Colleges and Schools, and Indiana Department of Education. Total enrollment: 645. Upper school average class size: 22. Upper school faculty-student ratio: 1:16. There are 180 required school days per year for Upper School students. Upper School students typically attend 5 days per week. The average school day consists of 7 hours and 5 minutes.

Upper School Student Profile Grade 9: 166 students (88 boys, 78 girls); Grade 10: 176 students (86 boys, 90 girls); Grade 11: 157 students (74 boys, 83 girls); Grade 12: 146 students (64 boys, 82 girls). 80% of students are Lutheran Church–Missouri Synod.

Faculty School total: 41. In upper school: 22 men, 19 women; 23 have advanced degrees.

Subjects Offered 3-dimensional art, Advanced Placement courses, algebra, American history, American literature, art, band, Bible studies, biology, biology-AP, broadcasting, business, calculus, calculus-AP, ceramics, chemistry, chemistry-AP, choir, computer science, creative writing, discrete mathematics, driver education, earth science, economics, English, English literature, English literature and composition-AP, entrepreneurship, environmental science, ethics, expository writing, family and consumer science, food and nutrition, French, geography, geometry, German, government/civics, grammar, health, health and safety, history, home economics, honors algebra, honors English, honors geometry, journalism, JROTC, JROTC or LEAD (Leadership Education and Development), keyboarding, Latin, marching band, mathematics, media arts, media communications, music, newspaper, painting, physical education, physics, physics-AP, psychology, religion, science, social sciences, social studies, sociology, Spanish, speech, statistics-AP, theater, theater arts, theology, typing, U.S. government, U.S. history-AP, video film production, weight training, world history, world literature, writing, yearbook.

Graduation Requirements English, foreign language, mathematics, physical education (includes health), religion (includes Bible studies and theology), science, social sciences, social studies (includes history). Community service is required.

Special Academic Programs Advanced Placement exam preparation; honors section; independent study; study at local college for college credit; programs in English, mathematics, general development for dyslexic students.

College Admission Counseling 183 students graduated in 2010; 169 went to college, including Ball State University; Indiana University–Purdue University Fort Wayne; Indiana University Bloomington; Purdue University; Valparaiso University. Other: 11 went to work, 3 entered military service. Mean SAT critical reading: 523, mean SAT math: 567, mean SAT writing: 511.

Student Life Upper grades have uniform requirement, student council. Discipline rests primarily with faculty. Attendance at religious services is required.

Summer Programs Session focuses on summer classes, drivers ed, summer conditioning and sports camps; held both on and off campus; held at various locations based on sport; accepts boys and girls; open to students from other schools.

Tuition and Aid Day student tuition: $6350–$7800. Tuition installment plan (FACTS Tuition Payment Plan, monthly payment plans, individually arranged payment plans, NBD bank loan). Tuition reduction for siblings, merit scholarship grants, need-based scholarship grants available.

Admissions Deadline for receipt of application materials: none. Application fee required: $35. On-campus interview recommended.

Athletics Interscholastic: baseball (boys), basketball (b,g), cheering (g), cross-country running (b,g), dance team (g), diving (b,g), football (b), golf (b,g), gymnastics (g), soccer (b,g), softball (g), swimming and diving (b,g), tennis (b,g), track and field (b,g), volleyball (g); coed interscholastic: bowling, crew, JROTC drill, riflery; coed intramural: volleyball. 3 PE instructors, 50 coaches, 1 athletic trainer.

Computers Computers are regularly used in English, mathematics, newspaper, religion, yearbook classes. Computer resources include on-campus library services, Internet access, wireless campus network. Computer access in designated common areas is available to students. Students grades are available online.

Contact Mrs. Krista Friend, Enrollment Management Coordinator. 219-483-1102. Fax: 219-471-0180. E-mail: kfriend@clhscadets.com. Web site: www.clhscadets.com.

CONVENT OF THE SACRED HEART
1177 King Street
Greenwich, Connecticut 06831
Head of School: Mrs. Pamela Juan Hayes

General Information Girls' day college-preparatory, arts, religious studies, and technology school, affiliated with Roman Catholic Church. Grades PS–12. Founded: 1848. Setting: suburban. Nearest major city is New York, NY. 110-acre campus. 10 buildings on campus. Approved or accredited by Connecticut Association of Independent Schools, Network of Sacred Heart Schools, New England Association of Schools and Colleges, and Connecticut Department of Education. Member of National Association of Independent Schools and Secondary School Admission Test Board. Endowment: $22.8 million. Total enrollment: 777. Upper school average class size: 13. Upper school faculty-student ratio: 1:7. There are 163 required school days per year for Upper School students. Upper School students typically attend 5 days per week. The average school day consists of 7 hours and 15 minutes.

Upper School Student Profile Grade 6: 66 students (66 girls); Grade 7: 77 students (77 girls); Grade 8: 75 students (75 girls); Grade 9: 67 students (67 girls); Grade 10: 84 students (84 girls); Grade 11: 60 students (60 girls); Grade 12: 79 students (79 girls). 70% of students are Roman Catholic.

Faculty School total: 112. In upper school: 15 men, 36 women; 45 have advanced degrees.

Subjects Offered 20th century world history, advanced biology, advanced chemistry, advanced math, Advanced Placement courses, advanced studio art-AP, algebra, American literature, American literature-AP, Arabic, biology, biology-AP, broadcast journalism, calculus, calculus-AP, Catholic belief and practice, chemistry, chemistry-AP, Chinese, choir, choral music, Christian and Hebrew scripture, Christian education, Christian ethics, Christianity, college counseling, community service, comparative government and politics-AP, concert bell choir, design, drama, drawing, English language and composition-AP, English literature, English literature and composition-AP, environmental science-AP, ethics, European history, European history-AP, fine arts, French, French language-AP, geometry, health, honors algebra, honors geometry, honors U.S. history, HTML design, instrumental music, journalism, Latin, literary magazine, photography, physical education, physics, physics-AP, pre-calculus, SAT/ACT preparation, Spanish, Spanish language-AP, Spanish literature-AP, statistics, theology, trigonometry, U.S. history, U.S. history-AP, world cultures, world literature.

Find your focus at Sacred Heart
Diana, Class of '12, Aspiring Broadcast Journalist

A Sacred Heart education can change a girl's view of herself. In our Broadcast Journalism classes, students work in a state-of-the-art studio writing, presenting, shooting, editing and composing PSAs, news shows, documentaries, and other video projects—regularly receiving local and national awards for their work. It's just one of the innovative learning experiences that enables our girls to discover their talents, grow in confidence, and achieve amazing success. They step up, they take aim, they produce—and never again do they see themselves in quite the same light.

Convent of the SacredHeart
An independent, Catholic school for girls from preschool through grade 12

Greenwich, CT • 203-532-3534 • www.cshgreenwich.org

Convent of the Sacred Heart

Graduation Requirements Arts and fine arts (art, music, dance, drama), electives, English, foreign language, mathematics, physical education (includes health), religion (includes Bible studies and theology), science, social studies (includes history). Community service is required.

Special Academic Programs 17 Advanced Placement exams for which test preparation is offered; honors section; independent study; term-away projects; domestic exchange program (with Network of Sacred Heart Schools); study abroad; academic accommodation for the gifted and the artistically talented.

College Admission Counseling 60 students graduated in 2010; all went to college, including Boston College; Elon University; Georgetown University; The Johns Hopkins University; Trinity College; Villanova University.

Student Life Upper grades have uniform requirement, student council, honor system. Discipline rests primarily with faculty. Attendance at religious services is required.

Tuition and Aid Day student tuition: $32,200. Tuition installment plan (Academic Management Services Plan). Need-based scholarship grants available. In 2010–11, 21% of upper-school students received aid. Total amount of financial aid awarded in 2010–11: $1,400,000.

Admissions Traditional secondary-level entrance grade is 9. ISEE or SSAT required. Deadline for receipt of application materials: February 1. Application fee required: $50. On-campus interview required.

Athletics Interscholastic: basketball, cooperative games, crew, cross-country running, dance, diving, field hockey, fitness, golf, jogging, lacrosse, physical fitness, running, soccer, softball, squash, swimming and diving, tennis, volleyball; intramural: equestrian sports, fitness, independent competitive sports, physical training, strength & conditioning. 4 PE instructors, 34 coaches, 1 athletic trainer.

Computers Computers are regularly used in all academic classes. Computer network features include on-campus library services, online commercial services, Internet access, wireless campus network, Internet filtering or blocking technology, course selection online, laptops mandatory for students in grades 7 to 12. Campus intranet, student e-mail accounts, and computer access in designated common areas are available to students. The school has a published electronic and media policy.

Contact Catherine Machir, Director of Admission. 203-532-3534. Fax: 203-532-3301. E-mail: admission@cshgreenwich.org. Web site: www.cshgreenwich.org.

See Display on page 203 and Close-Up on page 762.

CONVENT OF THE SACRED HEART

1 East 91st Street
New York, New York 10128-0689
Head of School: Dr. Joseph J. Ciancaglini

General Information Girls' day college-preparatory, arts, religious studies, bilingual studies, and technology school, affiliated with Roman Catholic Church. Grades PK–12. Founded: 1881. Setting: urban. 2 buildings on campus. Approved or accredited by Network of Sacred Heart Schools, New York State Association of Independent Schools, and New York Department of Education. Member of National Association of Independent Schools and Secondary School Admission Test Board. Endowment: $33.8 million. Total enrollment: 691. Upper school average class size: 16. Upper school faculty-student ratio: 1:16.

Upper School Student Profile Grade 8: 53 students (53 girls); Grade 9: 52 students (52 girls); Grade 10: 51 students (51 girls); Grade 11: 50 students (50 girls); Grade 12: 47 students (47 girls). 65% of students are Roman Catholic.

Faculty School total: 110. In upper school: 10 men, 30 women; 38 have advanced degrees.

Subjects Offered Advanced studio art-AP, algebra, American history, American literature, art, audio visual/media, biology, biology-AP, calculus, calculus-AP, campus ministry, ceramics, chemistry, chemistry-AP, chorus, computer applications, computer multimedia, creative writing, dance, desktop publishing, digital photography, drama, earth science, East European studies, English, English literature, English literature-AP, environmental science, ethics, European history, expository writing, film history, fine arts, finite math, forensics, French, French-AP, functions, geography, geometry, government/civics, handbells, health, history, journalism, Latin, madrigals, mathematics, model United Nations, multicultural literature, multimedia design, music, musical theater, performing arts, photography, physical education, physical science, physics, physics-AP, portfolio art, pottery, pre-calculus, religion, science, science research, social studies, Spanish, Spanish-AP, speech, statistics, statistics-AP, theater, theology, trigonometry, U.S. history-AP, visual arts, women's literature, world history, world issues, world literature, world religions, writing.

Graduation Requirements Arts and fine arts (art, music, dance, drama), computer science, English, foreign language, mathematics, physical education (includes health), religion (includes Bible studies and theology), science, social studies (includes history).

Special Academic Programs 15 Advanced Placement exams for which test preparation is offered; honors section; independent study; term-away projects; domestic exchange program (with Network of Sacred Heart Schools); study abroad.

College Admission Counseling 48 students graduated in 2010; all went to college, including Boston College; Georgetown University; Lehigh University; New York University; The George Washington University; University of Pennsylvania.

Student Life Upper grades have uniform requirement, student council. Discipline rests primarily with faculty. Attendance at religious services is required.

Summer Programs Sports, art/fine arts, computer instruction programs offered; session focuses on visual and performing arts; held on campus; accepts boys and girls; open to students from other schools. 200 students usually enrolled. 2011 schedule: June 30 to July 25. Application deadline: April 15.

Tuition and Aid Day student tuition: $30,970. Tuition installment plan (Key Tuition Payment Plan). Need-based scholarship grants, need-based loans available. In 2010–11, 37% of upper-school students received aid. Total amount of financial aid awarded in 2010–11: $1,800,000.

Admissions Traditional secondary-level entrance grade is 9. For fall 2010, 200 students applied for upper-level admission, 35 were accepted, 16 enrolled. ERB or ISEE required. Deadline for receipt of application materials: November 15. Application fee required: $65. On-campus interview required.

Athletics Interscholastic: basketball, cross-country running, indoor track & field, lacrosse, soccer, softball, swimming and diving, tennis, track and field, volleyball, winter (indoor) track; intramural: aerobics/dance, aquatics, ballet, basketball, dance, fitness, gymnastics, jogging, physical training, roller blading, running, soccer, softball, swimming and diving, tennis, volleyball, weight lifting, weight training. 8 PE instructors, 8 coaches, 1 athletic trainer.

Computers Computers are regularly used in all academic classes. Computer network features include on-campus library services, online commercial services, Internet access, wireless campus network, Internet filtering or blocking technology. Campus intranet, student e-mail accounts, and computer access in designated common areas are available to students. The school has a published electronic and media policy.

Contact Evin Watson, Admissions Office Coordinator. 212-722-4745 Ext. 105. Fax: 212-996-1784. E-mail: ewatson@cshnyc.org. Web site: www.cshnyc.org.

CONVENT OF THE VISITATION SCHOOL

2455 Visitation Drive
Mendota Heights, Minnesota 55120-1696
Head of School: Dawn Nichols

General Information Coeducational day college-preparatory, arts, religious studies, bilingual studies, and technology school, affiliated with Roman Catholic Church. Boys grades PK–6, girls grades PK–12. Founded: 1873. Setting: suburban. Nearest major city is St. Paul. 50-acre campus. 1 building on campus. Approved or accredited by Independent Schools Association of the Central States and Minnesota Department of Education. Member of National Association of Independent Schools and Secondary School Admission Test Board. Endowment: $10 million. Total enrollment: 568. Upper school average class size: 18. Upper school faculty-student ratio: 1:10. The average school day consists of 6 hours and 40 minutes.

Upper School Student Profile Grade 9: 89 students (89 girls); Grade 10: 75 students (75 girls); Grade 11: 71 students (71 girls); Grade 12: 77 students (77 girls). 85% of students are Roman Catholic.

Faculty School total: 59. In upper school: 7 men, 31 women; 31 have advanced degrees.

Subjects Offered Algebra, American history, American literature, anatomy, art, astronomy, ballet, biology, biology-AP, British literature, calculus, calculus-AP, ceramics, chamber groups, chemistry, Chinese, choir, choral music, Christian scripture, church history, composition, computer programming, computer science, creative writing, desktop publishing, drawing, economics, English, English literature, English literature-AP, environmental science, European history, French, French-AP, genetics, geometry, government, graphic design, health, history, history-AP, honors algebra, Latin, literary genres, math analysis, mathematics, music, orchestra, painting, peer ministry, photography, physical education, physical science, physics, physiology, prayer/spirituality, psychology, religion, science, senior seminar, sociology, Spanish, Spanish-AP, speech, theater, U.S. government and politics-AP, U.S. history, Web site design, women spirituality and faith, world cultures, world history, world religions.

Graduation Requirements Arts and fine arts (art, music, dance, drama), computer science, English, foreign language, mathematics, physical education (includes health), religion (includes Bible studies and theology), science, social sciences, social studies (includes history), two-week senior year service project.

Special Academic Programs Advanced Placement exam preparation; honors section; independent study; study at local college for college credit.

College Admission Counseling 87 students graduated in 2009; all went to college, including Creighton University; Marquette University; St. Olaf College; University of Minnesota, Twin Cities Campus; University of Notre Dame; University of St. Thomas. Median SAT critical reading: 608, median SAT math: 591, median SAT writing: 620, median combined SAT: 1819, median composite ACT: 27. 68% scored over 600 on SAT critical reading, 76% scored over 600 on SAT math, 85% scored over 600 on SAT writing, 71% scored over 1800 on combined SAT, 74% scored over 26 on composite ACT.

Student Life Upper grades have uniform requirement, student council, honor system. Discipline rests primarily with faculty. Attendance at religious services is required.

Tuition and Aid Day student tuition: $17,697. Tuition installment plan (monthly payment plans, individually arranged payment plans, semiannual payment plan). Need-based scholarship grants, funds allocated from the Archdiocese available. In 2009–10, 29% of upper-school students received aid. Total amount of financial aid awarded in 2009–10: $869,400.

Admissions Traditional secondary-level entrance grade is 9. For fall 2009, 97 students applied for upper-level admission, 72 were accepted, 50 enrolled. ERB and

Individual IQ required. Deadline for receipt of application materials: January 16. Application fee required: $25. Interview required.

Athletics Interscholastic: alpine skiing, basketball, cross-country running, diving, golf, hockey, ice hockey, lacrosse, nordic skiing, skiing (cross-country), skiing (downhill), soccer, softball, swimming and diving, tennis, track and field, volleyball; intramural: ballet, basketball. 1 PE instructor, 30 coaches, 1 athletic trainer.

Computers Computers are regularly used in all classes. Computer network features include on-campus library services, online commercial services, Internet access, wireless campus network, Internet filtering or blocking technology. Students grades are available online. The school has a published electronic and media policy.

Contact Katie Owens, Director of Admissions. 651-683-1706. Fax: 651-454-7144. E-mail: kowens@vischool.org. Web site: www.visitation.net.

COPPER CANYON ACADEMY

Rimrock, Arizona
See Special Needs Schools section.

COQUITLAM COLLEGE

516 Brookmere Avenue
Coquitlam, British Columbia V3J 1W9, Canada
Head of School: Mr. Will Eckford

General Information college-preparatory and general academic school. Founded: 1982. Setting: suburban. Nearest major city is Vancouver, Canada. Students are housed in homestay. 10-acre campus. 1 building on campus. Approved or accredited by Canadian Council of Montessori Administrators and British Columbia Department of Education. Upper school average class size: 20.

Student Life Upper grades have student council. Discipline rests primarily with faculty.

Admissions No application fee required.

Contact Ms. Aase Sylte, Administrative Assistant. 604-939-6633. Fax: 604-939-0336. E-mail: aase@coquitlamcollege.com. Web site: www.coquitlamcollege.com.

COTTER SCHOOLS

1115 West Broadway
Winona, Minnesota 55987-1399
Head of School: Mrs. Jennifer Elfering

General Information Coeducational boarding and day college-preparatory, general academic, arts, religious studies, technology, and ESL school, affiliated with Roman Catholic Church. Boarding grades 9–12, day grades 7–12. Founded: 1911. Setting: small town. Nearest major city is Minneapolis. Students are housed in single-sex by floor dormitories. 75-acre campus. 7 buildings on campus. Approved or accredited by Midwest Association of Boarding Schools, National Catholic Education Association, North Central Association of Colleges and Schools, The Association of Boarding Schools, and Minnesota Department of Education. Endowment: $15 million. Total enrollment: 380. Upper school average class size: 16. Upper school faculty-student ratio: 1:11. There are 176 required school days per year for Upper School students. Upper School students typically attend 5 days per week. The average school day consists of 5 hours and 40 minutes.

Upper School Student Profile Grade 7: 33 students (15 boys, 18 girls); Grade 8: 49 students (28 boys, 21 girls); Grade 9: 58 students (31 boys, 27 girls); Grade 10: 88 students (46 boys, 42 girls); Grade 11: 78 students (40 boys, 38 girls); Grade 12: 74 students (41 boys, 33 girls). 31% of students are boarding students. 65% are state residents. 4 states are represented in upper school student body. 30% are international students. International students from China, Japan, Mexico, Republic of Korea, Taiwan, and Viet Nam; 7 other countries represented in student body. 66% of students are Roman Catholic.

Faculty School total: 38. In upper school: 18 men, 20 women, 32 have advanced degrees; 2 reside on campus.

Subjects Offered Algebra, American history, anatomy, art, band, Bible, biology, calculus, calculus-AP, campus ministry, chemistry, chorus, Christian and Hebrew scripture, Christian ethics, community service, computer science, death and loss, economics, English, environmental science, ESL, German, health, Hebrew scripture, honors English, learning lab, linear algebra, literature and composition-AP, math analysis, mathematics, media, painting, physical education, physical science, physics, psychology, science, Spanish, statistics, U.S. history, U.S. history-AP, visual arts, world geography, world religions.

Graduation Requirements English, foreign language, mathematics, performing arts, physical education (includes health), religion (includes Bible studies and theology), science, social studies (includes history), visual arts, 80 hours of community service.

Special Academic Programs Honors section; accelerated programs; independent study; term-away projects; study at local college for college credit; study abroad; academic accommodation for the gifted, the musically talented, and the artistically talented; remedial reading and/or remedial writing; remedial math; programs in English, mathematics for dyslexic students; ESL (25 students enrolled).

College Admission Counseling 80 students graduated in 2010; 78 went to college, including Saint John's University; Saint Mary's University of Minnesota; University

of Illinois at Urbana–Champaign; University of Minnesota, Twin Cities Campus; University of St. Thomas; University of Wisconsin–Madison. Other: 1 went to work, 1 entered military service. Median composite ACT: 24. 50% scored over 26 on composite ACT.

Student Life Upper grades have specified standards of dress, student council. Discipline rests primarily with faculty. Attendance at religious services is required.

Tuition and Aid Day student tuition: $5975; 5-day tuition and room/board: $23,850; 7-day tuition and room/board: $27,700. Tuition installment plan (monthly payment plans, individually arranged payment plans). Tuition reduction for siblings, need-based scholarship grants available. In 2010–11, 60% of upper-school students received aid.

Admissions Traditional secondary-level entrance grade is 9. For fall 2010, 78 students applied for upper-level admission, 56 were accepted, 42 enrolled. SLEP for foreign students or TOEFL required. Deadline for receipt of application materials: none. Application fee required: $50. Interview required.

Athletics Interscholastic: aerobics/dance (girls), baseball (b), basketball (b,g), cheering (g), cross-country running (b,g), dance (g), dance team (g), danceline (g), football (b), golf (b,g), gymnastics (g), hockey (b,g), ice hockey (b,g), skiing (cross-country) (b,g), soccer (b,g), softball (g), swimming and diving (b,g), tennis (b,g), track and field (b,g), volleyball (g), wrestling (b); intramural: basketball (b,g), indoor soccer (b); coed intramural: badminton, basketball, canoeing/kayaking, indoor soccer. 2 PE instructors, 66 coaches, 1 athletic trainer.

Computers Computers are regularly used in art, technology classes. Computer network features include on-campus library services, Internet access, Internet filtering or blocking technology. Campus intranet, student e-mail accounts, and computer access in designated common areas are available to students. The school has a published electronic and media policy.

Contact Mr. Will Gibson, Director of Admissions and International Programs. 507-453-5403. Fax: 507-453-5013. E-mail: wgibson@cotterschools.org. Web site: www.cotterschools.org.

THE COUNTRY DAY SCHOOL

13415 Dufferin Street
King City, Ontario L7B 1K5, Canada
Head of School: Mr. Paul C. Duckett

General Information Coeducational day college-preparatory, arts, business, and technology school. Grades JK–12. Founded: 1972. Setting: rural. Nearest major city is Toronto, Canada. 100-acre campus. 2 buildings on campus. Approved or accredited by Canadian Association of Independent Schools, Canadian Educational Standards Institute, Conference of Independent Schools of Ontario, and Ontario Department of Education. Language of instruction: English. Total enrollment: 720. Upper school average class size: 17. Upper school faculty-student ratio: 1:10.

Upper School Student Profile Grade 9: 80 students (40 boys, 40 girls); Grade 10: 80 students (40 boys, 40 girls); Grade 11: 80 students (40 boys, 40 girls); Grade 12: 80 students (40 boys, 40 girls).

Faculty School total: 79. In upper school: 28 men, 20 women.

Subjects Offered Advanced chemistry, advanced computer applications, advanced math, algebra, American history, anatomy and physiology, ancient history, ancient/medieval philosophy, art and culture, art history, athletics, band, biology, business studies, Canadian geography, Canadian history, Canadian literature, career education, career/college preparation, choir, comparative politics, computer programming, creative writing, English, environmental geography, European history, French, government/civics, history, languages, mathematics, modern Western civilization, performing arts, philosophy, physical education, physics, politics, science, society, world history.

Graduation Requirements Ministry Grade 10 Literacy Test (Government of Ontario).

Special Academic Programs Advanced Placement exam preparation; study abroad.

College Admission Counseling 79 students graduated in 2010; all went to college, including McGill University; McMaster University; Queen's University at Kingston; The University of Western Ontario; University of Toronto; Wilfrid Laurier University.

Student Life Upper grades have uniform requirement, student council, honor system. Discipline rests primarily with faculty.

Summer Programs Advancement, sports, art/fine arts programs offered; session focuses on advancement; held both on and off campus; held at Costa Rica, England, and Galapagos Islands; accepts boys and girls; open to students from other schools. 20 students usually enrolled. 2011 schedule: July 2 to July 31. Application deadline: March 1.

Tuition and Aid Day student tuition: CAN$21,725.

Admissions Traditional secondary-level entrance grade is 9. For fall 2010, 97 students applied for upper-level admission, 58 were accepted, 37 enrolled. CAT 5 or SSAT required. Deadline for receipt of application materials: none. Application fee required: CAN$125. On-campus interview required.

Athletics Interscholastic: baseball (b,g), basketball (b,g), cross-country running (b,g), golf (b,g), hockey (b,g), ice hockey (b,g), rugby (b,g), running (b,g), soccer (b,g), softball (b,g), track and field (b,g), volleyball (b,g); intramural: badminton (b,g), basketball (b,g), bowling (b,g), ice hockey (b), ice skating (b,g), physical fitness (b,g), skiing (downhill) (b,g), snowboarding (b,g), soccer (b,g), softball (b,g), volleyball (b,g); coed intramural: curling, Frisbee, physical fitness, physical training, rock climbing, strength & conditioning, swimming and diving, table tennis. 5 PE instructors.

Computers Computers are regularly used in accounting, business, career education, English, geography, history, mathematics, media, music, writing, yearbook classes. Computer network features include on-campus library services, Internet access, wireless campus network, Internet filtering or blocking technology, access to online library resources from home, access to homework online via Blackboard Software. Campus intranet is available to students.

Contact Mr. David Huckvale, Director of Admission. 905-833-1220. Fax: 905-833-1350. E-mail: admissions@cds.on.ca. Web site: www.cds.on.ca/.

COUNTRY DAY SCHOOL OF THE SACRED HEART

480 Bryn Mawr Avenue

Bryn Mawr, Pennsylvania 19010

Head of School: Sr. Matthew Anita MacDonald, SSJ

General Information Girls' day college-preparatory, arts, religious studies, and technology school, affiliated with Roman Catholic Church. Grades PK–12. Founded: 1865. Setting: suburban. Nearest major city is Philadelphia. 16-acre campus. 3 buildings on campus. Approved or accredited by Middle States Association of Colleges and Schools, Network of Sacred Heart Schools, and Pennsylvania Department of Education. Member of National Association of Independent Schools. Total enrollment: 325. Upper school average class size: 15. Upper school faculty-student ratio: 1:8. There are 180 required school days per year for Upper School students. The average school day consists of 7 hours.

Upper School Student Profile Grade 9: 38 students (38 girls); Grade 10: 49 students (49 girls); Grade 11: 44 students (44 girls); Grade 12: 49 students (49 girls). 75% of students are Roman Catholic.

Faculty School total: 44. In upper school: 5 men, 29 women; 21 have advanced degrees.

Subjects Offered Algebra, American history, American history-AP, American literature, art, arts, Bible studies, biology, calculus, chemistry, composition, computer science, economics, English, English literature, environmental science, ethics, European history, film, fine arts, French, geometry, government/civics, health, Latin, mathematics, media studies, physical education, physics, pre-calculus, religion, science, social sciences, social studies, Spanish, trigonometry, word processing, world history, world literature.

Graduation Requirements Arts and fine arts (art, music, dance, drama), English, foreign language, mathematics, physical education (includes health), religion (includes Bible studies and theology), science, social studies (includes history), two weeks of senior independent study with a working professional, 25 hours of community service per year.

Special Academic Programs 7 Advanced Placement exams for which test preparation is offered; honors section; independent study; term-away projects; study at local college for college credit; domestic exchange program (with Network of Sacred Heart Schools); study abroad; academic accommodation for the musically talented.

College Admission Counseling 42 students graduated in 2010; all went to college, including Drexel University; Georgetown University; Saint Joseph's University; The Catholic University of America. Mean SAT critical reading: 600, mean SAT math: 580, mean SAT writing: 610. 43% scored over 600 on SAT critical reading, 40% scored over 600 on SAT math, 49% scored over 600 on SAT writing.

Student Life Upper grades have uniform requirement, student council. Discipline rests equally with students and faculty. Attendance at religious services is required.

Tuition and Aid Day student tuition: $15,500. Tuition installment plan (SMART Tuition Payment Plan). Tuition reduction for siblings, merit scholarship grants, need-based scholarship grants available. In 2010–11, 70% of upper-school students received aid; total upper-school merit-scholarship money awarded: $415,700. Total amount of financial aid awarded in 2010–11: $424,350.

Admissions Traditional secondary-level entrance grade is 9. For fall 2010, 100 students applied for upper-level admission, 60 were accepted, 30 enrolled. High School Placement Test required. Deadline for receipt of application materials: none. Application fee required: $35. Interview required.

Athletics Interscholastic: basketball, crew, cross-country running, field hockey, golf, lacrosse, softball, tennis, track and field, volleyball; intramural: fitness walking. 2 PE instructors, 12 coaches, 1 athletic trainer.

Computers Computers are regularly used in English, foreign language, history, mathematics, science, technology classes. Computer network features include on-campus library services, online commercial services, Internet access. The school has a published electronic and media policy.

Contact Mrs. Laurie Nowlan, Director of Admissions. 610-527-3915 Ext. 214. Fax: 610-527-0942. E-mail: lnowlan@cdssh.org. Web site: www.cdssh.org.

COVENANT CANADIAN REFORMED SCHOOL

3030 TWP Road 615A

PO Box 67

Neerlandia, Alberta T0G 1R0, Canada

Head of School: Mr. Harry VanDelden

General Information Coeducational day college-preparatory, general academic, business, religious studies, and technology school, affiliated with Reformed Church. Grades K–12. Founded: 1977. Setting: rural. Nearest major city is Edmonton, Canada. 5-acre campus. 2 buildings on campus. Approved or accredited by Association of Independent Schools and Colleges of Alberta and Alberta Department of Education. Language of instruction: English. Total enrollment: 177. Upper school average class size: 10. Upper school faculty-student ratio: 1:10. There are 171 required school days per year for Upper School students. Upper School students typically attend 4 days per week. The average school day consists of 6 hours and 10 minutes.

Upper School Student Profile Grade 10: 12 students (2 boys, 10 girls); Grade 11: 7 students (3 boys, 4 girls); Grade 12: 7 students (3 boys, 4 girls). 100% of students are Reformed.

Faculty School total: 16. In upper school: 5 men, 2 women.

Subjects Offered Accounting, architectural drawing, Bible studies, biology, Canadian geography, career and personal planning, career technology, chemistry, child development, Christian education, computer information systems, computer skills, computer studies, consumer law, desktop publishing, digital photography, drawing and design, early childhood, electronic publishing, English, ESL, French as a second language, geology, health education, history, HTML design, information processing, intro to computers, introduction to technology, keyboarding, mathematics, physical education, physics, prayer/spirituality, religious studies, science, sewing, social studies, theology and the arts, Web site design, Western religions, work experience, world geography, world religions, yearbook.

Graduation Requirements Student must pass religious studies courses offered, in grades 10, 11, and 12 for the years the student attended.

Special Academic Programs Independent study; remedial reading and/or remedial writing; remedial math.

College Admission Counseling 8 students graduated in 2010; 2 went to college, including University of Lethbridge. Other: 6 went to work.

Student Life Upper grades have specified standards of dress, student council. Discipline rests primarily with faculty.

Tuition and Aid Day student tuition: CAN$5100. Tuition installment plan (monthly payment plans, individually arranged payment plans). Tuition rates per family available.

Admissions Traditional secondary-level entrance grade is 10. Achievement tests required. Deadline for receipt of application materials: none. No application fee required. Interview required.

Athletics Interscholastic: track and field (boys, girls), volleyball (b,g); coed intramural: badminton, ball hockey, baseball, basketball, flag football, floor hockey, football, Frisbee, hockey, ice hockey, indoor hockey, indoor soccer, lacrosse, soccer, softball, volleyball. 1 PE instructor, 2 coaches.

Computers Computers are regularly used in all classes. Computer network features include on-campus library services, Internet access, Internet filtering or blocking technology. Computer access in designated common areas is available to students.

Contact Mr. Harry VanDelden, Principal. 780-674-4774. Fax: 780-401-3295. E-mail: hvd@xplornet.com.

COVINGTON CATHOLIC HIGH SCHOOL

1600 Dixie Highway

Park Hills, Kentucky 41011

Head of School: Mr. Robert Rowe

General Information Boys' day college-preparatory, arts, business, religious studies, bilingual studies, and technology school, affiliated with Roman Catholic Church. Grades 9–12. Founded: 1925. Setting: suburban. Nearest major city is Cincinnati, OH. 2 buildings on campus. Approved or accredited by Southern Association of Colleges and Schools and Kentucky Department of Education. Total enrollment: 499. Upper school faculty-student ratio: 1:14. Upper School students typically attend 5 days per week. The average school day consists of 6 hours and 40 minutes.

Upper School Student Profile Grade 9: 125 students (125 boys); Grade 10: 121 students (121 boys); Grade 11: 115 students (115 boys); Grade 12: 120 students (120 boys).

Faculty School total: 37. In upper school: 31 men, 5 women; 21 have advanced degrees.

Subjects Offered Algebra, American government, American history, American history-AP, anatomy and physiology, art, biology, business law, calculus-AP, career exploration, chemistry, chemistry-AP, chorus, church history, computer applications, computer programming, computer science, computer science-AP, creative writing, current events, drama, economics, English, film, geometry, German, health, journalism, Latin, modern European history, music appreciation, orchestra, personal finance, physical education, physical science, physics, pre-algebra, pre-calculus, probability and statistics, psychology, psychology-AP, reading, scripture, social justice, sociology, Spanish, speech, theology, Web site design, wood processing, world civilizations, world geography, writing workshop.

Graduation Requirements Arts and fine arts (art, music, dance, drama), electives, English, mathematics, physical education (includes health), science, social studies (includes history).

Special Academic Programs 8 Advanced Placement exams for which test preparation is offered; honors section; study at local college for college credit.

College Admission Counseling 127 students graduated in 2010; 124 went to college, including Bellarmine University; Miami University; University of Dayton; University of Kentucky; University of Louisville; Xavier University. Other: 2 went to work, 1 entered military service. Mean composite ACT: 25.

Student Life Upper grades have specified standards of dress, student council. Discipline rests primarily with faculty. Attendance at religious services is required.

Tuition and Aid Day student tuition: $5945–$6300. Tuition reduction for siblings, merit scholarship grants, paying campus jobs available.

Admissions Traditional secondary-level entrance grade is 9. Deadline for receipt of application materials: none. No application fee required.

Athletics Interscholastic: baseball, basketball, bowling, football, soccer, swimming and diving, tennis, track and field; intramural: basketball, lacrosse, skiing (downhill), ultimate Frisbee, whiffle ball. 1 PE instructor.

Computers Computer network features include Internet access. Students grades are available online.

Contact Mr. Tony Barczak, Freshman/Sophomore Counselor. 859-491-2247 Ext. 2257. Fax: 859-448-2242. E-mail: tbarczak@covcath.org. Web site: http://www.covcath.org/.

THE CRAIG SCHOOL

Mountain Lakes, New Jersey
See Special Needs Schools section.

CRANBROOK SCHOOLS

39221 Woodward Avenue
PO Box 801
Bloomfield Hills, Michigan 48303-0801
Head of School: Arlyce Seibert

General Information Coeducational boarding and day college-preparatory and arts school. Boarding grades 9–12, day grades PK–12. Founded: 1922. Setting: suburban. Nearest major city is Detroit. Students are housed in single-sex dormitories. 315-acre campus. 10 buildings on campus. Approved or accredited by Independent Schools Association of the Central States, Midwest Association of Boarding Schools, The Association of Boarding Schools, The College Board, and Michigan Department of Education. Member of National Association of Independent Schools and Secondary School Admission Test Board. Endowment: $218 million. Total enrollment: 1,636. Upper school average class size: 16. Upper school faculty-student ratio: 1:8. There are 164 required school days per year for Upper School students. Upper School students typically attend 5 days per week. The average school day consists of 5 hours and 15 minutes.

Upper School Student Profile Grade 9: 179 students (85 boys, 94 girls); Grade 10: 195 students (103 boys, 92 girls); Grade 11: 223 students (117 boys, 106 girls); Grade 12: 193 students (108 boys, 85 girls). 33% of students are boarding students. 51% are state residents. 19 states are represented in upper school student body. 12% are international students. International students from China, Germany, Pakistan, Republic of Korea, Taiwan, and Thailand; 15 other countries represented in student body.

Faculty School total: 191. In upper school: 51 men, 41 women; 74 have advanced degrees; 67 reside on campus.

Subjects Offered Acting, advanced biology, advanced chemistry, advanced computer applications, advanced math, Advanced Placement courses, African-American literature, algebra, American history, American history-AP, American literature, American studies, anatomy, ancient history, anthropology, art, art history, astronomy, band, Basic programming, biology, biology-AP, botany, British literature, calculus, ceramics, chamber groups, chemistry, chemistry-AP, choir, choral music, chorus, classical civilization, computer programming, computer science, computer science-AP, concert band, concert choir, creative dance, creative writing, dance, design, drama, drawing, earth science, economics, economics and history, English, English literature, environmental science, ESL, ethics, European history, European history-AP, expository writing, film and literature, fine arts, French, genetics, geology, geometry, government/civics, health, history, humanities, interdisciplinary studies, jazz band, jewelry making, Latin, mathematics, metalworking, model United Nations, orchestra, painting, philosophy, photography, physics, pre-calculus, printmaking, psychology, religion, science, sculpture, social sciences, social studies, Spanish, speech, statistics, theater, trigonometry, weaving, wilderness education, world history, writing.

Graduation Requirements Arts, arts and crafts, English, foreign language, health, history, mathematics, performing arts, religion (includes Bible studies and theology), science.

Special Academic Programs Advanced Placement exam preparation; honors section; independent study; term-away projects; study abroad; academic accommodation for the gifted, the musically talented, and the artistically talented; ESL (20 students enrolled).

College Admission Counseling 203 students graduated in 2009; 202 went to college, including Brown University; Harvard University; Michigan State University; University of Michigan; University of Pennsylvania. Other: 1 had other specific plans. Mean SAT critical reading: 624, mean SAT math: 649, mean SAT writing: 634, mean composite ACT: 28.

Cranbrook Schools

Student Life Upper grades have specified standards of dress, student council, honor system. Discipline rests primarily with faculty.

Tuition and Aid Day student tuition: $25,850; 7-day tuition and room/board: $35,450. Tuition installment plan (FACTS Tuition Payment Plan). Merit scholarship grants, need-based scholarship grants available. In 2009–10, 35% of upper-school students received aid; total upper-school merit-scholarship money awarded: $182,000. Total amount of financial aid awarded in 2009–10: $6,100,000.

Admissions Traditional secondary-level entrance grade is 9. For fall 2009, 470 students applied for upper-level admission, 225 were accepted, 150 enrolled. SSAT required. Deadline for receipt of application materials: none. Application fee required: $25. Interview required.

Athletics Interscholastic: alpine skiing (boys, girls), baseball (b), basketball (b,g), crew (b,g), cross-country running (b,g), diving (b,g), field hockey (g), football (b), golf (b,g), hockey (b,g), ice hockey (b,g), lacrosse (b,g), skiing (downhill) (b,g), soccer (b,g), softball (g), swimming and diving (b,g), tennis (b,g), track and field (b,g), volleyball (g); intramural: basketball (b), weight training (b,g); coed intramural: backpacking, bicycling, bowling, climbing, dance, fencing, fitness, fitness walking, Frisbee, hiking/backpacking, independent competitive sports, jogging, martial arts, modern dance, mountain biking, outdoor adventure, outdoor education, physical fitness, physical training, rock climbing, running, scuba diving, snowboarding, soccer, softball, strength & conditioning, tai chi, tennis, ultimate Frisbee, volleyball, walking, weight lifting, wilderness, wilderness survival, yoga. 18 coaches, 3 athletic trainers.

Computers Computers are regularly used in English, foreign language, history, mathematics, science classes. Computer network features include on-campus library services, online commercial services, Internet access, wireless campus network, Internet filtering or blocking technology, SmartBoards. Student e-mail accounts and computer access in designated common areas are available to students. The school has a published electronic and media policy.

Contact Drew Miller, Director of Admission. 248-645-3610. Fax: 248-645-3025. E-mail: admission@cranbrook.edu. Web site: schools.cranbrook.edu.

See Display on page 207 and Close-Up on page 764.

CRAWFORD ADVENTIST ACADEMY
531 Finch Avenue West
Willowdale, Ontario M2R 3X2, Canada
Head of School: Mr. Norman Brown

General Information Coeducational day college-preparatory, arts, business, religious studies, bilingual studies, and technology school, affiliated with Seventh-day Adventist Church. Grades JK–12. Founded: 1954. Setting: urban. Nearest major city is Toronto, Canada. 5-acre campus. 1 building on campus. Approved or accredited by National Council for Private School Accreditation, Ontario Ministry of Education, and Ontario Department of Education. Language of instruction: English. Upper school average class size: 25. Upper school faculty-student ratio: 1:16. There are 188 required school days per year for Upper School students. Upper School students typically attend 5 days per week. The average school day consists of 6 hours and 30 minutes.

Upper School Student Profile Grade 6: 35 students (19 boys, 16 girls); Grade 7: 40 students (21 boys, 19 girls); Grade 8: 41 students (20 boys, 21 girls); Grade 9: 52 students (26 boys, 26 girls); Grade 10: 49 students (27 boys, 22 girls); Grade 11: 47 students (22 boys, 25 girls); Grade 12: 37 students (18 boys, 19 girls). 90% of students are Seventh-day Adventists.

Faculty School total: 18. In upper school: 11 men, 6 women; 11 have advanced degrees.

Subjects Offered Advanced computer applications, band, Bible, biology, business, business technology, calculus, Canadian geography, Canadian history, chemistry, choir, civics, community service, computer applications, computer information systems, drama, dramatic arts, earth and space science, English, English composition, French, French as a second language, geography, guidance, independent study, information technology, marketing, mathematics, physical education, physics, religion, science, writing, yearbook.

Special Academic Programs Advanced Placement exam preparation; remedial reading and/or remedial writing; programs in English for dyslexic students; ESL (3 students enrolled).

College Admission Counseling 37 students graduated in 2010; 5 went to college, including Andrews University; Oakwood University; Ryerson University; University of Toronto; University of Waterloo; York University. Other: 2 went to work, 30 entered a postgraduate year. Median composite ACT: 20. 22% scored over 26 on composite ACT.

Student Life Upper grades have uniform requirement, student council, honor system. Discipline rests primarily with faculty. Attendance at religious services is required.

Tuition and Aid Day student tuition: CAN$7600. Guaranteed tuition plan. Tuition installment plan (monthly payment plans, individually arranged payment plans). Tuition reduction for siblings, need-based scholarship grants, paying campus jobs available. In 2010–11, 10% of upper-school students received aid. Total amount of financial aid awarded in 2010–11: CAN$15,000.

Admissions Traditional secondary-level entrance grade is 9. For fall 2010, 15 students applied for upper-level admission, 10 were accepted, 9 enrolled. CAT, CAT 2, CCAT or CTBS (or similar from their school) required. Deadline for receipt of application materials: none. Application fee required: CAN$25. On-campus interview required.

Athletics Interscholastic: weight lifting (boys, girls); coed interscholastic: badminton, basketball, cooperative games, flag football, floor hockey, outdoor recreation, soccer, volleyball; coed intramural: basketball, flag football, floor hockey, indoor soccer, outdoor education, outdoor recreation, physical fitness, soccer, table tennis, volleyball. 1 PE instructor, 1 coach.

Computers Computers are regularly used in accounting, business, computer applications, yearbook classes. Computer network features include Internet access, wireless campus network, Internet filtering or blocking technology. Student e-mail accounts and computer access in designated common areas are available to students. Students grades are available online. The school has a published electronic and media policy.

Contact Mr. Andrew Mark Thomas, Principal, 9-12. 416-633-0090 Ext. 223. Fax: 416-633-0467. E-mail: athomas@caasda.com.

CRESPI CARMELITE HIGH SCHOOL
5031 Alonzo Avenue
Encino, California 91316-3699
Head of School: Fr. Paul Henson, OCARM

General Information Boys' day college-preparatory, arts, and religious studies school, affiliated with Roman Catholic Church. Grades 9–12. Founded: 1959. Setting: suburban. Nearest major city is Los Angeles. 3-acre campus. 3 buildings on campus. Approved or accredited by Western Association of Schools and Colleges, Western Catholic Education Association, and California Department of Education. Total enrollment: 585. Upper school average class size: 23. Upper school faculty-student ratio: 1:23. There are 182 required school days per year for Upper School students. Upper School students typically attend 5 days per week. The average school day consists of 6 hours.

Upper School Student Profile Grade 9: 173 students (173 boys); Grade 10: 143 students (143 boys); Grade 11: 140 students (140 boys); Grade 12: 129 students (129 boys). 59% of students are Roman Catholic.

Faculty School total: 37. In upper school: 33 men, 4 women; 29 have advanced degrees.

Subjects Offered Advanced Placement courses, advanced studio art-AP, algebra, American history-AP, American literature-AP, anatomy and physiology, Ancient Greek, ancient world history, applied music, ASB Leadership, astronomy, athletic training, audio visual/media, baseball, Basic programming, basketball, biology, biology-AP, British literature, British literature-AP, business mathematics, calculus, calculus-AP, chemistry, Christian scripture, church history, classical Greek literature, computer graphics, constitutional law, drama performance, driver education, earth science, economics and history, economics-AP, English composition, English literature and composition-AP, environmental science, ethics, European history-AP, film studies, French language-AP, French-AP, geometry, golf, government, government and politics-AP, Greek, Greek culture, health, history of the Catholic Church, Holocaust, Holocaust studies, honors English, honors geometry, international studies, journalism, language and composition, Latin-AP, law, media arts, men's studies, model United Nations, moral and social development, music appreciation, music composition, photography, physical science, physics-AP, prayer/spirituality, precalculus, probability and statistics, psychology, Shakespeare, social justice, Spanish, Spanish language-AP, Spanish literature-AP, Spanish-AP, speech, sports, sports conditioning, statistics-AP, student government, student publications, U.S. history, U.S. history-AP, video film production, Vietnam War, visual arts, Web site design, weight training, Western civilization, Western religions, world cultures, world geography, world religions, yearbook, zoology.

Graduation Requirements Arts and fine arts (art, music, dance, drama), English, foreign language, mathematics, physical education (includes health), religion (includes Bible studies and theology), science, social sciences, social studies (includes history). Community service is required.

Special Academic Programs 13 Advanced Placement exams for which test preparation is offered; honors section.

College Admission Counseling 147 students graduated in 2010; 143 went to college, including California Polytechnic State University, San Luis Obispo; California State University, Northridge; University of California, Los Angeles; University of California, Santa Barbara; University of San Diego. Other: 3 entered military service, 1 had other specific plans. Median SAT critical reading: 520, median SAT math: 500, median SAT writing: 540, median composite ACT: 23.

Student Life Upper grades have specified standards of dress, student council, honor system. Discipline rests primarily with faculty. Attendance at religious services is required.

Summer Programs Remediation, enrichment, advancement, sports, art/fine arts programs offered; session focuses on remediation and/or enrichment in math, science, language, and social studies; held on campus; accepts boys and girls; open to students from other schools. 250 students usually enrolled. 2011 schedule: June 28 to July 30. Application deadline: June 25.

Tuition and Aid Day student tuition: $12,000. Tuition installment plan (FACTS Tuition Payment Plan, Tuition Management Systems Plan). Merit scholarship grants, need-based scholarship grants available. In 2010–11, 32% of upper-school students received aid; total upper-school merit-scholarship money awarded: $48,600. Total amount of financial aid awarded in 2010–11: $1,018,965.

Admissions Traditional secondary-level entrance grade is 9. For fall 2010, 295 students applied for upper-level admission, 286 were accepted, 173 enrolled. High

School Placement Test required. Deadline for receipt of application materials: February 4. Application fee required: $100. On-campus interview required.

Athletics Interscholastic: aquatics, baseball, basketball, cross-country running, football, golf, lacrosse, soccer, swimming and diving, tennis, track and field, volleyball, water polo, wrestling; intramural: basketball, floor hockey, Frisbee, table tennis. 4 PE instructors, 2 athletic trainers.

Computers Computers are regularly used in business applications, business studies, economics, English, foreign language, history, mathematics, media production, science, video film production, yearbook classes. Computer network features include on-campus library services, online commercial services, Internet access, wireless campus network. Students grades are available online. The school has a published electronic and media policy.

Contact Mrs. Anita Rezzo, Assistant Admissions Director. 818-345-1672 Ext. 329. Fax: 818-705-0209. E-mail: arezzo@crespi.org. Web site: www.crespi.org.

CRESTWOOD PREPARATORY COLLEGE
217 Brookbanks Drive
Toronto, Ontario M3A 2T7, Canada
Head of School: Mr. Vince Pagano

General Information Coeducational day college-preparatory school. Grades 7–12. Founded: 1980. Setting: urban. 5-acre campus. 1 building on campus. Approved or accredited by Ontario Department of Education. Language of instruction: English. Total enrollment: 525. Upper school average class size: 17. Upper school faculty-student ratio: 1:16. There are 190 required school days per year for Upper School students.

Faculty School total: 45. In upper school: 22 men, 23 women.

Special Academic Programs Advanced Placement exam preparation.

Student Life Upper grades have uniform requirement, student council. Discipline rests primarily with faculty.

Tuition and Aid Day student tuition: CAN$18,600. Tuition installment plan (The Tuition Plan). Tuition reduction for siblings available.

Admissions Writing sample required. Deadline for receipt of application materials: February 2. Application fee required: CAN$125. Interview required.

Athletics Interscholastic: ball hockey (boys), baseball (b,g), basketball (b,g), golf (b), hockey (b,g), indoor track & field (b,g), running (b,g), softball (b,g), swimming and diving (b,g), volleyball (b,g); intramural: ball hockey (b), flag football (b), tai chi (b,g); coed interscholastic: Frisbee, scuba diving. 5 PE instructors.

Contact Mr. David Hecock. 416-391-1441 Ext. 23. Fax: 416-444-0949. E-mail: dhecock@crestwoodprepco.com. Web site: www.crestwoodprepco.com.

CRETIN-DERHAM HALL
550 South Albert Street
Saint Paul, Minnesota 55116
Head of School: Mr. Richard Engler

General Information Coeducational day college-preparatory, general academic, arts, business, religious studies, technology, and Junior ROTC school, affiliated with Roman Catholic Church. Grades 9–12. Founded: 1987. Setting: urban. Nearest major city is St. Paul. 15-acre campus. 5 buildings on campus. Approved or accredited by North Central Association of Colleges and Schools. Total enrollment: 1,321. Upper school average class size: 20. Upper school faculty-student ratio: 1:15. The average school day consists of 5 hours and 25 minutes.

Upper School Student Profile Grade 9: 330 students (167 boys, 163 girls); Grade 10: 333 students (167 boys, 166 girls); Grade 11: 333 students (172 boys, 161 girls); Grade 12: 325 students (158 boys, 167 girls). 93% of students are Roman Catholic.

Faculty School total: 120. In upper school: 56 men, 64 women; 61 have advanced degrees.

Subjects Offered 3-dimensional art, aerobics, algebra, American history, American literature, analysis, art history, arts, audio visual/media, biology, business, chemistry, computer math, computer programming, computer science, drama, economics, English, environmental science, ethics, fine arts, French, geography, geometry, German, government/civics, history, JROTC, Latin, mathematics, music, physical education, physics, religion, science, social studies, Spanish, speech, theater, theology, trigonometry, U.S. government and politics-AP.

Graduation Requirements Arts and fine arts (art, music, dance, drama), English, foreign language, health science, mathematics, physical education (includes health), religion (includes Bible studies and theology), science, social studies (includes history).

Special Academic Programs Advanced Placement exam preparation; honors section; accelerated programs; independent study; study at local college for college credit; academic accommodation for the gifted; remedial reading and/or remedial writing; remedial math.

College Admission Counseling 329 students graduated in 2009; 309 went to college, including College of Saint Benedict; University of Minnesota, Twin Cities Campus; University of St. Thomas; University of Wisconsin–Madison. Other: 20 had other specific plans.

Student Life Upper grades have uniform requirement, student council. Discipline rests primarily with faculty. Attendance at religious services is required.

Tuition and Aid Day student tuition: $9600. Tuition installment plan (monthly payment plans, individually arranged payment plans, 2- and 3-payment plans). Need-based scholarship grants, paying campus jobs available. In 2009–10, 44% of upper-school students received aid. Total amount of financial aid awarded in 2009–10: $1,900,000.

Admissions Traditional secondary-level entrance grade is 9. For fall 2009, 510 students applied for upper-level admission, 360 were accepted, 330 enrolled. STS required. Deadline for receipt of application materials: none. No application fee required.

Athletics Interscholastic: baseball (boys), basketball (b,g), cross-country running (b,g), dance team (g), diving (b,g), figure skating (g), football (b), golf (b,g), gymnastics (g), ice hockey (b,g), lacrosse (g), riflery (b,g), skiing (downhill) (b,g), soccer (b,g), softball (g), swimming and diving (b,g), tennis (b,g), track and field (b,g), ultimate Frisbee (b,g), volleyball (g); coed interscholastic: alpine skiing, badminton, cheering, fencing, JROTC drill; coed intramural: basketball, volleyball. 5 PE instructors, 1 athletic trainer.

Computers Computers are regularly used in all academic, data processing, publications, yearbook classes. Computer network features include on-campus library services, online commercial services, Internet access, Internet filtering or blocking technology, check assignments and contact faculty. Campus intranet and student e-mail accounts are available to students. Students grades are available online. The school has a published electronic and media policy.

Contact Mary Jo Groeller, Administrator of Admissions. 651-696-3302. Fax: 651-696-3394. E-mail: mjgroeller@c-dh.org. Web site: www.c-dh.org.

CROSS CREEK PROGRAMS
LaVerkin, Utah
See Special Needs Schools section.

CROSSPOINT ACADEMY
4012 Chico Way NW
Bremerton, Washington 98312-1397
Head of School: Mr. James White

General Information Coeducational day college-preparatory, arts, religious studies, and technology school, affiliated with Christian faith. Grades K–12. Founded: 1991. Setting: small town. Nearest major city is Tacoma. 7-acre campus. 7 buildings on campus. Approved or accredited by Association of Christian Schools International, Northwest Accreditation Commission, and Washington Department of Education. Total enrollment: 242. Upper school average class size: 17. Upper school faculty-student ratio: 1:8. There are 171 required school days per year for Upper School students. Upper School students typically attend 5 days per week. The average school day consists of 6 hours and 45 minutes.

Upper School Student Profile Grade 7: 14 students (6 boys, 8 girls); Grade 8: 26 students (11 boys, 15 girls); Grade 9: 25 students (13 boys, 12 girls); Grade 10: 28 students (12 boys, 16 girls); Grade 11: 17 students (9 boys, 8 girls); Grade 12: 31 students (18 boys, 13 girls). 70% of students are Christian faith.

Faculty School total: 25. In upper school: 6 men, 10 women; 8 have advanced degrees.

Subjects Offered Algebra, American literature, art, band, Bible, biology, calculus-AP, chemistry, choir, computer animation, computers, creative writing, desktop publishing, digital photography, drama, drama performance, earth science, English, geography, geometry, health, introduction to theater, keyboarding, leadership, life science, life skills, physical fitness, physical science, physics, practical living, pre-algebra, pre-calculus, programming, religion, science, senior project, Spanish, speech, student government, technology, U.S. government and politics-AP, U.S. history, U.S. history-AP, video, vocal ensemble, Washington State and Northwest History, weight training, world history, world literature, world religions, world wide web design, yearbook.

Graduation Requirements Arts and fine arts (art, music, dance, drama), Bible, computer science, English, foreign language, mathematics, physical education (includes health), practical living, science, social studies (includes history), speech.

Special Academic Programs Study at local college for college credit.

College Admission Counseling 33 students graduated in 2010; 32 went to college, including Baylor University; Central Washington University; Georgia Institute of Technology; Olympic College; Seattle Pacific University; University of Washington. Other: 1 went to work. Mean SAT critical reading: 578, mean SAT math: 569, mean SAT writing: 557, mean combined SAT: 1704, mean composite ACT: 24. 36% scored over 600 on SAT critical reading, 24% scored over 600 on SAT math, 36% scored over 600 on SAT writing, 36% scored over 1800 on combined SAT, 14% scored over 26 on composite ACT.

Student Life Upper grades have specified standards of dress, student council, honor system. Discipline rests primarily with faculty. Attendance at religious services is required.

Tuition and Aid Day student tuition: $9430. Tuition installment plan (monthly payment plans, prepayment discount plan, active military discount, Pastor, church employee & Christian school employee discounts). Tuition reduction for siblings, need-based scholarship grants available. In 2010–11, 28% of upper-school students received aid. Total amount of financial aid awarded in 2010–11: $171,000.

Admissions Traditional secondary-level entrance grade is 7. For fall 2010, 21 students applied for upper-level admission, 20 were accepted, 19 enrolled. Comprehensive educational evaluation required. Deadline for receipt of application materials: none. Application fee required: $50. Interview required.

Athletics Interscholastic: basketball (boys, girls), cross-country running (b,g), golf (b), soccer (b,g), softball (g), track and field (b,g), volleyball (g), weight training (b,g).

Computers Computers are regularly used in animation, computer applications, desktop publishing, digital applications, graphics, keyboarding, photography, publications, technology, video film production, Web site design, yearbook classes. Computer network features include Internet access, wireless campus network, Internet filtering or blocking technology. Student e-mail accounts are available to students. Students grades are available online. The school has a published electronic and media policy.

Contact Ms. Sherri M. Miller, Admissions and Marketing Coordinator. 360-377-7700 Ext. 5004. Fax: 360-377-7795. E-mail: smiller@crista.net. Web site: www.crosspointacademy.org.

CROSSROADS COLLEGE PREPARATORY SCHOOL

500 DeBaliviere Avenue
St. Louis, Missouri 63112
Head of School: William B. Handmaker

General Information Coeducational day college-preparatory and arts school. Grades 7–12. Founded: 1974. Setting: urban. 20-acre campus. 1 building on campus. Approved or accredited by Independent Schools Association of the Central States and Missouri Department of Education. Member of National Association of Independent Schools and Secondary School Admission Test Board. Total enrollment: 215. Upper school average class size: 14. Upper school faculty-student ratio: 1:9. Upper School students typically attend 5 days per week. The average school day consists of 7 hours and 30 minutes.

Upper School Student Profile Grade 9: 40 students (25 boys, 15 girls); Grade 10: 46 students (23 boys, 23 girls); Grade 11: 40 students (17 boys, 23 girls); Grade 12: 26 students (11 boys, 15 girls).

Faculty School total: 29. In upper school: 10 men, 11 women; 14 have advanced degrees.

Subjects Offered 3-dimensional art, advanced chemistry, African American history, African-American history, algebra, American literature, anatomy, art, art history, art history-AP, Asian history, biology, biology-AP, botany, calculus, calculus-AP, ceramics, chemistry, chemistry-AP, community service, comparative religion, computer applications, creative writing, drama, ecology, English, English literature, environmental science, environmental science-AP, environmental studies, European history, fine arts, French, geography, geology, geometry, history, journalism, keyboarding, Latin, literature and composition-AP, mathematics, music, music theater, photography, physical education, physics, psychology, SAT/ACT preparation, social sciences, sociology, Spanish, speech, studio art-AP, theater, trigonometry, U.S. history-AP, women's studies, word processing, world history, world literature.

Graduation Requirements American literature, arts and fine arts (art, music, dance, drama), biology, chemistry, classics, computer science, creative writing, earth science, electives, English composition, English literature, environmental science, foreign language, interdisciplinary studies, mathematics, non-Western literature, physical education (includes health), political science, practical arts, social sciences, social studies (includes history), U.S. government and politics, world cultures, one course taken at a local university or college during senior year.

Special Academic Programs Advanced Placement exam preparation; honors section; independent study; study at local college for college credit.

College Admission Counseling 36 students graduated in 2010; all went to college, including Grinnell College; Knox College; Saint Louis University; University of Chicago; Washington University in St. Louis; Wesleyan University. Mean SAT critical reading: 650, mean SAT math: 660, mean SAT writing: 630, mean composite ACT: 27.

Student Life Upper grades have specified standards of dress, student council, honor system. Discipline rests equally with students and faculty.

Summer Programs Enrichment, sports, art/fine arts programs offered; held on campus; accepts boys and girls; open to students from other schools.

Tuition and Aid Day student tuition: $16,750. Tuition installment plan (FACTS Tuition Payment Plan, monthly payment plans, individually arranged payment plans). Merit scholarship grants, need-based scholarship grants available. In 2010–11, 43% of upper-school students received aid.

Admissions Traditional secondary-level entrance grade is 9. For fall 2010, 36 students applied for upper-level admission, 24 were accepted, 15 enrolled. SSAT required. Deadline for receipt of application materials: January 21. Application fee required: $40. On-campus interview required.

Athletics Interscholastic: baseball (boys), basketball (b,g), indoor soccer (b,g), soccer (b,g), tennis (b,g), track and field (b,g), volleyball (g); intramural: soccer (b,g); coed interscholastic: bicycling, dance, fitness, physical fitness, physical training, weight lifting, weight training; coed intramural: aquatics, basketball, bicycling, dance team, drill team, fencing, indoor soccer, table tennis, touch football, volleyball, wall climbing, weight training, yoga. 3 PE instructors, 10 coaches.

Computers Computers are regularly used in computer applications, English, foreign language, history, journalism, mathematics, newspaper, programming, science, Web site design, word processing, writing, yearbook classes. Computer network features include on-campus library services, Internet access, wireless campus network, Internet filtering or blocking technology, SmartBoard usage in every academic classroom. Computer access in designated common areas is available to students. Students grades are available online.

Contact Maggie Baisch, Director of Admission. 314-367-8101. Fax: 314-367-9711. E-mail: maggie@crossroadscollegeprep.org. Web site: www.crossroadscollegeprep.org.

CROSSROADS SCHOOL FOR ARTS & SCIENCES

1714 21st Street
Santa Monica, California 90404-3917
Head of School: Mr. Bob Riddle

General Information Coeducational day college-preparatory, arts, and technology school. Grades K–12. Founded: 1971. Setting: urban. Nearest major city is Los Angeles. 3-acre campus. 16 buildings on campus. Approved or accredited by California Association of Independent Schools, Western Association of Schools and Colleges, and California Department of Education. Member of National Association of Independent Schools. Endowment: $13 million. Total enrollment: 1,139. Upper school average class size: 15. Upper school faculty-student ratio: 1:11. There are 161 required school days per year for Upper School students. Upper School students typically attend 5 days per week. The average school day consists of 7 hours.

Upper School Student Profile Grade 6: 94 students (47 boys, 47 girls); Grade 7: 116 students (59 boys, 57 girls); Grade 8: 118 students (62 boys, 56 girls); Grade 9: 129 students (57 boys, 72 girls); Grade 10: 123 students (59 boys, 64 girls); Grade 11: 132 students (64 boys, 68 girls); Grade 12: 116 students (66 boys, 50 girls).

Faculty School total: 153. In upper school: 39 men, 39 women; 44 have advanced degrees.

Subjects Offered Algebra, American history, American studies, art history, biology, calculus, ceramics, chemistry, community service, computer programming, computer science, creative writing, critical studies in film, cultural arts, dance, earth and space science, English, environmental education, film studies, French, gender issues, geometry, graphic design, great books, Greek, human development, Japanese, jazz ensemble, jazz theory, journalism, Latin, marine biology, marine ecology, music appreciation, music theory, orchestra, photography, physical education, physics, physiology, pre-calculus, sculpture, Spanish, statistics, studio art, theater, trigonometry, video film production, world civilizations, yoga.

Graduation Requirements Arts and fine arts (art, music, dance, drama), English, foreign language, human development, mathematics, physical education (includes health), science, social studies (includes history). Community service is required.

Special Academic Programs Honors section; term-away projects; academic accommodation for the gifted, the musically talented, and the artistically talented.

College Admission Counseling 119 students graduated in 2009; all went to college, including Barnard College; New York University; University of California, Berkeley; University of Southern California; University of Wisconsin–Madison. Mean SAT critical reading: 625, mean SAT math: 614, mean SAT writing: 652, mean combined SAT: 1891, mean composite ACT: 26.

Student Life Upper grades have student council. Discipline rests primarily with faculty.

Tuition and Aid Day student tuition: $28,170. Tuition installment plan (individually arranged payment plans). Merit scholarship grants, Tuition Reduction Fund available. In 2009–10, 22% of upper-school students received aid; total upper-school merit-scholarship money awarded: $50,000. Total amount of financial aid awarded in 2009–10: $2,200,751.

Admissions Traditional secondary-level entrance grade is 9. For fall 2009, 155 students applied for upper-level admission, 63 were accepted, 44 enrolled. ISEE required. Deadline for receipt of application materials: December 12. Application fee required: $125. On-campus interview required.

Athletics Interscholastic: baseball (boys), basketball (b,g), cross-country running (b,g), soccer (b,g), softball (g), tennis (b,g), track and field (b,g), volleyball (b,g); coed interscholastic: flag football, golf, swimming and diving; coed intramural: canoeing/kayaking, climbing, hiking/backpacking, kayaking, outdoor activities, outdoor education, rock climbing, ropes courses, snowshoeing, table tennis. 10 PE instructors, 29 coaches, 1 athletic trainer.

Computers Computers are regularly used in college planning, creative writing, foreign language, graphic design, journalism, Latin, mathematics, music, newspaper, programming, science classes. Computer network features include on-campus library services, online commercial services, Internet access, wireless campus network. Student e-mail accounts and computer access in designated common areas are available to students. The school has a published electronic and media policy.

Contact Celia Lee, Director of Admissions. 310-829-7391 Ext. 704. Fax: 310-392-9011. E-mail: clee@xrds.org. Web site: www.xrds.org.

CRYSTAL SPRINGS UPLANDS SCHOOL

400 Uplands Drive
Hillsborough, California 94010
Head of School: Ms. Amy Richards

General Information Coeducational day college-preparatory school. Grades 6–12. Founded: 1952. Setting: suburban. Nearest major city is San Francisco. 10-acre campus. 4 buildings on campus. Approved or accredited by California Association of Independent Schools, Western Association of Schools and Colleges, and California Department of Education. Member of National Association of Independent Schools and Secondary School Admission Test Board. Endowment: $15 million. Total enrollment: 358. Upper school average class size: 14. Upper school faculty-student ratio: 1:9.

Faculty School total: 44. In upper school: 18 men, 26 women; 24 have advanced degrees.

Subjects Offered Acting, advanced computer applications, algebra, American history, American history-AP, American literature, art, art history-AP, art-AP, astronomy, biology, biology-AP, calculus, calculus-AP, ceramics, chamber groups, chemistry, chorus, comparative cultures, computer math, computer programming, computer science, concert bell choir, creative writing, dance, dance performance, drama, English, English literature, ensembles, environmental science-AP, European history, European history-AP, fine arts, French, French language-AP, French literature-AP, geometry, government and politics-AP, graphic design, health, history, mathematics, multicultural literature, music, music theory-AP, photography, physical education, physics, physics-AP, poetry, post-calculus, pre-calculus, science, Shakespeare, Spanish, Spanish language-AP, Spanish literature-AP, statistics, theater, U.S. government and politics-AP, video film production, wellness, world history, world literature, writing.

Graduation Requirements Arts and fine arts (art, music, dance, drama), English, foreign language, history, mathematics, physical education (includes health), science, senior project.

Special Academic Programs 16 Advanced Placement exams for which test preparation is offered; honors section; term-away projects; domestic exchange program; study abroad.

College Admission Counseling 61 students graduated in 2010; all went to college, including Stanford University; University of California, Los Angeles; University of California, San Diego; University of Pennsylvania; University of Southern California. Mean SAT critical reading: 674, mean SAT math: 703, mean SAT writing: 688, mean combined SAT: 2067, mean composite ACT: 29.

Student Life Upper grades have specified standards of dress, student council, honor system. Discipline rests equally with students and faculty.

Tuition and Aid Day student tuition: $32,700. Tuition installment plan (Insured Tuition Payment Plan, monthly payment plans, Tuition Management Systems Plan). Need-based scholarship grants available. In 2010–11, 22% of upper-school students received aid. Total amount of financial aid awarded in 2010–11: $2,000,000.

Admissions Traditional secondary-level entrance grade is 9. ISEE or SSAT required. Deadline for receipt of application materials: January 13. Application fee required: $85. On-campus interview required.

Athletics Interscholastic: baseball (boys), basketball (b,g), cross-country running (b,g), football (b), soccer (b,g), swimming and diving (b,g), tennis (b,g), track and field (b,g), volleyball (b,g); coed interscholastic: badminton, dance, golf; coed intramural: dance, fitness, outdoors, rock climbing. 3 PE instructors, 14 coaches, 1 athletic trainer.

Computers Computers are regularly used in all academic classes. Computer network features include on-campus library services, online commercial services, Internet access, wireless campus network, Internet filtering or blocking technology. Campus intranet, student e-mail accounts, and computer access in designated common areas are available to students. The school has a published electronic and media policy.

Contact Aaron Whitmore, Director of Admission. 650-342-4175 Ext. 1517. Fax: 650-342-7611. E-mail: admission@csus.org. Web site: www.csus.org.

THE CULVER ACADEMIES
1300 Academy Road
Culver, Indiana 46511
Head of School: Mr. John N. Buxton

General Information Coeducational boarding and day college-preparatory and arts school. Grades 9–PG. Founded: 1894. Setting: small town. Nearest major city is South Bend. Students are housed in single-sex dormitories. 1,800-acre campus. 38 buildings on campus. Approved or accredited by Independent Schools Association of the Central States, North Central Association of Colleges and Schools, and Indiana Department of Education. Member of National Association of Independent Schools and Secondary School Admission Test Board. Endowment: $285 million. Total enrollment: 792. Upper school average class size: 14. Upper school faculty-student ratio: 1:9. There are 185 required school days per year for Upper School students. Upper School students typically attend 5 days per week. The average school day consists of 6 hours.

Upper School Student Profile Grade 9: 148 students (93 boys, 55 girls); Grade 10: 210 students (122 boys, 88 girls); Grade 11: 225 students (124 boys, 101 girls); Grade 12: 207 students (110 boys, 97 girls); Postgraduate: 1 student (1 girl). 92% of students are boarding students. 30% are state residents. 39 states are represented in upper school student body. 24% are international students. International students from Canada, China, Mexico, Republic of Korea, Saudi Arabia, and Taiwan; 22 other countries represented in student body.

Faculty School total: 97. In upper school: 53 men, 44 women; 83 have advanced degrees; 16 reside on campus.

Subjects Offered Acting, advanced math, African-American history, algebra, American government, American history, American history-AP, American literature, anatomy, anatomy and physiology, art, art history, arts, ballet, Basic programming, biology, biology-AP, calculus, calculus-AP, career/college preparation, ceramics,

character education, chemistry, chemistry-AP, Chinese, choir, church history, college admission preparation, college placement, college planning, comparative government and politics-AP, comparative religion, computer math, computer programming, computer science, computer science-AP, dance, drama, dramatic arts, driver education, economics, economics-AP, English, English language-AP, English literature, entrepreneurship, equestrian sports, equine science, equitation, ESL, ethics and responsibility, European history, film studies, fine arts, fitness, French, French-AP, geology, geometry, German, German literature, German-AP, global studies, government, government-AP, government/civics, health and wellness, honors English, honors geometry, humanities, instrumental music, integrated mathematics, integrated science, jazz band, Latin, Latin-AP, leadership, library research, macro/microeconomics-AP, mathematics, mentorship program, music, music theory, music theory-AP, photography, physical education, physics, physics-AP, physiology, piano, play production, pottery, pre-algebra, pre-calculus, science, science research, Shakespeare, social studies, Spanish, Spanish language-AP, Spanish-AP, speech, statistics-AP, strings, theater, trigonometry, U.S. government and politics-AP, U.S. history-AP, world history, world religions.

Graduation Requirements Arts and fine arts (art, music, dance, drama), English, foreign language, health education, history, leadership, mathematics, science, senior community service project.

Special Academic Programs 20 Advanced Placement exams for which test preparation is offered; honors section; academic accommodation for the gifted, the musically talented, and the artistically talented; ESL (24 students enrolled).

College Admission Counseling 201 students graduated in 2010; 199 went to college, including Indiana University Bloomington; Purdue University; Southern Methodist University; The University of North Carolina at Chapel Hill; Vanderbilt University. Other: 2 had other specific plans.

Student Life Upper grades have uniform requirement, student council, honor system. Discipline rests equally with students and faculty. Attendance at religious services is required.

Summer Programs Enrichment, advancement, ESL, sports, art/fine arts, computer instruction programs offered; session focuses on leadership training, citizenship, lifetime interests and skills development; held on campus; accepts boys and girls; open to students from other schools. 1,300 students usually enrolled. 2011 schedule: June 25 to August 7. Application deadline: May 1.

Tuition and Aid Day student tuition: $26,000; 7-day tuition and room/board: $36,000. Guaranteed tuition plan. Tuition installment plan (Key Tuition Payment Plan). Merit scholarship grants, need-based scholarship grants available. In 2010–11, 46% of upper-school students received aid; total upper-school merit-scholarship money awarded: $7,850,000. Total amount of financial aid awarded in 2010–11: $8,900,000.

Admissions Traditional secondary-level entrance grade is 9. For fall 2010, 2,500 students applied for upper-level admission, 528 were accepted, 266 enrolled. SSAT or TOEFL required. Deadline for receipt of application materials: June 1. Application fee required: $30. Interview required.

Athletics Interscholastic: baseball (boys), basketball (b,g), cheering (g), crew (b,g), cross-country running (b,g), diving (b,g), equestrian sports (b,g), fencing (b,g), football (b), golf (b,g), hockey (b,g), horseback riding (b,g), ice hockey (b,g), indoor hockey (b,g), indoor track & field (b,g), lacrosse (b,g), polo (b,g), soccer (b,g), softball (g), swimming and diving (b,g), tennis (b,g), track and field (b,g), volleyball (g), winter (indoor) track (b,g), wrestling (b,g); intramural: aerobics (b,g), ballet (g), basketball (b,g), dance (b,g), dance squad (g), dance team (g), danceline (g), drill team (b,g), flag football (b), ice hockey (b,g), indoor soccer (b,g), marksmanship (b,g), modern dance (b,g), paint ball (b,g), racquetball (b,g), rugby (b,g), soccer (b,g); coed interscholastic: dressage, sailing; coed intramural: aerobics, aerobics/dance, alpine skiing, aquatics, archery, backpacking, badminton, broomball, climbing, combined training, cross-country running, figure skating, fitness, fitness walking, Frisbee, handball, hiking/backpacking, horseback riding, ice skating, independent competitive sports, indoor track & field, jogging, life saving, Nautilus, outdoor activities, outdoor adventure, outdoor skills, physical fitness, physical training, power lifting, project adventure, ropes courses, rowing, running, scuba diving, skeet shooting, skiing (downhill), snowboarding, strength & conditioning, swimming and diving, table tennis, tai chi, trap and skeet, ultimate Frisbee, volleyball, walking, wall climbing, weight lifting, weight training, wilderness, yoga. 8 PE instructors, 4 athletic trainers.

Computers Computers are regularly used in all classes. Computer network features include on-campus library services, online commercial services, Internet access, wireless campus network, Internet filtering or blocking technology, each student is issued a laptop. Campus intranet and student e-mail accounts are available to students. Students grades are available online. The school has a published electronic and media policy.

Contact Mr. Michael Turnbull, Director of Admissions. 574-842-7100. Fax: 574-842-8066. E-mail: turnbul@culver.org. Web site: culver.org.

CURREY INGRAM ACADEMY
6544 Murray Lane
Brentwood, Tennessee 37027
Head of School: Ms. Kathleen G. Rayburn

General Information Coeducational day college-preparatory, arts, bilingual studies, technology, ethics and character education, and service learning school; primarily serves students with learning disabilities, individuals with Attention Deficit Disorder, dyslexic students, non-verbal learning disabilities, and speech and language disabilities. Grades K–12. Founded: 1968. Setting: suburban. Nearest major city is Nashville. 83-acre campus. 2 buildings on campus. Approved or accredited by Council of Accreditation and School Improvement, Southern Association of Colleges and Schools, Southern Association of Independent Schools, Tennessee Association of Independent Schools, and Tennessee Department of Education. Total enrollment: 280. Upper school average class size: 7. Upper school faculty-student ratio: 1:4. There are 175 required school days per year for Upper School students. Upper School students typically attend 5 days per week. The average school day consists of 6 hours.

Upper School Student Profile Grade 9: 24 students (16 boys, 8 girls); Grade 10: 15 students (9 boys, 6 girls); Grade 11: 19 students (13 boys, 6 girls); Grade 12: 9 students (4 boys, 5 girls).

Faculty In upper school: 10 men, 11 women; 12 have advanced degrees.

Subjects Offered Algebra, American government, art, basic language skills, biology, British literature, character education, chemistry, cinematography, college admission preparation, college awareness, college counseling, college planning, community service, digital music, digital photography, drama performance, earth science, economics, electives, English composition, English literature, environmental science, ethics and responsibility, government, health, history, integrated technology fundamentals, learning strategies, life skills, literature, modern world history, music, newspaper, physical education, physics, pragmatics, pre-calculus, reading/study skills, social studies, sports, studio art, technology, video film production, vocal music, writing, writing workshop, yearbook.

Graduation Requirements Arts and fine arts (art, music, dance, drama), electives, English, ethics, foreign language, mathematics, physical education (includes health), science, social studies (includes history), students who need remediation in reading/writing take Reading/Writing Workshop instead of foreign language, seniors must complete Service Learning credit plus 30 hours of community service.

Special Academic Programs Honors section; independent study; academic accommodation for the gifted, the musically talented, and the artistically talented; remedial reading and/or remedial writing; programs in English, mathematics, general development for dyslexic students.

College Admission Counseling 22 students graduated in 2010; all went to college, including Belmont University; Denison University; Lesley University; Middle Tennessee State University; Western Kentucky University.

Student Life Upper grades have uniform requirement, student council, honor system. Discipline rests primarily with faculty.

Summer Programs Enrichment, sports, art/fine arts programs offered; session focuses on Camps for arts and athletics; held on campus; accepts boys and girls; open to students from other schools. 2011 schedule: June.

Tuition and Aid Day student tuition: $33,378. Tuition installment plan (monthly payment plans). Need-based scholarship grants available. In 2010–11, 35% of upper-school students received aid. Total amount of financial aid awarded in 2010–11: $1,200,000.

Admissions Traditional secondary-level entrance grade is 9. Psychoeducational evaluation required. Deadline for receipt of application materials: none. Application fee required: $250. Interview required.

Athletics Interscholastic: baseball (boys), basketball (b,g), cheering (g), cross-country running (b,g), football (b), softball (g), volleyball (g); intramural: dance (g); coed interscholastic: soccer.

Computers Computers are regularly used in all academic classes. Computer network features include on-campus library services, Internet access, wireless campus network, Internet filtering or blocking technology, iPods for instructional use in classrooms. Students grades are available online. The school has a published electronic and media policy.

Contact Ms. Amber Mogg, Director of Admission. 615-507-3173 Ext. 244. Fax: 615-507-3170. E-mail: amber.mogg@curreyingram.org. Web site: www.curreyingram.org.

CUSHING ACADEMY

39 School Street
PO Box 8000
Ashburnham, Massachusetts 01430-8000
Head of School: Dr. James Tracy

General Information Coeducational boarding and day college-preparatory, arts, and technology school. Grades 9–PG. Founded: 1865. Setting: small town. Nearest major city is Boston. Students are housed in single-sex dormitories. 162-acre campus. 31 buildings on campus. Approved or accredited by Association of Independent Schools in New England, New England Association of Schools and Colleges, and Massachusetts Department of Education. Member of National Association of Independent Schools and Secondary School Admission Test Board. Endowment: $22.6 million. Total enrollment: 445. Upper school average class size: 12. Upper school faculty-student ratio: 1:8. There are 152 required school days per year for Upper School students. Upper School students typically attend 5 days per week. The average school day consists of 7 hours.

Upper School Student Profile Grade 9: 65 students (41 boys, 24 girls); Grade 10: 107 students (67 boys, 40 girls); Grade 11: 140 students (71 boys, 69 girls); Grade 12: 110 students (70 boys, 40 girls); Postgraduate: 23 students (20 boys, 3 girls). 85% of students are boarding students. 31% are state residents. 28 states are represented in upper school student body. 30% are international students. International students from Canada, China, Japan, Republic of Korea, Spain, and Taiwan; 30 other countries represented in student body.

Faculty School total: 64. In upper school: 27 men, 37 women; 37 have advanced degrees; 47 reside on campus.

Subjects Offered Advanced biology, advanced math, Advanced Placement courses, aerobics, algebra, American government, American history, American literature, American literature-AP, anatomy, anatomy and physiology, architectural drawing, art, art history, athletic training, bioethics, biology, biology-AP, calculus, calculus-AP, career education internship, chemistry, chemistry-AP, Chinese, chorus, Civil War, community service, computer programming, computer science, creative arts, creative drama, creative writing, dance, developmental language skills, digital photography, discrete mathematics, drafting, drama, drawing, driver education, earth and space science, ecology, ecology, environmental systems, economics, economics and history, economics-AP, English, English literature, environmental science, ESL, ethics, European history, expository writing, fine arts, French, geometry, government/civics, grammar, graphic arts, health, health and wellness, history, honors algebra, honors English, honors geometry, honors U.S. history, honors world history, Latin, Latin-AP, Mandarin, marine biology, mathematics, mechanical drawing, music, music history, music theory, musical theater, photography, physics, physiology, pre-calculus, probability and statistics, psychology, SAT preparation, science, social studies, sociology, Spanish, Spanish-AP, speech, stagecraft, statistics-AP, student government, technology, The 20th Century, theater, theater history, trigonometry, U.S. government and politics-AP, U.S. history, United Nations and international issues, Vietnam War, visual arts, vocal music, wind instruments, world history, world literature, World-Wide-Web publishing, writing.

Graduation Requirements Arts and fine arts (art, music, dance, drama), English, foreign language, health and wellness, mathematics, science, social studies (includes history).

Special Academic Programs 14 Advanced Placement exams for which test preparation is offered; honors section; independent study; term-away projects; academic accommodation for the gifted, the musically talented, and the artistically talented; remedial reading and/or remedial writing; remedial math; programs in English, mathematics, general development for dyslexic students; ESL (75 students enrolled).

College Admission Counseling 128 students graduated in 2010; 125 went to college, including Boston University; Emory University; Roger Williams University; University of Massachusetts Amherst; Wheaton College. Other: 2 entered a postgraduate year.

Student Life Upper grades have specified standards of dress, student council, honor system. Discipline rests primarily with faculty.

Summer Programs Remediation, enrichment, advancement, ESL, sports, art/fine arts, computer instruction programs offered; session focuses on enrichment; held on campus; accepts boys and girls; open to students from other schools. 320 students usually enrolled. 2011 schedule: July 3 to August 5.

Tuition and Aid Day student tuition: $32,200; 7-day tuition and room/board: $44,600. Tuition installment plan (Academic Management Services Plan, monthly payment plans). Merit scholarship grants, need-based scholarship grants available. In 2010–11, 26% of upper-school students received aid; total upper-school merit-scholarship money awarded: $100,000. Total amount of financial aid awarded in 2010–11: $3,200,000.

Admissions Traditional secondary-level entrance grade is 9. For fall 2010, 804 students applied for upper-level admission, 505 were accepted, 185 enrolled. ACT, PSAT, SAT, SLEP, SSAT or TOEFL required. Deadline for receipt of application materials: February 1. Application fee required: $50. Interview required.

Athletics Interscholastic: baseball (boys), basketball (b,g), field hockey (g), football (b), hockey (b,g), ice hockey (b,g), lacrosse (b,g), running (b,g), skiing (downhill) (b,g), soccer (b,g), softball (g), tennis (b,g), track and field (b,g), volleyball (g); intramural: flag football (b); coed interscholastic: alpine skiing, cross-country running, golf, running; coed intramural: aerobics, aerobics/dance, alpine skiing, dance, equestrian sports, figure skating, fitness, horseback riding, ice hockey, ice skating, independent competitive sports, martial arts, modern dance, outdoor adventure, outdoor education, outdoor skills, physical training, ropes courses, skiing (downhill), snowboarding, strength & conditioning, wall climbing, weight training. 2 coaches, 2 athletic trainers.

Computers Computers are regularly used in art, English, history, mathematics, science classes. Computer network features include on-campus library services, online commercial services, Internet access, wireless campus network, Internet filtering or blocking technology, CushNet (on campus network). Campus intranet, student e-mail accounts, and computer access in designated common areas are available to students. Students grades are available online. The school has a published electronic and media policy.

Contact Mrs. Deborah Gustafson, Co-Director of Admissions. 978-827-7300. Fax: 978-827-6253. E-mail: admissions@cushing.org. Web site: www.cushing.org.

See Display on page 212 and Close-Up on page 766.

DADE CHRISTIAN SCHOOL

6601 NW 167 Street
Miami, Florida 33015
Head of School: Dr. Jim Virtue, EdD

General Information Coeducational day college-preparatory, arts, business, religious studies, bilingual studies, and technology school, affiliated with Baptist Church. Grades 1–12. Founded: 1961. Setting: suburban. 32-acre campus. 1 building on campus. Approved or accredited by CITA (Commission on International and Trans-Regional Accreditation), Southern Association of Colleges and Schools, and Florida Department of Education. Total enrollment: 863. Upper school average class size: 19. Upper school faculty-student ratio: 1:10. There are 180 required school days per year for Upper School students. Upper School students typically attend 5 days per week. The average school day consists of 6 hours and 20 minutes.

Upper School Student Profile Grade 9: 82 students (42 boys, 40 girls); Grade 10: 91 students (38 boys, 53 girls); Grade 11: 68 students (42 boys, 26 girls); Grade 12: 74 students (35 boys, 39 girls).

Faculty School total: 91. In upper school: 20 men, 26 women; 18 have advanced degrees.

Subjects Offered 20th century history, accounting, advanced chemistry, advanced math, algebra, American government, American studies, analysis and differential calculus, anatomy and physiology, ancient world history, art, art-AP, Bible, Bible studies, biology, British literature (honors), calculus, calculus-AP, chemistry, chemistry-AP, choir, choral music, Christian and Hebrew scripture, Christian doctrine, Christian ethics, Christian studies, computer applications, computer graphics, concert band, concert choir, contemporary history, drama, earth science, economics, English, English composition, English language and composition-AP, English language-AP, English literature, English literature and composition-AP, ethics, French, general math, geography, geometry, health and wellness, honors algebra, honors English, honors geometry, honors U.S. history, honors world history, keyboarding, Life of Christ, life science, linear algebra, marine biology, modern world history, orchestra, physical education, physics, pre-algebra, psychology, psychology-AP, Spanish, Spanish language-AP, studio art-AP, U.S. government and politics-AP, U.S. history, U.S. history-AP, vocal ensemble.

Graduation Requirements Arts and fine arts (art, music, dance, drama), Bible, English, foreign language, mathematics, physical education (includes health), science, social studies (includes history), performing/practical arts, requirements for scholars diploma differ.

Special Academic Programs Advanced Placement exam preparation; honors section; study at local college for college credit; academic accommodation for the gifted.

College Admission Counseling 77 students graduated in 2009; 76 went to college, including Broward College; Florida International University; Miami Dade College; Nova Southeastern University; University of Central Florida; University of Miami. Other: 1 entered military service. Median SAT critical reading: 470, median SAT math: 450, median SAT writing: 450, median combined SAT: 1390, median composite ACT: 20. 10% scored over 600 on SAT critical reading, 10% scored over 600 on SAT math, 15% scored over 600 on SAT writing, 6% scored over 1800 on combined SAT, 20% scored over 26 on composite ACT.

Student Life Upper grades have uniform requirement, student council. Discipline rests primarily with faculty.

Tuition and Aid Day student tuition: $10,200. Tuition installment plan (FACTS Tuition Payment Plan). Tuition reduction for siblings, need-based scholarship grants, paying campus jobs available.

Admissions Traditional secondary-level entrance grade is 9. For fall 2009, 75 students applied for upper-level admission, 35 were accepted, 32 enrolled. Admissions testing required. Deadline for receipt of application materials: August 1. Application fee required: $150. Interview required.

Athletics Interscholastic: baseball (boys, girls), basketball (b,g), cheering (g), cross-country running (b,g), football (b), golf (b,g), soccer (b,g), softball (g), tennis (b,g), track and field (b,g), volleyball (g), wrestling (b). 6 PE instructors, 6 coaches, 1 athletic trainer.

Computers Computers are regularly used in computer applications, graphics, keyboarding, Web site design classes. Computer resources include on-campus library services, online commercial services, Internet access. The school has a published electronic and media policy.

Contact Mrs. Santa Granda, School Office Secretary. 305-827-8767. Fax: 305-826-4072. E-mail: sgranda@dadechristian.org. Web site: www.dadechristian.org.

DAKOTA CHRISTIAN HIGH SCHOOL

37614 Highway 44
Corsica, South Dakota 57328
Head of School: Ivan Groothuis

General Information Coeducational day college-preparatory, general academic, business, religious studies, and technology school, affiliated with Christian faith. Grades 9–12. Founded: 1955. Setting: rural. Nearest major city is Mitchell. 17-acre campus. 1 building on campus. Approved or accredited by Christian Schools International and South Dakota Department of Education. Endowment: $475,000.

Dakota Christian High School

Total enrollment: 126. Upper school average class size: 15. Upper school faculty-student ratio: 1:8. There are 180 required school days per year for Upper School students.

Upper School Student Profile Grade 7: 10 students (5 boys, 5 girls); Grade 8: 7 students (3 boys, 4 girls); Grade 9: 12 students (7 boys, 5 girls); Grade 10: 9 students (3 boys, 6 girls); Grade 11: 11 students (2 boys, 9 girls); Grade 12: 18 students (10 boys, 8 girls). 80% of students are Christian faith.

Faculty School total: 9. In upper school: 5 men, 4 women; 4 have advanced degrees.

Subjects Offered Accounting, algebra, American history, American literature, ancient world history, Bible studies, biology, business law, chemistry, Christian ethics, church history, computer studies, concert band, concert choir, creative writing, earth science, English, English literature, fine arts, geometry, government/civics, grammar, history, home economics, keyboarding, mathematics, music, New Testament, personal finance, philosophy, physical education, physics, physiology, pre-calculus, psychology, religion, science, social studies, Spanish, speech, statistics, trigonometry, world history, world literature, yearbook.

Graduation Requirements Algebra, arts and fine arts (art, music, dance, drama), biology, computer studies, English, first aid, geography, geometry, keyboarding, music appreciation, philosophy, physical education (includes health), physical science, religion (includes Bible studies and theology), social sciences, sociology, speech, U.S. history, world history, writing, 10 hours of community service.

Special Academic Programs Independent study; study at local college for college credit.

College Admission Counseling 12 students graduated in 2010; 10 went to college, including Dordt College; South Dakota State University; The University of South Dakota; Trinity Christian College; University of Sioux Falls. Other: 2 went to work. Median composite ACT: 23.

Student Life Upper grades have specified standards of dress, student council, honor system. Discipline rests primarily with faculty. Attendance at religious services is required.

Tuition and Aid Day student tuition: $4700. Tuition installment plan (monthly payment plans, individually arranged payment plans). Tuition reduction for siblings, need-based scholarship grants available. In 2010–11, 100% of upper-school students received aid. Total amount of financial aid awarded in 2010–11: $300,000.

Admissions Traditional secondary-level entrance grade is 9. For fall 2010, 50 students applied for upper-level admission, 50 were accepted, 50 enrolled. Deadline for receipt of application materials: none. Application fee required: $100. Interview recommended.

Athletics Interscholastic: basketball (boys, girls); cheering (g), football (b), volleyball (g); intramural: baseball (b), kickball (b,g), softball (g); coed interscholastic: cross-country running, golf, track and field; coed intramural: archery, floor hockey, paddle tennis, soccer, touch football, volleyball. 5 coaches.

Computers Computers are regularly used in accounting, business applications, business skills, social studies, Spanish, typing, word processing, writing, yearbook classes. Computer network features include on-campus library services, Internet access, wireless campus network, Internet filtering or blocking technology. Students grades are available online. The school has a published electronic and media policy.

Contact Ivan Groothuis, Principal. 605-243-2211. Fax: 605-243-2379. Web site: www.dchs.net.

DALLAS ACADEMY

Dallas, Texas
See Special Needs Schools section.

DALLAS CHRISTIAN SCHOOL

1515 Republic Parkway
Mesquite, Texas 75150
Head of School: Dr. Colleen Netterville

General Information Coeducational day college-preparatory and religious studies school, affiliated with Church of Christ. Grades PK–12. Founded: 1957. Setting: suburban. Nearest major city is Dallas. 60-acre campus. 7 buildings on campus. Approved or accredited by National Christian School Association, Southern Association of Colleges and Schools, and Texas Department of Education. Total enrollment: 595. Upper school average class size: 25. Upper school faculty-student ratio: 1:12. There are 178 required school days per year for Upper School students. Upper School students typically attend 5 days per week. The average school day consists of 7 hours and 15 minutes.

Upper School Student Profile 36% of students are members of Church of Christ.

Faculty School total: 56. In upper school: 13 men, 17 women; 14 have advanced degrees.

Subjects Offered Algebra, American history, American literature, art, band, Bible studies, biology, calculus, cheerleading, chemistry, chorus, computer math, computer science, creative writing, drama, economics, English, English literature, fine arts, French, geography, geometry, government/civics, health, history, humanities, journalism, mathematics, newspaper, physical education, physics, religion, science, sign language, social studies, Spanish, speech, speech origins of English, theater, world history, world literature, yearbook.

Graduation Requirements Arts and fine arts (art, music, dance, drama), computer science, English, foreign language, mathematics, physical education (includes health), religion (includes Bible studies and theology), science, social studies (includes history), speech origins of English, seniors must take SAT or ACT.

Special Academic Programs Study at local college for college credit.

College Admission Counseling 71 students graduated in 2010; 70 went to college, including Abilene Christian University; Austin College; Baylor University; Dallas Baptist University; Pepperdine University; Texas A&M University. Mean SAT critical reading: 603, mean SAT math: 568, mean SAT writing: 595, mean composite ACT: 27.

Student Life Upper grades have uniform requirement, student council, honor system. Discipline rests primarily with faculty. Attendance at religious services is required.

Tuition and Aid Day student tuition: $12,450. Tuition installment plan (FACTS Tuition Payment Plan). Tuition reduction for siblings, need-based scholarship grants available. In 2010–11, 18% of upper-school students received aid. Total amount of financial aid awarded in 2010–11: $180,000.

Admissions Traditional secondary-level entrance grade is 9. For fall 2010, 32 students applied for upper-level admission, 20 were accepted, 18 enrolled. ERB IF, ERB Mathematics, ERB Reading and Math and Woodcock-Johnson Revised Achievement Test required. Deadline for receipt of application materials: none. Application fee required. On-campus interview required.

Athletics Interscholastic: baseball (boys), basketball (b,g), cheering (g), cross-country running (b,g), drill team (g), football (b), golf (b,g), soccer (b,g), softball (g), tennis (b,g), track and field (b,g), volleyball (g). 2 PE instructors.

Computers Computers are regularly used in computer applications, newspaper, Web site design, yearbook classes. Computer network features include on-campus library services, Internet access, Internet filtering or blocking technology. Student e-mail accounts are available to students. Students grades are available online.

Contact Mrs. Katie Neuroth, Admissions Assistant. 972-270-5495 Ext. 266. Fax: 972-686-9436. E-mail: kneuroth@dallaschristian.com. Web site: www.dallaschristian.com.

THE DALTON SCHOOL

108 East 89th Street
New York, New York 10128-1599
Head of School: Ellen C. Stein

General Information Coeducational day college-preparatory and arts school. Grades K–12. Founded: 1919. Setting: urban. 2 buildings on campus. Approved or accredited by New York State Association of Independent Schools. Member of National Association of Independent Schools and Secondary School Admission Test Board. Endowment: $65 million. Total enrollment: 1,306. Upper school average class size: 15. Upper school faculty-student ratio: 1:7.

Upper School Student Profile Grade 9: 116 students (59 boys, 57 girls); Grade 10: 119 students (61 boys, 58 girls); Grade 11: 117 students (59 boys, 58 girls); Grade 12: 109 students (52 boys, 57 girls).

Faculty School total: 203. In upper school: 60 men, 61 women; 58 have advanced degrees.

Subjects Offered Algebra, American history, American legal systems, American literature, architecture, art, art history, Asian literature, astronomy, biology, calculus, ceramics, chemistry, community service, computer programming, computer science, dance, earth science, ecology, economics, English, English literature, environmental science, ethics, European history, fine arts, French, geometry, government/civics, health, history, Latin, law, mathematics, music, philosophy, photography, physical education, physics, Russian literature, science, social studies, Spanish, theater, trigonometry, world history, world literature.

Graduation Requirements Arts and fine arts (art, music, dance, drama), computer science, English, foreign language, history, mathematics, physical education (includes health), science. Community service is required.

Special Academic Programs Advanced Placement exam preparation; honors section; independent study; study at local college for college credit.

College Admission Counseling 100 students graduated in 2010; all went to college, including Brown University; Cornell University; Harvard University; The George Washington University; University of Pennsylvania; Yale University. Median SAT critical reading: 690, median SAT math: 680, median SAT writing: 720.

Student Life Upper grades have student council. Discipline rests equally with students and faculty.

Tuition and Aid Day student tuition: $35,300. Tuition installment plan (FACTS Tuition Payment Plan, 2-payment plan). Need-based scholarship grants available. In 2010–11, 24% of upper-school students received aid. Total amount of financial aid awarded in 2010–11: $2,938,600.

Admissions Traditional secondary-level entrance grade is 9. For fall 2010, 394 students applied for upper-level admission, 50 were accepted, 30 enrolled. ISEE or SSAT required. Deadline for receipt of application materials: November 19. Application fee required: $50. On-campus interview required.

Athletics Interscholastic: baseball (boys), basketball (b,g), lacrosse (b,g), soccer (b,g), softball (g), tennis (b,g), track and field (b,g), wrestling (b); intramural: baseball (b), basketball (b,g); coed interscholastic: cross-country running, football, swimming and diving, volleyball; coed intramural: cheering, dance, football, modern dance, ultimate Frisbee. 10 PE instructors, 14 coaches, 1 athletic trainer.

Computers Computers are regularly used in English, foreign language, mathematics, science classes. Computer network features include on-campus library services, online commercial services, Internet access, wireless campus network, Internet filtering or blocking technology. Campus intranet, student e-mail accounts, and computer access in designated common areas are available to students.

Contact Eva Radó, Director, Middle and High School Admissions. 212-423-5262. Fax: 212-423-5259. E-mail: rado@dalton.org. Web site: www.dalton.org.

DAMIEN HIGH SCHOOL

2280 Damien Avenue
La Verne, California 91750
Head of School: Rev. Patrick Travers

General Information Boys' day college-preparatory school, affiliated with Roman Catholic Church. Grades 9–12. Founded: 1959. Setting: suburban. Nearest major city is Los Angeles. 23-acre campus. 9 buildings on campus. Approved or accredited by Western Association of Schools and Colleges, Western Catholic Education Association, and California Department of Education. Endowment: $2 million. Total enrollment: 980. Upper school average class size: 22. Upper school faculty-student ratio: 1:22. There are 180 required school days per year for Upper School students. Upper School students typically attend 5 days per week. The average school day consists of 7 hours.

Upper School Student Profile Grade 9: 230 students (230 boys); Grade 10: 240 students (240 boys); Grade 11: 240 students (240 boys); Grade 12: 270 students (270 boys). 65% of students are Roman Catholic.

Faculty School total: 70. In upper school: 60 men, 10 women; 60 have advanced degrees.

Subjects Offered 20th century American writers, 20th century history, 20th century physics, 20th century world history, 3-dimensional art, 3-dimensional design, acting, adolescent issues, advanced biology, advanced chemistry, advanced computer applications, advanced math, Advanced Placement courses, advanced studio art-AP, algebra, American Civil War, American democracy, American foreign policy, American government, American history, American history-AP, American literature, American literature-AP, analysis, analysis and differential calculus, analysis of data, analytic geometry, anatomy and physiology, ancient history, ancient world history, ancient/medieval philosophy, animation, applied arts, applied music, architectural drawing, architecture, art, art and culture, art appreciation, art education, art history, art history-AP, art-AP, arts, arts and crafts, arts appreciation, ASB Leadership, athletic training, athletics, audio visual/media, band, baseball, basic language skills, Basic programming, basketball, Bible, Bible as literature, Bible studies, biology, biology-AP, body human, bowling, British literature, British literature-AP, broadcasting, calculus, calculus-AP, campus ministry, Catholic belief and practice, chemistry, chemistry-AP, Chinese, choir, choral music, chorus, Christian and Hebrew scripture, Christian doctrine, Christian education, Christian ethics, Christian scripture, Christian studies, Christian testament, Christianity, church history, civics, civil rights, Civil War, civil war history, comparative government and politics, comparative government and politics-AP, comparative political systems-AP, comparative politics, comparative religion, composition, composition-AP, computer animation, computer applications, computer art, computer education, computer graphics, computer information systems, computer literacy, computer multimedia, computer processing, computer programming, computer programming-AP, computer resources, computer science, computer science-AP, computer skills, computer studies, computer technologies, computer tools, computer-aided design, computers, conceptual physics, concert band, constitutional history of U.S., constitutional law, contemporary art, creative writing, data analysis, data processing, debate, democracy in America, drama, drama performance, drama workshop, dramatic arts, drawing, drawing and design, economics, economics-AP, English, English composition, English language and composition-AP, English language-AP, English literature, English literature and composition-AP, English literature-AP, English-AP, English/composition-AP, environmental science-AP, equality and freedom, European history-AP, expository writing, film, film appreciation, film history, film studies, fine arts, foreign language, foreign policy, forensics, French, French language-AP, French literature-AP, French studies, French-AP, freshman seminar, functions, geometry, German, German literature, German-AP, global issues, government, government and politics-AP, government-AP, government/civics, government/civics-AP, grammar, guidance, health, health education, history, history of music, history of the Americas, history of the Catholic Church, history-AP, honors algebra, honors English, honors geometry, honors U.S. history, honors world history, HTML design, human anatomy, human biology, human geography—AP, human sexuality, Internet, intro to computers, jazz, jazz band, jazz ensemble, jazz theory, journalism, lab science, language, language and composition, language arts, language-AP, leadership and service, library, Life of Christ, life science, literature and composition-AP, literature-AP, logarithms, macro/microeconomics-AP, macroeconomics-AP, math applications, mathematical modeling, mathematics, mathematics-AP, mechanical drawing, medieval history, microeconomics, microeconomics-AP, modern European history, modern European history-AP, modern history, modern languages, modern political theory, modern politics, modern Western civilization, modern world history, moral and social development, moral reasoning, moral theology, music, music appreciation, music composition, music history, music performance, music theory, music theory-AP, music-AP, musical productions, Native American history, New Testament, newspaper, North American literature, philosophy, physical education, physics, physics-AP,

physiology, political science, politics, prayer/spirituality, pre-calculus, probability and statistics, programming, psychology, psychology-AP, reading, reading/study skills, religion, religion and culture, religious education, religious studies, science, scripture, social doctrine, social justice, social sciences, Spanish, Spanish language-AP, Spanish literature, Spanish literature-AP, Spanish-AP, speech, speech and debate, statistics, statistics-AP, stock market, student government, student publications, studio art, studio art-AP, swimming, technology, tennis, the Web, theater, theater arts, theater design and production, theater history, theater production, theology, track and field, trigonometry, U.S. government, U.S. government and politics, U.S. government and politics-AP, U.S. history, U.S. history-AP, U.S. literature, U.S. Presidents, United States government-AP, video, Vietnam War, visual arts, vocal jazz, vocal music, water polo, weight fitness, weight training, weightlifting, Western civilization, Western literature, Western religions, wind ensemble, wind instruments, world geography, world governments, world history, world history-AP, world literature, world religions, world religions, World War I, World War II, world wide web design, wrestling, writing, writing, yearbook.

Special Academic Programs 18 Advanced Placement exams for which test preparation is offered; honors section; accelerated programs; independent study; study at local college for college credit; study abroad; remedial reading and/or remedial writing; remedial math.

College Admission Counseling 270 students graduated in 2010; all went to college, including California State University, Fullerton. Median SAT critical reading: 470, median SAT math: 530. 30% scored over 600 on SAT critical reading, 40% scored over 600 on SAT math.

Student Life Upper grades have specified standards of dress, student council. Discipline rests primarily with faculty.

Summer Programs Remediation, enrichment, advancement, sports, art/fine arts, computer instruction programs offered; session focuses on academics; held on campus; accepts boys and girls; open to students from other schools. 600 students usually enrolled. 2011 schedule: June 21 to July 23. Application deadline: June 1.

Tuition and Aid Day student tuition: $6600. Guaranteed tuition plan. Tuition installment plan (The Tuition Plan, monthly payment plans, individually arranged payment plans). Tuition reduction for siblings, merit scholarship grants, need-based scholarship grants available. In 2010–11, 10% of upper-school students received aid; total upper-school merit-scholarship money awarded: $50,000. Total amount of financial aid awarded in 2010–11: $50,000.

Admissions Traditional secondary-level entrance grade is 9. For fall 2010, 270 students applied for upper-level admission, 260 were accepted, 230 enrolled. Scholastic Testing Service required. Deadline for receipt of application materials: none. Application fee required: $65.

Athletics Interscholastic: baseball, basketball, billiards, bowling, cross-country running, diving, fishing, football, golf, hockey, in-line hockey, indoor hockey, lacrosse, racquetball, roller hockey, running, soccer, surfing, swimming and diving, tennis, track and field, water polo, weight lifting, wrestling. 1 PE instructor, 30 coaches, 2 athletic trainers.

Computers Computers are regularly used in all classes. Computer network features include on-campus library services, online commercial services, Internet access. The school has a published electronic and media policy.

Contact Mrs. Kay Manning, Registrar. 909-596-1946. Fax: 909-596-6112. E-mail: kay@damien-hs.edu. Web site: www.damien-hs.edu.

DAMIEN MEMORIAL SCHOOL

1401 Houghtailing Street
Honolulu, Hawaii 96817-2797
Head of School: Mr. Bernard Ho

General Information Boys' day college-preparatory, arts, business, religious studies, and technology school, affiliated with Roman Catholic Church. Grades 6–12. Founded: 1962. Setting: urban. 8-acre campus. 9 buildings on campus. Approved or accredited by National Catholic Education Association and Western Association of Schools and Colleges. Total enrollment: 407. Upper school average class size: 25. Upper school faculty-student ratio: 1:10. There are 180 required school days per year for Upper School students. Upper School students typically attend 5 days per week. The average school day consists of 6 hours and 30 minutes.

Upper School Student Profile Grade 7: 20 students (20 boys); Grade 8: 24 students (24 boys); Grade 9: 103 students (103 boys); Grade 10: 72 students (72 boys); Grade 11: 90 students (90 boys); Grade 12: 100 students (100 boys). 75% of students are Roman Catholic.

Faculty School total: 35. In upper school: 27 men, 8 women; 24 have advanced degrees.

Subjects Offered Advanced Placement courses, algebra, American history, American literature, art, band, biology, business, business skills, calculus, chemistry, computer programming, economics, engineering, English, English literature, geometry, government, grammar, Hawaiian history, health, history, Japanese, journalism, JROTC, mathematics, photography, physical education, physics, pre-calculus, psychology, religion, SAT/ACT preparation, science, social sciences, social studies, Spanish, speech, trigonometry, world history.

Graduation Requirements Business skills (includes word processing), English, foreign language, mathematics, physical education (includes health), religion (includes Bible studies and theology), science, social sciences, social studies (includes history).

Damien Memorial School

Special Academic Programs Honors section; independent study; study at local college for college credit.

College Admission Counseling 120 students graduated in 2010; 116 went to college, including Pacific University. Other: 4 went to work.

Student Life Upper grades have specified standards of dress, student council. Discipline rests primarily with faculty. Attendance at religious services is required.

Summer Programs Remediation, enrichment, advancement programs offered; session focuses on Incoming 6th-9th grade orientation; held on campus; accepts boys, open to students from other schools. 120 students usually enrolled. 2011 schedule: June 6 to July 1. Application deadline: none.

Tuition and Aid Day student tuition: $9875. Tuition installment plan (FACTS Tuition Payment Plan, monthly payment plans, individually arranged payment plans, 2-payment plan, 10-payment plan). Tuition reduction for siblings, merit scholarship grants, need-based scholarship grants available. In 2010–11, 50% of upper-school students received aid; total upper-school merit-scholarship money awarded: $100,000. Total amount of financial aid awarded in 2010–11: $600,000.

Admissions Traditional secondary-level entrance grade is 9. Educational Development Series or High School Placement Test required. Deadline for receipt of application materials: none. Application fee required: $50. On-campus interview recommended.

Athletics Interscholastic: baseball, basketball, bowling, canoeing/kayaking, cheering (g), cross-country running, football, golf, judo, soccer, strength & conditioning, tennis, track and field, volleyball, weight training, wrestling; intramural: basketball. 2 PE instructors, 15 coaches, 2 athletic trainers.

Computers Computers are regularly used in English, science, yearbook classes. Computer network features include on-campus library services, Internet access, wireless campus network, Internet filtering or blocking technology. Student e-mail accounts and computer access in designated common areas are available to students. Students grades are available online. The school has a published electronic and media policy.

Contact Mr. Brent Limos, Director of Admissions. 808-841-0195. Fax: 808-847-1401. E-mail: limos@damien.edu. Web site: www.damien.edu/.

DANA HALL SCHOOL
45 Dana Road
Wellesley, Massachusetts 02482
Head of School: Ms. Caroline Erisman, JD

General Information Girls' boarding and day college-preparatory school. Boarding grades 9–12, day grades 6–12. Founded: 1881. Setting: suburban. Nearest major city is Boston. Students are housed in single-sex dormitories. 55-acre campus. 34 buildings on campus. Approved or accredited by Association of Independent Schools in New England, Massachusetts Department of Education, New England Association of Schools and Colleges, The Association of Boarding Schools, and Massachusetts Department of Education. Member of National Association of Independent Schools and Secondary School Admission Test Board. Endowment: $22 million. Total enrollment: 487. Upper school average class size: 12. Upper school faculty-student ratio: 1:9. There are 160 required school days per year for Upper School students. Upper School students typically attend 5 days per week. The average school day consists of 7 hours and 30 minutes.

Upper School Student Profile Grade 9: 78 students (78 girls); Grade 10: 92 students (92 girls); Grade 11: 100 students (100 girls); Grade 12: 90 students (90 girls). 37% of students are boarding students. 82% are state residents. 11 states are represented in upper school student body. 12% are international students. International students from China, Hong Kong, Japan, Republic of Korea, Taiwan, and Thailand; 11 other countries represented in student body.

Faculty School total: 71. In upper school: 22 men, 31 women; 36 have advanced degrees; 34 reside on campus.

Subjects Offered Acting, African history, African studies, algebra, American history, American literature, architecture, art, art history, art-AP, astronomy, biology, calculus, ceramics, chemistry, chorus, community service, computer programming, computer science, creative writing, dance, dance performance, drama, drama workshop, drawing, East Asian history, economics, electives, English, English composition, English language and composition-AP, English/composition-AP, European history, European history-AP, fitness, French, French language-AP, French literature-AP, freshman foundations, geometry, government, government/civics, health, journalism, Latin, Latin American history, Latin-AP, leadership education training, library, Mandarin, marine biology, mathematics-AP, Middle Eastern history, music, music composition, music performance, music theory, photography, physics, public speaking, Russian studies, Spanish, Spanish-AP, statistics-AP, trigonometry, U.S. history-AP, U.S. literature, weight training, Western civilization, women in the classical world.

Graduation Requirements American history, area studies, computer science, English, fitness, foreign language, mathematics, performing arts, science, social studies (includes history), visual arts, 20 hours of community service.

Special Academic Programs 14 Advanced Placement exams for which test preparation is offered; honors section; independent study; term-away projects; study abroad.

College Admission Counseling 88 students graduated in 2009; all went to college, including Boston College; Colby College; Syracuse University; Trinity College; University of Southern California; Vassar College. Mean SAT critical reading: 612,

---

mean SAT math: 634, mean SAT writing: 643, mean combined SAT: 1889, mean composite ACT: 27. 52% scored over 600 on SAT critical reading, 70% scored over 600 on SAT math, 73% scored over 600 on SAT writing, 67% scored over 1800 on combined SAT, 69% scored over 26 on composite ACT.

Student Life Upper grades have specified standards of dress, student council, honor system. Discipline rests equally with students and faculty.

Tuition and Aid Day student tuition: $35,340; 7-day tuition and room/board: $46,700. Tuition installment plan (monthly payment plans, K-12 Family Education Loan, AchieverLoan). Need-based scholarship grants, need-based loans available. In 2009–10, 19% of upper-school students received aid. Total amount of financial aid awarded in 2009–10: $2,885,183.

Admissions Traditional secondary-level entrance grade is 9. For fall 2009, 331 students applied for upper-level admission, 148 were accepted, 66 enrolled. ISEE, SSAT or TOEFL required. Deadline for receipt of application materials: February 1. Application fee required: $50. Interview required.

Athletics Interscholastic: basketball, cross-country running, equestrian sports, fencing, field hockey, golf, horseback riding, ice hockey, lacrosse, modern dance, soccer, softball, squash, swimming and diving, tennis, volleyball; intramural: aerobics, aerobics/dance, aquatics, ballet, crew, dance, equestrian sports, fitness, Frisbee, golf, hiking/backpacking, horseback riding, indoor track, life saving, martial arts, modern dance, Nautilus, outdoor activities, physical fitness, physical training, rock climbing, scuba diving, self defense, skiing (downhill), squash, strength & conditioning, swimming and diving, tennis, ultimate Frisbee, weight lifting, weight training, yoga. 5 PE instructors, 20 coaches, 1 athletic trainer.

Computers Computers are regularly used in art, English, French, history, Latin, mathematics, science, Spanish, Web site design, yearbook classes. Computer network features include on-campus library services, online commercial services, Internet access, wireless campus network, Internet filtering or blocking technology. Campus intranet, student e-mail accounts, and computer access in designated common areas are available to students.

Contact Mrs. Brenda Dowdell, Admission Office Manager. 781-235-3010 Ext. 2531. Fax: 781-239-1383. E-mail: admission@danahall.org. Web site: www.danahall.org.

DARLINGTON SCHOOL
1014 Cave Spring Road
Rome, Georgia 30161
Head of School: Thomas C. Whitworth III

General Information Coeducational boarding and day college-preparatory, arts, and technology school. Boarding grades 9–PG, day grades PK–PG. Founded: 1905. Setting: small town. Nearest major city is Atlanta. Students are housed in single-sex dormitories. 400-acre campus. 15 buildings on campus. Approved or accredited by Georgia Independent School Association, Southern Association of Colleges and Schools, Southern Association of Independent Schools, The Association of Boarding Schools, and Georgia Department of Education. Member of National Association of Independent Schools and Secondary School Admission Test Board. Endowment: $34.7 million. Total enrollment: 824. Upper school average class size: 14. Upper school faculty-student ratio: 1:13. There are 176 required school days per year for Upper School students. Upper School students typically attend 5 days per week. The average school day consists of 7 hours and 30 minutes.

Upper School Student Profile Grade 6: 50 students (31 boys, 19 girls); Grade 7: 49 students (25 boys, 24 girls); Grade 8: 56 students (30 boys, 26 girls); Grade 9: 86 students (48 boys, 38 girls); Grade 10: 123 students (62 boys, 61 girls); Grade 11: 123 students (65 boys, 58 girls); Grade 12: 133 students (76 boys, 57 girls). 36% of students are boarding students. 85% are state residents. 26 states are represented in upper school student body. 17% are international students. International students from Bermuda, China, Germany, Jamaica, Republic of Korea, and Taiwan; 21 other countries represented in student body.

Faculty School total: 92. In upper school: 34 men, 19 women; 33 have advanced degrees; 55 reside on campus.

Subjects Offered Advanced biology, advanced chemistry, Advanced Placement courses, advanced studio art-AP, algebra, ancient world history, art, art history, art history-AP, band, biology, biology-AP, calculus, calculus-AP, chemistry, chemistry-AP, choir, chorus, college counseling, computer programming, computer science, concert choir, creative writing, drama, drawing, economics, economics-AP, English, English language and composition-AP, English literature, English literature-AP, English-AP, ensembles, environmental science, environmental science-AP, ESL, fine arts, French, geometry, government-AP, graphic arts, graphic design, health, honors algebra, honors English, honors geometry, honors world history, humanities, jazz ensemble, journalism, lab science, macro/microeconomics-AP, macroeconomics-AP, modern European history-AP, music, music theory-AP, musical theater, newspaper, personal fitness, physical education, physics, physics-AP, pre-calculus, probability and statistics, psychology-AP, robotics, Spanish, Spanish language-AP, Spanish literature-AP, Spanish-AP, statistics-AP, studio art-AP, trigonometry, U.S. history, U.S. history-AP, video, video film production, vocal ensemble, wind ensemble, world cultures, world history, world history-AP, yearbook.

Graduation Requirements Arts and fine arts (art, music, dance, drama), English, foreign language, information technology, mathematics, physical education (includes health), science, social studies (includes history), community service/servant leadership program, after school activity.

Special Academic Programs 19 Advanced Placement exams for which test preparation is offered; honors section; ESL (8 students enrolled).
College Admission Counseling 140 students graduated in 2009; all went to college, including Auburn University; Georgia Institute of Technology; Georgia Southern University; The University of Alabama; University of Georgia; University of Mississippi.
Student Life Upper grades have uniform requirement, student council, honor system. Discipline rests equally with students and faculty.
Tuition and Aid Day student tuition: $16,300; 7-day tuition and room/board: $36,800. Tuition installment plan (monthly payment plans, individually arranged payment plans). Merit scholarship grants, need-based scholarship grants available. In 2009–10, 28% of upper-school students received aid; total upper-school merit-scholarship money awarded: $374,300. Total amount of financial aid awarded in 2009–10: $1,489,275.
Admissions Traditional secondary-level entrance grade is 9. For fall 2009, 299 students applied for upper-level admission, 153 were accepted, 87 enrolled. PSAT and SAT for applicants to grade 11 and 12, SSAT or WISC III or TOEFL required. Deadline for receipt of application materials: February 1. Application fee required: $50. Interview required.
Athletics Interscholastic: baseball (boys), basketball (b,g), cheering (g), crew (b,g), cross-country running (b,g), diving (b,g), football (b), golf (b,g), lacrosse (b,g), rowing (b,g), soccer (b,g), softball (g), swimming and diving (b,g), tennis (b,g), track and field (b,g), volleyball (g), wrestling (b); intramural: aquatics (b,g), basketball (b,g), cheering (g), dance squad (g), fitness (b,g), flag football (b,g), flagball (b,g), indoor soccer (b), running (b,g), tennis (b,g), volleyball (b,g); coed intramural: aerobics, fishing, fly fishing, Frisbee, independent competitive sports, outdoor activities, outdoor education, outdoor recreation, physical fitness, physical training, skeet shooting, soccer, speleology, strength & conditioning, table tennis, ultimate Frisbee, water volleyball, weight lifting, weight training. 2 PE instructors, 8 coaches, 2 athletic trainers.
Computers Computers are regularly used in computer applications, English, foreign language, history, mathematics, science, Web site design classes. Computer network features include on-campus library services, Internet access, wireless campus network, Internet filtering or blocking technology. Campus intranet, student e-mail accounts, and computer access in designated common areas are available to students. Students grades are available online. The school has a published electronic and media policy.
Contact Ms. Ivey Harrison, Assistant Director of Admission. 706-236-0407. Fax: 706-232-3600. E-mail: iharrison@darlingtonschool.org. Web site: www.darlingtonschool.org.

DARROW SCHOOL
110 Darrow Road
New Lebanon, New York 12125
Head of School: Mrs. Nancy Wolf
General Information Coeducational boarding and day college-preparatory, arts, hands-on learning, and sustainability school. Grades 9–12. Founded: 1932. Setting: rural. Nearest major city is Pittsfield, MA. Students are housed in single-sex dormitories. 365-acre campus. 26 buildings on campus. Approved or accredited by Middle States Association of Colleges and Schools, New York State Association of Independent Schools, and The Association of Boarding Schools. Member of National Association of Independent Schools and Secondary School Admission Test Board. Endowment: $2.5 million. Total enrollment: 107. Upper school average class size: 9. Upper school faculty-student ratio: 1:4. Upper School students typically attend 6 days per week. The average school day consists of 5 hours.
Upper School Student Profile Grade 9: 16 students (5 boys, 11 girls); Grade 10: 33 students (20 boys, 13 girls); Grade 11: 31 students (18 boys, 13 girls); Grade 12: 27 students (18 boys, 9 girls). 80% of students are boarding students. 52% are state residents. 13 states are represented in upper school student body. 20% are international students. International students from Angola, China, Jamaica, Japan, Nigeria, and Republic of Korea; 2 other countries represented in student body.
Faculty School total: 31. In upper school: 17 men, 14 women; 15 have advanced degrees; 30 reside on campus.
Subjects Offered 3-dimensional art, advanced math, African-American literature, algebra, American literature, art, art history, athletics, biology, calculus, ceramics, chemistry, civil rights, clayworking, computer graphics, creative writing, critical writing, culinary arts, design, digital art, drama, drawing, drawing and design, ecology, economics, English, English literature, ensembles, environmental education, environmental science, environmental studies, ESL, ethics, experiential education, fine arts, French, geometry, health and wellness, history, independent study, Latin American literature, leadership, literature, mathematics, microeconomics, multicultural studies, music appreciation, music theory, oil painting, ornithology, photo shop, photography, physics, play production, poetry, portfolio art, pottery, precalculus, reading/study skills, Russian literature, science, social studies, Spanish, Spanish literature, sports, studio art, study skills, theater, U.S. history, Western civilization, women's literature, woodworking, writing, yearbook.
Graduation Requirements Arts, arts and fine arts (art, music, dance, drama), electives, English, foreign language, history, mathematics, physical education (includes health), science.
Special Academic Programs Independent study; academic accommodation for the musically talented and the artistically talented; ESL (10 students enrolled).

College Admission Counseling 33 students graduated in 2009; all went to college, including Clarkson University; Hartwick College; Hobart and William Smith Colleges; Mount Holyoke College; New York University; Penn State University Park.
Student Life Upper grades have specified standards of dress, student council. Discipline rests equally with students and faculty.
Tuition and Aid Day student tuition: $24,150; 7-day tuition and room/board: $42,150. Tuition installment plan (Academic Management Services Plan, Key Tuition Payment Plan, individually arranged payment plans). Need-based scholarship grants available. In 2009–10, 32% of upper-school students received aid. Total amount of financial aid awarded in 2009–10: $920,000.
Admissions Traditional secondary-level entrance grade is 9. For fall 2009, 170 students applied for upper-level admission, 109 were accepted, 52 enrolled. SLEP for foreign students or TOEFL or SLEP required. Deadline for receipt of application materials: none. Application fee required: $50. On-campus interview required.
Athletics Interscholastic: baseball (boys), basketball (b,g), cross-country running (b,g), soccer (b,g), softball (g), tennis (b,g); coed interscholastic: cross-country running, Frisbee, lacrosse, tennis, ultimate Frisbee; coed intramural: alpine skiing, dance, fitness, freestyle skiing, hiking/backpacking, horseback riding, outdoor activities, outdoor education, physical fitness, rock climbing, skiing (cross-country), skiing (downhill), snowboarding, telemark skiing, weight lifting.
Computers Computers are regularly used in graphic design, photography classes. Computer network features include on-campus library services, Internet access, wireless campus network, Internet filtering or blocking technology. Campus intranet, student e-mail accounts, and computer access in designated common areas are available to students. The school has a published electronic and media policy.
Contact Ms. Jamie Hicks-Furgang, Director of Admission. 518-794-6008. Fax: 518-794-7065. E-mail: hicksj@darrowschool.org. Web site: www.darrowschool.org.

DAVID LIPSCOMB HIGH SCHOOL
3901 Granny White Pike
Nashville, Tennessee 37204-3951
Head of School: Dr. Michael P. Hammond
General Information Coeducational day college-preparatory and religious studies school, affiliated with Church of Christ. Grades PK–12. Founded: 1891. Setting: suburban. 10-acre campus. 4 buildings on campus. Approved or accredited by National Christian School Association, Southern Association of Colleges and Schools, Southern Association of Independent Schools, Tennessee Association of Independent Schools, and Tennessee Department of Education. Endowment: $95,000. Total enrollment: 1,386. Upper school average class size: 20. Upper school faculty-student ratio: 1:15. Upper School students typically attend 5 days per week.
Upper School Student Profile Grade 9: 137 students (65 boys, 72 girls); Grade 10: 119 students (69 boys, 50 girls); Grade 11: 135 students (73 boys, 62 girls); Grade 12: 147 students (72 boys, 75 girls). 64% of students are members of Church of Christ.
Faculty School total: 35. In upper school: 16 men, 19 women; 25 have advanced degrees.
Subjects Offered Accounting, advanced computer applications, algebra, American government, American history, anatomy and physiology, art, band, biology, biology-AP, calculus-AP, chemistry, chemistry-AP, chorus, computer science, current history, drama, economics, English, French, geography, geometry, health, home economics, honors algebra, honors English, honors geometry, interior design, journalism, keyboarding, Latin, mathematics, modern history, painting, photography, physical education, physics, pre-algebra, psychology, religion, science, science research, social studies, Spanish, Spanish-AP, speech, statistics, trigonometry, visual arts, world history.
Graduation Requirements Economics, English, foreign language, mathematics, physical education (includes health), religion (includes Bible studies and theology), science, social studies (includes history), research paper, 60 hours of community service.
Special Academic Programs 4 Advanced Placement exams for which test preparation is offered; honors section; accelerated programs; study at local college for college credit; programs in general development for dyslexic students.
College Admission Counseling 132 students graduated in 2010; 131 went to college, including Belmont University; Harding University; Lipscomb University; Middle Tennessee State University; The University of Alabama; The University of Tennessee. Other: 1 entered military service. Mean composite ACT: 24.
Student Life Upper grades have uniform requirement, student council. Discipline rests primarily with faculty. Attendance at religious services is required.
Summer Programs Remediation, enrichment, sports, art/fine arts programs offered; session focuses on mathematics and English remediation, Middle School Summer Academy; held on campus; accepts boys and girls; open to students from other schools. 100 students usually enrolled. 2011 schedule: June 1 to July 31. Application deadline: May 15.
Tuition and Aid Day student tuition: $9500. Tuition installment plan (monthly payment plans, individually arranged payment plans). Tuition reduction for siblings, need-based scholarship grants available. In 2010–11, 1% of upper-school students received aid. Total amount of financial aid awarded in 2010–11: $46,840.
Admissions Traditional secondary-level entrance grade is 9. For fall 2010, 41 students applied for upper-level admission, 35 were accepted, 30 enrolled. TOEFL required. Deadline for receipt of application materials: none. Application fee required: $100. Interview required.

David Lipscomb High School

Athletics Interscholastic: baseball (boys), basketball (b,g), bowling (b,g), cheering (g), cross-country running (b,g), football (b), golf (b,g), soccer (b,g), softball (g), tennis (b,g), track and field (b,g), volleyball (g), wrestling (b); intramural: basketball (b,g); coed intramural: basketball. 2 PE instructors, 16 coaches, 1 athletic trainer.
Computers Computer network features include on-campus library services, online commercial services, Internet access, wireless campus network, Internet filtering or blocking technology. Student e-mail accounts and computer access in designated common areas are available to students. Students grades are available online. The school has a published electronic and media policy.
Contact Mrs. Kim Schow, Administrative Assistant. 615-966-6409. Fax: 615-966-7639. E-mail: kim.schow@lipscomb.edu. Web site: www.dlcs.lipscomb.edu.

DAVIDSON ACADEMY
1414 Old Hickory Boulevard
Nashville, Tennessee 37207-1098
Head of School: Dr. Bill Chaney
General Information Coeducational day college-preparatory, arts, religious studies, technology, and science, mathematics school, affiliated with Christian faith. Grades PK–12. Founded: 1980. Setting: suburban. 66-acre campus. 1 building on campus. Approved or accredited by Association of Christian Schools International, Southern Association of Colleges and Schools, Tennessee Association of Independent Schools, and Tennessee Department of Education. Endowment: $25,000. Upper school average class size: 18. Upper school faculty-student ratio: 1:10. There are 180 required school days per year for Upper School students. Upper School students typically attend 5 days per week. The average school day consists of 7 hours.
Upper School Student Profile 99% of students are Christian faith.
Faculty School total: 62. In upper school: 15 men, 15 women; 19 have advanced degrees.
Subjects Offered 3-dimensional art, ACT preparation, advanced math, Advanced Placement courses, algebra, American government, American history, American history-AP, art, art appreciation, audio visual/media, band, Bible, Bible studies, biology, calculus, calculus-AP, cheerleading, chemistry, choral music, chorus, church history, college admission preparation, college counseling, college placement, composition-AP, computer applications, computer skills, conceptual physics, concert band, concert choir, consumer economics, creative writing, drama, drama performance, dramatic arts, earth science, economics, English, English literature-AP, English-AP, English/composition-AP, film and new technologies, geography, geometry, government-AP, health and wellness, history, honors algebra, honors English, honors geometry, human anatomy, independent study, Latin, leadership and service, Life of Christ, literature, marching band, mathematics, mathematics-AP, music, musical productions, New Testament, newspaper, physical education, physical fitness, physical science, physics, physics-AP, poetry, pre-algebra, pre-calculus, pre-college orientation, probability and statistics, psychology, reading, religious studies, science, senior project, Spanish, speech, speech communications, trigonometry, U.S. history, U.S. history-AP, video film production, wellness, world geography, world history, writing, yearbook.
Graduation Requirements Algebra, art, biology, calculus, chemistry, computer technologies, drama, economics, electives, English, English composition, English literature, foreign language, geometry, government, literature, physical science, physics, senior project, trigonometry, U.S. history, wellness, world history, senior math topics, Old Testament, New Testament.
Special Academic Programs Advanced Placement exam preparation; honors section; independent study; study at local college for college credit; programs in general development for dyslexic students.
College Admission Counseling 66 students graduated in 2010; all went to college, including Austin Peay State University; Middle Tennessee State University; Tennessee Technological University; The University of Tennessee; Western Kentucky University. Median composite ACT: 25.
Student Life Upper grades have uniform requirement, student council, honor system. Discipline rests primarily with faculty.
Summer Programs Enrichment, advancement, sports, art/fine arts programs offered; session focuses on physical and mental growth through a caring, Christian, and learning-enriched environment; held on campus; accepts boys and girls; open to students from other schools. 250 students usually enrolled. 2011 schedule: May 30 to July 30. Application deadline: April 15.
Tuition and Aid Day student tuition: $7745. Tuition installment plan (monthly payment plans, individually arranged payment plans). Tuition reduction for siblings, need-based scholarship grants, need-based financial aid, tuition reduction for children of faculty and staff available. In 2010–11, 10% of upper-school students received aid.
Admissions Traditional secondary-level entrance grade is 9. For fall 2010, 63 students applied for upper-level admission, 52 were accepted, 44 enrolled. Admissions testing, any standardized test and WRAT required. Deadline for receipt of application materials: none. Application fee required: $100.
Athletics Interscholastic: baseball (boys), basketball (b,g), cheering (g), cross-country running (b,g), dance team (g), football (b), golf (b,g), soccer (b,g), softball (g), tennis (b,g), track and field (b,g), volleyball (g); intramural: ballet (g), dance (g), weight training (b). 1 athletic trainer.
Computers Computers are regularly used in computer applications, English, graphic arts, history, mathematics, media production, newspaper, yearbook classes. Computer network features include on-campus library services, Internet access, wireless campus network, Internet filtering or blocking technology, RenWeb, Accelerated Reader, CollegeView. Computer access in designated common areas is available to students. Students grades are available online.
Contact Mrs. Darlyne Kent, Director of Admissions. 615-860-5307. Fax: 615-868-7918. E-mail: dkent@davidsonacademy.com. Web site: www.davidsonacademy.com.

DEERFIELD ACADEMY
7 Boyden Lane
Deerfield, Massachusetts 01342
Head of School: Dr. Margarita O'Byrne Curtis
General Information Coeducational boarding and day college-preparatory school. Grades 9–PG. Founded: 1797. Setting: small town. Nearest major city is Hartford, CT. Students are housed in single-sex dormitories. 280-acre campus. 81 buildings on campus. Approved or accredited by Association of Independent Schools in New England, National Independent Private Schools Association, New England Association of Schools and Colleges, and Massachusetts Department of Education. Member of National Association of Independent Schools and Secondary School Admission Test Board. Endowment: $315 million. Total enrollment: 630. Upper school average class size: 12. Upper school faculty-student ratio: 1:6. There are 150 required school days per year for Upper School students. Upper School students typically attend 5 days per week. The average school day consists of 5 hours and 25 minutes.
Upper School Student Profile Grade 9: 97 students (46 boys, 51 girls); Grade 10: 164 students (78 boys, 86 girls); Grade 11: 181 students (94 boys, 87 girls); Grade 12: 168 students (83 boys, 85 girls); Postgraduate: 20 students (17 boys, 3 girls). 88% of students are boarding students. 22% are state residents. 38 states are represented in upper school student body. 14% are international students. International students from Canada, China, Jamaica, Republic of Korea, Thailand, and Venezuela; 19 other countries represented in student body.
Faculty School total: 114. In upper school: 63 men, 47 women; 81 have advanced degrees; 110 reside on campus.
Subjects Offered Advanced chemistry, advanced computer applications, advanced math, advanced studio art-AP, algebra, American government, American history-AP, American studies, analytic geometry, anatomy, applied arts, applied music, Arabic, architectural drawing, architecture, art, art history, art history-AP, Asian history, Asian literature, Asian studies, astronomy, Basic programming, biochemistry, biology, biology-AP, Black history, calculus, calculus-AP, chemistry, chemistry-AP, Chinese, computer applications, computer math, computer programming, computer science, computer science-AP, concert band, creative writing, dance, dance performance, discrete mathematics, drama, drama performance, drama workshop, drawing and design, earth science, Eastern religion and philosophy, ecology, economics, economics-AP, English, English literature, English literature-AP, English-AP, environmental science, ethics, European history, expository writing, fine arts, French, geology, geometry, Greek, health, health education, history, instrumental music, journalism, Latin, literature, mathematics, modern European history, music, philosophy, photography, physics, physics-AP, physiology, probability and statistics, religion, science, social studies, Spanish, Spanish literature, studio art, studio art-AP, theater, theater arts, trigonometry, U.S. history, U.S. literature, video, vocal music, Western civilization, world civilizations, world governments, world history, world literature, world religions, writing.
Graduation Requirements Arts and fine arts (art, music, dance, drama), English, foreign language, history, mathematics, philosophy, science.
Special Academic Programs Advanced Placement exam preparation; honors section; independent study; term-away projects; study abroad; academic accommodation for the gifted, the musically talented, and the artistically talented.
College Admission Counseling 193 students graduated in 2010; 183 went to college, including Brown University; Dartmouth College; Georgetown University; Harvard University; Princeton University; Yale University. Other: 10 had other specific plans. Mean SAT critical reading: 660, mean SAT math: 670, mean SAT writing: 670.
Student Life Upper grades have specified standards of dress, student council, honor system. Discipline rests equally with students and faculty.
Tuition and Aid Day student tuition: $31,400; 7-day tuition and room/board: $43,800. Tuition installment plan (Educational Data Systems, Inc.). Need-based scholarship grants available. In 2010–11, 35% of upper-school students received aid. Total amount of financial aid awarded in 2010–11: $6,600,000.
Admissions Traditional secondary-level entrance grade is 9. For fall 2010, 2,069 students applied for upper-level admission, 287 were accepted, 187 enrolled. ACT, ISEE, PSAT, SAT, SSAT or TOEFL required. Deadline for receipt of application materials: January 15. Application fee required: $60. Interview required.
Athletics Interscholastic: alpine skiing (boys, girls), baseball (b), basketball (b,g), crew (b,g), cross-country running (b,g), diving (b,g), field hockey (g), football (b), golf (b), ice hockey (b,g), lacrosse (b,g), skiing (downhill) (b,g), soccer (b,g), softball (g), squash (b,g), swimming and diving (b,g), tennis (b,g), track and field (b,g), volleyball (g), water polo (b,g), wrestling (b); intramural: dance (b,g), fitness (b,g), modern dance (b,g); coed interscholastic: bicycling, diving, golf, indoor track & field, swimming and diving; coed intramural: aerobics, aerobics/dance, aerobics/Nautilus, alpine skiing, aquatics, ballet, canoeing/kayaking, dance, fitness, hiking/backpacking, life saving, modern dance, outdoor skills, paddle tennis, sailing, skiing (cross-country), skiing (downhill), snowboarding, soccer, squash, strength & conditioning, swimming and diving, tennis, volleyball, weight lifting. 1 coach, 2 athletic trainers.

DEERFIELD ACADEMY

Deerfield Academy, founded in 1797, is an independent, co-educational boarding school located in Western Massachusetts.

Deerfield Academy is an exceptional place. The students and faculty who fill its halls, play on its fields, perform on its stages, and pursue academic excellence in its classrooms are extraordinary people. We offer you the invitation to join them.

Deerfield prepares its students for both college and the world beyond, yet its graduates return often, remembering the Academy for the important role it played in their lives. Friendships that last a lifetime, teachers who made a difference, perspectives broadened and refined, pride in the Academy and loyalty to its tradition: these are the hallmarks of a Deerfield education.

deerfield.edu

Computers Computers are regularly used in architecture, mathematics, programming, science classes. Computer network features include on-campus library services, online commercial services, Internet access, wireless campus network. Campus intranet, student e-mail accounts, and computer access in designated common areas are available to students. Students grades are available online. The school has a published electronic and media policy.

Contact Patricia L. Gimbel, Dean of Admission and Financial Aid. 413-774-1400. Fax: 413-772-1100. E-mail: admission@deerfield.edu. Web site: www.deerfield.edu.

See Display on this page and Close-Up on page 768.

DEERFIELD-WINDSOR SCHOOL

2500 Nottingham Way
Albany, Georgia 31707
Head of School: Mr. David L. Davies

General Information Coeducational day college-preparatory, arts, and technology school. Grades PK–12. Founded: 1964. Setting: suburban. Nearest major city is Atlanta. 24-acre campus. 1 building on campus. Approved or accredited by Southern Association of Colleges and Schools, Southern Association of Independent Schools, and Georgia Department of Education. Endowment: $1 million. Total enrollment: 864. Upper school average class size: 18. Upper school faculty-student ratio: 1:18. There are 180 required school days per year for Upper School students. Upper School students typically attend 5 days per week. The average school day consists of 6 hours and 25 minutes.

Upper School Student Profile Grade 9: 61 students (35 boys, 26 girls); Grade 10: 68 students (33 boys, 35 girls); Grade 11: 61 students (28 boys, 33 girls); Grade 12: 55 students (32 boys, 23 girls).

Faculty School total: 56. In upper school: 9 men, 28 women; 22 have advanced degrees.

Subjects Offered Algebra, American history, American literature, art, art history, biology, calculus, chemistry, creative writing, drama, earth science, economics, English, English literature, environmental science, expository writing, French, geometry, government/civics, grammar, health, history, Latin, mathematics, music, physical education, physics, physiology, psychology, science, social sciences, social studies, Spanish, speech, theater, trigonometry, world history, world literature, writing, yearbook.

Graduation Requirements 55 volunteer hours of community service.

Special Academic Programs 10 Advanced Placement exams for which test preparation is offered; honors section; independent study; study at local college for college credit; academic accommodation for the gifted and the artistically talented; programs in general development for dyslexic students.

College Admission Counseling 68 students graduated in 2010; all went to college, including Georgia Institute of Technology; Georgia Southern University; University of Georgia; Valdosta State University. Mean SAT critical reading: 576, mean SAT math: 527, mean SAT writing: 587, mean combined SAT: 1690.

Student Life Upper grades have specified standards of dress, student council, honor system. Discipline rests primarily with faculty.

Tuition and Aid Day student tuition: $8400. Tuition installment plan (Insured Tuition Payment Plan, monthly payment plans, individually arranged payment plans, quarterly and semi-annual payment plans). Tuition reduction for siblings, merit scholarship grants, need-based scholarship grants, need-based tuition reduction available. In 2010–11, 7% of upper-school students received aid; total upper-school merit-scholarship money awarded: $25,200. Total amount of financial aid awarded in 2010–11: $250,000.

Admissions Traditional secondary-level entrance grade is 9. For fall 2010, 36 students applied for upper-level admission, 21 were accepted, 18 enrolled. ERB verbal, ERB math and Otis-Lennon Mental Ability Test required. Deadline for receipt of application materials: none. Application fee required: $50. On-campus interview recommended.

Athletics Interscholastic: baseball (boys), basketball (b,g), football (b), golf (b), running (b,g), soccer (b,g), softball (g), strength & conditioning (b,g), swimming and diving (b,g), tennis (b,g), track and field (b,g), wrestling (b); intramural: basketball (b,g), danceline (b,g), football (b), soccer (b,g), weight lifting (b,g); coed intramural: badminton. 4 PE instructors, 9 coaches, 1 athletic trainer.

Computers Computers are regularly used in mathematics, yearbook classes. Computer network features include on-campus library services, Internet access, wireless campus network.

Contact Mrs. DeeDee R. Willcox, College Counselor. 912-435-1301 Ext. 256. Fax: 912-888-6085. E-mail: deedee.willcox@deerfieldwindsor.com. Web site: www.deerfieldwindsor.com.

DE LA SALLE COLLEGE

131 Farnham Avenue
Toronto, Ontario M4V 1H7, Canada
Head of School: Br. Domenic Viggiani, FSC

General Information Coeducational day college-preparatory, arts, business, religious studies, bilingual studies, and technology school, affiliated with Roman Catholic Church. Grades 5–12. Founded: 1851. Setting: urban. 12-acre campus. 4 buildings on campus. Approved or accredited by Association of Independent Schools and Colleges of Alberta, Conference of Independent Schools of Ontario, and Ontario Department of Education. Language of instruction: English. Total enrollment: 592. Upper school average class size: 22. Upper school faculty-student ratio: 1:15.

Upper School Student Profile Grade 9: 101 students (38 boys, 63 girls); Grade 10: 124 students (62 boys, 62 girls); Grade 11: 102 students (51 boys, 51 girls); Grade 12: 97 students (50 boys, 47 girls). 90% of students are Roman Catholic.

Faculty School total: 44. In upper school: 30 men, 12 women.

Special Academic Programs Advanced Placement exam preparation; accelerated programs.

College Admission Counseling 100 students graduated in 2009; all went to college, including McGill University; McMaster University; Queen's University at Kingston; The University of Western Ontario; University of Toronto; York University.

Student Life Upper grades have uniform requirement, student council, honor system. Discipline rests primarily with faculty. Attendance at religious services is required.

Tuition and Aid Day student tuition: CAN$11,500. Tuition installment plan (monthly payment plans). Bursaries, merit scholarship grants, need-based scholarship grants available. In 2009–10, 10% of upper-school students received aid.

Admissions Traditional secondary-level entrance grade is 9. For fall 2009, 150 students applied for upper-level admission, 75 were accepted, 50 enrolled. SSAT required. Deadline for receipt of application materials: December 11. Application fee required: CAN$100. On-campus interview required.

Athletics Interscholastic: baseball (boys), basketball (b,g), field hockey (g), football (b), ice hockey (b,g), soccer (b,g), softball (g), volleyball (b,g); coed interscholastic: alpine skiing, aquatics, badminton, cross-country running, golf, track and field; coed intramural: ball hockey, fencing. 4 PE instructors.

Computers Computer network features include Internet access, Internet filtering or blocking technology. Student e-mail accounts are available to students.

Contact Mrs. Cathy Guastelluccia, President's Secretary/Admissions Secretary. 416-969-8771 Ext. 228. Fax: 416-969-9175. E-mail: cguastelluccia@delasalleoaklands.org. Web site: www.delasalleoaklands.org.

DE LA SALLE HIGH SCHOOL

1130 Winton Drive
Concord, California 94518-3528
Head of School: Br. Christopher Brady, FSC

General Information Boys' day college-preparatory, arts, and religious studies school, affiliated with Roman Catholic Church. Grades 9–12. Founded: 1965. Setting: suburban. Nearest major city is Oakland. 25-acre campus. 11 buildings on campus. Approved or accredited by Western Association of Schools and Colleges and Western Catholic Education Association. Endowment: $3.5 million. Total enrollment: 1,042. Upper school average class size: 30. Upper school faculty-student ratio: 1:28. There are 172 required school days per year for Upper School students. Upper School students typically attend 5 days per week. The average school day consists of 6 hours and 5 minutes.

Upper School Student Profile Grade 9: 266 students (266 boys); Grade 10: 259 students (259 boys); Grade 11: 258 students (258 boys); Grade 12: 259 students (259 boys). 80% of students are Roman Catholic.

Faculty School total: 73. In upper school: 49 men, 24 women; 44 have advanced degrees.

Subjects Offered Advanced studio art-AP, algebra, American history, anatomy, art, band, Bible studies, biology, calculus, chemistry, chorus, design, drafting, drawing, economics, English, English-AP, ethics, fine arts, first aid, French, geometry, government/civics, health, history, Italian, jazz, Latin, literature, marine biology, mathematics, music theory, painting, physical education, physics, physiology, pre-calculus, psychology, religion, science, sculpture, social studies, Spanish, Spanish-AP, sports medicine, statistics, statistics-AP, trigonometry, world history, world religions, writing.

Graduation Requirements Arts and fine arts (art, music, dance, drama), English, foreign language, mathematics, physical education (includes health), religion (includes Bible studies and theology), science, social studies (includes history).

Special Academic Programs Advanced Placement exam preparation; honors section; independent study; remedial math.

College Admission Counseling 251 students graduated in 2010; 247 went to college, including California Polytechnic State University, San Luis Obispo; California State University, Chico; Loyola Marymount University; Saint Mary's College of California; Santa Clara University; University of California, Davis. Other: 2 entered military service, 1 entered a postgraduate year, 1 had other specific plans. Mean SAT critical reading: 571, mean SAT math: 584, mean SAT writing: 556, mean combined SAT: 1711, mean composite ACT: 25. 36% scored over 600 on SAT critical reading, 42% scored over 600 on SAT math, 27% scored over 600 on SAT writing, 37% scored over 1800 on combined SAT, 39% scored over 26 on composite ACT.

Student Life Upper grades have specified standards of dress, student council, honor system. Discipline rests primarily with faculty. Attendance at religious services is required.

Summer Programs Remediation programs offered; session focuses on remediation for incoming and/or conditionally accepted freshmen only; held on campus; accepts boys; not open to students from other schools. 40 students usually enrolled. 2011 schedule: June 13 to July 1. Application deadline: June 1.

Tuition and Aid Day student tuition: $14,400. Tuition installment plan (10-month). Need-based grants available. In 2010–11, 30% of upper-school students received aid.

Admissions Traditional secondary-level entrance grade is 9. For fall 2010, 479 students applied for upper-level admission, 300 were accepted, 266 enrolled. High School Placement Test required. Deadline for receipt of application materials: December 3. Application fee required: $75. On-campus interview required.

Athletics Interscholastic: baseball, basketball, cross-country running, diving, football, golf, lacrosse, rugby, soccer, swimming and diving, tennis, track and field, volleyball, water polo, wrestling; intramural: bowling, flag football, floor hockey, football, ultimate Frisbee. 2 PE instructors, 85 coaches, 2 athletic trainers.

Computers Computers are regularly used in animation, Web site design, yearbook classes. Computer network features include on-campus library services, Internet access, wireless campus network, Internet filtering or blocking technology. Student e-mail accounts and computer access in designated common areas are available to students. Students grades are available online. The school has a published electronic and media policy.

Contact Mr. Joseph Grantham, Director of Admissions. 925-288-8102. Fax: 925-686-3474. E-mail: granthamj@dlshs.org. Web site: www.dlshs.org.

DELASALLE HIGH SCHOOL

One DeLaSalle Drive
Minneapolis, Minnesota 55401-1597
Head of School: Br. Michael Collins, FSC

General Information Coeducational day college-preparatory, arts, business, religious studies, and technology school, affiliated with Roman Catholic Church; primarily serves students with learning disabilities and specific support for some learning disabilities. Grades 9–12. Founded: 1900. Setting: urban. 10-acre campus. 3 buildings on campus. Approved or accredited by National Catholic Education Association, North Central Association of Colleges and Schools, and Minnesota Department of Education. Endowment: $2.8 million. Total enrollment: 620. Upper school average class size: 23. Upper school faculty-student ratio: 1:14. There are 175 required school days per year for Upper School students. Upper School students typically attend 5 days per week. The average school day consists of 6 hours and 30 minutes.

Upper School Student Profile Grade 9: 173 students (84 boys, 89 girls); Grade 10: 146 students (71 boys, 75 girls); Grade 11: 153 students (78 boys, 75 girls); Grade 12: 148 students (66 boys, 82 girls). 70% of students are Roman Catholic.

Faculty School total: 58. In upper school: 30 men, 28 women; 44 have advanced degrees.

Subjects Offered 20th century American writers, 20th century history, 20th century world history, advanced computer applications, advanced studio art-AP, African literature, African-American literature, algebra, American government, American history, American history-AP, American legal systems, American literature, ancient world history, anthropology, art, art-AP, ballet, band, Bible, biology, biology-AP, business applications, calculus, calculus-AP, campus ministry, Catholic belief and practice, Central and Eastern European history, chamber groups, chemistry, chemistry-AP, choir, choral music, Christian and Hebrew scripture, Christian ethics, comparative religion, composition, computer applications, computer graphics, computer programming, computer science, computer science-AP, concert band, concert choir, creative writing, drama workshop, economics, English, English language and composition-AP, English language-AP, English literature-AP, ethics, European history, European history-AP, first aid, fitness, forensics, French, French-AP, geography, geometry, government, graphic arts, graphic design, health and wellness, history of the Catholic Church, history-AP, honors algebra, honors English, honors geometry, honors U.S. history, honors world history, instrumental music, introduction to theater, journalism, keyboarding, mathematics, mathematics-AP, moral and social development, personal finance, philosophy, physical education, physical science, physics, physics-AP, pre-calculus, psychology, psychology-AP, Shakespeare, social justice, Spanish, Spanish language-AP, speech, street law, trigonometry, vocal music, Western civilization, world geography, world religions, World War II, writing.

Graduation Requirements Arts and fine arts (art, music, dance, drama), English, foreign language, mathematics, physical education (includes health), religious studies, science, social studies (includes history), 60 hours of documented Christian service.

Special Academic Programs Advanced Placement exam preparation; honors section; independent study; study at local college for college credit.

College Admission Counseling 152 students graduated in 2009; 150 went to college, including Carleton College; College of Saint Benedict; Saint John's University; Saint Mary's University of Minnesota; University of Minnesota, Twin Cities Campus; University of St. Thomas. Other: 1 went to work, 1 entered military service. Mean composite ACT: 25. 58% scored over 26 on composite ACT.

Student Life Upper grades have uniform requirement, student council, honor system. Discipline rests primarily with faculty. Attendance at religious services is required.

Tuition and Aid Day student tuition: $9950. Tuition installment plan (monthly payment plans). Merit scholarship grants, need-based scholarship grants, off-campus work programs for tuition benefit available. In 2009–10, 53% of upper-school students received aid; total upper-school merit-scholarship money awarded: $150,000. Total amount of financial aid awarded in 2009–10: $1,760,000.

Admissions Traditional secondary-level entrance grade is 9. For fall 2009, 383 students applied for upper-level admission, 279 were accepted, 173 enrolled.

Academic Profile Tests or High School Placement Test required. Deadline for receipt of application materials: none. No application fee required. Interview required.

Athletics Interscholastic: baseball (boys), basketball (b,g), cross-country running (b,g), football (b), golf (b,g), soccer (b,g), softball (g), swimming and diving (g), tennis (b,g), track and field (b,g), volleyball (g), wrestling (b); coed interscholastic: cheering, rowing, weight training; coed intramural: aerobics, archery, bowling, dance, dance team, strength & conditioning. 2 PE instructors, 47 coaches, 1 athletic trainer.

Computers Computers are regularly used in art, business, English, French, graphic design, independent study, journalism, media, media production, music, science, social studies, Spanish, writing classes. Computer network features include on-campus library services, Internet access, Internet filtering or blocking technology. Student e-mail accounts are available to students. Students grades are available online. The school has a published electronic and media policy.

Contact Mr. Mike O'Keefe, Vice President. 612-676-7679. Fax: 612-676-7699. E-mail: mike.okeefe@delasalle.com. Web site: www.delasalle.com.

DELAWARE COUNTY CHRISTIAN SCHOOL

462 Malin Road
Newtown Square, Pennsylvania 19073-3499
Head of School: Dr. Stephen P. Dill

General Information Coeducational day college-preparatory and arts school, affiliated with Protestant-Evangelical faith. Grades PK–12. Founded: 1950. Setting: suburban. Nearest major city is Philadelphia. 26-acre campus. 6 buildings on campus. Approved or accredited by Association of Christian Schools International, Middle States Association of Colleges and Schools, and Pennsylvania Department of Education. Endowment: $3.8 million. Total enrollment: 810. Upper school average class size: 21. Upper school faculty-student ratio: 1:12. The average school day consists of 6 hours and 30 minutes.

Upper School Student Profile Grade 9: 91 students (48 boys, 43 girls); Grade 10: 87 students (39 boys, 48 girls); Grade 11: 79 students (35 boys, 44 girls); Grade 12: 83 students (42 boys, 41 girls). 100% of students are Protestant-Evangelical faith.

Faculty School total: 100. In upper school: 28 men, 32 women; 45 have advanced degrees.

Subjects Offered Algebra, American history, American literature, art, Bible studies, biology, calculus, chemistry, choir, choral music, concert band, concert bell choir, concert choir, creative writing, digital art, discrete mathematics, drama, earth science, economics, English, English literature, English literature and composition-AP, European history-AP, fine arts, geography, geometry, German, German-AP, government/civics, grammar, graphics, handbells, journalism, literature, mathematics, music, music theory, physical education, physics, physics-AP, religion, science, social studies, Spanish, Spanish-AP, theater, trigonometry, U.S. history-AP, world history, writing workshop, yearbook.

Graduation Requirements Arts and fine arts (art, music, dance, drama), computer science, English, foreign language, mathematics, physical education (includes health), religion (includes Bible studies and theology), science, social studies (includes history).

Special Academic Programs Advanced Placement exam preparation; honors section; study abroad; academic accommodation for the gifted, the musically talented, and the artistically talented.

College Admission Counseling 95 students graduated in 2009; 86 went to college, including Eastern University; Messiah College; Temple University. Other: 2 went to work, 1 had other specific plans. Mean SAT critical reading: 577, mean SAT math: 555, mean SAT writing: 566, mean combined SAT: 1698.

Student Life Upper grades have uniform requirement, student council, honor system. Discipline rests primarily with faculty. Attendance at religious services is required.

Tuition and Aid Day student tuition: $11,319. Tuition installment plan (monthly payment plans). Tuition reduction for siblings, merit scholarship grants, need-based scholarship grants available. In 2009–10, 33% of upper-school students received aid; total upper-school merit-scholarship money awarded: $18,000. Total amount of financial aid awarded in 2009–10: $800,000.

Admissions Traditional secondary-level entrance grade is 9. ERB required. Deadline for receipt of application materials: none. Application fee required: $50. On-campus interview required.

Athletics Interscholastic: baseball (boys), basketball (b,g), cheering (g), cross-country running (b,g), field hockey (g), football (b), golf (b,g), ice hockey (b), lacrosse (b), soccer (b,g), softball (g), tennis (b,g), track and field (b,g), wrestling (b); intramural: ice hockey (b); coed interscholastic: life saving. 3 PE instructors.

Computers Computers are regularly used in art, English, journalism, library, literary magazine, mathematics, newspaper, photography, photojournalism, publications, SAT preparation, science, technology, video film production, writing, writing, yearbook classes. Computer network features include on-campus library services, Internet access, wireless campus network, Internet filtering or blocking technology. Students grades are available online. The school has a published electronic and media policy.

Contact Mrs. Arlene J. Warmhold, Admissions Administrative Assistant. 610-353-6522 Ext. 2285. Fax: 610-356-9684. E-mail: awarmhold@dccs.org. Web site: www.dccs.org.

DELAWARE VALLEY FRIENDS SCHOOL

Paoli, Pennsylvania
See Special Needs Schools section.

DELBARTON SCHOOL

230 Mendham Road
Morristown, New Jersey 07960
Head of School: Br. Paul Diveny, OSB

General Information Boys' day college-preparatory, arts, religious studies, and technology school, affiliated with Roman Catholic Church. Grades 7–12. Founded: 1939. Setting: suburban. Nearest major city is New York, NY. 200-acre campus. 7 buildings on campus. Approved or accredited by Middle States Association of Colleges and Schools, National Catholic Education Association, New Jersey Association of Independent Schools, and New Jersey Department of Education. Member of National Association of Independent Schools and Secondary School Admission Test Board. Endowment: $23.9 million. Total enrollment: 540. Upper school average class size: 15. Upper school faculty-student ratio: 1:10. There are 164 required school days per year for Upper School students. Upper School students typically attend 5 days per week. The average school day consists of 6 hours and 15 minutes.

Upper School Student Profile Grade 9: 120 students (120 boys); Grade 10: 122 students (122 boys); Grade 11: 113 students (113 boys); Grade 12: 118 students (118 boys). 80% of students are Roman Catholic.

Faculty School total: 84. In upper school: 69 men, 15 women; 53 have advanced degrees.

Subjects Offered Accounting, advanced chemistry, algebra, American history, American literature, art, art history, astronomy, biology, calculus, chemistry, computer math, computer programming, computer science, creative writing, driver education, economics, English, English literature, environmental science, ethics, European history, fine arts, French, geography, geometry, German, grammar, health, history, international relations, Latin, mathematics, music, philosophy, physical education, physics, religion, Russian, social studies, Spanish, speech, trigonometry, world history.

Graduation Requirements Arts and fine arts (art, music, dance, drama), computer science, English, foreign language, mathematics, physical education (includes health), religion (includes Bible studies and theology), science, social studies (includes history), speech.

Special Academic Programs Advanced Placement exam preparation; independent study.

College Admission Counseling 122 students graduated in 2009; all went to college, including Columbia University; Georgetown University; Villanova University.

Student Life Upper grades have specified standards of dress, student council, honor system. Discipline rests primarily with faculty. Attendance at religious services is required.

Tuition and Aid Day student tuition: $25,975. Tuition installment plan (monthly payment plans, individually arranged payment plans). Need-based scholarship grants available. In 2009–10, 15% of upper-school students received aid. Total amount of financial aid awarded in 2009–10: $1,370,000.

Admissions Traditional secondary-level entrance grade is 9. For fall 2009, 289 students applied for upper-level admission, 120 were accepted, 93 enrolled. Stanford Achievement Test, Otis-Lennon School Ability Test, school's own exam required. Deadline for receipt of application materials: November 27. Application fee required: $65. On-campus interview required.

Athletics Interscholastic: baseball, basketball, bowling, cross-country running, football, golf, ice hockey, indoor track, lacrosse, soccer, squash, swimming and diving, tennis, track and field, winter (indoor) track, wrestling; intramural: bicycling, combined training, fitness, flag football, Frisbee, independent competitive sports, mountain biking, skiing (downhill), strength & conditioning, ultimate Frisbee, weight lifting, weight training. 5 PE instructors.

Computers Computers are regularly used in music, science, word processing classes. Computer network features include on-campus library services, online commercial services, Internet access, wireless campus network. Student e-mail accounts are available to students. Students grades are available online.

Contact Mrs. Connie Curnow, Administrative Assistant, Office of Admissions. 973-538-3231 Ext. 3019. Fax: 973-538-8836. E-mail: ccurnow@delbarton.org. Web site: www.delbarton.org.

See Display on next page and Close-Up on page 770.

DELPHI ACADEMY OF LOS ANGELES

11341 Brainard Avenue
Lake View Terrace, California 91342
Head of School: Mrs. Karen Dale

General Information Coeducational day college-preparatory, general academic, arts, business, and technology school. Grades K–12. Founded: 1984. Setting: suburban. Nearest major city is Los Angeles. 10-acre campus. 4 buildings on campus. Approved or accredited by California Department of Education. Total enrollment: 178. Upper school average class size: 18. Upper school faculty-student ratio: 1:18. There

Delphi Academy of Los Angeles

are 176 required school days per year for Upper School students. Upper School students typically attend 5 days per week. The average school day consists of 7 hours and 45 minutes.

Upper School Student Profile Grade 9: 17 students (7 boys, 10 girls); Grade 10: 20 students (11 boys, 9 girls); Grade 11: 10 students (6 boys, 4 girls); Grade 12: 10 students (5 boys, 5 girls).

Faculty School total: 19. In upper school: 2 men, 2 women; 1 has an advanced degree.

Subjects Offered Acting, advanced chemistry, advanced computer applications, advanced math, algebra, American literature, anatomy and physiology, art, art history, ASB Leadership, Basic programming, biology, business skills, calculus, calligraphy, career and personal planning, career education internship, career/college preparation, ceramics, chemistry, choir, college counseling, communication skills, community service, comparative religion, competitive science projects, composition, computer applications, consumer economics, consumer mathematics, current events, decision making skills, drama, drawing, economics, education, electronics, English, English literature, ethical decision making, ethics and responsibility, expository writing, family living, fine arts, first aid, fitness, French, geography, geometry, government, grammar, health, history, honors English, intro to computers, language arts, leadership, literature seminar, logic, math applications, mathematics, music, nutrition, personal money management, philosophy, physical education, physical science, physics, pre-algebra, pre-calculus, public speaking, religion, research skills, SAT preparation, science, science project, senior career experience, Shakespeare, social studies, sociology, Spanish, student government, study skills, trigonometry, U.S. constitutional history, U.S. government, Western civilization, world history, yearbook.

Graduation Requirements Advanced chemistry, advanced computer applications, calculus, communication skills, comparative religion, constitutional history of U.S., current events, economics, English literature, foreign language, government/civics, health, physics, public speaking, Shakespeare, student government.

Special Academic Programs Accelerated programs; independent study; term-away projects; academic accommodation for the gifted; remedial reading and/or remedial writing; remedial math.

College Admission Counseling 10 students graduated in 2009; 5 went to college, including California State Polytechnic University, Pomona; California State University, Northridge; Occidental College. Other: 5 went to work. Mean SAT critical reading: 660, mean SAT math: 680. 100% scored over 600 on SAT critical reading, 100% scored over 600 on SAT math.

Student Life Upper grades have specified standards of dress, student council, honor system. Discipline rests primarily with faculty.

Tuition and Aid Day student tuition: $14,635. Tuition installment plan (monthly payment plans, individually arranged payment plans). Tuition reduction for siblings, need-based scholarship grants available. In 2009–10, 5% of upper-school students received aid.

Admissions Traditional secondary-level entrance grade is 9. For fall 2009, 6 students applied for upper-level admission, 3 were accepted, 3 enrolled. Admissions testing, OLSAT, Stanford Achievement Test and writing sample required. Deadline for receipt of application materials: none. Application fee required: $100. On-campus interview required.

Athletics Interscholastic: basketball (boys), softball (b,g), volleyball (g); intramural: basketball (b,g), football (b), softball (b,g), volleyball (b,g); coed interscholastic: baseball, equestrian sports, flag football, soccer, softball; coed intramural: aerobics, aerobics/dance, cooperative games, dance, field hockey, fitness, flag football, Frisbee, jogging, outdoor activities, outdoor recreation, physical fitness, running, soccer, tennis, ultimate Frisbee. 3 PE instructors, 3 coaches.

Computers Computers are regularly used in all academic, business, business applications, career exploration, college planning, data processing, desktop publishing, engineering, library skills, newspaper, photography, research skills, yearbook classes. Computer network features include Internet access, wireless campus network, Internet filtering or blocking technology.

Contact Mrs. Virginia Lindskog, Registrar. 818-583-1070 Ext. 111. Fax: 818-583-1082. E-mail: virginia_lindskog@delphila.org. Web site: www.delphila.org.

THE DELPHIAN SCHOOL

20950 Southwest Rock Creek Road
Sheridan, Oregon 97378
Head of School: Rosemary Didear

General Information Coeducational boarding and day college-preparatory, general academic, arts, business, technology, and computer technology, career orientation school. Boarding grades 3–12, day grades K–12. Founded: 1976. Setting: rural. Nearest major city is Salem. Students are housed in single-sex dormitories. 800-acre campus. Approved or accredited by Oregon Department of Education. Total enrollment: 266. Upper school average class size: 17. Upper School students typically attend 5 days per week. The average school day consists of 7 hours.

Upper School Student Profile 80% of students are boarding students. 10% are state residents. 15 states are represented in upper school student body. 15% are international students. International students from Canada, France, Japan, Mexico, Republic of Korea, and Taiwan; 6 other countries represented in student body.

Faculty School total: 55. In upper school: 48 reside on campus.

Subjects Offered Advanced chemistry, advanced computer applications, algebra, American history, American literature, anatomy and physiology, art, arts and crafts, biology, biology-AP, business, business applications, business skills, calculus, calculus-AP, career and personal planning, career/college preparation, ceramics, cheerleading, chemistry, choir, communication skills, comparative religion, computer

programming, computer science, computer skills, concert choir, creative writing, drama, drawing, economics, economics-AP, electronics, English, English composition, English language and composition-AP, English literature and composition-AP, ESL, ethical decision making, ethics, ethics and responsibility, fine arts, first aid, French, geography, geometry, government, grammar, health, language arts, leadership, logic, mathematics, music, music history, nutrition, personal money management, photography, physical education, physical fitness, physical science, physics, public speaking, research skills, SAT preparation, science, Shakespeare, social studies, Spanish, student government, study skills, trigonometry, U.S. constitutional history, U.S. government, volleyball, world history, yearbook, yoga.

Graduation Requirements American history, anatomy and physiology, business skills (includes word processing), career/college preparation, communication skills, composition, computer science, current events, economics, English, ethics, foreign language, leadership, literature, logic, mathematics, mathematics-AP, physical education (includes health), public speaking, science, social studies (includes history), student government, U.S. government, world history, the school has specific graduation requirements which students are required to meet in order to complete each equivalent grade level. Community service is required.

Special Academic Programs Accelerated programs; independent study; academic accommodation for the gifted, the musically talented, and the artistically talented; ESL (38 students enrolled).

College Admission Counseling 30 students graduated in 2009; 18 went to college, including Carnegie Mellon University; Cornell University; Parsons The New School for Design; University of Michigan; University of Oregon; University of Washington. Other: 7 went to work, 5 had other specific plans. 64% scored over 600 on SAT critical reading, 57% scored over 600 on SAT math.

Student Life Upper grades have specified standards of dress, student council, honor system. Discipline rests equally with students and faculty.

Tuition and Aid Day student tuition: $17,795; 7-day tuition and room/board: $32,620. Tuition installment plan (monthly payment plans, individually arranged payment plans). Tuition reduction for siblings, merit scholarship grants, need-based scholarship grants, need-based loans available. In 2009–10, 37% of upper-school students received aid; total upper-school merit-scholarship money awarded: $150,000. Total amount of financial aid awarded in 2009–10: $315,000.

Admissions Traditional secondary-level entrance grade is 9. Admissions testing and any standardized test required. Deadline for receipt of application materials: none. Application fee required: $100. On-campus interview required.

Athletics Interscholastic: baseball (boys), basketball (b,g), soccer (b), softball (g), tennis (b,g), volleyball (g); coed intramural: fitness, flag football, hiking/backpacking, jogging, jump rope, kickball, martial arts, outdoors, physical fitness, physical training, racquetball, running, strength & conditioning, tennis, walking, weight lifting, weight training, yoga. 4 PE instructors, 15 coaches.

Computers Computers are regularly used in art, business applications, business skills, career education, college planning, computer applications, creative writing, design, digital applications, foreign language, graphic design, mathematics, media arts, media production, multimedia, music, publications, research skills, technology, typing, video film production, Web site design, writing, yearbook classes. Computer network features include on-campus library services, Internet access, wireless campus network, Internet filtering or blocking technology. Campus intranet, student e-mail accounts, and computer access in designated common areas are available to students. The school has a published electronic and media policy.

Contact Sue MacKenzie, Admissions Assistant. 800-626-6610. Fax: 503-843-4158. E-mail: info@delphian.org. Web site: www.delphian.org.

DELPHOS SAINT JOHN'S HIGH SCHOOL

515 East Second Street
Delphos, Ohio 45833
Head of School: Mr. Donald P. Huysman

General Information Coeducational day college-preparatory, general academic, arts, business, and religious studies school, affiliated with Roman Catholic Church; primarily serves underachievers. Grades 9–12. Founded: 1912. Setting: rural. Nearest major city is Toledo. 2 buildings on campus. Approved or accredited by North Central Association of Colleges and Schools, Ohio Catholic Schools Accreditation Association (OCSAA), and Ohio Department of Education. Total enrollment: 284. Upper school average class size: 14. Upper school faculty-student ratio: 1:14. There are 182 required school days per year for Upper School students. Upper School students typically attend 5 days per week. The average school day consists of 6 hours and 30 minutes.

Upper School Student Profile Grade 9: 80 students (39 boys, 41 girls); Grade 10: 71 students (38 boys, 33 girls); Grade 11: 68 students (34 boys, 34 girls); Grade 12: 65 students (26 boys, 39 girls). 96% of students are Roman Catholic.

Faculty School total: 25. In upper school: 10 men, 15 women; 7 have advanced degrees.

College Admission Counseling 71 students graduated in 2009; 60 went to college, including University of Cincinnati; University of Dayton; Wright State University. Other: 5 went to work, 3 entered military service, 3 had other specific plans. Median composite ACT: 22. 12% scored over 26 on composite ACT.

Student Life Upper grades have uniform requirement. Discipline rests primarily with faculty. Attendance at religious services is required.

Tuition and Aid Day student tuition: $2500. Tuition installment plan (FACTS Tuition Payment Plan). Tuition reduction for siblings available. In 2009–10, 45% of upper-school students received aid.

Admissions Traditional secondary-level entrance grade is 9. Deadline for receipt of application materials: none. No application fee required. Interview required.

Athletics Interscholastic: basketball (boys, girls), cheering (g), cross-country running (b,g), football (b), golf (b,g), indoor track (b,g), soccer (g), strength & conditioning (b), volleyball (g), weight lifting (b,g), weight training (b,g); intramural: baseball (b), basketball (b), strength & conditioning (b,g), volleyball (b,g). 12 coaches, 1 athletic trainer.

Computers Computers are regularly used in all academic classes. Computer network features include Internet access, Internet filtering or blocking technology.

Contact Mr. Alan Unterbrink, Guidance Counselor. 419-692-5371 Ext. 1135. Fax: 419-879-6874. E-mail: unterbrink@dsj.noacsc.org.

DEMATHA CATHOLIC HIGH SCHOOL

4313 Madison Street
Hyattsville, Maryland 20781
Head of School: Daniel J. McMahon, PhD

General Information Boys' day college-preparatory, arts, business, religious studies, technology, and music (instrumental and choral) school, affiliated with Roman Catholic Church. Grades 9–12. Founded: 1946. Setting: suburban. Nearest major city is Washington, DC. 6-acre campus. 5 buildings on campus. Approved or accredited by Association of Independent Schools of Greater Washington, Middle States Association of Colleges and Schools, National Catholic Education Association, and Maryland Department of Education. Total enrollment: 954. Upper school average class size: 22. Upper school faculty-student ratio: 1:13. There are 174 required school days per year for Upper School students. Upper School students typically attend 5 days per week. The average school day consists of 6 hours.

Upper School Student Profile Grade 9: 278 students (278 boys); Grade 10: 232 students (232 boys); Grade 11: 212 students (212 boys); Grade 12: 232 students (232 boys). 61% of students are Roman Catholic.

Faculty School total: 81. In upper school: 59 men, 22 women; 42 have advanced degrees.

Subjects Offered Accounting, Advanced Placement courses, algebra, American government, American history, American history-AP, anatomy and physiology, art, art history, art-AP, astronomy, band, biology, biology-AP, British literature, British literature-AP, business, business law, calculus, calculus-AP, campus ministry, chemistry, chemistry-AP, Chinese, choral music, chorus, Christian ethics, church history, college admission preparation, community service, computer applications, computer programming, computer science, computer science-AP, computer skills, computer studies, contemporary art, digital photography, English, English composition, English literature, environmental science, film studies, French, French language-AP, geology, geometry, German, German-AP, government, government-AP, Greek, health, health education, history, history of religion, history of rock and roll, honors algebra, honors English, honors geometry, honors U.S. history, honors world history, instrumental music, jazz, journalism, Latin, Latin American studies, Latin-AP, literature-AP, mathematics, modern languages, music, music performance, mythology, newspaper, photography, photojournalism, physical education, physical science, physics, physics-AP, pre-calculus, psychology, SAT preparation, science, science research, social studies, Spanish, Spanish-AP, speech, sports medicine, statistics, studio art, studio art-AP, study skills, symphonic band, theology, trigonometry, U.S. government, U.S. government and politics-AP, U.S. history, U.S. literature, vocal music, world history, writing, yearbook.

Graduation Requirements Arts, computer science, English, foreign language, mathematics, physical education (includes health), science, social studies (includes history), theology, 55 hours of Christian service, Service reflection paper.

Special Academic Programs Advanced Placement exam preparation; honors section; independent study; academic accommodation for the gifted, the musically talented, and the artistically talented; remedial reading and/or remedial writing.

College Admission Counseling 223 students graduated in 2010; 218 went to college, including Howard University; Salisbury University; The Catholic University of America; Towson University; University of Maryland, Baltimore County; University of Maryland, College Park. Other: 2 went to work, 3 entered military service. Mean SAT critical reading: 521, mean SAT math: 527, mean SAT writing: 502.

Student Life Upper grades have uniform requirement, student council, honor system. Discipline rests primarily with faculty. Attendance at religious services is required.

Summer Programs Remediation, enrichment, sports, art/fine arts, computer instruction programs offered; session focuses on remediation/enrichment; held on campus; accepts boys and girls; open to students from other schools. 400 students usually enrolled. 2011 schedule: June 20 to July 22. Application deadline: June 10.

Tuition and Aid Day student tuition: $12,250. Tuition installment plan (FACTS Tuition Payment Plan). Tuition reduction for siblings, merit scholarship grants, need-based scholarship grants, paying campus jobs available. In 2010–11, 46% of upper-school students received aid; total upper-school merit-scholarship money awarded: $390,250. Total amount of financial aid awarded in 2010–11: $1,315,500.

Admissions Traditional secondary-level entrance grade is 9. For fall 2010, 650 students applied for upper-level admission, 451 were accepted, 278 enrolled. Archdiocese of Washington Entrance Exam, High School Placement Test or High

DeMatha Catholic High School

School Placement Test (closed version) from Scholastic Testing Service required. Deadline for receipt of application materials: December 15. Application fee required: $50.

Athletics Interscholastic: baseball, basketball, crew, cross-country running, diving, football, golf, hockey, ice hockey, indoor track, indoor track & field, lacrosse, rugby, soccer, swimming and diving, tennis, track and field, ultimate Frisbee, water polo, winter (indoor) track, wrestling; intramural: basketball, bowling, strength & conditioning. 2 PE instructors, 1 coach, 2 athletic trainers.

Computers Computers are regularly used in computer applications, digital applications, independent study, lab/keyboard, library, newspaper, publishing, science, technology, Web site design, word processing, yearbook classes. Computer network features include on-campus library services, Internet access, wireless campus network, Internet filtering or blocking technology, ProQuest, SIRS, World Book. Computer access in designated common areas is available to students. The school has a published electronic and media policy.

Contact Mrs. Christine Thomas, Assistant Director of Admissions. 240-764-2210. Fax: 240-764-2277. E-mail: cthomas@dematha.org. Web site: www.dematha.org.

DENVER ACADEMY
Denver, Colorado
See Special Needs Schools section.

DENVER CHRISTIAN HIGH SCHOOL
2135 South Pearl Street
Denver, Colorado 80210
Head of School: Mr. Mark H. Swalley

General Information Coeducational day college-preparatory, general academic, arts, business, religious studies, bilingual studies, and technology school, affiliated with Christian Reformed Church. Grades 9–12. Founded: 1950. Setting: urban. 4-acre campus. 1 building on campus. Approved or accredited by Association of Christian Schools International, North Central Association of Colleges and Schools, and Colorado Department of Education. Endowment: $1.3 million. Total enrollment: 199. Upper school average class size: 15. Upper school faculty-student ratio: 1:14. There are 181 required school days per year for Upper School students. Upper School students typically attend 5 days per week. The average school day consists of 6 hours and 45 minutes.

Upper School Student Profile Grade 9: 48 students (25 boys, 23 girls); Grade 10: 45 students (23 boys, 22 girls); Grade 11: 48 students (24 boys, 24 girls); Grade 12: 58 students (26 boys, 32 girls). 20% of students are members of Christian Reformed Church.

Faculty School total: 22. In upper school: 10 men, 12 women; 16 have advanced degrees.

Subjects Offered Acting, advanced chemistry, advanced computer applications, advanced math, algebra, American government, American history, American literature, art, band, Bible, biology, British literature, calculus, chamber groups, chemistry, choir, Christian doctrine, Christian scripture, church history, composition, computer applications, concert band, concert choir, consumer economics, drama, driver education, earth science, European history, general math, government, grammar, health, introduction to literature, jazz band, keyboarding, personal fitness, physical education, physical fitness, physics, poetry, pre-algebra, pre-calculus, psychology, research, senior seminar, Shakespeare, Spanish, speech, studio art, symphonic band, the Web, trigonometry, U.S. government, U.S. history, Web site design, weight fitness, Western civilization, world geography, world history, yearbook.

Graduation Requirements Bible studies.

Special Academic Programs Honors section; independent study; special instructional classes for deaf students.

College Admission Counseling 81 students graduated in 2009; 78 went to college, including Azusa Pacific University; Calvin College; Colorado State University; Dordt College; University of Colorado at Boulder. Other: 3 went to work. Mean SAT critical reading: 560, mean SAT math: 545, mean composite ACT: 24.

Student Life Upper grades have specified standards of dress, student council. Discipline rests primarily with faculty. Attendance at religious services is required.

Tuition and Aid Day student tuition: $90,000. Tuition installment plan (FACTS Tuition Payment Plan, monthly payment plans). Tuition reduction for siblings, merit scholarship grants, need-based scholarship grants available. In 2009–10, 45% of upper-school students received aid. Total amount of financial aid awarded in 2009–10: $72,000.

Admissions Traditional secondary-level entrance grade is 9. For fall 2009, 22 students applied for upper-level admission, 19 were accepted, 19 enrolled. WISC-III and Woodcock-Johnson, WISC/Woodcock-Johnson or Woodcock-Johnson Educational Evaluation, WISC III required. Deadline for receipt of application materials: none. Application fee required: $260. Interview required.

Athletics Interscholastic: baseball (boys), basketball (b,g), cheering (g), cross-country running (b,g), football (b), golf (b,g), soccer (b,g), track and field (b,g), volleyball (g); coed interscholastic: physical training, strength & conditioning. 1 PE instructor, 25 coaches.

Computers Computer network features include on-campus library services, Internet access, wireless campus network, Internet filtering or blocking technology. Student

e-mail accounts are available to students. Students grades are available online. The school has a published electronic and media policy.

Contact Sheryl Vriesman, Admissions Secretary. 303-733-2421 Ext. 110. Fax: 303-733-7734. E-mail: sherylv@denver-christian.org.

DENVER LUTHERAN HIGH SCHOOL
3201 West Arizona Avenue
Denver, Colorado 80219
Head of School: Mr. Daniel Gehrke

General Information Coeducational day college-preparatory, general academic, arts, religious studies, and technology school, affiliated with Lutheran Church–Missouri Synod. Grades 9–12. Founded: 1955. Setting: urban. 12-acre campus. 1 building on campus. Approved or accredited by National Lutheran School Accreditation, North Central Association of Colleges and Schools, and Colorado Department of Education. Total enrollment: 182. Upper school average class size: 18. Upper school faculty-student ratio: 1:17. There are 175 required school days per year for Upper School students. Upper School students typically attend 5 days per week. The average school day consists of 6 hours.

Upper School Student Profile Grade 9: 51 students (24 boys, 27 girls); Grade 10: 42 students (24 boys, 18 girls); Grade 11: 36 students (18 boys, 18 girls); Grade 12: 53 students (30 boys, 23 girls). 65% of students are Lutheran Church–Missouri Synod.

Faculty School total: 18. In upper school: 15 men, 3 women; 6 have advanced degrees.

Subjects Offered 20th century history, algebra, art, band, biology, calculus, chemistry, chorus, computer programming, computer science, consumer mathematics, creative writing, English, fine arts, geography, geometry, literature, mathematics, physical education, physics, psychology, reading, religion, science, social sciences, social studies, Spanish, speech, trigonometry.

Graduation Requirements Algebra, American government, arts and fine arts (art, music, dance, drama), biology, chemistry, computer applications, electives, English, English composition, English literature, geography, mathematics, physical education (includes health), science, social sciences, social studies (includes history), religion class for each year enrolled.

Special Academic Programs Advanced Placement exam preparation; honors section; independent study; remedial reading and/or remedial writing; remedial math.

College Admission Counseling 47 students graduated in 2010; 44 went to college, including Colorado State University; Concordia University; Metropolitan State College of Denver; University of Colorado at Boulder; University of Northern Colorado. Other: 2 went to work, 1 entered military service. Mean composite ACT: 23.

Student Life Upper grades have specified standards of dress, student council, honor system. Discipline rests primarily with faculty. Attendance at religious services is required.

Tuition and Aid Day student tuition: $7000. Need-based scholarship grants available. In 2010–11, 30% of upper-school students received aid.

Admissions Traditional secondary-level entrance grade is 9. High School Placement Test required. Deadline for receipt of application materials: none. Application fee required: $100. On-campus interview required.

Athletics Interscholastic: baseball (boys), basketball (b,g), floor hockey (b), football (b), golf (b,g), roller hockey (b), softball (g), tennis (g), track and field (b,g), volleyball (g), weight training (b,g), wrestling (b); intramural: field hockey (b). 3 PE instructors, 6 coaches, 1 athletic trainer.

Computers Computers are regularly used in art, geography, graphic arts, theater arts, Web site design, yearbook classes. Computer network features include online commercial services, Internet access. The school has a published electronic and media policy.

Contact Mr. Ryan Bredow, Admissions Director. 303-934-2345 Ext. 3306. Fax: 303-934-0455. Web site: www.denverlhs.org.

DEPAUL CATHOLIC HIGH SCHOOL
1512 Alps Road
Wayne, New Jersey 07470
Head of School: Fr. Mike Donovan

General Information Coeducational day college-preparatory, arts, and religious studies school, affiliated with Roman Catholic Church. Grades 9–12. Founded: 1956. Setting: suburban. Nearest major city is New York, NY. 5-acre campus. 2 buildings on campus. Approved or accredited by National Catholic Education Association and New Jersey Department of Education. Upper school average class size: 22. Upper school faculty-student ratio: 1:19. There are 185 required school days per year for Upper School students. Upper School students typically attend 5 days per week. The average school day consists of 7 hours.

Upper School Student Profile 90% of students are Roman Catholic.

Faculty School total: 65. In upper school: 25 men, 40 women; 40 have advanced degrees.

Special Academic Programs International Baccalaureate program; Advanced Placement exam preparation; honors section; accelerated programs; remedial reading and/or remedial writing; remedial math; programs in general development for dyslexic students; special instructional classes for deaf students, blind students.

College Admission Counseling 195 students graduated in 2010; all went to college.
Student Life Upper grades have uniform requirement, student council, honor system. Discipline rests equally with students and faculty. Attendance at religious services is required.
Summer Programs Sports programs offered; held on campus; accepts boys and girls; open to students from other schools. 300 students usually enrolled. 2011 schedule: June 20 to July 31.
Tuition and Aid Day student tuition: $9800. Tuition installment plan (SMART Tuition Payment Plan, monthly payment plans, individually arranged payment plans). Tuition reduction for siblings, merit scholarship grants, need-based scholarship grants available.
Admissions Cooperative Entrance Exam (McGraw-Hill) required. Deadline for receipt of application materials: December 1. No application fee required.
Athletics Interscholastic: baseball (boys), basketball (b,g), cheering (g); cross-country running (b,g), dance (g), dance squad (g), dance team (g), danceline (g), figure skating (g), football (b), gymnastics (g), ice skating (g), independent competitive sports (b,g), indoor track (b,g), indoor track & field (b,g), lacrosse (b,g), modern dance (g), soccer (b,g), softball (b), swimming and diving (b,g), tennis (b,g), track and field (b,g), volleyball (b,g), weight lifting (b,g), weight training (b,g), winter (indoor) track (b,g), wrestling (b); intramural: equestrian sports (g), strength & conditioning (b,g); coed interscholastic: alpine skiing, bowling, drill team, golf, ice hockey, skiing (downhill). 5 PE instructors, 40 coaches, 1 athletic trainer.
Computers Computer network features include on-campus library services, Internet access, wireless campus network, Internet filtering or blocking technology. Campus intranet, student e-mail accounts, and computer access in designated common areas are available to students. Students grades are available online. The school has a published electronic and media policy.
Contact Mr. John W. Merritt, Director of Admissions. 973-694-3702 Ext. 410. Fax: 973-694-3525. E-mail: merrittj@dpchs.org. Web site: www.depaulcatholic.org.

THE DERRYFIELD SCHOOL
2108 River Road
Manchester, New Hampshire 03104-1396
Head of School: Mr. Craig Sellers
General Information Coeducational day college-preparatory school. Grades 6–12. Founded: 1964. Setting: suburban. Nearest major city is Boston, MA. 84-acre campus. 3 buildings on campus. Approved or accredited by Association of Independent Schools in New England, Independent Schools of Northern New England, New England Association of Schools and Colleges, and New Hampshire Department of Education. Member of National Association of Independent Schools and Secondary School Admission Test Board. Endowment: $4.8 million. Total enrollment: 381. Upper school

average class size: 14. Upper school faculty-student ratio: 1:8. There are 159 required school days per year for Upper School students. Upper School students typically attend 5 days per week. The average school day consists of 6 hours and 45 minutes.
Upper School Student Profile Grade 9: 63 students (31 boys, 32 girls); Grade 10: 54 students (23 boys, 31 girls); Grade 11: 67 students (28 boys, 39 girls); Grade 12: 64 students (31 boys, 33 girls).
Faculty School total: 47. In upper school: 18 men, 14 women; 18 have advanced degrees.
Subjects Offered 3-dimensional art, African-American literature, algebra, American literature, anatomy and physiology, ancient world history, area studies, art, art history, biology, British literature, calculus, calculus-AP, chemistry, chemistry-AP, China/Japan history, Chinese, chorus, computer science, contemporary issues, creative writing, drafting, drama, driver education, earth science, economics, economics and history, engineering, English, English composition, English literature, English-AP, European history, expository writing, film, fine arts, French, French language-AP, French literature-AP, geography, geometry, global issues, government/civics, graphics, Greek, health, history, Holocaust, independent study, Latin, Latin-AP, mathematics, media, music, music theory, mythology, organic chemistry, philosophy, physical education, physics, physics-AP, pre-calculus, public speaking, robotics, science, Shakespeare, social studies, Spanish, Spanish language-AP, Spanish literature-AP, speech, statistics, statistics-AP, studio art, theater, trigonometry, U.S. history-AP, Western civilization, world history, world literature, writing.
Graduation Requirements Arts and fine arts (art, music, dance, drama), athletics, English, foreign language, health and wellness, history, mathematics, science.
Special Academic Programs Advanced Placement exam preparation; honors section; independent study; term-away projects.
College Admission Counseling 65 students graduated in 2010; all went to college, including Bates College; Colby College; Cornell University; Northeastern University; University of New Hampshire; University of Vermont.
Student Life Upper grades have specified standards of dress, student council. Discipline rests equally with students and faculty.
Summer Programs Art/fine arts programs offered; session focuses on theater camp; held on campus; accepts boys and girls; open to students from other schools. 50 students usually enrolled. 2011 schedule: July to August 4. Application deadline: June.
Tuition and Aid Day student tuition: $25,200. Tuition installment plan (FACTS Tuition Payment Plan, monthly payment plans). Merit scholarship grants, need-based scholarship grants available. In 2010–11, 24% of upper-school students received aid; total upper-school merit-scholarship money awarded: $77,500. Total amount of financial aid awarded in 2010–11: $744,000.
Admissions Traditional secondary-level entrance grade is 9. For fall 2010, 63 students applied for upper-level admission, 53 were accepted, 26 enrolled. SSAT required. Deadline for receipt of application materials: February 1. Application fee required: $50. On-campus interview required.

The Derryfield School

Athletics Interscholastic: alpine skiing (boys, girls), baseball (b), basketball (b,g), crew (b,g), cross-country running (b,g), field hockey (g), independent competitive sports (b,g), lacrosse (b,g), skiing (cross-country) (b,g), skiing (downhill) (b,g), soccer (b,g), softball (g), tennis (b,g); coed interscholastic: golf, physical training; coed intramural: aerobics, ropes courses, swimming and diving, weight training, yoga. 10 coaches, 1 athletic trainer.
Computers Computers are regularly used in geography, mathematics, media production, music, programming, science, Web site design classes. Computer network features include on-campus library services, online commercial services, Internet access, wireless campus network, online computer linked to New Hampshire State Library. Student e-mail accounts and computer access in designated common areas are available to students. The school has a published electronic and media policy.
Contact Ms. Allison Price, Director of Admission and Financial Aid. 603-669-4524 Ext. 6201. Fax: 603-641-9521. E-mail: aprice@derryfield.org. Web site: www.derryfield.org.

See Display on page 225 and Close-Up on page 772.

DESERT CHRISTIAN HIGH SCHOOL
7525 East Speedway Boulevard
Tucson, Arizona 85710
Head of School: Mr. Jon Self
General Information Coeducational day college-preparatory, general academic, arts, and religious studies school, affiliated with Christian faith. Grades 9–12. Founded: 1984. Setting: suburban. 6-acre campus. 10 buildings on campus. Approved or accredited by Association of Christian Schools International, Christian Schools International, North Central Association of Colleges and Schools, and Arizona Department of Education. Total enrollment: 219. Upper school average class size: 18. Upper school faculty-student ratio: 1:13. There are 180 required school days per year for Upper School students. The average school day consists of 5 hours and 55 minutes.
Upper School Student Profile Grade 9: 48 students (22 boys, 26 girls); Grade 10: 53 students (23 boys, 30 girls); Grade 11: 57 students (27 boys, 30 girls); Grade 12: 61 students (25 boys, 36 girls). 100% of students are Christian.
Faculty School total: 17. In upper school: 5 men, 12 women; 6 have advanced degrees.
Subjects Offered Advanced biology, advanced chemistry, algebra, American literature, American sign language, art, band, Bible, biology, calculus, chemistry, choir, chorus, Christian doctrine, Christian ethics, Christian scripture, communication skills, drama performance, English, English literature, ensembles, French, geometry, German, health science, history, honors English, musical theater, physical education, physics, senior seminar, Spanish, speech, U.S. government, U.S. history, Western civilization, writing, yearbook.
Graduation Requirements Bible, foreign language, language arts, mathematics, physical education (includes health), science, social studies (includes history), sociology, 15-30 community service hours required each year.
Special Academic Programs Advanced Placement exam preparation; honors section; independent study; term-away projects; study at local college for college credit; academic accommodation for the musically talented and the artistically talented.
College Admission Counseling 59 students graduated in 2009; 56 went to college, including Northern Arizona University; Pima Community College; The University of Arizona. Other: 2 went to work, 1 entered military service. Median SAT critical reading: 532, median SAT math: 541, median SAT writing: 533, median combined SAT: 1600, median composite ACT: 24.
Student Life Upper grades have specified standards of dress, student council, honor system. Discipline rests primarily with faculty. Attendance at religious services is required.
Tuition and Aid Day student tuition: $7400. Tuition installment plan (monthly payment plans). Need-based scholarship grants available. In 2009–10, 20% of upper-school students received aid. Total amount of financial aid awarded in 2009–10: $100,000.
Admissions Traditional secondary-level entrance grade is 9. For fall 2009, 65 students applied for upper-level admission, 55 were accepted, 48 enrolled. Deadline for receipt of application materials: March. Application fee required: $50. Interview recommended.
Athletics Interscholastic: baseball (boys), basketball (b,g), soccer (b,g), softball (g), tennis (b,g), track and field (b,g), volleyball (b,g); coed interscholastic: golf, swimming and diving; coed intramural: scuba diving. 1 PE instructor, 12 coaches.
Computers Computers are regularly used in yearbook classes. Computer network features include on-campus library services, online commercial services, Internet access, wireless campus network, Internet filtering or blocking technology. Campus intranet and computer access in designated common areas are available to students. Students grades are available online. The school has a published electronic and media policy.
Contact Mrs. Linda Self, Admissions Coordinator. 520-298-5817. Fax: 520-298-9312. E-mail: lself@desertchristian.org. Web site: www.desertchristian.org.

DE SMET JESUIT HIGH SCHOOL
233 North New Ballas Road
Creve Coeur, Missouri 63141
Head of School: Dr. Gregory A. Densberger
General Information Boys' day college-preparatory, arts, and religious studies school, affiliated with Roman Catholic Church; primarily serves students with learning disabilities. Grades 9–12. Founded: 1967. Setting: suburban. Nearest major city is St. Louis. 30-acre campus. 3 buildings on campus. Approved or accredited by North Central Association of Colleges and Schools. Endowment: $3 million. Upper school average class size: 24. Upper school faculty-student ratio: 1:14.
Upper School Student Profile 94% of students are Roman Catholic.
Faculty School total: 89. In upper school: 78 men, 11 women; 57 have advanced degrees.
Subjects Offered Algebra, American history, American literature, art, biology, broadcasting, business, calculus, chemistry, computer math, computer programming, computer science, creative writing, dance, drafting, drama, driver education, earth science, economics, English, English literature, ethics, European history, expository writing, fine arts, French, geography, geometry, German, government/civics, grammar, history, journalism, Latin, mathematics, mechanical drawing, music, physical education, physics, psychology, religion, science, social sciences, social studies, sociology, Spanish, speech, theater, theology, trigonometry, typing, world history, writing.
Graduation Requirements Arts and fine arts (art, music, dance, drama), business skills (includes word processing), computer science, English, foreign language, mathematics, physical education (includes health), religion (includes Bible studies and theology), science, social sciences, social studies (includes history). Community service is required.
Special Academic Programs Advanced Placement exam preparation; honors section; study at local college for college credit.
College Admission Counseling 254 students graduated in 2009; 253 went to college, including Saint Louis University; St. Louis Community College at Meramec; Truman State University; University of Missouri; University of Missouri–St. Louis. Other: 1 entered military service.
Student Life Upper grades have specified standards of dress, student council, honor system. Discipline rests primarily with faculty. Attendance at religious services is required.
Tuition and Aid Day student tuition: $9760. Tuition installment plan (monthly payment plans). Merit scholarship grants, need-based scholarship grants available. In 2009–10, 20% of upper-school students received aid.
Admissions Any standardized test or High School Placement Test required. Deadline for receipt of application materials: December 10. No application fee required. On-campus interview required.
Athletics Interscholastic: baseball, basketball, bowling, cross-country running, diving, football, Frisbee, golf, ice hockey, in-line hockey, lacrosse, racquetball, rugby, soccer, strength & conditioning, swimming and diving, team handball, tennis, track and field, volleyball, water polo, weight training, wrestling; intramural: floor hockey, Frisbee, in-line skating, outdoor recreation, paint ball, roller hockey, Special Olympics, ultimate Frisbee. 4 PE instructors, 25 coaches, 2 athletic trainers.
Computers Computers are regularly used in English, foreign language, history, mathematics, science classes.
Contact Mrs. Anne G. Gibbons, Admissions Director. 314-567-3500 Ext. 247. Fax: 314-567-1519. E-mail: agibbons@desmet.org. Web site: www.desmet.org.

DES MOINES CHRISTIAN SCHOOL
13007 Douglas Parkway
Urbandale, Iowa 50323
Head of School: Mr. John Steddom
General Information Coeducational day college-preparatory, arts, business, and religious studies school, affiliated with Christian faith. Grades PK–12. Founded: 1948. Setting: suburban. Nearest major city is Des Moines. 26-acre campus. 2 buildings on campus. Approved or accredited by Association of Christian Schools International, North Central Association of Colleges and Schools, and Iowa Department of Education. Endowment: $60,000. Total enrollment: 744. Upper school average class size: 20. Upper school faculty-student ratio: 1:18. There are 180 required school days per year for Upper School students. Upper School students typically attend 5 days per week. The average school day consists of 7 hours and 10 minutes.
Upper School Student Profile 90% of students are Christian faith.
Faculty School total: 27. In upper school: 11 men, 16 women; 13 have advanced degrees.
Subjects Offered 20th century world history, acting, advanced math, Advanced Placement courses, algebra, American government, American history, American history-AP, American literature, American literature-AP, applied music, art, Bible, biology, calculus-AP, chemistry, choir, choral music, chorus, Christian doctrine, Christian ethics, Christian scripture, Christian studies, Christian testament, Christianity, church history, civics, composition, composition-AP, computer applications, computer art, computer education, computer graphics, computer programming, concert band, concert choir, CPR, creative writing, decision making skills, drama, drawing, driver education, economics, economics and history, English, English literature, English literature and composition-AP, first aid, foreign language, general

math, geometry, government, guidance, health, health and safety, health education, history-AP, human anatomy, integrated mathematics, jazz band, keyboarding, physical science, pre-algebra, pre-calculus, psychology, Spanish, speech, speech communications, student government, student publications.

Graduation Requirements Arts and fine arts (art, music, dance, drama), Bible, language arts, mathematics, physical education (includes health), science, social studies (includes history), speech, technology.

Special Academic Programs Advanced Placement exam preparation; accelerated programs; independent study; study at local college for college credit.

College Admission Counseling 36 students graduated in 2010; 31 went to college, including Iowa State University of Science and Technology; The University of Iowa; University of Northern Iowa. Other: 1 went to work, 2 entered military service. Median composite ACT: 25. 45% scored over 26 on composite ACT.

Student Life Upper grades have specified standards of dress, student council, honor system. Discipline rests primarily with faculty. Attendance at religious services is required.

Tuition and Aid Day student tuition: $6715. Tuition installment plan (monthly payment plans, individually arranged payment plans). Tuition reduction for siblings, need-based scholarship grants available. In 2010–11, 30% of upper-school students received aid. Total amount of financial aid awarded in 2010–11: $250,000.

Admissions Traditional secondary-level entrance grade is 9. For fall 2010, 22 students applied for upper-level admission, 21 were accepted, 21 enrolled. Iowa Test of Educational Development or Iowa Tests of Basic Skills required. Deadline for receipt of application materials: none. Application fee required: $250. Interview required.

Athletics Interscholastic: baseball (boys), basketball (b,g), cheering (g), football (b), golf (b,g), soccer (b), softball (g), track and field (b,g), volleyball (g); coed interscholastic: bowling, JROTC drill. 1 PE instructor, 17 coaches, 1 athletic trainer.

Computers Computers are regularly used in computer applications, media classes. Computer network features include on-campus library services, Internet access, wireless campus network, Internet filtering or blocking technology. Students grades are available online. The school has a published electronic and media policy.

Contact Mrs. Melanie Carlson, Administrative Assistant. 515-252-2490. Fax: 515-252-6972. E-mail: mcarlson@dmcs.org.

DEVON PREPARATORY SCHOOL
363 Valley Forge Road
Devon, Pennsylvania 19333-1299
Head of School: Rev. James J. Shea, Sch.P

General Information Boys' day college-preparatory school, affiliated with Roman Catholic Church. Grades 6–12. Founded: 1956. Setting: suburban. Nearest major city is Philadelphia. 20-acre campus. 7 buildings on campus. Approved or accredited by Middle States Association of Colleges and Schools, Pennsylvania Association of Independent Schools, and Pennsylvania Department of Education. Endowment: $600,000. Total enrollment: 275. Upper school average class size: 15. Upper school faculty-student ratio: 1:10. There are 180 required school days per year for Upper School students. Upper School students typically attend 5 days per week. The average school day consists of 6 hours.

Upper School Student Profile Grade 9: 46 students (46 boys); Grade 10: 42 students (42 boys); Grade 11: 47 students (47 boys); Grade 12: 60 students (60 boys). 84% of students are Roman Catholic.

Faculty School total: 33. In upper school: 23 men, 9 women; 21 have advanced degrees.

Subjects Offered Accounting, ACT preparation, Advanced Placement courses, algebra, American history, American literature, anatomy and physiology, art, biology, biology-AP, British literature, calculus, calculus-AP, chemistry, chemistry-AP, community service, computer science, computer science-AP, economics, English, European history, forensics, French, French language-AP, geography, geometry, German, German-AP, health, language-AP, Latin, literature and composition-AP, mathematics, modern European history, music, performing arts, physical education, physics, physics-AP, political science, pre-calculus, religion, science, social studies, Spanish, Spanish-AP, trigonometry, U.S. history-AP, Vietnam War, world cultures, world literature.

Graduation Requirements Computer science, English, foreign language, geography, Latin, mathematics, physical education (includes health), political science, religion (includes Bible studies and theology), science, social studies (includes history). Community service is required.

Special Academic Programs 18 Advanced Placement exams for which test preparation is offered.

College Admission Counseling 56 students graduated in 2010; all went to college, including Lafayette College; Lehigh University; Penn State University Park; The Catholic University of America; University of Pennsylvania; University of Pittsburgh. Median SAT critical reading: 643, median SAT math: 635, median SAT writing: 633.

Student Life Upper grades have specified standards of dress, student council. Discipline rests primarily with faculty. Attendance at religious services is required.

Tuition and Aid Day student tuition: $17,500. Tuition installment plan (monthly payment plans). Tuition reduction for siblings, merit scholarship grants, need-based scholarship grants available. In 2010–11, 20% of upper-school students received aid; total upper-school merit-scholarship money awarded: $475,000. Total amount of financial aid awarded in 2010–11: $700,000.

Admissions Traditional secondary-level entrance grade is 9. For fall 2010, 200 students applied for upper-level admission, 75 were accepted, 25 enrolled. Math and English placement tests required. Deadline for receipt of application materials: none. Application fee required: $25. On-campus interview recommended.

Athletics Interscholastic: baseball, basketball, cross-country running, golf, indoor track & field, lacrosse, soccer, tennis, track and field; intramural: outdoor recreation, paint ball. 2 PE instructors, 8 coaches, 1 athletic trainer.

Computers Computers are regularly used in all academic, newspaper, technology, writing, yearbook classes. Computer network features include on-campus library services, Internet access, wireless campus network, Internet filtering or blocking technology. Students grades are available online. The school has a published electronic and media policy.

Contact Mr. Patrick Parsons, Director of Admissions. 610-688-7337 Ext. 129. Fax: 610-688-2409. E-mail: pparsons@devonprep.com. Web site: www.devonprep.com.

DEXTER SCHOOL
20 Newton Street
Brookline, Massachusetts 02445
Head of School: Mr. Todd A. Vincent

General Information Boys' day college-preparatory and arts school. Grades 1–12. Founded: 1926. Setting: suburban. Nearest major city is Boston. 36-acre campus. 4 buildings on campus. Approved or accredited by Massachusetts Department of Education. Endowment: $24 million. Total enrollment: 444. Upper school average class size: 16. Upper school faculty-student ratio: 1:7. There are 172 required school days per year for Upper School students. Upper School students typically attend 5 days per week. The average school day consists of 6 hours and 45 minutes.

Upper School Student Profile Grade 6: 36 students (36 boys); Grade 7: 28 students (28 boys); Grade 8: 36 students (36 boys); Grade 9: 42 students (42 boys); Grade 10: 42 students (42 boys); Grade 11: 31 students (31 boys); Grade 12: 39 students (39 boys).

Faculty School total: 110. In upper school: 26 men, 23 women; 31 have advanced degrees.

Subjects Offered Acting, advanced studio art-AP, algebra, American government, American history-AP, American literature, American literature-AP, analysis and differential calculus, Ancient Greek, ancient history, art, art history, art history-AP, art-AP, astronomy, biology, biology-AP, British literature, British literature-AP, calculus, calculus-AP, Central and Eastern European history, ceramics, character education, chemistry, chemistry-AP, Chinese history, choral music, community service, computer graphics, computer music, conceptual physics, constitutional law, digital photography, drama workshop, earth and space science, economics, electronic music, English, English language-AP, English literature-AP, environmental science, ethics, European history, European history-AP, European literature, Far Eastern history, French, French language-AP, French literature-AP, French-AP, geometry, grammar, graphic arts, history of China and Japan, history of England, history of music, honors algebra, honors English, honors geometry, honors U.S. history, independent study, instrumental music, jazz ensemble, Latin, Latin-AP, marine biology, medieval history, Middle Eastern history, modern European history, music, music composition, music history, music technology, music theory, music theory-AP, music-AP, photography, physics, physics-AP, probability and statistics, public speaking, robotics, Russian history, SAT preparation, Spanish, Spanish language-AP, Spanish literature-AP, Spanish-AP, statistics, studio art, studio art-AP, U.S. history, U.S. history-AP, vocal music, woodworking, writing workshop.

Graduation Requirements Latin I.

Special Academic Programs 11 Advanced Placement exams for which test preparation is offered; honors section.

College Admission Counseling 19 students graduated in 2010; 17 went to college, including Boston College; Harvard University; Northeastern University; St. Lawrence University; Trinity College; Tufts University. Other: 1 went to work, 1 entered a postgraduate year.

Student Life Upper grades have specified standards of dress, student council, honor system. Discipline rests primarily with faculty. Attendance at religious services is required.

Tuition and Aid Day student tuition: $36,795. Tuition installment plan (monthly payment plans). Need-based scholarship grants available. In 2010–11, 29% of upper-school students received aid.

Admissions Traditional secondary-level entrance grade is 9. For fall 2010, 53 students applied for upper-level admission, 33 were accepted, 22 enrolled. ISEE, PSAT and SAT for applicants to grade 11 and 12 or SSAT required. Deadline for receipt of application materials: February 1. No application fee required. Interview required.

Athletics Interscholastic: baseball, basketball, crew, cross-country running, curling, fitness, football, golf, ice hockey, lacrosse, soccer, squash, swimming and diving, tennis. 6 coaches, 2 athletic trainers.

Computers Computers are regularly used in all classes. Computer network features include on-campus library services, online commercial services, Internet access, wireless campus network, Internet filtering or blocking technology, one-to-one laptop program. Campus intranet and student e-mail accounts are available to students. The school has a published electronic and media policy.

Contact Mrs. Jennifer DaPonte, Admissions Office Manager. 617-454-2721. Fax: 617-928-7696. E-mail: admissions@dexter.org. Web site: http://www.dexter.org.

DICKINSON TRINITY

PO Box 1177
Dickinson, North Dakota 58601
Head of School: Sr. Dorothy Zeller

General Information Coeducational day and distance learning college-preparatory, arts, business, religious studies, and technology school, affiliated with Roman Catholic Church; primarily serves students with learning disabilities and speech/language deficits. Grades 7–12. Distance learning grades 9–12. Founded: 1961. Setting: small town. Nearest major city is Bismarck. 18-acre campus. 1 building on campus. Approved or accredited by National Catholic Education Association and North Dakota Department of Education. Total enrollment: 231. Upper school average class size: 40. Upper school faculty-student ratio: 1:11. There are 180 required school days per year for Upper School students. Upper School students typically attend 5 days per week. The average school day consists of 6 hours and 33 minutes.

Upper School Student Profile Grade 7: 39 students (17 boys, 22 girls); Grade 8: 47 students (29 boys, 18 girls); Grade 9: 47 students (21 boys, 26 girls); Grade 10: 36 students (16 boys, 20 girls); Grade 11: 40 students (18 boys, 22 girls); Grade 12: 45 students (22 boys, 23 girls). 97% of students are Roman Catholic.

Faculty School total: 21. In upper school: 8 men, 13 women; 2 have advanced degrees.

Subjects Offered Accounting, advanced chemistry, algebra, American history, art, biology, business, business law, business skills, chemistry, communications, computer programming, computer science, English, geography, geometry, government/civics, health, instrumental music, journalism, keyboarding, mathematics, music, organic chemistry, physical education, physical science, physics, pre-calculus, psychology, religion, religious education, science, social sciences, social studies, Spanish, statistics, trigonometry, world history.

Graduation Requirements Business skills (includes word processing), English, mathematics, physical education (includes health), religion (includes Bible studies and theology), science, social sciences, social studies (includes history), community service hours for grade 11 and grade 12 students.

Special Academic Programs Independent study; study at local college for college credit; academic accommodation for the gifted; remedial reading and/or remedial writing; remedial math; special instructional classes for students with physical handicaps that do not preclude mobility.

College Admission Counseling 45 students graduated in 2009; 38 went to college, including Dickinson State University; Minot State University; North Dakota State University; University of Mary; University of North Dakota; Valley City State University. Other: 7 went to work.

Student Life Upper grades have specified standards of dress, student council, honor system. Discipline rests primarily with faculty. Attendance at religious services is required.

Tuition and Aid Tuition installment plan (monthly payment plans, individually arranged payment plans, harvest season payments). Tuition reduction for siblings, need-based scholarship grants, paying campus jobs, partial tuition waver available.

Admissions Traditional secondary-level entrance grade is 9. For fall 2009, 6 students applied for upper-level admission, 6 were accepted, 6 enrolled. Deadline for receipt of application materials: none. No application fee required. On-campus interview required.

Athletics Interscholastic: baseball (boys), basketball (b,g), cheering (g), cross-country running (b,g), diving (b,g), football (b), golf (b,g), gymnastics (g), hockey (b,g), ice hockey (b,g), indoor track & field (b,g), softball (g), swimming and diving (b,g), track and field (b,g), volleyball (g), wrestling (b); coed intramural: archery, bowling, football. 2 PE instructors, 22 coaches.

Computers Computers are regularly used in business education, foreign language, mathematics classes. Computer network features include on-campus library services, Internet access, wireless campus network, Internet filtering or blocking technology. Campus intranet, student e-mail accounts, and computer access in designated common areas are available to students. Students grades are available online. The school has a published electronic and media policy.

Contact Rocklyn Cofer, Principal. 701-483-6081. Fax: 701-483-1450. E-mail: rocklyn.g.cofer@sendit.nodak.edu. Web site: www.trinityhighschool.com.

DOANE STUART SCHOOL

199 Washington Avenue
Rensselaer, New York 12144
Head of School: Dr. Richard D. Enemark

General Information Coeducational day college-preparatory, arts, religious studies, Irish and peace studies, and bioethics school, affiliated with Episcopal Church. Grades N–12. Founded: 1852. Setting: urban. Nearest major city is Albany. 27-acre campus. 3 buildings on campus. Approved or accredited by National Association of Episcopal Schools, New York State Association of Independent Schools, and New York Department of Education. Member of National Association of Independent Schools and Secondary School Admission Test Board. Endowment: $1 million. Total enrollment: 284. Upper school average class size: 14. Upper school faculty-student ratio: 1:7. Upper School students typically attend 5 days per week. The average school day consists of 7 hours and 30 minutes.

Upper School Student Profile Grade 9: 26 students (13 boys, 13 girls); Grade 10: 30 students (11 boys, 19 girls); Grade 11: 29 students (22 boys, 7 girls); Grade 12: 34 students (15 boys, 19 girls). 10% of students are members of Episcopal Church.

Faculty School total: 50. In upper school: 11 men, 9 women; 12 have advanced degrees.

Subjects Offered 3-dimensional art, 3-dimensional design, accounting, advanced biology, advanced chemistry, advanced math, advanced studio art-AP, African-American literature, algebra, American history, American literature, art, bioethics, biology, Buddhism, calculus, campus ministry, ceramics, chemistry, choral music, college admission preparation, college counseling, college placement, college planning, college writing, community service, computer science, creative writing, earth science, economics, English, English literature, environmental science, ethics, fencing, fine arts, French, geometry, government/civics, health, history, independent study, instrumental music, instruments, international studies, internship, Irish literature, Irish studies, jazz band, jazz ensemble, journalism, literature, mathematics, mechanical drawing, media arts, medieval/Renaissance history, mentorship program, microeconomics, Middle Eastern history, music, music composition, music performance, music theory, newspaper, oil painting, opera, oral communications, oral expression, organ, painting, peace and justice, peace education, peace studies, performing arts, photography, physical education, physical fitness, physical science, physics, play production, play/screen writing, playwriting, playwriting and directing, poetry, policy and value, political economy, political science, politics, portfolio art, portfolio writing, pre-algebra, pre-calculus, psychology, psychology-AP, public service, public speaking, religion, SAT preparation, science, senior humanities, senior seminar, Shakespeare, social studies, Spanish, theater, trigonometry, world history, writing.

Special Academic Programs 30 Advanced Placement exams for which test preparation is offered; independent study; term-away projects; study at local college for college credit; domestic exchange program; study abroad; academic accommodation for the gifted, the musically talented, and the artistically talented.

College Admission Counseling 23 students graduated in 2010; all went to college, including Carleton College; Cornell University; Kenyon College; Rensselaer Polytechnic Institute; The Johns Hopkins University; Vassar College.

Student Life Upper grades have uniform requirement, student council. Discipline rests primarily with faculty. Attendance at religious services is required.

Tuition and Aid Day student tuition: $19,330–$21,400. Tuition installment plan (Academic Management Services Plan). Need-based scholarship grants available. In 2010–11, 40% of upper-school students received aid. Total amount of financial aid awarded in 2010–11: $727,810.

Admissions Traditional secondary-level entrance grade is 9. For fall 2010, 58 students applied for upper-level admission, 30 were accepted, 17 enrolled. School's own test required. Deadline for receipt of application materials: none. Application fee required: $75. On-campus interview required.

Athletics Interscholastic: baseball (boys), basketball (b,g), crew (b,g), soccer (b,g), softball (g), volleyball (g); intramural: backpacking (b,g), independent competitive sports (b,g); coed interscholastic: crew, cross-country running, independent competitive sports, tennis; coed intramural: backpacking, crew, cross-country running, fencing, Frisbee, hiking/backpacking, independent competitive sports, jogging, outdoor adventure, outdoors, physical fitness, sailing, soccer, strength & conditioning, tai chi, ultimate Frisbee, walking, yoga. 2 PE instructors, 8 coaches.

Computers Computers are regularly used in accounting, architecture, art, basic skills, business, career exploration, college planning, creative writing, current events, data processing, desktop publishing, drawing and design, economics, English, ethics, foreign language, freshman foundations, geography, graphic arts, graphic design, graphics, health, historical foundations for arts, history, humanities, independent study, introduction to technology, journalism, keyboarding, language development, learning cognition, library science, library skills, literary magazine, mathematics, media arts, media production, mentorship program, multimedia, music, music technology, news writing, newspaper, philosophy, photography, programming, psychology, publications, publishing, reading, religion, religious studies, remedial study skills, research skills, SAT preparation, science, senior seminar, social sciences, social studies, study skills, technology, theater, theater arts, video film production, Web site design, writing, writing, yearbook classes. Computer resources include on-campus library services, online commercial services, Internet access, wireless campus network. Computer access in designated common areas is available to students. The school has a published electronic and media policy.

Contact Mr. Michael Green, Director of Admission. 518-465-5222 Ext. 241. Fax: 518-465-5230. E-mail: mgreen@doanestuart.org. Web site: www.doanestuart.org.

THE DOMINICAN ACADEMY OF THE CITY OF NEW YORK

44 East 68th Street
New York, New York 10065
Head of School: Sr. Barbara Kane, OP

General Information Girls' day college-preparatory, arts, religious studies, and technology school, affiliated with Roman Catholic Church. Grades 9–12. Founded: 1897. Setting: urban. 1 building on campus. Approved or accredited by Middle States Association of Colleges and Schools, National Catholic Education Association, New York State Board of Regents, and New York Department of Education. Total enrollment: 231. Upper school average class size: 22. Upper school faculty-student ratio: 1:9. There are 180 required school days per year for Upper School students. Upper School students typically attend 5 days per week. The average school day consists of 6 hours and 30 minutes.

Upper School Student Profile Grade 9: 61 students (61 girls); Grade 10: 52 students (52 girls); Grade 11: 66 students (66 girls); Grade 12: 52 students (52 girls). 90% of students are Roman Catholic.

Faculty School total: 26. In upper school: 6 men, 20 women; 24 have advanced degrees.

Subjects Offered Algebra, American history, American history-AP, American literature, art history-AP, biology, biology-AP, calculus, calculus-AP, chemistry, chemistry-AP, chorus, communications, computer science, creative writing, dance, debate, drama, economics, economics-AP, English, English literature, English-AP, European history-AP, forensics, French, French-AP, geometry, global studies, government and politics-AP, government/civics, health, history, Latin, Latin-AP, library studies, logic, mathematics, music, music theory, physical education, physics, physics-AP, pre-calculus, psychology, religion, science, social studies, Spanish, Spanish-AP, world history.

Graduation Requirements Alternative physical education, arts and fine arts (art, music, dance, drama), English, foreign language, Latin, mathematics, religion (includes Bible studies and theology), science, social studies (includes history).

Special Academic Programs 11 Advanced Placement exams for which test preparation is offered.

College Admission Counseling 53 students graduated in 2010; all went to college, including Boston University; Cornell University; Fordham University; New York University; Queens College of the City University of New York; Villanova University.

Student Life Upper grades have uniform requirement, student council. Discipline rests primarily with faculty. Attendance at religious services is required.

Summer Programs Remediation, advancement programs offered; session focuses on Integrated Algebra Regents prep; held on campus; accepts girls; not open to students from other schools. 15 students usually enrolled.

Tuition and Aid Day student tuition: $10,500. Tuition installment plan (FACTS Tuition Payment Plan, individually arranged payment plans, quarterly payment plan, semester payment plan). Tuition reduction for siblings, merit scholarship grants, need-based scholarship grants, paying campus jobs available. In 2010–11, 25% of upper-school students received aid; total upper-school merit-scholarship money awarded: $55,000. Total amount of financial aid awarded in 2010–11: $268,000.

Admissions Traditional secondary-level entrance grade is 9. For fall 2010, 350 students applied for upper-level admission, 200 were accepted, 61 enrolled. Catholic High School Entrance Examination required. Deadline for receipt of application materials: December 20. No application fee required.

Athletics Interscholastic: basketball, cross-country running, soccer, softball, tennis, track and field, volleyball; intramural: billiards, dance, soccer, volleyball. 1 PE instructor.

Computers Computers are regularly used in economics, health, history, Latin, library science, library studies, mathematics, science, technology classes. Computer network features include on-campus library services, online commercial services, Internet access, wireless campus network, Internet filtering or blocking technology, T1 fiber optic network. Campus intranet, student e-mail accounts, and computer access in designated common areas are available to students. The school has a published electronic and media policy.

Contact Mrs. Jo Ann Fannon, Associate Director of Admissions. 212-744-0195 Ext. 31. Fax: 212-744-0375. E-mail: jfannon@dominicanacademy.org. Web site: www.dominicanacademy.org.

DONELSON CHRISTIAN ACADEMY
300 Danyacrest Drive
Nashville, Tennessee 37214
Head of School: Dr. Daniel W. Kellum Sr.

General Information Coeducational day college-preparatory, arts, religious studies, and technology school, affiliated with Christian faith. Grades K4–12. Founded: 1971. Setting: suburban. 30-acre campus. 3 buildings on campus. Approved or accredited by Association of Christian Schools International, Southern Association of Colleges and Schools, Tennessee Association of Independent Schools, and Tennessee Department of Education. Endowment: $70,000. Total enrollment: 754. Upper school average class size: 16. Upper school faculty-student ratio: 1:16. There are 180 required school days per year for Upper School students. Upper School students typically attend 5 days per week. The average school day consists of 6 hours and 50 minutes.

Upper School Student Profile Grade 9: 67 students (32 boys, 35 girls); Grade 10: 77 students (35 boys, 42 girls); Grade 11: 68 students (35 boys, 33 girls); Grade 12: 67 students (34 boys, 33 girls). 95% of students are Christian faith.

Faculty School total: 31. In upper school: 9 men, 19 women; 16 have advanced degrees.

Subjects Offered Advanced Placement courses, algebra, American history, American literature, anatomy, art, Bible studies, biology, business, business skills, calculus, chemistry, community service, computer science, drama, earth science, ecology, economics, English, English literature, environmental science, fine arts, French, geography, geometry, government/civics, grammar, health, history, journalism, keyboarding, Latin, mathematics, music, physical education, physics, physi-

ology, psychology, religion, science, social sciences, social studies, sociology, Spanish, speech, theater, world history, world literature.

Graduation Requirements Arts and fine arts (art, music, dance, drama), Bible, chemistry, electives, English, foreign language, mathematics, physical education (includes health), science, social sciences, social studies (includes history), wellness, senior service (community service for 12th grade students).

Special Academic Programs 6 Advanced Placement exams for which test preparation is offered; honors section; independent study; study at local college for college credit; academic accommodation for the gifted.

College Admission Counseling 65 students graduated in 2010; all went to college, including Lipscomb University; Middle Tennessee State University; Tennessee Technological University; The University of Tennessee System; Trevecca Nazarene University; Western Kentucky University. Median SAT critical reading: 560, median SAT math: 505, median SAT writing: 525, median combined SAT: 1590, median composite ACT: 23. 50% scored over 600 on SAT critical reading, 25% scored over 600 on SAT math, 25% scored over 600 on SAT writing, 25% scored over 1800 on combined SAT, 22% scored over 26 on composite ACT.

Student Life Upper grades have uniform requirement, student council, honor system. Discipline rests primarily with faculty. Attendance at religious services is required.

Summer Programs Sports programs offered; session focuses on skill development; held on campus; accepts boys and girls; not open to students from other schools. 230 students usually enrolled. 2011 schedule: June 1 to August 1. Application deadline: none.

Tuition and Aid Day student tuition: $7785. Tuition installment plan (FACTS Tuition Payment Plan, monthly payment plans). Tuition reduction for siblings, need-based scholarship grants, paying campus jobs available. In 2010–11, 20% of upper-school students received aid. Total amount of financial aid awarded in 2010–11: $136,853.

Admissions Traditional secondary-level entrance grade is 9. For fall 2010, 30 students applied for upper-level admission, 27 were accepted, 22 enrolled. Achievement tests or Stanford Achievement Test required. Deadline for receipt of application materials: none. Application fee required: $40. On-campus interview required.

Athletics Interscholastic: baseball (boys), basketball (b,g), bowling (b,g), cheering (g), cross-country running (b,g), football (b), golf (b,g), soccer (b,g), softball (g), tennis (b,g), track and field (b,g), volleyball (g), wrestling (b); intramural: basketball (b,g); coed interscholastic: physical fitness, swimming and diving, weight training; coed intramural: fitness. 1 PE instructor, 2 coaches.

Computers Computers are regularly used in all academic, career exploration, college planning, creative writing, French, history, journalism, library, mathematics, newspaper, science, technology, yearbook classes. Computer network features include on-campus library services, Internet access, wireless campus network, Internet filtering or blocking technology. Campus intranet is available to students. Students grades are available online. The school has a published electronic and media policy.

Contact Mrs. Stephanie Craven, Admissions Assistant. 615-577-1215. Fax: 615-883-2998. E-mail: scraven@dcawildcats.org. Web site: www.dcawildcats.org.

DONNA KLEIN JEWISH ACADEMY
9801 Donna Klein Boulevard
Boca Raton, Florida 33428-1524
Head of School: Stephen Thompson, PhD

General Information Coeducational day college-preparatory, religious studies, and bilingual studies school, affiliated with Jewish faith. Grades K–12. Founded: 1979. Setting: suburban. 32-acre campus. 2 buildings on campus. Approved or accredited by Florida Council of Independent Schools, Southern Association of Colleges and Schools, and Florida Department of Education. Languages of instruction: English and Hebrew. Total enrollment: 694. Upper school average class size: 13. Upper school faculty-student ratio: 1:4. There are 172 required school days per year for Upper School students. Upper School students typically attend 5 days per week. The average school day consists of 7 hours and 30 minutes.

Upper School Student Profile Grade 6: 62 students (26 boys, 36 girls); Grade 7: 70 students (33 boys, 37 girls); Grade 8: 58 students (28 boys, 30 girls); Grade 9: 18 students (6 boys, 12 girls); Grade 10: 25 students (12 boys, 13 girls); Grade 11: 23 students (11 boys, 12 girls); Grade 12: 11 students (7 boys, 4 girls). 100% of students are Jewish.

Faculty School total: 84. In upper school: 10 men, 10 women; 17 have advanced degrees.

Subjects Offered Advanced biology, advanced chemistry, advanced math, Advanced Placement courses, art, baseball, basketball, Bible studies, biology, calculus, calculus-AP, chemistry, college counseling, computer programming, computer tools, debate, drama, economics, English, English language and composition-AP, English literature and composition-AP, environmental science, environmental science-AP, geometry, government, Hebrew, honors English, honors geometry, honors U.S. history, honors world history, Jewish history, Jewish studies, journalism, Judaic studies, literature and composition-AP, physical education, pre-calculus, SAT preparation, Spanish, statistics-AP, theater production, U.S. government and politics, U.S. history-AP, visual arts, world history, world history-AP, writing, yearbook.

Graduation Requirements Electives, English, foreign language, history, Judaic studies, mathematics, physical education (includes health), science, writing, completion of 225 hours of community service.

Donna Klein Jewish Academy

Special Academic Programs 7 Advanced Placement exams for which test preparation is offered.

College Admission Counseling 20 students graduated in 2009; 18 went to college, including Brandeis University; Florida State University; University of Central Florida; University of Florida. Other: 2 went to work. Median SAT critical reading: 495, median SAT math: 510, median SAT writing: 545, median composite ACT: 23. 32% scored over 600 on SAT critical reading, 19% scored over 600 on SAT math, 27% scored over 600 on SAT writing, 23% scored over 26 on composite ACT.

Student Life Upper grades have specified standards of dress, student council, honor system. Discipline rests primarily with faculty. Attendance at religious services is required.

Tuition and Aid Day student tuition: $17,615. Tuition installment plan (monthly payment plans, individually arranged payment plans). Need-based scholarship grants available. In 2009–10, 25% of upper-school students received aid.

Admissions Traditional secondary-level entrance grade is 9. For fall 2009, 5 students applied for upper-level admission, 3 were accepted, 2 enrolled. SSAT required. Deadline for receipt of application materials: none. Application fee required: $100. On-campus interview required.

Athletics Interscholastic: baseball (boys), basketball (b,g), golf (b), soccer (b,g), volleyball (g); intramural: basketball (b,g); coed interscholastic: cross-country running, tennis; coed intramural: dance team, fitness, scuba diving, self defense, swimming and diving, tennis, weight lifting, weight training. 2 PE instructors, 2 coaches.

Computers Computers are regularly used in all classes. Computer network features include Internet access, wireless campus network. Campus intranet and student e-mail accounts are available to students. Students grades are available online. The school has a published electronic and media policy.

Contact Mrs. Jodi Orshan, Assistant Director of Admissions, High School. 561-558-2583. Fax: 561-558-2581. E-mail: orshanj@dkja.org. Web site: www.dkja.org.

DOWLING CATHOLIC HIGH SCHOOL
1400 Buffalo Road
West Des Moines, Iowa 50265
Head of School: Dr. Jerry M. Deegan

General Information Coeducational day college-preparatory, general academic, arts, business, religious studies, bilingual studies, technology, performing arts, and Advanced Placement school, affiliated with Roman Catholic Church. Grades 9–12. Founded: 1918. Setting: suburban. 60-acre campus. 1 building on campus. Approved or accredited by North Central Association of Colleges and Schools and Iowa Department of Education. Endowment: $9 million. Total enrollment: 1,372. Upper school average class size: 25. Upper school faculty-student ratio: 1:17.

Upper School Student Profile 94.5% of students are Roman Catholic.

Faculty School total: 79. In upper school: 39 men, 40 women; 40 have advanced degrees.

Subjects Offered 20th century world history, accounting, ACT preparation, acting, advanced chemistry, advanced computer applications, advanced math, Advanced Placement courses, advertising design, algebra, American government, American history, American history-AP, American literature, American literature-AP, applied arts, aquatics, art, art history, athletics, band, baseball, Basic programming, biology, biology-AP, brass choir, British literature, business, business communications, business law, calculus, calculus-AP, career and personal planning, career planning, career/college preparation, ceramics, chamber groups, cheerleading, chemistry, chemistry-AP, choir, choral music, chorus, church history, college counseling, college planning, composition, composition-AP, computer applications, computer information systems, computer processing, computer programming, computers, concert band, concert choir, creative writing, digital photography, drama, economics, economics-AP, engineering, English, English composition, English language and composition-AP, English literature, environmental science, European history, European history-AP, finance, fine arts, foreign language, French, general business, general science, geography, geometry, German, government, government-AP, health, health education, history, history-AP, honors algebra, honors English, honors geometry, honors U.S. history, honors world history, humanities, information processing, integrated mathematics, jazz band, journalism, keyboarding, Latin, life saving, literature, literature-AP, marching band, metalworking, modern European history, newspaper, painting, personal finance, physical education, physics, physics-AP, play production, poetry, pottery, pre-algebra, pre-calculus, probability and statistics, programming, religion, SAT/ACT preparation, scuba diving, social justice, sociology, Spanish, Spanish language-AP, speech and debate, swimming, tennis, theater production, theology, U.S. government, U.S. government and politics-AP, U.S. history, U.S. history-AP, visual arts, vocal jazz, weight training, world religions, yearbook.

Graduation Requirements Arts, business, electives, English, mathematics, reading, science, social studies (includes history), theology, Reading Across the Curriculum (RAC), 10 service hours per semester/20 per year, 10.5 credits of electives. Community service is required.

Special Academic Programs Advanced Placement exam preparation; honors section; accelerated programs; independent study; study at local college for college credit; academic accommodation for the gifted, the musically talented, and the artistically talented; remedial reading and/or remedial writing; remedial math; special instructional classes for blind students.

College Admission Counseling 295 students graduated in 2010; 294 went to college, including Creighton University; Iowa State University of Science and Technology; Loras College; The University of Iowa; University of Northern Iowa. Other: 1 went to work. Median SAT critical reading: 613, median SAT math: 618, median SAT writing: 583, median combined SAT: 605, median composite ACT: 24.

Student Life Upper grades have uniform requirement, student council, honor system. Discipline rests primarily with faculty. Attendance at religious services is required.

Summer Programs Enrichment, advancement, sports, art/fine arts, computer instruction programs offered; session focuses on advancement for the purpose of freeing up a slot in the schedule to take an elective; held on campus; accepts boys and girls; not open to students from other schools. 250 students usually enrolled. 2011 schedule: June 3 to July 1.

Tuition and Aid Day student tuition: $5908. Tuition installment plan (monthly payment plans, individually arranged payment plans). Need-based scholarship grants, paying campus jobs available. In 2010–11, 45% of upper-school students received aid. Total amount of financial aid awarded in 2010–11: $1,000,000.

Admissions Traditional secondary-level entrance grade is 9. Placement test required. Deadline for receipt of application materials: none. Application fee required: $90.

Athletics Interscholastic: aerobics/dance (girls), aquatics (b,g), baseball (b), basketball (b,g), bowling (b,g), cheering (g), cross-country running (b,g), dance team (b,g), diving (g), drill team (g), football (b), golf (b,g), hockey (b), soccer (b,g), softball (g), swimming and diving (b,g), tennis (b,g), track and field (b,g), volleyball (g), wrestling (b); coed interscholastic: cheering; coed intramural: ultimate Frisbee.

Computers Computers are regularly used in keyboarding classes. Computer network features include on-campus library services, Internet access, wireless campus network, Internet filtering or blocking technology. Computer access in designated common areas is available to students. Students grades are available online.

Contact Mrs. Tatia Eischeid, Admissions Assistant. 515-222-1047. Fax: 515-222-1056. E-mail: teischei@dowlingcatholic.org. Web site: www.dowlingcatholic.org.

DUBAI AMERICAN ACADEMY
PO Box 32762
Dubai, United Arab Emirates
Head of School: Mrs. Robin Appleby

General Information Coeducational day college-preparatory school. Grades PK–12. Founded: 1997. Setting: urban. 23-acre campus. 2 buildings on campus. Approved or accredited by European Council of International Schools, International Baccalaureate Organization, and New England Association of Schools and Colleges. Language of instruction: English. Total enrollment: 2,269. Upper school average class size: 20. Upper school faculty-student ratio: 1:12.

Upper School Student Profile Grade 6: 152 students (81 boys, 71 girls); Grade 7: 148 students (81 boys, 67 girls); Grade 8: 157 students (71 boys, 86 girls); Grade 9: 140 students (63 boys, 77 girls); Grade 10: 142 students (63 boys, 79 girls); Grade 11: 139 students (60 boys, 79 girls); Grade 12: 136 students (65 boys, 71 girls).

Faculty School total: 172. In upper school: 51 men, 40 women; 35 have advanced degrees.

Subjects Offered 20th century history, algebra, ancient world history, biology, business, chemistry, choir, computer science, digital photography, drama, economics, ESL, geometry, guidance, history, HTML design, International Baccalaureate courses, language arts, life skills, modern languages, music, physics, pre-algebra, pre-calculus, psychology, robotics, science, sociology, theory of knowledge, visual arts.

Graduation Requirements Arts and fine arts (art, music, dance, drama), English, health, information technology, languages, physical education (includes health), physics, science, social studies (includes history).

Special Academic Programs International Baccalaureate program.

College Admission Counseling 126 students graduated in 2009; 118 went to college, including Columbia University; Cornell University; New York University; University of California, Berkeley; University of Pennsylvania; University of Toronto. Other: 1 went to work, 7 had other specific plans. Median SAT critical reading: 530, median SAT math: 605, median SAT writing: 590.

Student Life Upper grades have uniform requirement, student council, honor system. Discipline rests primarily with faculty.

Tuition and Aid Day student tuition: 65,270 United Arab Emirates dirhams. Tuition installment plan (individually arranged payment plans, 2-installment plan).

Admissions Traditional secondary-level entrance grade is 11. For fall 2009, 474 students applied for upper-level admission, 152 were accepted, 152 enrolled. Math Placement Exam, placement test, Stanford Test of Academic Skills or writing sample required. Deadline for receipt of application materials: none. Application fee required: 500 United Arab Emirates dirhams. On-campus interview required.

Athletics Interscholastic: aerobics (boys, girls), aerobics/Nautilus (b,g), aquatics (b,g), badminton (b,g), ball hockey (b,g), baseball (b,g), basketball (b,g), bocce (b,g), cooperative games (b,g), cross-country running (b,g), fitness (b,g), flag football (b,g), floor hockey (b,g), Frisbee (b,g), indoor soccer (b,g), jogging (b,g), jump rope (b,g), kickball (b,g), lacrosse (b,g), life saving (b,g), Nautilus (b,g), Newcombe ball (b,g), physical fitness (b,g), physical training (b,g), rugby (b,g), running (b,g), soccer (b,g), softball (b,g), strength & conditioning (b,g), swimming and diving (b,g), touch football (b,g), track and field (b,g), ultimate Frisbee (b,g), volleyball (b,g), walking (b,g), water polo (b,g), water volleyball (b,g), weight lifting (b,g), weight training (b,g); intramural: aquatics (b,g), basketball (b,g), cross country running (b,g), soccer (b,g), tennis (b,g), track and field (b,g), volleyball (b,g); coed intramural: badminton, field hockey, floor hockey, football, golf, soccer, softball, strength & conditioning, table tennis, touch football, ultimate Frisbee, weight training. 7 PE instructors.

Computers Computers are regularly used in all classes. Computer network features include on-campus library services, Internet access, wireless campus network, Internet filtering or blocking technology. Computer access in designated common areas is available to students. Students grades are available online.

Contact Mrs. Carla Fakhreddine, Registrar. 971-43479222. Fax: 971-43476070. E-mail: cfakhreddine@daa.sch.ae. Web site: www.gemsaa-dubai.com.

DUBLIN CHRISTIAN ACADEMY

106 Page Road
Box 521
Dublin, New Hampshire 03444
Head of School: Mr. Kevin E. Moody

General Information Coeducational boarding and day college-preparatory, arts, business, and religious studies school, affiliated with Christian faith, Baptist Church. Boarding grades 7–12, day grades K–12. Founded: 1964. Setting: rural. Nearest major city is Boston, MA. Students are housed in single-sex dormitories. 200-acre campus. 5 buildings on campus. Approved or accredited by American Association of Christian Schools and New Hampshire Department of Education. Total enrollment: 74. Upper school average class size: 15. Upper-school faculty-student ratio: 1:8. Upper School students typically attend 5 days per week. The average school day consists of 5 hours and 45 minutes.

Upper School Student Profile Grade 6: 3 students (2 boys, 1 girl); Grade 7: 5 students (4 boys, 1 girl); Grade 8: 2 students (1 boy, 1 girl); Grade 9: 4 students (1 boy, 3 girls); Grade 10: 15 students (9 boys, 6 girls); Grade 11: 11 students (6 boys, 5 girls); Grade 12: 13 students (8 boys, 5 girls). 33% of students are boarding students. 57% are state residents. 5 states are represented in upper school student body. 25% are international students. International students from China and Republic of Korea. 80% of students are Christian faith, Baptist.

Faculty School total: 23. In upper school: 6 men, 6 women; 7 have advanced degrees; 17 reside on campus.

Subjects Offered Accounting, algebra, art, Bible studies, biology, business, calculus, ceramics, chemistry, chorus, computer literacy, consumer mathematics, economics, English, geometry, history, home economics, instrumental music, law, mathematics, music, physics, piano, religion, science, social studies, Spanish, speech, studio art, study skills, U.S. history, voice, word processing, world history.

Graduation Requirements English, foreign language, mathematics, religion (includes Bible studies and theology), science, social studies (includes history), speech.

Special Academic Programs Advanced Placement exam preparation; academic accommodation for the musically talented and the artistically talented; remedial reading and/or remedial writing; remedial math.

College Admission Counseling 16 students graduated in 2009; 13 went to college, including Bob Jones University; Clearwater Christian College; Colorado Christian University; Liberty University; The Master's College and Seminary. Other: 1 went to work. Mean SAT critical reading: 620, mean SAT math: 560, mean composite ACT: 23.

Student Life Upper grades have uniform requirement, student council. Discipline rests primarily with faculty. Attendance at religious services is required.

Tuition and Aid Day student tuition: $6970; 7-day tuition and room/board: $13,200. Tuition installment plan (FACTS Tuition Payment Plan). Need-based scholarship grants available. In 2009–10, 20% of upper-school students received aid.

Admissions Deadline for receipt of application materials: May 1. Application fee required: $35. Interview recommended.

Athletics Interscholastic: basketball (boys, girls), soccer (b), volleyball (g); intramural: cheering (g), flag football (b); coed intramural: alpine skiing, ice skating, snowboarding, softball.

Computers Computers are regularly used in accounting, business, English, foreign language, history, mathematics, music, science classes. Computer network features include on-campus library services, Internet access, Internet filtering or blocking technology.

Contact Mrs. Jenny Schmidt, Admissions Secretary. 603-563-8505. Fax: 603-563-8008. E-mail: jschmidt@dublinchristian.org. Web site: www.dublinchristian.org.

DUBLIN SCHOOL

Box 522
18 Lehmann Way
Dublin, New Hampshire 03444-0522
Head of School: Bradford D. Bates

General Information Coeducational boarding and day college-preparatory school. Grades 9–12. Founded: 1935. Setting: rural. Nearest major city is Boston, MA. Students are housed in single-sex dormitories. 300-acre campus. 22 buildings on campus. Approved or accredited by Independent Schools of Northern New England, New England Association of Schools and Colleges, and The Association of Boarding Schools. Member of National Association of Independent Schools and Secondary School Admission Test Board. Total enrollment: 127. Upper school average class size: 8. Upper school faculty-student ratio: 1:4. Upper School students typically attend 5 days per week. The average school day consists of 6 hours and 35 minutes.

Upper School Student Profile Grade 9: 29 students (17 boys, 12 girls); Grade 10: 37 students (21 boys, 16 girls); Grade 11: 36 students (25 boys, 11 girls); Grade 12: 25 students (14 boys, 11 girls). 72% of students are boarding students. 35% are state residents. 16 states are represented in upper school student body. 23% are international students. International students from China, Egypt, Japan, Mexico, Republic of Korea, and Spain; 6 other countries represented in student body.

Faculty School total: 29. In upper school: 15 men, 14 women; 18 have advanced degrees; 23 reside on campus.

Subjects Offered Acting, advanced math, African-American history, algebra, American foreign policy, American literature, anatomy and physiology, ancient world history, art, arts, biology, biology-AP, British literature, calculus, calculus-AP, carpentry, ceramics, chemistry, choir, chorus, college counseling, college placement, community service, computer education, computer literacy, computer programming, costumes and make-up, creative arts, creative dance, creative drama, cultural arts, dance performance, digital music, drama, drama performance, dramatic arts, drawing and design, electronic music, English, English composition, English literature, ESL, European civilization, European history, film history, fine arts, foreign policy, French, geology, geometry, guitar, honors U.S. history, instrumental music, Latin, library research, library skills, literature, marine biology, mathematics, modern dance, modern European history, music, music composition, music performance, music technology, music theory, musical productions, musical theater, musical theater dance, painting, personal and social education, personal development, philosophy, photography, physics, poetry, pre-algebra, pre-calculus, psychology, research, science, senior project, Shakespeare, social studies, Spanish, Spanish literature, stagecraft, statistics, student government, studio art, study skills, theater, theater arts, U.S. government and politics, U.S. history, U.S. history-AP, video film production, vocal ensemble, voice, weight training, world literature, writing, yearbook.

Graduation Requirements Art, arts, computer skills, English, general science, history, languages, mathematics, independent study in selected disciplines (for seniors), graduation requirements for honors diploma differ.

Special Academic Programs Advanced Placement exam preparation; honors section; independent study; term-away projects; domestic exchange program (with The Network Program Schools); programs in general development for dyslexic students; ESL (10 students enrolled).

College Admission Counseling 35 students graduated in 2010; 33 went to college, including Goucher College; Mount Holyoke College; Sacred Heart University; Smith College; The Johns Hopkins University; University of New Hampshire. Mean SAT critical reading: 563, mean SAT math: 549, mean SAT writing: 510, mean combined SAT: 1622, mean composite ACT: 21.

Student Life Upper grades have specified standards of dress, student council, honor system. Discipline rests primarily with faculty.

Tuition and Aid Day student tuition: $25,000; 7-day tuition and room/board: $43,000. Tuition installment plan (monthly payment plans). Need-based scholarship grants, need-based financial aid available. In 2010–11, 32% of upper-school students received aid. Total amount of financial aid awarded in 2010–11: $1,600,000.

Admissions Traditional secondary-level entrance grade is 9. For fall 2010, 143 students applied for upper-level admission, 97 were accepted, 48 enrolled. English, French, and math proficiency, SSAT, SSAT, ERB, PSAT, SAT, PLAN or ACT or TOEFL or SLEP required. Deadline for receipt of application materials: January 31. Application fee required: $50. Interview required.

Athletics Interscholastic: basketball (boys, girls), crew (b,g), freestyle skiing (b,g), lacrosse (b,g), skiing (downhill) (b,g), snowboarding (b,g), soccer (b,g), tennis (b,g); coed interscholastic: aerobics/dance, alpine skiing, crew, cross-country running, dance, dance team, equestrian sports, modern dance, nordic skiing, rowing, running, sailing, skiing (cross-country), skiing (downhill), snowboarding; coed intramural: aerobics/dance, alpine skiing, backpacking, basketball, bicycling, bowling, canoeing/kayaking, climbing, cooperative games, fencing, fishing, fitness, flagball, freestyle skiing, Frisbee, golf, hiking/backpacking, horseback riding, ice hockey, indoor soccer, martial arts, mountain biking, outdoor activities, outdoor adventure, outdoor education, outdoor recreation, physical fitness, physical training, rock climbing, ropes courses, sailing, skateboarding, skiing (cross-country), skiing (downhill), snowshoeing, softball, strength & conditioning, table tennis, telemark skiing, tennis, ultimate Frisbee, volleyball, wall climbing, weight lifting, weight training, whiffle ball, wrestling, yoga.

Computers Computers are regularly used in all academic classes. Computer network features include on-campus library services, Internet access, wireless campus network, Internet filtering or blocking technology. Student e-mail accounts are available to students. The school has a published electronic and media policy.

Contact Sheila Bogan, Director of Admission and Financial Aid. 603-563-1233. Fax: 603-563-8671. E-mail: admission@dublinschool.org. Web site: www.dublinschool.org/.

DUBOIS CENTRAL CATHOLIC HIGH SCHOOL/ MIDDLE SCHOOL

PO Box 567
200 Central Christian Road
DuBois, Pennsylvania 15801
Head of School: Rev. Fr. Marc Stockton

General Information college-preparatory and general academic school, affiliated with Roman Catholic Church. Founded: 1961. Setting: small town. Nearest major city is Pittsburgh. 51-acre campus. 1 building on campus. Approved or accredited by Middle States Association of Colleges and Schools, Western Catholic Education Association, and Pennsylvania Department of Education. Endowment: $750,000. Upper school average class size: 20. Upper school faculty-student ratio: 1:14.

Upper School Student Profile 86% of students are Roman Catholic.

Faculty In upper school: 8 men, 13 women.

Student Life Upper grades have uniform requirement, student council. Discipline rests primarily with faculty.

Admissions No application fee required.

Contact Mrs. Joyce Taylor, Director of Development. 814-371-3060 Ext. 606. Fax: 814-371-3215. E-mail: jtaylor@duboiscatholic.com. Web site: www.duboiscatholic.com.

DUCHESNE ACADEMY OF THE SACRED HEART

3601 Burt Street
Omaha, Nebraska 68131
Head of School: Mrs. Sheila Haggas

General Information Girls' day college-preparatory school, affiliated with Roman Catholic Church. Grades 9–12. Founded: 1881. Setting: urban. 13-acre campus. 3 buildings on campus. Approved or accredited by Network of Sacred Heart Schools, North Central Association of Colleges and Schools, and Nebraska Department of Education. Endowment: $4 million. Total enrollment: 303. Upper school average class size: 15. Upper school faculty-student ratio: 1:9. There are 173 required school days per year for Upper School students. Upper School students typically attend 5 days per week. The average school day consists of 7 hours.

Upper School Student Profile Grade 9: 86 students (86 girls); Grade 10: 82 students (82 girls); Grade 11: 59 students (59 girls); Grade 12: 76 students (76 girls). 90% of students are Roman Catholic.

Faculty School total: 38. In upper school: 10 men, 28 women; 26 have advanced degrees.

Subjects Offered 20th century history, 3-dimensional art, ACT preparation, acting, advanced chemistry, advanced math, algebra, American history, American literature, American literature-AP, anatomy and physiology, art, art history, bell choir, Bible as literature, biology, British literature, business, calculus, chemistry, chemistry-AP, child development, choir, choral music, Christian and Hebrew scripture, Christian ethics, Christian scripture, Christian testament, Christianity, church history, college counseling, community service, comparative government and politics, computer skills, constitutional history of U.S., constitutional law, creative writing, dance, digital photography, driver education, economics, English, environmental science, ethics, forensics, French, geometry, health, healthful living, Hebrew scripture, independent study, instrumental music, introduction to theater, journalism, Latin, modern European history, music theory, personal finance, photography, physical education, physics, physics-AP, pre-calculus, publications, SAT preparation, senior seminar, sociology, Spanish, speech, technical theater, theater, theater production, U.S. government and politics, world cultures, world literature, world religions, yearbook.

Graduation Requirements Arts and fine arts (art, music, dance, drama), computer literacy, English, foreign language, mathematics, physical education (includes health), religion (includes Bible studies and theology), science, social studies (includes history). Community service is required.

Special Academic Programs Advanced Placement exam preparation; honors section; independent study; term-away projects; study at local college for college credit; domestic exchange program (with Network of Sacred Heart Schools); study abroad; academic accommodation for the gifted; special instructional classes for deaf students, blind students.

College Admission Counseling 59 students graduated in 2010; all went to college, including Creighton University; Iowa State University of Science and Technology; Saint Louis University; The University of Iowa; University of Nebraska–Lincoln; University of Nebraska at Omaha. Median combined SAT: 1810, median composite ACT: 27.

Student Life Upper grades have uniform requirement, student council, honor system. Discipline rests primarily with faculty. Attendance at religious services is required.

Summer Programs Sports programs offered; session focuses on open gym/fitness training; held on campus; accepts girls; not open to students from other schools. 100 students usually enrolled. 2011 schedule: June to July. Application deadline: May.

Tuition and Aid Day student tuition: $8800. Tuition installment plan (monthly payment plans, quarterly payment plan, semester payment plan). Tuition reduction for siblings, merit scholarship grants, need-based scholarship grants, minority scholarships, reduced tuition for children of Creighton University employees available. In

2010–11, 48% of upper-school students received aid; total upper-school merit-scholarship money awarded: $50,000. Total amount of financial aid awarded in 2010–11: $117,000.

Admissions Traditional secondary-level entrance grade is 9. For fall 2010, 332 students applied for upper-level admission, 313 were accepted, 303 enrolled. Scholastic Testing Service required. Deadline for receipt of application materials: January 26. Application fee required: $35. On-campus interview required.

Athletics Interscholastic: basketball, cheering, cross-country running, dance squad, dance team, diving, golf, soccer, softball, swimming and diving, tennis, track and field, volleyball; intramural: aerobics, aerobics/dance, cheering, yoga. 2 PE instructors, 12 coaches, 1 athletic trainer.

Computers Computers are regularly used in all academic classes. Computer network features include on-campus library services, Internet access, wireless campus network, Internet filtering or blocking technology, computer network with other Sacred Heart schools, mandatory laptop purchase by 10th, 11th, and 12th grade students. Campus intranet and student e-mail accounts are available to students. Students grades are available online. The school has a published electronic and media policy.

Contact Mrs. Meg Jones, Recruitment Director/Exchange Coordinator. 402-558-3800 Ext. 1070. Fax: 402-558-0051. E-mail: mjones@duchesneacademy.org. Web site: www.duchesneacademy.org.

DUCHESNE ACADEMY OF THE SACRED HEART

10202 Memorial Drive
Houston, Texas 77024
Head of School: Sr. Jan Dunn, RSCJ

General Information Girls' day college-preparatory, arts, religious studies, and technology school, affiliated with Roman Catholic Church. Grades PK–12. Founded: 1960. Setting: suburban. 14-acre campus. 2 buildings on campus. Approved or accredited by Independent Schools Association of the Southwest, National Catholic Education Association, Network of Sacred Heart Schools, Texas Catholic Conference, Texas Education Agency, and Texas Department of Education. Endowment: $7 million. Total enrollment: 675. Upper school average class size: 14. Upper school faculty-student ratio: 1:7. There are 180 required school days per year for Upper School students. Upper School students typically attend 5 days per week. The average school day consists of 7 hours and 25 minutes.

Upper School Student Profile Grade 6: 60 students (60 girls); Grade 7: 61 students (61 girls); Grade 8: 39 students (39 girls); Grade 9: 56 students (56 girls); Grade 10: 62 students (62 girls); Grade 11: 62 students (62 girls); Grade 12: 60 students (60 girls). 64% of students are Roman Catholic.

Faculty School total: 92. In upper school: 3 men, 33 women; 28 have advanced degrees.

Subjects Offered Algebra, American literature, art history, arts, band, Bible studies, bioethics, biology, British literature, calculus, calculus-AP, ceramics, chemistry, chemistry-AP, community service, composition, computer graphics, computer programming, creative writing, desktop publishing, drawing, economics, English, English literature, European history, fine arts, French, French-AP, geometry, government/civics, health, human sexuality, Internet, Latin, mathematics, music, photography, physical education, physical fitness, physics, prayer/spirituality, pre-calculus, psychology, religious studies, science, scripture, sexuality, Shakespeare, social justice, social studies, Spanish, Spanish-AP, speech, statistics, statistics-AP, studio art, theater, theater production, theology, U.S. government and politics-AP, U.S. history, U.S. history-AP, Western literature, women's studies, world history, world literature, world religions, writing.

Graduation Requirements Arts and fine arts (art, music, dance, drama), computer science, English, foreign language, history, mathematics, physical education (includes health), religion (includes Bible studies and theology), science, completion of social awareness program. Community service is required.

Special Academic Programs 15 Advanced Placement exams for which test preparation is offered; honors section; independent study; domestic exchange program (with Network of Sacred Heart Schools); academic accommodation for the musically talented and the artistically talented.

College Admission Counseling 67 students graduated in 2010; all went to college, including Duke University; Southern Methodist University; Texas Christian University; The University of Texas at Austin; Trinity University; University of Houston. Median SAT critical reading: 600, median SAT math: 585, median SAT writing: 640, median combined SAT: 1845, median composite ACT: 27. 61% scored over 600 on SAT critical reading, 48% scored over 600 on SAT math, 78% scored over 600 on SAT writing, 59% scored over 1800 on combined SAT, 54% scored over 26 on composite ACT.

Student Life Upper grades have uniform requirement, student council, honor system. Discipline rests primarily with faculty. Attendance at religious services is required.

Summer Programs Enrichment, art/fine arts, computer instruction programs offered; session focuses on high school credit, and math review, enrichment; held on campus; accepts girls; open to students from other schools. 225 students usually enrolled. 2011 schedule: June 7 to July 23.

Tuition and Aid Day student tuition: $18,340. Tuition installment plan (monthly payment plans). Merit scholarship grants, need-based scholarship grants available. In 2010–11, 21% of upper-school students received aid; total upper-school merit-scholarship money awarded: $46,300. Total amount of financial aid awarded in 2010–11: $641,530.

Admissions Traditional secondary-level entrance grade is 9. For fall 2010, 101 students applied for upper-level admission, 68 were accepted, 29 enrolled. ISEE required. Deadline for receipt of application materials: February 1. Application fee required: $80. On-campus interview required.

Athletics Interscholastic: basketball, combined training, cross-country running, dance team, diving, field hockey, golf, soccer, softball, swimming and diving, tennis, track and field, volleyball, winter soccer. 5 PE instructors, 25 coaches, 2 athletic trainers.

Computers Computers are regularly used in all academic classes. Computer network features include on-campus library services, online commercial services, Internet access, wireless campus network, Internet filtering or blocking technology. Student e-mail accounts are available to students. Students grades are available online. The school has a published electronic and media policy.

Contact Mrs. Beth Speck, Director of Admission. 713-468-8211 Ext. 133. Fax: 713-465-9809. E-mail: beth.speck@duchesne.org. Web site: www.duchesne.org.

DUNN SCHOOL
PO Box 98
2555 West Highway 154
Los Olivos, California 93441
Head of School: Michael Beck

General Information Coeducational boarding and day college-preparatory and arts school. Boarding grades 9–12, day grades 6–12. Founded: 1957. Setting: small town. Nearest major city is Santa Barbara. Students are housed in single-sex dormitories. 57-acre campus. 15 buildings on campus. Approved or accredited by California Association of Independent Schools, National Independent Private Schools Association, The Association of Boarding Schools, Western Association of Schools and Colleges, and California Department of Education. Member of National Association of Independent Schools and Secondary School Admission Test Board. Total enrollment: 218. Upper school average class size: 15. Upper school faculty-student ratio: 1:6. There are 158 required school days per year for Upper School students. Upper School students typically attend 5 days per week. The average school day consists of 7 hours and 15 minutes.

Upper School Student Profile Grade 9: 16 students (9 boys, 7 girls); Grade 10: 42 students (23 boys, 19 girls); Grade 11: 45 students (23 boys, 22 girls); Grade 12: 47 students (28 boys, 19 girls). 62% of students are boarding students. 65% are state residents. 12 states are represented in upper school student body. 25% are international students. International students from China, Ghana, Republic of Korea, Sudan, Taiwan, and Thailand; 4 other countries represented in student body.

Faculty School total: 37. In upper school: 13 men, 11 women; 24 have advanced degrees; 30 reside on campus.

Subjects Offered Algebra, American history, American history-AP, biology, biology-AP, calculus-AP, ceramics, chemistry, chemistry-AP, college counseling, conceptual physics, contemporary history, creative writing, economics, English, English language-AP, English literature-AP, environmental science, environmental science-AP, European history, experiential education, fine arts, French, French language-AP, guitar, human development, instrumental music, integrated mathematics, Mandarin, microeconomics, music, outdoor education, photography, physics, probability and statistics, science, Spanish, Spanish language-AP, statistics-AP, studio art, studio art-AP, world history.

Graduation Requirements Arts and fine arts (art, music, dance, drama), biology, chemistry, college counseling, English, foreign language, history, lab science, mathematics, outdoor education, physics, science, U.S. government, U.S. history, world cultures.

Special Academic Programs Advanced Placement exam preparation; honors section; independent study; special instructional classes for students with moderate to mild learning differences.

College Admission Counseling 42 students graduated in 2009; 41 went to college, including Claremont McKenna College; Saint Mary's College of California; University of California, Berkeley; University of California, Los Angeles; University of Colorado at Boulder. Other: 1 went to work.

Student Life Upper grades have specified standards of dress, student council, honor system. Discipline rests primarily with faculty.

Tuition and Aid Day student tuition: $19,200; 7-day tuition and room/board: $43,000. Tuition installment plan (Academic Management Services Plan, individually arranged payment plans, 2-payment plan). Need-based scholarship grants available. In 2009–10, 21% of upper-school students received aid. Total amount of financial aid awarded in 2009–10: $608,260.

Admissions Traditional secondary-level entrance grade is 9. For fall 2009, 92 students applied for upper-level admission, 58 were accepted, 25 enrolled. ISEE, SLEP for foreign students, SSAT or TOEFL required. Deadline for receipt of application materials: February 1. Application fee required: $50. Interview required.

Athletics Interscholastic: baseball (boys), basketball (b,g), football (b), lacrosse (b,g), soccer (b,g), tennis (b,g), volleyball (b,g); coed interscholastic: backpacking, canoeing/kayaking, climbing, cross-country running, dance, dance team, equestrian sports, fitness, fitness walking, golf, kayaking, modern dance, outdoor education, paddle tennis, physical fitness, physical training, rafting, rock climbing, ropes courses, strength & conditioning, surfing, swimming and diving, table tennis, track and field, walking, weight lifting, weight training; coed intramural: equestrian sports, Frisbee,

hiking/backpacking, horseback riding, horseshoes, indoor soccer, paddle tennis, rappelling, ropes courses, table tennis. 3 coaches, 1 athletic trainer.

Computers Computers are regularly used in art, college planning, English, history, mathematics, multimedia, music, publications, science, yearbook classes. Computer network features include on-campus library services, Internet access, wireless campus network, Internet filtering or blocking technology. Student e-mail accounts and computer access in designated common areas are available to students. The school has a published electronic and media policy.

Contact Ann E. Greenough, Director of Admission. 800-287-9197. Fax: 805-686-2078. E-mail: admissions@dunnschool.org. Web site: www.dunnschool.org.

DURHAM ACADEMY
3601 Ridge Road
Durham, North Carolina 27705
Head of School: Mr. Edward Costello

General Information Coeducational day college-preparatory, arts, and technology school. Grades PK–12. Founded: 1933. Setting: suburban. 75-acre campus. 11 buildings on campus. Approved or accredited by North Carolina Association of Independent Schools, Southern Association of Colleges and Schools, Southern Association of Independent Schools, and North Carolina Department of Education. Member of National Association of Independent Schools and Secondary School Admission Test Board. Endowment: $9.6 million. Total enrollment: 1,135. Upper school average class size: 15. Upper school faculty-student ratio: 1:12. There are 175 required school days per year for Upper School students. Upper School students typically attend 5 days per week. The average school day consists of 6 hours.

Upper School Student Profile Grade 9: 98 students (47 boys, 51 girls); Grade 10: 102 students (49 boys, 53 girls); Grade 11: 96 students (43 boys, 53 girls); Grade 12: 88 students (46 boys, 42 girls).

Faculty School total: 169. In upper school: 22 men, 21 women; 36 have advanced degrees.

Subjects Offered 3-dimensional art, accounting, acting, advanced biology, advanced chemistry, advanced computer applications, advanced math, Advanced Placement courses, advanced studio art-AP, algebra, American history, American literature, art, art history, astronomy, biology, calculus, ceramics, chemistry, chemistry-AP, Chinese, chorus, community service, computer graphics, computer programming, computer science, concert band, creative writing, dance, drama, ecology, economics, English, English literature, environmental science, fine arts, finite math, French, geometry, German, history, Latin, mathematics, music, outdoor education, physical education, physics, psychology, science, social studies, Spanish, statistics, theater.

Graduation Requirements Arts and fine arts (art, music, dance, drama), computer science, English, foreign language, mathematics, outdoor education, physical education (includes health), science, senior project, social studies (includes history), community service hours required for graduation.

Special Academic Programs Advanced Placement exam preparation; honors section; independent study; special instructional classes for students with learning disabilities and Attention Deficit Disorder.

College Admission Counseling Colleges students went to include Duke University; East Carolina University; Elon University; North Carolina State University; The University of North Carolina at Chapel Hill; Wake Forest University. Mean SAT critical reading: 659, mean SAT math: 663, mean SAT writing: 656.

Student Life Upper grades have specified standards of dress, student council, honor system. Discipline rests equally with students and faculty.

Summer Programs Remediation, enrichment, sports, art/fine arts, computer instruction programs offered; session focuses on academic enrichment, non-academic activities; held on campus; accepts boys and girls; open to students from other schools. 600 students usually enrolled. 2011 schedule: June 14 to July 30. Application deadline: none.

Tuition and Aid Day student tuition: $19,400. Tuition installment plan (Key Tuition Payment Plan, monthly payment plans). Need-based scholarship grants available. In 2010–11, 13% of upper-school students received aid. Total amount of financial aid awarded in 2010–11: $724,650.

Admissions Traditional secondary-level entrance grade is 9. For fall 2010, 75 students applied for upper-level admission, 47 were accepted, 29 enrolled. ISEE required. Deadline for receipt of application materials: January 14. Application fee required: $55. Interview required.

Athletics Interscholastic: aquatics (boys, girls), baseball (b), basketball (b,g), cross-country running (b,g), dance team (g), field hockey (g), golf (b), lacrosse (b,g), soccer (b,g), softball (g), swimming and diving (b,g), tennis (b,g), track and field (b,g), volleyball (g), weight training (b,g); coed interscholastic: golf, outdoor adventure, outdoor education, weight training; coed intramural: indoor soccer, judo, martial arts, modern dance, physical fitness, physical training, winter soccer. 1 PE instructor, 6 coaches, 1 athletic trainer.

Computers Computers are regularly used in all academic, animation, computer applications, graphic arts, graphic design, introduction to technology, video film production, Web site design classes. Computer network features include on-campus library services, online commercial services, Internet access, wireless campus network, Internet filtering or blocking technology. Student e-mail accounts and computer access in designated common areas are available to students. The school has a published electronic and media policy.

Contact Ms. S. Victoria Muradi, Director of Admission and Financial Aid. 919-493-5787. Fax: 919-489-4893. E-mail: admissions@da.org. Web site: www.da.org.

DWIGHT-ENGLEWOOD SCHOOL

315 East Palisade Avenue
Englewood, New Jersey 07631-0489
Head of School: Dr. Rodney V. De Jarnett

General Information Coeducational day college-preparatory, arts, and technology school. Grades PK–12. Founded: 1889. Setting: suburban. Nearest major city is New York, NY. 41-acre campus. 13 buildings on campus. Approved or accredited by Middle States Association of Colleges and Schools, New Jersey Association of Independent Schools, and New Jersey Department of Education. Member of National Association of Independent Schools and Secondary School Admission Test Board. Endowment: $10 million. Total enrollment: 959. Upper school average class size: 15. Upper school faculty-student ratio: 1:9. Upper School students typically attend 5 days per week. The average school day consists of 7 hours and 30 minutes.

Upper School Student Profile Grade 9: 116 students (54 boys, 62 girls); Grade 10: 114 students (62 boys, 52 girls); Grade 11: 111 students (61 boys, 50 girls); Grade 12: 106 students (54 boys, 52 girls).

Faculty School total: 130. In upper school: 32 men, 39 women; 60 have advanced degrees.

Subjects Offered Acting, advanced chemistry, advanced math, Advanced Placement courses, advanced studio art-AP, American history, American history-AP, American literature-AP, analysis, analysis and differential calculus, analysis of data, analytic geometry, ancient history, architecture, art, art history, art history-AP, bell choir, bioethics, bioethics, DNA and culture, biology, biology-AP, calculus-AP, ceramics, chemistry-AP, choir, chorus, community service, computer graphics, computer science-AP, concert bell choir, creative writing, critical thinking, data analysis, digital imaging, digital photography, drama, dramatic arts, drawing, drawing and design, economics and history, engineering, English, English language and composition-AP, English language-AP, English literature, English literature and composition-AP, English literature-AP, English-AP, environmental science, environmental science-AP, ethics, European history, evolution, fine arts, foreign language, fractal geometry, French, French language-AP, French literature-AP, French-AP, general science, genetics, geometry, government and politics-AP, government-AP, health, health education, history, history of jazz, independent study, Japanese, language-AP, Latin, law, literature and composition-AP, mathematics, orchestra, organic chemistry, painting, photography, physical education, physics-AP, printmaking, psychology, robotics, science, social studies, Spanish, statistics-AP, technology, U.S. government and politics-AP, world history.

Graduation Requirements Arts and fine arts (art, music, dance, drama), English, ethics, foreign language, mathematics, physical education (includes health), science, social studies (includes history), technology. Community service is required.

Special Academic Programs Advanced Placement exam preparation; honors section; independent study; study abroad.

College Admission Counseling 126 students graduated in 2009; all went to college, including Boston University; Columbia University; Cornell University; New York University; The George Washington University; University of Pennsylvania. Mean SAT critical reading: 652, mean SAT math: 648, mean SAT writing: 668. 44% scored over 600 on SAT critical reading, 54% scored over 600 on SAT math, 60% scored over 600 on SAT writing.

Student Life Upper grades have student council. Discipline rests equally with students and faculty.

Tuition and Aid Day student tuition: $27,777. Tuition installment plan (monthly payment plans). Need-based scholarship grants available. In 2009–10, 14% of upper-school students received aid. Total amount of financial aid awarded in 2009–10: $2,200,000.

Admissions Traditional secondary-level entrance grade is 9. For fall 2009, 206 students applied for upper-level admission, 113 were accepted, 61 enrolled. ISEE or SSAT required. Deadline for receipt of application materials: December 31. Application fee required: $65. On-campus interview required.

Athletics Interscholastic: baseball (boys), basketball (b,g), cross-country running (b,g), field hockey (g), football (b), lacrosse (b,g), soccer (b,g), softball (g), tennis (b,g), track and field (b,g), volleyball (g), wrestling (b); intramural: cheering (g), fencing (b,g), hockey (b); coed interscholastic: Frisbee, golf. 10 PE instructors, 15 coaches, 1 athletic trainer.

Computers Computers are regularly used in art, English, history, mathematics, science, technology classes. Computer network features include on-campus library services, online commercial services, Internet access, wireless campus network, Internet filtering or blocking technology, tablet PC program, Taub Tech Center. Student e-mail accounts and computer access in designated common areas are available to students. Students grades are available online. The school has a published electronic and media policy.

Contact Ms. Sherronda L. Brown, Director of Enrollment and External Relations. 201-569-9500 Ext. 3500. Fax: 201-568-9451. E-mail: browns@d-e.org. Web site: www.d-e.org.

THE DWIGHT SCHOOL

291 Central Park West
New York, New York 10024
Head of School: Mr. Stephen Spahn

General Information Coeducational day college-preparatory, arts, business, bilingual studies, and technology school. Grades PK–12. Founded: 1880. Setting: urban. 3 buildings on campus. Approved or accredited by European Council of International Schools, International Baccalaureate Organization, Middle States Association of Colleges and Schools, and New York Department of Education. Endowment: $5 million. Total enrollment: 435. Upper school average class size: 15. Upper school faculty-student ratio: 1:6.

Upper School Student Profile Grade 9: 64 students (36 boys, 28 girls); Grade 10: 67 students (39 boys, 28 girls); Grade 11: 61 students (40 boys, 21 girls); Grade 12: 62 students (38 boys, 24 girls).

Faculty School total: 93. In upper school: 24 men, 26 women; 32 have advanced degrees.

Subjects Offered Algebra, American history, American literature, art, art history, biology, calculus, chemistry, community service, computer math, computer science, creative writing, dance, drama, economics, English, English literature, environmental science, ethics, European history, expository writing, film, fine arts, French, geometry, government/civics, grammar, health, history, Italian, Japanese, journalism, Latin, mathematics, music, philosophy, photography, physical education, physics, physiology, psychology, science, social studies, Spanish, technology/design, theater, theory of knowledge, trigonometry, typing, world history, world literature, writing.

Graduation Requirements Arts and fine arts (art, music, dance, drama), computer science, English, foreign language, mathematics, physical education (includes health), science, social studies (includes history). Community service is required.

Special Academic Programs International Baccalaureate program; Advanced Placement exam preparation; honors section; independent study; term-away projects; study abroad; remedial reading and/or remedial writing; remedial math; special instructional classes for students with learning disabilities; ESL (15 students enrolled).

College Admission Counseling 65 students graduated in 2009; 61 went to college, including Brown University; Dartmouth College; New York University; Northwestern University; The George Washington University; Trinity College. Other: 4 went to work.

Student Life Upper grades have specified standards of dress, student council, honor system. Discipline rests equally with students and faculty.

Tuition and Aid Day student tuition: $26,250–$28,000. Tuition installment plan (The Tuition Plan, Insured Tuition Payment Plan, monthly payment plans, individually arranged payment plans). Need-based scholarship grants, prepGATE loans available. In 2009–10, 20% of upper-school students received aid. Total amount of financial aid awarded in 2009–10: $500,000.

Admissions Traditional secondary-level entrance grade is 9. ERB or ISEE required. Deadline for receipt of application materials: none. Application fee required: $50. On-campus interview required.

Athletics Interscholastic: baseball (boys), basketball (b,g), cross-country running (b,g), dance (g), dance team (g), fencing (b,g); intramural: basketball (b,g), boxing (b,g), fencing (b,g); coed interscholastic: fencing; coed intramural: boxing, fencing, golf. 6 PE instructors, 16 coaches.

Computers Computers are regularly used in foreign language, mathematics, music, science classes. Computer network features include on-campus library services, online commercial services, Internet access, wireless campus network, Internet filtering or blocking technology. Students grades are available online.

Contact Alicia P. Janiak, Co-Head of Admissions. 212-724-6360. Fax: 212-724-2539. E-mail: ajaniak@dwight.edu. Web site: www.dwight.edu.

EAGLEBROOK SCHOOL

Deerfield, Massachusetts
See Junior Boarding Schools section.

EAGLE HILL-SOUTHPORT

Southport, Connecticut
See Special Needs Schools section.

EAGLE ROCK SCHOOL

Estes Park, Colorado
See Special Needs Schools section.

EAST CATHOLIC HIGH SCHOOL

115 New State Road
Manchester, Connecticut 06042-1898
Head of School: Mr. Christian Joseph Cashman

General Information Coeducational day college-preparatory, arts, and religious studies school, affiliated with Roman Catholic Church. Grades 9–12. Founded: 1961. Setting: suburban. Nearest major city is Hartford. 47-acre campus. 2 buildings on campus. Approved or accredited by Connecticut Association of Independent Schools, New England Association of Schools and Colleges, and Connecticut Department of Education. Total enrollment: 684. Upper school average class size: 19. Upper school faculty-student ratio: 1:13. There are 177 required school days per year for Upper School students. Upper School students typically attend 5 days per week. The average school day consists of 5 hours and 33 minutes.

Upper School Student Profile Grade 9: 145 students (58 boys, 87 girls); Grade 10: 177 students (84 boys, 93 girls); Grade 11: 185 students (86 boys, 99 girls); Grade 12: 177 students (86 boys, 91 girls). 75% of students are Roman Catholic.

Faculty School total: 58. In upper school: 21 men, 37 women; 52 have advanced degrees.

Subjects Offered Algebra, American history, American history-AP, American literature, American literature-AP, anatomy, art, Bible studies, biology, biology-AP, business, calculus, calculus-AP, chemistry, chemistry-AP, computer programming, computer science, digital photography, economics, English, English literature, English literature-AP, environmental science, ethics, European history, expository writing, French, geography, geometry, government/civics, grammar, Greek culture, health, history, Latin, mathematics, music, music theory, music theory-AP, music-AP, philosophy, physical education, physics, physiology, psychology, religion, science, sculpture, social studies, sociology, Spanish, theology, trigonometry, world history, world literature, writing.

Graduation Requirements English, foreign language, health and wellness, mathematics, physical education (includes health), religion (includes Bible studies and theology), science, social studies (includes history), study skills, 10 hours of community service per year.

Special Academic Programs Advanced Placement exam preparation; honors section.

College Admission Counseling 171 students graduated in 2009; 158 went to college, including Central Connecticut State University; Fairfield University; Southern Connecticut State University; University of Connecticut; University of Hartford. Other: 1 went to work, 1 entered a postgraduate year, 1 had other specific plans.

Student Life Upper grades have uniform requirement, student council. Discipline rests primarily with faculty. Attendance at religious services is required.

Tuition and Aid Day student tuition: $10,500. Tuition installment plan (FACTS Tuition Payment Plan, July prepayment discount plan). Tuition reduction for siblings, merit scholarship grants, need-based scholarship grants available.

Admissions Traditional secondary-level entrance grade is 9. For fall 2009, 266 students applied for upper-level admission, 244 were accepted, 145 enrolled. High School Placement Test required. Deadline for receipt of application materials: none. Application fee required: $20.

Athletics Interscholastic: baseball (boys), basketball (b,g), cheering (g), cross-country running (b,g), dance team (g), football (b), golf (b,g), ice hockey (b), lacrosse (b,g), soccer (b,g), softball (g), swimming and diving (g), tennis (b,g), track and field (b,g), volleyball (g), weight lifting (b), winter (indoor) track (b,g), wrestling (b); intramural: volleyball (g); coed interscholastic: indoor track, table tennis. 2 PE instructors, 40 coaches, 1 athletic trainer.

Computers Computers are regularly used in all academic classes. Computer resources include on-campus library services, online commercial services, Internet access, wireless campus network, Internet filtering or blocking technology. The school has a published electronic and media policy.

Contact Ms. Jacqueline Gryphon, Director of Recruitment and Admissions. 860-649-5336 Ext. 238. Fax: 860-649-7191. E-mail: gryphonj@echs.com. Web site: www.echs.com.

EASTERN CHRISTIAN HIGH SCHOOL
50 Oakwood Avenue
North Haledon, New Jersey 07508
Head of School: Mr. Thomas Dykhouse

General Information Coeducational day college-preparatory, general academic, arts, and technology school, affiliated with Christian Reformed Church. Grades PK–12. Founded: 1892. Setting: suburban. Nearest major city is New York, NY. 27-acre campus. 1 building on campus. Approved or accredited by Association of Christian Schools International, Christian Schools International, Middle States Association of Colleges and Schools, New Jersey Department of Education, and New Jersey Department of Education. Endowment: $6 million. Total enrollment: 757. Upper school average class size: 20. Upper school faculty-student ratio: 1:10. There are 185 required school days per year for Upper School students. Upper School students typically attend 5 days per week. The average school day consists of 6 hours and 40 minutes.

Upper School Student Profile Grade 6: 43 students (23 boys, 20 girls); Grade 7: 54 students (31 boys, 23 girls); Grade 8: 61 students (24 boys, 37 girls); Grade 9: 90 students (39 boys, 51 girls); Grade 10: 94 students (44 boys, 50 girls); Grade 11: 81 students (37 boys, 44 girls); Grade 12: 88 students (38 boys, 50 girls). 40% of students are members of Christian Reformed Church.

Faculty School total: 85. In upper school: 11 men, 22 women; 21 have advanced degrees.

Subjects Offered Accounting, advanced biology, algebra, American history, American legal systems, American literature, art, band, Bible studies, biology, business, business skills, calculus, chemistry, chorus, community service, composition, computer programming, computer science, computer-aided design, contem-

porary math, creative writing, driver education, English, English composition, English literature, entrepreneurship, ESL, European history, fine arts, French, geometry, government/civics, health, history, humanities, journalism, Latin, mathematics, music, orchestra, personal finance, physical education, physical science, physics, pre-calculus, psychology, science, social studies, sociology, Spanish, study skills, technical education, trigonometry, Web site design, world history, writing, writing workshop, yearbook.

Graduation Requirements Arts and fine arts (art, music, dance, drama), Bible, English, foreign language, lab science, leadership, mathematics, physical education (includes health), social studies (includes history), 50 hours of community service.

Special Academic Programs 1 Advanced Placement exam for which test preparation is offered; honors section; independent study; academic accommodation for the gifted, the musically talented, and the artistically talented; remedial reading and/or remedial writing; remedial math; programs in English, mathematics for dyslexic students; ESL (20 students enrolled).

College Admission Counseling 81 students graduated in 2010; 76 went to college, including Calvin College; Liberty University; Messiah College; Montclair State University; Palm Beach Atlantic University; William Paterson University of New Jersey. Other: 5 went to work. Median SAT critical reading: 540, median SAT math: 510, median SAT writing: 510. Mean composite ACT: 20. 28% scored over 600 on SAT critical reading, 24% scored over 600 on SAT math, 25% scored over 600 on SAT writing.

Student Life Upper grades have specified standards of dress, student council. Discipline rests primarily with faculty. Attendance at religious services is required.

Tuition and Aid Day student tuition: $11,230. Tuition installment plan (SMART Tuition Payment Plan, monthly payment plans). Tuition reduction for siblings, need-based scholarship grants available.

Admissions Traditional secondary-level entrance grade is 9. For fall 2010, 63 students applied for upper-level admission, 50 were accepted, 50 enrolled. Deadline for receipt of application materials: none. Application fee required: $100. On-campus interview required.

Athletics Interscholastic: baseball (boys), basketball (b,g), bowling (b,g), cheering (g), cross-country running (b,g), golf (b,g), soccer (b,g), softball (g), tennis (b,g), track and field (b,g), volleyball (g); intramural: aerobics (b,g), badminton (b,g), basketball (b,g), fitness walking (b,g), flag football (b,g), flagball (b,g), football (b,g), Frisbee (b,g), golf (b,g), gymnastics (b,g), indoor soccer (b,g), lacrosse (b,g), paddle tennis (b,g), physical fitness (b,g), roller hockey (b,g), running (b,g), skateboarding (b,g), skiing (downhill) (b,g), soccer (b,g), softball (b,g), street hockey (b,g), table tennis (b,g), volleyball (b,g), weight lifting (b,g); coed intramural: aerobics, badminton, baseball, basketball, fitness walking, flag football, flagball, football, golf, gymnastics, indoor soccer, lacrosse, paddle tennis, physical fitness, roller hockey, running, skateboarding, skiing (downhill), soccer, softball, street hockey, table tennis, volleyball, weight lifting. 2 PE instructors, 18 coaches.

Computers Computers are regularly used in all academic classes. Computer network features include on-campus library services, Internet access, wireless campus network, Internet filtering or blocking technology, Microsoft Office, Microsoft Visual Studio, AutoCAD LT 2000, Adobe Photoshop, Adobe GoLive, Adobe Illustrator, Adobe LiveMotion, Macromedia Dreamweaver, Adobe Premiere, Lego Mindstorms NXT. Computer access in designated common areas is available to students. Students grades are available online. The school has a published electronic and media policy.

Contact Mr. G. Anthony Cantalupo, Admission Director. 973-427-6244 Ext. 207. Fax: 973-427-9775. E-mail: admissions@easternchristian.org. Web site: www.easternchristian.org.

EAST LINN CHRISTIAN ACADEMY
36883 Victory Drive
Lebanon, Oregon 97355
Head of School: Mr. Jim M. Hill

General Information Coeducational day college-preparatory and general academic school, affiliated with Christian faith. Grades PK–12. Founded: 1981. Setting: rural. Nearest major city is Salem. 25-acre campus. 5 buildings on campus. Approved or accredited by Association of Christian Schools International, Northwest Association of Schools and Colleges, and Oregon Department of Education. Total enrollment: 296. Upper school average class size: 29. Upper school faculty-student ratio: 1:11. There are 171 required school days per year for Upper School students. Upper School students typically attend 5 days per week. The average school day consists of 7 hours.

Upper School Student Profile Grade 9: 30 students (14 boys, 16 girls); Grade 10: 25 students (11 boys, 14 girls); Grade 11: 23 students (9 boys, 14 girls); Grade 12: 39 students (20 boys, 19 girls). 100% of students are Christian.

Faculty School total: 21. In upper school: 5 men, 6 women; 5 have advanced degrees.

Subjects Offered Algebra, American government, anatomy and physiology, art, ASB Leadership, Bible, biology, British literature, calculus, chemistry, choir, civics, college writing, computer processing, computer programming, computers, concert band, constitutional history of U.S., consumer economics, desktop publishing, drama, earth science, economics, English, English literature, family living, geometry, government/civics, health, home economics, industrial arts, keyboarding, language arts, leadership education training, Life of Christ, literature, North American literature, personal finance, physical education, physical science, physics, pre-algebra, pre-calculus, Spanish, U.S. government, U.S. history, Western civilization, work-study, world cultures, yearbook.

East Linn Christian Academy

Special Academic Programs Independent study; remedial reading and/or remedial writing; remedial math; ESL (6 students enrolled).

College Admission Counseling 24 students graduated in 2009; they went to Corban University; Linn-Benton Community College; Oregon State University; Western Oregon University.

Student Life Upper grades have specified standards of dress, student council, honor system. Discipline rests primarily with faculty. Attendance at religious services is required.

Tuition and Aid Day student tuition: $4732. Tuition installment plan (monthly payment plans, individually arranged payment plans). Tuition reduction for siblings, need-based scholarship grants available. In 2009–10, 5% of upper-school students received aid. Total amount of financial aid awarded in 2009–10: $1500.

Admissions Traditional secondary-level entrance grade is 9. Wide Range Achievement Test required. Deadline for receipt of application materials: none. Application fee required: $150. Interview required.

Athletics Interscholastic: basketball (boys, girls), cross-country running (b,g), equestrian sports (b,g), golf (b,g), soccer (b), track and field (b,g), volleyball (g). 2 PE instructors, 5 coaches.

Computers Computers are regularly used in keyboarding classes. Computer resources include Internet access, Internet filtering or blocking technology. Students grades are available online.

Contact Kim Warren, Administrative Secretary. 541-259-2324. Fax: 541-451-3800. E-mail: elca@peak.org. Web site: www.eastlinnchristian.com.

EASTSIDE CATHOLIC SCHOOL

232-228th Avenue SE
Sammamish, Washington 98074
Head of School: Sr. Mary E. Tracy

General Information Coeducational day college-preparatory, arts, religious studies, and technology school, affiliated with Roman Catholic Church. Grades 6–12. Founded: 1980. Setting: suburban. 50-acre campus. 2 buildings on campus. Approved or accredited by National Catholic Education Association, Northwest Association of Schools and Colleges, Pacific Northwest Association of Independent Schools, and Washington Department of Education. Total enrollment: 808. Upper school average class size: 20. Upper school faculty-student ratio: 1:14. There are 180 required school days per year for Upper School students. The average school day consists of 6 hours and 45 minutes.

Upper School Student Profile 60% of students are Roman Catholic.

Faculty School total: 78. In upper school: 22 men, 30 women; 38 have advanced degrees.

Subjects Offered Advanced Placement courses, algebra, American government, American history, American literature, anatomy and physiology, art, art-AP, ASB Leadership, athletic training, band, biology, biology-AP, British literature, calculus, calculus-AP, calligraphy, campus ministry, Catholic belief and practice, ceramics, chemistry, chemistry-AP, choir, church history, community service, computers, contemporary issues, creative writing, debate, digital photography, drama, drawing, economics, English, English literature, French, French-AP, geometry, government and politics-AP, graphic design, health, history, honors algebra, honors English, honors geometry, honors U.S. history, honors world history, journalism, law, math analysis, music, painting, performing arts, physical education, physics, physics-AP, religious education, social justice, Spanish, Spanish-AP, speech and debate, studio art, theology, trigonometry, U.S. history-AP, Web site design, world history, yearbook.

Graduation Requirements Arts and fine arts (art, music, dance, drama), business education, English, foreign language, mathematics, physical education (includes health), science, social sciences, theology, 100 hours of community service (over 4 years).

Special Academic Programs Advanced Placement exam preparation; honors section; study at local college for college credit; academic accommodation for the gifted and the musically talented; programs in English, mathematics, general development for dyslexic students.

College Admission Counseling 167 students graduated in 2010; 165 went to college, including Gonzaga University; Santa Clara University; Seattle University; University of Portland; University of Washington; Washington State University. Other: 1 entered a postgraduate year, 1 had other specific plans.

Student Life Upper grades have specified standards of dress, student council, honor system. Discipline rests primarily with faculty. Attendance at religious services is required.

Tuition and Aid Day student tuition: $17,300. Tuition installment plan (monthly payment plans). Tuition reduction for siblings, merit scholarship grants, need-based scholarship grants available. In 2010–11, 30% of upper-school students received aid. Total amount of financial aid awarded in 2010–11: $1,700,000.

Admissions Traditional secondary-level entrance grade is 9. For fall 2010, 287 students applied for upper-level admission, 259 were accepted, 159 enrolled. ISEE required. Deadline for receipt of application materials: January 14. Application fee required: $25. Interview recommended.

Athletics Interscholastic: baseball (boys), basketball (b,g), cheering (g), drill team (g), football (b), golf (b,g), lacrosse (b,g), soccer (b,g), softball (g), swimming and diving (b,g), tennis (b,g), track and field (b,g), volleyball (g), wrestling (b); coed interscholastic: cross-country running, Special Olympics; coed intramural: strength & conditioning, weight lifting, weight training. 2 PE instructors, 43 coaches, 2 athletic trainers.

Computers Computers are regularly used in business education, digital applications, graphic design, technology, Web site design, yearbook classes. Computer network features include on-campus library services, online commercial services, Internet access, wireless campus network, Internet filtering or blocking technology. Students grades are available online.

Contact Helene Johnson, Director of Admission. 425-295-3014. Fax: 425-392-5160. E-mail: hjohnson@eastsidecatholic.org. Web site: www.eastsidecatholic.org.

EASTSIDE CHRISTIAN ACADEMY

1320 Abbeydale Drive SE
Calgary, Alberta T2A 7L8, Canada
Head of School: Dr. Frank Moody

General Information Coeducational day and distance learning college-preparatory, general academic, religious studies, and music school, affiliated with Christian faith. Grades K–12. Distance learning grades 10–12. Founded: 1999. Setting: urban. Students are housed in host family homes. 4-acre campus. 1 building on campus. Approved or accredited by Alberta Department of Education. Language of instruction: English. Total enrollment: 97. Upper school average class size: 30. Upper school faculty-student ratio: 1:25. There are 180 required school days per year for Upper School students. Upper School students typically attend 5 days per week. The average school day consists of 6 hours.

Upper School Student Profile Grade 6: 6 students (6 girls); Grade 7: 10 students (3 boys, 7 girls); Grade 8: 8 students (4 boys, 4 girls); Grade 9: 4 students (3 boys, 1 girl); Grade 10: 11 students (3 boys, 8 girls); Grade 11: 5 students (3 boys, 2 girls); Grade 12: 7 students (4 boys, 3 girls). 100% of students are Christian faith.

Faculty School total: 4. In upper school: 2 men, 2 women; 1 has an advanced degree.

Subjects Offered Algebra, art, Bible studies, biology, business, business mathematics, Canadian geography, Canadian history, career/college preparation, chemistry, church history, civics, computer literacy, economics, English, etymology, French, geometry, Greek, Life of Christ, literature, music, natural history, physical education, physical science, physics, Spanish, speech, typing, world geography, world history.

Graduation Requirements Algebra, Bible studies, biology, business education, Canadian geography, Canadian history, chemistry, Christian scripture, Christian testament, church history, concert band, data processing, economics, electives, English, etymology, French, geometry, German, mathematics, music, physical education (includes health), physical science, physics, religious education, social studies (includes history), Spanish, speech and debate, vocal music, volleyball, world geography, world history.

Special Academic Programs Honors section; accelerated programs; independent study; study at local college for college credit; academic accommodation for the gifted and the musically talented; remedial reading and/or remedial writing; remedial math.

College Admission Counseling 6 students graduated in 2010. Other: 6 went to work.

Student Life Upper grades have uniform requirement, student council, honor system. Discipline rests primarily with faculty. Attendance at religious services is required.

Summer Programs Remediation, advancement programs offered; session focuses on remediation/make-up; held on campus; accepts boys and girls; not open to students from other schools. 10 students usually enrolled. 2011 schedule: July 1 to August 15. Application deadline: May 15.

Tuition and Aid Day student tuition: CAN$3600. Tuition installment plan (monthly payment plans, individually arranged payment plans). Tuition reduction for siblings, bursaries, need-based scholarship grants available.

Admissions Traditional secondary-level entrance grade is 10. For fall 2010, 26 students applied for upper-level admission, 26 were accepted, 26 enrolled. Cognitive Abilities Test, Diagnostic Achievement Battery-2 (for applicants from non-U.S. curriculum) and school placement exam required. Deadline for receipt of application materials: March 1. Application fee required: CAN$60. On-campus interview required.

Athletics Interscholastic: badminton (boys, girls), ball hockey (b,g), basketball (b,g), volleyball (b,g); coed interscholastic: soccer; coed intramural: badminton, ball hockey, basketball, floor hockey, volleyball. 1 PE instructor, 2 coaches.

Computers Computers are regularly used in career exploration, data processing, economics, English, French, geography, history, information technology, keyboarding, literacy, mathematics, media, reading, religion, religious studies, social studies, Spanish, speech, typing, word processing classes. Computer network features include Internet access, wireless campus network, Internet filtering or blocking technology. Computer access in designated common areas is available to students. Students grades are available online. The school has a published electronic and media policy.

Contact LaDawn Torgerson, Secretary. 403-569-1003 Ext. 200. Fax: 403-569-1023. E-mail: admin@ecaab.ca.

EASTSIDE COLLEGE PREPARATORY SCHOOL

1041 Myrtle Street
East Palo Alto, California 94303
Head of School: Chris Bischof

General Information Coeducational boarding and day college-preparatory school. Grades 6–12. Founded: 1996. Setting: suburban. Nearest major city is Oakland. Students are housed in single-sex dormitories. 6-acre campus. 7 buildings on campus. Approved or accredited by Western Association of Schools and Colleges and California Department of Education. Total enrollment: 258. Upper school average class size: 18. Upper school faculty-student ratio: 1:8. There are 180 required school days per year for Upper School students. Upper School students typically attend 5 days per week. The average school day consists of 6 hours.

Upper School Student Profile Grade 9: 47 students (18 boys, 29 girls); Grade 10: 45 students (18 boys, 27 girls); Grade 11: 39 students (19 boys, 20 girls); Grade 12: 33 students (12 boys, 21 girls). 20% of students are boarding students. 100% are state residents. 1 state is represented in upper school student body.

Faculty School total: 36. In upper school: 10 men, 20 women; 25 have advanced degrees; 4 reside on campus.

Special Academic Programs Advanced Placement exam preparation.

Student Life Upper grades have specified standards of dress, student council, honor system. Discipline rests primarily with faculty.

Tuition and Aid Financial aid available to upper-school students. In 2009–10, 100% of upper-school students received aid. Total amount of financial aid awarded in 2009–10: $3,061,000.

Admissions Traditional secondary-level entrance grade is 9. For fall 2009, 150 students applied for upper-level admission, 50 were accepted, 48 enrolled. Deadline for receipt of application materials: January 11. No application fee required. Interview required.

Athletics Interscholastic: basketball (boys, girls), cross-country running (b), soccer (b,g), track and field (b,g), volleyball (b,g). 1 PE instructor, 3 coaches.

Computers Computer network features include Internet access, wireless campus network, Internet filtering or blocking technology. Student e-mail accounts are available to students. Students grades are available online.

Contact Helen Kim, Vice Principal. 650-688-0850 Ext. 109. Fax: 650-688-0859. E-mail: helenk@eastside.org. Web site: www.eastside.org.

ECKERD YOUTH ALTERNATIVES

Clearwater, Florida
See Special Needs Schools section.

ECOLE D'HUMANITÉ

CH 6085 Hasliberg Goldern, Switzerland
Head of School: Mr. John Ashley Curtis

General Information Coeducational boarding and day college-preparatory, general academic, arts, vocational, and bilingual studies school. Ungraded, ages 12–19. Founded: 1934. Setting: rural. Nearest major city is Lucerne, Switzerland. Students are housed in coed dormitories. 5-acre campus. 13 buildings on campus. Approved or accredited by CITA (Commission on International and Trans-Regional Accreditation), Department of Education of Bern, North Central Association of Colleges and Schools, and Swiss Federation of Private Schools. Member of European Council of International Schools. Languages of instruction: English and German. Endowment: 1 million Swiss francs. Upper school average class size: 5. Upper school faculty-student ratio: 1:5. Upper School students typically attend 6 days per week. The average school day consists of 6 hours.

Upper School Student Profile 95% of students are boarding students. 49% are international students. International students from China, Germany, Italy, Russian Federation, Taiwan, and United States; 12 other countries represented in student body.

Faculty School total: 44. In upper school: 15 men, 19 women; 10 have advanced degrees; 37 reside on campus.

Subjects Offered Advanced Placement courses, algebra, American literature, art, art history, backpacking, band, batik, biology, biology-AP, calculus, calculus-AP, career and personal planning, carpentry, ceramics, chemistry, choir, choreography, chorus, college counseling, community service, computer programming, computer skills, costumes and make-up, crafts, creative dance, creative writing, culinary arts, cultural geography, current events, dance, dance performance, drama, drama workshop, drawing, ecology, environmental systems, English, English as a foreign language, English composition, English literature, English literature-AP, environmental science, ESL, European history, expository writing, fine arts, first aid, folk dance, French, French as a second language, gardening, geography, geometry, German, German-AP, grammar, guitar, gymnastics, health, history, home economics, independent study, jazz ensemble, jewelry making, Latin, mathematics, modern dance, music, music appreciation, music performance, musical productions, musical theater, musical theater dance, outdoor education, peer counseling, philosophy, photo shop, photography, physical education, physics, piano, poetry, pottery, pre-calculus, psychology, religion, research skills, SAT preparation, science, sewing, Shakespeare, single survival, social sciences, social studies, studio art, swimming, theater, TOEFL preparation, trigonometry, U.S. history, visual and performing arts, vocal ensemble, voice, volleyball, weaving, wind ensemble, women's studies, woodworking, world history, world history-AP, world literature, writing, yoga.

Graduation Requirements English, foreign language, independent study, mathematics, physical education (includes health), research skills, SAT preparation,

science, social sciences, social studies (includes history), 2x term paper methodology course, balance of courses in arts, sports, handcrafts. Community service is required.

Special Academic Programs 5 Advanced Placement exams for which test preparation is offered; honors section; accelerated programs; independent study; term-away projects; academic accommodation for the gifted, the musically talented, and the artistically talented; remedial reading and/or remedial writing; remedial math; ESL (40 students enrolled).

College Admission Counseling 10 students graduated in 2010; 6 went to college, including Brandeis University; Brown University; New York University; The Colorado College. Other: 2 went to work, 2 had other specific plans. Median SAT critical reading: 600, median SAT math: 650, median SAT writing: 580.

Student Life Upper grades have student council, honor system. Discipline rests equally with students and faculty.

Tuition and Aid Day student tuition: 22,000 Swiss francs; 7-day tuition and room/board: 44,000 Swiss francs–48,000 Swiss francs. Guaranteed tuition plan. Tuition installment plan (monthly payment plans, individually arranged payment plans). Need-based scholarship grants, need-based loans, middle-income loans available. In 2010–11, 20% of upper-school students received aid. Total amount of financial aid awarded in 2010–11: 180,000 Swiss francs.

Admissions Traditional secondary-level entrance age is 16. For fall 2010, 50 students applied for upper-level admission, 46 were accepted, 46 enrolled. Deadline for receipt of application materials: none. No application fee required. Interview recommended.

Athletics Interscholastic: basketball (boys); intramural: basketball (b,g); coed intramural: aerobics, aerobics/dance, alpine skiing, archery, backpacking, badminton, ballet, baseball, basketball, bicycling, canoeing/kayaking, climbing, dance, fitness, freestyle skiing, Frisbee, gymnastics, hiking/backpacking, horseback riding, indoor soccer, jogging, juggling, kayaking, martial arts, modern dance, mountaineering, physical fitness, rock climbing, skiing (downhill), snowboarding, snowshoeing, soccer, softball, strength & conditioning, swimming and diving, table tennis, tennis, ultimate Frisbee, volleyball, yoga.

Computers Computers are regularly used in career exploration, college planning, creative writing, data processing, English, graphic design, independent study, library, newspaper, photography, typing, yearbook classes. Computer resources include Internet access. Computer access in designated common areas is available to students.

Contact John Ashley Curtis, Director. 41-33-972-9272. Fax: 41-33-972-9272. E-mail: admissions@ecole.ch. Web site: www.ecole.ch.

See Display on page 237 and Close-Up on page 774.

ECOLE INTERNATIONALE DE BOSTON / INTERNATIONAL SCHOOL OF BOSTON

45 Matignon Road
Cambridge, Massachusetts 02140
Head of School: Dr. Richard Blumenthal

General Information Coeducational day college-preparatory, arts, and bilingual studies school. Grades PK–12. Founded: 1962. Setting: urban. Nearest major city is Boston. 5-acre campus. 2 buildings on campus. Approved or accredited by Association of Independent Schools in New England, European Council of International Schools, French Ministry of Education, International Baccalaureate Organization, New England Association of Schools and Colleges, and Massachusetts Department of Education. Member of National Association of Independent Schools. Languages of instruction: English and French. Endowment: $50,000. Total enrollment: 567. Upper school average class size: 10. Upper school faculty-student ratio: 1:6.

Upper School Student Profile Grade 9: 22 students (10 boys, 12 girls); Grade 10: 11 students (3 boys, 8 girls); Grade 11: 20 students (11 boys, 9 girls); Grade 12: 18 students (6 boys, 12 girls).

Faculty School total: 100. In upper school: 7 men, 20 women; 18 have advanced degrees.

Graduation Requirements French Baccalaureate requirements, International Baccalaureate requirements.

Special Academic Programs International Baccalaureate program; accelerated programs; independent study; ESL (50 students enrolled).

College Admission Counseling 18 students graduated in 2009; all went to college, including Boston University; Columbia University; McGill University; New York University; Northeastern University. Mean SAT critical reading: 621, mean SAT math: 619, mean SAT writing: 620.

Student Life Upper grades have specified standards of dress, student council. Discipline rests primarily with faculty.

Tuition and Aid Day student tuition: $21,700. Tuition installment plan (monthly payment plans, individually arranged payment plans). Bursaries, need-based scholarship grants available. In 2009–10, 55% of upper-school students received aid. Total amount of financial aid awarded in 2009–10: $594,000.

Admissions Traditional secondary-level entrance grade is 9. Placement test or PSAT or SAT required. Deadline for receipt of application materials: none. Application fee required: $75. Interview recommended.

Athletics Coed Interscholastic: aerobics/dance, archery, badminton, basketball, bicycling, fencing, fitness, gymnastics, handball, indoor track, martial arts, soccer, table tennis, tennis, volleyball; coed intramural: basketball, fencing, handball, martial arts, outdoors, soccer, table tennis. 2 PE instructors.

Computers Computers are regularly used in mathematics, science classes. Computer resources include on-campus library services, Internet access, wireless campus network, Internet filtering or blocking technology. Student e-mail accounts and computer access in designated common areas are available to students. Students grades are available online. The school has a published electronic and media policy.

Contact Barbara Saran-Brunner, Director of Admissions. 617-499-1459. Fax: 617-234-0064. E-mail: bsaran@isbos.org. Web site: www.isbos.org.

EDGEWOOD ACADEMY

5475 Elmore Road
PO Box 160
Elmore, Alabama 36025
Head of School: Mr. Frankie Mitchum

General Information college-preparatory, arts, business, religious studies, bilingual studies, and technology school. Founded: 1967. Setting: small town. Nearest major city is Montgomery. 30-acre campus. 4 buildings on campus. Approved or accredited by National Independent Private Schools Association, Southern Association of Colleges and Schools, and Alabama Department of Education. Total enrollment: 243. Upper school average class size: 15. Upper school faculty-student ratio: 1:11. There are 177 required school days per year for Upper School students. Upper School students typically attend 5 days per week. The average school day consists of 5 hours and 45 minutes.

Faculty School total: 20. In upper school: 4 men, 5 women; 7 have advanced degrees.

Graduation Requirements Advanced Diploma requires 100 hours of community service, Standard Diplomas requires 50 hours of community service.

Special Academic Programs Advanced Placement exam preparation; study at local college for college credit.

College Admission Counseling 23 students graduated in 2010; they went to Auburn University Montgomery. Median composite ACT: 25.

Student Life Upper grades have specified standards of dress, student council.

Summer Programs Session focuses on Driver education; held both on and off campus; held at Driving practice—random; accepts boys and girls; open to students from other schools. 15 students usually enrolled. 2011 schedule: June to July. Application deadline: May.

Tuition and Aid Day student tuition: $5500. Tuition installment plan (SMART Tuition Payment Plan). Tuition reduction for siblings available.

Admissions Admissions testing required. Deadline for receipt of application materials: none. No application fee required. Interview required.

Athletics Interscholastic: baseball (boys), basketball (b,g), cheering (g), football (b), physical fitness (b,g), physical training (b,g), softball (g), volleyball (g), weight lifting (b), weight training (b,g); coed interscholastic: track and field. 2 PE instructors, 3 coaches.

Computers Computers are regularly used in yearbook classes. Computer network features include on-campus library services, Internet access, wireless campus network, Internet filtering or blocking technology. Students grades are available online. The school has a published electronic and media policy.

Contact 334-567-5102. Fax: 334-567-8316. Web site: edgewoodacademy.org.

EDISON SCHOOL

Box 2, Site 11, RR2
Okotoks, Alberta T1S 1A2, Canada
Head of School: Mrs. Beth Chernoff

General Information Coeducational day college-preparatory and general academic school. Grades K–12. Founded: 1993. Setting: small town. Nearest major city is Calgary, Canada. 5-acre campus. 3 buildings on campus. Approved or accredited by Association of Independent Schools and Colleges of Alberta and Alberta Department of Education. Languages of instruction: English, Spanish, and French. Total enrollment: 198. Upper school average class size: 12. Upper school faculty-student ratio: 1:12.

Upper School Student Profile Grade 9: 12 students (6 boys, 6 girls); Grade 10: 12 students (6 boys, 6 girls); Grade 11: 12 students (6 boys, 6 girls); Grade 12: 12 students (6 boys, 6 girls).

Faculty School total: 18. In upper school: 5 men, 1 woman; 4 have advanced degrees.

Subjects Offered Advanced Placement courses, art, biology, chemistry, English, French, mathematics, physical education, physics, science, social studies, Spanish, standard curriculum.

Graduation Requirements Alberta Learning requirements.

Special Academic Programs Advanced Placement exam preparation; accelerated programs; independent study; study at local college for college credit; academic accommodation for the gifted.

College Admission Counseling 8 students graduated in 2009; 7 went to college, including The University of British Columbia; University of Alberta; University of Calgary; University of Waterloo. Other: 1 went to work. Median composite ACT: 26. 58% scored over 26 on composite ACT.

Student Life Upper grades have uniform requirement, student council, honor system. Discipline rests primarily with faculty.

Tuition and Aid Day student tuition: CAN$7000. Tuition installment plan (monthly payment plans). Tuition reduction for siblings available.

Admissions Traditional secondary-level entrance grade is 9. For fall 2009, 20 students applied for upper-level admission, 4 were accepted, 4 enrolled. Achievement tests or admissions testing required. Deadline for receipt of application materials: none. No application fee required. On-campus interview required.

Athletics Interscholastic: badminton (boys, girls), basketball (b,g), cross-country running (b,g); intramural: badminton (b,g), basketball (b,g), cross-country running (b,g); coed interscholastic: badminton, flag football; coed intramural: badminton, flag football, outdoor education. 1 PE instructor, 1 coach.

Computers Computers are regularly used in all classes. Computer resources include Internet access. Computer access in designated common areas is available to students.

Contact Mrs. Beth Chernoff, Headmistress. 403-938-7670. Fax: 403-938-7224. E-mail: office@edisonschool.ca. Web site: www.edisonschool.ca.

EDMUND BURKE SCHOOL
4101 Connecticut Avenue NW
Washington, District of Columbia 20008
Head of School: David Shapiro

General Information Coeducational day college-preparatory and arts school. Grades 6–12. Founded: 1968. Setting: urban. 2 buildings on campus. Approved or accredited by Association of Independent Maryland Schools, Association of Independent Schools of Greater Washington, Middle States Association of Colleges and Schools, and District of Columbia Department of Education. Member of National Association of Independent Schools and Secondary School Admission Test Board. Endowment: $829,556. Total enrollment: 275. Upper school average class size: 15. Upper school faculty-student ratio: 1:7. There are 185 required school days per year for Upper School students. Upper School students typically attend 5 days per week. The average school day consists of 5 hours.

Upper School Student Profile Grade 9: 42 students (19 boys, 23 girls); Grade 10: 52 students (29 boys, 23 girls); Grade 11: 53 students (30 boys, 23 girls); Grade 12: 60 students (29 boys, 31 girls).

Faculty School total: 41. In upper school: 19 men, 19 women; 20 have advanced degrees.

Subjects Offered African-American literature, algebra, American history, American literature, anatomy, anthropology, biology, calculus, ceramics, chemistry, computer science, creative writing, economics, English, English literature, European history, French, geography, geometry, health, history, journalism, Latin, linguistics, music, performing arts, philosophy, photography, physical education, physics, senior seminar, Spanish, theater, trigonometry, values and decisions, visual arts, women's studies, world history, writing.

Graduation Requirements English, foreign language, health, history, mathematics, physical education (includes health), science, social sciences, values and decisions, visual and performing arts, senior research seminar. Community service is required.

Special Academic Programs Advanced Placement exam preparation; independent study; term-away projects.

College Admission Counseling 65 students graduated in 2010; all went to college, including New York University; University of New Hampshire; University of Pittsburgh; University of Rhode Island; Wesleyan University. Median SAT critical reading: 651, median SAT math: 641, median SAT writing: 648.

Student Life Upper grades have student council, honor system. Discipline rests primarily with faculty.

Summer Programs Remediation, enrichment, advancement, ESL, art/fine arts, computer instruction programs offered; session focuses on academic programs and visual arts; held on campus; accepts boys and girls; open to students from other schools. 50 students usually enrolled. 2011 schedule: June 20 to August 21. Application deadline: none.

Tuition and Aid Day student tuition: $31,650. Tuition installment plan (The Tuition Plan, Insured Tuition Payment Plan, Academic Management Services Plan, individually arranged payment plans). Need-based scholarship grants available. In 2010–11, 29% of upper-school students received aid. Total amount of financial aid awarded in 2010–11: $978,185.

Admissions Traditional secondary-level entrance grade is 9. For fall 2010, 130 students applied for upper-level admission, 86 were accepted, 39 enrolled. ISEE or SSAT required. Deadline for receipt of application materials: January 15. Application fee required: $60. On-campus interview required.

Athletics Interscholastic: aquatics (boys, girls), basketball (b,g), cross-country running (b,g), golf (b,g), soccer (b,g), softball (g), swimming and diving (g), track and field (b,g), volleyball (b,g), wrestling (b,g); intramural: dance team (b,g), Frisbee (b,g), martial arts (b,g), physical fitness (b,g), weight lifting (b,g); coed interscholastic: swimming and diving; coed intramural: indoor soccer, jogging. 2 PE instructors, 2 coaches.

Computers Computers are regularly used in creative writing, English, foreign language, French, graphic arts, history, journalism, mathematics, science classes. Computer network features include on-campus library services, online commercial services, Internet access. Students grades are available online. The school has a published electronic and media policy.

Contact Admissions Office. 202-362-8882. Fax: 202-362-1914. E-mail: admissions@eburke.org. Web site: www.eburke.org.

ELAN SCHOOL
Poland, Maine
See Special Needs Schools section.

ELGIN ACADEMY
350 Park Street
Elgin, Illinois 60120
Head of School: Dr. John W. Cooper

General Information Coeducational day college-preparatory, arts, and technology school. Grades PS–12. Founded: 1839. Setting: suburban. Nearest major city is Chicago. 20-acre campus. 8 buildings on campus. Approved or accredited by Independent Schools Association of the Central States. Member of National Association of Independent Schools and Secondary School Admission Test Board. Endowment: $10 million. Total enrollment: 424. Upper school average class size: 12. Upper school faculty-student ratio: 1:5. There are 183 required school days per year for Upper School students. Upper School students typically attend 5 days per week. The average school day consists of 6 hours and 30 minutes.

Upper School Student Profile Grade 9: 43 students (21 boys, 22 girls); Grade 10: 32 students (17 boys, 15 girls); Grade 11: 37 students (17 boys, 20 girls); Grade 12: 25 students (15 boys, 10 girls).

Subjects Offered Algebra, American history, American literature, anatomy and physiology, art, art history, biology, calculus, ceramics, chemistry, computer programming, computer science, creative writing, drama, English, English literature, environmental science, European history, expository writing, fine arts, finite math, French, geometry, government/civics, grammar, history, Latin, Latin-AP, mathematics, music, painting, photography, physical education, psychology, psychology-AP, science, social studies, Spanish, statistics, theater, trigonometry, world history, world literature, writing.

Graduation Requirements 20th century history, arts and fine arts (art, music, dance, drama), English, foreign language, mathematics, science, social studies (includes history).

Special Academic Programs 16 Advanced Placement exams for which test preparation is offered; honors section; independent study.

College Admission Counseling 29 students graduated in 2010; all went to college, including Lawrence University; New York University; Northwestern University; University of Notre Dame; Washington University in St. Louis; Wellesley College. Median SAT critical reading: 650, median SAT math: 600, median SAT writing: 650, median combined SAT: 1910, median composite ACT: 27.

Student Life Upper grades have specified standards of dress, student council, honor system. Discipline rests primarily with faculty.

Summer Programs Enrichment, sports, art/fine arts programs offered; session focuses on College prep work, academics, athletics, art, music; held on campus; accepts boys and girls; open to students from other schools. 2011 schedule: June 1 to August 30.

Tuition and Aid Day student tuition: $17,725. Tuition installment plan (FACTS Tuition Payment Plan, 10-month payment plan). Tuition reduction for siblings, merit scholarship grants, need-based scholarship grants available. In 2010–11, 40% of upper-school students received aid; total upper-school merit-scholarship money awarded: $15,000.

Admissions Traditional secondary-level entrance grade is 9. ERB—verbal abilities, reading comprehension, quantitative abilities (level F, form 1) required. Deadline for receipt of application materials: none. Application fee required: $50. Interview required.

Athletics Interscholastic: field hockey (girls), golf (b); coed interscholastic: basketball, cross-country running, outdoors, soccer, tennis, track and field, volleyball, wilderness, wilderness survival; coed intramural: backpacking, canoeing/kayaking. 2 PE instructors.

Computers Computers are regularly used in art, English, foreign language, mathematics, science, social studies classes. Computer network features include on-campus library services, online commercial services, Internet access, wireless campus network. Campus intranet is available to students. Students grades are available online. The school has a published electronic and media policy.

Contact Mr. Shannon D. Howell, Director of Admission and Marketing. 847-695-0303. Fax: 847-695-5017. E-mail: showell@elginacademy.org. Web site: www.elginacademy.org.

ELIZABETH SETON HIGH SCHOOL
5715 Emerson Street
Bladensburg, Maryland 20710-1844
Head of School: Sr. Ellen Marie Hagar

General Information Girls' day college-preparatory, arts, religious studies, bilingual studies, technology, visual arts, and music school, affiliated with Roman Catholic Church. Grades 9–12. Founded: 1959. Setting: suburban. Nearest major city is Washington, DC. 24-acre campus. 2 buildings on campus. Approved or accredited by Middle States Association of Colleges and Schools, National Catholic Education Association, and Maryland Department of Education. Total enrollment: 654. Upper school average class size: 18. Upper school faculty-student ratio: 1:13. There are 180

Elizabeth Seton High School

required school days per year for Upper School students. Upper School students typically attend 5 days per week. The average school day consists of 6 hours and 30 minutes.

Upper School Student Profile Grade 9: 156 students (156 girls); Grade 10: 152 students (152 girls); Grade 11: 186 students (186 girls); Grade 12: 160 students (160 girls). 65% of students are Roman Catholic.

Faculty School total: 59. In upper school: 4 men, 55 women; 30 have advanced degrees.

Subjects Offered Accounting, advanced chemistry, advanced math, algebra, American history, American history-AP, American literature, analytic geometry, anatomy, art, art-AP, bioethics, biology, business, calculus, calculus-AP, ceramics, chemistry, choir, chorus, Christian and Hebrew scripture, Christianity, church history, community service, computer multimedia, computer programming, computer science, desktop publishing, earth science, economics, English, English literature, English literature and composition-AP, English literature-AP, environmental science, ethics, European history, film and literature, fine arts, French, geography, geometry, government-AP, government/civics, grammar, health, history, home economics, honors algebra, honors English, honors geometry, journalism, keyboarding, Latin, mathematics, music, newspaper, philosophy, photography, physical education, physics, physiology, pre-calculus, probability and statistics, psychology, psychology-AP, religion, science, social studies, sociology, Spanish, speech, symphonic band, theology, trigonometry, U.S. government and politics-AP, Web site design, world history, world literature, writing.

Graduation Requirements 1½ elective credits, arts and fine arts (art, music, dance, drama), English, foreign language, health education, mathematics, physical education (includes health), religion (includes Bible studies and theology), science, social studies (includes history), technology. Community service is required.

Special Academic Programs Advanced Placement exam preparation; honors section; independent study; academic accommodation for the gifted, the musically talented, and the artistically talented; programs in general development for dyslexic students; special instructional classes for students with mild learning disabilities, organizational deficiencies, Attention Deficit Disorder, and dyslexia.

College Admission Counseling 139 students graduated in 2010; all went to college, including Frostburg State University; Salisbury University; Temple University; Towson University; University of Maryland, Baltimore County; University of Maryland, College Park. Mean SAT critical reading: 520, mean SAT math: 500, mean SAT writing: 550.

Student Life Upper grades have uniform requirement, student council, honor system. Discipline rests equally with students and faculty. Attendance at religious services is required.

Summer Programs Remediation, enrichment, sports, art/fine arts programs offered; held on campus; accepts girls; open to students from other schools. 2011 schedule: June to August.

Tuition and Aid Day student tuition: $10,300. Tuition installment plan (FACTS Tuition Payment Plan, monthly payment plans, individually arranged payment plans, quarterly payment plan). Tuition reduction for siblings, merit scholarship grants, need-based scholarship grants, paying campus jobs available. In 2010–11, 50% of upper-school students received aid; total upper-school merit-scholarship money awarded: $75,000. Total amount of financial aid awarded in 2010–11: $400,000.

Admissions Traditional secondary-level entrance grade is 9. For fall 2010, 350 students applied for upper-level admission, 250 were accepted, 156 enrolled. High School Placement Test required. Deadline for receipt of application materials: December 7. Application fee required: $50. On-campus interview required.

Athletics Interscholastic: basketball, cheering, crew, cross-country running, dance squad, dance team, equestrian sports, field hockey, golf, horseback riding, indoor track, lacrosse, modern dance, pom squad, rowing, running, soccer, softball, swimming and diving, tennis, volleyball, winter (indoor) track; intramural: aerobics, aerobics/dance, aerobics/Nautilus, combined training, cooperative games, cross-country running, dance, fitness, fitness walking, flag football, martial arts, ocean paddling, outdoor recreation, physical fitness, strength & conditioning, walking, weight training. 4 PE instructors, 32 coaches, 1 athletic trainer.

Computers Computers are regularly used in computer applications, desktop publishing, English, graphic design, independent study, keyboarding, lab/keyboard, literary magazine, multimedia, photojournalism, programming, research skills, science, typing, Web site design, word processing, yearbook classes. Computer network features include on-campus library services, online commercial services, Internet access, wireless campus network, Internet filtering or blocking technology. Student e-mail accounts are available to students. Students grades are available online. The school has a published electronic and media policy.

Contact Ms. Melissa Davey, Director of Admissions. 301-864-4532 Ext. 7115. Fax: 301-864-8946. E-mail: mdavey@setonhs.org. Web site: www.setonhs.org.

ELK MOUNTAIN ACADEMY
PO Box 330
Heron, Montana 59844
Head of School: Mike Linderman

General Information Boys' boarding college-preparatory, general academic, arts, and technology school; primarily serves students with learning disabilities, individuals with Attention Deficit Disorder, individuals with emotional and behavioral problems, dyslexic students, and drug/alcohol addiction. Grades 9–12. Founded: 1994. Setting:

rural. Nearest major city is Sandpoint, ID. Students are housed in single-sex dormitories. 90-acre campus. 1 building on campus. Approved or accredited by Northwest Accreditation Commission and Northwest Association of Schools and Colleges. Total enrollment: 25. Upper school average class size: 10. Upper school faculty-student ratio: 1:8. There are 240 required school days per year for Upper School students. Upper School students typically attend 5 days per week. The average school day consists of 6 hours.

Upper School Student Profile Grade 9: 3 students (3 boys); Grade 10: 6 students (6 boys); Grade 11: 8 students (8 boys); Grade 12: 8 students (8 boys). 100% of students are boarding students. 6 states are represented in upper school student body. International students from Panama and United Kingdom.

Faculty School total: 3. In upper school: 2 men, 1 woman.

Subjects Offered Algebra, American government, American history, American literature, anatomy and physiology, art, biology, British literature, chemistry, earth science, economics, English, English literature, geography, geometry, government, grammar, health, history, independent living, literature, pre-algebra, pre-calculus, psychology, science, speech, world history.

Special Academic Programs Accelerated programs; independent study; study at local college for college credit; remedial reading and/or remedial writing; remedial math; programs in English, mathematics for dyslexic students.

College Admission Counseling 8 students graduated in 2009; 3 went to college. Other: 3 went to work, 2 entered military service.

Student Life Upper grades have student council, honor system. Discipline rests equally with students and faculty.

Tuition and Aid Guaranteed tuition plan. Tuition installment plan (monthly payment plans). Tuition reduction for siblings, need-based scholarship grants, paying campus jobs available. In 2009–10, 10% of upper-school students received aid. Total amount of financial aid awarded in 2009–10: $100,000.

Admissions Traditional secondary-level entrance grade is 11. Deadline for receipt of application materials: none. No application fee required. Interview required.

Athletics Intramural: alpine skiing, backpacking, basketball, billiards, blading, bowling, canoeing/kayaking, climbing, cross-country running, fishing, fitness, fitness walking, fly fishing, freestyle skiing, Frisbee, hiking/backpacking, kayaking, lacrosse, outdoor activities, paint ball, physical training, racquetball, rafting, roller blading, snowboarding, snowshoeing, soccer, strength & conditioning, table tennis, ultimate Frisbee, weight lifting, wilderness, winter soccer, yoga. 1 PE instructor.

Computers Computers are regularly used in all classes. Computer network features include on-campus library services, Internet access, Internet filtering or blocking technology. Campus intranet and student e-mail accounts are available to students. The school has a published electronic and media policy.

Contact Loretta Olding, Director of Admissions. 406-847-4400. Fax: 406-847-0034. E-mail: lolding@elkmountainacademy.org. Web site: www.elkmountainacademy.org.

ELMWOOD SCHOOL
261 Buena Vista Road
Ottawa, Ontario K1M 0V9, Canada
Head of School: Ms. Cheryl Boughton

General Information Girls' day college-preparatory, arts, business, bilingual studies, and technology school. Grades JK–12. Founded: 1915. Setting: suburban. 2-acre campus. 1 building on campus. Approved or accredited by Conference of Independent Schools of Ontario, International Baccalaureate Organization, Ontario Ministry of Education, Standards in Excellence And Learning (SEAL), and Ontario Department of Education. Language of instruction: English. Total enrollment: 340. Upper school average class size: 10. Upper school faculty-student ratio: 1:8. There are 178 required school days per year for Upper School students. The average school day consists of 6 hours and 45 minutes.

Faculty School total: 50. In upper school: 5 men, 25 women; 14 have advanced degrees.

Subjects Offered Algebra, art, art history, biology, business, calculus, Canadian geography, Canadian history, chemistry, communications, computer math, computer science, creative writing, drama, economics, English, English literature, environmental science, ESL, European history, fine arts, French, geography, geometry, German, grammar, health, history, Latin, mathematics, music, philosophy, physical education, physics, science, social studies, Spanish, theater, theory of knowledge, trigonometry, typing, world history, world literature.

Graduation Requirements Arts and fine arts (art, music, dance, drama), business skills (includes word processing), Canadian geography, Canadian history, English, foreign language, mathematics, physical education (includes health), science, social studies (includes history).

Special Academic Programs International Baccalaureate program; accelerated programs; independent study; term-away projects; study abroad; academic accommodation for the gifted; ESL.

College Admission Counseling 42 students graduated in 2009; all went to college, including McGill University; Queen's University at Kingston; The University of Western Ontario; University of Ottawa; University of Toronto; University of Waterloo.

Student Life Upper grades have uniform requirement, student council, honor system. Discipline rests primarily with faculty.

Tuition and Aid Day student tuition: CAN$14,300–CAN$19,900. Tuition installment plan (individually arranged payment plans, 4-payment plan and 11 month payment plan). Bursaries, merit scholarship grants, need-based scholarship grants available. In 2009–10, 10% of upper-school students received aid; total upper-school merit-scholarship money awarded: CAN$80,000. Total amount of financial aid awarded in 2009–10: CAN$250,000.

Admissions CAT and school's own exam required. Deadline for receipt of application materials: none. Application fee required: CAN$100. Interview required.

Athletics Interscholastic: aerobics, aerobics/dance, alpine skiing, aquatics, badminton, basketball, cheering, crew, cross-country running, field hockey, golf, handball, rugby, skiing (downhill), swimming and diving, team handball, tennis, touch football, ultimate Frisbee, volleyball, water polo; intramural: aerobics/Nautilus, badminton, ball hockey, ballet, basketball, dance, fitness walking, hiking/backpacking, ice hockey, outdoor adventure, ropes courses, snowboarding, wilderness, yoga. 4 PE instructors.

Computers Computers are regularly used in all classes. Computer network features include on-campus library services, Internet access, Internet filtering or blocking technology. Campus intranet, student e-mail accounts, and computer access in designated common areas are available to students.

Contact Ms. Donna Naufal Moffatt, Director of Admissions. 613-744-7783. Fax: 613-741-8210. E-mail: admissions@elmwood.ca. Web site: www.elmwood.ca.

ELYRIA CATHOLIC HIGH SCHOOL
725 Gulf Road
Elyria, Ohio 44035-3697
Head of School: Mrs. Amy Butler

General Information Coeducational day college-preparatory, arts, business, and religious studies school, affiliated with Roman Catholic Church. Grades 9–12. Founded: 1948. Setting: suburban. Nearest major city is Cleveland. 16-acre campus. 1 building on campus. Approved or accredited by North Central Association of Colleges and Schools, Ohio Catholic Schools Accreditation Association (OCSAA), and Ohio Department of Education. Endowment: $3 million. Total enrollment: 518. Upper school average class size: 24. Upper school faculty-student ratio: 1:14.

Upper School Student Profile Grade 9: 112 students (60 boys, 52 girls); Grade 10: 114 students (69 boys, 45 girls); Grade 11: 142 students (64 boys, 78 girls); Grade 12: 150 students (82 boys, 68 girls). 90% of students are Roman Catholic.

Faculty School total: 40. In upper school: 18 men, 15 women; 19 have advanced degrees.

Subjects Offered Accounting, advanced math, algebra, American government, American history, American history-AP, analysis of data, anatomy and physiology, art, band, biology, business, calculus, calculus-AP, campus ministry, Catholic belief and practice, chamber groups, chemistry, child development, choir, Christian and Hebrew scripture, Christian doctrine, Christian ethics, church history, computer applications, concert band, concert choir, current events, data analysis, drama, drama performance, earth science, English, fine arts, food and nutrition, French, French language-AP, geometry, German, health, history, honors English, industrial arts, introduction to theater, journalism, leadership, life issues, marching band, music appreciation, parent/child development, peer ministry, physical fitness, physics, prayer/spirituality, pre-calculus, psychology, reading/study skills, social justice, Spanish, Spanish language-AP, theater, world religions, yearbook.

Graduation Requirements Arts and fine arts (art, music, dance, drama), computers, English, mathematics, physical education (includes health), religion (includes Bible studies and theology), science, social studies (includes history), school and community service hours, Ohio Proficiency Test.

Special Academic Programs Advanced Placement exam preparation; honors section; study at local college for college credit; remedial reading and/or remedial writing; remedial math; special instructional classes for students with learning disabilities and Attention Deficit Disorder.

College Admission Counseling 121 students graduated in 2009; 119 went to college, including Bowling Green State University; Kent State University; Ohio University; The Ohio State University; The University of Toledo; University of Dayton. Other: 2 entered military service. Mean SAT critical reading: 570, mean SAT math: 557.

Student Life Upper grades have specified standards of dress, student council, honor system. Discipline rests primarily with faculty. Attendance at religious services is required.

Tuition and Aid Day student tuition: $6300. Tuition installment plan (monthly payment plans). Tuition reduction for siblings, merit scholarship grants, need-based scholarship grants, paying campus jobs available. In 2009–10, 24% of upper-school students received aid; total upper-school merit-scholarship money awarded: $20,000. Total amount of financial aid awarded in 2009–10: $200,000.

Admissions Traditional secondary-level entrance grade is 9. High School Placement Test (closed version) from Scholastic Testing Service required. Deadline for receipt of application materials: January 23. No application fee required. Interview recommended.

Athletics Interscholastic: baseball (boys), basketball (b,g), cross-country running (b,g), football (b), golf (b), ice hockey (b), rugby (b), soccer (b,g), softball (g), tennis (b,g), volleyball (g), wrestling (b); coed interscholastic: bowling, cheering, swimming and diving, track and field. 2 PE instructors, 47 coaches, 1 athletic trainer.

Computers Computers are regularly used in business studies, journalism, newspaper, typing, word processing, yearbook classes. Computer network features include on-campus library services, Internet access, Internet filtering or blocking technology. Students grades are available online. The school has a published electronic and media policy.

Contact Mr. Michael Wisnor, Director of Admissions/Dean of Students. 440-365-1821 Ext. 16. Fax: 440 365-7536. E-mail: wisnor@elyriacatholic.com. Web site: www.elyriacatholic.com.

EMERSON HONORS HIGH SCHOOLS
4100 East Walnut Street
Orange, California 92869
Head of School: Dr. Glory Ludwick

General Information Coeducational boarding and day college-preparatory, general academic, and arts school. Boarding grades 7–12, day grades K–12. Founded: 1958. Setting: suburban. Nearest major city is Los Angeles. Students are housed in homes of host families. 5-acre campus. 8 buildings on campus. Approved or accredited by Western Association of Schools and Colleges and California Department of Education. Total enrollment: 180. Upper school average class size: 18. Upper school faculty-student ratio: 1:18. There are 180 required school days per year for Upper School students. Upper School students typically attend 5 days per week. The average school day consists of 6 hours.

Upper School Student Profile Grade 7: 5 students (2 boys, 3 girls); Grade 8: 14 students (10 boys, 4 girls); Grade 9: 21 students (11 boys, 10 girls); Grade 10: 13 students (7 boys, 6 girls); Grade 11: 29 students (16 boys, 13 girls); Grade 12: 24 students (11 boys, 13 girls). 20% of students are boarding students. 80% are state residents. 3 states are represented in upper school student body. 20% are international students. International students from China, Japan, Republic of Korea, Taiwan, and Viet Nam; 5 other countries represented in student body.

Faculty School total: 25. In upper school: 7 men, 6 women; 11 have advanced degrees.

Subjects Offered Acting, advanced chemistry, advanced math, advanced TOEFL/grammar, algebra, American government, American history-AP, analysis and differential calculus, anatomy, ancient world history, applied arts, applied music, Arabic, art, art and culture, art appreciation, art education, art history, Basic programming, biology, biology-AP, calculus, calculus-AP, cell biology, ceramics, chemistry, chemistry-AP, Chinese, civil war history, classical civilization, classical Greek literature, classical music, classics, clayworking, computer processing, computer programming, computer skills, concert band, contemporary art, contemporary history, creative drama, creative writing, cultural geography, current events, current history, drama workshop, drawing, earth science, economics and history, Egyptian history, English, English literature, ESL, fine arts, gardening, general math, geography, geometry, grammar, jazz band, keyboarding, library skills, Mandarin, math analysis, physics, physics-AP, pre-algebra, pre-calculus, reading, SAT preparation, science, Shakespeare, Spanish, TOEFL preparation, U.S. government and politics-AP, U.S. history, world history.

Graduation Requirements Art, English, foreign language, mathematics, music, physical education (includes health), science, social studies (includes history). Community service is required.

Special Academic Programs Advanced Placement exam preparation; honors section; accelerated programs; independent study; study at local college for college credit; academic accommodation for the gifted, the musically talented, and the artistically talented; ESL (50 students enrolled).

College Admission Counseling 23 students graduated in 2009; 20 went to college, including California State University, Fullerton; Chapman University; Occidental College; Purdue University; The Johns Hopkins University; University of California, Santa Cruz. Other: 1 went to work, 1 entered military service, 1 had other specific plans. Mean SAT critical reading: 568, mean SAT math: 614, mean SAT writing: 590.

Student Life Upper grades have specified standards of dress, honor system. Discipline rests equally with students and faculty.

Tuition and Aid Day student tuition: $12,150; 7-day tuition and room/board: $20,000–$30,000. Tuition installment plan (monthly payment plans, individually arranged payment plans). Tuition reduction for siblings, need-based scholarship grants available. In 2009–10, 10% of upper-school students received aid. Total amount of financial aid awarded in 2009–10: $50,000.

Admissions Traditional secondary-level entrance grade is 10. For fall 2009, 100 students applied for upper-level admission, 80 were accepted, 75 enrolled. Achievement tests or any standardized test required. Deadline for receipt of application materials: none. Application fee required: $250. Interview required.

Athletics Coed Interscholastic: baseball, basketball, cross-country running, fitness, flag football, handball, kickball, physical fitness, soccer, softball, volleyball. 1 PE instructor, 1 coach.

Computers Computers are regularly used in desktop publishing, graphic design, keyboarding, Web site design, word processing, yearbook classes. Computer resources include Internet access, Internet filtering or blocking technology.

Contact Mrs. Cathie Peterson, Administration. 714-633-4774. E-mail: ryjeni@yahoo.com. Web site: www.eldorado-emerson.org.

THE EMERY WEINER SCHOOL

9825 Stella Link
Houston, Texas 77025
Head of School: Dr. David A. Portnoy

General Information Coeducational day college-preparatory, arts, religious studies, and bilingual studies school, affiliated with Jewish faith. Grades 6–12. Founded: 1978. Setting: urban. 12-acre campus. 2 buildings on campus. Approved or accredited by Independent Schools Association of the Southwest, Southern Association of Colleges and Schools, and Texas Department of Education. Total enrollment: 480. Upper School students typically attend 5 days per week. The average school day consists of 8 hours.

Faculty In upper school: 21 men, 19 women; 21 have advanced degrees.

Subjects Offered Acting, advanced chemistry, advanced math, algebra, art, biology, biology-AP, calculus, calculus-AP, ceramics, chemistry, chemistry-AP, civil war history, clayworking, composition, composition-AP, computer graphics, drama, drama performance, drawing, English, English-AP, foreign language, geometry, Hebrew, Hebrew scripture, history, history of religion, history-AP, honors English, honors U.S. history, Judaic studies, lab science, mathematics, mathematics-AP, newspaper, painting, physics, play production, play/screen writing, religion and culture, religious education, religious studies, Spanish, Spanish-AP, study skills, theater arts, theater design and production, U.S. history, U.S. history-AP, yearbook.

Graduation Requirements Arts, English, foreign language, history, Judaic studies, mathematics, physical education (includes health), science, one year Hebrew requirement for Upper School. Community service is required.

Special Academic Programs Advanced Placement exam preparation; honors section; independent study; academic accommodation for the gifted.

College Admission Counseling Colleges students went to include American University; Emory University; Indiana University Bloomington; The University of Texas at Austin; Trinity University; University of Michigan.

Student Life Upper grades have uniform requirement, student council, honor system. Discipline rests primarily with faculty. Attendance at religious services is required.

Tuition and Aid Day student tuition: $17,760. Tuition installment plan (monthly payment plans). Need-based scholarship grants available.

Admissions Traditional secondary-level entrance grade is 9. ISEE required. Deadline for receipt of application materials: January 22. Application fee required: $100. On-campus interview required.

Athletics Interscholastic: baseball (boys), basketball (b,g), football (b), golf (b), soccer (b,g), softball (g), tennis (b,g), track and field (b,g), volleyball (g); intramural: aerobics/dance (g), dance (g), yoga (g); coed intramural: outdoor activities.

Computers Computers are regularly used in graphic design, Web site design classes. Computer network features include on-campus library services, online commercial services, Internet access, wireless campus network, Adobe Creative Suite, Microsoft Publisher, Word, Excel, PowerPoint. Student e-mail accounts and computer access in designated common areas are available to students. Students grades are available online. The school has a published electronic and media policy.

Contact Mrs. Rosiland Ivie, Registrar. 832-204-5900 Ext. 106. Fax: 832-204-5910. Web site: www.emeryweiner.org.

EMMA WILLARD SCHOOL

285 Pawling Avenue
Troy, New York 12180
Head of School: Ms. Trudy E. Hall

General Information Girls' boarding and day college-preparatory and arts school. Grades 9–PG. Founded: 1814. Setting: suburban. Nearest major city is Albany. Students are housed in single-sex dormitories. 137-acre campus. 23 buildings on campus. Approved or accredited by New York State Association of Independent Schools, The Association of Boarding Schools, and New York Department of Education. Member of National Association of Independent Schools and Secondary School Admission Test Board. Endowment: $80 million. Total enrollment: 319. Upper school average class size: 12. Upper school faculty-student ratio: 1:5. The average school day consists of 7 hours and 20 minutes.

Upper School Student Profile Grade 9: 68 students (68 girls); Grade 10: 79 students (79 girls); Grade 11: 88 students (88 girls); Grade 12: 81 students (81 girls); Postgraduate: 3 students (3 girls). 64% of students are boarding students. 48% are state residents. 20 states are represented in upper school student body. 27% are international students. International students from China, Hong Kong, Japan, Mexico, Republic of Korea, and Taiwan; 24 other countries represented in student body.

Faculty School total: 69. In upper school: 16 men, 50 women; 51 have advanced degrees; 41 reside on campus.

Subjects Offered Advanced Placement courses, advanced studio art-AP, algebra, American history, American literature, ancient world history, art, art history, art history-AP, art-AP, ballet, bioethics, biology, biology-AP, calculus, calculus-AP, ceramics, chemistry, chemistry-AP, chorus, comparative government and politics-AP, computer programming, computer science, computer science-AP, conceptual physics, creative writing, dance, digital imaging, drama, drawing and design, economics, English, English literature, English literature and composition-AP, ESL, European history, expository writing, fiber arts, fine arts, forensics, French, French language-AP, geometry, government and politics-AP, government-AP, government/civics, health and wellness, history, internship, Latin-AP, mathematics, medieval/Renaissance history, music, neuroscience, orchestra, photography, physical education, physics, physics-AP, poetry, practicum, pre-calculus, SAT preparation, science, social sciences, Spanish, Spanish language-AP, Spanish-AP, statistics, statistics-AP, studio art-AP, theater, trigonometry, U.S. history-AP, weaving, world history, world literature.

Graduation Requirements Arts and fine arts (art, music, dance, drama), computer science, English, foreign language, mathematics, physical education (includes health), science, social studies (includes history). Community service is required.

Special Academic Programs 14 Advanced Placement exams for which test preparation is offered; independent study; term-away projects; study abroad; academic accommodation for the gifted, the musically talented, and the artistically talented; ESL (17 students enrolled).

College Admission Counseling 74 students graduated in 2010; all went to college, including Boston University; Carnegie Mellon University; Cornell University; Mount Holyoke College; Smith College; University of Rochester. Median SAT critical reading: 650, median SAT math: 650, median SAT writing: 670, median combined SAT: 1906, median composite ACT: 28. 74% scored over 600 on SAT critical reading, 66% scored over 600 on SAT math, 76% scored over 600 on SAT writing, 59% scored over 1800 on combined SAT, 61% scored over 26 on composite ACT.

Student Life Upper grades have specified standards of dress, student council, honor system. Discipline rests equally with students and faculty.

Tuition and Aid Day student tuition: $26,500; 7-day tuition and room/board: $41,550. Tuition installment plan (Key Tuition Payment Plan, monthly payment plans). Merit scholarship grants, need-based scholarship grants, Davis Scholars Program, Day Student /Capital District Scholarships available. In 2010–11, 53% of upper-school students received aid. Total amount of financial aid awarded in 2010–11: $3,855,950.

Admissions Traditional secondary-level entrance grade is 9. For fall 2010, 441 students applied for upper-level admission, 150 were accepted, 103 enrolled. ACT, PSAT or SAT, SAT, SSAT or TOEFL required. Deadline for receipt of application materials: February 1. Application fee required: $50. Interview required.

Athletics Interscholastic: aquatics, basketball, crew, cross-country running, diving, field hockey, lacrosse, rowing, soccer, softball, swimming and diving, tennis, track and field, volleyball; intramural: aerobics, aerobics/dance, ballet, basketball, dance, fencing, fitness, fitness walking, floor hockey, hiking/backpacking, jogging, martial arts, modern dance, outdoor activities, physical fitness, physical training, riflery, running, skiing (downhill), snowboarding, soccer, softball, strength & conditioning, swimming and diving, tennis, ultimate Frisbee, volleyball, water polo, weight training. 3 PE instructors, 3 coaches, 1 athletic trainer.

Computers Computers are regularly used in all classes. Computer network features include on-campus library services, online commercial services, Internet access, wireless campus network, Internet filtering or blocking technology. Campus intranet, student e-mail accounts, and computer access in designated common areas are available to students. Students grades are available online. The school has a published electronic and media policy.

Contact Ms. Sharon Busone, Officer Manager. 518-883-1327. Fax: 518-883-1805. E-mail: sbusone@emmawillard.org. Web site: www.emmawillard.org.

See Display on page 242 and Close-Up on page 776.

THE EPISCOPAL ACADEMY

1785 Bishop White Drive
Newtown Square, Pennsylvania 19073
Head of School: Mr. L. Hamilton Clark Jr.

General Information Coeducational day college-preparatory, arts, religious studies, and technology school, affiliated with Episcopal Church. Grades PK–12. Founded: 1785. Setting: suburban. Nearest major city is Philadelphia. 123-acre campus. 12 buildings on campus. Approved or accredited by Middle States Association of Colleges and Schools, Pennsylvania Association of Independent Schools, and Pennsylvania Department of Education. Member of National Association of Independent Schools and Secondary School Admission Test Board. Endowment: $16.5 million. Total enrollment: 1,223. Upper school average class size: 13. Upper school faculty-student ratio: 1:7. There are 172 required school days per year for Upper School students. Upper School students typically attend 5 days per week. The average school day consists of 9 hours and 30 minutes.

Upper School Student Profile Grade 9: 130 students (75 boys, 55 girls); Grade 10: 127 students (70 boys, 57 girls); Grade 11: 127 students (66 boys, 61 girls); Grade 12: 125 students (65 boys, 60 girls).

Faculty School total: 179. In upper school: 41 men, 38 women; 75 have advanced degrees.

Subjects Offered Algebra, American history, American history-AP, American literature, art, art history, biology, calculus, ceramics, chemistry, classical language, college counseling, computer art, computer graphics, computer information systems, computer programming, computer programming-AP, creative writing, drama, drawing, earth science, ecology, economics, English, English-AP, environmental science, ethics, European history, fine arts, French, French language-AP, French literature-AP, French studies, French-AP, geometry, government and politics-AP, Greek, health and safety, history, Latin, Latin-AP, mathematics, mechanical drawing, modern world history, music, painting, photography, physical education, physics, physics-AP, pre-calculus, psychology, religion, science, senior project, social studies, Spanish, Spanish language-AP, Spanish literature, Spanish literature-AP, Spanish-AP, statistics-AP, studio art, studio art-AP, theater history, theater production, theology, U.S. government and politics-AP, U.S. history, U.S. history-AP, Vietnam history, visual and performing arts, vocal ensemble, vocal music, water polo, weight training, woodworking, world cultures, world history, writing.

Graduation Requirements Arts and fine arts (art, music, dance, drama), English, foreign language, mathematics, physical education (includes health), religion (includes Bible studies and theology), science, senior project, social studies (includes history), participation in Outward Bound for 6 days.

Special Academic Programs Advanced Placement exam preparation; honors section; independent study; study abroad.

College Admission Counseling 122 students graduated in 2010; all went to college, including Bucknell University; Cornell University; Duke University; Georgetown University; Harvard University; University of Pennsylvania. Mean SAT critical reading: 664, mean SAT math: 660.

Student Life Upper grades have specified standards of dress, student council, honor system. Discipline rests primarily with faculty. Attendance at religious services is required.

Summer Programs Remediation, enrichment, advancement, art/fine arts, computer instruction programs offered; session focuses on acceleration, athletics, camp fun; held on campus; accepts boys and girls; open to students from other schools. 400 students usually enrolled. 2011 schedule: June 19 to July 28. Application deadline: none.

Tuition and Aid Day student tuition: $27,300. Tuition installment plan (Key Tuition Payment Plan, monthly payment plans, 60% due July 1—remainder by February 1). Need-based scholarship grants available. In 2010–11, 20% of upper-school students received aid. Total amount of financial aid awarded in 2010–11: $3,100,100.

Admissions Traditional secondary-level entrance grade is 9. For fall 2010, 235 students applied for upper-level admission, 107 were accepted, 46 enrolled. ISEE or SSAT required. Deadline for receipt of application materials: January 1. Application fee required: $50. On-campus interview required.

Athletics Interscholastic: baseball (boys), basketball (b,g), crew (b,g), cross-country running (b,g), dance (g), diving (b,g), field hockey (g), football (b), golf (b,g), indoor track (b,g), lacrosse (b,g), soccer (b,g), softball (g), squash (b,g), swimming and diving (b,g), tennis (b,g), track and field (b,g), winter (indoor) track (b,g); intramural: aerobics (g), aerobics/dance (g), dance (g), floor hockey (b); coed interscholastic: ice hockey, water polo; coed intramural: basketball, fencing, fitness, fitness walking, football, Frisbee, squash, trap and skeet, weight lifting, weight training. 1 PE instructor, 27 coaches, 2 athletic trainers.

Computers Computers are regularly used in art, English, foreign language, history, science, technology classes. Computer network features include on-campus library services, Internet access, wireless campus network, Internet filtering or blocking technology. Student e-mail accounts and computer access in designated common areas are available to students. The school has a published electronic and media policy.

Contact Ellen M. Hay, Director of Admission. 484-424-1400 Ext. 1444. Fax: 484-424-1604. E-mail: hay@episcopalacademy.org. Web site: www.episcopalacademy.org.

EPISCOPAL COLLEGIATE SCHOOL

1701 Cantrell Road
Little Rock, Arkansas 72201
Head of School: Mr. Steve Hickman

General Information Coeducational day college-preparatory, arts, and technology school, affiliated with Episcopal Church. Grades PK–12. Founded: 2000. Setting: suburban. Nearest major city is Memphis, TN. 34-acre campus. 3 buildings on campus. Approved or accredited by National Association of Episcopal Schools and Southwest Association of Episcopal Schools. Endowment: $31 million. Total enrollment: 676. Upper school average class size: 15. Upper school faculty-student ratio: 1:10. There are 179 required school days per year for Upper School students. Upper School students typically attend 5 days per week. The average school day consists of 7 hours and 30 minutes.

Upper School Student Profile Grade 6: 53 students (25 boys, 28 girls); Grade 7: 69 students (31 boys, 38 girls); Grade 8: 69 students (35 boys, 34 girls); Grade 9: 66 students (35 boys, 31 girls); Grade 10: 54 students (21 boys, 33 girls); Grade 11: 49 students (21 boys, 28 girls); Grade 12: 43 students (21 boys, 22 girls). 20% of students are members of Episcopal Church.

Faculty School total: 33. In upper school: 15 men, 18 women; 25 have advanced degrees.

Graduation Requirements Senior chapel talk.

Special Academic Programs 16 Advanced Placement exams for which test preparation is offered; honors section; independent study.

College Admission Counseling 51 students graduated in 2010; all went to college, including Hendrix College; Rhodes College; Sewanee: The University of the South; The University of Texas at Austin; Tulane University; University of Arkansas. Mean SAT critical reading: 637, mean SAT math: 610, mean SAT writing: 633, mean combined SAT: 1879, mean composite ACT: 27. 66% scored over 600 on SAT critical reading, 47% scored over 600 on SAT math, 63% scored over 600 on SAT writing, 63% scored over 1800 on combined SAT, 43% scored over 26 on composite ACT.

Student Life Upper grades have uniform requirement, student council, honor system. Discipline rests primarily with faculty. Attendance at religious services is required.

Summer Programs Enrichment, sports, art/fine arts, computer instruction programs offered; session focuses on enrichment; held on campus; accepts boys and girls; open to students from other schools. 150 students usually enrolled. 2011 schedule: June 1 to July 31. Application deadline: May 30.

Tuition and Aid Day student tuition: $9750. Tuition installment plan (monthly payment plans, individually arranged payment plans). Need-based scholarship grants available. In 2010–11, 25% of upper-school students received aid. Total amount of financial aid awarded in 2010–11: $436,000.

Admissions Traditional secondary-level entrance grade is 9. Stanford 9 required. Deadline for receipt of application materials: none. Application fee required: $50. Interview required.

Athletics Interscholastic: baseball (boys), basketball (b,g), cross-country running (b,g), fishing (b,g), fitness (b,g), football (b), golf (b,g), physical fitness (b,g), physical training (b,g), soccer (b,g), tennis (b,g), track and field (b,g), volleyball (g), weight training (b,g), wrestling (b,g); coed interscholastic: cheering. 2 PE instructors, 8 coaches, 2 athletic trainers.

Computers Computers are regularly used in all academic classes. Computer network features include on-campus library services, online commercial services, Internet access, wireless campus network, Internet filtering or blocking technology. Campus intranet and student e-mail accounts are available to students. Students grades are available online. The school has a published electronic and media policy.

Contact Ms. Ashley Honeywell, Director of Admission. 501-372-1194 Ext. 2406. Fax: 501-372-2160. E-mail: ahoneywell@episcopalcollegiate.org. Web site: www.episcopalcollegiate.org.

EPISCOPAL HIGH SCHOOL

4650 Bissonnet
Bellaire, Texas 77401
Head of School: Mr. C. Edward Smith

General Information Coeducational day college-preparatory, arts, religious studies, and technology school, affiliated with Episcopal Church. Grades 9–12. Founded: 1984. Setting: urban. Nearest major city is Houston. 35-acre campus. 7 buildings on campus. Approved or accredited by Independent Schools Association of the Southwest, National Association of Episcopal Schools, Texas Education Agency, and Texas Department of Education. Member of National Association of Independent Schools and Secondary School Admission Test Board. Total enrollment: 664. Upper school average class size: 15. Upper school faculty-student ratio: 1:9. Upper School students typically attend 5 days per week. The average school day consists of 8 hours.

Upper School Student Profile Grade 9: 163 students (69 boys, 94 girls); Grade 10: 169 students (79 boys, 90 girls); Grade 11: 160 students (69 boys, 91 girls); Grade 12: 156 students (68 boys, 88 girls). 25.6% of students are members of Episcopal Church.

Faculty School total: 102. In upper school: 43 men, 56 women; 57 have advanced degrees.

Subjects Offered Acting, algebra, anatomy, ancient history, art appreciation, art history, band, Bible studies, biology, biology-AP, calculus-AP, ceramics, chemistry, choir, civil rights, dance, debate, design, drawing, English, English-AP, ethics, European history, French, French-AP, geography, geology, geometry, government, government-AP, graphic design, health, history of science, instrumental music, journalism, Latin, Latin American studies, music theory, newspaper, oceanography, orchestra, painting, photography, physical education, physics, physics-AP, physiology, pre-calculus, sculpture, Spanish, Spanish-AP, speech, stagecraft, statistics, theater, theology, U.S. history, U.S. history-AP, video film production, Vietnam War, world religions, World War II, writing, yearbook.

Graduation Requirements Arts and fine arts (art, music, dance, drama), English, foreign language, mathematics, physical education (includes health), religion (includes Bible studies and theology), religious studies, science, social studies (includes history).

Special Academic Programs 14 Advanced Placement exams for which test preparation is offered; honors section; independent study; study at local college for college credit.

College Admission Counseling 161 students graduated in 2010; all went to college, including Baylor University; Southern Methodist University; Texas Christian University; The University of Texas at Austin.

Student Life Upper grades have uniform requirement, student council, honor system. Discipline rests equally with students and faculty. Attendance at religious services is required.

Summer Programs Remediation, enrichment, advancement, art/fine arts programs offered; session focuses on remediation, advancement, enrichment; held on campus; accepts boys and girls; open to students from other schools. 250 students usually enrolled. 2011 schedule: June 6 to July 16. Application deadline: May 10.

Tuition and Aid Day student tuition: $21,385. Tuition installment plan (Insured Tuition Payment Plan, SMART Tuition Payment Plan, monthly payment plans). Need-based scholarship grants, middle-income loans available. In 2010–11, 19% of upper-school students received aid. Total amount of financial aid awarded in 2010–11: $1,700,000.

Admissions Traditional secondary-level entrance grade is 9. For fall 2010, 610 students applied for upper-level admission, 394 were accepted, 179 enrolled. ISEE and Otis-Lennon Ability or Stanford Achievement Test required. Deadline for receipt of application materials: January 4. Application fee required: $60. On-campus interview required.

Athletics Interscholastic: ballet (boys, girls), baseball (b), basketball (b,g), cheering (b,g), cross-country running (b,g), dance (b,g), field hockey (b,g), football (b), golf (b,g), lacrosse (b,g), physical fitness (b,g), running (b,g), soccer (b,g), softball (g),

strength & conditioning (b,g), swimming and diving (b,g), tennis (b,g), track and field (b,g), volleyball (b,g), weight training (b,g), wrestling (b). 7 PE instructors, 8 coaches, 1 athletic trainer.

Computers Computers are regularly used in art, English, foreign language, history, mathematics, music, religion, science classes. Computer network features include on-campus library services, online commercial services, Internet access, wireless campus network, CollegeView. Student e-mail accounts are available to students. Students grades are available online. The school has a published electronic and media policy.

Contact Audrey Koehler, Director of Admission. 713-512-3400. Fax: 713-512-3603. E-mail: kpiper@ehshouston.org. Web site: www.ehshouston.org/.

EPISCOPAL HIGH SCHOOL

1200 North Quaker Lane
Alexandria, Virginia 22302
Head of School: Mr. F. Robertson Hershey

General Information Coeducational boarding college-preparatory, arts, religious studies, and technology school, affiliated with Episcopal Church. Grades 9–12. Founded: 1839. Setting: urban. Nearest major city is Washington, DC. Students are housed in single-sex dormitories. 130-acre campus. 26 buildings on campus. Approved or accredited by Association of Independent Schools of Greater Washington, National Association of Episcopal Schools, Southern Association of Colleges and Schools, Virginia Association of Independent Schools, and Virginia Department of Education. Member of National Association of Independent Schools and Secondary School Admission Test Board. Endowment: $153 million. Total enrollment: 435. Upper school average class size: 12. Upper school faculty-student ratio: 1:6.

Upper School Student Profile Grade 9: 95 students (52 boys, 43 girls); Grade 10: 112 students (62 boys, 50 girls); Grade 11: 112 students (62 boys, 50 girls); Grade 12: 116 students (64 boys, 52 girls). 100% of students are boarding students. 35% are state residents. 30 states are represented in upper school student body. 7% are international students. International students from China, Republic of Korea, Saudi Arabia, Thailand, United Kingdom, and Zimbabwe; 10 other countries represented in student body. 40% of students are members of Episcopal Church.

Faculty School total: 68. In upper school: 42 men, 26 women; 61 have advanced degrees; 54 reside on campus.

Subjects Offered 3-dimensional art, 3-dimensional design, advanced chemistry, advanced math, Advanced Placement courses, advanced studio art-AP, algebra, American history, American literature, art, art history, art-AP, astronomy, biology, biology-AP, calculus, calculus-AP, ceramics, chemistry, chemistry-AP, Chinese, choir, composition-AP, computer programming, computer programming-AP, computer science, computer science-AP, creative writing, dance, drama, economics, economics-AP, English, English literature, English literature and composition-AP, English literature-AP, English-AP, English/composition-AP, environmental science, environmental science-AP, ethics, European history, European history-AP, fine arts, forensics, French, French language-AP, French literature-AP, geometry, German, German-AP, government-AP, government/civics, Greek, history, honors algebra, honors English, honors geometry, honors U.S. history, honors world history, international relations, Latin, Latin-AP, mathematics, microeconomics-AP, Middle Eastern history, modern European history-AP, music, music theory-AP, photography, physical education, physics, physics-AP, pre-calculus, psychology-AP, religion, science, senior internship, Shakespeare, social sciences, social studies, Spanish, Spanish literature-AP, statistics-AP, theater, theology, trigonometry, U.S. history-AP, world history, world history-AP, writing.

Graduation Requirements Arts and fine arts (art, music, dance, drama), computer studies, English, foreign language, health, mathematics, physical education (includes health), science, social studies (includes history), theology.

Special Academic Programs Advanced Placement exam preparation; honors section; independent study; term-away projects; study abroad; academic accommodation for the gifted, the musically talented, and the artistically talented.

College Admission Counseling 105 students graduated in 2010; all went to college, including The University of North Carolina at Chapel Hill; University of Virginia; Washington and Lee University. 64% scored over 600 on SAT critical reading, 68% scored over 600 on SAT math, 71% scored over 600 on SAT writing.

Student Life Upper grades have specified standards of dress, student council, honor system. Discipline rests primarily with faculty. Attendance at religious services is required.

Summer Programs Enrichment, advancement, sports, art/fine arts programs offered; session focuses on academic enrichment and athletic skills; held on campus; accepts boys and girls; open to students from other schools.

Tuition and Aid 7-day tuition and room/board: $43,575. Tuition installment plan (Insured Tuition Payment Plan, monthly payment plans). Merit scholarship grants, need-based scholarship grants, paying campus jobs available. In 2010–11, 32% of upper-school students received aid; total upper-school merit-scholarship money awarded: $145,000. Total amount of financial aid awarded in 2010–11: $4,300,000.

Admissions Traditional secondary-level entrance grade is 9. For fall 2010, 589 students applied for upper-level admission, 237 were accepted, 138 enrolled. ISEE, PSAT or SAT or SSAT required. Deadline for receipt of application materials: January 15. Application fee required: $50. Interview required.

Athletics Interscholastic: baseball (boys), basketball (b,g), crew (g), cross-country running (b,g), field hockey (g), football (b), golf (b), indoor track (b,g), indoor track

& field (b,g), lacrosse (b,g), modern dance (g), rowing (g), soccer (b,g), softball (g), squash (b,g), tennis (b,g), track and field (b,g), volleyball (g), winter (indoor) track (b,g), wrestling (b); intramural: soccer (b), strength & conditioning (b,g); coed interscholastic: aerobics, aerobics/dance, aerobics/Nautilus, backpacking, ballet, canoeing/kayaking, climbing, dance, fitness, hiking/backpacking, kayaking, outdoor activities, outdoor adventure, outdoor education, outdoor recreation, outdoors, physical fitness, physical training, rock climbing, strength & conditioning, weight lifting, weight training; coed intramural: ballet, fitness, modern dance, outdoor activities, physical fitness, physical training, power lifting, wall climbing, weight lifting, weight training. 4 coaches, 2 athletic trainers.

Computers Computers are regularly used in all academic classes. Computer network features include on-campus library services, online commercial services, Internet access, wireless campus network, Internet filtering or blocking technology. Campus intranet and student e-mail accounts are available to students. Students grades are available online. The school has a published electronic and media policy.

Contact Ms. Emily M. Atkinson, Director of Admission. 703-933-4062. Fax: 703-933-3016. E-mail: admissions@episcopalhighschool.org. Web site: www.episcopalhighschool.org.

EPISCOPAL HIGH SCHOOL OF JACKSONVILLE

4455 Atlantic Boulevard
Jacksonville, Florida 32207
Head of School: Dale D. Regan

General Information Coeducational day college-preparatory, arts, religious studies, and technology school, affiliated with Episcopal Church. Grades 6–12. Founded: 1966. Setting: urban. 88-acre campus. 25 buildings on campus. Approved or accredited by Florida Council of Independent Schools, National Association of Episcopal Schools, Southern Association of Colleges and Schools, and Southern Association of Independent Schools. Member of National Association of Independent Schools. Endowment: $15.4 million. Total enrollment: 857. Upper school average class size: 17. Upper school faculty-student ratio: 1:10. There are 175 required school days per year for Upper School students. Upper School students typically attend 5 days per week. The average school day consists of 6 hours and 50 minutes.

Upper School Student Profile Grade 9: 140 students (76 boys, 64 girls); Grade 10: 142 students (73 boys, 69 girls); Grade 11: 140 students (73 boys, 67 girls); Grade 12: 144 students (77 boys, 67 girls). 25% of students are members of Episcopal Church.

Faculty School total: 93. In upper school: 35 men, 58 women; 53 have advanced degrees.

Subjects Offered Advanced studio art-AP, algebra, American history, American history-AP, American literature, ancient history, art, art history, art history-AP, band, Basic programming, biology, biology-AP, calculus, calculus-AP, ceramics, chemistry, chemistry-AP, Chinese, computer programming, computer science, computer science-AP, dance, drama, earth science, economics, electronic publishing, English, English language and composition-AP, English literature and composition-AP, English/composition-AP, environmental science-AP, European history-AP, fine arts, French, French language-AP, geography, geometry, German, German-AP, government and politics-AP, government/civics, health, history, journalism, Latin, Latin-AP, marine biology, mathematics, music, music history, music theory, music theory-AP, photography, physical education, physics, physics-AP, public speaking, religion, religious studies, science, social studies, Spanish, Spanish language-AP, statistics, statistics-AP, studio art-AP, technical theater, theater, theology, trigonometry, U.S. government and politics-AP, U.S. history-AP, world history, writing, yearbook.

Graduation Requirements Arts and fine arts (art, music, dance, drama), computer science, English, foreign language, leadership, library skills, mathematics, physical education (includes health), religion (includes Bible studies and theology), science, social studies (includes history), 75 community-service hours. Community service is required.

Special Academic Programs Advanced Placement exam preparation; honors section; independent study; study abroad; academic accommodation for the gifted.

College Admission Counseling 156 students graduated in 2010; all went to college, including Florida State University; University of Florida; University of North Florida. Median SAT critical reading: 579, median SAT math: 584, median SAT writing: 567, median combined SAT: 1729, median composite ACT: 26.

Student Life Upper grades have uniform requirement, student council, honor system. Discipline rests equally with students and faculty. Attendance at religious services is required.

Summer Programs Remediation, enrichment, advancement, sports, art/fine arts, rigorous outdoor training, computer instruction programs offered; session focuses on academics, athletics, fine arts, specialty programs; held on campus; accepts boys and girls; open to students from other schools. 500 students usually enrolled. 2011 schedule: May 27 to August 5. Application deadline: May 26.

Tuition and Aid Day student tuition: $17,400. Tuition installment plan (Insured Tuition Payment Plan, monthly payment plans). Need-based scholarship grants available. In 2010–11, 23% of upper-school students received aid. Total amount of financial aid awarded in 2010–11: $2,000,000.

Admissions Traditional secondary-level entrance grade is 9. For fall 2010, 89 students applied for upper-level admission, 58 were accepted, 38 enrolled. ISEE required. Deadline for receipt of application materials: January 11. Application fee required: $50. On-campus interview required.

Athletics Interscholastic: baseball (boys), basketball (b,g), crew (b,g), cross-country running (b,g), football (b), golf (b,g), lacrosse (b,g), modern dance (b,g), soccer (b,g), softball (g), swimming and diving (b,g), tennis (b,g), track and field (b,g), volleyball (g), weight lifting (b), weight training (b), wrestling (b); intramural: dance (g); coed interscholastic: cheering, dance, dance squad, dance team, wrestling; coed intramural: fencing. 7 PE instructors, 100 coaches, 4 athletic trainers.

Computers Computers are regularly used in all classes. Computer network features include on-campus library services, online commercial services, Internet access, wireless campus network, Internet filtering or blocking technology, Senior Systems: My BackPack online grading and student accounts, online parent portals, RSS feeds. Campus intranet, student e-mail accounts, and computer access in designated common areas are available to students. Students grades are available online. The school has a published electronic and media policy.

Contact Peggy P. Fox, Director of Admissions. 904-396-7104. Fax: 904-396-0981. E-mail: foxp@episcopalhigh.org. Web site: www.episcopalhigh.org.

THE EPISCOPAL SCHOOL OF DALLAS

4100 Merrell Road
Dallas, Texas 75229
Head of School: Rev. Stephen B. Swann

General Information Coeducational day college-preparatory, arts, religious studies, and technology school, affiliated with Episcopal Church. Grades PK–12. Founded: 1974. Setting: suburban. 36-acre campus. 5 buildings on campus. Approved or accredited by Independent Schools Association of the Southwest, National Association of Episcopal Schools, National Independent Private Schools Association, Southwest Association of Episcopal Schools, Texas Education Agency, and Texas Department of Education. Member of National Association of Independent Schools and Secondary School Admission Test Board. Endowment: $20.3 million. Total enrollment: 1,152. Upper school average class size: 15. Upper school faculty-student ratio: 1:8. There are 175 required school days per year for Upper School students. Upper School students typically attend 5 days per week. The average school day consists of 7 hours and 10 minutes.

Upper School Student Profile Grade 9: 101 students (53 boys, 48 girls); Grade 10: 99 students (45 boys, 54 girls); Grade 11: 100 students (42 boys, 58 girls); Grade 12: 99 students (52 boys, 47 girls). 52% of students are members of Episcopal Church.

Faculty School total: 154. In upper school: 36 men, 69 women; 69 have advanced degrees.

Subjects Offered Advanced Placement courses, algebra, American history, anatomy, art, art history, biology, calculus, chemistry, chorus, community service, computer math, computer science, creative writing, drama, earth science, ecology, economics, English, environmental science, ethics, European history, fine arts, French, geometry, government/civics, health, instrumental music, international relations, journalism, Latin, mathematics, Middle Eastern history, music, photography, physical education, physics, political science, pre-calculus, religion, science, social studies, Spanish, speech, theater, trigonometry, world history, world literature, writing.

Graduation Requirements Arts and fine arts (art, music, dance, drama), computer science, economics, English, foreign language, government, mathematics, physical education (includes health), religion (includes Bible studies and theology), science, social studies (includes history), participation in wilderness program, participation in community service. Community service is required.

Special Academic Programs Advanced Placement exam preparation; honors section; independent study; term-away projects.

College Admission Counseling 101 students graduated in 2009; all went to college, including Boston University; Stanford University; Texas Christian University; The University of Texas at Austin; University of Southern California; Vanderbilt University. 65% scored over 600 on SAT critical reading, 70% scored over 600 on SAT math, 73% scored over 600 on SAT writing, 76% scored over 26 on composite ACT.

Student Life Upper grades have uniform requirement, student council, honor system. Discipline rests equally with students and faculty. Attendance at religious services is required.

Tuition and Aid Day student tuition: $22,750. Tuition installment plan (Insured Tuition Payment Plan, FACTS Tuition Payment Plan, monthly payment plans). Need-based scholarship grants available. In 2009–10, 14% of upper-school students received aid. Total amount of financial aid awarded in 2009–10: $2,100,000.

Admissions Traditional secondary-level entrance grade is 9. For fall 2009, 121 students applied for upper-level admission, 65 were accepted, 34 enrolled. ISEE, SLEP for foreign students, SSAT or writing sample required. Deadline for receipt of application materials: January 30. Application fee required: $175. On-campus interview required.

Athletics Interscholastic: baseball (boys), basketball (b,g), cheering (g), crew (b,g), cross-country running (b,g), dance team (g), field hockey (g), football (b), golf (b,g), lacrosse (b,g), outdoor education (b,g), outdoor skills (b,g), rowing (b,g), soccer (b,g), softball (g), strength & conditioning (b,g), tennis (b,g), track and field (b,g), volleyball (g); coed interscholastic: crew. 2 PE instructors, 32 coaches, 2 athletic trainers.

Computers Computers are regularly used in English, journalism, mathematics, science classes. Computer network features include on-campus library services, online commercial services, Internet access. The school has a published electronic and media policy.

The Episcopal School of Dallas

Contact Ruth Burke, Director of Admission and Financial Aid. 214-353-5827. Fax: 214-353-5872. E-mail: burker@esdallas.org. Web site: www.esdallas.org.

ESCOLA AMERICANA DE CAMPINAS

Rua Cajamar, 35
Chácara da Barra
Campinas-SP 13090-860, Brazil
Head of School: Stephen A. Herrera

General Information Coeducational day college-preparatory, arts, bilingual studies, and technology school. Grades PK–12. Founded: 1956. Setting: urban. Nearest major city is São Paulo, Brazil. 4-acre campus. 4 buildings on campus. Approved or accredited by Association of American Schools in South America and Southern Association of Colleges and Schools. Member of European Council of International Schools. Languages of instruction: English and Portuguese. Endowment: $350,000. Total enrollment: 507. Upper school average class size: 17. Upper school faculty-student ratio: 1:7.

Upper School Student Profile Grade 6: 34 students (16 boys, 18 girls); Grade 7: 37 students (21 boys, 16 girls); Grade 8: 34 students (20 boys, 14 girls); Grade 9: 27 students (8 boys, 19 girls); Grade 10: 24 students (16 boys, 8 girls); Grade 11: 26 students (10 boys, 16 girls); Grade 12: 17 students (8 boys, 9 girls).

Faculty School total: 58. In upper school: 8 men, 16 women; 20 have advanced degrees.

Subjects Offered Algebra, American history, American literature, art, biology, calculus, chemistry, computer science, creative writing, drama, economics, English, English literature, fine arts, geography, geometry, government/civics, grammar, history, journalism, mathematics, music, physical education, physics, Portuguese, psychology, science, social studies, speech, trigonometry, world history, world literature, writing.

Graduation Requirements Arts and fine arts (art, music, dance, drama), computer science, English, foreign language, mathematics, physical education (includes health), science, social studies (includes history). Community service is required.

Special Academic Programs Advanced Placement exam preparation; honors section; term-away projects; study at local college for college credit; study abroad; special instructional classes for students with mild learning differences; ESL (5 students enrolled).

College Admission Counseling 17 students graduated in 2009; 16 went to college, including Emerson College; Northwestern University; Southwestern University; The University of Tampa. Other: 1 entered a postgraduate year. Median SAT critical reading: 610, median SAT math: 640, median SAT writing: 540, median combined SAT: 1790.

Student Life Upper grades have student council, honor system. Discipline rests equally with students and faculty.

Tuition and Aid Day student tuition: 45,611 Brazilian reals. Tuition installment plan (monthly payment plans). Need-based scholarship grants available. In 2009–10, 10% of upper-school students received aid. Total amount of financial aid awarded in 2009–10: $51,000.

Admissions Traditional secondary-level entrance grade is 9. For fall 2009, 35 students applied for upper-level admission, 24 were accepted, 22 enrolled. Admissions testing, English Composition Test for ESL students, ERB CTP IV, Iowa Test, CTBS, or TAP, SAT and writing sample required. Deadline for receipt of application materials: September 3. No application fee required. On-campus interview required.

Athletics Interscholastic: basketball (boys, girls), canoeing/kayaking (g), cheering (g), indoor soccer (b,g), soccer (b,g), volleyball (g); intramural: ballet (g), basketball (b,g), canoeing/kayaking (g), cheering (g), climbing (b,g), indoor soccer (b,g), soccer (b,g); coed intramural: aerobics, baseball, basketball, climbing, cooperative games, fitness, flag football, Frisbee, gymnastics, handball, indoor soccer, jogging, judo, kickball, martial arts, physical fitness, self defense, soccer, softball, strength & conditioning, table tennis, track and field, ultimate Frisbee, volleyball. 6 PE instructors, 11 coaches.

Computers Computers are regularly used in art, English, history, independent study, mathematics, science, yearbook classes. Computer network features include on-campus library services, online commercial services, Internet access. Campus intranet is available to students.

Contact Davi Sanchez, High School Principal. 55-19-2102-1006. Fax: 55-19-2102-1016. E-mail: davi_sanchez@eac.com.br. Web site: www.eac.com.br.

THE ETHEL WALKER SCHOOL

230 Bushy Hill Road
Simsbury, Connecticut 06070
Head of School: Mrs. Elizabeth Cromwell Speers

General Information Girls' boarding and day college-preparatory and arts school. Boarding grades 9–12, day grades 6–12. Founded: 1911. Setting: suburban. Nearest major city is Hartford. Students are housed in single-sex dormitories. 300-acre campus. 9 buildings on campus. Approved or accredited by Connecticut Association of Independent Schools, New England Association of Schools and Colleges, The Association of Boarding Schools, and Connecticut Department of Education. Member of National Association of Independent Schools and Secondary School Admission Test

Board. Endowment: $13 million. Total enrollment: 253. Upper school average class size: 13. Upper school faculty-student ratio: 1:9.

Upper School Student Profile Grade 6: 11 students (11 girls); Grade 7: 9 students (9 girls); Grade 8: 19 students (19 girls); Grade 9: 41 students (41 girls); Grade 10: 64 students (64 girls); Grade 11: 46 students (46 girls); Grade 12: 63 students (63 girls). 55% of students are boarding students. 40% are state residents. 16 states are represented in upper school student body. 19% are international students. International students from China, Germany, Japan, Mexico, Republic of Korea, and Spain; 7 other countries represented in student body.

Faculty School total: 45. In upper school: 11 men, 34 women; 27 have advanced degrees; 27 reside on campus.

Subjects Offered Acting, African drumming, algebra, American history, American literature, art, art history, Asian history, astronomy, ballet, bell choir, biology, calculus, calculus-AP, ceramics, chemistry, chemistry-AP, choir, choreography, college counseling, community service, computer science, computer science-AP, concert choir, creative writing, dance, dance performance, drama, drawing and design, driver education, earth science, English, English literature, English literature and composition-AP, environmental science, environmental science-AP, equestrian sports, ethics, ethics and responsibility, European history, fine arts, French, French language-AP, geography, geometry, health, history, history-AP, honors algebra, independent study, instrumental music, Latin, Latin American history, Latin-AP, mathematics, modern European history, music, music theory, musical theater, newspaper, peer counseling, personal fitness, photography, physical education, physics, poetry, pre-calculus, psychology-AP, SAT/ACT preparation, science, science project, science research, sculpture, senior project, set design, social sciences, Spanish, Spanish language-AP, Spanish literature-AP, Spanish-AP, student publications, studio art-AP, tap dance, the Web, trigonometry, U.S. history-AP, visual and performing arts, voice, women's health, world history, world literature, writing, yearbook.

Graduation Requirements Arts and fine arts (art, music, dance, drama), English, ethics, foreign language, history, leadership, mathematics, physical education (includes health), science, women's health, Junior/Senior project, Community service hours. Community service is required.

Special Academic Programs Advanced Placement exam preparation; honors section; independent study; term-away projects; study at local college for college credit; study abroad; academic accommodation for the gifted, the musically talented, and the artistically talented.

College Admission Counseling 56 students graduated in 2010; all went to college, including American University; Bates College; Georgetown University; Mount Holyoke College; The Johns Hopkins University; Washington and Lee University. Mean SAT critical reading: 573, mean SAT math: 560, mean SAT writing: 583, mean composite ACT: 24.

Student Life Upper grades have specified standards of dress, student council, honor system. Discipline rests equally with students and faculty.

Tuition and Aid Day student tuition: $32,950; 7-day tuition and room/board: $45,350. Tuition installment plan (monthly payment plans, individually arranged payment plans, 1-, 2-, and 10-payment plans). Financial aid available to upper-school students. In 2010–11, 46% of upper-school students received aid. Total amount of financial aid awarded in 2010–11: $3,000,000.

Admissions Traditional secondary-level entrance grade is 9. SSAT or TOEFL required. Deadline for receipt of application materials: February 1. Application fee required: $60. Interview required.

Athletics Interscholastic: alpine skiing, basketball, dance, dressage, equestrian sports, field hockey, golf, horseback riding, independent competitive sports, lacrosse, modern dance, nordic skiing, skiing (downhill), soccer, softball, tennis, volleyball; intramural: ballet, climbing, combined training, cross-country running, dance, dance team, equestrian sports, fitness, hiking/backpacking, jogging, kayaking, mountain biking, mountaineering, Nautilus, outdoor activities, physical fitness, physical training, rock climbing, ropes courses, running, strength & conditioning, swimming and diving, wall climbing, weight lifting, weight training, yoga. 3 PE instructors, 15 coaches, 1 athletic trainer.

Computers Computers are regularly used in English, foreign language, graphic design, history, mathematics, photography, science classes. Computer network features include on-campus library services, online commercial services, Internet access, wireless campus network, Internet filtering or blocking technology, Apple Share, Local Talk/Ethernet. Student e-mail accounts are available to students. Students grades are available online. The school has a published electronic and media policy.

Contact Ms. Margy Foulk, Director of Admission. 860-408-4200. Fax: 860-408-4202. E-mail: margy_foulk@ethelwalker.org. Web site: www.ethelwalker.org.

ETON ACADEMY

Birmingham, Michigan
See Special Needs Schools section.

EVANGELICAL CHRISTIAN SCHOOL

7600 Macon Road
PO Box 1030
Cordova, Tennessee 38088-1030
Head of School: Mr. Bryan Miller

General Information Coeducational day college-preparatory, arts, business, religious studies, and technology school, affiliated with Christian faith. Grades JK–12. Founded: 1964. Setting: suburban. Nearest major city is Memphis. 40-acre campus. 12 buildings on campus. Approved or accredited by Association of Christian Schools International, Southern Association of Colleges and Schools, Southern Association of Independent Schools, Tennessee Association of Independent Schools, The College Board, and Tennessee Department of Education. Endowment: $400,000. Total enrollment: 1,231. Upper school average class size: 14. Upper school faculty-student ratio: 1:11. There are 176 required school days per year for Upper School students. Upper School students typically attend 5 days per week. The average school day consists of 6 hours and 50 minutes.

Upper School Student Profile Grade 9: 112 students (54 boys, 58 girls); Grade 10: 108 students (57 boys, 51 girls); Grade 11: 119 students (65 boys, 54 girls); Grade 12: 123 students (62 boys, 61 girls). 100% of students are Christian faith.

Faculty School total: 168. In upper school: 15 men, 16 women; 18 have advanced degrees.

Subjects Offered Acting, Advanced Placement courses, algebra, American government, American history, American history-AP, anatomy, ancient history, art, art-AP, band, Bible studies, biology, business law, calculus, calculus-AP, chemistry, chorus, college placement, computer applications, computer science, concert choir, drama, economics, economics and history, English, English-AP, etymology, European history-AP, fine arts, French, general science, geometry, geometry with art applications, health, health and wellness, journalism, Latin, mathematics, newspaper, personal finance, physical education, physical fitness, physical science, physics, religion, science, social studies, Spanish, speech, speech communications, theater, theater arts, U.S. government and politics-AP, world civilizations, world history, yearbook.

Graduation Requirements Arts and fine arts (art, music, dance, drama), English, foreign language, mathematics, physical education (includes health), religion (includes Bible studies and theology), science, social studies (includes history), extracurricular activities.

Special Academic Programs Advanced Placement exam preparation; honors section; academic accommodation for the gifted, the musically talented, and the artistically talented; remedial reading and/or remedial writing; remedial math.

College Admission Counseling 141 students graduated in 2009; 140 went to college, including Auburn University; Samford University; The University of Alabama; The University of Tennessee; University of Memphis; University of Mississippi. Other: 1 entered military service. Mean SAT critical reading: 627, mean SAT math: 616, mean composite ACT: 26. 17% scored over 600 on SAT critical reading, 12% scored over 600 on SAT math, 32% scored over 26 on composite ACT.

Student Life Upper grades have uniform requirement, student council, honor system. Discipline rests primarily with faculty. Attendance at religious services is required.

Tuition and Aid Day student tuition: $11,695. Tuition installment plan (Insured Tuition Payment Plan, monthly payment plans, 2-payment plan (60% on June 1, 40% on December 1)). Need-based scholarship grants available. In 2009–10, 10% of upper-school students received aid. Total amount of financial aid awarded in 2009–10: $205,000.

Admissions Traditional secondary-level entrance grade is 9. For fall 2009, 36 students applied for upper-level admission, 30 were accepted, 28 enrolled. ISEE required. Deadline for receipt of application materials: January 15. Application fee required: $50. Interview required.

Athletics Interscholastic: baseball (boys), basketball (b,g), cheering (g), cross-country running (b,g), football (b), golf (b,g), physical fitness (b,g), soccer (b,g), softball (g), strength & conditioning (b,g), swimming and diving (b,g), tennis (b,g), track and field (b,g), volleyball (g), weight training (b,g). 3 PE instructors, 1 athletic trainer.

Computers Computers are regularly used in all classes. Computer network features include on-campus library services, online commercial services, Internet access, Internet filtering or blocking technology. Students grades are available online. The school has a published electronic and media policy.

Contact Mrs. Erin Dickson, Director of Admissions. 901-754-7217 Ext. 1101. Fax: 901-754-8123. E-mail: edickson@ecseagles.com. Web site: www.ecseagles.net.

EVANSVILLE DAY SCHOOL

3400 North Green River Road
Evansville, Indiana 47715
Head of School: Mr. Kendell Berry

General Information Coeducational day college-preparatory school. Grades PK–12. Founded: 1946. Setting: suburban. Nearest major city is St. Louis, MO. 55-acre campus. 1 building on campus. Approved or accredited by Independent Schools Association of the Central States and Indiana Department of Education. Member of National Association of Independent Schools. Endowment: $335,000. Total enrollment: 319. Upper school average class size: 15. Upper school faculty-

student ratio: 1:10. There are 180 required school days per year for Upper School students. Upper School students typically attend 5 days per week. The average school day consists of 7 hours.

Upper School Student Profile Grade 9: 21 students (11 boys, 10 girls); Grade 10: 26 students (15 boys, 11 girls); Grade 11: 26 students (14 boys, 12 girls); Grade 12: 11 students (5 boys, 6 girls).

Faculty School total: 42. In upper school: 11 men, 5 women; 12 have advanced degrees.

Subjects Offered Advanced Placement courses, algebra, American history, American literature, art, biology, calculus, ceramics, chemistry, computer programming, computer science, creative writing, drama, economics, English, English literature, environmental science, expository writing, fine arts, French, geography, geometry, government/civics, grammar, health, history, journalism, mathematics, music, music theory, philosophy, physical education, physics, psychology, science, social sciences, social studies, sociology, Spanish, speech, theater, trigonometry, world history, world literature, world religions, writing, zoology.

Graduation Requirements Arts and fine arts (art, music, dance, drama), computer science, English, foreign language, mathematics, physical education (includes health), science, social sciences, social studies (includes history), speech.

Special Academic Programs Advanced Placement exam preparation; honors section; study at local college for college credit; academic accommodation for the gifted.

College Admission Counseling 12 students graduated in 2009; all went to college, including Ball State University; Indiana University Bloomington; Purdue University; Rose-Hulman Institute of Technology; Saint Louis University. Median SAT critical reading: 575, median SAT math: 550, median SAT writing: 570, median combined SAT: 1690, median composite ACT: 24. 17% scored over 600 on SAT critical reading, 42% scored over 600 on SAT math, 25% scored over 600 on SAT writing, 17% scored over 1800 on combined SAT, 8% scored over 26 on composite ACT.

Student Life Upper grades have specified standards of dress, student council, honor system. Discipline rests primarily with faculty.

Tuition and Aid Day student tuition: $12,015. Tuition installment plan (Insured Tuition Payment Plan, monthly payment plans, pay in full: no fees, Pat semi-annually: no fees). Tuition reduction for siblings, merit scholarship grants, need-based scholarship grants, Professional Judgment scholarships available. In 2009–10, 20% of upper-school students received aid; total upper-school merit-scholarship money awarded: $112,000. Total amount of financial aid awarded in 2009–10: $183,000.

Admissions Traditional secondary-level entrance grade is 9. For fall 2009, 7 students applied for upper-level admission, 7 were accepted, 7 enrolled. English proficiency or ERB required. Deadline for receipt of application materials: none. Application fee required: $30. On-campus interview required.

Athletics Interscholastic: basketball (boys, girls), cheering (g), golf (b), outdoor adventure (b,g), physical fitness (b,g), pom squad (g), soccer (b,g), strength & conditioning (b,g), tennis (g), weight training (b); coed interscholastic: cheering, fitness walking. 3 PE instructors.

Computers Computers are regularly used in all academic, yearbook classes. Computer network features include on-campus library services, Internet access, Internet filtering or blocking technology. Student e-mail accounts and computer access in designated common areas are available to students. Students grades are available online. The school has a published electronic and media policy.

Contact Laura Cox, Director of Admission. 812-476-3039 Ext. 205. Fax: 812-476-4061. E-mail: lcox@evansvilledayschool.org. Web site: www.evansvilledayschool.org.

EXCEL ACADEMY, INC.

Newark, Ohio
See Special Needs Schools section.

EXCEL CHRISTIAN ACADEMY

325 Old Mill Road
Cartersville, Georgia 30120
Head of School: Mr. Tommy Harris

General Information Coeducational day college-preparatory school, affiliated with Church of God. Grades K–12. Founded: 1993. Setting: suburban. 15-acre campus. 3 buildings on campus. Approved or accredited by Association of Christian Schools International, Southern Association of Colleges and Schools, and Georgia Department of Education. Total enrollment: 373. Upper school average class size: 20. Upper school faculty-student ratio: 1:18.

Upper School Student Profile Grade 6: 34 students (17 boys, 17 girls); Grade 7: 37 students (20 boys, 17 girls); Grade 8: 39 students (21 boys, 18 girls); Grade 9: 40 students (14 boys, 26 girls); Grade 10: 24 students (14 boys, 10 girls); Grade 11: 17 students (3 boys, 14 girls); Grade 12: 29 students (11 boys, 18 girls). 29% of students are Church of God.

Faculty School total: 33. In upper school: 6 men, 14 women; 5 have advanced degrees.

Graduation Requirements Advanced Placement courses, Bible, computer technologies, electives, English, foreign language, history, mathematics, physical education (includes health), science.

Excel Christian Academy

Special Academic Programs 2 Advanced Placement exams for which test preparation is offered; honors section; study at local college for college credit.

College Admission Counseling 29 students graduated in 2009; 28 went to college, including Georgia Institute of Technology; Kennesaw State University; Valdosta State University. Other: 1 went to work. Median SAT critical reading: 530, median SAT math: 530, median SAT writing: 540, median combined SAT: 1600. 35% scored over 600 on SAT critical reading, 22% scored over 600 on SAT math, 22% scored over 600 on SAT writing, 22% scored over 1800 on combined SAT.

Student Life Upper grades have uniform requirement, student council, honor system. Discipline rests primarily with faculty.

Tuition and Aid Day student tuition: $8640. Tuition installment plan (monthly payment plans). Need-based loans available. In 2009–10, 30% of upper-school students received aid.

Admissions Traditional secondary-level entrance grade is 10. For fall 2009, 21 students applied for upper-level admission, 21 were accepted, 17 enrolled. Any standardized test required. Deadline for receipt of application materials: March. Application fee required: $100. Interview required.

Athletics Interscholastic: baseball (boys), basketball (b,g), cheering (g), cross-country running (b,g), softball (g), tennis (b,g); intramural: football (b); coed interscholastic: cross-country running, weight training. 2 PE instructors, 2 coaches.

Computers Computers are regularly used in business education, desktop publishing, journalism, newspaper, SAT preparation classes. Computer resources include Internet access.

Contact Mrs. Krista K. Keefe, Counselor. 770-382-9488. Fax: 770-606-9884. E-mail: kkeefe@excelacademy.cc. Web site: www.excelacademy.cc.

EXPLORATIONS ACADEMY
PO Box 3014
Bellingham, Washington 98227
Head of School: Daniel Kirkpatrick

General Information Coeducational day college-preparatory, experiential education, and international field study expeditions school. Ungraded, ages 11–18. Founded: 1995. Setting: urban. Nearest major city is Vancouver, BC, Canada. 1-acre campus. 1 building on campus. Approved or accredited by Northwest Accreditation Commission, Northwest Association of Schools and Colleges, Pacific Northwest Association of Independent Schools, and Washington Department of Education. Total enrollment: 26. Upper school average class size: 9. Upper school faculty-student ratio: 1:7. There are 177 required school days per year for Upper School students. Upper School students typically attend 5 days per week. The average school day consists of 6 hours.

Faculty School total: 7. In upper school: 4 men, 3 women; 5 have advanced degrees.

Subjects Offered Agriculture, American literature, anatomy and physiology, anthropology, archaeology, art, boat building, botany, calculus, carpentry, chemistry, computer graphics, computer programming, conflict resolution, construction, creative writing, desktop publishing, drawing, earth science, ecology, environmental science, first aid, French, gardening, gender issues, geology, government, health, horticulture, human relations, journalism, Latin American studies, leadership, marine biology, media, meteorology, microbiology, music, music history, painting, philosophy, photography, physical education, physics, poetry, political science, psychology, sculpture, sexuality, short story, Spanish, technology, theater design and production, video film production, world cultures, world geography, world history, world literature, writing.

Graduation Requirements Arts and fine arts (art, music, dance, drama), computer science, English, foreign language, human relations, lab science, mathematics, occupational education, physical education (includes health), science, social sciences, social studies (includes history), U.S. government and politics, Washington State and Northwest History, world history, one term of self-designed interdisciplinary studies. Community service is required.

Special Academic Programs Advanced Placement exam preparation; honors section; accelerated programs; independent study; term-away projects; academic accommodation for the gifted.

College Admission Counseling 5 students graduated in 2010; 4 went to college, including The Evergreen State College; University of Washington; Western Washington University. Other: 1 went to work.

Student Life Upper grades have honor system. Discipline rests primarily with faculty.

Summer Programs Enrichment, advancement, art/fine arts, rigorous outdoor training programs offered; session focuses on experiential learning; held both on and off campus; held at local urban and wilderness areas; accepts boys and girls; open to students from other schools. 12 students usually enrolled. 2011 schedule: July 6 to August 21. Application deadline: none.

Tuition and Aid Day student tuition: $10,500. Tuition installment plan (monthly payment plans, individually arranged payment plans, school's own payment plan). Tuition reduction for siblings, merit scholarship grants, need-based scholarship grants, need-based loans, low-interest loans with deferred payment available. In 2010–11, 40% of upper-school students received aid; total upper-school merit-scholarship money awarded: $35,000. Total amount of financial aid awarded in 2010–11: $81,000.

Admissions Traditional secondary-level entrance age is 14. For fall 2010, 30 students applied for upper-level admission, 25 were accepted, 24 enrolled. Non-standardized placement tests required. Deadline for receipt of application materials: none. Application fee required: $50. Interview required.

Computers Computers are regularly used in animation, art, English, French, graphics, mathematics, media production, publications, SAT preparation, science, writing, yearbook classes. Computer network features include online commercial services, Internet access, wireless campus network. Computer access in designated common areas is available to students. The school has a published electronic and media policy.

Contact Allison Roberts, Registrar. 360-671-8085. Fax: 360-671-2521. E-mail: info@explorationsacademy.org. Web site: www.ExplorationsAcademy.org.

FAIRFIELD COLLEGE PREPARATORY SCHOOL
1073 North Benson Road
Fairfield, Connecticut 06824-5157
Head of School: Rev. John J. Hanwell, SJ

General Information Boys' day college-preparatory, arts, religious studies, and technology school, affiliated with Roman Catholic Church. Grades 9–12. Founded: 1942. Setting: suburban. Nearest major city is Bridgeport. 220-acre campus. 4 buildings on campus. Approved or accredited by Connecticut Association of Independent Schools, Jesuit Secondary Education Association, New England Association of Schools and Colleges, and Connecticut Department of Education. Member of National Association of Independent Schools. Endowment: $7 million. Total enrollment: 917. Upper school average class size: 21. Upper school faculty-student ratio: 1:16. There are 183 required school days per year for Upper School students. Upper School students typically attend 5 days per week. The average school day consists of 5 hours and 50 minutes.

Upper School Student Profile Grade 9: 270 students (270 boys); Grade 10: 222 students (222 boys); Grade 11: 224 students (224 boys); Grade 12: 201 students (201 boys). 80% of students are Roman Catholic.

Faculty School total: 57. In upper school: 34 men, 23 women; 49 have advanced degrees.

Subjects Offered Advanced Placement courses, algebra, American history, American history-AP, American literature, American literature-AP, art, Asian studies, band, biology, biology-AP, British literature-AP, calculus, calculus-AP, career exploration, chemistry, choir, chorus, college admission preparation, college planning, community service, computer literacy, computer programming, computer science, constitutional law, creative writing, drama, drama workshop, drawing and design, driver education, economics, English, English literature, English literature-AP, English-AP, environmental science, European history, fine arts, French, French language-AP, French literature-AP, French-AP, geometry, graphics, guidance, history, honors algebra, honors English, honors geometry, honors U.S. history, journalism, language and composition, language arts, language structure, Latin, Latin-AP, mathematics, Middle East, moral theology, music, physics, physics-AP, pre-calculus, religion, SAT preparation, science, social justice, social studies, sociology, Spanish, Spanish language-AP, Spanish-AP, studio art, theater, theology, trigonometry, U.S. history-AP, United States government-AP, Web site design, Western civilization, word processing, world history, world literature, world religions, world wide web design, World-Wide-Web publishing.

Graduation Requirements Arts and fine arts (art, music, dance, drama), computer science, English, foreign language, mathematics, religion (includes Bible studies and theology), science, social studies (includes history), senior comprehensive exercises. Community service is required.

Special Academic Programs Advanced Placement exam preparation; honors section; study at local college for college credit.

College Admission Counseling 199 students graduated in 2009; 197 went to college, including Boston College; College of the Holy Cross; Fairfield University; Fordham University; Providence College; University of Connecticut. Other: 1 entered a postgraduate year, 1 had other specific plans. Mean SAT critical reading: 574, mean SAT math: 582, mean SAT writing: 567, mean combined SAT: 1723.

Student Life Upper grades have specified standards of dress, student council. Discipline rests primarily with faculty. Attendance at religious services is required.

Tuition and Aid Day student tuition: $14,985. Tuition installment plan (monthly payment plans). Need-based scholarship grants available. In 2009–10, 25% of upper-school students received aid. Total amount of financial aid awarded in 2009–10: $1,800,000.

Admissions Traditional secondary-level entrance grade is 9. For fall 2009, 487 students applied for upper-level admission, 374 were accepted, 252 enrolled. High School Placement Test required. Deadline for receipt of application materials: December 1. Application fee required: $60.

Athletics Interscholastic: alpine skiing, baseball, basketball, bowling, crew, cross-country running, diving, football, golf, ice hockey, indoor track & field, lacrosse, rugby, sailing, skiing (downhill), soccer, swimming and diving, tennis, track and field, winter (indoor) track, wrestling; intramural: basketball, bicycling, fitness, mountain biking, Nautilus, power lifting, skiing (downhill), strength & conditioning, table tennis, weight lifting. 33 coaches, 2 athletic trainers.

Computers Computers are regularly used in art, English, foreign language, history, mathematics, science, technology, theology classes. Computer network features include on-campus library services, online commercial services, Internet access, Internet filtering or blocking technology. The school has a published electronic and media policy.

Contact Mrs. Colleen H. Adams, Director of Communications. 203-254-4200 Ext. 2487. Fax: 203-254-4071. E-mail: cadams@fairfieldprep.org. Web site: www.fairfieldprep.org.

FAIRHILL SCHOOL
Dallas, Texas
See Special Needs Schools section.

FAIRMONT PRIVATE SCHOOLS AND PREPARATORY ACADEMY
2200 Sequoia Avenue
Anaheim, California 92801
Head of School: Mr. Robert Mendoza

General Information Coeducational day college-preparatory, arts, technology, International Baccalaureate, and medical magnet, engineering magnet school. Grades PK–12. Founded: 1953. Setting: suburban. Nearest major city is Los Angeles. 6-acre campus. 6 buildings on campus. Approved or accredited by International Baccalaureate Organization, National Independent Private Schools Association, and Western Association of Schools and Colleges. Member of Secondary School Admission Test Board. Total enrollment: 2,383. Upper school average class size: 15. Upper school faculty-student ratio: 1:11. There are 180 required school days per year for Upper School students. Upper School students typically attend 5 days per week. The average school day consists of 6 hours and 45 minutes.

Faculty School total: 120. In upper school: 20 men, 22 women; 23 have advanced degrees.

Subjects Offered Advanced Placement courses, advanced studio art-AP, algebra, all academic, American government, American history-AP, American literature-AP, analysis and differential calculus, anatomy, anatomy and physiology, art, art history-AP, arts, Asian literature, bioethics, DNA and culture, biology, biology-AP, British literature, British literature (honors), British literature-AP, calculus, calculus-AP, chemistry, chemistry-AP, Chinese, community service, computer science, creative writing, economics, economics and history, economics-AP, English, English literature and composition-AP, English-AP, environmental science, European history, European history-AP, expository writing, film and literature, film studies, filmmaking, fine arts, French, French language-AP, geometry, history, history-AP, International Baccalaureate courses, journalism, mathematics, music appreciation, music performance, music theory-AP, physical education, physical science, physics, physics-AP, pre-calculus, psychology-AP, science, social studies, Spanish, Spanish language-AP, speech and debate, statistics-AP, strings, student government, studio art-AP, TOEFL preparation, trigonometry, U.S. government, U.S. government and politics-AP, U.S. history, U.S. history-AP, world affairs, world history, writing, writing workshop, yearbook.

Graduation Requirements 3-dimensional design, arts and fine arts (art, music, dance, drama), computer science, electives, English, foreign language, health, mathematics, physical education (includes health), science, social sciences. Community service is required.

Special Academic Programs International Baccalaureate program; 17 Advanced Placement exams for which test preparation is offered; honors section; independent study; study at local college for college credit; academic accommodation for the gifted, the musically talented, and the artistically talented; ESL (30 students enrolled).

College Admission Counseling 153 students graduated in 2009; all went to college, including Boston University; Chapman University; University of California, Irvine; University of California, Los Angeles; University of California, Riverside; University of Southern California. Mean SAT critical reading: 549, mean SAT math: 668, mean SAT writing: 591, mean combined SAT: 1808. 33% scored over 600 on SAT critical reading, 79% scored over 600 on SAT math, 52% scored over 600 on SAT writing, 56% scored over 1800 on combined SAT.

Student Life Upper grades have specified standards of dress, student council. Discipline rests equally with students and faculty.

Tuition and Aid Day student tuition: $17,990. Tuition installment plan (monthly payment plans, individually arranged payment plans, annual and Semi-annual payment plans). Tuition reduction for siblings, need-based tuition assistance (applications available upon request) available. In 2009–10, 17% of upper-school students received aid. Total amount of financial aid awarded in 2009–10: $724,500.

Admissions Traditional secondary-level entrance grade is 9. ISEE or SSAT required. Deadline for receipt of application materials: none. Application fee required: $100. On-campus interview required.

Athletics Interscholastic: baseball (boys), basketball (b,g), cheering (g), football (b), soccer (b,g), softball (g), tennis (b,g), volleyball (g); intramural: roller hockey (b); coed interscholastic: cross-country running, golf, track and field; coed intramural: badminton, dance, swimming and diving, weight lifting. 2 PE instructors, 15 coaches.

Computers Computers are regularly used in all academic, business, foreign language, history, science classes. Computer resources include on-campus library services, online commercial services, Internet access, Internet filtering or blocking technology. Computer access in designated common areas is available to students. Students grades are available online. The school has a published electronic and media policy.

Contact Ms. Betty Petersen, Admissions Director. 714-999-5055. Fax: 714-999-0150. E-mail: bpetersen@fairmontschools.com. Web site: www.fairmontschools.com.

FAITH CHRISTIAN HIGH SCHOOL
3105 Colusa Highway
Yuba City, California 95993
Head of School: Mr. Stephen Finlay

General Information Coeducational day college-preparatory, arts, religious studies, and technology school, affiliated with Christian faith. Grades 9–12. Founded: 1975. Setting: small town. Nearest major city is Sacramento. 10-acre campus. 4 buildings on campus. Approved or accredited by Association of Christian Schools International, Western Association of Schools and Colleges, and California Department of Education. Total enrollment: 99. Upper school average class size: 25. Upper school faculty-student ratio: 1:12. There are 175 required school days per year for Upper School students. Upper School students typically attend 5 days per week. The average school day consists of 5 hours and 30 minutes.

Upper School Student Profile Grade 9: 22 students (12 boys, 10 girls); Grade 10: 27 students (10 boys, 17 girls); Grade 11: 24 students (13 boys, 11 girls); Grade 12: 26 students (11 boys, 15 girls). 99% of students are Christian.

Faculty School total: 15. In upper school: 11 men, 4 women; 4 have advanced degrees.

Subjects Offered Algebra, arts, Bible, biology, biology-AP, British literature, calculus-AP, chemistry, civics, computer science, computer studies, concert band, drama, economics, English, English composition, English literature, English-AP, geography, geometry, government, health, honors English, physical education, physical science, pre-calculus, senior project, Spanish, U.S. history, world geography, world history, yearbook.

Graduation Requirements Algebra, Bible, biology, civics, economics, English, geometry, health, physical science, senior project, U.S. history, world geography, world history.

Special Academic Programs Advanced Placement exam preparation; study at local college for college credit.

College Admission Counseling 28 students graduated in 2010; 26 went to college, including Azusa Pacific University; Biola University; California Polytechnic State University, San Luis Obispo; Simpson University; Vassar College. Other: 2 entered military service. Median SAT critical reading: 580, median SAT math: 540, median SAT writing: 550, median combined SAT: 1640, median composite ACT: 20. 30% scored over 600 on SAT critical reading, 20% scored over 600 on SAT math, 30% scored over 600 on SAT writing, 30% scored over 1800 on combined SAT, 25% scored over 26 on composite ACT.

Student Life Upper grades have specified standards of dress, student council, honor system. Discipline rests primarily with faculty. Attendance at religious services is required.

Tuition and Aid Day student tuition: $7460. Tuition installment plan (monthly payment plans). Tuition reduction for siblings, need-based scholarship grants available. In 2010–11, 20% of upper-school students received aid. Total amount of financial aid awarded in 2010–11: $50,000.

Admissions Traditional secondary-level entrance grade is 9. For fall 2010, 3 students applied for upper-level admission, 3 were accepted, 3 enrolled. Achievement tests required. Deadline for receipt of application materials: none. Application fee required: $50. Interview required.

Athletics Interscholastic: baseball (boys), basketball (b,g), cheering (g), cross-country running (b,g), soccer (b,g), volleyball (g); coed interscholastic: golf. 1 PE instructor, 8 coaches.

Computers Computers are regularly used in all academic classes. Computer network features include on-campus library services, Internet access, Internet filtering or blocking technology. Students grades are available online. The school has a published electronic and media policy.

Contact Mrs. Sue Shorey, Secretary. 530-674-5474. Fax: 530-674-0194. E-mail: sshorey@fcs-k12.org. Web site: www.fcs-k12.org.

FAITH LUTHERAN HIGH SCHOOL
2015 South Hualapai Way
Las Vegas, Nevada 89117-6949
Head of School: Mr. Kevin M. Dunning

General Information Coeducational day college-preparatory and religious studies school, affiliated with Lutheran Church–Missouri Synod, Evangelical Lutheran Church in America. Grades 6–12. Founded: 1979. Setting: suburban. 39-acre campus. 4 buildings on campus. Approved or accredited by Lutheran School Accreditation Commission, Northwest Accreditation Commission, Northwest Association of Schools and Colleges, and Nevada Department of Education. Endowment: $1 million. Total enrollment: 1,318. Upper school average class size: 25. Upper school faculty-student ratio: 1:17. There are 180 required school days per year for Upper School students. Upper School students typically attend 5 days per week. The average school day consists of 7 hours.

Upper School Student Profile Grade 9: 178 students (69 boys, 109 girls); Grade 10: 186 students (88 boys, 98 girls); Grade 11: 184 students (90 boys, 94 girls); Grade

Faith Lutheran High School

12: 156 students (71 boys, 85 girls). 26% of students are Lutheran Church–Missouri Synod, Evangelical Lutheran Church in America.

Faculty School total: 92. In upper school: 32 men, 54 women; 48 have advanced degrees.

Subjects Offered Algebra, American history, art, biology, chemistry, computer science, earth science, English, fine arts, fitness, geometry, German, health, mathematics, music, physical education, physical science, religion, SAT/ACT preparation, science, social studies, Spanish.

Graduation Requirements American history, arts and fine arts (art, music, dance, drama), computer science, English, foreign language, mathematics, physical education (includes health), religion (includes Bible studies and theology), science, social studies (includes history).

Special Academic Programs 7 Advanced Placement exams for which test preparation is offered; honors section; independent study; study at local college for college credit; academic accommodation for the musically talented.

College Admission Counseling 152 students graduated in 2010; 140 went to college, including Concordia University; University of Nevada, Las Vegas; University of Nevada, Reno. Other: 9 went to work, 3 entered military service. Median SAT critical reading: 540, median SAT math: 520, median SAT writing: 510, median combined SAT: 1570, median composite ACT: 23. 25% scored over 600 on SAT critical reading, 25% scored over 600 on SAT math, 20% scored over 600 on SAT writing, 23% scored over 1800 on combined SAT, 30% scored over 26 on composite ACT.

Student Life Upper grades have uniform requirement, student council. Discipline rests primarily with faculty. Attendance at religious services is required.

Tuition and Aid Day student tuition: $9100. Tuition installment plan (monthly payment plans, individually arranged payment plans). Tuition reduction for siblings, need-based scholarship grants available. In 2010–11, 12% of upper-school students received aid. Total amount of financial aid awarded in 2010–11: $460,000.

Admissions Traditional secondary-level entrance grade is 9. For fall 2010, 110 students applied for upper-level admission, 100 were accepted, 80 enrolled. High School Placement Test and Stanford 9 required. Deadline for receipt of application materials: none. Application fee required: $350. On-campus interview required.

Athletics Interscholastic: aerobics/dance (girls), aquatics (b,g), baseball (b), basketball (b,g), cheering (g), cross-country running (b,g), dance team (g), football (b), golf (b,g), lacrosse (b,g), soccer (b,g), softball (g), swimming and diving (b,g), tennis (b,g), track and field (b,g), volleyball (g), wrestling (b); intramural: strength & conditioning (b,g), weight training (b,g); coed interscholastic: strength & conditioning; coed intramural: fencing, skiing (downhill), snowboarding, ultimate Frisbee. 7 PE instructors, 26 coaches.

Computers Computers are regularly used in keyboarding, yearbook classes. Computer network features include on-campus library services, online commercial services, Internet access, wireless campus network, Internet filtering or blocking technology. Student e-mail accounts and computer access in designated common areas are available to students. Students grades are available online. The school has a published electronic and media policy.

Contact Julie Buuck, Admissions Coordinator. 702-562-7737. Fax: 702-804-4488. E-mail: NealC@faithlutheranlv.org. Web site: www.faithlutheranlv.org.

FALMOUTH ACADEMY

7 Highfield Drive
Falmouth, Massachusetts 02540

Head of School: Mr. David C. Faus

General Information Coeducational day college-preparatory and arts school. Grades 7–12. Founded: 1976. Setting: small town. Nearest major city is Boston. 34-acre campus. 3 buildings on campus. Approved or accredited by Association of Independent Schools in New England and New England Association of Schools and Colleges. Member of National Association of Independent Schools and Secondary School Admission Test Board. Endowment: $4 million. Total enrollment: 188. Upper school average class size: 12. Upper school faculty-student ratio: 1:4. There are 165 required school days per year for Upper School students. Upper School students typically attend 5 days per week. The average school day consists of 6 hours and 20 minutes.

Upper School Student Profile Grade 9: 26 students (11 boys, 15 girls); Grade 10: 30 students (10 boys, 20 girls); Grade 11: 31 students (14 boys, 17 girls); Grade 12: 36 students (17 boys, 19 girls).

Faculty School total: 35. In upper school: 14 men, 20 women; 26 have advanced degrees.

Subjects Offered Algebra, American history, American literature, art, biology, calculus, ceramics, chemistry, creative writing, drama, earth science, ecology, English, English literature, environmental science, European history, expository writing, fine arts, French, geography, geology, geometry, German, grammar, health, history, journalism, mathematics, music, photography, physical education, physics, science, sculpture, social studies, statistics, theater, trigonometry, woodworking, world history, world literature, writing.

Graduation Requirements Arts and fine arts (art, music, dance, drama), English, foreign language, history, mathematics, science.

Special Academic Programs 5 Advanced Placement exams for which test preparation is offered; independent study; term-away projects; study abroad.

College Admission Counseling 36 students graduated in 2010; 30 went to college, including Guilford College. Other: 6 had other specific plans. Mean SAT critical reading: 680, mean SAT math: 632, mean SAT writing: 669.

Student Life Upper grades have specified standards of dress, student council, honor system. Discipline rests primarily with faculty.

Tuition and Aid Day student tuition: $22,840. Merit scholarship grants, need-based scholarship grants, need-based loans available. In 2010–11, 40% of upper-school students received aid; total upper-school merit-scholarship money awarded: $6000. Total amount of financial aid awarded in 2010–11: $600,000.

Admissions Traditional secondary-level entrance grade is 9. For fall 2010, 25 students applied for upper-level admission, 15 were accepted, 10 enrolled. SSAT required. Deadline for receipt of application materials: March 1. Application fee required: $50. On-campus interview required.

Athletics Interscholastic: basketball (boys, girls), lacrosse (b,g), soccer (b,g). 1 PE instructor.

Computers Computers are regularly used in design, English, mathematics, science classes. Computer resources include on-campus library services, Internet access, Internet filtering or blocking technology. The school has a published electronic and media policy.

Contact Mr. Michael J. Earley, Director of Admissions. 508-457-9696 Ext. 224. Fax: 508-457-4112. E-mail: mearley@falmouthacademy.org. Web site: www.falmouthacademy.org.

THE FAMILY FOUNDATION SCHOOL

Hancock, New York
See Special Needs Schools section.

FATHER JUDGE HIGH SCHOOL

3301 Solly Avenue
Philadelphia, Pennsylvania 19136

Head of School: Dr. Kathleen Herpich

General Information Boys' day college-preparatory, arts, business, religious studies, and technology school, affiliated with Roman Catholic Church; primarily serves students with learning disabilities. Grades 9–12. Founded: 1953. Setting: suburban. 3 buildings on campus. Approved or accredited by Middle States Association of Colleges and Schools, National Catholic Education Association, and Pennsylvania Department of Education. Total enrollment: 1,143. Upper school average class size: 28. Upper school faculty-student ratio: 1:28. There are 180 required school days per year for Upper School students. Upper School students typically attend 5 days per week. The average school day consists of 7 hours.

Upper School Student Profile Grade 9: 210 students (210 boys); Grade 10: 341 students (341 boys); Grade 11: 291 students (291 boys); Grade 12: 301 students (301 boys). 98% of students are Roman Catholic.

Faculty School total: 65. In upper school: 46 men, 19 women.

Graduation Requirements 1½ elective credits, biology, English, foreign language, health education, mathematics, physical education (includes health), physical science, religion (includes Bible studies and theology), science, theology, U.S. government, world history.

Special Academic Programs 5 Advanced Placement exams for which test preparation is offered; honors section; study at local college for college credit.

College Admission Counseling 349 students graduated in 2009; 329 went to college, including Saint John's University; Temple University; The Catholic University of America; University of Delaware; University of Pennsylvania; West Chester University of Pennsylvania. Other: 7 went to work, 3 entered military service.

Student Life Upper grades have uniform requirement, student council, honor system. Discipline rests primarily with faculty. Attendance at religious services is required.

Tuition and Aid Tuition installment plan (monthly payment plans). Tuition reduction for siblings, need-based scholarship grants available. In 2009–10, 80% of upper-school students received aid.

Admissions Traditional secondary-level entrance grade is 10. Any standardized test or TerraNova required. Deadline for receipt of application materials: none. No application fee required.

Athletics Interscholastic: baseball, basketball, bowling, cheering (g), crew, cross-country running, dance (g), dance squad (g), dance team (g), danceline (g), golf, hockey, ice hockey, lacrosse, rugby, soccer, swimming and diving, tennis, track and field, winter (indoor) track, wrestling; intramural: flag football, touch football. 1 PE instructor, 30 coaches, 1 athletic trainer.

Computers Computers are regularly used in all classes. Computer network features include on-campus library services, Internet access, wireless campus network, Internet filtering or blocking technology. Student e-mail accounts are available to students. Students grades are available online. The school has a published electronic and media policy.

Contact Mr. Thomas Coyle, Admissions. 215-338-9494. Fax: 215-338-0250. E-mail: tcoyle@fatherjudge.com. Web site: www.fatherjudge.com.

FATHER LOPEZ HIGH SCHOOL

3918 LPGA Boulevard
Daytona Beach, Florida 32124
Head of School: Mr. Ted Petrucciani

General Information Coeducational day college-preparatory school, affiliated with Roman Catholic Church. Grades 9–12. Founded: 1959. Setting: suburban. 90-acre campus. 7 buildings on campus. Approved or accredited by National Catholic Education Association, Southern Association of Colleges and Schools, and Florida Department of Education. Total enrollment: 297. Upper school average class size: 23. Upper school faculty-student ratio: 1:20. There are 180 required school days per year for Upper School students. Upper School students typically attend 5 days per week. The average school day consists of 7 hours and 30 minutes.

Upper School Student Profile Grade 9: 67 students (35 boys, 32 girls); Grade 10: 92 students (46 boys, 46 girls); Grade 11: 65 students (30 boys, 35 girls); Grade 12: 73 students (36 boys, 37 girls). 80% of students are Roman Catholic.

Faculty School total: 25. In upper school: 10 men, 15 women; 14 have advanced degrees.

Subjects Offered Accounting, Advanced Placement courses, aerobics, algebra, American government, American history, American history-AP, American literature, anatomy and physiology, art, audio visual/media, biology, biology-AP, British literature, calculus-AP, chemistry, computer applications, computer graphics, consumer mathematics, culinary arts, digital photography, drama, drama performance, economics, English, English literature, English literature-AP, filmmaking, French, geometry, government, government-AP, graphic design, health education, honors algebra, honors English, honors geometry, honors U.S. history, marine science, photography, physical education, pre-calculus, psychology, social justice, Spanish, theology, U.S. government and politics-AP, U.S. history, U.S. history-AP, Web site design, weight training, world geography, world history, writing.

Graduation Requirements Algebra, American history, American literature, art, arts and fine arts (art, music, dance, drama), Bible, biology, British literature, calculus, chemistry, church history, computer skills, death and loss, economics, electives, English, English literature, fitness, foreign language, geometry, government, health and wellness, physical education (includes health), physics, social justice, U.S. government, world history, 100 hours of community service.

Special Academic Programs 7 Advanced Placement exams for which test preparation is offered; honors section; study at local college for college credit.

College Admission Counseling 66 students graduated in 2010; 65 went to college, including Florida State University; University of Central Florida; University of Florida; University of Miami; University of North Florida. Other: 1 had other specific plans. Mean SAT critical reading: 514, mean SAT math: 600, mean SAT writing: 492, mean combined SAT: 1506, mean composite ACT: 23.

Student Life Upper grades have uniform requirement, student council, honor system. Discipline rests primarily with faculty. Attendance at religious services is required.

Tuition and Aid Day student tuition: $9300. Tuition installment plan (SMART Tuition Payment Plan). Need-based scholarship grants, tuition subsidy for qualifying families available. In 2010–11, 50% of upper-school students received aid. Total amount of financial aid awarded in 2010–11: $600,000.

Admissions Traditional secondary-level entrance grade is 9. High School Placement Test required. Deadline for receipt of application materials: none. Application fee required: $325. Interview required.

Athletics Interscholastic: aerobics/dance (girls), baseball (b), basketball (b,g), cheering (g), cross-country running (b,g), dance (g), dance team (g), football (b), golf (b,g), lacrosse (b), soccer (b,g), softball (g), swimming and diving (b,g), tennis (b,g), track and field (b,g), volleyball (g). 1 PE instructor, 10 coaches, 1 athletic trainer.

Computers Computers are regularly used in accounting, computer applications, graphic design, media production, photography, video film production, yearbook classes. Computer network features include on-campus library services, Internet access, wireless campus network, Internet filtering or blocking technology. Student e-mail accounts and computer access in designated common areas are available to students. Students grades are available online. The school has a published electronic and media policy.

Contact Mr. Ted Petrucciani, Principal. 386-253-5213 Ext. 310. Fax: 386-252-6101. E-mail: tpetrucciani@fatherlopez.org. Web site: www.fatherlopez.org.

FATHER RYAN HIGH SCHOOL

700 Norwood Drive
Nashville, Tennessee 37204
Head of School: Mr. McIntyre Jim

General Information Coeducational day college-preparatory, arts, and religious studies school, affiliated with Roman Catholic Church. Grades 9–12. Founded: 1925. Setting: suburban. 40-acre campus. 9 buildings on campus. Approved or accredited by National Catholic Education Association, Southern Association of Colleges and Schools, Southern Association of Independent Schools, Tennessee Association of Independent Schools, and The College Board. Endowment: $5 million. Total enrollment: 920. Upper school average class size: 20. Upper school faculty-student ratio: 1:12. There are 180 required school days per year for Upper School students. Upper School students typically attend 5 days per week. The average school day consists of 7 hours and 10 minutes.

Upper School Student Profile Grade 9: 243 students (138 boys, 105 girls); Grade 10: 237 students (140 boys, 97 girls); Grade 11: 234 students (127 boys, 107 girls); Grade 12: 206 students (106 boys, 100 girls). 90% of students are Roman Catholic.

Faculty School total: 87. In upper school: 42 men, 43 women; 46 have advanced degrees.

Subjects Offered 3-dimensional design, Advanced Placement courses, aerobics, algebra, American government, American history, American history-AP, American literature, anatomy, art, art history, art-AP, Bible studies, biology, British literature, calculus, calculus-AP, Catholic belief and practice, chemistry, chemistry-AP, Chinese, Chinese studies, chorus, church history, college counseling, college planning, college writing, computer programming, computer science, computer studies, dance, dance performance, drama, drama performance, driver education, economics, English, English literature, English-AP, European history, European history-AP, film studies, French, French-AP, geography, geometry, government-AP, government/civics, grammar, health, history, honors geometry, honors U.S. history, journalism, Latin, mathematics, music, physical education, physics, physics-AP, physiology, psychology, psychology-AP, religion, SAT preparation, science, Shakespeare, social studies, Spanish, Spanish-AP, speech, statistics-AP, theater, theater production, theology, trigonometry, U.S. government and politics-AP, Web site design, wind ensemble, world history, world literature, world religions, writing.

Graduation Requirements Arts and fine arts (art, music, dance, drama), computer science, English, foreign language, health education, mathematics, physical education (includes health), religion (includes Bible studies and theology), science, social studies (includes history), service hours required each year.

Special Academic Programs Advanced Placement exam preparation; honors section; academic accommodation for the gifted, the musically talented, and the artistically talented; programs in English, mathematics for dyslexic students.

College Admission Counseling 202 students graduated in 2010; 200 went to college, including Belmont University; Middle Tennessee State University; Tennessee Technological University; The University of Tennessee; Western Kentucky University. Other: 2 went to work. Median SAT critical reading: 553, median SAT math: 524, median composite ACT: 24. 20% scored over 26 on composite ACT.

Student Life Upper grades have uniform requirement, student council. Discipline rests primarily with faculty. Attendance at religious services is required.

Summer Programs Remediation, enrichment, advancement, sports, art/fine arts, computer instruction programs offered; held on campus; accepts boys and girls; open to students from other schools. 210 students usually enrolled. 2011 schedule: June 1 to June 30. Application deadline: none.

Tuition and Aid Day student tuition: $10,185. Tuition installment plan (FACTS Tuition Payment Plan, individually arranged payment plans). Tuition reduction for siblings, need-based scholarship grants available. In 2010–11, 13% of upper-school students received aid. Total amount of financial aid awarded in 2010–11: $536,000.

Admissions Traditional secondary-level entrance grade is 9. For fall 2010, 328 students applied for upper-level admission, 278 were accepted, 243 enrolled. High School Placement Test required. Deadline for receipt of application materials: none. Application fee required: $80. On-campus interview required.

Athletics Interscholastic: aquatics (boys, girls), baseball (b,g), basketball (b,g), bowling (b,g), cheering (g), cross-country running (b,g), dance (g), dance squad (b), dance team (g), diving (b), football (b), golf (b,g), ice hockey (b), lacrosse (b,g), modern dance (g), power lifting (b), soccer (b,g), softball (g), Special Olympics (b,g), strength & conditioning (b,g), swimming and diving (b,g), tennis (b,g), track and field (b,g), volleyball (g), weight lifting (b,g), weight training (b,g), wrestling (b); intramural: fishing (b,g), indoor soccer (b,g), physical fitness (b,g). 1 athletic trainer.

Computers Computers are regularly used in all academic classes. Computer network features include on-campus library services, online commercial services, Internet access, Internet filtering or blocking technology. Computer access in designated common areas is available to students. Students grades are available online. The school has a published electronic and media policy.

Contact Ms. Kate Goetzinger, Director of Admissions. 615-383-4200, Fax: 615-783-0264. E-mail: goetzinfcrk@fatherryan.org. Web site: www.fatherryan.org.

FAYETTEVILLE ACADEMY

3200 Cliffdale Road
Fayetteville, North Carolina 28303
Head of School: Mr. Richard D. Cameron

General Information Coeducational day college-preparatory, arts, and technology school. Grades PK–12. Founded: 1969. Setting: suburban. 30-acre campus. 10 buildings on campus. Approved or accredited by North Carolina Association of Independent Schools, Southern Association of Colleges and Schools, Southern Association of Independent Schools, The College Board, and North Carolina Department of Education. Endowment: $287,052. Total enrollment: 403. Upper school average class size: 14. Upper school faculty-student ratio: 1:14. There are 175 required school days per year for Upper School students. Upper School students typically attend 5 days per week. The average school day consists of 6 hours and 55 minutes.

Upper School Student Profile Grade 9: 33 students (11 boys, 22 girls); Grade 10: 36 students (18 boys, 18 girls); Grade 11: 41 students (20 boys, 21 girls); Grade 12: 33 students (16 boys, 17 girls).

Faculty School total: 52. In upper school: 8 men, 15 women; 11 have advanced degrees.

Subjects Offered Algebra, American history, American literature, anatomy, art, band, biology, biology-AP, calculus, calculus-AP, chemistry, chemistry-AP, chorus, communications, ecology, English, English language and composition-AP, English literature, English literature-AP, European history, European history-AP, geography, geometry, government/civics, history, honors geometry, mathematics, music, physical education, physics, physiology, pre-calculus, psychology, science, social studies, Spanish, Spanish-AP, statistics-AP, trigonometry, typing, U.S. history-AP, weight training, world history, world history-AP, yearbook.

Graduation Requirements Arts and fine arts (art, music, dance, drama), English, foreign language, history, lab science, mathematics, physical education (includes health), senior projects.

Special Academic Programs Advanced Placement exam preparation; honors section; study at local college for college credit.

College Admission Counseling 37 students graduated in 2010; all went to college, including East Carolina University; Meredith College; North Carolina State University; The George Washington University; The University of North Carolina at Chapel Hill; The University of North Carolina Wilmington. Mean SAT critical reading: 569, mean SAT math: 586, mean SAT writing: 562, mean combined SAT: 1717, mean composite ACT: 24.

Student Life Upper grades have specified standards of dress, student council, honor system. Discipline rests primarily with faculty.

Summer Programs Enrichment, sports, art/fine arts, computer instruction programs offered; session focuses on enrichment; held on campus; accepts boys and girls; open to students from other schools. 350 students usually enrolled. 2011 schedule: June 13 to August 1.

Tuition and Aid Day student tuition: $12,500. Tuition installment plan (monthly payment plans, payment in full, 3-payment plan). Merit scholarship grants, need-based scholarship grants available. In 2010–11, 25% of upper-school students received aid; total upper-school merit-scholarship money awarded: $38,000. Total amount of financial aid awarded in 2010–11: $477,000.

Admissions Traditional secondary-level entrance grade is 9. For fall 2010, 32 students applied for upper-level admission, 29 were accepted, 20 enrolled. ERB and SSAT required. Deadline for receipt of application materials: none. Application fee required: $50. On-campus interview recommended.

Athletics Interscholastic: baseball (boys), basketball (b,g), cheering (g), cross-country running (b,g), golf (b), soccer (b,g), softball (g), tennis (b,g), track and field (b,g), volleyball (g), weight training (b,g); intramural: weight training (g); coed interscholastic: swimming and diving. 4 PE instructors, 10 coaches, 1 athletic trainer.

Computers Computers are regularly used in all classes. Computer network features include on-campus library services, online commercial services, Internet access. Students grades are available online.

Contact Ms. Barbara E. Lambert, Director of Admissions. 910-868-5131 Ext. 3311. Fax: 910-868-7351. E-mail: blambert@fayettevilleacademy.com. Web site: www.fayettevilleacademy.com.

FAY SCHOOL
Southborough, Massachusetts
See Junior Boarding Schools section.

FENWICK HIGH SCHOOL
505 West Washington Boulevard
Oak Park, Illinois 60302
Head of School: Mr. Richard A. Borsch
General Information Coeducational day college-preparatory school, affiliated with Roman Catholic Church. Grades 9–12. Founded: 1929. Setting: suburban. Nearest major city is Chicago. 1-acre campus. 4 buildings on campus. Approved or accredited by North Central Association of Colleges and Schools and Illinois Department of Education. Endowment: $4.5 million. Total enrollment: 1,196. Upper school average class size: 25. Upper school faculty-student ratio: 1:16. There are 180 required school days per year for Upper School students. Upper School students typically attend 5 days per week. The average school day consists of 2 hours and 20 minutes.

Upper School Student Profile Grade 9: 311 students (163 boys, 148 girls); Grade 10: 304 students (171 boys, 133 girls); Grade 11: 294 students (170 boys, 124 girls); Grade 12: 287 students (161 boys, 126 girls). 86% of students are Roman Catholic.

Faculty School total: 85. In upper school: 57 men, 28 women; 63 have advanced degrees.

Subjects Offered Algebra, American history, American history-AP, American literature, anatomy, art, art history, arts, astronomy, band, Bible studies, biology, British literature, British literature (honors), calculus, calculus-AP, chemistry, chemistry-AP, chorus, computer math, computer programming, computer science, creative writing, critical studies in film, critical writing, economics, economics-AP, English, English language and composition-AP, English literature, English literature and composition-AP, environmental science, European history, European history-AP, fine arts, French, French-AP, geometry, German, government/civics, health, history, humanities, Italian, Latin, Latin-AP, literature and composition-AP, literature-AP, marine biology, mathematics, music, music appreciation, physical education, physics,

physics-AP, religion, science, social studies, Spanish, Spanish-AP, speech, statistics, theology, trigonometry, U.S. history-AP, United States government-AP, world history, world history-AP, writing.

Graduation Requirements Arts and fine arts (art, music, dance, drama), computer science, English, foreign language, humanities, mathematics, physical education (includes health), religion (includes Bible studies and theology), science, social studies (includes history), speech, theology.

Special Academic Programs Advanced Placement exam preparation; honors section; study at local college for college credit; academic accommodation for the gifted.

College Admission Counseling 291 students graduated in 2010; all went to college, including DePaul University; Indiana University Bloomington; Loyola University Chicago; Marquette University; University of Illinois at Urbana–Champaign; University of Notre Dame. Median SAT critical reading: 580, median SAT math: 589, median SAT writing: 582, median combined SAT: 1750, median composite ACT: 27. 47% scored over 600 on SAT critical reading, 49% scored over 600 on SAT math, 46% scored over 600 on SAT writing, 48% scored over 1800 on combined SAT, 53% scored over 26 on composite ACT.

Student Life Upper grades have uniform requirement, student council. Discipline rests primarily with faculty. Attendance at religious services is required.

Summer Programs Remediation, enrichment, advancement, computer instruction programs offered; session focuses on enrichment; held on campus; accepts boys and girls; open to students from other schools. 300 students usually enrolled. 2011 schedule: June 19 to July 22. Application deadline: none.

Tuition and Aid Day student tuition: $10,950. Tuition installment plan (monthly payment plans, quarterly and semi-annual payment plans). Tuition reduction for siblings, merit scholarship grants, need-based scholarship grants available. In 2010–11, 33% of upper-school students received aid; total upper-school merit-scholarship money awarded: $91,500. Total amount of financial aid awarded in 2010–11: $1,336,049.

Admissions Traditional secondary-level entrance grade is 9. For fall 2010, 585 students applied for upper-level admission, 317 were accepted, 311 enrolled. Archdiocese of Boston or STS or High School Placement Test required. Deadline for receipt of application materials: January 8. Application fee required: $25.

Athletics Interscholastic: aquatics (boys, girls), baseball (b), basketball (b,g), bowling (b,g), cheering (g), cross-country running (b,g), diving (b,g), football (b), golf (b,g), ice hockey (b,g), lacrosse (b,g), soccer (b,g), softball (g), swimming and diving (b,g), tennis (b,g), track and field (b,g), volleyball (g), water polo (b,g), wrestling (b); intramural: basketball (b,g), bowling (b,g), indoor soccer (b,g), martial arts (b,g), pom squad (g), table tennis (b,g), touch football (b), volleyball (g); coed intramural: canoeing/kayaking, climbing, Nautilus, outdoor adventure, physical training, rock climbing, roller blading, strength & conditioning, wall climbing, weight lifting, weight training. 4 PE instructors, 1 athletic trainer.

Computers Computers are regularly used in English, journalism, literary magazine, mathematics, newspaper, science, yearbook classes. Computer network features include on-campus library services, online commercial services, Internet access, wireless campus network, Internet filtering or blocking technology. Student e-mail accounts are available to students. Students grades are available online. The school has a published electronic and media policy.

Contact Francesca Rabchuk, Director of Admissions. 708-386-0127 Ext. 115. Fax: 708-386-4323. E-mail: frabchuk@fenwickfriars.com. Web site: fenwickfriars.com.

THE FESSENDEN SCHOOL
West Newton, Massachusetts
See Junior Boarding Schools section.

THE FIELD SCHOOL
2301 Foxhall Road NW
Washington, District of Columbia 20007
Head of School: Dale T. Johnson
General Information Coeducational day college-preparatory and arts school. Grades 7–12. Founded: 1972. Setting: urban. 10-acre campus. 4 buildings on campus. Approved or accredited by Association of Independent Schools of Greater Washington and Middle States Association of Colleges and Schools. Member of National Association of Independent Schools and Secondary School Admission Test Board. Total enrollment: 320. Upper school average class size: 11. Upper school faculty-student ratio: 1:6.

Upper School Student Profile Grade 7: 28 students (13 boys, 15 girls); Grade 8: 32 students (16 boys, 16 girls); Grade 9: 68 students (33 boys, 35 girls); Grade 10: 65 students (32 boys, 33 girls); Grade 11: 67 students (33 boys, 34 girls); Grade 12: 61 students (30 boys, 31 girls).

Faculty School total: 63. In upper school: 30 men, 33 women; 28 have advanced degrees.

Subjects Offered Algebra, American history, American literature, ancient history, art, art history, biology, calculus, ceramics, chemistry, computer math, creative writing, drama, earth science, English, English literature, environmental science, European history, expository writing, fine arts, French, geometry, government/civics, grammar, history, journalism, Latin, literature, mathematics, music, photography, physical education, physics, pre-calculus, science, social studies, space and physical sciences, Spanish, theater, trigonometry, typing, world history, world literature, writing.

Graduation Requirements Arts and fine arts (art, music, dance, drama), English, foreign language, mathematics, physical education (includes health), science, social studies (includes history), winter internship (2 weeks annually).

Special Academic Programs Advanced Placement exam preparation; accelerated programs; independent study; academic accommodation for the gifted, the musically talented, and the artistically talented; remedial math.

College Admission Counseling 71 students graduated in 2009; 69 went to college, including College of Charleston; Columbia College; Kenyon College; Oberlin College; University of Virginia; Wesleyan University. Other: 1 went to work, 1 had other specific plans.

Student Life Upper grades have student council, honor system. Discipline rests primarily with faculty.

Tuition and Aid Day student tuition: $32,100. Tuition installment plan (Insured Tuition Payment Plan, Key Tuition Payment Plan, monthly payment plans). Need-based scholarship grants available. In 2009–10, 18% of upper-school students received aid. Total amount of financial aid awarded in 2009–10: $1,250,000.

Admissions Traditional secondary-level entrance grade is 9. For fall 2009, 195 students applied for upper-level admission, 77 were accepted, 44 enrolled. ISEE, SSAT or WISC-R or WISC-III required. Deadline for receipt of application materials: January 15. Application fee required: $80. On-campus interview required.

Athletics Interscholastic: baseball (boys), basketball (b,g), cross-country running (b,g), lacrosse (g), soccer (b,g), softball (g), swimming and diving (b,g), tennis (b,g), track and field (b,g), ultimate Frisbee (b,g), volleyball (g); intramural: basketball (b,g), bocce (b,g), bowling (b,g); coed interscholastic: Frisbee, swimming and diving; coed intramural: dance, fitness, Frisbee, indoor soccer, physical fitness, racquetball, ultimate Frisbee, volleyball, yoga.

Computers Computers are regularly used in English, foreign language, history, mathematics, media arts, science classes. Computer network features include on-campus library services, online commercial services, Internet access, Internet filtering or blocking technology. Campus intranet is available to students. The school has a published electronic and media policy.

Contact Ms. Michele Wiles, Admissions Assistant. 202-295-5839. Fax: 202-295-5850. E-mail: michelew@fieldschool.org. Web site: www.fieldschool.org.

FIELDSTONE DAY SCHOOL

2999 Dufferin Street
Toronto, Ontario M6B 3T4, Canada
Head of School: Ms. Josephine Parody

General Information Coeducational boarding and day college-preparatory and general academic school. Grades JK–12. Founded: 1997. Setting: urban. 6-acre campus. 1 building on campus. Approved or accredited by Ontario Department of Education. Languages of instruction: English and French. Total enrollment: 300. Upper school average class size: 20. Upper school faculty-student ratio: 1:16. Upper School students typically attend 5 days per week. The average school day consists of 7 hours.

Upper School Student Profile 20% of students are boarding students. 70% are province residents, 3 provinces are represented in upper school student body. 30% are international students. International students from China, Egypt, Japan, Mexico, Republic of Korea, and Viet Nam.

Faculty School total: 19. In upper school: 8 men, 11 women.

Special Academic Programs Advanced Placement exam preparation; academic accommodation for the gifted, the musically talented, and the artistically talented; ESL (60 students enrolled).

College Admission Counseling 12 students graduated in 2009; all went to college, including University of Toronto.

Student Life Upper grades have uniform requirement, student council. Discipline rests equally with students and faculty.

Tuition and Aid Day student tuition: CAN$18,000. Tuition installment plan (The Tuition Plan). Need-based scholarship grants available. In 2009–10, 5% of upper-school students received aid.

Admissions Traditional secondary-level entrance grade is 9. TOEFL and writing sample required. Deadline for receipt of application materials: January 30. Application fee required: CAN$150. Interview required.

Athletics Interscholastic: badminton (boys, girls), baseball (b,g), cross-country running (b,g), football (b,g), hockey (b,g), ice hockey (b,g), independent competitive sports (b,g), indoor hockey (b,g), indoor soccer (b,g), indoor track & field (b,g), jump rope (b,g), soccer (b,g), softball (b,g); intramural: cross-country running (b,g), dance (g), flag football (b,g), floor hockey (b,g), independent competitive sports (b,g), indoor hockey (b,g), indoor soccer (b,g), indoor track & field (b,g), jump rope (b,g), martial arts (b,g), mountain biking (b,g), soccer (b,g), volleyball (b,g); coed interscholastic: ballet, basketball, bicycling, cheering, cooperative games, dance, freestyle skiing, Frisbee, gymnastics, hockey, ice skating, modern dance, running, skiing (downhill); coed intramural: alpine skiing, ball hockey, baseball, basketball, Cosom hockey, Frisbee, golf, hockey, rugby, running, softball. 2 PE instructors.

Computers Computers are regularly used in accounting classes. Computer network features include on-campus library services, Internet access. The school has a published electronic and media policy.

Contact Ms. Sue Johnson, Director of Admissions. 416-487-7381 Ext. 227. Fax: 416-487-8190. E-mail: admissions@fieldstonedayschool.org. Web site: www.fieldstonedayschool.org.

THE FIRST ACADEMY

2667 Bruton Boulevard
Orlando, Florida 32805
Head of School: Dr. Steve D. Whitaker

General Information Coeducational day college-preparatory, arts, religious studies, and technology school, affiliated with Christian faith. Grades K4–12. Founded: 1986. Setting: suburban. 140-acre campus. 3 buildings on campus. Approved or accredited by Association of Christian Schools International, Southern Association of Colleges and Schools, Southern Association of Independent Schools, and Florida Department of Education. Endowment: $2.5 million. Total enrollment: 975. Upper school average class size: 17. Upper school faculty-student ratio: 1:10. There are 180 required school days per year for Upper School students. Upper School students typically attend 5 days per week. The average school day consists of 6 hours.

Upper School Student Profile Grade 9: 105 students (52 boys, 53 girls); Grade 10: 81 students (40 boys, 41 girls); Grade 11: 87 students (47 boys, 40 girls); Grade 12: 69 students (32 boys, 37 girls). 100% of students are Christian.

Faculty School total: 85. In upper school: 15 men, 18 women; 12 have advanced degrees.

Subjects Offered Advanced chemistry, advanced computer applications, advanced math, Advanced Placement courses, advanced studio art-AP, algebra, American government, American history, American history-AP, American literature, American literature-AP, analytic geometry, anatomy, ancient world history, art, art-AP, athletics, audio visual/media, band, Bible, Bible studies, biology, biology-AP, British history, British literature, British literature (honors), British literature-AP, broadcasting, calculus, calculus-AP, chemistry, chemistry-AP, choir, Christian doctrine, Christian ethics, Christian testament, church history, comparative government and politics, composition, computer graphics, computer programming, computer science, creative writing, drama, economics, economics and history, electives, English, English composition, English literature, English literature-AP, English-AP, ethics, European history, European history-AP, expository writing, fine arts, finite math, forensics, French language-AP, genetics, geometry, government, grammar, health, history, history-AP, honors algebra, honors English, honors geometry, honors U.S. history, honors world history, integrated mathematics, journalism, keyboarding, Latin, Latin-AP, life management skills, life skills, literature, literature-AP, marine biology, mathematics, media communications, music, newspaper, philosophy, physical education, physical science, physics, physiology, politics, pottery, pre-algebra, pre-calculus, religion, SAT/ACT preparation, science, social sciences, social studies, sociology, Spanish, Spanish-AP, speech, speech and debate, theater, trigonometry, U.S. government, U.S. government and politics-AP, world history, world history-AP, world literature, writing, yearbook.

Graduation Requirements Arts and fine arts (art, music, dance, drama), computer science, English, foreign language, mathematics, physical education (includes health), religion (includes Bible studies and theology), science, social sciences, social studies (includes history).

Special Academic Programs Advanced Placement exam preparation; honors section; independent study; study at local college for college credit; academic accommodation for the gifted.

College Admission Counseling 77 students graduated in 2010; all went to college, including Clemson University; Florida State University; Liberty University; Samford University; University of Central Florida; University of Florida.

Student Life Upper grades have uniform requirement, student council, honor system. Discipline rests primarily with faculty. Attendance at religious services is required.

Summer Programs Remediation, enrichment, sports, art/fine arts programs offered; session focuses on academics and athletic camps; held on campus; accepts boys and girls; open to students from other schools. 200 students usually enrolled. 2011 schedule: June 1 to July 3. Application deadline: March 1.

Tuition and Aid Day student tuition: $12,450–$12,750. Tuition installment plan (SMART Tuition Payment Plan, monthly payment plans). Need-based scholarship grants available.

Admissions Traditional secondary-level entrance grade is 9. Otis-Lennon School Ability Test and Stanford Achievement Test required. Deadline for receipt of application materials: none. Application fee required: $100. On-campus interview required.

Athletics Interscholastic: baseball (boys), basketball (b,g), cheering (g), cross-country running (b,g), diving (b,g), flag football (b), football (b), golf (b,g), lacrosse (b), physical fitness (b,g), physical training (b,g), power lifting (b), running (b,g), soccer (b,g), softball (g), strength & conditioning (b,g), swimming and diving (b,g), tennis (b,g), track and field (b,g), volleyball (g), weight lifting (b), wrestling (b); coed intramural: basketball. 6 PE instructors, 18 coaches, 1 athletic trainer.

Computers Computers are regularly used in art, computer applications, English, foreign language, history, journalism, keyboarding, library, library skills, media production, science, yearbook classes. Computer network features include on-campus library services, Internet access, Internet filtering or blocking technology. Students grades are available online. The school has a published electronic and media policy.

Contact Janie Weber, Admissions Assistant. 407-206-8602. Fax: 407-206-8700. E-mail: janieweber@thefirstacademy.org. Web site: www.TheFirstAcademy.org.

FIRST BAPTIST ACADEMY

PO Box 868
Dallas, Texas 75221
Head of School: Mr. Brian Littlefield

General Information Coeducational day college-preparatory, arts, religious studies, and technology school, affiliated with Baptist Church, Southern Baptist Convention. Grades K4–12. Founded: 1972. Setting: urban. 1 building on campus. Approved or accredited by Accreditation Commission of the Texas Association of Baptist Schools, Southern Association of Colleges and Schools, and Texas Department of Education. Endowment: $1.2 million. Total enrollment: 366. Upper school average class size: 18. Upper school faculty-student ratio: 1:8. There are 176 required school days per year for Upper School students. Upper School students typically attend 5 days per week. The average school day consists of 7 hours.

Upper School Student Profile 50% of students are Baptist, Southern Baptist Convention.

Faculty School total: 49. In upper school: 12 men, 16 women; 11 have advanced degrees.

Subjects Offered Algebra, American history, Bible, biology, calculus, calculus-AP, chemistry, choir, computer skills, concert band, desktop publishing, drawing, economics, English, English literature-AP, English-AP, fine arts, French, geometry, government-AP, history, Latin, math analysis, photography, physics, pre-calculus, Spanish, theater arts, world history.

Graduation Requirements Algebra, American history, arts and fine arts (art, music, dance, drama), Basic programming, Bible studies, biology, chemistry, economics, electives, English, French, government, history, keyboarding, Latin, mathematics, physical education (includes health), physics, science, Spanish, U.S. history, world geography, service hours are required for graduation. Community service is required.

Special Academic Programs 4 Advanced Placement exams for which test preparation is offered; honors section.

College Admission Counseling 50 students graduated in 2010; all went to college, including Baylor University; Texas A&M University; Texas Tech University; The University of Texas at Austin.

Student Life Upper grades have uniform requirement, student council, honor system. Discipline rests primarily with faculty. Attendance at religious services is required.

Tuition and Aid Day student tuition: $11,275. Tuition installment plan (FACTS Tuition Payment Plan). Need-based scholarship grants available. In 2010–11, 10% of upper-school students received aid.

Admissions Traditional secondary-level entrance grade is 9. ERB (grade level), ISEE or Stanford Achievement Test required. Deadline for receipt of application materials: none. Application fee required: $75. Interview required.

Athletics Interscholastic: aquatics (boys, girls), baseball (b), basketball (b,g), cheering (g), diving (b,g), football (b), golf (b,g), softball (g), strength & conditioning (b,g), swimming and diving (b,g), tennis (b,g), track and field (b,g), volleyball (g), wrestling (b). 2 PE instructors, 25 coaches.

Computers Computers are regularly used in desktop publishing classes. Computer resources include on-campus library services, Internet access. Students grades are available online. The school has a published electronic and media policy.

Contact Susan Money, Director of Public Relations. 214-969-7861. Fax: 214-969-7797. E-mail: smoney@firstdallas.org.

FIRST PRESBYTERIAN DAY SCHOOL

5671 Calvin Drive
Macon, Georgia 31210
Head of School: Mr. Gregg E. Thompson

General Information Coeducational day college-preparatory, arts, and religious studies school, affiliated with Christian faith, Presbyterian Church in America. Grades PK–12. Founded: 1970. Setting: suburban. Nearest major city is Atlanta. 64-acre campus. 7 buildings on campus. Approved or accredited by Christian Schools International, Georgia Independent School Association, Southern Association of Colleges and Schools, Southern Association of Independent Schools, and Georgia Department of Education. Endowment: $3.1 million. Total enrollment: 976. Upper school average class size: 18. Upper school faculty-student ratio: 1:12. There are 180 required school days per year for Upper School students. Upper School students typically attend 5 days per week. The average school day consists of 7 hours.

Upper School Student Profile Grade 9: 90 students (44 boys, 46 girls); Grade 10: 85 students (43 boys, 42 girls); Grade 11: 96 students (47 boys, 49 girls); Grade 12: 82 students (42 boys, 40 girls). 96% of students are Christian, Presbyterian Church in America.

Faculty School total: 73. In upper school: 24 men, 26 women; 40 have advanced degrees.

Subjects Offered 3-dimensional design, accounting, advanced biology, advanced chemistry, Advanced Placement courses, advanced studio art-AP, algebra, American literature, anatomy and physiology, art, art appreciation, art-AP, band, Bible, biology, biology-AP, British literature, calculus-AP, chemistry, chorus, comparative religion, computer applications, debate, economics, English, English language and composition-AP, English literature and composition-AP, family living, French, geometry, government, government-AP, honors algebra, honors English, honors geometry, journalism, Latin, Latin-AP, logic, model United Nations, modern European history, music appreciation, physical science, physics, pre-calculus, psychology, Spanish, statistics, studio art-AP, theater, U.S. government and politics-AP, U.S. history, U.S. history-AP, world history.

Graduation Requirements Arts and fine arts (art, music, dance, drama), Bible, computer skills, electives, English, foreign language, mathematics, physical education (includes health), science, social studies (includes history), service to distressed populations.

Special Academic Programs 12 Advanced Placement exams for which test preparation is offered; honors section.

College Admission Counseling 81 students graduated in 2010; all went to college, including Auburn University; Georgia College & State University; Georgia Institute of Technology; Mercer University; Samford University; University of Georgia. 34% scored over 600 on SAT critical reading, 43% scored over 600 on SAT math, 38% scored over 600 on SAT writing, 36% scored over 1800 on combined SAT.

Student Life Upper grades have uniform requirement, student council, honor system. Discipline rests primarily with faculty. Attendance at religious services is required.

Summer Programs Remediation, enrichment, sports, art/fine arts programs offered; session focuses on reading and study skills, mathematics enrichment, science, sports; held on campus; accepts boys and girls; open to students from other schools. 200 students usually enrolled. 2011 schedule: June 10 to July 30. Application deadline: May 15.

Tuition and Aid Day student tuition: $11,300. Tuition installment plan (monthly payment plans). Tuition reduction for siblings, merit scholarship grants, need-based scholarship grants available. In 2010–11, 31% of upper-school students received aid; total upper-school merit-scholarship money awarded: $4000. Total amount of financial aid awarded in 2010–11: $874,000.

Admissions Traditional secondary-level entrance grade is 9. CTP, Math Placement Exam or writing sample required. Deadline for receipt of application materials: February 1. Application fee required: $50. Interview recommended.

Athletics Interscholastic: baseball (boys), basketball (b,g), cheering (g), cross-country running (b,g), dance team (g), football (b), golf (b,g), soccer (b,g), softball (g), swimming and diving (b,g), tennis (b,g), track and field (b,g), volleyball (g), wrestling (b,g); intramural: football (b), indoor soccer (b,g), soccer (b,g), strength & conditioning (b,g), weight training (b,g). 3 PE instructors, 5 coaches, 1 athletic trainer.

Computers Computers are regularly used in all classes. Computer network features include on-campus library services, online commercial services, Internet access, Internet filtering or blocking technology. Campus intranet and computer access in designated common areas are available to students. Students grades are available online. The school has a published electronic and media policy.

Contact Mrs. Cheri Frame, Director of Admissions. 478-477-6505 Ext. 107. Fax: 478-477-2804. E-mail: admissions@fpdmacon.org. Web site: www.fpdmacon.org.

FISHBURNE MILITARY SCHOOL

225 South Wayne Avenue
Waynesboro, Virginia 22980
Head of School: Col. Roy F. Zinser

General Information Boys' boarding and day college-preparatory, Army Junior ROTC, and military school. Grades 7–PG. Founded: 1879. Setting: small town. Nearest major city is Washington, DC. Students are housed in single-sex dormitories. 10-acre campus. 4 buildings on campus. Approved or accredited by Southern Association of Colleges and Schools, Virginia Association of Independent Schools, and Virginia Department of Education. Endowment: $1.3 million. Total enrollment: 170. Upper school average class size: 9. Upper school faculty-student ratio: 1:9.

Upper School Student Profile Grade 9: 35 students (35 boys); Grade 10: 45 students (45 boys); Grade 11: 50 students (50 boys); Grade 12: 45 students (45 boys); Postgraduate: 15 students (15 boys). 90% of students are boarding students. 17 states are represented in upper school student body. 5% are international students. International students from Aruba, Mexico, Republic of Korea, Russian Federation, Saudi Arabia, and Taiwan; 5 other countries represented in student body.

Faculty School total: 24. In upper school: 20 men, 4 women; 5 have advanced degrees; 6 reside on campus.

Subjects Offered Algebra, American history, American literature, biology, calculus, chemistry, computer programming, computer science, computer technologies, creative writing, driver education, earth science, English, English literature, environmental science, French, geography, geology, geometry, government/civics, grammar, health, history, JROTC, mathematics, military science, music, physical education, physics, science, social studies, Spanish, speech, trigonometry, world history.

Graduation Requirements Computer science, English, foreign language, JROTC, mathematics, physical education (includes health), science, social studies (includes history).

Special Academic Programs Advanced Placement exam preparation; honors section; study at local college for college credit; remedial reading and/or remedial writing; remedial math.

College Admission Counseling 47 students graduated in 2010; all went to college, including Miami University; Penn State University Park; United States Military Academy; University of Virginia; Virginia Military Institute; Virginia Polytechnic Institute and State University. Median SAT critical reading: 470, median SAT math: 530, median SAT writing: 540, median combined SAT: 1535. 4.5% scored over 600 on SAT critical reading, 11.4% scored over 600 on SAT math, 4.5% scored over 600 on SAT writing, 2.3% scored over 1800 on combined SAT.

Student Life Upper grades have uniform requirement, student council, honor system. Discipline rests equally with students and faculty.

Admissions Traditional secondary-level entrance grade is 10. For fall 2010, 200 students applied for upper-level admission, 180 were accepted, 65 enrolled. Deadline for receipt of application materials: none. Application fee required: $50. Interview required.

Athletics Interscholastic: aquatics, baseball, basketball, canoeing/kayaking, cooperative games, cross-country running, drill team; intramural: baseball, basketball, billiards, bowling, fitness. 1 PE instructor, 15 coaches, 1 athletic trainer.

Computers Computers are regularly used in English, foreign language, history, mathematics, science classes. Computer network features include on-campus library services, Internet access, Internet filtering or blocking technology. Campus intranet and student e-mail accounts are available to students. The school has a published electronic and media policy.

Contact Mr. Brock Selkow, Director of Admissions. 800-946-7773. Fax: 540-946-7738. E-mail: bselkow@fishburne.org. Web site: www.fishburne.org.

FLINT HILL SCHOOL
3320 Jermantown Road
Oakton, Virginia 22124
Head of School: Mr. John Thomas

General Information Coeducational day college-preparatory, arts, technology, and athletics, community service school. Grades JK–12. Founded: 1956. Setting: suburban. Nearest major city is Washington, DC. 45-acre campus. 1 building on campus. Approved or accredited by Association of Independent Schools of Greater Washington, Virginia Association of Independent Schools, and Virginia Department of Education. Member of National Association of Independent Schools and Secondary School Admission Test Board. Endowment: $1.4 million. Total enrollment: 1,110. Upper school average class size: 18. Upper school faculty-student ratio: 1:8. There are 168 required school days per year for Upper School students. Upper School students typically attend 5 days per week. The average school day consists of 6 hours and 30 minutes.

Upper School Student Profile Grade 9: 118 students (65 boys, 53 girls); Grade 10: 122 students (77 boys, 45 girls); Grade 11: 120 students (71 boys, 49 girls); Grade 12: 125 students (60 boys, 65 girls).

Faculty School total: 114. In upper school: 22 men, 34 women; 49 have advanced degrees.

Subjects Offered 20th century history, advanced chemistry, algebra, anatomy, art, ballet, biology, biology-AP, British literature, calculus, calculus-AP, ceramics, chemistry, chemistry-AP, Chinese, choir, choral music, chorus, civil rights, community service, computer animation, computer graphics, computer programming, computer science-AP, concert band, concert choir, creative writing, digital imaging, discrete mathematics, drama, drawing, drawing and design, earth science, economics-AP, English, English literature, English literature and composition-AP, English-AP, environmental science, environmental science-AP, environmental studies, European civilization, European history, fine arts, French, French language-AP, French literature-AP, geometry, government-AP, history, history of music, honors English, improvisation, jazz band, jazz dance, Latin, Latin American studies, Latin-AP, macro/microeconomics-AP, marine science, modern European history-AP, music, music history, music theory, music theory-AP, orchestra, ornithology, photography, physical education, physics, physics-AP, physiology, playwriting, pre-calculus, psychology, psychology-AP, science, sculpture, senior project, Shakespeare, short story, Spanish, Spanish-AP, statistics-AP, studio art, study skills, symphonic band, theater, trigonometry, U.S. history, U.S. history-AP, world religions.

Graduation Requirements Arts and fine arts (art, music, dance, drama), athletics, English, foreign language, history, mathematics, physical education (includes health), science, senior project. Community service is required.

Special Academic Programs 23 Advanced Placement exams for which test preparation is offered; honors section; academic accommodation for the musically talented and the artistically talented.

College Admission Counseling 115 students graduated in 2010; 114 went to college, including Cornell University; James Madison University; The College of William and Mary; University of Virginia; Virginia Polytechnic Institute and State University; Wake Forest University. Other: 1 entered a postgraduate year. Median SAT critical reading: 590, median SAT math: 600, median SAT writing: 630, median combined SAT: 1840, median composite ACT: 27. 45% scored over 600 on SAT critical reading, 47% scored over 600 on SAT math, 57% scored over 600 on SAT writing, 53% scored over 1800 on combined SAT, 50% scored over 26 on composite ACT.

Student Life Upper grades have specified standards of dress, student council, honor system. Discipline rests primarily with faculty.

Summer Programs Remediation, enrichment, advancement, ESL, sports, art/fine arts, rigorous outdoor training, computer instruction programs offered; session focuses on academics, arts, enrichment, travel, athletics and service; held both on and off campus; held at various domestic and international locations; accepts boys and girls; open to students from other schools. 815 students usually enrolled. 2011 schedule: June 20 to July 29. Application deadline: none.

Tuition and Aid Day student tuition: $28,335. Tuition installment plan (Insured Tuition Payment Plan, FACTS Tuition Payment Plan, monthly payment plans, one

payment, two payments, or ten payments). Need-based scholarship grants available. In 2010–11, 17% of upper-school students received aid. Total amount of financial aid awarded in 2010–11: $1,661,780.

Admissions Traditional secondary-level entrance grade is 9. For fall 2010, 203 students applied for upper-level admission, 137 were accepted, 74 enrolled. ISEE, PSAT, SAT or SSAT required. Deadline for receipt of application materials: January 21. Application fee required: $75. On-campus interview required.

Athletics Interscholastic: aerobics/dance (girls), baseball (b), basketball (b,g), cross-country running (b,g), dance (g), dance team (g), diving (b,g), football (b), lacrosse (b,g), self defense (g), soccer (b,g), softball (g), swimming and diving (b,g), tennis (b,g), track and field (b,g), volleyball (g); coed interscholastic: golf, hockey, ice hockey, independent competitive sports, physical fitness, running, strength & conditioning, yoga; coed intramural: aerobics/dance, canoeing/kayaking, climbing, dance, fitness, modern dance, mountaineering, outdoor activities, outdoor education, physical fitness, physical training, strength & conditioning, wall climbing, weight training, winter soccer. 16 coaches, 2 athletic trainers.

Computers Computers are regularly used in all academic classes. Computer network features include on-campus library services, online commercial services, Internet access, wireless campus network, Internet filtering or blocking technology. Campus intranet, student e-mail accounts, and computer access in designated common areas are available to students. Students grades are available online. The school has a published electronic and media policy.

Contact Mr. Chris Pryor, Director of Admission and Financial Aid. 703-584-2300. Fax: 703-242-0718. E-mail: cpryor@flinthill.org. Web site: www.flinthill.org.

FLINTRIDGE PREPARATORY SCHOOL
4543 Crown Avenue
La Canada Flintridge, California 91011
Head of School: Peter H. Bachmann

General Information Coeducational day college-preparatory school. Grades 7–12. Founded: 1933. Setting: suburban. Nearest major city is Pasadena. 7-acre campus. 8 buildings on campus. Approved or accredited by California Association of Independent Schools, The College Board, and Western Association of Schools and Colleges. Member of National Association of Independent Schools. Total enrollment: 519. Upper school average class size: 15. Upper school faculty-student ratio: 1:8.

Upper School Student Profile Grade 9: 109 students (53 boys, 56 girls); Grade 10: 101 students (51 boys, 50 girls); Grade 11: 102 students (49 boys, 53 girls); Grade 12: 96 students (46 boys, 50 girls).

Faculty School total: 66. In upper school: 36 men, 29 women; 46 have advanced degrees.

Subjects Offered Algebra, American history, American literature, art, art history, biology, calculus, ceramics, chemistry, computer math, computer programming, computer science, creative writing, dance, drama, driver education, earth science, economics, English, English literature, European history, expository writing, fine arts, French, geometry, government/civics, grammar, history, Latin, mathematics, music, photography, physical education, physics, physiology, psychology, science, social studies, Spanish, statistics, theater, trigonometry, world history, world literature, writing.

Graduation Requirements Arts and fine arts (art, music, dance, drama), English, foreign language, mathematics, science, social studies (includes history).

Special Academic Programs Advanced Placement exam preparation; honors section; independent study; study abroad; academic accommodation for the gifted, the musically talented, and the artistically talented.

College Admission Counseling 88 students graduated in 2009; all went to college, including Cornell University; Princeton University; Stanford University; University of California, Berkeley; University of California, Los Angeles; University of Southern California. Median SAT critical reading: 680, median SAT math: 690, median SAT writing: 690. 87% scored over 600 on SAT critical reading, 87% scored over 600 on SAT math, 87% scored over 600 on SAT writing.

Student Life Upper grades have specified standards of dress, student council, honor system. Discipline rests equally with students and faculty.

Admissions Traditional secondary-level entrance grade is 9. For fall 2009, 231 students applied for upper-level admission, 107 were accepted, 59 enrolled. ISEE required. Deadline for receipt of application materials: January 31. Application fee required. On-campus interview required.

Athletics Interscholastic: aquatics (boys, girls), baseball (b), basketball (b,g), cheering (g), cross-country running (b,g), diving (b,g), football (b), soccer (b,g), softball (g), swimming and diving (b,g), tennis (b,g), track and field (b,g), volleyball (b,g), water polo (b,g), winter soccer (b,g); coed interscholastic: equestrian sports, golf. 4 PE instructors, 41 coaches, 1 athletic trainer.

Computers Computers are regularly used in foreign language, mathematics, science classes. Computer network features include on-campus library services, online commercial services, Internet access.

Contact Arthur Stetson, Director of Admissions. 818-949-5515. Fax: 818-952-6247. Web site: www.flintridgeprep.org.

FLINT RIVER ACADEMY

11556 East Highway 85
Woodbury, Georgia 30293
Head of School: Mrs. Michele Purvis
General Information Coeducational day college-preparatory, arts, and technology school. Grades PK–12. Founded: 1967. Setting: rural. Nearest major city is Atlanta. 8-acre campus. 3 buildings on campus. Approved or accredited by Georgia Accrediting Commission and Southern Association of Colleges and Schools. Total enrollment: 340. Upper school average class size: 18. Upper school faculty-student ratio: 1:14.
Upper School Student Profile Grade 9: 28 students (16 boys, 12 girls); Grade 10: 16 students (6 boys, 10 girls); Grade 11: 21 students (10 boys, 11 girls); Grade 12: 28 students (16 boys, 12 girls).
Faculty School total: 45. In upper school: 2 men, 12 women; 10 have advanced degrees.
Subjects Offered Accounting, algebra, American history, American literature, art, biology, business, business skills, calculus, chemistry, computer math, computer science, creative writing, drama, earth science, economics, English, fine arts, geography, geometry, government/civics, grammar, health, history, mathematics, music, physical education, physics, physiology, science, social sciences, social studies, Spanish, Spanish-AP, speech, theater, trigonometry, typing, world history, world literature.
Graduation Requirements Arts and fine arts (art, music, dance, drama), business skills (includes word processing), computer science, English, foreign language, mathematics, physical education (includes health), science, social sciences, social studies (includes history).
Special Academic Programs Advanced Placement exam preparation; honors section; study at local college for college credit; academic accommodation for the musically talented and the artistically talented; remedial math.
College Admission Counseling 21 students graduated in 2010; 16 went to college, including Auburn University; Columbus State University; Georgia Southern University; University of Georgia; Valdosta State University. Other: 5 went to work. Median SAT critical reading: 210, median SAT math: 527, median SAT writing: 513, median combined SAT: 1544, median composite ACT: 20.
Student Life Upper grades have specified standards of dress, student council, honor system. Discipline rests primarily with faculty.
Tuition and Aid Day student tuition: $6190. Tuition installment plan (monthly payment plans). Tuition reduction for third sibling available.
Admissions Traditional secondary-level entrance grade is 9. For fall 2010, 10 students applied for upper-level admission, 10 were accepted, 10 enrolled. ACT-Explore required. Deadline for receipt of application materials: none. Application fee required: $50. On-campus interview required.
Athletics Interscholastic: baseball (boys), basketball (b,g), cheering (g), cross-country running (b,g), football (b), golf (b,g), softball (g), tennis (b,g), track and field (b,g); intramural: baseball (b), basketball (b,g), cheering (g), dance team (g), golf (g), soccer (b), softball (g), tennis (b,g), volleyball (b,g), weight lifting (b,g), weight training (b); coed intramural: ropes courses. 2 coaches.
Computers Computer network features include on-campus library services, Internet access.
Contact Ms. Ida Ann Dunn, Guidance Counselor. 706-553-2541. Fax: 706-553-9777. E-mail: counselor@flinriveracademy.com. Web site: www.flinriveracademy.com.

FLORIDA AIR ACADEMY

1950 South Academy Drive
Melbourne, Florida 32901
Head of School: James Dwight
General Information Coeducational boarding and day college-preparatory, arts, technology, computer science, aerospace science, and military school. Grades 7–12. Founded: 1961. Setting: suburban. Nearest major city is Orlando. Students are housed in single-sex dormitories. 15-acre campus. 13 buildings on campus. Approved or accredited by Florida Council of Independent Schools, Southern Association of Colleges and Schools, and Florida Department of Education. Member of Secondary School Admission Test Board. Total enrollment: 237. Upper school average class size: 16. Upper school faculty-student ratio: 1:11.
Upper School Student Profile Grade 9: 19 students (13 boys, 6 girls); Grade 10: 52 students (40 boys, 12 girls); Grade 11: 61 students (49 boys, 12 girls); Grade 12: 66 students (49 boys, 17 girls). 65% of students are boarding students. 70% are state residents. 11 states are represented in upper school student body. 15% are international students. International students from Bahamas, Bermuda, Cayman Islands, China, Republic of Korea, and Taiwan; 34 other countries represented in student body.
Faculty School total: 28. In upper school: 18 men, 10 women; 5 have advanced degrees; 4 reside on campus.
Subjects Offered ACT preparation, advanced computer applications, aerospace education, aerospace science, algebra, American history, American literature, animation, applied music, art, band, biology, calculus, calculus-AP, chemistry, chorus, computer applications, computer art, computer graphics, computer programming, computer science, computer technology certification, driver education, economics, English, English literature and composition-AP, English literature-AP, English-AP, ESL, flight instruction, geometry, government/civics, graphic arts, graphic design,

health education, history, history-AP, honors algebra, honors English, honors geometry, honors U.S. history, honors world history, JROTC, mathematics, music, music appreciation, oceanography, physical education, physics, physics-AP, pre-calculus, psychology, SAT preparation, science, scuba diving, social studies, sociology, Spanish, Spanish language-AP, TOEFL preparation, trigonometry, U.S. government, world history, yearbook.
Graduation Requirements Aerospace education, arts and fine arts (art, music, dance, drama), computer education, English, mathematics, physical fitness, ROTC, science, social sciences, Spanish, 100 community service hours.
Special Academic Programs Advanced Placement exam preparation; honors section; study at local college for college credit; academic accommodation for the gifted; remedial reading and/or remedial writing; remedial math; ESL (20 students enrolled).
College Admission Counseling 84 students graduated in 2010; 82 went to college, including Florida Atlantic University; Florida Institute of Technology; Florida International University; Florida State University; University of Central Florida; University of Florida. Other: 2 entered military service.
Student Life Upper grades have uniform requirement, student council, honor system. Discipline rests primarily with faculty.
Summer Programs Remediation, enrichment, advancement, ESL, sports, computer instruction programs offered; session focuses on academics and activities; held on campus; accepts boys and girls; open to students from other schools. 120 students usually enrolled. 2011 schedule: June 18 to July 29. Application deadline: May 15.
Tuition and Aid Day student tuition: $10,500; 7-day tuition and room/board: $31,500. Tuition installment plan (individually arranged payment plans, student loan providers). Tuition reduction for siblings, need-based scholarship grants available. In 2010–11, 40% of upper-school students received aid. Total amount of financial aid awarded in 2010–11: $650,000.
Admissions Traditional secondary-level entrance grade is 9. For fall 2010, 310 students applied for upper-level admission, 261 were accepted, 237 enrolled. Achievement tests, admissions testing, any standardized test, PSAT and SAT for applicants to grade 11 and 12 or TOEFL required. Deadline for receipt of application materials: none. Application fee required: $100. Interview required.
Athletics Interscholastic: baseball (boys), basketball (b,g), cheering (g), cross-country running (b,g), football (b), golf (b), power lifting (b), soccer (b,g), softball (b,g), tennis (b,g), volleyball (b,g), weight lifting (b), winter soccer (b,g); intramural: aerobics/Nautilus (b), baseball (b), basketball (b,g), cooperative games (b), equestrian sports (b,g), flag football (b), floor hockey (b,g), football (b), Frisbee (b), golf (b), ice skating (b), power lifting (b), soccer (b,g), softball (b,g), touch football (b), volleyball (b,g), weight lifting (b), winter soccer (b,g); coed interscholastic: aerobics/dance, aquatics, climbing, drill team, JROTC drill, martial arts, Nautilus, physical fitness, physical training, rock climbing, running, scuba diving, strength & conditioning, swimming and diving, track and field, weight training, wrestling; coed intramural: billiards, bowling, canoeing/kayaking, independent competitive sports, jogging, JROTC drill, life saving, martial arts, Nautilus, outdoor activities, outdoor education, outdoor recreation, physical fitness, physical training, rock climbing, roller skating, ropes courses, running, scuba diving, self defense, skateboarding, street hockey, surfing, swimming and diving, table tennis, tai chi, tennis, ultimate Frisbee, weight training, windsurfing. 4 PE instructors, 6 coaches, 1 athletic trainer.
Computers Computers are regularly used in aerospace science, aviation, college planning, data processing, desktop publishing, English, foreign language, graphic arts, graphic design, information technology, mathematics, publishing, research skills, SAT preparation, science, social sciences, writing classes. Computer network features include on-campus library services, Internet access, wireless campus network, Internet filtering or blocking technology. Student e-mail accounts and computer access in designated common areas are available to students. Students grades are available online. The school has a published electronic and media policy.
Contact Tiffany D. Malcolm, Director of Admissions. 321-723-3211 Ext. 30012. Fax: 321-676-0422. E-mail: tmalcolm@flair.com. Web site: www.flair.com.

FONTBONNE ACADEMY

930 Brook Road
Milton, Massachusetts 02186
Head of School: Ms. Mary Ellen Barnes
General Information Girls' day college-preparatory, arts, religious studies, and technology school, affiliated with Roman Catholic Church. Grades 9–12. Founded: 1954. Setting: suburban. Nearest major city is Boston. 15-acre campus. 1 building on campus. Approved or accredited by Association of Independent Schools in New England, New England Association of Schools and Colleges, and Massachusetts Department of Education. Total enrollment: 385. Upper school average class size: 18. Upper school faculty-student ratio: 1:10. There are 180 required school days per year for Upper School students. Upper School students typically attend 5 days per week. The average school day consists of 7 hours and 25 minutes.
Upper School Student Profile 80% of students are Roman Catholic.
Faculty School total: 38. In upper school: 5 men, 33 women; 34 have advanced degrees.
Subjects Offered 20th century American writers, advanced computer applications, algebra, American history, American history-AP, American literature, analytic geometry, applied music, art, art-AP, biology, biology-AP, British literature (honors), calculus-AP, career/college preparation, Catholic belief and practice, chemistry, choral

music, chorus, church history, college admission preparation, college counseling, computer music, computer programming, conceptual physics, ecology, environmental systems, electronic music, English, English literature, English-AP, finance, fine arts, French, French-AP, freshman seminar, geometry, guidance, health, instrumental music, integrated mathematics, jazz ensemble, Latin, literature by women, media communications, physical education, physics, physiology, pre-calculus, research skills, science, social justice, social studies, sociology, Spanish, Spanish-AP, theater production, theology, trigonometry, vocal jazz, women's literature, world history.

Graduation Requirements Arts and fine arts (art, music, dance, drama), biology, English, foreign language, mathematics, physical education (includes health), physical science, theology, U.S. history, U.S. literature, world history, 100 hours of community service.

Special Academic Programs Advanced Placement exam preparation; honors section; independent study.

College Admission Counseling 136 students graduated in 2009; 115 went to college, including Boston University; Providence College; Saint Anselm College; Suffolk University; University of Massachusetts Amherst; University of New Hampshire. Other: 1 entered a postgraduate year, 2 had other specific plans.

Student Life Upper grades have uniform requirement, student council, honor system. Discipline rests primarily with faculty. Attendance at religious services is required.

Tuition and Aid Day student tuition: $12,000. Tuition installment plan (FACTS Tuition Payment Plan, 2-payment plan). Merit scholarship grants, need-based scholarship grants, tuition reduction for daughters of employees, work-study positions available.

Admissions Traditional secondary-level entrance grade is 9. For fall 2009, 570 students applied for upper-level admission, 310 were accepted, 100 enrolled. Archdiocese of Boston High School entrance exam provided by STS, High School Placement Test or standardized test scores required. Deadline for receipt of application materials: December 1. Application fee required: $30.

Athletics Interscholastic: alpine skiing, basketball, cheering, cross-country running, dance team, diving, golf, ice hockey, indoor track & field, lacrosse, skiing (downhill), soccer, softball, swimming and diving, tennis, track and field, volleyball, winter (indoor) track; intramural: basketball, dance, equestrian sports, flag football, floor hockey, horseback riding, lacrosse, Nautilus, physical fitness, physical training, strength & conditioning. 3 PE instructors, 26 coaches, 3 athletic trainers.

Computers Computers are regularly used in all classes. Computer network features include on-campus library services, online commercial services, Internet access, wireless campus network, Internet filtering or blocking technology. Student e-mail accounts are available to students. Students grades are available online. The school has a published electronic and media policy.

Contact Admissions. 617-696-3241. Fax: 617-696-7688. E-mail: bhiggins@fontbonneacademy.org. Web site: www.fontbonneacademy.org.

FONTBONNE HALL ACADEMY

9901 Shore Road
Brooklyn, New York 11209
Head of School: Sr. Dolores F. Crepeau, CSJ

General Information Girls' day college-preparatory, arts, religious studies, and technology school, affiliated with Roman Catholic Church. Grades 9–12. Founded: 1937. Nearest major city is New York. 5 buildings on campus. Approved or accredited by Middle States Association of Colleges and Schools and New York State Board of Regents. Total enrollment: 521. Upper school average class size: 20. Upper school faculty-student ratio: 1:14. There are 180 required school days per year for Upper School students. Upper School students typically attend 5 days per week. The average school day consists of 6 hours and 30 minutes.

Upper School Student Profile Grade 9: 130 students (130 girls); Grade 10: 134 students (134 girls); Grade 11: 134 students (134 girls); Grade 12: 123 students (123 girls). 90% of students are Roman Catholic.

Faculty School total: 40. In upper school: 4 men, 36 women; 34 have advanced degrees.

Subjects Offered Advanced chemistry, algebra, American literature-AP, anatomy and physiology, anthropology, art, biology-AP, calculus, calculus-AP, chemistry, chorus, computer multimedia, computers, earth science, economics, English, forensics, genetics, government, health, history-AP, Italian, Latin, marine science, mathematics, music, photography, physical education, physics, religion, Spanish, U.S. history, world geography, world history.

Graduation Requirements Algebra, American government, American history, American literature, art, biology, British literature, chemistry, college counseling, college writing, computer applications, economics, electives, English, European civilization, foreign language, geometry, government, guidance, health, Internet research, lab science, music, physical education (includes health), religion (includes Bible studies and theology), science, world civilizations, Board of Regents requirements, 60 hours of service.

Special Academic Programs Advanced Placement exam preparation; honors section; study at local college for college credit.

College Admission Counseling 143 students graduated in 2010; all went to college, including Columbia University; Fordham University; Manhattan College; New York University; The Catholic University of America; The Johns Hopkins University. Median SAT critical reading: 550, median SAT math: 550, median SAT writing: 600, median combined SAT: 1700.

Student Life Upper grades have uniform requirement, student council. Discipline rests primarily with faculty. Attendance at religious services is required.

Summer Programs Remediation, enrichment, sports programs offered; session focuses on preparation for Regents exams; held on campus; accepts girls; not open to students from other schools. 50 students usually enrolled. 2011 schedule: August 1 to August 12. Application deadline: June 27.

Tuition and Aid Day student tuition: $7850. Tuition installment plan (monthly payment plans, 3 payments per year). Tuition reduction for siblings, merit scholarship grants, need-based loans available. In 2010–11, 20% of upper-school students received aid; total upper-school merit-scholarship money awarded: $100,000. Total amount of financial aid awarded in 2010–11: $107,500.

Admissions Traditional secondary-level entrance grade is 9. For fall 2010, 437 students applied for upper-level admission, 296 were accepted, 136 enrolled. Diocesan Entrance Exam required. Deadline for receipt of application materials: February 4. Application fee required: $250. Interview required.

Athletics Interscholastic: aquatics, baseball, basketball, cheering, cross-country running, dance, dance squad, drill team, fishing, golf, running, soccer, softball, swimming and diving, tennis, track and field, volleyball. 2 PE instructors, 10 coaches, 2 athletic trainers.

Computers Computers are regularly used in all academic classes. Computer network features include on-campus library services, Internet access, wireless campus network, Internet filtering or blocking technology. Campus intranet and computer access in designated common areas are available to students. The school has a published electronic and media policy.

Contact Sr. Dolores F. Crepeau, CSJ, Principal. 718-748-2244. Fax: 718-745-3841. E-mail: crepeau@fontbonne.org. Web site: www.fontbonne.org.

FOOTHILLS ACADEMY

Calgary, Alberta, Canada
See Special Needs Schools section.

FORDHAM PREPARATORY SCHOOL

East Fordham Road
Bronx, New York 10458-5175
Head of School: Rev. Kenneth J. Boller, SJ

General Information Boys' day college-preparatory school, affiliated with Roman Catholic Church. Grades 9–12. Founded: 1841. Setting: urban. Nearest major city is New York. 5-acre campus. 2 buildings on campus. Approved or accredited by Jesuit Secondary Education Association, Middle States Association of Colleges and Schools, National Catholic Education Association, New York State Association of Independent Schools, and New York Department of Education. Endowment: $1.3 million. Total enrollment: 974. Upper school average class size: 24. Upper school faculty-student ratio: 1:11.

Upper School Student Profile Grade 9: 243 students (243 boys); Grade 10: 248 students (248 boys); Grade 11: 262 students (262 boys); Grade 12: 221 students (221 boys). 75% of students are Roman Catholic.

Faculty School total: 88. In upper school: 63 men, 25 women; 78 have advanced degrees.

Subjects Offered Advanced chemistry, algebra, American Civil War, American history, American history-AP, American literature, Ancient Greek, architectural drawing, art history-AP, biochemistry, biology, biology-AP, British literature, calculus, calculus-AP, chemistry, chemistry-AP, Chinese, computer programming, computer programming-AP, constitutional history of U.S., creative writing, economics, emerging technology, English, English language and composition-AP, English literature-AP, European history-AP, finite math, forensics, French, geometry, German, global studies, government and politics-AP, health, Italian, Latin, Latin-AP, macroeconomics-AP, media communications, modern history, modern world history, music, physical education, physics, physics-AP, poetry, pre-calculus, religious studies, science research, short story, Spanish, Spanish language-AP, Spanish literature-AP, statistics-AP, studio art, studio art-AP, trigonometry, world history-AP.

Graduation Requirements Arts and fine arts (art, music, dance, drama), English, foreign language, mathematics, physical education (includes health), religious studies, science, social studies (includes history), senior service project.

Special Academic Programs Advanced Placement exam preparation; honors section; study at local college for college credit.

College Admission Counseling 220 students graduated in 2010; all went to college, including Boston College; College of the Holy Cross; Fordham University; Loyola University Maryland; Manhattan College; Penn State University Park. Mean SAT critical reading: 610, mean SAT math: 598, mean SAT writing: 602.

Student Life Upper grades have specified standards of dress. Discipline rests primarily with faculty. Attendance at religious services is required.

Tuition and Aid Day student tuition: $15,060. Tuition installment plan (monthly payment plans). Merit scholarship grants, need-based scholarship grants available. In 2010–11, 35% of upper-school students received aid; total upper-school merit-scholarship money awarded: $400,000. Total amount of financial aid awarded in 2010–11: $1,750,000.

Admissions Traditional secondary-level entrance grade is 9. For fall 2010, 1,145 students applied for upper-level admission, 551 were accepted, 243 enrolled.

Fordham Preparatory School

Cooperative Entrance Exam (McGraw-Hill), Diocesan Entrance Exam, ISEE, SSAT or STS required. Deadline for receipt of application materials: December 15. No application fee required. On-campus interview recommended.

Athletics Interscholastic: baseball, basketball, bowling, crew, cross-country running, diving, football, golf, ice hockey, indoor track, lacrosse, soccer, swimming and diving, tennis, track and field, volleyball, winter (indoor) track, wrestling; intramural: basketball, fitness, Frisbee, rock climbing, weight training. 2 PE instructors, 16 coaches.

Computers Computers are regularly used in English, foreign language, history, mathematics, science classes. Computer network features include on-campus library services, online commercial services, Internet access, wireless campus network, Internet filtering or blocking technology. Student e-mail accounts are available to students. The school has a published electronic and media policy.

Contact Christopher D. Lauber, Director of Admissions. 718-584-8367. Fax: 718-367-7598. E-mail: lauberc@fordhamprep.org. Web site: www.fordhamprep.org.

FOREST HEIGHTS LODGE

Evergreen, Colorado
See Special Needs Schools section.

FOREST LAKE ACADEMY

500 Education Loop
Apopka, Florida 32703
Head of School: Gloria M. Becker

General Information Coeducational boarding and day and distance learning college-preparatory, arts, religious studies, and bilingual studies school, affiliated with Seventh-day Adventists. Grades 9–12. Distance learning grades 9–12. Founded: 1926. Setting: suburban. Nearest major city is Orlando. Students are housed in single-sex dormitories. 200-acre campus. 9 buildings on campus. Approved or accredited by CITA (Commission on International and Trans-Regional Accreditation), National Council for Private School Accreditation, Southern Association of Colleges and Schools, and Florida Department of Education. Total enrollment: 426. Upper school average class size: 22. Upper school faculty-student ratio: 1:15. There are 176 required school days per year for Upper School students. Upper School students typically attend 5 days per week. The average school day consists of 5 hours and 35 minutes.

Upper School Student Profile Grade 9: 114 students (54 boys, 60 girls); Grade 10: 104 students (47 boys, 57 girls); Grade 11: 102 students (53 boys, 49 girls); Grade 12: 106 students (43 boys, 63 girls). 10% of students are boarding students. 84% are state residents. 9 states are represented in upper school student body. 1% are international students. International students from Argentina, Bermuda, Mexico, Puerto Rico, and Republic of Korea. 95% of students are Seventh-day Adventists.

Faculty School total: 30. In upper school: 21 men, 9 women; 22 have advanced degrees; 7 reside on campus.

Subjects Offered Algebra, American government, American literature, art, band, Bible studies, biology, calculus, chemistry, choir, church history, computer applications, concert choir, desktop publishing, digital photography, economics, English, environmental science, geometry, health, honors algebra, honors English, honors geometry, honors world history, integrated mathematics, life management skills, music, physical science, physics, pre-calculus, psychology, SAT preparation, senior project, Spanish, strings, swimming, U.S. history, video film production, world history, world literature, writing, yearbook.

Graduation Requirements Arts and fine arts (art, music, dance, drama), computer science, English, foreign language, health, mathematics, physical education (includes health), religion (includes Bible studies and theology), science, social studies (includes history), 20 hours of community service activity for each year enrolled.

Special Academic Programs Honors section; study at local college for college credit.

College Admission Counseling 108 students graduated in 2010; 102 went to college, including Andrews University; Florida Hospital College of Health Sciences; Oakwood University; Southern Adventist University; University of Central Florida; University of Florida. Other: 3 went to work, 3 entered military service. Mean SAT critical reading: 501, mean SAT math: 478, mean SAT writing: 484, mean combined SAT: 487, mean composite ACT: 21.

Student Life Upper grades have uniform requirement, student council, honor system. Discipline rests primarily with faculty.

Tuition and Aid Day student tuition: $10,448; 7-day tuition and room/board: $20,058. Tuition installment plan (FACTS Tuition Payment Plan, monthly payment plans, individually arranged payment plans). Merit scholarship grants, need-based scholarship grants, paying campus jobs available. In 2010–11, 57% of upper-school students received aid; total upper-school merit-scholarship money awarded: $7940. Total amount of financial aid awarded in 2010–11: $378,500.

Admissions Traditional secondary-level entrance grade is 9. Deadline for receipt of application materials: none. Application fee required: $60. Interview recommended.

Athletics Interscholastic: basketball (boys, girls), golf (b), volleyball (g); intramural: golf (b); coed intramural: baseball, flag football, floor hockey, outdoor activities, outdoor recreation, soccer, softball, volleyball. 2 PE instructors, 1 coach.

Computers Computers are regularly used in computer applications, desktop publishing, photography, Web site design, writing, yearbook classes. Computer network

features include on-campus library services, Internet access, wireless campus network, Internet filtering or blocking technology, financial aid and grant search programs for college. Campus intranet, student e-mail accounts, and computer access in designated common areas are available to students. Students grades are available online. The school has a published electronic and media policy.

Contact Mrs. Claudia Dure C. Osorio, Admissions Officer. 407-862-8411 Ext. 729. Fax: 407-862-7050. E-mail: osorioc@forestlake.org. Web site: www. forestlakeacademy.org.

FOREST RIDGE SCHOOL OF THE SACRED HEART

4800 139th Avenue SE
Bellevue, Washington 98006
Head of School: Mark L. Pierotti

General Information Girls' day college-preparatory, arts, religious studies, and technology school, affiliated with Roman Catholic Church. Grades 5–12. Founded: 1907. Setting: suburban. Nearest major city is Seattle. 20-acre campus. 6 buildings on campus. Approved or accredited by National Catholic Education Association, Network of Sacred Heart Schools, Northwest Association of Schools and Colleges, Pacific Northwest Association of Independent Schools, and Washington Department of Education. Member of National Association of Independent Schools. Total enrollment: 388. Upper school average class size: 15. Upper school faculty-student ratio: 1:6. There are 170 required school days per year for Upper School students. Upper School students typically attend 5 days per week. The average school day consists of 7 hours.

Upper School Student Profile Grade 9: 53 students (53 girls); Grade 10: 45 students (45 girls); Grade 11: 40 students (40 girls); Grade 12: 39 students (39 girls). 34% of students are Roman Catholic.

Faculty School total: 58. In upper school: 10 men, 23 women; 29 have advanced degrees.

Subjects Offered American history, bell choir, biology, British history, British literature, British literature (honors), calculus, calculus-AP, Catholic belief and practice, ceramics, chamber groups, chemistry, chemistry-AP, choir, Christian and Hebrew scripture, Christianity, church history, civil war history, classical civilization, college counseling, computer skills, concert bell choir, critical thinking, critical writing, dance, digital photography, discrete mathematics, drama, drama performance, drama workshop, drawing, East European studies, English composition, English literature, ethics, fine arts, French, French-AP, geometry, government, government-AP, graphic design, handbells, health and wellness, history, history of religion, honors algebra, honors English, honors geometry, honors U.S. history, human relations, information processing, internship, Japanese, leadership, modern European history, outdoor education, painting, physics, pre-calculus, senior career experience, senior seminar, Shakespeare, social issues, social justice, Spanish, Spanish-AP, statistics, weight training, yoga.

Graduation Requirements Arts and fine arts (art, music, dance, drama), biology, computer science, English, foreign language, mathematics, physical education (includes health), religion (includes Bible studies and theology), science, social studies (includes history).

Special Academic Programs Advanced Placement exam preparation.

College Admission Counseling 55 students graduated in 2009; all went to college, including Gonzaga University; Harvey Mudd College; Santa Clara University; Seattle University; Stanford University; University of Washington. Mean SAT critical reading: 594, mean SAT math: 594, mean SAT writing: 587, mean combined SAT: 1775.

Student Life Upper grades have uniform requirement, student council, honor system. Discipline rests primarily with faculty. Attendance at religious services is required.

Tuition and Aid Day student tuition: $23,500. Tuition installment plan (SMART Tuition Payment Plan, monthly payment plans). Merit scholarship grants, need-based scholarship grants available. In 2009–10, 25% of upper-school students received aid; total upper-school merit-scholarship money awarded: $140,000. Total amount of financial aid awarded in 2009–10: $1,073,500.

Admissions Traditional secondary-level entrance grade is 9. ISEE required. Deadline for receipt of application materials: January 14. Application fee required: $50. Interview required.

Athletics Interscholastic: aerobics/dance, basketball, climbing, cross-country running, dance, dance team, golf, independent competitive sports, lacrosse, outdoor activities, outdoor adventure, outdoor education, physical fitness, physical training, rock climbing, soccer, softball, tennis, track and field, volleyball; intramural: basketball, cross-country running, golf, independent competitive sports, lacrosse, soccer, softball, tennis, track and field, volleyball. 2 PE instructors, 8 coaches.

Computers Computers are regularly used in all classes. Computer network features include on-campus library services, online commercial services, Internet access, wireless campus network, Internet filtering or blocking technology, all students use laptop computers in and outside of school. Campus intranet and student e-mail accounts are available to students. Students grades are available online. The school has a published electronic and media policy.

Contact Rosanne Tomich, Director of Admission. 425-201-2421. Fax: 425-643-3881. E-mail: rosanneto@forestridge.org. Web site: www.forestridge.org.

THE FORMAN SCHOOL
Litchfield, Connecticut
See Special Needs Schools section.

FORSYTH COUNTRY DAY SCHOOL
5501 Shallowford Road
PO Box 549
Lewisville, North Carolina 27023-0549
Head of School: Mr. Henry M. Battle Jr.

General Information Coeducational day college-preparatory school. Grades PK–12. Founded: 1970. Setting: suburban. Nearest major city is Winston-Salem. 80-acre campus. 7 buildings on campus. Approved or accredited by North Carolina Association of Independent Schools, Southern Association of Colleges and Schools, Southern Association of Independent Schools, The College Board, and North Carolina Department of Education. Member of National Association of Independent Schools. Endowment: $16 million. Total enrollment: 909. Upper school average class size: 15. Upper school faculty-student ratio: 1:12. There are 175 required school days per year for Upper School students. Upper School students typically attend 5 days per week. The average school day consists of 5 hours and 45 minutes.

Upper School Student Profile Grade 9: 85 students (51 boys, 34 girls); Grade 10: 76 students (41 boys, 35 girls); Grade 11: 116 students (70 boys, 46 girls); Grade 12: 110 students (71 boys, 39 girls).

Faculty School total: 175. In upper school: 18 men, 29 women; 24 have advanced degrees.

Subjects Offered Advanced Placement courses, advanced studio art-AP, algebra, American history, American history-AP, American literature, art, astronomy, biology, calculus, calculus-AP, ceramics, chemistry, Chinese studies, community service, computer math, computer programming, computer science, creative writing, digital art, drama, English, English literature, European history, fine arts, foreign policy, French, freshman seminar, geometry, grammar, health, history, history of science, humanities, international relations, Japanese studies, journalism, Latin, Mandarin, mathematics, Middle Eastern history, music, photography, physical education, physics, psychology, SAT/ACT preparation, science, social studies, Spanish, statistics-AP, theater, yearbook.

Graduation Requirements Arts and fine arts (art, music, dance, drama), English, foreign language, history, mathematics, physical education (includes health), physical fitness, science. Community service is required.

Special Academic Programs 18 Advanced Placement exams for which test preparation is offered; honors section; academic accommodation for the gifted; programs in English, general development for dyslexic students; ESL (2 students enrolled).

College Admission Counseling 114 students graduated in 2010; all went to college, including Duke University; Elon University; North Carolina State University; The University of North Carolina at Chapel Hill; The University of North Carolina Wilmington; Wake Forest University. Median SAT critical reading: 600, median SAT math: 610. 70% scored over 600 on SAT critical reading, 68% scored over 600 on SAT math.

Student Life Upper grades have specified standards of dress, student council, honor system. Discipline rests equally with students and faculty.

Summer Programs Enrichment programs offered; session focuses on leadership training; held both on and off campus; held at various businesses and offices throughout the community; accepts boys and girls; open to students from other schools. 50 students usually enrolled. 2011 schedule: June 15 to July 31.

Tuition and Aid Day student tuition: $17,800. Tuition installment plan (Insured Tuition Payment Plan, monthly payment plans, individually arranged payment plans). Need-based scholarship grants available. In 2010–11, 18% of upper-school students received aid. Total amount of financial aid awarded in 2010–11: $905,950.

Admissions Traditional secondary-level entrance grade is 9. For fall 2010, 84 students applied for upper-level admission, 77 were accepted, 57 enrolled. ERB CTP IV, WRAT and writing sample required. Deadline for receipt of application materials: none. Application fee required: $100. On-campus interview required.

Athletics Interscholastic: baseball (boys), basketball (b,g), cheering (g), cross-country running (b,g), field hockey (g), football (b), lacrosse (b,g), physical fitness (b,g), soccer (b,g), softball (g), tennis (b,g), track and field (b,g), volleyball (g), wrestling (b); coed interscholastic: golf, swimming and diving; coed intramural: sailing. 4 PE instructors, 4 coaches, 1 athletic trainer.

Computers Computers are regularly used in art, English, foreign language, history, mathematics, music, science classes. Computer network features include on-campus library services, online commercial services, Internet access, wireless campus network, Internet filtering or blocking technology. Campus intranet, student e-mail accounts, and computer access in designated common areas are available to students. Students grades are available online. The school has a published electronic and media policy.

Contact Cindy C. Kluttz, Director of Admission. 336-945-3151 Ext. 340. Fax: 336-945-2907. E-mail: cindykluttz@fcds.org. Web site: www.fcds.org.

FORT LAUDERDALE PREPARATORY SCHOOL
3275 West Oakland Park Boulevard
Fort Lauderdale, Florida 33311
Head of School: Dr. Lawrence Berkowitz, PhD

General Information Coeducational day college-preparatory, general academic, arts, and technology school. Grades PK–12. Founded: 1986. Setting: urban. 5-acre campus. 1 building on campus. Approved or accredited by CITA (Commission on International and Trans-Regional Accreditation), Florida Council of Independent Schools, National Independent Private Schools Association, Southern Association of Colleges and Schools, and Florida Department of Education. Member of European Council of International Schools. Languages of instruction: English and Spanish. Upper school average class size: 16. Upper school faculty-student ratio: 1:8. There are 178 required school days per year for Upper School students. Upper School students typically attend 5 days per week. The average school day consists of 8 hours.

Upper School Student Profile Grade 6: 16 students (9 boys, 7 girls); Grade 7: 16 students (8 boys, 8 girls); Grade 8: 18 students (10 boys, 8 girls); Grade 9: 13 students (7 boys, 6 girls); Grade 10: 13 students (6 boys, 7 girls); Grade 11: 15 students (7 boys, 8 girls); Grade 12: 16 students (8 boys, 8 girls).

Faculty School total: 28. In upper school: 11 men, 10 women; 9 have advanced degrees.

Subjects Offered Accounting, ACT preparation, advanced chemistry, advanced computer applications, advanced math, Advanced Placement courses, advanced studio art-AP, advanced TOEFL/grammar, algebra, American government, American history, American history-AP, American literature, American literature-AP, art, art appreciation, art history, art history-AP, art-AP, automated accounting, Basic programming, biology, biology-AP, bookkeeping, British literature, British literature (honors), business applications, business education, business mathematics, calculus, calculus-AP, career education, career/college preparation, character education, chemistry, chemistry-AP, U.S. government and politics-AP.

Special Academic Programs International Baccalaureate program; Advanced Placement exam preparation; honors section; accelerated programs; independent study; study at local college for college credit; academic accommodation for the gifted; remedial reading and/or remedial writing; remedial math; programs in English, mathematics, general development for dyslexic students; ESL (17 students enrolled).

College Admission Counseling 19 students graduated in 2010; 17 went to college, including Florida Atlantic University; Florida State University; Hunter College of the City University of New York; University of Florida; University of Miami; University of South Florida. Other: 1 went to work, 1 entered military service.

Student Life Upper grades have uniform requirement, student council, honor system. Discipline rests primarily with faculty.

Summer Programs Remediation, enrichment, advancement, ESL, computer instruction programs offered; session focuses on academics; held on campus; accepts boys and girls; open to students from other schools. 100 students usually enrolled. 2011 schedule: June 18 to July 26.

Tuition and Aid Day student tuition: $12,500. Tuition installment plan (monthly payment plans, individually arranged payment plans). Tuition reduction for siblings, merit scholarship grants, need-based scholarship grants available. In 2010–11, 50% of upper-school students received aid; total upper-school merit-scholarship money awarded: $200,000. Total amount of financial aid awarded in 2010–11: $1,000,000.

Admissions Traditional secondary-level entrance grade is 7. For fall 2010, 90 students applied for upper-level admission, 60 were accepted, 52 enrolled. Admissions testing, High School Placement Test, math and English placement tests, Math Placement Exam, school's own exam, standardized test scores, Stanford Achievement Test, TOEFL or writing sample required. Deadline for receipt of application materials: none. Application fee required: $50. Interview recommended.

Athletics 2 PE instructors.

Computers Computers are regularly used in all academic classes. Computer network features include on-campus library services, Internet access, wireless campus network, Internet filtering or blocking technology. Campus intranet is available to students. The school has a published electronic and media policy.

Contact Jonathan A. Lonstein, Director of Admissions. 954-485-7500. Fax: 954-485-1732. E-mail: admissions@flps.com. Web site: www.flps.com/.

FORT WORTH COUNTRY DAY SCHOOL
4200 Country Day Lane
Fort Worth, Texas 76109-4299
Head of School: Evan D. Peterson

General Information Coeducational day college-preparatory and arts school. Grades K–12. Founded: 1962. Setting: suburban. 100-acre campus. 13 buildings on campus. Approved or accredited by Independent Schools Association of the Southwest. Member of National Association of Independent Schools. Endowment: $38 million. Total enrollment: 1,116. Upper school average class size: 14. Upper school faculty-student ratio: 1:10. There are 174 required school days per year for Upper School students. Upper School students typically attend 5 days per week. The average school day consists of 8 hours.

Upper School Student Profile Grade 9: 95 students (48 boys, 47 girls); Grade 10: 100 students (50 boys, 50 girls); Grade 11: 99 students (41 boys, 58 girls); Grade 12: 94 students (49 boys, 45 girls).

Fort Worth Country Day School

Faculty School total: 128. In upper school: 16 men, 21 women; 29 have advanced degrees.

Subjects Offered Algebra, American history, American literature, art, art history, biology, calculus, ceramics, chemistry, comparative religion, computer math, computer programming, computer science, computer technologies, creative writing, dance, drama, driver education, earth science, ecology, economics, English, English literature, European history, expository writing, fine arts, French, geography, geology, geometry, government/civics, grammar, health, history, journalism, Latin, mathematics, modern problems, music, music history, photography, physical education, physics, psychology, science, social studies, Spanish, speech, study skills, technology, theater, trigonometry, typing, word processing, world history, writing.

Graduation Requirements Algebra, American government, arts and fine arts (art, music, dance, drama), biology, English, foreign language, lab science, mathematics, physical education (includes health), science, social studies (includes history), participation in athletics. Community service is required.

Special Academic Programs 22 Advanced Placement exams for which test preparation is offered; honors section; independent study; term-away projects; study at local college for college credit; study abroad; academic accommodation for the gifted, the musically talented, and the artistically talented.

College Admission Counseling 95 students graduated in 2009; all went to college, including Southern Methodist University; Texas A&M University; Texas Christian University; The University of Texas at Austin; University of Georgia; University of Oklahoma.

Student Life Upper grades have uniform requirement, student council, honor system. Discipline rests equally with students and faculty.

Tuition and Aid Day student tuition: $16,315. Tuition installment plan (Key Tuition Payment Plan, monthly payment plans, individually arranged payment plans). Merit scholarship grants, need-based scholarship grants, Malone Scholars Program available. In 2009–10, 20% of upper-school students received aid; total upper-school merit-scholarship money awarded: $151,000. Total amount of financial aid awarded in 2009–10: $820,000.

Admissions Traditional secondary-level entrance grade is 9. For fall 2009, 79 students applied for upper-level admission, 39 were accepted, 31 enrolled. ERB or ISEE required. Deadline for receipt of application materials: March 5. Application fee required: $75. Interview required.

Athletics Interscholastic: ballet (boys, girls), baseball (b), basketball (b,g), cheering (g), field hockey (g), football (b), lacrosse (b), swimming and diving (g), track and field (b,g), volleyball (b,g), winter soccer (b,g), wrestling (b); intramural: lacrosse (b); coed interscholastic: ballet, cross-country running, dance, dance team, fitness, golf, independent competitive sports, physical training, ropes courses, strength & conditioning, tennis. 12 PE instructors, 45 coaches, 2 athletic trainers.

Computers Computers are regularly used in architecture, college planning, computer applications, creative writing, desktop publishing, English, foreign language, history, humanities, introduction to technology, library skills, life skills, mathematics, music, newspaper, publications, reading, science, Web site design, writing, yearbook classes. Computer network features include on-campus library services, online commercial services, Internet access, wireless campus network, Internet filtering or blocking technology. Campus intranet, student e-mail accounts, and computer access in designated common areas are available to students. The school has a published electronic and media policy.

Contact Yolanda Espinoza, Admissions Associate. 817-302-3209. Fax: 817-377-3425. E-mail: yespinoza@fwcds.org. Web site: www.fwcds.org.

FOUNDATION ACADEMY

15304 Tilden Road
Winter Garden, Florida 34787
Head of School: Mr. Shawn Minks

General Information Coeducational day college-preparatory, general academic, and arts school, affiliated with Baptist Church. Grades 6–12. Founded: 1958. Setting: suburban. Nearest major city is Orlando. 75-acre campus. 3 buildings on campus. Approved or accredited by Association of Christian Schools International, European Council of International Schools, and Southern Association of Colleges and Schools. Total enrollment: 539. Upper school average class size: 16. Upper school faculty-student ratio: 1:16. There are 180 required school days per year for Upper School students. Upper School students typically attend 5 days per week. The average school day consists of 6 hours and 45 minutes.

Upper School Student Profile Grade 6: 52 students (24 boys, 28 girls); Grade 7: 46 students (21 boys, 25 girls); Grade 8: 49 students (23 boys, 26 girls); Grade 9: 28 students (17 boys, 11 girls); Grade 10: 27 students (18 boys, 9 girls); Grade 11: 27 students (16 boys, 11 girls); Grade 12: 27 students (14 boys, 13 girls). 20% of students are Baptist.

Faculty School total: 34. In upper school: 11 men, 23 women; 5 have advanced degrees.

Subjects Offered Advanced Placement courses, anatomy and physiology, art, band, Bible, biology, biology-AP, business law, business mathematics, calculus, calculus-AP, chemistry, college admission preparation, computer processing, drama, economics and history, English, English composition, English literature, English literature-AP, French, geometry, government, health education, history-AP, physical

education, physical fitness, SAT preparation, science, science project, social psychology, Spanish, speech, sports conditioning, studio art-AP, U.S. history, weight training.

Graduation Requirements Algebra, American government, American history, American literature, anatomy and physiology, arts and fine arts (art, music, dance, drama), Bible, biology, chemistry, college admission preparation, English, English composition, geography, geometry, government, history, human anatomy, languages, SAT preparation, science, U.S. history, 4 credits of Bible.

Special Academic Programs Advanced Placement exam preparation; honors section; independent study; study at local college for college credit; remedial reading and/or remedial writing; remedial math; programs in English, mathematics for dyslexic students.

College Admission Counseling 26 students graduated in 2010; 25 went to college, including Charleston Southern University; Florida Atlantic University; University of Central Florida; Valencia Community College. Other: 1 entered military service.

Student Life Upper grades have uniform requirement, student council. Discipline rests primarily with faculty. Attendance at religious services is required.

Summer Programs Sports, art/fine arts programs offered; session focuses on sports camps, art; held on campus; accepts boys and girls; open to students from other schools. 100 students usually enrolled. 2011 schedule: June 1 to July 31.

Tuition and Aid Day student tuition: $8000. Guaranteed tuition plan. Tuition installment plan (SMART Tuition Payment Plan). Tuition reduction for siblings, need-based scholarship grants available. In 2010–11, 10% of upper-school students received aid.

Admissions Traditional secondary-level entrance grade is 9. Admissions testing, Gates MacGinite Reading Tests, Math Placement Exam and Wide Range Achievement Test required. Deadline for receipt of application materials: none. Application fee required: $150. Interview required.

Athletics Interscholastic: baseball (boys), basketball (b,g), bowling (b,g), cheering (g), cross-country running (b,g), football (b), golf (b), soccer (b), softball (g), tennis (b,g), track and field (b,g), volleyball (g); intramural: bowling (b,g). 2 PE instructors, 50 coaches.

Computers Computers are regularly used in career exploration, college planning, computer applications, independent study, library skills, word processing, yearbook classes. Computer resources include on-campus library services, Internet access, Internet filtering or blocking technology. Campus intranet is available to students. Students grades are available online.

Contact Mrs. Stephanie Baysinger, Student Advisor. 407-877-2744. Fax: 407-877-1985. E-mail: sbaysinger@foundationacademy.net. Web site: www.foundationacademy.net.

FOUNTAIN VALLEY SCHOOL OF COLORADO

6155 Fountain Valley School Road
Colorado Springs, Colorado 80911
Head of School: Craig W. Larimer Jr.

General Information Coeducational boarding and day college-preparatory, arts, and technology school. Grades 9–12. Founded: 1930. Setting: suburban. Students are housed in single-sex dormitories. 1,100-acre campus. 42 buildings on campus. Approved or accredited by Association of Colorado Independent Schools, The Association of Boarding Schools, and Colorado Department of Education. Member of National Association of Independent Schools and Secondary School Admission Test Board. Endowment: $34 million. Total enrollment: 251. Upper school average class size: 12. Upper school faculty-student ratio: 1:6. Upper School students typically attend 5 days per week. The average school day consists of 9 hours and 15 minutes.

Upper School Student Profile Grade 9: 55 students (23 boys, 32 girls); Grade 10: 55 students (26 boys, 29 girls); Grade 11: 76 students (35 boys, 41 girls); Grade 12: 75 students (37 boys, 38 girls). 67% of students are boarding students. 53% are state residents. 27 states are represented in upper school student body. 22% are international students. International students from China, Germany, Mexico, Republic of Korea, Saudi Arabia, and Taiwan; 13 other countries represented in student body.

Faculty School total: 47. In upper school: 21 men, 15 women; 25 have advanced degrees; 27 reside on campus.

Subjects Offered 3-dimensional art, 3-dimensional design, acting, advanced chemistry, Advanced Placement courses, advanced studio art-AP, algebra, American history, American history-AP, American literature, biology, biology-AP, British literature, calculus, calculus-AP, ceramics, chamber groups, chemistry, chemistry-AP, college counseling, Colorado ecology, composition, computer applications, computer multimedia, computer programming, creative writing, drama, English, English literature and composition-AP, environmental science-AP, ESL, fiction, film and literature, French, French language-AP, geology, geometry, honors algebra, honors English, honors geometry, instrumental music, jewelry making, literature, Mandarin, musical productions, outdoor education, photography, physics, physics-AP, pre-calculus, probability and statistics, robotics, senior project, senior seminar, Shakespeare, Shakespearean histories, short story, Spanish, Spanish language-AP, statistics-AP, strings, student government, student publications, studio art, studio art-AP, U.S. government and politics-AP, visual and performing arts, vocal ensemble, Western civilization, wilderness education, wind ensemble, world history, world history-AP, world literature, writing.

Graduation Requirements Arts and fine arts (art, music, dance, drama), computer science, English, foreign language, history, mathematics, physical education (includes health), science, social studies (includes history), community service hours, senior seminar.

Special Academic Programs 19 Advanced Placement exams for which test preparation is offered; honors section; independent study; academic accommodation for the gifted, the musically talented, and the artistically talented; ESL (17 students enrolled).

College Admission Counseling 61 students graduated in 2010; 57 went to college, including Claremont McKenna College; Rollins College; Santa Clara University; Stanford University; University of Illinois at Urbana–Champaign; University of Pennsylvania. Other: 1 entered military service, 3 had other specific plans. Median SAT critical reading: 570, median SAT math: 610, median SAT writing: 540, median composite ACT: 25.

Student Life Upper grades have specified standards of dress, student council, honor system. Discipline rests equally with students and faculty.

Summer Programs Enrichment, ESL, sports, rigorous outdoor training, computer instruction programs offered; session focuses on outdoor education, natural sciences, leadership, sports camps, international student enrichment; held both on and off campus; held at FVS' 40-acre Mountain Campus and surrounding Mount Princeton region; accepts boys and girls; open to students from other schools. 100 students usually enrolled. 2011 schedule: June 5 to August 15. Application deadline: none.

Tuition and Aid Day student tuition: $22,800; 7-day tuition and room/board: $42,000. Tuition installment plan (Key Tuition Payment Plan, monthly payment plans, individually arranged payment plans). Merit scholarship grants, need-based scholarship grants available. In 2010–11, 36% of upper-school students received aid; total upper-school merit-scholarship money awarded: $322,600. Total amount of financial aid awarded in 2010–11: $1,800,000.

Admissions Traditional secondary-level entrance grade is 9. For fall 2010, 226 students applied for upper-level admission, 154 were accepted, 91 enrolled. SSAT or TOEFL required. Deadline for receipt of application materials: February 1. Application fee required: $50. Interview required.

Athletics Interscholastic: basketball (boys, girls), cross-country running (b,g), diving (g), field hockey (g), hockey (b), ice hockey (b), lacrosse (b,g), soccer (b,g), swimming and diving (g), tennis (b,g), track and field (b,g), volleyball (b,g); coed interscholastic: climbing, equestrian sports, golf, horseback riding, independent competitive sports, rock climbing, rodeo, skiing (downhill), snowboarding, telemark skiing; coed intramural: aerobics/dance, alpine skiing, backpacking, climbing, dance, equestrian sports, fitness, Frisbee, hiking/backpacking, horseback riding, modern dance, mountain biking, mountaineering, outdoor activities, outdoor adventure, outdoor education, outdoor recreation, outdoor skills, physical fitness, rock climbing, skiing (downhill), snowboarding, strength & conditioning, table tennis, telemark skiing, tennis, ultimate Frisbee, weight training. 2 coaches, 1 athletic trainer.

Computers Computers are regularly used in all academic, college planning, multimedia, news writing, newspaper, photography, publications, Web site design, yearbook classes. Computer network features include on-campus library services, online commercial services, Internet access, wireless campus network, Internet filtering or blocking technology. Campus intranet, student e-mail accounts, and computer access in designated common areas are available to students. Students grades are available online. The school has a published electronic and media policy.
Contact Mr. Randy Roach, Director of Admission. 719-390-7035 Ext. 251. Fax: 719-390-7762. E-mail: admission@fvs.edu. Web site: www.fvs.edu.

See Display below and Close-Up on page 778.

FOWLERS ACADEMY
PO Box 921
Guaynabo, Puerto Rico 00970-0921
Head of School: Mrs. Carmen Tuominen
General Information Coeducational day general academic, arts, religious studies, music, and graphic art design school, affiliated with Christian faith; primarily serves underachievers. Grades 7–12. Founded: 1986. Setting: suburban. 2-acre campus. 2 buildings on campus. Approved or accredited by Comisión Acreditadora de Instituciones Educativas, The College Board, and Puerto Rico Department of Education. Languages of instruction: English and Spanish. Total enrollment: 64. Upper school average class size: 15. Upper school faculty-student ratio: 1:15. Upper School students typically attend 5 days per week. The average school day consists of 6 hours and 45 minutes.

Upper School Student Profile Grade 7: 7 students (5 boys, 2 girls); Grade 8: 5 students (4 boys, 1 girl); Grade 9: 10 students (8 boys, 2 girls); Grade 10: 15 students (11 boys, 4 girls); Grade 11: 15 students (14 boys, 1 girl); Grade 12: 12 students (10 boys, 2 girls).

Faculty School total: 8. In upper school: 5 men, 2 women; 2 have advanced degrees.

Subjects Offered Algebra, American history, ancient world history, art, athletics, basketball, Bible, character education, chemistry, Christian education, Christian ethics, Christian scripture, computer applications, computer art, computer education, computer graphics, computer literacy, computer skills, culinary arts, dance, drama, drawing, earth science, electives, English, film appreciation, geometry, history, instrumental music, keyboarding, leadership, leadership and service, martial arts, mathematics, music, physical education, physics, pre-algebra, pre-college orientation, Puerto Rican history, science, sex education, Spanish, Spanish literature, theater, U.S. history, world history.

Fowlers Academy

Graduation Requirements Algebra, ancient world history, biology, chemistry, Christian education, electives, English, geometry, physical education (includes health), physical science, physics, pre-college orientation, Puerto Rican history, Spanish, U.S. history, world history.

Special Academic Programs Accelerated programs; special instructional classes for students with ADD and LD.

College Admission Counseling 12 students graduated in 2010; 9 went to college, including Johnson & Wales University; University of Puerto Rico, Mayagüez Campus. Other: 1 went to work, 2 entered a postgraduate year.

Student Life Upper grades have uniform requirement, student council, honor system. Discipline rests primarily with faculty.

Summer Programs Remediation, enrichment, advancement programs offered; session focuses on academic courses and remediation; held on campus; accepts boys and girls; open to students from other schools. 30 students usually enrolled. 2011 schedule: June 1 to June 28. Application deadline: May 31.

Tuition and Aid Day student tuition: $5900. Tuition installment plan (monthly payment plans, individually arranged payment plans). Tuition reduction for siblings, need-based scholarship grants available. In 2010–11, 4% of upper-school students received aid. Total amount of financial aid awarded in 2010–11: $7100.

Admissions Traditional secondary-level entrance grade is 9. For fall 2010, 15 students applied for upper-level admission, 13 were accepted, 12 enrolled. Psycho-educational evaluation required. Deadline for receipt of application materials: none. No application fee required. On-campus interview required.

Athletics Interscholastic: basketball (boys); intramural: basketball (b); coed interscholastic: archery, physical fitness; coed intramural: archery, fitness, physical fitness, soccer, table tennis, volleyball. 1 PE instructor.

Computers Computers are regularly used in English, graphic arts, graphic design, keyboarding, mathematics, religious studies, science, Spanish classes. Computer resources include Internet access, Internet filtering or blocking technology. Computer access in designated common areas is available to students.

Contact Mr. Lynette Montes, Registrar. 787-787-1350. Fax: 787-789-0055. E-mail: fowlersacademy@gmail.com.

FOXCROFT ACADEMY

975 West Main Street
Dover-Foxcroft, Maine 04426
Head of School: Dr. Vandy E. Hewett

General Information Coeducational boarding and day college-preparatory and technology school. Grades 9–12. Founded: 1823. Setting: small town. Nearest major city is Bangor. Students are housed in single-sex by floor dormitories, coed dormitories, and single-sex dormitories. 120-acre campus. 5 buildings on campus. Approved or accredited by Association of Independent Schools in New England, Independent Schools of Northern New England, New England Association of Schools and Colleges, and Maine Department of Education. Endowment: $6 million. Total enrollment: 439. Upper school average class size: 16. Upper school faculty-student ratio: 1:10. There are 177 required school days per year for Upper School students. The average school day consists of 6 hours and 50 minutes.

Upper School Student Profile Grade 9: 108 students (51 boys, 57 girls); Grade 10: 112 students (56 boys, 56 girls); Grade 11: 109 students (56 boys, 53 girls); Grade 12: 108 students (55 boys, 53 girls). 21% of students are boarding students. 79% are state residents. 2 states are represented in upper school student body. 21% are international students. International students from Austria, China, Germany, Japan, Republic of Korea, and Viet Nam; 6 other countries represented in student body.

Faculty School total: 42. In upper school: 23 men, 19 women; 24 have advanced degrees; 9 reside on campus.

Subjects Offered Advanced Placement courses, algebra, American literature, ancient history, art history, art-AP, auto mechanics, calculus-AP, career planning, cell biology, chemistry-AP, child development, Chinese, choral music, classical civilization, communication skills, computer art, computer programming, critical thinking, engineering, English, English-AP, ESL, ethics, family and consumer science, French, geometry, health, history-AP, home economics, honors algebra, honors English, honors U.S. history, jazz ensemble, Latin, literature-AP, mathematics-AP, model United Nations, modern history, multimedia, music, music composition, music theater, music theory, orchestra, parent/child development, peer counseling, personal fitness, physics-AP, poetry, political science, portfolio art, pre-calculus, SAT preparation, science project, Shakespeare, small engine repair, Spanish, statistics-AP, stock market, strings, student government, student publications, studio art-AP, swimming, technical drawing, theater arts, TOEFL preparation, U.S. government, U.S. history-AP, U.S. literature, video and animation, visual arts, vocal ensemble, woodworking, work-study, world arts, world cultures, world geography, world history, world wide web design, writing, yearbook.

Graduation Requirements Advanced math, algebra, American government, American history, analytic geometry, art, arts and fine arts (art, music, dance, drama), biology, chemistry, classical language, college admission preparation, communication skills, composition, computer skills, computer technologies, desktop publishing, economics, English literature, ethics, family and consumer science, foreign language, human biology, languages, music, physical education (includes health), physics, pre-calculus, statistics, visual arts, Western civilization, world cultures, writing, must meet performance standards in all core academic areas. Community service is required.

Special Academic Programs Advanced Placement exam preparation; honors section; independent study; academic accommodation for the gifted, the musically talented, and the artistically talented; remedial reading and/or remedial writing; remedial math; ESL (38 students enrolled).

College Admission Counseling 103 students graduated in 2009; 81 went to college, including Colby College; Cornell University; Michigan State University; Penn State University Park; University of Maine; University of Massachusetts Boston. Other: 8 went to work, 12 entered military service, 1 entered a postgraduate year, 1 had other specific plans. Median SAT critical reading: 580, median SAT math: 710, median SAT writing: 525, median combined SAT: 1815.

Student Life Upper grades have specified standards of dress, student council, honor system. Discipline rests primarily with faculty.

Tuition and Aid Day student tuition: $11,900; 5-day tuition and room/board: $27,500; 7-day tuition and room/board: $33,100. Tuition installment plan (The Tuition Plan, Key Tuition Payment Plan, monthly payment plans, individually arranged payment plans). Tuition reduction for siblings, merit scholarship grants, need-based scholarship grants available. In 2009–10, 10% of upper-school students received aid; total upper-school merit-scholarship money awarded: $13,000. Total amount of financial aid awarded in 2009–10: $56,000.

Admissions Traditional secondary-level entrance grade is 9. For fall 2009, 135 students applied for upper-level admission, 69 were accepted, 48 enrolled. TOEFL or SLEP or writing sample required. Deadline for receipt of application materials: none. Application fee required: $50. Interview required.

Athletics Interscholastic: baseball (boys); basketball (b,g); cheering (g); cross-country running (b,g), field hockey (g), football (b), golf (b,g), hockey (b), soccer (b,g), softball (g), tennis (b,g), winter (indoor) track (b,g), wrestling (b,g); coed interscholastic: aquatics, indoor track & field, swimming and diving, wrestling; coed intramural: fencing, floor hockey, outdoor activities, snowboarding. 2 PE instructors, 11 coaches.

Computers Computers are regularly used in all academic classes. Computer network features include on-campus library services, Internet access, wireless campus network, Internet filtering or blocking technology. Campus intranet, student e-mail accounts, and computer access in designated common areas are available to students. The school has a published electronic and media policy.

Contact Mrs. Hsi-Wen (Ruby Canning) You, Admissions Assistant. 207-564-8664. Fax: 207-564-8664. E-mail: ruby.canning@foxcroftacademy.org. Web site: www.foxcroftacademy.org.

FOXCROFT SCHOOL

22407 Foxhound Lane
P.O. Box 5555
Middleburg, Virginia 20118
Head of School: Mary Louise Leipheimer

General Information Girls' boarding and day college-preparatory school. Grades 9–12. Founded: 1914. Setting: rural. Nearest major city is Washington, DC. Students are housed in single-sex dormitories. 500-acre campus. 32 buildings on campus. Approved or accredited by National Association of Episcopal Schools, The Association of Boarding Schools, Virginia Association of Independent Schools, and Virginia Department of Education. Member of National Association of Independent Schools and Secondary School Admission Test Board. Endowment: $22.8 million. Total enrollment: 157. Upper school average class size: 10. Upper school faculty-student ratio: 1:7. There are 159 required school days per year for Upper School students. Upper School students typically attend 5 days per week. The average school day consists of 7 hours and 15 minutes.

Upper School Student Profile Grade 9: 36 students (36 girls); Grade 10: 32 students (32 girls); Grade 11: 42 students (42 girls); Grade 12: 47 students (47 girls). 64% of students are boarding students. 49% are state residents. 21 states are represented in upper school student body. 18% are international students. International students from China, France, Jamaica, Mexico, Republic of Korea, and Spain; 2 other countries represented in student body.

Faculty School total: 22. In upper school: 5 men, 17 women; 17 have advanced degrees; 16 reside on campus.

Subjects Offered 3-dimensional art, acting, advanced chemistry, algebra, American literature, anatomy and physiology, ancient world history, architecture, art, art history, astronomy, biology, British literature, calculus, calculus-AP, cell biology, ceramics, chemistry, chemistry-AP, choir, chorus, college counseling, community service, comparative religion, computer graphics, computer science, conceptual physics, constitutional law, creative dance, creative drama, creative writing, current events, dance, debate, digital photography, discrete mathematics, drama, drawing and design, economics, economics-AP, electives, English, English composition, English literature, English literature-AP, environmental science, European civilization, European history, European literature, expository writing, fine arts, fitness, French, French language-AP, general science, geology, geometry, grammar, health education, history, human anatomy, independent study, leadership, library, macroeconomics-AP, mathematics, microbiology, music, music theory, music theory-AP, painting, performing arts, photography, physical education, physics, piano, poetry, pottery, pre-calculus, probability and statistics, production, public speaking, SAT preparation, sculpture, senior project, social studies, Spanish, Spanish language-AP, Spanish literature, Spanish literature-AP, studio art, studio art-AP, technology, The 20th Century, trigonometry, U.S. history, U.S. history-AP, vocal ensemble, world cultures, world literature, writing, yearbook, yoga.

Graduation Requirements Arts and fine arts (art, music, dance, drama), English, foreign language, history, mathematics, physical education (includes health), science, senior thesis if student is not enrolled in AP English.

Special Academic Programs 11 Advanced Placement exams for which test preparation is offered; independent study; term-away projects; study abroad; academic accommodation for the gifted, the musically talented, and the artistically talented.

College Admission Counseling 53 students graduated in 2010; 52 went to college, including College of Charleston; Eckerd College; Furman University; James Madison University; Parsons The New School for Design; The College of William and Mary. Other: 1 had other specific plans.

Student Life Upper grades have specified standards of dress, student council, honor system. Discipline rests equally with students and faculty.

Tuition and Aid Day student tuition: $32,400; 7-day tuition and room/board: $43,200. Tuition installment plan (Insured Tuition Payment Plan, Tuition Management Systems Plan (Monthly Payment Plan)). Merit scholarship grants, need-based scholarship grants, merit-based scholarship grants are offered to prosepctive 9th grade students available. In 2010–11, 30% of upper-school students received aid; total upper-school merit-scholarship money awarded: $36,842. Total amount of financial aid awarded in 2010–11: $1,435,050.

Admissions Traditional secondary-level entrance grade is 9. For fall 2010, 137 students applied for upper-level admission, 122 were accepted, 51 enrolled. SSAT or TOEFL required. Deadline for receipt of application materials: February 15. Application fee required: $50. Interview required.

Athletics Interscholastic: basketball, cross-country running, dressage, equestrian sports, field hockey, horseback riding, lacrosse, running, soccer, softball, swimming and diving, tennis, volleyball; intramural: aerobics, aerobics/dance, basketball, climbing, combined training, dance, dance team, dressage, equestrian sports, field hockey, fitness, horseback riding, modern dance, physical fitness, physical training, rock climbing, strength & conditioning, weight lifting, weight training. 3 coaches, 1 athletic trainer.

Computers Computers are regularly used in all classes. Computer resources include on-campus library services, online commercial services, Internet access, wireless campus network, Internet filtering or blocking technology. Campus intranet, student e-mail accounts, and computer access in designated common areas are available to students. The school has a published electronic and media policy.

Contact Erica L. Ohanesian, Director of Admission and Financial Aid. 540-687-4341. Fax: 540-687-3627. E-mail: eohanesian@foxcroft.org. Web site: www.foxcroft.org.

FOX RIVER COUNTRY DAY SCHOOL

Elgin, Illinois
See Junior Boarding Schools section.

FOX VALLEY LUTHERAN HIGH SCHOOL

5300 North Meade Street
Appleton, Wisconsin 54913-8383
Head of School: Mr. Paul Hartwig

General Information Coeducational day college-preparatory, general academic, arts, business, vocational, religious studies, and technology school, affiliated with Wisconsin Evangelical Lutheran Synod. Grades 9–12. Founded: 1953. Setting: suburban. 63-acre campus. 1 building on campus. Approved or accredited by Wisconsin Department of Education. Endowment: $2.5 million. Total enrollment: 563. Upper school average class size: 23. Upper school faculty-student ratio: 1:14. There are 180 required school days per year for Upper School students. Upper School students typically attend 5 days per week. The average school day consists of 6 hours and 30 minutes.

Upper School Student Profile Grade 9: 129 students (52 boys, 77 girls); Grade 10: 139 students (74 boys, 65 girls); Grade 11: 156 students (87 boys, 69 girls); Grade 12: 139 students (71 boys, 68 girls). 85% of students are Wisconsin Evangelical Lutheran Synod.

Faculty School total: 44. In upper school: 32 men, 10 women; 18 have advanced degrees.

Subjects Offered Accounting, advanced chemistry, advanced computer applications, advanced math, algebra, American government, American history, American literature, art, athletics, band, basic language skills, Basic programming, Bible, Bible studies, biology, British literature, British literature (honors), British literature-AP, business, business law, calculus, calculus-AP, choir, Christian doctrine, church history, communication skills, comparative religion, composition, computer applications, computer programming, computer skills, computer-aided design, concert band, concert choir, construction, critical writing, digital photography, drama, earth science, economics, economics-AP, English, English composition, foods, general science, geometry, German, government, graphic arts, health and wellness, honors English, keyboarding, language and composition, Latin, Life of Christ, modern Western civilization, modern world history, personal fitness, physical fitness, physics, piano,

psychology, reading/study skills, religion, remedial/makeup course work, sewing, Spanish, statistics, symphonic band, woodworking, world geography, world history.

Graduation Requirements 1½ elective credits, arts and fine arts (art, music, dance, drama), English, mathematics, physical education (includes health), religion (includes Bible studies and theology), science.

Special Academic Programs Honors section; accelerated programs; study at local college for college credit; academic accommodation for the gifted; remedial reading and/or remedial writing; remedial math.

College Admission Counseling 169 students graduated in 2010; 160 went to college, including Marquette University; Martin Luther College; University of Wisconsin–Eau Claire; University of Wisconsin–Fox Valley; University of Wisconsin–Oshkosh. Other: 5 went to work, 2 entered military service, 1 had other specific plans.

Student Life Upper grades have specified standards of dress, student council, honor system. Discipline rests primarily with faculty. Attendance at religious services is required.

Tuition and Aid Day student tuition: $4750–$7000. Tuition installment plan (FACTS Tuition Payment Plan). Tuition reduction for siblings, need-based scholarship grants available. In 2010–11, 25% of upper-school students received aid. Total amount of financial aid awarded in 2010–11: $320,000.

Admissions Traditional secondary-level entrance grade is 9. ACT-Explore or Explore required. Deadline for receipt of application materials: none. Application fee required: $25. Interview required.

Athletics Interscholastic: baseball (boys), basketball (b,g), cheering (g), cross-country running (b,g), dance team (g), football (b), golf (b,g), hockey (b,g), ice hockey (b), softball (g), track and field (b,g), volleyball (g), wrestling (b). 2 PE instructors, 1 athletic trainer.

Computers Computers are regularly used in business, current events, economics, English, graphic arts, keyboarding, science classes. Computer network features include on-campus library services, Internet access, Internet filtering or blocking technology. Campus intranet and student e-mail accounts are available to students. Students grades are available online. The school has a published electronic and media policy.

Contact Mrs. Gloria Knoll, Guidance Assistant. 920-739-4441. E-mail: gknoll@fvlhs.org. Web site: www.fvlhs.org.

FRANCIS W. PARKER SCHOOL

330 West Webster Avenue
Chicago, Illinois 60614
Head of School: Dr. Daniel B. Frank

General Information Coeducational day college-preparatory school. Grades PK–12. Founded: 1901. Setting: urban. 5-acre campus. 1 building on campus. Approved or accredited by Independent Schools Association of the Central States, North Central Association of Colleges and Schools, and Illinois Department of Education. Member of National Association of Independent Schools. Endowment: $17.8 million. Total enrollment: 918. Upper school average class size: 16. Upper school faculty-student ratio: 1:6. There are 186 required school days per year for Upper School students. Upper School students typically attend 5 days per week. The average school day consists of 6 hours and 50 minutes.

Upper School Student Profile Grade 9: 85 students (43 boys, 42 girls); Grade 10: 81 students (45 boys, 36 girls); Grade 11: 80 students (39 boys, 41 girls); Grade 12: 75 students (35 boys, 40 girls).

Faculty School total: 120. In upper school: 27 men, 28 women; 44 have advanced degrees.

Subjects Offered Art, Chinese, community service, drama, English, French, health, history, journalism, Latin, leadership, mathematics, music, physical education, science, social sciences, Spanish, yearbook.

Graduation Requirements Arts and fine arts (art, music, dance, drama), English, foreign language, mathematics, physical education (includes health), science, social studics (includes history). Community service is required.

Special Academic Programs Independent study.

College Admission Counseling 80 students graduated in 2009; all went to college, including Columbia University; Duke University; University of Illinois at Urbana–Champaign; University of Michigan; University of Pennsylvania; Yale University.

Student Life Upper grades have specified standards of dress, student council, honor system. Discipline rests equally with students and faculty.

Tuition and Aid Day student tuition: $26,984. Tuition installment plan (Academic Management Services Plan, monthly payment plans, individually arranged payment plans). Need-based scholarship grants available. In 2009–10, 48% of upper-school students received aid. Total amount of financial aid awarded in 2009–10: $1,200,000.

Admissions Traditional secondary-level entrance grade is 9. For fall 2009, 175 students applied for upper-level admission, 36 were accepted, 27 enrolled. ISEE required. Deadline for receipt of application materials: none. Application fee required: $70. On-campus interview required.

Athletics Interscholastic: baseball (boys), basketball (b,g), cross-country running (b,g), field hockey (g), golf (b,g), soccer (b,g), softball (g), tennis (b,g), track and field (b,g), volleyball (g); coed interscholastic: aerobics/Nautilus, badminton, Cosom hockey, floor hockey, in-line hockey, in-line skating, indoor hockey, indoor track & field, jogging, Nautilus, roller blading, roller hockey, running, table tennis, ultimate Frisbee; coed intramural: strength & conditioning. 6 PE instructors, 26 coaches, 1 athletic trainer.

Francis W. Parker School

Computers Computers are regularly used in all academic, animation, design, engineering, music, video film production, Web site design classes. Computer network features include on-campus library services, online commercial services, Internet access, wireless campus network, Internet filtering or blocking technology, black/white and color printing. Student e-mail accounts are available to students. The school has a published electronic and media policy.

Contact Alexandra Springer, Admission Coordinator. 773-797-5107. Fax: 773-549-0587. E-mail: aspringer@fwparker.org. Web site: www.fwparker.org.

FRANKLIN ACADEMY

East Haddam, Connecticut
See Special Needs Schools section.

FRANKLIN ROAD ACADEMY

4700 Franklin Road
Nashville, Tennessee 37220
Head of School: Dr. Margaret Wade

General Information Coeducational day college-preparatory, arts, religious studies, and technology school. Grades PK–12. Founded: 1971. Setting: suburban. 57-acre campus. 5 buildings on campus. Approved or accredited by Southern Association of Colleges and Schools, Southern Association of Independent Schools, Tennessee Association of Independent Schools, and Tennessee Department of Education. Member of National Association of Independent Schools. Endowment: $10.4 million. Total enrollment: 816. Upper school average class size: 8. Upper school faculty-student ratio: 1:8. There are 185 required school days per year for Upper School students. Upper School students typically attend 5 days per week. The average school day consists of 6 hours and 30 minutes.

Upper School Student Profile Grade 9: 60 students (30 boys, 30 girls); Grade 10: 60 students (30 boys, 30 girls); Grade 11: 60 students (30 boys, 30 girls); Grade 12: 60 students (30 boys, 30 girls).

Faculty School total: 100. In upper school: 21 men, 14 women; 20 have advanced degrees.

Subjects Offered Advanced chemistry, Advanced Placement courses, algebra, American history, American literature, anatomy and physiology, art, art-AP, band, baseball, basketball, Bible, Bible studies, biology, biology-AP, calculus, calculus-AP, chemistry, chemistry-AP, choral music, Civil War, college counseling, computer education, computer music, computer programming, computer science, current events, dance, drama, dramatic arts, economics, economics and history, electronic music, English, English language-AP, English literature, English literature-AP, environmental science, European history, European history-AP, fine arts, French, French language-AP, French literature-AP, geometry, government/civics, grammar, history, history-AP, honors algebra, honors English, honors geometry, honors U.S. history, human anatomy, jazz band, keyboarding, Latin, Latin-AP, Life of Christ, mathematics, mathematics-AP, model United Nations, music, music theory, personal development, physical education, physics, physics-AP, pottery, pre-calculus, SAT preparation, SAT/ACT preparation, science, social sciences, social studies, Spanish, Spanish language-AP, Spanish literature-AP, speech, statistics, statistics-AP, student government, student publications, technical theater, theater, theater production, track and field, trigonometry, U.S. government, U.S. history, U.S. history-AP, vocal music, volleyball, weight training, world history, world literature, wrestling, writing.

Graduation Requirements Arts and fine arts (art, music, dance, drama), computer science, English, foreign language, mathematics, physical education (includes health), religion (includes Bible studies and theology), science, social studies (includes history). Community service is required.

Special Academic Programs Advanced Placement exam preparation; honors section; independent study; term-away projects; academic accommodation for the gifted, the musically talented, and the artistically talented.

College Admission Counseling 56 students graduated in 2010; all went to college, including Auburn University; Belmont University; Middle Tennessee State University; The University of Tennessee; University of Georgia. 40% scored over 600 on SAT critical reading, 50% scored over 600 on SAT math, 50% scored over 26 on composite ACT.

Student Life Upper grades have uniform requirement, student council, honor system. Discipline rests primarily with faculty.

Summer Programs Enrichment, sports, art/fine arts, computer instruction programs offered; session focuses on day camps, the arts, technology, and sports; held both on and off campus; held at area swimming pool; accepts boys and girls; open to students from other schools. 400 students usually enrolled. 2011 schedule: June 1 to July 22.

Tuition and Aid Day student tuition: $16,560. Tuition installment plan (Insured Tuition Payment Plan, FACTS Tuition Payment Plan, individually arranged payment plans). Need-based scholarship grants available. In 2010–11, 10% of upper-school students received aid. Total amount of financial aid awarded in 2010–11: $600,000.

Admissions Traditional secondary-level entrance grade is 9. For fall 2010, 104 students applied for upper-level admission, 65 were accepted, 23 enrolled. ISEE required. Deadline for receipt of application materials: none. Application fee required: $40. On-campus interview required.

Athletics Interscholastic: baseball (boys), basketball (b,g), bowling (b,g), cheering (g), cross-country running (b,g), dance (g), diving (b,g), football (b), golf (b,g), hockey (b), ice hockey (b), soccer (b,g), softball (g), swimming and diving (b,g), tennis (b,g), track and field (b,g), volleyball (g), wrestling (b); intramural: aerobics/dance (g), physical fitness (b,g), physical training (b,g), power lifting (b), strength & conditioning (b,g); coed intramural: aerobics/dance, riflery. 2 PE instructors, 2 coaches, 1 athletic trainer.

Computers Computers are regularly used in art, Bible studies, college planning, creative writing, economics, English, foreign language, French, history, journalism, keyboarding, Latin, library skills, literary magazine, mathematics, music, religious studies, science, social sciences, Spanish, technology, theater, theater arts, Web site design, writing, yearbook classes. Computer network features include on-campus library services, online commercial services, Internet access, wireless campus network, Internet filtering or blocking technology, networked instructional software. Campus intranet and student e-mail accounts are available to students. Students grades are available online. The school has a published electronic and media policy.

Contact Dr. Kenyetta Wynn, Director of Admissions. 615-832-8845. Fax: 615-834-4137. E-mail: wynnk@franklinroadacademy.com. Web site: www.franklinroadacademy.com.

FRASER ACADEMY

Vancouver, British Columbia, Canada
See Special Needs Schools section.

FREDERICA ACADEMY

200 Murray Way
St. Simons Island, Georgia 31522
Head of School: Ms. Ellen E. Fleming

General Information Coeducational day college-preparatory, arts, and technology school. Grades PK–12. Founded: 1970. Setting: small town. Nearest major city is Jacksonville, FL. 35-acre campus. 7 buildings on campus. Approved or accredited by Georgia Independent School Association, Southern Association of Colleges and Schools, and Georgia Department of Education. Member of National Association of Independent Schools. Endowment: $2 million. Total enrollment: 357. Upper school average class size: 18. Upper school faculty-student ratio: 1:9. There are 180 required school days per year for Upper School students. Upper School students typically attend 5 days per week. The average school day consists of 8 hours and 5 minutes.

Faculty School total: 50. In upper school: 6 men, 9 women; 10 have advanced degrees.

Subjects Offered Algebra, American history, American literature, anatomy, ancient history, art, biology, biology-AP, calculus-AP, chemistry, choral music, computer applications, drama, economics, English, English literature, environmental science, geometry, government/civics, grammar, keyboarding, literature-AP, photography, physical education, physical science, physics, pre-calculus, psychology, public speaking, science, Spanish, U.S. history-AP, world history, world literature, writing, yearbook.

Graduation Requirements Algebra, American government, American history, arts and fine arts (art, music, dance, drama), biology, chemistry, computer applications, economics, English literature, foreign language, geometry, physical education (includes health), world history.

Special Academic Programs Advanced Placement exam preparation; honors section.

College Admission Counseling 41 students graduated in 2010; all went to college, including Georgia Institute of Technology; University of Georgia. Mean SAT critical reading: 591, mean SAT math: 583, mean SAT writing: 584, mean combined SAT: 1758.

Student Life Upper grades have specified standards of dress, student council, honor system. Discipline rests primarily with faculty.

Summer Programs Enrichment, sports, art/fine arts, computer instruction programs offered; session focuses on enrichment; held on campus; accepts boys and girls; open to students from other schools. 200 students usually enrolled. 2011 schedule: June 15 to August 1. Application deadline: May 2.

Tuition and Aid Day student tuition: $14,440. Merit scholarship grants, need-based scholarship grants, local bank financing available. In 2010–11, 30% of upper-school students received aid. Total amount of financial aid awarded in 2010–11: $300,000.

Admissions Traditional secondary-level entrance grade is 9. Any standardized test, Cognitive Abilities Test, OLSAT/Stanford and writing sample required. Deadline for receipt of application materials: none. Application fee required: $75. On-campus interview required.

Athletics Interscholastic: baseball (boys), basketball (b,g), cheering (g), cross-country running (b,g), golf (b,g), lacrosse (b), outdoor education (b,g), physical fitness (b,g), soccer (b,g), tennis (b,g), volleyball (g), weight training (b,g); coed interscholastic: cross-country running, golf, swimming and diving. 2 PE instructors, 5 coaches, 1 athletic trainer.

Computers Computers are regularly used in library skills, photography, yearbook classes. Computer network features include on-campus library services, online commercial services, Internet access, wireless campus network. Students grades are available online. The school has a published electronic and media policy.

Contact Mrs. Jennifer D. Wall, Director of Admission. 912-638-9981 Ext. 106. Fax: 912-638-1442. E-mail: jwall@fredericaacademy.org. Web site: www.fredericaacademy.org.

FREEMAN ACADEMY
748 South Main Street
PO Box 1000
Freeman, South Dakota 57029
Head of School: Ms. Pam Tieszen

General Information Coeducational boarding and day college-preparatory, arts, and religious studies school, affiliated with Mennonite Church. Boarding grades 9–12, day grades 5–12. Founded: 1900. Setting: rural. Nearest major city is Sioux Falls. Students are housed in coed dormitories and host family homes. 80-acre campus. 6 buildings on campus. Approved or accredited by Mennonite Schools Council, North Central Association of Colleges and Schools, and South Dakota Department of Education. Endowment: $378,000. Total enrollment: 70. Upper school average class size: 12. Upper school faculty-student ratio: 1:5. There are 180 required school days per year for Upper School students. Upper School students typically attend 5 days per week. The average school day consists of 8 hours.

Upper School Student Profile Grade 9: 6 students (4 boys, 2 girls); Grade 10: 15 students (9 boys, 6 girls); Grade 11: 9 students (2 boys, 7 girls); Grade 12: 17 students (9 boys, 8 girls). 19% of students are boarding students. 85% are state residents. 1 state is represented in upper school student body. 15% are international students. International students from Democratic People's Republic of Korea, Paraguay, Taiwan, and Thailand. 63% of students are Mennonite.

Faculty School total: 10. In upper school: 4 men, 6 women; 2 have advanced degrees.
Subjects Offered Computer science, English, fine arts, humanities, mathematics, music, religion, science, social sciences.
Graduation Requirements Arts and fine arts (art, music, dance, drama), computer science, English, foreign language, mathematics, religion (includes Bible studies and theology), science, social studies (includes history), humanities.
Special Academic Programs Independent study; academic accommodation for the musically talented and the artistically talented.
College Admission Counseling 10 students graduated in 2010; all went to college, including Bethel College; Goshen College; Hesston College; University of Sioux Falls. Median composite ACT: 24. 50% scored over 26 on composite ACT.
Student Life Upper grades have specified standards of dress, honor system. Discipline rests primarily with faculty. Attendance at religious services is required.
Tuition and Aid Day student tuition: $5685; 7-day tuition and room/board: $14,500. Tuition installment plan (FACTS Tuition Payment Plan, monthly payment plans, semester payment plan). Tuition reduction for siblings, merit scholarship grants, need-based scholarship grants available. In 2010–11, 13% of upper-school students received aid; total upper-school merit-scholarship money awarded: $500. Total amount of financial aid awarded in 2010–11: $20,000.
Admissions Traditional secondary-level entrance grade is 9. For fall 2010, 9 students applied for upper-level admission, 8 were accepted, 8 enrolled. Deadline for receipt of application materials: none. No application fee required. Interview recommended.
Athletics Interscholastic: basketball (boys, girls), cheering (g), cross-country running (b,g), golf (b,g), soccer (b,g), track and field (b,g), volleyball (g). 3 coaches.
Computers Computers are regularly used in English, keyboarding, mathematics, religion, science, social studies, speech, yearbook classes. Computer network features include on-campus library services, Internet access, wireless campus network, Internet filtering or blocking technology. Student e-mail accounts and computer access in designated common areas are available to students. Students grades are available online. The school has a published electronic and media policy.
Contact Ms. Bonnie Young, Enrollment Director. 605-925-4237 Ext. 225. Fax: 605-925-4271. E-mail: byoung@freemanacademy.org. Web site: www.freemanacademy.org.

FRENCH-AMERICAN SCHOOL OF NEW YORK
525 Fenimore Road
Mamaroneck, New York 10543
Head of School: Mr. Robert Leonhardt

General Information Coeducational day college-preparatory and bilingual studies school. Grades N–12. Founded: 1980. Setting: suburban. Nearest major city is White Plains. 1 building on campus. Approved or accredited by Middle States Association of Colleges and Schools, New York State Association of Independent Schools, and New York Department of Education. Languages of instruction: English and French. Total enrollment: 825. Upper school average class size: 18. Upper school faculty-student ratio: 1:7. There are 167 required school days per year for Upper School students. Upper School students typically attend 5 days per week. The average school day consists of 6 hours and 11 minutes.
Upper School Student Profile Grade 9: 56 students (21 boys, 35 girls); Grade 10: 44 students (18 boys, 26 girls); Grade 11: 37 students (24 boys, 13 girls); Grade 12: 25 students (11 boys, 14 girls).
Faculty School total: 116. In upper school: 17 men, 35 women; 33 have advanced degrees.

Subjects Offered Algebra, American history, American literature, art, biology, choir, civics, computer applications, computer multimedia, current events, earth science, ecology, economics, English, ESL, European history, expository writing, French, French language-AP, French literature-AP, French studies, geometry, German, government, health, Latin, mathematics, multimedia, music, newspaper, philosophy, physical education, physics, public speaking, science, social studies, Spanish, Spanish language-AP, world history, world literature, writing, yearbook.
Graduation Requirements 20th century history, algebra, American history, biology, calculus, chemistry, civics, computer studies, current events, English, European history, foreign language, French, geography, geology, geometry, history, mathematics, music, philosophy, physical education (includes health), physics, pre-algebra, pre-calculus, research seminar, social studies (includes history). Community service is required.
Special Academic Programs Advanced Placement exam preparation; honors section; ESL (22 students enrolled).
College Admission Counseling 22 students graduated in 2010; 21 went to college, including McGill University. Other: 1 had other specific plans. Mean SAT critical reading: 624, mean SAT math: 642, mean SAT writing: 631.
Student Life Upper grades have specified standards of dress, student council. Discipline rests primarily with faculty.
Tuition and Aid Day student tuition: $22,600–$23,350. Tuition installment plan (Academic Management Services Plan). Need-based scholarship grants available. In 2010–11, 5% of upper-school students received aid. Total amount of financial aid awarded in 2010–11: $188,856.
Admissions Traditional secondary-level entrance grade is 9. For fall 2010, 25 students applied for upper-level admission, 19 were accepted, 16 enrolled. English, French, and math proficiency required. Deadline for receipt of application materials: none. Application fee required: $100. Interview recommended.
Athletics Interscholastic: baseball (boys), basketball (b,g), cross-country running (b,g), rugby (b,g), soccer (b,g), softball (g), tennis (b,g); coed intramural: fencing. 3 PE instructors, 3 coaches.
Computers Computers are regularly used in art, English, foreign language, French, history, mathematics, music, publications, science classes. Computer network features include on-campus library services, Internet access, Internet filtering or blocking technology, laptop use (in certain classes). Student e-mail accounts are available to students. The school has a published electronic and media policy.
Contact Mr. Antoine Agopian, Director of Admissions. 914-250-0400. Fax: 914-940-2214. E-mail: aagopian@fasny.org. Web site: www.fasny.org.

FRESNO ADVENTIST ACADEMY
5397 East Olive Avenue
Fresno, California 93727
Head of School: Pastor Daniel Kittle

General Information Coeducational day college-preparatory, general academic, arts, business, vocational, and religious studies school, affiliated with Seventh-day Adventist Church. Grades K–12. Founded: 1897. Setting: suburban. 40-acre campus. 7 buildings on campus. Approved or accredited by Board of Regents, General Conference of Seventh-day Adventists, Western Association of Schools and Colleges, and California Department of Education. Language of instruction: Spanish. Endowment: $875,000. Total enrollment: 193. Upper school average class size: 20. Upper school faculty-student ratio: 1:19. There are 147 required school days per year for Upper School students. Upper School students typically attend 4 days per week. The average school day consists of 7 hours and 35 minutes.
Upper School Student Profile Grade 9: 19 students (10 boys, 9 girls); Grade 10: 17 students (8 boys, 9 girls); Grade 11: 14 students (6 boys, 8 girls); Grade 12: 16 students (7 boys, 9 girls). 80% of students are Seventh-day Adventists.
Faculty School total: 23. In upper school: 6 men, 6 women; 7 have advanced degrees.
Subjects Offered Algebra, American government, American history, American literature, anatomy, art history, Bible, Bible studies, biology, business skills, ceramics, chemistry, choir, choral music, computer science, digital photography, economics, English, English literature, fine arts, geometry, government/civics, grammar, health, health education, history, home economics, industrial arts, keyboarding, life skills, mathematics, music, physical education, physical science, physics, physiology, pre-algebra, publications, religion, science, small engine repair, social sciences, social studies, Spanish, speech communications, typing, vocal ensemble, welding, work experience, world history.
Graduation Requirements Arts and fine arts (art, music, dance, drama), business skills (includes word processing), computer science, English, foreign language, mathematics, physical education (includes health), religion (includes Bible studies and theology), science, social sciences, social studies (includes history), work experience, service learning, work experience.
Special Academic Programs Advanced Placement exam preparation; honors section; accelerated programs; independent study; study at local college for college credit; programs in general development for dyslexic students; ESL (2 students enrolled).
College Admission Counseling 17 students graduated in 2010; 15 went to college, including Azusa Pacific University; California State University, Fresno; Fresno City College; La Sierra University; Oakwood University. Other: 2 went to work. 10% scored over 600 on SAT critical reading, 10% scored over 600 on SAT math, 10% scored over 26 on composite ACT.

Fresno Adventist Academy

Student Life Upper grades have specified standards of dress, student council, honor system. Discipline rests primarily with faculty. Attendance at religious services is required.

Summer Programs Remediation, enrichment, ESL programs offered; held on campus; accepts boys and girls; open to students from other schools. 24 students usually enrolled. 2011 schedule: June 21 to August 6. Application deadline: June 4.

Tuition and Aid Day student tuition: $8000. Tuition installment plan (monthly payment plans, individually arranged payment plans). Tuition reduction for siblings, merit scholarship grants, need-based scholarship grants, paying campus jobs available. In 2010–11, 80% of upper-school students received aid. Total amount of financial aid awarded in 2010–11: $102,000.

Admissions Traditional secondary-level entrance grade is 9. For fall 2010, 14 students applied for upper-level admission, 14 were accepted, 13 enrolled. 3-R Achievement Test, ITBS achievement test, school's own exam or Test of Achievement and Proficiency required. Deadline for receipt of application materials: none. Application fee required: $25. Interview required.

Athletics Interscholastic: basketball (boys, girls), flag football (b,g), volleyball (b,g); intramural: basketball (b,g), flag football (b,g), soccer (b,g), track and field (b,g), volleyball (b,g); coed interscholastic: volleyball; coed intramural: flag football, soccer, track and field, volleyball. 1 PE instructor, 4 coaches.

Computers Computers are regularly used in art, business skills, computer applications, economics, English, foreign language, keyboarding, life skills, photography, science, yearbook classes. Computer network features include on-campus library services, Internet access, wireless campus network, Internet filtering or blocking technology. Student e-mail accounts are available to students. Students grades are available online.

Contact Mrs. Sue Schramm, Executive Assistant. 559-251-5548. Fax: 559-252-6495. E-mail: sschramm@faa.org. Web site: www.faa.org.

FRESNO CHRISTIAN SCHOOLS
7280 North Cedar Avenue
Fresno, California 93720
Head of School: Mr. Todd Bennett

General Information Coeducational day college-preparatory, arts, religious studies, and technology school, affiliated with Protestant-Evangelical faith. Grades K–12. Founded: 1977. Setting: suburban. 27-acre campus. 4 buildings on campus. Approved or accredited by Association of Christian Schools International, Western Association of Schools and Colleges, and California Department of Education. Endowment: $50,000. Total enrollment: 612. Upper school average class size: 20. Upper school faculty-student ratio: 1:10. There are 176 required school days per year for Upper School students. Upper School students typically attend 5 days per week. The average school day consists of 5 hours and 45 minutes.

Upper School Student Profile Grade 6: 50 students (24 boys, 26 girls); Grade 7: 49 students (22 boys, 27 girls); Grade 8: 56 students (25 boys, 31 girls); Grade 9: 51 students (28 boys, 23 girls); Grade 10: 34 students (16 boys, 18 girls); Grade 11: 44 students (22 boys, 22 girls); Grade 12: 55 students (29 boys, 26 girls). 98% of students are Protestant-Evangelical faith.

Faculty School total: 30. In upper school: 8 men, 7 women; 5 have advanced degrees.

Subjects Offered Advanced Placement courses, algebra, alternative physical education, American government, American history-AP, art, ASB Leadership, athletics, band, baseball, basketball, Bible, Bible studies, biology, biology-AP, British literature, calculus-AP, cheerleading, chemistry, choir, choral music, Christian education, civics, composition-AP, computer applications, computer graphics, computer literacy, concert band, drama, economics, English, English language and composition-AP, English literature and composition-AP, English-AP, ensembles, geometry, golf, home economics, honors algebra, honors English, honors geometry, humanities, jazz band, journalism, leadership, marching band, mathematics, mathematics-AP, physical education, physics, pre-calculus, softball, Spanish, sports, statistics-AP, student government, tennis, track and field, trigonometry, U.S. history, video film production, vocal music, volleyball, woodworking, work experience, world history, yearbook.

Graduation Requirements Arts and fine arts (art, music, dance, drama), electives, English, mathematics, physical education (includes health), religion (includes Bible studies and theology), science, social studies (includes history).

Special Academic Programs 5 Advanced Placement exams for which test preparation is offered; honors section; independent study; study at local college for college credit; remedial reading and/or remedial writing; remedial math; special instructional classes for students with learning disabilities.

College Admission Counseling 67 students graduated in 2010; 58 went to college, including Azusa Pacific University; Biola University; California State University, Fresno; Fresno City College; Pepperdine University; Whitworth University. Other: 1 entered military service, 8 had other specific plans. Mean SAT critical reading: 544, mean SAT math: 546, mean SAT writing: 508, mean combined SAT: 1598.

Student Life Upper grades have specified standards of dress, student council, honor system. Discipline rests primarily with faculty. Attendance at religious services is required.

Tuition and Aid Day student tuition: $8274. Tuition installment plan (FACTS Tuition Payment Plan, monthly payment plans, individually arranged payment plans). Tuition reduction for siblings, merit scholarship grants, need-based scholarship grants

available. In 2010–11, 15% of upper-school students received aid; total upper-school merit-scholarship money awarded: $5000. Total amount of financial aid awarded in 2010–11: $300,000.

Admissions Traditional secondary-level entrance grade is 9. Any standardized test required. Deadline for receipt of application materials: none. Application fee required: $100. Interview required.

Athletics Interscholastic: baseball (boys), basketball (b,g), cheering (g), cross-country running (b,g), drill team (g), football (b), soccer (b,g), softball (g), strength & conditioning (b,g), tennis (b), track and field (b,g), volleyball (g), weight training (b,g); coed interscholastic: golf, physical training; coed intramural: badminton, basketball, outdoor recreation, volleyball. 2 PE instructors, 12 coaches, 1 athletic trainer.

Computers Computers are regularly used in media production, publications, yearbook classes. Computer network features include on-campus library services, online commercial services, Internet access, wireless campus network, Internet filtering or blocking technology. Computer access in designated common areas is available to students. Students grades are available online. The school has a published electronic and media policy.

Contact Mr. Todd Bennett, Principal. 559-299-1695. Fax: 559-299-2478. E-mail: tbennett@fresnochristian.com. Web site: www.fresnochristian.com.

FRIENDS ACADEMY
270 Duck Pond Road
Locust Valley, New York 11560
Head of School: Mr. William G. Morris Jr.

General Information Coeducational day college-preparatory school, affiliated with Society of Friends. Grades N–12. Founded: 1876. Setting: suburban. Nearest major city is New York. 65-acre campus. 8 buildings on campus. Approved or accredited by New York State Association of Independent Schools and New York Department of Education. Member of National Association of Independent Schools and Secondary School Admission Test Board. Endowment: $26 million. Total enrollment: 751. Upper school average class size: 15. Upper school faculty-student ratio: 1:6. There are 165 required school days per year for Upper School students. Upper School students typically attend 5 days per week. The average school day consists of 7 hours.

Upper School Student Profile Grade 9: 84 students (41 boys, 43 girls); Grade 10: 103 students (44 boys, 59 girls); Grade 11: 101 students (56 boys, 45 girls); Grade 12: 87 students (47 boys, 40 girls). 2% of students are members of Society of Friends.

Faculty School total: 92. In upper school: 28 men, 33 women; 49 have advanced degrees.

Subjects Offered Advanced Placement courses, African studies, algebra, American history, American literature, art, art history, Bible studies, biology, calculus, ceramics, chemistry, community service, computer literacy, computer programming, computer science, creative writing, drama, driver education, English, English literature, environmental science, ethics, European history, expository writing, fine arts, French, geography, geometry, grammar, Greek, health, history, Italian, Latin, logic, mathematics, mechanical drawing, music, outdoor education, photography, physical education, physics, psychology, religion, science, social sciences, social studies, Spanish, speech, theater, trigonometry, Western civilization, world literature, writing.

Graduation Requirements Arts and fine arts (art, music, dance, drama), computer literacy, English, foreign language, mathematics, outdoor education, physical education (includes health), religion (includes Bible studies and theology), science, social sciences, social studies (includes history), speech, participation in on-campus work crew program, independent service program. Community service is required.

Special Academic Programs Advanced Placement exam preparation; honors section; independent study.

College Admission Counseling 89 students graduated in 2010; all went to college, including Boston College; Connecticut College; Cornell University; Princeton University; The George Washington University; University of Pennsylvania. Mean SAT critical reading: 595, mean SAT math: 616.

Student Life Upper grades have specified standards of dress, student council. Discipline rests primarily with faculty. Attendance at religious services is required.

Summer Programs Art/fine arts programs offered; session focuses on using the arts to learn life skills and using life skills to explore the arts (via The Artist's Institute); held on campus; accepts boys and girls; open to students from other schools. 25 students usually enrolled. 2011 schedule: June 20 to July 22.

Tuition and Aid Day student tuition: $26,900. Tuition installment plan (Insured Tuition Payment Plan, monthly payment plans). Need-based scholarship grants, Quaker grants, Tuition remission for children of faculty and staff available. In 2010–11, 20% of upper-school students received aid. Total amount of financial aid awarded in 2010–11: $1,000,000.

Admissions Traditional secondary-level entrance grade is 9. For fall 2010, 114 students applied for upper-level admission, 71 were accepted, 44 enrolled. SSAT required. Deadline for receipt of application materials: January 15. Application fee required: $50. On-campus interview required.

Athletics Interscholastic: baseball (boys), basketball (b,g), crew (b,g), cross-country running (b,g), field hockey (g), football (b), golf (b), indoor track & field (b,g), lacrosse (b,g), soccer (b,g), softball (g), tennis (b,g), track and field (b,g), winter (indoor) track (b,g), wrestling (b); coed intramural: dance, volleyball. 7 PE instructors, 1 athletic trainer.

Computers Computers are regularly used in English, mathematics, science, technology classes. Computer network features include on-campus library services, online commercial services, Internet access, wireless campus network, Internet filtering or blocking technology. Campus intranet, student e-mail accounts, and computer access in designated common areas are available to students. The school has a published electronic and media policy.

Contact Joanna Kim, Admissions Assistant. 516-393-4244. Fax: 516-465-1718. E-mail: joanna_kim@fa.org. Web site: www.fa.org.

FRIENDS' CENTRAL SCHOOL

1101 City Avenue
Wynnewood, Pennsylvania 19096
Head of School: David Felsen
General Information Coeducational day college-preparatory school, affiliated with Society of Friends. Grades N–12. Founded: 1845. Setting: suburban. Nearest major city is Philadelphia. 23-acre campus. 7 buildings on campus. Approved or accredited by Pennsylvania Association of Independent Schools and Pennsylvania Department of Education. Member of National Association of Independent Schools. Endowment: $17.6 million. Total enrollment: 955. Upper school average class size: 18. Upper school faculty-student ratio: 1:9. Upper School students typically attend 5 days per week. The average school day consists of 6 hours and 40 minutes.

Upper School Student Profile Grade 9: 101 students (54 boys, 47 girls); Grade 10: 108 students (51 boys, 57 girls); Grade 11: 97 students (54 boys, 43 girls); Grade 12: 88 students (42 boys, 46 girls). 3% of students are members of Society of Friends.
Faculty School total: 130. In upper school: 26 men, 26 women; 38 have advanced degrees.
Subjects Offered Advanced biology, advanced chemistry, advanced math, algebra, American history, American literature, Bible, biology, calculus, ceramics, chemistry, chorus, computer applications, computer programming, conflict resolution, drama, English, French, geometry, instrumental music, Latin, life skills, media studies, modern European history, music history, music theory, philosophy, photography, physical education, physical science, physics, pre-calculus, psychology, sexuality, Spanish, studio art, study skills, Western literature, women in world history, woodworking, world history, writing workshop.
Graduation Requirements Arts and fine arts (art, music, dance, drama), English, foreign language, mathematics, science, service learning/internship, U.S. history, world cultures.
Special Academic Programs Honors section; independent study; term-away projects.
College Admission Counseling 97 students graduated in 2010; all went to college, including Boston University; Franklin & Marshall College; Oberlin College; Temple University; University of Pennsylvania; Washington University in St. Louis. Mean SAT critical reading: 669, mean SAT math: 633, mean SAT writing: 640.
Student Life Upper grades have specified standards of dress, student council. Discipline rests primarily with faculty. Attendance at religious services is required.
Summer Programs Remediation, advancement programs offered; held on campus; accepts boys and girls; open to students from other schools. 37 students usually enrolled. 2011 schedule: June 27 to August 5.
Tuition and Aid Day student tuition: $26,300. Tuition installment plan (monthly payment plans, Higher Education Service, Inc). Need-based scholarship grants available. In 2010–11, 31% of upper-school students received aid. Total amount of financial aid awarded in 2010–11: $2,059,947.
Admissions Traditional secondary-level entrance grade is 9. For fall 2010, 137 students applied for upper-level admission, 57 were accepted, 34 enrolled. ISEE, SSAT or Wechsler Intelligence Scale for Children required. Deadline for receipt of application materials: January 15. Application fee required: $50. On-campus interview required.
Athletics Interscholastic: aquatics (boys, girls), baseball (b), basketball (b,g), cross-country running (b,g), field hockey (g); coed interscholastic: cheering, golf, squash; coed intramural: aerobics/dance, aerobics/Nautilus, dance, fitness. 8 PE instructors, 10 coaches, 1 athletic trainer.
Computers Computers are regularly used in college planning, foreign language, French, health, information technology, introduction to technology, Latin, mathematics, publishing, science, Spanish, technology, Web site design, yearbook classes. Computer network features include on-campus library services, online commercial services, Internet access, wireless campus network, Internet filtering or blocking technology. Intranet collaboration. Campus intranet and student e-mail accounts are available to students. The school has a published electronic and media policy.
Contact Barbara Behar, Director of Admission and Financial Aid. 610-645-5032. Fax: 610-658-5644. E-mail: admission@friendscentral.org. Web site: www.friendscentral.org.

FRIENDSHIP CHRISTIAN SCHOOL

5400 Coles Ferry Pike
Lebanon, Tennessee 37087
Head of School: Mr. Jon Shoulders
General Information Coeducational day college-preparatory, arts, business, religious studies, technology, and dual enrollment with Cumberland University school,

affiliated with Christian faith. Grades PK–12. Founded: 1973. Setting: rural. Nearest major city is Nashville. 50-acre campus. 6 buildings on campus. Approved or accredited by National Christian School Association, Southern Association of Colleges and Schools, and Tennessee Department of Education. Endowment: $250. Total enrollment: 627. Upper school average class size: 20. Upper school faculty-student ratio: 1:15. There are 175 required school days per year for Upper School students. Upper School students typically attend 5 days per week. The average school day consists of 6 hours and 35 minutes.
Upper School Student Profile Grade 9: 56 students (27 boys, 29 girls); Grade 10: 50 students (23 boys, 27 girls); Grade 11: 50 students (29 boys, 21 girls); Grade 12: 47 students (20 boys, 27 girls). 80% of students are Christian faith.
Faculty School total: 50. In upper school: 9 men, 12 women; 18 have advanced degrees.
Subjects Offered Accounting, ACT preparation, advanced biology, advanced chemistry, advanced math, Advanced Placement courses, agriculture, algebra, American government, anatomy and physiology, Ancient Greek, art, athletic training, backpacking, band, Bible, Bible studies, biology, bowling, British literature (honors), business applications, calculus, calculus-AP, chemistry, choral music, chorus, college placement, college planning, computers, creative writing, drama, driver education, earth science, economics, English, English-AP, environmental science, geometry, honors algebra, honors English, honors geometry, Internet, journalism, keyboarding, mathematics, modern history, physical education, physical science, physics, physiology, pre-algebra, psychology, science project, science research, Spanish, speech, swimming, trigonometry, U.S. constitutional history, U.S. government, U.S. history, U.S. history-AP, U.S. Presidents, weight training, wellness, world geography, world history, yearbook.
Graduation Requirements ACT preparation, advanced chemistry, advanced math, Advanced Placement courses, algebra, American government, American history, American history-AP, applied arts, arts and fine arts (art, music, dance, drama), Bible, biology, chemistry, chemistry-AP, ecology, English language and composition-AP, English literature-AP, English-AP, foreign language, French, honors U.S. history, keyboarding, physical education (includes health), physics, pre-calculus, U.S. government and politics-AP, U.S. history-AP, weight training.
Special Academic Programs Advanced Placement exam preparation; honors section; study at local college for college credit.
College Admission Counseling 58 students graduated in 2010; all went to college, including Cumberland University; Lipscomb University; Tennessee Technological University; The University of Tennessee; United States Naval Academy; Vanderbilt University. Mean composite ACT: 23. 50% scored over 26 on composite ACT.
Student Life Upper grades have uniform requirement, student council, honor system. Discipline rests primarily with faculty.
Tuition and Aid Day student tuition: $7300. Tuition installment plan (FACTS Tuition Payment Plan). Tuition reduction for siblings, need-based scholarship grants, paying campus jobs available. In 2010–11, 2% of upper-school students received aid. Total amount of financial aid awarded in 2010–11: $5000.
Admissions Traditional secondary-level entrance grade is 9. For fall 2010, 163 students applied for upper-level admission, 160 were accepted, 117 enrolled. Otis-Lennon School Ability Test required. Deadline for receipt of application materials: none. Application fee required: $50. Interview recommended.
Athletics Interscholastic: baseball (boys), basketball (b,g), cheering (g), football (b), golf (b,g), physical fitness (b,g); coed interscholastic: bowling, cross-country running, golf, physical fitness. 2 PE instructors, 13 coaches, 1 athletic trainer.
Computers Computers are regularly used in accounting, all academic, business, college planning, creative writing, journalism, library, media, multimedia, newspaper, reading, remedial study skills, science, typing classes. Computer network features include on-campus library services, online commercial services, Internet access, wireless campus network, Internet filtering or blocking technology. Student e-mail accounts and computer access in designated common areas are available to students. Students grades are available online. The school has a published electronic and media policy.
Contact Terresia Williams, Director of Admissions. 615-449-1573 Ext. 207. Fax: 615-449-2769. E-mail: twilliams@friendshipchristian.org. Web site: www.friendshipchristian.org.

FRIENDS SELECT SCHOOL

17th & Benjamin Franklin Parkway
Philadelphia, Pennsylvania 19103-1284
Head of School: Rose Hagan
General Information Coeducational day college-preparatory, arts, and religious studies school, affiliated with Society of Friends. Grades PK–12. Founded: 1689. Setting: urban. 1-acre campus. 2 buildings on campus. Approved or accredited by Friends Council on Education. Member of National Association of Independent Schools and Secondary School Admission Test Board. Endowment: $8 million. Total enrollment: 536. Upper school average class size: 15. Upper school faculty-student ratio: 1:15. There are 167 required school days per year for Upper School students. Upper School students typically attend 5 days per week. The average school day consists of 6 hours and 20 minutes.
Upper School Student Profile Grade 9: 35 students (11 boys, 24 girls); Grade 10: 44 students (19 boys, 25 girls); Grade 11: 37 students (16 boys, 21 girls); Grade 12: 49 students (20 boys, 29 girls). 5% of students are members of Society of Friends.

Friends Select School

Faculty School total: 74. In upper school: 14 men, 18 women; 27 have advanced degrees.

Subjects Offered 20th century American writers, 3-dimensional art, algebra, American history, American literature, art, art history, biology, calculus, chemistry, computer math, computer programming, computer science, creative writing, drama, drawing, earth science, ecology, economics, electronics, English, English literature, ethics, European history, expository writing, fine arts, French, geography, geology, geometry, government/civics, grammar, health, history, Italian, Latin, marine biology, mathematics, music, photography, physical education, physics, religion, science, sculpture, social studies, Spanish, statistics, theater, trigonometry, world history, world literature, writing.

Graduation Requirements Arts and fine arts (art, music, dance, drama), English, foreign language, mathematics, physical education (includes health), religion (includes Bible studies and theology), science, senior project, social studies (includes history), junior internship.

Special Academic Programs Advanced Placement exam preparation; independent study; academic accommodation for the musically talented and the artistically talented; ESL (10 students enrolled).

College Admission Counseling 38 students graduated in 2010; 37 went to college, including Arcadia University; Boston University; Drexel University; Northeastern University; The George Washington University; University of Pennsylvania. Other: 1 had other specific plans.

Student Life Upper grades have student council. Discipline rests primarily with faculty. Attendance at religious services is required.

Summer Programs Remediation, enrichment, advancement, art/fine arts, computer instruction programs offered; session focuses on enrichment and advancement; held on campus; accepts boys and girls; open to students from other schools. 50 students usually enrolled. 2011 schedule: June 27 to August 5. Application deadline: June 6.

Tuition and Aid Day student tuition: $25,825. Tuition installment plan (10-month payment plan, 2-payment plan). Tuition reduction for siblings, need-based scholarship grants, need-based loans, K-12 Family Education Loan Program (SLM Financial Group), AchieverLoans (Key Education Resources), tuition reduction for 3-plus siblings from same family; 5% reduction for children of alumni/alumnae available. In 2010–11, 43% of upper-school students received aid. Total amount of financial aid awarded in 2010–11: $888,006.

Admissions Traditional secondary-level entrance grade is 9. For fall 2010, 73 students applied for upper-level admission, 55 were accepted, 21 enrolled. ERB CTP IV, ISEE, PSAT and SAT for applicants to grade 11 and 12, SSAT or WISC or WAIS required. Deadline for receipt of application materials: none. Application fee required: $40. On-campus interview required.

Athletics Interscholastic: baseball (boys), basketball (b,g), crew (b,g), cross-country running (b,g), field hockey (g), soccer (b,g), softball (g), wrestling (b); coed interscholastic: crew, cross-country running, swimming and diving, tennis. 5 PE instructors, 28 coaches, 1 athletic trainer.

Computers Computers are regularly used in all academic, English, foreign language, mathematics, science classes. Computer network features include on-campus library services, online commercial services, Internet access, online learning center. Campus intranet, student e-mail accounts, and computer access in designated common areas are available to students. The school has a published electronic and media policy.

Contact Roger Dillow, Director of Enrollment Management and Director of Admission PK-8. 215-561-5900 Ext. 102. Fax: 215-864-2979. E-mail: rogerd@ friends-select.org. Web site: friends-select.org.

FRIENDS SEMINARY

222 East 16th Street
New York, New York 10003
Head of School: Robert N. Lauder

General Information Coeducational day college-preparatory school, affiliated with Society of Friends. Grades K–12. Founded: 1786. Setting: urban. 8 buildings on campus. Approved or accredited by Friends Council on Education, New York State Association of Independent Schools, and New York Department of Education. Member of National Association of Independent Schools. Endowment: $8.4 million. Total enrollment: 695. Upper school average class size: 15. Upper school faculty-student ratio: 1:7.

Upper School Student Profile Grade 9: 70 students (33 boys, 37 girls); Grade 10: 71 students (31 boys, 40 girls); Grade 11: 69 students (35 boys, 34 girls); Grade 12: 69 students (32 boys, 37 girls). 3% of students are members of Society of Friends.

Faculty School total: 92. In upper school: 28 men, 29 women; 40 have advanced degrees.

Subjects Offered Acting, African-American studies, algebra, American history, American literature, anthropology, Arabic, architecture, art history, biology, calculus, chemistry, chorus, community service, creative writing, drama, driver education, ecology, English, English literature, environmental science, European history, experiential education, fabric arts, fine arts, French, genetics, geology, geometry, government/civics, Greek, health, history, Holocaust, human relations, international relations, Internet, Islamic history, jazz, Latin, law, marine biology, mathematics, media, music, musical productions, photography, physical education, physics, playwriting, science, sculpture, social studies, Spanish, statistics, theater, trigonometry, wilderness education, world history, world literature, world religions.

Graduation Requirements Arts and fine arts (art, music, dance, drama), computer science, English, experiential education, foreign language, human relations, mathematics, physical education (includes health), science, social studies (includes history), 7 hours in-school and 20 hours out-of-school community service per year.

Special Academic Programs Advanced Placement exam preparation; independent study; term-away projects; study at local college for college credit; domestic exchange program; study abroad.

College Admission Counseling 69 students graduated in 2009; all went to college, including Barnard College; Brown University; Columbia College; Cornell University; Syracuse University; Wesleyan University. Median SAT critical reading: 652, median SAT math: 647, median SAT writing: 675.

Student Life Upper grades have student council, honor system. Discipline rests primarily with faculty.

Tuition and Aid Day student tuition: $31,940. Tuition installment plan (The Tuition Plan, Insured Tuition Payment Plan, Key Tuition Payment Plan, monthly payment plans, individually arranged payment plans). Need-based scholarship grants available. In 2009–10, 25% of upper-school students received aid. Total amount of financial aid awarded in 2009–10: $3,485,274.

Admissions Traditional secondary-level entrance grade is 9. ISEE or SSAT required. Deadline for receipt of application materials: January 15. Application fee required: $75. On-campus interview required.

Athletics Interscholastic: baseball (boys), basketball (b,g), soccer (b,g), softball (g), tennis (b,g), volleyball (g); coed interscholastic: golf, squash, swimming and diving, track and field, volleyball, wilderness survival, yoga. 5 PE instructors, 5 coaches.

Computers Computers are regularly used in all academic classes. Computer network features include online commercial services, Internet access, Internet filtering or blocking technology. Student e-mail accounts are available to students. The school has a published electronic and media policy.

Contact Harriet O. Burnett, Director of Admissions. 212-979-5030 Ext. 141. Fax: 212-677-5543. E-mail: hburnett@friendsseminary.org. Web site: www. friendsseminary.org.

FRONT RANGE CHRISTIAN HIGH SCHOOL

6637 West Ottawa Avenue
Littleton, Colorado 80128
Head of School: Pres. Brian Meek

General Information Coeducational day college-preparatory, general academic, arts, business, vocational, religious studies, bilingual studies, technology, and science, math, language arts, media school, affiliated with Christian faith. Grades K–12. Founded: 1994. Setting: suburban. Nearest major city is Denver. 20-acre campus. 3 buildings on campus. Approved or accredited by Association of Christian Schools International, North Central Association of Colleges and Schools, and Colorado Department of Education. Total enrollment: 391. Upper school average class size: 25. Upper school faculty-student ratio: 1:12.

Upper School Student Profile Grade 9: 47 students (22 boys, 25 girls); Grade 10: 42 students (16 boys, 26 girls); Grade 11: 34 students (17 boys, 17 girls); Grade 12: 46 students (25 boys, 21 girls). 100% of students are Christian faith.

Faculty School total: 41. In upper school: 9 men, 11 women; 10 have advanced degrees.

Special Academic Programs Advanced Placement exam preparation; honors section; academic accommodation for the gifted; remedial reading and/or remedial writing; remedial math; programs in English, mathematics, general development for dyslexic students; special instructional classes for deaf students, blind students.

College Admission Counseling 36 students graduated in 2009; 31 went to college, including Arapahoe Community College; Colorado State University; University of Northern Colorado. Other: 2 went to work, 1 entered military service, 2 had other specific plans.

Student Life Upper grades have specified standards of dress, student council, honor system. Discipline rests primarily with faculty. Attendance at religious services is required.

Tuition and Aid Day student tuition: $7950. Tuition installment plan (FACTS Tuition Payment Plan, monthly payment plans). Tuition reduction for siblings, need-based scholarship grants, paying campus jobs available. In 2009–10, 100% of upper-school students received aid. Total amount of financial aid awarded in 2009–10: $180,000.

Admissions Traditional secondary-level entrance grade is 9. For fall 2009, 12 students applied for upper-level admission, 8 were accepted, 6 enrolled. English proficiency, essay or Math Placement Exam required. Deadline for receipt of application materials: none. Application fee required: $50. Interview required.

Athletics Interscholastic: baseball (boys), basketball (b,g), cheering (g), cross-country running (g), dance (b,g), football (b), golf (b), physical fitness (b,g), soccer (g), volleyball (g); intramural: basketball (b,g), soccer (b), volleyball (g). 1 PE instructor, 28 coaches.

Computers Computers are regularly used in basic skills, computer applications, data processing, information technology, introduction to technology, keyboarding, media arts, multimedia, yearbook classes. Computer network features include on-campus library services, Internet access, Internet filtering or blocking technology, Renweb Parents access. Computer access in designated common areas is available to students. Students grades are available online. The school has a published electronic and media policy.

Contact Karen Kay, Admissions Coordinator. 303-531-4541. Fax: 720-922-3296. E-mail: kkay@frcs.org. Web site: www.frontrangechristian.org.

THE FROSTIG SCHOOL
Pasadena, California
See Special Needs Schools section.

FRYEBURG ACADEMY
745 Main Street
Fryeburg, Maine 04037-1329
Head of School: Mr. Daniel G. Lee Jr.

General Information Coeducational boarding and day college-preparatory, general academic, arts, and technology school. Grades 9–PG. Founded: 1792. Setting: small town. Nearest major city is Portland. Students are housed in single-sex dormitories. 34-acre campus. 17 buildings on campus. Approved or accredited by Association of Independent Schools in New England, Independent Schools of Northern New England, New England Association of Schools and Colleges, The Association of Boarding Schools, The College Board, and Maine Department of Education. Member of National Association of Independent Schools and Secondary School Admission Test Board. Endowment: $8 million. Total enrollment: 681. Upper school average class size: 15. Upper school faculty-student ratio: 1:10. There are 170 required school days per year for Upper School students. Upper School students typically attend 5 days per week. The average school day consists of 6 hours and 30 minutes.

Upper School Student Profile Grade 9: 145 students (73 boys, 72 girls); Grade 10: 151 students (76 boys, 75 girls); Grade 11: 159 students (83 boys, 76 girls); Grade 12: 184 students (96 boys, 88 girls); Postgraduate: 2 students (2 boys). 20% of students are boarding students. 83% are state residents. 9 states are represented in upper school student body. 14% are international students. International students from China, Democratic People's Republic of Korea, Germany, Spain, Taiwan, and Viet Nam; 15 other countries represented in student body.

Faculty School total: 67. In upper school: 35 men, 32 women; 27 have advanced degrees; 25 reside on campus.

Subjects Offered Algebra, American literature, anatomy, art, art history, biology, botany, business, calculus, chemistry, computer math, computer programming, computer science, creative writing, drafting, drama, driver education, earth science, ecology, economics, English, English literature, ethics, European history, expository writing, fine arts, French, geography, geometry, government/civics, grammar, health, history, industrial arts, journalism, Latin, linear algebra, marine biology, mathematics, mechanical drawing, music, photography, physical education, physics, physiology, psychology, science, social studies, sociology, Spanish, speech, theater, trigonometry, typing, world history, world literature, writing.

Graduation Requirements Arts and fine arts (art, music, dance, drama), computer science, English, foreign language, mathematics, physical education (includes health), science, social studies (includes history). Community service is required.

Special Academic Programs 14 Advanced Placement exams for which test preparation is offered; honors section; independent study; study at local college for college credit; academic accommodation for the musically talented; remedial reading and/or remedial writing; remedial math; programs in English, mathematics, general development for dyslexic students; special instructional classes for students with learning disabilities, Attention Deficit Disorder, and dyslexia; ESL (45 students enrolled).

College Admission Counseling 191 students graduated in 2009; 153 went to college, including Boston University; Colby College; Northeastern University; University of Illinois at Urbana–Champaign; University of Maine; University of New Hampshire. Other: 29 went to work, 3 entered military service, 1 entered a postgraduate year, 5 had other specific plans.

Student Life Upper grades have specified standards of dress, student council. Discipline rests primarily with faculty.

Tuition and Aid Day student tuition: $18,650; 5-day tuition and room/board: $29,750; 7-day tuition and room/board: $37,300. Tuition installment plan (monthly payment plans, individually arranged payment plans). Need-based scholarship grants available. In 2009–10, 42% of upper-school students received aid. Total amount of financial aid awarded in 2009–10: $950,000.

Admissions Traditional secondary-level entrance grade is 10. For fall 2009, 175 students applied for upper level admission, 137 were accepted, 52 enrolled. Writing sample required. Deadline for receipt of application materials: none. Application fee required: $50. Interview required.

Athletics Interscholastic: baseball (boys), basketball (b,g), cross-country running (b,g), field hockey (g), football (b), golf (b), hockey (b,g), ice hockey (b), lacrosse (b,g), skiing (cross-country) (b,g), skiing (downhill) (b,g), soccer (b,g), softball (g), tennis (b,g), track and field (b,g), wrestling (b); intramural: ice hockey (g), strength & conditioning (b,g), table tennis (b,g); coed interscholastic: alpine skiing, cheering, mountain biking, nordic skiing; coed intramural: alpine skiing, archery, backpacking, badminton, ball hockey, basketball, bicycling, billiards, bowling, canoeing/kayaking, climbing, figure skating, fishing, fitness, fitness walking, flag football, floor hockey, fly fishing, freestyle skiing, Frisbee, golf, hiking/backpacking, ice skating, jogging, kayaking, mountain biking, mountaineering, paint ball, physical fitness, physical training, pistol, rock climbing, roller blading, skiing (downhill), snowboarding,

snowshoeing, swimming and diving, table tennis, tai chi, telemark skiing, tennis, ultimate Frisbee, volleyball, walking, wall climbing, weight lifting, whiffle ball, winter walking. 2 PE instructors, 3 coaches, 1 athletic trainer.

Computers Computers are regularly used in all classes. Computer network features include on-campus library services, Internet access, wireless campus network. Computer access in designated common areas is available to students. The school has a published electronic and media policy.

Contact Stephanie S. Morin, Director of Admission. 207-935-2013. Fax: 207-935-4292. E-mail: admissions@fryeburgacademy.org. Web site: www.fryeburgacademy.org.

FUQUA SCHOOL
605 Fuqua Drive
PO Drawer 328
Farmville, Virginia 23901
Head of School: Ms. Ruth S. Murphy

General Information Coeducational day college-preparatory, arts, and business school. Grades PK–12. Founded: 1959. Setting: small town. Nearest major city is Richmond. 60-acre campus. 19 buildings on campus. Approved or accredited by Southern Association of Colleges and Schools, Virginia Association of Independent Schools, and Virginia Department of Education. Member of Secondary School Admission Test Board. Endowment: $4.9 million. Total enrollment: 431. Upper school average class size: 16. Upper school faculty-student ratio: 1:16. There are 180 required school days per year for Upper School students. Upper School students typically attend 5 days per week. The average school day consists of 6 hours.

Upper School Student Profile Grade 9: 37 students (16 boys, 21 girls); Grade 10: 36 students (20 boys, 16 girls); Grade 11: 32 students (19 boys, 13 girls); Grade 12: 40 students (18 boys, 22 girls).

Faculty School total: 42. In upper school: 7 men, 12 women; 6 have advanced degrees.

Subjects Offered Agriculture, algebra, art, band, biology-AP, calculus-AP, chemistry, chemistry-AP, communications, composition, computer information systems, driver education, economics, English composition, English literature-AP, English-AP, environmental science, environmental studies, ethics, fitness, general business, geometry, government-AP, grammar, health, history-AP, industrial technology, personal finance, physics, pre-calculus, Spanish, theater, U.S. government, U.S. history-AP, United States government-AP, weight training, yearbook, zoology.

Graduation Requirements Arts and fine arts (art, music, dance, drama), communications, composition, computer information systems, driver education, English, fitness, foreign language, grammar, health education, mathematics, physical education (includes health), science, social studies (includes history). Community service is required.

Special Academic Programs Advanced Placement exam preparation; honors section; accelerated programs; independent study; study at local college for college credit.

College Admission Counseling 30 students graduated in 2010; all went to college, including James Madison University; Lynchburg College; The University of North Carolina Wilmington; University of Virginia; Virginia Polytechnic Institute and State University; Washington and Lee University. Median SAT critical reading: 570, median SAT math: 540, median SAT writing: 550, median composite ACT: 26. 42% scored over 600 on SAT critical reading, 41% scored over 600 on SAT math, 40% scored over 600 on SAT writing, 57% scored over 26 on composite ACT.

Student Life Upper grades have specified standards of dress, student council, honor system. Discipline rests primarily with faculty.

Summer Programs Sports programs offered; session focuses on sports and sport skills; held on campus; accepts boys and girls; open to students from other schools. 40 students usually enrolled. 2011 schedule: June 15 to July 31. Application deadline: May 15.

Tuition and Aid Day student tuition: $7180. Tuition installment plan (The Tuition Plan, Insured Tuition Payment Plan, monthly payment plans, individually arranged payment plans). Tuition reduction for siblings, merit scholarship grants, need-based scholarship grants available. In 2010–11, 41% of upper-school students received aid; total upper-school merit-scholarship money awarded: $7000. Total amount of financial aid awarded in 2010–11: $50,000.

Admissions Traditional secondary-level entrance grade is 9. For fall 2010, 9 students applied for upper-level admission, 9 were accepted, 9 enrolled. Placement test required. Deadline for receipt of application materials: none. Application fee required: $100. On-campus interview required.

Athletics Interscholastic: baseball (boys), basketball (b,g), cheering (g), football (b), softball (g), tennis (g), volleyball (g); coed interscholastic: cross-country running, golf, soccer, swimming and diving, track and field; coed intramural: basketball. 2 PE instructors, 38 coaches, 1 athletic trainer.

Computers Computers are regularly used in all classes. Computer network features include on-campus library services, online commercial services, Internet access, Internet filtering or blocking technology, video editing software, CD-ROM +RW and DVD +RW. Student e-mail accounts and computer access in designated common areas are available to students. The school has a published electronic and media policy.

Fuqua School

Contact Mrs. Christy M. Murphy, Director of Admissions and Special Events. 434-392-4131 Ext. 273. Fax: 434-392-5062. E-mail: murphycm@fuquaschool.com. Web site: www.fuquaschool.com.

GABLES ACADEMY
Stone Mountain, Georgia
See Special Needs Schools section.

GABRIEL RICHARD HIGH SCHOOL
15325 Pennsylvania Road
Riverview, Michigan 48193
Head of School: Br. James Rottenbucher, CSC
General Information Coeducational day college-preparatory school, affiliated with Roman Catholic Church. Grades 9–12. Founded: 1965. Setting: suburban. Nearest major city is Detroit. 23-acre campus. 1 building on campus. Approved or accredited by Michigan Association of Non-Public Schools, North Central Association of Colleges and Schools, and Michigan Department of Education. Total enrollment: 407. Upper school average class size: 25. Upper school faculty-student ratio: 1:15. There are 180 required school days per year for Upper School students. Upper School students typically attend 5 days per week. The average school day consists of 6 hours and 35 minutes.
Upper School Student Profile Grade 9: 94 students (30 boys, 64 girls); Grade 10: 92 students (54 boys, 38 girls); Grade 11: 106 students (52 boys, 54 girls); Grade 12: 115 students (65 boys, 50 girls); Postgraduate: 407 students (201 boys, 206 girls). 90% of students are Roman Catholic.
Faculty School total: 28. In upper school: 9 men, 19 women; 18 have advanced degrees.
Subjects Offered 1½ elective credits, 1968, 20th century American writers, 20th century history, 20th century world history, 3-dimensional art, accounting, acting, advanced chemistry, advanced math, Advanced Placement courses, advanced studio art-AP, algebra, American Civil War, American democracy, American government, American history, American history-AP, American literature, American literature-AP, anatomy, anatomy and physiology, ancient history, ancient world history, animal science, art, band, basic language skills, biology, biology-AP, British literature (honors), business, business law, calculus, calculus-AP, campus ministry, Catholic belief and practice, ceramics, chemistry, chemistry-AP, child development, Christian doctrine, Christian education, Christian scripture, Christian testament, Christianity, church history, Civil War, civil war history, clayworking, college planning, communications, comparative politics, comparative religion, computer information systems, constitutional history of U.S., constitutional law, desktop publishing, digital art, digital photography, drama, drawing, earth science, economics, English literature, English-AP, environmental science, European history-AP, family living, food and nutrition, foods, forensics, French, general business, general math, general science, geography, geometry, German, government, government-AP, health, history, history of the Catholic Church, history-AP, home economics, honors algebra, honors English, human anatomy, humanities, independent living, instrumental music, keyboarding, lab science, library assistant, logic, New Testament, participation in sports, peace and justice, peer ministry, photography, physical fitness, physics, physics-AP, portfolio art, pre-algebra, psychology-AP, publications, research, senior composition, sociology, Spanish, speech, sports, studio art-AP, theater arts, U.S. government and politics-AP, U.S. history, U.S. history-AP, United States government-AP, weight fitness, weight training, yearbook, zoology.
Graduation Requirements Arts and fine arts (art, music, dance, drama), English, mathematics, physical education (includes health), science, social studies (includes history), speech, theology.
Special Academic Programs Advanced Placement exam preparation; honors section; independent study.
College Admission Counseling 115 students graduated in 2009; all went to college, including Central Michigan University; Grand Valley State University; Michigan State University; University of Michigan; University of Michigan–Dearborn; Wayne State University. Median composite ACT: 22. 16.5% scored over 26 on composite ACT.
Student Life Upper grades have uniform requirement, student council, honor system. Discipline rests primarily with faculty. Attendance at religious services is required.
Tuition and Aid Tuition installment plan (The Tuition Plan, Academic Management Services Plan). Tuition reduction for siblings, merit scholarship grants, need-based scholarship grants available.
Admissions Traditional secondary-level entrance grade is 9. For fall 2009, 94 students applied for upper-level admission, 94 were accepted, 94 enrolled. High School Placement Test required. Deadline for receipt of application materials: none. Application fee required: $100. Interview required.
Athletics Interscholastic: baseball (boys), basketball (b,g), cheering (g), cross-country running (b,g), football (b), golf (b), ice hockey (b), pom squad (g), soccer (b,g), softball (g), tennis (b,g), track and field (b,g), volleyball (g), wrestling (b); coed interscholastic: bowling, figure skating. 2 PE instructors.
Computers Computers are regularly used in desktop publishing, digital applications, keyboarding, research skills, speech classes. Computer network features include on-campus library services, Internet access. Computer access in designated common areas is available to students. Students grades are available online.

Contact Mrs. Joan Fitzgerald, Assistant Principal. 734-284-1875 Ext. 13. Fax: 734-284-9304. E-mail: jfitzgerald@grriverview.org. Web site: www.grriverview.org.

THE GALLOWAY SCHOOL
215 West Wieuca Road NW
Atlanta, Georgia 30342
Head of School: Tom Brereton
General Information Coeducational day college-preparatory, arts, and technology school. Grades PK–12. Founded: 1969. Setting: suburban. 8-acre campus. 4 buildings on campus. Approved or accredited by Georgia Independent School Association, Southern Association of Colleges and Schools, Southern Association of Independent Schools, and Georgia Department of Education. Member of National Association of Independent Schools and Secondary School Admission Test Board. Endowment: $5 million. Total enrollment: 703. Upper school average class size: 12. Upper school faculty-student ratio: 1:8.
Upper School Student Profile Grade 9: 56 students (30 boys, 26 girls); Grade 10: 62 students (34 boys, 28 girls); Grade 11: 54 students (22 boys, 32 girls); Grade 12: 50 students (28 boys, 22 girls).
Faculty School total: 103. In upper school: 14 men, 20 women; 25 have advanced degrees.
Subjects Offered 3-dimensional design, advanced computer applications, Advanced Placement courses, algebra, American culture, American history, American literature, analytic geometry, animation, biology, biology-AP, British literature, calculus, calculus-AP, chemistry, computer animation, computer applications, computer graphics, desktop publishing, digital art, digital music, digital photography, drama, economics, electives, English, English-AP, filmmaking, fine arts, French, geometry, guidance, history, integrated physics, language arts, Latin, library, mathematics, music, physical education, physical science, political science, pre-calculus, public speaking, science, senior composition, social studies, Spanish, technology, U.S. government and politics-AP, visual arts, world geography, world history, world literature.
Graduation Requirements Arts and fine arts (art, music, dance, drama), computers, electives, English, foreign language, mathematics, science, social studies (includes history).
Special Academic Programs Advanced Placement exam preparation; accelerated programs; independent study; study at local college for college credit; academic accommodation for the gifted, the musically talented, and the artistically talented.
College Admission Counseling 55 students graduated in 2009; all went to college, including Emory University; Emory University, Oxford College; Georgia Institute of Technology; University of Georgia.
Student Life Upper grades have specified standards of dress, student council, honor system. Discipline rests primarily with faculty.
Tuition and Aid Day student tuition: $18,430. Tuition installment plan (50/50). Need-based scholarship grants available. In 2009–10, 14% of upper-school students received aid. Total amount of financial aid awarded in 2009–10: $312,130.
Admissions Traditional secondary-level entrance grade is 9. For fall 2009, 87 students applied for upper-level admission, 44 were accepted, 24 enrolled. SSAT required. Deadline for receipt of application materials: January 29. Application fee required: $75. Interview required.
Athletics Interscholastic: basketball (boys, girls), golf (b,g), soccer (b,g), softball (g), swimming and diving (b,g), tennis (b,g), volleyball (g); intramural: dance team (g); coed interscholastic: cross-country running, outdoor adventure, running, track and field, ultimate Frisbee. 1 PE instructor, 4 coaches, 1 athletic trainer.
Computers Computers are regularly used in art, desktop publishing, drawing and design, English, graphic arts, information technology, introduction to technology, journalism, keyboarding, literary magazine, mathematics, multimedia, music, newspaper, photography, publishing, research skills, science, technology, theater, Web site design, yearbook classes. Computer network features include on-campus library services, online commercial services, Internet access, wireless campus network, Internet filtering or blocking technology, print sharing. Campus intranet, student e-mail accounts, and computer access in designated common areas are available to students. Students grades are available online. The school has a published electronic and media policy.

Contact Rosetta Gooden, Director of Admission. 404-252-8389. Fax: 404-252-7770. E-mail: rgooden@gallowayschool.org. Web site: www.gallowayschool.org.

GANN ACADEMY (THE NEW JEWISH HIGH SCHOOL OF GREATER BOSTON)
333 Forest Street
Waltham, Massachusetts 02452
Head of School: Rabbi Marc A. Baker
General Information Coeducational day college-preparatory, arts, and religious studies school, affiliated with Jewish faith. Grades 9–12. Founded: 1997. Setting: suburban. Nearest major city is Boston. 20-acre campus. 2 buildings on campus. Approved or accredited by New England Association of Schools and Colleges and Massachusetts Department of Education. Total enrollment: 323. Upper school average class size: 14. Upper school faculty-student ratio: 1:5. There are 165 required school

days per year for Upper School students. Upper School students typically attend 5 days per week. The average school day consists of 8 hours.

Upper School Student Profile Grade 9: 89 students (44 boys, 45 girls); Grade 10: 67 students (29 boys, 38 girls); Grade 11: 85 students (41 boys, 44 girls); Grade 12: 82 students (42 boys, 40 girls). 100% of students are Jewish.

Faculty School total: 72. In upper school: 30 men, 42 women; 48 have advanced degrees.

Subjects Offered Advanced Placement courses, algebra, American history-AP, American literature-AP, art history, arts, Bible as literature, biology, calculus, calculus-AP, chemistry, creative arts, creative writing, drama, English, French, geometry, health and wellness, Hebrew, history, Jewish history, Judaic studies, Mandarin, music, photography, physics, pre-calculus, Rabbinic literature, Spanish.

Graduation Requirements Arts, athletics, Bible as literature, English, health, Hebrew, history, mathematics, Rabbinic literature, science, Jewish Thought, electives.

Special Academic Programs Advanced Placement exam preparation; study abroad.

College Admission Counseling 74 students graduated in 2010; all went to college, including Barnard College; Boston University; Cornell University; The George Washington University; University of Michigan; University of Vermont. Median SAT critical reading: 655, median SAT math: 650, median SAT writing: 665, median combined SAT: 1310, median composite ACT: 27. 71% scored over 600 on SAT critical reading, 66% scored over 600 on SAT math, 81% scored over 600 on SAT writing, 74% scored over 1800 on combined SAT, 56% scored over 26 on composite ACT.

Student Life Upper grades have specified standards of dress, student council, honor system. Discipline rests primarily with faculty. Attendance at religious services is required.

Tuition and Aid Day student tuition: $29,100. Tuition installment plan (FACTS Tuition Payment Plan). Need-based scholarship grants available. In 2010–11, 43% of upper-school students received aid.

Admissions Traditional secondary-level entrance grade is 9. For fall 2010, 146 students applied for upper-level admission, 132 were accepted, 85 enrolled. SSAT required. Deadline for receipt of application materials: January 31. Application fee required: $100. On-campus interview required.

Athletics Interscholastic: baseball (boys), basketball (b,g), cross-country running (b,g), lacrosse (b,g), soccer (b,g), softball (g), tennis (b,g); intramural: basketball (b,g), tennis (b,g); coed interscholastic: juggling, ultimate Frisbee; coed intramural: fitness, golf, modern dance, table tennis, yoga. 26 coaches, 1 athletic trainer.

Computers Computer network features include on-campus library services, Internet access, wireless campus network, Internet filtering or blocking technology, computer lab. Student e-mail accounts and computer access in designated common areas are available to students. Students grades are available online. The school has a published electronic and media policy.

Contact Efraim Yudewitz, Director of Admissions. 781-642-6800 Ext. 101. Fax: 781-642-6805. E-mail: eyudewitz@gannacademy.org. Web site: www.gannacademy.org/.

GARCES MEMORIAL HIGH SCHOOL

2800 Loma Linda Drive
Bakersfield, California 93305
Head of School: Mrs. Kathleen B. Bears

General Information Coeducational day college-preparatory school, affiliated with Roman Catholic Church. Grades 9–12. Founded: 1947. Setting: suburban. Nearest major city is Los Angeles. 32-acre campus. 16 buildings on campus. Approved or accredited by Western Association of Schools and Colleges and Western Catholic Education Association. Endowment: $460,000. Total enrollment: 627. Upper school average class size: 25. Upper school faculty-student ratio: 1:28. There are 180 required school days per year for Upper School students. Upper School students typically attend 5 days per week. The average school day consists of 6 hours.

Upper School Student Profile Grade 9: 152 students (75 boys, 77 girls); Grade 10: 158 students (80 boys, 78 girls); Grade 11: 166 students (81 boys, 85 girls); Grade 12: 151 students (79 boys, 72 girls). 75% of students are Roman Catholic.

Faculty School total: 56. In upper school: 22 men, 30 women; 26 have advanced degrees.

Subjects Offered Algebra, American history, American literature, anatomy, art, biology, calculus, chemistry, community service, computer science, creative writing, drama, driver education, economics, English, English literature, ethics, fine arts, French, geography, geometry, government/civics, graphic arts, health, history, journalism, mathematics, music, physical education, physics, physiology, psychology, religion, science, social studies, Spanish, theater, world history, world literature.

Graduation Requirements Arts and fine arts (art, music, dance, drama), computer literacy, English, foreign language, health education, mathematics, physical education (includes health), religion (includes Bible studies and theology), science, social studies (includes history), 40 hours of community service.

Special Academic Programs Advanced Placement exam preparation; honors section; study at local college for college credit.

College Admission Counseling 156 students graduated in 2010; all went to college, including Bakersfield College; California Polytechnic State University, San Luis Obispo; California State University, Bakersfield; Texas Christian University; University of California, Santa Barbara; University of California, Santa Cruz. Mean SAT

critical reading: 538, mean SAT math: 525, mean SAT writing: 529, mean composite ACT: 24. 15.3% scored over 600 on SAT critical reading, 16.9% scored over 600 on SAT math.

Student Life Upper grades have uniform requirement, student council. Discipline rests primarily with faculty. Attendance at religious services is required.

Summer Programs Remediation, enrichment, advancement, sports, art/fine arts, computer instruction programs offered; session focuses on mathematics and English; held on campus; accepts boys and girls; open to students from other schools. 800 students usually enrolled. 2011 schedule: June 7 to July 8. Application deadline: May 6.

Tuition and Aid Day student tuition: $7500–$8500. Tuition installment plan (monthly payment plans, individually arranged payment plans). Merit scholarship grants, need-based scholarship grants available. In 2010–11, 32% of upper-school students received aid; total upper-school merit-scholarship money awarded: $9035. Total amount of financial aid awarded in 2010–11: $312,000.

Admissions Traditional secondary-level entrance grade is 9. For fall 2010, 185 students applied for upper-level admission, 175 were accepted, 152 enrolled. CTBS/4 required. Deadline for receipt of application materials: none. Application fee required: $75. Interview required.

Athletics Interscholastic: baseball (boys), basketball (b,g), cheering (g), cross-country running (b,g), dance squad (g), dance team (g), diving (b,g), golf (b,g), soccer (b,g), softball (g), swimming and diving (b,g), tennis (b,g), track and field (b,g), volleyball (g), water polo (b,g), weight training (b); intramural: baseball (b), basketball (b,g), volleyball (b,g); coed intramural: basketball, volleyball. 3 PE instructors, 28 coaches, 1 athletic trainer.

Computers Computers are regularly used in graphic arts, journalism, keyboarding classes. Computer resources include Internet access.

Contact Mrs. Joan M. Richardson, Registrar. 661-327-2578 Ext. 109. Fax: 661-327-5427. E-mail: jrichardson@garces.org. Web site: www.garces.org.

GARRISON FOREST SCHOOL

300 Garrison Forest Road
Owings Mills, Maryland 21117
Head of School: Mr. G. Peter O'Neill Jr.

General Information Girls' boarding and day (coeducational in lower grades) college-preparatory, arts, and Women in Science & Engineering (WISE) school. Boarding girls grades 8–12, day boys grades N–K, day girls grades N–12. Founded: 1910. Setting: suburban. Nearest major city is Baltimore. Students are housed in single-sex dormitories. 110-acre campus. 18 buildings on campus. Approved or accredited by Association of Independent Maryland Schools, Middle States Association of Colleges and Schools, The Association of Boarding Schools, and Maryland Department of Education. Member of National Association of Independent Schools and Secondary School Admission Test Board. Endowment: $30 million. Total enrollment: 671. Upper school average class size: 14. Upper school faculty-student ratio: 1:7. The average school day consists of 6 hours and 45 minutes.

Upper School Student Profile Grade 6: 44 students (44 girls); Grade 7: 45 students (45 girls); Grade 8: 59 students (59 girls); Grade 9: 79 students (79 girls); Grade 10: 75 students (75 girls); Grade 11: 69 students (69 girls); Grade 12: 66 students (66 girls). 22% of students are boarding students. 7 states are represented in upper school student body. 12% are international students. International students from Bahamas, China, Mauritius, Mexico, Republic of Korea, and Taiwan.

Faculty School total: 104. In upper school: 6 men, 36 women; 39 have advanced degrees; 20 reside on campus.

Subjects Offered Algebra, American history, American literature, anatomy, animal behavior, art, art history, art history-AP, arts and crafts, biology, calculus, calculus-AP, ceramics, chemistry, chemistry-AP, child development, Chinese, Chinese studies, computer science, computer skills, creative writing, dance, decision making skills, design, drama, drawing, ecology, English, English literature, English-AP, ESL, ethics, fine arts, French, French-AP, geometry, history-AP, Latin, Latin-AP, life skills, mathematics, music, philosophy, photography, physical education, physics, physics-AP, portfolio art, science, Spanish, Spanish-AP, statistics, theater, trigonometry, U.S. history-AP, world history.

Graduation Requirements Arts and fine arts (art, music, dance, drama), decision making skills, English, foreign language, mathematics, physical education (includes health), science, social studies (includes history).

Special Academic Programs 11 Advanced Placement exams for which test preparation is offered; honors section; independent study; term-away projects; academic accommodation for the gifted, the musically talented, and the artistically talented; ESL (8 students enrolled).

College Admission Counseling 67 students graduated in 2010; all went to college, including Clemson University; Rensselaer Polytechnic Institute; University of Maryland, College Park; University of Vermont; University of Virginia; Washington and Lee University. 50% scored over 600 on SAT critical reading, 50% scored over 600 on SAT math, 50% scored over 600 on SAT writing.

Student Life Upper grades have uniform requirement, student council, honor system. Discipline rests equally with students and faculty.

Summer Programs Sports, art/fine arts programs offered; held on campus; accepts boys and girls; open to students from other schools. 650 students usually enrolled. 2011 schedule: June 13 to August 5. Application deadline: June.

Garrison Forest School

Tuition and Aid Day student tuition: $23,350; 7-day tuition and room/board: $42,160. Tuition installment plan (FACTS Tuition Payment Plan). Need-based scholarship grants, need-based loans available. In 2010–11, 32% of upper-school students received aid. Total amount of financial aid awarded in 2010–11: $1,377,360.
Admissions Traditional secondary-level entrance grade is 9. For fall 2010, 119 students applied for upper-level admission, 74 were accepted, 40 enrolled. ISEE or SSAT required. Deadline for receipt of application materials: January 7. Application fee required: $50. Interview required.
Athletics Interscholastic: badminton, basketball, cross-country running, equestrian sports, field hockey, golf, horseback riding, indoor soccer, lacrosse, polo, soccer, softball, tennis, track and field, winter soccer; intramural: aerobics, aerobics/dance, bowling, dance, fitness, horseback riding, modern dance, physical fitness, squash, strength & conditioning, swimming and diving, yoga. 5 PE instructors, 12 coaches, 1 athletic trainer.
Computers Computers are regularly used in art, English, foreign language, history, mathematics, science classes. Computer network features include on-campus library services, Internet access, wireless campus network, Internet filtering or blocking technology, Moodle. Student e-mail accounts are available to students. The school has a published electronic and media policy.
Contact Mrs. Leslie D. Tinati, Director of Admission and Financial Aid. 410-559-3111. Fax: 410-363-8441. E-mail: gfsinfo@gfs.org. Web site: www.gfs.org.

GASTON DAY SCHOOL
2001 Gaston Day School Road
Gastonia, North Carolina 28056
Head of School: Dr. Richard E. Rankin
General Information Coeducational day college-preparatory and arts school. Grades PS–12. Founded: 1967. Setting: suburban. Nearest major city is Charlotte. 60-acre campus. 4 buildings on campus. Approved or accredited by North Carolina Association of Independent Schools, Southern Association of Colleges and Schools, Southern Association of Independent Schools, and North Carolina Department of Education. Member of National Association of Independent Schools. Endowment: $1.9 million. Total enrollment: 480. Upper school average class size: 12. Upper school faculty-student ratio: 1:6. There are 180 required school days per year for Upper School students. Upper School students typically attend 5 days per week. The average school day consists of 7 hours and 15 minutes.
Upper School Student Profile Grade 9: 37 students (22 boys, 15 girls); Grade 10: 31 students (11 boys, 20 girls); Grade 11: 34 students (15 boys, 19 girls); Grade 12: 40 students (20 boys, 20 girls).
Faculty School total: 53. In upper school: 10 men, 15 women; 11 have advanced degrees.
Subjects Offered Advanced chemistry, Advanced Placement courses, advanced studio art-AP, algebra, American history-AP, American literature, anatomy and physiology, art, biology, biology-AP, British literature, British literature (honors), calculus-AP, chemistry, chemistry-AP, chorus, creative writing, drama, English language and composition-AP, English language-AP, English literature and composition-AP, environmental science, environmental science-AP, film and literature, fine arts, French, general science, geometry, government/civics, honors algebra, honors English, honors geometry, honors U.S. history, honors world history, jazz band, journalism, learning lab, physics, pre-calculus, senior internship, Spanish, Spanish-AP, statistics-AP, student government, studio art-AP, study skills, U.S. government, U.S. history, U.S. history-AP, United States government-AP, visual arts, weight training, world literature, yearbook.
Graduation Requirements Arts and fine arts (art, music, dance, drama), electives, English, foreign language, mathematics, physical education (includes health), science, social studies (includes history), 25 hours of community service per year, seniors must complete a senior project.
Special Academic Programs Advanced Placement exam preparation; honors section; independent study; academic accommodation for the gifted.
College Admission Counseling 27 students graduated in 2010; 25 went to college, including Clemson University; College of Charleston; High Point University; The University of North Carolina at Chapel Hill; Washington and Lee University; Wofford College. Other: 2 entered a postgraduate year. Mean SAT critical reading: 615, mean SAT math: 587, mean SAT writing: 598.
Student Life Upper grades have specified standards of dress, student council, honor system. Discipline rests primarily with faculty.
Summer Programs Remediation, enrichment, advancement, sports, art/fine arts programs offered; session focuses on academic enrichment, advancement in sports and arts; held on campus; accepts boys and girls; open to students from other schools. 200 students usually enrolled. 2011 schedule: June to August.
Tuition and Aid Day student tuition: $12,890. Tuition installment plan (monthly payment plans, individually arranged payment plans). Merit scholarship grants, need-based scholarship grants available. In 2010–11, 44% of upper-school students received aid; total upper-school merit-scholarship money awarded: $137,210. Total amount of financial aid awarded in 2010–11: $239,193.
Admissions Traditional secondary-level entrance grade is 9. For fall 2010, 38 students applied for upper-level admission, 24 were accepted, 18 enrolled. ISEE required. Deadline for receipt of application materials: none. Application fee required: $50. On-campus interview required.

Athletics Interscholastic: baseball (boys), basketball (b,g), cheering (g), cross-country running (b,g), soccer (b,g), softball (g), swimming and diving (b,g), tennis (b,g), track and field (b,g), volleyball (g); intramural: climbing (b,g), cooperative games (g), equestrian sports (g), fencing (b,g), fitness (b,g), floor hockey (b,g), physical fitness (b,g), physical training (b,g), strength & conditioning (b,g), ultimate Frisbee (b,g), weight lifting (b,g), weight training (b,g); coed interscholastic: golf; coed intramural: skeet shooting. 1 PE instructor, 25 coaches, 1 athletic trainer.
Computers Computers are regularly used in art, English, foreign language, history, journalism, mathematics, newspaper, science, yearbook classes. Computer network features include on-campus library services, online commercial services, Internet access, Internet filtering or blocking technology. Computer access in designated common areas is available to students. Students grades are available online.
Contact Mrs. Martha Jayne Rhyne, Director of Admission. 704-864-7744 Ext. 174. Fax: 704-865-3813. E-mail: martha.rhyne@gastonday.org. Web site: www.gastonday.org.

GATEWAY SCHOOL
Arlington, Texas
See Special Needs Schools section.

GEM STATE ADVENTIST ACADEMY
16115 Montana Avenue
Caldwell, Idaho 83607
Head of School: Peter McPherson
General Information Coeducational boarding and day and distance learning college-preparatory, arts, religious studies, and technology school, affiliated with Seventh-day Adventist Church. Grades 9–12. Distance learning grade 9. Founded: 1918. Setting: rural. Nearest major city is Boise. Students are housed in single-sex dormitories. 4 buildings on campus. Approved or accredited by Northwest Association of Schools and Colleges and Idaho Department of Education. Total enrollment: 104. Upper school average class size: 24. Upper school faculty-student ratio: 1:9. There are 175 required school days per year for Upper School students. Upper School students typically attend 5 days per week. The average school day consists of 6 hours.
Upper School Student Profile Grade 9: 21 students (5 boys, 16 girls); Grade 10: 25 students (11 boys, 14 girls); Grade 11: 29 students (15 boys, 14 girls); Grade 12: 29 students (15 boys, 14 girls). 45% of students are boarding students. 84% are state residents. 7 states are represented in upper school student body. 1% are international students. International students from China. 95% of students are Seventh-day Adventists.
Faculty School total: 12. In upper school: 9 men, 3 women; 6 have advanced degrees; 2 reside on campus.
Subjects Offered Advanced computer applications, algebra, art, bell choir, Bible studies, biology, calculus-AP, chemistry, chorus, computer applications, consumer mathematics, economics, English, general science, geometry, graphic arts, gymnastics, health, Internet, keyboarding, music history, music theory, physical education, physics, piano, pre-algebra, pre-calculus, Spanish, speech, U.S. government, U.S. history, voice, work experience, world history, yearbook.
Graduation Requirements Arts and fine arts (art, music, dance, drama), computer education, economics, English, foreign language, humanities, mathematics, physical education (includes health), religion (includes Bible studies and theology), science, social studies (includes history), speech, U.S. government, U.S. history, senior project.
Special Academic Programs Advanced Placement exam preparation; study at local college for college credit.
College Admission Counseling 42 students graduated in 2010; 38 went to college, including Boise State University; Pacific Union College; Southern Adventist University; Walla Walla University.
Student Life Upper grades have specified standards of dress, student council, honor system. Discipline rests primarily with faculty. Attendance at religious services is required.
Tuition and Aid Day student tuition: $9244; 5-day tuition and room/board: $13,078; 7-day tuition and room/board: $14,612. Tuition installment plan (FACTS Tuition Payment Plan, monthly payment plans, individually arranged payment plans). Tuition reduction for siblings, merit scholarship grants, need-based scholarship grants, paying campus jobs available.
Admissions Traditional secondary-level entrance grade is 9. TOEFL or SLEP required. Deadline for receipt of application materials: none. No application fee required. Interview required.
Athletics Interscholastic: basketball (boys, girls), flag football (b), volleyball (g); intramural: basketball (b,g), flag football (b,g), floor hockey (b,g), soccer (b,g), softball (b,g); coed intramural: gymnastics, softball. 1 PE instructor, 1 coach.
Computers Computers are regularly used in all academic, art, business education, English, graphic arts, health, history, science, typing, writing classes. Computer network features include on-campus library services, online commercial services, Internet access, Internet filtering or blocking technology. Student e-mail accounts are available to students. Students grades are available online. The school has a published electronic and media policy.
Contact Karen Davies, Registrar. 208-459-1627. Fax: 208-454-9079. E-mail: kdavies@gemstate.org. Web site: www.gemstate.org.

THE GENEVA SCHOOL

2025 State Road 436
Winter Park, Florida 32792
Head of School: Rev. Robert Forrest Ingram

General Information Coeducational day college-preparatory, arts, and religious studies school, affiliated with Christian faith. Grades K4–12. Founded: 1993. Setting: suburban. Nearest major city is Orlando. 3-acre campus. 1 building on campus. Approved or accredited by Florida Council of Independent Schools. Total enrollment: 474. Upper school average class size: 18. Upper school faculty-student ratio: 1:9. There are 170 required school days per year for Upper School students. Upper School students typically attend 5 days per week. The average school day consists of 6 hours and 45 minutes.

Upper School Student Profile Grade 9: 27 students (10 boys, 17 girls); Grade 10: 23 students (10 boys, 13 girls); Grade 11: 26 students (10 boys, 16 girls); Grade 12: 10 students (4 boys, 6 girls). 95% of students are Christian faith.

Faculty School total: 53. In upper school: 17 men, 12 women; 19 have advanced degrees.

Subjects Offered Advanced Placement courses, advanced studio art-AP, aesthetics, algebra, American government, anatomy and physiology, Ancient Greek, ancient world history, art, Bible, biology, British literature (honors), calculus, calculus-AP, chemistry, chemistry-AP, choir, choral music, Christian ethics, classical Greek literature, classics, comparative religion, critical writing, critical thinking, debate, drama, earth science, economics, English language and composition-AP, English literature and composition-AP, ethics, European history, foreign language, French, French-AP, history, honors algebra, honors English, honors geometry, honors U.S. history, honors world history, independent study, instrumental music, Irish literature, journalism, Latin, life management skills, mathematics, medieval literature, music appreciation, oral communications, philosophy, photography, photojournalism, physical education, physical fitness, physical science, physics, physics-AP, pre-algebra, pre-calculus, reading/study skills, rhetoric, science, senior thesis, Shakespeare, Spanish, speech and debate, studio art-AP, theater, theater arts, trigonometry, U.S. history, U.S. history-AP, world history, yearbook.

Graduation Requirements Arts and fine arts (art, music, dance, drama), athletics, Bible, electives, English, foreign language, history, mathematics, rhetoric, science, classics.

Special Academic Programs 12 Advanced Placement exams for which test preparation is offered; honors section; independent study; study at local college for college credit; academic accommodation for the gifted, the musically talented, and the artistically talented.

College Admission Counseling 22 students graduated in 2010; all went to college, including Florida State University; Furman University; Rollins College; University of Central Florida; University of Florida; University of Oklahoma. Median SAT critical reading: 625, median SAT math: 581, median SAT writing: 593, median combined SAT: 1830, median composite ACT: 26.

Student Life Upper grades have uniform requirement, student council, honor system. Discipline rests primarily with faculty. Attendance at religious services is required.

Summer Programs Enrichment, sports, art/fine arts programs offered; session focuses on sports, arts, discovery; held both on and off campus; held at Winter Park; accepts boys and girls; open to students from other schools. 200 students usually enrolled. 2011 schedule: June to August. Application deadline: May.

Tuition and Aid Day student tuition: $10,590. Tuition installment plan (The Tuition Plan, monthly payment plans). Need-based scholarship grants available. In 2010–11, 30% of upper-school students received aid.

Admissions Traditional secondary-level entrance grade is 9. For fall 2010, 64 students applied for upper-level admission, 25 were accepted, 24 enrolled. ISEE required. Deadline for receipt of application materials: none. Application fee required: $100. Interview required.

Athletics Interscholastic: baseball (boys), basketball (b,g), cross-country running (b,g), flag football (b), soccer (b,g), softball (g), tennis (b,g), volleyball (g); coed interscholastic: golf. 3 PE instructors, 10 coaches, 1 athletic trainer.

Computers Computers are regularly used in all academic, journalism, photography, yearbook classes. Computer network features include on-campus library services, Internet access, wireless campus network, Internet filtering or blocking technology. Students grades are available online. The school has a published electronic and media policy.

Contact Mrs. Patti Rader, Director of Admission. 407-332-6363 Ext. 204, Fax: 407-332-1664. E-mail: pnrader@genevaschool.org. Web site: www.genevaschool.org.

GEORGE SCHOOL

1690 Newtown Langhorne Road
PO Box 4460
Newtown, Pennsylvania 18940
Head of School: Nancy O. Starmer

General Information Coeducational boarding and day college-preparatory, arts, religious studies, bilingual studies, and technology school, affiliated with Society of Friends. Grades 9–12. Founded: 1893. Setting: suburban. Nearest major city is Philadelphia. Students are housed in single-sex dormitories. 265-acre campus. 19 buildings on campus. Approved or accredited by Friends Council on Education,

International Baccalaureate Organization, Middle States Association of Colleges and Schools, Pennsylvania Association of Independent Schools, The Association of Boarding Schools, The College Board, and Pennsylvania Department of Education. Member of National Association of Independent Schools and Secondary School Admission Test Board. Endowment: $7 million. Total enrollment: 539. Upper school average class size: 14. Upper school faculty-student ratio: 1:7. Upper School students typically attend 5 days per week. The average school day consists of 6 hours.

Upper School Student Profile Grade 9: 112 students (51 boys, 61 girls); Grade 10: 144 students (72 boys, 72 girls); Grade 11: 143 students (71 boys, 72 girls); Grade 12: 140 students (66 boys, 74 girls). 53% of students are boarding students. 21 states are represented in upper school student body. International students from China, Hong Kong, Japan, Republic of Korea, Taiwan, and United Kingdom; 31 other countries represented in student body. 13% of students are members of Society of Friends.

Faculty School total: 82. In upper school: 54 have advanced degrees; 49 reside on campus.

Subjects Offered African-American history, algebra, American history-AP, American literature, American literature-AP, art, Asian history, astronomy, athletics, Bible studies, biology, biology-AP, calculus, calculus-AP, ceramics, chemistry, chemistry-AP, Chinese, community service, composition, computer science, dance, drama, drawing, driver education, English, English literature, English literature and composition-AP, English literature-AP, English-AP, environmental science, ESL, fine arts, French, French language-AP, geometry, global studies, health, history-AP, horticulture, Latin, Latin American history, life science, literature, mathematics, Middle Eastern history, modern dance, modern European history, music theory, orchestra, painting, philosophy, photography, physical education, physics, pre-calculus, probability and statistics, religion, Russian history, science, science and technology, Spanish, Spanish language-AP, stagecraft, statistics-AP, theater, theory of knowledge, video film production, visual arts, vocal ensemble, woodworking, work camp program, world history, world literature.

Graduation Requirements Arts and fine arts (art, music, dance, drama), English, foreign language, geometry, mathematics, performing arts, religion (includes Bible studies and theology), science, social studies (includes history), 65 hours of community service.

Special Academic Programs International Baccalaureate program; Advanced Placement exam preparation; honors section; independent study; ESL.

College Admission Counseling 124 students graduated in 2010; 120 went to college, including American University; Boston University; Connecticut College; McGill University; New York University; The George Washington University. Other: 1 entered military service, 3 had other specific plans.

Student Life Upper grades have specified standards of dress, student council, honor system. Discipline rests equally with students and faculty. Attendance at religious services is required.

Summer Programs Enrichment, advancement, ESL programs offered; session focuses on academic and social preparation; held on campus; accepts boys and girls; not open to students from other schools.

Tuition and Aid Day student tuition: $30,850; 7-day tuition and room/board: $42,920. Tuition installment plan (monthly payment plans, individually arranged payment plans). Merit scholarship grants, need-based scholarship grants available. In 2010–11, 47% of upper-school students received aid; total upper-school merit-scholarship money awarded: $230,000. Total amount of financial aid awarded in 2010–11: $6,100,000.

Admissions Traditional secondary-level entrance grade is 9. For fall 2010, 538 students applied for upper-level admission, 261 were accepted, 148 enrolled. SSAT or TOEFL or SLEP required. Deadline for receipt of application materials: February 15. Application fee required: $50. Interview required.

Athletics Interscholastic: baseball (boys), basketball (b,g), cross-country running (b,g), field hockey (g), football (b), lacrosse (b,g), soccer (b,g), softball (g), swimming and diving (b,g), tennis (b,g), track and field (b,g), volleyball (g), wrestling (b,g); coed interscholastic: cheering, equestrian sports, golf, horseback riding, winter (indoor) track; coed intramural: aerobics/dance, aquatics, dance, horseback riding. 5 PE instructors, 5 coaches, 1 athletic trainer.

Computers Computers are regularly used in English, ESL, foreign language, history, mathematics, newspaper, photography, science, yearbook classes. Computer network features include on-campus library services, online commercial services, Internet access, wireless campus network, Internet filtering or blocking technology. Campus intranet and student e-mail accounts are available to students. The school has a published electronic and media policy.

Contact Christian Donovan, Director of Admission. 215-579-6547. Fax: 215-579-6549. E-mail: admission@georgeschool.org. Web site: www.georgeschool.org.

GEORGE STEVENS ACADEMY

23 Union Street
Blue Hill, Maine 04614
Head of School: Mr. Bayard Brokaw

General Information Coeducational boarding and day college-preparatory, general academic, arts, vocational, and technology school. Grades 9–12. Founded: 1803. Setting: small town. Nearest major city is Bangor. Students are housed in single-sex dormitories and host family homes. 20-acre campus. 6 buildings on campus. Approved or accredited by Independent Schools of Northern New England, New England Association of Schools and Colleges, The College Board, and Maine Department of

George Stevens Academy

Education. Endowment: $7 million. Total enrollment: 299. Upper school average class size: 15. Upper school faculty-student ratio: 1:10. There are 180 required school days per year for Upper School students. Upper School students typically attend 5 days per week. The average school day consists of 6 hours and 30 minutes.

Upper School Student Profile Grade 9: 61 students (37 boys, 24 girls); Grade 10: 78 students (43 boys, 35 girls); Grade 11: 76 students (29 boys, 47 girls); Grade 12: 84 students (34 boys, 50 girls). 7% of students are boarding students. 89% are state residents. 1 state is represented in upper school student body. 11% are international students. International students from China, Germany, Japan, Republic of Korea, Thailand, and Viet Nam.

Faculty School total: 32. In upper school: 14 men, 18 women; 17 have advanced degrees; 1 resides on campus.

Subjects Offered 20th century history, 3-dimensional design, advanced chemistry, advanced math, Advanced Placement courses, algebra, American literature, American literature-AP, art, art history, art-AP, arts and crafts, band, biology, British literature (honors), business mathematics, calculus-AP, carpentry, chamber groups, chemistry, computer applications, computer literacy, creative writing, critical thinking, desktop publishing, developmental language skills, drafting, drawing, driver education, earth science, electives, English, English-AP, environmental science, environmental science-AP, ESL, European history, fine arts, foreign language, forensics, French, general math, general science, geometry, German, health education, history, history-AP, honors algebra, honors English, honors geometry, honors U.S. history, human geography—AP, humanities, independent study, industrial arts, industrial technology, instrumental music, internship, jazz band, jazz ensemble, lab science, languages, Latin, literature, literature-AP, marine science, mathematics, mathematics-AP, mechanics, model United Nations, modern history, modern languages, modern problems, music, music theory, musical productions, mythology, personal fitness, photo shop, photography, physical education, physics, pre-algebra, pre-calculus, printmaking, psychology, reading/study skills, remedial study skills, science, senior project, shop, small engine repair, social issues, social sciences, Spanish, speech and debate, sports, statistics-AP, street law, student government, technology/design, TOEFL preparation, transportation technology, U.S. history, U.S. history-AP, Western civilization, wilderness education, woodworking, work-study, World-Wide-Web publishing, writing.

Graduation Requirements Arts and fine arts (art, music, dance, drama), electives, English, foreign language, history, mathematics, physical education (includes health), science, social sciences, U.S. history, senior debate.

Special Academic Programs Advanced Placement exam preparation; honors section; accelerated programs; independent study; term-away projects; academic accommodation for the gifted, the musically talented, and the artistically talented; remedial reading and/or remedial writing; remedial math; ESL (23 students enrolled).

College Admission Counseling 79 students graduated in 2010; 67 went to college, including College of the Atlantic; Husson University; Maine Maritime Academy; University of Maine; University of Southern Maine; Wellesley College. Other: 11 went to work, 1 entered military service. Median SAT critical reading: 470, median SAT math: 520, median SAT writing: 490, median combined SAT: 1360. 26% scored over 600 on SAT critical reading, 32% scored over 600 on SAT math, 25% scored over 600 on SAT writing, 24% scored over 1800 on combined SAT.

Student Life Upper grades have student council. Discipline rests primarily with faculty.

Summer Programs Remediation, enrichment, ESL, sports, art/fine arts programs offered; session focuses on ESL; held on campus; accepts boys and girls; open to students from other schools. 2011 schedule: August 1 to August 26. Application deadline: May 15.

Tuition and Aid 7-day tuition and room/board: $35,000. Tuition installment plan (monthly payment plans, individually arranged payment plans). Tuition reduction for siblings available.

Admissions Traditional secondary-level entrance grade is 9. International English Language Test, PSAT, SSAT or TOEFL or SLEP required. Deadline for receipt of application materials: none. Application fee required: $50. Interview required.

Athletics Interscholastic: baseball (boys), basketball (b,g), cheering (b,g), cross-country running (b,g), golf (b,g), independent competitive sports (b,g), indoor track & field (b,g), running (b,g), sailing (b,g), soccer (b,g), softball (g), swimming and diving (b,g), tennis (b,g), track and field (b,g), winter (indoor) track (b,g), wrestling (b,g); coed intramural: canoeing/kayaking, croquet, dance, dance team, fitness walking, flag football, floor hockey, hiking/backpacking, outdoor activities, outdoor adventure, outdoor education, outdoor skills, physical fitness, physical training, skateboarding, skiing (cross-country), skiing (downhill), snowboarding, snowshoeing, table tennis, ultimate Frisbee, volleyball, walking, weight training, wilderness. 2 PE instructors, 26 coaches.

Computers Computers are regularly used in all academic, computer applications, desktop publishing, photography, Web site design classes. Computer network features include on-campus library services, Internet access, wireless campus network, Internet filtering or blocking technology. Computer access in designated common areas is available to students. Students grades are available online. The school has a published electronic and media policy.

Contact Ms. Sheryl Cole Stearns, Director of International Student Program. 207-374-2808 Ext. 134. Fax: 207-374-2982. E-mail: s.stearns@georgestevens.org. Web site: www.georgestevensacademy.org.

See Display below and Close-Up on page 780.

GEORGETOWN PREPARATORY SCHOOL

10900 Rockville Pike
North Bethesda, Maryland 20852-3299
Head of School: Mr. Jeff Jones

General Information Boys' boarding and day college-preparatory, arts, religious studies, and technology school, affiliated with Roman Catholic Church. Grades 9–12. Founded: 1789. Setting: suburban. Nearest major city is Washington, DC. Students are housed in single-sex dormitories. 92-acre campus. 8 buildings on campus. Approved or accredited by Jesuit Secondary Education Association, Middle States Association of Colleges and Schools, National Catholic Education Association, The Association of Boarding Schools, and Maryland Department of Education. Member of National Association of Independent Schools and Secondary School Admission Test Board. Endowment: $20 million. Total enrollment: 484. Upper school average class size: 16. Upper school faculty-student ratio: 1:8. Upper School students typically attend 5 days per week. The average school day consists of 6 hours and 30 minutes.

Upper School Student Profile Grade 9: 127 students (127 boys); Grade 10: 119 students (119 boys); Grade 11: 121 students (121 boys); Grade 12: 117 students (117 boys). 20% of students are boarding students. 60% are state residents. 17 states are represented in upper school student body. 15% are international students. International students from China, Indonesia, Mexico, Nigeria, Republic of Korea, and Taiwan; 24 other countries represented in student body. 75% of students are Roman Catholic.

Faculty School total: 58. In upper school: 36 men, 22 women; 50 have advanced degrees; 17 reside on campus.

Subjects Offered Algebra, American history, American literature, art, art history, Bible studies, biology, calculus, chemistry, computer programming, computer science, drama, driver education, economics, English, English literature, ESL, ethics, European history, fine arts, French, geometry, German, government/civics, history, journalism, Latin, mathematics, music, philosophy, physical education, physics, psychology, religion, science, social studies, Spanish, speech, stained glass, theater, theology, trigonometry, world history, world literature.

Graduation Requirements Arts and fine arts (art, music, dance, drama), classics, English, foreign language, mathematics, music theory, religion (includes Bible studies and theology), science, social studies (includes history), two years of Latin. Community service is required.

Special Academic Programs 24 Advanced Placement exams for which test preparation is offered; honors section; independent study; term-away projects; study abroad; academic accommodation for the gifted; ESL (14 students enrolled).

College Admission Counseling 118 students graduated in 2010; all went to college, including Boston College; Georgetown University; Stanford University; University of Notre Dame; University of Pennsylvania; University of Virginia. Mean SAT critical reading: 620, mean SAT math: 643, mean SAT writing: 637, mean combined SAT: 1900, mean composite ACT: 27.

Student Life Upper grades have specified standards of dress, student council. Discipline rests primarily with faculty. Attendance at religious services is required.

Summer Programs Remediation, enrichment, advancement, ESL, sports programs offered; session focuses on ESL; held on campus; accepts boys and girls; open to students from other schools. 75 students usually enrolled. 2011 schedule: June 28 to August 6. Application deadline: March 1.

Tuition and Aid Day student tuition: $26,935; 7-day tuition and room/board: $46,020. Tuition installment plan (FACTS Tuition Payment Plan). Need-based scholarship grants, middle-income loans available. In 2010–11, 25% of upper-school students received aid. Total amount of financial aid awarded in 2010–11: $2,000,000.

Admissions Traditional secondary-level entrance grade is 9. For fall 2010, 392 students applied for upper-level admission, 170 were accepted, 135 enrolled. SSAT required. Deadline for receipt of application materials: January 16. Application fee required: $100. Interview required.

Athletics Interscholastic: baseball, basketball, cross-country running, diving, fencing, football, golf, ice hockey, indoor soccer, indoor track & field, lacrosse, rugby, running, soccer, swimming and diving, tennis, track and field, winter (indoor) track, wrestling; intramural: basketball, canoeing/kayaking, fitness, flag football, floor hockey, Frisbee, hiking/backpacking, ice skating, indoor hockey, kayaking, life saving, martial arts, mountain biking, Nautilus, ocean paddling, paddle tennis, paint ball, physical fitness, physical training, power lifting, racquetball, rappelling, rock climbing, ropes courses, scuba diving, skiing (downhill), snowboarding, soccer, softball, strength & conditioning, table tennis, tennis, ultimate Frisbee, volleyball, weight training. 16 coaches, 3 athletic trainers.

Computers Computers are regularly used in art, classics, data processing, English, French, history, Latin, mathematics, music, religious studies, science, Spanish, writing classes. Computer network features include on-campus library services, online commercial services, Internet access, wireless campus network, Internet filtering or blocking technology. Campus intranet, student e-mail accounts, and computer access in designated common areas are available to students. Students grades are available online. The school has a published electronic and media policy.

Contact Mr. Brian J. Gilbert, Dean of Admissions. 301-214-1215. Fax: 301-493-6128. E-mail: admissions@gprep.org. Web site: www.gprep.org.

GEORGETOWN VISITATION PREPARATORY SCHOOL

1524 35th Street NW
Washington, District of Columbia 20007
Head of School: Daniel M. Kerns Jr.

General Information Girls' day college-preparatory school, affiliated with Roman Catholic Church. Grades 9–12. Founded: 1799. Setting: urban. 23-acre campus. 7 buildings on campus. Approved or accredited by Association of Independent Schools of Greater Washington, Middle States Association of Colleges and Schools, National Independent Private Schools Association, and District of Columbia Department of Education. Member of National Association of Independent Schools. Endowment: $16.7 million. Total enrollment: 484. Upper school average class size: 15. Upper school faculty-student ratio: 1:10. There are 181 required school days per year for Upper School students. Upper School students typically attend 5 days per week. The average school day consists of 5 hours and 30 minutes.

Upper School Student Profile Grade 9: 124 students (124 girls); Grade 10: 117 students (117 girls); Grade 11: 121 students (121 girls); Grade 12: 122 students (122 girls). 93% of students are Roman Catholic.

Faculty School total: 54. In upper school: 12 men, 42 women; 39 have advanced degrees.

Subjects Offered Advanced Placement courses, advanced studio art-AP, algebra, American history, American literature, anthropology, art, art history, art history-AP, Bible studies, biology, biology-AP, calculus, calculus-AP, chemistry, comparative political systems-AP, computer programming, computer science, creative writing, dance, English, English language and composition-AP, English literature, English literature and composition-AP, environmental science, environmental science-AP, ethics, European history, European history-AP, expository writing, fine arts, French, French-AP, geography, geometry, government-AP, government/civics, health, history, Latin, mathematics, music, philosophy, physical education, physics, psychology, psychology-AP, religion, science, social sciences, social studies, Spanish, speech, theology, trigonometry, U.S. government and politics-AP, U.S. history-AP, world history.

Graduation Requirements Arts and fine arts (art, music, dance, drama), English, foreign language, mathematics, physical education (includes health), religion (includes Bible studies and theology), science, social sciences, social studies (includes history), 80 hours of community service.

Special Academic Programs Advanced Placement exam preparation; honors section; independent study; study at local college for college credit.

College Admission Counseling 122 students graduated in 2010; all went to college, including Boston College; Georgetown University; Princeton University; University of Notre Dame; University of Virginia. Mean SAT critical reading: 651, mean SAT math: 626.

Student Life Upper grades have uniform requirement, student council, honor system. Discipline rests primarily with faculty. Attendance at religious services is required.

Summer Programs Remediation, enrichment, sports, art/fine arts, computer instruction programs offered; held on campus; accepts girls; not open to students from other schools. 100 students usually enrolled. 2011 schedule: June to July. Application deadline: April.

Tuition and Aid Day student tuition: $22,500. Tuition installment plan (FACTS Tuition Payment Plan, individually arranged payment plans). Merit scholarship grants, need-based scholarship grants available. In 2010–11, 25% of upper-school students received aid; total upper-school merit-scholarship money awarded: $55,000. Total amount of financial aid awarded in 2010–11: $1,250,000.

Admissions Traditional secondary-level entrance grade is 9. For fall 2010, 430 students applied for upper-level admission, 160 were accepted, 126 enrolled. High School Placement Test or High School Placement Test (closed version) from Scholastic Testing Service required. Deadline for receipt of application materials: December 4. Application fee required: $50. On-campus interview required.

Athletics Interscholastic: basketball, crew, cross-country running, dance, diving, field hockey, fitness, indoor track, lacrosse, soccer, softball, swimming and diving, tennis, track and field, volleyball; intramural: cheering, flag football, strength & conditioning. 4 PE instructors, 23 coaches, 1 athletic trainer.

Computers Computers are regularly used in art, English, French, history, mathematics, religion, science, Spanish classes. Computer network features include on-campus library services, online commercial services, Internet access, wireless campus network, Internet filtering or blocking technology. Student e-mail accounts are available to students.

Contact Janet Keller, Director of Admissions. 202-337-3350 Ext. 2241. Fax: 202-333-3522. E-mail: jkeller@visi.org. Web site: www.visi.org.

See Display on next page.

GEORGE WALTON ACADEMY

One Bulldog Drive
Monroe, Georgia 30655
Head of School: William M. Nicholson

General Information Coeducational day college-preparatory, arts, and technology school. Grades K4–12. Founded: 1969. Setting: small town. Nearest major city is Atlanta. 54-acre campus. 8 buildings on campus. Approved or accredited by Southern

Association of Colleges and Schools and Georgia Department of Education. Total enrollment: 945. Upper school average class size: 17. Upper school faculty-student ratio: 1:12. There are 180 required school days per year for Upper School students. Upper School students typically attend 5 days per week. The average school day consists of 6 hours and 45 minutes.
Upper School Student Profile Grade 6: 63 students (32 boys, 31 girls); Grade 7: 70 students (38 boys, 32 girls); Grade 8: 74 students (37 boys, 37 girls); Grade 9: 81 students (38 boys, 43 girls); Grade 10: 82 students (41 boys, 41 girls); Grade 11: 80 students (38 boys, 42 girls); Grade 12: 97 students (55 boys, 42 girls).
Faculty School total: 83. In upper school: 15 men, 38 women; 20 have advanced degrees.
Subjects Offered Algebra, American history, American literature, anatomy, art, art history, Bible studies, biology, calculus, chemistry, creative writing, drama, economics, English, English literature, environmental science, European history, fine arts, geography, geometry, government/civics, grammar, health, history, journalism, Latin, mathematics, music, photography, physical education, physics, psychology, science, social sciences, social studies, sociology, Spanish, trigonometry, world history, world literature, writing.
Graduation Requirements Arts and fine arts (art, music, dance, drama), composition, English, foreign language, mathematics, physical education (includes health), science, social sciences, social studies (includes history), all students must be accepted to a college or university to graduate.
Special Academic Programs 11 Advanced Placement exams for which test preparation is offered; honors section; academic accommodation for the musically talented and the artistically talented.
College Admission Counseling 80 students graduated in 2010; all went to college, including Georgia College & State University; Georgia Institute of Technology; Georgia Southern University; Georgia State University; North Georgia College & State University; University of Georgia.
Student Life Upper grades have uniform requirement, student council, honor system. Discipline rests primarily with faculty.
Tuition and Aid Day student tuition: $8000. Tuition installment plan (monthly payment plans). Tuition reduction for siblings, need-based scholarship grants available. In 2010–11, 1% of upper-school students received aid.
Admissions Traditional secondary-level entrance grade is 9. ACT, CAT 5, CTBS, Stanford Achievement Test, any other standardized test, Otis-Lennon, Stanford Achievement Test, PSAT or SAT required. Deadline for receipt of application materials: none. Application fee required: $150. On-campus interview recommended.
Athletics Interscholastic: aquatics (boys, girls), baseball (b), basketball (b,g), cheering (g), cross-country running (b,g), dance squad (g), drill team (g), football (b), golf (b), physical fitness (b,g), soccer (b,g), softball (g), swimming and diving (b,g), tennis (b,g), track and field (b,g), volleyball (g), weight lifting (b), weight training (b,g), wrestling (b). 5 PE instructors, 12 coaches.
Computers Computers are regularly used in all academic classes. Computer network features include on-campus library services, Internet access, wireless campus network, Internet filtering or blocking technology. Computer access in designated common areas is available to students. Students grades are available online. The school has a published electronic and media policy.
Contact Ms. Chris Stancil, Director of Admissions. 770-207-5172 Ext. 234. Fax: 770-267-4023. E-mail: cstancil@gwa.com. Web site: www.gwa.com.

GEORGIA MILITARY COLLEGE HIGH SCHOOL
201 East Greene Street
Milledgeville, Georgia 31061
Head of School: Col. John Thornton
General Information Coeducational day college-preparatory and military school. Grades 6–12. Founded: 1879. Setting: small town. Nearest major city is Macon. 4 buildings on campus. Approved or accredited by Commission on Secondary and Middle Schools, Southern Association of Colleges and Schools, and Georgia Department of Education. Total enrollment: 500. Upper school average class size: 20.
Upper School Student Profile Grade 9: 62 students (31 boys, 31 girls); Grade 10: 62 students (31 boys, 31 girls); Grade 11: 62 students (31 boys, 31 girls); Grade 12: 62 students (31 boys, 31 girls).
Faculty School total: 29. In upper school: 10 men, 8 women.
Subjects Offered Computer science, English, general science, health, JROTC, keyboarding, mathematics, physical education, social studies.
Special Academic Programs 4 Advanced Placement exams for which test preparation is offered; study at local college for college credit.
College Admission Counseling 60 students graduated in 2009; 56 went to college, including Georgia College & State University; Georgia Southern University; University of Georgia; Valdosta State University. Other: 1 went to work, 3 entered military service. Median SAT critical reading: 509, median SAT math: 503.
Student Life Upper grades have uniform requirement, student council, honor system. Discipline rests equally with students and faculty.
Tuition and Aid Day student tuition: $4200. Tuition installment plan (monthly payment plans). Need-based scholarship grants available.
Admissions Traditional secondary-level entrance grade is 9. Deadline for receipt of application materials: none. Application fee required: $35.

Athletics Interscholastic: baseball (boys), basketball (b,g), cheering (g), danceline (g), football (b), soccer (b,g), softball (g); coed interscholastic: drill team, golf, JROTC drill, marksmanship, riflery, tennis, track and field, wrestling. 4 PE instructors, 2 coaches.

Computers Computers are regularly used in computer applications, media production, SAT preparation, yearbook classes. Computer network features include on-campus library services, Internet access, wireless campus network, Internet filtering or blocking technology. Student e-mail accounts and computer access in designated common areas are available to students. Students grades are available online. The school has a published electronic and media policy.

Contact Mrs. Kim Mountain, Administrative Assistant. 478-387-4852. Fax: 478-445-4536. E-mail: kmountain@gmc.cc.ga.us. Web site: www.gmc.cc.ga.us/prep.

GERMANTOWN FRIENDS SCHOOL

31 West Coulter Street
Philadelphia, Pennsylvania 19144
Head of School: Richard L. Wade

General Information Coeducational day college-preparatory, arts, and technology school, affiliated with Society of Friends. Grades K–12. Founded: 1845. Setting: urban. 21-acre campus. 21 buildings on campus. Approved or accredited by Friends Council on Education, Middle States Association of Colleges and Schools, and Pennsylvania Association of Independent Schools. Member of National Association of Independent Schools and Secondary School Admission Test Board. Endowment: $20 million. Total enrollment: 861. Upper school average class size: 18. Upper school faculty-student ratio: 1:9. There are 172 required school days per year for Upper School students. Upper School students typically attend 5 days per week. The average school day consists of 6 hours and 25 minutes.

Upper School Student Profile Grade 9: 93 students (41 boys, 52 girls); Grade 10: 85 students (50 boys, 35 girls); Grade 11: 78 students (39 boys, 39 girls); Grade 12: 90 students (41 boys, 49 girls). 6.3% of students are members of Society of Friends.

Faculty School total: 122. In upper school: 27 men, 34 women; 42 have advanced degrees.

Subjects Offered 3-dimensional art, advanced chemistry, advanced math, algebra, American history, ancient history, art, art history, biology, calculus, chemistry, choir, chorus, comparative cultures, computer applications, computer programming, creative writing, drama, dramatic arts, drawing, English, environmental education, environmental science, European history, French, geometry, graphic arts, Greek, health, human sexuality, independent study, instrumental music, jazz ensemble, Latin, Latin History, madrigals, mathematics, music, music theory, orchestra, painting, philosophy, photography, physical education, physics, pre-calculus, science, social studies, Spanish, sports, stagecraft, statistics, studio art, theater, trigonometry, vocal music.

Graduation Requirements English, foreign language, history, lab science, mathematics, music, physical education (includes health), month-long off-campus independent project.

Special Academic Programs Honors section; independent study; term-away projects; domestic exchange program (with The Network Program Schools, The Catlin Gabel School); study abroad; academic accommodation for the gifted, the musically talented, and the artistically talented; ESL (3 students enrolled).

College Admission Counseling 98 students graduated in 2010; 97 went to college, including Barnard College; New York University; Temple University; The George Washington University; Trinity College; University of Pennsylvania. Other: 1 had other specific plans. Mean SAT critical reading: 652, mean SAT math: 651, mean SAT writing: 665. 78% scored over 600 on SAT critical reading, 60% scored over 600 on SAT math, 70% scored over 600 on SAT writing.

Student Life Upper grades have student council. Discipline rests primarily with faculty. Attendance at religious services is required.

Tuition and Aid Day student tuition: $23,460–$25,900. Tuition installment plan (Academic Management Services Plan, Key Tuition Payment Plan, individually arranged payment plans). Need-based scholarship grants, need-based loans available. In 2010–11, 27% of upper-school students received aid. Total amount of financial aid awarded in 2010–11: $855,950.

Admissions Traditional secondary-level entrance grade is 9. For fall 2010, 77 students applied for upper-level admission, 53 were accepted, 27 enrolled. ISEE or SSAT required. Deadline for receipt of application materials: December 3. Application fee required: $40. On-campus interview required.

Athletics Interscholastic: baseball (boys), basketball (b,g), cross-country running (b,g), field hockey (g), indoor soccer (b,g), indoor track & field (b,g), lacrosse (g), soccer (b,g), softball (g), squash (b,g), tennis (b,g), track and field (b,g), wrestling (b); coed intramural: physical training, strength & conditioning, weight training. 5 PE instructors, 35 coaches, 1 athletic trainer.

Computers Computers are regularly used in art, English, foreign language, history, mathematics, music, photography, publications, science classes. Computer network features include on-campus library services, online commercial services, Internet access, wireless campus network, Internet filtering or blocking technology. Campus intranet, student e-mail accounts, and computer access in designated common areas are available to students.

Contact Laura Sharpless Myran, Director, Admissions and Financial Aid. 215-951-2346. Fax: 215-951-2370. E-mail: lauram@gfsnet.org. Web site: www.germantownfriends.org.

GILL ST. BERNARD'S SCHOOL

PO Box 604
St. Bernard's Road
Gladstone, New Jersey 07934
Head of School: Mr. S. A. Rowell

General Information Coeducational day college-preparatory school. Grades PK–12. Founded: 1900. Setting: small town. Nearest major city is New York, NY. 72-acre campus. 15 buildings on campus. Approved or accredited by Middle States Association of Colleges and Schools and New Jersey Association of Independent Schools. Member of National Association of Independent Schools and Secondary School Admission Test Board. Endowment: $5 million. Total enrollment: 703. Upper school average class size: 16. Upper school faculty-student ratio: 1:7. There are 175 required school days per year for Upper School students. Upper School students typically attend 5 days per week. The average school day consists of 7 hours.

Faculty School total: 105. In upper school: 21 men, 19 women; 28 have advanced degrees.

Subjects Offered 20th century world history, 3-dimensional art, advanced chemistry, advanced computer applications, advanced math, Advanced Placement courses, algebra, American democracy, American history, American history-AP, American literature, analysis and differential calculus, analytic geometry, art, astronomy, biology, biology-AP, British literature, British literature (honors), calculus, calculus-AP, chemistry, chemistry-AP, chorus, college counseling, comparative cultures, computer science, computer science-AP, contemporary issues, creative writing, earth science, economics, English, English literature, English literature-AP, environmental science, environmental science-AP, European history, European history-AP, fine arts, forensics, French, gender issues, geography, geometry, government/civics, health, history, honors English, human geography—AP, independent study, international relations, Latin, Latin American literature, literature, mathematics, music, oceanography, philosophy, photography, physical education, physics, portfolio art, psychology, science, social studies, Spanish, Spanish-AP, technology, theater, U.S. government and politics-AP, United States government-AP, woodworking, world history, world literature.

Graduation Requirements Arts and fine arts (art, music, dance, drama), English, foreign language, history, mathematics, science, The Unit: an intensive 2-week course each year of Upper School.

Special Academic Programs 14 Advanced Placement exams for which test preparation is offered; honors section; independent study; study abroad.

College Admission Counseling 48 students graduated in 2010; all went to college, including Boston College; Fairfield University; Georgetown University; Villanova University; Williams College. 65% scored over 600 on SAT critical reading, 65% scored over 600 on SAT math, 70% scored over 600 on SAT writing.

Student Life Upper grades have specified standards of dress, student council, honor system. Discipline rests primarily with faculty.

Summer Programs Enrichment, advancement, sports, art/fine arts programs offered; session focuses on academics, arts, sports, day and outdoor camping; held on campus; accepts boys and girls; open to students from other schools. 325 students usually enrolled. 2011 schedule: June 10 to August 20. Application deadline: none.

Tuition and Aid Day student tuition: $28,250. Tuition installment plan (The Tuition Plan, Insured Tuition Payment Plan). Merit scholarship grants, need-based scholarship grants available. In 2010–11, 12% of upper-school students received aid. Total amount of financial aid awarded in 2010–11: $1,000,000.

Admissions Traditional secondary-level entrance grade is 9. For fall 2010, 290 students applied for upper-level admission, 150 were accepted, 116 enrolled. ISEE or SSAT required. Deadline for receipt of application materials: January 25. Application fee required: $75. On-campus interview required.

Athletics Interscholastic: baseball (boys), basketball (b,g), cheering (g), cross-country running (b,g), fencing (b,g), ice hockey (b), indoor track & field (b,g), lacrosse (b,g), soccer (b,g), softball (g), tennis (b,g), track and field (b,g), winter (indoor) track (b,g); intramural: skiing (downhill) (b,g), strength & conditioning (b,g); coed interscholastic: golf, swimming and diving; coed intramural: backpacking, hiking/backpacking, outdoor adventure, outdoor recreation, physical fitness, physical training. 6 PE instructors, 37 coaches, 1 athletic trainer.

Computers Computers are regularly used in art, computer applications, design, desktop publishing, graphic arts, graphic design, independent study, information technology, introduction to technology, journalism, library, library skills, literary magazine, multimedia, news writing, newspaper, photography, programming, research skills, science, technology, Web site design, yearbook classes. Computer network features include on-campus library services, online commercial services, Internet access, wireless campus network, Internet filtering or blocking technology. Campus intranet and computer access in designated common areas are available to students. The school has a published electronic and media policy.

Contact Mrs. Ann Marie Blackman, Admission Office Manager. 908-234-1611 Ext. 245. Fax: 908-234-1712. E-mail: ablackman@gsbschool.org. Web site: www.gsbschool.org.

GILMAN SCHOOL

5407 Roland Avenue
Baltimore, Maryland 21210
Head of School: Mr. John E. Schmick

General Information Boys' day college-preparatory school. Grades K–12. Founded: 1897. Setting: suburban. 68-acre campus. 5 buildings on campus. Approved or accredited by Association of Independent Maryland Schools, Middle States Association of Colleges and Schools, and Maryland Department of Education. Member of National Association of Independent Schools and Secondary School Admission Test Board. Endowment: $83.5 million. Total enrollment: 1,012. Upper school average class size: 16. Upper school faculty-student ratio: 1:8. There are 172 required school days per year for Upper School students. Upper School students typically attend 5 days per week. The average school day consists of 9 hours.

Upper School Student Profile Grade 9: 119 students (119 boys); Grade 10: 115 students (115 boys); Grade 11: 115 students (115 boys); Grade 12: 105 students (105 boys).

Faculty School total: 142. In upper school: 58 men, 8 women; 50 have advanced degrees.

Subjects Offered Algebra, American history, American literature, anatomy, Arabic, art, art history, biology, calculus, chemistry, Chinese, community service, computer math, computer programming, computer science, creative writing, drafting, drama, ecology, economics, English, English literature, environmental science, European history, expository writing, fine arts, French, geometry, German, government/civics, Greek, history, industrial arts, Latin, mathematics, mechanical drawing, music, photography, physical education, physics, physiology, religion, Russian, science, social studies, Spanish, speech, statistics, theater, trigonometry, writing.

Graduation Requirements Art history, athletics, English, foreign language, history, mathematics, music appreciation, religion (includes Bible studies and theology), science, senior project.

Special Academic Programs 30 Advanced Placement exams for which test preparation is offered; honors section; independent study; term-away projects; academic accommodation for the gifted.

College Admission Counseling 120 students graduated in 2010; 118 went to college, including Dartmouth College; Dickinson College; University of Maryland, College Park; University of Virginia; Virginia Polytechnic Institute and State University; Wake Forest University. Other: 2 entered a postgraduate year. Mean SAT critical reading: 638, mean SAT math: 660, mean SAT writing: 637.

Student Life Upper grades have specified standards of dress, student council, honor system. Discipline rests primarily with faculty.

Summer Programs Remediation, enrichment, advancement, sports, art/fine arts, rigorous outdoor training programs offered; session focuses on remediation & enrichment; held on campus; accepts boys and girls; open to students from other schools. 250 students usually enrolled. 2011 schedule: June 20 to July 29. Application deadline: June 20.

Tuition and Aid Day student tuition: $23,290. Tuition installment plan (Insured Tuition Payment Plan, FACTS Tuition Payment Plan, monthly payment plans). Need-based scholarship grants, need-based loans available. In 2010–11, 25% of upper-school students received aid. Total amount of financial aid awarded in 2010–11: $1,840,900.

Admissions Traditional secondary-level entrance grade is 9. For fall 2010, 133 students applied for upper-level admission, 45 were accepted, 32 enrolled. ISEE required. Deadline for receipt of application materials: January 7. Application fee required: $50. On-campus interview required.

Athletics Interscholastic: baseball, basketball, cross-country running, football, golf, ice hockey, indoor track, lacrosse, soccer, squash, swimming and diving, tennis, track and field, volleyball, water polo, winter (indoor) track, wrestling; intramural: basketball, bicycling, cross-country running, fitness, flag football, Frisbee, golf, physical fitness, rugby, table tennis, tennis, touch football, weight lifting. 2 PE instructors, 2 athletic trainers.

Computers Computers are regularly used in computer applications, design, digital applications classes. Computer network features include on-campus library services, Internet access, wireless campus network, Internet filtering or blocking technology. Campus intranet, student e-mail accounts, and computer access in designated common areas are available to students. The school has a published electronic and media policy.

Contact Allison Conner, Admissions Assistant. 410-323-7169. Fax: 410-864-2825. E-mail: aconner@gilman.edu. Web site: www.gilman.edu.

GILMOUR ACADEMY

34001 Cedar Road
Gates Mills, Ohio 44040-9356
Head of School: Br. Robert E. Lavelle, CSC

General Information Coeducational boarding and day college-preparatory, arts, religious studies, and technology school, affiliated with Roman Catholic Church. Boarding grades 7–12, day grades PK–12. Founded: 1946. Setting: suburban. Nearest major city is Cleveland. Students are housed in coed dormitories and boy's wing and girl's wing dormitory. 144-acre campus. 15 buildings on campus. Approved or accredited by Independent Schools Association of the Central States, Midwest Association of Boarding Schools, National Catholic Education Association, North Central Association of Colleges and Schools, Ohio Association of Independent Schools, The Association of Boarding Schools, and Ohio Department of Education. Member of National Association of Independent Schools and Secondary School Admission Test Board. Endowment: $30 million. Total enrollment: 713. Upper school average class size: 14. Upper school faculty-student ratio: 1:10. Upper school students typically attend 5 days per week. The average school day consists of 7 hours and 20 minutes.

Upper School Student Profile Grade 9: 100 students (49 boys, 51 girls); Grade 10: 111 students (53 boys, 58 girls); Grade 11: 111 students (53 boys, 58 girls); Grade 12: 103 students (54 boys, 49 girls); Postgraduate: 3 students (2 boys, 1 girl). 12% of students are boarding students. 88% are state residents. 15 states are represented in upper school student body. 3% are international students. International students from Canada, China, and Republic of Korea; 1 other country represented in student body. 75% of students are Roman Catholic.

Faculty School total: 80. In upper school: 40 men, 33 women; 57 have advanced degrees; 4 reside on campus.

Subjects Offered Advanced Placement courses, advanced studio art-AP, algebra, American government, American history, American literature, art, band, Bible, biology, biology-AP, British literature, broadcast journalism, calculus, calculus-AP, ceramics, chemistry, chemistry-AP, chorus, community service, computer programming, computer science, computer science-AP, creative writing, drama, drawing, economics, English, English literature, English-AP, ensembles, ethics, European history, European history-AP, fine arts, French, French language-AP, French-AP, geometry, geometry with art applications, government, government-AP, government/civics, health, history, history of rock and roll, independent study, jazz ensemble, journalism, Latin, Latin-AP, law, leadership, mathematics, mathematics-AP, model United Nations, modern European history-AP, music, musical productions, oil painting, painting, photography, physical education, physical fitness, physics, physics-AP, pre-algebra, pre-calculus, religion, religious studies, SAT/ACT preparation, science, social studies, Spanish, Spanish language-AP, speech, speech and debate, statistics-AP, student government, student publications, studio art, studio art-AP, swimming, theater, trigonometry, U.S. history, U.S. history-AP, weight training, work-study, world history, writing, writing workshop, yearbook.

Graduation Requirements Arts and fine arts (art, music, dance, drama), English, foreign language, mathematics, physical education (includes health), religion (includes Bible studies and theology), science, social studies (includes history), speech, senior project. Community service is required.

Special Academic Programs Advanced Placement exam preparation; accelerated programs; independent study; study at local college for college credit; academic accommodation for the gifted, the musically talented, and the artistically talented.

College Admission Counseling 108 students graduated in 2010; 104 went to college, including Boston College; Case Western Reserve University; John Carroll University; Loyola University Chicago; Miami University; University of Dayton. Other: 4 entered a postgraduate year. Mean SAT critical reading: 562, mean SAT math: 587, mean SAT writing: 600, mean combined SAT: 1749, mean composite ACT: 25.

Student Life Upper grades have specified standards of dress, student council, honor system. Discipline rests equally with students and faculty. Attendance at religious services is required.

Summer Programs Sports programs offered; session focuses on athletics; held on campus; accepts boys and girls; open to students from other schools. 100 students usually enrolled. 2011 schedule: June to July. Application deadline: none.

Tuition and Aid Day student tuition: $9840–$23,755; 7-day tuition and room/board: $35,635. Tuition installment plan (monthly payment plans, Tuition Management System). Tuition reduction for siblings, merit scholarship grants, need-based scholarship grants, need-based loans, paying campus jobs, endowed scholarships with criteria specified by donors available. In 2010–11, 55% of upper-school students received aid; total upper-school merit-scholarship money awarded: $75,000. Total amount of financial aid awarded in 2010–11: $3,200,000.

Admissions Traditional secondary-level entrance grade is 9. For fall 2010, 200 students applied for upper-level admission, 170 were accepted, 87 enrolled. ACT, ACT-Explore, ISEE, PSAT, SAT, SSAT or TOEFL required. Deadline for receipt of application materials: none. Application fee required: $35. Interview required.

Athletics Interscholastic: baseball (boys), basketball (b,g), cross-country running (b,g), football (b), gymnastics (g), hockey (b,g), ice hockey (b,g), lacrosse (b,g), running (b,g), soccer (b,g), softball (g), swimming and diving (b,g), tennis (b,g), track and field (b,g), volleyball (g), winter soccer (b,g); intramural: cheering (g), indoor soccer (b,g); coed interscholastic: figure skating, golf, indoor track, indoor track & field, winter (indoor) track; coed intramural: aerobics, alpine skiing, aquatics, basketball, bowling, broomball, figure skating, fitness, golf, ice skating, indoor track, paddle tennis, physical fitness, physical training, skiing (downhill), snowboarding, soccer, strength & conditioning, swimming and diving, tennis, volleyball, weight training, winter (indoor) track, winter soccer. 9 coaches, 3 athletic trainers.

Computers Computers are regularly used in all academic classes. Computer network features include on-campus library services, online commercial services, Internet access, wireless campus network, Internet filtering or blocking technology. Campus intranet, student e-mail accounts, and computer access in designated common areas are available to students. Students grades are available online. The school has a published electronic and media policy.

Contact Mr. Steve M. Scheidt, Director of Middle and Upper School Admissions. 440-473-8050. Fax: 440-473-8010. E-mail: admissions@gilmour.org. Web site: www.gilmour.org.

GIRARD COLLEGE

2101 South College Avenue
Box #121
Philadelphia, Pennsylvania 19121-4857
Head of School: Mrs. Autumn A. Graves
General Information Coeducational boarding college-preparatory and general academic school. Grades 1–12. Founded: 1848. Setting: urban. Students are housed in single-sex dormitories. 43-acre campus. 10 buildings on campus. Approved or accredited by Middle States Association of Colleges and Schools, The Association of Boarding Schools, and Pennsylvania Department of Education. Member of National Association of Independent Schools. Endowment: $355 million. Total enrollment: 530. Upper school average class size: 22. Upper school faculty-student ratio: 1:16.
Upper School Student Profile Grade 7: 55 students (24 boys, 31 girls); Grade 8: 56 students (29 boys, 27 girls); Grade 9: 60 students (24 boys, 36 girls); Grade 10: 64 students (29 boys, 35 girls); Grade 11: 59 students (29 boys, 30 girls); Grade 12: 56 students (23 boys, 33 girls). 100% of students are boarding students. 90% are state residents. 6 states are represented in upper school student body.
Faculty School total: 71. In upper school: 12 men, 9 women; 9 have advanced degrees; 1 resides on campus.
Subjects Offered Algebra, American history, American literature, anatomy, art, biology, calculus, chemistry, choir, college counseling, community service, computer literacy, earth science, English, English literature, European history, French, geometry, government/civics, health, honors algebra, honors English, honors geometry, honors U.S. history, instrumental music, jazz band, life management skills, mathematics, multicultural studies, music appreciation, physical education, physics, poetry, pre-calculus, SAT preparation, senior project, social studies, sociology, Spanish, video film production, world cultures.
Graduation Requirements College counseling, computer literacy, English, foreign language, mathematics, physical education (includes health), science, senior career experience, senior project, social sciences, social studies (includes history). Community service is required.
Special Academic Programs Advanced Placement exam preparation; honors section; study at local college for college credit; remedial reading and/or remedial writing; remedial math.
College Admission Counseling 41 students graduated in 2010; 40 went to college, including Columbia College; Howard University; Penn State University Park; Rutgers, The State University of New Jersey, New Brunswick; Temple University; Villanova University. Other: 1 had other specific plans. Mean SAT critical reading: 490, mean SAT math: 477.
Student Life Upper grades have uniform requirement, student council. Discipline rests primarily with faculty.
Summer Programs Enrichment, advancement, sports, art/fine arts, computer instruction programs offered; session focuses on academic and recreation; held on campus; accepts boys and girls; open to students from other schools. 200 students usually enrolled. 2011 schedule: July to August.
Tuition and Aid Full scholarships (if admission requirements met) available. In 2010–11, 100% of upper-school students received aid.
Admissions Traditional secondary-level entrance grade is 9. Admissions testing and math, reading, and mental ability tests required. Deadline for receipt of application materials: none. No application fee required. On-campus interview required.
Athletics Interscholastic: baseball (boys), basketball (b,g), cross-country running (b,g), soccer (b,g), softball (g), tennis (g), track and field (b,g), winter (indoor) track (b,g), wrestling (b); intramural: bicycling (b), strength & conditioning (b,g), yoga (g); coed interscholastic: cheering; coed intramural: aerobics, aerobics/dance, aquatics, dance, fitness, flag football, indoor track & field, jogging, jump rope, life saving, martial arts, outdoor activities, outdoor adventure, physical fitness, running, swimming and diving, walking, weight training, winter walking. 1 PE instructor, 11 coaches.
Computers Computers are regularly used in college planning, English, foreign language, history, library, mathematics, newspaper, reading, research skills, SAT preparation, science, social studies, study skills, word processing, writing, yearbook classes. Computer network features include on-campus library services, online commercial services, Internet access, Internet filtering or blocking technology. Student e-mail accounts are available to students. The school has a published electronic and media policy.
Contact Joan McGovern, Admissions Representative. 215-787-2621. Fax: 215-787-4402. E-mail: admissions@girardcollege.com. Web site: www.girardcollege.com.

GIRLS PREPARATORY SCHOOL

205 Island Avenue
Chattanooga, Tennessee 37405
Head of School: Mr. Stanley R. Tucker
General Information Girls' day college-preparatory, arts, and technology school. Grades 6–12. Founded: 1906. Setting: suburban. Nearest major city is Atlanta, GA. 55-acre campus. 8 buildings on campus. Approved or accredited by Southern Association of Colleges and Schools and Southern Association of Independent Schools. Member of National Association of Independent Schools. Endowment: $24.2 million. Total enrollment: 607. Upper school average class size: 14. Upper school

faculty-student ratio: 1:8. There are 180 required school days per year for Upper School students. Upper School students typically attend 5 days per week. The average school day consists of 7 hours and 45 minutes.
Upper School Student Profile Grade 9: 102 students (102 girls); Grade 10: 94 students (94 girls); Grade 11: 97 students (97 girls); Grade 12: 83 students (83 girls).
Faculty School total: 76. In upper school: 13 men, 39 women; 29 have advanced degrees.
Subjects Offered Algebra, American history, American literature, art, art history, Basic programming, Bible studies, biology, calculus, chemistry, computer science, dance, drama, English, English literature, European history, fine arts, forensics, French, geometry, government/civics, graphic design, history, Latin, mathematics, music, orchestra, physical education, physics, pottery, pre-calculus, religion, science, Spanish, statistics, trigonometry, world history.
Graduation Requirements Arts and fine arts (art, music, dance, drama), electives, English, foreign language, history, mathematics, physical education (includes health), religion (includes Bible studies and theology), science.
Special Academic Programs 18 Advanced Placement exams for which test preparation is offered; honors section; independent study.
College Admission Counseling 108 students graduated in 2010; all went to college, including Furman University; Samford University; Savannah College of Art and Design; Sewanee: The University of the South; The University of Tennessee; Wake Forest University. Median SAT critical reading: 580, median SAT math: 580, median SAT writing: 590, median combined SAT: 1750, median composite ACT: 27. 40% scored over 600 on SAT critical reading, 38% scored over 600 on SAT math, 42% scored over 600 on SAT writing, 41% scored over 1800 on combined SAT, 42% scored over 26 on composite ACT.
Student Life Upper grades have uniform requirement, student council, honor system. Discipline rests primarily with faculty.
Summer Programs Remediation, enrichment, advancement, sports, art/fine arts, computer instruction programs offered; session focuses on summer fun and enrichment; held both on and off campus; held at Lupton Athletic fields & yacht club in Hixson; accepts boys and girls; open to students from other schools. 400 students usually enrolled. 2011 schedule: June 6 to July 22. Application deadline: June 1.
Tuition and Aid Day student tuition: $19,530. Tuition installment plan (Insured Tuition Payment Plan, FACTS Tuition Payment Plan, monthly payment plans, individually arranged payment plans, 60%/40% and 100% payment plans). Need-based scholarship grants available. In 2010–11, 38% of upper-school students received aid. Total amount of financial aid awarded in 2010–11: $1,183,294.
Admissions Traditional secondary-level entrance grade is 9. For fall 2010, 42 students applied for upper-level admission, 35 were accepted, 26 enrolled. Admissions testing required. Deadline for receipt of application materials: none. Application fee required: $75. Interview recommended.
Athletics Interscholastic: basketball, bowling, cheering, crew, cross-country running, diving, golf, lacrosse, rowing, soccer, softball, swimming and diving, tennis, track and field, volleyball; intramural: backpacking, bicycling, canoeing/kayaking, climbing, dance, dance squad, fitness, fitness walking, Frisbee, hiking/backpacking, jogging, kayaking, life saving, modern dance, mountain biking, outdoor activities, outdoor education, outdoor skills, paddle tennis, physical fitness, rafting, rock climbing, running, self defense, strength & conditioning, ultimate Frisbee, walking, weight training, wilderness, yoga; coed interscholastic: cheering. 6 PE instructors, 24 coaches, 1 athletic trainer.
Computers Computers are regularly used in Bible studies, computer applications, dance, English, foreign language, history, mathematics, science classes. Computer network features include on-campus library services, online commercial services, Internet access, wireless campus network, Internet filtering or blocking technology, network printing. Student e-mail accounts and computer access in designated common areas are available to students. Students grades are available online. The school has a published electronic and media policy.
Contact Debbie Bohner Young, Director of Admissions. 423-634-7647. Fax: 423-634-7643. E-mail: dyoung@gps.edu. Web site: www.gps.edu.

GLADES DAY SCHOOL

400 Gator Boulevard
Belle Glade, Florida 33430
Head of School: Dr. Robert Egley
General Information Coeducational day college-preparatory and general academic school. Grades PK–12. Founded: 1965. Setting: small town. Nearest major city is West Palm Beach. 21-acre campus. 4 buildings on campus. Approved or accredited by Florida Council of Independent Schools. Total enrollment: 395. Upper school average class size: 20. Upper school faculty-student ratio: 1:15. There are 180 required school days per year for Upper School students. Upper School students typically attend 5 days per week. The average school day consists of 6 hours and 35 minutes.
Upper School Student Profile Grade 9: 39 students (18 boys, 21 girls); Grade 10: 51 students (27 boys, 24 girls); Grade 11: 46 students (22 boys, 24 girls); Grade 12: 54 students (33 boys, 21 girls).
Faculty School total: 34. In upper school: 9 men, 14 women; 3 have advanced degrees.
Subjects Offered Agriculture, algebra, American government, American history, American literature, anatomy, ancient history, art, Bible studies, biology, calculus, computer applications, computer skills, computer technologies, earth

science, economics, English, English literature, English literature and composition-AP, European history, European history-AP, general math, geometry, government and politics-AP, grammar, health, health education, journalism, keyboarding, literature and composition-AP, macro/microeconomics-AP, macroeconomics-AP, modern world history, physical education, pre-calculus, SAT/ACT preparation, Spanish, trigonometry, U.S. government and politics-AP, U.S. history, U.S. history-AP, weightlifting, world history, yearbook.

Graduation Requirements Algebra, American government, American literature, anatomy, ancient world history, arts and fine arts (art, music, dance, drama), biology, calculus, chemistry, computer applications, economics, English, English composition, English literature, geometry, health education, keyboarding, macroeconomics-AP, marine biology, modern world history, physical education (includes health), physical fitness, physical science, physics, pre-calculus, Spanish, U.S. history, world history.

Special Academic Programs 6 Advanced Placement exams for which test preparation is offered; honors section; independent study; study at local college for college credit; programs in general development for dyslexic students.

College Admission Counseling 52 students graduated in 2010; 50 went to college, including Florida Gulf Coast University; Florida State University; Palm Beach State College; Santa Fe College; University of Central Florida; University of Florida. Other: 2 went to work.

Student Life Upper grades have uniform requirement, student council, honor system. Discipline rests primarily with faculty.

Summer Programs Remediation programs offered; session focuses on remediation; held on campus; accepts boys and girls; not open to students from other schools. 15 students usually enrolled. 2011 schedule: June 7 to July 15. Application deadline: June 4.

Tuition and Aid Day student tuition: $6900–$7650. Tuition installment plan (FACTS Tuition Payment Plan, monthly payment plans, individually arranged payment plans). Tuition reduction for siblings, need-based scholarship grants available. In 2010–11, 10% of upper-school students received aid.

Admissions Traditional secondary-level entrance grade is 9. For fall 2010, 34 students applied for upper-level admission, 25 were accepted, 25 enrolled. Deadline for receipt of application materials: none. Application fee required: $400. On-campus interview required.

Athletics Interscholastic: baseball (boys), basketball (b,g), cheering (g), cross-country running (b,g), football (b), golf (b), soccer (b,g), softball (g), track and field (b,g), volleyball (g); intramural: strength & conditioning (b,g), weight training (b,g). 3 PE instructors, 2 coaches, 1 athletic trainer.

Computers Computers are regularly used in English, journalism, science, Spanish, Web site design, word processing, yearbook classes. Computer network features include on-campus library services, Internet access, wireless campus network. Campus intranet and student e-mail accounts are available to students. Students grades are available online. The school has a published electronic and media policy.

Contact Mrs. Irene Tellechea, High School Secretary. 561-996-6769 Ext. 10. Fax: 561-992-9274. E-mail: admissions@gladesdayschool.com. Web site: www.gladesdayschool.com.

GLEN EDEN SCHOOL
Vancouver, British Columbia, Canada
See Special Needs Schools section.

GLENELG COUNTRY SCHOOL
12793 Folly Quarter Road
Ellicott City, Maryland 21042
Head of School: Gregory J. Ventre

General Information Coeducational day college-preparatory, arts, and technology school. Grades PK–12. Founded: 1954. Setting: suburban. Nearest major city is Baltimore. 87-acre campus. 1 building on campus. Approved or accredited by Association of Independent Maryland Schools, Middle States Association of Colleges and Schools, and Maryland Department of Education. Member of National Association of Independent Schools. Endowment: $900,000. Total enrollment: 797. Upper school average class size: 15. Upper school faculty-student ratio: 1:6. There are 175 required school days per year for Upper School students. Upper School students typically attend 5 days per week. The average school day consists of 7 hours.

Upper School Student Profile Grade 9: 69 students (37 boys, 32 girls); Grade 10: 82 students (44 boys, 38 girls); Grade 11: 74 students (39 boys, 35 girls); Grade 12: 71 students (35 boys, 36 girls).

Faculty School total: 131. In upper school: 26 men, 21 women; 35 have advanced degrees.

Subjects Offered Algebra, American history, American literature, art, art history, biology, biology-AP, calculus, calculus-AP, chemistry, chemistry-AP, Chinese, chorus, community service, computer science, creative writing, drama, English, English literature, English-AP, European history, expository writing, French, French-AP, geometry, history, humanities, integrative seminar, Latin, Latin-AP, mathematics, photography, physical education, physical science, physics, physics-AP, pre-calculus, psychology, publications, science, social studies, Spanish, Spanish-AP, statistics, studio art, theater, trigonometry, world affairs.

Graduation Requirements Civics, English, foreign language, integrative seminar, mathematics, physical education (includes health), science, social studies (includes history), participation in Civic Leadership Program, 25 hours of community service per year.

Special Academic Programs 17 Advanced Placement exams for which test preparation is offered; honors section; independent study; academic accommodation for the gifted.

College Admission Counseling 63 students graduated in 2010; 61 went to college, including Gettysburg College; University of Maryland, College Park; University of South Carolina; Wake Forest University. Other: 1 entered a postgraduate year, 1 had other specific plans. Median SAT critical reading: 604, median SAT math: 611, median SAT writing: 616, median combined SAT: 1831. 51% scored over 600 on SAT critical reading, 53% scored over 600 on SAT math, 56% scored over 600 on SAT writing, 57% scored over 1800 on combined SAT.

Student Life Upper grades have uniform requirement, student council, honor system. Discipline rests equally with students and faculty.

Summer Programs Sports programs offered; session focuses on athletics and CIT (Couselor-In-Training) programs; held on campus; accepts boys and girls; open to students from other schools. 300 students usually enrolled. 2011 schedule: June 20 to July 29. Application deadline: May 31.

Tuition and Aid Day student tuition: $22,450. Tuition installment plan (monthly payment plans, individually arranged payment plans, 2-payment plan). Merit scholarship grants, need-based scholarship grants available. In 2010–11, 40% of upper-school students received aid; total upper-school merit-scholarship money awarded: $120,000. Total amount of financial aid awarded in 2010–11: $1,600,000.

Admissions Traditional secondary-level entrance grade is 9. For fall 2010, 49 students applied for upper-level admission, 36 were accepted, 28 enrolled. ISEE or SSAT required. Deadline for receipt of application materials: January 15. Application fee required: $75. On-campus interview required.

Athletics Interscholastic: baseball (boys), basketball (b,g), cross-country running (b,g), field hockey (g), golf (b,g), ice hockey (b), indoor soccer (g), lacrosse (b,g), soccer (b,g), tennis (b,g), volleyball (g), winter soccer (g), wrestling (b); coed interscholastic: golf, ice hockey, strength & conditioning; coed intramural: aerobics, aerobics/dance, dance, fitness, flag football, Frisbee, physical fitness, physical training, skiing (downhill), strength & conditioning, ultimate Frisbee, weight training, yoga. 5 PE instructors, 12 coaches, 1 athletic trainer.

Computers Computers are regularly used in all academic classes. Computer network features include on-campus library services, Internet access, wireless campus network. Campus intranet, student e-mail accounts, and computer access in designated common areas are available to students. Students grades are available online. The school has a published electronic and media policy.

Contact Mrs. Karen K. Wootton, Director of Admission and Financial Aid. 410-531-7346 Ext. 2203. Fax: 410-531-7363. E-mail: wootton@glenelg.org. Web site: www.glenelg.org.

THE GLENHOLME SCHOOL, A DEVEREUX CENTER
Washington, Connecticut
See Special Needs Schools section.

GLENLYON NORFOLK SCHOOL
801 Bank Street
Victoria, British Columbia V8S 4A8, Canada
Head of School: Mr. Simon Bruce-Lockhart

General Information Coeducational day college-preparatory, arts, technology, and International Baccalaureate school. Grades JK–12. Founded: 1913. Setting: urban. 6-acre campus. 5 buildings on campus. Approved or accredited by International Baccalaureate Organization and British Columbia Department of Education. Affiliate member of National Association of Independent Schools. Language of instruction: English. Endowment: CAN$800,000. Upper school average class size: 18. Upper school faculty-student ratio: 1:8. There are 180 required school days per year for Upper School students. Upper School students typically attend 5 days per week. The average school day consists of 6 hours.

Upper School Student Profile Grade 9: 64 students (32 boys, 32 girls); Grade 10: 57 students (36 boys, 21 girls); Grade 11: 68 students (44 boys, 24 girls); Grade 12: 59 students (25 boys, 34 girls).

Faculty School total: 90. In upper school: 20 men, 21 women; 13 have advanced degrees.

Subjects Offered 20th century world history, art, band, biology, calculus, chemistry, choir, community service, comparative civilizations, concert band, creative writing, debate, directing, drama, English, English literature, European history, European literature, fine arts, French, geography, history, information technology, International Baccalaureate courses, jazz band, journalism, life skills, mathematics, music, newspaper, peer counseling, physical education, physics, public speaking, science, social studies, Spanish, stagecraft, theater arts, theory of knowledge, vocal jazz, world history, world literature, writing, yearbook.

Graduation Requirements Arts and fine arts (art, music, dance, drama), career planning, English, foreign language, information technology, mathematics, physical education (includes health), science, social studies (includes history). Community service is required.

Special Academic Programs International Baccalaureate program; honors section; term-away projects; ESL (15 students enrolled).

College Admission Counseling 81 students graduated in 2010; 71 went to college, including McGill University; The University of British Columbia; University of Calgary; University of Toronto; University of Victoria. Other: 2 went to work, 1 entered military service, 7 had other specific plans.

Student Life Upper grades have uniform requirement, student council, honor system. Discipline rests primarily with faculty.

Tuition and Aid Day student tuition: CAN$12,990–CAN$15,970. Guaranteed tuition plan. Tuition installment plan (monthly payment plans, individually arranged payment plans). Tuition reduction for siblings, bursaries, merit scholarship grants, tuition allowances for children of staff available. In 2010–11, 19% of upper-school students received aid; total upper-school merit-scholarship money awarded: CAN$23,050. Total amount of financial aid awarded in 2010–11: CAN$129,895.

Admissions Traditional secondary-level entrance grade is 9. SAT, SLEP, SSAT or writing sample required. Deadline for receipt of application materials: none. Application fee required: CAN$185. Interview recommended.

Athletics Interscholastic: backpacking (boys, girls), badminton (b,g), basketball (b,g), canoeing/kayaking (b,g), climbing (b,g), crew (b,g), cross-country running (b,g), field hockey (g), fitness (b,g), kayaking (b,g), rock climbing (b,g), rowing (b,g), rugby (b), soccer (b,g), squash (b,g), swimming and diving (b,g), tennis (b,g), track and field (b,g), volleyball (g); intramural: badminton (b,g), ball hockey (b), basketball (b,g), floor hockey (b), outdoor education (b,g), outdoor recreation (b,g), outdoor skills (b,g), swimming and diving (b,g), track and field (b,g), ultimate Frisbee (b,g); coed interscholastic: backpacking, badminton, canoeing/kayaking, crew, cross-country running, fitness, golf, kayaking, sailing, tennis; coed intramural: badminton, basketball, outdoor education, outdoor recreation, outdoor skills, swimming and diving, track and field, ultimate Frisbee. 4 PE instructors, 12 coaches.

Computers Computers are regularly used in all classes. Computer network features include on-campus library services, Internet access, wireless campus network, Internet filtering or blocking technology. Campus intranet and student e-mail accounts are available to students. The school has a published electronic and media policy.

Contact Ms. Andrea Hughes, Admissions Associate. 250-370-6801. Fax: 250-370-6811. E-mail: admissions@mygns.ca. Web site: www.glenlyonnorfolk.bc.ca.

GONZAGA COLLEGE HIGH SCHOOL

19 Eye Street NW
Washington, District of Columbia 20001
Head of School: Rev. Vincent Conti, SJ

General Information Boys' day college-preparatory, arts, religious studies, and technology school, affiliated with Roman Catholic Church. Grades 9–12. Founded: 1821. Setting: urban. 1-acre campus. 9 buildings on campus. Approved or accredited by Association of Independent Schools of Greater Washington, Jesuit Secondary Education Association, Middle States Association of Colleges and Schools, and District of Columbia Department of Education. Endowment: $9.1 million. Total enrollment: 957. Upper school average class size: 26. Upper school faculty-student ratio: 1:15. There are 173 required school days per year for Upper School students. Upper School students typically attend 5 days per week. The average school day consists of 6 hours and 35 minutes.

Upper School Student Profile Grade 9: 242 students (242 boys); Grade 10: 245 students (245 boys); Grade 11: 237 students (237 boys); Grade 12: 234 students (234 boys). 80% of students are Roman Catholic.

Faculty School total: 66. In upper school: 50 men, 16 women; 60 have advanced degrees.

Subjects Offered Advanced Placement courses, African-American literature, algebra, American history, American literature, applied music, art, band, biology, broadcasting, calculus, calculus-AP, Catholic belief and practice, chemistry, chemistry-AP, Chinese, choir, choral music, Christian and Hebrew scripture, Christian ethics, Christian scripture, communications, community service, computer applications, computer math, computer programming, computer science, concert band, concert choir, creative writing, driver education, earth science, economics, economics-AP, English, English literature, English literature and composition-AP, English literature-AP, English-AP, environmental science-AP, ethics, ethics and responsibility, European history, European history-AP, expository writing, film appreciation, film studies, fine arts, French, French-AP, functions, geometry, government, government/civics, grammar, Greek, health, health education, history, honors algebra, honors English, honors geometry, human geography—AP, independent study, Irish literature, jazz ensemble, Latin, Latin-AP, mathematics, media communications, music, musicianship, philosophy, photography, physical education, physics, physics-AP, piano, poetry, political science, political systems, psychology, psychology-AP, religion, Russian history, Russian studies, science, social justice, social sciences, social studies, Spanish, Spanish-AP, statistics, statistics-AP, studio art-AP, symphonic band, theology, trigonometry, U.S. government and politics-AP, Web site design, world history, world literature.

Graduation Requirements Accounting, arts and fine arts (art, music, dance, drama), English, ethics, foreign language, mathematics, physical education (includes health),

religion (includes Bible studies and theology), science, social justice, social sciences, social studies (includes history). Community service is required.

Special Academic Programs Advanced Placement exam preparation; honors section.

College Admission Counseling 229 students graduated in 2010; 226 went to college, including Fordham University; James Madison University; University of Maryland, College Park; University of Notre Dame; University of South Carolina; University of Virginia. Other: 1 entered a postgraduate year, 2 had other specific plans.

Student Life Upper grades have specified standards of dress, student council, honor system. Discipline rests primarily with faculty. Attendance at religious services is required.

Summer Programs Remediation, enrichment programs offered; session focuses on new student remediation, enrichment, and SAT preparation; held on campus; accepts boys and girls; open to students from other schools. 200 students usually enrolled. 2011 schedule: June 29 to July 24. Application deadline: June 1.

Tuition and Aid Day student tuition: $16,850. Tuition installment plan (Insured Tuition Payment Plan, monthly payment plans). Merit scholarship grants, need-based scholarship grants available. In 2010–11, 33% of upper-school students received aid; total upper-school merit-scholarship money awarded: $100,000. Total amount of financial aid awarded in 2010–11: $2,000,000.

Admissions Traditional secondary-level entrance grade is 9. For fall 2010, 707 students applied for upper-level admission, 300 were accepted, 242 enrolled. High School Placement Test (closed version) from Scholastic Testing Service required. Deadline for receipt of application materials: December 10. Application fee required: $35.

Athletics Interscholastic: baseball, basketball, crew, cross-country running, diving, football, golf, ice hockey, indoor track & field, lacrosse, rugby, soccer, squash, swimming and diving, tennis, track and field, water polo, winter (indoor) track, wrestling; intramural: basketball, bowling, fencing, fishing, football, Frisbee, hiking/backpacking, martial arts, physical training, skiing (downhill), softball, strength & conditioning, table tennis, volleyball, weight lifting, whiffle ball. 2 PE instructors, 30 coaches, 3 athletic trainers.

Computers Computer network features include on-campus library services, Internet access. Student e-mail accounts are available to students.

Contact Mr. Andrew C. Battaile, Director of Admission. 202-336-7101. Fax: 202-454-1188. E-mail: abattaile@gonzaga.org. Web site: www.gonzaga.org.

GORDON TECHNICAL HIGH SCHOOL

3633 North California Avenue
Chicago, Illinois 60618
Head of School: Ms. Kelly Jones

General Information Coeducational day college-preparatory, arts, business, vocational, religious studies, bilingual studies, and technology school, affiliated with Roman Catholic Church; primarily serves students with learning disabilities. Grades 9–12. Founded: 1952. Setting: urban. 4-acre campus. 1 building on campus. Approved or accredited by North Central Association of Colleges and Schools and Illinois Department of Education. Endowment: $5 million. Total enrollment: 505. Upper school average class size: 22. Upper school faculty-student ratio: 1:15. There are 180 required school days per year for Upper School students. Upper School students typically attend 5 days per week. The average school day consists of 7 hours.

Upper School Student Profile Grade 9: 121 students (71 boys, 50 girls); Grade 10: 149 students (81 boys, 68 girls); Grade 11: 101 students (55 boys, 46 girls); Grade 12: 137 students (76 boys, 61 girls). 66% of students are Roman Catholic.

Faculty School total: 40. In upper school: 24 men, 12 women; 34 have advanced degrees.

Special Academic Programs 9 Advanced Placement exams for which test preparation is offered; honors section; study at local college for college credit; academic accommodation for the gifted; remedial reading and/or remedial writing; remedial math.

College Admission Counseling 111 students graduated in 2009; all went to college, including DePaul University; Loyola University Chicago; Northeastern Illinois University; University of Illinois at Chicago; University of Illinois at Urbana–Champaign.

Student Life Upper grades have uniform requirement, student council, honor system. Discipline rests primarily with faculty. Attendance at religious services is required.

Tuition and Aid Day student tuition: $8250. Tuition installment plan (monthly payment plans). Tuition reduction for siblings, bursaries, merit scholarship grants, need-based scholarship grants, paying campus jobs available. In 2009–10, 60% of upper-school students received aid. Total amount of financial aid awarded in 2009–10: $950,000.

Admissions Traditional secondary-level entrance grade is 9. For fall 2009, 238 students applied for upper-level admission, 196 were accepted, 159 enrolled. Deadline for receipt of application materials: none. No application fee required. On-campus interview recommended.

Athletics Interscholastic: baseball (boys), basketball (b,g), cheering (g), cross-country running (b,g), dance team (g), football (b), indoor track (b,g), indoor track & field (b,g), pom squad (g), running (b,g), soccer (b,g), softball (g), volleyball (b,g), wrestling (b); intramural: baseball (b), basketball (b,g), power lifting (b), strength & conditioning (b,g), weight training (b,g); coed interscholastic: bowling; coed intramural: aerobics, aerobics/dance, aerobics/Nautilus, badminton, baseball, basketball, climbing, fitness, outdoor activities, outdoor adventure, outdoor recreation, physical fitness, physical training, ropes courses, track and field. 2 PE instructors, 1 coach.

Computers Computers are regularly used in all classes. Computer network features include on-campus library services, online commercial services, Internet access, wireless campus network. Students grades are available online. The school has a published electronic and media policy.

Contact Mr. Shay Boyle, Director of Admissions. 773-423-5014. Fax: 773-539-9158. E-mail: sboyle@gordontech.org. Web site: www.gordontech.org.

GOULD ACADEMY

PO Box 860
39 Church Street
Bethel, Maine 04217
Head of School: Daniel A. Kunkle

General Information Coeducational boarding and day college-preparatory, arts, and technology school. Grades 9–PG. Founded: 1836. Setting: small town. Nearest major city is Portland. Students are housed in single-sex dormitories. 456-acre campus. 30 buildings on campus. Approved or accredited by Association of Independent Schools in New England, Independent Schools of Northern New England, New England Association of Schools and Colleges, The Association of Boarding Schools, and Maine Department of Education. Member of National Association of Independent Schools and Secondary School Admission Test Board. Endowment: $9.5 million. Total enrollment: 249. Upper school average class size: 12. Upper school faculty-student ratio: 1:6. There are 175 required school days per year for Upper School students. Upper School students typically attend 5 days per week.

Upper School Student Profile Grade 9: 28 students (16 boys, 12 girls); Grade 10: 69 students (46 boys, 23 girls); Grade 11: 72 students (39 boys, 33 girls); Grade 12: 65 students (43 boys, 22 girls); Postgraduate: 4 students (4 boys). 71% of students are boarding students. 42% are state residents. 22 states are represented in upper school student body. 20% are international students. International students from China, Germany, Japan, Republic of Korea, Spain, and Taiwan; 2 other countries represented in student body.

Faculty School total: 44. In upper school: 23 men, 21 women; 25 have advanced degrees; 32 reside on campus.

Subjects Offered Acting, Advanced Placement courses, African-American literature, algebra, American foreign policy, American history, American literature, American literature-AP, analytic geometry, art, art history, athletic training, band, bioethics, DNA and culture, biology, biology-AP, British literature, British literature (honors), British literature-AP, calculus, calculus-AP, celestial navigation, ceramics, chemistry, chemistry-AP, chorus, Civil War, clayworking, college placement, computer information systems, computer music, computer programming, computer science, computers, conceptual physics, creative writing, debate, design, digital music, drama, drawing, earth science, Eastern religion and philosophy, ecology, economics, electives, electronic music, electronics, English, environmental science, environmental science-AP, ESL, European history, expository writing, foreign policy, French, geography, geometry, government and politics-AP, history, history-AP, honors algebra, honors English, honors world history, introduction to digital multitrack recording techniques, jazz band, jewelry making, Latin, learning strategies, literature by women, mathematics, music, music appreciation, music theory, musicianship, navigation, painting, philosophy, photography, physics, pottery, pre-calculus, printmaking, robotics, science, sculpture, Shakespeare, social studies, software design, Spanish, theater, U.S. government and politics-AP, video film production, women's literature, world history, writing.

Graduation Requirements English, foreign language, mathematics, physical education (includes health), science, social studies (includes history).

Special Academic Programs Advanced Placement exam preparation; honors section; independent study; term-away projects; study abroad; academic accommodation for the gifted, the musically talented, and the artistically talented; ESL (25 students enrolled).

College Admission Counseling 64 students graduated in 2010; all went to college, including Bentley University; Lewis & Clark College; Rochester Institute of Technology; Saint Michael's College; University of Illinois at Urbana–Champaign; University of Vermont.

Student Life Upper grades have specified standards of dress, student council, honor system. Discipline rests equally with students and faculty.

Tuition and Aid Day student tuition: $26,850; 7-day tuition and room/board: $45,500. Tuition installment plan (individually arranged payment plans, full payment by August 15, 2/3 payment by August 12, 1/3 by December 1). Need-based scholarship grants, need-based loans available. In 2010–11, 38% of upper-school students received aid. Total amount of financial aid awarded in 2010–11: $1,355,000.

Admissions Traditional secondary-level entrance grade is 9. For fall 2010, 168 students applied for upper-level admission, 149 were accepted, 78 enrolled. SSAT required. Deadline for receipt of application materials: February 1. Application fee required: $30. Interview required.

Athletics Interscholastic: alpine skiing (boys, girls), baseball (b), basketball (b,g), bicycling (b,g), cross-country running (b,g), field hockey (g), freestyle skiing (b,g); coed interscholastic: climbing, dance, dressage, equestrian sports, golf; coed intramural: golf. 11 coaches, 1 athletic trainer.

Computers Computers are regularly used in English, foreign language, history, mathematics, music, science, technology classes. Computer network features include on-campus library services, Internet access, wireless campus network. Student e-mail accounts are available to students. Students grades are available online. The school has a published electronic and media policy.

Contact Todd Ormiston, Director of Admission. 207-824-7777. Fax: 207-824-2926. E-mail: todd.ormiston@gouldacademy.org. Web site: www.gouldacademy.org.

THE GOVERNOR FRENCH ACADEMY

219 West Main Street
Belleville, Illinois 62220-1537
Head of School: Mr. Phillip E. Paeltz

General Information Coeducational boarding and day college-preparatory and bilingual studies school. Boarding grades 9–12, day grades K–12. Founded: 1983. Setting: small town. Nearest major city is St. Louis, MO. Students are housed in homes of local families. 3 buildings on campus. Approved or accredited by CITA (Commission on International and Trans-Regional Accreditation), North Central Association of Colleges and Schools, and Illinois Department of Education. Endowment: $100,000. Total enrollment: 182. Upper school average class size: 15. Upper school faculty-student ratio: 1:6. There are 176 required school days per year for Upper School students. Upper School students typically attend 5 days per week. The average school day consists of 7 hours and 15 minutes.

Upper School Student Profile Grade 9: 15 students (9 boys, 6 girls); Grade 10: 8 students (3 boys, 5 girls); Grade 11: 11 students (7 boys, 4 girls); Grade 12: 20 students (11 boys, 9 girls). 12% of students are boarding students. 88% are state residents. 1 state is represented in upper school student body. 12% are international students. International students from China, Republic of Korea, and Taiwan.

Faculty School total: 15. In upper school: 2 men, 5 women; 5 have advanced degrees.

Subjects Offered Algebra, American history, American literature, biology, calculus, chemistry, creative writing, earth science, ecology, economics, English, English literature, environmental science, European history, expository writing, geography, geometry, government/civics, grammar, history, mathematics, physical education, physics, science, social sciences, social studies, theater arts, trigonometry, world history, world literature.

Graduation Requirements English, foreign language, mathematics, physical education (includes health), science, social sciences, vote of faculty.

Special Academic Programs 6 Advanced Placement exams for which test preparation is offered; accelerated programs; independent study; academic accommodation for the gifted and the artistically talented; programs in English for dyslexic students; ESL (7 students enrolled).

College Admission Counseling 11 students graduated in 2010; all went to college, including Saint Louis University. Median composite ACT: 25.

Student Life Upper grades have uniform requirement, honor system. Discipline rests primarily with faculty.

Summer Programs Remediation, enrichment, advancement programs offered; session focuses on academics; held on campus; accepts boys and girls; open to students from other schools. 30 students usually enrolled. 2011 schedule: June 20 to July 29. Application deadline: none.

Tuition and Aid Day student tuition: $5500; 7-day tuition and room/board: $22,200. Tuition installment plan (monthly payment plans). Tuition reduction for siblings available.

Admissions Traditional secondary-level entrance grade is 9. For fall 2010, 15 students applied for upper-level admission, 15 were accepted, 13 enrolled. School placement exam required. Deadline for receipt of application materials: none. No application fee required. Interview required.

Athletics Interscholastic: martial arts (boys, girls), volleyball (g); intramural: basketball (b), martial arts (b,g); coed interscholastic: basketball, soccer; coed intramural: independent competitive sports, softball.

Computers Computers are regularly used in computer applications, science, yearbook classes. Computer network features include Internet access, wireless campus network, Internet filtering or blocking technology. Computer access in designated common areas is available to students. The school has a published electronic and media policy.

Contact Ms. Carol Wilson, Director of Admissions. 618-233-7542. Fax: 618-233-0541. E-mail: admiss@governorfrench.com. Web site: www.governorfrench.com.

THE GOVERNOR'S ACADEMY (FORMERLY GOVERNOR DUMMER ACADEMY)

1 Elm Street
Byfield, Massachusetts 01922
Head of School: John Martin Doggett Jr.

General Information Coeducational boarding and day college-preparatory and arts school. Grades 9–12. Founded: 1763. Setting: rural. Nearest major city is Boston. Students are housed in single-sex dormitories. 450-acre campus. 48 buildings on campus. Approved or accredited by Association of Independent Schools in New England, New England Association of Schools and Colleges, and The Association of Boarding Schools. Member of National Association of Independent Schools and Secondary School Admission Test Board. Endowment: $63 million. Total enrollment:

395. Upper school average class size: 12. Upper school faculty-student ratio: 1:5. There are 158 required school days per year for Upper School students. Upper School students typically attend 5 days per week.
Upper School Student Profile Grade 9: 89 students (44 boys, 45 girls); Grade 10: 108 students (59 boys, 49 girls); Grade 11: 102 students (58 boys, 44 girls); Grade 12: 91 students (47 boys, 44 girls). 65% of students are boarding students. 50% are state residents. 21 states are represented in upper school student body. 12% are international students. International students from Bermuda, China, Republic of Korea, Singapore, Taiwan, and Thailand; 6 other countries represented in student body.
Faculty In upper school: 46 men, 36 women; 40 have advanced degrees; 60 reside on campus.
Subjects Offered Advanced chemistry, algebra, American history, American history-AP, American literature, anatomy, art, band, biology, biology-AP, calculus-AP, ceramics, chemistry, chemistry-AP, Chinese, chorus, civics, computer graphics, computer math, computer programming, computer science, computer science-AP, constitutional law, creative writing, dance, drama, driver education, ecology, economics, economics-AP, English language-AP, English literature, English literature and composition-AP, environmental science, ESL, European history, European history-AP, expository writing, filmmaking, fine arts, French, French-AP, geometry, German, health, history, Holocaust and other genocides, honors algebra, jazz band, Latin, Latin-AP, marine biology, marine science, mathematics, Middle Eastern history, modern European history, modern European history-AP, music, music history, music theory, photography, physics, physics-AP, psychology, religion, science, social studies, Spanish, Spanish language-AP, Spanish literature-AP, statistics-AP, studio art-AP, theater, trigonometry, visual and performing arts, women's studies, writing.
Graduation Requirements Arts and fine arts (art, music, dance, drama), English, foreign language, history, mathematics, science, 50 hours of community service.
Special Academic Programs Advanced Placement exam preparation; honors section; independent study; study abroad; ESL (5 students enrolled).
College Admission Counseling 96 students graduated in 2010; all went to college, including Boston University; Colby College; Harvard University; New York University; Tufts University. Mean SAT critical reading: 602, mean SAT math: 633, mean SAT writing: 603, mean combined SAT: 1829. 38% scored over 600 on SAT critical reading, 50% scored over 600 on SAT math, 42% scored over 600 on SAT writing, 42% scored over 1800 on combined SAT.
Student Life Upper grades have specified standards of dress, student council, honor system. Discipline rests primarily with faculty.
Summer Programs Enrichment, advancement, ESL, sports, art/fine arts programs offered; session focuses on exploration and development of skills, talents, and interests; held on campus; accepts boys and girls; open to students from other schools. 500 students usually enrolled. 2011 schedule: June 15 to August 15. Application deadline: none.
Tuition and Aid Day student tuition: $35,250; 7-day tuition and room/board: $44,550. Tuition installment plan (The Tuition Plan, Academic Management Services Plan, monthly payment plans). Need-based scholarship grants available. In 2010–11, 28% of upper-school students received aid. Total amount of financial aid awarded in 2010–11: $32,000,000.
Admissions Traditional secondary-level entrance grade is 9. For fall 2010, 775 students applied for upper-level admission, 234 were accepted, 110 enrolled. ISEE, SSAT or TOEFL required. Deadline for receipt of application materials: January 31. Application fee required: $50. Interview required.
Athletics Interscholastic: baseball (boys), basketball (b,g), cross-country running (b,g), field hockey (g), football (b), ice hockey (b,g), indoor track & field (b,g), lacrosse (b,g), soccer (b,g), softball (g), tennis (b,g), track and field (b,g), volleyball (g), wrestling (b); intramural: dance (g); coed interscholastic: golf; coed intramural: aerobics/dance, alpine skiing, dance, outdoor activities, outdoor recreation, skiing (downhill), tennis, yoga. 2 athletic trainers.
Computers Computers are regularly used in art, English, foreign language, history, mathematics, music, science classes. Computer network features include on-campus library services, online commercial services, Internet access, wireless campus network, Internet filtering or blocking technology, laptop sign-out in student center and library, Moodle Website for teachers and students to share course data, events, and discussions. Campus intranet, student e-mail accounts, and computer access in designated common areas are available to students. The school has a published electronic and media policy.
Contact Michael Kinnealey, Director of Admission. 978-499-3120. Fax: 978-462-1278. E-mail: admissions@thegovernorsacademy.org. Web site: www.thegovernorsacademy.org.

THE GOW SCHOOL
South Wales, New York
See Special Needs Schools section.

GRACE BAPTIST ACADEMY
7815 Shallowford Road
Chattanooga, Tennessee 37421
Head of School: Mr. David Patrick
General Information Coeducational day college-preparatory and religious studies school, affiliated with Baptist Church. Grades K4–12. Founded: 1985. Setting: suburban. 2 buildings on campus. Approved or accredited by Association of Christian Schools International, Southern Association of Colleges and Schools, and Tennessee Department of Education. Total enrollment: 704. Upper school average class size: 22. Upper school faculty-student ratio: 1:20. Upper School students typically attend 5 days per week. The average school day consists of 7 hours and 15 minutes.
Upper School Student Profile Grade 9: 53 students (23 boys, 30 girls); Grade 10: 45 students (18 boys, 27 girls); Grade 11: 49 students (20 boys, 29 girls); Grade 12: 42 students (20 boys, 22 girls). 75% of students are Baptist.
Faculty School total: 47. In upper school: 10 men, 9 women; 5 have advanced degrees.
Subjects Offered Advanced computer applications, algebra, American government, American history, American literature, ancient world history, art, band, Bible, Bible studies, biology, biology-AP, calculus, chemistry, choir, Christian doctrine, Christian ethics, Christian testament, computer applications, drama performance, dramatic arts, economics, English, English composition, English literature, environmental studies, fitness, general math, general science, geometry, global studies, health, health and safety, honors English, honors world history, keyboarding, language arts, Life of Christ, mathematics, music, New Testament, physical education, physics, pre-algebra, pre-calculus, SAT/ACT preparation, Spanish, speech, state history, study skills, U.S. government and politics, U.S. history, weight training, weightlifting, world geography, yearbook.
Graduation Requirements Algebra, American history, Bible, biology, chemistry, economics, English, English literature, geometry, global studies, government, physical education (includes health), Spanish, speech, U.S. history, visual and performing arts, 1/2 unit of speech.
Special Academic Programs Honors section; study at local college for college credit.
College Admission Counseling 58 students graduated in 2010; 56 went to college, including Chattanooga State Community College; The University of Tennessee at Chattanooga. Other: 2 went to work. Mean composite ACT: 22.
Student Life Upper grades have uniform requirement, student council, honor system. Discipline rests primarily with faculty. Attendance at religious services is required.
Summer Programs Remediation programs offered; held on campus; accepts boys and girls; open to students from other schools. 75 students usually enrolled. 2011 schedule: June 20 to July 22. Application deadline: June 5.
Tuition and Aid Tuition installment plan (FACTS Tuition Payment Plan, bank draft). Tuition reduction for siblings, need-based scholarship grants available. In 2010–11, 5% of upper-school students received aid.
Admissions Traditional secondary-level entrance grade is 9. For fall 2010, 26 students applied for upper-level admission, 25 were accepted, 25 enrolled. Latest standardized score from previous school required. Deadline for receipt of application materials: none. Application fee required: $300. On-campus interview required.
Athletics Interscholastic: baseball (boys), basketball (b,g), cheering (g), cross-country running (b,g), football (b), soccer (b,g), softball (g), tennis (b,g), track and field (b,g), volleyball (g), weight training (b,g); intramural: physical training (b,g), strength & conditioning (b,g), weight lifting (b), weight training (b); coed interscholastic: archery, golf. 2 PE instructors, 5 coaches, 1 athletic trainer.
Computers Computers are regularly used in computer applications, keyboarding, Web site design classes. Computer resources include on-campus library services, Internet access, Internet filtering or blocking technology. Students grades are available online.
Contact Mrs. Janine McCurdy, Admissions Director. 423-892-8222 Ext. 115. Fax: 423-892-1194. E-mail: jmccurdy@gracechatt.org. Web site: www.gracechatt.org.

GRACE CHRISTIAN SCHOOL
12407 Pintail Street
Anchorage, Alaska 99516
Head of School: Mr. Nathan Davis
General Information Coeducational day college-preparatory, arts, religious studies, and technology school, affiliated with Christian faith. Grades K–12. Founded: 1980. Setting: urban. 7-acre campus. 1 building on campus. Approved or accredited by Association of Christian Schools International, Northwest Accreditation Commission, and Northwest Association of Schools and Colleges. Total enrollment: 631. Upper school average class size: 17. Upper school faculty-student ratio: 1:15. There are 180 required school days per year for Upper School students. Upper School students typically attend 5 days per week. The average school day consists of 6 hours and 50 minutes.
Upper School Student Profile Grade 7: 67 students (34 boys, 33 girls); Grade 8: 58 students (34 boys, 24 girls); Grade 9: 63 students (28 boys, 35 girls); Grade 10: 65 students (32 boys, 33 girls); Grade 11: 63 students (30 boys, 33 girls); Grade 12: 54 students (21 boys, 33 girls). 99% of students are Christian faith.
Faculty School total: 53. In upper school: 12 men, 17 women; 7 have advanced degrees.

Subjects Offered Algebra, American government, American history, art, Bible, biology, biology-AP, calculus-AP, chemistry, chemistry-AP, choir, computer skills, computer technologies, creative writing, drama, economics, English, English language and composition-AP, English literature and composition-AP, English literature-AP, English/composition-AP, film, fine arts, French, geometry, health, literature, media, music theory-AP, physical education, physical science, physics, psychology, publications, science, social studies, Spanish, speech, trigonometry, U.S. history, weightlifting, world history, yearbook.

Graduation Requirements Algebra, American government, American literature, biology, British literature, consumer economics, electives, English composition, English literature, geometry, literary genres, literature, physical education (includes health), physical science, practical arts, U.S. history, world history, one year of Bible for every year attending, Old Testament survey in 9th grade, 10th Grade-New Testament survey, 11th Grade-Life and Times of Christ/Marriage and Family, 12th Grade-Defending Your Faith/Understanding the Times.

Special Academic Programs Advanced Placement exam preparation.

College Admission Counseling 56 students graduated in 2009; 54 went to college, including Corban University; George Fox University; University of Alaska Anchorage; University of Alaska Fairbanks; Westmont College. Other: 2 went to work. Mean SAT critical reading: 551, mean SAT math: 512, mean SAT writing: 532, mean composite ACT: 25. 33% scored over 600 on SAT critical reading, 33% scored over 600 on SAT math, 37% scored over 600 on SAT writing.

Student Life Upper grades have specified standards of dress, student council, honor system. Discipline rests primarily with faculty. Attendance at religious services is required.

Tuition and Aid Day student tuition: $7500. Tuition installment plan (monthly payment plans, individually arranged payment plans). Tuition reduction for siblings, need-based scholarship grants available. In 2009–10, 15% of upper-school students received aid. Total amount of financial aid awarded in 2009–10: $200,000.

Admissions Traditional secondary-level entrance grade is 9. For fall 2009, 36 students applied for upper-level admission, 34 were accepted, 34 enrolled. School's own exam and Stanford Achievement Test required. Deadline for receipt of application materials: none. Application fee required: $50. Interview required.

Athletics Interscholastic: basketball (boys, girls), cheering (g), cross-country running (b,g), skiing (cross-country) (b,g), soccer (b,g), track and field (b,g), volleyball (g), wrestling (b). 2 PE instructors, 8 coaches.

Computers Computers are regularly used in career exploration, computer applications, media, publications, technology, yearbook classes. Computer network features include on-campus library services, online commercial services, Internet access, Internet filtering or blocking technology. Students grades are available online.

Contact Darlene Kuiper, Admissions. 907-345-4814. Fax: 907-644-2260. E-mail: admissions@gracechristianalaska.org. Web site: www.gracechristianalaska.org.

GRACE CHRISTIAN SCHOOL

50 Kirkdale Road
Charlottetown, Prince Edward Island C1E 1N6, Canada

Head of School: Mr. Jason Biech

General Information Coeducational day college-preparatory, arts, and religious studies school, affiliated with Baptist Church, Evangelical faith. Grades JK–12. Founded: 1980. Setting: small town. 6-acre campus. 1 building on campus. Approved or accredited by Christian Schools International and Prince Edward Island Department of Education. Language of instruction: English. Endowment: CAN$100,000. Total enrollment: 124. Upper school average class size: 10. Upper school faculty-student ratio: 1:10. There are 185 required school days per year for Upper School students. Upper School students typically attend 5 days per week. The average school day consists of 6 hours.

Upper School Student Profile Grade 6: 14 students (4 boys, 10 girls); Grade 7: 13 students (7 boys, 6 girls); Grade 8: 10 students (5 boys, 5 girls); Grade 9: 12 students (8 boys, 4 girls); Grade 10: 8 students (5 boys, 3 girls); Grade 11: 7 students (1 boy, 6 girls); Grade 12: 10 students (5 boys, 5 girls). 70% of students are Baptist, members of Evangelical faith.

Faculty School total: 12. In upper school: 4 men, 3 women.

Graduation Requirements Bible, language, mathematics, Christian service requirements.

College Admission Counseling 10 students graduated in 2010; 9 went to college, including Acadia University. Other: 1 went to work.

Student Life Upper grades have specified standards of dress, student council. Discipline rests primarily with faculty. Attendance at religious services is required.

Tuition and Aid Day student tuition: CAN$3600. Tuition installment plan (monthly payment plans). Tuition reduction for siblings, bursaries available. In 2010–11, 5% of upper-school students received aid. Total amount of financial aid awarded in 2010–11: CAN$4000.

Admissions Traditional secondary-level entrance grade is 10. For fall 2010, 6 students applied for upper-level admission, 6 were accepted, 6 enrolled. Deadline for receipt of application materials: June 25. Application fee required: CAN$200. On-campus interview required.

Athletics Interscholastic: basketball (boys, girls), cross-country running (b,g), soccer (b,g); coed interscholastic: cross-country running, golf, track and field; coed intramural: cross-country running, track and field.

Computers Computer resources include Internet access.

Contact Mr. Jason Biech, Administrator. 902-628-1668 Ext. 223. Fax: 902-628-1668. E-mail: principal@gracechristianschool.ca.

THE GRAUER SCHOOL

1500 South El Camino Real
Encinitas, California 92024

Head of School: Dr. Stuart Robert Grauer, EdD

General Information Coeducational day and distance learning college-preparatory, arts, and technology school. Grades 6–12. Distance learning grades 9–12. Founded: 1991. Setting: suburban. Nearest major city is San Diego. 5-acre campus. 6 buildings on campus. Approved or accredited by California Association of Independent Schools, Western Association of Schools and Colleges, and California Department of Education. Endowment: $150,000. Total enrollment: 150. Upper school average class size: 12. Upper school faculty-student ratio: 1:7. There are 178 required school days per year for Upper School students. Upper School students typically attend 5 days per week. The average school day consists of 6 hours and 30 minutes.

Upper School Student Profile Grade 6: 12 students (6 boys, 6 girls); Grade 7: 25 students (10 boys, 15 girls); Grade 8: 27 students (18 boys, 9 girls); Grade 9: 15 students (8 boys, 7 girls); Grade 10: 23 students (9 boys, 14 girls); Grade 11: 22 students (13 boys, 9 girls); Grade 12: 15 students (5 boys, 10 girls).

Faculty School total: 35. In upper school: 12 men, 13 women; 18 have advanced degrees.

Subjects Offered ACT preparation, advanced biology, advanced chemistry, advanced math, advanced TOEFL/grammar, African dance, algebra, alternative physical education, American government, American history, anatomy and physiology, ancient history, applied music, art, art appreciation, art history, art history-AP, ASB Leadership, athletic training, audio visual/media, backpacking, baseball, basketball, bell choir, biology, business mathematics, calculus, character education, chemistry, Chinese, choir, civics, classical music, college admission preparation, college planning, community service, computer applications, computer education, computer multimedia, computers, creative writing, culinary arts, drama, dramatic arts, earth and space science, economics, English literature, environmental education, ESL, ESL, experiential education, fencing, film studies, filmmaking, fitness, French, gardening, geography, geometry, global studies, health, high adventure outdoor program, honors algebra, honors English, honors geometry, honors U.S. history, honors world history, Japanese, keyboarding, Latin, leadership and service, marine science, multimedia, music, music appreciation, music performance, outdoor education, peace studies, personal fitness, photo shop, photography, physical education, physics, pre-algebra, pre-calculus, religion, religion and culture, robotics, SAT preparation, Spanish, speech and debate, studio art, study skills, surfing, tennis, theater arts, trigonometry, U.S. government, U.S. history, U.S. literature, world geography, world history, world religions.

Graduation Requirements Algebra, American history, art, biology, chemistry, college admission preparation, computer applications, computer skills, economics, English, experiential education, foreign language, French, geometry, life science, marine science, mathematics, non-Western literature, outdoor education, physical education (includes health), physical science, physics, science, senior project, social studies (includes history), studio art, U.S. government, U.S. history, U.S. literature, Western civilization, Western literature, wilderness education, world geography, world history, world literature, world religions, Expeditionary learning in the field and 50 hours community service.

Special Academic Programs Advanced Placement exam preparation; honors section; accelerated programs; independent study; study abroad; academic accommodation for the gifted, the musically talented, and the artistically talented; remedial math; special instructional classes for deaf students; ESL (7 students enrolled).

College Admission Counseling 18 students graduated in 2010; all went to college, including California State University, San Marcos; Florida Institute of Technology; Lehigh University; Occidental College; University of California, San Diego; University of Colorado at Boulder. Median SAT critical reading: 650, median SAT math: 600, median SAT writing: 600. 60% scored over 600 on SAT critical reading, 60% scored over 600 on SAT math, 60% scored over 600 on SAT writing.

Student Life Upper grades have specified standards of dress, student council, honor system. Discipline rests equally with students and faculty.

Summer Programs Remediation, enrichment, advancement, ESL, sports, art/fine arts, rigorous outdoor training, computer instruction programs offered; session focuses on academics and enrichment; held on campus; accepts boys and girls; open to students from other schools. 60 students usually enrolled. 2011 schedule: June 21 to July 30. Application deadline: June 1.

Tuition and Aid Day student tuition: $18,000. Tuition installment plan (individually arranged payment plans, 3 payment plans). Tuition reduction for siblings, merit scholarship grants, need-based scholarship grants available. In 2010–11, 10% of upper-school students received aid. Total amount of financial aid awarded in 2010–11: $90,000.

Admissions Traditional secondary-level entrance grade is 9. For fall 2010, 30 students applied for upper-level admission, 19 were accepted, 15 enrolled. Admissions testing, any standardized test and writing sample required. Deadline for receipt of application materials: February 7. Application fee required: $100. On-campus interview required.

Athletics Interscholastic: equestrian sports (girls), football (g), tennis (b,g), volleyball (g); intramural: baseball (b), basketball (b,g), equestrian sports (g), ice hockey (g),

martial arts (g), soccer (b,g), tennis (b,g), triathlon (b,g), volleyball (b,g); coed interscholastic: cross-country running, sailing, soccer, tennis, track and field; coed intramural: aerobics/dance, alpine skiing, backpacking, bicycling, bowling, canoeing/kayaking, climbing, cross-country running, dance, dressage, fitness, fitness walking, flag football, football, golf, hiking/backpacking, independent competitive sports, jogging, kayaking, marksmanship, mountain biking, outdoor education, physical fitness, physical training, rock climbing, running, sailing, self defense, skiing (downhill), snowboarding, soccer, strength & conditioning, surfing, tennis, track and field, triathlon, volleyball, weight training, yoga. 4 PE instructors, 2 coaches, 1 athletic trainer.
Computers Computers are regularly used in English, ESL, foreign language, graphic arts, journalism, keyboarding, multimedia, photography, programming, SAT preparation, video film production, yearbook classes. Computer network features include Internet access, wireless campus network, Internet filtering or blocking technology. Campus intranet and computer access in designated common areas are available to students. Students grades are available online. The school has a published electronic and media policy.
Contact Mrs. Elizabeth Braymen, JD, Admissions Coordinator. 760-274-2116. Fax: 760-944-6784. E-mail: admissions@grauerschool.com. Web site: www.grauerschool.com.

GREATER ATLANTA CHRISTIAN SCHOOLS
1575 Indian Trail Road
Norcross, Georgia 30093
Head of School: Dr. David Fincher
General Information Coeducational day college-preparatory, arts, religious studies, and technology school, affiliated with Christian faith, Christian faith. Grades P4–12. Founded: 1961. Setting: suburban. Nearest major city is Atlanta. 74-acre campus. 18 buildings on campus. Approved or accredited by Canadian Educational Standards Institute, Georgia Independent School Association, National Christian School Association, Southern Association of Colleges and Schools, Southern Association of Independent Schools, The College Board, and Georgia Department of Education. Endowment: $28.5 million. Total enrollment: 1,850. Upper school average class size: 13. Upper school faculty-student ratio: 1:13. There are 180 required school days per year for Upper School students. Upper School students typically attend 5 days per week. The average school day consists of 7 hours and 10 minutes.
Upper School Student Profile Grade 9: 186 students (96 boys, 90 girls); Grade 10: 201 students (99 boys, 102 girls); Grade 11: 177 students (97 boys, 80 girls); Grade 12: 155 students (78 boys, 77 girls).
Faculty School total: 150. In upper school: 35 men, 30 women; 39 have advanced degrees.
Subjects Offered 3-dimensional art, accounting, Advanced Placement courses, algebra, American history-AP, American literature, analysis, anatomy, art appreciation, art history, art-AP, audio visual/media, band, Bible, biology-AP, British literature, business, calculus-AP, chemistry-AP, chorus, composition, computer applications, computer math, computer programming, computer science-AP, dramatic arts, economics-AP, English language and composition-AP, environmental science, ethics, European history, European history-AP, expository writing, French, geometry, government-AP, graphic design, home economics, honors English, journalism, language arts, Latin, Latin-AP, music theory-AP, music-AP, newspaper, orchestra, painting, personal finance, philosophy, photography, physics-AP, physiology, pre-calculus, psychology-AP, religion, sculpture, sociology, Spanish, speech, speech communications, statistics, statistics-AP, studio art-AP, symphonic band, theology, trigonometry, U.S. history-AP, video film production, visual arts, Web site design, world history-AP, world literature, yearbook.
Graduation Requirements English, foreign language, mathematics, physical education (includes health), religious studies, science, social sciences, social studies (includes history), one year of Bible for each year of attendance.
Special Academic Programs 19 Advanced Placement exams for which test preparation is offered; honors section; study abroad; academic accommodation for the gifted, the musically talented, and the artistically talented.
College Admission Counseling 151 students graduated in 2010; all went to college, including Auburn University; Georgia Institute of Technology; Georgia Southern University; Lipscomb University; The University of Alabama; University of Georgia. Median SAT critical reading: 566, median SAT math: 581, median SAT writing: 568, median combined SAT: 1715, median composite ACT: 26.
Student Life Upper grades have uniform requirement, student council, honor system. Discipline rests primarily with faculty. Attendance at religious services is required.
Summer Programs Enrichment, sports, art/fine arts programs offered; session focuses on Recreation; held on campus; accepts boys and girls; open to students from other schools. 150 students usually enrolled. 2011 schedule: June 1 to August 1.
Tuition and Aid Day student tuition: $14,400. Tuition installment plan (monthly payment plans, quarterly payment plan). Need-based scholarship grants available.
Admissions Traditional secondary-level entrance grade is 9. For fall 2010, 123 students applied for upper-level admission, 85 were accepted, 69 enrolled. California Achievement Test or Stanford 9 required. Deadline for receipt of application materials: none. Application fee required: $160. On-campus interview required.
Athletics Interscholastic: baseball (boys), dance team (g), flag football (b), football (b), golf (b,g), lacrosse (b,g), soccer (b,g), softball (g), tennis (b,g), volleyball (g), wrestling (b); intramural: aerobics (g), ballet (g), cheering (g), physical fitness (b,g),

strength & conditioning (b,g), weight lifting (b), weight training (b,g); coed interscholastic: aquatics, basketball, cross-country running, diving, swimming and diving, track and field, water polo. 5 PE instructors, 1 athletic trainer.
Computers Computers are regularly used in college planning classes. Computer network features include on-campus library services, online commercial services, Internet access, wireless campus network, Internet filtering or blocking technology. Campus intranet is available to students. Students grades are available online. The school has a published electronic and media policy.
Contact Mrs. Linda Clovis, Director of Admissions. 770-243-2274. Fax: 770-243-2213. E-mail: lclovis@greateratlantachristian.org. Web site: www.greateratlantachristian.org.

GREAT LAKES CHRISTIAN HIGH SCHOOL
4875 King Street
Beamsville, Ontario L0R 1B6, Canada
Head of School: Mr. Don Rose
General Information Coeducational boarding and day college-preparatory, general academic, and religious studies school, affiliated with Church of Christ. Grades 9–12. Founded: 1952. Setting: small town. Nearest major city is Hamilton, Canada. Students are housed in single-sex dormitories. 15-acre campus. 6 buildings on campus. Approved or accredited by Ontario Ministry of Education and Ontario Department of Education. Language of instruction: English. Endowment: CAN$500,000. Total enrollment: 109. Upper school average class size: 22. Upper school faculty-student ratio: 1:10. There are 180 required school days per year for Upper School students. Upper School students typically attend 5 days per week. The average school day consists of 6 hours and 10 minutes.
Upper School Student Profile Grade 9: 30 students (18 boys, 12 girls); Grade 10: 28 students (11 boys, 17 girls); Grade 11: 25 students (15 boys, 10 girls); Grade 12: 26 students (12 boys, 14 girls). 55% of students are boarding students. 65% are province residents. 5 provinces are represented in upper school student body. 25% are international students. International students from China, Hong Kong, Japan, Republic of Korea, Taiwan, and United States; 3 other countries represented in student body. 40% of students are members of Church of Christ.
Faculty School total: 11. In upper school: 7 men, 4 women; 4 have advanced degrees; 3 reside on campus.
Subjects Offered 20th century world history, accounting, algebra, arts appreciation, Bible, biology, calculus, career and personal planning, chemistry, computer science, computer technologies, dramatic arts, economics, English, English composition, English language and composition-AP, English literature, English-AP, ESL, family studies, finite math, French, geography, history, mathematics, mathematics-AP, media, music, music composition, physical education, physics, society, technology, world issues.
Graduation Requirements 20th century history, advanced math, art, Bible, business, Canadian geography, Canadian history, Canadian literature, career planning, civics, computer information systems, conceptual physics, critical thinking, current events, economics, English, English composition, English literature, French as a second language, geography, mathematics, physical education (includes health), science, society challenge and change, world geography, world history.
Special Academic Programs Independent study; ESL (13 students enrolled).
College Admission Counseling 23 students graduated in 2009; 17 went to college, including Brock University; Carleton University; McMaster University; University of Toronto; Wilfrid Laurier University; York University. Other: 6 went to work.
Student Life Upper grades have uniform requirement, student council. Discipline rests primarily with faculty. Attendance at religious services is required.
Tuition and Aid Day student tuition: CAN$7300; 5-day tuition and room/board: CAN$12,200; 7-day tuition and room/board: CAN$13,850. Tuition installment plan (monthly payment plans, individually arranged payment plans). Tuition reduction for siblings, bursaries, merit scholarship grants, need-based scholarship grants, need-based loans, middle-income loans, paying campus jobs available. In 2009–10, 40% of upper-school students received aid; total upper-school merit-scholarship money awarded: CAN$12,000. Total amount of financial aid awarded in 2009–10: CAN$100,000.
Admissions Traditional secondary-level entrance grade is 9. For fall 2009, 140 students applied for upper-level admission, 130 were accepted, 110 enrolled. SLEP required. Deadline for receipt of application materials: none. Application fee required: CAN$100. Interview recommended.
Athletics Interscholastic: badminton (boys, girls), basketball (b,g), cross-country running (b,g), golf (b), hockey (b,g), ice hockey (b,g), soccer (b,g), tennis (b,g), track and field (b,g), volleyball (b,g); intramural: aerobics (g), badminton (b,g), basketball (b,g), cooperative games (b,g), fitness (b,g), ice hockey (b,g), volleyball (b,g); coed interscholastic: badminton, indoor hockey, indoor soccer, netball; coed intramural: badminton, ball hockey, baseball, basketball, cooperative games, floor hockey, hockey, volleyball. 2 PE instructors, 2 coaches.
Computers Computers are regularly used in accounting, business, music, technology, typing classes. Computer network features include Internet access, Internet filtering or blocking technology. Computer access in designated common areas is available to students.
Contact Mr. Tim E. Alexander, Director of Admissions. 905-563-5374 Ext. 212. Fax: 905-563-0818. E-mail: study@glchs.on.ca. Web site: www.glchs.on.ca.

GREENFIELD SCHOOL

PO Box 3525
Wilson, North Carolina 27895-3525
Head of School: Janet B. Beaman

General Information Coeducational day and distance learning college-preparatory school. Grades PS–12. Distance learning grades 11–12. Founded: 1969. Setting: small town. Nearest major city is Raleigh. 61-acre campus. 9 buildings on campus. Approved or accredited by North Carolina Association of Independent Schools, Southern Association of Colleges and Schools, and North Carolina Department of Education. Member of National Association of Independent Schools. Total enrollment: 298. Upper school average class size: 19. Upper school faculty-student ratio: 1:3. There are 180 required school days per year for Upper School students. Upper School students typically attend 5 days per week. The average school day consists of 6 hours and 45 minutes.

Upper School Student Profile Grade 9: 22 students (7 boys, 15 girls); Grade 10: 19 students (10 boys, 9 girls); Grade 11: 14 students (11 boys, 3 girls); Grade 12: 19 students (9 boys, 10 girls).

Faculty School total: 57. In upper school: 9 men, 13 women; 16 have advanced degrees.

Subjects Offered Advanced computer applications, advanced math, Advanced Placement courses, algebra, American history, American literature, ancient world history, art, athletics, biology, British literature, calculus, calculus-AP, chemistry, chorus, college awareness, community service, computer applications, computer education, computer graphics, computer information systems, computer math, computer multimedia, computer processing, computer programming, computer programming-AP, computer science, computer skills, computer technologies, desktop publishing, drama, earth science, economics, electives, English, English literature, fine arts, foreign language, geography, geometry, government/civics, grammar, health, history, honors algebra, honors English, honors geometry, honors world history, keyboarding, language arts, mathematics, music, physical education, physical science, physics, pre-algebra, pre-calculus, SAT preparation, science, social studies, Spanish, sports conditioning, trigonometry, Web site design, world geography, world history, writing, yearbook.

Graduation Requirements Arts and fine arts (art, music, dance, drama), computer science, English, foreign language, mathematics, physical education (includes health), science, social studies (includes history). Community service is required.

Special Academic Programs 5 Advanced Placement exams for which test preparation is offered; honors section; independent study; study at local college for college credit; academic accommodation for the gifted; remedial reading and/or remedial writing; remedial math; programs in English, general development for dyslexic students.

College Admission Counseling 24 students graduated in 2010; all went to college, including Appalachian State University; East Carolina University; Hampden-Sydney College; North Carolina State University; The University of North Carolina at Chapel Hill; The University of North Carolina Wilmington. Median SAT critical reading: 530, median SAT math: 550, median SAT writing: 550, median combined SAT: 1670, median composite ACT: 23. 25% scored over 600 on SAT critical reading, 33% scored over 600 on SAT math, 21% scored over 600 on SAT writing, 21% scored over 1800 on combined SAT, 27% scored over 26 on composite ACT.

Student Life Upper grades have specified standards of dress, student council, honor system. Discipline rests primarily with faculty.

Summer Programs Enrichment, sports, art/fine arts, computer instruction programs offered; session focuses on academic enrichment, athletic development, and relaxation; held on campus; accepts boys and girls; open to students from other schools. 200 students usually enrolled. 2011 schedule: June 1 to August 6. Application deadline: none.

Tuition and Aid Day student tuition: $8235. Tuition installment plan (monthly payment plans). Tuition reduction for siblings, merit scholarship grants, need-based scholarship grants available.

Admissions Traditional secondary-level entrance grade is 9. For fall 2010, 12 students applied for upper-level admission, 8 were accepted, 7 enrolled. Comprehensive Test of Basic Skills or CTP III required. Deadline for receipt of application materials: none. Application fee required: $100. On-campus interview required.

Athletics Interscholastic: baseball (boys), basketball (b,g), cheering (g), soccer (b,g), tennis (b,g), volleyball (g); coed interscholastic: golf. 3 PE instructors, 13 coaches.

Computers Computers are regularly used in all academic classes. Computer resources include on-campus library services, Internet access, wireless campus network, Internet filtering or blocking technology. Computer access in designated common areas is available to students. The school has a published electronic and media policy.

Contact Diane Oliphant Hamilton, Director of Admissions/Community Relations. 252-237-8046. Fax: 252-237-1825. E-mail: hamiltond@greenfieldschool.org. Web site: www.greenfieldschool.org.

GREEN FIELDS COUNTRY DAY SCHOOL

6000 North Camino de la Tierra
Tucson, Arizona 85741
Head of School: Dr. Matthew Teller

General Information Coeducational day college-preparatory and arts school. Grades K–12. Founded: 1933. Setting: suburban. 22-acre campus. 15 buildings on campus. Approved or accredited by Arizona Association of Independent Schools and North Central Association of Colleges and Schools. Member of National Association of Independent Schools. Total enrollment: 171. Upper school average class size: 12. Upper school faculty-student ratio: 1:4. The average school day consists of 7 hours.

Upper School Student Profile Grade 9: 23 students (13 boys, 10 girls); Grade 10: 5 students (2 boys, 3 girls); Grade 11: 11 students (5 boys, 6 girls); Grade 12: 19 students (9 boys, 10 girls).

Faculty School total: 29. In upper school: 9 men, 9 women; 12 have advanced degrees.

Subjects Offered 3-dimensional art, advanced chemistry, advanced computer applications, advanced math, Advanced Placement courses, advanced studio art-AP, algebra, American government, American history, American history-AP, American literature, anatomy and physiology, art, art-AP, Basic programming, biology, biology-AP, British literature (honors), British literature-AP, calculus, calculus-AP, ceramics, chemistry, chorus, college placement, computer programming, computer science, conceptual physics, drama, drama performance, English, environmental science-AP, European history, European history-AP, expository writing, fine arts, French, French language-AP, French literature-AP, French-AP, geography, geometry, government and politics-AP, government-AP, independent study, journalism, music theory, musical theater, newspaper, physical education, physics, political science, pre-calculus, probability and statistics, social studies, Spanish, Spanish-AP, studio art-AP, trigonometry, U.S. government and politics-AP, U.S. history-AP, Web site design, world history, writing, yearbook.

Graduation Requirements Advanced math, algebra, American history, American literature, arts and fine arts (art, music, dance, drama), biology, chemistry, computer skills, electives, English, English literature, foreign language, geometry, mathematics, physical education (includes health), science, social studies (includes history), world history, writing.

Special Academic Programs Advanced Placement exam preparation; independent study.

College Admission Counseling 12 students graduated in 2009; 11 went to college, including California Institute of Technology; Connecticut College; Northern Arizona University; The University of Arizona.

Student Life Upper grades have specified standards of dress, student council, honor system. Discipline rests primarily with faculty.

Tuition and Aid Day student tuition: $14,200. Guaranteed tuition plan. Tuition installment plan (FACTS Tuition Payment Plan, semester payment plan). Merit scholarship grants, need-based scholarship grants available. In 2009–10, 25% of upper-school students received aid; total upper-school merit-scholarship money awarded: $20,317. Total amount of financial aid awarded in 2009–10: $187,987.

Admissions Traditional secondary-level entrance grade is 9. Achievement tests or Achievement/Aptitude/Writing required. Deadline for receipt of application materials: none. Application fee required: $35. On-campus interview recommended.

Athletics Interscholastic: baseball (boys), basketball (b,g), softball (g), volleyball (g); coed interscholastic: physical fitness, physical training, soccer, track and field; coed intramural: climbing, outdoor adventure, outdoor skills, rock climbing, tennis, wall climbing. 2 PE instructors, 8 coaches.

Computers Computers are regularly used in English, mathematics, newspaper, science, yearbook classes. Computer resources include on-campus library services, online commercial services, Internet access, wireless campus network, Internet filtering or blocking technology. Computer access in designated common areas is available to students. The school has a published electronic and media policy.

Contact Carole Knapp, Director of Admission. 520-297-2288 Ext. 105. Fax: 520-297-2072. E-mail: admissions@greenfields.org. Web site: www.greenfields.org.

GREENHILL SCHOOL

4141 Spring Valley Road
Addison, Texas 75001
Head of School: Scott A. Griggs

General Information Coeducational day college-preparatory school. Grades PK–12. Founded: 1950. Setting: suburban. Nearest major city is Dallas. 78-acre campus. 8 buildings on campus. Approved or accredited by Independent Schools Association of the Southwest and Texas Department of Education. Member of National Association of Independent Schools and Secondary School Admission Test Board. Endowment: $22.8 million. Total enrollment: 1,273. Upper school average class size: 18. Upper school faculty-student ratio: 1:18.

Upper School Student Profile Grade 9: 113 students (55 boys, 58 girls); Grade 10: 118 students (59 boys, 59 girls); Grade 11: 118 students (59 boys, 59 girls); Grade 12: 104 students (47 boys, 57 girls).

Faculty School total: 140. In upper school: 37 men, 19 women; 41 have advanced degrees.

Subjects Offered Algebra, American history, American literature, art, art history, biology, calculus, ceramics, chemistry, Chinese, computer math, computer programming, computer science, creative writing, dance, drama, ecology, economics, English, English literature, European history, expository writing, fine arts, French, geometry, government/civics, grammar, health, history, journalism, Latin, Mandarin, mathematics, music, philosophy, photography, physical education, physics, science, social studies, Spanish, speech, theater, trigonometry, world history, world literature, writing.

Graduation Requirements Arts and fine arts (art, music, dance, drama), classical language, computer studies, English, history, mathematics, modern languages, physical education (includes health), science. Community service is required.

Special Academic Programs Advanced Placement exam preparation; honors section; independent study.

College Admission Counseling 102 students graduated in 2010; 100 went to college, including Indiana University Bloomington; Rice University; University of Pennsylvania; University of Southern California; Washington University in St. Louis. Other: 1 went to work, 1 entered military service. Mean SAT critical reading: 658, mean SAT math: 673, mean SAT writing: 643.

Student Life Upper grades have specified standards of dress, student council, honor system. Discipline rests primarily with faculty.

Summer Programs Enrichment, sports, art/fine arts, computer instruction programs offered; session focuses on enrichment and sports; held on campus; accepts boys and girls; open to students from other schools. 1,300 students usually enrolled. 2011 schedule: June 6 to August 12. Application deadline: none.

Tuition and Aid Day student tuition: $22,450. Need-based scholarship grants available. In 2010–11, 18% of upper-school students received aid. Total amount of financial aid awarded in 2010–11: $1,282,620.

Admissions Traditional secondary-level entrance grade is 9. For fall 2010, 173 students applied for upper-level admission, 67 were accepted, 41 enrolled. ISEE required. Deadline for receipt of application materials: January 14. Application fee required: $175. Interview required.

Athletics Interscholastic: aquatics (boys, girls), baseball (b), basketball (b,g), cheering (g), field hockey (g), football (b), golf (b,g), lacrosse (b,g), rowing (b,g), running (b,g), soccer (b,g), softball (g), swimming and diving (b,g), tennis (b,g), track and field (b,g), ultimate Frisbee (b,g), volleyball (b,g), weight training (b,g), winter soccer (b,g); intramural: baseball (b), power lifting (b); coed interscholastic: cross-country running; coed intramural: aquatics, ballet, basketball, dance, fitness, Frisbee, physical fitness, strength & conditioning, table tennis, tai chi, ultimate Frisbee, water volleyball, weight lifting, weight training, yoga. 11 PE instructors, 20 coaches, 2 athletic trainers.

Computers Computers are regularly used in English, mathematics, science classes. Computer network features include on-campus library services, online commercial services, Internet access, wireless campus network, Internet filtering or blocking technology. Campus intranet, student e-mail accounts, and computer access in designated common areas are available to students. Students grades are available online. The school has a published electronic and media policy.

Contact Angela H. Woodson, Director of Admission. 972-628-5910. Fax: 972-404-8217. E-mail: admission@greenhill.org. Web site: www.greenhill.org.

GREENHILLS SCHOOL
850 Greenhills Drive
Ann Arbor, Michigan 48105
Head of School: Peter B. Fayroian
General Information Coeducational day college-preparatory and arts school. Grades 6–12. Founded: 1968. Setting: suburban. Nearest major city is Detroit. 30-acre campus. 1 building on campus. Approved or accredited by Independent Schools Association of the Central States and Michigan Department of Education. Member of National Association of Independent Schools and Secondary School Admission Test Board. Endowment: $6 million. Total enrollment: 538. Upper school average class size: 15. Upper school faculty-student ratio: 1:7. There are 165 required school days per year for Upper School students. Upper School students typically attend 5 days per week. The average school day consists of 7 hours.

Upper School Student Profile Grade 9: 70 students (28 boys, 42 girls); Grade 10: 79 students (44 boys, 35 girls); Grade 11: 89 students (30 boys, 59 girls); Grade 12: 79 students (29 boys, 50 girls).

Faculty School total: 70. In upper school: 24 men, 24 women; 42 have advanced degrees.

Subjects Offered 3-dimensional art, advanced chemistry, Advanced Placement courses, African-American literature, algebra, American history, American literature, ancient history, art, astronomy, biology, calculus, calculus-AP, ceramics, chemistry, Chinese, Chinese studies, chorus, community service, creative writing, discrete mathematics, drama, drawing, economics, economics and history, English, English literature, ethics, European history, expository writing, fine arts, French, geometry, government, health, history, jazz, journalism, Latin, mathematics, music, orchestra, painting, photography, physical education, physical science, physics, science, social studies, Spanish, theater, trigonometry, world history, world literature, writing.

Graduation Requirements Arts and fine arts (art, music, dance, drama), English, foreign language, mathematics, physical education (includes health), science, social studies (includes history), senior project. Community service is required.

Special Academic Programs Advanced Placement exam preparation; honors section; independent study; study at local college for college credit; academic

accommodation for the gifted; programs in English, mathematics for dyslexic students; special instructional classes for blind students.

College Admission Counseling 80 students graduated in 2010; all went to college, including Pomona College; Princeton University; University of Michigan; Wesleyan University; Yale University. Median SAT critical reading: 659, median SAT math: 672, median SAT writing: 651, median combined SAT: 1982, median composite ACT: 29.

Student Life Upper grades have specified standards of dress, student council, honor system. Discipline rests equally with students and faculty.

Summer Programs Enrichment, sports, art/fine arts, rigorous outdoor training programs offered; session focuses on enrichment, academics, travel; held on campus; accepts boys and girls; open to students from other schools. 30 students usually enrolled. 2011 schedule: July 1 to July 30. Application deadline: none.

Tuition and Aid Day student tuition: $18,225. Tuition installment plan (FACTS Tuition Payment Plan, monthly payment plans). Need-based scholarship grants available. In 2010–11, 21% of upper-school students received aid. Total amount of financial aid awarded in 2010–11: $1,000,000.

Admissions Traditional secondary-level entrance grade is 9. For fall 2010, 86 students applied for upper-level admission, 55 were accepted, 31 enrolled. SSAT or TOEFL required. Deadline for receipt of application materials: none. Application fee required: $50. Interview required.

Athletics Interscholastic: baseball (boys), basketball (b,g), cross-country running (b,g), field hockey (g), golf (b,g), soccer (b,g), softball (g), tennis (b,g), track and field (b,g), volleyball (g); intramural: basketball (b,g), cross-country running (b,g), field hockey (g), soccer (b,g); coed interscholastic: equestrian sports, swimming and diving; coed intramural: hiking/backpacking, outdoor activities, outdoor education. 3 PE instructors, 1 athletic trainer.

Computers Computers are regularly used in all academic classes. Computer network features include on-campus library services, online commercial services, Internet access, wireless campus network, Internet filtering or blocking technology. Campus intranet, student e-mail accounts, and computer access in designated common areas are available to students. Students grades are available online. The school has a published electronic and media policy.

Contact Betsy Ellsworth, Director of Admission and Financial Aid. 734-205-4061. Fax: 734-205-4056. E-mail: admission@greenhillsschool.org. Web site: www. greenhillsschool.org.

GREEN MEADOW WALDORF SCHOOL
307 Hungry Hollow Road
Chestnut Ridge, New York 10977
Head of School: Kay Hoffman
General Information Coeducational day college-preparatory, general academic, and arts school. Grades N–12. Founded: 1950. Setting: suburban. Nearest major city is New York. 11-acre campus. 3 buildings on campus. Approved or accredited by Association of Waldorf Schools of North America, New York State Association of Independent Schools, and New York Department of Education. Total enrollment: 375. Upper school average class size: 25. Upper school faculty-student ratio: 1:9. There are 171 required school days per year for Upper School students. Upper School students typically attend 5 days per week. The average school day consists of 7 hours.

Upper School Student Profile Grade 9: 24 students (10 boys, 14 girls); Grade 10: 29 students (10 boys, 19 girls); Grade 11: 15 students (9 boys, 6 girls); Grade 12: 16 students (5 boys, 11 girls).

Faculty School total: 60. In upper school: 10 men, 9 women; 11 have advanced degrees.

Subjects Offered Algebra, American history, American literature, anatomy, architecture, art, art history, arts, batik, Bible studies, biology, botany, calculus, chemistry, computer math, computer science, creative writing, dance, drama, driver education, earth science, English, English literature, ethics, European history, expository writing, fine arts, French, geography, geology, geometry, German, government/civics, grammar, health, history, history of ideas, history of science, logic, marine biology, mathematics, music, orchestra, philosophy, physical education, physics, physiology, poetry, Russian literature, science, sculpture, social studies, Spanish, speech, theater, trigonometry, woodworking, world history, world literature, writing, zoology.

Graduation Requirements Arts and fine arts (art, music, dance, drama), English, foreign language, mathematics, physical education (includes health), science, social studies (includes history).

Special Academic Programs Honors section; independent study; term-away projects; study abroad; remedial reading and/or remedial writing; remedial math; programs in English for dyslexic students; ESL (7 students enrolled).

College Admission Counseling 29 students graduated in 2009; 27 went to college, including Bryn Mawr College; Loyola Marymount University; New York University; Parsons The New School for Design; The College of New Jersey; Trinity College. Other: 2 had other specific plans. 31% scored over 600 on SAT critical reading, 27% scored over 600 on SAT math.

Student Life Upper grades have specified standards of dress, student council. Discipline rests primarily with faculty.

Tuition and Aid Day student tuition: $17,400–$18,250. Guaranteed tuition plan. Tuition installment plan (Insured Tuition Payment Plan, monthly payment plans). Need-based scholarship grants available.

Green Meadow Waldorf School

Admissions Traditional secondary-level entrance grade is 9. Deadline for receipt of application materials: none. Application fee required: $50. On-campus interview required.

Athletics Interscholastic: baseball (boys), basketball (b,g), softball (g), tennis (g), volleyball (g); intramural: basketball (b,g); coed interscholastic: Circus, cross-country running, horseback riding, tennis, volleyball; coed intramural: volleyball. 2 PE instructors, 5 coaches.

Computers Computers are regularly used in mathematics classes. Computer resources include Internet access, Internet filtering or blocking technology. Computer access in designated common areas is available to students. The school has a published electronic and media policy.

Contact Patricia Owens, Admissions Coordinator. 845-356-2514 Ext. 302. Fax: 845-371-2358. E-mail: powens@gmws.org. Web site: www.gmws.org.

GREENSBORO DAY SCHOOL

5401 Lawndale Drive
Greensboro, North Carolina 27455
Head of School: Mr. Mark C. Hale

General Information Coeducational day college-preparatory, arts, and technology school. Grades K–12. Founded: 1970. Setting: suburban. 65-acre campus. 10 buildings on campus. Approved or accredited by North Carolina Association of Independent Schools and Southern Association of Colleges and Schools. Member of National Association of Independent Schools. Total enrollment: 904. Upper school average class size: 16. Upper school faculty-student ratio: 1:13. There are 182 required school days per year for Upper School students. Upper School students typically attend 5 days per week. The average school day consists of 6 hours and 15 minutes.

Upper School Student Profile Grade 9: 86 students (39 boys, 47 girls); Grade 10: 90 students (42 boys, 48 girls); Grade 11: 95 students (51 boys, 44 girls); Grade 12: 86 students (45 boys, 41 girls).

Faculty School total: 120. In upper school: 24 men, 26 women.

Subjects Offered Algebra, American government, American history, American literature, art, art appreciation, biology, biology-AP, calculus, calculus-AP, chemistry, chorus, college admission preparation, college counseling, college placement, computer programming, computer science-AP, creative writing, drama, economics, English, English language-AP, English literature, ESL, European history, European history-AP, fine arts, French, French language-AP, French literature-AP, geometry, government/civics, health, history, journalism, Latin, Latin-AP, mathematics, music, photography, physical education, physics, physics-AP, psychology, SAT preparation, science, social studies, Spanish, Spanish language-AP, Spanish literature-AP, sports medicine, statistics-AP, theater, trigonometry, U.S. history-AP, world history, writing, yearbook.

Graduation Requirements Arts and fine arts (art, music, dance, drama), English, foreign language, mathematics, physical education (includes health), science, social studies (includes history), senior project (four-week internship).

Special Academic Programs 11 Advanced Placement exams for which test preparation is offered; honors section; independent study; term-away projects; study abroad; academic accommodation for the gifted and the artistically talented; special instructional classes for students with learning disabilities and Attention Deficit Disorder; ESL (8 students enrolled).

College Admission Counseling 82 students graduated in 2010; all went to college, including Duke University; The University of North Carolina at Chapel Hill; The University of North Carolina at Charlotte; The University of North Carolina Wilmington; Wake Forest University. Median SAT critical reading: 600, median SAT math: 610, median SAT writing: 600.

Student Life Upper grades have specified standards of dress, student council, honor system. Discipline rests equally with students and faculty.

Summer Programs Remediation, enrichment, advancement, sports, art/fine arts, computer instruction programs offered; session focuses on enrichment and camps; held on campus; accepts boys and girls; open to students from other schools. 600 students usually enrolled.

Tuition and Aid Day student tuition: $8000–$18,650. Tuition installment plan (FACTS Tuition Payment Plan, monthly payment plans, individually arranged payment plans). Need-based scholarship grants available.

Admissions Traditional secondary-level entrance grade is 9. ERB (CTP-Verbal, Quantitative) required. Deadline for receipt of application materials: none. Application fee required: $50. On-campus interview required.

Athletics Interscholastic: baseball (boys), basketball (b,g), cheering (g), cross-country running (b,g), field hockey (g), lacrosse (b,g), soccer (b,g), swimming and diving (b,g), tennis (b,g), track and field (b,g), volleyball (g), wrestling (b); intramural: weight lifting (b,g); coed interscholastic: aquatics, golf; coed intramural: backpacking, badminton, basketball, ropes courses. 11 PE instructors, 20 coaches, 2 athletic trainers.

Computers Computers are regularly used in yearbook classes. Computer network features include on-campus library services, online commercial services, Internet access, wireless campus network, Internet filtering or blocking technology. Student e-mail accounts are available to students. Students grades are available online. The school has a published electronic and media policy.

Contact Robin Schenck, Director of Admission and Financial Aid. 336-288-8590 Ext. 106. Fax: 336-282-2905. E-mail: robinschenck@greensboroday.org. Web site: www.greensboroday.org.

GREENS FARMS ACADEMY

35 Beachside Avenue
PO Box 998
Greens Farms, Connecticut 06838-0998
Head of School: Janet M. Hartwell

General Information Coeducational day college-preparatory, arts, and technology school. Grades K–12. Founded: 1925. Setting: suburban. Nearest major city is New York, NY. 42-acre campus. 2 buildings on campus. Approved or accredited by Connecticut Association of Independent Schools, New England Association of Schools and Colleges, and Connecticut Department of Education. Member of National Association of Independent Schools and Secondary School Admission Test Board. Endowment: $27 million. Total enrollment: 652. Upper school average class size: 12. Upper school faculty-student ratio: 1:6. There are 170 required school days per year for Upper School students. Upper School students typically attend 5 days per week. The average school day consists of 7 hours.

Upper School Student Profile Grade 9: 75 students (35 boys, 40 girls); Grade 10: 68 students (36 boys, 32 girls); Grade 11: 71 students (35 boys, 36 girls); Grade 12: 70 students (38 boys, 32 girls).

Faculty School total: 99. In upper school: 23 men, 24 women; 25 have advanced degrees.

Subjects Offered Advanced studio art-AP, algebra, American history, American history-AP, American literature, American literature-AP, animation, architecture, art, art history, art-AP, biology, biology-AP, calculus, calculus-AP, chemistry, chemistry-AP, China/Japan history, Chinese, choral music, computer art, computer graphics, computer information systems, computer math, computer programming, computer science, concert choir, creative writing, digital art, digital music, digital photography, drama, earth science, ecology, economics, English, English literature, English literature-AP, environmental science, environmental science-AP, European history, European history-AP, expository writing, fine arts, French, French-AP, geography, geology, geometry, government, government/civics, grammar, health, health and wellness, history, honors algebra, honors English, honors geometry, jazz ensemble, keyboarding, Latin, Latin-AP, life skills, literature-AP, Mandarin, mathematics, music, music theory, music theory-AP, newspaper, orchestra, philosophy, photography, physical education, physics, physics-AP, play production, pre-calculus, public speaking, science, senior project, senior seminar, social studies, Spanish, Spanish-AP, speech, squash, statistics-AP, studio art-AP, tennis, theater, theater design and production, theater history, trigonometry, U.S. government, U.S. government and politics-AP, U.S. history-AP, video film production, vocal ensemble, Web site design, weight training, wind ensemble, world history, world literature, world wide web design, wrestling, writing.

Graduation Requirements Algebra, art, athletics, biology, English, foreign language, geometry, history, mathematics, physical science, science.

Special Academic Programs Advanced Placement exam preparation; honors section; independent study; term-away projects; study abroad.

College Admission Counseling 58 students graduated in 2009; all went to college, including Boston University; Brown University; Columbia College; Cornell University; Georgetown University; University of Pennsylvania. Mean SAT critical reading: 634, mean SAT math: 626, mean SAT writing: 657, mean composite ACT: 27. 68% scored over 600 on SAT critical reading, 66% scored over 600 on SAT math, 79% scored over 600 on SAT writing.

Student Life Upper grades have specified standards of dress, student council, honor system. Discipline rests equally with students and faculty.

Tuition and Aid Day student tuition: $32,450. Tuition installment plan (Key Tuition Payment Plan). Need-based scholarship grants available. In 2009–10, 14% of upper-school students received aid. Total amount of financial aid awarded in 2009–10: $1,233,350.

Admissions Traditional secondary-level entrance grade is 9. For fall 2009, 160 students applied for upper-level admission, 73 were accepted, 39 enrolled. ISEE or SSAT required. Deadline for receipt of application materials: January 15. Application fee required: $75. On-campus interview required.

Athletics Interscholastic: baseball (boys), basketball (b,g), climbing (b,g), crew (b,g), cross-country running (b,g), field hockey (g), fitness (b,g), golf (b,g), independent competitive sports (b,g), indoor hockey (b), lacrosse (b,g), physical fitness (b,g), physical training (b,g), running (b,g), soccer (b,g), softball (g), squash (b,g), tennis (b,g), volleyball (g), wrestling (b); intramural: aerobics/dance (g), dance (g); coed interscholastic: independent competitive sports, rock climbing, rowing, running, sailing, wall climbing; coed intramural: climbing, fencing, figure skating, fitness, Frisbee, ice skating, Nautilus, physical fitness, physical training, rock climbing, strength & conditioning, ultimate Frisbee, weight lifting, weight training, yoga. 6 PE instructors, 12 coaches, 1 athletic trainer.

Computers Computers are regularly used in animation, art, creative writing, English, foreign language, French, graphic arts, graphic design, graphics, history, independent study, Latin, library, literary magazine, mathematics, music, newspaper, photography, science, senior seminar, Spanish, video film production, Web site design, yearbook classes. Computer network features include on-campus library services, online commercial services, Internet access, wireless campus network, Internet filtering or blocking technology. Student e-mail accounts and computer access in designated common areas are available to students. Students grades are available online. The school has a published electronic and media policy.

Contact Peggy Harwood, Admission Assistant. 203-256-7514. Fax: 203-256-7591. E-mail: admissions@gfacademy.org. Web site: www.gfacademy.org.

GREENWICH ACADEMY
200 North Maple Avenue
Greenwich, Connecticut 06830-4799
Head of School; Molly H. King

General Information Girls' day college-preparatory and arts school. Grades PK–12. Founded: 1827. Setting: suburban. Nearest major city is New York, NY. 39-acre campus. 6 buildings on campus. Approved or accredited by Connecticut Association of Independent Schools, New England Association of Schools and Colleges, and Connecticut Department of Education. Member of National Association of Independent Schools and Secondary School Admission Test Board. Endowment: $61.9 million. Total enrollment: 802. Upper school average class size: 13. Upper school faculty-student ratio: 1:6. There are 164 required school days per year for Upper School students. Upper School students typically attend 5 days per week. The average school day consists of 5 hours.

Upper School Student Profile Grade 9: 77 students (77 girls); Grade 10: 92 students (92 girls); Grade 11: 90 students (90 girls); Grade 12: 80 students (80 girls).

Faculty School total: 139. In upper school: 29 men, 109 women; 41 have advanced degrees.

Subjects Offered Advanced Placement courses, advanced studio art-AP, African-American literature, algebra, American history, American history-AP, American literature, ancient history, Arabic, architecture, art, art history, art history-AP, art-AP, astronomy, biochemistry, biology, biology-AP, calculus, calculus-AP, ceramics, chemistry, chemistry-AP, Chinese, classics, computer science, creative writing, dance, dance performance, drama, drama performance, earth science, ecology, economics, economics-AP, English, English literature, environmental science, European history, European history-AP, expository writing, film, film and literature, fine arts, foreign language, French, French language-AP, French literature-AP, French-AP, geology, geometry, government and politics-AP, government/civics, health, history, history-AP, honors algebra, honors geometry, independent study, Italian, Latin, Latin-AP, mathematics, mathematics-AP, medieval history, microeconomics, microeconomics-AP, music, music performance, music theory-AP, oceanography, physical education, physics, pre-calculus, psychology, science, senior project, Spanish, Spanish-AP, speech, statistics, studio art-AP, theater, trigonometry, world history, world literature.

Graduation Requirements Arts and fine arts (art, music, dance, drama), English, foreign language, mathematics, physical education (includes health), science, social studies (includes history). Community service is required.

Special Academic Programs 26 Advanced Placement exams for which test preparation is offered; honors section; independent study; term-away projects; study abroad.

College Admission Counseling 77 students graduated in 2010; all went to college, including Boston College; Bowdoin College; New York University; Princeton University; Stanford University; Yale University. Mean SAT critical reading: 675, mean SAT math: 664, mean SAT writing: 700, mean combined SAT: 1900, mean composite ACT: 29. 84% scored over 600 on SAT critical reading, 82% scored over 600 on SAT math, 94% scored over 600 on SAT writing, 91% scored over 1800 on combined SAT, 91% scored over 26 on composite ACT.

Student Life Upper grades have uniform requirement, student council, honor system. Discipline rests equally with students and faculty.

Summer Programs Enrichment, sports, art/fine arts programs offered; session focuses on enrichment, arts/fine arts, and sports; held on campus; accepts boys and girls; open to students from other schools. 200 students usually enrolled. 2011 schedule: June 14 to August 15.

Tuition and Aid Day student tuition: $33,300. Tuition installment plan (Academic Management Services Plan, monthly payment plans). Need-based scholarship grants, middle-income loans, PLITT Loans, tuition reduction for children of faculty and staff available. In 2010–11, 20% of upper-school students received aid. Total amount of financial aid awarded in 2010–11: $1,351,850.

Admissions Traditional secondary-level entrance grade is 9. For fall 2010, 127 students applied for upper-level admission, 57 were accepted, 36 enrolled. ERB, ISEE or SSAT required. Deadline for receipt of application materials: December 15. Application fee required: $75. On-campus interview required.

Athletics Interscholastic: basketball, crew, cross-country running, dance, dance team, fencing, field hockey, golf, hockey, ice hockey, independent competitive sports, lacrosse, sailing, soccer, softball, squash, swimming and diving, tennis, volleyball; intramural: aerobics, aerobics/Nautilus, basketball, cooperative games, crew, dance, fitness, floor hockey, Frisbee, independent competitive sports, lacrosse, modern dance, Nautilus, physical fitness, physical training, running, self defense, soccer, strength & conditioning, tennis, volleyball, weight lifting, yoga. 7 PE instructors, 54 coaches, 1 athletic trainer.

Computers Computers are regularly used in art, English, foreign language, history, humanities, mathematics, music, science classes. Computer network features include on-campus library services, online commercial services, Internet access, wireless campus network, Internet filtering or blocking technology. Campus intranet and student e-mail accounts are available to students. The school has a published electronic and media policy.

Contact Irene Mann, Admission Associate, Registrar. 203-625-8990. Fax: 203-625-8912. E-mail: imann@greenwichacademy.org. Web site: www.greenwichacademy.org.

GREENWOOD LABORATORY SCHOOL
901 South National Avenue
Springfield, Missouri 65897
Head of School: Dr. Janice Duncan

General Information Coeducational day college-preparatory, arts, and technology school. Grades K–12. Founded: 1908. Setting: urban. 3-acre campus. 1 building on campus. Approved or accredited by North Central Association of Colleges and Schools and Missouri Department of Education. Total enrollment: 339. Upper school average class size: 30. Upper school faculty-student ratio: 1:28.

Upper School Student Profile Grade 6: 24 students (12 boys, 12 girls); Grade 7: 29 students (17 boys, 12 girls); Grade 8: 31 students (20 boys, 11 girls); Grade 9: 30 students (18 boys, 12 girls); Grade 10: 28 students (15 boys, 13 girls); Grade 11: 22 students (17 boys, 5 girls); Grade 12: 24 students (10 boys, 14 girls).

Faculty School total: 32. In upper school: 10 men, 10 women; 19 have advanced degrees.

Subjects Offered English, fine arts, foreign language, health, instrumental music, mathematics, physical education, science, social studies, state government, vocal music.

Graduation Requirements Students have to pass a Graduation Exhibition and achieve Public Affairs Merits.

Special Academic Programs Study at local college for college credit.

College Admission Counseling 18 students graduated in 2009; all went to college, including Missouri State University; University of Missouri. Median composite ACT: 27. 67% scored over 26 on composite ACT.

Student Life Upper grades have student council. Discipline rests primarily with faculty.

Tuition and Aid Day student tuition: $4060. Tuition installment plan (individually arranged payment plans, single payment plan).

Admissions Traditional secondary-level entrance grade is 9. For fall 2009, 11 students applied for upper-level admission, 11 were accepted, 11 enrolled. Deadline for receipt of application materials: none. No application fee required. On-campus interview required.

Athletics Interscholastic: basketball (boys, girls), golf (b,g), soccer (b,g), swimming and diving (b,g), tennis (b,g); coed interscholastic: cross-country running, physical fitness, track and field. 3 PE instructors, 5 coaches.

Computers Computers are regularly used in English, French, history, science, Spanish, yearbook classes. Computer network features include on-campus library services, wireless campus network, Internet filtering or blocking technology. Student e-mail accounts and computer access in designated common areas are available to students. Students grades are available online. The school has a published electronic and media policy.

Contact Ms. Ruth Ann Johnson, Counselor. 417-836-7667. Fax: 417-836-8449. E-mail: RuthAnnJohnson@MissouriState.edu. Web site: www.education.missouristate.edu/greenwood.

THE GREENWOOD SCHOOL
Putney, Vermont
See Junior Boarding Schools section.

THE GRIER SCHOOL
PO Box 308
Tyrone, Pennsylvania 16686-0308
Head of School: Mrs. Gina Borst

General Information Girls' boarding college-preparatory, general academic, and arts school. Grades 6–PG. Founded: 1853. Setting: rural. Nearest major city is Pittsburgh. Students are housed in single-sex dormitories. 320-acre campus. 12 buildings on campus. Approved or accredited by Middle States Association of Colleges and Schools, Pennsylvania Association of Independent Schools, and The Association of Boarding Schools. Member of National Association of Independent Schools and Secondary School Admission Test Board. Endowment: $10 million. Total enrollment: 220. Upper school average class size: 10. Upper school faculty-student ratio: 1:6.

Upper School Student Profile Grade 9: 37 students (37 girls); Grade 10: 50 students (50 girls); Grade 11: 53 students (53 girls); Grade 12: 50 students (50 girls). 100% of students are boarding students. 5% are state residents. 22 states are represented in upper school student body. 40% are international students. International students from China, Germany, Mexico, Republic of Korea, Taiwan, and Viet Nam; 7 other countries represented in student body.

Faculty School total: 40. In upper school: 14 men, 23 women; 11 have advanced degrees; 16 reside on campus.

Subjects Offered Algebra, American history, American literature, anatomy, art, art history, art history-AP, art-AP, biology, biology-AP, calculus, calculus-AP, ceramics, chemistry, choral music, choreography, community service, computer math, computer programming, computer-aided design, creative writing, dance, desktop publishing, drama, earth science, ecology, English, English literature, English-AP, environmental science, equine science, ESL, European history, fabric arts, fine arts, French, French-AP, geography, geometry, government/civics, health, history, journalism, linguistics, mathematics, music, photography, physical education, physics, physiology, piano, psychology, science, social studies, Spanish, theater, trigonometry, typing, video film production, voice, world history, writing, yearbook.

Graduation Requirements Arts and fine arts (art, music, dance, drama), computer science, English, foreign language, mathematics, physical education (includes health), science, social sciences, social studies (includes history).

Special Academic Programs 16 Advanced Placement exams for which test preparation is offered; honors section; independent study; study abroad; academic accommodation for the gifted, the musically talented, and the artistically talented; remedial reading and/or remedial writing; remedial math; programs in English, general development for dyslexic students; special instructional classes for students with learning disabilities, Attention Deficit Disorder, and dyslexia; ESL (39 students enrolled).

College Admission Counseling 45 students graduated in 2009; all went to college, including Lynn University; University of Illinois at Urbana–Champaign; University of Michigan; University of Wisconsin–Madison. Median SAT critical reading: 540, median SAT math: 570. 25% scored over 600 on SAT critical reading, 20% scored over 600 on SAT math.

Student Life Upper grades have specified standards of dress, student council, honor system. Discipline rests primarily with faculty.

Tuition and Aid 7-day tuition and room/board: $35,900. Tuition installment plan (individually arranged payment plans). Tuition reduction for siblings, merit scholarship grants, need-based scholarship grants, need-based loans, paying campus jobs available. In 2009–10, 45% of upper-school students received aid. Total amount of financial aid awarded in 2009–10: $1,150,000.

Admissions For fall 2009, 187 students applied for upper-level admission, 124 were accepted, 109 enrolled. SSAT or WISC III required. Deadline for receipt of application materials: none. Application fee required: $50. Interview recommended.

Athletics Interscholastic: basketball, dance team, drill team, equestrian sports, martial arts, skiing (downhill), soccer, softball, tennis, track and field; intramural: aerobics, aerobics/dance, alpine skiing, aquatics, ballet, bicycling, bowling, dance, hiking/backpacking, horseback riding, jogging, modern dance, mountain biking, nordic skiing, ropes courses, skiing (cross-country), skiing (downhill), swimming and diving, tennis, volleyball, walking, weight training, yoga. 3 PE instructors, 3 coaches, 3 athletic trainers.

Computers Computers are regularly used in English, foreign language, mathematics, science classes. Computer network features include on-campus library services, online commercial services, Internet access, wireless campus network, Internet filtering or blocking technology. The school has a published electronic and media policy.

Contact Andrew M. Wilson, Headmaster/Director of Admissions. 814-684-3000 Ext. 106. Fax: 814-684-2177. E-mail: admissions@grier.org. Web site: www.grier.org.

GRIGGS INTERNATIONAL ACADEMY

12501 Old Columbia Pike
Silver Spring, Maryland 20904-6600
Head of School: Dr. Donald R. Sahly

General Information Coeducational day and distance learning college-preparatory, general academic, and religious studies school, affiliated with Seventh-day Adventist Church. Grades PK–PG. Distance learning grades K–12. Founded: 1909. Setting: suburban. Nearest major city is Washington, DC. 1 building on campus. Approved or accredited by Board of Regents, General Conference of Seventh-day Adventists, CITA (Commission on International and Trans-Regional Accreditation), Distance Education and Training Council, Middle States Association of Colleges and Schools, and Maryland Department of Education. Total enrollment: 728.

Upper School Student Profile 60% of students are Seventh-day Adventists.

Faculty School total: 34. In upper school: 14 men, 20 women; 19 have advanced degrees.

Subjects Offered Accounting, algebra, American government, American history, American literature, art appreciation, art history, arts, Bible studies, biology, business skills, chemistry, digital photography, earth science, English, English literature, fine arts, food science, French, geography, geometry, government/civics, health, home economics, keyboarding, mathematics, music appreciation, physics, pre-algebra, science, social studies, Spanish, word processing, world history, writing.

Graduation Requirements American government, arts and fine arts (art, music, dance, drama), English, health, history, keyboarding, language, mathematics, religion (includes Bible studies and theology), science, social studies (includes history), requirements for basic diploma differ. Community service is required.

Special Academic Programs Accelerated programs; independent study; study at local college for college credit.

College Admission Counseling 27 students graduated in 2010; they went to Andrews University; Loma Linda University; Southern Adventist University; Towson University; University of Maryland, Baltimore County; Washington Adventist University.

Student Life Upper grades have honor system. Discipline rests primarily with faculty.

Summer Programs Remediation, enrichment programs offered; held on campus; accepts boys and girls; open to students from other schools.

Tuition and Aid Day student tuition: $1680–$2100. Tuition installment plan (monthly payment plans, individually arranged payment plans).

Admissions Deadline for receipt of application materials: none. Application fee required: $80.

Computers Computers are regularly used in word processing classes. Students grades are available online.

Contact Mrs. Angie Crews, Enrollment Services Director. 301-680-5170. Fax: 301-680-6577. E-mail: adeaver@griggs.edu. Web site: www.griggs.edu.

See Display on page 290 and Close-Up on page 782.

GROTON SCHOOL

Box 991
Farmers Row
Groton, Massachusetts 01450
Head of School: Richard B. Commons

General Information Coeducational boarding and day college-preparatory, arts, and religious studies school, affiliated with Episcopal Church. Grades 8–12. Founded: 1884. Setting: rural. Nearest major city is Boston. Students are housed in single-sex dormitories. 400-acre campus. 17 buildings on campus. Approved or accredited by Association of Independent Schools in New England, New England Association of Schools and Colleges, and The Association of Boarding Schools. Member of National Association of Independent Schools and Secondary School Admission Test Board. Endowment: $265 million. Total enrollment: 372. Upper school average class size: 13. Upper school faculty-student ratio: 1:6. Upper School students typically attend 6 days per week. The average school day consists of 6 hours and 30 minutes.

Upper School Student Profile Grade 9: 73 students (37 boys, 36 girls); Grade 10: 86 students (44 boys, 42 girls); Grade 11: 95 students (49 boys, 46 girls); Grade 12: 91 students (47 boys, 44 girls). 79% of students are boarding students. 27% are state residents. 32 states are represented in upper school student body. 16% are international students. International students from Bermuda, Canada, China, France, Republic of Korea, and United Arab Emirates; 4 other countries represented in student body.

Faculty School total: 87. In upper school: 49 men, 38 women; 63 have advanced degrees; 78 reside on campus.

Subjects Offered Advanced chemistry, advanced math, algebra, American literature, American literature-AP, analytic geometry, Ancient Greek, ancient world history, archaeology, art, art history, art history-AP, Bible studies, biology, biology-AP, botany, Buddhism, calculus, calculus-AP, cell biology, Central and Eastern European history, ceramics, chemistry, chemistry-AP, Chinese, choir, choral music, civil rights, Civil War, civil war history, classical Greek literature, classical language, classics, composition, composition-AP, creative writing, dance, discrete mathematics, drawing, earth science, ecology, environmental systems, economics, English, English composition, English-AP, environmental science, environmental science-AP, environmental studies, ethics, ethics and responsibility, European history, European history-AP, expository writing, fine arts, fractal geometry, French, French language-AP, French literature-AP, geography, geometry, government, grammar, Greek, health, history, Holocaust, honors algebra, honors English, honors geometry, honors U.S. history, honors world history, independent study, lab science, language-AP, Latin, Latin-AP, linear algebra, literature, literature and composition-AP, mathematics, mathematics-AP, modern European history, modern European history-AP, modern history, modern languages, modern world history, music, music history, music theory, organic biochemistry, painting, philosophy, photo shop, photography, physical science, physics, physics-AP, pre-algebra, pre-calculus, psychology, religion, religious education, religious studies, science, Shakespeare, social sciences, Spanish, Spanish language-AP, Spanish literature, Spanish literature-AP, sports medicine, statistics, studio art, studio art-AP, theology, trigonometry, U.S. constitutional history, U.S. government, U.S. government and politics, U.S. government and politics-AP, U.S. history, U.S. history-AP, vocal music, Western civilization, wood lab, woodworking, world history, world history-AP, writing.

Graduation Requirements Arts and fine arts (art, music, dance, drama), classical language, English, foreign language, mathematics, religious studies, science, social studies (includes history).

Special Academic Programs 13 Advanced Placement exams for which test preparation is offered; honors section; independent study; study abroad; academic accommodation for the gifted, the musically talented, and the artistically talented.

College Admission Counseling 83 students graduated in 2010; all went to college, including Georgetown University; Harvard University; Northwestern University; Stanford University; Tufts University; University of Virginia. Median SAT critical reading: 700, median SAT math: 700, median SAT writing: 710, median combined SAT: 2100, median composite ACT: 28. 92% scored over 600 on SAT critical reading, 95% scored over 600 on SAT math, 96% scored over 600 on SAT writing, 99% scored over 1800 on combined SAT, 78% scored over 26 on composite ACT.

Student Life Upper grades have specified standards of dress, student council, honor system. Discipline rests equally with students and faculty. Attendance at religious services is required.

Tuition and Aid Day student tuition: $37,020; 7-day tuition and room/board: $48,895. Tuition installment plan (Insured Tuition Payment Plan, Key Tuition Payment Plan, monthly payment plans, individually arranged payment plans). Need-based scholarship grants, Key Education Resources available. In 2010–11, 37% of upper-school students received aid. Total amount of financial aid awarded in 2010–11: $4,500,000.

Admissions Traditional secondary-level entrance grade is 9. For fall 2010, 1,001 students applied for upper-level admission, 158 were accepted, 90 enrolled. ISEE,

MIND, BODY, SPIRIT
Character, Intellect, Leadership
At Groton you can do it all.

At Groton you can be an actor and an athlete, a scholar and a musician. Now is a time to explore. Take the time to find your talents!

A small school with big opportunities, Groton offers distinguishing features such as an eighth grade, the chance to study two languages concurrently, and a diverse community that thrives through a deep commitment of one to another and each to the whole.

For more information contact:
GROTON SCHOOL
Admission Office
978-448-7510
www.groton.org

SSAT or TOEFL required. Deadline for receipt of application materials: January 15. Application fee required: $50. Interview required.

Athletics Interscholastic: baseball (boys), basketball (b,g), crew (b,g), cross-country running (b,g), field hockey (g), Fives (b,g), football (b), hockey (b,g), ice hockey (b,g), lacrosse (b,g), rowing (b,g), soccer (b,g), squash (b,g), tennis (b,g); intramural: physical training (b,g), self defense (g), weight training (b,g); coed interscholastic: dance team; coed intramural: aerobics/dance, alpine skiing, dance, fitness, Fives, Frisbee, golf, ice skating, jogging, modern dance, nordic skiing, outdoor activities, skeet shooting, skiing (cross-country), skiing (downhill), soccer, strength & conditioning, swimming and diving, track and field, trap and skeet, ultimate Frisbee, yoga. 2 coaches, 1 athletic trainer.

Computers Computers are regularly used in English, history, mathematics, science classes. Computer network features include on-campus library services, Internet access, wireless campus network, Internet filtering or blocking technology, campus-wide wireless environment. Campus intranet and student e-mail accounts are available to students. The school has a published electronic and media policy.

Contact Mr. Ian Gracey, Director of Admission. 978-448-7510. Fax: 978-448-9623. E-mail: igracey@groton.org. Web site: www.groton.org.

See Display on page 291 and Close-Up on page 784.

GUAMANI PRIVATE SCHOOL

PO Box 3000
Guayama, Puerto Rico 00785
Head of School: Mr. Eduardo Delgado

General Information Coeducational day college-preparatory and bilingual studies school. Grades 1–12. Founded: 1914. Setting: urban. Nearest major city is Caguas. 1-acre campus. 1 building on campus. Approved or accredited by Middle States Association of Colleges and Schools, National Catholic Education Association, and Puerto Rico Department of Education. Languages of instruction: English and Spanish. Total enrollment: 606. Upper school average class size: 20. Upper school faculty-student ratio: 1:13.

Faculty School total: 32. In upper school: 10 men, 10 women; 3 have advanced degrees.

Subjects Offered Advanced math, Advanced Placement courses, algebra, American government, American history, analysis and differential calculus, chemistry, civics, pre-algebra, pre-calculus, science project, science research, social sciences, social studies, sociology, Spanish, Spanish language-AP, U.S. literature, visual arts, world geography, world history.

Graduation Requirements Mathematics, science, social sciences, Spanish, acceptance into a college or university. Community service is required.

Special Academic Programs Advanced Placement exam preparation; honors section; independent study.

College Admission Counseling 23 students graduated in 2009; they went to Embry-Riddle Aeronautical University; Syracuse University; University of Puerto Rico, Cayey University College; University of Puerto Rico, Mayagüez Campus; University of Puerto Rico, Río Piedras. Other: 23 entered a postgraduate year.

Student Life Upper grades have uniform requirement, student council, honor system. Discipline rests primarily with faculty.

Admissions Traditional secondary-level entrance grade is 9. For fall 2009, 30 students applied for upper-level admission, 21 were accepted, 20 enrolled. School's own test or Test of Achievement and Proficiency required. Deadline for receipt of application materials: none. Application fee required: $30. Interview required.

Athletics Interscholastic: aerobics/dance (girls), basketball (b,g), cheering (g), dance squad (g), volleyball (b,g); coed interscholastic: dance team. 3 PE instructors, 2 coaches.

Computers Computers are regularly used in English, mathematics, science, social sciences, Spanish, word processing classes. Computer resources include on-campus library services, Internet access, wireless campus network, Internet filtering or blocking technology. The school has a published electronic and media policy.

Contact Mrs. Digna Torres, Secretary. 787-864-6880. Fax: 787-866-4947. Web site: www.guamani.com.

GUERIN COLLEGE PREPARATORY HIGH SCHOOL

8001 West Belmont
River Grove, Illinois 60171-1096
Head of School: Mr. Anthony Tinerella

General Information Coeducational day college-preparatory, arts, religious studies, and technology school, affiliated with Roman Catholic Church. Grades 9–12. Founded: 1962. Setting: suburban. Nearest major city is Chicago. 22-acre campus. 2 buildings on campus. Approved or accredited by National Catholic Education Association, North Central Association of Colleges and Schools, and Illinois Department of Education. Endowment: $2 million. Total enrollment: 620. Upper school average class size: 25. Upper school faculty-student ratio: 1:16. There are 176 required school days per year for Upper School students. Upper School students typically attend 5 days per week. The average school day consists of 7 hours.

Upper School Student Profile Grade 9: 153 students (75 boys, 78 girls); Grade 10: 149 students (80 boys, 69 girls); Grade 11: 148 students (68 boys, 80 girls); Grade 12: 170 students (66 boys, 104 girls). 92% of students are Roman Catholic.

Faculty School total: 54. In upper school: 15 men, 38 women; 27 have advanced degrees.

Subjects Offered 3-dimensional art, 3-dimensional design, accounting, ACT preparation, acting, advanced biology, advanced chemistry, advanced math, Advanced Placement courses, advanced studio art-AP, advertising design, algebra, American government, American history, American history-AP, American literature, American literature-AP, anatomy and physiology, applied arts, applied music, art, athletics, band, baseball, Bible, biology, biology-AP, British literature, British literature (honors), British literature-AP, calculus, calculus-AP, campus ministry, career education, career/college preparation, Catholic belief and practice, cheerleading, chemistry, chemistry-AP, child development, choir, choral music, chorus, Christian and Hebrew scripture, Christian doctrine, Christian ethics, Christian scripture, Christian studies, Christian testament, church history, college counseling, college placement, college planning, college writing, comparative religion, competitive science projects, computer information systems, computer literacy, computers, concert band, concert choir, constitutional history of U.S., constitutional law.

Graduation Requirements Arts and fine arts (art, music, dance, drama), computers, electives, English, mathematics, physical education (includes health), science, social sciences, speech, theology, theology and the arts, a minimum of four service-learning classes.

Special Academic Programs 12 Advanced Placement exams for which test preparation is offered; honors section; study at local college for college credit; academic accommodation for the gifted, the musically talented, and the artistically talented; ESL (1 student enrolled).

College Admission Counseling 155 students graduated in 2009; 150 went to college, including DePaul University; Dominican University; Illinois State University; Loyola University Chicago; Northeastern Illinois University; Northern Illinois University. Other: 5 entered a postgraduate year. Median composite ACT: 21.

Student Life Upper grades have uniform requirement, student council. Discipline rests primarily with faculty. Attendance at religious services is required.

Tuition and Aid Day student tuition: $7850. Tuition installment plan (monthly payment plans, individually arranged payment plans, TMS). Tuition reduction for siblings, merit scholarship grants, need-based scholarship grants, paying campus jobs available. In 2009–10, 48% of upper-school students received aid; total upper-school merit-scholarship money awarded: $100,000. Total amount of financial aid awarded in 2009–10: $400,000.

Admissions Traditional secondary-level entrance grade is 9. Explore required. Deadline for receipt of application materials: none. Application fee required: $200.

Athletics Interscholastic: baseball (boys), basketball (b,g), dance (g), dance team (g), football (b), gymnastics (g), hockey (b), ice hockey (b), soccer (b,g), softball (g), strength & conditioning (b,g), volleyball (g), weight training (b,g); coed interscholastic: cheering, cross-country running, dance, golf, ice hockey, physical fitness, strength & conditioning, track and field, wrestling; coed intramural: fitness walking. 3 PE instructors, 30 coaches, 1 athletic trainer.

Computers Computers are regularly used in all academic, computer applications classes. Computer network features include Internet access, wireless campus network, Internet filtering or blocking technology, all 9th, 10th graders and 11th graders lease a laptop computer and bring to all classes. Student e-mail accounts and computer access in designated common areas are available to students. Students grades are available online. The school has a published electronic and media policy.

Contact Mrs. Valerie Reiss, Director of Admissions. 708-453-6233 Ext. 4732. Fax: 708-453-6296. E-mail: vreiss@guerinprep.org. Web site: www.guerinprep.org.

GULLIVER PREPARATORY SCHOOL

6575 North Kendall Drive
Miami, Florida 33156
Head of School: John W. Krutulis

General Information Coeducational day college-preparatory, arts, technology, International Baccalaureate, architectural design, and pre-engineering, law and litigation, biomedical sciences school. Grades PK–12. Founded: 1926. Setting: suburban. 14-acre campus. 3 buildings on campus. Approved or accredited by CITA (Commission on International and Trans-Regional Accreditation), European Council of International Schools, Florida Council of Independent Schools, Southern Association of Colleges and Schools, and Florida Department of Education. Member of Secondary School Admission Test Board. Total enrollment: 1,834. Upper school average class size: 14. Upper school faculty-student ratio: 1:8.

Faculty School total: 126. In upper school: 58 men, 68 women; 69 have advanced degrees.

Subjects Offered Algebra, American history, American literature, anatomy, architectural drawing, architecture, art, art history, biology, calculus, ceramics, chemistry, college admission preparation, college writing, computer animation, computer applications, computer processing, computer programming, computer programming-AP, computer science, computer science-AP, computer skills, computer studies, concert band, concert choir, creative writing, dance, desktop publishing, drafting, drama, economics, engineering, English, English literature, European history, fine arts, French, geometry, government/civics, history, Italian, keyboarding, Latin, marine biology, mathematics, mechanical drawing, music, newspaper, physical education, physics, psychology, science, social studies, Spanish, speech, statistics, theater, trigonometry, video, world history, world literature, yearbook, zoology.

Graduation Requirements Arts and fine arts (art, music, dance, drama), computer science, English, foreign language, mathematics, physical education (includes health), science, social studies (includes history). Community service is required.

Special Academic Programs International Baccalaureate program; Advanced Placement exam preparation; honors section; study at local college for college credit; academic accommodation for the gifted, the musically talented, and the artistically talented.

College Admission Counseling 180 students graduated in 2010; all went to college, including Boston University; Duke University; Florida International University; Florida State University; University of Florida; University of Miami. Mean SAT critical reading: 575, mean SAT math: 590, mean SAT writing: 578.

Student Life Upper grades have specified standards of dress, student council, honor system. Discipline rests primarily with faculty.

Summer Programs Remediation, enrichment, advancement, art/fine arts, rigorous outdoor training, computer instruction programs offered; session focuses on enrichment and reinforcement; held on campus; accepts boys and girls; not open to students from other schools. 175 students usually enrolled. 2011 schedule: June 7 to July 16. Application deadline: June 7.

Tuition and Aid Day student tuition: $8500–$24,520. Tuition installment plan (monthly payment plans, school's own tuition recovery plan). Tuition reduction for siblings, need-based scholarship grants, application and matriculation fee waived for children of alumni available.

Admissions Traditional secondary-level entrance grade is 9. For fall 2010, 340 students applied for upper-level admission, 242 were accepted, 134 enrolled. School's own exam and SSAT required. Deadline for receipt of application materials: February 19. Application fee required: $100. Interview recommended.

Athletics Interscholastic: aerobics/Nautilus (girls), baseball (b), basketball (b,g), cross-country running (b,g), dance (g), dance squad (g), dance team (g), diving (b,g), football (b), golf (b,g), gymnastics (b,g), lacrosse (b), physical training (b,g), running (b,g), soccer (b,g), softball (g), swimming and diving (b,g), tennis (b,g), track and field (b,g), volleyball (g), water polo (b,g); intramural: boxing (b,g), weight training (b,g); coed interscholastic: aerobics, bowling, cheering, modern dance, yoga; coed intramural: aerobics/dance, aerobics/Nautilus, badminton, dance, dance squad, dance team, fitness, flag football, Frisbee, kickball, modern dance, netball, physical fitness, running, strength & conditioning, touch football, yoga. 6 PE instructors, 55 coaches, 2 athletic trainers.

Computers Computers are regularly used in architecture, art, college planning, drafting, English, graphic arts, graphic design, keyboarding, newspaper, programming, science, technology, word processing, yearbook classes. Computer network features include on-campus library services, online commercial services, Internet access, wireless campus network, Internet filtering or blocking technology, modified laptop program, SMART Boards and Audio enhancement systems. Students grades are available online. The school has a published electronic and media policy.

Contact Carol A. Bowen, Director of Admission. 305-666-7937 Ext. 1408. Fax: 305-665-3791. E-mail: bowc@gulliverschools.org. Web site: www.gulliverschools.org.

GUNSTON DAY SCHOOL

911 Gunston Road
PO Box 200
Centreville, Maryland 21617
Head of School: Mr. John A. Lewis, IV

General Information Coeducational day college-preparatory, arts, and technology school. Grades 9–12. Founded: 1911. Setting: rural. Nearest major city is Annapolis. 32-acre campus. 4 buildings on campus. Approved or accredited by Association of Independent Maryland Schools, Middle States Association of Colleges and Schools, and Maryland Department of Education. Member of National Association of Independent Schools and Secondary School Admission Test Board. Endowment: $1 million. Total enrollment: 147. Upper school average class size: 8. Upper school faculty-student ratio: 1:6. There are 170 required school days per year for Upper School students. Upper School students typically attend 5 days per week. The average school day consists of 8 hours.

Upper School Student Profile Grade 9: 30 students (7 boys, 23 girls); Grade 10: 31 students (17 boys, 14 girls); Grade 11: 44 students (23 boys, 21 girls); Grade 12: 42 students (22 boys, 20 girls).

Faculty School total: 25. In upper school: 16 men, 9 women; 14 have advanced degrees.

Subjects Offered Advanced biology, advanced chemistry, advanced math, Advanced Placement courses, advanced studio art-AP, algebra, American government, American history, American literature, anatomy and physiology, ancient history, applied arts, art, art history, art history-AP, biology, biology-AP, British literature, British literature (honors), calculus, calculus-AP, calligraphy, ceramics, chemistry, chemistry-AP, Chesapeake Bay studies, chorus, college counseling, college placement, college planning, community service, computer applications, computer science, digital photography, drama performance, economics, English, English as a foreign language, English literature, environmental science, environmental science-AP, equestrian sports, ethical decision making, ethics, European history-AP, fine arts, fitness, French, freshman seminar, geometry, golf, government, government-AP, government/civics, health, health and wellness, history, history-AP, honors algebra, honors English,

honors geometry, ideas, lab science, Latin, Latin-AP, mathematics, mathematics-AP, medieval history, Microsoft, music, music appreciation, music composition, music theory, painting, performing arts, photography, physics, physics-AP, play production, poetry, pottery, pre-calculus, pre-college orientation, printmaking, psychology, SAT preparation, SAT/ACT preparation, science, sculpture, senior internship, senior project, senior thesis, short story, silk screening, Spanish, Spanish-AP, sports, studio art, studio art-AP, swimming, tennis, trigonometry, U.S. government, U.S. government and politics-AP, U.S. history, U.S. history-AP, weight training, wellness, woodworking, world history, writing workshop.

Graduation Requirements Arts and fine arts (art, music, dance, drama), athletics, computer science, English, foreign language, history, mathematics, science, social sciences. Community service is required.

Special Academic Programs Advanced Placement exam preparation; honors section; independent study; term-away projects; study at local college for college credit; study abroad; academic accommodation for the gifted, the musically talented, and the artistically talented; ESL (14 students enrolled).

College Admission Counseling 25 students graduated in 2010; all went to college, including Davidson College; Dickinson College; Lehigh University; University of Maryland, College Park; Virginia Polytechnic Institute and State University; Washington College.

Student Life Upper grades have specified standards of dress, student council, honor system. Discipline rests primarily with faculty.

Summer Programs Advancement programs offered; session focuses on geometry; held on campus; accepts boys and girls; not open to students from other schools. 3 students usually enrolled. 2011 schedule: June 17 to July 22. Application deadline: none.

Tuition and Aid Day student tuition: $21,730. Tuition installment plan (monthly payment plans, individually arranged payment plans, Sallie Mae, Tuition Management Solutions). Merit scholarship grants, need-based scholarship grants available. In 2010–11, 50% of upper-school students received aid; total upper-school merit-scholarship money awarded: $32,595. Total amount of financial aid awarded in 2010–11: $700,000.

Admissions Traditional secondary-level entrance grade is 9. For fall 2010, 65 students applied for upper-level admission, 63 were accepted, 46 enrolled. ISEE or SSAT required. Deadline for receipt of application materials: February 1. Application fee required: $50. On-campus interview required.

Athletics Interscholastic: basketball (boys, girls), field hockey (g), lacrosse (b,g), soccer (b,g), swimming and diving (b,g), tennis (b,g); intramural: independent competitive sports (b,g), tennis (b,g); coed interscholastic: crew, equestrian sports, golf, horseback riding, sailing, swimming and diving, tennis; coed intramural: equestrian sports, fitness, independent competitive sports, strength & conditioning, tennis, weight training. 4 coaches.

Computers Computers are regularly used in English, foreign language, history, mathematics, science classes. Computer network features include online commercial services, Internet access, wireless campus network, Internet filtering or blocking technology, Gale Library. Campus intranet, student e-mail accounts, and computer access in designated common areas are available to students.

Contact David Henry, Director of Admission and Financial Aid. 410-758-0620. Fax: 410-758-0628. E-mail: dhenry@gunstondayschool.org. Web site: www.gunstondayschool.org/.

GWYNEDD MERCY ACADEMY

1345 Sumneytown Pike
PO Box 902
Gwynedd Valley, Pennsylvania 19437-0902
Head of School: Sr. Kathleen Boyce, RSM

General Information Girls' day college-preparatory, arts, religious studies, and technology school, affiliated with Roman Catholic Church. Grades 9–12. Founded: 1861. Setting: suburban. Nearest major city is Philadelphia. 48-acre campus. 1 building on campus. Approved or accredited by Mercy Secondary Education Association, Middle States Association of Colleges and Schools, National Catholic Education Association, and Pennsylvania Department of Education. Total enrollment: 387. Upper school average class size: 18. Upper school faculty-student ratio: 1:11. There are 178 required school days per year for Upper School students. Upper School students typically attend 5 days per week. The average school day consists of 6 hours and 5 minutes.

Upper School Student Profile Grade 9: 101 students (101 girls); Grade 10: 90 students (90 girls); Grade 11: 105 students (105 girls); Grade 12: 91 students (91 girls). 99% of students are Roman Catholic.

Faculty School total: 36. In upper school: 6 men, 30 women; 26 have advanced degrees.

Subjects Offered Accounting, Advanced Placement courses, algebra, American history, American history-AP, American literature, art, art appreciation, athletics, biology, business law, business, skills, calculus, calculus-AP, chemistry, college counseling, computer science, computer skills, English, fine arts, French, geometry, health, health education, history, honors English, human development, Latin, library studies, mathematics, music, music theory, physical education, physical science, physics, piloting, post-calculus, pre-calculus, religion, social studies, Spanish,

Gwynedd Mercy Academy

statistics-AP, study skills, theology, trigonometry, U.S. government and politics-AP, word processing, world cultures, zoology.
Graduation Requirements English, foreign language, mathematics, physical education (includes health), religion (includes Bible studies and theology), science, social studies (includes history).
Special Academic Programs Advanced Placement exam preparation; honors section; study at local college for college credit; academic accommodation for the musically talented and the artistically talented.
College Admission Counseling 95 students graduated in 2010; all went to college, including Fordham University; Penn State University Park; Saint Joseph's University; Temple University; The University of Scranton. Mean SAT critical reading: 578, mean SAT math: 563, mean SAT writing: 579, mean combined SAT: 1710. 36% scored over 600 on SAT critical reading, 26% scored over 600 on SAT math, 43% scored over 600 on SAT writing, 35% scored over 1800 on combined SAT.
Student Life Upper grades have uniform requirement, student council, honor system. Discipline rests primarily with faculty. Attendance at religious services is required.
Summer Programs Sports programs offered; session focuses on sports; held on campus; accepts girls; open to students from other schools. 85 students usually enrolled. 2011 schedule: June 18 to August 2. Application deadline: May 31.
Tuition and Aid Day student tuition: $13,500. Tuition installment plan (monthly payment plans, individually arranged payment plans, quarterly and semi-annual payment plans). Tuition reduction for siblings, merit scholarship grants, need-based scholarship grants available. In 2010–11, 5% of upper-school students received aid; total upper-school merit-scholarship money awarded: $141,680. Total amount of financial aid awarded in 2010–11: $217,680.
Admissions Traditional secondary-level entrance grade is 9. For fall 2010, 272 students applied for upper-level admission, 230 were accepted, 103 enrolled. Scholastic Testing Service High School Placement Test (open version) required. Deadline for receipt of application materials: November 6. Application fee required: $50.
Athletics Interscholastic: basketball, cross-country running, diving, field hockey, golf, indoor track, lacrosse, soccer, softball, swimming and diving, tennis, track and field, volleyball; intramural: dance. 2 PE instructors, 24 coaches, 1 athletic trainer.
Computers Computers are regularly used in art, business, English, foreign language, French, history, Latin, library skills, mathematics, music, newspaper, publications, religion, science, technology, word processing, writing, yearbook classes. Computer network features include on-campus library services, online commercial services, Internet access, wireless campus network, Internet filtering or blocking technology. Student e-mail accounts and computer access in designated common areas are available to students. The school has a published electronic and media policy.
Contact Mrs. Kimberly Dunphy Scott, Director of Admissions. 215-646-8815 Ext. 329. Fax: 215-646-4361. E-mail: kscott@gmahs.org. Web site: www.gmahs.org.

HACKLEY SCHOOL
293 Benedict Avenue
Tarrytown, New York 10591
Head of School: Mr. Walter C. Johnson
General Information Coeducational boarding and day college-preparatory, arts, technology, and liberal arts; math and science school. Boarding grades 9–12, day grades K–12. Founded: 1899. Setting: suburban. Nearest major city is New York. Students are housed in single-sex dormitories. 285-acre campus. 15 buildings on campus. Approved or accredited by Middle States Association of Colleges and Schools, New York State Association of Independent Schools, New York State Board of Regents, and The Association of Boarding Schools. Member of National Association of Independent Schools and Secondary School Admission Test Board. Endowment: $28 million. Total enrollment: 841. Upper school average class size: 15. Upper school faculty-student ratio: 1:6. There are 169 required school days per year for Upper School students. Upper School students typically attend 5 days per week. The average school day consists of 7 hours.
Upper School Student Profile Grade 9: 100 students (53 boys, 47 girls); Grade 10: 97 students (48 boys, 49 girls); Grade 11: 91 students (46 boys, 45 girls); Grade 12: 96 students (46 boys, 50 girls). 3% of students are boarding students. 96% are state residents. 3 states are represented in upper school student body.
Faculty School total: 128. In upper school: 30 men, 34 women; 53 have advanced degrees; 43 reside on campus.
Subjects Offered 20th century world history, 3-dimensional art, addiction, algebra, American history, American history-AP, American literature, ancient history, anthropology, architectural drawing, art, art history-AP, biology, biology-AP, British literature, calculus-AP, ceramics, chemistry, chemistry-AP, Chinese, chorus, computer graphics, computer programming, computer science, computer science-AP, concert band, contemporary issues, creative writing, driver education, ecology, economics, electronic publishing, English, environmental science-AP, European history, fine arts, finite math, French, French language-AP, French literature-AP, geometry, Greek, history, Italian, Latin, Latin-AP, marine biology, mathematics, modern European history, music, music theory, music theory-AP, orchestra, organic chemistry, performing arts, photography, physical education, physics, physics-AP, pre-calculus, science, Spanish, Spanish language-AP, Spanish literature-AP, statistics-AP, studio art-AP, trigonometry, U.S. government and politics-AP, world history.

Graduation Requirements Arts and fine arts (art, music, dance, drama), English, foreign language, health, history, mathematics, physical education (includes health), science.
Special Academic Programs 21 Advanced Placement exams for which test preparation is offered; honors section; independent study.
College Admission Counseling 95 students graduated in 2010; all went to college, including Colgate University; Columbia University; Dartmouth College; Harvard University; University of Pennsylvania; Vanderbilt University. 90% scored over 600 on SAT critical reading, 90% scored over 600 on SAT math, 90% scored over 600 on SAT writing.
Student Life Upper grades have specified standards of dress, student council. Discipline rests primarily with faculty.
Summer Programs Sports programs offered; session focuses on sports (football and basketball); held on campus; accepts boys and girls; open to students from other schools. 50 students usually enrolled. 2011 schedule: June to June.
Tuition and Aid Day student tuition: $34,400; 5-day tuition and room/board: $45,000. Tuition installment plan (Insured Tuition Payment Plan, Academic Management Services Plan, Key Tuition Payment Plan, monthly payment plans). Need-based scholarship grants, need-based loans available. In 2010–11, 15% of upper-school students received aid. Total amount of financial aid awarded in 2010–11: $2,513,880.
Admissions Traditional secondary-level entrance grade is 9. For fall 2010, 200 students applied for upper-level admission, 81 were accepted, 48 enrolled. ERB, ISEE or SSAT required. Deadline for receipt of application materials: January 14. Application fee required: $65. On-campus interview required.
Athletics Interscholastic: baseball (boys), basketball (b,g), field hockey (g), football (b), golf (b,g), lacrosse (b,g), soccer (b,g), softball (g), squash (b,g), tennis (b,g), wrestling (b); intramural: squash (b,g); coed interscholastic: cross-country running, fencing, indoor track, strength & conditioning, swimming and diving, track and field; coed intramural: aerobics, aerobics/Nautilus, climbing, cooperative games, fitness, Frisbee, kayaking, life saving, martial arts, outdoor education, outdoor recreation, physical fitness, physical training, ropes courses, scuba diving, weight training, yoga. 6 PE instructors, 9 coaches, 1 athletic trainer.
Computers Computers are regularly used in computer applications, desktop publishing, drawing and design, graphic arts, independent study, keyboarding, literary magazine, music, newspaper, photography, programming, Web site design, yearbook classes. Computer network features include on-campus library services, online commercial services, Internet access, wireless campus network, laptop loaner program. Campus intranet and computer access in designated common areas are available to students.
Contact Mrs. Lynn Hooley, Admissions Associate. 914-366-2642. Fax: 914-366-2636. E-mail: lhooley@hackleyschool.org. Web site: www.hackleyschool.org.

HALSTROM HIGH SCHOOL
380 South Melrose Drive
Suite 416
Vista, California 92081
Head of School: Ms. Gabe Azzaro
General Information Coeducational day and distance learning college-preparatory and general academic school; primarily serves dyslexic students. Grades 7–12. Distance learning grades 7–12. Founded: 1985. Setting: suburban. Nearest major city is San Diego. 1-acre campus. 1 building on campus. Approved or accredited by Western Association of Schools and Colleges and California Department of Education. Total enrollment: 30. Upper school average class size: 1. Upper school faculty-student ratio: 1:1. There are 280 required school days per year for Upper School students. Upper School students typically attend 5 days per week. The average school day consists of 5 hours.
Upper School Student Profile Grade 8: 3 students (2 boys, 1 girl); Grade 9: 5 students (1 boy, 4 girls); Grade 10: 6 students (3 boys, 3 girls); Grade 11: 8 students (5 boys, 3 girls); Grade 12: 10 students (7 boys, 3 girls).
Faculty School total: 15. In upper school: 3 men, 12 women; 4 have advanced degrees.
Subjects Offered Adolescent issues, advanced computer applications, algebra, American literature, anatomy and physiology, anthropology, art appreciation, astronomy, biology, calculus, chemistry, composition, creative writing, earth and space science, economics, English, English literature, French, geography, geometry, integrated mathematics, journalism, marine biology, math analysis, music appreciation, mythology, oceanography, physics, pre-calculus, printmaking, probability and statistics, psychology, reading, sociology, Spanish, theater, trigonometry, U.S. history, world history, world literature.
Graduation Requirements Arts and fine arts (art, music, dance, drama), English, foreign language, mathematics, personal development, practical arts, science, social sciences, 2 semesters of cultural geography, one semester of business math, 75 hours of volunteer service.
Special Academic Programs Accelerated programs; independent study; term-away projects; academic accommodation for the gifted, the musically talented, and the artistically talented; remedial reading and/or remedial writing; remedial math; programs in English, mathematics, general development for dyslexic students; special instructional classes for deaf students, blind students.

College Admission Counseling Colleges students went to include California State University, San Marcos; MiraCosta College; Palomar College; The University of Arizona; University of Southern California.

Student Life Upper grades have student council, honor system. Discipline rests primarily with faculty.

Tuition and Aid Day student tuition: $7000–$10,000. Guaranteed tuition plan. Tuition installment plan (monthly payment plans, individually arranged payment plans). Tuition reduction for siblings, need-based scholarship grants, discount for teachers' sons/daughters available. In 2009–10, 5% of upper-school students received aid. Total amount of financial aid awarded in 2009–10: $10,000.

Admissions Traditional secondary-level entrance grade is 10. For fall 2009, 27 students applied for upper-level admission, 27 were accepted, 27 enrolled. Achievement/Aptitude/Writing required. Deadline for receipt of application materials: none. Application fee required: $150. On-campus interview required.

Computers Computers are regularly used in all academic, computer applications classes. Computer network features include Internet access, Internet filtering or blocking technology.

Contact Ms. Gabrielle Kathleen Azzaro, Director. 760-732-1200. Fax: 760-643-1849. E-mail: gabeazzaro@halstromhs.org. Web site: www.halstromhs.org.

HAMDEN HALL COUNTRY DAY SCHOOL

1108 Whitney Avenue
Hamden, Connecticut 06517
Head of School: Mr. Robert J. Izzo

General Information Coeducational day college-preparatory school. Grades PS–12. Founded: 1912. Setting: suburban. Nearest major city is New Haven. 42-acre campus. 8 buildings on campus. Approved or accredited by Connecticut Association of Independent Schools, New England Association of Schools and Colleges, and Connecticut Department of Education. Member of National Association of Independent Schools. Endowment: $8.2 million. Total enrollment: 563. Upper school average class size: 15. Upper school faculty-student ratio: 1:8. There are 165 required school days per year for Upper School students. Upper School students typically attend 5 days per week. The average school day consists of 4 hours and 45 minutes.

Upper School Student Profile Grade 9: 54 students (33 boys, 21 girls); Grade 10: 62 students (34 boys, 28 girls); Grade 11: 81 students (46 boys, 35 girls); Grade 12: 70 students (39 boys, 31 girls).

Faculty School total: 80. In upper school: 22 men, 21 women; 31 have advanced degrees.

Subjects Offered African-American history, algebra, American literature, anatomy, art history, astronomy, biology, British literature, calculus, ceramics, chamber groups, chemistry, chorus, computer graphics, computer multimedia, computer programming, computer science, constitutional law, creative writing, digital photography, drama, drawing, electronics, English language and composition-AP, European history-AP, expository writing, French, genetics, geology, geometry, improvisation, independent study, jazz, Latin, life science, Mandarin, marine biology, meteorology, multimedia design, music appreciation, music history, music theory, oceanography, painting, peer counseling, performing arts, physiology, playwriting, poetry, printmaking, sculpture, Spanish, speech, statistics, theater, trigonometry, U.S. history, video film production, Western civilization, women in literature, world history, world literature, zoology.

Graduation Requirements Arts and fine arts (art, music, dance, drama), computer science, English, foreign language, mathematics, physical education (includes health), science, social studies (includes history), participation in 2 athletic seasons each year.

Special Academic Programs Advanced Placement exam preparation; honors section; independent study.

College Admission Counseling 65 students graduated in 2010; all went to college, including Boston College; Brown University; Dickinson College; Emory University; Franklin & Marshall College; Princeton University. Median SAT critical reading: 600, median SAT math: 600, median SAT writing: 600, median combined SAT: 1800, median composite ACT: 26.

Student Life Upper grades have specified standards of dress, student council, honor system. Discipline rests equally with students and faculty.

Summer Programs Remediation, enrichment, advancement, sports, art/fine arts, computer instruction programs offered; held on campus; accepts boys and girls; open to students from other schools. 450 students usually enrolled. 2011 schedule: June 13 to August 19. Application deadline: none.

Tuition and Aid Day student tuition: $28,990. Tuition installment plan (Tuition Management Services). Need-based scholarship grants, need-based loans, paying campus jobs, Key Education Resources available. In 2010–11, 30% of upper-school students received aid. Total amount of financial aid awarded in 2010–11: $1,421,655.

Admissions Traditional secondary-level entrance grade is 9. For fall 2010, 120 students applied for upper-level admission, 80 were accepted, 27 enrolled. ISEE or SSAT required. Deadline for receipt of application materials: January 15. Application fee required: $50. Interview required.

Athletics Interscholastic: baseball (boys), basketball (b,g), field hockey (g), football (b), ice hockey (b), lacrosse (b,g), soccer (b,g), softball (g), tennis (b,g), volleyball (g), wrestling (b); coed interscholastic: cross-country running, golf, outdoors, physical fitness, swimming and diving; coed intramural: outdoors, physical fitness, running, weight training. 3 PE instructors, 15 coaches, 1 athletic trainer.

Computers Computers are regularly used in all academic, art, digital applications, graphic arts, graphic design, information technology, video film production, yearbook

classes. Computer network features include on-campus library services, Internet access, wireless campus network, Internet filtering or blocking technology. Student e-mail accounts are available to students. The school has a published electronic and media policy.

Contact Janet B. Izzo, Director of Admissions. 203-752-2610. Fax: 203-752-2611. E-mail: jizzo@hamdenhall.org. Web site: www.hamdenhall.org.

HAMILTON DISTRICT CHRISTIAN HIGH

92 Glancaster Road
Ancaster, Ontario L9G 3K9, Canada
Head of School: Mr. George Van Kampen

General Information Coeducational day college-preparatory, general academic, arts, business, vocational, religious studies, and technology school, affiliated with Christian faith. Grades 9–12. Founded: 1956. Setting: suburban. Nearest major city is Hamilton, Canada. 22-acre campus. 1 building on campus. Approved or accredited by Christian Schools International, Ontario Ministry of Education, and Ontario Department of Education. Language of instruction: English. Total enrollment: 480. Upper school average class size: 19. Upper school faculty-student ratio: 1:19. There are 180 required school days per year for Upper School students. Upper School students typically attend 5 days per week. The average school day consists of 6 hours.

Upper School Student Profile Grade 9: 120 students (60 boys, 60 girls); Grade 10: 100 students (50 boys, 50 girls); Grade 11: 130 students (65 boys, 65 girls); Grade 12: 130 students (65 boys, 65 girls). 100% of students are Christian faith.

Faculty School total: 37. In upper school: 24 men, 13 women; 9 have advanced degrees.

Subjects Offered 20th century history, 3-dimensional art, 3-dimensional design, accounting, acting, adolescent issues, advanced chemistry, advanced computer applications, advanced math, ancient history, ancient world history, applied arts, architectural drawing, art, art history, Bible, biology, business technology, calculus, Canadian geography, Canadian history, Canadian law, career experience, carpentry, chemistry, choir, civics, computer applications, computer multimedia, computer programming, computer technologies, computer-aided design, concert band, creative writing, drafting, drama, economics, English literature, environmental science, ESL, family and consumer science, finite math, food and nutrition, French, geometry, guidance, history, instrumental music, keyboarding, leadership, mathematics, media, modern Western civilization, music, peer counseling, personal finance, physical education, physics, religious studies, science, sociology, trigonometry, woodworking.

Graduation Requirements Art, Bible, Canadian geography, Canadian history, career education, civics, English, French, history, keyboarding, mathematics, science, 40 hours of community service.

Special Academic Programs 6 Advanced Placement exams for which test preparation is offered; independent study; term-away projects; academic accommodation for the musically talented and the artistically talented; remedial reading and/or remedial writing; remedial math; ESL (20 students enrolled).

College Admission Counseling 108 students graduated in 2010; 95 went to college, including McMaster University; Queen's University at Kingston; Redeemer University College; The University of Western Ontario; University of Waterloo; Wilfrid Laurier University. Other: 8 went to work, 5 had other specific plans. Median composite ACT: 23. 25% scored over 26 on composite ACT.

Student Life Upper grades have uniform requirement, student council. Discipline rests primarily with faculty.

Tuition and Aid Day student tuition: CAN$11,360. Tuition installment plan (monthly payment plans, individually arranged payment plans). Merit scholarship grants, need-based scholarship grants, tuition assistance fund, family rate tuition: additional children at no extra charge, reduced rate for two-school tuition families and home school families available. In 2010–11, 6% of upper-school students received aid; total upper-school merit-scholarship money awarded: CAN$4000. Total amount of financial aid awarded in 2010–11: CAN$95,000.

Admissions Traditional secondary-level entrance grade is 9. For fall 2010, 140 students applied for upper-level admission, 139 were accepted, 130 enrolled. Deadline for receipt of application materials: none. No application fee required. Interview required.

Athletics Interscholastic: badminton (boys, girls), baseball (g), basketball (b,g), cross-country running (b,g), golf (b,g), hockey (b), ice hockey (b), lacrosse (b,g), running (b,g), soccer (b,g), softball (g), touch football (b), track and field (b,g), volleyball (b,g); intramural: ball hockey (b,g), basketball (b,g), flag football (b,g), floor hockey (b,g), volleyball (b,g), wallyball (b,g), whiffle ball (b,g); coed interscholastic: badminton, ultimate Frisbee; coed intramural: floor hockey, horseback riding, indoor soccer, mountain biking, weight lifting, weight training. 5 PE instructors, 6 coaches.

Computers Computers are regularly used in art, business studies, career education, career exploration, college planning, current events, desktop publishing, drafting, economics, English, ESL, ethics, geography, graphic arts, graphic design, history, independent study, keyboarding, library, literary magazine, mathematics, media production, music, news writing, newspaper, photography, religious studies, research skills, science, video film production, Web site design, writing, yearbook classes. Computer network features include on-campus library services, online commercial services, Internet access, wireless campus network, Internet filtering or blocking technology, course Web pages, course chat rooms. Campus intranet, student e-mail

Hamilton District Christian High

accounts, and computer access in designated common areas are available to students. Students grades are available online. The school has a published electronic and media policy.

Contact Ms. Janet Hagen, Office Manager. 905-648-6655 Ext. 103. Fax: 905-648-3139. E-mail: jhagen@hdch.org. Web site: www.hdch.org.

HAMPSHIRE COUNTRY SCHOOL

Rindge, New Hampshire
See Junior Boarding Schools section.

HAMPTON ROADS ACADEMY

739 Academy Lane
Newport News, Virginia 23602
Head of School: Mr. Thomas D. Harvey

General Information Coeducational day college-preparatory school. Grades PK–12. Founded: 1959. Setting: suburban. 53-acre campus. 4 buildings on campus. Approved or accredited by Virginia Association of Independent Schools and Virginia Department of Education. Member of National Association of Independent Schools. Total enrollment: 585. Upper school average class size: 16. Upper school faculty-student ratio: 1:10. Upper School students typically attend 5 days per week. The average school day consists of 6 hours and 30 minutes.

Upper School Student Profile Grade 9: 65 students (37 boys, 28 girls); Grade 10: 70 students (34 boys, 36 girls); Grade 11: 72 students (40 boys, 32 girls); Grade 12: 74 students (45 boys, 29 girls).

Faculty School total: 70. In upper school: 13 men, 17 women; 19 have advanced degrees.

Subjects Offered African studies, algebra, American history, American literature, anatomy, art, biology, calculus, ceramics, chemistry, creative writing, drama, driver education, earth science, economics, English, English literature, European history, expository writing, fine arts, French, geography, geometry, government/civics, grammar, health, history, Latin, mathematics, music, photography, physical education, physics, physiology, science, social studies, Spanish, speech, statistics, theater, trigonometry, typing, world history, world literature, writing.

Graduation Requirements Arts and fine arts (art, music, dance, drama), English, foreign language, mathematics, physical education (includes health), science, social studies (includes history), community service. Community service is required.

Special Academic Programs 21 Advanced Placement exams for which test preparation is offered; honors section; independent study.

College Admission Counseling 67 students graduated in 2010; all went to college, including James Madison University; Roanoke College; The College of William and Mary; University of Virginia; Virginia Polytechnic Institute and State University. Median SAT critical reading: 600, median SAT math: 600, median SAT writing: 600, median combined SAT: 1800, median composite ACT: 22. 60% scored over 600 on SAT critical reading, 54% scored over 600 on SAT math, 56% scored over 600 on SAT writing, 57% scored over 1800 on combined SAT, 36% scored over 26 on composite ACT.

Student Life Upper grades have specified standards of dress, student council, honor system. Discipline rests primarily with faculty.

Summer Programs Enrichment, sports, art/fine arts, computer instruction programs offered; session focuses on K-8 students; held on campus; accepts boys and girls; open to students from other schools. 75 students usually enrolled. 2011 schedule: June 10 to July 30. Application deadline: none.

Tuition and Aid Day student tuition: $14,800. Tuition installment plan (SMART Tuition Payment Plan). Need-based scholarship grants available. In 2010–11, 18% of upper-school students received aid.

Admissions Traditional secondary-level entrance grade is 9. For fall 2010, 43 students applied for upper-level admission, 39 were accepted, 36 enrolled. ERB, school's own test and writing sample required. Deadline for receipt of application materials: none. Application fee required: $100. On-campus interview required.

Athletics Interscholastic: baseball (boys), basketball (b,g), cheering (g), cross-country running (b,g), field hockey (g), football (b), golf (b,g), lacrosse (b), physical training (b,g), sailing (b,g), soccer (b,g), softball (g), swimming and diving (b,g), tennis (b,g), track and field (b,g), volleyball (b,g), weight training (b,g); coed interscholastic: aquatics; coed intramural: equestrian sports, fitness, physical fitness, physical training, ropes courses, strength & conditioning, ultimate Frisbee, weight training. 3 PE instructors, 44 coaches, 1 athletic trainer.

Computers Computers are regularly used in English, mathematics, music, science, writing, yearbook classes. Computer network features include on-campus library services, online commercial services, Internet access, wireless campus network, Internet filtering or blocking technology. Student e-mail accounts are available to students. Students grades are available online. The school has a published electronic and media policy.

Contact Rebecca Bresee, Director of Admission. 757-884-9148. Fax: 757-884-9137. E-mail: RBrese@hra.org. Web site: www.hra.org.

HANALANI SCHOOLS

94-294 Anania Drive
Mililani, Hawaii 96789
Head of School: Mr. Mark Y. Sugimoto

General Information Coeducational day college-preparatory, arts, religious studies, bilingual studies, and technology school, affiliated with Christian faith. Grades PK–12. Founded: 1952. Setting: suburban. 6-acre campus. 6 buildings on campus. Approved or accredited by The Hawaii Council of Private Schools, Western Association of Schools and Colleges, and Hawaii Department of Education. Total enrollment: 769. Upper school average class size: 16. Upper school faculty-student ratio: 1:16. There are 175 required school days per year for Upper School students. Upper-School students typically attend 5 days per week. The average school day consists of 7 hours and 5 minutes.

Upper School Student Profile Grade 6: 59 students (30 boys, 29 girls); Grade 7: 58 students (32 boys, 26 girls); Grade 8: 63 students (35 boys, 28 girls); Grade 9: 61 students (36 boys, 25 girls); Grade 10: 63 students (31 boys, 32 girls); Grade 11: 51 students (26 boys, 25 girls); Grade 12: 46 students (23 boys, 23 girls). 98% of students are Christian faith.

Faculty School total: 62. In upper school: 18 men, 14 women; 10 have advanced degrees.

Subjects Offered Advanced math, Advanced Placement courses, algebra, American government, American literature, art, band, basketball, Bible, Bible studies, biology, British literature, calculus, calculus-AP, cheerleading, chemistry, chemistry-AP, choir, chorus, Christian doctrine, Christian ethics, computer skills, concert band, consumer mathematics, drafting, drama, earth science, English composition, English literature, English-AP, ethics, geography, geometry, golf, grammar, handbells, intro to computers, Japanese, Japanese as Second Language, Japanese studies, journalism, keyboarding, language development, leadership, Life of Christ, life science, music, paleontology, physical education, physical science, physics, piano, pre-algebra, pre-calculus, robotics, SAT preparation, sign language, Spanish, speech, student government, student publications, study skills, theology, transition mathematics, trigonometry, U.S. history, U.S. history-AP, video, voice, volleyball, world history, writing, yearbook.

Graduation Requirements Arts and fine arts (art, music, dance, drama), Bible, Bible studies, electives, English, foreign language, guidance, mathematics, physical education (includes health), science, social studies (includes history), technology. Community service is required.

Special Academic Programs Advanced Placement exam preparation; honors section; independent study; remedial reading and/or remedial writing; remedial math.

College Admission Counseling 48 students graduated in 2010; 47 went to college, including Chaminade University of Honolulu; Hawai'i Pacific University; Pacific University; University of California, Davis; University of California, Irvine; University of Hawaii at Manoa. Other: 1 went to work.

Student Life Upper grades have uniform requirement, student council, honor system. Discipline rests primarily with faculty. Attendance at religious services is required.

Summer Programs Remediation, enrichment, advancement, sports, art/fine arts, computer instruction programs offered; session focuses on enrichment and advancement; held both on and off campus; held at a variety of outdoor places; accepts boys and girls; open to students from other schools. 60 students usually enrolled. 2011 schedule: June 6 to July 15. Application deadline: May 15.

Tuition and Aid Day student tuition: $8600. Tuition installment plan (SMART Tuition Payment Plan, monthly payment plans, lump sum payment, biannual payment). Tuition reduction for siblings, need-based scholarship grants, student referral credit available. In 2010–11, 14% of upper-school students received aid. Total amount of financial aid awarded in 2010–11: $164,045.

Admissions Traditional secondary-level entrance grade is 9. For fall 2010, 98 students applied for upper-level admission, 88 were accepted, 69 enrolled. SAT or SSAT required. Deadline for receipt of application materials: none. Application fee required: $75. Interview required.

Athletics Interscholastic: archery (boys), baseball (b), basketball (b,g), bowling (b,g), cheering (g), cross-country running (b,g), football (b), golf (b,g), outdoor education (b,g), soccer (b,g), track and field (b,g), volleyball (b,g), water polo (b); intramural: basketball (b,g), fitness (b,g), flag football (b,g), football (b,g), physical fitness (b,g), soccer (b,g), strength & conditioning (b,g), table tennis (b,g), track and field (b,g), volleyball (b,g), weight lifting (b,g), weight training (b,g); coed intramural: indoor soccer, jump rope, kickball, ropes courses, touch football. 3 PE instructors, 2 coaches.

Computers Computers are regularly used in all academic, journalism, newspaper, science, social sciences, yearbook classes. Computer network features include on-campus library services, online commercial services, Internet access, wireless campus network, Internet filtering or blocking technology, desktop publishing applications, Ebsco, Moodle. Campus intranet and student e-mail accounts are available to students. Students grades are available online. The school has a published electronic and media policy.

Contact Ms. Nancy J. Cowley, Admissions Director. 808-625-0737 Ext. 456. Fax: 808-625-0691. E-mail: admissions@hanalani.org. Web site: www.hanalani.org.

HANK HANEY INTERNATIONAL JUNIOR GOLF ACADEMY

55 Hospital Center Common
Hilton Head Island, South Carolina 29926
Head of School: Tina Sprouse

General Information Coeducational boarding and day college-preparatory, arts, business, and bilingual studies school. Grades 5–PG. Founded: 1995. Setting: suburban. Nearest major city is Savannah, GA. Students are housed in single-sex cottages. 5-acre campus. 2 buildings on campus. Approved or accredited by South Carolina Department of Education. Candidate for accreditation by Southern Association of Colleges and Schools. Total enrollment: 140. Upper school average class size: 9. Upper school faculty-student ratio: 1:10. Upper School students typically attend 5 days per week. The average school day consists of 4 hours and 30 minutes.

Upper School Student Profile 95% of students are boarding students. 28 states are represented in upper school student body. 50% are international students. International students from Canada, Denmark, Japan, Mexico, Republic of Korea, and United Kingdom; 28 other countries represented in student body.

Faculty School total: 14. In upper school: 2 men, 12 women; 5 have advanced degrees.

Special Academic Programs Advanced Placement exam preparation; honors section; ESL.

Student Life Upper grades have specified standards of dress, student council, honor system. Discipline rests equally with students and faculty.

Summer Programs ESL, sports programs offered; session focuses on golf; held on campus; accepts boys and girls; open to students from other schools. 350 students usually enrolled. 2011 schedule: June 6 to August 12. Application deadline: June 1.

Tuition and Aid Day student tuition: $38,900; 7-day tuition and room/board: $51,900. Guaranteed tuition plan. Tuition installment plan (individually arranged payment plans). Tuition reduction for siblings, Sallie Mae loans available.

Admissions Deadline for receipt of application materials: none. Application fee required: $50. Interview recommended.

Athletics Interscholastic: golf (boys, girls). 13 coaches.

Computers Computer resources include Internet access, wireless campus network. Computer access in designated common areas is available to students. Students grades are available online.

Contact Matt Bashaw, Director of Admissions. 843-686-1500. Fax: 843-785-5116. E-mail: admissions@ijga.com. Web site: www.ijga.com.

HANSON MEMORIAL HIGH SCHOOL

903 Anderson Street
Franklin, Louisiana 70538-0000
Head of School: Dr. Vincent Miholic

General Information Coeducational day and distance learning college-preparatory, general academic, arts, business, vocational, religious studies, and technology school, affiliated with Roman Catholic Church. Grades 6–12. Distance learning grades 9–12. Founded: 1925. Setting: rural. Nearest major city is Lafayette. 14-acre campus. 4 buildings on campus. Approved or accredited by National Catholic Education Association, Southern Association of Colleges and Schools, and Louisiana Department of Education. Total enrollment: 275. Upper school average class size: 27. Upper school faculty-student ratio: 1:13. There are 178 required school days per year for Upper School students.

Upper School Student Profile 80% of students are Roman Catholic.

Faculty School total: 20. In upper school: 4 men, 16 women; 5 have advanced degrees.

Subjects Offered 3-dimensional art, 3-dimensional design, addiction, ADL skills, Advanced Placement courses, advanced studio art-AP, advanced TOEFL/grammar, advertising design, aerobics, aerospace education, aerospace science, aesthetics, African American history, African American studies, African dance, African drumming, African history, African literature, African studies, African-American history, African-American literature, African-American studies, agriculture, agroecology, Alabama history and geography, algebra, alternative physical education, American biography, American Civil War, American culture, American democracy, American foreign policy, American government, American history-AP, American legal systems, American literature-AP, American minority experience, American politics in film, American sign language, American studies, anatomy, anatomy and physiology, Ancient Greek, ancient history, ancient/medieval philosophy, animal behavior, animal husbandry, animal science, animation, anthropology, applied arts, applied music, applied skills, aquatics, Arabic, Arabic studies, archaeology, architectural drawing, architecture, area studies, art and culture, art appreciation, art education, art history, art history-AP, art in New York, art-AP, arts, arts and crafts, arts appreciation, ASB Leadership, Asian history, Asian literature, Asian studies, astronomy, astrophysics, athletic training, athletics, atomic theory, audio visual/media, audition methods, auto mechanics, automated accounting, aviation, backpacking, bacteriology, ballet, ballet technique, band, banking, basic imaging, basic language skills, Basic programming, basic skills, batik, biochemistry, bioethics, bioethics, DNA and culture, biology-AP, biotechnology, bivouac, Black history, boat building, boating, body human, Bolivian history, Bolivian social studies, bookbinding, bookkeeping, bookmaking, botany, bowling, brass choir, Brazilian history, Brazilian social studies, Brazilian studies, British history, British literature (honors), British literature-AP,

British National Curriculum, broadcast journalism, broadcasting, Broadway dance, Buddhism, business applications, business communications, business education, business law, business skills, business studies, cabinet making, calculus-AP, California writers, calligraphy, Canadian geography, Canadian history, Canadian law, Canadian literature, Cantonese, career and technology systems, career education, career education internship, career experience, career exploration, Career Passport, career planning, career technology, careers, Caribbean history, carpentry, cartography, cartooning/animation, celestial navigation, cell biology, Central and Eastern European history, ceramics, ceremonies of life, chamber groups, chaplaincy, chemistry-AP, Cherokee, Chesapeake Bay studies, Cheyenne history, Cheyenne language, child development, China/Japan history, Chinese, Chinese history, Chinese literature, Chinese studies, choral music, choreography, chorus, cinematography, circus acts, civics/free enterprise, civil rights, Civil War, classical Greek literature, classical language, classical music, classical studies, classics, clayworking, clinical chemistry, collage and assemblage, college counseling, college writing, Colorado ecology, comedy, Coming of Age in the 20th Century, commercial art, communication skills, communications, community garden, community service, comparative civilizations, comparative cultures, comparative government and politics, comparative government and politics-AP, comparative political systems-AP, comparative politics, comparative religion, competitive science projects, composition-AP, computer animation, computer applications, computer art, computer education, computer graphics, computer literacy, computer math, computer multimedia, computer music, computer processing, computer programming, computer programming-AP, computer resources, computer science, computer science-AP, computer studies, computer technologies, computer technology certification, computer tools, computer-aided design, computers, conceptual physics, concert band, concert bell choir, concert choir, conflict resolution, conservation, constitutional history of U.S., constitutional law, construction, consumer economics, consumer education, consumer law, consumer mathematics, contemporary art, contemporary issues, contemporary issues in science, contemporary math, contemporary problems, contemporary studies, contemporary technique, contemporary women writers, costumes and make-up, CPR, crafts, creation science, creative arts, creative dance, creative drama, criminal justice, criminology, critical studies in film, critical thinking, critical writing, culinary arts, cultural arts, cultural criticism, cultural geography, current events, dance, dance performance, Danish, data analysis, data processing, death and loss, debate, design, desktop publishing, desktop publishing, ESL, developmental language skills, developmental math, digital applications, digital art, digital imaging, digital music, digital photography, directing, discrete mathematics, diversity studies, DNA, DNA research, DNA science lab, drafting, drama workshop, dramatic arts, drawing, drawing and design, driver education, Dutch, early childhood, earth and space science, earth systems analysis, East Asian history, East European studies, Eastern religion and philosophy, Eastern world civilizations, Easterner in the West, ecology, environmental systems, economics, economics and history, economics-AP, education, Egyptian history, electronic imagery, electronic music, electronic publishing, electronic research, electronics, emergency medicine, emerging technology, engineering, English as a foreign language, English language and composition-AP, English language-AP, English literature and composition-AP, English literature-AP, English-AP, English/composition-AP, ensembles, entomology, entrepreneurship, environmental education, environmental geography, environmental science-AP, environmental studies, environmental systems, epic literature, equestrian sports, equine management, equine science, equitation, ESL, ESL, essential learning systems, ethical decision making, ethics, ethics and responsibility, ethnic literature, ethnic studies, ethology, etymology, European civilization, European history, European history-AP, European literature, eurythmics (guard), eurythmy, evolution, exercise science, existentialism, experiential education, experimental science, expository writing, expressive arts, fabric arts, family and consumer science, family living, family studies, Far Eastern history, Farsi, fashion, female experience in America, fencing, fiber arts, fiction, field ecology, Filipino, film, film and literature, film and new technologies, film appreciation, film history, film series, film studies, filmmaking, finance, fine arts, Finnish, first aid, fitness, flight instruction, folk art, folk dance, folk music, food and nutrition.

Special Academic Programs Study at local college for college credit.

College Admission Counseling 38 students graduated in 2010; 36 went to college, including Louisiana State University and Agricultural and Mechanical College; Nicholls State University. Other: 2 went to work.

Student Life Upper grades have uniform requirement, student council, honor system. Discipline rests primarily with faculty. Attendance at religious services is required.

Tuition and Aid Guaranteed tuition plan. Tuition installment plan (monthly payment plans). Tuition reduction for siblings, need-based scholarship grants available. In 2010–11, 10% of upper-school students received aid.

Admissions Traditional secondary-level entrance grade is 9. ACT required. Deadline for receipt of application materials: February. Application fee required. On-campus interview required.

Athletics Interscholastic: baseball (boys), basketball (b,g), cheering (b,g), cross-country running (b,g), drill team (g), football (b), golf (b,g), softball (g), strength & conditioning (b,g), track and field (b,g), weight lifting (b,g); intramural: tennis (b,g); coed interscholastic: cheering, cross-country running, golf; coed intramural: tennis. 7 coaches.

Computers Computers are regularly used in all academic classes. Computer network features include on-campus library services, online commercial services, Internet access, wireless campus network, Internet filtering or blocking technology. Students grades are available online. The school has a published electronic and media policy.

Hanson Memorial High School

Contact Mrs. Kim Adams, Dean of Students. 337-828-3487. Fax: 337-828-0787. E-mail: kadams@hansonmemorial.com. Web site: www.hansonmemorial.com.

HAPPY HILL FARM ACADEMY

3846 North Highway 144
Granbury, Texas 76048
Head of School: Dr. Marc Evans

General Information Coeducational boarding and day and distance learning college-preparatory, arts, and agriculture and horticulture school, affiliated with Christian faith. Grades K–12. Distance learning grade X. Founded: 1975. Setting: rural. Nearest major city is Dallas. Students are housed in single-sex residences. 500-acre campus. 1 building on campus. Approved or accredited by Association of Christian Schools International, Southern Association of Colleges and Schools, and The Association of Boarding Schools. Total enrollment: 125. Upper school average class size: 8. Upper school faculty-student ratio: 1:7. There are 186 required school days per year for Upper School students. Upper School students typically attend 5 days per week. The average school day consists of 6 hours and 30 minutes.

Upper School Student Profile 90% of students are boarding students. 80% are state residents. 8 states are represented in upper school student body. 2% are international students. International students from China, Hong Kong, Russian Federation, and Taiwan. 65% of students are Christian.

Faculty School total: 25. In upper school: 4 men, 17 women; 6 have advanced degrees; 7 reside on campus.

Subjects Offered 1½ elective credits, advanced math, Advanced Placement courses, agriculture, algebra, all academic, American history, American literature, animal husbandry, animal science, applied music, art, athletics, basketball, Bible, biology, calculus, cheerleading, chemistry, choir, classical music, computer education, computer literacy, computer skills, concert choir, desktop publishing, drawing, economics, economics-AP, electives, English, English literature, English-AP, fine arts, gardening, general math, general science, geometry, golf, government, government-AP, guitar, health, history, horticulture, instruments, journalism, language arts, library, life science, mathematics, mathematics-AP, music, music appreciation, music performance, music theory, newspaper, physical education, physics, pottery, pre-algebra, pre-calculus, science, scripture, social studies, Spanish, speech, sports, tennis, track and field, trigonometry, U.S. government, U.S. history, vocal ensemble, volleyball, weight training, woodworking, world history, yearbook.

Special Academic Programs Honors section; independent study; academic accommodation for the musically talented; ESL (6 students enrolled).

College Admission Counseling 11 students graduated in 2010; 10 went to college, including Southwestern University; Texas A&M University; Texas Christian University; Texas State University–San Marcos; United States Air Force Academy. Other: 1 entered military service.

Student Life Upper grades have uniform requirement, student council, honor system. Discipline rests primarily with faculty. Attendance at religious services is required.

Summer Programs Remediation, enrichment, ESL, sports, art/fine arts programs offered; session focuses on Enrichment; held on campus; accepts boys and girls; not open to students from other schools. 118 students usually enrolled. 2011 schedule: June 6 to July 15.

Tuition and Aid Day student tuition: $1200–$8000; 7-day tuition and room/board: $1200–$36,000. Tuition installment plan (monthly payment plans, individually arranged payment plans). Tuition reduction for siblings, need-based scholarship grants available. In 2010–11, 98% of upper-school students received aid.

Admissions Traditional secondary-level entrance grade is 10. Achievement tests, English for Non-native Speakers, Stanford Achievement Test or writing sample required. Deadline for receipt of application materials: none. Application fee required: $40. On-campus interview required.

Athletics Interscholastic: baseball (boys), basketball (b,g), cheering (g), cross-country running (b,g), football (b), golf (b,g), horseback riding (b,g), outdoor education (b,g), physical fitness (b,g), running (b,g), soccer (g), softball (g), strength & conditioning (b,g), tennis (b,g), track and field (b,g), volleyball (g), weight training (b,g). 2 PE instructors, 4 coaches.

Computers Computers are regularly used in computer applications, creative writing, desktop publishing, English, journalism, library, newspaper, yearbook classes. Computer resources include on-campus library services, Internet access, wireless campus network, Internet filtering or blocking technology. Computer access in designated common areas is available to students. Students grades are available online.

Contact Mr. Todd L. Shipman, President/Chief Financial Officer. 254-897-4822. Fax: 254-897-7650. E-mail: todd@happyhillfarm.org. Web site: www.happyhillfarm.org.

HARDING ACADEMY

Box 10775, Harding University
1529 East Park Avenue
Searcy, Arkansas 72149
Head of School: James Simmons

General Information Coeducational boarding and day college-preparatory, vocational, and religious studies school, affiliated with Church of Christ. Boarding grades 9–12, day grades K–12. Founded: 1924. Setting: small town. Nearest major city is Little Rock. Students are housed in single-sex dormitories. 15-acre campus. 1 building on campus. Approved or accredited by National Christian School Association, North Central Association of Colleges and Schools, and Arkansas Department of Education. Total enrollment: 589. Upper school average class size: 25. Upper school faculty-student ratio: 1:11. There are 180 required school days per year for Upper School students. Upper School students typically attend 5 days per week. The average school day consists of 7 hours and 25 minutes.

Upper School Student Profile Grade 7: 53 students (28 boys, 25 girls); Grade 8: 48 students (20 boys, 28 girls); Grade 9: 39 students (16 boys, 23 girls); Grade 10: 44 students (22 boys, 22 girls); Grade 11: 48 students (26 boys, 22 girls); Grade 12: 55 students (30 boys, 25 girls). 9% of students are boarding students. 91% are state residents. 2 states are represented in upper school student body. 9% are international students. International students from China and Japan. 78% of students are members of Church of Christ.

Faculty School total: 55. In upper school: 16 men, 12 women; 21 have advanced degrees; 1 resides on campus.

Subjects Offered Accounting, ACT preparation, advanced math, algebra, American history, anatomy, art, Bible, Bible studies, biology, calculus-AP, chemistry, chorus, civics, computer applications, computer programming, consumer education, English, English-AP, family living, geography, geometry, health, history, history-AP, human anatomy, journalism, keyboarding, life skills, mathematics, modern world history, music appreciation, physical education, physical science, physics-AP, pre-calculus, psychology, science, Spanish, speech, statistics, study skills, wellness.

Special Academic Programs Advanced Placement exam preparation; study at local college for college credit; academic accommodation for the gifted.

College Admission Counseling 52 students graduated in 2009; 50 went to college, including Arkansas State University—Jonesboro; Harding University; Henderson State University. Other: 2 went to work. Median composite ACT: 24.

Student Life Upper grades have specified standards of dress, student council, honor system. Discipline rests primarily with faculty. Attendance at religious services is required.

Tuition and Aid Day student tuition: $3250–$5250; 7-day tuition and room/board: $9500–$11,000. Tuition installment plan (monthly payment plans).

Admissions Traditional secondary-level entrance grade is 9. Any standardized test or TOEFL required. Deadline for receipt of application materials: none. Application fee required: $100. Interview recommended.

Athletics Interscholastic: baseball (boys), basketball (b,g), cheering (g), cross-country running (b,g), football (b), golf (b,g), softball (g), tennis (b,g), track and field (b,g), volleyball (g), weight lifting (b). 4 PE instructors, 8 coaches, 1 athletic trainer.

Computers Computers are regularly used in all academic classes. Computer network features include on-campus library services, Internet access. Students grades are available online. The school has a published electronic and media policy.

Contact Darren Mathews, Dean of High School. 501-279-7201. Fax: 501-279-7213. E-mail: dmathews@harding.edu. Web site: www.harding.edu/hacademy/.

HARDING ACADEMY

1100 Cherry Road
Memphis, Tennessee 38117
Head of School: Ms. Pamela Womack

General Information Coeducational day college-preparatory, arts, and religious studies school, affiliated with Church of Christ. Grades PS–12. Founded: 1952. Setting: suburban. 28-acre campus. 3 buildings on campus. Approved or accredited by National Christian School Association, Southern Association of Colleges and Schools, and Tennessee Department of Education. Endowment: $2 million. Total enrollment: 1,276. Upper school average class size: 19. Upper school faculty-student ratio: 1:13. There are 180 required school days per year for Upper School students. Upper School students typically attend 5 days per week. The average school day consists of 6 hours and 30 minutes.

Upper School Student Profile Grade 7: 92 students (47 boys, 45 girls); Grade 8: 89 students (42 boys, 47 girls); Grade 9: 77 students (36 boys, 41 girls); Grade 10: 100 students (55 boys, 45 girls); Grade 11: 105 students (56 boys, 49 girls); Grade 12: 65 students (27 boys, 38 girls). 47% of students are members of Church of Christ.

Faculty School total: 45. In upper school: 18 men, 27 women; 23 have advanced degrees.

Subjects Offered Accounting, algebra, American government, American history, American history-AP, American literature, art, art-AP, band, Bible, biology, biology-AP, British literature, British literature-AP, calculus-AP, chemistry, chorus, computer applications, concert band, drama, earth science, English, English language and composition-AP, English literature and composition-AP, etymology, French, geography, geometry, grammar, journalism, keyboarding, physical fitness, Spanish, Spanish language-AP, speech, statistics, world history.

Graduation Requirements Algebra, American government, American history, American literature, arts and fine arts (art, music, dance, drama), Bible, biology, British literature, English, fitness, foreign language, geometry, speech, world history.

Special Academic Programs 8 Advanced Placement exams for which test preparation is offered; honors section.

College Admission Counseling 98 students graduated in 2010; all went to college, including Harding University; Lipscomb University; The University of Tennessee;

The University of Tennessee at Chattanooga; University of Memphis. Mean SAT critical reading: 534, mean SAT math: 499, mean SAT writing: 540, mean composite ACT: 24.

Student Life Upper grades have uniform requirement, honor system. Discipline rests primarily with faculty. Attendance at religious services is required.

Summer Programs Remediation, enrichment, sports, art/fine arts, computer instruction programs offered; held on campus; accepts boys and girls; open to students from other schools.

Tuition and Aid Day student tuition: $9495–$10,395. Tuition installment plan (monthly payment plans, individually arranged payment plans). Tuition reduction for siblings, need-based scholarship grants available. In 2010–11, 18% of upper-school students received aid. Total amount of financial aid awarded in 2010–11: $191,824.

Admissions Traditional secondary-level entrance grade is 7. For fall 2010, 74 students applied for upper-level admission, 62 were accepted, 56 enrolled. Metropolitan Achievement Short Form and Otis-Lennon School Ability Test required. Deadline for receipt of application materials: none. Application fee required: $50. Interview required.

Athletics Interscholastic: baseball (boys), basketball (b,g), bowling (b,g), cheering (g), cross-country running (b,g), fitness (b,g), football (b), golf (b,g), soccer (b,g), softball (g), tennis (b,g), track and field (b,g), volleyball (g). 2 PE instructors, 45 coaches, 1 athletic trainer.

Computers Computers are regularly used in keyboarding classes. Computer network features include on-campus library services, online commercial services, Internet access. Students grades are available online. The school has a published electronic and media policy.

Contact Mrs. Karen Sills, Administrative Assistant in Admissions. 901-767-4494 Ext. 113. Fax: 901-763-4949. E-mail: sills.karen@hardinglions.org. Web site: www.hardinglions.org.

HARDING ACADEMY

170 Windsor Drive
Nashville, Tennessee 37205
Head of School: Ian Craig

General Information Coeducational day college-preparatory, general academic, arts, and technology school. Grades K–8. Founded: 1971. Setting: suburban. 15-acre campus. Approved or accredited by Southern Association of Colleges and Schools, Southern Association of Independent Schools, Tennessee Association of Independent Schools, and Tennessee Department of Education. Endowment: $2.2 million. Total enrollment: 480.

Upper School Student Profile Grade 6: 50 students (25 boys, 25 girls); Grade 7: 50 students (25 boys, 25 girls); Grade 8: 50 students (25 boys, 25 girls).

Faculty School total: 61.

Subjects Offered Algebra, art, chorus, civics, computers, dance, drama, English, French, history, jazz band, lab science, library, mathematics, music, physical education, pre-algebra, science.

Student Life Upper grades have specified standards of dress, honor system. Discipline rests primarily with faculty.

Tuition and Aid Day student tuition: $14,725. Tuition installment plan (Key Tuition Payment Plan, monthly payment plans). Need-based scholarship grants available.

Admissions Achievement/Aptitude/Writing, CTP III, ERB, Gates MacGinite (vocab) and Stanford Achievement Test (math), ISEE, Otis-Lennon School Ability Test or writing sample required. Deadline for receipt of application materials: December 1. Application fee required: $100. On-campus interview required.

Athletics Interscholastic: baseball (boys), basketball (b,g), cheering (g), football (b), lacrosse (b,g), soccer (b,g), tennis (b,g), track and field (b,g), volleyball (g), wrestling (b); coed interscholastic: cross-country running, diving, golf, swimming and diving; coed intramural: ballet, climbing, dance, floor hockey, Frisbee, indoor soccer, modern dance, table tennis, ultimate Frisbee. 4 PE instructors, 15 coaches.

Computers Computer resources include on-campus library services, online commercial services, Internet access, wireless campus network, Internet filtering or blocking technology. Campus intranet is available to students. Students grades are available online.

Contact Rebecca Arnold, Director of Admission and Financial Aid. 615-356-2974. Fax: 615-356-0441. E-mail: arnoldb@hardingacademy.org. Web site: www.hardingacademy.org.

HARGRAVE MILITARY ACADEMY

200 Military Drive
Chatham, Virginia 24531
Head of School: Col. Wheeler Baker, USMC (ret.), PhD

General Information Boys' boarding and day college-preparatory, general academic, arts, religious studies, technology, academic post-graduate, leadership and ethics, and military school, affiliated with Baptist General Association of Virginia. Grades 7–PG. Founded: 1909. Setting: small town. Nearest major city is Danville. Students are housed in single-sex dormitories. 276-acre campus. 13 buildings on campus. Approved or accredited by Southern Association of Colleges and Schools, The Association of Boarding Schools, and Virginia Association of Independent Schools. Member of National Association of Independent Schools. Endowment: $3.5

million. Total enrollment: 310. Upper school average class size: 11. Upper school faculty-student ratio: 1:12. Upper School students typically attend 5 days per week.

Upper School Student Profile 94% of students are boarding students. 24% are state residents. 31 states are represented in upper school student body. 10% are international students. International students from China, Egypt, Republic of Korea, and Venezuela; 8 other countries represented in student body. 20% of students are Baptist General Association of Virginia.

Faculty School total: 30. In upper school: 18 men, 12 women; all have advanced degrees; 12 reside on campus.

Subjects Offered 3-dimensional design, advanced biology, advanced chemistry, advanced math, Advanced Placement courses, algebra, American government, American history, American literature, art, astronomy, Bible studies, biology, calculus, chemistry, creative writing, debate, drama, driver education, English, English literature, environmental science, ESL, French, geography, geometry, government/civics, health, history, journalism, leadership, leadership and service, leadership education training, mathematics, media production, meteorology, physical education, physics, psychology, reading, religion, SAT/ACT preparation, science, social studies, sociology, Spanish, speech, study skills, TOEFL preparation, trigonometry.

Graduation Requirements Computer science, English, foreign language, mathematics, physical education (includes health), religion (includes Bible studies and theology), science, social studies (includes history).

Special Academic Programs Advanced Placement exam preparation; honors section; independent study; study at local college for college credit; remedial reading and/or remedial writing; remedial math; programs in general development for dyslexic students; special instructional classes for students with Attention Deficit Disorder; ESL (8 students enrolled).

College Admission Counseling 74 students graduated in 2010; all went to college, including The University of North Carolina at Charlotte; United States Military Academy; United States Naval Academy; Virginia Military Institute; Virginia Polytechnic Institute and State University.

Student Life Upper grades have uniform requirement, student council, honor system. Discipline rests equally with students and faculty. Attendance at religious services is required.

Summer Programs Remediation, enrichment, advancement, ESL, sports, rigorous outdoor training, computer instruction programs offered; session focuses on academics/sports camps; held on campus; accepts boys; open to students from other schools. 150 students usually enrolled. 2011 schedule: June 26 to July 23. Application deadline: June 25.

Tuition and Aid Day student tuition: $12,750; 5-day tuition and room/board: $30,800; 7-day tuition and room/board: $30,800. Tuition installment plan (monthly payment plans, individually arranged payment plans). Tuition reduction for siblings, merit scholarship grants, need-based scholarship grants, need-based loans, Sallie Mae available. In 2010–11, 32% of upper-school students received aid; total upper-school merit-scholarship money awarded: $150,000. Total amount of financial aid awarded in 2010–11: $525,000.

Admissions Traditional secondary-level entrance grade is 10. Math and English placement tests required. Deadline for receipt of application materials: none. Application fee required: $75. Interview recommended.

Athletics Interscholastic: aquatics, baseball, basketball, cross-country running, diving, football, golf, lacrosse, marksmanship, riflery, soccer, swimming and diving, tennis, wrestling; intramural: aquatics, backpacking, billiards, canoeing/kayaking, climbing, cross-country running, drill team, fishing, fitness, fitness walking, hiking/backpacking, independent competitive sports, jogging, jump rope, kayaking, lacrosse, life saving, marksmanship, mountaineering, Nautilus, outdoor activities, paint ball, physical fitness, physical training, rappelling, riflery, rock climbing, ropes courses, running, scuba diving, skeet shooting, skiing (downhill), strength & conditioning, swimming and diving, table tennis, tennis, trap and skeet, walking, water polo, weight lifting, weight training. 1 PE instructor, 10 coaches, 1 athletic trainer.

Computers Computers are regularly used in all academic classes. Computer network features include on-campus library services, online commercial services, Internet access, wireless campus network, Internet filtering or blocking technology. Campus intranet, student e-mail accounts, and computer access in designated common areas are available to students. Students grades are available online. The school has a published electronic and media policy.

Contact Mrs. Amy Walker, Director of Admissions. 434-432-2481 Ext. 2130. Fax: 434-432-3129. E-mail: admissions@hargrave.edu. Web site: www.hargrave.edu.

THE HARKER SCHOOL

500 Saratoga Avenue
San Jose, California 95129
Head of School: Christopher Nikoloff

General Information Coeducational day college-preparatory, arts, technology, and gifted students school. Grades K–12. Founded: 1893. Setting: urban. 16-acre campus. 7 buildings on campus. Approved or accredited by California Association of Independent Schools, Western Association of Schools and Colleges, and California Department of Education. Member of National Association of Independent Schools. Total enrollment: 1,750. Upper school average class size: 16. Upper school faculty-student ratio: 1:16. Upper School students typically attend 5 days per week.

The Harker School

Upper School Student Profile Grade 9: 179 students (99 boys, 80 girls); Grade 10: 178 students (87 boys, 91 girls); Grade 11: 174 students (95 boys, 79 girls); Grade 12: 164 students (78 boys, 86 girls).
Faculty School total: 192. In upper school: 39 men, 37 women; 59 have advanced degrees.
Subjects Offered Acting, advanced math, aerobics, algebra, American literature, anatomy and physiology, architecture, art history-AP, Asian history, Asian literature, astronomy, baseball, basketball, biology, biology-AP, British literature, British literature (honors), calculus-AP, ceramics, chemistry, chemistry-AP, choir, college counseling, community service, computer programming, computer science-AP, contemporary women writers, dance, dance performance, debate, discrete mathematics, drawing, ecology, economics, electronics, engineering, English literature and composition-AP, environmental science-AP, ethics, European history-AP, evolution, expository writing, fencing, film and literature, fitness, French, French language-AP, French literature-AP, golf, graphic arts, honors algebra, honors geometry, instrumental music, international affairs, Japanese, Latin, Latin-AP, linear algebra, literary magazine, macro/microeconomics-AP, macroeconomics-AP, Mandarin, medieval literature, mentorship program, music, music theory-AP, newspaper, orchestra, organic chemistry, painting, physics, physics-AP, play production, political thought, pre-calculus, psychology-AP, public policy, public speaking, radio broadcasting, robotics, scene study, sculpture, self-defense, Shakespeare, softball, Spanish, Spanish language-AP, Spanish literature-AP, statistics, stone carving, student government, studio art-AP, study skills, swimming, technical theater, tennis, theater arts, track and field, trigonometry, U.S. government and politics-AP, U.S. history, U.S. history-AP, video and animation, visual arts, vocal ensemble, volleyball, weight training, Western philosophy, women in world history, world history, wrestling, yearbook, yoga.
Graduation Requirements Algebra, arts and fine arts (art, music, dance, drama), biology, chemistry, computer science, English, foreign language, geometry, physical education (includes health), physics, public speaking, trigonometry, U.S. history, world history, 30 total hours of community service.
Special Academic Programs Advanced Placement exam preparation; honors section; independent study; academic accommodation for the gifted.
College Admission Counseling 166 students graduated in 2010; all went to college, including Harvard University; Stanford University; University of California, Berkeley; University of California, Los Angeles; University of California, San Diego; University of Southern California. Mean SAT critical reading: 693, mean SAT math: 715, mean SAT writing: 712.
Student Life Upper grades have specified standards of dress, student council, honor system. Discipline rests primarily with faculty.
Summer Programs Enrichment, advancement programs offered; session focuses on academics; held both on and off campus; held at venues abroad for upper school students; accepts boys and girls; open to students from other schools. 700 students usually enrolled. 2011 schedule: June 20 to August 12.

Tuition and Aid Day student tuition: $35,372. Need-based scholarship grants, need-based loans available. In 2010–11, 10% of upper-school students received aid.
Admissions Traditional secondary-level entrance grade is 9. ERB CTP IV, essay, ISEE or SSAT required. Deadline for receipt of application materials: January 14. Application fee required: $75. Interview required.
Athletics Interscholastic: baseball (boys), basketball (b,g), cross-country running (b,g), football (b), golf (b,g), lacrosse (g), soccer (b,g), softball (g), swimming and diving (b,g), tennis (b,g), track and field (b,g), volleyball (b,g), water polo (b,g), wrestling (b,g); coed interscholastic: cheering, football; coed intramural: aerobics/dance, dance, fencing, fitness, physical fitness, tennis, yoga. 4 PE instructors, 62 coaches, 1 athletic trainer.
Computers Computers are regularly used in all academic, graphic arts, newspaper, programming, yearbook classes. Computer network features include on-campus library services, online commercial services, Internet access, wireless campus network, Internet filtering or blocking technology, ProQuest, Gale Group, InfoTrac, Facts On File. Student e-mail accounts are available to students. The school has a published electronic and media policy.
Contact Ruth Tebo, Assistant to the Director of Admission. 408-249-2510. Fax: 408-984-2325. E-mail: rutht@harker.org. Web site: www.harker.org.

See Display below and Close-Up on page 786.

THE HARLEY SCHOOL

1981 Clover Street
Rochester, New York 14618
Head of School: Dr. Timothy Cottrell

General Information Coeducational day college-preparatory and arts school. Grades N–12. Founded: 1917. Setting: suburban. 25-acre campus. 3 buildings on campus. Approved or accredited by National Independent Private Schools Association and New York State Association of Independent Schools. Member of National Association of Independent Schools. Endowment: $8.5 million. Total enrollment: 492. Upper school average class size: 7. Upper school faculty-student ratio: 1:7. Upper School students typically attend 5 days per week. The average school day consists of 6 hours and 50 minutes.
Upper School Student Profile Grade 9: 32 students (17 boys, 15 girls); Grade 10: 37 students (14 boys, 23 girls); Grade 11: 46 students (24 boys, 22 girls); Grade 12: 45 students (19 boys, 26 girls).
Faculty School total: 90. In upper school: 14 men, 14 women; 28 have advanced degrees.
Subjects Offered 3-dimensional art, Advanced Placement courses, algebra, American history, anthropology, art, art history, art-AP, band, biology, calculus, calculus-AP, ceramics, chamber groups, chemistry, Chinese, choir, chorus, community

service, comparative government and politics-AP, computer graphics, computer math, computer programming, computer science, creative writing, debate, desktop publishing, drama, drawing, driver education, economics AP, English, English language and composition-AP, English literature, environmental science, ethics, European history, expository writing, film, fine arts, foreign language, French, gardening, geometry, graphic arts, Greek, health, jazz band, language-AP, Latin, mathematics, multimedia, music, music theory, orchestra, organic gardening, outdoor education, photography, physical education, physics, psychology, SAT preparation, science, Shakespeare, social studies, Spanish, speech, student government, study skills, theater, theater arts, theater production, U.S. history-AP, voice, world history, writing, yoga.

Graduation Requirements Arts and fine arts (art, music, dance, drama), computer science, English, foreign language, internship, mathematics, physical education (includes health), science, social studies (includes history), participation in team sports. Community service is required.

Special Academic Programs 17 Advanced Placement exams for which test preparation is offered; honors section; independent study; study abroad.

College Admission Counseling 42 students graduated in 2010; all went to college, including Carnegie Mellon University; Cornell University; New York University; Pomona College; Rhode Island School of Design; University of Rochester. Mean SAT critical reading: 619, mean SAT math: 607, mean SAT writing: 590.

Student Life Upper grades have student council, honor system. Discipline rests primarily with faculty.

Summer Programs Remediation, enrichment, sports, art/fine arts, computer instruction programs offered; session focuses on day camp, outdoor skills, swimming, tennis, writing, college prep; held both on and off campus; held at field house, classrooms, grounds, field trips; accepts boys and girls; open to students from other schools. 125 students usually enrolled. 2011 schedule: June 6 to July 29. Application deadline: May.

Tuition and Aid Day student tuition: $16,850–$19,500. Tuition installment plan (Insured Tuition Payment Plan, Key Tuition Payment Plan, monthly payment plans, 2-payment plan, prepaid discount plan). Tuition reduction for siblings, need-based scholarship grants available. In 2010–11, 36% of upper-school students received aid.

Admissions Traditional secondary-level entrance grade is 9. For fall 2010, 28 students applied for upper-level admission, 23 were accepted, 21 enrolled. Essay and Math Placement Exam required. Deadline for receipt of application materials: none. Application fee required: $50. On-campus interview required.

Athletics Interscholastic: baseball (boys), basketball (b,g), bowling (b,g), golf (b), skiing (downhill) (b,g), soccer (b,g), softball (b,g), swimming and diving (b,g), tennis (b,g), track and field (b,g), volleyball (b,g); coed interscholastic: cross-country running, outdoor education, running, yoga. 3 PE instructors, 11 coaches.

Computers Computers are regularly used in all academic, art classes. Computer network features include Internet access, wireless campus network. The school has a published electronic and media policy.

Contact Ms. Valerie Myntti, Director of Admissions. 585-442-1770. Fax: 585-442-5758. E-mail: vmyntti@harleyschool.org. Web site: www.harleyschool.org.

HARMONY HEIGHTS RESIDENTIAL AND DAY SCHOOL

Oyster Bay, New York
See Special Needs Schools section.

HARRELLS CHRISTIAN ACADEMY

360 Tomahawk Highway
PO Box 88
Harrells, North Carolina 28444
Head of School: Dr. Ronald L. Montgomery

General Information Coeducational day college-preparatory, arts, religious studies, and technology school, affiliated with Christian faith. Grades K–12. Founded: 1969. Setting: rural. Nearest major city is Wilmington. 32-acre campus. 7 buildings on campus. Approved or accredited by North Carolina Association of Independent Schools, Southern Association of Colleges and Schools, Southern Association of Independent Schools, and North Carolina Department of Education. Total enrollment: 452. Upper school average class size: 13. Upper school faculty-student ratio: 1:9. There are 179 required school days per year for Upper School students. Upper School students typically attend 5 days per week. The average school day consists of 6 hours and 32 minutes.

Upper School Student Profile Grade 9: 40 students (20 boys, 20 girls); Grade 10: 33 students (19 boys, 14 girls); Grade 11: 40 students (24 boys, 16 girls); Grade 12: 33 students (19 boys, 14 girls). 96% of students are Christian.

Faculty School total: 17. In upper school: 5 men, 11 women; 5 have advanced degrees.

Subjects Offered Algebra, animal science, art, art education, biology, biotechnology, botany, British literature, calculus, ceramics, chemistry, computer art, earth science, English, English language and composition-AP, English literature, English literature and composition-AP, government/civics, history, journalism, keyboarding, Latin, mathematics, photography, physical education, physical science, religion, social studies, Spanish, weightlifting, yearbook.

Graduation Requirements Biology, computer applications, electives, English, environmental science, foreign language, mathematics, physical education (includes health), physical science, religious studies, social studies (includes history). Community service is required.

Special Academic Programs 2 Advanced Placement exams for which test preparation is offered; honors section; study at local college for college credit; programs in English, mathematics, general development for dyslexic students.

College Admission Counseling 40 students graduated in 2010; all went to college, including East Carolina University; North Carolina State University; The University of North Carolina at Chapel Hill; The University of North Carolina Wilmington. Median SAT critical reading: 480, median SAT math: 480, median SAT writing: 490, median combined SAT: 1420, median composite ACT: 20. 16% scored over 600 on SAT critical reading, 1% scored over 600 on SAT writing, 15% scored over 26 on composite ACT.

Student Life Upper grades have specified standards of dress, student council, honor system. Discipline rests primarily with faculty. Attendance at religious services is required.

Tuition and Aid Day student tuition: $7470. Tuition installment plan (FACTS Tuition Payment Plan, individually arranged payment plans). Tuition reduction for siblings available. In 2010–11, 10% of upper-school students received aid. Total amount of financial aid awarded in 2010–11: $27,800.

Admissions Traditional secondary-level entrance grade is 9. For fall 2010, 14 students applied for upper-level admission, 13 were accepted, 12 enrolled. Admissions testing and Iowa Tests of Basic Skills required. Deadline for receipt of application materials: none. Application fee required: $35. On-campus interview required.

Athletics Interscholastic: baseball (boys), basketball (b,g), cheering (g), football (b), soccer (b,g), softball (g), tennis (g), volleyball (g); coed interscholastic: golf, swimming and diving; coed intramural: basketball. 1 PE instructor, 1 coach.

Computers Computers are regularly used in art, computer applications, English, journalism, keyboarding, yearbook classes. Computer network features include Internet access, Internet filtering or blocking technology. The school has a published electronic and media policy.

Contact Mrs. Susan Frederick, Administrative Assistant. 910-532-4575 Ext. 221. Fax: 910-532-2958. E-mail: sfrederick@harrellsca.org. Web site: www.harrellschristianacademy.com.

THE HARRISBURG ACADEMY

10 Erford Road
Wormleysburg, Pennsylvania 17043
Head of School: Dr. James Newman

General Information Coeducational day college-preparatory and arts school. Grades N–12. Founded: 1784. Setting: suburban. Nearest major city is Harrisburg. 23-acre campus. 1 building on campus. Approved or accredited by International Baccalaureate Organization, Middle States Association of Colleges and Schools, Pennsylvania Association of Independent Schools, and Pennsylvania Department of Education. Member of National Association of Independent Schools. Endowment: $4 million. Total enrollment: 416. Upper school average class size: 9. Upper school faculty-student ratio: 1:8. There are 172 required school days per year for Upper School students. Upper School students typically attend 5 days per week. The average school day consists of 7 hours.

Upper School Student Profile Grade 9: 25 students (13 boys, 12 girls); Grade 10: 33 students (14 boys, 19 girls); Grade 11: 30 students (17 boys, 13 girls); Grade 12: 35 students (17 boys, 18 girls).

Faculty School total: 60. In upper school: 8 men, 13 women; 9 have advanced degrees.

Subjects Offered Advanced Placement courses, algebra, American history, American literature, art, biology, business skills, calculus, ceramics, chemistry, computer science, creative writing, drama, economics, English, English literature, environmental science, European history, expository writing, fine arts, French, geography, geometry, grammar, health, history, International Baccalaureate courses, Latin, mathematics, music, philosophy, physical education, physics, psychology, science, social studies, Spanish, speech, typing, world history, world literature, writing.

Graduation Requirements Arts and fine arts (art, music, dance, drama), business skills (includes word processing), college planning, English, foreign language, mathematics, physical education (includes health), public speaking, science, social studies (includes history). Community service is required.

Special Academic Programs International Baccalaureate program; Advanced Placement exam preparation; honors section; independent study; study at local college for college credit.

College Admission Counseling 21 students graduated in 2009; all went to college, including Dickinson College; Drexel University; Penn State University Park; Syracuse University; University of Pittsburgh; University of Richmond. 50% scored over 600 on SAT critical reading, 50% scored over 600 on SAT math.

Student Life Upper grades have specified standards of dress, student council, honor system. Discipline rests primarily with faculty.

Tuition and Aid Day student tuition: $15,626. Tuition installment plan (Insured Tuition Payment Plan, monthly payment plans). Need-based scholarship grants, need-based loans available. In 2009–10, 8% of upper-school students received aid. Total amount of financial aid awarded in 2009–10: $450,811.

The Harrisburg Academy

Admissions Traditional secondary-level entrance grade is 9. Admissions testing required. Deadline for receipt of application materials: none. Application fee required: $65. On-campus interview required.

Athletics Interscholastic: basketball (boys, girls), field hockey (g), golf (b), lacrosse (b), soccer (b,g), tennis (b,g); coed interscholastic: swimming and diving; coed intramural: cross-country running, skiing (downhill). 3 PE instructors, 18 coaches, 1 athletic trainer.

Computers Computers are regularly used in art, English, mathematics, music, science classes. Computer network features include on-campus library services, Internet access, wireless campus network, Internet filtering or blocking technology. Campus intranet and student e-mail accounts are available to students. Students grades are available online. The school has a published electronic and media policy.

Contact Mrs. Jessica Warren, Director of Admissions. 717-763-7811 Ext. 313. Fax: 717-975-0894. E-mail: warren.j@harrisburgacademy.org. Web site: www.harrisburgacademy.org.

HARROW SCHOOL

5 High Street
Harrow on the Hill
Middlesex HAI 3HT, United Kingdom
Head of School: Barnaby J. Lenon

General Information Boys' boarding college-preparatory school, affiliated with Church of England (Anglican). Grades 9–13. Founded: 1572. Setting: suburban. Nearest major city is London, United Kingdom. Students are housed in individual or double rooms. 250-acre campus. 50 buildings on campus. Approved or accredited by Boarding Schools Association (UK). Language of instruction: English. Total enrollment: 820. Upper school average class size: 10. Upper school faculty-student ratio: 1:8.

Upper School Student Profile Grade 9: 160 students (160 boys); Grade 10: 160 students (160 boys); Grade 11: 160 students (160 boys); Grade 12: 175 students (175 boys); Grade 13: 175 students (175 boys). 100% of students are boarding students. 20% are international students. International students from Australia, China, Germany, Malaysia, Republic of Korea, and United States; 32 other countries represented in student body. 70% of students are members of Church of England (Anglican).

Faculty School total: 100. In upper school: 85 men, 15 women; all reside on campus.

Subjects Offered Advanced chemistry, advanced math, algebra, ancient history, Arabic, art, art history, Bible studies, biology, British literature, business studies, calculus, calculus-AP, career education internship, ceramics, character education, chemistry, chemistry-AP, computer science, creative writing, drama, ecology, economics, English, English literature, European history, French, geography, geometry, German, grammar, Greek, history, Italian, Japanese, Latin, mathematics, music, photography, physics, religion, Spanish, statistics, theater, trigonometry, zoology.

Graduation Requirements Completion of at least three advanced level (AP) courses.

Special Academic Programs Advanced Placement exam preparation; academic accommodation for the gifted, the musically talented, and the artistically talented; programs in general development for dyslexic students; ESL (15 students enrolled).

College Admission Counseling 160 students graduated in 2010.

Student Life Upper grades have uniform requirement, honor system. Discipline rests primarily with faculty.

Summer Programs ESL, sports programs offered; session focuses on English as a foreign language; held on campus; accepts boys and girls; open to students from other schools. 800 students usually enrolled. 2011 schedule: July 20 to August 20. Application deadline: March 18.

Tuition and Aid 7-day tuition and room/board: £30,000. Tuition installment plan (individually arranged payment plans). Tuition reduction for siblings, bursaries, merit scholarship grants available. In 2010–11, 20% of upper-school students received aid.

Admissions Traditional secondary-level entrance grade is 12. For fall 2010, 200 students applied for upper-level admission, 26 were accepted, 26 enrolled. Cognitive Abilities Test and common entrance examinations required. Deadline for receipt of application materials: January. Application fee required: £250. On-campus interview required.

Athletics Interscholastic: alpine skiing, archery, badminton, ball hockey, basketball, biathlon, climbing, cricket, croquet, cross-country running, equestrian sports, fencing, field hockey, fishing, fitness, Fives, fly fishing, golf, hockey, indoor soccer, jogging, judo, life saving, marksmanship, martial arts, physical fitness, physical training, pistol, polo, riflery, rock climbing, rugby, running, sailing, scuba diving, skiing (downhill), soccer, squash, strength & conditioning, swimming and diving, table tennis, tennis, track and field, triathlon, volleyball, wall climbing, water polo, weight training, winter soccer; intramural: alpine skiing, archery, backpacking, badminton, biathlon, canoeing/kayaking, climbing, cricket, croquet, cross-country running, drill team, fencing, field hockey, fishing, fly fishing, golf, hiking/backpacking, hockey, independent competitive sports, jogging, kayaking, life saving, marksmanship, martial arts, mountaineering, outdoor adventure, physical fitness, rock climbing, rugby, running, soccer, squash, strength & conditioning, swimming and diving, tennis, track and field, wall climbing, water polo, weight training. 1 PE instructor, 8 coaches, 2 athletic trainers.

Computers Computers are regularly used in all academic classes. Computer network features include on-campus library services, online commercial services, Internet access, wireless campus network, Internet filtering or blocking technology. Student e-mail accounts are available to students. Students grades are available online. The school has a published electronic and media policy.

Contact Mr. Rob Taylor, Registrar. 44-208-8728007. Fax: 44-208-8728012. E-mail: admissions@harrowschool.org.uk. Web site: www.harrowschool.org.uk.

HARVARD-WESTLAKE SCHOOL

3700 Coldwater Canyon
North Hollywood, California 91604
Head of School: Thomas C. Hudnut

General Information Coeducational day college-preparatory school, affiliated with Episcopal Church. Grades 7–12. Founded: 1989. Setting: urban. Nearest major city is Los Angeles. 26-acre campus. 12 buildings on campus. Approved or accredited by Western Association of Schools and Colleges. Member of National Association of Independent Schools. Endowment: $39.5 million. Total enrollment: 1,609. Upper school average class size: 16. Upper school faculty-student ratio: 1:8. Upper School students typically attend 5 days per week. The average school day consists of 6 hours and 35 minutes.

Upper School Student Profile Grade 10: 297 students (152 boys, 145 girls); Grade 11: 296 students (158 boys, 138 girls); Grade 12: 282 students (154 boys, 128 girls).

Faculty School total: 122. In upper school: 72 men, 50 women; 85 have advanced degrees.

Subjects Offered 3-dimensional art, advanced studio art-AP, algebra, American history, American literature, American literature-AP, anatomy, architecture, art, art history, art history-AP, Asian studies, astronomy, biology, biology-AP, calculus, calculus-AP, ceramics, chemistry, chemistry-AP, Chinese, choreography, chorus, classics, community service, comparative government and politics-AP, computer animation, computer programming, computer science, computer science-AP, creative writing, dance, drama, drawing, economics, economics-AP, electronics, English, English language and composition-AP, English literature, English literature-AP, environmental science, environmental science-AP, European history, expository writing, film, film studies, fine arts, French, French language-AP, French literature-AP, geography, geology, geometry, government and politics-AP, government/civics, grammar, health, human development, human geography—AP, Japanese, jazz, journalism, Latin, Latin-AP, logic, macro/microeconomics-AP, Mandarin, mathematics, music, music history, music theory-AP, oceanography, orchestra, painting, photography, physical education, physics, physics-AP, physiology, political science, pre-calculus, psychology, Russian, science, senior project, Shakespeare, social studies, Spanish, Spanish language-AP, Spanish literature-AP, statistics, statistics-AP, studio art-AP, technical theater, theater, trigonometry, U.S. government and politics-AP, U.S. history-AP, video, women's studies, world history, world history-AP, world literature, yearbook, zoology.

Graduation Requirements English, foreign language, history, human development, mathematics, performing arts, physical education (includes health), science, visual arts. Community service is required.

Special Academic Programs 30 Advanced Placement exams for which test preparation is offered; honors section; independent study; term-away projects; study at local college for college credit; study abroad; academic accommodation for the gifted, the musically talented, and the artistically talented.

College Admission Counseling 280 students graduated in 2010; 278 went to college, including Columbia University; Cornell University; New York University; University of Michigan; University of Pennsylvania; University of Southern California. Other: 2 had other specific plans. Mean SAT critical reading: 663, mean SAT math: 681, mean SAT writing: 676. 90% scored over 600 on SAT critical reading, 91% scored over 600 on SAT math.

Student Life Upper grades have specified standards of dress, student council, honor system. Discipline rests primarily with faculty.

Summer Programs Enrichment, sports, art/fine arts, rigorous outdoor training, computer instruction programs offered; session focuses on enrichment and sports; held on campus; accepts boys and girls; open to students from other schools. 500 students usually enrolled. 2011 schedule: June 13 to August 12. Application deadline: none.

Tuition and Aid Day student tuition: $29,200. Tuition installment plan (monthly payment plans, semiannual payment plan, triennial payment plan). Need-based scholarship grants, short-term loans (payable by end of year in which loan is made) available. In 2010–11, 16% of upper-school students received aid. Total amount of financial aid awarded in 2010–11: $6,846,600.

Admissions Traditional secondary-level entrance grade is 10. For fall 2010, 56 students applied for upper-level admission, 17 were accepted, 15 enrolled. ISEE required. Deadline for receipt of application materials: January 24. Application fee required: $200. On-campus interview required.

Athletics Interscholastic: baseball (boys), basketball (b,g), cross-country running (b,g), field hockey (g), football (b), golf (b,g), gymnastics (g), lacrosse (b), soccer (b,g), softball (g), swimming and diving (b,g), tennis (b,g), track and field (b,g), volleyball (b,g), water polo (b,g), wrestling (b); coed interscholastic: diving, equestrian sports, fencing, martial arts; coed intramural: badminton. 6 PE instructors, 32 coaches, 3 athletic trainers.

Computers Computers are regularly used in art, foreign language, history, mathematics, music, science classes. Computer resources include on-campus library services, Internet access, wireless campus network, music composition and editing, foreign language lab, science lab. Campus intranet, student e-mail accounts, and computer access in designated common areas are available to students. Students grades are available online.

Contact Elizabeth Gregory, Director of Admission. 310-274-7281. Fax: 310-288-3212. E-mail: egregory@hw.com. Web site: www.harvardwestlake.com.

THE HARVEY SCHOOL
260 Jay Street
Katonah, New York 10536
Head of School: Mr. Barry W. Fenstermacher

General Information Coeducational boarding and day and distance learning college-preparatory school. Boarding grades 9–12, day grades 6–12. Distance learning grades 6–12. Founded: 1916. Setting: suburban. Students are housed in single-sex dormitories. 125-acre campus. 14 buildings on campus. Approved or accredited by New York State Association of Independent Schools. Member of National Association of Independent Schools. Endowment: $1.9 million. Total enrollment: 330. Upper school average class size: 12. Upper school faculty-student ratio: 1:7. There are 165 required school days per year for Upper School students. Upper School students typically attend 5 days per week. The average school day consists of 8 hours and 50 minutes.

Upper School Student Profile Grade 9: 69 students (40 boys, 29 girls); Grade 10: 56 students (32 boys, 24 girls); Grade 11: 65 students (37 boys, 28 girls); Grade 12: 63 students (34 boys, 29 girls). 7% of students are boarding students. 75% are state residents. 3 states are represented in upper school student body.

Faculty School total: 64. In upper school: 22 men, 20 women; 22 have advanced degrees; 16 reside on campus.

Subjects Offered Algebra, American history, American literature, art, art history, biology, calculus, ceramics, chemistry, composition AP, computer programming-AP, creative writing, drama, English, English literature, European history, expository writing, fine arts, French, general science, geology, geometry, government/civics, grammar, Greek, history, Japanese, Latin, mathematics, music, photography, physics, religion, science, social studies, Spanish, theater, trigonometry, world history, writing.

Graduation Requirements Arts and fine arts (art, music, dance, drama), computer literacy, English, foreign language, mathematics, science, social sciences, social studies (includes history).

Special Academic Programs 11 Advanced Placement exams for which test preparation is offered; honors section; independent study.

College Admission Counseling 55 students graduated in 2010; all went to college, including Barnard College; Bentley University; Cornell University; University of Connecticut; Villanova University.

Student Life Upper grades have specified standards of dress, student council. Discipline rests primarily with faculty.

Summer Programs Remediation, advancement programs offered; session focuses on on-line academic course; held off campus; held at via distance learning; accepts boys and girls; open to students from other schools. 20 students usually enrolled. 2011 schedule: June 20 to August 10. Application deadline: May 1.

Tuition and Aid Day student tuition: $31,700; 5-day tuition and room/board: $7000. Tuition installment plan (FACTS Tuition Payment Plan, individually arranged payment plans). Need-based scholarship grants available. In 2010–11, 28% of upper-school students received aid. Total amount of financial aid awarded in 2010–11: $1,965,000.

Admissions Traditional secondary-level entrance grade is 9. For fall 2010, 140 students applied for upper-level admission, 70 were accepted, 46 enrolled. Deadline for receipt of application materials: none. Application fee required: $50. Interview required.

Athletics Interscholastic: baseball (boys), basketball (b,g), football (b), ice hockey (b), lacrosse (b,g), rugby (b), soccer (b,g), softball (g), volleyball (g); coed interscholastic: baseball, cross-country running, dance, figure skating, fitness, golf, tennis, weight lifting, yoga; coed intramural: aerobics, fitness walking, Frisbee, mountain biking. 1 athletic trainer.

Computers Computers are regularly used in English, foreign language, history, mathematics, science classes. Computer resources include on-campus library services, online commercial services, Internet access. The school has a published electronic and media policy.

Contact Mr. William Porter, Director of Admissions. 914-232-3161 Ext. 113. Fax: 914-232-6034. E-mail: wporter@harveyschool.org. Web site: www.harveyschool.org.

HATHAWAY BROWN SCHOOL
19600 North Park Boulevard
Shaker Heights, Ohio 44122
Head of School: H. William Christ

General Information Coeducational day (boys' only in lower grades) college-preparatory school. Boys grade PS, girls grades PS–12. Founded: 1876. Setting: suburban. Nearest major city is Cleveland. 18-acre campus. 1 building on campus. Approved or accredited by Independent Schools Association of the Central States and Ohio Association of Independent Schools. Member of National Association of Independent Schools. Endowment: $31.8 million. Total enrollment: 860. Upper school

average class size: 13. Upper school faculty-student ratio: 1:8. Upper School students typically attend 5 days per week. The average school day consists of 7 hours and 17 minutes.

Upper School Student Profile Grade 9: 91 students (91 girls); Grade 10: 85 students (85 girls); Grade 11: 93 students (93 girls); Grade 12: 82 students (82 girls).

Faculty School total: 129. In upper school: 18 men, 43 women; 32 have advanced degrees.

Subjects Offered Advanced Placement courses, algebra, American history, American literature, anatomy, art, art history, biology, biology-AP, calculus, ceramics, chemistry, chemistry-AP, communications, community service, computer math, computer programming, computer science, creative writing, dance, drama, economics, engineering, English, English literature, environmental science, ethics, European history, expository writing, fine arts, French, geography, geometry, government/civics, graphic design, health, history, international relations, journalism, Latin, mathematics, microbiology, music, outdoor education, photography, physical education, physics, physics-AP, physiology, psychology, research seminar, science, social studies, Spanish, statistics, statistics-AP, theater, trigonometry, U.S. history, U.S. history-AP, woodworking, world history, writing.

Graduation Requirements Arts and fine arts (art, music, dance, drama), computer applications, computer science, English, foreign language, history, mathematics, physical education (includes health), science, senior speech, senior project.

Special Academic Programs 16 Advanced Placement exams for which test preparation is offered; honors section; independent study; term-away projects; study at local college for college credit; study abroad; academic accommodation for the gifted and the musically talented; remedial reading and/or remedial writing; remedial math; programs in general development for dyslexic students; special instructional classes for deaf students.

College Admission Counseling 85 students graduated in 2009; all went to college, including Bates College; Brown University; Columbia College; Miami University; Yale University. Mean SAT critical reading: 633, mean SAT math: 631, mean SAT writing: 653, mean combined SAT: 1917.

Student Life Upper grades have specified standards of dress, student council, honor system. Discipline rests equally with students and faculty.

Tuition and Aid Day student tuition: $3530–$22,880. Tuition installment plan (Academic Management Services Plan, Key Tuition Payment Plan). Need-based scholarship grants available. In 2009–10, 30% of upper-school students received aid. Total amount of financial aid awarded in 2009–10: $3,100,000.

Admissions Traditional secondary-level entrance grade is 9. For fall 2009, 130 students applied for upper-level admission, 25 enrolled. ISEE required. Deadline for receipt of application materials: none. Application fee required: $35. Interview required.

Athletics Interscholastic: basketball, cross-country running, diving, field hockey, golf, lacrosse, soccer, softball, swimming and diving, tennis, track and field, volleyball; intramural: modern dance, outdoor adventure, physical fitness, ropes courses, strength & conditioning. 6 PE instructors, 22 coaches, 1 athletic trainer.

Computers Computers are regularly used in all academic classes. Computer network features include on-campus library services, online commercial services, Internet access, wireless campus network, Internet filtering or blocking technology. Student e-mail accounts and computer access in designated common areas are available to students. The school has a published electronic and media policy.

Contact Ms. Denise Burks, Administrative Assistant. 216-932-4214 Ext. 244. Fax: 216-397-0992. E-mail: dburks@hb.edu. Web site: www.hb.edu.

THE HAVERFORD SCHOOL
450 Lancaster Avenue
Haverford, Pennsylvania 19041
Head of School: Dr. Joseph T. Cox

General Information Boys' day college-preparatory and arts school. Grades PK–12. Founded: 1884. Setting: suburban. Nearest major city is Philadelphia. 32-acre campus. 7 buildings on campus. Approved or accredited by Middle States Association of Colleges and Schools, Pennsylvania Association of Independent Schools, and Pennsylvania Department of Education. Member of National Association of Independent Schools and Secondary School Admission Test Board. Endowment: $32.5 million. Total enrollment: 981. Upper school average class size: 16. Upper school faculty-student ratio: 1:7. Upper School students typically attend 5 days per week.

Upper School Student Profile Grade 9: 109 students (109 boys); Grade 10: 100 students (100 boys); Grade 11: 92 students (92 boys); Grade 12: 97 students (97 boys).

Faculty School total: 117. In upper school: 36 men, 11 women; 31 have advanced degrees.

Subjects Offered Algebra, American history, American literature, animal behavior, art, astronomy, biology, calculus, ceramics, chemistry, Chinese, Chinese studies, drama, ecology, economics, economics and history, English, English literature, European history, fine arts, French, geology, geometry, German, government/civics, history, Latin, mathematics, music, photography, physical education, physics, physiology, science, social studies, Spanish, statistics, theater, trigonometry, world affairs, world history, world literature.

Graduation Requirements Arts and fine arts (art, music, dance, drama), English, foreign language, mathematics, physical education (includes health), science, social studies (includes history).

The Haverford School

Special Academic Programs Honors section; independent study; term-away projects; academic accommodation for the gifted; remedial reading and/or remedial writing; remedial math.

College Admission Counseling 96 students graduated in 2010; 94 went to college, including Cornell University; Franklin & Marshall College; Penn State University Park; Princeton University; University of Pennsylvania; University of Pittsburgh. Other: 1 entered a postgraduate year, 1 had other specific plans. Mean SAT critical reading: 630, mean SAT math: 640, mean SAT writing: 640, mean combined SAT: 1910, mean composite ACT: 26. 41% scored over 600 on SAT critical reading, 48% scored over 600 on SAT math, 42% scored over 600 on SAT writing.

Student Life Upper grades have specified standards of dress, student council, honor system. Discipline rests equally with students and faculty.

Tuition and Aid Day student tuition: $29,900. Tuition installment plan (Insured Tuition Payment Plan, monthly payment plans, individually arranged payment plans). Merit scholarship grants, need-based scholarship grants available. In 2010–11, 31% of upper-school students received aid; total upper-school merit-scholarship money awarded: $20,000. Total amount of financial aid awarded in 2010–11: $2,117,550.

Admissions Traditional secondary-level entrance grade is 9. For fall 2010, 162 students applied for upper-level admission, 78 were accepted, 52 enrolled. ISEE, SSAT or Wechsler Intelligence Scale for Children required. Deadline for receipt of application materials: none. Application fee required: $50. Interview required.

Athletics Interscholastic: aquatics, baseball, basketball, crew, cross-country running, football, golf, ice hockey, indoor track, lacrosse, rowing, soccer, squash, swimming and diving, tennis, track and field, water polo, winter (indoor) track, wrestling; intramural: fitness, physical fitness, physical training, soccer, strength & conditioning, weight training. 6 PE instructors, 2 coaches, 2 athletic trainers.

Computers Computers are regularly used in art, English, history, mathematics, music, science classes. Computer network features include on-campus library services, online commercial services, Internet access. Computer access in designated common areas is available to students. Students grades are available online. The school has a published electronic and media policy.

Contact Mr. Kevin P. Seits, Director of Admissions and Tuition Assistance. 610-642-3020 Ext. 1457. Fax: 610-642-8724. E-mail: kseits@haverford.org. Web site: www.haverford.org.

HAWAIIAN MISSION ACADEMY

1438 Pensacola Street
Honolulu, Hawaii 96822
Head of School: Mr. Hugh P. Winn

General Information Coeducational boarding and day college-preparatory, general academic, arts, business, religious studies, bilingual studies, and technology school, affiliated with Seventh-day Adventist Church. Grades 9–12. Founded: 1895. Setting: urban. Students are housed in single-sex by floor dormitories. 4-acre campus. 4 buildings on campus. Approved or accredited by The Hawaii Council of Private Schools, Western Association of Schools and Colleges, and Hawaii Department of Education. Total enrollment: 110. Upper school average class size: 25. Upper school faculty-student ratio: 1:15. The average school day consists of 6 hours and 50 minutes.

Upper School Student Profile Grade 9: 25 students (17 boys, 8 girls); Grade 10: 31 students (19 boys, 12 girls); Grade 11: 27 students (10 boys, 17 girls); Grade 12: 30 students (16 boys, 14 girls). 20% of students are boarding students. 46% are state residents. 2 states are represented in upper school student body. 50% are international students. International students from Hong Kong, Japan, Republic of Korea, and Taiwan. 80% of students are Seventh-day Adventists.

Faculty School total: 13. In upper school: 8 men, 5 women; 9 have advanced degrees; 2 reside on campus.

Subjects Offered Algebra, anatomy and physiology, art, Bible, biology, business, business education, business skills, calculus, chemistry, choir, Christianity, community service, computer literacy, computer science, conceptual physics, concert choir, desktop publishing, digital art, economics, electives, English, English literature, ESL, family and consumer science, family living, general science, geometry, grammar, Hawaiian history, health, independent living, interactive media, journalism, keyboarding, lab science, library, Microsoft, personal finance, physical education, pre-algebra, pre-calculus, Spanish, student government, student publications, U.S. government, U.S. history, video film production, weight training, work experience, work-study, world history, yearbook.

Graduation Requirements Algebra, arts and fine arts (art, music, dance, drama), biology, chemistry, computer literacy, English, foreign language, geometry, Hawaiian history, keyboarding, physical education (includes health), physics, practical arts, religion (includes Bible studies and theology), social studies (includes history), U.S. government, work experience, world history, 25 hours of community service per year, 100 hours of work experience throughout the 4 years combined.

Special Academic Programs Honors section; ESL (8 students enrolled).

College Admission Counseling 23 students graduated in 2010; 22 went to college, including Kapiolani Community College; La Sierra University; Pacific Union College; University of Hawaii at Manoa. Other: 1 entered military service. Mean SAT critical reading: 505, mean SAT math: 535.

Student Life Upper grades have uniform requirement, student council. Discipline rests primarily with faculty.

Tuition and Aid Day student tuition: $10,245; 7-day tuition and room/board: $11,120. Tuition installment plan (Insured Tuition Payment Plan, monthly payment plans, individually arranged payment plans). Tuition reduction for siblings, need-based scholarship grants, paying campus jobs available. In 2010–11, 25% of upper-school students received aid.

Admissions Placement test and TOEFL required. Deadline for receipt of application materials: none. Application fee required: $25. Interview recommended.

Athletics Interscholastic: basketball (boys, girls), golf (b,g), volleyball (b,g). 2 PE instructors, 6 coaches.

Computers Computers are regularly used in desktop publishing, economics, graphic arts, journalism, keyboarding, media production, newspaper, publications, science, video film production, word processing, yearbook classes. Computer network features include on-campus library services, Internet access, wireless campus network. Students grades are available online.

Contact Mrs. Nenny Safotu, Registrar. 808-536-2207 Ext. 202. Fax: 808-524-3294. E-mail: registrar@hawaiianmissionacademy.org. Web site: www.hawaiianmissionacademy.org.

HAWAII BAPTIST ACADEMY

2429 Pali Highway
Honolulu, Hawaii 96817
Head of School: Richard Bento

General Information Coeducational day college-preparatory and Christian education school, affiliated with Southern Baptist Convention. Grades K–12. Founded: 1949. Setting: urban. 13-acre campus. 6 buildings on campus. Approved or accredited by Western Association of Schools and Colleges. Member of National Association of Independent Schools and Secondary School Admission Test Board. Endowment: $4 million. Total enrollment: 1,099. Upper school average class size: 20. Upper school faculty-student ratio: 1:12. There are 176 required school days per year for Upper School students. Upper School students typically attend 5 days per week. The average school day consists of 6 hours.

Upper School Student Profile Grade 9: 131 students (70 boys, 61 girls); Grade 10: 117 students (56 boys, 61 girls); Grade 11: 112 students (53 boys, 59 girls); Grade 12: 110 students (63 boys, 47 girls). 14% of students are Southern Baptist Convention.

Faculty School total: 78. In upper school: 17 men, 21 women; 23 have advanced degrees.

Subjects Offered Advanced Placement courses, algebra, American history, American history-AP, American literature, analytic geometry, ancient world history, art, Asian history, astronomy, Basic programming, Bible studies, biology, biology-AP, British literature, calculus-AP, ceramics, chemistry, chemistry-AP, Chinese, Christian education, Christian ethics, Christian studies, communication skills, computer applications, concert band, drama, drama performance, drawing, earth science, economics, English, English language and composition-AP, English literature, English literature-AP, fine arts, forensics, French, geography, geometry, Hawaiian history, Japanese, journalism, marine biology, mathematics, mechanical drawing, modern world history, music, music theory-AP, photography, physical education, physics, physics-AP, political science, psychology, psychology-AP, religion, science, social studies, Spanish, speech, statistics, statistics-AP, trigonometry, world history, world literature, writing.

Graduation Requirements Algebra, arts and fine arts (art, music, dance, drama), Asian history, Bible studies, biology, communication skills, computer applications, economics, English, foreign language, Hawaiian history, mathematics, physical education (includes health), political science, science, social studies (includes history).

Special Academic Programs Advanced Placement exam preparation; independent study.

College Admission Counseling 102 students graduated in 2010; all went to college, including Creighton University; George Fox University; Hawai'i Pacific University; Oregon State University; Saint Louis University; University of Hawaii at Manoa. Mean SAT critical reading: 542, mean SAT math: 599, mean SAT writing: 551, mean combined SAT: 1692, mean composite ACT: 24.

Student Life Upper grades have uniform requirement, student council. Discipline rests primarily with faculty. Attendance at religious services is required.

Summer Programs Remediation, enrichment, sports, art/fine arts, computer instruction programs offered; session focuses on academic/social preparation for entrance to regular school, instruction/remediation, and personal growth; held both on and off campus; held at various recreation sites; accepts boys and girls; open to students from other schools. 315 students usually enrolled. 2011 schedule: June 13 to July 18. Application deadline: May 13.

Tuition and Aid Day student tuition: $12,090. Guaranteed tuition plan. Tuition installment plan (Insured Tuition Payment Plan, monthly payment plans). Need-based scholarship grants available. In 2010–11, 11% of upper-school students received aid. Total amount of financial aid awarded in 2010–11: $192,133.

Admissions Traditional secondary-level entrance grade is 9. For fall 2010, 70 students applied for upper-level admission, 31 were accepted, 19 enrolled. Achievement tests and SSAT required. Deadline for receipt of application materials: January 31. Application fee required: $60. On-campus interview required.

Athletics Interscholastic: aquatics (boys, girls), baseball (b), basketball (b,g), bowling (b,g), canoeing/kayaking (b,g), cheering (g), cross-country running (b,g), diving (b,g), football (b), golf (b,g), judo (b,g), kayaking (b,g), riflery (b,g), soccer (b,g), softball (g), swimming and diving (b,g), tennis (b,g), track and field (b,g), volleyball (b,g), water polo (b,g), wrestling (b,g); coed interscholastic: canoeing/kayaking, cheering, golf, sailing. 3 PE instructors, 30 coaches, 2 athletic trainers.

Computers Computers are regularly used in keyboarding, newspaper, programming, word processing, yearbook classes. Computer resources include Internet access, Internet filtering or blocking technology. The school has a published electronic and media policy.

Contact Mrs. Katherine Lee, Director of Admissions. 808-595-7585. Fax: 808-564-0332. E-mail: klee@hba.net. Web site: www.hba.net.

HAWAI'I PREPARATORY ACADEMY

65-1692 Kohala Mountain Road
Kamuela, Hawaii 96743-8476
Head of School: Mr. Lindsay Barnes Jr.

General Information Coeducational boarding and day college-preparatory school. Boarding grades 6–PG, day grades K–12. Founded: 1949. Setting: small town. Nearest major city is Kona. Students are housed in single-sex by floor dormitories and single-sex dormitories. 220-acre campus. 22 buildings on campus. Approved or accredited by The Association of Boarding Schools and Western Association of Schools and Colleges. Member of National Association of Independent Schools and Secondary School Admission Test Board. Endowment: $16.4 million. Total enrollment: 575. Upper school average class size: 12.

Upper School Student Profile 50% of students are boarding students. 14 states are represented in upper school student body. 20% are international students.

Subjects Offered 3-dimensional art, advanced computer applications, Advanced Placement courses, algebra, American literature, art history-AP, astronomy, band, biology, biology-AP, calculus, calculus-AP, ceramics, chemistry, chemistry-AP, choir, composition-AP, computer literacy, creative writing, digital photography, drama, drama performance, drawing, driver education, economics, English, environmental science, environmental science-AP, ESL, film, fine arts, forensics, French, French-AP, geology, geometry, guitar, Hawaiian history, honors world history, instrumental music, Japanese, literary genres, literature-AP, marine biology, math applications, mathematics, music theory, orchestra, photography, physical education, physical science, physics, physics-AP, pre-calculus, probability and statistics, psychology, psychology-AP, robotics, science research, Spanish, Spanish-AP, statistics-AP, strings, studio art, theater production, trigonometry, U.S. history, U.S. history-AP, video film production, visual arts, vocal music, Web site design, world cultures, world history, world history-AP, world literature, yearbook.

Graduation Requirements Arts and fine arts (art, music, dance, drama), electives, English, mathematics, modern languages, science, social studies (includes history), sports, technology.

Special Academic Programs Advanced Placement exam preparation; honors section; independent study; ESL (15 students enrolled).

Student Life Upper grades have specified standards of dress, student council, honor system. Discipline rests equally with students and faculty.

Tuition and Aid Day student tuition: $19,200; 7-day tuition and room/board: $37,900. Guaranteed tuition plan. Tuition installment plan (Key Tuition Payment Plan, monthly payment plans, prepayment plan, 2-payment plan). Need-based scholarship grants, Hawaii residential boarding grants available. In 2009–10, 36% of upper-school students received aid. Total amount of financial aid awarded in 2009–10: $1,500,000.

Admissions Traditional secondary-level entrance grade is 9. Any standardized test, ISEE or SSAT required. Deadline for receipt of application materials: February 1. Application fee required: $25. Interview required.

Athletics Interscholastic: baseball (boys), basketball (b,g), cross-country running (b,g), ocean paddling (b,g), soccer (b,g), softball (g), swimming and diving (b,g), tennis (b,g), track and field (b,g), volleyball (b,g), water polo (g); wrestling (b,g); intramural: baseball (b); coed interscholastic: dressage, football, golf, horseback riding; coed intramural: badminton, basketball, dance, dressage, golf, horseback riding, scuba diving, soccer, strength & conditioning, surfing, swimming and diving, tennis, ultimate Frisbee, volleyball, weight lifting, yoga. 1 athletic trainer.

Computers Computers are regularly used in computer applications, digital applications, science, video film production, yearbook classes. Computer network features include on-campus library services, online commercial services, Internet access, wireless campus network, Internet filtering or blocking technology. Campus intranet, student e-mail accounts, and computer access in designated common areas are available to students. Students grades are available online. The school has a published electronic and media policy.

Contact Mr. Joshua D. Clark, Director of Admission. 808-881-4074. Fax: 808-881-4003. E-mail: admissions@hpa.edu. Web site: www.hpa.edu/.

HAWKEN SCHOOL

12465 County Line Road
PO Box 8002
Gates Mills, Ohio 44040-8002
Head of School: D. Scott Looney

General Information Coeducational day college-preparatory, arts, business, STEMM (Science, Technology, Engineering, Math, Medicine), and writing school. Grades PS–12. Founded: 1915. Setting: suburban. Nearest major city is Cleveland. 325-acre campus. 5 buildings on campus. Approved or accredited by Independent Schools Association of the Central States, Ohio Association of Independent Schools, and Ohio Department of Education. Member of National Association of Independent Schools. Endowment: $36.1 million. Total enrollment: 942. Upper school average class size: 15. Upper school faculty-student ratio: 1:9. Upper School students typically attend 5 days per week. The average school day consists of 4 hours and 33 minutes.

Upper School Student Profile Grade 9: 112 students (64 boys, 48 girls); Grade 10: 103 students (53 boys, 50 girls); Grade 11: 117 students (59 boys, 58 girls); Grade 12: 93 students (45 boys, 48 girls).

Faculty School total: 115. In upper school: 35 men, 22 women; 42 have advanced degrees.

Subjects Offered 20th century world history, accounting, acting, advanced chemistry, advanced math, Advanced Placement courses, advanced studio art-AP, African-American literature, algebra, American Civil War, American history, American history-AP, American literature, animal science, art, art appreciation, art history, band, Bible as literature, biology, botany, business, business mathematics, calculus, calculus-AP, ceramics, chemistry, chemistry-AP, Chinese, choir, choral music, chorus, Civil War, classical Greek literature, community service, computer applications, computer math, computer programming, computer science, computer science-AP, computer skills, concert band, creative dance, creative writing, dance, dance performance, drama, drawing, driver education, ecology, economics, economics and history, electronic music, English, English literature, English-AP, environmental science-AP, ethics, European history, field ecology, film, film studies, fine arts, first aid, French, French studies, French-AP, geography, geometry, government/civics, grammar, graphic design, health, history, history of jazz, history of rock and roll, Holocaust and other genocides, humanities, improvisation, Latin, Latin-AP, mathematics, mathematics-AP, music, music theory, outdoor education, painting, performing arts, philosophy, photography, physical education, physics, physics-AP, physiology, poetry, probability and statistics, qualitative analysis, science, science research, sculpture, senior project, social sciences, social studies, Spanish, Spanish literature-AP, speech, statistics-AP, strings, studio art-AP, swimming, theater, theater arts, theater design and production, theater production, trigonometry, U.S. history, U.S. history-AP, world history, world literature, World War I, World War II, writing.

Graduation Requirements Arts and fine arts (art, music, dance, drama), computer science, English, foreign language, history, mathematics, physical education (includes health), science. Community service is required.

Special Academic Programs Advanced Placement exam preparation; honors section; accelerated programs; independent study; term-away projects; study at local college for college credit; study abroad; academic accommodation for the gifted and the musically talented.

College Admission Counseling 116 students graduated in 2010; all went to college, including Case Western Reserve University; Miami University; Southern Methodist University; The Ohio State University; University of Michigan; University of Pennsylvania. Median SAT critical reading: 610, median SAT math: 635, median SAT writing: 625, median combined SAT: 1245, median composite ACT: 27. 58% scored over 600 on SAT critical reading, 72% scored over 600 on SAT math, 62% scored over 600 on SAT writing, 60% scored over 1800 on combined SAT, 63% scored over 26 on composite ACT.

Student Life Upper grades have specified standards of dress, student council, honor system. Discipline rests equally with students and faculty.

Summer Programs Remediation, enrichment, advancement, computer instruction programs offered; session focuses on credit, review, preview and enrichment in English, math, computer studies, and health; held on campus; accepts boys and girls; open to students from other schools. 100 students usually enrolled. 2011 schedule: June 13 to July 22. Application deadline: none.

Tuition and Aid Day student tuition: $24,371–$26,146. Tuition installment plan (Key Tuition Payment Plan, installment payment plan (60 percent by 8/15 and 40 percent by 1/15), AchieverLoans (Key Education Resources)). Merit scholarship grants, need-based scholarship grants, need-based loans available. In 2010–11, 33% of upper-school students received aid; total upper-school merit-scholarship money awarded: $96,000. Total amount of financial aid awarded in 2010–11: $2,600,000.

Admissions Traditional secondary-level entrance grade is 9. For fall 2010, 119 students applied for upper-level admission, 90 were accepted, 58 enrolled. ISEE required. Deadline for receipt of application materials: December 17. Application fee required: $25. On-campus interview required.

Athletics Interscholastic: baseball (boys), basketball (b,g), cross-country running (b,g), diving (b,g), field hockey (g), football (b), golf (b,g), lacrosse (b,g), soccer (b,g), softball (g), swimming and diving (b,g), tennis (b,g), track and field (b,g); intramural: basketball (b); coed intramural: dance, drill team, outdoor skills. 3 PE instructors, 33 coaches, 1 athletic trainer.

Computers Computers are regularly used in all classes. Computer network features include on-campus library services, Internet access, wireless campus network, Internet filtering or blocking technology. Campus intranet and student e-mail accounts are available to students. Students grades are available online. The school has a published electronic and media policy.

Contact Heather Daly, Director of Admission and Financial Assistance. 440-423-2955. Fax: 440-423-2994. E-mail: hdaly@hawken.edu. Web site: www.hawken.edu/.

HAWTHORNE CHRISTIAN ACADEMY
2000 Route 208
Hawthorne, New Jersey 07506
Head of School: Mr. Donald J. Klingen
General Information Coeducational day college-preparatory, arts, religious studies, technology, music, and missions school, affiliated with Christian faith, Christian faith. Grades PS–12. Founded: 1981. Setting: suburban. Nearest major city is New York, NY. 22-acre campus. 4 buildings on campus. Approved or accredited by Association of Christian Schools International, Middle States Association of Colleges and Schools, and New Jersey Department of Education. Total enrollment: 456. Upper school average class size: 21. Upper school faculty-student ratio: 1:7. There are 180 required school days per year for Upper School students. Upper School students typically attend 5 days per week. The average school day consists of 6 hours and 40 minutes.
Upper School Student Profile Grade 9: 43 students (22 boys, 21 girls); Grade 10: 39 students (14 boys, 25 girls); Grade 11: 32 students (14 boys, 18 girls); Grade 12: 29 students (20 boys, 9 girls). 100% of students are Christian faith, Christian.
Faculty School total: 60. In upper school: 10 men, 12 women; 6 have advanced degrees.
Subjects Offered Accounting, advanced computer applications, Advanced Placement courses, algebra, anatomy and physiology, art and culture, band, Basic programming, bell choir, Bible, biology, business applications, calculus, calculus-AP, chemistry, choir, choral music, chorus, composition, computer information systems, computer programming, computers, contemporary issues, creative writing, current events, drama, electives, English literature, English literature-AP, ensembles, foreign language, geometry, government, guidance, handbells, health, home economics, information technology, instrumental music, instruments, intro to computers, law, mathematics, music, music history, music theory, physical education, physical science, physics, politics, pre-calculus, psychology, Spanish, Spanish-AP, studio art, U.S. government, U.S. government and politics-AP, U.S. history-AP, video, visual arts, voice, Web site design, world history, yearbook.
Graduation Requirements Algebra, Bible, biology, chemistry, English literature, English literature-AP, geometry, intro to computers, mathematics, physical education (includes health), physical science, pre-calculus, Spanish, U.S. government, U.S. history, U.S. history-AP, world history, Christian service hours, Apologetics and Current Issues, specified number of Academic Elective Courses.
College Admission Counseling 45 students graduated in 2010; 41 went to college, including Liberty University; Montclair State University; New Jersey Institute of Technology; Philadelphia Biblical University; Ramapo College of New Jersey; William Paterson University of New Jersey. Mean SAT critical reading: 569, mean SAT math: 534, mean SAT writing: 601, mean combined SAT: 1103.
Student Life Upper grades have specified standards of dress, student council. Discipline rests primarily with faculty. Attendance at religious services is required.
Tuition and Aid Day student tuition: $10,030. Tuition installment plan (monthly payment plans). Tuition reduction for siblings, merit scholarship grants, need-based scholarship grants, pastoral discounts, teacher/employee discounts available. In 2010–11, 51% of upper-school students received aid; total upper-school merit-scholarship money awarded: $20,500. Total amount of financial aid awarded in 2010–11: $26,124.
Admissions Traditional secondary-level entrance grade is 9. Admissions testing, Otis-Lennon School Ability Test or WRAT required. Deadline for receipt of application materials: none. Application fee required: $100. On-campus interview required.
Athletics Interscholastic: baseball (boys), basketball (b,g), soccer (b,g), softball (g), strength & conditioning (b), volleyball (g); coed interscholastic: bowling, cross-country running, golf, track and field. 2 PE instructors.
Computers Computers are regularly used in business applications, computer applications, information technology, introduction to technology, lab/keyboard, library, technology, Web site design, yearbook classes. Computer network features include on-campus library services, Internet access, Internet filtering or blocking technology. Campus intranet is available to students. Students grades are available online. The school has a published electronic and media policy.
Contact Mrs. Judith De Boer, Admissions Coordinator. 973-423-3331 Ext. 261. Fax: 973-238-1718. E-mail: jdeboer@hca.org.

HAWTHORN SCHOOL FOR GIRLS
101 Scarsdale Road
North York, Ontario M3B 2R2, Canada
General Information Girls' day college-preparatory school, affiliated with Roman Catholic Church. Grades PS–12. Founded: 1989. Setting: urban. Nearest major city is Toronto, Canada. 1 building on campus. Approved or accredited by Canadian Educational Standards Institute, Conference of Independent Schools of Ontario, and Ontario Department of Education. Language of instruction: English. Total enrollment: 145.
Upper School Student Profile 75% of students are Roman Catholic.
Faculty School total: 40.
College Admission Counseling 5 students graduated in 2010; all went to college.
Student Life Upper grades have uniform requirement, student council, honor system. Discipline rests primarily with faculty.

Tuition and Aid Day student tuition: CAN$14,800. Need-based scholarship grants available.
Admissions Traditional secondary-level entrance grade is 7. Deadline for receipt of application materials: none. Application fee required: CAN$100. Interview required.
Computers Computer resources include Internet access. Computer access in designated common areas is available to students. The school has a published electronic and media policy.
Contact 416-444-3054. Fax: 416-449-2891. Web site: www.hawthornschool.com.

HEAD-ROYCE SCHOOL
4315 Lincoln Avenue
Oakland, California 94602
Head of School: Robert Lake
General Information Coeducational day college-preparatory, arts, technology, and STEM, robotics school. Grades K–12. Founded: 1887. Setting: urban. 14-acre campus. 8 buildings on campus. Approved or accredited by California Association of Independent Schools, Western Association of Schools and Colleges, and California Department of Education. Member of National Association of Independent Schools. Endowment: $15 million. Total enrollment: 815. Upper school average class size: 16. Upper school faculty-student ratio: 1:9. There are 175 required school days per year for Upper School students. Upper School students typically attend 5 days per week. The average school day consists of 7 hours.
Upper School Student Profile Grade 9: 92 students (50 boys, 42 girls); Grade 10: 80 students (43 boys, 37 girls); Grade 11: 83 students (39 boys, 44 girls); Grade 12: 84 students (34 boys, 50 girls).
Faculty School total: 95. In upper school: 24 men, 19 women; 29 have advanced degrees.
Subjects Offered Algebra, American history, American literature, art, art history, astronomy, biology, calculus, ceramics, chemistry, Chinese, community service, computer programming, computer science, creative writing, debate, drama, ecology, English, English literature, European history, expository writing, fine arts, French, geometry, graphic arts, health, history, journalism, Latin, marine biology, mathematics, music, neurobiology, photography, physical education, physics, psychology, science, social studies, Spanish, theater, trigonometry, typing, video, world history, world literature, writing.
Graduation Requirements Art history, arts and fine arts (art, music, dance, drama), computer science, English, foreign language, mathematics, physical education (includes health), science, social studies (includes history), 40 hours of community service.
Special Academic Programs 20 Advanced Placement exams for which test preparation is offered; honors section; independent study; term-away projects; study at local college for college credit; study abroad; academic accommodation for the gifted, the musically talented, and the artistically talented.
College Admission Counseling 85 students graduated in 2010; all went to college, including Dartmouth College; University of California, Davis; University of California, Los Angeles; University of Michigan; University of Southern California; Yale University. Mean SAT critical reading: 650, mean SAT math: 661, mean SAT writing: 664.
Student Life Upper grades have specified standards of dress, student council, honor system. Discipline rests primarily with faculty.
Summer Programs Remediation, enrichment, advancement programs offered; session focuses on sports and enrichment; held on campus; accepts boys and girls; open to students from other schools. 600 students usually enrolled. 2011 schedule: June 20 to July 29. Application deadline: February.
Tuition and Aid Day student tuition: $29,200. Tuition installment plan (SMART Tuition Payment Plan, monthly payment plans). Need-based scholarship grants, paying campus jobs, tuition remission for children of faculty and staff available. In 2010–11, 27% of upper-school students received aid. Total amount of financial aid awarded in 2010–11: $1,652,800.
Admissions Traditional secondary-level entrance grade is 9. For fall 2010, 179 students applied for upper-level admission, 83 were accepted, 28 enrolled. ISEE or SSAT required. Deadline for receipt of application materials: January 13. Application fee required: $100. On-campus interview required.
Athletics Interscholastic: baseball (boys), basketball (b,g), cross-country running (b,g), dance squad (g), golf (b,g), lacrosse (b), modern dance (g), outdoor education (b,g), physical fitness (b,g), soccer (b,g), softball (g), strength & conditioning (b,g), swimming and diving (b,g), tennis (b,g), volleyball (b,g), weight lifting (b,g), weight training (b,g); coed interscholastic: cross-country running, golf, outdoor education, physical fitness, strength & conditioning, swimming and diving; coed intramural: bicycling, dance, ultimate Frisbee. 6 PE instructors, 39 coaches.
Computers Computers are regularly used in all academic, English, graphics, mathematics, science, yearbook classes. Computer network features include on-campus library services, online commercial services, Internet access, wireless campus network, laptop carts, smartboards. Student e-mail accounts and computer access in designated common areas are available to students. Students grades are available online. The school has a published electronic and media policy.
Contact Catherine Epstein, Director of Admissions. 510-531-1300. Fax: 510-530-8329. E-mail: cepstein@headroyce.org. Web site: www.headroyce.org.

HEBREW ACADEMY-THE FIVE TOWNS

635 Central Avenue
Cedarhurst, New York 11516

Head of School: Ms. Naomi Lippman

General Information Coeducational day college-preparatory, arts, business, and religious studies school, affiliated with Jewish faith. Grades 9–12. Founded: 1978. Setting: suburban. Nearest major city is New York. 1 building on campus. Approved or accredited by Middle States Association of Colleges and Schools, The College Board, and New York Department of Education. Languages of instruction: English and Hebrew. Total enrollment: 488. Upper school average class size: 20. The average school day consists of 9 hours and 15 minutes.

Upper School Student Profile 100% of students are Jewish.

Faculty School total: 60.

Subjects Offered Advanced Placement courses, arts, English, fine arts, foreign language, Jewish studies, Judaic studies, mathematics, physical education, religion, science, social sciences, social studies.

Graduation Requirements Arts and fine arts (art, music, dance, drama), English, foreign language, Judaic studies, mathematics, physical education (includes health), religion (includes Bible studies and theology), science, social sciences, social studies (includes history).

Special Academic Programs 11 Advanced Placement exams for which test preparation is offered; honors section; independent study; study abroad; academic accommodation for the artistically talented.

College Admission Counseling 95 students graduated in 2010; all went to college, including Columbia University; New York University; Queens College of the City University of New York; State University of New York at Binghamton; University of Maryland, College Park; Yeshiva University. Median SAT critical reading: 590, median SAT math: 610, median SAT writing: 570. 48% scored over 600 on SAT critical reading, 56% scored over 600 on SAT math, 41% scored over 600 on SAT writing.

Student Life Upper grades have specified standards of dress, student council, honor system. Discipline rests primarily with faculty. Attendance at religious services is required.

Tuition and Aid Tuition installment plan (monthly payment plans, individually arranged payment plans). Need-based scholarship grants available.

Admissions Traditional secondary-level entrance grade is 9. Board of Jewish Education Entrance Exam required. Deadline for receipt of application materials: March 15. Application fee required. On-campus interview required.

Athletics Interscholastic: baseball (boys, girls), basketball (b,g), field hockey (b), softball (b,g), tennis (b,g), volleyball (g); coed intramural: skiing (downhill). 2 PE instructors, 8 coaches.

Computers Computers are regularly used in computer applications classes. Computer resources include on-campus library services, online commercial services, Internet access, Internet filtering or blocking technology. Student e-mail accounts are available to students. The school has a published electronic and media policy.

Contact Ms. Naomi Lippman, Principal, General Studies. 516-569-3807. Fax: 516-374-5761. Web site: www.haftr.org.

HEBRON ACADEMY

PO Box 309
Hebron, Maine 04238

Head of School: Mr. John J. King

General Information Coeducational boarding and day college-preparatory, arts, business, religious studies, technology, creative writing, and honors and AP courses school. Boarding grades 9–PG, day grades 6–PG. Founded: 1804. Setting: rural. Nearest major city is Portland. Students are housed in single-sex dormitories. 1,500-acre campus. 22 buildings on campus. Approved or accredited by Independent Schools of Northern New England, New England Association of Schools and Colleges, The Association of Boarding Schools, and Maine Department of Education. Member of National Association of Independent Schools and Secondary School Admission Test Board. Endowment: $13 million. Total enrollment: 256. Upper school average class size: 12. Upper school faculty-student ratio: 1:7. There are 175 required school days per year for Upper School students. Upper School students typically attend 5 days per week. The average school day consists of 7 hours and 15 minutes.

Upper School Student Profile Grade 9: 32 students (20 boys, 12 girls); Grade 10: 46 students (29 boys, 17 girls); Grade 11: 64 students (30 boys, 34 girls); Grade 12: 64 students (50 boys, 14 girls); Postgraduate: 8 students (8 boys). 70% of students are boarding students. 50% are state residents. 21 states are represented in upper school student body. 20% are international students. International students from Canada, China, Germany, Japan, Republic of Korea, and Spain; 6 other countries represented in student body.

Faculty School total: 42. In upper school: 21 men, 21 women; 16 have advanced degrees; 35 reside on campus.

Subjects Offered Algebra, anatomy and physiology, art, art-AP, astronomy, biology, business studies, calculus, calculus-AP, chemistry, chemistry-AP, college counseling, composition, composition-AP, computer multimedia, computer programming, computer science, computer studies, current events, digital photography, drama, drawing, drawing and design, English, ESL, ethics, French, functions, geology, geometry, health and wellness, history, independent study, international relations, jazz, Latin,

leadership, music, music theory, painting, personal fitness, photography, physics, piano, portfolio art, pottery, programming, psychology, sculpture, Spanish, studio art, trigonometry, U.S. history, wilderness education, world history, world religions.

Graduation Requirements Algebra, art, biology, chemistry, English, foreign language, geometry, U.S. history.

Special Academic Programs Advanced Placement exam preparation; honors section; independent study; academic accommodation for the gifted, the musically talented, and the artistically talented; ESL (12 students enrolled).

College Admission Counseling 79 students graduated in 2009; 75 went to college, including Colby College; Elmira College; University of Maine; University of New Hampshire; University of Pennsylvania. Other: 3 had other specific plans. Median SAT critical reading: 500, median SAT math: 580, median SAT writing: 550, median combined SAT: 1680. 24% scored over 600 on SAT critical reading, 45% scored over 600 on SAT math, 33% scored over 600 on SAT writing, 38% scored over 1800 on combined SAT.

Student Life Upper grades have specified standards of dress, student council, honor system. Discipline rests primarily with faculty.

Tuition and Aid Day student tuition: $23,250; 7-day tuition and room/board: $43,995. Tuition installment plan (Insured Tuition Payment Plan, monthly payment plans). Merit scholarship grants, need-based scholarship grants, prepGATE loans available. In 2009–10, 49% of upper-school students received aid; total upper-school merit-scholarship money awarded: $15,000. Total amount of financial aid awarded in 2009–10: $2,000,000.

Admissions Traditional secondary-level entrance grade is 9. For fall 2009, 305 students applied for upper-level admission, 207 were accepted, 97 enrolled. PSAT or SAT for applicants to grade 11 and 12, SSAT or TOEFL or SLEP required. Deadline for receipt of application materials: February 1. Application fee required: $50. Interview required.

Athletics Interscholastic: alpine skiing (boys, girls), baseball (b), basketball (b,g), cross-country running (b,g), dance (g), field hockey (g), football (b), golf (b,g), ice hockey (b,g), lacrosse (b,g), mountain biking (b,g), outdoor education (b,g), outdoor skills (b,g), physical fitness (b,g), running (b,g), skiing (downhill) (b,g), soccer (b,g), softball (b,g), tennis (b,g), track and field (b,g), wall climbing (b,g); coed intramural: outdoor education, outdoor skills, roller hockey. 2 coaches, 2 athletic trainers.

Computers Computers are regularly used in art, graphic design, introduction to technology classes. Computer network features include on-campus library services, online commercial services, Internet access, wireless campus network, Internet filtering or blocking technology. Campus intranet, student e-mail accounts, and computer access in designated common areas are available to students. Students grades are available online. The school has a published electronic and media policy.

Contact Mr. Joseph M. Hemmings, Director of Admission. 207-966-2100 Ext. 225. Fax: 207-966-1111. E-mail: admissions@hebronacademy.org. Web site: www.hebronacademy.org.

HERITAGE CHRISTIAN ACADEMY

2003 McKnight Boulevard NE
Calgary, Alberta T2E 6L2, Canada

Head of School: Mrs. LaVerne Pue

General Information Coeducational day college-preparatory, general academic, arts, religious studies, bilingual studies, and technology school, affiliated with Christian faith, Evangelical faith. Grades K–12. Founded: 1979. Setting: urban. 10-acre campus. 1 building on campus. Approved or accredited by Association of Christian Schools International, Association of Independent Schools and Colleges of Alberta, and Alberta Department of Education. Language of instruction: English. Total enrollment: 568. Upper school average class size: 27. Upper school faculty-student ratio: 1:9. There are 200 required school days per year for Upper School students. Upper School students typically attend 5 days per week. The average school day consists of 7 hours.

Upper School Student Profile Grade 10: 31 students (13 boys, 18 girls); Grade 11: 29 students (16 boys, 13 girls); Grade 12: 34 students (20 boys, 14 girls). 100% of students are Christian, members of Evangelical faith.

Faculty School total: 34. In upper school: 5 men, 4 women; 2 have advanced degrees.

Subjects Offered Art, band, Bible, biology, career and personal planning, chemistry, choir, choral music, Christian education, computer applications, computer multimedia, creative writing, English, essential learning systems, French as a second language, health, language arts, mathematics, physical education, physics, psychology, religious studies, science, sewing, social studies, sports medicine, work experience.

Graduation Requirements Career and personal planning, English, mathematics, physical education (includes health), religious studies, science, social studies (includes history).

Special Academic Programs Independent study; remedial reading and/or remedial writing; remedial math; special instructional classes for deaf students, students with dyslexia addressed through IPPs and classroom accommodations.

College Admission Counseling 28 students graduated in 2010; 22 went to college, including Mount Royal University; The University of British Columbia; University of Calgary; University of Lethbridge; Wilfrid Laurier University. Other: 5 went to work, 1 had other specific plans.

Student Life Upper grades have uniform requirement, student council, honor system. Discipline rests primarily with faculty. Attendance at religious services is required.

Tuition and Aid Day student tuition: CAN$2765. Tuition installment plan (monthly payment plans, individually arranged payment plans). Tuition reduction for siblings available.

Admissions Traditional secondary-level entrance grade is 10. For fall 2010, 11 students applied for upper-level admission, 10 were accepted, 10 enrolled. CTBS (or similar from their school) required. Deadline for receipt of application materials: none. Application fee required: CAN$100. Interview required.

Athletics Interscholastic: badminton (boys, girls), basketball (b,g), cross-country running (b,g), floor hockey (b), golf (b,g), track and field (b,g), volleyball (b,g), wrestling (b,g); coed interscholastic: track and field; coed intramural: basketball, climbing, floor hockey, indoor soccer, indoor track & field, outdoor activities, physical fitness, project adventure, soccer, touch football, track and field, volleyball, wall climbing. 1 PE instructor.

Computers Computers are regularly used in animation, Bible studies, career education, data processing, English, graphics, information technology, keyboarding, mathematics, multimedia, photography, science, social studies classes. Computer network features include Internet access, Internet filtering or blocking technology. Student e-mail accounts are available to students. The school has a published electronic and media policy.

Contact Office. 403-219-3201. Fax: 403-219-3210. E-mail: heritage_info@ pallisersd.ab.ca. Web site: www.hcacalgary.com.

HERITAGE CHRISTIAN SCHOOL

2850 Fourth Avenue
PO Box 400
Jordan, Ontario L0R 1S0, Canada
Head of School: Mr. A. Ben Harsevoort

General Information Coeducational day college-preparatory, general academic, arts, and religious studies school, affiliated with Reformed Church. Grades K–12. Founded: 1992. Setting: rural. Nearest major city is St. Catharines, Canada. 26-acre campus. 1 building on campus. Approved or accredited by Ontario Department of Education. Language of instruction: English. Total enrollment: 571. Upper school average class size: 50. Upper school faculty-student ratio: 1:15.

Upper School Student Profile Grade 9: 31 students (21 boys, 10 girls); Grade 10: 49 students (23 boys, 26 girls); Grade 11: 41 students (20 boys, 21 girls); Grade 12: 43 students (22 boys, 21 girls). 95% of students are Reformed.

Faculty School total: 30. In upper school: 11 men, 4 women; 4 have advanced degrees.

Subjects Offered 20th century American writers, 20th century physics, 20th century world history, advanced chemistry, advanced math, algebra, analysis and differential calculus, art, Bible, biology, bookkeeping, British literature, business mathematics, business studies, calculus, Canadian geography, Canadian history, Canadian law, Canadian literature, career education, chemistry, choral music, Christian and Hebrew scripture, Christian doctrine, Christian education, Christian ethics, Christian studies, Christian testament, Christianity, church history, civics, classical civilization, computer education, computer programming, computer skills, consumer mathematics, creative writing, culinary arts, drafting, English, English composition, English literature, entrepreneurship, environmental education, ethics, European civilization, European history, family studies, finite math, foods, foundations of civilization, French as a second language, general math, geography, geometry, grammar, health, history, honors algebra, honors English, honors geometry, honors world history, humanities, independent living, keyboarding, language and composition, language arts, law and the legal system, life science, literature, marketing, mathematics, media literacy, modern civilization, modern European history, modern Western civilization, music, music appreciation, novels, personal finance, physical education, physics, practicum, public speaking, religion and culture, religious education, religious studies, Shakespeare, society challenge and change, speech communications, technical drawing, vocal music, word processing, world civilizations, world literature, writing.

Graduation Requirements Ontario Secondary School Diploma requirements.

Special Academic Programs Independent study; remedial reading and/or remedial writing; remedial math.

College Admission Counseling 38 students graduated in 2010; 30 went to college, including Calvin College; Covenant College. Other: 8 went to work.

Student Life Upper grades have uniform requirement, student council. Discipline rests primarily with faculty. Attendance at religious services is required.

Tuition and Aid Day student tuition: CAN$12,500. Tuition installment plan (monthly payment plans).

Admissions Traditional secondary-level entrance grade is 9. Deadline for receipt of application materials: none. No application fee required. On-campus interview required.

Athletics Interscholastic: badminton (boys, girls), basketball (b,g), ice hockey (b), soccer (b,g), volleyball (b,g). 3 coaches.

Computers Computers are regularly used in accounting, business, economics, information technology, keyboarding, mathematics, newspaper, typing, yearbook classes. The school has a published electronic and media policy.

Contact Mrs. Mariam Sinke, Administrative Assistant. 905-562-7303 Ext. 221. Fax: 905-562-0020. E-mail: heritage@hcsjordan.ca. Web site: www.hcsjordan.ca.

HERITAGE HALL

1800 Northwest 122nd Street
Oklahoma City, Oklahoma 73120-9524
Head of School: Guy A. Bramble

General Information Coeducational day college-preparatory, arts, and ESL school. Grades PS–12. Founded: 1969. Setting: suburban. 97-acre campus. 3 buildings on campus. Approved or accredited by Independent Schools Association of the Southwest and Oklahoma Department of Education. Member of National Association of Independent Schools and Secondary School Admission Test Board. Endowment: $1.4 million. Total enrollment: 924. Upper school average class size: 16. Upper school faculty-student ratio: 1:16. Upper School students typically attend 5 days per week. The average school day consists of 7 hours.

Upper School Student Profile Grade 9: 88 students (42 boys, 46 girls); Grade 10: 120 students (66 boys, 54 girls); Grade 11: 98 students (61 boys, 37 girls); Grade 12: 95 students (47 boys, 48 girls).

Faculty School total: 116. In upper school: 13 men, 30 women; 27 have advanced degrees.

Subjects Offered Advanced chemistry, algebra, American history, American literature, art, art history, biology, calculus, ceramics, chemistry, community service, computer science, debate, earth science, economics, English, English literature, environmental science, ethics, European history, film and literature, French, geography, geometry, government/civics, grammar, history, journalism, mathematics, music, photography, physical education, physics, play production, psychology, science, social studies, Spanish, speech, trigonometry, world history, world literature, writing.

Graduation Requirements Arts and fine arts (art, music, dance, drama), computer education, English, foreign language, mathematics, physical education (includes health), science, social studies (includes history), 32 hours of documented community service each year in grades 9 through 12.

Special Academic Programs Advanced Placement exam preparation; honors section; independent study; academic accommodation for the gifted, the musically talented, and the artistically talented; programs in English, mathematics, general development for dyslexic students; ESL (12 students enrolled).

College Admission Counseling 92 students graduated in 2009; all went to college, including Oklahoma State University; Southern Methodist University; Texas Christian University; University of Oklahoma. Mean SAT critical reading: 649, mean SAT math: 634, mean SAT writing: 627, mean composite ACT: 26.

Student Life Upper grades have specified standards of dress, student council, honor system. Discipline rests equally with students and faculty.

Tuition and Aid Day student tuition: $14,665. Tuition installment plan (Insured Tuition Payment Plan, monthly payment plans). Merit scholarship grants, need-based scholarship grants, need-based loans available. In 2009–10, 22% of upper-school students received aid; total upper-school merit-scholarship money awarded: $92,000. Total amount of financial aid awarded in 2009–10: $5,110,000.

Admissions Traditional secondary-level entrance grade is 9. For fall 2009, 81 students applied for upper-level admission, 66 were accepted, 53 enrolled. ERB CTP (level F), ERB CTP IV, essay, Math Placement Exam, WISC-III and Woodcock-Johnson and writing sample required. Deadline for receipt of application materials: none. Application fee required: $35. On-campus interview required.

Athletics Interscholastic: baseball (boys), basketball (b,g), cheering (g), cross-country running (b,g), field hockey (g), fitness (b,g), football (b), golf (b,g), physical fitness (b,g), soccer (b,g), softball (g), strength & conditioning (b,g), swimming and diving (b,g), tennis (b,g), track and field (b,g), volleyball (g), weight training (b,g), wrestling (b); intramural: Frisbee (b); coed intramural: bowling, rowing. 5 PE instructors, 15 coaches, 1 athletic trainer.

Computers Computers are regularly used in art, college planning, computer applications, desktop publishing, English, ESL, foreign language, library, mathematics, multimedia, newspaper, programming, publishing, SAT preparation, science, speech, Web site design, word processing, writing, yearbook classes. Computer network features include on-campus library services, online commercial services, Internet access, wireless campus network, Internet filtering or blocking technology, homework assignments and test schedules available online. Campus intranet and computer access in designated common areas are available to students. Students grades are available online. The school has a published electronic and media policy.

Contact Mr. Paul O. Arceneaux, Director of Admission. 405-749-3000. Fax: 405-751-7372. E-mail: parceneaux@heritagehall.com. Web site: www. heritagehall.com.

THE HERITAGE SCHOOL

2093 Highway 29 North
Newnan, Georgia 30263
Head of School: Judith Griffith

General Information Coeducational day college-preparatory, arts, and technology school. Grades PK–12. Founded: 1970. Setting: suburban. Nearest major city is Atlanta. 62-acre campus. 10 buildings on campus. Approved or accredited by Georgia Independent School Association, Southern Association of Colleges and Schools, Southern Association of Independent Schools, and Georgia Department of Education. Member of National Association of Independent Schools. Endowment: $1.1 million. Total enrollment: 424. Upper school average class size: 18. Upper school faculty-student ratio: 1:7. There are 180 required school days per year for Upper School students. Upper School students typically attend 5 days per week.

Upper School Student Profile Grade 9: 41 students (29 boys, 12 girls); Grade 10: 41 students (25 boys, 16 girls); Grade 11: 42 students (20 boys, 22 girls); Grade 12: 20 students (13 boys, 7 girls).

Faculty School total: 49. In upper school: 5 men, 15 women; 3 have advanced degrees.

Subjects Offered Advanced Placement courses, algebra, American history, American literature, art, art history, biology, calculus, chemistry, computer applications, drama, earth science, economics, English, English literature, environmental science, European history, French, geography, geometry, government/civics, grammar, health, history, mathematics, music, physical education, public speaking, science, social sciences, social studies, Spanish, speech, theater, world history, world literature.

Graduation Requirements Arts and fine arts (art, music, dance, drama), computer science, electives, English, foreign language, mathematics, physical education (includes health), public speaking, science, social studies (includes history).

Special Academic Programs 16 Advanced Placement exams for which test preparation is offered; independent study.

College Admission Counseling 38 students graduated in 2010; 37 went to college, including Georgia Institute of Technology; Georgia Southern University; Mercer University; Savannah College of Art and Design; University of Georgia; Wake Forest University. Other: 1 entered military service. Mean SAT critical reading: 555, mean SAT math: 550, mean SAT writing: 525, mean combined SAT: 1620, mean composite ACT: 24.

Student Life Upper grades have specified standards of dress, student council, honor system. Discipline rests primarily with faculty.

Tuition and Aid Day student tuition: $6860–$12,980. Tuition installment plan (monthly payment plans). Tuition reduction for siblings, need-based scholarship grants available. In 2010–11, 20% of upper-school students received aid. Total amount of financial aid awarded in 2010–11: $175,000.

Admissions Traditional secondary-level entrance grade is 9. For fall 2010, 37 students applied for upper-level admission, 27 were accepted, 24 enrolled. Otis-Lennon School Ability Test required. Deadline for receipt of application materials: none. Application fee required: $50. On-campus interview required.

Athletics Interscholastic: aerobics/dance (girls), baseball (b), basketball (b,g), cheering (g), cross-country running (b,g), dance team (g), football (b), golf (b,g), soccer (b,g), softball (g), swimming and diving (b,g), tennis (b,g), weight training (b); intramural: cheering (g), football (b); coed interscholastic: physical fitness, skeet shooting; coed intramural: backpacking, basketball, canoeing/kayaking, climbing, equestrian sports, flag football, hiking/backpacking, juggling, kayaking, mountaineering, outdoor adventure, outdoor education, ropes courses, wilderness survival. 3 PE instructors, 1 athletic trainer.

Computers Computers are regularly used in college planning, creative writing, English, foreign language, publications, science, yearbook classes. Computer network features include on-campus library services, online commercial services, Internet access, wireless campus network, Internet filtering or blocking technology. Campus intranet, student e-mail accounts, and computer access in designated common areas are available to students. Students grades are available online. The school has a published electronic and media policy.

Contact Amy Riley, Advancement Director. 678-423-5393. Fax: 770-253-4850. E-mail: ariley@heritagehawks.org. Web site: www.heritagehawks.org.

THE HEWITT SCHOOL

45 East 75th Street
New York, New York 10021
Head of School: Ms. Joan Z. Lonergan

General Information Girls' day college-preparatory school. Grades K–12. Founded: 1920. Setting: urban. 1 building on campus. Approved or accredited by Middle States Association of Colleges and Schools, National Independent Private Schools Association, and New York State Association of Independent Schools. Member of National Association of Independent Schools and Secondary School Admission Test Board. Total enrollment: 498. Upper school average class size: 11. Upper school faculty-student ratio: 1:7. Upper School students typically attend 5 days per week. The average school day consists of 7 hours.

Upper School Student Profile Grade 9: 31 students (31 girls); Grade 10: 29 students (29 girls); Grade 11: 25 students (25 girls); Grade 12: 30 students (30 girls).

Faculty School total: 82. In upper school: 14 men, 16 women; 24 have advanced degrees.

Subjects Offered Algebra, American history, American literature, anatomy and physiology, art, biology, calculus, chemistry, computers, drama, earth science, English, English literature, European history, fine arts, French, genetics, geometry, history, Latin, mathematics, music, photography, physical education, physics, pre-calculus, science, Spanish, world history.

Graduation Requirements Creative arts, English, foreign language, history, mathematics, physical education (includes health), science, technology.

Special Academic Programs Advanced Placement exam preparation; honors section; independent study; term-away projects; study abroad.

College Admission Counseling 33 students graduated in 2010; 32 went to college, including Connecticut College; Cornell University; Duke University; Harvard University; Syracuse University; University of Michigan. Other: 1 had other specific plans.

Student Life Upper grades have uniform requirement, student council. Discipline rests primarily with faculty.

Tuition and Aid Day student tuition: $36,650. Guaranteed tuition plan. Tuition installment plan (Insured Tuition Payment Plan, Key Tuition Payment Plan, monthly payment plans). Need-based scholarship grants available. In 2010–11, 22% of upper-school students received aid. Total amount of financial aid awarded in 2010–11: $1,394,709.

Admissions Traditional secondary-level entrance grade is 9. ERB and ISEE required. Deadline for receipt of application materials: December 1. Application fee required: $60. On-campus interview required.

Athletics Interscholastic: badminton, basketball, cross-country running, soccer, swimming and diving, tennis, track and field, volleyball; intramural: badminton, basketball, crew, cross-country running, lacrosse, soccer, swimming and diving, tennis, track and field, volleyball. 4 PE instructors.

Computers Computers are regularly used in all academic, art, English, foreign language, history, humanities, mathematics, music, science classes. Computer network features include on-campus library services, online commercial services, Internet access, wireless campus network, Internet filtering or blocking technology. Student e-mail accounts are available to students. The school has a published electronic and media policy.

Contact Ms. Kathleen P. Kaminsky, Director of Admissions, Middle and Upper School. 212-288-1919. Fax: 212-472-7531. E-mail: kkaminsky@hewittschool.org. Web site: hewittschool.org.

HIGHLAND HALL WALDORF SCHOOL

17100 Superior Street
Northridge, California 91325
Head of School: Jim Pedroja

General Information Coeducational day college-preparatory and arts school. Grades N–12. Founded: 1955. Setting: suburban. Nearest major city is Los Angeles. 11-acre campus. 4 buildings on campus. Approved or accredited by Association of Waldorf Schools of North America and Western Association of Schools and Colleges. Total enrollment: 360. Upper school average class size: 25. Upper school faculty-student ratio: 1:6. There are 170 required school days per year for Upper School students. Upper School students typically attend 5 days per week. The average school day consists of 7 hours and 10 minutes.

Upper School Student Profile Grade 9: 22 students (10 boys, 12 girls); Grade 10: 22 students (9 boys, 13 girls); Grade 11: 24 students (12 boys, 12 girls); Grade 12: 21 students (9 boys, 12 girls).

Faculty School total: 59. In upper school: 16 men, 14 women; 3 have advanced degrees.

Subjects Offered Algebra, American history, American literature, anatomy, ancient history, architecture, art, art history, astronomy, biology, bookbinding, botany, calculus, career/college preparation, cell biology, chemistry, choral music, chorus, clayworking, conflict resolution, CPR, creative writing, drama, drawing, earth science, economics, English, English literature, ethnic studies, European history, eurythmy, expository writing, geography, geology, geometry, German, government/civics, grammar, guidance, guitar, handbells, health, history, honors U.S. history, jazz ensemble, marine biology, mathematics, metalworking, music, music history, Native American history, orchestra, painting, physical education, physics, physiology, pre-algebra, pre-calculus, SAT preparation, sculpture, sewing, social studies, Spanish, speech, stained glass, stone carving, theater, trigonometry, woodworking, world history, world literature, writing, yearbook, zoology.

Graduation Requirements Ancient history, art, art history, crafts, earth science, economics, English, foreign language, government, history of music, human sexuality, mathematics, music, physical education (includes health), science, sculpture, society and culture, U.S. history, world history. Community service is required.

Special Academic Programs Honors section; independent study; study abroad.

College Admission Counseling 23 students graduated in 2010; 22 went to college, including Berklee College of Music; Lewis & Clark College; Marlboro College; Middlebury College; Sarah Lawrence College; Vassar College. Other: 1 went to work. Mean SAT critical reading: 645, mean SAT math: 550, mean composite ACT: 27. 50% scored over 600 on SAT critical reading, 60% scored over 600 on SAT math, 50% scored over 26 on composite ACT.

Student Life Upper grades have specified standards of dress, student council. Discipline rests primarily with faculty.

Tuition and Aid Day student tuition: $19,225. Tuition installment plan (Insured Tuition Payment Plan, FACTS Tuition Payment Plan, monthly payment plans). Need-based scholarship grants available. In 2010–11, 19% of upper-school students received aid. Total amount of financial aid awarded in 2010–11: $204,600.

Admissions Traditional secondary-level entrance grade is 9. For fall 2010, 30 students applied for upper-level admission, 24 were accepted, 11 enrolled. Essay, math and English placement tests and writing sample required. Deadline for receipt of application materials: January 31. Application fee required: $100. On-campus interview required.

Highland Hall Waldorf School

Athletics Interscholastic: baseball (boys), basketball (b,g), softball (g), volleyball (b,g); coed interscholastic: soccer; coed intramural: golf. 2 PE instructors, 3 coaches.
Computers Computers are regularly used in newspaper, yearbook classes. Computer network features include on-campus library services, Internet access, wireless campus network.
Contact Lynn van Schilfgaarde, Enrollment Director. 818-349-1394 Ext. 211. Fax: 818-349-2390. E-mail: lvs@highlandhall.org. Web site: www.highlandhall.org.

HIGH MOWING SCHOOL

222 Isaac Frye Highway
Wilton, New Hampshire 03086
Head of School: Douglas Powers

General Information Coeducational boarding and day college-preparatory and arts school. Grades 9–12. Founded: 1942. Setting: rural. Nearest major city is Boston, MA. Students are housed in single-sex dormitories. 125-acre campus. 17 buildings on campus. Approved or accredited by Association of Independent Schools in New England, Association of Waldorf Schools of North America, Independent Schools of Northern New England, New England Association of Schools and Colleges, The Association of Boarding Schools, and New Hampshire Department of Education. Member of National Association of Independent Schools and Secondary School Admission Test Board. Endowment: $1 million. Total enrollment: 94. Upper school average class size: 10. Upper school faculty-student ratio: 1:5. There are 180 required school days per year for Upper School students. Upper School students typically attend 5 days per week. The average school day consists of 6 hours and 25 minutes.
Upper School Student Profile Grade 9: 18 students (7 boys, 11 girls); Grade 10: 21 students (9 boys, 12 girls); Grade 11: 25 students (9 boys, 16 girls); Grade 12: 30 students (14 boys, 16 girls). 50% of students are boarding students. 50% are state residents. 12 states are represented in upper school student body. 10% are international students. International students from France, Germany, Japan, Mexico, Republic of Korea, and Switzerland; 1 other country represented in student body.
Faculty School total: 26. In upper school: 10 men, 12 women; 16 have advanced degrees; 15 reside on campus.
Subjects Offered Advanced chemistry, algebra, American history, American literature, anatomy, ancient history, ancient world history, art, art appreciation, art history, arts, batik, biochemistry, biology, botany, calculus, ceramics, chemistry, chorus, community service, computer programming, creative writing, digital art, drama, driver education, earth science, ecology, economics, English, English literature, environmental science, ESL, ethics, European history, eurythmy, expository writing, fiber arts, filmmaking, fine arts, French, geography, geology, geometry, German, government/civics, grammar, graphic arts, graphic design, health, health education, history, history of science, jazz band, mathematics, meteorology, music, mythology, nature study, optics, philosophy, photography, physical education, physics, physiology, probability and statistics, projective geometry, Russian literature, science, social sciences, social studies, Spanish, speech, studio art, theater, theory of knowledge, trigonometry, wilderness education, world history, world literature, writing, zoology.
Graduation Requirements Algebra, arts and fine arts (art, music, dance, drama), economics, English, foreign language, geometry, government, health, language arts, mathematics, performing arts, physical education (includes health), physics, science, social sciences, social studies (includes history), studio art, U.S. history. Community service is required.
Special Academic Programs Advanced Placement exam preparation; honors section; independent study; term-away projects; study abroad; academic accommodation for the musically talented and the artistically talented; remedial math; programs in mathematics for dyslexic students; ESL (4 students enrolled).
College Admission Counseling 35 students graduated in 2009; 25 went to college, including Bard College; Bennington College; Berklee College of Music; Mount Holyoke College; New York University; University of Vermont. Other: 1 entered military service, 2 had other specific plans. Median SAT critical reading: 602, median SAT math: 518, median SAT writing: 583.
Student Life Upper grades have specified standards of dress, student council. Discipline rests equally with students and faculty.
Tuition and Aid Day student tuition: $25,600; 5-day tuition and room/board: $38,500; 7-day tuition and room/board: $40,800. Tuition installment plan (FACTS Tuition Payment Plan). Need-based scholarship grants available. In 2009–10, 45% of upper-school students received aid. Total amount of financial aid awarded in 2009–10: $554,000.
Admissions Traditional secondary-level entrance grade is 9. Deadline for receipt of application materials: none. Application fee required: $50. Interview required.
Athletics Interscholastic: baseball (boys), basketball (b,g), cross-country running (b,g), lacrosse (g), soccer (b,g); coed intramural: aerobics, alpine skiing, backpacking, bicycling, billiards, Circus, climbing, cross-country running, dance, fitness, fitness walking, Frisbee, hiking/backpacking, jogging, juggling, outdoor activities, physical fitness, physical training, rock climbing, running, skiing (cross-country), skiing (downhill), snowboarding, snowshoeing, tennis, ultimate Frisbee, walking, wall climbing, wilderness, wilderness survival, wildernessways, yoga. 1 PE instructor, 8 coaches.

Computers Computers are regularly used in graphic arts, graphic design, mathematics, science, technology classes. Computer resources include on-campus library services, Internet access, wireless campus network. The school has a published electronic and media policy.
Contact Patricia Meissner, Director of Admissions. 603-654-2391 Ext. 109. Fax: 603-654-6588. E-mail: admissions@highmowing.org. Web site: www.highmowing.org.

HIGHROAD ACADEMY

46641 Chilliwack Central Road
Chilliwack, British Columbia V2P 1K3, Canada
Head of School: Mr. David Shinness

General Information college-preparatory school, affiliated with Christian faith. Founded: 1978. Setting: small town. Nearest major city is Vancouver, Canada. 45-acre campus. 1 building on campus. Approved or accredited by Association of Christian Schools International and British Columbia Department of Education. Upper school average class size: 25. Upper school faculty-student ratio: 1:10.
Upper School Student Profile 100% of students are Christian.
Faculty School total: 25. In upper school: 5 men, 5 women.
Student Life Upper grades have uniform requirement, student council, honor system. Discipline rests primarily with faculty. Attendance at religious services is required.
Admissions No application fee required.
Contact Mrs. Kit Kristjanson, Office Manager. 604-792-4680. Fax: 604-792-2465. E-mail: kkristjanson@highroadacademy.com. Web site: www.highroadacademy.com.

THE HILL CENTER, DURHAM ACADEMY

Durham, North Carolina
See Special Needs Schools section.

HILLCREST CHRISTIAN SCHOOL

17531 Rinaldi Street
Granada Hills, California 91344
Head of School: Mr. David Kendrick

General Information Coeducational day college-preparatory, general academic, arts, and religious studies school, affiliated with Christian faith. Grades K–12. Founded: 1976. Setting: suburban. Nearest major city is Los Angeles. 4-acre campus. 3 buildings on campus. Approved or accredited by Association of Christian Schools International, Western Association of Schools and Colleges, and California Department of Education. Total enrollment: 619. Upper school average class size: 25. Upper school faculty-student ratio: 1:15. There are 175 required school days per year for Upper School students. Upper School students typically attend 5 days per week. The average school day consists of 5 hours and 48 minutes.
Upper School Student Profile Grade 9: 52 students (20 boys, 32 girls); Grade 10: 63 students (23 boys, 40 girls); Grade 11: 46 students (19 boys, 27 girls); Grade 12: 63 students (26 boys, 37 girls).
Faculty School total: 40. In upper school: 8 men, 11 women; 7 have advanced degrees.
Subjects Offered Accounting, algebra, American literature, art, Bible studies, biology, British literature, calculus-AP, chemistry, choir, choral music, computer applications, drama, dramatic arts, economics, economics-AP, English, English literature and composition-AP, English literature-AP, foreign language, general math, geometry, journalism, keyboarding, leadership and service, Life of Christ, microeconomics-AP, physical education, physics, pre-algebra, pre-calculus, psychology, Spanish, U.S. government, U.S. history, U.S. history-AP, world history.
Graduation Requirements Advanced math, algebra, Bible, biology, chemistry, economics, English, geometry, physical education (includes health), physical science, Spanish, U.S. government, U.S. history, visual and performing arts, world history, cumulative GPA of 2.0 or higher.
Special Academic Programs Advanced Placement exam preparation; independent study; academic accommodation for the musically talented; programs in general development for dyslexic students.
College Admission Counseling 39 students graduated in 2009; 37 went to college, including Azusa Pacific University; California State University, Northridge; Pepperdine University; University of California, Irvine; University of California, Riverside; Westmont College. Other: 1 went to work, 1 entered military service. Mean SAT critical reading: 496, mean SAT math: 466, mean SAT writing: 486, mean composite ACT: 21. 24% scored over 600 on SAT critical reading, 12% scored over 600 on SAT math.
Student Life Upper grades have uniform requirement, student council. Discipline rests primarily with faculty. Attendance at religious services is required.
Tuition and Aid Day student tuition: $6578. Tuition installment plan (SMART Tuition Payment Plan). Tuition reduction for siblings, need-based scholarship grants available. In 2009–10, 5% of upper-school students received aid. Total amount of financial aid awarded in 2009–10: $35,000.
Admissions Traditional secondary-level entrance grade is 9. For fall 2009, 46 students applied for upper-level admission, 35 were accepted, 29 enrolled. 3-R

Achievement Test, Math Placement Exam and Stanford 9 required. Deadline for receipt of application materials: none. Application fee required: $275. On-campus interview required.

Athletics Interscholastic: baseball (boys), basketball (b,g), cheering (g), cross-country running (b,g), football (b), softball (g), volleyball (b,g); intramural: dance (g); coed interscholastic: golf, soccer; coed intramural: hiking/backpacking, physical training, strength & conditioning. 2 PE instructors, 10 coaches, 1 athletic trainer.

Computers Computers are regularly used in accounting, Bible studies, Christian doctrine, computer applications, economics, English, independent study, journalism, SAT preparation, social sciences, yearbook classes. Computer network features include on-campus library services, Internet access, Internet filtering or blocking technology. Students grades are available online. The school has a published electronic and media policy.

Contact Mrs. Krista Joyner, Registrar. 818-368-7071. Fax: 818-363-4455. E-mail: kjoyner@hillcrestchristianschool.org.

HILLCREST CHRISTIAN SCHOOL
4060 South Siwell Road
Jackson, Mississippi 39212
Head of School: Dr. Tom Prather

General Information Coeducational day college-preparatory, arts, business, religious studies, and technology school. Grades 1–12. Founded: 1971. Setting: urban. 36-acre campus. 5 buildings on campus. Approved or accredited by Association of Christian Schools International, Mississippi Private School Association, and Southern Association of Colleges and Schools. Total enrollment: 595. Upper school average class size: 15. Upper school faculty-student ratio: 1:11. There are 175 required school days per year for Upper School students. Upper School students typically attend 5 days per week. The average school day consists of 5 hours and 50 minutes.

Upper School Student Profile Grade 7: 53 students (30 boys, 23 girls); Grade 8: 57 students (25 boys, 32 girls); Grade 9: 32 students (15 boys, 17 girls); Grade 10: 47 students (32 boys, 15 girls); Grade 11: 44 students (21 boys, 23 girls); Grade 12: 34 students (16 boys, 18 girls).

Faculty School total: 63. In upper school: 12 men, 14 women; 11 have advanced degrees.

Subjects Offered Advanced biology, advanced math, Advanced Placement courses, algebra, American government, American history-AP, American literature, American literature-AP, anatomy and physiology, art, band, baseball, basketball, Bible, biology, biology-AP, British literature, business communications, calculus, chemistry, chemistry-AP, choir, choral music, comparative government and politics-AP, computer applications, computer graphics, critical writing, current events, desktop publishing, earth science, economics, electives, English, English language and composition-AP, English literature, English literature and composition-AP, geography, geometry, health, library assistant, life science, pre-algebra, reading/study skills, social studies, Spanish, sports, state history, transition mathematics, trigonometry, U.S. government, U.S. government and politics-AP, U.S. history, U.S. history-AP, world geography, world history.

Graduation Requirements Bible, electives, English, history, language, mathematics, science, must complete 10 community service hours per school year attended, must apply and be accepted to a college.

Special Academic Programs 7 Advanced Placement exams for which test preparation is offered; honors section; independent study; study at local college for college credit.

College Admission Counseling 31 students graduated in 2010; 30 went to college, including Hinds Community College; Holmes Community College; Mississippi College; Mississippi State University; University of Mississippi; University of Southern Mississippi. Other: 1 entered military service. Median composite ACT: 22. 3% scored over 26 on composite ACT.

Student Life Upper grades have uniform requirement, student council, honor system. Discipline rests primarily with faculty.

Tuition and Aid Day student tuition: $5628. Tuition installment plan (monthly payment plans). Tuition reduction for siblings, need-based scholarship grants available. In 2010–11, 8% of upper-school students received aid. Total amount of financial aid awarded in 2010–11: $42,824.

Admissions Traditional secondary-level entrance grade is 7. For fall 2010, 64 students applied for upper-level admission, 42 were accepted, 39 enrolled. Admissions testing and Stanford Achievement Test, Otis-Lennon School Ability Test required. Deadline for receipt of application materials: none. Application fee required: $50. Interview recommended.

Athletics Interscholastic: baseball (boys), basketball (b,g), cheering (g), drill team (g), football (b), golf (b), softball (g), weight lifting (b); intramural: basketball (b,g), dance team (g), football (b), softball (g); coed interscholastic: cross-country running, soccer, tennis; coed intramural: cheering, cross-country running, golf, tennis, track and field, weight lifting, weight training. 2 coaches.

Computers Computers are regularly used in computer applications, desktop publishing, graphic design, yearbook classes. Computer resources include Internet access. Students grades are available online.

Contact Mrs. Melissa Jones, Director of Admissions. 601-372-0149 Ext. 300. Fax: 601-371-8061. E-mail: mjones@hillcrestchristian.org. Web site: www.hillcrestchristian.org.

HILLCREST SCHOOL
Midland, Texas
See Special Needs Schools section.

THE HILL SCHOOL
717 East High Street
Pottstown, Pennsylvania 19464-5791
Head of School: Mr. David R. Dougherty

General Information Coeducational boarding and day college-preparatory school, affiliated with Christian faith. Boarding grades 9–PG, day grades 9–12. Founded: 1851. Setting: small town. Nearest major city is Philadelphia. Students are housed in single-sex dormitories. 200-acre campus. 58 buildings on campus. Approved or accredited by Middle States Association of Colleges and Schools, The Association of Boarding Schools, and Pennsylvania Department of Education. Member of National Association of Independent Schools and Secondary School Admission Test Board. Endowment: $10 million. Total enrollment: 494. Upper school average class size: 13. Upper school faculty-student ratio: 1:7. Upper School students typically attend 6 days per week. The average school day consists of 5 hours and 33 minutes.

Upper School Student Profile Grade 9: 84 students (49 boys, 35 girls); Grade 10: 117 students (57 boys, 60 girls); Grade 11: 149 students (88 boys, 61 girls); Grade 12: 123 students (69 boys, 54 girls); Postgraduate: 19 students (15 boys, 4 girls). 80% of students are boarding students. 48% are state residents. 30 states are represented in upper school student body. 11% are international students. International students from China, Germany, Hong Kong, Republic of Korea, Spain, and Venezuela; 14 other countries represented in student body.

Faculty School total: 86. In upper school: 56 men, 30 women; 61 have advanced degrees; 80 reside on campus.

Subjects Offered Acting, advanced chemistry, advanced computer applications, advanced math, Advanced Placement courses, advanced studio art-AP, algebra, American Civil War, American history, American history-AP, American literature-AP, American studies, anatomy and physiology, Ancient Greek, ancient world history, art, art history, art-AP, arts, astronomy, athletic training, basic language skills, Basic programming, Bible studies, biochemistry, biology, biology-AP, boat building, botany, British literature-AP, calculus, calculus-AP, chamber groups, chemistry, chemistry-AP, Chinese, choral music, Christian ethics, Christian scripture, Christian testament, college admission preparation, college counseling, college placement, college planning, college writing, composition-AP, computer math, computer programming, computer science, computer science-AP, concert choir, creative writing, digital art, earth science, ecology, economics, economics-AP, English, English language and composition-AP, English literature, English literature and composition-AP, environmental science, European history, European history-AP, expository writing, French, French language-AP, French literature-AP, geography, geometry, German, government/civics, grammar, Greek, history, honors algebra, honors English, honors geometry, humanities, independent study, instrumental music, jazz band, journalism, lab science, Latin, Latin-AP, life issues, linear algebra, mathematics, music, oral communications, orchestra, participation in sports, photography, physics, physics-AP, pre-calculus, pre-college orientation, psychology, psychology-AP, radio broadcasting, religion, SAT/ACT preparation, science, sex education, sexuality, social studies, sociology, Spanish, speech, sports medicine, theater, theology, trigonometry, typing, U.S. history-AP, woodworking, world history, world literature.

Graduation Requirements Art, English, foreign language, mathematics, religion (includes Bible studies and theology), science, social studies (includes history).

Special Academic Programs Advanced Placement exam preparation; honors section; independent study; study abroad.

College Admission Counseling 130 students graduated in 2009; all went to college, including Brown University; Cornell University; Georgetown University; Trinity College; United States Naval Academy; University of Pennsylvania. Mean SAT critical reading: 625, mean SAT math: 633, mean SAT writing: 625, mean composite ACT: 26. 62% scored over 600 on SAT critical reading, 66% scored over 600 on SAT math, 53% scored over 26 on composite ACT.

Student Life Upper grades have specified standards of dress, student council, honor system. Discipline rests equally with students and faculty. Attendance at religious services is required.

Tuition and Aid Day student tuition: $30,400; 7-day tuition and room/board: $44,000. Tuition installment plan (Insured Tuition Payment Plan, monthly payment plans, individually arranged payment plans). Need-based scholarship grants available. In 2009–10, 38% of upper-school students received aid. Total amount of financial aid awarded in 2009–10: $4,800,000.

Admissions Traditional secondary-level entrance grade is 9. For fall 2009, 702 students applied for upper-level admission, 286 were accepted, 154 enrolled. ACT, ISEE, PSAT or SAT for applicants to grade 11 and 12, SSAT or TOEFL required. Deadline for receipt of application materials: January 31. Application fee required: $50. Interview required.

Athletics Interscholastic: baseball (boys), basketball (b,g), cross-country running (b,g), field hockey (g), football (b), ice hockey (b,g), indoor track (b,g), lacrosse (b,g), soccer (b,g), softball (g), squash (b,g), swimming and diving (b,g), tennis (b,g), water polo (b,g), winter (indoor) track (b,g), wrestling (b); coed interscholastic: diving, golf, track and field; coed intramural: aerobics, basketball, golf, martial arts, riflery, soccer, squash, strength & conditioning, tennis, volleyball, weight lifting. 2 coaches, 2 athletic trainers.

Computers Computers are regularly used in all classes. Computer network features include on-campus library services, online commercial services, Internet access, wireless campus network. Student e-mail accounts are available to students. The school has a published electronic and media policy.

Contact Mr. Thomas Eccleston, IV, Director of Admission and Enrollment Management. 610-326-1000. Fax: 610-705-1753. E-mail: teccleston@thehill.org. Web site: www.thehill.org.

See Display below and Close-Up on page 788.

HILL SCHOOL OF FORT WORTH

4817 Odessa Avenue
Fort Worth, Texas 76133-1640
Head of School: Greg Owens

General Information Coeducational day college-preparatory, general academic, and arts school. Grades 2–12. Founded: 1973. Setting: suburban. 1 building on campus. Approved or accredited by Southern Association of Colleges and Schools and Texas Department of Education. Upper school average class size: 9.

Special Academic Programs Special instructional classes for students with learning differences.

Student Life Upper grades have uniform requirement.

Admissions No application fee required.

Contact 817-923-9482. Web site: www.hillschool.org.

HILLSIDE SCHOOL

Marlborough, Massachusetts
See Junior Boarding Schools section.

THE HILL TOP PREPARATORY SCHOOL

Rosemont, Pennsylvania
See Special Needs Schools section.

HILTON HEAD PREPARATORY SCHOOL

8 Fox Grape Road
Hilton Head Island, South Carolina 29928
Head of School: Dr. Anthony Kandel

General Information Coeducational day college-preparatory, arts, and technology school. Grades JK–12. Founded: 1965. Setting: small town. Nearest major city is Savannah, GA. 25-acre campus. 7 buildings on campus. Approved or accredited by South Carolina Independent School Association, Southern Association of Colleges and Schools, Southern Association of Independent Schools, The College Board, and South Carolina Department of Education. Member of National Association of Independent Schools and Secondary School Admission Test Board. Total enrollment: 439. Upper school average class size: 12. Upper school faculty-student ratio: 1:12.

Upper School Student Profile Grade 9: 47 students (22 boys, 25 girls); Grade 10: 45 students (22 boys, 23 girls); Grade 11: 43 students (23 boys, 20 girls); Grade 12: 45 students (27 boys, 18 girls).

Faculty School total: 66. In upper school: 14 men, 14 women; 12 have advanced degrees.

Subjects Offered Advanced studio art-AP, algebra, American literature-AP, art, biology-AP, British literature, calculus, calculus-AP, chemistry, chemistry-AP, Chinese, chorus, college counseling, community service, computer science-AP, computer studies, drama, English literature and composition-AP, geography, geometry, guidance, guitar, health education, history-AP, journalism, leadership and service, library, literature and composition-AP, marine biology, marine science, newspaper, peer counseling, performing arts, physical education, physical fitness, physics-AP, piano, pre-calculus, probability and statistics, SAT/ACT preparation, senior career experience, senior thesis, Spanish language-AP, Spanish-AP, statistics-AP, strings, student government, studio art, trigonometry, U.S. history, U.S. history-AP, visual and performing arts, world history, world literature, yearbook.

Graduation Requirements Arts and fine arts (art, music, dance, drama), computer literacy, English, foreign language, internship, mathematics, physical education (includes health), science, social studies (includes history), senior speech, 10 hours of community service per school year.

Special Academic Programs Advanced Placement exam preparation; honors section.

College Admission Counseling 42 students graduated in 2010; all went to college, including Clemson University; Dartmouth College; Furman University; Northwestern University; Notre Dame de Namur University; Wake Forest University. Median SAT critical reading: 612, median SAT math: 633, median SAT writing: 630.

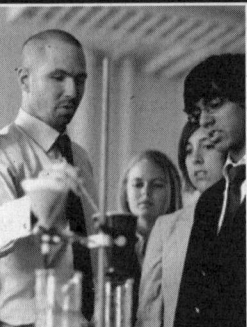   

Student Life Upper grades have specified standards of dress, student council, honor system. Discipline rests equally with students and faculty.

Summer Programs Enrichment, sports, art/fine arts, computer instruction programs offered; held on campus; accepts boys and girls; open to students from other schools. 25 students usually enrolled. 2011 schedule: June 7 to July 31. Application deadline: none.

Tuition and Aid Day student tuition: $11,875–$15,295. Tuition installment plan (Insured Tuition Payment Plan, FACTS Tuition Payment Plan, monthly payment plans, individually arranged payment plans, bank-arranged plan, self-insured tuition refund plan). Tuition reduction for siblings, need-based scholarship grants, tuition discounts for children of faculty available. In 2010–11, 23% of upper-school students received aid. Total amount of financial aid awarded in 2010–11: $250,000.

Admissions Traditional secondary-level entrance grade is 9. For fall 2010, 25 students applied for upper-level admission, 20 were accepted, 17 enrolled. ERB, PSAT, PSAT or SAT, PSAT, SAT, or ACT for applicants to grade 11 and 12, SAT, school's own exam or writing sample required. Deadline for receipt of application materials: none. Application fee required: $75. Interview required.

Athletics Interscholastic: aerobics/dance (girls), baseball (b), basketball (b,g), cheering (g), dance team (g), football (b), running (b,g), soccer (b,g), swimming and diving (b,g), tennis (b,g), volleyball (g); intramural: aerobics/dance (g), basketball (b,g), dance team (g), soccer (b,g); coed interscholastic: aquatics, cross-country running, golf, running, swimming and diving; coed intramural: outdoor activities, physical fitness, strength & conditioning. 4 PE instructors, 4 coaches, 1 athletic trainer.

Computers Computers are regularly used in all academic, art, college planning, drawing and design, graphic arts, graphic design, library science, media arts, music, newspaper, photography, research skills, SAT preparation, senior seminar, speech, stock market, technical drawing, theater, theater arts, yearbook classes. Computer network features include on-campus library services, Internet access, wireless campus network, Internet filtering or blocking technology. Campus intranet is available to students. The school has a published electronic and media policy.

Contact Bobbie C. Somerville, Director of Admissions. 843-671-2286. Fax: 843-671-7624. E-mail: bsomerville@hhprep.org. Web site: www.hhprep.org.

THE HOCKADAY SCHOOL
11600 Welch Road
Dallas, Texas 75229-2999
Head of School: Jeanne P. Whitman

General Information Girls' boarding and day college-preparatory school. Boarding grades 8–12, day grades PK–12. Founded: 1913. Setting: suburban. Students are housed in single-sex dormitories. 100-acre campus. 12 buildings on campus. Approved or accredited by Independent Schools Association of the Southwest and The Association of Boarding Schools. Member of National Association of Independent Schools and Secondary School Admission Test Board. Endowment: $92 million. Total enrollment: 1,046. Upper school average class size: 14. Upper school faculty-student ratio: 1:14. Upper School students typically attend 5 days per week. The average school day consists of 6 hours and 40 minutes.

Upper School Student Profile Grade 9: 114 students (114 girls); Grade 10: 105 students (105 girls); Grade 11: 118 students (118 girls); Grade 12: 106 students (106 girls). 15% of students are boarding students. 33% are state residents. 9 states are represented in upper school student body. 3% are international students. International students from China, Japan, Mexico, Norway, Republic of Korea, and Saudi Arabia; 1 other country represented in student body.

Faculty School total: 129. In upper school: 17 men, 44 women; 48 have advanced degrees.

Subjects Offered Acting, advanced math, advanced studio art-AP, algebra, American history, American history-AP, American literature, analytic geometry, anatomy, applied arts, applied music, art history, astronomy, athletics, audio visual/media, basketball, biology, biology-AP, body human, British literature, broadcast journalism, broadcasting, Broadway dance, calculus, calculus-AP, cell biology, ceramics, chemistry, chemistry-AP, comparative religion, computer applications, computer science, computer science-AP, concert choir, consumer economics, CPR, creative writing, current events, dance, dance performance, debate, digital art, digital imaging, digital music, digital photography, directing, discrete mathematics, drawing and design, ecology, environmental systems, economics-AP, English, English literature, English literature and composition-AP, environmental science, environmental science-AP, ESL, fencing, finite math, French, French language-AP, French literature-AP, genetics, geometry, guitar, health, health and wellness, honors English, humanities, information technology, interdisciplinary studies, journalism, Latin, Latin-AP, madrigals, Mandarin, microbiology, modern European history-AP, newspaper, non-Western literature, orchestra, philosophy, photography, physical education, physical fitness, physics, physics-AP, piano, pre-calculus, printmaking, probability and statistics, psychology, psychology-AP, self-defense, senior internship, set design, short story, Spanish,

The Hockaday School

Spanish language-AP, Spanish literature-AP, stagecraft, studio art, studio art-AP, swimming, tennis, track and field, U.S. government, U.S. history, U.S. history-AP, voice, volleyball, Web site design, wellness, world history, yearbook.

Graduation Requirements Algebra, American literature, art history, audio visual/media, biology-AP, chemistry, computer literacy, computer skills, English, English literature, geometry, history of music, information technology, languages, physical education (includes health), physics, senior project, U.S. government, U.S. history, world history, one semester of History of Art and Music, 60 hours of community service.

Special Academic Programs Advanced Placement exam preparation; honors section; independent study; term-away projects; study abroad; ESL (12 students enrolled).

College Admission Counseling 100 students graduated in 2009; all went to college, including Cornell University; Georgetown University; Harvard University; Northwestern University; Stanford University; Vanderbilt University.

Student Life Upper grades have uniform requirement, student council, honor system. Discipline rests primarily with faculty.

Tuition and Aid Day student tuition: $21,970–$22,580; 7-day tuition and room/board: $40,101–$44,810. Need-based scholarship grants, need-based financial aid available. In 2009–10, 17% of upper-school students received aid. Total amount of financial aid awarded in 2009–10: $1,582,900.

Admissions Traditional secondary-level entrance grade is 9. For fall 2009, 194 students applied for upper-level admission, 57 were accepted, 40 enrolled. Admissions testing required. Deadline for receipt of application materials: none. Application fee required: $175. Interview required.

Athletics Interscholastic: basketball, cheering, crew, cross-country running, diving, fencing, field hockey, golf, lacrosse, rowing, soccer, softball, swimming and diving, tennis, track and field, volleyball, winter soccer; intramural: aerobics, aerobics/dance, aquatics, archery, badminton, bicycling, cooperative games, crew, dance, fitness, fitness walking, Frisbee, golf, hiking/backpacking, in-line hockey, in-line skating, independent competitive sports, jogging, life saving, martial arts, mountain biking, outdoor activities, outdoor adventure, paddle tennis, physical fitness, physical training, project adventure, racquetball, roller blading, ropes courses, running, self defense, strength & conditioning, swimming and diving, table tennis, tennis, ultimate Frisbee, walking, wallyball, weight lifting, weight training, yoga. 7 PE instructors, 5 coaches, 1 athletic trainer.

Computers Computers are regularly used in animation, art, computer applications, creative writing, dance, engineering, English, French, health, history, humanities, information technology, introduction to technology, journalism, Latin, mathematics, media, media production, media services, multimedia, music, newspaper, photography, photojournalism, psychology, publications, publishing, science, Spanish, technology, Web site design, yearbook classes. Computer network features include on-campus library services, online commercial services, Internet access, wireless campus network, Internet filtering or blocking technology. Student e-mail accounts and computer access in designated common areas are available to students. Students grades are available online. The school has a published electronic and media policy.

Contact Jen Liggitt, Director of Admission. 214-363-6311. Fax: 214-265-1649. E-mail: admissions@mail.hockaday.org. Web site: www.hockaday.org.

See Display on page 313 and Close-Up on page 790.

HOKKAIDO INTERNATIONAL SCHOOL

1-55 5-jo 19-chome
Hiragishi, Toyohira-ku
Sapporo 062-0935, Japan
Head of School: Mr. Richard Branson

General Information Coeducational boarding and day and distance learning college-preparatory school. Boarding grades 7–12, day grades PK–12. Distance learning grades 10–12. Founded: 1958. Setting: urban. Students are housed in coed dormitories. 4-acre campus. 2 buildings on campus. Approved or accredited by CITA (Commission on International and Trans-Regional Accreditation) and Western Association of Schools and Colleges. Member of Secondary School Admission Test Board. Language of instruction: English. Endowment: $10 million. Total enrollment: 198. Upper school average class size: 14. Upper school faculty-student ratio: 1:10. There are 180 required school days per year for Upper School students. Upper School students typically attend 5 days per week. The average school day consists of 7 hours.

Upper School Student Profile Grade 10: 14 students (5 boys, 9 girls); Grade 11: 13 students (1 boy, 12 girls); Grade 12: 18 students (8 boys, 10 girls). 24% of students are boarding students. 44% are international students. International students from Republic of Korea, Russian Federation, Taiwan, and United States; 10 other countries represented in student body.

Faculty School total: 25. In upper school: 8 men, 4 women; 5 have advanced degrees; 2 reside on campus.

Subjects Offered Algebra, art, arts, biology, calculus, calculus-AP, chemistry, English, English literature-AP, fine arts, geography, history, Japanese, language arts, mathematics, music, physical education, physics, physics-AP, pre-calculus, science, social studies, Spanish, U.S. history.

Graduation Requirements Arts and fine arts (art, music, dance, drama), English, foreign language, mathematics, physical education (includes health), science, social sciences, social studies (includes history), extracurricular involvement requirement (EIR).

Special Academic Programs Advanced Placement exam preparation; independent study; ESL (20 students enrolled).

College Admission Counseling 17 students graduated in 2009; 15 went to college. Other: 1 went to work, 1 entered military service. Mean SAT critical reading: 500, mean SAT math: 610, mean SAT writing: 500.

Student Life Upper grades have student council. Discipline rests primarily with faculty.

Tuition and Aid Day student tuition: ¥1,055,000; 7-day tuition and room/board: ¥1,700,000. Tuition reduction for siblings, need-based scholarship grants available. In 2009–10, 20% of upper-school students received aid. Total amount of financial aid awarded in 2009–10: ¥2,000,000.

Admissions Traditional secondary-level entrance grade is 10. For fall 2009, 10 students applied for upper-level admission, 9 were accepted, 9 enrolled. School's own exam required. Deadline for receipt of application materials: none. Application fee required: ¥17,300. Interview required.

Athletics Interscholastic: basketball (boys, girls), indoor soccer (b), soccer (b), volleyball (g); coed intramural: backpacking, freestyle skiing, hiking/backpacking, outdoor activities, outdoor recreation, skiing (downhill), snowboarding. 1 PE instructor.

Computers Computers are regularly used in English, foreign language, geography, history, mathematics, science classes. Computer network features include Internet access, wireless campus network. Students grades are available online.

Contact Mrs. Shimako Abe, Administrative Assistant. 81-11-816-5000. Fax: 81-11-816-2500. E-mail: shimakoa@his.ac.jp. Web site: www.his.ac.jp.

HOLDERNESS SCHOOL

Chapel Lane
PO Box 1879
Plymouth, New Hampshire 03264-1879
Head of School: Mr. R. Phillip Peck

General Information Coeducational boarding and day college-preparatory, arts, religious studies, bilingual studies, and technology school, affiliated with Episcopal Church. Grades 9–PG. Founded: 1879. Setting: small town. Nearest major city is Boston, MA. Students are housed in single-sex dormitories. 620-acre campus. 35 buildings on campus. Approved or accredited by Association of Independent Schools in New England, New England Association of Schools and Colleges, The Association of Boarding Schools, and New Hampshire Department of Education. Member of National Association of Independent Schools and Secondary School Admission Test Board. Endowment: $44 million. Total enrollment: 281. Upper school average class size: 12. Upper school faculty-student ratio: 1:6. Upper School students typically attend 6 days per week.

Upper School Student Profile Grade 9: 49 students (27 boys, 22 girls); Grade 10: 66 students (42 boys, 24 girls); Grade 11: 87 students (47 boys, 40 girls); Grade 12: 76 students (48 boys, 28 girls); Postgraduate: 3 students (3 boys). 79% of students are boarding students. 36% are state residents. 24 states are represented in upper school student body. 13% are international students. International students from Canada, China, Lithuania, Republic of Korea, Saudi Arabia, and Spain; 7 other countries represented in student body. 20% of students are members of Episcopal Church.

Faculty School total: 49. In upper school: 29 men, 20 women; 29 have advanced degrees; 29 reside on campus.

Subjects Offered Advanced chemistry, Advanced Placement courses, algebra, anatomy and physiology, art, art history, Bible studies, biology, calculus, ceramics, chemistry, chorus, community service, drama, drawing, driver education, economics, economics and history, English, environmental science, ethics, ethics and responsibility, European history, fine arts, French, geometry, government/civics, history, human anatomy, human development, humanities, jazz band, Latin, mathematics, music, music composition, music theory, music theory-AP, painting, photography, physics, pre-calculus, religion, science, society and culture, Spanish, statistics, theater, theater arts, theater production, theology, trigonometry, U.S. history, women in world history, women's studies, world history, world religions, writing.

Graduation Requirements Arts and fine arts (art, music, dance, drama), English, foreign language, history, human development, humanities, mathematics, science, theology. Community service is required.

Special Academic Programs Advanced Placement exam preparation; honors section; independent study; term-away projects; study abroad; academic accommodation for the gifted, the musically talented, and the artistically talented.

College Admission Counseling 78 students graduated in 2009; 77 went to college, including Bates College; Dartmouth College; St. Lawrence University; University of New Hampshire; University of Vermont. Other: 1 entered a postgraduate year. Mean SAT critical reading: 555, mean SAT math: 577, mean SAT writing: 555. 37% scored over 600 on SAT critical reading, 39% scored over 600 on SAT math.

Student Life Upper grades have specified standards of dress, student council, honor system. Discipline rests equally with students and faculty. Attendance at religious services is required.

Tuition and Aid Day student tuition: $25,360; 7-day tuition and room/board: $42,670. Tuition installment plan (Insured Tuition Payment Plan, Key Tuition Payment Plan, monthly payment plans). Need based scholarship grants available. In 2009–10, 41% of upper-school students received aid. Total amount of financial aid awarded in 2009–10: $2,577,890.

Admissions Traditional secondary-level entrance grade is 9. For fall 2009, 425 students applied for upper-level admission, 204 were accepted, 104 enrolled. SSAT or WISC III or TOEFL required. Deadline for receipt of application materials: February 1. Application fee required: $50. Interview required.

Athletics Interscholastic: alpine skiing (boys, girls), baseball (b), basketball (b,g), bicycling (b,g), cross-country running (b,g), field hockey (g), football (b), freestyle skiing (b,g), ice hockey (b,g), lacrosse (b,g), nordic skiing (b,g), skiing (cross-country) (b,g), skiing (downhill) (b,g), snowboarding (b,g), soccer (b,g), softball (g), tennis (b,g); coed interscholastic: golf, running, ski jumping; coed intramural: aerobics/dance, backpacking, canoeing/kayaking, climbing, dance, equestrian sports, fishing, fly fishing, Frisbee, hiking/backpacking, horseback riding, ice hockey, kayaking, mountain biking, mountaineering, outdoor activities, outdoor skills, physical fitness, rock climbing, skiing (cross-country), skiing (downhill), snowboarding, snowshoeing, softball, squash, strength & conditioning, table tennis, ultimate Frisbee, wall climbing, weight lifting, weight training, wilderness, wilderness survival. 21 coaches, 1 athletic trainer.

Computers Computers are regularly used in Bible studies, creative writing, English, foreign language, graphic arts, history, library, mathematics, music, photography, religious studies, science, technology, theater, video film production, Web site design, yearbook classes. Computer network features include on-campus library services, Internet access, wireless campus network, Internet filtering or blocking technology, four computer labs (3 PC, 1 Mac). Campus intranet, student e-mail accounts, and computer access in designated common areas are available to students. The school has a published electronic and media policy.

Contact Ms. Nancy Dalley, Director of Financial Aid and Admission Operations. 603-536-1747. Fax: 603-536-2125. E-mail: admissions@holderness.org. Web site: www.holderness.org.

THE HOLTON-ARMS SCHOOL

7303 River Road
Bethesda, Maryland 20817
Head of School: Susanna A. Jones

General Information Girls' day college-preparatory school. Grades 3–12. Founded: 1901. Setting: suburban. Nearest major city is Washington, DC. 57-acre campus. 8 buildings on campus. Approved or accredited by Association of Independent Maryland Schools, Middle States Association of Colleges and Schools, and Maryland Department of Education. Member of National Association of Independent Schools and Secondary School Admission Test Board. Endowment: $51 million. Total enrollment: 638. Upper school average class size: 15. Upper school faculty-student ratio: 1:7. There are 173 required school days per year for Upper School students. Upper School students typically attend 5 days per week. The average school day consists of 7 hours and 30 minutes.

Upper School Student Profile Grade 9: 91 students (91 girls); Grade 10: 73 students (73 girls); Grade 11: 76 students (76 girls); Grade 12: 76 students (76 girls).

Faculty School total: 64. In upper school: 20 men, 44 women; 47 have advanced degrees.

Subjects Offered Acting, algebra, American history, American history-AP, American literature, ancient world history, art, art history, art history-AP, Asian studies, biology, biology-AP, calculus, calculus-AP, ceramics, chemistry, Chinese, community service, contemporary history, creative writing, dance, drama, drawing, ecology, economics, economics and history, economics-AP, engineering, English, English literature, environmental science, environmental science-AP, European history, European history-AP, expository writing, forensics, French, French-AP, geography, government/civics, grammar, health, history, history-AP, Latin, Latin American history, Latin-AP, macro/microeconomics-AP, mathematics, medieval history, Middle Eastern history, music, music technology, painting, philosophy, photography, physical education, physics, physics-AP, psychology, science, science research, social studies, Spanish, Spanish-AP, speech, statistics, theater, trigonometry, U.S. government and politics-AP, world history, world literature, writing.

Graduation Requirements Arts, English, foreign language, history, mathematics, physical education (includes health), science. Community service is required.

Special Academic Programs Advanced Placement exam preparation; honors section; independent study; academic accommodation for the gifted and the artistically talented.

College Admission Counseling 88 students graduated in 2009; all went to college, including Cornell University; Georgetown University; Harvard University; Middlebury College; Princeton University; Stanford University. Mean SAT critical reading: 673, mean SAT math: 673, mean SAT writing: 696, mean combined SAT: 2042, mean composite ACT: 29.

Student Life Upper grades have uniform requirement, student council, honor system. Discipline rests equally with students and faculty.

Tuition and Aid Day student tuition: $28,150–$29,450. Tuition installment plan (Key Tuition Payment Plan, monthly payment plans). Need-based scholarship grants available. In 2009–10, 24% of upper-school students received aid. Total amount of financial aid awarded in 2009–10: $2,912,000.

Admissions Traditional secondary-level entrance grade is 9. ISEE or SSAT required. Deadline for receipt of application materials: February 1. Application fee required: $60. Interview required.

Athletics Interscholastic: basketball, crew, cross-country running, diving, field hockey, ice hockey, indoor track, lacrosse, soccer, softball, swimming and diving, tennis, track and field, volleyball, winter (indoor) track; intramural: dance, life saving, modern dance, physical fitness, strength & conditioning; coed intramural: water polo. 9 PE instructors, 10 coaches, 1 athletic trainer.

Computers Computers are regularly used in all classes. Computer network features include on-campus library services, online commercial services, Internet access, wireless campus network, laptop program (grades 7-12). Campus intranet and student e-mail accounts are available to students. Students grades are available online. The school has a published electronic and media policy.

Contact Sharron Rodgers, Director of Enrollment and Marketing. 301-365-5300. Fax: 301-365-6071. E-mail: admit@holton-arms.edu. Web site: www.holton-arms.edu.

HOLY CROSS HIGH SCHOOL

587 Oronoke Road
Waterbury, Connecticut 06708
Head of School: Mr. Timothy McDonald

General Information Coeducational day college-preparatory and religious studies school, affiliated with Roman Catholic Church. Grades 9–12. Founded: 1968. Setting: suburban. 37-acre campus. 1 building on campus. Approved or accredited by Commission on Independent Schools, European Council of International Schools, New England Association of Schools and Colleges, and Connecticut Department of Education. Total enrollment: 730. Upper school average class size: 21. Upper school faculty-student ratio: 1:15. There are 160 required school days per year for Upper School students. Upper School students typically attend 5 days per week. The average school day consists of 6 hours.

Upper School Student Profile Grade 9: 168 students (90 boys, 78 girls); Grade 10: 184 students (100 boys, 84 girls); Grade 11: 201 students (106 boys, 95 girls); Grade 12: 178 students (84 boys, 94 girls). 85% of students are Roman Catholic.

Faculty School total: 60. In upper school: 28 men, 32 women; 37 have advanced degrees.

Subjects Offered Advanced biology, advanced math, Advanced Placement courses, advanced studio art-AP, algebra, American history, American history-AP, American literature, American literature-AP, American studies, anatomy, anatomy and physiology, art, art-AP, arts, band, Basic programming, biology, biology-AP, British literature, British literature-AP, business, business law, calculus, calculus-AP, campus ministry, Catholic belief and practice, chamber groups, chemistry, chemistry-AP, choir, computer applications, computer programming, computer science, concert band, concert choir, CPR, creative writing, drama, driver education, economics, economics and history, English, English literature, English-AP, environmental science, French, geometry, history, mathematics, music, physical education, physics, physiology, psychology, religion, science, social studies, Spanish, statistics, theater, theology, trigonometry, word processing, world history, world literature.

Graduation Requirements English, foreign language, mathematics, physical education (includes health), religion (includes Bible studies and theology), science, social studies (includes history).

Special Academic Programs Advanced Placement exam preparation; honors section; independent study; study at local college for college credit.

College Admission Counseling 196 students graduated in 2010; 190 went to college, including Central Connecticut State University; Naugatuck Valley Community College; Southern Connecticut State University; University of Connecticut; Western Connecticut State University. Other: 2 went to work, 1 entered military service, 3 had other specific plans.

Student Life Upper grades have specified standards of dress, student council. Discipline rests primarily with faculty. Attendance at religious services is required.

Tuition and Aid Day student tuition: $9200. Tuition installment plan (monthly payment plans, individually arranged payment plans, Tuition Management Systems (TMS)). Merit scholarship grants, need-based scholarship grants available In 2010–11, 30% of upper-school students received aid; total upper-school merit-scholarship money awarded: $135,000. Total amount of financial aid awarded in 2010–11: $550,000.

Admissions Traditional secondary-level entrance grade is 9. For fall 2010, 384 students applied for upper-level admission, 326 were accepted, 168 enrolled. ETS HSPT (closed) required. Deadline for receipt of application materials: none. Application fee required: $20.

Athletics Interscholastic: baseball (boys), basketball (b,g), cheering (g), cross-country running (b,g), diving (b,g), football (b), golf (b,g), gymnastics (g), soccer (b,g), softball (g), swimming and diving (b,g), tennis (b,g), track and field (b,g), volleyball (g), winter (indoor) track (b,g), wrestling (b); intramural: basketball (b), skiing (downhill) (b,g), weight lifting (b); coed intramural: bowling, table tennis, ultimate Frisbee, yoga. 4 PE instructors, 20 coaches, 1 athletic trainer.

Computers Computer network features include Internet access, wireless campus network. Campus intranet and computer access in designated common areas are available to students. Students grades are available online.

Holy Cross High School

Contact Mrs. Jodie LaCava McGarrity, Director of Admissions. 203-757-9248. Fax: 203-757-3423. E-mail: jmcgarrity@holycrosshs-ct.com. Web site: www.holycrosshs-ct.com.

HOLY GHOST PREPARATORY SCHOOL

2429 Bristol Pike
Bensalem, Pennsylvania 19020
Head of School: Rev. Jeffrey T. Duaime, CSSP

General Information Boys' day college-preparatory, arts, and technology school, affiliated with Roman Catholic Church. Grades 9–12. Founded: 1897. Setting: suburban. Nearest major city is Philadelphia. 53-acre campus. 4 buildings on campus. Approved or accredited by Middle States Association of Colleges and Schools, National Catholic Education Association, and Pennsylvania Association of Independent Schools. Member of National Association of Independent Schools. Endowment: $2 million. Total enrollment: 502. Upper school average class size: 17. Upper school faculty-student ratio: 1:11. The average school day consists of 6 hours and 30 minutes.

Upper School Student Profile Grade 9: 125 students (125 boys); Grade 10: 127 students (127 boys); Grade 11: 124 students (124 boys); Grade 12: 126 students (126 boys). 94% of students are Roman Catholic.

Faculty School total: 50. In upper school: 32 men, 18 women; 34 have advanced degrees.

Subjects Offered 3-dimensional art, Advanced Placement courses, advanced studio art-AP, algebra, American government, American history, American history-AP, American literature, analysis, anatomy and physiology, art, Bible, biology, biology-AP, calculus, calculus-AP, campus ministry, career/college preparation, careers, ceremonies of life, chemistry, Chinese history, choral music, church history, college admission preparation, college counseling, communication arts, communication skills, computer programming-AP, computer science, computer science-AP, creative writing, drama performance, earth science, economics, English, English language and composition-AP, English literature, English literature and composition-AP, environmental science, European history, European history-AP, film, fine arts, French, French language-AP, geometry, government and politics-AP, government/civics, health, history, journalism, language-AP, Latin, Latin-AP, mathematics, modern European history-AP, music, music theory-AP, oral communications, physical education, physics, public speaking, religion, science, sexuality, social studies, Spanish, Spanish language-AP, Spanish-AP, speech, statistics, trigonometry, U.S. history-AP, United States government-AP, world cultures, world history, world history-AP, world literature, writing, yearbook.

Graduation Requirements Arts and fine arts (art, music, dance, drama), computer science, English, foreign language, mathematics, physical education (includes health), religion (includes Bible studies and theology), science, social studies (includes history), summer reading. Community service is required.

Special Academic Programs Advanced Placement exam preparation; honors section; independent study; study abroad.

College Admission Counseling 117 students graduated in 2010; all went to college, including Boston College; Drexel University; Duquesne University; Saint Joseph's University; University of Pennsylvania; Villanova University. Median SAT critical reading: 610, median SAT math: 640.

Student Life Upper grades have specified standards of dress, student council, honor system. Discipline rests primarily with faculty.

Summer Programs Enrichment, advancement, sports, computer instruction programs offered; session focuses on entrance exam preparation; held on campus; accepts boys and girls; open to students from other schools. 100 students usually enrolled. 2011 schedule: June 29 to July 24. Application deadline: June 1.

Tuition and Aid Day student tuition: $15,500. Tuition installment plan (monthly payment plans, quarterly and semi-annual payment plans). Merit scholarship grants, need-based scholarship grants, music scholarships, minority scholarships, art scholarships available. In 2010–11, 35% of upper-school students received aid; total upper-school merit-scholarship money awarded: $200,000. Total amount of financial aid awarded in 2010–11: $350,000.

Admissions Traditional secondary-level entrance grade is 9. For fall 2010, 398 students applied for upper-level admission, 158 were accepted, 125 enrolled. High School Placement Test (closed version) from Scholastic Testing Service required. Deadline for receipt of application materials: December 12. Application fee required: $60. On-campus interview required.

Athletics Interscholastic: baseball, basketball, bowling, cross-country running, golf, ice hockey, indoor track & field, lacrosse, soccer, Special Olympics, swimming and diving, tennis, track and field; intramural: basketball, fitness walking, flag football, football, Frisbee, soccer, street hockey, tennis. 10 coaches, 1 athletic trainer.

Computers Computers are regularly used in college planning, English, foreign language, mathematics, programming, publications, science, speech, yearbook classes. Computer network features include on-campus library services, online commercial services, Internet access, wireless campus network, Internet filtering or blocking technology. Student e-mail accounts are available to students.

Contact Mr. Ryan T. Abramson, Director of Admissions. 215-639-0811. Fax: 215-639-4225. E-mail: rabramson@holyghostprep.org. Web site: www.holyghostprep.org.

HOLY INNOCENTS' EPISCOPAL SCHOOL

805 Mount Vernon Highway NW
Atlanta, Georgia 30327
Head of School: Mr. Rick Betts

General Information Coeducational day college-preparatory, arts, religious studies, and technology school, affiliated with Episcopal Church. Grades PS–12. Founded: 1959. Setting: suburban. 46-acre campus. 4 buildings on campus. Approved or accredited by Southern Association of Colleges and Schools and Georgia Department of Education. Member of National Association of Independent Schools and Secondary School Admission Test Board. Endowment: $13.4 million. Total enrollment: 1,330. Upper school average class size: 18. Upper school faculty-student ratio: 1:10. There are 173 required school days per year for Upper School students. Upper School students typically attend 5 days per week. The average school day consists of 7 hours and 15 minutes.

Upper School Student Profile Grade 6: 112 students (51 boys, 61 girls); Grade 7: 123 students (58 boys, 65 girls); Grade 8: 119 students (47 boys, 72 girls); Grade 9: 119 students (60 boys, 59 girls); Grade 10: 102 students (45 boys, 57 girls); Grade 11: 97 students (43 boys, 54 girls); Grade 12: 106 students (46 boys, 60 girls). 27% of students are members of Episcopal Church.

Faculty School total: 158. In upper school: 25 men, 29 women; 45 have advanced degrees.

Subjects Offered 3-dimensional art, 3-dimensional design, advanced biology, advanced chemistry, advanced math, Advanced Placement courses, advanced studio art-AP, algebra, American government, American history, American history-AP, American literature, American literature-AP, anatomy, anatomy and physiology, ancient world history, applied music, art, art-AP, athletics, band, baseball, basketball, Bible, Bible studies, biology, biology-AP, calculus, calculus-AP, cheerleading, chemistry, chemistry-AP, choir, choral music, chorus, college counseling, college placement, community service, composition, computer animation, computer education, computer graphics, computer resources, concert band, concert choir, creative writing, drama, drama performance, drawing and design, earth science, economics, electives, English, English composition, English language-AP, English literature, English literature-AP, English-AP, environmental studies, ethics, European history, European history-AP, fine arts, French, French language-AP, French-AP, geometry, golf, government, government and politics-AP, government/civics, guidance, health and wellness, history, honors algebra, honors English, honors geometry, honors U.S. history, honors world history, language arts, Latin, Latin-AP, mathematics, New Testament, orchestra, peer counseling, performing arts, personal finance, photography, physical education, physics, physics-AP, pre-calculus, psychology, religion, religious studies, SAT preparation, science, science project, sex education, social studies, Spanish, Spanish language-AP, speech and debate, sports, study skills, swimming, U.S. history, U.S. history-AP, visual arts, world history, writing workshop, yearbook.

Graduation Requirements Arts and fine arts (art, music, dance, drama), electives, English, foreign language, history, mathematics, physical education (includes health), physical fitness, religion (includes Bible studies and theology), science, 10 hours of community service each year, plus additional hours for NHS students.

Special Academic Programs Advanced Placement exam preparation; honors section; term-away projects; study abroad.

College Admission Counseling 98 students graduated in 2010; 97 went to college, including Auburn University; College of Charleston; The University of Alabama; The University of North Carolina at Chapel Hill; University of Georgia; University of Virginia. Other: 1 had other specific plans. Mean SAT critical reading: 575, mean SAT math: 590, mean SAT writing: 600, mean combined SAT: 588, mean composite ACT: 25.

Student Life Upper grades have uniform requirement, student council, honor system. Discipline rests primarily with faculty. Attendance at religious services is required.

Summer Programs Enrichment, sports, art/fine arts programs offered; session focuses on athletics, fine arts, and academics; held on campus; accepts boys and girls; open to students from other schools. 725 students usually enrolled. 2011 schedule: June 2 to August 14. Application deadline: February 12.

Tuition and Aid Day student tuition: $18,960. Tuition installment plan (Insured Tuition Payment Plan). Need-based scholarship grants available. In 2010–11, 17% of upper-school students received aid. Total amount of financial aid awarded in 2010–11: $956,160.

Admissions Traditional secondary-level entrance grade is 9. For fall 2010, 144 students applied for upper-level admission, 78 were accepted, 31 enrolled. Essay, mathematics proficiency exam, school's own test and SSAT required. Deadline for receipt of application materials: February 18. Application fee required: $95. Interview required.

Athletics Interscholastic: baseball (boys), basketball (b,g), cheering (g), cross-country running (b,g), equestrian sports (g), football (b), golf (b,g), lacrosse (b,g), physical fitness (b,g), physical training (b,g), soccer (b,g), softball (g), swimming and diving (b,g), tennis (b,g), track and field (b,g), volleyball (g), wrestling (b); intramural: combined training (b,g), fitness (b,g); coed intramural: combined training, fitness. 9 PE instructors, 63 coaches, 1 athletic trainer.

Computers Computers are regularly used in all academic classes. Computer network features include on-campus library services, Internet access, wireless campus network, Internet filtering or blocking technology, 1-to-1 student laptops (grades 5-12), two computer labs and various individual classroom computers. Campus intranet and student e-mail accounts are available to students. Students grades are available online. The school has a published electronic and media policy.

Contact Mr. Chris Pomar, Director of Admissions. 404-255-4026. Fax: 404-847-1156. E-mail: chris.pomar@hies.org. Web site: www.hies.org.

HOLY NAME HIGH SCHOOL

955 East Wyomissing Boulevard
Reading, Pennsylvania 19611
Head of School: Rev. John A. Frink

General Information Coeducational day college-preparatory school, affiliated with Roman Catholic Church. Grades 9–12. Founded: 1964. Setting: suburban. 18-acre campus. 1 building on campus. Approved or accredited by Middle States Association of Colleges and Schools and Pennsylvania Department of Education. Total enrollment: 461. Upper school average class size: 25. Upper school faculty-student ratio: 1:13. There are 180 required school days per year for Upper School students.

Upper School Student Profile Grade 9: 118 students (56 boys, 62 girls); Grade 10: 124 students (59 boys, 65 girls); Grade 11: 112 students (57 boys, 55 girls); Grade 12: 107 students (56 boys, 51 girls). 94% of students are Roman Catholic.

Faculty School total: 35. In upper school: 18 men, 17 women; 14 have advanced degrees.

Graduation Requirements 4 years of theology.

Special Academic Programs Advanced Placement exam preparation; honors section; study at local college for college credit.

College Admission Counseling 111 students graduated in 2010; all went to college.

Student Life Upper grades have uniform requirement, student council. Discipline rests primarily with faculty. Attendance at religious services is required.

Summer Programs Sports programs offered; session focuses on basketball and volleyball; held on campus; accepts boys and girls; not open to students from other schools. 300 students usually enrolled. 2011 schedule: June 12 to August 11. Application deadline: none.

Tuition and Aid Day student tuition: $5700. Tuition installment plan (FACTS Tuition Payment Plan). Tuition reduction for siblings, need-based scholarship grants available. In 2010–11, 34% of upper-school students received aid. Total amount of financial aid awarded in 2010–11: $24,522.

Admissions Traditional secondary-level entrance grade is 9. For fall 2010, 128 students applied for upper-level admission, 125 were accepted, 125 enrolled. Math and English placement tests required. Deadline for receipt of application materials: none. Application fee required: $100. On-campus interview recommended.

Athletics Interscholastic: baseball (boys), basketball (b,g), cheering (g), field hockey (g), football (b), ice hockey (b), lacrosse (b,g), soccer (b,g), softball (g), swimming and diving (b,g), tennis (b,g), track and field (b,g), volleyball (g); coed interscholastic: cross-country running, golf; coed intramural: ice hockey. 1 PE instructor, 52 coaches, 1 athletic trainer.

Computers Computers are regularly used in all academic classes. Computer resources include on-campus library services, online commercial services, Internet access, Internet filtering or blocking technology. Student e-mail accounts are available to students. Students grades are available online.

Contact Mr. Josh Ditsky, Director of College Counseling. 610-374-8361 Ext. 46. Fax: 610-374-4398. E-mail: jditsky@gohnhs.org. Web site: www.gohnhs.org.

HOLY NAMES HIGH SCHOOL

4660 Harbord Drive
Oakland, California 94618
Head of School: Sr. Sally Slyngstad

General Information Girls' day college-preparatory, arts, religious studies, and technology school, affiliated with Roman Catholic Church. Grades 9–12. Founded: 1868. Setting: urban. 5-acre campus. 1 building on campus. Approved or accredited by Western Association of Schools and Colleges and California Department of Education. Endowment: $5 million. Total enrollment: 300. Upper school average class size: 21. Upper school faculty-student ratio: 1:11. There are 180 required school days per year for Upper School students. Upper School students typically attend 5 days per week. The average school day consists of 5 hours and 50 minutes.

Upper School Student Profile Grade 9: 75 students (75 girls); Grade 10: 75 (75 girls); Grade 11: 79 students (79 girls); Grade 12: 71 students (71 girls). 51% of students are Roman Catholic.

Faculty School total: 29. In upper school: 4 men, 25 women; all have advanced degrees.

Subjects Offered Advanced Placement courses, algebra, American history, American literature, art, biology, business skills, calculus, chemistry, computer programming, computer science, creative writing, drama, driver education, economics, English, English literature, fine arts, French, geometry, government/civics, health, history, mathematics, music, photography, physical education, physics, physiology, psychology, religion, science, social sciences, social studies, Spanish, speech, statistics, theater, theology, trigonometry, typing, world history, world literature.

Graduation Requirements Arts and fine arts (art, music, dance, drama), computer science, English, foreign language, mathematics, physical education (includes health), religion (includes Bible studies and theology), science, social sciences, social studies (includes history), technology.

Special Academic Programs 8 Advanced Placement exams for which test preparation is offered; honors section; independent study; term-away projects; study at local college for college credit; academic accommodation for the gifted, the musically talented, and the artistically talented.

College Admission Counseling 71 students graduated in 2009; all went to college, including California State University; Howard University; Saint Mary's College of California; University of California, Berkeley; University of Southern California. Mean SAT critical reading: 632, mean SAT math: 658. 99% scored over 600 on SAT critical reading, 99% scored over 600 on SAT math.

Student Life Upper grades have uniform requirement, student council, honor system. Discipline rests equally with students and faculty. Attendance at religious services is required.

Tuition and Aid Day student tuition: $10,800. Tuition installment plan (SMART Tuition Payment Plan, FACTS Tuition Payment Plan, monthly payment plans, individually arranged payment plans). Merit scholarship grants, need-based scholarship grants available. In 2009–10, 49% of upper-school students received aid; total upper-school merit-scholarship money awarded: $89,000. Total amount of financial aid awarded in 2009–10: $324,466.

Admissions For fall 2009, 225 students applied for upper-level admission, 175 were accepted, 75 enrolled. Catholic High School Entrance Examination and STS required. Deadline for receipt of application materials: January 9. Application fee required: $75. On-campus interview required.

Athletics Interscholastic: backpacking, basketball, cross-country running, dance squad, golf, indoor track & field, physical fitness, soccer, softball, swimming and diving, tennis, track and field, volleyball; intramural: backpacking, basketball, cross-country running, dance squad, golf, indoor track & field, physical fitness, soccer, softball, swimming and diving, tennis, track and field, volleyball. 2 PE instructors, 25 coaches, 8 athletic trainers.

Computers Computers are regularly used in English, foreign language, mathematics, religious studies, science classes. Computer network features include on-campus library services, Internet access, wireless campus network, Internet filtering or blocking technology. Campus intranet, student e-mail accounts, and computer access in designated common areas are available to students. Students grades are available online. The school has a published electronic and media policy.

Contact Sandra Carrillo, Director of Admissions. 510-450-1110 Ext. 119. Fax: 510-547-3111. E-mail: scarrillo@hnhsoakland.org. Web site: www.hnhsoakland.org/.

HOLYOKE CATHOLIC HIGH SCHOOL

134 Springfield Street
Chicopee, Massachusetts 01013
Head of School: Dr. Michael Griffin

General Information Coeducational day college-preparatory and arts school, affiliated with Roman Catholic Church. Grades 9–12. Founded: 1963. Setting: small town. Nearest major city is Springfield. .5-acre campus. 2 buildings on campus. Approved or accredited by National Catholic Education Association, New England Association of Schools and Colleges, and Massachusetts Department of Education. Upper school average class size: 15. Upper school faculty-student ratio: 1:12. There are 180 required school days per year for Upper School students. Upper School students typically attend 5 days per week. The average school day consists of 6 hours and 30 minutes.

Upper School Student Profile 90% of students are Roman Catholic.

Faculty School total: 26. In upper school: 12 men, 14 women; 19 have advanced degrees.

Subjects Offered U.S. history, U.S. history-AP.

Graduation Requirements U.S. literature, community service hours at each grade level.

Special Academic Programs 5 Advanced Placement exams for which test preparation is offered; honors section; independent study; study at local college for college credit.

College Admission Counseling 85 students graduated in 2010; 83 went to college. Other: 1 went to work, 1 entered military service.

Student Life Upper grades have uniform requirement, student council. Discipline rests primarily with faculty. Attendance at religious services is required.

Tuition and Aid Day student tuition: $7000. Tuition installment plan (FACTS Tuition Payment Plan, individually arranged payment plans). Need-based scholarship grants available. In 2010–11, 24% of upper-school students received aid. Total amount of financial aid awarded in 2010–11: $87,000.

Admissions Traditional secondary-level entrance grade is 9. For fall 2010, 90 students applied for upper-level admission, 85 were accepted, 79 enrolled. Scholastic Testing Service High School Placement Test and SSTS Placement Test required. Deadline for receipt of application materials: none. Application fee required: $100. Interview required.

Athletics Interscholastic: baseball (boys), basketball (b,g), cheering (g), cross-country running (b,g), flag football (g), football (b), indoor track (b,g), lacrosse (b,g), soccer (b,g), softball (g), tennis (g), wrestling (b); coed interscholastic: alpine skiing, dance, Frisbee, golf, hiking/backpacking, outdoor adventure, skiing (downhill), swimming and diving, track and field; coed intramural: volleyball, weight training. 18 coaches, 2 athletic trainers.

Computers Computers are regularly used in all classes. Computer network features include on-campus library services, Internet access, Internet filtering or blocking technology. Campus intranet and student e-mail accounts are available to students. Students grades are available online. The school has a published electronic and media policy.

Contact Mrs. Theresa Marie Zaborowski, Director of Admissions. 413-331-2480 Ext. 1132. Fax: 413-331-2708. E-mail: tzaborowski@gaels.org. Web site: www. gaels.org.

HOLY SAVIOR MENARD CATHOLIC HIGH SCHOOL

4603 Coliseum Boulevard
Alexandria, Louisiana 71303
Head of School: Mr. Joel Desselle

General Information Coeducational day college-preparatory and religious studies school, affiliated with Roman Catholic Church. Grades 7–12. Founded: 1930. Setting: suburban. 5-acre campus. 5 buildings on campus. Approved or accredited by National Catholic Education Association, Southern Association of Colleges and Schools, and Louisiana Department of Education. Total enrollment: 465. Upper school average class size: 18. Upper school faculty-student ratio: 1:14. There are 178 required school days per year for Upper School students. Upper School students typically attend 5 days per week. The average school day consists of 7 hours and 15 minutes.

Upper School Student Profile Grade 9: 86 students (34 boys, 52 girls); Grade 10: 70 students (26 boys, 44 girls); Grade 11: 72 students (42 boys, 30 girls); Grade 12: 80 students (47 boys, 33 girls). 87% of students are Roman Catholic.

Faculty School total: 37. In upper school: 16 men, 16 women; 11 have advanced degrees.

Subjects Offered Advanced math, algebra, American history, anatomy and physiology, art, athletics, biology, biology-AP, British literature, British literature (honors), calculus-AP, campus ministry, Catholic belief and practice, cheerleading, chemistry, civics/free enterprise, computer applications, computer science, digital photography, English, English composition, English literature, English literature-AP, fine arts, French, general science, geometry, health, honors algebra, honors English, honors geometry, honors U.S. history, honors world history, journalism, language arts, moral reasoning, New Testament, newspaper, philosophy, physical education, physical science, physics, pre-algebra, pre-calculus, psychology, publications, reading/study skills, religion, sociology, Spanish, world geography, world history, yearbook.

Graduation Requirements Algebra, American history, arts and fine arts (art, music, dance, drama), biology, chemistry, civics/free enterprise, computer applications, English, foreign language, geometry, physical science, religion (includes Bible studies and theology), world history, 26 credits required.

Special Academic Programs 4 Advanced Placement exams for which test preparation is offered; honors section; study at local college for college credit.

College Admission Counseling 91 students graduated in 2010; 88 went to college, including Baylor University; Louisiana State University and Agricultural and Mechanical College; Louisiana Tech University; Northwestern State University of Louisiana; Tulane University; University of Louisiana at Lafayette. Other: 2 went to work, 1 entered military service. Mean composite ACT: 23. 33% scored over 26 on composite ACT.

Student Life Upper grades have uniform requirement, student council, honor system. Discipline rests primarily with faculty. Attendance at religious services is required.

Summer Programs Remediation programs offered; session focuses on summer school for credit recovery; held on campus; accepts boys and girls; not open to students from other schools. 10 students usually enrolled. 2011 schedule: June 1 to June 30. Application deadline: May 31.

Tuition and Aid Day student tuition: $5400. Tuition installment plan (FACTS Tuition Payment Plan, monthly payment plans, individually arranged payment plans). Tuition reduction for siblings, merit scholarship grants, need-based scholarship grants available. In 2010–11, 13% of upper-school students received aid; total upper-school merit-scholarship money awarded: $5000. Total amount of financial aid awarded in 2010–11: $135,000.

Admissions Traditional secondary-level entrance grade is 9. For fall 2010, 29 students applied for upper-level admission, 29 were accepted, 29 enrolled. CTBS, Stanford Achievement Test, any other standardized test required. Deadline for receipt of application materials: March 15. Application fee required: $250. On-campus interview required.

Athletics Interscholastic: baseball (boys), basketball (b,g), cheering (g), cross-country running (b,g), danceline (g), football (b), golf (b,g), power lifting (b), running (b,g), soccer (b,g), softball (g), tennis (b,g), track and field (b,g); coed interscholastic: swimming and diving. 2 coaches.

Computers Computers are regularly used in computer applications, English, journalism, photography, publications, science, Web site design classes. Computer network features include on-campus library services, Internet access, wireless campus network, Internet filtering or blocking technology. Computer access in designated common areas is available to students. Students grades are available online.

Contact Mrs. Ashley Meadows, Guidance Secretary. 318-445-8233. Fax: 318-448-8170. E-mail: ameadows@holysaviormenard.com. Web site: www. holysaviormenard.com.

HOLY TRINITY DIOCESAN HIGH SCHOOL

98 Cherry Lane
Hicksville, New York 11801
Head of School: Mr. Gene Fennell

General Information Coeducational day college-preparatory school, affiliated with Roman Catholic Church. Grades 9–12. Founded: 1967. Setting: suburban. Nearest major city is New York. 1 building on campus. Approved or accredited by National Council for Private School Accreditation, National Private School Accreditation Alliance, New York State Board of Regents, and The College Board. Total enrollment: 1,496. Upper school average class size: 28.

Upper School Student Profile Grade 9: 382 students (190 boys, 192 girls); Grade 10: 389 students (185 boys, 204 girls); Grade 11: 340 students (137 boys, 203 girls); Grade 12: 385 students (157 boys, 228 girls). 90% of students are Roman Catholic.

Faculty School total: 110. In upper school: 43 men, 67 women; 91 have advanced degrees.

Subjects Offered Accounting, advanced math, Advanced Placement courses, American government, American history, American history-AP, American literature, American literature-AP, anatomy and physiology, architectural drawing, art, band, biology, biology-AP, British literature, British literature (honors), business law, calculus, calculus-AP, campus ministry, ceramics, chemistry, chemistry-AP, chorus, Christian scripture, Christian studies, Christian testament, comparative religion, composition, concert band, criminology, critical studies in film, dance, desktop publishing, earth science, economics, English, English composition, English language and composition-AP, English literature, English literature-AP, environmental science, film, food and nutrition, French, government and politics-AP, health, honors English, honors U.S. history, honors world history, intro to computers, jazz theory, keyboarding, literature and composition-AP, mathematics, music, performing arts, physical education, physics, physics-AP, pre-calculus, public speaking, religion, Spanish, Spanish language-AP, stagecraft, statistics, theater arts, theology, U.S. government and politics, U.S. government and politics-AP, U.S. history, U.S. history-AP, world wide web design.

Graduation Requirements Arts and fine arts (art, music, dance, drama), economics, English, foreign language, mathematics, physical education (includes health), religion (includes Bible studies and theology), science, U.S. government and politics.

Special Academic Programs Advanced Placement exam preparation; honors section; study at local college for college credit.

College Admission Counseling 431 students graduated in 2009; all went to college, including Adelphi University; Hofstra University; Nassau Community College; Stony Brook University, State University of New York. Mean SAT critical reading: 514, mean SAT math: 522, mean SAT writing: 520.

Student Life Upper grades have uniform requirement, student council. Discipline rests primarily with faculty.

Tuition and Aid Day student tuition: $7375. Tuition installment plan (monthly payment plans, individually arranged payment plans, 10-month tuition plan, 3-payment plan). Need-based scholarship grants available.

Admissions Traditional secondary-level entrance grade is 9. Catholic High School Entrance Examination required. Deadline for receipt of application materials: none. Application fee required. Interview recommended.

Athletics Interscholastic: badminton (girls), baseball (b), basketball (b,g), cheering (g), cross-country running (b,g), dance team (g), football (b), golf (b), gymnastics (g), indoor track (b,g), lacrosse (b,g), soccer (b,g), softball (g), swimming and diving (b,g), tennis (b,g), track and field (b,g), volleyball (b,g), weight lifting (b), weight training (b), winter (indoor) track (b,g), wrestling (b); intramural: physical training (b), weight training (b); coed interscholastic: bowling, fitness. 6 PE instructors, 1 athletic trainer.

Computers Computers are regularly used in college planning, computer applications, desktop publishing, drawing and design, economics, English, foreign language, graphic design, history, journalism, library, music technology, newspaper, occupational education, programming, research skills, SAT preparation, science, social studies, theater, Web site design, writing, yearbook classes. Computer network features include on-campus library services, Internet access, Internet filtering or blocking technology. Student e-mail accounts and computer access in designated common areas are available to students. Students grades are available online. The school has a published electronic and media policy.

Contact Admissions. 516-433-2900. Fax: 516-433-2827. E-mail: hths98@ holytrinityhs.echalk.com. Web site: www.holytrinityhs.org.

HOLY TRINITY HIGH SCHOOL

1443 West Division Street
Chicago, Illinois 60642
Head of School: Mr. Timothy M. Bopp

General Information Coeducational day college-preparatory, arts, business, religious studies, bilingual studies, and technology school, affiliated with Roman Catholic Church. Grades 9–12. Founded: 1910. Setting: urban. 1 building on campus. Approved or accredited by North Central Association of Colleges and Schools and Illinois

Department of Education. Total enrollment: 300. Upper school average class size: 20. Upper school faculty-student ratio: 1:11. The average school day consists of 5 hours and 52 minutes.

Upper School Student Profile Grade 9: 71 students (40 boys, 31 girls); Grade 10: 82 students (53 boys, 29 girls); Grade 11: 72 students (40 boys, 32 girls); Grade 12: 75 students (33 boys, 42 girls). 50% of students are Roman Catholic.

Faculty School total: 28. In upper school: 13 men, 15 women; 14 have advanced degrees.

Graduation Requirements Business, English, mathematics, modern languages, physical education (includes health), religion (includes Bible studies and theology), science, social studies (includes history), visual and performing arts.

Special Academic Programs Advanced Placement exam preparation; honors section; study at local college for college credit; remedial reading and/or remedial writing; ESL.

College Admission Counseling 65 students graduated in 2010; all went to college, including Adelphi University.

Student Life Upper grades have uniform requirement, student council, honor system. Discipline rests equally with students and faculty. Attendance at religious services is required.

Tuition and Aid Day student tuition: $6750. Tuition installment plan (monthly payment plans). Tuition reduction for siblings, merit scholarship grants, need-based scholarship grants available. In 2010–11, 95% of upper-school students received aid; total upper-school merit-scholarship money awarded: $126,500. Total amount of financial aid awarded in 2010–11: $1,547,085.

Admissions Traditional secondary-level entrance grade is 9. For fall 2010, 165 students applied for upper-level admission, 157 were accepted, 80 enrolled. Deadline for receipt of application materials: January 8. Application fee required: $25.

Athletics Interscholastic: baseball (boys), basketball (b,g), cross-country running (b,g), soccer (b,g), softball (g), track and field (b,g), volleyball (b,g); coed interscholastic: bowling, flag football; coed intramural: cheering, dance. 2 PE instructors.

Computers Computers are regularly used in animation, business education, business skills, college planning, keyboarding classes. Computer network features include on-campus library services, Internet access, wireless campus network, Internet filtering or blocking technology. Computer access in designated common areas is available to students. The school has a published electronic and media policy.

Contact Ms. Maura E. Daly, Director of Recruitment. 773-278-4212 Ext. 3023. Fax: 773-278-0144. E-mail: mdaly@holytrinity-hs.org. Web site: www.holytrinity-hs.org.

HOOSAC SCHOOL

PO Box 9
Hoosick, New York 12089
Head of School: Richard J. Lomuscio

General Information Coeducational boarding and day college-preparatory and arts school, affiliated with Episcopal Church. Grades 8–PG. Founded: 1889. Setting: rural. Nearest major city is Albany. Students are housed in single-sex dormitories. 350-acre campus. 16 buildings on campus. Approved or accredited by Middle States Association of Colleges and Schools, National Association of Episcopal Schools, New York State Association of Independent Schools, New York State Board of Regents, The Association of Boarding Schools, and New York Department of Education. Member of National Association of Independent Schools and Secondary School Admission Test Board. Endowment: $1.5 million. Total enrollment: 125. Upper school average class size: 8. Upper school faculty-student ratio: 1:5.

Upper School Student Profile Grade 8: 7 students (5 boys, 2 girls); Grade 9: 20 students (10 boys, 10 girls); Grade 10: 23 students (16 boys, 7 girls); Grade 11: 29 students (17 boys, 12 girls); Grade 12: 41 students (29 boys, 12 girls); Postgraduate: 5 students (5 boys). 88% of students are boarding students. 29% are state residents. 17 states are represented in upper school student body. 27% are international students. International students from Canada, China, Hungary, India, Jamaica, and Republic of Korea; 13 other countries represented in student body.

Faculty School total: 23. In upper school: 13 men, 10 women; 10 have advanced degrees; 15 reside on campus.

Subjects Offered Advertising design, algebra, American history, American literature, art, art history, astronomy, biology, calculus, calculus-AP, ceramics, chemistry, computer science, creative writing, criminology, dance, drama, driver education, earth science, English, English literature, English-AP, ethics, European history, expository writing, fine arts, French, geometry, government/civics, grammar, history, history-AP, marketing, mathematics, music, photography, physical education, physics, science, social studies, theater, world history, world literature, writing.

Graduation Requirements Arts and fine arts (art, music, dance, drama), computer literacy, English, ethics, foreign language, mathematics, physical education (includes health), science, social studies (includes history), ethics.

Special Academic Programs Advanced Placement exam preparation; honors section; accelerated programs; independent study; study at local college for college credit; academic accommodation for the musically talented and the artistically talented; remedial reading and/or remedial writing; remedial math; programs in English, mathematics, general development for dyslexic students; ESL (15 students enrolled).

Hoosac School is a coeducational boarding school enrolling students in grades 8-12 and PG. Hoosac Students receive individual attention with a 5:1 student/teacher ratio. The college preparatory curriculum includes AP courses and an ESL program.

Facilities include a technology lab, athletic center with indoor pool, observatory, and arts center. The rural campus setting is ideal for camping, skiing and snowboarding. Hoosac fields strong teams in many sports and its represented especially well in ice hockey, baseball, soccer, and lacrosse.

To receive information contact:
Asst. Headmaster Dean S. Foster
Hoosac School
Hoosick, NY 12089
(518) 686-7331

admissions@hoosac.com

www.hoosac.com

Hoosac School

College Admission Counseling 45 students graduated in 2010; all went to college, including Boston College; Boston University; Bowdoin College; Hamilton College; Penn State University Park; University of Michigan.

Student Life Upper grades have specified standards of dress, student council, honor system. Discipline rests primarily with faculty. Attendance at religious services is required.

Tuition and Aid Day student tuition: $16,000; 7-day tuition and room/board: $35,000. Tuition installment plan (Academic Management Services Plan, Key Tuition Payment Plan, monthly payment plans, individually arranged payment plans). Merit scholarship grants, need-based scholarship grants available. In 2010–11, 30% of upper-school students received aid. Total amount of financial aid awarded in 2010–11: $500,000.

Admissions Traditional secondary-level entrance grade is 9. For fall 2010, 168 students applied for upper-level admission, 108 were accepted, 56 enrolled. Deadline for receipt of application materials: none. Application fee required: $30. Interview required.

Athletics Interscholastic: baseball (boys), basketball (b,g), cross-country running (b,g), ice hockey (b), lacrosse (b); intramural: bicycling (b,g), flag football (b,g), floor hockey (b,g); coed intramural: alpine skiing, aquatics, backpacking, ball hockey, billiards, bowling, cross-country running, dance, deck hockey, fishing, freestyle skiing, golf, indoor hockey, indoor soccer, life saving. 1 PE instructor, 15 coaches.

Computers Computers are regularly used in computer applications, journalism, literary magazine, media arts, media production, multimedia, news writing, newspaper, photography, photojournalism classes. Computer network features include on-campus library services, Internet access, wireless campus network, Internet filtering or blocking technology. Campus intranet, student e-mail accounts, and computer access in designated common areas are available to students. The school has a published electronic and media policy.

Contact Dean S. Foster, Assistant Headmaster. 800-822-0159. Fax: 518-686-3370. E-mail: admissions@hoosac.com. Web site: www.hoosac.com.

See Display on page 319 and Close-Up on page 792.

HOPKINS SCHOOL

986 Forest Road
New Haven, Connecticut 06515

Head of School: Ms. Barbara M. Riley

General Information Coeducational day college-preparatory school. Grades 7–12. Founded: 1660. Setting: urban. Nearest major city is New York, NY. 108-acre campus. 9 buildings on campus. Approved or accredited by Connecticut Association of Independent Schools, New England Association of Schools and Colleges, and Connecticut Department of Education. Member of National Association of Independent Schools. Endowment: $55 million. Total enrollment: 681. Upper school average class size: 12. Upper school faculty-student ratio: 1:6. There are 170 required school days per year for Upper School students. Upper School students typically attend 5 days per week. The average school day consists of 7 hours and 30 minutes.

Upper School Student Profile Grade 9: 138 students (68 boys, 70 girls); Grade 10: 139 students (75 boys, 64 girls); Grade 11: 120 students (62 boys, 58 girls); Grade 12: 129 students (58 boys, 71 girls).

Faculty School total: 123. In upper school: 52 men, 71 women; 97 have advanced degrees.

Subjects Offered African-American history, algebra, American history, American literature, anatomy and physiology, ancient history, art, art history, art history-AP, art-AP, Asian studies, biochemistry, biology, biology-AP, calculus, calculus-AP, ceramics, chemistry, chemistry-AP, chorus, classical music, computer math, computer programming, computer science, computer science-AP, creative writing, drama, earth science, economics, English, English literature, environmental science-AP, European history, expository writing, film, fine arts, French, French-AP, geometry, government/civics, Greek, history, Holocaust studies, HTML design, human geography—AP, human sexuality, Islamic history, Italian, jazz, Latin, Latin American history, Latin-AP, mathematics, military history, music, music theory, philosophy, photography, physics, physics-AP, politics, psychology, Russian history, Spanish, Spanish-AP, studio art, studio art-AP, theater, trigonometry, U.S. history-AP, urban studies, video, Web site design, woodworking, world history, world literature, writing.

Graduation Requirements Arts and fine arts (art, music, dance, drama), English, foreign language, mathematics, physical education (includes health), science, social studies (includes history), swimming, grade 12 community service project.

Special Academic Programs Advanced Placement exam preparation; honors section; independent study; term-away projects; study abroad.

College Admission Counseling 131 students graduated in 2010; all went to college, including Brown University; Colgate University; Georgetown University; The Johns Hopkins University; Wesleyan University; Yale University. Mean SAT critical reading: 688, mean SAT math: 698, mean SAT writing: 703, mean combined SAT: 2090, mean composite ACT: 29.

Student Life Upper grades have specified standards of dress, student council, honor system. Discipline rests equally with students and faculty.

Summer Programs Remediation, enrichment, advancement, ESL, sports, art/fine arts, rigorous outdoor training, computer instruction programs offered; session focuses on academics and athletics; held on campus; accepts boys and girls; open to students from other schools. 220 students usually enrolled. 2011 schedule: June 27 to August 5. Application deadline: none.

Tuition and Aid Day student tuition: $30,650. Tuition installment plan (Academic Management Services Plan, Key Tuition Payment Plan). Need-based scholarship grants available. In 2010–11, 18% of upper-school students received aid. Total amount of financial aid awarded in 2010–11: $2,400,000.

Admissions Traditional secondary-level entrance grade is 9. For fall 2010, 264 students applied for upper-level admission, 131 were accepted, 74 enrolled. ISEE or SSAT required. Deadline for receipt of application materials: January 15. Application fee required: $60. On-campus interview required.

Athletics Interscholastic: baseball (boys), basketball (b,g), crew (b,g), cross-country running (b,g), diving (b,g), fencing (b,g), field hockey (g), football (b), independent competitive sports (b,g), indoor track (b), lacrosse (b,g), soccer (b,g), softball (g), swimming and diving (b,g), tennis (b,g), track and field (b,g), volleyball (g), wrestling (b); intramural: independent competitive sports (b,g); coed interscholastic: aquatics, golf, independent competitive sports, skydiving, squash, water polo, winter (indoor) track; coed intramural: aerobics, aerobics/dance, aerobics/Nautilus, ballet, basketball, climbing, cooperative games, dance, fencing, fitness, floor hockey, Frisbee, independent competitive sports, Nautilus, outdoor adventure, project adventure, ropes courses, running, soccer, swimming and diving, tennis, volleyball, weight lifting, weight training, wilderness, yoga. 5 coaches, 3 athletic trainers.

Computers Computers are regularly used in art, English, foreign language, history, mathematics, science classes. Computer network features include on-campus library services, Internet access, wireless campus network, Internet filtering or blocking technology. Campus intranet and student e-mail accounts are available to students. The school has a published electronic and media policy.

Contact Ms. Gena Eggert, Administrative Assistant to Director of Admissions. 203-397-1001 Ext. 211. Fax: 203-389-2249. E-mail: admissions@hopkins.edu. Web site: www.hopkins.edu.

THE HORACE MANN SCHOOL

231 West 246th Street
Bronx, New York 10471

Head of School: Dr. Thomas M. Kelly

General Information Coeducational day college-preparatory, arts, and technology school. Grades N–12. Founded: 1887. Setting: suburban. Nearest major city is New York. 18-acre campus. 6 buildings on campus. Approved or accredited by New York State Association of Independent Schools and New York Department of Education. Member of National Association of Independent Schools and Secondary School Admission Test Board. Endowment: $93 million. Total enrollment: 1,784. Upper school average class size: 17. Upper school faculty-student ratio: 1:9. Upper School students typically attend 5 days per week. The average school day consists of 6 hours and 35 minutes.

Upper School Student Profile Grade 9: 194 students (104 boys, 90 girls); Grade 10: 173 students (87 boys, 86 girls); Grade 11: 179 students (92 boys, 87 girls); Grade 12: 177 students (89 boys, 88 girls).

Faculty School total: 245.

Subjects Offered Advanced Placement courses, algebra, American history, anthropology, art, art history, astronomy, biology, business, calculus, ceramics, chemistry, community service, computer math, computer programming, computer science, creative writing, dance, drama, driver education, economics, English, English literature, environmental science, European history, expository writing, fine arts, French, French-AP, geology, geometry, German, government/civics, grammar, health, history, history of science, Italian, Japanese, journalism, Latin, logic, Mandarin, mathematics, music, philosophy, photography, physical education, physics, psychology, religion, Russian, science, social studies, Spanish, statistics, television, theater, trigonometry, typing, video, world history, writing.

Graduation Requirements Algebra, arts and fine arts (art, music, dance, drama), biology, computer science, CPR, English, foreign language, geometry, health and wellness, mathematics, physical education (includes health), science, trigonometry, U.S. history, world history. Community service is required.

Special Academic Programs Advanced Placement exam preparation; honors section; independent study.

College Admission Counseling 175 students graduated in 2009; 174 went to college, including Brown University; Columbia College; Cornell University; Georgetown University; New York University; University of Pennsylvania. Other: 1 had other specific plans.

Student Life Upper grades have student council, honor system. Discipline rests equally with students and faculty.

Tuition and Aid Day student tuition: $34,050. Tuition installment plan (Academic Management Services Plan, individually arranged payment plans, 3-payment plan). Need-based scholarship grants available. In 2009–10, 17% of upper-school students received aid. Total amount of financial aid awarded in 2009–10: $3,622,000.

Admissions Traditional secondary-level entrance grade is 9. ERB, ISEE or SSAT required. Deadline for receipt of application materials: December 1. Application fee required: $50. On-campus interview required.

Athletics Interscholastic: baseball (boys), basketball (b,g), crew (b,g), cross-country running (b,g), field hockey (g), football (b), gymnastics (g), lacrosse (b,g), soccer (b,g), softball (g), swimming and diving (b,g), tennis (b,g), track and field (b,g), volleyball (g), wrestling (b); intramural: baseball (b), basketball (b,g), field hockey (g), football (b), lacrosse (b,g), soccer (b,g), tennis (b,g); coed interscholastic: fencing, golf, indoor track & field, skiing (downhill), squash, water polo, winter (indoor) track; coed intramural: bowling, climbing, cross-country running, dance squad, dance team, fitness, Frisbee, golf, modern dance, outdoor education, paddle tennis, physical fitness, physical training, rock climbing, ropes courses, softball, strength & conditioning, swimming and diving, table tennis, track and field, ultimate Frisbee, volleyball, water polo, weight lifting, weight training. 14 PE instructors, 22 coaches, 2 athletic trainers.

Computers Computers are regularly used in English, foreign language, library skills, mathematics, media production, photography, science classes. Computer network features include on-campus library services, online commercial services, Internet access, wireless campus network. Campus intranet, student e-mail accounts, and computer access in designated common areas are available to students. The school has a published electronic and media policy.

Contact Lisa J. Moreira, Director of Admissions and Financial Aid. 718-432-4100. Fax: 718-432-3610. E-mail: admissions@horacemann.org. Web site: www.horacemann.org/.

HOSANNA CHRISTIAN SCHOOL

5000 Hosanna Way
Kamath Falls, Oregon 97603
Head of School: Mr. Jeff Mudrow

General Information Coeducational day college-preparatory, general academic, and religious studies school, affiliated with Evangelical faith. Grades PK–12. Founded: 1989. Setting: small town. Nearest major city is Klamath Falls. 26-acre campus. 1 building on campus. Approved or accredited by Association of Christian Schools International, Northwest Accreditation Commission, and Oregon Department of Education. Endowment: $120,000. Total enrollment: 265. Upper school average class size: 20. Upper school faculty-student ratio: 1:15. There are 180 required school days per year for Upper School students. Upper School students typically attend 5 days per week. The average school day consists of 4 hours.

Upper School Student Profile Grade 6: 12 students (5 boys, 7 girls); Grade 7: 17 students (5 boys, 12 girls); Grade 8: 14 students (7 boys, 7 girls); Grade 9: 20 students (8 boys, 12 girls); Grade 10: 20 students (7 boys, 13 girls); Grade 11: 14 students (6 boys, 8 girls); Grade 12: 22 students (7 boys, 15 girls). 100% of students are members of Evangelical faith.

Faculty School total: 24. In upper school: 10 men, 2 women; 2 have advanced degrees.

Subjects Offered Algebra, American government, American history, American literature, anatomy, art, Bible, biology, British literature, chemistry, choir, Christian doctrine, Christian ethics, Christian testament, college writing, computer skills, computers, consumer economics, creative drama, critical thinking, dance, drama, economics, English, English literature, geometry, government/civics, intro to computers, keyboarding, leadership, Life of Christ, Microsoft, personal finance, physical education, pre-algebra, reading/study skills, religious studies, service learning/ internship, Spanish, speech, sports, track and field, trigonometry, U.S. government, U.S. history, volleyball, world history, yearbook.

Special Academic Programs Accelerated programs; study at local college for college credit; remedial reading and/or remedial writing; remedial math.

College Admission Counseling 15 students graduated in 2009; 13 went to college, including George Fox University; Oregon Institute of Technology; Portland State University; Southern Oregon University; University of Nevada, Reno; Western Oregon University. Other: 1 went to work, 1 had other specific plans.

Student Life Upper grades have specified standards of dress, student council, honor system. Discipline rests primarily with faculty. Attendance at religious services is required.

Tuition and Aid Day student tuition: $5000. Tuition installment plan (monthly payment plans). Tuition reduction for siblings, need-based scholarship grants available. In 2009–10, 10% of upper-school students received aid. Total amount of financial aid awarded in 2009–10: $20,000.

Admissions Traditional secondary-level entrance grade is 9. For fall 2009, 20 students applied for upper-level admission, 13 were accepted, 12 enrolled. Deadline for receipt of application materials: none. No application fee required. Interview required.

Athletics Interscholastic: basketball (boys, girls), cheering (g), cross-country running (b,g), dance team (g), track and field (b,g), volleyball (g); intramural: basketball (b,g); coed interscholastic: golf, soccer, track and field. 2 PE instructors, 8 coaches.

Computers Computers are regularly used in computer applications, economics, yearbook classes. Computer network features include on-campus library services, online commercial services, Internet access, Internet filtering or blocking technology. Computer access in designated common areas is available to students. Students grades are available online. The school has a published electronic and media policy.

Contact Mrs. Christi Garrison, Assistant. 541-882-7732. Fax: 541-882-6940. E-mail: admin@hosannachristian.org. Web site: www.hosannachristian.org.

THE HOTCHKISS SCHOOL

11 Interlaken Road
PO Box 800
Lakeville, Connecticut 06039
Head of School: Mr. Malcolm H. McKenzie

General Information Coeducational boarding and day college-preparatory school. Grades 9–PG. Founded: 1891. Setting: rural. Nearest major city is Hartford. Students are housed in single-sex dormitories. 810-acre campus. 80 buildings on campus. Approved or accredited by Connecticut Association of Independent Schools, New England Association of Schools and Colleges, The Association of Boarding Schools, and Connecticut Department of Education. Member of National Association of Independent Schools and Secondary School Admission Test Board. Endowment: $333 million. Total enrollment: 598. Upper school average class size: 12. Upper school faculty-student ratio: 1:6. There are 170 required school days per year for Upper School students. Upper School students typically attend 6 days per week. The average school day consists of 6 hours and 50 minutes.

Upper School Student Profile Grade 9: 107 students (52 boys, 55 girls); Grade 10: 157 students (73 boys, 84 girls); Grade 11: 162 students (79 boys, 83 girls); Grade 12: 154 students (75 boys, 79 girls); Postgraduate: 18 students (17 boys, 1 girl). 92% of students are boarding students. 20% are state residents. 39 states are represented in upper school student body. 18% are international students. International students from Canada, China, Ghana, Hong Kong, Jamaica, and Republic of Korea; 24 other countries represented in student body.

Faculty School total: 115. In upper school: 63 men, 52 women; 91 have advanced degrees; 103 reside on campus.

Subjects Offered 3-dimensional design, acting, advanced math, Advanced Placement courses, advanced studio art-AP, algebra, American history, American history-AP, American literature, American studies, anatomy and physiology, Ancient Greek, ancient history, architecture, art, art history-AP, astronomy, bioethics, biology, biology-AP, calculus, calculus-AP, ceramics, chemistry, chemistry-AP, China/Japan history, Chinese, chorus, classics, college counseling, comparative government and politics-AP, computer programming, computer science, computer science-AP, conceptual physics, constitutional history of U.S., creative writing, dance, digital photography, discrete mathematics, drama, drawing, economics, economics-AP, English, English-AP, environmental science, environmental science-AP, ethics, European history, European history-AP, expository writing, fine arts, French, French language-AP, French literature-AP, geometry, German, history of music, Holocaust, humanities, independent study, jazz dance, jazz ensemble, Latin, Latin American history, Latin-AP, limnology, mathematics, music, music history, music technology, music theory, music theory-AP, musical productions, non-Western literature, orchestra, organic chemistry, philosophy, photography, physics, physics-AP, playwriting, pre-calculus, public speaking, religion, science, Spanish, Spanish language-AP, Spanish literature-AP, statistics-AP, studio art, theater, trigonometry, video, voice, world literature, writing.

Graduation Requirements American history, arts and fine arts (art, music, dance, drama), English, foreign language, mathematics, science.

Special Academic Programs Advanced Placement exam preparation; honors section; independent study; term-away projects; study abroad; academic accommodation for the gifted, the musically talented, and the artistically talented.

College Admission Counseling 169 students graduated in 2010; all went to college, including Colgate University; Columbia University; Dartmouth College; New York University; Princeton University; University of Pennsylvania. Median SAT critical reading: 620, median SAT math: 640, median SAT writing: 630, median combined SAT: 1890, median composite ACT: 29. 61% scored over 600 on SAT critical reading, 70% scored over 600 on SAT math, 65% scored over 600 on SAT writing, 64% scored over 1800 on combined SAT, 75% scored over 26 on composite ACT.

Student Life Upper grades have specified standards of dress, student council. Discipline rests equally with students and faculty.

Summer Programs Art/fine arts programs offered; session focuses on chamber music, environmental studies; held on campus; accepts boys and girls; open to students from other schools. 92 students usually enrolled. 2011 schedule: June 26 to July 17. Application deadline: none.

Tuition and Aid Day student tuition: $37,065; 7-day tuition and room/board: $43,500. Tuition installment plan (Tuition Management Systems (formerly Key Tuition Plan)). Need-based scholarship grants, need-based loans available. In 2010–11, 37% of upper-school students received aid. Total amount of financial aid awarded in 2010–11: $7,687,883.

Admissions Traditional secondary-level entrance grade is 9. For fall 2010, 1,628 students applied for upper-level admission, 370 were accepted, 210 enrolled. ACT, ISEE, PSAT, SAT, or ACT for applicants to grade 11 and 12, SSAT or TOEFL required. Deadline for receipt of application materials: January 15. Application fee required: $65. Interview required.

Athletics Interscholastic: baseball (boys), basketball (b,g), cross-country running (b,g), diving (b,g), field hockey (g), football (b), golf (b,g), ice hockey (b,g), lacrosse (b,g), soccer (b,g), softball (g), squash (b,g), swimming and diving (b,g), tennis (b,g), touch football (b), track and field (b,g), volleyball (g), water polo (b), wrestling (b); coed interscholastic: Frisbee, sailing, ultimate Frisbee; coed intramural: aerobics, aerobics/Nautilus, ballet, basketball, canoeing/kayaking, climbing, combined training, dance, drill team, fitness, fitness walking, Frisbee, golf, hiking/backpacking, ice hockey, jogging, Nautilus, outdoor education, paddle tennis, physical fitness, physical training, rock climbing, running, squash, strength & conditioning, tennis, ultimate Frisbee, volleyball, walking, wall climbing, water polo, weight lifting, yoga. 2 coaches, 2 athletic trainers.

Computers Computers are regularly used in all academic classes. Computer network features include on-campus library services, online commercial services, Internet access, wireless campus network, Internet filtering or blocking technology. Campus intranet, student e-mail accounts, and computer access in designated common areas are available to students. Students grades are available online. The school has a published electronic and media policy.

Contact Ms. Rachael N. Beare, Dean of Admission and Financial Aid. 860-435-3102. Fax: 860-435-0042. E-mail: admission@hotchkiss.org. Web site: www.hotchkiss.org.

HOUGHTON ACADEMY
9790 Thayer Street
Houghton, New York 14744
Head of School: Mr. Philip G. Stockin

General Information Coeducational boarding and day college-preparatory, arts, religious studies, and ESL school, affiliated with Wesleyan Church. Boarding grades 9–PG, day grades 6–PG. Founded: 1883. Setting: rural. Nearest major city is Buffalo. Students are housed in single-sex dormitories and staff homes. 25-acre campus. 6 buildings on campus. Approved or accredited by Association of Christian Schools International, Middle States Association of Colleges and Schools, The Association of Boarding Schools, and New York Department of Education. Endowment: $90,000. Total enrollment: 142. Upper school average class size: 16. Upper school faculty-student ratio: 1:8. There are 177 required school days per year for Upper School students. Upper School students typically attend 5 days per week. The average school day consists of 6 hours and 30 minutes.

Upper School Student Profile Grade 9: 15 students (8 boys, 7 girls); Grade 10: 24 students (17 boys, 7 girls); Grade 11: 35 students (20 boys, 15 girls); Grade 12: 42 students (15 boys, 27 girls). 44% of students are boarding students. 40% are state residents. 3 states are represented in upper school student body. 46% are international students. International students from China, Republic of Korea, and Viet Nam; 4 other countries represented in student body. 25% of students are members of Wesleyan Church.

Faculty School total: 22. In upper school: 11 men, 11 women; 14 have advanced degrees; 3 reside on campus.

Subjects Offered Algebra, American history, American literature, art, band, Bible, Bible studies, biology, business, business skills, calculus, chemistry, chorus, community service, computer science, creative writing, desktop publishing, driver education, earth science, economics, English, English literature, environmental science, ESL, ethics, fine arts, geography, geometry, government/civics, grammar, history, home economics, industrial arts, international relations, mathematics, music, photography, physical education, physics, science, social sciences, social studies, Spanish, speech, trigonometry, word processing, world history, writing.

Graduation Requirements Arts and fine arts (art, music, dance, drama), Bible, electives, English, mathematics, physical education (includes health), science, social studies (includes history).

Special Academic Programs 3 Advanced Placement exams for which test preparation is offered; honors section; independent study; study at local college for college credit; ESL.

College Admission Counseling 40 students graduated in 2010; 37 went to college, including Boston University; Houghton College; Johnson & Wales University; Michigan State University; State University of New York at Binghamton; Syracuse University. Other: 1 went to work, 2 had other specific plans. Median SAT critical reading: 500, median SAT math: 645. 23% scored over 600 on SAT critical reading, 63% scored over 600 on SAT math.

Student Life Upper grades have specified standards of dress, student council. Discipline rests primarily with faculty. Attendance at religious services is required.

Tuition and Aid Day student tuition: $6750; 7-day tuition and room/board: $24,115. Tuition installment plan (FACTS Tuition Payment Plan). Need-based scholarship grants available. In 2010–11, 25% of upper-school students received aid. Total amount of financial aid awarded in 2010–11: $95,000.

Admissions Traditional secondary-level entrance grade is 9. For fall 2010, 102 students applied for upper-level admission, 57 were accepted, 32 enrolled. PSAT or SAT for applicants to grade 11 and 12, SLEP, SSAT or TOEFL required. Deadline for receipt of application materials: February 18. Application fee required: $50. Interview required.

Athletics Interscholastic: basketball (boys, girls), cheering (g), soccer (b), volleyball (g); intramural: badminton (b,g), basketball (b,g), floor hockey (b,g), golf (b,g), indoor soccer (b,g), paddle tennis (b,g), racquetball (b,g), skiing (downhill) (b,g), soccer (b,g), table tennis (b,g), tennis (b,g), volleyball (b,g); coed interscholastic: golf; coed intramural: badminton, ball hockey, indoor soccer, paddle tennis, skiing (downhill), softball, table tennis. 2 PE instructors, 11 coaches, 1 athletic trainer.

Computers Computers are regularly used in accounting, Bible studies, college planning, English, graphic design, keyboarding, mathematics, multimedia, SAT preparation, science, word processing, yearbook classes. Computer network features include on-campus library services, Internet access, Internet filtering or blocking technology, electronic access to Houghton College Library holdings. Computer access

in designated common areas is available to students. Students grades are available online. The school has a published electronic and media policy.

Contact Ronald J. Bradbury, Director of Admissions. 585-567-8115. Fax: 585-567-8048. E-mail: admissions@houghtonacademy.org. Web site: www.houghtonacademy.org.

THE HOWARD SCHOOL
Atlanta, Georgia
See Special Needs Schools section.

THE HOWE SCHOOL
PO Box 240
Howe, Indiana 46746
Head of School: Mr. David Watson

General Information Coeducational boarding and day college-preparatory, religious studies, bilingual studies, Junior ROTC, and military school, affiliated with Episcopal Church. Grades 5–12. Founded: 1884. Setting: rural. Nearest major city is South Bend. Students are housed in single-sex dormitories. 100-acre campus. 15 buildings on campus. Approved or accredited by Independent Schools Association of the Central States, North Central Association of Colleges and Schools, The Association of Boarding Schools, and Indiana Department of Education. Member of National Association of Independent Schools. Total enrollment: 114. Upper school average class size: 10. Upper school faculty-student ratio: 1:9. There are 180 required school days per year for Upper School students. Upper School students typically attend 5 days per week. The average school day consists of 5 hours and 50 minutes.

Upper School Student Profile Grade 9: 14 students (14 boys); Grade 10: 22 students (18 boys, 4 girls); Grade 11: 31 students (24 boys, 7 girls); Grade 12: 22 students (18 boys, 4 girls). 99% of students are boarding students. 18% are state residents. 13 states are represented in upper school student body. 17% are international students. International students from Barbados, China, Republic of Korea, and Rwanda. 4% of students are members of Episcopal Church.

Faculty School total: 25. In upper school: 11 men, 9 women; 5 have advanced degrees; 6 reside on campus.

Subjects Offered Accounting, algebra, American history, American literature, band, biology, biology-AP, broadcasting, cabinet making, calculus, calculus-AP, chemistry, chemistry-AP, chorus, comparative religion, computer graphics, computer programming, drafting, economics, English, English language and composition-AP, English literature, environmental science, French, geography, geometry, German, government/civics, grammar, history, industrial arts, journalism, JROTC, leadership, mathematics, music, physical education, physics, pre-algebra, pre-calculus, religion, science, social studies, sociology, Spanish, speech, speech communications, trigonometry, world geography, world history, world literature, yearbook.

Graduation Requirements Computer education, English, foreign language, JROTC, leadership, mathematics, physical education (includes health), religion (includes Bible studies and theology), science, social studies (includes history).

Special Academic Programs Advanced Placement exam preparation; honors section; accelerated programs; study at local college for college credit; ESL (9 students enrolled).

College Admission Counseling 28 students graduated in 2010; 26 went to college, including Adrian College; Lake Superior State University; Michigan State University; Rose-Hulman Institute of Technology; The Citadel, The Military College of South Carolina; The College of Wooster. Other: 2 had other specific plans.

Student Life Upper grades have uniform requirement, student council, honor system. Discipline rests primarily with faculty. Attendance at religious services is required.

Summer Programs Remediation, advancement programs offered; session focuses on academics with a blend of recreation; held off campus; held at Cedar Lake, IN; accepts boys; open to students from other schools. 75 students usually enrolled. 2011 schedule: June 19 to July 29. Application deadline: July 8.

Tuition and Aid Day student tuition: $16,160; 7-day tuition and room/board: $26,800. Tuition installment plan (monthly payment plans). Tuition reduction for siblings, need-based scholarship grants available. In 2010–11, 38% of upper-school students received aid. Total amount of financial aid awarded in 2010–11: $187,865.

Admissions Traditional secondary-level entrance grade is 9. For fall 2010, 62 students applied for upper-level admission, 47 were accepted, 33 enrolled. OLSAT, Stanford Achievement Test and TOEFL or SLEP required. Deadline for receipt of application materials: none. Application fee required: $100. Interview recommended.

Athletics Interscholastic: baseball (boys), basketball (b,g), football (b), tennis (b,g), track and field (b,g), volleyball (g), wrestling (b); intramural: baseball (b), football (b), physical training (b), softball (b); coed interscholastic: basketball, golf, JROTC drill, riflery, soccer; coed intramural: basketball, horseback riding, physical fitness, soccer, swimming and diving, volleyball. 1 PE instructor, 1 coach.

Computers Computers are regularly used in English, foreign language, JROTC, mathematics, newspaper, science, yearbook classes. Computer network features include on-campus library services, Internet access, wireless campus network, Internet filtering or blocking technology, CAD, Microsoft Office. Campus intranet and student e-mail accounts are available to students. Students grades are available online.

Contact Mr. Charles Grady, Director of Admissions. 260-562-2131 Ext. 221. Fax: 260-562-3678. E-mail: cgrady@thehoweschool.org. Web site: www.thehoweschool.org.

THE HUDSON SCHOOL
601 Park Avenue
Hoboken, New Jersey 07030
Head of School: Mrs. Suellen F. Newman
General Information Coeducational day college-preparatory, arts, and music, theater, foreign languages school. Grades 5–12. Founded: 1978. Setting: urban. Nearest major city is New York, NY. 1 building on campus. Approved or accredited by Middle States Association of Colleges and Schools, New Jersey Association of Independent Schools, and New Jersey Department of Education. Member of National Association of Independent Schools. Endowment: $1.8 million. Total enrollment: 195. Upper school average class size: 18. Upper school faculty-student ratio: 1:20. There are 175 required school days per year for Upper School students. Upper School students typically attend 5 days per week. The average school day consists of 8 hours.
Upper School Student Profile Grade 9: 26 students (11 boys, 15 girls); Grade 10: 20 students (7 boys, 13 girls); Grade 11: 23 students (9 boys, 14 girls); Grade 12: 16 students (5 boys, 11 girls).
Faculty School total: 50. In upper school: 12 men, 15 women; 16 have advanced degrees.
Subjects Offered African drumming, algebra, American government, American literature, anatomy and physiology, art, biology, British literature, calculus, chemistry, computer science, computer science-AP, computers, conceptual physics, contemporary issues, creative writing, English, English literature, English literature-AP, English-AP, environmental science, ethnic literature, film, French, gender issues, German, health, Japanese, Latin, learning strategies, mathematics, media studies, microbiology, music, music theory, mythology, personal finance, physical education, physics-AP, psychology-AP, social sciences, Spanish, Spanish-AP, U.S. history, U.S. history-AP, world civilizations, world literature.
Graduation Requirements Arts and fine arts (art, music, dance, drama), computer science, English, foreign language, Latin, mathematics, physical education (includes health), science, social studies (includes history). Community service is required.
Special Academic Programs Advanced Placement exam preparation; honors section; accelerated programs; independent study; study at local college for college credit; study abroad; academic accommodation for the gifted, the musically talented, and the artistically talented; remedial reading and/or remedial writing; remedial math; ESL (6 students enrolled).
College Admission Counseling 18 students graduated in 2009; all went to college, including Bennington College; Drew University; New York University; Pace University; Rensselaer Polytechnic Institute; University of Pennsylvania. Median SAT critical reading: 610, median SAT math: 570, median SAT writing: 590, median combined SAT: 1670. 56% scored over 600 on SAT critical reading, 33% scored over 600 on SAT math, 50% scored over 600 on SAT writing, 39% scored over 1800 on combined SAT.
Student Life Upper grades have student council, honor system. Discipline rests primarily with faculty.
Tuition and Aid Day student tuition: $15,270. Tuition installment plan (monthly payment plans, individually arranged payment plans, semiannual and annual payment plans, quarterly by special arrangement). Need-based scholarship grants available. In 2009–10, 35% of upper-school students received aid. Total amount of financial aid awarded in 2009–10: $292,000.
Admissions Traditional secondary-level entrance grade is 9. For fall 2009, 95 students applied for upper-level admission, 65 were accepted, 54 enrolled. ERB, ISEE or SSAT required. Deadline for receipt of application materials: December 15. Application fee required: $50. On-campus interview required.
Athletics Interscholastic: basketball (boys, girls), soccer (b,g), softball (g); intramural: dance (g), modern dance (g); coed interscholastic: bowling, cheering, track and field; coed intramural: aerobics/dance, fencing, Frisbee, outdoor education, physical fitness, ultimate Frisbee, yoga. 3 PE instructors, 4 coaches.
Computers Computers are regularly used in college planning, creative writing, desktop publishing, ESL, English, ethics, French, humanities, music, newspaper, philosophy, photography, photojournalism, programming, publications, Spanish, technology, theater, video film production, Web site design, word processing, writing, yearbook classes. Computer network features include Internet access, Internet filtering or blocking technology.
Contact Mrs. Suellen F. Newman, Director. 201-659-8335 Ext. 107. Fax: 201-222-3669. E-mail: admissions@thehudsonschool.org. Web site: www.thehudsonschool.org.

HUMANEX ACADEMY
Englewood, Colorado
See Special Needs Schools section.

THE HUN SCHOOL OF PRINCETON
176 Edgerstoune Road
Princeton, New Jersey 08540
Head of School: Jonathan Brougham
General Information Coeducational boarding and day college-preparatory school. Boarding grades 9–PG, day grades 6–PG. Founded: 1914. Setting: small town. Nearest major city is New York, NY. Students are housed in single-sex dormitories. 45-acre campus. 7 buildings on campus. Approved or accredited by Middle States Association of Colleges and Schools, New Jersey Association of Independent Schools, and The Association of Boarding Schools. Member of National Association of Independent Schools and Secondary School Admission Test Board. Endowment: $12 million. Total enrollment: 597. Upper school average class size: 13. Upper school faculty-student ratio: 1:8.
Upper School Student Profile Grade 9: 106 students (56 boys, 50 girls); Grade 10: 128 students (73 boys, 55 girls); Grade 11: 134 students (84 boys, 50 girls); Grade 12: 121 students (75 boys, 46 girls); Postgraduate: 13 students (12 boys, 1 girl). 30% of students are boarding students. 14 states are represented in upper school student body. 13% are international students. International students from Bahrain, Republic of Korea, Russian Federation, Saudi Arabia, Taiwan, and Venezuela; 20 other countries represented in student body.
Faculty School total: 117. In upper school: 60 men, 57 women; 48 have advanced degrees; 29 reside on campus.
Subjects Offered 3-dimensional art, 3-dimensional design, advanced computer applications, Advanced Placement courses, advanced TOEFL/grammar, algebra, American government, American history, American history-AP, American literature, anatomy, architectural drawing, architecture, art, art history, art history-AP, astrophysics, biology, biology-AP, calculus, calculus-AP, ceramics, chemistry, chemistry-AP, chorus, community service, computer programming, computer science, drama, driver education, economics, engineering, English, English-AP, ESL, European history, fine arts, forensics, French, French-AP, geometry, government/civics, health, history, interdisciplinary studies, jazz band, Latin, Latin-AP, marine biology, mathematics, mechanical drawing, music, photography, physical education, physics, physics-AP, physiology, public speaking, science, social studies, Spanish, Spanish-AP, statistics-AP, television, theater, trigonometry, U.S. history-AP, video, video film production, world history.
Graduation Requirements Arts and fine arts (art, music, dance, drama), computer science, English, foreign language, health, history, mathematics, science, 10-20 hours of community service per year, summer reading, extra-curricular activities.
Special Academic Programs Advanced Placement exam preparation; honors section; academic accommodation for the gifted; ESL (35 students enrolled).
College Admission Counseling 151 students graduated in 2010; 149 went to college, including Boston University; Lehigh University; Penn State University Park; Princeton University; Syracuse University. Other: 2 entered military service. Median SAT critical reading: 590, median SAT math: 620, median SAT writing: 610, median composite ACT: 27.
Student Life Upper grades have specified standards of dress, student council, honor system. Discipline rests equally with students and faculty.
Summer Programs Remediation, enrichment, advancement, ESL, art/fine arts, computer instruction programs offered; session focuses on make-up courses, enrichment, SAT and TOEFL preparation; held on campus; accepts boys and girls; open to students from other schools. 110 students usually enrolled. 2011 schedule: June 28 to July 23. Application deadline: none.
Tuition and Aid Day student tuition: $30,560; 7-day tuition and room/board: $44,420. Tuition installment plan (Academic Management Services Plan). Merit scholarship grants, need-based scholarship grants, prepGATE loans available. In 2010–11, 25% of upper-school students received aid; total upper-school merit-scholarship money awarded: $50,000. Total amount of financial aid awarded in 2010–11: $2,500,000.
Admissions Traditional secondary-level entrance grade is 9. PSAT or SAT for applicants to grade 11 and 12, SSAT or TOEFL required. Deadline for receipt of application materials: January 31. Application fee required: $50. Interview required.
Athletics Interscholastic: baseball (boys), basketball (b,g), crew (b,g), cross-country running (b,g), fencing (b,g), field hockey (g), football (b), lacrosse (b,g), soccer (b,g), softball (g), tennis (b,g); intramural: dance squad (g), soccer (b,g), weight training (b,g); coed interscholastic: golf, ice hockey, swimming and diving, track and field; coed intramural: aerobics/dance, aerobics/Nautilus, ballet, basketball, cross-country running, dance, fitness, flag football, Frisbee, jogging, Nautilus, paint ball, physical fitness, running, skiing (downhill), strength & conditioning, touch football, ultimate Frisbee, volleyball, weight lifting. 3 coaches, 1 athletic trainer.
Computers Computers are regularly used in all academic classes. Computer network features include on-campus library services, online commercial services, Internet access, wireless campus network, Internet filtering or blocking technology. Campus intranet and student e-mail accounts are available to students. The school has a published electronic and media policy.
Contact Mr. Steven C. Bristol, Director of Admissions. 609-921-7600. Fax: 609-279-9398. E-mail: admiss@hunschool.org. Web site: www.hunschool.org.

HUNTINGTON-SURREY SCHOOL

4804 Grover Avenue
Austin, Texas 78756
Head of School: Dr. Light Bailey German

General Information Coeducational day college-preparatory, arts, and writing, thearter arts school. Grades 9–12. Founded: 1973. Setting: urban. .5-acre campus. 1 building on campus. Approved or accredited by Southern Association of Colleges and Schools and Texas Department of Education. Total enrollment: 46. Upper school average class size: 8. Upper school faculty-student ratio: 1:4. There are 160 required school days per year for Upper School students. Upper School students typically attend 5 days per week. The average school day consists of 4 hours and 45 minutes.

Upper School Student Profile Grade 9: 4 students (2 boys, 2 girls); Grade 10: 11 students (7 boys, 4 girls); Grade 11: 12 students (9 boys, 3 girls); Grade 12: 19 students (7 boys, 12 girls).

Faculty School total: 20. In upper school: 7 men, 13 women; 10 have advanced degrees.

Subjects Offered Algebra, art, biology, calculus, chemistry, college planning, comparative religion, creative drama, discrete mathematics, drama, ecology, environmental systems, English, film history, French, geometry, German, history, Latin, literature, math analysis, math review, mathematics, philosophy, physical science, physics, portfolio art, pre-algebra, pre-calculus, SAT preparation, senior science survey, social studies, Spanish, student publications, study skills, theater arts, trigonometry, U.S. history, work-study, world history, writing.

Graduation Requirements American literature, biology, British literature, mathematics, world history, world literature, writing, senior research project, school exit examinations: assertion with proof essay exam and mathematical competency exam, senior advisory course.

Special Academic Programs Accelerated programs; academic accommodation for the gifted.

College Admission Counseling 16 students graduated in 2010; 14 went to college, including Occidental College; Schreiner University; St. Edward's University; Texas State University–San Marcos; Texas Tech University; The University of Texas at Austin. Other: 2 went to work. Median SAT critical reading: 540, median SAT math: 550, median SAT writing: 540, median combined SAT: 1630. 25% scored over 600 on SAT critical reading, 25% scored over 600 on SAT math, 25% scored over 600 on SAT writing, 25% scored over 1800 on combined SAT.

Student Life Upper grades have student council, honor system. Discipline rests primarily with faculty.

Summer Programs Remediation, enrichment, advancement programs offered; session focuses on one-on-one teaching, or small classes; held on campus; accepts boys and girls; open to students from other schools. 12 students usually enrolled. 2011 schedule: June 13 to July 22. Application deadline: May 10.

Tuition and Aid Day student tuition: $9000. Tuition installment plan (monthly payment plans).

Admissions Traditional secondary-level entrance grade is 9. For fall 2010, 14 students applied for upper-level admission, 12 were accepted, 12 enrolled. Deadline for receipt of application materials: none. No application fee required. On-campus interview required.

Computers Computers are regularly used in study skills, writing classes. Computer resources include study hall computers and printers (available for student use). Computer access in designated common areas is available to students.

Contact Ms. Johni Walker-Little, Assistant Director. 512-478-4743. Fax: 512-457-0235. Web site: www.huntingtonsurrey.com.

HUTCHISON SCHOOL

1740 Ridgeway Road
Memphis, Tennessee 38119-5397
Head of School: Dr. Annette C. Smith

General Information Girls' day college-preparatory, arts, and technology school. Grades PK–12. Founded: 1902. Setting: suburban. 52-acre campus. 10 buildings on campus. Approved or accredited by Southern Association of Colleges and Schools, Southern Association of Independent Schools, and Tennessee Association of Independent Schools. Member of National Association of Independent Schools. Endowment: $14 million. Total enrollment: 926. Upper school average class size: 16. Upper school faculty-student ratio: 1:16.

Upper School Student Profile Grade 9: 69 students (69 girls); Grade 10: 59 students (59 girls); Grade 11: 58 students (58 girls); Grade 12: 59 students (59 girls).

Faculty School total: 122. In upper school: 3 men, 21 women; 19 have advanced degrees.

Subjects Offered Acting, advanced studio art-AP, algebra, American government, American history, American history-AP, American literature, American literature-AP, anatomy and physiology, art, biology, biology-AP, British literature, British literature (honors), British literature-AP, calculus, calculus-AP, chemistry, chemistry-AP, choral music, college writing, contemporary issues, creative writing, dance, digital photography, drama, earth science, economics, English, English language-AP, English literature, English literature-AP, environmental education, environmental science, European history, European history-AP, film and literature, film history, fine arts, foreign language, French, French language-AP, genetics, geography, geometry, global issues, government/civics, health, health and wellness, history, honors algebra, honors

English, honors geometry, independent study, Latin, mathematics, music, music theory-AP, physical education, physics, physics-AP, pre-calculus, psychology, science, social studies, Spanish, speech, studio art, studio art-AP, theater, video film production, women's studies, world history, world history-AP, writing.

Graduation Requirements Alternative physical education, arts and fine arts (art, music, dance, drama), English, foreign language, humanities, mathematics, physical education (includes health), science, social studies (includes history), world history, annual community service, senior speaker program.

Special Academic Programs 20 Advanced Placement exams for which test preparation is offered; honors section; independent study; study abroad; academic accommodation for the gifted.

College Admission Counseling 48 students graduated in 2009; 45 went to college, including The University of Alabama; The University of Tennessee; University of Georgia; University of Mississippi; University of Virginia; Vanderbilt University. Mean SAT critical reading: 572, mean SAT math: 582, mean SAT writing: 597, mean combined SAT: 1759, mean composite ACT: 26. 33% scored over 600 on SAT critical reading, 41% scored over 600 on SAT math, 31% scored over 600 on SAT writing, 33% scored over 1800 on combined SAT, 47% scored over 26 on composite ACT.

Student Life Upper grades have uniform requirement, student council, honor system. Discipline rests equally with students and faculty.

Tuition and Aid Day student tuition: $15,652. Tuition installment plan (Insured Tuition Payment Plan, monthly payment plans, individually arranged payment plans, 4-payment plan). Need-based scholarship grants available. In 2009–10, 12% of upper-school students received aid. Total amount of financial aid awarded in 2009–10: $138,774.

Admissions Traditional secondary-level entrance grade is 9. For fall 2009, 37 students applied for upper-level admission, 22 were accepted, 17 enrolled. Admissions testing, ERB CTP IV, ISEE, school's own test or writing sample required. Deadline for receipt of application materials: none. Application fee required: $50. Interview required.

Athletics Interscholastic: basketball (girls), bowling (g), cross-country running (g), dance (g), dance team (g), fitness (g), golf (g), lacrosse (g), soccer (g), swimming and diving (g), tennis (g), volleyball (g); intramural: basketball (g), bowling (g), cross-country running (g), lacrosse (g), soccer (g), softball (g), volleyball (g). 4 PE instructors, 17 coaches, 1 athletic trainer.

Computers Computers are regularly used in all academic, video film production classes. Computer network features include on-campus library services, online commercial services, Internet access, wireless campus network, Internet filtering or blocking technology. Campus intranet and student e-mail accounts are available to students. Students grades are available online. The school has a published electronic and media policy.

Contact Candy Covington, Advancement Director. 901-762-6672. Fax: 901-432-6655. E-mail: ccovington@hutchisonschool.org. Web site: www.hutchisonschool.org.

HYDE SCHOOL

PO Box 237
Woodstock, Connecticut 06281
Head of School: Laura Gauld

General Information Coeducational boarding and day college-preparatory and general academic school. Grades 9–12. Founded: 1996. Setting: rural. Nearest major city is Hartford. Students are housed in single-sex dormitories. 120-acre campus. 7 buildings on campus. Approved or accredited by Association of Independent Schools in New England, New England Association of Schools and Colleges, The Association of Boarding Schools, and Connecticut Department of Education. Endowment: $8 million. Total enrollment: 151. Upper school average class size: 12. Upper school faculty-student ratio: 1:12.

Upper School Student Profile Grade 9: 9 students (8 boys, 1 girl); Grade 10: 28 students (18 boys, 10 girls); Grade 11: 52 students (36 boys, 16 girls); Grade 12: 60 students (38 boys, 22 girls); Postgraduate: 2 students (2 boys). 98% of students are boarding students. 24% are state residents. 21 states are represented in upper school student body. 2% are international students. International students from Canada, China, Japan, and Republic of Korea.

Faculty School total: 27. In upper school: 17 men, 10 women; 9 have advanced degrees; all reside on campus.

Subjects Offered 20th century history, advanced chemistry, Advanced Placement courses, algebra, athletics, biology, calculus, calculus-AP, character education, chemistry, English, English language and composition-AP, English language-AP, English literature, environmental science-AP, ethics, geometry, global issues, independent study, media arts, physics, pre-calculus, Spanish, Spanish-AP, sports, U.S. history, U.S. history-AP, wilderness education, wilderness experience.

Graduation Requirements Electives, English, foreign language, mathematics, science, social studies (includes history), Hyde's graduation requirements embody academic achievement and character development. Character growth is determined through an intense 40-hour, evaluation process involving all members of the senior class and faculty. All students make a speech at graduation representing their principles.

Special Academic Programs 5 Advanced Placement exams for which test preparation is offered; honors section; independent study; remedial reading and/or remedial writing; remedial math; ESL (6 students enrolled).

College Admission Counseling 47 students graduated in 2009; 44 went to college, including Abilene Christian University; Northeastern University. Other: 1 went to work, 1 entered military service, 1 entered a postgraduate year. Median SAT critical reading: 550, median SAT math: 525, median SAT writing: 530, median combined SAT: 1605, median composite ACT: 20.

Student Life Upper grades have specified standards of dress, honor system. Discipline rests equally with students and faculty.

Tuition and Aid Day student tuition: $24,200; 5-day tuition and room/board: $46,700; 7-day tuition and room/board: $46,700. Tuition reduction for siblings, need-based scholarship grants available. In 2009–10, 25% of upper-school students received aid. Total amount of financial aid awarded in 2009–10: $258,000.

Admissions Traditional secondary-level entrance grade is 11. For fall 2009, 151 students applied for upper-level admission, 106 were accepted, 94 enrolled. Deadline for receipt of application materials: none. Application fee required: $100. Interview required.

Athletics Interscholastic: basketball (boys, girls), cross-country running (b,g), football (b), lacrosse (b,g), soccer (b,g), tennis (b,g), track and field (b,g), wrestling (b); coed interscholastic: equestrian sports, martial arts, ropes courses, wilderness, wrestling; coed intramural: backpacking, canoeing/kayaking, climbing, hiking/backpacking, outdoor adventure, outdoor skills, ropes courses, wilderness. 2 athletic trainers.

Computers Computer network features include on-campus library services, online commercial services, Internet access, Internet filtering or blocking technology. Student e-mail accounts are available to students. The school has a published electronic and media policy.

Contact MaryAnn Tingley, Admission Assistant. 860-963-4736. Fax: 860-928-0612. E-mail: mtingley@hyde.edu. Web site: www.hyde.edu.

HYDE SCHOOL

616 High Street
Bath, Maine 04530
Head of School: Don MacMillan

General Information Coeducational boarding and day college-preparatory and arts school. Grades 9–12. Founded: 1966. Setting: small town. Nearest major city is Portland. Students are housed in single-sex dormitories. 145-acre campus. 32 buildings on campus. Approved or accredited by Association of Independent Schools in New England, Independent Schools of Northern New England, New England Association of Schools and Colleges, and The Association of Boarding Schools. Member of National Association of Independent Schools. Endowment: $9 million. Total enrollment: 143. Upper school average class size: 12. Upper school faculty-student ratio: 1:6. Upper School students typically attend 6 days per week. The average school day consists of 7 hours.

Upper School Student Profile Grade 9: 7 students (3 boys, 4 girls); Grade 10: 20 students (15 boys, 5 girls); Grade 11: 52 students (38 boys, 14 girls); Grade 12: 46 students (24 boys, 22 girls); Postgraduate: 4 students (3 boys, 1 girl). 99% of students are boarding students. 21% are state residents. 27 states are represented in upper school student body. 21% are international students. International students from Canada, China, Democratic People's Republic of Korea, Rwanda, Spain, and United Kingdom; 7 other countries represented in student body.

Faculty School total: 23. In upper school: 12 men, 7 women; 16 have advanced degrees; 21 reside on campus.

Subjects Offered Algebra, American history, ancient history, art, biology, calculus, chemistry, composition-AP, creative writing, early childhood, economics, English, European history, geometry, government, history, music, physical education, physics-AP, pre-calculus, public policy, religion and culture, Spanish, statistics, technical theater, U.S. history, U.S. history-AP.

Graduation Requirements Electives, English, foreign language, history, mathematics, science, Hyde's graduation requirements embody academic achievement and character development. Character growth is determined through an intense 40-hour, evaluation process involving all members of the senior class and faculty. All students make a speech at graduation representing their principles.

Special Academic Programs Honors section; independent study; study at local college for college credit; remedial reading and/or remedial writing; remedial math; ESL (18 students enrolled).

College Admission Counseling 53 students graduated in 2010; 51 went to college, including Rhodes College; Southern Methodist University; Stanford University; The University of Texas at Austin; University of Denver; University of Maryland, College Park. Other: 1 went to work, 1 entered military service. Mean SAT critical reading: 530, mean SAT math: 520, mean SAT writing: 520, mean combined SAT: 1570, mean composite ACT: 21. 25% scored over 600 on SAT critical reading, 17% scored over 600 on SAT math, 14% scored over 600 on SAT writing, 18% scored over 1800 on combined SAT, 16% scored over 26 on composite ACT.

Student Life Upper grades have specified standards of dress, honor system. Discipline rests equally with students and faculty.

Summer Programs Enrichment, sports, art/fine arts, rigorous outdoor training programs offered; session focuses on Orientation for the school year; held both on and off campus; held at wilderness preserve in Eustis, ME and on Seguin Island off the coast of Maine; accepts boys and girls; open to students from other schools. 80 students usually enrolled. 2011 schedule: May 31 to August 31. Application deadline: none.

Tuition and Aid Day student tuition: $24,000; 7-day tuition and room/board: $45,200. Tuition installment plan (monthly payment plans, individually arranged payment plans). Tuition reduction for siblings, need-based scholarship grants available. In 2010–11, 33% of upper-school students received aid. Total amount of financial aid awarded in 2010–11: $820,000.

Admissions Traditional secondary-level entrance grade is 9. For fall 2010, 137 students applied for upper-level admission, 83 were accepted, 68 enrolled. Deadline for receipt of application materials: none. Application fee required: $100. Interview required.

Athletics Interscholastic: basketball (boys, girls), crew (b,g), cross-country running (b,g), football (b), lacrosse (b,g), soccer (b,g), swimming and diving (b,g), tennis (b,g), track and field (b,g), ultimate Frisbee (b); coed interscholastic: dance, hiking/backpacking, indoor track, nordic skiing, rock climbing, ropes courses, wrestling; coed intramural: hiking/backpacking, kayaking, life saving, outdoor adventure, outdoor skills, physical fitness, physical training, project adventure, ropes courses, snowshoeing, strength & conditioning, ultimate Frisbee, walking, weight lifting, weight training, wilderness, wilderness survival. 8 coaches, 1 athletic trainer.

Computers Computer network features include on-campus library services, online commercial services, Internet access, wireless campus network, Internet filtering or blocking technology. Student e-mail accounts are available to students. The school has a published electronic and media policy.

Contact Wanda Smith, Admission Assistant. 207-443-7101. Fax: 207-442-9346. E-mail: wsmith@hyde.edu. Web site: www.hyde.edu.

HYMAN BRAND HEBREW ACADEMY OF GREATER KANSAS CITY

5801 West 115th Street
Overland Park, Kansas 66211
Head of School: Mr. Howard Haas

General Information Coeducational day college-preparatory, general academic, and religious studies school, affiliated with Jewish faith. Grades K–12. Founded: 1966. Setting: suburban. Nearest major city is Kansas City, MO. 32-acre campus. 1 building on campus. Approved or accredited by Independent Schools Association of the Central States and North Central Association of Colleges and Schools. Languages of instruction: English and Hebrew. Endowment: $4.7 million. Total enrollment: 233. Upper school average class size: 15. Upper school faculty-student ratio: 1:5. There are 165 required school days per year for Upper School students. Upper School students typically attend 5 days per week. The average school day consists of 7 hours and 45 minutes.

Upper School Student Profile Grade 9: 14 students (7 boys, 7 girls); Grade 10: 11 students (7 boys, 4 girls); Grade 11: 10 students (5 boys, 5 girls); Grade 12: 15 students (6 boys, 9 girls). 100% of students are Jewish.

Faculty School total: 36. In upper school: 9 men, 9 women; 14 have advanced degrees.

Subjects Offered 3-dimensional design, algebra, American government, American history, American history-AP, American literature, anatomy and physiology, art, art history, Bible studies, biology, British literature, calculus-AP, chemistry, community service, computer applications, computer science, digital art, economics, English, English language and composition-AP, English literature, English literature and composition-AP, environmental science, ethics, European history, fine arts, geometry, health, Hebrew, Hebrew scripture, Holocaust seminar, Jewish studies, model United Nations, physical education, physics, statistics-AP, Talmud, trigonometry, U.S. government and politics-AP, world history, world literature, yearbook.

Graduation Requirements Arts and fine arts (art, music, dance, drama), English, foreign language, mathematics, physical education (includes health), religion (includes Bible studies and theology), science, social studies (includes history). Community service is required.

Special Academic Programs 22 Advanced Placement exams for which test preparation is offered; study at local college for college credit; academic accommodation for the gifted.

College Admission Counseling 12 students graduated in 2010; 7 went to college, including Boston University; Brandeis University; Hampshire College; Indiana University Bloomington; The University of Kansas; Tulane University. Other: 5 entered a postgraduate year.

Student Life Upper grades have specified standards of dress, student council. Discipline rests primarily with faculty. Attendance at religious services is required.

Tuition and Aid Day student tuition: $6700. Tuition installment plan (FACTS Tuition Payment Plan). Need-based scholarship grants available. In 2010–11, 38% of upper-school students received aid. Total amount of financial aid awarded in 2010–11: $80,945.

Admissions Traditional secondary-level entrance grade is 9. For fall 2010, 1 student applied for upper-level admission, 1 was accepted, 1 enrolled. Writing sample required. Deadline for receipt of application materials: none. Application fee required: $50. Interview recommended.

Athletics Interscholastic: basketball (boys, girls), soccer (b,g), tennis (b,g); coed interscholastic: cross-country running; coed intramural: tennis. 2 PE instructors, 6 coaches.

Computers Computers are regularly used in computer applications, desktop publishing, digital applications, economics, English, humanities, mathematics, news-

paper, psychology, religious studies, science, social studies, writing, yearbook classes. Computer network features include on-campus library services, online commercial services, Internet access, wireless campus network. Student e-mail accounts and computer access in designated common areas are available to students. Students grades are available online. The school has a published electronic and media policy.
Contact Mrs. Tamara Lawson Schuster, Director of Admissions. 913-327-8135. Fax: 913-327-8180. E-mail: tschuster@hbha.edu. Web site: www.hbha.edu.

IDYLLWILD ARTS ACADEMY

52500 Temecula Road
PO Box 38
Idyllwild, California 92549
Head of School: William Lowman

General Information Coeducational boarding and day college-preparatory and arts school. Grades 9–PG. Founded: 1986. Setting: rural. Nearest major city is Los Angeles. Students are housed in single-sex dormitories. 205-acre campus. 44 buildings on campus. Approved or accredited by California Association of Independent Schools and Western Association of Schools and Colleges. Member of National Association of Independent Schools and Secondary School Admission Test Board. Endowment: $3 million. Total enrollment: 278. Upper school average class size: 16. Upper school faculty-student ratio: 1:12.

Upper School Student Profile Grade 9: 49 students (18 boys, 31 girls); Grade 10: 61 students (28 boys, 33 girls); Grade 11: 77 students (37 boys, 40 girls); Grade 12: 83 students (41 boys, 42 girls); Postgraduate: 4 students (2 boys, 2 girls). 92% of students are boarding students. 38% are state residents. 35 states are represented in upper school student body. 44% are international students. International students from Australia, China, Japan, Mexico, Republic of Korea, and Taiwan; 16 other countries represented in student body.

Faculty School total: 65. In upper school: 24 men, 20 women; 30 have advanced degrees; 23 reside on campus.

Subjects Offered 3-dimensional art, 3-dimensional design, acting, advanced math, algebra, American government, American history, American literature, anatomy, art, art history, audio visual/media, audition methods, ballet, biology, Broadway dance, calculus, career/college preparation, ceramics, chemistry, choir, choral music, choreography, computer graphics, computer science, creative writing, critical studies in film, dance, digital art, directing, drama, drawing and design, economics, English, English literature, ensembles, environmental science, ESL, fiction, film and literature, film and new technologies, film appreciation, film history, film studies, filmmaking, fine arts, French, geography, geometry, government/civics, grammar, history, illustration, improvisation, jazz dance, jazz ensemble, jazz theory, mathematics, multimedia, music, music theater, music theory, musical productions, musical theater dance, orchestra, performing arts, photography, physical education, physics, play production, playwriting and directing, poetry, pottery, printmaking, science, social sciences, social studies, Spanish, tap dance, technical theater, technology/design, theater, video film production, vocal music, voice and diction, voice ensemble, world history, world literature, writing.

Graduation Requirements Art, arts and fine arts (art, music, dance, drama), English, foreign language, mathematics, performing arts, physical education (includes health), science, social sciences, social studies (includes history).

Special Academic Programs Advanced Placement exam preparation; honors section; ESL (45 students enrolled).

College Admission Counseling 68 students graduated in 2010; 66 went to college, including California Institute of the Arts; New York University; The Johns Hopkins University; The Juilliard School; University of California, Los Angeles; University of Rochester. Other: 2 went to work.

Student Life Upper grades have student council. Discipline rests equally with students and faculty.

Summer Programs ESL, art/fine arts programs offered; session focuses on visual and performing arts; held on campus; accepts boys and girls; open to students from other schools. 600 students usually enrolled. 2011 schedule: July 10 to August 19. Application deadline: none.

Tuition and Aid Day student tuition: $33,385; 7-day tuition and room/board: $49,875. Tuition installment plan (Key Tuition Payment Plan, monthly payment plans, individually arranged payment plans, school's own payment plan). Need-based scholarship grants available. In 2010–11, 68% of upper-school students received aid. Total amount of financial aid awarded in 2010–11: $5,054,332.

Admissions Traditional secondary-level entrance grade is 10. For fall 2010, 400 students applied for upper-level admission, 320 were accepted, 278 enrolled. SLEP, SSAT or TOEFL required. Deadline for receipt of application materials: none. Application fee required: $50. Interview required.

Athletics Intramural: aerobics (boys, girls); coed intramural: aerobics, aerobics/dance, aerobics/Nautilus, ballet, basketball, bicycling, billiards, bowling, climbing, combined training, cooperative games, cross-country running, dance, fencing, fitness, Frisbee, hiking/backpacking, jogging, judo, martial arts, modern dance, mountain biking, outdoor activities, outdoor adventure, outdoor education, outdoor recreation, outdoors, physical fitness, physical training, rock climbing, soccer, swimming and diving, tennis, ultimate Frisbee, volleyball, walking, weight training, yoga. 1 PE instructor.

Computers Computers are regularly used in art, design, drafting, drawing and design, English, ESL, graphic design, media production, science classes. Computer resources include on-campus library services, Internet access, wireless campus network, Internet filtering or blocking technology. Computer access in designated common areas is available to students. Students grades are available online. The school has a published electronic and media policy.

Contact Mr. Marek Pramuka, Dean of Admission and Financial Aid. 951-659-2171 Ext. 2223. Fax: 951-659-3168. E-mail: admission@idyllwildarts.org. Web site: www.idyllwildarts.org.

See Display on page 326 and Close-Up on page 794.

ILLIANA CHRISTIAN HIGH SCHOOL
2261 Indiana Avenue
Lansing, Illinois 60438
Head of School: Peter Boonstra
General Information Coeducational day college-preparatory, general academic, arts, business, vocational, religious studies, and technology school, affiliated with Christian Reformed Church, Reformed Church in America. Grades 9–12. Founded: 1945. Setting: suburban. Nearest major city is Chicago. 15-acre campus. 1 building on campus. Approved or accredited by Association of Christian Schools International, Christian Schools International, North Central Association of Colleges and Schools, and Illinois Department of Education. Endowment: $17 million. Total enrollment: 630. Upper school average class size: 23. Upper school faculty-student ratio: 1:18.
Upper School Student Profile Grade 9: 155 students (87 boys, 68 girls); Grade 10: 187 students (97 boys, 90 girls); Grade 11: 170 students (92 boys, 78 girls); Grade 12: 163 students (75 boys, 88 girls). 70% of students are members of Christian Reformed Church, Reformed Church in America.
Faculty School total: 41. In upper school: 20 men, 21 women; 32 have advanced degrees.
Subjects Offered Algebra, American history, American literature, art, arts, Bible studies, biology, botany, business, business skills, calculus, ceramics, chemistry, computer programming, computer science, drama, earth science, economics, English, environmental science, European history, expository writing, fine arts, geometry, German, government/civics, history, home economics, industrial arts, journalism, mathematics, music, physical education, physics, psychology, social studies, sociology, Spanish, theater, typing, world history, world literature, zoology.
Graduation Requirements Arts and fine arts (art, music, dance, drama), business skills (includes word processing), English, foreign language, mathematics, physical education (includes health), practical arts, religion (includes Bible studies and theology), science, social studies (includes history).
Special Academic Programs Advanced Placement exam preparation; honors section; remedial reading and/or remedial writing; remedial math; programs in English, mathematics for dyslexic students.
College Admission Counseling 155 students graduated in 2009; 121 went to college, including Calvin College; Dordt College; Hope College; Olivet Nazarene University; Purdue University; Trinity Christian College. Other: 3 entered military service, 31 had other specific plans.
Student Life Upper grades have specified standards of dress, student council. Discipline rests primarily with faculty. Attendance at religious services is required.
Tuition and Aid Day student tuition: $7100. Tuition installment plan (monthly payment plans). Need-based scholarship grants available. In 2009–10, 1% of upper-school students received aid.
Admissions Traditional secondary-level entrance grade is 9. For fall 2009, 163 students applied for upper-level admission, 162 were accepted, 155 enrolled. ACT-Explore required. No application fee required. On-campus interview required.
Athletics Interscholastic: baseball (boys), basketball (b,g), cheering (g), cross-country running (b,g), golf (b), indoor track & field (b,g), soccer (b,g), softball (g), tennis (b,g), track and field (b,g), volleyball (b,g), wrestling (b); coed intramural: bowling. 3 PE instructors, 37 coaches, 1 athletic trainer.
Computers Computers are regularly used in business applications, drawing and design, information technology classes. Computer network features include on-campus library services, online commercial services, Internet access.
Contact Peter Boonstra, Principal. 708-474-0515. Fax: 708-474-0581. E-mail: peter.boonstra@illianachristian.org. Web site: www.ichs.pvt.k12.il.us.

IMMACULATA ACADEMY
5138 South Park Avenue
Hamburg, New York 14075
Head of School: Mrs. Mary Lou Stahl
General Information Girls' day college-preparatory, arts, business, religious studies, bilingual studies, and technology school, affiliated with Roman Catholic Church. Grades 9–12. Founded: 1928. Setting: suburban. Nearest major city is Buffalo. 25-acre campus. 1 building on campus. Approved or accredited by Middle States Association of Colleges and Schools, National Catholic Education Association, New York State Association of Independent Schools, New York State Board of Regents, and New York Department of Education. Endowment: $325,000. Total enrollment: 208. Upper school average class size: 12. Upper school faculty-student ratio: 1:10. Upper School students typically attend 5 days per week. The average school day consists of 4 hours and 40 minutes.
Upper School Student Profile Grade 9: 55 students (55 girls); Grade 10: 45 students (45 girls); Grade 11: 53 students (53 girls); Grade 12: 55 students (55 girls). 90% of students are Roman Catholic.
Faculty School total: 29. In upper school: 7 men, 22 women; 23 have advanced degrees.

Subjects Offered Advanced math, Advanced Placement courses, algebra, American government, American history, American history-AP, American literature, art, art appreciation, art-AP, athletics, biology, biology-AP, business, business skills, calculus, chemistry, chemistry-AP, chorus, computer science, earth science, economics, English, English literature, English-AP, fine arts, French, geometry, government/civics, health, instrumental music, Latin, marketing, mathematics, music, physical education, physics, psychology, religion, religious education, science, social sciences, social studies, sociology, Spanish, studio art, studio art-AP, trigonometry, world literature.
Graduation Requirements Advanced studio art-AP, arts and fine arts (art, music, dance, drama), computer science, English, foreign language, mathematics, physical education (includes health), religion (includes Bible studies and theology), science, social studies (includes history), 80 hours of community service (minimum of 20 hours per year), reflection paper about service each year, senior year synthesis paper on service and subsequent interview.
Special Academic Programs Advanced Placement exam preparation; honors section; independent study; study at local college for college credit; academic accommodation for the musically talented and the artistically talented.
College Admission Counseling 50 students graduated in 2009; 49 went to college, including Canisius College; Niagara University; Rochester Institute of Technology; St. Bonaventure University; The College at Brockport, State University of New York; University at Buffalo, the State University of New York. Other: 1 entered military service. Mean SAT critical reading: 530, mean SAT math: 509, mean SAT writing: 526, mean composite ACT: 23. 24% scored over 600 on SAT critical reading, 10% scored over 600 on SAT math, 23% scored over 600 on SAT writing, 14% scored over 1800 on combined SAT, 22% scored over 26 on composite ACT.
Student Life Upper grades have uniform requirement, student council, honor system. Discipline rests primarily with faculty. Attendance at religious services is required.
Tuition and Aid Day student tuition: $7210. Tuition installment plan (FACTS Tuition Payment Plan, individually arranged payment plans). Merit scholarship grants, need-based scholarship grants, need-based loans, tuition reduction for daughters of alumnae, tuition reduction for Diocesan employees available. In 2009–10, 49% of upper-school students received aid; total upper-school merit-scholarship money awarded: $155,000. Total amount of financial aid awarded in 2009–10: $346,000.
Admissions Traditional secondary-level entrance grade is 9. For fall 2009, 121 students applied for upper-level admission, 101 were accepted, 55 enrolled. Catholic High School Entrance Examination or High School Placement Test required. Deadline for receipt of application materials: none. No application fee required. On-campus interview recommended.
Athletics Interscholastic: aerobics/dance, badminton, basketball, bowling, cross-country running, dance team, golf, soccer, softball, track and field, volleyball; intramural: basketball, dance squad, floor hockey, indoor track & field, tennis, winter (indoor) track. 1 PE instructor, 14 coaches.
Computers Computers are regularly used in business applications, desktop publishing, newspaper, typing, word processing classes. Computer network features include on-campus library services, Internet access, Internet filtering or blocking technology, remote access to homework assignments through Learning Village. The school has a published electronic and media policy.
Contact Mrs. Andrea Drabik, Director of Admissions and Recruitment. 716-646-9942. Fax: 716-646-1782. E-mail: adrabik@immaculataacademy.com. Web site: www.immaculataacademy.com.

IMMACULATA HIGH SCHOOL
600 Shawnee
Leavenworth, Kansas 66048
Head of School: Mrs. Helen C. Schwinn
General Information Coeducational day college-preparatory, arts, business, religious studies, and technology school, affiliated with Roman Catholic Church (Jesuit order). Grades 9–12. Founded: 1924. Setting: suburban. Nearest major city is Kansas City. 2-acre campus. 1 building on campus. Approved or accredited by North Central Association of Colleges and Schools and Kansas Department of Education. Total enrollment: 122. Upper school average class size: 15. Upper school faculty-student ratio: 1:9. There are 171 required school days per year for Upper School students. Upper School students typically attend 5 days per week. The average school day consists of 7 hours.
Upper School Student Profile Grade 9: 34 students (21 boys, 13 girls); Grade 10: 25 students (15 boys, 10 girls); Grade 11: 34 students (21 boys, 13 girls); Grade 12: 30 students (11 boys, 19 girls). 85% of students are Roman Catholic Church (Jesuit order).
Faculty School total: 15. In upper school: 4 men, 10 women; 7 have advanced degrees.
Special Academic Programs Honors section; study at local college for college credit.
College Admission Counseling 22 students graduated in 2009; 20 went to college. Other: 2 went to work.
Student Life Upper grades have uniform requirement, student council. Discipline rests primarily with faculty. Attendance at religious services is required.
Admissions Traditional secondary-level entrance grade is 9. Achievement tests required. Deadline for receipt of application materials: none. No application fee required.

Immaculata High School

Athletics Interscholastic: baseball (boys), basketball (b,g), cheering (g), football (b), golf (b), power lifting (b,g), soccer (b,g), softball (g), swimming and diving (b), tennis (b,g), track and field (b,g), volleyball (g), wrestling (b). 1 PE instructor, 4 coaches.
Computers Computers are regularly used in business education classes. Computer network features include Internet access, wireless campus network. Campus intranet is available to students. Students grades are available online.
Contact Paula Hyde, Academic Adviser. 913-682-3900. Fax: 913-682-9036. E-mail: phyde@archkckcs.org. Web site: www.archkckcs.org/immaculata.

IMMACULATA HIGH SCHOOL
240 Mountain Avenue
Somerville, New Jersey 08876
Head of School: Sr. Regina Havens
General Information Coeducational day college-preparatory and religious studies school, affiliated with Roman Catholic Church. Grades 9–12. Founded: 1962. Setting: suburban. 19-acre campus. 3 buildings on campus. Approved or accredited by Middle States Association of Colleges and Schools, National Catholic Education Association, and New Jersey Department of Education. Total enrollment: 813. Upper school average class size: 22. Upper school faculty-student ratio: 1:13. There are 180 required school days per year for Upper School students. Upper School students typically attend 5 days per week. The average school day consists of 6 hours and 30 minutes.
Upper School Student Profile Grade 9: 210 students (112 boys, 98 girls); Grade 10: 203 students (89 boys, 114 girls); Grade 11: 228 students (131 boys, 97 girls); Grade 12: 203 students (109 boys, 94 girls). 92% of students are Roman Catholic.
Faculty School total: 80. In upper school: 20 men, 60 women; 48 have advanced degrees.
Subjects Offered Accounting, advanced chemistry, advanced math, Advanced Placement courses, algebra, American literature, American history, anatomy, ancient world history, art, art history-AP, biology, British literature, business, calculus, calculus-AP, chemistry, chemistry-AP, creative writing, drama, drawing and design, driver education, Eastern world civilizations, ecology, English-AP, environmental science, environmental studies, European history-AP, film history, foreign language, French language-AP, geometry, global issues, global studies, graphic design, health, honors algebra, honors English, honors geometry, marching band, music theory, religious education, science, social studies, speech, trigonometry, U.S. history-AP.
Graduation Requirements Algebra, American literature, biology, British literature, chemistry, driver education, foreign language, geometry, health education, physical education (includes health), physical science, theology, U.S. history.
Special Academic Programs Advanced Placement exam preparation; honors section; academic accommodation for the musically talented.
College Admission Counseling 184 students graduated in 2009; 183 went to college, including Loyola University Maryland; Penn State University Park; Rutgers, The State University of New Jersey, New Brunswick; Saint Joseph's University; Seton Hall University; The University of Scranton. Other: 1 had other specific plans. Mean SAT critical reading: 535, mean SAT math: 542, mean SAT writing: 560.
Student Life Upper grades have uniform requirement. Discipline rests primarily with faculty. Attendance at religious services is required.
Tuition and Aid Day student tuition: $8350. Tuition installment plan (FACTS Tuition Payment Plan).
Admissions Traditional secondary-level entrance grade is 9. For fall 2009, 300 students applied for upper-level admission, 240 were accepted, 210 enrolled. High School Placement Test required. Deadline for receipt of application materials: December 31. Application fee required: $150. On-campus interview required.
Athletics Interscholastic: baseball (boys), basketball (b,g), cheering (g), cross-country running (b,g), football (b), lacrosse (b,g), soccer (b,g), softball (g), tennis (b,g); coed interscholastic: bowling, golf, swimming and diving. 5 PE instructors, 50 coaches, 1 athletic trainer.
Computers Computers are regularly used in graphic design, journalism classes. Computer network features include on-campus library services, online commercial services, Internet access. Students grades are available online.
Contact Sr. Anne Brigid Gallagher, Assistant Principal/Academic Dean. 908-722-0200 Ext. 118. Fax: 908-218-7765. E-mail: sannebrigid@immaculatahighschool.org. Web site: www.immaculatahighschool.org.

IMMACULATA-LA SALLE HIGH SCHOOL
3601 South Miami Avenue
Miami, Florida 33133
Head of School: Sr. Patricia Roche, FMA
General Information Coeducational day college-preparatory, arts, business, religious studies, and technology school, affiliated with Roman Catholic Church. Grades 9–12. Founded: 1958. Setting: urban. 13-acre campus. 7 buildings on campus. Approved or accredited by Southern Association of Colleges and Schools, The College Board, and Florida Department of Education. Endowment: $71,000. Total enrollment: 751. Upper school average class size: 24. Upper school faculty-student ratio: 1:15. There are 180 required school days per year for Upper School students. Upper School students typically attend 5 days per week. The average school day consists of 6 hours and 30 minutes.

Upper School Student Profile Grade 9: 202 students (70 boys, 132 girls); Grade 10: 179 students (58 boys, 121 girls); Grade 11: 197 students (59 boys, 138 girls); Grade 12: 173 students (68 boys, 105 girls). 95% of students are Roman Catholic.
Faculty School total: 49. In upper school: 17 men, 31 women; 27 have advanced degrees.
Subjects Offered Advanced Placement courses, African American studies, algebra, American history, American history-AP, analytic geometry, anatomy, art, automated accounting, band, Bible studies, biology, calculus, chemistry, Chinese, choral music, computer programming, computer programming-AP, computer science, desktop publishing, drama, economics, English, European history, fine arts, French, geometry, government/civics, health, history, humanities, Italian, marine biology, mathematics, music appreciation, physical education, physics, psychology, religion, science, social studies, sociology, Spanish, speech, trigonometry, U.S. government and politics-AP, world history.
Graduation Requirements Arts and fine arts (art, music, dance, drama), business skills (includes word processing), computer science, English, foreign language, mathematics, physical education (includes health), religion (includes Bible studies and theology), science, social studies (includes history), 20 hours of community service for each of the 4 years.
Special Academic Programs Advanced Placement exam preparation; honors section; independent study; study at local college for college credit; academic accommodation for the gifted.
College Admission Counseling 173 students graduated in 2010; 170 went to college, including Barry University; Florida International University; Florida State University; Miami Dade College; University of Central Florida; University of Miami. Other: 3 had other specific plans. Mean SAT critical reading: 509, mean SAT math: 491, mean SAT writing: 515, mean combined SAT: 1515, mean composite ACT: 22. 16% scored over 600 on SAT critical reading, 11% scored over 600 on SAT math, 16% scored over 600 on SAT writing, 43% scored over 1800 on combined SAT, 20% scored over 26 on composite ACT.
Student Life Upper grades have uniform requirement, student council. Discipline rests equally with students and faculty. Attendance at religious services is required.
Summer Programs Remediation, enrichment programs offered; session focuses on remediation and enrichment; held on campus; accepts boys and girls; open to students from other schools. 150 students usually enrolled. 2011 schedule: June 20 to July 15. Application deadline: June 13.
Tuition and Aid Day student tuition: $11,000. Tuition installment plan (FACTS Tuition Payment Plan, monthly payment plans, individually arranged payment plans). Paying campus jobs available. In 2010–11, 9% of upper-school students received aid. Total amount of financial aid awarded in 2010–11: $260,000.
Admissions Traditional secondary-level entrance grade is 9. For fall 2010, 450 students applied for upper-level admission, 330 were accepted, 255 enrolled. Catholic High School Entrance Examination or PSAT and SAT for applicants to grade 11 and 12 required. Deadline for receipt of application materials: none. Application fee required: $500. On-campus interview required.
Athletics Interscholastic: baseball (boys), basketball (b,g), bicycling (b,g), cheering (b,g), cross-country running (b,g), dance team (g), football (b), lacrosse (b), soccer (b,g), softball (g), swimming and diving (b,g), tennis (b,g), track and field (b,g), trap and skeet (b,g), volleyball (g), weight training (b,g), winter soccer (b,g); intramural: football (b), volleyball (g); coed interscholastic: tennis, track and field; coed intramural: aerobics/dance, bicycling, dance, dance team, mountain biking, physical fitness, sailing, table tennis, weight training. 3 PE instructors, 15 coaches, 1 athletic trainer.
Computers Computers are regularly used in business, business applications, economics, French, journalism, mathematics, programming, science, technology, word processing, yearbook classes. Computer network features include on-campus library services, Internet access. Students grades are available online.
Contact Ms. Nancy Toruno, Admissions Director. 305-854-2334 Ext. 130. Fax: 305-858-5971. E-mail: admissions@ilsroyals.com. Web site: www.ilsroyals.com.

IMMACULATE CONCEPTION HIGH SCHOOL
258 South Main Street
Lodi, New Jersey 07644-2199
Head of School: Sr. Mary Alicia Adametz, CSSF
General Information Girls' day college-preparatory, arts, and religious studies school, affiliated with Roman Catholic Church. Grades 9–12. Founded: 1915. Setting: suburban. Nearest major city is Paterson. 3-acre campus. 1 building on campus. Approved or accredited by Middle States Association of Colleges and Schools, National Catholic Education Association, and New Jersey Department of Education. Total enrollment: 167. Upper school average class size: 17. Upper school faculty-student ratio: 1:10. There are 180 required school days per year for Upper School students. Upper School students typically attend 5 days per week. The average school day consists of 6 hours and 8 minutes.
Upper School Student Profile Grade 9: 37 students (37 girls); Grade 10: 35 students (35 girls); Grade 11: 36 students (36 girls); Grade 12: 45 students (45 girls). 85% of students are Roman Catholic.
Faculty School total: 16. In upper school: 3 men, 13 women.
Subjects Offered Advanced math, algebra, American government, American history, American history-AP, American literature, anatomy and physiology, art, Bible studies, biology, British literature, character education, chemistry, communications, computer

graphics, computer skills, driver education, English, French, genetics, geometry, health and safety, honors algebra, honors English, honors geometry, honors U.S. history, lab science, musical productions, organic chemistry, performing arts, photography, physical education, physical science, pre-calculus, psychology, religious education, social psychology, Spanish, women in society, world cultures, writing.

Graduation Requirements English, foreign language, lab science, mathematics, physical education (includes health), religious studies, social studies (includes history). Community service is required.

Special Academic Programs 1 Advanced Placement exam for which test preparation is offered; honors section; study at local college for college credit.

College Admission Counseling 38 students graduated in 2010; 37 went to college, including Bergen Community College; Felician College; Ramapo College of New Jersey; Rutgers, The State University of New Jersey, New Brunswick; Seton Hall University; William Paterson University of New Jersey. Other: 1 had other specific plans. Mean SAT critical reading: 500, mean SAT math: 450, mean SAT writing: 520, mean combined SAT: 1470.

Student Life Upper grades have uniform requirement, student council. Discipline rests primarily with faculty. Attendance at religious services is required.

Summer Programs Enrichment, advancement programs offered; session focuses on Jump Start Program for incoming freshmen; held on campus; accepts girls; not open to students from other schools. 25 students usually enrolled. 2011 schedule: August to August. Application deadline: February.

Tuition and Aid Day student tuition: $8750. Tuition installment plan (FACTS Tuition Payment Plan, annual payment plan). Tuition reduction for siblings, merit scholarship grants, need-based scholarship grants available. In 2010–11, 27% of upper-school students received aid; total upper-school merit-scholarship money awarded: $54,500. Total amount of financial aid awarded in 2010–11: $73,250.

Admissions Traditional secondary-level entrance grade is 9. For fall 2010, 251 students applied for upper-level admission, 240 were accepted, 37 enrolled. Cooperative Entrance Exam (McGraw-Hill) required. Deadline for receipt of application materials: none. Application fee required: $300. Interview recommended.

Athletics Interscholastic: basketball, cheering, cross-country running, soccer, softball, swimming and diving, tennis, volleyball; intramural: aerobics, basketball, fitness, fitness walking, floor hockey, physical fitness, tennis, volleyball, walking. 2 PE instructors, 12 coaches, 1 athletic trainer.

Computers Computers are regularly used in graphics, newspaper, photography, word processing, yearbook classes. Computer resources include on-campus library services, Internet access, Internet filtering or blocking technology. Computer access in designated common areas is available to students. Students grades are available online. The school has a published electronic and media policy.

Contact Mrs. Sara Simon, Director of Enrollment Management. 973-773-2665. Fax: 973-614-0893. E-mail: ssimon@ichslodi.org. Web site: www.ichslodi.org.

IMMACULATE CONCEPTION HIGH SCHOOL AND MIDDLE SCHOOL

1725 Central Avenue
Memphis, Tennessee 38104
Head of School: Mrs. Sally S. Hermsdorfer

General Information Coeducational day college-preparatory, arts, religious studies, bilingual studies, and technology school, affiliated with Roman Catholic Church, Christian faith; primarily serves students with learning disabilities and individuals with Attention Deficit Disorder. Boys grades 7–8, girls grades 7–12. Founded: 1950. Setting: urban. 4 buildings on campus. Approved or accredited by Commission on Secondary and Middle Schools and Southern Association of Colleges and Schools. Total enrollment: 218. Upper school average class size: 20. Upper school faculty-student ratio: 1:16. There are 183 required school days per year for Upper School students. Upper School students typically attend 5 days per week. The average school day consists of 7 hours and 55 minutes.

Upper School Student Profile Grade 7: 50 students (24 boys, 26 girls); Grade 8: 48 students (25 boys, 23 girls); Grade 9: 28 students (28 boys); Grade 10: 34 students (34 boys); Grade 11: 26 students (26 boys); Grade 12: 25 students (25 boys). 70% of students are Roman Catholic, Christian.

Faculty School total: 18. In upper school: 3 men, 14 women; 8 have advanced degrees.

Subjects Offered Algebra, American history-AP, anatomy, arts, biology, business law, business skills, calculus-AP, chemistry, chorus, community service, computer science, drama, economics, English, English-AP, European history-AP, fine arts, French, French-AP, geography, geometry, government/civics, history, mathematics, physical education, physics, psychology, religion, science, social sciences, social studies, Spanish, theater, trigonometry, word processing, world history.

Graduation Requirements American government, arts and fine arts (art, music, dance, drama), business skills (includes word processing), computer science, English, foreign language, mathematics, physical education (includes health), religion (includes Bible studies and theology), science, social sciences, social studies (includes history), students must have completed 34 extra curricular service hours. Community service is required.

Special Academic Programs 4 Advanced Placement exams for which test preparation is offered; honors section; independent study; term-away projects; study at local

college for college credit; academic accommodation for the gifted; remedial reading and/or remedial writing; remedial math; programs in English, mathematics, general development for dyslexic students.

College Admission Counseling 34 students graduated in 2009; 33 went to college, including Christian Brothers University; Rhodes College; Saint Mary's College; The University of Tennessee; University of Memphis; University of Mississippi. Other: 1 went to work. Median composite ACT: 24. 20% scored over 26 on composite ACT.

Student Life Upper grades have uniform requirement, student council, honor system. Discipline rests equally with students and faculty. Attendance at religious services is required.

Tuition and Aid Day student tuition: $8570. Tuition installment plan (FACTS Tuition Payment Plan, monthly payment plans, individually arranged payment plans, small discount offered for one lump sum, or two annual payments). Merit scholarship grants, need-based scholarship grants available. In 2009–10, 28% of upper-school students received aid; total upper-school merit-scholarship money awarded: $35. Total amount of financial aid awarded in 2009–10: $85.

Admissions Traditional secondary-level entrance grade is 9. For fall 2009, 190 students applied for upper-level admission, 120 were accepted, 120 enrolled. High School Placement Test, and High School Placement Test (closed version) from Scholastic Testing Service required. Deadline for receipt of application materials: none. Application fee required: $100. On-campus interview required.

Athletics Interscholastic: aquatics (girls), basketball (g), bowling (g), cheering (g), cross-country running (g), fitness walking (g), golf (g), indoor soccer (g), martial arts (g), physical fitness (g), soccer (g), softball (g), swimming and diving (g), tennis (g), track and field (g), volleyball (g). 1 PE instructor.

Computers Computers are regularly used in English, foreign language, history, mathematics, science classes. Computer network features include on-campus library services, online commercial services, Internet access, Internet filtering or blocking technology. Campus intranet and computer access in designated common areas are available to students. Students grades are available online. The school has a published electronic and media policy.

Contact Mrs. Betsy McKay, Director of Admissions. 901-435-5309. Fax: 901-725-2701. E-mail: betsy.mckay@ic.cdom.org. Web site: www.myiccs.org.

IMMACULATE CONCEPTION SCHOOL

217 Cottage Hill Avenue
Elmhurst, Illinois 60126
Head of School: Pamela M. Levar

General Information Coeducational day college-preparatory, arts, religious studies, and technology school, affiliated with Roman Catholic Church. Grades 9–12. Founded: 1936. Setting: suburban. Nearest major city is Chicago. 2 buildings on campus. Approved or accredited by North Central Association of Colleges and Schools and Illinois Department of Education. Total enrollment: 344. Upper school average class size: 17. Upper school faculty-student ratio: 1:14. There are 176 required school days per year for Upper School students. Upper School students typically attend 5 days per week. The average school day consists of 6 hours and 25 minutes.

Upper School Student Profile Grade 9: 88 students (49 boys, 39 girls); Grade 10: 79 students (43 boys, 36 girls); Grade 11: 91 students (45 boys, 46 girls); Grade 12: 86 students (44 boys, 42 girls). 88% of students are Roman Catholic.

Faculty School total: 25. In upper school: 7 men, 18 women; 12 have advanced degrees.

Subjects Offered 3-dimensional art, advanced chemistry, advanced math, algebra, American government, American history, anatomy and physiology, ancient world history, art, biology, biology-AP, British literature, business law, calculus, calculus-AP, campus ministry, career/college preparation, Catholic belief and practice, ceramics, chemistry, college counseling, computer applications, computer programming, constitutional history of U.S., consumer education, current events, drawing, ecology, environmental systems, economics, English, English-AP, environmental science, fitness, foreign language, French, geometry, government/civics, health education, honors algebra, honors English, honors geometry, honors U.S. history, humanities, keyboarding, library, musical theater, newspaper, painting, physical education, physics, pre-calculus, psychology, SAT/ACT preparation, sociology, Spanish, speech, student government, trigonometry, U.S. history-AP, yearbook.

Graduation Requirements Algebra, American government, American literature, anatomy and physiology, art, biology, British literature, calculus, Catholic belief and practice, chemistry, computer applications, constitutional history of U.S., consumer education, English, environmental science, foreign language, geometry, grammar, health, history, human biology, language and composition, mathematics, physical science, political science, pre-calculus, trigonometry, U.S. history, world history, 40 hours of Christian Service, Attendance at retreat.

Special Academic Programs 4 Advanced Placement exams for which test preparation is offered; honors section; study at local college for college credit.

College Admission Counseling 84 students graduated in 2010; 83 went to college, including Illinois State University; Lewis University; St. Norbert College; The University of Iowa; Triton College; University of Illinois at Urbana–Champaign. Other: 1 had other specific plans. Median composite ACT: 22. 23% scored over 26 on composite ACT.

Student Life Upper grades have uniform requirement, student council. Discipline rests primarily with faculty. Attendance at religious services is required.

Immaculate Conception School

Summer Programs Sports programs offered; session focuses on sports; held on campus; accepts boys and girls; not open to students from other schools. 150 students usually enrolled. 2011 schedule: June 15 to July 28.

Tuition and Aid Day student tuition: $8300. Tuition installment plan (SMART Tuition Payment Plan). Tuition reduction for siblings, merit scholarship grants, need-based scholarship grants, merit scholarships (for placement test top scorers), externally funded scholarships (alumni, memorials), Catholic school teacher grants (1/3 reduction) available. In 2010–11, 33% of upper-school students received aid; total upper-school merit-scholarship money awarded: $15,000. Total amount of financial aid awarded in 2010–11: $150,000.

Admissions Traditional secondary-level entrance grade is 9. For fall 2010, 138 students applied for upper-level admission, 133 were accepted, 106 enrolled. High School Placement Test (closed version) from Scholastic Testing Service required. Deadline for receipt of application materials: none. No application fee required.

Athletics Interscholastic: baseball (boys), basketball (b,g), bowling (b), cheering (g), cross-country running (b,g), dance team (g), football (b), lacrosse (b), pom squad (g), soccer (g), softball (g), track and field (b,g), volleyball (g), weight lifting (b), weight training (b,g); coed interscholastic: fishing, golf, winter (indoor) track. 2 PE instructors, 30 coaches, 2 athletic trainers.

Computers Computers are regularly used in business applications, career exploration, college planning, computer applications, library, news writing, science, stock market, yearbook classes. Computer network features include on-campus library services, online commercial services, Internet access, Internet filtering or blocking technology. Computer access in designated common areas is available to students. Students grades are available online. The school has a published electronic and media policy.

Contact Mrs. Kathy Kowieski, Director of Admissions. 630-530-3484. Fax: 630-530-2290. E-mail: kkowieski@ichsknights.org. Web site: www.ichsknights.org.

IMMANUEL CHRISTIAN HIGH SCHOOL

802 6th Avenue N
Lethbridge, Alberta T1H 0S1, Canada
Head of School: Mr. Rob van Spronsen

General Information Coeducational day college-preparatory, general academic, and religious studies school, affiliated with Christian Reformed Church, Reformed Church. Grades 7–12. Founded: 1962. Setting: urban. 4-acre campus. 1 building on campus. Approved or accredited by Christian Schools International and Alberta Department of Education. Language of instruction: English. Total enrollment: 228. Upper school average class size: 22. Upper school faculty-student ratio: 1:19. There are 188 required school days per year for Upper School students. Upper School students typically attend 5 days per week. The average school day consists of 5 hours and 30 minutes.

Upper School Student Profile 70% of students are members of Christian Reformed Church, Reformed.

Faculty School total: 18. In upper school: 10 men, 8 women; 4 have advanced degrees.

Subjects Offered Algebra, art, athletics, basketball, Bible, biology, business applications, calculus, career planning, carpentry, chemistry, choral music, Christian education, Christian ethics, Christian studies, computer applications, drama, English, first aid, food and nutrition, French as a second language, global issues, guidance, health, history, industrial arts, mathematics, science, social studies.

Graduation Requirements Alberta Learning requirements.

Special Academic Programs Independent study.

College Admission Counseling 41 students graduated in 2010; 18 went to college, including Calvin College; Dordt College; Redeemer University College; Trinity Western University; University of Alberta; University of Lethbridge. Other: 22 went to work.

Student Life Upper grades have specified standards of dress, student council, honor system. Discipline rests primarily with faculty. Attendance at religious services is required.

Tuition and Aid Day student tuition: CAN$6500–CAN$7200. Tuition installment plan (monthly payment plans, individually arranged payment plans). Tuition reduction for siblings available. In 2010–11, 0% of upper-school students received aid.

Admissions Traditional secondary-level entrance grade is 10. Deadline for receipt of application materials: none. No application fee required. Interview required.

Athletics Interscholastic: badminton (boys, girls), basketball (b,g), golf (b,g), running (b,g), track and field (b,g), volleyball (b,g); intramural: badminton (b,g), basketball (b,g), outdoor education (b,g), track and field (b,g), volleyball (b,g); coed interscholastic: badminton, cross-country running; coed intramural: badminton, outdoor education, scuba diving. 2 PE instructors.

Computers Computers are regularly used in all classes. Computer network features include on-campus library services, Internet access, wireless campus network, Internet filtering or blocking technology. Student e-mail accounts and computer access in designated common areas are available to students. Students grades are available online. The school has a published electronic and media policy.

Contact Mr. Rob van Spronsen, Principal. 403-328-4783. Fax: 403-327-6333. E-mail: rvanspronsen@immanuelcs.ca. Web site: ichs.icssa.ca.

IMPERIAL COLLEGE OF TORONTO

20 Queen Elizabeth Boulevard
Etobicoke, Ontario M8Z 1L8, Canada
Head of School: Mr. Daniel Crabb

General Information Coeducational boarding college-preparatory and general academic school. Grades 11–12. Founded: 1990. Setting: urban. Nearest major city is Toronto, Canada. Students are housed in coed dormitories. 2-acre campus. 1 building on campus. Approved or accredited by Ontario Ministry of Education and Ontario Department of Education. Language of instruction: English. Total enrollment: 210. Upper school average class size: 22. Upper school faculty-student ratio: 1:22. The average school day consists of 6 hours.

Upper School Student Profile Grade 11: 38 students (20 boys, 18 girls); Grade 12: 172 students (88 boys, 84 girls). 25% of students are boarding students. 5% are province residents. 1 province is represented in upper school student body. 95% are international students. International students from China, Hong Kong, Malaysia, Republic of Korea, Taiwan, and Viet Nam; 2 other countries represented in student body.

Faculty School total: 17. In upper school: 10 men, 7 women; 6 have advanced degrees; 2 reside on campus.

Subjects Offered Accounting, advanced TOEFL/grammar, algebra, biology, chemistry, Chinese, college placement, computer applications, economics, finite math, geography, geometry, mathematics, physics.

Graduation Requirements Accounting, calculus, computer science, economics, English, mathematics, physics.

Special Academic Programs Accelerated programs; independent study; special instructional classes for students with emotional and behavioral problems; ESL (85 students enrolled).

College Admission Counseling 181 students graduated in 2009; 162 went to college, including McMaster University; Queen's University at Kingston; Simon Fraser University; University of Manitoba; University of Toronto; University of Waterloo. Other: 10 had other specific plans.

Student Life Upper grades have honor system. Discipline rests primarily with faculty.

Tuition and Aid Guaranteed tuition plan.

Admissions Deadline for receipt of application materials: none. Application fee required: CAN$200.

Computers Computers are regularly used in accounting, business education, college planning, computer applications, creative writing, current events, data processing, design, desktop publishing, digital applications, economics, English, ESL, foreign language, geography, information technology, multimedia, science, study skills, Web site design, word processing, writing classes. Computer network features include Internet access. Campus intranet and computer access in designated common areas are available to students.

Contact Mr. Isaac Kuo, Executive Assistant to Director. 416-251-4970. Fax: 416-251-0259. E-mail: info@imperialcollege.org. Web site: www.imperialcollege.org.

INCARNATE WORD ACADEMY

609 Crawford
Houston, Texas 77002-3668
Head of School: Ms. Mary Getschow

General Information Girls' day college-preparatory, arts, and religious studies school, affiliated with Roman Catholic Church. Grades 9–12. Founded: 1873. Setting: urban. 2 buildings on campus. Approved or accredited by Southern Association of Colleges and Schools, Texas Catholic Conference, Texas Education Agency, and Texas Department of Education. Total enrollment: 272. Upper school average class size: 13. Upper school faculty-student ratio: 1:13. There are 180 required school days per year for Upper School students. Upper School students typically attend 5 days per week. The average school day consists of 7 hours.

Upper School Student Profile Grade 9: 82 students (82 girls); Grade 10: 69 students (69 girls); Grade 11: 72 students (72 girls); Grade 12: 51 students (51 girls). 85.7% of students are Roman Catholic.

Faculty School total: 26. In upper school: 6 men, 16 women; 15 have advanced degrees.

Subjects Offered Algebra, American government, American history, American history-AP, American literature, American literature-AP, art, biology, biology-AP, British literature, British literature-AP, calculus, chemistry, chemistry-AP, concert choir, drama, English composition, English literature, English literature and composition-AP, English literature-AP, English-AP, English/composition-AP, environmental science-AP, French, government and politics-AP, government-AP, health, history-AP, honors algebra, honors English, honors geometry, honors U.S. history, honors world history, Latin, literature and composition-AP, literature-AP, microeconomics, microeconomics-AP, newspaper, physical education, physics, pre-calculus, psychology, publications, SAT/ACT preparation, social studies, Spanish, Spanish language-AP, Spanish literature-AP, Spanish-AP, theater arts, theater production, theology, trigonometry, U.S. government and politics, U.S. government and politics-AP, U.S. history, U.S. history-AP, U.S. literature, United States government-AP, video and animation, Web site design, world geography, world history, world literature, world religions, world studies, world wide web design, World-Wide-Web publishing, yearbook.

Graduation Requirements 100 hours of community service.

Special Academic Programs Advanced Placement exam preparation; honors section; study at local college for college credit.

College Admission Counseling 54 students graduated in 2010; all went to college, including Baylor University; Texas A&M University; The University of Texas at Austin; University of Houston.

Student Life Upper grades have uniform requirement, student council, honor system. Discipline rests primarily with faculty. Attendance at religious services is required.

Summer Programs Sports programs offered; session focuses on sports conditioning camp; held both on and off campus; held at University of St. Thomas and St. Thomas High School; accepts girls; open to students from other schools. 45 students usually enrolled. 2011 schedule: July 28 to August 1.

Tuition and Aid Day student tuition: $8600. Tuition installment plan (monthly payment plans). Merit scholarship grants, need-based scholarship grants, paying campus jobs available. In 2010–11, 30% of upper-school students received aid; total upper-school merit-scholarship money awarded: $43,850. Total amount of financial aid awarded in 2010–11: $119,606.

Admissions Traditional secondary-level entrance grade is 9. High School Placement Test (closed version) from Scholastic Testing Service or ISEE required. Deadline for receipt of application materials: January 15. Application fee required: $50. On-campus interview recommended.

Athletics Interscholastic: basketball, cheering, cross-country running, dance, dance team, golf, running, soccer, softball, track and field, volleyball; intramural: fitness, physical fitness. 2 PE instructors, 6 coaches, 1 athletic trainer.

Computers Computers are regularly used in computer applications, economics, history, keyboarding, mathematics, research skills, science, social studies, technology, Web site design, yearbook classes. Computer network features include on-campus library services, online commercial services, Internet access, wireless campus network, Internet filtering or blocking technology. Students grades are available online. The school has a published electronic and media policy.

Contact Ms. Gianna Leggio, Director of Admissions. 713-227-3637 Ext. 117. Fax: 713-227-1014. E-mail: gleggio@incarnateword.org. Web site: www. incarnateword.org.

INDEPENDENT SCHOOL

8317 East Douglas
Wichita, Kansas 67207

Head of School: Mr. Chris Taylor

General Information Coeducational day college-preparatory school. Grades PK–12. Founded: 1980. Setting: suburban. 22-acre campus. 2 buildings on campus. Approved or accredited by National Christian School Association and North Central Association of Colleges and Schools. Candidate for accreditation by Independent Schools Association of the Central States. Endowment: $1.8 million. Total enrollment: 616. Upper school average class size: 18. Upper school faculty-student ratio: 1:10. Upper School students typically attend 5 days per week. The average school day consists of 6 hours.

Upper School Student Profile Grade 9: 64 students (42 boys, 22 girls); Grade 10: 52 students (26 boys, 26 girls); Grade 11: 56 students (28 boys, 28 girls); Grade 12: 53 students (25 boys, 28 girls).

Faculty In upper school: 14 men, 11 women; 14 have advanced degrees.

Subjects Offered 3-dimensional art, advanced math, Advanced Placement courses, algebra, American government, American history, American history-AP, American literature, anatomy and physiology, art, biology, biology-AP, British literature, British literature (honors), calculus, calculus-AP, ceramics, chemistry, chemistry-AP, choir, computer applications, computer art, debate, English literature-AP, film and new technologies, foreign language, forensics, geometry, health, health and wellness, keyboarding, Latin, music, music theory-AP, newspaper, physics, physics-AP, Spanish, Spanish-AP, statistics-AP, theater, theater arts, trigonometry, U.S. government and politics-AP, Web site design, weight training, yearbook.

Graduation Requirements Algebra, American government, American history, American literature, arts and fine arts (art, music, dance, drama), biology, British literature, chemistry, computer applications, computer literacy, English, foreign language, geography, geometry, humanities, physical education (includes health), world history, world literature, 50 hours of community service.

Special Academic Programs Advanced Placement exam preparation; honors section; academic accommodation for the gifted, the musically talented, and the artistically talented.

College Admission Counseling 53 students graduated in 2009; they went to Creighton University; Kansas State University; Oklahoma State University; The University of Kansas. Mean SAT critical reading: 580, mean SAT math: 590, mean SAT writing: 560, mean combined SAT: 1730, mean composite ACT: 25.

Student Life Upper grades have specified standards of dress, student council. Discipline rests primarily with faculty.

Tuition and Aid Day student tuition: $9150. Tuition installment plan (monthly payment plans, individually arranged payment plans). Need-based scholarship grants available. In 2009–10, 22% of upper-school students received aid.

Admissions Traditional secondary-level entrance grade is 9. Admissions testing, non-standardized placement tests and Otis-Lennon Ability or Stanford Achievement Test required. Deadline for receipt of application materials: none. Application fee required: $40. On-campus interview required.

Athletics Interscholastic: baseball (boys), basketball (b,g), cheering (g), cross-country running (b,g), dance team (g), football (b), golf (b,g), soccer (b,g), softball (g), strength & conditioning (b,g), swimming and diving (b,g), tennis (b,g), track and field (b,g), volleyball (g), weight training (b,g), wrestling (b); coed interscholastic: strength & conditioning, weight training. 2 PE instructors, 5 coaches, 1 athletic trainer.

Computers Computers are regularly used in art, college planning, economics, English, humanities, introduction to technology, keyboarding, library, literary magazine, mathematics, newspaper, photography, publications, Web site design, yearbook classes. Computer network features include on-campus library services, Internet access, Internet filtering or blocking technology, homework online. Students grades are available online. The school has a published electronic and media policy.

Contact Ms. Danielle T. Veltz, Director of Admissions. 316-686-0152 Ext. 405. Fax: 316-686-3918. E-mail: danielle.veltz@theindependentschool.com. Web site: www. theindependentschool.com.

INDIAN MOUNTAIN SCHOOL

Lakeville, Connecticut
See Junior Boarding Schools section.

INDIAN SPRINGS SCHOOL

190 Woodward Drive
Indian Springs, Alabama 35124

Head of School: Mr. Gareth Vaughan

General Information Coeducational boarding and day college-preparatory, arts, and technology school. Boarding grades 9–12, day grades 8–12. Founded: 1952. Setting: suburban. Nearest major city is Birmingham. Students are housed in single-sex dormitories. 350-acre campus. 38 buildings on campus. Approved or accredited by Southern Association of Colleges and Schools, Southern Association of Independent Schools, The Association of Boarding Schools, and Alabama Department of Education. Member of National Association of Independent Schools and Secondary School Admission Test Board. Endowment: $18 million. Total enrollment: 281. Upper school average class size: 12. Upper school faculty-student ratio: 1:8. There are 175 required school days per year for Upper School students. Upper School students typically attend 5 days per week. The average school day consists of 6 hours and 20 minutes.

Upper School Student Profile Grade 8: 28 students (16 boys, 12 girls); Grade 9: 46 students (25 boys, 21 girls); Grade 10: 63 students (28 boys, 35 girls); Grade 11: 74 students (39 boys, 35 girls); Grade 12: 70 students (32 boys, 38 girls). 27% of students are boarding students. 83% are state residents. 9 states are represented in upper school student body. 10% are international students. International students from Australia, Canada, China, Germany, Republic of Korea, and Saudi Arabia.

Faculty School total: 43. In upper school: 20 men, 21 women; 34 have advanced degrees; 23 reside on campus.

Subjects Offered Advanced Placement courses, algebra, American history, American literature, art, art history, astronomy, athletics, biology, biology-AP, calculus, calculus-AP, ceramics, chemistry, chemistry-AP, Chinese, computer applications, computer multimedia, concert choir, constitutional law, contemporary issues, creative writing, drama, economics, economics-AP, English, English literature, English-AP, environmental science-AP, European history, expository writing, film studies, fine arts, French, French-AP, geology, geometry, government-AP, government/civics, history, jazz, jazz ensemble, keyboarding, Latin, Latin-AP, mathematics, music, painting, philosophy, photo shop, physical education, physical fitness, physics, play production, pre-calculus, science, Shakespeare, social studies, Spanish, Spanish-AP, statistics-AP, theater, trigonometry, U.S. government and politics-AP, world history, world literature, world religions, writing, yearbook.

Graduation Requirements Arts and fine arts (art, music, dance, drama), English, foreign language, mathematics, physical education (includes health), science, social studies (includes history), art or music history.

Special Academic Programs Advanced Placement exam preparation; independent study; academic accommodation for the gifted and the musically talented.

College Admission Counseling 65 students graduated in 2009; all went to college, including Georgetown University; Princeton University; Sewanee: The University of the South; The Johns Hopkins University; The University of Alabama; University of Illinois at Urbana–Champaign. Median SAT critical reading: 660, median SAT math: 655. Mean SAT writing: 671, mean composite ACT: 27. 77% scored over 600 on SAT critical reading, 72% scored over 600 on SAT math, 65% scored over 26 on composite ACT.

Student Life Upper grades have student council, honor system. Discipline rests equally with students and faculty.

Tuition and Aid Day student tuition: $16,960; 5-day tuition and room/board: $29,260; 7-day tuition and room/board: $31,560. Tuition installment plan (FACTS Tuition Payment Plan, monthly payment plans). Need-based scholarship grants, paying campus jobs available. In 2009–10, 27% of upper-school students received aid. Total amount of financial aid awarded in 2009–10: $1,008,973.

Indian Springs School

Admissions Traditional secondary-level entrance grade is 9. For fall 2009, 163 students applied for upper-level admission, 99 were accepted, 71 enrolled. SSAT or TOEFL required. Deadline for receipt of application materials: none. Application fee required: $65. Interview required.

Athletics Interscholastic: baseball (boys), basketball (b,g), soccer (b,g), softball (g), tennis (b,g), volleyball (g); intramural: basketball (b,g), flag football (b), soccer (b,g); coed interscholastic: cross-country running, golf, ultimate Frisbee; coed intramural: aerobics, aerobics/Nautilus, outdoor activities, paint ball, physical fitness, strength & conditioning, table tennis, ultimate Frisbee, yoga. 2 PE instructors, 5 coaches, 1 athletic trainer.

Computers Computers are regularly used in English, keyboarding, photography, technology classes. Computer network features include on-campus library services, online commercial services, Internet access, wireless campus network, Internet filtering or blocking technology. Campus intranet, student e-mail accounts, and computer access in designated common areas are available to students. Students grades are available online.

Contact Mrs. Christine Copeland, Assistant Director of Admission and Financial Aid. 205-332-0582. Fax: 205-988-3797. E-mail: ccopeland@indiansprings.org. Web site: www.indiansprings.org.

INSTITUTE OF NOTRE DAME
901 Aisquith Street
Baltimore, Maryland 21202-5499
Head of School: Sr. Kathleen Feeley

General Information Girls' day college-preparatory, arts, business, religious studies, bilingual studies, and technology school, affiliated with Roman Catholic Church. Grades 9–12. Founded: 1847. Setting: urban. 2-acre campus. 1 building on campus. Approved or accredited by Association of Independent Maryland Schools, Middle States Association of Colleges and Schools, and Maryland Department of Education. Endowment: $5 million. Total enrollment: 318. Upper school average class size: 17. Upper school faculty-student ratio: 1:12. There are 180 required school days per year for Upper School students. Upper School students typically attend 5 days per week. The average school day consists of 6 hours and 20 minutes.

Upper School Student Profile Grade 9: 95 students (95 girls); Grade 10: 90 students (90 girls); Grade 11: 68 students (68 girls); Grade 12: 65 students (65 girls). 70% of students are Roman Catholic.

Faculty School total: 27. In upper school: 5 men, 22 women; 20 have advanced degrees.

Subjects Offered Accounting, algebra, American history, American literature, anatomy, art, Bible studies, biology, business, calculus, chemistry, Christianity, computer applications, computer math, computer programming, computer science, creative writing, criminal justice, dance, design, drama, drawing, driver education, earth science, English, English literature, environmental science, finance, fine arts, French, freshman seminar, geography, geology, geometry, government/civics, health, history, journalism, Latin, marine biology, mathematics, music, music history, physical education, physics, physiology, psychology, religion, science, social studies, sociology, Spanish, speech, theater, theology, trigonometry, women's studies, world history, world literature.

Graduation Requirements Arts and fine arts (art, music, dance, drama), business skills (includes word processing), computer science, English, foreign language, mathematics, physical education (includes health), religion (includes Bible studies and theology), science, social studies (includes history), 80 hours of community service.

Special Academic Programs 10 Advanced Placement exams for which test preparation is offered; honors section; accelerated programs; independent study; study at local college for college credit; academic accommodation for the gifted; remedial reading and/or remedial writing; remedial math.

College Admission Counseling 88 students graduated in 2010; all went to college, including College of Notre Dame of Maryland; Loyola University Maryland; Stevenson University; Towson University; University of Maryland, Baltimore; University of Maryland, Baltimore County.

Student Life Upper grades have uniform requirement, student council, honor system. Discipline rests primarily with faculty. Attendance at religious services is required.

Summer Programs Enrichment, sports, art/fine arts, rigorous outdoor training, computer instruction programs offered; session focuses on community; held both on and off campus; held at Patterson Park, Herring Run Park, and Meadowood Regional Park; accepts girls; open to students from other schools. 150 students usually enrolled. 2011 schedule: June to July. Application deadline: none.

Tuition and Aid Day student tuition: $12,225. Tuition installment plan (monthly payment plans). Tuition reduction for siblings, merit scholarship grants, need-based scholarship grants, paying campus jobs, bank loans available. In 2010–11, 47% of upper-school students received aid; total upper-school merit-scholarship money awarded: $180,000. Total amount of financial aid awarded in 2010–11: $300,000.

Admissions Traditional secondary-level entrance grade is 9. For fall 2010, 227 students applied for upper-level admission, 90 enrolled. High School Placement Test required. Deadline for receipt of application materials: December 17. Application fee required: $30. On-campus interview required.

Athletics Interscholastic: aerobics/dance, badminton, basketball, cheering, crew, cross-country running, field hockey, golf, independent competitive sports, lacrosse, outdoor adventure, outdoors, physical training, pom squad, rowing, running, soccer, softball, strength & conditioning, swimming and diving, track and field, volleyball,

winter (indoor) track, winter soccer; intramural: aerobics/dance, ballet, dance, dance squad, dance team, horseback riding, modern dance, outdoor adventure, self defense, weight training. 1 PE instructor, 16 coaches, 1 athletic trainer.

Computers Computers are regularly used in all academic classes. Computer network features include on-campus library services, online commercial services, Internet access, wireless campus network, Internet filtering or blocking technology. Campus intranet, student e-mail accounts, and computer access in designated common areas are available to students. Students grades are available online. The school has a published electronic and media policy.

Contact Mrs. Amy Conly '93, Director of Admissions. 410-522-7800 Ext. 220. Fax: 410-522-7810. E-mail: aconly@indofmd.org. Web site: www.indofmd.org.

INTERLOCHEN ARTS ACADEMY
PO Box 199
4000 Highway M-137
Interlochen, Michigan 49643-0199
Head of School: Mr. Jeffrey S. Kimpton

General Information Coeducational boarding and day college-preparatory and arts school. Grades 9–PG. Founded: 1962. Setting: rural. Nearest major city is Traverse City. Students are housed in single-sex dormitories. 1,200-acre campus. 225 buildings on campus. Approved or accredited by Independent Schools Association of the Central States, North Central Association of Colleges and Schools, The Association of Boarding Schools, and Michigan Department of Education. Member of National Association of Independent Schools and Secondary School Admission Test Board. Endowment: $32 million. Total enrollment: 455. Upper school average class size: 12. Upper school faculty-student ratio: 1:6. There are 151 required school days per year for Upper School students. Upper School students typically attend 5 days per week. The average school day consists of 9 hours.

Upper School Student Profile Grade 9: 27 students (14 boys, 13 girls); Grade 10: 62 students (18 boys, 44 girls); Grade 11: 160 students (71 boys, 89 girls); Grade 12: 188 students (95 boys, 93 girls); Postgraduate: 18 students (10 boys, 8 girls). 92% of students are boarding students. 20% are state residents. 48 states are represented in upper school student body. 23% are international students. International students from Canada, China, Germany, Japan, Republic of Korea, and Taiwan; 19 other countries represented in student body.

Faculty School total: 77. In upper school: 49 men, 28 women; 60 have advanced degrees; 36 reside on campus.

Subjects Offered Algebra, American history, American literature, art, ballet, ballet technique, biology, British literature, British literature (honors), calculus, ceramics, chamber groups, chemistry, chemistry-AP, choir, choral music, choreography, civil war history, computer math, computer science, contemporary art, creative writing, current events, dance, dance performance, drafting, drama, dramatic arts, earth science, ecology, English, English literature, environmental science, European history, expository writing, fine arts, French, geometry, German, government/civics, health, history, mathematics, music, philosophy, photography, physical education, physics, science, social studies, Spanish, speech, statistics, theater, trigonometry, world history, world literature, writing.

Graduation Requirements Arts and fine arts (art, music, dance, drama), English, mathematics, physical education (includes health), science, social studies (includes history).

Special Academic Programs Advanced Placement exam preparation; accelerated programs; independent study; term-away projects; academic accommodation for the gifted, the musically talented, and the artistically talented; ESL (54 students enrolled).

College Admission Counseling Colleges students went to include Cleveland Institute of Music; Eastman School of Music; Oberlin College; Peabody Conservatory of The Johns Hopkins University; The Juilliard School; University of Michigan. Mean SAT critical reading: 627, mean SAT math: 555, mean SAT writing: 612, mean composite ACT: 25.

Student Life Upper grades have uniform requirement, student council, honor system. Discipline rests primarily with faculty.

Summer Programs Art/fine arts programs offered; session focuses on fine and performing arts; held on campus; accepts boys and girls; open to students from other schools. 2,500 students usually enrolled. 2011 schedule: June 25 to August 8. Application deadline: February 1.

Tuition and Aid Day student tuition: $28,200; 7-day tuition and room/board: $44,750. Tuition installment plan (Key Tuition Payment Plan, payment plan). Merit scholarship grants, need-based scholarship grants available. In 2010–11, 70% of upper-school students received aid. Total amount of financial aid awarded in 2010–11: $7,000,000.

Admissions Traditional secondary-level entrance grade is 11. Achievement tests, any standardized test, audition, essay, placement test or SSAT required. Deadline for receipt of application materials: none. Application fee required: $50. Interview recommended.

Athletics Intramural: baseball (boys); coed intramural: aerobics, aerobics/dance, archery, badminton, ballet, basketball, canoeing/kayaking, climbing, cooperative games, cross-country running, fishing, fitness, fitness walking, flag football, floor hockey, fly fishing, Frisbee, hiking/backpacking, indoor soccer, jogging, modern dance, Newcombe ball, outdoor activities, physical fitness, pillo polo, project adventure, rappelling, ropes courses, running, skiing (cross-country), skiing (downhill), snowshoeing, soccer, softball, table tennis, touch football, ultimate Frisbee, volleyball, wall climbing, whiffle ball, yoga. 1 PE instructor.

Computers Computers are regularly used in graphic arts, mathematics, music, science, video film production classes. Computer network features include on-campus library services, online commercial services, Internet access, wireless campus network. Campus intranet and student e-mail accounts are available to students. The school has a published electronic and media policy.

Contact Jim Bekkering, Director of Admission. 231-276-7472. Fax: 231-276-7464. E-mail: admission@interlochen.org. Web site: www.interlochen.org.

INTERMOUNTAIN CHRISTIAN SCHOOL

6515 South Lion Lane
Salt Lake City, Utah 84121
Head of School: Adm. Layne Billings

General Information Coeducational day college-preparatory, general academic, arts, business, and religious studies school, affiliated with Evangelical Free Church of America, Christian faith. Grades PK–12. Founded: 1982. Setting: suburban. 6-acre campus. 1 building on campus. Approved or accredited by Association of Christian Schools International, Northwest Association of Schools and Colleges, and Utah Department of Education. Endowment: $25,000. Total enrollment: 300. Upper school average class size: 26. Upper school faculty-student ratio: 1:15. There are 180 required school days per year for Upper School students. Upper School students typically attend 5 days per week. The average school day consists of 6 hours.

Upper School Student Profile Grade 9: 25 students (14 boys, 11 girls); Grade 10: 12 students (2 boys, 10 girls); Grade 11: 22 students (14 boys, 8 girls); Grade 12: 22 students (11 boys, 11 girls). 90% of students are members of Evangelical Free Church of America, Christian.

Faculty School total: 28. In upper school: 8 men, 9 women; 4 have advanced degrees.

Subjects Offered Advanced Placement courses, algebra, American government, American history, American literature, art, ASB Leadership, athletics, baseball, basketball, bell choir, Bible, biology, calculus, career education, ceramics, chemistry, choir, chorus, Christian doctrine, church history, civics, community service, composition, computer programming, computer science, computer skills, concert band, concert bell choir, concert choir, current events, debate, drama, drama performance, economics and history, electives, English, English literature-AP, European history, European literature, fine arts, food science, geometry, government, health, history, instrumental music, keyboarding, mathematics, peer ministry, photo shop, photography, physical education, physics, pre-calculus, reading/study skills, science, sex education, social studies, Spanish, trigonometry, U.S. government, U.S. history, vocal ensemble, volleyball, world geography, world history.

Graduation Requirements Arts and fine arts (art, music, dance, drama), Bible, computer science, English, foreign language, mathematics, physical education (includes health), science, social sciences, social studies (includes history). Community service is required.

Special Academic Programs 3 Advanced Placement exams for which test preparation is offered; honors section; study at local college for college credit.

College Admission Counseling 22 students graduated in 2009; all went to college, including Salt Lake Community College; University of Utah; Whitworth University. Mean SAT critical reading: 563, mean SAT math: 569, mean SAT writing: 572, mean combined SAT: 1719, mean composite ACT: 26. 26% scored over 600 on SAT critical reading, 37% scored over 600 on SAT math, 26% scored over 600 on SAT writing, 26% scored over 1800 on combined SAT, 63% scored over 26 on composite ACT.

Student Life Upper grades have specified standards of dress, student council, honor system. Discipline rests primarily with faculty. Attendance at religious services is required.

Tuition and Aid Day student tuition: $5655. Tuition installment plan (Insured Tuition Payment Plan, monthly payment plans, discounted up-front tuition payment). Tuition reduction for siblings, need-based scholarship grants available. In 2009–10, 11% of upper-school students received aid. Total amount of financial aid awarded in 2009–10: $15,140.

Admissions Traditional secondary-level entrance grade is 9. For fall 2009, 20 students applied for upper-level admission, 14 were accepted, 14 enrolled. WISC/Woodcock-Johnson and Woodcock Language Proficiency Test required. Deadline for receipt of application materials: none. Application fee required: $90. On-campus interview required.

Athletics Interscholastic: baseball (boys), basketball (b,g), golf (b,g), soccer (b,g), volleyball (g), wrestling (b); coed intramural: skiing (downhill), snowboarding. 2 PE instructors, 4 coaches.

Computers Computers are regularly used in art, English, history, mathematics, science, Spanish classes. Computer network features include Internet access, wireless campus network, Internet filtering or blocking technology. Computer access in designated common areas is available to students. Students grades are available online. The school has a published electronic and media policy.

Contact Eileen Rocco, Registrar. 801-942-8811. Fax: 801-942-8813. E-mail: rocco_e@slcics.org. Web site: www.slcics.org.

INTERNATIONAL COLLEGE SPAIN

Calle Vereda Norte, #3
La Moraleja
Madrid 28109, Spain
Head of School: Dr. Peter Southern

General Information Coeducational day college-preparatory and bilingual studies school. Grades PK–12. Founded: 1980. Setting: suburban. 3-hectare campus. 2 buildings on campus. Approved or accredited by European Council of International Schools, International Baccalaureate Organization, Mennonite Schools Council, and New England Association of Schools and Colleges. Language of instruction: English. Total enrollment: 709. Upper school average class size: 18. Upper school faculty-student ratio: 1:9. There are 176 required school days per year for Upper School students. Upper School students typically attend 5 days per week. The average school day consists of 6 hours.

Upper School Student Profile Grade 6: 47 students (22 boys, 25 girls); Grade 7: 52 students (19 boys, 33 girls); Grade 8: 55 students (26 boys, 29 girls); Grade 9: 55 students (26 boys, 29 girls); Grade 10: 57 students (34 boys, 23 girls); Grade 11: 53 students (22 boys, 31 girls); Grade 12: 57 students (28 boys, 29 girls).

Faculty School total: 48. In upper school: 12 men, 27 women; 22 have advanced degrees.

Subjects Offered 20th century world history, advanced math, art, biology, chemistry, Danish, design, drama, Dutch, economics, English, English literature, European history, expressive arts, French, geography, global studies, history, humanities, information technology, interdisciplinary studies, International Baccalaureate courses, Italian, Japanese, mathematics, model United Nations, music, personal and social education, physical education, physics, science, social education, social studies, Spanish, Spanish literature, Swedish, technology, theory of knowledge, world literature.

Graduation Requirements English, foreign language, mathematics, science, social sciences, social studies (includes history), 90% minimum attendance, minimum average effort grade of satisfactory. Community service is required.

Special Academic Programs International Baccalaureate program; ESL (45 students enrolled).

College Admission Counseling 53 students graduated in 2010; 50 went to college, including Duke University; Northeastern University; The Johns Hopkins University. Other: 1 entered military service. 75% scored over 600 on SAT critical reading, 100% scored over 600 on SAT math.

Student Life Upper grades have specified standards of dress, student council. Discipline rests equally with students and faculty.

Tuition and Aid Day student tuition: €14,280–€14,970. Tuition installment plan (Insured Tuition Payment Plan). Tuition reduction for siblings, bursaries, merit scholarship grants, need-based scholarship grants available. In 2010–11, 4% of upper-school students received aid; total upper-school merit-scholarship money awarded: €20,613. Total amount of financial aid awarded in 2010–11: €39,000.

Admissions Traditional secondary-level entrance grade is 11. For fall 2010, 87 students applied for upper-level admission, 43 were accepted, 35 enrolled. Admissions testing and math and English placement tests required. Deadline for receipt of application materials: none. Application fee required: €550. On-campus interview recommended.

Athletics Interscholastic: basketball (boys, girls), cross-country running (b,g), soccer (b,g), volleyball (b,g); intramural: aerobics/dance (b,g), badminton (b,g), ballet (b,g), field hockey (b,g), gymnastics (b,g), physical fitness (b,g), soccer (b,g), softball (b,g), swimming and diving (b,g), table tennis (b,g), tennis (b,g), volleyball (b,g); coed interscholastic: track and field; coed intramural: alpine skiing, dance, fencing, golf, horseback riding, judo, martial arts, modern dance, skiing (downhill), snowboarding. 2 PE instructors, 2 coaches.

Computers Computers are regularly used in art, career education, career exploration, college planning, economics, English, ESL, information technology, mathematics, science classes. Computer network features include on-campus library services, online commercial services, Internet access, wireless campus network, Internet filtering or blocking technology. Campus intranet, student e-mail accounts, and computer access in designated common areas are available to students. Students grades are available online. The school has a published electronic and media policy.

Contact Mrs. Eunice Amondaray, Admissions Officer. 34-9-1-650-2398. Fax: 34-9-1-650-1035. E-mail: admissions@icsmadrid.org. Web site: www.icsmadrid.org.

INTERNATIONAL HIGH SCHOOL

150 Oak Street
San Francisco, California 94102
Head of School: Ms. Jane Camblin

General Information Coeducational day college-preparatory, arts, bilingual studies, and technology school. Grades PK–12. Founded: 1962. Setting: urban. 3-acre campus. 2 buildings on campus. Approved or accredited by California Association of Independent Schools, European Council of International Schools, French Ministry of Education, International Baccalaureate Organization, Western Association of Schools and Colleges, and California Department of Education. Member of National Association of Independent Schools and Secondary School Admission Test Board. Languages of instruction: English and French. Endowment: $4.9 million. Total enrollment: 1,003. Upper school average class size: 17. Upper school faculty-student

International High School

ratio: 1:10. There are 165 required school days per year for Upper School students. The average school day consists of 7 hours.

Upper School Student Profile Grade 9: 77 students (35 boys, 42 girls); Grade 10: 83 students (36 boys, 47 girls); Grade 11: 87 students (37 boys, 50 girls); Grade 12: 94 students (40 boys, 54 girls).

Faculty School total: 139. In upper school: 33 men, 30 women; 35 have advanced degrees.

Subjects Offered Advanced chemistry, advanced math, algebra, American history, American literature, art, biology, calculus, chemistry, community service, computer science, creative writing, current events, drama, earth science, economics, English, English literature, environmental science, ESL, European history, expository writing, fine arts, French, geography, geometry, German, government/civics, history, International Baccalaureate courses, Mandarin, mathematics, music, philosophy, physical education, physics, science, social studies, Spanish, theater, theory of knowledge, trigonometry, world history, world literature, writing.

Graduation Requirements Arts and fine arts (art, music, dance, drama), English, foreign language, International Baccalaureate courses, mathematics, physical education (includes health), science, social studies (includes history), theory of knowledge, extended essay, 150 hours of CAS.

Special Academic Programs International Baccalaureate program; honors section; independent study; term-away projects; study abroad; academic accommodation for the gifted, the musically talented, and the artistically talented; ESL (18 students enrolled).

College Admission Counseling 68 students graduated in 2010; 64 went to college, including Boston University; McGill University; New York University; Skidmore College; University of California, Berkeley; University of California, Davis. Other: 4 had other specific plans. Mean SAT critical reading: 631, mean SAT math: 610, mean SAT writing: 616.

Student Life Upper grades have student council. Discipline rests equally with students and faculty.

Summer Programs Remediation, enrichment, advancement, art/fine arts programs offered; session focuses on enrichment; held both on and off campus; held at France; accepts boys and girls; open to students from other schools.

Tuition and Aid Day student tuition: $30,360. Tuition installment plan (FACTS Tuition Payment Plan). Need-based scholarship grants, French bourse available. In 2010–11, 25% of upper-school students received aid. Total amount of financial aid awarded in 2010–11: $748,000.

Admissions Traditional secondary-level entrance grade is 9. For fall 2010, 350 students applied for upper-level admission, 234 were accepted, 65 enrolled. Any standardized test, SSAT or writing sample required. Deadline for receipt of application materials: January 13. Application fee required: $75. Interview required.

Athletics Interscholastic: baseball (boys, girls), basketball (b,g), football (b), soccer (b,g), volleyball (b,g); intramural: ballet (b,g), baseball (b), basketball (b,g), floor hockey (b,g), soccer (b,g), softball (g), tennis (b,g), volleyball (b,g); coed interscholastic: badminton, cross-country running, golf, swimming and diving, tennis, track and field; coed intramural: badminton, ballet, cross-country running, fencing, flagball, golf, handball, indoor hockey, outdoor activities, outdoor adventure, physical fitness, physical training, swimming and diving, water polo, weight training. 4 PE instructors, 8 coaches, 3 athletic trainers.

Computers Computers are regularly used in all academic classes. Computer network features include on-campus library services, online commercial services, Internet access, wireless campus network, video editing, Web page creation. Computer access in designated common areas is available to students. The school has a published electronic and media policy.

Contact Ms. Erin Cronin, Associate Director of Admission. 415-558-2093. Fax: 415-558-2085. E-mail: erinc@internationalsf.org. Web site: www.internationalsf.org.

INTERNATIONAL SCHOOL BANGKOK
39/7 Soi Nichada Thani, Samakee Road
Pakkret 11120, Thailand
Head of School: Dr. William Gerritz

General Information Coeducational day college-preparatory, arts, and technology school. Grades PK–12. Founded: 1951. Setting: suburban. Nearest major city is Bangkok, Thailand. 37-acre campus. 2 buildings on campus. Approved or accredited by Western Association of Schools and Colleges and state department of education. Affiliate member of National Association of Independent Schools; member of European Council of International Schools. Language of instruction: English. Total enrollment: 1,818. Upper school average class size: 18. Upper school faculty-student ratio: 1:10. There are 183 required school days per year for Upper School students. Upper School students typically attend 5 days per week. The average school day consists of 6 hours.

Upper School Student Profile Grade 9: 185 students (93 boys, 92 girls); Grade 10: 162 students (83 boys, 79 girls); Grade 11: 178 students (100 boys, 78 girls); Grade 12: 180 students (77 boys, 103 girls).

Faculty School total: 229. In upper school: 50 men, 42 women; 70 have advanced degrees.

Subjects Offered Algebra, American history, American literature, art, art history, biology, business, calculus, calculus-AP, ceramics, chemistry, computer math, computer programming, computer science, creative writing, dance, drafting, drama, earth science, ecology, economics, electives, English, English literature, environ-

mental science, ESL, European history, expository writing, fine arts, French, geography, geology, geometry, German, government/civics, health, history, home economics, humanities, industrial arts, Japanese, journalism, language arts, languages, mathematics, mechanical drawing, music, performing arts, philosophy, photography, physical education, physics, psychology, reading, science, social studies, sociology, Spanish, speech, statistics, Thai, theater, theory of knowledge, trigonometry, typing, world history, world literature, writing.

Graduation Requirements Arts and fine arts (art, music, dance, drama), computers, English, mathematics, physical education (includes health), science, social studies (includes history), Community Service hours. Community service is required.

Special Academic Programs International Baccalaureate program; Advanced Placement exam preparation; ESL.

College Admission Counseling 179 students graduated in 2010; 177 went to college, including Boston University; Brigham Young University; Stanford University; Syracuse University; University of Illinois at Urbana–Champaign; University of Southern California. Other: 1 entered military service, 1 had other specific plans.

Student Life Upper grades have uniform requirement, student council, honor system. Discipline rests primarily with faculty.

Summer Programs Remediation, enrichment, ESL, art/fine arts programs offered; held on campus; accepts boys and girls; open to students from other schools. 400 students usually enrolled. 2011 schedule: June 6 to July 29. Application deadline: June 3.

Tuition and Aid Day student tuition: 721,000 Thai bahts. Tuition installment plan (individually arranged payment plans).

Admissions Math and English placement tests and school's own exam required. Deadline for receipt of application materials: none. Application fee required: 4500 Thai bahts. On-campus interview required.

Athletics Interscholastic: aquatics (boys, girls), badminton (b,g), basketball (b,g), cross-country running (b,g), dance (b,g), football (b,g), rugby (b,g), running (b,g), soccer (b,g), softball (b,g), swimming and diving (b,g), tennis (b,g), track and field (b,g), volleyball (b,g); intramural: aquatics (b,g), badminton (b,g), basketball (b,g), cross-country running (b,g), dance (b,g), fencing (b), rugby (b,g), running (b,g), swimming and diving (b,g), track and field (b,g), volleyball (b,g). 5 PE instructors.

Computers Computers are regularly used in all academic, business, computer applications, creative writing, current events, design, desktop publishing, economics, English, ESL, foreign language, French, geography, graphic arts, graphic design, health, history, humanities, information technology, journalism, library, literary magazine, mathematics, photography, psychology, publications, research skills, science, social studies, Spanish, technology, yearbook classes. Computer network features include on-campus library services, Internet access, wireless campus network, Internet filtering or blocking technology. Campus intranet, student e-mail accounts, and computer access in designated common areas are available to students. Students grades are available online. The school has a published electronic and media policy.

Contact Ms. Wendy Van Bramer, Admissions Director. 662-963-5800. Fax: 662-960-4103. E-mail: register@isb.ac.th. Web site: www.isb.ac.th.

INTERNATIONAL SCHOOL HAMBURG
Hemmingstedter Weg 130
Hamburg 22609, Germany
Head of School: Dr. Vladimir Kuskovski

General Information Coeducational day college-preparatory, arts, and technology school. Grades PK–12. Founded: 1957. Setting: suburban. 3-acre campus. 1 building on campus. Approved or accredited by European Council of International Schools and New England Association of Schools and Colleges. Language of instruction: English. Total enrollment: 669. Upper school average class size: 20. Upper school faculty-student ratio: 1:8. Upper School students typically attend 5 days per week.

Upper School Student Profile Grade 9: 69 students (43 boys, 26 girls); Grade 10: 51 students (29 boys, 22 girls); Grade 11: 46 students (25 boys, 21 girls); Grade 12: 47 students (22 boys, 25 girls).

Faculty School total: 85. In upper school: 47 men, 25 women; 25 have advanced degrees.

Subjects Offered Art, biology, chemistry, computer math, drama, English, ESL, European history, fine arts, French, geography, German, history, mathematics, model United Nations, music, photography, physical education, physics, science, social studies, Spanish, theater, theory of knowledge, world history.

Graduation Requirements Arts and fine arts (art, music, dance, drama), English, foreign language, mathematics, physical education (includes health), science, social studies (includes history).

Special Academic Programs International Baccalaureate program; ESL (80 students enrolled).

College Admission Counseling 47 students graduated in 2010; 43 went to college, including Columbia University; McGill University; University of Edinburgh; Yale University. Other: 1 entered military service, 3 had other specific plans.

Student Life Upper grades have student council. Discipline rests primarily with faculty.

Tuition and Aid Day student tuition: €13,950–€17,450. Tuition installment plan (2-payment plan).

Admissions Traditional secondary-level entrance grade is 9. For fall 2010, 50 students applied for upper-level admission, 45 were accepted, 44 enrolled. ACT, CTBS, Stanford Achievement Test, any other standardized test or PSAT and SAT for applicants to grade 11 and 12 required. Deadline for receipt of application materials: none. Application fee required: €100. On-campus interview required.

Athletics Interscholastic: badminton (boys, girls), basketball (b,g), canoeing/kayaking (b,g), climbing (b,g), cross-country running (b,g), floor hockey (b,g), football (b,g), indoor hockey (b,g), indoor soccer (b,g), netball (b,g), physical training (b,g), rowing (b,g), running (b,g), sailing (b,g), soccer (b,g), tennis (b,g), track and field (b,g), volleyball (b,g); intramural: basketball (b,g), cross-country running (b,g), field hockey (b,g), football (b,g), soccer (b,g), tennis (b,g), track and field (b,g), volleyball (b,g); coed interscholastic: badminton, canoeing/kayaking, climbing, cross-country running, floor hockey, football, indoor hockey, indoor soccer, netball, running, sailing, soccer, tennis, track and field, volleyball; coed intramural: cross-country running, football, soccer, tennis, track and field, volleyball. 5 PE instructors, 4 coaches.

Computers Computers are regularly used in business studies, English, ESL, foreign language, French, geography, history, humanities, library, mathematics, music, science, Spanish, yearbook classes. Computer network features include on-campus library services, online commercial services, Internet access, Internet filtering or blocking technology. Campus intranet and student e-mail accounts are available to students. The school has a published electronic and media policy.

Contact Catherine Bissonnet, Director of Admissions. 49-40-883-00-133. Fax: 49-40-881-1405. E-mail: cbissonnet@ishamburg.org. Web site: www.ishamburg.org.

INTERNATIONAL SCHOOL MANILA

University Parkway
Fort Bonifacio
1634 Taguig City, Philippines
Head of School: Mr. David Toze

General Information Coeducational day college-preparatory, arts, business, bilingual studies, and technology school. Grades PS–12. Founded: 1920. Setting: urban. Nearest major city is Manila, Philippines. 7-hectare campus. 1 building on campus. Approved or accredited by European Council of International Schools and Western Association of Schools and Colleges. Affiliate member of National Association of Independent Schools; member of Secondary School Admission Test Board. Language of instruction: English. Total enrollment: 1,966. Upper school average class size: 16. Upper school faculty-student ratio: 1:9. There are 181 required school days per year for Upper School students.

Upper School Student Profile Grade 6: 142 students (68 boys, 74 girls); Grade 7: 156 students (80 boys, 76 girls); Grade 8: 168 students (89 boys, 79 girls); Grade 9: 188 students (98 boys, 90 girls); Grade 10: 172 students (82 boys, 90 girls); Grade 11: 188 students (86 boys, 102 girls); Grade 12: 174 students (86 boys, 88 girls).

Faculty School total: 200. In upper school: 42 men, 38 women; 35 have advanced degrees.

Subjects Offered Acting, anthropology, art, athletic training, band, Basic programming, biology, business, calculus-AP, chemistry, Chinese, choir, college admission preparation, college awareness, college counseling, college placement, college planning, computer applications, computer graphics, computer literacy, computer multimedia, computer programming, computer science, creative writing, critical writing, dance, desktop publishing, digital photography, economics, economics and history, English, environmental science, ESL, film, filmmaking, foreign language, French, French as a second language, general science, geography, graphic design, health, health and wellness, health education, information technology, integrated mathematics, International Baccalaureate courses, international relations, Japanese, Japanese as Second Language, jazz band, leadership, math applications, math methods, mathematics, media studies, music, orchestra, parenting, peer counseling, personal fitness, Philippine culture, physical science, physics, political science, pre-calculus, programming, psychology, reading/study skills, remedial study skills, research, service learning/internship, sex education, Spanish, theater, theater arts, theory of knowledge, track and field, U.S. history, U.S. history-AP, video film production, visual and performing arts, visual arts, weight fitness, weight training, world history, world religions, writing.

Special Academic Programs International Baccalaureate program; Advanced Placement exam preparation; honors section; accelerated programs; independent study; ESL (166 students enrolled).

College Admission Counseling 166 students graduated in 2010; 161 went to college, including New York University; Penn State University Park; Purdue University; The University of British Columbia; University of California, Berkeley; University of Southern California. Other: 2 went to work, 3 had other specific plans. Mean SAT critical reading: 581, mean SAT math: 649, mean SAT writing: 603, mean combined SAT: 1832, mean composite ACT: 26.

Student Life Upper grades have uniform requirement, student council, honor system. Discipline rests equally with students and faculty.

Summer Programs ESL programs offered; session focuses on academics for ESL; held on campus; accepts boys and girls; open to students from other schools. 2011 schedule: June to July. Application deadline: none.

Tuition and Aid Day student tuition: $1997–$7280. Tuition installment plan (monthly payment plans, individually arranged payment plans, quarterly payment plan). Scholarships for low-income local students available.

Admissions Traditional secondary-level entrance grade is 9. For fall 2010, 273 students applied for upper-level admission, 170 were accepted, 148 enrolled. Deadline for receipt of application materials: none. Application fee required: $200. On-campus interview recommended.

Athletics Interscholastic: badminton (boys, girls), basketball (b,g), bowling (b,g), cheering (g), cross-country running (b,g), dance (b,g), golf (b,g), gymnastics (b,g), martial arts (b,g), rugby (b,g), soccer (b,g), softball (b,g), swimming and diving (b,g), table tennis (b,g), tennis (b,g), track and field (b,g), volleyball (b,g), wall climbing (b,g); intramural: rugby (b,g), wall climbing (b,g), water polo (b,g); coed interscholastic: wall climbing; coed intramural: volleyball, wall climbing. 4 PE instructors, 10 coaches.

Computers Computers are regularly used in art, English, foreign language, history, mathematics, music, science classes. Computer network features include on-campus library services, online commercial services, Internet access, wireless campus network, Internet filtering or blocking technology. Campus intranet and student e-mail accounts are available to students. Students grades are available online. The school has a published electronic and media policy.

Contact Gary Jerome, Director of Admission. 63-2-840-8488. Fax: 63-2-840-8489. E-mail: admission@ismanila.org. Web site: www.ismanila.org.

THE INTERNATIONAL SCHOOL OF ABERDEEN

296 North Deeside Road
Milltimber
Aberdeen AB13 OAB, United Kingdom
Head of School: Dr. Daniel A. Hovde

General Information Coeducational day college-preparatory and general academic school. Grades PK–12. Founded: 1972. Setting: suburban. 10-acre campus. 2 buildings on campus. Approved or accredited by European Council of International Schools, Independent Schools Council (UK), International Baccalaureate Organization, and Middle States Association of Colleges and Schools. Language of instruction: English. Total enrollment: 417. Upper school average class size: 15. Upper school faculty-student ratio: 1:3. There are 170 required school days per year for Upper School students. Upper School students typically attend 5 days per week. The average school day consists of 5 hours and 40 minutes.

Upper School Student Profile Grade 9: 31 students (12 boys, 19 girls); Grade 10: 22 students (13 boys, 9 girls); Grade 11: 25 students (12 boys, 13 girls); Grade 12: 33 students (19 boys, 14 girls).

Faculty School total: 73. In upper school: 13 men, 25 women; 22 have advanced degrees.

Subjects Offered Art, biology, chemistry, computer science, drama, economics, English, French, geography, government/civics, history, international relations, mathematics, music, physical education, physics, science, social studies, Spanish.

Graduation Requirements Arts and fine arts (art, music, dance, drama), computer science, economics, English, foreign language, mathematics, physical education (includes health), science, social studies (includes history).

Special Academic Programs International Baccalaureate program; independent study; ESL (45 students enrolled).

College Admission Counseling 33 students graduated in 2009. Mean SAT critical reading: 554, mean SAT math: 591, mean SAT writing: 545, mean combined SAT: 1690, mean composite ACT: 25.

Student Life Upper grades have student council, honor system. Discipline rests equally with students and faculty.

Tuition and Aid Day student tuition: £17,445. Tuition installment plan (individually arranged payment plans). Bursaries, merit scholarship grants, need-based scholarship grants available.

Admissions For fall 2009, 34 students applied for upper-level admission, 27 were accepted, 23 enrolled. Deadline for receipt of application materials: none. Application fee required: £500. On-campus interview required.

Athletics Interscholastic: badminton (boys, girls), basketball (b,g), football (b,g), golf (b,g), soccer (b,g), volleyball (b,g); intramural: aerobics (g), aerobics/dance (g), badminton (b,g), ball hockey (b,g), ballet (g), baseball (b), basketball (b,g), Circus (b,g), climbing (b,g), football (b,g), handball (b,g), hockey (b,g), lacrosse (b,g), soccer (b,g), softball (b,g), table tennis (b,g), track and field (b,g), ultimate Frisbee (b,g), unicycling (b,g), volleyball (b,g); coed interscholastic: badminton, basketball, softball; coed intramural: archery, badminton, ball hockey, basketball, bocce, Circus, climbing, croquet, cross-country running, fitness, Frisbee, gymnastics, indoor hockey, juggling, jump rope, lacrosse, roller blading, roller hockey, roller skating, soccer, softball, table tennis, tennis, ultimate Frisbee, volleyball, wall climbing. 4 PE instructors, 10 coaches.

Computers Computers are regularly used in English, foreign language, mathematics, science classes. Computer network features include on-campus library services, Internet access, Internet filtering or blocking technology. Student e-mail accounts are available to students. The school has a published electronic and media policy.

Contact Mrs. Sheila Sibley, Admissions. 44-1224 732267. Fax: 44-1224 735648. E-mail: sheila.sibley@isa.aberdeen.sch.uk. Web site: www.isa.aberdeen.sch.uk.

INTERNATIONAL SCHOOL OF AMSTERDAM

Sportlaan 45
Amstelveen 1185 TB, Netherlands
Head of School: Dr. Ed Greene

General Information Coeducational day college-preparatory, arts, bilingual studies, and technology school. Grades PS–12. Founded: 1964. Setting: suburban. Nearest major city is Amsterdam, Netherlands. 1-acre campus. 2 buildings on campus. Approved or accredited by European Council of International Schools and New England Association of Schools and Colleges. Language of instruction: English. Total enrollment: 895. Upper school average class size: 18. Upper school faculty-student ratio: 1:6. There are 177 required school days per year for Upper School students. Upper School students typically attend 5 days per week. The average school day consists of 7 hours.

Upper School Student Profile Grade 9: 67 students (27 boys, 40 girls); Grade 10: 56 students (30 boys, 26 girls); Grade 11: 51 students (28 boys, 23 girls); Grade 12: 44 students (23 boys, 21 girls).

Faculty School total: 165. In upper school: 33 men, 43 women; 24 have advanced degrees.

Subjects Offered Addiction, advanced math, algebra, American literature, art, biology, calculus, chemistry, community service, computer programming, computer science, drama, Dutch, economics, English, English literature, ESL, European history, food science, French, geography, geometry, German, history, Japanese, mathematics, music, photography, physical education, physics, science, social sciences, social studies, Spanish, technology, theater, theory of knowledge, trigonometry, world history, world literature.

Graduation Requirements Arts, computer science, English, foreign language, mathematics, physical education (includes health), science, social sciences, social studies (includes history). Community service is required.

Special Academic Programs International Baccalaureate program; independent study; academic accommodation for the gifted, the musically talented, and the artistically talented; remedial reading and/or remedial writing; remedial math; programs in English, mathematics, general development for dyslexic students; ESL (56 students enrolled).

College Admission Counseling 45 students graduated in 2010; 37 went to college, including Boston University; Emory University; New York University; University of Colorado at Boulder. Other: 8 had other specific plans. Median SAT critical reading: 560, median SAT math: 570, median SAT writing: 600, median combined SAT: 1680. 44% scored over 600 on SAT critical reading, 54% scored over 600 on SAT math, 54% scored over 600 on SAT writing, 51% scored over 1800 on combined SAT.

Student Life Upper grades have student council, honor system. Discipline rests primarily with faculty.

Tuition and Aid Day student tuition: €20,430–€21,055. Tuition installment plan (monthly payment plans, individually arranged payment plans).

Admissions Traditional secondary-level entrance grade is 9. For fall 2010, 58 students applied for upper-level admission, 40 were accepted, 29 enrolled. Deadline for receipt of application materials: none. No application fee required. On-campus interview required.

Athletics Interscholastic: basketball (boys, girls); coed intramural: aerobics, aerobics/dance, badminton, ballet, basketball, cricket. 7 PE instructors, 14 coaches, 14 athletic trainers.

Computers Computers are regularly used in art, drawing and design, English, foreign language, information technology, keyboarding, library, mathematics, music, science, yearbook classes. Computer network features include on-campus library services, online commercial services, Internet access, Internet filtering or blocking technology. Campus intranet and student e-mail accounts are available to students.

Contact Julia True, Director of Admissions. 31-20-347-1111. Fax: 31-20-347-1105. E-mail: admissions@isa.nl. Web site: www.isa.nl.

INTERNATIONAL SCHOOL OF ARUBA

Wayaca 238A
Oranjestad, Aruba
Head of School: Paul D. Sibley

General Information Coeducational day college-preparatory, business, and bilingual studies school. Grades PK–12. Founded: 1985. Setting: suburban. Nearest major city is Oranjestad, Aruba. 5-acre campus. 2 buildings on campus. Approved or accredited by Association of American Schools in South America, Southern Association of Colleges and Schools, The College Board, and US Department of State. Language of instruction: English. Total enrollment: 150. Upper school average class size: 12. Upper school faculty-student ratio: 1:8. There are 181 required school days per year for Upper School students. Upper School students typically attend 5 days per week. The average school day consists of 5 hours and 40 minutes.

Upper School Student Profile Grade 6: 12 students (9 boys, 3 girls); Grade 7: 13 students (8 boys, 5 girls); Grade 8: 12 students (6 boys, 6 girls); Grade 9: 16 students (9 boys, 7 girls); Grade 10: 12 students (10 boys, 2 girls); Grade 11: 9 students (1 boy, 8 girls); Grade 12: 12 students (4 boys, 8 girls).

Faculty School total: 22. In upper school: 4 men, 10 women; 3 have advanced degrees.

Subjects Offered Advanced Placement courses, algebra, American history, art, biology, calculus, chemistry, computer science, Dutch, English, English literature,

environmental science, geometry, mathematics, oceanography, physical education, physics, science, social sciences, social studies, Spanish, world history.

Graduation Requirements Arts and fine arts (art, music, dance, drama), computer science, English, foreign language, mathematics, physical education (includes health), science, social sciences, social studies (includes history). Community service is required.

Special Academic Programs Advanced Placement exam preparation; independent study; remedial reading and/or remedial writing; ESL (18 students enrolled).

College Admission Counseling 10 students graduated in 2009; 9 went to college, including Florida International University; Lynn University; University of Florida; York University. Other: 1 went to work. Median SAT critical reading: 500, median SAT math: 625. 25% scored over 600 on SAT critical reading, 50% scored over 600 on SAT math.

Student Life Upper grades have uniform requirement, student council, honor system. Discipline rests primarily with faculty.

Tuition and Aid Day student tuition: $10,000–$17,000. Tuition installment plan (5-payment plan). Tuition reduction for siblings available.

Admissions Traditional secondary-level entrance grade is 10. For fall 2009, 10 students applied for upper-level admission, 7 were accepted, 6 enrolled. Any standardized test and SLEP required. Deadline for receipt of application materials: none. Application fee required: 100 Arubian guilders. On-campus interview required.

Athletics Interscholastic: basketball (boys, girls), scuba diving (b,g), soccer (b,g), softball (b,g), tennis (b,g), volleyball (b,g); intramural: aerobics/dance (b,g), basketball (b,g), soccer (b,g), track and field (b,g), volleyball (b,g); coed interscholastic: softball, tennis. 1 PE instructor.

Computers Computers are regularly used in college planning, computer applications, yearbook classes. Computer resources include Internet access, Internet filtering or blocking technology. Computer access in designated common areas is available to students. The school has a published electronic and media policy.

Contact Mary B. Sibley, Dean of Academics/Counselor. 297-583-5040. Fax: 297-583-6020. E-mail: info@isaruba.com.

INTERNATIONAL SCHOOL OF ATHENS

Xenias and Artemidos Streets
PO Box 51051
Kifissia—Athens GR-145 10, Greece
Head of School: Mr. C. N. Dardoufas

General Information Coeducational day and distance learning college-preparatory and arts school. Grades N–12. Distance learning grades 9–12. Founded: 1972. Setting: suburban. Nearest major city is Athens, Greece. 2-acre campus. 1 building on campus. Approved or accredited by CITA (Commission on International and Trans-Regional Accreditation), Department of Defense Dependents Schools, International Baccalaureate Organization, and Middle States Association of Colleges and Schools. Language of instruction: English. Total enrollment: 358. Upper school average class size: 15. Upper school faculty-student ratio: 1:9. There are 174 required school days per year for Upper School students. Upper School students typically attend 5 days per week. The average school day consists of 6 hours.

Upper School Student Profile Grade 10: 35 students (20 boys, 15 girls); Grade 11: 31 students (20 boys, 11 girls); Grade 12: 57 students (33 boys, 24 girls).

Faculty School total: 69. In upper school: 13 men, 24 women; 24 have advanced degrees.

Subjects Offered American literature, Arabic, art, art history, biology, business studies, calculus, chemistry, drama, English, English literature, ESL, French, geography, Greek, history, information technology, mathematics, modern world history, music, physical education, physics, science, sociology, Spanish, studio art, theory of knowledge, world history, world literature, writing.

Graduation Requirements Art history, arts and fine arts (art, music, dance, drama), English, foreign language, history, information technology, mathematics, physical education (includes health), science, requirements for students in IB diploma program differ. Community service is required.

Special Academic Programs International Baccalaureate program; independent study; academic accommodation for the gifted; remedial reading and/or remedial writing; remedial math; programs in English, mathematics, general development for dyslexic students; ESL.

Student Life Upper grades have uniform requirement, student council. Discipline rests primarily with faculty.

Summer Programs ESL, sports, art/fine arts, computer instruction programs offered; session focuses on ESL; held both on and off campus; held at archaeological sites, beaches, and pool; accepts boys and girls; open to students from other schools. 100 students usually enrolled. 2011 schedule: June 27 to July 23. Application deadline: none.

Tuition and Aid Day student tuition: €11,200–€12,350. Tuition installment plan (monthly payment plans, individually arranged payment plans). Tuition reduction for siblings, need-based scholarship grants, prepayment discount available.

Admissions Traditional secondary-level entrance grade is 10. For fall 2010, 22 students applied for upper-level admission, 19 were accepted, 17 enrolled. Math Placement Exam, Secondary Level English Proficiency or writing sample required. Deadline for receipt of application materials: none. Application fee required: €1200. On-campus interview required.

Athletics Interscholastic: basketball (boys, girls), cross-country running (b,g), jogging (b,g), soccer (b,g), track and field (b,g), volleyball (b,g); intramural: basketball (b,g), cross-country running (b,g), jogging (b,g), soccer (b,g), swimming and diving (b,g), volleyball (b,g); coed intramural: tennis, water volleyball. 4 PE instructors.

Computers Computers are regularly used in English, foreign language, information technology, library, mathematics, science, social studies, yearbook classes. Computer resources include on-campus library services, online commercial services, Internet access, wireless campus network, Internet filtering or blocking technology. Computer access in designated common areas is available to students.

Contact Ms. Helen Haniotakis, Admissions Officer. 30-210-623-3888. Fax: 30-210-623-3160. E-mail: ehaniotaki@isa.edu.gr. Web site: www.isa.edu.gr/home.htm.

INTERNATIONAL SCHOOL OF BERNE

Mattenstrasse 3
Guemligen 3073, Switzerland
Head of School: Mr. Kevin Thomas Page

General Information Coeducational day college-preparatory school. Grades PK–12. Founded: 1961. Setting: suburban. Nearest major city is Berne, Switzerland. 1-hectare campus. 4 buildings on campus. Approved or accredited by European Council of International Schools, International Baccalaureate Organization, New England Association of Schools and Colleges, and Swiss Federation of Private Schools. Language of instruction: English. Total enrollment: 246. Upper school average class size: 21. Upper school faculty-student ratio: 1:5. There are 180 required school days per year for Upper School students. Upper School students typically attend 5 days per week. The average school day consists of 6 hours.

Upper School Student Profile Grade 6: 21 students (14 boys, 7 girls); Grade 7: 21 students (10 boys, 11 girls); Grade 8: 20 students (13 boys, 7 girls); Grade 9: 21 students (10 boys, 11 girls); Grade 10: 22 students (11 boys, 11 girls); Grade 11: 28 students (17 boys, 11 girls); Grade 12: 19 students (12 boys, 7 girls).

Faculty School total: 42. In upper school: 16 men, 12 women; 19 have advanced degrees.

Subjects Offered Biology, chemistry, economics, English, English literature, ESL, European history, French, geography, German, history, mathematics, music, physical education, physics, science, technology, theater arts, visual arts, world history, world literature.

Graduation Requirements Biology, chemistry, economics, English, foreign language, French, geography, German, history, mathematics, music, physical education (includes health), physics, technology, theater arts, theory of knowledge, visual arts, extended essay, Creativity Action Service (CAS), Theory of Knowledge.

Special Academic Programs International Baccalaureate program; academic accommodation for the gifted; ESL (17 students enrolled).

College Admission Counseling 23 students graduated in 2010; 14 went to college, including Brown University; Northeastern University; University of California, Los Angeles. Other: 4 went to work, 5 had other specific plans. Mean SAT critical reading: 571, mean SAT math: 647, mean SAT writing: 581. 45% scored over 600 on SAT critical reading, 73% scored over 600 on SAT math, 45% scored over 600 on SAT writing, 45% scored over 1800 on combined SAT.

Student Life Upper grades have specified standards of dress, student council. Discipline rests primarily with faculty.

Tuition and Aid Day student tuition: 26,820 Swiss francs–30,140 Swiss francs. Tuition installment plan (monthly payment plans, individually arranged payment plans).

Admissions For fall 2010, 38 students applied for upper-level admission, 38 were accepted, 38 enrolled. Math and English placement tests required. Deadline for receipt of application materials: none. Application fee required: 250 Swiss francs. On-campus interview required.

Athletics Interscholastic: alpine skiing (boys, girls), basketball (b,g), cross-country running (b,g), indoor hockey (b,g), indoor soccer (b,g), running (b,g), skiing (downhill) (b,g), snowboarding (b,g), soccer (b,g), swimming and diving (b,g), track and field (b,g), volleyball (b,g); intramural: alpine skiing (b,g), basketball (b,g), cross-country running (b,g), ice skating (b,g), indoor hockey (b,g), indoor soccer (b,g), running (b,g), skiing (downhill) (b,g), snowboarding (b,g), soccer (b,g), swimming and diving (b,g), track and field (b,g), volleyball (b,g); coed interscholastic: alpine skiing, swimming and diving; coed intramural: alpine skiing, ice skating, swimming and diving. 1 PE instructor, 4 coaches.

Computers Computers are regularly used in English, French, information technology, library skills, mathematics, science classes. Computer network features include on-campus library services, online commercial services, Internet access, wireless campus network, Internet filtering or blocking technology. Student e-mail accounts and computer access in designated common areas are available to students. Students grades are available online. The school has a published electronic and media policy.

Contact Mr. Tobin Bechtel, Secondary School Principal. 41-(0) 31-951-23-58. Fax: 41-(0)31-951-1710. E-mail: tobin.bechtel@isberne.ch. Web site: www.isberne.ch.

See Display below and Close-Up on page 796.

THE INTERNATIONAL SCHOOL OF GENEVA

62 Route de Chene
Geneva 1208, Switzerland
Head of School: Dr. Nicholas Tate, PhD

General Information Coeducational day college-preparatory, general academic, and bilingual studies school. Grades PK–13. Founded: 1924. Setting: urban. 15-acre

The International School of Geneva

campus. 16 buildings on campus. Approved or accredited by European Council of International Schools, Headmasters' Conference, International Baccalaureate Organization, Middle States Association of Colleges and Schools, Swiss Federation of Private Schools, and The College Board. Member of Secondary School Admission Test Board. Languages of instruction: English and French. Total enrollment: 4,010. Upper school average class size: 20. Upper school faculty-student ratio: 1:10. Upper School students typically attend 5 days per week. The average school day consists of 6 hours and 30 minutes.

Upper School Student Profile Grade 9: 320 students (150 boys, 170 girls); Grade 10: 340 students (180 boys, 160 girls); Grade 11: 325 students (165 boys, 160 girls); Grade 12: 365 students (180 boys, 185 girls); Grade 13: 355 students (175 boys, 180 girls).

Faculty School total: 430.

Subjects Offered Advanced chemistry, advanced math, art, biology, chemistry, computer skills, computer-aided design, drama, economics, English, English literature, ESL, fine arts, French, French as a second language, French literature-AP, general science, geography, German, history, International Baccalaureate courses, Italian, mathematics, music, performing arts, physical education, physics, psychology, science, social studies, Spanish, theater, theory of knowledge, world literature.

Graduation Requirements English, foreign language, lab science, mathematics, social studies (includes history).

Special Academic Programs International Baccalaureate program; academic accommodation for the musically talented and the artistically talented; remedial reading and/or remedial writing; remedial math; programs in general development for dyslexic students; ESL (150 students enrolled).

College Admission Counseling 365 students graduated in 2009; 350 went to college. Other: 4 went to work, 8 entered military service.

Student Life Upper grades have student council. Discipline rests primarily with faculty.

Tuition and Aid Day student tuition: 28,235 Swiss francs. Tuition installment plan (monthly payment plans, trimester payment plan). Tuition reduction for siblings, bursaries available.

Admissions Deadline for receipt of application materials: none. No application fee required. On-campus interview recommended.

Athletics Interscholastic: alpine skiing (boys, girls), basketball (b,g), cross-country running (b,g), indoor soccer (b,g), rugby (b,g), running (b,g), skiing (downhill) (b,g), soccer (b,g), swimming and diving (b,g), tennis (b,g), track and field (b,g); intramural: alpine skiing (b,g), badminton (b,g), basketball (b,g), climbing (b,g), crew (b,g), cross-country running (b,g), field hockey (b,g), indoor soccer (b,g), rugby (b,g), running (b,g), skiing (downhill) (b,g), soccer (b,g), swimming and diving (b,g), table tennis (b,g), tennis (b,g), track and field (b,g). 10 PE instructors, 25 coaches.

Computers Computers are regularly used in all academic classes. Computer network features include on-campus library services, Internet access, wireless campus network, Internet filtering or blocking technology. Campus intranet is available to students. Students grades are available online. The school has a published electronic and media policy.

Contact Mr. John Douglas, Director of Admissions. 41-22-787-26-30. Fax: 41-22-787 26 32. E-mail: admissions@ecolint.ch. Web site: www.ecolint.ch.

THE INTERNATIONAL SCHOOL OF KUALA LUMPUR

Jalan Kolam Air
Ampang, Selangor 68000, Malaysia
Head of School: Mr. Paul B. Chmelik

General Information Coeducational day college-preparatory school. Grades PK–12. Founded: 1965. Setting: suburban. Nearest major city is Kuala Lumpur, Malaysia. 7-acre campus. 1 building on campus. Approved or accredited by European Council of International Schools and Western Association of Schools and Colleges. Affiliate member of National Association of Independent Schools. Language of instruction: English. Total enrollment: 1,588. Upper school average class size: 20. Upper school faculty-student ratio: 1:9.

Upper School Student Profile Grade 9: 141 students (75 boys, 66 girls); Grade 10: 155 students (71 boys, 84 girls); Grade 11: 156 students (92 boys, 64 girls); Grade 12: 152 students (73 boys, 79 girls).

Faculty School total: 169. In upper school: 28 men, 22 women; 40 have advanced degrees.

Subjects Offered Advanced chemistry, advanced math, Advanced Placement courses, anthropology, applied arts, architecture, art, Asian history, biology, calculus-AP, ceramics, chemistry, computer multimedia, computer science, concert band, concert choir, economics, English, English literature, English-AP, environmental science, ESL, film studies, fine arts, French, graphic design, guitar, health, history, information technology, integrated mathematics, integrated science, International Baccalaureate courses, Japanese, jazz band, journalism, Korean, Malay, Mandarin, math analysis, mathematics, music theory, photography, physical education, physics, pre-calculus, psychology, science, Spanish, stagecraft, statistics-AP, theater, theory of knowledge, U.S. history-AP, vocal ensemble, world studies, world wide web design, yearbook.

Graduation Requirements Art, English, foreign language, health, mathematics, physical education (includes health), science, social studies (includes history).

Special Academic Programs International Baccalaureate program; Advanced Placement exam preparation; honors section; independent study; special instructional classes for students with mild learning disabilities; ESL (100 students enrolled).

College Admission Counseling 131 students graduated in 2010; 122 went to college, including McGill University; Northwestern University; Texas A&M University; The Ohio State University; The University of British Columbia; University of Victoria. Other: 2 went to work, 3 entered military service, 3 entered a postgraduate year, 1 had other specific plans. Mean SAT critical reading: 554, mean SAT math: 643, mean SAT writing: 553, mean combined SAT: 1750, mean composite ACT: 27. 37% scored over 600 on SAT critical reading, 73% scored over 600 on SAT math, 47% scored over 600 on SAT writing, 73% scored over 26 on composite ACT.

Student Life Upper grades have uniform requirement, student council, honor system. Discipline rests primarily with faculty.

Summer Programs Enrichment, ESL, sports, art/fine arts, rigorous outdoor training, computer instruction programs offered; session focuses on enrichment and basic skills; held both on and off campus; held at various locations, including science center; accepts boys and girls; open to students from other schools. 40 students usually enrolled. 2011 schedule: June 12 to July 1. Application deadline: May 31.

Tuition and Aid Day student tuition: 64,600 Malaysian ringgits. Tuition installment plan (individually arranged payment plans). IB Scholarships to Malaysian students available.

Admissions Traditional secondary-level entrance grade is 9. For fall 2010, 95 students applied for upper-level admission, 93 were accepted, 93 enrolled. English for Non-native Speakers, Gates MacGinite Reading Tests or Math Placement Exam required. Deadline for receipt of application materials: none. Application fee required: 800 Malaysian ringgits.

Athletics Interscholastic: aerobics/dance (boys, girls), aquatics (b,g), badminton (b,g), basketball (b,g), climbing (b,g), cross-country running (b,g), dance (b,g), dance team (b,g), equestrian sports (b,g), golf (b,g), rugby (b), running (b,g), soccer (b,g), softball (b,g), swimming and diving (b,g), tennis (b,g), touch football (b,g), track and field (b,g), volleyball (b,g); intramural: aerobics/dance (b,g), aquatics (b,g), badminton (b,g), basketball (b,g), climbing (b,g), cooperative games (b,g), dance (b,g), fitness (b,g), Frisbee (b,g), judo (b,g), martial arts (b,g), outdoor education (b,g), paddle tennis (b,g), physical fitness (b,g), rock climbing (b,g), rugby (b), soccer (b,g), softball (b,g), swimming and diving (b,g), tennis (b,g), touch football (b,g), track and field (b,g), ultimate Frisbee (b,g), volleyball (b,g), water polo (b,g), water volleyball (b,g), weight training (b,g); coed interscholastic: aerobics/dance, aquatics, badminton, dance, dance team, swimming and diving, track and field, wall climbing; coed intramural: aerobics/dance, aquatics, badminton, baseball, basketball, climbing, cooperative games, Cosom hockey, dance, field hockey, fitness, floor hockey, football, golf, kickball, outdoor education, paddle tennis, physical fitness, rock climbing, self defense, soccer, softball, strength & conditioning, swimming and diving, touch football, track and field, ultimate Frisbee, wall climbing, weight training, yoga. 3 PE instructors, 2 coaches.

Computers Computers are regularly used in all academic, computer applications, graphic design, multimedia, newspaper, photography, programming, publications, video film production, Web site design, yearbook classes. Computer network features include on-campus library services, online commercial services, Internet access, wireless campus network, Internet filtering or blocking technology, Microsoft Office. Campus intranet, student e-mail accounts, and computer access in designated common areas are available to students. The school has a published electronic and media policy.

Contact Ms. Amina O'Kane, Director of Admissions. 011-603-4259-5600 Ext. 5626. Fax: 011-603-4259-5738. E-mail: aokane@iskl.edu.my. Web site: www.iskl.edu.my.

INTERNATIONAL SCHOOL OF LAUSANNE

Chemin de la Grangette 2
Le Mont-sur-Lausanne 1052, Switzerland
Head of School: Ms. Lyn Cheetham

General Information Coeducational day college-preparatory school. Grades PK–12. Founded: 1962. Setting: suburban. Nearest major city is Lausanne, Switzerland. 8-acre campus. 1 building on campus. Approved or accredited by European Council of International Schools, International Baccalaureate Organization, and New England Association of Schools and Colleges. Language of instruction: English. Total enrollment: 608. Upper school average class size: 20. Upper school faculty-student ratio: 1:7.

Upper School Student Profile Grade 6: 43 students (26 boys, 17 girls); Grade 7: 45 students (26 boys, 19 girls); Grade 8: 45 students (25 boys, 20 girls); Grade 9: 46 students (26 boys, 20 girls); Grade 10: 50 students (27 boys, 23 girls); Grade 11: 52 students (27 boys, 25 girls); Grade 12: 53 students (29 boys, 24 girls).

Faculty School total: 85. In upper school: 18 men, 17 women; 4 have advanced degrees.

Subjects Offered Art, biology, chemistry, community service, design, drama, economics, English, ESL, French, geography, German, history, information technology, International Baccalaureate courses, library skills, mathematics, music, personal and social education, physics, science, Spanish, sports, Swedish, swimming, theory of knowledge.

Graduation Requirements English, foreign language, mathematics, physical education (includes health), science, social sciences. Community service is required.

Special Academic Programs International Baccalaureate program; special instructional classes for students with learning disabilities, dyslexia, etc.; ESL (20 students enrolled).

College Admission Counseling 51 students graduated in 2009; 48 went to college, including Connecticut College; Dartmouth College; Emerson College; McGill University; University of Pennsylvania; Villanova University. Other: 1 entered military service, 2 had other specific plans.

Student Life Upper grades have specified standards of dress, student council. Discipline rests equally with students and faculty.

Tuition and Aid Day student tuition: 30,850 Swiss francs. Bursaries available.

Admissions Traditional secondary-level entrance grade is 9. English for Non-native Speakers required. Deadline for receipt of application materials: none. Application fee required: 2500 Swiss francs. On-campus interview recommended.

Athletics Interscholastic: alpine skiing (boys, girls), aquatics (b,g), badminton (b,g), basketball (b), cross-country running (b,g), football (b,g), indoor soccer (b,g), netball (g), rugby (b), skiing (downhill) (b,g), soccer (b,g), swimming and diving (b,g), tennis (b,g), track and field (b,g), volleyball (g); intramural: artistic gym (g), dance (g), gymnastics (g); coed interscholastic: outdoor activities, running, tennis; coed intramural: aerobics/dance, badminton, basketball, climbing, dance, field hockey, fitness, floor hockey, indoor soccer, jogging, kayaking, mountain biking, nordic skiing, outdoor activities, rock climbing, rugby, skiing (downhill), soccer, softball, squash, swimming and diving, track and field, ultimate Frisbee, volleyball, water polo. 3 PE instructors, 3 coaches.

Computers Computers are regularly used in all classes. Computer network features include on-campus library services, Internet access, wireless campus network, Internet filtering or blocking technology. Campus intranet and student e-mail accounts are available to students. The school has a published electronic and media policy.

Contact Ms. Susy Weill, Admissions Office. 41-21-560 02 02. Fax: 41-21-560 02 03. E-mail: admissions@isl.ch. Web site: www.isl.ch.

THE INTERNATIONAL SCHOOL OF LONDON

139 Gunnersbury Avenue
London W3 8LG, United Kingdom
Head of School: Mr. Huw Davies

General Information Coeducational day college-preparatory school, affiliated with Community of Christ. Grades K–13. Founded: 1972. Setting: urban. 2 buildings on campus. Approved or accredited by European Council of International Schools. Language of instruction: English. Total enrollment: 340. Upper school average class size: 18. Upper school faculty-student ratio: 1:8. Upper School students typically attend 5 days per week.

Faculty School total: 67. In upper school: 15 men, 16 women; 21 have advanced degrees.

Subjects Offered Art, economics, English, French, geography, history, languages, mathematics, music, physical education, science, social sciences, Spanish, world affairs.

Graduation Requirements Foreign language, mathematics, science, social sciences. Community service is required.

Special Academic Programs International Baccalaureate program; ESL (47 students enrolled).

College Admission Counseling 22 students graduated in 2010; all went to college, including University of London; University of Oxford.

Student Life Upper grades have student council. Discipline rests primarily with faculty.

Tuition and Aid Day student tuition: £18,250.

Admissions For fall 2010, 36 students applied for upper-level admission, 30 were accepted, 30 enrolled. Deadline for receipt of application materials: July 30. Application fee required: £150. Interview recommended.

Athletics Interscholastic: basketball (boys, girls), soccer (b); intramural: badminton (b,g), softball (b,g), swimming and diving (b,g), table tennis (b,g), tennis (b,g); coed interscholastic: soccer; coed intramural: softball, swimming and diving, table tennis, tennis. 2 PE instructors, 2 coaches.

Computers Computers are regularly used in English, foreign language, mathematics, science classes. Computer network features include on-campus library services, Internet access, wireless campus network, Internet filtering or blocking technology. Student e-mail accounts are available to students. The school has a published electronic and media policy.

Contact Yoel Gordon, Director of Admissions. 20-8992-5823. Fax: 44-8993-7012. E-mail: mail@islondon.com. Web site: www.islondon.com.

THE INTERNATIONAL SCHOOL OF PARIS

6, rue Beethoven
Paris 75016, France
Head of School: Mrs. Audrey Peverelli

General Information Coeducational day college-preparatory, general academic, arts, bilingual studies, and all programs of the IBO (PYP, MYP and IB Diploma) school. Grades N–12. Founded: 1964. Setting: urban. 4 buildings on campus. Approved or accredited by European Council of International Schools, International Baccalaureate Organization, New England Association of Schools and Colleges, and

Northwest Association of Schools and Colleges. Affiliate member of National Association of Independent Schools. Language of instruction: English. Endowment: €50,000. Total enrollment: 660. Upper school average class size: 14. Upper school faculty-student ratio: 1:6. There are 175 required school days per year for Upper School students. Upper School students typically attend 5 days per week. The average school day consists of 6 hours and 30 minutes.

Faculty School total: 100. In upper school: 29 men, 36 women; 36 have advanced degrees.

Subjects Offered Algebra, art, biology, calculus, ceramics, chemistry, computer science, ecology, environmental systems, economics, English, English literature, ESL, fine arts, French, geography, geometry, Hindi, Japanese, Korean, mathematics, music, physical education, physics, Russian, science, social sciences, social studies, Swedish, theory of knowledge, trigonometry, world history.

Graduation Requirements English, foreign language, mathematics, science, social studies (includes history), theory of knowledge, extended essay (IB diploma requirements). Community service is required.

Special Academic Programs International Baccalaureate program; ESL (65 students enrolled).

College Admission Counseling 72 students graduated in 2009; 68 went to college, including Columbia University; McGill University; Waseda University. Other: 4 had other specific plans. Median SAT critical reading: 565, median SAT math: 590, median SAT writing: 570.

Student Life Upper grades have student council. Discipline rests primarily with faculty.

Tuition and Aid Day student tuition: €23,000. Tuition installment plan (individually arranged payment plans). Need-based scholarship grants available. In 2009–10, 5% of upper-school students received aid. Total amount of financial aid awarded in 2009–10: $200,000.

Admissions Traditional secondary-level entrance grade is 7. For fall 2009, 50 students applied for upper-level admission, 44 were accepted, 44 enrolled. Deadline for receipt of application materials: none. Application fee required: €700. Interview recommended.

Athletics Interscholastic: baseball (boys, girls), basketball (b,g), soccer (b,g), swimming and diving (b,g); intramural: baseball (b,g), basketball (b,g), lacrosse (b,g), skiing (downhill) (b,g), soccer (b,g), tennis (b,g), track and field (b,g), volleyball (b,g); coed intramural: aerobics/dance, badminton, ball hockey, field hockey, indoor hockey, indoor soccer, juggling, physical fitness, running, swimming and diving, table tennis. 3 PE instructors.

Computers Computers are regularly used in design, English, foreign language, mathematics, science classes. Computer network features include on-campus library services, online commercial services, Internet access, wireless campus network. Campus intranet and student e-mail accounts are available to students. The school has a published electronic and media policy.

Contact Mrs. Catherine Hard, Director of Admissions. 33-1-42-24-09-54. Fax: 33-1-45-27-15-93. E-mail: chard@isparis.edu. Web site: www.isparis.edu.

INTERNATIONAL SCHOOL OF ZUG AND LUZERN (ISZL)

Walterswil
Baar 6340, Switzerland
Head of School: Dominic Currer

General Information Coeducational day college-preparatory, International Baccalaureate (PYP, MYP, DP), and Advanced Placement school. Founded: 1961. Setting: small town. Nearest major city is Zurich, Switzerland. 5-hectare campus. 1 building on campus. Approved or accredited by International Baccalaureate Organization and The College Board. Member of European Council of International Schools. Language of instruction: English. Total enrollment: 1,189. Upper school average class size: 11. Upper school faculty-student ratio: 1:6. There are 180 required school days per year for Upper School students. Upper School students typically attend 5 days per week. The average school day consists of 7 hours.

Faculty School total: 200. In upper school: 16 men, 28 women.

Subjects Offered Art, art history-AP, biology, biology-AP, calculus-AP, chemistry, chemistry-AP, computer graphics, computer science-AP, dance, drama, English, English language and composition-AP, English literature and composition-AP, environmental science-AP, ESL, European history-AP, French, French language-AP, German, German-AP, human geography—AP, humanities, integrated mathematics, integrated science, macro/microeconomics-AP, music, physical education, physics, physics-AP, pre-calculus, studio art-AP, technology/design.

Graduation Requirements Art, art history-AP, biology-AP, calculus-AP, chemistry-AP, choir, college counseling, computer programming-AP, computer science-AP, computers, dance, drama, economics-AP, English, English language-AP, English literature-AP, environmental science-AP, ESL, European history-AP, foreign language, French, French language-AP, German, German-AP, health education, human geography—AP, International Baccalaureate courses, lab science, macro/microeconomics-AP, macroeconomics-AP, mathematics, model United Nations, modern European history-AP, music, physical education (includes health), physics-AP, pre-calculus, SAT/ACT preparation, social sciences, Spanish, studio art-AP, yearbook. Community service is required.

International School of Zug and Luzern (ISZL)

Special Academic Programs International Baccalaureate program; Advanced Placement exam preparation; accelerated programs; independent study; ESL (40 students enrolled).

College Admission Counseling 33 students graduated in 2010; 26 went to college, including Pace University; Pepperdine University; Stanford University; Villanova University; Yale University. Other: 3 entered a postgraduate year, 4 had other specific plans.

Student Life Upper grades have specified standards of dress, student council. Discipline rests primarily with faculty.

Summer Programs ESL, sports, rigorous outdoor training programs offered; session focuses on sports and language; held both on and off campus; held at Outdoor Activity Centre; accepts boys and girls; not open to students from other schools.

Tuition and Aid Day student tuition: 21,500 Swiss francs–32,000 Swiss francs. Tuition installment plan (monthly payment plans, individually arranged payment plans, semester payment plan). Discounts for children of staff and reciprocal arrangements with international primary school available.

Admissions English for Non-native Speakers or math and English placement tests required. Deadline for receipt of application materials: none. Application fee required: 5000 Swiss francs. Interview recommended.

Athletics Interscholastic: aerobics/dance (girls), alpine skiing (b,g), basketball (b,g), cross-country running (b,g), golf (b,g), indoor soccer (b,g), rugby (b), skiing (downhill) (b,g), soccer (b,g), swimming and diving (b,g), track and field (b,g), volleyball (b,g); intramural: alpine skiing (b,g), basketball (b,g), cross-country running (b,g), indoor soccer (b,g), soccer (b,g), track and field (b,g); coed interscholastic: canoeing/kayaking, climbing, softball; coed intramural: aerobics/dance, backpacking, badminton, ball hockey, bicycling, canoeing/kayaking, climbing, dance, field hockey, golf, hiking/backpacking, ice skating, kayaking, martial arts, mountain biking, outdoor activities, outdoor education, racquetball, rowing, running, sailing, skiing (downhill), snowboarding, soccer, softball, swimming and diving, tennis, walking, winter walking. 2 PE instructors, 2 coaches, 2 athletic trainers.

Computers Computers are regularly used in college planning classes. Computer network features include Internet access, Internet filtering or blocking technology. Campus intranet, student e-mail accounts, and computer access in designated common areas are available to students. The school has a published electronic and media policy.

Contact Urs Kappeler, Business Director. 41-41-768 2950. Fax: 41-41-768 2951. E-mail: urs.kappeler@iszl.ch. Web site: www.iszl.ch.

IOLANI SCHOOL

563 Kamoku Street
Honolulu, Hawaii 96826
Head of School: Dr. Val T. Iwashita

General Information Coeducational day college-preparatory, arts, and technology school, affiliated with Episcopal Church. Grades K–12. Founded: 1863. Setting: urban. 25-acre campus. 7 buildings on campus. Approved or accredited by National Association of Episcopal Schools, Western Association of Schools and Colleges, and Hawaii Department of Education. Member of National Association of Independent Schools and Secondary School Admission Test Board. Endowment: $100 million. Total enrollment: 1,867. Upper school average class size: 17. Upper school faculty-student ratio: 1:12. There are 178 required school days per year for Upper School students. Upper School students typically attend 5 days per week. The average school day consists of 6 hours.

Upper School Student Profile Grade 7: 181 students (84 boys, 97 girls); Grade 8: 196 students (99 boys, 97 girls); Grade 9: 244 students (120 boys, 124 girls); Grade 10: 242 students (113 boys, 129 girls); Grade 11: 233 students (109 boys, 124 girls); Grade 12: 230 students (114 boys, 116 girls).

Faculty School total: 185. In upper school: 63 men, 68 women; 90 have advanced degrees.

Subjects Offered 3-dimensional design, Advanced Placement courses, advanced studio art-AP, African American history, algebra, American history, American history-AP, American literature, American literature-AP, art, Asian studies, band, Basic programming, Bible, Bible studies, biology, biology-AP, British literature, calculus, calculus-AP, ceramics, chemistry, chemistry-AP, Chinese, chorus, computer programming, computer programming-AP, computer science, computer science-AP, conceptual physics, concert band, creative writing, dance, drama, earth science, economics, economics-AP, English, English as a foreign language, English language and composition-AP, English literature, English literature and composition-AP, English literature-AP, European history, European history-AP, expository writing, film and literature, fine arts, French, French language-AP, French literature-AP, geography, geometry, government-AP, government/civics, Hawaiian history, health, health education, history, Japanese, Japanese studies, jazz band, jazz ensemble, journalism, Latin, Latin-AP, leadership, macro/microeconomics-AP, macroeconomics-AP, Mandarin, marching band, mathematics, money management, music, newspaper, orchestra, photography, physical education, physics, physics-AP, pre-calculus, psychology, psychology-AP, religion, science, Shakespeare, social studies, Spanish, Spanish-AP, speech, statistics, statistics-AP, studio art-AP, theater, trigonometry, U.S. government and politics-AP, Web site design, world affairs, world history, world literature, writing.

Graduation Requirements Algebra, arts and fine arts (art, music, dance, drama), Bible, biology, chemistry, computer science, English, European history, foreign language, geometry, literature, physical education (includes health), physics, U.S. history.

Special Academic Programs Advanced Placement exam preparation; honors section; independent study; academic accommodation for the gifted, the musically talented, and the artistically talented; ESL (15 students enrolled).

College Admission Counseling 223 students graduated in 2010; all went to college, including Oregon State University; Santa Clara University; University of Hawaii at Manoa; University of Southern California; University of Washington.

Student Life Upper grades have specified standards of dress, student council. Discipline rests primarily with faculty. Attendance at religious services is required.

Summer Programs Enrichment, advancement, ESL, sports, art/fine arts, computer instruction programs offered; session focuses on reinforcement, enrichment, recreation, and sports; held on campus; accepts boys and girls; open to students from other schools. 3,000 students usually enrolled. 2011 schedule: June 13 to July 22. Application deadline: March 28.

Tuition and Aid Day student tuition: $16,150. Tuition installment plan (monthly payment plans, semester and annual payment plans). Need-based scholarship grants available. In 2010–11, 12% of upper-school students received aid. Total amount of financial aid awarded in 2010–11: $3,000,500.

Admissions Traditional secondary-level entrance grade is 7. For fall 2010, 696 students applied for upper-level admission, 188 were accepted, 132 enrolled. SSAT required. Deadline for receipt of application materials: December 1. Application fee required: $125. On-campus interview recommended.

Athletics Interscholastic: aerobics/dance (girls), baseball (b), basketball (b,g), bowling (b,g), canoeing/kayaking (b,g), cheering (g), cross-country running (b,g), dance (g), dance team (g), diving (b,g), football (b), kayaking (b,g), modern dance (g), ocean paddling (b,g), soccer (b,g), softball (g), strength & conditioning (b,g), swimming and diving (b,g), tennis (b,g), track and field (b,g), volleyball (b,g), water polo (b,g), weight training (b,g), wrestling (b,g); coed interscholastic: ballet, golf, judo, tennis. 6 PE instructors, 170 coaches, 3 athletic trainers.

Computers Computers are regularly used in all academic classes. Computer network features include on-campus library services, online commercial services, Internet access, wireless campus network, Internet filtering or blocking technology. Student e-mail accounts and computer access in designated common areas are available to students. The school has a published electronic and media policy.

Contact Patricia N. Liu, Director of Admission. 808-943-2222. Fax: 808-943-2375. E-mail: admission@iolani.org. Web site: www.iolani.org.

IONA PREPARATORY SCHOOL

255 Wilmot Road
New Rochelle, New York 10804
Head of School: Mrs. Maureen B. Kiers

General Information Boys' day college-preparatory, arts, religious studies, and technology school, affiliated with Roman Catholic Church. Grades 9–12. Founded: 1916. Setting: suburban. Nearest major city is New York. 29-acre campus. 3 buildings on campus. Approved or accredited by Christian Brothers Association, European Council of International Schools, Middle States Association of Colleges and Schools, National Catholic Education Association, New York State Association of Independent Schools, and New York State Board of Regents. Endowment: $6 million. Total enrollment: 741. Upper school average class size: 26. Upper school faculty-student ratio: 1:13. There are 180 required school days per year for Upper School students. Upper School students typically attend 5 days per week. The average school day consists of 6 hours and 30 minutes.

Upper School Student Profile Grade 9: 203 students (203 boys); Grade 10: 178 students (178 boys); Grade 11: 187 students (187 boys); Grade 12: 173 students (173 boys). 87% of students are Roman Catholic.

Faculty School total: 67. In upper school: 47 men, 18 women; 65 have advanced degrees.

Subjects Offered Accounting, Advanced Placement courses, algebra, American history, American history-AP, American literature, anatomy, art, astronomy, biology, biology-AP, British literature, calculus, chemistry, chemistry-AP, communications, community service, composition-AP, computer programming, computer science, economics, English, English literature-AP, English/composition-AP, environmental science, European history, European history-AP, European literature, fine arts, French, French as a second language, geometry, government-AP, graphic design, health, health and safety, history, Italian, Latin, media, music, painting, physical education, physics, physiology, psychology, psychology-AP, religion, science, social sciences, social studies, Spanish, trigonometry, U.S. government and politics-AP, word processing, world literature, world religions.

Graduation Requirements Art, computer science, English, foreign language, mathematics, music, physical education (includes health), religion (includes Bible studies and theology), science, social studies (includes history), 75 hours of community service (senior year).

Special Academic Programs Advanced Placement exam preparation; honors section; study at local college for college credit; study abroad; academic accommodation for the gifted.

College Admission Counseling 168 students graduated in 2010; all went to college, including Boston College; Fairfield University; Fordham University; Iona College;

Loyola University Maryland. Mean SAT critical reading: 610, mean SAT math: 620. 30% scored over 600 on SAT critical reading, 39% scored over 600 on SAT math.
Student Life Upper grades have specified standards of dress, student council, honor system. Discipline rests primarily with faculty. Attendance at religious services is required.
Tuition and Aid Day student tuition: $14,200. Tuition installment plan (monthly payment plans, individually arranged payment plans, 10-payment plan, semester payment plan). Tuition reduction for siblings, merit scholarship grants, need-based scholarship grants available. In 2010–11, 31% of upper-school students received aid; total upper-school merit-scholarship money awarded: $187,000. Total amount of financial aid awarded in 2010–11: $325,000.
Admissions Traditional secondary-level entrance grade is 9. For fall 2010, 830 students applied for upper-level admission, 560 were accepted, 203 enrolled. Admissions testing, Catholic High School Entrance Examination, ISEE, SSAT, Test of Achievement and Proficiency or writing sample required. Deadline for receipt of application materials: none. No application fee required. Interview recommended.
Athletics Interscholastic: badminton, baseball, basketball, bowling, climbing, crew, cross-country running, diving, field hockey, flag football, football, golf, ice hockey, indoor track, indoor track & field, lacrosse, paint ball, physical fitness, rock climbing, running, soccer, swimming and diving, tennis, track and field, ultimate Frisbee, volleyball, weight lifting, weight training, winter (indoor) track, wrestling; intramural: baseball, basketball, climbing, fitness, flag football, floor hockey, Frisbee, physical fitness, physical training, rock climbing, soccer, strength & conditioning, tennis, volleyball, wall climbing, weight lifting. 3 PE instructors, 40 coaches, 1 athletic trainer.
Computers Computers are regularly used in all classes. Computer network features include on-campus library services, online commercial services, Internet access, wireless campus network, Internet filtering or blocking technology. Campus intranet and student e-mail accounts are available to students. The school has a published electronic and media policy.
Contact Mrs. Ann V. Slocum, Director of Admissions. 914-632-0714 Ext. 215. Fax: 914-632-9760. E-mail: aslocum@ionaprep.org. Web site: www.ionaprep.org.

ISIDORE NEWMAN SCHOOL

1903 Jefferson Avenue
New Orleans, Louisiana 70115
Head of School: Dr. Thomas J. Locke
General Information Coeducational day college-preparatory school. Grades PK–12. Founded: 1903. Setting: urban. 11-acre campus. 10 buildings on campus. Approved or accredited by Independent Schools Association of the Southwest, Southern Association of Colleges and Schools, and Louisiana Department of Education. Member of National Association of Independent Schools. Endowment: $24 million. Total enrollment: 921. Upper school average class size: 16. Upper school faculty-student ratio: 1:17. There are 175 required school days per year for Upper School students. Upper School students typically attend 5 days per week. The average school day consists of 7 hours and 50 minutes.
Upper School Student Profile Grade 9: 73 students (41 boys, 32 girls); Grade 10: 70 students (44 boys, 26 girls); Grade 11: 83 students (52 boys, 31 girls); Grade 12: 80 students (50 boys, 30 girls).
Faculty School total: 117. In upper school: 19 men, 26 women.
Subjects Offered Advanced computer applications, Advanced Placement courses, algebra, American history, American history-AP, American literature, anatomy, art, art history, biology, biology-AP, calculus, calculus-AP, ceramics, chemistry, Chinese, choral music, chorus, civics, communications, computer science-AP, dance, drama, English, English literature, environmental science, European history-AP, film, film history, fine arts, French, French language-AP, French literature-AP, French-AP, genetics, geometry, government/civics, history, human development, humanities, Latin, Latin-AP, mathematics, modern European history, modern European history-AP, music, music theory, peer counseling, photojournalism, physical education, physics, physics-AP, physiology, science, sculpture, social studies, Spanish, Spanish language-AP, Spanish literature-AP, speech, statistics-AP, technical theater, theater, trigonometry, U.S. government and politics-AP, U.S. history, U.S. history-AP, world history.
Graduation Requirements Arts and fine arts (art, music, dance, drama), computer science, English, foreign language, mathematics, physical education (includes health), science, social studies (includes history), speech, senior Capstone Elective-one class each semester of senior year.
Special Academic Programs Advanced Placement exam preparation; honors section; independent study; term-away projects.
College Admission Counseling 86 students graduated in 2010; all went to college, including Louisiana State University and Agricultural and Mechanical College; Loyola University New Orleans; Rhodes College; The University of Texas at Austin; Tulane University; University of Georgia.
Student Life Upper grades have specified standards of dress, student council, honor system. Discipline rests equally with students and faculty.
Summer Programs Remediation, enrichment, sports, art/fine arts, computer instruction programs offered; held on campus; accepts boys and girls; open to students from other schools. 433 students usually enrolled. 2011 schedule: June to July. Application deadline: none.

Tuition and Aid Day student tuition: $18,467. Tuition installment plan (Sallie Mae tuition loans). Need-based scholarship grants, Sallie Mae Loans available. In 2010–11, 25% of upper-school students received aid. Total amount of financial aid awarded in 2010–11: $847,872.
Admissions Traditional secondary-level entrance grade is 9. ERB (CTP-Verbal, Quantitative), ERB CTP III, independent norms, Individual IQ, Achievement and behavior rating scale, ISEE, school's own test and writing sample required. Deadline for receipt of application materials: none. Application fee required: $35. Interview required.
Athletics Interscholastic: aquatics (boys, girls), baseball (b), basketball (b,g), cross-country running (b,g), football (b), golf (b,g), gymnastics (b,g), indoor track & field (b), soccer (b,g), softball (g), swimming and diving (b,g), tennis (b,g), track and field (b,g), volleyball (g); coed interscholastic: cheering. 16 coaches, 2 athletic trainers.
Computers Computers are regularly used in all academic classes. Computer network features include on-campus library services, online commercial services, Internet access, wireless campus network, Internet filtering or blocking technology. Campus intranet and student e-mail accounts are available to students. Students grades are available online. The school has a published electronic and media policy.
Contact Mrs. Ladd Sheets, Admission Assistant. 504-896-6323. Fax: 504-896-8597. E-mail: lsheets@newmanschool.org. Web site: www.newmanschool.org.

ISLAND SCHOOL

3-1875 Kaumualii Highway
Lihue, Hawaii 96766-9597
Head of School: Mr. Robert Springer
General Information Coeducational day college-preparatory, arts, bilingual studies, and technology school. Grades PK–12. Founded: 1977. Setting: small town. 38-acre campus. 11 buildings on campus. Approved or accredited by Academy of Orton-Gillingham Practitioners and Educators, The Hawaii Council of Private Schools, Western Association of Schools and Colleges, and Hawaii Department of Education. Endowment: $800,000. Total enrollment: 362. Upper school average class size: 15. Upper school faculty-student ratio: 1:11. There are 174 required school days per year for Upper School students. Upper School students typically attend 5 days per week. The average school day consists of 7 hours and 45 minutes.
Upper School Student Profile Grade 6: 27 students (11 boys, 16 girls); Grade 7: 40 students (17 boys, 23 girls); Grade 8: 34 students (18 boys, 16 girls); Grade 9: 30 students (18 boys, 12 girls); Grade 10: 23 students (8 boys, 15 girls); Grade 11: 34 students (11 boys, 23 girls); Grade 12: 23 students (10 boys, 13 girls).
Faculty School total: 46. In upper school: 6 men, 17 women; 9 have advanced degrees.
Subjects Offered Calculus, calculus-AP, chemistry, chemistry-AP, Chinese, intro to computers, introduction to literature, keyboarding, language structure, literature, marine ecology, marine science, mathematics, medieval history, medieval literature, microeconomics, modern Western civilization, modern world history, money management, music, news writing, organic gardening, performing arts, photo shop, photography, physical education, physical fitness, physics, physics-AP, poetry, pre-algebra, pre-calculus, religious studies, robotics, SAT/ACT preparation, scuba diving, sex education, Shakespeare, Shakespearean histories, short story, social studies, stagecraft, stock market, student government, theater, theater design and production, trigonometry, U.S. government, U.S. government and politics, U.S. government and politics-AP, U.S. history, U.S. literature, world history, world religions, world studies, world wide web design, writing, writing workshop, yearbook.
Graduation Requirements Drama, electives, English, foreign language, life skills, mathematics, music, physical education (includes health), science, social studies (includes history), visual arts.
Special Academic Programs 3 Advanced Placement exams for which test preparation is offered; honors section; independent study; study at local college for college credit; academic accommodation for the gifted.
College Admission Counseling 24 students graduated in 2010; all went to college, including Pepperdine University; University of Denver; University of Hawaii at Manoa. Mean SAT critical reading: 526, mean SAT math: 519, mean SAT writing: 511.
Student Life Upper grades have specified standards of dress, student council, honor system. Discipline rests primarily with faculty.
Summer Programs Remediation, advancement, sports programs offered; session focuses on broadening of students' academic abilities; held on campus; accepts boys and girls; open to students from other schools. 30 students usually enrolled. 2011 schedule: June 14 to July 31. Application deadline: June.
Tuition and Aid Day student tuition: $11,580. Tuition installment plan (FACTS Tuition Payment Plan). Need-based scholarship grants available. In 2010–11, 41% of upper-school students received aid. Total amount of financial aid awarded in 2010–11: $15,000.
Admissions Traditional secondary-level entrance grade is 9. For fall 2010, 100 students applied for upper-level admission, 65 were accepted, 55 enrolled. Admissions testing, any standardized test, essay, Math Placement Exam and Stanford Achievement Test required. Deadline for receipt of application materials: none. Application fee required: $40. Interview required.
Athletics Interscholastic: basketball (boys, girls), cross-country running (b,g), golf (b,g), marksmanship (b,g), riflery (b,g), soccer (b,g), swimming and diving (b,g), tennis (b,g), track and field (b,g), volleyball (b,g); intramural: basketball (b,g), cross-country running (b,g), physical fitness (b,g), physical training (b,g), scuba diving

(b,g), soccer (b,g), softball (b,g), volleyball (b,g), weight lifting (b,g); coed interscholastic: riflery; coed intramural: baseball, basketball, combined training, dance, flag football, floor hockey, football, jogging, kickball, physical fitness, physical training, running, scuba diving, self defense, soccer, softball, volleyball, weight lifting, yoga. 1 PE instructor, 11 coaches.

Computers Computers are regularly used in business, data processing, desktop publishing, English, history, information technology, introduction to technology, mathematics classes. Computer network features include on-campus library services, Internet access, wireless campus network. Student e-mail accounts are available to students. Students grades are available online.

Contact Mr. Sean Magoun, Admission Director. 808-246-0233 Ext. 241. Fax: 808-245-6053. E-mail: sean@ischool.org. Web site: www.ischool.org.

JACK M. BARRACK HEBREW ACADEMY (FORMERLY AKIBA HEBREW ACADEMY)
272 South Bryn Mawr Avenue
Bryn Mawr, Pennsylvania 19010
Head of School: Dr. Steven M. Brown

General Information Coeducational day college-preparatory and religious studies school, affiliated with Jewish faith. Grades 6–12. Founded: 1946. Setting: suburban. Nearest major city is Philadelphia. 35-acre campus. 2 buildings on campus. Approved or accredited by Middle States Association of Colleges and Schools and Pennsylvania Department of Education. Member of National Association of Independent Schools. Languages of instruction: English and Hebrew. Total enrollment: 315. Upper school average class size: 16. Upper school faculty-student ratio: 1:16. There are 168 required school days per year for Upper School students. Upper School students typically attend 5 days per week. The average school day consists of 7 hours.

Upper School Student Profile Grade 9: 56 students (22 boys, 34 girls); Grade 10: 53 students (21 boys, 32 girls); Grade 11: 53 students (18 boys, 35 girls); Grade 12: 59 students (25 boys, 34 girls). 100% of students are Jewish.

Faculty School total: 55. In upper school: 18 men, 30 women; 40 have advanced degrees.

Subjects Offered Algebra, American history, American literature, art, astronomy, Bible studies, biology, calculus, chemistry, community service, computer math, computer programming, computer science, creative writing, earth science, English, English literature, environmental science, environmental science-AP, ethics, European history, French, geometry, government/civics, grammar, health, Hebrew, history, Jewish studies, Latin, mathematics, music, physical education, physics, public speaking, religion, science, social studies, Spanish, trigonometry, world history, writing.

Graduation Requirements English, foreign language, mathematics, physical education (includes health), religion (includes Bible studies and theology), science, social studies (includes history), senior community service project: 150 hours in the senior year in, order to graduate.

Special Academic Programs 8 Advanced Placement exams for which test preparation is offered; accelerated programs; independent study; term-away projects; study at local college for college credit; study abroad; academic accommodation for the gifted; remedial reading and/or remedial writing; remedial math; special instructional classes for deaf students.

College Admission Counseling 56 students graduated in 2009; all went to college, including Brandeis University; New York University; University of Maryland, College Park; University of Pennsylvania; University of Pittsburgh. Median SAT critical reading: 650, median SAT math: 650, median SAT writing: 650.

Student Life Upper grades have specified standards of dress, student council. Discipline rests primarily with faculty.

Tuition and Aid Day student tuition: $23,700. Tuition installment plan (Key Tuition Payment Plan, monthly payment plans, individually arranged payment plans). Merit scholarship grants, need-based scholarship grants available. In 2009–10, 44% of upper-school students received aid; total upper-school merit-scholarship money awarded: $40,000. Total amount of financial aid awarded in 2009–10: $1,500,000.

Admissions Traditional secondary-level entrance grade is 9. For fall 2009, 96 students applied for upper-level admission, 83 were accepted, 74 enrolled. ISEE required. Deadline for receipt of application materials: none. Application fee required: $75. On-campus interview required.

Athletics Interscholastic: baseball (boys), basketball (b,g), soccer (b,g), softball (g), tennis (b,g), track and field (g); intramural: basketball (b,g), field hockey (b,g), golf (b,g), lacrosse (g), running (b,g), soccer (b,g), track and field (g), volleyball (b,g); coed interscholastic: cross-country running, soccer, swimming and diving. 2 PE instructors, 16 coaches.

Computers Computers are regularly used in foreign language, French, health, history, humanities, independent study, information technology, introduction to technology, journalism, keyboarding, Latin, library, literary magazine, mathematics, media production, multimedia, news writing, newspaper, photojournalism, programming, publications, remedial study skills, research skills, SAT preparation, science, social sciences, Spanish, study skills, technology, video film production, Web site design, word processing, writing, yearbook classes. Computer network features include on-campus library services, online commercial services, Internet access, wireless campus network, Internet filtering or blocking technology. Campus intranet,

student e-mail accounts, and computer access in designated common areas are available to students. Students grades are available online. The school has a published electronic and media policy.

Contact Vivian Young, Director of Admissions. 610-922-2350. Fax: 610-922-2301. E-mail: vyoung@jbha.org. Web site: www.jbha.org.

JACKSON ACADEMY
4908 Ridgewood Road
PO Box 14978
Jackson, Mississippi 39236-4978
Head of School: Dr. Pat Taylor

General Information Coeducational day college-preparatory and technology school. Grades PK–12. Founded: 1959. Setting: urban. 48-acre campus. 6 buildings on campus. Approved or accredited by Canadian Council of Montessori Administrators, Mississippi Private School Association, Southern Association of Colleges and Schools, and Southern Association of Independent Schools. Member of National Association of Independent Schools. Endowment: $100,500. Total enrollment: 1,271. Upper school average class size: 21. Upper school faculty-student ratio: 1:15. There are 178 required school days per year for Upper School students. Upper School students typically attend 5 days per week. The average school day consists of 6 hours and 45 minutes.

Upper School Student Profile Grade 9: 88 students (37 boys, 51 girls); Grade 10: 80 students (48 boys, 32 girls); Grade 11: 85 students (47 boys, 38 girls); Grade 12: 87 students (42 boys, 45 girls).

Faculty School total: 100. In upper school: 15 men, 30 women; 20 have advanced degrees.

Subjects Offered Accounting, algebra, American government, American history, American history-AP, American literature, anatomy and physiology, art, art history, band, Bible, biology, biology-AP, calculus, calculus-AP, chemistry, chemistry-AP, chorus, computer applications, computer programming, creative writing, driver education, economics, English, English language-AP, English literature, English literature-AP, film history, forensics, French, geography, geometry, Latin, physical education, physical science, physics, physics-AP, pre-calculus, sociology, Spanish, speech, state government, studio art, U.S. government and politics-AP, world history, world literature.

Graduation Requirements Electives, English, foreign language, mathematics, science, social studies (includes history).

Special Academic Programs Advanced Placement exam preparation; honors section; independent study; study at local college for college credit.

College Admission Counseling 98 students graduated in 2009; 97 went to college, including Belhaven University; Millsaps College; Mississippi College; Mississippi State University; University of Mississippi; Vanderbilt University. Other: 1 had other specific plans. Median SAT critical reading: 650, median SAT math: 650, median SAT writing: 650, median combined SAT: 1860, median composite ACT: 30. 49% scored over 600 on SAT critical reading, 71% scored over 600 on SAT math, 60% scored over 600 on SAT writing, 62% scored over 1800 on combined SAT.

Student Life Upper grades have uniform requirement, student council. Discipline rests primarily with faculty.

Tuition and Aid Day student tuition: $10,380. Tuition installment plan (monthly bank draft, biannual payment plan). Tuition reduction for siblings, need-based scholarship grants available. In 2009–10, 13% of upper-school students received aid. Total amount of financial aid awarded in 2009–10: $145,881.

Admissions Traditional secondary-level entrance grade is 10. For fall 2009, 18 students applied for upper-level admission, 16 were accepted, 14 enrolled. Otis-Lennon, Stanford Achievement Test required. Deadline for receipt of application materials: none. Application fee required: $50. On-campus interview required.

Athletics Interscholastic: baseball (boys), basketball (b,g), cheering (g), cross-country running (b,g), drill team (g), football (b), golf (b,g), soccer (b,g), softball (g), tennis (b,g), track and field (b,g); intramural: basketball (b,g); coed interscholastic: outdoor activities, swimming and diving. 1 PE instructor, 5 coaches.

Computers Computers are regularly used in English, history, mathematics, publishing, science classes. Computer network features include on-campus library services, Internet access, Internet filtering or blocking technology. Students grades are available online.

Contact Mrs. Linda C. Purviance, Director of Admissions. 601-362-9677. Fax: 601-364-5722. E-mail: lpurviance@jacksonacademy.org. Web site: www.jacksonacademy.org.

JACKSON CHRISTIAN SCHOOL
832 Country Club Lane
Jackson, Tennessee 38305
Head of School: Dr. Rick Brooks

General Information Coeducational day college-preparatory, arts, religious studies, bilingual studies, and technology school, affiliated with Church of Christ. Grades JK–12. Founded: 1976. Setting: suburban. 30-acre campus. 6 buildings on campus. Approved or accredited by National Christian School Association, Southern Association of Colleges and Schools, and Tennessee Department of Education. Endowment: $875,000. Total enrollment: 857. Upper school average class size: 19.

Upper school faculty-student ratio: 1:19. There are 180 required school days per year for Upper School students. Upper School students typically attend 5 days per week. The average school day consists of 6 hours.

Upper School Student Profile Grade 6: 86 students (39 boys, 47 girls); Grade 7: 72 students (41 boys, 31 girls); Grade 8: 58 students (30 boys, 28 girls); Grade 9: 79 students (40 boys, 39 girls); Grade 10: 60 students (28 boys, 32 girls); Grade 11: 77 students (38 boys, 39 girls); Grade 12: 70 students (40 boys, 30 girls). 34% of students are members of Church of Christ.

Faculty School total: 65. In upper school: 14 men, 24 women; 13 have advanced degrees.

Subjects Offered ACT preparation, advanced chemistry, advanced computer applications, advanced studio art-AP, algebra, American government, American history, anatomy and physiology, art, baseball, basketball, Bible, Bible studies, biology, calculus, chemistry, choir, chorus, current events, ecology, economics, English, English composition, geometry, government, government/civics, honors English, journalism, keyboarding, life science, physical education, physical science, physics, pre-calculus, psychology, Spanish, state history, theater, theater arts, trigonometry, U.S. government, U.S. history, word processing, world geography, world history.

Graduation Requirements 20th century world history, 3-dimensional art, 3-dimensional design, ACT preparation, arts and fine arts (art, music, dance, drama), English, foreign language, mathematics, physical education (includes health), religion (includes Bible studies and theology), science, social studies (includes history), must take the ACT test.

Special Academic Programs Honors section; study at local college for college credit; programs in English, mathematics for dyslexic students.

College Admission Counseling 81 students graduated in 2010; 79 went to college, including Freed-Hardeman University; Harding University; Jackson State Community College; Middle Tennessee State University; The University of Tennessee; Union University. Other: 2 went to work. Median composite ACT: 24. 35% scored over 26 on composite ACT.

Student Life Upper grades have uniform requirement, student council, honor system. Discipline rests primarily with faculty.

Summer Programs Remediation programs offered; session focuses on make-up failed courses; held on campus; accepts boys and girls; not open to students from other schools. 8 students usually enrolled. 2011 schedule: June to July.

Tuition and Aid Day student tuition: $7200. Guaranteed tuition plan. Tuition installment plan (monthly payment plans, individually arranged payment plans, quarterly payment plan, semester payment plan, pay-in-full discount). Tuition reduction for siblings, need-based scholarship grants available. In 2010–11, 15% of upper-school students received aid. Total amount of financial aid awarded in 2010–11: $15,218.

Admissions Traditional secondary-level entrance grade is 9. For fall 2010, 40 students applied for upper-level admission, 32 were accepted, 31 enrolled. Math and English placement tests required. Deadline for receipt of application materials: none. Application fee required: $100. Interview required.

Athletics Interscholastic: baseball (boys), basketball (b,g), cheering (g), cross-country running (b,g), football (b), golf (b,g), soccer (b,g), softball (g), tennis (b,g), track and field (b,g); coed interscholastic: cheering. 3 PE instructors, 10 coaches.

Computers Computers are regularly used in business applications, computer applications, desktop publishing, library, multimedia, programming, science, Web site design classes. Computer network features include online commercial services, Internet access, wireless campus network, Internet filtering or blocking technology. Campus intranet, student e-mail accounts, and computer access in designated common areas are available to students. Students grades are available online.

Contact Chris Brush, Director of Admissions. 731-668-8055. Fax: 731-668-8055. E-mail: cbrush@jcseagles.org. Web site: www.jcseagles.org.

JACKSON PREPARATORY SCHOOL

3100 Lakeland Drive
Jackson, Mississippi 39232
Head of School: Susan R. Lindsay

General Information Coeducational day college-preparatory school. Grades 6–12. Founded: 1970. Setting: urban. 74-acre campus. 6 buildings on campus. Approved or accredited by Mississippi Private School Association, Southern Association of Colleges and Schools, Southern Association of Independent Schools, and The College Board. Member of National Association of Independent Schools. Endowment: $993,373. Total enrollment: 801. Upper school average class size: 16. Upper school faculty-student ratio: 1:13. There are 176 required school days per year for Upper School students. Upper School students typically attend 5 days per week. The average school day consists of 6 hours and 45 minutes.

Upper School Student Profile Grade 10: 126 students (68 boys, 58 girls); Grade 11: 142 students (68 boys, 74 girls); Grade 12: 122 students (67 boys, 55 girls).

Faculty School total: 90. In upper school: 26 men, 47 women; 42 have advanced degrees.

Subjects Offered Accounting, advanced chemistry, Advanced Placement courses, algebra, American government, American history, American history-AP, American literature, art, Asian studies, Bible as literature, biology, biology-AP, British literature, calculus, calculus-AP, chemistry, chemistry-AP, choral music, civics, classical studies, computer science, creative writing, debate, discrete mathematics, drama, driver education, earth science, economics, English, English literature, English literature-AP,

European history, film, fine arts, finite math, French, geography, geometry, government-AP, government/civics, grammar, Greek, Greek culture, history, honors algebra, honors English, honors geometry, journalism, Latin, Latin-AP, mathematics, music, physical education, physics, physics-AP, pre-algebra, pre-calculus, science, social studies, Spanish, trigonometry, U.S. government, U.S. government and politics-AP, U.S. history, U.S. history-AP, world history, world literature.

Graduation Requirements Arts and fine arts (art, music, dance, drama), computer applications, English, foreign language, mathematics, science, social studies (includes history).

Special Academic Programs Advanced Placement exam preparation; honors section; academic accommodation for the gifted, the musically talented, and the artistically talented; programs in English, mathematics, general development for dyslexic students.

College Admission Counseling 98 students graduated in 2010; all went to college, including Louisiana State University in Shreveport; Mississippi State University; The University of Alabama; University of Mississippi. Mean SAT critical reading: 632, mean SAT math: 624, mean SAT writing: 614, mean composite ACT: 26.

Student Life Upper grades have uniform requirement, student council, honor system. Discipline rests primarily with faculty.

Summer Programs Remediation, enrichment, art/fine arts, computer instruction programs offered; session focuses on enrichment; held on campus; accepts boys and girls; open to students from other schools. 200 students usually enrolled. 2011 schedule: June 7 to July 16. Application deadline: May 1.

Tuition and Aid Day student tuition: $10,750. Tuition installment plan (monthly payment plans). Need-based scholarship grants available. In 2010–11, 12% of upper-school students received aid. Total amount of financial aid awarded in 2010–11: $195,000.

Admissions Traditional secondary-level entrance grade is 10. For fall 2010, 26 students applied for upper-level admission, 18 were accepted, 16 enrolled. Non-standardized placement tests and OLSAT, Stanford Achievement Test required. Deadline for receipt of application materials: none. Application fee required: $40. Interview required.

Athletics Interscholastic: baseball (boys), basketball (b,g), cheering (g), cross-country running (b,g), dance team (g), football (b), Frisbee (b), soccer (b,g), softball (g), swimming and diving (b,g), tennis (b,g), track and field (b,g), ultimate Frisbee (b); intramural: basketball (b,g), Frisbee (b), soccer (b,g), volleyball (b,g); coed interscholastic: cheering, golf. 4 coaches.

Computers Computers are regularly used in all classes. Computer network features include on-campus library services, online commercial services, Internet access, Electric Library, EBSCOhost®, GaleNet, Grolier Online, NewsBank, online subscription services. The school has a published electronic and media policy.

Contact Lesley W. Morton, Director of Admission. 601-932-8106 Ext. 1. Fax: 601-936-4068. E-mail: lmorton@jacksonprep.net. Web site: www.jacksonprep.net.

JESUIT COLLEGE PREPARATORY SCHOOL

12345 Inwood Road
Dallas, Texas 75244
Head of School: Mr. Mike Earsing

General Information Boys' day college-preparatory school, affiliated with Roman Catholic Church (Jesuit order). Grades 9–12. Founded: 1942. Setting: suburban. 27-acre campus. 2 buildings on campus. Approved or accredited by Jesuit Secondary Education Association, National Catholic Education Association, Southern Association of Colleges and Schools, Texas Catholic Conference, and Texas Department of Education. Endowment: $25.6 million. Total enrollment: 1,064. Upper school average class size: 17. Upper school faculty-student ratio: 1:11. There are 190 required school days per year for Upper School students. Upper School students typically attend 5 days per week. The average school day consists of 6 hours.

Upper School Student Profile Grade 9: 272 students (272 boys); Grade 10: 270 students (270 boys); Grade 11: 270 students (270 boys); Grade 12: 252 students (252 boys). 80.5% of students are Roman Catholic Church (Jesuit order).

Faculty School total: 115. In upper school: 85 men, 30 women; 56 have advanced degrees.

Subjects Offered Advanced chemistry, advanced computer applications, advanced math, American literature-AP, American studies, art, art appreciation, art-AP, arts, band, Bible, biology, biology-AP, British literature, British literature-AP, calculus, calculus-AP, Catholic belief and practice, ceramics, chemistry, chemistry-AP, choir, Christian ethics, church history, civics, college counseling, community service, composition, composition-AP, computer applications, computer graphics, computer science, computer science-AP, contemporary issues, discrete mathematics, drama, drama performance, drama workshop, drawing, drawing and design, driver education, earth science, economics, economics-AP, English, English composition, English language and composition-AP, English language-AP, English literature, English literature and composition-AP, English literature-AP, English-AP, English/composition-AP, ethical decision making, European history, fine arts, French, French-AP, general science, geometry, government, government-AP, grammar, guitar, health, history, history-AP, honors algebra, honors English, honors geometry, honors U.S. history, honors world history, instrumental music, jazz band, journalism, Latin, literature and composition-AP, marching band, mathematics, mathematics-AP, microcomputer technology applications, music, music appreciation, musical productions, orchestra, peace and justice, peer ministry, performing arts, physical education, physics, physics-AP, pottery, prayer/spirituality, pre-calculus, psychology, public speaking, publications, religion, scripture, social studies, Spanish, Spanish language-AP, Spanish literature-AP, Spanish-AP, speech, speech and debate, speech and oral interpretations, statistics, student government, student publications, studio art, studio art-AP, symphonic band, theater, theology, U.S. government, U.S. government and politics-AP, U.S. history, U.S. history-AP, U.S. literature, world history, world history-AP.

Graduation Requirements Arts and fine arts (art, music, dance, drama), computer science, English, foreign language, mathematics, physical education (includes health), science, social studies (includes history), theology. Community service is required.

Special Academic Programs 18 Advanced Placement exams for which test preparation is offered; honors section; independent study; study at local college for college credit.

College Admission Counseling 248 students graduated in 2010; 246 went to college, including Saint Louis University; Southern Methodist University; Texas A&M University; Texas Christian University; The University of Alabama; The University of Texas at Austin. Other: 2 had other specific plans. Mean SAT critical reading: 598, mean SAT math: 618, mean SAT writing: 595.

Student Life Upper grades have specified standards of dress, student council, honor system. Discipline rests primarily with faculty. Attendance at religious services is required.

Summer Programs Remediation, enrichment, advancement, sports, art/fine arts, computer instruction programs offered; session focuses on youth recreation; held on campus; accepts boys and girls; open to students from other schools. 800 students usually enrolled. 2011 schedule: June 15 to July 10. Application deadline: May 30.

Tuition and Aid Day student tuition: $13,200. Tuition installment plan (FACTS Tuition Payment Plan, individually arranged payment plans). Merit scholarship grants, need-based scholarship grants, paying campus jobs available. In 2010–11, 25% of upper-school students received aid; total upper-school merit-scholarship money awarded: $56,000. Total amount of financial aid awarded in 2010–11: $1,233,850.

Admissions Traditional secondary-level entrance grade is 9. For fall 2010, 484 students applied for upper-level admission, 318 were accepted, 274 enrolled. ISEE required. Deadline for receipt of application materials: January 7. Application fee required: $75. Interview required.

Athletics Interscholastic: baseball, basketball, bowling, crew, cross-country running, diving, fencing, football, golf, ice hockey, lacrosse, power lifting, rugby, soccer, swimming and diving, tennis, track and field, water polo, wrestling; intramural: basketball, bicycling, broomball, flagball, floor hockey, indoor soccer, ultimate Frisbee, volleyball; coed interscholastic: cheering, drill team. 6 PE instructors, 30 coaches, 2 athletic trainers.

Computers Computers are regularly used in college planning, desktop publishing, digital applications, engineering, English, foreign language, graphic design, graphics, humanities, introduction to technology, journalism, literary magazine, mathematics, media production, multimedia, newspaper, programming, publications, science, social studies, technology, video film production, Web site design, writing, yearbook classes. Computer network features include on-campus library services, online commercial services, Internet access, wireless campus network, Internet filtering or blocking technology. Campus intranet, student e-mail accounts, and computer access in designated common areas are available to students. Students grades are available online. The school has a published electronic and media policy.

Contact Mrs. Susie Herrmann, Admissions Assistant. 972-387-8700 Ext. 453. Fax: 972-980-6707. E-mail: sherrmann@jesuitcp.org. Web site: www.jesuitcp.org.

JESUIT HIGH SCHOOL

1200 Jacob Lane
Carmichael, California 95608
Head of School: Ms. Brianna Latko

General Information Boys' day college-preparatory and religious studies school, affiliated with Roman Catholic Church. Grades 9–12. Founded: 1963. Setting: suburban. Nearest major city is Sacramento. 46-acre campus. 12 buildings on campus. Approved or accredited by Jesuit Secondary Education Association, National Catholic Education Association, Western Association of Schools and Colleges, and California Department of Education. Member of Secondary School Admission Test Board. Total enrollment: 1,076. Upper school average class size: 25. Upper school faculty-student ratio: 1:18.

Upper School Student Profile Grade 9: 279 students (279 boys); Grade 10: 264 students (264 boys); Grade 11: 274 students (274 boys); Grade 12: 259 students (259 boys). 80% of students are Roman Catholic.

Faculty School total: 81. In upper school: 58 men, 23 women; 48 have advanced degrees.

Subjects Offered Advanced Placement courses, algebra, American history, American literature, art, art history, arts, biology, business, calculus, chemistry, computer programming, computer science, drama, driver education, earth science, economics, English, English literature, environmental science, ethics, European history, fine arts, French, geography, geometry, German, government/civics, grammar, health, history, honors algebra, honors English, honors U.S. history, journalism, Latin, mathematics, music, music theory-AP, physical education, physics, pre-calculus, religion, science, social justice, social sciences, social studies, Spanish, speech, studio art, theater, theology, trigonometry, typing, U.S. government and politics-AP, U.S. history-AP, world history, world literature, writing.

Graduation Requirements Arts and fine arts (art, music, dance, drama), English, foreign language, mathematics, physical education (includes health), science, social studies (includes history), theology, 60 hours of community service.

Special Academic Programs Advanced Placement exam preparation; honors section.

College Admission Counseling 252 students graduated in 2009; 247 went to college, including California Polytechnic State University, San Luis Obispo; California State University, Sacramento; Loyola Marymount University; Santa Clara University; University of California System; University of Southern California. Other: 2 went to work, 3 entered military service. Mean SAT critical reading: 574, mean SAT math: 592, mean SAT writing: 577, mean composite ACT: 24.

Student Life Upper grades have specified standards of dress, student council, honor system. Discipline rests primarily with faculty. Attendance at religious services is required.

Tuition and Aid Day student tuition: $11,510. Tuition installment plan (monthly payment plans). Need-based scholarship grants, paying campus jobs available. In 2009–10, 15% of upper-school students received aid. Total amount of financial aid awarded in 2009–10: $740,000.

Admissions Traditional secondary-level entrance grade is 9. For fall 2009, 465 students applied for upper-level admission, 290 were accepted, 280 enrolled. High School Placement Test required. Deadline for receipt of application materials: February 5. Application fee required: $30. On-campus interview required.

Athletics Interscholastic: baseball, basketball, cross-country running, diving, football, golf, lacrosse, rugby, soccer, swimming and diving, tennis, track and field, volleyball, water polo, wrestling; intramural: baseball, basketball, bowling, football, soccer, volleyball. 6 PE instructors, 15 coaches, 1 athletic trainer.

Computers Computers are regularly used in English, mathematics, social studies classes. Computer resources include on-campus library services, online commercial services, Internet access.

Contact Mr. Gerry Lane, Director of Admissions. 916-482-6060 Ext. 227. Fax: 916-482-2310. E-mail: admissions@jhssac.org. Web site: www.jhssac.org.

JESUIT HIGH SCHOOL OF NEW ORLEANS

4133 Banks Street
New Orleans, Louisiana 70119-6883
Head of School: Fr. Anthony McGinn, SJ

General Information Boys' day college-preparatory school, affiliated with Roman Catholic Church. Grades 8–12. Founded: 1847. Setting: urban. Nearest major city is Baton Rouge. 8-acre campus. 3 buildings on campus. Approved or accredited by Jesuit Secondary Education Association, National Catholic Education Association, Southern Association of Colleges and Schools, and Louisiana Department of Education. Endowment: $17.5 million. Total enrollment: 1,346. Upper school average class size: 22. Upper school faculty-student ratio: 1:12. There are 180 required school days per year for Upper School students. Upper School students typically attend 5 days per week. The average school day consists of 5 hours and 30 minutes.

Upper School Student Profile Grade 9: 279 students (279 boys); Grade 10: 271 students (271 boys); Grade 11: 270 students (270 boys); Grade 12: 267 students (267 boys). 88% of students are Roman Catholic.

Faculty School total: 110. In upper school: 74 men, 36 women; 57 have advanced degrees.

Subjects Offered Algebra, American history, American literature, analysis, art history, arts, band, Bible studies, biology, biology-AP, calculus, calculus-AP, chemistry, chemistry-AP, Christianity, church history, civics, community service, comparative government and politics-AP, computer applications, computer literacy, computer programming, computer science, creative writing, economics, English, English literature, English literature and composition-AP, environmental science, fine arts, French, French language-AP, geography, geometry, government/civics, grammar, Greek, health, history, JROTC, Latin, Latin-AP, law, mathematics, military history, military science, music, physical education, physical science, physics, physics-AP, politics, psychology, public speaking, religion, ROTC (for boys), SAT/ACT preparation, science, scripture, social studies, sociology, Spanish, Spanish language-AP, speech, study skills, theology, trigonometry, U.S. government and politics-AP, U.S. history-AP, Western civilization, world literature, writing.

Graduation Requirements Arts and fine arts (art, music, dance, drama), computer science, English, foreign language, mathematics, physical education (includes health), religion (includes Bible studies and theology), science, social sciences, social studies (includes history), speech. Community service is required.

Special Academic Programs Advanced Placement exam preparation; honors section.

College Admission Counseling 259 students graduated in 2010; 254 went to college, including Louisiana State University and Agricultural and Mechanical College; Loyola University New Orleans; The University of Alabama; University of Louisiana at Lafayette; University of New Orleans. Other: 2 entered military service, 3 had other specific plans. Median SAT critical reading: 600, median SAT math: 610, median SAT writing: 590, median combined SAT: 1790, median composite ACT: 26. 65% scored over 600 on SAT critical reading, 69% scored over 600 on SAT math, 69% scored over 600 on SAT writing, 67% scored over 1800 on combined SAT, 50% scored over 26 on composite ACT.

Student Life Upper grades have uniform requirement, student council, honor system. Discipline rests primarily with faculty. Attendance at religious services is required.

Summer Programs Enrichment programs offered; held on campus; accepts boys; not open to students from other schools. 120 students usually enrolled. 2011 schedule: May 31 to July 1. Application deadline: May 27.

Tuition and Aid Day student tuition: $7000. Tuition installment plan (monthly payment plans, individually arranged payment plans, Monthly, quarterly as arranged with parents on an individual basis.). Need-based scholarship grants, paying campus jobs available. In 2010–11, 8% of upper-school students received aid. Total amount of financial aid awarded in 2010–11: $371,265.

Admissions Traditional secondary-level entrance grade is 9. For fall 2010, 89 students applied for upper-level admission, 66 were accepted, 47 enrolled. High School Placement Test required. Deadline for receipt of application materials: January 12. Application fee required: $20.

Athletics Interscholastic: baseball, basketball, bowling, cross-country running, football, golf, in-line hockey, indoor track & field, JROTC drill, lacrosse, marksmanship, physical fitness, riflery, rugby, soccer, swimming and diving, tennis, track and field, wrestling; intramural: baseball, basketball, bicycling, bowling, cheering, flag football, football, Frisbee, golf, table tennis, touch football. 9 PE instructors, 41 coaches, 1 athletic trainer.

Computers Computers are regularly used in library skills, mathematics, reading, science, yearbook classes. Computer network features include on-campus library services, online commercial services, Internet access, Internet filtering or blocking technology. Computer access in designated common areas is available to students. The school has a published electronic and media policy.

Contact Mr. Jack S. Truxillo, Director of Admissions. 504-483-3936. Fax: 504-483-3942. E-mail: truxillo@jesuitnola.org. Web site: www.jesuitnola.org.

JESUIT HIGH SCHOOL OF TAMPA
4701 North Himes Avenue
Tampa, Florida 33614-6694
Head of School: Mr. Joseph Sabin

General Information Boys' day college-preparatory school, affiliated with Roman Catholic Church. Grades 9–12. Founded: 1899. Setting: urban. 40-acre campus. 9 buildings on campus. Approved or accredited by Jesuit Secondary Education Association, National Catholic Education Association, Southern Association of Colleges and Schools, and Florida Department of Education. Total enrollment: 709. Upper school average class size: 24. Upper school faculty-student ratio: 1:13. There are 175 required school days per year for Upper School students. Upper School students typically attend 5 days per week. The average school day consists of 7 hours and 23 minutes.

Upper School Student Profile Grade 9: 196 students (196 boys); Grade 10: 191 students (191 boys); Grade 11: 170 students (170 boys); Grade 12: 152 students (152 boys). 75% of students are Roman Catholic.

Faculty School total: 55. In upper school: 40 men, 15 women; 40 have advanced degrees.

Subjects Offered Algebra, American foreign policy, American government, American history, analytic geometry, anatomy, art, biology, calculus, calculus-AP, chemistry, chemistry-AP, chorus, computer science, economics, English, English language and composition-AP, English literature and composition-AP, ethics, European history, French, geometry, global studies, health, Latin, marine biology, math analysis, music, physical education, physics, physics-AP, physiology, pre-calculus, psychology, Spanish, Spanish language-AP, speech, studio art-AP, theology, trigonometry, U.S. government and politics-AP, U.S. history-AP, world history, world history-AP, writing.

Graduation Requirements Arts and fine arts (art, music, dance, drama), English, foreign language, mathematics, physical education (includes health), science, social studies (includes history), theology, 150 hours of community service (additional 20 hours for National Honor Society members).

Special Academic Programs 10 Advanced Placement exams for which test preparation is offered; honors section.

College Admission Counseling 149 students graduated in 2010; all went to college, including Florida Gulf Coast University; Florida State University; Georgia Institute of Technology; University of Florida; University of South Florida. Mean SAT critical reading: 600, mean SAT math: 610, mean SAT writing: 590, mean combined SAT: 1800, mean composite ACT: 26.

Student Life Upper grades have specified standards of dress, student council. Discipline rests primarily with faculty. Attendance at religious services is required.

Summer Programs Remediation programs offered; session focuses on remediation only; held on campus; accepts boys; not open to students from other schools. 2011 schedule: June 13 to July 15.

Tuition and Aid Day student tuition: $12,000. Tuition installment plan (FACTS Tuition Payment Plan). Need-based scholarship grants available. In 2010–11, 25% of upper-school students received aid. Total amount of financial aid awarded in 2010–11: $1,200,000.

Admissions Traditional secondary-level entrance grade is 9. For fall 2010, 349 students applied for upper-level admission, 305 were accepted, 196 enrolled. High School Placement Test (closed version) from Scholastic Testing Service required. Deadline for receipt of application materials: January 8. Application fee required: $50.

Athletics Interscholastic: baseball, basketball, bowling, cross-country running, diving, football, golf, soccer, swimming and diving, tennis, track and field, wrestling; intramural: basketball, football, Frisbee, ice hockey, lacrosse, sailing, softball, ultimate Frisbee. 2 PE instructors, 1 athletic trainer.

Computers Computer network features include on-campus library services, online commercial services, Internet access, Internet filtering or blocking technology. Campus intranet and computer access in designated common areas are available to students. Students grades are available online. The school has a published electronic and media policy.

Contact Mr. Steve Matesich, Director of Admissions. 813-877-5344 Ext. 509. Fax: 813-872-1853. E-mail: smatesich@jesuittampa.org. Web site: www.jesuittampa.org.

J. K. MULLEN HIGH SCHOOL
3601 South Lowell Boulevard
Denver, Colorado 80236
Head of School: Mrs. Linda Brady

General Information Coeducational day college-preparatory school, affiliated with Roman Catholic Church. Grades 9–12. Founded: 1931. Setting: suburban. 38-acre campus. 7 buildings on campus. Approved or accredited by Christian Brothers Association, North Central Association of Colleges and Schools, and Colorado Department of Education. Total enrollment: 1,010. Upper school average class size: 24. Upper school faculty-student ratio: 1:17.

Upper School Student Profile Grade 9: 265 students (143 boys, 122 girls); Grade 10: 250 students (115 boys, 135 girls); Grade 11: 250 students (123 boys, 127 girls); Grade 12: 245 students (116 boys, 129 girls). 70% of students are Roman Catholic.

Faculty School total: 60. In upper school: 32 men, 28 women; 40 have advanced degrees.

Subjects Offered 3-dimensional art, 3-dimensional design, accounting, advanced chemistry, advanced computer applications, advanced math, algebra, analysis and differential calculus, anatomy, art, Basic programming, Bible as literature, Bible studies, biology, British literature, British literature (honors), British literature-AP, business, calculus, calculus-AP, cartooning/animation, chemistry, choir, comparative religion, computer animation, computer applications, computer graphics, computer math, computer programming, computer science, computer-aided design, CPR, creative writing, debate, drafting, drama, ecology, economics, English, English literature, ethics, European history, expository writing, first aid, French, geography, geology, geometry, German, government, government/civics, grammar, health, history, history of the Catholic Church, honors algebra, honors English, honors geometry, honors U.S. history, honors world history, human relations, human sexuality, law studies, leadership, mathematics, mechanical drawing, music, mythology, philosophy, physical education, physical science, physics, physiology, pre-calculus, probability and statistics, psychology, religion, scripture, Shakespeare, social studies, Spanish, Spanish language-AP, Spanish literature-AP, speech, speech and debate, street law, student publications, theology, trigonometry, U.S. government, U.S. government and politics-AP, U.S. history, U.S. history-AP, U.S. literature, weight fitness, world geography, world history, world literature, writing.

Graduation Requirements English, foreign language, mathematics, physical education (includes health), religion (includes Bible studies and theology), science, social sciences, social studies (includes history), speech, 70 hours of community service.

Special Academic Programs Advanced Placement exam preparation; honors section; independent study; academic accommodation for the gifted; remedial reading and/or remedial writing.

College Admission Counseling 241 students graduated in 2010; all went to college, including Colorado School of Mines; Colorado State University; Creighton University; University of Colorado at Boulder; University of Northern Colorado. Mean SAT critical reading: 568, mean SAT math: 555, mean composite ACT: 24.

Student Life Upper grades have uniform requirement, student council. Attendance at religious services is required.

Tuition and Aid Day student tuition: $9250. Tuition installment plan (monthly payment plans, individually arranged payment plans). Tuition reduction for siblings, merit scholarship grants, need-based scholarship grants available. In 2010–11, 33% of upper-school students received aid; total upper-school merit-scholarship money awarded: $30,000. Total amount of financial aid awarded in 2010–11: $808,000.

Admissions Traditional secondary-level entrance grade is 9. For fall 2010, 530 students applied for upper-level admission, 310 were accepted, 281 enrolled. High School Placement Test required. Deadline for receipt of application materials: none. No application fee required. On-campus interview required.

Athletics Interscholastic: baseball (boys), basketball (b,g), cheering (g), cross-country running (b,g), diving (b,g), football (b), golf (b,g), ice hockey (b,g), lacrosse (b,g), power lifting (b,g), running (b,g), soccer (b,g), softball (g), swimming and diving (b,g), tennis (b,g), track and field (b,g), volleyball (g), wrestling (b); intramural: bowling (b,g), skiing (downhill) (b,g), weight lifting (b,g).

Computers Computers are regularly used in art, English, foreign language, history, mathematics, science classes. Computer network features include on-campus library services, online commercial services, Internet access.

Contact Frank Cawley, Director of Admissions. 303-761-1764 Ext. 3304. Fax: 303-761-0502. E-mail: cawley@mullenhigh.com. Web site: www.mullenhigh.com.

JOHN BURROUGHS SCHOOL
755 South Price Road
St. Louis, Missouri 63124
Head of School: Andy Abbott
General Information Coeducational day college-preparatory school. Grades 7–12. Founded: 1923. Setting: suburban. 47-acre campus. 7 buildings on campus. Approved or accredited by Independent Schools Association of the Central States. Member of National Association of Independent Schools and Secondary School Admission Test Board. Endowment: $36.2 million. Total enrollment: 600. Upper school average class size: 13. Upper school faculty-student ratio: 1:7. There are 166 required school days per year for Upper School students. Upper School students typically attend 5 days per week. The average school day consists of 8 hours.
Upper School Student Profile Grade 7: 95 students (44 boys, 51 girls); Grade 8: 95 students (46 boys, 49 girls); Grade 9: 106 students (53 boys, 53 girls); Grade 10: 103 students (52 boys, 51 girls); Grade 11: 98 students (43 boys, 55 girls); Grade 12: 103 students (52 boys, 51 girls).
Faculty School total: 107. In upper school: 48 men, 59 women; 84 have advanced degrees.
Subjects Offered Acting, Advanced Placement courses, African American history, algebra, American history, American literature, Ancient Greek, ancient world history, applied arts, architectural drawing, art, art history, art history-AP, astronomy, bioethics, biology, biology-AP, calculus, calculus-AP, ceramics, chemistry, chemistry-AP, Chinese, choral music, chorus, classical language, community service, comparative religion, computer math, computer science, computer skills, computer-aided design, creative writing, dance, debate, drama, earth science, ecology, engineering, English, English literature, environmental science, environmental systems, expository writing, fine arts, finite math, foreign language, French, French language-AP, geology, geometry, German, global issues, global studies, Greek, Greek culture, health, history, home economics, honors English, industrial arts, jazz, jazz band, keyboarding, lab science, Latin, Latin-AP, mathematics, mechanical drawing, meteorology, model United Nations, music, orchestra, organic chemistry, personal finance, photography, physical education, physics, poetry, pre-algebra, pre-calculus, probability and statistics, psychology, public speaking, reading/study skills, religion, Russian, science, social sciences, social studies, Spanish, Spanish-AP, speech and debate, statistics, trigonometry, vocal music, word processing, world civilizations, world history, world literature, world religions, writing.
Graduation Requirements Arts and fine arts (art, music, dance, drama), English, foreign language, history, mathematics, performing arts, physical education (includes health), practical arts, science, Senior May project.
Special Academic Programs Advanced Placement exam preparation; honors section; independent study.
College Admission Counseling 103 students graduated in 2010; all went to college, including Harvard University; Indiana University Bloomington; Northwestern University; University of Missouri; Washington University in St. Louis; Yale University. Median SAT critical reading: 680, median SAT math: 710, median SAT writing: 710, median combined SAT: 2100, median composite ACT: 32. 88% scored over 600 on SAT critical reading, 97% scored over 600 on SAT math, 88% scored over 600 on SAT writing, 94% scored over 1800 on combined SAT, 90% scored over 26 on composite ACT.
Student Life Upper grades have student council, honor system. Discipline rests equally with students and faculty.
Tuition and Aid Day student tuition: $21,200. Tuition installment plan (monthly payment plans). Need-based scholarship grants, need-based loans available. In 2010–11, 21% of upper-school students received aid. Total amount of financial aid awarded in 2010–11: $1,892,000.
Admissions Traditional secondary-level entrance grade is 9. For fall 2010, 271 students applied for upper-level admission, 130 were accepted, 110 enrolled. SSAT required. Deadline for receipt of application materials: January 21. Application fee required: $40. On-campus interview required.
Athletics Interscholastic: baseball (boys), basketball (b,g), cheering (b,g), cross-country running (b,g), dance (b,g), dance squad (b,g), diving (b,g), field hockey (g), fitness (b,g), football (b), golf (b,g), ice hockey (b), independent competitive sports (b,g), lacrosse (b,g), modern dance (b,g), outdoor education (b,g), physical fitness (b,g), physical training (b,g), racquetball (b,g), soccer (b,g), swimming and diving (b,g), tennis (b,g), track and field (b,g), volleyball (b), water polo (b), wrestling (b), yoga (b,g); coed interscholastic: cheering, dance squad. 48 coaches, 1 athletic trainer.
Computers Computers are regularly used in all academic, animation, architecture, art, basic skills, cabinet making, college planning, current events, desktop publishing, drafting, drawing and design, industrial technology, keyboarding, lab/keyboard, library, library skills, media production, music, photography, photojournalism, remedial study skills, research skills, study skills, technical drawing, theater, video film production, Web site design, yearbook classes. Computer network features include on-campus library services, online commercial services, Internet access, wireless campus network, monitoring software. Campus intranet and computer access in designated common areas are available to students. The school has a published electronic and media policy.
Contact Caroline LaVigne, Director of Admissions and Tuition Aid. 314-993-4040. Fax: 314-567-2896. E-mail: clavigne@jburroughs.org. Web site: www.jburroughs.org.

THE JOHN COOPER SCHOOL
One John Cooper Drive
The Woodlands, Texas 77381
Head of School: Mr. Michael F. Maher
General Information Coeducational day college-preparatory, arts, and technology school. Grades PK–12. Founded: 1988. Setting: suburban. Nearest major city is Houston. 43-acre campus. 7 buildings on campus. Approved or accredited by Independent Schools Association of the Southwest. Member of National Association of Independent Schools. Endowment: $1.5 million. Total enrollment: 985. Upper school average class size: 16. Upper school faculty-student ratio: 1:12. There are 176 required school days per year for Upper School students. Upper School students typically attend 5 days per week. The average school day consists of 7 hours and 30 minutes.
Upper School Student Profile Grade 9: 92 students (43 boys, 49 girls); Grade 10: 82 students (39 boys, 43 girls); Grade 11: 81 students (39 boys, 42 girls); Grade 12: 84 students (42 boys, 42 girls).
Faculty School total: 110. In upper school: 10 men, 29 women; 31 have advanced degrees.
Subjects Offered 3-dimensional art, 3-dimensional design, acting, advanced chemistry, Advanced Placement courses, advanced studio art-AP, algebra, American history, American history-AP, American literature, anatomy and physiology, ancient history, ancient world history, art history, art history-AP, art-AP, athletics, band, biology, biology-AP, British literature, British literature (honors), business technology, calculus, calculus-AP, ceramics, character education, chemistry, chemistry-AP, choral music, college admission preparation, college counseling, college planning, comparative religion, computer art, computer information systems, computer programming, computer resources, computer science, computer science-AP, conceptual physics, concert band, concert choir, contemporary issues, creative dance, creative writing, dance, dance performance, digital imaging, digital photography, drama, drama performance, dramatic arts, drawing, economics, economics-AP, English, English literature and composition-AP, English literature-AP, environmental science, environmental studies, European history, European history-AP, filmmaking, fine arts, foreign language, French, French language-AP, French-AP, geometry, health, health and wellness, Holocaust, Holocaust studies, honors geometry, human anatomy, information technology, instrumental music, Latin, Latin-AP, linear algebra, literature-AP, modern European history-AP, modern political theory, musical theater, painting, photography, physical education, physics, physics-AP, pre-calculus, psychology, psychology-AP, Spanish, Spanish language-AP, Spanish-AP, speech, statistics-AP, student publications, symphonic band, theater, trigonometry, U.S. history-AP, video film production, volleyball, world history, world literature, world religions, yearbook.
Graduation Requirements Arts and fine arts (art, music, dance, drama), English, foreign language, mathematics, physical education (includes health), science, social studies (includes history).
Special Academic Programs 18 Advanced Placement exams for which test preparation is offered.
College Admission Counseling 81 students graduated in 2010; all went to college, including Baylor University; Columbia University; Louisiana State University and Agricultural and Mechanical College; Southern Methodist University; Texas Christian University; University of Chicago. Mean SAT critical reading: 661, mean SAT math: 674, mean SAT writing: 642, mean combined SAT: 1978, mean composite ACT: 28.
Student Life Upper grades have specified standards of dress, student council, honor system. Discipline rests primarily with faculty.
Summer Programs Enrichment, advancement, sports, art/fine arts, computer instruction programs offered; session focuses on academic enrichment; held on campus; accepts boys and girls; open to students from other schools. 980 students usually enrolled. 2011 schedule: June 1 to July 3. Application deadline: none.
Tuition and Aid Day student tuition: $18,420. Tuition installment plan (monthly payment plans, 2-part, 4-part). Need-based scholarship grants available. In 2010–11, 12% of upper-school students received aid. Total amount of financial aid awarded in 2010–11: $306,970.
Admissions Traditional secondary-level entrance grade is 9. For fall 2010, 95 students applied for upper-level admission, 49 were accepted, 41 enrolled. CTP III, ISEE, Otis-Lennon School Ability Test or writing sample required. Deadline for receipt of application materials: none. Application fee required: $125. Interview required.
Athletics Interscholastic: baseball (boys), basketball (b,g), cross-country running (b,g), golf (b,g), softball (g), swimming and diving (b,g), tennis (b,g), track and field (b,g), volleyball (g), winter soccer (b,g). 7 PE instructors, 8 coaches, 1 athletic trainer.
Computers Computers are regularly used in all academic, art, computer applications, desktop publishing, drawing and design, foreign language, journalism, media production, music, publications, video film production, Web site design, yearbook classes. Computer network features include on-campus library services, online commercial services, Internet access, wireless campus network, Internet filtering or blocking technology. Campus intranet and computer access in designated common areas are available to students. Students grades are available online. The school has a published electronic and media policy.
Contact Mr. Craig Meredith, Director of Admission. 281-367-0900 Ext. 308. Fax: 281-298-5715. E-mail: cmeredith@johncooper.org. Web site: www.johncooper.org.

346 ⓕ www.facebook.com/sec.schools

THE JOHN DEWEY ACADEMY

Great Barrington, Massachusetts
See Special Needs Schools section.

JOHN F. KENNEDY MEMORIAL HIGH SCHOOL

140 South 140th Street
Burien, Washington 98168-3496
Head of School: Mr. Michael L. Prato

General Information Coeducational boarding and day college-preparatory and religious studies school, affiliated with Roman Catholic Church. Grades 9–12. Founded: 1966. Setting: suburban. Nearest major city is Seattle. Students are housed in single-sex dormitories and one dorm for international boys. 25-acre campus. 4 buildings on campus. Approved or accredited by CITA (Commission on International and Trans-Regional Accreditation), National Catholic Education Association, Northwest Association of Schools and Colleges, and Washington Department of Education. Languages of instruction: English and Spanish. Endowment: $1.7 million. Total enrollment: 948. Upper school average class size: 23. Upper school faculty-student ratio: 1:17. The average school day consists of 6 hours.

Upper School Student Profile Grade 9: 220 students (108 boys, 112 girls); Grade 10: 231 students (123 boys, 108 girls); Grade 11: 268 students (131 boys, 137 girls); Grade 12: 229 students (122 boys, 107 girls). 2% of students are boarding students. 91% are state residents. 1 state is represented in upper school student body. 9% are international students. International students from China, Japan, Republic of Korea, Taiwan, Thailand, and Viet Nam; 5 other countries represented in student body. 70% of students are Roman Catholic.

Faculty School total: 70. In upper school: 37 men, 33 women; 25 have advanced degrees.

Subjects Offered Accounting, acting, advanced TOEFL/grammar, algebra, American sign language, art, art appreciation, art history, astronomy, basic skills, Bible, biology, business mathematics, calculus, carpentry, Catholic belief and practice, chemistry, Christian doctrine, Christian ethics, Christian scripture, clayworking, community service, comparative religion, composition-AP, computer applications, computer-aided design, concert band, concert choir, construction, contemporary issues, creative writing, current events, drafting, drama, economics, English, English composition, English language and composition-AP, English literature, ESL, ethical decision making, fiction, fine arts, French, French-AP, general business, geometry, German, health, Hebrew scripture, honors algebra, honors English, honors geometry, honors U.S. history, ideas, integrated science, interdisciplinary studies, international studies, jazz ensemble, journalism, keyboarding, language arts, Latin, Latin-AP, law, leadership, marine biology, mathematics, media, physical education, physics, public policy, public service, publications, sculpture, sign language, social justice, Spanish, speech, symphonic band, trigonometry, U.S. history, U.S. history-AP, video, Washington State and Northwest History, woodworking, world history, world religions, yearbook.

Graduation Requirements Arts and fine arts (art, music, dance, drama), English, foreign language, mathematics, physical education (includes health), religion (includes Bible studies and theology), religious education, science, social studies (includes history), culminating project, education plan (high school-college) or alternative.

Special Academic Programs International Baccalaureate program; Advanced Placement exam preparation; honors section; accelerated programs; independent study; study at local college for college credit; study abroad; academic accommodation for the gifted, the musically talented, and the artistically talented; remedial reading and/or remedial writing; remedial math; programs in English, mathematics, general development for dyslexic students; ESL (41 students enrolled).

College Admission Counseling 203 students graduated in 2009; 186 went to college, including Central Washington University; Gonzaga University; Seattle University; University of Washington; Washington State University; Western Washington University. Other: 2 went to work, 1 entered military service, 14 had other specific plans.

Student Life Upper grades have specified standards of dress, student council. Discipline rests primarily with faculty. Attendance at religious services is required.

Tuition and Aid Day student tuition: $8360–$9020; 7-day tuition and room/board: $16,800. Tuition installment plan (monthly payment plans, individually arranged payment plans). Tuition reduction for siblings, merit scholarship grants, need-based scholarship grants, paying campus jobs available. In 2009–10, 19% of upper-school students received aid; total upper-school merit-scholarship money awarded: $9780. Total amount of financial aid awarded in 2009–10: $390,000.

Admissions Traditional secondary-level entrance grade is 9. Scholastic Testing Service High School Placement Test required. Deadline for receipt of application materials: none. Application fee required: $25. Interview recommended.

Athletics Interscholastic: aquatics (boys, girls), baseball (b), basketball (b,g), cheering (g), cross-country running (b,g), diving (b,g), drill team (g), football (b), golf (b,g), gymnastics (g), soccer (b,g), softball (g), swimming and diving (b,g), tennis (b,g), track and field (b,g), volleyball (b,g), wrestling (b); intramural: basketball (b,g), combined training (b), Frisbee (b,g), physical training (b,g), scuba diving (b,g), strength & conditioning (b,g), table tennis (b,g), ultimate Frisbee (b,g), volleyball (b,g), weight lifting (b,g), weight training (b,g); coed intramural: table tennis, ultimate Frisbee. 3 PE instructors, 53 coaches, 1 athletic trainer.

Computers Computers are regularly used in English, foreign language, history, science, technology, video film production classes. Computer network features include on-campus library services, Internet access. Students grades are available online. The school has a published electronic and media policy.

Contact Mr. James Mesick, Director of Admissions, Marketing, and Public Relations. 206-246-0500 Ext. 306. Fax: 206-242-0831. E-mail: mesickj@ kennedyhs.org. Web site: www.kennedyhs.org.

JOHN PAUL II CATHOLIC HIGH SCHOOL

5100 Terrebone Drive
Tallahassee, Florida 32311-7848
Head of School: Sr. Ellen Cronan

General Information Coeducational day college-preparatory and religious studies school, affiliated with Roman Catholic Church. Grades 9–12. Founded: 2001. Setting: suburban. 37-acre campus. 3 buildings on campus. Approved or accredited by Academy of Orton-Gillingham Practitioners and Educators, Accreditation Commission of the Texas Association of Baptist Schools, American Association of Christian Schools, Arizona Association of Independent Schools, Association for Experiential Education, Association of American Schools in South America, Association of Christian Schools International, Association of Colorado Independent Schools, Association of Independent Maryland Schools, Association of Independent Schools and Colleges of Alberta, Association of Independent Schools in New England, Association of Independent Schools of Florida, Association of Independent Schools of Greater Washington, Southern Association of Colleges and Schools, and Florida Department of Education. Total enrollment: 119. Upper school average class size: 12. Upper school faculty-student ratio: 1:8. There are 180 required school days per year for Upper School students. Upper School students typically attend 5 days per week. The average school day consists of 7 hours.

Upper School Student Profile Grade 9: 30 students (11 boys, 19 girls); Grade 10: 20 students (8 boys, 12 girls); Grade 11: 32 students (14 boys, 18 girls); Grade 12: 37 students (22 boys, 15 girls). 83% of students are Roman Catholic.

Faculty School total: 16. In upper school: 5 men, 11 women; 14 have advanced degrees.

Subjects Offered All academic, Bible, English language and composition-AP, English literature and composition-AP, history of the Catholic Church, Latin, music, Spanish, Spanish language-AP, strings.

Graduation Requirements Algebra, American government, American history, biology, Christian doctrine, economics, English, fitness, foreign language, health.

Special Academic Programs 6 Advanced Placement exams for which test preparation is offered; honors section; study at local college for college credit.

College Admission Counseling 21 students graduated in 2010; all went to college, including Florida State University; Georgia Institute of Technology; Mount St. Mary's University; Tallahassee Community College; University of South Florida. Mean SAT critical reading: 558, mean SAT math: 544, mean SAT writing: 535. 43% scored over 600 on SAT critical reading, 57% scored over 600 on SAT math.

Student Life Upper grades have uniform requirement, student council. Discipline rests primarily with faculty. Attendance at religious services is required.

Tuition and Aid Day student tuition: $8700. Tuition installment plan (FACTS Tuition Payment Plan). Need-based scholarship grants available. In 2010–11, 17% of upper-school students received aid. Total amount of financial aid awarded in 2010–11: $40,000.

Admissions Traditional secondary-level entrance grade is 9. Explore, High School Placement Test or High School Placement Test (closed version) from Scholastic Testing Service required. Deadline for receipt of application materials: none. Application fee required: $200. On-campus interview recommended.

Athletics Interscholastic: baseball (boys), basketball (b,g), cheering (g), cross-country running (b,g), football (b), golf (b), soccer (b,g), tennis (b,g), volleyball (g). 1 PE instructor, 8 coaches, 1 athletic trainer.

Computers Computers are regularly used in drawing and design, technology classes. Computer network features include on-campus library services, Internet access, Internet filtering or blocking technology. Student e-mail accounts are available to students. Students grades are available online. The school has a published electronic and media policy.

Contact Mrs. Sharon Strohl, Office Administrator. 850-201-5744. Fax: 850-205-3299. E-mail: sstrohl@jpiichs.org. Web site: www.jpiichs.org.

JOSEPHINUM HIGH SCHOOL

1501 North Oakley Boulevard
Chicago, Illinois 60622
Head of School: Mrs. Lourdes Weber

General Information Girls' day college-preparatory, general academic, arts, religious studies, and technology school, affiliated with Roman Catholic Church. Grades 7–12. Founded: 1890. Setting: urban. 2-acre campus. 1 building on campus. Approved or accredited by Network of Sacred Heart Schools, North Central Association of Colleges and Schools, and Illinois Department of Education. Endowment: $1.5 million. Total enrollment: 150. Upper school average class size: 18. Upper school faculty-student ratio: 1:10. There are 176 required school days per year for Upper

School students. Upper School students typically attend 5 days per week. The average school day consists of 7 hours and 30 minutes.

Upper School Student Profile Grade 7: 14 students (14 girls); Grade 8: 8 students (8 girls); Grade 9: 40 students (40 girls); Grade 10: 19 students (19 girls); Grade 11: 35 students (35 girls); Grade 12: 21 students (21 girls). 50% of students are Roman Catholic.

Faculty School total: 18. In upper school: 4 men, 14 women; 11 have advanced degrees.

Subjects Offered Algebra, American literature, applied arts, art, Bible, biology, biology-AP, British literature, chemistry, community service, computer education, constitutional history of U.S., consumer education, English, English-AP, global studies, health, health and wellness, library research, peer counseling, physical education, scripture, senior project, social justice, softball, Spanish, Spanish-AP, U.S. history, volleyball, Web authoring, women's studies, world geography, world religions, yearbook.

Graduation Requirements Arts and fine arts (art, music, dance, drama), biology, computer science, English, foreign language, mathematics, physical education (includes health), religion (includes Bible studies and theology), science, social sciences, social studies (includes history), completion of a senior capstone project. Community service is required.

Special Academic Programs Advanced Placement exam preparation; honors section; independent study; remedial reading and/or remedial writing; remedial math.

College Admission Counseling 21 students graduated in 2009; 20 went to college, including DePaul University; Dominican University; Loyola University Chicago; Northeastern Illinois University; University of Illinois at Chicago; University of Illinois at Urbana–Champaign. Other: 1 entered military service.

Student Life Upper grades have uniform requirement, student council, honor system. Discipline rests primarily with faculty. Attendance at religious services is required.

Tuition and Aid Day student tuition: $4100. Tuition installment plan (monthly payment plans, individually arranged payment plans, Tuition Management Systems Plan). Tuition reduction for siblings, merit scholarship grants, need-based scholarship grants available. In 2009–10, 89% of upper-school students received aid; total upper-school merit-scholarship money awarded: $20,200. Total amount of financial aid awarded in 2009–10: $400,000.

Admissions Traditional secondary-level entrance grade is 9. For fall 2009, 50 students applied for upper-level admission, 48 were accepted, 43 enrolled. ACT, ACT-Explore, Catholic High School Entrance Examination or Scholastic Testing Service High School Placement Test (open version) required. Deadline for receipt of application materials: none. Application fee required: $25. Interview required.

Athletics Interscholastic: basketball, soccer, softball, volleyball; intramural: cheering. 1 PE instructor, 3 coaches.

Computers Computers are regularly used in all academic, creative writing classes. Computer resources include Internet access, Internet filtering or blocking technology. Student e-mail accounts are available to students. Students grades are available online. The school has a published electronic and media policy.

Contact Ms. Melissa Michaels, Admissions Director. 773-276-1261. Fax: 773-292-3963. E-mail: melissa.michaels@josephinum.org. Web site: www.josephinum.org.

THE JOURNEYS SCHOOL OF TETON SCIENCE SCHOOL

700 Coyote Canyon Road
Jackson, Wyoming 83001
Head of School: Mr. Nate McClennen

General Information Coeducational day college-preparatory school. Grades K–12. Founded: 2001. Setting: rural. 800-acre campus. 1 building on campus. Approved or accredited by Pacific Northwest Association of Independent Schools and Wyoming Department of Education. Upper school average class size: 7.

Special Academic Programs International Baccalaureate program.

Student Life Discipline rests equally with students and faculty.

Admissions No application fee required. Interview required.

Contact Tammie VanHolland, Director of Admissions. 307-734-3710. Fax: 307-733-3340. E-mail: tammie.vanholland@journeysschool.org.

THE JUDGE ROTENBERG EDUCATIONAL CENTER

Canton, Massachusetts
See Special Needs Schools section.

JUNIPERO SERRA HIGH SCHOOL

14830 South Van Ness Avenue
Gardena, California 90249
Head of School: Mr. Michael Wagner, JD

General Information Coeducational day college-preparatory, arts, and religious studies school, affiliated with Roman Catholic Church. Grades 9–12. Founded: 1950. Setting: urban. 24-acre campus. 10 buildings on campus. Approved or accredited by California Association of Independent Schools, National Catholic Education Association, Western Association of Schools and Colleges, Western Catholic Education Association, and California Department of Education. Member of Secondary School

Admission Test Board. Endowment: $200,000. Total enrollment: 686. Upper school average class size: 26. Upper school faculty-student ratio: 1:25. There are 180 required school days per year for Upper School students. Upper School students typically attend 5 days per week. The average school day consists of 5 hours and 45 minutes.

Upper School Student Profile Grade 9: 210 students (146 boys, 64 girls); Grade 10: 191 students (120 boys, 71 girls); Grade 11: 133 students (76 boys, 57 girls); Grade 12: 152 students (87 boys, 65 girls). 51% of students are Roman Catholic.

Faculty School total: 36. In upper school: 22 men, 14 women; 25 have advanced degrees.

Subjects Offered Acting, advanced math, advanced studio art-AP, algebra, American history-AP, American literature, anatomy, biology, biology-AP, calculus-AP, chemistry, choir, computer science, drama, economics, English, English literature, English literature-AP, fine arts, geometry, government, journalism, mathematics, music, photography, physical education, physics, physiology, pre-calculus, religion, science, social studies, Spanish, Spanish-AP, theater, theology, U.S. history, world history, writing.

Graduation Requirements Arts and fine arts (art, music, dance, drama), computer science, English, foreign language, mathematics, physical education (includes health), religion (includes Bible studies and theology), science, social studies (includes history), Completion of an SAT or ACT test preperation program, Complete 100 Service Hours, The school does not accept D and F grades as passing. Community service is required.

Special Academic Programs Advanced Placement exam preparation; honors section; study at local college for college credit; remedial reading and/or remedial writing; remedial math.

College Admission Counseling 147 students graduated in 2010; all went to college, including California State University; El Camino College; Loyola Marymount University; University of California, Los Angeles. Mean SAT critical reading: 464, mean SAT math: 452, mean SAT writing: 455, mean composite ACT: 21. 10% scored over 600 on SAT critical reading, 10% scored over 600 on SAT math, 10% scored over 600 on SAT writing, 7% scored over 26 on composite ACT.

Student Life Upper grades have uniform requirement, student council, honor system. Discipline rests primarily with faculty. Attendance at religious services is required.

Summer Programs Remediation, enrichment, advancement, sports, art/fine arts, rigorous outdoor training, computer instruction programs offered; session focuses on advancement and remediation; held on campus; accepts boys and girls; open to students from other schools. 200 students usually enrolled. 2011 schedule: June 14 to July 30. Application deadline: June 1.

Tuition and Aid Day student tuition: $6000. Tuition installment plan (FACTS Tuition Payment Plan). Tuition reduction for siblings, merit scholarship grants, need-based scholarship grants available. In 2010–11, 50% of upper-school students received aid; total upper-school merit-scholarship money awarded: $15,000. Total amount of financial aid awarded in 2010–11: $400,000.

Admissions Traditional secondary-level entrance grade is 9. For fall 2010, 400 students applied for upper-level admission, 300 were accepted, 210 enrolled. High School Placement Test required. Deadline for receipt of application materials: none. Application fee required: $75. On-campus interview recommended.

Athletics Interscholastic: baseball (boys), basketball (b,g), cheering (g), cross-country running (b,g), football (b), golf (b,g), soccer (b,g), softball (g), track and field (b,g), volleyball (b,g), winter soccer (b,g), wrestling (b); coed interscholastic: swimming and diving, track and field; coed intramural: basketball, volleyball. 2 PE instructors, 23 coaches, 2 athletic trainers.

Computers Computers are regularly used in art, English, foreign language, history, mathematics, music, science classes. Computer network features include on-campus library services, Internet access, Internet filtering or blocking technology. Computer access in designated common areas is available to students. Students grades are available online. The school has a published electronic and media policy.

Contact Mrs. Denise Harris, Admissions Coordinator. 310-324-6675 Ext. 222. Fax: 310-352-4953. E-mail: dharris@serrahighschool.com. Web site: www.serrahighschool.com.

KALAMAZOO CHRISTIAN HIGH SCHOOL

2121 Stadium Drive
Kalamazoo, Michigan 49008-1692
Head of School: Ms. Linda Dahnke

General Information Coeducational day college-preparatory, general academic, arts, business, vocational, religious studies, bilingual studies, and technology school, affiliated with Christian Reformed Church, Reformed Church in America. Grades 9–12. Founded: 1877. Setting: urban. 3-acre campus. 1 building on campus. Approved or accredited by Christian Schools International, North Central Association of Colleges and Schools, and Michigan Department of Education. Endowment: $1 million. Total enrollment: 811. Upper school average class size: 22. Upper school faculty-student ratio: 1:11. There are 172 required school days per year for Upper School students. Upper School students typically attend 5 days per week. The average school day consists of 6 hours and 45 minutes.

Upper School Student Profile 50% of students are members of Christian Reformed Church, Reformed Church in America.

Faculty School total: 25. In upper school: 17 men, 8 women; 10 have advanced degrees.

Graduation Requirements 50 hours community service.

Special Academic Programs Advanced Placement exam preparation; honors section; study at local college for college credit.

College Admission Counseling 100 students graduated in 2010; 90 went to college, including Calvin College; Hope College; University of Michigan; Western Michigan University. Other: 2 entered military service. Median composite ACT: 24.

Student Life Upper grades have specified standards of dress, student council, honor system. Discipline rests primarily with faculty. Attendance at religious services is required.

Tuition and Aid Day student tuition: $8952. Tuition installment plan (FACTS Tuition Payment Plan, monthly payment plans, individually arranged payment plans). Tuition reduction for siblings, need-based scholarship grants available. In 2010–11, 50% of upper-school students received aid.

Admissions Traditional secondary-level entrance grade is 9. Deadline for receipt of application materials: none. Application fee required: $100. Interview required.

Athletics Interscholastic: baseball (boys), basketball (b,g), bowling (b,g), cheering (g), cross-country running (b,g), football (b), golf (b), hockey (b), physical fitness (b,g), soccer (b,g), softball (g), strength & conditioning (b,g), tennis (b,g), track and field (b,g), volleyball (b,g), weight lifting (b,g), weight training (b,g). 2 PE instructors, 32 coaches, 1 athletic trainer.

Computers Computers are regularly used in accounting, business, business applications, business skills, data processing, graphic arts, graphic design, keyboarding, lab/keyboard classes. Computer network features include on-campus library services, online commercial services, Internet access.

Contact Ms. Linda Dahnke, Principal. 269-381-2250 Ext. 220. Fax: 269-381-0319. E-mail: ldahnke@kcsa.org. Web site: www.kcsa.org.

KAPLAN COLLEGE PREPARATORY SCHOOL

4601 Sheridan Street
Suite 600
Hollywood, Florida 33021
Head of School: Miriam Rube

General Information college-preparatory school. Distance learning grades 6–12. Founded: 2001. Setting: suburban. Nearest major city is Fort Lauderdale. Approved or accredited by Southern Association of Colleges and Schools, The College Board, and Florida Department of Education. Total enrollment: 256.

Upper School Student Profile Grade 9: 48 students (29 boys, 19 girls); Grade 10: 53 students (27 boys, 26 girls); Grade 11: 66 students (37 boys, 29 girls); Grade 12: 66 students (39 boys, 27 girls).

Faculty School total: 22. In upper school: 5 men, 17 women; 12 have advanced degrees.

Subjects Offered Advanced Placement courses, algebra, American government, American history, American history-AP, American literature, American literature-AP, art history, biology, biology-AP, business technology, chemistry, chemistry-AP, computer applications, earth and space science, economics, emerging technology, English, English language and composition-AP, English literature and composition-AP, English literature-AP, French, geometry, health, honors algebra, language, life management skills, marine science, mathematics, mathematics-AP, physical education, physical fitness, physics, pre-algebra, pre-calculus, psychology, SAT preparation, science, Spanish, U.S. government and politics-AP, U.S. history, world history, world literature.

Graduation Requirements American government, American history, American literature, biology, British literature, chemistry, economics, electives, English literature, foreign language, general science, life management skills, personal fitness, physical education (includes health), world history, world literature, the last six courses must be with KCPS for a Kaplan College Preparatory School diploma.

Special Academic Programs Advanced Placement exam preparation; honors section; accelerated programs; ESL.

College Admission Counseling 30 students graduated in 2010; 27 went to college, including Dartmouth College; Duke University; University of Miami; University of Michigan; University of South Carolina; Wake Forest University. Other: 1 went to work, 2 had other specific plans.

Student Life Upper grades have student council, honor system. Discipline rests primarily with faculty.

Summer Programs Remediation, enrichment, advancement, art/fine arts, computer instruction programs offered; session focuses on credit recovery and academic enhancement; held off campus; held at online; accepts boys and girls; open to students from other schools. 650 students usually enrolled. 2011 schedule: May 1 to August 31.

Tuition and Aid Tuition installment plan (monthly payment plans, individually arranged payment plans).

Admissions Traditional secondary-level entrance grade is 9. School placement exam required. Deadline for receipt of application materials: none. Application fee required: $100. Interview recommended.

Athletics 1 PE instructor.

Computers Computers are regularly used in all classes. Students grades are available online. The school has a published electronic and media policy.

Contact Alison Cohen, Registrar. 954-964-6502. Fax: 800-878-3152. E-mail: acohen2@kaplan.edu. Web site: www.kaplancollegepreparatory.com.

KARACHI AMERICAN SCHOOL

Amir Khusro Road, KDA Scheme No. 1
Karachi 75350, Pakistan
Head of School: Peter L. Pelosi, PhD

General Information college-preparatory, arts, bilingual studies, and technology school. Founded: 1953. Setting: urban. 14-acre campus. 8 buildings on campus. Approved or accredited by European Council of International Schools and Middle States Association of Colleges and Schools. Language of instruction: English. Endowment: $9 million. Total enrollment: 334. Upper school average class size: 16. Upper school faculty-student ratio: 1:6. There are 180 required school days per year for Upper School students. Upper School students typically attend 5 days per week. The average school day consists of 7 hours.

Upper School Student Profile Grade 6: 23 students (13 boys, 10 girls); Grade 7: 24 students (10 boys, 14 girls); Grade 8: 23 students (17 boys, 6 girls); Grade 9: 36 students (24 boys, 12 girls); Grade 10: 27 students (15 boys, 12 girls); Grade 11: 33 students (22 boys, 11 girls); Grade 12: 30 students (16 boys, 14 girls).

Faculty School total: 39. In upper school: 11 men, 16 women; 24 have advanced degrees.

Subjects Offered Advanced Placement courses, band, biology, chemistry, chemistry-AP, computer science, concert band, desktop publishing, drama workshop, English, English-AP, French, general science, geometry, health, journalism, mathematics, physical education, physics-AP, psychology, science research, social studies, Spanish, Spanish-AP, studio art.

Graduation Requirements Arts and fine arts (art, music, dance, drama), computer studies, English, foreign language, mathematics, physical education (includes health), science, social studies (includes history), speech, writing, 26 credits are required. Community service is required.

Special Academic Programs Advanced Placement exam preparation; ESL (18 students enrolled).

College Admission Counseling 25 students graduated in 2009; all went to college, including Clark University; Hamilton College; McGill University; University of Massachusetts Amherst. Median composite ACT: 25. Mean SAT critical reading: 577, mean SAT math: 600, mean SAT writing: 583. 31% scored over 600 on SAT critical reading, 59% scored over 600 on SAT math, 44% scored over 600 on SAT writing, 25% scored over 1800 on combined SAT, 33% scored over 26 on composite ACT.

Student Life Upper grades have specified standards of dress, student council. Discipline rests primarily with faculty.

Tuition and Aid Day student tuition: $9830–$12,035. Tuition installment plan (pay in May and September (70%-30%)).

Admissions For fall 2009, 102 students applied for upper-level admission, 53 were accepted, 53 enrolled. Achievement tests, admissions testing, any standardized test, English proficiency, ESL, Iowa Test of Educational Development, Iowa Tests of Basic Skills, latest standardized score from previous school, PSAT or SAT, psychoeducational evaluation, SLEP for foreign students or writing sample required. Deadline for receipt of application materials: April 15. Application fee required: $250. On-campus interview required.

Athletics Interscholastic: badminton (boys, girls), baseball (b,g), basketball (b,g), cheering (b,g), cricket (b,g), cross-country running (b,g), flag football (b,g), floor hockey (b,g), football (b,g), physical fitness (b,g), physical training (b,g), running (b,g), soccer (b,g), softball (b,g), squash (b,g), swimming and diving (b,g), table tennis (b,g), tennis (b,g), track and field (b,g), volleyball (b,g); intramural: running (b,g); coed interscholastic: archery, badminton, baseball, cheering, cross-country running, floor hockey, football, physical fitness, physical training, running, soccer, softball, squash, swimming and diving, table tennis, tennis, track and field, volleyball; coed intramural: running. 5 PE instructors, 12 coaches, 3 athletic trainers.

Computers Computers are regularly used in all academic classes. Computer network features include on-campus library services, online commercial services, Internet access, wireless campus network, Internet filtering or blocking technology. Campus intranet, student e-mail accounts, and computer access in designated common areas are available to students. Students grades are available online. The school has a published electronic and media policy.

Contact Afshan Waris, Admission Officer. 92-21-453-9096. Fax: 92-21-454-7305. E-mail: admission@kas.edu.pk. Web site: www.kas.edu.pk.

THE KARAFIN SCHOOL

Mount Kisco, New York
See Special Needs Schools section.

KAUAI CHRISTIAN ACADEMY

PO Box 1121
4000 Kilauea Road
Kilauea, Hawaii 96754
Head of School: Adm. Daniel A. Moore

General Information Coeducational day college-preparatory, general academic, and religious studies school, affiliated with Protestant-Evangelical faith, Christian faith. Grades PS–12. Founded: 1973. Setting: small town. Nearest major city is Lihue. 10-acre campus. 1 building on campus. Approved or accredited by American

Kauai Christian Academy

Association of Christian Schools and Hawaii Department of Education. Endowment: $1,000. Total enrollment: 80. Upper school average class size: 10. Upper school faculty-student ratio: 1:11. There are 168 required school days per year for Upper School students. Upper School students typically attend 5 days per week. The average school day consists of 6 hours and 30 minutes.

Upper School Student Profile Grade 6: 6 students (2 boys, 4 girls); Grade 7: 9 students (7 boys, 2 girls); Grade 8: 8 students (3 boys, 5 girls); Grade 9: 1 student (1 girl); Grade 10: 5 students (2 boys, 3 girls); Grade 11: 2 students (2 boys); Grade 12: 3 students (2 boys, 1 girl). 75% of students are Protestant-Evangelical faith, Christian faith.

Faculty School total: 9. In upper school: 3 men, 3 women; 3 have advanced degrees.

Subjects Offered Advanced math, agriculture, algebra, American government, American history, ancient history, art, arts, athletics, Basic programming, Bible, Bible as literature, Bible studies, biology, botany, calculus, chemistry, Christian and Hebrew scripture, economics, economics-AP, electives, English, English literature, English literature and composition-AP, family living, geography, geometry, government, history, Latin, music, physical science, pre-algebra, speech, world geography, world history.

Graduation Requirements Arts and fine arts (art, music, dance, drama), computer science, English, Latin, mathematics, science, social studies (includes history), speech, one year of Bible for each year enrolled.

Special Academic Programs Advanced Placement exam preparation; accelerated programs; independent study.

Student Life Upper grades have specified standards of dress. Discipline rests primarily with faculty.

Summer Programs Remediation, enrichment, computer instruction programs offered; session focuses on Enrichment; held on campus; accepts boys and girls; open to students from other schools. 2011 schedule: June 13 to July 8. Application deadline: May 31.

Tuition and Aid Day student tuition: $5000. Tuition installment plan (monthly payment plans, 10-month payment plan). Tuition reduction for siblings, need-based scholarship grants, paying campus jobs, contact school for financial aid available. In 2010–11, 40% of upper-school students received aid. Total amount of financial aid awarded in 2010–11: $40,000.

Admissions Traditional secondary-level entrance grade is 7. For fall 2010, 30 students applied for upper-level admission, 28 were accepted, 28 enrolled. Deadline for receipt of application materials: none. Application fee required: $75. Interview required.

Athletics 1 PE instructor.

Computers Computers are regularly used in computer applications classes. Computer resources include Internet access, wireless campus network, Internet filtering or blocking technology. Campus intranet and computer access in designated common areas are available to students.

Contact Adm. Daniel A. Moore, Principal. 808-828-0047. Fax: 808-828-1850. E-mail: dmoore@kcaschool.net. Web site: www.kcatoday.org.

KEITH COUNTRY DAY SCHOOL

1 Jacoby Place
Rockford, Illinois 61107
Head of School: Mr. Alan W. Gibby

General Information Coeducational day college-preparatory and arts school. Grades PK–12. Founded: 1916. Setting: suburban. Nearest major city is Chicago. 15-acre campus. 1 building on campus. Approved or accredited by Independent Schools Association of the Central States and Illinois Department of Education. Member of National Association of Independent Schools. Endowment: $985,000. Total enrollment: 307. Upper school average class size: 16. Upper school faculty-student ratio: 1:6. There are 176 required school days per year for Upper School students. Upper School students typically attend 5 days per week. The average school day consists of 7 hours and 15 minutes.

Upper School Student Profile Grade 9: 27 students (15 boys, 12 girls); Grade 10: 31 students (18 boys, 13 girls); Grade 11: 22 students (8 boys, 14 girls); Grade 12: 33 students (16 boys, 17 girls).

Faculty School total: 50. In upper school: 19 men, 13 women; 15 have advanced degrees.

Subjects Offered Advanced math, Advanced Placement courses, algebra, American history, American literature, Ancient Greek, art, arts, Bible as literature, biology, biology-AP, calculus, ceramics, chemistry, chemistry-AP, college counseling, community service, computer science, design, drama, drawing, economics, English, English literature, English-AP, environmental science, European history, fine arts, French, geography, geometry, government/civics, health, history, Latin, mathematics, music, painting, photography, physical education, physics, pre-calculus, research skills, science, social studies, speech, study skills, theater, trigonometry, world history, world literature.

Graduation Requirements Arts and fine arts (art, music, dance, drama), college counseling, computer science, English, foreign language, mathematics, physical education (includes health), research skills, science, senior project, social studies (includes history), speech, 90 hours of community service.

Special Academic Programs Advanced Placement exam preparation; honors section; study at local college for college credit; study abroad; academic accommo-

dation for the gifted, the musically talented, and the artistically talented; remedial reading and/or remedial writing; programs in general development for dyslexic students.

College Admission Counseling 31 students graduated in 2010; all went to college, including Brown University; DePaul University; Marquette University; University of Illinois at Urbana–Champaign; University of Michigan. 60% scored over 600 on SAT math, 70% scored over 600 on SAT writing, 70% scored over 1800 on combined SAT, 63% scored over 26 on composite ACT.

Student Life Upper grades have specified standards of dress, student council, honor system. Discipline rests equally with students and faculty.

Summer Programs Enrichment, sports, art/fine arts programs offered; session focuses on sports skills camps, math camp, music camp; held on campus; accepts boys and girls; open to students from other schools. 65 students usually enrolled. 2011 schedule: June 10 to August 10.

Tuition and Aid Day student tuition: $14,050. Tuition installment plan (monthly payment plans, school's own payment plan). Tuition reduction for siblings, merit scholarship grants, need-based scholarship grants available. In 2010–11, 53% of upper-school students received aid; total upper-school merit-scholarship money awarded: $117,300. Total amount of financial aid awarded in 2010–11: $363,566.

Admissions Traditional secondary-level entrance grade is 9. For fall 2010, 86 students applied for upper-level admission, 58 were accepted, 11 enrolled. ERB, placement test and school's own exam required. Deadline for receipt of application materials: none. Application fee required: $50. On-campus interview required.

Athletics Interscholastic: basketball (boys, girls), physical fitness (b,g), soccer (b,g), tennis (b,g), volleyball (g); coed interscholastic: cross-country running, golf, table tennis; coed intramural: crew. 3 PE instructors, 6 coaches.

Computers Computers are regularly used in English, foreign language, history, mathematics, science, social studies, Spanish, writing, yearbook classes. Computer network features include on-campus library services, Internet access, wireless campus network, Internet filtering or blocking technology. Student e-mail accounts are available to students. Students grades are available online. The school has a published electronic and media policy.

Contact Marcia Aramovich, Director of Admissions. 815-399-8850 Ext. 144. Fax: 815-399-2470. E-mail: marcia.aramovich@keithschool.net. Web site: www.keithschool.com.

KENT DENVER SCHOOL

4000 East Quincy Avenue
Englewood, Colorado 80113
Head of School: Todd Horn

General Information Coeducational day college-preparatory and arts school. Grades 6–12. Founded: 1922. Setting: suburban. Nearest major city is Denver. 220-acre campus. 6 buildings on campus. Approved or accredited by Association of Colorado Independent Schools and Colorado Department of Education. Member of National Association of Independent Schools and Secondary School Admission Test Board. Endowment: $35 million. Total enrollment: 664. Upper school average class size: 15. Upper school faculty-student ratio: 1:7. Upper School students typically attend 5 days per week. The average school day consists of 7 hours.

Faculty School total: 85. In upper school: 30 men, 29 women; 41 have advanced degrees.

Subjects Offered African-American literature, algebra, American history, American history-AP, American literature, ancient history, anthropology, art, art history, art history-AP, Asian studies, biology, calculus, calculus-AP, career education internship, ceramics, chemistry, choir, clayworking, college counseling, community service, computer math, computer programming, computer programming-AP, computer science, creative writing, drama, earth science, economics, English, English language and composition-AP, English language-AP, English literature, English literature and composition-AP, environmental science, European history, European history-AP, fine arts, French, French language-AP, French literature-AP, French-AP, general science, genetics, geography, geology, geometry, government/civics, grammar, guitar, health and wellness, history, history-AP, human development, independent study, jazz band, Latin, mathematics, music, music performance, mythology, photography, physical education, physics, pre-calculus, science, social studies, Spanish, Spanish language-AP, Spanish literature-AP, statistics, studio art-AP, theater, Web site design, world history, world literature, writing.

Graduation Requirements Arts and fine arts (art, music, dance, drama), computer science, English, foreign language, history, internship, mathematics, participation in sports, physical education (includes health), science. Community service is required.

Special Academic Programs 16 Advanced Placement exams for which test preparation is offered; honors section; independent study; programs in general development for dyslexic students.

College Admission Counseling 105 students graduated in 2009; all went to college, including Claremont McKenna College; Dartmouth College; Middlebury College; Stanford University; The Colorado College; University of Southern California. Mean SAT critical reading: 619, mean SAT math: 628, mean SAT writing: 623.

Student Life Upper grades have specified standards of dress, student council. Discipline rests equally with students and faculty.

Tuition and Aid Day student tuition: $19,630. Tuition installment plan (Insured Tuition Payment Plan, Key Tuition Payment Plan, monthly payment plans).

Need-based scholarship grants available. In 2009–10, 21% of upper-school students received aid. Total amount of financial aid awarded in 2009–10: $2,000,000.

Admissions Traditional secondary-level entrance grade is 9. For fall 2009, 172 students applied for upper-level admission, 81 were accepted, 57 enrolled. ISEE or SSAT required. Deadline for receipt of application materials: January 29. Application fee required: $60. Interview required.

Athletics Interscholastic: basketball (boys, girls), cross-country running (b,g), diving (g), field hockey (g), football (b), golf (b,g), hockey (b), ice hockey (b), lacrosse (b,g), soccer (b,g), swimming and diving (g), tennis (b,g), track and field (b,g), volleyball (g), wrestling (b); coed interscholastic: baseball, outdoor education; coed intramural: aerobics/Nautilus, bicycling, fitness, mountain biking, outdoor adventure, outdoor education, outdoor skills, physical fitness, physical training, strength & conditioning, weight lifting. 3 PE instructors, 17 coaches, 1 athletic trainer.

Computers Computers are regularly used in art, English, foreign language, history, mathematics, science classes. Computer network features include on-campus library services, online commercial services, Internet access, wireless campus network, Internet filtering or blocking technology. Student e-mail accounts and computer access in designated common areas are available to students. The school has a published electronic and media policy.

Contact Susan Green, Admission Office Manager. 303-770-7660 Ext. 237. Fax: 303-770-1398. E-mail: sgreen@kentdenver.org. Web site: www.kentdenver.org.

KENT PLACE SCHOOL

42 Norwood Avenue
Summit, New Jersey 07902-0308
Head of School: Mrs. Susan C. Bosland

General Information Coeducational day (boys' only in lower grades) college-preparatory school. Boys grades N–PK, girls grades N–12. Founded: 1894. Setting: suburban. Nearest major city is New York, NY. 25-acre campus. 6 buildings on campus. Approved or accredited by Middle States Association of Colleges and Schools and New Jersey Association of Independent Schools. Member of National Association of Independent Schools and Secondary School Admission Test Board. Endowment: $14.2 million. Total enrollment: 636. Upper school average class size: 17. Upper school faculty-student ratio: 1:7. Upper School students typically attend 5 days per week.

Upper School Student Profile Grade 9: 70 students (70 girls); Grade 10: 65 students (65 girls); Grade 11: 62 students (62 girls); Grade 12: 72 students (72 girls).

Faculty School total: 81. In upper school: 5 men, 28 women; 27 have advanced degrees.

Subjects Offered Advanced Placement courses, algebra, American history, American history-AP, American literature, anatomy and physiology, art, art history-AP, biology, biology-AP, calculus, calculus-AP, ceramics, chemistry, chemistry-AP, computer literacy, computer programming-AP, computer science, creative writing, dance, drama, driver education, economics, English, English language-AP, English literature, English literature-AP, environmental science, environmental science-AP, European history, expository writing, fine arts, French, French language-AP, French literature-AP, geometry, government/civics, grammar, health, history, independent study, Latin, Latin-AP, macroeconomics-AP, mathematics, modern European history-AP, music, music theory-AP, photography, physical education, physics, science, social studies, Spanish, Spanish language-AP, Spanish literature-AP, statistics, statistics-AP, theater, trigonometry, world history.

Graduation Requirements Arts and fine arts (art, music, dance, drama), computer science, English, foreign language, mathematics, physical education (includes health), science, social studies (includes history).

Special Academic Programs Advanced Placement exam preparation; independent study.

College Admission Counseling 61 students graduated in 2009; all went to college, including Boston College; Bucknell University; Cornell University; Princeton University; University of Pennsylvania; Yale University. Median SAT critical reading: 660, median SAT math: 670. Mean SAT writing: 710. 78% scored over 600 on SAT critical reading, 88% scored over 600 on SAT math.

Student Life Upper grades have specified standards of dress, student council, honor system. Discipline rests equally with students and faculty.

Tuition and Aid Day student tuition: $29,516. Tuition installment plan (Insured Tuition Payment Plan, Key Tuition Payment Plan, monthly payment plans). Need-based scholarship grants available. In 2009–10, 20% of upper-school students received aid. Total amount of financial aid awarded in 2009–10: $921,243.

Admissions Traditional secondary-level entrance grade is 9. ISEE or SSAT required. Deadline for receipt of application materials: January 8. Application fee required: $70. On-campus interview required.

Athletics Interscholastic: basketball, cross-country running, field hockey, indoor track, lacrosse, soccer, softball, swimming and diving, tennis, track and field, volleyball, winter (indoor) track; intramural: dance, fencing, modern dance, physical fitness, squash. 4 PE instructors, 19 coaches, 1 athletic trainer.

Computers Computers are regularly used in all classes. Computer network features include on-campus library services, online commercial services, Internet access, wireless campus network, Internet filtering or blocking technology. Student e-mail accounts are available to students. The school has a published electronic and media policy.

Contact Mrs. Nancy J. Humick, Director of Admission and Financial Aid. 908-273-0900 Ext. 254, Fax: 908-273 9390. E-mail: admission@kentplace.org. Web site: www.kentplace.org.

KENT SCHOOL

PO Box 2006
Kent, Connecticut 06757
Head of School: Rev. Richardson W. Schell

General Information Coeducational boarding and day college-preparatory, arts, religious studies, technology, and pre-engineering school, affiliated with Episcopal Church. Grades 9–PG. Founded: 1906. Setting: small town. Nearest major city is Hartford. Students are housed in single-sex dormitories. 1,200-acre campus. 17 buildings on campus. Approved or accredited by Association of Independent Schools in New England, Connecticut Association of Independent Schools, National Association of Episcopal Schools, New England Association of Schools and Colleges, New York State Association of Independent Schools, The Association of Boarding Schools, and Connecticut Department of Education. Member of National Association of Independent Schools and Secondary School Admission Test Board. Endowment: $73.5 million. Total enrollment: 560. Upper school average class size: 12. Upper school faculty-student ratio: 1:8.

Upper School Student Profile Grade 9: 70 students (35 boys, 35 girls); Grade 10: 147 students (70 boys, 77 girls); Grade 11: 155 students (80 boys, 75 girls); Grade 12: 188 students (98 boys, 90 girls). 90% of students are boarding students. 31% are state residents. 37 states are represented in upper school student body. 31% are international students. International students from Canada, China, Germany, Hong Kong, Republic of Korea, and Thailand; 44 other countries represented in student body.

Faculty School total: 73. In upper school: 43 men, 30 women; 55 have advanced degrees; 66 reside on campus.

Subjects Offered Advanced studio art-AP, African-American history, algebra, American history, American history-AP, American literature, architecture, art, art history-AP, Asian history, astronomy, Bible studies, biology, biology-AP, biotechnology, calculus, calculus-AP, ceramics, chemistry, chemistry-AP, Chinese, classical Greek literature, classical studies, composition-AP, computer math, computer programming, computer science, computer science-AP, digital imaging, drama, ecology, economics, English, English literature, English literature-AP, environmental science-AP, environmental studies, European history, European history-AP, expository writing, fine arts, French, French language-AP, French literature-AP, genetics, geology, geometry, German, German-AP, government and politics-AP, Greek, history, Latin, Latin American history, Latin-AP, law and the legal system, mathematics, meteorology, Middle Eastern history, modern European history-AP, music, music theory-AP, photography, physical education, physics, physics-AP, probability and statistics, psychology-AP, religion, science, sculpture, social studies, Spanish, Spanish language-AP, Spanish literature-AP, statistics-AP, theater, theology, trigonometry, U.S. government and politics-AP, world geography, world history, world literature.

Graduation Requirements Arts and fine arts (art, music, dance, drama), English, foreign language, history, mathematics, music, religion (includes Bible studies and theology), science, U.S. history.

Special Academic Programs 26 Advanced Placement exams for which test preparation is offered; honors section; independent study; academic accommodation for the gifted, the musically talented, and the artistically talented; ESL.

College Admission Counseling 171 students graduated in 2010; all went to college, including Boston University; Carnegie Mellon University; Colgate University; Cornell University; Princeton University; St. Lawrence University.

Student Life Upper grades have specified standards of dress, student council. Discipline rests equally with students and faculty. Attendance at religious services is required.

Tuition and Aid Day student tuition: $35,900; 7-day tuition and room/board: $45,300. Tuition installment plan (Key Tuition Payment Plan, monthly payment plans, individually arranged payment plans). Merit scholarship grants, need-based scholarship grants, need-based loans available. In 2010–11, 37% of upper-school students received aid. Total amount of financial aid awarded in 2010–11: $7,300,000

Admissions Traditional secondary-level entrance grade is 9. For fall 2010, 1,200 students applied for upper-level admission, 450 were accepted, 190 enrolled. PSAT or SAT for applicants to grade 11 and 12, SSAT or TOEFL required. Deadline for receipt of application materials: January 15. Application fee required: $65. Interview required.

Athletics Interscholastic: baseball (boys), basketball (b,g), crew (b,g), cross-country running (b,g), diving (b,g), field hockey (g), football (b), golf (b,g), hockey (b,g), ice hockey (b,g), lacrosse (b,g), rowing (b,g), soccer (b,g), softball (g), squash (b,g), swimming and diving (b,g), tennis (b,g); intramural: basketball (b), crew (b,g), rowing (b,g); coed interscholastic: crew, dressage, equestrian sports, golf, horseback riding; coed intramural: aerobics/dance, aerobics/Nautilus, alpine skiing, ballet, bicycling, combined training, dance, dressage, equestrian sports, figure skating, fitness, hockey, horseback riding, ice skating, life saving, modern dance, mountain biking, physical fitness, physical training, ropes courses, sailing, skiing (downhill), snowboarding, soccer, squash, strength & conditioning, swimming and diving, tennis, ultimate Frisbee, weight training, yoga. 2 athletic trainers.

Computers Computers are regularly used in all academic, journalism, newspaper, yearbook classes. Computer network features include on-campus library services, online commercial services, Internet access, wireless campus network, all students receive a Tablet PC, students have online storage for schoolwork, Adobe Creative Suite, Autodesk, Mathcad and Microsoft Office Software for all students. Campus intranet, student e-mail accounts, and computer access in designated common areas are available to students. The school has a published electronic and media policy.
Contact Ms. Kathryn F. Sullivan, Director of Admissions. 860-927-6111. Fax: 860-927-6109. E-mail: admissions@kent-school.edu. Web site: www.kent-school.edu.

KENTS HILL SCHOOL
PO Box 257
1614 Main Street, Route 17
Kents Hill, Maine 04349-0257
Head of School: Mr. Rist Bonnefond
General Information Coeducational boarding and day college-preparatory, arts, technology, environmental studies, and ESL school, affiliated with Methodist Church. Grades 9–PG. Founded: 1824. Setting: rural. Nearest major city is Portland. Students are housed in single-sex dormitories. 400-acre campus. 24 buildings on campus. Approved or accredited by Association of Independent Schools in New England, Independent Schools of Northern New England, New England Association of Schools and Colleges, The Association of Boarding Schools, and Maine Department of Education. Member of National Association of Independent Schools and Secondary School Admission Test Board. Endowment: $4.9 million. Total enrollment: 235. Upper school average class size: 12. Upper school faculty-student ratio: 1:5. The average school day consists of 7 hours.
Upper School Student Profile Grade 9: 35 students (23 boys, 12 girls); Grade 10: 56 students (32 boys, 24 girls); Grade 11: 70 students (48 boys, 22 girls); Grade 12: 51 students (31 boys, 20 girls); Postgraduate: 16 students (14 boys, 2 girls). 75% of students are boarding students. 33% are state residents. 22 states are represented in upper school student body. 20% are international students. International students from Canada, China, France, Germany, Japan, and Republic of Korea; 12 other countries represented in student body. 3% of students are Methodist.
Faculty School total: 46. In upper school: 26 men, 20 women; 18 have advanced degrees; 42 reside on campus.
Subjects Offered Acting, advanced math, Advanced Placement courses, advanced studio art-AP, African-American literature, algebra, American history, American literature, art, art history, astronomy, biology, biotechnology, calculus, calculus-AP, ceramics, chemistry, college counseling, computer graphics, computer science-AP, computer-aided design, concert choir, creative writing, dance, drama, Eastern religion and philosophy, ecology, economics, English, English literature, environmental science, environmental science-AP, environmental studies, ESL, ethics, ethics and responsibility, European history, filmmaking, fine arts, French, geology, geometry, government/civics, health, history, Holocaust, jazz ensemble, journalism, mathematics, music, photography, physics, psychology, religion, science, Shakespeare, Spanish, theater, U.S. history-AP, Western religions, woodworking, world history, writing.
Graduation Requirements English, environmental studies, foreign language, health, mathematics, science, social studies (includes history), visual and performing arts.
Special Academic Programs 11 Advanced Placement exams for which test preparation is offered; honors section; independent study; term-away projects; study abroad; academic accommodation for the gifted and the artistically talented; programs in general development for dyslexic students; special instructional classes for students with learning differences (through the Learning Skills Center); ESL (20 students enrolled).
College Admission Counseling 76 students graduated in 2009; 69 went to college. Other: 1 entered military service, 5 entered a postgraduate year, 1 had other specific plans.
Student Life Upper grades have specified standards of dress, student council, honor system. Discipline rests equally with students and faculty.
Tuition and Aid Day student tuition: $23,800; 7-day tuition and room/board: $42,800. Tuition installment plan (Insured Tuition Payment Plan, FACTS Tuition Payment Plan, monthly payment plans, individually arranged payment plans, 2-payment plan). Need-based scholarship grants available. In 2009–10, 41% of upper-school students received aid. Total amount of financial aid awarded in 2009–10: $1,900,000.
Admissions Traditional secondary-level entrance grade is 9. Deadline for receipt of application materials: none. Application fee required: $50. Interview required.
Athletics Interscholastic: baseball (boys), basketball (b,g), field hockey (g), football (b), hockey (b,g), ice hockey (b,g), lacrosse (b,g), soccer (b,g), softball (g), tennis (b,g); coed interscholastic: alpine skiing, cross-country running, equestrian sports, fencing, golf, horseback riding, independent competitive sports, mountain biking, physical training, skiing (cross-country), skiing (downhill), snowboarding; coed intramural: alpine skiing, canoeing/kayaking, dance, equestrian sports, fencing, figure skating, fitness, freestyle skiing, hiking/backpacking, horseback riding, ice skating, kayaking, mountain biking, nordic skiing, outdoor activities, outdoor recreation, outdoor skills,

rock climbing, skiing (cross-country), skiing (downhill), snowboarding, snowshoeing, soccer, strength & conditioning, tennis. 4 coaches, 1 athletic trainer.
Computers Computers are regularly used in all academic, college planning, desktop publishing, graphic design, media production, newspaper, photojournalism, publications, SAT preparation, video film production, Web site design, yearbook classes. Computer network features include on-campus library services, online commercial services, Internet access, Internet filtering or blocking technology. Student e-mail accounts and computer access in designated common areas are available to students. The school has a published electronic and media policy.
Contact Mrs. Amy Smucker, Director of Admissions. 207-685-4914 Ext. 152. Fax: 207-685-9529. E-mail: asmucker@kentshill.org. Web site: www.kentshill.org.

KENTUCKY COUNTRY DAY SCHOOL
4100 Springdale Road
Louisville, Kentucky 40241
Head of School: Mr. Bradley E. Lyman
General Information Coeducational day college-preparatory, arts, technology, honors program, independent study, and advanced programs for academically exceptional students school. Grades JK–12. Founded: 1972. Setting: suburban. 85-acre campus. 3 buildings on campus. Approved or accredited by Independent Schools Association of the Central States. Member of National Association of Independent Schools. Endowment: $10.3 million. Total enrollment: 921. Upper school average class size: 15. Upper school faculty-student ratio: 1:7. There are 170 required school days per year for Upper School students. Upper School students typically attend 5 days per week. The average school day consists of 7 hours and 5 minutes.
Upper School Student Profile Grade 9: 66 students (29 boys, 37 girls); Grade 10: 77 students (37 boys, 40 girls); Grade 11: 75 students (36 boys, 39 girls); Grade 12: 81 students (40 boys, 41 girls).
Faculty School total: 112. In upper school: 22 men, 18 women; 32 have advanced degrees.
Subjects Offered Algebra, American history, American literature, art, biology, calculus, ceramics, chemistry, collage and assemblage, communications, computer math, computer programming, computer science, drama, economics, English, English literature, European history, fine arts, French, geology, geometry, government/civics, history, humanities, instrumental music, Latin, law, mathematics, multimedia, music, physical education, physics, play production, psychology, psychology-AP, science, sculpture, senior internship, senior project, social sciences, social studies, Spanish, Spanish language-AP, speech, stagecraft, statistics, studio art-AP, technical theater, theater, trigonometry, U.S. government and politics-AP, U.S. history-AP.
Graduation Requirements Arts and fine arts (art, music, dance, drama), communications, English, foreign language, mathematics, physical education (includes health), science, social studies (includes history).
Special Academic Programs 20 Advanced Placement exams for which test preparation is offered; honors section; independent study; term-away projects; study abroad; academic accommodation for the gifted, the musically talented, and the artistically talented.
College Admission Counseling 58 students graduated in 2010; all went to college, including Davidson College; Miami University; University of Kentucky; University of Louisville; Vanderbilt University; Wake Forest University. Median SAT critical reading: 590, median SAT math: 610, median SAT writing: 610, median combined SAT: 1790, median composite ACT: 27. 50% scored over 600 on SAT critical reading, 61% scored over 600 on SAT math, 57% scored over 600 on SAT writing, 49% scored over 1800 on combined SAT, 59% scored over 26 on composite ACT.
Student Life Upper grades have specified standards of dress, student council, honor system. Discipline rests equally with students and faculty.
Summer Programs Remediation, enrichment, advancement, sports, art/fine arts, rigorous outdoor training, computer instruction programs offered; session focuses on enrichment; held on campus; accepts boys and girls; open to students from other schools. 200 students usually enrolled. 2011 schedule: June 7 to August 20. Application deadline: none.
Tuition and Aid Day student tuition: $16,800. Tuition installment plan (FACTS Tuition Payment Plan). Merit scholarship grants, need-based scholarship grants available. In 2010–11, 23% of upper-school students received aid; total upper-school merit-scholarship money awarded: $27,750. Total amount of financial aid awarded in 2010–11: $734,962.
Admissions Traditional secondary-level entrance grade is 9. For fall 2010, 60 students applied for upper-level admission, 34 were accepted, 28 enrolled. ERB Reading and Math required. Deadline for receipt of application materials: none. Application fee required: $75. On-campus interview required.
Athletics Interscholastic: baseball (boys), basketball (b,g), cross-country running (b,g), diving (b,g), field hockey (g), football (b), golf (b,g), lacrosse (b,g), soccer (b,g), softball (g), swimming and diving (b,g), tennis (b,g), track and field (b,g), volleyball (g), wrestling (b); coed interscholastic: weight training; coed intramural: bowling, project adventure, ropes courses, weight lifting. 7 PE instructors, 86 coaches, 1 athletic trainer.
Computers Computers are regularly used in all classes. Computer network features include on-campus library services, online commercial services, Internet access, wireless campus network, Internet filtering or blocking technology. Campus intranet and student e-mail accounts are available to students. Students grades are available online. The school has a published electronic and media policy.

Contact Mr. Jeff Holbrook, Director of Admissions. 502-814-4375. Fax: 502-814-4381. E-mail: admissions@kcd.org. Web site: www.kcd.org.

KERR-VANCE ACADEMY

700 Vance Academy Road
Henderson, North Carolina 27537
Head of School: Mr. Paul Villatico

General Information Coeducational day college-preparatory school. Grades PK–12. Founded: 1968. Setting: rural. Nearest major city is Raleigh. 25-acre campus. 8 buildings on campus. Approved or accredited by North Carolina Association of Independent Schools, Southern Association of Colleges and Schools, and North Carolina Department of Education. Endowment: $40,000. Total enrollment: 472. Upper school average class size: 16. Upper school faculty-student ratio: 1:10. There are 180 required school days per year for Upper School students. Upper School students typically attend 5 days per week. The average school day consists of 6 hours.
Upper School Student Profile Grade 9: 32 students (20 boys, 12 girls); Grade 10: 40 students (16 boys, 24 girls); Grade 11: 30 students (17 boys, 13 girls); Grade 12: 45 students (25 boys, 20 girls).
Faculty School total: 41. In upper school: 5 men, 13 women; 12 have advanced degrees.
Subjects Offered Advanced Placement courses, algebra, American history, American literature, art, art history, biology, calculus, chemistry, computer programming, computer science, creative writing, driver education, earth science, economics, English, English literature, environmental science, French, geography, geometry, government/civics, grammar, Latin, mathematics, music, physical education, physics, psychology, SAT/ACT preparation, science, social sciences, social studies, sociology, Spanish, speech, trigonometry, world history, world literature, writing.
Graduation Requirements Computer science, English, English composition, English literature, foreign language, mathematics, physical education (includes health), science, social sciences, social studies (includes history), writing. Community service is required.
Special Academic Programs International Baccalaureate program; Advanced Placement exam preparation; honors section.
College Admission Counseling 34 students graduated in 2010; all went to college, including East Carolina University; Meredith College; North Carolina State University; The University of North Carolina at Chapel Hill; The University of North Carolina at Greensboro; The University of North Carolina Wilmington. Mean SAT critical reading: 508, mean SAT math: 517, mean composite ACT: 25. 16% scored over 600 on SAT critical reading, 21% scored over 600 on SAT math, 33% scored over 26 on composite ACT.
Student Life Upper grades have specified standards of dress, student council. Discipline rests primarily with faculty.
Summer Programs Enrichment, advancement programs offered; session focuses on academic advancement; held on campus; accepts boys and girls; open to students from other schools. 50 students usually enrolled. 2011 schedule: July 10 to August 11. Application deadline: May 15.
Tuition and Aid Day student tuition: $8100. Tuition installment plan (monthly payment plans). Tuition reduction for siblings, need-based scholarship grants available. In 2010–11, 5% of upper-school students received aid. Total amount of financial aid awarded in 2010–11: $15,000.
Admissions Admissions testing or writing sample required. Deadline for receipt of application materials: none. Application fee required: $50. On-campus interview required.
Athletics Interscholastic: baseball (boys), basketball (b,g), cheering (g), cross-country running (b,g), golf (b), lacrosse (b), soccer (b,g), softball (g), tennis (b,g), volleyball (g), weight training (b,g), wrestling (b); intramural: soccer (b,g), weight lifting (b); coed intramural: swimming and diving, volleyball. 3 PE instructors, 7 coaches, 1 athletic trainer.
Computers Computers are regularly used in art, English, history, library, literary magazine, newspaper, programming, reading, research skills, SAT preparation, science, technology, writing, yearbook classes. Computer network features include on-campus library services, online commercial services, Internet access.
Contact Shannon T. Gwynn, Admissions Coordinator. 252-492-0018. Fax: 252-438-4652. E-mail: sgwynn@kerrvance.com. Web site: www.kerrvance.com.

THE KEW-FOREST SCHOOL

119-17 Union Turnpike
Forest Hills, New York 11375
Head of School: Mr. Mark P. Fish

General Information Coeducational day college-preparatory and arts school. Grades PK–12. Founded: 1918. Setting: urban. Nearest major city is New York. 1-acre campus. 1 building on campus. Approved or accredited by Middle States Association of Colleges and Schools, New York Department of Education, New York State Association of Independent Schools, and New York Department of Education. Member of National Association of Independent Schools. Total enrollment: 237. Upper school average class size: 15. Upper school faculty-student ratio: 1:6. There are

162 required school days per year for Upper School students. Upper School students typically attend 5 days per week. The average school day consists of 6 hours.
Faculty School total: 34. In upper school: 14 men, 7 women; 14 have advanced degrees.
Subjects Offered Algebra, American history, ancient history, art, biology, biology-AP, calculus, calculus-AP, chemistry, English, English composition, English language and composition-AP, English literature, French, French-AP, geometry, health, history, honors geometry, Latin, Latin-AP, marine biology, modern European history, philosophy, physical education, physics, physics-AP, pre-calculus, Spanish, Spanish-AP, trigonometry, U.S. government and politics.
Graduation Requirements Art, English, health, history, history of the Catholic Church, mathematics, modern languages, music appreciation, physical education (includes health), science, computer competency.
Special Academic Programs International Baccalaureate program; Advanced Placement exam preparation; academic accommodation for the gifted.
College Admission Counseling 40 students graduated in 2010; all went to college, including New York University. Median SAT critical reading: 520, median SAT math: 575. 25% scored over 600 on SAT critical reading, 40% scored over 600 on SAT math.
Student Life Upper grades have uniform requirement, student council, honor system. Discipline rests primarily with faculty.
Summer Programs Remediation, enrichment, advancement programs offered; session focuses on Summer Institute; held on campus; accepts boys and girls; open to students from other schools. 50 students usually enrolled. 2011 schedule: July to August.
Tuition and Aid Day student tuition: $25,750. Tuition installment plan (FACTS Tuition Payment Plan, Tuition Management Systems Plan). Need-based scholarship grants available. In 2010–11, 25% of upper-school students received aid. Total amount of financial aid awarded in 2010–11: $841,000.
Admissions Traditional secondary-level entrance grade is 9. ISEE or SSAT required. Deadline for receipt of application materials: February 15. Application fee required: $75. On-campus interview required.
Athletics Interscholastic: basketball (boys, girls), cross-country running (b,g), soccer (b,g), tennis (b,g), volleyball (g); intramural: baseball (b), basketball (b,g), soccer (b,g), tennis (b,g); coed intramural: cross-country running, volleyball. 2 PE instructors, 5 coaches.
Computers Computers are regularly used in all academic classes. Computer network features include on-campus library services, Internet access, wireless campus network, Internet filtering or blocking technology. Students grades are available online.
Contact Mr. Rene A. Bolanos, Director of Admission. 718-268-4667 Ext. 125. Fax: 718-268-9121. E-mail: rbolanos@kewforest.org. Web site: www.kewforest.org.

THE KEY SCHOOL

534 Hillsmere Drive
Annapolis, Maryland 21403
Head of School: Marcella M. Yedid

General Information Coeducational day college-preparatory, arts, and outdoor education school. Grades PK–12. Founded: 1958. Setting: suburban. Nearest major city is Baltimore. 15-acre campus. 10 buildings on campus. Approved or accredited by Association of Independent Maryland Schools and Maryland Department of Education. Member of National Association of Independent Schools. Endowment: $4.4 million. Total enrollment: 690. Upper school average class size: 14. Upper school faculty-student ratio: 1:8.
Upper School Student Profile Grade 9: 53 students (26 boys, 27 girls); Grade 10: 47 students (19 boys, 28 girls); Grade 11: 43 students (17 boys, 26 girls); Grade 12: 53 students (28 boys, 25 girls).
Faculty School total: 111. In upper school: 15 men, 25 women; 28 have advanced degrees.
Subjects Offered Acting, algebra, American studies, ancient history, art, art history, biology, calculus, ceramics, chemistry, Chesapeake Bay studies, choir, computer science, conceptual physics, creative writing, dance, digital art, digital photography, drama, drama performance, drawing, economics, English, English literature, European history, fine arts, French, geometry, journalism, Latin, literature by women, music, photography, physical education, physics, physiology, playwriting, pre-calculus, printmaking, Russian literature, sculpture, Shakespeare, Spanish, Spanish literature, statistics, studio art, theater, theater production, trigonometry.
Graduation Requirements Arts and fine arts (art, music, dance, drama), English, foreign language, history, mathematics, performing arts, physical education (includes health), science.
Special Academic Programs Advanced Placement exam preparation; honors section; independent study; academic accommodation for the gifted.
College Admission Counseling 49 students graduated in 2009; all went to college, including Bryn Mawr College; Oberlin College; St. Mary's College of Maryland; University of Chicago; University of Maryland, Baltimore County; University of Maryland, College Park.
Student Life Upper grades have student council. Discipline rests equally with students and faculty.
Tuition and Aid Day student tuition: $22,250. Tuition installment plan (monthly payment plans, TuitionPay Plan from Sallie Mae, Management Services Plan). Tuition

reduction for siblings, need-based scholarship grants available. In 2009–10, 23% of upper-school students received aid. Total amount of financial aid awarded in 2009–10: $439,397.

Admissions Traditional secondary-level entrance grade is 9. For fall 2009, 63 students applied for upper-level admission, 39 were accepted, 29 enrolled. ERB or ISEE required. Deadline for receipt of application materials: none. Application fee required: $45. Interview required.

Athletics Interscholastic: baseball (boys), basketball (b,g), field hockey (g), indoor soccer (g), lacrosse (b,g), soccer (b,g); intramural: field hockey (g), lacrosse (b,g); coed interscholastic: cross-country running, equestrian sports, golf, sailing, tennis; coed intramural: backpacking, basketball, canoeing/kayaking, climbing, cooperative games, dance, fitness, fitness walking, golf, hiking/backpacking, kayaking, kickball, modern dance, Newcombe ball, outdoor activities, project adventure, roller blading, running. 1 PE instructor, 44 coaches, 1 athletic trainer.

Computers Computers are regularly used in all academic classes. Computer network features include on-campus library services, online commercial services, Internet access, wireless campus network, online supplementary course materials. Campus intranet, student e-mail accounts, and computer access in designated common areas are available to students. The school has a published electronic and media policy.

Contact Jessie D. Dunleavy, Assistant Head of School for Enrollment Management. 410-263-9231. Fax: 410-280-5516. E-mail: jdunleavy@keyschool.org. Web site: www.keyschool.org.

KEY SCHOOL
Fort Worth, Texas
See Special Needs Schools section.

KILDONAN SCHOOL
Amenia, New York
See Special Needs Schools section.

KIMBALL UNION ACADEMY
PO Box 188
Main Street
Meriden, New Hampshire 03770
Head of School: Mr. Michael J. Schafer

General Information Coeducational boarding and day college-preparatory, arts, and environmental science school. Grades 9–PG. Founded: 1813. Setting: small town. Nearest major city is Boston, MA. Students are housed in single-sex dormitories. 1,300-acre campus. 35 buildings on campus. Approved or accredited by Independent Schools of Northern New England, New England Association of Schools and Colleges, The Association of Boarding Schools, The College Board, and New Hampshire Department of Education. Member of National Association of Independent Schools and Secondary School Admission Test Board. Endowment: $11 million. Total enrollment: 317. Upper school average class size: 12. Upper school faculty-student ratio: 1:9. There are 159 required school days per year for Upper School students. Upper School students typically attend 6 days per week. The average school day consists of 5 hours and 8 minutes.

Upper School Student Profile Grade 9: 46 students (27 boys, 19 girls); Grade 10: 80 students (47 boys, 33 girls); Grade 11: 90 students (49 boys, 41 girls); Grade 12: 83 students (48 boys, 35 girls); Postgraduate: 18 students (18 boys). 66% of students are boarding students. 32% are state residents. 21 states are represented in upper school student body. 27% are international students. International students from Canada, China, Germany, Republic of Korea, Spain, and United Kingdom; 12 other countries represented in student body.

Faculty School total: 47. In upper school: 32 men, 15 women; 33 have advanced degrees; 25 reside on campus.

Subjects Offered 3-dimensional design, acting, Advanced Placement courses, algebra, American history, American literature, anatomy, anthropology, architecture, art, art history, art history-AP, biology, biology-AP, calculus, calculus-AP, ceramics, chemistry, chemistry-AP, composition-AP, computer programming, creative writing, dance, digital photography, drama, driver education, English, English language and composition-AP, English literature, English literature and composition-AP, English-AP, environmental science, environmental science-AP, environmental studies, European history, fine arts, French, French language-AP, French literature-AP, geology, geometry, government/civics, grammar, health, history, history-AP, honors English, honors geometry, human geography—AP, independent study, international relations, jazz band, jazz ensemble, language-AP, Latin, Latin-AP, Mandarin, mathematical modeling, mathematics, modern European history-AP, modern world history, music, music history, music theory, music theory-AP, peer counseling, photo shop, photography, physics, physics-AP, physiology, playwriting, pottery, probability and statistics, programming, psychology, public speaking, science, social studies, Spanish, Spanish-AP, stagecraft, statistics-AP, student publications, studio art, studio art-AP, theater, theater arts, theater design and production, trigonometry, U.S. government, U.S. history, U.S. history-AP, video film production, visual arts, woodworking, world history, world literature, writing.

Graduation Requirements Art, English, foreign language, history, mathematics, science.

Special Academic Programs 19 Advanced Placement exams for which test preparation is offered; honors section; independent study; term-away projects; study abroad.

College Admission Counseling 105 students graduated in 2010; 101 went to college, including Boston University; Dartmouth College; Hobart and William Smith Colleges; Northeastern University; St. Lawrence University; Suffolk University. Other: 4 had other specific plans. Median SAT critical reading: 560, median SAT math: 570, median SAT writing: 560, median combined SAT: 1680, median composite ACT: 23. 27% scored over 600 on SAT critical reading, 41% scored over 600 on SAT math, 35% scored over 600 on SAT writing, 27% scored over 1800 on combined SAT, 21% scored over 26 on composite ACT.

Student Life Upper grades have specified standards of dress, student council, honor system. Discipline rests equally with students and faculty.

Summer Programs Enrichment, ESL, sports, art/fine arts programs offered; session focuses on environmental leadership (EE Just Institute) and ALPS (Accelerated Language Program) with Dartmouth College; held both on and off campus; held at Costa Rica; accepts boys and girls; open to students from other schools. 200 students usually enrolled. 2011 schedule: July 2 to July 30. Application deadline: April 15.

Tuition and Aid Day student tuition: $28,850; 7-day tuition and room/board: $44,970. Tuition installment plan (Insured Tuition Payment Plan, Academic Management Services Plan, Key Tuition Payment Plan, monthly payment plans). Need-based scholarship grants, paying campus jobs available. In 2010–11, 47% of upper-school students received aid. Total amount of financial aid awarded in 2010–11: $2,400,000.

Admissions Traditional secondary-level entrance grade is 9. For fall 2010, 475 students applied for upper-level admission, 268 were accepted, 124 enrolled. ACT, PSAT or SAT, SLEP, SSAT or TOEFL required. Deadline for receipt of application materials: February 1. Application fee required: $50. Interview required.

Athletics Interscholastic: alpine skiing (boys, girls), baseball (b), basketball (b,g), cross-country running (b,g), equestrian sports (b,g), field hockey (g), football (b), freestyle skiing (b,g), golf (b,g), hockey (b,g), horseback riding (b,g), ice hockey (b,g), lacrosse (b,g), nordic skiing (b,g), rugby (b), running (b,g), skiing (cross-country) (b,g), skiing (downhill) (b,g), snowboarding (b,g), soccer (b,g), softball (g), swimming and diving (b,g), tennis (b,g); coed intramural: alpine skiing, backpacking, canoeing/kayaking, dance, equestrian sports, fitness, freestyle skiing, hiking/backpacking, modern dance, outdoor activities, physical fitness, rock climbing, strength & conditioning, surfing, weight lifting, yoga. 1 coach, 2 athletic trainers.

Computers Computers are regularly used in architecture, literary magazine, theater arts, woodworking classes. Computer network features include on-campus library services, Internet access, wireless campus network, Internet filtering or blocking technology, computer music studio/audio recording. Campus intranet, student e-mail accounts, and computer access in designated common areas are available to students. Students grades are available online. The school has a published electronic and media policy.

Contact Mr. Rich Ryerson, Director of Admissions and Financial Aid. 603-469-2100. Fax: 603-469-2041. E-mail: admissions@kua.org. Web site: www.kua.org.

KING GEORGE SCHOOL
Sutton, Vermont
See Special Needs Schools section.

KING LOW HEYWOOD THOMAS
1450 Newfield Avenue
Stamford, Connecticut 06905
Head of School: Thomas B. Main

General Information Coeducational day college-preparatory school. Grades PK–12. Founded: 1865. Setting: suburban. Nearest major city is New York, NY. 40-acre campus. 4 buildings on campus. Approved or accredited by Connecticut Association of Independent Schools and New England Association of Schools and Colleges. Member of National Association of Independent Schools. Endowment: $16.1 million. Total enrollment: 685. Upper school average class size: 12. Upper school faculty-student ratio: 1:7. The average school day consists of 7 hours and 15 minutes.

Upper School Student Profile Grade 9: 88 students (50 boys, 38 girls); Grade 10: 85 students (48 boys, 37 girls); Grade 11: 69 students (45 boys, 24 girls); Grade 12: 66 students (38 boys, 28 girls).

Faculty School total: 105. In upper school: 23 men, 24 women; 35 have advanced degrees.

Subjects Offered Acting, advanced chemistry, advanced computer applications, advanced math, Advanced Placement courses, algebra, American history, ancient history, ancient world history, art, biology, British literature, calculus, calculus-AP, chemistry, chemistry-AP, choral music, college counseling, college placement, computer applications, computer graphics, computer multimedia, computer programming, computer programming-AP, computer science, creative writing, discrete mathematics, dramatic arts, economics, economics-AP, English, English literature, English literature-AP, ethics, ethics and responsibility, European history, European history-AP, expository writing, fine arts, French, French language-AP, general science, geometry, health, history, Holocaust, honors algebra, honors English, honors geometry, honors U.S. history, honors world history, independent study, introduction to theater, macroeconomics-AP, mathematics, mathematics-AP, microeconomics-AP, model United Nations, modern European history-AP, modern languages, musical productions, musical theater, performing arts, philosophy, physics, physics-AP, play production, pre-calculus, SAT preparation, science, social studies, Spanish, Spanish literature, Spanish literature-AP, statistics, statistics-AP, student government, student publications, studio art, theater arts, trigonometry, U.S. history-AP, U.S. literature, world history, writing workshop.

Graduation Requirements Arts and fine arts (art, music, dance, drama), English, ethics, foreign language, history, life skills, mathematics, science, sports, participation in one theater performance before graduation.

Special Academic Programs 19 Advanced Placement exams for which test preparation is offered; honors section; independent study; academic accommodation for the gifted, the musically talented, and the artistically talented.

College Admission Counseling 68 students graduated in 2010; 66 went to college, including Boston University; Bucknell University; Colgate University; Northeastern University; University of Richmond; Wake Forest University. Other: 2 entered a postgraduate year. Median SAT critical reading: 580, median SAT math: 605, median SAT writing: 600, median combined SAT: 1750, median composite ACT: 25. 48% scored over 600 on SAT critical reading, 55% scored over 600 on SAT math, 55% scored over 600 on SAT writing, 46% scored over 1800 on combined SAT, 36% scored over 26 on composite ACT.

Student Life Upper grades have specified standards of dress, student council, honor system. Discipline rests primarily with faculty.

Summer Programs Remediation, enrichment, advancement, sports, art/fine arts, computer instruction programs offered; session focuses on academics (grades 6-12), enrichment (elementary school), and sports (grades 4-8) enrichment; held on campus; accepts boys and girls; open to students from other schools. 250 students usually enrolled. 2011 schedule: June 20 to August 5. Application deadline: May 27.

Tuition and Aid Day student tuition: $31,400. Tuition installment plan (Key Tuition Payment Plan). Need-based scholarship grants available. In 2010–11, 14% of upper-school students received aid. Total amount of financial aid awarded in 2010–11: $765,875.

Admissions Traditional secondary-level entrance grade is 9. For fall 2010, 200 students applied for upper-level admission, 67 were accepted, 47 enrolled. ISEE, school's own test or SSAT required. Deadline for receipt of application materials: January 1. Application fee required: $75. On-campus interview required.

Athletics Interscholastic: baseball (boys), basketball (b,g), cross-country running (b,g), field hockey (g), football (b), golf (b,g), ice hockey (b), independent competitive sports (b,g), lacrosse (b,g), soccer (b,g), softball (g), tennis (b,g), volleyball (g); intramural: dance (g), physical training (b,g); coed interscholastic: hockey, ice hockey, independent competitive sports, squash, weight training; coed intramural: aerobics, aerobics/dance, dance, fitness, physical training, strength & conditioning, weight lifting, weight training, yoga. 34 coaches, 2 athletic trainers.

Computers Computers are regularly used in college planning, creative writing, economics, English, ethics, foreign language, French, history, mathematics, science, technology, writing, yearbook classes. Computer network features include on-campus library services, online commercial services, Internet access, wireless campus network, Internet filtering or blocking technology. Campus intranet, student e-mail accounts, and computer access in designated common areas are available to students. The school has a published electronic and media policy.

Contact Carrie Salvatore, Director of Admission and Financial Aid. 203-322-3496 Ext. 352. Fax: 203-505-6288. E-mail: csalvatore@klht.org. Web site: www.klht.org.

THE KING'S ACADEMY

202 Smothers Road
Seymour, Tennessee 37865
Head of School: Walter Grubb

General Information Coeducational boarding and day and distance learning college-preparatory and religious studies school, affiliated with Southern Baptist Convention. Boarding boys grades 6–12, boarding girls grades 7–12, day boys grades K4–12, day girls grades K4–12. Distance learning grades 9–12. Founded: 1880. Setting: suburban. Nearest major city is Knoxville. Students are housed in single-sex dormitories. 67-acre campus. 8 buildings on campus. Approved or accredited by Southern Association of Colleges and Schools and Tennessee Department of Education. Endowment: $1.1 million. Total enrollment: 402. Upper school average class size: 14. Upper school faculty-student ratio: 1:14. There are 180 required school days per year for Upper School students. Upper School students typically attend 5 days per week. The average school day consists of 7 hours.

Upper School Student Profile Grade 9: 38 students (19 boys, 19 girls); Grade 10: 35 students (19 boys, 16 girls); Grade 11: 37 students (16 boys, 21 girls); Grade 12: 33 students (20 boys, 13 girls). 20% of students are boarding students. 79% are state residents. 1 state is represented in upper school student body. 28% are international students. International students from Bahamas, Brazil, China, Iraq, Republic of Korea, and Thailand; 9 other countries represented in student body. 80% of students are Southern Baptist Convention.

Faculty School total: 44. In upper school: 8 men, 13 women; 11 have advanced degrees; 5 reside on campus.

Subjects Offered Advanced Placement courses, algebra, American history, anatomy, art, Bible studies, biology, calculus, chemistry, Chinese, choir, drama, economics, English, English-AP, ESL, fine arts, geometry, government/civics, grammar, health, health and wellness, history, keyboarding, mathematics, music, orchestra, physical education, physics, physiology, religion, science, social studies, Spanish, world history.

Graduation Requirements Arts and fine arts (art, music, dance, drama), computer science, English, foreign language, mathematics, religion (includes Bible studies and theology), science, social studies (includes history), wellness.

Special Academic Programs Advanced Placement exam preparation; honors section; independent study; study at local college for college credit; ESL (20 students enrolled).

College Admission Counseling 43 students graduated in 2010; 41 went to college, including Middle Tennessee State University; The University of Tennessee; University of Illinois at Urbana–Champaign; University of Minnesota, Twin Cities Campus; University of Mississippi; University of Washington. Other: 2 entered military service.

Student Life Upper grades have uniform requirement, student council. Discipline rests primarily with faculty. Attendance at religious services is required.

Tuition and Aid Day student tuition: $5180–$6220; 5-day tuition and room/board: $15,140–$15,810; 7-day tuition and room/board: $21,525–$25,495. Tuition installment plan (monthly payment plans, individually arranged payment plans). Need-based scholarship grants, paying campus jobs available. In 2010–11, 23% of upper-school students received aid. Total amount of financial aid awarded in 2010–11: $136,615.

Admissions Traditional secondary-level entrance grade is 9. For fall 2010, 36 students applied for upper-level admission, 32 were accepted, 26 enrolled. Deadline for receipt of application materials: none. Application fee required: $50. Interview recommended.

Athletics Interscholastic: baseball (boys), basketball (b,g), cheering (g), football (b), golf (b,g), soccer (b,g), tennis (b,g), volleyball (g), weight lifting (b), weight training (b); intramural: basketball (b,g), billiards (b,g), table tennis (b,g), tennis (b,g), volleyball (g), weight lifting (b,g), weight training (b,g); coed interscholastic: backpacking, bowling, cross-country running, rappelling, rock climbing, strength & conditioning, track and field; coed intramural: canoeing/kayaking, cross-country running, outdoor education, physical fitness, volleyball.

Computers Computers are regularly used in business applications, computer applications, keyboarding, yearbook classes. Computer network features include Internet access.

Contact Janice Mink, Director of Admissions. 865-573-8321. Fax: 865-573-8323. E-mail: jmink@thekingsacademy.net. Web site: www.thekingsacademy.net.

THE KING'S CHRISTIAN HIGH SCHOOL

5 Carnegie Plaza
Cherry Hill, New Jersey 08003-1020
Head of School: Rebecca B. Stiegel, EdD

General Information Coeducational day and distance learning college-preparatory and religious studies school, affiliated with Christian faith. Grades P3–12. Distance learning grades 6–12. Founded: 1946. Setting: suburban. Nearest major city is Philadelphia, PA. 11-acre campus. 1 building on campus. Approved or accredited by Association of Christian Schools International, Middle States Association of Colleges and Schools, and New Jersey Department of Education. Total enrollment: 276. Upper school average class size: 18. Upper school faculty-student ratio: 1:6. There are 180 required school days per year for Upper School students. Upper School students typically attend 5 days per week. The average school day consists of 6 hours and 30 minutes.

Upper School Student Profile Grade 9: 30 students (14 boys, 16 girls); Grade 10: 29 students (15 boys, 14 girls); Grade 11: 26 students (12 boys, 14 girls); Grade 12: 29 students (12 boys, 17 girls). 100% of students are Christian faith.

Faculty School total: 31. In upper school: 7 men, 11 women; 2 have advanced degrees.

Subjects Offered Accounting, Advanced Placement courses, algebra, American history, American literature, anatomy, anatomy and physiology, art, art appreciation, art history, art history-AP, band, bell choir, Bible, Bible studies, biology, biology-AP, British literature, business mathematics, calculus, calculus-AP, career and personal planning, career education, career/college preparation, chemistry, choir, Christian ethics, church history, college admission preparation, composition, computer education, computer graphics, computer skills, concert band, concert bell choir, concert choir, consumer mathematics, drama, economics, English literature, environmental science, ESL, fine arts, foreign language, general math, geometry, government-AP, handbells, health and safety, health and wellness, health education, honors algebra, honors English, honors geometry, honors U.S. history, instrumental music, jazz band, keyboarding, language arts, library assistant, Life of Christ, marine science, music appreciation, music theory, music theory-AP, New Testament, physical education, physics, SAT preparation, SAT/ACT preparation, senior project, Shakespeare, Spanish, speech, study skills, U.S. government, U.S. history, vocal ensemble, Web site design, world cultures, world history, yearbook.

Graduation Requirements Algebra, arts and fine arts (art, music, dance, drama), Bible, biology, British literature, career education, career technology, chemistry, Christian ethics, church history, computer technologies, English composition, English literature, ethics, human biology, Life of Christ, physical education (includes health),

The King's Christian High School

physical science, public speaking, SAT preparation, senior project, Spanish, study skills, U.S. government, U.S. history, world literature, writing, required volunteer service hours each year for grades 6-12.

Special Academic Programs 7 Advanced Placement exams for which test preparation is offered; honors section; independent study; study at local college for college credit; programs in English, mathematics, general development for dyslexic students; special instructional classes for students with learning disabilities, Attention Deficit Disorder; ESL (4 students enrolled).

College Admission Counseling 44 students graduated in 2009; all went to college, including Cedarville University; Eastern University; Gordon College; Liberty University; Taylor University. Mean SAT critical reading: 540, mean SAT math: 515, mean SAT writing: 522, mean combined SAT: 1577. 21% scored over 600 on SAT critical reading, 18% scored over 600 on SAT math, 15% scored over 600 on SAT writing.

Student Life Upper grades have specified standards of dress, student council, honor system. Discipline rests primarily with faculty. Attendance at religious services is required.

Tuition and Aid Day student tuition: $8900. Tuition installment plan (FACTS Tuition Payment Plan, annual and semi-annual payments). Need-based scholarship grants available. In 2009–10, 46% of upper-school students received aid. Total amount of financial aid awarded in 2009–10: $139,000.

Admissions Traditional secondary-level entrance grade is 9. For fall 2009, 19 students applied for upper-level admission, 17 were accepted, 16 enrolled. Deadline for receipt of application materials: none. Application fee required: $200. On-campus interview required.

Athletics Interscholastic: baseball (boys), basketball (b,g), physical fitness (b,g), soccer (b,g), softball (g), track and field (b,g); intramural: basketball (b), flag football (b), golf (b,g). 2 PE instructors.

Computers Computers are regularly used in career education, career exploration, college planning, computer applications, desktop publishing, ESL, graphic design, keyboarding, lab/keyboard, Latin, library, library skills, life skills, music, SAT preparation, Web site design, writing, yearbook classes. Computer network features include on-campus library services, Internet access, Internet filtering or blocking technology. Campus intranet and computer access in designated common areas are available to students. Students grades are available online. The school has a published electronic and media policy.

Contact Mrs. Jamie Sellers, Director of Admissions. 856-489-6720 Ext. 117. Fax: 856-489-6727. E-mail: jsellers@tkcs.org. Web site: www.tkcs.org.

KINGS CHRISTIAN SCHOOL
900 East D Street
Lemoore, California 93245
Head of School: Mr. Duane E. Daniel

General Information Coeducational day college-preparatory, general academic, arts, business, religious studies, and technology school. Grades PK–12. Founded: 1979. Setting: small town. Nearest major city is Fresno. 17-acre campus. 12 buildings on campus. Approved or accredited by Association of Christian Schools International and Western Association of Schools and Colleges. Total enrollment: 283. Upper school average class size: 20. Upper school faculty-student ratio: 1:11. There are 180 required school days per year for Upper School students. Upper School students typically attend 5 days per week. The average school day consists of 6 hours and 45 minutes.

Upper School Student Profile Grade 6: 14 students (10 boys, 4 girls); Grade 7: 25 students (15 boys, 10 girls); Grade 8: 26 students (17 boys, 9 girls); Grade 9: 19 students (10 boys, 9 girls); Grade 10: 24 students (14 boys, 10 girls); Grade 11: 28 students (11 boys, 17 girls); Grade 12: 27 students (13 boys, 14 girls).

Faculty School total: 24. In upper school: 4 men, 5 women; 3 have advanced degrees.

Subjects Offered Accounting, advanced math, algebra, American government, art, Bible studies, biology, business, calculus-AP, career education, chemistry, choir, chorus, community service, computer literacy, computer programming, drama, drama performance, drawing, driver education, economics, English, English literature-AP, finance, fine arts, geography, geometry, health, home economics, keyboarding, life skills, literature, mathematics, music, music theory, novels, physical education, physical science, physics, pre-algebra, religion, SAT preparation, science, Shakespeare, social sciences, social studies, Spanish, speech, U.S. history, weight training, word processing, yearbook.

Graduation Requirements Arts and fine arts (art, music, dance, drama), English, foreign language, mathematics, physical education (includes health), portfolio writing, science, social sciences, successfully pass Bible every year of attendance, proof of at least 9th grade proficiency (SAT Test).

Special Academic Programs 2 Advanced Placement exams for which test preparation is offered; honors section; accelerated programs; independent study; remedial reading and/or remedial writing; remedial math.

College Admission Counseling 27 students graduated in 2010; 22 went to college, including Biola University; California State University, Fresno; Point Loma Nazarene University; The Master's College and Seminary; Vanguard University of Southern California; West Hills Community College. Other: 2 went to work, 3 entered military service. Median SAT critical reading: 570, median SAT math: 490, median SAT writing: 540, median combined SAT: 1600. 22% scored over 600 on SAT critical reading, 22% scored over 600 on SAT math, 22% scored over 600 on SAT writing, 10% scored over 1800 on combined SAT.

Student Life Upper grades have specified standards of dress, student council. Discipline rests primarily with faculty.

Tuition and Aid Day student tuition: $5610. Tuition installment plan (monthly payment plans). Tuition reduction for siblings, need-based scholarship grants, paying campus jobs available. In 2010–11, 18% of upper-school students received aid. Total amount of financial aid awarded in 2010–11: $150,000.

Admissions Traditional secondary-level entrance grade is 9. For fall 2010, 19 students applied for upper-level admission, 16 were accepted, 15 enrolled. PSAT or Stanford Achievement Test required. Deadline for receipt of application materials: none. Application fee required: $75.

Athletics Interscholastic: baseball (boys), basketball (b,g), football (b), softball (g), track and field (b,g), volleyball (g); intramural: physical fitness (b,g), physical training (b,g), power lifting (b), strength & conditioning (b,g), track and field (b,g), weight training (b,g); coed interscholastic: cheering, cross-country running, track and field; coed intramural: badminton, fitness, Frisbee, physical fitness, strength & conditioning, table tennis, track and field, volleyball. 5 PE instructors, 9 coaches, 2 athletic trainers.

Computers Computers are regularly used in Bible studies, college planning, English, introduction to technology, journalism, library skills, programming, SAT preparation, technical drawing, yearbook classes. Computer network features include on-campus library services, Internet access, wireless campus network, Internet filtering or blocking technology.

Contact Leslie Reynolds, Registrar. 559-924-8301 Ext. 107. Fax: 559-924-0607. E-mail: lreynolds@kcsnet.com. Web site: www.kcsnet.com.

KING'S-EDGEHILL SCHOOL
254 College Road
Windsor, Nova Scotia B0N 2T0, Canada
Head of School: Mr. Joseph Seagram

General Information Coeducational boarding and day college-preparatory school. Grades 6–12. Founded: 1788. Setting: small town. Nearest major city is Halifax, Canada. Students are housed in single-sex dormitories. 65-acre campus. 17 buildings on campus. Approved or accredited by Nova Scotia Department of Education. Language of instruction: English. Total enrollment: 290. Upper school average class size: 15. Upper school faculty-student ratio: 1:10.

Upper School Student Profile Grade 10: 60 students (28 boys, 32 girls); Grade 11: 70 students (37 boys, 33 girls); Grade 12: 70 students (38 boys, 32 girls). 68% of students are boarding students. 55% are province residents. 13 provinces are represented in upper school student body. 30% are international students. International students from Germany, Hong Kong, Mexico, Republic of Korea, and Taiwan; 13 other countries represented in student body.

Faculty School total: 46. In upper school: 19 men, 23 women; 15 have advanced degrees; 22 reside on campus.

Subjects Offered Art, biology, calculus, chemistry, current events, drama, economics, English, French, geography, geology, history, mathematics, music, physics, political science, religion, science, social sciences, social studies, theater, theory of knowledge, world history.

Graduation Requirements English, foreign language, mathematics, science, social sciences, social studies (includes history).

Special Academic Programs International Baccalaureate program; honors section; term-away projects; study abroad; academic accommodation for the gifted; ESL (22 students enrolled).

College Admission Counseling 78 students graduated in 2010; 77 went to college, including Dalhousie University; McGill University; Queen's University at Kingston; The University of British Columbia; The University of Western Ontario. Other: 1 went to work.

Student Life Upper grades have uniform requirement, student council, honor system. Discipline rests primarily with faculty. Attendance at religious services is required.

Tuition and Aid Day student tuition: CAN$11,900; 5-day tuition and room/board: CAN$31,000; 7-day tuition and room/board: CAN$31,000–CAN$40,000. Tuition installment plan (monthly payment plans, individually arranged payment plans). Bursaries, merit scholarship grants available. In 2010–11, 35% of upper-school students received aid. Total amount of financial aid awarded in 2010–11: CAN$700,000.

Admissions Traditional secondary-level entrance grade is 10. OLSAT and English Exam required. Deadline for receipt of application materials: none. Application fee required: CAN$100. Interview required.

Athletics Interscholastic: alpine skiing (boys, girls), aquatics (b,g), badminton (b,g), baseball (b,g), basketball (b,g), biathlon (b,g), bicycling (b,g), cross-country running (b,g), equestrian sports (b,g), fitness (b,g), Frisbee (b,g), golf (b,g), ice hockey (b,g), outdoor recreation (b,g), outdoor skills (b,g), physical fitness (b,g), rugby (b,g), skiing (cross-country) (b,g), skiing (downhill) (b,g), snowboarding (b,g), soccer (b,g), softball (b,g), table tennis (b,g), tennis (b,g), track and field (b,g), ultimate Frisbee (b,g), volleyball (b,g), weight lifting (b,g), wrestling (b,g); intramural: basketball (b,g), bicycling (b,g), cross-country running (b,g), golf (b,g), rugby (b,g), skiing (cross-country) (b,g), skiing (downhill) (b,g), snowboarding (b,g), soccer (b,g), softball (b,g), table tennis (b,g), tennis (b,g), track and field (b,g), weight lifting (b,g), yoga (b,g); coed interscholastic: alpine skiing, aquatics, bicycling, equestrian sports, fitness, Frisbee, outdoor recreation, outdoor skills, physical fitness, table tennis; coed intramural: bowling, curling, field hockey, table tennis, yoga. 2 PE instructors, 30 coaches.

Computers Computers are regularly used in computer applications, English, foreign language, mathematics, music, science classes. Computer network features include on-campus library services, online commercial services, Internet access, Internet filtering or blocking technology. Campus intranet, student e-mail accounts, and computer access in designated common areas are available to students.

Contact Mr. Chris B. Strickey, Director of Admission. 902-798-2278. Fax: 902-798-2105. E-mail: strickey@kes.ns.ca. Web site: www.kes.ns.ca.

KING'S HIGH SCHOOL

19303 Fremont Avenue North
Seattle, Washington 98133
Head of School: Bob Ruhlman

General Information Coeducational day college-preparatory, arts, business, religious studies, and technology school, affiliated with Christian faith. Grades PK–12. Founded: 1950. Setting: suburban. 55-acre campus. 6 buildings on campus. Approved or accredited by Association of Christian Schools International, Northwest Association of Schools and Colleges, and Washington Department of Education. Total enrollment: 1,130. Upper school average class size: 25. Upper school faculty-student ratio: 1:15. There are 171 required school days per year for Upper School students. Upper School students typically attend 5 days per week. The average school day consists of 5 hours and 47 minutes.

Upper School Student Profile Grade 9: 127 students (58 boys, 69 girls); Grade 10: 113 students (61 boys, 52 girls); Grade 11: 120 students (62 boys, 58 girls); Grade 12: 111 students (52 boys, 59 girls). 80% of students are Christian faith.

Faculty School total: 89. In upper school: 11 men, 22 women; 20 have advanced degrees.

Subjects Offered Advanced Placement courses, algebra, American history, American literature, anatomy, anatomy and physiology, art, Bible, biology, business, calculus, calculus-AP, ceramics, chemistry, chemistry-AP, choir, choral music, computer science, culinary arts, drama, earth science, English, English literature, English-AP, environmental science, European history, European history-AP, expository writing, fine arts, geography, geometry, health, history, history-AP, honors algebra, honors English, honors geometry, honors U.S. history, journalism, leadership, mathematics, music, orchestra, photography, physical education, physics, pre-calculus, psychology, religion, SAT preparation, science, social studies, Spanish, speech, theater, trigonometry, U.S. history, U.S. history-AP, video film production, vocal ensemble, vocal jazz, world history, writing.

Graduation Requirements Arts and fine arts (art, music, dance, drama), computer science, English, foreign language, mathematics, physical education (includes health), religion (includes Bible studies and theology), science, social studies (includes history), speech, senior thesis, senior project, senior retreat.

Special Academic Programs Advanced Placement exam preparation; honors section.

College Admission Counseling 102 students graduated in 2009; 100 went to college, including Central Washington University; Seattle Pacific University; University of Washington. Other: 2 went to work. Mean SAT critical reading: 546, mean SAT math: 587, mean SAT writing: 538, mean combined SAT: 1671, mean composite ACT: 24.

Student Life Upper grades have specified standards of dress, student council. Discipline rests primarily with faculty. Attendance at religious services is required.

Tuition and Aid Day student tuition: $10,660. Tuition installment plan (monthly payment plans). Tuition reduction for siblings, need-based scholarship grants, paying campus jobs available. In 2009–10, 16% of upper-school students received aid. Total amount of financial aid awarded in 2009–10: $572,000.

Admissions Traditional secondary-level entrance grade is 9. For fall 2009, 59 students applied for upper-level admission, 54 were accepted, 50 enrolled. Gates MacGinite Placement Test or TOEFL required. Deadline for receipt of application materials: none. Application fee required: $50. On-campus interview required.

Athletics Interscholastic: basketball (boys, girls), cross-country running (b,g), football (b), golf (b,g), soccer (b,g), track and field (b,g), volleyball (g); coed interscholastic: cheering, physical fitness, physical training, power lifting, strength & conditioning, weight training. 3 PE instructors, 26 coaches, 1 athletic trainer.

Computers Computers are regularly used in English, introduction to technology, journalism, keyboarding, media production, photography, science, study skills, technology, video film production, Web site design, yearbook classes. Computer network features include on-campus library services, online commercial services, Internet access, Internet filtering or blocking technology. Students grades are available online. The school has a published electronic and media policy.

Contact Krista Feyma, Secondary Admissions Coordinator. 206-289-7783. Fax: 206-546-7214. E-mail: kfeyma@crista.net. Web site: www.kingsschools.org.

KINGSHILL SCHOOL

St. Croix, Virgin Islands
See Special Needs Schools section.

KING'S RIDGE CHRISTIAN SCHOOL

2765 Bethany Bend
Alpharetta, Georgia 30004
Head of School: Mr. C. David Rhodes III

General Information Coeducational day college-preparatory school, affiliated with Christian faith. Grades K–12. Founded: 2001. Setting: suburban. Nearest major city is Atlanta. 70-acre campus. 3 buildings on campus. Approved or accredited by Georgia Accrediting Commission, Georgia Independent School Association, Southern Association of Colleges and Schools, and Southern Association of Independent Schools. Total enrollment: 650. Upper school average class size: 12. Upper school faculty-student ratio: 1:8. There are 180 required school days per year for Upper School students. Upper School students typically attend 5 days per week. The average school day consists of 6 hours and 45 minutes.

Faculty School total: 110. In upper school: 12 men, 12 women; 14 have advanced degrees.

Subjects Offered Advanced Placement courses, algebra, American government, American history, art, astronomy, biology, calculus-AP, chemistry, Christian doctrine, Christian education, Christian ethics, civics, communication skills, computer programming, drama performance, drawing, English composition, English literature, European history, finance, French, geometry, honors algebra, honors English, honors geometry, honors U.S. history, Life of Christ, music composition, physical fitness, physics, public speaking, SAT preparation, Spanish, speech, statistics, studio art, video film production, yearbook.

Graduation Requirements 50 hours of community service between grades 9-12.

Special Academic Programs Advanced Placement exam preparation; honors section.

College Admission Counseling 16 students graduated in 2010; all went to college, including American University; Auburn University; Elon University; Georgia College & State University; Georgia Institute of Technology; Samford University.

Student Life Upper grades have uniform requirement, student council, honor system. Discipline rests primarily with faculty. Attendance at religious services is required.

Tuition and Aid Day student tuition: $14,134. Tuition installment plan (Insured Tuition Payment Plan, FACTS Tuition Payment Plan). Tuition reduction for siblings, need-based scholarship grants available. In 2010–11, 30% of upper-school students received aid.

Admissions SSAT, ERB, PSAT, SAT, PLAN or ACT required. Deadline for receipt of application materials: none. Application fee required: $75. Interview required.

Athletics Interscholastic: baseball (boys), basketball (b,g), cheering (g), football (b), lacrosse (b), soccer (b,g), softball (g), strength & conditioning (b), swimming and diving (b,g), tennis (b,g), volleyball (g); coed interscholastic: cross-country running, equestrian sports, golf, horseback riding, track and field; coed intramural: weight training. 3 PE instructors, 3 coaches.

Computers Computers are regularly used in all academic classes. Computer network features include online commercial services, Internet access, wireless campus network, Internet filtering or blocking technology, online collaboration of classroom activities. Campus intranet, student e-mail accounts, and computer access in designated common areas are available to students. Students grades are available online. The school has a published electronic and media policy.

Contact Lisa K. McGuire, Director of Admission/Marketing. 770-754-5738 Ext. 118. Fax: 770-754-5544. E-mail: lmcguire@kingsridgecs.org. Web site: www. kingsridgecs.org/.

KINGSWAY COLLEGE

1200 Leland Road
Oshawa, Ontario L1K 2H4, Canada
Head of School: Mr. Scott Bowes

General Information Coeducational boarding and day college-preparatory, general academic, religious studies, and bilingual studies school, affiliated with Seventh-day Adventists. Grades 9–12. Founded: 1903. Setting: small town. Nearest major city is Toronto, Canada. Students are housed in single-sex dormitories. 100-acre campus. 9 buildings on campus. Approved or accredited by Ontario Ministry of Education and Ontario Department of Education. Language of instruction: English. Endowment: CAN$1.6 million. Total enrollment: 185. Upper school average class size: 25. Upper school faculty-student ratio: 1:11. There are 180 required school days per year for Upper School students. Upper School students typically attend 5 days per week. The average school day consists of 5 hours and 50 minutes.

Upper School Student Profile Grade 9: 40 students (19 boys, 21 girls); Grade 10: 51 students (22 boys, 29 girls); Grade 11: 50 students (27 boys, 23 girls); Grade 12: 44 students (27 boys, 17 girls). 45% of students are boarding students. 85% are province residents. 9 provinces are represented in upper school student body. 4% are international students. International students from Bahamas, Bermuda, Democratic People's Republic of Korea, Japan, United Kingdom, and United States. 90% of students are Seventh-day Adventists.

Faculty School total: 16. In upper school: 9 men, 7 women; 2 have advanced degrees; 8 reside on campus.

Subjects Offered Accounting, advanced chemistry, advanced computer applications, advanced math, algebra, American history, anthropology, band, biology, business studies, calculus, Canadian geography, Canadian history, Canadian law, career education, ceramics, chemistry, choir, civics, computer applications, computer information systems, computer programming, computer studies, concert band, English, English literature, ESL, French, healthful living, information processing, intro to computers, music, music performance, physical education, physics, psychology, religious education, science, sociology, U.S. history, visual arts, work-study, world civilizations, world religions.

Graduation Requirements Art, Canadian geography, Canadian history, careers, civics, English, French, mathematics, physical education (includes health), science, all students must take one religion course per year.

Special Academic Programs ESL (2 students enrolled).

College Admission Counseling 45 students graduated in 2010; 37 went to college, including Andrews University; McGill University; Southern Adventist University; University of Michigan; University of Toronto; Walla Walla University. Other: 1 entered military service, 2 had other specific plans.

Student Life Upper grades have specified standards of dress, student council. Discipline rests primarily with faculty. Attendance at religious services is required.

Tuition and Aid Day student tuition: CAN$9430; 7-day tuition and room/board: CAN$16,013. Tuition installment plan (monthly payment plans, individually arranged payment plans). Tuition reduction for siblings, merit scholarship grants, need-based scholarship grants, paying campus jobs available. In 2010–11, 45% of upper-school students received aid; total upper-school merit-scholarship money awarded: CAN$24,000. Total amount of financial aid awarded in 2010–11: CAN$156,000.

Admissions Traditional secondary-level entrance grade is 9. For fall 2010, 189 students applied for upper-level admission, 187 were accepted, 185 enrolled. Deadline for receipt of application materials: none. No application fee required. Interview recommended.

Athletics Interscholastic: basketball (boys, girls); intramural: basketball (b,g), flag football (b,g), floor hockey (b,g), ice hockey (b), indoor hockey (b,g), soccer (b,g), softball (b,g), volleyball (b,g); coed intramural: backpacking, badminton, bicycling, canoeing/kayaking, gymnastics, hiking/backpacking, outdoor education, roller skating, skiing (downhill), snowboarding, volleyball. 1 PE instructor.

Computers Computers are regularly used in accounting, business, career education, computer applications, data processing, English, ESL, history, programming, science, social sciences classes. Computer network features include Internet access, Internet filtering or blocking technology. Student e-mail accounts are available to students. Students grades are available online. The school has a published electronic and media policy.

Contact Ms. Remy Guenin, Director of Enrollment Services. 905-433-1144 Ext. 212. Fax: 905-433-1156. E-mail: gueninr@kingswaycollege.on.ca. Web site: www.kingswaycollege.on.ca.

KINGSWOOD-OXFORD SCHOOL

170 Kingswood Road
West Hartford, Connecticut 06119-1430
Head of School: Mr. Dennis Bisgaard

General Information Coeducational day college-preparatory school. Grades 6–12. Founded: 1909. Setting: suburban. Nearest major city is Hartford. 30-acre campus. 11 buildings on campus. Approved or accredited by Connecticut Association of Independent Schools, New England Association of Schools and Colleges, and Connecticut Department of Education. Member of National Association of Independent Schools and Secondary School Admission Test Board. Endowment: $23.8 million. Total enrollment: 508. Upper school average class size: 13. Upper school faculty-student ratio: 1:8. There are 160 required school days per year for Upper School students. Upper School students typically attend 5 days per week. The average school day consists of 7 hours.

Upper School Student Profile Grade 9: 89 students (46 boys, 43 girls); Grade 10: 76 students (42 boys, 34 girls); Grade 11: 101 students (48 boys, 53 girls); Grade 12: 98 students (51 boys, 47 girls).

Faculty School total: 66. In upper school: 30 men, 36 women; 29 have advanced degrees.

Subjects Offered Algebra, American history, American literature, art, art history-AP, band, biology, biology-AP, calculus, calculus-AP, chemistry, chemistry-AP, Chinese, Chinese studies, chorus, composition-AP, computer science, computer science-AP, concert band, concert choir, creative writing, digital music, digital photography, dramatic arts, drawing, economics, economics-AP, English, English language-AP, English literature, English literature-AP, environmental science, fine arts, forensics, French, French language-AP, geography, geometry, government/civics, jazz band, jazz ensemble, journalism, Latin, marine biology, mathematics, media, music, orchestra, photography, physics, physics-AP, political science, public speaking, social studies, Spanish, Spanish language-AP, Spanish-AP, statistics, statistics-AP, theater, U.S. history-AP, visual arts, world history, world literature, writing.

Graduation Requirements Computer science, English, foreign language, mathematics, performing arts, science, social studies (includes history), technology, visual arts, participation on athletic teams, senior thesis in English, 30 hours of community service. Community service is required.

Special Academic Programs 17 Advanced Placement exams for which test preparation is offered; honors section; independent study; term-away projects; study at local college for college credit; study abroad.

College Admission Counseling 91 students graduated in 2010; all went to college, including Gettysburg College; Skidmore College; Syracuse University; Tufts Uni-

versity; University of Connecticut; Williams College. Median SAT critical reading: 595, median SAT math: 600, median SAT writing: 605, median combined SAT: 1810, median composite ACT: 24.

Student Life Upper grades have specified standards of dress, student council, honor system. Discipline rests equally with students and faculty.

Tuition and Aid Day student tuition: $31,210. Tuition installment plan (Academic Management Services Plan). Merit scholarship grants, need-based scholarship grants available. In 2010–11, 34% of upper-school students received aid; total upper-school merit-scholarship money awarded: $225,000. Total amount of financial aid awarded in 2010–11: $2,700,000.

Admissions Traditional secondary-level entrance grade is 9. For fall 2010, 181 students applied for upper-level admission, 97 were accepted, 44 enrolled. SSAT required. Deadline for receipt of application materials: February 1. Application fee required: $55. On-campus interview required.

Athletics Interscholastic: baseball (boys), basketball (b,g), cross-country running (b,g), dance (b,g), diving (b,g), field hockey (g), football (b), ice hockey (b,g), lacrosse (b,g), soccer (b,g), softball (g), squash (b,g), strength & conditioning (b,g), swimming and diving (b,g), tennis (b,g), track and field (b,g), volleyball (g); intramural: basketball (b), soccer (b), yoga (g); coed interscholastic: golf, skiing (downhill); coed intramural: dance, strength & conditioning. 5 coaches, 2 athletic trainers.

Computers Computers are regularly used in English, foreign language, history, mathematics, music technology, photography, science classes. Computer resources include on-campus library services, Internet access, wireless campus network. Student e-mail accounts and computer access in designated common areas are available to students. Students grades are available online. The school has a published electronic and media policy.

Contact Mr. James E. O¿Donnell, Director of Enrollment Management. 860-727-5000. Fax: 860-236-3651. E-mail: odonnell.j@k-o.org. Web site: www.kingswoodoxford.org.

KIROV ACADEMY OF BALLET OF WASHINGTON, D.C.

4301 Harewood Road NE
Washington, District of Columbia 20017
Head of School: Mr. Michael Beard

General Information Coeducational boarding and day college-preparatory, arts, and classical ballet; Vaganova method school. Grades 6–12. Founded: 1990. Setting: urban. Students are housed in single-sex by floor dormitories. 3-acre campus. 1 building on campus. Approved or accredited by Middle States Association of Colleges and Schools and District of Columbia Department of Education. Total enrollment: 63. Upper school average class size: 10. Upper school faculty-student ratio: 1:8. There are 160 required school days per year for Upper School students. Upper School students typically attend 5 days per week. The average school day consists of 9 hours.

Upper School Student Profile Grade 6: 4 students (4 girls); Grade 7: 1 student (1 boy); Grade 8: 5 students (5 girls); Grade 9: 5 students (1 boy, 4 girls); Grade 10: 13 students (4 boys, 9 girls); Grade 11: 16 students (2 boys, 14 girls); Grade 12: 14 students (2 boys, 12 girls); Postgraduate: 4 students (2 boys, 2 girls). 90% of students are boarding students. 15 states are represented in upper school student body. International students from Italy, Japan, Mexico, Republic of Korea, and Taiwan.

Faculty School total: 9. In upper school: 3 men, 5 women; 6 have advanced degrees.

Subjects Offered 20th century physics, aesthetics, algebra, American government, American history, American literature, analytic geometry, anatomy, art history, ballet, ballet technique, biology, career planning, chemistry, dance, dance performance, English, ESL, European literature, French, health and wellness, mathematics, music appreciation, nutrition, personal finance, science, senior career experience, world history.

Special Academic Programs ESL (6 students enrolled).

College Admission Counseling 10 students graduated in 2010; 2 went to college, including Indiana University of Pennsylvania; New York University. Other: 8 went to work.

Student Life Upper grades have specified standards of dress, student council. Discipline rests primarily with faculty.

Summer Programs Art/fine arts programs offered; session focuses on classical ballet; held on campus; accepts boys and girls; open to students from other schools. 300 students usually enrolled. 2011 schedule: June 17 to July 29. Application deadline: March 15.

Tuition and Aid Tuition installment plan (monthly payment plans). Merit scholarship grants, paying campus jobs available.

Admissions Iowa Tests of Basic Skills required. Deadline for receipt of application materials: none. No application fee required. On-campus interview required.

Athletics Interscholastic: ballet (boys, girls), dance (b,g); intramural: ballet (b,g); coed interscholastic: ballet, dance; coed intramural: ballet.

Computers Computer network features include Internet access, wireless campus network, Internet filtering or blocking technology. Campus intranet and computer access in designated common areas are available to students. Students grades are available online.

Contact Ms. Rebecca Rorke, Director of Programs. 202-636-0635. Fax: 202-832-8995. E-mail: rorke@kirovacademydc.org. Web site: www.kirovacademydc.org.

THE KISKI SCHOOL
1888 Brett Lane
Saltsburg, Pennsylvania 15681
Head of School: Mr. Christopher A. Brueningsen
General Information Boys' boarding and day and distance learning college-preparatory, technology, and liberal arts and sciences school. Boarding grades 9–PG, day grades 9–12. Distance learning grades 9–12. Founded: 1888. Setting: rural. Nearest major city is Pittsburgh. Students are housed in single-sex dormitories. 350-acre campus. 42 buildings on campus. Approved or accredited by Middle States Association of Colleges and Schools, Pennsylvania Association of Independent Schools, The Association of Boarding Schools, and Pennsylvania Department of Education. Member of National Association of Independent Schools and Secondary School Admission Test Board. Endowment: $10 million. Total enrollment: 200. Upper school average class size: 10. Upper school faculty-student ratio: 1:6.
Upper School Student Profile Grade 9: 31 students (31 boys); Grade 10: 43 students (43 boys); Grade 11: 69 students (69 boys); Grade 12: 56 students (56 boys); Postgraduate: 11 students (11 boys). 95% of students are boarding students. 45% are state residents. 13 states are represented in upper school student body. 38% are international students. International students from Germany, Jamaica, Mexico, Republic of Korea, Spain, and Taiwan; 14 other countries represented in student body.
Faculty School total: 42. In upper school: 34 men, 8 women; 18 have advanced degrees; 38 reside on campus.
Subjects Offered Advanced chemistry, advanced math, algebra, American history-AP, analytic geometry, art, art history, biology, calculus, calculus-AP, ceramics, chemistry, chorus, computer programming, computer science, drama, drama performance, earth science, economics and history, English, English language-AP, English literature, ESL, European history, European history-AP, fine arts, foreign policy, French, French literature-AP, French-AP, geology, geometry, health, history, introduction to theater, music, organic chemistry, physics, physics-AP, political thought, pre-calculus, probability and statistics, psychology, SAT/ACT preparation, senior project, Spanish, speech and debate, The 20th Century, theater arts, theater production, trigonometry, U.S. history, U.S. history-AP, U.S. literature, wellness, world history, writing.
Graduation Requirements Arts and fine arts (art, music, dance, drama), English, ethics, foreign language, lab science, mathematics, personal development, physical education (includes health), social studies (includes history), senior research paper.
Special Academic Programs Advanced Placement exam preparation; honors section; academic accommodation for the gifted; ESL (8 students enrolled).
College Admission Counseling 54 students graduated in 2009; all went to college, including Carnegie Mellon University; Duquesne University; Muhlenberg College; Penn State University Park; The Johns Hopkins University; United States Naval Academy. Mean SAT critical reading: 513, mean SAT math: 591, mean SAT writing: 481.
Student Life Upper grades have specified standards of dress, student council, honor system. Discipline rests primarily with faculty.
Tuition and Aid Day student tuition: $21,300; 7-day tuition and room/board: $36,300. Tuition installment plan (Key Tuition Payment Plan, FACTS Tuition Payment Plan). Merit scholarship grants, need-based scholarship grants, Sallie Mae loans available. Total upper-school merit-scholarship money awarded for 2009–10: $50,000. Total amount of financial aid awarded in 2009–10: $1,900,000.
Admissions Traditional secondary-level entrance grade is 9. For fall 2009, 200 students applied for upper-level admission, 142 were accepted, 89 enrolled. ISEE or SSAT required. Deadline for receipt of application materials: none. Application fee required: $50. Interview required.
Athletics Interscholastic: baseball, basketball, cross-country running, diving, football, golf, hockey, ice hockey, lacrosse, soccer, swimming and diving, tennis, track and field, wrestling; intramural: alpine skiing, basketball, canoeing/kayaking, fishing, fitness, fitness walking, flag football, fly fishing, Frisbee, golf, hiking/backpacking, indoor track & field, jogging, martial arts, mountain biking, outdoor activities, outdoor recreation, paint ball, physical training, power lifting, rafting, skiing (downhill), snowboarding, strength & conditioning, swimming and diving, table tennis, ultimate Frisbee, weight lifting, weight training. 2 PE instructors, 24 coaches, 1 athletic trainer.
Computers Computers are regularly used in computer applications, economics, English, ESL, French, history, library skills, life skills, mathematics, psychology, science classes. Computer network features include on-campus library services, online commercial services, Internet access, wireless campus network, Internet filtering or blocking technology. Campus intranet and student e-mail accounts are available to students. Students grades are available online. The school has a published electronic and media policy.
Contact Mr. William W. Ellis, Assistant Headmaster for Enrollment Management. 724-639-3586 Ext. 237. Fax: 724-639-8467. E-mail: bill.ellis@kiski.org. Web site: www.kiski.org.

THE KNOX SCHOOL
541 Long Beach Road
St. James, New York 11780
Head of School: Mr. George K. Allison
General Information Coeducational boarding and day college-preparatory, arts, bilingual studies, and technology school. Boarding grades 7–12, day grades 6–12.

Founded: 1904. Setting: suburban. Nearest major city is New York. Students are housed in single-sex dormitories. 48-acre campus. 12 buildings on campus. Approved or accredited by Middle States Association of Colleges and Schools, New York State Association of Independent Schools, The Association of Boarding Schools, and New York Department of Education. Member of National Association of Independent Schools. Endowment: $1 million. Total enrollment: 120. Upper school average class size: 12. Upper school faculty-student ratio: 1:5.
Upper School Student Profile Grade 7: 7 students (5 boys, 2 girls); Grade 8: 8 students (5 boys, 3 girls); Grade 9: 22 students (12 boys, 10 girls); Grade 10: 30 students (13 boys, 17 girls); Grade 11: 21 students (7 boys, 14 girls); Grade 12: 31 students (21 boys, 10 girls). 82% of students are boarding students. 47% are state residents. 5 states are represented in upper school student body. 52% are international students. International students from Belarus, China, Japan, Mexico, Republic of Korea, and Spain; 2 other countries represented in student body.
Faculty School total: 29. In upper school: 9 men, 20 women; 14 have advanced degrees; 20 reside on campus.
Subjects Offered 20th century history, algebra, American literature, art history, biology, British literature, calculus, calculus-AP, chemistry, chemistry-AP, computer art, computer science, creative writing, earth science, economics, English, English composition, environmental science, ESL, European history, French, geometry, government, health and wellness, Italian, Latin, music, music history, photo shop, photography, physics, physics-AP, pre-algebra, pre-calculus, psychology, Spanish, studio art, theater, U.S. history, vocal music, world history, world literature.
Graduation Requirements Art, computer education, electives, English, foreign language, health, history, lab science, mathematics, senior project, community service.
Special Academic Programs Advanced Placement exam preparation; honors section; independent study; term-away projects; study at local college for college credit; study abroad; academic accommodation for the gifted; ESL (32 students enrolled).
College Admission Counseling 22 students graduated in 2009; 21 went to college, including Boston University; Hofstra University; Lynn University; New York University; The George Washington University; University of Michigan. Other: 1 had other specific plans.
Student Life Upper grades have uniform requirement, student council, honor system. Discipline rests primarily with faculty.
Tuition and Aid Day student tuition: $23,175; 5-day tuition and room/board: $39,860; 7-day tuition and room/board: $42,025. Tuition installment plan (individually arranged payment plans). Need-based scholarship grants available. In 2009–10, 25% of upper-school students received aid. Total amount of financial aid awarded in 2009–10: $503,670.
Admissions Traditional secondary-level entrance grade is 9. For fall 2009, 96 students applied for upper-level admission, 68 were accepted, 29 enrolled. CCAT, ERB, SLEP, SSAT or TOEFL required. Deadline for receipt of application materials: none. Application fee required: $75. On-campus interview required.
Athletics Interscholastic: baseball (boys), basketball (b,g), soccer (b), softball (g), tennis (b,g), volleyball (g); coed interscholastic: crew, cross-country running, equestrian sports, golf, horseback riding, soccer; coed intramural: combined training, dance, dressage, equestrian sports, fitness, golf, horseback riding, outdoor activities, physical training, yoga. 19 coaches.
Computers Computers are regularly used in computer applications, graphic arts, graphic design classes. Computer network features include on-campus library services, Internet access, wireless campus network. Computer access in designated common areas is available to students. Students grades are available online. The school has a published electronic and media policy.
Contact Ms. Jenna Skarda, Associate Director of Admission/Director of Financial Aid. 631-686-1600 Ext. 413. Fax: 631-686-1650. E-mail: jskarda@knoxschool.org. Web site: www.knoxschool.org.

KNOXVILLE CATHOLIC HIGH SCHOOL
9245 Fox Lonas Road
Knoxville, Tennessee 37923
Head of School: Mr. Dickie Sompayrac
General Information Coeducational day college-preparatory, arts, and religious studies school, affiliated with Roman Catholic Church. Grades 9–12. Founded: 1932. Setting: suburban. 20-acre campus. 3 buildings on campus. Approved or accredited by Southern Association of Colleges and Schools and Tennessee Department of Education. Total enrollment: 662. Upper school average class size: 19. Upper school faculty-student ratio: 1:13.
Upper School Student Profile Grade 9: 187 students (92 boys, 95 girls); Grade 10: 154 students (79 boys, 75 girls); Grade 11: 167 students (71 boys, 96 girls); Grade 12: 154 students (82 boys, 72 girls). 83% of students are Roman Catholic.
Faculty School total: 50. In upper school: 23 men, 26 women; 27 have advanced degrees.
Subjects Offered Accounting, ACT preparation, Advanced Placement courses, algebra, American government, American history, American history-AP, anatomy and physiology, art, art-AP, band, biology, biology-AP, business, calculus, calculus-AP, ceramics, chemistry, chemistry-AP, computers, current events, drama, drama performance, drawing, driver education, ecology, economics, English, English language and composition-AP, English language-AP, English literature, English literature and composition-AP, English literature-AP, English-AP, ESL, European history, forensics,

French, French language-AP, French-AP, geography, geometry, government, government-AP, government/civics, health and wellness, honors algebra, honors English, honors geometry, honors U.S. history, independent study, journalism, Latin, library assistant, music appreciation, newspaper, painting, personal finance, physical education, physical fitness, physical science, physics, physiology, pottery, pre-algebra, pre-calculus, psychology, religion, sociology, Spanish, Spanish-AP, speech, speech communications, statistics, statistics-AP, theater, theater arts, theater production, theology, U.S. government, U.S. government and politics-AP, U.S. history, U.S. history-AP, United States government-AP, Web site design, weight training, weight-lifting, wellness, world geography, world history, writing workshop, yearbook.
Graduation Requirements Arts and fine arts (art, music, dance, drama), electives, English, foreign language, mathematics, science, social studies (includes history), speech, theology, wellness.
Special Academic Programs Advanced Placement exam preparation; honors section; study at local college for college credit; ESL (9 students enrolled).
College Admission Counseling 132 students graduated in 2009; 125 went to college, including Middle Tennessee State University; The University of Tennessee; The University of Tennessee at Chattanooga. Other: 7 went to work.
Student Life Upper grades have uniform requirement, student council, honor system. Discipline rests primarily with faculty. Attendance at religious services is required.
Tuition and Aid Day student tuition: $7450–$9000. Tuition installment plan (FACTS Tuition Payment Plan).
Admissions Traditional secondary-level entrance grade is 9. High School Placement Test or High School Placement Test (closed version) from Scholastic Testing Service required. Deadline for receipt of application materials: February 15. Application fee required: $100. Interview required.
Athletics Interscholastic: aquatics (boys, girls), baseball (b), basketball (b,g), bowling (b,g), cheering (g), cross-country running (b,g), dance team (g), diving (b,g), football (b), golf (b,g), ice hockey (b), in-line hockey (b), rugby (b), soccer (b,g), softball (g), swimming and diving (b,g), tennis (b,g), track and field (b,g), volleyball (g), wrestling (b); intramural: dance (g). 2 PE instructors, 4 coaches, 1 athletic trainer.
Computers Computer network features include on-campus library services, Internet access. Students grades are available online. The school has a published electronic and media policy.
Contact Ms. Barrie Smith, Dean of Admissions. 865-560-0502. Fax: 865-560-0314. E-mail: bsmith@knoxvillecatholic.com. Web site: www.knoxvillecatholic.com.

KODAIKANAL INTERNATIONAL SCHOOL
PO Box 25
Seven Roads Junction
Kodaikanal 624 101, India
Head of School: Mr. Arthur Geoffrey Fisher
General Information Coeducational boarding and day college-preparatory, arts, business, religious studies, technology, music, and drama school, affiliated with Christian faith. Boarding grades 4–12, day grades PS–12. Founded: 1901. Setting: small town. Nearest major city is Madurai, India. Students are housed in single-sex dormitories. 111-acre campus. 23 buildings on campus. Approved or accredited by Middle States Association of Colleges and Schools. Member of Secondary School Admission Test Board and European Council of International Schools. Language of instruction: English. Total enrollment: 577. Upper school average class size: 18. Upper school faculty-student ratio: 1:6. The average school day consists of 6 hours and 20 minutes.
Upper School Student Profile Grade 11: 109 students (55 boys, 54 girls); Grade 12: 138 students (70 boys, 68 girls). 91% of students are boarding students. 41% are international students. International students from Bhutan, Nepal, Republic of Korea, Thailand, United Kingdom, and United States; 20 other countries represented in student body. 47% of students are Christian faith.
Faculty School total: 154. In upper school: 30 men, 36 women; 57 have advanced degrees; 143 reside on campus.
Subjects Offered Accounting, art, art history, biology, biotechnology, business, chemistry, community service, computer programming, computer science, dance, economics, English, English literature, environmental science, ESL, ethics, European history, fine arts, French, geography, German, health, history, home economics, industrial arts, journalism, mathematics, music, photography, physical education, physics, political science, religion, science, social studies, Spanish, technology/design, theory of knowledge, trigonometry, world literature, writing, yearbook.
Graduation Requirements Arts and fine arts (art, music, dance, drama), business skills (includes word processing), computer science, electives, English, foreign language, mathematics, physical education (includes health), religion (includes Bible studies and theology), science, social studies (includes history). Community service is required.
Special Academic Programs International Baccalaureate program; honors section; accelerated programs; independent study; term-away projects; study abroad; academic accommodation for the gifted, the musically talented, and the artistically talented; remedial reading and/or remedial writing; remedial math; programs in English, mathematics, general development for dyslexic students; ESL (67 students enrolled).
College Admission Counseling 105 students graduated in 2009; 98 went to college, including Carleton College; McGill University; The University of British Columbia;

University of Toronto. Other: 7 had other specific plans. Mean SAT critical reading: 528, mean SAT math: 569, mean SAT writing: 539, mean composite ACT: 21.
Student Life Upper grades have specified standards of dress, student council, honor system. Discipline rests primarily with faculty.
Tuition and Aid Day student tuition: $12,250; 7-day tuition and room/board: $13,000. Tuition installment plan (monthly payment plans, individually arranged payment plans). Merit scholarship grants, need-based scholarship grants available. In 2009–10, 29% of upper-school students received aid. Total amount of financial aid awarded in 2009–10: $154,475.
Admissions Traditional secondary-level entrance grade is 11. For fall 2009, 102 students applied for upper-level admission, 83 were accepted, 50 enrolled. Admissions testing, Iowa Tests of Basic Skills or school's own exam required. Deadline for receipt of application materials: none. Application fee required: $70. On-campus interview recommended.
Athletics Interscholastic: badminton (boys, girls), basketball (b,g), cricket (b), cross-country running (b,g), field hockey (b,g), football (b,g), Frisbee (b,g), golf (b,g), hockey (b,g), indoor hockey (g), soccer (b), tennis (b,g), track and field (b,g), volleyball (b,g); intramural: archery (b,g), badminton (b,g), baseball (b,g), basketball (b,g), bicycling (b,g), billiards (b,g), canoeing/kayaking (b,g), climbing (b,g), cooperative games (b,g), cricket (b), cross-country running (b,g), dance (g), field hockey (b,g), football (b,g), Frisbee (b,g), golf (b,g), gymnastics (b,g), hockey (b,g), independent competitive sports (b,g), indoor hockey (b,g), indoor soccer (b,g), physical fitness (b,g), racquetball (b,g), rappelling (b,g), rowing (b,g), rugby (b), running (b,g), soccer (b,g), softball (b,g), squash (b,g), table tennis (b,g), team handball (b,g), tennis (b,g), track and field (b,g), volleyball (b,g), weight training (b,g); coed interscholastic: ultimate Frisbee; coed intramural: hiking/backpacking, independent competitive sports, kayaking, outdoor activities, outdoor education, physical training, ultimate Frisbee, wall climbing, yoga. 5 PE instructors.
Computers Computers are regularly used in art classes. Computer network features include on-campus library services, Internet access, wireless campus network, Internet filtering or blocking technology. Campus intranet, student e-mail accounts, and computer access in designated common areas are available to students. Students grades are available online. The school has a published electronic and media policy.
Contact Mrs. Helen Haeusler, Admissions Coordinator. 91-4542 247 217. Fax: 91-4542 241 109. E-mail: admissions@kis.in. Web site: www.kis.in.

LA CHEIM SCHOOL
Antioch, California
See Special Needs Schools section.

LADYWOOD HIGH SCHOOL
14680 Newburgh Road
Livonia, Michigan 48154
Head of School: Sr. Mary Ann Smith, CSSF
General Information Girls' day college-preparatory, arts, business, and religious studies school, affiliated with Roman Catholic Church. Grades 9–12. Founded: 1950. Setting: suburban. Nearest major city is Detroit. 17-acre campus. 1 building on campus. Approved or accredited by National Catholic Education Association, North Central Association of Colleges and Schools, and Michigan Department of Education. Total enrollment: 347. Upper school average class size: 24. Upper school faculty-student ratio: 1:12. There are 179 required school days per year for Upper School students. Upper School students typically attend 5 days per week.
Upper School Student Profile Grade 9: 69 students (69 girls); Grade 10: 84 students (84 girls); Grade 11: 107 students (107 girls); Grade 12: 87 students (87 girls). 93% of students are Roman Catholic.
Faculty School total: 34. In upper school: 6 men, 25 women; 14 have advanced degrees.
Subjects Offered Advanced chemistry, algebra, American government, American history, American history-AP, American literature, anatomy and physiology, art, Asian history, Bible studies, biology, biology-AP, calculus-AP, career and personal planning, career exploration, Catholic belief and practice, ceramics, child development, choir, Christian and Hebrew scripture, college writing, composition, computer education, culinary arts, discrete mathematics, drama performance, drawing and design, economics, English, English composition, English literature and composition-AP, environmental science, environmental science-AP, film appreciation, food science, French, French language-AP, French-AP, geometry, global issues, graphic arts, health, history of the Catholic Church, independent living, Italian, keyboarding, language and composition, language arts, leadership and service, library assistant, life management skills, oil painting, orchestra, parent/child development, physical education, physics, poetry, prayer/spirituality, pre-calculus, probability and statistics, psychology, religion, scripture, sewing, short story, sociology, Spanish, Spanish language-AP, Spanish-AP, speech, studio art-AP, theater, theater arts, visual and performing arts, water color painting, world studies, writing, yearbook.
Graduation Requirements Algebra, American government, American history, American literature, arts and fine arts (art, music, dance, drama), biology, British literature, Catholic belief and practice, chemistry, computer science, economics, English composition, foreign language, geometry, global studies, health education,

keyboarding, literature, mathematics, physical education (includes health), religion (includes Bible studies and theology), science, social sciences, speech communications, world literature.

Special Academic Programs Advanced Placement exam preparation; study at local college for college credit.

College Admission Counseling 96 students graduated in 2010; all went to college, including Central Michigan University; Michigan State University; University of Michigan; University of Notre Dame; Wayne State University; Western Michigan University. Median composite ACT: 23. Mean SAT critical reading: 532, mean SAT math: 586, mean SAT writing: 532, mean combined SAT: 1650. 26% scored over 26 on composite ACT.

Student Life Upper grades have uniform requirement, student council, honor system. Discipline rests primarily with faculty. Attendance at religious services is required.

Tuition and Aid Day student tuition: $7400. Tuition installment plan (The Tuition Plan, monthly payment plans, individually arranged payment plans). Tuition reduction for siblings, merit scholarship grants, need-based scholarship grants available. In 2010–11, 29% of upper-school students received aid. Total amount of financial aid awarded in 2010–11: $100,000.

Admissions Traditional secondary-level entrance grade is 9. High School Placement Test required. Deadline for receipt of application materials: none. Application fee required: $500. Interview recommended.

Athletics Interscholastic: basketball, bowling, cheering, cross-country running, diving, equestrian sports, field hockey, figure skating, flag football, golf, ice hockey, lacrosse, pom squad, skiing (cross-country), skiing (downhill), snowboarding, soccer, softball, strength & conditioning, swimming and diving, tennis, track and field, volleyball, weight training; intramural: flagball. 1 PE instructor, 30 coaches, 1 athletic trainer.

Computers Computers are regularly used in accounting, computer applications, data processing, graphic design, keyboarding, Web site design, word processing, yearbook classes. Computer network features include on-campus library services, Internet access, Internet filtering or blocking technology. Campus intranet is available to students. Students grades are available online. The school has a published electronic and media policy.

Contact Guidance Counselors. 734-591-5492 Ext. 226. Fax: 734-591-4214. Web site: www.ladywood.org.

LAGUNA BLANCA SCHOOL

4125 Paloma Drive
Santa Barbara, California 93110
Head of School: Paul Slocombe

General Information Coeducational day college-preparatory, arts, and technology school. Grades K–12. Founded: 1933. Setting: suburban. 33-acre campus. 10 buildings on campus. Approved or accredited by California Association of Independent Schools, Western Association of Schools and Colleges, and California Department of Education. Member of National Association of Independent Schools. Endowment: $5.5 million. Total enrollment: 417. Upper school average class size: 12. Upper school faculty-student ratio: 1:5.

Upper School Student Profile Grade 9: 35 students (12 boys, 23 girls); Grade 10: 45 students (22 boys, 23 girls); Grade 11: 56 students (26 boys, 30 girls); Grade 12: 46 students (22 boys, 24 girls).

Faculty School total: 68. In upper school: 17 men, 19 women; 26 have advanced degrees.

Subjects Offered Advanced chemistry, Advanced Placement courses, algebra, American history, American history-AP, art, art history, athletics, biology, biology-AP, calculus-AP, ceramics, chemistry, chemistry-AP, chorus, community service, computer science, computer science-AP, creative writing, drama, economics-AP, English, English-AP, French, French-AP, geometry, government/civics, Latin, Latin-AP, music, photography, physical education, physics, public speaking, Spanish, Spanish-AP, speech, statistics AP, studio art-AP, theater, U.S. government and politics-AP, Western civilization, world history, yearbook.

Graduation Requirements Arts and fine arts (art, music, dance, drama), computer science, English, foreign language, mathematics, physical education (includes health), science, social studies (includes history), speech, senior internship project. Community service is required.

Special Academic Programs Honors section; independent study, special instructional classes for deaf students, blind students.

College Admission Counseling 54 students graduated in 2009; all went to college, including New York University; University of California, Berkeley; University of California, Santa Barbara; University of Southern California; Wheaton College; Yale University. Mean SAT critical reading: 642, mean SAT math: 628, mean SAT writing: 663, mean combined SAT: 1933, mean composite ACT: 27. 65% scored over 600 on SAT critical reading, 62% scored over 600 on SAT math, 77% scored over 600 on SAT writing, 77% scored over 1800 on combined SAT, 43% scored over 26 on composite ACT.

Student Life Upper grades have specified standards of dress, student council, honor system. Discipline rests primarily with faculty.

Tuition and Aid Day student tuition: $21,900. Tuition installment plan (Insured Tuition Payment Plan, monthly payment plans, individually arranged payment plans). Merit scholarship grants, need-based scholarship grants available. In 2009–10, 25%

of upper-school students received aid; total upper-school merit-scholarship money awarded: $21,900. Total amount of financial aid awarded in 2009–10: $566,465.

Admissions Traditional secondary-level entrance grade is 9. For fall 2009, 37 students applied for upper-level admission, 34 were accepted, 22 enrolled. ISEE, QUIC, SSAT or WRAT required. Deadline for receipt of application materials: February 1. Application fee required: $100. Interview required.

Athletics Interscholastic: baseball (boys), basketball (b,g), cross-country running (b,g), football (b), independent competitive sports (b,g), lacrosse (b,g), racquetball (b), soccer (b,g), softball (g), tennis (b,g), track and field (b,g), volleyball (b,g); coed interscholastic: golf, sailing; coed intramural: backpacking, hiking/backpacking, juggling, skiing (downhill), surfing, yoga. 3 PE instructors, 30 coaches, 1 athletic trainer.

Computers Computers are regularly used in art, college planning, creative writing, French, geography, history, journalism, lab/keyboard, library, literary magazine, mathematics, music, newspaper, publications, science, theater, theater arts, typing, word processing, yearbook classes. Computer network features include on-campus library services, online commercial services, Internet access, library database access from the home. The school has a published electronic and media policy.

Contact Joyce Balak, Director of Admission and Financial Aid. 805-687-2461 Ext. 210. Fax: 805-682-2553. E-mail: jbalak@lagunablanca.org. Web site: www.lagunablanca.org.

LA JOLLA COUNTRY DAY SCHOOL

9490 Genesee Avenue
La Jolla, California 92037
Head of School: Mr. Christopher Schuck

General Information Coeducational day college-preparatory, arts, and technology school. Grades N–12. Founded: 1926. Setting: suburban. Nearest major city is San Diego. 24-acre campus. 8 buildings on campus. Approved or accredited by California Association of Independent Schools, Western Association of Schools and Colleges, and California Department of Education. Member of National Association of Independent Schools and Secondary School Admission Test Board. Endowment: $2.4 million. Total enrollment: 1,136. Upper school average class size: 16. Upper school faculty-student ratio: 1:15. There are 171 required school days per year for Upper School students. Upper School students typically attend 5 days per week. The average school day consists of 7 hours.

Upper School Student Profile Grade 9: 118 students (59 boys, 59 girls); Grade 10: 123 students (70 boys, 53 girls); Grade 11: 117 students (59 boys, 58 girls); Grade 12: 113 students (60 boys, 53 girls).

Faculty School total: 123. In upper school: 22 men, 24 women; 30 have advanced degrees.

Subjects Offered Advanced studio art-AP, algebra, Arabic, art, art appreciation, art history, art history-AP, astronomy, biology, biology-AP, calculus-AP, chemistry, chemistry-AP, chorus, comparative religion, computer graphics, computer multimedia, computer programming, computer science, computer science-AP, conceptual physics, creative writing, dance, drama, drama performance, drama workshop, economics, English, English language-AP, English literature, English literature and composition-AP, English literature-AP, environmental science, European history, European history-AP, expository writing, film studies, French, French literature-AP, French-AP, freshman seminar, geometry, geometry with art applications, government, government-AP, history of drama, honors algebra, honors geometry, independent study, instrumental music, linear algebra, madrigals, multimedia, music appreciation, music history, music-AP, painting, performing arts, photography, physical education, physical science, physics, physics-AP, portfolio art, pre-calculus, programming, psychology, Spanish, Spanish literature-AP, Spanish-AP, speech, statistics-AP, strings, studio art, studio art-AP, technical theater, theater, theater arts, theater history, theater production, theory of knowledge, U.S. history-AP, wellness, women's studies, world cultures, writing.

Graduation Requirements Arts and fine arts (art, music, dance, drama), English, foreign language, mathematics, performing arts, physical education (includes health), science, senior project, social sciences, speech, 40 hours of community service.

Special Academic Programs Advanced Placement exam preparation; honors section; study abroad.

College Admission Counseling 103 students graduated in 2010; 102 went to college, including Boston University; Santa Clara University; Stanford University; University of Southern California; Villanova University. Other: 1 had other specific plans. Mean SAT critical reading: 627, mean SAT math: 628, mean SAT writing: 644.

Student Life Upper grades have specified standards of dress, student council. Discipline rests equally with students and faculty.

Summer Programs Remediation, enrichment, advancement, sports, art/fine arts, computer instruction programs offered; session focuses on academics, summer camp, sports camps; held on campus; accepts boys and girls; open to students from other schools. 300 students usually enrolled. 2011 schedule: June 22 to July 31. Application deadline: none.

Tuition and Aid Day student tuition: $25,737. Tuition installment plan (FACTS Tuition Payment Plan, monthly payment plans). Need-based scholarship grants available. In 2010–11, 26% of upper-school students received aid. Total amount of financial aid awarded in 2010–11: $1,849,552.

La Jolla Country Day School

Admissions Traditional secondary-level entrance grade is 9. ISEE required. Deadline for receipt of application materials: February 1. Application fee required: $125. On-campus interview required.

Athletics Interscholastic: aquatics (boys, girls), baseball (b), basketball (b,g), cheering (g), cross-country running (b,g), dance (b,g), fencing (b,g), football (b), golf (b,g), independent competitive sports (b,g), lacrosse (b,g), roller hockey (b), soccer (b,g), softball (g), swimming and diving (b,g), tennis (b,g), track and field (b,g), volleyball (b,g), water polo (b,g); coed interscholastic: physical fitness, physical training, strength & conditioning, surfing, ultimate Frisbee, weight lifting, weight training; coed intramural: dance team, outdoor education, snowboarding. 8 PE instructors, 50 coaches, 1 athletic trainer.

Computers Computers are regularly used in art, English, French, history, mathematics, science, Spanish, technology classes. Computer network features include on-campus library services, online commercial services, Internet access, wireless campus network, e-mail connection from home. The school has a published electronic and media policy.

Contact Mr. Vincent Travaglione, Director of Admission. 858-453-3440 Ext. 117. Fax: 858-453-8210. E-mail: vtravaglione@ljcds.org. Web site: www.ljcds.org.

LAKEFIELD COLLEGE SCHOOL

4391 County Road, #29
Lakefield, Ontario K0L 2H0, Canada

Head of School: Ms. Sarah J. McMahon

General Information Coeducational boarding and day college-preparatory, arts, technology, and distance learning, outdoor education program school, affiliated with Church of England (Anglican). Boarding grades 9–12, day grades 7–12. Founded: 1879. Setting: small town. Nearest major city is Toronto, Canada. Students are housed in single-sex dormitories. 315-acre campus. 25 buildings on campus. Approved or accredited by Canadian Association of Independent Schools, Canadian Educational Standards Institute, The Association of Boarding Schools, and Ontario Department of Education. Affiliate member of National Association of Independent Schools; member of Secondary School Admission Test Board. Language of instruction: English. Endowment: CAN$17 million. Total enrollment: 371. Upper school average class size: 17. Upper school faculty-student ratio: 1:7. The average school day consists of 5 hours.

Upper School Student Profile Grade 7: 17 students (12 boys, 5 girls); Grade 8: 21 students (15 boys, 6 girls); Grade 9: 46 students (25 boys, 21 girls); Grade 10: 84 students (41 boys, 43 girls); Grade 11: 82 students (39 boys, 43 girls); Grade 12: 101 students (49 boys, 52 girls). 73% of students are boarding students. 75% are province residents. 16 provinces are represented in upper school student body. 28% are international students. International students from Barbados, China, Germany, Saudi Arabia, U.S. Virgin Islands, and United States; 24 other countries represented in student body. 40% of students are members of Church of England (Anglican).

Faculty School total: 54. In upper school: 27 men, 26 women; 11 have advanced degrees; 22 reside on campus.

Subjects Offered Algebra, art, art history, biology, calculus, chemistry, computer science, creative writing, drama, driver education, earth science, economics, English, English literature, environmental science, fine arts, French, geography, geometry, government/civics, health, history, kinesiology, mathematics, music, outdoor education, physical education, physics, science, social studies, sociology, Spanish, theater, trigonometry, vocal music, world history, world literature.

Graduation Requirements English, foreign language, mathematics, physical education (includes health), science, social studies (includes history).

Special Academic Programs Advanced Placement exam preparation; honors section; accelerated programs; independent study; term-away projects; study at local college for college credit; study abroad; academic accommodation for the gifted, the musically talented, and the artistically talented.

College Admission Counseling 100 students graduated in 2010; 95 went to college, including McGill University; Queen's University at Kingston; The University of British Columbia; The University of Western Ontario; Trent University; University of Toronto. Other: 5 had other specific plans.

Student Life Upper grades have uniform requirement, student council, honor system. Discipline rests equally with students and faculty.

Summer Programs Session focuses on on-line courses for current students; held off campus; held at via distance learning; accepts boys and girls; not open to students from other schools. 100 students usually enrolled. 2011 schedule: June 22 to August 30.

Tuition and Aid Day student tuition: CAN$26,700; 7-day tuition and room/board: CAN$44,550. Tuition installment plan (Insured Tuition Payment Plan, monthly payment plans, individually arranged payment plans, 3-payment plan). Bursaries, need-based scholarship grants available. In 2010–11, 33% of upper-school students received aid. Total amount of financial aid awarded in 2010–11: CAN$170,500.

Admissions Traditional secondary-level entrance grade is 9. For fall 2010, 203 students applied for upper-level admission, 156 were accepted, 146 enrolled. Otis-Lennon School Ability Test or SSAT required. Deadline for receipt of application materials: none. Application fee required: CAN$100. Interview required.

Athletics Interscholastic: alpine skiing (boys, girls), baseball (b), basketball (g), crew (g), cross-country running (b,g), field hockey (g), golf (b,g), hockey (b,g), ice hockey (b,g), nordic skiing (b,g), outdoor education (b,g), ropes courses (b,g), rowing (b,g), rugby (b,g), skiing (cross-country) (b,g), skiing (downhill) (b,g), snowboarding (b,g), soccer (b,g), softball (b); intramural: aerobics/dance (g), basketball (b,g), cross-country running (b,g), skiing (cross-country) (b,g); coed interscholastic: alpine skiing,

cross-country running, equestrian sports, Frisbee, golf, hockey, horseback riding, ice hockey, nordic skiing, outdoor education, sailing, skiing (cross-country), skiing (downhill), snowboarding; coed intramural: aerobics/Nautilus, baseball, basketball, bicycling, canoeing/kayaking, climbing, cross-country running, dance, equestrian sports, fitness, ice hockey, kayaking, sailing, skiing (cross-country), skiing (downhill), softball.

Computers Computers are regularly used in art, English, foreign language, history, mathematics, music, science classes. Computer network features include on-campus library services, online commercial services, Internet access, Internet filtering or blocking technology. Student e-mail accounts are available to students. Students grades are available online. The school has a published electronic and media policy.

Contact Mrs. Barbara M. Rutherford, Assistant Director of Admissions. 705-652-3324 Ext. 345. Fax: 705-652-6320. E-mail: admissions@lcs.on.ca. Web site: www.lcs.on.ca.

LAKE FOREST ACADEMY

1500 West Kennedy Road
Lake Forest, Illinois 60045

Head of School: Dr. John Strudwick

General Information Coeducational boarding and day college-preparatory and arts school. Grades 9–12. Founded: 1857. Setting: suburban. Nearest major city is Chicago. Students are housed in single-sex dormitories. 160-acre campus. 30 buildings on campus. Approved or accredited by Independent Schools Association of the Central States, Midwest Association of Boarding Schools, The Association of Boarding Schools, The College Board, and Illinois Department of Education. Member of National Association of Independent Schools and Secondary School Admission Test Board. Endowment: $25.8 million. Total enrollment: 391. Upper school average class size: 12. Upper school faculty-student ratio: 1:7. The average school day consists of 7 hours.

Upper School Student Profile Grade 9: 80 students (48 boys, 32 girls); Grade 10: 104 students (56 boys, 48 girls); Grade 11: 108 students (60 boys, 48 girls); Grade 12: 94 students (52 boys, 42 girls); Postgraduate: 5 students (4 boys, 1 girl). 50% of students are boarding students. 71% are state residents. 20 states are represented in upper school student body. 30% are international students. International students from Canada, China, Germany, Republic of Korea, Taiwan, and Thailand; 30 other countries represented in student body.

Faculty School total: 69. In upper school: 36 men, 33 women; 46 have advanced degrees; 53 reside on campus.

Subjects Offered 20th century history, 20th century world history, 3-dimensional art, 3-dimensional design, acting, advanced chemistry, advanced computer applications, advanced math, Advanced Placement courses, advanced studio art-AP, algebra, American government, American history, American history-AP, American literature, American literature-AP, American studies, anatomy and physiology, anthropology, applied arts, applied music, art, art appreciation, art education, art history, art history-AP, art-AP, astronomy, bioethics, bioethics, DNA and culture, biology, biology-AP, calculus, calculus-AP, ceramics, chemistry, chemistry-AP, Chinese, choir, choral music, chorus, cinematography, comparative government and politics-AP, computer applications, computer graphics, computer information systems, computer programming, computer science, computer science-AP, creative writing, drama, ecology, English, English literature, environmental science, ESL, fine arts, French, geometry, health and wellness, history, journalism, Latin, Latin American literature, Latin-AP, literature and composition-AP, mathematics, music, mythology, photography, physics, poetry, pre-calculus, science, Shakespeare, social studies, Spanish, speech, statistics-AP, theater, U.S. government and politics-AP, world history.

Graduation Requirements Arts and fine arts (art, music, dance, drama), athletics, English, foreign language, mathematics, science, social studies (includes history). Community service is required.

Special Academic Programs Advanced Placement exam preparation; honors section; independent study; study abroad; academic accommodation for the gifted, the musically talented, and the artistically talented; ESL (16 students enrolled).

College Admission Counseling 105 students graduated in 2010; all went to college, including Duke University; Miami University; Northwestern University; University of Illinois at Urbana–Champaign; University of Michigan. Mean SAT critical reading: 580, mean SAT math: 640, mean SAT writing: 590, mean combined SAT: 1800, mean composite ACT: 27.

Student Life Upper grades have specified standards of dress, student council. Discipline rests equally with students and faculty.

Summer Programs ESL programs offered; session focuses on ESL; held on campus; accepts boys and girls; open to students from other schools. 85 students usually enrolled. 2011 schedule: July 13 to August 15. Application deadline: June 1.

Tuition and Aid Day student tuition: $31,000; 7-day tuition and room/board: $42,000. Tuition installment plan (FACTS Tuition Payment Plan). Merit scholarship grants, need-based scholarship grants available. In 2010–11, 30% of upper-school students received aid. Total amount of financial aid awarded in 2010–11: $3,100,000.

Admissions Traditional secondary-level entrance grade is 9. For fall 2010, 463 students applied for upper-level admission, 197 were accepted, 124 enrolled. SSAT or TOEFL required. Deadline for receipt of application materials: January 31. Application fee required: $50. Interview required.

Athletics Interscholastic: baseball (boys), basketball (b,g), cross-country running (b,g), field hockey (g), football (b), ice hockey (b,g), soccer (b,g), softball (g), swimming and diving (b,g), tennis (b,g), track and field (b,g), volleyball (b,g), wrestling (b); intramural: lacrosse (b,g); coed interscholastic: cheering, golf; coed intramural: bowling, dance, dance squad, fitness, martial arts, racquetball, sailing, squash, water polo, weight training, yoga. 3 coaches, 1 athletic trainer.

Computers Computers are regularly used in English, foreign language, history, mathematics, science classes. Computer network features include on-campus library services, online commercial services, Internet access, wireless campus network, Internet filtering or blocking technology, iPods, Smart Boards in classrooms. Campus intranet, student e-mail accounts, and computer access in designated common areas are available to students. The school has a published electronic and media policy.

Contact Admissions Office. 847-615-3267. Fax: 847-295-8149. E-mail: info@lfanet.org. Web site: www.lfanet.org.

LAKEHILL PREPARATORY SCHOOL
2720 Hillside Drive
Dallas, Texas 75214
Head of School: Roger L. Perry

General Information Coeducational day college-preparatory, arts, bilingual studies, and technology school. Grades K–12. Founded: 1971. Setting: urban. 23-acre campus. 4 buildings on campus. Approved or accredited by Independent Schools Association of the Southwest, Southern Association of Colleges and Schools, Texas Private School Accreditation Commission, The College Board, and Texas Department of Education. Endowment: $30,000. Total enrollment: 400. Upper school average class size: 15. Upper school faculty-student ratio: 1:10. There are 175 required school days per year for Upper School students. Upper School students typically attend 5 days per week. The average school day consists of 7 hours and 30 minutes.
Upper School Student Profile Grade 9: 31 students (15 boys, 16 girls); Grade 10: 23 students (10 boys, 13 girls); Grade 11: 20 students (11 boys, 9 girls); Grade 12: 33 students (11 boys, 22 girls).
Faculty School total: 44. In upper school: 9 men, 14 women; 15 have advanced degrees.
Subjects Offered Advanced Placement courses, advanced studio art-AP, algebra, American history, American history-AP, American literature, art, art history, biology, calculus, calculus-AP, chemistry, college counseling, computer math, computer programming, computer programming-AP, computer science, digital photography, drama, earth science, economics, English, English language and composition-AP, English literature, environmental science-AP, European history, French, French language-AP, geography, geometry, government/civics, grammar, health, history, journalism, Latin, mathematics, music, music theater, physical education, physics, psychology, public speaking, publications, science, senior career experience, Shakespeare, social sciences, social studies, Spanish, Spanish language-AP, Spanish literature-AP, speech, statistics, theater, trigonometry, Western civilization, world history, world literature, writing.
Graduation Requirements Arts and fine arts (art, music, dance, drama), computer science, electives, English, foreign language, mathematics, physical education (includes health), science, social sciences, social studies (includes history), senior internship program.
Special Academic Programs Advanced Placement exam preparation; honors section; independent study; study abroad.
College Admission Counseling 23 students graduated in 2010; all went to college, including Southern Methodist University; Texas A&M University; The University of Texas at Austin; University of Southern California; Vanderbilt University; Vassar College. Median combined SAT: 1664, median composite ACT: 24.
Student Life Upper grades have specified standards of dress, student council, honor system. Discipline rests primarily with faculty.
Summer Programs Enrichment, sports, art/fine arts, computer instruction programs offered; session focuses on enrichment; held on campus; accepts boys and girls; open to students from other schools. 200 students usually enrolled. 2011 schedule: June 6 to July 29. Application deadline: May 15.
Tuition and Aid Day student tuition: $16,238. Tuition installment plan (monthly payment plans). Tuition reduction for siblings, need-based scholarship grants available. In 2010–11, 18% of upper-school students received aid.
Admissions Traditional secondary-level entrance grade is 9. ERB CTP IV, ISEE or Stanford Achievement Test required. Deadline for receipt of application materials: January 7. Application fee required: $150. On-campus interview recommended.
Athletics Interscholastic: baseball (boys), basketball (b,g), cheering (g), cross-country running (b,g), football (b), golf (b,g), jogging (b,g), rock climbing (b,g), softball (g), tennis (b,g), track and field (b,g), volleyball (g), weight training (b,g); coed interscholastic: tennis; coed intramural: bowling. 3 PE instructors, 12 coaches, 1 athletic trainer.
Computers Computers are regularly used in college planning, creative writing, English, graphic design, journalism, mathematics, science, speech, Web site design, word processing, writing, yearbook classes. Computer network features include on-campus library services, online commercial services, Internet access, wireless campus network, Internet filtering or blocking technology. Student e-mail accounts are available to students. Students grades are available online. The school has a published electronic and media policy.
Contact Holly Walker, Director of Admission. 214-826-2931. Fax: 214-826-4623. E-mail: hwalker@lakehillprep.org. Web site: www.lakehillprep.org.

LAKELAND CHRISTIAN ACADEMY
1093 South 250 East
Winona Lake, Indiana 46590
Head of School: Mrs. Joy Lavender

General Information Coeducational day college-preparatory, arts, religious studies, bilingual studies, and technology school, affiliated with Christian faith; primarily serves students with learning disabilities and individuals with Attention Deficit Disorder. Grades 7–12. Founded: 1974. Setting: small town. Nearest major city is Fort Wayne. 40-acre campus. 1 building on campus. Approved or accredited by North Central Association of Colleges and Schools and Indiana Department of Education. Endowment: $750,000. Total enrollment: 149. Upper school average class size: 24. Upper school faculty-student ratio: 1:15. There are 180 required school days per year for Upper School students. Upper School students typically attend 5 days per week. The average school day consists of 7 hours and 20 minutes.
Upper School Student Profile Grade 9: 35 students (17 boys, 18 girls); Grade 10: 24 students (11 boys, 13 girls); Grade 11: 17 students (11 boys, 6 girls); Grade 12: 30 students (10 boys, 20 girls). 100% of students are Christian faith.
Faculty School total: 15. In upper school: 3 men, 12 women; 7 have advanced degrees.
Subjects Offered ACT preparation, acting, advanced biology, advanced chemistry, advanced math, algebra, American government, American history, analysis and differential calculus, analytic geometry, anatomy, art, band, baseball, Basic programming, basketball, Bible, biology, calculus, career and personal planning, chemistry, choir, computer applications, computer education, consumer economics, consumer education, consumer mathematics, CPR, desktop publishing, economics, electives, English, English literature, food science, government, grammar, health education, history, human anatomy, human biology, keyboarding, mathematics, physical fitness, physics, poetry, pre-algebra, pre-calculus, psychology, Shakespeare, Spanish, speech, U.S. government, U.S. history, world geography.
Graduation Requirements Anatomy, anatomy and physiology, ancient world history, arts and fine arts (art, music, dance, drama), Basic programming, Bible, biochemistry, biology, calculus, character education, chemistry, civil war history, college planning, composition, constitutional law, consumer economics, desktop publishing, earth science, economics, electives, English, foreign language, geography, geometry, government, health, keyboarding, physical science, physics, pre-algebra, pre-calculus, publications, speech, U.S. government, U.S. history.
Special Academic Programs Independent study; study at local college for college credit; programs in general development for dyslexic students.
College Admission Counseling 30 students graduated in 2009; 20 went to college, including Indiana University–Purdue University Fort Wayne; Wheaton College. Other: 8 went to work, 2 entered military service.
Student Life Upper grades have specified standards of dress, student council, honor system. Discipline rests primarily with faculty. Attendance at religious services is required.
Tuition and Aid Day student tuition: $5500. Tuition installment plan (monthly payment plans, individually arranged payment plans). Need-based scholarship grants available. In 2009–10, 22% of upper-school students received aid. Total amount of financial aid awarded in 2009–10: $98,000.
Admissions Traditional secondary-level entrance grade is 9. For fall 2009, 25 students applied for upper-level admission, 24 were accepted, 24 enrolled. ACT, CTBS, Stanford Achievement Test, any other standardized test, latest standardized score from previous school, PSAT, SAT or Stanford Achievement Test required. Deadline for receipt of application materials: none. Application fee required: $75. Interview required.
Athletics Interscholastic: basketball (boys, girls), cheering (g), soccer (b,g), softball (g), track and field (b,g), volleyball (g); intramural: basketball (b,g), physical training (b); coed interscholastic: baseball, soccer, track and field. 2 PE instructors, 8 coaches.
Computers Computers are regularly used in all academic classes. Computer network features include on-campus library services, online commercial services, Internet access, wireless campus network, Internet filtering or blocking technology. Campus intranet, student e-mail accounts, and computer access in designated common areas are available to students. Students grades are available online. The school has a published electronic and media policy.
Contact Joy Lavender, Administrator. 574-267-7265. Fax: 574-267-5687. E-mail: jlavender@lcacougars.com. Web site: www.lcacougars.com.

LAKE MARY PREPARATORY SCHOOL
650 Rantoul Lane
Lake Mary, Florida 32746
Head of School: Dr. Spencer Taintor

General Information Coeducational boarding and day and distance learning college-preparatory, arts, business, and technology school. Boarding grades 7–12, day grades PK–12. Distance learning grade X. Founded: 1999. Setting: suburban. Nearest major city is Orlando. Students are housed in single-sex dormitories. 48-acre campus. 1 building on campus. Approved or accredited by European Council of International Schools, Florida Council of Independent Schools, and Florida Department of Education. Total enrollment: 644. Upper school average class size: 20. Upper school faculty-student ratio: 1:22. There are 180 required school days per year for Upper

Lake Mary Preparatory School

School students. Upper School students typically attend 5 days per week. The average school day consists of 7 hours and 30 minutes.

Upper School Student Profile Grade 6: 53 students (35 boys, 18 girls); Grade 7: 40 students (20 boys, 20 girls); Grade 8: 46 students (24 boys, 22 girls); Grade 9: 61 students (41 boys, 20 girls); Grade 10: 59 students (35 boys, 24 girls); Grade 11: 74 students (43 boys, 31 girls); Grade 12: 56 students (30 boys, 26 girls). 7% of students are boarding students. 93% are state residents. 2 states are represented in upper school student body. 7% are international students. International students from Brazil, China, Republic of Korea, Russian Federation, Turkey, and Viet Nam.

Faculty School total: 62. In upper school: 18 men, 21 women; 13 have advanced degrees; 8 reside on campus.

Subjects Offered .

Special Academic Programs Advanced Placement exam preparation; honors section; study abroad; ESL (52 students enrolled).

College Admission Counseling 52 students graduated in 2010; all went to college, including Florida State University; Penn State University Park; University of Central Florida; University of Florida; University of Miami. Median SAT critical reading: 490, median SAT math: 560, median SAT writing: 500, median combined SAT: 1050, median composite ACT: 23. 15% scored over 600 on SAT critical reading, 30% scored over 600 on SAT math, 10% scored over 600 on SAT writing, 18% scored over 1800 on combined SAT, 15% scored over 26 on composite ACT.

Student Life Upper grades have uniform requirement, student council, honor system. Discipline rests primarily with faculty.

Tuition and Aid Day student tuition: $11,950; 7-day tuition and room/board: $34,850. Tuition installment plan (monthly payment plans). Tuition reduction for siblings, need-based scholarship grants available. In 2010–11, 10% of upper-school students received aid.

Admissions Traditional secondary-level entrance grade is 9. ISEE required. Deadline for receipt of application materials: none. Application fee required: $100. Interview required.

Athletics Interscholastic: aerobics/dance (girls), aquatics (g), ballet (g), baseball (b), basketball (b,g), bowling (b), cheering (g), cross-country running (b,g), dance (b), dance squad (b), dance team (b), fitness (b,g), fitness walking (b,g), football (g), golf (b,g), gymnastics (b), jogging (b,g), lacrosse (g), physical fitness (b,g), physical training (b,g), pom squad (b), running (b,g), soccer (b,g), softball (b), strength & conditioning (b,g), swimming and diving (b), tennis (b,g), track and field (b,g), volleyball (b), winter soccer (b,g), yoga (b,g). 4 PE instructors, 22 coaches, 1 athletic trainer.

Computers Computers are regularly used in all academic classes. Computer network features include on-campus library services, Internet access, wireless campus network, Internet filtering or blocking technology. Students grades are available online. The school has a published electronic and media policy.

Contact Mrs. Laura Lykins, Director of Admissions. 407-805-0095 Ext. 105. Fax: 407-322-3872. E-mail: laura.lykins@lakemaryprep.com.

LAKE RIDGE ACADEMY

37501 Center Ridge Road
North Ridgeville, Ohio 44039
Head of School: Mrs. Carol L. Klimas

General Information Coeducational day college-preparatory, arts, technology, entrepreneurial studies, and environmental studies school. Grades K–12. Founded: 1963. Setting: suburban. Nearest major city is Cleveland. 88-acre campus. 12 buildings on campus. Approved or accredited by Independent Schools Association of the Central States and Ohio Department of Education. Member of National Association of Independent Schools. Endowment: $1.2 million. Total enrollment: 339. Upper school average class size: 12. Upper school faculty-student ratio: 1:8. There are 172 required school days per year for Upper School students. Upper School students typically attend 5 days per week. The average school day consists of 6 hours.

Upper School Student Profile Grade 9: 33 students (18 boys, 15 girls); Grade 10: 35 students (14 boys, 21 girls); Grade 11: 52 students (28 boys, 24 girls); Grade 12: 39 students (22 boys, 17 girls).

Faculty School total: 48. In upper school: 17 men, 28 women; 33 have advanced degrees.

Subjects Offered Algebra, American history, American literature, art, biology, biology-AP, calculus, calculus-AP, ceramics, chemistry, chemistry-AP, choir, computer applications, creative writing, design, digital imaging, discrete mathematics, ecology, environmental systems, economics, electronic publishing, English, English-AP, entrepreneurship, ethics, expository writing, fine arts, French, French-AP, functions, geometry, graphic arts, health, humanities, instrumental music, interactive media, journalism, literature, mathematics, music composition, music theory, physical education, physics, physics-AP, portfolio writing, pre-calculus, senior seminar, Shakespeare, social studies, Spanish, Spanish-AP, statistics, theater, U.S. history-AP, video film production, world civilizations, world history, world literature, writing.

Graduation Requirements Arts and fine arts (art, music, dance, drama), English, ethics, foreign language, mathematics, physical education (includes health), science, social studies (includes history), U.S. history.

Special Academic Programs Advanced Placement exam preparation; honors section; independent study; study at local college for college credit; academic accommodation for the gifted, the musically talented, and the artistically talented;

---

programs in general development for dyslexic students; special instructional classes for deaf students; ESL (8 students enrolled).

College Admission Counseling 33 students graduated in 2010; all went to college, including Haverford College; Northwestern University; Ohio Wesleyan University; Purdue University; Rochester Institute of Technology; The George Washington University. Median SAT critical reading: 600, median SAT math: 630, median SAT writing: 600, median composite ACT: 26. 60% scored over 600 on SAT critical reading, 65% scored over 600 on SAT math, 40% scored over 600 on SAT writing, 50% scored over 1800 on combined SAT, 50% scored over 26 on composite ACT.

Student Life Upper grades have specified standards of dress, student council, honor system. Discipline rests primarily with faculty.

Summer Programs Remediation, enrichment, advancement, sports, art/fine arts, computer instruction programs offered; session focuses on academics, arts, athletics; held both on and off campus; held at various locations (for field trips); accepts boys and girls; open to students from other schools. 180 students usually enrolled. 2011 schedule: June 7 to July 16. Application deadline: June.

Tuition and Aid Day student tuition: $22,000–$24,250. Tuition installment plan (The Tuition Plan, Insured Tuition Payment Plan, monthly payment plans, individually arranged payment plans). Tuition reduction for siblings, merit scholarship grants, need-based scholarship grants available. In 2010–11, 50% of upper-school students received aid; total upper-school merit-scholarship money awarded: $472,095. Total amount of financial aid awarded in 2010–11: $841,475.

Admissions Traditional secondary-level entrance grade is 9. For fall 2010, 69 students applied for upper-level admission, 45 were accepted, 28 enrolled. CTBS, OLSAT, essay, ISEE, mathematics proficiency exam, school's own exam, TOEFL or SLEP and writing sample required. Deadline for receipt of application materials: none. Application fee required: $35. Interview required.

Athletics Interscholastic: baseball (boys), basketball (b,g), cross-country running (b,g), golf (b,g), indoor track & field (b), soccer (b,g), softball (g), tennis (b,g), track and field (b,g), volleyball (g), winter (indoor) track (b), wrestling (b); intramural: indoor soccer (b,g), strength & conditioning (b,g), winter soccer (b,g); coed intramural: backpacking, indoor soccer, outdoor adventure, outdoor recreation, physical fitness, physical training, strength & conditioning, ultimate Frisbee, weight lifting, weight training. 2 PE instructors, 12 coaches, 1 athletic trainer.

Computers Computers are regularly used in college planning, creative writing, drawing and design, English, foreign language, history, journalism, mathematics, media production, research skills, science classes. Computer network features include on-campus library services, online commercial services, Internet access, wireless campus network, Internet filtering or blocking technology. Campus intranet and student e-mail accounts are available to students. Students grades are available online. The school has a published electronic and media policy.

Contact Mrs. Edie Sweeterman, Associate Director of Admission. 440-327-1175 Ext. 106. Fax: 440-327-3641. E-mail: admission@lakeridgeacademy.org. Web site: www.lakeridgeacademy.org.

LAKESIDE SCHOOL

14050 First Avenue NE
Seattle, Washington 98125-3099
Head of School: Mr. Bernard Noe

General Information Coeducational day college-preparatory, arts, and technology school. Grades 5–12. Founded: 1919. Setting: urban. 34-acre campus. 19 buildings on campus. Approved or accredited by Northwest Association of Schools and Colleges, Pacific Northwest Association of Independent Schools, and Washington Department of Education. Member of National Association of Independent Schools. Endowment: $159 million. Total enrollment: 793. Upper school average class size: 16. Upper school faculty-student ratio: 1:9. There are 169 required school days per year for Upper School students. Upper School students typically attend 5 days per week. The average school day consists of 6 hours and 50 minutes.

Upper School Student Profile Grade 9: 131 students (66 boys, 65 girls); Grade 10: 144 students (72 boys, 72 girls); Grade 11: 132 students (68 boys, 64 girls); Grade 12: 127 students (67 boys, 60 girls).

Faculty School total: 94. In upper school: 33 men, 23 women; 41 have advanced degrees.

Subjects Offered Algebra, American history, American literature, art, biology, calculus, ceramics, chemistry, community service, computer programming, computer science, creative writing, drama, driver education, economics, English, English literature, environmental science, European history, expository writing, fine arts, French, geometry, government/civics, health, history, journalism, Latin, mathematics, music, outdoor education, philosophy, photography, physical education, physics, pre-calculus, science, social studies, Spanish, theater, trigonometry, world history, world literature, writing.

Graduation Requirements Arts, English, foreign language, history, mathematics, outdoor education, physical education (includes health), science. Community service is required.

Special Academic Programs Honors section; independent study; term-away projects; study abroad.

College Admission Counseling 123 students graduated in 2010; 113 went to college, including Columbia University; Occidental College; Scripps College; University of Southern California; University of Washington; Wesleyan University. Other: 10 had

other specific plans. Median SAT critical reading: 705, median SAT math: 720, median SAT writing: 690, median combined SAT: 2095, median composite ACT: 31.
Student Life Upper grades have student council. Discipline rests equally with students and faculty.
Summer Programs Enrichment, advancement, sports, art/fine arts, computer instruction programs offered; session focuses on enrichment and advancement for students from public middle schools; held on campus; accepts boys and girls; open to students from other schools. 264 students usually enrolled. 2011 schedule: June 27 to August 5. Application deadline: June 1.
Tuition and Aid Day student tuition: $25,250. Tuition installment plan (monthly payment plans). Need-based scholarship grants available. In 2010–11, 28% of upper-school students received aid. Total amount of financial aid awarded in 2010–11: $2,778,078.
Admissions Traditional secondary-level entrance grade is 9. For fall 2010, 312 students applied for upper-level admission, 78 were accepted, 60 enrolled. ISEE or PSAT or SAT for applicants to grade 11 and 12 required. Deadline for receipt of application materials: January 28. Application fee required: $40. Interview required.
Athletics Interscholastic: baseball (boys), basketball (b,g), crew (b,g), cross-country running (b,g), diving (b,g), football (b), golf (b,g), lacrosse (b,g), soccer (b,g), softball (g), swimming and diving (b,g), tennis (b,g), track and field (b,g), volleyball (g); coed interscholastic: ultimate Frisbee, wrestling; coed intramural: outdoor education, skiing (cross-country), squash. 5 PE instructors, 71 coaches.
Computers Computers are regularly used in all academic classes. Computer network features include on-campus library services, online commercial services, Internet access, wireless campus network, Internet filtering or blocking technology, class schedule search, online course registration, online directory. Campus intranet, student e-mail accounts, and computer access in designated common areas are available to students. The school has a published electronic and media policy.
Contact Ms. Christy Gallotte, Admissions and Financial Aid Assistant. 206-368-3605. Fax: 206-440-2777. E-mail: admissions@lakesideschool.org. Web site: www.lakesideschool.org.

LA LUMIERE SCHOOL
6801 North Wilhelm Road
La Porte, Indiana 46350
Head of School: Michael H. Kennedy
General Information Coeducational boarding and day college-preparatory, arts, and religious studies school, affiliated with Roman Catholic Church. Boarding grades 9–PG, day grades 9–12. Founded: 1963. Setting: rural. Nearest major city is Chicago, IL. Students are housed in single-sex dormitories. 144-acre campus. 18 buildings on campus. Approved or accredited by Independent Schools Association of the Central States, Midwest Association of Boarding Schools, North Central Association of Colleges and Schools, and The Association of Boarding Schools. Member of National Association of Independent Schools. Total enrollment: 209. Upper school average class size: 12. Upper school faculty-student ratio: 1:8. The average school day consists of 7 hours and 30 minutes.
Upper School Student Profile Grade 9: 40 students (23 boys, 17 girls); Grade 10: 52 students (25 boys, 27 girls); Grade 11: 61 students (39 boys, 22 girls); Grade 12: 52 students (30 boys, 22 girls); Postgraduate: 2 students (2 boys). 35% of students are boarding students. 57% are state residents. 8 states are represented in upper school student body. 13% are international students. International students from China, Croatia, Iran, Republic of Korea, Serbia and Montenegro, and Spain; 3 other countries represented in student body. 40% of students are Roman Catholic.
Faculty School total: 27. In upper school: 14 men, 11 women; 13 have advanced degrees; 18 reside on campus.
Subjects Offered Advanced Placement courses, algebra, American history-AP, American literature, art, art history, biology, biology-AP, British literature, calculus, calculus-AP, chemistry, Christian and Hebrew scripture, college counseling, computer programming, conceptual physics, creative writing, drama, economics, English, English literature, English-AP, ESL, ethics, French, French-AP, geography, geometry, government/civics, graphic design, health, Latin, physics, physics-AP, pre-calculus, SAT/ACT preparation, Spanish, Spanish-AP, speech, study skills, trigonometry, U.S. history, U.S. history-AP, Web site design, world history, world literature, world religions.
Graduation Requirements American government, American history, American literature, arts and fine arts (art, music, dance, drama), Bible as literature, British literature, college writing, computer science, economics, electives, English, English composition, English literature, ethics, foreign language, government, health education, leadership, mathematics, public service, science, social studies (includes history), theology, U.S. history, world history. Community service is required.
Special Academic Programs Advanced Placement exam preparation; honors section; independent study; study at local college for college credit; academic accommodation for the gifted and the artistically talented; ESL (2 students enrolled).
College Admission Counseling 38 students graduated in 2010; all went to college, including DePaul University; Indiana University Bloomington; Loyola University Chicago; Michigan State University; Purdue University; University of Notre Dame. Mean SAT critical reading: 531, mean SAT math: 613, mean SAT writing: 522, mean composite ACT: 23.
Student Life Upper grades have uniform requirement, student council, honor system. Discipline rests primarily with faculty.

Summer Programs Enrichment, advancement, ESL programs offered; session focuses on academics; held on campus; accepts boys and girls; open to students from other schools. 25 students usually enrolled. Application deadline: June 1.
Tuition and Aid Day student tuition: $9495; 7-day tuition and room/board: $31,475. Tuition installment plan (Academic Management Services Plan, Key Tuition Payment Plan, FACTS Tuition Payment Plan, individually arranged payment plans). Tuition reduction for siblings, merit scholarship grants, need-based scholarship grants available. In 2010–11, 26% of upper-school students received aid; total upper-school merit-scholarship money awarded: $15,000. Total amount of financial aid awarded in 2010–11: $580,000.
Admissions Traditional secondary-level entrance grade is 9. For fall 2010, 127 students applied for upper-level admission, 71 were accepted, 59 enrolled. Achievement tests, English proficiency, ISEE, school's own exam or SLEP for foreign students required. Deadline for receipt of application materials: none. Application fee required: $50. Interview required.
Athletics Interscholastic: baseball (boys), basketball (b,g), football (b), golf (b,g), hockey (b), independent competitive sports (b,g), lacrosse (b), softball (g), tennis (b,g), track and field (b,g), volleyball (g); intramural: aerobics/dance (g), volleyball (b,g); coed interscholastic: cross-country running, running, soccer; coed intramural: aerobics/Nautilus, basketball, billiards, bowling, canoeing/kayaking, combined training, cooperative games, cross-country running, dance, fishing, fitness, flag football, floor hockey, Frisbee, hiking/backpacking, jogging, kayaking, martial arts, Nautilus, outdoor adventure, outdoor recreation, physical fitness, physical training, power lifting, ropes courses, skateboarding, strength & conditioning, table tennis, touch football, ultimate Frisbee, weight lifting, weight training, yoga. 10 coaches, 1 athletic trainer.
Computers Computers are regularly used in all academic, college planning, creative writing, programming, yearbook classes. Computer network features include on-campus library services, Internet access, wireless campus network, Internet filtering or blocking technology. Student e-mail accounts and computer access in designated common areas are available to students. Students grades are available online. The school has a published electronic and media policy.
Contact Ms. Mary C. O'Malley, Director of Admissions. 219-326-7450. Fax: 219-325-3185. E-mail: admissions@lalumiere.org. Web site: www.lalumiere.org.

LANCASTER MENNONITE HIGH SCHOOL
2176 Lincoln Highway East
Lancaster, Pennsylvania 17602
Head of School: Mr. Elvin Kennel
General Information Coeducational boarding and day college-preparatory, general academic, arts, vocational, religious studies, and agriculture school, affiliated with Mennonite Church. Boarding grades 9–12, day grades 6–12. Founded: 1942. Setting: suburban. Nearest major city is Philadelphia. Students are housed in coed dormitories and single-sex by wings. 100-acre campus. 9 buildings on campus. Approved or accredited by Mennonite Education Agency, Mennonite Schools Council, Middle States Association of Colleges and Schools, and Pennsylvania Department of Education. Endowment: $12 million. Total enrollment: 1,481. Upper school average class size: 18. Upper school faculty-student ratio: 1:15. There are 182 required school days per year for Upper School students. Upper School students typically attend 5 days per week. The average school day consists of 6 hours and 30 minutes.
Upper School Student Profile Grade 9: 135 students (72 boys, 63 girls); Grade 10: 162 students (87 boys, 75 girls); Grade 11: 156 students (76 boys, 80 girls); Grade 12: 186 students (89 boys, 97 girls). 8% of students are boarding students. 89% are state residents. 7 states are represented in upper school student body. 11% are international students. International students from China, Ethiopia, Germany, Japan, Kenya, and Republic of Korea; 2 other countries represented in student body. 36% of students are Mennonite.
Faculty School total: 77. In upper school: 38 men, 37 women; 50 have advanced degrees; 4 reside on campus.
Subjects Offered 1½ elective credits, Advanced Placement courses.
Graduation Requirements A certain amount of credits is needed in various academic areas.
Special Academic Programs Advanced Placement exam preparation; honors section; independent study; study at local college for college credit; remedial reading and/or remedial writing; remedial math; special instructional classes for deaf students, blind students; ESL (40 students enrolled).
College Admission Counseling 168 students graduated in 2010; 121 went to college, including Eastern Mennonite University; Goshen College; Hesston College; Messiah College; Penn State University Park; York College of Pennsylvania. Other: 28 went to work, 17 had other specific plans. Mean SAT critical reading: 556, mean SAT math: 552, mean SAT writing: 533, mean combined SAT: 1641.
Student Life Upper grades have specified standards of dress, student council. Discipline rests primarily with faculty. Attendance at religious services is required.
Summer Programs Enrichment, sports programs offered; held on campus; accepts boys and girls; open to students from other schools. 200 students usually enrolled. 2011 schedule: June to August. Application deadline: none.
Tuition and Aid Day student tuition: $6900; 5-day tuition and room/board: $9816; 7-day tuition and room/board: $13,140. Tuition installment plan (monthly payment plans). Tuition reduction for siblings, merit scholarship grants, need-based scholarship grants, paying campus jobs available. In 2010–11, 30% of upper-school students

received aid; total upper-school merit-scholarship money awarded: $20,000. Total amount of financial aid awarded in 2010–11: $1,200,000.

Admissions Traditional secondary-level entrance grade is 9. For fall 2010, 185 students applied for upper-level admission, 155 were accepted, 117 enrolled. Deadline for receipt of application materials: none. Application fee required: $100. Interview recommended.

Athletics Interscholastic: ball hockey (girls), baseball (b), basketball (b,g), cross-country running (b,g), field hockey (g), golf (b), lacrosse (b), soccer (b,g), softball (g), tennis (b,g), track and field (b,g); coed interscholastic: baseball. 4 PE instructors, 20 coaches, 1 athletic trainer.

Computers Computers are regularly used in all academic classes. Computer network features include on-campus library services, Internet access, Internet filtering or blocking technology. The school has a published electronic and media policy.

Contact Christy L. Horst, Administrative Assistant for Admissions. 717-299-0436 Ext. 312. Fax: 717-299-0823. E-mail: horstcl@lancastermennonite.org. Web site: www.lancastermennonite.org.

LANDMARK CHRISTIAN ACADEMY

6502 Johnsontown Road
Louisville, Kentucky 40272
Head of School: Mr. Monte L. Ashworth

General Information Coeducational day college-preparatory and religious studies school, affiliated with Baptist Church. Grades K4–12. Founded: 1977. Setting: suburban. 5-acre campus. 1 building on campus. Total enrollment: 121. Upper school average class size: 10. Upper school faculty-student ratio: 1:11. There are 177 required school days per year for Upper School students. Upper School students typically attend 5 days per week. The average school day consists of 6 hours and 50 minutes.

Upper School Student Profile Grade 9: 3 students (3 boys); Grade 10: 6 students (4 boys, 2 girls); Grade 11: 11 students (5 boys, 6 girls); Grade 12: 5 students (4 boys, 1 girl). 80% of students are Baptist.

Faculty School total: 11. In upper school: 3 men, 3 women; 3 have advanced degrees.

Subjects Offered Advanced math, algebra, American history, American literature, analytic geometry, ancient history, ancient world history, Bible, biology, business mathematics, chemistry, choir, computer technologies, consumer economics, consumer mathematics, economics, English composition, English literature, general science, geography, geometry, grammar, health, history, home economics, keyboarding, modern history, physical education, physics, pre-algebra, pre-calculus, speech, trigonometry, world geography, world history.

Graduation Requirements Bible, computers, English, foreign language, history, mathematics, science, social sciences.

College Admission Counseling 55 students graduated in 2010; 5 went to college, including Jefferson Community and Technical College. Other: 5 went to work.

Student Life Upper grades have uniform requirement. Discipline rests primarily with faculty.

Tuition and Aid Day student tuition: $3250. Tuition installment plan (FACTS Tuition Payment Plan). Tuition reduction for siblings available.

Admissions Traditional secondary-level entrance grade is 9. For fall 2010, 3 students applied for upper-level admission, 3 were accepted, 3 enrolled. Math and English placement tests required. Deadline for receipt of application materials: none. Application fee required: $275. On-campus interview required.

Athletics Interscholastic: basketball (boys), soccer (b), track and field (b,g), volleyball (g).

Computers Computers are regularly used in computer applications, keyboarding classes. The school has a published electronic and media policy.

Contact Mr. Monte Ashworth, Administrator. 502-933-3000. Fax: 502-933-5179. E-mail: info@libcky.com.

LANDMARK EAST SCHOOL

Wolfville, Nova Scotia, Canada
See Special Needs Schools section.

LANDMARK SCHOOL

Prides Crossing, Massachusetts
See Special Needs Schools section.

LANDON SCHOOL

6101 Wilson Lane
Bethesda, Maryland 20817
Head of School: Mr. David M. Armstrong

General Information Boys' day college-preparatory, arts, and music school. Grades 3–12. Founded: 1929. Setting: suburban. Nearest major city is Washington, DC. 75-acre campus. 13 buildings on campus. Approved or accredited by Association of Independent Maryland Schools, Middle States Association of Colleges and Schools, and Maryland Department of Education. Member of National Association of Independent Schools. Endowment: $10.4 million. Total enrollment: 685. Upper school average class size: 15. Upper school faculty-student ratio: 1:8. There are 160 required

school days per year for Upper School students. Upper School students typically attend 5 days per week. The average school day consists of 7 hours and 10 minutes.

Upper School Student Profile Grade 9: 88 students (88 boys); Grade 10: 87 students (87 boys); Grade 11: 81 students (81 boys); Grade 12: 83 students (83 boys).

Faculty School total: 118. In upper school: 48 men, 14 women; 40 have advanced degrees.

Subjects Offered Acting, algebra, American Civil War, American foreign policy, American history, American literature, American studies, architecture, art, art history-AP, biology, biology-AP, calculus, calculus-AP, ceramics, chemistry, chemistry-AP, Chinese, Chinese history, classics, computer science, computer science-AP, conceptual physics, constitutional law, creative writing, digital art, drama, drawing, earth science, economics-AP, engineering, English, English literature, environmental science-AP, environmental studies, ethics, European history, expository writing, fine arts, foreign policy, forensics, French, French language-AP, French literature-AP, French studies, freshman foundations, geography, geology, geometry, government/civics, grammar, handbells, health, history, humanities, international relations, jazz band, justice seminar, Latin, mathematics, meteorology, Middle Eastern history, music, music history, music theory, music theory-AP, oceanography, painting, performing arts, photography, photojournalism, physical education, physics, physics-AP, pre-calculus, science, sculpture, senior project, Shakespeare, social studies, Spanish, Spanish language-AP, Spanish literature, statistics-AP, strings, technological applications, theater, trigonometry, typing, U.S. history, U.S. history-AP, world history, world literature, writing.

Graduation Requirements American Civil War, American government, arts and fine arts (art, music, dance, drama), biology, chemistry, English, ethics, foreign language, government, humanities, mathematics, music, physical education (includes health), pre-calculus, science, social studies (includes history), senior project & community service requirement, 2 year arts requirement.

Special Academic Programs Advanced Placement exam preparation; honors section; independent study; term-away projects; study abroad.

College Admission Counseling 81 students graduated in 2010; all went to college, including Cornell University; Davidson College; University of Denver; University of Virginia. Mean SAT critical reading: 644, mean SAT math: 645, mean SAT writing: 632, mean combined SAT: 1920, mean composite ACT: 28.

Student Life Upper grades have specified standards of dress, student council, honor system. Discipline rests equally with students and faculty.

Summer Programs Remediation, enrichment, advancement, art/fine arts programs offered; session focuses on enrichment, advancement, remediation, expanded time in art studios and music, and travel abroad; held both on and off campus; held at locations in France, China, Europe, Italy/Greece, and Spain; accepts boys and girls; open to students from other schools. 200 students usually enrolled. 2011 schedule: June 20 to July 29. Application deadline: none.

Tuition and Aid Day student tuition: $30,123. Tuition installment plan (FACTS Tuition Payment Plan, 2 payment plan (June and December)). Need-based scholarship grants available. In 2010–11, 19% of upper-school students received aid. Total amount of financial aid awarded in 2010–11: $1,240,100.

Admissions Traditional secondary-level entrance grade is 9. For fall 2010, 121 students applied for upper-level admission, 63 were accepted, 25 enrolled. ISEE or SSAT required. Deadline for receipt of application materials: January 31. Application fee required: $75. On-campus interview required.

Athletics Interscholastic: baseball, basketball, cross-country running, diving, fencing, football, golf, ice hockey, indoor track, indoor track & field, lacrosse, riflery, rugby, soccer, squash, strength & conditioning, swimming and diving, tennis, track and field, ultimate Frisbee, water polo, winter (indoor) track, wrestling; intramural: basketball, climbing, football, Frisbee, physical fitness, softball, strength & conditioning, tennis, ultimate Frisbee, weight lifting. 12 coaches, 1 athletic trainer.

Computers Computer network features include on-campus library services, online commercial services, Internet access, wireless campus network, Internet filtering or blocking technology, password-accessed Web portals. Campus intranet, student e-mail accounts, and computer access in designated common areas are available to students. Students grades are available online. The school has a published electronic and media policy.

Contact Mr. George C. Mulligan, Director of Admissions. 301-320-1067. Fax: 301-320-1133. E-mail: george_mulligan@landon.net. Web site: www.landon.net.

LANSDALE CATHOLIC HIGH SCHOOL

700 Lansdale Avenue
Lansdale, Pennsylvania 19446-2995
Head of School: Mr. Timothy Quinn

General Information Coeducational day college-preparatory, general academic, and religious studies school, affiliated with Roman Catholic Church. Grades 9–12. Founded: 1949. Setting: suburban. Nearest major city is Philadelphia. 1 building on campus. Approved or accredited by Middle States Association of Colleges and Schools, National Catholic Education Association, and Pennsylvania Department of Education. Total enrollment: 815. Upper school average class size: 30. There are 183 required school days per year for Upper School students. Upper School students typically attend 5 days per week. The average school day consists of 6 hours and 45 minutes.

Upper School Student Profile Grade 9: 178 students (74 boys, 104 girls); Grade 10: 190 students (104 boys, 86 girls); Grade 11: 222 students (107 boys, 115 girls); Grade 12: 225 students (110 boys, 115 girls). 99% of students are Roman Catholic.

Faculty School total: 42. In upper school: 21 men, 21 women; 21 have advanced degrees.

Subjects Offered Algebra, American government, American history, American history-AP, American literature, analytic geometry, art, art history-AP, art-AP, band, Basic programming, biology-AP, business law, calculus, calculus-AP, career education, career planning, career/college preparation, Catholic belief and practice, chemistry, choir, chorus, church history, classical language, college counseling, college placement, college planning, composition-AP, computer education, computer programming, drama, English language and composition-AP, English literature and composition-AP, English literature-AP, English/composition-AP, environmental science, European history, European history-AP, French, government and politics-AP, government-AP, Greek, health education, Italian, Latin, macro/microeconomics-AP, mathematics-AP, physical fitness, physical science, physics, pre-calculus, SAT/ACT preparation, Spanish, statistics, statistics-AP, student government, studio art, studio art-AP, The 20th Century, trigonometry, U.S. government and politics, U.S. government and politics-AP, U.S. history, U.S. history-AP, United States government-AP, Western civilization.

Graduation Requirements Service requirement : 30 hours by the end of junior year.

Special Academic Programs 15 Advanced Placement exams for which test preparation is offered; honors section; study at local college for college credit.

College Admission Counseling 184 students graduated in 2009; 180 went to college, including Montgomery County Community College; Penn State University Park; Temple University; The University of Scranton. Other: 3 went to work, 1 entered military service.

Student Life Upper grades have uniform requirement, student council, honor system. Discipline rests primarily with faculty. Attendance at religious services is required.

Tuition and Aid Day student tuition: $5200. Tuition installment plan (monthly payment plans, individually arranged payment plans). Tuition reduction for siblings, merit scholarship grants, need-based scholarship grants, TAP Program available. In 2009–10, 20% of upper-school students received aid.

Admissions Traditional secondary-level entrance grade is 9. Deadline for receipt of application materials: none. Application fee required. Interview recommended.

Athletics Interscholastic: baseball (boys), basketball (b,g), cheering (g), cross-country running (b,g), dance squad (b,g), field hockey (g), football (b), golf (b,g), ice hockey (b,g), lacrosse (b,g), rugby (b,g), soccer (b,g), softball (g), swimming and diving (b,g), tennis (b,g), track and field (b,g), volleyball (g), weight lifting (b), winter (indoor) track (b,g); intramural: flag football (b), ice hockey (b,g); coed interscholastic: bowling, diving, indoor track, indoor track & field. 2 PE instructors, 1 coach.

Computers Computers are regularly used in all classes. Computer network features include on-campus library services, online commercial services, Internet access, wireless campus network, Internet filtering or blocking technology. Computer access in designated common areas is available to students. Students grades are available online. The school has a published electronic and media policy.

Contact Mr. James Casey, President. 215-362-6160 Ext. 133. Fax: 215-362-5746. E-mail: jcasey@lansdalecatholic.com. Web site: www.lansdalecatholic.com.

LA SALLE ACADEMY

612 Academy Avenue
Providence, Rhode Island 02908
Head of School: Br. Michael McKenery, FSC

General Information Coeducational day college-preparatory, arts, religious studies, and technology school, affiliated with Roman Catholic Church. Grades 7–12. Founded: 1874. Setting: urban. 60-acre campus. 5 buildings on campus. Approved or accredited by New England Association of Schools and Colleges. Member of National Association of Independent Schools. Total enrollment: 1,460. Upper school average class size: 20. Upper school faculty-student ratio: 1:12.

Upper School Student Profile 85% of students are Roman Catholic.

Faculty School total: 108. In upper school: 59 men, 49 women; 76 have advanced degrees.

Subjects Offered Algebra, American history, American literature, anatomy, art, astronomy, biology, business, calculus, ceramics, chemistry, community service, computer programming, computer science, creative writing, dance, drama, drawing, economics, electronics, engineering, English, English literature, environmental science, ESL, film, fine arts, French, geology, geometry, history, Italian, journalism, law, mathematics, microbiology, music, painting, photography, physical education, physical science, physics, physiology, psychology, religion, science, social studies, sociology, Spanish, statistics, theater, trigonometry, world history, world literature, writing.

Graduation Requirements Arts and fine arts (art, music, dance, drama), computer science, English, foreign language, mathematics, physical education (includes health), religion (includes Bible studies and theology), science, social studies (includes history). Community service is required.

Special Academic Programs Advanced Placement exam preparation; honors section; study at local college for college credit; academic accommodation for the gifted, the musically talented, and the artistically talented.

College Admission Counseling 292 students graduated in 2009; 285 went to college, including Boston College; Brown University; Harvard University; United States Military Academy; University of Rhode Island; Yale University. Other: 6 went to work, 1 entered military service.

Student Life Upper grades have uniform requirement, student council, honor system. Discipline rests equally with students and faculty.

Tuition and Aid Day student tuition: $11,900. Tuition installment plan (FACTS Tuition Payment Plan). Merit scholarship grants, need-based scholarship grants available. In 2009–10, 35% of upper-school students received aid; total upper-school merit-scholarship money awarded: $600,000. Total amount of financial aid awarded in 2009–10: $1,500,000.

Admissions Traditional secondary-level entrance grade is 9. For fall 2009, 850 students applied for upper-level admission, 400 were accepted, 350 enrolled. STS, Diocese Test required. Deadline for receipt of application materials: December 31. Application fee required: $25.

Athletics Interscholastic: baseball (boys), basketball (b,g), cross-country running (b,g), football (b), golf (b,g), gymnastics (b,g), ice hockey (b,g), lacrosse (b,g), sailing (b,g), soccer (b,g), softball (g), swimming and diving (b,g), tennis (b,g), track and field (b,g), volleyball (b,g), wrestling (b,g); coed intramural: fencing, modern dance, physical fitness, physical training, table tennis, touch football, volleyball, walking, whiffle ball. 5 PE instructors, 61 coaches, 4 athletic trainers.

Computers Computers are regularly used in English, foreign language, history, mathematics, music, science classes. Computer network features include online commercial services, Internet access.

Contact Mr. George Aldrich, Director of Admissions and Public Relations. 401-351-7750 Ext. 122. Fax: 401-444-1782. E-mail: galdrich@lasalle-academy.org. Web site: www.lasalle-academy.org.

LA SALLE HIGH SCHOOL

3880 East Sierra Madre Boulevard
Pasadena, California 91107-1996
Head of School: Mr. Patrick Bonacci

General Information Coeducational day college-preparatory, arts, and religious studies school, affiliated with Roman Catholic Church. Grades 9–12. Founded: 1956. Setting: suburban. Nearest major city is Los Angeles. 10-acre campus. 3 buildings on campus. Approved or accredited by Christian Brothers Association, Western Association of Schools and Colleges, Western Catholic Education Association, and California Department of Education. Total enrollment: 740. Upper school average class size: 26. Upper school faculty-student ratio: 1:11. There are 180 required school days per year for Upper School students. Upper School students typically attend 5 days per week. The average school day consists of 6 hours and 15 minutes.

Upper School Student Profile Grade 9: 171 students (85 boys, 86 girls); Grade 10: 185 students (93 boys, 92 girls); Grade 11: 196 students (98 boys, 98 girls); Grade 12: 188 students (98 boys, 90 girls). 66% of students are Roman Catholic.

Faculty School total: 72. In upper school: 43 men, 28 women; 40 have advanced degrees.

Subjects Offered 20th century history, acting, advanced computer applications, Advanced Placement courses, advanced studio art-AP, algebra, American Civil War, American government, American literature-AP, ancient world history, art, art-AP, ASB Leadership, band, biology-AP, business law, calculus, calculus-AP, campus ministry, Catholic belief and practice, chemistry-AP, chorus, Christian and Hebrew scripture, church history, civics, Civil War, classical civilization, community service, comparative religion, composition, composition-AP, computer applications, computer education, computer graphics, computer literacy, computer programming, concert choir, constitutional history of U.S., creative writing, dance, dance performance, digital photography, drama, dramatic arts, drawing, ecology, environmental systems, economics, economics-AP, education, electives, English, English composition, English language-AP, English literature, English literature and composition-AP, English-AP, fiction, film, fine arts, foreign language, French, general math, general science, geometry, government, government/civics, government/civics-AP, health and safety, health education, Hispanic literature, history, history-AP, honors algebra, honors English, honors U.S. history, honors world history, integrated mathematics, introduction to theater, jazz, jazz band, jazz dance, jazz ensemble, journalism, keyboarding, lab science, lab/keyboard, law and the legal system, leadership, leadership and service, mathematics, mathematics-AP, microbiology, modern European history-AP, musical productions, newspaper, photo shop, photography, physics, physics-AP, play production, pottery, pre-calculus, religion, religion and culture, religious studies, Roman civilization, science, social justice, Spanish, Spanish-AP, statistics, student government, studio art, studio art-AP, study skills, tap dance, technical theater, television, theater, theater arts, theater design and production, theater production, trigonometry, U.S. government, U.S. government and politics-AP, U.S. history, U.S. history-AP, U.S. literature, video communication, visual and performing arts, visual arts, wind instruments, world history, writing, yearbook.

Graduation Requirements Algebra, arts and fine arts (art, music, dance, drama), biology, British literature, campus ministry, chemistry, Christian and Hebrew scripture, Christian doctrine, church history, civics, computer literacy, economics, English, English composition, English literature, foreign language, geometry, integrated mathematics, physical education (includes health), physics, religious studies, U.S. history.

La Salle High School

Special Academic Programs 14 Advanced Placement exams for which test preparation is offered; honors section.

College Admission Counseling 176 students graduated in 2010; all went to college, including California State Polytechnic University, Pomona; Loyola Marymount University; University of Colorado at Boulder; University of Southern California. Mean composite ACT: 25.

Student Life Upper grades have uniform requirement, student council, honor system. Discipline rests primarily with faculty. Attendance at religious services is required.

Summer Programs Remediation, enrichment, advancement, sports, art/fine arts, computer instruction programs offered; session focuses on academics and sports camps; held both on and off campus; held at Some students do classes online and Some students do classes at local Junior Colleges; accepts boys and girls; open to students from other schools. 460 students usually enrolled. 2011 schedule: June 13 to July 22. Application deadline: June 3.

Tuition and Aid Day student tuition: $13,250. Tuition installment plan (monthly payment plans, biannual). Merit scholarship grants, need-based scholarship grants available. In 2010–11, 38% of upper-school students received aid; total upper-school merit-scholarship money awarded: $75,000. Total amount of financial aid awarded in 2010–11: $1,200,000.

Admissions For fall 2010, 500 students applied for upper-level admission, 253 were accepted, 171 enrolled. STS required. Deadline for receipt of application materials: January 7. Application fee required: $70. Interview required.

Athletics Interscholastic: baseball (boys), basketball (b,g), cross-country running (b,g), equestrian sports (g), football (b), golf (b,g), soccer (b,g), softball (g), swimming and diving (b,g), tennis (b,g), track and field (b,g), volleyball (b,g), water polo (b,g); intramural: basketball (b,g), dance team (g), flag football (b); coed interscholastic: cheering, physical fitness, weight training; coed intramural: fitness, Frisbee, physical fitness, weight training. 2 PE instructors, 42 coaches, 2 athletic trainers.

Computers Computers are regularly used in all academic, computer applications, video film production classes. Computer resources include on-campus library services, online commercial services, Internet access. Campus intranet and computer access in designated common areas are available to students. Students grades are available online. The school has a published electronic and media policy.

Contact Mrs. Norma J. Wong, Admissions Secretary. 626-351-8951. Fax: 626-696-4411. E-mail: nwong@lasallehs.org. Web site: www.lasallehs.org.

THE LATIN SCHOOL OF CHICAGO

59 West North Boulevard
Chicago, Illinois 60610-1492

Head of School: Shelley Greenwood

General Information Coeducational day college-preparatory school. Grades JK–12. Founded: 1888. Setting: urban. 1-acre campus. 1 building on campus. Approved or accredited by Independent Schools Association of the Central States and Illinois Department of Education. Member of National Association of Independent Schools and Secondary School Admission Test Board. Endowment: $14.5 million. Total enrollment: 1,107. Upper school average class size: 15. Upper school faculty-student ratio: 1:8. There are 165 required school days per year for Upper School students. Upper School students typically attend 5 days per week. The average school day consists of 6 hours and 30 minutes.

Upper School Student Profile Grade 6: 67 students (32 boys, 35 girls); Grade 7: 78 students (37 boys, 41 girls); Grade 8: 80 students (39 boys, 41 girls); Grade 9: 106 students (49 boys, 57 girls); Grade 10: 111 students (52 boys, 59 girls); Grade 11: 107 students (47 boys, 60 girls); Grade 12: 111 students (54 boys, 57 girls).

Faculty School total: 150. In upper school: 40 men, 38 women; 61 have advanced degrees.

Subjects Offered Advanced Placement courses, advanced studio art-AP, African studies, African-American literature, algebra, American history, American history-AP, American literature, anatomy, animal behavior, art, art history, Asian studies, astronomy, biochemistry, biology, biology-AP, calculus, calculus-AP, chemistry, chemistry-AP, chorus, community service, composition, computer graphics, computer programming, computer science, creative writing, dance, drama, ecology, electives, electronics, English, English literature, environmental science, environmental science-AP, ethics, European civilization, European history, fine arts, French, French language-AP, French literature-AP, geography, geometry, history, history of ideas, honors U.S. history, human relations, human sexuality, humanities, independent study, instrumental music, Latin, Latin American history, Latin American literature, Latin-AP, literature by women, Mandarin, mathematical modeling, mathematics, mathematics-AP, Middle East, Middle Eastern history, music theory, photography, physical education, physics, physics-AP, physiology, poetry, probability and statistics, psychology, religion, science, social studies, Spanish, Spanish language-AP, Spanish literature, Spanish literature-AP, speech, stage design, statistics, studio art-AP, theater, trigonometry, women's literature, world history, world literature, writing.

Graduation Requirements Arts and fine arts (art, music, dance, drama), English, ethics, foreign language, human relations, human sexuality, mathematics, performing arts, physical education (includes health), science, social studies (includes history), technology, one-week non-credit course each year, Service Learning requirement. Community service is required.

Special Academic Programs Advanced Placement exam preparation; honors section; independent study; study abroad; academic accommodation for the gifted; remedial reading and/or remedial writing; remedial math; programs in general development for dyslexic students.

College Admission Counseling 110 students graduated in 2010; all went to college, including Miami University; Northwestern University; Tufts University; University of Chicago; University of Wisconsin–Madison; Yale University.

Student Life Upper grades have specified standards of dress, student council, honor system. Discipline rests equally with students and faculty.

Summer Programs Remediation, enrichment, advancement, sports, art/fine arts, rigorous outdoor training, computer instruction programs offered; session focuses on enrichment, remediation, sports, travel, and adventure; held both on and off campus; held at lakefront, city parks, wilderness experiences in the United States and abroad; accepts boys and girls; open to students from other schools. 180 students usually enrolled. 2011 schedule: June 14 to August 6. Application deadline: none.

Tuition and Aid Day student tuition: $26,985. Tuition installment plan (Insured Tuition Payment Plan, Key Tuition Payment Plan, FACTS Tuition Payment Plan, monthly payment plans, individually arranged payment plans). Need-based scholarship grants, need-based loans, middle-income loans, Key Education Achiever Loans available. In 2010–11, 21% of upper-school students received aid. Total amount of financial aid awarded in 2010–11: $1,997,189.

Admissions Traditional secondary-level entrance grade is 9. For fall 2010, 256 students applied for upper-level admission, 109 were accepted, 54 enrolled. ISEE required. Deadline for receipt of application materials: January 3. Application fee required: $80. On-campus interview required.

Athletics Interscholastic: aquatics (boys, girls), badminton (g), baseball (b), basketball (b,g), cross-country running (b,g), field hockey (g), golf (b,g), ice hockey (b,g), soccer (b,g), softball (g), swimming and diving (b,g), tennis (b,g), track and field (b,g), volleyball (b,g), water polo (b,g); intramural: life saving (b,g); coed intramural: dance, kayaking, outdoor activities, outdoor adventure, outdoor education, outdoor recreation, physical fitness, physical training, skiing (downhill). 6 PE instructors, 12 coaches, 2 athletic trainers.

Computers Computers are regularly used in art, English, foreign language, mathematics, science classes. Computer network features include on-campus library services, online commercial services, Internet access, wireless campus network. Campus intranet, student e-mail accounts, and computer access in designated common areas are available to students. The school has a published electronic and media policy.

Contact Frankie Brown, Director of Admissions and Financial Aid. 312-582-6060. Fax: 312-582-6061. E-mail: fbrown@latinschool.org. Web site: www.latinschool.org.

THE LAUREATE ACADEMY

Winnipeg, Manitoba, Canada
See Special Needs Schools section.

LAUREL SPRINGS SCHOOL

302 West El Paseo Road
Ojai, California 93023

Head of School: Marilyn Mosley

General Information Distance learning only college-preparatory, arts, vocational, technology, and distance learning school. Distance learning grades K–12. Founded: 1991. Setting: small town. Nearest major city is Los Angeles. 1 building on campus. Approved or accredited by Western Association of Schools and Colleges and California Department of Education. Total enrollment: 2,869. Upper school average class size: 1. Upper school faculty-student ratio: 1:1.

Faculty School total: 72. In upper school: 15 men, 57 women; 30 have advanced degrees.

Subjects Offered Algebra, American literature, art appreciation, art history, biology, biology-AP, British literature, British literature (honors), calculus, calculus-AP, calligraphy, career/college preparation, cartooning/animation, chemistry, chemistry-AP, college admission preparation, college counseling, driver education, earth science, economics, electives, English composition, English language and composition-AP, English literature and composition-AP, environmental education, environmental studies, French, French-AP, geometry, German, health, history of music, honors algebra, honors English, honors geometry, honors U.S. history, honors world history, Latin, macroeconomics-AP, Mandarin, microeconomics-AP, music history, mythology, photo shop, physical education, physics, physics-AP, pre-calculus, psychology, psychology-AP, SAT/ACT preparation, Shakespeare, sociology, Spanish, Spanish language-AP, statistics-AP, trigonometry, U.S. government, U.S. government and politics-AP, U.S. history, U.S. history-AP, world cultures, world history, world literature.

Graduation Requirements Arts and fine arts (art, music, dance, drama), electives, English, foreign language, mathematics, physical education (includes health), science, social studies (includes history).

Special Academic Programs Honors section; accelerated programs; independent study; term-away projects; academic accommodation for the gifted, the musically talented, and the artistically talented; remedial reading and/or remedial writing;

remedial math; programs in English, mathematics, general development for dyslexic students; special instructional classes for students needing customized learning options; ESL.

College Admission Counseling Colleges students went to include Pace University; San Jose State University; Stanford University; The University of Texas at Austin; University of California, Santa Barbara; University of California, Santa Cruz.

Student Life Upper grades have honor system. Discipline rests equally with students and faculty.

Summer Programs Remediation, enrichment, advancement, ESL, art/fine arts, computer instruction programs offered; session focuses on remediation and dual enrollment options; held both on and off campus; held at individual homes of enrolled students; accepts boys and girls; open to students from other schools. 1,231 students usually enrolled. 2011 schedule: July 1 to August 15. Application deadline: June 15.

Tuition and Aid Guaranteed tuition plan. Tuition installment plan (monthly payment plans, individually arranged payment plans). Tuition reduction for siblings, need-based scholarship grants available.

Admissions Traditional secondary-level entrance grade is 9. Deadline for receipt of application materials: none. Application fee required: $100. Interview required.

Computers Computers are regularly used in art, economics, English, foreign language, geography, health, history, independent study, information technology, language development, life skills, mathematics, psychology, SAT preparation, science, social studies, writing classes. Computer network features include on-campus library services, Internet access, 100 online courses. Student e-mail accounts are available to students. Students grades are available online.

Contact Ms. Tamara Honrado, Head of Enrollments. 805-646-2473 Ext. 121. Fax: 805-646-0186. E-mail: thonrado@laurelsprings.com. Web site: www.laurelsprings.com.

LAUREL VIEW ACADEMY

140 Mapleton Avenue
Barrie, Ontario L4N 9N7, Canada
Head of School: Mrs. Susi Rumney

General Information Coeducational day college-preparatory, general academic, arts, business, and technology school. Grades JK–12. Founded: 2001. Setting: suburban. 3-acre campus. 1 building on campus. Approved or accredited by Ontario Ministry of Education and Ontario Department of Education. Language of instruction: English. Upper school average class size: 10. Upper school faculty-student ratio: 1:5. There are 174 required school days per year for Upper School students. Upper School students typically attend 5 days per week. The average school day consists of 6 hours.

Faculty School total: 3. In upper school: 1 man, 1 woman; 2 have advanced degrees.

Subjects Offered 20th century history, 20th century physics, 20th century world history, advanced chemistry, advanced math, algebra, analysis of data, analytic geometry, anthropology, art, biology, business, calculus, Canadian geography, Canadian history, Canadian law, Canadian literature, career education, character education, chemistry, discrete mathematics, English, English as a foreign language, ESL, French as a second language, general science, geography, government and politics-AP, grammar, health education, history, language arts, law, leadership, linear algebra, literature, math analysis, math applications, math methods, math review, mathematical modeling, mathematics, media, novels, oral communications, oral expression, parent/child development, performing arts, philosophy, physical education, physics, political science, politics, pre-algebra, pre-calculus, pre-college orientation, probability and statistics, projective geometry, psychology, reading, reading/study skills, research, research and reference, research skills, science, science and technology, sex education, Shakespeare, short story, social education, social issues, social justice, social psychology, social sciences, social skills, social studies, society, society and culture, society challenge and change, society, politics and law, socioeconomic problems, sociology, statistics, student government, study skills, technical education, The 20th Century, visual arts, world geography, world history, world issues, world literature, World War I, World War II, writing.

Graduation Requirements 20th century history, arts, careers, civics, English, French as a second language, general science, geography, mathematics, physical education (includes health).

Special Academic Programs Independent study; ESL.

College Admission Counseling 2 students graduated in 2009; 1 went to college, including McMaster University. Other: 1 entered military service.

Student Life Upper grades have uniform requirement. Discipline rests primarily with faculty.

Tuition and Aid Day student tuition: CAN$9000. Tuition installment plan (monthly payment plans). Tuition reduction for siblings, need-based scholarship grants available.

Admissions For fall 2009, 2 students applied for upper-level admission, 2 were accepted. Deadline for receipt of application materials: none. Application fee required: CAN$150. Interview recommended.

Athletics Coed Interscholastic: alpine skiing, basketball, bowling, combined training, cooperative games, cross-country running, equestrian sports, horseback riding, outdoor activities, physical fitness, skiing (downhill), soccer.

Computers Computer resources include Internet access, wireless campus network.

Contact Mrs. Susi Rumney. 705-796-8295. Fax: 705-458-8296. E-mail: laurelview.academy@sympatico.ca. Web site: www.laurelviewacademy.ca.

LAUSANNE COLLEGIATE SCHOOL

1381 West Massey Road
Memphis, Tennessee 38120
Head of School: Mr. Stuart McCathie

General Information Coeducational day college-preparatory, arts, bilingual studies, technology, AP courses, honors curriculum, and sports education, electives school. Grades PK–12. Founded: 1926. Setting: suburban. 28-acre campus. 5 buildings on campus. Approved or accredited by National Independent Private Schools Association, Southern Association of Colleges and Schools, Southern Association of Independent Schools, Tennessee Association of Independent Schools, and Tennessee Department of Education. Member of National Association of Independent Schools. Endowment: $700,000. Total enrollment: 735. Upper school average class size: 15. Upper school faculty-student ratio: 1:9. There are 175 required school days per year for Upper School students. Upper School students typically attend 5 days per week. The average school day consists of 6 hours and 30 minutes.

Upper School Student Profile Grade 9: 71 students (30 boys, 41 girls); Grade 10: 56 students (24 boys, 32 girls); Grade 11: 80 students (32 boys, 48 girls); Grade 12: 64 students (25 boys, 39 girls).

Faculty School total: 105. In upper school: 11 men, 14 women; 19 have advanced degrees.

Subjects Offered Acting, algebra, American government, ancient world history, art, art-AP, biology, biology-AP, calculus, chemistry, choir, college admission preparation, comparative government and politics-AP, computer programming, creative writing, discrete mathematics, economics, English, English-AP, French, French-AP, geometry, health and wellness, honors algebra, honors English, honors geometry, humanities, instrumental music, international studies, journalism, Latin, Latin-AP, modern world history, photography, physical education, physical science, physics, physics-AP, play production, pre-calculus, public policy, short story, Spanish, Spanish-AP, statistics, U.S. history, U.S. history-AP, World War II, writing workshop.

Graduation Requirements Arts and fine arts (art, music, dance, drama), English, foreign language, mathematics, physical education (includes health), science, social studies (includes history).

Special Academic Programs 12 Advanced Placement exams for which test preparation is offered; honors section; academic accommodation for the gifted, the musically talented, and the artistically talented; ESL (19 students enrolled).

College Admission Counseling 54 students graduated in 2009; all went to college, including Birmingham-Southern College; Mississippi State University; Rhodes College; Sewanee: The University of the South; The University of Tennessee; University of Memphis.

Student Life Upper grades have specified standards of dress, student council, honor system. Discipline rests primarily with faculty.

Tuition and Aid Day student tuition: $14,400. Tuition installment plan (monthly payment plans, Tuition Refund Plan (TRP)). Need-based scholarship grants, tuition remission for children of faculty available. In 2009–10, 10% of upper-school students received aid. Total amount of financial aid awarded in 2009–10: $247,177.

Admissions Traditional secondary-level entrance grade is 9. For fall 2009, 63 students applied for upper-level admission, 41 were accepted, 34 enrolled. ISEE required. Deadline for receipt of application materials: none. Application fee required: $75. Interview required.

Athletics Interscholastic: basketball (boys, girls), cheering (g), cross-country running (b,g), dance squad (g), dance team (g), golf (b,g), gymnastics (g), lacrosse (b,g), pom squad (g), soccer (b,g), swimming and diving (b,g), tennis (b,g), track and field (b,g), volleyball (g); intramural: backpacking (b,g), ballet (g), basketball (b,g), bowling (b,g), canoeing/kayaking (b,g), climbing (b,g), dance team (g), flag football (b,g), floor hockey (b,g), Frisbee (b,g), hiking/backpacking (b,g), indoor soccer (b,g), kayaking (b,g), lacrosse (b,g), mountain biking (b,g), mountaineering (b,g), outdoor activities (b,g), physical fitness (b,g), rafting (b,g), rappelling (b,g), rock climbing (b,g), ropes courses (b,g), rugby (b), soccer (b,g), strength & conditioning (b,g), tennis (b,g), track and field (b,g), ultimate Frisbee (b,g), volleyball (b,g), wall climbing (b,g), weight lifting (b,g), wilderness (b,g); coed interscholastic: swimming and diving; coed intramural: backpacking, basketball, bowling, canoeing/kayaking, climbing, fishing, flag football, floor hockey, Frisbee, hiking/backpacking, indoor soccer, kayaking, lacrosse, martial arts, mountain biking, mountaineering, outdoor activities, physical fitness, rafting, rappelling, rock climbing, ropes courses, soccer, strength & conditioning, tennis, track and field, ultimate Frisbee, volleyball, wall climbing, weight lifting, wilderness, yoga. 4 coaches, 1 athletic trainer.

Computers Computers are regularly used in all academic, technology classes. Computer network features include on-campus library services, online commercial services, Internet access, wireless campus network, Internet filtering or blocking technology, homework assignments available online. Student e-mail accounts are available to students. Students grades are available online. The school has a published electronic and media policy.

Contact Mrs. Ashley Davis, Admission Coordinator. 901-474-1030. Fax: 901-474-1010. E-mail: adavis@lausanneschool.com. Web site: www.lausanneschool.com.

LAWRENCE ACADEMY

Powderhouse Road
Groton, Massachusetts 01450
Head of School: D. Scott Wiggins, Esq.

General Information Coeducational boarding and day college-preparatory, interdisciplinary ninth grade curriculum, and student-centered learning school; primarily serves students with learning disabilities. Grades 9–12. Founded: 1793. Setting: small town. Nearest major city is Boston. Students are housed in single-sex dormitories. 100-acre campus. 31 buildings on campus. Approved or accredited by Association of Independent Schools in New England, New England Association of Schools and Colleges, The Association of Boarding Schools, and Massachusetts Department of Education. Member of National Association of Independent Schools and Secondary School Admission Test Board. Endowment: $16 million. Total enrollment: 399. Upper school average class size: 15. Upper school faculty-student ratio: 1:8. Upper School students typically attend 5 days per week. The average school day consists of 6 hours and 20 minutes.

Upper School Student Profile Grade 9: 79 students (40 boys, 39 girls); Grade 10: 111 students (61 boys, 50 girls); Grade 11: 108 students (59 boys, 49 girls); Grade 12: 101 students (51 boys, 50 girls). 50% of students are boarding students. 60% are state residents. 18 states are represented in upper school student body. 14% are international students. International students from China, Germany, Republic of Korea, Russian Federation, and Spain; 15 other countries represented in student body.

Faculty School total: 75. In upper school: 41 men, 34 women; 50 have advanced degrees; 35 reside on campus.

Subjects Offered Advanced Placement courses, African-American literature, algebra, American history, anatomy, art, astronomy, biology, biology-AP, botany, calculus, calculus-AP, ceramics, chemistry, composition, creative writing, criminal justice, dance, drawing, ecology, electives, electronics, English, English literature, entomology, environmental science-AP, ESL, European history, fine arts, finite math, fractal geometry, French, French-AP, government/civics, history, independent study, John F. Kennedy, Latin, Latin American literature, limnology, marine science, mathematics, microbiology, music, music composition, music technology, music theory, music-AP, ornithology, painting, photography, physics, physics-AP, playwriting, pre-calculus, psychology, scene study, science, sculpture, Shakespeare, social psychology, Spanish, Spanish-AP, studio art, theater, tropical biology, U.S. government and politics-AP, writing.

Graduation Requirements Arts and fine arts (art, music, dance, drama), English, foreign language, history, mathematics, science, Winterim participation.

Special Academic Programs Advanced Placement exam preparation; honors section; independent study; study abroad; academic accommodation for the musically talented and the artistically talented; special instructional classes for deaf students, blind students; ESL (20 students enrolled).

College Admission Counseling 105 students graduated in 2009; all went to college, including Boston College; Boston University; Skidmore College; Syracuse University; University of New Hampshire; University of Vermont. Median SAT critical reading: 560, median SAT math: 580, median SAT writing: 570. 34% scored over 600 on SAT critical reading, 46% scored over 600 on SAT math, 40% scored over 600 on SAT writing, 37% scored over 1800 on combined SAT.

Student Life Upper grades have specified standards of dress, student council, honor system. Discipline rests primarily with faculty.

Tuition and Aid Day student tuition: $35,575; 7-day tuition and room/board: $46,200. Tuition installment plan (Key Tuition Payment Plan, monthly payment plans). Need-based scholarship grants, need-based loans, prepGATE loans available. In 2009–10, 29% of upper-school students received aid. Total amount of financial aid awarded in 2009–10: $3,100,000.

Admissions Traditional secondary-level entrance grade is 9. For fall 2009, 602 students applied for upper-level admission, 269 were accepted, 132 enrolled. PSAT or SAT, SSAT or TOEFL required. Deadline for receipt of application materials: February 1. Application fee required: $50. Interview required.

Athletics Interscholastic: baseball (boys), basketball (b,g), cross-country running (b,g), field hockey (g), football (b), golf (b,g), ice hockey (b,g), lacrosse (b,g), soccer (b,g), softball (g), tennis (b,g), volleyball (g), wrestling (b); intramural: snowboarding (b,g), tennis (b,g); coed interscholastic: alpine skiing, independent competitive sports, skiing (downhill); coed intramural: dance, fitness, independent competitive sports, modern dance, outdoors, physical fitness, physical training, rappelling, skiing (downhill), strength & conditioning, volleyball, weight training. 5 coaches, 2 athletic trainers.

Computers Computers are regularly used in college planning, computer applications, ESL, library, media production, music, photography, SAT preparation, video film production, yearbook classes. Computer network features include on-campus library services, online commercial services, Internet access, wireless campus network, Internet filtering or blocking technology. Student e-mail accounts and computer access in designated common areas are available to students. Students grades are available online. The school has a published electronic and media policy.

Contact Tony Hawgood, Director of Admissions. 978-448-6535. Fax: 978-448-1519. E-mail: admiss@lacademy.edu. Web site: www.lacademy.edu.

LAWRENCE SCHOOL

Sagamore Hills, Ohio
See Special Needs Schools section.

THE LAWRENCEVILLE SCHOOL

PO Box 6008
2500 Main Street
Lawrenceville, New Jersey 08648
Head of School: Elizabeth A. Duffy

General Information Coeducational boarding and day college-preparatory, arts, religious studies, and technology school. Grades 9–PG. Founded: 1810. Setting: small town. Nearest major city is Philadelphia, PA. Students are housed in single-sex dormitories. 700-acre campus. 39 buildings on campus. Approved or accredited by Middle States Association of Colleges and Schools, New Jersey Association of Independent Schools, The Association of Boarding Schools, and New Jersey Department of Education. Member of National Association of Independent Schools and Secondary School Admission Test Board. Endowment: $279. Total enrollment: 810. Upper school average class size: 12. Upper school faculty-student ratio: 1:8. Upper School students typically attend 6 days per week. The average school day consists of 7 hours.

Upper School Student Profile Grade 9: 144 students (71 boys, 73 girls); Grade 10: 221 students (113 boys, 108 girls); Grade 11: 216 students (113 boys, 103 girls); Grade 12: 214 students (118 boys, 96 girls); Postgraduate: 15 students (13 boys, 2 girls). 68% of students are boarding students. 45% are state residents. 32 states are represented in upper school student body. 15% are international students. International students from Canada, China, Hong Kong, Japan, Republic of Korea, and Saudi Arabia; 26 other countries represented in student body.

Faculty School total: 142. In upper school: 76 men, 66 women; 107 have advanced degrees.

Subjects Offered Acting, advanced chemistry, advanced computer applications, advanced studio art-AP, African-American literature, algebra, American Civil War, American foreign policy, American government, American history, American history-AP, American literature, American studies, architecture, art, art history, art history-AP, art-AP, arts, Asian history, astronomy, Basic programming, Bible, Bible studies, bioethics, bioethics, DNA and culture, biology, biology-AP, British literature, Buddhism, calculus, calculus-AP, Central and Eastern European history, ceramics, chamber groups, chemistry, chemistry-AP, China/Japan history, Chinese, Chinese studies, choir, chorus, Christian studies, Civil War, civil war history, classical Greek literature, classical language, comparative government and politics, conceptual physics, constitutional history of U.S., contemporary women writers, critical writing, dance, data analysis, design, digital applications, digital art, drama, dramatic arts, drawing, drawing and design, driver education, Eastern religion and philosophy, economics, electronic music, English, English literature, English literature-AP, English/composition-AP, environmental science, environmental studies, ethics, European history, European history-AP, European literature, evolution, field ecology, film and new technologies, film appreciation, filmmaking, foreign language, foreign policy, French, French language-AP, French literature-AP, French studies, French-AP, geometry, global science, Greek, health and wellness, Hebrew scripture, Hindi, historical foundations for arts, history of China and Japan, Holocaust, human biology, humanities, independent study, instruments, interdisciplinary studies, introduction to literature, introduction to theater, Irish literature, Irish studies, Islamic studies, Japanese, Japanese history, jazz, Jewish studies, John F. Kennedy, journalism, Latin, linear algebra, literature, medieval history, medieval literature, Middle East, Middle Eastern history, nature study, orchestra, organic chemistry, painting, participation in sports, personal development, philosophy, photography, physics, physics-AP, physiology, poetry, pre-algebra, pre-calculus, printmaking, probability and statistics, research seminar, robotics, science, set design, Shakespeare, short story, Southern literature, Spanish, Spanish language-AP, Spanish literature, studio art, the Presidency, the Sixties, theater, theater arts, U.S. constitutional history, U.S. government, U.S. government and politics, U.S. history, visual arts, water color painting, women in world history, world history, world religions, world religions, writing.

Graduation Requirements Arts and fine arts (art, music, dance, drama), English, foreign language, interdisciplinary studies, mathematics, religion (includes Bible studies and theology), science, social sciences, social studies (includes history). Community service is required.

Special Academic Programs Honors section; independent study; term-away projects; study abroad.

College Admission Counseling 232 students graduated in 2010; 230 went to college, including Columbia College; New York University; Princeton University; University of Pennsylvania; Yale University. Other: 1 went to work, 1 entered a postgraduate year. Median SAT critical reading: 676, median SAT math: 697, median SAT writing: 687.

Student Life Upper grades have specified standards of dress, student council, honor system. Discipline rests equally with students and faculty.

Tuition and Aid Day student tuition: $38,050; 7-day tuition and room/board: $46,475. Tuition installment plan (one, two, and nine month installment plans are available). Need-based scholarship grants available. In 2010–11, 29% of upper-school students received aid. Total amount of financial aid awarded in 2010–11: $9,100,000.

Admissions Traditional secondary-level entrance grade is 9. For fall 2010, 1,929 students applied for upper-level admission, 244 enrolled. ISEE, PSAT and SAT for applicants to grade 11 and 12, SSAT or TOEFL or SLEP required. Deadline for receipt of application materials: January 31. Application fee required: $50. Interview required.

Athletics Interscholastic: baseball (boys), basketball (b,g), crew (b,g), cross-country running (b,g), fencing (b,g), field hockey (g), football (b), golf (b,g), hockey (b,g), ice hockey (b,g), indoor track (b,g), indoor track & field (b,g), lacrosse (b,g), rowing (b,g), soccer (b,g), softball (g), squash (b,g), swimming and diving (b,g), tennis (b,g), track and field (b,g), volleyball (b,g), water polo (b,g), winter (indoor) track (b,g); intramural: basketball (b,g), Frisbee (g), handball (b,g), team handball (b,g), ultimate Frisbee (g), weight lifting (b,g), weight training (b,g); coed interscholastic: wrestling; coed intramural: backpacking, bicycling, broomball, canoeing/kayaking, climbing, cricket, dance, fitness, hiking/backpacking, ice skating, kayaking, modern dance, Nautilus, outdoor activities, physical fitness, physical training, rock climbing, ropes courses, squash, strength & conditioning, wall climbing, yoga. 72 coaches, 4 athletic trainers.

Computers Computers are regularly used in art, English, mathematics, music, science, technology classes. Computer network features include on-campus library services, online commercial services, Internet access, wireless campus network, Internet filtering or blocking technology. Campus intranet, student e-mail accounts, and computer access in designated common areas are available to students. Students grades are available online. The school has a published electronic and media policy.

Contact Gregg W.M. Maloberti, Dean of Admission. 800-735-2030. Fax: 609-895-2217. E-mail: admissions@lawrenceville.org. Web site: www.lawrenceville.org.

See Display on this page and Close-Up on page 798.

LEE ACADEMY

26 Winn Road
Lee, Maine 04455
Head of School: Mr. Bruce Lindberg

General Information Coeducational boarding and day college-preparatory, arts, and vocational school. Boarding grades 9–PG, day grades 9–12. Founded: 1845. Setting: rural. Nearest major city is Bangor. Students are housed in single-sex dormitories. 400-acre campus. 15 buildings on campus. Approved or accredited by Independent Schools of Northern New England, New England Association of Schools and Colleges, and Maine Department of Education. Endowment: $1. Total enrollment: 272. Upper school average class size: 12. Upper school faculty-student ratio: 1:10. Upper School students typically attend 5 days per week. The average school day consists of 7 hours and 30 minutes.

Upper School Student Profile Grade 9: 49 students (27 boys, 22 girls); Grade 10: 61 students (41 boys, 20 girls); Grade 11: 80 students (52 boys, 28 girls); Grade 12: 74 students (40 boys, 34 girls); Postgraduate: 8 students (8 boys). 30% of students are boarding students. 70% are state residents. 7 states are represented in upper school student body. 30% are international students. International students from China, Democratic People's Republic of Korea, Hong Kong, Israel, Taiwan, and Thailand; 3 other countries represented in student body.

Faculty School total: 29. In upper school: 15 men, 14 women; 9 have advanced degrees; 13 reside on campus.

Subjects Offered ACT preparation, advanced chemistry, Advanced Placement courses, advanced studio art-AP, architectural drawing, art, band, calculus, chemistry, chemistry-AP, choir, chorus, civics, civil rights, drama, electives, English, English language and composition-AP, English literature and composition-AP, English-AP, ESL, ESL, foreign language, forensics, French, general math, geometry, government-AP, government/civics, health and wellness, honors algebra, honors geometry, honors U.S. history, integrated mathematics, mathematics, mathematics-AP, music, music appreciation, musical productions, musical theater, peer counseling, physical education, physics, physics-AP, pre-algebra, pre-calculus, pre-college orientation, SAT/ACT preparation, Spanish, stagecraft, theater, theater arts, TOEFL preparation, U.S. government, U.S. government and politics, U.S. government and politics-AP, U.S. history, U.S. history-AP, United States government-AP, white-water trips, world cultures, world history, yearbook.

Graduation Requirements Algebra, American history, arts, biology, civics, computer skills, English, foreign language, health and wellness, mathematics, physical education (includes health), science.

Special Academic Programs Advanced Placement exam preparation; honors section; independent study; ESL (52 students enrolled).

College Admission Counseling 48 students graduated in 2009; 44 went to college, including Bates College; University of Maine. Other: 2 went to work, 2 entered military service. Median SAT critical reading: 560, median SAT math: 622, median SAT writing: 570, median composite ACT: 26.

Student Life Upper grades have specified standards of dress, student council. Discipline rests primarily with faculty.

Tuition and Aid Day student tuition: $8000; 5-day tuition and room/board: $21,800; 7-day tuition and room/board: $30,400. Guaranteed tuition plan. Tuition installment plan (monthly payment plans, individually arranged payment plans). Merit scholarship grants, need-based scholarship grants available. In 2009–10, 40% of upper-school students received aid.

Admissions Traditional secondary-level entrance grade is 9. For fall 2009, 92 students applied for upper-level admission, 65 were accepted, 57 enrolled. SAT,

---

Learning at Lawrenceville:

Building on the Past, Preparing for the Future

Founded in 1810, The Lawrenceville School offers a comprehensive, coeducational program for 815 students in grades nine through post-graduate, who come from 32 states and 32 countries. The School is located on 700 acres in the historic village of Lawrenceville, N.J.

www.lawrenceville.org

THE LAWRENCEVILLE SCHOOL

P.O. Box 6008 Lawrenceville, NJ 08648 800-735-2030

TOEFL or SLEP or writing sample required. Deadline for receipt of application materials: none. No application fee required. Interview recommended.

Athletics Interscholastic: baseball (boys), basketball (b,g), cross-country running (b,g), nordic skiing (b,g); intramural: backpacking (b,g); coed interscholastic: alpine skiing, cheering, golf; coed intramural: aerobics, aerobics/dance, aerobics/Nautilus, archery, badminton, ball hockey, bicycling, billiards, bowling, canoeing/kayaking, cooperative games, cross-country running, fishing, fitness, fitness walking, floor hockey, freestyle skiing, Frisbee, golf, hiking/backpacking, horseback riding, horseshoes, in-line skating, indoor soccer, jogging, kayaking, kickball, life saving, mountain biking, Nautilus, outdoor activities. 2 PE instructors, 11 coaches, 2 athletic trainers.

Computers Computers are regularly used in architecture, drafting, English, ESL, independent study, library, literary magazine, SAT preparation, yearbook classes. Computer resources include on-campus library services, Internet access, wireless campus network, Internet filtering or blocking technology. Campus intranet, student e-mail accounts, and computer access in designated common areas are available to students. Students grades are available online. The school has a published electronic and media policy.

Contact Mrs. Deborah Jacobs, Director of Admission. 207-738-2252. Fax: 207-738-3257. E-mail: admissions@leeacademy.org. Web site: www.leeacademy.org.

LEE ACADEMY
415 Lee Drive
Clarksdale, Mississippi 38614
Head of School: Ricky Weiss

General Information college-preparatory, arts, and business school. Founded: 1970. Setting: small town. Nearest major city is Memphis, TN. 4 buildings on campus. Approved or accredited by Mississippi Private School Association, Southern Association of Colleges and Schools, and Mississippi Department of Education. Total enrollment: 386. Upper school average class size: 22. Upper school faculty-student ratio: 1:20. There are 185 required school days per year for Upper School students. Upper School students typically attend 5 days per week. The average school day consists of 6 hours and 30 minutes.

Upper School Student Profile Grade 6: 21 students (10 boys, 11 girls); Grade 7: 45 students (25 boys, 20 girls); Grade 8: 45 students (28 boys, 17 girls); Grade 9: 36 students (16 boys, 20 girls); Grade 10: 50 students (28 boys, 22 girls); Grade 11: 50 students (26 boys, 24 girls); Grade 12: 38 students (20 boys, 18 girls).

Faculty School total: 45. In upper school: 4 men, 15 women; 8 have advanced degrees.

Subjects Offered ACT preparation, American government, American history, ancient world history, art, athletics, baseball, basketball, Bible, biology, bookkeeping, business, business law, calculus, cheerleading, chemistry, choral music, computer applications, earth and space science, earth science, English, English composition, English literature, foreign language, geography, geometry, guidance, health, Spanish, speech, U.S. history, writing workshop, yearbook.

Graduation Requirements Math methods.

College Admission Counseling 44 students graduated in 2010; all went to college, including Mississippi State University; University of Mississippi.

Student Life Upper grades have uniform requirement, student council. Discipline rests primarily with faculty.

Tuition and Aid Day student tuition: $5000. Tuition installment plan (monthly payment plans). Tuition reduction for siblings, need-based scholarship grants available. In 2010–11, 10% of upper-school students received aid. Total amount of financial aid awarded in 2010–11: $25,000.

Admissions Traditional secondary-level entrance grade is 9. For fall 2010, 174 students applied for upper-level admission, 174 were accepted, 174 enrolled. Deadline for receipt of application materials: February 28. No application fee required.

Athletics Interscholastic: baseball (boys), basketball (b), cheering (g), football (b); coed interscholastic: cross-country running, golf, soccer. 1 PE instructor.

Computers Computer resources include on-campus library services. Computer access in designated common areas is available to students. Students grades are available online.

Contact Ricky Weiss, Headmaster. 662-627-7891. Fax: 662-627-7896. E-mail: leeoffice@acbleone.net.

THE LEELANAU SCHOOL
Glen Arbor, Michigan
See Special Needs Schools section.

LEE-SCOTT ACADEMY
1601 Academy Drive
Auburn, Alabama 36830
Head of School: Dr. Don Roberts

General Information Coeducational day college-preparatory school, affiliated with Christian faith. Grades PK–12. Founded: 1967. Setting: small town. Nearest major city is Montgomery. 65-acre campus. 4 buildings on campus. Approved or accredited by Southern Association of Colleges and Schools and Alabama Department of Education. Endowment: $1 million. Total enrollment: 606. Upper school average class size: 15.

Upper school faculty-student ratio: 1:12. There are 176 required school days per year for Upper School students. Upper School students typically attend 5 days per week. The average school day consists of 7 hours and 10 minutes.

Upper School Student Profile Grade 7: 34 students (19 boys, 15 girls); Grade 8: 48 students (21 boys, 27 girls); Grade 9: 49 students (25 boys, 24 girls); Grade 10: 53 students (32 boys, 21 girls); Grade 11: 53 students (29 boys, 24 girls); Grade 12: 51 students (31 boys, 20 girls). 97% of students are Christian.

Faculty School total: 56. In upper school: 12 men, 16 women; 12 have advanced degrees.

Subjects Offered Algebra, anatomy, art, band, Bible studies, biology, calculus-AP, chemistry, chorus, computer applications, drama, driver education, economics, English, English literature and composition-AP, French, geometry, government, health, history-AP, honors English, HTML design, jazz band, keyboarding, Latin, macroeconomics-AP, physical education, physical science, physics-AP, pre-calculus, Spanish, speech, trigonometry, U.S. history, U.S. history-AP, world history.

Graduation Requirements Arts and fine arts (art, music, dance, drama), computer science, English, foreign language, health education, mathematics, physical education (includes health), science, social studies (includes history).

Special Academic Programs 5 Advanced Placement exams for which test preparation is offered; honors section; study at local college for college credit.

College Admission Counseling 50 students graduated in 2009; 48 went to college, including Auburn University; Georgia Institute of Technology; Southern Union State Community College; The University of Alabama; Troy University; University of Montevallo. Other: 2 went to work.

Student Life Upper grades have specified standards of dress, student council, honor system. Discipline rests primarily with faculty.

Tuition and Aid Day student tuition: $5660. Tuition installment plan (monthly payment plans, quarterly, bi-annual, and annual payment plans). Tuition reduction for siblings available.

Admissions Traditional secondary-level entrance grade is 7. Stanford Achievement Test required. Deadline for receipt of application materials: none. Application fee required: $250. On-campus interview required.

Athletics Interscholastic: baseball (boys), basketball (b,g), cheering (g), football (b), pom squad (g), softball (g), tennis (b,g), track and field (b,g), volleyball (g); intramural: basketball (b,g); coed interscholastic: golf, soccer. 4 PE instructors, 6 coaches, 1 athletic trainer.

Computers Computers are regularly used in English, history, mathematics, science classes. Computer network features include on-campus library services, Internet access, Internet filtering or blocking technology. Computer access in designated common areas is available to students. Students grades are available online.

Contact Mary Jane Pointer, Receptionist/Secretary. 334-821-2430. Fax: 334-821-0876. E-mail: mpointer@lee-scott.org. Web site: www.lee-scott.org.

LEHIGH VALLEY CHRISTIAN HIGH SCHOOL
330 Howertown Road
Catasauqua, Pennsylvania 18032
Head of School: Mr. Robert J. Brennan Jr.

General Information Coeducational day college-preparatory and general academic school, affiliated with Protestant-Evangelical faith. Grades 9–12. Founded: 1988. Setting: urban. Nearest major city is Allentown. 2-acre campus. 1 building on campus. Approved or accredited by Association of Christian Schools International, Middle States Association of Colleges and Schools, and Pennsylvania Department of Education. Total enrollment: 143. Upper school average class size: 20. Upper school faculty-student ratio: 1:12. There are 180 required school days per year for Upper School students. Upper School students typically attend 5 days per week. The average school day consists of 6 hours and 45 minutes.

Upper School Student Profile Grade 9: 27 students (6 boys, 21 girls); Grade 10: 31 students (10 boys, 21 girls); Grade 11: 39 students (16 boys, 23 girls); Grade 12: 46 students (17 boys, 29 girls). 90% of students are Protestant-Evangelical faith.

Faculty School total: 17. In upper school: 10 men, 7 women; 9 have advanced degrees.

Subjects Offered Accounting, Advanced Placement courses, algebra, American history, ancient world history, art, Bible, biology, biology-AP, calculus-AP, chemistry, chemistry-AP, chorus, computer applications, consumer mathematics, economics, English, English language and composition-AP, English literature and composition-AP, environmental science, geometry, government, health, history, keyboarding, physical education, physical science, physics, physics-AP, pre-algebra, pre-calculus, Spanish, state history, U.S. history, Western civilization, yearbook.

Graduation Requirements Algebra, American history, American literature, art, Bible, Bible studies, biology, British literature, chemistry, choir, civics, computer applications, English, foreign language, geometry, mathematics, physical education (includes health), physical science, science, social sciences, Western civilization, general lifestyle not harmful to the testimony of the school as a Christian institution, minimum one year of full-time enrollment in LVCH or another Christian high school.

Special Academic Programs Advanced Placement exam preparation; honors section; accelerated programs; independent study; study at local college for college credit; academic accommodation for the gifted; programs in English, mathematics, general development for dyslexic students; special instructional classes for students needing learning support; ESL (2 students enrolled).

College Admission Counseling 28 students graduated in 2010; 26 went to college, including Eastern University; Lehigh University; Liberty University; Moravian College; Penn State University Park; Philadelphia Biblical University. Other: 1 entered military service, 1 had other specific plans. Mean SAT critical reading: 520, mean SAT math: 528, mean SAT writing: 529, mean combined SAT: 1577.

Student Life Upper grades have uniform requirement, student council. Discipline rests primarily with faculty.

Summer Programs Remediation, advancement programs offered; session focuses on make-up courses; held both on and off campus; held at students' homes (for independent credit); accepts boys and girls; not open to students from other schools. 12 students usually enrolled. 2011 schedule: June 18 to August 11.

Tuition and Aid Day student tuition: $7250. Tuition installment plan (FACTS Tuition Payment Plan, individually arranged payment plans). Tuition reduction for siblings, need-based scholarship grants available. In 2010–11, 34% of upper-school students received aid. Total amount of financial aid awarded in 2010–11: $100,000.

Admissions Traditional secondary-level entrance grade is 9. For fall 2010, 42 students applied for upper-level admission, 40 were accepted, 39 enrolled. Achievement tests, Gates MacGinite Reading Tests or Wide Range Achievement Test required. Deadline for receipt of application materials: none. Application fee required: $250. On-campus interview required.

Athletics Interscholastic: baseball (boys), basketball (b,g), cheering (g), soccer (b,g), volleyball (g); coed interscholastic: track and field; coed intramural: fitness walking. 1 PE instructor, 10 coaches.

Computers Computers are regularly used in graphic arts, keyboarding, library, life skills, multimedia, science, technology, writing, yearbook classes. Computer network features include on-campus library services, Internet access, Internet filtering or blocking technology. Students grades are available online. The school has a published electronic and media policy.

Contact Dr. Alan H. Russell, Director of Admissions. 610-403-1000 Ext. 42. Fax: 610-403-1004. E-mail: a.russell@lvchs.org. Web site: www.lvchs.org.

LEHMAN HIGH SCHOOL

2400 Saint Mary Avenue
Sidney, Ohio 45365

Head of School: Mr. David Michael Barhorst

General Information Coeducational day and distance learning college-preparatory, arts, business, religious studies, and technology school, affiliated with Roman Catholic Church. Grades 9–12. Distance learning grades 10–12. Founded: 1970. Setting: small town. Nearest major city is Dayton. 50-acre campus. 1 building on campus. Approved or accredited by North Central Association of Colleges and Schools, Ohio Catholic Schools Accreditation Association (OCSAA), and Ohio Department of Education. Endowment: $800,000. Total enrollment: 230. Upper school average class size: 16. Upper school faculty-student ratio: 1:16. There are 179 required school days per year for Upper School students. Upper School students typically attend 5 days per week. The average school day consists of 7 hours.

Upper School Student Profile Grade 9: 74 students (34 boys, 40 girls); Grade 10: 48 students (24 boys, 24 girls); Grade 11: 49 students (17 boys, 32 girls); Grade 12: 59 students (36 boys, 23 girls). 90% of students are Roman Catholic.

Faculty School total: 22. In upper school: 11 men, 11 women; 14 have advanced degrees.

Subjects Offered Accounting, algebra, American government, American literature, anatomy and physiology, art, art history, biology, biology-AP, British literature, British literature (honors), business, calculus, calculus-AP, ceramics, chemistry, chemistry-AP, choir, computer applications, computer-aided design, concert band, earth science, English, English literature and composition-AP, environmental science, geography, geometry, government, health education, history of the Catholic Church, integrated science, intro to computers, Latin, moral theology, newspaper, painting, peace and justice, physical education, physics, pre-algebra, pre-calculus, psychology, sociology, Spanish, studio art, U.S. history, vocal music, world history, yearbook.

Graduation Requirements Biology, business, chemistry, computer applications, electives, English composition, English literature, health education, mathematics, physical education (includes health), physical science, religion (includes Bible studies and theology), U.S. government, U.S. history, must attend a senior retreat.

Special Academic Programs Advanced Placement exam preparation; honors section; independent study; study at local college for college credit.

College Admission Counseling 59 students graduated in 2010; all went to college, including Ohio University; The Ohio State University; University of Cincinnati; University of Dayton; Wright State University. Mean composite ACT: 24. 32% scored over 26 on composite ACT.

Student Life Upper grades have uniform requirement, student council, honor system. Discipline rests primarily with faculty. Attendance at religious services is required.

Tuition and Aid Day student tuition: $6760. Tuition installment plan (FACTS Tuition Payment Plan). Tuition reduction for siblings, need-based scholarship grants available. In 2010–11, 41% of upper-school students received aid. Total amount of financial aid awarded in 2010–11: $372,565.

Admissions Traditional secondary-level entrance grade is 9. For fall 2010, 2 students applied for upper-level admission, 2 were accepted, 2 enrolled. Achievement tests or any standardized test required. Deadline for receipt of application materials: none. Application fee required: $100. Interview recommended.

Athletics Interscholastic: aquatics (boys, girls), baseball (b), basketball (b,g), cheering (g), cross-country running (b,g), diving (b,g), football (b), golf (b), soccer (b,g), softball (g), swimming and diving (b,g), tennis (b,g), track and field (b,g), volleyball (g), wrestling (b); intramural: strength & conditioning (b,g); coed intramural: indoor track. 46 coaches, 1 athletic trainer.

Computers Computers are regularly used in accounting, computer applications, industrial technology, newspaper, yearbook classes. Computer resources include on-campus library services, Internet access, Internet filtering or blocking technology. Computer access in designated common areas is available to students. Students grades are available online. The school has a published electronic and media policy.

Contact Mrs. Denise Stauffer, Principal. 937-498-1161 Ext. 115. Fax: 937-492-9877. E-mail: d.stauffer@lehmancatholic.com.

LEIPZIG INTERNATIONAL SCHOOL E.V.

Konneritzstrasse 47
Leipzig 04229, Germany

Head of School: Mr. Roel Scheepens

General Information Coeducational day college-preparatory and general academic school. Grades K–12. Founded: 1992. Setting: urban. 1-hectare campus. 2 buildings on campus. Member of European Council of International Schools. Language of instruction: English. Endowment: €15 million. Total enrollment: 580. Upper school average class size: 17. Upper school faculty-student ratio: 1:9. There are 182 required school days per year for Upper School students. Upper School students typically attend 5 days per week. The average school day consists of 7 hours and 25 minutes.

Faculty School total: 68. In upper school: 9 men, 15 women; 7 have advanced degrees.

Special Academic Programs International Baccalaureate program; ESL (60 students enrolled).

Student Life Upper grades have student council. Discipline rests primarily with faculty.

Tuition and Aid Tuition reduction for siblings, need-based scholarship grants available. In 2009–10, 25% of upper-school students received aid.

Admissions English proficiency required. Deadline for receipt of application materials: none. Application fee required: €300. Interview recommended.

Athletics 2 PE instructors.

Computers Computer network features include on-campus library services, online commercial services, Internet access, wireless campus network, Internet filtering or blocking technology. Campus intranet and computer access in designated common areas are available to students.

Contact Ms. Marlene Cailleau. E-mail: admin@intschool-leipzig.com. Web site: www.intschool-leipzig.com.

LE LYCEE FRANCAIS DE LOS ANGELES

3261 Overland Avenue
Los Angeles, California 90034-3589

Head of School: Mrs. Clara-Lisa Kabbaz

General Information Coeducational day college-preparatory, general academic, arts, and bilingual studies school. Grades PS–12. Founded: 1964. Setting: suburban. Nearest major city is West Los Angeles. 12-acre campus. 7 buildings on campus. Approved or accredited by French Ministry of Education and Western Association of Schools and Colleges. Member of European Council of International Schools. Languages of instruction: English and French. Endowment: $4.8 million. Total enrollment: 732. Upper school average class size: 16. Upper school faculty-student ratio: 1:15. There are 170 required school days per year for Upper School students. Upper School students typically attend 5 days per week. The average school day consists of 7 hours and 45 minutes.

Upper School Student Profile Grade 6: 48 students (12 boys, 36 girls); Grade 7: 37 students (15 boys, 22 girls); Grade 8: 52 students (23 boys, 29 girls); Grade 9: 22 students (8 boys, 14 girls); Grade 10: 27 students (7 boys, 20 girls); Grade 11: 39 students (18 boys, 21 girls); Grade 12: 41 students (21 boys, 20 girls).

Faculty School total: 85. In upper school: 16 men, 26 women; 31 have advanced degrees.

Subjects Offered 20th century history, algebra, American history, American literature, anatomy, art, biology, calculus, ceramics, chemistry, computer programming, computer science, creative writing, dance, drama, earth science, economics, English, English literature, environmental science, ESL, European history, expository writing, fine arts, French, geography, geology, geometry, German, government/civics, grammar, history, Latin, mathematics, music, philosophy, photography, physical education, physics, science, social sciences, social studies, Spanish, statistics, theater, trigonometry, typing, world history, world literature, writing.

Graduation Requirements Arts and fine arts (art, music, dance, drama), English, foreign language, mathematics, physical education (includes health), science, social sciences, social studies (includes history).

Special Academic Programs International Baccalaureate program; Advanced Placement exam preparation; honors section; remedial reading and/or remedial writing; remedial math; ESL (25 students enrolled).

College Admission Counseling 36 students graduated in 2010; all went to college, including Loyola Marymount University; New York University; University of

Le Lycee Francais de Los Angeles

California, Berkeley; University of California, Los Angeles; University of California, Santa Cruz; University of Southern California. Median SAT critical reading: 600, median SAT math: 590, median SAT writing: 600, median combined SAT: 1720, median composite ACT: 25.

Student Life Upper grades have uniform requirement, student council, honor system. Discipline rests primarily with faculty.

Summer Programs Session focuses on social activities, sports, foreign languages; held both on and off campus; held at field trips, local parks; accepts boys and girls; open to students from other schools. 2011 schedule: June 20 to July 29. Application deadline: April 1.

Tuition and Aid Day student tuition: $12,880–$20,350. Bursaries, need-based scholarship grants available. In 2010–11, 12% of upper-school students received aid. Total amount of financial aid awarded in 2010–11: $63,000.

Admissions Traditional secondary-level entrance grade is 9. For fall 2010, 45 students applied for upper-level admission, 32 were accepted, 28 enrolled. School's own exam required. Deadline for receipt of application materials: February 28. Application fee required: $1000. Interview required.

Athletics Interscholastic: basketball (boys); intramural: ballet (g), baseball (g), fencing (b,g), outdoor activities (b,g), outdoor recreation (b,g), physical fitness (b,g); coed intramural: archery, martial arts. 6 PE instructors, 5 coaches, 4 athletic trainers.

Computers Computers are regularly used in English, foreign language, mathematics, science classes. Computer resources include on-campus library services, Internet access, wireless campus network, Internet filtering or blocking technology, Internet Café. Computer access in designated common areas is available to students. The school has a published electronic and media policy.

Contact Mme. Sophie Darmon, Admissions. 310-836-3464 Ext. 315. Fax: 310-558-8069. E-mail: admissions@lyceela.org. Web site: www.LyceeLA.org.

LEO CATHOLIC HIGH SCHOOL

7901 South Sangamon Street
Chicago, Illinois 60620
Head of School: Mr. Philip G. Mesina

General Information college-preparatory and religious studies school, affiliated with Roman Catholic Church. Founded: 1926. Setting: urban. Students are housed in Male Only Day School. 1 building on campus. Approved or accredited by North Central Association of Colleges and Schools and Illinois Department of Education. Total enrollment: 141. Upper school average class size: 12. Upper school faculty-student ratio: 1:12. There are 178 required school days per year for Upper School students. Upper School students typically attend 5 days per week. The average school day consists of 7 hours.

Upper School Student Profile 10% of students are Roman Catholic.

Faculty School total: 13. In upper school: 9 men, 3 women; 4 have advanced degrees.

Subjects Offered ACT preparation, advanced biology, advanced chemistry, advanced computer applications, advanced math, African American history, African American studies, algebra, American Civil War, American government, American history, applied arts, applied music, art, art appreciation, art education, athletic training, athletics, band, baseball, Basic programming, basketball, Bible, Bible as literature, Bible studies, biology, Black history, bowling, business applications, calculus, campus ministry, career and personal planning, Catholic belief and practice, character education, chemistry, choir, choral music, church history, civics, civil rights, Civil War, civil war history, classics, college awareness, college counseling, college placement, college planning, college writing, comparative religion, composition, computer education, computer multimedia, computer skills, computers, consumer economics, consumer education, economics, English, environmental science, ethics, foreign language, geometry, golf, health education, history, honors algebra, honors English, honors U.S. history, honors world history, Internet, jazz band, journalism, library, music, public speaking, reading, religion and culture, science, social sciences, Spanish, sports conditioning, sports nutrition, student government, student publications, theology, track and field, trigonometry, typing, U.S. government, vocal music, word processing, yearbook.

Special Academic Programs Honors section.

Student Life Upper grades have uniform requirement, student council, honor system. Discipline rests primarily with faculty. Attendance at religious services is required.

Summer Programs Remediation, sports programs offered; held on campus; accepts boys; open to students from other schools.

Tuition and Aid Day student tuition: $7000. Tuition installment plan (monthly payment plans). Tuition reduction for siblings, need-based scholarship grants available.

Admissions ACT-Explore required. Deadline for receipt of application materials: none. No application fee required. Interview recommended.

Athletics Interscholastic: baseball (boys), basketball (b), bowling (b), cross-country running (b), football (b), indoor track & field (b), track and field (b); intramural: boxing (b), golf (b), physical fitness (b), physical training (b), weight training (b).

Computers Computers are regularly used in art, college planning, computer applications, economics, English, health, history, humanities, journalism, mathematics, music, newspaper, reading, religion, social sciences, Spanish, theology, word processing, yearbook classes. Computer network features include on-campus library services, Internet access, wireless campus network, Internet filtering or blocking

technology. Computer access in designated common areas is available to students. Students grades are available online. The school has a published electronic and media policy.

Contact Mr. Michael Holmes, Director of Admissions. 773-224-9600 Ext. 212. Fax: 773-224-3856. E-mail: mholmes@leohighschool.org. Web site: www.leohighschool.org.

LESTER B. PEARSON UNITED WORLD COLLEGE OF THE PACIFIC

650 Pearson College Drive
Victoria, British Columbia V9C 4H7, Canada
Head of School: Dr. David Hawley

General Information Coeducational boarding and day college-preparatory and International Baccalaureate school. Grades 13–PG. Founded: 1974. Setting: rural. Approved or accredited by British Columbia Department of Education. Languages of instruction: English and French. Upper school average class size: 15.

Upper School Student Profile 100% of students are boarding students. 75% are international students.

Special Academic Programs International Baccalaureate program.

Tuition and Aid Financial aid available to upper-school students. In 2009–10, 100% of upper-school students received aid.

Admissions Deadline for receipt of application materials: February 15. Application fee required: CAN$50. Interview required.

Contact Canadian Selection Coordinator. 250-391-2411. E-mail: admin@pearsoncollege.ca. Web site: www.pearsoncollege.ca.

LEXINGTON CATHOLIC HIGH SCHOOL

2250 Clays Mill Road
Lexington, Kentucky 40503-1797
Head of School: Dr. Steven Angelucci

General Information Coeducational day college-preparatory and religious studies school, affiliated with Roman Catholic Church. Grades 9–12. Founded: 1823. Setting: urban. 6-acre campus. 3 buildings on campus. Approved or accredited by National Catholic Education Association, Southern Association of Colleges and Schools, and Kentucky Department of Education. Endowment: $600,000. Total enrollment: 842. Upper school average class size: 22. Upper school faculty-student ratio: 1:14. There are 177 required school days per year for Upper School students. Upper School students typically attend 5 days per week. The average school day consists of 6 hours and 15 minutes.

Upper School Student Profile Grade 9: 219 students (114 boys, 105 girls); Grade 10: 210 students (104 boys, 106 girls); Grade 11: 207 students (100 boys, 107 girls); Grade 12: 206 students (111 boys, 95 girls). 80% of students are Roman Catholic.

Faculty School total: 63. In upper school: 33 men, 30 women; 53 have advanced degrees.

Subjects Offered Accounting, advanced chemistry, Advanced Placement courses, advanced studio art-AP, algebra, American government, American history, American history-AP, American literature, anatomy and physiology, art, astronomy, band, Bible as literature, biology, biology-AP, British literature, British literature (honors), calculus, calculus-AP, Catholic belief and practice, ceramics, chemistry, chemistry-AP, choral music, Christian and Hebrew scripture, church history, comparative religion, computer applications, computer programming, creative writing, drama, economics, English-AP, ethics, film, French, French-AP, geography, geology, geometry, government and politics-AP, health, history of the Catholic Church, honors English, honors geometry, honors U.S. history, honors world history, humanities, introduction to literature, Latin, Latin-AP, physical education, physics, psychology, religious studies, sociology, Spanish, Spanish language-AP, U.S. government, U.S. government and politics-AP, U.S. history, U.S. history-AP, world history, world literature.

Graduation Requirements American history, American literature, arts and fine arts (art, music, dance, drama), biology, British literature, Catholic belief and practice, chemistry, Christian and Hebrew scripture, church history, comparative religion, computer applications, English, foreign language, mathematics, physical education (includes health), religion (includes Bible studies and theology), science, U.S. government, U.S. government and politics, U.S. history, world history.

Special Academic Programs Advanced Placement exam preparation; honors section.

College Admission Counseling 210 students graduated in 2009; 200 went to college, including University of Kentucky. Other: 8 went to work, 2 entered military service. Median SAT critical reading: 550, median SAT math: 570, median SAT writing: 530, median composite ACT: 23. 33% scored over 600 on SAT critical reading, 37% scored over 600 on SAT math, 28% scored over 600 on SAT writing, 24% scored over 26 on composite ACT.

Student Life Upper grades have uniform requirement, student council, honor system. Discipline rests primarily with faculty. Attendance at religious services is required.

Tuition and Aid Day student tuition: $6100. Tuition installment plan (monthly payment plans, individually arranged payment plans). Merit scholarship grants, need-based scholarship grants available. In 2009–10, 10% of upper-school students received aid; total upper-school merit-scholarship money awarded: $5000. Total amount of financial aid awarded in 2009–10: $450,000.

Admissions Traditional secondary-level entrance grade is 9. For fall 2009, 240 students applied for upper-level admission, 240 were accepted, 219 enrolled. Scholastic Testing Service High School Placement Test required. Deadline for receipt of application materials: none. Application fee required: $275.

Athletics Interscholastic: baseball (boys), basketball (b,g), cheering (g), cross-country running (b,g), dance team (g), diving (b,g), football (b), golf (b,g), ice hockey (b), power lifting (b), soccer (b,g), softball (g), swimming and diving (b,g), tennis (b,g), track and field (b,g), volleyball (g); intramural: basketball (b,g), flag football (g), lacrosse (b), physical training (b,g); coed interscholastic: ultimate Frisbee; coed intramural: bowling, hiking/backpacking, outdoor activities. 2 PE instructors, 2 athletic trainers.

Computers Computers are regularly used in all academic classes. Computer network features include on-campus library services, Internet access, wireless campus network. Students grades are available online. The school has a published electronic and media policy.

Contact Ms. Susie Fryer, Admissions Director. 859-277-7183 Ext. 231. Fax: 859-276-5086. E-mail: sfryer@lexingtoncatholic.com. Web site: www.lexingtoncatholic.com.

LEXINGTON CHRISTIAN ACADEMY

48 Bartlett Avenue
Lexington, Massachusetts 02420
Head of School: Mr. Mark R. Davis

General Information Coeducational day college-preparatory, arts, religious studies, and technology school, affiliated with Christian faith. Grades 6–12. Founded: 1946. Setting: suburban. Nearest major city is Boston. 30-acre campus. 1 building on campus. Approved or accredited by Association of Christian Schools International, Association of Independent Schools in New England, Christian Schools International, New England Association of Schools and Colleges, and Massachusetts Department of Education. Member of National Association of Independent Schools. Endowment: $3.6 million. Total enrollment: 311. Upper school average class size: 16. Upper school faculty-student ratio: 1:11. There are 168 required school days per year for Upper School students. Upper School students typically attend 5 days per week. The average school day consists of 7 hours.

Upper School Student Profile Grade 9: 54 students (25 boys, 29 girls); Grade 10: 51 students (28 boys, 23 girls); Grade 11: 61 students (32 boys, 29 girls); Grade 12: 54 students (27 boys, 27 girls).

Faculty School total: 42. In upper school: 22 men, 20 women; 29 have advanced degrees.

Subjects Offered Advanced Placement courses, algebra, American history-AP, anatomy, ancient history, art, Bible studies, biology, biology-AP, British literature, British literature-AP, calculus-AP, chemistry, choral music, Christian ethics, college counseling, community service, computer graphics, computer information systems, computers, concert band, creative writing, drama, economics, English, English literature, English literature-AP, ESL, European history-AP, French, general science, geography, geometry, health, history, independent study, journalism, Latin, mathematics, modern world history, music, music theory, physical education, physical science, physics, physiology, psychology, religion, science, science research, senior internship, senior project, social studies, Spanish, theater, trigonometry, U.S. government and politics, world history, world literature, writing.

Graduation Requirements Algebra, American history, American literature, ancient world history, Bible, Bible studies, biology, British history, British literature, chemistry, college counseling, college planning, computer literacy, electives, English, English literature, ethics, European history, European literature, foreign language, geometry, health education, keyboarding, lab science, mathematics, physical education (includes health), physics, religion (includes Bible studies and theology), science, senior internship, service learning/internship, social studies (includes history), U.S. history, senior internship (3-week work experience in career of student's choice, including a journal of the experience), Interim (participation each year in one week of special Interim courses). Community service is required.

Special Academic Programs Advanced Placement exam preparation; honors section; independent study; term-away projects; study at local college for college credit; ESL (26 students enrolled).

College Admission Counseling 53 students graduated in 2009; 52 went to college, including Boston University; Furman University; Gordon College; Northeastern University; Wheaton College. Other: 1 had other specific plans. Mean SAT critical reading: 603, mean SAT math: 625, mean SAT writing: 587.

Student Life Upper grades have specified standards of dress, student council. Discipline rests primarily with faculty. Attendance at religious services is required.

Tuition and Aid Day student tuition: $21,250. Tuition installment plan (Tuition Management Systems). Merit scholarship grants, need-based scholarship grants available. In 2009–10, 45% of upper-school students received aid; total upper-school merit-scholarship money awarded: $223,973. Total amount of financial aid awarded in 2009–10: $739,135.

Admissions Traditional secondary-level entrance grade is 9. ISEE or SSAT required. Deadline for receipt of application materials: February 15. Application fee required: $50. Interview required.

Athletics Interscholastic: baseball (boys), basketball (b,g), cross-country running (b,g), field hockey (g), lacrosse (b,g), soccer (b,g), softball (g), wrestling (b); intramural: basketball (b,g), gymnastics (b,g), lacrosse (b,g), physical training (b,g), soccer (b,g), tennis (b,g), volleyball (b,g), wrestling (b); coed interscholastic: golf; coed intramural: climbing, fitness, outdoor activities, rock climbing, skiing (downhill), snowboarding, strength & conditioning, ultimate Frisbee, volleyball, wall climbing, weight training. 2 PE instructors, 10 coaches, 1 athletic trainer.

Computers Computers are regularly used in all academic, graphic design, library science, literary magazine, mathematics, media arts, music, photography, publications, science, yearbook classes. Computer network features include on-campus library services, online commercial services, Internet access, wireless campus network, Internet filtering or blocking technology. Campus intranet and computer access in designated common areas are available to students. The school has a published electronic and media policy.

Contact Mrs. Cynthia Torjesen, Director of Admission. 781-862-7850 Ext. 152. Fax: 781-863-8503. E-mail: cindy.torjesen@lca.edu. Web site: www.lca.edu.

LEYSIN AMERICAN SCHOOL IN SWITZERLAND

Admissions Office
Beau Site
Leysin 1854, Switzerland
Head of School: Dr. Marc-Frédéric Ott

General Information Coeducational boarding college-preparatory school. Grades 8–PG. Founded: 1961. Setting: small town. Nearest major city is Geneva, Switzerland. Students are housed in single-sex dormitories. 14 buildings on campus. Approved or accredited by European Council of International Schools, International Baccalaureate Organization, Middle States Association of Colleges and Schools, Swiss Federation of Private Schools, and The Association of Boarding Schools. Member of Secondary School Admission Test Board. Language of instruction: English. Total enrollment: 380. Upper school average class size: 14. Upper school faculty-student ratio: 1:8. There are 180 required school days per year for Upper School students. Upper School students typically attend 5 days per week. The average school day consists of 5 hours and 55 minutes.

Upper School Student Profile 100% of students are boarding students. 98% are international students. International students from Brazil, Kazakhstan, Mexico, Russian Federation, Saudi Arabia, and United States; 55 other countries represented in student body.

Faculty School total: 72. In upper school: 40 men, 32 women; 42 have advanced degrees; 67 reside on campus.

Subjects Offered Algebra, American history, American literature, ancient history, art, band, biology, business, business studies, calculus, calculus-AP, chemistry, chorus, college counseling, computer programming, computer science, computer technologies, creative arts, current events, dance, drama, ecology, environmental systems, economics, English, English literature, ensembles, ESL, European history, fine arts, fitness, French, French studies, geometry, German, health education, history, history of the Americas, humanities, information technology, International Baccalaureate courses, intro to computers, journalism, language arts, math analysis, math methods, mathematics, mathematics-AP, model United Nations, modern languages, music, music appreciation, performing arts, physical education, physical science, physics, piano, pre-algebra, pre-calculus, psychology, SAT preparation, science, social sciences, social studies, Spanish, Spanish literature, stagecraft, studio art, study skills, theater, theory of knowledge, TOEFL preparation, trigonometry, United Nations and international issues, weightlifting, world history, yearbook.

Graduation Requirements Arts and fine arts (art, music, dance, drama), computer science, English, foreign language, mathematics, physical education (includes health), science, senior humanities, social studies (includes history), Swiss and European cultural trip reports.

Special Academic Programs International Baccalaureate program; honors section; independent study; study abroad; academic accommodation for the gifted, the musically talented, and the artistically talented; ESL (110 students enrolled).

College Admission Counseling 104 students graduated in 2009; 102 went to college, including Boston University; Mount Holyoke College; New York University; Northeastern University; The University of Texas at Austin; University of Virginia. Other: 2 entered a postgraduate year. Mean SAT critical reading: 496, mean SAT math: 548, mean SAT writing: 509.

Student Life Upper grades have specified standards of dress, student council, honor system. Discipline rests equally with students and faculty.

Tuition and Aid 5-day tuition and room/board: 51,000 Swiss francs; 7-day tuition and room/board: 69,500 Swiss francs. Tuition installment plan (individually arranged payment plans, Corporate payment plan). Tuition reduction for siblings, bursaries, merit scholarship grants, need-based scholarship grants, paying campus jobs available. In 2009–10, 10% of upper-school students received aid; total upper-school merit-scholarship money awarded: 250,000 Swiss francs. Total amount of financial aid awarded in 2009–10: 600,000 Swiss francs.

Admissions Traditional secondary-level entrance grade is 10. Achievement/Aptitude/Writing or essay required. Deadline for receipt of application materials: none. Application fee required: 200 Swiss francs. Interview recommended.

Athletics Interscholastic: alpine skiing (boys, girls), basketball (b,g), hockey (b), ice hockey (b), soccer (b,g), tennis (b,g), volleyball (b,g); intramural: basketball (b,g), soccer (b,g), tennis (b,g), volleyball (b,g); coed interscholastic: bicycling, cross-country running, equestrian sports, golf, skiing (cross-country), skiing (downhill), snowboarding, squash, swimming and diving, track and field; coed intramural: aerobics, aerobics/dance, alpine skiing, backpacking, ball hockey, ballet, bicycling, canoeing/kayaking, climbing, cross-country running, curling, dance, dance team, equestrian sports, figure skating, fitness, flag football, floor hockey, freestyle skiing, golf, hiking/backpacking, horseback riding, ice skating, indoor hockey, indoor soccer, jogging, juggling, martial arts, mountain biking, mountaineering, nordic skiing, outdoor activities, outdoor adventure, outdoor education, outdoor recreation, paddle tennis, paint ball, physical fitness, physical training, rafting, rappelling, rock climbing, ropes courses, running, sailing, skiing (cross-country), skiing (downhill), snow-boarding, snowshoeing, squash, street hockey, strength & conditioning, swimming and diving, table tennis, track and field, unicycling, walking, wall climbing, weight lifting, weight training, yoga. 1 PE instructor, 2 athletic trainers.

Computers Computers are regularly used in all classes. Computer network features include on-campus library services, online commercial services, Internet access, wireless campus network, Internet filtering or blocking technology. Campus intranet and student e-mail accounts are available to students. Students grades are available online. The school has a published electronic and media policy.

Contact Mr. Aaron L. Schmidtberger, Director of Admissions, North America. 603-431-7654. Fax: 41-24-494-1585. E-mail: admissions@las.ch. Web site: www. las.ch.

See Display below and Close-Up on page 800.

LIBERTY CHRISTIAN SCHOOL

7661 Warner Avenue
Huntington Beach, California 92647
Head of School: Mr. Chris Herring
General Information Coeducational day college-preparatory and religious studies school, affiliated with Baptist Church. Grades K–12. Founded: 1970. Setting: suburban. Nearest major city is Los Angeles. 5-acre campus. 3 buildings on campus. Approved or accredited by Accrediting Commission for Schools, Western Association of Schools and Colleges, and California Department of Education. Total enrollment: 348. Upper school average class size: 25. Upper school faculty-student ratio: 1:7. There are 180 required school days per year for Upper School students. Upper School students typically attend 5 days per week. The average school day consists of 6 hours and 30 minutes.
Upper School Student Profile Grade 9: 24 students (12 boys, 12 girls); Grade 10: 15 students (3 boys, 12 girls); Grade 11: 34 students (15 boys, 19 girls); Grade 12: 18 students (5 boys, 13 girls). 75% of students are Baptist.

Faculty School total: 25. In upper school: 6 men, 7 women; 3 have advanced degrees.
Subjects Offered American literature.
Special Academic Programs Advanced Placement exam preparation; honors section; independent study.
College Admission Counseling Colleges students went to include Azusa Pacific University; California State University, Long Beach; Golden West College; Orange Coast College.
Student Life Upper grades have specified standards of dress, student council, honor system. Discipline rests primarily with faculty. Attendance at religious services is required.
Admissions Traditional secondary-level entrance grade is 9. For fall 2010, 29 students applied for upper-level admission, 29 were accepted, 29 enrolled. Woodcock-Johnson required. Deadline for receipt of application materials: none. Application fee required: $225. On-campus interview required.
Athletics Interscholastic: baseball (boys), basketball (b,g), cheering (b), flag football (b,g), football (b,g), physical training (b,g); intramural: baseball (b), basketball (b); coed interscholastic: cheering. 1 PE instructor, 4 coaches.
Computers Computer network features include on-campus library services, Internet access. Students grades are available online.
Contact Clarice Burkholder, Registrar. 714-842-5992. Fax: 714-848-7484. Web site: www.libertychristian.org.

LICK-WILMERDING HIGH SCHOOL

755 Ocean Avenue
San Francisco, California 94112
Head of School: Dr. Albert M. Adams II
General Information Coeducational day college-preparatory, technology, performing arts, and visual arts school. Grades 9–12. Founded: 1895. Setting: urban. 4-acre campus. 6 buildings on campus. Approved or accredited by California Association of Independent Schools, Western Association of Schools and Colleges, and California Department of Education. Member of National Association of Independent Schools and Secondary School Admission Test Board. Endowment: $43 million. Total enrollment: 440. Upper school average class size: 15. Upper school faculty-student ratio: 1:9. Upper School students typically attend 5 days per week. The average school day consists of 7 hours and 30 minutes.
Upper School Student Profile Grade 9: 113 students (51 boys, 62 girls); Grade 10: 113 students (54 boys, 59 girls); Grade 11: 111 students (52 boys, 59 girls); Grade 12: 106 students (55 boys, 51 girls).
Faculty School total: 63. In upper school: 26 men, 35 women; 42 have advanced degrees.

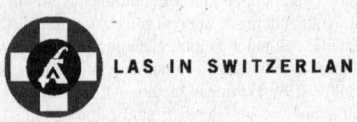

Subjects Offered Acting, adolescent issues, advanced chemistry, advanced math, Advanced Placement courses, advanced studio art-AP, African-American literature, algebra, American history, American literature, anatomy and physiology, architectural drawing, architecture, art, biology, biology-AP, calculus, calculus-AP, chemistry, chemistry-AP, choral music, computer music, computer science, computer science-AP, creative writing, critical thinking, dance, digital imaging, drafting, drama, electronics, English, English literature, European history, fine arts, French, French language-AP, French literature-AP, French-AP, geometry, history, industrial arts, jazz band, jewelry making, journalism, mathematics, mechanical drawing, music, music theory-AP, .music-AP, peer counseling, photography, physical education, physics, physics-AP, psychology, psychology-AP, science, social studies, Spanish, Spanish literature, Spanish-AP, stagecraft, statistics-AP, studio art-AP, technical arts, theater, trigonometry, U.S. history, woodworking, word processing, world history, world history-AP, world literature, writing, yoga.

Graduation Requirements Arts and fine arts (art, music, dance, drama), English, foreign language, mathematics, physical education (includes health), science, social studies (includes history), technical arts, technology/design, junior project with technical arts.

Special Academic Programs Advanced Placement exam preparation; honors section; independent study.

College Admission Counseling 101 students graduated in 2010; all went to college, including Cornell University; Occidental College; Stanford University; University of California, Berkeley; University of California, Los Angeles; Vassar College. Median SAT critical reading: 660, median SAT math: 680, median SAT writing: 700. 86% scored over 600 on SAT critical reading, 85% scored over 600 on SAT math, 89% scored over 600 on SAT writing.

Student Life Upper grades have student council. Discipline rests primarily with faculty.

Tuition and Aid Day student tuition: $34,395. Tuition installment plan (FACTS Tuition Payment Plan, 3- or 10-installment plans). Need-based scholarship grants available. In 2010–11, 42% of upper-school students received aid. Total amount of financial aid awarded in 2010–11: $4,300,000.

Admissions Traditional secondary-level entrance grade is 9. For fall 2010, 736 students applied for upper-level admission, 150 were accepted, 111 enrolled. ISEE or SSAT required. Deadline for receipt of application materials: January 14. Application fee required: $95. Interview required.

Athletics Interscholastic: baseball (boys), basketball (b,g), cross-country running (b,g), lacrosse (b,g), soccer (b,g), swimming and diving (b,g), tennis (b,g), track and field (b,g), volleyball (b,g); coed interscholastic: badminton, wrestling; coed intramural: dance, fitness, modern dance, physical fitness, rock climbing, ultimate Frisbee, yoga. 1 PE instructor, 25 coaches.

Computers Computers are regularly used in architecture, digital applications, drafting, history, journalism, library, literary magazine, mathematics, media, science, writing, yearbook classes. Computer network features include on-campus library services, online commercial services, Internet access, wireless campus network, Internet filtering or blocking technology. Campus intranet, student e-mail accounts, and computer access in designated common areas are available to students. Students grades are available online.

Contact Lisa Wu, Director of Admissions. 415-337-9990. Fax: 415-239-1230. E-mail: admissions@lwhs.org. Web site: www.lwhs.org.

LIFEGATE SCHOOL

1052 Fairfield Avenue
Eugene, Oregon 97402-2053
Head of School: Mr. Tom Gregersen

General Information Coeducational boarding and day and distance learning college-preparatory, general academic, arts, and religious studies school, affiliated with Church of Christ, Scientist. Grades 6–12. Distance learning grade X. Founded: 1994. Setting: suburban. 1-acre campus. 1 building on campus. Approved or accredited by Association of Christian Schools International, Northwest Association of Schools and Colleges, Texas Private School Accreditation Commission, and Oregon Department of Education. Total enrollment: 44. Upper school average class size: 8. Upper school faculty-student ratio: 1:10. Upper School students typically attend 5 days per week. The average school day consists of 7 hours.

Upper School Student Profile Grade 6: 5 students (4 boys, 1 girl); Grade 7: 4 students (2 boys, 2 girls); Grade 8: 5 students (2 boys, 3 girls); Grade 9: 7 students (4 boys, 3 girls); Grade 10: 10 students (5 boys, 5 girls); Grade 11: 9 students (4 boys, 5 girls); Grade 12: 6 students (3 boys, 3 girls). 100% are state residents. 50 states are represented in upper school student body. 95% of students are members of Church of Christ, Scientist.

Faculty School total: 16. In upper school: 5 men, 2 women; 5 have advanced degrees.

Subjects Offered Advanced biology, advanced chemistry, advanced math, Advanced Placement courses, algebra, American government, American history, ancient world history, art, band, Bible, Bible studies, biology, biology-AP, British literature (honors), British literature-AP, calculus, calculus-AP, career and personal planning, chemistry, computer applications, computer graphics, computer processing, cultural geography, drama, economics, English, English composition, English language and composition-AP, English literature-AP, geometry, health education, independent

study, journalism, keyboarding, leadership, life skills, physical education, physical science, physics, pre-algebra, pre-calculus, reading/study skills, Spanish, world history, writing, yearbook.

Graduation Requirements Bible, English, government, history, keyboarding, life skills, mathematics, physical education (includes health), 25 hours of volunteer work per year.

Special Academic Programs Advanced Placement exam preparation; honors section; accelerated programs; independent study; academic accommodation for the gifted and the artistically talented; remedial reading and/or remedial writing; remedial math; programs in mathematics, general development for dyslexic students.

College Admission Counseling 12 students graduated in 2010; 9 went to college, including George Fox University; Georgia State University; Lane Community College; Oregon Institute of Technology; Oregon State University; University of Oregon. Other: 1 went to work, 2 entered military service.

Student Life Upper grades have specified standards of dress, student council. Discipline rests primarily with faculty. Attendance at religious services is required.

Tuition and Aid Day student tuition: $5550. Tuition installment plan (monthly payment plans). Tuition reduction for siblings, need-based scholarship grants available. In 2010–11, 14% of upper-school students received aid. Total amount of financial aid awarded in 2010–11: $50,000.

Admissions Traditional secondary-level entrance grade is 9. For fall 2010, 9 students applied for upper-level admission, 9 were accepted, 9 enrolled. Deadline for receipt of application materials: none. No application fee required. On-campus interview required.

Athletics Interscholastic: basketball (boys), outdoor activities (b,g), outdoor education (b,g), volleyball (g); coed interscholastic: track and field. 1 PE instructor, 1 coach.

Computers Computers are regularly used in desktop publishing, English, freshman foundations, lab/keyboard, media arts, Web site design, writing, yearbook classes. Computer network features include on-campus library services, Internet access, wireless campus network, Internet filtering or blocking technology. Campus intranet and student e-mail accounts are available to students. Students grades are available online.

Contact Ms. Donna Wickwire, Assistant Administrator. 541-689-5847. Fax: 541-689-6028. E-mail: donnaw@lifegatechristian.org. Web site: www.lifegatechristian.org.

LIGHTHOUSE CHRISTIAN SCHOOL

4290-50th Street
Sylvan Lake, Alberta T4S 0H3, Canada
Head of School: Dion Krause

General Information Coeducational day college-preparatory, general academic, arts, and religious studies school. Grades PK–12. Nearest major city is Red Deer, Canada. Approved or accredited by Alberta Department of Education. Language of instruction: English. Total enrollment: 84. Upper school faculty-student ratio: 1:15.

Upper School Student Profile Grade 10: 5 students (3 boys, 2 girls); Grade 11: 5 students (2 boys, 3 girls); Grade 12: 12 students (4 boys, 8 girls).

Faculty School total: 11. In upper school: 1 man, 10 women.

College Admission Counseling 5 students graduated in 2010. Other: 2 went to work, 3 had other specific plans.

Student Life Upper grades have specified standards of dress, honor system.

Admissions Traditional secondary-level entrance grade is 10. For fall 2010, 2 students applied for upper-level admission, 2 were accepted, 2 enrolled. Deadline for receipt of application materials: none. No application fee required. Interview required.

Contact Dion Krause, Principal. 403-887-2166. Fax: 403-887-5729. E-mail: lightca@telusplanet.net.

LIMA CENTRAL CATHOLIC HIGH SCHOOL

720 South Cable Road
Lima, Ohio 45805-3496
Head of School: Mr. Richard Mitterholzer

General Information Coeducational day college-preparatory and religious studies school, affiliated with Roman Catholic Church. Grades 9–12. Founded: 1956. Setting: small town. Nearest major city is Columbus. 78-acre campus. 2 buildings on campus. Approved or accredited by North Central Association of Colleges and Schools, Ohio Catholic Schools Accreditation Association (OCSAA), and Ohio Department of Education. Endowment: $4 million. Total enrollment: 350. Upper school average class size: 20. Upper school faculty-student ratio: 1:13. There are 178 required school days per year for Upper School students. Upper School students typically attend 5 days per week. The average school day consists of 6 hours.

Upper School Student Profile 80% of students are Roman Catholic.

Faculty School total: 30. In upper school: 16 men, 14 women; 15 have advanced degrees.

Subjects Offered Advanced Placement courses, arts, calculus-AP, chemistry, computer literacy, English, English-AP, German, health, Italian, mathematics, physical education, physics, pre-calculus, religion, science, social studies, Spanish, statistics-AP, Web site design, world history-AP.

Lima Central Catholic High School

Graduation Requirements Computer literacy, English, mathematics, physical education (includes health), religion (includes Bible studies and theology), science, social studies (includes history), requirements for academic and honors diplomas differ.

Special Academic Programs Advanced Placement exam preparation; honors section; study at local college for college credit.

College Admission Counseling 80 students graduated in 2010; 77 went to college, including The Ohio State University; University of Cincinnati; Wright State University; Xavier University. Other: 2 went to work, 1 had other specific plans. Mean composite ACT: 23.

Student Life Upper grades have uniform requirement, student council. Discipline rests primarily with faculty. Attendance at religious services is required.

Summer Programs Enrichment, sports programs offered; held on campus; accepts boys and girls; open to students from other schools. 50 students usually enrolled.

Tuition and Aid Day student tuition: $4200. Tuition installment plan (FACTS Tuition Payment Plan, prepaid tuition through Union Bank). Merit scholarship grants, need-based scholarship grants available. In 2010–11, 35% of upper-school students received aid; total upper-school merit-scholarship money awarded: $10,000. Total amount of financial aid awarded in 2010–11: $75,000.

Admissions Traditional secondary-level entrance grade is 9. For fall 2010, 120 students applied for upper-level admission, 110 were accepted, 100 enrolled. ACT-Explore required. Deadline for receipt of application materials: none. Application fee required: $125. Interview recommended.

Athletics Interscholastic: aquatics (boys, girls), baseball (b), basketball (b,g), bowling (b,g), cross-country running (b,g), football (b), golf (b,g), soccer (b,g), softball (g), swimming and diving (b,g), track and field (b,g), volleyball (g), wrestling (b); intramural: bowling (b,g).

Computers Computer network features include Internet access.

Contact Mr. Robert Seggerson. 419-222-4276. Fax: 419-222-6933. Web site: www.lcchs.edu.

LINCOLN ACADEMY

81 Academy Hill
Newcastle, Maine 04553
Head of School: Mr. John B. Pinkerton

General Information Coeducational day college-preparatory, general academic, arts, business, vocational, technology, Advanced Placement, and world languages school. Grades 9–12. Founded: 1801. Setting: small town. Nearest major city is Portland. 85-acre campus. 4 buildings on campus. Approved or accredited by New England Association of Schools and Colleges and Maine Department of Education. Endowment: $5.5 million. Total enrollment: 547. Upper school average class size: 18. Upper school faculty-student ratio: 1:8. There are 181 required school days per year for Upper School students. Upper School students typically attend 5 days per week. The average school day consists of 6 hours and 40 minutes.

Subjects Offered 20th century history, 20th century world history, 3-dimensional art, 3-dimensional design, accounting, acting, advanced biology, advanced chemistry, advanced math, Advanced Placement courses, advanced studio art-AP, algebra, American history, American history-AP, American literature, American literature-AP, architectural drawing, art and culture, art-AP, athletics, audio visual/media, auto mechanics, band, basic language skills, biology, biology-AP, bookkeeping, business, business skills, calculus, calculus-AP, career/college preparation, chemistry, chemistry-AP, chorus, computer skills, conceptual physics, concert band, concert choir, desktop publishing, developmental language skills, developmental math, drafting, drama, English composition, English language-AP, English literature-AP, English-AP, English/composition-AP, environmental science-AP, filmmaking, foreign language, French, French-AP, general math, geography, geometry, healthful living, history, history of rock and roll, honors algebra, honors English, honors geometry, honors U.S. history, honors world history, industrial arts, instrumental music, integrated physics, Italian, Japanese, jazz band, language arts, language development, marine science, mechanical drawing, music theory, music theory-AP, musical productions, performing arts, physical education, play production, play/screen writing, poetry, portfolio art, pre-algebra, pre-calculus, psychology, Russian, sculpture, social studies, Spanish, Spanish language-AP, studio art, technical drawing, technical education, U.S. history, U.S. history-AP, U.S. literature, visual and performing arts, work-study, world history, yearbook.

Graduation Requirements Job shadow experiences, community service.

Special Academic Programs 12 Advanced Placement exams for which test preparation is offered; honors section; independent study.

Student Life Upper grades have specified standards of dress, student council. Discipline rests primarily with faculty.

Tuition and Aid Day student tuition: $10,046.

Admissions Traditional secondary-level entrance grade is 9. Deadline for receipt of application materials: none. No application fee required. On-campus interview required.

Athletics Interscholastic: baseball (boys), basketball (b,g), cheering (g), cross-country running (b,g), field hockey (g), golf (b), lacrosse (b,g), soccer (b,g), softball (g), swimming and diving (b,g), tennis (b,g), track and field (b,g), wrestling (g); coed interscholastic: indoor track, Special Olympics; coed intramural: dance team, outdoor activities.

Computers Computers are regularly used in all classes. Computer network features include on-campus library services, online commercial services, Internet access, wireless campus network. Campus intranet, student e-mail accounts, and computer access in designated common areas are available to students. Students grades are available online. The school has a published electronic and media policy.

Contact Sarah Wills-Viega, Director of Counseling Services. 207-563-3596 Ext. 126. E-mail: wills-viega@lincolnacademy.org. Web site: www.lincolnacademy.org.

LINCOLN SCHOOL

301 Butler Avenue
Providence, Rhode Island 02906-5556
Head of School: Julia Russell Eells

General Information Coeducational day (boys' only in lower grades) college-preparatory, arts, and technology school, affiliated with Society of Friends. Boys grades N–PK, girls grades N–12. Founded: 1884. Setting: urban. 46-acre campus. 5 buildings on campus. Approved or accredited by Association of Independent Schools in New England, Friends Council on Education, National Association of Episcopal Schools, New England Association of Schools and Colleges, and Rhode Island Department of Education. Member of National Association of Independent Schools and Secondary School Admission Test Board. Endowment: $7 million. Total enrollment: 378. Upper school average class size: 13. Upper school faculty-student ratio: 1:4. Upper School students typically attend 5 days per week. The average school day consists of 7 hours and 13 minutes.

Upper School Student Profile Grade 9: 39 students (39 girls); Grade 10: 47 students (47 girls); Grade 11: 28 students (28 girls); Grade 12: 41 students (41 girls). 1% of students are members of Society of Friends.

Faculty School total: 75. In upper school: 11 men, 35 women; 24 have advanced degrees.

Subjects Offered Algebra, American history, American literature, anatomy, Arabic, art, biology, biology-AP, calculus, calculus-AP, ceramics, chemistry, chemistry-AP, college awareness, community service, computer science, creative writing, dance, English, English literature, environmental science, ethics, European history, European history-AP, French, French-AP, geometry, health, history, Latin, music, photography, physical education, physics, pre-calculus, Spanish, Spanish language-AP, statistics-AP, theater, trigonometry, U.S. history-AP, visual literacy, women's studies, world history, world literature.

Graduation Requirements Arts and fine arts (art, music, dance, drama), college planning, computer science, English, ethics, foreign language, mathematics, physical education (includes health), science, social studies (includes history), senior service trip. Community service is required.

Special Academic Programs Advanced Placement exam preparation; honors section; independent study; term-away projects; study at local college for college credit; study abroad; programs in general development for dyslexic students.

College Admission Counseling 40 students graduated in 2009; all went to college, including Boston University; Brown University; Hobart and William Smith Colleges; Lehigh University; Trinity College; Vanderbilt University. Median SAT critical reading: 590, median SAT math: 570, median SAT writing: 609.

Student Life Upper grades have uniform requirement, student council. Discipline rests equally with students and faculty.

Tuition and Aid Day student tuition: $26,045. Tuition installment plan (monthly payment plans, individually arranged payment plans, Tuition Management Systems Plan). Need-based scholarship grants available. In 2009–10, 25% of upper-school students received aid. Total amount of financial aid awarded in 2009–10: $1,000,000.

Admissions Traditional secondary-level entrance grade is 9. For fall 2009, 77 students applied for upper-level admission, 53 were accepted, 24 enrolled. ISEE or SSAT required. Deadline for receipt of application materials: February 16. Application fee required: $50. Interview required.

Athletics Interscholastic: basketball, crew, cross-country running, field hockey, lacrosse, soccer, squash, swimming and diving, tennis. 3 PE instructors, 17 coaches, 1 athletic trainer.

Computers Computers are regularly used in English, history, science classes. Computer network features include on-campus library services, Internet access. The school has a published electronic and media policy.

Contact Mrs. Diane Mota, Admission Office Administrative Assistant. 401-331-9696 Ext. 3157. Fax: 401-751-6670. E-mail: dmota@lincolnschool.org. Web site: www.lincolnschool.org.

LINDEN CHRISTIAN SCHOOL

877 Wilkes Avenue
Winnipeg, Manitoba R3P 1B8, Canada
Head of School: Mr. Robert Charach

General Information Coeducational day college-preparatory, arts, religious studies, and technology school, affiliated with Baptist Church. Grades 9–12. Founded: 1987. Setting: suburban. 1 building on campus. Approved or accredited by Association of Christian Schools International and Manitoba Department of Education. Language of instruction: English. Total enrollment: 875. Upper school average class size: 25. Upper school faculty-student ratio: 1:13.

Upper School Student Profile Grade 9: 80 students (36 boys, 44 girls); Grade 10: 72 students (34 boys, 38 girls); Grade 11: 64 students (28 boys, 36 girls); Grade 12: 73 students (30 boys, 43 girls).

Faculty School total: 61. In upper school: 14 men, 9 women.

Subjects Offered Choir, choral music, computer applications, computer information systems, computer science, computer studies, computer technologies, concert band, drama, dramatic arts, independent study, jazz band, jazz ensemble, leadership, leadership and service, music theater, religious studies, vocal jazz, voice ensemble.

Graduation Requirements Bible studies, English, mathematics, physical education (includes health), science, social studies (includes history).

College Admission Counseling 53 students graduated in 2009; 45 went to college, including Providence College; The University of Winnipeg; University of Manitoba. Other: 8 went to work.

Student Life Upper grades have specified standards of dress, student council, honor system. Discipline rests primarily with faculty. Attendance at religious services is required.

Tuition and Aid Day student tuition: CAN$2940. Tuition installment plan (monthly payment plans). Tuition reduction for siblings, bursaries available. In 2009–10, 8% of upper-school students received aid.

Admissions Traditional secondary-level entrance grade is 9. PSAT required. Application fee required: CAN$25. Interview required.

Athletics Interscholastic: badminton (boys, girls), basketball (b,g), broomball (b,g), cooperative games (b,g), cross-country running (b,g), fitness (b,g), flag football (b,g), floor hockey (b,g), football (b,g), golf (b,g), physical fitness (b,g), volleyball (b,g); intramural: badminton (b,g), basketball (b,g), cross-country running (b,g), soccer (b,g), volleyball (b,g). 4 PE instructors.

Computers Computers are regularly used in all classes. Computer network features include on-campus library services, Internet access, wireless campus network, Internet filtering or blocking technology. Student e-mail accounts are available to students. Students grades are available online. The school has a published electronic and media policy.

Contact Mrs. Terrie Bell, Registrar. 204-989-6739. Fax: 204-487-7068. E-mail: tbell@lindenchristian.org.

LINDEN HILL SCHOOL
Northfield, Massachusetts
See Junior Boarding Schools section.

THE LINDEN SCHOOL
10 Rosehill Avenue
Toronto, Ontario M4T 1G5, Canada
Head of School: Ms. Dawn Chan

General Information Girls' day college-preparatory, arts, technology, humanities, and science school. Grades 1–12. Founded: 1993. Setting: urban. 2 buildings on campus. Approved or accredited by Ontario Department of Education. Language of instruction: English. Total enrollment: 144. Upper school average class size: 12. Upper school faculty-student ratio: 1:3. There are 180 required school days per year for Upper School students. Upper School students typically attend 5 days per week. The average school day consists of 7 hours.

Upper School Student Profile Grade 9: 13 students (13 girls); Grade 10: 18 students (18 girls); Grade 11: 17 students (17 girls); Grade 12: 9 students (9 girls).

Faculty School total: 30. In upper school: 3 men, 26 women; 10 have advanced degrees.

Subjects Offered Algebra, biology, calculus, chemistry, computer science, dramatic arts, English, English literature, French, geography, geometry, history, information technology, Latin, physics, Spanish, visual arts, writing workshop.

Graduation Requirements Canadian geography, Canadian history, career education, English, French, mathematics, science and technology, Ontario Secondary School Diploma requirements.

Special Academic Programs Advanced Placement exam preparation; honors section; independent study; academic accommodation for the gifted; ESL (6 students enrolled).

College Admission Counseling 5 students graduated in 2009; 3 went to college, including University of Toronto. Other: 1 entered a postgraduate year, 1 had other specific plans.

Student Life Upper grades have specified standards of dress, honor system. Discipline rests equally with students and faculty.

Tuition and Aid Day student tuition: CAN$14,500. Tuition installment plan (monthly payment plans, individually arranged payment plans). Bursaries, merit scholarship grants, need-based scholarship grants, paying campus jobs available. In 2009–10, 20% of upper-school students received aid; total upper-school merit-scholarship money awarded: CAN$100,000. Total amount of financial aid awarded in 2009–10: CAN$150,000.

Admissions Traditional secondary-level entrance grade is 9. School's own test required. Deadline for receipt of application materials: none. Application fee required: CAN$100. Interview required.

Athletics Interscholastic: cross-country running, dance, fitness, fitness walking, flag football, floor hockey, indoor hockey, indoor soccer, running, track and field, ultimate Frisbee, volleyball; intramural: alpine skiing, backpacking, badminton, ball hockey, baseball, basketball, boxing, canoeing/kayaking, climbing, combined training, cooperative games, cross-country running, dance, fitness, floor hockey, Frisbee, hiking/backpacking, ice skating, indoor hockey, indoor soccer, kickball, modern dance, outdoor activities, physical fitness, rock climbing, ropes courses, running, skiing (cross-country), skiing (downhill), snowboarding, soccer, track and field, ultimate Frisbee, volleyball, yoga. 2 PE instructors.

Computers Computers are regularly used in all classes. Computer network features include on-campus library services, Internet access, wireless campus network, Internet filtering or blocking technology. Computer access in designated common areas is available to students. The school has a published electronic and media policy.

Contact Ms. Ina Szekely, Co-Principal. 416-966-4406 Ext. 26. Fax: 416-966-9736. E-mail: admissions@lindenschool.ca. Web site: www.lindenschool.ca.

LINFIELD CHRISTIAN SCHOOL
31950 Pauba Road
Temecula, California 92592
Head of School: Karen Raftery

General Information Coeducational day college-preparatory, arts, religious studies, and technology school, affiliated with Christian faith. Grades K–12. Founded: 1936. Setting: suburban. Nearest major city is San Diego. 105-acre campus. 6 buildings on campus. Approved or accredited by Association of Christian Schools International, Western Association of Schools and Colleges, and California Department of Education. Total enrollment: 750. Upper school average class size: 20. Upper school faculty-student ratio: 1:14. There are 173 required school days per year for Upper School students. Upper School students typically attend 5 days per week. The average school day consists of 6 hours and 55 minutes.

Upper School Student Profile 70% of students are Christian faith.

Faculty School total: 54. In upper school: 9 men, 17 women; 8 have advanced degrees.

Subjects Offered Advanced math, algebra, American sign language, anatomy and physiology, art, ASB Leadership, athletics, band, Bible, biology, calculus-AP, career/college preparation, chemistry, chemistry-AP, choir, computers, economics, English, English-AP, European history-AP, film, filmmaking, French, freshman foundations, general science, geometry, government, government-AP, health, physical education, physics, pre-calculus, public policy, senior seminar, service learning/internship, Spanish, Spanish-AP, speech and debate, sports medicine, theater, U.S. history, U.S. history-AP, world history, world religions, yearbook.

Graduation Requirements Arts and fine arts (art, music, dance, drama), computer science, economics, English, foreign language, freshman foundations, government, mathematics, physical education (includes health), religion (includes Bible studies and theology), science, senior seminar, social sciences, social studies (includes history), speech and debate. Community service is required.

Special Academic Programs 12 Advanced Placement exams for which test preparation is offered; honors section.

College Admission Counseling 88 students graduated in 2010; all went to college, including Azusa Pacific University; California State University, San Marcos; University of California, Riverside; University of California, San Diego. Median SAT critical reading: 560, median SAT math: 540, median SAT writing: 520.

Student Life Upper grades have uniform requirement, student council, honor system. Discipline rests primarily with faculty. Attendance at religious services is required.

Summer Programs Sports, art/fine arts programs offered; held on campus; accepts boys and girls; open to students from other schools.

Tuition and Aid Day student tuition: $8580. Tuition installment plan (monthly payment plans). Merit scholarship grants, need-based scholarship grants available. In 2010–11, 30% of upper-school students received aid.

Admissions 3-R Achievement Test, SLEP and USC/UC Math Diagnostic Test required. Deadline for receipt of application materials: none. Application fee required: $50. On-campus interview required.

Athletics Interscholastic: baseball (boys), basketball (b,g), cheering (g), cross-country running (b,g), equestrian sports (g), football (b), soccer (b,g), softball (g), tennis (b,g), track and field (b,g), volleyball (g); intramural: volleyball (g); coed interscholastic: golf; coed intramural: cross-country running. 3 PE instructors, 16 coaches, 1 athletic trainer.

Computers Computers are regularly used in computer applications, keyboarding, science, senior seminar, yearbook classes. Computer network features include on-campus library services, Internet access, wireless campus network, Internet filtering or blocking technology. Computer access in designated common areas is available to students. Students grades are available online. The school has a published electronic and media policy.

Contact Mrs. Becky Swanson, Admissions Assistant. 951-676-8111 Ext. 1402. Fax: 951-695-1291. E-mail: bswanson@linfield.com. Web site: www.linfield.com.

THE LINSLY SCHOOL

60 Knox Lane
Wheeling, West Virginia 26003-6489
Head of School: Mr. Chad Barnett

General Information Coeducational boarding and day college-preparatory, arts, technology, and science, mathematics, humanities, foreign language school. Boarding grades 7–12, day grades 5–12. Founded: 1814. Setting: suburban. Nearest major city is Pittsburgh, PA. Students are housed in single-sex dormitories. 60-acre campus. 19 buildings on campus. Approved or accredited by Independent Schools Association of the Central States, North Central Association of Colleges and Schools, The Association of Boarding Schools, and West Virginia Department of Education. Member of National Association of Independent Schools. Endowment: $16 million. Total enrollment: 444. Upper school average class size: 15. Upper school faculty-student ratio: 1:9.

Upper School Student Profile Grade 9: 65 students (38 boys, 27 girls); Grade 10: 70 students (40 boys, 30 girls); Grade 11: 85 students (46 boys, 39 girls); Grade 12: 64 students (32 boys, 32 girls). 40% of students are boarding students. 50% are state residents. 20 states are represented in upper school student body. 9% are international students. International students from Bahamas, China, Mexico, Republic of Korea, South Africa, and Thailand; 15 other countries represented in student body.

Faculty School total: 48. In upper school: 23 men, 12 women; 18 have advanced degrees; 23 reside on campus.

Subjects Offered Algebra, American history, American literature, art, art history, biology, biology-AP, calculus-AP, character education, chemistry, chemistry-AP, Chinese, chorus, college counseling, communications, computer programming, computer science, concert band, contemporary issues, creative writing, drama, earth science, economics, English, English language-AP, English literature, English literature-AP, environmental science, expository writing, film, fine arts, French, geometry, German, government/civics, health, history, human geography—AP, humanities, Latin, mathematics, model United Nations, music, newspaper, physical education, physics, physics-AP, psychology, psychology-AP, science, social studies, Spanish, speech, statistics, technology/design, theater, U.S. history-AP, world history, writing, yearbook, zoology.

Graduation Requirements Arts and fine arts (art, music, dance, drama), computer science, English, foreign language, mathematics, physical education (includes health), science, social studies (includes history).

Special Academic Programs 12 Advanced Placement exams for which test preparation is offered; academic accommodation for the gifted.

College Admission Counseling 60 students graduated in 2010; all went to college, including Columbia University; Cornell University; Northwestern University; United States Air Force Academy; University of Pennsylvania; West Virginia University. Mean SAT critical reading: 580, mean SAT math: 580, mean SAT writing: 570, mean combined SAT: 1730, mean composite ACT: 26.

Student Life Upper grades have uniform requirement, student council, honor system. Discipline rests primarily with faculty.

Summer Programs Enrichment, advancement, computer instruction programs offered; held on campus; accepts boys and girls; open to students from other schools. 100 students usually enrolled. 2011 schedule: June 12 to July 12. Application deadline: June 12.

Tuition and Aid Day student tuition: $13,600; 5-day tuition and room/board: $27,750; 7-day tuition and room/board: $27,750. Tuition installment plan (Academic Management Services Plan). Need-based scholarship grants available. In 2010–11, 40% of upper-school students received aid. Total amount of financial aid awarded in 2010–11: $900,000.

Admissions Traditional secondary-level entrance grade is 9. Otis-Lennon, Stanford Achievement Test or SSAT required. Deadline for receipt of application materials: January 31. No application fee required. Interview required.

Athletics Interscholastic: baseball (boys), basketball (b,g), cheering (g), cross-country running (b,g), diving (b,g), football (b), golf (b,g), ice hockey (b,g), lacrosse (b), soccer (b,g), softball (g), wrestling (b); intramural: flag football (b,g), floor hockey (b), football (b), hiking/backpacking (b,g), indoor soccer (b,g), indoor track (b,g), indoor track & field (b,g), life saving (b,g), mountain biking (b,g), outdoor activities (b,g), physical fitness (b,g), power lifting (b), rappelling (b,g), rock climbing (b,g), roller blading (b,g), ropes courses (b,g), running (b,g), street hockey (b); coed intramural: backpacking, badminton, bowling, canoeing/kayaking, climbing, combined training, cooperative games, cross-country running, fitness, Frisbee, ice skating, in-line skating, jogging, kayaking, kickball, life saving, mountain biking, Nautilus, physical fitness, physical training, rafting, rock climbing, ropes courses, running, scuba diving, soccer, softball. 4 PE instructors, 4 coaches, 1 athletic trainer.

Computers Computers are regularly used in economics, English, foreign language, humanities, mathematics, music, psychology, science classes. Computer network features include on-campus library services, Internet access, wireless campus network, Internet filtering or blocking technology. Student e-mail accounts are available to students.

Never, Never, Never Quit.

Learn more about Linsly...
Join Us for a Campus Visit Day!
Register online at
www.linsly.org/admissions

From a family's first Campus Visit to Graduation Day, these words echo throughout the Linsly Experience. To persevere through adversity. To show grace in victory and defeat. To respect the opposition. These values serve students well while they are at Linsly and through their college and professional lives.

phone **304-233-1436**
www.**linsly**.org

The Linsly School
BRINGING YOUNG MINDS TO LIFE.

©2009, The Linsly School, 60 Knox Lane, Wheeling, WV 26003. *The Linsly School is an equal opportunity school.*

Contact Mr. Craig Tredenick, Director of Admissions. 304-233-1436. Fax: 304-234-4614. E-mail: admit@linsly.org. Web site: www.linsly.org.

See Display on page 380.

LITTLE KESWICK SCHOOL

Keswick, Virginia
See Special Needs Schools section.

LODI ACADEMY

1230 South Central Avenue
Lodi, California 95242
Head of School: Mr. Doug Brown

General Information Coeducational day college-preparatory, general academic, arts, and religious studies school, affiliated with Seventh-day Adventist Church. Boys grade 9, girls grade 12. Founded: 1908. Setting: small town. Nearest major city is Sacramento. 30-acre campus. 9 buildings on campus. Approved or accredited by Western Association of Schools and Colleges and California Department of Education. Endowment: $1.1 million. Total enrollment: 101. Upper school average class size: 13. Upper school faculty-student ratio: 1:11. Upper School students typically attend 5 days per week. The average school day consists of 6 hours and 50 minutes.

Upper School Student Profile Grade 9: 24 students (12 boys, 12 girls); Grade 10: 30 students (15 boys, 15 girls); Grade 11: 26 students (9 boys, 17 girls); Grade 12: 21 students (15 boys, 6 girls). 82% of students are Seventh-day Adventists.

Faculty School total: 9. In upper school: 5 men, 4 women; 4 have advanced degrees.

Subjects Offered Accounting, algebra, American history, American literature, art, auto mechanics, band, Bible, biology, chemistry, choir, chorus, community service, computer applications, economics, English, English literature, general math, geography, geometry, government, health, life skills, music appreciation, physical education, physical science, physics, piano, pre-algebra, pre-calculus, Spanish, student publications, U.S. history, U.S. history-AP, work experience, world history, yearbook.

Graduation Requirements Algebra, American history, American literature, applied arts, arts and fine arts (art, music, dance, drama), Bible, biology, chemistry, computer applications, economics, English, English literature, geography, geometry, keyboarding, life skills, physical education (includes health), physical science, Spanish, U.S. government, U.S. history, work experience, world history, 100 hours of community service, 100 hours of paid work experience. Community service is required.

College Admission Counseling 21 students graduated in 2010; 20 went to college, including Grand Canyon University; Pacific Union College; Walla Walla University. Other: 1 had other specific plans.

Student Life Upper grades have specified standards of dress, student council. Discipline rests equally with students and faculty. Attendance at religious services is required.

Tuition and Aid Day student tuition: $750. Tuition installment plan (monthly payment plans, individually arranged payment plans). Tuition reduction for siblings, merit scholarship grants, need-based scholarship grants, paying campus jobs available. In 2010–11, 30% of upper-school students received aid; total upper-school merit-scholarship money awarded: $8000. Total amount of financial aid awarded in 2010–11: $25,000.

Admissions Achievement tests or Iowa Tests of Basic Skills required. Deadline for receipt of application materials: none. Application fee required: $300. Interview required.

Athletics Interscholastic: basketball (boys, girls), flag football (b,g), soccer (g), volleyball (g); intramural: basketball (b,g), flag football (b,g), volleyball (g); coed interscholastic: golf. 1 PE instructor.

Computers Computers are regularly used in accounting, Bible studies, computer applications, English, mathematics classes. Computer network features include Internet access, Internet filtering or blocking technology. Student e-mail accounts and computer access in designated common areas are available to students. Students grades are available online. The school has a published electronic and media policy.

Contact Mrs. Dorene Hackett, Registrar. 209-369-2781 Ext. 102. Fax: 209-747-6689. E-mail: dorene@lodiacademy.net. Web site: www.lodiacademy.net.

LONG ISLAND LUTHERAN MIDDLE AND HIGH SCHOOL

131 Brookville Road
Brookville, New York 11545-3399
Head of School: Dr. David Hahn

General Information Coeducational day and distance learning college-preparatory, arts, business, and religious studies school, affiliated with Lutheran Church. Grades 6–12. Distance learning grades 11–12. Founded: 1960. Setting: suburban. Nearest major city is New York. 32-acre campus. 6 buildings on campus. Approved or accredited by Evangelical Lutheran Church in America, Middle States Association of Colleges and Schools, New York State Association of Independent Schools, US Department of State, and New York Department of Education. Endowment: $6 million. Total enrollment: 600. Upper school average class size: 18. Upper school

faculty-student ratio: 1:9. There are 161 required school days per year for Upper School students. Upper School students typically attend 5 days per week. The average school day consists of 6 hours and 30 minutes.

Upper School Student Profile Grade 9: 102 students (54 boys, 48 girls); Grade 10: 109 students (67 boys, 42 girls); Grade 11: 106 students (58 boys, 48 girls); Grade 12: 103 students (54 boys, 49 girls). 34% of students are Lutheran.

Faculty School total: 56. In upper school: 18 men, 27 women; 45 have advanced degrees.

Subjects Offered Accounting, algebra, American history, American literature, anatomy, art, band, biology, biology-AP, business, business communications, business skills, calculus, calculus-AP, ceramics, choir, communication skills, computer programming, computer science, computer science-AP, creative writing, dance, driver education, earth science, economics-AP, English, English language-AP, English literature, English literature-AP, environmental science, ethics, European history, European history-AP, fine arts, French, French language-AP, geography, geometry, government/civics, grammar, graphic arts, health, history, marketing, mathematics, music, physical education, physics, physics-AP, physiology, psychology, religion, social studies, Spanish, Spanish language-AP, trigonometry, U.S. government and politics-AP, U.S. history-AP, video film production, word processing, world history, writing.

Graduation Requirements Arts and fine arts (art, music, dance, drama), business skills (includes word processing), computer science, English, foreign language, mathematics, physical education (includes health), religion (includes Bible studies and theology), science, social studies (includes history).

Special Academic Programs 14 Advanced Placement exams for which test preparation is offered; honors section; term-away projects; study at local college for college credit.

College Admission Counseling 101 students graduated in 2010; all went to college, including Fordham University; Georgetown University; Hofstra University; New York University; Quinnipiac University; Stony Brook University, State University of New York. Mean SAT critical reading: 581, mean SAT math: 567, mean SAT writing: 572, mean combined SAT: 1720, mean composite ACT: 24. 25% scored over 26 on composite ACT.

Student Life Upper grades have uniform requirement, student council, honor system. Discipline rests primarily with faculty. Attendance at religious services is required.

Summer Programs Sports, art/fine arts, computer instruction programs offered; session focuses on sports, recreation, and education; held both on and off campus; held at local satellite facilities; accepts boys and girls; open to students from other schools. 6,000 students usually enrolled. 2011 schedule: June 27 to August 19. Application deadline: January.

Tuition and Aid Day student tuition: $9625–$11,550. Tuition installment plan (monthly payment plans, school's own payment plan). Tuition reduction for siblings, merit scholarship grants, need-based scholarship grants available. In 2010–11, 28% of upper-school students received aid; total upper-school merit-scholarship money awarded: $10,000. Total amount of financial aid awarded in 2010–11: $250,000.

Admissions Traditional secondary-level entrance grade is 9. For fall 2010, 144 students applied for upper-level admission, 82 were accepted, 55 enrolled. Cognitive Abilities Test, Math Placement Exam and writing sample required. Deadline for receipt of application materials: none. Application fee required: $100. On-campus interview required.

Athletics Interscholastic: baseball (boys, girls), basketball (b), cheering (g), dance team (g), football (b), lacrosse (b,g), roller hockey (b), soccer (b,g), softball (g), tennis (b,g), volleyball (g), wrestling (b); intramural: dance team (g), flag football (b), horseback riding (b,g); coed interscholastic: cross-country running, golf, running, track and field, winter (indoor) track; coed intramural: bowling, equestrian sports, physical training, skiing (downhill). 3 PE instructors, 30 coaches.

Computers Computers are regularly used in accounting, art, business, business skills, college planning, design, English, graphic design, history, library skills, mathematics, science classes. Computer network features include on-campus library services, Internet access, wireless campus network, Internet filtering or blocking technology. Student e-mail accounts and computer access in designated common areas are available to students. Students grades are available online. The school has a published electronic and media policy.

Contact Barbara Ward, Director of Admissions. 516-626-1700 Ext. 546. Fax: 516-622-7459. E-mail: barbara.ward@luhi.org. Web site: www.luhi.org.

THE LOOMIS CHAFFEE SCHOOL

4 Batchelder Road
Windsor, Connecticut 06095
Head of School: Dr. Sheila Culbert

General Information Coeducational boarding and day college-preparatory and arts school. Grades 9–PG. Founded: 1914. Setting: rural. Nearest major city is Hartford. Students are housed in single-sex dormitories. 300-acre campus. 65 buildings on campus. Approved or accredited by Connecticut Association of Independent Schools, New England Association of Schools and Colleges, The Association of Boarding Schools, and Connecticut Department of Education. Member of National Association of Independent Schools and Secondary School Admission Test Board. Endowment: $172 million. Total enrollment: 690. Upper school average class size: 12. Upper school faculty-student ratio: 1:5. There are 167 required school days per year for Upper School students. Upper School students typically attend 6 days per week. The average school day consists of 8 hours.

Upper School Student Profile Grade 9: 118 students (66 boys, 52 girls); Grade 10: 194 students (98 boys, 96 girls); Grade 11: 174 students (98 boys, 76 girls); Grade 12: 181 students (87 boys, 94 girls); Postgraduate: 23 students (22 boys, 1 girl). 57% of students are boarding students. 54% are state residents. 26 states are represented in upper school student body. 8% are international students. International students from Canada, China, Republic of Korea, Thailand, United Kingdom, and Viet Nam; 14 other countries represented in student body.

Faculty School total: 149. In upper school: 68 men, 81 women; 106 have advanced degrees; 70 reside on campus.

Subjects Offered Algebra, American history, American literature, anatomy, art, art history, astronomy, biology, calculus, ceramics, chemistry, creative writing, dance, drama, ecology, economics, English, English literature, environmental science, ethics, European history, expository writing, fine arts, French, geology, geometry, history, history of ideas, history of science, Latin, library studies, logic, Mandarin, mathematics, music, philosophy, photography, physical education, physics, physiology, religion, science, Spanish, statistics, theater, video film production, world history, world literature, writing.

Graduation Requirements Arts and fine arts (art, music, dance, drama), English, foreign language, history, mathematics, philosophy, physical education (includes health), science.

Special Academic Programs Advanced Placement exam preparation; honors section; independent study; term-away projects; study at local college for college credit; study abroad; academic accommodation for the gifted, the musically talented, and the artistically talented.

College Admission Counseling 209 students graduated in 2009; all went to college, including Bates College; Middlebury College; New York University; Skidmore College; The George Washington University; University of Connecticut. 71% scored over 600 on SAT critical reading, 75% scored over 600 on SAT math, 78% scored over 600 on SAT writing, 75% scored over 1800 on combined SAT.

Student Life Upper grades have specified standards of dress, student council. Discipline rests primarily with faculty.

Tuition and Aid Day student tuition: $32,600; 7-day tuition and room/board: $43,000. Tuition installment plan (Insured Tuition Payment Plan, Key Tuition Payment Plan, monthly payment plans). Need-based scholarship grants, need-based loans available. In 2009–10, 33% of upper-school students received aid. Total amount of financial aid awarded in 2009–10: $6,400,000.

Admissions Traditional secondary-level entrance grade is 9. For fall 2009, 1,412 students applied for upper-level admission, 482 were accepted, 209 enrolled. ISEE, PSAT, SAT, SSAT or TOEFL required. Deadline for receipt of application materials: January 15. Application fee required: $75. Interview required.

Athletics Interscholastic: baseball (boys), basketball (b,g), cross-country running (b,g), field hockey (g), football (b), golf (b,g), ice hockey (b,g), lacrosse (b,g), soccer (b,g), softball (g), squash (b,g), swimming and diving (b,g), tennis (b,g), track and field (b,g), volleyball (g), water polo (b,g), wrestling (b); intramural: ice hockey (b,g), soccer (b,g), volleyball (b,g), yoga (b,g); coed interscholastic: alpine skiing, diving, skiing (downhill); coed intramural: aerobics, aerobics/dance, aerobics/Nautilus, backpacking, ballet, basketball, bicycling, canoeing/kayaking, climbing, dance, fencing, fitness, Frisbee, hiking/backpacking, jogging, kayaking, life saving, modern dance, mountain biking, Nautilus, outdoor activities, outdoor adventure, physical fitness, physical training, ropes courses, running, scuba diving, soccer, softball, squash, strength & conditioning, swimming and diving, ultimate Frisbee, weight training. 5 PE instructors, 2 athletic trainers.

Computers Computers are regularly used in all academic classes. Computer network features include on-campus library services, online commercial services, Internet access, wireless campus network. Campus intranet, student e-mail accounts, and computer access in designated common areas are available to students. Students grades are available online. The school has a published electronic and media policy.

Contact Mr. Erby Mitchell, Assistant Head of School for Enrollment. 860-687-6400. Fax: 860-298-8756. E-mail: erby_mitchell@loomis.org. Web site: www.loomis.org.

LORETTO ACADEMY

1300 Hardaway Street
El Paso, Texas 79903
Head of School: Sr. Mary E. (Buffy) Boesen, SL

General Information Coeducational day (boys' only in lower grades) college-preparatory, arts, religious studies, and technology school, affiliated with Roman Catholic Church. Boys grades PK–5, girls grades PK–12. Founded: 1923. Setting: urban. 17-acre campus. 3 buildings on campus. Approved or accredited by Southern Association of Colleges and Schools and Texas Catholic Conference. Endowment: $3.3 million. Total enrollment: 659. Upper school average class size: 20. Upper school faculty-student ratio: 1:13. There are 180 required school days per year for Upper School students. Upper School students typically attend 5 days per week. The average school day consists of 7 hours.

Upper School Student Profile 81% of students are Roman Catholic.

Faculty School total: 53. In upper school: 4 men, 21 women; 16 have advanced degrees.

Subjects Offered Acting, advanced math, Advanced Placement courses, algebra, American government, American history, art, art appreciation, art-AP, arts, arts and crafts, Bible, biology, body human, business mathematics, calculus, calculus-AP, chemistry, choir, choral music, Christian and Hebrew scripture, college writing, computer applications, computer programming, computer science, English, environmental science, fine arts, French, geology, geometry, government, government-AP, health, honors algebra, honors English, honors geometry, integrated science, Internet, jewelry making, journalism, keyboarding, life issues, literature, literature-AP, mathematics, modern dance, moral theology, music appreciation, photo shop, physical education, physics, physics-AP, religion, science, social studies, Spanish, Spanish language-AP, Spanish-AP, speech, speech and debate, student government, study skills, technical writing, theater production, world geography, world history, world religions, yearbook, zoology.

Graduation Requirements Algebra, American government, arts and fine arts (art, music, dance, drama), biology, Christian and Hebrew scripture, Christian ethics, Christian studies, computer science, economics, English, English composition, English literature, environmental science, foreign language, geography, lab/keyboard, life issues, mathematics, moral reasoning, physical education (includes health), physical science, psychology, religion (includes Bible studies and theology), science, social studies (includes history), speech communications, world geography, world religions, Service Learning .5.

Special Academic Programs Advanced Placement exam preparation.

College Admission Counseling 93 students graduated in 2010; all went to college, including New Mexico State University; St. Edward's University; St. Mary's University; The University of Texas at El Paso; The University of Texas at San Antonio. Mean SAT critical reading: 491, mean SAT math: 466, mean SAT writing: 509. 11% scored over 600 on SAT critical reading, 13% scored over 600 on SAT math, 28% scored over 600 on SAT writing, 16% scored over 1800 on combined SAT, 12% scored over 26 on composite ACT.

Student Life Upper grades have uniform requirement, student council, honor system. Discipline rests primarily with faculty.

Summer Programs Remediation programs offered; session focuses on remediation; held on campus; accepts girls; not open to students from other schools. 25 students usually enrolled. 2011 schedule: June 1 to July 2.

Tuition and Aid Day student tuition: $6350. Tuition installment plan (FACTS Tuition Payment Plan). Tuition reduction for siblings, need-based scholarship grants, paying campus jobs, need-based financial aid available. In 2010–11, 26% of upper-school students received aid. Total amount of financial aid awarded in 2010–11: $203,000.

Admissions Traditional secondary-level entrance grade is 9. For fall 2010, 104 students applied for upper-level admission, 97 were accepted, 81 enrolled. High School Placement Test required. Deadline for receipt of application materials: none. Application fee required: $30. On-campus interview required.

Athletics Interscholastic: aquatics (girls), basketball (g), cheering (g), cross-country running (g), dance squad (g), dance team (g), golf (g), soccer (g), softball (g), swimming and diving (g), tennis (g), track and field (g), volleyball (g). 2 PE instructors, 10 coaches.

Computers Computers are regularly used in all academic classes. Computer network features include Internet access, Internet filtering or blocking technology. The school has a published electronic and media policy.

Contact Mrs. Lily Miranda, Director of Admissions. 915-566-8400. Fax: 915-566-0636. E-mail: lmiranda@loretto.org. Web site: www.loretto.org.

LOS ANGELES BAPTIST MIDDLE SCHOOL/HIGH SCHOOL

9825 Woodley Avenue
North Hills, California 91343
Head of School: Mr. Scott Marshall

General Information Coeducational day college-preparatory, arts, religious studies, and technology school, affiliated with Baptist Church. Grades 6–12. Founded: 1962. Setting: suburban. Nearest major city is Los Angeles. 11-acre campus. 5 buildings on campus. Approved or accredited by Association of Christian Schools International and Western Association of Schools and Colleges. Total enrollment: 829. Upper school average class size: 30. Upper school faculty-student ratio: 1:22. There are 180 required school days per year for Upper School students. Upper School students typically attend 5 days per week. The average school day consists of 6 hours and 45 minutes.

Upper School Student Profile Grade 9: 122 students (64 boys, 58 girls); Grade 10: 144 students (63 boys, 81 girls); Grade 11: 117 students (60 boys, 57 girls); Grade 12: 158 students (80 boys, 78 girls).

Faculty School total: 40. In upper school: 20 men, 20 women; 24 have advanced degrees.

Subjects Offered 3-dimensional design, advanced computer applications, algebra, American history, American literature, American literature-AP, analysis and differential calculus, anatomy and physiology, art, art appreciation, ASB Leadership, band, Bible studies, biology, biology-AP, calculus-AP, ceramics, chemistry, chemistry-AP, choir, choral music, Christian doctrine, Christian education, Christian ethics, Civil War, computer applications, computer education, computer graphics, computer programming, computer science, computer skills, computer technologies, digital photography, drama, drama performance, earth science, economics, English, English literature, English-AP, European history-AP, expository writing, fine arts, French,

French-AP, geography, geometry, government/civics, home economics, HTML design, intro to computers, jazz band, journalism, keyboarding, mathematics, music, photography, physical education, physics, physics-AP, practical arts, pre-calculus, psychology, psychology-AP, religion, science, social studies, Spanish, Spanish-AP, speech, statistics, statistics-AP, studio art, theater arts, trigonometry, typing, U.S. history-AP, world history, world history-AP.

Graduation Requirements Arts and fine arts (art, music, dance, drama), English, foreign language, mathematics, physical education (includes health), practical arts, religion (includes Bible studies and theology), science, social studies (includes history).

Special Academic Programs Advanced Placement exam preparation; honors section.

College Admission Counseling 152 students graduated in 2010; 149 went to college, including Azusa Pacific University; California State University, Northridge; University of California, Irvine; University of California, Los Angeles; University of California, Riverside. Other: 2 entered military service, 1 had other specific plans. Median SAT critical reading: 531, median SAT math: 542, median SAT writing: 500, median combined SAT: 1590, median composite ACT: 22. 25.8% scored over 600 on SAT critical reading, 31.2% scored over 600 on SAT math, 23.7% scored over 600 on SAT writing, 21.5% scored over 1800 on combined SAT, 8.6% scored over 26 on composite ACT.

Student Life Upper grades have uniform requirement, student council, honor system. Discipline rests primarily with faculty. Attendance at religious services is required.

Summer Programs Remediation, advancement, sports, computer instruction programs offered; session focuses on remediation and enrichment; held both on and off campus; held at Internet based learning can be done from any computer.; accepts boys and girls; open to students from other schools. 350 students usually enrolled. 2011 schedule: June 1 to July 30.

Tuition and Aid Day student tuition: $7850. Tuition installment plan (FACTS Tuition Payment Plan, 2-semester payment plan, annual payment plan). Merit scholarship grants, need-based scholarship grants available. In 2010–11, 36% of upper-school students received aid; total upper-school merit-scholarship money awarded: $2000. Total amount of financial aid awarded in 2010–11: $977,525.

Admissions Traditional secondary-level entrance grade is 9. For fall 2010, 197 students applied for upper-level admission, 186 were accepted, 181 enrolled. QUIC required. Deadline for receipt of application materials: August 1. Application fee required: $100. On-campus interview required.

Athletics Interscholastic: baseball (boys), basketball (b,g), cheering (g), cross-country running (b,g), football (b), golf (b), soccer (b,g), softball (g), tennis (g), track and field (b,g), volleyball (b,g). 3 PE instructors, 44 coaches.

Computers Computers are regularly used in animation, business applications, career technology, French, graphic design, graphics, introduction to technology, keyboarding, lab/keyboard, library, programming, Spanish, technology, typing, Web site design, word processing classes. Computer network features include on-campus library services, Internet access, Internet filtering or blocking technology. The school has a published electronic and media policy.

Contact Mrs. Karnel Watkins, Admissions/Recruitment Coordinator. 818-894-5742 Ext. 322. Fax: 818-892-5018. E-mail: kwatkins@labaptist.org. Web site: www.labaptist.org/.

LOS ANGELES LUTHERAN HIGH SCHOOL

13570 Eldridge Avenue
Sylmar, California 91342
Head of School: Mr. Edward R. Amey

General Information Coeducational day and distance learning college-preparatory, arts, and religious studies school, affiliated with Lutheran Church–Missouri Synod, Lutheran Church. Grades 6–12. Distance learning grades 11–12. Founded: 1953. Setting: urban. Nearest major city is Los Angeles. 4-acre campus. 1 building on campus. Approved or accredited by National Lutheran School Accreditation, Western Association of Schools and Colleges, and California Department of Education. Endowment: $450,000. Total enrollment: 190. Upper school average class size: 22. Upper school faculty-student ratio: 1:12. There are 180 required school days per year for Upper School students. Upper School students typically attend 5 days per week. The average school day consists of 6 hours and 30 minutes.

Upper School Student Profile Grade 6: 4 students (2 boys, 2 girls); Grade 7: 24 students (8 boys, 16 girls); Grade 8: 34 students (20 boys, 14 girls); Grade 9: 24 students (9 boys, 15 girls); Grade 10: 29 students (18 boys, 11 girls); Grade 11: 33 students (18 boys, 15 girls); Grade 12: 41 students (17 boys, 24 girls). 30% of students are Lutheran Church–Missouri Synod, Lutheran.

Faculty School total: 17. In upper school: 9 men, 8 women; 5 have advanced degrees.

Subjects Offered 3-dimensional art, Advanced Placement courses, algebra, American literature, anatomy and physiology, ancient history, band, bell choir, Bible, Bible studies, biology, biology-AP, British literature (honors), business applications, business law, business mathematics, calculus, career/college preparation, chemistry, choir, choral music, Christian doctrine, Christian scripture, classical music, composition, concert band, drawing, economics, English literature, English-AP, ESL, ethics, family studies, film appreciation, geography, geometry, German, government, jazz, jazz band, journalism, Life of Christ, math analysis, music theory, painting, physics, psychology, Spanish, U.S. history, world history, yearbook.

Graduation Requirements Advanced math, algebra, American government, American history, American literature, analytic geometry, ancient world history, biology, British literature, career education, chemistry, Christian doctrine, Christian testament, comparative religion, composition, economics, English composition, English literature, geometry, government, keyboarding, physical education (includes health), religious education, Spanish, U.S. government, U.S. history, world history.

Special Academic Programs 4 Advanced Placement exams for which test preparation is offered; honors section; study at local college for college credit; academic accommodation for the gifted, the musically talented, and the artistically talented; ESL (15 students enrolled).

College Admission Counseling 23 students graduated in 2009; 20 went to college, including California State University, Northridge; Concordia University; Loyola Marymount University; University of California, Davis; University of California, Irvine; University of Southern California. Other: 3 went to work.

Student Life Upper grades have uniform requirement, student council. Discipline rests primarily with faculty. Attendance at religious services is required.

Tuition and Aid Day student tuition: $6825. Tuition installment plan (SMART Tuition Payment Plan, monthly payment plans). Merit scholarship grants, need-based scholarship grants available. In 2009–10, 20% of upper-school students received aid; total upper-school merit-scholarship money awarded: $10,000. Total amount of financial aid awarded in 2009–10: $25,000.

Admissions Traditional secondary-level entrance grade is 9. For fall 2009, 40 students applied for upper-level admission, 30 were accepted, 29 enrolled. Achievement/Aptitude/Writing or placement test required. Deadline for receipt of application materials: none. Application fee required: $300. Interview required.

Athletics Interscholastic: baseball (boys), basketball (b,g), cheering (g), drill team (g), flag football (b), football (b), volleyball (b,g); intramural: aerobics (b,g), fitness (b,g), jogging (b,g), lacrosse (b), physical fitness (b,g), physical training (b,g), ropes courses (b,g), strength & conditioning (b), tennis (b,g), track and field (b,g), ultimate Frisbee (b,g), walking (b,g), weight training (b,g); coed interscholastic: flag football, soccer; coed intramural: golf. 2 PE instructors, 8 coaches.

Computers Computers are regularly used in business, business applications, college planning, computer applications, desktop publishing, digital applications, journalism, keyboarding, lab/keyboard, media production, science, yearbook classes. Computer network features include on-campus library services, online commercial services, Internet access, Internet filtering or blocking technology. Students grades are available online. The school has a published electronic and media policy.

Contact Ms. Barbara Winslow, Admissions Counselor. 818-362-5861. Fax: 818-367-0043. E-mail: barbara.winslow@lalhs.org. Web site: www.lalutheran.org.

LOUISVILLE COLLEGIATE SCHOOL

2427 Glenmary Avenue
Louisville, Kentucky 40204
Head of School: Junius Scott Prince

General Information Coeducational day college-preparatory, arts, and technology school. Grades JK–12. Founded: 1915. Setting: urban. 24-acre campus. 2 buildings on campus. Approved or accredited by Independent Schools Association of the Central States. Member of National Association of Independent Schools and Secondary School Admission Test Board. Endowment: $5.4 million. Total enrollment: 650. Upper school average class size: 13. Upper school faculty-student ratio: 1:8.

Faculty School total: 80. In upper school: 12 men, 10 women; 20 have advanced degrees.

Subjects Offered Algebra, American history, American literature, ancient history, art, art history, biology, calculus, chemistry, Chinese, chorus, community service, composition, computer science, creative writing, discrete mathematics, drama, economics, English, English literature, ensembles, environmental science, European history, fine arts, French, geometry, German, history, mathematics, media, music, music history, physical education, physics, physiology, pre-calculus, science, social studies, Spanish, statistics, studio art, theater, trigonometry, world history, world literature, writing.

Graduation Requirements Arts and fine arts (art, music, dance, drama), English, foreign language, mathematics, physical education (includes health), science, social studies (includes history), senior symposium in leadership and service, individual and class service projects, senior speech.

Special Academic Programs Advanced Placement exam preparation; honors section; independent study; term-away projects; study abroad.

College Admission Counseling 53 students graduated in 2010; all went to college, including Centre College; Miami University; Northwestern University; University of Colorado at Boulder; Vanderbilt University. Median SAT critical reading: 623, median SAT math: 619, median SAT writing: 627, median combined SAT: 1869, median composite ACT: 27.

Student Life Upper grades have uniform requirement, student council, honor system. Discipline rests equally with students and faculty.

Summer Programs Enrichment, advancement, sports, art/fine arts, computer instruction programs offered; session focuses on educational enrichment and sports; held both on and off campus; held at Champion's Trace Athletic Fields; accepts boys and girls; open to students from other schools. 350 students usually enrolled. 2011 schedule: June 1 to July 31. Application deadline: none.

Louisville Collegiate School

Tuition and Aid Day student tuition: $18,750. Tuition installment plan (The Tuition Plan, monthly payment plans, individually arranged payment plans). Merit scholarship grants, need-based scholarship grants available. In 2010–11, 28% of upper-school students received aid.

Admissions Traditional secondary-level entrance grade is 9. School's own exam and SSAT required. Deadline for receipt of application materials: none. Application fee required: $50. Interview required.

Athletics Interscholastic: basketball (boys, girls), crew (g), cross-country running (b,g), field hockey (g), golf (b,g), indoor track (b,g), lacrosse (b,g), rowing (b,g), soccer (b,g), softball (g), strength & conditioning (b,g), swimming and diving (b,g), tennis (b,g), track and field (b,g), winter (indoor) track (b,g); intramural: basketball (b,g), soccer (b,g), tennis (b,g); coed interscholastic: soccer, strength & conditioning; coed intramural: soccer. 4 PE instructors, 60 coaches, 1 athletic trainer.

Computers Computers are regularly used in art, English, foreign language, history, mathematics, science classes. Computer network features include on-campus library services, online commercial services, Internet access, wireless campus network, Internet filtering or blocking technology. Student e-mail accounts and computer access in designated common areas are available to students. Students grades are available online. The school has a published electronic and media policy.

Contact Lynne Age, Admission Office Administrative Assistant. 502-479-0378. Fax: 502-454-0549. E-mail: lynne_age@loucol.com. Web site: www.loucol.com.

LOUISVILLE HIGH SCHOOL

22300 Mulholland Drive
Woodland Hills, California 91364
Head of School: Mrs. Kathleen Vercillo

General Information Girls' day college-preparatory, arts, religious studies, and technology school, affiliated with Roman Catholic Church. Grades 9–12. Founded: 1960. Setting: suburban. Nearest major city is Encino. 17-acre campus. 7 buildings on campus. Approved or accredited by National Catholic Education Association, Western Association of Schools and Colleges, Western Catholic Education Association, and California Department of Education. Total enrollment: 439. Upper school average class size: 25. Upper school faculty-student ratio: 1:25. There are 180 required school days per year for Upper School students. Upper School students typically attend 5 days per week. The average school day consists of 6 hours.

Upper School Student Profile Grade 9: 137 students (137 girls); Grade 10: 117 students (117 girls); Grade 11: 84 students (84 girls); Grade 12: 101 students (101 girls). 78% of students are Roman Catholic.

Faculty School total: 45. In upper school: 7 men, 29 women; 28 have advanced degrees.

Subjects Offered Advanced Placement courses, advanced studio art-AP, algebra, American history, American literature, anatomy, art, Bible studies, biology, calculus, calculus-AP, campus ministry, ceramics, chemistry, computer science, creative writing, dance, drama, earth science, economics, English, English literature, European history, fine arts, French, geography, geometry, government/civics, grammar, history, journalism, law, mathematics, music, photography, physical education, physics, physiology, psychology, religion, science, social sciences, social studies, Spanish, speech, statistics, theater, trigonometry, video film production, Web site design, world history, world literature.

Graduation Requirements Arts and fine arts (art, music, dance, drama), computer science, English, foreign language, mathematics, performing arts, physical education (includes health), religion (includes Bible studies and theology), science, social sciences, social studies (includes history), visual arts. Community service is required.

Special Academic Programs Advanced Placement exam preparation.

College Admission Counseling 130 students graduated in 2010; all went to college, including California State University, Northridge; Chapman University; Loyola Marymount University; University of California, Los Angeles; University of Portland; University of Southern California.

Student Life Upper grades have uniform requirement, student council, honor system. Discipline rests equally with students and faculty. Attendance at religious services is required.

Summer Programs Sports programs offered; session focuses on skill development; held both on and off campus; held at Los Angeles Pierce Community College and Balboa Park; accepts girls; open to students from other schools. 200 students usually enrolled. 2011 schedule: June 13 to August 19. Application deadline: May 27.

Tuition and Aid Day student tuition: $11,900. Tuition installment plan (FACTS Tuition Payment Plan). Merit scholarship grants, need-based scholarship grants available. In 2010–11, 28% of upper-school students received aid; total upper-school merit-scholarship money awarded: $60,000. Total amount of financial aid awarded in 2010–11: $424,000.

Admissions Traditional secondary-level entrance grade is 9. For fall 2010, 189 students applied for upper-level admission, 150 were accepted, 137 enrolled. High School Placement Test required. Deadline for receipt of application materials: January 19. Application fee required: $100. On-campus interview required.

Athletics Interscholastic: basketball, cross-country running, equestrian sports, field hockey, fitness walking, golf, soccer, softball, swimming and diving, tennis, track and field, volleyball, water polo, yoga. 2 PE instructors, 31 coaches, 1 athletic trainer.

Computers Computers are regularly used in all academic, college planning, computer applications, creative writing, economics, English, foreign language, French, graphic design, graphics, health, journalism, library, literary magazine,

mathematics, media, media production, photography, religion, religious studies, science, social studies, Spanish, speech, technology, Web site design, yearbook classes. Computer network features include on-campus library services, online commercial services, Internet access, wireless campus network, Internet filtering or blocking technology. Student e-mail accounts are available to students. Students grades are available online. The school has a published electronic and media policy.

Contact Mrs. Linda Klarin, Admissions Coordinator. 818-346-8812. Fax: 818-346-9483. E-mail: lklarin@louisvillehs.org. Web site: www.louisvillehs.org.

THE LOVETT SCHOOL

4075 Paces Ferry Road NW
Atlanta, Georgia 30327
Head of School: William S. Peebles

General Information Coeducational day college-preparatory school. Grades K–12. Founded: 1926. Setting: suburban. 100-acre campus. 8 buildings on campus. Approved or accredited by Southern Association of Colleges and Schools, Southern Association of Independent Schools, and Georgia Department of Education. Member of National Association of Independent Schools and Secondary School Admission Test Board. Endowment: $50.9 million. Total enrollment: 1,587. Upper school average class size: 15. Upper school faculty-student ratio: 1:15. There are 175 required school days per year for Upper School students. Upper School students typically attend 5 days per week.

Upper School Student Profile Grade 9: 155 students (72 boys, 83 girls); Grade 10: 152 students (74 boys, 78 girls); Grade 11: 151 students (71 boys, 80 girls); Grade 12: 141 students (64 boys, 77 girls).

Faculty School total: 154. In upper school: 28 men, 30 women; 45 have advanced degrees.

Subjects Offered Advanced chemistry, advanced computer applications, advanced math, Advanced Placement courses, African American history, African history, African literature, African-American literature, algebra, American government, American history, American history-AP, American legal systems, American literature, ancient history, ancient world history, architecture, art, art history, Asian history, Asian studies, band, biology, botany, calculus, calculus-AP, career and personal planning, career/college preparation, ceramics, character education, chemistry, chorus, computer art, computer education, computer graphics, computer programming, computer science, creative writing, dance, debate, drama, driver education, earth science, ecology, economics, electronic music, English, English literature, English-AP, environmental science, ethics, European history, fiction, film history, fine arts, French, French language-AP, French literature-AP, French studies, French-AP, gender issues, genetics, geometry, German, history, human development, jazz dance, journalism, Latin, Latin-AP, leadership, marine biology, mathematics, medieval history, music theory, music theory-AP, newspaper, orchestra, painting, philosophy, photography, physical education, physics, portfolio art, pre-calculus, public speaking, religion, robotics, science, sculpture, social studies, Spanish, Spanish language-AP, Spanish literature-AP, speech, statistics, technical theater, theater, theater arts, trigonometry, U.S. government and politics-AP, video, Western civilization, Western philosophy, world cultures, world history, world literature, world religions, writing workshop, yearbook, zoology.

Graduation Requirements Algebra, American studies, arts and fine arts (art, music, dance, drama), biology, English, foreign language, geometry, history, mathematics, physical education (includes health), religion (includes Bible studies and theology), science, Western civilization.

Special Academic Programs Advanced Placement exam preparation; honors section; independent study; term-away projects; study abroad; academic accommodation for the gifted, the musically talented, and the artistically talented.

College Admission Counseling 139 students graduated in 2010; all went to college, including Auburn University; College of Charleston; Georgia Institute of Technology; The University of Alabama; The University of North Carolina at Chapel Hill; University of Georgia.

Student Life Upper grades have uniform requirement, student council, honor system. Discipline rests primarily with faculty. Attendance at religious services is required.

Summer Programs Remediation, enrichment, advancement programs offered; session focuses on academic course work; held on campus; accepts boys and girls; open to students from other schools. 35 students usually enrolled. 2011 schedule: June 6 to July 22. Application deadline: June 6.

Tuition and Aid Day student tuition: $17,535–$20,935. Tuition installment plan (The Tuition Plan, Key Tuition Payment Plan, monthly payment plans, individually arranged payment plans, 1/2 paid in July and 1/2 paid in November). Need-based scholarship grants, local bank loans available. In 2010–11, 14% of upper-school students received aid. Total amount of financial aid awarded in 2010–11: $2,560,000.

Admissions Traditional secondary-level entrance grade is 9. SSAT required. Deadline for receipt of application materials: February 4. Application fee required: $75. On-campus interview required.

Athletics Interscholastic: artistic gym (girls), baseball (b), basketball (b,g), cheering (g), cross-country running (b,g), dance (g), diving (b,g), football (b), golf (b,g), gymnastics (g), lacrosse (b,g), modern dance (g), soccer (b,g), softball (g), swimming and diving (b,g), tennis (b,g), track and field (b,g), volleyball (g), wrestling (b); intramural: aerobics/dance (g), dance (g), in-line hockey (b), modern dance (g), roller hockey (b); coed intramural: backpacking, bicycling, bowling, canoeing/kayaking, climbing, fitness, flag football, Frisbee, hiking/backpacking, kayaking, mountain

biking, outdoor activities, physical fitness, physical training, rappelling, rock climbing, ropes courses, strength & conditioning, ultimate Frisbee, wall climbing, weight lifting, weight training, yoga. 3 PE instructors, 26 coaches, 2 athletic trainers.
Computers Computers are regularly used in all academic classes. Computer network features include on-campus library services, online commercial services, Internet access, wireless campus network, Internet filtering or blocking technology, central file storage. Student e-mail accounts and computer access in designated common areas are available to students. Students grades are available online.
Contact Ms. Debbie Lange, Director of Admission. 404-262-3032. Fax: 404-479-8463. E-mail: dlange@lovett.org. Web site: www.lovett.org.

THE LOWELL WHITEMAN SCHOOL

42605 County Road 36
Steamboat Springs, Colorado 80487
Head of School: Mr. Walt Daub

General Information Coeducational boarding and day college-preparatory school. Grades 9–12. Founded: 1957. Setting: rural. Nearest major city is Denver. Students are housed in single-sex dormitories. 192-acre campus. 10 buildings on campus. Approved or accredited by Association of Colorado Independent Schools, The Association of Boarding Schools, and Colorado Department of Education. Member of National Association of Independent Schools and Secondary School Admission Test Board. Endowment: $1 million. Total enrollment: 80. Upper school average class size: 8. Upper school faculty-student ratio: 1:7. There are 175 required school days per year for Upper School students. Upper School students typically attend 5 days per week. The average school day consists of 7 hours.
Upper School Student Profile Grade 9: 16 students (9 boys, 7 girls); Grade 10: 15 students (10 boys, 5 girls); Grade 11: 21 students (13 boys, 8 girls); Grade 12: 25 students (9 boys, 16 girls). 47% of students are boarding students. 65% are state residents. 24 states are represented in upper school student body. 6% are international students. International students from Canada, China, Germany, Mexico, United Arab Emirates, and United Kingdom.
Faculty School total: 20. In upper school: 8 men, 8 women; 7 have advanced degrees; 16 reside on campus.
Subjects Offered 20th century history, algebra, American history, American literature, American studies, anatomy, art, art history, biology, calculus, chemistry, computer math, computer programming, computer science, creative writing, drama, economics, English, English literature, expository writing, film, fine arts, French, geography, geology, geometry, government/civics, grammar, mathematics, physical education, physics, science, social sciences, social studies, Spanish, theater, trigonometry, typing, world history, writing.
Graduation Requirements Algebra, arts and fine arts (art, music, dance, drama), chemistry, computer science, English, foreign language, geography, geometry, mathematics, physical education (includes health), science, social sciences, social studies (includes history), Western civilization, foreign travel program, competitive ski/snowboarding program, outdoor program.
Special Academic Programs Advanced Placement exam preparation; honors section; independent study; study abroad; academic accommodation for the gifted.
College Admission Counseling 32 students graduated in 2009; 30 went to college, including Colorado State University; Middlebury College; Sierra College; The Colorado College; University of Colorado at Boulder; University of Denver. Other: 2 had other specific plans.
Student Life Upper grades have student council, honor system. Discipline rests equally with students and faculty.
Tuition and Aid Day student tuition: $17,700; 5-day tuition and room/board: $32,900; 7-day tuition and room/board: $32,900. Tuition installment plan (individually arranged payment plans, school's own payment plan). Merit scholarship grants, need-based scholarship grants available. In 2009–10, 36% of upper-school students received aid; total upper-school merit-scholarship money awarded: $10,000. Total amount of financial aid awarded in 2009–10: $440,000.
Admissions Traditional secondary-level entrance grade is 9. For fall 2009, 45 students applied for upper-level admission, 30 were accepted, 26 enrolled. Deadline for receipt of application materials: none. Application fee required: $50. Interview required.
Athletics Interscholastic: alpine skiing (boys, girls), baseball (b), basketball (b,g), biathlon (b,g), cross-country running (b,g), dance team (g), freestyle skiing (b,g), golf (b,g), hockey (b,g), ice hockey (b,g), indoor hockey (b,g), mountain biking (b,g), mountaineering (b,g), nordic skiing (b,g), outdoor adventure (b,g), ski jumping (b,g), skiing (cross-country) (b,g), skiing (downhill) (b,g), snowboarding (b,g), soccer (b,g), tennis (b,g), wrestling (b); intramural: backpacking (b,g), basketball (b,g), bicycling (b,g), ice hockey (b,g), ice skating (b,g), independent competitive sports (b,g), indoor hockey (b,g), indoor soccer (b,g), jogging (b,g), lacrosse (g), mountain biking (b,g), mountaineering (b,g), outdoor adventure (b,g), rock climbing (b,g), skiing (cross-country) (b,g), skiing (downhill) (b,g), snowboarding (b,g), soccer (b,g); coed interscholastic: alpine skiing, biathlon, climbing, cross-country running, freestyle skiing, golf, ice hockey, indoor hockey, kayaking, mountain biking, mountaineering, nordic skiing, outdoor adventure, outdoor education, outdoor recreation, outdoor skills, rock climbing, ski jumping, skiing (cross-country), skiing (downhill), snowboarding, soccer, telemark skiing, wall climbing; coed intramural: aerobics, backpacking, badminton, bicycling, billiards, canoeing/kayaking, climbing, figure skating, fitness, flag football, Frisbee, golf, hiking/backpacking, horseback riding, ice hockey, ice skating, independent competitive sports, indoor hockey, indoor soccer, jogging, judo, juggling, kayaking, lacrosse, mountain biking, mountaineering, outdoor adventure, outdoor education, outdoor recreation, outdoor skills, paint ball, physical fitness, physical training, rafting, rappelling, rock climbing, rugby, running, skateboarding, skiing (cross-country), skiing (downhill), snowboarding, snowshoeing, soccer, strength & conditioning, swimming and diving, table tennis, telemark skiing, tennis, volleyball, wall climbing, weight lifting, weight training, wilderness, wilderness survival, wildernessways, winter soccer, winter walking, yoga.
Computers Computers are regularly used in all academic classes. Computer network features include on-campus library services, online commercial services, Internet access, wireless campus network, Internet filtering or blocking technology. Campus intranet and student e-mail accounts are available to students. The school has a published electronic and media policy.
Contact Mr. Walt Daub, Head of School and Director of Admissions. 970-879-1350 Ext. 12. Fax: 970-879-0506. E-mail: admissions@lws.edu. Web site: www.lws.edu.

LOWER BRULE HIGH SCHOOL

PO Box 245
Lower Brule, South Dakota 57548
Head of School: Tara Thomas

General Information Coeducational day college-preparatory, general academic, arts, vocational, and bilingual studies school; primarily serves underachievers. Grades 7–12. Founded: 1971. Setting: rural. Nearest major city is Pierre. 25-acre campus. 1 building on campus. Approved or accredited by South Dakota Department of Education. Total enrollment: 258. Upper school average class size: 10.
Upper School Student Profile Grade 9: 25 students (13 boys, 12 girls); Grade 10: 18 students (6 boys, 12 girls); Grade 11: 12 students (5 boys, 7 girls); Grade 12: 12 students (5 boys, 7 girls).
Faculty School total: 23. In upper school: 9 men, 12 women.
Subjects Offered Advanced computer applications, advanced math, algebra, American government, American history, American literature, ancient world history, art, athletics, basketball, biology, career experience, careers, carpentry, cheerleading, chemistry, college admission preparation, college awareness, college planning, composition, computer applications, computer literacy, computer studies, construction, creative writing, current events, drawing, driver education, English literature, general math, geography, geometry, government, grammar, health, health and wellness, human anatomy, human biology, independent living, JROTC, JROTC or LEAD (Leadership Education and Development), keyboarding, lab science, language arts, library, literature, mathematics, metalworking, Native American arts and crafts, Native American history, Native American studies, newspaper, painting, photography, physical education, physical science, physics, pre-algebra, pre-college orientation, psychology, reading, reading/study skills, SAT/ACT preparation, short story, social sciences, sociology, speech, sports, state history, study skills, substance abuse, track and field, U.S. government, U.S. history, vocational-technical courses, volleyball, welding, woodworking, world geography, world history, writing, yearbook.
Graduation Requirements Advanced math, algebra, American history, American literature, anatomy and physiology, arts, biology, British literature, chemistry, composition, computer science, computer skills, computer studies, electives, English, English composition, English-AP, geography, government, Internet, JROTC, keyboarding, Native American studies, research and reference, short story, speech, U.S. government, U.S. history, world geography.
Special Academic Programs Accelerated programs; study at local college for college credit; remedial reading and/or remedial writing; programs in English for dyslexic students; special instructional classes for students with learning disabilities, ADD, emotional and behavioral problems.
College Admission Counseling 13 students graduated in 2009; 1 went to college, including Abilene Christian University. Other: 2 entered military service, 10 had other specific plans.
Student Life Upper grades have student council. Discipline rests primarily with faculty.
Admissions CTBS, Stanford Achievement Test, any other standardized test required. Deadline for receipt of application materials: none. No application fee required.
Athletics Interscholastic: basketball (boys, girls), cheering (g), cross-country running (b,g), football (b), JROTC drill (b,g), physical fitness (b,g), rodeo (b,g), running (b,g), track and field (b,g), volleyball (g); coed interscholastic: running. 2 PE instructors, 5 coaches.
Computers Computers are regularly used in accounting, career exploration, college planning, creative writing, current events, desktop publishing, history, library, mathematics, photography, social sciences, social studies, typing, yearbook classes. Computer network features include on-campus library services, Internet access, Internet filtering or blocking technology. Student e-mail accounts are available to students. Students grades are available online.
Contact Tara Thomas, Principal. 605-473-5510. Fax: 605-473-5207. E-mail: TaraThomas@brule.bia.edu

Body school directory.

LOYOLA ACADEMY

1100 Laramie Avenue
Wilmette, Illinois 60091
Head of School: Rev. Patrick E. McGrath, SJ

General Information Coeducational day college-preparatory and comprehensive college preparation in the Jesuit tradition school, affiliated with Roman Catholic Church (Jesuit order). Grades 9–12. Founded: 1909. Setting: suburban. Nearest major city is Chicago. 26-acre campus. 1 building on campus. Approved or accredited by North Central Association of Colleges and Schools and Illinois Department of Education. Endowment: $40 million. Total enrollment: 2,000. Upper school average class size: 24. Upper school faculty-student ratio: 1:17. The average school day consists of 7 hours and 12 minutes.

Upper School Student Profile 88% of students are Roman Catholic Church (Jesuit order).

Faculty School total: 160. In upper school: 80 men, 70 women; 130 have advanced degrees.

Subjects Offered Advanced Placement courses, algebra, American history, American history-AP, American literature, American literature-AP, anatomy, Ancient Greek, art, art history, Asian history, band, biology, biology-AP, calculus, chemistry, chemistry-AP, Chinese, chorus, communications, computer math, computer programming, computer science, creative writing, dance, design, drama, drawing, earth science, economics, English, English literature, ethics, European history-AP, expository writing, fine arts, finite math, French, general science, genetics, geography, geometry, German, government and politics-AP, health, history, history-AP, humanities, instrumental music, justice seminar, keyboarding, Latin, literature, mathematics, music, musicianship, painting, physical education, physics, physics-AP, physiology, political science, psychology, psychology-AP, religious studies, science, sculpture, social studies, Spanish, Spanish-AP, speech, statistics, statistics-AP, theater, theology, theology and the arts, trigonometry, word processing, world history, world literature, writing.

Graduation Requirements Arts and fine arts (art, music, dance, drama), English, foreign language, mathematics, physical education (includes health), religion (includes Bible studies and theology), science, social studies (includes history), attendance at Freshman and Junior Retreats.

Special Academic Programs Advanced Placement exam preparation; honors section; independent study; study abroad; academic accommodation for the gifted; programs in English, mathematics, general development for dyslexic students; special instructional classes for students with mild learning challenges.

College Admission Counseling 479 students graduated in 2010; 478 went to college, including Boston College; DePaul University; Loyola University Chicago; Marquette University; University of Illinois; University of Notre Dame. Other: 1 went to work. Mean SAT critical reading: 569, mean SAT math: 579, mean composite ACT: 25. 27% scored over 600 on SAT critical reading, 29% scored over 600 on SAT math, 25% scored over 26 on composite ACT.

Student Life Upper grades have specified standards of dress, student council, honor system. Discipline rests primarily with faculty. Attendance at religious services is required.

Summer Programs Remediation, enrichment, advancement, sports, art/fine arts, computer instruction programs offered; session focuses on enrichment; held both on and off campus; held at 60-acre state-of-the-art athletic campus in Glenview (3.1 miles away); accepts boys and girls; open to students from other schools. 850 students usually enrolled. 2011 schedule: June 20 to July 28. Application deadline: June 2.

Tuition and Aid Day student tuition: $12,500. Tuition installment plan (monthly payment plans, 1-, 2-, 4- and monthly payment plans). Need-based scholarship grants available. In 2010–11, 30% of upper-school students received aid. Total amount of financial aid awarded in 2010–11: $3,750,000.

Admissions Traditional secondary-level entrance grade is 9. For fall 2010, 920 students applied for upper-level admission, 700 were accepted, 535 enrolled. STS Examination required. Deadline for receipt of application materials: January 26. Application fee required: $25.

Athletics Interscholastic: baseball (boys), basketball (b,g), crew (b,g), cross-country running (b,g), diving (b,g), field hockey (g), football (b), golf (b,g), ice hockey (b,g), indoor track & field (b,g), lacrosse (b,g), rowing (b,g), soccer (b,g), softball (g), swimming and diving (b,g), tennis (b,g), track and field (b,g), volleyball (b,g), water polo (b,g), wrestling (b); intramural: cheering (g), dance (b,g), dance squad (g), dance team (g), drill team (g), modern dance (b,g), pom squad (g); coed interscholastic: bowling, sailing; coed intramural: aerobics, aerobics/dance, ballet, basketball, bicycling, billiards, bowling, canoeing/kayaking, climbing, fitness, Frisbee, golf, hiking/backpacking, kayaking, martial arts, mountain biking, outdoor education, physical fitness, scuba diving, skateboarding, skiing (downhill), snowboarding, strength & conditioning, table tennis, ultimate Frisbee, wall climbing, weight lifting, weight training, yoga. 6 PE instructors, 2 athletic trainers.

Computers Computers are regularly used in all academic classes. Computer network features include on-campus library services, Internet access, wireless campus network, Internet filtering or blocking technology. Campus intranet is available to students. Students grades are available online. The school has a published electronic and media policy.

Contact Mrs. Genevieve B. Atwood, Director of Admissions. 847-920-2480. Fax: 847-920-2552. E-mail: gatwood@loy.org. Web site: www.goramblers.org.

LOYOLA-BLAKEFIELD

PO Box 6819
Baltimore, Maryland 21285-6819
Head of School: Mr. Anthony I. Day

General Information Boys' day college-preparatory, arts, and religious studies school, affiliated with Roman Catholic Church. Grades 6–12. Founded: 1852. Setting: suburban. 60-acre campus. 7 buildings on campus. Approved or accredited by Association of Independent Maryland Schools and Jesuit Secondary Education Association. Endowment: $9.9 million. Total enrollment: 1,002. Upper school average class size: 19. Upper school faculty-student ratio: 1:11. There are 175 required school days per year for Upper School students. Upper School students typically attend 5 days per week. The average school day consists of 6 hours and 55 minutes.

Upper School Student Profile Grade 9: 202 students (202 boys); Grade 10: 190 students (190 boys); Grade 11: 169 students (169 boys); Grade 12: 197 students (197 boys). 80% of students are Roman Catholic.

Faculty School total: 88. In upper school: 52 men, 16 women; 55 have advanced degrees.

Subjects Offered Accounting, algebra, American government, American literature, American literature-AP, art, art history, band, biology, biology-AP, biotechnology, British literature, British literature (honors), calculus, calculus-AP, ceramics, chemistry, chemistry-AP, Chesapeake Bay studies, chorus, civil war history, composition, composition-AP, computer graphics, computer science, concert band, drawing, driver education, English, English language-AP, English literature-AP, European history-AP, film studies, fine arts, forensics, French, French language-AP, German, German-AP, government and politics-AP, Greek, history, history of music, honors algebra, honors English, honors geometry, honors U.S. history, honors world history, instrumental music, jazz ensemble, journalism, Latin, Latin-AP, mathematics, music history, oil painting, painting, photography, physical education, physics, physics-AP, poetry, pre-calculus, psychology, public speaking, religion, science, Spanish, Spanish language-AP, stagecraft, statistics-AP, U.S. government and politics-AP, U.S. history, U.S. history-AP, yearbook.

Graduation Requirements Arts and fine arts (art, music, dance, drama), computer science, English, foreign language, mathematics, physical education (includes health), religion (includes Bible studies and theology), science, social studies (includes history), 40 hours of Christian service.

Special Academic Programs Advanced Placement exam preparation; honors section; independent study; academic accommodation for the gifted, the musically talented, and the artistically talented.

College Admission Counseling 204 students graduated in 2009; all went to college, including Randolph-Macon College; Saint Joseph's University; Towson University; University of Maryland, Baltimore County; University of Maryland, College Park; Virginia Polytechnic Institute and State University. Mean SAT critical reading: 612, mean SAT math: 618.

Student Life Upper grades have specified standards of dress, student council, honor system. Discipline rests primarily with faculty. Attendance at religious services is required.

Tuition and Aid Day student tuition: $14,630. Tuition installment plan (Key Tuition Payment Plan). Merit scholarship grants, need-based scholarship grants available. In 2009–10, 25% of upper-school students received aid; total upper-school merit-scholarship money awarded: $267,420. Total amount of financial aid awarded in 2009–10: $1,200,000.

Admissions Traditional secondary-level entrance grade is 9. For fall 2009, 358 students applied for upper-level admission, 220 were accepted, 130 enrolled. High School Placement Test or ISEE required. Deadline for receipt of application materials: December 15. Application fee required: $35. On-campus interview required.

Athletics Interscholastic: baseball, basketball, cross-country running, diving, football, golf, ice hockey, indoor track & field, lacrosse, rugby, soccer, squash, swimming and diving, tennis, track and field, volleyball, water polo, winter (indoor) track, wrestling; intramural: badminton, basketball, fishing, flag football, football, indoor soccer, lacrosse, martial arts, sailing, tennis, ultimate Frisbee. 4 PE instructors, 30 coaches, 1 athletic trainer.

Computers Computers are regularly used in all classes. Computer network features include on-campus library services, online commercial services, Internet access, wireless campus network, Internet filtering or blocking technology. Campus intranet, student e-mail accounts, and computer access in designated common areas are available to students. Students grades are available online. The school has a published electronic and media policy.

Contact Ms. Paddy M. London, Admissions Assistant. 443-841-3680. Fax: 443-841-3105. E-mail: plondon@loyolablakefield.org. Web site: www.loyolablakefield.org.

LOYOLA HIGH SCHOOL, JESUIT COLLEGE PREPARATORY

1901 Venice Boulevard
Los Angeles, California 90006-4496
Head of School: Mr. Frank P. Kozakowski

General Information Boys' day college-preparatory, arts, religious studies, bilingual studies, and technology school, affiliated with Roman Catholic Church. Grades 9–12. Founded: 1865. Setting: urban. 23-acre campus. 12 buildings on campus. Approved or accredited by California Association of Independent Schools and Western Association of Schools and Colleges. Endowment: $20 million. Total enrollment: 1,224. Upper school average class size: 26. Upper school faculty-student ratio: 1:15.

Upper School Student Profile Grade 9: 315 students (315 boys); Grade 10: 320 students (320 boys); Grade 11: 298 students (298 boys); Grade 12: 291 students (291 boys). 84% of students are Roman Catholic.

Faculty School total: 95. In upper school: 62 men, 33 women; 75 have advanced degrees.

Subjects Offered African-American studies, algebra, American history, American history-AP, American literature, anatomy and physiology, art, art history, Bible studies, biology, biology-AP, calculus, calculus-AP, ceramics, chemistry, chemistry-AP, community service, composition, computer math, computer programming, computer science, computer science-AP, creative writing, drama, earth science, economics-AP, English, English literature, English-AP, environmental science-AP, ethics, European history, European history-AP, expository writing, fine arts, French, French-AP, geometry, German, German-AP, government/civics, grammar, health, history, Latin, Latin-AP, mathematics, Mexican history, music, music theory-AP, oceanography, philosophy, photography, physical education, physics, physics-AP, pre-calculus, psychology-AP, religion, rhetoric, science, Shakespeare, social studies, Spanish, Spanish language-AP, Spanish literature-AP, theater, theology, trigonometry, typing, Western civilization, world history, world literature, writing.

Graduation Requirements Arts and fine arts (art, music, dance, drama), English, foreign language, mathematics, physical education (includes health), religion (includes Bible studies and theology), science, social sciences, social studies (includes history), three-week internship in senior year. Community service is required.

Special Academic Programs Advanced Placement exam preparation; honors section; independent study; special instructional classes for deaf students.

College Admission Counseling 292 students graduated in 2009; all went to college, including Loyola Marymount University; University of California, Berkeley; University of California, Irvine; University of California, Los Angeles; University of California, Santa Barbara; University of Southern California. Mean SAT critical reading: 612, mean SAT math: 618, mean SAT writing: 616, mean combined SAT: 1846. 54% scored over 600 on SAT critical reading, 52% scored over 600 on SAT math, 53% scored over 600 on SAT writing.

Student Life Upper grades have specified standards of dress, student council, honor system. Discipline rests primarily with faculty. Attendance at religious services is required.

Tuition and Aid Day student tuition: $13,240. Tuition installment plan (FACTS Tuition Payment Plan, semester payment plan). Merit scholarship grants, need-based scholarship grants available. In 2009–10, 24% of upper school students received aid; total upper-school merit-scholarship money awarded: $165,000. Total amount of financial aid awarded in 2009–10: $2,100,000.

Admissions Traditional secondary-level entrance grade is 9. For fall 2009, 720 students applied for upper-level admission, 355 were accepted, 315 enrolled. High School Placement Test required. Deadline for receipt of application materials: January 8. Application fee required: $75.

Athletics Interscholastic: baseball, basketball, cross-country running, diving, football, golf, lacrosse, soccer, swimming and diving, tennis, track and field, volleyball, water polo; intramural: baseball, basketball, diving, football, paddle tennis, soccer, swimming and diving, tennis, volleyball, water polo. 2 PE instructors, 3 coaches, 2 athletic trainers.

Computers Computers are regularly used in English, history, journalism, keyboarding, mathematics, science, yearbook classes. Computer network features include on-campus library services, Internet access, wireless campus network, Internet filtering or blocking technology. The school has a published electronic and media policy.

Contact Heath B. Utley, Director of Admissions. 213-381-5121 Ext. 219. Fax: 213-368-3819. E-mail: hutley@loyolahs.edu. Web site: www.loyolahs.edu.

LOYOLA SCHOOL

980 Park Avenue
New York, New York 10028-0020
Head of School: Mr. James F.X. Lyness

General Information Coeducational day college-preparatory school, affiliated with Roman Catholic Church (Jesuit order). Grades 9–12. Founded: 1900. Setting: urban. 2 buildings on campus. Approved or accredited by Jesuit Secondary Education Association, Middle States Association of Colleges and Schools, National Catholic Education Association, New York State Association of Independent Schools, and New York State Board of Regents. Member of National Association of Independent Schools. Total enrollment: 202. Upper school average class size: 17. Upper school faculty-student ratio: 1:9. There are 180 required school days per year for Upper School students. Upper School students typically attend 5 days per week. The average school day consists of 6 hours and 20 minutes.

Upper School Student Profile Grade 9: 49 students (25 boys, 24 girls); Grade 10: 45 students (20 boys, 25 girls); Grade 11: 53 students (25 boys, 28 girls); Grade 12: 55 students (24 boys, 31 girls). 85% of students are Roman Catholic Church (Jesuit order).

Faculty School total: 30. In upper school: 16 men, 14 women; 28 have advanced degrees.

Subjects Offered Advanced Placement courses, algebra, American government, American history, American literature, art, art history, biology, calculus, chemistry, chorus, college counseling, community service, comparative religion, computer programming, computer science, creative writing, death and loss, discrete mathematics, drama, economics, English, English literature, ethics, European history, expository writing, film, film history, fine arts, French, geometry, grammar, health, history, instrumental music, Italian, journalism, language-AP, Latin, mathematics, music history, philosophy, photography, physical education, physics, political science, pre-calculus, religion, science, social studies, Spanish, speech, statistics-AP, student government, student publications, theater, theology, trigonometry, world history, writing.

Graduation Requirements Art history, computer literacy, English, foreign language, guidance, mathematics, music history, physical education (includes health), science, social studies (includes history), speech, theology, Christian service program hours each year.

Special Academic Programs 9 Advanced Placement exams for which test preparation is offered; study at local college for college credit.

College Admission Counseling 55 students graduated in 2010; all went to college, including Cornell University; Fordham University; Georgetown University; Gettysburg College; Lafayette College; Northwestern University. Median SAT critical reading: 620, median SAT math: 600, median SAT writing: 630.

Student Life Upper grades have specified standards of dress, student council, honor system. Discipline rests primarily with faculty. Attendance at religious services is required.

Tuition and Aid Day student tuition: $28,000. Tuition installment plan (Academic Management Services Plan). Merit scholarship grants, need-based scholarship grants available. In 2010–11, 33% of upper-school students received aid; total upper-school merit-scholarship money awarded: $200,000. Total amount of financial aid awarded in 2010–11: $1,194,000.

Admissions Traditional secondary-level entrance grade is 9. ISEE, school's own exam or SSAT required. Deadline for receipt of application materials: November 19. Application fee required: $75. On-campus interview recommended.

Athletics Interscholastic: baseball (boys), basketball (b,g), cross-country running (b,g), soccer (b), softball (g), track and field (b,g), volleyball (g); intramural: basketball (b,g), dance (g); coed interscholastic: golf, physical fitness, soccer; coed intramural: Frisbee, hiking/backpacking, outdoor activities, outdoor adventure, paddle tennis, physical fitness, physical training, track and field. 1 PE instructor, 9 coaches.

Computers Computers are regularly used in all academic classes. Computer network features include on-campus library services, online commercial services, Internet access, wireless campus network, Internet filtering or blocking technology. Campus intranet, student e-mail accounts, and computer access in designated common areas are available to students. The school has a published electronic and media policy.

Contact Mr. Gabriel Rotman, Associate Director of Admissions. 646-346-8131. Fax: 646-346-8175. E-mail: grotman@loyola-nyc.org. Web site: www.loyola-nyc.org.

LUSTRE CHRISTIAN HIGH SCHOOL

HC 66, Box 57
Lustre, Montana 59225
Head of School: Al Leland

General Information Coeducational boarding and day college-preparatory, general academic, and religious studies school, affiliated with Mennonite Brethren Church. Grades 9–12. Founded: 1948. Setting: rural. Nearest major city is Glasgow. Students are housed in single-sex by floor dormitories. 20-acre campus. 1 building on campus. Approved or accredited by Association of Christian Schools International and Montana Department of Education. Endowment: $220,000. Total enrollment: 25. Upper school average class size: 7. Upper school faculty-student ratio: 1:4. There are 180 required school days per year for Upper School students. Upper School students typically attend 5 days per week. The average school day consists of 6 hours and 58 minutes.

Upper School Student Profile Grade 9: 3 students (3 girls); Grade 10: 10 students (7 boys, 3 girls); Grade 11: 6 students (5 boys, 1 girl); Grade 12: 6 students (5 boys, 1 girl). 56% of students are boarding students. 44% are state residents. 5 states are represented in upper school student body. 36% are international students. International students from China and Republic of Korea; 1 other country represented in student body. 8% of students are members of Mennonite Brethren Church.

Faculty School total: 6. In upper school: 1 man, 5 women; 1 has an advanced degree; 4 reside on campus.

Subjects Offered Algebra, American literature, band, Bible studies, biology, British literature, chemistry, choir, Christian studies, computer science, computers, current events, English, fine arts, foreign language, geometry, health, journalism, mathematics, physical education, physical science, pre-calculus, religion, science, social sciences, social studies, U.S. government, U.S. history, world history.

Graduation Requirements Arts and fine arts (art, music, dance, drama), Bible, computer science, English, mathematics, physical education (includes health), science, social studies (includes history), senior chapel message (as part of senior Bible program).

Special Academic Programs Independent study.

College Admission Counseling 3 students graduated in 2009; all went to college, including Montana State University. Median composite ACT: 16.

Lustre Christian High School

Student Life Upper grades have specified standards of dress, student council. Discipline rests primarily with faculty. Attendance at religious services is required.
Tuition and Aid Day student tuition: $1750; 7-day tuition and room/board: $3300. Tuition installment plan (monthly payment plans, individually arranged payment plans). Need-based scholarship grants available. In 2009–10, 12% of upper-school students received aid.
Admissions Traditional secondary-level entrance grade is 9. For fall 2009, 16 students applied for upper-level admission, 13 were accepted, 10 enrolled. ITBS achievement test, PSAT, SLEP for foreign students or TOEFL or SLEP required. Deadline for receipt of application materials: none. No application fee required. Interview recommended.
Athletics Interscholastic: basketball (boys, girls), football (b), track and field (b,g), volleyball (g). 1 PE instructor, 1 coach.
Computers Computers are regularly used in Bible studies, English, history, journalism, mathematics, religious studies, science, yearbook classes. Computer network features include Internet access, wireless campus network.
Contact Al Leland, Supervising Teacher. 406-392-5735. Fax: 406-392-5765. E-mail: aleland@nemont.net. Web site: www.lustrechristian.org.

LUTHERAN HIGH NORTH

1130 West 34th Street
Houston, Texas 77018
Head of School: Mr. Mychal Thom
General Information Coeducational day college-preparatory, arts, religious studies, bilingual studies, and technology school, affiliated with Lutheran Church–Missouri Synod. Grades 9–12. Founded: 1982. Setting: urban. 10-acre campus. 3 buildings on campus. Approved or accredited by National Lutheran School Accreditation, Southern Association of Colleges and Schools, Texas Education Agency, and Texas Private School Accreditation Commission. Endowment: $1.5 million. Total enrollment: 295. Upper school average class size: 22. Upper school faculty-student ratio: 1:22.
Upper School Student Profile Grade 9: 68 students (33 boys, 35 girls); Grade 10: 82 students (33 boys, 49 girls); Grade 11: 71 students (30 boys, 41 girls); Grade 12: 70 students (33 boys, 37 girls). 50% of students are Lutheran Church–Missouri Synod.
Faculty School total: 26. In upper school: 13 men, 12 women; 11 have advanced degrees.
Subjects Offered 20th century American writers, 20th century history, 20th century physics, 20th century world history, 3-dimensional art, 3-dimensional design, ACT preparation, acting, advanced chemistry, advanced computer applications, advanced math, Advanced Placement courses, algebra, American Civil War, American government, American history, American literature, anatomy and physiology, ancient world history, applied arts, applied music, art, athletic training, athletics, band, baseball, Basic programming, basketball, Bible, Bible studies, biology, British literature, British literature (honors), business technology, cabinet making, calculus, calculus-AP, ceramics, cheerleading, chemistry, choir, choral music, chorus, Christian doctrine, Christian education, Christian scripture, Christian testament, civil war history, college counseling, college placement, college planning, college writing, computer applications, computer information systems, computer multimedia, computer programming, concert band, concert choir, digital imaging, digital photography, drafting, drama, drama performance, economics, English, English composition, English literature, English-AP, environmental science, foreign language, geometry, golf, government, health, history, honors algebra, honors English, honors geometry, human anatomy, human biology, instrumental music, jazz band, journalism, keyboarding, language, Latin, marching band, music theory, musical productions, novels, oil painting, photojournalism, physical education, physics, pre-calculus, psychology, public speaking, SAT preparation, SAT/ACT preparation, senior career experience, social issues, softball, Spanish, swimming, travel, U.S. government, visual arts, volleyball, Web site design, weight training, weightlifting, woodworking, world history, yearbook.
Graduation Requirements Algebra, anatomy and physiology, art education, arts and fine arts (art, music, dance, drama), computer science, economics, electives, English, foreign language, geography, geometry, government, human biology, mathematics, physical education (includes health), public speaking, religion (includes Bible studies and theology), science, social studies (includes history), U.S. history, world history. Distinguished Diploma students must have an additional credit in foreign language, 2½ credits electives, 5 credits honors work, and 4 advanced measures with approved college courses with A or B.
Special Academic Programs Advanced Placement exam preparation; honors section; study at local college for college credit; programs in English, mathematics for dyslexic students.
College Admission Counseling 70 students graduated in 2009; 67 went to college, including Sam Houston State University; Texas A&M University; The University of Texas at Austin; The University of Texas at San Antonio; University of Houston. Other: 1 went to work, 2 entered military service. Mean SAT writing: 522, mean combined SAT: 1013, mean composite ACT: 21.
Student Life Upper grades have uniform requirement, student council, honor system. Discipline rests primarily with faculty. Attendance at religious services is required.
Tuition and Aid Day student tuition: $9950. Tuition installment plan (FACTS Tuition Payment Plan, individually arranged payment plans, special tuition arrangements-full, half, semester or monthly). Tuition reduction for siblings, merit scholarship grants, need-based scholarship grants available. In 2009–10, 30% of upper-school students

received aid; total upper-school merit-scholarship money awarded: $8000. Total amount of financial aid awarded in 2009–10: $175,000.
Admissions Traditional secondary-level entrance grade is 9. For fall 2009, 110 students applied for upper-level admission, 83 were accepted, 75 enrolled. Admissions testing and High School Placement Test (closed version) from Scholastic Testing Service required. Deadline for receipt of application materials: none. Application fee required: $50. Interview required.
Athletics Interscholastic: aquatics (boys, girls), baseball (b), basketball (b,g), football (b), soccer (b,g), softball (g), volleyball (g), winter soccer (b,g); coed interscholastic: cheering, cross-country running, golf, outdoor activities, physical fitness, physical training, power lifting, swimming and diving, track and field, weight lifting, weight training. 3 PE instructors, 8 coaches, 2 athletic trainers.
Computers Computers are regularly used in current events, desktop publishing, drafting, English, graphic arts, graphic design, information technology, journalism, keyboarding, media arts, multimedia, news writing, publications, publishing, research skills, Spanish, theology, Web site design, word processing, writing, yearbook classes. Computer network features include on-campus library services, Internet access, Internet filtering or blocking technology. Student e-mail accounts are available to students. Students grades are available online. The school has a published electronic and media policy.
Contact Melissa White, Admissions Director. 713-880-3131 Ext. 330. Fax: 713-880-5447. E-mail: melissawhite@lea-hou.org. Web site: www. lutheranhighnorth.org/default.htm.

LUTHERAN HIGH SCHOOL

3960 Fruit Street
La Verne, California 91750
Head of School: Lance E. Ebel
General Information Coeducational day college-preparatory, general academic, arts, religious studies, and technology school, affiliated with Lutheran Church–Missouri Synod. Grades 9–12. Founded: 1973. Setting: suburban. Nearest major city is Los Angeles. 10-acre campus. 7 buildings on campus. Approved or accredited by Association of Christian Schools International, Lutheran School Accreditation Commission, National Lutheran School Accreditation, and Western Association of Schools and Colleges. Total enrollment: 130. Upper school average class size: 15. Upper school faculty-student ratio: 1:9. There are 180 required school days per year for Upper School students. Upper School students typically attend 5 days per week. The average school day consists of 6 hours and 40 minutes.
Upper School Student Profile Grade 9: 35 students (18 boys, 17 girls); Grade 10: 34 students (21 boys, 13 girls); Grade 11: 24 students (16 boys, 8 girls); Grade 12: 37 students (20 boys, 17 girls). 29% of students are Lutheran Church–Missouri Synod.
Faculty School total: 14. In upper school: 5 men, 9 women; 9 have advanced degrees.
Subjects Offered Advanced math, Advanced Placement courses, algebra, American government, American history, American history-AP, American literature, anatomy, anatomy and physiology, art, ASB Leadership, athletics, biology, biology-AP, British literature, calculus, calculus-AP, chemistry, choir, college counseling, community service, comparative religion, composition, computer literacy, computer programming, computer science, computer science-AP, computers, conceptual physics, drama, economics, English, English literature and composition-AP, English literature-AP, fine arts, geography, geometry, government, history-AP, honors algebra, honors English, honors geometry, honors U.S. history, honors world history, human anatomy, keyboarding, mathematics, naval science, NJROTC, physical education, physics, physics-AP, pre-calculus, psychology, religion, science, sign language, social sciences, social studies, Spanish, Spanish language-AP, theology, U.S. government, U.S. government and politics-AP, U.S. history-AP, word processing, world history, world literature, yearbook.
Graduation Requirements Arts and fine arts (art, music, dance, drama), business skills (includes word processing), computer science, English, foreign language, mathematics, physical education (includes health), religion (includes Bible studies and theology), science, social sciences, social studies (includes history), 24 hours per year of service to the community, senior project completion.
Special Academic Programs Advanced Placement exam preparation; honors section; accelerated programs; study at local college for college credit.
College Admission Counseling 31 students graduated in 2010; 30 went to college, including Azusa Pacific University; California State University, Fullerton; Columbia University; Concordia University; University of California, Berkeley. Other: 1 entered military service. Median SAT critical reading: 485, median SAT math: 495, median SAT writing: 515, median combined SAT: 1465. 18% scored over 600 on SAT critical reading, 14% scored over 600 on SAT math, 9% scored over 600 on SAT writing, 14% scored over 1800 on combined SAT.
Student Life Upper grades have specified standards of dress, student council, honor system. Discipline rests primarily with faculty. Attendance at religious services is required.
Summer Programs Remediation, enrichment, advancement, sports programs offered; session focuses on athletics and academic remediation; held on campus; accepts boys and girls; open to students from other schools. 20 students usually enrolled. 2011 schedule: June 13 to August 15. Application deadline: June 1.
Tuition and Aid Day student tuition: $6200–$6950. Tuition installment plan (SMART Tuition Payment Plan, monthly payment plans, individually arranged payment plans, advance payment discounts, credit card payments). Tuition reduction

for siblings, merit scholarship grants, need-based scholarship grants available. In 2010–11, 31% of upper-school students received aid; total upper-school merit-scholarship money awarded: $21,650. Total amount of financial aid awarded in 2010–11: $109,150.

Admissions Traditional secondary-level entrance grade is 9. High School Placement Test required. Deadline for receipt of application materials: none. Application fee required: $75. Interview required.

Athletics Interscholastic: aerobics/dance (girls), baseball (b), basketball (b,g), cheering (g), cross-country running (b,g), dance squad (g), dance team (g), drill team (b,g), football (b), golf (b,g), softball (g), volleyball (g), wrestling (b); coed interscholastic: golf, JROTC drill, soccer, track and field. 1 PE instructor, 20 coaches.

Computers Computers are regularly used in all academic, English, geography, history, information technology, mathematics, NJROTC, programming, science, Spanish, yearbook classes. Computer network features include online commercial services, Internet access, wireless campus network, Internet filtering or blocking technology. Campus intranet is available to students. Students grades are available online. The school has a published electronic and media policy.

Contact Kathy Johnson, Office Manager. 909-593-4494 Ext. 221. Fax: 909-596-3744. E-mail: kjohnson@lhslv.org. Web site: www.lhslv.org.

LUTHERAN HIGH SCHOOL
5555 South Arlington Avenue
Indianapolis, Indiana 46237-2366
Head of School: Mr. David Sommermeyer

General Information Coeducational day college-preparatory, general academic, and religious studies school, affiliated with Lutheran Church–Missouri Synod. Grades 9–12. Founded: 1975. Setting: suburban. 18-acre campus. 1 building on campus. Approved or accredited by National Lutheran School Accreditation, North Central Association of Colleges and Schools, and Indiana Department of Education. Endowment: $450,000. Total enrollment: 246. Upper school average class size: 18. Upper school faculty-student ratio: 1:15. There are 180 required school days per year for Upper School students. Upper School students typically attend 5 days per week. The average school day consists of 7 hours and 15 minutes.

Upper School Student Profile Grade 9: 53 students (24 boys, 29 girls); Grade 10: 48 students (26 boys, 22 girls); Grade 11: 74 students (39 boys, 35 girls); Grade 12: 70 students (30 boys, 40 girls). 64% of students are Lutheran Church–Missouri Synod.

Faculty School total: 17. In upper school: 13 men, 4 women; 15 have advanced degrees.

Subjects Offered Accounting, advanced biology, advanced chemistry, advanced computer applications, advanced math, Advanced Placement courses, algebra, American government, American history, American literature-AP, American sign language, anatomy, anatomy and physiology, Basic programming, Bible, Bible studies, biology, biology-AP, bookkeeping, business, calculus-AP, ceramics, chemistry, chemistry-AP, choir, Christian doctrine, Christian ethics, church history, comparative religion, computer applications, computer graphics, computer programming, computer science-AP, concert band, concert choir, desktop publishing, developmental language skills, drawing, driver education, economics, English, English language and composition-AP, English literature and composition-AP, environmental studies, family living, general business, general math, geometry, German, graphic design, health and wellness, humanities, independent study, jazz band, music theory, oil painting, personal fitness, physical fitness, physics, precalculus, printmaking, probability and statistics, psychology, publishing, sculpture, sociology, Spanish, speech, sports conditioning, student teaching, theater arts, U.S. government, vocational-technical courses, Web site design, world history, writing workshop.

Graduation Requirements Algebra, anatomy and physiology, arts and fine arts (art, music, dance, drama), biology-AP, chemistry-AP, computer applications, economics, English, foreign language, geometry, health and safety, physical education (includes health), physics, religious studies, U.S. government, U.S. history, world geography, world history.

Special Academic Programs 8 Advanced Placement exams for which test preparation is offered; honors section; independent study; study at local college for college credit; remedial reading and/or remedial writing; remedial math.

College Admission Counseling 60 students graduated in 2010; 59 went to college, including Ball State University; Indiana University Bloomington; Purdue University; University of Indianapolis; Valparaiso University. Other: 1 went to work. Mean SAT critical reading: 507, mean SAT math: 560, mean SAT writing: 497, mean combined SAT: 1564, mean composite ACT: 23.

Student Life Upper grades have uniform requirement, student council, honor system. Discipline rests primarily with faculty. Attendance at religious services is required.

Tuition and Aid Day student tuition: $8500. Tuition installment plan (FACTS Tuition Payment Plan). Tuition reduction for siblings, need-based scholarship grants, paying campus jobs, Simply Giving (Thrivent), church worker grants available. In 2010–11, 30% of upper-school students received aid. Total amount of financial aid awarded in 2010–11: $181,700.

Admissions Traditional secondary-level entrance grade is 9. Deadline for receipt of application materials: none. Application fee required: $150. On-campus interview required.

Athletics Interscholastic: baseball (boys), basketball (b,g), cheering (b,g), cross-country running (b,g), football (b), golf (b,g), soccer (b,g), softball (g), strength &

conditioning (b,g), tennis (b,g), track and field (b,g), volleyball (g), weight lifting (b,g), weight training (b,g); coed interscholastic: physical fitness, weight training; coed intramural: basketball, bowling, football. 22 coaches.

Computers Computers are regularly used in accounting, art, Bible studies, business applications, career exploration, current events, design, desktop publishing, drawing and design, economics, English, foreign language, graphic design, historical foundations for arts, history, independent study, keyboarding, library skills, media production, publications, science, social sciences, yearbook classes. Computer network features include on-campus library services, online commercial services, Internet access, wireless campus network, Internet filtering or blocking technology, shared library catalog and Internet databases with Indianapolis-Marion County Public Library. Computer access in designated common areas is available to students. Students grades are available online. The school has a published electronic and media policy.

Contact Mrs. Margo Korb, Administrative Assistant. 317-787-5474 Ext. 211. Fax: 317-787-2794. E-mail: mkorb@lhsi.org. Web site: www.lhsi.org.

LUTHERAN HIGH SCHOOL
12411 Wornall Road
Kansas City, Missouri 64145-1736
Head of School: Mr. Chris Domsch

General Information Coeducational day college-preparatory and religious studies school, affiliated with Lutheran Church–Missouri Synod. Grades 9–12. Founded: 1980. Setting: suburban. 29-acre campus. 1 building on campus. Approved or accredited by Missouri Independent School Association, National Lutheran School Accreditation, North Central Association of Colleges and Schools, and Missouri Department of Education. Endowment: $97,000. Total enrollment: 120. Upper school average class size: 15. Upper school faculty-student ratio: 1:12. There are 172 required school days per year for Upper School students. Upper School students typically attend 5 days per week. The average school day consists of 6 hours and 45 minutes.

Upper School Student Profile Grade 9: 41 students (30 boys, 11 girls); Grade 10: 19 students (6 boys, 13 girls); Grade 11: 27 students (19 boys, 8 girls); Grade 12: 32 students (17 boys, 15 girls). 80% of students are Lutheran Church–Missouri Synod.

Faculty School total: 14. In upper school: 5 men, 9 women; 5 have advanced degrees.

Subjects Offered Advanced math, algebra, American government, American literature, analysis, analytic geometry, anatomy and physiology, ancient world history, applied music, art, athletics, baseball, Basic programming, basketball, Bible studies, biology, biology-AP, calculus, cheerleading, chemistry, choir, Christian doctrine, Christian education, Christian ethics, Christian scripture, Christianity, church history, college counseling, communication skills, comparative religion, composition, contemporary art, earth science, English composition, English literature, geometry, government, graphic arts, health education, history, history of religion, instrumental music, Internet, Internet research, introduction to literature, keyboarding, Life of Christ, math analysis, New Testament, photography, physical education, physical science, physics, pre-algebra, psychology, sociology, Spanish, speech and oral interpretations, state history, statistics, student government, theater, theater production, track and field, trigonometry, U.S. government, volleyball, weightlifting.

Graduation Requirements Algebra, American government, American history, American literature, analytic geometry, art, arts and fine arts (art, music, dance, drama), Bible studies, biology, British literature, calculus, chemistry, church history, electives, geometry, health education, math analysis, modern world history, trigonometry, U.S. history.

Special Academic Programs Honors section; independent study; study at local college for college credit; remedial math.

College Admission Counseling 21 students graduated in 2010; 19 went to college, including Johnson County Community College; Kansas State University; Missouri State University; University of Central Missouri; University of Missouri. Other: 2 went to work. Mean SAT critical reading: 550, mean SAT math: 480, mean composite ACT: 24. 50% scored over 600 on SAT critical reading, 50% scored over 600 on SAT math, 25% scored over 26 on composite ACT.

Student Life Upper grades have specified standards of dress, student council, honor system. Discipline rests primarily with faculty.

Tuition and Aid Day student tuition: $6140–$9000. Tuition installment plan (monthly payment plans, individually arranged payment plans). Tuition reduction for siblings, need-based scholarship grants available. In 2010–11, 20% of upper-school students received aid. Total amount of financial aid awarded in 2010–11: $15,000.

Admissions Traditional secondary-level entrance grade is 9. For fall 2010, 120 students applied for upper-level admission, 120 were accepted, 120 enrolled. SLEP for foreign students required. Deadline for receipt of application materials: none. Application fee required: $275. On-campus interview required.

Athletics Interscholastic: baseball (boys), basketball (b,g), cheering (g), cross-country running (b,g), dance (g), dance team (g), fitness (b,g), golf (b), physical training (b,g), soccer (b,g), tennis (b,g), track and field (b,g), volleyball (g), weight lifting (b,g), weight training (b,g); coed intramural: basketball, bowling, golf, gymnastics, physical fitness, softball, volleyball, weight training. 2 coaches.

Computers Computers are regularly used in data processing, desktop publishing, journalism, photography, word processing classes. Computer network features include on-campus library services, Internet access, wireless campus network, Internet

filtering or blocking technology. Student e-mail accounts are available to students. Students grades are available online. The school has a published electronic and media policy.
Contact Mrs. Paula Meier, Registrar. 816-241-5478. Fax: 816-876-2069. E-mail: pmeier@lhskc.com. Web site: www.lhskc.com.

LUTHERAN HIGH SCHOOL IN MAYER
305 5th Street NE
Mayer, Minnesota 55360
Head of School: Joel Philip Landskroener
General Information Coeducational day college-preparatory, arts, religious studies, and technology school, affiliated with Lutheran Church–Missouri Synod; primarily serves students with learning disabilities and individuals with Attention Deficit Disorder. Grades 9–12. Founded: 1961. Setting: small town. Nearest major city is Minneapolis. 54-acre campus. 3 buildings on campus. Approved or accredited by National Lutheran School Accreditation, North Central Association of Colleges and Schools, and Minnesota Department of Education. Endowment: $3.9 million. Total enrollment: 252. Upper school average class size: 17. Upper school faculty-student ratio: 1:14. There are 174 required school days per year for Upper School students. Upper School students typically attend 5 days per week. The average school day consists of 6 hours and 20 minutes.
Upper School Student Profile Grade 9: 70 students (43 boys, 27 girls); Grade 10: 62 students (30 boys, 32 girls); Grade 11: 56 students (23 boys, 33 girls); Grade 12: 64 students (30 boys, 34 girls). 92% of students are Lutheran Church–Missouri Synod.
Faculty School total: 21. In upper school: 12 men, 9 women; 17 have advanced degrees.
Subjects Offered 1½ elective credits, algebra, American history, American history-AP, art, band, biology, ceramics, chemistry, choir, computer science, drawing, earth science, English, environmental science, fine arts, geometry, health, history, music, music appreciation, painting, physical education, physical science, physics, pre-calculus, psychology, religion, science, sculpture, Spanish, world geography, writing.
Graduation Requirements Arts and fine arts (art, music, dance, drama), computer science, English, foreign language, mathematics, physical education (includes health), religion (includes Bible studies and theology), science, social sciences, social studies (includes history).
Special Academic Programs 2 Advanced Placement exams for which test preparation is offered; honors section; accelerated programs; independent study; study at local college for college credit; academic accommodation for the gifted and the musically talented; remedial reading and/or remedial writing; remedial math; programs in English, mathematics for dyslexic students.
College Admission Counseling 44 students graduated in 2009; 40 went to college, including Grove City College; North Dakota State University; University of Minnesota, Duluth; University of Minnesota, Twin Cities Campus; University of Wisconsin–Stevens Point; Valparaiso University. Other: 1 went to work, 2 entered military service, 1 had other specific plans. Median composite ACT: 23. 11% scored over 26 on composite ACT.
Student Life Upper grades have specified standards of dress, student council. Discipline rests primarily with faculty. Attendance at religious services is required.
Tuition and Aid Day student tuition: $8200. Tuition installment plan (monthly payment plans, individually arranged payment plans, guaranteed tuition pre-payment plan). Need-based scholarship grants available. In 2009–10, 40% of upper-school students received aid. Total amount of financial aid awarded in 2009–10: $200,000.
Admissions Traditional secondary-level entrance grade is 9. For fall 2009, 76 students applied for upper-level admission, 76 were accepted, 73 enrolled. TOEFL or writing sample required. Application fee required: $100. Interview required.
Athletics Interscholastic: baseball (boys), basketball (b,g), cross-country running (b,g), dance (g), dance squad (g), dance team (g), danceline (g), football (b), golf (b,g), soccer (g), softball (g), swimming and diving (b,g), track and field (b,g), volleyball (g), wrestling (b); intramural: weight lifting (b,g); coed interscholastic: bowling. 1 PE instructor, 5 coaches, 1 athletic trainer.
Computers Computers are regularly used in all classes. Computer network features include on-campus library services, online commercial services, Internet access, wireless campus network, Internet filtering or blocking technology. Computer access in designated common areas is available to students. Students grades are available online. The school has a published electronic and media policy.
Contact Kevin W. Wilaby, Principal. 952-657-2251 Ext. 317. Fax: 952-657-2344. E-mail: kwilaby@lhsmayer.org. Web site: www.lhsmayer.org.

LUTHERAN HIGH SCHOOL NORTH
5401 Lucas Hunt Road
St. Louis, Missouri 63121
Head of School: Mr. William Lucas
General Information Coeducational day college-preparatory, arts, business, religious studies, bilingual studies, and technology school, affiliated with Lutheran Church. Grades 9–12. Founded: 1946. Setting: urban. 47-acre campus. 1 building on campus. Approved or accredited by Lutheran School Accreditation Commission, National Lutheran School Accreditation, North Central Association of Colleges and

Schools, and Missouri Department of Education. Endowment: $5.8 million. Total enrollment: 341. Upper school average class size: 20. Upper school faculty-student ratio: 1:10. There are 176 required school days per year for Upper School students. Upper School students typically attend 5 days per week. The average school day consists of 6 hours and 20 minutes.
Upper School Student Profile Grade 9: 76 students (42 boys, 34 girls); Grade 10: 85 students (33 boys, 52 girls); Grade 11: 86 students (52 boys, 34 girls); Grade 12: 94 students (43 boys, 51 girls). 47% of students are Lutheran.
Faculty School total: 33. In upper school: 22 men, 11 women; 26 have advanced degrees.
Subjects Offered Accounting, advanced chemistry, Advanced Placement courses, algebra, American history, American history-AP, American literature, anatomy, art, Bible studies, biology, business, business law, business skills, calculus, calculus-AP, ceramics, chemistry, child development, choir, Christian doctrine, Christian education, Christian ethics, Christian scripture, Christian studies, Christianity, church history, computer applications, computer multimedia, computer science, concert band, concert choir, data analysis, design, drawing, drawing and design, economics, English, English composition, English literature, English literature-AP, entrepreneurship, European history, family and consumer science, fashion, fine arts, finite math, food and nutrition, foods, French, geography, geometry, government, government/civics, health education, history, human anatomy, keyboarding, literature-AP, marketing, mathematics, media studies, multimedia design, music, organic chemistry, painting, physical education, physics, physiology, practical arts, pre-calculus, printmaking, probability and statistics, psychology, religion, research, science, social studies, society and culture, Spanish, speech, statistics, student publications, theology, U.S. government, U.S. history-AP, world geography, world history, world literature, world religions, writing.
Graduation Requirements American history, arts and fine arts (art, music, dance, drama), English, mathematics, physical education (includes health), practical arts, religion (includes Bible studies and theology), science, social studies (includes history), Saved to Serve (community service hours).
Special Academic Programs Advanced Placement exam preparation; honors section; independent study; study at local college for college credit.
College Admission Counseling 94 students graduated in 2010; 77 went to college, including Ball State University; Concordia University, Nebraska; Southeast Missouri State University; Truman State University; University of Central Missouri; University of Missouri. Other: 1 went to work, 2 entered military service, 2 entered a postgraduate year. 50% scored over 26 on composite ACT.
Student Life Upper grades have uniform requirement, student council, honor system. Discipline rests primarily with faculty. Attendance at religious services is required.
Summer Programs Enrichment, sports programs offered; session focuses on fundamentals and enrichment; held on campus; accepts boys and girls; not open to students from other schools. 150 students usually enrolled. 2011 schedule: June 1 to July 31.
Tuition and Aid Day student tuition: $9225–$10,425. Tuition installment plan (FACTS Tuition Payment Plan, monthly payment plans, individually arranged payment plans, semester payment plan, full-year payment plan with discount). Tuition reduction for siblings, merit scholarship grants, need-based scholarship grants available. In 2010–11, 60% of upper-school students received aid; total upper-school merit-scholarship money awarded: $22,000. Total amount of financial aid awarded in 2010–11: $600,000.
Admissions Traditional secondary-level entrance grade is 9. For fall 2010, 98 students applied for upper-level admission, 95 were accepted, 76 enrolled. ACT-Explore required. Deadline for receipt of application materials: none. Application fee required: $250. Interview recommended.
Athletics Interscholastic: baseball (boys), basketball (b,g), cheering (g), cross-country running (b,g), dance squad (g), football (b), golf (b), pom squad (g), soccer (b,g), softball (g), tennis (b,g), track and field (b,g), volleyball (g). 2 PE instructors.
Computers Computers are regularly used in art, business education, English, history, mathematics, science, social studies, yearbook classes. Computer network features include on-campus library services, Internet access, wireless campus network, Internet filtering or blocking technology, Internet College Work Program. Campus intranet and computer access in designated common areas are available to students. Students grades are available online. The school has a published electronic and media policy.
Contact Judy Knight, Records Clerk. 314-389-3100 Ext. 420. Fax: 314-389-3103. E-mail: jknight@lhsn.org. Web site: www.lhsn.org.

LUTHERAN HIGH SCHOOL NORTHWEST
1000 Bagley Avenue
Rochester Hills, Michigan 48309
Head of School: Mr. Paul Looker
General Information Coeducational day college-preparatory and religious studies school, affiliated with Lutheran Church–Missouri Synod. Grades 9–12. Founded: 1978. Setting: suburban. Nearest major city is Detroit. 30-acre campus. 1 building on campus. Approved or accredited by Michigan Association of Non-Public Schools, National Lutheran School Accreditation, North Central Association of Colleges and Schools, and Michigan Department of Education. Endowment: $1 million. Total enrollment: 284. Upper school average class size: 25. Upper school faculty-student

ratio: 1:16. There are 185 required school days per year for Upper School students. Upper School students typically attend 5 days per week. The average school day consists of 7 hours and 20 minutes.

Upper School Student Profile Grade 9: 79 students (49 boys, 30 girls); Grade 10: 69 students (38 boys, 31 girls); Grade 11: 69 students (35 boys, 34 girls); Grade 12: 67 students (30 boys, 37 girls). 75% of students are Lutheran Church–Missouri Synod.

Faculty School total: 19. In upper school: 12 men, 7 women; 15 have advanced degrees.

Subjects Offered Accounting, advanced chemistry, algebra, American history, American history-AP, art, audio visual/media, band, Basic programming, biology, biology-AP, bookkeeping, business, business mathematics, calculus, chemistry, chorus, computer science, drawing, drawing and design, Eastern world civilizations, economics, English, English-AP, geography, geometry, German, government/civics, graphic arts, law, mathematics, music, painting, physical education, physical science, physics-AP, psychology, Spanish, statistics-AP, theology, trigonometry, U.S. government and politics-AP, world history.

Graduation Requirements Arts and fine arts (art, music, dance, drama), English, mathematics, physical education (includes health), religion (includes Bible studies and theology), science, social sciences, social studies (includes history). Community service is required.

Special Academic Programs 6 Advanced Placement exams for which test preparation is offered; honors section; independent study; study at local college for college credit.

College Admission Counseling 67 students graduated in 2010; 65 went to college, including Central Michigan University; Concordia College; Michigan State University; Oakland University; University of Michigan; Western Michigan University. Other: 2 went to work. Median composite ACT: 24. 20% scored over 26 on composite ACT.

Student Life Upper grades have specified standards of dress, student council. Discipline rests primarily with faculty. Attendance at religious services is required.

Tuition and Aid Day student tuition: $7550. Tuition installment plan (monthly payment plans). Merit scholarship grants, need-based scholarship grants available. In 2010–11, 2% of upper-school students received aid; total upper-school merit-scholarship money awarded: $2000. Total amount of financial aid awarded in 2010–11: $2000.

Admissions Traditional secondary-level entrance grade is 9. For fall 2010, 79 students applied for upper-level admission, 79 were accepted, 79 enrolled. High School Placement Test required. Deadline for receipt of application materials: none. Application fee required: $350. On-campus interview required.

Athletics Interscholastic: baseball (boys), basketball (b,g), cheering (g), cross-country running (b,g), football (b), golf (b,g), soccer (b,g), softball (g), track and field (b,g), volleyball (g), wrestling (b); intramural: indoor soccer (b,g); coed intramural: badminton, fitness, physical fitness, physical training, tennis, weight training.

Computers Computers are regularly used in journalism, keyboarding, mathematics, media, research skills, word processing, yearbook classes. Computer network features include Internet access, Internet filtering or blocking technology. Students grades are available online. The school has a published electronic and media policy.

Contact Mr. Paul Looker, Principal. 248-852-6677. Fax: 248-852-2667. E-mail: plooker@lhsa.com. Web site: www.lhnw.lhsa.com.

LUTHERAN HIGH SCHOOL OF HAWAII

1404 University Avenue
Honolulu, Hawaii 96822-2494
Head of School: Arthur Gundell

General Information Coeducational day college-preparatory school, affiliated with Lutheran Church–Missouri Synod. Grades 9–12. Founded: 1988. Setting: urban. 1-acre campus. 3 buildings on campus. Approved or accredited by Lutheran School Accreditation Commission, The Hawaii Council of Private Schools, Western Association of Schools and Colleges, and Hawaii Department of Education. Member of Secondary School Admission Test Board. Endowment: $35,000. Total enrollment: 98. Upper school average class size: 12. Upper school faculty-student ratio: 1:7. There are 175 required school days per year for Upper School students. Upper School students typically attend 5 days per week. The average school day consists of 7 hours and 15 minutes.

Upper School Student Profile Grade 9: 26 students (11 boys, 15 girls); Grade 10: 20 students (11 boys, 9 girls); Grade 11: 33 students (19 boys, 14 girls); Grade 12: 19 students (12 boys, 7 girls). 13% of students are Lutheran Church–Missouri Synod.

Faculty School total: 14. In upper school: 8 men, 6 women; 7 have advanced degrees.

Subjects Offered 20th century history, 3-dimensional art, advanced math, Advanced Placement courses, algebra, American government, American history, American literature, analytic geometry, art, art-AP, Bible studies, biology, British literature, calculus, calculus-AP, chemistry, choir, computer applications, computer programming, computer science, concert band, consumer economics, drama, earth science, economics, English, English literature, European history, expository writing, fine arts, food and nutrition, geometry, government/civics, grammar, health, history, home economics, Japanese, journalism, keyboarding, life skills, marine biology, mathematics, music, oceanography, photography, physical education, physics, psychology, religion, science, social sciences, social studies, Spanish, speech, theater, world history, world literature.

Graduation Requirements Arts and fine arts (art, music, dance, drama), computer science, English, mathematics, physical education (includes health), religion (includes Bible studies and theology), science, social studies (includes history).

Special Academic Programs Advanced Placement exam preparation; honors section; study at local college for college credit; academic accommodation for the musically talented and the artistically talented.

College Admission Counseling 33 students graduated in 2010; all went to college, including Kapiolani Community College; University of Hawaii at Manoa. Median composite ACT: 23. Mean SAT critical reading: 525, mean SAT math: 530, mean SAT writing: 525. 10% scored over 600 on SAT critical reading, 15% scored over 600 on SAT math.

Student Life Upper grades have specified standards of dress, student council, honor system. Discipline rests primarily with faculty. Attendance at religious services is required.

Tuition and Aid Day student tuition: $8290–$10,250. Tuition installment plan (Insured Tuition Payment Plan). Tuition reduction for siblings, merit scholarship grants, need-based scholarship grants available. In 2010–11, 25% of upper-school students received aid; total upper-school merit-scholarship money awarded: $40,075. Total amount of financial aid awarded in 2010–11: $50,000.

Admissions Traditional secondary-level entrance grade is 9. For fall 2010, 57 students applied for upper-level admission, 56 were accepted, 34 enrolled. SSAT required. Deadline for receipt of application materials: none. Application fee required: $30. Interview recommended.

Athletics Interscholastic: baseball (boys), basketball (b,g), bowling (b,g), canoeing/kayaking (b,g), cross-country running (b,g), diving (b,g), golf (b,g), judo (b,g), kayaking (b,g), paddling (b,g), soccer (b,g), softball (g), swimming and diving (b,g), tennis (b,g), track and field (b,g), volleyball (b,g), water polo (b,g), wrestling (b,g); coed interscholastic: cheering, football, sailing, strength & conditioning; coed intramural: dance. 1 PE instructor, 5 coaches, 1 athletic trainer.

Computers Computers are regularly used in art, desktop publishing, English, history, journalism, library, mathematics, newspaper, photography, photojournalism, science, yearbook classes. Computer network features include on-campus library services, Internet access, Internet filtering or blocking technology. Students grades are available online. The school has a published electronic and media policy.

Contact Arthur Gundell, Principal. 808-949-5302. Fax: 808-947-3701. E-mail: gundell@lhshawaii.org. Web site: lhshawaii.org.

LUTHERAN HIGH SCHOOL OF SAN DIEGO

810 Buena Vista Way
Chula Vista, California 91910-6853
Head of School: Mr. Scott Dufresne

General Information Coeducational day and distance learning college-preparatory, arts, religious studies, and technology school, affiliated with Lutheran Church. Grades 9–12. Distance learning grades 9–12. Founded: 1975. Setting: urban. Nearest major city is San Diego. 9-acre campus. 6 buildings on campus. Approved or accredited by National Lutheran School Accreditation, Western Association of Schools and Colleges, and California Department of Education. Total enrollment: 78. Upper school average class size: 12. Upper school faculty-student ratio: 1:12. There are 180 required school days per year for Upper School students. Upper School students typically attend 5 days per week. The average school day consists of 6 hours and 30 minutes.

Upper School Student Profile Grade 9: 15 students (7 boys, 8 girls); Grade 10: 18 students (9 boys, 9 girls); Grade 11: 18 students (12 boys, 6 girls); Grade 12: 27 students (12 boys, 15 girls). 50% of students are Lutheran.

Faculty School total: 9. In upper school: 5 men, 4 women; 6 have advanced degrees.

Subjects Offered Accounting, acting, Advanced Placement courses, algebra, American government, American history, American literature, American literature-AP, analytic geometry, anatomy and physiology, applied arts, applied music, art, art appreciation, art history-AP, ASB Leadership, athletics, band, baseball, basketball, bell choir, Bible, biology, biology-AP, British literature, British literature-AP, calculus-AP, campus ministry, chemistry, choir, choral music, Christian education, Christian ethics, comparative religion, computer literacy, creative writing, drama, driver education, economics, English, English language and composition-AP, English language-AP, English literature and composition-AP, English literature-AP, English-AP, English/composition-AP, European history-AP, French, geometry, government, health education, history, music appreciation, physical education, physics, pre-calculus, softball, Spanish, Spanish language-AP, speech, student government, U.S. government and politics, yearbook.

Special Academic Programs Advanced Placement exam preparation.

College Admission Counseling 18 students graduated in 2010; 17 went to college, including Concordia University; Point Loma Nazarene University; San Diego State University; University of California, Irvine; University of California, Riverside. Other: 1 went to work. Mean SAT critical reading: 520, mean SAT math: 540, mean SAT writing: 550, mean combined SAT: 1522.

Student Life Upper grades have specified standards of dress, student council, honor system. Discipline rests primarily with faculty. Attendance at religious services is required.

Tuition and Aid Day student tuition: $7500. Tuition installment plan (monthly payment plans, individually arranged payment plans, Simply Giving—Thrivent Financial for Lutherans, Tuition Solution). Tuition reduction for siblings, merit scholarship grants, need-based scholarship grants available. In 2010–11, 31% of upper-school students received aid; total upper-school merit-scholarship money awarded: $8000. Total amount of financial aid awarded in 2010–11: $30,000.

Admissions Traditional secondary-level entrance grade is 9. Admissions testing required. Application fee required: $250. On-campus interview required.

Athletics Interscholastic: baseball (boys), basketball (b,g), cross-country running (b,g), football (b), softball (g), volleyball (g). 1 PE instructor, 10 coaches.

Computers Computer network features include on-campus library services, Internet access. Students grades are available online.

Contact Debbie Heien, Office Manager. 619-262-4444 Ext. 120. Fax: 603-691-0424. E-mail: debbie.heien@lhssd.org. Web site: www.lutheranhighsandiego.org.

LUTHERAN HIGH SCHOOL SOUTH

9515 Tesson Ferry Road
St. Louis, Missouri 63123-4317
Head of School: Mr. Brian Ryherd

General Information Coeducational day college-preparatory, arts, business, religious studies, and technology school, affiliated with Lutheran Church–Missouri Synod. Grades 9–12. Founded: 1957. Setting: suburban. 35-acre campus. 1 building on campus. Approved or accredited by National Lutheran School Accreditation, North Central Association of Colleges and Schools, and Missouri Department of Education. Endowment: $6.5 million. Total enrollment: 544. Upper school average class size: 21. Upper school faculty-student ratio: 1:14. There are 178 required school days per year for Upper School students. Upper School students typically attend 5 days per week. The average school day consists of 7 hours.

Upper School Student Profile Grade 9: 137 students (66 boys, 71 girls); Grade 10: 137 students (72 boys, 65 girls); Grade 11: 138 students (69 boys, 69 girls); Grade 12: 132 students (70 boys, 62 girls). 83% of students are Lutheran Church–Missouri Synod.

Faculty School total: 41. In upper school: 27 men, 14 women; 30 have advanced degrees.

Subjects Offered Accounting, algebra, American history, American history-AP, American literature, anatomy, art, art history, band, biology, biology-AP, business, business skills, calculus, calculus-AP, ceramics, chemistry, chorus, community service, composition, composition-AP, computer programming, computer science, consumer economics, creative writing, current events, drafting, drama, drawing, earth science, economics, English, English literature, English literature-AP, family studies, fine arts, food science, French, geography, geometry, German, government/civics, health, jazz, journalism, keyboarding, leadership, literature, mathematics, music history, music theory, nutrition, physical education, physics, physiology, psychology, reading, religion, robotics, science, sculpture, social sciences, sociology, Spanish, speech, technology, theater, theology, trigonometry, woodworking, world history, world literature, writing, yearbook.

Graduation Requirements Arts and fine arts (art, music, dance, drama), business skills (includes word processing), English, mathematics, physical education (includes health), religion (includes Bible studies and theology), science, social sciences, social studies (includes history), service component (30 hours per year).

Special Academic Programs Advanced Placement exam preparation; honors section; independent study; study at local college for college credit; remedial reading and/or remedial writing; remedial math; programs in English, mathematics, general development for dyslexic students.

College Admission Counseling 106 students graduated in 2010; all went to college, including Missouri State University; Saint Louis University; Southeast Missouri State University; Truman State University; University of Missouri; Webster University. Median composite ACT: 25. 33% scored over 26 on composite ACT.

Student Life Upper grades have uniform requirement, student council. Discipline rests primarily with faculty. Attendance at religious services is required.

Tuition and Aid Day student tuition: $10,425. Tuition installment plan (FACTS Tuition Payment Plan, monthly payment plans, individually arranged payment plans, 3% discount for paying in full by July 1 prior to the start of school). Tuition reduction for siblings, merit scholarship grants, need-based scholarship grants, paying campus jobs available. In 2010–11, 34% of upper-school students received aid; total upper-school merit-scholarship money awarded: $13,000. Total amount of financial aid awarded in 2010–11: $750,000.

Admissions Traditional secondary-level entrance grade is 9. For fall 2010, 159 students applied for upper-level admission, 157 were accepted, 137 enrolled. Explore required. Deadline for receipt of application materials: none. Application fee required: $250. On-campus interview required.

Athletics Interscholastic: baseball (boys), basketball (b,g), cheering (g), cross-country running (b,g), dance squad (g), diving (g), field hockey (g), football (b), golf (b,g), hockey (b), ice hockey (b), soccer (b,g), softball (g), swimming and diving (g), tennis (b,g), track and field (b,g), volleyball (g); coed intramural: bowling, table tennis, tennis. 1 PE instructor, 10 coaches, 1 athletic trainer.

Computers Computers are regularly used in accounting, drafting, drawing and design, English, industrial technology, journalism, keyboarding, mathematics, religion, science, social sciences classes. Computer network features include on-campus library services, online commercial services, Internet access, wireless campus network, Internet filtering or blocking technology. Student e-mail accounts and computer access in designated common areas are available to students. Students grades are available online. The school has a published electronic and media policy.

Contact Mrs. Jayne Lauer, Director of Recruitment and Public Relations. 314-631-1400 Ext. 426. Fax: 314-631-7762. E-mail: jlauer@lhssonline.org. Web site: www.lhssonline.org.

LUTHER COLLEGE HIGH SCHOOL

1500 Royal Street
Regina, Saskatchewan S4T 5A5, Canada
Head of School: Mr. Mark Anderson

General Information Coeducational boarding and day college-preparatory, general academic, arts, religious studies, International Baccalaureate, and ESL school, affiliated with Lutheran Church. Grades 9–12. Founded: 1913. Setting: urban. Nearest major city is Winnipeg, MB, Canada. Students are housed in single-sex dormitories. 27-acre campus. 5 buildings on campus. Approved or accredited by Saskatchewan Department of Education. Language of instruction: English. Endowment: CAN$600,000. Total enrollment: 370. Upper school average class size: 20. Upper school faculty-student ratio: 1:16. There are 190 required school days per year for Upper School students. Upper School students typically attend 5 days per week. The average school day consists of 7 hours.

Upper School Student Profile 20% of students are boarding students. 84% are province residents. 5 provinces are represented in upper school student body. 16% are international students. International students from China, Germany, Hong Kong, Republic of Korea, Taiwan, and Thailand; 7 other countries represented in student body. 22% of students are Lutheran.

Faculty School total: 34. In upper school: 20 men, 14 women; 5 have advanced degrees; 2 reside on campus.

Subjects Offered Band, biology, calculus, chemistry, choir, Christian ethics, computer science, drama, English, ESL, French, German, handbells, history, information processing, International Baccalaureate courses, Latin, mathematics, music, orchestra, physical fitness, physics, psychology, science, video film production.

Graduation Requirements Christian ethics, English, mathematics, science, social studies (includes history).

Special Academic Programs International Baccalaureate program; independent study; study at local college for college credit; study abroad; academic accommodation for the gifted; ESL (15 students enrolled).

College Admission Counseling 115 students graduated in 2010; 98 went to college, including Queen's University at Kingston; University of Alberta; University of Regina; University of Saskatchewan; University of Toronto. Other: 10 went to work, 7 had other specific plans.

Student Life Upper grades have specified standards of dress, student council. Discipline rests primarily with faculty. Attendance at religious services is required.

Tuition and Aid Day student tuition: CAN$10,360; 7-day tuition and room/board: CAN$18,210. Tuition installment plan (monthly payment plans, individually arranged payment plans). Tuition reduction for siblings, bursaries, merit scholarship grants, need-based scholarship grants available. In 2010–11, 20% of upper-school students received aid; total upper-school merit-scholarship money awarded: CAN$30,000. Total amount of financial aid awarded in 2010–11: CAN$165,000.

Admissions Traditional secondary-level entrance grade is 9. For fall 2010, 134 students applied for upper-level admission, 118 were accepted, 118 enrolled. English entrance exam required. Deadline for receipt of application materials: none. Application fee required: CAN$300.

Athletics Interscholastic: badminton (boys, girls), baseball (b), basketball (b,g), bicycling (b,g), cheering (g), cross-country running (b,g), curling (b,g), football (b), golf (b,g), hockey (b,g), pom squad (g), rugby (b,g), soccer (b,g), softball (g), volleyball (g); intramural: basketball (b,g), floor hockey (b,g), soccer (b,g), volleyball (g); coed interscholastic: badminton, curling, pom squad, track and field; coed intramural: aerobics/dance, basketball, curling, floor hockey, football, outdoor education, table tennis, ultimate Frisbee. 4 PE instructors, 28 coaches, 2 athletic trainers.

Computers Computers are regularly used in all academic, yearbook classes. Computer network features include Internet access, wireless campus network, Internet filtering or blocking technology. Student e-mail accounts and computer access in designated common areas are available to students.

Contact Ms. Alanna Kalyniuk, Registrar. 306-791-9154. Fax: 306-359-6962. E-mail: lutherhs@luthercollege.edu. Web site: www.luthercollege.edu.

LUTHER HIGH SCHOOL NORTH

5700 West Berteau Avenue
Chicago, Illinois 60634
Head of School: Mr. Thomas E. Wiemann

General Information Coeducational day and distance learning college-preparatory, general academic, arts, business, religious studies, and technology school, affiliated with Lutheran Church–Missouri Synod, Evangelical Lutheran Church in America. Grades 9–12. Distance learning grades 10–12. Founded: 1909. Setting: urban. 10-acre campus. 1 building on campus. Approved or accredited by Evangelical Lutheran Church in America, National Lutheran School Accreditation, North Central Association of Colleges and Schools, and Illinois Department of Education. Endowment: $20,000. Total enrollment: 180. Upper school average class size: 16. Upper school faculty-student ratio: 1:16. There are 179 required school days per year for Upper School students. Upper School students typically attend 5 days per week. The average school day consists of 7 hours.

Upper School Student Profile Grade 9: 45 students (25 boys, 20 girls); Grade 10: 40 students (20 boys, 20 girls); Grade 11: 54 students (29 boys, 25 girls); Grade 12: 41 students (21 boys, 20 girls). 47% of students are Lutheran Church–Missouri Synod, Evangelical Lutheran Church in America.

Faculty School total: 17. In upper school: 7 men, 10 women; 14 have advanced degrees.

Subjects Offered 20th century history, 3-dimensional art, accounting, ACT preparation, advanced computer applications, algebra, American legal systems, anatomy, art, astronomy, band, biology, business, calculus, ceramics, chemistry, chorus, composition, computer science, crafts, drawing, economics, English, English-AP, fine arts, geography, geometry, German, government-AP, government/civics, health, keyboarding, law, mathematics, music, painting, photography, physical education, physics, physiology, psychology, public speaking, reading, science, sewing, social sciences, social studies, Spanish, study skills, theology, trigonometry, U.S. history, word processing.

Graduation Requirements Arts and fine arts (art, music, dance, drama), English, foreign language, mathematics, physical education (includes health), religion (includes Bible studies and theology), science, social sciences, social studies (includes history), word processing, summative portfolio demonstration of faculty selected, extra and co-curricular participation annually.

Special Academic Programs Advanced Placement exam preparation; honors section; accelerated programs; independent study; study at local college for college credit; academic accommodation for the gifted, the musically talented, and the artistically talented; remedial reading and/or remedial writing; remedial math; programs in general development for dyslexic students; special instructional classes for students with learning differences.

College Admission Counseling 54 students graduated in 2010; 48 went to college, including Concordia University; DePaul University; Northeastern Illinois University; University of Illinois at Chicago; University of Illinois at Urbana–Champaign; Valparaiso University. Other: 2 went to work, 2 entered military service, 2 had other specific plans. Median composite ACT: 23. 20% scored over 26 on composite ACT.

Student Life Upper grades have specified standards of dress, student council. Discipline rests primarily with faculty. Attendance at religious services is required.

Summer Programs Remediation, enrichment, advancement, sports, computer instruction programs offered; session focuses on academics and enrichment for credit; held on campus; accepts boys and girls; open to students from other schools. 300 students usually enrolled. 2011 schedule: June 21 to July 29. Application deadline: June 20.

Tuition and Aid Day student tuition: $7600. Tuition installment plan (Insured Tuition Payment Plan, Academic Management Services Plan, monthly payment plans, individually arranged payment plans). Tuition reduction for siblings, merit scholarship grants, need-based scholarship grants, paying campus jobs available. In 2010–11, 70% of upper-school students received aid; total upper-school merit-scholarship money awarded: $30,000.

Admissions Traditional secondary-level entrance grade is 9. For fall 2010, 75 students applied for upper-level admission, 64 were accepted, 62 enrolled. Admissions testing and Stanford Achievement Test, Otis-Lennon School Ability Test required. Deadline for receipt of application materials: none. Application fee required: $175. On-campus interview recommended.

Athletics Interscholastic: baseball (boys), basketball (b,g), cross-country running (b,g), football (b), indoor track & field (b,g), softball (g), track and field (b,g), volleyball (g); coed interscholastic: indoor track; coed intramural: bowling. 2 PE instructors, 10 coaches, 1 athletic trainer.

Computers Computers are regularly used in all academic classes. Computer network features include on-campus library services, online commercial services, Internet access, wireless campus network, Internet filtering or blocking technology, workshops for students and parents in technology. Student e-mail accounts and computer access in designated common areas are available to students. Students grades are available online. The school has a published electronic and media policy.

Contact Mr. Sam Radom, Admissions Assistant. 773-286-3600. Fax: 773-286-0304. E-mail: sradom@luthernorth.org. Web site: www.luthernorth.org.

LYCEE CLAUDEL

1635 Promenade Riverside
Ottawa, Ontario K1G 0E5, Canada

Head of School: Mme. Joëlle Emorine

General Information Coeducational day and distance learning college-preparatory school. Grades 1–12. Distance learning grade X. Founded: 1962. Setting: suburban. 2-hectare campus. 1 building on campus. Approved or accredited by French Ministry of Education and Ontario Department of Education. Language of instruction: French. Endowment: CAN$6 million. Total enrollment: 976. Upper school average class size: 24. Upper school faculty-student ratio: 1:18. There are 174 required school days per year for Upper School students. Upper School students typically attend 5 days per week. The average school day consists of 6 hours and 30 minutes.

Upper School Student Profile Grade 6: 71 students (33 boys, 38 girls); Grade 7: 68 students (34 boys, 34 girls); Grade 8: 77 students (38 boys, 39 girls); Grade 9: 78 students (39 boys, 39 girls); Grade 10: 68 students (31 boys, 37 girls); Grade 11: 70 students (38 boys, 32 girls); Grade 12: 46 students (21 boys, 25 girls).

Faculty School total: 45. In upper school: 15 men, 30 women; 30 have advanced degrees.

Subjects Offered Advanced biology, advanced chemistry, advanced math, Advanced Placement courses, algebra, all academic, anatomy, anatomy and physiology, ancient world history, applied arts, applied music, archaeology, art and culture, art history, arts, arts and crafts, band, biology, botany, calculus, Canadian geography, Canadian history, Canadian literature, chemistry, classics, composition, computer education, computer technologies, consumer economics, current events, current history, drawing, ecology, ecology, environmental systems, economics, economics and history, English, English composition, English language and composition-AP, English language-AP, English literature, English literature-AP, English-AP, equality and freedom, ESL, European civilization, European history, experimental science, film and literature, fitness, foreign language, French, French as a second language, French studies, general math, general science, geography, geology, geometry, grammar, gymnastics, health and safety, health education, history, human anatomy, human biology, human development, human issues, human relations, human sexuality, lab science, language-AP, Latin, Latin History, literacy, literature and composition-AP, literature-AP, math analysis, math applications, mathematics, music, music history, music performance, oral communications, oral expression, organic biochemistry, organic chemistry, painting, philosophy, physical education, physics, political economy, reading, reading/study skills, science, science and technology, science project, social education, society, society and culture, sports, technology.

Special Academic Programs International Baccalaureate program; Advanced Placement exam preparation; academic accommodation for the musically talented; ESL (50 students enrolled).

College Admission Counseling 50 students graduated in 2009; all went to college, including Carleton University; McGill University; Queen's University at Kingston; University of Ottawa; University of Toronto; Wellesley College.

Student Life Upper grades have student council. Discipline rests primarily with faculty.

Tuition and Aid Day student tuition: CAN$6500–CAN$7000. Tuition installment plan (monthly payment plans). Bursaries available. In 2009–10, 4% of upper-school students received aid.

Admissions Traditional secondary-level entrance grade is 10. For fall 2009, 100 students applied for upper-level admission, 100 were accepted, 100 enrolled. Deadline for receipt of application materials: June 15. Application fee required: CAN$100. Interview required.

Athletics Interscholastic: badminton (boys), judo (b,g); coed intramural: badminton, basketball, handball, jogging, judo. 4 PE instructors.

Computers Computer resources include on-campus library services, online commercial services, Internet access.

Contact Mme. Jacqueline Hessel, Registrar. 613-733-8522 Ext. 606. Fax: 613-733-3782. E-mail: secretariat.lycee@claudel.org.

LYCEE FRANÇAIS DE NEW YORK

505 East 75th Street
New York, New York 10021

Head of School: Yves Thézé

General Information Coeducational day college-preparatory and bilingual studies school. Grades N–12. Founded: 1935. Setting: urban. 7-acre campus. 1 building on campus. Approved or accredited by French Ministry of Education, New York State Association of Independent Schools, and New York Department of Education. Languages of instruction: English and French. Endowment: $11 million. Total enrollment: 1,371. Upper school average class size: 22. Upper school faculty-student ratio: 1:9.

Upper School Student Profile Grade 6: 94 students (37 boys, 57 girls); Grade 7: 90 students (48 boys, 42 girls); Grade 8: 86 students (35 boys, 51 girls); Grade 9: 81 students (37 boys, 44 girls); Grade 10: 96 students (38 boys, 58 girls); Grade 11: 93 students (46 boys, 47 girls); Grade 12: 100 students (45 boys, 55 girls).

Faculty School total: 143. In upper school: 28 men, 45 women; 65 have advanced degrees.

Subjects Offered Algebra, American history, American literature, art, art history, biology, calculus, chemistry, computer science, creative writing, earth science, economics, English, English literature, English literature-AP, European history, fine arts, French, French language-AP, French literature-AP, geography, geometry, German, German-AP, government/civics, Greek, health, history, Italian, Latin, Mandarin, mathematics, music, philosophy, physical education, physics, science, social sciences, social studies, Spanish, Spanish language-AP, Spanish literature-AP, trigonometry, world history, world literature, writing.

Graduation Requirements Arts and fine arts (art, music, dance, drama), computer science, English, foreign language, French, Latin, mathematics, physical education (includes health), physical fitness, science, social sciences, requirements for the French baccalaureate differ.

Special Academic Programs International Baccalaureate program; Advanced Placement exam preparation; honors section; accelerated programs; independent study; term-away projects; study abroad; ESL (57 students enrolled).

College Admission Counseling 94 students graduated in 2009; 91 went to college, including Bard College; Columbia University; McGill University; New York

University; The Johns Hopkins University; University of Chicago. Other: 3 had other specific plans. Median SAT critical reading: 580, median SAT math: 615, median SAT writing: 620, median combined SAT: 1820. 48% scored over 600 on SAT critical reading, 58% scored over 600 on SAT math, 57% scored over 600 on SAT writing, 55% scored over 1800 on combined SAT.

Student Life Upper grades have specified standards of dress, student council, honor system. Discipline rests primarily with faculty.

Tuition and Aid Day student tuition: $22,650. Tuition installment plan (Academic Management Services Plan, individually arranged payment plans). Need-based scholarship grants, French government financial assistance available. In 2009–10, 25% of upper-school students received aid.

Admissions For fall 2009, 134 students applied for upper-level admission, 108 were accepted, 84 enrolled. Deadline for receipt of application materials: none. Application fee required: $200. On-campus interview recommended.

Athletics Interscholastic: basketball (boys, girls), gymnastics (g), soccer (b,g), tennis (b,g), volleyball (g); coed interscholastic: cross-country running, golf, running, softball, swimming and diving, track and field; coed intramural: alpine skiing, badminton, ballet, basketball, dance, fencing, fitness, gymnastics, ice skating, in-line skating, indoor soccer, judo, martial arts, modern dance, physical fitness, physical training, roller blading, rugby, skiing (downhill), snowboarding, soccer, strength & conditioning, table tennis, tennis, volleyball, weight lifting, weight training, yoga. 8 PE instructors, 5 coaches.

Computers Computers are regularly used in all academic, yearbook classes. Computer network features include on-campus library services, online commercial services, Internet access, wireless campus network, Internet filtering or blocking technology.

Contact Martine Lala, Director of Admissions. 212-439-3827. Fax: 212-439-4215. E-mail: mlala@lfny.org. Web site: www.lfny.org.

THE LYCEE INTERNATIONAL, AMERICAN SECTION

rue du Fer-a-Cheval
BP 70107
Saint-Germain-en-Laye Cedex 78101, France
Head of School: Mr. Sean Lynch

General Information Coeducational day college-preparatory and bilingual studies school. Grades PK–12. Founded: 1952. Setting: suburban. Nearest major city is Paris, France. 10-acre campus. 6 buildings on campus. Approved or accredited by French Ministry of Education and The College Board. Member of European Council of International Schools. Languages of instruction: English and French. Total enrollment: 705. Upper school average class size: 20. Upper school faculty-student ratio: 1:18. Upper School students typically attend 5 days per week. The average school day consists of 8 hours and 30 minutes.

Upper School Student Profile Grade 10: 63 students (27 boys, 36 girls); Grade 11: 54 students (19 boys, 35 girls); Grade 12: 55 students (19 boys, 36 girls).

Faculty School total: 20. In upper school: 5 men, 4 women; 6 have advanced degrees.

Subjects Offered Algebra, American history, American literature, art, biology, botany, calculus, chemistry, computer math, computer programming, computer science, drama, Dutch, economics, English, English literature, English-AP, European history, French, geography, geometry, German, grammar, Greek, health, history, Italian, Latin, mathematics, music, philosophy, physical education, physics, Russian, science, social sciences, social studies, Spanish, statistics, theater, trigonometry, world history, world literature, writing, zoology.

Graduation Requirements English, foreign language, French, mathematics, physical education (includes health), science, social sciences, social studies (includes history), examination (French Baccalaureate with International option).

Special Academic Programs Advanced Placement exam preparation; honors section.

College Admission Counseling 63 students graduated in 2010; all went to college, including Duke University; Harvard University; McGill University; New York University; Rhode Island School of Design; Tufts University. 73.4% scored over 600 on SAT critical reading, 73.4% scored over 600 on SAT math.

Student Life Upper grades have student council. Discipline rests primarily with faculty.

Tuition and Aid Day student tuition: €3250–€7500. Tuition installment plan (monthly payment plans). Tuition reduction for siblings, need-based scholarship grants available. In 2010–11, 5% of upper-school students received aid. Total amount of financial aid awarded in 2010–11: €30,000.

Admissions Traditional secondary-level entrance grade is 10. For fall 2010, 34 students applied for upper-level admission, 10 were accepted, 8 enrolled. Admissions testing required. Deadline for receipt of application materials: none. Application fee required: $250. On-campus interview recommended.

Athletics Intramural: badminton (boys, girls), basketball (b,g), climbing (b,g), judo (b), martial arts (b), rugby (b), soccer (b,g), tennis (b,g), track and field (b,g), volleyball (b,g), wall climbing (b,g); coed intramural: swimming and diving, table tennis. 9 PE instructors.

Computers Computers are regularly used in mathematics, technology classes. Computer resources include on-campus library services, Internet access.

Contact Mrs. Mary Friel, Director of Admissions. 33-1-34-51-90-92. Fax: 33-1 30 87 00 49. E-mail: admissions@americansection.org. Web site: www.americansection.org.

LYDIA PATTERSON INSTITUTE

517 South Florence Street
El Paso, Texas 79901-2998
Head of School: Mr. Hector Lachica

General Information Coeducational day college-preparatory, arts, religious studies, bilingual studies, and technology school, affiliated with United Methodist Church. Grades 9–12. Founded: 1913. Setting: urban. 1-acre campus. 5 buildings on campus. Approved or accredited by Southern Association of Colleges and Schools, University Senate of United Methodist Church, and Texas Department of Education. Languages of instruction: English and Spanish. Endowment: $5 million. Total enrollment: 399. Upper school average class size: 20. Upper school faculty-student ratio: 1:20. There are 183 required school days per year for Upper School students. Upper School students typically attend 5 days per week. The average school day consists of 6 hours and 45 minutes.

Upper School Student Profile Grade 9: 40 students (21 boys, 19 girls); Grade 10: 49 students (24 boys, 25 girls); Grade 11: 56 students (24 boys, 32 girls); Grade 12: 86 students (39 boys, 47 girls). 2% of students are United Methodist Church.

Faculty School total: 26. In upper school: 16 men, 10 women; 5 have advanced degrees.

Subjects Offered Computer science, economics, English, fine arts, foreign language, health, mathematics, physical education, religion, U.S. government, U.S. history, world geography, world history.

Graduation Requirements Arts and fine arts (art, music, dance, drama), computer science, economics, English, foreign language, mathematics, physical education (includes health), religion (includes Bible studies and theology), science, U.S. government, U.S. history, world history, world history, world geography.

Special Academic Programs International Baccalaureate program; Advanced Placement exam preparation; honors section; accelerated programs; independent study; study at local college for college credit; academic accommodation for the gifted; special instructional classes for deaf students; ESL (182 students enrolled).

College Admission Counseling 82 students graduated in 2010; 79 went to college, including El Paso Community College; MacMurray College; The University of Texas at El Paso. Other: 3 went to work. Median SAT critical reading: 400, median SAT math: 401, median SAT writing: 380, median combined SAT: 1170.

Student Life Upper grades have uniform requirement, student council. Discipline rests equally with students and faculty. Attendance at religious services is required.

Summer Programs Remediation, advancement, ESL programs offered; session focuses on advancement; held on campus; accepts boys and girls; open to students from other schools. 165 students usually enrolled. 2011 schedule: May 31 to July 5. Application deadline: May 27.

Tuition and Aid Day student tuition: $2430. Tuition installment plan (monthly payment plans). Need-based scholarship grants available. In 2010–11, 30% of upper-school students received aid. Total amount of financial aid awarded in 2010–11: $157,950.

Admissions Traditional secondary-level entrance grade is 9. English entrance exam required. Deadline for receipt of application materials: none. Application fee required: $270. On-campus interview required.

Athletics Interscholastic: basketball (boys, girls), cross-country running (b,g), dance (b), soccer (b,g), track and field (b,g), volleyball (b,g), weight lifting (b,g); intramural: baseball (b), basketball (b,g), dance (b), soccer (b,g), track and field (b,g), volleyball (b,g); coed interscholastic: dance team. 2 PE instructors, 4 coaches.

Computers Computers are regularly used in yearbook classes. Computer network features include on-campus library services, online commercial services, Internet access, wireless campus network. Campus intranet and student e-mail accounts are available to students.

Contact Mr. Hector Lachica, Vice President for Academic Affairs. 915-533-8286 Ext. 20. Fax: 915-533-5236. E-mail: hlachica@lydiapattersoninstitute.org. Web site: www.lydiapattersoninstitute.org.

LYMAN WARD MILITARY ACADEMY

PO Box 550 P
174 Ward Circle
Camp Hill, Alabama 36850-0550
Head of School: Col. Albert W. Jenrette

General Information Boys' boarding and distance learning college-preparatory and military school, affiliated with Christian faith; primarily serves underachievers. Grades 6–12. Distance learning grades 11–12. Founded: 1898. Setting: small town. Nearest major city is Birmingham. Students are housed in single-sex dormitories. 300-acre campus. 23 buildings on campus. Approved or accredited by Southern Association of Colleges and Schools and Alabama Department of Education. Total enrollment: 115. Upper school average class size: 15. Upper school faculty-student ratio: 1:15. There are 180 required school days per year for Upper School students. Upper School students typically attend 5 days per week. The average school day consists of 7 hours.

Upper School Student Profile Grade 6: 15 students (15 boys); Grade 7: 15 students (15 boys); Grade 8: 15 students (15 boys); Grade 9: 15 students (15 boys); Grade 10: 20 students (20 boys); Grade 11: 15 students (15 boys); Grade 12: 25 students (25 boys). 100% of students are boarding students. 25% are state residents. 15 states are represented in upper school student body. 1% are international students. International students from Colombia, Germany, Guatemala, and Mexico; 4 other countries represented in student body. 85% of students are Christian faith.

Faculty School total: 14. In upper school: 8 men, 4 women; 6 have advanced degrees; 2 reside on campus.

Subjects Offered Advanced Placement courses, algebra, band, biology, chemistry, computers, economics, English, geometry, government, health, JROTC, physical science, physiology, pre-algebra, pre-calculus, reading, Spanish, trigonometry, U.S. history, world history.

Special Academic Programs Advanced Placement exam preparation; honors section; remedial reading and/or remedial writing; remedial math.

College Admission Counseling 18 students graduated in 2010; 15 went to college, including Auburn University; Clemson University; Florida State University; North Georgia College & State University; The Citadel, The Military College of South Carolina; The University of Alabama. Other: 1 went to work, 2 entered military service. 5% scored over 600 on SAT critical reading, 5% scored over 600 on SAT math, 5% scored over 26 on composite ACT.

Student Life Upper grades have uniform requirement, student council, honor system. Discipline rests primarily with faculty. Attendance at religious services is required.

Summer Programs Remediation, enrichment, advancement, rigorous outdoor training programs offered; session focuses on leadership training through challenging exercises; held both on and off campus; held at Lake Martin, Natahalla River, and Mt. Cheaha; accepts boys; open to students from other schools. 25 students usually enrolled. 2011 schedule: June 16 to July 11. Application deadline: none.

Tuition and Aid 7-day tuition and room/board: $16,000. Tuition installment plan (monthly payment plans). Tuition reduction for siblings, merit scholarship grants, need-based scholarship grants available. In 2010–11, 10% of upper-school students received aid. Total amount of financial aid awarded in 2010–11: $50,000.

Admissions Traditional secondary-level entrance grade is 10. Star-9 required. Deadline for receipt of application materials: none. Application fee required: $250. Interview recommended.

Athletics Interscholastic: baseball, basketball, drill team, football, JROTC drill, marksmanship, riflery, soccer; intramural: aquatics, archery, basketball, billiards, canoeing/kayaking, cross-country running, drill team, fishing, fitness, flag football, football, Frisbee, hiking/backpacking, JROTC drill, life saving, marksmanship, outdoor activities, physical fitness, physical training, project adventure, rafting, rappelling, riflery, ropes courses, running, soccer, softball, strength & conditioning, swimming and diving, table tennis, tennis, ultimate Frisbee, volleyball. 2 PE instructors, 3 coaches, 1 athletic trainer.

Computers Computer resources include on-campus library services, Internet access, Internet filtering or blocking technology. Student e-mail accounts are available to students. The school has a published electronic and media policy.

Contact Maj. Joe C. Watson, Assistant to the President/Admissions. 256-896-4127. Fax: 256-896-4661. E-mail: info@lwma.org. Web site: www.lwma.org.

LYNDON INSTITUTE

PO Box 127
College Road
Lyndon Center, Vermont 05850-0127

General Information Coeducational boarding and day college-preparatory, general academic, arts, business, technology, and ESL school. Boarding grades 8–12, day grades 9–12. Founded: 1867. Setting: small town. Nearest major city is Burlington. Students are housed in single-sex dormitories. 150-acre campus. 27 buildings on campus. Approved or accredited by Independent Schools of Northern New England, New England Association of Schools and Colleges, The Association of Boarding Schools, and Vermont Department of Education. Endowment: $8 million. Upper school average class size: 15. Upper school faculty-student ratio: 1:10.

Tuition and Aid Day student tuition: $14,004; 5-day tuition and room/board: $28,280; 7-day tuition and room/board: $39,600. Tuition installment plan (monthly payment plans, individually arranged payments). Need-based scholarships/grants, prepGATE loans available. In 2010–11, 2% of upper-school students received aid. Total amount of financial aid awarded in 2010–11: $14,150.

Admissions Traditional secondary-level entrance grade is 9. TOEFL or SLEP, SSAT, ERB, PSAT, SAT, PLAN, or ACT required. Deadline for receipt of application materials: March 31. Application fee required: $50. Interview recommended.

See Display on this page and Close-Up on page 802.

Discover

Lyndon
INSTITUTE

*A co-educational,
day and boarding school offering
a college preparatory course of study
in a campus-style setting in
Northeastern Vermont.*

*Lyndon Institute is large enough
to offer a comprehensive education,
but small enough to involve each student
meaningfully in school life.*

Mary B. Thomas, *Assistant Head for Admissions*
College Road, P.O. Box 127, Lyndon Center, VT 05850
phone: 802-626-5232
website: www.LyndonInstitute.org
email: Mary.Thomas@LyndonInstitute.org

MA'AYANOT YESHIVA HIGH SCHOOL FOR GIRLS OF BERGAN COUNTY

1650 Palisade Avenue
Teaneck, New Jersey 07666
Head of School: Mrs. Rookie Billet
General Information Girls' day college-preparatory and religious studies school, affiliated with Jewish faith. Grades 9–12. Founded: 1995. Setting: suburban. 1 building on campus. Approved or accredited by Middle States Association of Colleges and Schools and New Jersey Department of Education. Languages of instruction: English and Hebrew. Total enrollment: 221. Upper school average class size: 18. Upper school faculty-student ratio: 1:5. There are 155 required school days per year for Upper School students. Upper School students typically attend 5 days per week. The average school day consists of 9 hours and 15 minutes.
Upper School Student Profile Grade 9: 46 students (46 girls); Grade 10: 60 students (60 girls); Grade 11: 64 students (64 girls); Grade 12: 51 students (51 girls). 100% of students are Jewish.
Faculty School total: 45. In upper school: 6 men, 39 women.
Subjects Offered 20th century world history, advanced biology, advanced chemistry, advanced math, Advanced Placement courses, algebra, American culture, American government, American literature, American sign language, Bible, Bible studies, biology, biology-AP, calculus, calculus-AP, chemistry, chemistry-AP, college writing, computer programming, computer skills, creative writing, desktop publishing, geometry, health education, Hebrew, Hebrew scripture, history, honors English, Jewish history, Jewish studies, Judaic studies, lab science, language and composition, literature, model United Nations, physical education, physics, pre-calculus, psychology-AP, senior internship, Spanish, speech, statistics-AP, Talmud, the Sixties, U.S. government, world history.
Graduation Requirements Algebra, art, biology, chemistry, English, geometry, Hebrew, history, physical education (includes health), physics, technology.
Special Academic Programs Advanced Placement exam preparation.
College Admission Counseling 68 students graduated in 2009; all went to college, including Queens College of the City University of New York; Rutgers, The State University of New Jersey, New Brunswick; Yeshiva University.
Student Life Upper grades have specified standards of dress, student council. Discipline rests primarily with faculty. Attendance at religious services is required.
Tuition and Aid Day student tuition: $18,500. Tuition installment plan (FACTS Tuition Payment Plan). Need-based scholarship grants available. In 2009–10, 22% of upper-school students received aid.
Admissions Traditional secondary-level entrance grade is 9. For fall 2009, 100 students applied for upper-level admission, 80 were accepted, 52 enrolled. Board of Jewish Education Entrance Exam required. Deadline for receipt of application materials: none. Application fee required: $75. Interview required.
Athletics Interscholastic: basketball, indoor soccer, softball, swimming and diving, track and field, volleyball. 2 PE instructors, 8 coaches.
Computers Computers are regularly used in all academic classes. Computer resources include on-campus library services, Internet access, wireless campus network, Internet filtering or blocking technology. Student e-mail accounts and computer access in designated common areas are available to students.
Contact Mrs. Rivka Kahan, Assistant Principal/Director of Admissions. 201-833-4307 Ext. 202. Fax: 201-833-0816. E-mail: kahanr@maayanot.org.

MACLACHLAN COLLEGE

337 Trafalgar Road
Oakville, Ontario L6J 3H3, Canada
Head of School: Mr. Michael Piening
General Information Coeducational day college-preparatory, arts, business, and technology school. Grades PK–12. Founded: 1978. Setting: suburban. Nearest major city is Toronto, Canada. 2-acre campus. 1 building on campus. Approved or accredited by Canadian Association of Independent Schools, Canadian Educational Standards Institute, Conference of Independent Schools of Ontario, Ontario Ministry of Education, and Ontario Department of Education. Language of instruction: English. Total enrollment: 344. Upper school average class size: 18. Upper school faculty-student ratio: 1:10. Upper School students typically attend 5 days per week. The average school day consists of 6 hours and 45 minutes.
Upper School Student Profile Grade 9: 28 students (17 boys, 11 girls); Grade 10: 36 students (21 boys, 15 girls); Grade 11: 37 students (21 boys, 16 girls); Grade 12: 32 students (23 boys, 9 girls).
Faculty School total: 30. In upper school: 2 men, 12 women; 7 have advanced degrees.
Subjects Offered 20th century history, accounting, algebra, band, business, business law, business mathematics, calculus, Canadian geography, Canadian history, Canadian law, Canadian literature, career education, chemistry, civics, computer multimedia, computer programming, computer science, drama, economics, English, environmental science, ESL, finite math, French, geography, geometry, health, history, law, marketing, mathematics, multimedia, physical education, physics, science, society challenge and change, TOEFL preparation, visual arts.
Graduation Requirements Arts, careers, civics, English, French, geography, history, mathematics, physical education (includes health), science, pass the grade 10 Ontario Literacy test, 40 hours of community service.

Special Academic Programs Advanced Placement exam preparation; accelerated programs; independent study; ESL (30 students enrolled).
College Admission Counseling 36 students graduated in 2010; they went to Carleton University; Ryerson University; The University of Western Ontario; University of Toronto; University of Waterloo; York University. Other: 36 entered a postgraduate year.
Student Life Upper grades have uniform requirement, student council, honor system. Discipline rests primarily with faculty.
Tuition and Aid Day student tuition: CAN$18,350. Tuition installment plan (monthly payment plans). Tuition reduction for siblings, bursaries available. In 2010–11, 1% of upper-school students received aid. Total amount of financial aid awarded in 2010–11: CAN$9000.
Admissions Traditional secondary-level entrance grade is 11. Deadline for receipt of application materials: none. Application fee required: CAN$250. Interview required.
Athletics Interscholastic: aerobics (boys), wrestling (b); intramural: ball hockey (b), baseball (b,g), basketball (b,g), flag football (b,g), floor hockey (b,g), soccer (b,g), softball (b,g), touch football (b,g), ultimate Frisbee (b,g), volleyball (b,g), wilderness survival (b,g); coed interscholastic: aerobics, archery, backpacking, badminton, ball hockey, baseball, basketball, bowling, canoeing/kayaking, cooperative games, cricket, cross-country running, curling, field hockey, fitness, fitness walking, flag football, flagball, floor hockey, football, golf, gymnastics, hiking/backpacking, ice skating, lacrosse, outdoor activities, outdoor adventure, outdoor education, physical fitness, racquetball, running, soccer, softball, touch football, ultimate Frisbee, volleyball, wilderness survival; coed intramural: football, hiking/backpacking, independent competitive sports. 2 PE instructors.
Computers Computers are regularly used in accounting, art, basic skills, business, business applications, business education, business studies, career education, career exploration, career technology, commercial art, computer applications, creative writing, data processing, design, desktop publishing, digital applications, economics, English, ESL, French, geography, graphic arts, health, history, humanities, information technology, library, mathematics, media arts, multimedia, music, programming, reading, research skills, science, theology, Web site design, wilderness education, writing, writing, yearbook classes. Computer network features include on-campus library services, Internet access, wireless campus network, Internet filtering or blocking technology. Campus intranet, student e-mail accounts, and computer access in designated common areas are available to students. The school has a published electronic and media policy.
Contact Ms. Nancy Norcross, Director of Admissions. 905-844-0372 Ext. 235. Fax: 905-844-9369. E-mail: nnorcross@maclachlan.ca. Web site: www.maclachlan.ca.

MADISON ACADEMY

325 Slaughter Road
Madison, Alabama 35758
Head of School: Dr. Robert F. Burton
General Information Coeducational day college-preparatory and religious studies school, affiliated with Church of Christ. Grades PS–12. Founded: 1955. Setting: suburban. Nearest major city is Huntsville. 160-acre campus. 5 buildings on campus. Approved or accredited by Southern Association of Colleges and Schools. Endowment: $800,000. Total enrollment: 860. Upper school average class size: 20. Upper school faculty-student ratio: 1:15.
Upper School Student Profile 35% of students are members of Church of Christ.
Faculty School total: 70. In upper school: 14 men, 20 women; 14 have advanced degrees.
Subjects Offered Accounting, advanced math, Alabama history and geography, algebra, American literature, anatomy, art, art history, arts, band, Bible studies, biology, calculus, calculus-AP, chemistry, choral music, chorus, Christian education, Christian ethics, Christian scripture, Christian studies, church history, community service, computer science, concert choir, consumer mathematics, creative writing, drama, earth science, economics, English, English literature, English/composition-AP, environmental science, European history, expository writing, French, general math, geography, geology, geometry, government/civics, health, human anatomy, journalism, keyboarding, music, photography, physical education, physical science, physics, physics-AP, physiology, pre-algebra, religion, Spanish, speech, studio art, trigonometry, U.S. government, U.S. government and politics, U.S. history, world geography, world history, world literature.
Graduation Requirements English, foreign language, mathematics, religion (includes Bible studies and theology), science, social sciences.
Special Academic Programs Honors section; accelerated programs; study at local college for college credit.
College Admission Counseling 70 students graduated in 2010; 69 went to college, including Abilene Christian University; Auburn University; Freed-Hardeman University; Lipscomb University; The University of Alabama. Other: 1 entered military service. Mean composite ACT: 23.
Student Life Upper grades have uniform requirement, student council, honor system. Discipline rests primarily with faculty. Attendance at religious services is required.
Tuition and Aid Day student tuition: $4450. Tuition installment plan (monthly payment plans). Tuition reduction for siblings, need-based scholarship grants available. In 2010–11, 10% of upper-school students received aid. Total amount of financial aid awarded in 2010–11: $100,000.

Admissions Traditional secondary-level entrance grade is 9. For fall 2010, 100 students applied for upper-level admission, 50 were accepted, 41 enrolled. Stanford Achievement Test required. Deadline for receipt of application materials: none. Application fee required: $200. On-campus interview required.

Athletics Interscholastic: baseball (boys), basketball (b,g), cheering (g), football (b), golf (b), softball (g), volleyball (g). 3 PE instructors, 36 coaches, 1 athletic trainer.

Computers Computers are regularly used in art, foreign language, science classes. Computer network features include on-campus library services, Internet access.

Contact Dr. Michael Weimer, High School Principal. 256-971-1624. Fax: 256-971-1436. E-mail: mweimer@macademy.org. Web site: www.macademy.org.

MADISON-RIDGELAND ACADEMY

7601 Old Canton Road
Madison, Mississippi 39110
Head of School: Tommy Thompson

General Information Coeducational day college-preparatory school. Grades 1–12. Founded: 1969. Setting: suburban. Nearest major city is Jackson. 25-acre campus. 6 buildings on campus. Approved or accredited by Mississippi Private School Association, Southern Association of Colleges and Schools, and Mississippi Department of Education. Endowment: $1 million. Total enrollment: 926. Upper school average class size: 20. Upper school faculty-student ratio: 1:13. There are 180 required school days per year for Upper School students. Upper School students typically attend 5 days per week. The average school day consists of 7 hours and 15 minutes.

Upper School Student Profile Grade 9: 75 students (35 boys, 40 girls); Grade 10: 56 students (28 boys, 28 girls); Grade 11: 61 students (30 boys, 31 girls); Grade 12: 54 students (26 boys, 28 girls).

Faculty School total: 64. In upper school: 14 men, 23 women; 14 have advanced degrees.

Subjects Offered Accounting, algebra, American government, American history, American history-AP, anatomy and physiology, art, Bible, biology, biology-AP, chemistry, chemistry-AP, chorus, civics, communications, computer applications, computer programming, creative writing, debate, drama, driver education, economics, English, European history-AP, forensics, French, French-AP, geography, geometry, global studies, government, graphic arts, health, journalism, keyboarding, music, newspaper, physical fitness, physics, physics-AP, pre-calculus, probability and statistics, psychology, sociology, Spanish, Spanish-AP, speech, trigonometry, U.S. government and politics-AP, Web site design, world history, yearbook.

Graduation Requirements ACT preparation, advanced math, algebra, American government, biology, chemistry, civics, computer applications, economics, electives, English, foreign language, geometry, health, keyboarding, science, social studies (includes history).

Special Academic Programs Advanced Placement exam preparation; honors section; study at local college for college credit; academic accommodation for the gifted.

College Admission Counseling 64 students graduated in 2010; all went to college, including Belhaven University; Millsaps College; Mississippi College; Mississippi State University; University of Mississippi; University of Southern Mississippi. Median SAT critical reading: 705, median SAT math: 620, median composite ACT: 24. 100% scored over 600 on SAT critical reading, 100% scored over 600 on SAT math, 25% scored over 26 on composite ACT.

Student Life Upper grades have specified standards of dress, student council. Discipline rests primarily with faculty. Attendance at religious services is required.

Summer Programs Enrichment, sports programs offered; held on campus; accepts boys and girls; open to students from other schools. 300 students usually enrolled. 2011 schedule: June 1 to July 30. Application deadline: May 15.

Tuition and Aid Day student tuition: $7500. Tuition installment plan (monthly payment plans, semiannual payment plan). Tuition reduction for siblings, merit scholarship grants, need-based scholarship grants available. In 2010–11, 3% of upper-school students received aid; total upper-school merit-scholarship money awarded: $21,300. Total amount of financial aid awarded in 2010–11: $170,000.

Admissions Traditional secondary-level entrance grade is 9. For fall 2010, 60 students applied for upper-level admission, 54 were accepted, 38 enrolled. Admissions testing, BASIS or Otis-Lennon Ability or Stanford Achievement Test required. Deadline for receipt of application materials: none. Application fee required: $35. On-campus interview required.

Athletics Interscholastic: aquatics (boys, girls), baseball (b), basketball (b,g), cheering (g), cross-country running (b,g), dance team (b,g), football (b), golf (b), soccer (b,g), softball (g), strength & conditioning (b,g), tennis (b,g), track and field (b,g); coed interscholastic: aquatics, golf, tennis. 4 PE instructors, 12 coaches, 1 athletic trainer.

Computers Computers are regularly used in accounting, art, journalism, media, media services, Web site design classes. Computer network features include on-campus library services, Internet access, Internet filtering or blocking technology. Students grades are available online. The school has a published electronic and media policy.

Contact Mrs. Tammy Synder, Registrar. 601-856-4455. Fax: 601-853-3835. Web site: www.mrapats.com.

MAGNIFICAT HIGH SCHOOL

20770 Hilliard Boulevard
Rocky River, Ohio 44116
Head of School: Sr. Carol Anne Smith, HM

General Information Girls' day college-preparatory school, affiliated with Roman Catholic Church. Grades 9–12. Founded: 1955. Setting: suburban. Nearest major city is Cleveland. 20-acre campus. 1 building on campus. Approved or accredited by North Central Association of Colleges and Schools, Ohio Catholic Schools Accreditation Association (OCSAA), and Ohio Department of Education. Total enrollment: 800. Upper school average class size: 22. Upper school faculty-student ratio: 1:12. The average school day consists of 5 hours and 55 minutes.

Upper School Student Profile 93% of students are Roman Catholic.

Faculty School total: 77. In upper school: 5 men, 72 women; 50 have advanced degrees.

Subjects Offered Accounting, algebra, American literature, Arabic, art, art history, art history-AP, arts, band, biology, biology-AP, British literature, business, business technology, calculus-AP, chemistry, chemistry-AP, Chinese, choir, chorus, clay-working, comparative religion, computer applications, computer science-AP, CPR, dance, design, drama, drawing, earth science, economics, economics-AP, electives, English, film and literature, first aid, French, French-AP, geometry, government, health, keyboarding, life issues, mathematics, metalworking, modern languages, music, oral communications, orchestra, painting, photography, physical education, physics, pre-calculus, probability and statistics, programming, psychology, science, social studies, sociology, Spanish, Spanish-AP, statistics, statistics-AP, theology, trigonometry, U.S. history, U.S. history-AP, Web site design, world history, world history-AP, world literature, writing.

Graduation Requirements Art appreciation, electives, English, health education, keyboarding, mathematics, modern languages, physical education (includes health), social studies (includes history), theology, word processing, service requirements and senior Genesis Project.

Special Academic Programs 12 Advanced Placement exams for which test preparation is offered; honors section.

College Admission Counseling 200 students graduated in 2010; all went to college, including John Carroll University; Loyola University Chicago; The Ohio State University; University of Dayton; University of Notre Dame; Xavier University. Mean SAT critical reading: 562, mean SAT math: 548, mean SAT writing: 561, mean composite ACT: 25.

Student Life Upper grades have uniform requirement, student council. Attendance at religious services is required.

Tuition and Aid Day student tuition: $10,300. Tuition installment plan (SMART Tuition Payment Plan). Merit scholarship grants, need-based scholarship grants available. In 2010–11, 42% of upper-school students received aid; total upper-school merit-scholarship money awarded: $82,500. Total amount of financial aid awarded in 2010–11: $900,000.

Admissions Traditional secondary-level entrance grade is 9. High School Placement Test (closed version) from Scholastic Testing Service required. Deadline for receipt of application materials: January 28. No application fee required.

Athletics Interscholastic: basketball, cross-country running, dance team, diving, field hockey, golf, gymnastics, lacrosse, soccer, softball, swimming and diving, tennis, track and field, volleyball. 3 PE instructors, 53 coaches, 1 athletic trainer.

Computers Computers are regularly used in all academic classes. Computer network features include on-campus library services, Internet access. Computer access in designated common areas is available to students. Students grades are available online. The school has a published electronic and media policy.

Contact Mrs. Maggie Gibbons Gedeon, Director of Admissions. 440-331-1572 Ext. 248. Fax: 440-331-7257. E-mail: mgedeon@magnificaths.org. Web site: www. magnificaths.org.

MAGNOLIA HEIGHTS SCHOOL

One Chiefs Drive
Senatobia, Mississippi 38668
Head of School: Dr. Marvin Lishman

General Information Coeducational day college-preparatory school. Grades PK–12. Founded: 1970. Setting: rural. Nearest major city is Memphis, TN. 35-acre campus. 5 buildings on campus. Approved or accredited by Mississippi Private School Association, Southern Association of Colleges and Schools, and Mississippi Department of Education. Endowment: $100,000. Total enrollment: 685. Upper school average class size: 22. Upper school faculty-student ratio: 1:10. There are 180 required school days per year for Upper School students. Upper School students typically attend 5 days per week. The average school day consists of 7 hours and 15 minutes.

Upper School Student Profile Grade 6: 59 students (28 boys, 31 girls); Grade 7: 56 students (20 boys, 36 girls); Grade 8: 55 students (27 boys, 28 girls); Grade 9: 55 students (30 boys, 25 girls); Grade 10: 49 students (25 boys, 24 girls); Grade 11: 47 students (24 boys, 23 girls); Grade 12: 54 students (27 boys, 27 girls).

Faculty School total: 35. In upper school: 10 men, 20 women; 20 have advanced degrees.

Subjects Offered Accounting, algebra, American history, art, Bible studies, biology, calculus, chemistry, computer programming, computer science, consumer economics,

Magnolia Heights School

creative writing, current events, driver education, economics, English, geography, geometry, government/civics, keyboarding, physical education, physics, psychology, Spanish, speech, trigonometry, world history.
College Admission Counseling 55 students graduated in 2009; 53 went to college, including Christian Brothers University; Delta State University; Mississippi College; Mississippi State University; University of Arkansas; University of Mississippi. Other: 2 entered military service.
Student Life Upper grades have uniform requirement, student council. Discipline rests primarily with faculty.
Tuition and Aid Day student tuition: $5500. Tuition installment plan (FACTS Tuition Payment Plan, monthly payment plans). Need-based scholarship grants available. In 2009–10, 3% of upper-school students received aid. Total amount of financial aid awarded in 2009–10: $12,000.
Admissions Traditional secondary-level entrance grade is 10. For fall 2009, 40 students applied for upper-level admission, 30 were accepted, 30 enrolled. Achievement tests, ACT, admissions testing, CTBS, OLSAT, CTBS, Stanford Achievement Test, any other standardized test, MAT 7 Metropolitan Achievement Test, PSAT, SAT or Stanford Achievement Test required. Deadline for receipt of application materials: none. Application fee required: $200. On-campus interview required.
Athletics Interscholastic: baseball (boys), basketball (b,g), cheering (g), football (b), golf (b,g), soccer (b,g), softball (g), tennis (b,g), track and field (b,g).
Computers Computer network features include online commercial services, Internet access, Internet filtering or blocking technology. Campus intranet and student e-mail accounts are available to students. Students grades are available online. The school has a published electronic and media policy.
Contact Mrs. Allyson Mitchell, Director of Admissions. 662-562-4491. Fax: 662-562-0386. E-mail: allyson.mitchell@magnoliaheights.com. Web site: www.magnoliaheights.com.

MAHARISHI SCHOOL OF THE AGE OF ENLIGHTENMENT

804 Dr. Robert Keith Wallace Drive
Fairfield, Iowa 52556-2200
Head of School: Dr. Richard Beall
General Information Coeducational day college-preparatory, arts, Science of Creative Intelligence: the study of Natural Law, and Transcendental Meditation: Research in Consciousness school. Grades PS–12. Founded: 1972. Setting: small town. Nearest major city is Iowa City. 10-acre campus. 5 buildings on campus. Approved or accredited by Independent Schools Association of the Central States and Iowa Department of Education. Member of National Association of Independent Schools. Total enrollment: 198. Upper school average class size: 11. There are 186 required school days per year for Upper School students. Upper School students typically attend 5 days per week. The average school day consists of 9 hours.
Upper School Student Profile Grade 10: 16 students (8 boys, 8 girls); Grade 11: 15 students (10 boys, 5 girls); Grade 12: 21 students (9 boys, 12 girls).
Faculty School total: 54. In upper school: 11 men, 17 women; 12 have advanced degrees.
Subjects Offered American government, American history, American literature, art, art history, basketball, British literature, business mathematics, chemistry, computer science, desktop publishing, digital photography, drama performance, driver education, economics, electives, environmental education, ESL, general math, integrated mathematics, photography, physical education, physiology, pre-calculus, Sanskrit, science project, senior thesis, track and field, Vedic science, vocal music, volleyball, world history, world literature, writing, yoga.
Graduation Requirements Art history, computer science, economics, electives, English, foreign language, mathematics, physical education (includes health), science, senior thesis, social studies (includes history), writing, Science of Creative Intelligence course, student etiquette.
Special Academic Programs Honors section; academic accommodation for the gifted, the musically talented, and the artistically talented; remedial reading and/or remedial writing; remedial math.
College Admission Counseling 20 students graduated in 2010; all went to college, including California College of the Arts; Cornell College; Maharishi University of Management; Mount Holyoke College; St. Olaf College; The University of Iowa. Median SAT critical reading: 590, median SAT math: 530, median SAT writing: 545, median combined SAT: 1740, median composite ACT: 25. 40% scored over 600 on SAT critical reading, 30% scored over 600 on SAT math, 30% scored over 600 on SAT writing, 50% scored over 1800 on combined SAT, 37.5% scored over 26 on composite ACT.
Student Life Upper grades have uniform requirement, student council. Discipline rests primarily with faculty.
Summer Programs Enrichment, sports, art/fine arts programs offered; session focuses on interscholastic sports, arts; held both on and off campus; held at Neighboring schools and universities; accepts boys and girls; not open to students from other schools. 40 students usually enrolled. 2011 schedule: June 15 to August 15. Application deadline: June 12.

Tuition and Aid Day student tuition: $13,900. Tuition installment plan (two semester payments). Tuition reduction for siblings, need-based scholarship grants available. In 2010–11, 85% of upper-school students received aid.
Admissions Traditional secondary-level entrance grade is 10. For fall 2010, 5 students applied for upper-level admission, 5 were accepted, 5 enrolled. Deadline for receipt of application materials: none. No application fee required. Interview required.
Athletics Interscholastic: basketball (boys, girls), cheering (b,g), dance team (g), golf (b), indoor track & field (b,g), soccer (b), tennis (b,g), track and field (b,g), volleyball (g); intramural: badminton (b,g), ballet (g), basketball (b,g), canoeing/kayaking (b,g), fitness walking (g), jogging (b,g), outdoor activities (b,g), physical fitness (b,g), physical training (b,g), strength & conditioning (b,g), table tennis (b,g), tennis (b,g), volleyball (g), yoga (b,g). 3 PE instructors, 11 coaches.
Computers Computers are regularly used in business education, creative writing, desktop publishing, economics, English, ESL, geography, graphic design, history, independent study, library, library science, library skills, literacy, mathematics, multimedia, photography, programming, publications, science, senior seminar, social sciences, social studies, stock market, typing, video film production, writing classes. Computer network features include Internet access, Internet filtering or blocking technology, file and portfolio management. Campus intranet and computer access in designated common areas are available to students. Students grades are available online. The school has a published electronic and media policy.
Contact Ms. Tere Cutler, Director of Admissions. 641-472-9400 Ext. 5064. Fax: 641-472-1211. E-mail: tcutler@msae.edu. Web site: www.maharishischooliowa.org.

MAINE CENTRAL INSTITUTE

295 Main Street
Pittsfield, Maine 04967
Head of School: Christopher Hopkins
General Information Coeducational boarding and day college-preparatory, general academic, arts, vocational, bilingual studies, technology, humanities, and mathematics, the sciences school. Grades 9–PG. Founded: 1866. Setting: small town. Nearest major city is Portland. Students are housed in single-sex dormitories and honors dorm is coed. 23-acre campus. Approved or accredited by Independent Schools of Northern New England, Massachusetts Department of Education, New England Association of Schools and Colleges, The Association of Boarding Schools, and Maine Department of Education. Member of National Association of Independent Schools and Secondary School Admission Test Board. Total enrollment: 462. Upper school average class size: 16. Upper school faculty-student ratio: 1:14. There are 175 required school days per year for Upper School students. Upper School students typically attend 5 days per week. The average school day consists of 7 hours and 15 minutes.
Upper School Student Profile Grade 9: 88 students (49 boys, 39 girls); Grade 10: 105 students (48 boys, 57 girls); Grade 11: 130 students (73 boys, 57 girls); Grade 12: 127 students (68 boys, 59 girls); Postgraduate: 13 students (12 boys, 1 girl). 71% are state residents. 11 states are represented in upper school student body. 85% are international students.
Faculty School total: 41. In upper school: 20 men, 21 women; 14 have advanced degrees; 25 reside on campus.
Subjects Offered Algebra, American history, American literature, anatomy, art, art-AP, Asian studies, astronomy, audio visual/media, ballet, biology, botany, calculus, calculus-AP, career exploration, chemistry, chemistry-AP, child development, civil rights, computer science, concert band, concert choir, contemporary issues, creative writing, drafting, drama, earth science, ecology, economics, electronic publishing, English, English literature, environmental science, ESL, ethics, fine arts, French, geology, geometry, government/civics, health, history, humanities, integrated science, jazz band, jazz dance, jazz ensemble, Latin, life management skills, literature-AP, mathematics, meteorology, music, music appreciation, music composition, music theory, personal finance, philosophy, photography, physical education, physics, physics-AP, piano, psychology, reading/study skills, SAT preparation, science, social sciences, social studies, sociology, Spanish, statistics, theater, trigonometry, video film production, Web site design, world history.
Graduation Requirements Arts and fine arts (art, music, dance, drama), computer skills, English, mathematics, physical education (includes health), science, senior project, social studies (includes history), Manson essay.
Special Academic Programs Advanced Placement exam preparation; honors section; accelerated programs; independent study; study at local college for college credit; study abroad; academic accommodation for the musically talented; remedial reading and/or remedial writing; remedial math; programs in English, mathematics, general development for dyslexic students; ESL (46 students enrolled).
College Admission Counseling 115 students graduated in 2010; 90 went to college, including Husson University; Maine Maritime Academy; University of Maine; University of Maine at Farmington; University of Southern Maine. Other: 15 went to work, 3 entered military service, 1 entered a postgraduate year, 6 had other specific plans. Median SAT critical reading: 428, median SAT math: 444, median SAT writing: 442, median combined SAT: 1314.
Student Life Upper grades have specified standards of dress, student council, honor system. Discipline rests primarily with faculty.
Summer Programs ESL, art/fine arts programs offered; session focuses on basic ESL, summer ballet; held on campus; accepts boys and girls; open to students from other schools. 35 students usually enrolled. 2011 schedule: July to August. Application deadline: none.

Tuition and Aid Day student tuition: $10,000; 7-day tuition and room/board: $38,000. Tuition installment plan (Key Tuition Payment Plan, SMART Tuition Payment Plan, school's own payment plan). Merit scholarship grants, need-based scholarship grants available. In 2010–11, 25% of upper-school students received aid; total upper-school merit-scholarship money awarded: $24,430. Total amount of financial aid awarded in 2010–11: $705,450.

Admissions Traditional secondary-level entrance grade is 9. For fall 2010, 378 students applied for upper-level admission, 344 were accepted, 136 enrolled. Deadline for receipt of application materials: none. Application fee required: $50. Interview recommended.

Athletics Interscholastic: baseball (boys), basketball (b,g), field hockey (g), football (b), riflery (b,g); intramural: football (b); coed interscholastic: aerobics/dance, alpine skiing, ballet, cheering, cross-country running, dance, fencing, golf, modern dance, physical training; coed intramural: alpine skiing, backpacking, basketball, billiards, canoeing/kayaking, climbing, cooperative games, fencing, fishing, flagball, floor hockey, handball, outdoor activities, rafting. 1 PE instructor, 30 coaches, 1 athletic trainer.

Computers Computer network features include on-campus library services, Internet access, wireless campus network, Internet filtering or blocking technology. Student e-mail accounts are available to students. Students grades are available online.

Contact Mr. Clint M. Williams, Director of Admission. 207-487-2282 Ext. 128. Fax: 207-487-3512. E-mail: cwilliams@mci-school.org. Web site: www.mci-school.org.

See Display below and Close-Up on page 804.

MALASPINA INTERNATIONAL HIGH SCHOOL

900 Fifth Street
Nanaimo, British Columbia V9R 5S5, Canada
Head of School: Mr. Keith Watson

General Information Coeducational boarding and day college-preparatory, general academic, arts, and business school; primarily serves dyslexic students. Grades 10–12. Founded: 1996. Setting: small town. Nearest major city is Vancouver, Canada. Students are housed in host family homes. 110-acre campus. 6 buildings on campus. Approved or accredited by British Columbia Department of Education. Language of instruction: English. Total enrollment: 155. Upper school average class size: 12. Upper school faculty-student ratio: 1:13.

Upper School Student Profile Grade 10: 9 students (5 boys, 4 girls); Grade 11: 62 students (27 boys, 35 girls); Grade 12: 84 students (45 boys, 39 girls).

Faculty School total: 12. In upper school: 3 men, 9 women; 4 have advanced degrees.

Subjects Offered 20th century history, accounting, advanced chemistry, advanced math, art, biology, biology-AP, Canadian geography, chemistry, chemistry-AP, communication skills, communications, composition, composition-AP, computer studies, developmental math, drawing, English, English/composition-AP, ESL, European history, French, geography, Japanese, Mandarin, mathematics, physical science, physics, SAT preparation, yearbook.

Graduation Requirements Applied skills, career and personal planning, English, mathematics, science, social studies (includes history).

Special Academic Programs Advanced Placement exam preparation; accelerated programs; independent study; study at local college for college credit; academic accommodation for the gifted; remedial reading and/or remedial writing; programs in English, mathematics, general development for dyslexic students; ESL (70 students enrolled).

College Admission Counseling 45 students graduated in 2009; 42 went to college, including Simon Fraser University; The University of British Columbia; University of Victoria. Other: 2 went to work, 1 had other specific plans.

Student Life Upper grades have specified standards of dress, student council, honor system. Discipline rests equally with students and faculty.

Tuition and Aid Day student tuition: CAN$12,000; 7-day tuition and room/board: CAN$21,000. Tuition installment plan (individually arranged payment plans). Tuition reduction for siblings, bursaries, merit scholarship grants, need-based scholarship grants available.

Admissions Traditional secondary-level entrance grade is 11. For fall 2009, 61 students applied for upper-level admission, 56 were accepted, 51 enrolled. Achievement tests and math and English placement tests required. Deadline for receipt of application materials: none. Application fee required: CAN$150.

Athletics Interscholastic: basketball (girls), soccer (g); intramural: ice hockey (b); coed interscholastic: aerobics/dance, alpine skiing, badminton, ball hockey, basketball, bowling, canoeing/kayaking, dance, floor hockey, golf, gymnastics, modern dance, physical fitness, physical training, rock climbing, roller blading, skateboarding, skiing (cross-country), skiing (downhill), surfing, swimming and diving, table tennis, tennis, volleyball, walking, weight training, winter soccer; coed intramural: aerobics, aerobics/dance, alpine skiing, aquatics, badminton, basketball, bicycling, bowling, canoeing/kayaking, climbing, cross-country running, fitness, golf, ice skating, kayaking, outdoor skills, paint ball, rock climbing, rowing, skiing (cross-country), skiing (downhill), snowboarding, soccer, swimming and diving, walking. 2 PE instructors.

Computers Computers are regularly used in all classes. Computer network features include on-campus library services, Internet access, wireless campus network.

Contact Mr. Tom Lewis, Principal. 604-740-6317. Fax: 604-740-6470. E-mail: lewist@mala.bc.ca. Web site: www.mala.bc.ca/www/discover/intercol/index.htm.

MALDEN CATHOLIC HIGH SCHOOL

99 Crystal Street
Malden, Massachusetts 02148
Head of School: Mr. Edward Tyrrell

General Information Boys' day college-preparatory, arts, business, religious studies, bilingual studies, and technology school, affiliated with Roman Catholic Church; primarily serves students with learning disabilities and individuals with Attention Deficit Disorder. Grades 9–12. Founded: 1932. Setting: urban. Nearest major city is Boston. 15-acre campus. 1 building on campus. Approved or accredited by New England Association of Schools and Colleges and Massachusetts Department of Education. Endowment: $2 million. Total enrollment: 700. Upper school average class size: 23. Upper school faculty-student ratio: 1:13. The average school day consists of 6 hours.

Upper School Student Profile Grade 9: 214 students (214 boys); Grade 10: 154 students (154 boys); Grade 11: 162 students (162 boys); Grade 12: 157 students (157 boys). 85% of students are Roman Catholic.

Faculty School total: 52. In upper school: 40 men, 12 women; 43 have advanced degrees.

Subjects Offered 20th century history, 3-dimensional art, accounting, advanced chemistry, advanced math, Advanced Placement courses, algebra, American government, American history-AP, American literature, ancient world history, art, art appreciation, art history, Asian history, athletics, basic language skills, Bible studies, biology, British literature, British literature (honors), British literature-AP, business, calculus-AP, campus ministry, Chinese history, Christian and Hebrew scripture, Christian testament, college admission preparation, community service, computer programming, computer skills, desktop publishing, English language and composition-AP, English-AP, European history, European history-AP, fine arts, foreign language, French, French language-AP, genetics, geometry, global studies, government, health and safety, honors algebra, honors English, honors geometry, honors U.S. history, honors world history, independent study, integrated science, language arts, leadership and service, library studies, marine biology, marine science, math analysis, modern European history, music appreciation, physical education, psychology, religion, SAT preparation, Spanish, Spanish language-AP, studio art, the Sixties, U.S. history, U.S. history-AP, world history, world history-AP.

Graduation Requirements Algebra, American literature, arts and fine arts (art, music, dance, drama), biology, British literature, Catholic belief and practice, chemistry, computer skills, foreign language, geometry, global studies, mathematics, physical education (includes health), religion (includes Bible studies and theology), science, social studies (includes history), Christian service.

Special Academic Programs 12 Advanced Placement exams for which test preparation is offered; honors section; independent study.

College Admission Counseling 175 students graduated in 2009; 170 went to college, including Assumption College; Boston College; Boston University; Merrimack College; Northeastern University; Salem State University. Other: 3 went to work, 2 entered military service.

Student Life Upper grades have specified standards of dress, student council, honor system. Discipline rests primarily with faculty. Attendance at religious services is required.

Tuition and Aid Day student tuition: $10,650. Tuition installment plan (FACTS Tuition Payment Plan, monthly payment plans). Merit scholarship grants, need-based scholarship grants, paying campus jobs available. In 2009–10, 40% of upper-school students received aid; total upper-school merit-scholarship money awarded: $300,000. Total amount of financial aid awarded in 2009–10: $300,000.

Admissions Traditional secondary-level entrance grade is 9. For fall 2009, 400 students applied for upper-level admission, 300 were accepted, 170 enrolled. Archdiocese of Boston High School entrance exam provided by STS required. Deadline for receipt of application materials: December 15. No application fee required. Interview recommended.

Athletics Interscholastic: baseball, basketball, cross-country running, football, golf, hockey, ice hockey, indoor track, indoor track & field, lacrosse, soccer, swimming and diving, tennis, track and field, winter (indoor) track, wrestling; intramural: alpine skiing, badminton, ball hockey, basketball, fitness, flag football, floor hockey, Frisbee, jogging, lacrosse, life saving, nordic skiing, physical fitness, physical training, rugby, skiing (downhill), snowboarding, strength & conditioning, table tennis, weight lifting, weight training. 2 PE instructors, 15 coaches, 1 athletic trainer.

Computers Computers are regularly used in all academic, basic skills, business applications, business studies, design, desktop publishing, graphic arts, graphic design, graphics, information technology, journalism, library, library skills, multimedia, news writing, photography, photojournalism, religion, study skills, technology, theology, Web site design, word processing classes. Computer network features include on-campus library services, online commercial services, Internet access, wireless campus network, Internet filtering or blocking technology. Students grades are available online. The school has a published electronic and media policy.

Contact Mr. Matthew O'Neil, Associate Director of Admissions. 781-322-3098 Ext. 308. Fax: 781-397-0573. E-mail: oneilm@maldencatholic.org. Web site: www.maldencatholic.org.

MANHATTAN CHRISTIAN HIGH SCHOOL

8000 Churchill Road
Manhattan, Montana 59741

General Information Coeducational day and distance learning college-preparatory, general academic, arts, business, religious studies, and technology school, affiliated with Christian Reformed Church, Christian faith. Grades PK–12. Distance learning grades 9–12. Founded: 1907. Setting: rural. Nearest major city is Bozeman. 20-acre campus. 1 building on campus. Approved or accredited by Christian Schools International, Office for Standards in Education (OFSTED), The College Board, home study, and Montana Department of Education. Endowment: $3 million. Total enrollment: 268. Upper school average class size: 15. Upper school faculty-student ratio: 1:10. There are 175 required school days per year for Upper School students. Upper School students typically attend 5 days per week. The average school day consists of 6 hours and 19 minutes.

Upper School Student Profile Grade 9: 19 students (14 boys, 5 girls); Grade 10: 19 students (7 boys, 12 girls); Grade 11: 38 students (21 boys, 17 girls); Grade 12: 9 students (9 girls). 50% of students are members of Christian Reformed Church, Christian faith.

Faculty In upper school: 6 men, 5 women; 3 have advanced degrees.

Subjects Offered Art, Bible studies, business, community service, English, general science, internship, mathematics, music, physical education, senior project, social studies, Spanish.

Graduation Requirements Arts and fine arts (art, music, dance, drama), business skills (includes word processing), English, mathematics, physical education (includes health), religion (includes Bible studies and theology), science, senior project, social studies (includes history), speech. Community service is required.

Special Academic Programs Advanced Placement exam preparation; honors section; independent study; term-away projects; study at local college for college credit; remedial reading and/or remedial writing; remedial math; programs in English, mathematics, general development for dyslexic students.

College Admission Counseling 32 students graduated in 2010; 28 went to college, including Dordt College; Montana State University. Other: 3 went to work, 1 entered military service. Mean composite ACT: 23.

Student Life Upper grades have specified standards of dress, student council, honor system. Discipline rests primarily with faculty. Attendance at religious services is required.

Tuition and Aid Day student tuition: $5500. Guaranteed tuition plan. Tuition installment plan (monthly payment plans, individually arranged payment plans). Tuition reduction for siblings, need-based scholarship grants available. In 2010–11, 80% of upper-school students received aid.

Admissions Traditional secondary-level entrance grade is 9. For fall 2010, 13 students applied for upper-level admission, 13 were accepted, 13 enrolled. Academic Profile Tests or any standardized test required. Deadline for receipt of application materials: none. Application fee required. Interview required.

Athletics Interscholastic: basketball (boys, girls), cheering (b,g), cross-country running (b,g), football (b), golf (b,g), track and field (b,g), volleyball (g). 1 PE instructor, 19 coaches.

Computers Computers are regularly used in business, English, science, senior seminar, social studies classes. Computer network features include on-campus library services, online commercial services, Internet access, Internet filtering or blocking technology. Student e-mail accounts are available to students. Students grades are available online. The school has a published electronic and media policy.

Contact Eleanor Den Hartigh, Admissions Director. 406-282-7261. Fax: 406-282-7701. E-mail: edenhartigh@manhattanchristian.org. Web site: www.manhattanchristian.org.

MANLIUS PEBBLE HILL SCHOOL

5300 Jamesville Road
DeWitt, New York 13214
Head of School: Baxter F. Ball

General Information Coeducational day college-preparatory school. Grades PK–PG. Founded: 1869. Setting: suburban. Nearest major city is Syracuse. 25-acre campus. 10 buildings on campus. Approved or accredited by Middle States Association of Colleges and Schools. Member of National Association of Independent Schools. Endowment: $2.7 million. Total enrollment: 588. Upper school average class size: 13. Upper school faculty-student ratio: 1:6. There are 160 required school days per year for Upper School students. Upper School students typically attend 5 days per week. The average school day consists of 6 hours and 55 minutes.

Upper School Student Profile Grade 9: 51 students (25 boys, 26 girls); Grade 10: 61 students (29 boys, 32 girls); Grade 11: 63 students (29 boys, 34 girls); Grade 12: 75 students (32 boys, 43 girls).

Faculty School total: 81. In upper school: 20 men, 28 women; 25 have advanced degrees.

Subjects Offered 3-dimensional design, advanced chemistry, advanced math, Advanced Placement courses, advanced studio art-AP, algebra, American history, American history-AP, American literature, American literature-AP, ancient world history, art history, ballet, Basic programming, biology, biology-AP, calculus, calculus-AP, ceramics, chemistry, chemistry-AP, Chinese, college counseling, comedy, computer math, computer science, creative writing, drama, driver education, earth science, English, English literature, environmental science, European history, expository writing, fine arts, French, geometry, government/civics, health, information technology, Latin, literature, marketing, mathematics, music, philosophy, photography, physical education, physics, science, social studies, sociology, Spanish, statistics, theater, trigonometry, world history.

Graduation Requirements Arts and fine arts (art, music, dance, drama), computer science, electives, English, foreign language, health and wellness, history, mathematics, performing arts, physical education (includes health), science.

Special Academic Programs 18 Advanced Placement exams for which test preparation is offered; honors section; independent study; term-away projects; study at local college for college credit; study abroad; academic accommodation for the gifted; ESL (5 students enrolled).

College Admission Counseling 72 students graduated in 2010; 71 went to college, including Cornell University; Hamilton College; New York University; Princeton University; Syracuse University; Tufts University. Other: 1 had other specific plans. Mean SAT critical reading: 613, mean SAT math: 602, mean SAT writing: 616.

Student Life Upper grades have specified standards of dress, student council, honor system. Discipline rests primarily with faculty.

Summer Programs Enrichment, advancement, sports, art/fine arts, computer instruction programs offered; session focuses on summer camp; held on campus; accepts boys and girls; open to students from other schools. 900 students usually enrolled. 2011 schedule: June 29 to August 21. Application deadline: none.

Tuition and Aid Day student tuition: $16,500–$17,875. Tuition installment plan (Insured Tuition Payment Plan, FACTS Tuition Payment Plan). Merit scholarship grants, need-based scholarship grants available. In 2010–11, 40% of upper-school students received aid; total upper-school merit-scholarship money awarded: $740,000. Total amount of financial aid awarded in 2010–11: $880,000.

Admissions Traditional secondary-level entrance grade is 9. For fall 2010, 54 students applied for upper-level admission, 44 were accepted, 30 enrolled. ERB or PSAT or SAT for applicants to grade 11 and 12 required. Deadline for receipt of application materials: none. Application fee required: $50. On-campus interview required.

Athletics Interscholastic: basketball (boys), diving (g), lacrosse (b,g), soccer (b,g), softball (g), swimming and diving (g), tennis (b,g), volleyball (g); intramural: lacrosse (g); coed interscholastic: alpine skiing, ballet, cheering, cross-country running, dance, equestrian sports, fitness, golf, indoor track, modern dance, outdoor education, skiing (downhill), snowboarding, strength & conditioning, track and field, winter (indoor) track; coed intramural: outdoor education, trap and skeet. 4 PE instructors, 9 coaches, 1 athletic trainer.

Computers Computers are regularly used in English, foreign language, graphic design, history, information technology, library skills, literary magazine, mathematics, newspaper, science, Web site design, yearbook classes. Computer network features include on-campus library services, online commercial services, Internet access, wireless campus network, Internet filtering or blocking technology. Campus intranet, student e-mail accounts, and computer access in designated common areas are available to students. The school has a published electronic and media policy.

Contact Lynne E. Allard, Director of Admission. 315-446-2452 Ext. 131. Fax: 315-446-2620. E-mail: lallard@mph.net. Web site: www.mph.net.

MAPLEBROOK SCHOOL
Amenia, New York
See Special Needs Schools section.

MARET SCHOOL
3000 Cathedral Avenue NW
Washington, District of Columbia 20008
Head of School: Marjo Talbott

General Information Coeducational day college-preparatory, arts, and technology school. Grades K–12. Founded: 1911. Setting: urban. 7-acre campus. 6 buildings on campus. Approved or accredited by Association of Independent Maryland Schools, Association of Independent Schools of Greater Washington, Middle States Association of Colleges and Schools, and District of Columbia Department of Education. Member of National Association of Independent Schools and Secondary School Admission Test Board. Endowment: $12 million. Total enrollment: 636. Upper school average class size: 18. Upper school faculty-student ratio: 1:7. The average school day consists of 7 hours.

Upper School Student Profile Grade 9: 81 students (40 boys, 41 girls); Grade 10: 83 students (47 boys, 36 girls); Grade 11: 76 students (39 boys, 37 girls); Grade 12: 69 students (35 boys, 34 girls).

Faculty School total: 102. In upper school: 31 men, 44 women; 57 have advanced degrees.

Subjects Offered Acting, advanced computer applications, advanced studio art-AP, African-American literature, algebra, American history, American literature, anatomy, art, astronomy, biology, calculus-AP, ceramics, chemistry, civil rights, classical civilization, classical Greek literature, classical language, classics, computer graphics, computer math, computer programming, computer science, creative writing, drama, earth science, ecology, English, English literature, European history, film history, fine arts, French, gender issues, geometry, government/civics, history, humanities, Latin,

marine biology, mathematics, music, philosophy, photography, physical education, physics, physiology, psychology, science, Spanish, statistics, technology, trigonometry, women in world history, world history, world literature, writing.

Graduation Requirements Arts and fine arts (art, music, dance, drama), English, foreign language, history, mathematics, music, performing arts, physical education (includes health), science, 15 hours of community service in grades 9 and 10, additional 15 hours in grades 11 and 12.

Special Academic Programs 15 Advanced Placement exams for which test preparation is offered; honors section; independent study; study at local college for college credit; study abroad; academic accommodation for the gifted, the musically talented, and the artistically talented.

College Admission Counseling 73 students graduated in 2010; 71 went to college, including Stanford University; Tufts University; Tulane University; University of Notre Dame; University of Pennsylvania; Washington University in St. Louis. Other: 2 entered a postgraduate year.

Student Life Upper grades have student council. Discipline rests primarily with faculty.

Summer Programs Advancement, sports, art/fine arts programs offered; session focuses on academics, athletics, and performing arts; held both on and off campus; held at locations in Honduras, Florida, France and China; accepts boys and girls; open to students from other schools. 100 students usually enrolled. 2011 schedule: June 15 to August 15. Application deadline: June 1.

Tuition and Aid Day student tuition: $30,600. Tuition installment plan (Key Tuition Payment Plan). Need-based scholarship grants available. In 2010–11, 21% of upper-school students received aid. Total amount of financial aid awarded in 2010–11: $2,800,000.

Admissions Traditional secondary-level entrance grade is 9. For fall 2010, 270 students applied for upper-level admission, 45 were accepted, 30 enrolled. ISEE, PSAT or SSAT required. Deadline for receipt of application materials: January 7. Application fee required: $65. On-campus interview required.

Athletics Interscholastic: baseball (boys), basketball (b,g), football (b), lacrosse (b,g), soccer (b,g), softball (g), tennis (b,g), volleyball (g), wrestling (b); intramural: ice hockey (b), squash (b,g); coed interscholastic: aerobics, cross-country running, diving, flag football, golf, independent competitive sports, martial arts, swimming and diving, track and field, ultimate Frisbee; coed intramural: indoor soccer, ultimate Frisbee, weight lifting, weight training, yoga. 6 PE instructors, 25 coaches, 1 athletic trainer.

Computers Computers are regularly used in graphic design, graphics, programming, publications, Web site design classes. Computer network features include on-campus library services, online commercial services, Internet access, wireless campus network, Internet filtering or blocking technology. Campus intranet and student e-mail accounts are available to students. The school has a published electronic and media policy.

Contact Annie M. Farquhar, Director of Admission and Financial Aid. 202-939-8814. Fax: 202-939-8845. E-mail: admissions@maret.org. Web site: www.maret.org.

MARIANAPOLIS PREPARATORY SCHOOL
PO Box 304
26 Chase Road
Thompson, Connecticut 06277-0304
Head of School: Mrs. Marilyn S. Ebbitt

General Information Coeducational boarding and day college-preparatory, religious studies, and ESL school, affiliated with Roman Catholic Church. Grades 9–PG. Founded: 1926. Setting: small town. Nearest major city is Boston, MA. Students are housed in single-sex dormitories. 300-acre campus. 11 buildings on campus. Approved or accredited by Connecticut Association of Independent Schools, New England Association of Schools and Colleges, The Association of Boarding Schools, and Connecticut Department of Education. Member of Secondary School Admission Test Board. Total enrollment: 315. Upper school average class size: 15. Upper school faculty-student ratio: 1:10.

Upper School Student Profile Grade 9: 70 students (35 boys, 35 girls); Grade 10: 75 students (35 boys, 40 girls); Grade 11: 85 students (45 boys, 40 girls); Grade 12: 80 students (35 boys, 45 girls); Postgraduate: 5 students (3 boys, 2 girls). 38% of students are boarding students. 30% are state residents. 4 states are represented in upper school student body. 33% are international students. International students from China, Colombia, Mexico, Republic of Korea, Venezuela, and Viet Nam; 11 other countries represented in student body. 60% of students are Roman Catholic.

Faculty School total: 34. In upper school: 19 men, 15 women; 10 have advanced degrees; 14 reside on campus.

Subjects Offered Algebra, American government, American literature, art, Bible studies, biology, calculus, calculus-AP, chemistry, chemistry-AP, chorus, Christian and Hebrew scripture, Christian doctrine, Christian ethics, church history, comparative religion, computer programming, computer science, contemporary studies, drawing, English, English literature, English literature-AP, English-AP, environmental science, ESL, fine arts, French, geometry, government/civics, guitar, history, honors algebra, honors English, honors geometry, Mandarin, mathematics, modern European history, moral theology, music, physics, physics-AP, piano, pre-calculus, probability and statistics, psychology, religion, science, social studies, Spanish, theology, trigonometry, U.S. history, world literature.

Marianapolis Preparatory School

Graduation Requirements Arts and fine arts (art, music, dance, drama), computer science, electives, English, foreign language, mathematics, religion (includes Bible studies and theology), science, social studies (includes history). Community service is required.

Special Academic Programs Advanced Placement exam preparation; honors section; independent study; ESL (90 students enrolled).

College Admission Counseling 67 students graduated in 2009; all went to college, including Boston College; College of the Holy Cross; University of Connecticut; University of Illinois at Urbana–Champaign; Wake Forest University; Worcester Polytechnic Institute.

Student Life Upper grades have specified standards of dress, student council. Discipline rests equally with students and faculty. Attendance at religious services is required.

Tuition and Aid Day student tuition: $10,995; 7-day tuition and room/board: $33,470. Tuition installment plan (Key Tuition Payment Plan, monthly payment plans, individually arranged payment plans). Tuition reduction for siblings, merit scholarship grants, need-based scholarship grants, tuition reduction for Diocese of Norwich affiliation available. In 2009–10, 62% of upper-school students received aid; total upper-school merit-scholarship money awarded: $100,000. Total amount of financial aid awarded in 2009–10: $800,000.

Admissions For fall 2009, 250 students applied for upper-level admission, 175 were accepted, 115 enrolled. Common entrance examinations, PSAT, SAT, SLEP, SSAT or TOEFL required. Deadline for receipt of application materials: none. Application fee required: $100. Interview required.

Athletics Interscholastic: baseball (boys), basketball (b,g), cross-country running (b,g), lacrosse (b,g), soccer (b,g), softball (g), tennis (b,g), volleyball (g); intramural: basketball (b,g), dance (g), modern dance (g); coed interscholastic: Frisbee, golf, running, track and field, ultimate Frisbee, wrestling; coed intramural: aerobics/dance, alpine skiing, cross-country running, dance, flag football, Frisbee, independent competitive sports, jogging, judo, martial arts, mountain biking, skiing (cross-country), skiing (downhill), snowboarding, snowshoeing, swimming and diving, table tennis, tennis, ultimate Frisbee, volleyball, weight lifting, weight training, yoga. 24 coaches, 1 athletic trainer.

Computers Computers are regularly used in all academic, ESL classes. Computer network features include Internet access, wireless campus network, Internet filtering or blocking technology. Student e-mail accounts are available to students. The school has a published electronic and media policy.

Contact Mr. Dan Harrop, Director of Admissions and Financial Aid. 860-923-9565 Ext. 233. Fax: 860-923-3730. E-mail: dharrop@marianapolis.org. Web site: www.marianapolis.org.

MARIAN CATHOLIC HIGH SCHOOL

166 Marian Avenue
Tamaqua, Pennsylvania 18252-9789
Head of School: Sr. Bernard Agnes Smith, IHM

General Information Coeducational day college-preparatory, general academic, business, and technology school, affiliated with Roman Catholic Church. Grades 9–12. Founded: 1954. Setting: rural. Nearest major city is Hazleton. 1 building on campus. Approved or accredited by Middle States Association of Colleges and Schools, National Catholic Education Association, and Pennsylvania Department of Education. Total enrollment: 354. Upper school average class size: 23. Upper school faculty-student ratio: 1:11.

Upper School Student Profile Grade 9: 78 students (40 boys, 38 girls); Grade 10: 86 students (43 boys, 43 girls); Grade 11: 82 students (35 boys, 47 girls); Grade 12: 108 students (56 boys, 52 girls). 95% of students are Roman Catholic.

Faculty School total: 31. In upper school: 12 men, 19 women; 15 have advanced degrees.

Special Academic Programs Advanced Placement exam preparation; study at local college for college credit.

College Admission Counseling Colleges students went to include La Salle University.

Student Life Upper grades have uniform requirement, student council. Discipline rests primarily with faculty. Attendance at religious services is required.

Tuition and Aid Day student tuition: $4350. Tuition installment plan (FACTS Tuition Payment Plan, monthly payment plans). Tuition reduction for siblings, merit scholarship grants, need-based scholarship grants available. In 2009–10, 45% of upper-school students received aid. Total amount of financial aid awarded in 2009–10: $102,000.

Admissions Traditional secondary-level entrance grade is 9. Deadline for receipt of application materials: none. Application fee required: $100. Interview recommended.

Athletics Interscholastic: baseball (boys), basketball (b,g), cheering (g), cross-country running (b,g), football (b), golf (b,g), softball (g), volleyball (g). 2 PE instructors, 20 coaches, 1 athletic trainer.

Computers Computer resources include on-campus library services, Internet access, Internet filtering or blocking technology. Student e-mail accounts are available to students. The school has a published electronic and media policy.

Contact Sr. Eileen McGuigan, IHM, Studies Director. 570-467-3335 Ext. 217. Fax: 570-467-0186. Web site: www.mariancatholichs.org.

MARIAN CENTRAL CATHOLIC HIGH SCHOOL

1001 McHenry Avenue
Woodstock, Illinois 60098
Head of School: Mr. Charles D. Rakers

General Information Coeducational day college-preparatory, arts, business, religious studies, bilingual studies, and technology school, affiliated with Roman Catholic Church. Grades 9–12. Founded: 1959. Setting: suburban. 42-acre campus. 1 building on campus. Approved or accredited by National Catholic Education Association, North Central Association of Colleges and Schools, and Illinois Department of Education. Endowment: $941,524. Total enrollment: 717. Upper school average class size: 24. Upper school faculty-student ratio: 1:16. There are 177 required school days per year for Upper School students. Upper School students typically attend 5 days per week. The average school day consists of 6 hours and 25 minutes.

Upper School Student Profile Grade 9: 175 students (91 boys, 84 girls); Grade 10: 173 students (97 boys, 76 girls); Grade 11: 176 students (92 boys, 84 girls); Grade 12: 193 students (103 boys, 90 girls). 89.3% of students are Roman Catholic.

Faculty School total: 54. In upper school: 29 men, 25 women; 37 have advanced degrees.

Subjects Offered Accounting, advanced biology, advanced chemistry, advanced math, Advanced Placement courses, algebra, American government, art, band, biology, business law, calculus, calculus-AP, chemistry, chemistry-AP, chorus, comparative government and politics-AP, composition, computer programming, consumer economics, English, English composition, English literature-AP, first aid, French, general science, geography, geometry, global issues, government, health, honors algebra, honors English, honors geometry, honors U.S. history, information processing, integrated science, marketing, physical education, physical fitness, physical science, physics, pre-calculus, psychology, psychology-AP, publications, religious studies, Spanish, speech, U.S. history, U.S. history-AP, world history-AP.

Graduation Requirements Art, biology, consumer economics, electives, English, first aid, foreign language, government, health, mathematics, music, physical education (includes health), religious studies, science, U.S. history.

Special Academic Programs 7 Advanced Placement exams for which test preparation is offered; honors section; remedial reading and/or remedial writing; remedial math.

College Admission Counseling 175 students graduated in 2010; 172 went to college, including DePaul University; Marquette University; Saint Louis University; St. Norbert College; The University of Iowa; University of Illinois at Urbana–Champaign. Other: 1 went to work, 1 entered a postgraduate year, 1 had other specific plans. Mean composite ACT: 25. 40% scored over 26 on composite ACT.

Student Life Upper grades have uniform requirement, student council. Discipline rests primarily with faculty. Attendance at religious services is required.

Summer Programs Sports programs offered; session focuses on sports camps; held on campus; accepts boys and girls; open to students from other schools. 2011 schedule: June to August.

Tuition and Aid Day student tuition: $5570–$7450. Tuition installment plan (monthly payment plans, quarterly payment plan, semester payment plans, yearly payment plans). Tuition reduction for siblings, need-based scholarship grants, paying campus jobs available. In 2010–11, 18% of upper-school students received aid. Total amount of financial aid awarded in 2010–11: $289,203.

Admissions Traditional secondary-level entrance grade is 9. High School Placement Test (closed version) from Scholastic Testing Service required. Deadline for receipt of application materials: none. No application fee required.

Athletics Interscholastic: baseball (boys), basketball (b,g), cheering (g), cross-country running (b,g), dance team (g), football (b), golf (b,g), pom squad (g), soccer (b,g), softball (g), tennis (b,g), track and field (b,g), volleyball (g), wrestling (b); intramural: floor hockey (b,g); coed interscholastic: fencing, fishing. 3 PE instructors, 47 coaches, 1 athletic trainer.

Computers Computers are regularly used in information technology, programming, publications classes. Computer resources include on-campus library services, online commercial services, Internet access, Internet filtering or blocking technology. Students grades are available online. The school has a published electronic and media policy.

Contact Mrs. Barbara Villont, Director of Curriculum and Technology. 815-338-4220 Ext. 105. Fax: 815-338-4253. E-mail: bvillont@marian.com. Web site: www.marian.com.

MARIAN HIGH SCHOOL

1311 South Logan Street
Mishawaka, Indiana 46544
Head of School: Carl Loesch

General Information Coeducational day college-preparatory, arts, business, vocational, religious studies, bilingual studies, and technology school, affiliated with Roman Catholic Church. Grades 9–12. Founded: 1965. Setting: suburban. 135-acre campus. 1 building on campus. Approved or accredited by North Central Association of Colleges and Schools, The College Board, and Indiana Department of Education. Total enrollment: 676. Upper school average class size: 27. Upper school faculty-student ratio: 1:22. There are 180 required school days per year for Upper School students. Upper School students typically attend 5 days per week. The average school day consists of 6 hours and 30 minutes.

Upper School Student Profile Grade 9: 178 students (90 boys, 88 girls); Grade 10: 177 students (88 boys, 89 girls); Grade 11: 172 students (87 boys, 85 girls); Grade 12: 149 students (75 boys, 74 girls). 85% of students are Roman Catholic.

Faculty School total: 46. In upper school: 18 men, 28 women; 23 have advanced degrees.

Subjects Offered 20th century history, 20th century physics, 20th century world history, 3-dimensional art, 3-dimensional design, accounting, acting, advanced chemistry, advanced computer applications, advanced math, algebra, alternative physical education, American government, American literature, analysis and differential calculus, analytic geometry, anatomy, ancient world history, art, art history, arts and crafts, arts appreciation, business law, calculus, Catholic belief and practice, chemistry, drama, drawing, drawing and design, economics, English composition, English literature-AP, environmental science, environmental studies, environmental systems, family and consumer science, family living, fashion, fine arts, food and nutrition, foods, French, French language-AP, general business, general math, geography, geometry, German, government and politics-AP, government-AP, government/civics, guidance, health, histology, honors world history, independent living, integrated science, keyboarding, Latin, Life of Christ, media, media arts, moral theology, music, music appreciation, nutrition, physics, physics-AP, pre-algebra, pre-calculus, psychology, religion, scripture, senior project, sewing, sociology, Spanish, Spanish language-AP, Spanish-AP, study skills, theology, U.S. government and politics-AP, U.S. history, U.S. history-AP, visual arts, vocal music, Western civilization.

Graduation Requirements Algebra, American government, American history, analytic geometry, arts and fine arts (art, music, dance, drama), biology, chemistry, computer information systems, computer skills, economics, English, English composition, English literature, French, keyboarding, languages, mathematics, science, scripture, writing, four years of theology.

Special Academic Programs Advanced Placement exam preparation; study at local college for college credit; remedial reading and/or remedial writing; remedial math.

College Admission Counseling 165 students graduated in 2010; 157 went to college, including Ball State University; DePaul University; Indiana University–Purdue University Fort Wayne; Indiana University Bloomington; Purdue University; University of Notre Dame. Other: 5 went to work, 2 entered military service, 1 had other specific plans. Mean SAT critical reading: 524, mean SAT math: 539, mean SAT writing: 513, mean composite ACT: 22.

Student Life Upper grades have specified standards of dress, student council, honor system. Discipline rests equally with students and faculty. Attendance at religious services is required.

Summer Programs Sports, art/fine arts, computer instruction programs offered; session focuses on enrichment; held on campus; accepts boys and girls; open to students from other schools.

Tuition and Aid Day student tuition: $5575–$6575. Tuition installment plan (The Tuition Plan, FACTS Tuition Payment Plan, individually arranged payment plans). Tuition reduction for siblings, need-based loans available. In 2010–11, 45% of upper-school students received aid. Total amount of financial aid awarded in 2010–11: $350,000.

Admissions Traditional secondary-level entrance grade is 9. For fall 2010, 189 students applied for upper-level admission, 189 were accepted, 178 enrolled. High School Placement Test, Math Placement Exam or placement test required. Deadline for receipt of application materials: August 13. Application fee required: $100. Interview required.

Athletics Interscholastic: aerobics/dance (girls), aquatics (b,g), baseball (b); basketball (b,g), cheering (b,g), Cosom hockey (b), cross-country running (b,g), dance team (g), diving (b,g), flag football (g), football (b), golf (b,g), gymnastics (g), hockey (b), ice hockey (b), indoor hockey (b), lacrosse (b,g), power lifting (b,g), rugby (b), soccer (b,g), softball (g), swimming and diving (b,g), tennis (b,g), track and field (b,g), volleyball (g), weight training (b,g), wrestling (b,g); intramural: basketball (b), flag football (g), pom squad (g); coed interscholastic: cheering, wrestling; coed intramural: alpine skiing, bowling. 2 PE instructors, 42 coaches, 1 athletic trainer.

Computers Computers are regularly used in business education, business skills, career education, commercial art, economics, foreign language, graphic arts, history, library, media arts, occupational education, publications, religion, yearbook classes. Computer network features include on-campus library services, online commercial services, Internet access, Internet filtering or blocking technology. Students grades are available online. The school has a published electronic and media policy.

Contact Janet M. Hatfield, Dean. 574-259-5257. Fax: 574-258-7668. E-mail: jhatfield@marianhs.org. Web site: www.marianhs.org/.

MARIN ACADEMY

1600 Mission Avenue
San Rafael, California 94901-1859
Head of School: Travis Brownley

General Information Coeducational day college-preparatory, arts, technology, and outdoor education program school. Grades 9–12. Founded: 1971. Setting: suburban. Nearest major city is San Francisco. 10-acre campus. 11 buildings on campus. Approved or accredited by California Association of Independent Schools, The College Board, and Western Association of Schools and Colleges. Member of National Association of Independent Schools and Secondary School Admission Test Board. Endowment: $9.1 billion. Total enrollment: 406. Upper school average class size: 15.

Upper school faculty-student ratio: 1:9. There are 180 required school days per year for Upper School students. Upper School students typically attend 5 days per week. The average school day consists of 6 hours and 45 minutes.

Upper School Student Profile Grade 9: 100 students (48 boys, 52 girls); Grade 10: 102 students (53 boys, 49 girls); Grade 11: 103 students (49 boys, 54 girls); Grade 12: 102 students (51 boys, 51 girls).

Faculty School total: 55. In upper school: 23 men, 32 women; 36 have advanced degrees.

Subjects Offered 20th century history, 20th century world history, 3-dimensional art, acting, adolescent issues, Advanced Placement courses, African history, algebra, American culture, American government, American history, American literature, American minority experience, American studies, ancient world history, art, Asian history, Asian literature, biology, British literature (honors), calculus, ceramics, chemistry, chorus, college counseling, community service, creative writing, dance, digital imaging, digital photography, English, English literature, environmental science, European history, fine arts, French, geology, geometry, government/civics, health, history, honors U.S. history, human development, Islamic history, Islamic studies, Japanese, journalism, Mandarin, mathematics, music, oceanography, photography, physical education, physics, pre-calculus, science, social studies, Spanish, theater, trigonometry, world cultures, world history-AP.

Graduation Requirements Arts and fine arts (art, music, dance, drama), English, foreign language, health and wellness, health education, mathematics, physical education (includes health), science, social studies (includes history), annual one-week experiential education course. Community service is required.

Special Academic Programs Advanced Placement exam preparation; honors section; independent study; term-away projects; study at local college for college credit; study abroad; academic accommodation for the gifted, the musically talented, and the artistically talented.

College Admission Counseling 99 students graduated in 2010; 92 went to college, including New York University; Oberlin College; Stanford University; University of California, Berkeley; University of California, Los Angeles; University of Southern California. Other: 1 had other specific plans. Median SAT critical reading: 670, median SAT math: 645, median SAT writing: 675, median combined SAT: 2000, median composite ACT: 28.

Student Life Upper grades have student council, honor system. Discipline rests primarily with faculty.

Tuition and Aid Day student tuition: $33,360. Tuition installment plan (Key Tuition Payment Plan). Need-based scholarship grants, need-based loans available. In 2010–11, 21% of upper-school students received aid. Total amount of financial aid awarded in 2010–11: $2,400,000.

Admissions Traditional secondary-level entrance grade is 9. For fall 2010, 470 students applied for upper-level admission, 170 were accepted, 100 enrolled. CTBS or ERB, ISEE, SSAT or Star-9 required. Deadline for receipt of application materials: January 13. Application fee required: $100. On-campus interview required.

Athletics Interscholastic: aquatics (boys, girls), baseball (b), basketball (b,g), combined training (b,g), cross-country running (b,g), fencing (b,g), golf (b,g), independent competitive sports (b,g), lacrosse (b), mountain biking (b,g), outdoor activities (b,g), rock climbing (b,g), sailing (b,g), soccer (b,g), softball (g), swimming and diving (b,g), tennis (b,g), track and field (b,g), volleyball (g), water polo (b,g); coed interscholastic: dance, golf; coed intramural: bicycling, climbing, fitness, flag football, Frisbee, hiking/backpacking, kayaking, martial arts, Nautilus, outdoor skills, physical fitness, rock climbing, scuba diving, ultimate Frisbee. 28 coaches, 1 athletic trainer.

Computers Computers are regularly used in art, English, foreign language, history, library skills, mathematics, music, photography, science, yearbook classes. Computer network features include on-campus library services, online commercial services, Internet access, wireless campus network, multimedia hardware and production applications. Student e-mail accounts and computer access in designated common areas are available to students.

Contact Dan Babior, Director of Admissions and Financial Aid. 415-453-4550 Ext. 216. Fax: 415-453-8905. E-mail: dbabior@ma.org. Web site: www.ma.org.

MARINE MILITARY ACADEMY

320 Iwo Jima Boulevard
Harlingen, Texas 78550
Head of School: Brig. Gen. Stephen A. Cheney, USMC-Retd.

General Information Boys' boarding college-preparatory and military school. Grades 8–PG. Founded: 1965. Setting: small town. Nearest major city is Brownsville. Students are housed in single-sex dormitories. 142-acre campus. 43 buildings on campus. Approved or accredited by European Council of International Schools, Military High School and College Association, Southern Association of Colleges and Schools, Southern Association of Independent Schools, and Texas Department of Education. Endowment: $18 million. Total enrollment: 402. Upper school average class size: 12. Upper school faculty-student ratio: 1:12.

Upper School Student Profile Grade 8: 23 students (23 boys); Grade 9: 46 students (46 boys); Grade 10: 56 students (56 boys); Grade 11: 61 students (61 boys); Grade 12: 61 students (61 boys); Postgraduate: 2 students (2 boys). 100% of students are boarding students. 46% are state residents. 31 states are represented in upper school student body. 16% are international students. International students from China, Germany, Japan, Mexico, Panama, and United Arab Emirates; 9 other countries represented in student body.

Faculty School total: 34. In upper school: 17 men, 17 women; 16 have advanced degrees; 1 resides on campus.

Subjects Offered Aerospace science, algebra, American history, band, biology, calculus, calculus-AP, chemistry, computer programming, computer science, economics, English, environmental science, French, French-AP, geography, geometry, German, German-AP, government/civics, history, journalism, JROTC, keyboarding, marine science, mathematics, military science, physics, physics-AP, political science, SAT preparation, science, social sciences, social studies, Spanish, Spanish-AP, speech, world history.

Graduation Requirements Business skills (includes word processing), computer science, English, foreign language, mathematics, military science, physical education (includes health), science, social sciences, social studies (includes history).

Special Academic Programs Advanced Placement exam preparation; honors section; academic accommodation for the gifted; ESL (55 students enrolled).

College Admission Counseling 46 students graduated in 2010; they went to Texas A&M University; Texas Tech University; The Citadel, The Military College of South Carolina; United States Military Academy; United States Naval Academy; Virginia Military Institute. 11.7% scored over 600 on SAT critical reading, 14% scored over 600 on SAT math.

Student Life Upper grades have uniform requirement, student council, honor system. Discipline rests equally with students and faculty.

Summer Programs ESL, rigorous outdoor training programs offered; session focuses on military training and physical fitness; held on campus; accepts boys; open to students from other schools. 300 students usually enrolled. 2011 schedule: July 2 to July 30. Application deadline: none.

Tuition and Aid 7-day tuition and room/board: $33,000. Tuition installment plan (monthly payment plans, individually arranged payment plans, Chief Financial Officer authorization required). Tuition reduction for siblings available. In 2010–11, 12% of upper-school students received aid. Total amount of financial aid awarded in 2010–11: $490,950.

Admissions For fall 2010, 167 students applied for upper-level admission, 151 were accepted, 125 enrolled. Deadline for receipt of application materials: none. Application fee required: $100. On-campus interview recommended.

Athletics Interscholastic: baseball, basketball, bicycling, boxing, cross-country running, football, golf, JROTC drill, judo, marksmanship, physical fitness, riflery, running, soccer, swimming and diving, tennis, track and field; intramural: basketball, climbing, paint ball, physical fitness, physical training, racquetball, rappelling, running, sailing, soccer, softball, swimming and diving, track and field, volleyball, wall climbing, weight lifting. 15 coaches, 1 athletic trainer.

Computers Computers are regularly used in English, foreign language, mathematics, science, yearbook classes. Computer network features include on-campus library services, online commercial services, Internet access, Internet filtering or blocking technology. Student e-mail accounts and computer access in designated common areas are available to students. Students grades are available online.

Contact Mrs. Jay Perez, Admissions Officer. 956-423-6006 Ext. 251. Fax: 956-421-9273. E-mail: admissions@mma-tx.org. Web site: www.marinemilitaryacademy.com.

THE MARIN SCHOOL

100 Ebbtide Avenue #300
Sausalito, California 94965
Head of School: Peter Esty

General Information Coeducational day college-preparatory, arts, and film, technology, photography school. Grades 9–12. Founded: 1980. Setting: small town. Nearest major city is San Francisco. 4 buildings on campus. Approved or accredited by California Association of Independent Schools, Western Association of Schools and Colleges, and California Department of Education. Total enrollment: 100. Upper school average class size: 7. Upper school faculty-student ratio: 1:7. There are 174 required school days per year for Upper School students. Upper School students typically attend 5 days per week. The average school day consists of 7 hours.

Faculty School total: 17. In upper school: 5 men, 12 women.

Subjects Offered Algebra, American literature, arts, biology, British literature (honors), calculus, chemistry, chorus, civics, community service, composition, drama, earth science, ecology, economics, English, environmental science, ESL, fine arts, French, general math, general science, geography, geometry, health, life science, literature, mathematics, physical education, physics, pre-algebra, pre-calculus, science, social sciences, social studies, Spanish, trigonometry, typing, U.S. history, visual arts, Western civilization, women's literature, word processing.

Graduation Requirements Arts and fine arts (art, music, dance, drama), foreign language, mathematics, physical education (includes health), science, social sciences. Community service is required.

College Admission Counseling 25 students graduated in 2010; all went to college, including Bard College; Eugene Lang College The New School for Liberal Arts; Goucher College; Lewis & Clark College; Reed College; The Evergreen State College.

Student Life Upper grades have honor system. Discipline rests primarily with faculty.

Tuition and Aid Day student tuition: $33,420. Tuition installment plan (FACTS Tuition Payment Plan). Need-based scholarship grants available. In 2010–11, 51% of upper-school students received aid.

Admissions Traditional secondary-level entrance grade is 9. ERB, SSAT, Star-9 or STS required. Deadline for receipt of application materials: none. Application fee required: $75. Interview required.

Athletics Coed Interscholastic: basketball, sailing, soccer; coed intramural: basketball, bicycling, mountain biking, sailing, soccer.

Computers Computer network features include on-campus library services, online commercial services, Internet access, wireless campus network, Internet filtering or blocking technology. Campus intranet and student e-mail accounts are available to students. Students grades are available online. The school has a published electronic and media policy.

Contact 415-339-9336.

MARION ACADEMY

2002 Prier Drive
Marion, Alabama 36756
Head of School: Mr. Anthony L. Yelverton

General Information Coeducational day college-preparatory, general academic, arts, religious studies, bilingual studies, and technology school, affiliated with Christian faith. Grades K–12. Founded: 1987. Setting: small town. Nearest major city is Tuscaloosa. 5-acre campus. 1 building on campus. Approved or accredited by Alabama Department of Education. Total enrollment: 83. Upper school average class size: 8. Upper school faculty-student ratio: 1:8. There are 180 required school days per year for Upper School students. Upper School students typically attend 5 days per week. The average school day consists of 6 hours and 30 minutes.

Upper School Student Profile Grade 6: 9 students (6 boys, 3 girls); Grade 7: 6 students (4 boys, 2 girls); Grade 8: 9 students (2 boys, 7 girls); Grade 9: 7 students (3 boys, 4 girls); Grade 10: 5 students (1 boy, 4 girls); Grade 11: 11 students (5 boys, 6 girls); Grade 12: 8 students (3 boys, 5 girls). 98% of students are Christian.

Faculty School total: 14. In upper school: 3 men, 2 women; 2 have advanced degrees.

Subjects Offered 20th century history, 20th century world history, advanced math, Alabama history and geography, algebra, American government, anatomy and physiology, art, athletics, basic language skills, Bible studies, biology, cheerleading, college planning, creative writing, drama, earth science, economics, English language and composition-AP, English language-AP, English literature, English literature and composition-AP, foreign language, general math, geography, government, grammar, health education, history, honors algebra, honors English, human anatomy, Internet, language, language and composition, language arts, library, math applications, math methods, math review, mathematics, mathematics-AP, physical education, SAT/ACT preparation, speech, U.S. government, U.S. history.

College Admission Counseling 10 students graduated in 2010; 8 went to college. Other: 1 went to work, 1 entered military service.

Student Life Upper grades have specified standards of dress, student council, honor system. Discipline rests primarily with faculty.

Tuition and Aid Guaranteed tuition plan.

Admissions Traditional secondary-level entrance grade is 9. Deadline for receipt of application materials: none. Application fee required. Interview required.

Athletics Interscholastic: baseball (boys), basketball (b,g), cheering (g), football (b), softball (g), track and field (b,g), volleyball (g); coed interscholastic: track and field. 1 PE instructor, 1 coach.

Computers Computers are regularly used in career education, library skills classes. Computer network features include Internet access. Student e-mail accounts are available to students.

Contact Mrs. Margaret S. Hallmon, Secretary. 334-683-8204. Fax: 334-683-4938. E-mail: marionacademy@hotmail.com. Web site: www.marionacademy.org.

MARIST HIGH SCHOOL

4200 West 115th Street
Chicago, Illinois 60655-4306
Head of School: Br. Patrick McNamara, FMS

General Information Coeducational day college-preparatory, arts, religious studies, and technology school, affiliated with Roman Catholic Church; primarily serves students with learning disabilities. Grades 9–12. Founded: 1963. Setting: suburban. 55-acre campus. 1 building on campus. Approved or accredited by National Catholic Education Association and Illinois Department of Education. Total enrollment: 1,800. Upper school average class size: 29. Upper school faculty-student ratio: 1:18. The average school day consists of 6 hours and 30 minutes.

Upper School Student Profile 93% of students are Roman Catholic.

Faculty School total: 102. In upper school: 63 men, 39 women; 74 have advanced degrees.

Subjects Offered Accounting, algebra, American legal systems, anatomy, architecture, art, band, biology, biology-AP, business mathematics, calculus, calculus-AP, chemistry, chemistry-AP, chorus, computer graphics, computer science, computer science-AP, creative writing, drafting, drawing, economics, English, English-AP, environmental science, film and literature, film studies, forensics, French, French language-AP, geometry, information technology, journalism, painting, peer counseling, philosophy, physics, physics-AP, pottery, psychology, reading, religious studies, rhetoric, senior humanities, Spanish, Spanish-AP, studio art, U.S. history, U.S. history-AP, Web site design, wellness, Western civilization, world geography.

Graduation Requirements Electives, English, foreign language, mathematics, performing arts, physical education (includes health), religion (includes Bible studies and theology), science, social studies (includes history), technology, visual arts.

Special Academic Programs Advanced Placement exam preparation; honors section; study at local college for college credit; remedial reading and/or remedial writing; programs in English, mathematics, general development for dyslexic students.

College Admission Counseling 422 students graduated in 2009; 416 went to college, including DePaul University; Eastern Illinois University; Illinois State University; Loyola University Chicago; Marquette University; University of Illinois at Urbana–Champaign. Other: 3 went to work, 3 entered military service. Mean composite ACT: 23.

Student Life Upper grades have uniform requirement, student council, honor system. Discipline rests primarily with faculty. Attendance at religious services is required.

Tuition and Aid Day student tuition: $8700. Tuition installment plan (monthly payment plans). Tuition reduction for siblings, merit scholarship grants, need-based scholarship grants, paying campus jobs available. In 2009–10, 31% of upper-school students received aid.

Admissions High School Placement Test required. Deadline for receipt of application materials: January 10. Application fee required: $25.

Athletics Interscholastic: baseball (boys), basketball (b,g), bordenball (b,g), boxing (b), cheering (b), cross-country running (b,g), dance team (g), flag football (g), football (b), golf (b,g), hockey (b), ice hockey (b), pom squad (b), soccer (b,g), softball (g), swimming and diving (g), tennis (b,g), track and field (b,g), volleyball (b,g), wrestling (b); intramural: basketball (b,g), boxing (b); coed interscholastic: billiards; coed intramural: bicycling, bowling, flag football, Frisbee, skiing (downhill). 8 PE instructors, 3 coaches, 1 athletic trainer.

Computers Computers are regularly used in architecture, drafting, graphic design, newspaper, Web site design classes. Computer network features include on-campus library services, online commercial services, Internet access, wireless campus network, Internet filtering or blocking technology. Campus intranet, student e-mail accounts, and computer access in designated common areas are available to students. Students grades are available online. The school has a published electronic and media policy.

Contact Mrs. Alex Brown, Director of Admissions. 773-881-5300 Ext. 5330. Fax: 773-881-0595. E-mail: alex@marist.net. Web site: www.marist.net.

MARIST HIGH SCHOOL
1241 Kennedy Boulevard
Bayonne, New Jersey 07002
Head of School: Br. Steve Schlitte, FMS

General Information Coeducational day college-preparatory, religious studies, and technology school, affiliated with Roman Catholic Church; primarily serves students with learning disabilities. Grades 9–12. Founded: 1954. Setting: urban. 1 building on campus. Approved or accredited by Middle States Association of Colleges and Schools, National Catholic Education Association, and New Jersey Department of Education. Upper school average class size: 25. Upper school faculty-student ratio: 1:25.

Upper School Student Profile Grade 9: 143 students (94 boys, 49 girls); Grade 10: 113 students (70 boys, 43 girls); Grade 11: 114 students (72 boys, 42 girls); Grade 12: 142 students (82 boys, 60 girls). 30% of students are Roman Catholic.

Faculty School total: 55. In upper school: 30 men, 25 women; 20 have advanced degrees.

Subjects Offered Advanced Placement courses, algebra, American history, American history-AP, art education, art history-AP, athletics, baseball, basketball, biology, biology-AP, bowling, British literature (honors), business education, calculus-AP, campus ministry, career/college preparation, character education, college awareness, college counseling, college placement, college planning, college writing, composition-AP, computer education, computer graphics, computer programming, computer skills, economics, English, geometry, health, history, history-AP, independent study, Internet, mathematics, mathematics-AP, programming, social sciences, Spanish, Spanish language-AP.

Graduation Requirements Advanced Placement courses, art, computer skills, driver education, English, foreign language, mathematics, physical education (includes health), religion (includes Bible studies and theology), SAT preparation, science, social studies (includes history), writing workshop.

Special Academic Programs Advanced Placement exam preparation; honors section; independent study; study at local college for college credit; academic accommodation for the gifted; remedial reading and/or remedial writing; remedial math; programs in English, mathematics, general development for dyslexic students; special instructional classes for students with learning disabilities.

College Admission Counseling Colleges students went to include New Jersey Institute of Technology; Pace University; Saint Peter's College; Seton Hall University; The College of New Jersey.

Student Life Upper grades have uniform requirement, student council, honor system. Discipline rests primarily with faculty. Attendance at religious services is required.

Tuition and Aid Day student tuition: $6600. Tuition installment plan (FACTS Tuition Payment Plan). Tuition reduction for siblings, merit scholarship grants, need-based scholarship grants available.

Admissions Traditional secondary-level entrance grade is 9. For fall 2009, 600 students applied for upper-level admission, 110 enrolled. Cooperative Entrance Exam (McGraw-Hill) or Terra Nova-CTB required. Deadline for receipt of application materials: none. Application fee required: $425. On-campus interview recommended.

Athletics Interscholastic: baseball (b,g), basketball (b,g), football (b), soccer (b,g), softball (g), tennis (b,g), volleyball (g); coed interscholastic: bowling, cheering, cross-country running, swimming and diving, track and field, weight lifting; coed intramural: weight lifting, whiffle ball. 1 PE instructor.

Computers Computers are regularly used in all academic classes. Computer network features include on-campus library services, Internet access, wireless campus network, Internet filtering or blocking technology. The school has a published electronic and media policy.

Contact Mr. John A. Taormina, Director of Marketing and Admissions. 201-437-4544 Ext. 202. Fax: 201-437-6013. E-mail: admissions@marist.org. Web site: www.marist.org.

MARIST SCHOOL
3790 Ashford-Dunwoody Road NE
Atlanta, Georgia 30319-1899
Head of School: Rev. Joel M. Konzen, SM

General Information Coeducational day college-preparatory, arts, business, religious studies, and technology school, affiliated with Roman Catholic Church. Grades 7–12. Founded: 1901. Setting: suburban. 77-acre campus. 18 buildings on campus. Approved or accredited by Southern Association of Colleges and Schools, Southern Association of Independent Schools, and Georgia Department of Education. Member of National Association of Independent Schools and Secondary School Admission Test Board. Endowment: $12.8 million. Total enrollment: 1,079. Upper school average class size: 18. Upper school faculty-student ratio: 1:12. There are 177 required school days per year for Upper School students. Upper School students typically attend 5 days per week. The average school day consists of 5 hours and 30 minutes.

Upper School Student Profile Grade 7: 147 students (74 boys, 73 girls); Grade 8: 144 students (72 boys, 72 girls); Grade 9: 205 students (108 boys, 97 girls); Grade 10: 198 students (99 boys, 99 girls); Grade 11: 203 students (102 boys, 101 girls); Grade 12: 182 students (93 boys, 89 girls). 75% of students are Roman Catholic.

Faculty School total: 98. In upper school: 51 men, 47 women; 71 have advanced degrees.

Subjects Offered Algebra, American history, American literature, ancient history, art, art history, biology, business skills, calculus, ceramics, chemistry, community service, computer programming, computer science, creative writing, dance, drama, driver education, economics, English, English literature, European history, fine arts, French, general science, geography, geology, geometry, German, government/civics, health, history, humanities, journalism, Latin, mathematics, music, peace and justice, philosophy, photography, physical education, physics, religion, science, social studies, Spanish, speech, statistics, studio art, theater, theology, world history, world literature, world religions, writing.

Graduation Requirements Arts and fine arts (art, music, dance, drama), business skills (includes word processing), computer science, English, foreign language, mathematics, physical education (includes health), religion (includes Bible studies and theology), science, social studies (includes history), community service requirements in all grades. Community service is required.

Special Academic Programs Advanced Placement exam preparation; honors section; independent study.

College Admission Counseling 197 students graduated in 2010; 196 went to college, including Auburn University; Clemson University; Georgia Institute of Technology; The University of Alabama; University of Georgia. Other: 1 had other specific plans.

Student Life Upper grades have uniform requirement, student council, honor system. Discipline rests primarily with faculty. Attendance at religious services is required.

Summer Programs Enrichment, sports, art/fine arts programs offered; held on campus; accepts boys and girls; open to students from other schools.

Tuition and Aid Day student tuition: $15,475. Tuition installment plan (individually arranged payment plans, Tuition Management System). Need-based scholarship grants available. In 2010–11, 18% of upper-school students received aid. Total amount of financial aid awarded in 2010–11: $16,976,775.

Admissions Traditional secondary-level entrance grade is 7. SSAT required. Deadline for receipt of application materials: January 28. Application fee required: $75. On-campus interview required.

Athletics Interscholastic: baseball (boys), basketball (b,g), cheering (g), cross-country running (b,g), diving (b,g), football (b), golf (b,g), lacrosse (b,g), soccer (b,g), softball (g), swimming and diving (b,g), tennis (b,g), track and field (b,g), volleyball (g), weight lifting (b,g), wrestling (b); coed interscholastic: drill team; coed intramural: outdoor education, ultimate Frisbee. 6 PE instructors.

Computers Computers are regularly used in accounting, business applications, computer applications, drawing and design, English, foreign language, mathematics, music, science classes. Computer network features include on-campus library services, online commercial services, Internet access, wireless campus network, Internet filtering or blocking technology. Student e-mail accounts and computer access in designated common areas are available to students. Students grades are available online. The school has a published electronic and media policy.

Contact Mr. Jim Byrne, Director of Admissions. 770-936-2214. Fax: 770-457-8402. E-mail: admissions@marist.com. Web site: www.marist.com.

MARLBOROUGH SCHOOL
250 South Rossmore Avenue
Los Angeles, California 90004
Head of School: Ms. Barbara E. Wagner

General Information Girls' day college-preparatory school. Grades 7–12. Founded: 1889. Setting: urban. 4-acre campus. 5 buildings on campus. Approved or accredited by California Association of Independent Schools, Western Association of Schools and Colleges, and California Department of Education. Member of National Association of Independent Schools. Endowment: $34.8 million. Total enrollment: 530. Upper school average class size: 12. Upper school faculty-student ratio: 1:8. There are 166 required school days per year for Upper School students. Upper School students typically attend 5 days per week. The average school day consists of 6 hours and 20 minutes.

Faculty School total: 72. In upper school: 15 men, 24 women; 30 have advanced degrees.

Subjects Offered Algebra, American literature, American studies, architecture, art history-AP, astronomy, athletic training, ballet technique, biology, biology-AP, calculus, calculus-AP, ceramics, chemistry, chemistry-AP, Chinese history, choral music, choreography, community service, computer programming, creative writing, dance, digital art, drawing, earth systems analysis, economics, English, English literature, English literature and composition-AP, environmental science, environmental science-AP, European history, European history-AP, French, French language-AP, gender issues, geometry, global studies, health, Hispanic literature, instrumental music, internship, journalism, Latin, Latin American literature, Latin-AP, linear algebra, Mandarin, metalworking, modern world history, music theory, newspaper, painting, photography, physical education, physics, physics-AP, political thought, psychology, research, robotics, Russian literature, sculpture, self-defense, social sciences, Spanish, Spanish language-AP, statistics, statistics-AP, studio art-AP, theater, trigonometry, U.S. history, U.S. history-AP, video and animation, world history, world history-AP, world literature, yearbook, yoga.

Graduation Requirements Arts and fine arts (art, music, dance, drama), English, foreign language, history, mathematics, science, social sciences, typing.

Special Academic Programs 21 Advanced Placement exams for which test preparation is offered; honors section; independent study.

College Admission Counseling 87 students graduated in 2010; all went to college, including Columbia University; Cornell University; Dartmouth College; Princeton University; Stanford University; University of Pennsylvania. Median SAT critical reading: 670, median SAT math: 670, median SAT writing: 700.

Student Life Upper grades have uniform requirement, student council, honor system. Discipline rests equally with students and faculty.

Summer Programs Remediation, enrichment, advancement, sports, art/fine arts, computer instruction programs offered; session focuses on Art, Smart, and Heart; held on campus; accepts boys and girls; open to students from other schools. 500 students usually enrolled. 2011 schedule: June 27 to July 29. Application deadline: June 1.

Tuition and Aid Day student tuition: $29,850. Tuition installment plan (FACTS Tuition Payment Plan, monthly payment plans). Need-based scholarship grants available. In 2010–11, 18% of upper-school students received aid. Total amount of financial aid awarded in 2010–11: $2,043,254.

Admissions For fall 2010, 142 students applied for upper-level admission, 41 were accepted, 20 enrolled. ISEE required. Deadline for receipt of application materials: January 15. Application fee required: $150. On-campus interview required.

Athletics Interscholastic: basketball, cross-country running, equestrian sports, golf, independent competitive sports, soccer, softball, swimming and diving, tennis, track and field, volleyball, water polo. 7 PE instructors, 31 coaches, 1 athletic trainer.

Computers Computers are regularly used in all academic classes. Computer network features include on-campus library services, online commercial services, Internet access, wireless campus network, Internet filtering or blocking technology, videoconferencing. Student e-mail accounts are available to students. Students grades are available online. The school has a published electronic and media policy.

Contact Ms. Jeanette Woo Chitjian, Director of Admissions. 323-964-8450. Fax: 323-933-0542. E-mail: jeanette.woochitjian@marlboroughschool.org. Web site: www.marlboroughschool.org.

MARMION ACADEMY
1000 Butterfield Road
Aurora, Illinois 60502
Head of School: John K. Milroy

General Information Boys' day college-preparatory, business, religious studies, Junior ROTC, and LEAD (Leadership Education and Development) school, affiliated with Roman Catholic Church. Grades 9–12. Founded: 1933. Setting: suburban. Nearest major city is Chicago. 325-acre campus. 5 buildings on campus. Approved or accredited by National Catholic Education Association, North Central Association of Colleges and Schools, and Illinois Department of Education. Member of Secondary School Admission Test Board. Endowment: $9 million. Total enrollment: 499. Upper school average class size: 27. Upper school faculty-student ratio: 1:11. The average school day consists of 7 hours and 25 minutes.

Upper School Student Profile Grade 9: 113 students (113 boys); Grade 10: 125 students (125 boys); Grade 11: 118 students (118 boys); Grade 12: 143 students (143 boys). 88% of students are Roman Catholic.

Faculty School total: 50. In upper school: 40 men, 10 women; 31 have advanced degrees.

Subjects Offered 1½ elective credits, accounting, algebra, American history, American literature, anatomy, art, astronomy, band, biology, biology-AP, botany, calculus, calculus-AP, chemistry, community service, computer science, computer science-AP, computer-aided design, creative writing, driver education, ecology, economics, English, English literature, English-AP, fine arts, French, general science, geometry, government/civics, history, history-AP, Italian, JROTC, Latin, leadership, leadership education training, mathematics, mathematics-AP, meteorology, music, philosophy, physical education, physics, physics-AP, physiology, psychology, religion, science, social sciences, social studies, sociology, Spanish, Spanish language-AP, theology, trigonometry, Western civilization, zoology.

Graduation Requirements Arts and fine arts (art, music, dance, drama), English, foreign language, JROTC, leadership education training, mathematics, music appreciation, physical education (includes health), religion (includes Bible studies and theology), science, social sciences, social studies (includes history). Community service is required.

Special Academic Programs Advanced Placement exam preparation; honors section; independent study; academic accommodation for the gifted.

College Admission Counseling 121 students graduated in 2010; all went to college, including Loyola University Chicago; Marquette University; Northern Illinois University; Saint Louis University; University of Illinois. Mean composite ACT: 25.

Student Life Upper grades have uniform requirement, student council. Discipline rests primarily with faculty. Attendance at religious services is required.

Tuition and Aid Day student tuition: $9100. Tuition installment plan (Tuition Management Systems). Merit scholarship grants, need-based scholarship grants, paying campus jobs available. In 2010–11, 30% of upper-school students received aid; total upper-school merit-scholarship money awarded: $144,000. Total amount of financial aid awarded in 2010–11: $323,000.

Admissions Traditional secondary-level entrance grade is 9. For fall 2010, 210 students applied for upper-level admission, 186 were accepted, 143 enrolled. High School Placement Test (closed version) from Scholastic Testing Service required. Deadline for receipt of application materials: none. Application fee required: $50. On-campus interview required.

Athletics Interscholastic: baseball, basketball, cross-country running, diving, football, golf, lacrosse, riflery, soccer, swimming and diving, tennis, track and field, wrestling; intramural: baseball, basketball, fencing, floor hockey, football, JROTC drill, outdoor activities, outdoors, soccer, swimming and diving, table tennis, tennis, volleyball, water polo, weight lifting. 2 PE instructors, 3 coaches, 1 athletic trainer.

Computers Computers are regularly used in design, science classes. Computer network features include on-campus library services, Internet access. The school has a published electronic and media policy.

Contact William J. Dickson Jr., Director of Admissions. 630-897-6936. Fax: 630-897-7086. Web site: www.marmion.org.

MARQUETTE HIGH SCHOOL
1000 Paul Street
Ottawa, Illinois 61350
Head of School: Supt. Ronald James Spandet

General Information Coeducational day college-preparatory and religious studies school, affiliated with Roman Catholic Church; primarily serves students with learning disabilities and individuals with Attention Deficit Disorder. Grades 9–12. Founded: 1854. Setting: small town. Nearest major city is Aurora. 10-acre campus. 1 building on campus. Approved or accredited by National Catholic Education Association, North Central Association of Colleges and Schools, and Illinois Department of Education. Endowment: $1.6 million. Total enrollment: 200. Upper school average class size: 20. Upper school faculty-student ratio: 1:20. There are 180 required school days per year for Upper School students. Upper School students typically attend 5 days per week. The average school day consists of 7 hours.

Upper School Student Profile Grade 9: 56 students (27 boys, 29 girls); Grade 10: 43 students (14 boys, 29 girls); Grade 11: 51 students (27 boys, 24 girls); Grade 12: 50 students (37 boys, 13 girls). 90% of students are Roman Catholic.

Faculty School total: 23. In upper school: 13 men, 10 women; 10 have advanced degrees.

Subjects Offered .

Graduation Requirements 120 hours of community service.

Special Academic Programs Honors section; accelerated programs; independent study; study at local college for college credit; academic accommodation for the gifted; remedial reading and/or remedial writing; remedial math; special instructional classes for deaf students.

College Admission Counseling 51 students graduated in 2009; 50 went to college. Other: 1 went to work. Median composite ACT: 22. 13% scored over 26 on composite ACT.

Student Life Upper grades have specified standards of dress, student council, honor system. Discipline rests primarily with faculty. Attendance at religious services is required.

Tuition and Aid Tuition installment plan (FACTS Tuition Payment Plan, individually arranged payment plans, full payments, semi-annual, and quarterly payments are paid at the office). Need-based scholarship grants available. In 2009–10, 40% of upper-school students received aid. Total amount of financial aid awarded in 2009–10: $170,000.

Admissions Traditional secondary-level entrance grade is 9. Explore or TerraNova required. Deadline for receipt of application materials: none. No application fee required. On-campus interview required.

Athletics Interscholastic: baseball (boys), basketball (b,g), bowling (b,g), cheering (g), cross-country running (b,g), dance squad (g), football (b), golf (b), physical fitness (b,g), physical training (b,g), pom squad (g), power lifting (b), running (b,g), softball (g), strength & conditioning (b,g), track and field (b,g), volleyball (g), weight lifting (b,g), weight training (b,g). 2 PE instructors, 5 coaches, 1 athletic trainer.

Computers Computers are regularly used in all classes. Computer resources include on-campus library services, Internet access, Internet filtering or blocking technology. Computer access in designated common areas is available to students. The school has a published electronic and media policy.

Contact Mrs. Mindy McConnaughhy, Student Relations Director. 815-433-0125 Ext. 615. Fax: 815-433-2632. Web site: www.marquettehs.com.

MARQUETTE UNIVERSITY HIGH SCHOOL

3401 West Wisconsin Avenue
Milwaukee, Wisconsin 53208
Head of School: Mr. Jeff Monday

General Information Boys' day college-preparatory school, affiliated with Roman Catholic Church. Grades 9–12. Founded: 1857. Setting: urban. 1 building on campus. Approved or accredited by National Catholic Education Association, North Central Association of Colleges and Schools, and Wisconsin Department of Education. Total enrollment: 1,067. Upper school average class size: 22. Upper school faculty-student ratio: 1:13. Upper School students typically attend 5 days per week.

Upper School Student Profile Grade 9: 278 students (278 boys); Grade 10: 272 students (272 boys); Grade 11: 267 students (267 boys); Grade 12: 250 students (250 boys). 85% of students are Roman Catholic.

Faculty School total: 86. In upper school: 57 men, 29 women; 64 have advanced degrees.

Subjects Offered Algebra, American history, American literature, architectural drawing, architecture, art, art-AP, Bible studies, biology, biology-AP, calculus, calculus-AP, ceramics, chemistry, chemistry-AP, choral music, computer math, computer programming, computer science, computer science-AP, creative writing, drama, driver education, economics, English, English language-AP, English literature, English literature-AP, ethics, European history, European history-AP, expository writing, geography, geometry, German, government/civics, grammar, graphic design, health, history, jazz band, Latin, Latin-AP, macroeconomics-AP, mathematics, microeconomics-AP, music, philosophy, photography, physical education, physics, psychology, psychology-AP, religion, social studies, sociology, Spanish, Spanish language-AP, statistics-AP, studio art-AP, theology, trigonometry, U.S. government and politics-AP, U.S. history-AP, world history, world literature, World War I, World War II, writing.

Graduation Requirements Arts and fine arts (art, music, dance, drama), English, foreign language, mathematics, science, social studies (includes history), theology, retreats, community service hours. Community service is required.

Special Academic Programs Advanced Placement exam preparation; honors section.

College Admission Counseling 250 students graduated in 2010; 248 went to college, including Creighton University; Marquette University; Saint Louis University; University of Minnesota, Twin Cities Campus; University of Wisconsin Madison; University of Wisconsin–Milwaukee. Other: 2 entered military service. Median composite ACT: 27. Mean SAT critical reading: 670, mean SAT math: 690.

Student Life Upper grades have specified standards of dress, student council, honor system. Discipline rests primarily with faculty.

Tuition and Aid Day student tuition: $9785. Tuition installment plan (monthly payment plans, prepaid tuition loan program). Need-based scholarship grants, paying campus jobs, state-sponsored voucher program available. In 2010–11, 27% of upper-school students received aid. Total amount of financial aid awarded in 2010–11: $1,400,000.

Admissions Traditional secondary-level entrance grade is 9. Essay and STS—Educational Development Series required. Deadline for receipt of application materials: November 25. Application fee required: $25.

Athletics Interscholastic: baseball, basketball, cross-country running, diving, fitness, football, golf, hockey, ice hockey, indoor track, indoor track & field, lacrosse, physical fitness, physical training, power lifting, rugby, sailing, skiing (downhill), soccer, strength & conditioning, swimming and diving, tennis, track and field, volleyball, weight lifting, weight training, wrestling; intramural: basketball, bowling, soccer, softball, volleyball.

Computers Computers are regularly used in architecture, college planning, creative writing, data processing, desktop publishing, economics, English, graphic design, literary magazine, mathematics, music, newspaper, research skills, stock market, Web

site design, word processing, writing, yearbook classes. Computer network features include on-campus library services, online commercial services, Internet access, Internet filtering or blocking technology, university and county library systems link. Student e-mail accounts are available to students.

Contact Mr. Casey Kowalewski, Director of Admissions. 414-933-7220 Ext. 3046. Fax: 414-937-6002. E-mail: admissions@muhs.edu. Web site: www.muhs.edu.

MARS HILL BIBLE SCHOOL

698 Cox Creek Parkway
Florence, Alabama 35630
Head of School: Dr. Kenny D. Barfield

General Information Coeducational day college-preparatory, arts, and religious studies school, affiliated with Church of Christ. Grades K–12. Founded: 1947. Setting: suburban. Nearest major city is Huntsville. 80-acre campus. 7 buildings on campus. Approved or accredited by National Christian School Association and Southern Association of Colleges and Schools. Endowment: $2.7 million. Total enrollment: 600. Upper school average class size: 22. Upper school faculty-student ratio: 1:14. There are 180 required school days per year for Upper School students. Upper School students typically attend 5 days per week. The average school day consists of 6 hours.

Upper School Student Profile Grade 9: 54 students (18 boys, 36 girls); Grade 10: 71 students (27 boys, 44 girls); Grade 11: 67 students (34 boys, 33 girls); Grade 12: 48 students (29 boys, 19 girls). 82% of students are members of Church of Christ.

Faculty School total: 43. In upper school: 11 men, 12 women; 15 have advanced degrees.

Subjects Offered ACT preparation, algebra, American government, American literature, American literature-AP, anatomy and physiology, ancient world history, band, Bible studies, biology, biology-AP, calculus, calculus-AP, chemistry, chorus, computer literacy, computer programming, computer science, concert band, concert choir, debate, drama, drama performance, driver education, ecology, economics, English, English composition, English literature, English literature and composition-AP, English literature-AP, ensembles, forensics, geometry, health, honors English, human anatomy, Internet research, jazz band, Life of Christ, marine biology, musical productions, physical education, physical science, physics, pre-algebra, pre-calculus, psychology, Spanish, speech, speech and debate, student government, student publications, U.S. history, U.S. history-AP, word processing, world geography, world history, yearbook.

Graduation Requirements Algebra, American government, American history, American literature, ancient world history, Bible, biology, British literature, chemistry, college writing, computer applications, computer literacy, economics, English composition, foreign language, geometry, health and wellness, introduction to literature, mathematics, physical education (includes health), physical science, science, social studies (includes history), speech communications. Community service is required.

Special Academic Programs 3 Advanced Placement exams for which test preparation is offered; honors section; independent study; study at local college for college credit; special instructional classes for students with learning disabilities, Attention Deficit Disorder, and dyslexia.

College Admission Counseling 48 students graduated in 2010; all went to college, including Auburn University; Freed-Hardeman University; Harding University; The University of Alabama; The University of Alabama at Birmingham; University of North Alabama. Median composite ACT: 24. 43% scored over 26 on composite ACT.

Student Life Upper grades have specified standards of dress, student council. Discipline rests primarily with faculty. Attendance at religious services is required.

Summer Programs Enrichment, sports, art/fine arts programs offered; session focuses on Athletics, driver education, forensics, show choir, band; held on campus; accepts boys and girls; open to students from other schools. 200 students usually enrolled. 2011 schedule: June 1 to July 31. Application deadline: June 1.

Tuition and Aid Day student tuition: $5230. Tuition installment plan (FACTS Tuition Payment Plan, monthly payment plans). Tuition reduction for siblings, need-based scholarship grants available. In 2010–11, 20% of upper-school students received aid. Total amount of financial aid awarded in 2010–11: $150,000.

Admissions Traditional secondary-level entrance grade is 9. For fall 2010, 24 students applied for upper-level admission, 19 were accepted, 16 enrolled. Achievement tests, ACT-Explore, PSAT or Stanford Achievement Test required. Deadline for receipt of application materials: none. Application fee required: $100. Interview required.

Athletics Interscholastic: baseball (boys), basketball (b,g), cheering (g), cross-country running (b,g), football (b), golf (b,g), soccer (b,g), softball (g), tennis (b,g), track and field (b,g), volleyball (g); intramural: basketball (b,g). 3 PE instructors, 7 coaches.

Computers Computers are regularly used in all academic, Bible studies, English, history, remedial study skills, yearbook classes. Computer resources include on-campus library services, online commercial services, Internet access, wireless campus network, Internet filtering or blocking technology. Campus intranet and computer access in designated common areas are available to students. Students grades are available online. The school has a published electronic and media policy.

Contact Mrs. Jeannie Garrett, Director of Admissions. 256-767-1203 Ext. 205. Fax: 256-767-6304. E-mail: jgarrett@mhbs.org. Web site: www.mhbs.org.

MARTIN LUTHER HIGH SCHOOL

60-02 Maspeth Avenue
Maspeth, New York 11378
Head of School: Randy Gast

General Information Coeducational day college-preparatory, arts, and business school, affiliated with Lutheran Church. Grades 9–12. Founded: 1960. Setting: urban. Nearest major city is New York. 1-acre campus. 1 building on campus. Approved or accredited by Middle States Association of Colleges and Schools and New York Department of Education. Endowment: $2.2 million. Total enrollment: 211. Upper school average class size: 22. Upper school faculty-student ratio: 1:12.

Upper School Student Profile Grade 9: 42 students (19 boys, 23 girls); Grade 10: 39 students (20 boys, 19 girls); Grade 11: 52 students (30 boys, 22 girls); Grade 12: 78 students (34 boys, 44 girls). 16% of students are Lutheran.

Faculty School total: 18. In upper school: 7 men, 11 women; 8 have advanced degrees.

Subjects Offered Algebra, American history, art, Bible studies, biology, business, business skills, calculus, chemistry, chemistry-AP, computer programming, computer science, drama, driver education, earth science, economics, English, English literature, English literature-AP, environmental science-AP, ethics, European history, fine arts, French, geography, geometry, German, government/civics, grammar, health, history, journalism, marine biology, mathematics, music, philosophy, photography, physical education, physics, psychology, religion, science, social studies, Spanish, Spanish-AP, speech, theater, theology, trigonometry, U.S. history-AP, world history.

Graduation Requirements Arts and fine arts (art, music, dance, drama), business skills (includes word processing), English, foreign language, mathematics, physical education (includes health), religion (includes Bible studies and theology), science, social studies (includes history), service hours.

Special Academic Programs Advanced Placement exam preparation; honors section; accelerated programs; independent study; study at local college for college credit; programs in general development for dyslexic students.

College Admission Counseling 76 students graduated in 2010; 74 went to college, including John Jay College of Criminal Justice of the City University of New York; Queens College of the City University of New York; St. Francis College; St. John's University; St. Joseph's College, New York. Other: 1 entered military service.

Student Life Upper grades have uniform requirement, student council. Discipline rests primarily with faculty. Attendance at religious services is required.

Summer Programs Remediation, computer instruction programs offered; held on campus; accepts boys and girls; open to students from other schools. 250 students usually enrolled. 2011 schedule: July 2 to August 16. Application deadline: none.

Tuition and Aid Day student tuition: $8000–$9200. Tuition installment plan (monthly payment plans). Tuition reduction for siblings, merit scholarship grants, need-based scholarship grants available. In 2010–11, 50% of upper-school students received aid; total upper-school merit-scholarship money awarded: $73,125. Total amount of financial aid awarded in 2010–11: $195,182.

Admissions Traditional secondary-level entrance grade is 9. School's own exam required. Deadline for receipt of application materials: none. Application fee required: $50. On-campus interview required.

Athletics Interscholastic: baseball (boys), basketball (b,g), cheering (g), cross-country running (b,g), fitness (b,g), soccer (b), softball (g), tennis (b,g), track and field (b,g), volleyball (g), wrestling (b,g); intramural: basketball (b,g), cross-country running (b,g), floor hockey (b,g), indoor hockey (b,g), soccer (b,g), weight lifting (b,g), wrestling (b); coed interscholastic: cheering, cross-country running, fitness, soccer; coed intramural: archery, badminton, cross-country running, fitness, handball, paddle tennis, racquetball, track and field, volleyball, wrestling. 3 PE instructors, 18 coaches.

Computers Computers are regularly used in business education, career education, Christian doctrine, history, keyboarding, newspaper, yearbook classes. Computer resources include on-campus library services, Internet access.

Contact Ms. Patricia Dee, Admissions Administrator. 718-894-4000 Ext. 122. Fax: 718-894-1469. E-mail: pdee@martinluthernyc.org. Web site: www.martinluthernyc.org.

THE MARVELWOOD SCHOOL

476 Skiff Mountain Road
PO Box 3001
Kent, Connecticut 06757-3001
Head of School: Mr. Scott E. Pottbecker

General Information Coeducational boarding and day college-preparatory, arts, technology, field science, and community service, and ESL school; primarily serves underachievers, students with learning disabilities, individuals with Attention Deficit Disorder, and dyslexic students. Grades 9–12. Founded: 1957. Setting: rural. Nearest major city is Hartford. Students are housed in single-sex dormitories. 83-acre campus. 10 buildings on campus. Approved or accredited by Connecticut Association of Independent Schools, New England Association of Schools and Colleges, The Association of Boarding Schools, and Connecticut Department of Education. Member of National Association of Independent Schools. Endowment: $1.4 million. Total enrollment: 165. Upper school average class size: 8. Upper school faculty-student ratio: 1:4. Upper School students typically attend 6 days per week.

Upper School Student Profile Grade 9: 15 students (10 boys, 5 girls); Grade 10: 36 students (20 boys, 16 girls); Grade 11: 62 students (44 boys, 18 girls); Grade 12: 52

students (32 boys, 20 girls). 94% of students are boarding students. 21% are state residents. 14 states are represented in upper school student body. 33% are international students. International students from China, Jamaica, Mexico, Republic of Korea, Spain, and United Kingdom; 7 other countries represented in student body.

Faculty School total: 48. In upper school: 19 men, 27 women; 24 have advanced degrees; 35 reside on campus.

Subjects Offered Algebra, American history, American literature, anatomy and physiology, art, art history, biology, calculus, ceramics, chemistry, chorus, college writing, community service, creative writing, drama, driver education, English, English literature, ESL, ethology, European history, film, fine arts, French, geography, geometry, history of China and Japan, limnology, mathematics, music, ornithology, photography, physics, pre-algebra, psychology, religion, science, Shakespeare, social studies, Spanish, studio art, trigonometry, world cultures, world history, world literature.

Graduation Requirements Arts and fine arts (art, music, dance, drama), English, foreign language, mathematics, science, social studies (includes history), senior service project, daily participation in sports, weekly community service program.

Special Academic Programs Advanced Placement exam preparation; honors section; remedial reading and/or remedial writing; remedial math; programs in general development for dyslexic students; ESL (38 students enrolled).

College Admission Counseling 47 students graduated in 2009; 44 went to college, including Lynn University; Pace University; Savannah College of Art and Design; Syracuse University; University of Hartford; Washington College. Other: 3 had other specific plans. Median SAT critical reading: 458, median SAT math: 424, median SAT writing: 458.

Student Life Upper grades have uniform requirement, student council. Discipline rests primarily with faculty.

Tuition and Aid Day student tuition: $26,500; 7-day tuition and room/board: $43,000. Tuition installment plan (Insured Tuition Payment Plan, Academic Management Services Plan, Key Tuition Payment Plan, individually arranged payment plans). Merit scholarship grants, need-based scholarship grants available. In 2009–10, 30% of upper-school students received aid; total upper-school merit-scholarship money awarded: $43,000. Total amount of financial aid awarded in 2009–10: $806,000.

Admissions Traditional secondary-level entrance grade is 9. For fall 2009, 222 students applied for upper-level admission, 122 were accepted, 57 enrolled. Deadline for receipt of application materials: none. Application fee required: $50. Interview required.

Athletics Interscholastic: baseball (boys), basketball (b,g), cross-country running (b,g), lacrosse (b), soccer (b,g), softball (g), tennis (b,g), volleyball (g), wrestling (b); intramural: lacrosse (g); coed interscholastic: alpine skiing, golf, skiing (downhill); coed intramural: bicycling, canoeing/kayaking, climbing, dance, fishing, fly fishing, Frisbee, hiking/backpacking, horseback riding, kayaking, mountain biking, mountaineering, outdoor activities, physical training, rock climbing, ropes courses, skiing (downhill), snowboarding, strength & conditioning, weight training, wilderness, wildernessways, yoga. 1 athletic trainer.

Computers Computers are regularly used in mathematics, newspaper, photography, science, writing classes. Computer network features include on-campus library services, Internet access, wireless campus network, Internet filtering or blocking technology. Campus intranet, student e-mail accounts, and computer access in designated common areas are available to students. The school has a published electronic and media policy.

Contact Mrs. Maureen Smith, Admissions Associate. 860-927-0047 Ext. 1005. Fax: 860-927-0021. E-mail: maureen.smith@marvelwood.org. Web site: www.marvelwood.org.

MARY INSTITUTE AND ST. LOUIS COUNTRY DAY SCHOOL (MICDS)

101 North Warson Road
St. Louis, Missouri 63124
Head of School: Lisa Lyle

General Information Coeducational day college-preparatory, arts, and technology school. Grades JK–12. Founded: 1859. Setting: suburban. 100-acre campus. 5 buildings on campus. Approved or accredited by Independent Schools Association of the Central States, Missouri Independent School Association, and Missouri Department of Education. Member of National Association of Independent Schools and Secondary School Admission Test Board. Endowment: $62.3 million. Total enrollment: 1,210. Upper school average class size: 15. Upper school faculty-student ratio: 1:8. There are 165 required school days per year for Upper School students. Upper School students typically attend 5 days per week. The average school day consists of 7 hours and 10 minutes.

Upper School Student Profile Grade 9: 148 students (73 boys, 75 girls); Grade 10: 157 students (84 boys, 73 girls); Grade 11: 139 students (65 boys, 74 girls); Grade 12: 154 students (76 boys, 78 girls).

Faculty School total: 159. In upper school: 37 men, 34 women; 56 have advanced degrees.

Subjects Offered Acting, advanced chemistry, algebra, American literature, animal behavior, architecture, art history-AP, band, biology, biology-AP, calculus, calculus-AP, chemistry, chemistry-AP, chorus, civil rights, composition, creative writing, digital art, directing, economics, economics-AP, English language-AP, English literature and composition-AP, ethics, European history-AP, French, geometry, global studies, government-AP, Latin, literature, music theory-AP, painting, photography, physics, physics-AP, physiology, playwriting and directing, political science, pre-calculus, psychology, sculpture, Shakespeare, Spanish, Spanish language-AP, statistics, statistics-AP, studio art, studio art-AP, trigonometry, U.S. history, U.S. history-AP, utopia, Web site design, world history.

Graduation Requirements Arts and fine arts (art, music, dance, drama), English, foreign language, mathematics, physical education (includes health), science, social studies (includes history). Community service is required.

Special Academic Programs Advanced Placement exam preparation; honors section; independent study; term-away projects; study abroad; academic accommodation for the gifted.

College Admission Counseling 137 students graduated in 2009; all went to college, including Miami University; Southern Methodist University; University of Michigan; University of Missouri; University of Southern California; Washington University in St. Louis. Mean SAT critical reading: 608, mean SAT math: 630, mean SAT writing: 607, mean combined SAT: 1845, mean composite ACT: 28.

Student Life Upper grades have specified standards of dress, student council, honor system. Discipline rests equally with students and faculty.

Tuition and Aid Day student tuition: $20,040. Tuition installment plan (Monthly Plan through FACTS Management, Your Tuition Solution (Loan), credit card payment). Need-based scholarship grants available. In 2009–10, 23% of upper-school students received aid. Total amount of financial aid awarded in 2009–10: $1,741,895.

Admissions Traditional secondary-level entrance grade is 9. For fall 2009, 66 students applied for upper-level admission, 35 were accepted, 25 enrolled. ISEE or SSAT required. Deadline for receipt of application materials: January 15. Application fee required: $40. Interview required.

Athletics Interscholastic: baseball (boys), cheering (g), crew (b,g), cross-country running (b,g), dance (b,g), diving (b,g), field hockey (g), football (b), golf (b,g), ice hockey (b), lacrosse (b,g), soccer (b,g), swimming and diving (b,g), tennis (b,g), track and field (b,g), volleyball (g), water polo (b), wrestling (b); intramural: fitness (b,g), independent competitive sports (b,g), jogging (b,g), modern dance (b,g), physical fitness (b,g), physical training (b,g), strength & conditioning (b,g), weight training (b,g); coed interscholastic: dance, water polo, wrestling; coed intramural: fitness, independent competitive sports, modern dance, physical fitness, physical training, strength & conditioning, ultimate Frisbee, weight training. 45 coaches.

Computers Computers are regularly used in art, English, foreign language, history, mathematics, music, science classes. Computer network features include on-campus library services, online commercial services, Internet access, wireless campus network, Internet filtering or blocking technology. Student e-mail accounts and computer access in designated common areas are available to students. Students grades are available online. The school has a published electronic and media policy.

Contact Peggy B. Laramie, Director of Admission and Financial Aid. 314-995-7367. Fax: 314-872-3257. E-mail: plaramie@micds.org.

MARYKNOLL SCHOOL
1526 Alexander Street
Honolulu, Hawaii 96822
Head of School: Perry K. Martin

General Information Coeducational day college-preparatory school, affiliated with Roman Catholic Church. Grades K–12. Founded: 1927. Setting: urban. 3-acre campus. 3 buildings on campus. Approved or accredited by National Catholic Education Association, Western Association of Schools and Colleges, Western Catholic Education Association, and Hawaii Department of Education. Member of National Association of Independent Schools and Secondary School Admission Test Board. Endowment: $3.5 million. Total enrollment: 1,465. Upper school average class size: 18. Upper school faculty-student ratio: 1:11.

Upper School Student Profile Grade 6: 95 students (59 boys, 36 girls); Grade 7: 102 students (46 boys, 56 girls); Grade 8: 100 students (50 boys, 50 girls); Grade 9: 171 students (77 boys, 94 girls); Grade 10: 154 students (69 boys, 85 girls); Grade 11: 147 students (72 boys, 75 girls); Grade 12: 136 students (67 boys, 69 girls). 50% of students are Roman Catholic.

Faculty School total: 104. In upper school: 26 men, 28 women; 30 have advanced degrees.

Subjects Offered Adolescent issues, advanced chemistry, algebra, American literature, art, art history-AP, biology, biology-AP, biotechnology, calculus-AP, chemistry, chemistry-AP, college counseling, college placement, computer programming, creative writing, drawing, economics, English language and composition-AP, English literature and composition-AP, ethics, European history-AP, geography, geometry, global science, golf, government, government-AP, guitar, Hawaiian history, Hawaiian language, human development, Japanese, journalism, library assistant, marine science, media, mythology, novels, Pacific art, painting, philosophy, physical education, physics, physics-AP, poetry, pre-calculus, psychology, psychology-AP, religion, religious studies, research, Russian history, science fiction, senior project, Shakespeare, sociology, Spanish, speech, statistics, studio art-AP, theater, U.S. history, U.S. history-AP, Web site design, weight training, world history, world literature, yearbook.

Graduation Requirements Arts and fine arts (art, music, dance, drama), English, foreign language, mathematics, physical education (includes health), religion

(includes Bible studies and theology), science, senior project, social sciences, social studies (includes history), portfolio of student works. Community service is required.

Special Academic Programs Advanced Placement exam preparation; honors section; independent study.

College Admission Counseling 125 students graduated in 2010; all went to college, including Loyola Marymount University; Santa Clara University; University of Hawaii at Manoa; University of San Francisco; University of Southern California; University of Washington.

Student Life Upper grades have uniform requirement, student council. Discipline rests equally with students and faculty. Attendance at religious services is required.

Summer Programs Remediation, enrichment, advancement, sports, art/fine arts, computer instruction programs offered; session focuses on advancement and enrichment; held on campus; accepts boys and girls; open to students from other schools. 800 students usually enrolled. 2011 schedule: June 16 to July 28. Application deadline: May 15.

Tuition and Aid Day student tuition: $13,010. Tuition installment plan (Insured Tuition Payment Plan, monthly payment plans). Merit scholarship grants, need-based scholarship grants, paying campus jobs available. In 2010–11, 18% of upper-school students received aid; total upper-school merit-scholarship money awarded: $73,000. Total amount of financial aid awarded in 2010–11: $550,000.

Admissions Traditional secondary-level entrance grade is 9. PSAT or SSAT required. Deadline for receipt of application materials: December 15. Application fee required: $75. On-campus interview required.

Athletics Interscholastic: aerobics/dance (girls), baseball (b), basketball (b,g), bowling (b,g), canoeing/kayaking (b,g), cross-country running (b,g), dance (g), diving (b,g), football (b), golf (b,g), gymnastics (b,g), judo (b,g), kayaking (b,g), martial arts (b,g), ocean paddling (b,g), paddling (b,g), power lifting (b,g), riflery (b,g), sailing (b,g), soccer (b,g), softball (g), strength & conditioning (b,g), swimming and diving (b,g), tennis (b,g), track and field (b,g), volleyball (b,g), water polo (b,g), weight lifting (b,g), weight training (b,g), wrestling (b,g); intramural: basketball (b,g), volleyball (b,g); coed interscholastic: canoeing/kayaking, cheering, football, ocean paddling, paddling, strength & conditioning, weight training, wrestling; coed intramural: basketball, bowling, floor hockey. 4 PE instructors, 50 coaches, 2 athletic trainers.

Computers Computers are regularly used in English, foreign language, history, mathematics, science classes. Computer network features include on-campus library services, online commercial services, Internet access, wireless campus network, Internet filtering or blocking technology. Student e-mail accounts are available to students. The school has a published electronic and media policy.

Contact Mrs. Lori Carlos, Director of Admission. 808-952-7330. Fax: 808-952-7306. E-mail: admission@maryknollschool.org. Web site: www.maryknollschool.org.

MARYLAWN OF THE ORANGES
445 Scotland Road
South Orange, New Jersey 07079
Head of School: Mrs. Christine H. Lopez

General Information Girls' day college-preparatory, arts, business, religious studies, bilingual studies; and technology school, affiliated with Roman Catholic Church. Grades 7–12. Founded: 1935. Setting: suburban. Nearest major city is Newark. 2 buildings on campus. Approved or accredited by Middle States Association of Colleges and Schools and New Jersey Department of Education. Total enrollment: 143. Upper school average class size: 15. Upper school faculty-student ratio: 1:15. There are 183 required school days per year for Upper School students. Upper School students typically attend 5 days per week. The average school day consists of 7 hours and 15 minutes.

Upper School Student Profile Grade 7: 8 students (8 girls); Grade 8: 8 students (8 girls); Grade 9: 20 students (20 girls); Grade 10: 39 students (39 girls); Grade 11: 33 students (33 girls); Grade 12: 35 students (35 girls). 25% of students are Roman Catholic.

Faculty School total: 21. In upper school: 9 men, 12 women; 8 have advanced degrees.

Subjects Offered Advanced chemistry, advanced math, algebra, American literature, anatomy and physiology, art, art history, athletics, biology, British literature (honors), calculus, campus ministry, career/college preparation, Catholic belief and practice, cheerleading, chemistry, choir, choral music, Christian ethics, Christian scripture, civics, classical studies, community service, constitutional law, dramatic arts, English, English-AP, fine arts, French, geometry, global studies, grammar, guidance, health education, honors algebra, honors English, honors geometry, honors U.S. history, Internet research, language arts, Latin, mathematics, moral theology, music theory, physical education, physics, pre-calculus, psychology, SAT/ACT preparation, social studies, Spanish, trigonometry, U.S. history, world history, world religions, writing workshop, yearbook.

Graduation Requirements Arts and fine arts (art, music, dance, drama), electives, English, foreign language, guidance, health education, mathematics, physical education (includes health), religious studies, science, social studies (includes history), 20 hours of community service (sophomore year), 25 hours of community service (junior year), 40 hours of community service (senior year).

Marylawn of the Oranges

Special Academic Programs 1 Advanced Placement exam for which test preparation is offered; honors section; independent study; academic accommodation for the gifted, the musically talented, and the artistically talented; remedial reading and/or remedial writing; remedial math; ESL.

College Admission Counseling 41 students graduated in 2010; all went to college, including Johnson & Wales University; Kean University; Pace University; Rutgers, The State University of New Jersey, New Brunswick; Seton Hall University; Temple University. Median SAT critical reading: 450, median SAT math: 420, median SAT writing: 450. 10% scored over 600 on SAT critical reading, 2% scored over 600 on SAT math, 10% scored over 600 on SAT writing.

Student Life Upper grades have uniform requirement, student council. Discipline rests primarily with faculty. Attendance at religious services is required.

Summer Programs Remediation, enrichment, advancement, computer instruction programs offered; session focuses on prep and advancement for secondary school courses, make-up for failed classes; held on campus; accepts boys and girls; open to students from other schools. 75 students usually enrolled. 2011 schedule: June 27 to July 26. Application deadline: June 20.

Tuition and Aid Day student tuition: $8300. Tuition installment plan (monthly payment plans, Tuition Management Systems). Tuition reduction for siblings, merit scholarship grants, need-based scholarship grants available. In 2010–11, 45% of upper-school students received aid; total upper-school merit-scholarship money awarded: $20,000. Total amount of financial aid awarded in 2010–11: $111,850.

Admissions Traditional secondary-level entrance grade is 9. For fall 2010, 130 students applied for upper-level admission, 98 were accepted, 46 enrolled. Cooperative Entrance Exam (McGraw-Hill) required. Deadline for receipt of application materials: none. Application fee required: $125. On-campus interview recommended.

Athletics Interscholastic: basketball, cheering, dance team, drill team, softball, track and field, volleyball; intramural: basketball, physical fitness, soccer, softball, tennis, weight training. 2 PE instructors, 6 coaches.

Computers Computers are regularly used in all classes. Computer resources include on-campus library services, Internet access, Internet filtering or blocking technology. Student e-mail accounts are available to students. The school has a published electronic and media policy.

Contact Ms. Fiana Muhlberger, Admissions Officer. 973-762-9222 Ext. 15. Fax: 973-378-7975. E-mail: fmuhlberger@marylawn.us. Web site: www.marylawn.us.

MARYMOUNT HIGH SCHOOL

10643 Sunset Boulevard
Los Angeles, California 90077
Head of School: Ms. Jacqueline Landry

General Information Girls' day college-preparatory and religious studies school, affiliated with Roman Catholic Church. Grades 9–12. Founded: 1923. Setting: suburban. 6-acre campus. 6 buildings on campus. Approved or accredited by California Association of Independent Schools, National Catholic Education Association, The College Board, Western Association of Schools and Colleges, and California Department of Education. Member of National Association of Independent Schools and Secondary School Admission Test Board. Endowment: $5.3 million. Total enrollment: 366. Upper school average class size: 15. Upper school faculty-student ratio: 1:7. There are 170 required school days per year for Upper School students. Upper School students typically attend 5 days per week. The average school day consists of 7 hours.

Upper School Student Profile Grade 9: 89 students (89 girls); Grade 10: 93 students (93 girls); Grade 11: 89 students (89 girls); Grade 12: 95 students (95 girls). 68% of students are Roman Catholic.

Faculty School total: 54. In upper school: 13 men, 41 women; 42 have advanced degrees.

Subjects Offered Acting, advanced studio art-AP, aerobics, African literature, algebra, American history, American legal systems, American literature, anatomy, art, art history, art-AP, biology, biology-AP, British literature, calculus, calculus-AP, ceramics, chemistry, choir, Christian testament, community service, computer literacy, computer science, contemporary issues, dance, death and loss, design, drama, drawing, ecology, economics, English, English literature, environmental science, environmental science-AP, ethics, fencing, fine arts, French, French-AP, gender and religion, geography, geometry, government/civics, Hebrew scripture, human development, Japanese literature, jazz ensemble, journalism, language and composition, literary magazine, literature, literature-AP, music, musical productions, painting, peace studies, performing arts, photography, physical education, physics, physiology, pre-calculus, printmaking, psychology, religion, religious studies, robotics, science, self-defense, social justice, social studies, softball, Spanish, Spanish language-AP, Spanish literature-AP, speech, swimming, theology, trigonometry, U.S. government and politics-AP, U.S. history, U.S. history-AP, vocal music, volleyball, women's studies, world religions, writing.

Graduation Requirements Arts and fine arts (art, music, dance, drama), English, foreign language, mathematics, physical education (includes health), religion (includes Bible studies and theology), science, social studies (includes history), 100 hours of community service.

Special Academic Programs 17 Advanced Placement exams for which test preparation is offered; honors section; independent study.

College Admission Counseling 105 students graduated in 2010; all went to college, including New York University; Santa Clara University; University of California,
Berkeley; University of California, Los Angeles; University of California, Santa Barbara; University of Southern California. Median SAT critical reading: 615, median SAT math: 609, median SAT writing: 668, median combined SAT: 1892. Mean composite ACT: 27.

Student Life Upper grades have uniform requirement, student council, honor system. Discipline rests equally with students and faculty. Attendance at religious services is required.

Summer Programs Remediation, enrichment, advancement, sports, art/fine arts, computer instruction programs offered; session focuses on enrichment, advancement; held on campus; accepts girls; open to students from other schools. 180 students usually enrolled. 2011 schedule: June 20 to July 22. Application deadline: May 20.

Tuition and Aid Day student tuition: $25,600. Tuition installment plan (FACTS Tuition Payment Plan). Merit scholarship grants, need-based scholarship grants available. In 2010–11, 25% of upper-school students received aid; total upper-school merit-scholarship money awarded: $15,000. Total amount of financial aid awarded in 2010–11: $1,200,000.

Admissions Traditional secondary-level entrance grade is 9. For fall 2010, 216 students applied for upper-level admission, 164 were accepted, 84 enrolled. ISEE required. Deadline for receipt of application materials: January 10. Application fee required: $100. On-campus interview required.

Athletics Interscholastic: basketball, cross-country running, equestrian sports, fencing, golf, soccer, softball, swimming and diving, tennis, track and field, volleyball, water polo; intramural: aerobics, aerobics/dance, archery, crew, dance, physical fitness, self defense, strength & conditioning. 1 PE instructor, 24 coaches, 1 athletic trainer.

Computers Computers are regularly used in all academic classes. Computer network features include on-campus library services, online commercial services, Internet access, wireless campus network, Internet filtering or blocking technology, one-to-one student laptop program, access to UCLA Library, Loyola Marymount University Library, 14 independent high school libraries. Campus intranet, student e-mail accounts, and computer access in designated common areas are available to students. Students grades are available online. The school has a published electronic and media policy.

Contact Mrs. Erica Huebner, Director of Admission. 310-472-1205 Ext. 220. Fax: 310-440-4316. E-mail: ehuebner@mhs-la.org. Web site: www.mhs-la.org.

MARYMOUNT INTERNATIONAL SCHOOL

Via di Villa Lauchli 180
Rome 00191, Italy
Head of School: Ms. Maire McNamara

General Information Coeducational day college-preparatory school, affiliated with Roman Catholic Church. Grades PK–12. Founded: 1946. Setting: suburban. 16-acre campus. 3 buildings on campus. Approved or accredited by European Council of International Schools and New England Association of Schools and Colleges. Language of instruction: English. Total enrollment: 637. Upper school average class size: 18. Upper school faculty-student ratio: 1:15. There are 171 required school days per year for Upper School students. Upper School students typically attend 5 days per week. The average school day consists of 6 hours and 45 minutes.

Upper School Student Profile Grade 9: 48 students (24 boys, 24 girls); Grade 10: 52 students (31 boys, 21 girls); Grade 11: 54 students (16 boys, 38 girls); Grade 12: 47 students (31 boys, 16 girls). 75% of students are Roman Catholic.

Faculty School total: 98. In upper school: 12 men, 35 women; 40 have advanced degrees.

Subjects Offered Algebra, American history, American literature, art, art history, art history-AP, biology, calculus, ceramics, chemistry, computer science, current events, drama, English, English literature, environmental science, ESL, European history, fine arts, French, geography, geometry, health, history, International Baccalaureate courses, international relations, Italian, Latin, mathematics, music, photography, physical education, physics, pre-calculus, psychology, religious education, science, social studies, Spanish, study skills, theater arts, theory of knowledge, trigonometry, world history.

Graduation Requirements Arts and fine arts (art, music, dance, drama), English, foreign language, mathematics, religion (includes Bible studies and theology), science, social studies (includes history).

Special Academic Programs International Baccalaureate program; ESL (24 students enrolled).

College Admission Counseling 46 students graduated in 2010; 40 went to college, including Bentley University; Dickinson College; New York University; Northeastern University; Penn State University Park; University of Illinois at Chicago. Other: 1 went to work, 1 entered a postgraduate year, 2 had other specific plans. Median SAT critical reading: 500, median SAT math: 500, median SAT writing: 520. 15% scored over 600 on SAT critical reading, 15% scored over 600 on SAT math, 15% scored over 600 on SAT writing.

Student Life Upper grades have specified standards of dress, student council, honor system. Discipline rests primarily with faculty. Attendance at religious services is required.

Tuition and Aid Day student tuition: €17,200.

Admissions Traditional secondary-level entrance grade is 9. For fall 2010, 53 students applied for upper-level admission, 41 were accepted, 30 enrolled. Deadline for receipt of application materials: none. Application fee required. €350. On-campus interview recommended.

Athletics Interscholastic: basketball (boys, girls), cheering (g), cross-country running (b,g), soccer (b,g), tennis (b,g), track and field (b,g), volleyball (b,g). 2 PE instructors, 9 coaches.

Computers Computers are regularly used in graphic arts classes. Computer network features include on-campus library services, Internet access, wireless campus network, Internet filtering or blocking technology. Student e-mail accounts are available to students.

Contact Ms. Deborah Woods, Admissions Director. 39-063629101 Ext. 212. Fax: 39-36301738. E-mail: admissions@marymountrome.org. Web site: www.marymountrome.org.

MARYMOUNT INTERNATIONAL SCHOOL

George Road
Kingston upon Thames
Surrey KT2 7PE, United Kingdom
Head of School: Ms. Sarah Gallagher

General Information Girls' boarding and day college-preparatory, general academic, arts, religious studies, and International Baccalaureate school, affiliated with Roman Catholic Church. Grades 6–12. Founded: 1955. Setting: suburban. Nearest major city is London, United Kingdom. Students are housed in single-sex dormitories. 7-acre campus. 9 buildings on campus. Approved or accredited by Boarding Schools Association (UK), Department for Education and Skills (UK), European Council of International Schools, Independent Schools Council (UK), International Baccalaureate Organization, and Middle States Association of Colleges and Schools. Member of Secondary School Admission Test Board. Language of instruction: English. Total enrollment: 212. Upper school average class size: 12. Upper school faculty-student ratio: 1:7. There are 176 required school days per year for Upper School students. Upper School students typically attend 5 days per week. The average school day consists of 7 hours and 30 minutes.

Upper School Student Profile Grade 9: 29 students (29 girls); Grade 10: 47 students (47 girls); Grade 11: 45 students (45 girls); Grade 12: 48 students (48 girls). 46% of students are boarding students. 41% are international students. International students from China, Germany, Japan, Republic of Korea, Spain, and United States; 40 other countries represented in student body. 37% of students are Roman Catholic.

Faculty School total: 44. In upper school: 11 men, 33 women; 20 have advanced degrees.

Subjects Offered Advanced biology, advanced chemistry, advanced math, algebra, art, biology, chemistry, Chinese, Chinese literature, drama, economics, English, English literature, ESL, European history, French, general science, geography, German, German literature, history, information technology, Japanese, Japanese literature, mathematics, music, personal and social education, physical education, physics, religion, Spanish, theater, theory of knowledge, world history, world literature.

Graduation Requirements English, foreign language, mathematics, physical education (includes health), religion (includes Bible studies and theology), science, social studies (includes history), IB Diploma requirements-3 Higher Level, 3 Standard Level courses, additional IB Diploma requirements—CAS program hours (Creativity, Action, Service), Theory of Knowledge Course, and Extended Essay.

Special Academic Programs International Baccalaureate program; honors section; independent study; ESL (32 students enrolled).

College Admission Counseling 57 students graduated in 2010; 53 went to college. Other: 4 had other specific plans.

Student Life Upper grades have uniform requirement, student council, honor system. Discipline rests primarily with faculty. Attendance at religious services is required.

Tuition and Aid Day student tuition: £15,950; 5-day tuition and room/board: £12,370; 7-day tuition and room/board: £11,070. Tuition installment plan (individually arranged payment plans, two semester payments, three term payments). Tuition reduction for siblings, bursaries, merit scholarship grants, need-based scholarship grants available. In 2010–11, 6% of upper-school students received aid. Total amount of financial aid awarded in 2010–11: £85,000.

Admissions Traditional secondary level entrance grade is 11. For fall 2010, 94 students applied for upper-level admission, 72 were accepted, 58 enrolled. English proficiency, mathematics proficiency exam, school's own test or writing sample required. Deadline for receipt of application materials: none. Application fee required: £100. Interview recommended.

Athletics Interscholastic: badminton, basketball, fitness, soccer, softball, tennis, volleyball; intramural: aerobics/dance, badminton, basketball, dance, fencing, fitness, horseback riding, indoor soccer, modern dance, physical fitness, physical training, soccer, softball, strength & conditioning, tennis, volleyball, weight training. 3 PE instructors, 2 coaches.

Computers Computers are regularly used in all academic, information technology classes. Computer network features include on-campus library services, Internet access, wireless campus network, Internet filtering or blocking technology. Campus intranet, student e-mail accounts, and computer access in designated common areas are available to students. The school has a published electronic and media policy.

Contact Mr. Chris Hiscock, Marketing and Admissions Officer. 44-(0) 20 8949 0571. Fax: 44-(0) 20 8336 2485. E-mail: admissions@marymountlondon.com. Web site: www.marymountlondon.com.

MARYMOUNT SCHOOL

1026 Fifth Avenue
New York, New York 10028
Head of School: Mrs. Concepcion Alvar, EdD

General Information Coeducational day (boys' only in lower grades) college-preparatory, arts, religious studies, and technology school, affiliated with Roman Catholic Church. Boys grades N–PK, girls grades N–12. Founded: 1926. Setting: urban. 3 buildings on campus. Approved or accredited by New York State Association of Independent Schools. Member of National Association of Independent Schools. Endowment: $800,000. Total enrollment: 608. Upper school average class size: 15. Upper school faculty-student ratio: 1:6. The average school day consists of 7 hours and 30 minutes.

Upper School Student Profile Grade 8: 34 students (34 girls); Grade 9: 57 students (57 girls); Grade 10: 47 students (47 girls); Grade 11: 48 students (48 girls); Grade 12: 49 students (49 girls). 69% of students are Roman Catholic.

Faculty School total: 104. In upper school: 16 men, 35 women; 43 have advanced degrees.

Subjects Offered Advanced studio art-AP, algebra, American history, American literature, art, art history, astronomy, bell choir, Bible studies, biology, calculus, chemistry, chorus, community service, computer science, dance, economics, English, English literature, ethics, European history, fine arts, French, geometry, Greek, health, Latin, mathematics, music, music history, physical education, physics, political science, religion, science, Spanish, speech, statistics, studio art, studio art-AP, technological applications, technology, theater history, trigonometry, world history, world literature, writing.

Graduation Requirements Arts and fine arts (art, music, dance, drama), computer science, English, foreign language, history, mathematics, physical education (includes health), religion (includes Bible studies and theology), science, speech, senior internships, senior seminars, Class XII Retreat. Community service is required.

Special Academic Programs Advanced Placement exam preparation; honors section; study abroad; academic accommodation for the gifted.

College Admission Counseling 44 students graduated in 2009; all went to college, including American University; Boston University; Harvard University; Haverford College; Trinity College; University of Pennsylvania. Mean SAT critical reading: 660, mean SAT math: 630, mean SAT writing: 690.

Student Life Upper grades have uniform requirement, student council, honor system. Discipline rests primarily with faculty. Attendance at religious services is required.

Tuition and Aid Day student tuition: $19,595–$34,000. Tuition installment plan (Key Tuition Payment Plan). Need-based scholarship grants available. In 2009–10, 20% of upper-school students received aid.

Admissions Traditional secondary-level entrance grade is 9. ISEE or SSAT required. Deadline for receipt of application materials: November 30. Application fee required: $70. On-campus interview required.

Athletics Interscholastic: aerobics, badminton, basketball, bicycling, cross-country running, dance, fencing, field hockey, fitness, gymnastics, jogging, lacrosse, modern dance, physical fitness, soccer, softball, swimming and diving, tennis, track and field, volleyball, yoga; intramural: aerobics, badminton, basketball, bicycling, cross-country running, dance, fitness, gymnastics, lacrosse, martial arts, modern dance, outdoor adventure, physical fitness, soccer, softball, volleyball, yoga. 3 PE instructors, 18 coaches, 1 athletic trainer.

Computers Computers are regularly used in all classes. Computer network features include on-campus library services, Internet access, wireless campus network, Internet filtering or blocking technology. Student e-mail accounts and computer access in designated common areas are available to students. The school has a published electronic and media policy.

Contact Mrs. Lillian Issa, Director of Admissions. 212-744-4486 Ext. 152. Fax: 212-744-0716. E-mail: lissa@marymountnyc.org. Web site: www.marymountnyc.org.

See Display on next page and Close-Up on page 806.

MARY STAR OF THE SEA HIGH SCHOOL

2500 North Taper Avenue
San Pedro, California 90731
Head of School: Ms. Rita Dever

General Information Coeducational day college-preparatory and religious studies school, affiliated with Roman Catholic Church. Grades 9–12. Founded: 1954. Setting: urban. 1-acre campus. 2 buildings on campus. Approved or accredited by Western Association of Schools and Colleges and California Department of Education. Total enrollment: 519. Upper school average class size: 25. Upper school faculty-student ratio: 1:17. There are 180 required school days per year for Upper School students. Upper School students typically attend 5 days per week. The average school day consists of 6 hours and 20 minutes.

Mary Star of the Sea High School

Upper School Student Profile Grade 9: 133 students (61 boys, 72 girls); Grade 10: 125 students (59 boys, 66 girls); Grade 11: 123 students (53 boys, 70 girls); Grade 12: 138 students (75 boys, 63 girls). 96% of students are Roman Catholic.

Faculty School total: 31. In upper school: 19 men, 12 women; 27 have advanced degrees.

Subjects Offered Advanced Placement courses, algebra, American government, American literature, American literature-AP, anatomy and physiology, art, art history, biology, British literature, calculus, calculus-AP, chemistry, choir, consumer mathematics, economics, English, European history-AP, geometry, government, government-AP, health education, honors algebra, honors English, honors geometry, honors U.S. history, honors world history, human anatomy, Latin, marine biology, physics, pre-algebra, psychology, religion, Spanish, U.S. government and politics-AP, U.S. history, U.S. history-AP, Western civilization.

Graduation Requirements American literature, biology, British literature, chemistry, economics, English, foreign language, geography, geometry, government, religion (includes Bible studies and theology), world history, world literature, service hours.

Special Academic Programs Advanced Placement exam preparation; honors section.

College Admission Counseling 117 students graduated in 2010; 116 went to college, including California State University, Dominguez Hills; California State University, Fullerton; California State University, Long Beach; El Camino College; University of California, Irvine; University of California, San Diego. Other: 1 entered military service.

Student Life Upper grades have uniform requirement, student council. Discipline rests primarily with faculty. Attendance at religious services is required.

Summer Programs Remediation, art/fine arts programs offered; session focuses on remediation; held on campus; accepts boys and girls; open to students from other schools. 250 students usually enrolled. 2011 schedule: June 20 to July 22. Application deadline: June 20.

Tuition and Aid Day student tuition: $7000. Tuition installment plan (SMART Tuition Payment Plan). Tuition reduction for siblings, merit scholarship grants, need-based scholarship grants available. In 2010–11, 15% of upper-school students received aid. Total amount of financial aid awarded in 2010–11: $145,000.

Admissions Traditional secondary-level entrance grade is 9. For fall 2010, 225 students applied for upper-level admission, 165 were accepted, 165 enrolled. Catholic High School Entrance Examination required. Deadline for receipt of application materials: January 18. Application fee required: $75. Interview required.

Athletics Interscholastic: baseball (boys), basketball (b,g), cheering (g), cross-country running (b,g), dance squad (g), football (b), soccer (b,g), softball (g), track and field (b,g), volleyball (b,g); coed interscholastic: swimming and diving. 1 PE instructor, 20 coaches.

Computers Computer resources include on-campus library services, Internet access, wireless campus network, Internet filtering or blocking technology. Computer access in designated common areas is available to students. Students grades are available online. The school has a published electronic and media policy.

Contact Mrs. Josephine Ludders, Registrar. 310-547-1130. Fax: 310-547-1827. E-mail: registrar@marystarhigh.com.

MARYVALE PREPARATORY SCHOOL

11300 Falls Road
Brooklandville, Maryland 21022

Head of School: Sr. Shawn Marie Maguire, SND

General Information Girls' day college-preparatory, arts, religious studies, bilingual studies, and technology school, affiliated with Roman Catholic Church. Grades 6–12. Founded: 1945. Setting: suburban. Nearest major city is Baltimore. 113-acre campus. 4 buildings on campus. Approved or accredited by Association of Independent Maryland Schools, Middle States Association of Colleges and Schools, National Catholic Education Association, and Maryland Department of Education. Member of National Association of Independent Schools. Endowment: $1 million. Total enrollment: 362. Upper school average class size: 15. Upper school faculty-student ratio: 1:8. Upper School students typically attend 5 days per week. The average school day consists of 6 hours.

Upper School Student Profile Grade 6: 23 students (23 girls); Grade 7: 32 students (32 girls); Grade 8: 27 students (27 girls); Grade 9: 70 students (70 girls); Grade 10: 64 students (64 girls); Grade 11: 67 students (67 girls); Grade 12: 79 students (79 girls). 80% of students are Roman Catholic.

Faculty School total: 50. In upper school: 5 men, 34 women; 27 have advanced degrees.

Subjects Offered Algebra, American history, American literature, anatomy and physiology, anthropology, art, art history, band, biology, biology-AP, British literature (honors), calculus, calculus-AP, chemistry, chorus, community service, computer science, digital photography, drama, economics, English, English literature, English literature-AP, English-AP, forensics, French, French-AP, geography, geometry, grammar, health, history, Holocaust, honors algebra, honors English, honors U.S. history, honors world history, journalism, keyboarding, Latin, literary magazine, marine biology, mathematics, model United Nations, music, newspaper, physical education, physics, piano, pre-algebra, pre-calculus, psychology, public speaking, religion, research, science, Shakespeare, social studies, Spanish, Spanish-AP, speech, statistics, theater, theology, trigonometry, U.S. history-AP, voice, Web site design, world history, world literature, writing, yearbook.

Graduation Requirements Arts and fine arts (art, music, dance, drama), computer science, English, foreign language, mathematics, physical education (includes health),

We look different. We feel different. We *are* different.

Discover
Marymount
Marymount School of New York

religion (includes Bible studies and theology), science, social studies (includes history), 100 hours of community service.

Special Academic Programs Advanced Placement exam preparation; honors section; accelerated programs; study at local college for college credit.

College Admission Counseling 76 students graduated in 2010; 75 went to college, including Salisbury University; Towson University; University of Delaware; University of Maryland, Baltimore County; University of Maryland, College Park. Other: 1 entered military service. Mean SAT critical reading: 569, mean SAT math: 532, mean SAT writing: 602, mean combined SAT: 1703. 31% scored over 600 on SAT critical reading, 21% scored over 600 on SAT math, 43% scored over 600 on SAT writing, 30% scored over 1800 on combined SAT, 26% scored over 26 on composite ACT.

Student Life Upper grades have uniform requirement, student council, honor system. Discipline rests equally with students and faculty. Attendance at religious services is required.

Summer Programs Enrichment, sports, art/fine arts, computer instruction programs offered; session focuses on enrichment in a unique setting for girls in grades 4-9; held on campus; accepts girls; open to students from other schools. 150 students usually enrolled. 2011 schedule: June 20 to July 8. Application deadline: June 1.

Tuition and Aid Tuition installment plan (Academic Management Services Plan). Bursaries, need-based scholarship grants available. In 2010–11, 29% of upper-school students received aid. Total amount of financial aid awarded in 2010–11: $496,585.

Admissions Traditional secondary-level entrance grade is 9. For fall 2010, 152 students applied for upper-level admission, 119 were accepted, 42 enrolled. High School Placement Test required. Deadline for receipt of application materials: January 7. Application fee required: $50. On-campus interview required.

Athletics Interscholastic: basketball, cross-country running, field hockey, indoor soccer, indoor track, indoor track & field, lacrosse, physical fitness, soccer, softball, track and field, volleyball, winter soccer, yoga. 3 PE instructors, 26 coaches, 1 athletic trainer.

Computers Computers are regularly used in all academic classes. Computer network features include on-campus library services, online commercial services, Internet access, wireless campus network, Internet filtering or blocking technology. Student e-mail accounts and computer access in designated common areas are available to students. Students grades are available online. The school has a published electronic and media policy.

Contact Monica C. Graham, Director of Admissions. 410-560-3243. Fax: 410-561-1826. E-mail: grahamm@maryvale.com. Web site: www.maryvale.com.

MARYWOOD—PALM VALLEY SCHOOL

35-525 DaVall Drive
Rancho Mirage, California 92270
Head of School: Mr. Vincent Downey

General Information Coeducational day college-preparatory school. Grades PK–12. Founded: 1952. Setting: suburban. Nearest major city is Palm Springs. 38-acre campus. 3 buildings on campus. Approved or accredited by California Association of Independent Schools and Western Association of Schools and Colleges. Endowment: $500,000. Total enrollment: 435. Upper school average class size: 15. Upper school faculty-student ratio: 1:9. There are 175 required school days per year for Upper School students. Upper School students typically attend 5 days per week. The average school day consists of 7 hours.

Faculty School total: 34. In upper school: 7 men, 4 women; 9 have advanced degrees.

Subjects Offered Algebra, American history, American history-AP, American literature, anatomy, ancient history, art, art history, art history-AP, astronomy, biology, biology-AP, calculus-AP, chemistry, chorus, computer science, drama, English, English-AP, European history, European history-AP, European literature, fine arts, French, French-AP, geometry, history, humanities, Latin, mathematics, physical education, physics, physiology, pre-calculus, science, social sciences, social studies, Spanish, Spanish-AP, theater, yearbook.

Graduation Requirements Arts and fine arts (art, music, dance, drama), English, foreign language, mathematics, physical education (includes health), science, social studies (includes history), 36 hours per year of community service.

Special Academic Programs Advanced Placement exam preparation; honors section; independent study.

College Admission Counseling 11 students graduated in 2009; all went to college, including Boston University; Pitzer College; The George Washington University; University of California, San Diego; University of Southern California; Wellesley College.

Student Life Upper grades have uniform requirement, student council, honor system. Discipline rests primarily with faculty.

Tuition and Aid Day student tuition: $16,000. Tuition installment plan (Insured Tuition Payment Plan, monthly payment plans). Bursaries, merit scholarship grants, need-based scholarship grants available. In 2009–10, 25% of upper-school students received aid; total upper-school merit-scholarship money awarded: $30,000. Total amount of financial aid awarded in 2009–10: $200,000.

Admissions Traditional secondary-level entrance grade is 9. For fall 2009, 42 students applied for upper-level admission, 29 were accepted, 21 enrolled. ERB CTP III and independent norms required. Deadline for receipt of application materials: none. Application fee required: $100. Interview required.

Athletics Interscholastic: baseball (boys), basketball (b,g), flag football (b), football (b), golf (g), softball (g), volleyball (g); coed interscholastic: golf, soccer, tennis; coed

intramural: backpacking, bowling, hiking/backpacking, outdoor activities, outdoor adventure, outdoor education. 3 PE instructors.

Computers Computers are regularly used in English, foreign language, history, mathematics, science classes. Computer network features include on-campus library services, online commercial services, Internet access, wireless campus network, Internet filtering or blocking technology. Students grades are available online. The school has a published electronic and media policy.

Contact Mr. Vincent Downey, Head of School. 760-328-0861. Fax: 760-770-4541. E-mail: vdowney@mwpv.org. Web site: www.mwpv.org.

THE MASTERS SCHOOL

49 Clinton Avenue
Dobbs Ferry, New York 10522
Head of School: Dr. Maureen Fonseca

General Information Coeducational boarding and day college-preparatory, arts, and technology school. Boarding grades 9–12, day grades 5–12. Founded: 1877. Setting: suburban. Nearest major city is New York. Students are housed in single-sex dormitories. 96-acre campus. 13 buildings on campus. Approved or accredited by Middle States Association of Colleges and Schools, New York State Association of Independent Schools, The Association of Boarding Schools, and New York Department of Education. Member of National Association of Independent Schools and Secondary School Admission Test Board. Endowment: $27.5 million. Total enrollment: 580. Upper school average class size: 14. Upper school faculty-student ratio: 1:6. Upper School students typically attend 5 days per week. The average school day consists of 6 hours.

Upper School Student Profile Grade 9: 97 students (50 boys, 47 girls); Grade 10: 103 students (50 boys, 53 girls); Grade 11: 109 students (45 boys, 64 girls); Grade 12: 105 students (43 boys, 62 girls). 40% of students are boarding students. 70% are state residents. 18 states are represented in upper school student body. 14% are international students. International students from China, Germany, Republic of Korea, Russian Federation, Switzerland, and Taiwan; 12 other countries represented in student body.

Faculty School total: 97. In upper school: 37 men, 50 women; 70 have advanced degrees; 60 reside on campus.

Subjects Offered Acting, algebra, American history, American literature, art history, biology, biology-AP, calculus, calculus-AP, ceramics, chemistry, chemistry-AP, computer math, computer programming, computer science, creative writing, dance, drama, driver education, earth science, electronics, English, English language-AP, English literature, English literature-AP, environmental science, ESL, ethics, European history, European history-AP, expository writing, fine arts, French, French language-AP, French literature-AP, geography, geometry, grammar, health, health and wellness, health education, jazz, jazz band, journalism, Latin, Latin-AP, mathematics, meteorology, music, music theory-AP, performing arts, photography, physical education, physics, physics-AP, pre-calculus, religion, science, senior thesis, social studies, Spanish, Spanish language-AP, Spanish literature-AP, speech, statistics, statistics-AP, studio art, studio art-AP, theater, trigonometry, U.S. history, U.S. history-AP, world history, world literature, world religions, writing, yearbook, yoga.

Graduation Requirements Arts and fine arts (art, music, dance, drama), computer science, English, foreign language, health, mathematics, physical education (includes health), public speaking, science, U.S. history, world history, world religions.

Special Academic Programs 19 Advanced Placement exams for which test preparation is offered; honors section; independent study; term-away projects; study at local college for college credit; study abroad; academic accommodation for the gifted, the musically talented, and the artistically talented; ESL (20 students enrolled).

College Admission Counseling 95 students graduated in 2010; all went to college, including Cornell University; Middlebury College; New York University; The Johns Hopkins University; University of Chicago; Williams College. Mean SAT critical reading: 660, mean SAT math: 630, mean SAT writing: 700, mean combined SAT: 1990. 61% scored over 600 on SAT critical reading, 57% scored over 600 on SAT math, 68% scored over 600 on SAT writing, 58% scored over 1800 on combined SAT.

Student Life Upper grades have specified standards of dress, student council. Discipline rests equally with students and faculty.

Tuition and Aid Day student tuition: $32,220; 7-day tuition and room/board: $45,500. Tuition installment plan (Insured Tuition Payment Plan, Key Tuition Payment Plan, monthly payment plans, individually arranged payment plans). Need-based scholarship grants available. In 2010–11, 33% of upper-school students received aid. Total amount of financial aid awarded in 2010–11: $3,800,000.

Admissions Traditional secondary-level entrance grade is 9. For fall 2010, 520 students applied for upper-level admission, 243 were accepted, 156 enrolled. ISEE, SSAT or TOEFL required. Deadline for receipt of application materials: February 1. Application fee required: $50. Interview required.

Athletics Interscholastic: baseball (boys), basketball (b,g), cross-country running (b,g), fencing (b,g), field hockey (g), lacrosse (b,g), soccer (b,g), softball (g), tennis (b,g), volleyball (g); coed interscholastic: dance, dance team, golf; coed intramural: aerobics, aerobics/dance, aerobics/Nautilus, combined training, dance squad, dance team, fitness, Frisbee, martial arts, modern dance, outdoor activities, physical fitness, physical training, strength & conditioning, ultimate Frisbee, weight lifting, weight training, yoga. 2 PE instructors, 13 coaches, 1 athletic trainer.

Computers Computers are regularly used in computer applications, English, foreign language, graphic arts, graphic design, history, mathematics, newspaper, photography,

The Masters School

programming, publications, science, senior seminar, study skills, video film production, Web site design, writing, yearbook classes. Computer network features include on-campus library services, online commercial services, Internet access, wireless campus network, Internet filtering or blocking technology. Student e-mail accounts and computer access in designated common areas are available to students. The school has a published electronic and media policy.

Contact The Office of Admission. 914-479-6420. Fax: 914-693-7295. E-mail: admission@mastersny.org. Web site: www.mastersny.org.

MATER DEI HIGH SCHOOL

1300 Harmony Way
Evansville, Indiana 47720-6199
Head of School: Mr. Timothy Anderson Dickel

General Information Coeducational day college-preparatory, arts, business, religious studies, and technology school, affiliated with Roman Catholic Church; primarily serves students with learning disabilities, individuals with Attention Deficit Disorder, and dyslexic students. Grades 9–12. Founded: 1948. Setting: urban. 25-acre campus. 1 building on campus. Approved or accredited by National Christian School Association, North Central Association of Colleges and Schools, and Indiana Department of Education. Total enrollment: 536. Upper school average class size: 25. Upper school faculty-student ratio: 1:15. There are 180 required school days per year for Upper School students. Upper School students typically attend 5 days per week. The average school day consists of 7 hours.

Upper School Student Profile Grade 9: 128 students (69 boys, 59 girls); Grade 10: 148 students (80 boys, 68 girls); Grade 11: 132 students (65 boys, 67 girls); Grade 12: 129 students (63 boys, 66 girls). 98% of students are Roman Catholic.

Faculty School total: 40. In upper school: 18 men, 21 women; 28 have advanced degrees.

Subjects Offered American legal systems.

Graduation Requirements Service hours to church and community, religion credits.

Special Academic Programs Advanced Placement exam preparation; honors section; study at local college for college credit; programs in English, mathematics for dyslexic students; special instructional classes for students with LD, ADD, emotional and behavioral problems.

College Admission Counseling 134 students graduated in 2009; 114 went to college, including Purdue University; University of Evansville. Other: 4 went to work, 1 entered military service, 14 entered a postgraduate year, 1 had other specific plans. Median SAT math: 513, median SAT writing: 511, median combined SAT: 1024, median composite ACT: 23.

Student Life Upper grades have uniform requirement, student council, honor system. Discipline rests primarily with faculty. Attendance at religious services is required.

Tuition and Aid Guaranteed tuition plan. Need-based scholarship grants available. In 2009–10, 30% of upper-school students received aid.

Admissions Traditional secondary-level entrance grade is 9. Deadline for receipt of application materials: none. Application fee required: $170. Interview recommended.

Athletics Interscholastic: baseball (boys), basketball (b,g), cheering (g), cross-country running (b,g), dance squad (g), diving (b,g), football (b), golf (b,g), soccer (b,g), softball (g), swimming and diving (b,g), tennis (b,g), track and field (b,g), volleyball (g), weight training (b,g), wrestling (b); coed interscholastic: bowling. 2 athletic trainers.

Computers Computers are regularly used in economics classes. Computer network features include on-campus library services, Internet access, wireless campus network, Internet filtering or blocking technology. Students grades are available online. The school has a published electronic and media policy.

Contact Admissions. 812-426-2258. Fax: 812-421-5717. E-mail: materdeiwildcats@evansville.net.

MATIGNON HIGH SCHOOL

One Matignon Road
Cambridge, Massachusetts 02140
Head of School: Mr. Thomas Galligani

General Information Coeducational day college-preparatory, arts, business, religious studies, and technology school, affiliated with Roman Catholic Church. Grades 9–12. Founded: 1945. Setting: suburban. Nearest major city is Boston. 10-acre campus. 3 buildings on campus. Approved or accredited by Association of Independent Schools in New England, National Catholic Education Association, New England Association of Schools and Colleges, and Massachusetts Department of Education. Endowment: $253,000. Total enrollment: 418. Upper school average class size: 18. Upper school faculty-student ratio: 1:15. Upper School students typically attend 5 days per week. The average school day consists of 7 hours.

Upper School Student Profile Grade 9: 104 students (42 boys, 62 girls); Grade 10: 101 students (46 boys, 55 girls); Grade 11: 113 students (56 boys, 57 girls); Grade 12: 96 students (35 boys, 61 girls). 75% of students are Roman Catholic.

Faculty School total: 37. In upper school: 14 men, 23 women; 18 have advanced degrees.

Subjects Offered 3-dimensional art, 3-dimensional design, accounting, adolescent issues, Advanced Placement courses, algebra, American history, American literature, anatomy and physiology, art, art history, Bible studies, biology, calculus, chemistry,

community service, computer science, drawing and design, economics, English, English literature, environmental science, fine arts, French, geometry, government/civics, grammar, health, history, Latin, law, mathematics, physical education, physics, psychology, religion, science, social sciences, social studies, Spanish, theology, trigonometry, world history, writing.

Graduation Requirements 20th century history, accounting, Advanced Placement courses, algebra, American history, anatomy and physiology, arts and fine arts (art, music, dance, drama), chemistry, computer science, English-AP, French, French-AP, geometry, health education, honors algebra, honors English, honors geometry, honors world history, Latin, law, physical education (includes health), psychology, religious studies, SAT preparation, senior internship, Spanish, Spanish-AP, U.S. history, U.S. history-AP, world cultures, world history, Christian service, forty-five hours of community service (before junior year).

Special Academic Programs Advanced Placement exam preparation; honors section; independent study; study at local college for college credit; study abroad; ESL (10 students enrolled).

College Admission Counseling 62 students graduated in 2010; 61 went to college, including Boston University; Northeastern University; Saint Anselm College; Suffolk University; University of Massachusetts Amherst; University of Massachusetts Boston. Other: 1 entered military service. Mean SAT critical reading: 529, mean SAT math: 550, mean SAT writing: 540, mean combined SAT: 1619. 21% scored over 600 on SAT critical reading, 23% scored over 600 on SAT math, 14% scored over 600 on SAT writing, 20% scored over 1800 on combined SAT.

Student Life Upper grades have uniform requirement, student council, honor system. Discipline rests primarily with faculty. Attendance at religious services is required.

Summer Programs Remediation, enrichment programs offered; held on campus; accepts boys and girls; open to students from other schools. 80 students usually enrolled. 2011 schedule: June 27 to August 12. Application deadline: none.

Tuition and Aid Day student tuition: $8300. Tuition installment plan (FACTS Tuition Payment Plan, monthly payment plans). Merit scholarship grants, need-based scholarship grants available. In 2010–11, 50% of upper-school students received aid; total upper-school merit-scholarship money awarded: $50,000. Total amount of financial aid awarded in 2010–11: $110,000.

Admissions Traditional secondary-level entrance grade is 9. Catholic High School Entrance Examination, SSAT or TOEFL or SLEP required. Deadline for receipt of application materials: none. No application fee required. On-campus interview recommended.

Athletics Interscholastic: baseball (boys), basketball (b,g), cheering (g), cross-country running (b,g), football (b), golf (b,g), ice hockey (b,g), lacrosse (b,g), soccer (b,g), softball (g), swimming and diving (b,g), tennis (b,g), track and field (b,g), volleyball (g); intramural: aerobics/dance (b,g), dance (g), dance squad (g), dance team (g), figure skating (g), Frisbee (b,g), physical training (b,g), strength & conditioning (b,g), weight lifting (b,g), weight training (b,g); coed intramural: yoga. 1 PE instructor, 20 coaches, 1 athletic trainer.

Computers Computers are regularly used in all academic classes. Computer network features include on-campus library services, Internet access, wireless campus network, Internet filtering or blocking technology, all academic homework is provided online. Student e-mail accounts and computer access in designated common areas are available to students. Students grades are available online.

Contact Mr. Joseph DiSarcina, Principal. 617-876-1212 Ext. 14. Fax: 617-661-3905. E-mail: jdisarcina@matignon-hs.org. Web site: www.matignon-hs.org.

MAUI PREPARATORY ACADEMY

5095 Napilihau Street, #109B
PMB #186
Lahaina, Hawaii 96761,
Head of School: Mr. George C. Baker

General Information Coeducational day college-preparatory school. Grades PK–12. Founded: 2005. Approved or accredited by European Council of International Schools and Western Association of Schools and Colleges. Language of instruction: English.

Subjects Offered Art, biology, calculus, chemistry, English, environmental science, foreign language, health, history, mathematics, physics, social studies, technology.

Graduation Requirements Science project.

Special Academic Programs Advanced Placement exam preparation.

Admissions ERB required.

Athletics Interscholastic: aquatics (boys, girls), canoeing/kayaking (b,g), cross-country running (b,g), golf (b), independent competitive sports (b,g), indoor track (b,g), ocean paddling (b,g), surfing (b,g), swimming and diving (b,g), tennis (b,g), track and field (b,g), volleyball (g); intramural: basketball (b,g), marksmanship (b,g), ropes courses (b,g), surfing (b,g), windsurfing (b,g); coed interscholastic: aquatics, canoeing/kayaking, cross-country running, independent competitive sports, indoor track, ocean paddling, surfing, swimming and diving, tennis, track and field; coed intramural: basketball, marksmanship, ropes courses, surfing, windsurfing.

Contact Mrs. Cathi Minami, Admissions Coordinator. 808-665-9966. Fax: 808-665-1075. E-mail: cminami@mauiprep.org.

MAUMEE VALLEY COUNTRY DAY SCHOOL

1715 South Reynolds Road
Toledo, Ohio 43614-1499
Head of School: Gary Boehm
General Information Coeducational day college-preparatory and arts school. Grades P3–12. Founded: 1884. Setting: suburban. 72-acre campus. 4 buildings on campus. Approved or accredited by Independent Schools Association of the Central States, Ohio Association of Independent Schools, and Ohio Department of Education. Member of National Association of Independent Schools. Endowment: $10.5 million. Total enrollment: 488. Upper school average class size: 10. Upper school faculty-student ratio: 1:10. Upper School students typically attend 5 days per week. The average school day consists of 7 hours.
Upper School Student Profile Grade 9: 46 students (28 boys, 18 girls); Grade 10: 46 students (27 boys, 19 girls); Grade 11: 45 students (23 boys, 22 girls); Grade 12: 54 students (33 boys, 21 girls).
Faculty School total: 58. In upper school: 16 men, 11 women; 21 have advanced degrees.
Subjects Offered Algebra, American government, American history, anthropology, art, biology, biology-AP, calculus-AP, chemistry, choir, computer graphics, computer science, creative writing, design, drama, earth science, ecology, English, environmental science, European history, expository writing, fine arts, French, geology, geometry, government/civics, grammar, health, history, human development, humanities, mathematics, microbiology, music, physical education, physics, science, social studies, Spanish, Spanish-AP, speech, statistics, statistics-AP, theater, trigonometry, women's studies, world history.
Graduation Requirements American government, arts and fine arts (art, music, dance, drama), English, foreign language, mathematics, physical education (includes health), science, social studies (includes history). Community service is required.
Special Academic Programs Advanced Placement exam preparation; honors section; independent study; term-away projects; study at local college for college credit; domestic exchange program (with The Athenian School, The Network Program Schools); study abroad; academic accommodation for the gifted, the musically talented, and the artistically talented; ESL (5 students enrolled).
College Admission Counseling 49 students graduated in 2009; 48 went to college, including Indiana University Bloomington; Miami University; Purdue University; The George Washington University; The University of Toledo. Other: 1 went to work. Mean SAT critical reading: 634, mean SAT math: 632, mean SAT writing: 621, mean combined SAT: 1887, mean composite ACT: 29. 50% scored over 600 on SAT critical reading, 50% scored over 600 on SAT math.
Student Life Upper grades have specified standards of dress, student council, honor system. Discipline rests equally with students and faculty.
Tuition and Aid Day student tuition: $14,550–$15,550. Tuition installment plan (FACTS Tuition Payment Plan, monthly payment plans, individually arranged payment plans). Merit scholarship grants, need-based scholarship grants available. In 2009–10, 35% of upper-school students received aid; total upper-school merit-scholarship money awarded: $136,000. Total amount of financial aid awarded in 2009–10: $454,900.
Admissions Traditional secondary-level entrance grade is 9. For fall 2009, 34 students applied for upper-level admission, 27 were accepted, 22 enrolled. Brigance Test of Basic Skills, CTP, ERB—verbal abilities, reading comprehension, quantitative abilities (level F, form 1), OLSAT, ERB, Otis-Lennon Ability or Stanford Achievement Test, Otis-Lennon and 2 sections of ERB, Slosson Intelligence or writing sample required. Deadline for receipt of application materials: none. Application fee required: $50. On-campus interview required.
Athletics Interscholastic: baseball (boys), basketball (b,g), cheering (b,g), cross-country running (b,g), field hockey (g), golf (b,g), lacrosse (g), soccer (b,g), tennis (b,g), track and field (b,g); intramural: indoor soccer (g), lacrosse (g); coed intramural: strength & conditioning, weight training. 3 PE instructors, 10 coaches, 1 athletic trainer.
Computers Computers are regularly used in English, foreign language, graphic design, history, information technology, library skills, literary magazine, mathematics, music, newspaper, science, yearbook classes. Computer network features include on-campus library services, online commercial services, Internet access, wireless campus network, Internet filtering or blocking technology. Student e-mail accounts are available to students. Students grades are available online. The school has a published electronic and media policy.
Contact Sarah Bigenho, Assistant Director of Admission Operations. 419-381-1313 Ext. 105. Fax: 419-381-9941. E-mail: sbigenho@mvcds.org. Web site: www.mvcds.org.

MAUR HILL-MOUNT ACADEMY

1000 Green Street
Atchison, Kansas 66002
Head of School: Mr. Phil Baniewicz
General Information Coeducational boarding and day college-preparatory, arts, religious studies, bilingual studies, and English as a Second language school, affiliated with Roman Catholic Church. Grades 9–12. Founded: 1863. Setting: small town. Nearest major city is Kansas City, MO. Students are housed in single-sex dormitories. 90-acre campus. 7 buildings on campus. Approved or accredited by National Catholic Education Association, North Central Association of Colleges and Schools, The Association of Boarding Schools, and Kansas Department of Education. Member of Secondary School Admission Test Board. Total enrollment: 198. Upper school average class size: 17. Upper school faculty-student ratio: 1:9. There are 182 required school days per year for Upper School students. Upper School students typically attend 5 days per week. The average school day consists of 6 hours and 30 minutes.
Upper School Student Profile Grade 9: 53 students (29 boys, 24 girls); Grade 10: 45 students (24 boys, 21 girls); Grade 11: 56 students (32 boys, 24 girls); Grade 12: 54 students (27 boys, 27 girls). 40% of students are boarding students. 50% are state residents. 7 states are represented in upper school student body. 25% are international students. International students from China, Mexico, Republic of Korea, Saudi Arabia, Sweden, and Taiwan; 5 other countries represented in student body. 65% of students are Roman Catholic.
Faculty School total: 21. In upper school: 13 men, 8 women; 11 have advanced degrees; 3 reside on campus.
Subjects Offered Algebra, American history, American literature, anatomy, art, basketball, Bible studies, biology, business, business skills, calculus, chemistry, computer math, computer programming, computer science, current events, drama, economics, English, English literature, ESL, ethics, fine arts, French, geography, geometry, government/civics, grammar, health, history, humanities, journalism, mathematics, music, photography, physical education, physics, physiology, psychology, religion, science, social sciences, social studies, sociology, Spanish, speech, theater, theology, trigonometry, typing, world history, world literature, writing.
Graduation Requirements Arts and fine arts (art, music, dance, drama), business skills (includes word processing), computer science, English, foreign language, mathematics, physical education (includes health), religion (includes Bible studies and theology), science, social sciences, social studies (includes history).
Special Academic Programs Honors section; study at local college for college credit; academic accommodation for the gifted; special instructional classes for students with Attention Deficit Disorder; ESL (19 students enrolled).
College Admission Counseling 57 students graduated in 2010; 56 went to college, including Benedictine College; Creighton University; Penn State University Park; Saint Louis University; The University of Kansas. Other: 1 went to work.
Student Life Upper grades have uniform requirement, student council, honor system. Discipline rests primarily with faculty. Attendance at religious services is required.
Summer Programs ESL programs offered; session focuses on activities camp, ESL program; held on campus; accepts boys and girls; open to students from other schools. 17 students usually enrolled. 2011 schedule: July 5 to August 12. Application deadline: June 1.
Tuition and Aid 5-day tuition and room/board: $16,000; 7-day tuition and room/board: $18,650. Tuition installment plan (FACTS Tuition Payment Plan, monthly payment plans, individually arranged payment plans). Tuition reduction for siblings, merit scholarship grants, need-based scholarship grants, paying campus jobs available. In 2010–11, 40% of upper-school students received aid. Total amount of financial aid awarded in 2010–11: $225,000.
Admissions Traditional secondary-level entrance grade is 10. For fall 2010, 134 students applied for upper-level admission, 65 were accepted, 54 enrolled. High School Placement Test required. Deadline for receipt of application materials: none. Application fee required: $50. Interview required.
Athletics Interscholastic: aquatics (girls), baseball (b), basketball (b,g), cheering (g), cross-country running (b,g), dance (g), dance squad (g), dance team (g), drill team (g), football (b), swimming and diving (g), tennis (b,g), track and field (b,g), volleyball (g); intramural: boxing (b), field hockey (b), fitness (b), flag football (b), floor hockey (b), football (b), running (b,g), skateboarding (b), skiing (downhill) (b,g), soccer (b,g), swimming and diving (g), touch football (b), track and field (b,g), weight lifting (b,g), weight training (b,g); coed interscholastic: golf, physical fitness, physical training, running, soccer, wrestling; coed intramural: baseball, basketball, bowling, Nautilus, physical fitness, physical training, roller blading, table tennis, tennis, volleyball, walking. 2 PE instructors, 10 coaches, 2 athletic trainers.
Computers Computer network features include on-campus library services, Internet access, Internet filtering or blocking technology. Students grades are available online.
Contact Mr. Deke Nolan, Admissions Director. 913-367-5482 Ext. 210. Fax: 913-367-5096. E-mail: admissions@mh-ma.com. Web site: www.mh-ma.com.

MAYFIELD SENIOR SCHOOL

500 Bellefontaine Street
Pasadena, California 91105
Head of School: Mrs. Rita Curasi McBride
General Information Girls' day college-preparatory, arts, and religious studies school, affiliated with Roman Catholic Church. Grades 9–12. Founded: 1931. Setting: suburban. Nearest major city is Los Angeles. 8-acre campus. 4 buildings on campus. Approved or accredited by California Association of Independent Schools, National Catholic Education Association, and Western Association of Schools and Colleges. Member of National Association of Independent Schools. Endowment: $5.8 million. Total enrollment: 300. Upper school average class size: 16. Upper school faculty-student ratio: 1:8. There are 166 required school days per year for Upper School students. Upper School students typically attend 5 days per week. The average school day consists of 7 hours and 15 minutes.

Mayfield Senior School

Upper School Student Profile Grade 9: 75 students (75 girls); Grade 10: 75 students (75 girls); Grade 11: 75 students (75 girls); Grade 12: 75 students (75 girls). 80% of students are Roman Catholic.

Faculty School total: 39. In upper school: 9 men, 30 women; 26 have advanced degrees.

Subjects Offered Algebra, American history, American history-AP, American literature, anatomy, art, art history-AP, bioethics, biology, biology-AP, calculus, calculus-AP, ceramics, chemistry, community service, computer programming, computer science, creative writing, dance, drama, economics, English, English language-AP, English literature, English-AP, European history, European history-AP, fine arts, French, French language-AP, French literature-AP, French-AP, geography, geometry, government/civics, health, history, journalism, Latin, Latin-AP, marine biology, mathematics, music, music theory-AP, mythology, philosophy, photography, physical education, physics, physics-AP, physiology, psychology, religion, science, social sciences, social studies, Spanish, Spanish language-AP, Spanish literature-AP, Spanish-AP, speech, studio art-AP, theater, theology, trigonometry, world history, writing.

Graduation Requirements Arts and fine arts (art, music, dance, drama), computer science, English, foreign language, mathematics, physical education (includes health), religion (includes Bible studies and theology), science, social sciences, social studies (includes history). Community service is required.

Special Academic Programs 14 Advanced Placement exams for which test preparation is offered; honors section; academic accommodation for the gifted, the musically talented, and the artistically talented.

College Admission Counseling 75 students graduated in 2009; all went to college, including Boston University; Georgetown University; Harvard University; Stanford University; University of California, Los Angeles; University of Southern California. Mean SAT critical reading: 602, mean SAT math: 578, mean SAT writing: 596.

Student Life Upper grades have uniform requirement, student council, honor system. Discipline rests primarily with faculty. Attendance at religious services is required.

Tuition and Aid Day student tuition: $19,995. Tuition installment plan (monthly payment plans, 2-payment plan). Merit scholarship grants, need-based scholarship grants available. In 2009–10, 24% of upper-school students received aid; total upper-school merit-scholarship money awarded: $81,990. Total amount of financial aid awarded in 2009–10: $593,339.

Admissions Traditional secondary-level entrance grade is 9. For fall 2009, 226 students applied for upper-level admission, 142 were accepted, 85 enrolled. ISEE required. Deadline for receipt of application materials: January 15. Application fee required: $100. On-campus interview required.

Athletics Interscholastic: badminton, basketball, cross-country running, dance, diving, equestrian sports, fencing, fitness, fitness walking, golf, jogging, jump rope, physical training, ropes courses, soccer, softball, swimming and diving, tennis, track and field, volleyball, water polo, winter soccer, yoga; intramural: fencing. 3 PE instructors, 17 coaches.

Computers Computers are regularly used in foreign language, history, mathematics, religious studies, science classes. Computer network features include on-campus library services, online commercial services, Internet access, wireless campus network, Internet filtering or blocking technology. Campus intranet, student e-mail accounts, and computer access in designated common areas are available to students. Students grades are available online. The school has a published electronic and media policy.

Contact Mrs. Clemmie Phillips, Director of Admissions. 626-799-9121 Ext. 210. Fax: 626-799-8576. E-mail: clemmie.phillips@mayfieldsenior.org. Web site: www. mayfieldsenior.org.

MAZAPAN SCHOOL

Standard Fruit de Honduras
Zona de Mazapan
La Ceiba, Honduras
Head of School: Ms. Martha Counsil

General Information Coeducational day college-preparatory, bilingual studies, and technology school. Grades 1–12. Founded: 1928. Setting: urban. Nearest major city is San Pedro Sula, Honduras. 5-acre campus. 10 buildings on campus. Approved or accredited by European Council of International Schools, National Private School Accreditation Alliance, Southern Association of Colleges and Schools, The College Board, and state department of education. Languages of instruction: English and Spanish. Endowment: $1 million. Upper school average class size: 25. Upper school faculty-student ratio: 1:12. There are 180 required school days per year for Upper School students. Upper School students typically attend 5 days per week. The average school day consists of 6 hours and 45 minutes.

Upper School Student Profile Grade 9: 26 students (10 boys, 16 girls); Grade 10: 16 students (6 boys, 10 girls); Grade 11: 21 students (12 boys, 9 girls); Grade 12: 23 students (12 boys, 11 girls).

Faculty School total: 23. In upper school: 7 men, 7 women; 7 have advanced degrees.

Subjects Offered Algebra, American history, American literature, art, band, biology, calculus, calculus-AP, chemistry, college counseling, computer science, earth science, economics, English, English literature, geometry, government/civics, grammar,

health, history, Honduran history, mathematics, music, philosophy, physical education, physics, pre-calculus, psychology, science, social studies, sociology, Spanish, trigonometry, world history.

Graduation Requirements Algebra, arts and fine arts (art, music, dance, drama), biology, calculus, computer science, economics, English, foreign language, mathematics, physical education (includes health), science, social sciences, social studies (includes history), complete the credits for the Honduran Bachillerato.

Special Academic Programs Independent study.

College Admission Counseling 24 students graduated in 2009; all went to college, including Louisiana State University and Agricultural and Mechanical College; The University of North Carolina at Greensboro; The University of Texas at Austin; University of Miami; University of New Orleans; University of the Ozarks. Median SAT critical reading: 570, median SAT math: 500, median composite ACT: 21.

Student Life Upper grades have uniform requirement, student council, honor system. Discipline rests primarily with faculty.

Tuition and Aid Day student tuition: $4264. Tuition installment plan (monthly payment plans). Merit scholarship grants, need-based scholarships/grants for children of Dole employees available. In 2009–10, 40% of upper-school students received aid. Total amount of financial aid awarded in 2009–10: $97,461.

Admissions For fall 2009, 6 students applied for upper-level admission, 4 were accepted, 4 enrolled. Admissions testing and Stanford Achievement Test required. Deadline for receipt of application materials: none. Application fee required: $50. On-campus interview required.

Athletics Interscholastic: baseball (girls), basketball (b,g), cheering (g), soccer (b,g), volleyball (b,g); intramural: baseball (b,g), basketball (b,g), dance (g), paddle tennis (b,g), soccer (b,g), table tennis (b,g), volleyball (b,g), weight lifting (b,g); coed intramural: cheering, paddle tennis, soccer, swimming and diving, tennis. 1 PE instructor, 3 coaches, 1 athletic trainer.

Computers Computers are regularly used in all academic, career exploration, journalism, library skills, music, newspaper classes. Computer resources include on-campus library services, Internet access, Internet filtering or blocking technology. **Contact** Enma Nufio, Guidance Counselor. 504-443-2716 Ext. 14. Fax: 504-443-3559. E-mail: enma.nufio@dole.com. Web site: www.mazapanschool.org.

MCAULEY HIGH SCHOOL

6000 Oakwood Avenue
Cincinnati, Ohio 45224-2398
Head of School: Mr. Christopher Pastura

General Information Girls' day college-preparatory school, affiliated with Roman Catholic Church. Grades 9–12. Founded: 1964. Approved or accredited by North Central Association of Colleges and Schools and Ohio Department of Education. Total enrollment: 699.

Upper School Student Profile 96% of students are Roman Catholic.

Special Academic Programs 12 Advanced Placement exams for which test preparation is offered; study at local college for college credit.

Student Life Upper grades have uniform requirement. Discipline rests equally with students and faculty. Attendance at religious services is required.

Admissions High School Placement Test required. Application fee required: $500. **Contact** Mrs. Kristina A. Schwartz, Director of Guidance. 513-681-1800 Ext. 1143. Fax: 513-681-1802. E-mail: schwartzk@mcauleyhs.net. Web site: www. mcauleyhs.net.

THE MCCALLIE SCHOOL

500 Dodds Avenue
Chattanooga, Tennessee 37404
Head of School: Dr. R. Kirk Walker

General Information Boys' boarding and day college-preparatory, arts, business, and religious studies school, affiliated with Christian faith. Boarding grades 9–12, day grades 6–12. Founded: 1905. Setting: suburban. Nearest major city is Atlanta, GA. Students are housed in single-sex dormitories. 110-acre campus. 19 buildings on campus. Approved or accredited by Southern Association of Colleges and Schools, Southern Association of Independent Schools, Tennessee Association of Independent Schools, The Association of Boarding Schools, and Tennessee Department of Education. Member of National Association of Independent Schools and Secondary School Admission Test Board. Endowment: $68 million. Total enrollment: 913. Upper school average class size: 14. Upper school faculty-student ratio: 1:8. Upper School students typically attend 5 days per week. The average school day consists of 8 hours and 30 minutes.

Upper School Student Profile Grade 9: 163 students (163 boys); Grade 10: 162 students (162 boys); Grade 11: 170 students (170 boys); Grade 12: 158 students (158 boys). 42% of students are boarding students. 28 states are represented in upper school student body. 7% are international students. International students from Cayman Islands, Germany, Jamaica, Republic of Korea, Spain, and Switzerland; 3 other countries represented in student body.

Faculty School total: 133. In upper school: 93 men, 15 women; 77 have advanced degrees; 58 reside on campus.

Subjects Offered Algebra, American Civil War, American history, American literature, American studies, art, Bible studies, bioethics, biology, calculus, ceramics, chemistry, Chinese, computer science, creative writing, design, drama, economics, English, English literature, environmental science, European history, fine arts, French, geometry, German, government/civics, Greek, health, history, human development, Japanese, journalism, keyboarding, Latin, mathematics, music, music theory, photography, physical education, physical science, physics, poetry, political science, pottery, printmaking, public speaking, religion, rhetoric, science, social sciences, social studies, Spanish, speech, theater, trigonometry, world history, world literature, writing.

Graduation Requirements Arts and fine arts (art, music, dance, drama), English, foreign language, mathematics, physical education (includes health), public speaking, religion (includes Bible studies and theology), science, social sciences, social studies (includes history).

Special Academic Programs Advanced Placement exam preparation; honors section; independent study; study abroad; academic accommodation for the gifted, the musically talented, and the artistically talented.

College Admission Counseling 146 students graduated in 2009; all went to college, including Georgia Institute of Technology; North Carolina State University; The University of North Carolina at Chapel Hill; The University of Tennessee; University of Georgia; Vanderbilt University. Mean SAT critical reading: 602, mean SAT math: 641, mean SAT writing: 607, mean combined SAT: 1849, mean composite ACT: 27.

Student Life Upper grades have specified standards of dress, student council, honor system. Discipline rests equally with students and faculty. Attendance at religious services is required.

Tuition and Aid Day student tuition: $18,795; 7-day tuition and room/board: $36,850. Tuition installment plan (Insured Tuition Payment Plan, monthly payment plans, individually arranged payment plans). Merit scholarship grants, need-based scholarship grants, need-based loans available. In 2009–10, 38% of upper-school students received aid; total upper-school merit-scholarship money awarded: $850,000. Total amount of financial aid awarded in 2009–10: $3,500,000.

Admissions Traditional secondary-level entrance grade is 9. ISEE or SSAT required. Deadline for receipt of application materials: March 1. Application fee required: $50. On-campus interview required.

Athletics Interscholastic: baseball, basketball, bowling, climbing, crew, cross-country running, diving, football, golf, indoor track, indoor track & field, lacrosse, physical training, rock climbing, rowing, skeet shooting, soccer, swimming and diving, tennis, track and field, trap and skeet, ultimate Frisbee, wall climbing, wrestling; intramural: backpacking, baseball, basketball, bicycling, billiards, bowling, canoeing/kayaking, climbing, fencing, fishing, fitness, flag football, fly fishing, football, Frisbee, golf, hiking/backpacking, indoor soccer, juggling, kayaking, lacrosse, martial arts, mountain biking, mountaineering, outdoor activities, paint ball, physical fitness, physical training, power lifting, racquetball, rappelling, rock climbing, ropes courses, scuba diving, soccer, softball, strength & conditioning, swimming and diving, table tennis, tennis, touch football, ultimate Frisbee, volleyball, wall climbing, water polo, weight lifting, weight training, whiffle ball, wilderness, wilderness survival, wrestling, yoga; coed interscholastic: cheering. 1 coach, 3 athletic trainers.

Computers Computers are regularly used in Bible studies, economics, English, foreign language, mathematics, science, writing classes. Computer network features include on-campus library services, online commercial services, Internet access, wireless campus network, Internet filtering or blocking technology. Campus intranet, student e-mail accounts, and computer access in designated common areas are available to students. Students grades are available online. The school has a published electronic and media policy.

Contact Mr. David L. Hughes, Director of Boarding Admissions. 423-624-8300. Fax: 423-493-5426. E-mail: admissions@mccallie.org. Web site: www.mccallie.org.

MCCURDY SCHOOL

261 McCurdy Road
Espanola, New Mexico 87532
Head of School: Rev. Daniel Garcia

General Information Coeducational day college-preparatory, general academic, arts, business, religious studies, and technology school, affiliated with United Methodist Church. Grades PK–12. Founded: 1912. Setting: small town. Nearest major city is Albuquerque. 44-acre campus. 8 buildings on campus. Approved or accredited by North Central Association of Colleges and Schools, University Senate of United Methodist Church, and New Mexico Department of Education. Endowment: $1 million. Total enrollment: 342. Upper school average class size: 14. Upper school faculty-student ratio: 1:14.

Upper School Student Profile Grade 9: 47 students (25 boys, 22 girls); Grade 10: 29 students (16 boys, 13 girls); Grade 11: 38 students (18 boys, 20 girls); Grade 12: 30 students (14 boys, 16 girls). 8% of students are United Methodist Church.

Faculty School total: 32. In upper school: 5 men, 9 women; 9 have advanced degrees.

Subjects Offered Advanced Placement courses, algebra, American history-AP, anatomy, art, athletic training, athletics, biology, business, calculus-AP, chemistry, choral music, Christian studies, computer applications, computer science, drama, English, English-AP, general science, geometry, government/civics, grammar, health, health education, journalism, Life of Christ, mathematics, physical education, religion, social studies, Spanish, speech.

Graduation Requirements Arts and fine arts (art, music, dance, drama), English, mathematics, physical education (includes health), religion (includes Bible studies and theology), science, social studies (includes history).

Special Academic Programs Advanced Placement exam preparation; honors section; independent study; study at local college for college credit.

College Admission Counseling 27 students graduated in 2009; all went to college, including New Mexico State University; Northern New Mexico College; Tufts University; University of New Mexico. Mean composite ACT: 20. 10% scored over 26 on composite ACT.

Student Life Upper grades have specified standards of dress, student council. Discipline rests primarily with faculty. Attendance at religious services is required.

Tuition and Aid Day student tuition: $4612. Tuition installment plan (FACTS Tuition Payment Plan, monthly payment plans). Tuition reduction for siblings, merit scholarship grants, need-based scholarship grants, paying campus jobs available. In 2009–10, 30% of upper-school students received aid; total upper-school merit-scholarship money awarded: $28,664. Total amount of financial aid awarded in 2009–10: $37,664.

Admissions Traditional secondary-level entrance grade is 9. For fall 2009, 12 students applied for upper-level admission, 10 were accepted, 10 enrolled. Deadline for receipt of application materials: none. Application fee required: $25. Interview required.

Athletics Interscholastic: baseball (boys), basketball (b,g), cheering (g), cross-country running (b,g), football (b), softball (b); intramural: physical fitness (b,g), physical training (b,g); coed intramural: bowling, skiing (downhill). 2 PE instructors, 15 coaches.

Computers Computers are regularly used in accounting, business applications, computer applications, English, science classes. Computer resources include on-campus library services, Internet access.

Contact Ms. Pamela Miller, Business Manager. 505-753-7221. Fax: 505-753-7830. E-mail: busmgr@mccurdy.org. Web site: www.McCurdy.org.

MCDONOGH SCHOOL

8600 McDonogh Road
Owings Mills, Maryland 21117-0380
Head of School: Charles W. Britton

General Information Coeducational boarding and day college-preparatory school. Boarding grades 9–12, day grades K–12. Founded: 1873. Setting: suburban. Nearest major city is Baltimore. Students are housed in single-sex dormitories. 800-acre campus. 44 buildings on campus. Approved or accredited by Association of Independent Maryland Schools. Member of National Association of Independent Schools. Endowment: $72 million. Total enrollment: 1,297. Upper school average class size: 15. Upper school faculty-student ratio: 1:9. There are 172 required school days per year for Upper School students. Upper School students typically attend 5 days per week. The average school day consists of 6 hours and 10 minutes.

Upper School Student Profile Grade 9: 145 students (79 boys, 66 girls); Grade 10: 151 students (76 boys, 75 girls); Grade 11: 147 students (78 boys, 69 girls); Grade 12: 142 students (80 boys, 62 girls). 9% of students are boarding students. 98% are state residents. 3 states are represented in upper school student body. 1% are international students.

Faculty School total: 197. In upper school: 41 men, 48 women; 66 have advanced degrees; 31 reside on campus.

Subjects Offered 20th century American writers, acting, advanced chemistry, Advanced Placement courses, African history, African literature, African-American studies, algebra, American history, American history-AP, American literature, American literature-AP, anatomy, area studies, art, art history, art-AP, Asian studies, band, bioethics, biology, biology-AP, botany, calculus, calculus AP, ceramics, chemistry, chemistry-AP, Chesapeake Bay studies, classical Greek literature, composition-AP, computer animation, computer graphics, computer music, computer programming, computer science, computer science-AP, concert band, concert choir, creative writing, dance, drama, drawing, ecology, economics, economics-AP, electives, engineering, English, English composition, English literature, English literature and composition-AP, English literature-AP, English-AP, English/composition-AP, environmental science, environmental science-AP, ethics, European history, film, film and literature, fine arts, fitness, foreign language, French, French language-AP, French literature-AP, French-AP, genetics, geology, geometry, German, German-AP, government and politics-AP, government-AP, government/civics, health and wellness, history, history-AP, honors algebra, honors English, honors geometry, honors U.S. history, honors world history, Irish literature, jazz band, jazz dance, journalism, language-AP, languages, Latin, Latin American literature, linguistics, literature and composition-AP, literature by women, marine biology, mathematics, Middle Eastern history, music, music theory, music theory-AP, oceanography, photography, physical education, physical fitness, physics, poetry, pre-calculus, psychology, religion, Russian history, science, senior project, set design, Shakespeare, short story, Spanish, Spanish language-AP, Spanish literature, Spanish literature-AP, Spanish-AP, speech, speech communications, statistics-AP, tap dance, theater, trigonometry, tropical ecology, U.S. government and politics-AP, U.S. history, U.S. history-AP, video, visual arts, Web site design, woodworking, world history, world history-AP, world religions, world wide web design, writing workshop, yearbook.

McDonogh School

Graduation Requirements Arts and fine arts (art, music, dance, drama), English, foreign language, mathematics, physical education (includes health), science, senior project, social studies (includes history). Community service is required.

Special Academic Programs Advanced Placement exam preparation; honors section; independent study; term-away projects.

College Admission Counseling 143 students graduated in 2010; all went to college, including Boston University; Franklin & Marshall College; Penn State University Park; University of Delaware; University of Maryland, College Park. Mean SAT critical reading: 611, mean SAT math: 647, mean SAT writing: 620, mean combined SAT: 1878, mean composite ACT: 28.

Student Life Upper grades have uniform requirement, student council, honor system. Discipline rests primarily with faculty.

Summer Programs Enrichment, sports, art/fine arts, computer instruction programs offered; session focuses on recreation and sports camps; held both on and off campus; held at Gunpowder Falls State Park and Chesapeake Bay; accepts boys and girls; open to students from other schools. 1,800 students usually enrolled. 2011 schedule: June 20 to July 29. Application deadline: May 1.

Tuition and Aid Day student tuition: $23,370; 5-day tuition and room/board: $31,420. Tuition installment plan (Key Tuition Payment Plan, monthly payment plans, individually arranged payment plans). Need-based scholarship grants, need-based loans, middle-income loans available. In 2010–11, 24% of upper-school students received aid. Total amount of financial aid awarded in 2010–11: $2,415,935.

Admissions Traditional secondary-level entrance grade is 9. For fall 2010, 295 students applied for upper-level admission, 91 were accepted, 51 enrolled. ISEE required. Deadline for receipt of application materials: December 15. Application fee required: $50. On-campus interview required.

Athletics Interscholastic: aquatics (boys, girls), baseball (b), basketball (b,g), cross-country running (b,g), equestrian sports (b,g), field hockey (g), football (b), golf (b,g), lacrosse (b,g), soccer (b,g), softball (g), swimming and diving (b,g), tennis (b,g), volleyball (g), water polo (b,g), winter (indoor) track (b,g), wrestling (b); coed interscholastic: cheering, equestrian sports, horseback riding, squash, track and field; coed intramural: badminton, ballet, dance, fencing, fitness, squash. 10 PE instructors, 92 coaches, 2 athletic trainers.

Computers Computers are regularly used in all classes. Computer network features include on-campus library services, online commercial services, Internet access, wireless campus network, Internet filtering or blocking technology. Campus intranet, student e-mail accounts, and computer access in designated common areas are available to students. Students grades are available online. The school has a published electronic and media policy.

Contact Anita Hilson, Director of Admissions. 410-581-4719. Fax: 410-998-3537. E-mail: ahilson@mcdonogh.org. Web site: www.mcdonogh.org.

MCGILL-TOOLEN CATHOLIC HIGH SCHOOL

1501 Old Shell Road
Mobile, Alabama 36604-2291
Head of School: Mrs. Michelle T. Haas

General Information Coeducational day college-preparatory, arts, religious studies, and technology school, affiliated with Roman Catholic Church. Grades 9–12. Founded: 1896. Setting: urban. 18-acre campus. 5 buildings on campus. Approved or accredited by Southern Association of Colleges and Schools and Alabama Department of Education. Total enrollment: 1,078. Upper school average class size: 21. Upper school faculty-student ratio: 1:14. There are 180 required school days per year for Upper School students. Upper School students typically attend 5 days per week. The average school day consists of 6 hours and 40 minutes.

Upper School Student Profile Grade 9: 266 students (132 boys, 134 girls); Grade 10: 278 students (141 boys, 137 girls); Grade 11: 301 students (144 boys, 157 girls); Grade 12: 233 students (123 boys, 110 girls). 90.4% of students are Roman Catholic.

Faculty School total: 79. In upper school: 36 men, 42 women; 51 have advanced degrees.

Subjects Offered 3-dimensional art, 3-dimensional design, ACT preparation, advanced biology, advanced chemistry, advanced math, Advanced Placement courses, American government, American history, American history-AP, American literature, analytic geometry, anatomy and physiology, athletic training, band, baseball, basketball, Bible studies, biology, biology-AP, British literature, British literature (honors), calculus, calculus-AP, campus ministry, Catholic belief and practice, ceramics, cheerleading, chemistry, chemistry-AP, choir, choral music, chorus, church history, conceptual physics, concert choir, current events, driver education, economics, English, English composition, English language and composition-AP, English-AP, French, geography, geometry, government, government and politics-AP, graphic design, health, health and wellness, history of the Catholic Church, honors algebra, honors English, honors geometry, honors U.S. history, honors world history, independent study, keyboarding, Latin, marine biology, modern European history-AP, modern world history, multimedia, music appreciation, painting, physical education, physical fitness, physics, physics-AP, pre-algebra, pre-calculus, psychology, reading, reading/study skills, softball, Spanish, Spanish language-AP, speech, studio art, studio art-AP, U.S. government, U.S. government and politics, U.S. government and politics-AP, U.S. history, U.S. history-AP, U.S. literature, video film production, vocal ensemble, volleyball, Web site design, weight fitness, weight training, world geography, world history, world history-AP, world literature, yearbook.

Graduation Requirements Electives, English, keyboarding, mathematics, physical education (includes health), religion (includes Bible studies and theology), science, social studies (includes history), must complete 1 cultural unit each semeseter enrolled at McGill-Toolen.

Special Academic Programs 14 Advanced Placement exams for which test preparation is offered; honors section; remedial reading and/or remedial writing; remedial math.

College Admission Counseling 239 students graduated in 2010; 220 went to college, including Auburn University; Louisiana State University and Agricultural and Mechanical College; Spring Hill College; The University of Alabama; University of South Alabama; University of Southern Mississippi. Other: 17 went to work, 2 entered military service. Median composite ACT: 23. 19% scored over 26 on composite ACT.

Student Life Upper grades have uniform requirement, student council. Discipline rests primarily with faculty. Attendance at religious services is required.

Summer Programs Remediation, enrichment programs offered; session focuses on Math/Reading/English transition to high school. Remediation for Religion courses; held on campus; accepts boys and girls; not open to students from other schools. 25 students usually enrolled. 2011 schedule: July 11 to July 23. Application deadline: June 10.

Tuition and Aid Day student tuition: $6000–$7200. Tuition installment plan (FACTS Tuition Payment Plan). Tuition reduction for siblings, merit scholarship grants, need-based scholarship grants available. In 2010–11, 25% of upper-school students received aid; total upper-school merit-scholarship money awarded: $25,000. Total amount of financial aid awarded in 2010–11: $335,000.

Admissions ACT-Explore required. Deadline for receipt of application materials: none. Application fee required: $100. On-campus interview recommended.

Athletics Interscholastic: baseball (boys), basketball (b,g), cheering (g), cross-country running (b,g), diving (b,g), football (b), golf (b,g), indoor track (b,g), soccer (b,g), softball (g), swimming and diving (b,g), tennis (b,g), track and field (b,g), volleyball (g); intramural: outdoor adventure (b,g), table tennis (b,g), ultimate Frisbee (b,g); coed intramural: hiking/backpacking. 4 PE instructors, 3 coaches, 1 athletic trainer.

Computers Computers are regularly used in current events, graphic design, keyboarding, reading, technology, video film production, Web site design, yearbook classes. Computer network features include on-campus library services, Internet access, wireless campus network, Internet filtering or blocking technology. Campus intranet is available to students. Students grades are available online. The school has a published electronic and media policy.

Contact Mr. Paul Knapstein, Director of Enrollment. 251-445-2934. Fax: 251-433-8356. E-mail: knapstp@mcgill-toolen.org.

MCQUAID JESUIT

1800 South Clinton Avenue
Rochester, New York 14618
Head of School: Fr. James K. Coughlin, SJ

General Information Boys' day college-preparatory, arts, religious studies, and technology school, affiliated with Roman Catholic Church (Jesuit order). Grades 7–12. Founded: 1954. Setting: suburban. 33-acre campus. 1 building on campus. Approved or accredited by Jesuit Secondary Education Association, Middle States Association of Colleges and Schools, National Catholic Education Association, and New York State Board of Regents. Endowment: $9 million. Total enrollment: 843. Upper school average class size: 20. Upper school faculty-student ratio: 1:14. There are 166 required school days per year for Upper School students. Upper School students typically attend 5 days per week. The average school day consists of 6 hours and 40 minutes.

Upper School Student Profile Grade 9: 172 students (172 boys); Grade 10: 159 students (159 boys); Grade 11: 175 students (175 boys); Grade 12: 153 students (153 boys). 79% of students are Roman Catholic Church (Jesuit order).

Faculty School total: 67. In upper school: 42 men, 19 women; 54 have advanced degrees.

Subjects Offered 3-dimensional art, advanced computer applications, advanced math, algebra, American government, American history, American literature, art, band, Bible studies, biology, biology-AP, biotechnology, calculus, calculus-AP, Catholic belief and practice, chemistry, chemistry-AP, choir, classical language, community service, computer literacy, computer math, computer programming, computer programming-AP, computer science, creative writing, drama, dramatic arts, driver education, earth science, economics, economics-AP, English, English literature, English literature and composition, English literature-AP, environmental science, environmental science-AP, European history, European history-AP, expository writing, fine arts, foreign language, French, geography, geometry, global studies, government/civics, grammar, health, history, honors English, instrumental music, Irish studies, Italian, jazz band, keyboarding, Latin, mathematics, modern European history-AP, music, musical theater, novels, physical education, physics, physics-AP, poetry, portfolio writing, pre-calculus, psychology, psychology-AP, religion, religious studies, robotics, Russian, science, senior seminar, Shakespeare, social studies, Spanish, Spanish language-AP, speech and debate, statistics-AP, studio art-AP, theology, U.S. history-AP, vocal ensemble, vocal music, word processing, world history-AP, writing.

Graduation Requirements Arts and fine arts (art, music, dance, drama), English, foreign language, health education, mathematics, physical education (includes health), religion (includes Bible studies and theology), science, social studies (includes history). Community service is required.

Special Academic Programs 18 Advanced Placement exams for which test preparation is offered; honors section.

College Admission Counseling 148 students graduated in 2009; 142 went to college, including Boston College; John Carroll University; Le Moyne College; Rochester Institute of Technology; State University of New York at Binghamton; State University of New York College at Geneseo. Other: 1 went to work, 2 entered military service, 3 had other specific plans. Mean SAT critical reading: 602, mean SAT math: 598.

Student Life Upper grades have specified standards of dress, student council, honor system. Discipline rests primarily with faculty. Attendance at religious services is required.

Tuition and Aid Day student tuition: $9650. Tuition installment plan (monthly payment plans, individually arranged payment plans). Merit scholarship grants, need-based scholarship grants available. In 2009–10, 40% of upper-school students received aid; total upper-school merit-scholarship money awarded: $14,000. Total amount of financial aid awarded in 2009–10: $1,340,000.

Admissions Traditional secondary-level entrance grade is 9. For fall 2009, 118 students applied for upper-level admission, 109 were accepted, 101 enrolled. STS required. Deadline for receipt of application materials: none. No application fee required.

Athletics Interscholastic: alpine skiing, baseball, basketball, bowling, crew, cross-country running, football, golf, ice hockey, indoor track, indoor track & field, lacrosse, rowing, rugby, sailing, skiing (downhill), soccer, swimming and diving, tennis, track and field, volleyball, winter (indoor) track, wrestling; intramural: baseball, basketball, bicycling, billiards, bocce, fencing, flag football, floor hockey, football, Frisbee, handball, hiking/backpacking, juggling, martial arts, mountain biking, paint ball, physical fitness, physical training, power lifting, ropes courses, self defense, skiing (cross-country), soccer, softball, strength & conditioning, table tennis, tennis, touch football, ultimate Frisbee, volleyball, water polo, weight lifting, weight training, wrestling, yoga. 4 PE instructors, 19 coaches, 1 athletic trainer.

Computers Computers are regularly used in art, English, foreign language, graphic design, history, journalism, lab/keyboard, library, literary magazine, mathematics, music, newspaper, religious studies, research skills, science, word processing, yearbook classes. Computer network features include on-campus library services, online commercial services, Internet access, wireless campus network, Internet filtering or blocking technology. Computer access in designated common areas is available to students. The school has a published electronic and media policy.

Contact Mr. Christopher Parks, Dean of Admissions. 585-256-6117. Fax: 585-256-6171. E-mail: cparks@mcquaid.org. Web site: www.mcquaid.org.

MEADOWRIDGE SCHOOL

12224 240th Street
Maple Ridge, British Columbia V4R 1N1, Canada

Head of School: Mr. Hugh Burke

General Information Coeducational day college-preparatory, arts, and technology school. Grades JK–12. Founded: 1985. Setting: rural. Nearest major city is Vancouver, Canada. 16-acre campus. 1 building on campus. Approved or accredited by Canadian Association of Independent Schools, Canadian Educational Standards Institute, European Council of International Schools, International Baccalaureate Organization, and British Columbia Department of Education. Language of instruction: English. Total enrollment: 511. Upper school average class size: 18. Upper school faculty-student ratio: 1:9. The average school day consists of 6 hours.

Upper School Student Profile Grade 8: 44 students (19 boys, 25 girls); Grade 9: 31 students (12 boys, 19 girls); Grade 10: 38 students (13 boys, 25 girls); Grade 11: 42 students (18 boys, 24 girls); Grade 12: 28 students (16 boys, 12 girls).

Faculty School total: 46. In upper school: 11 men, 9 women; 6 have advanced degrees.

Subjects Offered Accounting, Advanced Placement courses, art, biology, biology-AP, calculus, calculus-AP, career and personal planning, chemistry, comparative civilizations, computer science-AP, computer technologies, drama, English, English literature, English-AP, filmmaking, forensics, French, geography, history, humanities, marketing, mathematics, photography, physical education, physics, science, Spanish, weight training.

Graduation Requirements 3 provincially examinable courses.

Special Academic Programs International Baccalaureate program; study abroad; academic accommodation for the gifted.

College Admission Counseling 34 students graduated in 2010; all went to college, including McGill University; Queen's University at Kingston; Simon Fraser University; The University of British Columbia; University of Toronto; University of Victoria.

Student Life Upper grades have uniform requirement, student council, honor system. Discipline rests equally with students and faculty.

Tuition and Aid Day student tuition: CAN$13,800. Tuition installment plan (Insured Tuition Payment Plan, monthly payment plans). Tuition reduction for siblings, bursaries, merit scholarship grants available. In 2010–11, 1% of upper-school students received aid; total upper-school merit-scholarship money awarded: CAN$22,000.

Admissions Traditional secondary-level entrance grade is 8. For fall 2010, 39 students applied for upper-level admission, 28 were accepted, 26 enrolled. Admissions testing and writing sample required. Deadline for receipt of application materials: none. Application fee required: CAN$150. On-campus interview required.

Athletics Interscholastic: aerobics/dance (boys, girls), badminton (b,g), basketball (b,g), physical fitness (b,g), rugby (b,g), soccer (b,g), volleyball (b,g); intramural: aerobics/dance (b,g), basketball (b,g); coed interscholastic: aerobics/dance, cross-country running, flag football, outdoor activities, swimming and diving, track and field; coed intramural: aerobics/dance. 2 PE instructors.

Computers Computers are regularly used in information technology, journalism, video film production, yearbook classes. Computer network features include on-campus library services, Internet access, wireless campus network, Internet filtering or blocking technology. Student e-mail accounts and computer access in designated common areas are available to students.

Contact Ms. Christine Bickle, Director of Admissions. 604-476-3040. Fax: 604-467-4989. E-mail: christine.bickle@meadowridge.bc.ca. Web site: www.meadowridge.bc.ca.

THE MEADOWS SCHOOL

8601 Scholar Lane
Las Vegas, Nevada 89128-7302

Head of School: Mr. Henry L. Chanin

General Information Coeducational day college-preparatory, arts, technology, and debate, foreign languages school. Grades PK–12. Founded: 1981. Setting: suburban. 42-acre campus. 10 buildings on campus. Approved or accredited by CITA (Commission on International and Trans-Regional Accreditation), Northwest Association of Schools and Colleges, Pacific Northwest Association of Independent Schools, and Nevada Department of Education. Member of National Association of Independent Schools and Secondary School Admission Test Board. Endowment: $12 million. Total enrollment: 897. Upper school average class size: 18. Upper school faculty-student ratio: 1:11. There are 180 required school days per year for Upper School students. Upper School students typically attend 5 days per week. The average school day consists of 7 hours.

Upper School Student Profile Grade 9: 74 students (37 boys, 37 girls); Grade 10: 74 students (38 boys, 36 girls); Grade 11: 74 students (37 boys, 37 girls); Grade 12: 45 students (24 boys, 21 girls).

Faculty School total: 86. In upper school: 18 men, 18 women; 26 have advanced degrees.

Subjects Offered 20th century American writers, 3-dimensional art, acting, advanced chemistry, advanced math, Advanced Placement courses, advanced studio art-AP, American literature, anatomy and physiology, ancient history, anthropology, architectural drawing, architecture, art, art history, art history-AP, athletics, band, banking, Basic programming, biology, biology-AP, British literature, British literature (honors), calculus, calculus-AP, ceramics, chemistry, chemistry-AP, choir, choral music, chorus, comparative religion, composition, computer animation, computer applications, computer graphics, computer literacy, computer programming, computer programming-AP, computer science, computer science-AP, concert choir, constitutional law, creative writing, dance, digital art, digital photography, drama, drama performance, drawing, drawing and design, economics, economics-AP, English, English composition, English language and composition-AP, English literature, English literature and composition-AP, European history, European history-AP, film studies, finance, fine arts, finite math, foreign language, forensics, French, French language-AP, genetics, geometry, government-AP, health, honors English, honors geometry, honors U.S. history, honors world history, human anatomy, instrumental music, integrated mathematics, international relations, journalism, keyboarding, Latin, Latin-AP, law, literature and composition-AP, microeconomics-AP, money management, music theater, painting, philosophy, photography, physics, physics-AP, pre-calculus, psychology-AP, sculpture, Shakespeare, social justice, social sciences, Spanish, Spanish language-AP, Spanish literature, Spanish literature-AP, Spanish-AP, speech, speech and debate, speech and oral interpretations, statistics, statistics-AP, studio art, studio art-AP, technical theater, technology, theater production, trigonometry, U.S. government, U.S. government and politics-AP, U.S. history, U.S. history-AP, yearbook.

Graduation Requirements American literature, ancient world history, arts and fine arts (art, music, dance, drama), biology, English, English composition, English literature, European history, foreign language, geometry, mathematics, physical education (includes health), physics, pre-calculus, science, social studies (includes history), technical skills, U.S. government, U.S. history, seniors have a 24-hour per semester community service requirement, grades 9-11 have a 16-hour per semester community service requirement.

Special Academic Programs 24 Advanced Placement exams for which test preparation is offered; honors section; academic accommodation for the gifted, the musically talented, and the artistically talented.

College Admission Counseling 58 students graduated in 2010; all went to college, including Chapman University; Loyola Marymount University; The George Washington University; University of Oregon; University of San Francisco; University of Southern California. Median SAT critical reading: 620, median SAT math: 650, median SAT writing: 630, median combined SAT: 1900, median composite ACT: 28.

The Meadows School

57% scored over 600 on SAT critical reading, 64% scored over 600 on SAT math, 70% scored over 600 on SAT writing, 63% scored over 1800 on combined SAT, 64% scored over 26 on composite ACT.

Student Life Upper grades have uniform requirement, student council, honor system. Discipline rests equally with students and faculty.

Summer Programs Enrichment programs offered; session focuses on enrichment; held on campus; accepts boys and girls; open to students from other schools. 50 students usually enrolled. 2011 schedule: June 6 to July 1. Application deadline: May 27.

Tuition and Aid Day student tuition: $19,650. Tuition installment plan (Insured Tuition Payment Plan, monthly payment plans, individually arranged payment plans, 2-payment plan, 70% by July 15 and 30% by February 15, 10 monthly payment plan using electronic withdrawal only). Need-based scholarship grants, need-based loans available. In 2010–11, 17% of upper-school students received aid. Total amount of financial aid awarded in 2010–11: $597,540.

Admissions Traditional secondary-level entrance grade is 9. ERB, ISEE, PSAT, SAT or SSAT required. Deadline for receipt of application materials: none. Application fee required: $100. On-campus interview required.

Athletics Interscholastic: baseball (boys), basketball (b,g), bowling (b,g), cheering (g), cross-country running (b,g), dance team (g), diving (b,g), football (b), golf (b), softball (g), swimming and diving (b,g), tennis (b,g), track and field (b,g), volleyball (g), wrestling (b); coed interscholastic: soccer. 1 PE instructor, 1 athletic trainer.

Computers Computers are regularly used in architecture, college planning, desktop publishing, English, foreign language, graphic design, history, independent study, information technology, introduction to technology, library, mathematics, music, news writing, photography, photojournalism, programming, publications, publishing, science, speech, technology, yearbook classes. Computer network features include on-campus library services, online commercial services, Internet access, wireless campus network, Internet filtering or blocking technology, Neon, SMART boards, three wireless mobile computer labs with notebook computers, course syllabus and homework for upper and middle school. Computer access in designated common areas is available to students. The school has a published electronic and media policy.

Contact Web site: www.themeadowsschool.org.

MEMORIAL HALL SCHOOL

5400 Mitchelldale, Ste,A-1
Houston, Texas 77092
Head of School: Rev. George C. Aurich

General Information Coeducational day college-preparatory, general academic, and bilingual studies school. Grades 4–12. Founded: 1966. Setting: urban. 1 building on campus. Approved or accredited by Southern Association of Colleges and Schools, Southern Association of Independent Schools, Texas Education Agency, and Texas Department of Education. Total enrollment: 80. Upper school average class size: 14. Upper school faculty-student ratio: 1:14. Upper School students typically attend 4 days per week. The average school day consists of 7 hours and 30 minutes.

Faculty School total: 11. In upper school: 4 men, 7 women; 3 have advanced degrees.

Subjects Offered Algebra, American history, art, biology, business mathematics, business skills, chemistry, computer science, economics, English, ESL, fine arts, geography, geometry, government/civics, health, history, journalism, mathematics, physical education, physics, psychology, science, social sciences, social studies, sociology, Spanish, trigonometry, world history.

Graduation Requirements Arts and crafts, arts and fine arts (art, music, dance, drama), business skills (includes word processing), computer science, English, foreign language, mathematics, physical education (includes health), science, social sciences, social studies (includes history), community service, foreign credit accepted upon completion.

Special Academic Programs Honors section; accelerated programs; independent study; study at local college for college credit; academic accommodation for the gifted; remedial reading and/or remedial writing; remedial math; programs in English, mathematics, general development for dyslexic students; special instructional classes for students with learning disabilities, Attention Deficit Disorder, and dyslexia; ESL (60 students enrolled).

College Admission Counseling 28 students graduated in 2010; all went to college, including Baylor University; Sam Houston State University; St. Thomas University; Texas A&M University; The University of Texas at Austin; University of Houston.

Student Life Upper grades have uniform requirement, student council, honor system. Discipline rests equally with students and faculty.

Summer Programs Remediation, enrichment, advancement, ESL, computer instruction programs offered; session focuses on additional credit enrichment, study skills; held on campus; accepts boys and girls; open to students from other schools. 55 students usually enrolled. 2011 schedule: June 15 to July 30. Application deadline: none.

Tuition and Aid Day student tuition: $11,400. Tuition installment plan (Insured Tuition Payment Plan, monthly payment plans, individually arranged payment plans). Tuition reduction for siblings available. In 2010–11, 5% of upper-school students received aid.

Admissions Traditional secondary-level entrance grade is 9. Stanford Achievement Test required. Deadline for receipt of application materials: none. Application fee required: $300. Interview required.

Athletics Interscholastic: aerobics (boys, girls), aerobics/dance (b,g), fitness (b,g), fitness walking (b,g), jump rope (b,g), yoga (b,g); intramural: cheering (g); coed intramural: dance, outdoor activities, physical fitness. 2 PE instructors.

Computers Computers are regularly used in all academic, basic skills, foreign language classes. Computer network features include Internet access.

Contact Kimberly Smith, Coordinator. 713-688-5566. Fax: 713-956-9751. E-mail: memhallsch@aol.com. Web site: www.memorialhall.org.

MEMPHIS UNIVERSITY SCHOOL

6191 Park Avenue
Memphis, Tennessee 38119-5399
Head of School: Mr. Ellis L. Haguewood

General Information Boys' day college-preparatory school. Grades 7–12. Founded: 1893. Setting: suburban. 94-acre campus. 8 buildings on campus. Approved or accredited by Southern Association of Colleges and Schools, Southern Association of Independent Schools, and Tennessee Association of Independent Schools. Member of National Association of Independent Schools. Endowment: $21 million. Total enrollment: 658. Upper school average class size: 14. Upper school faculty-student ratio: 1:8. There are 176 required school days per year for Upper School students. Upper School students typically attend 5 days per week. The average school day consists of 7 hours.

Upper School Student Profile Grade 9: 117 students (117 boys); Grade 10: 133 students (133 boys); Grade 11: 88 students (88 boys); Grade 12: 94 students (94 boys).

Faculty School total: 71. In upper school: 43 men, 13 women; 40 have advanced degrees.

Subjects Offered Algebra, American government, American literature, art, art history, art history-AP, arts and crafts, Bible, biology, biology-AP, British literature, calculus, calculus-AP, chemistry, chemistry-AP, choral music, college counseling, college placement, comparative government and politics-AP, comparative religion, composition-AP, computer education, computer programming, computer science, computer science-AP, driver education, earth science, economics, economics and history, English, English composition, English literature, English literature and composition-AP, environmental science, ethics, ethics and responsibility, European history, European history-AP, expository writing, fine arts, foreign language, French, geometry, global studies, government and politics-AP, government/civics, grammar, health, history, humanities, introduction to theater, keyboarding, language and composition, Latin, library skills, literature, mathematics, music, music appreciation, music composition, music theory, physical education, physical science, physics, physics-AP, pre-algebra, pre-calculus, probability and statistics, psychology, religion, research skills, science, social sciences, social studies, Spanish, studio art, study skills, trigonometry, U.S. history, U.S. history-AP, United States government-AP, Western civilization, world history, writing.

Graduation Requirements Arts and fine arts (art, music, dance, drama), English, foreign language, mathematics, physical education (includes health), religion (includes Bible studies and theology), science, social sciences, social studies (includes history).

Special Academic Programs 18 Advanced Placement exams for which test preparation is offered; honors section; study abroad; remedial reading and/or remedial writing; remedial math.

College Admission Counseling 112 students graduated in 2010; all went to college, including Southern Methodist University; The University of Alabama at Birmingham; The University of Tennessee; University of Arkansas; University of Mississippi; Vanderbilt University. Median composite ACT: 29. Mean SAT critical reading: 615, mean SAT math: 638, mean SAT writing: 614. 59% scored over 600 on SAT critical reading, 65% scored over 600 on SAT math, 61% scored over 600 on SAT writing, 61% scored over 1800 on combined SAT, 68% scored over 26 on composite ACT.

Student Life Upper grades have specified standards of dress, student council, honor system. Discipline rests primarily with faculty.

Summer Programs Remediation, enrichment, advancement, sports programs offered; session focuses on academics and athletics; held on campus; accepts boys and girls; open to students from other schools. 460 students usually enrolled. 2011 schedule: June 6 to July 29. Application deadline: none.

Tuition and Aid Day student tuition: $16,750. Tuition installment plan (FACTS Tuition Payment Plan, monthly payment plans, individually arranged payment plans). Need-based scholarship grants available. In 2010–11, 31% of upper-school students received aid. Total amount of financial aid awarded in 2010–11: $1,300,000.

Admissions Traditional secondary-level entrance grade is 9. For fall 2010, 38 students applied for upper-level admission, 35 were accepted, 30 enrolled. ISEE required. Deadline for receipt of application materials: December 10. Application fee required: $50. On-campus interview recommended.

Athletics Interscholastic: baseball, basketball, cross-country running, football, golf, lacrosse, soccer, swimming and diving, tennis, track and field, trap and skeet, weight training, wrestling. 5 PE instructors, 9 coaches, 1 athletic trainer.

Computers Computers are regularly used in all academic, career exploration, college planning, graphic design, library science, newspaper, publications, yearbook classes. Computer network features include on-campus library services, online commercial services, Internet access, wireless campus network, Internet filtering or blocking technology. Campus intranet, student e-mail accounts, and computer access in designated common areas are available to students. Students grades are available online. The school has a published electronic and media policy.

Contact Mrs. Peggy E. Williamson, Director of Admissions. 901-260-1349. Fax: 901-260-1301. E-mail: peggy.williamson@musowls.org. Web site: www.musowls.org.

MENAUL SCHOOL

301 Menaul Boulevard NE
Albuquerque, New Mexico 87107
Head of School: Mr. Lindsey R. Gilbert

General Information Coeducational boarding and day college-preparatory and arts school, affiliated with Presbyterian Church. Boarding grades 9–12, day grades 6–12. Founded: 1896. Setting: urban. Students are housed in single-sex dormitories. 35-acre campus. 10 buildings on campus. Approved or accredited by Independent Schools Association of the Southwest, North Central Association of Colleges and Schools, The College Board, and New Mexico Department of Education. Endowment: $3.3 million. Total enrollment: 175. Upper school average class size: 12. Upper school faculty-student ratio: 1:9. There are 180 required school days per year for Upper School students. Upper School students typically attend 5 days per week. The average school day consists of 6 hours.

Upper School Student Profile Grade 9: 21 students (17 boys, 4 girls); Grade 10: 26 students (20 boys, 6 girls); Grade 11: 30 students (12 boys, 18 girls); Grade 12: 26 students (15 boys, 11 girls). 8% of students are boarding students. 10% are state residents. 1 state is represented in upper school student body. 90% are international students. International students from China and Viet Nam. 20% of students are Presbyterian.

Faculty School total: 25. In upper school: 13 men, 11 women; 16 have advanced degrees; 5 reside on campus.

Subjects Offered ACT preparation, Advanced Placement courses, algebra, American government, American history, American literature, art, arts and crafts, band, Bible studies, biology, calculus-AP, chemistry, clayworking, communications, computer graphics, computer programming, computer science, earth science, economics, English, English literature, English-AP, ethics, fine arts, geography, geometry, government/civics, history, Life of Christ, mathematics, music, Native American arts and crafts, physical education, physics, psychology, religion, science, social sciences, social studies, sociology, Spanish, theology, trigonometry, U.S. government and politics-AP, world history, world literature, writing, yearbook.

Graduation Requirements Arts and fine arts (art, music, dance, drama), communications, computer science, English, foreign language, mathematics, physical education (includes health), religion (includes Bible studies and theology), science, social sciences, social studies (includes history), 100 hours of community service.

Special Academic Programs Advanced Placement exam preparation; honors section; independent study; study at local college for college credit; academic accommodation for the gifted and the artistically talented; ESL (3 students enrolled).

College Admission Counseling 14 students graduated in 2010; all went to college, including New Mexico State University; University of New Mexico. Median SAT critical reading: 500, median SAT math: 450, median composite ACT: 21. 20% scored over 600 on SAT critical reading, 15% scored over 600 on SAT math, 5% scored over 26 on composite ACT.

Student Life Upper grades have uniform requirement, student council. Discipline rests primarily with faculty. Attendance at religious services is required.

Tuition and Aid Day student tuition: $13,100; 7-day tuition and room/board: $28,000. Tuition installment plan (FACTS Tuition Payment Plan). Need-based scholarship grants available. In 2010–11, 60% of upper-school students received aid. Total amount of financial aid awarded in 2010–11: $307,000.

Admissions Traditional secondary-level entrance grade is 9. For fall 2010, 20 students applied for upper-level admission, 15 were accepted, 15 enrolled. Achievement tests, ERB, Gates MacGinitie Reading Tests, ISEE or SSAT required. Deadline for receipt of application materials: none. Application fee required: $30. Interview required.

Athletics Interscholastic: basketball (boys, girls), flag football (b), football (b), soccer (g), softball (g), volleyball (g); coed interscholastic: golf, outdoor education, running, track and field. 2 PE instructors, 6 coaches, 1 athletic trainer.

Computers Computers are regularly used in art, college planning, English, graphics, history, mathematics, psychology, science, yearbook classes. Computer network features include on-campus library services, online commercial services, Internet access, wireless campus network, Internet filtering or blocking technology. Campus intranet, student e-mail accounts, and computer access in designated common areas are available to students. Students grades are available online. The school has a published electronic and media policy.

Contact Rebecca Toevs, PhD, Director of Admission and Financial Aid. 505-341-7223. Fax: 505-344-2517. E-mail: rtoevs@menaulschool.com. Web site: www.menaulschool.com.

MENLO SCHOOL

50 Valparaiso Avenue
Atherton, California 94027
Head of School: Norman M. Colb

General Information Coeducational day college-preparatory school. Grades 6–12. Founded: 1915. Setting: suburban. Nearest major city is San Jose. 35-acre campus. 23 buildings on campus. Approved or accredited by California Association of Independent Schools, Western Association of Schools and Colleges, and California Department of Education. Member of National Association of Independent Schools. Endowment: $22 million. Total enrollment: 810. Upper school average class size: 15. Upper school faculty-student ratio: 1:10. There are 170 required school days per year for Upper School students. Upper School students typically attend 5 days per week. The average school day consists of 7 hours.

Faculty School total: 86. In upper school: 29 men, 45 women; 58 have advanced degrees.

Subjects Offered 20th century American writers, advanced biology, advanced chemistry, advanced computer applications, advanced math, algebra, American history, American history-AP, American literature, American literature-AP, analytic geometry, anatomy and physiology, ancient world history, art, art history, art-AP, Asian studies, biology, biology-AP, British literature-AP, calculus, calculus-AP, chemistry, chemistry-AP, chorus, computer graphics, computer literacy, computer multimedia, computer programming, computer science, computer science-AP, creative writing, dance, debate, drama, earth science, economics, economics-AP, engineering, English, English language and composition-AP, English literature, English literature-AP, English-AP, environmental science, ethics, European history, European history-AP, film studies, fine arts, French, French as a second language, French language-AP, French literature-AP, French-AP, freshman seminar, geometry, government and politics-AP, history, honors English, honors geometry, honors U.S. history, intro to computers, Japanese, jazz band, jazz dance, jazz ensemble, journalism, Latin, Latin-AP, law, literature-AP, Mandarin, mathematics, mathematics-AP, methods of research, modern European history, modern world history, multimedia, music, music theory, music theory-AP, music-AP, musical productions, newspaper, orchestra, performing arts, philosophy, photography, physical education, physics, physics-AP, play production, poetry, pre-calculus, rhetoric, robotics, science, science fiction, science research, senior project, Shakespeare, society and culture, Spanish, Spanish language-AP, Spanish literature-AP, Spanish-AP, statistics, statistics-AP, student government, student publications, studio art, studio art-AP, swimming, U.S. government and politics-AP, U.S. history-AP, video film production, wellness, women's literature, world history, world religions, writing, yearbook.

Graduation Requirements Arts and fine arts (art, music, dance, drama), English, foreign language, mathematics, physical education (includes health), science, social studies (includes history), freshman seminar, Knight School, senior project (3-week project at the end of senior year). Community service is required.

Special Academic Programs Advanced Placement exam preparation; honors section; independent study.

College Admission Counseling 136 students graduated in 2010; 133 went to college, including Princeton University; Stanford University; University of California, Berkeley; University of California, Los Angeles; University of California, Santa Barbara; University of Southern California. Other: 1 entered a postgraduate year, 2 had other specific plans. Mean SAT critical reading: 655, mean SAT math: 681, mean SAT writing: 673. 74% scored over 600 on SAT critical reading, 88% scored over 600 on SAT math, 80% scored over 600 on SAT writing, 86% scored over 26 on composite ACT.

Student Life Upper grades have student council. Discipline rests equally with students and faculty.

Summer Programs Enrichment programs offered; session focuses on academic enrichment; held on campus; accepts boys and girls; open to students from other schools. 70 students usually enrolled. 2011 schedule: June 14 to July 2. Application deadline: April 30.

Tuition and Aid Day student tuition: $33,600. Tuition installment plan (Key Tuition Payment Plan). Need-based scholarship grants, paying campus jobs available. In 2010–11, 20% of upper-school students received aid. Total amount of financial aid awarded in 2010–11: $4,200,000.

Admissions Traditional secondary-level entrance grade is 9. For fall 2010, 400 students applied for upper-level admission, 84 enrolled. ISEE, SSAT or TOEFL required. Deadline for receipt of application materials: January 13. Application fee required: $85. On-campus interview required.

Athletics Interscholastic: aerobics/dance (girls), baseball (b), basketball (b,g), cross-country running (b,g), dance (g), football (b), golf (b,g), lacrosse (b,g), soccer (b,g), softball (g), swimming and diving (b,g), tennis (b,g), track and field (b,g), volleyball (b,g), water polo (b,g); coed interscholastic: aerobics/dance, dance, martial arts. 67 coaches, 2 athletic trainers.

Computers Computers are regularly used in English, foreign language, history, journalism, mathematics, media arts, multimedia, newspaper, science, yearbook classes. Computer network features include on-campus library services, online commercial services, Internet access, wireless campus network, Internet filtering or blocking technology. Student e-mail accounts and computer access in designated common areas are available to students.

Contact Mary Emery, Admissions and Financial Aid Assistant. 650-330-2000 Ext. 2601. Fax: 650-330-2012. Web site: www.menloschool.org.

MENNONITE COLLEGIATE INSTITUTE

Box 250
Gretna, Manitoba R0G 0V0, Canada
Head of School: Mr. Darryl K. Loewen
General Information Coeducational boarding and day college-preparatory, general academic, arts, business, and religious studies school, affiliated with Mennonite Church, Mennonite Brethren Church; primarily serves students with learning disabilities, individuals with Attention Deficit Disorder, individuals with emotional and behavioral problems, dyslexic students, and physical disabilities. Grades 9–12. Founded: 1889. Setting: small town. Nearest major city is Winnipeg, Canada. Students are housed in single-sex dormitories. 12-acre campus. 5 buildings on campus. Approved or accredited by The College Board and Manitoba Department of Education. Language of instruction: English. Endowment: CAN$500,000. Total enrollment: 153. Upper school average class size: 20. Upper school faculty-student ratio: 1:13. There are 196 required school days per year for Upper School students. Upper School students typically attend 5 days per week. The average school day consists of 5 hours and 35 minutes.
Upper School Student Profile Grade 9: 23 students (10 boys, 13 girls); Grade 10: 42 students (17 boys, 25 girls); Grade 11: 43 students (25 boys, 18 girls); Grade 12: 49 students (23 boys, 26 girls). 42% of students are boarding students. 95% are province residents. 3 provinces are represented in upper school student body. 3% are international students. International students from Congo, Democratic People's Republic of Korea, Hong Kong, Japan, Kenya, and Mexico; 1 other country represented in student body. 70% of students are Mennonite, members of Mennonite Brethren Church.
Faculty School total: 12. In upper school: 7 men, 5 women; 2 have advanced degrees; 1 resides on campus.
Subjects Offered All academic.
Graduation Requirements Bible, English, mathematics, physical education (includes health), compulsory religion courses at each grade level, compulsory religious history courses at one level.
Special Academic Programs 2 Advanced Placement exams for which test preparation is offered; academic accommodation for the musically talented; remedial reading and/or remedial writing; remedial math; special instructional classes for blind students; ESL (4 students enrolled).
College Admission Counseling 42 students graduated in 2009; 25 went to college, including The University of Winnipeg; University of Manitoba. Other: 15 went to work, 2 had other specific plans.
Student Life Upper grades have uniform requirement, student council, honor system. Discipline rests primarily with faculty. Attendance at religious services is required.
Tuition and Aid Day student tuition: CAN$4300; 7-day tuition and room/board: CAN$8100. Tuition installment plan (monthly payment plans, individually arranged payment plans). Tuition reduction for siblings, bursaries, merit scholarship grants, need-based scholarship grants, need-based loans, middle-income loans available. In 2009–10, 30% of upper-school students received aid; total upper-school merit-scholarship money awarded: CAN$9000. Total amount of financial aid awarded in 2009–10: CAN$40,000.
Admissions Traditional secondary-level entrance grade is 9. For fall 2009, 157 students applied for upper-level admission, 157 were accepted, 153 enrolled. Deadline for receipt of application materials: none. Application fee required: CAN$200. Interview required.
Athletics Interscholastic: badminton (boys, girls), baseball (b,g), basketball (b,g), cross-country running (b,g), curling (b,g), golf (b,g), ice hockey (b,g), soccer (b,g), track and field (b,g), volleyball (b,g); intramural: floor hockey (b,g); coed interscholastic: badminton, cross-country running, curling, golf, track and field; coed intramural: floor hockey. 1 PE instructor, 2 athletic trainers.
Computers Computers are regularly used in all academic classes. Computer network features include on-campus library services, Internet access, Internet filtering or blocking technology. The school has a published electronic and media policy.
Contact Mr. Jeremy Siemens, Admissions Counselor. 204-327-5891. Fax: 204-327-5872. E-mail: admissions@mciblues.net. Web site: www.mciblues.net.

MENTOR COLLEGE

40 Forest Avenue
Mississauga, Ontario L5G 1L1, Canada
Head of School: Mr. Ken Philbrook
General Information Coeducational day college-preparatory school. Grades JK–12. Founded: 1981. Setting: suburban. 20-hectare campus. 1 building on campus. Approved or accredited by Ontario Department of Education. Language of instruction: English. Total enrollment: 1,497. Upper school average class size: 16. Upper school faculty-student ratio: 1:14.
Faculty School total: 59. In upper school: 26 men, 33 women.
Subjects Offered Accounting, advanced chemistry, algebra, biology, business, calculus, Canadian geography, Canadian history, careers, chemistry, civics, computer multimedia, computer programming, data analysis, discrete mathematics, earth and space science, economics, English/composition-AP, environmental science, ESL, European history, exercise science, fine arts, French as a second language, history, law, literature, marine biology, mathematics, music, philosophy, physical education, physical science, physics, science, Spanish, visual arts, world issues.

Special Academic Programs Advanced Placement exam preparation; ESL (50 students enrolled).
College Admission Counseling 142 students graduated in 2009; 137 went to college, including McGill University; McMaster University; Queen's University at Kingston; University of Toronto; University of Waterloo; Wilfrid Laurier University. Other: 4 went to work, 1 had other specific plans.
Student Life Upper grades have uniform requirement, student council. Discipline rests primarily with faculty.
Tuition and Aid Day student tuition: CAN$14,000. Merit scholarship grants available. Total upper-school merit-scholarship money awarded for 2009–10: CAN$3002. Total amount of financial aid awarded in 2009–10: CAN$3002.
Admissions Traditional secondary-level entrance grade is 9. School's own exam required. Deadline for receipt of application materials: none. Application fee required: CAN$100. Interview required.
Athletics Interscholastic: alpine skiing (boys, girls), aquatics (b,g), badminton (b,g), basketball (b,g), cheering (b,g), cricket (b), cross-country running (b,g), golf (b,g), hockey (b), indoor soccer (b,g), rowing (b,g), rugby (b,g), skiing (downhill) (b,g), soccer (b,g), swimming and diving (b,g), table tennis (b,g), tennis (b,g), track and field (b,g), volleyball (b,g), wrestling (b,g); intramural: badminton (b,g), basketball (b,g), floor hockey (b,g), indoor hockey (b,g), indoor soccer (b,g), lacrosse (b,g), soccer (b,g), volleyball (b,g); coed interscholastic: archery, mountain biking, softball, ultimate Frisbee; coed intramural: cricket, dance, outdoor education, physical fitness, physical training, scuba diving, table tennis. 4 PE instructors.
Computers Computers are regularly used in business, computer applications, French as a second language, geography, technology classes. Computer network features include online commercial services, Internet access, Internet filtering or blocking technology, Edline. The school has a published electronic and media policy.
Contact Anna Penney, Registrar. 905-271-3393. Fax: 905-271-8367. E-mail: admin@mentorcollege.edu. Web site: www.mentorcollege.edu.

MERCEDES COLLEGE

540 Fullarton Road
Springfield 5062, Australia
Head of School: Mr. Peter Howard Daw
General Information Coeducational day college-preparatory, general academic, arts, business, vocational, religious studies, and bilingual studies school, affiliated with Roman Catholic Church. Grades 1–12. Founded: 1954. Setting: suburban. Nearest major city is Adelaide, Australia. 7-hectare campus. 10 buildings on campus. Approved or accredited by International Baccalaureate Organization. Member of European Council of International Schools. Language of instruction: English. Total enrollment: 1,201. Upper school average class size: 16. Upper school faculty-student ratio: 1:12.
Upper School Student Profile Grade 10: 149 students (78 boys, 71 girls); Grade 11: 154 students (76 boys, 78 girls); Grade 12: 154 students (82 boys, 72 girls). 90% of students are Roman Catholic.
Faculty School total: 132. In upper school: 24 men, 38 women; 14 have advanced degrees.
Special Academic Programs International Baccalaureate program; academic accommodation for the gifted; remedial reading and/or remedial writing; programs in general development for dyslexic students; ESL.
College Admission Counseling 154 students graduated in 2009.
Student Life Upper grades have uniform requirement, student council, honor system. Discipline rests primarily with faculty. Attendance at religious services is required.
Admissions For fall 2009, 66 students applied for upper-level admission, 52 were accepted, 52 enrolled. Deadline for receipt of application materials: none. Application fee required. Interview required.
Athletics Interscholastic: cricket (boys), football (b), netball (g), water polo (b); coed interscholastic: alpine skiing, badminton, basketball, canoeing/kayaking, climbing, cross-country running, fitness, hiking/backpacking, hockey, outdoor education, physical fitness, physical training, rock climbing, running, soccer, swimming and diving, table tennis, tennis, track and field, triathlon, volleyball, winter soccer. 6 PE instructors.
Computers Computers are regularly used in all classes. Computer network features include on-campus library services, Internet access, wireless campus network, Internet filtering or blocking technology. Student e-mail accounts are available to students. The school has a published electronic and media policy.
Contact Mrs. Shirley Smith, Registrar. 618-83723200. Fax: 618-83799540 Ext. 252. E-mail: ssmith@mercedes.adl.catholic.edu.au. Web site: www.mercedes.adl.catholic.edu.au.

MERCERSBURG ACADEMY

300 East Seminary Street
Mercersburg, Pennsylvania 17236
Head of School: Mr. Doug Hale
General Information Coeducational boarding and day college-preparatory school. Boarding grades 9–PG, day grades 9–11. Founded: 1893. Setting: small town. Nearest major city is Washington, DC. Students are housed in single-sex dormitories. 300-acre campus. 30 buildings on campus. Approved or accredited by Association of

Independent Schools of Greater Washington, Middle States Association of Colleges and Schools, Pennsylvania Association of Independent Schools, The Association of Boarding Schools, and Pennsylvania Department of Education. Member of National Association of Independent Schools and Secondary School Admission Test Board. Endowment: $160 million. Total enrollment: 430. Upper school average class size: 12. Upper school faculty-student ratio: 1:5. Upper School students typically attend 5 days per week. The average school day consists of 7 hours and 30 minutes.

Upper School Student Profile Grade 9: 82 students (43 boys, 39 girls); Grade 10: 107 students (49 boys, 58 girls); Grade 11: 113 students (65 boys, 48 girls); Grade 12: 110 students (63 boys, 47 girls); Postgraduate: 18 students (14 boys, 4 girls). 85% of students are boarding students. 30% are state residents. 33 states are represented in upper school student body. 18% are international students. International students from China, Germany, Republic of Korea, Saudi Arabia, Spain, and Thailand; 28 other countries represented in student body.

Faculty School total: 97. In upper school: 64 men, 33 women; 63 have advanced degrees; 29 reside on campus.

Subjects Offered 20th century American writers, 20th century world history, 3-dimensional art, acting, advanced chemistry, advanced computer applications, Advanced Placement courses, African American history, African dance, African drumming, algebra, American Civil War, American history, American history-AP, American literature, American literature-AP, art, art history, art history-AP, Asian history, astronomy, ballet, band, biology, biology-AP, botany, British literature-AP, Buddhism, calculus, calculus-AP, ceramics, chemistry, chemistry-AP, Chinese, choral music, chorus, comparative government and politics-AP, computer graphics, computer math, computer programming-AP, computer science, computer science-AP, concert band, creative writing, dance, digital art, drama, drawing, economics-AP, English, English literature, English literature and composition-AP, environmental science-AP, ethics, European history, European history-AP, film studies, fine arts, French, French language-AP, French literature-AP, genetics, geometry, German, German-AP, government and politics-AP, health, history, history of music, honors algebra, honors English, honors geometry, honors U.S. history, honors world history, humanities, Islamic studies, jazz band, journalism, Latin, Latin-AP, mathematics, modern European history-AP, music, music composition, music history, musical theater dance, orchestra, painting, personal fitness, physical education, physical science, physics, physics-AP, poetry, public speaking, religion, robotics, SAT preparation, science, sculpture, social studies, Spanish, Spanish language-AP, speech, stagecraft, statistics-AP, strings, studio art, theater, theater design and production, trigonometry, U.S. government and politics-AP, U.S. history-AP, United States government-AP, world history, world history-AP, world literature, yoga.

Graduation Requirements Arts and fine arts (art, music, dance, drama), English, foreign language, history, mathematics, physical education (includes health), religion (includes Bible studies and theology), science, participation in sports, performing arts, or other activities.

Special Academic Programs Advanced Placement exam preparation; honors section; independent study; term-away projects; study abroad; academic accommodation for the gifted.

College Admission Counseling 125 students graduated in 2009; all went to college, including Bryn Mawr College; Bucknell University; Georgetown University; Sewanee: The University of the South; United States Naval Academy; University of Pennsylvania.

Student Life Upper grades have specified standards of dress, student council, honor system. Discipline rests primarily with faculty.

Tuition and Aid Day student tuition: $32,750; 7-day tuition and room/board: $42,900. Tuition installment plan (Insured Tuition Payment Plan, Key Tuition Payment Plan, monthly payment plans). Merit scholarship grants, need-based scholarship grants, need-based loans available. In 2009–10, 44% of upper-school students received aid; total upper-school merit-scholarship money awarded: $400,000. Total amount of financial aid awarded in 2009–10: $4,600,000.

Admissions Traditional secondary-level entrance grade is 9. For fall 2009, 605 students applied for upper-level admission, 314 were accepted, 166 enrolled. ACT, ISEE, PSAT and SAT for applicants to grade 11 and 12, SSAT or TOEFL required. Deadline for receipt of application materials: January 31. Application fee required: $50. Interview required.

Athletics Interscholastic: baseball (boys), basketball (b,g), cross-country running (b,g), diving (b,g), field hockey (g), football (b), lacrosse (b,g), soccer (b,g), softball (g), squash (b,g), swimming and diving (b,g), tennis (b,g), track and field (b,g), volleyball (g), winter (indoor) track (b,g), wrestling (b); coed interscholastic: alpine skiing, golf; coed intramural: aerobics/dance, alpine skiing, backpacking, ballet, bicycling, canoeing/kayaking, climbing, dance, equestrian sports, freestyle skiing, Frisbee, golf, hiking/backpacking, horseback riding, kayaking, martial arts, modern dance, mountain biking, outdoor education, physical fitness, physical training, rafting, rappelling, rock climbing, skiing (downhill), snowboarding, strength & conditioning, table tennis, ultimate Frisbee, wall climbing, weight lifting, weight training, wilderness survival, yoga. 4 PE instructors, 22 coaches, 2 athletic trainers.

Computers Computers are regularly used in art, English, foreign language, history, mathematics, music, science classes. Computer network features include on-campus library services, online commercial services, Internet access, wireless campus network. Student e-mail accounts and computer access in designated common areas are available to students. The school has a published electronic and media policy.

Contact Mr. Tommy W. Adams, Assistant Head of School for Enrollment. 717-328-6173. Fax: 717-328-6319. E-mail: admission@mercersburg.edu. Web site: www.mercersburg.edu.

MERCHISTON CASTLE SCHOOL

Colinton

Edinburgh EH13 0PU, United Kingdom

Head of School: Mr. A. R. Hunter

General Information Boys' boarding and day college-preparatory school, affiliated with Christian faith. Ungraded, ages 8–18. Founded: 1833. Setting: suburban. Students are housed in single-sex dormitories. 100-acre campus. 11 buildings on campus. Approved or accredited by Headmasters' Conference. Language of instruction: English. Upper school average class size: 9. Upper school faculty-student ratio: 1:9.

Upper School Student Profile 76% of students are boarding students. 20% are international students. International students from Belgium, Brazil, China, Germany, and United States; 10 other countries represented in student body. 50% of students are Christian faith.

Faculty School total: 61. In upper school: 38 men, 23 women; 37 have advanced degrees; 30 reside on campus.

Subjects Offered Algebra, art, biology, calculus, chemistry, Chinese, computer science, creative writing, design, drama, electronics, English, English literature, European history, French, geography, geometry, German, government/civics, grammar, history, Italian, Japanese, Latin, mathematics, music, physical education, physics, religion, Russian, science, social studies, Spanish, trigonometry, world history.

Graduation Requirements Any three A-level courses.

Special Academic Programs Study abroad; academic accommodation for the gifted, the musically talented, and the artistically talented; remedial reading and/or remedial writing; remedial math; special instructional classes for deaf students, blind students; ESL (10 students enrolled).

College Admission Counseling 65 students graduated in 2010; 62 went to college. Other: 3 had other specific plans.

Student Life Upper grades have specified standards of dress, student council, honor system. Discipline rests equally with students and faculty.

Tuition and Aid Day student tuition: £17,460; 5-day tuition and room/board: £24,120; 7-day tuition and room/board: £24,120. Tuition reduction for siblings, bursaries, merit scholarship grants available.

Admissions Achievement/Aptitude/Writing and school's own exam required. Deadline for receipt of application materials: none. Application fee required: £150. Interview recommended.

Athletics Interscholastic: basketball (boys), cricket (b), cross-country running (b), fencing (b), football (b), golf (b), riflery (b), rugby (b), sailing (b), scuba diving (b), skiing (downhill) (b), soccer (b), squash (b), swimming and diving (b), tennis (b), track and field (b); intramural: badminton (b), basketball (b), bicycling (b), cricket (b), cross-country running (b), diving (b), fencing (b), Fives (b), football (b), golf (b), gymnastics (b), martial arts (b), mountain biking (b), outdoor activities (b), riflery (b), rugby (b), sailing (b), scuba diving (b), skiing (downhill) (b), soccer (b), squash (b), swimming and diving (b), table tennis (b), tennis (b), track and field (b), volleyball (b). 2 PE instructors, 1 coach.

Computers Computer network features include Internet access. Campus intranet and student e-mail accounts are available to students. The school has a published electronic and media policy.

Contact Mrs. Anne Rickard, Director of Admissions. 44-131-312-2201. Fax: 44-131-441 Ext. 6060. E-mail: admissions@merchiston.co.uk. Web site: www.merchiston.co.uk.

MERCY HIGH SCHOOL

233 Riverside Way

Red Bluff, California 96080

Head of School: Mrs. Cheryl A. Ramirez

General Information Coeducational day college preparatory, arts, and religious studies school, affiliated with Roman Catholic Church. Grades 9–12. Founded: 1882. Setting: small town. Nearest major city is Chico. 1 building on campus. Approved or accredited by Western Association of Schools and Colleges and California Department of Education. Total enrollment: 91. Upper school average class size: 15. Upper school faculty-student ratio: 1:10. There are 180 required school days per year for Upper School students. Upper School students typically attend 5 days per week. The average school day consists of 6 hours and 58 minutes.

Upper School Student Profile Grade 9: 23 students (12 boys, 11 girls); Grade 10: 13 students (4 boys, 9 girls); Grade 11: 32 students (18 boys, 14 girls); Grade 12: 23 students (14 boys, 9 girls). 70% of students are Roman Catholic.

Faculty School total: 10. In upper school: 4 men, 6 women; 2 have advanced degrees.

Subjects Offered Advanced Placement courses, algebra, art, biology, biology-AP, calculus-AP, chemistry, choral music, computer science, economics, English, English language and composition-AP, English literature and composition-AP, geometry, honors English, language and composition, physical education, physics, pre-calculus, religious studies, social justice, Spanish, Spanish language-AP, theater arts, U.S.

Mercy High School

government and politics, U.S. government and politics-AP, U.S. history, U.S. history-AP, world geography, world history, world religions, yearbook.

Graduation Requirements 20 community service hours per year.

Special Academic Programs Advanced Placement exam preparation; honors section; study at local college for college credit.

College Admission Counseling 35 students graduated in 2009; 33 went to college, including California State University, Chico; University of California, Berkeley; University of California, San Diego; University of San Diego.

Student Life Upper school grades have specified standards of dress, student council. Discipline rests primarily with faculty. Attendance at religious services is required.

Tuition and Aid Tuition installment plan (FACTS Tuition Payment Plan, 2-payment plan, prepayment discount plan). Need-based scholarship grants available.

Admissions Traditional secondary-level entrance grade is 9. For fall 2009, 33 students applied for upper-level admission, 33 were accepted, 33 enrolled. Deadline for receipt of application materials: none. Application fee required: $50.

Athletics Interscholastic: baseball (boys), basketball (b,g), cheering (g), football (b), softball (g), tennis (b,g), volleyball (g); intramural: basketball (b,g), volleyball (b,g); coed interscholastic: cross-country running, golf, skiing (downhill), snowboarding, soccer, swimming and diving, track and field; coed intramural: badminton. 1 PE instructor, 2 coaches.

Computers Computer resources include Internet access. Students grades are available online.

Contact Mrs. Cheryl Ramirez, Principal/Counselor. 916-527-8313. Fax: 916-527-3058. E-mail: mercy@mercy-high.org. Web site: www.mercy-high.org.

MERCY HIGH SCHOOL
1740 Randolph Road
Middletown, Connecticut 06457-5155
Head of School: Sr. Mary McCarthy, RSM

General Information Girls' day college-preparatory, arts, and religious studies school, affiliated with Roman Catholic Church. Grades 9–12. Founded: 1963. Setting: rural. Nearest major city is Hartford. 26-acre campus. 1 building on campus. Approved or accredited by Mercy Secondary Education Association, National Catholic Education Association, New England Association of Schools and Colleges, and Connecticut Department of Education. Total enrollment: 683. Upper school average class size: 21. Upper school faculty-student ratio: 1:13. There are 172 required school days per year for Upper School students. Upper School students typically attend 5 days per week. The average school day consists of 6 hours and 30 minutes.

Upper School Student Profile Grade 9: 176 students (176 girls); Grade 10: 162 students (162 girls); Grade 11: 173 students (173 girls); Grade 12: 172 students (172 girls). 85% of students are Roman Catholic.

Faculty School total: 53. In upper school: 9 men, 44 women; 39 have advanced degrees.

Subjects Offered Accounting, advanced math, algebra, American government, American literature, American literature-AP, art, art history, arts and crafts, biology, biology-AP, business, calculus, calculus-AP, Catholic belief and practice, ceramics, chamber groups, chemistry, chemistry-AP, choir, chorus, civics, comparative government and politics, computer applications, concert band, concert choir, creative writing, drama workshop, drawing and design, English, English literature, English-AP, European history, expository writing, French, French language-AP, French literature-AP, French-AP, geometry, government/civics, grammar, health, history, honors algebra, honors English, honors geometry, honors U.S. history, honors world history, humanities, independent study, Italian, journalism, keyboarding, Latin, law, literature-AP, mathematics, modern history, music, musical theater, neuroscience, photography, physical education, physics, physics-AP, physiology, pottery, pre-algebra, pre-calculus, psychology, public speaking, religious studies, science, social studies, Spanish, Spanish language-AP, Spanish-AP, statistics, statistics-AP, theater arts, trigonometry, U.S. history, U.S. history-AP, wind ensemble, word processing, world history, world literature, writing.

Graduation Requirements Civics, computer applications, English, foreign language, mathematics, physical education (includes health), religion (includes Bible studies and theology), science, social studies (includes history), 70 hours of community service.

Special Academic Programs 10 Advanced Placement exams for which test preparation is offered; honors section; independent study; study at local college for college credit.

College Admission Counseling 169 students graduated in 2010; 168 went to college, including Central Connecticut State University; Curry College; Salve Regina University; Southern Connecticut State University; University of Connecticut; Western New England College. Other: 1 had other specific plans. Median SAT critical reading: 530, median SAT math: 510, median SAT writing: 540, median combined SAT: 1580, median composite ACT: 23. 26% scored over 600 on SAT critical reading, 22% scored over 600 on SAT math, 25% scored over 600 on SAT writing, 21% scored over 1800 on combined SAT, 24% scored over 26 on composite ACT.

Student Life Upper grades have uniform requirement, student council. Discipline rests primarily with faculty. Attendance at religious services is required.

Tuition and Aid Day student tuition: $9850–$10,350. Tuition installment plan (FACTS Tuition Payment Plan, individually arranged payment plans). Tuition reduction for siblings, merit scholarship grants, need-based scholarship grants available.

Admissions Traditional secondary-level entrance grade is 9. For fall 2010, 338 students applied for upper-level admission, 304 were accepted, 190 enrolled. High School Placement Test (closed version) from Scholastic Testing Service required. Deadline for receipt of application materials: none. Application fee required: $50.

Athletics Interscholastic: basketball, cheering, cross-country running, diving, field hockey, golf, gymnastics, indoor track, lacrosse, soccer, softball, swimming and diving, tennis, track and field, volleyball; intramural: basketball, floor hockey, golf, soccer, tennis, volleyball. 1 PE instructor, 24 coaches, 1 athletic trainer.

Computers Computers are regularly used in accounting, all academic, computer applications, desktop publishing, journalism, word processing classes. Computer network features include on-campus library services, Internet access, Internet filtering or blocking technology. Campus intranct, student e-mail accounts, and computer access in designated common areas are available to students.

Contact Mrs. Diane Santostefano, Director of Admissions. 860-346-6659. Fax: 860-344-9887. E-mail: dsantostefano@mercyhigh.com. Web site: www.mercyhigh.com.

MERCY HIGH SCHOOL
1501 South 48th Street
Omaha, Nebraska 68106-2598
Head of School: Ms. Carolyn Jaworski

General Information Girls' day college-preparatory, general academic, arts, business, religious studies, and technology school, affiliated with Roman Catholic Church. Grades 9–12. Founded: 1955. Setting: urban. 2-acre campus. 1 building on campus. Approved or accredited by Mercy Secondary Education Association, National Catholic Education Association, North Central Association of Colleges and Schools, and Nebraska Department of Education. Total enrollment: 360. Upper school average class size: 20. Upper school faculty-student ratio: 1:12. There are 180 required school days per year for Upper School students. Upper School students typically attend 5 days per week. The average school day consists of 7 hours and 15 minutes.

Upper School Student Profile Grade 9: 100 students (100 girls); Grade 10: 106 students (106 girls); Grade 11: 82 students (82 girls); Grade 12: 72 students (72 girls). 90% of students are Roman Catholic.

Faculty School total: 33. In upper school: 6 men, 27 women; 20 have advanced degrees.

Subjects Offered Accounting, algebra, American government, American history, American history-AP, American literature, anatomy and physiology, art, ballet, biology, British literature, British literature-AP, business applications, calculus, calculus-AP, chemistry, chemistry-AP, child development, choir, computer education, consumer mathematics, culinary arts, debate, drama, drawing, ecology, English, French, general math, geometry, health, honors English, honors geometry, journalism, keyboarding, math review, moral theology, painting, participation in sports, peace and justice, physics, physics-AP, play production, pottery, pre-algebra, pre-calculus, psychology, social justice, Spanish, Spanish-AP, speech, speech and debate, sports medicine, stagecraft, statistics, theology, theology and the arts, trigonometry, U.S. government, U.S. history, U.S. history-AP, vocal music, world history, yearbook.

Graduation Requirements Advanced math, algebra, American government, anatomy and physiology, arts and fine arts (art, music, dance, drama), biology, chemistry, computer applications, debate, English, foreign language, geometry, mathematics, physical education (includes health), physics, social studies (includes history), speech, theology, U.S. history, world history, service hours.

Special Academic Programs Advanced Placement exam preparation; honors section; study at local college for college credit; remedial reading and/or remedial writing; remedial math; programs in general development for dyslexic students; special instructional classes for deaf students, blind students, students with LD, ADD, emotional and behavioral problems.

College Admission Counseling 99 students graduated in 2010; 96 went to college, including Creighton University; University of Nebraska–Lincoln; University of Nebraska at Omaha. Other: 3 went to work.

Student Life Upper grades have uniform requirement, student council, honor system. Discipline rests primarily with faculty. Attendance at religious services is required.

Tuition and Aid Day student tuition: $7300. Tuition installment plan (individually arranged payment plans, each family has an individualized tuition based upon their income). Tuition reduction for siblings, merit scholarship grants, need-based scholarship grants, paying campus jobs available. In 2010–11, 85% of upper-school students received aid; total upper-school merit-scholarship money awarded: $100,000. Total amount of financial aid awarded in 2010–11: $1,000,000.

Admissions Traditional secondary-level entrance grade is 9. For fall 2010, 115 students applied for upper-level admission, 102 were accepted, 100 enrolled. STS Examination required. Deadline for receipt of application materials: March 31. Application fee required: $100. Interview required.

Athletics Interscholastic: aerobics, archery, badminton, ballet, basketball, bowling, cheering, cross-country running, dance squad, dance team, diving, fitness walking, golf, independent competitive sports, physical fitness, self defense, soccer, softball, strength & conditioning, swimming and diving, tennis, track and field, volleyball, weight training; intramural: indoor soccer. 2 PE instructors, 15 coaches, 1 athletic trainer.

Computers Computers are regularly used in accounting, business, business applications, business education, business studies, history, journalism, keyboarding, lab/keyboard, library, library skills, mathematics, music, photojournalism, publica-

tions, religion, science, yearbook classes. Computer network features include on-campus library services, online commercial services, Internet access, wireless campus network, Internet filtering or blocking technology. Student e-mail accounts and computer access in designated common areas are available to students. Students grades are available online. The school has a published electronic and media policy.
Contact Ms. Anne Zadina, Recruitment Director. 402-553-9424. Fax: 402-553-0394. E-mail: zadinaa@mercyhigh.org. Web site: www.mercyhigh.org.

MERCY HIGH SCHOOL COLLEGE PREPARATORY
3250 19th Avenue
San Francisco, California 94132-2000
Head of School: Dr. Dorothy McCrea
General Information Girls' day college-preparatory, arts, business, religious studies, and technology school, affiliated with Roman Catholic Church. Grades 9–12. Founded: 1952. Setting: urban. Nearest major city is Daly City. 6-acre campus. 2 buildings on campus. Approved or accredited by European Council of International Schools, Western Association of Schools and Colleges, Western Catholic Education Association, and California Department of Education. Endowment: $2 million. Total enrollment: 486. Upper school average class size: 26. Upper school faculty-student ratio: 1:15. There are 181 required school days per year for Upper School students. Upper School students typically attend 5 days per week. The average school day consists of 7 hours and 5 minutes.
Upper School Student Profile Grade 9: 116 students (116 girls); Grade 10: 114 students (114 girls); Grade 11: 128 students (128 girls); Grade 12: 128 students (128 girls). 64.6% of students are Roman Catholic.
Faculty School total: 33. In upper school: 6 men, 27 women; 21 have advanced degrees.
Subjects Offered Algebra, American history, American literature, art, biology, business, calculus, ceramics, chemistry, chorus, computer applications, computer programming, creative writing, dance, drama, English, English literature, environmental science, ethnic studies, expository writing, French, geometry, government/ civics, keyboarding, mathematics, physical education, physics, physics-AP, religious studies, social justice, social studies, Spanish, speech, statistics, theater, trigonometry, visual and performing arts, world history, world literature.
Graduation Requirements 50 volunteer hours and a senior culminating project or 100 hours of volunteer service, Intersession.
Special Academic Programs Advanced Placement exam preparation; honors section.
College Admission Counseling 112 students graduated in 2010; 107 went to college, including College of San Mateo; Notre Dame de Namur University; San Francisco State University; Skyline College; University of San Francisco. Other: 1 entered military service, 1 had other specific plans. Mean SAT critical reading: 488, mean SAT math: 482, mean SAT writing: 508, mean combined SAT: 1478, mean composite ACT: 22. 9% scored over 600 on SAT critical reading, 11.5% scored over 600 on SAT math, 15% scored over 600 on SAT writing, 11.5% scored over 1800 on combined SAT, 27% scored over 26 on composite ACT.
Student Life Upper grades have uniform requirement, student council, honor system. Discipline rests primarily with faculty. Attendance at religious services is required.
Summer Programs Enrichment programs offered; session focuses on pre-high program—enrichment only, secondary program—enrichment and remediation; held on campus; accepts boys and girls; open to students from other schools. 400 students usually enrolled. 2011 schedule: June 20 to July 15. Application deadline: June 16.
Tuition and Aid Day student tuition: $14,045. Tuition installment plan (FACTS Tuition Payment Plan, full payment, 10 months payment (July-April), semiannual payment (July & December)). Need-based scholarship grants available. In 2010–11, 48% of upper-school students received aid. Total amount of financial aid awarded in 2010–11: $1,600,000.
Admissions Traditional secondary-level entrance grade is 9. For fall 2010, 298 students applied for upper-level admission, 249 were accepted, 116 enrolled. Comprehensive Test of Basic Skills required. Deadline for receipt of application materials: December 7. Application fee required: $80. On-campus interview required.
Athletics Interscholastic: basketball, cross-country running, dance, dance squad, self defense, soccer, softball, swimming and diving, tennis, track and field, volleyball. 2 PE instructors, 10 coaches.
Computers Computers are regularly used in all academic classes. Computer network features include on-campus library services, Internet access, wireless campus network, Internet filtering or blocking technology, Hunter Systems. Campus intranet and computer access in designated common areas are available to students. Students grades are available online. The school has a published electronic and media policy.
Contact Liz Belonogoff, Admissions Director. 415-584-5929. Fax: 415-334-9726. E-mail: lbelonogoff@mercyhs.org. Web site: www.mercyhs.org.

MERCYHURST PREPARATORY SCHOOL
538 East Grandview Boulevard
Erie, Pennsylvania 16504-2697
Head of School: Ms. Margaret M. Aste
General Information Coeducational day college-preparatory, arts, religious studies, and technology school, affiliated with Roman Catholic Church. Grades 9–12.

Founded: 1926. Setting: urban. 5-acre campus. 1 building on campus. Approved or accredited by International Baccalaureate Organization, Middle States Association of Colleges and Schools, and Pennsylvania Department of Education. Total enrollment: 595. Upper school average class size: 25. Upper school faculty-student ratio: 1:13. There are 180 required school days per year for Upper School students. Upper School students typically attend 5 days per week. The average school day consists of 6 hours and 45 minutes.
Upper School Student Profile Grade 9: 145 students (54 boys, 91 girls); Grade 10: 149 students (49 boys, 100 girls); Grade 11: 145 students (50 boys, 95 girls); Grade 12: 156 students (61 boys, 95 girls). 81% of students are Roman Catholic.
Faculty School total: 45. In upper school: 17 men, 28 women; 19 have advanced degrees.
Subjects Offered Accounting, algebra, American Civil War, American government, American history, American literature, anatomy, art, art appreciation, art education, art history, astronomy, athletic training, ballet, biology, business skills, calculus, campus ministry, career exploration, ceramics, chemistry, chorus, Christian ethics, civil war history, communications, community service, computer applications, computer programming, computer science, creative arts, dance, digital photography, drama, drama performance, drawing, drawing and design, earth science, English, English literature, environmental science, ethics, European history, expository writing, fine arts, first aid, French, geology, geometry, government/civics, guitar, health, Hebrew scripture, history, Holocaust, humanities, Internet, journalism, keyboarding, leadership, mathematics, multimedia, music, music appreciation, music theory-AP, musical productions, orchestra, painting, photography, physical education, physics, physiology, piano, psychology, public speaking, publications, reading/study skills, religion, SAT preparation, SAT/ACT preparation, science, senior internship, set design, social studies, Spanish, speech, speech and debate, study skills, tap dance, technical theater, technology/design, theater, theater arts, theology, theory of knowledge, trigonometry, typing, U.S. government, U.S. history, visual and performing arts, weight fitness, weightlifting, word processing, world cultures, world history, writing, yearbook.
Graduation Requirements Arts and fine arts (art, music, dance, drama), arts appreciation, business skills (includes word processing), computer science, creative arts, English, foreign language, mathematics, physical education (includes health), public speaking, religion (includes Bible studies and theology), science, social studies (includes history), technological applications, 25 service hours per year.
Special Academic Programs International Baccalaureate program; honors section; independent study; study at local college for college credit; academic accommodation for the gifted, the musically talented, and the artistically talented; remedial reading and/or remedial writing; remedial math; special instructional classes for deaf students.
College Admission Counseling 136 students graduated in 2009; 135 went to college, including Edinboro University of Pennsylvania; Gannon University; John Carroll University; Mercyhurst College; Penn State University Park. Other: 1 went to work. Mean SAT critical reading: 512, mean SAT math: 491, mean SAT writing: 505, mean composite ACT: 22.
Student Life Upper grades have uniform requirement, student council, honor system. Discipline rests primarily with faculty. Attendance at religious services is required.
Tuition and Aid Day student tuition: $6600. Tuition installment plan (FACTS Tuition Payment Plan). Merit scholarship grants, need-based scholarship grants, creative arts scholarships, alumni scholarships, endowment scholarships available. In 2009–10, 52% of upper-school students received aid; total upper-school merit-scholarship money awarded: $188,175. Total amount of financial aid awarded in 2009–10: $678,510.
Admissions For fall 2009, 235 students applied for upper-level admission, 210 were accepted, 145 enrolled. Achievement tests, High School Placement Test or Iowa Tests of Basic Skills required. Deadline for receipt of application materials: none. Application fee required: $10.
Athletics Interscholastic: baseball (boys), basketball (b,g), bowling (g), cheering (g), crew (b,g), cross-country running (b,g), dance team (g), football (b), golf (b,g), modern dance (g), rowing (b,g), skiing (downhill) (g), soccer (b,g), softball (g), swimming and diving (b,g), tennis (b,g), track and field (b,g), volleyball (g); coed interscholastic: tennis, weight training; coed intramural: weight lifting, weight training. 2 PE instructors, 40 coaches, 1 athletic trainer.
Computers Computers are regularly used in college planning, English, foreign language, history, journalism, mathematics, media, newspaper, photography, photo journalism, publications, publishing, SAT preparation, science, typing, word processing, writing, yearbook classes. Computer network features include on-campus library services, online commercial services, Internet access, wireless campus network, Internet filtering or blocking technology. Campus intranet is available to students. Students grades are available online. The school has a published electronic and media policy.
Contact Mrs. Marcia E. DiTullio, Administrative Assistant. 814-824-2323. Fax: 814-824-2116. E-mail: mditullio@mpslakers.com. Web site: www.mpslakers.com.

MERCY VOCATIONAL HIGH SCHOOL
2900 West Hunting Park Avenue
Philadelphia, Pennsylvania 19129
Head of School: Sr. Rosemary Herron, RSM
General Information Coeducational day college-preparatory and vocational school, affiliated with Roman Catholic Church. Grades 9–12. Founded: 1950. Setting: urban.

Mercy Vocational High School

2 buildings on campus. Approved or accredited by Middle States Association of Colleges and Schools and Pennsylvania Department of Education. Upper school average class size: 26. Upper school faculty-student ratio: 1:16. There are 180 required school days per year for Upper School students. Upper School students typically attend 5 days per week. The average school day consists of 7 hours and 5 minutes.

Upper School Student Profile Grade 9: 125 students (71 boys, 54 girls); Grade 10: 89 students (50 boys, 39 girls); Grade 11: 90 students (50 boys, 40 girls); Grade 12: 78 students (37 boys, 41 girls).

Faculty School total: 38. In upper school: 14 men, 24 women.

Graduation Requirements ACT preparation, Community Service.

Special Academic Programs Remedial reading and/or remedial writing.

College Admission Counseling 75 students graduated in 2010.

Student Life Upper grades have uniform requirement, student council, honor system. Discipline rests primarily with faculty. Attendance at religious services is required.

Summer Programs Advancement programs offered; session focuses on incoming freshmen; held on campus; accepts boys and girls; not open to students from other schools. 40 students usually enrolled. 2011 schedule: June 27 to July 15.

Tuition and Aid Tuition installment plan (SMART Tuition Payment Plan). Need-based scholarship grants available. In 2010–11, 74% of upper-school students received aid.

Admissions Traditional secondary-level entrance grade is 9. For fall 2010, 179 students applied for upper-level admission, 125 were accepted, 125 enrolled. School's own test required. Deadline for receipt of application materials: none. No application fee required.

Athletics Interscholastic: baseball (boys), basketball (b,g), biathlon (g), cheering (g), cross-country running (b,g), soccer (b,g), softball (g), track and field (b,g); intramural: weight lifting (b), weight training (b). 1 PE instructor, 6 coaches.

Computers Computers are regularly used in aerospace science, animation, architecture, art, aviation, classics, commercial art, dance, design, desktop publishing, desktop publishing, ESL, digital applications, drafting, drawing and design, economics, engineering, ESL, ethics, foreign language, French, French as a second language, freshman foundations, geography, graphic arts, graphic design, graphics, historical foundations for arts, human geography—AP, humanities, independent study, journalism, JROTC, language development, Latin, learning cognition, library, library science, literacy, literary magazine, media, media arts, media production, media services, mentorship program, multimedia, music, music technology, news writing, newspaper, NJROTC, occupational education, philosophy, photography, photojournalism, programming, psychology, publications, publishing, SAT preparation, senior seminar, Spanish, speech, stock market, technical drawing, theater, theater arts, typing, video film production, Web site design, wilderness education classes. Computer network features include wireless campus network, Internet filtering or blocking technology. Campus intranet and student e-mail accounts are available to students. Students grades are available online.

Contact Director of Admissions. 215-226-1225 Ext. 115. Fax: 215-228-6337. E-mail: wdonahue@mercyvhs.org. Web site: www.mercyvocational.org.

MERION MERCY ACADEMY

511 Montgomery Avenue
Merion Station, Pennsylvania 19066
Head of School: Sr. Barbara Buckley

General Information Girls' day college-preparatory, arts, and religious studies school, affiliated with Roman Catholic Church. Grades 9–12. Founded: 1884. Setting: suburban. Nearest major city is Philadelphia. 35-acre campus. 7 buildings on campus. Approved or accredited by Middle States Association of Colleges and Schools. Endowment: $350,000. Total enrollment: 484. Upper school average class size: 17. Upper school faculty-student ratio: 1:9.

Upper School Student Profile Grade 9: 118 students (118 girls); Grade 10: 131 students (131 girls); Grade 11: 118 students (118 girls); Grade 12: 117 students (117 girls). 90% of students are Roman Catholic.

Faculty School total: 53. In upper school: 6 men, 47 women; 41 have advanced degrees.

Subjects Offered Algebra, American history, American literature, art, art history, biology, business, calculus, chemistry, computer programming, creative writing, drama, economics, English, English literature, environmental science, European history, fine arts, French, geometry, government/civics, grammar, health, history, journalism, Latin, mathematics, music, music history, physical education, physics, physiology, psychology, religion, science, social studies, Spanish, speech, theater, theology, trigonometry, women's studies, world history, world literature, writing.

Graduation Requirements Arts and fine arts (art, music, dance, drama), English, foreign language, mathematics, physical education (includes health), religion (includes Bible studies and theology), science, social studies (includes history).

Special Academic Programs Advanced Placement exam preparation; honors section; study at local college for college credit; academic accommodation for the gifted, the musically talented, and the artistically talented; remedial reading and/or remedial writing; remedial math.

College Admission Counseling 119 students graduated in 2010; all went to college, including Boston College; Georgetown University; Penn State University Park; Saint Joseph's University; The University of Scranton; Villanova University. Mean SAT critical reading: 601, mean SAT math: 573, mean SAT writing: 620.

Student Life Upper grades have uniform requirement, student council, honor system. Discipline rests primarily with faculty. Attendance at religious services is required.

Summer Programs Enrichment, advancement, sports, art/fine arts programs offered; session focuses on enrichment; held on campus; accepts boys and girls; open to students from other schools. 150 students usually enrolled. 2011 schedule: June 21 to July 23. Application deadline: May 1.

Tuition and Aid Day student tuition: $14,150. Tuition installment plan (The Tuition Plan, monthly payment plans, 2 equal payments plan). Tuition reduction for siblings, merit scholarship grants, need-based scholarship grants, middle-income loans, alumnae, Mercy, and music scholarships available. In 2010–11, 36% of upper-school students received aid; total upper-school merit-scholarship money awarded: $452,150. Total amount of financial aid awarded in 2010–11: $857,600.

Admissions Traditional secondary-level entrance grade is 9. For fall 2010, 300 students applied for upper-level admission, 180 were accepted, 118 enrolled. High School Placement Test required. Deadline for receipt of application materials: November 15. Application fee required: $30. On-campus interview required.

Athletics Interscholastic: basketball, cheering, crew, cross-country running, field hockey, golf, lacrosse, soccer, softball, swimming and diving, tennis, track and field, volleyball, winter (indoor) track; intramural: basketball, dance, tennis. 2 PE instructors, 19 coaches, 1 athletic trainer.

Computers Computers are regularly used in all academic classes. Computer network features include on-campus library services, online commercial services, Internet access, Internet filtering or blocking technology.

Contact Eileen Killeen, Director of Admissions. 610-664-6655 Ext. 116. Fax: 610-664-6322. E-mail: ekilleen@merion-mercy.com. Web site: www.merion-mercy.com.

MESA GRANDE SEVENTH-DAY ACADEMY

975 South Fremont Street
Calimesa, California 92320
Head of School: Alfred J. Riddle

General Information Coeducational day college-preparatory, arts, religious studies, and technology school, affiliated with Seventh-day Adventists, Christian faith. Grades K–12. Founded: 1928. Setting: rural. Nearest major city is San Bernardino. 14-acre campus. 3 buildings on campus. Approved or accredited by Western Association of Schools and Colleges and California Department of Education. Endowment: $650,000. Total enrollment: 288. Upper school average class size: 30. Upper school faculty-student ratio: 1:10. There are 180 required school days per year for Upper School students. Upper School students typically attend 5 days per week. The average school day consists of 8 hours.

Upper School Student Profile Grade 9: 131 students (75 boys, 56 girls); Grade 10: 48 students (20 boys, 28 girls); Grade 11: 28 students (16 boys, 12 girls); Grade 12: 29 students (17 boys, 12 girls). 90% of students are Seventh-day Adventists, Christian.

Faculty School total: 25. In upper school: 9 men, 7 women; 9 have advanced degrees.

Subjects Offered Algebra, American literature, animal behavior, arts, ASB Leadership, auto mechanics, bell choir, biology, British literature, career education, chemistry, choral music, community service, composition, computer applications, computer-aided design, computers, concert choir, desktop publishing, drama, economics, economics and history, English, English composition, family living, fine arts, geometry, government/civics, graphic arts, handbells, health, instrumental music, keyboarding, lab science, marine biology, mathematics, music composition, music theory, physical education, physical science, physics, pre-calculus, religion, religious education, science, social sciences, social studies, Spanish, U.S. government, U.S. history, video film production, world history, world literature, yearbook.

Graduation Requirements Algebra, American government, applied skills, arts and fine arts (art, music, dance, drama), biology, British literature, career education, chemistry, computer education, computer technologies, economics, English, English composition, family living, industrial technology, keyboarding, mathematics, modern languages, physical education (includes health), physical fitness, physical science, physics, religious studies, science, social studies (includes history), Spanish, technical skills, work experience, community service.

College Admission Counseling 38 students graduated in 2009; 37 went to college, including Andrews University; California State University, San Bernardino; La Sierra University; Pacific Union College; University of California, Riverside; Walla Walla University. Other: 1 went to work. Median SAT critical reading: 540, median SAT math: 567, median composite ACT: 24. 10% scored over 600 on SAT critical reading, 10% scored over 600 on SAT math, 5% scored over 26 on composite ACT.

Student Life Upper grades have uniform requirement, student council, honor system. Discipline rests primarily with faculty. Attendance at religious services is required.

Tuition and Aid Day student tuition: $7980. Tuition installment plan (monthly payment plans, individually arranged payment plans). Need-based loans, middle-income loans available. In 2009–10, 25% of upper-school students received aid. Total amount of financial aid awarded in 2009–10: $35,000.

Admissions Traditional secondary-level entrance grade is 9. For fall 2009, 55 students applied for upper-level admission, 45 were accepted, 45 enrolled. Any standardized test, ITBS-TAP or Math Placement Exam required. Deadline for receipt of application materials: none. Application fee required: $50. On-campus interview required.

Athletics Interscholastic: baseball (boys), basketball (b,g), flag football (b,g), softball (g), volleyball (b,g); coed interscholastic: cross-country running, golf, physical fitness, weight lifting. 3 PE instructors, 12 coaches, 2 athletic trainers.

Computers Computers are regularly used in design, graphic design, library skills, science, technical drawing, technology, typing, video film production, writing, yearbook classes. Computer network features include on-campus library services, online commercial services, Internet access, Internet filtering or blocking technology. Student e-mail accounts and computer access in designated common areas are available to students. Students grades are available online. The school has a published electronic and media policy.

Contact Lois M. Myhre, Admissions Office. 909-795-1112 Ext. 257. Fax: 909-795-1653. E-mail: lois.myhre@mgak-12.org. Web site: www.mesagrandeacademy.org.

METRO-EAST LUTHERAN HIGH SCHOOL

6305 Center Grove Road
Edwardsville, Illinois 62025
Head of School: Daniel S. Kostencki

General Information Coeducational day college-preparatory and general academic school, affiliated with Lutheran Church–Missouri Synod. Grades 9–12. Founded: 1977. Setting: urban. Nearest major city is St. Louis. 15-acre campus. 1 building on campus. Approved or accredited by National Lutheran School Accreditation, North Central Association of Colleges and Schools, and Illinois Department of Education. Total enrollment: 232. Upper school average class size: 15. Upper school faculty-student ratio: 1:15. There are 176 required school days per year for Upper School students. Upper School students typically attend 5 days per week. The average school day consists of 6 hours and 30 minutes.

Upper School Student Profile Grade 9: 43 students (28 boys, 15 girls); Grade 10: 51 students (30 boys, 21 girls); Grade 11: 68 students (30 boys, 38 girls); Grade 12: 70 students (37 boys, 33 girls). 70% of students are Lutheran Church–Missouri Synod.

Faculty School total: 20. In upper school: 13 men, 7 women; 10 have advanced degrees.

Subjects Offered Accounting, advanced biology, advanced chemistry, advanced math, algebra, American history, analytic geometry, anatomy and physiology, art, arts and crafts, band, bioethics, DNA and culture, biology, calculus, chemistry, choir, Christian doctrine, Christian ethics, Christian studies, civics, communications, computer applications, concert band, drawing, earth and space science, economics, English, English literature, fine arts, general science, geography, geometry, health, honors English, honors geometry, honors U.S. history, independent study, journalism, mathematics, microbiology, modern history, New Testament, newspaper, oral communications, organic chemistry, physical education, physics, pottery, pre-calculus, psychology, religion, social studies, Spanish, Spanish language-AP, studio art, theology, world history.

Graduation Requirements Algebra, biology, civics, economics, foreign language, geography, geometry, health, religion (includes Bible studies and theology).

Special Academic Programs Honors section.

College Admission Counseling 62 students graduated in 2009.

Student Life Upper grades have specified standards of dress, student council, honor system. Discipline rests primarily with faculty. Attendance at religious services is required.

Tuition and Aid Day student tuition: $6700. Tuition installment plan (monthly payment plans). Tuition reduction for siblings, need-based scholarship grants available. Total amount of financial aid awarded in 2009–10: $30,000.

Admissions School's own exam required. Deadline for receipt of application materials: none. Application fee required: $250. On-campus interview recommended.

Athletics Interscholastic: baseball (boys), basketball (b,g), bowling (b,g), cheering (g), cross-country running (b,g), dance team (g), fishing (b), football (b), golf (b,g), indoor track & field (b,g), soccer (b,g), softball (g), tennis (b,g), track and field (b,g), volleyball (g). 2 PE instructors.

Computers Computers are regularly used in accounting, business, computer applications, journalism, science classes. Computer network features include on-campus library services, Internet access, Internet filtering or blocking technology. Student e-mail accounts and computer access in designated common areas are available to students. Students grades are available online. The school has a published electronic and media policy.

Contact Mrs. Deborah Wudtke, Office Manager. 618-656-0043 Ext. 132. Fax: 618-656-3315. E-mail: deb.wudtke@melhs.org. Web site: www.melhs.org.

MIAMI COUNTRY DAY SCHOOL

601 Northeast 107th Street
Miami, Florida 33161
Head of School: Dr. John P. Davies

General Information Coeducational day college-preparatory school. Grades PK–12. Founded: 1938. Setting: suburban. 16-acre campus. 6 buildings on campus. Approved or accredited by Florida Council of Independent Schools, Southern Association of Colleges and Schools, Southern Association of Independent Schools, The College Board, and Florida Department of Education. Member of National Association of Independent Schools and Secondary School Admission Test Board.

Endowment: $4.5 million. Total enrollment: 900. Upper school average class size: 18. Upper school faculty-student ratio: 1:8. There are 179 required school days per year for Upper School students. Upper School students typically attend 5 days per week. The average school day consists of 6 hours and 15 minutes.

Upper School Student Profile Grade 9: 88 students (63 boys, 25 girls); Grade 10: 79 students (40 boys, 39 girls); Grade 11: 90 students (48 boys, 42 girls); Grade 12: 80 students (45 boys, 35 girls).

Faculty School total: 90. In upper school: 23 men, 26 women; 33 have advanced degrees.

Subjects Offered Advanced Placement courses, African-American studies, algebra, American history, American history-AP, American literature, ancient history, art, art history, backpacking, band, biology, calculus, calculus-AP, ceramics, chemistry, community service, composition, computer programming, computer science, conflict resolution, creative writing, design, desktop publishing, DNA science lab, drama, drawing, economics, English, English language and composition-AP, English literature, English literature-AP, environmental science-AP, ESL, European history, film, film and literature, fine arts, French, geography, geometry, government/civics, health, instrumental music, jewelry making, journalism, law, life management skills, literature, marine biology, mathematics, music theory, orchestra, painting, philosophy, photography, physical education, physical science, physics, physics-AP, post-calculus, psychology, public speaking, religion, science, sculpture, social sciences, social studies, Spanish, Spanish language-AP, Spanish literature-AP, theater, trigonometry, U.S. government and politics-AP, video film production, world history, world literature, writing, yearbook.

Graduation Requirements Arts and fine arts (art, music, dance, drama), computer science, electives, English, foreign language, mathematics, philosophy, physical education (includes health), religion (includes Bible studies and theology), science, social studies (includes history), speech and debate, 80 hours of community service.

Special Academic Programs Advanced Placement exam preparation; honors section; independent study; study at local college for college credit; ESL (9 students enrolled).

College Admission Counseling 97 students graduated in 2009; all went to college, including Florida International University; Florida State University; Harvard University; University of Florida; University of Miami; University of Pennsylvania. Median SAT critical reading: 630, median SAT math: 660, median SAT writing: 630.

Student Life Upper grades have uniform requirement, student council, honor system. Discipline rests equally with students and faculty.

Tuition and Aid Day student tuition: $21,661–$22,169. Tuition installment plan (Academic Management Services Plan). Need-based scholarship grants available. In 2009–10, 18% of upper-school students received aid. Total amount of financial aid awarded in 2009–10: $816,000.

Admissions Traditional secondary-level entrance grade is 9. For fall 2009, 91 students applied for upper-level admission, 51 were accepted, 42 enrolled. ISEE, OLSAT, ERB, PSAT and SAT for applicants to grade 11 and 12 or writing sample required. Deadline for receipt of application materials: February 2. Application fee required: $85. On-campus interview required.

Athletics Interscholastic: baseball (boys), basketball (b,g), cheering (g), cross-country running (b,g), football (b), golf (b,g), lacrosse (b), soccer (b,g), softball (g), swimming and diving (b,g), tennis (b,g), track and field (b,g), volleyball (g), water polo (b,g), yoga (b,g); intramural: baseball (b), basketball (b,g), cheering (g), cross-country running (b,g), dance (g), lacrosse (b), volleyball (b), yoga (g); coed intramural: crew, flag football, outdoor education, outdoor skills, physical fitness, physical training, soccer, strength & conditioning, weight training. 3 PE instructors, 24 coaches, 1 athletic trainer.

Computers Computers are regularly used in all academic, graphic design, journalism, media, research skills, Web site design, yearbook classes. Computer network features include on-campus library services, online commercial services, Internet access, wireless campus network, Internet filtering or blocking technology, The Homework Site, faculty access via the Web (faweb). Student e-mail accounts and computer access in designated common areas are available to students. Students grades are available online. The school has a published electronic and media policy.

Contact Jasmine A. Lake, Director of Admission and Financial Aid. 305-779-7230. Fax: 305-758-5107. E-mail: admissions@miamicountryday.org. Web site: www.miamicountryday.org.

THE MIAMI VALLEY SCHOOL

5151 Denise Drive
Dayton, Ohio 45429
Head of School: Peter B. Benedict II

General Information Coeducational day college-preparatory, arts, religious studies, and technology school. Grades PK–12. Founded: 1964. Setting: suburban. 22-acre campus. 3 buildings on campus. Approved or accredited by Independent Schools Association of the Central States, Ohio Association of Independent Schools, and Ohio Department of Education. Member of National Association of Independent Schools. Endowment: $2.1 million. Total enrollment: 439. Upper school average class size: 16. Upper school faculty-student ratio: 1:9. Upper School students typically attend 5 days per week. The average school day consists of 7 hours and 15 minutes.

Faculty School total: 82. In upper school: 13 men, 12 women; 21 have advanced degrees.

The Miami Valley School

Subjects Offered Algebra, American history, American literature, anatomy, art, art history, biology, calculus, ceramics, chemistry, Chinese, Chinese history, community service, computer programming, computer science, creative writing, drama, earth science, ecology, economics, English, English literature, environmental science, European history, fine arts, French, gender issues, genetics, geology, geometry, government/civics, grammar, health, history, instrumental music, journalism, Latin, marine biology, mathematics, microbiology, music, philosophy, photography, physical education, physics, physiology, psychology, religion, science, social sciences, social studies, sociology, Spanish, speech, statistics, theater, trigonometry, word processing, world history, world literature, writing.

Graduation Requirements Alternative physical education, arts and fine arts (art, music, dance, drama), English, foreign language, mathematics, science, social sciences, social studies (includes history), Immersion Term. Community service is required.

Special Academic Programs Advanced Placement exam preparation; honors section; independent study; study at local college for college credit; study abroad; academic accommodation for the gifted, the musically talented, and the artistically talented.

College Admission Counseling 55 students graduated in 2010; all went to college, including Dartmouth College; Duke University; Emory University, Oxford College; Haverford College; The George Washington University; Vanderbilt University. Mean SAT critical reading: 625, mean SAT math: 608, mean SAT writing: 623, mean composite ACT: 26.

Student Life Upper grades have specified standards of dress, student council, honor system. Discipline rests equally with students and faculty.

Tuition and Aid Day student tuition: $17,400. Tuition installment plan (FACTS Tuition Payment Plan). Merit scholarship grants, need-based scholarship grants available. In 2010–11, 36% of upper-school students received aid; total upper-school merit-scholarship money awarded: $60,000. Total amount of financial aid awarded in 2010–11: $500,000.

Admissions Traditional secondary-level entrance grade is 9. For fall 2010, 30 students applied for upper-level admission, 25 were accepted, 23 enrolled. Achievement/Aptitude/Writing, school's own test, SSAT, Stanford Achievement Test, Otis-Lennon School Ability Test, TOEFL or SLEP or writing sample required. Deadline for receipt of application materials: February 15. Application fee required: $70. On-campus interview required.

Athletics Interscholastic: baseball (boys), basketball (b,g), cheering (g), lacrosse (b,g), soccer (b,g), softball (g), strength & conditioning (b,g), tennis (b,g), track and field (b,g), volleyball (g), weight training (b,g), wrestling (b); coed interscholastic: cross-country running, golf, running, squash, swimming and diving; coed intramural: crew. 2 PE instructors, 25 coaches, 1 athletic trainer.

Computers Computers are regularly used in literary magazine, mathematics, media production, multimedia, music technology, newspaper, photography, programming, science, social sciences, technology, yearbook classes. Computer network features include on-campus library services, online commercial services, Internet access, wireless campus network, Internet filtering or blocking technology. Campus intranet and student e-mail accounts are available to students. Students grades are available online. The school has a published electronic and media policy.

Contact Mr. C.S. Adams III, Director of Enrollment and Financial Aid. 937-434-4444 Ext. 125. Fax: 937-434-1033. E-mail: trey.adams@mvschool.com. Web site: www.mvschool.com.

MIDDLESEX SCHOOL

1400 Lowell Road
Concord, Massachusetts 01742
Head of School: Kathleen C. Giles

General Information Coeducational boarding and day college-preparatory and arts school. Grades 9–12. Founded: 1901. Setting: suburban. Nearest major city is Boston. Students are housed in single-sex dormitories. 350-acre campus. 31 buildings on campus. Approved or accredited by New England Association of Schools and Colleges. Member of National Association of Independent Schools and Secondary School Admission Test Board. Endowment: $137 million. Total enrollment: 374. Upper school average class size: 12. Upper school faculty-student ratio: 1:6. There are 178 required school days per year for Upper School students. Upper School students typically attend 6 days per week. The average school day consists of 7 hours and 7 minutes.

Upper School Student Profile Grade 9: 82 students (42 boys, 40 girls); Grade 10: 104 students (47 boys, 57 girls); Grade 11: 102 students (53 boys, 49 girls); Grade 12: 85 students (40 boys, 45 girls); Postgraduate: 1 student (1 girl). 67% of students are boarding students. 56% are state residents. 32 states are represented in upper school student body. 8% are international students. International students from Bermuda, Canada, China, Republic of Korea, Russian Federation, and Thailand; 9 other countries represented in student body.

Faculty School total: 60. In upper school: 32 men, 28 women; 45 have advanced degrees; 52 reside on campus.

Subjects Offered Acting, advanced biology, advanced chemistry, advanced computer applications, Advanced Placement courses, advanced studio art-AP, African American history, African history, African-American history, algebra, American literature, analytic geometry, art, art history, art history-AP, art-AP, Asian literature, astronomy, biology, biology-AP, British literature, calculus, calculus-AP, ceramics,

chemistry, chemistry-AP, Chinese, classical Greek literature, computer programming, computer programming-AP, computer science, computer science-AP, creative writing, discrete mathematics, DNA, drama, economics, economics-AP, English, English literature, English literature and composition-AP, environmental science, environmental science-AP, ethics, European history, European history-AP, finite math, forensics, French, French language-AP, French literature-AP, geometry, Greek, history, history of jazz, Holocaust studies, independent study, jazz band, Latin, Latin American history, marine studies, mathematics, media, Middle East, Middle Eastern history, model United Nations, music, music theory, music theory-AP, philosophy, photography, physics, physics-AP, political science, religion, Shakespeare, Spanish, Spanish language-AP, Spanish literature-AP, statistics, statistics-AP, studio art-AP, theater, trigonometry, U.S. government and politics-AP, U.S. history, U.S. history-AP, video film production, Vietnam history, Vietnam War, vocal ensemble, women in world history, woodworking, world history, writing, writing workshop.

Graduation Requirements Algebra, analytic geometry, arts, English, English literature and composition-AP, European history, foreign language, geometry, science, trigonometry, U.S. history, completion of a wooden plaque.

Special Academic Programs 22 Advanced Placement exams for which test preparation is offered; honors section; independent study; academic accommodation for the gifted.

College Admission Counseling 93 students graduated in 2010; all went to college, including Bates College; Bucknell University; Columbia University; Dartmouth College; Harvard University; Trinity College. Median SAT critical reading: 660, median SAT math: 670, median SAT writing: 690, median combined SAT: 2020. 81% scored over 600 on SAT critical reading, 90% scored over 600 on SAT math, 90% scored over 600 on SAT writing, 89% scored over 1800 on combined SAT.

Student Life Upper grades have specified standards of dress, student council, honor system. Discipline rests equally with students and faculty.

Summer Programs Art/fine arts programs offered; session focuses on arts; held on campus; accepts boys and girls; open to students from other schools. 180 students usually enrolled. 2011 schedule: June 27 to August 30.

Tuition and Aid Day student tuition: $36,870; 7-day tuition and room/board: $46,090. Guaranteed tuition plan. Tuition installment plan (Insured Tuition Payment Plan, monthly payment plans, semiannual payment plan). Need-based scholarship grants, need-based loans available. In 2010–11, 32% of upper-school students received aid. Total amount of financial aid awarded in 2010–11: $4,100,000.

Admissions Traditional secondary-level entrance grade is 9. For fall 2010, 1,038 students applied for upper-level admission, 114 enrolled. ISEE or SSAT required. Deadline for receipt of application materials: January 15. Application fee required: $50. Interview recommended.

Athletics Interscholastic: alpine skiing (boys, girls), baseball (b), basketball (b,g), crew (b,g), cross-country running (b,g), field hockey (g), football (b), ice hockey (b,g), lacrosse (b,g), skiing (downhill) (b,g), soccer (b,g), softball (g), squash (b,g), tennis (b,g), wrestling (b); coed interscholastic: golf, physical training, track and field; coed intramural: dance, fitness, strength & conditioning, yoga. 1 PE instructor, 18 coaches, 2 athletic trainers.

Computers Computers are regularly used in all classes. Computer network features include on-campus library services, online commercial services, Internet access, wireless campus network, Internet filtering or blocking technology. Campus intranet, student e-mail accounts, and computer access in designated common areas are available to students. The school has a published electronic and media policy.

Contact Douglas C. Price, Director of Admissions. 978-371-6524. Fax: 978-402-1400. E-mail: admissions@mxschool.edu. Web site: www.mxschool.edu.

MIDLAND SCHOOL

PO Box 8
5100 Figueroa Mountain Road
Los Olivos, California 93441
Head of School: Will Graham

General Information Coeducational boarding and day college-preparatory and environmental studies school. Boarding grades 9–12, day grades 9–11. Founded: 1932. Setting: rural. Nearest major city is Santa Barbara. Students are housed in single-sex cabins. 2,860-acre campus. Approved or accredited by California Association of Independent Schools, The Association of Boarding Schools, The College Board, US Department of State, and Western Association of Schools and Colleges. Member of National Association of Independent Schools and Secondary School Admission Test Board. Endowment: $8.5 million. Total enrollment: 80. Upper school average class size: 12. Upper school faculty-student ratio: 1:5.

Upper School Student Profile Grade 9: 23 students (13 boys, 10 girls); Grade 10: 22 students (11 boys, 11 girls); Grade 11: 21 students (14 boys, 7 girls); Grade 12: 14 students (10 boys, 4 girls). 98% of students are boarding students. 70% are state residents. 6 states are represented in upper school student body. 12% are international students. International students from China, Hong Kong, and Republic of Korea.

Faculty School total: 22. In upper school: 12 men, 10 women; 9 have advanced degrees; 20 reside on campus.

Subjects Offered 3-dimensional art, adolescent issues, advanced chemistry, advanced math, agroecology, algebra, American history, American literature, American studies, anthropology, backpacking, basketball, biology, calculus-AP, ceramics, character education, chemistry, Chinese history, clayworking, community service, composition, creative writing, drama, economics, environmental education, environmental studies, equestrian sports, film and literature, foreign language, gardening, geology, geometry, health education, human sexuality, hydrology, integrated science, land and ranch management, leadership, literature by women, metalworking, music, painting, physics, physics-AP, pre-calculus, senior project, senior seminar, senior thesis, sex education, Spanish, Spanish literature, Spanish-AP, statistics, U.S. history, utopia, volleyball, wilderness education, wilderness experience, world studies.

Graduation Requirements Arts and fine arts (art, music, dance, drama), English, foreign language, history, mathematics, science, senior thesis, independent senior thesis.

Special Academic Programs 6 Advanced Placement exams for which test preparation is offered; honors section; independent study.

College Admission Counseling 22 students graduated in 2009; 19 went to college. Other: 3 entered a postgraduate year.

Student Life Upper grades have specified standards of dress, student council. Discipline rests equally with students and faculty.

Tuition and Aid Day student tuition: $20,200; 7-day tuition and room/board: $36,000. Need-based scholarship grants, need-based loans available. In 2009–10, 42% of upper-school students received aid. Total amount of financial aid awarded in 2009–10: $873,000.

Admissions Traditional secondary-level entrance grade is 9. For fall 2009, 58 students applied for upper-level admission, 50 were accepted, 31 enrolled. SSAT required. Deadline for receipt of application materials: February 15. Application fee required: $30. On-campus interview required.

Athletics Interscholastic: cross-country running (boys, girls), lacrosse (b,g), soccer (b,g), volleyball (g); intramural: table tennis (b,g); coed interscholastic: basketball; coed intramural: backpacking, bicycling, dance, equestrian sports, hiking/backpacking, horseback riding, mountain biking, outdoor adventure, outdoor education, outdoor skills, surfing, touch football, ultimate Frisbee. 10 coaches.

Computers Computer network features include on-campus library services, Internet access, Internet filtering or blocking technology. Student e-mail accounts are available to students. The school has a published electronic and media policy.

Contact Derek Svennungsen, Director of Admissions. 805-688-5114 Ext. 14. Fax: 805-686-2470. E-mail: dsvennungsen@midland-school.org. Web site: www.midland-school.org.

MID-PACIFIC INSTITUTE

2445 Kaala Street
Honolulu, Hawaii 96822-2299
Head of School: Mr. Joe C. Rice

General Information Coeducational day college-preparatory, arts, bilingual studies, technology, and International Baccalaureate school, affiliated with Christian faith. Grades K–12. Founded: 1864. Setting: urban. 38-acre campus. 31 buildings on campus. Approved or accredited by International Baccalaureate Organization and Western Association of Schools and Colleges. Member of National Association of Independent Schools and Secondary School Admission Test Board. Endowment: $10 million. Total enrollment: 1,525. Upper school average class size: 20. Upper school faculty-student ratio: 1:20. Upper School students typically attend 5 days per week. The average school day consists of 6 hours and 15 minutes.

Upper School Student Profile 60% of students are Christian faith.

Faculty School total: 104. In upper school: 42 men, 54 women; 20 have advanced degrees.

Subjects Offered Algebra, American history, American literature, art, art history, astronomy, ballet, band, biology, business skills, calculus, career education, ceramics, chemistry, computer programming, computer science, creative writing, dance, debate, drama, drawing, economics, English, English literature, ESL, film, fine arts, first aid, French, general science, geography, geometry, Hawaiian history, health, history, instrumental music, Japanese, Latin, law, mathematics, oceanography, oral communications, painting, philosophy, photography, physical education, physics, printmaking, psychology, religion, science, sculpture, social sciences, social studies, Spanish, speech, swimming, swimming competency, technological applications, technology, theater, video, weight training, world history, world literature, writing.

Graduation Requirements Arts and fine arts (art, music, dance, drama), business skills (includes word processing), career education, computer science, English, foreign language, mathematics, oral communications, physical education (includes health), religion (includes Bible studies and theology), science, social sciences, social studies (includes history), speech, swimming competency.

Special Academic Programs International Baccalaureate program; Advanced Placement exam preparation; honors section; study at local college for college credit; academic accommodation for the gifted and the artistically talented; ESL (41 students enrolled).

College Admission Counseling 200 students graduated in 2010; all went to college, including Hawai'i Pacific University; Pacific University; University of Hawaii at Manoa; University of Southern California; University of Washington.

Student Life Upper grades have specified standards of dress, student council, honor system. Discipline rests primarily with faculty. Attendance at religious services is required.

Summer Programs Enrichment, advancement, ESL, art/fine arts, computer instruction programs offered; session focuses on physical fitness and skills; held on campus; accepts boys and girls; open to students from other schools. 950 students usually enrolled. 2011 schedule: June 5 to July 26. Application deadline: April 5.

Tuition and Aid Day student tuition: $17,000. Tuition installment plan (Insured Tuition Payment Plan, FACTS Tuition Payment Plan, monthly payment plans, semiannual payment plan). Merit scholarship grants, need-based scholarship grants, paying campus jobs, tuition reduction for children of employees available. In 2010–11, 17% of upper-school students received aid; total upper-school merit-scholarship money awarded: $305,000. Total amount of financial aid awarded in 2010–11: $644,000.

Admissions Traditional secondary-level entrance grade is 9. For fall 2010, 700 students applied for upper-level admission, 220 were accepted, 150 enrolled. SAT, SSAT and TOEFL required. Deadline for receipt of application materials: December 1. Application fee required: $100. Interview required.

Athletics Interscholastic: aquatics (boys, girls), baseball (b), basketball (b,g), bowling (b,g), canoeing/kayaking (b,g), cheering (g), cross-country running (b,g), football (b), golf (b,g), gymnastics (g), independent competitive sports (b,g), kayaking (b,g), ocean paddling (b,g), physical fitness (b,g), physical training (b,g), riflery (b,g), soccer (b,g), softball (g), strength & conditioning (b,g), surfing (b,g), swimming and diving (b,g), tennis (b,g), track and field (b,g), volleyball (b,g), water polo (b,g), wrestling (b,g); intramural: badminton (b,g), weight lifting (b,g), weight training (b,g); coed interscholastic: fitness, modern dance; coed intramural: badminton. 6 PE instructors, 20 coaches, 2 athletic trainers.

Computers Computers are regularly used in English, foreign language, mathematics, media arts, science classes. Computer network features include on-campus library services, online commercial services, Internet access, wireless campus network, Internet filtering or blocking technology. Campus intranet, student e-mail accounts, and computer access in designated common areas are available to students. Students grades are available online. The school has a published electronic and media policy.

Contact Mrs. Linda Oshio, Admissions Secretary. 808-973-5005. Fax: 808-973-5099. E-mail: admissions@midpac.edu. Web site: www.midpac.edu.

MID-PENINSULA HIGH SCHOOL

1340 Willow Road
Menlo Park, California 94025-1516
Head of School: Douglas C. Thompson, PhD

General Information Coeducational day college-preparatory, general academic, and arts school; primarily serves underachievers, students with learning disabilities, individuals with Attention Deficit Disorder, individuals with emotional and behavioral problems, dyslexic students, and Asberger's Syndrome. Grades 9–12. Founded: 1979. Setting: suburban. Nearest major city is San Jose. 2-acre campus. 1 building on campus. Approved or accredited by California Association of Independent Schools, Western Association of Schools and Colleges, and California Department of Education. Endowment: $1.4 million. Total enrollment: 117. Upper school average class size: 12. Upper school faculty-student ratio: 1:8. Upper School students typically attend 5 days per week. The average school day consists of 6 hours and 10 minutes.

Upper School Student Profile Grade 9: 25 students (11 boys, 14 girls); Grade 10: 30 students (17 boys, 13 girls); Grade 11: 34 students (22 boys, 12 girls); Grade 12: 27 students (19 boys, 8 girls).

Faculty School total: 17. In upper school: 9 men, 8 women; 6 have advanced degrees.

Subjects Offered Algebra, American sign language, art, biology, calculus, calculus-AP, chemistry, composition, contemporary issues, drama, driver education, English, geometry, government, human relations, mathematics, music performance, physical education, physics, SAT/ACT preparation, science, Spanish, sports, study skills, trigonometry, U.S. history, world studies.

Graduation Requirements American government, government, human relations, mathematics, physical education (includes health), science, social sciences, U.S. history. Community service is required.

Special Academic Programs Accelerated programs; independent study; remedial reading and/or remedial writing; remedial math.

College Admission Counseling 27 students graduated in 2009; 26 went to college, including California State University, Chico; California State University, East Bay; California State University, Monterey Bay; Pacific Lutheran University; University of San Francisco; Whittier College. Other: 1 went to work.

Student Life Discipline rests primarily with faculty.

Tuition and Aid Day student tuition: $25,462. Tuition installment plan (monthly payment plans, individually arranged payment plans, 2-payment plan). Tuition reduction for siblings, need-based scholarship grants available. In 2009–10, 34% of upper-school students received aid. Total amount of financial aid awarded in 2009–10: $772,487.

Admissions Traditional secondary-level entrance grade is 9. For fall 2009, 88 students applied for upper-level admission, 83 were accepted, 58 enrolled. Deadline for receipt of application materials: none. No application fee required. On-campus interview required.

Athletics Interscholastic: baseball (boys), basketball (b,g), softball (g), volleyball (b,g); coed interscholastic: cross-country running, soccer, track and field. 1 PE instructor, 4 coaches.

Computers Computers are regularly used in desktop publishing, English, mathematics, music, publications, social sciences classes. Computer network features include Internet access, wireless campus network, Internet filtering or blocking technology. Computer access in designated common areas is available to students. The school has a published electronic and media policy.

Contact Ms. Barbara Brown, Director of Admissions. 650-321-1991 Ext. 147. Fax: 650-321-9921. E-mail: barbara@mid-pen.com. Web site: www.mid-pen.com.

MILFORD ACADEMY

7 School Street
PO Box 878
New Berlin, New York 13411
Head of School: Mr. William Chaplick

General Information Coeducational boarding and day college-preparatory and general academic school. Boarding grades 9–PG, day grades 7–PG. Founded: 1916. Setting: small town. Nearest major city is Syracuse. Students are housed in single-sex dormitories. 26-acre campus. 4 buildings on campus. Approved or accredited by New York Department of Education. Upper school average class size: 9. Upper school faculty-student ratio: 1:10. There are 150 required school days per year for Upper School students. Upper School students typically attend 6 days per week. The average school day consists of 7 hours and 30 minutes.

Upper School Student Profile 100% of students are boarding students. 18% are state residents. 20 states are represented in upper school student body. International students from Canada, Japan, Republic of Korea, Russian Federation, and Sweden.

Faculty School total: 12. In upper school: 6 reside on campus.

Graduation Requirements Arts and fine arts (art, music, dance, drama), computer science, English, foreign language, mathematics, physical education (includes health), science, social studies (includes history).

Special Academic Programs ESL (8 students enrolled).

College Admission Counseling 45 students graduated in 2009; all went to college.

Student Life Upper grades have uniform requirement, student council. Discipline rests primarily with faculty.

Tuition and Aid Day student tuition: $12,500; 7-day tuition and room/board: $19,965. Tuition installment plan (monthly payment plans, individually arranged payment plans). Tuition reduction for siblings, paying campus jobs available. In 2009–10, 16% of upper-school students received aid.

Admissions ACT required. Deadline for receipt of application materials: none. Application fee required: $65. On-campus interview required.

Athletics Interscholastic: baseball (boys, girls), basketball (b), football (b), ice hockey (b). 4 coaches, 1 athletic trainer.

Contact Mr. Warren Prohaska, Director of Admissions. 607-847-9280. Fax: 607-847-9250. Web site: www.milfordacademy.org.

MILLBROOK SCHOOL

131 Millbrook School Road
Millbrook, New York 12545
Head of School: Mr. Drew Casertano

General Information Coeducational boarding and day college-preparatory, arts, environmental stewardship, and community service school. Grades 9–12. Founded: 1931. Setting: rural. Nearest major city is New York. Students are housed in single-sex dormitories. 800-acre campus. 40 buildings on campus. Approved or accredited by National Independent Private Schools Association, New York State Association of Independent Schools, The Association of Boarding Schools, and New York Department of Education. Member of National Association of Independent Schools and Secondary School Admission Test Board. Endowment: $22 million. Total enrollment: 260. Upper school average class size: 14. Upper school faculty-student ratio: 1:5. There are 179 required school days per year for Upper School students. Upper School students typically attend 6 days per week. The average school day consists of 7 hours.

Upper School Student Profile Grade 9: 44 students (22 boys, 22 girls); Grade 10: 71 students (37 boys, 34 girls); Grade 11: 77 students (47 boys, 30 girls); Grade 12: 64 students (39 boys, 25 girls); Postgraduate: 2 students (2 boys). 80% of students are boarding students. 40% are state residents. 20 states are represented in upper school student body. 15% are international students. International students from Canada, China, Costa Rica, Germany, Republic of Korea, and Viet Nam; 7 other countries represented in student body.

Faculty School total: 59. In upper school: 29 men, 30 women; 29 have advanced degrees; 45 reside on campus.

Subjects Offered Acting, advanced biology, advanced chemistry, advanced math, Advanced Placement courses, advanced studio art-AP, aesthetics, algebra, American history, American literature, ancient history, ancient world history, animal behavior, animal science, anthropology, art, art history, astronomy, biology, calculus, calculus-AP, ceramics, chemistry, choral music, constitutional law, creative writing, dance, dance performance, digital photography, drama, drama performance, drawing, ecology, English, English language-AP, English literature, English-AP, environmental science, European history, fine arts, forensics, French, French language-AP, French-AP, geometry, global studies, history, honors English, honors geometry, human biology, human development, independent study, instrumental music, jazz band, jazz ensemble, journalism, Mandarin, mathematics, medieval history, Middle Eastern history, music, music appreciation, music history, painting, philosophy, photography,

physics, pre-calculus, psychology, science, senior project, social sciences, social studies, Spanish, Spanish-AP, studio art, study skills, theater, trigonometry, world history.

Graduation Requirements Biology, English, foreign language, history, mathematics, science, visual and performing arts, Culminating Experience for Seniors.

Special Academic Programs 8 Advanced Placement exams for which test preparation is offered; honors section; independent study; term-away projects; study abroad.

College Admission Counseling 78 students graduated in 2010; 76 went to college, including Connecticut College; Hamilton College; The Colorado College; The George Washington University; Williams College. Other: 2 had other specific plans. Mean SAT critical reading: 563, mean SAT math: 575, mean SAT writing: 564, mean combined SAT: 1701, mean composite ACT: 23.

Student Life Upper grades have specified standards of dress, student council, honor system. Discipline rests primarily with faculty.

Tuition and Aid Day student tuition: $32,550; 7-day tuition and room/board: $44,775. Tuition installment plan (individually arranged payment plans, Tuition Management Services). Need-based scholarship grants, need-based loans available. In 2010–11, 27% of upper-school students received aid. Total amount of financial aid awarded in 2010–11: $2,000,000.

Admissions Traditional secondary-level entrance grade is 9. For fall 2010, 469 students applied for upper-level admission, 254 were accepted, 99 enrolled. ISEE, PSAT or SAT for applicants to grade 11 and 12, SSAT, TOEFL or writing sample required. Deadline for receipt of application materials: January 15. Application fee required: $50. Interview required.

Athletics Interscholastic: baseball (boys), basketball (b,g), cross-country running (b,g), field hockey (g), ice hockey (b,g), lacrosse (b,g), soccer (b,g), softball (g), squash (b,g), tennis (b,g); coed interscholastic: golf; coed intramural: aerobics/dance, aerobics/Nautilus, badminton, bicycling, dance, equestrian sports, fitness, horseback riding, modern dance, outdoor education, physical training, running, skiing (downhill), snowboarding, strength & conditioning, weight training, yoga. 1 coach, 1 athletic trainer.

Computers Computers are regularly used in foreign language, history, journalism, mathematics, photography, science, study skills, video film production, yearbook classes. Computer network features include on-campus library services, online commercial services, Internet access, wireless campus network, Internet filtering or blocking technology. Campus intranet, student e-mail accounts, and computer access in designated common areas are available to students. Students grades are available online. The school has a published electronic and media policy.

Contact Mrs. Wendy Greenfield, Admission Office Assistant. 845-677-8261 Ext. 138. Fax: 845-677-1265. E-mail: admissions@millbrook.org. Web site: www.millbrook.org.

MILLER SCHOOL

1000 Samuel Miller Loop
Charlottesville, Virginia 22903-9328
Head of School: Mr. Walter "Winn" Price

General Information Coeducational boarding and day college-preparatory and arts school. Grades 8–12. Founded: 1878. Setting: rural. Students are housed in single-sex dormitories. 1,600-acre campus. 6 buildings on campus. Approved or accredited by The Association of Boarding Schools and Virginia Association of Independent Schools. Member of National Association of Independent Schools. Endowment: $14 million. Total enrollment: 145. Upper school average class size: 10. Upper school faculty-student ratio: 1:6.

Upper School Student Profile Grade 8: 8 students (3 boys, 5 girls); Grade 9: 27 students (17 boys, 10 girls); Grade 10: 28 students (15 boys, 13 girls); Grade 11: 40 students (26 boys, 14 girls); Grade 12: 40 students (16 boys, 24 girls); Postgraduate: 1 student (1 boy). 68% of students are boarding students. 55% are state residents. 9 states are represented in upper school student body. 26% are international students. International students from Cameroon, China, Kazakhstan, Lithuania, Republic of Korea, and Ukraine; 6 other countries represented in student body.

Faculty School total: 26. In upper school: 15 men, 11 women; 19 have advanced degrees; 23 reside on campus.

Subjects Offered Algebra, American government, American literature, ancient history, art, arts, baseball, basketball, biology, calculus, calculus-AP, carpentry, chemistry, civics, CPR, creative writing, drama performance, driver education, earth science, economics, economics and history, electives, English, English composition, English language and composition-AP, English language-AP, English literature, English literature and composition-AP, English literature-AP, English-AP, English/composition-AP, environmental science, environmental science-AP, environmental studies, environmental systems, ESL, European history, European history-AP, fine arts, fitness, foreign language, French, French language-AP, French literature-AP, French studies, French-AP, geography, geometry, government, government and politics-AP, government-AP, government/civics, history-AP, independent study, instrumental music, Latin, macroeconomics-AP, mathematics-AP, modern European history, modern European history-AP, music, music performance, musical productions, musical theater, participation in sports, photography, physical education, physical fitness, physical science, physics, poetry, pre-algebra, pre-calculus, reading/study skills, Spanish, Spanish language-AP, Spanish literature-AP, Spanish-AP, sports conditioning, statistics, student government, studio art, studio art-AP, study skills, tennis, trigonometry, U.S. government, U.S. government and politics-AP, U.S. history, U.S. history-AP, visual arts, volleyball, woodworking, wrestling, yearbook.

Graduation Requirements Arts and fine arts (art, music, dance, drama), English, foreign language, mathematics, physical education (includes health), science, social studies (includes history). Community service is required.

Special Academic Programs Advanced Placement exam preparation; honors section; accelerated programs; independent study; academic accommodation for the gifted, the musically talented, and the artistically talented; ESL (8 students enrolled).

College Admission Counseling 42 students graduated in 2009; 40 went to college, including Duke University; James Madison University; Longwood University; Penn State University Park; University of Virginia; Virginia Polytechnic Institute and State University. Other: 2 had other specific plans. Mean SAT critical reading: 561, mean SAT math: 568, mean SAT writing: 542. 35% scored over 600 on SAT critical reading, 35% scored over 600 on SAT math.

Student Life Upper grades have specified standards of dress, student council, honor system. Discipline rests equally with students and faculty.

Tuition and Aid Day student tuition: $14,950; 5-day tuition and room/board: $31,200; 7-day tuition and room/board: $34,200. Tuition installment plan (Insured Tuition Payment Plan, SMART Tuition Payment Plan, individually arranged payment plans). Tuition reduction for siblings, need-based scholarship grants available. In 2009–10, 33% of upper-school students received aid. Total amount of financial aid awarded in 2009–10: $525,000.

Admissions Traditional secondary-level entrance grade is 9. For fall 2009, 130 students applied for upper-level admission, 94 were accepted, 58 enrolled. ACT, any standardized test, California Achievement Test, Iowa Tests of Basic Skills, PSAT or SAT, SSAT, Stanford Achievement Test or TOEFL or SLEP required. Deadline for receipt of application materials: none. Application fee required: $50. Interview required.

Athletics Interscholastic: baseball (boys), basketball (b,g), cross-country running (b,g), lacrosse (b), soccer (b,g), tennis (b,g), volleyball (g), wrestling (b); coed interscholastic: equestrian sports, golf, horseback riding; coed intramural: basketball, bicycling, canoeing/kayaking, cross-country running, fishing, fitness, Frisbee, hiking/backpacking, indoor soccer, jogging, mountain biking, outdoor activities, paint ball, physical fitness, physical training, power lifting, running, skateboarding, soccer, softball, street hockey, strength & conditioning, swimming and diving, table tennis, tennis, touch football, ultimate Frisbee, volleyball, walking, weight lifting, weight training. 5 coaches, 1 athletic trainer.

Computers Computers are regularly used in English, foreign language, history, mathematics, science classes. Computer network features include on-campus library services, online commercial services, Internet access, wireless campus network, Internet filtering or blocking technology. Campus intranet and student e-mail accounts are available to students. The school has a published electronic and media policy.

Contact Ms. Dee Gregory, Assistant Director of Admissions. 434-823-4805 Ext. 248. Fax: 434-205-5007. E-mail: dgregory@millerschool.org. Web site: www.millerschool.org.

MILO ADVENTIST ACADEMY

PO Box 278
Days Creek, Oregon 97429-0278
Head of School: Mr. Randall S. Bovee

General Information Coeducational boarding and day and distance learning college-preparatory, general academic, religious studies, and English for Academic Achievement (English Language Learning) school, affiliated with Seventh-day Adventist Church. Grades 9–12. Distance learning grades 9–12. Founded: 1955. Setting: rural. Nearest major city is Roseburg. Students are housed in single-sex dormitories. 475-acre campus. 8 buildings on campus. Approved or accredited by Board of Regents, General Conference of Seventh-day Adventists, National Council for Private School Accreditation, Northwest Association of Schools and Colleges, and Oregon Department of Education. Endowment: $15,000. Total enrollment: 103. Upper school average class size: 20. Upper school faculty-student ratio: 1:10. There are 176 required school days per year for Upper School students. Upper School students typically attend 5 days per week. The average school day consists of 5 hours and 45 minutes.

Upper School Student Profile Grade 9: 25 students (9 boys, 16 girls); Grade 10: 25 students (9 boys, 16 girls); Grade 11: 32 students (15 boys, 17 girls); Grade 12: 30 students (15 boys, 15 girls). 80% of students are boarding students. 70% are state residents. 6 states are represented in upper school student body. 6% are international students. International students from China, Japan, Republic of Korea, and Taiwan. 85% of students are Seventh-day Adventists.

Faculty School total: 12. In upper school: 7 men, 5 women; 7 have advanced degrees; 11 reside on campus.

Subjects Offered Advanced Placement courses, algebra, American government, American history-AP, American literature, anatomy and physiology, art, art appreciation, band, bell choir, Bible, Bible studies, biology, British literature, calculus-AP, career planning, chemistry, choir, choral music, Christian education, church history, college admission preparation, college counseling, college planning, communication skills, community service, computer literacy, computer skills, conceptual physics, drama performance, earth science, economics, English, English literature and composition-AP, ensembles, ESL, family and consumer science, folk art, food and nutrition, foreign language, general math, geometry, global studies, government,

graphic arts, graphic design, guidance, guitar, handbells, health, keyboarding, music appreciation, participation in sports, peer ministry, photography, physical education, physics, play production, pottery, pre-algebra, pre-calculus, sewing, Spanish, technology, U.S. government, U.S. history, U.S. history-AP, wind instruments, woodworking, word processing, work-study, writing workshop, yearbook.

Graduation Requirements Algebra, American literature, arts and fine arts (art, music, dance, drama), Bible, computer literacy, computer skills, economics, English, foreign language, geometry, global studies, health, lab science, mathematics, physical education (includes health), religion (includes Bible studies and theology), science, technology, U.S. government, U.S. history, enrollment in Bible every year in school.

Special Academic Programs 5 Advanced Placement exams for which test preparation is offered; independent study; ESL (6 students enrolled).

College Admission Counseling 40 students graduated in 2009; 34 went to college, including Lane Community College; Pacific Union College; Southern Adventist University; University of Michigan; University of Oregon; Walla Walla University. Other: 5 went to work, 1 had other specific plans. Median SAT critical reading: 530, median SAT math: 500, median SAT writing: 510, median combined SAT: 1610, median composite ACT: 24. 38% scored over 600 on SAT critical reading, 30% scored over 600 on SAT math, 23% scored over 600 on SAT writing, 21% scored over 1800 on combined SAT, 20% scored over 26 on composite ACT.

Student Life Upper grades have specified standards of dress, student council, honor system. Discipline rests primarily with faculty. Attendance at religious services is required.

Tuition and Aid Day student tuition: $7500; 7-day tuition and room/board: $14,500. Tuition installment plan (monthly payment plans, individually arranged payment plans). Tuition reduction for siblings, merit scholarship grants, paying campus jobs, work sponsorship program available. In 2009–10, 70% of upper-school students received aid; total upper-school merit-scholarship money awarded: $9000. Total amount of financial aid awarded in 2009–10: $211,775.

Admissions Traditional secondary-level entrance grade is 11. For fall 2009, 107 students applied for upper-level admission, 105 were accepted, 103 enrolled. TOEFL required. Deadline for receipt of application materials: none. Application fee required: $25. Interview required.

Athletics Interscholastic: baseball (boys), basketball (b,g), flag football (b), softball (g), volleyball (g); intramural: aerobics (g), baseball (b), basketball (b,g), bicycling (b,g), cooperative games (b,g), field hockey (b), flag football (b), floor hockey (b,g), hiking/backpacking (b,g), horseback riding (b,g), indoor hockey (b,g), jogging (b,g), mountain biking (b), outdoor activities (b,g), outdoor recreation (b,g), skateboarding (b), soccer (b,g), softball (b,g), swimming and diving (b,g), walking (b,g), weight lifting (b); coed interscholastic: soccer; coed intramural: basketball, cooperative games, field hockey, floor hockey, indoor hockey, outdoor activities, outdoor recreation, soccer, softball, swimming and diving, track and field, volleyball. 1 PE instructor.

Computers Computers are regularly used in computer applications, English, graphic design, keyboarding, mathematics, photography, publications, Web site design, word processing, writing, yearbook classes. Computer network features include on-campus library services, Internet access, Internet filtering or blocking technology. Student e-mail accounts and computer access in designated common areas are available to students. Students grades are available online. The school has a published electronic and media policy.

Contact Mrs. Nancy Starr, Administrative Assistant. 541-825-3200 Ext. 3321. Fax: 541-825-3723. E-mail: info@miloacademy.org. Web site: www.miloacademy.net.

MILTON ACADEMY

170 Centre Street
Milton, Massachusetts 02186
Head of School: Todd Bland

General Information Coeducational boarding and day college-preparatory school. Boarding grades 9–12, day grades K–12. Founded: 1798. Setting: suburban. Nearest major city is Boston. Students are housed in single-sex dormitories. 125-acre campus. 24 buildings on campus. Approved or accredited by Association of Independent Schools in New England, New England Association of Schools and Colleges, The Association of Boarding Schools, and Massachusetts Department of Education. Member of National Association of Independent Schools and Secondary School Admission Test Board. Endowment: $167 million. Total enrollment: 980. Upper school average class size: 14. Upper school faculty-student ratio: 1:5. There are 162 required school days per year for Upper School students. Upper School students typically attend 5 days per week. The average school day consists of 7 hours.

Upper School Student Profile 50% of students are boarding students. 64% are state residents. 25 states are represented in upper school student body. 10% are international students. International students from Hong Kong, Jamaica, Japan, Malaysia, Republic of Korea, and Taiwan; 18 other countries represented in student body.

Faculty School total: 180. In upper school: 62 men, 65 women; 99 have advanced degrees; 102 reside on campus.

Subjects Offered Algebra, American history, American literature, anatomy, architecture, art, art history, astronomy, biology, calculus, ceramics, chemistry, Chinese, computer math, computer programming, computer science, creative writing, current events, dance, drama, earth science, economics, English, English literature, ethics, European history, expository writing, fine arts, French, geography, geometry, government/civics, grammar, Greek, health, history, Latin, mathematics, music, philosophy, photography, physical education, physics, physiology, psychology, religion, science, social studies, sociology, Spanish, speech, statistics, theater, trigonometry, world history, world literature, writing.

Graduation Requirements Arts and fine arts (art, music, dance, drama), current events, English, foreign language, leadership, mathematics, physical education (includes health), public speaking, science, social studies (includes history).

Special Academic Programs Advanced Placement exam preparation; honors section; independent study; term-away projects; study abroad; academic accommodation for the gifted, the musically talented, and the artistically talented.

College Admission Counseling 164 students graduated in 2010; all went to college, including Boston College; Brown University; Columbia University; Georgetown University; Harvard University; Tufts University. Mean SAT critical reading: 680, mean SAT math: 692, mean SAT writing: 693.

Student Life Upper grades have student council, honor system. Discipline rests equally with students and faculty.

Tuition and Aid Day student tuition: $36,100; 7-day tuition and room/board: $43,975. Tuition installment plan (The Tuition Management Systems (TMS)). Need-based scholarship grants available. In 2010–11, 32% of upper-school students received aid. Total amount of financial aid awarded in 2010–11: $7,650,000.

Admissions Traditional secondary-level entrance grade is 9. For fall 2010, 1,000 students applied for upper-level admission, 275 were accepted, 155 enrolled. ISEE, PSAT, SAT, SSAT or TOEFL required. Deadline for receipt of application materials: January 15. Application fee required: $50. Interview required.

Athletics Interscholastic: baseball (boys), basketball (b,g), cross-country running (b,g), field hockey (g), football (b), ice hockey (b,g), lacrosse (b,g), soccer (b,g), softball (g), squash (b,g), tennis (b,g), track and field (b,g), volleyball (g); intramural: basketball (b,g), soccer (b,g), strength & conditioning (b,g); coed interscholastic: alpine skiing, diving, golf, sailing, skiing (downhill), swimming and diving, wrestling; coed intramural: climbing, outdoor activities, outdoor education, project adventure, rock climbing, skiing (downhill), squash, tennis, ultimate Frisbee, yoga. 6 PE instructors, 107 coaches, 3 athletic trainers.

Computers Computers are regularly used in mathematics, science classes. Computer network features include on-campus library services, online commercial services, Internet access, wireless campus network, Internet filtering or blocking technology. Student e-mail accounts and computer access in designated common areas are available to students.

Contact Mrs. Patricia Finn, Admission Assistant. 617-898-2227. Fax: 617-898-1701. E-mail: admissions@milton.edu. Web site: www.milton.edu.

See Close-Up on page 808.

MINOT BISHOP RYAN

316 11th Avenue NW
Minot, North Dakota 58703
Head of School: Mr. Richard Limke

General Information Coeducational day college-preparatory and religious studies school, affiliated with Roman Catholic Church. Grades 7–12. Founded: 1958. 3-acre campus. 1 building on campus. Approved or accredited by North Central Association of Colleges and Schools and North Dakota Department of Education. Total enrollment: 400. Upper school average class size: 17. Upper school faculty-student ratio: 1:17. The average school day consists of 7 hours.

Upper School Student Profile 90% of students are Roman Catholic.

Faculty School total: 24. In upper school: 8 men, 16 women.

Subjects Offered Accounting, algebra, American literature, art, arts and crafts, band, Basic programming, biology, calculus, career exploration, chemistry, choir, computer programming, computer science, creative writing, earth science, economics, English, English literature, food science, geography, geometry, German, government, health, home economics, human biology, keyboarding, law, life science, mathematics, parent/child development, physical science, physics, play production, pre-algebra, psychology, religion, social studies, sociology, Spanish, speech, trigonometry, U.S. history, world history, writing.

Student Life Upper grades have specified standards of dress, student council. Discipline rests primarily with faculty. Attendance at religious services is required.

Tuition and Aid Tuition installment plan (FACTS Tuition Payment Plan). Tuition reduction for siblings, merit scholarship grants, need-based scholarship grants available. In 2009–10, 60% of upper-school students received aid. Total amount of financial aid awarded in 2009–10: $5000.

Admissions Deadline for receipt of application materials: none. No application fee required. On-campus interview required.

Athletics Interscholastic: baseball (boys), basketball (b,g), cross-country running (b,g), dance squad (g), dance team (g), football (b), golf (b,g), gymnastics (g), hockey (b), ice hockey (b), soccer (b,g), swimming and diving (b,g), tennis (b,g), track and field (b,g), volleyball (g), wrestling (b). 2 PE instructors, 8 coaches.

Computers Computer resources include on-campus library services, wireless campus network, Internet filtering or blocking technology. Campus intranet and student e-mail accounts are available to students. Students grades are available online.

Contact Mr. Terry Voiles, Principal. 701-852-4004. Fax: 701-839-4651. E-mail: tvoiles@brhs.com. Web site: www.minotcatholic.org.

MISS EDGAR'S AND MISS CRAMP'S SCHOOL

525 Mount Pleasant Avenue
Montreal, Quebec H3Y 3H6, Canada
Head of School: Ms. Katherine Nikidis

General Information Girls' day college-preparatory, arts, bilingual studies, and technology school. Grades K–11. Founded: 1909. Setting: urban. 4-acre campus. 1 building on campus. Approved or accredited by Canadian Association of Independent Schools, Quebec Association of Independent Schools, and Quebec Department of Education. Affiliate member of National Association of Independent Schools; member of Secondary School Admission Test Board. Languages of instruction: English and French. Total enrollment: 335. Upper school average class size: 19. Upper school faculty-student ratio: 1:9. There are 180 required school days per year for Upper School students. Upper School students typically attend 5 days per week. The average school day consists of 5 hours.

Upper School Student Profile Grade 9: 39 students (39 girls); Grade 10: 40 students (40 girls); Grade 11: 36 students (36 girls).

Faculty School total: 40. In upper school: 3 men, 15 women; 8 have advanced degrees.

Subjects Offered Art, art history, biology, calculus, career exploration, chemistry, computer science, creative writing, drama, ecology, economics, English, environmental science, European history, French, geography, history, mathematics, media, music, physical education, physics, science, social studies, Spanish, theater, women's studies, world history.

Graduation Requirements English, foreign language, mathematics, science, social studies (includes history).

Special Academic Programs 2 Advanced Placement exams for which test preparation is offered; honors section.

College Admission Counseling 43 students graduated in 2010; all went to college, including John Abbott College; Lower Canada College; Marianopolis College.

Student Life Upper grades have uniform requirement, student council, honor system. Discipline rests primarily with faculty.

Tuition and Aid Day student tuition: CAN$15,000. Tuition installment plan (individually arranged payment plans). Bursaries, merit scholarship grants available. In 2010–11, 18% of upper-school students received aid; total upper-school merit-scholarship money awarded: CAN$80,000. Total amount of financial aid awarded in 2010–11: CAN$105,000.

Admissions Traditional secondary-level entrance grade is 9. For fall 2010, 22 students applied for upper-level admission, 15 were accepted, 8 enrolled. CCAT, SSAT or writing sample required. Deadline for receipt of application materials: none. Application fee required: CAN$50. On-campus interview required.

Athletics Interscholastic: badminton, basketball, cross-country running, golf, hockey, ice hockey, running, soccer, swimming and diving, tennis, touch football, track and field, volleyball; intramural: badminton, baseball, basketball, crew, cross-country running, curling, dance, field hockey, gymnastics, ice hockey, outdoor adventure, outdoor education, outdoor skills, physical fitness, rugby, running, skiing (cross-country), soccer, softball, touch football, track and field, volleyball. 3 PE instructors, 11 coaches.

Computers Computers are regularly used in art, English, French, history, newspaper, writing, yearbook classes. Computer network features include on-campus library services, Internet access, wireless campus network, Internet filtering or blocking technology. Campus intranet, student e-mail accounts, and computer access in designated common areas are available to students. The school has a published electronic and media policy.

Contact Ms. Carla Bolsius, Admissions Coordinator. 514-935-6357 Ext. 254. Fax: 514-935-1099. E-mail: bolsiusc@ecs.qc.ca. Web site: www.ecs.qc.ca.

MISS HALL'S SCHOOL

492 Holmes Road
Pittsfield, Massachusetts 01201
Head of School: Ms. Jeannie Norris

General Information Girls' boarding and day college-preparatory, arts, technology, community service, and leadership development school. Grades 9–12. Founded: 1898. Setting: suburban. Nearest major city is Albany, NY. Students are housed in single-sex dormitories. 80-acre campus. 9 buildings on campus. Approved or accredited by Association of Independent Schools in New England, New England Association of Schools and Colleges, The Association of Boarding Schools, and Massachusetts Department of Education. Member of National Association of Independent Schools and Secondary School Admission Test Board. Endowment: $12 million. Total enrollment: 180. Upper school average class size: 11. Upper school faculty-student ratio: 1:6.

Upper School Student Profile Grade 9: 40 students (40 girls); Grade 10: 40 students (40 girls); Grade 11: 50 students (50 girls); Grade 12: 50 students (50 girls). 75% of students are boarding students. 34% are state residents. 20 states are represented in upper school student body. 30% are international students. International students from China, India, Mexico, Pakistan, Republic of Korea, and Taiwan; 14 other countries represented in student body.

Faculty School total: 35. In upper school: 8 men, 27 women; 26 have advanced degrees; 18 reside on campus.

Subjects Offered Advanced Placement courses, algebra, American government, American history, American literature, anatomy, art, art history, biology, business skills, calculus, ceramics, chamber groups, chemistry, college counseling, community service, computer science, CPR, dance, drama, drawing, driver education, ecology, economics, English, English literature, English-AP, environmental science, ESL, ethics, ethics and responsibility, European history, European history-AP, expressive arts, fine arts, forensics, French, geometry, government/civics, health, history, Latin, mathematics, music, music history, painting, photography, physics, physiology, political science, psychology, science, social studies, Spanish, theater, trigonometry, world cultures, world history.

Graduation Requirements Arts and fine arts (art, music, dance, drama), English, foreign language, history, mathematics, physical education (includes health), science. Community service is required.

Special Academic Programs Advanced Placement exam preparation; honors section; independent study; academic accommodation for the gifted, the musically talented, and the artistically talented; special instructional classes for students with mild learning disabilities and Attention Deficit Disorder; ESL (20 students enrolled).

College Admission Counseling 51 students graduated in 2009; all went to college, including Babson College; Denison University; Northeastern University; Williams College; Yale University.

Student Life Upper grades have specified standards of dress, student council, honor system. Discipline rests equally with students and faculty.

Tuition and Aid Day student tuition: $26,375; 7-day tuition and room/board: $42,650. Tuition installment plan (Insured Tuition Payment Plan, Academic Management Services Plan, Key Tuition Payment Plan, monthly payment plans, individually arranged payment plans). Merit scholarship grants, need-based scholarship grants available. In 2009–10, 47% of upper-school students received aid; total upper-school merit-scholarship money awarded: $275,000. Total amount of financial aid awarded in 2009–10: $2,000,000.

Admissions Traditional secondary-level entrance grade is 9. For fall 2009, 225 students applied for upper-level admission, 99 were accepted, 52 enrolled. SSAT or TOEFL required. Deadline for receipt of application materials: February 15. Application fee required: $40. Interview required.

Athletics Interscholastic: alpine skiing, basketball, cross-country running, field hockey, lacrosse, skiing (downhill), soccer, softball, tennis, volleyball; intramural: aerobics, aerobics/dance, alpine skiing, dance, equestrian sports, fitness, jogging, modern dance, outdoor activities, outdoor education, outdoor skills, physical fitness, rock climbing, ropes courses, running, skiing (cross-country), skiing (downhill), snowboarding, tennis, walking, wall climbing, wilderness, yoga. 3 coaches, 1 athletic trainer.

Computers Computers are regularly used in computer applications, English, foreign language, history, music, newspaper, photography, science, yearbook classes. Computer network features include on-campus library services, online commercial services, Internet access, wireless campus network. Student e-mail accounts and computer access in designated common areas are available to students. The school has a published electronic and media policy.

Contact Ms. Kimberly B. Boland, Director of Admission. 413-499-1300. Fax: 413-448-2994. E-mail: info@misshalls.org. Web site: www.misshalls.org.

MISS PORTER'S SCHOOL

60 Main Street
Farmington, Connecticut 06032
Head of School: Dr. Katherine G. Windsor

General Information Girls' boarding and day college-preparatory and arts school. Grades 9–12. Founded: 1843. Setting: suburban. Nearest major city is Hartford. Students are housed in single-sex dormitories. 50-acre campus. 56 buildings on campus. Approved or accredited by New England Association of Schools and Colleges and Connecticut Department of Education. Member of National Association of Independent Schools and Secondary School Admission Test Board. Endowment: $85 million. Upper school average class size: 11. Upper school faculty-student ratio: 1:8.

Upper School Student Profile Grade 9: 66 students (66 girls); Grade 10: 78 students (78 girls); Grade 11: 89 students (89 girls); Grade 12: 89 students (89 girls). 60% of students are boarding students. 23 states are represented in upper school student body. 9% are international students. International students from China, Hong Kong, Mexico, and Republic of Korea; 23 other countries represented in student body.

Faculty School total: 57. In upper school: 22 men, 35 women; 36 have advanced degrees.

Subjects Offered Acting, advanced chemistry, advanced computer applications, advanced math, Advanced Placement courses, advanced studio art-AP, African history, algebra, American history, American literature, anatomy and physiology, aquatics, area studies, art history, art history-AP, arts, astronomy, athletics, ballet, biology, biology-AP, British literature, calculus, calculus-AP, career/college preparation, ceramics, chemistry, chemistry-AP, Chinese, Chinese history, classical language, college counseling, college planning, community service, computer applications, computer graphics, computer programming, computer science, creative writing, dance, dance performance, desktop publishing, drama, drama performance, economics, economics and history, engineering, English, English literature, environmental science, environmental science-AP, ethical decision making, ethics, European history, European history-AP, experiential education, expository writing, fitness, foreign language, forensics, French, French language-AP, French literature-AP,

Our Foundation Her Future

Our graduates will shape a changing world.

www.porters.org/admission

PORTER'S
FARMINGTON
Miss Porter's School
Farmington, CT • Since 1843

Miss Porter's School admits students of any race, color, national origin or any other class protected by relevant law.

geometry, global issues, golf, graphic design, health and wellness, history, honors geometry, human rights, international relations, intro to computers, Japanese history, jazz, jewelry making, languages, Latin, Latin American literature, Latin-AP, leadership, mathematics, Middle Eastern history, model United Nations, modern dance, modern European history-AP, multicultural literature, music, music history, music performance, music theory, participation in sports, performing arts, personal finance, photography, physics, physics-AP, pre-calculus, printmaking, psychology, public speaking, science, Shakespeare, social studies, Spanish, Spanish language-AP, Spanish literature-AP, sports, squash, statistics, statistics-AP, student government, studio art, studio art-AP, swimming, swimming test, tennis, textiles, theater, trigonometry, U.S. history, U.S. history-AP, video film production, visual arts, vocal music, Web site design, Western civilization, writing, yoga.

Graduation Requirements Arts and fine arts (art, music, dance, drama), athletics, computer science, English, experiential education, foreign language, leadership, mathematics, science, social studies (includes history). Community service is required.

Special Academic Programs 20 Advanced Placement exams for which test preparation is offered; honors section; independent study; term-away projects; study abroad; ESL.

College Admission Counseling 85 students graduated in 2010; all went to college, including Georgetown University; New York University; Northeastern University; Smith College; Tufts University; Wellesley College. Mean SAT critical reading: 635, mean SAT math: 620, mean SAT writing: 646, mean combined SAT: 1901, mean composite ACT: 27.

Student Life Upper grades have specified standards of dress, student council, honor system. Discipline rests equally with students and faculty.

Summer Programs Enrichment, advancement, sports, art/fine arts programs offered; session focuses on athletics—rowing, soccer, Model UN, leadership; held on campus; accepts girls; open to students from other schools. 60 students usually enrolled. Application deadline: none.

Tuition and Aid Day student tuition: $35,450; 7-day tuition and room/board: $45,100. Tuition installment plan (monthly payment plans, individually arranged payment plans). Merit scholarship grants, need-based scholarship grants available. In 2010–11, 40% of upper-school students received aid. Total amount of financial aid awarded in 2010–11: $3,700,000.

Admissions Traditional secondary-level entrance grade is 9. For fall 2010, 456 students applied for upper-level admission, 192 were accepted, 98 enrolled. ISEE, PSAT and SAT for applicants to grade 11 and 12, SSAT or TOEFL required. Deadline for receipt of application materials: January 15. Application fee required: $50. Interview required.

Athletics Interscholastic: alpine skiing, badminton, basketball, crew, cross-country running, dance, diving, equestrian sports, field hockey, golf, horseback riding, independent competitive sports, lacrosse, skiing (downhill), soccer, softball, squash, swimming and diving, tennis, track and field, ultimate Frisbee, volleyball; intramural: aerobics, aerobics/Nautilus, ballet, climbing, dance, equestrian sports, fencing, fitness, fitness walking, golf, horseback riding, jogging, life saving, martial arts, modern dance, physical fitness, self defense, skiing (downhill), snowboarding, squash, strength & conditioning, swimming and diving, tennis, walking, wall climbing, yoga.

Computers Computers are regularly used in computer applications, desktop publishing, graphic design, graphics, introduction to technology, publications, Web site design classes. Computer network features include on-campus library services, online commercial services, Internet access, wireless campus network, Internet filtering or blocking technology. Campus intranet, student e-mail accounts, and computer access in designated common areas are available to students. Students grades are available online. The school has a published electronic and media policy.

Contact Liz Schmitt, Director of Admission. 860-409-3530. Fax: 860-409-3531. E-mail: liz_schmitt@missporters.org. Web site: www.porters.org.

See Display on page 433 and Close-Up on page 810.

MMI PREPARATORY SCHOOL

154 Centre Street
Freeland, Pennsylvania 18224
Head of School: Mr. Thomas G. Hood

General Information Coeducational day college-preparatory, arts, and technology school. Grades 6–12. Founded: 1879. Setting: small town. Nearest major city is Hazleton. 20-acre campus. 1 building on campus. Approved or accredited by Middle States Association of Colleges and Schools and Pennsylvania Department of Education. Member of National Association of Independent Schools. Endowment: $17 million. Total enrollment: 250. Upper school average class size: 16. Upper school faculty-student ratio: 1:12. Upper School students typically attend 5 days per week. The average school day consists of 6 hours and 30 minutes.

Faculty School total: 28. In upper school: 12 men, 16 women; all have advanced degrees.

Subjects Offered Algebra, American history, American literature, anatomy, art, biology, calculus, chemistry, Chinese, computer programming, computer science, consumer education, creative writing, earth science, economics, English, English literature, environmental science, European history, expository writing, fine arts, geography, geometry, German, government/civics, grammar, health, history, key-

boarding, Latin, mathematics, music, physical education, physics, physiology, psychology, science, social studies, Spanish, speech, statistics, trigonometry, world history, world literature.

Graduation Requirements Analysis and differential calculus, arts and fine arts (art, music, dance, drama), college counseling, computer science, consumer education, economics, English, foreign language, mathematics, physical education (includes health), science, social studies (includes history), speech, independent research project presentation every spring, public speaking assembly project every year.

Special Academic Programs 9 Advanced Placement exams for which test preparation is offered; honors section; independent study; study at local college for college credit; academic accommodation for the gifted; special instructional classes for blind students.

College Admission Counseling 34 students graduated in 2010; all went to college, including Carnegie Mellon University; New York University; Penn State University Park; Saint Joseph's University; Temple University; The University of Scranton. Mean SAT critical reading: 610, mean SAT math: 620, mean SAT writing: 613, mean combined SAT: 1843.

Student Life Upper grades have specified standards of dress, student council, honor system. Discipline rests primarily with faculty.

Summer Programs Remediation, enrichment, advancement, computer instruction programs offered; session focuses on academics; held on campus; accepts boys and girls; open to students from other schools. 100 students usually enrolled. 2011 schedule: June 6 to July 8. Application deadline: May 15.

Tuition and Aid Day student tuition: $11,775. Tuition installment plan (monthly payment plans). Merit scholarship grants, need-based scholarship grants, paying campus jobs available. In 2010–11, 63% of upper-school students received aid; total upper-school merit-scholarship money awarded: $46,500. Total amount of financial aid awarded in 2010–11: $853,000.

Admissions Traditional secondary-level entrance grade is 9. Cognitive Abilities Test and Iowa Tests of Basic Skills required. Deadline for receipt of application materials: none. Application fee required: $25. On-campus interview required.

Athletics Interscholastic: baseball (boys), basketball (b,g), cheering (g), cross-country running (b,g), soccer (b,g), softball (g), tennis (b,g), volleyball (g); intramural: bowling (b,g); coed interscholastic: golf; coed intramural: skiing (downhill), snowboarding. 2 PE instructors.

Computers Computers are regularly used in all classes. Computer network features include on-campus library services, Internet access, Internet filtering or blocking technology. Computer access in designated common areas is available to students. Students grades are available online. The school has a published electronic and media policy.

Contact Kim McNulty, Director of Admissions and Financial Aid. 570-636-1108 Ext. 138. Fax: 570-636-0742. E-mail: kmcnulty@mmiprep.org. Web site: www.mmiprep.org.

MODESTO CHRISTIAN SCHOOL

5901 Sisk Road
Modesto, California 95356
Head of School: Rev. Ralph Sudfeld

General Information Coeducational day college-preparatory, arts, and religious studies school, affiliated with Assembly of God Church. Grades K–12. Founded: 1962. Setting: suburban. Nearest major city is Sacramento. 55-acre campus. 6 buildings on campus. Approved or accredited by Association of Christian Schools International, Western Association of Schools and Colleges, and California Department of Education. Total enrollment: 580. Upper school average class size: 20. Upper school faculty-student ratio: 1:11. There are 177 required school days per year for Upper School students. The average school day consists of 6 hours and 45 minutes.

Upper School Student Profile Grade 9: 65 students (41 boys, 24 girls); Grade 10: 66 students (41 boys, 25 girls); Grade 11: 71 students (37 boys, 34 girls); Grade 12: 78 students (43 boys, 35 girls). 10% of students are members of Assembly of God Church.

Faculty School total: 26. In upper school: 10 men, 16 women; 4 have advanced degrees.

Subjects Offered Advanced biology, algebra, American literature, American sign language, anatomy and physiology, arts, band, biology, biology-AP, calculus-AP, career education, chemistry, church history, consumer education, digital photography, drama, economics, English, English literature, environmental science, fine arts, French language-AP, general math, geometry, grammar, health, history, honors English, keyboarding, mathematics, physical education, physics, political science, pre-algebra, pre-calculus, religion, science, social sciences, social studies, Spanish, Spanish language-AP, speech, studio art-AP, study skills, U.S. government, U.S. history, U.S. history-AP, word processing, world history.

Graduation Requirements Arts and fine arts (art, music, dance, drama), English, foreign language, mathematics, physical education (includes health), religion (includes Bible studies and theology), science, social studies (includes history), speech.

Special Academic Programs 7 Advanced Placement exams for which test preparation is offered; honors section; remedial reading and/or remedial writing; remedial math; programs in English, mathematics, general development for dyslexic students.

College Admission Counseling 68 students graduated in 2009; 66 went to college, including Azusa Pacific University; California Polytechnic State University, San Luis

Obispo; California State University, Stanislaus; Modesto Junior College. Other: 1 went to work, 1 entered military service. Median SAT critical reading: 524, median SAT math: 513, median SAT writing: 505.

Student Life Upper grades have specified standards of dress, student council. Discipline rests primarily with faculty. Attendance at religious services is required.

Tuition and Aid Day student tuition: $7295. Tuition installment plan (monthly payment plans, individually arranged payment plans). Tuition reduction for siblings available. In 2009–10, 5% of upper-school students received aid.

Admissions Traditional secondary-level entrance grade is 9. Admissions testing or Stanford Achievement Test required. Deadline for receipt of application materials: none. Application fee required: $200. On-campus interview required.

Athletics Interscholastic: baseball (boys), basketball (b,g), football (b), golf (b,g), soccer (b,g), softball (g), strength & conditioning (b,g), volleyball (g), wrestling (b); coed interscholastic: fitness, tennis, track and field, weight lifting. 2 PE instructors, 20 coaches.

Computers Computers are regularly used in career education, college planning, typing, yearbook classes. Computer resources include on-campus library services, Internet filtering or blocking technology. Students grades are available online. The school has a published electronic and media policy.

Contact Mrs. Lynn Olson, Admissions Office. 209-343-2225. Fax: 209-543-9930. E-mail: lolson@modestochristian.org. Web site: www.modestochristian.org.

MONSIGNOR DONOVAN HIGH SCHOOL

711 Hooper Avenue
Toms River, New Jersey 08753
Head of School: Edward Gere

General Information Coeducational day college-preparatory school, affiliated with Roman Catholic Church. Grades 9–12. Founded: 1962. Setting: suburban. 1 building on campus. Approved or accredited by Middle States Association of Colleges and Schools, National Catholic Education Association, and New Jersey Department of Education. Total enrollment: 836. Upper school average class size: 30. Upper school faculty-student ratio: 1:15.

Upper School Student Profile Grade 9: 177 students (88 boys, 89 girls); Grade 10: 219 students (103 boys, 116 girls); Grade 11: 218 students (109 boys, 109 girls); Grade 12: 222 students (110 boys, 112 girls). 85% of students are Roman Catholic.

Faculty School total: 54. In upper school: 22 men, 32 women.

Special Academic Programs Advanced Placement exam preparation; honors section; independent study; study at local college for college credit; academic accommodation for the gifted, the musically talented, and the artistically talented; remedial reading and/or remedial writing; remedial math.

College Admission Counseling 232 students graduated in 2010; 218 went to college. Other: 8 went to work, 4 entered military service, 2 had other specific plans.

Student Life Upper grades have uniform requirement, student council, honor system. Discipline rests equally with students and faculty. Attendance at religious services is required.

Tuition and Aid Day student tuition: $10,075. Tuition installment plan (SMART Tuition Payment Plan, monthly payment plans). Merit scholarship grants, need-based scholarship grants, paying campus jobs available. In 2010–11, 20% of upper-school students received aid.

Admissions Traditional secondary-level entrance grade is 9. High School Placement Test (closed version) from Scholastic Testing Service or Scholastic Testing Service High School Placement Test required. Deadline for receipt of application materials: November 10. Application fee required: $50. On-campus interview recommended.

Athletics Interscholastic: baseball (boys), cheering (g), dance (g), football (b), golf (b), ice hockey (b), lacrosse (g), softball (g), wrestling (b); coed interscholastic: basketball, bowling, cross-country running, hiking/backpacking, sailing, skiing (cross-country), snowboarding, soccer, strength & conditioning, surfing, swimming and diving, tennis. 5 PE instructors, 22 coaches, 1 athletic trainer.

Computers Computers are regularly used in all academic classes. Computer network features include on-campus library services, Internet access, wireless campus network, Internet filtering or blocking technology. Student e-mail accounts are available to students. Students grades are available online.

Contact Mrs. Carol A. Gaspartich, Registrar. 732-349-8801 Ext. 2426. Fax: 732-505-8014. E-mail: cgaspartich@mondonhs.com. Web site: www.mondonhs.com.

MONTANA ACADEMY

Marion, Montana
See Special Needs Schools section.

MONTCLAIR COLLEGE PREPARATORY SCHOOL

8071 Sepulveda Boulevard
Van Nuys, California 91402-4420
Head of School: Mr. Mark Simpson

General Information Coeducational boarding and day college-preparatory, arts, and technology school. Grades 7–12. Founded: 1956. Setting: urban. Nearest major city is Los Angeles. Students are housed in coed dormitories. 5-acre campus. 5 buildings on campus. Approved or accredited by Western Association of Schools and Colleges.

Total enrollment: 254. Upper school average class size: 20. Upper school faculty-student ratio: 1:15. Upper School students typically attend 5 days per week. The average school day consists of 6 hours and 30 minutes.

Upper School Student Profile 5% of students are boarding students. 5% are international students. International students from Cameroon, China, Japan, Republic of Korea, and Taiwan; 1 other country represented in student body.

Faculty School total: 45. In upper school: 23 men, 22 women; 12 have advanced degrees; 2 reside on campus.

Subjects Offered Advanced Placement courses.

Graduation Requirements Arts and fine arts (art, music, dance, drama), computer science, English, foreign language, lab science, mathematics, U.S. government, U.S. history.

Special Academic Programs Advanced Placement exam preparation; honors section; independent study; study at local college for college credit; ESL (64 students enrolled).

College Admission Counseling 78 students graduated in 2010; 75 went to college, including Loyola Marymount University; San Francisco State University; University of California, Berkeley; University of California, Los Angeles; University of California, Santa Barbara. Other: 3 had other specific plans.

Student Life Upper grades have uniform requirement, student council, honor system. Discipline rests primarily with faculty.

Summer Programs Remediation, advancement, sports, computer instruction programs offered; session focuses on review courses; held on campus; accepts boys and girls; open to students from other schools. 75 students usually enrolled. 2011 schedule: June 28 to August 4.

Tuition and Aid Day student tuition: $15,000; 7-day tuition and room/board: $39,950. Tuition installment plan (monthly payment plans, 1- and 2-payment plans). Limited need-based financial aid available. In 2010–11, 8% of upper-school students received aid. Total amount of financial aid awarded in 2010–11: $250,000.

Admissions Traditional secondary-level entrance grade is 9. For fall 2010, 150 students applied for upper-level admission, 100 were accepted, 50 enrolled. ISEE or school's own exam required. Deadline for receipt of application materials: none. Application fee required: $100.

Athletics Interscholastic: baseball (boys), basketball (b,g), cross-country running (b,g), flag football (b), football (b), golf (b,g), soccer (b,g), softball (g), volleyball (b,g); coed interscholastic: cheering, cross-country running, golf, horseback riding, tennis; coed intramural: alpine skiing, badminton, dance, dance squad, dance team, skiing (downhill), snowboarding, surfing, weight lifting. 2 PE instructors, 10 coaches, 1 athletic trainer.

Computers Computers are regularly used in all academic, desktop publishing classes. Computer network features include Internet access, wireless campus network, Internet filtering or blocking technology. Campus intranet and computer access in designated common areas are available to students. Students grades are available online.

Contact Mrs. Kandice Neumann, Director of Admissions. 818-787-5290 Ext. 10. Fax: 818-786-3382. E-mail: kneumann@montclairprep.com. Web site: www. montclairprep.org.

MONTCLAIR KIMBERLEY ACADEMY

201 Valley Road
Montclair, New Jersey 07042
Head of School: Mr. Thomas W. Nammack

General Information Coeducational day college-preparatory, arts, and technology school. Grades PK–12. Founded: 1887. Setting: suburban. Nearest major city is New York, NY. 28-acre campus. 1 building on campus. Approved or accredited by Middle States Association of Colleges and Schools and National Lutheran School Accreditation. Member of National Association of Independent Schools and Secondary School Admission Test Board. Endowment: $12 million. Total enrollment: 997. Upper school average class size: 12. Upper school faculty-student ratio: 1:6. Upper School students typically attend 5 days per week. The average school day consists of 6 hours and 30 minutes.

Upper School Student Profile Grade 9: 118 students (56 boys, 62 girls); Grade 10: 113 students (62 boys, 51 girls); Grade 11: 107 students (64 boys, 43 girls); Grade 12: 107 students (48 boys, 59 girls).

Faculty School total: 73. In upper school: 40 men, 33 women; 64 have advanced degrees.

Subjects Offered Acting, advanced chemistry, advanced math, algebra, American history, American literature, architecture, art, astronomy, biology, biology-AP, British literature, calculus, calculus-AP, chemistry, chemistry-AP, Chinese, chorus, communications, concert band, creative writing, dance, digital photography, drama, driver education, ecology, economics, economics-AP, English, English literature, environmental science, ethics, European history, expository writing, fine arts, French, French language-AP, French literature-AP, geometry, government/civics, health, history, Latin, mathematics, music, photography, physical education, physics, physics-AP, post-calculus, Spanish, Spanish language-AP, Spanish literature-AP, statistics-AP, theater, trigonometry, world history, world literature, world wide web design, writing.

Graduation Requirements Arts and fine arts (art, music, dance, drama), English, foreign language, history, mathematics, physical education (includes health), science, swimming, citizenship.

Montclair Kimberley Academy

Special Academic Programs Advanced Placement exam preparation; honors section; independent study; term-away projects; academic accommodation for the gifted.

College Admission Counseling 112 students graduated in 2010; 111 went to college, including Boston College; Boston University; Brown University; Columbia University; Georgetown University; University of Pennsylvania. Other: 1 entered a postgraduate year. Mean SAT critical reading: 630, mean SAT math: 647. 60% scored over 600 on SAT critical reading, 65% scored over 600 on SAT math.

Student Life Upper grades have specified standards of dress, student council, honor system. Discipline rests equally with students and faculty.

Summer Programs Enrichment, sports, art/fine arts, computer instruction programs offered; held on campus; accepts boys and girls; open to students from other schools. 250 students usually enrolled. 2011 schedule: June 27 to August 5. Application deadline: none.

Tuition and Aid Day student tuition: $29,700. Tuition installment plan (Insured Tuition Payment Plan, monthly payment plans, individually arranged payment plans). Need-based scholarship grants available. In 2010–11, 15% of upper-school students received aid. Total amount of financial aid awarded in 2010–11: $1,281,308.

Admissions Traditional secondary-level entrance grade is 9. ISEE or SSAT required. Deadline for receipt of application materials: January 31. Application fee required: $50. On-campus interview required.

Athletics Interscholastic: baseball (boys), basketball (b,g), cheering (g); cross-country running (b,g), dance (b,g), dance team (b,g), fencing (b,g), field hockey (g), football (b), ice hockey (b), lacrosse (b,g), outdoor activities (b,g), physical fitness (b,g), soccer (b,g), softball (g), swimming and diving (b,g), tennis (b,g), track and field (b,g), volleyball (g), winter (indoor) track (b,g), wrestling (b); coed interscholastic: golf. 5 PE instructors, 9 coaches, 2 athletic trainers.

Computers Computer network features include on-campus library services, online commercial services, Internet access, wireless campus network, Internet filtering or blocking technology, 1:1 laptop school, community intranet. Campus intranet and student e-mail accounts are available to students. The school has a published electronic and media policy.

Contact Sarah Rowland, Director of Admissions and Financial Aid. 973-509-7930. Fax: 973-509-4526. E-mail: srowland@mka.org. Web site: www.mka.org.

MONTEREY BAY ACADEMY

783 San Andreas Road
La Selva Beach, California 95076-1907
Head of School: Mr. Timothy Kubrock

General Information Coeducational boarding and day college-preparatory and religious studies school, affiliated with Seventh-day Adventist Church. Grades 9–12. Founded: 1949. Setting: rural. Nearest major city is San Jose. Students are housed in single-sex dormitories. 379-acre campus. 12 buildings on campus. Approved or accredited by Western Association of Schools and Colleges and California Department of Education. Total enrollment: 211. Upper school average class size: 20. Upper school faculty-student ratio: 1:13. There are 180 required school days per year for Upper School students. Upper School students typically attend 5 days per week. The average school day consists of 7 hours.

Upper School Student Profile Grade 9: 29 students (14 boys, 15 girls); Grade 10: 45 students (27 boys, 18 girls); Grade 11; 70 students (34 boys, 36 girls); Grade 12: 67 students (37 boys, 30 girls). 75% of students are boarding students. 75% are state residents. 7 states are represented in upper school student body. 10% are international students. International students from China, Germany, Hong Kong, Japan, Republic of Korea, and Russian Federation. 80% of students are Seventh-day Adventists.

Faculty School total: 16. In upper school: 12 men, 4 women; 7 have advanced degrees; all reside on campus.

Subjects Offered Accounting, Advanced Placement courses, algebra, American literature, biology, calculus, chemistry, choir, Christianity, computer applications, computer literacy, drama, economics, English, English language and composition-AP, geography, geometry, graphics, health, instrumental music, keyboarding, marine biology, photography, physical education, physical science, physics, physiology, piano, pre-algebra, pre-calculus, religion, Spanish, statistics, technology, typing, U.S. government, U.S. history, U.S. history-AP, voice, weight training, woodworking, world history.

Graduation Requirements Arts and fine arts (art, music, dance, drama), business skills (includes word processing), computer science, English, life skills, mathematics, physical education (includes health), science, social studies (includes history), work experience, religious studies for each year in a Seventh-day Adventist School.

Special Academic Programs Advanced Placement exam preparation; ESL (15 students enrolled).

College Admission Counseling 51 students graduated in 2010; 47 went to college, including La Sierra University; Pacific Union College; Southern Adventist University; University of California System; Walla Walla University. Other: 3 went to work, 1 entered military service.

Student Life Upper grades have specified standards of dress, student council. Discipline rests primarily with faculty. Attendance at religious services is required.

Tuition and Aid Day student tuition: $8600–$10,100; 7-day tuition and room/board: $14,700–$23,050. Tuition installment plan (monthly payment plans). Need-based scholarship grants, paying campus jobs available. In 2010–11, 30% of upper-school students received aid. Total amount of financial aid awarded in 2010–11: $300,000.

Admissions Traditional secondary-level entrance grade is 9. For fall 2010, 225 students applied for upper-level admission, 220 were accepted, 211 enrolled. TOEFL required. Deadline for receipt of application materials: July 15. Application fee required: $50. Interview recommended.

Athletics Interscholastic: basketball (boys, girls), flag football (b,g), softball (b,g), volleyball (b,g). 2 PE instructors, 7 coaches.

Computers Computers are regularly used in accounting, mathematics, science, typing, yearbook classes. Computer resources include Internet access, Internet filtering or blocking technology. Students grades are available online. The school has a published electronic and media policy.

Contact Ms. Donna J. Baerg, Vice Principal for Academic Affairs. 831-728-1481 Ext. 1218. Fax: 831-728-1485. E-mail: academics@montereybayacademy.org. Web site: www.montereybayacademy.org.

MONTE VISTA CHRISTIAN SCHOOL

2 School Way
Watsonville, California 95076
Head of School: Mr. Stephen Sharp

General Information Coeducational boarding and day college-preparatory, arts, religious studies, technology, and ESL school, affiliated with Christian faith. Boarding grades 9–12, day grades 6–12. Founded: 1926. Setting: rural. Nearest major city is San Jose. Students are housed in single-sex dormitories. 100-acre campus. 27 buildings on campus. Approved or accredited by Association of Christian Schools International, The Association of Boarding Schools, and Western Association of Schools and Colleges. Endowment: $1 million. Total enrollment: 808. Upper school average class size: 17. Upper school faculty-student ratio: 1:9. There are 180 required school days per year for Upper School students. Upper School students typically attend 5 days per week. The average school day consists of 7 hours and 5 minutes.

Upper School Student Profile Grade 9: 150 students (75 boys, 75 girls); Grade 10: 153 students (75 boys, 78 girls); Grade 11: 145 students (75 boys, 70 girls); Grade 12: 150 students (73 boys, 77 girls). 22% of students are boarding students. 80% are state residents. 1 state is represented in upper school student body. 20% are international students. International students from China, Hong Kong, Japan, Republic of Korea, Taiwan, and Thailand; 4 other countries represented in student body. 80% of students are Christian faith.

Faculty School total: 68. In upper school: 23 men, 23 women; 15 have advanced degrees; 15 reside on campus.

Subjects Offered 3-dimensional art, 3-dimensional design, advanced chemistry, advanced computer applications, advanced TOEFL/grammar, algebra, American government, American literature, anatomy, art, ASB Leadership, auto mechanics, band, basic skills, Bible studies, biology, biology-AP, calculus, calculus-AP, calligraphy, campus ministry, career/college preparation, carpentry, ceramics, chemistry, chemistry-AP, choir, choral music, Christian doctrine, Christian ethics, Christian scripture, Christian studies, Christianity, computer applications, computer education, computer graphics, computer literacy, computer science, computer skills, culinary arts, desktop publishing, digital imaging, drafting, drama, drama performance, drawing, drawing and design, earth science, economics, English, English literature, English-AP, environmental science, equestrian sports, ESL, European history-AP, fine arts, French, geology, geometry, government/civics, grammar, guitar, health, history, honors algebra, honors English, honors geometry, honors world history, human anatomy, industrial arts, Japanese, keyboarding, learning lab, marine biology, mathematics, music, orchestra, photography, physical education, physics, physiology, pre-calculus, psychology, religion, SAT preparation, science, social studies, Spanish, statistics-AP, student government, trigonometry, U.S. government and politics-AP, U.S. history, U.S. history-AP, vocal music, Web site design, woodworking, world history, world literature, wrestling, yearbook.

Graduation Requirements American government, arts and fine arts (art, music, dance, drama), Bible, biology, computer science, economics, English, foreign language, geometry, health education, keyboarding, mathematics, physical education (includes health), science, U.S. history, world history.

Special Academic Programs Advanced Placement exam preparation; honors section; special instructional classes for students with mild learning differences; ESL (12 students enrolled).

College Admission Counseling 138 students graduated in 2010; 136 went to college, including University of California, Berkeley; University of California, Davis; University of California, Los Angeles; University of California, San Diego; University of Wisconsin–Madison. Other: 2 went to work. Median SAT critical reading: 513, median SAT math: 571, median SAT writing: 528, median composite ACT: 23.

Student Life Upper grades have specified standards of dress, student council. Discipline rests primarily with faculty. Attendance at religious services is required.

Summer Programs Remediation, enrichment, ESL, sports programs offered; session focuses on academics, ESL, and equestrian sports; held on campus; accepts boys and girls; open to students from other schools. 200 students usually enrolled. 2011 schedule: July 10 to August 19. Application deadline: May 15.

Tuition and Aid Day student tuition: $8700; 7-day tuition and room/board: $34,550–$35,550. Tuition installment plan (FACTS Tuition Payment Plan, individually arranged payment plans, three payments (enrollment, 7/1 and 12/1)). Tuition reduction for siblings, need-based scholarship grants available. In 2010–11, 5% of upper-school students received aid. Total amount of financial aid awarded in 2010–11: $500,000.

Admissions Traditional secondary-level entrance grade is 9. SSAT or TOEFL required. Deadline for receipt of application materials: February 15. Application fee required: $80. Interview required.

Athletics Interscholastic: baseball (boys), basketball (b,g), cheering (g), cross-country running (b,g), football (b), golf (b,g), soccer (b,g), softball (g), swimming and diving (b,g), tennis (b,g), track and field (b,g), volleyball (b,g), wrestling (b); intramural: baseball (b), basketball (b,g), cross-country running (b,g), equestrian sports (b,g), field hockey (b,g), football (b), golf (b,g), soccer (b,g), swimming and diving (b,g), tennis (b,g), track and field (b,g), volleyball (b,g), weight lifting (b,g), wrestling (b); coed interscholastic: aquatics, diving, drill team, horseback riding. 6 PE instructors, 14 coaches, 2 athletic trainers.

Computers Computers are regularly used in desktop publishing, ESL, foreign language, mathematics, writing classes. Computer network features include on-campus library services, Internet access, wireless campus network, Internet filtering or blocking technology, iPads. Student e-mail accounts and computer access in designated common areas are available to students. Students grades are available online. The school has a published electronic and media policy.

Contact Mr. Peter C. Gieseke, Director of Admission. 831-722-8178 Ext. 194. Fax: 831-722-0361. E-mail: petergieseke@mvcs.com. Web site: mvcs.org.

MONTGOMERY BELL ACADEMY

4001 Harding Road
Nashville, Tennessee 37205
Head of School: Bradford Gioia

General Information Boys' day college-preparatory and arts school. Grades 7–12. Founded: 1867. Setting: urban. 43-acre campus. 9 buildings on campus. Approved or accredited by Southern Association of Colleges and Schools, Southern Association of Independent Schools, and Tennessee Association of Independent Schools. Member of National Association of Independent Schools and Secondary School Admission Test Board. Endowment: $60.1 million. Total enrollment: 712. Upper school average class size: 14. Upper school faculty-student ratio: 1:8. There are 180 required school days per year for Upper School students. Upper School students typically attend 5 days per week. The average school day consists of 7 hours and 20 minutes.

Upper School Student Profile Grade 9: 135 students (135 boys); Grade 10: 124 students (124 boys); Grade 11: 113 students (113 boys); Grade 12: 117 students (117 boys).

Faculty School total: 90. In upper school: 67 men, 21 women; 71 have advanced degrees.

Subjects Offered Advanced Placement courses, algebra, American history, American history-AP, American literature, American literature-AP, art, art history, art history-AP, biology, biology-AP, calculus, calculus-AP, chemistry, chemistry-AP, Chinese, computer programming, computer science, computer science-AP, drama, earth science, economics, English, English literature, environmental science-AP, European history, European history-AP, fine arts, French, French language-AP, French literature-AP, French-AP, geography, geology, geometry, German, German-AP, government/civics, grammar, Greek, history, Latin, Latin-AP, mathematics, music, music history, music theory, music theory-AP, physical education, physics, physics-AP, science, social studies, Spanish, Spanish-AP, speech, statistics, statistics-AP, theater, trigonometry, U.S. government and politics-AP, U.S. history-AP, world history, world history-AP, writing.

Graduation Requirements Arts and fine arts (art, music, dance, drama), English, foreign language, mathematics, physical education (includes health), science, social studies (includes history).

Special Academic Programs Advanced Placement exam preparation; honors section; term-away projects; study abroad.

College Admission Counseling 99 students graduated in 2009; 98 went to college, including Auburn University; Sewanee: The University of the South; Southern Methodist University; The University of Tennessee; University of Georgia; Vanderbilt University. Other: 1 had other specific plans. Mean SAT critical reading: 636, mean SAT math: 651, mean SAT writing: 648, mean combined SAT: 1935, mean composite ACT: 28.

Student Life Upper grades have specified standards of dress, student council, honor system. Discipline rests primarily with faculty.

Tuition and Aid Day student tuition: $18,900. Tuition installment plan (monthly payment plans, Dewar Tuition Refund Plan). Need-based scholarship grants available. In 2009–10, 21% of upper-school students received aid. Total amount of financial aid awarded in 2009–10: $1,480,000.

Admissions Traditional secondary-level entrance grade is 9. For fall 2009, 96 students applied for upper-level admission, 35 were accepted, 28 enrolled. ISEE required. Deadline for receipt of application materials: February 1. Application fee required: $50. On-campus interview required.

Athletics Interscholastic: baseball, basketball, bowling, crew, cross-country running, diving, football, Frisbee, golf, hockey, ice hockey, lacrosse, riflery, rock climbing, rowing, soccer, track and field, wrestling; intramural: backpacking, baseball, basketball, cheering, climbing, crew, flag football, football, Frisbee, hiking/backpacking, independent competitive sports, outdoor activities, paddle tennis, soccer, strength & conditioning, table tennis, track and field, weight training. 2 PE instructors, 6 coaches, 2 athletic trainers.

Computers Computers are regularly used in all academic classes. Computer network features include on-campus library services, online commercial services, Internet

access, wireless campus network, Internet filtering or blocking technology. Student e-mail accounts are available to students. Students grades are available online.

Contact Mr. Greg Ferrell, Director, Admission and Financial Aid. 615-369-5311 Ext. 251. Fax: 615-297-0271. E-mail: ferrelg@montgomerybell.com. Web site: www.montgomerybell.com.

MONT'KIARA INTERNATIONAL SCHOOL

22 Jalan Kiara
Mont Kiara
Kuala Lumpur 50480, Malaysia
Head of School: Linda Moran

General Information Coeducational day college-preparatory school. Grades 1–12. Founded: 1994. Setting: suburban. 6-acre campus. 3 buildings on campus. Approved or accredited by Western Association of Schools and Colleges. Language of instruction: English. Total enrollment: 933. Upper school average class size: 20. Upper school faculty-student ratio: 1:6.

Upper School Student Profile Grade 9: 56 students (18 boys, 38 girls); Grade 10: 53 students (21 boys, 32 girls); Grade 11: 55 students (35 boys, 20 girls); Grade 12: 44 students (26 boys, 18 girls).

Faculty School total: 102. In upper school: 24 men, 23 women; 28 have advanced degrees.

Special Academic Programs International Baccalaureate program; ESL (9 students enrolled).

College Admission Counseling 58 students graduated in 2009; 45 went to college, including The University of British Columbia; University of Richmond. Other: 5 went to work, 5 entered military service, 3 had other specific plans. Mean SAT critical reading: 565, mean SAT math: 595, mean SAT writing: 532, mean combined SAT: 1692. 85% scored over 600 on SAT critical reading, 76% scored over 600 on SAT math, 91% scored over 600 on SAT writing, 84% scored over 1800 on combined SAT.

Student Life Upper grades have uniform requirement, student council. Discipline rests primarily with faculty.

Tuition and Aid Day student tuition: 71,990 Malaysian ringgits.

Admissions Traditional secondary-level entrance grade is 9. For fall 2009, 14 students applied for upper-level admission, 9 were accepted, 9 enrolled. Admissions testing, any standardized test and Math Placement Exam required. Deadline for receipt of application materials: none. Application fee required: 650 Malaysian ringgits. On-campus interview required.

Athletics Interscholastic: baseball (boys, girls), basketball (b,g), danceline (b,g), martial arts (b,g), rugby (g), soccer (b,g), softball (b,g), swimming and diving (b,g), tennis (b,g), track and field (b,g), volleyball (b,g), wall climbing (b,g); coed interscholastic: aerobics/dance, aquatics. 4 PE instructors.

Computers Computer network features include on-campus library services, online commercial services, Internet access, wireless campus network, Internet filtering or blocking technology. Student e-mail accounts are available to students. Students grades are available online. The school has a published electronic and media policy.

Contact Mohanaeswari Nadarajah, Executive Secretary, Admissions. 603-2093 8604. Fax: 603-2903 6045. E-mail: mohana@mkis.edu.my. Web site: www.mkis.edu.my.

MONTVERDE ACADEMY

17235 Seventh Street
Montverde, Florida 34756
Head of School: Mr. Kasey C. Kesselring

General Information Coeducational boarding and day college-preparatory and arts school. Boarding grades 7–PG, day grades PK–PG. Founded: 1912. Setting: small town. Nearest major city is Orlando. Students are housed in single-sex dormitories. 125-acre campus. 25 buildings on campus. Approved or accredited by Florida Council of Independent Schools, Southern Association of Colleges and Schools, Southern Association of Independent Schools, and The Association of Boarding Schools. Member of National Association of Independent Schools. Endowment: $8 million. Total enrollment: 700. Upper school average class size: 20. Upper school faculty-student ratio: 1:12. Upper School students typically attend 5 days per week.

Upper School Student Profile Grade 9: 46 students (19 boys, 27 girls); Grade 10: 77 students (42 boys, 35 girls); Grade 11: 133 students (91 boys, 42 girls); Grade 12: 136 students (85 boys, 51 girls); Postgraduate: 2 students (2 boys). 65% of students are boarding students. 30% are state residents. 9 states are represented in upper school student body. 65% are international students. International students from China, Germany, Puerto Rico, Republic of Korea, Thailand, and Viet Nam; 34 other countries represented in student body.

Faculty School total: 57. In upper school: 14 men, 19 women; 20 have advanced degrees; 38 reside on campus.

Subjects Offered 20th century history, 3-dimensional art, accounting, acting, advanced computer applications, algebra, American history, American literature, anatomy, anatomy and physiology, ancient world history, art, art history, art history-AP, biology, biology-AP, business, business law, calculus, calculus-AP, ceramics, chemistry, chemistry-AP, choral music, clayworking, computer applications, computer graphics, computer science, concert choir, crafts, desktop publishing, drama, East Asian history, economics, English, English language and composition-AP,

English literature, English literature and composition-AP, ESL, ethics, European history, European history-AP, finance, fitness, forensics, French, French language-AP, geography, geometry, government, health, history, history of music, honors algebra, honors English, honors geometry, honors U.S. history, international affairs, introduction to theater, jazz band, keyboarding, marine biology, marketing, mathematics, modern world history, music appreciation, music theory-AP, photo shop, photography, physical education, physics, physics-AP, physiology, piano, politics, pre-calculus, programming, SAT/ACT preparation, science, Spanish, Spanish language-AP, statistics-AP, studio art, studio art-AP, study skills, symphonic band, technical theater, theater history, trigonometry, U.S. government and politics-AP, U.S. history, U.S. history-AP, Web site design, woodworking, world history, world history-AP.

Graduation Requirements Arts and fine arts (art, music, dance, drama), computer science, electives, English, foreign language, mathematics, physical education (includes health), science, social studies (includes history), international students are not required to take a foreign language if their native language is not English.

Special Academic Programs Advanced Placement exam preparation; honors section; ESL (106 students enrolled).

College Admission Counseling 71 students graduated in 2009; 70 went to college. Other: 1 entered military service. Median SAT critical reading: 423, median SAT math: 542, median SAT writing: 442, median combined SAT: 1364, median composite ACT: 18.

Student Life Upper grades have uniform requirement, student council, honor system. Discipline rests equally with students and faculty.

Tuition and Aid Day student tuition: $10,170; 7-day tuition and room/board: $29,500. Tuition installment plan (monthly payment plans). Tuition reduction for siblings, need-based scholarship grants available. In 2009–10, 18% of upper-school students received aid. Total amount of financial aid awarded in 2009–10: $1,000,000.

Admissions Traditional secondary-level entrance grade is 9. ISEE or SSAT required. Deadline for receipt of application materials: none. Application fee required: $50. Interview recommended.

Athletics Interscholastic: baseball (boys), basketball (b,g), cheering (g), cross-country running (b,g), golf (b,g), soccer (b,g), tennis (b,g), track and field (b,g), volleyball (g), weight lifting (b,g); intramural: basketball (b,g), dance team (b,g), flag football (b), paddle tennis (b,g), soccer (b,g), softball (b,g), table tennis (b,g), tennis (b,g); coed interscholastic: equestrian sports, horseback riding, track and field, weight lifting; coed intramural: aerobics/dance, aquatics, basketball, bicycling, billiards, canoeing/kayaking, equestrian sports, fishing, fitness, fitness walking, Frisbee, horseback riding, jogging, juggling, kayaking, paddle tennis, physical fitness, physical training, running, soccer, strength & conditioning, ultimate Frisbee, walking, water skiing, yoga. 3 PE instructors, 16 coaches, 7 athletic trainers.

Computers Computers are regularly used in all academic, computer applications, desktop publishing, information technology, introduction to technology, keyboarding, language development, library skills, newspaper, programming, publications classes. Computer network features include on-campus library services, online commercial services, Internet access, wireless campus network, Internet filtering or blocking technology. Computer access in designated common areas is available to students. Students grades are available online. The school has a published electronic and media policy.

Contact Mrs. Robin Revis-Pyke, Dean of Admission and Financial Aid. 407-469-2561 Ext. 204. Fax: 407-469-3711. E-mail: robin.pyke@montverde.org. Web site: www.montverde.org.

MOORESTOWN FRIENDS SCHOOL

110 East Main Street
Moorestown, New Jersey 08057
Head of School: Mr. Laurence Van Meter

General Information Coeducational day college-preparatory, arts, religious studies, and technology school, affiliated with Society of Friends. Grades PS–12. Founded: 1785. Setting: suburban. Nearest major city is Philadelphia, PA. 48-acre campus. 9 buildings on campus. Approved or accredited by Middle States Association of Colleges and Schools and New Jersey Department of Education. Member of National Association of Independent Schools. Endowment: $6.8 million. Total enrollment: 708. Upper school average class size: 18. Upper school faculty-student ratio: 1:9. There are 169 required school days per year for Upper School students. Upper School students typically attend 5 days per week.

Upper School Student Profile Grade 9: 70 students (33 boys, 37 girls); Grade 10: 71 students (30 boys, 41 girls); Grade 11: 74 students (33 boys, 41 girls); Grade 12: 74 students (39 boys, 35 girls). 3% of students are members of Society of Friends.

Faculty School total: 90. In upper school: 23 men, 36 women; 43 have advanced degrees.

Subjects Offered Algebra, American history, American literature, art, art history, biology, calculus, ceramics, chemistry, Chinese, community service, computer programming, computer science, creative writing, drama, driver education, earth science, economics, English, English literature, environmental science, ethics, European history, expository writing, fine arts, French, geometry, government/civics, grammar, health, history, mathematics, music, philosophy, photography, physical education, physics, psychology, religion, science, social studies, Spanish, theater, trigonometry, world history, writing.

Graduation Requirements Arts and fine arts (art, music, dance, drama), English, foreign language, mathematics, physical education (includes health), science, senior project, social studies (includes history). Community service is required.

Special Academic Programs Advanced Placement exam preparation; honors section; independent study; term-away projects; study abroad.

College Admission Counseling 72 students graduated in 2010; all went to college, including Dickinson College; Drexel University; Lehigh University; Syracuse University; The George Washington University; Villanova University. Mean SAT critical reading: 616, mean SAT math: 627, mean SAT writing: 631, mean combined SAT: 1874.

Student Life Upper grades have specified standards of dress, student council, honor system. Discipline rests primarily with faculty. Attendance at religious services is required.

Tuition and Aid Day student tuition: $22,350. Tuition installment plan (Academic Management Services Plan, Tuition Refund Plan). Need-based scholarship grants, need-based loans, tuition reduction for children of faculty and staff available. In 2010–11, 35% of upper-school students received aid. Total amount of financial aid awarded in 2010–11: $1,372,175.

Admissions Traditional secondary-level entrance grade is 9. For fall 2010, 72 students applied for upper-level admission, 41 were accepted, 30 enrolled. ERB CTP required. Deadline for receipt of application materials: none. Application fee required: $45. On-campus interview required.

Athletics Interscholastic: baseball (boys), basketball (b,g), crew (b,g), cross-country running (b,g), fencing (b,g), field hockey (g), independent competitive sports (b,g), lacrosse (g), physical training (b,g), soccer (b,g), swimming and diving (b,g), tennis (b,g); intramural: floor hockey (b), roller hockey (b), street hockey (b), weight training (b,g); coed interscholastic: golf. 5 PE instructors, 24 coaches, 1 athletic trainer.

Computers Computers are regularly used in English, foreign language, mathematics, music, science classes. Computer network features include on-campus library services, Internet access, wireless campus network, Internet filtering or blocking technology. Campus intranet, student e-mail accounts, and computer access in designated common areas are available to students. Students grades are available online.

Contact Karin B. Miller, Director of Admission and Financial Aid. 856-235-2900 Ext. 227. Fax: 856-235-6684. E-mail: kmiller@mfriends.org. Web site: www.mfriends.org.

MOOSEHEART HIGH SCHOOL

255 James J. Davis Drive
Mooseheart, Illinois 60539
Head of School: Mr. Gary Lee Urwiler

General Information Coeducational boarding and day college-preparatory, general academic, arts, business, vocational, religious studies, bilingual studies, technology, nursing, and cosmetology school, affiliated with Protestant faith, Roman Catholic Church; primarily serves underachievers and students in dysfunctional family situations. Grades K–12. Founded: 1913. Setting: small town. Nearest major city is Aurora. Students are housed in family homes. 1,000-acre campus. 40 buildings on campus. Approved or accredited by North Central Association of Colleges and Schools and Illinois Department of Education. Total enrollment: 206. Upper school average class size: 13. Upper school faculty-student ratio: 1:6. There are 176 required school days per year for Upper School students. Upper School students typically attend 5 days per week. The average school day consists of 6 hours and 45 minutes.

Upper School Student Profile Grade 6: 6 students (3 boys, 3 girls); Grade 7: 22 students (14 boys, 8 girls); Grade 8: 20 students (17 boys, 3 girls); Grade 9: 35 students (23 boys, 12 girls); Grade 10: 25 students (12 boys, 13 girls); Grade 11: 29 students (9 boys, 20 girls); Grade 12: 25 students (14 boys, 11 girls). 95% of students are Protestant, Roman Catholic.

Faculty School total: 45. In upper school: 9 men, 11 women; 5 have advanced degrees.

Special Academic Programs Remedial reading and/or remedial writing; remedial math.

College Admission Counseling 25 students graduated in 2009.

Student Life Upper grades have specified standards of dress, student council, honor system. Discipline rests primarily with faculty. Attendance at religious services is required.

Admissions Traditional secondary-level entrance grade is 9. Mathematics proficiency exam required. Deadline for receipt of application materials: March. No application fee required. Interview recommended.

Athletics Interscholastic: basketball (boys, girls), drill team (b,g), football (b), JROTC drill (b,g), track and field (b,g), volleyball (g). 2 PE instructors, 10 coaches.

Computers Computers are regularly used in word processing classes. Computer resources include on-campus library services, Internet access, wireless campus network, Internet filtering or blocking technology. The school has a published electronic and media policy.

Contact Kyle Rife, Director of Admission. 630-906-3631 Ext. 3631. Fax: 630-906-3634 Ext. 3634. E-mail: krife@mooseheart.org.

MORAVIAN ACADEMY

4313 Green Pond Road
Bethlehem, Pennsylvania 18020
Head of School: George N. King Jr.

General Information Coeducational day college-preparatory school, affiliated with Moravian Church. Grades PK–12. Founded: 1742. Setting: rural. Nearest major city is Philadelphia. 120-acre campus. 8 buildings on campus. Approved or accredited by Middle States Association of Colleges and Schools, Pennsylvania Association of Independent Schools, and Pennsylvania Department of Education. Member of National Association of Independent Schools and Secondary School Admission Test Board. Endowment: $9.7 million. Total enrollment: 764. Upper school average class size: 15. Upper school faculty-student ratio: 1:7. There are 173 required school days per year for Upper School students. Upper School students typically attend 5 days per week. The average school day consists of 7 hours and 15 minutes.

Upper School Student Profile Grade 9: 78 students (37 boys, 41 girls); Grade 10: 74 students (35 boys, 39 girls); Grade 11: 65 students (22 boys, 43 girls); Grade 12: 70 students (30 boys, 40 girls).

Faculty School total: 100. In upper school: 21 men, 20 women; 40 have advanced degrees.

Subjects Offered Acting, advanced biology, advanced chemistry, Advanced Placement courses, algebra, American history, American history-AP, American literature, anatomy, ancient history, ancient world history, art, bell choir, biology, biology-AP, botany, calculus, calculus-AP, ceramics, chemistry, chemistry-AP, Chinese, Chinese history, community service, drama, drawing, driver education, ecology, economics, English, English language-AP, English literature, English literature-AP, environmental science, ethics, European history, European history-AP, film, fine arts, French, French language-AP, geometry, government, health, history, honors geometry, Latin American history, mathematics, Middle East, music, painting, photography, physical education, physics, playwriting, poetry, probability and statistics, religion, science, short story, Spanish, Spanish language-AP, statistics, statistics-AP, theater, trigonometry, U.S. history-AP, woodworking, world history, world literature, zoology.

Graduation Requirements Arts and fine arts (art, music, dance, drama), English, foreign language, mathematics, physical education (includes health), religion (includes Bible studies and theology), science, social studies (includes history), service project.

Special Academic Programs 11 Advanced Placement exams for which test preparation is offered; honors section; independent study; study at local college for college credit.

College Admission Counseling 77 students graduated in 2010; 75 went to college, including Bucknell University; Columbia University; Cornell University; Lehigh University; Muhlenberg College; Wellesley College. Other: 2 had other specific plans. Mean SAT critical reading: 655, mean SAT math: 676, mean SAT writing: 653.

Student Life Upper grades have specified standards of dress, student council. Discipline rests equally with students and faculty. Attendance at religious services is required.

Summer Programs Remediation, enrichment, art/fine arts programs offered; session focuses on enrichment; held on campus; accepts boys and girls; open to students from other schools. 2011 schedule: June 20 to July 29.

Tuition and Aid Day student tuition: $21,570. Tuition installment plan (monthly payment plans). Need-based scholarship grants available. In 2010–11, 23% of upper-school students received aid. Total amount of financial aid awarded in 2010–11: $907,000.

Admissions Traditional secondary-level entrance grade is 9. For fall 2010, 55 students applied for upper-level admission, 51 were accepted, 34 enrolled. ERB and Otis-Lennon School Ability Test required. Deadline for receipt of application materials: none. Application fee required: $65. On-campus interview required.

Athletics Interscholastic: baseball (boys), basketball (b,g), field hockey (g), football (b), lacrosse (b), soccer (b,g), softball (g), tennis (b,g), track and field (b,g), wrestling (b); coed interscholastic: cross-country running, golf, swimming and diving. 3 PE instructors, 15 coaches, 1 athletic trainer.

Computers Computers are regularly used in all academic, art, English, foreign language, history, mathematics, music, science classes. Computer resources include on-campus library services, Internet access, wireless campus network. The school has a published electronic and media policy.

Contact Daniel Axford, Director of Upper School Admissions. 610-691-1600. Fax: 610-691-3354. E-mail: daxford@moravianacademy.org. Web site: www.moravianacademy.org.

See Display below and Close-Up on page 812.

MOREAU CATHOLIC HIGH SCHOOL

27170 Mission Boulevard
Hayward, California 94544
Head of School: Mr. Terry Lee

General Information Coeducational day college-preparatory, arts, business, religious studies, and technology school, affiliated with Roman Catholic Church. Grades

Moreau Catholic High School

9–12. Founded: 1965. Setting: suburban. Nearest major city is Oakland. 14-acre campus. 6 buildings on campus. Approved or accredited by National Catholic Education Association, Western Association of Schools and Colleges, Western Catholic Education Association, and California Department of Education. Endowment: $2.5 million. Total enrollment: 930. Upper school average class size: 27. Upper school faculty-student ratio: 1:18. Upper School students typically attend 5 days per week. The average school day consists of 6 hours and 35 minutes.

Upper School Student Profile Grade 9: 227 students (104 boys, 123 girls); Grade 10: 227 students (107 boys, 120 girls); Grade 11: 242 students (124 boys, 118 girls); Grade 12: 234 students (124 boys, 110 girls). 72% of students are Roman Catholic.

Faculty School total: 60. In upper school: 25 men, 32 women; 34 have advanced degrees.

Subjects Offered Advanced Placement courses, aerobics, algebra, American Civil War, American history, American literature, anatomy, art, art history, ASB Leadership, astronomy, athletics, biology, biology-AP, business, business law, business skills, calculus, calculus-AP, campus ministry, ceramics, cheerleading, chemistry, choral music, Christian ethics, Christian scripture, Christianity, church history, community service, computer education, computer math, computer programming, computer science, concert band, creative writing, drafting, drama, drama performance, driver education, earth science, economics, electronics, engineering, English, English literature, English/composition-AP, ethics, ethics and responsibility, European history, expository writing, fine arts, French, French-AP, geometry, government-AP, government/civics, grammar, health, health education, history, history of the Catholic Church, home economics, honors algebra, honors English, honors geometry, honors U.S. history, honors world history, human biology, instrumental music, jazz band, jazz ensemble, journalism, marching band, mathematics, mechanical drawing, media studies, moral and social development, moral theology, music, music appreciation, newspaper, physical education, physics, physics-AP, physiology, psychology, religion, science, sculpture, social sciences, social studies, Spanish, Spanish language-AP, speech, sports medicine, sports science, student government, student publications, symphonic band, the Sixties, theater, theology, trigonometry, typing, U.S. government, U.S. government and politics-AP, U.S. history, U.S. history-AP, weight training, world history, world literature, writing, yearbook.

Graduation Requirements Arts and fine arts (art, music, dance, drama), computer science, English, foreign language, mathematics, physical education (includes health), religion (includes Bible studies and theology), science, social sciences, social studies (includes history). Community service is required.

Special Academic Programs Advanced Placement exam preparation; honors section; special instructional classes for Saints and Scholars program for students with documented learning disabilities who require accommodations.

College Admission Counseling 232 students graduated in 2010; 230 went to college, including California State University; Saint Mary's College of California; Santa Clara University; Stanford University; University of California, Berkeley; University of San Francisco. Other: 2 entered military service. Mean SAT critical reading: 555, mean SAT math: 559, mean composite ACT: 23.

Student Life Upper grades have specified standards of dress, student council, honor system. Discipline rests primarily with faculty. Attendance at religious services is required.

Summer Programs Remediation, enrichment, sports programs offered; session focuses on enrichment and remediation; held on campus; accepts boys and girls; open to students from other schools. 245 students usually enrolled. 2011 schedule: June 21 to July 30. Application deadline: May 31.

Tuition and Aid Day student tuition: $10,944. Tuition installment plan (FACTS Tuition Payment Plan). Tuition reduction for siblings, merit scholarship grants, need-based scholarship grants, paying campus jobs available. In 2010–11, 35% of upper-school students received aid. Total amount of financial aid awarded in 2010–11: $775,000.

Admissions Traditional secondary-level entrance grade is 9. For fall 2010, 312 students applied for upper-level admission, 295 were accepted, 232 enrolled. Scholastic Testing Service High School Placement Test required. Deadline for receipt of application materials: January 8. Application fee required: $90. On-campus interview required.

Athletics Interscholastic: aquatics (boys, girls), badminton (b,g), baseball (b), basketball (b,g), cheering (g), cross-country running (b,g), dance squad (g), football (b), golf (b,g), soccer (b,g), softball (g), swimming and diving (b,g), tennis (b,g), track and field (b,g), volleyball (b,g); intramural: lacrosse (g); coed interscholastic: aerobics/dance, modern dance; coed intramural: equestrian sports, skiing (downhill), strength & conditioning. 5 PE instructors, 50 coaches, 1 athletic trainer.

Computers Computers are regularly used in career exploration, college planning, English, foreign language, history, journalism, keyboarding, mathematics, newspaper, religious studies, science, technology, theology, yearbook classes. Computer network features include on-campus library services, online commercial services, Internet access, wireless campus network, PowerSchool grade program, 1:1 student laptop program (every student at Moreau has a laptop). Campus intranet, student e-mail accounts, and computer access in designated common areas are available to students. Students grades are available online. The school has a published electronic and media policy.

Contact Patricia Bevilacqua, Admissions Assistant. 510-881-4320. Fax: 510-581-5669. E-mail: apply@moreaucatholic.org. Web site: www.moreaucatholic.org.

MORGAN PARK ACADEMY

2153 West 111th Street
Chicago, Illinois 60643
Head of School: Dr. Catherine Raaflaub

General Information Coeducational day college-preparatory, arts, and technology school. Grades PK–12. Founded: 1873. Setting: urban. 20-acre campus. 5 buildings on campus. Approved or accredited by Independent Schools Association of the Central States and Illinois Department of Education. Member of National Association of Independent Schools. Endowment: $905,450. Total enrollment: 449. Upper school average class size: 14. Upper school faculty-student ratio: 1:6. There are 170 required school days per year for Upper School students. Upper School students typically attend 5 days per week. The average school day consists of 6 hours and 50 minutes.

Upper School Student Profile Grade 9: 31 students (11 boys, 20 girls); Grade 10: 37 students (13 boys, 24 girls); Grade 11: 37 students (19 boys, 18 girls); Grade 12: 37 students (13 boys, 24 girls).

Faculty School total: 59. In upper school: 9 men, 13 women; 15 have advanced degrees.

Subjects Offered Accounting, algebra, American history, American literature, art, art history, biology, calculus, chemistry, computer programming, computer science, creative writing, current events, drama, driver education, English, English language-AP, English literature, English literature-AP, expository writing, fine arts, French, general science, geography, geometry, health, history, humanities, journalism, mathematics, music, physical education, physics, political science, science, social studies, Spanish, speech, studio art, trigonometry, word processing, world history, world literature, writing.

Graduation Requirements Arts and fine arts (art, music, dance, drama), English, foreign language, history, lab science, mathematics, physical education (includes health).

Special Academic Programs Advanced Placement exam preparation; honors section; independent study; study abroad; academic accommodation for the gifted, the musically talented, and the artistically talented.

College Admission Counseling 39 students graduated in 2009; 38 went to college, including Brown University; Northwestern University; University of Illinois; University of Michigan; Washington University in St. Louis. Other: 1 went to work. Median composite ACT: 27. 50% scored over 600 on SAT critical reading, 80% scored over 600 on SAT math, 57% scored over 26 on composite ACT.

Student Life Upper grades have specified standards of dress, student council, honor system. Discipline rests equally with students and faculty.

Tuition and Aid Day student tuition: $17,800. Tuition installment plan (FACTS Tuition Payment Plan). Tuition reduction for siblings, merit scholarship grants, need-based scholarship grants available. In 2009–10, 25% of upper-school students received aid; total upper-school merit-scholarship money awarded: $55,000. Total amount of financial aid awarded in 2009–10: $400,000.

Admissions Traditional secondary-level entrance grade is 9. For fall 2009, 65 students applied for upper-level admission, 40 were accepted, 30 enrolled. Admissions testing, ISEE and writing sample required. Deadline for receipt of application materials: none. Application fee required: $50. On-campus interview required.

Athletics Interscholastic: baseball (boys), basketball (b,g), cheering (b,g), golf (b,g), soccer (b,g), softball (g), tennis (b,g), volleyball (g); coed interscholastic: golf; coed intramural: archery, badminton, bowling, football, paddle tennis, skiing (cross-country), weight lifting. 4 PE instructors, 4 coaches.

Computers Computers are regularly used in art, economics, English, foreign language, graphic arts, history, humanities, journalism, mathematics, news writing, newspaper, science, Spanish, yearbook classes. Computer network features include on-campus library services, online commercial services, Internet access.

Contact Adriana Mourgelas, Director of Admissions. 773-881-6700 Ext. 246. Fax: 773-881-8409. E-mail: amourgelas@morganparkacademy.org. Web site: www.MorganParkAcademy.org.

MORRISTOWN-BEARD SCHOOL

70 Whippany Road
Morristown, New Jersey 07960
Head of School: Dr. Alex D. Curtis, PhD

General Information Coeducational day college-preparatory and arts school. Grades 6–12. Founded: 1891. Setting: suburban. Nearest major city is New York, NY. 22-acre campus. 11 buildings on campus. Approved or accredited by Middle States Association of Colleges and Schools, New Jersey Association of Independent Schools, and New Jersey Department of Education. Member of National Association of Independent Schools and Secondary School Admission Test Board. Endowment: $10 million. Total enrollment: 548. Upper school average class size: 12. Upper school faculty-student ratio: 1:7. Upper School students typically attend 5 days per week. The average school day consists of 7 hours.

Upper School Student Profile Grade 6: 42 students (23 boys, 19 girls); Grade 7: 54 students (31 boys, 23 girls); Grade 8: 55 students (34 boys, 21 girls); Grade 9: 95 students (49 boys, 46 girls); Grade 10: 106 students (58 boys, 48 girls); Grade 11: 97 students (50 boys, 47 girls); Grade 12: 94 students (43 boys, 51 girls).

Faculty School total: 93. In upper school: 54 have advanced degrees.

Subjects Offered 20th century history, acting, advanced chemistry, advanced math, Advanced Placement courses, advanced studio art-AP, African history, African literature, African studies, algebra, American history, American legal systems, American studies, anatomy and physiology, ancient world history, architecture, art, art history, Asian studies, astronomy, astrophysics, Bible as literature, biology, biology-AP, calculus, calculus-AP, career exploration, ceramics, chemistry, chemistry-AP, choir, chorus, community service, computer programming, computer science, computer science-AP, computer skills, computer studies, constitutional law, creative writing, dance, drama, drawing, earth science, ecology, engineering, English, English-AP, fine arts, French, geometry, health, instrumental music, journalism, Latin, Middle Eastern history, mythology, nature writers, painting, photography, physical education, physical science, physics, physics-AP, public speaking, regional literature, rite of passage, Spanish, Spanish-AP, speech, statistics, statistics-AP, studio art-AP, the comic tradition, theater, trigonometry, U.S. history-AP, women in literature, world history.

Graduation Requirements Arts and fine arts (art, music, dance, drama), English, foreign language, mathematics, physical education (includes health), science, service learning/internship, social studies (includes history). Community service is required.

Special Academic Programs Advanced Placement exam preparation; honors section; independent study; term-away projects; study abroad.

College Admission Counseling 102 students graduated in 2010; 100 went to college, including Muhlenberg College. Other: 2 entered a postgraduate year. Mean SAT critical reading: 572, mean SAT math: 598, mean SAT writing: 595, mean composite ACT: 24.

Student Life Upper grades have specified standards of dress, student council, honor system. Discipline rests equally with students and faculty.

Summer Programs Enrichment, advancement, sports, art/fine arts, computer instruction programs offered; session focuses on traditional day camp; held on campus; accepts boys and girls; open to students from other schools. 700 students usually enrolled. 2011 schedule: June 22 to August 4.

Tuition and Aid Day student tuition: $30,140. Tuition installment plan (Tuition Management Services). Merit scholarship grants, need-based scholarship grants available. In 2010–11, 13% of upper-school students received aid; total upper-school merit-scholarship money awarded: $85,500. Total amount of financial aid awarded in 2010–11: $1,000,000.

Admissions Traditional secondary-level entrance grade is 9. For fall 2010, 340 students applied for upper-level admission, 202 were accepted, 128 enrolled. ISEE or SSAT required. Deadline for receipt of application materials: February 7. Application fee required: $55. On-campus interview required.

Athletics Interscholastic: baseball (boys), basketball (b,g), field hockey (g), football (b), ice hockey (b,g), lacrosse (b,g), skiing (downhill) (b,g), soccer (b,g), softball (g), swimming and diving (b,g), tennis (b,g), track and field (b,g), volleyball (g); coed interscholastic: alpine skiing, cross-country running, dance, golf, swimming and diving, track and field, yoga; coed intramural: dance, figure skating, fitness, mountain biking, Nautilus, physical fitness. 4 PE instructors, 3 coaches, 1 athletic trainer.

Computers Computers are regularly used in architecture, art, English, foreign language, history, mathematics, music, science classes. Computer network features include on-campus library services, online commercial services, Internet access, wireless campus network, Internet filtering or blocking technology, Jstor, Jerseycat. Student e-mail accounts are available to students.

Contact Mrs. Barbara Luperi, Admission Assistant. 973-539-3032. Fax: 973-539-1590. E-mail: bluperi@mbs.net. Web site: www.mbs.net.

MOTHER CABRINI HIGH SCHOOL

701 Fort Washington Avenue
New York, New York 10040
Head of School: Mrs. Rose K. McTague

General Information Girls' day college-preparatory school, affiliated with Roman Catholic Church. Grades 9–12. Founded: 1899. Setting: urban. 2-acre campus. 1 building on campus. Approved or accredited by Middle States Association of Colleges and Schools, National Catholic Education Association, New York State Board of Regents, and New York Department of Education. Total enrollment: 296. Upper school average class size: 22. Upper school faculty-student ratio: 1:13. There are 180 required school days per year for Upper School students. Upper School students typically attend 5 days per week. The average school day consists of 6 hours and 22 minutes.

Upper School Student Profile Grade 9: 64 students (64 girls); Grade 10: 69 students (69 girls); Grade 11: 87 students (87 girls); Grade 12: 76 students (76 girls). 75% of students are Roman Catholic.

Faculty School total: 28. In upper school: 7 men, 21 women; 20 have advanced degrees.

Subjects Offered Accounting, algebra, American literature, anatomy and physiology, art, art history, basketball, chemistry, computer applications, computer science, English literature, environmental science, forensics, geometry, guidance, health, honors algebra, honors geometry, literature, peer counseling, photo shop, physics, pre-algebra, pre-calculus, religion, softball, Spanish, Spanish literature, Spanish-AP, speech, U.S. government, U.S. history-AP, volleyball, world literature.

Graduation Requirements Art, electives, English, language, mathematics, music, physical education (includes health), science, social studies (includes history).

Special Academic Programs 3 Advanced Placement exams for which test preparation is offered; honors section; study at local college for college credit.

College Admission Counseling 88 students graduated in 2009; all went to college, including Cornell University; Dartmouth College; Fairfield University; Fordham University; John Jay College of Criminal Justice of the City University of New York.

Student Life Upper grades have uniform requirement, student council. Discipline rests equally with students and faculty. Attendance at religious services is required.

Tuition and Aid Day student tuition: $7490. Tuition installment plan (SMART Tuition Payment Plan). Tuition reduction for siblings, merit scholarship grants, need-based scholarship grants, paying campus jobs available. Total upper-school merit-scholarship money awarded for 2009–10: $109,000.

Admissions Traditional secondary-level entrance grade is 9. For fall 2009, 364 students applied for upper-level admission, 306 were accepted, 64 enrolled. Catholic High School Entrance Examination, Gates MacGinite Reading Tests and Otis-Lennon School Ability Test required. Deadline for receipt of application materials: none. No application fee required. Interview recommended.

Athletics Interscholastic: basketball, cheering, softball, volleyball; intramural: aerobics/dance, running.

Computers Computers are regularly used in computer applications, introduction to technology, Web site design classes. Computer resources include on-campus library services, Internet access, Internet filtering or blocking technology. Campus intranet and student e-mail accounts are available to students. The school has a published electronic and media policy.

Contact Director of Recruitment and Public Relations. 212-923-9114. Fax: 212-923-3960. E-mail: info@cabrinihs.org. Web site: www.cabrinihs.com.

MOTHER MCAULEY HIGH SCHOOL

3737 West 99th Street
Chicago, Illinois 60655-3133
Head of School: Dr. Christine M. Melone

General Information Girls' day college-preparatory, arts, religious studies, and technology school, affiliated with Roman Catholic Church. Grades 9–12. Founded: 1846. Setting: urban. 21-acre campus. 2 buildings on campus. Approved or accredited by Mercy Secondary Education Association, National Catholic Education Association, North Central Association of Colleges and Schools, The College Board, and Illinois Department of Education. Endowment: $2 million. Total enrollment: 1,362. Upper school average class size: 25. Upper school faculty-student ratio: 1:17. There are 180 required school days per year for Upper School students. Upper School students typically attend 5 days per week. The average school day consists of 6 hours and 30 minutes.

Upper School Student Profile Grade 9: 319 students (319 girls); Grade 10: 350 students (350 girls); Grade 11: 323 students (323 girls); Grade 12: 370 students (370 girls). 87% of students are Roman Catholic.

Faculty School total: 92. In upper school: 12 men, 80 women; 56 have advanced degrees.

Subjects Offered Anatomy and physiology, art history, art history-AP, calculus-AP, ceramics, chemistry-AP, English, English literature, English literature and composition-AP, European history-AP, first aid, French, French-AP, general science, geography, geometry, geometry with art applications, global issues, graphic design, history of the Catholic Church, honors algebra, honors English, honors geometry, honors U.S. history, honors world history, introduction to theater, journalism, Latin, Latin-AP, Life of Christ, marching band, media literacy, music appreciation, newspaper, orchestra, painting, photography, physical education, physics, play production, scripture, Spanish, Spanish-AP, speech, studio art, studio art-AP, theater, theology, U.S. history, U.S. history-AP, U.S. literature, Web site design, wind ensemble, world history, world history-AP, yearbook.

Graduation Requirements Art history, English, lab science, language, mathematics, music, physical education (includes health), social sciences, speech, technology, theology.

Special Academic Programs Advanced Placement exam preparation; honors section; study at local college for college credit.

College Admission Counseling 363 students graduated in 2010; 362 went to college, including Eastern Illinois University; Illinois State University; Loyola University Chicago; University of Illinois at Chicago; University of Illinois at Urbana–Champaign. Other: 1 went to work. Mean composite ACT: 23.

Student Life Upper grades have uniform requirement, student council. Discipline rests primarily with faculty. Attendance at religious services is required.

Summer Programs Remediation, enrichment, advancement, sports, art/fine arts, computer instruction programs offered; session focuses on academics; held on campus; accepts girls; open to students from other schools. 200 students usually enrolled. 2011 schedule: June 13 to July 23. Application deadline: June 10.

Tuition and Aid Day student tuition: $8500. Tuition installment plan (monthly payment plans, individually arranged payment plans). Tuition reduction for siblings, merit scholarship grants, need-based scholarship grants, paying campus jobs available. In 2010–11, 30% of upper-school students received aid; total upper-school merit-scholarship money awarded: $30,000. Total amount of financial aid awarded in 2010–11: $550,000.

Admissions Traditional secondary-level entrance grade is 9. For fall 2010, 364 students applied for upper-level admission, 360 were accepted, 319 enrolled. ACT-Explore required. Deadline for receipt of application materials: August 15. Application fee required: $150.

Athletics Interscholastic: basketball, cross-country running, diving, golf, independent competitive sports, soccer, softball, swimming and diving, tennis, track and field, volleyball, water polo; intramural: aerobics, basketball, bowling, Frisbee, softball, touch football, ultimate Frisbee, volleyball. 2 PE instructors, 20 coaches, 1 athletic trainer.

Computers Computers are regularly used in accounting, art, basic skills, business education, drafting, drawing and design, English, foreign language, French, graphics, journalism, Latin, mathematics, music, newspaper, photography, science, social sciences, Spanish, theater, Web site design, writing, yearbook classes. Computer network features include on-campus library services, Internet access, wireless campus network, Internet filtering or blocking technology. Student e-mail accounts and computer access in designated common areas are available to students. Students grades are available online. The school has a published electronic and media policy. **Contact** Mrs. Kathryn Klyczek, Director of Admissions and Financial Aid. 773-881-6534. Fax: 773-429-4235. E-mail: kklyczek@mothermcauley.org. Web site: www.mothermcauley.org.

MOUNDS PARK ACADEMY

2051 Larpenteur Avenue East
St. Paul, Minnesota 55109
Head of School: Michael Downs
General Information Coeducational day college-preparatory, arts, bilingual studies, and technology school. Grades PK–12. Founded: 1982. Setting: suburban. 32-acre campus. 1 building on campus. Approved or accredited by Independent Schools Association of the Central States and Minnesota Department of Education. Member of National Association of Independent Schools. Endowment: $2.6 million. Total enrollment: 625. Upper school average class size: 16. Upper school faculty-student ratio: 1:9.
Upper School Student Profile Grade 9: 64 students (33 boys, 31 girls); Grade 10: 65 students (38 boys, 27 girls); Grade 11: 52 students (21 boys, 31 girls); Grade 12: 69 students (35 boys, 34 girls).
Faculty School total: 76. In upper school: 11 men, 23 women; 16 have advanced degrees.
Subjects Offered Algebra, American history, American literature, anatomy, area studies, art, biology, calculus, ceramics, chemistry, chorus, contemporary women writers, creative writing, debate, design, drama, drawing, economics, English literature, fine arts, French, geometry, health, history, independent study, instrumental music, law, literature, mathematics, media, men's studies, multicultural literature, music, painting, photography, physical education, physical science, physics, physiology, psychology, public policy issues and action, science, senior seminar, social sciences, social studies, Spanish, speech, statistics, theater, trigonometry, vocal music, Western civilization, world literature, writing.
Graduation Requirements Arts and fine arts (art, music, dance, drama), English, foreign language, health education, mathematics, physical education (includes health), science, senior seminar, social studies (includes history), senior performance. Community service is required.
Special Academic Programs 4 Advanced Placement exams for which test preparation is offered; honors section; independent study; study at local college for college credit.
College Admission Counseling 69 students graduated in 2009; 66 went to college, including Carleton College; Princeton University; St. Olaf College; The Colorado College; University of Minnesota, Twin Cities Campus; University of Wisconsin–Madison. Other: 3 had other specific plans. Mean SAT critical reading: 628, mean SAT math: 613, mean SAT writing: 607, mean combined SAT: 1848, mean composite ACT: 27.
Student Life Upper grades have specified standards of dress, student council. Discipline rests equally with students and faculty.
Tuition and Aid Day student tuition: $19,960. Tuition installment plan (monthly payment plans, 2-payment plan, 3-payment plan, 8-payment plan, 12-payment plan). Need-based scholarship grants available. In 2009–10, 10% of upper-school students received aid.
Admissions Traditional secondary-level entrance grade is 9. For fall 2009, 31 students applied for upper-level admission, 20 were accepted, 13 enrolled. Writing sample required. Deadline for receipt of application materials: March 2. Application fee required: $50. Interview required.
Athletics Interscholastic: baseball (boys), basketball (b,g), cross-country running (b,g), dance team (g), equestrian sports (g), football (b), golf (b,g), hockey (b), nordic skiing (b,g), skiing (cross-country) (b,g), soccer (b,g), softball (g), swimming and diving (g), tennis (b,g), track and field (b,g), volleyball (g). 6 PE instructors.
Computers Computers are regularly used in English, foreign language, mathematics, science, social studies classes. Computer network features include on-campus library services, online commercial services, Internet access, wireless campus network, Internet filtering or blocking technology. Student e-mail accounts are available to students. Students grades are available online. The school has a published electronic and media policy. **Contact** Linda Hoopes, Director of Admission. 651-748-5577. Fax: 651-748-5534. E-mail: lhoopes@moundsparkacademy.org. Web site: www. moundsparkacademy.org.

MOUNTAIN VIEW ACADEMY

360 South Shoreline Boulevard
Mountain View, California 94041
Head of School: Mr. Dan Meidinger
General Information Coeducational day college-preparatory, arts, business, religious studies, bilingual studies, and technology school, affiliated with Seventh-day Adventist Church. Grades 9–12. Founded: 1923. Setting: urban. Nearest major city is San Jose. 3-acre campus. 4 buildings on campus. Approved or accredited by Western Association of Schools and Colleges and California Department of Education. Total enrollment: 142. Upper school average class size: 20. Upper school faculty-student ratio: 1:12. There are 180 required school days per year for Upper School students. Upper School students typically attend 5 days per week. The average school day consists of 7 hours.
Upper School Student Profile Grade 9: 32 students (15 boys, 17 girls); Grade 10: 38 students (18 boys, 20 girls); Grade 11: 40 students (17 boys, 23 girls); Grade 12: 34 students (22 boys, 12 girls). 70% of students are Seventh-day Adventists.
Faculty School total: 13. In upper school: 6 men, 6 women; 6 have advanced degrees.
Graduation Requirements Algebra, American government, American history, arts and fine arts (art, music, dance, drama), biology, computer literacy, economics, electives, English, English composition, English literature, foreign language, geometry, health, home economics, religion (includes Bible studies and theology), world history, community service-25 hours per year.
Special Academic Programs Advanced Placement exam preparation; honors section; accelerated programs; remedial math.
College Admission Counseling 55 students graduated in 2009; 54 went to college, including De Anza College; Foothill College; La Sierra University; Pacific Union College; San Jose State University; University of California, San Diego. Other: 1 went to work. Median SAT critical reading: 525, median SAT math: 570, median composite ACT: 22. 21% scored over 600 on SAT critical reading, 28% scored over 600 on SAT math.
Student Life Upper grades have specified standards of dress, student council, honor system. Discipline rests primarily with faculty. Attendance at religious services is required.
Tuition and Aid Day student tuition: $10,950–$11,725. Tuition installment plan (monthly payment plans). Merit scholarship grants, need-based scholarship grants, paying campus jobs available. In 2009–10, 35% of upper-school students received aid; total upper-school merit-scholarship money awarded: $15,000. Total amount of financial aid awarded in 2009–10: $48,500.
Admissions Traditional secondary-level entrance grade is 9. For fall 2009, 160 students applied for upper-level admission, 143 were accepted, 142 enrolled. SLEP for foreign students or TOEFL required. Deadline for receipt of application materials: April 30. No application fee required. Interview required.
Athletics Interscholastic: basketball (boys, girls), flag football (b,g), soccer (b,g), softball (b,g), volleyball (b,g); intramural: basketball (b,g), flag football (b,g), softball (b,g), volleyball (b,g). 1 PE instructor.
Computers Computers are regularly used in basic skills classes. Computer network features include Internet access. The school has a published electronic and media policy. **Contact** Alyce Schales, Registrar. 650-967-2324 Ext. 24. Fax: 650-967-6886. E-mail: aschales@mtnviewacademy.org. Web site: www.mtnviewacademy.org.

MOUNT CARMEL HIGH SCHOOL

6410 South Dante
Chicago, Illinois 60637
Head of School: Rev. Carl J. Markelz, O. Carm.
General Information Boys' day college-preparatory, arts, business, religious studies, and technology school, affiliated with Roman Catholic Church. Grades 9–12. Founded: 1900. Setting: urban. 3-acre campus. 5 buildings on campus. Approved or accredited by National Catholic Education Association, North Central Association of Colleges and Schools, The College Board, and Illinois Department of Education. Endowment: $5.1 million. Total enrollment: 790. Upper school average class size: 25. Upper school faculty-student ratio: 1:19. There are 176 required school days per year for Upper School students. Upper School students typically attend 5 days per week. The average school day consists of 6 hours and 15 minutes.
Upper School Student Profile Grade 9: 194 students (194 boys); Grade 10: 201 students (201 boys); Grade 11: 202 students (202 boys); Grade 12: 193 students (193 boys). 89% of students are Roman Catholic.
Faculty School total: 59. In upper school: 42 men, 11 women; 44 have advanced degrees.
Subjects Offered Art appreciation, art history, business, computer science, economics, English, French, general science, geography, government/civics, health, history of music, Latin, mathematics, physical education, psychology, religion, science, social sciences, social studies, Spanish, speech, theology.
Graduation Requirements Computer science, English, foreign language, mathematics, physical education (includes health), religion (includes Bible studies and theology), science, social sciences, social studies (includes history). Community service is required.
Special Academic Programs Advanced Placement exam preparation; honors section; remedial reading and/or remedial writing; remedial math.

College Admission Counseling 195 students graduated in 2010; 191 went to college, including DePaul University; Eastern Illinois University; Marquette University; Northern Illinois University; University of Illinois; University of Illinois at Chicago. Other: 1 went to work, 1 entered military service, 2 entered a postgraduate year. Mean SAT critical reading: 556, mean SAT math: 528, mean SAT writing: 569, mean combined SAT: 1654, mean composite ACT: 22. 35% scored over 600 on SAT critical reading, 35% scored over 600 on SAT math, 35% scored over 600 on SAT writing, 35% scored over 1800 on combined SAT, 14% scored over 26 on composite ACT.
Student Life Upper grades have specified standards of dress, student council. Discipline rests primarily with faculty. Attendance at religious services is required.
Summer Programs Remediation programs offered; session focuses on make-up credits for failed classes, skills refresher courses; held on campus; accepts boys; not open to students from other schools. 170 students usually enrolled. 2011 schedule: June 11 to July 19.
Tuition and Aid Day student tuition: $8600. Tuition installment plan (The Tuition Plan, FACTS Tuition Payment Plan). Tuition reduction for siblings, bursaries, merit scholarship grants, need-based scholarship grants, paying campus jobs available. In 2010–11, 33% of upper-school students received aid; total upper-school merit-scholarship money awarded: $100,000. Total amount of financial aid awarded in 2010–11: $500,000.
Admissions Traditional secondary-level entrance grade is 9. For fall 2010, 279 students applied for upper-level admission, 264 were accepted, 195 enrolled. ACT-Explore required. Deadline for receipt of application materials: none. Application fee required: $300. Interview recommended.
Athletics Interscholastic: baseball, basketball, bowling, cross-country running, football, golf, ice hockey, lacrosse, rugby, soccer, swimming and diving, tennis, track and field, volleyball, water polo, weight training, wrestling; intramural: basketball, football, soccer, softball, volleyball, weight lifting. 3 PE instructors, 27 coaches, 1 athletic trainer.
Computers Computers are regularly used in art, business, business education, college planning, data processing, desktop publishing, economics, English, foreign language, geography, graphic design, humanities, journalism, library, mathematics, psychology, science, technology classes. Computer network features include on-campus library services, Internet access, numerous databases, word processing, PowerPoint, spreadsheet training.
Contact Mr. John Stimler, Principal. 773-324-1020 Ext. 272. Fax: 773-324-9235. E-mail: jstimler@mchs.org. Web site: www.mchs.org.

MOUNT CARMEL SCHOOL

PO Box 500006
Saipan, Northern Mariana Islands 96950
Head of School: Margaret C. DelaCruz
General Information Coeducational day college-preparatory, general academic, religious studies, and technology school, affiliated with Roman Catholic Church. Grades 1–12. Founded: 1952. Setting: rural. Nearest major city is Hagatna, GU, Guam. 5-acre campus. 1 building on campus. Approved or accredited by Western Association of Schools and Colleges and Northern Mariana Islands Department of Education. Total enrollment: 378. Upper school average class size: 25. Upper school faculty-student ratio: 1:20. There are 180 required school days per year for Upper School students. Upper School students typically attend 5 days per week. The average school day consists of 6 hours and 5 minutes.
Upper School Student Profile Grade 9: 41 students (19 boys, 22 girls); Grade 10: 28 students (16 boys, 12 girls); Grade 11: 40 students (19 boys, 21 girls); Grade 12: 37 students (21 boys, 16 girls). 95% of students are Roman Catholic.
Faculty School total: 20. In upper school: 3 men, 6 women; 4 have advanced degrees.
Subjects Offered Advanced math, algebra, American government, American history, American history-AP, art, biology, British literature, calculus, calculus-AP, campus ministry, Catholic belief and practice, chemistry, Christian doctrine, Christian scripture, civics, composition, computer applications, computer science, drama, English, English literature, English literature-AP, foreign language, gardening, geometry, history of the Catholic Church, HTML design, independent study, Japanese, literature, media production, moral theology, physical education, physics, pre-calculus, Spanish, state history, theology, trigonometry, world history, world literature, world religions, yearbook.
Graduation Requirements Algebra, American history, art, biology, British literature, Catholic belief and practice, chemistry, Christian ethics, Christian scripture, church history, civics, composition, computer applications, English, English literature, foreign language, geometry, physical education (includes health), physics, theology, U.S. literature, world history.
Special Academic Programs 3 Advanced Placement exams for which test preparation is offered; independent study.
College Admission Counseling 45 students graduated in 2009; 37 went to college, including Kapiolani Community College. Other: 4 went to work, 3 entered military service.
Student Life Upper grades have uniform requirement, student council, honor system. Discipline rests primarily with faculty. Attendance at religious services is required.
Tuition and Aid Day student tuition: $3530. Tuition installment plan (monthly payment plans). Tuition reduction for siblings, merit scholarship grants, need-based scholarship grants available. In 2009–10, 4% of upper-school students received aid;

total upper-school merit-scholarship money awarded: $1000. Total amount of financial aid awarded in 2009–10: $3000.
Admissions Traditional secondary-level entrance grade is 9. For fall 2009, 79 students applied for upper-level admission, 79 were accepted, 78 enrolled. Deadline for receipt of application materials: none. Application fee required: $50.
Athletics Interscholastic: aquatics (boys, girls), basketball (b,g), canoeing/kayaking (b,g), flag football (b), ocean paddling (b,g), softball (g), track and field (b,g), volleyball (b,g); intramural: badminton (b,g), basketball (b,g), flag football (b,g), floor hockey (b,g), soccer (b,g), volleyball (b,g); coed interscholastic: aquatics, ocean paddling, volleyball; coed intramural: badminton, soccer, volleyball. 1 PE instructor.
Computers Computers are regularly used in all academic, computer applications classes. Computer network features include on-campus library services, online commercial services, Internet access, wireless campus network, Internet filtering or blocking technology. Campus intranet is available to students. Students grades are available online. The school has a published electronic and media policy.
Contact Mrs. Lourdes T. Mendiola, Principal. 670-234-6184. Fax: 670-235-4751. E-mail: mendiola.lou@gmail.com. Web site: www.mtcarmel-edu.net.

MT. DE SALES ACADEMY

851 Orange Street
Macon, Georgia 31201
Head of School: Mr. David Held
General Information Coeducational day college-preparatory, arts, and technology school, affiliated with Roman Catholic Church. Grades 6–12. Founded: 1876. Setting: urban. 10 buildings on campus. Approved or accredited by Georgia Independent School Association, Mercy Secondary Education Association, Southern Association of Colleges and Schools, Southern Association of Independent Schools, and Georgia Department of Education. Endowment: $400,000. Total enrollment: 656. Upper school average class size: 17. Upper school faculty-student ratio: 1:10. There are 180 required school days per year for Upper School students. Upper School students typically attend 5 days per week. The average school day consists of 7 hours.
Upper School Student Profile Grade 6: 43 students (23 boys, 20 girls); Grade 7: 91 students (41 boys, 50 girls); Grade 8: 77 students (41 boys, 36 girls); Grade 9: 123 students (50 boys, 73 girls); Grade 10: 112 students (51 boys, 61 girls); Grade 11: 108 students (58 boys, 50 girls); Grade 12: 102 students (47 boys, 55 girls). 42% of students are Roman Catholic.
Faculty School total: 68. In upper school: 34 men, 34 women; 41 have advanced degrees.
Subjects Offered 20th century world history, advanced biology, advanced chemistry, advanced computer applications, advanced math, Advanced Placement courses, advanced studio art-AP, African American studies, algebra, American Civil War, American government, American history, American history-AP, American literature, American literature-AP, anatomy and physiology, art history-AP, astronomy, athletic training, band, biology, biology-AP, British literature, calculus, calculus-AP, chemistry, chemistry-AP, choral music, chorus, Christian education, Christian scripture, computer applications, computer multimedia, computer programming-AP, drawing and design, economics, English, English language and composition-AP, English literature and composition-AP, European history-AP, forensics, French, government, government and politics-AP, health, Holocaust studies, honors algebra, honors English, honors geometry, New Testament, physical education, physics-AP, portfolio art, pre-calculus, programming, psychology, psychology-AP, Spanish-AP, speech, statistics, statistics-AP, studio art, U.S. government, U.S. government and politics-AP, U.S. history, U.S. history-AP, visual arts, World War II, yearbook.
Special Academic Programs Honors section.
College Admission Counseling 101 students graduated in 2010; all went to college, including Georgia Institute of Technology; Georgia Southern University; Macon State College; University of Georgia. Mean SAT critical reading: 670, mean SAT math: 660, mean SAT writing: 650, mean combined SAT: 1980.
Student Life Upper grades have specified standards of dress, student council, honor system. Discipline rests primarily with faculty. Attendance at religious services is required.
Tuition and Aid Tuition installment plan (FACTS Tuition Payment Plan). Merit scholarship grants, need-based scholarship grants available. In 2010–11, 30% of upper-school students received aid; total upper-school merit-scholarship money awarded: $122,000. Total amount of financial aid awarded in 2010–11: $813,771.
Admissions Traditional secondary-level entrance grade is 9. For fall 2010, 214 students applied for upper-level admission, 174 were accepted, 132 enrolled. Stanford Achievement Test or Terra Nova-CTB required. Deadline for receipt of application materials: none. Application fee required: $50.
Athletics Interscholastic: baseball (boys), basketball (b,g), cheering (g), cross-country running (b,g), dance team (g), fitness (b,g), football (b), physical fitness (b,g), physical training (b,g), soccer (b,g), softball (g), swimming and diving (b,g), track and field (b,g), weight training (b,g).
Computers Computers are regularly used in all classes. Computer network features include on-campus library services, Internet access, wireless campus network. Campus intranet and student e-mail accounts are available to students. Students grades are available online. The school has a published electronic and media policy.
Contact 912-751-3240. Fax: 912-751-3241. Web site: www.mountdesales.net.

MOUNT MERCY ACADEMY

88 Red Jacket Parkway
Buffalo, New York 14220
Head of School: Mrs. Paulette C. Gaske
General Information Girls' day college-preparatory, arts, and religious studies school, affiliated with Roman Catholic Church. Grades 9–12. Founded: 1904. Setting: urban. 2 buildings on campus. Approved or accredited by Middle States Association of Colleges and Schools and New York Department of Education. Total enrollment: 273. Upper school average class size: 20. Upper school faculty-student ratio: 1:20. There are 180 required school days per year for Upper School students. Upper School students typically attend 5 days per week. The average school day consists of 6 hours and 43 minutes.
Upper School Student Profile Grade 9: 75 students (75 girls); Grade 10: 54 students (54 girls); Grade 11: 76 students (76 girls); Grade 12: 68 students (68 girls). 97% of students are Roman Catholic.
Faculty School total: 39. In upper school: 6 men, 30 women.
Special Academic Programs Advanced Placement exam preparation; honors section; independent study.
College Admission Counseling 108 students graduated in 2010; 97 went to college. Other: 1 entered military service.
Student Life Upper grades have uniform requirement, student council, honor system. Discipline rests equally with students and faculty. Attendance at religious services is required.
Summer Programs Enrichment programs offered; session focuses on Regents Review; held on campus; accepts boys and girls; open to students from other schools. 2011 schedule: August.
Tuition and Aid Day student tuition: $7800. Tuition installment plan (FACTS Tuition Payment Plan). Tuition reduction for siblings, merit scholarship grants, need-based scholarship grants, paying campus jobs available.
Admissions Admissions testing or High School Placement Test (closed version) from Scholastic Testing Service required. Deadline for receipt of application materials: none. Application fee required: $20. On-campus interview required.
Athletics Interscholastic: aquatics, basketball, bowling, cross-country running, golf, lacrosse, modern dance, skiing (downhill), soccer, softball, swimming and diving, tennis, volleyball. 2 PE instructors, 13 coaches.
Computers Computers are regularly used in art, business, desktop publishing, keyboarding, study skills, yearbook classes. Computer network features include on-campus library services, Internet access, wireless campus network, Internet filtering or blocking technology. Campus intranet, student e-mail accounts, and computer access in designated common areas are available to students. Students grades are available online. The school has a published electronic and media policy.
Contact Mrs. Jeanne Burvid, Director of Admissions. 716-825-8796 Ext. 511. Fax: 716-825-0976. E-mail: jburvid@mtmercy.org. Web site: www.mtmercy.org.

MOUNT MICHAEL BENEDICTINE SCHOOL

22520 Mount Michael Road
Elkhorn, Nebraska 68022-3400
Head of School: Mr. Tom Ridder
General Information Boys' boarding and day college-preparatory, arts, religious studies, and technology school, affiliated with Roman Catholic Church. Grades 9–12. Founded: 1970. Setting: suburban. Nearest major city is Omaha. Students are housed in single-sex dormitories and private homes. 440-acre campus. 1 building on campus. Approved or accredited by European Council of International Schools, National Catholic Education Association, North Central Association of Colleges and Schools, The College Board, and Nebraska Department of Education. Endowment: $275,000. Total enrollment: 206. Upper school average class size: 12. Upper school faculty-student ratio: 1:7. There are 180 required school days per year for Upper School students. Upper School students typically attend 5 days per week. The average school day consists of 7 hours and 25 minutes.
Upper School Student Profile Grade 9: 48 students (48 boys); Grade 10: 43 students (43 boys); Grade 11: 60 students (60 boys); Grade 12: 48 students (48 boys). 8% of students are boarding students. 79% are state residents. 4 states are represented in upper school student body. 9% are international students. International students from Bahamas, China, Republic of Korea, Rwanda, and Spain. 84% of students are Roman Catholic.
Faculty School total: 28. In upper school: 20 men, 8 women; 26 have advanced degrees; 9 reside on campus.
Subjects Offered Accounting, Advanced Placement courses, algebra, American history, American history-AP, American literature, architectural drawing, art, band, Basic programming, basketball, bioethics, DNA and culture, biology, biology-AP, business, business skills, calculus-AP, ceramics, chemistry, chemistry-AP, chorus, Christian doctrine, Christian ethics, Christian scripture, Christianity, community service, computer programming, computer science, critical writing, drafting, drama, economics, English, English language-AP, English literature, English literature and composition-AP, European history, European history-AP, French, French language-AP, geography, geometry, government/civics, health education, Hebrew scripture, history of the Catholic Church, journalism, keyboarding, Latin, math applications, mathematics, music, physical education, physics, physics-AP,

psychology-AP, reading, science, social sciences, social studies, Spanish, speech, theater, theology, trigonometry, weight training, Western civilization, world religions, wrestling, writing, yearbook.
Graduation Requirements Advanced math, algebra, American government, American history, anatomy and physiology, biology, biology-AP, career/college preparation, chemistry, Christian studies, computer science, economics, economics and history, English, foreign language, geometry, government, mathematics, physical education (includes health), physics, pre-calculus, social studies (includes history), speech, Western civilization, world cultures, world religions, service hours requirement. Community service is required.
Special Academic Programs 11 Advanced Placement exams for which test preparation is offered; honors section; independent study; study at local college for college credit.
College Admission Counseling 46 students graduated in 2010; all went to college, including Creighton University; Saint John's University; University of Missouri; University of Nebraska–Lincoln; University of Nebraska at Omaha; University of Wisconsin–Madison. Median SAT critical reading: 660, median SAT math: 740, median SAT writing: 640, median combined SAT: 1990, median composite ACT: 27. 75% scored over 600 on SAT critical reading, 100% scored over 600 on SAT math, 100% scored over 600 on SAT writing, 92% scored over 1800 on combined SAT, 58% scored over 26 on composite ACT.
Student Life Upper grades have specified standards of dress, student council, honor system. Discipline rests primarily with faculty. Attendance at religious services is required.
Tuition and Aid Day student tuition: $7720–$7995; 5-day tuition and room/board: $12,790–$13,065; 7-day tuition and room/board: $14,890–$15,165. Tuition installment plan (FACTS Tuition Payment Plan). Tuition reduction for siblings, bursaries, merit scholarship grants, need-based loans, paying campus jobs available. In 2010–11, 48% of upper-school students received aid; total upper-school merit-scholarship money awarded: $101,900. Total amount of financial aid awarded in 2010–11: $240,000.
Admissions Traditional secondary-level entrance grade is 9. For fall 2010, 78 students applied for upper-level admission, 58 were accepted, 48 enrolled. California Achievement Test, Explore, High School Placement Test, Iowa Tests of Basic Skills, Stanford Achievement Test or TOEFL required. Deadline for receipt of application materials: July 1. Application fee required: $30. Interview required.
Athletics Interscholastic: baseball, basketball, bowling, cheering, cross-country running, diving, football, golf, soccer, swimming and diving, tennis, wrestling; intramural: ball hockey, basketball, flag football, floor hockey, physical fitness, physical training, soccer, strength & conditioning, ultimate Frisbee, weight lifting, weight training. 1 PE instructor, 21 coaches, 2 athletic trainers.
Computers Computers are regularly used in architecture, career education, career exploration, career technology, college planning, drafting, economics, French, geography, history, journalism, keyboarding, library, mathematics, newspaper, science, Spanish, stock market, Web site design, yearbook classes. Computer network features include on-campus library services, online commercial services, Internet access, wireless campus network, Internet filtering or blocking technology. Campus intranet, student e-mail accounts, and computer access in designated common areas are available to students. Students grades are available online. The school has a published electronic and media policy.
Contact Mr. Eric Crawford, Director of Admissions. 402-253-0946. Fax: 402-289-4539. E-mail: ecrawford@mountmichael.org. Web site: www.mountmichaelhs.com.

MOUNT SAINT CHARLES ACADEMY

800 Logee Street
Woonsocket, Rhode Island 02895-5599
Head of School: Mr. Herve E. Richer Jr.
General Information Coeducational day college-preparatory, arts, and religious studies school, affiliated with Roman Catholic Church. Grades 7–12. Founded: 1924. Setting: suburban. Nearest major city is Providence. 22-acre campus. 2 buildings on campus. Approved or accredited by New England Association of Schools and Colleges and Rhode Island Department of Education. Total enrollment: 993. Upper school average class size: 25. Upper school faculty-student ratio: 1:18. There are 180 required school days per year for Upper School students. The average school day consists of 6 hours and 15 minutes.
Upper School Student Profile Grade 7: 73 students (38 boys, 35 girls); Grade 8: 105 students (62 boys, 43 girls); Grade 9: 191 students (78 boys, 113 girls); Grade 10: 169 students (69 boys, 100 girls); Grade 11: 196 students (90 boys, 106 girls); Grade 12: 175 students (79 boys, 96 girls). 85% of students are Roman Catholic.
Faculty School total: 55. In upper school: 26 men, 26 women; 30 have advanced degrees.
Subjects Offered Advanced computer applications, algebra, American literature, architecture, art, art-AP, band, biology, biology-AP, British literature, calculus, calculus-AP, chemistry, chorus, computer science, creative writing, dance, drama, economics, English, English language and composition-AP, English literature, English literature and composition-AP, English literature-AP, environmental science, environmental science-AP, European history, European history-AP, fine arts, forensics, French, geography, geometry, government, government and politics-AP, government/civics, handbells, health education, history, history of the Catholic Church, honors U.S. history, honors world history, jazz band, mathematics, mathematics-AP, modern

European history, music, music theory-AP, physical education, physics, physiology, psychology, psychology-AP, religion, science, social studies, Spanish, theater, trigonometry, U.S. history, U.S. history-AP, world history, world literature, writing, yearbook.

Graduation Requirements Arts and fine arts (art, music, dance, drama), computer science, English, foreign language, mathematics, physical education (includes health), religion (includes Bible studies and theology), science, social studies (includes history).

Special Academic Programs 14 Advanced Placement exams for which test preparation is offered; honors section; study at local college for college credit.

College Admission Counseling 167 students graduated in 2010; 165 went to college. Other: 2 entered a postgraduate year.

Student Life Upper grades have uniform requirement, student council. Discipline rests primarily with faculty. Attendance at religious services is required.

Summer Programs Sports, art/fine arts programs offered; session focuses on fine arts, soccer, hockey, basketball; held on campus; accepts boys and girls; open to students from other schools. 220 students usually enrolled. 2011 schedule: July. Application deadline: none.

Tuition and Aid Day student tuition: $10,600. Tuition installment plan (FACTS Tuition Payment Plan, full payment discount plan). Need-based scholarship grants available. In 2010–11, 30% of upper-school students received aid. Total amount of financial aid awarded in 2010–11: $700,000.

Admissions Traditional secondary-level entrance grade is 7. For fall 2010, 300 students applied for upper-level admission, 225 were accepted, 178 enrolled. Diocesan Entrance Exam, ISEE, SAS, STS-HSPT, SSAT or STS required. Deadline for receipt of application materials: none. Application fee required: $25.

Athletics Interscholastic: baseball (boys), basketball (b,g), cross-country running (b,g), gymnastics (g), ice hockey (b,g), indoor track (b,g), lacrosse (b,g), sailing (b,g), soccer (b,g), softball (g), swimming and diving (b,g), tennis (b,g), track and field (b,g), volleyball (b,g), winter (indoor) track (b,g); intramural: aerobics/dance (g), basketball (b,g), dance (g); coed interscholastic: cheering, golf; coed intramural: billiards, bowling, dance team, flag football, indoor soccer, lacrosse, physical training, soccer, strength & conditioning, touch football. 4 PE instructors, 15 coaches, 1 athletic trainer.

Computers Computers are regularly used in accounting, architecture, art, computer applications, desktop publishing, graphic design, science, yearbook classes. Computer network features include on-campus library services, online commercial services, Internet access, Internet filtering or blocking technology, college/financial aid searches. Campus intranet, student e-mail accounts, and computer access in designated common areas are available to students. Students grades are available online. The school has a published electronic and media policy.

Contact Joseph J. O'Neill Jr., Registrar/Director of Admissions. 401-769-0310 Ext. 137. Fax: 401-762-2327. E-mail: admissions@mountsaintcharles.org. Web site: www.mountsaintcharles.org.

MT. SAINT DOMINIC ACADEMY

3 Ryerson Avenue
Caldwell, New Jersey 07006

Head of School: Sr. Frances Sullivan, OP

General Information Girls' day college-preparatory, arts, religious studies, and technology school, affiliated with Roman Catholic Church. Grades 9–12. Founded: 1892. Setting: suburban. Nearest major city is Newark. 70-acre campus. 3 buildings on campus. Approved or accredited by Middle States Association of Colleges and Schools, New Jersey Association of Independent Schools, and New Jersey Department of Education. Endowment: $1.5 million. Total enrollment: 315. Upper school average class size: 12. Upper school faculty-student ratio: 1:12. There are 180 required school days per year for Upper School students. Upper School students typically attend 5 days per week. The average school day consists of 6 hours.

Upper School Student Profile Grade 9: 98 students (98 girls); Grade 10: 65 students (65 girls); Grade 11: 86 students (86 girls); Grade 12: 66 students (66 girls). 88% of students are Roman Catholic.

Faculty School total: 39. In upper school: 5 men, 34 women; 16 have advanced degrees.

Subjects Offered Advanced math, advanced studio art-AP, algebra, American history-AP, American literature, American literature-AP, anatomy and physiology, art, Bible studies, biology, biology-AP, British literature, British literature (honors), calculus, calculus-AP, Catholic belief and practice, chemistry, choir, college counseling, college placement, college planning, communication skills, composition, composition-AP, computer applications, computer science, computer skills, computer technologies, concert choir, contemporary history, creative arts, creative writing, dance, debate, desktop publishing, digital photography, drama, drama workshop, drawing and design, driver education, ecology, environmental systems, English, English language and composition-AP, English literature, English literature and composition-AP, environmental science, forensics, French, geometry, health, history, Holocaust studies, literature, mathematics, music, photography, physical education, physics, pre-calculus, psychology, public speaking, religion, SAT preparation, science, Spanish, studio art-AP, U.S. history, U.S. history-AP, U.S. literature, word processing, world history, world literature, world wide web design.

Graduation Requirements 4 years of community service.

Special Academic Programs Advanced Placement exam preparation; honors section; independent study; academic accommodation for the gifted, the musically talented, and the artistically talented.

College Admission Counseling 99 students graduated in 2010; 96 went to college, including Loyola University Maryland; Montclair State University; Ramapo College of New Jersey; Rutgers, The State University of New Jersey, New Brunswick; Seton Hall University. Median SAT critical reading: 557, median SAT math: 541, median SAT writing: 573. 19% scored over 600 on SAT critical reading, 21% scored over 600 on SAT math, 18% scored over 600 on SAT writing.

Student Life Upper grades have uniform requirement, student council, honor system. Discipline rests primarily with faculty. Attendance at religious services is required.

Summer Programs Enrichment, advancement, sports programs offered; session focuses on mathematics advancement, English and math enrichment; held on campus; accepts girls; open to students from other schools. 15 students usually enrolled. 2011 schedule: June to July. Application deadline: May.

Tuition and Aid Day student tuition: $14,150. Tuition installment plan (individually arranged payment plans, one payment in full, or otherwise monthly, quarterly, or semi-annually). Tuition reduction for siblings, merit scholarship grants, need-based scholarship grants available. In 2010–11, 16% of upper-school students received aid; total upper-school merit-scholarship money awarded: $95,000. Total amount of financial aid awarded in 2010–11: $192,000.

Admissions Traditional secondary-level entrance grade is 9. For fall 2010, 215 students applied for upper-level admission, 211 were accepted, 99 enrolled. Cooperative Entrance Exam (McGraw-Hill) required. Deadline for receipt of application materials: December 15. Application fee required: $40.

Athletics Interscholastic: aerobics/dance, aquatics, basketball, cross-country running, golf, indoor track, indoor track & field, lacrosse, soccer, softball, swimming and diving, tennis, track and field, volleyball; intramural: ballet, cheering, dance, dance squad, dance team, field hockey, modern dance. 1 PE instructor, 20 coaches, 1 athletic trainer.

Computers Computers are regularly used in English, foreign language, history, mathematics, music, science classes. Computer network features include on-campus library services, online commercial services, Internet access, wireless campus network, Internet filtering or blocking technology. Student e-mail accounts are available to students. Students grades are available online. The school has a published electronic and media policy.

Contact Maryann Feuerstein, Director of Admission. 973-226-0660 Ext. 1114. Fax: 973-226-2135. E-mail: mfeuerstein@msdacademy.org. Web site: www.msdacademy.org.

MOUNT SAINT JOSEPH ACADEMY

120 West Wissahickon Avenue
Flourtown, Pennsylvania 19031

Head of School: Sr. Kathleen Brabson, SSJ

General Information Girls' day college-preparatory school, affiliated with Roman Catholic Church. Grades 9–12. Founded: 1858. Setting: suburban. Nearest major city is Philadelphia. 78-acre campus. 1 building on campus. Approved or accredited by Middle States Association of Colleges and Schools, National Catholic Education Association, Pennsylvania Association of Independent Schools, and Pennsylvania Department of Education. Member of National Association of Independent Schools. Endowment: $3 million. Total enrollment: 568. Upper school average class size: 19. Upper school faculty-student ratio: 1:10. There are 180 required school days per year for Upper School students. Upper School students typically attend 5 days per week. The average school day consists of 6 hours and 45 minutes.

Upper School Student Profile Grade 9: 137 students (137 girls); Grade 10: 140 students (140 girls); Grade 11: 144 students (144 girls); Grade 12: 147 students (147 girls). 95% of students are Roman Catholic.

Faculty School total: 61. In upper school: 14 men, 47 women; 41 have advanced degrees.

Subjects Offered Accounting, algebra, American history, American history-AP, American literature, American studies, art, art history, astronomy, biochemistry, biology, calculus, calculus-AP, chemistry, chorus, communications, computer science, design, desktop publishing, drama, drawing, economics, English, English literature, English literature-AP, ethics, European history, film, fine arts, French, French-AP, geography, geometry, government/civics, health, history, human sexuality, instrumental music, journalism, keyboarding, Latin, literature, mathematics, music, music-AP, painting, physical education, physics, physics-AP, physiology, pre-calculus, psychology, religion, science, social studies, Spanish, Spanish-AP, speech, technology, theater, theology, trigonometry, word processing, world history, world literature, writing.

Graduation Requirements Arts and fine arts (art, music, dance, drama), computer science, English, foreign language, mathematics, physical education (includes health), religion (includes Bible studies and theology), science, social studies (includes history).

Special Academic Programs 13 Advanced Placement exams for which test preparation is offered; honors section; independent study; study at local college for college credit; academic accommodation for the gifted, the musically talented, and the artistically talented.

College Admission Counseling 140 students graduated in 2010; all went to college, including Penn State University Park; Saint Joseph's University; Temple University;

The University of Scranton; University of Delaware; University of Pennsylvania. Mean SAT critical reading: 623, mean SAT math: 603, mean SAT writing: 645, mean combined SAT: 1871. 55% scored over 600 on SAT critical reading, 47% scored over 600 on SAT math, 68% scored over 600 on SAT writing, 60% scored over 1800 on combined SAT.

Student Life Upper grades have uniform requirement, student council, honor system. Discipline rests primarily with faculty. Attendance at religious services is required.

Tuition and Aid Day student tuition: $13,400. Tuition installment plan (Higher Education Service, Inc., semester payment plan). Tuition reduction for siblings, merit scholarship grants, need-based scholarship grants available. In 2010–11, 17% of upper-school students received aid; total upper-school merit-scholarship money awarded: $341,700. Total amount of financial aid awarded in 2010–11: $564,400.

Admissions Traditional secondary-level entrance grade is 9. For fall 2010, 311 students applied for upper-level admission, 137 enrolled. High School Placement Test, SAS, STS-HSPT or school's own test required. Deadline for receipt of application materials: October 29. Application fee required: $75.

Athletics Interscholastic: basketball, cheering, crew, cross-country running, diving, field hockey, golf, indoor track, lacrosse, soccer, softball, swimming and diving, tennis, track and field, volleyball. 2 PE instructors, 24 coaches, 1 athletic trainer.

Computers Computers are regularly used in art, business studies, career exploration, college planning, commercial art, computer applications, desktop publishing, English, foreign language, graphic design, history, mathematics, music, science, theater arts, writing, writing, yearbook classes. Computer network features include on-campus library services, online commercial services, Internet access, wireless campus network, Internet filtering or blocking technology, video conferencing, SmartBoards. Campus intranet, student e-mail accounts, and computer access in designated common areas are available to students. Students grades are available online. The school has a published electronic and media policy.

Contact Ms. Carol Finney, Director of Admissions. 215-233-9133. Fax: 215-233-5887. E-mail: cfinney@msjacad.org. Web site: www.msjacad.org.

MOUNT SAINT MARY ACADEMY

1645 Highway 22
Watchung, New Jersey 07069
Head of School: Sr. Lisa D. Gambacorto, Ed.S

General Information Girls' day college-preparatory, religious studies, and technology school, affiliated with Roman Catholic Church. Grades 9–12. Founded: 1908. Setting: suburban. Nearest major city is New York, NY. 84-acre campus. 5 buildings on campus. Approved or accredited by Mercy Secondary Education Association, Middle States Association of Colleges and Schools, National Catholic Education Association, New Jersey Association of Independent Schools, The College Board, and New Jersey Department of Education. Member of National Association of Independent Schools. Endowment: $1.3 million. Total enrollment: 352. Upper school average class size: 20. Upper school faculty-student ratio: 1:8. The average school day consists of 6 hours and 45 minutes.

Upper School Student Profile Grade 9: 69 students (69 girls); Grade 10: 82 students (82 girls); Grade 11: 117 students (117 girls); Grade 12: 84 students (84 girls). 90% of students are Roman Catholic.

Faculty School total: 47. In upper school: 6 men, 41 women; 36 have advanced degrees.

Subjects Offered Algebra, American history, American literature, art, art history, Bible studies, biology, business skills, calculus, career exploration, chemistry, computer programming, computer science, driver education, English, English literature, fine arts, French, geometry, government/civics, health, history, Italian, Latin, mathematics, music, physical education, physics, psychology, religion, science, social studies, Spanish, study skills, theology, trigonometry, world history, writing.

Graduation Requirements Arts and fine arts (art, music, dance, drama), business skills (includes word processing), computer science, English, foreign language, mathematics, physical education (includes health), religion (includes Bible studies and theology), science, self-defense, social sciences, social studies (includes history).

Special Academic Programs Advanced Placement exam preparation; honors section; independent study; remedial reading and/or remedial writing; remedial math.

College Admission Counseling 94 students graduated in 2009; all went to college, including Boston College; New York University; Rutgers, The State University of New Jersey, New Brunswick; Seton Hall University. Mean SAT critical reading: 592, mean SAT math: 578.

Student Life Upper grades have uniform requirement, student council. Discipline rests primarily with faculty. Attendance at religious services is required.

Tuition and Aid Day student tuition: $17,100. Tuition installment plan (FACTS Tuition Payment Plan). Tuition reduction for siblings, merit scholarship grants, need-based scholarship grants, scholarships/grants for children of faculty available. In 2009–10, 35% of upper-school students received aid; total upper-school merit-scholarship money awarded: $60,000. Total amount of financial aid awarded in 2009–10: $165,000.

Admissions Traditional secondary-level entrance grade is 9. For fall 2009, 135 students applied for upper-level admission, 120 were accepted, 80 enrolled. ACT-Explore required. Deadline for receipt of application materials: June 1. Application fee required: $50. On-campus interview required.

Athletics Interscholastic: basketball, cheering, cross-country running, field hockey, indoor track, lacrosse, soccer, softball, swimming and diving, tennis, track and field; intramural: dance, golf, tai chi, volleyball. 2 PE instructors, 3 coaches.

Computers Computers are regularly used in all classes. Computer network features include on-campus library services, online commercial services, Internet access, wireless campus network, Internet filtering or blocking technology. Student e-mail accounts are available to students. Students grades are available online. The school has a published electronic and media policy.

Contact Ms. Donna Venezia Toryak, Director of Admissions. 908-757-0108 Ext. 4506. Fax: 908-756-8085. E-mail: dtoryak@mountsaintmary.org. Web site: www.mountsaintmary.org.

MOUNT ST. MICHAEL ACADEMY

4300 Murdock Avenue
Bronx, New York 10466
Head of School: Dr. Anthony D. Miserandino

General Information Boys' day college-preparatory, religious studies, and technology school, affiliated with Roman Catholic Church. Grades 6–12. Founded: 1926. Setting: urban. Nearest major city is New York. 22-acre campus. 3 buildings on campus. Approved or accredited by Middle States Association of Colleges and Schools and New York Department of Education. Endowment: $3.5 million. Total enrollment: 1,144. Upper school average class size: 27. Upper school faculty-student ratio: 1:18. The average school day consists of 6 hours.

Upper School Student Profile Grade 9: 272 students (272 boys); Grade 10: 256 students (256 boys); Grade 11: 223 students (223 boys); Grade 12: 227 students (227 boys). 75% of students are Roman Catholic.

Faculty School total: 62. In upper school: 46 men, 14 women; 54 have advanced degrees.

Subjects Offered Algebra, American history, American history-AP, American literature, art, arts, biology, business, calculus, chemistry, computer programming, computer science, creative writing, driver education, economics, English, environmental science, ethics, European history, fine arts, geometry, government/civics, health, history, Italian, Latin, mathematics, music, physical education, physics, psychology, science, social sciences, social studies, Spanish, theology, trigonometry, world history.

Graduation Requirements Arts and fine arts (art, music, dance, drama), computer science, English, foreign language, mathematics, physical education (includes health), religion (includes Bible studies and theology), science, social sciences, social studies (includes history).

Special Academic Programs Advanced Placement exam preparation; honors section; academic accommodation for the gifted, the musically talented, and the artistically talented.

College Admission Counseling 177 students graduated in 2009; 160 went to college, including Fordham University; Iona College; Manhattan College; St. John's University. Other: 13 went to work, 4 entered military service.

Student Life Upper grades have specified standards of dress, student council. Discipline rests primarily with faculty.

Tuition and Aid Day student tuition: $6000. Tuition installment plan (monthly payment plans). Tuition reduction for siblings, merit scholarship grants, need-based scholarship grants available. In 2009–10, 40% of upper-school students received aid; total upper-school merit-scholarship money awarded: $240,000. Total amount of financial aid awarded in 2009–10: $750,000.

Admissions Traditional secondary-level entrance grade is 9. For fall 2009, 1,020 students applied for upper-level admission, 450 were accepted, 305 enrolled. Diocesan Entrance Exam required. Deadline for receipt of application materials: none. Application fee required: $20. On-campus interview recommended.

Athletics Interscholastic: baseball, basketball, bowling, cross-country running, football, golf, ice hockey, lacrosse, physical training, power lifting, soccer, tennis, track and field, volleyball, weight lifting, weight training, wrestling. 3 PE instructors, 30 coaches, 1 athletic trainer.

Computers Computer network features include on-campus library services, Internet access, Internet filtering or blocking technology. Student e-mail accounts are available to students. Students grades are available online. The school has a published electronic and media policy.

Contact Thomas Fraher, Director of Admissions. 718-515-6400 Ext. 231. Fax: 718-994-7729. E-mail: thomas.fraher@mtstmichael.org. Web site: www.mountstmichael.org.

MPS ETOBICOKE

30 Barrhead Crescent
Toronto, Ontario M9W 3Z7, Canada
Head of School: Mrs. Gabrielle Bush

General Information Coeducational day college-preparatory, arts, business, and technology school. Grades JK–12. Founded: 1977. Setting: urban. 1 building on campus. Approved or accredited by Ontario Ministry of Education and Ontario Department of Education. Language of instruction: English. Total enrollment: 318. Upper school average class size: 18. Upper school faculty-student ratio: 1:14. There are 192 required school days per year for Upper School students. Upper School students typically attend 5 days per week. The average school day consists of 6 hours and 30 minutes.

Upper School Student Profile Grade 9: 21 students (12 boys, 9 girls); Grade 10: 31 students (23 boys, 8 girls); Grade 11: 43 students (28 boys, 15 girls); Grade 12: 40 students (27 boys, 13 girls).

Faculty School total: 37. In upper school: 6 men, 7 women; 5 have advanced degrees.

Subjects Offered Accounting, anthropology, biology, Canadian geography, Canadian history, Canadian law, chemistry, civics, communications, data processing, discrete mathematics, dramatic arts, English, film, French, functions, geometry, healthful living, information technology, learning strategies, mathematics, organizational studies, personal finance, physics, psychology, reading, science, society challenge and change, sociology, visual arts, world history, writing.

Graduation Requirements English, Ontario Ministry of Education requirements.

Special Academic Programs ESL (15 students enrolled).

College Admission Counseling 34 students graduated in 2010; 32 went to college, including McMaster University; Ryerson University; University of Guelph; University of Toronto; York University.

Student Life Upper grades have uniform requirement, student council, honor system. Discipline rests primarily with faculty.

Summer Programs Remediation, enrichment, advancement, ESL, sports, art/fine arts, computer instruction programs offered; session focuses on academics; held on campus; accepts boys and girls; open to students from other schools. 100 students usually enrolled. 2011 schedule: July 6 to July 30. Application deadline: June 25.

Tuition and Aid Day student tuition: CAN$13,000. Tuition installment plan (individually arranged payment plans, MPS Payment Plan). Tuition reduction for siblings available.

Admissions Traditional secondary-level entrance grade is 9. For fall 2010, 15 students applied for upper-level admission, 13 were accepted, 13 enrolled. Admissions testing required. Deadline for receipt of application materials: October 31. No application fee required. Interview required.

Athletics Interscholastic: baseball (boys, girls), basketball (b,g), flag football (b,g), football (b), indoor track & field (b,g), running (b,g), soccer (b,g), swimming and diving (b,g), track and field (b,g), volleyball (b,g); intramural: basketball (b,g), flag football (b,g), floor hockey (b,g), Frisbee (b,g), indoor hockey (b,g), physical fitness (b,g), rhythmic gymnastics (b,g), running (b,g), soccer (b,g), swimming and diving (b,g), touch football (b,g), track and field (b,g), ultimate Frisbee (b,g), volleyball (b,g), winter (indoor) track (b,g), winter soccer (b,g); coed interscholastic: aquatics, bowling, cross-country running, field hockey, flag football; coed intramural: badminton, baseball, basketball, bowling, cooperative games, cross-country running, flag football, table tennis, tennis. 2 PE instructors, 12 coaches.

Computers Computers are regularly used in art, business education, computer applications, graphic arts, media arts classes. Computer resources include Internet access, Internet filtering or blocking technology. The school has a published electronic and media policy.

Contact Mrs. Gabrielle Bush, Director. 416-745-1328. Fax: 416-745-4168. E-mail: gbushmps@rogers.com. Web site: www.mpsontario.com.

MU HIGH SCHOOL

136 Clark Hall
Columbia, Missouri 65211
Head of School: Ms. Kristi D. Smalley

General Information Coeducational day college-preparatory, general academic, and distance learning school. Grades 9–12. Founded: 1999. Setting: small town. Nearest major city is St. Louis. Approved or accredited by Missouri Independent School Association and North Central Association of Colleges and Schools.

Subjects Offered 20th century American writers, 20th century physics, 20th century world history, 3-dimensional art, accounting, adolescent issues, advanced math, Advanced Placement courses, aerospace science, African-American literature, algebra, American history, ancient world history, art, art appreciation, astronomy, basic language skills, Basic programming, biology, business applications, business mathematics, business skills, business studies, career exploration, career planning, career/college preparation, careers, character education, chemistry, child development, civics, college planning, communication arts, comparative politics, comparative religion, computer applications, computer literacy, computer programming, conservation, consumer education, consumer mathematics, contemporary history, contemporary issues, contemporary math, creative writing, decision making skills, economics, English, English literature and composition-AP, entrepreneurship, environmental science, European literature, family and consumer science, family living, family studies, female experience in America, fiction, film and literature, fitness, food and nutrition, French, general science, geography, geology, geometry, German, government, grammar, health and wellness, history, independent study, integrated mathematics, interpersonal skills, Japanese, keyboarding, language, language arts, Latin, law and the legal system, literature, literature by women, math applications, mathematics, media studies, medieval history, modern history, modern world history, music appreciation, mythology, newspaper, North American literature, novels, parent/child development, personal and social education, personal development, personal fitness, personal money management, photography, poetry, political science, pre-algebra, pre-calculus, psychology, reading/study skills, religious studies, science fiction, Shakespeare, short story, skills for success, social studies, sociology, Spanish,

state history, statistics, study skills, trigonometry, U.S. constitutional history, U.S. government and politics, U.S. literature, women's literature, world geography, world religions, writing.

Graduation Requirements Missouri Department of Elementary and Secondary Education requirements.

Special Academic Programs Advanced Placement exam preparation; accelerated programs; independent study; academic accommodation for the gifted; remedial reading and/or remedial writing.

College Admission Counseling 69 students graduated in 2010.

Admissions Deadline for receipt of application materials: none. No application fee required.

Computers Computers are regularly used in accounting, aerospace science, art, business, business applications, business education, business skills, business studies, career education, career exploration, classics, college planning, computer applications, creative writing, current events, digital applications, economics, English, foreign language, French, French as a second language, geography, health, historical foundations for arts, history, humanities, independent study, information technology, journalism, keyboarding, language development, Latin, life skills, mathematics, media, music, news writing, occupational education, photography, programming, psychology, reading, religious studies, research skills, science, social sciences, social studies, Spanish, study skills, theater, theater arts, typing, writing, writing classes. Computer resources include INET Library, Britannica Online School Edition, course access. Computer access in designated common areas is available to students. Students grades are available online.

Contact Alicia Bixby, Counselor. 800-609-3727. Fax: 573-882-6808. E-mail: cdis@missouri.edu. Web site: cdis.missouri.edu/.

MUNICH INTERNATIONAL SCHOOL

Schloss Buchhof
Starnberg D-82319, Germany
Head of School: Simon Taylor

General Information Coeducational day college-preparatory, arts, business, bilingual studies, and technology school. Grades PK–12. Founded: 1966. Setting: rural. Nearest major city is Munich, Germany. 26-acre campus. 5 buildings on campus. Approved or accredited by European Council of International Schools, International Baccalaureate Organization, and New England Association of Schools and Colleges. Affiliate member of National Association of Independent Schools; member of Secondary School Admission Test Board. Language of instruction: English. Total enrollment: 1,215. Upper school average class size: 21. Upper school faculty-student ratio: 1:6. There are 185 required school days per year for Upper School students. Upper School students typically attend 5 days per week. The average school day consists of 6 hours and 55 minutes.

Upper School Student Profile Grade 9: 110 students (57 boys, 53 girls); Grade 10: 110 students (61 boys, 49 girls); Grade 11: 106 students (54 boys, 52 girls); Grade 12: 90 students (45 boys, 45 girls).

Faculty School total: 160. In upper school: 27 men, 42 women; 28 have advanced degrees.

Subjects Offered Adolescent issues, algebra, art, biology, business, calculus, chemistry, community service, computer science, computer-aided design, design, drama, Dutch, earth science, economics, English, English literature, ESL, European history, film studies, fine arts, French, geography, geometry, German, grammar, health, health education, history, home economics, information technology, instrumental music, integrated mathematics, International Baccalaureate courses, Japanese, journalism, lab/keyboard, library skills, math methods, mathematics, model United Nations, music, personal and social education, physical education, physics, Russian, SAT preparation, science, senior thesis, social sciences, social studies, Spanish, speech and debate, student government, Swedish, technology/design, theater, theory of knowledge, trigonometry, world history, world literature, writing, yearbook.

Graduation Requirements Arts and fine arts (art, music, dance, drama), English, foreign language, mathematics, philosophy, physical education (includes health), science, social sciences, social studies (includes history), theory of knowledge, extended essay. Community service is required.

Special Academic Programs International Baccalaureate program; academic accommodation for the gifted; remedial math; ESL (36 students enrolled).

College Admission Counseling 97 students graduated in 2010; 72 went to college, including Columbia University; Duke University; McGill University; Middlebury College. Other: 1 went to work, 2 entered military service, 22 had other specific plans. Mean SAT critical reading: 587, mean SAT math: 589, mean SAT writing: 596, mean combined SAT: 1772, mean composite ACT: 27. 40% scored over 600 on SAT critical reading, 40% scored over 600 on SAT math, 47% scored over 600 on SAT writing, 40% scored over 1800 on combined SAT, 50% scored over 26 on composite ACT.

Student Life Upper grades have specified standards of dress, student council, honor system. Discipline rests equally with students and faculty.

Summer Programs Sports, rigorous outdoor training programs offered; held both on and off campus; held at Lake Garda (Italy); accepts boys and girls; open to students from other schools. 120 students usually enrolled. 2011 schedule: June 30 to August 13. Application deadline: May 31.

Munich International School

Tuition and Aid Day student tuition: €16,210. Tuition installment plan (monthly payment plans, individually arranged payment plans). Tuition reduction for siblings, need-based tuition remission for current students available. In 2010–11, 8% of upper-school students received aid.

Admissions Traditional secondary-level entrance grade is 9. For fall 2010, 92 students applied for upper-level admission, 57 were accepted, 41 enrolled. English for Non-native Speakers, Math Placement Exam or Secondary Level English Proficiency required. Deadline for receipt of application materials: none. Application fee required: €80. On-campus interview recommended.

Athletics Interscholastic: alpine skiing (boys, girls), basketball (b,g), cross-country running (b,g), freestyle skiing (b,g), golf (b,g), skiing (downhill) (b,g), soccer (b,g), softball (g), swimming and diving (b,g), tennis (b,g), track and field (b,g), volleyball (b,g); intramural: alpine skiing (b,g), badminton (b,g), ballet (b,g), basketball (b,g), canoeing/kayaking (b,g), climbing (b,g), cross-country running (b,g), dance (b,g), freestyle skiing (b,g), gymnastics (b,g), indoor hockey (b,g), indoor soccer (b,g), kayaking (b,g), outdoor skills (b,g), skiing (downhill) (b,g), soccer (b,g), softball (g), strength & conditioning (b,g), swimming and diving (b,g), table tennis (b,g), tennis (b,g), track and field (b,g), volleyball (b,g), wall climbing (b,g); coed interscholastic: alpine skiing, golf, track and field; coed intramural: alpine skiing, ballet, canoeing/ kayaking, climbing, dance, gymnastics, kayaking, outdoor skills, swimming and diving, wall climbing. 5 PE instructors, 8 coaches.

Computers Computers are regularly used in all academic, current events, library skills, newspaper, research skills, yearbook classes. Computer network features include on-campus library services, Internet access, wireless campus network, Internet filtering or blocking technology. Campus intranet and student e-mail accounts are available to students. Students grades are available online. The school has a published electronic and media policy.

Contact Ms. Manuela Black, Director of Admissions. 49-8151-366 Ext. 120. Fax: 49-8151-366 Ext. 129. E-mail: admissions@mis-munich.de. Web site: www.mis-munich.de.

See Close-Up on page 814.

NARDIN ACADEMY

135 Cleveland Avenue
Buffalo, New York 14222-1699
Head of School: Rebecca R. Reeder

General Information Coeducational day college-preparatory, arts, religious studies, and technology school, affiliated with Roman Catholic Church. Boys grades PK–8, girls grades PK–12. Founded: 1857. Setting: urban. 6-acre campus. 1 building on campus. Approved or accredited by Middle States Association of Colleges and Schools, New York State Board of Regents, and New York Department of Education. Endowment: $1.3 million. Upper school average class size: 18. Upper school faculty-student ratio: 1:9. There are 165 required school days per year for Upper School students. Upper School students typically attend 5 days per week. The average school day consists of 6 hours and 30 minutes.

Upper School Student Profile Grade 9: 121 students (121 girls); Grade 10: 115 students (115 girls); Grade 11: 114 students (114 girls); Grade 12: 106 students (106 girls). 85% of students are Roman Catholic.

Faculty School total: 115. In upper school: 5 men, 45 women; 32 have advanced degrees.

Subjects Offered American history, American literature, art, biology, biology-AP, calculus, calculus-AP, chemistry, chemistry-AP, computer science, creative writing, dance, death and loss, economics, economics and history, English, English language and composition-AP, English literature, English literature and composition-AP, environmental science, European history, European history-AP, fine arts, French, French language-AP, government/civics, history, journalism, Latin, literature and composition-AP, mathematics, music, philosophy, photography, physical education, physics, pre-calculus, religion, Spanish, Spanish language-AP, speech, statistics, U.S. government and politics-AP, U.S. history-AP, world history, world literature.

Graduation Requirements Arts and fine arts (art, music, dance, drama), computer science, English, foreign language, health, mathematics, physical education (includes health), religion (includes Bible studies and theology), science, social studies (includes history). Community service is required.

Special Academic Programs 12 Advanced Placement exams for which test preparation is offered; honors section; independent study; term-away projects; academic accommodation for the gifted, the musically talented, and the artistically talented; remedial reading and/or remedial writing; remedial math; programs in English, mathematics for dyslexic students; special instructional classes for deaf students, blind students.

College Admission Counseling 116 students graduated in 2009; all went to college, including Buffalo State College, State University of New York; Canisius College; Loyola University Chicago; The George Washington University; University at Buffalo, the State University of New York; University of Pittsburgh. Mean SAT critical reading: 621, mean SAT math: 614, mean SAT writing: 651, mean combined SAT: 1886. 64% scored over 600 on SAT critical reading, 63% scored over 600 on SAT math, 76% scored over 600 on SAT writing, 66% scored over 1800 on combined SAT.

Student Life Upper grades have specified standards of dress, student council. Discipline rests primarily with faculty. Attendance at religious services is required.

Tuition and Aid Day student tuition: $8665. Tuition installment plan (monthly payment plans, individually arranged payment plans, quarterly payment plan). Merit scholarship grants, need-based scholarship grants, paying campus jobs available. In 2009–10, 24% of upper-school students received aid; total upper-school merit-scholarship money awarded: $105,285. Total amount of financial aid awarded in 2009–10: $233,895.

Admissions Traditional secondary-level entrance grade is 9. For fall 2009, 250 students applied for upper-level admission, 171 were accepted, 124 enrolled. High School Placement Test (closed version) from Scholastic Testing Service required. Deadline for receipt of application materials: none. Application fee required: $20.

Athletics Interscholastic: basketball, bowling, crew, cross-country running, golf, indoor track, lacrosse, rowing, running, soccer, softball, squash, swimming and diving, tennis, track and field, volleyball; intramural: aerobics, aerobics/dance, badminton, ballet, basketball, bowling, dance, equestrian sports, fitness, fitness walking, hiking/ backpacking, horseback riding, ice hockey, modern dance, outdoor adventure, physical fitness, rafting, skiing (downhill), snowboarding, strength & conditioning, volleyball, walking, weight training. 3 PE instructors, 27 coaches, 4 athletic trainers.

Computers Computers are regularly used in all academic, art, career education, career exploration, college planning, computer applications, creative writing, desktop publishing, digital applications, economics, English, foreign language, French, graphic arts, health, history, journalism, keyboarding, Latin, literary magazine, mathematics, media production, music, newspaper, philosophy, photography, publications, religion, SAT preparation, science, social studies, Spanish, speech, stock market, technology, theater, video film production, word processing, writing, yearbook classes. Computer network features include on-campus library services, online commercial services, Internet access, wireless campus network, Internet filtering or blocking technology. Students grades are available online. The school has a published electronic and media policy.

Contact Mrs. Rebecca R. Reeder, Principal. 716-881-6262 Ext. 1230. Fax: 716-881-0086. E-mail: rreeder@nardin.org. Web site: www.nardin.org.

NASHVILLE CHRISTIAN SCHOOL

7555 Sawyer Brown Road
Nashville, Tennessee 37221
Head of School: Mrs. Connie Jo Shelton

General Information Coeducational day college-preparatory, arts, and religious studies school, affiliated with Christian faith, Church of Christ. Grades K–12. Founded: 1971. Setting: suburban. 45-acre campus. 2 buildings on campus. Approved or accredited by National Christian School Association, Southern Association of Colleges and Schools, and Tennessee Department of Education. Total enrollment: 483. Upper school average class size: 18. Upper school faculty-student ratio: 1:18. There are 176 required school days per year for Upper School students. Upper School students typically attend 5 days per week. The average school day consists of 7 hours and 15 minutes.

Upper School Student Profile Grade 9: 66 students (33 boys, 33 girls); Grade 10: 39 students (22 boys, 17 girls); Grade 11: 35 students (17 boys, 18 girls); Grade 12: 41 students (25 boys, 16 girls). 60% of students are Christian, members of Church of Christ.

Faculty School total: 40. In upper school: 12 men, 9 women; 15 have advanced degrees.

Subjects Offered Advanced Placement courses, algebra, American history, art, Bible, Bible studies, biology, calculus, chemistry, chorus, computer science, economics, English, fine arts, general science, geometry, government/civics, health, journalism, keyboarding, Latin, Mandarin, mathematics, music, physical education, physical science, physics, pre-algebra, pre-calculus, science, social sciences, social studies, Spanish, speech.

Graduation Requirements American history, American history-AP, arts and fine arts (art, music, dance, drama), Bible, computer science, English, foreign language, mathematics, physical education (includes health), science, social sciences, social studies (includes history).

Special Academic Programs Advanced Placement exam preparation; honors section; independent study; study at local college for college credit; remedial reading and/or remedial writing; remedial math; programs in English, mathematics, general development for dyslexic students; special instructional classes for students with Attention Deficit Disorder.

College Admission Counseling 48 students graduated in 2010; 45 went to college, including Belmont University; Lipscomb University; Middle Tennessee State University; Tennessee Technological University; The University of Tennessee at Chattanooga; Western Kentucky University. Other: 2 went to work, 1 entered military service.

Student Life Upper grades have uniform requirement, student council, honor system. Discipline rests primarily with faculty. Attendance at religious services is required.

Summer Programs Held on campus; accepts boys and girls; open to students from other schools.

Tuition and Aid Day student tuition: $7790. Guaranteed tuition plan. Tuition installment plan (SMART Tuition Payment Plan). Tuition reduction for siblings, need-based scholarship grants, paying campus jobs available. In 2010–11, 3% of upper-school students received aid. Total amount of financial aid awarded in 2010–11: $3000.

Admissions Traditional secondary-level entrance grade is 9. For fall 2010, 30 students applied for upper-level admission, 29 were accepted, 28 enrolled. Stanford Diagnostic Test required. Deadline for receipt of application materials: none. Application fee required: $100. Interview required.

Athletics Interscholastic: baseball (boys), basketball (b,g), bowling (b,g), cheering (g), cross-country running (g), football (b), golf (b,g), riflery (b,g), soccer (g), softball (g), strength & conditioning (b,g), track and field (b,g), volleyball (g), weight lifting (b,g), weight training (b,g), wrestling (b); intramural: aerobics/dance (g); coed interscholastic: fitness, physical fitness, physical training. 2 PE instructors, 6 coaches, 1 athletic trainer.

Computers Computers are regularly used in all academic classes. Computer network features include on-campus library services, Internet access, wireless campus network, Internet filtering or blocking technology. Student e-mail accounts and computer access in designated common areas are available to students. Students grades are available online.

Contact Mr. Phillip Montgomery, Director of Admissions. 615-356-5600 Ext. 117. Fax: 615-352-1324. E-mail: montgomeryp@nashvillechristian.org. Web site: www.nashvillechristian.org.

NATIONAL HIGH SCHOOL

6685 Peachtree Industrial Boulevard
Atlanta, Georgia 30360
Head of School: Alex Mithani

General Information Distance learning only college-preparatory, general academic, arts, and business school. Distance learning grades 9–12. Founded: 2000. Setting: urban. 1 building on campus. Approved or accredited by CITA (Commission on International and Trans-Regional Accreditation), Southern Association of Colleges and Schools, and Georgia Department of Education. Total enrollment: 396. Upper school faculty-student ratio: 1:10.

Faculty School total: 64.

Subjects Offered 1½ elective credits, advanced biology, advanced chemistry, advanced computer applications, advanced math, Advanced Placement courses, American history, American history-AP, American literature, American literature-AP, biology, biology-AP, British literature, chemistry, chemistry-AP, electives, English, French, general math, geography, geometry, German, health, keyboarding, language arts, mathematical modeling, physical education, physical science, physics, physics-AP, pre-algebra, pre-calculus, U.S. history, world geography.

Graduation Requirements Algebra, American government, American history, American literature, biology, chemistry, earth science, economics and history, electives, English, English literature, foreign language, geography, geometry, grammar, history, physical fitness, physical science, physics, pre-calculus, U.S. government, U.S. history, world history, world literature, two elective credits.

Special Academic Programs Advanced Placement exam preparation; honors section; accelerated programs; academic accommodation for the gifted, the musically talented, and the artistically talented; remedial reading and/or remedial writing; remedial math.

Student Life Upper grades have student council, honor system. Discipline rests primarily with faculty.

Summer Programs Remediation, enrichment, advancement, art/fine arts, computer instruction programs offered; held off campus; held at via distance learning; accepts boys and girls; open to students from other schools. 2011 schedule: June to August. Application deadline: May.

Tuition and Aid Guaranteed tuition plan. Tuition installment plan (The Tuition Plan).

Admissions Traditional secondary-level entrance grade is 11. Admissions testing required. Deadline for receipt of application materials: none. No application fee required. Interview required.

Computers Computers are regularly used in all classes. Computer resources include Internet access, wireless campus network, Internet filtering or blocking technology. Campus intranet and student e-mail accounts are available to students. Students grades are available online. The school has a published electronic and media policy.

Contact Ms. Dona Mathews, Director of Admissions. 404-214-6014 Ext. 6010. Fax: 678-387-5289. E-mail: dmathews@nationalhighschool.com. Web site: www.nationalhighschool.com.

NAVAJO PREPARATORY SCHOOL, INC.

1220 West Apache Street
Farmington, New Mexico 87401
Head of School: Mr. John C. Tohtsoni Jr.

General Information Coeducational boarding and day college-preparatory, arts, and bilingual studies school. Grades 9–12. Founded: 1991. Setting: suburban. Nearest major city is Albuquerque. Students are housed in single-sex dormitories. 84-acre campus. 12 buildings on campus. Approved or accredited by National Council for Nonpublic Schools, North Central Association of Colleges and Schools, and New Mexico Department of Education. Upper school average class size: 10. Upper school faculty-student ratio: 1:15. There are 181 required school days per year for Upper School students. Upper School students typically attend 5 days per week. The average school day consists of 7 hours.

Upper School Student Profile Grade 9: 52 students (19 boys, 33 girls); Grade 10: 49 students (19 boys, 30 girls); Grade 11: 40 students (19 boys, 21 girls); Grade 12: 42 students (14 boys, 28 girls). 65% of students are boarding students. 60% are state residents. 6 states are represented in upper school student body.

Faculty School total: 19. In upper school: 10 men, 9 women; 16 have advanced degrees.

Graduation Requirements Navajo language, Navajo history, Navajo culture.

College Admission Counseling 39 students graduated in 2010; 36 went to college, including Fort Lewis College; San Juan College; The University of Arizona; University of New Mexico; Whittier College. Other: 2 went to work, 1 entered military service.

Student Life Upper grades have specified standards of dress, student council, honor system. Discipline rests primarily with faculty.

Tuition and Aid Tuition installment plan (SMART Tuition Payment Plan). Merit scholarship grants available.

Admissions ACT-Explore required. Deadline for receipt of application materials: none. Application fee required: $20. Interview required.

Athletics Interscholastic: baseball (boys, girls), basketball (b,g), cheering (b,g), cross-country running (b,g), football (b,g), golf (b,g), softball (b,g), volleyball (b,g). 1 PE instructor, 19 coaches.

Computers Computer network features include on-campus library services, Internet access, wireless campus network. Student e-mail accounts are available to students. The school has a published electronic and media policy.

Contact Ms. Sandra Westbrook, Admissions. 505-326-6571 Ext. 129. Fax: 505-564-8099. E-mail: sandra.westbrook@bie.edu. Web site: www.navajoprep.com.

NAWA ACADEMY

French Gulch, California
See Special Needs Schools section.

NAZARETH ACADEMY

1209 West Ogden Avenue
LaGrange Park, Illinois 60526
Head of School: Ms. Deborah A. Vondrasek

General Information Coeducational day college-preparatory school, affiliated with Roman Catholic Church. Grades 9–12. Founded: 1900. Setting: suburban. Nearest major city is Chicago. 15-acre campus. 2 buildings on campus. Approved or accredited by North Central Association of Colleges and Schools and Illinois Department of Education. Total enrollment: 824. Upper school average class size: 24. Upper school faculty-student ratio: 1:17. There are 180 required school days per year for Upper School students. Upper School students typically attend 5 days per week. The average school day consists of 7 hours.

Upper School Student Profile Grade 9: 222 students (119 boys, 103 girls); Grade 10: 212 students (100 boys, 112 girls); Grade 11: 203 students (102 boys, 101 girls); Grade 12: 187 students (96 boys, 91 girls). 90% of students are Roman Catholic.

Faculty School total: 47. In upper school: 19 men, 28 women; 40 have advanced degrees.

Subjects Offered 3-dimensional design, acting, algebra, American government, American literature, art, biology, biology-AP, calculus-AP, chemistry, computer programming, computer science-AP, concert band, concert choir, creative writing, drawing and design, economics, English, English language and composition-AP, English literature and composition-AP, environmental science, French, geometry, health, Italian, journalism, music theory, photography, physical education, physics, pre-calculus, psychology, religion, scripture, Spanish, speech, studio art, theater, trigonometry, U.S. history, U.S. history-AP, Western civilization, wind ensemble, world history, world literature, world religions.

Graduation Requirements Advanced math, algebra, American literature, arts and fine arts (art, music, dance, drama), biology, chemistry, church history, English, foreign language, geometry, physical education (includes health), physics, religion (includes Bible studies and theology), scripture, U.S. history, Western civilization, world literature, world religions, world studies, service hours, off-campus retreat for juniors.

Special Academic Programs 10 Advanced Placement exams for which test preparation is offered; honors section.

College Admission Counseling 172 students graduated in 2010; 171 went to college, including Loyola University Chicago; Marquette University; Northwestern University; University of Illinois at Chicago; University of Illinois at Urbana–Champaign; University of Notre Dame. Other: 1 entered military service. Median composite ACT: 25. 34% scored over 26 on composite ACT.

Student Life Upper grades have uniform requirement, student council, honor system. Discipline rests primarily with faculty. Attendance at religious services is required.

Summer Programs Sports programs offered; session focuses on athletic camps; held on campus; accepts boys and girls; open to students from other schools.

Tuition and Aid Day student tuition: $9980. Tuition installment plan (monthly payment plans). Tuition reduction for siblings, merit scholarship grants, need-based scholarship grants available. In 2010–11, 22% of upper-school students received aid; total upper-school merit-scholarship money awarded: $40,000. Total amount of financial aid awarded in 2010–11: $300,000.

Nazareth Academy

Admissions Traditional secondary-level entrance grade is 9. For fall 2010, 350 students applied for upper-level admission, 222 enrolled. High School Placement Test (closed version) from Scholastic Testing Service required. Deadline for receipt of application materials: June 30. No application fee required.

Athletics Interscholastic: baseball (boys), basketball (b,g), cheering (g), cross-country running (b,g), football (b), golf (b,g), hockey (b), lacrosse (b,g), pom squad (g), soccer (b,g), softball (g), swimming and diving (g), tennis (b,g), track and field (b,g), volleyball (b,g), wrestling (b). 2 PE instructors, 1 coach, 1 athletic trainer.

Computers Computers are regularly used in English, foreign language, history, mathematics, science classes. Computer network features include on-campus library services, Internet access, wireless campus network, Internet filtering or blocking technology. Students grades are available online. The school has a published electronic and media policy.

Contact Mr. John Bonk, Recruitment Director. 708-387-8538. Fax: 708-354-0109. E-mail: jbonk@nazarethacademy.com. Web site: www.nazarethacademy.com.

NEBRASKA CHRISTIAN SCHOOLS

1847 Inskip Avenue
Central City, Nebraska 68826
Head of School: Mr. Daniel R. Woods

General Information Coeducational boarding and day college-preparatory school, affiliated with Protestant-Evangelical faith. Boarding grades 7–12, day grades K–12. Founded: 1959. Setting: rural. Nearest major city is Lincoln. Students are housed in single-sex dormitories. 27-acre campus. 7 buildings on campus. Approved or accredited by Association of Christian Schools International and Nebraska Department of Education. Endowment: $35,000. Total enrollment: 215. Upper school average class size: 20. Upper school faculty-student ratio: 1:10. There are 155 required school days per year for Upper School students. Upper School students typically attend 4 days per week. The average school day consists of 8 hours.

Upper School Student Profile Grade 9: 28 students (9 boys, 19 girls); Grade 10: 35 students (14 boys, 21 girls); Grade 11: 27 students (15 boys, 12 girls); Grade 12: 26 students (15 boys, 11 girls). 38% of students are boarding students. 72% are state residents. 2 states are represented in upper school student body. 28% are international students. International students from China, Hong Kong, Republic of Korea, Taiwan, Thailand, and Viet Nam; 1 other country represented in student body. 90% of students are Protestant-Evangelical faith.

Faculty School total: 18. In upper school: 9 men, 9 women; 5 have advanced degrees; 5 reside on campus.

Subjects Offered Accounting, advanced math, algebra, American government, American history, American literature, anatomy and physiology, ancient world history, art, band, Bible, biology, business, business law, chemistry, choir, Christian doctrine, Christian ethics, Christian studies, composition, computer applications, computer programming, concert band, consumer mathematics, creation science, desktop publishing, economics, English, English composition, ESL, family living, fitness, general math, geography, geometry, health and safety, history, keyboarding, lab science, language arts, Life of Christ, life science, literature, mathematics, music, music theory, physical education, physical fitness, physical science, physics, pre-calculus, science, science project, social studies, Spanish, speech, trigonometry, vocal ensemble, vocal music, Web site design, word processing, world geography, world history, writing, yearbook.

Graduation Requirements Algebra, American government, American history, American literature, art, Bible, biology, Christian doctrine, economics, English, family living, geometry, history, keyboarding, Life of Christ, physical education (includes health), physical science, world history.

Special Academic Programs Independent study; study at local college for college credit; ESL (16 students enrolled).

College Admission Counseling 27 students graduated in 2010; 24 went to college, including Hillsdale College; LeTourneau University; Trinity Christian College; University of Nebraska–Lincoln; University of Nebraska at Kearney. Other: 2 entered military service, 1 had other specific plans. Median composite ACT: 24. 21% scored over 26 on composite ACT.

Student Life Upper grades have specified standards of dress, student council, honor system. Discipline rests primarily with faculty. Attendance at religious services is required.

Tuition and Aid Day student tuition: $5000; 5-day tuition and room/board: $8000; 7-day tuition and room/board: $24,000. Guaranteed tuition plan. Tuition installment plan (FACTS Tuition Payment Plan, individually arranged payment plans). Tuition reduction for siblings, merit scholarship grants, need-based scholarship grants available. In 2010–11, 44% of upper-school students received aid. Total amount of financial aid awarded in 2010–11: $100,000.

Admissions Traditional secondary-level entrance grade is 9. For fall 2010, 28 students applied for upper-level admission, 23 were accepted, 14 enrolled. SLEP for foreign students or TOEFL or SLEP required. Deadline for receipt of application materials: none. Application fee required: $300. Interview recommended.

Athletics Interscholastic: basketball (boys, girls), cross-country running (b,g), football (b), track and field (b,g), volleyball (g), wrestling (b). 2 PE instructors, 7 coaches.

Computers Computers are regularly used in business applications, desktop publishing, programming, Web site design, yearbook classes. Computer network features

include Internet access, wireless campus network, Internet filtering or blocking technology. Students grades are available online.

Contact Mr. Larry Hoff, Director, International Programs. 308-946-3836. Fax: 308-946-3837. E-mail: lhoff@nebraskachristian.org. Web site: www.nebraskachristian.org.

NERINX HALL

530 East Lockwood Avenue
Webster Groves, Missouri 63119
Head of School: Sr. Barbara Roche, SL

General Information Girls' day college-preparatory and arts school, affiliated with Roman Catholic Church. Grades 9–12. Founded: 1924. Setting: suburban. Nearest major city is St. Louis. 4 buildings on campus. Approved or accredited by North Central Association of Colleges and Schools and Missouri Department of Education. Endowment: $2.7 million. Total enrollment: 631. Upper school average class size: 20. Upper school faculty-student ratio: 1:10. The average school day consists of 6 hours and 25 minutes.

Upper School Student Profile Grade 9: 165 students (165 girls); Grade 10: 164 students (164 girls); Grade 11: 153 students (153 girls); Grade 12: 149 students (149 girls). 92% of students are Roman Catholic.

Faculty School total: 62. In upper school: 14 men, 48 women; 49 have advanced degrees.

Subjects Offered Acting, advanced math, American government, American history, American literature, anatomy, anthropology, art, astronomy, athletics, biology, business, calculus, ceramics, chemistry, computer applications, computer graphics, conceptual physics, creative writing, death and loss, desktop publishing, drawing and design, Eastern world civilizations, economics, English composition, English literature, film appreciation, French, geology, German, graphics, health, history, Holocaust, honors algebra, honors English, honors geometry, honors U.S. history, instrumental music, jazz band, keyboarding, lab science, Latin, media, Middle East, model United Nations, multimedia, orchestra, painting, performing arts, personal finance, physics, pre-calculus, psychology, public speaking, religious education, Spanish, theology, Web site design, Western civilization.

Graduation Requirements Algebra, arts and fine arts (art, music, dance, drama), biology, chemistry, foreign language, geometry, physical education (includes health), physical fitness, physics, public speaking, theology, U.S. government and politics, U.S. history, U.S. literature, world history, writing. Community service is required.

Special Academic Programs Honors section; study at local college for college credit.

College Admission Counseling 147 students graduated in 2010; 146 went to college, including DePaul University; Missouri State University; Saint Louis University; Truman State University; University of Dayton; University of Missouri. Other: 1 had other specific plans. Mean composite ACT: 27.

Student Life Upper grades have uniform requirement, student council, honor system. Discipline rests primarily with faculty. Attendance at religious services is required.

Summer Programs Advancement programs offered; session focuses on advancement; held on campus; accepts girls; not open to students from other schools. 175 students usually enrolled.

Tuition and Aid Day student tuition: $10,400. Tuition installment plan (individually arranged payment plans). Tuition reduction for siblings, merit scholarship grants, need-based scholarship grants, paying campus jobs available. In 2010–11, 25% of upper-school students received aid. Total amount of financial aid awarded in 2010–11: $505,000.

Admissions Traditional secondary-level entrance grade is 9. For fall 2010, 218 students applied for upper-level admission, 177 were accepted, 164 enrolled. Any standardized test or CTBS (or similar from their school) required. Deadline for receipt of application materials: November 22. Application fee required: $10. On-campus interview required.

Athletics Interscholastic: basketball, cross-country running, diving, field hockey, golf, lacrosse, racquetball, soccer, softball, swimming and diving, tennis, track and field, volleyball. 3 PE instructors, 25 coaches.

Computers Computers are regularly used in graphics, humanities, mathematics, science, speech, writing, writing classes. Computer network features include on-campus library services, Internet access, wireless campus network, Internet filtering or blocking technology. Student e-mail accounts are available to students. Students grades are available online. The school has a published electronic and media policy.

Contact Mrs. Mary Ann Gentry. 314-968-1505 Ext. 151. Fax: 314-968-0604. E-mail: mgentry@nerinxhs.org. Web site: www.nerinxhs.org.

NEUCHATEL JUNIOR COLLEGE

Cret-Taconnet 4
Neuchâtel 2002, Switzerland
Head of School: Mr. Bill Boyer

General Information Coeducational boarding college-preparatory, arts, business, bilingual studies, and international development school. Grade 12. Founded: 1956. Setting: urban. Nearest major city is Berne, Switzerland. Students are housed in homes of host families. 1-acre campus. 3 buildings on campus. Approved or accredited by state department of education. Languages of instruction: English and French. Endowment: CAN$400,000. Total enrollment: 87. Upper school average class size: 15. Upper school faculty-student ratio: 1:10. Upper School students typically attend 5 days per week. The average school day consists of 5 hours and 15 minutes.

Upper School Student Profile Grade 12: 70 students (17 boys, 53 girls); Postgraduate: 17 students (10 boys, 7 girls). 100% of students are boarding students. 4% are international students. International students from Bermuda, Canada, Germany, Saudi Arabia, United Kingdom, and United States.

Faculty School total: 10. In upper school: 4 men, 6 women; 7 have advanced degrees; 1 resides on campus.

Subjects Offered 20th century world history, advanced chemistry, advanced math, Advanced Placement courses, advanced studio art-AP, algebra, analysis and differential calculus, ancient world history, applied arts, art, art history, art history-AP, athletics, biology, biology-AP, British history, calculus, calculus-AP, Canadian history, Canadian law, Canadian literature, chemistry, chemistry-AP, classical civilization, comparative government and politics-AP, comparative politics, debate, dramatic arts, earth science, economics, economics-AP, English, English language and composition-AP, English literature-AP, environmental science, European history, European history-AP, finite math, French as a second language, French language-AP, French literature-AP, German-AP, government and politics-AP, human geography—AP, law, personal and social education, physics, physics-AP, public speaking, studio art-AP, United Nations and international issues, world history-AP, world issues.

Graduation Requirements Minimum of 6 senior year university prep level courses.

Special Academic Programs Advanced Placement exam preparation; study abroad.

College Admission Counseling 98 students graduated in 2009; 97 went to college, including Dalhousie University; McGill University; McMaster University; Queen's University at Kingston; The University of Western Ontario; University of Toronto. Other: 1 had other specific plans.

Student Life Upper grades have specified standards of dress, student council, honor system. Discipline rests primarily with faculty.

Tuition and Aid 7-day tuition and room/board: 41,500 Swiss francs. Bursaries, merit scholarship grants available. In 2009–10, 8% of upper-school students received aid; total upper-school merit-scholarship money awarded: 10,000 Swiss francs. Total amount of financial aid awarded in 2009–10: 52,500 Swiss francs.

Admissions Traditional secondary-level entrance grade is 12. For fall 2009, 123 students applied for upper-level admission, 115 were accepted, 97 enrolled. Deadline for receipt of application materials: December 7. Application fee required: CAN$175. Interview recommended.

Athletics Interscholastic: field hockey (boys, girls), rugby (b,g), soccer (b,g); intramural: hockey (b,g), ice hockey (b,g), indoor hockey (b,g), rugby (b,g), soccer (b,g); coed interscholastic: alpine skiing, aquatics, snowboarding, swimming and diving; coed intramural: alpine skiing, aquatics, basketball, bicycling, cross-country running, curling, floor hockey, jogging, sailing, snowboarding, volleyball.

Computers Computer network features include on-campus library services, Internet access, wireless campus network. Student e-mail accounts are available to students. The school has a published electronic and media policy.

Contact Ms. Anne Hamilton, Admission Officer. 416-368-8169 Ext. 222. Fax: 416-368-0956. E-mail: admissions@neuchatel.org. Web site: www.njc.ch/school/.

NEWARK ACADEMY

91 South Orange Avenue
Livingston, New Jersey 07039-4989
Head of School: M. Donald M. Austin

General Information Coeducational day college-preparatory, arts, technology, and International Baccalaureate school. Grades 6–12. Founded: 1774. Setting: suburban. Nearest major city is Morristown. 68-acre campus. 1 building on campus. Approved or accredited by Middle States Association of Colleges and Schools, New Jersey Association of Independent Schools, and New Jersey Department of Education. Member of National Association of Independent Schools and Secondary School Admission Test Board. Endowment: $16.8 million. Total enrollment: 557. Upper school average class size: 13. Upper school faculty-student ratio: 1:12. There are 165 required school days per year for Upper School students. The average school day consists of 6 hours and 30 minutes.

Upper School Student Profile Grade 9: 100 students (49 boys, 51 girls); Grade 10: 106 students (53 boys, 53 girls); Grade 11: 91 students (46 boys, 45 girls); Grade 12: 99 students (51 boys, 48 girls).

Faculty School total: 74. In upper school: 36 men, 34 women; 58 have advanced degrees.

Subjects Offered Algebra, American history, American literature, anatomy, art, art history, arts, biology, botany, calculus, ceramics, chemistry, chorus, communications, community service, computer programming, computer science, creative writing, drama, driver education, ecology, economics, English, English literature, European history, finance, fine arts, French, geometry, government/civics, grammar, health, history, humanities, Latin, leadership, Mandarin, mathematics, music, philosophy, physical education, physics, religion, SAT/ACT preparation, science, social studies, Spanish, theater, theory of knowledge, trigonometry, typing, world history, world literature, writing.

Graduation Requirements Arts and fine arts (art, music, dance, drama), computer science, English, foreign language, mathematics, physical education (includes health), science, social studies (includes history), 40-hour senior service project, community service.

Special Academic Programs International Baccalaureate program; Advanced Placement exam preparation; honors section; accelerated programs; independent study; term-away projects; study at local college for college credit; study abroad; academic accommodation for the gifted, the musically talented, and the artistically talented.

College Admission Counseling 98 students graduated in 2010; all went to college, including Cornell University; Lafayette College; The George Washington University; University of Chicago; University of Pennsylvania; Villanova University. Median SAT math: 660, median SAT writing: 650, median composite ACT: 26. 83% scored over 600 on SAT math, 82% scored over 600 on SAT writing, 36% scored over 26 on composite ACT.

Student Life Upper grades have specified standards of dress, student council, honor system. Discipline rests equally with students and faculty.

Summer Programs Remediation, enrichment, advancement, ESL, sports, art/fine arts, computer instruction programs offered; session focuses on enrichment and advancement; held on campus; accepts boys and girls; open to students from other schools. 850 students usually enrolled. 2011 schedule: June 27 to August 5. Application deadline: May 1.

Tuition and Aid Day student tuition: $28,775. Tuition installment plan (Insured Tuition Payment Plan, Key Tuition Payment Plan, monthly payment plans, individually arranged payment plans). Need-based scholarship grants available. In 2010–11, 15% of upper-school students received aid. Total amount of financial aid awarded in 2010–11: $1,388,542.

Admissions Traditional secondary-level entrance grade is 9. For fall 2010, 256 students applied for upper-level admission, 82 were accepted, 58 enrolled. ISEE or SSAT required. Deadline for receipt of application materials: January 8. Application fee required: $65. Interview required.

Athletics Interscholastic: baseball (boys), basketball (b,g), cross-country running (b,g), fencing (b,g), field hockey (g), football (b), golf (b,g), lacrosse (b,g), running (b,g), skiing (downhill) (b,g), soccer (b,g), softball (g), swimming and diving (b,g), tennis (b,g), track and field (b,g), volleyball (g), wrestling (b); intramural: aerobics/dance (b,g), aerobics/Nautilus (b,g), baseball (b), basketball (b,g), bicycling (b,g), cross-country running (b,g), dance (b,g), dance team (b,g), field hockey (g), fitness (b,g), football (b), golf (b,g), hockey (b), ice hockey (b), lacrosse (b,g), modern dance (b,g), soccer (b,g), softball (g), swimming and diving (b,g), tennis (b,g), track and field (b,g), volleyball (g), weight lifting (b,g), wrestling (b), yoga (b,g); coed intramural: aerobics/dance, aerobics/Nautilus, bicycling, cricket, dance, dance team, fitness, modern dance, mountain biking, skiing (downhill), table tennis, ultimate Frisbee, weight lifting, yoga. 5 PE instructors, 10 coaches, 1 athletic trainer.

Computers Computers are regularly used in all academic classes. Computer network features include on-campus library services, online commercial services, Internet access, wireless campus network. Student e-mail accounts are available to students. The school has a published electronic and media policy.

Contact Mrs. Jennifer Blythe, Admissions Office Manager. 973-992-7000 Ext. 323. Fax: 973-993-8962. E-mail: jblythe@newarka.edu. Web site: www.newarka.edu.

NEW COVENANT ACADEMY

3304 South Cox Road
Springfield, Missouri 65807
Head of School: Mr. Matt Searson

General Information Coeducational day college-preparatory, arts, business, religious studies, technology, and Science, Math, Foreign Language, Language Arts school, affiliated with Christian faith. Grades JK–12. Founded: 1979. Setting: suburban. 22-acre campus. 1 building on campus. Approved or accredited by Association of Christian Schools International and North Central Association of Colleges and Schools. Total enrollment: 337. Upper school average class size: 15. Upper school faculty-student ratio: 1:10. There are 167 required school days per year for Upper School students. Upper School students typically attend 5 days per week. The average school day consists of 7 hours and 30 minutes.

Upper School Student Profile 99% of students are Christian.

Faculty School total: 30. In upper school: 5 men, 7 women.

Subjects Offered Advanced math, algebra, American government, American history, American literature, anatomy and physiology, ancient world history, art, athletics, Bible, biology, British literature, business, calculus, chemistry, Christianity, comparative government and politics, computer processing, computer technologies, computers, concert choir, economics, English, English composition, geology, geometry, health, history, independent study, Life of Christ, literature, mathematics, music appreciation, New Testament, oceanography, physical education, physics, pre-algebra, robotics, science, scripture, Spanish, trigonometry, world history, yearbook.

Special Academic Programs Independent study; study at local college for college credit.

College Admission Counseling 27 students graduated in 2010; 26 went to college, including Evangel University; Missouri State University; University of Missouri. Median composite ACT: 24. 17% scored over 26 on composite ACT.

New Covenant Academy

Student Life Upper grades have specified standards of dress, student council, honor system. Discipline rests primarily with faculty. Attendance at religious services is required.

Tuition and Aid Guaranteed tuition plan. Tuition installment plan (monthly payment plans). Need-based scholarship grants available. Total amount of financial aid awarded in 2010–11: $150,000.

Admissions Otis-Lennon School Ability Test or Stanford Achievement Test required. Deadline for receipt of application materials: none. Application fee required: $50. Interview required.

Athletics Interscholastic: basketball (boys, girls), cheering (g), golf (b), soccer (b,g), track and field (b,g), volleyball (g); coed interscholastic: golf. 2 PE instructors, 11 coaches.

Computers Computers are regularly used in computer applications, journalism, technology, word processing, yearbook classes. Computer network features include Internet access, Internet filtering or blocking technology. Computer access in designated common areas is available to students. Students grades are available online. **Contact** Mrs. Delana Reynolds, Admissions Officer. 417-887-9848 Ext. 3. Fax: 417-887-2419. E-mail: dreynolds@newcovenant.net. Web site: www.newcovenant.net.

NEW ENGLISH SCHOOL
PO Box 6156
Hawalli 32036, Kuwait
Head of School: Dr. Ziad S. Rajab

General Information Coeducational day college-preparatory, arts, business, bilingual studies, and technology school. Grades K–13. Founded: 1969. Setting: urban. Nearest major city is Kuwait City, Kuwait. 1-hectare campus. 5 buildings on campus. Approved or accredited by Kuwait Ministry of Education. Language of instruction: English. Total enrollment: 2,249. Upper school average class size: 25. Upper school faculty-student ratio: 1:12. There are 175 required school days per year for Upper School students. Upper School students typically attend 5 days per week. The average school day consists of 6 hours and 30 minutes.

Upper School Student Profile Grade 6: 150 students (89 boys, 61 girls); Grade 7: 167 students (92 boys, 75 girls); Grade 8: 204 students (122 boys, 82 girls); Grade 9: 218 students (114 boys, 104 girls); Grade 10: 238 students (141 boys, 97 girls); Grade 11: 254 students (146 boys, 108 girls); Grade 12: 103 students (63 boys, 40 girls); Grade 13: 25 students (13 boys, 12 girls).

Faculty School total: 215. In upper school: 48 men, 43 women; 10 have advanced degrees.

Subjects Offered Accounting, advanced math, art, biology, business studies, chemistry, computer science, drama, economics, French, geography, history, information technology, mathematics, music, physical education.

Special Academic Programs ESL (60 students enrolled).

College Admission Counseling 225 students graduated in 2010.

Student Life Upper grades have uniform requirement. Discipline rests primarily with faculty.

Tuition and Aid Day student tuition: 1400 Kuwaiti dinars–3570 Kuwaiti dinars.

Admissions Traditional secondary-level entrance grade is 7. For fall 2010, 400 students applied for upper-level admission, 250 were accepted, 250 enrolled. School's own exam required. Application fee required: 10 Kuwaiti dinars. Interview required.

Athletics Interscholastic: netball (girls); intramural: netball (g); coed interscholastic: basketball, cricket, football, track and field; coed intramural: badminton, ball hockey, basketball, cricket, football, gymnastics, hockey, outdoor adventure, paint ball, sailing, table tennis, tennis, track and field, walking, yoga.

Computers Computer network features include on-campus library services, Internet access.

Contact Ms. Hasmiq Hagop, Admissions. 965-25318061. Fax: 965-25319924. E-mail: hagop@neskt.com. Web site: www.neskt.com.

NEW HAMPTON SCHOOL
70 Main Street
New Hampton, New Hampshire 03256
Head of School: Andrew Menke

General Information Coeducational boarding and day college-preparatory, general academic, and arts school. Grades 9–PG. Founded: 1821. Setting: small town. Nearest major city is Boston, MA. Students are housed in single-sex dormitories. 350-acre campus. 35 buildings on campus. Approved or accredited by Association of Independent Schools in New England, Independent Schools of Northern New England, New England Association of Schools and Colleges, The Association of Boarding Schools, and New Hampshire Department of Education. Member of National Association of Independent Schools and Secondary School Admission Test Board. Endowment: $10 million. Total enrollment: 310. Upper school average class size: 11. Upper school faculty-student ratio: 1:5. Upper School students typically attend 5 days per week.

Upper School Student Profile Grade 9: 44 students (21 boys, 23 girls); Grade 10: 62 students (36 boys, 26 girls); Grade 11: 90 students (55 boys, 35 girls); Grade 12: 84 students (56 boys, 28 girls); Postgraduate: 30 students (25 boys, 5 girls). 77% of students are boarding students. 30% are state residents. 28 states are represented in upper school student body. 18% are international students. International students from Bermuda, Canada, China, Germany, Republic of Korea, and Spain; 12 other countries represented in student body.

Faculty School total: 82. In upper school: 38 men, 40 women; 55 have advanced degrees; 51 reside on campus.

Subjects Offered Algebra, American history, American literature, anatomy, art, art history, biochemistry, biology, broadcasting, calculus, chemistry, community service, computer programming, computer science, creative writing, dance, drama, driver education, earth science, ecology, economics, English, English literature, environmental science, European history, fine arts, French, geometry, health, history, journalism, Latin, mathematics, music, photography, physics, physics-AP, physiology, psychology, science, social studies, Spanish, speech, theater, trigonometry, world history, world literature, writing.

Graduation Requirements Arts and fine arts (art, music, dance, drama), computer science, English, foreign language, mathematics, performing arts, science, social studies (includes history), speech, Experiential Learning. Community service is required.

Special Academic Programs Advanced Placement exam preparation; honors section; independent study; academic accommodation for the gifted, the musically talented, and the artistically talented; remedial reading and/or remedial writing; remedial math; programs in English, mathematics, general development for dyslexic students; ESL (15 students enrolled).

College Admission Counseling 98 students graduated in 2009; 96 went to college, including Colby College; Ithaca College; Northeastern University; St. Lawrence University; University of New Hampshire; University of Vermont. Other: 1 entered a postgraduate year, 1 had other specific plans. Median SAT critical reading: 500, median SAT math: 530. 15% scored over 600 on SAT critical reading, 25% scored over 600 on SAT math.

Student Life Upper grades have specified standards of dress, student council, honor system. Discipline rests primarily with faculty.

Tuition and Aid Day student tuition: $25,200; 7-day tuition and room/board: $42,500. Tuition installment plan (Insured Tuition Payment Plan, Academic Management Services Plan, Key Tuition Payment Plan, monthly payment plans). Need-based scholarship grants available. In 2009–10, 30% of upper-school students received aid. Total amount of financial aid awarded in 2009–10: $2,400,000.

Admissions Traditional secondary-level entrance grade is 9. For fall 2009, 424 students applied for upper-level admission, 300 were accepted, 137 enrolled. SSAT or TOEFL or SLEP required. Deadline for receipt of application materials: February 1. Application fee required: $50. Interview required.

Athletics Interscholastic: alpine skiing (boys, girls), baseball (b), basketball (b,g), bicycling (b,g), cross-country running (b,g), field hockey (g), football (b), golf (b,g), hockey (b,g), ice hockey (b,g), lacrosse (b,g), skiing (downhill) (b,g), soccer (b,g), softball (g), tennis (b,g); coed interscholastic: alpine skiing, bicycling, canoeing/kayaking, equestrian sports, horseback riding, kayaking, mountain biking, snowboarding; coed intramural: aerobics/dance, ballet, bicycling, canoeing/kayaking, climbing, cross-country running, dance, equestrian sports, fitness, golf, hiking/backpacking, horseback riding, ice hockey, kayaking, modern dance, nordic skiing, outdoor activities, outdoor adventure, outdoor education, outdoor recreation, outdoor skills, physical training, rock climbing, ropes courses, skiing (downhill), snowboarding, tennis, volleyball, wall climbing, weight lifting, weight training, yoga. 3 athletic trainers.

Computers Computers are regularly used in English, graphic design, introduction to technology, journalism, mathematics, media production, music, science, video film production, yearbook classes. Computer resources include on-campus library services, online commercial services, Internet access, wireless campus network, Internet filtering or blocking technology. Campus intranet, student e-mail accounts, and computer access in designated common areas are available to students. Students grades are available online. The school has a published electronic and media policy. **Contact** Ms. Suzanne Walker Buck, Director of Admission. 603-677-3402. Fax: 603-677-3481. E-mail: sbuck@newhampton.org. Web site: www.newhampton.org.

NEW HAVEN
2172 East 7200 South
Spanish Fork, Utah 84660
Head of School: Laurie Laird

General Information Girls' boarding college-preparatory and general academic school; primarily serves students with learning disabilities, individuals with Attention Deficit Disorder, and individuals with emotional and behavioral problems. Grades 8–12. Founded: 1995. Setting: rural. Students are housed in single-sex dormitories. 20-acre campus. 4 buildings on campus. Approved or accredited by CITA (Commission on International and Trans-Regional Accreditation), Joint Commission on Accreditation of Healthcare Organizations, Northwest Association of Schools and Colleges, The College Board, and Utah Department of Education. Total enrollment: 64. Upper school average class size: 10. Upper school faculty-student ratio: 1:7.

Upper School Student Profile Grade 10: 20 students (20 girls); Grade 11: 20 students (20 girls); Grade 12: 14 students (14 girls). 100% of students are boarding students. 10% are state residents. 21 states are represented in upper school student body. 15% are international students. International students from Canada and Spain.

Faculty School total: 8. In upper school: 6 women; 2 have advanced degrees.

Special Academic Programs Honors section; accelerated programs; independent study.

College Admission Counseling 12 students graduated in 2009; 10 went to college, including Whittier College. Other: 2 went to work. Median SAT critical reading: 590, median SAT math: 545, median SAT writing: 590, median composite ACT: 25.

Student Life Upper grades have specified standards of dress, student council, honor system. Discipline rests primarily with faculty.

Admissions Deadline for receipt of application materials: none. No application fee required. Interview recommended.

Athletics Interscholastic: aerobics (girls), baseball (g), basketball (g), combined training (g), cooperative games (g), dance (g), equestrian sports (g), fitness (g), fitness walking (g), flag football (g), Frisbee (g), gymnastics (g), hiking/backpacking (g), horseback riding (g), jogging (g), outdoor activities (g), outdoor adventure (g), outdoor recreation (g), physical fitness (g), physical training (g), soccer (g), softball (g), strength & conditioning (g), volleyball (g), walking (g), weight training (g), winter soccer (g), yoga (g). 2 PE instructors.

Computers Computers are regularly used in history classes. Computer network features include on-campus library services, Internet access, wireless campus network, Internet filtering or blocking technology. Students grades are available online. The school has a published electronic and media policy.

Contact Irene Kotter, Admissions Director. 801-794-1220 Ext. 5271. Fax: 801-794-9558. E-mail: Irenek@newhavenrtc.com. Web site: www.newhavenrtc.com.

NEW HORIZON YOUTH MINISTRIES
Marion, Indiana
See Special Needs Schools section.

NEWMAN HIGH SCHOOL
1130 West Bridge
Wausau, Wisconsin 54401
Head of School: Mr. Lawrence P. Theiss

General Information Coeducational day college-preparatory and religious studies school, affiliated with Roman Catholic Church. Grades 9–12. Founded: 1951. Setting: urban. 80-acre campus. 1 building on campus. Approved or accredited by National Catholic Education Association, North Central Association of Colleges and Schools, and Wisconsin Department of Education. Upper school average class size: 15. Upper school faculty-student ratio: 1:15. There are 180 required school days per year for Upper School students. Upper School students typically attend 5 days per week. The average school day consists of 6 hours and 40 minutes.

Upper School Student Profile Grade 9: 60 students (26 boys, 34 girls); Grade 10: 60 students (22 boys, 38 girls); Grade 11: 54 students (28 boys, 26 girls); Grade 12: 37 students (18 boys, 19 girls). 96% of students are Roman Catholic.

Faculty School total: 21. In upper school: 13 men, 8 women; 12 have advanced degrees.

Special Academic Programs Advanced Placement exam preparation; independent study.

College Admission Counseling 59 students graduated in 2009; 58 went to college, including Carroll University; Concordia University Wisconsin; University of Wisconsin–La Crosse; University of Wisconsin–Madison; University of Wisconsin–Milwaukee. Other: 1 entered a postgraduate year. Mean composite ACT: 23. 34% scored over 26 on composite ACT.

Student Life Upper grades have specified standards of dress, student council, honor system. Discipline rests primarily with faculty. Attendance at religious services is required.

Admissions Traditional secondary-level entrance grade is 9. For fall 2009, 211 students applied for upper-level admission, 211 were accepted, 211 enrolled. Deadline for receipt of application materials: none. No application fee required. On-campus interview required.

Athletics Interscholastic: baseball (boys), basketball (b,g), football (b); intramural: ice hockey (b,g); coed interscholastic: alpine skiing. 1 PE instructor, 19 coaches, 1 athletic trainer.

Computers Computers are regularly used in accounting, basic skills, business applications, business education, business skills, photography, publications, publishing, research skills, senior seminar, stock market, technology, typing, word processing, writing, yearbook classes. Computer resources include on-campus library services, Internet access, Internet filtering or blocking technology.

Contact Mr. Lawrence P. Theiss, Principal. 715-845-8274. Fax: 715-842-1302. E-mail: ltheiss@newmancatholicschools.com.

THE NEWMAN SCHOOL
247 Marlborough Street
Boston, Massachusetts 02116
General Information Coeducational day college-preparatory and ESL school. Grades 9–PG. Founded: 1945. Setting: urban. 2 buildings on campus. Approved or accredited by Association of Independent Schools in New England, New England Association of Schools and Colleges, and Massachusetts Department of Education.

Member of Secondary School Admission Test Board. Total enrollment: 230. Upper school average class size: 14. Upper school faculty-student ratio: 1:14.

See Display on page 453 and Close-Up on page 816.

NEW MEXICO MILITARY INSTITUTE

101 West College Boulevard
Roswell, New Mexico 88201
Head of School: Maj. Gen. Jerry W. Grizzle
General Information Coeducational boarding college-preparatory, arts, Junior Reserve Officer Training Corps (JROTC), and military school. Grades 9–12. Founded: 1891. Setting: small town. Nearest major city is Albuquerque. Students are housed in coed dormitories. 300-acre campus. 17 buildings on campus. Approved or accredited by Council of Accreditation and School Improvement, North Central Association of Colleges and Schools, and New Mexico Department of Education. Member of Secondary School Admission Test Board. Endowment: $130 million. Total enrollment: 380. Upper school average class size: 14. Upper school faculty-student ratio: 1:14. There are 180 required school days per year for Upper School students. Upper School students typically attend 7 days per week. The average school day consists of 9 hours.
Upper School Student Profile Grade 9: 96 students (82 boys, 14 girls); Grade 10: 88 students (73 boys, 15 girls); Grade 11: 111 students (94 boys, 17 girls); Grade 12: 86 students (68 boys, 18 girls). 100% of students are boarding students. 45% are state residents. 44 states are represented in upper school student body. 14% are international students. International students from China, Mexico, Poland, Republic of Korea, United Arab Emirates, and United States Minor Outlying Islands; 14 other countries represented in student body.
Faculty School total: 77. In upper school: 37 men, 31 women; 66 have advanced degrees.
Subjects Offered Algebra, American history, American literature, Arabic, art, art history, biology, business, business skills, calculus, chemistry, computer programming, computer science, creative writing, drafting, drama, driver education, earth science, ecology, economics, English, English literature, European history, fine arts, French, geology, geometry, government/civics, grammar, health, history, journalism, JROTC, mathematics, mechanical drawing, music, physical education, physics, science, social sciences, social studies, sociology, Spanish, speech, theater, trigonometry, typing, world history, writing.
Graduation Requirements Arts and fine arts (art, music, dance, drama), business skills (includes word processing), computer science, English, foreign language, JROTC, mathematics, physical education (includes health), science, social sciences, social studies (includes history), all graduates take the ACT as a condition of graduation.
Special Academic Programs Honors section; study at local college for college credit.
College Admission Counseling 62 students graduated in 2009; 61 went to college, including New Mexico Military Institute; New Mexico State University; United States Air Force Academy; United States Naval Academy; University of New Mexico. Other: 1 went to work. Median composite ACT: 22. 24% scored over 26 on composite ACT.
Student Life Upper grades have uniform requirement, student council, honor system. Discipline rests primarily with students.
Tuition and Aid 7-day tuition and room/board: $12,301. Tuition installment plan (monthly payment plans, individually arranged payment plans). Merit scholarship grants, need-based scholarship grants available. In 2009–10, 70% of upper-school students received aid; total upper-school merit-scholarship money awarded: $450,000. Total amount of financial aid awarded in 2009–10: $750,000.
Admissions Traditional secondary-level entrance grade is 9. For fall 2009, 678 students applied for upper-level admission, 305 were accepted, 249 enrolled. Common entrance examinations required. Deadline for receipt of application materials: none. Application fee required: $85. Interview required.
Athletics Interscholastic: baseball (boys), basketball (b,g), cheering (b,g), cross-country running (b,g), diving (b,g), football (b), strength & conditioning (b,g), tennis (b,g), track and field (g), volleyball (g), weight training (b,g); coed interscholastic: drill team, fitness, golf, JROTC drill, life saving, marksmanship, physical fitness, physical training, riflery, running, soccer, swimming and diving, tennis; coed intramural: aerobics/Nautilus, alpine skiing, aquatics, archery, bowling, climbing, combined training, fencing, fitness, flag football, Frisbee, martial arts, Nautilus, paint ball, physical fitness, physical training, racquetball, ropes courses, running, self defense, skiing (downhill), softball, strength & conditioning, swimming and diving, touch football, ultimate Frisbee, weight lifting, weight training, yoga. 3 PE instructors, 11 coaches, 2 athletic trainers.
Computers Computers are regularly used in all classes. Computer network features include on-campus library services, online commercial services, Internet access, wireless campus network, Internet filtering or blocking technology. Campus intranet, student e-mail accounts, and computer access in designated common areas are available to students. Students grades are available online. The school has a published electronic and media policy.
Contact Maj. Sonya Rodriguez, Director of Admissions and Financial Aid. 575-624-8065. Fax: 575-624-8058. E-mail: admissions@nmmi.edu. Web site: www.nmmi.edu.

NEW TRIBES MISSION ACADEMY

PO Box 707
Durham, Ontario N0G 1R0, Canada
Head of School: Helmut Penner
General Information Coeducational day college-preparatory school, affiliated with Baptist Bible Fellowship, Brethren Church. Boys grades 3–11, girls grades 7–10. Founded: 1992. Setting: small town. 1-acre campus. 1 building on campus. Approved or accredited by Association of Christian Schools International. Language of instruction: English. Total enrollment: 21. Upper school average class size: 6. Upper school faculty-student ratio: 1:3. There are 168 required school days per year for Upper School students. Upper School students typically attend 5 days per week.
Upper School Student Profile Grade 6: 2 students (2 boys); Grade 7: 5 students (3 boys, 2 girls); Grade 8: 2 students (1 boy, 1 girl); Grade 9: 1 student (1 boy); Grade 10: 3 students (1 boy, 2 girls); Grade 11: 2 students (2 boys). 80% of students are Baptist Bible Fellowship, Brethren.
Faculty School total: 8. In upper school: 3 men, 2 women.
Subjects Offered Algebra, art, Bible studies, biology, computer applications, English language and composition-AP, French, geography, history, literature, physical education.
Graduation Requirements Advanced math, algebra, Bible studies, biology, Canadian geography, Canadian history, chemistry, computer skills, consumer mathematics, English, English language and composition-AP, English literature and composition-AP, French, history, mathematics, physical education (includes health), physics, science.
College Admission Counseling 1 student graduated in 2009 and went to college.
Student Life Upper grades have specified standards of dress. Discipline rests equally with students and faculty.
Tuition and Aid Day student tuition: CAN$1200. Tuition installment plan (monthly payment plans).
Admissions CAT or SAT required. Deadline for receipt of application materials: August 24. No application fee required. Interview recommended.
Athletics Coed Intramural: archery, badminton, basketball, floor hockey, indoor soccer, soccer, track and field, volleyball. 1 PE instructor.
Computers Computer access in designated common areas is available to students.
Contact Helmut Penner, Principal. 519-369-2622. Fax: 519-369-5828. E-mail: academy@ntmc.ca.

NEW WAY LEARNING ACADEMY

Scottsdale, Arizona
See Special Needs Schools section.

NEW YORK MILITARY ACADEMY

78 Academy Avenue
Cornwall-on-Hudson, New York 12520
Head of School: Capt. Robert D. Watts
General Information Coeducational boarding and day college-preparatory, Junior ROTC, ESL, and military school. Grades 7–12. Founded: 1889. Setting: small town. Nearest major city is New York. Students are housed in single-sex dormitories. 165-acre campus. 11 buildings on campus. Approved or accredited by Middle States Association of Colleges and Schools, New York State Association of Independent Schools, The Association of Boarding Schools, and New York Department of Education. Member of National Association of Independent Schools and Secondary School Admission Test Board. Languages of instruction: English, Spanish, and French. Endowment: $2.6 million. Total enrollment: 141. Upper school average class size: 10. Upper school faculty-student ratio: 1:10. There are 180 required school days per year for Upper School students. Upper School students typically attend 5 days per week. The average school day consists of 6 hours and 30 minutes.
Upper School Student Profile Grade 9: 17 students (13 boys, 4 girls); Grade 10: 28 students (22 boys, 6 girls); Grade 11: 38 students (31 boys, 7 girls); Grade 12: 41 students (29 boys, 12 girls); Grade 13: 124 students (95 boys, 29 girls). 82% of students are boarding students. 66% are state residents. 8 states are represented in upper school student body. 13% are international students. International students from Ethiopia, Guadeloupe, Hong Kong, Mexico, Republic of Korea, and Venezuela; 3 other countries represented in student body.
Faculty School total: 20. In upper school: 8 men, 12 women; 15 have advanced degrees; 16 reside on campus.
Subjects Offered Algebra, American history, American history-AP, art, biology, business mathematics, chemistry, computer literacy, criminology, earth science, economics, English, English-AP, environmental science, geography, geometry, government, health, JROTC, physical science, physics, pre-calculus, social studies, Spanish, trigonometry, world history.
Graduation Requirements American history, art, biology, calculus, chemistry, computer science, economics, English, English composition, English literature, foreign language, global studies, government, JROTC or LEAD (Leadership Education and Development), mathematics, physical education (includes health), science, trigonometry. Community service is required.

Special Academic Programs 2 Advanced Placement exams for which test preparation is offered; honors section; study at local college for college credit; ESL (12 students enrolled)

College Admission Counseling 40 students graduated in 2009; 38 went to college, including American University; Boston University; Drexel University; Embry-Riddle Aeronautical University; Stony Brook University, State University of New York; United States Military Academy. Other: 2 had other specific plans.

Student Life Upper grades have uniform requirement, student council, honor system. Discipline rests equally with students and faculty. Attendance at religious services is required.

Tuition and Aid Day student tuition: $8200; 7-day tuition and room/board: $27,825. Tuition installment plan (individually arranged payment plans). Tuition reduction for siblings, merit scholarship grants, need-based scholarship grants, Sallie Mae loans available. In 2009–10, 74% of upper-school students received aid; total upper-school merit-scholarship money awarded: $36,000. Total amount of financial aid awarded in 2009–10: $355,000.

Admissions Traditional secondary-level entrance grade is 10. For fall 2009, 51 students applied for upper-level admission, 42 were accepted, 36 enrolled. California Achievement Test, Cooperative Entrance Exam (McGraw-Hill), Iowa Tests of Basic Skills, Otis-Lennon School Ability Test, PSAT and SAT for applicants to grade 11 and 12, SLEP, SSAT, Stanford Achievement Test or TOEFL required. Deadline for receipt of application materials: none. Application fee required: $100. On-campus interview required.

Athletics Interscholastic: baseball (boys), basketball (b,g), football (b), ice hockey (b), lacrosse (b), soccer (b), softball (g), volleyball (g), wrestling (b); intramural: hockey (b); coed interscholastic: cross-country running, drill team, fencing, golf, JROTC drill, marksmanship, martial arts, paint ball, project adventure, riflery, tennis, track and field, weight lifting; coed intramural: dance, dance team, equestrian sports, handball, ice skating, martial arts. 1 PE instructor, 1 coach, 1 athletic trainer.

Computers Computers are regularly used in all academic classes. Computer network features include on-campus library services, Internet access, Internet filtering or blocking technology. Student e-mail accounts are available to students. Students grades are available online. The school has a published electronic and media policy.

Contact Ms. Maureen T. Kelly, Assistant Director of Admissions. 845-534-3710 Ext. 4249. Fax: 845-534-7699. E-mail: mkelly@nyma.org. Web site: www.nyma.org.

NIAGARA CHRISTIAN COMMUNITY OF SCHOOLS
2619 Niagara Boulevard
Fort Erie, Ontario L2A 5M4, Canada
Head of School: Mr. Mark Thiessen

General Information Coeducational boarding and day college-preparatory, general academic, arts, business, and religious studies school, affiliated with Brethren in Christ Church. Boarding grades 9–12, day grades JK–12. Founded: 1932. Setting: rural. Nearest major city is Niagara Falls, Canada. Students are housed in single-sex dormitories. 121-acre campus. 15 buildings on campus. Approved or accredited by Association of Christian Schools International and Ontario Department of Education. Language of instruction: English. Total enrollment: 266. Upper school average class size: 17. Upper school faculty-student ratio: 1:17. There are 177 required school days per year for Upper School students. Upper School students typically attend 5 days per week. The average school day consists of 7 hours.

Upper School Student Profile Grade 9: 28 students (16 boys, 12 girls); Grade 10: 22 students (11 boys, 11 girls); Grade 11: 66 students (43 boys, 23 girls); Grade 12: 75 students (38 boys, 37 girls). 70% of students are boarding students. 25% are province residents. 2 provinces are represented in upper school student body. 75% are international students. International students from Cayman Islands, Hong Kong, Japan, Mexico, Republic of Korea, and Taiwan; 4 other countries represented in student body. 17% of students are Brethren in Christ Church.

Faculty School total: 22. In upper school: 11 men, 11 women; 4 have advanced degrees; 1 resides on campus.

Subjects Offered Accounting, advanced chemistry, advanced computer applications, advanced math, Advanced Placement courses, advanced TOEFL/grammar, algebra, American history, analysis and differential calculus, analysis of data, analytic geometry, anatomy, ancient history, anthropology, art, art history, athletics, Bible, biology, biology-AP, business, business applications, business education, business mathematics, business technology, calculus, calculus-AP, Canadian geography, Canadian history, Canadian literature, career education, chemistry, choir, civics, computer applications, computer programming, concert choir, CPR, data processing, discrete mathematics, dramatic arts, early childhood, economics, English, English literature, ESL, European history, exercise science, family studies, French as a second language, general math, geography, geometry, guidance, health education, history, information technology, instrumental music, integrated science, international affairs, leadership education training, Life of Christ, mathematics, media studies, medieval history, modern world history, music, parenting, physical education, physics, politics, pre-calculus, science, Spanish, TOEFL preparation, world history, world history-AP, world issues, world religions, writing, writing.

Special Academic Programs Special instructional classes for students with learning disabilities; ESL (125 students enrolled).

The Nichols School

College Admission Counseling 88 students graduated in 2010; 80 went to college, including Brock University; McMaster University; The University of Western Ontario; University of Toronto; University of Waterloo; Wilfrid Laurier University. Other: 8 had other specific plans.

Student Life Upper grades have uniform requirement, student council, honor system. Discipline rests primarily with faculty. Attendance at religious services is required.

Tuition and Aid Day student tuition: CAN$7695; 5-day tuition and room/board: CAN$16,990; 7-day tuition and room/board: CAN$29,890. Tuition installment plan (monthly payment plans, individually arranged payment plans, quarterly payment plan). Tuition reduction for siblings, bursaries, merit scholarship grants, need-based scholarship grants, paying campus jobs available. In 2010–11, 40% of upper-school students received aid; total upper-school merit-scholarship money awarded: CAN$50,000. Total amount of financial aid awarded in 2010–11: CAN$400,000.

Admissions Traditional secondary-level entrance grade is 9. For fall 2010, 61 students applied for upper-level admission, 53 were accepted, 50 enrolled. Admissions testing and English proficiency required. Deadline for receipt of application materials: none. Application fee required: CAN$100. Interview required.

Athletics Interscholastic: badminton (boys, girls), basketball (b,g), cross-country running (b,g), golf (b), hockey (b,g), ice hockey (b,g); intramural: basketball (b,g), indoor soccer (b,g); coed interscholastic: badminton; coed intramural: aerobics, alpine skiing, badminton, ball hockey, baseball, bowling, canoeing/kayaking, cross-country running, fitness, fitness walking, floor hockey, golf, ice skating. 1 PE instructor, 1 coach.

Computers Computers are regularly used in accounting, business, data processing, economics, ESL, mathematics, science, yearbook classes. Computer network features include on-campus library services, Internet access, wireless campus network, Internet filtering or blocking technology. Computer access in designated common areas is available to students. Students grades are available online. The school has a published electronic and media policy.

Contact Mr. Tom Auld, Director of Student Life. 905-871-6980 Ext. 2280. Fax: 905-871-9260. E-mail: tomauld@niagaracc.com. Web site: www.niagaracc.com.

THE NICHOLS SCHOOL
1250 Amherst Street
Buffalo, New York 14216
Head of School: Richard C. Bryan Jr.

General Information Coeducational day college-preparatory, arts, and technology school. Grades 5–12. Founded: 1892. Setting: urban. 32-acre campus. 8 buildings on campus. Approved or accredited by New York Department of Education, New York State Association of Independent Schools, and New York Department of Education. Member of National Association of Independent Schools. Endowment: $21 million. Total enrollment: 556. Upper school average class size: 14. Upper school faculty-student ratio: 1:8. Upper School students typically attend 5 days per week. The average school day consists of 7 hours.

Upper School Student Profile Grade 9: 98 students (57 boys, 41 girls); Grade 10: 94 students (45 boys, 49 girls); Grade 11: 82 students (37 boys, 45 girls); Grade 12: 102 students (51 boys, 51 girls).

Faculty School total: 73. In upper school: 28 men, 19 women; 45 have advanced degrees.

Subjects Offered Algebra, American history, American literature, anatomy, art, art history, biology, calculus, chemistry, Chinese, community service, computer graphics, computer math, computer programming, computer science, creative writing, dance, drama, driver education, earth science, economics, English, English literature, environmental science, European history, expository writing, fine arts, French, geology, geometry, government/civics, history, Latin, mathematics, music, photography, physical education, physics, science, social studies, Spanish, speech, theater, trigonometry, world history, world literature.

Graduation Requirements Arts and fine arts (art, music, dance, drama), English, foreign language, mathematics, physical education (includes health), science, social studies (includes history).

Special Academic Programs Advanced Placement exam preparation; honors section; independent study; study abroad.

College Admission Counseling 103 students graduated in 2010; 102 went to college, including Hobart and William Smith Colleges; Rochester Institute of Technology; St. Lawrence University; The George Washington University; University at Buffalo, the State University of New York; University of Rochester. Other: 1 had other specific plans. Median SAT critical reading: 590, median SAT math: 610, median SAT writing: 580. 46% scored over 600 on SAT critical reading, 56% scored over 600 on SAT math, 42% scored over 600 on SAT writing.

Student Life Upper grades have specified standards of dress, student council, honor system. Discipline rests equally with students and faculty.

Summer Programs Remediation, enrichment, advancement, art/fine arts programs offered; session focuses on academic enrichment; held on campus; accepts boys and girls; open to students from other schools. 68 students usually enrolled. 2011 schedule: June 15 to August 15. Application deadline: none.

Tuition and Aid Day student tuition: $17,200–$18,800. Tuition installment plan (Insured Tuition Payment Plan, monthly payment plans). Need-based scholarship grants available. In 2010–11, 30% of upper-school students received aid. Total amount of financial aid awarded in 2010–11: $1,500,000.

The Nichols School

Admissions Traditional secondary-level entrance grade is 9. For fall 2010, 205 students applied for upper-level admission, 185 were accepted, 115 enrolled. Otis-Lennon and 2 sections of ERB required. Deadline for receipt of application materials: none. Application fee required: $35. On-campus interview required.

Athletics Interscholastic: baseball (boys), basketball (b,g), crew (b,g), cross-country running (b,g), field hockey (g), football (b), golf (b,g), hockey (b,g), ice hockey (b,g), lacrosse (b,g), soccer (b,g), softball (g), squash (b,g), tennis (b,g), volleyball (g), wrestling (b); coed interscholastic: aerobics, aerobics/dance, dance, modern dance; coed intramural: aerobics/dance. 21 coaches, 1 athletic trainer.

Computers Computers are regularly used in art, library skills, newspaper, photography, science, technology, yearbook classes. Computer network features include on-campus library services, online commercial services, Internet access. Student e-mail accounts are available to students. The school has a published electronic and media policy.

Contact Mrs. Heather Newton, Director of Admissions. 716-332-6325. Fax: 716-875-6474. E-mail: hnewton@nicholsschool.org. Web site: www.nicholsschool.org.

NOAH WEBSTER CHRISTIAN SCHOOL

3411 Cleveland Avenue
PO Box 21239
Cheyenne, Wyoming 82003
Head of School: Miss Shirley Falk

General Information Coeducational day college-preparatory and general academic school, affiliated with Evangelical/Fundamental faith. Grades K–12. Founded: 1987. Setting: small town. Nearest major city is Denver, CO. 1 building on campus. Approved or accredited by Association of Christian Schools International. Total enrollment: 87. Upper school average class size: 11. Upper school faculty-student ratio: 1:11. There are 176 required school days per year for Upper School students. Upper School students typically attend 5 days per week. The average school day consists of 6 hours and 30 minutes.

Upper School Student Profile Grade 9: 5 students (2 boys, 3 girls); Grade 10: 4 students (2 boys, 2 girls); Grade 11: 2 students (1 boy, 1 girl).

Faculty School total: 15. In upper school: 1 man, 7 women; 1 has an advanced degree.

Special Academic Programs Independent study; study at local college for college credit.

College Admission Counseling 2 students graduated in 2009; all went to college.

Student Life Upper grades have specified standards of dress. Discipline rests primarily with faculty.

Admissions Deadline for receipt of application materials: none. Application fee required. On-campus interview required.

Athletics 1 PE instructor.

Computers Computer network features include Internet access, Internet filtering or blocking technology. Computer access in designated common areas is available to students.

Contact 307-635-2175. Fax: 307-773-8523. Web site: www.cheyennenoahwebster.com.

NOBLE ACADEMY

Greensboro, North Carolina
See Special Needs Schools section.

NOBLE AND GREENOUGH SCHOOL

10 Campus Drive
Dedham, Massachusetts 02026-4099
Head of School: Mr. Robert P. Henderson Jr.

General Information Coeducational boarding and day college-preparatory school. Boarding grades 9–12, day grades 7–12. Founded: 1866. Setting: suburban. Nearest major city is Boston. Students are housed in single-sex dormitories. 187-acre campus. 12 buildings on campus. Approved or accredited by Association of Independent Schools in New England, New England Association of Schools and Colleges, The College Board, and Massachusetts Department of Education. Member of National Association of Independent Schools and Secondary School Admission Test Board. Endowment: $80 million. Total enrollment: 581. Upper school average class size: 14. Upper school faculty-student ratio: 1:7. There are 162 required school days per year for Upper School students. Upper School students typically attend 5 days per week. The average school day consists of 7 hours and 5 minutes.

Upper School Student Profile Grade 9: 118 students (54 boys, 64 girls); Grade 10: 113 students (61 boys, 52 girls); Grade 11: 121 students (57 boys, 64 girls); Grade 12: 115 students (56 boys, 59 girls). 8% of students are boarding students. 99% are state residents. 5 states are represented in upper school student body.

Faculty School total: 116. In upper school: 59 men, 57 women; 35 reside on campus.

Subjects Offered 20th century history, Advanced Placement courses, African-American literature, algebra, American history, American literature, anatomy, ancient history, art, art history, astronomy, biology, calculus, ceramics, chemistry, community service, computer programming, computer science, concert band, creative writing, drama, drawing, earth science, ecology, economics, English, English literature,

environmental science, ethics, European history, expository writing, fine arts, French, genetics, geography, geometry, government/civics, grammar, health, history, independent study, Japanese, journalism, Latin, Latin American history, marine biology, mathematics, music, painting, philosophy, photography, physics, physiology, printmaking, psychology, Roman civilization, science, senior internship, senior project, social studies, Spanish, speech, statistics, theater, trigonometry, Vietnam, world history, world literature, writing.

Graduation Requirements Arts and fine arts (art, music, dance, drama), computer science, English, foreign language, mathematics, performing arts, physical education (includes health), science, social studies (includes history), 80 hours of community service must be completed.

Special Academic Programs Advanced Placement exam preparation; honors section; independent study; term-away projects; study abroad; academic accommodation for the gifted, the musically talented, and the artistically talented.

College Admission Counseling 117 students graduated in 2009; all went to college, including Boston College; Brown University; Dartmouth College; Duke University; Harvard University; Princeton University. 72% scored over 600 on SAT critical reading, 75% scored over 600 on SAT math, 80% scored over 600 on SAT writing.

Student Life Upper grades have specified standards of dress, student council, honor system. Discipline rests equally with students and faculty.

Tuition and Aid Day student tuition: $33,900; 5-day tuition and room/board: $38,900. Tuition installment plan (Tuition Management Systems). Need-based scholarship grants, need-based loans available. In 2009–10, 20% of upper-school students received aid. Total amount of financial aid awarded in 2009–10: $2,531,050.

Admissions Traditional secondary-level entrance grade is 9. For fall 2009, 527 students applied for upper-level admission, 126 were accepted, 70 enrolled. ISEE or SSAT required. Deadline for receipt of application materials: January 15. Application fee required: $50. On-campus interview required.

Athletics Interscholastic: baseball (boys), basketball (b,g), crew (b,g), cross-country running (b,g), field hockey (g), football (b); coed intramural: aerobics/dance, dance. 12 coaches, 2 athletic trainers.

Computers Computers are regularly used in English, foreign language, history, journalism, Latin, mathematics, music, science classes. Computer network features include on-campus library services, online commercial services, Internet access, Internet filtering or blocking technology, NoblesNet (first class e-mail and bulletin board with electronic conferencing capability), wireless iBooks. Campus intranet, student e-mail accounts, and computer access in designated common areas are available to students. The school has a published electronic and media policy.

Contact Ms. Jennifer Hines, Dean of Enrollment Management. 781-320-7100. Fax: 781-320-1329. E-mail: admission@nobles.edu. Web site: www.nobles.edu.

THE NORA SCHOOL

955 Sligo Avenue
Silver Spring, Maryland 20910
Head of School: David E. Mullen

General Information Coeducational day college-preparatory, arts, and technology school. Grades 9–12. Founded: 1964. Setting: urban. Nearest major city is Washington, DC. 1-acre campus. 1 building on campus. Approved or accredited by Association of Independent Schools of Greater Washington, Middle States Association of Colleges and Schools, and Maryland Department of Education. Endowment: $208,000. Total enrollment: 60. Upper school average class size: 8. Upper school faculty-student ratio: 1:5. There are 175 required school days per year for Upper School students. Upper School students typically attend 5 days per week. The average school day consists of 5 hours and 35 minutes.

Upper School Student Profile Grade 9: 6 students (1 boy, 5 girls); Grade 10: 21 students (14 boys, 7 girls); Grade 11: 15 students (10 boys, 5 girls); Grade 12: 17 students (9 boys, 8 girls).

Faculty School total: 12. In upper school: 9 men, 3 women; 11 have advanced degrees.

Subjects Offered African-American literature, algebra, American literature, American studies, art, art history, astronomy, biology, British literature, calculus, ceramics, chemistry, college writing, community service, computer graphics, conceptual physics, conflict resolution, crafts, creative writing, English composition, environmental science, expository writing, film and literature, forensics, geography, geometry, German, graphic design, illustration, integrated science, peace studies, peer counseling, photo shop, photography, physical education, physics, political science, pre-algebra, pre-calculus, psychology, sculpture, Shakespeare, social justice, Spanish, street law, studio art, trigonometry, U.S. history, wilderness education, women's literature, world history, world religions, writing.

Graduation Requirements Arts and fine arts (art, music, dance, drama), English, foreign language, lab science, mathematics, personal fitness, science, social studies (includes history), sports, U.S. history, wilderness education, writing, graduation portfolio. Community service is required.

Special Academic Programs Independent study; term-away projects; study at local college for college credit; academic accommodation for the gifted and the artistically talented; remedial reading and/or remedial writing; remedial math; programs in English, mathematics, general development for dyslexic students; special instructional classes for students with Attention Deficit Disorder and learning disabilities, students who have been unsuccessful in a traditional learning environment.

College Admission Counseling 15 students graduated in 2010; 14 went to college, including Dickinson College; Drew University; Florida Gulf Coast University; Goucher College; Loyola University Maryland; Mount Holyoke College. Other: 1 went to work.

Student Life Upper grades have student council. Discipline rests primarily with faculty.

Tuition and Aid Day student tuition: $21,450. Tuition installment plan (Key Tuition Payment Plan, monthly payment plans, individually arranged payment plans). Need-based scholarship grants, Black Student Fund, Latino Student Fund, Washington Scholarship Fund available. In 2010–11, 18% of upper-school students received aid. Total amount of financial aid awarded in 2010–11: $115,000.

Admissions Traditional secondary-level entrance grade is 9. For fall 2010, 41 students applied for upper-level admission, 32 were accepted, 19 enrolled. Writing sample required. Deadline for receipt of application materials: none. Application fee required: $75. On-campus interview required.

Athletics Interscholastic: basketball (boys, girls); intramural: cheering (g); coed interscholastic: soccer, softball; coed intramural: alpine skiing, backpacking, bicycling, bowling, canoeing/kayaking, climbing, cooperative games, hiking/backpacking, ice skating, kayaking, outdoor activities, outdoor adventure, rafting, rock climbing, ropes courses, skiing (downhill), table tennis, tennis, volleyball, wilderness. 2 coaches.

Computers Computers are regularly used in art, college planning, creative writing, design, drawing and design, English, graphic arts, graphic design, independent study, literary magazine, mathematics, photography, SAT preparation, writing, writing, yearbook classes. Computer network features include on-campus library services, online commercial services, Internet access, wireless campus network, Internet filtering or blocking technology. Students grades are available online. The school has a published electronic and media policy.

Contact Janette Patterson, Director of Admissions. 301-495-6672. Fax: 301-495-7829. E-mail: janette@nora-school.org. Web site: www.nora-school.org.

NORFOLK ACADEMY

1585 Wesleyan Drive
Norfolk, Virginia 23502
Head of School: Mr. Dennis G. Manning

General Information Coeducational day college-preparatory school. Grades 1–12. Founded: 1728. Setting: suburban. 70-acre campus. 14 buildings on campus. Approved or accredited by Southern Association of Colleges and Schools, Virginia Association of Independent Schools, and Virginia Department of Education. Member of National Association of Independent Schools. Endowment: $3.2 million. Total enrollment: 1,230. Upper school average class size: 20. Upper school faculty-student ratio: 1:10.

Upper School Student Profile Grade 10: 124 students (69 boys, 55 girls); Grade 11: 117 students (61 boys, 56 girls); Grade 12: 106 students (52 boys, 54 girls).

Faculty School total: 124. In upper school: 39 men, 13 women; 32 have advanced degrees.

Subjects Offered Algebra, American history, American literature, art, art history, band, biology, calculus, chemistry, chorus, computer math, computer programming, computer science, dance, driver education, economics, English, English literature, environmental science, European history, film studies, fine arts, French, geography, geometry, German, government/civics, health, history, instrumental music, Italian, Latin, mathematics, music, music history, music theory, physical education, physics, science, social studies, Spanish, speech, statistics, studio art, theater arts, world history.

Graduation Requirements Arts and fine arts (art, music, dance, drama), English, foreign language, mathematics, physical education (includes health), science, social studies (includes history), 8-minute senior speech, seminar program. Community service is required.

Special Academic Programs Advanced Placement exam preparation; study abroad; academic accommodation for the gifted, the musically talented, and the artistically talented.

College Admission Counseling 115 students graduated in 2010; all went to college, including The College of William and Mary; The Johns Hopkins University; University of Virginia; Virginia Polytechnic Institute and State University. Mean SAT critical reading: 634, mean SAT math: 660, mean SAT writing: 645.

Student Life Upper grades have specified standards of dress, student council, honor system. Discipline rests primarily with students.

Summer Programs Enrichment, advancement, sports, art/fine arts programs offered; session focuses on academics and athletics; held on campus; accepts boys and girls; open to students from other schools. 500 students usually enrolled. 2011 schedule: June 22 to July 31.

Tuition and Aid Day student tuition: $19,650. Tuition installment plan (Key Tuition Payment Plan, monthly payment plans). Need-based scholarship grants, need-based loans available. In 2010–11, 17% of upper-school students received aid.

Admissions Traditional secondary-level entrance grade is 10. For fall 2010, 19 students applied for upper-level admission, 6 were accepted, 4 enrolled. ERB Achievement Test, ERB CTP IV and Otis-Lennon School Ability Test required. Deadline for receipt of application materials: January 29. Application fee required: $35. Interview required.

Athletics Interscholastic: baseball (boys), basketball (b,g), cheering (g), crew (b,g), cross-country running (b,g), diving (b,g), field hockey (g), football (b), golf (b,g),

indoor track (b,g), lacrosse (b,g), sailing (b,g), soccer (b,g), softball (g), swimming and diving (b,g), tennis (b,g), volleyball (g), winter (indoor) track (b,g), wrestling (b); intramural: ballet (g), dance (g), dance team (g), modern dance (g), physical fitness (b,g), physical training (b,g), weight training (b,g). 2 PE instructors, 2 coaches, 3 athletic trainers.

Computers Computers are regularly used in all academic classes. Computer network features include on-campus library services, Internet access, Internet filtering or blocking technology, online library resources, video production, curriculum-based software, desktop publishing, campus-wide media distribution system. Student e-mail accounts and computer access in designated common areas are available to students. The school has a published electronic and media policy.

Contact Mrs. Linda Gorsline, Director of Upper School. 757-461-6236 Ext. 5362. Fax: 757-455-3186. E-mail: lgorsline@norfolkacademy.org. Web site: www.norfolkacademy.org.

NORFOLK COLLEGIATE SCHOOL

7336 Granby Street
Norfolk, Virginia 23505
Head of School: Mr. Scott G. Kennedy

General Information Coeducational day college-preparatory school. Grades K–12. Founded: 1948. Setting: urban. 10-acre campus. 1 building on campus. Approved or accredited by Southern Association of Colleges and Schools, Southern Association of Independent Schools, Virginia Association of Independent Schools, and Virginia Department of Education. Member of National Association of Independent Schools. Total enrollment: 855. Upper school average class size: 17. Upper school faculty-student ratio: 1:10. There are 178 required school days per year for Upper School students. Upper School students typically attend 5 days per week. The average school day consists of 6 hours and 30 minutes.

Upper School Student Profile Grade 9: 74 students (32 boys, 42 girls); Grade 10: 72 students (40 boys, 32 girls); Grade 11: 88 students (52 boys, 36 girls); Grade 12: 82 students (43 boys, 39 girls).

Faculty School total: 95. In upper school: 13 men, 34 women; 29 have advanced degrees.

Subjects Offered Algebra, American history, American literature, analysis, ancient world history, art, art history, band, biology, biology-AP, calculus-AP, chemistry, chemistry-AP, chorus, computer-aided design, concert band, cultural geography, drawing, driver education, English, English language-AP, English literature, English literature-AP, environmental science-AP, European history-AP, expository writing, family living, film studies, first aid, French, geometry, German, global issues, government-AP, government/civics, graphic arts, history, human geography—AP, independent study, jazz band, journalism, Latin, Latin-AP, linear algebra, marine biology, mathematics, music, oceanography, painting, photography, physical education, physics, pottery, pre-calculus, psychology-AP, public speaking, publications, science, social studies, Spanish, statistics-AP, trigonometry, U.S. and Virginia government-AP, U.S. government and politics-AP, U.S. history-AP, video communication, video film production, world geography, world history-AP, yearbook.

Graduation Requirements Algebra, arts and fine arts (art, music, dance, drama), biology, chemistry, computer literacy, English composition, English literature, family living, first aid, foreign language, geometry, health education, mathematics, physical education (includes health), science, senior project, social studies (includes history), U.S. and Virginia government, U.S. and Virginia history, Western civilization.

Special Academic Programs 15 Advanced Placement exams for which test preparation is offered; honors section; independent study; academic accommodation for the gifted; programs in English, mathematics, general development for dyslexic students.

College Admission Counseling 89 students graduated in 2009; 88 went to college, including George Mason University; James Madison University; Old Dominion University; The College of William and Mary; University of Virginia; Virginia Polytechnic Institute and State University. Other: 1 entered a postgraduate year. Median SAT critical reading: 600, median SAT math: 610, median SAT writing: 610, median combined SAT: 1800, median composite ACT: 27. 43% scored over 600 on SAT critical reading, 47% scored over 600 on SAT math, 42% scored over 600 on SAT writing, 50% scored over 1800 on combined SAT, 54% scored over 26 on composite ACT.

Student Life Upper grades have specified standards of dress, student council, honor system. Discipline rests primarily with faculty.

Tuition and Aid Day student tuition: $13,200. Tuition installment plan (monthly payment plans, individually arranged payment plans, semiannual payment plan, The Tuition Refund Plan). Merit scholarship grants, need-based scholarship grants available. In 2009–10, 26% of upper-school students received aid; total upper-school merit-scholarship money awarded: $14,525. Total amount of financial aid awarded in 2009–10: $586,310.

Admissions Traditional secondary-level entrance grade is 9. For fall 2009, 53 students applied for upper-level admission, 42 were accepted, 22 enrolled. ERB CTP IV, ERB Reading and Math, essay and Otis-Lennon School Ability Test required. Deadline for receipt of application materials: February 13. Application fee required: $50. On-campus interview required.

Athletics Interscholastic: baseball (boys), basketball (b,g), cross-country running (b,g), field hockey (g), lacrosse (b,g), soccer (b,g), softball (g), swimming and diving (b,g), tennis (b,g), track and field (b,g), volleyball (b,g), wrestling (b); coed interscholastic: cheering, crew, golf, sailing; coed intramural: sailing. 3 PE instructors, 42 coaches, 1 athletic trainer.

Computers Computers are regularly used in art, career exploration, college planning, computer applications, current events, desktop publishing, drawing and design, English, foreign language, graphic arts, health, history, human geography—AP, humanities, independent study, journalism, library skills, literary magazine, mathematics, music, newspaper, photojournalism, publishing, research skills, SAT preparation, science, senior seminar, social sciences, stock market, video film production, Web site design, yearbook classes. Computer network features include on-campus library services, online commercial services, Internet access, Internet filtering or blocking technology, ProQuest, Biography Resource Center, Contemporary Literary Criticism, Expanded Academic ASAP, ELibrary, Health and Wellness Resource Center, InfoTrac. Students grades are available online. The school has a published electronic and media policy.

Contact Brenda H. Waters, Director of Admissions. 757-480-1495. Fax: 757-588-8655. E-mail: bwaters@norfolkcollegiate.org. Web site: www.norfolkcollegiate.org.

THE NORTH BROWARD PREPARATORY UPPER SCHOOL

7600 Lyons Road
Coconut Creek, Florida 33073
Head of School: Thomas L. Marcy, EdD

General Information Coeducational boarding and day college-preparatory, arts, and technology school, Boarding grades 8–12, day grades PK–12. Founded: 1957. Setting: suburban. Students are housed in single-sex dormitories. 75-acre campus. 10 buildings on campus. Approved or accredited by Florida Council of Independent Schools and Southern Association of Colleges and Schools. Total enrollment: 1,375. Upper school average class size: 16. Upper school faculty-student ratio: 1:18. There are 177 required school days per year for Upper School students. Upper School students typically attend 5 days per week. The average school day consists of 6 hours and 20 minutes.

Upper School Student Profile Grade 6: 92 students (56 boys, 36 girls); Grade 7: 119 students (74 boys, 45 girls); Grade 8: 108 students (66 boys, 42 girls); Grade 9: 131 students (63 boys, 68 girls); Grade 10: 166 students (85 boys, 81 girls); Grade 11: 230 students (150 boys, 80 girls); Grade 12: 169 students (93 boys, 76 girls). 15% of students are boarding students. 85% are state residents. 3 states are represented in upper school student body. 1% are international students. International students from Brazil, China, Germany, Italy, Republic of Korea, and Russian Federation; 6 other countries represented in student body.

Faculty School total: 104. In upper school: 39 men, 65 women; 45 have advanced degrees; 7 reside on campus.

Subjects Offered Algebra, American history-AP, analysis and differential calculus, analytic geometry, ancient world history, art, art history, audio visual/media, Basic programming, biology, biology-AP, British literature, broadcast journalism, business, calculus, calculus-AP, chemistry, chemistry-AP, choir, choral music, college counseling, computer applications, computer graphics, computer programming, computer programming-AP, computers, concert band, concert choir, contemporary women writers, drama workshop, dramatic arts, ecology, environmental systems, economics, English, English composition, English literature, English literature and composition-AP, environmental science, environmental science-AP, ESL, European history, European history-AP, forensics, French, French language-AP, French literature-AP, geometry, guitar, honors algebra, honors English, honors geometry, honors U.S. history, honors world history, jazz band, jazz dance, jazz ensemble, keyboarding, Latin, model United Nations, modern European history, modern European history-AP, music, music appreciation, performing arts, physical education, physical fitness, physics-AP, psychology-AP, robotics, SAT preparation, Shakespeare, skills for success, sociology, Spanish, Spanish language-AP, Spanish literature, Spanish literature-AP, U.S. government, U.S. government and politics-AP, U.S. history, U.S. literature, wind ensemble, wind instruments, women in literature, women's literature, world history-AP.

Graduation Requirements Algebra, American history, American literature, biology, calculus, chemistry, computer applications, electives, English, European history, foreign language, geometry, performing arts, physical education (includes health), physics, U.S. government, U.S. literature, world cultures. Community service is required.

Special Academic Programs International Baccalaureate program; Advanced Placement exam preparation; honors section; independent study; study at local college for college credit; academic accommodation for the gifted, the musically talented, and the artistically talented; remedial reading and/or remedial writing; remedial math; programs in English, mathematics, general development for dyslexic students; ESL (80 students enrolled).

College Admission Counseling 197 students graduated in 2009; 193 went to college, including Boston University; Duke University; Florida State University; University of Florida; University of Miami; University of Pennsylvania. Other: 4 had other specific plans. Mean SAT critical reading: 532, mean SAT math: 531, mean SAT writing: 538. 27% scored over 600 on SAT critical reading, 29% scored over 600 on SAT math, 25% scored over 600 on SAT writing, 23% scored over 1800 on combined SAT, 26% scored over 26 on composite ACT.

Student Life Upper grades have uniform requirement, student council, honor system. Discipline rests equally with students and faculty.

Tuition and Aid Day student tuition: $18,000–$20,400; 7-day tuition and room/board: $38,950. Tuition installment plan (monthly payment plans). Tuition reduction for siblings, merit scholarship grants, need-based scholarship grants available. In 2009–10, 22% of upper-school students received aid; total upper-school merit-scholarship money awarded: $1,300,000. Total amount of financial aid awarded in 2009–10: $2,400,000.

Admissions Traditional secondary-level entrance grade is 9. For fall 2009, 160 students applied for upper-level admission, 121 were accepted, 70 enrolled. SSAT required. Deadline for receipt of application materials: none. Application fee required: $150. Interview required.

Athletics Interscholastic: aquatics (boys, girls), baseball (b), basketball (b,g), bowling (g), cross-country running (b,g), dance (g), dance squad (g), dance team (g), flag football (g), football (b), golf (b,g), ice hockey (b), lacrosse (b,g), physical fitness (b,g), rugby (b), soccer (b,g), softball (g), swimming and diving (b,g), tennis (b,g), track and field (b,g), volleyball (g), water polo (b,g), winter soccer (b,g); coed interscholastic: aquatics, bowling, cheering, cross-country running, dressage, fencing, golf, physical fitness; coed intramural: basketball, flag football, scuba diving, strength & conditioning. 4 PE instructors, 18 coaches, 1 athletic trainer.

Computers Computers are regularly used in all academic classes. Computer network features include on-campus library services, online commercial services, Internet access, wireless campus network, Internet filtering or blocking technology. Campus intranet, student e-mail accounts, and computer access in designated common areas are available to students. Students grades are available online. The school has a published electronic and media policy.

Contact Jackie Fagan, Director of Admissions. 954-247-0011 Ext. 303. Fax: 954-247-0012. E-mail: faganj@nbps.org. Web site: www.nbps.org.

NORTH CLACKAMAS CHRISTIAN SCHOOL

19575 Sebastian Way
Oregon City, Oregon 97045
Head of School: Mr. Bruce Reinhardt

General Information Coeducational day college-preparatory, arts, religious studies, bilingual studies, and technology school, affiliated with Christian faith. Grades PK–12. Founded: 1973. Setting: suburban. Nearest major city is Portland. 5-acre campus. 3 buildings on campus. Approved or accredited by Association of Christian Schools International, Northwest Accreditation Commission, and Oregon Department of Education. Total enrollment: 170. Upper school average class size: 25. Upper school faculty-student ratio: 1:20. There are 168 required school days per year for Upper School students. Upper School students typically attend 5 days per week. The average school day consists of 6 hours and 30 minutes.

Upper School Student Profile Grade 7: 17 students (8 boys, 9 girls); Grade 8: 11 students (8 boys, 3 girls); Grade 9: 13 students (8 boys, 5 girls); Grade 10: 13 students (9 boys, 4 girls); Grade 11: 16 students (11 boys, 5 girls); Grade 12: 12 students (8 boys, 4 girls). 100% of students are Christian faith.

Faculty School total: 18. In upper school: 5 men, 8 women; 5 have advanced degrees.

Special Academic Programs Honors section; study at local college for college credit.

College Admission Counseling 16 students graduated in 2009; 15 went to college, including Corban University; George Fox University; Oregon State University; University of Oregon; University of Portland; Whitworth University. Other: 1 entered military service.

Student Life Upper grades have specified standards of dress, student council, honor system. Discipline rests primarily with faculty. Attendance at religious services is required.

Tuition and Aid Day student tuition: $6245. Tuition installment plan (monthly payment plans, individually arranged payment plans). Tuition reduction for siblings, need-based scholarship grants available.

Admissions Stanford Achievement Test required. Deadline for receipt of application materials: none. Application fee required: $75. On-campus interview required.

Athletics Interscholastic: basketball (boys, girls), cheering (g), cross-country running (b,g), track and field (b,g), volleyball (g); intramural: basketball (b,g), cheering (g), cross-country running (b,g), track and field (b,g), volleyball (g); coed interscholastic: soccer; coed intramural: soccer.

Computers Computers are regularly used in all academic, Bible studies classes. Computer resources include on-campus library services, Internet access, Internet filtering or blocking technology. Computer access in designated common areas is available to students. Students grades are available online.

Contact Mrs. Sherrie Fillis, Office Manager/Registrar. 503-655-5961 Ext. 100. Fax: 503-655-4875. E-mail: sherrie_fillis@ncchristianschool.com. Web site: ncchristianschool.com.

NORTH COBB CHRISTIAN SCHOOL

4500 Lakeview Drive
Kennesaw, Georgia 30144
Head of School: Mr. Todd Clingman

General Information Coeducational day college-preparatory, arts, business, and religious studies school, affiliated with Christian faith. Grades PK–12. Founded: 1983. Setting: suburban. Nearest major city is Atlanta. 16-acre campus. 3 buildings on campus. Approved or accredited by Association of Christian Schools International, Georgia Accrediting Commission, and Southern Association of Colleges and Schools. Endowment: $102,225. Total enrollment: 780. Upper school average class size: 13. Upper school faculty-student ratio: 1:10. There are 180 required school days per year for Upper School students. Upper School students typically attend 5 days per week. The average school day consists of 7 hours.

Upper School Student Profile Grade 9: 57 students (35 boys, 22 girls); Grade 10: 71 students (33 boys, 38 girls); Grade 11: 48 students (24 boys, 24 girls); Grade 12: 73 students (33 boys, 40 girls). 95% of students are Christian.

Faculty School total: 66. In upper school: 11 men, 13 women; 11 have advanced degrees.

Subjects Offered Acting, Advanced Placement courses, algebra, American literature, analysis, analysis and differential calculus, anatomy and physiology, band, Bible, Bible studies, biology, British literature, British literature (honors), British literature-AP, calculus, calculus-AP, chemistry, choral music, composition, computer graphics, computer programming, computer skills, computer technology certification, computers, concert band, concert choir, dance, desktop publishing, drama, ecology, economics, economics-AP, electives, English, English literature-AP, English-AP, English/composition-AP, fine arts, French, French-AP, geometry, government, graphic arts, health, honors algebra, honors geometry, honors U.S. history, HTML design, instrumental music, journalism, keyboarding, leadership, life management skills, literature, marching band, math analysis, physical education, physical science, physics, psychology, Spanish, Spanish-AP, statistics, student government, theater, trigonometry, U.S. government, U.S. government and politics-AP, U.S. history, U.S. history-AP, U.S. literature, weight training, word processing, world governments, world history, world history-AP, world literature, world wide web design.

Graduation Requirements Arts and fine arts (art, music, dance, drama), Bible, computers, electives, English, foreign language, mathematics, physical education (includes health), science, social studies (includes history), Community Service, Leadership Practicum. Community service is required.

Special Academic Programs Advanced Placement exam preparation; honors section; study at local college for college credit; academic accommodation for the musically talented and the artistically talented.

College Admission Counseling 34 students graduated in 2010; all went to college, including Covenant College; Georgia College & State University; Georgia State University; Kennesaw State University; University of Georgia; Young Harris College. Median SAT critical reading: 570, median SAT math: 550, median SAT writing: 530, median combined SAT: 1570, median composite ACT: 24. 39% scored over 600 on SAT critical reading, 43% scored over 600 on SAT math, 22% scored over 600 on SAT writing, 35% scored over 1800 on combined SAT, 60% scored over 26 on composite ACT.

Student Life Upper grades have specified standards of dress, student council. Discipline rests primarily with faculty. Attendance at religious services is required.

Summer Programs Remediation, enrichment, sports, art/fine arts, computer instruction programs offered; session focuses on advancing skills and pleasure; held both on and off campus; held at other college campus for sports purposes; accepts boys and girls; open to students from other schools. 125 students usually enrolled. 2011 schedule: June 6 to July 22. Application deadline: May 1.

Tuition and Aid Day student tuition: $10,620–$11,151. Tuition installment plan (FACTS Tuition Payment Plan). Tuition reduction for siblings, need-based scholarship grants available. In 2010–11, 29% of upper-school students received aid. Total amount of financial aid awarded in 2010–11: $272,370.

Admissions Traditional secondary-level entrance grade is 9. For fall 2010, 36 students applied for upper-level admission, 25 were accepted, 21 enrolled. Otis-Lennon, Stanford Achievement Test required. Deadline for receipt of application materials: none. Application fee required: $100. Interview required.

Athletics Interscholastic: aerobics (boys, girls), aerobics/dance (g), ballet (g), baseball (b), basketball (b,g), cheering (g), cross-country running (b,g), dance (g), equestrian sports (b,g), football (b), physical fitness (b,g), soccer (b,g), softball (g), swimming and diving (b,g), tennis (b,g), track and field (b,g), volleyball (g); coed interscholastic: aquatics, archery, golf, strength & conditioning, weight training. 6 PE instructors, 6 coaches, 2 athletic trainers.

Computers Computers are regularly used in art, basic skills, desktop publishing, drawing and design, graphic arts, graphic design, keyboarding, library skills, media production, video film production, word processing, yearbook classes. Computer network features include on-campus library services, Internet access, wireless campus network. Computer access in designated common areas is available to students. Students grades are available online. The school has a published electronic and media policy.

Contact Mrs. Joan Carver, Admissions Assistant. 770-975-0252 Ext. 501. Fax: 770-874-9978. E-mail: jcarver@ncchristian.org. Web site: www.ncchristian.org.

NORTH COUNTRY SCHOOL

Lake Placid, New York
See Junior Boarding Schools section.

NORTH SHORE COUNTRY DAY SCHOOL

310 Green Bay Road
Winnetka, Illinois 60093-4094
Head of School: Mr. Tom Doar III

General Information Coeducational day college-preparatory, arts, technology, global, and service-learning school. Grades PK–12. Founded: 1919. Setting: suburban. Nearest major city is Chicago. 16-acre campus. 6 buildings on campus. Approved or accredited by Independent Schools Association of the Central States and Illinois Department of Education. Member of National Association of Independent Schools and Secondary School Admission Test Board. Endowment: $17 million. Total enrollment: 500. Upper school average class size: 14. Upper school faculty-student ratio: 1:8. Upper School students typically attend 5 days per week.

Upper School Student Profile Grade 9: 51 students (23 boys, 28 girls); Grade 10: 51 students (28 boys, 23 girls); Grade 11: 51 students (27 boys, 24 girls); Grade 12: 47 students (24 boys, 23 girls).

Faculty School total: 80. In upper school: 27 men, 35 women; 42 have advanced degrees.

Subjects Offered Algebra, American history, American literature, anatomy, art, art history, Asian studies, biology, biology-AP, calculus, calculus-AP, ceramics, chemistry, chemistry-AP, computer math, computer programming, computer science, creative writing, drama, earth science, ecology, economics, English, English literature, English-AP, environmental science, European history, expository writing, fine arts, French, French-AP, geography, geometry, government/civics, grammar, industrial arts, journalism, Mandarin, marine biology, mathematics, music, photography, physical education, physics, physics-AP, science, social studies, Spanish, Spanish-AP, speech, statistics, statistics-AP, technology, theater, trigonometry, U.S. history-AP, world history, world literature, writing.

Graduation Requirements Arts and fine arts (art, music, dance, drama), computer science, English, foreign language, mathematics, physical education (includes health), physical fitness, science, service learning/internship, social studies (includes history), technology, one stage performance in four years, completion of senior service project in May, completion of one-week community service project in four years.

Special Academic Programs Advanced Placement exam preparation; independent study; term-away projects; study at local college for college credit; study abroad.

College Admission Counseling 43 students graduated in 2010; all went to college, including Claremont McKenna College; Rice University; University of Michigan; Vanderbilt University.

Student Life Upper grades have specified standards of dress, student council, honor system. Discipline rests primarily with faculty.

Summer Programs Enrichment, sports, art/fine arts, rigorous outdoor training, computer instruction programs offered; session focuses on academic and artistic enrichment, outdoor expedition, soccer, basketball, field hockey; held both on and off campus; held at lakefront and local preserves and camp sites; accepts boys and girls; open to students from other schools. 750 students usually enrolled. 2011 schedule: June 13 to August 5. Application deadline: none.

Tuition and Aid Day student tuition: $22,422–$23,485. Tuition installment plan (Insured Tuition Payment Plan, Key Tuition Payment Plan, monthly payment plans, individually arranged payment plans, trimester payment plan). Merit scholarship grants, need-based scholarship grants, need-based loans, middle-income loans available. In 2010–11, 15% of upper-school students received aid. Total amount of financial aid awarded in 2010–11: $1,000,000.

Admissions Traditional secondary-level entrance grade is 9. ERB and writing sample required. Deadline for receipt of application materials: March 1. Application fee required: $50. On-campus interview required.

Athletics Interscholastic: baseball (boys), basketball (b,g), cross-country running (b,g), field hockey (g), football (b), golf (b,g), indoor track & field (b,g), soccer (b,g), tennis (b,g), track and field (b,g), volleyball (g); intramural: physical training (b,g), weight lifting (b,g); coed intramural: dance, sailing. 4 PE instructors, 24 coaches, 1 athletic trainer.

Computers Computers are regularly used in accounting, all academic classes. Computer network features include on-campus library services, online commercial services, Internet access, wireless campus network, Internet filtering or blocking technology. Campus intranet and student e-mail accounts are available to students. The school has a published electronic and media policy.

Contact Ms. Hannah Ruddock, Admissions Associate. 847-441-3313. Fax: 847-446-0675. E-mail: hruddock@nscds.org. Web site: www.nscds.org.

THE NORTHWEST ACADEMY

1130 Southwest Main Street
Portland, Oregon 97205
Head of School: Mary Vinton Folberg

General Information Coeducational day college-preparatory and arts school. Grades 6–12. Founded: 1995. Setting: urban. 4 buildings on campus. Approved or accredited by Northwest Association of Schools and Colleges, Pacific Northwest

The Northwest Academy

Association of Independent Schools, and Oregon Department of Education. Total enrollment: 122. Upper school average class size: 15. Upper school faculty-student ratio: 1:10. Upper School students typically attend 5 days per week. The average school day consists of 6 hours and 30 minutes.

Upper School Student Profile Grade 6: 15 students (6 boys, 9 girls); Grade 7: 25 students (11 boys, 14 girls); Grade 8: 22 students (10 boys, 12 girls); Grade 9: 15 students (6 boys, 9 girls); Grade 10: 17 students (9 boys, 8 girls); Grade 11: 9 students (5 boys, 4 girls); Grade 12: 19 students (9 boys, 10 girls).

Faculty School total: 34. In upper school: 18 men, 16 women; 7 have advanced degrees.

Subjects Offered 20th century history, acting, algebra, anatomy and physiology, animation, art history, ballet, biology, calculus, career/college preparation, chamber groups, chemistry, comparative government and politics, comparative politics, comparative religion, computer animation, computer literacy, computer music, creative writing, critical thinking, dance performance, desktop publishing, digital art, drama workshop, drawing, earth and space science, ecology, environmental systems, English literature, European civilization, film studies, French, geometry, history of music, Holocaust studies, human anatomy, humanities, illustration, independent study, internship, introduction to digital multitrack recording techniques, jazz band, jazz dance, jazz ensemble, journalism, keyboarding, martial arts, media arts, medieval/Renaissance history, multimedia design, music composition, music history, music performance, musical theater, painting, photo shop, physics, play/screen writing, political systems, pre-calculus, printmaking, senior thesis, Shakespeare, social sciences, Spanish, student publications, tap dance, theater, trigonometry, U.S. government and politics, U.S. history, video film production, visual arts, vocal ensemble, vocal jazz, world cultures, world history, world wide web design, writing.

Graduation Requirements 4 years of English/humanities, senior thesis seminar, 3 years of both math and science, 2 years of foreign language, 6 units of credit of arts electives, community service, computer literacy, PE.

Special Academic Programs Accelerated programs; independent study; study at local college for college credit; academic accommodation for the gifted, the musically talented, and the artistically talented.

College Admission Counseling 16 students graduated in 2009; 15 went to college, including Bennington College; California College of the Arts; Hampshire College; Reed College; Trinity University; Whitman College. Other: 1 went to work. 77% scored over 600 on SAT critical reading, 52% scored over 600 on SAT math, 67% scored over 600 on SAT writing.

Student Life Upper grades have student council, honor system. Discipline rests primarily with faculty.

Tuition and Aid Day student tuition: $17,850. Tuition installment plan (FACTS Tuition Payment Plan). Need-based scholarship grants available. In 2009–10, 25% of upper-school students received aid.

Admissions Traditional secondary-level entrance grade is 9. For fall 2009, 12 students applied for upper-level admission, 10 were accepted, 8 enrolled. Admissions testing, placement test and writing sample required. Deadline for receipt of application materials: February 5. Application fee required: $100. Interview required.

Athletics Coed Intramural: aerobics/dance, artistic gym, ballet, cooperative games, dance, modern dance, tai chi, yoga.

Computers Computers are regularly used in all academic classes. Computer network features include Internet access, wireless campus network, film and audio editing, sound design, animation, Flash. Campus intranet and computer access in designated common areas are available to students. The school has a published electronic and media policy.

Contact Lainie Keslin Ettinger, Director of Admissions. 503-223-3367 Ext. 104. Fax: 503-402-1043. E-mail: lettinger@nwacademy.org. Web site: www.nwacademy.org.

NORTHWEST CATHOLIC HIGH SCHOOL

29 Wampanoag Drive
West Hartford, Connecticut 06117
Head of School: Mrs. Margaret Williamson

General Information Coeducational day college-preparatory school, affiliated with Roman Catholic Church. Grades 9–12. Founded: 1961. Setting: suburban. Nearest major city is Hartford. 1 building on campus. Approved or accredited by New England Association of Schools and Colleges and Connecticut Department of Education. Total enrollment: 623. Upper school average class size: 18. Upper school faculty-student ratio: 1:12. There are 180 required school days per year for Upper School students. Upper School students typically attend 5 days per week. The average school day consists of 6 hours and 18 minutes.

Upper School Student Profile Grade 9: 151 students (69 boys, 82 girls); Grade 10: 175 students (87 boys, 88 girls); Grade 11: 167 students (72 boys, 95 girls); Grade 12: 130 students (58 boys, 72 girls). 80% of students are Roman Catholic.

Faculty School total: 56. In upper school: 42 have advanced degrees.

Graduation Requirements Arts and fine arts (art, music, dance, drama), English, foreign language, health education, mathematics, physical education (includes health), religion (includes Bible studies and theology), science, social studies (includes history), 25 hours of community service.

Special Academic Programs 15 Advanced Placement exams for which test preparation is offered; honors section; study at local college for college credit.

College Admission Counseling 160 students graduated in 2010; 159 went to college. Other: 1 entered military service. Mean SAT critical reading: 552, mean SAT math: 559, mean SAT writing: 560.

Student Life Upper grades have uniform requirement, student council, honor system. Discipline rests primarily with faculty. Attendance at religious services is required.

Tuition and Aid Day student tuition: $12,335. Tuition installment plan (monthly payment plans). Tuition reduction for siblings, merit scholarship grants, need-based scholarship grants available. Total amount of financial aid awarded in 2010–11: $1,300,000.

Admissions Traditional secondary-level entrance grade is 9. High School Placement Test required. Deadline for receipt of application materials: March. Application fee required: $25.

Athletics Interscholastic: baseball (boys), basketball (b,g), cheering (g), cross-country running (b,g), field hockey (g), golf (b,g), ice hockey (b), indoor track & field (b,g), lacrosse (b,g), soccer (b,g), softball (g), tennis (b,g), track and field (b,g), volleyball (g), winter (indoor) track (b,g); intramural: basketball (b,g); coed interscholastic: diving, football, swimming and diving; coed intramural: dance team, flag football, indoor soccer, outdoor adventure, rafting, rappelling, rock climbing, ropes courses, scuba diving, skiing (downhill), snowboarding, strength & conditioning, ultimate Frisbee, weight training, whiffle ball. 1 PE instructor, 1 athletic trainer.

Computers Computers are regularly used in all academic classes. Computer network features include on-campus library services, Internet access, Internet filtering or blocking technology. Student e-mail accounts and computer access in designated common areas are available to students. Students grades are available online. The school has a published electronic and media policy.

Contact Mrs. Nancy Scully Bannon, Director of Admissions. 860-236-4221 Ext. 124. Fax: 860-570-0080. E-mail: nbannon@nwcath.org. Web site: www.northwestcatholic.org.

THE NORTHWEST SCHOOL

1415 Summit Avenue
Seattle, Washington 98122
Head of School: Ellen Taussig

General Information Coeducational boarding and day college-preparatory, arts, and ESL school. Boarding grades 9–12, day grades 6–12. Founded: 1978. Setting: urban. Students are housed in coed dormitories. 1-acre campus. 4 buildings on campus. Approved or accredited by Northwest Accreditation Commission, Pacific Northwest Association of Independent Schools, and Washington Department of Education. Member of National Association of Independent Schools. Endowment: $788,915. Total enrollment: 462. Upper school average class size: 16. Upper school faculty-student ratio: 1:9. There are 168 required school days per year for Upper School students. Upper School students typically attend 5 days per week. The average school day consists of 7 hours and 20 minutes.

Upper School Student Profile Grade 9: 71 students (38 boys, 33 girls); Grade 10: 85 students (47 boys, 38 girls); Grade 11: 90 students (41 boys, 49 girls); Grade 12: 80 students (42 boys, 38 girls). 11% of students are boarding students. 79% are state residents. 1 state is represented in upper school student body. 21% are international students. International students from China, Japan, Republic of Korea, Spain, Taiwan, and Thailand; 3 other countries represented in student body.

Faculty School total: 70. In upper school: 21 men, 33 women; 36 have advanced degrees.

Subjects Offered Advanced chemistry, algebra, astronomy, biology, calculus, ceramics, chemistry, Chinese, chorus, computer skills, contemporary problems, dance, drama, drawing, earth science, English, ESL, evolution, fiber arts, film, fine arts, French, geometry, health, history, humanities, illustration, improvisation, jazz dance, jazz ensemble, journalism, life science, literature, math analysis, mathematics, mentorship program, musical theater, orchestra, outdoor education, painting, performing arts, philosophy, photography, physical education, physical science, physics, play production, pre-algebra, pre-calculus, printmaking, Spanish, statistics, strings, textiles, theater, trigonometry, U.S. government and politics, U.S. history, visual arts, Washington State and Northwest History, water color painting, wilderness education, world history, writing.

Graduation Requirements English, foreign language, history, humanities, mathematics, physical education (includes health), science, senior project, social studies (includes history), visual and performing arts, participation in environmental maintenance program.

Special Academic Programs ESL (42 students enrolled).

College Admission Counseling 87 students graduated in 2010; 83 went to college, including Cornish College of the Arts; Oberlin College; University of California, Berkeley; University of Southern California; University of Washington; Whitman College. Other: 2 went to work, 2 had other specific plans.

Student Life Upper grades have honor system. Discipline rests primarily with faculty.

Summer Programs Enrichment, ESL, sports, art/fine arts, computer instruction programs offered; session focuses on global connections with international students; held on campus; accepts boys and girls; open to students from other schools. 325 students usually enrolled. 2011 schedule: July 5 to August 11. Application deadline: June 17.

Tuition and Aid Day student tuition: $27,405; 7-day tuition and room/board: $38,975. Tuition installment plan (school's own payment plan). Need-based scholarship grants available. In 2010–11, 18% of upper-school students received aid. Total amount of financial aid awarded in 2010–11: $1,180,555.

Admissions Traditional secondary-level entrance grade is 9. For fall 2010, 226 students applied for upper-level admission, 127 were accepted, 50 enrolled. IELTS, ISEE, or TOEFL required. Deadline for receipt of application materials: January 13. Application fee required: $65. Interview required.

Athletics Interscholastic: basketball (boys, girls), cross-country running (b,g), soccer (b,g), track and field (b,g), ultimate Frisbee (b,g), volleyball (g); coed intramural: fitness, hiking/backpacking, outdoor education, physical fitness, rock climbing, ropes courses, skiing (cross-country), skiing (downhill). 2 PE instructors, 20 coaches.

Computers Computers are regularly used in art, English, ESL, foreign language, graphic design, health, history, humanities, journalism, library, mathematics, music, science, social studies, theater, video film production, writing, yearbook classes. Computer network features include on-campus library services, Internet access, wireless campus network, ProQuest, ABC-Cleo, JSTOR, eLibrary, CultureGrams, World Conflicts and Online Encyclopedias. Computer access in designated common areas is available to students. The school has a published electronic and media policy.

Contact Anne Smith, Director of Admissions. 206-682-7309. Fax: 206-467-7353. E-mail: anne.smith@northwestschool.org. Web site: www.northwestschool.org.

NORTHWEST YESHIVA HIGH SCHOOL

5017 90th Avenue Southeast
Mercer Island, Washington 98040
Head of School: Rabbi Bernie Fox

General Information Coeducational day college-preparatory and religious studies school, affiliated with Jewish faith. Grades 9–12. Founded: 1974. Setting: suburban. Nearest major city is Seattle. 2-acre campus. 3 buildings on campus. Approved or accredited by Northwest Association of Schools and Colleges and Washington Department of Education. Languages of instruction: English and Hebrew. Endowment: $841,000. Total enrollment: 79. Upper school average class size: 12. Upper school faculty-student ratio: 1:4. There are 180 required school days per year for Upper School students. Upper School students typically attend 5 days per week. The average school day consists of 7 hours.

Upper School Student Profile Grade 9: 19 students (12 boys, 7 girls); Grade 10: 23 students (12 boys, 11 girls); Grade 11: 22 students (12 boys, 10 girls); Grade 12: 16 students (9 boys, 7 girls). 100% of students are Jewish.

Faculty School total: 30. In upper school: 15 men, 13 women; 15 have advanced degrees.

Subjects Offered 20th century history, algebra, American legal systems, art, art history, biology, calculus, chemistry, college admission preparation, college counseling, drama, economics, English, film appreciation, fine arts, geometry, Hebrew, Hebrew scripture, integrated mathematics, Jewish history, Judaic studies, lab science, language arts, modern Western civilization, newspaper, philosophy, physical education, physics, prayer/spirituality, pre-algebra, pre-calculus, psychology, Rabbinic literature, religious studies, Spanish, Talmud, U.S. government, U.S. history, U.S. literature, Western civilization, world history, writing, yearbook.

Graduation Requirements Advanced math, arts and fine arts (art, music, dance, drama), biology, conceptual physics, Hebrew, integrated mathematics, Judaic studies, language arts, physics, Spanish, Talmud, U.S. government, U.S. history, world history. Community service is required.

Special Academic Programs Independent study; academic accommodation for the gifted; remedial reading and/or remedial writing; remedial math; special instructional classes for deaf students; ESL (1 student enrolled).

College Admission Counseling 26 students graduated in 2010; 13 went to college, including Brandeis University; University of Washington; Yeshiva University. Other: 13 had other specific plans. Median SAT critical reading: 620, median SAT math: 550, median SAT writing: 590, median combined SAT: 1780. 40% scored over 600 on SAT critical reading, 53% scored over 600 on SAT math, 47% scored over 600 on SAT writing, 40% scored over 1800 on combined SAT.

Student Life Upper grades have specified standards of dress, student council, honor system. Discipline rests primarily with faculty. Attendance at religious services is required.

Tuition and Aid Day student tuition: $13,500. Tuition installment plan (monthly payment plans, individually arranged payment plans). Need-based scholarship grants available. In 2010–11, 45% of upper-school students received aid. Total amount of financial aid awarded in 2010–11: $328,331.

Admissions Traditional secondary-level entrance grade is 9. Deadline for receipt of application materials: none. Application fee required: $250. Interview required.

Athletics Interscholastic: basketball (boys, girls), cross-country running (b,g), golf (b,g), volleyball (g); coed interscholastic: cross-country running, softball. 5 PE instructors, 5 coaches.

Computers Computer network features include Internet access.

Contact Mr. Ian Weiner, Director of Student Services. 206-232-5272. Fax: 206-232-2711. E-mail: iw@nyhs.com. Web site: www.nyhs.net.

NORTHWOOD SCHOOL

PO Box 1070
92 Northwood Road
Lake Placid, New York 12946
Head of School: Edward M. Good

General Information Coeducational boarding and day college-preparatory and arts school. Grades 9–PG. Founded: 1905. Setting: small town. Nearest major city is

Northwood School

Albany. Students are housed in single-sex dormitories. 80-acre campus. 8 buildings on campus. Approved or accredited by New York State Association of Independent Schools and The Association of Boarding Schools. Member of National Association of Independent Schools and Secondary School Admission Test Board. Endowment: $8 million. Total enrollment: 181. Upper school average class size: 9. Upper school faculty-student ratio: 1:6. Upper School students typically attend 5 days per week.

Upper School Student Profile Grade 9: 20 students (12 boys, 8 girls); Grade 10: 34 students (21 boys, 13 girls); Grade 11: 57 students (34 boys, 23 girls); Grade 12: 57 students (40 boys, 17 girls); Postgraduate: 12 students (11 boys, 1 girl). 79% of students are boarding students. 39% are state residents. 22 states are represented in upper school student body. 33% are international students. International students from Canada, China, Finland, Norway, Republic of Korea, and Spain; 6 other countries represented in student body.

Faculty School total: 33. In upper school: 24 men, 9 women; 17 have advanced degrees; 16 reside on campus.

Subjects Offered Algebra, American history, American literature, art, biology, calculus, ceramics, chemistry, computer science, drama, earth science, English, English literature, ensembles, environmental science, expository writing, fiber arts, French, geography, geology, geometry, government/civics, great issues, health, history, journalism, mathematics, music, photography, physical education, physics, psychology, SAT preparation, science, social studies, sociology, Spanish, theater, trigonometry, world history.

Graduation Requirements Arts and fine arts (art, music, dance, drama), English, foreign language, mathematics, physical education (includes health), science, social studies (includes history).

Special Academic Programs 5 Advanced Placement exams for which test preparation is offered; honors section; independent study; remedial reading and/or remedial writing; ESL (25 students enrolled).

College Admission Counseling 57 students graduated in 2010; 48 went to college, including Queen's University at Kingston; St. Lawrence University. Other: 1 entered military service, 2 entered a postgraduate year, 6 had other specific plans. Median SAT critical reading: 520, median SAT math: 500, median SAT writing: 510.

Student Life Upper grades have specified standards of dress, student council, honor system. Discipline rests primarily with faculty.

Tuition and Aid Day student tuition: $24,000; 7-day tuition and room/board: $42,500. Tuition installment plan (The Tuition Plan, monthly payment plans). Need-based scholarship grants available. In 2010–11, 55% of upper-school students received aid.

Admissions Traditional secondary-level entrance grade is 11. For fall 2010, 186 students applied for upper-level admission, 120 were accepted, 82 enrolled. TOEFL or SLEP required. Deadline for receipt of application materials: none. Application fee required: $50. Interview required.

Athletics Interscholastic: crew (boys, girls), hockey (b,g), ice hockey (b,g), ice skating (b,g), lacrosse (b,g), nordic skiing (b,g), ski jumping (b,g), skiing (downhill) (b,g), soccer (b,g), telemark skiing (b,g), tennis (b,g); intramural: hockey (b,g), ice hockey (b,g), ice skating (b,g), skiing (downhill) (b,g), snowboarding (b,g); coed interscholastic: alpine skiing, figure skating, fitness, freestyle skiing, golf, nordic skiing, skiing (cross-country), snowboarding, telemark skiing; coed intramural: alpine skiing, backpacking, bicycling, canoeing/kayaking, climbing, combined training, cross-country running, figure skating, fishing, fitness, fly fishing, freestyle skiing, golf, hiking/backpacking, jogging, kayaking, luge, mountain biking, mountaineering, nordic skiing, outdoor adventure, physical training, rafting, rappelling, rock climbing, ropes courses, rowing, running, skiing (cross-country), skiing (downhill), snowboarding, street hockey, strength & conditioning, tennis, walking, wall climbing, weight training, wilderness, wilderness survival, wildernessways, winter walking. 1 coach, 1 athletic trainer.

Computers Computers are regularly used in English, foreign language, history, mathematics, science classes. Computer network features include on-campus library services, online commercial services, Internet access, wireless campus network, Internet filtering or blocking technology. Students grades are available online. The school has a published electronic and media policy.

Contact Timothy Weaver, Director of Admissions. 518-523-3382 Ext. 205. Fax: 518-523-3405. E-mail: weavert@northwoodschool.com. Web site: www.northwoodschool.com.

See Display on page 461 and Close-Up on page 818.

THE NORWICH FREE ACADEMY

305 Broadway
Norwich, Connecticut 06360
Head of School: Mrs. Jacqueline M. Sullivan

General Information Coeducational day college-preparatory, general academic, arts, business, vocational, bilingual studies, and technology school. Grades 9–12. Founded: 1856. Setting: suburban. 15-acre campus. 11 buildings on campus. Approved or accredited by New England Association of Schools and Colleges and Connecticut Department of Education. Upper school average class size: 22. Upper school faculty-student ratio: 1:22. There are 180 required school days per year for Upper School students. Upper School students typically attend 5 days per week. The average school day consists of 7 hours.

Faculty School total: 85. In upper school: 30 men, 55 women; 75 have advanced degrees.

Subjects Offered ACT preparation.

Special Academic Programs Advanced Placement exam preparation; honors section; study at local college for college credit; remedial reading and/or remedial writing; remedial math; special instructional classes for students with learning disabilities, Attention Deficit Disorder, emotional and behavioral problems, and dyslexia; ESL (90 students enrolled).

College Admission Counseling 507 students graduated in 2010; 396 went to college. Other: 56 went to work, 45 entered military service, 3 had other specific plans.

Student Life Upper grades have specified standards of dress, honor system. Discipline rests equally with students and faculty.

Summer Programs Remediation, ESL, sports programs offered; held on campus; accepts boys and girls; open to students from other schools. 250 students usually enrolled. 2011 schedule: July 1 to July 29. Application deadline: June 1.

Tuition and Aid Day student tuition: $11,400.

Admissions ACT-Explore required. Deadline for receipt of application materials: none. No application fee required. Interview required.

Athletics Interscholastic: baseball (boys), basketball (b,g), cheering (b,g), cross-country running (b,g), drill team (g), fencing (b,g), field hockey (g), football (b), golf (b,g), gymnastics (g), ice hockey (b), indoor track (b,g), indoor track & field (b,g), lacrosse (b,g), running (b,g), soccer (b,g), softball (g), Special Olympics (b,g), swimming and diving (b,g), tennis (b,g), track and field (b,g), volleyball (b,g), weight lifting (b), winter (indoor) track (b,g), wrestling (b); intramural: hockey (b), ice hockey (b), ice skating (b), skiing (downhill) (b,g), snowboarding (b,g), table tennis (b); coed intramural: dance, dance team, physical fitness. 4 PE instructors, 25 coaches, 5 athletic trainers.

Computers Computer network features include on-campus library services, Internet access, Internet filtering or blocking technology. The school has a published electronic and media policy.

Contact Mrs. Jacqueline M. Sullivan, Interim Superintendent/Head of School. 860-425-5501. E-mail: sullivanj@norwichfreeacademy.com. Web site: www.norwichfreeacademy.com.

NOTRE DAME ACADEMY

2851 Overland Avenue
Los Angeles, California 90064
Head of School: Mrs. Joan Gumaer Tyhurst

General Information Girls' day college-preparatory, arts, religious studies, technology, and fine arts school, affiliated with Roman Catholic Church. Grades 9–12. Founded: 1949. Setting: urban. 1 building on campus. Approved or accredited by Western Association of Schools and Colleges, Western Catholic Education Association, and California Department of Education. Total enrollment: 400. Upper school average class size: 23. Upper school faculty-student ratio: 1:14.

Upper School Student Profile 86% of students are Roman Catholic.

Faculty School total: 28. In upper school: 4 men, 24 women.

Subjects Offered Advanced chemistry, advanced studio art-AP, algebra, American history, art, art history-AP, art-AP, athletic training, biology, biology-AP, calculus, calculus-AP, campus ministry, chemistry, choir, Christian and Hebrew scripture, community service, computer science, dance, design, digital photography, drama, drama performance, earth science, economics, English, English language and composition-AP, English literature and composition-AP, fine arts, French, French-AP, geometry, global studies, government and politics-AP, government/civics, health, history, honors geometry, Japanese, law, leadership, photography, physical education, physics, pre-calculus, psychology, psychology-AP, religion, Spanish, Spanish language-AP, speech and oral interpretations, statistics, trigonometry, U.S. government and politics-AP, U.S. history-AP, world civilizations, world history-AP.

Graduation Requirements Arts and fine arts (art, music, dance, drama), computer science, English, foreign language, mathematics, physical education (includes health), religion (includes Bible studies and theology), science, social studies (includes history), speech. Community service is required.

Special Academic Programs Advanced Placement exam preparation; honors section.

College Admission Counseling 117 students graduated in 2010; all went to college, including Loyola Marymount University; Santa Clara University; University of California, Berkeley; University of California, Los Angeles; University of California, Santa Barbara; University of Southern California. Mean SAT critical reading: 613, mean SAT math: 597, mean SAT writing: 638.

Student Life Upper grades have uniform requirement, student council, honor system. Discipline rests primarily with faculty. Attendance at religious services is required.

Summer Programs Remediation, enrichment, advancement, art/fine arts, rigorous outdoor training programs offered; session focuses on assisting students in attaining grade level or advancing grade level; held on campus; accepts girls; not open to students from other schools. 200 students usually enrolled. 2011 schedule: June 13 to July 15. Application deadline: May 27.

Tuition and Aid Day student tuition: $10,350. Tuition installment plan (FACTS Tuition Payment Plan, monthly payment plans, quarterly and semester payment plans). Merit scholarship grants, need-based scholarship grants, paying campus jobs available. In 2010–11, 29% of upper-school students received aid.

Admissions For fall 2010, 230 students applied for upper-level admission, 150 were accepted, 100 enrolled. High School Placement Test (closed version) from Scholastic Testing Service required. Deadline for receipt of application materials: January 14. Application fee required: $75. On-campus interview required.

Athletics Interscholastic: basketball, cross-country running, dance, soccer, softball, swimming and diving, track and field, volleyball. 1 PE instructor, 8 coaches.

Computers Computers are regularly used in art, design, English, history, journalism, photography, yearbook classes. Computer network features include on-campus library services, online commercial services, Internet access, wireless campus network. Student e-mail accounts are available to students. Students grades are available online. The school has a published electronic and media policy.

Contact Ms. Brigid Williams, Director of Admissions. 310-839-5289 Ext. 218. Fax: 310-839-7957. E-mail: bwilliams@ndala.com. Web site: www.ndala.com.

NOTRE DAME ACADEMY
1073 Main Street
Hingham, Massachusetts 02043
Head of School: Sr. Barbara A. Barry, SND

General Information Girls' day college-preparatory, arts, business, religious studies, and technology school, affiliated with Roman Catholic Church. Grades 9–12. Founded: 1853. Setting: suburban. Nearest major city is Boston. 68-acre campus. 1 building on campus. Approved or accredited by Association of Independent Schools in New England, National Catholic Education Association, New England Association of Schools and Colleges, and Massachusetts Department of Education. Endowment: $4.9 million. Total enrollment: 568. Upper school average class size: 20. Upper school faculty-student ratio: 1:11. There are 180 required school days per year for Upper School students. Upper School students typically attend 5 days per week. The average school day consists of 6 hours and 30 minutes.

Upper School Student Profile Grade 9: 146 students (146 girls); Grade 10: 138 students (138 girls); Grade 11: 142 students (142 girls); Grade 12: 142 students (142 girls). 94% of students are Roman Catholic.

Faculty School total: 54. In upper school: 10 men, 44 women; 45 have advanced degrees.

Subjects Offered Acting, advanced chemistry, Advanced Placement courses, advanced studio art-AP, algebra, American history, American history-AP, American literature, anatomy, anatomy and physiology, art, art history, Bible studies, bioethics, biology, biology-AP, business, business skills, calculus, calculus-AP, campus ministry, Catholic belief and practice, ceramics, chemistry, community service, computer science, driver education, economics, English, English literature, ethics, European history, fine arts, French, geometry, government/civics, history, Latin, mathematics, music, photography, physical education, physics, physiology, psychology, religion, science, social sciences, social studies, Spanish, trigonometry, U.S. government and politics-AP, world history, world literature.

Graduation Requirements Art, computer applications, English, foreign language, guidance, mathematics, music, physical education (includes health), religion (includes Bible studies and theology), science, social studies (includes history).

Special Academic Programs 17 Advanced Placement exams for which test preparation is offered; honors section; independent study.

College Admission Counseling 144 students graduated in 2009; all went to college, including Holy Cross College; Loyola University Maryland; Northeastern University; Providence College; Saint Anselm College; University of Massachusetts Amherst.

Student Life Upper grades have uniform requirement, student council, honor system. Discipline rests primarily with faculty. Attendance at religious services is required.

Tuition and Aid Day student tuition: $14,490. Tuition installment plan (FACTS Tuition Payment Plan). Merit scholarship grants, need-based scholarship grants available. In 2009–10, 33% of upper-school students received aid; total upper-school merit-scholarship money awarded: $200,000. Total amount of financial aid awarded in 2009–10: $600,000.

Admissions Traditional secondary-level entrance grade is 9. For fall 2009, 350 students applied for upper-level admission, 275 were accepted, 146 enrolled. Diocesan Entrance Exam required. Deadline for receipt of application materials: December 1. Application fee required: $30.

Athletics Interscholastic: alpine skiing, basketball, cheering, cross-country running, dance team, diving, field hockey, golf, gymnastics, ice hockey, indoor track & field, lacrosse, sailing, skiing (downhill), soccer, softball, strength & conditioning, swimming and diving, tennis, track and field, volleyball, weight training, winter (indoor) track; intramural: crew, dance team. 1 PE instructor, 26 coaches, 1 athletic trainer.

Computers Computers are regularly used in art, college planning, English, foreign language, history, mathematics, music, religion, science classes. Computer network features include on-campus library services, Internet access, wireless campus network, Internet filtering or blocking technology. Computer access in designated common areas is available to students. Students grades are available online. The school has a published electronic and media policy.

Contact Mrs. Patricia Spatola, Director of Admissions. 781-749-5930 Ext. 235. Fax: 781-749-8366. E-mail: pspatola@ndahingham.com. Web site: www.ndahingham.com.

NOTRE DAME ACADEMY
425 Salisbury Street
Worcester, Massachusetts 01609
Head of School: Sr. Ann E. Morrison, SND

General Information Girls' day and distance learning college-preparatory, arts, and religious studies school, affiliated with Roman Catholic Church. Grades 9–12. Distance learning grades 9–12. Founded: 1951. Setting: suburban. Nearest major city is Boston. 13-acre campus. 3 buildings on campus. Approved or accredited by Association of Independent Schools in New England and National Catholic Education Association. Member of National Association of Independent Schools. Total enrollment: 283. Upper school average class size: 17. Upper school faculty-student ratio: 1:11. The average school day consists of 6 hours.

Upper School Student Profile 85% of students are Roman Catholic.

Faculty School total: 39. In upper school: 4 men, 32 women; 27 have advanced degrees.

Subjects Offered 20th century history, advanced chemistry, advanced math, advanced studio art-AP, algebra, American history, American literature, analysis and differential calculus, anatomy and physiology, ancient world history, art, art history, art history-AP, Bible studies, biology, British literature, British literature (honors), British literature-AP, calculus, calculus-AP, career exploration, Catholic belief and practice, chamber groups, chemistry, chemistry-AP, choral music, Christian and Hebrew scripture, Christian doctrine, college planning, communication skills, community service, computer skills, creative writing, dance, drama, drawing and design, economics and history, English, English composition, English literature, English literature and composition-AP, English-AP, ethics, European history, European history-AP, expository writing, fine arts, French, French language-AP, geometry, grammar, graphic design, health, history, honors geometry, keyboarding, Latin, literature seminar, mathematics, mathematics-AP, music, music theory-AP, photography, physical education, physics, pre-calculus, psychology, public service, religion, science, senior project, Shakespeare, social studies, sociology, Spanish, Spanish language-AP, studio art-AP, theater, theology, trigonometry, world history, world literature, world religions, writing.

Graduation Requirements Arts and fine arts (art, music, dance, drama), computer science, English, foreign language, Latin, mathematics, physical education (includes health), public service, religion (includes Bible studies and theology), science, social studies (includes history), guidance seminar. Community service is required.

Special Academic Programs Advanced Placement exam preparation; honors section.

College Admission Counseling 63 students graduated in 2009; all went to college, including Boston College; Boston University; Northeastern University; Providence College. Mean SAT critical reading: 580, mean SAT math: 530, mean SAT writing: 600.

Student Life Upper grades have specified standards of dress, student council. Discipline rests equally with students and faculty. Attendance at religious services is required.

Tuition and Aid Day student tuition: $10,800. Tuition installment plan (Insured Tuition Payment Plan, monthly payment plans). Need-based scholarship grants available. In 2009–10, 7% of upper-school students received aid.

Admissions Traditional secondary-level entrance grade is 9. For fall 2009, 123 students applied for upper-level admission, 102 were accepted, 6 enrolled. Admissions testing and High School Placement Test required. Deadline for receipt of application materials: December 1. Application fee required: $50. On-campus interview recommended.

Athletics Interscholastic: alpine skiing (girls), aquatics (g), basketball (g), cross-country running (g), curling (g), diving (g), field hockey (g), fitness walking (g), freestyle skiing (g), golf (g), indoor track (g), indoor track & field (g), Nautilus (g), physical fitness (g), physical training (g), running (g), skiing (downhill) (g), softball (g), swimming and diving (g), tennis (g), track and field (g), winter (indoor) track (g); intramural: dance (g), fitness walking (g). 1 PE instructor, 20 coaches.

Computers Computers are regularly used in English, foreign language, graphic design, history, library skills, literary magazine, mathematics, newspaper, psychology, religious studies, research skills, science, yearbook classes. Computer network features include on-campus library services, Internet access, wireless campus network. Computer access in designated common areas is available to students. The school has a published electronic and media policy.

Contact Mrs. Mary F. Riordan, Admissions Director. 508-757-6200. Fax: 508-757-1800. E-mail: mriordan@nda-worc.org. Web site: www.nda-worc.org.

NOTRE DAME ACADEMY
35321 Notre Dame Lane
Middleburg, Virginia 20117-3621
Head of School: Ms. Elizabeth Manley Murray

General Information Coeducational day college-preparatory, arts, religious studies, and technology school, affiliated with Roman Catholic Church. Grades 9–12. Founded: 1965. Setting: rural. Nearest major city is Washington, DC. 90-acre campus. 8 buildings on campus. Approved or accredited by Association of Independent Schools of Greater Washington, Southern Association of Colleges and Schools, and Southern Association of Independent Schools. Endowment: $425,000. Total enrollment: 180. Upper school average class size: 14. Upper school faculty-student ratio: 1:9.

Notre Dame Academy

Upper School Student Profile Grade 9: 30 students (14 boys, 16 girls); Grade 10: 53 students (26 boys, 27 girls); Grade 11: 54 students (26 boys, 28 girls); Grade 12: 44 students (20 boys, 24 girls). 25% of students are Roman Catholic.

Faculty School total: 28. In upper school: 17 men, 11 women; 18 have advanced degrees.

Subjects Offered Accounting, Advanced Placement courses, advanced studio art-AP, algebra, American history-AP, American literature, anatomy, anthropology, archaeology, architectural drawing, architecture, art, biology, biology-AP, calculus, Catholic belief and practice, ceramics, chemistry, chemistry-AP, chorus, comparative government and politics-AP, composition-AP, computer applications, computer math, computer programming, computer-aided design, creative writing, design, drama, drama performance, drawing, English, English composition, English literature, English literature and composition-AP, English-AP, environmental science, fine arts, French, French-AP, geometry, government and politics-AP, government/civics, graphic arts, health, history, honors algebra, honors English, honors geometry, honors world history, human anatomy, independent study, instrumental music, keyboarding, Latin, literature, mathematics, music, music appreciation, painting, photography, physical education, physics, religion, SAT preparation, science, social sciences, social studies, Spanish, Spanish-AP, statistics, theater, U.S. government and politics-AP, writing.

Graduation Requirements Art, drama, English, foreign language, mathematics, music, science, social studies (includes history), theology, acceptance at a college or university, at least 25 hours of community service per year.

Special Academic Programs Advanced Placement exam preparation; honors section; study at local college for college credit; academic accommodation for the gifted, the musically talented, and the artistically talented.

College Admission Counseling 67 students graduated in 2009; all went to college, including James Madison University; Lynchburg College; The College of William and Mary; University of Virginia; Virginia Polytechnic Institute and State University. Mean SAT critical reading: 560, mean SAT math: 550, mean SAT writing: 560, mean combined SAT: 1670. 25% scored over 600 on SAT critical reading, 25% scored over 600 on SAT math, 28% scored over 600 on SAT writing, 27% scored over 1800 on combined SAT.

Student Life Upper grades have specified standards of dress, student council, honor system. Discipline rests primarily with faculty.

Tuition and Aid Day student tuition: $18,100. Tuition installment plan (FACTS Tuition Payment Plan, semiannual payment plan). Merit scholarship grants, need-based scholarship grants available. In 2009–10, 40% of upper-school students received aid; total upper-school merit-scholarship money awarded: $50,000. Total amount of financial aid awarded in 2009–10: $728,502.

Admissions Traditional secondary-level entrance grade is 9. For fall 2009, 90 students applied for upper-level admission, 80 were accepted, 60 enrolled. High School Placement Test, SLEP for foreign students, SSAT, WISC III or other aptitude measures; standardized achievement test or writing sample required. Deadline for receipt of application materials: none. Application fee required: $50. On-campus interview required.

Athletics Interscholastic: baseball (boys), basketball (b,g), field hockey (g), indoor soccer (b,g), lacrosse (b,g), soccer (b,g), softball (g), tennis (b,g), volleyball (g); intramural: strength & conditioning (b,g), weight training (b,g); coed interscholastic: cross-country running, golf, mountain biking, swimming and diving; coed intramural: flag football, outdoor activities, table tennis. 8 coaches, 1 athletic trainer.

Computers Computers are regularly used in all academic, art, literary magazine, music, newspaper, programming, yearbook classes. Computer network features include on-campus library services, Internet access, Internet filtering or blocking technology. Campus intranet and computer access in designated common areas are available to students. Students grades are available online. The school has a published electronic and media policy.

Contact Mr. Archie A. Catalfamo, Director of Admission. 540-687-5581 Ext. 3008. Fax: 540-687-3103. E-mail: acatalfamo@notredameva.org. Web site: www.notredameva.org.

NOTRE DAME COLLEGE PREP

7655 West Dempster Street
Niles, Illinois 60714-2098

Head of School: Mr. Daniel Tully

General Information Boys' day college-preparatory, arts, business, religious studies, and technology school, affiliated with Roman Catholic Church. Grades 9–12. Founded: 1955. Setting: suburban. Nearest major city is Chicago. 28-acre campus. 1 building on campus. Approved or accredited by National Catholic Education Association, North Central Association of Colleges and Schools, and Illinois Department of Education. Endowment: $1.2 million. Total enrollment: 831. Upper school average class size: 17. Upper school faculty-student ratio: 1:17. There are 174 required school days per year for Upper School students. Upper School students typically attend 5 days per week. The average school day consists of 6 hours and 50 minutes.

Upper School Student Profile Grade 9: 208 students (208 boys); Grade 10: 184 students (184 boys); Grade 11: 226 students (226 boys); Grade 12: 213 students (213 boys). 87% of students are Roman Catholic.

Faculty School total: 58. In upper school: 33 men, 25 women; 33 have advanced degrees.

Subjects Offered 3-dimensional art, accounting, advanced biology, advanced chemistry, advanced math, algebra, American literature, art, art history, art history-AP, band, Bible as literature, Bible studies, bioethics, biology, biology-AP, British literature, British literature (honors), calculus, calculus-AP, Catholic belief and practice, chemistry, chemistry-AP, choir, comedy, computer literacy, computer programming, concert band, contemporary history, creative writing, drama, dramatic arts, economics, English, English-AP, environmental science, ESL, ethics, European history-AP, film appreciation, fine arts, geography, geometry, government-AP, health, history, honors algebra, honors English, honors geometry, Italian, jazz, jazz band, journalism, Latin, Latin-AP, leadership, mathematics, music, music appreciation, music theory, philosophy, physical education, physics, pre-calculus, psychology, reading/study skills, religion, social studies, sociology, Spanish, Spanish-AP, speech, statistics, statistics-AP, theology, trigonometry, U.S. history, U.S. history-AP, Web site design, weight training, weightlifting, Western civilization, world literature, world religions.

Graduation Requirements Algebra, arts and fine arts (art, music, dance, drama), biology, computer literacy, English, foreign language, geometry, health, mathematics, physical education (includes health), religion (includes Bible studies and theology), science, social studies (includes history), U.S. history, Western civilization, four years of religious retreats and community services.

Special Academic Programs 11 Advanced Placement exams for which test preparation is offered; honors section; study at local college for college credit; academic accommodation for the gifted; remedial reading and/or remedial writing; remedial math; special instructional classes for remedial social studies and science; ESL (3 students enrolled).

College Admission Counseling 179 students graduated in 2010; 176 went to college, including Eastern Illinois University; Illinois State University; Marquette University; Northeastern Illinois University; University of Illinois at Chicago; University of Illinois at Urbana–Champaign. Other: 1 went to work, 2 had other specific plans. Mean composite ACT: 24. 39% scored over 26 on composite ACT.

Student Life Upper grades have specified standards of dress, student council, honor system. Discipline rests primarily with faculty. Attendance at religious services is required.

Summer Programs Remediation, enrichment, sports, art/fine arts, computer instruction programs offered; session focuses on remediation/make up; held on campus; accepts boys and girls; open to students from other schools. 200 students usually enrolled. 2011 schedule: June 1 to July 30.

Tuition and Aid Day student tuition: $8850. Tuition installment plan (The Tuition Plan, monthly payment plans). Tuition reduction for siblings, need-based scholarship grants, paying campus jobs available. In 2010–11, 32% of upper-school students received aid. Total amount of financial aid awarded in 2010–11: $3,600,000.

Admissions Traditional secondary-level entrance grade is 9. For fall 2010, 235 students applied for upper-level admission, 228 were accepted, 208 enrolled. ACT-Explore or TOEFL or SLEP required. Deadline for receipt of application materials: June 1. Application fee required: $25. Interview recommended.

Athletics Interscholastic: baseball, basketball, bowling, cross-country running, diving, football, golf, ice hockey, lacrosse, soccer, swimming and diving, tennis, track and field, volleyball, wrestling; intramural: baseball, basketball, boxing, combined training, flag football, floor hockey, football, lacrosse, outdoor adventure, paddle tennis, physical fitness, softball, table tennis, ultimate Frisbee, volleyball, weight lifting, weight training, wrestling. 4 PE instructors, 25 coaches, 1 athletic trainer.

Computers Computers are regularly used in accounting, art, computer applications, English, geography, health, history, science, Web site design classes. Computer network features include on-campus library services, Internet access, Internet filtering or blocking technology, college search and scholarships. Computer access in designated common areas is available to students. Students grades are available online. The school has a published electronic and media policy.

Contact Mr. Paul W. Tokarz, Director of Enrollment. 847-779-8616. Fax: 847-965-2975. E-mail: ptokarz@nddons.org. Web site: www.nddons.org.

NOTRE DAME HIGH SCHOOL

1540 Ralston Avenue
Belmont, California 94002-1995

Head of School: Ms. Rita Gleason

General Information Girls' day college-preparatory, arts, religious studies, technology, and visual and performing arts school, affiliated with Roman Catholic Church. Grades 9–12. Founded: 1851. Setting: suburban. Nearest major city is San Francisco. 11-acre campus. 1 building on campus. Approved or accredited by Western Association of Schools and Colleges and California Department of Education. Upper school average class size: 23. Upper school faculty-student ratio: 1:16. The average school day consists of 5 hours and 30 minutes.

Upper School Student Profile Grade 9: 150 students (150 girls); Grade 10: 124 students (124 girls); Grade 11: 133 students (133 girls); Grade 12: 139 students (139 girls). 75% of students are Roman Catholic.

Faculty School total: 43. In upper school: 9 men, 33 women; 32 have advanced degrees.

Subjects Offered Advanced chemistry, advanced computer applications, advanced math, Advanced Placement courses, advanced studio art-AP, algebra, American government, American history, American literature, art, art history, art history-AP, band, bioethics, biology, biology-AP, British literature, British literature-AP, calculus, calculus-AP, chemistry, chemistry-AP, choir, choral music, chorus, Christian and

Hebrew scripture, church history, computer applications, computer literacy, computer science, creative writing, dance, decision making skills, digital photography, driver education, economics, economics and history, economics-AP, English, English literature, English literature-AP, environmental science, ethics, European history, French, French language-AP, geometry, government and politics-AP, government-AP, health, Hebrew scripture, history, honors English, honors geometry, honors U.S. history, honors world history, integrated science, jazz band, journalism, leadership, leadership and service, modern world history, moral reasoning, newspaper, orchestra, photography, physical education, physical science, physics, pre-calculus, psychology, relationships, religion, science, sculpture, self-defense, social justice, social sciences, Spanish, Spanish language-AP, Spanish-AP, sports conditioning, sports medicine, studio art-AP, television, trigonometry, U.S. government, U.S. government and politics-AP, U.S. history-AP, video film production, weight training, world history, world literature, world religions, yearbook.

Graduation Requirements Arts and fine arts (art, music, dance, drama), English, foreign language, mathematics, physical education (includes health), religion (includes Bible studies and theology), science, social sciences, social studies (includes history), 100 hours community service.

Special Academic Programs Advanced Placement exam preparation; honors section; independent study; study at local college for college credit; special instructional classes for deaf students, blind students, students with learning differences.

College Admission Counseling 166 students graduated in 2009; all went to college, including Loyola Marymount University; San Jose State University; Santa Clara University; The University of Arizona; University of California, Davis; University of California, Santa Barbara. Mean SAT critical reading: 543, mean SAT math: 533, mean SAT writing: 558.

Student Life Upper grades have uniform requirement, student council, honor system. Discipline rests primarily with faculty. Attendance at religious services is required.

Tuition and Aid Day student tuition: $15,975. Tuition installment plan (Key Tuition Payment Plan, FACTS Tuition Payment Plan, individually arranged payment plans). Merit scholarship grants, need-based scholarship grants available. In 2009–10, 18% of upper-school students received aid; total upper-school merit-scholarship money awarded: $100,000. Total amount of financial aid awarded in 2009–10: $830,000.

Admissions Traditional secondary-level entrance grade is 9. For fall 2009, 400 students applied for upper-level admission, 224 were accepted, 160 enrolled. High School Placement Test (closed version) from Scholastic Testing Service and writing sample required. Deadline for receipt of application materials: January 8. Application fee required: $100. On-campus interview required.

Athletics Interscholastic: aquatics, basketball, cheering, cross-country running, dance team, golf, physical training, soccer, softball, strength & conditioning, swimming and diving, tennis, track and field, volleyball, water polo; intramural: cheering, touch football. 1 PE instructor, 33 coaches, 2 athletic trainers.

Computers Computers are regularly used in college planning, creative writing, English, foreign language, health, history, independent study, journalism, mathematics, media production, newspaper, photography, publishing, religious studies, SAT preparation, science, social studies, video film production, yearbook classes. Computer network features include on-campus library services, Internet access, wireless campus network, Internet filtering or blocking technology. Student e-mail accounts and computer access in designated common areas are available to students. Students grades are available online. The school has a published electronic and media policy.

Contact Alison Bianchetti, Director of Admissions. 650-595-1913 Ext. 320. Fax: 650-595-2643. E-mail: abianchetti@ndhsb.org. Web site: www.ndhsb.org.

NOTRE DAME HIGH SCHOOL

596 South Second Street
San Jose, California 95112

Head of School: Mrs. Mary Elizabeth Riley

General Information Girls' day college-preparatory, arts, religious studies, and technology school, affiliated with Roman Catholic Church. Grades 9–12. Founded: 1851. Setting: urban. 2-acre campus. 4 buildings on campus. Approved or accredited by Western Association of Schools and Colleges, Western Catholic Education Association, and California Department of Education. Total enrollment: 620. Upper school average class size: 27. Upper school faculty-student ratio: 1:13. There are 173 required school days per year for Upper School students. Upper School students typically attend 5 days per week. The average school day consists of 6 hours.

Upper School Student Profile Grade 9: 155 students (155 girls); Grade 10: 168 students (168 girls); Grade 11: 146 students (146 girls); Grade 12: 151 students (151 girls). 66% of students are Roman Catholic.

Faculty School total: 46. In upper school: 5 men, 41 women; 37 have advanced degrees.

Subjects Offered Advanced biology, advanced chemistry, Advanced Placement courses, algebra, art, ASB Leadership, athletics, Basic programming, biology, biology-AP, calculus, calculus-AP, campus ministry, ceramics, chemistry, Christian and Hebrew scripture, computer programming, computer science, creative writing, dance, decision making skills, digital photography, drama, drama performance, economics, English, English language and composition-AP, English literature, English literature and composition-AP, environmental science-AP, film and literature, fine arts, French, French language-AP, French literature-AP, geography, geometry, global

studies, government/civics, healthful living, honors algebra, honors English, honors geometry, honors U.S. history, honors world history, journalism, library research, library skills, mathematics, modern world history, moral and social development, musical theater, painting, peer counseling, peer ministry, philosophy, photography, physical education, physical fitness, physics, post-calculus, pre-calculus, psychology, psychology-AP, public speaking, religion, research skills, robotics, science, service learning/internship, social justice, social psychology, social studies, Spanish, Spanish language-AP, Spanish literature-AP, speech and debate, statistics, study skills, theater, trigonometry, U.S. government, U.S. government and politics-AP, U.S. history, U.S. history-AP, video film production, Web site design, women in society, world history, world history-AP, world religions, yearbook.

Graduation Requirements Arts and fine arts (art, music, dance, drama), computer science, English, foreign language, mathematics, physical education (includes health), religion (includes Bible studies and theology), science, social studies (includes history), community service learning program.

Special Academic Programs 10 Advanced Placement exams for which test preparation is offered; honors section; independent study; study at local college for college credit.

College Admission Counseling 148 students graduated in 2010; all went to college, including Loyola Marymount University; Saint Mary's College of California; San Jose State University; Santa Clara University; University of California, Davis; University of San Francisco. Median SAT critical reading: 570, median SAT math: 575, median SAT writing: 580. 41% scored over 600 on SAT critical reading, 43% scored over 600 on SAT math, 45% scored over 600 on SAT writing.

Student Life Upper grades have uniform requirement, student council, honor system. Discipline rests primarily with faculty. Attendance at religious services is required.

Summer Programs Enrichment, advancement programs offered; held on campus; accepts boys and girls; open to students from other schools. 2011 schedule: June to July.

Tuition and Aid Day student tuition: $14,250. Tuition installment plan (FACTS Tuition Payment Plan, monthly payment plans, annual payment plan, 2-payment plan). Merit scholarship grants, need-based scholarship grants, paying campus jobs, individual sponsored grants available. In 2010–11, 22% of upper-school students received aid; total upper-school merit-scholarship money awarded: $6600. Total amount of financial aid awarded in 2010–11: $700,000.

Admissions Traditional secondary-level entrance grade is 9. For fall 2010, 388 students applied for upper-level admission, 273 were accepted, 155 enrolled. High School Placement Test required. Deadline for receipt of application materials: January 26. Application fee required: $60.

Athletics Interscholastic: basketball, cross-country running, golf, lacrosse, soccer, softball, swimming and diving, tennis, track and field, volleyball; intramural: badminton, basketball, volleyball. 1 PE instructor, 25 coaches, 1 athletic trainer.

Computers Computers are regularly used in all academic, English, foreign language, history, mathematics, science classes. Computer network features include on-campus library services, online commercial services, Internet access, wireless campus network, Internet filtering or blocking technology. Student e-mail accounts are available to students. Students grades are available online. The school has a published electronic and media policy.

Contact Ms. Diana Hernandez, Director of Admissions. 408-294-1113. Fax: 408-293-9779. E-mail: dhernandez@ndsj.org. Web site: ndsj.org.

NOTRE DAME HIGH SCHOOL

910 North Eastern Avenue
Crowley, Louisiana 70526

Head of School: Mrs. Cindy Istre

General Information Coeducational day college-preparatory, arts, vocational, religious studies, and technology school, affiliated with Roman Catholic Church. Grades 9–12. Founded: 1967. Setting: small town. Nearest major city is Lafayette. 10-acre campus. 7 buildings on campus. Approved or accredited by Southern Association of Colleges and Schools and Louisiana Department of Education. Total enrollment: 450. Upper school average class size: 25. Upper school faculty-student ratio: 1:25. There are 178 required school days per year for Upper School students. Upper School students typically attend 5 days per week.

Upper School Student Profile 99% of students are Roman Catholic.

Faculty School total: 38. In upper school: 13 men, 25 women; 9 have advanced degrees.

Subjects Offered Accounting, adolescent issues, advanced math, agriculture, algebra, American history, anatomy and physiology, ancient world history, art, athletics, baseball, basketball, biology, calculus, chemistry, civics/free enterprise, computer applications, computer technologies, dance, drama, driver education, early childhood, English, environmental science, family and consumer science, fine arts, food and nutrition, French, geometry, health education, honors algebra, honors English, honors geometry, honors U.S. history, honors world history, keyboarding, physical education, physical science, physics, pre-calculus, psychology, publications, religion, softball, Spanish, speech, study skills, swimming, tennis, theater, track and field, U.S. history, volleyball, world history, yearbook.

Special Academic Programs Honors section; independent study; study at local college for college credit; academic accommodation for the gifted.

Notre Dame High School

College Admission Counseling 108 students graduated in 2009; 104 went to college, including Louisiana State University and Agricultural and Mechanical College; Louisiana State University at Eunice; University of Louisiana at Lafayette. Other: 3 went to work, 1 entered military service.

Student Life Upper grades have uniform requirement, student council. Discipline rests primarily with faculty. Attendance at religious services is required.

Tuition and Aid Tuition installment plan (The Tuition Plan, monthly payment plans). Tuition reduction for siblings available.

Admissions Explore or Iowa Test of Educational Development required. Deadline for receipt of application materials: none. No application fee required. Interview required.

Athletics Interscholastic: baseball (boys), basketball (b,g), cheering (g), cross-country running (b,g), dance squad (g), football (b), softball (g), tennis (b,g), track and field (b,g), volleyball (g); coed interscholastic: drill team, golf, soccer, swimming and diving. 12 coaches, 2 athletic trainers.

Computers Computers are regularly used in computer applications, English classes. Computer network features include on-campus library services, Internet access, Internet filtering or blocking technology. Students grades are available online.

Contact Mr. Nolan Theriot, Dean of Students. 337-783-3519. Fax: 337-788-2115. Web site: www.ndpios.com.

NOTRE DAME HIGH SCHOOL
320 East Ripa Avenue
St. Louis, Missouri 63125-2897
Head of School: Sr. Gail Guelker, SSND

General Information Girls' day college-preparatory, arts, business, religious studies, bilingual studies, and technology school, affiliated with Roman Catholic Church; primarily serves students with learning disabilities, individuals with Attention Deficit Disorder, and individuals with emotional and behavioral problems. Grades 9–12. Founded: 1934. Setting: suburban. 40-acre campus. 3 buildings on campus. Approved or accredited by North Central Association of Colleges and Schools and Missouri Department of Education. Total enrollment: 320. Upper school faculty-student ratio: 1:10. The average school day consists of 7 hours.

Upper School Student Profile Grade 9: 63 students (63 girls); Grade 10: 61 students (61 girls); Grade 11: 84 students (84 girls); Grade 12: 110 students (110 girls). 97% of students are Roman Catholic.

Faculty School total: 44. In upper school: 8 men, 36 women; 20 have advanced degrees.

Subjects Offered 3-dimensional art, ACT preparation, acting, advanced biology, advanced chemistry, advanced math, African-American literature, algebra, American history, American history-AP, American literature, analytic geometry, anatomy and physiology, applied music, art, arts, astronomy, basketball, Bible studies, biology, botany, British literature, broadcast journalism, business, business education, business law, calculus, calculus-AP, career/college preparation, ceramics, chemistry, chemistry-AP, child development, choir, choral music, chorus, Christian and Hebrew scripture, Christian studies, communication skills, communications, community service, composition-AP, computer art, computer programming, computer science, concert choir, creative writing, culinary arts, dance, death and loss, debate, developmental language skills, developmental math, digital art, digital photography, drama, drama workshop, early childhood, earth science, ecology, economics, English, English literature, English literature and composition-AP, English literature-AP, ethics, expository writing, family and consumer science, family living, fashion, film and literature, fine arts, food and nutrition, foreign language, French, French as a second language, French-AP, gardening, geography, geology, geometry, global studies, government and politics-AP, government/civics, grammar, graphic design, health, health education, history, history-AP, home economics, honors English, honors U.S. history, human sexuality, independent study, interdisciplinary studies, intro to computers, journalism, keyboarding, leadership, literary genres, mathematics, media literacy, music, musical theater, newspaper, photography, physical education, physics, public speaking, religion, science, social studies, sociology, Spanish, Spanish-AP, speech, speech and debate, theater, trigonometry, typing, U.S. history-AP, volleyball, world history, world literature, world religions, world studies, writing, writing, yearbook, zoology.

Graduation Requirements Arts and fine arts (art, music, dance, drama), athletics, business skills (includes word processing), computer science, English, mathematics, physical education (includes health), religion (includes Bible studies and theology), science, social studies (includes history). Community service is required.

Special Academic Programs Advanced Placement exam preparation; honors section; accelerated programs; independent study; study at local college for college credit; academic accommodation for the gifted, the musically talented, and the artistically talented; remedial reading and/or remedial writing; remedial math.

College Admission Counseling 99 students graduated in 2009; all went to college, including Missouri State University; Saint Louis University; Southeast Missouri State University; St. Louis Community College at Meramec; Truman State University; University of Missouri.

Student Life Upper grades have uniform requirement, student council, honor system. Discipline rests primarily with faculty.

Tuition and Aid Day student tuition: $9200. Tuition installment plan (FACTS Tuition Payment Plan, monthly payment plans, individually arranged payment plans, quarterly payment plan). Tuition reduction for siblings, merit scholarship grants, need-based scholarship grants, paying campus jobs, tuition reduction for children of faculty and

staff, reciprocal tuition agreement consortium available. In 2009–10, 30% of upper-school students received aid; total upper-school merit-scholarship money awarded: $10,000. Total amount of financial aid awarded in 2009–10: $90,000.

Admissions Traditional secondary-level entrance grade is 9. Any standardized test or Iowa Tests of Basic Skills required. Deadline for receipt of application materials: none. No application fee required.

Athletics Interscholastic: basketball, cheering, cross-country running, diving, golf, racquetball, soccer, softball, swimming and diving, track and field, volleyball; intramural: aerobics/dance, cheering, dance. 2 PE instructors, 9 coaches.

Computers Computers are regularly used in business skills, English, journalism, mathematics, newspaper, writing, yearbook classes. Computer network features include on-campus library services, online commercial services, Internet access, wireless campus network, Internet filtering or blocking technology. Campus intranet, student e-mail accounts, and computer access in designated common areas are available to students. Students grades are available online. The school has a published electronic and media policy.

Contact Mrs. Meredith Metzger, Marketing and Special Events Coordinator. 314-544-1015 Ext. 1104. Fax: 314-544-8003. E-mail: metzm@ndhs.net. Web site: www.ndhs.net.

NOTRE DAME HIGH SCHOOL
601 Lawrence Road
Lawrenceville, New Jersey 08648
Head of School: Mr. Barry Edward Breen and Ms. Mary Liz Ivins

General Information Coeducational day college-preparatory school, affiliated with Roman Catholic Church. Grades 9–12. Founded: 1957. Setting: suburban. Nearest major city is Trenton. 100-acre campus. 1 building on campus. Approved or accredited by Middle States Association of Colleges and Schools, National Catholic Education Association, and New Jersey Department of Education. Total enrollment: 1,266. Upper school average class size: 24. Upper school faculty-student ratio: 1:23. There are 180 required school days per year for Upper School students. Upper School students typically attend 5 days per week. The average school day consists of 6 hours and 30 minutes.

Upper School Student Profile Grade 9: 327 students (168 boys, 159 girls); Grade 10: 333 students (170 boys, 163 girls); Grade 11: 288 students (156 boys, 132 girls); Grade 12: 318 students (177 boys, 141 girls). 88% of students are Roman Catholic.

Faculty School total: 96. In upper school: 35 men, 61 women; 42 have advanced degrees.

Subjects Offered 20th century history, 3-dimensional art, 3-dimensional design, accounting, acting, advanced chemistry, advanced computer applications, advanced math, Advanced Placement courses, algebra, American history, American history-AP, American literature, ancient world history, applied music, art, art and culture, athletics, Basic programming, Bible studies, biology, biology-AP, British literature, business, business applications, business studies, calculus, calculus-AP, Catholic belief and practice, ceramics, chemistry, chemistry-AP, choir, Christian doctrine, comparative religion, computer applications, computer science, concert band, concert choir, constitutional law, contemporary issues, creative writing, dance, dance performance, discrete mathematics, drama, driver education, ecology, environmental systems, economics, English, English composition, English literature-AP, environmental science-AP, etymology, European history-AP, film studies, first aid, French, geometry, German, German literature, health education, honors algebra, honors English, honors world history, Italian, Japanese, journalism, language-AP, Latin, law, leadership and service, leadership education training, literature-AP, madrigals, math review, peer ministry, philosophy, photography, physical education, physics, physics-AP, piano, portfolio art, pre-algebra, pre-calculus, probability and statistics, psychology, psychology-AP, public speaking, reading/study skills, SAT preparation, scripture, senior internship, senior project, sociology, Spanish, Spanish literature, speech and debate, sports medicine, U.S. government, U.S. government and politics-AP, U.S. literature, women spirituality and faith, world history, world literature, writing.

Graduation Requirements Biology, English, foreign language, integrated technology fundamentals, lab science, mathematics, physical education (includes health), religion (includes Bible studies and theology), U.S. history, world history, service-learning. Community service is required.

Special Academic Programs 14 Advanced Placement exams for which test preparation is offered; honors section; independent study; study at local college for college credit; remedial reading and/or remedial writing; remedial math.

College Admission Counseling 315 students graduated in 2010; 312 went to college, including Duquesne University; Penn State University Park; Rutgers, The State University of New Jersey, New Brunswick; Saint Joseph's University; The College of New Jersey. Other: 1 went to work, 2 entered military service. Mean SAT critical reading: 556, mean SAT math: 557, mean SAT writing: 554, mean combined SAT: 1667. 30% scored over 600 on SAT critical reading, 34% scored over 600 on SAT math, 28% scored over 600 on SAT writing, 26% scored over 1800 on combined SAT.

Student Life Upper grades have uniform requirement, student council, honor system. Discipline rests primarily with faculty. Attendance at religious services is required.

Summer Programs Remediation, enrichment, sports, art/fine arts programs offered; session focuses on sports, arts and writing camps; held on campus; accepts boys and

girls; open to students from other schools. 775 students usually enrolled. 2011 schedule: June 21 to August 5. Application deadline: June 21.
Tuition and Aid Day student tuition: $9900. Tuition installment plan (Tuition Management Systems Plan). Tuition reduction for siblings, need-based scholarship grants available: In 2010–11, 10% of upper-school students received aid. Total amount of financial aid awarded in 2010–11: $180,000.
Admissions Traditional secondary-level entrance grade is 9. For fall 2010, 500 students applied for upper-level admission, 400 were accepted, 327 enrolled. Scholastic Testing Service High School Placement Test required. Deadline for receipt of application materials: November 30. Application fee required: $50. On-campus interview required.
Athletics Interscholastic: baseball (boys), basketball (b,g), cheering (g), cross-country running (b,g), dance (b,g), field hockey (g), football (b), golf (b,g), ice hockey (b), indoor track (b,g), lacrosse (b,g), soccer (b,g), softball (g), swimming and diving (b,g), tennis (b,g), track and field (b,g), winter (indoor) track (b,g), wrestling (b); intramural: touch football (g), volleyball (b,g); coed interscholastic: cheering, diving, fitness, strength & conditioning; coed intramural: Frisbee, outdoor activities, outdoor recreation, physical fitness, ultimate Frisbee, volleyball, weight lifting, weight training. 9 PE instructors, 65 coaches, 1 athletic trainer.
Computers Computers are regularly used in all academic classes. Computer network features include on-campus library services, online commercial services, Internet access, wireless campus network, Internet filtering or blocking technology. Campus intranet and computer access in designated common areas are available to students. Students grades are available online. The school has a published electronic and media policy.
Contact Ms. Peggy Miller, Director of Enrollment Management. 609-882-7900 Ext. 139. Fax: 609-882-6599. E-mail: miller@ndnj.org. Web site: www.ndnj.org.

NOTRE DAME HIGH SCHOOL
1400 Maple Avenue
Elmira, New York 14904
Head of School: Sr. Mary Walter Hickey
General Information Coeducational day college-preparatory, arts, and religious studies school, affiliated with Roman Catholic Church. Grades 9–12. Founded: 1954. Setting: suburban. Nearest major city is Rochester. 30-acre campus. 1 building on campus. Approved or accredited by Mercy Secondary Education Association, Middle States Association of Colleges and Schools, and New York Department of Education. Member of Secondary School Admission Test Board. Endowment: $500,000. Total enrollment: 222. Upper school average class size: 20. Upper school faculty-student ratio: 1:15. There are 180 required school days per year for Upper School students. Upper School students typically attend 5 days per week. The average school day consists of 5 hours and 30 minutes.
Upper School Student Profile Grade 9: 53 students (28 boys, 25 girls); Grade 10: 56 students (27 boys, 29 girls); Grade 11: 48 students (25 boys, 23 girls); Grade 12: 64 students (36 boys, 28 girls). 80% of students are Roman Catholic.
Faculty School total: 26. In upper school: 12 men, 14 women; 19 have advanced degrees.
Subjects Offered Accounting, art, arts, band, biology, calculus, ceramics, chemistry, chemistry-AP, choir, computer literacy, creative writing, drama, drawing, earth science, English, English-AP, fine arts, French, government/civics, health, human development, mathematics, multimedia, music composition, music history, music theory, painting, physical education, physics, portfolio art, pre-calculus, psychology, public speaking, religion, science, social studies, Spanish, studio art, theology.
Graduation Requirements Arts and fine arts (art, music, dance, drama), English, language, mathematics, physical education (includes health), religion (includes Bible studies and theology), science, social studies (includes history).
Special Academic Programs Advanced Placement exam preparation; honors section; accelerated programs; independent study; study at local college for college credit; academic accommodation for the gifted and the artistically talented; remedial reading and/or remedial writing; remedial math.
College Admission Counseling 82 students graduated in 2009; 81 went to college, including Cornell University; James Madison University; Mercyhurst College; Penn State University Park; State University of New York at Binghamton; State University of New York College at Geneseo. Other: 1 had other specific plans. Median SAT critical reading: 550, median SAT math: 530, median composite ACT: 22. 25% scored over 600 on SAT critical reading, 25% scored over 600 on SAT math, 25% scored over 26 on composite ACT.
Student Life Upper grades have uniform requirement, student council. Discipline rests primarily with faculty. Attendance at religious services is required.
Tuition and Aid Day student tuition: $7250. Tuition installment plan (monthly payment plans, individually arranged payment plans, local bank-arranged plan). Tuition reduction for siblings, merit scholarship grants, need-based scholarship grants, paying campus jobs available. In 2009–10, 40% of upper-school students received aid; total upper-school merit-scholarship money awarded: $2000. Total amount of financial aid awarded in 2009–10: $275,000.
Admissions Traditional secondary-level entrance grade is 9. For fall 2009, 60 students applied for upper-level admission, 58 were accepted, 58 enrolled. Scholastic Testing Service High School Placement Test required. Deadline for receipt of application materials: none. Application fee required: $75. Interview recommended.

Athletics Interscholastic: baseball (boys), basketball (b,g), cheering (g), football (b), golf (b), lacrosse (b), soccer (b,g), softball (g), tennis (b,g), track and field (b,g), wrestling (b); coed intramural: bicycling, bowling, skiing (downhill). 2 PE instructors, 27 coaches, 1 athletic trainer.
Computers Computer network features include on-campus library services, Internet access, wireless campus network, Internet filtering or blocking technology. Campus intranet, student e-mail accounts, and computer access in designated common areas are available to students. Students grades are available online. The school has a published electronic and media policy.
Contact Sr. Nancy Kelly, Director of Admissions. 607-734-2267 Ext. 318. Fax: 607-737-8903. E-mail: kellyn@notredamehighschool.com. Web site: www.notredamehighschool.com.

NOTRE DAME HIGH SCHOOL
2701 Vermont Avenue
Chattanooga, Tennessee 37404
Head of School: Mr. Perry L. Storey
General Information Coeducational day college-preparatory, arts, religious studies, and technology school, affiliated with Roman Catholic Church. Grades 9–12. Founded: 1876. Setting: urban. 20-acre campus. 5 buildings on campus. Approved or accredited by Southern Association of Colleges and Schools and Tennessee Department of Education. Endowment: $1.5 million. Total enrollment: 413. Upper school average class size: 18. Upper school faculty-student ratio: 1:10. Upper School students typically attend 5 days per week.
Upper School Student Profile Grade 9: 81 students (43 boys, 38 girls); Grade 10: 104 students (49 boys, 55 girls); Grade 11: 101 students (54 boys, 47 girls); Grade 12: 127 students (61 boys, 66 girls). 77% of students are Roman Catholic.
Faculty School total: 40. In upper school: 16 men, 24 women; 28 have advanced degrees.
Subjects Offered 3-dimensional art, ACT preparation, Advanced Placement courses, algebra, American history-AP, American literature, anatomy, anatomy and physiology, art-AP, band, biology, biology-AP, British literature, calculus, Catholic belief and practice, chemistry, choir, civics, conceptual physics, creative dance, criminal justice, drama, economics, electives, English composition, English literature, English-AP, environmental science-AP, European history-AP, foreign language, French, geometry, government, government/civics, health and wellness, history-AP, honors algebra, honors English, honors geometry, honors U.S. history, honors world history, Latin, physics, religion, Spanish, U.S. government and politics-AP, weight training, wellness, world geography, world history, world history-AP, writing, yoga.
Special Academic Programs Advanced Placement exam preparation; honors section; independent study; study at local college for college credit.
College Admission Counseling 120 students graduated in 2010; all went to college, including Auburn University; Middle Tennessee State University; The University of Tennessee; The University of Tennessee at Chattanooga; University of Georgia.
Student Life Upper grades have uniform requirement, student council, honor system. Discipline rests primarily with faculty. Attendance at religious services is required.
Summer Programs Enrichment, sports, art/fine arts programs offered; session focuses on enrichment; held both on and off campus; held at various sites in Chattanooga; accepts boys and girls; open to students from other schools. 250 students usually enrolled. 2011 schedule: June 1 to July 31. Application deadline: April 1.
Tuition and Aid Day student tuition: $9287–$12,249. Tuition installment plan (Insured Tuition Payment Plan, monthly payment plans). Tuition reduction for siblings, need-based scholarship grants, paying campus jobs available. In 2010–11, 28% of upper-school students received aid. Total amount of financial aid awarded in 2010–11: $526,521.
Admissions Traditional secondary-level entrance grade is 9. ACT-Explore required. Deadline for receipt of application materials: none. Application fee required: $100. On-campus interview required.
Athletics Interscholastic: aerobics/dance (girls), baseball (b), basketball (b,g), bowling (b,g), cross-country running (b,g), dance (g), dance squad (g), dance team (g), diving (b,g), football (b), golf (b,g), modern dance (g), physical training (b,g), running (b,g), soccer (b,g), softball (g), swimming and diving (b,g), tennis (b,g), track and field (b,g), volleyball (g), weight training (b,g), wrestling (b); intramural: aerobics/dance (g), cheering (g), indoor soccer (b,g), indoor track (b,g), lacrosse (b,g); coed interscholastic: cheering, yoga; coed intramural: backpacking, canoeing/kayaking, climbing, crew, hiking/backpacking, kayaking, mountaineering, outdoors, rafting, rappelling, rock climbing, rowing, skiing (downhill), snowboarding, wall climbing. 5 PE instructors, 30 coaches, 2 athletic trainers.
Computers Computer network features include on-campus library services, Internet access, wireless campus network, Internet filtering or blocking technology, language software labs. Computer access in designated common areas is available to students. Students grades are available online. The school has a published electronic and media policy.
Contact Ms. Jenny Rittgers, Admissions Director. 423-624-4618 Ext. 1004. Fax: 423-624-4621. E-mail: admissions@myndhs.com. Web site: www.myndhs.com.

NOTRE DAME HIGH SCHOOL FOR GIRLS

3115 North Mason Avenue
Chicago, Illinois 60634
Head of School: Ms. Denise Pikarski
General Information Girls' day college-preparatory, arts, business, religious studies, and technology school, affiliated with Roman Catholic Church; primarily serves students with learning disabilities, individuals with Attention Deficit Disorder, and individuals with emotional and behavioral problems. Grades 9–12. Founded: 1938. Setting: urban. 1 building on campus. Approved or accredited by National Catholic Education Association, North Central Association of Colleges and Schools, and Illinois Department of Education. Total enrollment: 142. Upper school average class size: 18. Upper school faculty-student ratio: 1:14. There are 180 required school days per year for Upper School students. Upper School students typically attend 5 days per week. The average school day consists of 7 hours and 15 minutes.
Upper School Student Profile Grade 9: 15 students (15 girls); Grade 10: 38 students (38 girls); Grade 11: 39 students (39 girls); Grade 12: 50 students (50 girls); Postgraduate: 142 students (142 girls). 65% of students are Roman Catholic.
Faculty School total: 25. In upper school: 10 men, 13 women; 16 have advanced degrees.
Subjects Offered Accounting, advanced computer applications, advanced math, algebra, American government, American history-AP, American literature, American studies, anatomy and physiology, art, astronomy, audio visual/media, band, Basic programming, biology, British literature, British literature-AP, calculus, career and personal planning, chemistry, chemistry-AP, chorus, composition, computer applications, computer programming, computer-aided design, concert band, consumer economics, consumer education, consumer mathematics, drawing, driver education, English, English-AP, family living, family studies, first aid, French, French-AP, geography, geometry, government-AP, health education, honors algebra, honors English, honors geometry, honors U.S. history, humanities, internship, journalism, keyboarding, literature, mathematics, music theory, painting, peer ministry, physical education, physical science, physics, pre-algebra, pre-calculus, public speaking, reading, SAT/ACT preparation, scripture, sculpture, sociology, Spanish, Spanish-AP, theater arts, theology, U.S. government and politics-AP, U.S. history, word processing, world civilizations, world history, writing.
Graduation Requirements Arts and fine arts (art, music, dance, drama), electives, English, foreign language, mathematics, physical education (includes health), science, social studies (includes history), theology, word processing, 60 hours of Christian service per school year.
Special Academic Programs Advanced Placement exam preparation; honors section; remedial reading and/or remedial writing; remedial math; special instructional classes for students with IEPs.
College Admission Counseling 70 students graduated in 2009; all went to college, including DePaul University; Dominican University; Loyola University Chicago; Northeastern Illinois University; Northern Illinois University; University of Illinois at Chicago.
Student Life Upper grades have uniform requirement, student council, honor system. Discipline rests equally with students and faculty. Attendance at religious services is required.
Tuition and Aid Day student tuition: $6800. Tuition installment plan (monthly payment plans, individually arranged payment plans). Tuition reduction for siblings, need-based scholarship grants, paying campus jobs available.
Admissions Traditional secondary-level entrance grade is 9. For fall 2009, 142 students applied for upper-level admission, 142 were accepted, 142 enrolled. TerraNova required. Deadline for receipt of application materials: none. Application fee required: $300. Interview required.
Athletics Interscholastic: basketball, dance, soccer, softball, track and field, volleyball. 1 PE instructor, 8 coaches.
Computers Computers are regularly used in art, basic skills, business education, career exploration, college planning, data processing, desktop publishing, English, foreign language, geography, graphic arts, health, history, humanities, independent study, information technology, journalism, library skills, mathematics, publications, religious studies, research skills, social studies, study skills, technology, theater arts, vocational-technical courses, Web site design, word processing, writing, writing, yearbook classes. Computer network features include on-campus library services, online commercial services, Internet access, wireless campus network. The school has a published electronic and media policy.
Contact Ms. Julie Raino, Director of Recruitment. 773-622-9494. Fax: 773-622-2807. E-mail: jraino@ndhs4girls.org. Web site: www.ndhs4girls.org.

NOTRE DAME JUNIOR/SENIOR HIGH SCHOOL

60 Spangenburg Avenue
East Stroudsburg, Pennsylvania 18301-2799
Head of School: Mr. Jeffrey Neill Lyons
General Information Coeducational day college-preparatory, arts, and religious studies school, affiliated with Roman Catholic Church. Grades 7–12. Founded: 1967. Setting: suburban. 40-acre campus. 4 buildings on campus. Approved or accredited by Middle States Association of Colleges and Schools, National Catholic Education Association, and Pennsylvania Department of Education. Total enrollment: 258. Upper school average class size: 25. Upper school faculty-student ratio: 1:15. There

are 180 required school days per year for Upper School students. Upper School students typically attend 5 days per week. The average school day consists of 6 hours and 30 minutes.
Upper School Student Profile Grade 7: 39 students (19 boys, 20 girls); Grade 8: 28 students (15 boys, 13 girls); Grade 9: 44 students (18 boys, 26 girls); Grade 10: 45 students (19 boys, 26 girls); Grade 11: 41 students (16 boys, 25 girls); Grade 12: 61 students (31 boys, 30 girls). 88% of students are Roman Catholic.
Faculty School total: 25. In upper school: 12 men, 13 women; 14 have advanced degrees.
Graduation Requirements Lab/keyboard, mathematics, moral theology, physical education (includes health), physical science, religion (includes Bible studies and theology), senior project, U.S. history, U.S. literature, word processing, world cultures, world religions.
Special Academic Programs Advanced Placement exam preparation; honors section; study at local college for college credit.
College Admission Counseling 63 students graduated in 2010; 61 went to college, including Marywood University; Mount St. Mary's University; Penn State University Park; Saint Joseph's University; Temple University; The University of Scranton. Other: 2 went to work. Median SAT critical reading: 500, median SAT math: 460, median SAT writing: 500, median combined SAT: 1460. 10% scored over 600 on SAT critical reading, 15% scored over 600 on SAT math, 10% scored over 600 on SAT writing, 25% scored over 1800 on combined SAT.
Student Life Upper grades have uniform requirement, student council. Discipline rests primarily with faculty. Attendance at religious services is required.
Tuition and Aid Tuition installment plan (FACTS Tuition Payment Plan). Tuition reduction for siblings, need-based scholarship grants available. In 2010–11, 30% of upper-school students received aid.
Admissions Traditional secondary-level entrance grade is 7. Achievement tests or TerraNova required. Deadline for receipt of application materials: May 1. No application fee required. Interview required.
Athletics Interscholastic: baseball (boys), basketball (b,g), cheering (g), field hockey (g), soccer (b,g), softball (g), swimming and diving (b,g), tennis (b,g), winter soccer (b,g); coed interscholastic: golf, soccer; coed intramural: cross-country running, indoor soccer, jogging, strength & conditioning. 2 PE instructors, 15 coaches, 1 athletic trainer.
Computers Computer network features include on-campus library services, Internet access, Internet filtering or blocking technology. The school has a published electronic and media policy.
Contact Mr. Jeffrey Neill Lyons, Principal. 570-421-0466. Fax: 570-476-0629. E-mail: principal@ndhigh.org. Web site: www.ndhigh.org.

NOTRE DAME PREPARATORY SCHOOL

815 Hampton Lane
Towson, Maryland 21286
Head of School: Sr. Patricia McCarron, SSND
General Information Girls' day college-preparatory school, affiliated with Roman Catholic Church. Grades 6–12. Founded: 1873. Setting: suburban. Nearest major city is Baltimore. 60-acre campus. 3 buildings on campus. Approved or accredited by Association of Independent Maryland Schools, Middle States Association of Colleges and Schools, National Catholic Education Association, and Maryland Department of Education. Member of National Association of Independent Schools. Endowment: $7 million. Total enrollment: 758. Upper school average class size: 16. Upper school faculty-student ratio: 1:9. There are 180 required school days per year for Upper School students. Upper School students typically attend 5 days per week. The average school day consists of 7 hours and 10 minutes.
Upper School Student Profile Grade 9: 152 students (152 girls); Grade 10: 153 students (153 girls); Grade 11: 134 students (134 girls); Grade 12: 147 students (147 girls). 85% of students are Roman Catholic.
Faculty School total: 90. In upper school: 13 men, 77 women; 75 have advanced degrees.
Subjects Offered Algebra, American history, American literature, anatomy, architectural drawing, art, Bible studies, biology, calculus, calculus-AP, ceramics, chemistry, community service, computer science, creative writing, drama, economics, English, English literature, environmental science, European history, fine arts, French, geometry, government/civics, grammar, history, Japanese, journalism, Latin, marine biology, mathematics, music, philosophy, photography, physical education, physics, religion, science, social issues, social justice, social studies, Spanish, statistics, swimming, theater, trigonometry, world history, world literature, writing.
Graduation Requirements Arts and fine arts (art, music, dance, drama), English, foreign language, mathematics, physical education (includes health), religion (includes Bible studies and theology), science, social studies (includes history), swimming. Community service is required.
Special Academic Programs 20 Advanced Placement exams for which test preparation is offered; honors section; independent study.
College Admission Counseling 134 students graduated in 2009; all went to college, including Franklin & Marshall College; Loyola University Maryland; St. Mary's College of Maryland; University of Maryland, College Park; University of Virginia; Virginia Polytechnic Institute and State University. Median SAT critical reading: 620, median SAT math: 610, median SAT writing: 630, median combined SAT: 1860, median composite ACT: 26. 58% scored over 600 on SAT critical reading, 55% scored

over 600 on SAT math, 66% scored over 600 on SAT writing, 65% scored over 1800 on combined SAT, 50% scored over 26 on composite ACT.

Student Life Upper grades have uniform requirement, student council, honor system. Discipline rests equally with students and faculty. Attendance at religious services is required.

Tuition and Aid Day student tuition: $15,250. Tuition installment plan (FACTS Tuition Payment Plan). Need-based scholarship grants available. In 2009–10, 24% of upper-school students received aid. Total amount of financial aid awarded in 2009–10: $811,400.

Admissions Traditional secondary-level entrance grade is 9. For fall 2009, 275 students applied for upper-level admission, 211 were accepted, 154 enrolled. High School Placement Test and ISEE required. Deadline for receipt of application materials: December 1. Application fee required: $75. On-campus interview required.

Athletics Interscholastic: badminton, basketball, crew, cross-country running, field hockey, golf, indoor soccer, indoor track, lacrosse, soccer, softball, swimming and diving, tennis, track and field, volleyball, winter (indoor) track, winter soccer; intramural: aerobics, badminton, basketball, cheering, cooperative games, dance team, field hockey, skiing (downhill), soccer, tennis, volleyball, yoga. 6 PE instructors, 28 coaches, 1 athletic trainer.

Computers Computers are regularly used in all classes. Computer network features include on-campus library services, online commercial services, Internet access, wireless campus network, Internet filtering or blocking technology, computer-based science, music, language, publications and art labs, Microsoft Office, laptop program for grades 9-12, laptop carts for grades 6-8, automated library research databases, Internet-based learning management systems. Student e-mail accounts and computer access in designated common areas are available to students. The school has a published electronic and media policy.

Contact Mrs. Katherine Goetz, Director of Admission. 410-825-0590. Fax: 410-825-0982. E-mail: goetzk@notredameprep.com. Web site: www.notredameprep.com.

OAK CREEK RANCH SCHOOL

West Sedona, Arizona
See Special Needs Schools section.

OAKCREST SCHOOL

850 Balls Hill Road
McLean, Virginia 22101
Head of School: Ms. Ellen M. Cavanagh

General Information Girls' day college-preparatory school. Grades 6–12. Founded: 1976. Setting: urban. Approved or accredited by Virginia Department of Education. Total enrollment: 187. Upper school average class size: 14.

Upper School Student Profile Grade 6: 19 students (19 girls); Grade 7: 25 students (25 girls); Grade 8: 23 students (23 girls); Grade 9: 31 students (31 girls); Grade 10: 31 students (31 girls); Grade 11: 28 students (28 girls); Grade 12: 31 students (31 girls).

College Admission Counseling 23 students graduated in 2010; all went to college. Mean SAT critical reading: 660, mean SAT math: 597, mean SAT writing: 640, mean combined SAT: 1897, mean composite ACT: 24.

Tuition and Aid Tuition installment plan (SMART Tuition Payment Plan).

Admissions Deadline for receipt of application materials: February 1. Application fee required: $50. Interview required.

Contact Mrs. Terri Collins, Director of Admission. 703-790-5450. Fax: 703-790-5380. E-mail: admissions@oakcrest.org. Web site: www.oakcrest.org.

OAK GROVE LUTHERAN SCHOOL

124 North Terrace
Fargo, North Dakota 58102
Head of School: Dr. Marilyn J. Guy

General Information Coeducational day college-preparatory, general academic, religious studies, and music school, affiliated with Evangelical Lutheran Church in America. Grades K–12. Founded: 1906. Setting: suburban. Nearest major city is Minneapolis, MN. 5.3-acre campus. 5 buildings on campus. Approved or accredited by North Central Association of Colleges and Schools and North Dakota Department of Education. Endowment: $4.8 million. Total enrollment: 430. Upper school average class size: 17. Upper school faculty-student ratio: 1:12.

Upper School Student Profile 75% of students are Evangelical Lutheran Church in America.

Faculty School total: 40. In upper school: 10 men, 12 women; 6 have advanced degrees.

Subjects Offered Accounting, algebra, American history, American literature, art, band, Bible studies, biology, British literature, business law, business skills, calculus, chemistry, chorus, civics, computer programming, computer science, consumer mathematics, driver education, Eastern world civilizations, economics, English, ensembles, family studies, food science, geography, geometry, German, government, health, history, keyboarding, mathematics, music appreciation, nutrition, physical education, physical science, physics, pre-calculus, psychology, religion, science,

social sciences, social studies, sociology, Spanish, speech, textiles, trigonometry, weight training, world affairs, world cultures, world history.

Graduation Requirements Business skills (includes word processing), English, mathematics, physical education (includes health), religion (includes Bible studies and theology), science, social sciences, social studies (includes history).

Special Academic Programs Advanced Placement exam preparation; honors section; independent study; study at local college for college credit; study abroad; academic accommodation for the gifted and the musically talented; remedial reading and/or remedial writing; remedial math; programs in English, mathematics, general development for dyslexic students; special instructional classes for students with learning disabilities, Attention Deficit Disorder; ESL (15 students enrolled).

College Admission Counseling 62 students graduated in 2009; 61 went to college, including Concordia College; North Dakota State University; South Dakota State University; University of North Dakota. Other: 1 went to work.

Student Life Upper grades have specified standards of dress, student council, honor system. Discipline rests equally with students and faculty. Attendance at religious services is required.

Tuition and Aid Day student tuition: $7100. Tuition installment plan (FACTS Tuition Payment Plan). Tuition reduction for siblings, merit scholarship grants, need-based scholarship grants, paying campus jobs, work-study tuition reduction plan available. In 2009–10, 46% of upper-school students received aid; total upper-school merit-scholarship money awarded: $12,000. Total amount of financial aid awarded in 2009–10: $250,000.

Admissions Traditional secondary-level entrance grade is 9. Achievement tests, ACT, Iowa Test, CTBS, or TAP, PSAT or SAT, Stanford Achievement Test, TOEFL or Woodcock-Johnson required. Deadline for receipt of application materials: none. Application fee required: $45. Interview recommended.

Athletics Interscholastic: aquatics (boys, girls), baseball (b,g), basketball (b,g), cross-country running (b,g), diving (b,g), football (b), golf (b,g), ice hockey (b,g), physical training (b,g), soccer (b,g), softball (g), swimming and diving (b,g), tennis (b,g), track and field (b,g), volleyball (g); coed intramural: billiards, table tennis. 2 PE instructors, 2 coaches, 1 athletic trainer.

Computers Computers are regularly used in business, college planning, English, history, independent study, library skills, mathematics, religious studies, science classes. Computer network features include on-campus library services, online commercial services, Internet access, wireless campus network, Internet filtering or blocking technology. Campus intranet, student e-mail accounts, and computer access in designated common areas are available to students. Students grades are available online. The school has a published electronic and media policy.

Contact Terry J. Haus, Director of Admissions. 701-373-7114. Fax: 701-297-1993. E-mail: terry.haus@oakgrovelutheran.com. Web site: www.oakgrovelutheran.com.

OAK GROVE SCHOOL

220 West Lomita Avenue
Ojai, California 93023
Head of School: Meredy Benson Rice

General Information Coeducational boarding and day college-preparatory and arts school. Boarding grades 7–12, day grades PK–12. Founded: 1975. Setting: small town. Nearest major city is Los Angeles. Students are housed in coed dormitories. 150-acre campus. 6 buildings on campus. Approved or accredited by California Association of Independent Schools, The Association of Boarding Schools, Western Association of Schools and Colleges, and California Department of Education. Member of Secondary School Admission Test Board. Endowment: $700,000. Total enrollment: 180. Upper school average class size: 12. Upper school faculty-student ratio: 1:7. There are 170 required school days per year for Upper School students. Upper School students typically attend 5 days per week. The average school day consists of 8 hours and 30 minutes.

Upper School Student Profile Grade 7: 7 students (6 boys, 1 girl); Grade 8: 12 students (6 boys, 6 girls); Grade 9: 7 students (4 boys, 3 girls); Grade 10: 14 students (10 boys, 4 girls); Grade 11: 9 students (4 boys, 5 girls); Grade 12: 6 students (3 boys, 3 girls). 35% of students are boarding students. 83% are state residents. 2 states are represented in upper school student body. 23% are international students. International students from China, India, Japan, Mexico, Republic of Korea, and Viet Nam.

Faculty School total: 30. In upper school: 6 men, 5 women; 5 have advanced degrees; 1 resides on campus.

Subjects Offered Algebra, American history, American literature, anatomy, art, art history, biology, calculus, ceramics, chemistry, communications, community service, comparative religion, computer science, drama, earth science, economics, English, English literature, ethics, film and new technologies, fine arts, gardening, geography, geometry, global studies, history, horticulture, human development, inquiry into relationship, mathematics, music, permaculture, photography, physical education, physics, relationships, religion and culture, science, social studies, Spanish, studio art, theater, world cultures, world history, world literature.

Graduation Requirements Algebra, American history, arts and fine arts (art, music, dance, drama), backpacking, biology, chemistry, college admission preparation, comparative religion, economics and history, English, ethics and responsibility, foreign language, geometry, mathematics, science, social studies (includes history), Spanish, world religions, participation in camping and travel programs and sports, one year of visual and performing arts. Community service is required.

Special Academic Programs 3 Advanced Placement exams for which test preparation is offered; honors section; ESL (4 students enrolled).

College Admission Counseling 12 students graduated in 2010; 11 went to college, including California Institute of the Arts; New York University; Pace University; The Colorado College; University of California, Berkeley. Other: 1 had other specific plans. Mean SAT critical reading: 627, mean SAT math: 580, mean SAT writing: 617. 57% scored over 600 on SAT critical reading, 28% scored over 600 on SAT math, 42% scored over 600 on SAT writing.

Student Life Upper grades have student council, honor system. Discipline rests equally with students and faculty.

Summer Programs ESL programs offered; held on campus; accepts boys and girls; open to students from other schools. 15 students usually enrolled. 2011 schedule: July to August. Application deadline: June.

Tuition and Aid Day student tuition: $15,650; 7-day tuition and room/board: $37,900. Tuition installment plan (FACTS Tuition Payment Plan, annual and semiannual payment plans). Need-based scholarship grants, African-American scholarships available. In 2010–11, 40% of upper-school students received aid. Total amount of financial aid awarded in 2010–11: $60,000.

Admissions Traditional secondary-level entrance grade is 9. For fall 2010, 31 students applied for upper-level admission, 22 were accepted, 8 enrolled. SSAT or TOEFL or SLEP required. Deadline for receipt of application materials: none. Application fee required: $50. Interview required.

Athletics Interscholastic: soccer (boys, girls), volleyball (b,g); intramural: equestrian sports (g), soccer (b,g), volleyball (b,g); coed intramural: backpacking, fitness, hiking/backpacking, outdoor activities, outdoor education, outdoor skills, physical fitness, ropes courses, skiing (downhill), table tennis, tennis, wilderness. 1 PE instructor, 3 coaches.

Computers Computers are regularly used in art, ESL, graphic arts, history, independent study, library, mathematics, multimedia, photography, SAT preparation, science, technology, typing, writing, yearbook classes. Computer network features include on-campus library services, online commercial services, Internet access, wireless campus network, Internet filtering or blocking technology. Computer access in designated common areas is available to students.

Contact Joy Maguire-Parsons, Director of Admissions and Financial Aid. 805-646-8236 Ext. 109. Fax: 805-646-6509. E-mail: enroll@oakgroveschool.com. Web site: www.oakgroveschool.com.

OAK HILL ACADEMY

2635 Oak Hill Road
Mouth of Wilson, Virginia 24363

Head of School: Dr. Michael D. Groves

General Information Coeducational boarding and day college-preparatory, general academic, dual-credit courses, and Honors classes school, affiliated with Baptist Church. Grades 8–12. Founded: 1878. Setting: rural. Nearest major city is Charlotte, NC. Students are housed in single-sex dormitories. 300-acre campus. 22 buildings on campus. Approved or accredited by Southern Association of Colleges and Schools, Southern Association of Independent Schools, The Association of Boarding Schools, Virginia Association of Independent Schools, and Virginia Department of Education. Member of Secondary School Admission Test Board. Endowment: $1.5 million. Total enrollment: 142. Upper school average class size: 10. Upper school faculty-student ratio: 1:10. There are 180 required school days per year for Upper School students. Upper School students typically attend 6 days per week. The average school day consists of 7 hours.

Upper School Student Profile Grade 8: 5 students (1 boy, 4 girls); Grade 9: 15 students (12 boys, 3 girls); Grade 10: 28 students (20 boys, 8 girls); Grade 11: 38 students (21 boys, 17 girls); Grade 12: 56 students (37 boys, 19 girls). 98% of students are boarding students. 16% are state residents. 25 states are represented in upper school student body. 20% are international students. International students from Bahamas, Canada, China, Japan, Republic of Korea, and Taiwan; 6 other countries represented in student body. 22% of students are Baptist.

Faculty School total: 19. In upper school: 10 men, 9 women; 15 have advanced degrees; 13 reside on campus.

Subjects Offered Advanced math, algebra, anatomy and physiology, art, art history, Bible as literature, biology, business, business mathematics, calculus, chemistry, choir, computer programming, creative writing, desktop publishing, digital photography, earth science, English, environmental science, equine science, fine arts, geometry, health, honors algebra, honors English, honors geometry, honors U.S. history, honors world history, instrumental music, intro to computers, keyboarding, mathematics, Microsoft, modern world history, physical education, physics, psychology, reading/study skills, religion, science, social sciences, social studies, Spanish, study skills, trigonometry, U.S. government, U.S. history, world geography, world history, world religions, world studies, yearbook.

Graduation Requirements Arts and fine arts (art, music, dance, drama), computer science, English, foreign language, mathematics, physical education (includes health), religion (includes Bible studies and theology), science, social sciences, social studies (includes history).

Special Academic Programs Honors section; study at local college for college credit; remedial reading and/or remedial writing; special instructional classes for students with Attention Deficit Disorder; ESL (20 students enrolled).

College Admission Counseling 50 students graduated in 2010; 47 went to college, including George Mason University; Indiana University Bloomington; The University of Arizona; The University of Iowa; University of Illinois at Urbana–Champaign; University of Kentucky. Other: 1 entered military service, 1 entered a postgraduate year, 1 had other specific plans. Median SAT critical reading: 480, median SAT math: 470. 10% scored over 600 on SAT critical reading, 5% scored over 600 on SAT math, 5% scored over 26 on composite ACT.

Student Life Upper grades have uniform requirement, student council, honor system. Discipline rests primarily with faculty. Attendance at religious services is required.

Summer Programs Remediation, advancement programs offered; session focuses on advancement and remediation; held on campus; accepts boys and girls; open to students from other schools. 50 students usually enrolled. 2011 schedule: June 21 to July 25. Application deadline: none.

Tuition and Aid Day student tuition: $9000; 7-day tuition and room/board: $27,400. Tuition installment plan (monthly payment plans, individually arranged payment plans, 12-month interest-free payment plan for those students accepted by June 1). Tuition reduction for siblings, need-based scholarship grants available. In 2010–11, 30% of upper-school students received aid. Total amount of financial aid awarded in 2010–11: $400,000.

Admissions Traditional secondary-level entrance grade is 11. For fall 2010, 92 students applied for upper-level admission, 82 were accepted, 55 enrolled. TOEFL or SLEP required. Deadline for receipt of application materials: none. Application fee required: $50. On-campus interview recommended.

Athletics Interscholastic: baseball (boys), basketball (b,g), cheering (g), tennis (b,g), volleyball (g); intramural: aquatics (g), baseball (b), basketball (b,g), billiards (b,g), bowling (b,g), canoeing/kayaking, equestrian sports (b,g), fishing (b), golf (b,g), hiking/backpacking (b,g), horseback riding (b,g), jogging (b,g), Nautilus (b,g), outdoor recreation (b,g), running (b,g), softball (g), strength & conditioning (b,g), table tennis (b,g), tennis (b,g), walking (g), weight lifting (b,g); coed interscholastic: cross-country running, soccer, track and field; coed intramural: fitness walking, flag football, paint ball, skiing (downhill), snowboarding, soccer, swimming and diving, ultimate Frisbee, volleyball, yoga. 1 PE instructor, 1 coach, 1 athletic trainer.

Computers Computers are regularly used in business education, creative writing, desktop publishing, English, ESL, mathematics, science, yearbook classes. Computer resources include on-campus library services, Internet access, wireless campus network, Internet filtering or blocking technology. Student e-mail accounts are available to students. Students grades are available online. The school has a published electronic and media policy.

Contact Mrs. Maureen Curran, Director of Admissions. 276-579-2619. Fax: 276-579-4722. E-mail: mcurran@oak-hill.net. Web site: www.oak-hill.net.

OAK HILL SCHOOL

86397 Eldon Schafer Drive
Eugene, Oregon 97405-9647

Head of School: Elliott Grey

General Information Coeducational day college-preparatory, arts, and technology school. Grades K–12. Founded: 1994. Setting: small town. Nearest major city is Portland. 72-acre campus. 2 buildings on campus. Approved or accredited by Northwest Association of Schools and Colleges, Pacific Northwest Association of Independent Schools, and Oregon Department of Education. Total enrollment: 115. Upper school average class size: 10. Upper school faculty-student ratio: 1:8. There are 175 required school days per year for Upper School students. Upper School students typically attend 5 days per week. The average school day consists of 7 hours.

Upper School Student Profile Grade 6: 6 students (2 boys, 4 girls); Grade 9: 7 students (4 boys, 3 girls); Grade 10: 7 students (3 boys, 4 girls); Grade 11: 9 students (5 boys, 4 girls); Grade 12: 6 students (3 boys, 3 girls).

Faculty School total: 23. In upper school: 5 men, 9 women; 9 have advanced degrees.

Subjects Offered Acting, advanced math, algebra, American literature, analytic geometry, anatomy, art, arts, band, calculus-AP, ceramics, chemistry, comparative government and politics, composition, computer education, drama performance, drawing and design, economics, English composition, English literature, English literature-AP, fitness, French, geometry, health education, history, independent study, Latin, outdoor education, physical education, pre-calculus, probability and statistics, Spanish, Spanish language-AP, Spanish literature-AP, speech communications, theater arts, U.S. government and politics, U.S. history, world history, writing.

Graduation Requirements American government, American history, arts, computer skills, economics, English, English composition, foreign language, French, lab science, mathematics, physical education (includes health), science, Spanish, world history, 70 community service hours.

Special Academic Programs Advanced Placement exam preparation; honors section; academic accommodation for the gifted.

College Admission Counseling 6 students graduated in 2010; all went to college, including Dominican University; Sarah Lawrence College; University of Oregon; Whittier College; Worcester Polytechnic Institute. Median SAT critical reading: 560, median SAT math: 610. 27% scored over 600 on SAT critical reading, 27% scored over 600 on SAT math.

Student Life Upper grades have specified standards of dress, student council, honor system. Discipline rests equally with students and faculty.

Tuition and Aid Day student tuition: $13,800. Tuition installment plan (monthly payment plans). Merit scholarship grants, need-based scholarship grants available. In 2010–11, 40% of upper-school students received aid.

Admissions Traditional secondary-level entrance grade is 9. For fall 2010, 55 students applied for upper-level admission, 34 were accepted, 28 enrolled. Comprehensive educational evaluation required. Deadline for receipt of application materials: February 15. Application fee required: $100. Interview required.

Athletics Interscholastic: basketball (boys); intramural: basketball (g), volleyball (g); coed interscholastic: cross-country running, indoor track & field, running, track and field; coed intramural: golf, outdoor education, physical training, strength & conditioning. 1 PE instructor, 1 coach.

Computers Computers are regularly used in desktop publishing, graphic arts, graphic design, information technology, introduction to technology, multimedia, publications, technology, Web site design, writing classes. Computer network features include Internet access, wireless campus network, Internet filtering or blocking technology, online homework calendars for each upper school class. Campus intranet, student e-mail accounts, and computer access in designated common areas are available to students. The school has a published electronic and media policy.

Contact Lauren Moody, Admissions Director. 541-744-0954. Fax: 541-741-6968. E-mail: admission@oakhillschool.com. Web site: oakhillschool.net.

OAK KNOLL SCHOOL OF THE HOLY CHILD

44 Blackburn Road
Summit, New Jersey 07901
Head of School: Timothy J. Saburn

General Information Girls' day college-preparatory, arts, and religious studies school, affiliated with Roman Catholic Church. Grades K–12. Founded: 1924. Setting: suburban. Nearest major city is New York, NY. 11-acre campus. 4 buildings on campus. Approved or accredited by Middle States Association of Colleges and Schools and New Jersey Department of Education. Member of National Association of Independent Schools and Secondary School Admission Test Board. Endowment: $8.5 million. Total enrollment: 544. Upper school average class size: 15. Upper school faculty-student ratio: 1:8.

Upper School Student Profile Grade 7: 35 students (35 girls); Grade 8: 38 students (38 girls); Grade 9: 63 students (63 girls); Grade 10: 63 students (63 girls); Grade 11: 52 students (52 girls); Grade 12: 63 students (63 girls). 86% of students are Roman Catholic.

Faculty School total: 72. In upper school: 5 men, 47 women; 38 have advanced degrees.

Subjects Offered 20th century American writers, addiction, adolescent issues, advanced studio art-AP, African American studies, African-American literature, algebra, alternative physical education, American history, American literature, American studies, anatomy, ancient world history, art, art appreciation, Asian studies, ballet, Basic programming, Bible studies, biology, biology-AP, British literature, calculus, calculus-AP, calligraphy, campus ministry, career/college preparation, Catholic belief and practice, chemistry, chemistry-AP, Christian and Hebrew scripture, church history, college counseling, computer graphics, computer literacy, computer programming-AP, computer science, computer science-AP, concert choir, creative writing, dance, dance performance, decision making skills, desktop publishing, digital photography, driver education, engineering, English, English literature, English literature-AP, English-AP, ensembles, ethics, ethnic studies, European history, European history-AP, expository writing, fine arts, French, French-AP, genetics, geometry, health and wellness, history, Latin, leadership and service, marine science, mathematics, modern world history, music, Native American history, oceanography, peer ministry, physical education, physics, physics-AP, physiology, pre-calculus, probability and statistics, psychology, SAT preparation, science, social psychology, Spanish, Spanish-AP, studio art-AP, theology, trigonometry, U.S. history-AP, word processing, world history, world literature, writing.

Graduation Requirements Arts and fine arts (art, music, dance, drama), computer science, English, foreign language, mathematics, physical education (includes health), religion (includes Bible studies and theology), science, U.S. history, world history.

Special Academic Programs Advanced Placement exam preparation; honors section; independent study.

College Admission Counseling 63 students graduated in 2010; all went to college, including Boston College; Colgate University; Georgetown University; Princeton University; University of Notre Dame; Villanova University. Mean SAT critical reading: 615, mean SAT math: 624, mean SAT writing: 656.

Student Life Upper grades have uniform requirement, student council. Discipline rests primarily with faculty. Attendance at religious services is required.

Summer Programs Enrichment, sports programs offered; held on campus; accepts boys and girls; open to students from other schools. 2011 schedule: June 20 to August. Application deadline: April.

Tuition and Aid Day student tuition: $30,800. Tuition installment plan (Key Tuition Payment Plan). Merit scholarship grants, need-based scholarship grants available. In 2010–11, 16% of upper-school students received aid; total upper-school merit-scholarship money awarded: $98,600. Total amount of financial aid awarded in 2010–11: $1,400,000.

Admissions Traditional secondary-level entrance grade is 9. For fall 2010, 107 students applied for upper-level admission, 84 were accepted, 44 enrolled. ISEE required. Deadline for receipt of application materials: January 26. Application fee required: $50. Interview required.

Athletics Interscholastic: basketball, cross-country running, fencing, field hockey, golf, lacrosse, soccer, softball, swimming and diving, tennis, track and field,

Oak Knoll SCHOOL OF THE HOLY CHILD

A Catholic independent school, coeducational from kindergarten through grade 6 and for young women only in grades 7-12.

CONTACT ADMISSIONS AT 908-522-8109 OR ADMISSIONS@OAKKNOLL.ORG
44 BLACKBURN ROAD, SUMMIT, NJ 07901 | WWW.OAKKNOLL.ORG | FACEBOOK.COM/OAKKNOLLSHC

Oak Knoll School of the Holy Child

volleyball, winter (indoor) track; intramural: dance squad, deck hockey, fitness, yoga. 3 PE instructors, 14 coaches, 1 athletic trainer.

Computers Computers are regularly used in all academic classes. Computer network features include on-campus library services, Internet access, wireless campus network, campus-wide laptop program grades 7-12. Campus intranet, student e-mail accounts, and computer access in designated common areas are available to students. Students grades are available online. The school has a published electronic and media policy.

Contact Suzanne Kimm Lewis, Admissions Director. 908-522-8109. Fax: 908-277-1838. E-mail: okadmissions@oakknoll.org. Web site: www.oakknoll.org.

See Display on page 471 and Close-Up on page 820.

THE OAKLAND SCHOOL

362 McKee Place
Pittsburgh, Pennsylvania 15213
Head of School: Mr. Jack C. King

General Information Coeducational day college-preparatory and arts school. Grades 8–12. Founded: 1982. Setting: urban. 1 building on campus. Approved or accredited by Pennsylvania Department of Education. Candidate for accreditation by Middle States Association of Colleges and Schools. Total enrollment: 53. Upper school average class size: 6. Upper school faculty-student ratio: 1:6. There are 180 required school days per year for Upper School students. Upper School students typically attend 5 days per week. The average school day consists of 5 hours and 30 minutes.

Upper School Student Profile Grade 8: 2 students (1 boy, 1 girl); Grade 9: 11 students (5 boys, 6 girls); Grade 10: 13 students (6 boys, 7 girls); Grade 11: 16 students (8 boys, 8 girls); Grade 12: 11 students (6 boys, 5 girls).

Faculty School total: 10. In upper school: 3 men, 7 women; 5 have advanced degrees.

Subjects Offered Advanced math, algebra, American history, American literature, art, art history, biology, business skills, calculus, chemistry, computer math, computer science, creative writing, drama, earth science, ecology, economics, English, English literature, environmental science, ESL, expository writing, fine arts, French, geography, geometry, German, government/civics, history, mathematics, physical education, physics, pre-calculus, psychology, SAT/ACT preparation, science, social studies, Spanish, speech, trigonometry, world history, world literature, writing.

Graduation Requirements Arts and fine arts (art, music, dance, drama), computer literacy, English, mathematics, physical education (includes health), science, social studies (includes history), community service.

Special Academic Programs Honors section; accelerated programs; independent study; study at local college for college credit; academic accommodation for the gifted and the artistically talented; remedial reading and/or remedial writing; remedial math; ESL (2 students enrolled).

College Admission Counseling 21 students graduated in 2010; 18 went to college, including The University of Kansas; University of Pittsburgh. Other: 3 had other specific plans. Mean SAT critical reading: 560, mean SAT math: 512, mean SAT writing: 580.

Student Life Upper grades have student council. Discipline rests primarily with faculty.

Tuition and Aid Day student tuition: $9400. Tuition installment plan (monthly payment plans, individually arranged payment plans, quarterly payment plan, semiannual payment plan). Tuition reduction for siblings, merit scholarship grants, need-based scholarship grants available. In 2010–11, 25% of upper-school students received aid; total upper-school merit-scholarship money awarded: $6000. Total amount of financial aid awarded in 2010–11: $45,000.

Admissions Traditional secondary-level entrance grade is 10. For fall 2010, 34 students applied for upper-level admission, 24 were accepted, 22 enrolled. WRAT required. Deadline for receipt of application materials: none. Application fee required: $100. On-campus interview required.

Athletics Intramural: aerobics/dance (girls), dance (g); coed intramural: baseball, basketball, bicycling, billiards, bowling, cooperative games, cross-country running, fitness, fitness walking, flag football, Frisbee, golf, hiking/backpacking, ice skating, jogging, jump rope, kickball, martial arts, racquetball, running, skateboarding, skiing (cross-country), skiing (downhill), snowboarding, softball, swimming and diving, tai chi, tennis, volleyball, walking. 1 PE instructor.

Computers Computers are regularly used in all academic classes. Computer network features include Internet access, wireless campus network. Student e-mail accounts and computer access in designated common areas are available to students. Students grades are available online.

Contact Admissions Desk. 412-621-7878. Fax: 412-621-7881. E-mail: oschool@stargate.net. Web site: www.theoaklandschool.org.

OAKLAND SCHOOL

Keswick, Virginia
See Special Needs Schools section.

OAK MOUNTAIN ACADEMY

222 Cross Plains Road
Carrollton, Georgia 30116
Head of School: Mrs. Paula J. Gillispie

General Information Coeducational day college-preparatory school, affiliated with Christian faith. Grades K4–12. Founded: 1962. Setting: small town. Nearest major city is Atlanta. 88-acre campus. 2 buildings on campus. Approved or accredited by Georgia Accrediting Commission, Southern Association of Colleges and Schools, and Georgia Department of Education. Total enrollment: 191. Upper school average class size: 10. Upper school faculty-student ratio: 1:5. There are 180 required school days per year for Upper School students. Upper School students typically attend 5 days per week. The average school day consists of 7 hours and 15 minutes.

Upper School Student Profile Grade 6: 6 students (1 boy, 5 girls); Grade 7: 10 students (6 boys, 4 girls); Grade 8: 20 students (7 boys, 13 girls); Grade 9: 18 students (7 boys, 11 girls); Grade 10: 17 students (7 boys, 10 girls); Grade 11: 17 students (10 boys, 7 girls); Grade 12: 17 students (9 boys, 8 girls).

Faculty School total: 28. In upper school: 5 men, 6 women; 8 have advanced degrees.

Subjects Offered Advanced math, Advanced Placement courses, algebra, American government, American history, American literature, anatomy, ancient world history, art, athletic training, athletics, Bible, biology, biology-AP, calculus, calculus-AP, chemistry, chemistry-AP, chorus, college counseling, community service, computer graphics, computer science, discrete mathematics, drama, economics, electives, English composition, English language-AP, English literature, English literature-AP, English-AP, expository writing, geometry, government, graphic arts, guidance, independent study, Latin, modern civilization, music, physical fitness, physical science, physics, pre-calculus, public speaking, research skills, senior internship, senior project, Spanish, statistics, student government, U.S. history, U.S. history-AP, world literature, yearbook.

Graduation Requirements Algebra, ancient world history, Bible, biology, calculus, chemistry, economics, electives, English, foreign language, geometry, modern civilization, physical education (includes health), physical science, public speaking, senior internship, senior project, U.S. government, U.S. history, senior project, including research paper, oral presentation, creating a product and 50-hour internship. Community service is required.

Special Academic Programs 5 Advanced Placement exams for which test preparation is offered; honors section; independent study; study at local college for college credit.

College Admission Counseling 17 students graduated in 2010; all went to college, including Georgia College & State University; Samford University; University of Georgia; University of West Georgia; Vanderbilt University. Median SAT critical reading: 540, median SAT math: 620, median SAT writing: 580, median combined SAT: 1760, median composite ACT: 27. 41% scored over 600 on SAT critical reading, 65% scored over 600 on SAT math, 47% scored over 600 on SAT writing, 47% scored over 1800 on combined SAT, 67% scored over 26 on composite ACT.

Student Life Upper grades have specified standards of dress, student council, honor system. Discipline rests primarily with faculty.

Summer Programs Enrichment, sports, art/fine arts programs offered; session focuses on Enrichment and discovery; held on campus; accepts boys and girls; open to students from other schools. 75 students usually enrolled. 2011 schedule: June 6 to July 29. Application deadline: April 29.

Tuition and Aid Day student tuition: $10,848. Tuition installment plan (monthly payment plans, three payment plan). Tuition reduction for siblings, need-based scholarship grants available. In 2010–11, 15% of upper-school students received aid. Total amount of financial aid awarded in 2010–11: $38,000.

Admissions Traditional secondary-level entrance grade is 9. For fall 2010, 18 students applied for upper-level admission, 11 were accepted, 11 enrolled. Deadline for receipt of application materials: none. Application fee required: $75. Interview required.

Athletics Interscholastic: baseball (boys), basketball (b,g), cheering (b,g), cross-country running (b,g), running (b,g), soccer (b,g), softball (g), swimming and diving (b,g), tennis (b,g), volleyball (g), weight training (b,g); coed interscholastic: golf. 2 PE instructors, 6 coaches.

Computers Computers are regularly used in Bible studies, college planning, English, foreign language, graphic arts, independent study, lab/keyboard, Latin, programming, religion, science, senior seminar, Spanish, yearbook classes. Computer network features include on-campus library services, online commercial services, Internet access, Internet filtering or blocking technology. Student e-mail accounts and computer access in designated common areas are available to students. Students grades are available online. The school has a published electronic and media policy.

Contact Mrs. Kristen Glauner, Director of Admissions. 770-834-6651. Fax: 770-834-6785. E-mail: kristenglauner@oakmountain.us. Web site: www.oakmountain.us.

OAK RIDGE MILITARY ACADEMY

2317 Oak Ridge Road
PO Box 498
Oak Ridge, North Carolina 27310
Head of School: Mr. David Johnson

General Information Coeducational boarding and day college-preparatory, leadership, and military school. Grades 7–12. Founded: 1852. Setting: small town. Nearest major city is Greensboro. Students are housed in single-sex dormitories. 101-acre campus. 22 buildings on campus. Approved or accredited by North Carolina Association of Independent Schools, Southern Association of Colleges and Schools, Southern Association of Independent Schools, and North Carolina Department of Education. Member of National Association of Independent Schools. Total enrollment: 65. Upper school average class size: 9. Upper school faculty-student ratio: 1:11. Upper School students typically attend 5 days per week. The average school day consists of 7 hours.

Upper School Student Profile 84% of students are boarding students. 49% are state residents. 16 states are represented in upper school student body. 14% are international students. International students from Bermuda, China, Honduras, Mexico, Philippines, and Republic of Korea; 4 other countries represented in student body.

Faculty School total: 25. In upper school: 12 men, 13 women; 8 have advanced degrees; 9 reside on campus.

Subjects Offered Algebra, American history, American literature, biology, calculus, chemistry, college writing, computer math, computer science, creative writing, driver education, earth science, English, English literature, environmental science, ESL, French, geometry, German, government/civics, grammar, health, JROTC, JROTC or LEAD (Leadership Education and Development), mathematics, military science, music, physical education, physics, SAT preparation, science, social studies, Spanish, trigonometry, world history, writing.

Graduation Requirements Computer science, English, foreign language, mathematics, physical education (includes health), ROTC, SAT preparation, science, social studies (includes history), writing, complete three college applications, 20 hours of community service.

Special Academic Programs Honors section; accelerated programs; study at local college for college credit; academic accommodation for the gifted; special instructional classes for students with Attention Deficit Disorder and Attention Deficit Hyperactivity Disorder; ESL (6 students enrolled).

College Admission Counseling 28 students graduated in 2010; 27 went to college, including Appalachian State University; East Carolina University; North Carolina State University; The Citadel, The Military College of South Carolina; The University of North Carolina at Chapel Hill; The University of North Carolina at Charlotte. Other: 1 entered military service.

Student Life Upper grades have uniform requirement, student council, honor system. Discipline rests equally with students and faculty. Attendance at religious services is required.

Summer Programs Remediation, enrichment, advancement, ESL programs offered; session focuses on leadership, adventure, academics, confidence building; held both on and off campus; held at Carowinds, Wet and Wild and white water rafting in WV; accepts boys and girls; open to students from other schools. 200 students usually enrolled. 2011 schedule: June 24 to August 5. Application deadline: June 1.

Tuition and Aid Day student tuition: $12,815; 5-day tuition and room/board: $22,195; 7-day tuition and room/board: $25,095. Tuition installment plan (Key Tuition Payment Plan, SMART Tuition Payment Plan, monthly payment plans). Tuition reduction for siblings, merit scholarship grants, USS Education Loan Program available. In 2010–11, 24% of upper-school students received aid.

Admissions Traditional secondary-level entrance grade is 10. Deadline for receipt of application materials: none. Application fee required: $100. Interview recommended.

Athletics Interscholastic: baseball (boys), basketball (b,g), football (b), golf (b), soccer (b,g), swimming and diving (b,g), tennis (b), track and field (b,g), volleyball (g), wrestling (b); intramural: basketball (b,g), flag football (b), outdoor adventure (b,g), paint ball (b,g), rappelling (b,g), scuba diving (b,g), skydiving (b,g), strength & conditioning (b,g), weight lifting (b,g); coed interscholastic: cross-country running, drill team, JROTC drill, marksmanship, riflery, swimming and diving, track and field; coed intramural: outdoor adventure, paint ball, pistol, rappelling, scuba diving, skydiving, softball, strength & conditioning, weight lifting. 1 PE instructor, 10 coaches, 1 athletic trainer.

Computers Computers are regularly used in English, mathematics, science classes. Computer resources include on-campus library services, Internet access, Internet filtering or blocking technology. Students grades are available online. The school has a published electronic and media policy.

Contact Mr. Bob Lipke, Director of Admissions. 336-643-4131 Ext. 196. Fax: 336-643-1797. E-mail: blipke@ormila.com. Web site: www.oakridgemilitary.com.

THE OAKRIDGE SCHOOL

5900 West Pioneer Parkway
Arlington, Texas 76013-2899
Head of School: Mr. Jonathan Kellam

General Information Coeducational day college-preparatory, arts, and technology school. Grades PS–12. Founded: 1979. Setting: suburban. 90-acre campus. 6 buildings on campus. Approved or accredited by Independent Schools Association of the Southwest and Texas Department of Education. Member of National Association of Independent Schools. Total enrollment: 870. Upper school average class size: 16. Upper school faculty-student ratio: 1:10. There are 176 required school days per year for Upper School students. Upper School students typically attend 5 days per week. The average school day consists of 7 hours and 30 minutes.

Faculty School total: 80. In upper school: 14 men, 13 women; 23 have advanced degrees.

Subjects Offered 3-dimensional art, acting, Advanced Placement courses, advanced studio art-AP, algebra, American history, American history-AP, American literature, anatomy, ancient world history, anthropology, archaeology, art, art history-AP, athletics, biology, British literature, calculus, calculus-AP, chemistry, chemistry-AP, Chinese, choir, choral music, classical civilization, college admission preparation, college counseling, college writing, community service, comparative religion, composition-AP, computer animation, computer applications, computer art, computer graphics, computer information systems, computer literacy, computer multimedia, computer processing, computer programming-AP, computer science-AP, computer skills, concert choir, creative writing, current events, desktop publishing, digital applications, digital art, digital imaging, digital music, digital photography, discrete mathematics, drafting, drama, drama performance, drama workshop, dramatic arts, drawing, drawing and design, economics, economics and history, English, English language and composition-AP, English literature and composition-AP, environmental science-AP, European civilization, European history-AP, expository writing, film and literature, fine arts, fractal geometry, French, French language-AP, French-AP, geometry, golf, government, government and politics-AP, government-AP, government/civics, graphic arts, graphic design, graphics, health, honors algebra, honors English, honors geometry, honors world history, human biology, independent study, keyboarding, language and composition, language arts, Latin, literature and composition-AP, media literacy, modern European history-AP, modern world history, music theory, music theory-AP, musical productions, organic chemistry, physics, physics-AP, play production, poetry, portfolio art, portfolio writing, pre-algebra, pre-calculus, printmaking, probability and statistics, programming, public service, public speaking, reading/study skills, SAT preparation, SAT/ACT preparation, Spanish, Spanish-AP, strings, theater, track and field, U.S. government, U.S. government and politics, U.S. government and politics-AP, U.S. history, U.S. history-AP, United States government-AP, video, video and animation, video communication, video film production, visual and performing arts, voice, voice ensemble, Web site design, weightlifting, world history.

Graduation Requirements Arts and fine arts (art, music, dance, drama), English, foreign language, mathematics, physical education (includes health), science, social studies (includes history), participation in six seasons of athletics. Community service is required.

Special Academic Programs Advanced Placement exam preparation; honors section; independent study; study at local college for college credit; study abroad; academic accommodation for the gifted, the musically talented, and the artistically talented.

College Admission Counseling 74 students graduated in 2010; all went to college, including Texas A&M University; Texas Christian University; Texas Tech University; The University of Texas at Austin; University of Notre Dame; University of Oklahoma. Mean SAT critical reading: 602, mean SAT math: 627, mean SAT writing: 591, mean combined SAT: 1820, mean composite ACT: 27.

Student Life Upper grades have uniform requirement, student council, honor system. Discipline rests primarily with faculty.

Summer Programs Remediation, enrichment, advancement, sports, art/fine arts, rigorous outdoor training, computer instruction programs offered; session focuses on enrichment; held both on and off campus; held at museums and recreational facilities; accepts boys and girls; open to students from other schools. 200 students usually enrolled. 2011 schedule: June 6 to July 15. Application deadline: none.

Tuition and Aid Day student tuition: $16,200. Tuition installment plan (FACTS Tuition Payment Plan, early discount option). Need-based scholarship grants available.

Admissions Traditional secondary-level entrance grade is 9. For fall 2010, 196 students applied for upper-level admission, 144 were accepted, 124 enrolled. ERB Reading and Math, ISEE or Otis-Lennon School Ability Test required. Deadline for receipt of application materials: March 1. Application fee required: $65. Interview required.

Athletics Interscholastic: ball hockey (girls), baseball (b), basketball (b,g), cheering (g), cross-country running (b,g), field hockey (g), football (b), golf (b,g), physical fitness (b,g), physical training (b,g), power lifting (b), soccer (b,g), softball (g), strength & conditioning (b,g), tennis (b,g), track and field (b,g), volleyball (g), weight lifting (b), winter soccer (b,g), wrestling (b); intramural: strength & conditioning (b,g), weight training (b); coed interscholastic: aquatics; coed intramural: fitness, fitness walking, judo, outdoor activities, physical fitness, physical training, running, winter walking. 5 PE instructors, 10 coaches, 1 athletic trainer.

Computers Computers are regularly used in art, English, foreign language, history, mathematics, programming, science, stock market, technology, video film production, Web site design, writing, yearbook classes. Computer network features include on-campus library services, online commercial services, Internet access, wireless campus network, Internet filtering or blocking technology. Campus intranet, student e-mail accounts, and computer access in designated common areas are available to students. Students grades are available online. The school has a published electronic and media policy.

The Oakridge School

Contact Dr. Jerry A. Davis Jr., Director of Admissions. 817-451-4994 Ext. 2708. Fax: 817-457-6681. E-mail: jadavis@theoakridgeschool.org. Web site: www.theoakridgeschool.org.

OAKWOOD FRIENDS SCHOOL

22 Spackenkill Road
Poughkeepsie, New York 12603
Head of School: Peter F. Baily

General Information Coeducational boarding and day college-preparatory and arts school, affiliated with Society of Friends. Boarding grades 9–12, day grades 6–12. Founded: 1796. Setting: suburban. Nearest major city is New York. Students are housed in single-sex by floor dormitories and coed dormitories. 63-acre campus. 22 buildings on campus. Approved or accredited by Friends Council on Education, New York State Association of Independent Schools, The Association of Boarding Schools, and New York Department of Education. Member of National Association of Independent Schools and Secondary School Admission Test Board. Endowment: $3 million. Total enrollment: 170. Upper school average class size: 15. Upper school faculty-student ratio: 1:5. Upper School students typically attend 5 days per week. The average school day consists of 5 hours.

Upper School Student Profile Grade 9: 25 students (15 boys, 10 girls); Grade 10: 39 students (16 boys, 23 girls); Grade 11: 45 students (24 boys, 21 girls); Grade 12: 44 students (20 boys, 24 girls). 49% of students are boarding students. 74% are state residents. 7 states are represented in upper school student body. 20% are international students. International students from China, Republic of Korea, Russian Federation, Taiwan, and Viet Nam. 4% of students are members of Society of Friends.

Faculty School total: 34. In upper school: 16 men, 13 women; 22 have advanced degrees; 24 reside on campus.

Subjects Offered Acting, algebra, American history, American literature, American sign language, anthropology, art, art history, biology, calculus, ceramics, chemistry, collage and assemblage, community service, computer applications, conceptual physics, creative writing, critical thinking, directing, drama, drawing, ecology, English, English literature, ensembles, environmental science, ESL, European history, existentialism, expository writing, fashion, fine arts, French, geometry, health, history, history of jazz, interdisciplinary studies, mathematics, media arts, music, music theater, painting, photography, physical education, physics, playwriting and directing, pre-calculus, printmaking, psychology, public speaking, Quakerism and ethics, robotics, science, sculpture, social studies, Spanish, theater, world history, writing.

Graduation Requirements Advanced math, algebra, American history, arts and fine arts (art, music, dance, drama), biology, chemistry, computer literacy, conceptual physics, English, foreign language, geometry, health, interdisciplinary studies, physical education (includes health), Quakerism and ethics, world history. Community service is required.

Special Academic Programs 8 Advanced Placement exams for which test preparation is offered; independent study; special instructional classes for students with mild learning differences; ESL (28 students enrolled).

College Admission Counseling 38 students graduated in 2009; all went to college, including Lehigh University; New York University; Rutgers, The State University of New Jersey, New Brunswick; School of the Art Institute of Chicago; Vassar College. Median SAT critical reading: 550, median SAT math: 580, median SAT writing: 520, median combined SAT: 1680. 32% scored over 600 on SAT critical reading, 21% scored over 600 on SAT math, 26% scored over 600 on SAT writing, 26% scored over 1800 on combined SAT.

Student Life Upper grades have specified standards of dress, student council, honor system. Discipline rests equally with students and faculty. Attendance at religious services is required.

Tuition and Aid Day student tuition: $21,725; 5-day tuition and room/board: $32,625; 7-day tuition and room/board: $37,625. Tuition installment plan (monthly payment plans, individually arranged payment plans). Tuition reduction for siblings, need-based scholarship grants available. In 2009–10, 37% of upper-school students received aid. Total amount of financial aid awarded in 2009–10: $750,000.

Admissions Traditional secondary-level entrance grade is 9. For fall 2009, 123 students applied for upper-level admission, 82 were accepted, 59 enrolled. SLEP for foreign students, TOEFL or writing sample required. Deadline for receipt of application materials: none. Application fee required: $40. Interview required.

Athletics Interscholastic: baseball (boys), basketball (b,g), cross-country running (b,g), soccer (b,g), softball (g), tennis (b,g), volleyball (g); coed interscholastic: aquatics, independent competitive sports, swimming and diving, ultimate Frisbee; coed intramural: bowling, cooperative games, cross-country running, fitness, fitness walking, jogging, martial arts, outdoor activities, physical training, ropes courses, running, strength & conditioning, table tennis, ultimate Frisbee, walking, weight lifting, yoga. 1 coach.

Computers Computers are regularly used in computer applications, English, foreign language, history, science, writing classes. Computer network features include on-campus library services, online commercial services, Internet access, wireless campus network, Internet filtering or blocking technology. Student e-mail accounts are available to students. The school has a published electronic and media policy.

Contact Susan Masciale-Lynch, Director of Admissions. 845-462-4200 Ext. 213. Fax: 845-462-4251. E-mail: smascialelynch@oakwoodfriends.org. Web site: www.oakwoodfriends.org.

OAKWOOD SCHOOL

11600 Magnolia Boulevard
North Hollywood, California 91601-3015
Head of School: Dr. James Alan Astman

General Information Coeducational day college-preparatory and arts school. Grades K–12. Founded: 1951. Setting: urban. Nearest major city is Los Angeles. 5-acre campus. 6 buildings on campus. Approved or accredited by California Association of Independent Schools and Western Association of Schools and Colleges. Member of National Association of Independent Schools and Secondary School Admission Test Board. Total enrollment: 763. Upper school average class size: 15. Upper school faculty-student ratio: 1:8. There are 170 required school days per year for Upper School students. Upper School students typically attend 5 days per week. The average school day consists of 6 hours and 30 minutes.

Upper School Student Profile Grade 7: 72 students (37 boys, 35 girls); Grade 8: 79 students (40 boys, 39 girls); Grade 9: 82 students (41 boys, 41 girls); Grade 10: 82 students (42 boys, 40 girls); Grade 11: 75 students (43 boys, 32 girls); Grade 12: 75 students (36 boys, 39 girls).

Faculty School total: 69. In upper school: 40 men, 29 women; 36 have advanced degrees.

Subjects Offered Algebra, American history, American literature, art, art history-AP, astronomy, ballet, Basic programming, biology, biology-AP, botany, calculus, calculus-AP, ceramics, chemistry, chemistry-AP, choir, community service, comparative religion, composition, computer literacy, computer math, computer programming, computer programming-AP, computer science, computer science-AP, computer skills, conceptual physics, constitutional law, creative writing, critical studies in film, dance, discrete mathematics, drama, earth and space science, earth science, ecology, economics, English, English language and composition-AP, English literature, English literature and composition-AP, environmental science, ethics, European civilization, expository writing, film studies, fine arts, French, French language-AP, geography, geology, geometry, government and politics-AP, government/civics, grammar, health, health and wellness, history, history of jazz, honors algebra, honors English, honors geometry, honors U.S. history, HTML design, human development, human geography—AP, human sexuality, independent study, introduction to theater, Japanese, jazz band, jazz ensemble, keyboarding, lab science, Latin, life science, Mandarin, marine biology, mathematics, medieval/Renaissance history, modern dance, music, music composition, music theory, music theory-AP, musical theater, philosophy, photography, physical education, physics, physics-AP, pre-algebra, pre-calculus, psychology, psychology-AP, science, science fiction, senior project, Shakespeare, social studies, Spanish, Spanish language-AP, statistics, statistics-AP, theater, trigonometry, U.S. government and politics-AP, world history, world literature, writing.

Graduation Requirements Winter Immersion.

Special Academic Programs 14 Advanced Placement exams for which test preparation is offered; academic accommodation for the gifted.

College Admission Counseling 72 students graduated in 2009; all went to college, including Brown University; California Institute of the Arts; Reed College; University of California, Berkeley; University of Southern California; Wesleyan University. Mean SAT critical reading: 643, mean SAT math: 634, mean SAT writing: 639, mean combined SAT: 1917, mean composite ACT: 26. 80% scored over 600 on SAT critical reading, 75% scored over 600 on SAT math, 76% scored over 600 on SAT writing.

Student Life Upper grades have specified standards of dress, student council. Discipline rests primarily with faculty.

Tuition and Aid Day student tuition: $28,680. Tuition installment plan (monthly payment plans, individually arranged payment plans, 2- and 10-payment plans). Need-based scholarship grants, middle-income loans, Your Tuition Solution available. In 2009–10, 17% of upper-school students received aid. Total amount of financial aid awarded in 2009–10: $2,390,000.

Admissions Traditional secondary-level entrance grade is 7. For fall 2009, 298 students applied for upper-level admission, 139 were accepted, 57 enrolled. ISEE required. Deadline for receipt of application materials: January 8. Application fee required: $100. On-campus interview required.

Athletics Interscholastic: baseball (boys, girls), cross-country running (b,g), flag football (b), soccer (b,g), softball (g), tennis (b,g), track and field (b,g), volleyball (b,g); intramural: baseball (b,g), dance (b,g), golf (b,g); coed interscholastic: equestrian sports, horseback riding, track and field; coed intramural: aerobics, aerobics/dance, aerobics/Nautilus, combined training, Cosom hockey, fitness, floor hockey, Frisbee, jogging, lacrosse, martial arts, modern dance, Nautilus, outdoor activities, paddle tennis, physical fitness, physical training, power lifting, ropes courses, running, self defense, softball, speedball, street hockey, strength & conditioning, team handball, tennis, touch football, ultimate Frisbee, volleyball, walking, weight lifting, weight training, yoga. 4 PE instructors, 20 coaches, 1 athletic trainer.

Computers Computers are regularly used in history, humanities, mathematics, programming, science, video film production classes. Computer resources include on-campus library services, online commercial services, Internet access, Internet filtering or blocking technology. Campus intranet and student e-mail accounts are available to students. Students grades are available online. The school has a published electronic and media policy.

Contact Margie Llinas, 7-12 Admission Coordinator. 818-752-5277. Fax: 818-766-1285. E-mail: mllinas@oakwoodschool.org. Web site: www.oakwoodschool.org.

THE OAKWOOD SCHOOL
4000 MacGregor Downs Road
Greenville, North Carolina 27834
Head of School: Mr. Robert R. Peterson

General Information Coeducational day college-preparatory, arts, and technology school. Grades PK–12. Founded: 1996. Setting: small town. Nearest major city is Raleigh. 41-acre campus. 1 building on campus. Approved or accredited by Southern Association of Colleges and Schools, Southern Association of Independent Schools, and North Carolina Department of Education. Languages of instruction: English and Spanish. Total enrollment: 341. Upper school average class size: 15. Upper school faculty-student ratio: 1:8. There are 175 required school days per year for Upper School students. Upper School students typically attend 5 days per week. The average school day consists of 6 hours and 45 minutes.

Upper School Student Profile Grade 8: 19 students (9 boys, 10 girls); Grade 9: 17 students (10 boys, 7 girls); Grade 10: 18 students (12 boys, 6 girls); Grade 11: 10 students (5 boys, 5 girls); Grade 12: 7 students (4 boys, 3 girls).

Faculty School total: 39. In upper school: 1 man, 19 women; 10 have advanced degrees.

Subjects Offered Algebra, American literature, American literature-AP, band, biology, biology-AP, calculus, calculus-AP, chemistry, chorus, conceptual physics, discrete mathematics, English language and composition-AP, environmental studies, European history, European literature, forensics, geometry, graphic design, health and wellness, history of drama, journalism, Latin, physics-AP, pottery, pre-calculus, psychology-AP, research and reference, Spanish, strings, studio art, U.S. history-AP, Western civilization, Western literature, world history, world literature, yearbook.

Graduation Requirements Arts and fine arts (art, music, dance, drama), English, foreign language, history, mathematics, physical education (includes health), science, electives such as art, music, orchestra, journalism, creative writing, computer graphics.

Special Academic Programs Advanced Placement exam preparation; honors section; independent study; academic accommodation for the gifted and the musically talented.

College Admission Counseling Colleges students went to include East Carolina University; Guilford College; Oberlin College; The University of North Carolina at Chapel Hill, The University of North Carolina Wilmington. Mean SAT critical reading: 630, mean SAT math: 606, mean SAT writing: 630.

Student Life Upper grades have specified standards of dress, student council, honor system. Discipline rests primarily with faculty.

Tuition and Aid Day student tuition: $9949. Tuition installment plan (Insured Tuition Payment Plan, monthly payment plans, individually arranged payment plans). Merit scholarship grants, need-based scholarship grants available. In 2009–10, 9% of upper-school students received aid; total upper-school merit-scholarship money awarded: $20,000. Total amount of financial aid awarded in 2009–10: $91,500.

Admissions Traditional secondary-level entrance grade is 8. For fall 2009, 23 students applied for upper-level admission, 20 were accepted, 18 enrolled. OLSAT, ERB, Woodcock-Johnson Revised Achievement Test and writing sample required. Deadline for receipt of application materials: none. Application fee required: $75. On-campus interview required.

Athletics Interscholastic: baseball (boys), basketball (b,g), cheering (g), independent competitive sports (b,g), soccer (b,g), softball (g), volleyball (g); intramural: softball (g); coed interscholastic: cross-country running, golf, physical fitness, swimming and diving, tennis; coed intramural: basketball, cross-country running. 2 PE instructors, 5 coaches.

Computers Computers are regularly used in all classes. Computer network features include on-campus library services, online commercial services, Internet access, wireless campus network, Internet filtering or blocking technology. Student e-mail accounts and computer access in designated common areas are available to students. Students grades are available online. The school has a published electronic and media policy.

Contact Mrs. Louise Haney, Director of Admissions. 252-931-0760 Ext. 228. Fax: 252-931-0964. E-mail: lhaney@theoakwoodschool.org. Web site: www.theoakwoodschool.org.

O'DEA HIGH SCHOOL
802 Terry Avenue
Seattle, Washington 98104-2018
Head of School: Br. Dominic Murray, CFC

General Information Boys' day college-preparatory, general academic, and religious studies school, affiliated with Roman Catholic Church. Grades 9–12. Founded: 1923. Setting: urban. 1-acre campus. 1 building on campus. Approved or accredited by National Catholic Education Association, Northwest Association of Schools and Colleges, and Washington Department of Education. Endowment: $3.5 million. Total enrollment: 466. Upper school average class size: 25. Upper school faculty-student ratio: 1:13. There are 183 required school days per year for Upper School students. Upper School students typically attend 5 days per week. The average school day consists of 6 hours.

Upper School Student Profile Grade 9: 138 students (138 boys); Grade 10: 127 students (127 boys); Grade 11: 106 students (106 boys); Grade 12: 95 students (95 boys). 81% of students are Roman Catholic.

Faculty School total: 38. In upper school: 32 men, 6 women; 25 have advanced degrees.

Subjects Offered Advanced chemistry, Advanced Placement courses, African-American history, algebra, American history, American literature, art, art appreciation, art education, art history, arts, band, biology, calculus, chemistry, Christian doctrine, Christian ethics, Christian scripture, church history, civics, college counseling, community service, computer music, computer programming, computer-aided design, contemporary problems, digital photography, drama performance, driver education, economics, English, fine arts, geometry, health, history, humanities, independent study, Japanese, jazz band, Latin, leadership, math analysis, mathematics, mathematics-AP, photography, physical education, physics, publications, science, social sciences, Spanish, trigonometry, world literature, writing.

Graduation Requirements Arts and fine arts (art, music, dance, drama), English, foreign language, mathematics, physical education (includes health), religion (includes Bible studies and theology), science, social studies (includes history). Community service is required.

Special Academic Programs 5 Advanced Placement exams for which test preparation is offered; honors section; study at local college for college credit; academic accommodation for the gifted; remedial reading and/or remedial writing.

College Admission Counseling 108 students graduated in 2009; 104 went to college, including Gonzaga University; Seattle University; University of Portland; University of Washington; Washington State University; Western Washington University. Other: 3 went to work, 1 entered military service.

Student Life Upper grades have specified standards of dress, student council, honor system. Discipline rests primarily with faculty. Attendance at religious services is required.

Tuition and Aid Day student tuition: $8173–$9372. Tuition installment plan (monthly payment plans). Tuition reduction for siblings, need-based scholarship grants available. In 2009–10, 29% of upper-school students received aid. Total amount of financial aid awarded in 2009–10: $340,000.

Admissions Traditional secondary-level entrance grade is 9. For fall 2009, 265 students applied for upper-level admission, 220 were accepted, 140 enrolled. Metropolitan Achievement Test required. Deadline for receipt of application materials: January 14. Application fee required: $25.

Athletics Interscholastic: baseball, basketball, cross-country running, football, golf, soccer, swimming and diving, tennis, track and field, weight training, wrestling; intramural: basketball, bicycling, flag football, indoor soccer, physical training, soccer, touch football, volleyball, weight training. 1 PE instructor.

Computers Computers are regularly used in accounting, desktop publishing, ESL, English, graphic design, mathematics, photography, publications, SAT preparation, science, study skills, technical drawing, yearbook classes. Computer network features include on-campus library services, Internet access, Internet filtering or blocking technology. Students grades are available online. The school has a published electronic and media policy.

Contact Mrs. Jeanne Flohr, Director of Admission. 206-622-1308. Fax: 206-340-4110. E-mail: jflohr@odea.org. Web site: www.odea.org.

OJAI VALLEY SCHOOL
723 El Paseo Road
Ojai, California 93023
Head of School: Mr. Michael J. Hall-Mounsey

General Information Coeducational boarding and day college-preparatory, arts, and technology school; primarily serves students with learning disabilities, individuals with Attention Deficit Disorder, and dyslexic students. Boarding grades 3–12, day grades PK–12. Founded: 1911. Setting: rural. Nearest major city is Los Angeles. Students are housed in single-sex dormitories. 200-acre campus. 13 buildings on campus. Approved or accredited by California Association of Independent Schools, The Association of Boarding Schools, Western Association of Schools and Colleges, and California Department of Education. Member of National Association of Independent Schools and Secondary School Admission Test Board. Endowment: $1 million. Total enrollment: 287. Upper school average class size: 12. Upper school faculty-student ratio: 1:6.

Upper School Student Profile Grade 9: 20 students (11 boys, 9 girls); Grade 10: 29 students (18 boys, 11 girls); Grade 11: 23 students (12 boys, 11 girls); Grade 12: 31 students (14 boys, 17 girls). 76% of students are boarding students. 52% are state residents. 6 states are represented in upper school student body. 43% are international students. International students from China, Japan, Mexico, Republic of Korea, Taiwan, and Thailand; 2 other countries represented in student body.

Faculty School total: 54. In upper school: 11 men, 12 women; 10 have advanced degrees; 10 reside on campus.

Subjects Offered 20th century history, algebra, American history, American literature, art, art history, biology, biology-AP, calculus-AP, chemistry, chemistry-AP, community service, computer science, conceptual physics, creative writing, drama, ecology, economics, English, English literature, English-AP, environmental science, equestrian sports, ESL, fine arts, geography, geometry, government/civics, grammar, history, honors English, humanities, independent study, mathematics, music, music theory-AP, photography, physical education, physics, psychology, science, social studies, Spanish, Spanish-AP, speech, statistics, studio art, studio art-AP, theater, trigonometry, wilderness education, world history, writing.

Graduation Requirements Arts and fine arts (art, music, dance, drama), economics, English, foreign language, government, mathematics, science, social studies (includes history).

Special Academic Programs 11 Advanced Placement exams for which test preparation is offered; honors section; accelerated programs; independent study; study abroad; academic accommodation for the gifted and the artistically talented; remedial reading and/or remedial writing; remedial math; ESL (12 students enrolled).

College Admission Counseling 40 students graduated in 2010; all went to college, including Boston University; New York University; The Johns Hopkins University; University of California, Riverside; University of California, Santa Barbara. Median SAT critical reading: 491, median SAT math: 580, median SAT writing: 518, median combined SAT: 1589. 25% scored over 600 on SAT math.

Student Life Upper grades have specified standards of dress, student council, honor system. Discipline rests equally with students and faculty.

Summer Programs Remediation, enrichment, advancement, ESL, art/fine arts, computer instruction programs offered; session focuses on academic and course credit; held on campus; accepts boys and girls; open to students from other schools. 300 students usually enrolled. 2011 schedule: June 20 to July 31. Application deadline: none.

Tuition and Aid Day student tuition: $19,720; 7-day tuition and room/board: $44,150. Tuition installment plan (individually arranged payment plans). Need-based scholarship grants, need-based loans available. In 2010–11, 15% of upper-school students received aid. Total amount of financial aid awarded in 2010–11: $256,750.

Admissions Traditional secondary-level entrance grade is 9. For fall 2010, 116 students applied for upper-level admission, 63 were accepted, 32 enrolled. Any standardized test, SSAT or TOEFL required. Deadline for receipt of application materials: none. Application fee required: $50. Interview required.

Athletics Interscholastic: baseball (boys), basketball (b,g), cross-country running (b,g), dressage (b,g), football (b), lacrosse (b,g), soccer (b,g), volleyball (b,g); coed interscholastic: equestrian sports, golf, track and field; coed intramural: backpacking, basketball, bicycling, climbing, cross-country running, equestrian sports, fencing, fitness, fitness walking, golf, hiking/backpacking, horseback riding, kayaking, martial arts, mountain biking, outdoor education, physical fitness, rappelling, rock climbing, ropes courses, surfing, swimming and diving, weight training, yoga. 2 PE instructors, 2 coaches, 2 athletic trainers.

Computers Computers are regularly used in economics, English, ESL, geography, history, humanities, journalism, mathematics, music, photography, SAT preparation, science, social sciences, yearbook classes. Computer resources include on-campus library services, online commercial services, Internet access, wireless campus network, Internet filtering or blocking technology. The school has a published electronic and media policy.

Contact Ms. Tracy Wilson, Director of Admission. 805-646-1423. Fax: 805-646-0362. E-mail: admission@ovs.org. Web site: www.ovs.org.

OLDENBURG ACADEMY

1 Twister Circle
Oldenburg, Indiana 47036
Head of School: Sr. Therese Gillman, OSF

General Information Coeducational day college-preparatory, arts, and religious studies school, affiliated with Roman Catholic Church. Grades 9–12. Founded: 1852. Setting: small town. Nearest major city is Cincinnati, OH. 23-acre campus. 3 buildings on campus. Approved or accredited by North Central Association of Colleges and Schools and Indiana Department of Education. Total enrollment: 209. Upper school average class size: 15. Upper school faculty-student ratio: 1:12. There are 180 required school days per year for Upper School students. The average school day consists of 6 hours.

Upper School Student Profile Grade 9: 38 students (12 boys, 26 girls); Grade 10: 71 students (32 boys, 39 girls); Grade 11: 44 students (15 boys, 29 girls); Grade 12: 55 students (23 boys, 32 girls). 80% of students are Roman Catholic.

Faculty School total: 18. In upper school: 5 men, 13 women; 13 have advanced degrees.

Graduation Requirements 40 hours of community service.

Special Academic Programs Advanced Placement exam preparation; honors section.

College Admission Counseling Colleges students went to include Butler University; Indiana University Bloomington; Purdue University.

Student Life Upper grades have uniform requirement, student council, honor system. Discipline rests primarily with faculty. Attendance at religious services is required.

Tuition and Aid Day student tuition: $6700. Tuition installment plan (FACTS Tuition Payment Plan). Tuition reduction for siblings, merit scholarship grants, need-based scholarship grants available. In 2010–11, 35% of upper-school students received aid. Total amount of financial aid awarded in 2010–11: $60,000.

Admissions Traditional secondary-level entrance grade is 9. High School Placement Test (closed version) from Scholastic Testing Service required. Deadline for receipt of application materials: none. Application fee required: $350. Interview recommended.

Athletics Interscholastic: baseball (boys), basketball (b,g), cheering (g), cross-country running (b,g), dance team (g), wrestling (b). 1 PE instructor, 9 coaches.

Computers Computers are regularly used in all academic classes. Computer network features include on-campus library services, Internet access, wireless campus network,

---

Internet filtering or blocking technology. Student e-mail accounts and computer access in designated common areas are available to students. Students grades are available online. The school has a published electronic and media policy.

Contact Mrs. Bettina Rose, Principal. 812-934-4440 Ext. 223. Fax: 812-934-4838. E-mail: brose@oldenburgacademy.org.

OLDFIELDS SCHOOL

1500 Glencoe Road
Glencoe, Maryland 21152
Head of School: Mr. Taylor Smith

General Information Girls' boarding and day college-preparatory, arts, and technology school. Grades 8–PG. Founded: 1867. Setting: rural. Nearest major city is Baltimore. Students are housed in single-sex dormitories. 230-acre campus. 14 buildings on campus. Approved or accredited by Association of Independent Maryland Schools, Middle States Association of Colleges and Schools, The Association of Boarding Schools, and Maryland Department of Education. Member of National Association of Independent Schools and Secondary School Admission Test Board. Endowment: $6.5 million. Total enrollment: 164. Upper school average class size: 10. Upper school faculty-student ratio: 1:6. The average school day consists of 8 hours.

Upper School Student Profile Grade 8: 12 students (12 girls); Grade 9: 28 students (28 girls); Grade 10: 47 students (47 girls); Grade 11: 30 students (30 girls); Grade 12: 47 students (47 girls). 70% of students are boarding students. 20% are state residents. 17 states are represented in upper school student body. 10% are international students. International students from Brazil, China, El Salvador, Germany, Mexico, and United Kingdom; 5 other countries represented in student body.

Faculty School total: 32. In upper school: 4 men, 28 women; 21 have advanced degrees; 24 reside on campus.

Subjects Offered 20th century history, 3-dimensional design, acting, advanced chemistry, algebra, American history, anatomy and physiology, art history, astronomy, biology, calculus, ceramics, chemistry, choreography, college counseling, computer science, dance, directing, drawing, English, equine science, ethics, French, geometry, government, graphic design, health, honors algebra, honors English, honors geometry, honors U.S. history, honors world history, HTML design, international relations, painting, photography, physics, pre-algebra, pre-calculus, psychology, publications, science, sociology, Spanish, technical theater, theater, trigonometry, voice, world history.

Graduation Requirements Arts and fine arts (art, music, dance, drama), computer literacy, English, foreign language, mathematics, physical education (includes health), science, social studies (includes history), participation in May Program, senior presentation.

Special Academic Programs Advanced Placement exam preparation; honors section; independent study; study abroad; academic accommodation for the gifted.

College Admission Counseling 39 students graduated in 2009; 38 went to college, including Rutgers, The State University of New Jersey, Newark; Syracuse University; The Johns Hopkins University; University of Maryland, College Park; University of Michigan; University of Virginia. Other: 1 had other specific plans.

Student Life Upper grades have specified standards of dress, student council, honor system. Discipline rests equally with students and faculty.

Tuition and Aid Day student tuition: $25,075; 5-day tuition and room/board: $37,948; 7-day tuition and room/board: $42,475. Tuition installment plan (Key Tuition Payment Plan, additional bank loans). Merit scholarship grants, need-based scholarship grants, middle-income loans available. In 2009–10, 27% of upper-school students received aid. Total amount of financial aid awarded in 2009–10: $1,200,000.

Admissions Traditional secondary-level entrance grade is 9. For fall 2009, 270 students applied for upper-level admission, 127 were accepted, 46 enrolled. ISEE, PSAT and SAT for applicants to grade 11 and 12, SSAT, TOEFL, Wechsler Intelligence Scale for Children or WISC/Woodcock-Johnson required. Deadline for receipt of application materials: February 1. Application fee required: $50. Interview recommended.

Athletics Interscholastic: badminton, basketball, cross-country running, equestrian sports, field hockey, horseback riding, indoor soccer, lacrosse, soccer, softball, tennis, volleyball, winter soccer; intramural: aerobics, aerobics/dance, aerobics/Nautilus, backpacking, ballet, dance, dance squad, dance team, dressage, equestrian sports, fitness, hiking/backpacking, horseback riding, jogging, modern dance, mountaineering, outdoor activities, physical fitness, running, sailing, strength & conditioning, surfing, table tennis, ultimate Frisbee, walking, weight lifting, weight training, wilderness, wilderness survival, yoga. 3 PE instructors, 8 coaches, 1 athletic trainer.

Computers Computers are regularly used in all academic classes. Computer network features include on-campus library services, online commercial services, Internet access, wireless campus network, Internet filtering or blocking technology. Campus intranet, student e-mail accounts, and computer access in designated common areas are available to students. Students grades are available online. The school has a published electronic and media policy.

Contact Dr. Parnell Hagerman, Associate Head of School. 410-472-4800. Fax: 410-472-6839. E-mail: hagermanp@oldfieldsschool.org. Web site: www.oldfieldsschool.org.

THE OLIVERIAN SCHOOL

Haverhill, New Hampshire
See Special Needs Schools section.

OLNEY FRIENDS SCHOOL

61830 Sandy Ridge Road
Barnesville, Ohio 43713
Head of School: Richard F. Sidwell

General Information Coeducational boarding and day college-preparatory and religious studies school, affiliated with Society of Friends. Grades 9–12. Founded: 1837. Setting: rural. Nearest major city is Pittsburgh, PA. Students are housed in single-sex dormitories. 350-acre campus. 10 buildings on campus. Approved or accredited by Friends Council on Education, Independent Schools Association of the Central States, Midwest Association of Boarding Schools, Ohio Association of Independent Schools, The Association of Boarding Schools, and Ohio Department of Education. Member of National Association of Independent Schools. Endowment: $600,000. Total enrollment: 57. Upper school average class size: 8. Upper school faculty-student ratio: 1:5. There are 181 required school days per year for Upper School students. Upper School students typically attend 5 days per week. The average school day consists of 6 hours and 15 minutes.

Upper School Student Profile Grade 9: 9 students (2 boys, 7 girls); Grade 10: 12 students (6 boys, 6 girls); Grade 11: 16 students (12 boys, 4 girls); Grade 12: 20 students (10 boys, 10 girls). 97% of students are boarding students. 15% are state residents. 14 states are represented in upper school student body. 44% are international students. International students from China, Ethiopia, Germany, Republic of Korea, Rwanda, and Viet Nam; 4 other countries represented in student body. 21% of students are members of Society of Friends.

Faculty School total: 13. In upper school: 4 men, 5 women; 2 have advanced degrees; 11 reside on campus.

Subjects Offered Advanced math, agriculture, agroecology, algebra, alternative physical education, ancient history, art, astronomy, biology, calculus, calculus-AP, ceramics, chemistry, chorus, clayworking, college counseling, community service, drawing, English, English literature, English literature-AP, environmental science, ESL, fine arts, folk art, gardening, general science, geometry, global issues, government/civics, health, history, library research, library skills, mathematics, photography, physical education, physics, religion, social studies, Spanish, Western civilization, woodworking, world literature.

Graduation Requirements Algebra, arts and fine arts (art, music, dance, drama), English, foreign language, general science, geometry, humanities, lab science, mathematics, physical education (includes health), pre-calculus, religion (includes Bible studies and theology), science, social studies (includes history), research graduation essay, practical skills and religion electives. Community service is required.

Special Academic Programs Advanced Placement exam preparation; independent study; term-away projects; ESL (20 students enrolled).

College Admission Counseling 16 students graduated in 2009; 15 went to college, including Drexel University; Earlham College; Georgia Institute of Technology; Haverford College; Ohio Wesleyan University. Other: 1 went to work. Median SAT critical reading: 540, median SAT math: 560. 33% scored over 600 on SAT critical reading, 33% scored over 600 on SAT math.

Student Life Upper grades have student council, honor system. Discipline rests equally with students and faculty. Attendance at religious services is required.

Tuition and Aid Day student tuition: $13,900; 7-day tuition and room/board: $27,800. Tuition installment plan (FACTS Tuition Payment Plan, monthly payment plans, individually arranged payment plans). Merit scholarship grants, need based scholarship grants, tuition discounts for children of faculty, tuition discounts for children of alumni and Quakers available. In 2009–10, 65% of upper-school students received aid; total upper-school merit-scholarship money awarded: $4000. Total amount of financial aid awarded in 2009–10: $411,900.

Admissions Traditional secondary-level entrance grade is 9. For fall 2009, 41 students applied for upper-level admission, 35 were accepted, 22 enrolled. TOEFL or SLEP required. Deadline for receipt of application materials: none. Application fee required: $50. On campus interview required.

Athletics Interscholastic: basketball (boys); intramural: basketball (b,g), volleyball (b,g); coed interscholastic: soccer; coed intramural: aerobics/dance, artistic gym, backpacking, ball hockey, bicycling, cooperative games, cross-country running, dance, field hockey, fitness, fitness walking, Frisbee, gymnastics, hiking/backpacking, indoor soccer, jump rope, outdoor activities, outdoor education, outdoor skills, outdoors, running, skiing (cross-country), soccer, softball, tennis, ultimate Frisbee, walking, wall climbing, yoga. 5 PE instructors, 3 coaches.

Computers Computers are regularly used in art, college planning, English, ESL, history, humanities, music, photography, social studies classes. Computer network features include on-campus library services, online commercial services, Internet access, wireless campus network, PC computer classroom with a multimedia presentation system, Mac computers in designated areas. Campus intranet, student e-mail accounts, and computer access in designated common areas are available to students. Students grades are available online. The school has a published electronic and media policy.

Contact Mary Ellen A Newport, Director of Admissions. 740-425-3655 Ext. 214. Fax: 740-425-3202. E-mail: admissions@olneyfriends.org. Web site: www.olneyfriends.org.

THE O'NEAL SCHOOL

3300 Airport Road
PO Box 290
Southern Pines, North Carolina 28388-0290
Head of School: Mr. Alan Barr

General Information Coeducational day college-preparatory school. Grades PK–12. Founded: 1971. Setting: small town. Nearest major city is Raleigh. 40-acre campus. 3 buildings on campus. Approved or accredited by North Carolina Association of Independent Schools, Southern Association of Colleges and Schools, Southern Association of Independent Schools, and North Carolina Department of Education. Member of National Association of Independent Schools. Endowment: $1.1 million. Total enrollment: 410. Upper school average class size: 15. Upper school faculty-student ratio: 1:12. There are 175 required school days per year for Upper School students. Upper School students typically attend 5 days per week. The average school day consists of 7 hours.

Upper School Student Profile Grade 9: 33 students (15 boys, 18 girls); Grade 10: 40 students (15 boys, 25 girls); Grade 11: 33 students (14 boys, 19 girls); Grade 12: 43 students (24 boys, 19 girls).

Faculty School total: 55. In upper school: 9 men, 10 women; 8 have advanced degrees.

Subjects Offered Algebra, American history, American literature, art, art history, art history-AP, biology, biology-AP, calculus-AP, chemistry, community service, computer science, creative writing, drama, economics, English, English language-AP, English literature, English literature-AP, environmental science, environmental science-AP, ethics, European history, European history-AP, expository writing, film, film appreciation, fine arts, French, geometry, government-AP, jazz band, Latin, logic, mathematics, music, philosophy, photography, physical education, physics-AP, political science, pottery, pre-calculus, public speaking, science, social studies, Spanish, speech, statistics-AP, U.S. history-AP, world history, world literature, yearbook.

Graduation Requirements Arts and fine arts (art, music, dance, drama), English, foreign language, mathematics, physical education (includes health), science, social studies (includes history), 36 hours of community service.

Special Academic Programs 13 Advanced Placement exams for which test preparation is offered; independent study; study at local college for college credit.

College Admission Counseling 46 students graduated in 2010; all went to college, including Appalachian State University; High Point University; North Carolina State University; The University of North Carolina at Chapel Hill; University of San Diego; Washington University in St. Louis. Median SAT critical reading: 590, median SAT math: 630, median SAT writing: 600, median combined SAT: 1830. 40% scored over 600 on SAT critical reading, 57% scored over 600 on SAT math, 52% scored over 600 on SAT writing, 45% scored over 1800 on combined SAT, 55% scored over 26 on composite ACT.

Student Life Upper grades have specified standards of dress, student council, honor system. Discipline rests primarily with faculty.

Tuition and Aid Day student tuition: $14,900. Tuition installment plan (Insured Tuition Payment Plan, monthly payment plans, individually arranged payment plans). Merit scholarship grants, need-based scholarship grants available. In 2010–11, 29% of upper-school students received aid; total upper-school merit-scholarship money awarded: $33,525. Total amount of financial aid awarded in 2010–11: $304,685.

Admissions Traditional secondary-level entrance grade is 9. For fall 2010, 27 students applied for upper-level admission, 23 were accepted, 17 enrolled. Admissions testing, essay, OLSAT, Stanford Achievement Test, PSAT and SAT for applicants to grade 11 and 12, WRAT or writing sample required. Deadline for receipt of application materials: none. Application fee required: $75. On-campus interview required.

Athletics Interscholastic: baseball (boys), basketball (b,g), cheering (g), cross-country running (b,g), soccer (b,g), swimming and diving (b,g), tennis (b,g), track and field (b,g), volleyball (g); intramural: cheering (g); coed interscholastic: golf; coed intramural: martial arts. 2 PE instructors, 2 coaches.

Computers Computers are regularly used in all academic classes. Computer network features include on-campus library services, Internet access, wireless campus network, Internet filtering or blocking technology, EBSCO, World Book Online. Student e-mail accounts and computer access in designated common areas are available to students. The school has a published electronic and media policy.

Contact Mrs. Alice Droppers, Director of Admissions and Financial Aid. 910-692-6920 Ext. 103. Fax: 910-692-6930. E-mail: adroppers@onealschool.org. Web site: www.onealschool.org.

ONEIDA BAPTIST INSTITUTE

11 Mulberry Street
Oneida, Kentucky 40972
Head of School: Dr. W. F. Underwood

General Information Coeducational boarding and day college-preparatory, general academic, arts, vocational, religious studies, bilingual studies, and agriculture school,

affiliated with Southern Baptist Convention. Grades 6–12. Founded: 1899. Setting: rural. Nearest major city is Lexington. Students are housed in single-sex dormitories. 200-acre campus. 15 buildings on campus. Approved or accredited by The Kentucky Non-Public School Commission, The National Non-Public School Commission, and Kentucky Department of Education. Endowment: $15 million. Total enrollment: 300. Upper school average class size: 11. Upper school faculty-student ratio: 1:11. There are 174 required school days per year for Upper School students. Upper School students typically attend 5 days per week. The average school day consists of 7 hours.
Upper School Student Profile Grade 9: 45 students (20 boys, 25 girls); Grade 10: 65 students (35 boys, 30 girls); Grade 11: 55 students (30 boys, 25 girls); Grade 12: 60 students (25 boys, 35 girls). 82% of students are boarding students. 65% are state residents. 20 states are represented in upper school student body. 22% are international students. International students from China, Ethiopia, India, Nigeria, and Thailand; 8 other countries represented in student body. 25% of students are Southern Baptist Convention.
Faculty School total: 43. In upper school: 21 men, 13 women; 10 have advanced degrees; all reside on campus.
Subjects Offered Agriculture, algebra, art, auto mechanics, band, Bible, biology, biology-AP, calculus, calculus-AP, chemistry, child development, choir, commercial art, computers, cultural geography, drama, earth and space science, English, English-AP, ESL, foods, geography, geometry, government-AP, guitar, health, language arts, life skills, literature, mathematics, physical education, piano, political science, pre-algebra, pre-calculus, science, social sciences, social studies, Spanish, stagecraft, U.S. history, U.S. history-AP, weight training, world history.
Graduation Requirements Arts and fine arts (art, music, dance, drama), Bible, computer literacy, English, foreign language, health, mathematics, physical education (includes health), science, social studies (includes history), field placement.
Special Academic Programs Advanced Placement exam preparation; independent study; remedial reading and/or remedial writing; remedial math; ESL (28 students enrolled).
College Admission Counseling 50 students graduated in 2010; 40 went to college, including Asbury University; Berea College; Lindsey Wilson College; Union College; University of Kentucky; University of the Cumberlands. Other: 9 went to work, 1 entered military service.
Student Life Upper grades have specified standards of dress. Discipline rests primarily with faculty. Attendance at religious services is required.
Summer Programs Remediation, enrichment, advancement, ESL programs offered; session focuses on remediation and make-up courses; held on campus; accepts boys and girls; open to students from other schools. 125 students usually enrolled. 2011 schedule: June 5 to July 15. Application deadline: none.
Tuition and Aid 7-day tuition and room/board: $5050–$10,000. Tuition installment plan (monthly payment plans). Need-based scholarship grants available. In 2010–11, 100% of upper-school students received aid.
Admissions Traditional secondary-level entrance grade is 9. Deadline for receipt of application materials: none. Application fee required: $35. On-campus interview required.
Athletics Interscholastic: baseball (boys), basketball (b,g), cheering (g), cross-country running (b,g), softball (g), swimming and diving (b,g), tennis (b,g), track and field (b,g), volleyball (g); coed interscholastic: soccer.
Computers Computers are regularly used in commercial art classes. Computer resources include Internet access, Internet filtering or blocking technology.
Contact Admissions. 606-847-4111 Ext. 233. Fax: 606-847-4496. E-mail: admissions4obi@yahoo.com. Web site: www.oneidaschool.org.

ORANGEWOOD ADVENTIST ACADEMY

13732 Clinton Street
Garden Grove, California 92843
Head of School: Mr. Ruben A. Escalante
General Information Coeducational day college-preparatory and religious studies school, affiliated with Seventh-day Adventist Church. Grades PK–12. Founded: 1956. Setting: urban. Nearest major city is Anaheim. 11-acre campus. 6 buildings on campus. Approved or accredited by Board of Regents, General Conference of Seventh-day Adventists, Western Association of Schools and Colleges, and California Department of Education. Total enrollment: 251. Upper school average class size: 24. Upper school faculty-student ratio: 1:10. There are 180 required school days per year for Upper School students. Upper School students typically attend 5 days per week. The average school day consists of 6 hours and 55 minutes.
Upper School Student Profile Grade 9: 20 students (11 boys, 9 girls); Grade 10: 17 students (7 boys, 10 girls); Grade 11: 21 students (7 boys, 14 girls); Grade 12: 26 students (12 boys, 14 girls). 80% of students are Seventh-day Adventists.
Faculty School total: 20. In upper school: 5 men, 5 women; 4 have advanced degrees.
Subjects Offered Algebra, arts, biology, calculus, career education, chemistry, choir, computer science, computers, drama, English, family studies, fine arts, geometry, government, health, journalism, life skills, mathematics, physical education, physical science, physics, pre-calculus, religion, science, social studies, Spanish, typing, U.S. history, world history, yearbook.
Graduation Requirements Arts and fine arts (art, music, dance, drama), business skills (includes word processing), computer science, English, foreign language, mathematics, physical education (includes health), religion (includes Bible studies and theology), science, social studies (includes history), work experience.

Special Academic Programs Advanced Placement exam preparation; honors section; ESL (21 students enrolled).
College Admission Counseling 24 students graduated in 2009; 22 went to college, including California State University; Loma Linda University; Pacific Union College. Other: 1 went to work, 1 had other specific plans. 4% scored over 600 on SAT critical reading, 3% scored over 600 on SAT math, 2% scored over 26 on composite ACT.
Student Life Upper grades have uniform requirement, student council, honor system. Discipline rests primarily with faculty. Attendance at religious services is required.
Tuition and Aid Day student tuition: $10,193. Tuition installment plan (monthly payment plans). Tuition reduction for siblings, merit scholarship grants, need-based scholarship grants, paying campus jobs available. In 2009–10, 52% of upper-school students received aid; total upper-school merit-scholarship money awarded: $150,000. Total amount of financial aid awarded in 2009–10: $200,000.
Admissions Traditional secondary-level entrance grade is 9. For fall 2009, 15 students applied for upper-level admission, 14 were accepted, 14 enrolled. TOEFL required. Deadline for receipt of application materials: none. No application fee required. Interview required.
Athletics Interscholastic: basketball (boys, girls), cheering (g), flag football (b), soccer (b), softball (g), volleyball (b,g); intramural: basketball (b,g), flag football (b), volleyball (b,g); coed interscholastic: soccer; coed intramural: gymnastics. 1 PE instructor, 5 coaches.
Computers Computers are regularly used in all academic classes. Computer network features include on-campus library services, online commercial services, Internet access, wireless campus network, Internet filtering or blocking technology, One-to-One Apple Program. Student e-mail accounts are available to students. The school has a published electronic and media policy.
Contact Mrs. Martha Machado, Director of Admissions and Records. 714-534-4694 Ext. 214. Fax: 714-534-5931. E-mail: mrsmach57@aol.com. Web site: www. orangewoodacademy.com.

ORANGEWOOD CHRISTIAN SCHOOL

1300 West Maitland Boulevard
Maitland, Florida 32751
Head of School: Mrs. LuAnne Schendel
General Information Coeducational day college-preparatory, arts, and technology school, affiliated with Presbyterian Church in America, Christian faith. Grades K–12. Founded: 1980. Setting: suburban. Nearest major city is Orlando. 2 buildings on campus. Approved or accredited by Association of Christian Schools International, Christian Schools of Florida, National Council for Private School Accreditation, and Southern Association of Colleges and Schools. Total enrollment: 711. Upper school average class size: 14. Upper school faculty-student ratio: 1:11. The average school day consists of 7 hours.
Upper School Student Profile 100% of students are Presbyterian Church in America, Christian.
Faculty School total: 65. In upper school: 13 men, 12 women; 14 have advanced degrees.
Subjects Offered Advanced Placement courses, algebra, American culture, American government, American history, American history-AP, anatomy and physiology, art, art-AP, astronomy, Bible, biology, biology-AP, calculus-AP, career exploration, ceramics, chemistry, choir, commercial art, computer applications, computer graphics, creative writing, drama, economics, English, English language and composition-AP, English literature and composition-AP, environmental science, foreign language, geometry, graphic design, honors algebra, honors English, honors geometry, honors U.S. history, honors world history, Latin, life management skills, marine science, meteorology, oceanography, painting, personal fitness, photography, physics, physics-AP, pre-calculus, psychology, SAT preparation, sculpture, senior seminar, Spanish, Spanish language-AP, speech, studio art-AP, television, trigonometry, weight training, world geography, world history, world religions, yearbook.
Graduation Requirements Algebra, American government, American history, arts and fine arts (art, music, dance, drama), Bible, biology, computer applications, economics, electives, English, foreign language, life management skills, mathematics, personal fitness, physical education (includes health), science, senior seminar, world history.
Special Academic Programs Advanced Placement exam preparation; honors section; accelerated programs; independent study; study at local college for college credit.
College Admission Counseling 60 students graduated in 2010; all went to college, including Covenant College; Florida State University; Palm Beach Atlantic University; University of Central Florida; University of Florida; University of North Florida. Median SAT critical reading: 550, median SAT math: 550. 32% scored over 600 on SAT critical reading, 27% scored over 600 on SAT math.
Student Life Upper grades have specified standards of dress, student council, honor system. Discipline rests primarily with faculty. Attendance at religious services is required.
Summer Programs Remediation, enrichment, advancement, sports, art/fine arts, rigorous outdoor training, computer instruction programs offered; session focuses on enrichment, sports, fine arts; held both on and off campus; held at various team camps; accepts boys and girls; open to students from other schools. 200 students usually enrolled. 2011 schedule: June to August. Application deadline: April.

Tuition and Aid Day student tuition: $8280. Tuition installment plan (SMART Tuition Payment Plan, 4% discount if paid in full). Tuition reduction for siblings, need-based scholarship grants available. In 2010–11, 10% of upper-school students received aid. Total amount of financial aid awarded in 2010–11: $91,461.

Admissions Traditional secondary-level entrance grade is 9. For fall 2010, 28 students applied for upper-level admission, 23 were accepted, 21 enrolled. Admissions testing or Iowa Tests of Basic Skills required. Deadline for receipt of application materials: none. Application fee required: $100. Interview required.

Athletics Interscholastic: baseball (boys), basketball (b,g), cheering (g), cross-country running (b,g), flag football (b), football (b), golf (b), physical fitness (b,g), physical training (b,g), soccer (b,g), softball (g), strength & conditioning (b,g), swimming and diving (g), tennis (b,g), track and field (b,g), volleyball (g), weight training (b,g), wrestling (b); coed intramural: bowling, sailing, table tennis, ultimate Frisbee. 2 PE instructors, 8 coaches, 2 athletic trainers.

Computers Computers are regularly used in all classes. Computer network features include on-campus library services, Internet access, wireless campus network, Internet filtering or blocking technology. Campus intranet, student e-mail accounts, and computer access in designated common areas are available to students. Students grades are available online. The school has a published electronic and media policy.

Contact Mrs. Joyce McDonald, Director of Admissions. 407-339-0223. Fax: 407-339-4148. E-mail: jmcdonald@orangewoodchristian.org. Web site: www.orangewoodchristian.org.

OREGON EPISCOPAL SCHOOL
6300 Southwest Nicol Road
Portland, Oregon 97223-7566
Head of School: Mrs. Kathy Layendecker

General Information Coeducational boarding and day college-preparatory, arts, religious studies, technology, and science school, affiliated with Episcopal Church. Boarding grades 9–12, day grades PK–12. Founded: 1869. Setting: suburban. Students are housed in single-sex dormitories. 59-acre campus. 9 buildings on campus. Approved or accredited by National Association of Episcopal Schools, Northwest Association of Schools and Colleges, Pacific Northwest Association of Independent Schools, and Oregon Department of Education. Member of National Association of Independent Schools and Secondary School Admission Test Board. Endowment: $17.7 million. Total enrollment: 849. Upper school average class size: 14. Upper school faculty-student ratio: 1:7. There are 175 required school days per year for Upper School students. Upper School students typically attend 5 days per week. The average school day consists of 7 hours.

Upper School Student Profile Grade 9: 85 students (43 boys, 42 girls); Grade 10: 70 students (33 boys, 37 girls); Grade 11: 80 students (43 boys, 37 girls); Grade 12: 79 students (38 boys, 41 girls). 18% of students are boarding students. 83% are state residents. 4 states are represented in upper school student body. 16% are international students. International students from China, Hong Kong, Indonesia, Republic of Korea, Taiwan, and Thailand; 7 other countries represented in student body. 14% of students are members of Episcopal Church.

Faculty School total: 127. In upper school: 26 men, 29 women; 40 have advanced degrees; 7 reside on campus.

Subjects Offered Advanced chemistry, advanced math, Advanced Placement courses, algebra, American history, American literature, American studies, anatomy, anatomy and physiology, Arabic studies, art, Asian history, astronomy, athletic training, Basic programming, biology, Buddhism, calculus, calculus-AP, ceramics, chemistry, Chinese, chorus, Christian studies, Christianity, college counseling, college planning, college writing, community service, computer graphics, computer science, computer science-AP, constitutional law, creative writing, dance, debate, discrete mathematics, drama, drawing, driver education, East Asian history, ecology, electronics, engineering, English, English literature, environmental science, ESL, ESL, European history, fencing, film, film and literature, filmmaking, fine arts, finite math, foreign language, foreign policy, French, French language-AP, French-AP, freshman seminar, functions, gardening, geology, geometry, graphic arts, graphic design, graphics, health, health and wellness, history, history of China and Japan, history of ideas, history of rock and roll, history-AP, human anatomy, human relations, human sexuality, humanities, independent study, international affairs, international relations, Japanese, jazz band, jazz dance, jazz ensemble, journalism, literature, marine biology, marine ecology, mathematics, mathematics-AP, microbiology, model United Nations, modern Chinese history, music, music history, music technology, musical productions, musical theater, newspaper, painting, personal finance, personal fitness, philosophy, photography, photojournalism, physical education, physical fitness, physics, playwriting and directing, poetry, pre-algebra, pre-calculus, psychology, psychology-AP, religion, religion and culture, research, science, science project, science research, service learning/internship, sex education, sexuality, Shakespeare, social studies, Spanish, Spanish language-AP, Spanish literature, Spanish-AP, speech, stagecraft, statistics, statistics-AP, tennis, theater, theater design and production, theology, track and field, trigonometry, U.S. history, U.S. history-AP, urban studies, video and animation, video film production, visual arts, vocal ensemble, vocal music, weight training, weightlifting, wellness, wilderness education, wilderness experience, world history, world literature, world religions, world religions, world wide web design, yearbook, yoga, zoology.

Graduation Requirements Arts and fine arts (art, music, dance, drama), electives, English, foreign language, health education, humanities, mathematics, philosophy,

physical education (includes health), religion (includes Bible studies and theology), science, U.S. history, Winterim, College Decisions (for juniors), 120 hours of service learning.

Special Academic Programs Advanced Placement exam preparation; honors section; independent study; term-away projects; study abroad; academic accommodation for the gifted; ESL (13 students enrolled).

College Admission Counseling 69 students graduated in 2010; all went to college, including Macalester College; New York University; Stanford University; The Colorado College; University of Illinois at Chicago; University of Oregon. Median SAT critical reading: 640, median SAT math: 670, median SAT writing: 640, median combined SAT: 1950. 56% scored over 600 on SAT critical reading, 81% scored over 600 on SAT math, 60% scored over 600 on SAT writing, 71% scored over 1800 on combined SAT, 72% scored over 26 on composite ACT.

Student Life Upper grades have specified standards of dress, student council. Discipline rests equally with students and faculty. Attendance at religious services is required.

Summer Programs Remediation, enrichment, advancement, sports, art/fine arts, computer instruction programs offered; session focuses on a variety of academic, sports, and artistic enrichment programs; held on campus; accepts boys and girls; open to students from other schools. 1,000 students usually enrolled. 2011 schedule: June 20 to August 21.

Tuition and Aid Day student tuition: $23,240; 7-day tuition and room/board: $42,200. Tuition installment plan (Insured Tuition Payment Plan, monthly payment plans). Need-based scholarship grants available. In 2010–11, 17% of upper-school students received aid. Total amount of financial aid awarded in 2010–11: $110,000.

Admissions Traditional secondary-level entrance grade is 9. For fall 2010, 146 students applied for upper-level admission, 88 were accepted, 50 enrolled. SSAT or TOEFL required. Deadline for receipt of application materials: February 1. Application fee required: $75. Interview required.

Athletics Interscholastic: alpine skiing (boys, girls), basketball (b,g), cross-country running (b,g), fencing (b,g), golf (b,g), lacrosse (b,g), skiing (downhill) (b,g), soccer (b,g), tennis (b,g), track and field (b,g), volleyball (g); intramural: backpacking (b,g), dance (b,g), hiking/backpacking (b,g), outdoor activities (b,g), snowboarding (b,g), yoga (b,g); coed intramural: outdoor education, physical fitness, physical training, rock climbing, ropes courses. 2 PE instructors, 22 coaches, 1 athletic trainer.

Computers Computers are regularly used in art, English, foreign language, history, humanities, independent study, mathematics, music, philosophy, religion, science, social sciences, technology classes. Computer network features include on-campus library services, online commercial services, Internet access, wireless campus network, Internet filtering or blocking technology. Campus intranet, student e-mail accounts, and computer access in designated common areas are available to students. The school has a published electronic and media policy.

Contact Ms. Jen Bash, Admissions Associate. 503-768-3115. Fax: 503-768-3140. E-mail: admit@oes.edu. Web site: www.oes.edu.

ORINDA ACADEMY
19 Altarinda Road
Orinda, California 94563-2602
Head of School: Ron Graydon

General Information Coeducational day college-preparatory, general academic, arts, and technology school. Grades 7–12. Founded: 1982. Setting: suburban. Nearest major city is Walnut Creek. 1-acre campus. 2 buildings on campus. Approved or accredited by East Bay Independent Schools Association, The College Board, and Western Association of Schools and Colleges. Total enrollment: 69. Upper school average class size: 10. Upper school faculty-student ratio: 1:9. There are 175 required school days per year for Upper School students. Upper School students typically attend 5 days per week. The average school day consists of 6 hours and 50 minutes.

Upper School Student Profile Grade 9: 21 students (9 boys, 12 girls); Grade 10: 12 students (8 boys, 4 girls); Grade 11: 15 students (6 boys, 9 girls); Grade 12: 16 students (9 boys, 7 girls).

Faculty School total: 15. In upper school: 7 men, 8 women; 9 have advanced degrees.

Subjects Offered Algebra, American history, American literature, art, basketball, biology, British literature, calculus, chemistry, chorus, community service, computer graphics, computer literacy, computer multimedia, computer music, computer processing, computer programming, contemporary issues, creative writing, dance, drama, earth science, economics, English, English literature, English literature and composition-AP, ensembles, environmental science, ESL, European history, film history, fine arts, French, geography, geometry, government/civics, health, history, history of music, introduction to theater, journalism, keyboarding, mathematics, music, music performance, musical productions, performing arts, physical education, physics, science, social studies, Spanish, Spanish language-AP, theater, trigonometry, visual arts, women's literature, yearbook.

Graduation Requirements Algebra, biology, civics, composition, economics, English, foreign language, geometry, physical education (includes health), science, trigonometry, U.S. history, visual and performing arts. Community service is required.

Special Academic Programs 2 Advanced Placement exams for which test preparation is offered; honors section; accelerated programs; academic accommodation for the gifted; ESL (2 students enrolled).

College Admission Counseling 24 students graduated in 2010; 22 went to college, including Carnegie Mellon University; Saint Mary's College of California; Sonoma

State University; University of California, Davis; University of California, Los Angeles; Whitman College. Other: 2 had other specific plans. Mean SAT critical reading: 549, mean SAT math: 516, mean SAT writing: 553, mean combined SAT: 1618, mean composite ACT: 24. 29% scored over 600 on SAT critical reading, 19% scored over 600 on SAT math, 43% scored over 600 on SAT writing, 14% scored over 1800 on combined SAT, 67% scored over 26 on composite ACT.

Student Life Upper grades have specified standards of dress, student council, honor system. Discipline rests primarily with faculty.

Summer Programs Remediation, enrichment, advancement programs offered; session focuses on academics; held on campus; accepts boys and girls; open to students from other schools. 50 students usually enrolled. 2011 schedule: June 20 to August 5. Application deadline: none.

Tuition and Aid Day student tuition: $26,975. Tuition installment plan (FACTS Tuition Payment Plan). Tuition reduction for siblings, need-based scholarship grants available. In 2010–11, 25% of upper-school students received aid. Total amount of financial aid awarded in 2010–11: $300,000.

Admissions Traditional secondary-level entrance grade is 9. For fall 2010, 75 students applied for upper-level admission, 33 were accepted, 21 enrolled. ISEE or SSAT required. Deadline for receipt of application materials: January 13. Application fee required: $75. On-campus interview required.

Athletics Interscholastic: baseball (boys), basketball (b,g); coed interscholastic: soccer; coed intramural: soccer, softball. 1 PE instructor, 1 coach.

Computers Computers are regularly used in English, journalism, social sciences, typing, writing, yearbook classes. Computer network features include Internet access. Student e-mail accounts are available to students. The school has a published electronic and media policy.

Contact Ron Graydon, Head of School/Director of Admissions. 925-250-7659 Ext. 302. Fax: 925-254-4768. E-mail: ron@orindaacademy.org. Web site: www.orindaacademy.org.

THE ORME SCHOOL

HC 63, Box 3040
Mayer, Arizona 86333
Head of School: Mr. KC Cassell

General Information Coeducational boarding and day college-preparatory, arts, bilingual studies, ESL program, and horsemanship school. Boarding grades 8–PG, day grades 1–PG. Founded: 1929. Setting: rural. Nearest major city is Phoenix. Students are housed in single-sex dormitories. 360-acre campus. 30 buildings on campus. Approved or accredited by Arizona Association of Independent Schools, North Central Association of Colleges and Schools, The Association of Boarding Schools, and Arizona Department of Education. Member of National Association of Independent Schools and Secondary School Admission Test Board. Endowment: $1 million. Total enrollment: 124. Upper school average class size: 12. Upper school faculty-student ratio: 1:6. There are 179 required school days per year for Upper School students. Upper School students typically attend 5 days per week. The average school day consists of 7 hours.

Upper School Student Profile Grade 9: 16 students (10 boys, 6 girls); Grade 10: 28 students (16 boys, 12 girls); Grade 11: 36 students (13 boys, 23 girls); Grade 12: 34 students (21 boys, 13 girls). 80% of students are boarding students. 60% are state residents. 15 states are represented in upper school student body. 30% are international students. International students from China, Germany, Hong Kong, Republic of Korea, Taiwan, and Turkey; 5 other countries represented in student body.

Faculty School total: 25. In upper school: 10 men, 12 women; 15 have advanced degrees; 20 reside on campus.

Subjects Offered Advanced Placement courses, advanced TOEFL/grammar, algebra, American history, American history-AP, American literature, American literature-AP, ancient world history, art, art history, astronomy, band, biology, British literature (honors), calculus, calculus-AP, ceramics, chemistry, choir, college admission preparation, college counseling, community service, computer programming, computer science, creative writing, drama, drama performance, ecology, English, English language and composition-AP, English literature, English literature and composition-AP, European history, European history-AP, fine arts, French, geography, geology, geometry, government, grammar, history, history of music, honors English, honors U.S. history, humanities, Latin, mathematics, music, performing arts, photography, physics, physics-AP, psychology, science, social sciences, social studies, Spanish, statistics-AP, student government, theater, trigonometry, U.S. history, U.S. history-AP, weightlifting, world cultures, world history, world literature, writing.

Graduation Requirements Arts and fine arts (art, music, dance, drama), computer science, English, foreign language, humanities, mathematics, science, social sciences, social studies (includes history), students must participate in annual outdoor programs such as Fall outing and Caravan. Community service is required.

Special Academic Programs Advanced Placement exam preparation; honors section; independent study; remedial reading and/or remedial writing; remedial math; programs in English, mathematics, general development for dyslexic students; ESL (27 students enrolled).

College Admission Counseling 33 students graduated in 2010; 32 went to college, including Arizona State University; Boston University; Columbia University; Cornell University; Dartmouth College; Northern Arizona University. Other: 1 went to work. Mean SAT critical reading: 500, mean SAT math: 533, mean SAT writing: 495, mean

combined SAT: 1528, mean composite ACT: 21. 19% scored over 600 on SAT critical reading, 12% scored over 1800 on combined SAT, 9% scored over 26 on composite ACT.

Student Life Upper grades have specified standards of dress, student council, honor system. Discipline rests equally with students and faculty.

Summer Programs Remediation, advancement, ESL programs offered; session focuses on advancement; held on campus; accepts boys and girls; open to students from other schools. 12 students usually enrolled. 2011 schedule: June 27 to July 25. Application deadline: none.

Tuition and Aid Day student tuition: $18,900; 5-day tuition and room/board: $26,290; 7-day tuition and room/board: $37,900. Tuition installment plan (monthly payment plans, individually arranged payment plans). Tuition reduction for siblings, need-based scholarship grants, need-based loans available. In 2010–11, 31% of upper-school students received aid. Total amount of financial aid awarded in 2010–11: $1,400,000.

Admissions Traditional secondary-level entrance grade is 9. For fall 2010, 91 students applied for upper-level admission, 66 were accepted, 33 enrolled. PSAT and SAT for applicants to grade 11 and 12 or TOEFL or SLEP required. Deadline for receipt of application materials: February 15. Application fee required: $50. Interview required.

Athletics Interscholastic: baseball (boys), basketball (b,g), cheering (g), cross-country running (b,g), equestrian sports (b,g), football (b), pom squad (g), rodeo (b,g), softball (g), tennis (b,g), track and field (b,g), volleyball (g); intramural: aerobics/dance (g), climbing (b,g), fitness (b,g), physical training (b,g), rappelling (b,g), rock climbing (b,g), rodeo (b,g), strength & conditioning (b,g), tennis (b,g), wall climbing (b,g), weight lifting (b,g), weight training (b,g), wilderness (b,g), wilderness survival (b,g), wrestling (b); coed interscholastic: equestrian sports, horseback riding, rodeo; coed intramural: backpacking, climbing, fitness, fitness walking, hiking/backpacking, horseback riding, mountain biking, mountaineering, outdoor activities, outdoor adventure, outdoor recreation, outdoor skills, outdoors, physical training, power lifting, rappelling, rock climbing, rodeo, skiing (downhill), snowboarding, soccer, strength & conditioning, walking, wall climbing, weight lifting, weight training, wilderness, wilderness survival.

Computers Computers are regularly used in all academic classes. Computer network features include on-campus library services, Internet access, wireless campus network, Internet filtering or blocking technology. Campus intranet and computer access in designated common areas are available to students. Students grades are available online. The school has a published electronic and media policy.

Contact Mrs. Johanna Hendrikse, Assistant Director of Admissions. 928-632-7601 Ext. 2224. Fax: 928-632-7605. E-mail: jhendrikse@ormeschool.org. Web site: www.ormeschool.org.

OUR LADY ACADEMY

222 South Beach Boulevard
Bay St. Louis, Mississippi 38520-4320
Head of School: Mrs. Susan Goggins

General Information Girls' day college-preparatory and religious studies school, affiliated with Roman Catholic Church. Grades 7–12. Founded: 1971. Setting: small town. Nearest major city is New Orleans, LA. 3-acre campus. 4 buildings on campus. Approved or accredited by Mercy Secondary Education Association, National Catholic Education Association, and Southern Association of Colleges and Schools. Endowment: $2 million. Total enrollment: 237. Upper school average class size: 22. Upper school faculty-student ratio: 1:13. There are 180 required school days per year for Upper School students. Upper School students typically attend 5 days per week. The average school day consists of 7 hours.

Upper School Student Profile Grade 9: 57 students (57 girls); Grade 10: 26 students (26 girls); Grade 11: 38 students (38 girls); Grade 12: 26 students (26 girls). 85% of students are Roman Catholic.

Faculty School total: 25. In upper school: 2 men, 23 women; 5 have advanced degrees.

Subjects Offered Accounting, ACT preparation, advanced biology, advanced math, Advanced Placement courses, algebra, aquatics, art, band, biology, biology-AP, calculus, Catholic belief and practice, ceramics, chemistry, choral music, Christian ethics, Christian studies, computers, desktop publishing, economics, English, English composition, English language-AP, English literature, entrepreneurship, environmental science, ESL, European history, European history-AP, fine arts, French, genetics, geology, geometry, graphic design, health, human anatomy, integrated science, journalism, Latin, law and the legal system, learning strategies, marine science, mathematics, minority studies, moral reasoning, music, mythology, oral communications, personal finance, physical education, physical science, physics, physics-AP, physiology, pre-algebra, pre-calculus, probability and statistics, psychology, reading, religious studies, scripture, service learning/internship, short story, Spanish, theater, theater arts, trigonometry, U.S. government, U.S. history, visual arts, word processing, world geography, world history, world religions.

Graduation Requirements Art, computers, English, foreign language, health, mathematics, religious studies, science, social sciences.

Special Academic Programs 9 Advanced Placement exams for which test preparation is offered; honors section; independent study; ESL (9 students enrolled).

College Admission Counseling 45 students graduated in 2009; all went to college, including Louisiana State University and Agricultural and Mechanical College;

Mississippi State University; University of Mississippi; University of South Alabama; University of Southern Mississippi. Median composite ACT: 21. 29% scored over 26 on composite ACT.

Student Life Upper grades have uniform requirement, student council, honor system. Discipline rests primarily with faculty. Attendance at religious services is required.

Tuition and Aid Day student tuition: $5200. Tuition installment plan (The Tuition Plan, monthly payment plans, individually arranged payment plans). Need-based scholarship grants available. In 2009–10, 5% of upper-school students received aid. Total amount of financial aid awarded in 2009–10: $40,000.

Admissions Traditional secondary-level entrance grade is 9. Metropolitan Achievement Short Form required. Deadline for receipt of application materials: none. No application fee required. On-campus interview required.

Athletics Interscholastic: basketball, cheering, cross-country running, dance squad, drill team, sailing, soccer, softball, track and field, volleyball; coed interscholastic: swimming and diving, tennis. 1 PE instructor, 8 coaches, 1 athletic trainer.

Computers Computers are regularly used in accounting, business, college planning, creative writing, desktop publishing, English, foreign language, keyboarding, library science, newspaper, typing, Web site design, word processing, writing, yearbook classes. Computer network features include Internet access, wireless campus network, Internet filtering or blocking technology. Campus intranet and computer access in designated common areas are available to students. Students grades are available online. The school has a published electronic and media policy.

Contact Mrs. Susan Goggins, Principal. 228-467-7048 Ext. 12. Fax: 228-467-1666. E-mail: sue.goggins@ourladyacademy.com. Web site: www.ourladyacademy.com.

OUR LADY OF GOOD COUNSEL HIGH SCHOOL

17301 Old Vic Boulevard
Olney, Maryland 20832
Head of School: Arthur Raimo

General Information Coeducational day college-preparatory, arts, religious studies, technology, and International Baccalaureate school, affiliated with Roman Catholic Church. Grades 9–12. Founded: 1958. Setting: suburban. Nearest major city is Washington, DC. 52-acre campus. 1 building on campus. Approved or accredited by Middle States Association of Colleges and Schools and Maryland Department of Education. Total enrollment: 1,200. Upper school average class size: 22. Upper school faculty-student ratio: 1:14. There are 185 required school days per year for Upper School students. The average school day consists of 6 hours and 45 minutes.

Upper School Student Profile 79% of students are Roman Catholic.

Faculty School total: 86. In upper school: 48 men, 38 women; 57 have advanced degrees.

Subjects Offered 20th century world history, accounting, algebra, American history, American history-AP, American literature, American literature-AP, art, art history, athletic training, Bible studies, biology, biology-AP, business law, business skills, calculus, calculus-AP, chemistry, chemistry-AP, choral music, college admission preparation, comparative government and politics-AP, composition-AP, computer applications, computer math, computer programming, computer science, creative writing, drama, economics, economics-AP, English, English literature, English literature and composition-AP, environmental science, ethics, European history, European history-AP, fine arts, French, French language-AP, general science, geometry, government/civics, health, health education, history, HTML design, International Baccalaureate courses, keyboarding, Latin, Latin American history, mathematics, music, music performance, physical education, physics, programming, psychology, religion, science, social sciences, social studies, Spanish, Spanish language-AP, speech, trigonometry, typing, world history, world literature.

Graduation Requirements Service requirements for each grade.

Special Academic Programs International Baccalaureate program; 16 Advanced Placement exams for which test preparation is offered; honors section; academic accommodation for the gifted; remedial reading and/or remedial writing; programs in English, mathematics for dyslexic students; special instructional classes for students with learning disabilities (Ryken Program).

College Admission Counseling 287 students graduated in 2009; all went to college, including James Madison University; Towson University; University of Dayton; University of Delaware; University of Maryland, College Park.

Student Life Upper grades have uniform requirement, student council, honor system. Discipline rests primarily with faculty. Attendance at religious services is required.

Tuition and Aid Day student tuition: $15,500. Tuition installment plan (FACTS Tuition Payment Plan). Merit scholarship grants, need-based scholarship grants available. In 2009–10, 25% of upper-school students received aid. Total amount of financial aid awarded in 2009–10: $1,975,000.

Admissions Traditional secondary-level entrance grade is 9. For fall 2009, 800 students applied for upper-level admission, 450 were accepted, 322 enrolled. Deadline for receipt of application materials: December 11. Application fee required: $50.

Athletics Interscholastic: baseball (boys), basketball (b,g), cheering (g), cross-country running (b,g), dance team (g), diving (b,g), field hockey (g), football (b), indoor track & field (b,g), lacrosse (b,g), pom squad (g), rugby (b), soccer (b,g), softball (g), swimming and diving (b,g), tennis (b,g), track and field (b,g), volleyball (g); intramural: basketball (b,g), equestrian sports (g), softball (b); coed interscholastic: golf, ice hockey, indoor track & field, winter (indoor) track, wrestling; coed intramural: paint ball, physical training, rugby, strength & conditioning, weight training. 5 PE instructors, 73 coaches, 2 athletic trainers.

Computers Computer network features include on-campus library services, online commercial services, Internet access, wireless campus network. Students grades are available online. The school has a published electronic and media policy.

Contact Emmy McNamara, Assistant Director of Admissions. 240-283-3235. Fax: 240-283-3250. E-mail: admissions@olgchs.org. Web site: www.olgchs.org.

OUR LADY OF MERCY ACADEMY

1001 Main Road
Newfield, New Jersey 08344
Head of School: Sr. Grace Marie Scandale

General Information Girls' day college-preparatory, arts, religious studies, and technology school, affiliated with Roman Catholic Church. Grades 9–12. Founded: 1962. Setting: rural. Nearest major city is Vineland. 58-acre campus. 2 buildings on campus. Approved or accredited by Middle States Association of Colleges and Schools and National Catholic Education Association. Endowment: $250,000. Total enrollment: 177. Upper school average class size: 20. Upper school faculty-student ratio: 1:11.

Upper School Student Profile Grade 9: 46 students (46 girls); Grade 10: 38 students (38 girls); Grade 11: 35 students (35 girls); Grade 12: 50 students (50 girls); Postgraduate: 169 students (169 girls). 90% of students are Roman Catholic.

Faculty School total: 22. In upper school: 1 man, 21 women; 10 have advanced degrees.

Subjects Offered Algebra, American history, American literature, art, biology, botany, British literature (honors), career and personal planning, Catholic belief and practice, chemistry, choral music, chorus, Christian ethics, Christian scripture, Christian testament, Christianity, college counseling, computer technologies, CPR, current events, death and loss, driver education, economics, electronic publishing, English literature, first aid, food and nutrition, French, graphic design, honors algebra, honors geometry, horticulture, Middle Eastern history, physics, pre-calculus, probability and statistics, psychology, publications, religion, remedial/makeup course work, social justice, sociology, technology, Western civilization.

Graduation Requirements Algebra, biology, chemistry, English, geometry, physical education (includes health), religion (includes Bible studies and theology), technology, U.S. history, Western civilization.

Special Academic Programs Honors section; study at local college for college credit.

College Admission Counseling 50 students graduated in 2010; all went to college, including La Salle University; Rutgers, The State University of New Jersey, New Brunswick; Saint Joseph's University; Seton Hall University; University of Pennsylvania.

Student Life Upper grades have uniform requirement, student council, honor system. Discipline rests primarily with faculty. Attendance at religious services is required.

Tuition and Aid Day student tuition: $8100. Tuition installment plan (SMART Tuition Payment Plan, monthly payment plans, individually arranged payment plans). Tuition reduction for siblings, merit scholarship grants, need-based scholarship grants, paying campus jobs available. In 2010–11, 15% of upper-school students received aid; total upper-school merit-scholarship money awarded: $35,000. Total amount of financial aid awarded in 2010–11: $40,000.

Admissions Traditional secondary-level entrance grade is 9. For fall 2010, 62 students applied for upper-level admission, 50 were accepted, 44 enrolled. High School Placement Test (closed version) from Scholastic Testing Service required. Deadline for receipt of application materials: none. Application fee required: $200.

Athletics Interscholastic: basketball, cheering, crew, cross-country running, diving, indoor track & field, lacrosse, running, soccer, softball, strength & conditioning, swimming and diving, tennis, track and field, volleyball, winter (indoor) track; intramural: badminton, basketball, flag football, golf, gymnastics, physical fitness, soccer, softball, synchronized swimming, volleyball. 2 PE instructors, 12 coaches.

Computers Computers are regularly used in all academic, career exploration, college planning, creative writing, graphic design, graphics, library, library skills, photography, publications, research skills, technology, typing, Web site design, word processing, yearbook classes. Computer network features include on-campus library services, online commercial services, Internet access, wireless campus network, Internet filtering or blocking technology. Students grades are available online. The school has a published electronic and media policy.

Contact Sr. Grace Marie Scandale, Principal. 856-697-2008. Fax: 856-697-2887. E-mail: srgrace@olmanj.org. Web site: www.olmanj.org.

OUR LADY OF MERCY HIGH SCHOOL

1437 Blossom Road
Rochester, New York 14610
Head of School: Mr. Terence Quinn

General Information Girls' day college-preparatory, arts, business, religious studies, and technology school, affiliated with Roman Catholic Church. Grades 7–12. Founded: 1928. Setting: suburban. 1 building on campus. Approved or accredited by Mercy Secondary Education Network, Middle States Association of Colleges and Schools, National Catholic Education Association, and New York State Board of Regents. Total enrollment: 707. Upper school average class size: 22. Upper school faculty-student ratio: 1:12. There are 183 required school days per year for Upper

School students. Upper School students typically attend 5 days per week. The average school day consists of 6 hours and 35 minutes.

Upper School Student Profile Grade 9: 139 students (139 girls); Grade 10: 143 students (143 girls); Grade 11: 150 students (150 girls); Grade 12: 125 students (125 girls). 78% of students are Roman Catholic.

Faculty School total: 60. In upper school: 11 men, 49 women; 54 have advanced degrees.

Subjects Offered Accounting, algebra, American history, American history-AP, American literature, art, biology, biology-AP, business, calculus-AP, ceramics, chemistry, chemistry-AP, creative writing, drama, earth science, economics, English, English literature, English literature-AP, entrepreneurship, European history-AP, finance, French, French-AP, geometry, government/civics, health, Latin, Latin-AP, mathematics, music, orchestra, photography, physical education, physics, physics-AP, prayer/spirituality, pre-calculus, psychology, psychology-AP, science, scripture, social justice, Spanish, Spanish-AP, speech, studio art, theater, theater arts, theology, world history, world history-AP, world literature, writing.

Graduation Requirements Arts and fine arts (art, music, dance, drama), English, foreign language, mathematics, physical education (includes health), science, social studies (includes history), theology.

Special Academic Programs 12 Advanced Placement exams for which test preparation is offered; honors section; study at local college for college credit; ESL (5 students enrolled).

College Admission Counseling 111 students graduated in 2010; all went to college, including Buffalo State College, State University of New York; State University of New York College at Geneseo; University of Notre Dame; University of Rochester. Mean SAT critical reading: 564, mean SAT math: 555, mean SAT writing: 600. 39% scored over 26 on composite ACT.

Student Life Upper grades have specified standards of dress, student council, honor system. Discipline rests primarily with faculty. Attendance at religious services is required.

Summer Programs Remediation, sports, art/fine arts, computer instruction programs offered; held on campus; accepts girls; open to students from other schools.

Tuition and Aid Day student tuition: $8100. Tuition installment plan (monthly payment plans, individually arranged payment plans, 2-payment plan). Merit scholarship grants, need-based scholarship grants available. In 2010–11, 20% of upper-school students received aid; total upper-school merit-scholarship money awarded: $1,200,000. Total amount of financial aid awarded in 2010–11: $1,200,000.

Admissions Traditional secondary-level entrance grade is 9. For fall 2010, 110 students applied for upper-level admission, 98 were accepted, 73 enrolled. Educational Development Series, High School Placement Test (closed version) from Scholastic Testing Service or Scholastic Testing Service High School Placement Test required. Deadline for receipt of application materials: none. Application fee required: $200. On-campus interview recommended.

Athletics Interscholastic: basketball, bowling, cheering, crew, cross-country running, diving, golf, indoor track, lacrosse, sailing, skiing (downhill), soccer, softball, swimming and diving, tennis, track and field, volleyball. 3 PE instructors, 12 coaches, 1 athletic trainer.

Computers Computers are regularly used in accounting, all academic, business, business education, career exploration, college planning, English, keyboarding, library skills, literary magazine, mathematics, newspaper, photography, publications, research skills, science, technology, yearbook classes. Computer resources include on-campus library services, Internet access. The school has a published electronic and media policy.

Contact Mary Elizabeth McCahill, Director of Admissions. 585-288-7120 Ext. 310. Fax: 585-288-7966. E-mail: mmccahill@mercyhs.com. Web site: www.mercyhs.com.

OUR LADY OF THE SACRED HEART

1504 Woodcrest Avenue
Coraopolis, Pennsylvania 15108
Head of School: Sr. Francine Horos, CSSF

General Information Coeducational day college-preparatory, arts, and vocational school, affiliated with Roman Catholic Church. Grades 9–12. Founded: 1932. Setting: suburban. Nearest major city is Pittsburgh. 75-acre campus. 2 buildings on campus. Approved or accredited by Middle States Association of Colleges and Schools, National Catholic Education Association, and Pennsylvania Department of Education. Endowment: $1 million. Total enrollment: 360. Upper school average class size: 25. Upper school faculty-student ratio: 1:13. There are 180 required school days per year for Upper School students. Upper School students typically attend 5 days per week. The average school day consists of 7 hours and 30 minutes.

Upper School Student Profile Grade 9: 93 students (34 boys, 59 girls); Grade 10: 91 students (41 boys, 50 girls); Grade 11: 90 students (40 boys, 50 girls); Grade 12: 86 students (37 boys, 49 girls). 95% of students are Roman Catholic.

Faculty School total: 28. In upper school: 13 men, 15 women; 6 have advanced degrees.

Subjects Offered Acting, advanced chemistry, advanced computer applications, algebra, American government, American history, American literature, American literature-AP, anatomy and physiology, art appreciation, band, Basic programming, biology, British literature, calculus, campus ministry, ceramics, chemistry, chorus, church history, communications, computer applications, computer tools, consumer mathematics, digital photography, economics-AP, environmental science, French,

geography, geometry, government, health, health education, Holocaust, honors English, keyboarding, Latin, modern history, music appreciation, physics, reading, religion, scripture, sociology, Spanish, statistics, studio art, theater arts, U.S. history, world history.

Graduation Requirements Arts and fine arts (art, music, dance, drama), computers, electives, English, grammar, language, mathematics, physical education (includes health), reading, religion (includes Bible studies and theology), science, social studies (includes history).

Special Academic Programs Advanced Placement exam preparation; honors section; study at local college for college credit; remedial reading and/or remedial writing.

College Admission Counseling 75 students graduated in 2009; all went to college, including Duquesne University; Edinboro University of Pennsylvania; Penn State Erie, The Behrend College; Penn State University Park; University of Pittsburgh. Mean SAT critical reading: 521, mean SAT math: 477, mean SAT writing: 527. 16% scored over 1800 on combined SAT.

Student Life Upper grades have uniform requirement, student council. Discipline rests primarily with faculty. Attendance at religious services is required.

Tuition and Aid Day student tuition: $6995. Tuition installment plan (monthly payment plans, individually arranged payment plans, quarterly payment plan). Tuition reduction for siblings, merit scholarship grants, need-based scholarship grants, paying campus jobs available. In 2009–10, 60% of upper-school students received aid; total upper-school merit-scholarship money awarded: $3000. Total amount of financial aid awarded in 2009–10: $700,000.

Admissions Traditional secondary-level entrance grade is 9. For fall 2009, 120 students applied for upper-level admission, 100 were accepted, 93 enrolled. High School Placement Test (closed version) from Scholastic Testing Service required. Deadline for receipt of application materials: none. Application fee required: $25. On-campus interview required.

Athletics Interscholastic: baseball (boys), basketball (b,g), bowling (b,g), cheering (g), cross-country running (b,g), football (b), hockey (b), horseback riding (g), soccer (b,g), softball (g), swimming and diving (b,g), track and field (b,g), volleyball (b,g); intramural: basketball (b,g), flag football (b,g), floor hockey (b,g), soccer (b,g), street hockey (b,g), volleyball (b,g); coed interscholastic: golf; coed intramural: tennis, walking. 1 PE instructor, 10 coaches, 1 athletic trainer.

Computers Computers are regularly used in basic skills, computer applications, data processing, multimedia, programming, yearbook classes. Computer network features include on-campus library services, Internet access, wireless campus network, Internet filtering or blocking technology. Computer access in designated common areas is available to students. Students grades are available online.

Contact Mr. Michael Cerchiaro, Director of Admissions. 412-264-5140. Fax: 412-264-4143. E-mail: mcerchiaro@olsh.org. Web site: www.olsh.org.

OUT-OF-DOOR-ACADEMY

5950 Deer Drive
Sarasota, Florida 34240
Head of School: Mr. David Mahler

General Information Coeducational day college-preparatory school. Grades PK–12. Founded: 1924. Setting: suburban. Nearest major city is Tampa. 85-acre campus. 9 buildings on campus. Approved or accredited by Florida Council of Independent Schools. Member of National Association of Independent Schools. Endowment: $370,000. Total enrollment: 580. Upper school average class size: 16. Upper school faculty-student ratio: 1:8. There are 172 required school days per year for Upper School students. Upper School students typically attend 5 days per week. The average school day consists of 7 hours.

Upper School Student Profile Grade 9: 57 students (28 boys, 29 girls); Grade 10: 52 students (21 boys, 31 girls); Grade 11: 57 students (34 boys, 23 girls); Grade 12: 53 students (28 boys, 25 girls).

Faculty School total: 78. In upper school: 17 men, 17 women; 19 have advanced degrees.

Subjects Offered Advanced Placement courses, advanced studio art-AP, algebra, American history-AP, art history, biology, biology-AP, British literature, calculus, calculus-AP, chemistry, chemistry-AP, college counseling, computers, drama, drama performance, dramatic arts, English, English composition, English language and composition-AP, English literature, English literature and composition-AP, English-AP, European history-AP, expository writing, French, French language-AP, geometry, graphic design, health and wellness, history-AP, honors algebra, honors geometry, Latin, Latin-AP, literature, literature and composition-AP, music, newspaper, photography, portfolio art, Spanish, Spanish language-AP, studio art, studio art-AP, U.S. government, U.S. history, U.S. history-AP, women's studies, world cultures, world literature, world studies, yearbook, zoology.

Graduation Requirements Arts and fine arts (art, music, dance, drama), electives, English, foreign language, health, history, mathematics, performing arts, personal fitness, science. Community service is required.

Special Academic Programs 21 Advanced Placement exams for which test preparation is offered; honors section; independent study.

College Admission Counseling 55 students graduated in 2010; all went to college, including Boston College; Rollins College; Stanford University; Syracuse University; The Johns Hopkins University; University of Miami. Mean SAT critical reading: 622, mean SAT math: 618, mean SAT writing: 613, mean combined SAT: 1854. 59% scored over 600 on SAT critical reading, 59% scored over 600 on SAT math, 61% scored over 600 on SAT writing, 61% scored over 1800 on combined SAT.

Student Life Upper grades have specified standards of dress, student council, honor system. Discipline rests equally with students and faculty.

Summer Programs Enrichment, sports, art/fine arts programs offered; held on campus; accepts boys and girls; open to students from other schools. 150 students usually enrolled. 2011 schedule: June to August. Application deadline: May.

Tuition and Aid Day student tuition: $17,750. Tuition installment plan (FACTS Tuition Payment Plan). Need-based scholarship grants, faculty/staff tuition remission available. In 2010–11, 17% of upper-school students received aid. Total amount of financial aid awarded in 2010–11: $410,000.

Admissions Traditional secondary-level entrance grade is 9. For fall 2010, 53 students applied for upper-level admission, 37 were accepted, 31 enrolled. PSAT, SAT or SSAT required. Deadline for receipt of application materials: March 4. Application fee required: $100. Interview required.

Athletics Interscholastic: baseball (boys), basketball (b,g), cheering (g), cross-country running (b,g), football (b), golf (b,g), independent competitive sports (b,g), soccer (b,g), softball (g), swimming and diving (b,g), tennis (b,g), track and field (b,g), volleyball (g); intramural: fitness (b,g); coed interscholastic: sailing; coed intramural: physical fitness, physical training, strength & conditioning, weight training. 3 PE instructors, 20 coaches, 1 athletic trainer.

Computers Computers are regularly used in computer applications, English, foreign language, French, graphic design, history, Latin, mathematics, newspaper, science, senior seminar, social studies, Spanish, yearbook classes. Computer network features include on-campus library services, online commercial services, Internet access, wireless campus network, Internet filtering or blocking technology, digital video production. Student e-mail accounts are available to students. The school has a published electronic and media policy.

Contact Mr. Jamie Carver, Director of Middle and Upper School Admissions. 941-554-5954. Fax: 941-907-1251. E-mail: jcarver@oda.edu. Web site: www.oda.edu.

THE OVERLAKE SCHOOL
20301 Northeast 108th Street
Redmond, Washington 98053
Head of School: Francisco J. Grijalva, EdD

General Information Coeducational day college-preparatory, arts, and technology school. Grades 5–12. Founded: 1967. Setting: rural. Nearest major city is Seattle. 75-acre campus. 22 buildings on campus. Approved or accredited by Northwest Accreditation Commission, Pacific Northwest Association of Independent Schools, The College Board, and Washington Department of Education. Member of National Association of Independent Schools. Endowment: $15 million. Total enrollment: 531. Upper school average class size: 13. Upper school faculty-student ratio: 1:9. There are 173 required school days per year for Upper School students. Upper School students typically attend 5 days per week.

Upper School Student Profile Grade 9: 80 students (37 boys, 43 girls); Grade 10: 70 students (38 boys, 32 girls); Grade 11: 75 students (48 boys, 27 girls); Grade 12: 69 students (34 boys, 35 girls).

Faculty School total: 58. In upper school: 17 men, 22 women; 28 have advanced degrees.

Subjects Offered African studies, algebra, American history, American history-AP, American literature, art-AP, bioethics, biology-AP, botany, calculus, calculus-AP, ceramics, chamber groups, chemistry-AP, Chinese, chorus, community service, comparative religion, computer programming, computer science, concert band, constitutional law, creative writing, dance, drama, economics, economics and history, English, English literature, English-AP, environmental science, ethics, European history-AP, European literature, film, fine arts, French, French-AP, geometry, global issues, graphic design, Holocaust and other genocides, integrated science, Japanese, jazz band, journalism, lab science, Latin, Latin American literature, Latin-AP, life skills, literature, math review, mathematics, metalworking, Middle East, music, music theater, outdoor education, painting, performing arts, photography, physical education, physics, physics-AP, pre-calculus, printmaking, psychology, science, social studies, Spanish, Spanish-AP, stagecraft, statistics, studio art, study skills, theater, video film production, Vietnam history, Vietnam War, woodworking, world history, world literature, World-Wide-Web publishing, yearbook.

Graduation Requirements Arts and fine arts (art, music, dance, drama), English, foreign language, history, lab science, mathematics, outdoor education, physical education (includes health), senior project, annual Project Week, 3 co-curricular activities, 15 hours of community service per year (60 total).

Special Academic Programs 14 Advanced Placement exams for which test preparation is offered; honors section; independent study; term-away projects; study abroad; academic accommodation for the gifted, the musically talented, and the artistically talented.

College Admission Counseling 73 students graduated in 2010; 72 went to college, including Santa Clara University; Scripps College; University of Southern California; University of Washington; Western Washington University; Whitman College. Other: 1 had other specific plans. Median SAT critical reading: 660, median SAT math: 660, median SAT writing: 650. 82% scored over 600 on SAT critical reading, 77% scored over 600 on SAT math, 77% scored over 600 on SAT writing.

Student Life Upper grades have student council. Discipline rests equally with students and faculty.

Summer Programs Sports programs offered; session focuses on skill-building sports camps; held on campus; accepts boys and girls; not open to students from other schools. 75 students usually enrolled. 2011 schedule: August 1 to August 15. Application deadline: June 30.

Tuition and Aid Day student tuition: $24,677. Tuition installment plan (Insured Tuition Payment Plan, monthly payment plans). Need-based scholarship grants, 50% tuition remission for faculty and staff, Malone Scholarship available. In 2010–11, 22% of upper-school students received aid. Total amount of financial aid awarded in 2010–11: $792,912.

Admissions Traditional secondary-level entrance grade is 9. For fall 2010, 73 students applied for upper-level admission, 42 were accepted, 28 enrolled. ISEE required. Deadline for receipt of application materials: January 13. Application fee required: $60. Interview required.

Athletics Interscholastic: baseball (boys), basketball (b,g), cross-country running (b,g), golf (b,g), lacrosse (b,g), outdoor education (b,g), physical fitness (b,g), rock climbing (b,g), ropes courses (b,g), soccer (b,g), tennis (b,g), track and field (b,g), volleyball (g); intramural: baseball (b), basketball (b,g), cross-country running (b,g), lacrosse (b,g), outdoor education (b,g), physical fitness (b,g), rock climbing (b,g), ropes courses (b,g), skiing (cross-country) (b,g), skiing (downhill) (b,g), soccer (b,g), strength & conditioning (b,g), tennis (b,g), track and field (b,g), ultimate Frisbee (b,g), volleyball (b,g), weight lifting (b,g), weight training (b,g); coed interscholastic: outdoor education, rock climbing, ropes courses, squash, tennis, ultimate Frisbee; coed intramural: backpacking, basketball, bicycling, canoeing/kayaking, climbing, cross-country running, dance, golf, hiking/backpacking, kayaking, mountain biking, mountaineering, outdoor activities, outdoor education, outdoor skills, rafting, rock climbing, ropes courses, skiing (cross-country), skiing (downhill), snowshoeing, table tennis, tennis, wall climbing, wilderness. 4 PE instructors, 22 coaches, 1 athletic trainer.

Computers Computers are regularly used in all classes. Computer network features include on-campus library services, online commercial services, Internet access, wireless campus network. Campus intranet and computer access in designated common areas are available to students. The school has a published electronic and media policy.

Contact Lori Maughan, Director of Admission. 425-868-1000. Fax: 425-868-5771. E-mail: lmaughan@overlake.org. Web site: www.overlake.org.

THE OXFORD ACADEMY
1393 Boston Post Road
Westbrook, Connecticut 06498-0685
Head of School: Philip B. Cocchiola

General Information Boys' boarding college-preparatory, general academic, arts, bilingual studies, and ESL school. Grades 9–PG. Founded: 1906. Setting: small town. Nearest major city is New Haven. Students are housed in single-sex dormitories. 13-acre campus. 8 buildings on campus. Approved or accredited by Connecticut Association of Independent Schools, New England Association of Schools and Colleges, The Association of Boarding Schools, and Connecticut Department of Education. Member of National Association of Independent Schools and Secondary School Admission Test Board. Endowment: $250,000. Total enrollment: 38. Upper school average class size: 1. Upper school faculty-student ratio: 1:1.

Upper School Student Profile Grade 9: 4 students (4 boys); Grade 10: 5 students (5 boys); Grade 11: 10 students (10 boys); Grade 12: 17 students (17 boys). 100% of students are boarding students. 35% are state residents. 8 states are represented in upper school student body. 33% are international students. International students from Bahamas, Bermuda, France, Mexico, Republic of Korea, and Saudi Arabia.

Faculty School total: 22. In upper school: 15 men, 7 women; 10 have advanced degrees; 12 reside on campus.

Subjects Offered Algebra, American history, American literature, anatomy, astronomy, biology, botany, calculus, chemistry, creative writing, earth science, ecology, economics, English, English literature, environmental science, ESL, European history, expository writing, French, geography, geology, geometry, German, government/civics, grammar, history, Latin, marine biology, mathematics, oceanography, paleontology, philosophy, physical education, physics, physiology, psychology, science, social studies, sociology, Spanish, study skills, trigonometry, world history, world literature, writing, zoology.

Graduation Requirements English, foreign language, mathematics, science, social studies (includes history). Community service is required.

Special Academic Programs Advanced Placement exam preparation; honors section; accelerated programs; independent study; academic accommodation for the gifted; remedial reading and/or remedial writing; remedial math; special instructional classes for students with mild ADD and learning differences; ESL (6 students enrolled).

College Admission Counseling 17 students graduated in 2010; all went to college, including Bucknell University; Georgia Southern University; Lynn University; Rhode Island School of Design; Suffolk University; Wheaton College. 20% scored over 600 on SAT critical reading, 20% scored over 600 on SAT math, 20% scored over 600 on SAT writing.

Student Life Upper grades have specified standards of dress, student council, honor system. Discipline rests equally with students and faculty.

Summer Programs Remediation, enrichment, advancement, ESL programs offered; session focuses on acceleration of academics, study skills; held on campus; accepts boys; open to students from other schools. 25 students usually enrolled. 2011 schedule: June 19 to July 22. Application deadline: none.

Tuition and Aid 7-day tuition and room/board: $52,474. Tuition installment plan (monthly payment plans, individually arranged payment plans).

Admissions For fall 2010, 22 students applied for upper-level admission, 19 were accepted, 13 enrolled. SLEP for foreign students, Stanford Achievement Test, Otis-Lennon School Ability Test, TOEFL, WISC or WAIS or Woodcock-Johnson required. Deadline for receipt of application materials: none. Application fee required: $65. Interview recommended.

Athletics Interscholastic: basketball, soccer, tennis; intramural: basketball, flag football, Frisbee, hiking/backpacking, paint ball, power lifting, roller blading, strength & conditioning, table tennis, weight lifting, weight training. 6 coaches.

Computers Computers are regularly used in mathematics classes. Computer network features include Internet access. Student e-mail accounts are available to students. The school has a published electronic and media policy.

Contact Mrs. Patricia Davis, Director of Admissions. 860-399-6247 Ext. 100. Fax: 860-399-6805. E-mail: admissions@oxfordacademy.net. Web site: www.oxfordacademy.net.

PACE ACADEMY

966 West Paces Ferry Road NW
Atlanta, Georgia 30327
Head of School: Mr. Frederick G. Assaf

General Information Coeducational day college-preparatory, arts, and technology school. Grades K–12. Founded: 1958. Setting: suburban. 63-acre campus. 7 buildings on campus. Approved or accredited by Southern Association of Colleges and Schools and Southern Association of Independent Schools. Member of National Association of Independent Schools and Secondary School Admission Test Board. Endowment: $32.1 million. Total enrollment: 1,015. Upper school average class size: 12. Upper school faculty-student ratio: 1:7. There are 180 required school days per year for Upper School students. Upper School students typically attend 5 days per week. The average school day consists of 6 hours and 50 minutes.

Upper School Student Profile Grade 9: 102 students (49 boys, 53 girls); Grade 10: 91 students (48 boys, 43 girls); Grade 11: 86 students (40 boys, 46 girls); Grade 12: 93 students (47 boys, 46 girls).

Faculty School total: 136. In upper school: 32 men, 26 women; 39 have advanced degrees.

Subjects Offered Acting, adolescent issues, advanced math, advanced studio art-AP, algebra, American history, American history-AP, American literature, ancient world history, architectural drawing, art, art history, art history-AP, arts, band, biology, biology-AP, British literature, British literature (honors), calculus, calculus-AP, ceramics, chemistry, chemistry-AP, Chinese history, chorus, community service, comparative government and politics-AP, comparative politics, computer science-AP, computer skills, creative writing, debate, digital imaging, digital photography, directing, drawing, earth science, economics, English, English literature, English-AP, environmental science-AP, European history, fine arts, French, French language-AP, geometry, history, honors algebra, honors English, honors geometry, honors U.S. history, honors world history, Japanese history, keyboarding, Latin, Latin-AP, leadership education training, mathematics, modern European history-AP, music history, music theory-AP, painting, photography, physical education, physics, physics-AP, political science, pre-algebra, psychology, public speaking, religion, science, social sciences, Spanish, Spanish language-AP, stagecraft, statistics-AP, student publications, trigonometry, world history, world literature, yearbook.

Graduation Requirements Arts and fine arts (art, music, dance, drama), English, foreign language, mathematics, physical education (includes health), science, social sciences, social studies (includes history), 40 hours of community service, one semester of public speaking.

Special Academic Programs 17 Advanced Placement exams for which test preparation is offered; honors section; independent study; term-away projects; study abroad; academic accommodation for the gifted, the musically talented, and the artistically talented.

College Admission Counseling 98 students graduated in 2009; all went to college, including College of Charleston; Georgia Institute of Technology; Southern Methodist University; University of Georgia; University of Southern California; Vanderbilt University. Mean SAT critical reading: 663, mean SAT math: 656, mean SAT writing: 657, mean combined SAT: 1976.

Student Life Upper grades have specified standards of dress, student council, honor system. Discipline rests equally with students and faculty.

Tuition and Aid Day student tuition: $20,200. Tuition installment plan (FACTS Tuition Payment Plan). Need-based scholarship grants available. In 2009–10, 10% of upper-school students received aid. Total amount of financial aid awarded in 2009–10: $1,100,000.

Admissions Traditional secondary-level entrance grade is 9. For fall 2009, 101 students applied for upper-level admission, 62 were accepted, 30 enrolled. SSAT required. Deadline for receipt of application materials: February 16. Application fee required: $75. On-campus interview required.

Athletics Interscholastic: baseball (boys), basketball (b,g), cheering (g), cross-country running (b,g), diving (b,g), fitness (b,g), football (b), golf (b,g), gymnastics (g), lacrosse (b,g), soccer (b,g), softball (g), swimming and diving (b,g), tennis (b,g), track and field (b,g), volleyball (g), wrestling (b); intramural: squash (b,g), water polo (b); coed intramural: squash, ultimate Frisbee. 8 PE instructors, 6 coaches, 4 athletic trainers.

Computers Computers are regularly used in all classes. Computer network features include on-campus library services, online commercial services, Internet access, wireless campus network, classroom SmartBoards and ActivBoards, student laptop loaner program. Campus intranet, student e-mail accounts, and computer access in designated common areas are available to students. Students grades are available online. The school has a published electronic and media policy.

Contact Mrs. Jennifer McGurn, Associate Director of Admissions. 404-926-3710. Fax: 404-240-9124. E-mail: jmcgurn@paceacademy.org. Web site: www.paceacademy.org.

PACE/BRANTLEY HALL HIGH SCHOOL

Longwood, Florida
See Special Needs Schools section.

PACIFIC CREST COMMUNITY SCHOOL

116 Northeast 29th Street
Portland, Oregon 97232
Head of School: Becky Lukens

General Information Coeducational day college-preparatory and arts school. Grades 7–12. Founded: 1993. Setting: urban. 1 building on campus. Approved or accredited by Northwest Accreditation Commission, Northwest Association of Schools and Colleges, and Oregon Department of Education. Total enrollment: 85. Upper school average class size: 10. Upper school faculty-student ratio: 1:9. There are 180 required school days per year for Upper School students. Upper School students typically attend 5 days per week. The average school day consists of 6 hours.

Faculty School total: 10. In upper school: 4 men, 6 women; 9 have advanced degrees.

Graduation Requirements Senior seminar/dissertation.

Special Academic Programs Independent study; study at local college for college credit; academic accommodation for the gifted.

College Admission Counseling 13 students graduated in 2010; 10 went to college. Other: 3 had other specific plans.

Student Life Discipline rests equally with students and faculty.

Tuition and Aid Day student tuition: $10,600. Tuition installment plan (monthly payment plans). Tuition reduction for siblings, need-based scholarship grants available. In 2010–11, 15% of upper-school students received aid. Total amount of financial aid awarded in 2010–11: $50,000.

Admissions Traditional secondary-level entrance grade is 9. For fall 2010, 17 students applied for upper-level admission, 17 were accepted, 17 enrolled. Deadline for receipt of application materials: none. Application fee required: $100. Interview required.

Athletics Coed Intramural: artistic gym, basketball, bicycling, bowling, canoeing/kayaking, hiking/backpacking, outdoor adventure, outdoor education, outdoor skills, rock climbing, running, skiing (cross-country). 2 PE instructors.

Computers Computer network features include Internet access, wireless campus network. Student e-mail accounts are available to students.

Contact Jenny Osborne, Co-Director. 503-234-2826. Fax: 503-234-3186. E-mail: Jenny@pcrest.org. Web site: www.pcrest.org.

PACIFIC HILLS SCHOOL

8628 Holloway Drive
West Hollywood, California 90069
Head of School: Mr. Richard S. Makoff

General Information Coeducational day college-preparatory school. Grades 6–12. Founded: 1983. Setting: urban. Nearest major city is Beverly Hills. 2-acre campus. 2 buildings on campus. Approved or accredited by California Association of Independent Schools, Western Association of Schools and Colleges, and California Department of Education. Member of National Association of Independent Schools. Total enrollment: 207. Upper school average class size: 15. Upper school faculty-student ratio: 1:10. There are 175 required school days per year for Upper School students. Upper School students typically attend 5 days per week. The average school day consists of 6 hours and 35 minutes.

Upper School Student Profile Grade 9: 23 students (13 boys, 10 girls); Grade 10: 41 students (22 boys, 19 girls); Grade 11: 35 students (23 boys, 12 girls); Grade 12: 51 students (33 boys, 18 girls).

Faculty School total: 27. In upper school: 16 men, 11 women; 9 have advanced degrees.

Subjects Offered Advanced Placement courses, aerobics, algebra, American history, American literature, anatomy, art, biology, calculus-AP, cheerleading, chemistry, computers, economics, English, English literature, film, French, geometry, government, human development, music, newspaper, photography, physical education, physics, pre-calculus, Spanish, speech, theater arts, yearbook.

Graduation Requirements Arts and fine arts (art, music, dance, drama), English, foreign language, mathematics, outdoor education, physical education (includes health), science, social sciences, social studies (includes history). Community service is required.

Special Academic Programs 6 Advanced Placement exams for which test preparation is offered; honors section.

College Admission Counseling 32 students graduated in 2009; all went to college, including California State University, Northridge; Loyola Marymount University; University of California, Irvine; University of California, Los Angeles; University of California, San Diego; University of Southern California. Mean SAT critical reading: 525, mean SAT math: 510, mean SAT writing: 532. 17% scored over 600 on SAT critical reading, 15% scored over 600 on SAT math, 15% scored over 600 on SAT writing.

Student Life Upper grades have specified standards of dress, student council, honor system. Discipline rests primarily with faculty.

Tuition and Aid Day student tuition: $20,950. Tuition installment plan (Insured Tuition Payment Plan, monthly payment plans, individually arranged payment plans). Tuition reduction for siblings, need-based scholarship grants, need-based loans available. In 2009–10, 52% of upper-school students received aid.

Admissions Traditional secondary-level entrance grade is 9. For fall 2009, 118 students applied for upper-level admission, 61 were accepted, 54 enrolled. CTBS (or similar from their school), ERB or ISEE required. Deadline for receipt of application materials: none. Application fee required: $100. On-campus interview required.

Athletics Interscholastic: baseball (boys), basketball (b,g), cheering (g), flag football (b), softball (g), volleyball (b,g); coed interscholastic: cross-country running, dance team, outdoor education, soccer, track and field. 3 PE instructors, 7 coaches.

Computers Computers are regularly used in graphic design, journalism, yearbook classes. Computer network features include Internet access, wireless campus network, Internet filtering or blocking technology. Students grades are available online. The school has a published electronic and media policy.

Contact Ms. Lynne Bradshaw, Admissions Assistant. 310-276-3068 Ext. 112. Fax: 310-657-3831. E-mail: lbradshaw@phschool.org. Web site: www.phschool.org.

THE PACKER COLLEGIATE INSTITUTE

170 Joralemon Street
Brooklyn, New York 11201
Head of School: Dr. Bruce L. Dennis

General Information Coeducational day college-preparatory school. Grades PK–12. Founded: 1845. Setting: urban. Nearest major city is New York. 5 buildings on campus. Approved or accredited by New York State Association of Independent Schools and New York Department of Education. Member of National Association of Independent Schools and Secondary School Admission Test Board. Endowment: $13 million. Total enrollment: 941. Upper school average class size: 15. Upper school faculty-student ratio: 1:7.

Upper School Student Profile Grade 9: 66 students (34 boys, 32 girls); Grade 10: 87 students (45 boys, 42 girls); Grade 11: 70 students (36 boys, 34 girls); Grade 12: 83 students (38 boys, 45 girls).

Faculty School total: 149. In upper school: 27 men, 42 women; 48 have advanced degrees.

Subjects Offered African literature, algebra, American history, American literature, art, art history, biology, calculus, chemistry, community service, computer math, computer programming, computer science, creative writing, dance, drama, English, English literature, ethics, European history, expository writing, fine arts, French, geometry, government/civics, health, history, Latin, music, philosophy, photography, physical education, physics, science, sociology, Spanish, theater, trigonometry, women's studies, world history, world literature.

Graduation Requirements Arts and fine arts (art, music, dance, drama), English, foreign language, mathematics, physical education (includes health), science, social studies (includes history). Community service is required.

Special Academic Programs Advanced Placement exam preparation; honors section; independent study; term-away projects; study at local college for college credit; study abroad.

College Admission Counseling Colleges students went to include Brown University; Skidmore College; Wesleyan College; Williams College; Yale University.

Student Life Upper grades have student council. Discipline rests equally with students and faculty.

Admissions Traditional secondary-level entrance grade is 9. For fall 2009, 220 students applied for upper-level admission, 80 were accepted, 35 enrolled. ISEE or SSAT required. Deadline for receipt of application materials: December 1. Application fee required: $50. On-campus interview required.

Athletics Interscholastic: baseball (boys), basketball (b,g), cross-country running (b,g), dance (b,g). 10 PE instructors, 4 coaches, 2 athletic trainers.

Computers Computers are regularly used in mathematics, science, writing classes. Computer network features include on-campus library services, online commercial services, Internet access, laptop program (grades 6-12).

Contact Kati Crowley, Admissions Coordinator. 718-250-0385. Fax: 718-875-1363. E-mail: kcrowley@packer.edu. Web site: www.packer.edu.

PADUA FRANCISCAN HIGH SCHOOL

6740 State Road
Parma, Ohio 44134-4598
Head of School: Mr. David Stec

General Information Coeducational day college-preparatory, arts, business, religious studies, and technology school, affiliated with Roman Catholic Church. Grades 9–12. Founded: 1961. Setting: suburban. Nearest major city is Cleveland. 40-acre campus. 1 building on campus. Approved or accredited by North Central Association of Colleges and Schools, Ohio Catholic Schools Accreditation Association (OCSAA), and Ohio Department of Education. Endowment: $1.5 million. Total enrollment: 833. Upper school average class size: 25. Upper school faculty-student ratio: 1:19. The average school day consists of 6 hours and 30 minutes.

Upper School Student Profile Grade 9: 191 students (104 boys, 87 girls); Grade 10: 208 students (111 boys, 97 girls); Grade 11: 233 students (107 boys, 126 girls); Grade 12: 201 students (87 boys, 114 girls). 90% of students are Roman Catholic.

Faculty School total: 60. In upper school: 27 men, 31 women; 30 have advanced degrees.

Subjects Offered Accounting, algebra, American government, art appreciation, biology-AP, business, calculus-AP, chemistry, child development, Christian ethics, church history, computers, concert band, concert choir, consumer economics, current events, design, drawing, earth science, economics, English, English language-AP, ensembles, fitness, food and nutrition, French, French-AP, geography, geometry, German, German-AP, honors English, honors geometry, honors U.S. history, integrated science, interior design, Italian, Latin, Latin-AP, marching band, marketing, math analysis, music appreciation, music theory, orchestra, painting, photography, physics, pre-calculus, programming, psychology, social issues, social justice, sociology, Spanish, Spanish-AP, stagecraft, symphonic band, theater, trigonometry, U.S. history, U.S. history-AP, world cultures, world history.

Graduation Requirements Arts and fine arts (art, music, dance, drama), computer science, English, foreign language, lab science, mathematics, physical education (includes health), social studies (includes history), theology, four years of service projects.

Special Academic Programs Advanced Placement exam preparation; honors section; accelerated programs; study at local college for college credit; study abroad; remedial reading and/or remedial writing; remedial math; special instructional classes for students with learning disabilities.

College Admission Counseling 236 students graduated in 2010; 232 went to college, including Bowling Green State University; Kent State University; Miami University; The University of Akron; The University of Toledo; University of Dayton. Other: 4 went to work. Median SAT critical reading: 537, median SAT math: 530, median composite ACT: 23.

Student Life Upper grades have uniform requirement, student council, honor system. Discipline rests primarily with faculty. Attendance at religious services is required.

Summer Programs Enrichment, sports, art/fine arts, computer instruction programs offered; session focuses on introducing students to school, programs, coaches, and other students; held on campus; accepts boys and girls; open to students from other schools. 175 students usually enrolled. 2011 schedule: June 20 to June 24. Application deadline: May 27.

Tuition and Aid Day student tuition: $8750. Tuition installment plan (monthly payment plans, individually arranged payment plans). Tuition reduction for siblings, merit scholarship grants, need-based scholarship grants, paying campus jobs available. In 2010–11, 48% of upper-school students received aid; total upper-school merit-scholarship money awarded: $181,000. Total amount of financial aid awarded in 2010–11: $12,500,000.

Admissions Traditional secondary-level entrance grade is 9. For fall 2010, 250 students applied for upper-level admission, 245 were accepted, 210 enrolled. STS required. Deadline for receipt of application materials: January 21. Application fee required: $100.

Athletics Interscholastic: aquatics (boys, girls), baseball (b), basketball (b,g), cheering (g), combined training (b,g), cross-country running (b,g), dance team (g), diving (b,g), football (b), golf (b,g), hockey (b), ice hockey (b), lacrosse (b), physical fitness (b,g), soccer (b,g), softball (g), strength & conditioning (b,g), swimming and diving (b,g), tennis (b,g), track and field (b,g), volleyball (g), wrestling (b); intramural: basketball (b), flag football (b), football (b), freestyle skiing (b,g), golf (g), gymnastics (g), power lifting (b), touch football (b), weight lifting (b), weight training (b,g), winter soccer (b); coed intramural: alpine skiing, backpacking, canoeing/kayaking, fishing, hiking/backpacking, skiing (downhill), snowboarding, wilderness, wilderness survival, wildernessways. 3 PE instructors, 30 coaches, 5 athletic trainers.

Computers Computers are regularly used in all academic classes. Computer network features include on-campus library services, online commercial services, Internet access, wireless campus network. Computer access in designated common areas is available to students. Students grades are available online. The school has a published electronic and media policy.

Contact Mrs. Nancy Hodas, Admissions Coordinator. 440-845-2444 Ext. 112. Fax: 440-845-5710. E-mail: nhodas@paduafranciscan.com. Web site: www. paduafranciscan.com.

THE PAIDEIA SCHOOL

1509 Ponce de Leon Avenue
Atlanta, Georgia 30307
Head of School: Paul F. Bianchi
General Information Coeducational day college-preparatory, arts, and technology school. Grades PK–12. Founded: 1971. Setting: urban. 28-acre campus. 13 buildings on campus. Approved or accredited by Georgia Independent School Association, Southern Association of Colleges and Schools, Southern Association of Independent Schools, and Georgia Department of Education. Endowment: $15 million. Total enrollment: 972. Upper school average class size: 12. Upper school faculty-student ratio: 1:9. There are 179 required school days per year for Upper School students. Upper School students typically attend 5 days per week. The average school day consists of 6 hours and 45 minutes.
Upper School Student Profile Grade 9: 106 students (52 boys, 54 girls); Grade 10: 109 students (49 boys, 60 girls); Grade 11: 98 students (51 boys, 47 girls); Grade 12: 95 students (44 boys, 51 girls).
Faculty School total: 135. In upper school: 32 men, 33 women; 54 have advanced degrees.
Subjects Offered African-American history, algebra, American culture, American government, American history, American literature, anatomy, archaeology, art, art history, Asian history, Asian studies, auto mechanics, bioethics, biology, biology-AP, calculus, ceramics, chemistry, chemistry-AP, chorus, community service, comparative religion, computer programming, creative writing, drama, drawing, ecology, environmental systems, economics, English, English literature, environmental science, ethics, European history-AP, expository writing, fine arts, forensics, French, French studies, geography, geology, geometry, government/civics, health, history, humanities, jazz, journalism, literature, mathematics, medieval history, organic chemistry, photography, physical education, physics, physics-AP, physiology, poetry, pre-calculus, psychology, psychology-AP, Shakespeare, social studies, sociology, Spanish, Spanish literature, speech, statistics, statistics-AP, theater, trigonometry, U.S. history, Web site design, weight training, women's health, women's studies, world history, world literature, writing.
Graduation Requirements Arts and fine arts (art, music, dance, drama), English, foreign language, mathematics, physical education (includes health), science, social studies (includes history). Community service is required.
Special Academic Programs 8 Advanced Placement exams for which test preparation is offered; honors section; independent study.
College Admission Counseling 97 students graduated in 2010; 96 went to college, including Emory University; Harvard University; Oberlin College; University of Chicago; University of Georgia; Washington University in St. Louis. Other: 1 entered a postgraduate year.
Student Life Upper grades have student council, honor system. Discipline rests equally with students and faculty.
Summer Programs Enrichment programs offered; session focuses on Two-week Urban Institute for students in grades 10-12; held both on and off campus; held at various government buildings around Atlanta; accepts boys and girls; open to students from other schools. 10 students usually enrolled. 2011 schedule: June 13 to June 24. Application deadline: February 28.
Tuition and Aid Day student tuition: $18,900. Tuition installment plan (bank-arranged tuition loan program). Need-based tuition assistance available. In 2010–11, 18% of upper-school students received aid. Total amount of financial aid awarded in 2010–11: $1,086,153.
Admissions Traditional secondary-level entrance grade is 9. Deadline for receipt of application materials: February 1. Application fee required: $75. On-campus interview required.
Athletics Interscholastic: baseball (boys), basketball (b,g), cross-country running (b,g), diving (b,g), soccer (b,g), softball (g), swimming and diving (b,g), tennis (b,g), track and field (b,g), ultimate Frisbee (b,g), volleyball (g); coed interscholastic: ultimate Frisbee; coed intramural: aerobics, basketball, bicycling, bowling, fitness, flag football, hiking/backpacking, lacrosse, outdoor education, soccer, softball, tai chi, ultimate Frisbee, yoga. 2 PE instructors, 1 athletic trainer.
Computers Computers are regularly used in art, English, foreign language, graphic arts, history, journalism, mathematics, music, science classes. Computer network features include on-campus library services, Internet access, wireless campus network, Internet filtering or blocking technology, technology assistant program, computer borrowing program for students, technology courses. Campus intranet, student e-mail accounts, and computer access in designated common areas are available to students. The school has a published electronic and media policy.
Contact Florence Henry, Admissions Office Administrator. 404-270-2312. Fax: 404-270-2312. E-mail: henry.flo@paideiaschool.org. Web site: www.paideiaschool.org.

PALMA SCHOOL

919 Iverson Street
Salinas, California 93901
Head of School: Br. Patrick D. Dunne, CFC
General Information Boys' day college-preparatory and religious studies school, affiliated with Roman Catholic Church. Grades 7–12. Founded: 1951. Setting: suburban. Nearest major city is San Jose. 25-acre campus. 16 buildings on campus.
Approved or accredited by Western Association of Schools and Colleges, Western Catholic Education Association, and California Department of Education. Endowment: $200,000. Total enrollment: 575. Upper school average class size: 25. Upper school faculty-student ratio: 1:15. Upper School students typically attend 5 days per week.
Upper School Student Profile Grade 9: 121 students (121 boys); Grade 10: 81 students (81 boys); Grade 11: 119 students (119 boys); Grade 12: 113 students (113 boys). 69% of students are Roman Catholic.
Faculty School total: 37. In upper school: 28 men, 9 women; 21 have advanced degrees.
Subjects Offered Algebra, American history, American literature, anatomy, art, art history, band, biology, business, calculus, calculus-AP, chemistry, Chinese, Christian and Hebrew scripture, church history, civics, community service, computer applications, computer art, computer math, computer multimedia, computer programming, computer programming-AP, computer science, computer-aided design, creative writing, debate, digital art, driver education, earth science, economics, English, English language and composition-AP, English literature, English literature-AP, ethics, European history, European history-AP, expository writing, film, film studies, fine arts, French, geography, geometry, government/civics, grammar, health, health education, history, honors algebra, honors geometry, Japanese, jazz ensemble, journalism, Latin, mathematics, music, participation in sports, physical education, physical science, physics, pre-calculus, psychology, religion, Russian, Russian literature, science, social studies, Spanish, Spanish language-AP, speech, statistics-AP, student government, theology, trigonometry, typing, U.S. government and politics-AP, U.S. history-AP, video film production, world history, world literature, world religions, writing.
Graduation Requirements Advanced biology, arts and fine arts (art, music, dance, drama), English, foreign language, mathematics, physical education (includes health), religion (includes Bible studies and theology), science, social studies (includes history), religious retreat (8th, 9th, 10th grades), 60 hours of community service.
Special Academic Programs Advanced Placement exam preparation; honors section; study at local college for college credit.
College Admission Counseling 117 students graduated in 2009; 113 went to college, including California Polytechnic State University, San Luis Obispo; California State University, Fresno; California State University, Monterey Bay; Saint Mary's College of California; Santa Clara University; University of California, Davis. Other: 2 went to work, 2 entered military service.
Student Life Upper grades have specified standards of dress, student council, honor system. Discipline rests primarily with faculty. Attendance at religious services is required.
Tuition and Aid Day student tuition: $9900. Tuition installment plan (Insured Tuition Payment Plan, monthly payment plans, 2-payment plan). Merit scholarship grants, need-based scholarship grants available. In 2009–10, 15% of upper-school students received aid. Total amount of financial aid awarded in 2009–10: $229,000.
Admissions Traditional secondary-level entrance grade is 9. For fall 2009, 50 students applied for upper-level admission, 40 were accepted, 30 enrolled. ETS high school placement exam required. Deadline for receipt of application materials: January 14. Application fee required: $75. On-campus interview required.
Athletics Interscholastic: baseball, basketball, cross-country running, diving, football, golf, soccer, swimming and diving, track and field, volleyball, water polo, wrestling; intramural: basketball, indoor soccer. 4 PE instructors, 15 coaches, 1 athletic trainer.
Computers Computers are regularly used in art, desktop publishing, economics, English, foreign language, history, mathematics, multimedia, music, newspaper, photography, science, social sciences, technical drawing, video film production, Web site design, word processing, writing, yearbook classes. Computer network features include on-campus library services, online commercial services, Internet access, wireless campus network, Internet filtering or blocking technology. Computer access in designated common areas is available to students. Students grades are available online. The school has a published electronic and media policy.
Contact Mr. Chris Dalman, Director of Admissions. 831-422-6391. Fax: 831-422-5065. E-mail: dalman@palmahs.org. Web site: www.palmahs.org.

PARADISE ADVENTIST ACADEMY

5699 Academy Drive
PO Box 2169
Paradise, California 95969
Head of School: Mr. Ken Preston
General Information Coeducational day college-preparatory school, affiliated with Seventh-day Adventists. Grades K–12. Founded: 1908. Setting: small town. Nearest major city is Sacramento. 12-acre campus. 6 buildings on campus. Approved or accredited by Western Association of Schools and Colleges and California Department of Education. Endowment: $200,000. Total enrollment: 191. Upper school average class size: 20. Upper school faculty-student ratio: 1:8. There are 180 required school days per year for Upper School students. Upper School students typically attend 5 days per week. The average school day consists of 8 hours and 5 minutes.
Upper School Student Profile Grade 9: 19 students (12 boys, 7 girls); Grade 10: 24 students (14 boys, 10 girls); Grade 11: 23 students (11 boys, 12 girls); Grade 12: 18 students (10 boys, 8 girls). 80% of students are Seventh-day Adventists.

Faculty School total: 20. In upper school: 7 men, 3 women; 6 have advanced degrees.

Subjects Offered Advanced biology, advanced computer applications, advanced math, algebra, American government, American history, auto mechanics, band, basketball, Bible, biology, career education, carpentry, chemistry, choir, computer applications, computers, drama, earth science, English, geometry, health, keyboarding, military history, physical education, physical science, physics, pre-algebra, pre-calculus, Spanish, speech, U.S. government, U.S. history, volleyball, weight-lifting, woodworking, world history, yearbook.

Graduation Requirements Advanced computer applications, algebra, American government, American history, arts and fine arts (art, music, dance, drama), Bible, biology, career and personal planning, career education, chemistry, computer literacy, electives, English, health, keyboarding, languages, life skills, physical education (includes health), physics, Spanish, world history, 100 hours of community service, 20 credits of fine arts, career development portfolio.

Special Academic Programs Accelerated programs; independent study.

College Admission Counseling 17 students graduated in 2010; all went to college, including Azusa Pacific University; Pacific Union College; Walla Walla University. Median SAT critical reading: 550, median SAT math: 570, median SAT writing: 545, median combined SAT: 1565, median composite ACT: 23. 20% scored over 600 on SAT critical reading, 40% scored over 600 on SAT math, 20% scored over 600 on SAT writing, 27% scored over 1800 on combined SAT, 31% scored over 26 on composite ACT.

Student Life Upper grades have specified standards of dress, student council. Discipline rests primarily with faculty. Attendance at religious services is required.

Summer Programs Sports programs offered; session focuses on basketball; held on campus; accepts boys and girls; open to students from other schools. 15 students usually enrolled. 2011 schedule: June 20 to June 24. Application deadline: June 17.

Tuition and Aid Day student tuition: $7940. Tuition installment plan (FACTS Tuition Payment Plan, monthly payment plans, individually arranged payment plans). Tuition reduction for siblings, need-based scholarship grants, paying campus jobs available. In 2010–11, 25% of upper-school students received aid. Total amount of financial aid awarded in 2010–11: $50,000.

Admissions Traditional secondary-level entrance grade is 9. For fall 2010, 7 students applied for upper-level admission, 7 were accepted, 7 enrolled. Any standardized test required. Deadline for receipt of application materials: August 16. Application fee required: $35. Interview required.

Athletics Interscholastic: basketball (boys, girls), football (b,g), soccer (b), volleyball (g). 1 PE instructor, 2 coaches.

Computers Computers are regularly used in all academic classes. Computer network features include on-campus library services, Internet access, Internet filtering or blocking technology. Campus intranet, student e-mail accounts, and computer access in designated common areas are available to students. Students grades are available online. The school has a published electronic and media policy.

Contact Mrs. Brenda Muth, Registrar. 530-877-6540 Ext. 3010. Fax: 530-877-0870. E-mail: bmuth@mypaa.net. Web site: www.mypaa.net.

PARISH EPISCOPAL SCHOOL

4101 Sigma Road
Dallas, Texas 75244

Head of School: Mr. Dave Monaco

General Information Coeducational day college-preparatory school, affiliated with Episcopal Church. Grades PK–12. Founded: 1972. Setting: suburban. 50-acre campus. 1 building on campus. Approved or accredited by Independent Schools Association of the Southwest, Southwest Association of Episcopal Schools, and Texas Department of Education. Total enrollment: 1,190. Upper school average class size: 18.

Upper School Student Profile Grade 9: 89 students (32 boys, 57 girls); Grade 10: 65 students (29 boys, 36 girls); Grade 11: 75 students (34 boys, 41 girls); Grade 12: 49 students (24 boys, 25 girls). 25% of students are members of Episcopal Church.

Special Academic Programs Honors section.

Student Life Upper grades have uniform requirement, student council, honor system. Discipline rests primarily with faculty. Attendance at religious services is required.

Tuition and Aid Day student tuition: $14,400. Guaranteed tuition plan. Tuition installment plan (Insured Tuition Payment Plan, monthly payment plans). Need-based scholarship grants available.

Admissions Traditional secondary-level entrance grade is 9. ISEE required. Deadline for receipt of application materials: January 15. Application fee required: $150. Interview required.

Athletics Interscholastic: baseball (boys), basketball (b,g), cheering (g), field hockey (g), lacrosse (b,g), soccer (b,g), softball (g), winter soccer (b,g); intramural: aerobics/dance (g), dance (g); coed interscholastic: cross-country running, golf, tennis; coed intramural: physical fitness, strength & conditioning, weight training. 6 PE instructors, 12 coaches, 2 athletic trainers.

Computers Computer resources include Internet filtering or blocking technology. Campus intranet and computer access in designated common areas are available to students. Students grades are available online. The school has a published electronic and media policy.

Contact Ms. Laurel Ruff, Associate Director of Admission. 972-852-8769. Fax: 972-991-1237. E-mail: lruff@parishepiscopal.org. Web site: www.parishepiscopal.org.

PARKLANE ACADEMY

1115 Parklane Road
McComb, Mississippi 39648

Head of School: Mr. Jack Henderson

General Information Coeducational day college-preparatory school, affiliated with Christian faith. Grades PK–12. Founded: 1970. Setting: small town. Nearest major city is Jackson. 44-acre campus. 4 buildings on campus. Approved or accredited by Southern Association of Colleges and Schools and Mississippi Department of Education. Total enrollment: 976. Upper school average class size: 25. Upper school faculty-student ratio: 1:16.

Upper School Student Profile Grade 7: 72 students (42 boys, 30 girls); Grade 8: 69 students (40 boys, 29 girls); Grade 9: 95 students (41 boys, 54 girls); Grade 10: 53 students (36 boys, 17 girls); Grade 11: 85 students (43 boys, 42 girls); Grade 12: 51 students (22 boys, 29 girls). 80% of students are Christian faith.

Faculty School total: 54. In upper school: 9 men, 18 women; 9 have advanced degrees.

Subjects Offered 20th century world history, advanced chemistry, algebra, ancient world history, art, band, basic language skills, Bible, biology, calculus, choral music, choreography, civics, composition, computer applications, computer science, concert band, consumer economics, creative writing, driver education, economics, economics and history, English composition, English language-AP, English literature and composition-AP, English-AP, French, geography, government, government and politics-AP, government-AP, grammar, health, history-AP, honors geometry, honors U.S. history, human anatomy, keyboarding, lab science, library, literature, literature and composition-AP, literature-AP, media services, musical productions, physical science, physics, public speaking, reading, SAT/ACT preparation, science, Spanish, speech, state government, U.S. history, U.S. literature, world history, world literature.

Graduation Requirements Algebra, American history, American literature, analytic geometry, applied music, biology, British literature, chemistry, civics/free enterprise, computer applications, economics, electives, English, English composition, foreign language, geometry, government, honors algebra, honors English, honors geometry, honors U.S. history, honors world history, human biology, lab science, language and composition, music appreciation, U.S. government, world history.

Special Academic Programs Advanced Placement exam preparation; honors section; study at local college for college credit.

College Admission Counseling 59 students graduated in 2009; 50 went to college, including Belhaven University; Mississippi College; Mississippi State University; University of Mississippi; University of Southern Mississippi. Other: 2 entered military service. Median composite ACT: 23. 19% scored over 26 on composite ACT.

Student Life Upper grades have specified standards of dress, student council, honor system. Discipline rests primarily with faculty.

Tuition and Aid Day student tuition: $2700. Tuition installment plan (monthly payment plans). Tuition reduction for siblings available. In 2009–10, 1% of upper-school students received aid. Total amount of financial aid awarded in 2009–10: $3000.

Admissions Traditional secondary-level entrance grade is 9. Admissions testing required. Deadline for receipt of application materials: none. Application fee required: $150. On-campus interview required.

Athletics Interscholastic: baseball (boys), basketball (b,g), cheering (b,g), danceline (g), football (b), golf (b), soccer (b), softball (g), tennis (b), track and field (b,g), weight training (b,g). 1 PE instructor, 10 coaches.

Computers Computers are regularly used in computer applications, data processing, desktop publishing, keyboarding, science, typing, word processing, yearbook classes. Computer network features include on-campus library services, Internet access, wireless campus network. Campus intranet is available to students. Students grades are available online. The school has a published electronic and media policy.

Contact Mrs. Emma Lampton, Registrar/Technology Coordinator. 601-684-8113 Ext. 223. Fax: 601-684-4166 Ext. 256. E-mail: parklane@cableone.net. Web site: www.parklaneacademy.net.

THE PARK SCHOOL OF BALTIMORE

2425 Old Court Road
P.O. Box 8200
Brooklandville, Maryland 21022

Head of School: Mr. Daniel Paradis

General Information Coeducational day college-preparatory school. Grades PK–12. Founded: 1912. Setting: suburban. Nearest major city is Baltimore. 100-acre campus. 4 buildings on campus. Approved or accredited by Association of Independent Maryland Schools and Maryland Department of Education. Member of National Association of Independent Schools. Endowment: $24.2 million. Total enrollment: 879. Upper school average class size: 13. Upper school faculty-student ratio: 1:7. There are 170 required school days per year for Upper School students. Upper School students typically attend 5 days per week. The average school day consists of 4 hours and 15 minutes.

Upper School Student Profile Grade 9: 85 students (37 boys, 48 girls); Grade 10: 81 students (33 boys, 48 girls); Grade 11: 83 students (38 boys, 45 girls); Grade 12: 81 students (46 boys, 35 girls).

Faculty School total: 112. In upper school: 26 men, 23 women; 33 have advanced degrees.

The Park School of Baltimore

Subjects Offered 20th century history, 20th century world history, 3-dimensional art, 3-dimensional design, acting, advanced biology, advanced chemistry, advanced computer applications, advanced math, advanced studio art-AP, African-American literature, algebra, American history, American literature, American studies, analysis and differential calculus, analytic geometry, ancient world history, animal behavior, art, art history, astronomy, Bible as literature, biology, botany, British literature, calculus, calculus-AP, ceramics, chamber groups, chemistry, Chesapeake Bay studies, Chinese, choral music, chorus, civil rights, computer graphics, computer science, contemporary history, creative writing, criminal justice, design, drama, drama performance, drawing, earth science, ecology, economics, English, English literature, environmental science, environmental studies, equality and freedom, European history, expository writing, film studies, fine arts, food science, foreign language, forensics, French, French studies, genetics, geometry, global studies, government/civics, health, health and wellness, history, history of science, jazz ensemble, Latin American history, Latin American literature, marine biology, mathematics, mechanical drawing, music, music technology, music theory, musical theater, newspaper, painting, philosophy, photography, physical education, physics, science, sculpture, short story, social studies, Spanish, Spanish literature, technical theater, theater design and production, trigonometry, woodworking, world history, world literature, writing, yearbook.
Graduation Requirements Arts and fine arts (art, music, dance, drama), electives, English, foreign language, history, mathematics, physical education (includes health), science.
Special Academic Programs 14 Advanced Placement exams for which test preparation is offered; independent study; term-away projects; academic accommodation for the gifted, the musically talented, and the artistically talented.
College Admission Counseling 91 students graduated in 2010; 90 went to college, including Brown University; Dickinson College; Emory University; New York University; Oberlin College; The Johns Hopkins University. Other: 1 had other specific plans. 73% scored over 600 on SAT critical reading, 71% scored over 600 on SAT math, 79% scored over 600 on SAT writing, 80% scored over 1800 on combined SAT, 79% scored over 26 on composite ACT.
Student Life Upper grades have student council. Discipline rests equally with students and faculty.
Tuition and Aid Tuition installment plan (The Tuition Plan, Insured Tuition Payment Plan, monthly payment plans). Need-based scholarship grants available. In 2010–11, 19% of upper-school students received aid. Total amount of financial aid awarded in 2010–11: $1,129,365.
Admissions Traditional secondary-level entrance grade is 9. For fall 2010, 82 students applied for upper-level admission, 50 were accepted, 26 enrolled. ISEE required. Deadline for receipt of application materials: January 1. Application fee required: $50. Interview required.
Athletics Interscholastic: baseball (boys), basketball (b,g), cross-country running (b,g), field hockey (g), indoor soccer (g), lacrosse (b,g), soccer (b,g), softball (g), squash (b,g), tennis (b,g), winter soccer (g); coed intramural: climbing, Frisbee, strength & conditioning, ultimate Frisbee, wall climbing, yoga. 3 PE instructors, 30 coaches, 1 athletic trainer.
Computers Computers are regularly used in art, computer applications, creative writing, desktop publishing, English, foreign language, French, graphic design, history, journalism, library skills, mathematics, media production, music, music technology, news writing, newspaper, photojournalism, programming, publications, science, Spanish, theater, theater arts, video film production, woodworking, writing, writing, yearbook classes. Computer network features include on-campus library services, online commercial services, Internet access, wireless campus network, Internet filtering or blocking technology, Access to course materials and assignments through faculty web pages and wikis, Discounted software purchase plan. Campus intranet and computer access in designated common areas are available to students. Students grades are available online. The school has a published electronic and media policy.
Contact Rachel Hockett, Admission Receptionist. 410-339-4130. Fax: 410-339-4127. E-mail: admission@parkschool.net. Web site: www.parkschool.net.

THE PARK SCHOOL OF BUFFALO

4625 Harlem Road
Snyder, New York 14226
Head of School: Christopher J. Lauricella
General Information Coeducational day college-preparatory and arts school. Grades N–12. Founded: 1912. Setting: suburban. Nearest major city is Buffalo. 34-acre campus. 15 buildings on campus. Approved or accredited by National Independent Private Schools Association, New York Department of Education, New York State Association of Independent Schools, and New York Department of Education. Member of National Association of Independent Schools. Endowment: $1.3 million. Total enrollment: 242. Upper school average class size: 14. Upper school faculty-student ratio: 1:8. There are 166 required school days per year for Upper School students. Upper School students typically attend 5 days per week. The average school day consists of 7 hours.
Upper School Student Profile Grade 9: 20 students (11 boys, 9 girls); Grade 10: 21 students (9 boys, 12 girls); Grade 11: 32 students (15 boys, 17 girls); Grade 12: 33 students (14 boys, 19 girls).

Faculty School total: 39. In upper school: 11 men, 13 women; 20 have advanced degrees.
Subjects Offered Advanced studio art-AP, algebra, American history, American history-AP, American literature, American literature-AP, art, band, biology, biology-AP, calculus, calculus-AP, ceramics, chemistry, chorus, college admission preparation, college counseling, community service, computer applications, computer programming, critical thinking, drama, drawing, economics, English, environmental science, fine arts, forensics, French, French language-AP, freshman seminar, geometry, government/civics, health, junior and senior seminars, marine biology, media, media production, metalworking, music, orchestra, organic chemistry, photography, physical education, physics, senior project, senior seminar, senior thesis, Spanish, Spanish-AP, studio art-AP, trigonometry, U.S. government and politics-AP, woodworking, world history, yearbook.
Graduation Requirements Arts and fine arts (art, music, dance, drama), computer science, English, foreign language, mathematics, physical education (includes health), science, senior project, senior thesis, social sciences, social studies (includes history). Community service is required.
Special Academic Programs Advanced Placement exam preparation; honors section; accelerated programs; independent study; study at local college for college credit; study abroad; academic accommodation for the gifted; ESL (13 students enrolled).
College Admission Counseling 34 students graduated in 2010; all went to college, including Bard College; Bowdoin College; Purchase College, State University of New York; Purdue University; The George Washington University; University of Toronto. Median SAT critical reading: 587, median SAT math: 581, median SAT writing: 577, median combined SAT: 1968, median composite ACT: 25. 48% scored over 600 on SAT critical reading, 40% scored over 600 on SAT math, 44% scored over 600 on SAT writing, 44% scored over 1800 on combined SAT, 50% scored over 26 on composite ACT.
Student Life Upper grades have specified standards of dress, student council, honor system. Discipline rests equally with students and faculty.
Summer Programs Remediation, enrichment, advancement, ESL, sports programs offered; session focuses on recreational day camp, basketball camps, soccer camp, ESL, summer scholars; held on campus; accepts boys and girls; open to students from other schools. 585 students usually enrolled. 2011 schedule: July 6 to August 14. Application deadline: January 16.
Tuition and Aid Day student tuition: $16,700–$17,750. Tuition installment plan (Insured Tuition Payment Plan, FACTS Tuition Payment Plan). Tuition reduction for siblings, merit scholarship grants, need-based scholarship grants available. In 2010–11, 59% of upper-school students received aid; total upper-school merit-scholarship money awarded: $35,500. Total amount of financial aid awarded in 2010–11: $900,000.
Admissions Traditional secondary-level entrance grade is 9. For fall 2010, 56 students applied for upper-level admission, 26 were accepted, 25 enrolled. ERB Reading and Math, Otis-Lennon School Ability Test or TOEFL required. Deadline for receipt of application materials: none. Application fee required: $50. Interview required.
Athletics Interscholastic: basketball (boys, girls), bowling (b,g), golf (b), lacrosse (b), soccer (b,g), softball (g), tennis (b,g); coed intramural: aerobics, badminton, ball hockey, bicycling, cooperative games, cross-country running, fishing, fitness, flag football, floor hockey, Frisbee, hiking/backpacking, indoor soccer, outdoor activities, outdoor adventure, outdoor education, outdoor recreation, outdoor skills, outdoors, physical fitness, running, skiing (downhill), snowboarding, snowshoeing, soccer, strength & conditioning, weight lifting, weight training, winter walking, yoga. 2 PE instructors, 14 coaches.
Computers Computers are regularly used in creative writing, current events, data processing, English, graphic arts, independent study, mathematics, media, media arts, media services, newspaper, photography, science, word processing, yearbook classes. Computer network features include on-campus library services, online commercial services, Internet access, wireless campus network, Internet filtering or blocking technology. Campus intranet, student e-mail accounts, and computer access in designated common areas are available to students. Students grades are available online. The school has a published electronic and media policy.
Contact Jennifer A. Brady, Director of Admissions. 716-839-1242 Ext. 107. Fax: 716-408-9511. E-mail: jbrady@theparkschool.org. Web site: www.theparkschool.org.

PARK TUDOR SCHOOL

7200 North College Avenue
Indianapolis, Indiana 46240-3016
Head of School: Mr. Douglas S. Jennings
General Information Coeducational day college-preparatory, arts, and bilingual studies school. Grades PK–12. Founded: 1902. Setting: suburban. 55-acre campus. 6 buildings on campus. Approved or accredited by Independent Schools Association of the Central States and Indiana Department of Education. Member of National Association of Independent Schools and Secondary School Admission Test Board. Endowment: $89.6 million. Total enrollment: 985. Upper school average class size: 14. Upper school faculty-student ratio: 1:9. Upper school students typically attend 5 days per week.
Upper School Student Profile Grade 6: 60 students (28 boys, 32 girls); Grade 7: 69 students (39 boys, 30 girls); Grade 8: 72 students (33 boys, 39 girls); Grade 9: 104

students (54 boys, 50 girls); Grade 10: 108 students (55 boys, 53 girls); Grade 11: 109 students (54 boys, 55 girls); Grade 12: 105 students (58 boys, 47 girls).

Faculty School total: 128. In upper school: 26 men, 30 women; 39 have advanced degrees.

Subjects Offered 3-dimensional design, acting, advanced chemistry, advanced math, Advanced Placement courses, algebra, American history, American history-AP, American literature-AP, art, art history, art history-AP, ballet, biology, biology-AP, calculus, calculus-AP, ceramics, chemistry, chemistry-AP, choir, computer science, computer science-AP, creative writing, dance, drama, economics, economics-AP, electives, English, English language-AP, English literature-AP, English-AP, English/composition-AP, environmental science, environmental science-AP, ethics, etymology, film history, fine arts, French, French language-AP, French studies, geography, geometry, government/civics, health, history, history-AP, jazz band, jazz ensemble, journalism, Latin, Latin-AP, madrigals, Mandarin, mathematics, multicultural literature, music, music history, music theory, music theory-AP, philosophy, photography, physical education, physics, physics-AP, physiology, printmaking, science, social sciences, social studies, sociology, Spanish, Spanish language-AP, Spanish-AP, speech, speech and debate, statistics, statistics-AP, studio art, theater, theater design and production, theater history, trigonometry, U.S. government, U.S. history, U.S. history-AP, world history, world history-AP, world wide web design.

Graduation Requirements Arts and fine arts (art, music, dance, drama), English, foreign language, mathematics, physical education (includes health), science, social sciences, social studies (includes history).

Special Academic Programs 16 Advanced Placement exams for which test preparation is offered; honors section; accelerated programs; independent study; study abroad; academic accommodation for the gifted, the musically talented, and the artistically talented.

College Admission Counseling 100 students graduated in 2009; all went to college, including Bowdoin College; DePauw University; Emory University, Oxford College; Indiana University Bloomington; Purdue University; Vanderbilt University. Mean SAT critical reading: 627, mean SAT math: 617, mean SAT writing: 620, mean combined SAT: 1864, mean composite ACT: 28.

Student Life Upper grades have specified standards of dress, student council, honor system. Discipline rests equally with students and faculty.

Tuition and Aid Day student tuition: $16,570. Tuition installment plan (annual, biannual, or quarterly payment plans). Merit scholarship grants, need-based scholarship grants available. In 2009–10, 39% of upper-school students received aid; total upper-school merit-scholarship money awarded: $646,000. Total amount of financial aid awarded in 2009–10: $1,478,000.

Admissions Traditional secondary-level entrance grade is 9. For fall 2009, 112 students applied for upper-level admission, 81 were accepted, 52 enrolled. ERB CTP IV required. Deadline for receipt of application materials: December 12. Application fee required: $50. On-campus interview required.

Athletics Interscholastic: baseball (boys), basketball (b,g), crew (b,g), cross-country running (b,g), football (b), golf (b,g), ice hockey (b), lacrosse (b,g), soccer (b,g), softball (g), swimming and diving (b,g), tennis (b,g), track and field (b,g), volleyball (g), wrestling (b); intramural: basketball (b,g); coed interscholastic: cheering; coed intramural: running, soccer. 5 PE instructors, 21 coaches, 1 athletic trainer.

Computers Computers are regularly used in newspaper, yearbook classes. Computer network features include on-campus library services, online commercial services, Internet access, wireless campus network, Internet filtering or blocking technology. Campus intranet, student e-mail accounts, and computer access in designated common areas are available to students. Students grades are available online. The school has a published electronic and media policy.

Contact Mr. David Amstutz, Assistant Head and Director of Admissions. 317-415-2777. Fax: 317-254-2714. E-mail: damstutz@parktudor.org. Web site: www.parktudor.org.

PARKVIEW ADVENTIST ACADEMY

5505 College Avenue
Lacombe, Alberta T4L 2E7, Canada
Head of School: Angie Bishop

General Information Coeducational boarding and day college-preparatory, general academic, arts, vocational, religious studies, and technology school, affiliated with Seventh-day Adventist Church. Grades 10–12. Founded: 1907. Setting: small town. Nearest major city is Calgary, Canada. Students are housed in coed dormitories. Approved or accredited by Board of Regents, General Conference of Seventh-day Adventists and Alberta Department of Education. Language of instruction: English. Upper school average class size: 20. Upper school faculty-student ratio: 1:12.

Upper School Student Profile Grade 10: 30 students (16 boys, 14 girls); Grade 11: 32 students (17 boys, 15 girls); Grade 12: 45 students (24 boys, 21 girls). 80% of students are Seventh-day Adventists.

Faculty School total: 9. In upper school: 6 men, 3 women; 5 have advanced degrees; 1 resides on campus.

Subjects Offered Advanced math, art, arts, band, biology, business, career and technology systems, chemistry, choir, choral music, computer science, driver education, English, ESL, fine arts, foods, French, home economics, industrial arts, information processing, instrumental music, language arts, mathematics, mechanics,

metalworking, music, photography, physical education, physics, publications, religion, religious studies, science, social sciences, social studies, welding, woodworking.

Graduation Requirements Computer processing, English, keyboarding, mathematics, physical education (includes health), religious studies, science, social studies (includes history), word processing.

Special Academic Programs ESL (6 students enrolled).

Student Life Upper grades have specified standards of dress, student council, honor system. Discipline rests primarily with faculty. Attendance at religious services is required.

Tuition and Aid Day student tuition: CAN$5657; 7-day tuition and room/board: CAN$11,724. Tuition installment plan (monthly payment plans, individually arranged payment plans). Tuition reduction for siblings, merit scholarship grants available.

Admissions Deadline for receipt of application materials: none. Application fee required: CAN$20.

Athletics Interscholastic: basketball (boys), hockey (b), soccer (b), volleyball (b,g); intramural: basketball (b), football (b), softball (g); coed interscholastic: soccer. 1 PE instructor.

Computers Computer resources include Internet access.

Contact Rodney Jamieson, Vice Principal. 403-782-3381 Ext. 4111. Fax: 403-782-7308. E-mail: rjamieso@cauc.ca. Web site: www.paa.ca/.

THE PATHWAY SCHOOL

Norristown, Pennsylvania
See Special Needs Schools section.

PATTEN ACADEMY OF CHRISTIAN EDUCATION

2433 Coolidge Avenue
Oakland, California 94601
Head of School: Dr. Sharon Anderson

General Information Coeducational day college-preparatory, arts, religious studies, and bilingual studies school, affiliated with Christian faith. Founded: 1944. Setting: urban. Nearest major city is San Francisco. 3 buildings on campus. Approved or accredited by Western Association of Schools and Colleges and California Department of Education. Total enrollment: 187. Upper school average class size: 14. Upper school faculty-student ratio: 1:8. There are 182 required school days per year for Upper School students. Upper School students typically attend 5 days per week. The average school day consists of 6 hours and 45 minutes.

Upper School Student Profile Grade 9: 19 students (8 boys, 11 girls); Grade 10: 13 students (8 boys, 5 girls); Grade 11: 14 students (6 boys, 8 girls); Grade 12: 13 students (9 boys, 4 girls). 9% of students are Christian faith.

Faculty School total: 14. In upper school: 6 men, 2 women; 6 have advanced degrees.

Subjects Offered Algebra, American literature, art, arts, band, Bible studies, biology, chemistry, choir, community service, computer science, economics, English, English literature, fine arts, geometry, health, instrumental music, introduction to literature, language arts, life skills, mathematics, music, physical education, physical science, physics, piano, pre-calculus, religion, science, social studies, Spanish, strings, U.S. government, U.S. history, vocal music, world geography, world history, world literature, writing.

Graduation Requirements Arts and fine arts (art, music, dance, drama), business skills (includes word processing), computer science, foreign language, mathematics, science, social studies (includes history). Community service is required.

College Admission Counseling 17 students graduated in 2009; they went to California State University, East Bay; Morehouse College; Patten University; Saint Mary's College of California; University of California, Berkeley. Other: 3 entered military service.

Student Life Upper grades have uniform requirement, student council, honor system. Discipline rests primarily with faculty. Attendance at religious services is required.

Tuition and Aid Day student tuition: $5554. Tuition installment plan (monthly payment plans). Need-based scholarship grants available.

Admissions Traditional secondary-level entrance grade is 9. For fall 2009, 20 students applied for upper-level admission, 14 were accepted, 10 enrolled. Deadline for receipt of application materials: none. Application fee required: $40. Interview required.

Athletics Interscholastic: baseball (boys), basketball (b,g), flag football (b), soccer (b), volleyball (g). 1 PE instructor, 2 coaches.

Computers Computer network features include Internet access.

Contact Mrs. Sharon Moncher, Coordinator. 510-533-3121. Fax: 510-535-9381. Web site: www.pattenacademy.org.

PAUL VI HIGH SCHOOL

901 Hopkins Road, Suite B
Haddonfield, New Jersey 08033
Head of School: Sr. Marianne McMann

General Information Coeducational day college-preparatory, general academic, arts, business, religious studies, and technology school, affiliated with Roman Catholic Church. Grades 9–12. Founded: 1966. Setting: suburban. Nearest major city is

Philadelphia, PA. 35-acre campus. 1 building on campus. Approved or accredited by Middle States Association of Colleges and Schools and New Jersey Department of Education. Total enrollment: 1,200. Upper school average class size: 22. Upper school faculty-student ratio: 1:20. There are 180 required school days per year for Upper School students. Upper School students typically attend 5 days per week. The average school day consists of 6 hours and 30 minutes.

Upper School Student Profile Grade 9: 250 students (121 boys, 129 girls); Grade 10: 345 students (158 boys, 187 girls); Grade 11: 326 students (153 boys, 173 girls); Grade 12: 275 students (121 boys, 154 girls). 91.5% of students are Roman Catholic.

Faculty School total: 68. In upper school: 26 men, 34 women; 21 have advanced degrees.

Subjects Offered Accounting, algebra, anatomy and physiology, art, art appreciation, ballet, band, biology, biology-AP, business, business law, calculus-AP, ceramics, chemistry, chemistry-AP, chorus, comparative government and politics, computer literacy, computer programming, computer-aided design, creative writing, culinary arts, dance, drama, earth science, economics, English, English literature and composition-AP, film appreciation, French, geometry, honors algebra, honors English, honors geometry, humanities, intro to computers, Italian, keyboarding, Latin, marketing, math analysis, music, physical science, physics, pre-calculus, psychology, religious education, sociology, Spanish, study skills, technical drawing, U.S. history, world history, writing.

Graduation Requirements Algebra, biology, chemistry, English, geometry, language, physical education (includes health), physical science, practical arts, religion (includes Bible studies and theology), U.S. history, 20 hours of community service required in grade 12, 10 hours of community service required in grade 11, community service encouraged for grades 9 and 10.

Special Academic Programs International Baccalaureate program; Advanced Placement exam preparation; honors section; academic accommodation for the musically talented and the artistically talented; remedial reading and/or remedial writing; remedial math; programs in general development for dyslexic students; ESL (4 students enrolled).

College Admission Counseling 260 students graduated in 2009; 254 went to college, including La Salle University; Loyola University Maryland; Rutgers, The State University of New Jersey, Rutgers College; Saint Joseph's University; The College of New Jersey; The University of Scranton. Other: 3 went to work, 2 entered military service, 1 had other specific plans. Mean SAT critical reading: 566, mean SAT math: 565.

Student Life Upper grades have uniform requirement, student council, honor system. Discipline rests primarily with faculty. Attendance at religious services is required.

Tuition and Aid Day student tuition: $6775. Tuition installment plan (FACTS Tuition Payment Plan). Tuition reduction for siblings, merit scholarship grants, need-based scholarship grants available. In 2009–10, 20% of upper-school students received aid; total upper-school merit-scholarship money awarded: $17,000. Total amount of financial aid awarded in 2009–10: $130,000.

Admissions Traditional secondary-level entrance grade is 9. For fall 2009, 320 students applied for upper-level admission, 314 were accepted, 250 enrolled. Any standardized test or High School Placement Test required. Deadline for receipt of application materials: none. No application fee required.

Athletics Interscholastic: baseball (boys), basketball (b,g), cheering (g), cross-country running (b,g), field hockey (g), football (g), ice hockey (b), lacrosse (b,g), soccer (b,g), softball (g), swimming and diving (b,g), tennis (g), wrestling (b); coed interscholastic: golf, track and field; coed intramural: bowling, dance, dance team, volleyball. 2 PE instructors, 10 coaches, 1 athletic trainer.

Computers Computers are regularly used in business education, career exploration, college planning, creative writing, journalism, keyboarding, literary magazine, mathematics, science, technical drawing, word processing classes. Computer network features include on-campus library services, Internet access, wireless campus network, Internet filtering or blocking technology, each student has his/her own laptop supplied by the school. Students grades are available online.

Contact Mrs. Stefanie Markellos, Director of Development. 856-858-4900 Ext. 36. Fax: 856-858-5058. E-mail: smarkellos@pvihs.org. Web site: www.pvihs.org.

PEDDIE SCHOOL

201 South Main Street
Hightstown, New Jersey 08520
Head of School: John F. Green

General Information Coeducational boarding and day college-preparatory, arts, and technology school. Grades 9–PG. Founded: 1864. Setting: small town. Nearest major city is Princeton. Students are housed in single-sex dormitories. 230-acre campus. 53 buildings on campus. Approved or accredited by Middle States Association of Colleges and Schools, New Jersey Association of Independent Schools, The Association of Boarding Schools, and New Jersey Department of Education. Member of National Association of Independent Schools and Secondary School Admission Test Board. Endowment: $228 million. Total enrollment: 550. Upper school average class size: 12. Upper school faculty-student ratio: 1:6. Upper School students typically attend 6 days per week.

Upper School Student Profile Grade 9: 116 students (57 boys, 59 girls); Grade 10: 143 students (70 boys, 73 girls); Grade 11: 150 students (76 boys, 74 girls); Grade 12: 128 students (68 boys, 60 girls); Postgraduate: 14 students (7 boys, 7 girls). 62% of students are boarding students. 17 states are represented in upper school student body. 11% are international students. International students from China, Hong Kong, Japan, Republic of Korea, Thailand, and United Kingdom; 23 other countries represented in student body.

Faculty School total: 94. In upper school: 50 men, 35 women; 75 have advanced degrees; 76 reside on campus.

Subjects Offered Acting, African studies, algebra, American history, American literature, American studies, anatomy, architecture, art, art history, art history-AP, Asian studies, astronomy, Bible studies, biology, biology-AP, calculus, calculus-AP, chemistry, Chinese, comedy, comparative religion, computer programming, computer science, creative writing, debate, digital imaging, DNA, DNA science lab, drama, earth science, ecology, economics, English, English literature, environmental science, environmental science-AP, European history, European history-AP, expository writing, film history, fine arts, forensics, French, French language-AP, French literature-AP, geometry, global issues, global science, government/civics, health, history, information technology, Latin, Latin-AP, mathematics, Middle East, music, music theory-AP, neuroscience, philosophy, photography, physical education, physics, physics-AP, psychology, psychology-AP, robotics, science, Shakespeare, social studies, Spanish, Spanish language-AP, Spanish literature-AP, speech, statistics, statistics-AP, studio art-AP, theater, trigonometry, U.S. history, U.S. history-AP, video film production, world history, world literature, World War I, World War II, writing.

Graduation Requirements Arts and fine arts (art, music, dance, drama), computer science, English, foreign language, history, mathematics, physical education (includes health), science. Community service is required.

Special Academic Programs Advanced Placement exam preparation; honors section; independent study; term-away projects; study abroad.

College Admission Counseling 132 students graduated in 2010; all went to college, including Carnegie Mellon University; Cornell University; Georgetown University; The George Washington University; University of Pennsylvania; University of Richmond.

Student Life Upper grades have specified standards of dress, student council. Discipline rests primarily with faculty.

Summer Programs Enrichment, advancement, sports, art/fine arts programs offered; session focuses on enrichment; held on campus; accepts boys and girls; open to students from other schools. 175 students usually enrolled. 2011 schedule: June 21 to August 2. Application deadline: none.

Tuition and Aid Day student tuition: $33,000; 7-day tuition and room/board: $43,000. Tuition installment plan (Academic Management Services Plan, monthly payment plans, individually arranged payment plans). Merit scholarship grants, need-based scholarship grants, need-based loans available. In 2010–11, 40% of upper-school students received aid; total upper-school merit-scholarship money awarded: $70,000. Total amount of financial aid awarded in 2010–11: $5,000,000.

Admissions Traditional secondary-level entrance grade is 9. For fall 2010, 1,400 students applied for upper-level admission, 323 were accepted, 169 enrolled. ISEE or SSAT required. Deadline for receipt of application materials: January 15. Application fee required: $50. Interview required.

Athletics Interscholastic: baseball (boys), basketball (b,g), crew (b,g), cross-country running (b,g), diving (b,g), field hockey (g), fitness (b,g), football (b), golf (b,g), indoor track & field (b,g), lacrosse (b,g), soccer (b,g), softball (g), strength & conditioning (b,g), swimming and diving (b,g), tennis (b,g), track and field (b,g), winter (indoor) track (b,g), wrestling (b), yoga (b,g); intramural: weight lifting (b,g), weight training (b,g); coed intramural: bicycling, bowling, softball. 9 coaches, 3 athletic trainers.

Computers Computers are regularly used in English, foreign language, history, mathematics, science classes. Computer network features include on-campus library services, online commercial services, Internet access, wireless campus network, Internet filtering or blocking technology, NewsBank, Britannica, GaleNet, Electric Library. Student e-mail accounts are available to students. Students grades are available online. The school has a published electronic and media policy.

Contact Raymond H. Cabot, Director of Admissions. 609-944-7501. Fax: 609-944-7901. E-mail: admission@peddie.org. Web site: www.peddie.org.

PENINSULA CATHOLIC HIGH SCHOOL

600 Harpersville Road
Newport News, Virginia 23601-1813
Head of School: Dr. Francine Gagne

General Information Coeducational day college-preparatory, arts, religious studies, and technology school, affiliated with Roman Catholic Church. Grades 8–12. Founded: 1903. Setting: suburban. Nearest major city is Newport News/Norfolk. 15-acre campus. 1 building on campus. Approved or accredited by National Catholic Education Association, Southern Association of Colleges and Schools, and Virginia Department of Education. Endowment: $180,000. Total enrollment: 305. Upper school average class size: 18. Upper school faculty-student ratio: 1:16. There are 183 required school days per year for Upper School students. Upper School students typically attend 5 days per week. The average school day consists of 6 hours.

Upper School Student Profile Grade 8: 26 students (12 boys, 14 girls); Grade 9: 101 students (48 boys, 53 girls); Grade 10: 66 students (25 boys, 41 girls); Grade 11: 79 students (39 boys, 40 girls); Grade 12: 66 students (28 boys, 38 girls). 75% of students are Roman Catholic.

Faculty School total: 29. In upper school: 10 men, 18 women; 20 have advanced degrees.

Subjects Offered 20th century American writers, 20th century history, 20th century world history, advanced chemistry, advanced math, algebra, American Civil War, American foreign policy, American government, American history, American history-AP, American literature, American literature-AP, analysis and differential calculus, anatomy and physiology, art, Bible as literature, Bible studies, biology, biology-AP, calculus, calculus-AP, campus ministry, Christian ethics, Christian testament, church history, college admission preparation, college placement, college planning, college writing, drama, driver education, English, English composition, English language and composition-AP, English language-AP, English literature, English literature and composition-AP, English-AP, foreign language, French, geography, geology, geometry, German, government, history, history of the Catholic Church, honors algebra, honors English, honors U.S. history, keyboarding, studio art-AP, U.S. government and politics-AP.

Graduation Requirements Arts and fine arts (art, music, dance, drama), English, foreign language, mathematics, physical education (includes health), religion (includes Bible studies and theology), science, social studies (includes history).

Special Academic Programs Advanced Placement exam preparation; honors section.

College Admission Counseling 70 students graduated in 2010; all went to college, including James Madison University; Longwood University; Old Dominion University; The College of William and Mary; University of Virginia; Virginia Polytechnic Institute and State University. Mean SAT critical reading: 543, mean SAT math: 537, mean SAT writing: 539.

Student Life Upper grades have uniform requirement, student council, honor system. Discipline rests primarily with faculty. Attendance at religious services is required.

Tuition and Aid Day student tuition: $8540. Tuition installment plan (FACTS Tuition Payment Plan). Tuition reduction for siblings, need-based scholarship grants available. In 2010–11, 25% of upper-school students received aid.

Admissions Traditional secondary-level entrance grade is 9. High School Placement Test (closed version) from Scholastic Testing Service or placement test required. Deadline for receipt of application materials: none. Application fee required: $100. Interview recommended.

Athletics Interscholastic: baseball (boys), basketball (b,g), cross-country running (b,g), soccer (b,g), softball (g), swimming and diving (b,g), tennis (b,g), track and field (b,g), volleyball (b,g), wrestling (b); coed interscholastic: cheering, golf. 2 PE instructors, 1 athletic trainer.

Computers Computers are regularly used in journalism, programming, yearbook classes. Computer resources include on-campus library services, Internet access.

Contact Mrs. Christine Miller, Guidance Counselor. 757-596-7247 Ext. 14. Fax: 757-591-9718. E-mail: guidance@peninsulacatholic.com. Web site: www.peninsulacatholic.com.

THE PENNINGTON SCHOOL

112 West Delaware Avenue
Pennington, New Jersey 08534-1601
Head of School: Mrs. Stephanie (Penny) G. Townsend

General Information Coeducational boarding and day college-preparatory and arts school, affiliated with Methodist Church; primarily serves students with learning disabilities and dyslexic students. Boarding grades 7–12, day grades 6–12. Founded: 1838. Setting: small town. Nearest major city is Philadelphia, PA. Students are housed in single-sex by floor dormitories and single-sex dormitories. 54-acre campus. 17 buildings on campus. Approved or accredited by Middle States Association of Colleges and Schools, National Independent Private Schools Association, New Jersey Association of Independent Schools, The Association of Boarding Schools, The College Board, University Senate of United Methodist Church, and New Jersey Department of Education. Member of National Association of Independent Schools and Secondary School Admission Test Board. Endowment: $24.5 million. Total enrollment: 485. Upper school average class size: 13. Upper school faculty-student ratio: 1:8. Upper School students typically attend 5 days per week.

Upper School Student Profile Grade 9: 89 students (44 boys, 45 girls); Grade 10: 104 students (58 boys, 46 girls); Grade 11: 95 students (56 boys, 39 girls); Grade 12: 100 students (57 boys, 43 girls). 26% of students are boarding students. 66% are state residents. 8 states are represented in upper school student body. 13% are international students. International students from China, Germany, Republic of Korea, South Africa, Taiwan, and Thailand; 18 other countries represented in student body. 5% of students are Methodist.

Faculty School total: 87. In upper school: 31 men, 38 women; 55 have advanced degrees; 49 reside on campus.

Subjects Offered Advanced studio art-AP, advanced TOEFL/grammar, African-American history, algebra, American history, American literature, anatomy, anatomy and physiology, art, bioethics, DNA and culture, biology, British literature-AP, calculus-AP, cheerleading, chemistry, chemistry-AP, Chinese, chorus, computer applications, computer skills, drama, economics, English, English literature, English literature-AP, English-AP, environmental science, ESL, fine arts, forensics, French, French language-AP, genetics, geometry, German, government and politics-AP, Greek, Greek culture, health, history-AP, honors algebra, honors English, honors geometry, honors U.S. history, jazz ensemble, Latin, macroeconomics-AP, music, music history, music theory, organic chemistry, photography, physics, physics-AP, pottery, pre-calculus, psychology, public speaking, religion, robotics, senior internship, Spanish, Spanish literature, Spanish-AP, stage design, stagecraft, technical theater, U.S. government and politics-AP, Web site design, weight training, world history, world history-AP.

Graduation Requirements Algebra, American history, arts and fine arts (art, music, dance, drama), athletics, biology, chemistry, computer education, English, foreign

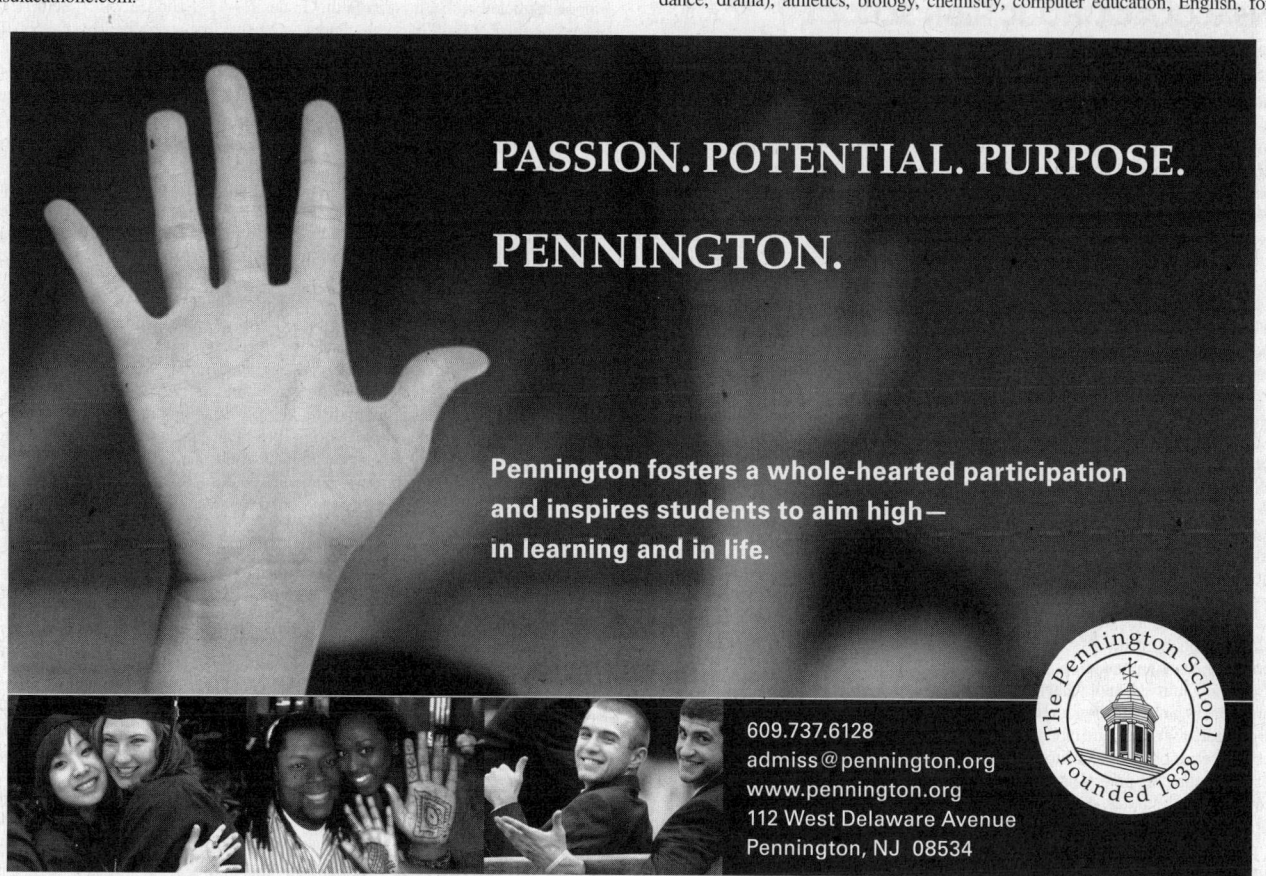

PASSION. POTENTIAL. PURPOSE.

PENNINGTON.

Pennington fosters a whole-hearted participation
and inspires students to aim high—
in learning and in life.

609.737.6128
admiss@pennington.org
www.pennington.org
112 West Delaware Avenue
Pennington, NJ 08534

The Pennington School · Founded 1838

language, geometry, health education, public speaking, religion (includes Bible studies and theology), religion and culture, world history.

Special Academic Programs Advanced Placement exam preparation; honors section; independent study; term-away projects; study at local college for college credit; academic accommodation for the gifted; programs in English for dyslexic students; ESL (41 students enrolled).

College Admission Counseling 99 students graduated in 2009; all went to college, including Carnegie Mellon University; Georgetown University; Muhlenberg College; New York University; Penn State University Park; Quinnipiac University.

Student Life Upper grades have specified standards of dress, student council. Discipline rests equally with students and faculty. Attendance at religious services is required.

Tuition and Aid Day student tuition: $27,300; 7-day tuition and room/board: $40,600. Tuition installment plan (Key Tuition Payment Plan). Merit scholarship grants, need-based scholarship grants available. In 2009–10, 28% of upper-school students received aid; total upper-school merit-scholarship money awarded: $201,600. Total amount of financial aid awarded in 2009–10: $2,000,000.

Admissions Traditional secondary-level entrance grade is 9. For fall 2009, 501 students applied for upper-level admission, 154 were accepted, 130 enrolled. Secondary Level English Proficiency, SLEP for foreign students, SSAT or TOEFL required. Deadline for receipt of application materials: February 1. Application fee required: $50. Interview required.

Athletics Interscholastic: baseball (boys), basketball (b,g), field hockey (g), football (b), ice hockey (b), lacrosse (b,g), soccer (b,g), softball (g), tennis (b,g), weight training (b); coed interscholastic: cheering, cross-country running, golf, indoor track, judo, swimming and diving, track and field, water polo, winter (indoor) track; coed intramural: fitness, strength & conditioning, weight training. 3 coaches, 2 athletic trainers.

Computers Computers are regularly used in art, college planning, computer applications, creative writing, desktop publishing, graphic design, library, literary magazine, mathematics, music, newspaper, research skills, science, video film production, yearbook classes. Computer network features include on-campus library services, online commercial services, Internet access, wireless campus network, Internet filtering or blocking technology, The Homework Site. Campus intranet, student e-mail accounts, and computer access in designated common areas are available to students. Students grades are available online. The school has a published electronic and media policy.

Contact Mr. Mark Saunders, Director of Admission. 609-737-6128. Fax: 609-730-1405. E-mail: msaunders@pennington.org. Web site: www.pennington.org.

See Display on page 491 and Close-Up on page 822.

PENSACOLA CATHOLIC HIGH SCHOOL

3043 West Scott Street
Pensacola, Florida 32505
Head of School: Sr. Kierstin Martin

General Information Coeducational day college-preparatory and technology school, affiliated with Roman Catholic Church. Grades 9–12. Founded: 1941. Setting: urban. 25-acre campus. 5 buildings on campus. Approved or accredited by Southern Association of Colleges and Schools. Total enrollment: 571. Upper school average class size: 22. Upper school faculty-student ratio: 1:18.

Upper School Student Profile Grade 9: 164 students (92 boys, 72 girls); Grade 10: 146 students (83 boys, 63 girls); Grade 11: 128 students (66 boys, 62 girls); Grade 12: 133 students (72 boys, 61 girls). 70% of students are Roman Catholic.

Faculty School total: 50. In upper school: 15 men, 35 women; 15 have advanced degrees.

Subjects Offered Advanced math, Advanced Placement courses, algebra, American government, American history, American history-AP, American literature, analysis and differential calculus, analytic geometry, anatomy and physiology, art, art appreciation, arts and crafts, athletics, band, baseball, basketball, Bible, Bible studies, biology, botany, British literature, broadcast journalism, business law, calculus, calculus-AP, campus ministry, Catholic belief and practice, chemistry, Christian ethics, Christian scripture, Christian studies, Christian testament, church history, civics, college counseling, comparative religion, composition, composition-AP, computer applications, computer graphics, consumer mathematics, CPR, creative arts, criminal justice, desktop publishing, digital photography, drawing, earth science, economics, electives, English, English composition, English language and composition-AP, English literature, English literature and composition-AP, environmental science, fabric arts, film appreciation, film history, filmmaking, foreign language, French, general science, genetics, geography, geometry, government, government-AP, grammar, graphic arts, guidance, health education, history, history of the Catholic Church, honors algebra, honors English, honors geometry, honors U.S. history, honors world history, human sexuality, journalism, keyboarding, lab science, library, library assistant, Life of Christ, literature and composition-AP, marine biology, music appreciation, music history, physical education, physical science, physics, pottery, pre-algebra, pre-calculus, probability and statistics, reading, religion, sex education, social studies, Spanish, student government, student publications, telecommunications and the Internet, television, the Web, trigonometry, U.S. government, U.S. government and politics-AP, U.S. history, U.S. literature, vocal music, weight training, Western civilization, world geography, world history, world religions.

Special Academic Programs Advanced Placement exam preparation; honors section; study at local college for college credit; academic accommodation for the gifted; remedial reading and/or remedial writing; remedial math; programs in English, mathematics, general development for dyslexic students; special instructional classes for deaf students, blind students.

College Admission Counseling 120 students graduated in 2010; 117 went to college, including Florida State University; Mississippi State University; Pensacola Junior College; The University of Alabama; University of Florida. Other: 2 entered military service, 1 had other specific plans. Mean SAT critical reading: 512, mean SAT math: 535, mean SAT writing: 511, mean combined SAT: 1557, mean composite ACT: 23.

Student Life Upper grades have specified standards of dress, student council. Discipline rests primarily with faculty. Attendance at religious services is required.

Summer Programs Remediation programs offered; session focuses on Religion courses; held on campus; accepts boys and girls; not open to students from other schools. 5 students usually enrolled.

Tuition and Aid Tuition reduction for siblings, need-based scholarship grants available.

Admissions Traditional secondary-level entrance grade is 9. ETS high school placement exam required. Deadline for receipt of application materials: none. Application fee required. On-campus interview required.

Athletics Interscholastic: baseball (boys), basketball (b,g), cheering (b,g), golf (b,g), physical training (b), soccer (b,g), softball (g), swimming and diving (b,g), wrestling (b).

Computers Computers are regularly used in Bible studies, computer applications, creative writing, desktop publishing, foreign language, French, geography, graphic design, history, independent study, keyboarding, mathematics, publications, reading, religion, science, social studies, Spanish, stock market, study skills, video film production, Web site design, word processing, yearbook classes. Computer network features include on-campus library services, online commercial services, Internet access, wireless campus network, Internet filtering or blocking technology. Student e-mail accounts and computer access in designated common areas are available to students. Students grades are available online. The school has a published electronic and media policy.

Contact Mary Kyte, Senior Guidance Counselor. 850-436-6400 Ext. 119. Fax: 850-436-6405. E-mail: mkyte@pensacolachs.org. Web site: www.pensacolachs.org.

PEOPLES CHRISTIAN ACADEMY

374 Sheppard Avenue East
Toronto, Ontario M2N 3B6, Canada
Head of School: Mr. Reg Andrews

General Information Coeducational day college-preparatory and religious studies school, affiliated with Christian faith. Grades JK–12. Founded: 1971. Setting: urban. 5-acre campus. 2 buildings on campus. Approved or accredited by Association of Christian Schools International, Christian Schools International, Ontario Ministry of Education, and Ontario Department of Education. Language of instruction: English. Endowment: CAN$15,000. Total enrollment: 417. Upper school average class size: 20. Upper school faculty-student ratio: 1:10. There are 176 required school days per year for Upper School students. Upper School students typically attend 5 days per week. The average school day consists of 7 hours.

Upper School Student Profile Grade 7: 40 students (22 boys, 18 girls); Grade 8: 30 students (16 boys, 14 girls); Grade 9: 41 students (16 boys, 25 girls); Grade 10: 28 students (18 boys, 10 girls); Grade 11: 27 students (11 boys, 16 girls); Grade 12: 31 students (18 boys, 13 girls). 85% of students are Christian.

Faculty School total: 45. In upper school: 7 men, 13 women; 4 have advanced degrees.

Subjects Offered Accounting, Bible, biology, calculus, Canadian geography, Canadian history, Canadian law, careers, chemistry, civics, discrete mathematics, dramatic arts, economics, English, exercise science, family studies, French, functions, geography, geometry, health education, healthful living, ideas, information technology, instrumental music, journalism, keyboarding, literature, mathematics, media arts, organizational studies, philosophy, physical education, physics, psychology, science, sociology, visual arts, vocal music, world history, world religions, writing.

Graduation Requirements Arts, Canadian geography, Canadian history, careers, civics, English, French as a second language, mathematics, physical education (includes health), science, must complete Bible course curriculum for all grades.

College Admission Counseling 42 students graduated in 2009; 40 went to college, including McMaster University; The University of Western Ontario; University of Guelph; University of Toronto; Wilfrid Laurier University; York University. Other: 2 had other specific plans.

Student Life Upper grades have uniform requirement, student council, honor system. Discipline rests primarily with faculty. Attendance at religious services is required.

Tuition and Aid Day student tuition: CAN$8284. Tuition installment plan (monthly payment plans). Tuition reduction for siblings, bursaries, need-based scholarship grants, alumni scholarships, prepayment tuition reduction available. In 2009–10, 2% of upper-school students received aid. Total amount of financial aid awarded in 2009–10: CAN$30,000.

Admissions Traditional secondary-level entrance grade is 9. For fall 2009, 15 students applied for upper-level admission, 10 were accepted, 10 enrolled. CTBS (or similar from their school) required. Deadline for receipt of application materials: none. Application fee required: CAN$295. On-campus interview required.

Athletics Interscholastic: badminton (boys, girls), baseball (b,g), basketball (b,g), cross-country running (b,g), running (b,g), track and field (b,g), volleyball (b,g); intramural: badminton (b,g), basketball (b,g), cross-country running (b,g), floor hockey (b,g), running (b,g); coed interscholastic: badminton, baseball, basketball, cross-country running, running, swimming and diving, track and field; coed intramural: badminton, basketball, cross-country running, floor hockey, running, volleyball. 2 PE instructors, 5 coaches.

Computers Computers are regularly used in business studies, drawing and design, graphics, information technology, introduction to technology, journalism, mathematics, yearbook classes. Computer network features include Internet access, Internet filtering or blocking technology. The school has a published electronic and media policy.

Contact School Office. 416-222-3341 Ext. 146. Fax: 416-222-3344. E-mail: admissions@pca.ca. Web site: www.pca.ca.

PERKIOMEN SCHOOL

200 Seminary Street
Pennsburg, Pennsylvania 18073
Head of School: Mr. Christopher R. Tompkins

General Information Coeducational boarding and day college-preparatory school, affiliated with Schwenkfelder Church. Boarding grades 7–PG, day grades 5–PG. Founded: 1875. Setting: small town. Nearest major city is Philadelphia. Students are housed in single-sex dormitories. 165-acre campus. 23 buildings on campus. Approved or accredited by Middle States Association of Colleges and Schools, Pennsylvania Association of Independent Schools, The Association of Boarding Schools, The College Board, and Pennsylvania Department of Education. Member of National Association of Independent Schools and Secondary School Admission Test Board. Endowment: $6 million. Total enrollment: 281. Upper school average class size: 12. Upper school faculty-student ratio: 1:7. There are 180 required school days per year for Upper School students. Upper School students typically attend 5 days per week. The average school day consists of 6 hours and 25 minutes.

Upper School Student Profile Grade 9: 41 students (27 boys, 14 girls); Grade 10: 63 students (39 boys, 24 girls); Grade 11: 88 students (59 boys, 29 girls); Grade 12: 65 students (38 boys, 27 girls); Postgraduate: 1 student (1 boy). 64% of students are boarding students. 65% are state residents. 8 states are represented in upper school student body. 18% are international students. International students from China, Democratic People's Republic of Korea, Germany, Hong Kong, Spain, and Taiwan; 9 other countries represented in student body. 1% of students are members of Schwenkfelder Church.

Faculty School total: 49. In upper school: 26 men, 23 women; 31 have advanced degrees; 36 reside on campus.

Subjects Offered African history, algebra, American history, American literature, art, art history, astronomy, Bible studies, biology, calculus, ceramics, chemistry, computer graphics, computer programming, computer science, creative writing, current events, dance, developmental language skills, drama, driver education, earth science, economics, English, English literature, environmental science, ESL, ethics, European history, fine arts, French, gender issues, geography, geology, geometry, government/civics, grammar, health, history, humanities, journalism, Latin, library studies, mathematics, music, painting, philosophy, photography, physical education, physics, physics-AP, psychology, religion, science, social studies, sociology, Spanish, speech, statistics, textiles, theater, trigonometry, world history, world literature.

Graduation Requirements Arts and fine arts (art, music, dance, drama), computer studies, English, foreign language, mathematics, physical education (includes health), religion (includes Bible studies and theology), science, social studies (includes history). Community service is required.

Special Academic Programs Advanced Placement exam preparation; honors section; independent study; academic accommodation for the gifted, the musically talented, and the artistically talented; programs in English, general development for dyslexic students; ESL (36 students enrolled).

College Admission Counseling 70 students graduated in 2009; all went to college, including Bryn Mawr College; Cornell University; Haverford College; Lehigh University; Northwestern University; University of Chicago. Mean SAT critical reading: 550, mean SAT math: 600, mean SAT writing: 560.

Student Life Upper grades have uniform requirement, student council. Discipline rests primarily with faculty. Attendance at religious services is required.

Tuition and Aid Day student tuition: $22,400; 7-day tuition and room/board: $41,900. Tuition installment plan (monthly payment plans). Merit scholarship grants, need-based scholarship grants available. In 2009–10, 33% of upper-school students received aid. Total amount of financial aid awarded in 2009–10: $1,399,000.

Admissions Traditional secondary-level entrance grade is 10. For fall 2009, 392 students applied for upper-level admission, 201 were accepted, 88 enrolled. SSAT or TOEFL or SLEP required. Deadline for receipt of application materials: February 10. Application fee required: $50. Interview required.

Athletics Interscholastic: baseball (boys), basketball (b,g), field hockey (g), football (b), golf (b), lacrosse (b,g), power lifting (b), soccer (b,g), softball (g), tennis (b,g), weight lifting (b), wrestling (b); coed interscholastic: cheering, cross-country running, dance, martial arts, swimming and diving; coed intramural: dance, skateboarding. 1 PE instructor, 7 coaches, 1 athletic trainer.

Computers Computers are regularly used in all academic, art classes. Computer network features include on-campus library services, online commercial services,

Internet access, Internet filtering or blocking technology. Campus intranet, student e-mail accounts, and computer access in designated common areas are available to students. The school has a published electronic and media policy.

Contact Mrs. Stormy S. Johnson, Director of Admissions. 215-679-9511. Fax: 215-679-1146. E-mail: sjohnson@perkiomen.org. Web site: www.perkiomen.org.

THE PHELPS SCHOOL

583 Sugartown Road
Malvern, Pennsylvania 19355
Head of School: Mr. Michael J. Reardon

General Information Boys' boarding and day college-preparatory, general academic, academic support program, and ESL program school; primarily serves underachievers. Grades 7–PG. Founded: 1946. Setting: suburban. Nearest major city is Philadelphia. Students are housed in single-sex dormitories. 75-acre campus. 18 buildings on campus. Approved or accredited by Academy of Orton-Gillingham Practitioners and Educators, Middle States Association of Colleges and Schools, Pennsylvania Association of Independent Schools, The Association of Boarding Schools, and Pennsylvania Department of Education. Total enrollment: 138. Upper school average class size: 7. Upper school faculty-student ratio: 1:5.

Upper School Student Profile Grade 7: 3 students (3 boys); Grade 8: 6 students (6 boys); Grade 9: 22 students (22 boys); Grade 10: 33 students (33 boys); Grade 11: 34 students (34 boys); Grade 12: 31 students (31 boys); Postgraduate: 9 students (9 boys). 87% of students are boarding students. 39% are state residents. 16 states are represented in upper school student body. 41% are international students. International students from China, Lithuania, Republic of Korea, Spain, Sweden, and Taiwan; 14 other countries represented in student body.

Faculty School total: 28. In upper school: 20 men, 8 women; 9 have advanced degrees; 24 reside on campus.

Subjects Offered Algebra, American history, art, biology, calculus, calculus-AP, chemistry, college admission preparation, earth science, English, environmental science, ESL, fitness, general math, geometry, government, health, learning strategies, mathematics, participation in sports, photography, physical education, physical science, physics, pre-algebra, pre-calculus, psychology, reading, reading/study skills, remedial study skills, SAT preparation, scuba diving, shop, Spanish, study skills, weight training, world history, yearbook.

Graduation Requirements English, mathematics, physical education (includes health), science, social studies (includes history). Community service is required.

Special Academic Programs Advanced Placement exam preparation; independent study; academic accommodation for the gifted, the musically talented, and the artistically talented; remedial reading and/or remedial writing; remedial math; programs in English, mathematics, general development for dyslexic students; ESL (42 students enrolled).

College Admission Counseling 44 students graduated in 2010; 43 went to college, including College of Charleston; Drexel University; Lynn University; Rochester Institute of Technology; University of Oregon; University of Rochester. Other: 1 went to work.

Student Life Upper grades have specified standards of dress, student council. Discipline rests primarily with faculty.

Summer Programs Sports programs offered; session focuses on Sports; held on campus; accepts boys and girls; open to students from other schools. 20 students usually enrolled. 2011 schedule: June 10 to August 15.

Tuition and Aid Day student tuition: $21,250; 5-day tuition and room/board: $36,200; 7-day tuition and room/board: $40,200. Tuition installment plan (individually arranged payment plans). Tuition reduction for siblings, need-based scholarship grants available. In 2010–11, 36% of upper-school students received aid. Total amount of financial aid awarded in 2010–11: $1,193,650.

Admissions Traditional secondary-level entrance grade is 7. For fall 2010, 156 students applied for upper-level admission, 110 were accepted, 65 enrolled. Deadline for receipt of application materials: none. Application fee required: $50. Interview required.

Athletics Interscholastic: baseball, basketball, cross-country running, golf, lacrosse, roller hockey, soccer, street hockey, tennis; intramural: bowling, climbing, fitness, flag football, Frisbee, golf, horseback riding, in-line skating, independent competitive sports, indoor soccer, martial arts, physical fitness, rock climbing, roller blading, ropes courses, scuba diving, softball, strength & conditioning, tennis, volleyball, wall climbing, weight lifting, weight training, winter soccer. 3 PE instructors.

Computers Computers are regularly used in all classes. Computer network features include Internet access, wireless campus network, Internet filtering or blocking technology, all students are provided a laptop with the option to buy. Campus intranet, student e-mail accounts, and computer access in designated common areas are available to students. Students grades are available online. The school has a published electronic and media policy.

Contact Mrs. Julie Wells Romain, Assistant Director of Admissions. 610-644-1754. Fax: 610-644-6679. E-mail: admis@thephelpsschool.org. Web site: www.thephelpsschool.org.

PHILADELPHIA-MONTGOMERY CHRISTIAN ACADEMY

35 Hillcrest Avenue
Erdenheim, Pennsylvania 19038
Head of School: Mr. Donald B. Beebe

General Information Coeducational day college-preparatory, arts, religious studies, and bilingual studies school, affiliated with Christian faith. Grades PK–12. Founded: 1943. Setting: suburban. Nearest major city is Philadelphia. 1-acre campus. 1 building on campus. Approved or accredited by Christian Schools International and Middle States Association of Colleges and Schools. Endowment: $150,205. Total enrollment: 342. Upper school average class size: 18. Upper school faculty-student ratio: 1:10. There are 178 required school days per year for Upper School students. Upper School students typically attend 5 days per week. The average school day consists of 6 hours and 50 minutes.

Upper School Student Profile Grade 9: 23 students (14 boys, 9 girls); Grade 10: 36 students (18 boys, 18 girls); Grade 11: 40 students (22 boys, 18 girls); Grade 12: 44 students (21 boys, 23 girls). 99% of students are Christian.

Faculty School total: 35. In upper school: 11 men, 8 women; 10 have advanced degrees.

Subjects Offered Algebra, American history, American literature, art, art history, biology, calculus, ceramics, chemistry, creative writing, drama, English, English literature, ethics, European history, fine arts, geography, geometry, German, government/civics, grammar, health, history, mathematics, music, physical education, physics, religion, science, social studies, sociology, Spanish, theater, trigonometry, typing, world history, writing.

Graduation Requirements Arts and fine arts (art, music, dance, drama), Bible, English, mathematics, physical education (includes health), science, social studies (includes history).

Special Academic Programs 3 Advanced Placement exams for which test preparation is offered; honors section; academic accommodation for the gifted, the musically talented, and the artistically talented.

College Admission Counseling 37 students graduated in 2009; 36 went to college, including Covenant College; Grove City College; Penn State University Park; Saint Joseph's University; Temple University; University of Pittsburgh. Other: 1 went to work. Mean SAT critical reading: 548, mean SAT math: 562, mean SAT writing: 538. 34% scored over 600 on SAT critical reading, 34% scored over 600 on SAT math, 26% scored over 600 on SAT writing.

Student Life Upper grades have uniform requirement, student council. Discipline rests primarily with faculty. Attendance at religious services is required.

Tuition and Aid Day student tuition: $10,995. Tuition installment plan (FACTS Tuition Payment Plan). Tuition reduction for siblings, need-based scholarship grants available.

Admissions Traditional secondary-level entrance grade is 9. For fall 2009, 28 students applied for upper-level admission, 17 were accepted, 15 enrolled. Iowa Tests of Basic Skills required. Deadline for receipt of application materials: February 6. Application fee required: $100. On-campus interview required.

Athletics Interscholastic: baseball (boys), basketball (b,g), soccer (b,g), softball (g), tennis (b,g), track and field (b,g), wrestling (b); coed interscholastic: cross-country running. 2 PE instructors.

Computers Computers are regularly used in art, English, mathematics classes. Computer resources include on-campus library services, Internet access, Internet filtering or blocking technology, online college search. The school has a published electronic and media policy.

Contact Mrs. Peggy Oliphint, Director of Admissions and Marketing. 215-233-0782 Ext. 408. Fax: 215-233-0829. E-mail: admissions@phil-mont.com. Web site: www.phil-mont.com.

PHILLIPS ACADEMY (ANDOVER)

180 Main Street
Andover, Massachusetts 01810-4161
Head of School: Barbara L. Chase

General Information Coeducational boarding and day college-preparatory school. Grades 9–PG. Founded: 1778. Setting: suburban. Nearest major city is Boston. Students are housed in single-sex dormitories and 9th graders housed separately from other students. 500-acre campus. 160 buildings on campus. Approved or accredited by New England Association of Schools and Colleges and The Association of Boarding Schools. Member of National Association of Independent Schools and Secondary School Admission Test Board. Endowment: $695 million. Total enrollment: 1,109. Upper school average class size: 13. Upper school faculty-student ratio: 1:5. There are 157 required school days per year for Upper School students. Upper School students typically attend 5 days per week. The average school day consists of 8 hours.

Upper School Student Profile Grade 9: 203 students (103 boys, 100 girls); Grade 10: 290 students (142 boys, 148 girls); Grade 11: 282 students (137 boys, 145 girls); Grade 12: 315 students (155 boys, 160 girls); Postgraduate: 19 students (16 boys, 3 girls). 74% of students are boarding students. 42% are state residents. 44 states are represented in upper school student body. 9% are international students. International students from Canada, China, Hong Kong, Republic of Korea, Thailand, and United Kingdom; 31 other countries represented in student body.

Faculty School total: 206. In upper school: 106 men, 100 women; 147 have advanced degrees; 190 reside on campus.

Subjects Offered Algebra, American history, American literature, ancient history, animal behavior, animation, Arabic, Arabic studies, architecture, art, art history, astronomy, band, Bible studies, biology, calculus, ceramics, chamber groups, chemistry, Chinese, chorus, computer graphics, computer programming, computer science, creative writing, dance, drama, driver education, ecology, economics, English, English literature, environmental science, ethics, European history, expository writing, film, fine arts, French, geology, geometry, German, government/civics, grammar, Greek, health, history, international relations, Japanese, jazz, Latin, Latin American studies, life issues, literature, mathematics, Middle Eastern history, music, mythology, oceanography, painting, philosophy, photography, physical education, physics, physiology, printmaking, psychology, religion, Russian, Russian studies, science, sculpture, social sciences, social studies, sociology, Spanish, speech, swimming, theater, trigonometry, video, world history, writing.

Graduation Requirements Arts and fine arts (art, music, dance, drama), English, foreign language, history, life issues, mathematics, philosophy, physical education (includes health), religion (includes Bible studies and theology), science, social sciences, swimming test.

Special Academic Programs Advanced Placement exam preparation; honors section; independent study; term-away projects; study abroad; academic accommodation for the gifted, the musically talented, and the artistically talented; programs in English, mathematics, general development for dyslexic students; special instructional classes for deaf students, blind students.

College Admission Counseling 293 students graduated in 2010; 282 went to college, including Brown University; Dartmouth College; Harvard University; Stanford University; University of Pennsylvania; Yale University. Other: 11 had other specific plans. Mean SAT critical reading: 683, mean SAT math: 694, mean SAT writing: 677.

Student Life Upper grades have student council, honor system. Discipline rests primarily with faculty.

Summer Programs Remediation, enrichment, advancement, ESL, art/fine arts, computer instruction programs offered; session focuses on academics; held both on and off campus; held at Colorado; accepts boys and girls; open to students from other schools. 550 students usually enrolled. 2011 schedule: June 28 to August 3. Application deadline: none.

Tuition and Aid Day student tuition: $32,200; 7-day tuition and room/board: $41,300. Tuition installment plan (individually arranged payment plans, The Andover Plan). Need-based scholarship grants, middle-income loans available. In 2010–11, 45% of upper-school students received aid. Total amount of financial aid awarded in 2010–11: $16,412,000.

Admissions For fall 2010, 2,910 students applied for upper-level admission, 414 were accepted, 323 enrolled. ISEE or SSAT required. Deadline for receipt of application materials: February 1. Application fee required: $30. Interview required.

Athletics Interscholastic: baseball (boys), basketball (b,g), bicycling (b,g), crew (b,g), cross-country running (b,g), diving (b,g), field hockey (g), football (b), golf (b,g), ice hockey (b,g), indoor track & field (b,g), lacrosse (b,g), nordic skiing (b,g), skiing (cross-country) (b,g), soccer (b,g), softball (g), squash (b,g), swimming and diving (b,g), tennis (b,g), track and field (b,g), volleyball (b,g), water polo (b,g), winter (indoor) track (b,g), wrestling (b); intramural: aerobics/dance (b,g), backpacking (b,g), basketball (b,g), crew (b,g), martial arts (b,g), physical fitness (b,g), physical training (b,g); coed interscholastic: bicycling, Frisbee, golf, ultimate Frisbee, wrestling; coed intramural: badminton, ballet, canoeing/kayaking, cheering, cross-country running, dance, fencing, fitness, fitness walking, hiking/backpacking, martial arts, modern dance, outdoor adventure, outdoor education, physical fitness, physical training, rappelling, rock climbing, ropes courses, soccer, softball, strength & conditioning, tennis, wall climbing. 7 PE instructors, 25 coaches, 3 athletic trainers.

Computers Computers are regularly used in animation, architecture, art, classics, computer applications, digital applications, English, foreign language, history, mathematics, music, photography, psychology, religious studies, science, theater, video film production classes. Computer network features include on-campus library services, online commercial services, Internet access, wireless campus network. Campus intranet and student e-mail accounts are available to students. The school has a published electronic and media policy.

Contact Jane F. Fried, Dean of Admission. 978-749-4050. Fax: 978-749-4068. E-mail: admissions@andover.edu. Web site: www.andover.edu.

PHOENIX CHRISTIAN UNIFIED SCHOOLS

1751 West Indian School Road
Phoenix, Arizona 85015
Head of School: Mr. James H. Koan II

General Information Coeducational day college-preparatory, general academic, religious studies, and AP/Honors school, affiliated with Christian faith. Grades PS–12. Founded: 1949. Setting: suburban. 12-acre campus. 10 buildings on campus. Approved or accredited by Association of Christian Schools International, North Central Association of Colleges and Schools, and Arizona Department of Education. Total enrollment: 476. Upper school average class size: 20. Upper school faculty-student ratio: 1:20. There are 180 required school days per year for Upper School students. Upper School students typically attend 5 days per week. The average school day consists of 6 hours and 40 minutes.

Upper School Student Profile Grade 6: 17 students (10 boys, 7 girls); Grade 7: 35 students (13 boys, 22 girls); Grade 8: 40 students (19 boys, 21 girls); Grade 9: 61 students (31 boys, 30 girls); Grade 10: 39 students (21 boys, 18 girls); Grade 11: 57 students (30 boys, 27 girls); Grade 12: 64 students (31 boys, 33 girls).

Faculty School total: 43. In upper school: 12 men, 14 women.

Subjects Offered Advanced computer applications, algebra, American literature, American literature-AP, anatomy, art, arts, band, Bible, biology, biology-AP, calculus, calculus-AP, career and personal planning, chemistry, choir, choral music, computer applications, computers, creative writing, culinary arts, drama, drama performance, drawing, economics, English, English literature, English literature-AP, English-AP, geometry, government, government-AP, home economics, instrumental music, integrated science, internship, intro to computers, language-AP, library, literature, literature-AP, marching band, photography, physical education, physics, pre-algebra, pre-calculus, psychology, religious education, sociology, Spanish, Spanish language-AP, statistics, student government, study skills, U.S. government, U.S. history, U.S. history-AP, Web site design, world history, yearbook.

Graduation Requirements Advanced math, Advanced Placement courses, algebra, American literature, arts and fine arts (art, music, dance, drama), biology, British literature, chemistry, computer education, economics, English, English composition, English literature, foreign language, geometry, government, integrated science, pre-calculus, religious studies, study skills, U.S. history, world history, world literature.

Special Academic Programs Advanced Placement exam preparation; honors section; independent study; study at local college for college credit; ESL (12 students enrolled).

College Admission Counseling 58 students graduated in 2010; 49 went to college, including Arizona State University; Glendale Community College; Grand Canyon University; Northern Arizona University; The University of Arizona. Other: 1 entered military service, 4 entered a postgraduate year, 1 had other specific plans. Mean SAT critical reading: 544, mean SAT math: 544, mean SAT writing: 532.

Student Life Upper grades have uniform requirement, student council. Discipline rests primarily with faculty. Attendance at religious services is required.

Tuition and Aid Day student tuition: $8560. Tuition installment plan (monthly payment plans, individually arranged payment plans). Tuition reduction for siblings, need-based scholarship grants available.

Admissions Traditional secondary-level entrance grade is 9. Achievement tests or any standardized test required. Deadline for receipt of application materials: none. Application fee required: $200. Interview required.

Athletics Interscholastic: baseball (boys), basketball (b,g), cheering (g), drill team (g), football (b), softball (g), volleyball (g), wrestling (b); coed interscholastic: cross-country running, diving, golf, soccer, swimming and diving, tennis, track and field, weight lifting, weight training. 24 coaches.

Computers Computers are regularly used in career exploration, college planning, computer applications, keyboarding, library, media services, Web site design, yearbook classes. Computer resources include on-campus library services, Internet access, Internet filtering or blocking technology. Campus intranet and computer access in designated common areas are available to students. Students grades are available online. The school has a published electronic and media policy.

Contact Mrs. Nancy L. Smith, Student Recruitment Coordinator. 602-265-4707 Ext. 221. Fax: 602-277-7170. E-mail: nsmith@phoenixchristian.org. Web site: www.phoenixchristian.org.

PHOENIX COUNTRY DAY SCHOOL

3901 East Stanford Drive
Paradise Valley, Arizona 85253

Head of School: Dr. Lee Pierson

General Information Coeducational day college-preparatory, arts, performing and studio arts and extensive athletics, and community service and international travel school. Grades PK–12. Founded: 1961. Setting: suburban. Nearest major city is Phoenix. 40-acre campus. 8 buildings on campus. Approved or accredited by Independent Schools Association of the Southwest, National Independent Private Schools Association, and North Central Association of Colleges and Schools. Member of National Association of Independent Schools. Endowment: $13.3 million. Total enrollment: 681. Upper school average class size: 15. Upper school faculty-student ratio: 1:9. There are 178 required school days per year for Upper School students. Upper School students typically attend 5 days per week. The average school day consists of 7 hours.

Upper School Student Profile Grade 9: 57 students (23 boys, 34 girls); Grade 10: 67 students (26 boys, 41 girls); Grade 11: 61 students (29 boys, 32 girls); Grade 12: 57 students (29 boys, 28 girls).

Faculty School total: 89. In upper school: 18 men, 16 women; 21 have advanced degrees.

Subjects Offered Acting, advanced biology, advanced chemistry, advanced math, Advanced Placement courses, African-American literature, algebra, American government, American history, American history-AP, American literature, anatomy, anatomy and physiology, anthropology, art, art history, art history-AP, astronomy, band, baseball, basketball, biology, biology-AP, British literature, calculus, calculus-AP, ceramics, chemistry, chemistry-AP, Chinese, Chinese studies, choir, chorus, computer programming, computer science, creative writing, digital photography, directing, discrete mathematics, drawing, ecology, English, English compo-

sition, English literature, environmental science, environmental science-AP, ethics, European history, evolution, fine arts, French, French-AP, geography, geology, geometry, government/civics, history, Holocaust studies, jazz band, journalism, Latin, Latin American literature, Latin-AP, literature, Mandarin, marine biology, mathematics, music, oceanography, orchestra, painting, photography, physical education, physics, physics-AP, physiology, pre-calculus, probability and statistics, psychology, scene study, science, Shakespeare, social sciences, social studies, Spanish, Spanish-AP, speech, statistics, statistics-AP, theater, theater arts, trigonometry, world history, world literature, world religions.

Graduation Requirements Advanced biology, American history, American literature, ancient world history, arts and fine arts (art, music, dance, drama), biology, chemistry, English, foreign language, mathematics, physical education (includes health), physics, science, U.S. history, Western civilization, world history, 40 hours of community service.

Special Academic Programs 15 Advanced Placement exams for which test preparation is offered; honors section; independent study; study abroad.

College Admission Counseling 63 students graduated in 2010; all went to college, including Duke University; Northwestern University; The University of Arizona; Tulane University; University of Southern California; Vanderbilt University. Median SAT critical reading: 670, median SAT math: 660, median SAT writing: 680, median combined SAT: 2000, median composite ACT: 28. 88% scored over 600 on SAT critical reading, 85% scored over 600 on SAT math, 83% scored over 600 on SAT writing, 86% scored over 1800 on combined SAT, 76% scored over 26 on composite ACT.

Student Life Upper grades have specified standards of dress, student council, honor system. Discipline rests primarily with faculty.

Summer Programs Enrichment, advancement, sports, art/fine arts, computer instruction programs offered; session focuses on academics/sports camp/arts program; held on campus; accepts boys and girls; open to students from other schools. 450 students usually enrolled. 2011 schedule: June 6 to July 15. Application deadline: none.

Tuition and Aid Day student tuition: $21,800. Tuition installment plan (Insured Tuition Payment Plan, monthly payment plans, individually arranged payment plans, 10 months, quarterly, semiannual, and yearly payment plans). Need-based scholarship grants available. In 2010–11, 21% of upper-school students received aid. Total amount of financial aid awarded in 2010–11: $1,707,800.

Admissions Traditional secondary-level entrance grade is 9. For fall 2010, 63 students applied for upper-level admission, 44 were accepted, 28 enrolled. Achievement/Aptitude/Writing, ERB CTP IV, Math Placement Exam, Otis-Lennon IQ and writing sample required. Deadline for receipt of application materials: March 1. Application fee required: $100. Interview required.

Athletics Interscholastic: baseball (boys), basketball (b,g), cheering (g), diving (b,g), flag football (b), golf (b,g), lacrosse (b,g), soccer (b,g), softball (g), winter soccer (g); intramural: archery (b,g), badminton (b,g), basketball (b,g), lacrosse (b,g), outdoor education (b,g), outdoor recreation (b,g), physical fitness (b,g), softball (g), strength & conditioning (b,g), yoga (b,g); coed interscholastic: cheering, diving, swimming and diving, tennis, volleyball; coed intramural: basketball, cross-country running, flag football, golf, running, soccer, swimming and diving, tennis, volleyball, winter soccer. 5 PE instructors, 20 coaches, 1 athletic trainer.

Computers Computers are regularly used in art, college planning, creative writing, data processing, desktop publishing, economics, engineering, English, foreign language, French, history, humanities, independent study, information technology, keyboarding, library, library skills, literary magazine, mathematics, news writing, newspaper, photography, programming, publications, research skills, science, social sciences, social studies, Spanish, stock market, Web site design, writing, yearbook classes. Computer network features include on-campus library services, online commercial services, Internet access, wireless campus network, Internet filtering or blocking technology. Campus intranet, student e-mail accounts, and computer access in designated common areas are available to students. Students grades are available online. The school has a published electronic and media policy.

Contact Sandy Orrick, Admissions Assistant. 602-955-8200 Ext. 2255. Fax: 602-381-4554. E-mail: sandy.orrick@pcds.org. Web site: www.pcds.org.

PICKENS ACADEMY

225 Ray Bass Road
Carrollton, Alabama 35447

Head of School: Mr. Brach White

General Information Coeducational day college-preparatory and general academic school. Grades K4–12. Founded: 1970. Setting: rural. Nearest major city is Tuscaloosa. 3 buildings on campus. Approved or accredited by Distance Education and Training Council, Southern Association of Colleges and Schools, and Alabama Department of Education. Total enrollment: 309. Upper school average class size: 25. Upper school faculty-student ratio: 1:20. There are 180 required school days per year for Upper School students. Upper School students typically attend 5 days per week. The average school day consists of 7 hours.

Upper School Student Profile Grade 7: 17 students (7 boys, 10 girls); Grade 8: 24 students (13 boys, 11 girls); Grade 9: 15 students (8 boys, 7 girls); Grade 10: 32 students (14 boys, 18 girls); Grade 11: 18 students (10 boys, 8 girls); Grade 12: 24 students (15 boys, 9 girls).

Faculty School total: 21. In upper school: 5 men, 16 women; 8 have advanced degrees.

Subjects Offered 20th century history, 20th century world history, advanced chemistry, advanced computer applications, advanced math, Alabama history and geography, algebra, American democracy, American government, American history, American literature, anatomy and physiology, ancient history, ancient world history, applied music, art, band, baseball, basketball, biology, British literature, business mathematics, calculus, career/college preparation, cheerleading, chemistry, civics, college admission preparation, composition, computer literacy, consumer economics, CPR, creative writing, desktop publishing, economics, English composition, English literature, environmental science, family and consumer science, French, geography, government, grammar, health education, history, keyboarding, land management, leadership education training, library assistant, Microsoft, music, music appreciation, physical education, physical science, physics, research skills, science, student government, trigonometry, U.S. government and politics, Web site design, weight training, weightlifting.

Graduation Requirements 20th century world history, advanced math, American government, American history, anatomy and physiology, calculus, economics, English, English composition, English literature, physics, research skills, trigonometry.

Special Academic Programs Honors section; study at local college for college credit.

College Admission Counseling 25 students graduated in 2010; 24 went to college, including Auburn University; The University of Alabama. Other: 1 went to work. Mean composite ACT: 21. 8% scored over 26 on composite ACT.

Student Life Upper grades have specified standards of dress, student council. Discipline rests primarily with faculty.

Tuition and Aid Day student tuition: $3000. Guaranteed tuition plan. Tuition installment plan (Insured Tuition Payment Plan, monthly payment plans).

Admissions Traditional secondary-level entrance grade is 9. PSAT or Stanford Achievement Test, Otis-Lennon School Ability Test required. Deadline for receipt of application materials: none. No application fee required. On-campus interview required.

Athletics Interscholastic: baseball (boys), basketball (b,g), cheering (g), cross-country running (b,g), danceline (g), football (b), golf (b,g), softball (g), volleyball (g), weight lifting (b,g); coed interscholastic: tennis, track and field. 1 PE instructor, 2 coaches.

Computers Computers are regularly used in all academic classes. Computer network features include on-campus library services, Internet access, Internet filtering or blocking technology. Student e-mail accounts are available to students. The school has a published electronic and media policy.

Contact Admissions. 205-367-8144. Fax: 205-367-8145. Web site: www.pickensacademy.com.

PICKERING COLLEGE
16945 Bayview Avenue
Newmarket, Ontario L3Y 4X2, Canada
Head of School: Mr. Peter C. Sturrup

General Information Coeducational boarding and day college-preparatory, arts, technology, film studies and radio station, and leadership school. Boarding grades 7–12, day grades JK–12. Founded: 1842. Setting: suburban. Nearest major city is Toronto, Canada. Students are housed in single-sex dormitories. 42-acre campus. 6 buildings on campus. Approved or accredited by Canadian Association of Independent Schools, Canadian Educational Standards Institute, National Independent Private Schools Association, Ontario Ministry of Education, The Association of Boarding Schools, and Ontario Department of Education. Affiliate member of National Association of Independent Schools. Language of instruction: English. Total enrollment: 400. Upper school average class size: 18. Upper school faculty-student ratio: 1:9. There are 164 required school days per year for Upper School students. Upper School students typically attend 5 days per week. The average school day consists of 8 hours.

Upper School Student Profile Grade 6: 26 students (12 boys, 14 girls); Grade 7: 22 students (9 boys, 13 girls); Grade 8: 35 students (22 boys, 13 girls); Grade 9: 49 students (28 boys, 21 girls); Grade 10: 51 students (24 boys, 27 girls); Grade 11: 60 students (32 boys, 28 girls); Grade 12: 69 students (31 boys, 38 girls). 40% of students are boarding students. 60% are province residents. 3 provinces are represented in upper school student body. 40% are international students. International students from Barbados, China, Germany, Mexico, Republic of Korea, and Spain; 14 other countries represented in student body.

Faculty School total: 42. In upper school: 17 men, 12 women; 7 have advanced degrees; 10 reside on campus.

Subjects Offered Algebra, art, art history, biology, business, business skills, business studies, calculus, Canadian geography, Canadian history, careers, chemistry, community service, computer applications, computer multimedia, computer programming, computer science, concert band, creative writing, drama, dramatic arts, economics, English, English composition, English literature, entrepreneurship, environmental science, ESL, experiential education, family studies, filmmaking, fine arts, finite math, French, geography, geometry, government/civics, guitar, health, health education, history, instrumental music, jazz band, law, leadership, literature, mathematics, media studies, music, physical education, physics, politics, science, social sciences, social studies, Spanish, theater, video film production, visual arts, vocal music, world history.

Graduation Requirements English, 60 hours of community service completed over 4 years before graduation.

Special Academic Programs Independent study; ESL (31 students enrolled).

College Admission Counseling 69 students graduated in 2010; 62 went to college, including Carleton University; McMaster University; Queen's University at Kingston; The University of Western Ontario; University of Toronto; Wilfrid Laurier University. Other: 1 went to work, 1 entered military service, 4 had other specific plans.

Student Life Upper grades have uniform requirement, student council, honor system. Discipline rests equally with students and faculty.

Summer Programs Remediation, advancement, ESL programs offered; session focuses on on-line math; held both on and off campus; held at via distance learning; accepts boys and girls; open to students from other schools. 30 students usually enrolled. 2011 schedule: June 26 to August 23. Application deadline: May.

Tuition and Aid Day student tuition: CAN$17,810–CAN$21,725; 7-day tuition and room/board: CAN$42,400–CAN$42,700. Tuition installment plan (Insured Tuition Payment Plan, monthly payment plans). Tuition reduction for siblings, bursaries, merit scholarship grants, need-based scholarship grants available. In 2010–11, 1% of upper-school students received aid.

Admissions Traditional secondary-level entrance grade is 9. For fall 2010, 92 students applied for upper-level admission, 61 enrolled. SSAT, ERB, PSAT, SAT, PLAN or ACT or TOEFL required. Deadline for receipt of application materials: none. Application fee required: CAN$200. Interview required.

Athletics Interscholastic: badminton (boys), basketball (b,g), cross-country running (b,g), figure skating (g), hockey (b,g), horseback riding (b,g), ice hockey (b), ice skating (b,g), mountain biking (b), skiing (downhill) (b,g), snowboarding (b,g), softball (b,g), swimming and diving (b,g), tennis (b,g), track and field (b,g), volleyball (b,g); intramural: badminton (b,g), ball hockey (b,g), basketball (b,g), combined training (b,g), floor hockey (b,g), hockey (b,g), horseback riding (b,g), ice hockey (b), ice skating (b,g), mountain biking (b,g), outdoor activities (b,g), outdoor adventure (b,g), outdoor recreation (b,g), paddle tennis (b,g), physical training (b,g), rock climbing (b,g), running (b,g), skiing (downhill) (b,g), strength & conditioning (b,g), swimming and diving (b,g), tennis (b,g), track and field (b,g), volleyball (b,g); coed interscholastic: alpine skiing, aquatics, bicycling, cross-country running, equestrian sports, hockey, horseback riding, ice hockey, ice skating, skiing (downhill), snowboarding, swimming and diving, tennis, track and field, volleyball; coed intramural: ball hockey, bowling, cross-country running, dance squad, equestrian sports, figure skating, floor hockey, Frisbee, golf, hockey, horseback riding, ice hockey, ice skating, mountain biking, outdoor adventure, skiing (downhill), strength & conditioning, swimming and diving, tennis, track and field, volleyball. 3 PE instructors, 2 coaches, 1 athletic trainer.

Computers Computers are regularly used in all classes. Computer network features include on-campus library services, Internet access, wireless campus network, Internet filtering or blocking technology. Student e-mail accounts are available to students. Students grades are available online. The school has a published electronic and media policy.

Contact Ms. Susan Hundert, Admission Administrator. 905-895-1700 Ext. 259. Fax: 905-895-1306. E-mail: admission@pickeringcollege.on.ca. Web site: www.pickeringcollege.on.ca.

PIC RIVER PRIVATE HIGH SCHOOL
21 Rabbit Drive
PO Box 217
Heron Bay, Ontario P0T 1R0, Canada
Head of School: Mrs. Lisa Michano-Courchene

General Information Coeducational day college-preparatory school. Grades K–12. Founded: 1993. Setting: rural. 2-acre campus. 1 building on campus. Approved or accredited by Ontario Department of Education. Language of instruction: English. Upper school faculty-student ratio: 1:10. There are 194 required school days per year for Upper School students. Upper School students typically attend 5 days per week. The average school day consists of 3 hours.

Faculty School total: 1. In upper school: 1 man.

Student Life Discipline rests primarily with faculty.

Admissions No application fee required.

Computers Computer network features include on-campus library services, Internet access, Internet filtering or blocking technology. Campus intranet and student e-mail accounts are available to students.

Contact Mr. Douglas Leslie Vollett, Teacher. 807-229-3726. Fax: 807-229-3727. E-mail: dvollett@picriver.com.

PIEDMONT ACADEMY

PO Box 231
126 Highway 212 West
Monticello, Georgia 31064
Head of School: Mr. Tony Tanner

General Information Coeducational day college-preparatory, arts, business, vocational, religious studies, bilingual studies, technology, and dual enrollment with Georgia Military College school, affiliated with Protestant faith. Grades PK–12. Founded: 1970. Setting: small town. Nearest major city is Atlanta. 25-acre campus. 8 buildings on campus. Approved or accredited by Georgia Accrediting Commission and Georgia Independent School Association. Total enrollment: 314. Upper school average class size: 17. Upper school faculty-student ratio: 1:13. There are 180 required school days per year for Upper School students. Upper School students typically attend 5 days per week. The average school day consists of 7 hours.
Upper School Student Profile Grade 6: 29 students (16 boys, 13 girls); Grade 7: 23 students (15 boys, 8 girls); Grade 8: 28 students (18 boys, 10 girls); Grade 9: 33 students (11 boys, 22 girls); Grade 10: 18 students (4 boys, 14 girls); Grade 11: 18 students (14 boys, 4 girls); Grade 12: 26 students (14 boys, 12 girls). 98% of students are Protestant.
Faculty School total: 31. In upper school: 6 men, 15 women; 15 have advanced degrees.
Subjects Offered Advanced chemistry, advanced computer applications, advanced math, algebra, American government, American history, American history-AP, anatomy and physiology, band, biology, business law, calculus, calculus-AP, chemistry, chemistry-AP, civics, computer science, computer science-AP, computers, concert band, concert choir, consumer economics, consumer law, economics, English, English-AP, geometry, government and politics-AP, government-AP, government/civics, grammar, health education, honors algebra, honors English, honors geometry, Internet, intro to computers, keyboarding, language arts, leadership and service, literature, mathematics, performing arts, personal finance, physical fitness, physical science, physics, pre-calculus, science, sociology, Spanish, student government, wind instruments, world history, yearbook.
Graduation Requirements Algebra, American government, American literature, biology, calculus, chemistry, civics, English composition, English literature, geometry, government, grammar, history, keyboarding, mathematics, physical education (includes health), physical science, science, Spanish.
Special Academic Programs Study at local college for college credit.
College Admission Counseling 25 students graduated in 2010; all went to college, including Georgia Perimeter College; North Georgia College & State University; University of Georgia.
Student Life Upper grades have uniform requirement, student council, honor system. Discipline rests primarily with faculty.
Summer Programs Sports, art/fine arts, rigorous outdoor training programs offered; session focuses on preparation for school year competition; held on campus; accepts boys and girls; open to students from other schools. 130 students usually enrolled. 2011 schedule: June 1 to August 2.
Tuition and Aid Day student tuition: $6000. Guaranteed tuition plan. Tuition installment plan (monthly payment plans, individually arranged payment plans). Tuition reduction for siblings, need-based scholarship grants available. In 2010–11, 10% of upper-school students received aid. Total amount of financial aid awarded in 2010–11: $25,000.
Admissions For fall 2010, 45 students applied for upper-level admission, 37 were accepted, 37 enrolled. OLSAT, Stanford Achievement Test required. Deadline for receipt of application materials: February 1. Application fee required: $75. Interview required.
Athletics Interscholastic: baseball (boys), basketball (b,g), cheering (b,g), fitness (b,g), flag football (b,g), football (b), golf (b,g), power lifting (b,g), soccer (b,g), softball (g), strength & conditioning (b,g), tennis (b,g), weight lifting (b,g), weight training (b,g), wrestling (b,g); coed interscholastic: track and field; coed intramural: flag football. 6 PE instructors, 10 coaches.
Computers Computers are regularly used in all academic classes. Computer network features include on-campus library services, online commercial services, Internet access, wireless campus network, Internet filtering or blocking technology. Campus intranet is available to students. Students grades are available online. The school has a published electronic and media policy.
Contact Judy M. Nelson, Director of Admissions/Public and Alumni Relations. 706-468-8818 Ext. 19. Fax: 706-468-2409. E-mail: judy_nelson@piedmontacademy.com. Web site: www.piedmontacademy.com.

PINECREST ACADEMY

955 Peachtree Parkway
Cumming, Georgia 30041
Head of School: Dr. John H. Tarpley

General Information Coeducational day college-preparatory and technology school, affiliated with Roman Catholic Church. Grades PK–12. Founded: 1993. Setting: suburban. Nearest major city is Atlanta. 70-acre campus. 4 buildings on campus. Approved or accredited by Georgia Accrediting Commission, Georgia Independent School Association, National Catholic Education Association, Southern Association of Colleges and Schools, and Georgia Department of Education. Total

enrollment: 892. Upper school average class size: 20. Upper school faculty-student ratio: 1:8. There are 180 required school days per year for Upper School students. Upper School students typically attend 5 days per week. The average school day consists of 7 hours and 30 minutes.
Upper School Student Profile Grade 6: 72 students (35 boys, 37 girls); Grade 7: 78 students (32 boys, 46 girls); Grade 8: 59 students (29 boys, 30 girls); Grade 9: 52 students (28 boys, 24 girls); Grade 10: 59 students (24 boys, 35 girls); Grade 11: 45 students (17 boys, 28 girls); Grade 12: 52 students (24 boys, 28 girls). 88% of students are Roman Catholic.
Faculty School total: 40. In upper school: 15 men, 25 women; 30 have advanced degrees.
Subjects Offered Advanced Placement courses.
Special Academic Programs 10 Advanced Placement exams for which test preparation is offered.
College Admission Counseling 33 students graduated in 2010; 24 went to college, including Emory University; Georgia Institute of Technology; University of Georgia. Other: 9 entered a postgraduate year.
Student Life Upper grades have uniform requirement, student council, honor system. Discipline rests primarily with faculty. Attendance at religious services is required.
Tuition and Aid Tuition reduction for siblings, need-based scholarship grants available.
Admissions Traditional secondary-level entrance grade is 9. Admissions testing, English for Non-native Speakers, PSAT, SLEP for foreign students, SSAT or TOEFL required. Deadline for receipt of application materials: none. Application fee required: $150. Interview required.
Athletics Interscholastic: baseball (boys), basketball (b,g), cheering (g), cross-country running (b,g), equestrian sports (g), football (b), soccer (b,g), softball (g), swimming and diving (b,g); intramural: baseball (b), basketball (b,g), cross-country running (b,g), dance squad (g), football (b), running (b,g), soccer (b,g), softball (b,g). 3 PE instructors, 13 coaches.
Computers Computer resources include on-campus library services, online commercial services, Internet access, wireless campus network, Internet filtering or blocking technology. Campus intranet and computer access in designated common areas are available to students. Students grades are available online. The school has a published electronic and media policy.
Contact Mrs. Jill Lagomasino, Admissions. 770-888-4477 Ext. 216. Fax: 770-886-5584. E-mail: jlagomasino@pinecrestacademy.org. Web site: http://www.pinecrestacademy.org/.

PINE CREST SCHOOL

1501 Northeast 62nd Street
Fort Lauderdale, Florida 33334-5116
Head of School: Dr. Lourdes Cowgill

General Information Coeducational day college-preparatory school. Grades PK–12, Founded: 1934. Setting: urban. 49-acre campus. 22 buildings on campus. Approved or accredited by Florida Council of Independent Schools, Southern Association of Colleges and Schools, and Southern Association of Independent Schools. Member of National Association of Independent Schools and Secondary School Admission Test Board. Endowment: $36.2 million. Total enrollment: 1,691. Upper school average class size: 17. Upper school faculty-student ratio: 1:10.
Upper School Student Profile Grade 9: 199 students (113 boys, 86 girls); Grade 10: 180 students (92 boys, 88 girls); Grade 11: 208 students (103 boys, 105 girls); Grade 12: 208 students (102 boys, 106 girls).
Faculty School total: 123. In upper school: 29 men, 45 women; 45 have advanced degrees.
Subjects Offered Algebra, American history, art, art history, ballet, band, biology, calculus, ceramics, chemistry, Chinese, chorus, comparative government and politics-AP, computer graphics, computer programming, computer science, dance, drama, economics, English, environmental science, ethics, European history, fine arts, forensics, French, geometry, German, government/civics, history, mathematics, music, orchestra, photography, physical education, physics, psychology, Spanish, speech, statistics.
Graduation Requirements Arts and fine arts (art, music, dance, drama), English, ethics, foreign language, humanities, mathematics, physical education (includes health), science, social studies (includes history), speech.
Special Academic Programs Advanced Placement exam preparation; honors section.
College Admission Counseling 196 students graduated in 2010; all went to college, including Florida State University; Harvard University; University of Florida; University of Miami; University of Pennsylvania; Vanderbilt University. Mean SAT critical reading: 640, mean SAT math: 659, mean SAT writing: 651, mean composite ACT: 29.
Student Life Upper grades have uniform requirement, student council, honor system. Discipline rests primarily with faculty.
Summer Programs Enrichment, advancement, sports programs offered; session focuses on competitive swimming, dance, summer school (grades 9-12); held on campus; accepts boys and girls; open to students from other schools. 300 students usually enrolled. 2011 schedule: June 7 to July 30. Application deadline: none.

Pine Crest School

Tuition and Aid Day student tuition: $22,650. Tuition installment plan (The Tuition Refund Plan). Need-based scholarship grants available. In 2010–11, 19% of upper-school students received aid. Total amount of financial aid awarded in 2010–11: $1,893,657.

Admissions Traditional secondary-level entrance grade is 9. For fall 2010, 158 students applied for upper-level admission, 106 were accepted, 69 enrolled. SSAT required. Deadline for receipt of application materials: none. Application fee required: $100. Interview required.

Athletics Interscholastic: aquatics (boys, girls), baseball (b), basketball (b,g), crew (b,g), cross-country running (b,g), diving (b,g), football (b), golf (b,g), lacrosse (b,g), physical fitness (b,g), soccer (b,g), softball (g), strength & conditioning (b,g), swimming and diving (b,g), tennis (b,g), track and field (b,g), volleyball (b,g), weight lifting (b,g); intramural: aquatics (b,g), swimming and diving (b,g); coed interscholastic: ballet, cheering; coed intramural: ballet, physical training, strength & conditioning. 8 PE instructors, 1 athletic trainer.

Computers Computer network features include on-campus library services, Internet access, wireless campus network, laptop program (grades 6-12), SmartBoards in classrooms.

Contact Mrs. Elena Del Alamo, Vice President for Admission. 954-492-4103. Fax: 954-492-4188. E-mail: pcadmit@pinecrest.edu. Web site: www.pinecrest.edu.

PINEHURST SCHOOL

St. Catharines, Ontario, Canada
See Special Needs Schools section.

PINEWOOD PREPARATORY SCHOOL

1114 Orangeburg Road
Summerville, South Carolina 29483
Head of School: Dr. Glyn Cowlishaw

General Information Coeducational day college-preparatory and arts school. Grades PS–12. Founded: 1952. Setting: suburban. 43-acre campus. 9 buildings on campus. Approved or accredited by South Carolina Independent School Association, Southern Association of Colleges and Schools, Southern Association of Independent Schools, and South Carolina Department of Education. Endowment: $1 million. Total enrollment: 784. Upper school average class size: 15. Upper school faculty-student ratio: 1:11. There are 175 required school days per year for Upper School students. Upper School students typically attend 5 days per week. The average school day consists of 7 hours and 20 minutes.

Upper School Student Profile Grade 6: 50 students (25 boys, 25 girls); Grade 7: 54 students (25 boys, 29 girls); Grade 8: 52 students (29 boys, 23 girls); Grade 9: 75 students (32 boys, 43 girls); Grade 10: 68 students (38 boys, 30 girls); Grade 11: 75 students (42 boys, 33 girls); Grade 12: 56 students (28 boys, 28 girls).

Faculty School total: 90. In upper school: 14 men, 22 women; 23 have advanced degrees.

Graduation Requirements Community service hour requirement.

Special Academic Programs Advanced Placement exam preparation; honors section; independent study; study at local college for college credit; academic accommodation for the gifted.

College Admission Counseling 83 students graduated in 2009; all went to college, including Charleston Southern University; Clemson University; College of Charleston; Furman University; University of South Carolina.

Student Life Upper grades have specified standards of dress, student council, honor system. Discipline rests primarily with faculty.

Tuition and Aid Tuition reduction for siblings, need-based scholarship grants available.

Admissions Application fee required. Interview recommended.

Athletics Interscholastic: aquatics (boys, girls), baseball (b), basketball (b,g), cheering (b,g), cross-country running (b,g), football (b,g), golf (b,g), soccer (b,g), softball (g), tennis (b,g), trap and skeet (b,g), volleyball (g); intramural: dance team (b,g), flag football (b), running (b,g); coed intramural: aerobics, aerobics/dance, running. 4 PE instructors.

Computers Computers are regularly used in all academic classes. Computer network features include on-campus library services, Internet access, wireless campus network, Internet filtering or blocking technology. Campus intranet and computer access in designated common areas are available to students. Students grades are available online. The school has a published electronic and media policy.

Contact Mrs. Nicole Bailey, Director of Admissions. 843-873-1643. Fax: 843-821-4257. E-mail: nbailey@pinewoodprep.com. Web site: www.pinewoodprep.com/.

THE PINGRY SCHOOL

Martinsville Road
PO Box 366
Martinsville, New Jersey 08836
Head of School: Mr. Nathaniel Conard

General Information Coeducational day college-preparatory and arts school. Grades K–12. Founded: 1861. Setting: suburban. Nearest major city is New York, NY. 240-acre campus. 1 building on campus. Approved or accredited by Middle States Association of Colleges and Schools, New Jersey Association of Independent Schools, and New Jersey Department of Education. Member of National Association of Independent Schools. Endowment: $57 million. Total enrollment: 1,065. Upper school average class size: 14. Upper school faculty-student ratio: 1:8. There are 168 required school days per year for Upper School students. Upper School students typically attend 5 days per week. The average school day consists of 6 hours and 15 minutes.

Upper School Student Profile Grade 9: 139 students (75 boys, 64 girls); Grade 10: 136 students (74 boys, 62 girls); Grade 11: 132 students (72 boys, 60 girls); Grade 12: 131 students (66 boys, 65 girls).

Faculty School total: 120. In upper school: 47 men, 37 women; 61 have advanced degrees.

Subjects Offered Algebra, American literature, analysis, analysis and differential calculus, anatomy, architecture, art, art history-AP, biology, biology-AP, brass choir, calculus, chemistry, chemistry-AP, Chinese, clayworking, comparative cultures, computer science-AP, creative writing, drafting, drama, driver education, English, ethics, European literature, filmmaking, French, French-AP, geometry, German, German-AP, Greek drama, health, jazz band, jewelry making, Latin, literature by women, macro/microeconomics-AP, macroeconomics-AP, modern European history, music theory, mythology, orchestra, painting, peer counseling, photography, physics, physics-AP, physiology, psychology, psychology-AP, sculpture, Shakespeare, Spanish, Spanish-AP, studio art-AP, trigonometry, U.S. government and politics-AP, U.S. history-AP, wind ensemble, world literature, yearbook.

Graduation Requirements Arts and fine arts (art, music, dance, drama), English, foreign language, mathematics, physical education (includes health), science, social studies (includes history). Community service is required.

Special Academic Programs 20 Advanced Placement exams for which test preparation is offered; honors section; independent study; term-away projects; study abroad; academic accommodation for the gifted.

College Admission Counseling 130 students graduated in 2010; 125 went to college, including Boston College; Cornell University; Georgetown University; Hamilton College; Princeton University; University of Pennsylvania. Other: 5 had other specific plans. Mean SAT critical reading: 686, mean SAT math: 693, mean SAT writing: 698, mean composite ACT: 30.

Student Life Upper grades have specified standards of dress, student council, honor system. Discipline rests equally with students and faculty.

Summer Programs Enrichment, sports programs offered; session focuses on enrichment, writing, and study skills; held on campus; accepts boys and girls; open to students from other schools. 30 students usually enrolled. 2011 schedule: June 27 to August 5.

Tuition and Aid Day student tuition: $25,670–$30,225. Tuition installment plan (individually arranged payment plans, My Tuition Solutions). Need-based scholarship grants available. In 2010–11, 14% of upper-school students received aid. Total amount of financial aid awarded in 2010–11: $1,864,385.

Admissions Traditional secondary-level entrance grade is 9. For fall 2010, 239 students applied for upper-level admission, 115 were accepted, 72 enrolled. ERB, ISEE, SSAT or Wechsler Intelligence Scale for Children required. Deadline for receipt of application materials: January 3. Application fee required: $75. On-campus interview required.

Athletics Interscholastic: alpine skiing (boys, girls), baseball (b), basketball (b,g), cross-country running (b,g), fencing (b,g), field hockey (g), football (b), golf (b,g), ice hockey (b,g), indoor track & field (b,g), lacrosse (b,g), skiing (downhill) (b,g), soccer (b,g), softball (g), squash (b,g), swimming and diving (b,g), tennis (b,g), track and field (b,g), wrestling (b); intramural: fitness (b,g), yoga (b,g); coed interscholastic: dance, physical fitness, physical training, water polo. 3 PE instructors, 15 coaches, 1 athletic trainer.

Computers Computers are regularly used in all academic classes. Computer network features include on-campus library services, online commercial services, Internet access, wireless campus network, Internet filtering or blocking technology. Campus intranet, student e-mail accounts, and computer access in designated common areas are available to students. The school has a published electronic and media policy.

Contact Ms. Victoria Adamo, Admission Coordinator. 908-647-5555 Ext. 1228. Fax: 908-647-4395. E-mail: vadamo@pingry.org. Web site: www.pingry.org.

PIONEER VALLEY CHRISTIAN SCHOOL

965 Plumtree Road
Springfield, Massachusetts 01119
Head of School: Mr. Timothy L. Duff

General Information Coeducational day college-preparatory, religious studies, bilingual studies, and technology school, affiliated with Protestant faith, Evangelical faith. Grades PS–12. Founded: 1972. Setting: suburban. 25-acre campus. 1 building on campus. Approved or accredited by Association of Christian Schools International, New England Association of Schools and Colleges, and Massachusetts Department of Education. Total enrollment: 263. Upper school average class size: 15. Upper school faculty-student ratio: 1:5. There are 173 required school days per year for Upper School students. Upper School students typically attend 5 days per week. The average school day consists of 6 hours and 40 minutes.

Upper School Student Profile Grade 9: 14 students (3 boys, 11 girls); Grade 10: 20 students (10 boys, 10 girls); Grade 11: 32 students (16 boys, 16 girls); Grade 12: 21 students (10 boys, 11 girls). 95% of students are Protestant, members of Evangelical faith.

Faculty School total: 31. In upper school: 5 men, 12 women; 10 have advanced degrees.

Subjects Offered Advanced math, algebra, American literature, American literature-AP, anatomy, art, athletics, baseball, basketball, bell choir, Bible studies, biology, British literature, British literature-AP, calculus-AP, chemistry, choir, choral music, Christian education, drama, economics, English, English-AP, French, geometry, government, history, instrumental music, music, physical education, physical science, physics, pre-algebra, sociology, softball, Spanish, speech, sports, technology, tennis, U.S. history, volleyball, weight training, Western civilization, world history, yearbook.

Graduation Requirements Algebra, American literature, arts and fine arts (art, music, dance, drama), Bible, biology, British literature, economics, English, foreign language, government, physical education (includes health), physical science, sociology, speech, U.S. history, Christian/community service hours.

Special Academic Programs Advanced Placement exam preparation; honors section; remedial reading and/or remedial writing; remedial math; programs in English, mathematics, general development for dyslexic students; special instructional classes for students with learning disabilities, Attention Deficit Disorder, and dyslexia.

College Admission Counseling 35 students graduated in 2010; 34 went to college, including American International College; Holyoke Community College; Mount Holyoke College; University of Massachusetts Amherst. Other: 1 went to work. Median SAT critical reading: 530, median SAT math: 480, median SAT writing: 520.

Student Life Upper grades have uniform requirement, honor system. Discipline rests primarily with faculty. Attendance at religious services is required.

Tuition and Aid Day student tuition: $9500. Tuition installment plan (monthly payment plans, Electronic Funds Transfer, weekly, biweekly, monthly). Need-based scholarship grants, need-based financial aid and scholarship available. In 2010–11, 54% of upper-school students received aid. Total amount of financial aid awarded in 2010–11: $72,350.

Admissions Traditional secondary-level entrance grade is 9. For fall 2010, 16 students applied for upper-level admission, 11 were accepted, 11 enrolled. Admissions testing required. Deadline for receipt of application materials: none. Application fee required: $80. Interview required.

Athletics Interscholastic: baseball (boys), basketball (b,g), softball (g), tennis (b,g), volleyball (g); intramural: soccer (b,g); coed interscholastic: soccer, weight training; coed intramural: combined training, golf, physical training, soccer, strength & conditioning. 2 PE instructors, 12 coaches.

Computers Computers are regularly used in all academic classes. Computer network features include Internet access, Internet filtering or blocking technology, homework assignments available online.

Contact Mr. Pat Sterlacci, Director of Admissions. 413-782-8031. Fax: 413-782-8033. E-mail: psterlacci@pvcs.org. Web site: www.pvcs.org.

POLY PREP COUNTRY DAY SCHOOL

9216 Seventh Avenue
Brooklyn, New York 11228
Head of School: Mr. David B. Harman

General Information Coeducational day college-preparatory school. Grades N–12. Founded: 1854. Setting: urban. 24-acre campus. 3 buildings on campus. Approved or accredited by Middle States Association of Colleges and Schools and New York State Association of Independent Schools. Member of National Association of Independent Schools and Secondary School Admission Test Board. Endowment: $16.8 million. Total enrollment: 1,080. Upper school average class size: 17. Upper school faculty-student ratio: 1:7.

Upper School Student Profile Grade 9: 120 students (68 boys, 52 girls); Grade 10: 116 students (60 boys, 56 girls); Grade 11: 108 students (58 boys, 50 girls); Grade 12: 129 students (71 boys, 58 girls).

Faculty School total: 196. In upper school: 38 men, 38 women; 68 have advanced degrees.

Subjects Offered 20th century world history, Advanced Placement courses, African American history, algebra, American history, American literature, art, art history, art history-AP, astronomy, bioethics, biology, biology-AP, biotechnology, calculus, calculus-AP, Caribbean history, ceramics, chemistry, chemistry-AP, choral music, classics, computer programming, computer programming-AP, computer science, computer-aided design, creative writing, drama, drawing, earth science, ecology, economics, English, English language-AP, English literature-AP, environmental science, environmental studies, European history, European history-AP, film and literature, filmmaking, fine arts, forensics, French, French language-AP, French literature-AP, geology, geometry, history, international relations, jazz band, Latin, Latin-AP, mathematics, music, music theory-AP, paleontology, philosophy, physical education, physics, physics-AP, politics, psychology, science, senior project, social studies, Spanish, Spanish language-AP, Spanish literature-AP, speech, theater, theater arts, trigonometry, U.S. history-AP, world history, world history-AP, writing.

Graduation Requirements Arts and fine arts (art, music, dance, drama), English, foreign language, history, mathematics, music, physical education (includes health), science, speech, senior thesis with oral presentation. Community service is required.

Special Academic Programs 16 Advanced Placement exams for which test preparation is offered; honors section; independent study; term-away projects; academic accommodation for the gifted and the artistically talented.

College Admission Counseling 116 students graduated in 2009; 115 went to college, including Brown University; Dickinson College; Fordham University; The George Washington University; The Johns Hopkins University; Wesleyan University. Other: 1 entered a postgraduate year. Median SAT critical reading: 640, median SAT math: 650, median SAT writing: 675, median combined SAT: 1960, median composite ACT: 26.

Student Life Upper grades have specified standards of dress, student council, honor system. Discipline rests equally with students and faculty.

Tuition and Aid Day student tuition: $9450–$31,300. Tuition installment plan (Sallie Mae TuitionPay). Merit scholarship grants, need-based scholarship grants available. In 2009–10, 26% of upper-school students received aid. Total amount of financial aid awarded in 2009–10: $4,600,000.

Admissions Traditional secondary-level entrance grade is 9. ERB, ISEE or SSAT required. Deadline for receipt of application materials: December 1. Application fee required: $50. On-campus interview required.

Athletics Interscholastic: baseball (boys), basketball (b,g), cross-country running (b,g), football (b), lacrosse (b,g), soccer (b,g), softball (g), squash (b,g), swimming and diving (b,g), tennis (b,g), track and field (b,g), volleyball (g), winter (indoor) track (b,g), wrestling (b); coed interscholastic: golf; coed intramural: ballet, cheering, dance, dance team, fitness, Frisbee, outdoor adventure, physical fitness, physical training, strength & conditioning, ultimate Frisbee, weight training, yoga. 12 PE instructors, 24 coaches, 1 athletic trainer.

Computers Computers are regularly used in all academic, publications, yearbook classes. Computer network features include on-campus library services, Internet access, wireless campus network, Internet filtering or blocking technology. Campus intranet, student e-mail accounts, and computer access in designated common areas are available to students. The school has a published electronic and media policy.

Contact Ms. Lori W. Redell, Assistant Head for Admissions and Financial Aid. 718-663-6060. Fax: 718-238-3393. E-mail: polyadmissions@polyprep.org. Web site: www.polyprep.org.

POLYTECHNIC SCHOOL

1030 East California Boulevard
Pasadena, California 91106-4099
Head of School: Mrs. Deborah E. Reed

General Information Coeducational day college-preparatory school. Grades K–12. Founded: 1907. Setting: suburban. 15-acre campus. 7 buildings on campus. Approved or accredited by California Association of Independent Schools, The College Board, Western Association of Schools and Colleges, and California Department of Education. Member of National Association of Independent Schools. Endowment: $47 million. Total enrollment: 860. Upper school average class size: 17. Upper school faculty-student ratio: 1:17. Upper School students typically attend 5 days per week. The average school day consists of 7 hours.

Upper School Student Profile Grade 9: 99 students (49 boys, 50 girls); Grade 10: 93 students (43 boys, 50 girls); Grade 11: 91 students (52 boys, 39 girls); Grade 12: 91 students (45 boys, 46 girls).

Faculty School total: 99. In upper school: 12 men, 25 women; 28 have advanced degrees.

Subjects Offered Acting, algebra, American history, American history-AP, analytic geometry, art history, athletics, audio visual/media, Basic programming, batik, biology, biology-AP, calculus, calculus-AP, ceramics, chamber groups, chemistry, chemistry-AP, choral music, communications, computer art, computer science, constitutional law, data analysis, drama, drama performance, drawing, East Asian history, economics, English, English language and composition-AP, English literature and composition-AP, ensembles, ethics, filmmaking, French, French literature-AP, functions, geometry, guitar, improvisation, jazz dance, jazz ensemble, Latin, Latin-AP, madrigals, math analysis, mathematical modeling, music history, music theory, musical productions, musical theater, orchestra, painting, photography, physical science, physics, physics-AP, Roman civilization, sculpture, silk screening, society, Spanish, Spanish literature-AP, statistics, tap dance, technical theater, theater, theater design and production, theater history, trigonometry, U.S. government and politics, U.S. history-AP, Vietnam War, visual arts, Western civilization, woodworking, world cultures, world religions.

Special Academic Programs 12 Advanced Placement exams for which test preparation is offered; honors section; independent study; study abroad.

College Admission Counseling 92 students graduated in 2010; all went to college, including Dartmouth College; Harvard University; Princeton University; University of California, Berkeley; University of Southern California; Wesleyan University.

Student Life Upper grades have specified standards of dress, student council, honor system. Discipline rests equally with students and faculty.

Tuition and Aid Day student tuition: $26,600. Tuition installment plan (monthly payment plans). Need-based scholarship grants available. In 2010–11, 20% of upper-school students received aid. Total amount of financial aid awarded in 2010–11: $2,800,000.

Admissions Traditional secondary-level entrance grade is 9. For fall 2010, 202 students applied for upper-level admission, 52 were accepted, 38 enrolled. ISEE required. Deadline for receipt of application materials: January 8. Application fee required: $100. On-campus interview required.

Athletics Interscholastic: aquatics (boys, girls), baseball (b), basketball (b,g), cross-country running (b,g), diving (b,g), golf (b,g), soccer (b,g), softball (g), swimming and diving (b,g), tennis (b,g), track and field (b,g), volleyball (b,g), water polo (b,g); coed interscholastic: badminton, dance squad, equestrian sports, fencing, football, outdoor education, physical fitness, physical training, strength & conditioning, weight lifting, weight training, yoga. 3 PE instructors, 27 coaches, 2 athletic trainers.

Computers Computers are regularly used in all classes. Computer network features include on-campus library services, Internet access, Internet filtering or blocking technology. Student e-mail accounts are available to students.

Contact Ms. Sally Jeanne McKenna, Director of Admissions. 626-396-6300. Fax: 626-396-6591. E-mail: sjmckenna@polytechnic.org. Web site: www.polytechnic.org.

POMFRET SCHOOL

PO Box 128
398 Pomfret Street
Pomfret, Connecticut 06258-0128

General Information Coeducational boarding and day college-preparatory, arts, religious studies, and technology school, affiliated with Episcopal Church. Grades 9–PG. Founded: 1894. Setting: rural. Nearest major city is Hartford. Students are housed in single-sex dormitories. 500-acre campus. 62 buildings on campus. Approved or accredited by Connecticut Association of Independent Schools, New England Association of Schools and Colleges, The Association of Boarding Schools, and Connecticut Department of Education. Member of National Association of Independent Schools and Secondary School Admission Test Board. Total enrollment: 355. Upper school average class size: 11. Upper school faculty-student ratio: 1:6.

See Display on this page and Close-Up on page 824.

POPE JOHN XXIII REGIONAL HIGH SCHOOL

28 Andover Road
Sparta, New Jersey 07871
Head of School: Mrs. Gloria Shope

General Information Coeducational day college-preparatory, arts, business, religious studies, and technology school, affiliated with Roman Catholic Church. Grades 8–12. Founded: 1956. Setting: suburban. Nearest major city is New York, NY. 15-acre campus. 2 buildings on campus. Approved or accredited by Department of Defense Dependents Schools, Middle States Association of Colleges and Schools, and New Jersey Department of Education. Total enrollment: 961. Upper school average class size: 20. Upper school faculty-student ratio: 1:13. There are 180 required school days per year for Upper School students. Upper School students typically attend 5 days per week. The average school day consists of 5 hours and 42 minutes.

Upper School Student Profile Grade 8: 29 students (20 boys, 9 girls); Grade 9: 219 students (109 boys, 110 girls); Grade 10: 225 students (120 boys, 105 girls); Grade 11: 256 students (129 boys, 127 girls); Grade 12: 232 students (126 boys, 106 girls). 82% of students are Roman Catholic.

Faculty School total: 79. In upper school: 36 men, 43 women; 35 have advanced degrees.

Subjects Offered Advanced chemistry, advanced computer applications, advanced math, Advanced Placement courses, algebra, American literature, American studies, anatomy and physiology, art, biology, biology-AP, British literature, business, business law, calculus, calculus-AP, chemistry, chemistry-AP, choral music, computer literacy, computer science, computer science-AP, conceptual physics, concert choir, earth science, economics, English, English language-AP, English literature, English literature and composition-AP, environmental science, environmental science-AP, European history-AP, fine arts, French, French-AP, geometry, German, global issues, government and politics-AP, graphic arts, health and safety, history-AP, honors algebra, honors English, honors geometry, honors U.S. history, honors world history, Italian, Japanese, jazz band, journalism, lab science, Latin, macroeconomics-AP, microeconomics-AP, modern politics, music theory, physical education, physics, physics-AP, pre-calculus, psychology, public speaking, reading/study skills, Spanish, Spanish language-AP, statistics, theater arts, theology, U.S. government, U.S. government and politics-AP, U.S. history, U.S. history-AP, world cultures, world history-AP, writing, zoology.

Graduation Requirements Arts and fine arts (art, music, dance, drama), English, foreign language, health and safety, mathematics, science, social studies (includes history), theology, 60 hours of community service (15 hours per year).

Special Academic Programs Honors section; ESL (20 students enrolled).

College Admission Counseling 193 students graduated in 2010; all went to college, including Loyola University Maryland; Rutgers, The State University of New Jersey, New Brunswick; Susquehanna University; The College of New Jersey; The University of Scranton; Villanova University. Mean SAT critical reading: 538, mean SAT math: 538, mean SAT writing: 532, mean combined SAT: 1608.

Student Life Upper grades have uniform requirement, student council. Discipline rests primarily with faculty. Attendance at religious services is required.

Summer Programs Remediation, enrichment, sports programs offered; session focuses on sports; held on campus; accepts boys and girls; open to students from other schools. 200 students usually enrolled.

Tuition and Aid Day student tuition: $13,000. Guaranteed tuition plan. Tuition installment plan (SMART Tuition Payment Plan). Need-based scholarship grants available.

Admissions Traditional secondary-level entrance grade is 9. CTB/McGraw-Hill/Macmillan Co-op Test, Math Placement Exam, placement test and writing sample required. Deadline for receipt of application materials: none. No application fee required.

Athletics Interscholastic: baseball (boys), basketball (b,g), cheering (g), cross-country running (b,g), field hockey (g), football (b), ice hockey (b), indoor track & field (b,g), lacrosse (b,g), running (b,g), skiing (downhill) (b,g), softball (g), swimming and diving (b,g), tennis (b,g), track and field (b,g), volleyball (b,g), winter (indoor) track (b,g), wrestling (b); coed interscholastic: golf.

Computers Computers are regularly used in graphic arts, programming classes. Computer network features include Internet access, Internet filtering or blocking technology. The school has a published electronic and media policy.

Contact Mrs. Anne Kaiser, Administrative Assistant for Admissions. 973-729-6125 Ext. 255. Fax: 973-729-4536. E-mail: annekaiser@popejohn.org. Web site: www.popejohn.org.

PORTER-GAUD SCHOOL
300 Albemarle Road
Charleston, South Carolina 29407
Head of School: Mr. David DuBose Egleston Jr.
General Information Coeducational day college-preparatory, arts, religious studies, and technology school, affiliated with Christian faith, Episcopal Church. Grades 1–12. Founded: 1867. Setting: suburban. 80-acre campus. 13 buildings on campus. Approved or accredited by National Association of Episcopal Schools, South Carolina Independent School Association, Southern Association of Colleges and Schools, Southern Association of Independent Schools, and South Carolina Department of Education. Member of National Association of Independent Schools. Endowment: $7 million. Total enrollment: 896. Upper school average class size: 14. Upper school faculty-student ratio: 1:15. There are 175 required school days per year for Upper School students. Upper School students typically attend 5 days per week. The average school day consists of 7 hours.

Upper School Student Profile Grade 9: 91 students (59 boys, 32 girls); Grade 10: 80 students (47 boys, 33 girls); Grade 11: 88 students (57 boys, 31 girls); Grade 12: 95 students (54 boys, 41 girls). 80% of students are Christian, members of Episcopal Church.

Faculty School total: 95. In upper school: 15 men, 25 women; 30 have advanced degrees.

Subjects Offered Advanced Placement courses, algebra, American history, American literature, art, art history, biology, calculus, chemistry, computer programming, computer science, drama, economics, English, English literature, ethics, European history, expository writing, fine arts, French, geometry, government/civics, health, Latin, music, music appreciation, physical education, physics, Spanish, world history, world literature.

Graduation Requirements Algebra, American literature, art education, arts and fine arts (art, music, dance, drama), biology, chemistry, computer science, English, English composition, English literature, European history, foreign language, geometry, physical education (includes health), physics, pre-calculus, religion (includes Bible studies and theology), trigonometry, U.S. history, world history.

Special Academic Programs 17 Advanced Placement exams for which test preparation is offered; honors section; independent study; ESL (2 students enrolled).

College Admission Counseling 85 students graduated in 2010; all went to college, including Clemson University; College of Charleston; The Citadel, The Military College of South Carolina; The University of North Carolina at Chapel Hill; University of Georgia; University of South Carolina. Mean SAT critical reading: 620, mean SAT math: 608, mean SAT writing: 629, mean combined SAT: 1857, mean composite ACT: 26.

Student Life Upper grades have uniform requirement, student council, honor system. Discipline rests equally with students and faculty. Attendance at religious services is required.

Tuition and Aid Day student tuition: $17,830. Tuition installment plan (monthly payment plans, individually arranged payment plans, 60/40 payment plan). Need-based scholarship grants available. In 2010–11, 21% of upper-school students received aid. Total amount of financial aid awarded in 2010–11: $1,639,000.

Admissions Traditional secondary-level entrance grade is 9. For fall 2010, 80 students applied for upper-level admission, 70 were accepted, 40 enrolled. ISEE or PSAT or SAT required. Deadline for receipt of application materials: none. Application fee required: $75. Interview required.

Athletics Interscholastic: baseball (boys), basketball (b,g), football (b), ice hockey (b), physical training (b,g), soccer (b,g), swimming and diving (b,g), tennis (b,g), track and field (b,g), volleyball (g), weight lifting (b,g), weight training (b,g); intramural: basketball (b,g), Frisbee (b,g), lacrosse (b); coed interscholastic: cheering, cross-country running, golf, Nautilus, sailing, strength & conditioning; coed intramural: Frisbee, ultimate Frisbee. 4 PE instructors, 26 coaches, 1 athletic trainer.

Computers Computers are regularly used in English, foreign language, history, mathematics, music, programming, science, video film production, yearbook classes. Computer network features include on-campus library services, Internet access, wireless campus network, Internet filtering or blocking technology. Campus intranet, student e-mail accounts, and computer access in designated common areas are available to students. Students grades are available online. The school has a published electronic and media policy.

Contact Mrs. Eleanor W. Hurtes, Director of Admissions. 843-402-4775. Fax: 843-556-7404. E-mail: eleanor.hurtes@portergaud.edu. Web site: www.portergaud.edu.

PORTLEDGE SCHOOL
355 Duck Pond Road
Locust Valley, New York 11560
Head of School: Steven L. Hahn
General Information Coeducational day college-preparatory school. Grades N–12. Founded: 1965. Setting: suburban. Nearest major city is New York. 62-acre campus. 4 buildings on campus. Approved or accredited by New York State Association of Independent Schools and New York State Board of Regents. Member of National Association of Independent Schools and Secondary School Admission Test Board. Endowment: $1.8 million. Total enrollment: 375. Upper school average class size: 12. Upper school faculty-student ratio: 1:5. There are 164 required school days per year for Upper School students. Upper School students typically attend 5 days per week. The average school day consists of 6 hours and 55 minutes.

Upper School Student Profile Grade 9: 38 students (16 boys, 22 girls); Grade 10: 41 students (25 boys, 16 girls); Grade 11: 48 students (29 boys, 19 girls); Grade 12: 41 students (19 boys, 22 girls).

Faculty School total: 71. In upper school: 13 men, 23 women; 21 have advanced degrees.

Subjects Offered 3-dimensional art, advanced biology, advanced chemistry, advanced computer applications, advanced math, Advanced Placement courses, advanced studio art-AP, algebra, American history, American history-AP, American literature, American literature-AP, ancient history, architectural drawing, architecture, art, art appreciation, art history, art-AP, Basic programming, biology, calculus, calculus-AP, ceramics, chemistry, chemistry-AP, chorus, community service, computer programming, computer science, computers, creative writing, digital music, drama, drama workshop, driver education, earth science, economics, English, English literature, English literature-AP, environmental science, European history, expository writing, fine arts, foreign language, French, French-AP, geography, geometry, government/civics, grammar, graphic design, health, health education, history, honors algebra, honors English, honors geometry, honors U.S. history, independent study, instrumental music, jazz ensemble, journalism, keyboarding, mathematics, music, Native American history, photography, physical education, physics, psychology, public policy, public service, public speaking, science, senior project, social sciences, social studies, Spanish, Spanish-AP, theater, trigonometry, U.S. history-AP, world history.

Graduation Requirements Arts and fine arts (art, music, dance, drama), computer science, English, foreign language, mathematics, performing arts, physical education (includes health), public speaking, science, senior project, social sciences, social studies (includes history). Community service is required.

Special Academic Programs Advanced Placement exam preparation; honors section; independent study; term-away projects; academic accommodation for the gifted, the musically talented, and the artistically talented.

College Admission Counseling 35 students graduated in 2009; all went to college. Median SAT critical reading: 580, median SAT math: 610, median SAT writing: 590, median composite ACT: 28.

Student Life Upper grades have specified standards of dress, student council, honor system. Discipline rests primarily with faculty.

Tuition and Aid Day student tuition: $28,000. Tuition installment plan (Tuition Management Systems). Tuition reduction for siblings, need-based scholarship grants available. In 2009–10, 30% of upper-school students received aid. Total amount of financial aid awarded in 2009–10: $922,500.

Admissions Traditional secondary-level entrance grade is 9. For fall 2009, 140 students applied for upper-level admission, 111 were accepted, 66 enrolled. SSAT required. Deadline for receipt of application materials: February 10. Application fee required: $75. On-campus interview required.

Athletics Interscholastic: baseball (boys), basketball (b,g), fencing (b,g), hockey (b,g), ice hockey (b,g), lacrosse (b,g), soccer (b,g), softball (g), tennis (b,g); intramural: tennis (g); coed interscholastic: cross-country running, golf, squash. 2 PE instructors, 2 coaches.

Computers Computers are regularly used in art, English, foreign language, history, mathematics, music, science classes. Computer network features include on-campus library services, online commercial services, Internet access, wireless campus network, Internet filtering or blocking technology. Computer access in designated common areas is available to students. The school has a published electronic and media policy.

Contact Susan Simon, Director of Admissions. 516-750-3203. Fax: 516-674-7063. E-mail: ssimon@portledge.org. Web site: www.portledge.org.

PORTSMOUTH ABBEY SCHOOL
285 Cory's Lane
Portsmouth, Rhode Island 02871
Head of School: Dr. James De Vecchi
General Information Coeducational boarding and day college-preparatory, arts, religious studies, and music, classics, humanities school, affiliated with Roman

Portsmouth Abbey School

Catholic Church. Grades 9–12. Founded: 1926. Setting: small town. Nearest major city is Providence. Students are housed in single-sex dormitories. 500-acre campus. 36 buildings on campus. Approved or accredited by Association of Independent Schools in New England, National Independent Private Schools Association, New England Association of Schools and Colleges, and The Association of Boarding Schools. Member of National Association of Independent Schools and Secondary School Admission Test Board. Endowment: $30 million. Total enrollment: 373. Upper school average class size: 13. Upper school faculty-student ratio: 1:8. There are 180 required school days per year for Upper School students. Upper School students typically attend 6 days per week. The average school day consists of 7 hours.

Upper School Student Profile Grade 9: 62 students (34 boys, 28 girls); Grade 10: 86 students (42 boys, 44 girls); Grade 11: 102 students (53 boys, 49 girls); Grade 12: 105 students (47 boys, 58 girls). 70% of students are boarding students. 41% are state residents. 23 states are represented in upper school student body. 11% are international students. International students from Canada, Dominican Republic, Germany, Guatemala, Republic of Korea, and Spain; 11 other countries represented in student body. 62% of students are Roman Catholic.

Faculty School total: 45. In upper school: 30 men, 15 women; 41 have advanced degrees; 34 reside on campus.

Subjects Offered Algebra, American literature, art, art history, art history-AP, art-AP, biology, biology-AP, calculus, calculus-AP, chemistry, chemistry-AP, Chinese, Christian doctrine, Christian ethics, church history, computer programming, computer programming-AP, computer science, computer science-AP, drama, economics, English, English language and composition-AP, English literature, English literature and composition-AP, ethics, European history, European history-AP, fine arts, French, French language-AP, French literature-AP, geometry, government/civics, Greek, health, history, history-AP, humanities, international relations, Latin, Latin-AP, Mandarin, marine biology, mathematics, mathematics-AP, modern European history, modern European history-AP, music, music appreciation, music composition, music history, music theory, music theory-AP, philosophy, photography, physical education, physics, physics-AP, physiology, political science, probability and statistics, religion, science, social sciences, Spanish, Spanish language-AP, Spanish literature-AP, statistics-AP, studio art-AP, theater, theology, trigonometry, U.S. history, U.S. history-AP, world history, writing workshop.

Graduation Requirements Arts and fine arts (art, music, dance, drama), English, foreign language, history, Latin, mathematics, religion (includes Bible studies and theology), science, humanities.

Special Academic Programs Advanced Placement exam preparation; honors section; independent study; academic accommodation for the gifted.

College Admission Counseling 101 students graduated in 2010; all went to college, including Boston College; Cornell University; Georgetown University; New York University; Northeastern University; The Catholic University of America. Median SAT critical reading: 600, median SAT math: 590, median SAT writing: 600, median combined SAT: 1830. 50% scored over 600 on SAT critical reading, 54% scored over 600 on SAT math, 44% scored over 600 on SAT writing, 46% scored over 1800 on combined SAT, 32% scored over 26 on composite ACT.

Student Life Upper grades have specified standards of dress, student council, honor system. Discipline rests primarily with faculty. Attendance at religious services is required.

Summer Programs Enrichment, advancement programs offered; held on campus; accepts boys and girls; open to students from other schools. 80 students usually enrolled. 2011 schedule: June 27 to July 24. Application deadline: none.

Tuition and Aid Day student tuition: $30,680; 7-day tuition and room/board: $44,850. Tuition installment plan (monthly payment plans, individually arranged payment plans, Tuition Management Systems Plan). Merit scholarship grants, need-based scholarship grants available. In 2010–11, 35% of upper-school students received aid; total upper-school merit-scholarship money awarded: $180,000. Total amount of financial aid awarded in 2010–11: $3,000,000.

Admissions Traditional secondary-level entrance grade is 9. For fall 2010, 380 students applied for upper-level admission, 215 were accepted, 108 enrolled. PSAT or SAT for applicants to grade 11 and 12, SSAT and SSAT or WISC III required. Deadline for receipt of application materials: January 31. Application fee required: $50. Interview required.

Athletics Interscholastic: baseball (boys), basketball (b,g), cross-country running (b,g), field hockey (g), football (b), golf (b,g), ice hockey (b,g), lacrosse (b,g), soccer (b,g), softball (g), squash (b,g), swimming and diving (b,g), track and field (b,g); coed interscholastic: cross-country running, sailing, tennis, track and field, weight training; coed intramural: ballet, dance, equestrian sports, fitness, horseback riding, modern dance. 2 athletic trainers.

Computers Computers are regularly used in science classes. Computer network features include on-campus library services, Internet access, wireless campus network. Student e-mail accounts are available to students.

Contact Mrs. Ann Motta, Admissions Coordinator. 401-643-1248. Fax: 401-643-1355. E-mail: admissions@portsmouthabbey.org. Web site: www.portsmouthabbey.org.

PORTSMOUTH CHRISTIAN ACADEMY

20 Seaborne Drive
Dover, New Hampshire 03820
Head of School: Mr. Brian Bell

General Information Coeducational day college-preparatory, arts, religious studies, technology, science/mathematics, and communication school, affiliated with Christian faith. Grades K–12. Founded: 1979. Setting: rural. Nearest major city is Portsmouth. 50-acre campus. 3 buildings on campus. Approved or accredited by Association of Christian Schools International, New England Association of Schools and Colleges, and New Hampshire Department of Education. Total enrollment: 617. Upper school average class size: 17. Upper school faculty-student ratio: 1:13. There are 180 required school days per year for Upper School students. Upper School students typically attend 5 days per week. The average school day consists of 7 hours and 5 minutes.

Upper School Student Profile Grade 9: 46 students (21 boys, 25 girls); Grade 10: 51 students (25 boys, 26 girls); Grade 11: 36 students (21 boys, 15 girls); Grade 12: 48 students (15 boys, 33 girls). 70% of students are Christian faith.

Faculty School total: 71. In upper school: 11 men, 13 women; 14 have advanced degrees.

Subjects Offered 20th century American writers, 20th century history, 3-dimensional art, 3-dimensional design, ACT preparation, advanced chemistry, advanced computer applications, advanced math, Advanced Placement courses, advanced studio art-AP, African drumming, algebra, alternative physical education, American history, American literature, American literature-AP, analysis and differential calculus, anatomy and physiology, applied music, art, art appreciation, art education, art history, art history-AP, arts appreciation, athletic training, athletics, band, baseball, basketball, Bible, Bible studies, biochemistry, biology, British literature, British literature (honors), calculus, calculus-AP, chemistry, chemistry-AP, choir, choral music, chorus, Christian doctrine, Christian education, Christian ethics, Christian scripture, Christian studies, Christian testament, Christianity, church history, civics, college admission preparation, college awareness, college counseling, college placement, college planning, college writing, comparative religion, composition, composition-AP, computer applications, computer education, computer graphics, computer processing, computer resources, computer skills, computer-aided design, contemporary issues, current history, digital photography, drama, drama performance, drama workshop, drawing, economics, economics and history, English, English composition, English language and composition-AP, English literature and composition-AP, English literature-AP, environmental science, European history, film and literature, foreign language, French, French language-AP, French studies, geometry, government, government/civics, guitar, health, health and wellness, honors algebra, honors English, honors geometry, instrumental music, jazz band, law studies, literature, literature and composition-AP, literature-AP, marine science, math review, mathematics, microbiology, modern history, music, music appreciation, musical productions, musical theater, New Testament, novels, performing arts, photography, physics, physics-AP, political economy, pre-calculus, religion and culture, rhetoric, SAT preparation, SAT/ACT preparation, Shakespeare, Spanish, Spanish language-AP, Spanish-AP, student government, symphonic band, theater arts, theology, U.S. history, U.S. literature, world history, World War II, writing, writing workshop, yearbook.

Graduation Requirements 20th century history, algebra, arts and fine arts (art, music, dance, drama), biology, chemistry, comparative cultures, composition, computer skills, foreign language, geometry, physical education (includes health), physical science, U.S. history, writing, one Bible course for each year of Upper School attendance, service hours.

Special Academic Programs Advanced Placement exam preparation; honors section; accelerated programs; independent study; study at local college for college credit; academic accommodation for the gifted and the musically talented; special instructional classes for students with Attention Deficit Disorder and dyslexia.

College Admission Counseling 47 students graduated in 2010; 44 went to college, including Pepperdine University; Rochester Institute of Technology; Seattle Pacific University; Texas A&M University; University of Massachusetts Amherst; University of New Hampshire. Other: 3 had other specific plans. Mean SAT critical reading: 562, mean SAT math: 536, mean SAT writing: 551.

Student Life Upper grades have specified standards of dress, student council, honor system. Discipline rests primarily with faculty.

Summer Programs Remediation, enrichment, sports programs offered; session focuses on soccer, basketball, and volleyball; held on campus; accepts boys and girls; open to students from other schools. 40 students usually enrolled. 2011 schedule: July 10 to August 10. Application deadline: June 1.

Tuition and Aid Day student tuition: $9350. Tuition installment plan (FACTS Tuition Payment Plan). Tuition reduction for siblings, merit scholarship grants, need-based scholarship grants available. In 2010–11, 20% of upper-school students received aid. Total amount of financial aid awarded in 2010–11: $165,000.

Admissions Traditional secondary-level entrance grade is 9. Achievement tests, PSAT or SAT, PSAT or SAT for applicants to grade 11 and 12, PSAT, SAT, or ACT for applicants to grade 11 and 12, SAT, standardized test scores, Stanford Achievement Test, Test of Achievement and Proficiency, TOEFL, TOEFL or SLEP or writing sample required. Deadline for receipt of application materials: none. Application fee required: $100. Interview required.

Athletics Interscholastic: baseball (boys), basketball (b,g), cross-country running (b,g), indoor track & field (b,g), soccer (b,g), softball (g), tennis (b,g), track and field (b,g), volleyball (g), winter (indoor) track (b,g); intramural: golf (b,g), skiing (cross-country) (b,g); coed interscholastic: alpine skiing, cross-country running, fitness, indoor track & field, winter (indoor) track. 1 PE instructor, 14 coaches.

Computers Computers are regularly used in art, Bible studies, career education, Christian doctrine, classics, college planning, desktop publishing, economics, English, foreign language, graphic design,. history, humanities, independent study, library, library skills, mathematics, media arts, photography, religion, religious studies, SAT preparation, science, social studies, writing, yearbook classes. Computer network features include on-campus library services, online commercial services, Internet access, Internet filtering or blocking technology. Computer access in designated common areas is available to students. Students grades are available online. The school has a published electronic and media policy.

Contact Mrs. Diane Sipp, Director of Admissions. 603-742-3617 Ext. 116, Fax: 603-750-0490. E-mail: dsipp@pcaschool.org. Web site: www.pcaschool.org.

THE POTOMAC SCHOOL
1301 Potomac School Road
McLean, Virginia 22101
Head of School: Geoffrey Jones

General Information Coeducational day college-preparatory and liberal arts, arts, athletics, and character education school. Grades K–12. Founded: 1904. Setting: suburban. Nearest major city is Washington, DC. 90-acre campus. Approved or accredited by Association of Independent Schools of Greater Washington and Virginia Association of Independent Schools. Member of National Association of Independent Schools and Secondary School Admission Test Board. Endowment: $23 million. Total enrollment: 1,005. Upper school average class size: 14. Upper school faculty-student ratio: 1:6.

Upper School Student Profile Grade 9: 101 students (50 boys, 51 girls); Grade 10: 98 students (54 boys, 44 girls); Grade 11: 110 students (54 boys, 56 girls); Grade 12: 98 students (56 boys, 42 girls).

Faculty School total: 148. In upper school: 27 men, 36 women; 46 have advanced degrees.

Subjects Offered 20th century American writers, 20th century history, 20th century world history, 3-dimensional art, 3-dimensional design, acting, advanced computer applications, advanced math, Advanced Placement courses, advanced studio art-AP, African history, African-American literature, African-American studies, algebra, American foreign policy, American literature, anatomy and physiology, ancient history, art, art history, Asian studies, athletics, band, bell choir, Bible as literature, bioethics, biology, British literature, calculus, calculus-AP, cell biology, ceramics, chamber groups, character education, chemistry, chemistry-AP, Chinese history, choral music, civil war history, college counseling, community service, comparative religion, computer programming, computer programming-AP, computer science, conceptual physics, concert band, creative writing, debate, directing, drama, drama performance, drawing and design, economics and history, electives, engineering, English, English literature, environmental science, ethics, European history, expository writing, film and literature, fine arts, French, French language-AP, French literature-AP, functions, geometry, global studies, government/civics, handbells, Harlem Renaissance, historical research, history of jazz, history of music, independent study, jazz band, Latin, Latin American literature, Latin-AP, literary magazine, madrigals, mathematics, medieval history, Middle Eastern history, model United Nations, modern European history, music, music composition, music theory-AP, newspaper, painting, participation in sports, performing arts, photography, physical education, physics, physics-AP, portfolio art, pre-calculus, robotics, science, science and technology, sculpture, senior project, Shakespeare, short story, Spanish, Spanish language-AP, Spanish literature-AP, squash, stagecraft, statistics-AP, strings, student government, studio art-AP, theater arts, trigonometry, U.S. government and politics-AP, U.S. history-AP, vocal music, World War II, yearbook.

Graduation Requirements Arts and fine arts (art, music, dance, drama), English, ethics, foreign language, history, mathematics, physical education (includes health), science, senior project, month-long senior project.

Special Academic Programs Advanced Placement exam preparation; honors section; independent study.

College Admission Counseling 92 students graduated in 2010; all went to college, including Colby College; Dickinson College; The College of William and Mary; University of Pennsylvania; University of Virginia; Yale University. Median SAT critical reading: 670, median SAT math: 690.

Student Life Upper grades have specified standards of dress, student council, honor system. Discipline rests equally with students and faculty.

Summer Programs Enrichment, advancement, sports, art/fine arts programs offered; session focuses on academics and enrichment; held on campus; accepts boys and girls; open to students from other schools. 2011 schedule: June 27 to August 19. Application deadline: none.

Tuition and Aid Day student tuition: $28,915. Tuition installment plan (Insured Tuition Payment Plan, monthly payment plans). Need-based scholarship grants available. In 2010–11, 15% of upper-school students received aid. Total amount of financial aid awarded in 2010–11: $1,298,967.

Admissions Traditional secondary-level entrance grade is 9. ISEE or SSAT required. Deadline for receipt of application materials: January 10. Application fee required: $65. On-campus interview required.

Athletics Interscholastic: baseball (boys), basketball (b,g), cross-country running (b,g), field hockey (g), football (b), lacrosse (b,g), soccer (b,g), softball (g), squash

(b,g), tennis (b,g), track and field (b,g), wrestling (b); intramural: weight lifting (b,g); coed interscholastic: fitness, golf, swimming and diving, weight training, winter (indoor) track; coed intramural: canoeing/kayaking, hiking/backpacking, ice hockey, outdoor education, physical fitness, physical training, sailing, strength & conditioning. 5 PE instructors, 33 coaches, 2 athletic trainers.

Computers Computers are regularly used in all academic, computer applications, drawing and design, independent study, literary magazine, newspaper, photography, programming, yearbook classes. Computer network features include on-campus library services, online commercial services, Internet access, wireless campus network, Internet filtering or blocking technology. Campus intranet and student e-mail accounts are available to students. The school has a published electronic and media policy.

Contact Leslie Vorndran, Admission Services Coordinator. 703-749-6313. Fax: 703-356-1764. Web site: www.potomacschool.org.

POUGHKEEPSIE DAY SCHOOL
260 Boardman Road
Poughkeepsie, New York 12603
Head of School: Josie Holford

General Information Coeducational day college-preparatory and arts school. Grades PK–12. Founded: 1934. Setting: suburban. Nearest major city is New York. 35-acre campus. 2 buildings on campus. Approved or accredited by New York State Association of Independent Schools and New York Department of Education. Member of National Association of Independent Schools. Endowment: $4.1 million. Total enrollment: 290. Upper school average class size: 12. Upper school faculty-student ratio: 1:7. There are 165 required school days per year for Upper School students. Upper School students typically attend 5 days per week. The average school day consists of 7 hours.

Upper School Student Profile Grade 9: 27 students (14 boys, 13 girls); Grade 10: 21 students (11 boys, 10 girls); Grade 11: 21 students (6 boys, 15 girls); Grade 12: 26 students (11 boys, 15 girls).

Faculty School total: 44. In upper school: 5 men, 12 women; 13 have advanced degrees.

Subjects Offered 3-dimensional art, acting, advanced math, Advanced Placement courses, African drumming, algebra, American literature, American literature-AP, analysis and differential calculus, analytic geometry, anatomy, anatomy and physiology, ancient history, ancient world history, art history, arts, Basic programming, bioethics, biology, calculus, calculus-AP, chamber groups, chemistry, collage and assemblage, college admission preparation, college planning, community service, computer programming, computer science, computer-aided design, conflict resolution, contemporary art, creative arts, creative drama, creative writing, decision making skills, desktop publishing, digital art, digital photography, discrete mathematics, drama, drama performance, drawing, ecology, economics, English, English literature, English literature-AP, English-AP, ensembles, European civilization, European history, fiction, filmmaking, fine arts, French, French language-AP, French-AP, geology, geometry, guitar, history, Holocaust and other genocides, Holocaust studies, independent study, instrumental music, integrated arts, interdisciplinary studies, Islamic studies, jazz band, jazz ensemble, lab science, leadership, life saving, life skills, linear algebra, literary magazine, literature, literature-AP, mathematics, modern European history, multicultural literature, multicultural studies, music, music appreciation, music composition, music performance, music theory, music theory-AP, musical productions, oil painting, painting, peer counseling, performing arts, photography, physical education, physical science, physics, physiology, play production, playwriting and directing, pre-calculus, printmaking, probability and statistics, religion and culture, SAT preparation, science, senior internship, service learning/internship, social issues, social studies, Spanish, Spanish language-AP, Spanish-AP, stained glass, statistics, strings, studio art, theater arts, theater production, trigonometry, U.S. history, video film production, visual arts, voice ensemble, Web site design, Western civilization, wind ensemble, writing workshop, yearbook, zoology.

Graduation Requirements Algebra, arts, biology, chemistry, classical Greek literature, college planning, electives, English, English literature, foreign language, geometry, interdisciplinary studies, life skills, mathematics, music, performing arts, physical education (includes health), physics, physiology, pre-calculus, SAT preparation, senior internship, senior thesis, trigonometry, visual arts, four-week off-campus senior internship. Community service is required.

Special Academic Programs Advanced Placement exam preparation; honors section; independent study; term-away projects; study at local college for college credit; academic accommodation for the gifted, the musically talented, and the artistically talented.

College Admission Counseling 19 students graduated in 2010; 17 went to college, including Barnard College; Clark University; Hampshire College; Smith College; Stanford University; The Johns Hopkins University. Other: 2 entered a postgraduate year. Mean SAT critical reading: 660, mean SAT math: 600, mean SAT writing: 640, mean combined SAT: 1900. 79% scored over 600 on SAT critical reading, 53% scored over 600 on SAT math, 63% scored over 600 on SAT writing, 74% scored over 1800 on combined SAT.

Student Life Upper grades have student council, honor system. Discipline rests primarily with faculty.

Summer Programs Art/fine arts programs offered; session focuses on visual and performing arts; held on campus; accepts boys and girls; open to students from other schools. 45 students usually enrolled. 2011 schedule: June 14 to August 7. Application deadline: May 15.

Tuition and Aid Day student tuition: $21,675. Tuition installment plan (FACTS Tuition Payment Plan, The Tuition Refund Plan). Need-based scholarship grants, tuition reduction for children of full-time faculty and staff available. In 2010–11, 34% of upper-school students received aid. Total amount of financial aid awarded in 2010–11: $281,560.

Admissions Traditional secondary-level entrance grade is 9. For fall 2010, 27 students applied for upper-level admission, 17 were accepted, 15 enrolled. School's own exam required. Deadline for receipt of application materials: January 15. Application fee required: $50. On-campus interview required.

Athletics Interscholastic: baseball (boys), basketball (b,g), cross-country running (b,g), soccer (b,g), softball (g); intramural: basketball (b,g), softball (g); coed interscholastic: cross-country running, Frisbee, soccer, ultimate Frisbee; coed intramural: alpine skiing, basketball, bicycling, cooperative games, cross-country running, dance, figure skating, fitness, fitness walking, Frisbee, hiking/backpacking, ice skating, jogging, life saving, outdoor education, outdoor skills, skiing (downhill), snowboarding, soccer, swimming and diving, tennis, ultimate Frisbee, volleyball, walking, yoga. 2 PE instructors, 5 coaches.

Computers Computers are regularly used in all academic, college planning, desktop publishing, journalism, library skills, literary magazine, media, music, newspaper, photography, photojournalism, programming, SAT preparation, video film production, Web site design, yearbook classes. Computer network features include on-campus library services, online commercial services, Internet access, wireless campus network, EBSCOhost®, Maps101, Web Feet Guides, Gale databases, ProQuest, unitedstreaming, Britannica Online, World Book Online, Grolier Online. Campus intranet, student e-mail accounts, and computer access in designated common areas are available to students. The school has a published electronic and media policy.

Contact Tammy Reilly, Admissions Assistant. 845-462-7600 Ext. 201. Fax: 845-462-7602. E-mail: treilly@poughkeepsieday.org. Web site: www.poughkeepsieday.org/.

POWERS CATHOLIC HIGH SCHOOL
G-2040 West Carpenter Road
Flint, Michigan 48505-1028
Head of School: Mr. Thomas H. Furnas

General Information Coeducational day college-preparatory, arts, and religious studies school, affiliated with Roman Catholic Church. Grades 9–12. Founded: 1970. Setting: urban. 67-acre campus. 1 building on campus. Approved or accredited by North Central Association of Colleges and Schools and Michigan Department of Education. Endowment: $3 million. Total enrollment: 539. Upper school average class size: 25. Upper school faculty-student ratio: 1:19. There are 188 required school days per year for Upper School students. Upper School students typically attend 5 days per week. The average school day consists of 6 hours and 40 minutes.

Upper School Student Profile Grade 9: 122 students (58 boys, 64 girls); Grade 10: 136 students (81 boys, 55 girls); Grade 11: 148 students (66 boys, 82 girls); Grade 12: 133 students (70 boys, 63 girls). 75% of students are Roman Catholic.

Faculty School total: 28. In upper school: 9 men, 19 women; 20 have advanced degrees.

Subjects Offered Art, art-AP, biology, biology-AP, calculus-AP, ceramics, chemistry, choir, computer skills, concert band, drafting, economics, English, English literature and composition-AP, European history-AP, French, geometry, government, government-AP, health, honors algebra, honors English, honors geometry, integrated science, interdisciplinary studies, macroeconomics-AP, marching band, math analysis, math applications, mechanical drawing, orchestra, physics, pre-algebra, pre-calculus, psychology, psychology-AP, public speaking, religion, social justice, Spanish, state history, studio art-AP, theology, trigonometry, U.S. history, wind ensemble, world geography, world history, world religions, yearbook.

Graduation Requirements American history, English, government, health, mathematics, science, theology, world history, 40 hours of community service.

Special Academic Programs 9 Advanced Placement exams for which test preparation is offered; honors section; remedial reading and/or remedial writing; remedial math.

College Admission Counseling 183 students graduated in 2010; 182 went to college, including Central Michigan University; Grand Valley State University; Michigan State University; Saginaw Valley State University; University of Michigan. Other: 1 entered military service. Mean SAT critical reading: 592, mean SAT math: 590, mean SAT writing: 599, mean composite ACT: 22.

Student Life Upper grades have specified standards of dress, student council. Discipline rests primarily with faculty. Attendance at religious services is required.

Tuition and Aid Day student tuition: $7500. Tuition installment plan (monthly payment plans, individually arranged payment plans). Tuition reduction for siblings, merit scholarship grants, need-based scholarship grants available. In 2010–11, 33% of upper-school students received aid; total upper-school merit-scholarship money awarded: $11,000. Total amount of financial aid awarded in 2010–11: $450,300.

Admissions Traditional secondary-level entrance grade is 9. ACT-Explore required. Deadline for receipt of application materials: none. Application fee required: $50. Interview required.

Athletics Interscholastic: alpine skiing (boys, girls), baseball (b), basketball (b,g), bowling (b,g), cross-country running (b,g), dance squad (g), dance team (g), diving (b,g), football (b), golf (b,g), ice hockey (b), lacrosse (b,g), Nautilus (b,g), skiing (downhill) (b,g), soccer (b,g), softball (g), swimming and diving (b,g), tennis (b,g), track and field (b,g), volleyball (g), wrestling (b); coed interscholastic: cheering, equestrian sports, indoor track, power lifting, skeet shooting, strength & conditioning, weight lifting; coed intramural: ultimate Frisbee, weight training. 2 PE instructors.

Computers Computers are regularly used in accounting, business applications, drafting, graphic design, keyboarding, yearbook classes. Computer resources include on-campus library services, Internet access, wireless campus network, Internet filtering or blocking technology. Computer access in designated common areas is available to students. Students grades are available online. The school has a published electronic and media policy.

Contact Ms. Sally Bartos, Assistant Principal for Instruction. 810-591-4741. Fax: 810-591-0383. E-mail: sbartos@powerscatholic.org. Web site: www.powerscatholic.org.

THE PRAIRIE SCHOOL
4050 Lighthouse Drive
Racine, Wisconsin 53402
Head of School: Mr. Wm. Mark H. Murphy

General Information Coeducational day college-preparatory, arts, and technology school. Grades PK–12. Founded: 1965. Setting: small town. Nearest major city is Milwaukee. 33-acre campus. 2 buildings on campus. Approved or accredited by Independent Schools Association of the Central States and Wisconsin Department of Education. Member of National Association of Independent Schools. Endowment: $38 million. Total enrollment: 696. Upper school average class size: 17. Upper school faculty-student ratio: 1:17. There are 175 required school days per year for Upper School students. Upper School students typically attend 5 days per week. The average school day consists of 7 hours.

Upper School Student Profile Grade 9: 65 students (34 boys, 31 girls); Grade 10: 74 students (38 boys, 36 girls); Grade 11: 71 students (32 boys, 39 girls); Grade 12: 57 students (28 boys, 29 girls).

Faculty School total: 75. In upper school: 18 men, 14 women; 18 have advanced degrees.

Subjects Offered Algebra, American history, American history-AP, American literature, art, astronomy, athletic training, biology, biology-AP, calculus, calculus-AP, ceramics, chemistry, chemistry-AP, choir, community service, comparative religion, computer science, CPR, creative writing, dance, digital imaging, drama, drawing and design, earth and space science, ecology, economics, English, English literature, English-AP, environmental science, environmental science-AP, European history, European history-AP, fine arts, French, French language-AP, geometry, glassblowing, government/civics, health, history, international relations, jazz ensemble, mathematics, multicultural literature, music, music theory-AP, orchestra, photography, physical education, physics, physics-AP, pre-calculus, probability and statistics, public speaking, science, social studies, Spanish, Spanish language-AP, speech, study skills, theater, trigonometry, Western literature, world history, world literature.

Graduation Requirements Arts and fine arts (art, music, dance, drama), English, foreign language, mathematics, physical education (includes health), science, social studies (includes history), study skills, Spring Interim program (including on-campus seminars, community service, off-campus internships), 100-hour service requirement.

Special Academic Programs 13 Advanced Placement exams for which test preparation is offered; honors section; independent study; term-away projects; academic accommodation for the gifted, the musically talented, and the artistically talented; remedial reading and/or remedial writing; ESL (2 students enrolled).

College Admission Counseling 63 students graduated in 2009; all went to college, including Arizona State University; Marquette University; Northwestern University; University of Minnesota, Twin Cities Campus; University of Wisconsin–Madison. Median SAT math: 570, median SAT writing: 580, median combined SAT: 1150, median composite ACT: 28.

Student Life Upper grades have specified standards of dress, student council, honor system. Discipline rests primarily with faculty.

Tuition and Aid Day student tuition: $13,095. Tuition installment plan (FACTS Tuition Payment Plan). Tuition reduction for siblings, merit scholarship grants, need-based scholarship grants available. In 2009–10, 43% of upper-school students received aid; total upper-school merit-scholarship money awarded: $138,000. Total amount of financial aid awarded in 2009–10: $720,000.

Admissions Traditional secondary-level entrance grade is 9. For fall 2009, 39 students applied for upper-level admission, 34 were accepted, 13 enrolled. Admissions testing, school's own exam or TerraNova required. Deadline for receipt of application materials: none. Application fee required: $50. On-campus interview required.

Athletics Interscholastic: baseball (boys), basketball (b,g), soccer (b,g), tennis (b,g), volleyball (g); coed interscholastic: cross-country running, golf, modern dance, outdoor activities, track and field. 7 PE instructors, 13 coaches, 1 athletic trainer.

Computers Computers are regularly used in all academic classes. Computer network features include on-campus library services, Internet access, wireless campus network, Internet filtering or blocking technology. Campus intranet and computer access in designated common areas are available to students. Students grades are available online. The school has a published electronic and media policy.

Contact Ms. Molly Lofquist Johnson, Director of Admissions. 262-260-4393. Fax: 262-260-3790. E-mail: mlofquist@prairieschool.com. Web site: www.prairieschool.com.

PRESBYTERIAN PAN AMERICAN SCHOOL

PO Box 1578
223 North FM Road 772
Kingsville, Texas 78364-1578
Head of School: Dr. James H. Matthews

General Information Coeducational boarding and day and distance learning college-preparatory school, affiliated with Presbyterian Church (U.S.A.). Grades 9–12. Distance learning grades 9–12. Founded: 1912. Setting: rural. Nearest major city is Corpus Christi. Students are housed in single-sex dormitories. 670-acre campus. 22 buildings on campus. Approved or accredited by Southern Association of Colleges and Schools, Texas Private School Accreditation Commission, and Texas Department of Education. Endowment: $5.3 million. Total enrollment: 130. Upper school average class size: 16. Upper school faculty-student ratio: 1:9. There are 180 required school days per year for Upper School students. Upper School students typically attend 5 days per week. The average school day consists of 8 hours.

Upper School Student Profile Grade 9: 54 students (23 boys, 31 girls); Grade 10: 5 students (3 boys, 2 girls); Grade 11: 40 students (25 boys, 15 girls); Grade 12: 36 students (18 boys, 18 girls); Grade 13: 1 student (1 girl). 100% of students are boarding students. 8% are state residents. 1 state is represented in upper school student body. 92% are international students. International students from China, Democratic People's Republic of Korea, Equatorial Guinea, Guatemala, Mexico, and Taiwan; 3 other countries represented in student body. 40% of students are Presbyterian Church (U.S.A.).

Faculty School total: 16. In upper school: 5 men, 11 women; 5 have advanced degrees; 3 reside on campus.

Subjects Offered Algebra, American history, American literature, art, arts, Bible studies, biology, calculus, chemistry, computer math, computer science, English, English literature, ESL, fine arts, geography, geometry, government/civics, health, history, mathematics, music, physical education, physics, pre-calculus, religion, science, social sciences, social studies, Spanish, speech, trigonometry, world history, world literature, writing.

Graduation Requirements Arts and fine arts (art, music, dance, drama), computer science, economics, English, foreign language, mathematics, physical education (includes health), religion (includes Bible studies and theology), science, social sciences, social studies (includes history).

Special Academic Programs Study at local college for college credit; ESL (59 students enrolled).

College Admission Counseling 43 students graduated in 2010; 29 went to college, including Schreiner University; Texas A&M University; The University of Texas at Austin; The University of Texas at San Antonio; Trinity University; University of Houston. Other: 14 had other specific plans. Median SAT critical reading: 400, median SAT math: 440, median SAT writing: 420. 3% scored over 600 on SAT math.

Student Life Upper grades have specified standards of dress, student council, honor system. Discipline rests primarily with faculty. Attendance at religious services is required.

Tuition and Aid Day student tuition: $8500; 7-day tuition and room/board: $14,500. Guaranteed tuition plan. Tuition installment plan (monthly payment plans, individually arranged payment plans, quarterly payment plan, semester payment plan). Tuition reduction for siblings, merit scholarship grants, need-based scholarship grants, need-based financial aid available. In 2010–11, 85% of upper-school students received aid. Total amount of financial aid awarded in 2010–11: $907,340.

Admissions Traditional secondary-level entrance grade is 9. For fall 2010, 117 students applied for upper-level admission, 98 were accepted, 59 enrolled. Secondary Level English Proficiency required. Deadline for receipt of application materials: none. Application fee required: $35. On-campus interview recommended.

Athletics Interscholastic: basketball (boys, girls), cross-country running (b,g), jogging (b,g), life saving (b,g), physical fitness (b,g), physical training (b,g), soccer (b), table tennis (b), tennis (b,g), track and field (b,g), volleyball (g), walking (b,g); coed interscholastic: cheering. 2 PE instructors, 3 coaches, 1 athletic trainer.

Computers Computers are regularly used in all academic, English, ESL, mathematics classes. Computer resources include on-campus library services, Internet access, Internet filtering or blocking technology. Campus intranet and computer access in designated common areas are available to students. Students grades are available online. The school has a published electronic and media policy.

Contact Joe L. Garcia, Director of Admission/Registrar. 361-592-4307. Fax: 361-592-6126. E-mail: jlgarcia@ppas.org. Web site: www.ppas.org.

PRESTON HIGH SCHOOL

2780 Schurz Avenue
Bronx, New York 10465
Head of School: Mrs. Jane Grendell

General Information Girls' day college-preparatory, arts, religious studies, and technology school, affiliated with Roman Catholic Church. Grades 9–12. Founded: 1947. Setting: urban. Nearest major city is New York. 5-acre campus. 2 buildings on campus. Approved or accredited by Middle States Association of Colleges and Schools and New York Department of Education. Total enrollment: 600. Upper school average class size: 25. Upper school faculty-student ratio: 1:15. Upper School students typically attend 5 days per week. The average school day consists of 5 hours and 20 minutes.

Upper School Student Profile Grade 9: 173 students (173 girls); Grade 10: 142 students (142 girls); Grade 11: 135 students (135 girls); Grade 12: 150 students (150 girls). 83% of students are Roman Catholic.

Faculty School total: 44. In upper school: 14 men, 30 women; 37 have advanced degrees.

Subjects Offered Advanced computer applications, advanced math, Advanced Placement courses, algebra, American history, American history-AP, anatomy and physiology, art, biology, biology-AP, British literature, British literature (honors), calculus-AP, Catholic belief and practice, chemistry, chorus, communication skills, computer education, computer graphics, computer programming, creative writing, earth science, economics and history, English, English literature and composition-AP, film history, foreign language, geometry, global studies, government-AP, graphic design, health, honors algebra, honors English, honors geometry, honors U.S. history, honors world history, Italian, Latin, law, media studies, moral theology, music, peer counseling, philosophy, physical education, physics, play/screen writing, religious studies, service learning/internship, Spanish, Spanish language-AP, Spanish literature-AP, U.S. government and politics-AP, women in world history, world literature.

Graduation Requirements All academic, service, independent senior project.

Special Academic Programs Advanced Placement exam preparation; honors section; independent study; study at local college for college credit.

College Admission Counseling 168 students graduated in 2009; 167 went to college, including Fordham University; Iona College; Manhattan College; New York University; State University of New York at Binghamton; University at Albany, State University of New York. Other: 1 entered military service.

Student Life Upper grades have uniform requirement, student council, honor system. Discipline rests equally with students and faculty. Attendance at religious services is required.

Tuition and Aid Day student tuition: $6915. Tuition installment plan (monthly payment plans, individually arranged payment plans). Tuition reduction for siblings, merit scholarship grants, need-based scholarship grants available.

Admissions Traditional secondary-level entrance grade is 9. Math, reading, and mental ability tests, school placement exam and writing sample required. Deadline for receipt of application materials: December 15. Application fee required: $75. Interview recommended.

Athletics Interscholastic: basketball, cheering, fitness, soccer, softball, swimming and diving, volleyball. 2 PE instructors, 9 coaches.

Computers Computers are regularly used in graphic design, Web site design classes. Computer network features include on-campus library services, Internet access, Internet filtering or blocking technology. The school has a published electronic and media policy.

Contact Mrs. Julia Wall, Director of Admissions. 718-863-9134 Ext. 132. Fax: 718-863-6125. E-mail: jwall@prestonhs.org. Web site: www.prestonhs.org.

PRESTONWOOD CHRISTIAN ACADEMY

6801 West Park Boulevard
Plano, Texas 75093
Head of School: Mr. Larry Taylor

General Information Coeducational day college-preparatory and Bible courses school, affiliated with Southern Baptist Convention. Grades PK–12. Founded: 1997. Setting: suburban. Nearest major city is Dallas. 44-acre campus. 2 buildings on campus. Approved or accredited by Southern Association of Colleges and Schools and Texas Department of Education. Total enrollment: 1,410. Upper school average class size: 18. Upper school faculty-student ratio: 1:18. There are 176 required school days per year for Upper School students. Upper School students typically attend 5 days per week. The average school day consists of 7 hours and 35 minutes.

Upper School Student Profile Grade 9: 121 students (58 boys, 63 girls); Grade 10: 115 students (59 boys, 56 girls); Grade 11: 122 students (63 boys, 59 girls); Grade 12: 122 students (57 boys, 65 girls). 65% of students are Southern Baptist Convention.

Faculty School total: 107. In upper school: 16 men, 22 women; 20 have advanced degrees.

Subjects Offered 20th century history, 20th century physics, advanced chemistry, advanced math, Advanced Placement courses, algebra, American history-AP, American literature, anatomy and physiology, art, art-AP, band, Bible, biology, biology-AP, British literature, calculus-AP, ceramics, chemistry, choir, Christian doctrine, computer applications, conceptual physics, debate, drama, drawing, economics, ethics, fine arts, fitness, geometry, government, government-AP, health, honors algebra, honors English, honors geometry, honors U.S. history, honors world history, internship, language-AP, leadership education training, learning lab, literature-AP, logic, multimedia, multimedia design, newspaper, painting, performing arts, personal fitness, philosophy, photo shop, physical fitness, physics, physics-AP, pre-calculus, printmaking, sculpture, service learning/internship, Spanish, Spanish-AP, speech, statistics, student government, studio art, U.S. government and politics-AP, U.S. history, Web site design, Western literature, world history, world religions, yearbook.

Prestonwood Christian Academy

Graduation Requirements 1½ elective credits, algebra, arts and fine arts (art, music, dance, drama), Bible, biology, British literature, chemistry, Christian doctrine, computer applications, economics, English, English literature, ethics, foreign language, geometry, government, health, mathematics, philosophy, physical education (includes health), physics, speech, U.S. history, Western literature, world history, mission trip.

Special Academic Programs Advanced Placement exam preparation; honors section; academic accommodation for the gifted.

College Admission Counseling 118 students graduated in 2010; all went to college, including Baylor University; Ouachita Baptist University; Southern Methodist University; Texas A&M University; Texas Christian University; University of Oklahoma. Mean SAT critical reading: 568, mean SAT math: 554, mean SAT writing: 564, mean combined SAT: 1696, mean composite ACT: 24. 43% scored over 600 on SAT critical reading, 38% scored over 600 on SAT math, 38% scored over 600 on SAT writing, 39% scored over 1800 on combined SAT, 34% scored over 26 on composite ACT.

Student Life Upper grades have uniform requirement, student council, honor system. Discipline rests primarily with faculty.

Summer Programs Remediation, enrichment, advancement, sports, art/fine arts, rigorous outdoor training, computer instruction programs offered; held on campus; accepts boys and girls; open to students from other schools. 800 students usually enrolled. 2011 schedule: June 1 to August 5. Application deadline: May 1.

Tuition and Aid Day student tuition: $15,615–$16,364. Tuition installment plan (FACTS Tuition Payment Plan, monthly payment plans, individually arranged payment plans). Tuition reduction for siblings, need-based scholarship grants available. In 2010–11, 25% of upper-school students received aid. Total amount of financial aid awarded in 2010–11: $444,807.

Admissions Traditional secondary-level entrance grade is 9. For fall 2010, 91 students applied for upper-level admission, 56 were accepted, 45 enrolled. ISEE or Stanford Achievement Test required. Deadline for receipt of application materials: none. Application fee required: $100. Interview required.

Athletics Interscholastic: baseball (boys), basketball (b,g), cheering (g), cross-country running (b,g), drill team (g), football (b), golf (b,g), soccer (b,g), softball (g), swimming and diving (b,g), tennis (b,g), track and field (b,g), volleyball (g). 22 coaches.

Computers Computers are regularly used in all academic, technology classes. Computer network features include on-campus library services, Internet access, wireless campus network, Internet filtering or blocking technology. Students grades are available online. The school has a published electronic and media policy.

Contact Mrs. Marsha Backof, Admissions Assistant. 972-930-4010. Fax: 972-930-4008. E-mail: mbackof@prestonwoodchristian.org. Web site: www.prestonwoodchristian.org.

PROCTOR ACADEMY
PO Box 500
204 Main Street
Andover, New Hampshire 03216
Head of School: Mr. Michael Henriques

General Information Coeducational boarding and day college-preparatory, arts, technology, environmental studies, and experiential learning programs school. Grades 9–12. Founded: 1848. Setting: small town. Nearest major city is Concord. Students are housed in single-sex dormitories. 3,000-acre campus. 45 buildings on campus. Approved or accredited by Association for Experiential Education, Association of Independent Schools in New England, Independent Schools of Northern New England, New England Association of Schools and Colleges, The Association of Boarding Schools, and New Hampshire Department of Education. Member of National Association of Independent Schools and Secondary School Admission Test Board. Endowment: $25 million. Total enrollment: 355. Upper school average class size: 12. Upper school faculty-student ratio: 1:5. There are 170 required school days per year for Upper School students. Upper School students typically attend 5 days per week. The average school day consists of 5 hours and 35 minutes.

Upper School Student Profile Grade 9: 70 students (37 boys, 33 girls); Grade 10: 92 students (49 boys, 43 girls); Grade 11: 93 students (59 boys, 34 girls); Grade 12: 94 students (60 boys, 34 girls); Postgraduate: 4 students (4 boys). 77% of students are boarding students. 31% are state residents. 30 states are represented in upper school student body. 7% are international students. International students from Bermuda, Canada, Germany, Hong Kong, Mexico, and Republic of Korea; 6 other countries represented in student body.

Faculty School total: 85. In upper school: 39 men, 46 women; 54 have advanced degrees; 35 reside on campus.

Subjects Offered Algebra, American history, American literature, art, art history, biology, boat building, calculus, ceramics, chemistry, computer math, computer programming, creative writing, drama, economics, English, English literature, environmental science, European history, fine arts, finite math, forestry, French, geometry, health, history, industrial arts, mathematics, Middle Eastern history, music, music history, music technology, Native American history, performing arts, photography, physical education, physics, piano, play/screen writing, poetry, political thought, probability and statistics, psychology, public speaking, publications, robotics, science, senior project, social sciences, Spanish, sports medicine, studio art, study

skills, the Web, theater, theater history, U.S. government and politics-AP, U.S. history-AP, Vietnam history, voice, voice ensemble, wilderness experience, woodworking, world literature, writing, writing workshop.

Graduation Requirements Arts and fine arts (art, music, dance, drama), English, foreign language, mathematics, science, social sciences.

Special Academic Programs 11 Advanced Placement exams for which test preparation is offered; honors section; independent study; term-away projects; study at local college for college credit; study abroad; academic accommodation for the gifted; programs in general development for dyslexic students; ESL (5 students enrolled).

College Admission Counseling 98 students graduated in 2009; 90 went to college, including Bates College; Mount Holyoke College; St. Lawrence University; The Colorado College; Trinity College; University of New Hampshire. Other: 8 had other specific plans. Mean SAT critical reading: 555, mean SAT math: 560, mean SAT writing: 545, mean combined SAT: 1660, mean composite ACT: 23. 20% scored over 600 on SAT critical reading, 24% scored over 600 on SAT math, 22% scored over 600 on SAT writing, 24% scored over 26 on composite ACT.

Student Life Upper grades have student council, honor system. Discipline rests equally with students and faculty.

Tuition and Aid Day student tuition: $26,200; 7-day tuition and room/board: $43,400. Tuition installment plan (Academic Management Services Plan, monthly payment plans). Need-based scholarship grants available. In 2009–10, 28% of upper-school students received aid. Total amount of financial aid awarded in 2009–10: $2,800,000.

Admissions Traditional secondary-level entrance grade is 9. For fall 2009, 445 students applied for upper-level admission, 221 were accepted, 121 enrolled. ISEE, PSAT or SAT for applicants to grade 11 and 12, SSAT, TOEFL or SLEP, WISC/Woodcock-Johnson or writing sample required. Deadline for receipt of application materials: February 1. Application fee required: $50. Interview required.

Athletics Interscholastic: alpine skiing (boys, girls), baseball (b), basketball (b,g), bicycling (b,g), canoeing/kayaking (b,g), cross-country running (b,g), field hockey (g), football (b), hockey (b,g), ice hockey (b,g), lacrosse (b,g), nordic skiing (b,g), skiing (downhill) (b,g), snowboarding (b,g), soccer (b,g), softball (g), tennis (b,g); intramural: alpine skiing (b,g), snowboarding (b,g); coed interscholastic: dance, freestyle skiing, golf, horseback riding, kayaking, ski jumping, skiing (cross-country); coed intramural: aerobics/dance, aerobics/Nautilus, backpacking, ballet, broomball, canoeing/kayaking, climbing, combined training, dance, equestrian sports, fencing, fitness, Frisbee, hiking/backpacking, horseback riding, kayaking, martial arts, modern dance, mountain biking, mountaineering, outdoor activities, outdoor adventure, outdoor education, outdoor recreation, outdoor skills, outdoors, paint ball, rock climbing, running, skiing (downhill), snowshoeing, strength & conditioning, ultimate Frisbee, wall climbing, weight lifting, weight training, wilderness, yoga. 5 coaches, 3 athletic trainers.

Computers Computers are regularly used in all academic classes. Computer network features include on-campus library services, online commercial services, Internet access, wireless campus network, Internet filtering or blocking technology. Campus intranet and student e-mail accounts are available to students. Students grades are available online. The school has a published electronic and media policy.

Contact Charlie Durell, Admissions Coordinator. 603-735-6312. Fax: 603-735-6284. E-mail: charlie_durell@proctornet.com. Web site: www.proctoracademy.org.

PROFESSIONAL CHILDREN'S SCHOOL
132 West 60th Street
New York, New York 10023
Head of School: Dr. James Dawson

General Information Coeducational day college-preparatory school. Grades 6–12. Founded: 1914. Setting: urban. 1 building on campus. Approved or accredited by New York State Association of Independent Schools. Member of National Association of Independent Schools. Endowment: $2.7 million. Total enrollment: 183. Upper school average class size: 10. Upper school faculty-student ratio: 1:8. There are 165 required school days per year for Upper School students. Upper School students typically attend 5 days per week. The average school day consists of 7 hours.

Upper School Student Profile Grade 9: 24 students (8 boys, 16 girls); Grade 10: 45 students (13 boys, 32 girls); Grade 11: 45 students (12 boys, 33 girls); Grade 12: 38 students (9 boys, 29 girls).

Faculty School total: 27. In upper school: 11 men, 15 women; 24 have advanced degrees.

Subjects Offered Advanced math, algebra, American government, American history, biology, calculus, chemistry, chorus, computer education, constitutional history of U.S., constitutional law, creative writing, drama, English, English literature, environmental science, ESL, foreign language, French, general math, geometry, health education, introduction to literature, keyboarding, library research, library skills, physical education, physics, pre-algebra, pre-calculus, Spanish, studio art, U.S. government, U.S. history.

Graduation Requirements Art, English, foreign language, health, history, mathematics, science.

Special Academic Programs ESL (20 students enrolled).

College Admission Counseling 54 students graduated in 2010; 42 went to college, including Barnard College; Emory University; Fordham University; Manhattan School of Music; New York University; The Juilliard School. Other: 12 went to work.

Student Life Upper grades have student council, honor system. Discipline rests primarily with faculty.

Tuition and Aid Day student tuition: $29,665. Tuition installment plan (Academic Management Services Plan, Tuition Management Systems). Need-based scholarship grants available. In 2010–11, 27% of upper-school students received aid. Total amount of financial aid awarded in 2010–11: $606,500.

Admissions Traditional secondary-level entrance grade is 9. For fall 2010, 145 students applied for upper-level admission, 117 were accepted, 55 enrolled. ERB, ISEE or Stanford Achievement Test required. Deadline for receipt of application materials: none. Application fee required: $75. On-campus interview recommended.

Athletics 1 PE instructor.

Computers Computers are regularly used in all academic classes. Computer network features include on-campus library services, Internet access, wireless campus network, Internet filtering or blocking technology. Student e-mail accounts are available to students. The school has a published electronic and media policy.

Contact Sherrie A. Hinkle, Director of Admissions. 212-582-3116 Ext. 112. Fax: 212-307-6542. E-mail: info@pcs-nyc.org. Web site: www.pcs-nyc.org.

THE PROUT SCHOOL

4640 Tower Hill Road
Wakefield, Rhode Island 02879
Head of School: Mr. Gary Delneo

General Information Coeducational day college-preparatory, arts, religious studies, and technology school, affiliated with Roman Catholic Church. Grades 9–12. Founded: 1966. Setting: small town. Nearest major city is Providence. 25-acre campus. 1 building on campus. Approved or accredited by International Baccalaureate Organization, New England Association of Schools and Colleges, Rhode Island State Certified Resource Progam, and Rhode Island Department of Education. Total enrollment: 640. Upper school average class size: 21. Upper school faculty-student ratio: 1:18. There are 182 required school days per year for Upper School students. Upper School students typically attend 5 days per week. The average school day consists of 6 hours and 30 minutes.

Upper School Student Profile 75% of students are Roman Catholic.

Faculty School total: 53. In upper school: 25 men, 28 women; 40 have advanced degrees.

Subjects Offered Acting, American literature, anatomy and physiology, art education, art history, athletic training, ballet, ballet technique, band, biology, calculus, chemistry, Chinese, choir, chorus, Christian doctrine, Christian education, Christian ethics, Christian scripture, Christian studies, Christianity, church history, clayworking, college planning, college writing, community service, comparative religion, computer applications, computer art, computer education, computer graphics, computer multimedia, computer programming, computer science, computer skills, computer studies, contemporary history, contemporary issues, costumes and make-up, CPR, creative dance, creative drama, creative thinking, critical studies in film, critical writing, dance performance, drama performance, drama workshop, dramatic arts, drawing, drawing and design, earth science, economics, economics and history, English, English composition, English literature, environmental science, environmental studies, first aid, fitness, food and nutrition, foreign language, French, general science, government, graphic arts, graphic design, health, health and wellness, history, history of the Catholic Church, honors English, honors U.S. history, honors world history, human anatomy, instruments, introduction to theater, Italian, jazz band, keyboarding, lab science, language, language and composition, law and the legal system, life science, marine science, mathematics, modern history, music performance, music theater, musical theater, musical theater dance, oceanography, personal fitness, physical fitness, physics, play production, portfolio art, pre-calculus, public service, religion, religion and culture, religious education, religious studies, scene study, science, science research, scripture, set design, Spanish, sports nutrition, stage and body movement, stage design, theater, theater arts, theater design and production, theater history, visual and performing arts, yearbook.

Graduation Requirements Computers, English, foreign language, health education, history, lab science, mathematics, oceanography, physical education (includes health), religion (includes Bible studies and theology), science.

Special Academic Programs International Baccalaureate program; Advanced Placement exam preparation; honors section.

College Admission Counseling 158 students graduated in 2010; 152 went to college, including Coker College; Johnson & Wales University; Providence College; Salve Regina University; University of New Hampshire; University of Rhode Island. Other: 1 went to work, 2 entered military service, 3 entered a postgraduate year.

Student Life Upper grades have uniform requirement, student council, honor system. Discipline rests primarily with faculty. Attendance at religious services is required.

Tuition and Aid Day student tuition: $10,750. Tuition installment plan (FACTS Tuition Payment Plan). Tuition reduction for siblings, need-based scholarship grants available. In 2010–11, 28% of upper-school students received aid. Total amount of financial aid awarded in 2010–11: $225,000.

Admissions Traditional secondary-level entrance grade is 9. For fall 2010, 310 students applied for upper-level admission, 228 were accepted, 167 enrolled. Admissions testing and essay required. Deadline for receipt of application materials: December 22. Application fee required: $25.

Athletics Interscholastic: baseball (boys), basketball (b,g), cheering (g), cross-country running (b,g), gymnastics (g), lacrosse (b,g), soccer (b,g), softball (g),

swimming and diving (b,g), tennis (b,g), track and field (b,g), volleyball (g); intramural: dance (g), outdoor recreation (b,g); coed interscholastic: aquatics, golf, ice hockey; coed intramural: aerobics, aerobics/dance, ballet, bicycling, fitness, outdoor recreation, sailing, strength & conditioning, table tennis, weight lifting, weight training. 3 PE instructors, 14 coaches.

Computers Computers are regularly used in all academic classes. Computer resources include on-campus library services, Internet access, Internet filtering or blocking technology. Computer access in designated common areas is available to students. The school has a published electronic and media policy.

Contact Ms. Kristen Need, Director of Admissions. 401-789-9262 Ext. 515. Fax: 401-782-2262. E-mail: kneed@theproutschool.org. Web site: www.theproutschool.org.

PROVIDENCE CATHOLIC SCHOOL, THE COLLEGE PREPARATORY SCHOOL FOR GIRLS GRADES 6-12

1215 North St. Mary's
San Antonio, Texas 78215-1787
Head of School: Sr. Antoinette Billeaud, CDP

General Information Girls' day college-preparatory, arts, and religious studies school, affiliated with Roman Catholic Church. Grades 6–12. Founded: 1951. Setting: urban. 3-acre campus. 4 buildings on campus. Approved or accredited by Southern Association of Colleges and Schools, Southern Association of Independent Schools, Texas Catholic Conference, and Texas Education Agency. Total enrollment: 346. Upper school average class size: 22. Upper school faculty-student ratio: 1:11. There are 186 required school days per year for Upper School students. Upper School students typically attend 5 days per week. The average school day consists of 7 hours.

Upper School Student Profile Grade 6: 55 students (55 girls); Grade 7: 43 students (43 girls); Grade 8: 42 students (42 girls); Grade 9: 49 students (49 girls); Grade 10: 50 students (50 girls); Grade 11: 57 students (57 girls); Grade 12: 50 students (50 girls). 80% of students are Roman Catholic.

Faculty School total: 34. In upper school: 5 men, 26 women; 28 have advanced degrees.

Subjects Offered Acting, advanced biology, advanced chemistry, advanced math, Advanced Placement courses, aerobics, algebra, American history, American history-AP, American literature, American literature-AP, anatomy, ancient world history, art, athletics, audio visual/media, band, biology, biology-AP, British literature, British literature-AP, broadcast journalism, broadcasting, calculus-AP, career education internship, Catholic belief and practice, cheerleading, chemistry, choir, choral music, church history, composition-AP, computer information systems, concert band, concert choir, conflict resolution, creative writing, dance, dance performance, desktop publishing, drama, drama performance, drama workshop, economics, English, English language and composition-AP, English language-AP, English literature, English literature and composition-AP, English literature-AP, English-AP, film, fitness, foreign language, French, geography, government, government and politics-AP, history, history-AP, human anatomy, jazz band, journalism, JROTC, JROTC or LEAD (Leadership Education and Development), Latin, law, leadership, literature and composition-AP, music theory, newspaper, peer ministry, personal fitness, photography, photojournalism, physical education, physical fitness, physical science, physics, play production, psychology, social justice, sociology, softball, Spanish, Spanish language-AP, Spanish-AP, speech, sports, statistics-AP, student government, student publications, swimming, swimming competency, tennis, Texas history, the Web, theater, theater arts, theater design and production, theater production, theology, track and field, U.S. government and politics, U.S. government and politics-AP, U.S. history, U.S. history-AP, volleyball, Web site design, world geography, world history, yearbook.

Graduation Requirements All academic, 100 hours of community service completed by grade 12, Senior Retreat participation.

Special Academic Programs International Baccalaureate program; 13 Advanced Placement exams for which test preparation is offered; honors section; independent study; study at local college for college credit.

College Admission Counseling 42 students graduated in 2010; all went to college, including St. Mary's University; Texas A&M University; The University of Texas at Austin; The University of Texas at San Antonio; University of the Incarnate Word.

Student Life Upper grades have uniform requirement, student council, honor system. Discipline rests primarily with faculty. Attendance at religious services is required.

Summer Programs Remediation, enrichment, advancement, sports, art/fine arts, computer instruction programs offered; session focuses on getting ahead (improvement); held on campus; accepts girls; open to students from other schools. 100 students usually enrolled. 2011 schedule: June 6 to July 14. Application deadline: May 25.

Tuition and Aid Day student tuition: $7035. Tuition installment plan (monthly payment plans, Middle School Tuition $4,202). Tuition reduction for siblings, merit scholarship grants, need-based scholarship grants available. In 2010–11, 20% of upper-school students received aid; total upper-school merit-scholarship money awarded: $55,500. Total amount of financial aid awarded in 2010–11: $200,000.

Admissions Traditional secondary-level entrance grade is 9. High School Placement Test or QUIC required. Deadline for receipt of application materials: none. No application fee required. On-campus interview recommended.

Providence Catholic School, The College Preparatory School for Girls Grades 6-12

Athletics Interscholastic: aerobics, aerobics/dance, basketball, bowling, cheering, cross-country running, dance, dance team, drill team, JROTC drill, physical fitness, physical training, running, soccer, softball, tennis, track and field, volleyball, weight training, winter soccer; coed interscholastic: aquatics. 2 PE instructors, 7 coaches, 1 athletic trainer.

Computers Computers are regularly used in desktop publishing, journalism, newspaper, Web site design, yearbook classes. Computer network features include on-campus library services, online commercial services, Internet access, Internet filtering or blocking technology, online classrooms. Campus intranet and student e-mail accounts are available to students. Students grades are available online. The school has a published electronic and media policy.

Contact Mrs. Nora Walsh, Enrollment Director. 210-224-6651 Ext. 210. Fax: 210-224-6214. E-mail: nwalsh@providencehs.net. Web site: www.providencehs.net.

PROVIDENCE CHRISTIAN SCHOOL

P.O. Box 240
Monarch, Alberta T0L 1M0, Canada
Head of School: Mr. Gerrit van de Haar

General Information Coeducational day college-preparatory, general academic, and religious studies school, affiliated with Calvinist faith, Reformed Church. Grades K–12. Founded: 1994. Setting: rural. Nearest major city is Lethbridge, Canada. 5-acre campus. 1 building on campus. Approved or accredited by Alberta Department of Education. Language of instruction: English. Total enrollment: 134. Upper school average class size: 12. Upper school faculty-student ratio: 1:11. There are 180 required school days per year for Upper School students. Upper School students typically attend 4 days per week. The average school day consists of 6 hours and 25 minutes.

Upper School Student Profile Grade 10: 9 students (5 boys, 4 girls); Grade 11: 12 students (6 boys, 6 girls); Grade 12: 8 students (3 boys, 5 girls). 90% of students are Calvinist, Reformed.

Faculty School total: 10. In upper school: 3 men, 2 women.

Subjects Offered Accounting, advanced biology, advanced math, Bible, Bible studies, bookkeeping, business applications, business education, business law, business studies, career and personal planning, career and technology systems, Christian doctrine, Christian scripture, church history, civil rights, computer technologies, critical thinking, English, ESL, finance, first aid, French, general science, health education, human sexuality, information processing, information technology, integrated mathematics, integrated physics, integrated science, keyboarding, language arts, library, life skills, mathematics, music, music appreciation, participation in sports, personal finance, physics, reading, religious education, science project, sewing, sex education, social studies, sports, Web site design.

Graduation Requirements Alberta Ministry of Education requirements.

Special Academic Programs International Baccalaureate program; ESL (6 students enrolled).

College Admission Counseling 6 students graduated in 2010; 1 went to college. Other: 3 went to work, 2 entered a postgraduate year.

Student Life Upper grades have specified standards of dress, student council, honor system. Discipline rests primarily with faculty. Attendance at religious services is required.

Tuition and Aid Day student tuition: CAN$5100. Tuition installment plan (The Tuition Plan). Tuition reduction for siblings available.

Admissions Traditional secondary-level entrance grade is 10. For fall 2010, 29 students applied for upper-level admission, 29 were accepted, 29 enrolled. Deadline for receipt of application materials: September 30. No application fee required. Interview required.

Athletics 2 PE instructors.

Computers Computers are regularly used in all classes. Computer network features include Internet access, wireless campus network, Internet filtering or blocking technology. The school has a published electronic and media policy.

Contact Mr. Gerrit van de Haar, Principal. 403-381-4418. Fax: 403-381-4428. E-mail: vandehaar.g@pcsmonarch.com. Web site: http://www.pcsmonarch.com/.

PROVIDENCE COUNTRY DAY SCHOOL

660 Waterman Avenue
East Providence, Rhode Island 02914-1724
Head of School: Mrs. Susan M. Haberlandt

General Information Coeducational day college-preparatory and arts school. Grades 6–12. Founded: 1923. Setting: suburban. Nearest major city is Providence. 42-acre campus. 6 buildings on campus. Approved or accredited by Association of Independent Schools in New England, New England Association of Schools and Colleges, The College Board, and Rhode Island Department of Education. Member of National Association of Independent Schools and Secondary School Admission Test Board. Endowment: $1.5 million. Total enrollment: 233. Upper school average class size: 12. Upper school faculty-student ratio: 1:7. The average school day consists of 6 hours and 50 minutes.

Upper School Student Profile Grade 6: 9 students (6 boys, 3 girls); Grade 7: 18 students (13 boys, 5 girls); Grade 8: 23 students (12 boys, 11 girls); Grade 9: 41 students (23 boys, 18 girls); Grade 10: 47 students (32 boys, 15 girls); Grade 11: 49 students (33 boys, 16 girls); Grade 12: 46 students (32 boys, 14 girls).

Faculty School total: 40. In upper school: 14 men, 15 women; 26 have advanced degrees.

Subjects Offered Advanced Placement courses, algebra, American government, American history, American history-AP, American literature, ancient history, art, art history-AP, Asian studies, Bible as literature, bioethics, biology, biology-AP, British literature, calculus, calculus-AP, ceramics, chemistry, choir, computer graphics, conceptual physics, creative writing, drama, earth science, electives, English, English literature, English literature-AP, environmental science, European civilization, European history, expository writing, fine arts, foreign language, forensics, French, geography, geometry, government/civics, graphic design, health, history, independent study, jazz ensemble, journalism, Latin, mathematics, media production, modern European history, music, performing arts, photography, physical education, physics, pottery, pre-algebra, pre-calculus, public speaking, science, senior internship, social studies, Spanish, Spanish language-AP, studio art, theater, trigonometry, U.S. government and politics-AP, visual arts, world history, writing.

Graduation Requirements Arts and fine arts (art, music, dance, drama), English, foreign language, history, mathematics, physical education (includes health), science, senior independent project.

Special Academic Programs 8 Advanced Placement exams for which test preparation is offered; honors section; independent study; term-away projects; study abroad; academic accommodation for the gifted, the musically talented, and the artistically talented.

College Admission Counseling 47 students graduated in 2010; 46 went to college, including Colby College; Connecticut College; Gettysburg College; Skidmore College; University of Rhode Island; Worcester Polytechnic Institute. Other: 1 entered a postgraduate year. Mean SAT critical reading: 575, mean SAT math: 576, mean SAT writing: 585.

Student Life Upper grades have specified standards of dress, student council, honor system. Discipline rests primarily with faculty.

Tuition and Aid Day student tuition: $27,100–$27,400. Tuition installment plan (monthly payment plans). Need-based scholarship grants available. In 2010–11, 41% of upper-school students received aid. Total amount of financial aid awarded in 2010–11: $1,500,000.

Admissions Traditional secondary-level entrance grade is 9. ISEE or SSAT required. Deadline for receipt of application materials: February 1. Application fee required: $55. On-campus interview required.

Athletics Interscholastic: baseball (boys), basketball (b,g), cross-country running (b,g), football (b), golf (b,g), ice hockey (b), indoor track & field (b,g), lacrosse (b,g), sailing (b,g), soccer (b,g), swimming and diving (b,g), tennis (b,g), track and field (b,g), winter (indoor) track (b,g), wrestling (b); coed interscholastic: physical fitness, yoga; coed intramural: strength & conditioning, weight training. 2 PE instructors, 8 coaches, 1 athletic trainer.

Computers Computers are regularly used in art, English, foreign language, history, mathematics, music, science classes. Computer network features include on-campus library services, online commercial services, Internet access, Internet filtering or blocking technology. Computer access in designated common areas is available to students. The school has a published electronic and media policy.

Contact Ms. Whitney H. Russell, Director of Admissions and Financial Aid. 401-438-5170 Ext. 102. Fax: 401-435-4514. E-mail: russell@providencecountryday.org. Web site: www.providencecountryday.org.

PROVIDENCE DAY SCHOOL

5800 Sardis Road
Charlotte, North Carolina 28270
Head of School: Mr. Steve Barker

General Information Coeducational day college-preparatory and global studies diploma program school. Grades PK–12. Founded: 1970. Setting: suburban. 44-acre campus. 18 buildings on campus. Approved or accredited by North Carolina Association of Independent Schools, Southern Association of Colleges and Schools, Southern Association of Independent Schools, and North Carolina Department of Education. Member of National Association of Independent Schools. Endowment: $4 million. Total enrollment: 1,501. Upper school average class size: 15. Upper school faculty-student ratio: 1:12. There are 177 required school days per year for Upper School students. Upper School students typically attend 5 days per week. The average school day consists of 7 hours and 10 minutes.

Upper School Student Profile Grade 6: 116 students (57 boys, 59 girls); Grade 7: 133 students (60 boys, 73 girls); Grade 8: 125 students (64 boys, 61 girls); Grade 9: 148 students (76 boys, 72 girls); Grade 10: 129 students (68 boys, 61 girls); Grade 11: 120 students (55 boys, 65 girls); Grade 12: 137 students (81 boys, 56 girls).

Faculty School total: 148. In upper school: 46 men, 34 women; 56 have advanced degrees.

Subjects Offered 3-dimensional design, accounting, African-American history, algebra, American history, American literature, art, art history-AP, Asian history, band, biology, biology-AP, calculus-AP, chemistry, chemistry-AP, chorus, Civil War, composition, computer graphics, computer programming, computer science, computer science-AP, drama, economics, English, English literature, English-AP, environmental science, environmental science-AP, fine arts, French, French-AP, geometry, German, German-AP, government-AP, government/civics, health, history, history-AP, instrumental music, international relations, journalism, Judaic studies, keyboarding, Latin, Latin-AP, literature, Mandarin, mathematics, music-AP, photography, physical education, physical science, physics, physics-AP, political science, pre-calculus, psychology, science, set design, social studies, Spanish, Spanish-AP, sports medicine, statistics-AP, theater, word processing, world history, writing, yearbook.

Graduation Requirements Arts and fine arts (art, music, dance, drama), computer science, English, foreign language, mathematics, physical education (includes health), science, social studies (includes history).

Special Academic Programs 24 Advanced Placement exams for which test preparation is offered; honors section; accelerated programs; study abroad; academic accommodation for the gifted, the musically talented, and the artistically talented.

College Admission Counseling 122 students graduated in 2010; 121 went to college, including Appalachian State University; Duke University; North Carolina State University; The University of North Carolina at Chapel Hill; University of Virginia; Wake Forest University. Other: 1 entered a postgraduate year. Median SAT critical reading: 650, median SAT math: 660, median SAT writing: 650, median combined SAT: 1960, median composite ACT: 28. 73% scored over 600 on SAT critical reading, 80% scored over 600 on SAT math, 71% scored over 600 on SAT writing, 73% scored over 1800 on combined SAT.

Student Life Upper grades have specified standards of dress, student council, honor system. Discipline rests equally with students and faculty.

Summer Programs Remediation, enrichment, advancement, sports, art/fine arts, computer instruction programs offered; session focuses on academics, enrichment; held both on and off campus; held at various parks, recreation centers, museums; accepts boys and girls; open to students from other schools. 2,500 students usually enrolled. 2011 schedule: June 7 to August 6. Application deadline: none.

Tuition and Aid Day student tuition: $20,026. Tuition installment plan (Academic Management Services Plan, monthly payment plans). Need-based scholarship grants available. In 2010–11, 14% of upper-school students received aid. Total amount of financial aid awarded in 2010–11: $1,056,585.

Admissions Traditional secondary-level entrance grade is 9. For fall 2010, 113 students applied for upper-level admission, 65 were accepted, 39 enrolled. Cognitive Abilities Test, ERB CTP IV, ISEE or Woodcock-Johnson Educational Evaluation, WISC III required. Deadline for receipt of application materials: January 15. Application fee required: $90. On-campus interview required.

Athletics Interscholastic: aerobics/dance (girls), baseball (b), basketball (b,g), cheering (g), cross-country running (b,g), dance squad (g), field hockey (g), football (b), golf (b,g), lacrosse (b;g), soccer (b,g), softball (g), swimming and diving (b,g), tennis (b,g), track and field (b,g), volleyball (g), wrestling (b); intramural: indoor hockey (b,g), indoor soccer (b,g), Newcombe ball (b,g), physical fitness (b,g), pillo polo (b,g), soccer (b,g), softball (b,g), strength & conditioning (b,g), volleyball (b,g); coed intramural: indoor hockey, indoor soccer, Newcombe ball, physical fitness, pillo polo, soccer, softball, strength & conditioning, tennis, volleyball. 4 PE instructors, 36 coaches, 2 athletic trainers.

Computers Computers are regularly used in English, mathematics, science, technology, word processing classes. Computer network features include on-campus library services, online commercial services, Internet access, wireless campus network, Internet filtering or blocking technology, wireless iBook lab available for individual student check-out. Student e-mail accounts and computer access in designated common areas are available to students. Students grades are available online. The school has a published electronic and media policy.

Contact Mrs. Carissa Goddard, Admissions Assistant. 704-887-7040. Fax: 704-887-7520 Ext. 7041. E-mail: carissa.goddard@providenceday.org. Web site: www.providenceday.org.

PROVIDENCE HIGH SCHOOL

511 South Buena Vista Street
Burbank, California 91505-4865
Head of School: Mr. Michael Collins

General Information Coeducational day college-preparatory, arts, religious studies, and technology school, affiliated with Roman Catholic Church. Grades 9–12. Founded: 1955. Setting: urban. Nearest major city is Los Angeles. 4-acre campus. 6 buildings on campus. Approved or accredited by National Catholic Education Association, The College Board, Western Association of Schools and Colleges, Western Catholic Education Association, and California Department of Education. Endowment: $100,000. Total enrollment: 375. Upper school average class size: 22. Upper school faculty-student ratio: 1:12. There are 183 required school days per year for Upper School students. Upper School students typically attend 5 days per week. The average school day consists of 6 hours.

Upper School Student Profile Grade 9: 80 students (44 boys, 36 girls); Grade 10: 97 students (40 boys, 57 girls); Grade 11: 102 students (55 boys, 47 girls); Grade 12: 96 students (34 boys, 62 girls). 72% of students are Roman Catholic.

Faculty School total: 33. In upper school: 11 men, 22 women; 29 have advanced degrees.

Subjects Offered 3-dimensional art, accounting, advanced computer applications, Advanced Placement courses, advanced studio art-AP, algebra, American history, American history-AP, American literature, American literature-AP, Basic programming, Bible studies, biology, biology-AP, calculus, Catholic belief and practice, ceramics, chemistry, chorus, church history, community service, computer animation, computer art, computer programming, computer science, digital photography, drama, economics, economics-AP, English, English literature, English literature and composition-AP, environmental science, ethics, film, fine arts, French, geography,

geometry, graphic arts, health, history, journalism, language-AP, law, mathematics, media studies, music, photography, physical education, physics, pre-calculus, psychology, religion, robotics, science, social studies, Spanish, Spanish-AP, theater, trigonometry, U.S. government, U.S. government and politics-AP, U.S. history-AP, United States government-AP, video, video and animation, video film production, visual and performing arts, volleyball, weight fitness, weight training, world cultures, world geography, world history, world religions, world religions, writing, yearbook, yoga.

Graduation Requirements American government, American history, American literature, art, biology, British literature, chemistry, comparative religion, computer science, cultural geography, economics, electives, English, ethics, foreign language, mathematics, physical education (includes health), religion (includes Bible studies and theology), science, social studies (includes history), world literature, completion of Christian Service hours.

Special Academic Programs 9 Advanced Placement exams for which test preparation is offered; honors section; academic accommodation for the musically talented and the artistically talented.

College Admission Counseling 108 students graduated in 2010; 104 went to college, including California State University, Los Angeles; California State University, Northridge; Loyola Marymount University; University of California, Irvine; University of California, Los Angeles; University of California, Riverside. Other: 4 had other specific plans. Median SAT critical reading: 530, median SAT math: 525, median SAT writing: 537, median composite ACT: 24.

Student Life Upper grades have uniform requirement, student council. Discipline rests equally with students and faculty. Attendance at religious services is required.

Summer Programs Remediation, enrichment, advancement, sports, art/fine arts, computer instruction programs offered; session focuses on enrichment, remediation, and extracurricular activities; held on campus; accepts boys and girls; open to students from other schools. 250 students usually enrolled. 2011 schedule: June 28 to July 29. Application deadline: June 1.

Tuition and Aid Day student tuition: $10,400. Tuition installment plan (The Tuition Plan, 1-payment plan: payment in full due July 1st, 2-payment plan-60% due July 1st, 40% due January 1st, 10-payment plan: monthly beginning July 1, ending April 1). Tuition reduction for siblings, merit scholarship grants, need-based scholarship grants available. In 2010–11, 31% of upper-school students received aid; total upper-school merit-scholarship money awarded: $56,500. Total amount of financial aid awarded in 2010–11: $219,000.

Admissions Admissions testing or ETS high school placement exam required. Deadline for receipt of application materials: March 8. Application fee required: $65. On-campus interview recommended.

Athletics Interscholastic: baseball (boys), basketball (b,g), combined training (b), cross-country running (b,g), fitness (b,g), physical fitness (b,g), soccer (b,g), softball (g), strength & conditioning (b,g), volleyball (b,g), weight training (b); coed interscholastic: cheering, cross-country running, dance team, track and field, yoga; coed intramural: volleyball. 3 PE instructors, 10 coaches.

Computers Computers are regularly used in accounting, animation, computer applications, desktop publishing, digital applications, information technology, journalism, library, literary magazine, media, media production, newspaper, photography, publications, video film production, Web site design, word processing, yearbook classes. Computer network features include on-campus library services, online commercial services, Internet access, wireless campus network, Microsoft Office Suite XP Professional, extranet portal. Student e-mail accounts are available to students. Students grades are available online. The school has a published electronic and media policy.

Contact Mrs. Judy Umeck, Director of Admissions. 818-846-8141 Ext. 501. Fax: 818-843-8421. E-mail: judy.umeck@providencehigh.org. Web site: www.providencehigh.org.

PULASKI ACADEMY

12701 Hinson Road
Little Rock, Arkansas 72212
Head of School: Dr. Bill R. Mott

General Information Coeducational day college-preparatory and arts school. Grades PK–12. Founded: 1971. Setting: suburban. 32-acre campus. 4 buildings on campus. Approved or accredited by Independent Schools Association of the Central States. Member of National Association of Independent Schools and Secondary School Admission Test Board. Endowment: $2.5 million. Total enrollment: 1,315. Upper school average class size: 13. Upper school faculty-student ratio: 1:13. There are 178 required school days per year for Upper School students. Upper School students typically attend 5 days per week. The average school day consists of 5 hours and 45 minutes.

Upper School Student Profile Grade 9: 94 students (48 boys, 46 girls); Grade 10: 86 students (43 boys, 43 girls); Grade 11: 91 students (43 boys, 48 girls); Grade 12: 104 students (54 boys, 50 girls).

Faculty School total: 137. In upper school: 19 men, 42 women; 14 have advanced degrees.

Subjects Offered Algebra, American history-AP, American literature, anatomy, art, art history, athletics, band, biology, biology-AP, calculus, calculus-AP, chemistry, chemistry-AP, chorus, community service, comparative government and politics-AP, composition-AP, computer programming-AP, creative writing, debate, design, desktop publishing, drama, drawing, English, English literature, English literature-AP, European history-AP, fine arts, French, French-AP, geometry, German, government and politics-AP, grammar, health, honors algebra, honors geometry, humanities, independent study, journalism, Latin, Latin-AP, learning lab, learning strategies, Mandarin, mathematics, music, music history, music theory, physical education, physical science, physics, physics-AP, physiology, pre-calculus, reading, science, social studies, Spanish, Spanish-AP, speech, statistics, theater, trigonometry, U.S. government and politics-AP, world civilizations, world history, yearbook.

Graduation Requirements Arts and fine arts (art, music, dance, drama), English, foreign language, history, mathematics, physical education (includes health), science. Community service is required.

Special Academic Programs Advanced Placement exam preparation; honors section; independent study.

College Admission Counseling 86 students graduated in 2009; all went to college, including Harvard University; Princeton University; Rhode Island School of Design; Stanford University; The University of North Carolina at Chapel Hill; University of Arkansas. Mean SAT critical reading: 582, mean SAT math: 587, mean SAT writing: 620, mean combined SAT: 1789, mean composite ACT: 27.

Student Life Upper grades have specified standards of dress, student council, honor system. Discipline rests primarily with faculty.

Tuition and Aid Day student tuition: $3200–$9700. Tuition installment plan (monthly payment plans, individually arranged payment plans, school's own payment plan). Tuition reduction for siblings, need-based scholarship grants available. In 2009–10, 13% of upper-school students received aid. Total amount of financial aid awarded in 2009–10: $300,000.

Admissions Traditional secondary-level entrance grade is 9. For fall 2009, 35 students applied for upper-level admission, 29 were accepted, 21 enrolled. Stanford Achievement Test required. Deadline for receipt of application materials: none. Application fee required: $50. On-campus interview recommended.

Athletics Interscholastic: aerobics/dance (girls), aerobics/Nautilus (b), aquatics (b,g), baseball (b), basketball (b,g), cheering (g), cross-country running (b,g), dance (g), dance squad (g), dance team (g), diving (b,g), drill team (g), football (b), golf (b,g), pom squad (g), soccer (b,g), softball (g), swimming and diving (b,g), tennis (b,g); intramural: fitness (b,g); coed interscholastic: aerobics. 4 PE instructors, 10 coaches, 1 athletic trainer.

Computers Computers are regularly used in business, career exploration, college planning, creative writing, current events, data processing, economics, English, foreign language, geography, human geography—AP, information technology, introduction to technology, mathematics, newspaper, publications, SAT preparation, science, yearbook classes. Computer network features include on-campus library services, Internet access. The school has a published electronic and media policy.

Contact Gregg R. Ledbetter, JD, Head of Enrollment and Financial Aid. 501-604-1923. Fax: 501-255-1801. E-mail: gregg.ledbetter@pulaskiacademy.org. Web site: www.pulaskiacademy.org.

PUNAHOU SCHOOL

1601 Punahou Street
Honolulu, Hawaii 96822

Head of School: Dr. James K. Scott

General Information Coeducational day college-preparatory, arts, bilingual studies, and technology school. Grades K–12. Founded: 1841. Setting: urban. 76-acre campus. 21 buildings on campus. Approved or accredited by Western Association of Schools and Colleges. Member of National Association of Independent Schools and Secondary School Admission Test Board. Endowment: $163.8 million. Total enrollment: 3,764. Upper school average class size: 21. Upper school faculty-student ratio: 1:12. There are 175 required school days per year for Upper School students. Upper School students typically attend 5 days per week. The average school day consists of 6 hours.

Upper School Student Profile Grade 9: 440 students (215 boys, 225 girls); Grade 10: 432 students (218 boys, 214 girls); Grade 11: 429 students (209 boys, 220 girls); Grade 12: 432 students (219 boys, 213 girls).

Faculty School total: 340. In upper school: 78 men, 79 women; 107 have advanced degrees.

Subjects Offered 20th century history, acting, algebra, American culture, American literature, American studies, anatomy and physiology, anthropology, Asian history, astronomy, Bible as literature, bioethics, biology, biology-AP, British literature, Buddhism, calculus-AP, ceramics, character education, chemistry, chemistry-AP, child development, chorus, college counseling, composition, computer science, computer science-AP, concert band, contemporary issues, creative writing, dance, digital art, drawing, driver education, economics, English, English composition, environmental science-AP, European history, European history-AP, film and literature, French, French language-AP, French studies, geometry, glassblowing, government and politics-AP, guidance, guitar, Hawaiian history, Hawaiian language, history of jazz, humanities, independent study, integrated science, Japanese, Japanese history, jewelry making, journalism, JROTC or LEAD (Leadership Education and Development), law, linguistics, Mandarin, marching band, marine biology, mechanical drawing, medieval history, men's studies, money management, music theory, oceanography, painting, peer counseling, photography, physical education, physics, physics-AP, pre-calculus, psychology, psychology-AP, religion, robotics, sculpture, Shakespeare, social studies, Spanish, Spanish-AP, sports psychology, statistics-AP, studio art, studio art-AP, symphonic band, technical theater, theater design and

production, trigonometry, U.S. government and politics-AP, U.S. history, U.S. history-AP, video, video film production, Western literature, wind ensemble, world civilizations, world literature, writing, yoga.

Graduation Requirements Electives, English, foreign language, mathematics, physical education (includes health), science, social studies (includes history), visual and performing arts, required sophomore English course, one course with the Spiritual, Ethical, Community Responsibility (SECR) designation.

Special Academic Programs 32 Advanced Placement exams for which test preparation is offered; honors section; independent study; study abroad.

College Admission Counseling 423 students graduated in 2009; 418 went to college, including Loyola Marymount University; Santa Clara University; University of Hawaii at Manoa; University of Puget Sound; University of Southern California; University of Washington. Other: 5 had other specific plans. Median SAT critical reading: 615, median SAT math: 666, median SAT writing: 619, median composite ACT: 27. 58% scored over 600 on SAT critical reading, 83% scored over 600 on SAT math, 60% scored over 600 on SAT writing, 54% scored over 26 on composite ACT.

Student Life Upper grades have specified standards of dress, student council, honor system. Discipline rests primarily with faculty. Attendance at religious services is required.

Tuition and Aid Day student tuition: $17,300. Tuition installment plan (Insured Tuition Payment Plan, monthly payment plans, semester payment plan). Merit scholarship grants, need-based scholarship grants available. In 2009–10, 13% of upper-school students received aid; total upper-school merit-scholarship money awarded: $212,600. Total amount of financial aid awarded in 2009–10: $2,084,059.

Admissions Traditional secondary-level entrance grade is 9. For fall 2009, 427 students applied for upper-level admission, 136 were accepted, 93 enrolled. SAT or SSAT required. Deadline for receipt of application materials: December 1. Application fee required: $100. Interview required.

Athletics Interscholastic: baseball (boys), basketball (b,g), bowling (b,g), canoeing/kayaking (b,g), cheering (g), cross-country running (b,g), football (b), golf (b,g), judo (b,g), kayaking (b,g), paddling (b,g), riflery (b,g), sailing (b,g), soccer (b,g), softball (g), swimming and diving (b,g), tennis (b,g), track and field (b,g), volleyball (b,g), water polo (b,g), wrestling (b,g); coed interscholastic: canoeing/kayaking, paddling. 4 PE instructors, 196 coaches, 3 athletic trainers.

Computers Computers are regularly used in all academic classes. Computer network features include on-campus library services, Internet access, wireless campus network, Internet filtering or blocking technology. Campus intranet, student e-mail accounts, and computer access in designated common areas are available to students. The school has a published electronic and media policy.

Contact Mrs. Betsy S. Hata, Director of Admission and Financial Aid. 808-944-5714. Fax: 808-943-3602. E-mail: admission@punahou.edu. Web site: www.punahou.edu.

PURNELL SCHOOL

Pottersville, New Jersey
See Special Needs Schools section.

THE PUTNEY SCHOOL

Elm Lea Farm
418 Houghton Brook Road
Putney, Vermont 05346-8675

Head of School: Emily Jones

General Information Coeducational boarding and day college-preparatory, arts, environmental science, and ESL school; primarily serves students with learning disabilities, individuals with Attention Deficit Disorder, and dyslexic students. Grades 9–12. Founded: 1935. Setting: rural. Nearest major city is Boston, MA. Students are housed in single-sex dormitories. 500-acre campus. 37 buildings on campus. Approved or accredited by Association of Independent Schools in New England, Independent Schools of Northern New England, New England Association of Schools and Colleges, The Association of Boarding Schools, and Vermont Department of Education. Member of National Association of Independent Schools and Secondary School Admission Test Board. Endowment: $18 million. Total enrollment: 226. Upper school average class size: 15. Upper school faculty-student ratio: 1:7.

Upper School Student Profile Grade 9: 39 students (18 boys, 21 girls); Grade 10: 58 students (21 boys, 37 girls); Grade 11: 65 students (32 boys, 33 girls); Grade 12: 64 students (31 boys, 33 girls); Postgraduate: 1 student (1 boy). 75% of students are boarding students. 30% are state residents. 22 states are represented in upper school student body. 20% are international students. International students from China, France, Germany, Japan, Republic of Korea, and Russian Federation; 9 other countries represented in student body.

Faculty School total: 42. In upper school: 20 men, 22 women; 29 have advanced degrees; 26 reside on campus.

Subjects Offered Advanced chemistry, African dance, African drumming, African studies, agroecology, algebra, American history, American literature, anatomy, ancient history, art, art history, astronomy, biology, calculus, cartooning/animation, ceramics, chamber groups, chemistry, chorus, college placement, comparative religion, computer science, conservation, creative writing, dance, design, digital photography, drama, drawing, ecology, economics, English, English literature, ensembles, environmental science, environmental systems, ESL, European history, expository writing, fabric arts, fiber arts, fine arts, foods, French, genetics, geometry, history, human development, instruments, jazz, jazz ensemble, Latin American history, literature, mathematics, Middle Eastern history, music, music appreciation, music composition, music history, music theory, musical theater, orchestra, painting, philosophy, photography, physical education, physics, physiology, post-calculus, printmaking, science, sculpture, sewing, Shakespeare, social studies, Spanish, stained glass, statistics, theater, U.S. history, video film production, vocal jazz, voice, weaving, women's studies, woodworking, work experience, world history, world literature, writing, yearbook, yoga.

Graduation Requirements Arts and fine arts (art, music, dance, drama), electives, English, foreign language, history, human development, lab science, mathematics, physical education (includes health), science, one trimester each of 6 required jobs, including lunch, dinner, barn, dishwashing, general substitute, and a land-use activity, Project Week: two projects each semester of dedicated work, one academic and one non-academic, participation in annual Long Spring camping/backpacking trips.

Special Academic Programs Advanced Placement exam preparation; independent study; term-away projects; academic accommodation for the gifted, the musically talented, and the artistically talented; ESL (17 students enrolled).

College Admission Counseling 62 students graduated in 2009; 60 went to college, including Columbia College; Dartmouth College; Earlham College; Hampshire College; Mount Holyoke College; New York University. Other: 2 had other specific plans. Mean SAT critical reading: 632, mean SAT math: 570, mean composite ACT: 25. 59% scored over 600 on SAT critical reading, 33% scored over 600 on SAT math, 50% scored over 26 on composite ACT.

Student Life Upper grades have student council, honor system. Discipline rests equally with students and faculty.

Tuition and Aid Day student tuition: $27,700; 7-day tuition and room/board: $42,500. Tuition installment plan (Academic Management Services Plan, Key Tuition Payment Plan, monthly payment plans, Tuition Management Systems Plan, pre-payment discount plan). Need-based scholarship grants available. In 2009–10, 42% of upper-school students received aid. Total amount of financial aid awarded in 2009–10: $1,200,000.

Admissions Traditional secondary-level entrance grade is 9. For fall 2009, 157 students applied for upper-level admission, 137 were accepted, 81 enrolled. SSAT required. Deadline for receipt of application materials: January 15. Application fee required: $40. Interview required.

Athletics Interscholastic: bicycling (boys, girls), crew (b,g), cross-country running (b,g), lacrosse (b,g), nordic skiing (b,g), rowing (b,g), running (b,g), skiing (cross-country) (b,g), soccer (b,g); coed interscholastic: alpine skiing, basketball, Frisbee, skiing (downhill), ultimate Frisbee; coed intramural: aerobics/dance, aerobics/Nautilus, alpine skiing, backpacking, badminton, ballet, basketball, bicycling, boxing, broomball, canoeing/kayaking, Circus, climbing, crew, cross-country running, dance, equestrian sports, fencing, fitness, fitness walking, freestyle skiing, Frisbee, hiking/backpacking, horseback riding, ice hockey, jogging, modern dance, mountain biking, nordic skiing, outdoor activities, outdoor adventure, outdoor education, outdoor recreation, outdoor skills, outdoors, paddling, physical fitness, rappelling, rock climbing, running, sailboarding, skiing (cross-country), skiing (downhill), snowboarding, snowshoeing, soccer, strength & conditioning, table tennis, tennis, ultimate Frisbee, volleyball, walking, wall climbing, weight training, wilderness, wilderness survival, windsurfing, winter walking, yoga. 3 coaches.

Computers Computers are regularly used in English, foreign language, history, mathematics, music, science classes. Computer network features include on-campus library services, online commercial services, Internet access, wireless campus network, Internet filtering or blocking technology. Student e-mail accounts are available to students. The school has a published electronic and media policy.

Contact Ann McBroom, Admission Assistant. 802-387-6219. Fax: 802-387-6278. E-mail: admission@putneyschool.org. Web site: www.putneyschool.org.

QUEEN ANNE SCHOOL

14111 Oak Grove Road
Upper Marlboro, Maryland 20774
Head of School: Ms. Christiana Holyer

General Information Coeducational day college-preparatory, arts, business, and technology school, affiliated with Episcopal Church. Grades 6–12. Founded: 1964. Setting: suburban. Nearest major city is Washington, DC. 60-acre campus. 8 buildings on campus. Approved or accredited by Association of Independent Maryland Schools, National Association of Episcopal Schools, and Maryland Department of Education. Member of National Association of Independent Schools and Secondary School Admission Test Board. Total enrollment: 92. Upper school average class size: 9. Upper school faculty-student ratio: 1:7. There are 180 required school days per year for Upper School students. Upper School students typically attend 5 days per week. The average school day consists of 7 hours and 30 minutes.

Upper School Student Profile Grade 6: 6 students (2 boys, 4 girls); Grade 7: 12 students (4 boys, 8 girls); Grade 8: 9 students (4 boys, 5 girls); Grade 9: 10 students (5 boys, 5 girls); Grade 10: 13 students (5 boys, 8 girls); Grade 11: 10 students (7 boys, 3 girls); Grade 12: 32 students (16 boys, 16 girls). 15% of students are members of Episcopal Church.

Faculty School total: 18. In upper school: 7 men, 11 women; 7 have advanced degrees.

Subjects Offered Algebra, American history, American history-AP, art, art history, arts, biology, biology-AP, calculus, calculus-AP, ceramics, chemistry, chemistry-AP, computer programming, computer science, creative writing, drama, earth science, economics, English, English literature, English literature and composition-AP, environmental science, ethics, fine arts, French, geography, geometry, government/civics, grammar, history, journalism, mathematics, music, philosophy, physical education, physics, physiology, psychology, religion, science, social studies, Spanish, theater, trigonometry, world history, world literature.

Graduation Requirements Arts and fine arts (art, music, dance, drama), English, foreign language, mathematics, physical education (includes health), religion (includes Bible studies and theology), science, social studies (includes history).

Special Academic Programs 10 Advanced Placement exams for which test preparation is offered.

College Admission Counseling 19 students graduated in 2010; all went to college, including Frostburg State University; University of Maryland, College Park; University of Virginia.

Student Life Upper grades have specified standards of dress, student council, honor system. Discipline rests equally with students and faculty.

Tuition and Aid Day student tuition: $15,000. Tuition installment plan (FACTS Tuition Payment Plan, monthly payment plans, full payment discount plan, 2- and 10-payment plans). Merit scholarship grants, need-based scholarship grants available. In 2010–11, 58% of upper-school students received aid; total upper-school merit-scholarship money awarded: $45,000. Total amount of financial aid awarded in 2010–11: $350,000.

Admissions Traditional secondary-level entrance grade is 9. For fall 2010, 28 students applied for upper-level admission, 14 were accepted, 6 enrolled. ISEE required. Deadline for receipt of application materials: none. Application fee required: $50. On-campus interview required.

Athletics Interscholastic: baseball (boys), basketball (b,g), cheering (g), soccer (b,g), softball (g), volleyball (g); coed interscholastic: cross-country running, outdoor education, track and field. 1 PE instructor, 2 coaches.

Computers Computers are regularly used in art, English, foreign language, mathematics, music, science classes. Computer network features include on-campus library services, online commercial services, Internet access, wireless campus network, Internet filtering or blocking technology. Student e-mail accounts are available to students. Students grades are available online. The school has a published electronic and media policy.

Contact Mr. Glenn Singer, Director of Admissions and Development. 301-249-5000 Ext. 305. Fax: 301-249-3838. E-mail: gsinger@queenanne.org. Web site: www.queenanne.org.

QUEEN MARGARET'S SCHOOL

660 Brownsey Avenue
Duncan, British Columbia V9L 1C2, Canada
Head of School: Pat Rowantree

General Information Girls' boarding and coeducational day college-preparatory, general academic, arts, and athletics and equestrian studies school. Boarding girls grades 7–12, day boys grades JK–7, day girls grades JK–12. Founded: 1921. Setting: small town. Nearest major city is Victoria, Canada. Students are housed in single-sex dormitories. 27-acre campus. 8 buildings on campus. Approved or accredited by Pacific Northwest Association of Independent Schools, Standards in Excellence And Learning (SEAL), The Association of Boarding Schools, and British Columbia Department of Education. Member of Canadian Association of Independent Schools. Language of instruction: English. Endowment: CAN$500,000. Total enrollment: 310. Upper school average class size: 18. Upper school faculty-student ratio: 1:7.

Upper School Student Profile 65% of students are boarding students. 50% are province residents. 11 provinces are represented in upper school student body. 50% are international students. International students from Hong Kong, Japan, Mexico, Republic of Korea, Taiwan, and United States; 18 other countries represented in student body.

Faculty School total: 36. In upper school: 8 men, 12 women; 8 have advanced degrees; 4 reside on campus.

Subjects Offered Advanced math, algebra, animal husbandry, animal science, applied skills, art, biology, business education, business skills, calculus, calculus-AP, Canadian history, career and personal planning, career exploration, chemistry, chemistry-AP, chorus, college planning, computer science, creative writing, drama, English, English literature, equine science, ESL, fine arts, French, geography, geometry, grammar, health, history, home economics, instrumental music, Japanese, journalism, mathematics, photography, physical education, physics, SAT preparation, science, social studies, speech, sports, sports psychology, theater, TOEFL preparation, trigonometry, visual arts, world history, writing.

Graduation Requirements Arts and fine arts (art, music, dance, drama), career and personal planning, computer science, English, finance, foreign language, mathematics, media production, physical education (includes health), science, social studies (includes history), women's studies. Community service is required.

Special Academic Programs Independent study; academic accommodation for the gifted, the musically talented, and the artistically talented; ESL (30 students enrolled).

College Admission Counseling 28 students graduated in 2009; 26 went to college, including McGill University; Queen's University at Kingston; The University of

British Columbia; University of Toronto; University of Victoria; Washington State University. Other: 1 went to work, 1 had other specific plans.

Student Life Upper grades have uniform requirement, student council. Discipline rests primarily with faculty. Attendance at religious services is required.

Tuition and Aid Day student tuition: CAN$9400–CAN$12,500; 5-day tuition and room/board: CAN$25,700; 7-day tuition and room/board: CAN$28,500–CAN$40,000. Tuition installment plan (Insured Tuition Payment Plan, monthly payment plans, individually arranged payment plans). Tuition reduction for siblings, bursaries, merit scholarship grants, tuition reduction for children of staff available. In 2009–10, 30% of upper-school students received aid; total upper-school merit-scholarship money awarded: CAN$50,000. Total amount of financial aid awarded in 2009–10: CAN$100,000.

Admissions Traditional secondary-level entrance grade is 8. Otis-Lennon School Ability Test, SLEP or Stanford Achievement Test required. Deadline for receipt of application materials: none. Application fee required: CAN$200. Interview required.

Athletics Interscholastic: badminton (girls), basketball (g), canoeing/kayaking (g), cooperative games (g), cross-country running (g), dressage (g), equestrian sports (g), field hockey (g), golf (g), horseback riding (g), ocean paddling (g), outdoor activities (g), outdoor recreation (g), paddling (g), rugby (g), soccer (g), tennis (g), track and field (g), volleyball (g); intramural: aerobics (g), aerobics/dance (g), alpine skiing (g), aquatics (g), backpacking (g), badminton (g), ball hockey (g), basketball (g), canoeing/kayaking (g), cooperative games (g), Cosom hockey (g), cross-country running (g), dressage (g), equestrian sports (g), field hockey (g), floor hockey (g), Frisbee (g), golf (g), horseback riding (g), indoor hockey (g), indoor soccer (g), jogging (g), nordic skiing (g), ocean paddling (g), outdoor activities (g), outdoor recreation (g), paddling (g), physical fitness (g), physical training (g), rugby (g), skiing (downhill) (g), snowboarding (g), soccer (g), tennis (g), track and field (g), ultimate Frisbee (g), volleyball (g). 2 PE instructors, 2 coaches, 2 athletic trainers.

Computers Computers are regularly used in career education, career exploration, college planning, creative writing, English, ESL, French, information technology, introduction to technology, journalism, mathematics, media arts, media production, science, social sciences, technology classes. Computer network features include on-campus library services, Internet access, wireless campus network, Internet filtering or blocking technology. Student e-mail accounts are available to students. The school has a published electronic and media policy.

Contact Admissions Coordinator. 250-746-4185. Fax: 250-746-4187. E-mail: admissions@qms.bc.ca. Web site: www.qms.bc.ca.

QUEEN OF PEACE HIGH SCHOOL

7659 South Linder Avenue
Burbank, Illinois 60459

Head of School: Dr. Kathleen Hanlon

General Information Girls' day college-preparatory school, affiliated with Roman Catholic Church. Grades 9–12. Founded: 1962. Setting: suburban. Nearest major city is Chicago. Approved or accredited by Illinois Department of Education. Upper school average class size: 19. Upper school faculty-student ratio: 1:16.

Faculty School total: 42.

Student Life Upper grades have uniform requirement, student council. Attendance at religious services is required.

Admissions No application fee required.

Contact Ms. Sharon Geinosky, Director of Counseling. 708-458-7600 Ext. 290. Fax: 708-458-5734. Web site: www.queenofpeacehs.org.

QUEEN OF PEACE HIGH SCHOOL

191 Rutherford Place
North Arlington, New Jersey 07031-6091

Head of School: Br. Larry Lavallee, FMS

General Information Coeducational day college-preparatory, arts, business, religious studies, and technology school, affiliated with Roman Catholic Church. Grades 9–12. Founded: 1930. Setting: suburban. Nearest major city is Newark. 3 buildings on campus. Approved or accredited by Christian Brothers Association, Middle States Association of Colleges and Schools, and New Jersey Department of Education. Endowment: $2 million. Total enrollment: 525. Upper school average class size: 20. Upper school faculty-student ratio: 1:15. There are 180 required school days per year for Upper School students. Upper School students typically attend 5 days per week. The average school day consists of 6 hours and 35 minutes.

Upper School Student Profile Grade 9: 115 students (62 boys, 53 girls); Grade 10: 108 students (54 boys, 54 girls); Grade 11: 128 students (56 boys, 72 girls); Grade 12: 174 students (74 boys, 100 girls). 90% of students are Roman Catholic.

Faculty School total: 44. In upper school: 20 men, 24 women; 28 have advanced degrees.

Subjects Offered Accounting, adolescent issues, advanced chemistry, advanced computer applications, advanced math, algebra, American history, American history-AP, American literature, anatomy and physiology, area studies, art, art appreciation, biology, British literature, British literature (honors), business applications, business technology, calculus, calculus-AP, campus ministry, career education, chemistry, Christian and Hebrew scripture, computer applications, computer graphics, computer programming, contemporary issues, drama, driver education, English,

English-AP, ESL, European history, French, general science, geometry, history-AP, honors algebra, honors English, honors geometry, honors U.S. history, honors world history, introduction to technology, keyboarding, modern European history, music appreciation, physical education, physics, pre-calculus, psychology, religion, religious studies, Spanish, speech, trigonometry, U.S. history, U.S. history-AP, Western civilization, writing.

Special Academic Programs Advanced Placement exam preparation; honors section; study at local college for college credit; remedial reading and/or remedial writing; remedial math; ESL (14 students enrolled).

College Admission Counseling 171 students graduated in 2010; 168 went to college, including Caldwell College; Kean University; Montclair State University; Rutgers, The State University of New Jersey, New Brunswick; Seton Hall University; William Paterson University of New Jersey. Other: 1 went to work, 2 entered military service.

Student Life Upper grades have uniform requirement, student council. Discipline rests primarily with faculty. Attendance at religious services is required.

Summer Programs Remediation, enrichment, ESL, computer instruction programs offered; session focuses on study skills improvement; held on campus; accepts boys and girls; open to students from other schools. 300 students usually enrolled. 2011 schedule: June 28 to July 30. Application deadline: June 20.

Tuition and Aid Day student tuition: $8250. Tuition installment plan (monthly payment plans, individually arranged payment plans, plans vary depending upon family needs/abilities). Tuition reduction for siblings, merit scholarship grants, need-based scholarship grants, limited financial aid available. In 2010–11, 20% of upper-school students received aid; total upper-school merit-scholarship money awarded: $100,000.

Admissions Traditional secondary-level entrance grade is 9. For fall 2010, 505 students applied for upper-level admission, 260 were accepted, 115 enrolled. CTB/McGraw-Hill/Macmillan Co-op Test required. Deadline for receipt of application materials: none. No application fee required.

Athletics Interscholastic: baseball (boys), basketball (b,g), cheering (g), cross-country running (b,g), football (b), indoor track (b,g), soccer (b,g), softball (g), tennis (b,g), track and field (b,g), volleyball (g), wrestling (b); intramural: roller hockey (b), skiing (downhill) (b), snowboarding (b), street hockey (b), strength & conditioning (b), weight training (b,g); coed interscholastic: bowling, dance team, golf, riflery; coed intramural: aerobics/dance, alpine skiing, ball hockey, dance team, fitness, floor hockey, freestyle skiing, in-line hockey, strength & conditioning. 3 PE instructors, 53 coaches, 1 athletic trainer.

Computers Computers are regularly used in accounting, animation, business applications, career exploration, college planning, computer applications, creative writing, current events, English, foreign language, French, graphic arts, graphic design, introduction to technology, keyboarding, library, literary magazine, mathematics, newspaper, remedial study skills, Spanish, study skills, technology, word processing, yearbook classes. Computer network features include on-campus library services, online commercial services, Internet access, wireless campus network, Internet filtering or blocking technology, parent computer access to daily grading system. Computer access in designated common areas is available to students. Students grades are available online. The school has a published electronic and media policy.

Contact Mr. Edmund G. McKeown, Admissions Director. 201-998-8227 Ext. 30. Fax: 201-998-3040. E-mail: admissions@qphs.org. Web site: www.qphs.org.

QUEENSWOOD

Shepherd's Way
Brookmans Park
Hatfield, Hertfordshire AL9 6NS, United Kingdom

Head of School: Mrs. Pauline Edgar

General Information Girls' boarding and day college-preparatory, general academic, arts, business, and technology school, affiliated with Christian faith, Methodist Church. Grades 6–12. Founded: 1894. Setting: rural. Nearest major city is London, United Kingdom. Students are housed in single-sex dormitories. 210-acre campus. 22 buildings on campus. Approved or accredited by British Accreditation Council. Language of instruction: English. Endowment: £50 million. Total enrollment: 430. Upper school average class size: 14. Upper school faculty-student ratio: 1:7.

Upper School Student Profile 53% of students are boarding students. 20% are international students. International students from Bermuda, China, Hong Kong, Malaysia, Nigeria, and Singapore; 21 other countries represented in student body. 80% of students are Christian, Methodist.

Faculty School total: 66. In upper school: 43 men, 14 women; 18 have advanced degrees; 15 reside on campus.

Subjects Offered 20th century physics, 20th century world history, 3-dimensional art, 3-dimensional design, accounting, acting, adolescent issues, advanced chemistry, advanced computer applications, advanced math, anatomy and physiology, applied music, art, art appreciation, art history, arts and crafts, ballet, band, biology, British history, British National Curriculum, business, business studies, career experience, career/college preparation, chemistry, choir, clayworking, collage and assemblage, community service, comparative cultures, computer applications, computer skills, conservation, contemporary art, contemporary issues, crafts, creative arts, creative dance, creative drama, creative thinking, creative writing, critical thinking, critical writing, culinary arts, cultural arts, current events, dance, data analysis, data processing, decision making skills, design, desktop publishing, digital photography, drama, drama performance, drama workshop, dramatic arts, drawing and design, driver education, earth science, ecology, environmental systems, economics, English, English composition, English literature, environmental geography, equestrian sports, ESL, European history, expressive arts, fabric arts, fashion, finance, first aid, fitness, food and nutrition, French, gender issues, general science, German, global issues, government, grammar, guitar, health, history of England, human biology, human relations, independent study, independent living, instrumental music, integrated mathematics, integrated physics, integrated science, international affairs, Internet, interpersonal skills, jazz band, jazz dance, jewelry making, keyboarding, Latin, leadership and service, library, life issues, literature, logarithms, logic, rhetoric, and debate, marketing, mathematics, medieval history, modern dance, modern politics, money management, moral and social development, moral reasoning, multicultural studies, music, music appreciation, music composition, music technology, music theory, news writing, oral communications, oral expression, orchestra, organ, outdoor education, parent/child development, peer counseling, personal fitness, personal growth, personal money management, photography, physical education, physical fitness, physics, piano, play production, poetry, printmaking, public speaking, reading/study skills, relationships, religion, religion and culture, religious studies, research skills, Roman civilization, scripture, sculpture, self-defense, sex education, Shakespeare, shop, skills for success, society and culture, society challenge and change, Spanish, speech and debate, sports science, statistics, strings, student government, technology/design, textiles, theater arts, theater design and production, typing, United Nations and international issues, values and decisions, voice, Web site design, weight fitness, wind instruments, word processing, world affairs, world cultures, world governments, world history, World War I, World War II, World-Wide-Web publishing, writing.

Graduation Requirements English, geography, health education, history, languages, mathematics, science, social education, information and communications technology.

Special Academic Programs Independent study; term-away projects; academic accommodation for the gifted and the musically talented; programs in English, mathematics, general development for dyslexic students; special instructional classes for deaf students; ESL (30 students enrolled).

Student Life Upper grades have uniform requirement, student council, honor system. Discipline rests equally with students and faculty. Attendance at religious services is required.

Tuition and Aid Day student tuition: £6155–£6725; 7-day tuition and room/board: £7985–£8705. Tuition reduction for siblings, bursaries, merit scholarship grants available. In 2009–10, 18% of upper-school students received aid; total upper-school merit-scholarship money awarded: £52,300. Total amount of financial aid awarded in 2009–10: £266,500.

Admissions Traditional secondary-level entrance grade is 11. For fall 2009, 140 students applied for upper-level admission, 106 were accepted, 66 enrolled. School's own test required. Deadline for receipt of application materials: none. Application fee required: £100. Interview required.

Athletics Interscholastic: badminton, cross-country running, dance, handball, hockey, life saving, netball, physical fitness, rounders, running, soccer, softball, strength & conditioning, swimming and diving, tennis, volleyball; intramural: aerobics, aerobics/dance, alpine skiing, archery, artistic gym, backpacking, badminton, ballet, basketball, canoeing/kayaking, cross-country running, dance, equestrian sports, fencing, fitness, fitness walking, golf, gymnastics, hockey, horseback riding, ice skating, indoor hockey, indoor soccer, lacrosse, life saving, modern dance, netball, outdoor activities, outdoor adventure, outdoor recreation, outdoor skills, physical fitness, rounders, running, self defense, skiing (downhill), soccer, softball, speleology, strength & conditioning, swimming and diving, tennis, volleyball, weight training. 7 coaches.

Computers Computers are regularly used in all classes. Computer network features include on-campus library services, Internet access, laptops.

Contact Mrs. Suzie Blackmore, Assistant Registrar. 440-1707602500. Fax: 440-1707602561. E-mail: registry@queenswood.org. Web site: www.queenswood.org.

QUIGLEY CATHOLIC HIGH SCHOOL
200 Quigley Drive
Baden, Pennsylvania 15005-1295
Head of School: Dr. Madonna J. Helbling
General Information Coeducational day college-preparatory, religious studies, and technology school, affiliated with Roman Catholic Church. Grades 9–12. Founded: 1967. Setting: suburban. Nearest major city is Pittsburgh. 19-acre campus. 1 building on campus. Approved or accredited by Middle States Association of Colleges and Schools, National Catholic Education Association, and Pennsylvania Department of Education. Endowment: $2.5 million. Total enrollment: 203. Upper school average class size: 20. Upper school faculty-student ratio: 1:12. There are 180 required school days per year for Upper School students. Upper School students typically attend 5 days per week. The average school day consists of 6 hours and 30 minutes.
Upper School Student Profile Grade 9: 47 students (16 boys, 31 girls); Grade 10: 40 students (18 boys, 22 girls); Grade 11: 66 students (34 boys, 32 girls); Grade 12: 50 students (20 boys, 30 girls). 95% of students are Roman Catholic.
Faculty School total: 17. In upper school: 8 men, 9 women; 14 have advanced degrees.

Subjects Offered Advanced Placement courses, algebra, American government, American history-AP, American literature, anatomy and physiology, art, athletics, band, baseball, Basic programming, basketball, biology, bookbinding, bowling, British literature, British literature (honors), calculus, calculus-AP, campus ministry, ceramics, cheerleading, chemistry, choir, chorus, church history, composition-AP, computer programming, computer science, concert choir, debate, drawing, ecology, English-AP, European history-AP, French language-AP, geometry, government, guitar, health education, honors algebra, honors world history, library, physical education, physical science, physics, piano, play production, pottery, pre-algebra, pre-calculus, printmaking, religious education, SAT preparation, Spanish, speech and debate, sports, student government, studio art, trigonometry, yearbook.
Graduation Requirements Algebra, American government, American history, American history-AP, British literature, British literature (honors), chemistry, church history, computer science, English, English literature, European history, European history-AP, French, geometry, government, health, math review, music, physical science, physics, religion (includes Bible studies and theology), Spanish, U.S. history, 125 hours of service completed by end of senior year.
Special Academic Programs Advanced Placement exam preparation; honors section; study at local college for college credit.
College Admission Counseling 38 students graduated in 2009; 37 went to college, including Duquesne University; John Carroll University; Penn State University Park; University of Pittsburgh. Other: 1 had other specific plans.
Student Life Upper grades have uniform requirement, student council, honor system. Discipline rests primarily with faculty. Attendance at religious services is required.
Tuition and Aid Day student tuition: $8350. Tuition installment plan (SMART Tuition Payment Plan, individually arranged payment plans, one-time payment in full). Tuition reduction for siblings, merit scholarship grants, need-based scholarship grants available. In 2009–10, 48% of upper-school students received aid; total upper-school merit-scholarship money awarded: $33,660. Total amount of financial aid awarded in 2009–10: $299,953.
Admissions Traditional secondary-level entrance grade is 9. For fall 2009, 9 students applied for upper-level admission, 9 were accepted, 8 enrolled. Iowa Test, CTBS, or TAP, Math Placement Exam or PSAT required. Deadline for receipt of application materials: none. Application fee required: $30. Interview required.
Athletics Interscholastic: baseball (boys), basketball (b,g), bowling (b,g), cheering (g), cross-country running (b,g), dance team (g), golf (b), gymnastics (g), ice hockey (b), soccer (b,g), softball (g), swimming and diving (g), tennis (g), volleyball (g), wrestling (b); intramural: aerobics (g); coed interscholastic: aquatics. 1 PE instructor, 11 coaches, 1 athletic trainer.
Computers Computers are regularly used in newspaper, programming, yearbook classes. Computer resources include on-campus library services, Internet access.
Contact Sr. Bridget Reilly, Guidance Counselor. 724-869-2188. Fax: 724-869-2188. E-mail: reillyb@qchs.org. Web site: www.qchs.org.

QUINTE CHRISTIAN HIGH SCHOOL
138 Wallbridge-Loyalist Road
RR 2
Belleville, Ontario K8N 4Z2, Canada
Head of School: Mr. Johan Cooke
General Information Coeducational day college-preparatory, general academic, arts, business, vocational, religious studies, bilingual studies, and technology school, affiliated with Christian faith, Protestant faith. Grades 9–12. Founded: 1977. Setting: suburban. Nearest major city is Toronto, Canada. 25-acre campus. 1 building on campus. Approved or accredited by Christian Schools International, Ontario Ministry of Education, and Ontario Department of Education. Language of instruction: English. Total enrollment: 161. Upper school average class size: 15. Upper school faculty-student ratio: 1:15. There are 176 required school days per year for Upper School students. Upper School students typically attend 5 days per week. The average school day consists of 6 hours and 10 minutes.
Upper School Student Profile Grade 9: 36 students (22 boys, 14 girls); Grade 10: 35 students (16 boys, 19 girls); Grade 11: 37 students (13 boys, 24 girls); Grade 12: 45 students (25 boys, 20 girls). 90% of students are Christian, Protestant.
Faculty School total: 16. In upper school: 9 men, 7 women; 2 have advanced degrees.
Subjects Offered Accounting, art, Bible, biology, calculus, careers, chemistry, Christian education, civics, computers, drama, English, English literature, ESL, French, geography, history, law, leadership education training, mathematics, mathematics-AP, media, music, peer counseling, physical education, physics, religious education, science, shop, society challenge and change, technical education, transportation technology, world issues, world religions.
Graduation Requirements Accounting, applied arts, careers, Christian education, civics, computers, English, French, geography, mathematics, physical education (includes health), religious education, science, social studies (includes history), world religions, Ontario Christian School diploma requirements.
Special Academic Programs Special instructional classes for students with learning disabilities.
College Admission Counseling 39 students graduated in 2010; 20 went to college, including Calvin College; Dordt College; Queen's University at Kingston; Redeemer University College; University of Guelph; University of Waterloo. 100% scored over 26 on composite ACT.

Quinte Christian High School

Student Life Upper grades have specified standards of dress, student council, honor system. Discipline rests primarily with faculty. Attendance at religious services is required.

Tuition and Aid Day student tuition: CAN$11,900. Tuition installment plan (monthly payment plans, individually arranged payment plans). Tuition reduction for siblings, need-based scholarship grants available. In 2010–11, 18% of upper-school students received aid.

Admissions Traditional secondary-level entrance grade is 9. Deadline for receipt of application materials: March 31. Application fee required: CAN$250. Interview required.

Athletics Interscholastic: badminton (boys, girls), basketball (b,g), cross-country running (b,g), track and field (b,g), volleyball (b,g); coed interscholastic: badminton; coed intramural: badminton, basketball, fitness walking, indoor soccer, physical training, volleyball. 3 PE instructors.

Computers Computers are regularly used in all classes. Computer network features include on-campus library services, Internet access, wireless campus network, Internet filtering or blocking technology. Campus intranet, student e-mail accounts, and computer access in designated common areas are available to students. The school has a published electronic and media policy.

Contact Mrs. Hermien Hogewoning, Administrative Assistant. 613-968-7870. Fax: 613-968-7970. E-mail: admin@qchs.ca. Web site: www.qchs.ca.

RABBI ALEXANDER S. GROSS HEBREW ACADEMY

2425 Pine Tree Drive
Miami Beach, Florida 33140
Head of School: Dr. Roni Raab

General Information Coeducational day college-preparatory, general academic, religious studies, and technology school, affiliated with Jewish faith. Grades N–12. Founded: 1948. Setting: urban. 4-acre campus. 1 building on campus. Approved or accredited by Massachusetts Office of Child Care Services, Southern Association of Colleges and Schools, and Florida Department of Education. Member of Secondary School Admission Test Board. Languages of instruction: English and Hebrew. Endowment: $650,000. Total enrollment: 499. Upper school average class size: 18. Upper school faculty-student ratio: 1:4.

Upper School Student Profile Grade 9: 39 students (19 boys, 20 girls); Grade 10: 42 students (25 boys, 17 girls); Grade 11: 66 students (30 boys, 36 girls); Grade 12: 45 students (26 boys, 19 girls). 100% of students are Jewish.

Faculty School total: 70. In upper school: 21 men, 18 women; 23 have advanced degrees.

Subjects Offered Algebra, audio visual/media, Bible studies, biology, biology-AP, calculus, calculus-AP, chemistry, chemistry-AP, computers, economics, English, English-AP, environmental science, geometry, Jewish studies, life science, physical education, physics, political science, pre-calculus, SAT preparation, social studies, Spanish, Talmud, technology.

Graduation Requirements Arts and fine arts (art, music, dance, drama), business skills (includes word processing), computer science, English, foreign language, mathematics, physical education (includes health), religion (includes Bible studies and theology), science, social sciences, social studies (includes history). Community service is required.

Special Academic Programs Advanced Placement exam preparation; honors section; independent study; study at local college for college credit; academic accommodation for the gifted; ESL (3 students enrolled).

College Admission Counseling 51 students graduated in 2009; 50 went to college, including Florida International University; New York University; University of Florida; University of Maryland, College Park; Yeshiva University. Other: 1 went to work. Mean SAT critical reading: 545, mean SAT math: 568, mean SAT writing: 526, mean combined SAT: 1639, mean composite ACT: 24.

Student Life Upper grades have specified standards of dress, student council, honor system. Discipline rests primarily with faculty. Attendance at religious services is required.

Tuition and Aid Day student tuition: $14,000. Tuition installment plan (monthly payment plans, individually arranged payment plans). Tuition reduction for siblings, need-based scholarship grants available. In 2009–10, 46% of upper-school students received aid. Total amount of financial aid awarded in 2009–10: $300,000.

Admissions Traditional secondary-level entrance grade is 9. For fall 2009, 40 students applied for upper-level admission, 33 were accepted, 30 enrolled. SSAT required. Deadline for receipt of application materials: none. No application fee required. On-campus interview required.

Athletics Interscholastic: basketball (boys, girls), soccer (b), tennis (b,g), volleyball (g); intramural: basketball (b,g), soccer (b), tennis (b,g), volleyball (g). 2 PE instructors, 3 coaches.

Computers Computers are regularly used in English, mathematics, religion, science classes. Computer network features include Internet access. Student e-mail accounts are available to students.

Contact Rabbi Mordechai Shifman, Principal. 305-532-6421. E-mail: mshifman@rasg.org. Web site: www.rasg.org.

RABUN GAP-NACOOCHEE SCHOOL

339 Nacoochee Drive
Rabun Gap, Georgia 30568
Head of School: Mr. John D. Marshall

General Information Coeducational boarding and day college-preparatory, arts, ESL, and performing arts school, affiliated with Presbyterian Church. Boarding grades 7–12, day grades 6–12. Founded: 1903. Setting: rural. Nearest major city is Atlanta. Students are housed in single-sex dormitories. 1,400-acre campus. 14 buildings on campus. Approved or accredited by Evangelical Lutheran Church in America, North Carolina Association of Independent Schools, Southern Association of Colleges and Schools, Southern Association of Independent Schools, The Association of Boarding Schools, and Georgia Department of Education. Member of National Association of Independent Schools and Secondary School Admission Test Board. Endowment: $50 million. Total enrollment: 357. Upper school average class size: 16. Upper school faculty-student ratio: 1:8. Upper School students typically attend 5 days per week.

Upper School Student Profile Grade 9: 56 students (29 boys, 27 girls); Grade 10: 76 students (39 boys, 37 girls); Grade 11: 72 students (35 boys, 37 girls); Grade 12: 61 students (30 boys, 31 girls). 58% of students are boarding students. 41% are state residents. 18 states are represented in upper school student body. 19% are international students. International students from China, Germany, Mexico, Republic of Korea, Taiwan, and Turks and Caicos Islands; 9 other countries represented in student body. 10% of students are Presbyterian.

Faculty School total: 52. In upper school: 19 men, 21 women; 26 have advanced degrees; 39 reside on campus.

Subjects Offered Advanced Placement courses, algebra, American literature, anatomy, ancient world history, art, art history, art history-AP, band, Bible studies, biology, biology-AP, botany, calculus-AP, chemistry, chemistry-AP, chorus, computer-aided design, creative writing, economics, English language-AP, English literature-AP, environmental science, environmental science-AP, ESL, European history-AP, French, French-AP, geography, geometry, government, government-AP, health, health education, history-AP, honors algebra, honors English, honors U.S. history, honors world history, industrial arts, journalism, life science, mathematics, modern European history-AP, modern world history, music, orchestra, physical education, physical science, physics, physics-AP, pre-algebra, pre-calculus, probability and statistics, psychology, science, Spanish, Spanish language-AP, Spanish-AP, studio art-AP, theater, U.S. government and politics-AP, U.S. history, U.S. history-AP, wind ensemble, world geography, world history, world literature, yearbook.

Graduation Requirements Algebra, ancient world history, arts and fine arts (art, music, dance, drama), biology, chemistry, English, foreign language, geometry, mathematics, modern world history, physical education (includes health), physics, religion (includes Bible studies and theology), science, social studies (includes history), U.S. history, participation in Intersession/G.A.P. Week.

Special Academic Programs Advanced Placement exam preparation; honors section; independent study; study abroad; ESL (16 students enrolled).

College Admission Counseling 69 students graduated in 2009; all went to college, including College of Charleston; Emory University; Georgia Institute of Technology; The University of North Carolina at Asheville; United States Naval Academy; University of Georgia.

Student Life Upper grades have uniform requirement, student council, honor system. Discipline rests primarily with faculty. Attendance at religious services is required.

Tuition and Aid Day student tuition: $15,675; 7-day tuition and room/board: $34,700. Tuition installment plan (Insured Tuition Payment Plan, monthly payment plans, semester payment plan). Merit scholarship grants, need-based scholarship grants, tuition remission for children of faculty and staff available. In 2009–10, 65% of upper-school students received aid; total upper-school merit-scholarship money awarded: $266,930. Total amount of financial aid awarded in 2009–10: $2,572,695.

Admissions Traditional secondary-level entrance grade is 9. For fall 2009, 308 students applied for upper-level admission, 196 were accepted, 117 enrolled. ISEE, SLEP for foreign students, SSAT or TOEFL required. Deadline for receipt of application materials: February 1. Application fee required: $85. Interview required.

Athletics Interscholastic: baseball (boys), basketball (b,g), cross-country running (b,g), football (b), soccer (b,g), softball (g), swimming and diving (b,g), tennis (b,g), volleyball (g); intramural: soccer (b,g), swimming and diving (b,g), tennis (b,g); coed interscholastic: Circus, dance team, golf, tennis; coed intramural: aerobics/dance, ballet, basketball, bicycling, canoeing/kayaking, Circus, climbing, combined training, dance, dance team, fitness, fitness walking, hiking/backpacking, kayaking, modern dance, mountain biking, Nautilus, outdoor activities, physical training, rafting, rock climbing, strength & conditioning, swimming and diving, tennis, triathlon, ultimate Frisbee, wall climbing, weight lifting, yoga. 1 PE instructor, 22 coaches, 1 athletic trainer.

Computers Computers are regularly used in English, library skills, literary magazine, technical drawing, theater arts, writing, yearbook classes. Computer network features include on-campus library services, online commercial services, Internet access, wireless campus network, Internet filtering or blocking technology, application and re-enrollment online services. Campus intranet, student e-mail accounts, and computer access in designated common areas are available to students. The school has a published electronic and media policy.

Contact Mrs. Kathy Watts, Admission Assistant. 706-746-7720. Fax: 706-746-7797. E-mail: kwatts@rabungap.org. Web site: www.rabungap.org.

RAMBAM MESIVTA

15 Frost Lane

Lawrence, New York 11559

Head of School: Rabbi Zev Meir Friedman

General Information Boys' day college-preparatory, religious studies, bilingual studies, and technology school, affiliated with Jewish faith. Grades 9–12. Founded: 1991. Setting: suburban. Nearest major city is New York. 1-acre campus. 1 building on campus. Approved or accredited by Middle States Association of Colleges and Schools, New York Department of Education, New York State Board of Regents, and The College Board. Languages of instruction: English and Hebrew. Total enrollment: 156. Upper school average class size: 23. Upper school faculty-student ratio: 1:3. There are 180 required school days per year for Upper School students. Upper School students typically attend 5 days per week.

Upper School Student Profile Grade 9: 45 students (45 boys); Grade 10: 40 students (40 boys); Grade 11: 34 students (34 boys); Grade 12: 37 students (37 boys). 100% of students are Jewish.

Faculty School total: 46. In upper school: 41 men, 4 women; 40 have advanced degrees.

Subjects Offered Accounting, Advanced Placement courses, algebra, Bible studies, biology-AP, business, business applications, business mathematics, calculus-AP, chemistry-AP, computer literacy, economics, emergency medicine, English, English-AP, ethics, European history, European history-AP, freshman seminar, geometry, Hebrew, Hebrew scripture, Holocaust studies, independent study, Israeli studies, Jewish history, Jewish studies, Judaic studies, Middle Eastern history, moral reasoning, moral theology, philosophy, physical education, physics-AP, prayer/spirituality, pre-calculus, psychology-AP, Rabbinic literature, robotics, SAT preparation, Spanish, Talmud, trigonometry, U.S. history, U.S. history-AP, Web site design.

Graduation Requirements Algebra, American history, Bible studies, biology, chemistry, computer science, English, English literature, general science, geometry, global studies, health, Hebrew, Hebrew scripture, Holocaust studies, integrated mathematics, Israeli studies, Jewish history, mathematics, music, physical education (includes health), Rabbinic literature, religious studies, U.S. history, world history.

Special Academic Programs 9 Advanced Placement exams for which test preparation is offered; honors section; independent study; study at local college for college credit; academic accommodation for the gifted.

College Admission Counseling 43 students graduated in 2009; they went to Columbia College; Harvard University; New York University; Queens College of the City University of New York; University of Pennsylvania; Yeshiva University. Other: 36 entered a postgraduate year. Median SAT critical reading: 570, median SAT math: 620, median SAT writing: 570.

Student Life Upper grades have specified standards of dress, student council, honor system. Discipline rests primarily with faculty. Attendance at religious services is required.

Tuition and Aid Day student tuition: $18,000. Tuition installment plan (monthly payment plans, individually arranged payment plans). Merit scholarship grants, need-based scholarship grants, need-based loans available. In 2009–10, 50% of upper-school students received aid; total upper-school merit-scholarship money awarded: $15,000. Total amount of financial aid awarded in 2009–10: $400,000.

Admissions Traditional secondary-level entrance grade is 9. For fall 2009, 110 students applied for upper-level admission, 45 were accepted, 45 enrolled. Board of Jewish Education Entrance Exam required. Deadline for receipt of application materials: March. Application fee required: $100. On-campus interview required.

Athletics Interscholastic: ball hockey, basketball, bowling, floor hockey, soccer, softball, tennis; intramural: basketball, table tennis, touch football. 6 coaches.

Computers Computers are regularly used in basic skills, college planning, computer applications, data processing, media, media production, publications, video film production, Web site design, yearbook classes. Computer resources include Internet access, wireless campus network, Internet filtering or blocking technology. Campus intranet and student e-mail accounts are available online. Students grades are available online.

Contact Shirley Levy. 516-371-5824 Ext. 100. Fax: 516-371-4706. E-mail: info@rambam.org. Web site: www.rambam.org.

RAMONA CONVENT SECONDARY SCHOOL

1701 West Ramona Road

Alhambra, California 91803-3080

Head of School: Ms. Kathleen Pillon

General Information Girls' day college-preparatory, arts, business, religious studies, bilingual studies, and technology school, affiliated with Roman Catholic Church. Grades 7–12. Founded: 1889. Setting: suburban. Nearest major city is Los Angeles. 15-acre campus. 10 buildings on campus. Approved or accredited by Western Association of Schools and Colleges, Western Catholic Education Association, and California Department of Education. Endowment: $2 million. Total enrollment: 392. Upper school average class size: 22. Upper school faculty-student ratio: 1:10. There are 180 required school days per year for Upper School students. Upper School students typically attend 5 days per week. The average school day consists of 6 hours and 30 minutes.

Upper School Student Profile Grade 9: 78 students (78 girls); Grade 10: 88 students (88 girls); Grade 11: 101 students (101 girls); Grade 12: 91 students (91 girls). 90% of students are Roman Catholic.

Faculty School total: 38. In upper school: 13 men, 25 women; 25 have advanced degrees.

Subjects Offered Advanced Placement courses, advanced studio art-AP, algebra, American history, American literature, art history, Bible studies, biology, biology-AP, calculus, calculus-AP, ceramics, chemistry, chemistry-AP, computer programming, computer science, dance, drama, economics, English, English literature, environmental science, European history, European history-AP, fine arts, French, French-AP, geography, geometry, government/civics, grammar, graphic arts, health, history, honors English, honors geometry, mathematics, music, photography, physical education, physics, pre-calculus, religion, science, social sciences, social studies, Spanish, Spanish language-AP, Spanish literature-AP, speech, theater, theology, trigonometry, U.S. government and politics-AP, visual arts, word processing, world history, world literature.

Graduation Requirements Arts and fine arts (art, music, dance, drama), business skills (includes word processing), computer science, English, foreign language, mathematics, physical education (includes health), religion (includes Bible studies and theology), science, social studies (includes history), speech, passing grade in the Ramona Arithmetic Proficiency Test.

Special Academic Programs Advanced Placement exam preparation; honors section; independent study; study abroad; academic accommodation for the gifted, the musically talented, and the artistically talented.

College Admission Counseling 89 students graduated in 2009; all went to college, including California State University, Los Angeles; Loyola Marymount University; Mount St. Mary's College; Pitzer College; University of California, Irvine; University of California, Los Angeles. Mean SAT critical reading: 535, mean SAT math: 493, mean SAT writing: 557.

Student Life Upper grades have uniform requirement, student council, honor system. Discipline rests primarily with faculty. Attendance at religious services is required.

Tuition and Aid Day student tuition: $9480. Tuition installment plan (monthly payment plans, quarterly and semester payment plans). Merit scholarship grants, need-based scholarship grants, paying campus jobs available. In 2009–10, 26% of upper-school students received aid; total upper-school merit-scholarship money awarded: $18,000. Total amount of financial aid awarded in 2009–10: $285,000.

Admissions Traditional secondary-level entrance grade is 9. For fall 2009, 190 students applied for upper-level admission, 150 were accepted, 78 enrolled. High School Placement Test required. Deadline for receipt of application materials: January 6. Application fee required: $60. On-campus interview required.

Athletics Interscholastic: basketball, cross-country running, soccer, softball, swimming and diving, tennis, track and field, volleyball. 1 PE instructor, 9 coaches.

Computers Computers are regularly used in all academic classes. Computer network features include on-campus library services, Internet access, wireless campus network, Internet filtering or blocking technology. Student e-mail accounts and computer access in designated common areas are available to students. Students grades are available online. The school has a published electronic and media policy.

Contact Laura Dumas, Recruitment. 626-282-4151 Ext. 145. Fax: 626-281-0797. Web site: www.ramonaconvent.org.

RANDOLPH-MACON ACADEMY

200 Academy Drive

Front Royal, Virginia 22630

Head of School: Maj. Gen. Henry M. Hobgood

General Information Coeducational boarding and day college-preparatory, religious studies, technology, Air Force Junior ROTC, ESL, and military school, affiliated with Methodist Church. Grades 6–PG. Founded: 1892. Setting: small town. Nearest major city is Washington, DC. Students are housed in single-sex dormitories. 135-acre campus. 9 buildings on campus. Approved or accredited by Southern Association of Colleges and Schools, The Association of Boarding Schools, University Senate of United Methodist Church, Virginia Association of Independent Schools, and Virginia Department of Education. Member of National Association of Independent Schools. Endowment: $3.8 million. Total enrollment: 358. Upper school average class size: 15. Upper school faculty-student ratio: 1:9. Upper School students typically attend 5 days per week. The average school day consists of 7 hours.

Upper School Student Profile Grade 9: 59 students (39 boys, 20 girls); Grade 10: 67 students (46 boys, 21 girls); Grade 11: 83 students (64 boys, 19 girls); Grade 12: 76 students (50 boys, 26 girls). 85% of students are boarding students. 48% are state residents. 20 states are represented in upper school student body. 21% are international students. International students from China, Ecuador, Hong Kong, Republic of Korea, Russian Federation, and Viet Nam; 12 other countries represented in student body. 12% of students are Methodist.

Faculty School total: 39. In upper school: 23 men, 9 women; 19 have advanced degrees; 15 reside on campus.

Subjects Offered Advanced math, aerospace science, algebra, American government, American history, American history-AP, American literature, American literature-AP, anatomy, anatomy and physiology, art, art history-AP, Asian history, aviation, band, Bible studies, biology, biology-AP, British literature, calculus, calculus-AP, career education, chemistry, chorus, college counseling, comparative religion, composition-AP, computer applications, computer literacy, conceptual physics, concert band, concert choir, critical thinking, desktop publishing, discrete mathematics, drama, English, English composition, English literature, English literature and composition-AP, English-AP, epic literature, ESL, European history-AP, flight instruction, geometry, German, German-AP, government/civics, handbells, history, honors algebra, honors English, honors geometry, honors U.S. history, independent study, journalism, JROTC, keyboarding, life management skills, mathematics, music, music appreciation, New Testament, personal finance, personal fitness, photography, physical education, physics, physics-AP, physiology, pre-algebra, pre-calculus, psychology, religion, SAT preparation, science, senior seminar, Shakespeare, social studies, Spanish, Spanish literature-AP, speech and debate, statistics-AP, studio art, theater arts, trigonometry, U.S. government, U.S. history, world history, yearbook.

Graduation Requirements Aerospace science, arts and fine arts (art, music, dance, drama), computer science, English, foreign language, mathematics, physical education (includes health), religion (includes Bible studies and theology), science, social studies (includes history), Air Force Junior ROTC for each year student is enrolled.

Special Academic Programs Advanced Placement exam preparation; honors section; independent study; study at local college for college credit; study abroad; academic accommodation for the gifted; ESL (18 students enrolled).

College Admission Counseling 87 students graduated in 2010; all went to college, including Arizona State University; Longwood University; Michigan State University; Purdue University; University of Pittsburgh; Virginia Military Institute. Median SAT critical reading: 510, median SAT math: 565, median SAT writing: 525, median combined SAT: 1625. 25% scored over 600 on SAT critical reading, 30% scored over 600 on SAT math, 16% scored over 600 on SAT writing, 22% scored over 1800 on combined SAT, 13% scored over 26 on composite ACT.

Student Life Upper grades have uniform requirement, student council, honor system. Discipline rests equally with students and faculty. Attendance at religious services is required.

Summer Programs Remediation, enrichment, advancement, ESL, art/fine arts, computer instruction programs offered; session focuses on remediation, new courses, ESL, flight, college counseling; held on campus; accepts boys and girls; open to students from other schools. 180 students usually enrolled. 2011 schedule: June 26 to July 22. Application deadline: June 23.

Tuition and Aid Day student tuition: $14,672; 7-day tuition and room/board: $29,532. Tuition installment plan (monthly payment plans, 2-payment plan). Tuition reduction for siblings, merit scholarship grants, need-based scholarship grants, paying campus jobs, Methodist Church scholarships available. In 2010–11, 14% of upper-school students received aid; total upper-school merit-scholarship money awarded: $20,000. Total amount of financial aid awarded in 2010–11: $300,000.

Admissions Traditional secondary-level entrance grade is 9. For fall 2010, 213 students applied for upper-level admission, 199 were accepted, 133 enrolled. Any standardized test or SSAT required. Deadline for receipt of application materials: none. Application fee required: $75. Interview required.

Athletics Interscholastic: baseball (boys), basketball (b,g), cross-country running (b,g), football (b), lacrosse (b), soccer (b,g), softball (g), swimming and diving (b,g), tennis (b,g), track and field (b,g), volleyball (b,g), wrestling (b); intramural: basketball (b,g), horseback riding (g), independent competitive sports (b,g), soccer (b,g), softball (g), strength & conditioning (b,g), swimming and diving (b,g), tennis (b,g), track and field (b,g), volleyball (b,g); coed interscholastic: cheering, drill team, golf, JROTC drill; coed intramural: golf, horseback riding, indoor soccer, jogging, JROTC drill, outdoor activities, outdoor recreation, physical fitness, soccer, strength & conditioning, swimming and diving, table tennis, volleyball, weight lifting, weight training. 2 PE instructors, 1 athletic trainer.

Computers Computers are regularly used in aerospace science, aviation, English, ESL, foreign language, independent study, mathematics, science, yearbook classes. Computer network features include on-campus library services, online commercial services, Internet access, Internet filtering or blocking technology. Campus intranet and student e-mail accounts are available to students. Students grades are available online. The school has a published electronic and media policy.

Contact Mrs. Paula Brady, Admissions Coordinator. 540-636-5200 Ext. 5484. Fax: 540-636-5419. E-mail: paulab@rma.edu. Web site: www.rma.edu.

RANDOLPH SCHOOL

1005 Drake Avenue SE
Huntsville, Alabama 35802
Head of School: Dr. Byron C. Hulsey

General Information Coeducational day college-preparatory and arts school. Grades K–12. Founded: 1959. Setting: suburban. 67-acre campus. 3 buildings on campus. Approved or accredited by Southern Association of Colleges and Schools, Southern Association of Independent Schools, and The College Board. Member of National Association of Independent Schools. Endowment: $12 million. Total enrollment: 939. Upper school average class size: 13. Upper school faculty-student ratio: 1:10. The average school day consists of 7 hours.

Faculty School total: 102. In upper school: 13 men, 20 women; 21 have advanced degrees.

Subjects Offered 3-dimensional art, acting, algebra, American history, American history-AP, American literature, anatomy, art, art-AP, band, biology, biology-AP, calculus, calculus-AP, ceramics, chemistry, chemistry-AP, comparative government and politics-AP, computer math, concert choir, consumer economics, creative writing,

drama, drama workshop, economics, English, English literature, English-AP, environmental science, European history, European history-AP, film appreciation, film-making, fine arts, forensics, French, French-AP, geometry, history, Homeric Greek, journalism, Latin, marine biology, mathematics, music, music theory-AP, physical education, physics, physics-AP, physiology, psychology, science, social studies, Southern literature, Spanish, Spanish-AP, speech, stage design, stagecraft, student publications, studio art-AP, theater, trigonometry, U.S. government and politics-AP, U.S. history-AP, world history, world history-AP, world literature, writing, yearbook.

Graduation Requirements Algebra, American literature, arts and fine arts (art, music, dance, drama), biology, British literature, chemistry, computer science, English, European history, foreign language, geometry, literature, mathematics, science, social studies (includes history), world literature.

Special Academic Programs 12 Advanced Placement exams for which test preparation is offered; honors section; independent study; study at local college for college credit.

College Admission Counseling 61 students graduated in 2010; all went to college, including Auburn University; Birmingham-Southern College; Sewanee: The University of the South; The University of Alabama; The University of Alabama at Birmingham; Vanderbilt University. Median SAT critical reading: 640, median SAT math: 670, median SAT writing: 640, median combined SAT: 1940, median composite ACT: 29. 65% scored over 600 on SAT critical reading, 72% scored over 600 on SAT math, 63% scored over 600 on SAT writing, 77% scored over 1800 on combined SAT, 67% scored over 26 on composite ACT.

Student Life Upper grades have specified standards of dress, student council, honor system. Discipline rests primarily with faculty.

Summer Programs Enrichment, sports programs offered; session focuses on sports, science, art, foreign language; held on campus; accepts boys and girls; open to students from other schools. 140 students usually enrolled. 2011 schedule: June 1 to July 31. Application deadline: April 30.

Tuition and Aid Day student tuition: $11,850–$14,785. Tuition installment plan (Insured Tuition Payment Plan, 2- and 10-payment plans). Merit scholarship grants, need-based scholarship grants available. In 2010–11, 4% of upper-school students received aid; total upper-school merit-scholarship money awarded: $21,932. Total amount of financial aid awarded in 2010–11: $88,875.

Admissions Traditional secondary-level entrance grade is 9. For fall 2010, 31 students applied for upper-level admission, 19 were accepted, 15 enrolled. ERB, ISEE or writing sample required. Deadline for receipt of application materials: none. Application fee required: $75. On-campus interview required.

Athletics Interscholastic: baseball (boys), basketball (b,g), cheering (g), cross-country running (b,g), diving (b,g), football (b), golf (b,g), indoor track & field (b,g), physical fitness (b,g), physical training (b,g), soccer (b,g), softball (g), swimming and diving (b,g), tennis (b,g), track and field (b,g), volleyball (g), winter (indoor) track (b,g); coed interscholastic: diving; coed intramural: flag football. 6 PE instructors, 5 coaches, 1 athletic trainer.

Computers Computers are regularly used in all academic classes. Computer network features include on-campus library services, online commercial services, Internet access, wireless campus network, Internet filtering or blocking technology, laptops. Campus intranet, student e-mail accounts, and computer access in designated common areas are available to students. Students grades are available online. The school has a published electronic and media policy.

Contact Glynn Below, Director of Admissions. 256-799-6104. Fax: 256-881-1784. E-mail: gbelow@randolphschool.net. Web site: www.randolphschool.net.

RANNEY SCHOOL

235 Hope Road
Tinton Falls, New Jersey 07724
Head of School: Dr. Lawrence S. Sykoff

General Information Coeducational day college-preparatory school. Grades N–12. Founded: 1960. Setting: suburban. Nearest major city is New York, NY. 60-acre campus. 3 buildings on campus. Approved or accredited by Middle States Association of Colleges and Schools and New Jersey Department of Education. Member of National Association of Independent Schools. Total enrollment: 807. Upper school average class size: 15. Upper school faculty-student ratio: 1:9.

Upper School Student Profile Grade 9: 61 students (31 boys, 30 girls); Grade 10: 52 students (25 boys, 27 girls); Grade 11: 61 students (31 boys, 30 girls); Grade 12: 57 students (24 boys, 33 girls).

Faculty School total: 94.

Subjects Offered Advanced Placement courses, algebra, American history, American literature, art, art history, art history-AP, biology, biology-AP, calculus, calculus-AP, ceramics, chemistry, chemistry-AP, computer programming, computer science, computer science-AP, economics, economics-AP, English, English language-AP, English literature, English literature-AP, European history, European history-AP, fine arts, French, French-AP, geometry, grammar, health, history, journalism, mathematics, music, physical education, physics, psychology, science, Spanish, Spanish language-AP, world history, world literature, writing.

Graduation Requirements Arts and fine arts (art, music, dance, drama), English, foreign language, history, mathematics, physical education (includes health), science.

Special Academic Programs Advanced Placement exam preparation; honors section.

College Admission Counseling 56 students graduated in 2010; all went to college, including Barnard College; Columbia University; Duke University; Emory University; Lehigh University; New York University. Mean SAT critical reading: 626, mean SAT math: 621, mean SAT writing: 638, mean combined SAT: 1884.

Student Life Upper grades have specified standards of dress, student council, honor system. Discipline rests equally with students and faculty.

Summer Programs Enrichment, sports, art/fine arts, computer instruction programs offered; session focuses on mathematics and English; held on campus; accepts boys and girls; open to students from other schools. 2011 schedule: July 1 to August 23. Application deadline: March 30.

Tuition and Aid Day student tuition: $21,650–$24,100. Tuition installment plan (Tuiton Management Systems (TMS)). Need-based scholarship grants, reduced tuition for children of employees available.

Admissions Traditional secondary-level entrance grade is 9. For fall 2010, 57 students applied for upper-level admission, 43 were accepted, 26 enrolled. ERB required. Deadline for receipt of application materials: none. Application fee required: $75. On-campus interview required.

Athletics Interscholastic: baseball (boys), basketball (b,g), cheering (g), field hockey (g), lacrosse (b), soccer (b,g), softball (g), tennis (b,g); coed interscholastic: aquatics, cross-country running, golf, swimming and diving, track and field; coed intramural: aquatics, crew, fencing, fitness, weight training. 6 PE instructors, 16 coaches, 1 athletic trainer.

Computers Computer resources include on-campus library services, Internet access, Internet filtering or blocking technology. The school has a published electronic and media policy.

Contact Heather Rudisi, Associate Head for Admission and Marketing. 732-542-4777 Ext. 107. Fax: 732-460-1078. E-mail: hrudisi@ranneyschool.org. Web site: www.ranneyschool.org.

See Close-Up on page 826.

RANSOM EVERGLADES SCHOOL

3575 Main Highway
Miami, Florida 33133
Head of School: Mrs. Ellen Y. Moceri

General Information Coeducational day college-preparatory school. Grades 6–12. Founded: 1903. Setting: urban. 11-acre campus. 19 buildings on campus. Approved or accredited by Southern Association of Colleges and Schools, Southern Association of Independent Schools, and Florida Department of Education. Member of National Association of Independent Schools and Secondary School Admission Test Board. Endowment: $23.2 million. Total enrollment: 1,069. Upper school average class size: 14. Upper school faculty-student ratio: 1:10. There are 175 required school days per year for Upper School students. Upper School students typically attend 5 days per week. The average school day consists of 7 hours and 30 minutes.

Upper School Student Profile Grade 9: 161 students (80 boys, 81 girls); Grade 10: 157 students (89 boys, 68 girls); Grade 11: 143 students (65 boys, 78 girls); Grade 12: 141 students (60 boys, 81 girls).

Faculty School total: 95. In upper school: 32 men, 28 women; 43 have advanced degrees.

Subjects Offered Advanced Placement courses, algebra, American history, American history-AP, American literature, anatomy and physiology, art, art history, art history-AP, Asian studies, astronomy, band, biology, calculus, calculus-AP, ceramics, chemistry, chemistry-AP, Chinese, choir, chorus, college counseling, comparative government and politics-AP, computer math, computer programming, computer science, computer science-AP, computer-aided design, concert band, creative writing, dance, dance performance, debate, digital photography, drama, earth science, ecology, economics, economics-AP, engineering, English, English literature, English literature and composition-AP, English-AP, environmental science, environmental science-AP, environmental studies, ethical decision making, ethics, ethics and responsibility, European history, European history-AP, experiential education, fine arts, French, French language-AP, French-AP, geography, geology, geometry, government and politics-AP, government/civics, grammar, graphic design, guitar, health, health and wellness, history, history-AP, human anatomy, interdisciplinary studies, jazz ensemble, journalism, macro/microeconomics-AP, macroeconomics-AP, Mandarin, marine biology, mathematics, mathematics-AP, music, music theory, music theory-AP, music-AP, mythology, philosophy, photography, physical education, physics, physics-AP, probability and statistics, psychology, psychology-AP, robotics, science, sculpture, social studies, sociology, Spanish, Spanish language-AP, Spanish literature-AP, speech, speech and debate, statistics, statistics-AP, theater, theory of knowledge, trigonometry, U.S. government and politics-AP, U.S. history, U.S. history-AP, world history, world history-AP, world literature, writing, yearbook.

Graduation Requirements Arts and fine arts (art, music, dance, drama), computer science, English, foreign language, mathematics, physical education (includes health), science, social studies (includes history).

Special Academic Programs 23 Advanced Placement exams for which test preparation is offered; honors section.

College Admission Counseling 154 students graduated in 2010; all went to college, including Boston College; Cornell University; Tufts University; University of Miami; University of Pennsylvania; Washington University in St. Louis. Median SAT critical reading: 660, median SAT math: 680, median SAT writing: 670.

Student Life Upper grades have specified standards of dress, student council, honor system. Discipline rests primarily with faculty.

Summer Programs Enrichment, advancement, computer instruction programs offered; session focuses on enrichment to reinforce basic skills and advancement for credit; held on campus; accepts boys and girls; open to students from other schools. 130 students usually enrolled. 2011 schedule: June 13 to July 22. Application deadline: June 6.

Tuition and Aid Day student tuition: $25,150. Tuition installment plan (monthly payment plans, 60%/40% payment plan). Need-based scholarship grants available. In 2010–11, 17% of upper-school students received aid. Total amount of financial aid awarded in 2010–11: $3,329,170.

Admissions Traditional secondary-level entrance grade is 9. For fall 2010, 143 students applied for upper-level admission, 32 were accepted, 22 enrolled. SSAT required. Deadline for receipt of application materials: February 15. Application fee required: $100. On-campus interview required.

Athletics Interscholastic: baseball (boys), basketball (b,g), canoeing/kayaking (b,g), cheering (g), crew (b,g), cross-country running (b,g), dance (g), dance team (g), football (b), golf (b,g), kayaking (b,g), lacrosse (b), physical training (b,g), sailing (b,g), soccer (b,g), softball (g), swimming and diving (b,g), tennis (b,g), track and field (b,g), volleyball (b,g), water polo (b,g), wrestling (b); coed interscholastic: crew, kayaking, sailing. 5 PE instructors, 75 coaches, 2 athletic trainers.

Computers Computers are regularly used in all classes. Computer network features include on-campus library services, online commercial services, Internet access, wireless campus network, Internet filtering or blocking technology. Student e-mail accounts and computer access in designated common areas are available to students. Students grades are available online. The school has a published electronic and media policy.

Contact Amy Sayfie, Director of Admission. 305-250-6875. Fax: 305-854-1846. E-mail: asayfie@ransomeverglades.org. Web site: www.ransomeverglades.org.

RAVENSCROFT SCHOOL

7409 Falls of the Neuse Road
Raleigh, North Carolina 27615
Head of School: Mrs. Doreen C. Kelly

General Information Coeducational day college-preparatory, arts, and technology school. Grades PK–12. Founded: 1862. Setting: suburban. 127-acre campus. 13 buildings on campus. Approved or accredited by Southern Association of Colleges and Schools, Southern Association of Independent Schools, and North Carolina Department of Education. Member of National Association of Independent Schools. Endowment: $12 million. Total enrollment: 1,235. Upper school average class size: 16. Upper school faculty-student ratio: 1:6.

Upper School Student Profile Grade 9: 106 students (62 boys, 44 girls); Grade 10: 115 students (63 boys, 52 girls); Grade 11: 107 students (58 boys, 49 girls); Grade 12: 117 students (58 boys, 59 girls).

Faculty School total: 182. In upper school: 32 men, 38 women; 49 have advanced degrees.

Subjects Offered Advanced Placement courses, algebra, American history, American literature, anatomy, art, art history, astronomy, biology, biotechnology, calculus, chemistry, computer programming, computer science, discrete mathematics, drama, economics, engineering, English, English literature, environmental science, environmental science-AP, European history, expository writing, fine arts, French, geometry, government/civics, Greek, health, history, journalism, Latin, mathematics, music, photography, physical education, physics, psychology, science, social sciences, social studies, Spanish, speech, sports medicine, stagecraft, statistics-AP, theater, world history, writing.

Graduation Requirements Arts and fine arts (art, music, dance, drama), composition, English, foreign language, mathematics, physical education (includes health), science, social sciences, social studies (includes history). Community service is required.

Special Academic Programs 24 Advanced Placement exams for which test preparation is offered; honors section; independent study; term-away projects; study at local college for college credit; study abroad; academic accommodation for the gifted, the musically talented, and the artistically talented.

College Admission Counseling 113 students graduated in 2009; all went to college, including Clemson University; East Carolina University; North Carolina State University; The University of North Carolina at Chapel Hill; The University of North Carolina Wilmington; University of South Carolina. Median SAT critical reading: 610, median SAT math: 650, median SAT writing: 640, median combined SAT: 1890, median composite ACT: 26. 56% scored over 600 on SAT critical reading, 70% scored over 600 on SAT math, 67% scored over 600 on SAT writing, 63% scored over 1800 on combined SAT, 50% scored over 26 on composite ACT.

Student Life Upper grades have specified standards of dress, student council, honor system. Discipline rests equally with students and faculty.

Tuition and Aid Day student tuition: $17,250. Tuition installment plan (individually arranged payment plans). Merit scholarship grants, need-based scholarship grants, need-based loans available. In 2009–10, 19% of upper-school students received aid; total upper-school merit-scholarship money awarded: $37,625. Total amount of financial aid awarded in 2009–10: $82,907.

Admissions Traditional secondary-level entrance grade is 9. For fall 2009, 127 students applied for upper-level admission, 69 were accepted, 45 enrolled. ERB and

SSAT required. Deadline for receipt of application materials: none. Application fee required: $70. On-campus interview required.

Athletics Interscholastic: baseball (boys), basketball (b,g), cheering (g), cross-country running (b,g), dance squad (g), field hockey (g), fitness (b,g), football (b), golf (b,g), lacrosse (b,g), physical training (b,g), soccer (b,g), softball (g), strength & conditioning (b,g), swimming and diving (b,g), tennis (b,g), track and field (b,g), volleyball (g), weight training (b,g), wrestling (b); intramural: baseball (b), basketball (b,g), cheering (g), dance team (g), football (b,g), lacrosse (b), soccer (b,g), softball (g), strength & conditioning (b,g), swimming and diving (b,g), tennis (b,g), track and field (b,g), volleyball (g), wrestling (b); coed interscholastic: life saving. 10 PE instructors, 68 coaches, 2 athletic trainers.

Computers Computers are regularly used in economics, English, foreign language, history, mathematics, science, social studies, writing classes. Computer network features include on-campus library services, online commercial services, Internet access, wireless campus network, Internet filtering or blocking technology. Campus intranet, student e-mail accounts, and computer access in designated common areas are available to students. Students grades are available online. The school has a published electronic and media policy.

Contact Mrs. Pamela J. Jamison, Director of Admissions. 919-847-0900 Ext. 2226. Fax: 919-846-2371. E-mail: pjamison@ravenscroft.org. Web site: www.ravenscroft.org.

THE RECTORY SCHOOL

Pomfret, Connecticut
See Junior Boarding Schools section.

REDWOOD ADVENTIST ACADEMY

385 Mark West Springs Road
Santa Rosa, California 95404
Head of School: Mr. Robert Fenderson

General Information Coeducational day college-preparatory school, affiliated with Seventh-day Adventists. Grades K–12. Founded: 1931. Setting: suburban. Nearest major city is San Francisco. 10-acre campus. 3 buildings on campus. Approved or accredited by Board of Regents, General Conference of Seventh-day Adventists, Western Association of Schools and Colleges, and California Department of Education. Total enrollment: 107. Upper school average class size: 18. Upper school faculty-student ratio: 1:6. There are 180 required school days per year for Upper School students. Upper School students typically attend 5 days per week. The average school day consists of 7 hours and 45 minutes.

Upper School Student Profile Grade 9: 13 students (5 boys, 8 girls); Grade 10: 7 students (3 boys, 4 girls); Grade 11: 11 students (6 boys, 5 girls); Grade 12: 8 students (3 boys, 5 girls). 81% of students are Seventh-day Adventists.

Faculty School total: 12. In upper school: 5 men, 2 women; 2 have advanced degrees.

Subjects Offered All academic.

Graduation Requirements Engineering.

Special Academic Programs Accelerated programs; study at local college for college credit.

College Admission Counseling 15 students graduated in 2010; 13 went to college, including La Sierra University; Pacific Union College; University of California, Davis; Walla Walla University. Other: 1 went to work.

Student Life Upper grades have specified standards of dress, student council, honor system. Discipline rests primarily with faculty.

Tuition and Aid Day student tuition: $9500. Tuition reduction for siblings, need-based scholarship grants, paying campus jobs available. In 2010–11, 24% of upper-school students received aid. Total amount of financial aid awarded in 2010–11: $50,000.

Admissions Traditional secondary-level entrance grade is 9. For fall 2010, 4 students applied for upper-level admission, 4 were accepted, 4 enrolled. TOEFL or WRAT required. Deadline for receipt of application materials: none. Application fee required: $30. Interview recommended.

Athletics Interscholastic: basketball (boys, girls), flag football (b,g), softball (b,g), volleyball (g); intramural: outdoor education (b,g), physical fitness (b,g). 1 PE instructor.

Computers Computers are regularly used in computer applications, desktop publishing, keyboarding, life skills, mathematics, Spanish, video film production, word processing, yearbook classes. Computer network features include Internet access, wireless campus network, Internet filtering or blocking technology. Computer access in designated common areas is available to students. Students grades are available online. The school has a published electronic and media policy.

Contact Mrs. Glenda Purdy, Registrar. 707-545-1697 Ext. 45. Fax: 707-545-8020. E-mail: glendapurdy@gmail.com. Web site: www.redwoodaa.com.

REDWOOD CHRISTIAN SCHOOLS

4200 James Avenue
Castro Valley, California 94546
Head of School: Mr. Bruce D. Johnson

General Information Coeducational day college-preparatory and religious studies school, affiliated with Christian faith. Grades K–12. Founded: 1970. Setting: urban. Nearest major city is Oakland. 10-acre campus. 11 buildings on campus. Approved or accredited by Association of Christian Schools International, Western Association of Schools and Colleges, and California Department of Education. Total enrollment: 593. Upper school average class size: 18. Upper school faculty-student ratio: 1:15. There are 175 required school days per year for Upper School students. Upper School students typically attend 5 days per week. The average school day consists of 5 hours and 15 minutes.

Upper School Student Profile Grade 6: 49 students (25 boys, 24 girls); Grade 7: 60 students (32 boys, 28 girls); Grade 8: 55 students (29 boys, 26 girls); Grade 9: 56 students (31 boys, 25 girls); Grade 10: 51 students (22 boys, 29 girls); Grade 11: 57 students (32 boys, 25 girls); Grade 12: 53 students (27 boys, 26 girls). 50% of students are Christian.

Faculty School total: 26. In upper school: 15 men, 10 women; 9 have advanced degrees.

Subjects Offered Advanced math, Advanced Placement courses, algebra, art, athletics, band, baseball, basketball, Bible studies, biology, calculus, chemistry, choir, computer literacy, concert band, data processing, drama, economics, English, English-AP, European history-AP, fitness, geometry, honors English, keyboarding, macro/microeconomics-AP, physical education, physical science, physics, softball, Spanish, speech, track and field, trigonometry, U.S. government, U.S. history, vocal music, woodworking, world history, yearbook.

Graduation Requirements Arts and fine arts (art, music, dance, drama), Bible, computer literacy, electives, English, foreign language, mathematics, physical education (includes health), science, speech, world history.

Special Academic Programs Advanced Placement exam preparation; honors section; study at local college for college credit; remedial reading and/or remedial writing; remedial math; programs in English, mathematics, general development for dyslexic students.

College Admission Counseling 60 students graduated in 2010; 57 went to college, including Azusa Pacific University; Biola University; California State University, East Bay; Simpson University; University of California, Davis; University of California, Irvine. Other: 3 went to work. Mean SAT critical reading: 586, mean SAT math: 597, mean SAT writing: 581. 53% scored over 600 on SAT critical reading, 50% scored over 600 on SAT math, 53% scored over 600 on SAT writing, 47% scored over 1800 on combined SAT.

Student Life Upper grades have specified standards of dress, student council, honor system. Discipline rests primarily with faculty.

Tuition and Aid Day student tuition: $9507–$14,261. Tuition installment plan (monthly payment plans, individually arranged payment plans). Tuition reduction for siblings, need-based scholarship grants, paying campus jobs available. In 2010–11, 60% of upper-school students received aid. Total amount of financial aid awarded in 2010–11: $350,000.

Admissions Traditional secondary-level entrance grade is 9. For fall 2010, 38 students applied for upper-level admission, 34 were accepted, 27 enrolled. Stanford Achievement Test required. Deadline for receipt of application materials: none. Application fee required: $100. On-campus interview required.

Athletics Interscholastic: baseball (boys), basketball (b,g), cross-country running (b,g), soccer (b,g), softball (g), tennis (b,g), track and field (b,g), volleyball (b,g). 2 PE instructors, 1 coach.

Computers Computers are regularly used in keyboarding, yearbook classes. Students grades are available online.

Contact Mrs. Deborah Wright, Registrar. 510-889-7526. Fax: 510-881-0127. E-mail: deborahwright@rcs.edu. Web site: www.rcs.edu.

REGIS HIGH SCHOOL

55 East 84th Street
New York, New York 10028-0884
Head of School: Dr. Gary J. Tocchet, PhD

General Information Boys' day college-preparatory school, affiliated with Roman Catholic Church. Grades 9–12. Founded: 1914. Setting: urban. 3-acre campus. 1 building on campus. Approved or accredited by Jesuit Secondary Education Association, Middle States Association of Colleges and Schools, New York State Association of Independent Schools, and New York Department of Education. Total enrollment: 535. Upper school average class size: 14. Upper school faculty-student ratio: 1:15. There are 180 required school days per year for Upper School students. Upper School students typically attend 5 days per week. The average school day consists of 6 hours and 50 minutes.

Upper School Student Profile Grade 9: 136 students (136 boys); Grade 10: 134 students (134 boys); Grade 11: 130 students (130 boys); Grade 12: 135 students (135 boys). 100% of students are Roman Catholic.

Faculty School total: 62. In upper school: 39 men, 19 women; 53 have advanced degrees.

Subjects Offered Algebra, American history, American literature, art, art history, band, biology, calculus, chemistry, Chinese, computer programming, computer science, creative writing, drama, driver education, economics, English, English literature, ethics, European history, expository writing, film, French, geometry, German, health, history, Latin, mathematics, music, physical education, physics, psychology, social studies, Spanish, speech, statistics, theater, theology, trigonometry, writing.

Graduation Requirements Art, computer literacy, English, foreign language, history, mathematics, music, physical education (includes health), science, theology, Christian service program.

Special Academic Programs Advanced Placement exam preparation; independent study; study abroad.

College Admission Counseling 125 students graduated in 2010; all went to college, including Colgate University; College of the Holy Cross; Columbia University; Dartmouth College; Fordham University; Georgetown University. Mean SAT critical reading: 705, mean SAT math: 707, mean SAT writing: 709, mean combined SAT: 2120.

Student Life Upper grades have specified standards of dress, student council. Discipline rests primarily with faculty. Attendance at religious services is required.

Tuition and Aid Tuition-free school available.

Admissions Traditional secondary-level entrance grade is 9. For fall 2010, 792 students applied for upper-level admission, 146 were accepted, 136 enrolled. Admissions testing required. Deadline for receipt of application materials: October 22. Application fee required: $50. On-campus interview required.

Athletics Interscholastic: baseball, basketball, bowling, cross-country running; intramural: basketball, floor hockey. 2 PE instructors, 16 coaches.

Computers Computers are regularly used in all academic classes. Computer network features include on-campus library services, Internet access.

Contact Mr. Eric P. DiMichele, Director of Admissions. 212-288-1100 Ext. 2057. Fax: 212-794-1221. E-mail: edimiche@regis-nyc.org. Web site: www.regis-nyc.org.

REITZ MEMORIAL HIGH SCHOOL

1500 Lincoln Avenue

Evansville, Indiana 47714

Head of School: Mrs. Gwen Godsey

General Information Coeducational day college-preparatory and religious studies school, affiliated with Roman Catholic Church. Grades 9–12. Founded: 1924. Setting: urban. Nearest major city is Indianapolis. 2 buildings on campus. Approved or accredited by North Central Association of Colleges and Schools, The College Board, and Indiana Department of Education. Total enrollment: 790. Upper school average class size: 25. Upper school faculty-student ratio: 1:16. There are 180 required school days per year for Upper School students. Upper School students typically attend 5 days per week. The average school day consists of 7 hours.

Upper School Student Profile 90% of students are Roman Catholic.

Faculty School total: 52. In upper school: 17 men, 35 women; 27 have advanced degrees.

Subjects Offered 20th century American writers, 20th century history, 3-dimensional art, accounting, advanced biology, advanced chemistry, advanced computer applications, Advanced Placement courses, algebra, American government, American history, American literature, anthropology, applied music, art, art appreciation, art history, band, Basic programming, biology, biology-AP, British literature, business, business communications, business law, business skills, calculus-AP, Catholic belief and practice, ceramics, chemistry, chemistry-AP, choir, chorus, church history, composition, computer applications, computer programming, consumer economics, current events, digital photography, dramatic arts, drawing, driver education, earth and space science, ecology, environmental science, English, English composition, English literature and composition-AP, entomology, environmental science, etymology, foreign language, forensics, French, French language-AP, geometry, German, government, grammar, guitar, health and wellness, history of the Catholic Church, honors algebra, honors English, honors geometry, honors U.S. history, honors world history, jewelry making, journalism, keyboarding, law, law and the legal system, library assistant, Life of Christ, literary genres, marching band, media arts, music appreciation, music composition, music history, New Testament, newspaper, oil painting, painting, peace and justice, personal finance, physical education, physics, physics-AP, piano, portfolio art, prayer/spirituality, pre-calculus, printmaking, psychology, Spanish, Spanish language-AP, studio art, theater arts, trigonometry, U.S. history, weight training, world history, world history-AP, yearbook.

Graduation Requirements Service hours.

Special Academic Programs 8 Advanced Placement exams for which test preparation is offered; honors section; study at local college for college credit.

College Admission Counseling 205 students graduated in 2010; 204 went to college, including Indiana University Bloomington; Purdue University; University of Evansville; University of Kentucky; University of Mississippi; Western Kentucky University. Other: 1 entered military service.

Student Life Upper grades have uniform requirement, student council. Discipline rests primarily with faculty. Attendance at religious services is required.

Summer Programs Remediation, sports programs offered; held both on and off campus; held at city-owned local schools and fields; accepts boys and girls; open to students from other schools. 400 students usually enrolled. 2011 schedule: May 26 to July 31.

Tuition and Aid Day student tuition: $4500–$7050. Tuition installment plan (ETFCU Loans). Tuition reduction for siblings, need-based scholarship grants, need-based loans available. In 2010–11, 12% of upper-school students received aid. Total amount of financial aid awarded in 2010–11: $264,840.

Admissions Traditional secondary-level entrance grade is 9. For fall 2010, 805 students applied for upper-level admission, 805 were accepted, 790 enrolled. ACT-Explore required. Deadline for receipt of application materials: none. Application fee required: $180.

Athletics Interscholastic: baseball (boys), basketball (b,g), cheering (g), dance squad (g), dance team (g), diving (b,g), drill team (g), football (b), golf (b,g), soccer (b,g), softball (g), swimming and diving (b,g), tennis (b,g), track and field (b,g), volleyball (g), wrestling (b); intramural: bowling (b,g), lacrosse (b,g), paint ball (b); coed intramural: ice hockey, table tennis. 4 PE instructors, 1 athletic trainer.

Computers Computers are regularly used in all classes. Computer network features include on-campus library services, Internet access, wireless campus network, Internet filtering or blocking technology. Campus intranet and computer access in designated common areas are available to students. Students grades are available online. The school has a published electronic and media policy.

Contact Mrs. Lisa Popham, Assistant Principal. 812-476-4973 Ext. 205. Fax: 812-474-2942. E-mail: lisapopham@reitzmemorial.org. Web site: www.reitzmemorial.org.

REJOICE CHRISTIAN SCHOOLS

12200 East 86th Street North

Owasso, Oklahoma 74055

Head of School: Dr. Craig D. Shaw

General Information Coeducational day college-preparatory school, affiliated with Free Will Baptist Church. Grades P3–12. Founded: 1992. Setting: suburban. Nearest major city is Tulsa. 1 building on campus. Approved or accredited by Association of Christian Schools International, European Council of International Schools, and Oklahoma Department of Education. Total enrollment: 713. Upper school average class size: 12. Upper school faculty-student ratio: 1:12.

Upper School Student Profile Grade 6: 36 students (14 boys, 22 girls); Grade 7: 40 students (17 boys, 23 girls); Grade 8: 37 students (20 boys, 17 girls); Grade 9: 35 students (14 boys, 21 girls); Grade 10: 17 students (8 boys, 9 girls); Grade 11: 17 students (10 boys, 7 girls); Grade 12: 15 students (9 boys, 6 girls). 30% of students are Free Will Baptist Church.

Faculty School total: 22. In upper school: 5 men, 17 women; 8 have advanced degrees.

Subjects Offered Advanced biology, advanced chemistry, Advanced Placement courses, algebra, American democracy, American government, American history, American history-AP, anatomy, anatomy and physiology, art, art appreciation, art education, art history, athletic training, athletics, band, basketball, Bible, Bible studies, biology, biology-AP, business, business education, calculus, calculus-AP, cheerleading, chemistry, chemistry-AP, choir, chorus, Christian education, civics, computer skills, electives, English, English language-AP, English literature and composition-AP, English literature-AP, English-AP, English/composition-AP, fitness, general business, general math, geography, geometry, golf, government, government and politics-AP, government-AP, government/civics, government/civics-AP, history, honors algebra, honors English, honors geometry, honors U.S. history, honors world history, journalism, language, language arts, library, mathematics, mathematics-AP, media, music, novels, physical education, physical fitness, physical science, pre-algebra, pre-calculus, Spanish, Spanish language-AP, speech, speech and debate, sports, sports conditioning, state history, technology, track and field, trigonometry, U.S. government, U.S. government and politics-AP, U.S. history, U.S. history-AP, weight training, world history, world history-AP, yearbook.

Special Academic Programs Honors section; study at local college for college credit.

Student Life Upper grades have student council, honor system. Discipline rests primarily with faculty.

Tuition and Aid Tuition installment plan (SMART Tuition Payment Plan, monthly payment plans). Need-based scholarship grants available.

Admissions Gates MacGinite Reading Tests, Gates MacGinite Reading/Key Math or Stanford Achievement Test required. Deadline for receipt of application materials: none. Application fee required: $160. Interview required.

Athletics Interscholastic: basketball (boys, girls), cheering (g), cross-country running (b,g), fitness (b,g), flag football (b,g), football (b), golf (b,g), jogging (b,g), outdoor activities (b,g), outdoor recreation (b,g), physical fitness (b,g), physical training (b,g), ropes courses (b,g), running (b,g), strength & conditioning (b,g), track and field (b,g), volleyball (g), weight lifting (b), weight training (b,g). 2 PE instructors, 15 coaches, 2 athletic trainers.

Computers Computers are regularly used in English, journalism, library, media, newspaper, yearbook classes. Computer network features include on-campus library services, Internet access, wireless campus network, Internet filtering or blocking technology. Campus intranet is available to students. Students grades are available online. The school has a published electronic and media policy.

Contact Mrs. Julie Long, High School Registrar. 918-516-0050. Fax: 918-516-0299. E-mail: jlong@rejoiceschool.com. Web site: www.rejoiceschool.com.

RIBÉT ACADEMY

2911 San Fernando Road
Los Angeles, California 90065
Head of School: Mr. Ronald Dauzat

General Information Coeducational day college-preparatory, arts, and science school, affiliated with Open Bible Standard Churches, Worldwide Church of God. Grades 1–12. Founded: 1982. Setting: urban. 9-acre campus. 2 buildings on campus. Approved or accredited by Western Association of Schools and Colleges and California Department of Education. Total enrollment: 408. Upper school average class size: 18. Upper school faculty-student ratio: 1:10. There are 185 required school days per year for Upper School students. Upper School students typically attend 5 days per week. The average school day consists of 7 hours and 30 minutes.

Upper School Student Profile 10% of students are Open Bible Standard Churches, Worldwide Church of God.

Faculty School total: 39. In upper school: 12 men, 12 women; 15 have advanced degrees.

Subjects Offered Advanced chemistry, advanced math, Advanced Placement courses, advanced studio art-AP, African American history, African-American history, algebra, American history-AP, American literature, art history-AP, art-AP, band, Basic programming, basic skills, biology, biology-AP, British literature, business law, calculus, calculus-AP, chemistry, chemistry-AP, choir, civics, Civil War, college planning, composition-AP, computer literacy, concert band, creative writing, debate, English, English language-AP, English literature-AP, ESL, European history-AP, French, French-AP, geometry, journalism, marine biology, oral communications, physics, physics-AP, pre-calculus, SAT preparation, Spanish, Spanish-AP, studio art, theater arts, U.S. government and politics, U.S. history-AP, world history-AP, yearbook.

Graduation Requirements Arts and fine arts (art, music, dance, drama), computers, electives, English, foreign language, mathematics, physical education (includes health), science, social studies (includes history). Community service is required.

Special Academic Programs Advanced Placement exam preparation; honors section; independent study; term-away projects; study abroad; academic accommodation for the musically talented and the artistically talented; ESL (40 students enrolled).

College Admission Counseling 56 students graduated in 2009; all went to college, including University of California, Berkeley; University of California, Los Angeles; University of California, Riverside; University of California, San Diego; University of California, Santa Barbara; University of Southern California. 98% scored over 600 on SAT critical reading, 100% scored over 600 on SAT math, 88% scored over 600 on SAT writing, 72% scored over 1800 on combined SAT, 90% scored over 26 on composite ACT.

Student Life Upper grades have uniform requirement, student council, honor system. Discipline rests primarily with faculty.

Tuition and Aid Day student tuition: $14,400. Tuition installment plan (individually arranged payment plans). Tuition reduction for siblings, need-based scholarship grants, Reduction In Tuition Exchange (RITE) available. In 2009–10, 33% of upper-school students received aid. Total amount of financial aid awarded in 2009–10: $100,000.

Admissions Traditional secondary-level entrance grade is 9. For fall 2009, 75 students applied for upper-level admission, 60 were accepted, 50 enrolled. Essay, ISEE or latest standardized score from previous school required. Deadline for receipt of application materials: none. Application fee required: $100. Interview required.

Athletics Interscholastic: baseball (boys), basketball (b,g), flag football (b), football (b), physical fitness (b,g), softball (g), strength & conditioning (b,g), volleyball (b,g); intramural: paint ball (b), physical fitness (b,g), strength & conditioning (b,g), volleyball (b,g); coed interscholastic: aerobics/dance, archery, cheering, dance squad, dance team, golf, physical fitness, soccer, track and field; coed intramural: aerobics/dance, basketball, cheering, cooperative games, dance, dance squad, dance team, flag football, football, golf, jogging, jump rope, kickball, martial arts, outdoor activities, outdoor adventure, paddle tennis, physical fitness, power lifting, rock climbing, running, soccer, softball, strength & conditioning, table tennis, touch football, track and field, volleyball, walking. 3 PE instructors, 16 coaches, 1 athletic trainer.

Computers Computer network features include on-campus library services, Internet access, wireless campus network, Internet filtering or blocking technology. Student e-mail accounts are available to students. Students grades are available online.

Contact Ms. Julia Haberman, Marketing Director. 323-344-4330 Ext. 117. Fax: 323-344-4339. E-mail: jhaberman@ribetacademy.com. Web site: www.ribetacademy.com.

RICE HIGH SCHOOL

74 West 124th Street
New York, New York 10027
Head of School: Br. Michael Segvich, CFC

General Information Boys' day college-preparatory and religious studies school, affiliated with Roman Catholic Church. Grades 9–12. Founded: 1938. Setting: urban. 1 building on campus. Approved or accredited by Middle States Association of Colleges and Schools, National Catholic Education Association, and New York Department of Education. Languages of instruction: English and Spanish. Endowment: $2 million. Total enrollment: 285. Upper school average class size: 23.

Upper school faculty-student ratio: 1:15. Upper School students typically attend 5 days per week. The average school day consists of 6 hours and 20 minutes.

Upper School Student Profile Grade 9: 65 students (65 boys); Grade 10: 89 students (89 boys); Grade 11: 66 students (66 boys); Grade 12: 65 students (65 boys). 40% of students are Roman Catholic.

Faculty School total: 24. In upper school: 17 men, 7 women; 16 have advanced degrees.

Subjects Offered Algebra, American history, art, Bible studies, biology, business, business mathematics, calculus, computer applications, electives, English, film, geometry, health, human biology, mathematics, physical science, pre-calculus, religion, Spanish, U.S. history.

Graduation Requirements Algebra, American history, art, biology, chemistry, earth science, English, global studies, health education, mathematics, physical education (includes health), religion (includes Bible studies and theology), Spanish, U.S. history, 125 hours of community service.

Special Academic Programs Study at local college for college credit.

College Admission Counseling 39 students graduated in 2009; all went to college, including Cornell University; Fairfield University; Fordham University; New York University.

Student Life Upper grades have specified standards of dress, student council, honor system. Discipline rests primarily with faculty. Attendance at religious services is required.

Tuition and Aid Day student tuition: $5750. Tuition installment plan (The Tuition Plan, monthly payment plans). Merit scholarship grants, need-based scholarship grants available. In 2009–10, 75% of upper-school students received aid. Total amount of financial aid awarded in 2009–10: $600,000.

Admissions Traditional secondary-level entrance grade is 9. For fall 2009, 200 students applied for upper-level admission, 115 were accepted, 65 enrolled. Admissions testing required. Deadline for receipt of application materials: none. No application fee required. Interview recommended.

Athletics Interscholastic: baseball, basketball, bowling, cross-country running, flag football, indoor track & field, jogging, soccer, track and field; intramural: baseball, flag football, tennis. 1 PE instructor, 7 coaches.

Computers Computer network features include on-campus library services, Internet access, wireless campus network, Internet filtering or blocking technology. Campus intranet and student e-mail accounts are available to students. Students grades are available online.

Contact Mr. W. Eric Crawford, Director of Admissions. 212-369-4100 Ext. 208. Fax: 212-369-5408. E-mail: wcrawford@ricehighschool.com. Web site: www.ricehighschool.com.

RIDGECROFT SCHOOL

420 NC 11 North
PO Box 1008
Ahoskie, North Carolina 27910
Head of School: Mr. Elton L. Winslow Sr.

General Information Coeducational day college-preparatory, arts, and technology school. Grades PK–12. Founded: 1968. Setting: rural. Nearest major city is Norfolk, VA. 52-acre campus. 3 buildings on campus. Approved or accredited by North Carolina Association of Independent Schools and Southern Association of Colleges and Schools. Endowment: $519,067. Total enrollment: 314. Upper school average class size: 15. Upper school faculty-student ratio: 1:9. There are 180 required school days per year for Upper School students. Upper School students typically attend 5 days per week. The average school day consists of 6 hours and 45 minutes.

Upper School Student Profile Grade 6: 23 students (16 boys, 7 girls); Grade 7: 17 students (12 boys, 5 girls); Grade 8: 22 students (10 boys, 12 girls); Grade 9: 17 students (11 boys, 6 girls); Grade 10: 22 students (8 boys, 14 girls); Grade 11: 24 students (18 boys, 6 girls); Grade 12: 20 students (11 boys, 9 girls).

Faculty School total: 31. In upper school: 3 men, 13 women; 5 have advanced degrees.

Subjects Offered Accounting, algebra, art, band, biology, business, calculus-AP, chemistry, computer skills, computers, earth science, English, English-AP, environmental science, forensics, functions, geometry, health, modeling, physical education, physical science, physics, pre-algebra, pre-calculus, Spanish, sports science, U.S. history, U.S. history-AP, weightlifting, world history, yearbook.

Graduation Requirements Algebra, American history, American legal systems, American literature, biology, British literature, chemistry, computer applications, earth science, economics, English, English composition, English literature, European literature, geometry, mathematics, physical education (includes health), Spanish, world history, community service-70 hours.

Special Academic Programs 3 Advanced Placement exams for which test preparation is offered; honors section; independent study; special instructional classes for students with learning disabilities and Attention Deficit Disorder.

College Admission Counseling Colleges students went to include East Carolina University; Meredith College; North Carolina State University. Other: 1 went to work, 18 entered a postgraduate year. Median SAT critical reading: 510, median SAT math: 540, median SAT writing: 560, median combined SAT: 1530. 7.1% scored over 600 on SAT critical reading, 7.1% scored over 600 on SAT math, 14.3% scored over 600 on SAT writing, 14.3% scored over 1800 on combined SAT.

Student Life Upper grades have specified standards of dress, student council, honor system. Discipline rests primarily with faculty.

Tuition and Aid Day student tuition: $4750. Tuition installment plan (monthly payment plans, individually arranged payment plans). Tuition reduction for siblings available.

Admissions Deadline for receipt of application materials: none. No application fee required. Interview recommended.

Athletics Interscholastic: baseball (boys), basketball (b,g), cheering (g), soccer (b,g), softball (g), tennis (g), volleyball (g); coed interscholastic: archery, golf, marksmanship, riflery, weight training. 1 coach.

Computers Computers are regularly used in accounting, English, history, science classes. Computer network features include on-campus library services, Internet access, wireless campus network, Internet filtering or blocking technology. Campus intranet and computer access in designated common areas are available to students. The school has a published electronic and media policy.

Contact Mrs. Cindy Burgess, Business Manager. 252-332-2964 Ext. 224. Fax: 252-332-7586. E-mail: cburgess@ridgecroft.org. Web site: www.ridgecroft.org.

RIDLEY COLLEGE

2 Ridley Road
St. Catharines, Ontario L2R7C3, Canada
Head of School: Mr. Jonathan Leigh

General Information Coeducational boarding and day college-preparatory, arts, business, and technology school, affiliated with Church of England (Anglican). Boarding grades 5–PG, day grades JK–PG. Founded: 1889. Setting: suburban. Nearest major city is Buffalo, NY. Students are housed in single-sex dormitories. 100-acre campus. 13 buildings on campus. Approved or accredited by Canadian Association of Independent Schools, Canadian Educational Standards Institute, Conference of Independent Schools of Ontario, The Association of Boarding Schools, and Ontario Department of Education. Affiliate member of National Association of Independent Schools; member of Secondary School Admission Test Board. Language of instruction: English. Endowment: CAN$25 million. Total enrollment: 591. Upper school average class size: 17. Upper school faculty-student ratio: 1:8. There are 222 required school days per year for Upper School students. Upper School students typically attend 6 days per week. The average school day consists of 6 hours.

Upper School Student Profile Grade 9: 69 students (39 boys, 30 girls); Grade 10: 91 students (48 boys, 43 girls); Grade 11: 111 students (70 boys, 41 girls); Grade 12: 139 students (67 boys, 72 girls); Postgraduate: 6 students (6 boys). 61% of students are boarding students. 62% are province residents. 17 provinces are represented in upper school student body. 36% are international students. International students from China, Germany, Hong Kong, Mexico, Republic of Korea, and United States; 25 other countries represented in student body. 20% of students are members of Church of England (Anglican).

Faculty School total: 70. In upper school: 40 men, 30 women; 27 have advanced degrees; 40 reside on campus.

Subjects Offered Accounting, Advanced Placement courses, algebra, American history, anthropology, art, art history, biology, business mathematics, business skills, calculus, Canadian history, Canadian law, chemistry, computer programming, computer science, creative writing, drafting, drama, dramatic arts, driver education, economics, English, English literature, ESL, fine arts, French, geography, German, kinesiology, Latin, Mandarin, mathematics, music, physical education, physics, science, social sciences, social studies, Spanish, theater, world history.

Graduation Requirements Arts and fine arts (art, music, dance, drama), business skills (includes word processing), English, foreign language, mathematics, physical education (includes health), science, social sciences, social studies (includes history).

Special Academic Programs 12 Advanced Placement exams for which test preparation is offered; honors section; independent study; study abroad; academic accommodation for the musically talented and the artistically talented; ESL (20 students enrolled).

College Admission Counseling 150 students graduated in 2010; 140 went to college, including Brock University; Queen's University at Kingston; The University of British Columbia; The University of Western Ontario; University of Toronto; University of Waterloo. Other: 4 entered a postgraduate year, 6 had other specific plans. Mean SAT critical reading: 570, mean SAT math: 590.

Student Life Upper grades have uniform requirement, student council, honor system. Discipline rests primarily with faculty. Attendance at religious services is required.

Tuition and Aid Day student tuition: CAN$24,750; 5-day tuition and room/board: CAN$33,820; 7-day tuition and room/board: CAN$44,500. Tuition installment plan (monthly payment plans, individually arranged payment plans). Bursaries, merit scholarship grants, need-based scholarship grants, need-based loans available. In 2010–11, 33% of upper-school students received aid; total upper-school merit-scholarship money awarded: CAN$300,000. Total amount of financial aid awarded in 2010–11: CAN$3,000,000.

Admissions Traditional secondary-level entrance grade is 9. For fall 2010, 287 students applied for upper-level admission, 203 were accepted, 138 enrolled. Deadline for receipt of application materials: none. Application fee required: CAN$150. Interview required.

Athletics Interscholastic: aerobics/dance (girls), artistic gym (g), baseball (b,g), basketball (b,g), crew (b,g), cross-country running (b,g), dance (g), dance squad (g), dance team (g), field hockey (g), fitness walking (g), gymnastics (g), hockey (b,g),

ice hockey (b,g), rowing (b,g), rugby (b,g), running (b,g), soccer (b,g), softball (b,g), squash (b,g), swimming and diving (b,g), tennis (b,g), track and field (b,g), volleyball (g); intramural: aerobics (g), aerobics/dance (g), ball hockey (b), ballet (g), Cosom hockey (g), hockey (b,g), ice hockey (b,g), running (b,g); coed interscholastic: golf, tennis; coed intramural: alpine skiing, aquatics, backpacking, badminton, baseball, basketball, bicycling, bowling, canoeing/kayaking, climbing, cooperative games, curling, drill team, equestrian sports, fencing, fitness, Frisbee, golf, hiking/ backpacking, horseback riding, ice skating, jogging, life saving, martial arts, modern dance, outdoor activities, outdoor education, outdoor recreation, outdoor skills, physical fitness, physical training, power lifting, racquetball, rock climbing, ropes courses, sailing, scuba diving, self defense, skiing (cross-country), skiing (downhill), snowboarding, snowshoeing, soccer, softball, squash, strength & conditioning, swimming and diving, table tennis, tennis, track and field, trap and skeet, ultimate Frisbee, volleyball, walking, wall climbing, weight lifting, weight training, yoga. 8 coaches, 3 athletic trainers.

Computers Computers are regularly used in all academic classes. Computer network features include on-campus library services, online commercial services, Internet access, wireless campus network, Internet filtering or blocking technology. Student e-mail accounts are available to students. Students grades are available online. The school has a published electronic and media policy.

Contact Mrs. Stephanie Park, Admissions Administrative Assistant. 905-684-1889 Ext. 2207. Fax: 905-684-8875. E-mail: admissions@ridleycollege.com. Web site: www.ridleycollege.com.

RIO HONDO PREPARATORY SCHOOL

5150 Farna Avenue
PO Box 662080
Arcadia, California 91066-2080
Head of School: Mrs. Leslie Orsburn

General Information Coeducational day college-preparatory and arts school. Grades 6–12. Founded: 1964. Setting: suburban. Nearest major city is Los Angeles. 6-acre campus. 5 buildings on campus. Approved or accredited by Western Association of Schools and Colleges and California Department of Education. Total enrollment: 187. Upper school average class size: 24. Upper school faculty-student ratio: 1:4. Upper School students typically attend 5 days per week. The average school day consists of 6 hours.

Upper School Student Profile Grade 6: 16 students (10 boys, 6 girls); Grade 7: 26 students (17 boys, 9 girls); Grade 8: 19 students (10 boys, 9 girls); Grade 9: 34 students (17 boys, 17 girls); Grade 10: 25 students (16 boys, 9 girls); Grade 11: 22 students (11 boys, 11 girls); Grade 12: 19 students (8 boys, 11 girls).

Faculty School total: 28. In upper school: 13 men, 9 women; 4 have advanced degrees.

Subjects Offered Advanced biology, Advanced Placement courses, algebra, American history, American history-AP, American literature, art, art appreciation, astronomy, athletics, band, baseball, basketball, bell choir, biology, biology-AP, calculus, calculus-AP, chemistry, chorus, college planning, comparative government and politics-AP, computer applications, driver education, earth science, economics, English, English literature, English literature and composition-AP, ESL, European history, fine arts, geology, geometry, government/civics, history, instrumental music, Internet research, Latin, mathematics, music, physical education, physics, physiology, psychology, psychology-AP, reading, science, social studies, softball, Spanish, statistics, theater production, travel, world history, yearbook.

Graduation Requirements Arts and fine arts (art, music, dance, drama), English, foreign language, mathematics, physical education (includes health), science, social studies (includes history), participation in one school summer tour (U.S. or Europe).

Special Academic Programs Advanced Placement exam preparation; honors section; study abroad; ESL (3 students enrolled).

College Admission Counseling 19 students graduated in 2010; all went to college, including California State Polytechnic University, Pomona; California State University, Fullerton; California State University, Long Beach; Citrus College; Pasadena City College; Penn State University Park. Median composite ACT: 20. Mean SAT critical reading: 457, mean SAT math: 517, mean SAT writing: 458, mean combined SAT: 1432.

Student Life Upper grades have uniform requirement, student council, honor system. Discipline rests equally with students and faculty.

Summer Programs Enrichment, sports programs offered; session focuses on educational tours; held off campus; held at sites in U.S. or Europe; accepts boys and girls; not open to students from other schools. 40 students usually enrolled. 2011 schedule: June to August.

Tuition and Aid Day student tuition: $8175. Tuition installment plan (individually arranged payment plans). Tuition reduction for siblings, need-based scholarship grants available. In 2010–11, 20% of upper-school students received aid.

Admissions Traditional secondary-level entrance grade is 9. Iowa Tests of Basic Skills required. Deadline for receipt of application materials: April 1. Application fee required: $25. On-campus interview required.

Athletics Interscholastic: baseball (boys), basketball (b,g), cheering (g), football (b), soccer (b,g), softball (g). 2 PE instructors, 5 coaches, 1 athletic trainer.

Computers Computers are regularly used in design, English, ESL, history, keyboarding, mathematics, science, word processing, writing, yearbook classes. Computer network features include on-campus library services, Internet access, wireless campus network, Internet filtering or blocking technology. Students grades are available online.

Contact Dina Loomis, Admissions Office. 626-444-9531. Fax: 626-442-1113. Web site: www.rhprep.org.

RIPON CHRISTIAN SCHOOLS

435 North Maple Avenue
Ripon, California 95366
Head of School: Mrs. Mary Ann Sybesma

General Information Coeducational day college-preparatory, arts, business, vocational, religious studies, and technology school, affiliated with Calvinist faith; primarily serves students with learning disabilities. Grades K–12. Founded: 1946. Setting: small town. Nearest major city is San Francisco. 34-acre campus. 5 buildings on campus. Approved or accredited by Association of Christian Schools International, Christian Schools International, Western Association of Schools and Colleges, and California Department of Education. Endowment: $2.5 million. Total enrollment: 679. Upper school average class size: 22. Upper school faculty-student ratio: 1:18. There are 177 required school days per year for Upper School students. Upper School students typically attend 5 days per week. The average school day consists of 6 hours.
Upper School Student Profile 60% of students are Calvinist.
Faculty School total: 48. In upper school: 12 men, 10 women; 11 have advanced degrees.
Subjects Offered 20th century American writers, accounting, advanced computer applications, algebra, American history, anatomy and physiology, animal science, art, band, Bible studies, biology, business, business mathematics, calculus, calculus-AP, ceramics, chemistry, choir, computer applications, computer education, computer science, computer-aided design, drafting, English, English language and composition-AP, English literature and composition-AP, environmental education, environmental science, ethics, family living, fine arts, geography, geometry, government/civics, grammar, health, history, keyboarding, leadership, life skills, mathematics, music, physical education, physics, psychology, science, social sciences, social studies, Spanish, Spanish-AP, U.S. history-AP, weightlifting, welding, woodworking, world history, yearbook.
Graduation Requirements Computer science, English, mathematics, physical education (includes health), religion (includes Bible studies and theology), science, social sciences, social studies (includes history), 10 service hours per semester are required of all students.
Special Academic Programs 4 Advanced Placement exams for which test preparation is offered; independent study; academic accommodation for the musically talented and the artistically talented; remedial math.
College Admission Counseling 56 students graduated in 2009; 54 went to college, including Azusa Pacific University; California Polytechnic State University, San Luis Obispo; California State University, Stanislaus; Calvin College; Dordt College; Modesto Junior College. Other: 2 entered military service.
Student Life Upper grades have specified standards of dress, student council. Discipline rests primarily with faculty. Attendance at religious services is required.
Tuition and Aid Day student tuition: $6885. Tuition installment plan (FACTS Tuition Payment Plan, individually arranged payment plans, 1-payment plan, biannual payment plan, quarterly payment plan). Tuition reduction for siblings, need-based scholarship grants, need-based financial assistance, TRIP program available. In 2009–10, 10% of upper-school students received aid. Total amount of financial aid awarded in 2009–10: $20,000.
Admissions Traditional secondary-level entrance grade is 9. For fall 2009, 22 students applied for upper-level admission, 21 were accepted, 21 enrolled. Kaufman Test of Educational Achievement or Woodcock-Johnson required. Deadline for receipt of application materials: none. No application fee required. On-campus interview required.
Athletics Interscholastic: baseball (boys), basketball (b,g), football (b), golf (b,g), physical fitness (b,g), physical training (b,g), soccer (b,g), softball (g), tennis (b,g), volleyball (g), weight training (b,g); intramural: indoor soccer (b); coed interscholastic: tennis; coed intramural: tennis. 2 PE instructors, 15 coaches.
Computers Computers are regularly used in business skills classes. Computer network features include on-campus library services, Internet access, wireless campus network, Internet filtering or blocking technology. Students grades are available online. The school has a published electronic and media policy.
Contact Mrs. Mary Ann Sybesma, Principal. 209-599-2155. Fax: 209-599-2170. E-mail: msybesma@rcschools.com. Web site: www.rcschools.com.

RIVERDALE COUNTRY SCHOOL

5250 Fieldston Road
Bronx, New York 10471-2999
Head of School: Dominic A.A. Randolph

General Information Coeducational day college-preparatory school. Grades PK–12. Founded: 1907. Setting: suburban. Nearest major city is New York. 27-acre campus. 9 buildings on campus. Approved or accredited by New York State Association of Independent Schools and New York Department of Education. Member of National Association of Independent Schools and Secondary School Admission Test

Board. Endowment: $50 million. Total enrollment: 1,127. Upper school average class size: 16. Upper school faculty-student ratio: 1:8. Upper School students typically attend 5 days per week.
Faculty School total: 185.
Subjects Offered Algebra, American literature, anatomy, art, art history, biology, calculus, ceramics, chemistry, community service, computer math, computer programming, computer science, creative writing, drama, driver education, earth science, ecology, economics, English, English literature, environmental science, European history, expository writing, fine arts, French, geology, geometry, government/civics, grammar, health, history, history of science, introduction to liberal studies, Japanese, journalism, Latin, Mandarin, marine biology, mathematics, music, oceanography, philosophy, photography, physical education, physics, psychology, science, social studies, Spanish, speech, statistics, theater, theory of knowledge, trigonometry, world history, writing.
Graduation Requirements American studies, arts and fine arts (art, music, dance, drama), computer science, English, foreign language, mathematics, physical education (includes health), science, social studies (includes history), integrated liberal studies. Community service is required.
Special Academic Programs Honors section; independent study; term-away projects; study abroad; academic accommodation for the gifted, the musically talented, and the artistically talented.
College Admission Counseling 120 students graduated in 2010; all went to college, including Brown University; Columbia University; Duke University; Stanford University; Tulane University; University of Pennsylvania.
Student Life Upper grades have student council, honor system. Discipline rests equally with students and faculty.
Tuition and Aid Day student tuition: $38,800. Tuition installment plan (monthly payment plans). Need-based scholarship grants available. In 2010–11, 20% of upper-school students received aid.
Admissions Traditional secondary-level entrance grade is 9. ISEE or SSAT required. Deadline for receipt of application materials: December 1. Application fee required: $60. On-campus interview required.
Athletics Interscholastic: baseball (boys), basketball (b,g), field hockey (g), football (b), gymnastics (g), lacrosse (b,g), soccer (b,g), softball (g), tennis (b,g), volleyball (g), wrestling (b); intramural: baseball (b), basketball (b,g), field hockey (g), football (b), gymnastics (g), lacrosse (b,g), soccer (b,g), softball (g), tennis (b,g), volleyball (g), wrestling (b); coed interscholastic: cross-country running, fencing, golf, squash, swimming and diving, track and field, ultimate Frisbee; coed intramural: cross-country running, dance, fencing, fitness, physical fitness, squash, swimming and diving, tennis, track and field, ultimate Frisbee, yoga. 7 PE instructors, 31 coaches, 1 athletic trainer.
Computers Computers are regularly used in art, English, foreign language, history, mathematics, music, science classes. Computer network features include on-campus library services, online commercial services, Internet access, Internet filtering or blocking technology, off-campus e-mail, off-campus library services. Student e-mail accounts and computer access in designated common areas are available to students. The school has a published electronic and media policy.
Contact Jenna Rogers King, Director of Middle and Upper School Admission. 718-519-2715. Fax: 718-519-2793. E-mail: jrking@riverdale.edu. Web site: www.riverdale.edu.

RIVERFIELD ACADEMY

115 Wood Street
Rayville, Louisiana 71269
Head of School: Marie D. Miller

General Information college-preparatory school. Founded: 1970. Setting: small town. Nearest major city is Monroe. 15-acre campus. 5 buildings on campus. Approved or accredited by Louisiana Department of Education. Language of instruction: Spanish. Total enrollment: 280. Upper school faculty-student ratio: 1:10. There are 180 required school days per year for Upper School students. Upper School students typically attend 5 days per week. The average school day consists of 7 hours and 10 minutes.
Upper School Student Profile Grade 6: 18 students (12 boys, 6 girls); Grade 7: 15 students (10 boys, 5 girls); Grade 8: 27 students (9 boys, 18 girls); Grade 9: 23 students (10 boys, 13 girls); Grade 10: 34 students (18 boys, 16 girls); Grade 11: 23 students (12 boys, 11 girls); Grade 12: 22 students (11 boys, 11 girls).
Faculty School total: 25. In upper school: 5 men, 5 women; 5 have advanced degrees.
Special Academic Programs International Baccalaureate program.
College Admission Counseling 34 students graduated in 2010; 32 went to college. Other: 2 went to work.
Student Life Upper grades have specified standards of dress, student council. Discipline rests primarily with faculty.
Admissions For fall 2010, 149 students applied for upper-level admission, 14 were accepted, 14 enrolled. Deadline for receipt of application materials: August 16. No application fee required. Interview recommended.
Athletics Interscholastic: baseball (boys), basketball (b), softball (g), tennis (b,g). 4 PE instructors, 4 coaches, 1 athletic trainer.
Computers Computer network features include on-campus library services, Internet access, wireless campus network. Campus intranet and computer access in designated common areas are available to students.

Contact Karen Smith, Secretary. 318-728-3281. Fax: 318-728-3285. Web site: riverfieldacademy.net.

RIVERMONT COLLEGIATE

1821 Sunset Drive
Bettendorf, Iowa 52722
Head of School: Mr. Richard E. St. Laurent

General Information Coeducational day college-preparatory, arts, and technology school. Grades PS–12. Founded: 1884. Setting: suburban. Nearest major city is Davenport. 16-acre campus. 6 buildings on campus. Approved or accredited by Independent Schools Association of the Central States and Iowa Department of Education. Member of National Association of Independent Schools and Secondary School Admission Test Board. Endowment: $1.9 million. Total enrollment: 194. Upper school average class size: 10. Upper school faculty-student ratio: 1:4.

Upper School Student Profile Grade 9: 7 students (2 boys, 5 girls); Grade 10: 9 students (3 boys, 6 girls); Grade 11: 8 students (2 boys, 6 girls); Grade 12: 11 students (7 boys, 4 girls).

Faculty School total: 26. In upper school: 4 men, 11 women; 6 have advanced degrees.

Subjects Offered Acting, advanced chemistry, advanced math, algebra, anatomy and physiology, ancient world history, art, arts, band, biology, business law, calculus, calculus-AP, chemistry, chemistry-AP, Chinese, computer multimedia, computer programming, computer science, creative writing, drama, earth science, economics, English, English literature, English-AP, European history, fine arts, French, French language-AP, French literature-AP, French-AP, geography, geometry, German, global science, government/civics, grammar, health, health education, history, history-AP, Holocaust studies, honors algebra, honors English, HTML design, humanities, independent study, jazz band, Latin, Latin American history, life science, mathematics, music, photography, physical education, physical fitness, physics, piano, psychology, public speaking, science, senior project, social studies, Spanish, Spanish literature-AP, Spanish-AP, speech, speech and debate, theater, theater arts, theater design and production, U.S. government, U.S. history, U.S. history-AP, vocal ensemble, Web site design, writing.

Graduation Requirements Arts and fine arts (art, music, dance, drama), computer science, English, foreign language, mathematics, physical education (includes health), science, senior project, social studies (includes history).

Special Academic Programs Advanced Placement exam preparation; honors section; independent study; study at local college for college credit; academic accommodation for the gifted and the musically talented.

College Admission Counseling Median SAT critical reading: 670, median SAT math: 640, median composite ACT: 28.

Student Life Upper grades have specified standards of dress, student council. Discipline rests primarily with faculty.

Summer Programs Enrichment, sports programs offered; session focuses on enrichment; held on campus; accepts boys and girls; open to students from other schools. 75 students usually enrolled. 2011 schedule: June 21 to August 6. Application deadline: May 28.

Tuition and Aid Day student tuition: $10,220. Tuition installment plan (Insured Tuition Payment Plan, Key Tuition Payment Plan, monthly payment plans). Tuition reduction for siblings, merit scholarship grants, need-based scholarship grants available. In 2010–11, 45% of upper-school students received aid; total upper-school merit-scholarship money awarded: $13,240. Total amount of financial aid awarded in 2010–11: $309,755.

Admissions Traditional secondary-level entrance grade is 11. For fall 2010, 2 students applied for upper-level admission, 2 were accepted, 2 enrolled. Any standardized test, Iowa Tests of Basic Skills or Wide Range Achievement Test required. Deadline for receipt of application materials: none. Application fee required: $50. Interview recommended.

Athletics Interscholastic: basketball (boys, girls), cheering (g), cross-country running (b,g), golf (b,g), soccer (b), swimming and diving (g), track and field (b,g), volleyball (g); intramural: basketball (b,g), cheering (g), table tennis (b,g); coed interscholastic: soccer; coed intramural: bowling, floor hockey, indoor soccer, table tennis, volleyball. 1 PE instructor, 3 coaches.

Computers Computers are regularly used in English, foreign language, history, independent study, mathematics classes. Computer network features include on-campus library services, Internet access, wireless campus network, Internet filtering or blocking technology. Student e-mail accounts are available to students. The school has a published electronic and media policy.

Contact Miss Cindy M. Murray, Director of Admission/Marketing Coordinator. 563-359-1366 Ext. 302. Fax: 563-359-7576. E-mail: murray@rvmt.org. Web site: www.rivermontcollegiate.org.

RIVERSIDE MILITARY ACADEMY

2001 Riverside Drive
Gainesville, Georgia 30501
Head of School: Dr. James H. Benson, Col., USMC-Retd.

General Information Boys' boarding and day college-preparatory, arts, technology, JROTC (grades 9-12), and military school, affiliated with Christian faith. Grades 7–12.

Founded: 1907. Setting: suburban. Nearest major city is Atlanta. Students are housed in single-sex dormitories. 206-acre campus. 9 buildings on campus. Approved or accredited by Southern Association of Colleges and Schools, Southern Association of Independent Schools, and Georgia Department of Education. Member of National Association of Independent Schools. Endowment: $54 million. Total enrollment: 300. Upper school average class size: 14. Upper school faculty-student ratio: 1:14. There are 180 required school days per year for Upper School students. Upper School students typically attend 5 days per week. The average school day consists of 5 hours and 45 minutes.

Upper School Student Profile Grade 9: 50 students (50 boys); Grade 10: 60 students (60 boys); Grade 11: 70 students (70 boys); Grade 12: 75 students (75 boys). 90% of students are boarding students. 60% are state residents. 30 states are represented in upper school student body. 29% are international students. International students from Bahamas, Canada, Dominican Republic, Mexico, Republic of Korea, and Taiwan; 8 other countries represented in student body. 80% of students are Christian faith.

Faculty School total: 45. In upper school: 30 men, 10 women; 30 have advanced degrees; 20 reside on campus.

Subjects Offered Advanced chemistry, algebra, American literature, American literature-AP, art, art appreciation, astronomy, band, biology, biology-AP, British literature-AP, calculus, calculus-AP, ceramics, chemistry, chemistry-AP, chorus, computer applications, computer education, computer programming, computer science, computer skills, computer studies, computer technologies, desktop publishing, drama, drawing, earth science, economics, English, English literature, ESL, ethics, European history, fine arts, French, geography, geometry, German, government/civics, grammar, health, history-AP, honors English, honors geometry, honors U.S. history, honors world history, JROTC, keyboarding, leadership, mathematics, military science, modern world history, music, music technology, music theory, painting, photography, physical education, physics, physics-AP, pre-algebra, pre-calculus, science, social studies, Spanish, statistics, theater, U.S. government, U.S. government and politics-AP, U.S. history, U.S. history-AP, U.S. literature, visual arts, weight training, world geography, world history, world history-AP, world literature, yearbook.

Graduation Requirements Arts and fine arts (art, music, dance, drama), computer science, English, foreign language, JROTC, mathematics, physical education (includes health), science, social studies (includes history).

Special Academic Programs 8 Advanced Placement exams for which test preparation is offered; honors section; ESL (24 students enrolled).

College Admission Counseling 68 students graduated in 2009; all went to college, including Clemson University; Georgia Institute of Technology; The Citadel, The Military College of South Carolina; The University of Alabama; University of California, Berkeley; University of Georgia. Median SAT critical reading: 460, median SAT math: 510, median SAT writing: 490, median combined SAT: 1508. Mean composite ACT: 21. 15.2% scored over 600 on SAT critical reading, 22.8% scored over 600 on SAT math, 7.6% scored over 600 on SAT writing, 11.4% scored over 26 on composite ACT.

Student Life Upper grades have uniform requirement, student council, honor system. Discipline rests equally with students and faculty. Attendance at religious services is required.

Tuition and Aid Day student tuition: $16,500; 7-day tuition and room/board: $27,500. Tuition installment plan (Key Tuition Payment Plan, FACTS Tuition Payment Plan, monthly payment plans). Tuition reduction for siblings, merit scholarship grants, need-based scholarship grants available. In 2009–10, 27% of upper-school students received aid; total upper-school merit-scholarship money awarded: $77,820. Total amount of financial aid awarded in 2009–10: $603,215.

Admissions Traditional secondary-level entrance grade is 9. Any standardized test required. Deadline for receipt of application materials: none. Application fee required: $100. Interview required.

Athletics Interscholastic: aquatics, baseball, basketball, cross-country running, drill team, football, golf, JROTC drill, lacrosse, marksmanship, riflery, soccer, swimming and diving, tennis, track and field, wrestling; intramural: aquatics, backpacking, baseball, basketball, billiards, canoeing/kayaking, cheering, climbing, combined training, crew, cross-country running, flag football, football, hiking/backpacking, indoor soccer, indoor track, indoor track & field, jogging, kayaking, marksmanship, mountaineering, outdoor activities, paddle tennis, paint ball, physical training, rappelling, rock climbing, ropes courses, running, skateboarding, soccer, softball, strength & conditioning, swimming and diving, table tennis, tennis, volleyball, wall climbing, water polo, water volleyball, weight lifting, weight training. 5 PE instructors, 12 coaches, 1 athletic trainer.

Computers Computers are regularly used in college planning, desktop publishing, English, ESL, foreign language, French, journalism, library, mathematics, music, newspaper, photography, SAT preparation, science, Spanish, technology, theater, yearbook classes. Computer network features include on-campus library services, Internet access, Internet filtering or blocking technology. Campus intranet, student e-mail accounts, and computer access in designated common areas are available to students. Students grades are available online. The school has a published electronic and media policy.

Contact Admissions Office. 800-462-2338. Fax: 678-291-3364. E-mail: admissions@riversidemilitary.com. Web site: www.riversidemilitary.com.

THE RIVERS SCHOOL
333 Winter Street
Weston, Massachusetts 02493-1040
Head of School: Thomas P. Olverson
General Information Coeducational day college-preparatory and arts school. Grades 6–12. Founded: 1915. Setting: suburban. Nearest major city is Boston. 53-acre campus. 8 buildings on campus. Approved or accredited by Association of Independent Schools in New England and New England Association of Schools and Colleges. Member of National Association of Independent Schools and Secondary School Admission Test Board. Endowment: $17.5 million. Total enrollment: 457. Upper school average class size: 12. Upper school faculty-student ratio: 1:6. The average school day consists of 7 hours and 15 minutes.
Upper School Student Profile Grade 9: 86 students (52 boys, 34 girls); Grade 10: 82 students (43 boys, 39 girls); Grade 11: 91 students (46 boys, 45 girls); Grade 12: 84 students (43 boys, 41 girls).
Faculty School total: 78. In upper school: 31 men, 31 women; 43 have advanced degrees.
Subjects Offered Advanced Placement courses, algebra, American history, American literature, art, art history, art history-AP, astronomy, biology, biology-AP, calculus, calculus-AP, ceramics, chamber groups, chemistry, chemistry-AP, chorus, civil rights, Civil War, computer graphics, computer science, computer science-AP, creative writing, drama, earth science, economics-AP, English, English language and composition-AP, English literature, English literature and composition-AP, environmental science-AP, European history, expository writing, film studies, filmmaking, fine arts, French, French-AP, geography, geometry, history, Holocaust, jazz band, journalism, kinesiology, Latin, Latin-AP, Mandarin, mathematics, modern European history-AP, music, photography, physics, physics-AP, playwriting, science, Spanish, Spanish-AP, statistics-AP, the Presidency, theater, theater arts, trigonometry, U.S. history-AP, world history, world literature.
Graduation Requirements Algebra, athletics, English, foreign language, geometry, history, mathematics, modern European history, science, U.S. history, visual and performing arts, participation in athletics. Community service is required.
Special Academic Programs Advanced Placement exam preparation; honors section; independent study; study at local college for college credit.
College Admission Counseling 79 students graduated in 2010; 78 went to college, including Hamilton College; Trinity College; Tufts University; Union College; University of Richmond; Wesleyan University. Other: 1 entered a postgraduate year. Median SAT critical reading: 652, median SAT math: 683, median SAT writing: 668. 75% scored over 600 on SAT critical reading, 90% scored over 600 on SAT math, 87% scored over 600 on SAT writing, 84% scored over 1800 on combined SAT.
Student Life Upper grades have specified standards of dress, student council, honor system. Discipline rests primarily with faculty.
Tuition and Aid Day student tuition: $35,400. Tuition installment plan (Academic Management Services Plan, Key Tuition Payment Plan, monthly payment plans). Need-based scholarship grants available. In 2010–11, 26% of upper-school students received aid. Total amount of financial aid awarded in 2010–11: $3,083,000.
Admissions Traditional secondary-level entrance grade is 9. For fall 2010, 349 students applied for upper-level admission, 150 were accepted, 59 enrolled. ISEE or SSAT required. Deadline for receipt of application materials: February 1. Application fee required: $40. On-campus interview required.
Athletics Interscholastic: alpine skiing (boys, girls), baseball (b), basketball (b,g), cross-country running (b,g), field hockey (g), football (b), ice hockey (b,g), lacrosse (b,g), skiing (downhill) (b,g), soccer (b,g), softball (g), strength & conditioning (b,g), tennis (b,g); intramural: basketball (b,g), tennis (g); coed interscholastic: fitness, physical training, track and field, weight lifting, weight training; coed intramural: strength & conditioning. 4 coaches, 2 athletic trainers.
Computers Computers are regularly used in art, aviation, English, foreign language, history, humanities, language development, mathematics, newspaper, publications, science, writing, yearbook classes. Computer network features include on-campus library services, online commercial services, Internet access, wireless campus network, Internet filtering or blocking technology, language lab. Campus intranet, student e-mail accounts, and computer access in designated common areas are available to students. Students grades are available online. The school has a published electronic and media policy.
Contact Gillian Lloyd, Director of Admissions. 781-235-9300. Fax: 781-239-3614. E-mail: g.lloyd@rivers.org. Web site: www.rivers.org.

RIVERSTONE INTERNATIONAL SCHOOL
55213 Warm Springs Avenue
Boise, Idaho 83716
Head of School: Mr. Andrew Derry
General Information Coeducational day college-preparatory school. Grades PS–12. Founded: 1997. Setting: suburban. 14-acre campus. 1 building on campus. Approved or accredited by European Council of International Schools, International Baccalaureate Organization, Northwest Association of Schools and Colleges, Pacific Northwest Association of Independent Schools, Western Catholic Education Association, and Idaho Department of Education. Total enrollment: 314. Upper school average class size: 12. Upper school faculty-student ratio: 1:6. There are 169 required school days

per year for Upper School students. Upper School students typically attend 5 days per week. The average school day consists of 7 hours and 20 minutes.
Upper School Student Profile Grade 9: 20 students (12 boys, 8 girls); Grade 10: 21 students (9 boys, 12 girls); Grade 11: 35 students (22 boys, 13 girls); Grade 12: 31 students (21 boys, 10 girls).
Faculty School total: 45. In upper school: 8 men, 14 women; 12 have advanced degrees.
Graduation Requirements Art, English, foreign language, history, mathematics, science.
Special Academic Programs International Baccalaureate program; independent study; study abroad; ESL (15 students enrolled).
College Admission Counseling 22 students graduated in 2010; all went to college, including Barnard College; Brown University; Colby College; Smith College; Stanford University; Whitman College. Median SAT critical reading: 660, median SAT math: 620, median SAT writing: 650, median combined SAT: 1940. 82% scored over 600 on SAT critical reading, 64% scored over 600 on SAT math, 73% scored over 600 on SAT writing, 73% scored over 1800 on combined SAT.
Student Life Upper grades have specified standards of dress, student council, honor system. Discipline rests equally with students and faculty.
Summer Programs Enrichment, ESL, art/fine arts, rigorous outdoor training programs offered; session focuses on camps, ESL, and outdoor education; held both on and off campus; held at Boise River, Boise foothills, and Sawtooth and White Cloud Mountains; accepts boys and girls; open to students from other schools. 100 students usually enrolled. 2011 schedule: July 11 to August 5. Application deadline: June 1.
Tuition and Aid Day student tuition: $14,550. Tuition installment plan (monthly payment plans). Need-based scholarship grants available. In 2010–11, 20% of upper-school students received aid.
Admissions Traditional secondary-level entrance grade is 9. For fall 2010, 43 students applied for upper-level admission, 30 were accepted, 18 enrolled. Deadline for receipt of application materials: none. Application fee required: $75. Interview required.
Athletics Interscholastic: volleyball (girls); intramural: fitness (g); coed interscholastic: alpine skiing, basketball, indoor soccer, nordic skiing, skiing (cross-country), skiing (downhill), snowboarding; coed intramural: backpacking, golf, hiking/backpacking, ice skating, kayaking, lacrosse, nordic skiing, outdoor activities, outdoor education, outdoor skills, physical fitness, rafting, rock climbing, ropes courses, running, skiing (cross-country), skiing (downhill), snowboarding, snowshoeing, soccer. 1 PE instructor, 3 coaches.
Computers Computers are regularly used in art, college planning, data processing, English, ESL, foreign language, French, history, lab/keyboard, music, research skills, Spanish, writing, yearbook classes. Computer network features include online commercial services, Internet access, wireless campus network. The school has a published electronic and media policy.
Contact Ms. Rachel Pusch, Director of Admissions and Marketing. 208-424-5000 Ext. 2104. Fax: 208-424-0033. E-mail: rpusch@riverstoneschool.org. Web site: www.riverstoneschool.org.

RIVERVIEW SCHOOL
East Sandwich, Massachusetts
See Special Needs Schools section.

ROBERT LAND ACADEMY
Wellandport, Ontario, Canada
See Special Needs Schools section.

ROBERT LOUIS STEVENSON SCHOOL
New York, New York
See Special Needs Schools section.

ROBINSON SCHOOL
5 Nairn Street
San Juan, Puerto Rico 00907, Puerto Rico
Head of School: Dr. Nan Wodarz, EdD
General Information Coeducational boarding and day and distance learning college-preparatory, arts, religious studies, bilingual studies, technology, and music/drama school, affiliated with United Methodist Church. Boarding grades 7–12, day grades PK–12. Distance learning grades 11–12. Founded: 1902. Setting: urban. Nearest major city is San Juan/Carolina/Bayamon, Puerto Rico. Students are housed in coed dormitories. 5-acre campus. 1 building on campus. Approved or accredited by Middle States Association of Colleges and Schools, The College Board, and Puerto Rico Department of Education. Member of National Association For Equal Opportunity in Higher Education's (NAFEO) historically/predominantly black colleges and universities (HBCU). Languages of instruction: English and Spanish. Total enrollment: 604. Upper school average class size: 18. Upper school faculty-student

ratio: 1:18. There are 168 required school days per year for Upper School students. Upper School students typically attend 5 days per week. The average school day consists of 7 hours and 30 minutes.

Upper School Student Profile Grade 7: 45 students (24 boys, 21 girls); Grade 8: 49 students (33 boys, 16 girls); Grade 9: 68 students (45 boys, 23 girls); Grade 10: 54 students (29 boys, 25 girls); Grade 11: 42 students (27 boys, 15 girls); Grade 12: 47 students (21 boys, 26 girls). 2% of students are United Methodist Church.

Faculty School total: 84. In upper school: 16 men, 27 women; 12 have advanced degrees; 2 reside on campus.

Subjects Offered Algebra, art, biology, biology-AP, calculus, chemistry, computer science, economics, English, English literature, English-AP, general science, geometry, health, history-AP, journalism, mathematics, music, physical education, physical science, physics, physics-AP, pre-calculus, Puerto Rican history, religion, SAT preparation, social studies, Spanish, Spanish-AP, writing.

Graduation Requirements Computers, electives, English, mathematics, physical education (includes health), religion (includes Bible studies and theology), science, social studies (includes history), Spanish.

Special Academic Programs Advanced Placement exam preparation; honors section; independent study; domestic exchange program; academic accommodation for the gifted; remedial reading and/or remedial writing; remedial math; programs in English, mathematics, general development for dyslexic students; special instructional classes for students with specific learning disabilities.

College Admission Counseling 37 students graduated in 2010; all went to college, including Boston College; Boston University; Manhattanville College; Syracuse University; University of Florida; University of Miami. Median SAT critical reading: 550, median SAT math: 535.

Student Life Upper grades have uniform requirement, student council, honor system. Discipline rests primarily with faculty. Attendance at religious services is required.

Summer Programs Remediation, enrichment, advancement, ESL, sports, art/fine arts, rigorous outdoor training, computer instruction programs offered; session focuses on remediation and/or advancement; held on campus; accepts boys and girls; open to students from other schools. 300 students usually enrolled. 2011 schedule: June 5 to July 2. Application deadline: none.

Tuition and Aid Tuition installment plan (monthly payment plans, individually arranged payment plans, annual and semi-annual payment plans, Semi-annually and anually). Tuition reduction for siblings, need-based scholarship grants available. In 2010–11, 11% of upper-school students received aid. Total amount of financial aid awarded in 2010–11: $78,820.

Admissions For fall 2010, 47 students applied for upper-level admission, 38 were accepted, 35 enrolled. Achievement tests, Iowa Tests of Basic Skills, Math Placement Exam, Otis-Lennon Mental Ability Test or PSAT required. Deadline for receipt of application materials: none. No application fee required. On-campus interview required.

Athletics Interscholastic: aquatics (boys, girls), basketball (b,g), cross-country running (b,g), indoor soccer (b,g), running (b,g), soccer (b,g), swimming and diving (b,g), track and field (b,g), volleyball (b,g); intramural: combined training (b,g), cooperative games (b,g), fitness (b,g), flag football (b,g), floor hockey (b,g), gymnastics (b,g), handball (b,g), indoor soccer (b,g), jogging (b,g), jump rope (b,g), kickball (b,g), outdoor recreation (b,g), physical fitness (b,g), physical training (b,g), running (b,g), soccer (b,g), strength & conditioning (b,g), table tennis (b,g), volleyball (b,g); coed interscholastic: soccer; coed intramural: basketball, combined training, cooperative games, fitness, flag football, floor hockey, gymnastics, handball, horseshoes, indoor soccer, jogging, jump rope, kickball, outdoor recreation, paddling, physical fitness, physical training, running, soccer, strength & conditioning, table tennis, tennis, volleyball. 4 PE instructors, 4 coaches, 4 athletic trainers.

Computers Computers are regularly used in English, mathematics, science classes. Computer network features include on-campus library services, Internet access. The school has a published electronic and media policy.

Contact Admissions Officer. 787-999-4604 Ext. 4618. Fax: 787-999-4618. E-mail: mtorres1@robinsonschool.org. Web site: www.robinsonschool.org.

ROCKLAND COUNTRY DAY SCHOOL

34 Kings Highway
Congers, New York 10920-2253
Head of School: Dr. Brian Mahoney

General Information Coeducational day college-preparatory and arts school. Grades PK–12. Founded: 1959. Setting: suburban. Nearest major city is New York. 20-acre campus. 5 buildings on campus. Approved or accredited by New York State Association of Independent Schools and New York Department of Education. Member of National Association of Independent Schools. Total enrollment: 130. Upper school average class size: 14. Upper school faculty-student ratio: 1:8. There are 163 required school days per year for Upper School students. Upper School students typically attend 5 days per week. The average school day consists of 5 hours and 2 minutes.

Upper School Student Profile Grade 9: 9 students (3 boys, 6 girls); Grade 10: 20 students (9 boys, 11 girls); Grade 11: 14 students (8 boys, 6 girls); Grade 12: 18 students (10 boys, 8 girls).

Faculty School total: 31. In upper school: 10 men, 11 women; 8 have advanced degrees.

Subjects Offered Algebra, American history, American literature, art, art history, band, biology, biology-AP, calculus, calculus-AP, career exploration, ceramics,

chemistry, chorus, college admission preparation, college counseling, college placement, community service, computers, creative arts, creative writing, dance, debate, digital photography, drama, drama performance, dramatic arts, drawing, earth science, economics, electives, English, English literature, English-AP, environmental science, environmental studies, European history, European history-AP, fine arts, forensics, French, French-AP, gardening, geometry, global studies, guitar, health, health education, history, honors English, humanities, independent study, instrumental music, internship, jazz ensemble, lab science, language-AP, literature-AP, madrigals, mathematics, mathematics-AP, modern European history-AP, music, music theory-AP, painting, performing arts, philosophy, photography, photojournalism, physical education, physics, physics-AP, pre-algebra, pre-calculus, science, social studies, Spanish, Spanish-AP, student government, studio art, theater, theater arts, U.S. history-AP, visual arts, voice ensemble, world history, world literature, writing, yearbook.

Graduation Requirements Arts and fine arts (art, music, dance, drama), computer science, English, experiential education, foreign language, mathematics, music, physical education (includes health), science, social studies (includes history), WISE Program, off-campus senior independent senior project. Community service is required.

Special Academic Programs 15 Advanced Placement exams for which test preparation is offered; honors section; independent study; study at local college for college credit; academic accommodation for the gifted, the musically talented, and the artistically talented.

College Admission Counseling 15 students graduated in 2010; all went to college, including Boston University; Ithaca College; New York University; Purchase College, State University of New York; Quinnipiac University; Smith College. Median SAT critical reading: 580, median SAT math: 550, median SAT writing: 560, median combined SAT: 1690.

Student Life Upper grades have specified standards of dress, student council, honor system. Discipline rests primarily with faculty.

Tuition and Aid Day student tuition: $14,900–$29,475. Tuition installment plan (Insured Tuition Payment Plan, monthly payment plans, individually arranged payment plans). Tuition reduction for siblings, need-based scholarship grants available. In 2010–11, 33% of upper-school students received aid. Total amount of financial aid awarded in 2010–11: $360,930.

Admissions Traditional secondary-level entrance grade is 9. For fall 2010, 20 students applied for upper-level admission, 12 were accepted, 4 enrolled. Any standardized test and writing sample required. Deadline for receipt of application materials: none. Application fee required: $50. Interview required.

Athletics Interscholastic: basketball (boys, girls), cheering (g); intramural: cheering (g); coed interscholastic: aerobics/dance, soccer; coed intramural: bowling, dance, golf, lacrosse, tennis. 1 PE instructor.

Computers Computers are regularly used in art, desktop publishing, English, foreign language, history, humanities, keyboarding, lab/keyboard, mathematics, newspaper, photography, research skills, science, video film production, word processing, yearbook classes. Computer network features include online commercial services, Internet access, wireless campus network, Internet filtering or blocking technology, E-Library. The school has a published electronic and media policy.

Contact Ms. Lorraine Greenwell, Admissions Director. 845-268-6802 Ext. 201. Fax: 845-268-4644. E-mail: lgreenwell@rocklandcds.org. Web site: www. rocklandcds.org.

ROCKLYN ACADEMY

Meaford, Ontario, Canada
See Special Needs Schools section.

ROCK POINT SCHOOL

1 Rock Point Road
Burlington, Vermont 05408
Head of School: John Rouleau

General Information Coeducational boarding and day college-preparatory and arts school, affiliated with Episcopal Church. Grades 9–12. Founded: 1928. Setting: small town. Students are housed in single-sex by floor dormitories. 130-acre campus. 3 buildings on campus. Approved or accredited by Association of Independent Schools in New England, Independent Schools of Northern New England, National Association of Episcopal Schools, New England Association of Schools and Colleges, The Association of Boarding Schools, and Vermont Department of Education. Endowment: $2.5 million. Total enrollment: 29. Upper school average class size: 10. Upper school faculty-student ratio: 1:5. There are 167 required school days per year for Upper School students. Upper School students typically attend 5 days per week. The average school day consists of 6 hours and 45 minutes.

Upper School Student Profile Grade 9: 2 students (1 boy, 1 girl); Grade 10: 8 students (4 boys, 4 girls); Grade 11: 9 students (5 boys, 4 girls); Grade 12: 10 students (7 boys, 3 girls). 90% of students are boarding students. 21% are state residents. 15 states are represented in upper school student body. 3% are international students. International students from India and Puerto Rico. 12% of students are members of Episcopal Church.

Faculty School total: 9. In upper school: 2 men, 6 women; 3 have advanced degrees.

Rock Point School

Subjects Offered Algebra, American history, American literature, ancient history, animation, art, art history, biology, calculus, chemistry, community service, creative thinking, critical thinking, drawing, earth science, English, geometry, health, historical foundations for arts, history, mathematics, painting, photography, physical education, poetry, portfolio art, pre-calculus, science, stained glass, Western civilization, world history, world literature.

Graduation Requirements Art, art history, English, history, mathematics, physical education (includes health), science. Community service is required.

Special Academic Programs Independent study; term-away projects; study at local college for college credit; special instructional classes for students who need structure and personal attention; ESL.

College Admission Counseling 11 students graduated in 2010; 9 went to college, including Hartwick College; Knox College; McDaniel College; University of California, Santa Cruz. Other: 1 entered military service, 1 had other specific plans. Median SAT critical reading: 540, median SAT math: 490, median SAT writing: 490, median combined SAT: 1500. 29% scored over 600 on SAT critical reading, 14% scored over 600 on SAT math, 14% scored over 600 on SAT writing, 29% scored over 1800 on combined SAT.

Student Life Upper grades have specified standards of dress. Discipline rests primarily with faculty.

Tuition and Aid Day student tuition: $25,200; 7-day tuition and room/board: $48,510. Tuition installment plan (individually arranged payment plans, deposit and two installment plan (September 1 and December 1)). Need-based scholarship grants available. In 2010–11, 31% of upper-school students received aid. Total amount of financial aid awarded in 2010–11: $114,750.

Admissions Traditional secondary-level entrance grade is 10. For fall 2010, 20 students applied for upper-level admission, 17 were accepted, 15 enrolled. Writing sample required. Deadline for receipt of application materials: none. Application fee required: $45. On-campus interview required.

Athletics Coed Interscholastic: basketball; coed intramural: alpine skiing, backpacking, ball hockey, basketball, bicycling, billiards, broomball, climbing, cooperative games, fitness, fitness walking, Frisbee, hiking/backpacking, jogging, kickball, martial arts, outdoor activities, outdoor adventure, outdoor recreation, physical fitness, physical training, rock climbing, ropes courses, running, skateboarding, skiing (downhill), snowboarding, soccer, softball, touch football, walking, weight training, winter walking, yoga. 7 PE instructors.

Computers Computers are regularly used in all academic, animation, art, college planning, creative writing, media, music, photography, video film production, word processing classes. Computer network features include Internet access, Internet filtering or blocking technology. Student e-mail accounts are available to students.

Contact Hillary Kramer, Director of Admissions. 802-863-1104 Ext. 12. Fax: 802-863-6628. E-mail: hkramer@rockpoint.org. Web site: www.rockpoint.org.

ROCKWAY MENNONITE COLLEGIATE

110 Doon Road
Kitchener, Ontario N2G 3C8, Canada
Head of School: Mr. Dennis Wikerd

General Information Coeducational boarding and day college-preparatory, arts, religious studies, and technology school, affiliated with Mennonite Church USA. Grades 6–12. Founded: 1945. Setting: suburban. Nearest major city is Toronto, Canada. Students are housed in host family homes. 14-acre campus. 7 buildings on campus. Approved or accredited by Mennonite Schools Council and Ontario Department of Education. Language of instruction: English. Endowment: CAN$450,000. Total enrollment: 300. Upper school average class size: 17. Upper school faculty-student ratio: 1:10. Upper School students typically attend 5 days per week. The average school day consists of 5 hours and 55 minutes.

Upper School Student Profile 1% of students are boarding students. 85% are province residents. 1 province is represented in upper school student body. 15% are international students. International students from China, Germany, Hong Kong, Japan, Republic of Korea, and Taiwan; 2 other countries represented in student body. 38% of students are Mennonite Church USA.

Faculty School total: 45. In upper school: 20 men, 20 women; 8 have advanced degrees.

Subjects Offered Algebra, auto mechanics, Bible, biology, calculus, Canadian history, career education, chemistry, choral music, civics, computer science, computer studies, construction, dramatic arts, English, entrepreneurship, ESL, family studies, finite math, food and nutrition, French, functions, geography, geometry, German, guidance, health, healthful living, history, information technology, instrumental music, integrated technology fundamentals, Mandarin, mathematics, music, orchestra, parenting, personal finance, philosophy, physical education, physics, religious studies, science, strings, technology/design, transportation technology, visual arts, vocal music, wind instruments, world history, world religions.

Graduation Requirements Ontario Ministry of Education requirements, 2 credits in a language other than English, religious studies courses through grade 11.

Special Academic Programs Independent study; academic accommodation for the gifted; ESL (34 students enrolled).

College Admission Counseling 79 students graduated in 2009; 60 went to college, including Carleton University; The University of Western Ontario; University of Guelph; University of Toronto; University of Waterloo; Wilfrid Laurier University. Other: 8 went to work, 11 had other specific plans.

Student Life Upper grades have specified standards of dress, student council. Discipline rests primarily with faculty. Attendance at religious services is required.

Tuition and Aid Day student tuition: CAN$9965; 7-day tuition and room/board: CAN$16,965. Tuition installment plan (monthly payment plans, individually arranged payment plans). Tuition reduction for siblings, bursaries, need-based scholarship grants, paying campus jobs available. In 2009–10, 17% of upper-school students received aid. Total amount of financial aid awarded in 2009–10: CAN$120,000.

Admissions Traditional secondary-level entrance grade is 9. For fall 2009, 40 students applied for upper-level admission, 38 were accepted, 36 enrolled. Deadline for receipt of application materials: none. Application fee required: CAN$100.

Athletics Interscholastic: badminton (boys, girls), baseball (b,g), basketball (b,g), cross-country running (b,g), soccer (b), softball (b,g), track and field (b,g), volleyball (b,g), wrestling (b,g); intramural: ball hockey (b,g), baseball (b,g), basketball (b,g), cooperative games (b,g), dance (b,g), field hockey (b,g), flag football (b,g), flagball (b,g), floor hockey (b,g), football (b,g), indoor soccer (b,g), nordic skiing (b,g), outdoor education (b,g), physical training (b,g), power lifting (b,g), rock climbing (b,g), rugby (b,g), skiing (downhill) (b,g), soccer (b,g), strength & conditioning (b,g), volleyball (b,g); coed interscholastic: soccer; coed intramural: baseball, canoeing/kayaking, cooperative games, outdoor education, roller skating, skiing (downhill), street hockey, table tennis, track and field. 2 PE instructors.

Computers Computers are regularly used in Bible studies, business, career technology, college planning, construction, drafting, English, geography, library, mathematics, religious studies, science, typing, Web site design classes. Computer resources include on-campus library services, Internet access, Internet filtering or blocking technology.

Contact Mr. Tom Bileski, Director of Community Relations. 519-342-0007 Ext. 3029. Fax: 519-743-5935. E-mail: admin@rockway.ca. Web site: www.rockway.ca.

THE ROEPER SCHOOL

41190 Woodward Avenue
Bloomfield Hills, Michigan 48304
Head of School: Randall C. Dunn

General Information Coeducational day college-preparatory school. Grades PK–12. Founded: 1941. Setting: urban. Nearest major city is Birmingham. 1-acre campus. 1 building on campus. Approved or accredited by Independent Schools Association of the Central States. Member of National Association of Independent Schools. Endowment: $4.9 million. Total enrollment: 625. Upper school average class size: 14. Upper school faculty-student ratio: 1:6. There are 165 required school days per year for Upper School students. Upper School students typically attend 5 days per week. The average school day consists of 7 hours and 10 minutes.

Upper School Student Profile Grade 9: 51 students (25 boys, 26 girls); Grade 10: 48 students (27 boys, 21 girls); Grade 11: 49 students (25 boys, 24 girls); Grade 12: 44 students (24 boys, 20 girls).

Faculty School total: 90. In upper school: 14 men, 24 women; 21 have advanced degrees.

Subjects Offered Algebra, American history, American literature, art, art history, biology, calculus, chemistry, computer programming, computer science, creative writing, dance, drama, English, English literature, European history, fine arts, French, geometry, government/civics, health, history, journalism, Latin, mathematics, music, philosophy, photography, physical education, physics, science, social studies, Spanish, speech, statistics, theater, trigonometry, world history, world literature, writing.

Graduation Requirements Arts and fine arts (art, music, dance, drama), computer science, English, foreign language, government, health, mathematics, science, social studies (includes history).

Special Academic Programs Advanced Placement exam preparation; independent study; academic accommodation for the gifted, the musically talented, and the artistically talented; programs in English, mathematics, general development for dyslexic students.

College Admission Counseling 51 students graduated in 2010; all went to college, including Eastern Michigan University; Kalamazoo College; Northwestern University; Oakland University; University of Michigan.

Student Life Upper grades have student council, honor system. Discipline rests primarily with faculty.

Summer Programs Art/fine arts programs offered; session focuses on theater; held on campus; accepts boys and girls; open to students from other schools. 40 students usually enrolled. 2011 schedule: June 20 to August 12.

Tuition and Aid Day student tuition: $21,650. Tuition installment plan (FACTS Tuition Payment Plan, individually arranged payment plans). Need-based scholarship grants available. In 2010–11, 40% of upper-school students received aid. Total amount of financial aid awarded in 2010–11: $862,775.

Admissions Traditional secondary-level entrance grade is 9. For fall 2010, 40 students applied for upper-level admission, 27 were accepted, 19 enrolled. Individual IQ required. Deadline for receipt of application materials: none. Application fee required: $75. On-campus interview required.

Athletics Interscholastic: baseball (boys), basketball (b,g), cross-country running (b,g), physical training (b,g), soccer (b,g), strength & conditioning (b,g), track and field (b,g), volleyball (g), weight lifting (b,g); intramural: indoor soccer (b,g); coed intramural: physical training, strength & conditioning, weight lifting.

Computers Computers are regularly used in English, journalism, library, mathematics, publishing, science, yearbook classes. Computer network features include on-campus library services, online commercial services, Internet access.

Contact Lori Zinser, Director of Admissions. 248-203-7302. Fax: 248-203-7310. E-mail: lori.zinser@roeper.org. Web site: www.roeper.org.

ROLAND PARK COUNTRY SCHOOL

5204 Roland Avenue
Baltimore, Maryland 21210
Head of School: Mrs. Jean Waller Brune

General Information Girls' day college-preparatory and arts school. Grades K–12. Founded: 1901. Setting: suburban. 21-acre campus. 1 building on campus. Approved or accredited by Association of Independent Maryland Schools. Member of National Association of Independent Schools and Secondary School Admission Test Board. Endowment: $44.3 million. Total enrollment: 675. Upper school average class size: 14. Upper school faculty-student ratio: 1:7. There are 172 required school days per year for Upper School students. Upper School students typically attend 5 days per week. The average school day consists of 7 hours and 45 minutes.

Upper School Student Profile Grade 9: 71 students (71 girls); Grade 10: 80 students (80 girls); Grade 11: 62 students (62 girls); Grade 12: 76 students (76 girls).

Faculty School total: 98. In upper school: 6 men, 42 women; 40 have advanced degrees.

Subjects Offered 3-dimensional art, advanced biology, advanced chemistry, advanced math, Advanced Placement courses, advanced studio art-AP, algebra, American history-AP, American literature, American literature-AP, anatomy, ancient world history, Arabic, art, art history, art history-AP, astronomy, biology, biology-AP, calculus, calculus-AP, ceramics, chemistry, chemistry-AP, Chesapeake Bay studies, Chinese, community service, computer programming, computer science, creative writing, dance, drama, ecology, economics, engineering, English, English language-AP, English literature, English literature-AP, English-AP, environmental science, environmental studies, European civilization, European history, European history-AP, French, French language-AP, French literature-AP, geometry, German, government/civics, Greek, health, integrated mathematics, Latin, music, philosophy, photography, physical education, physics, physiology, religion, Russian, science, social studies, Spanish, speech, statistics, theater, trigonometry, world history.

Graduation Requirements Adolescent issues, arts and fine arts (art, music, dance, drama), biology, chemistry, English, foreign language, history, mathematics, physical education (includes health), physics, public speaking, science. Community service is required.

Special Academic Programs Advanced Placement exam preparation; honors section; independent study; term-away projects; study abroad.

College Admission Counseling 71 students graduated in 2010; all went to college, including Dickinson College; Georgetown University; University of Maryland, College Park; University of Pennsylvania; University of Virginia; Washington and Lee University. Mean SAT critical reading: 607, mean SAT math: 603, mean SAT writing: 632, mean combined SAT: 1841, mean composite ACT: 23. 56% scored over 600 on SAT critical reading, 52% scored over 600 on SAT math, 69% scored over 600 on SAT writing, 54% scored over 1800 on combined SAT, 69% scored over 26 on composite ACT.

Student Life Upper grades have uniform requirement, student council, honor system. Discipline rests equally with students and faculty.

Summer Programs Remediation, enrichment, advancement, sports, art/fine arts programs offered; session focuses on summer camp, arts, some academics; held both on and off campus; held at off-site pool and venues for outdoor education programs and various sites around Baltimore for art projects; accepts boys and girls; open to students from other schools. 484 students usually enrolled. 2011 schedule: June 20 to August 26. Application deadline: none.

Tuition and Aid Day student tuition: $22,895. Tuition installment plan (FACTS Tuition Payment Plan, individually arranged payment plans). Need-based scholarship grants, paying campus jobs available. In 2010–11, 25% of upper-school students received aid. Total amount of financial aid awarded in 2010–11: $996,080.

Admissions Traditional secondary-level entrance grade is 9. For fall 2010, 93 students applied for upper-level admission, 57 were accepted, 25 enrolled. CTP, ERB CTP IV or ISEE required. Deadline for receipt of application materials: January 15. Application fee required: $50. Interview required.

Athletics Interscholastic: badminton, basketball, crew, cross-country running, field hockey, golf, independent competitive sports, indoor soccer, indoor track, lacrosse, soccer, softball, squash, swimming and diving, tennis, volleyball, winter (indoor) track, winter soccer; intramural: dance, fitness, modern dance, outdoor education, physical fitness, rock climbing, strength & conditioning. 7 PE instructors, 1 athletic trainer.

Computers Computers are regularly used in all classes. Computer network features include on-campus library services, online commercial services, Internet access, wireless campus network, Internet filtering or blocking technology, online database. Campus intranet, student e-mail accounts, and computer access in designated common areas are available to students. Students grades are available online. The school has a published electronic and media policy.

Contact Peggy Wolf, Director of Admissions. 410-323-5500. Fax: 410-323-2164. E-mail: admissions@rpcs.org. Web site: www.rpcs.org.

ROLLING HILLS PREPARATORY SCHOOL

One Rolling Hills Prep Way
San Pedro, California 90732
Head of School: Peter McCormack

General Information Coeducational day college-preparatory, arts, and technology school. Grades 6–12. Founded: 1981. Setting: suburban. Nearest major city is Los Angeles. 20-acre campus. 20 buildings on campus. Approved or accredited by California Association of Independent Schools, Western Association of Schools and Colleges, and California Department of Education. Member of National Association of Independent Schools. Endowment: $10,000. Total enrollment: 235. Upper school average class size: 16. Upper school faculty-student ratio: 1:9. There are 180 required school days per year for Upper School students. Upper School students typically attend 5 days per week. The average school day consists of 6 hours.

Upper School Student Profile Grade 9: 36 students (21 boys, 15 girls); Grade 10: 47 students (26 boys, 21 girls); Grade 11: 46 students (28 boys, 18 girls); Grade 12: 33 students (19 boys, 14 girls).

Faculty School total: 37. In upper school: 6 men, 21 women; 14 have advanced degrees.

Subjects Offered Algebra, American history, American literature, American sign language, anatomy, art, biology, calculus, ceramics, chemistry, Chinese, computer science, creative writing, drama, economics, English, English literature, European history, fine arts, French, geography, geometry, government/civics, history, mathematics, music, photography, physical education, physics, pre-calculus, robotics, science, social studies, Spanish, speech, statistics, theater, trigonometry, world history.

Graduation Requirements Arts and fine arts (art, music, dance, drama), English, foreign language, mathematics, outdoor education, physical education (includes health), science, social studies (includes history), two-week senior internship, senior speech.

Special Academic Programs Advanced Placement exam preparation; honors section; independent study; academic accommodation for the gifted; programs in general development for dyslexic students; ESL (21 students enrolled).

College Admission Counseling 33 students graduated in 2010; 32 went to college, including Dartmouth College; University of California, Berkeley; University of California, Los Angeles; University of California, Santa Barbara; University of Southern California. Other: 1 had other specific plans. Mean SAT critical reading: 590, mean SAT math: 590, mean SAT writing: 620. 45% scored over 600 on SAT critical reading, 40% scored over 600 on SAT math, 45% scored over 600 on SAT writing.

Student Life Upper grades have specified standards of dress, student council. Discipline rests primarily with faculty.

Tuition and Aid Day student tuition: $22,100. Tuition installment plan (Insured Tuition Payment Plan, Key Tuition Payment Plan, monthly payment plans). Merit scholarship grants, need-based scholarship grants available. In 2010–11, 35% of upper-school students received aid. Total amount of financial aid awarded in 2010–11: $500,000.

Admissions Traditional secondary-level entrance grade is 9. For fall 2010, 20 students applied for upper-level admission, 14 were accepted, 9 enrolled. ISEE required. Deadline for receipt of application materials: none. Application fee required: $150. On-campus interview required.

Athletics Interscholastic: baseball (boys), basketball (b,g), cheering (g), football (b), soccer (g), softball (g), track and field (g), volleyball (b,g); intramural: cheering (g), dance (g); coed interscholastic: cross-country running, golf, roller hockey, running, soccer, track and field; coed intramural: backpacking, climbing, hiking/backpacking, outdoor education, rock climbing, ropes courses. 4 PE instructors, 9 coaches, 1 athletic trainer.

Computers Computers are regularly used in English, foreign language, history, mathematics, science classes. Computer network features include on-campus library services, Internet access, wireless campus network. The school has a published electronic and media policy.

Contact Bryonna Fisco, Director of Admission. 310-791-1101 Ext. 148. Fax: 310-373-4931. E-mail: bfisco@rollinghillsprep.org. Web site: www. rollinghillsprep.org.

RONCALLI HIGH SCHOOL

3300 Prague Road
Indianapolis, Indiana 46227
Head of School: Mr. Joseph D. Hollowell

General Information Coeducational day college-preparatory and religious studies school, affiliated with Roman Catholic Church. Grades 9–12. Founded: 1969. Setting: suburban. 38-acre campus. 3 buildings on campus. Approved or accredited by National Catholic Education Association, North Central Association of Colleges and Schools, and Indiana Department of Education. Total enrollment: 1,142. Upper school average class size: 22. Upper school faculty-student ratio: 1:14.

Upper School Student Profile Grade 9: 317 students (172 boys, 145 girls); Grade 10: 266 students (141 boys, 125 girls); Grade 11: 292 students (144 boys, 148 girls); Grade 12: 268 students (134 boys, 134 girls). 96% of students are Roman Catholic.

Faculty School total: 78. In upper school: 31 men, 47 women; 42 have advanced degrees.

Subjects Offered ACT preparation, addiction, ADL skills, adolescent issues, advanced TOEFL/grammar, advertising design, aerobics, African American history,

Roncalli High School

African American studies, African dance, African drumming, African history, African literature, African studies, African-American history, African-American literature, African-American studies, agriculture, agroecology, Alabama history and geography, American biography, American culture, American democracy, American foreign policy.

Graduation Requirements Biology, computer applications, English, mathematics, physical education (includes health), physical science, religious studies, U.S. government, U.S. history, service requirements each year of school.

Special Academic Programs 13 Advanced Placement exams for which test preparation is offered; honors section; independent study; study at local college for college credit; study abroad; academic accommodation for the gifted, the musically talented, and the artistically talented; remedial reading and/or remedial writing; remedial math; programs in English, mathematics, general development for dyslexic students; special instructional classes for blind students, students with autism, learning disabilities, Attention Deficit Disorder.

College Admission Counseling 278 students graduated in 2009; 264 went to college, including Ball State University; Indiana University Bloomington; Purdue University. Other: 10 went to work, 4 entered military service. Mean SAT critical reading: 510, mean SAT math: 540, mean SAT writing: 510, mean combined SAT: 1560, mean composite ACT: 23. 25.3% scored over 600 on SAT critical reading, 26% scored over 600 on SAT math, 18% scored over 600 on SAT writing, 19.5% scored over 1800 on combined SAT, 23% scored over 26 on composite ACT.

Student Life Upper grades have uniform requirement, student council. Discipline rests primarily with faculty. Attendance at religious services is required.

Tuition and Aid Day student tuition: $7500. Tuition installment plan (monthly payment plans). Tuition reduction for siblings, merit scholarship grants, need-based scholarship grants, paying campus jobs available. In 2009–10, 24% of upper-school students received aid; total upper-school merit-scholarship money awarded: $10,000. Total amount of financial aid awarded in 2009–10: $725,000.

Admissions Traditional secondary-level entrance grade is 9. High School Placement Test or High School Placement Test (closed version) from Scholastic Testing Service required. Deadline for receipt of application materials: none. Application fee required: $100. On-campus interview required.

Athletics Interscholastic: baseball (boys), basketball (b,g), bowling (b,g), cheering (g), cross-country running (b,g), diving (b,g), football (b), golf (b,g), gymnastics (g), soccer (b,g), softball (g), strength & conditioning (b); intramural: backpacking (b,g), boxing (b,g), dance team (g), ice hockey (b), lacrosse (b), power lifting (b), rugby (b); coed intramural: climbing, Frisbee, hiking/backpacking, mountaineering, rock climbing. 5 PE instructors, 2 athletic trainers.

Computers Computer network features include on-campus library services, Internet access, wireless campus network, Internet filtering or blocking technology. Campus intranet, student e-mail accounts, and computer access in designated common areas are available to students. Students grades are available online. The school has a published electronic and media policy.

Contact Mr. James Kedra, Assistant Principal for Academic Affairs. 317-787-8277 Ext. 222. Fax: 317-788-4095. E-mail: jkedra@roncallihs.org. Web site: www.roncalli.org.

RON PETTIGREW CHRISTIAN SCHOOL

1761 110th Avenue
Dawson Creek, British Columbia V1G 4X4, Canada
Head of School: Phyllis L. Roch

General Information Coeducational day college-preparatory and general academic school, affiliated with Christian faith. Grades K–12. Founded: 1989. Setting: small town. Nearest major city is Prince George, Canada. 1-acre campus. 1 building on campus. Approved or accredited by Association of Christian Schools International and British Columbia Department of Education. Language of instruction: English. Total enrollment: 88. Upper school faculty-student ratio: 1:5.

Upper School Student Profile 76% of students are Christian faith.

Faculty School total: 6. In upper school: 2 men, 4 women.

College Admission Counseling 2 students graduated in 2010. Other: 2 went to work.

Student Life Upper grades have uniform requirement, student council, honor system. Discipline rests primarily with faculty. Attendance at religious services is required.

Admissions No application fee required. Interview required.

Computers Computer network features include Internet access, wireless campus network, Internet filtering or blocking technology.

Contact Phyllis L. Roch, Head of School. 250-782-4580. Fax: 250-782-9805. E-mail: rpcs@pris.ca.

ROSARY HIGH SCHOOL

1340 North Acacia Avenue
Fullerton, California 92831
Head of School: Mrs. Terry Gonzalez

General Information Girls' day college-preparatory, arts, religious studies, and technology school, affiliated with Roman Catholic Church. Grades 9–12. Founded: 1965. Setting: suburban. Nearest major city is Los Angeles. 4-acre campus. 4 buildings on campus. Approved or accredited by Western Association of Schools and Colleges, Western Catholic Education Association, and California Department of Education.

Total enrollment: 628. Upper school average class size: 21. Upper school faculty-student ratio: 1:15. There are 180 required school days per year for Upper School students. Upper School students typically attend 5 days per week. The average school day consists of 6 hours and 15 minutes.

Upper School Student Profile Grade 9: 179 students (179 girls); Grade 10: 178 students (178 girls); Grade 11: 157 students (157 girls); Grade 12: 166 students (166 girls). 87% of students are Roman Catholic.

Faculty School total: 47. In upper school: 8 men, 39 women; 19 have advanced degrees.

Subjects Offered Advanced Placement courses, algebra, American government, American history, animation, art, ASB Leadership, bell choir, Bible studies, biology, biology-AP, calculus-AP, career exploration, Catholic belief and practice, chamber groups, chemistry, chemistry-AP, child development, choir, church history, college counseling, comparative religion, computer applications, computer education, computer graphics, concert choir, creative writing, digital photography, drama, dramatic arts, drawing, drawing and design, economics, electives, English, English language-AP, English literature-AP, environmental science, fiber arts, film and literature, fine arts, finite math, French, French language-AP, geography, geometry, grammar, graphic arts, handbells, health, history of rock and roll, honors algebra, honors English, honors geometry, honors U.S. history, human biology, instrumental music, Internet, journalism, mathematics, multimedia, music performance, musical theater, orchestra, painting, parent/child development, peace and justice, performing arts, photography, physical education, physical science, physics, pre-calculus, psychology, religion, science, social justice, social studies, Spanish, Spanish language-AP, speech, sports conditioning, sports medicine, statistics, theater, theater design and production, U.S. government, U.S. government and politics-AP, U.S. history-AP, visual and performing arts, visual arts, water color painting, world geography, world history, world religions, world wide web design.

Graduation Requirements Arts and fine arts (art, music, dance, drama), computer science, English, foreign language, mathematics, physical education (includes health), religion (includes Bible studies and theology), science, social studies (includes history), speech communications.

Special Academic Programs 10 Advanced Placement exams for which test preparation is offered; honors section; remedial math.

College Admission Counseling 146 students graduated in 2009; all went to college, including California State University, Fullerton; Chapman University; Loyola Marymount University; Santa Clara University; Sonoma State University; University of California, Santa Barbara. Mean SAT critical reading: 534, mean SAT math: 518, mean SAT writing: 546. 31% scored over 600 on SAT critical reading, 27% scored over 600 on SAT math, 33% scored over 600 on SAT writing.

Student Life Upper grades have uniform requirement, student council, honor system. Discipline rests primarily with faculty. Attendance at religious services is required.

Tuition and Aid Day student tuition: $10,320. Tuition installment plan (FACTS Tuition Payment Plan). Merit scholarship grants, need-based scholarship grants available. In 2009–10, 17% of upper-school students received aid; total upper-school merit-scholarship money awarded: $14,500. Total amount of financial aid awarded in 2009–10: $221,000.

Admissions Traditional secondary-level entrance grade is 9. High School Placement Test required. Deadline for receipt of application materials: January 10. Application fee required: $70.

Athletics Interscholastic: basketball, cheering, cross-country running, dance team, golf, soccer, softball, swimming and diving, tennis, track and field, volleyball, water polo. 2 PE instructors, 25 coaches, 1 athletic trainer.

Computers Computers are regularly used in animation, business, geography, graphic design, journalism, media arts, multimedia, newspaper, religious studies, science, social studies, technology, video film production, Web site design, yearbook classes. Computer network features include on-campus library services, online commercial services, Internet access, graphics catalog, server access for saving files, networked access to laser printer. Students grades are available online. The school has a published electronic and media policy.

Contact Ms. Linda Simpson, Office Manager. 714-879-6302. Fax: 714-879-0853. E-mail: lsimpson@rosaryhs.org. Web site: www.rosaryhs.org.

ROSSEAU LAKE COLLEGE

1967 Bright Street
Rosseau, Ontario P0C 1J0, Canada
Head of School: Mr. Graham Hookey

General Information Coeducational boarding and day college-preparatory, arts, business, and technology school. Grades 7–12. Founded: 1967. Setting: rural. Nearest major city is Toronto, Canada. Students are housed in single-sex dormitories. 53-acre campus. 13 buildings on campus. Approved or accredited by Canadian Association of Independent Schools, Canadian Educational Standards Institute, The Association of Boarding Schools, and Ontario Department of Education. Languages of instruction: English and French. Endowment: CAN$100,000. Total enrollment: 105. Upper school average class size: 12. Upper school faculty-student ratio: 1:6. There are 176 required school days per year for Upper School students. Upper School students typically attend 5 days per week. The average school day consists of 5 hours and 30 minutes.

Upper School Student Profile Grade 9: 18 students (12 boys, 6 girls); Grade 10: 16 students (13 boys, 3 girls); Grade 11: 19 students (13 boys, 6 girls); Grade 12: 28 students (17 boys, 11 girls). 45% of students are boarding students. 80% are province residents. 2 provinces are represented in upper school student body. 20% are international students. International students from China, Democratic People's Republic of Korea, Japan, Mexico, Russian Federation, and Spain; 4 other countries represented in student body.

Faculty School total: 19. In upper school: 8 men, 11 women; 5 have advanced degrees; 11 reside on campus.

Subjects Offered Accounting, algebra, art, art history, biology, business, calculus, Canadian law, career and personal planning, chemistry, civics, computer programming, computer science, data analysis, economics, English, entrepreneurship, ESL, European history, experiential education, fine arts, French, geography, geometry, health, history, information technology, marketing, mathematics, music, outdoor education, physical education, physics, political science, science, social sciences, trigonometry, visual arts, world governments, writing.

Graduation Requirements Arts and fine arts (art, music, dance, drama), business skills (includes word processing), career planning, civics, computer science, English, foreign language, mathematics, physical education (includes health), science, social studies (includes history).

Special Academic Programs Accelerated programs; independent study; term-away projects; study abroad; academic accommodation for the gifted; remedial reading and/or remedial writing; remedial math; ESL (18 students enrolled).

College Admission Counseling 16 students graduated in 2010; all went to college, including McMaster University; Queen's University at Kingston; The University of Western Ontario; University of Guelph; University of Toronto; York University.

Student Life Upper grades have uniform requirement, student council, honor system. Discipline rests primarily with faculty.

Summer Programs Remediation, enrichment, advancement programs offered; session focuses on academics; held on campus; accepts boys and girls; open to students from other schools. 10 students usually enrolled. 2011 schedule: July 1 to July 30. Application deadline: June 15.

Tuition and Aid Day student tuition: CAN$17,700; 7-day tuition and room/board: CAN$40,500. Tuition installment plan (monthly payment plans, individually arranged payment plans). Merit scholarship grants, need-based scholarship grants available. In 2010–11, 10% of upper-school students received aid; total upper-school merit-scholarship money awarded: CAN$40,000. Total amount of financial aid awarded in 2010–11: CAN$160,000.

Admissions Traditional secondary-level entrance grade is 9. For fall 2010, 87 students applied for upper-level admission, 42 were accepted, 40 enrolled. Admissions testing and English Composition Test for ESL students required. Deadline for receipt of application materials: none. Application fee required: CAN$150. Interview required.

Athletics Interscholastic: baseball (boys), basketball (b,g), cross-country running (b,g), field hockey (g), hockey (b), ice hockey (b), mountain biking (b,g), nordic skiing (b,g), rugby (b), running (b,g), skiing (cross-country) (b,g), snowboarding (b,g), soccer (b,g), softball (b), swimming and diving (b,g), tennis (b,g), track and field (b,g), volleyball (b,g); intramural: alpine skiing (b,g), baseball (b), basketball (b,g), cross-country running (b,g), field hockey (g), hockey (b,g), ice hockey (b,g), rugby (b), running (b,g), skiing (cross-country) (b,g), snowboarding (b,g); coed interscholastic: bicycling, canoeing/kayaking, climbing, golf, kayaking, mountain biking, nordic skiing, running, skiing (cross-country), skiing (downhill), snowboarding, softball, track and field; coed intramural: aerobics, aerobics/dance, aquatics, backpacking, ball hockey, baseball, basketball, bicycling, bowling, broomball, canoeing/kayaking, climbing, combined training, cooperative games, Cosom hockey, cross-country running, equestrian sports, fishing, fitness, fitness walking, flag football, floor hockey, fly fishing, freestyle skiing, Frisbee, golf, hiking/backpacking, horseback riding, ice skating, indoor hockey, indoor soccer, jogging, kayaking, life saving, mountain biking, mountaineering, nordic skiing, outdoor activities, paddle tennis, paddling, physical fitness, physical training, rappelling, rock climbing, ropes courses, sailboarding, sailing, scuba diving, skateboarding, skiing (cross-country), skiing (downhill), snowboarding, snowshoeing, soccer, softball, squash, street hockey, strength & conditioning, swimming and diving, table tennis, tennis, track and field, triathlon, ultimate Frisbee, volleyball, walking, wall climbing, water skiing, weight lifting, weight training, wilderness, wilderness survival, wildernessways, windsurfing, winter walking, yoga. 2 PE instructors, 2 coaches.

Computers Computers are regularly used in geography, graphic arts, information technology classes. Computer network features include on-campus library services, Internet access, wireless campus network, Internet filtering or blocking technology. Campus intranet, student e-mail accounts, and computer access in designated common areas are available to students. The school has a published electronic and media policy.

Contact Ms. Jeanette Turvey, Admissions Assistant. 705-732-4351 Ext. 21. Fax: 705-732-6319. E-mail: admissions@rlc.on.ca. Web site: www.rosseaulakecollege.com.

ROSS SCHOOL

18 Goodfriend Drive
East Hampton, New York 11937
Head of School: Michele Claeys

General Information Coeducational boarding and day college-preparatory, globally-focused, integrated curriculum, and ESL curriculum school. Boarding grades 7–12, day grades N–12. Founded: 1991. Setting: small town. Nearest major city is New York. Students are housed in single-sex dormitories. 100-acre campus. 7

buildings on campus. Approved or accredited by Middle States Association of Colleges and Schools, New York State Association of Independent Schools, and New York Department of Education. Upper school faculty-student ratio: 1:7. There are 164 required school days per year for Upper School students. Upper School students typically attend 5 days per week. The average school day consists of 7 hours and 25 minutes.

Upper School Student Profile 34% of students are boarding students. 71% are state residents. 3 states are represented in upper school student body. 28% are international students. International students from China, Germany, Japan, Qatar, Republic of Korea, and Taiwan; 6 other countries represented in student body.

Faculty School total: 93. In upper school: 27 reside on campus.

Subjects Offered Advanced biology, advanced chemistry, advanced math, art history, athletics, Chinese, college counseling, computer multimedia, English literature, ESL, French, health and wellness, independent study, jazz band, media studies, model United Nations, music, philosophy, physics, SAT preparation, senior internship, senior project, Spanish, theater arts, United Nations and international issues, visual arts, world history.

Graduation Requirements 30 hours of community service.

Special Academic Programs 9 Advanced Placement exams for which test preparation is offered; honors section; independent study; term-away projects; ESL (30 students enrolled).

College Admission Counseling 49 students graduated in 2010; 48 went to college, including Duke University; New York University; Oberlin College; University of Chicago; Vassar College; Wesleyan University. Other: 1 had other specific plans.

Student Life Upper grades have uniform requirement, student council, honor system. Discipline rests primarily with faculty.

Summer Programs ESL, sports, art/fine arts programs offered; session focuses on sports and fine arts; held on campus; accepts boys and girls; open to students from other schools. 2011 schedule: June 27 to August 19. Application deadline: none.

Tuition and Aid Day student tuition: $31,100; 5-day tuition and room/board: $45,600. Tuition installment plan (monthly payment plans). Tuition reduction for siblings, need-based scholarship grants available. In 2010–11, 45% of upper-school students received aid.

Admissions Traditional secondary-level entrance grade is 9. Any standardized test required. Deadline for receipt of application materials: January 31. Application fee required: $50. Interview required.

Athletics Interscholastic: baseball (boys), basketball (b,g), lacrosse (b,g), soccer (b,g), softball (g), tennis (b,g), track and field (b,g), volleyball (b,g); coed interscholastic: cheering, golf, sailing; coed intramural: ballet, dance, fitness, kayaking, modern dance, mountain biking, sailing, surfing, tai chi, yoga.

Computers Computers are regularly used in all classes. Computer network features include on-campus library services, online commercial services, Internet access, wireless campus network, Internet filtering or blocking technology. Campus intranet and student e-mail accounts are available to students. Students grades are available online. The school has a published electronic and media policy.

Contact Ms. Kristen Kaschub, Director of International Recruitment. 631-907-5205. Fax: 631-907-5563. E-mail: kkaschub@ross.org. Web site: www.ross.org/.

ROTHESAY NETHERWOOD SCHOOL

40 College Hill Road
Rothesay, New Brunswick E2E 5H1, Canada
Head of School: Mr. Paul G. Kitchen

General Information Coeducational boarding and day college-preparatory, arts, and technology school, affiliated with Anglican Church of Canada. Grades 6–12. Founded: 1877. Setting: small town. Nearest major city is Saint John, Canada. Students are housed in single-sex dormitories. 180-acre campus. 26 buildings on campus. Approved or accredited by Canadian Association of Independent Schools, Canadian Educational Standards Institute, Conference of Independent Schools of Ontario, International Baccalaureate Organization, The Association of Boarding Schools, and New Brunswick Department of Education. Languages of instruction: English and French. Endowment: CAN$2.6 million. Total enrollment: 244. Upper school average class size: 16. Upper school faculty-student ratio: 1:8. There are 176 required school days per year for Upper School students. Upper School students typically attend 5 days per week. The average school day consists of 7 hours and 45 minutes.

Upper School Student Profile Grade 9: 23 students (15 boys, 8 girls); Grade 10: 51 students (34 boys, 17 girls); Grade 11: 65 students (28 boys, 37 girls); Grade 12: 48 students (19 boys, 29 girls). 57% of students are boarding students. 66% are province residents. 9 provinces are represented in upper school student body. 17% are international students. International students from Bermuda, China, Dominica, Germany, Jamaica, and Mexico; 4 other countries represented in student body. 30% of students are members of Anglican Church of Canada.

Faculty School total: 31. In upper school: 16 men, 11 women; 6 have advanced degrees; 22 reside on campus.

Subjects Offered Advanced chemistry, art, art history, biology, Canadian history, chemistry, computer programming, computer science, CPR, digital art, drama, driver education, English, English literature, ESL, European history, fine arts, French, geography, geometry, health, history, information technology, International Baccalaureate courses, leadership, math applications, mathematics, music, outdoor education, physical education, physics, science, social studies, Spanish, theater arts, world history, writing.

Graduation Requirements Arts and fine arts (art, music, dance, drama), computer science, English, foreign language, mathematics, physical education (includes health), science, social sciences, social studies (includes history), IB Theory of Knowledge, IB designation CAS hours (creativity, action, service), Extended Essay, Outward Bound adventure.

Special Academic Programs International Baccalaureate program; honors section; independent study; term-away projects; study at local college for college credit; academic accommodation for the gifted, the musically talented, and the artistically talented; ESL (10 students enrolled).

College Admission Counseling 40 students graduated in 2010; 39 went to college, including Acadia University; Dalhousie University; Mount Allison University; St. Francis Xavier University; University of Toronto. Other: 1 had other specific plans.

Student Life Upper grades have uniform requirement, student council, honor system. Discipline rests primarily with faculty. Attendance at religious services is required.

Tuition and Aid Day student tuition: CAN$18,800; 7-day tuition and room/board: CAN$38,650. Tuition installment plan (monthly payment plans, individually arranged payment plans). Tuition reduction for siblings, bursaries, merit scholarship grants, need-based scholarship grants available. In 2010–11, 35% of upper-school students received aid; total upper-school merit-scholarship money awarded: CAN$141,000. Total amount of financial aid awarded in 2010–11: CAN$857,000.

Admissions Traditional secondary-level entrance grade is 9. For fall 2010, 91 students applied for upper-level admission, 82 were accepted, 63 enrolled. School's own exam required. Deadline for receipt of application materials: none. Application fee required: CAN$200. Interview required.

Athletics Interscholastic: badminton (boys, girls), basketball (b,g), crew (b,g), cross-country running (b,g), field hockey (g), ice hockey (b,g), rowing (b,g), rugby (b,g), running (b,g), soccer (b,g), squash (b,g), tennis (b,g), track and field (b,g), volleyball (b,g); intramural: aerobics (g), badminton (b,g), cross-country running (b,g), golf (b,g), ice hockey (b,g), indoor soccer (b), squash (b,g), tennis (b,g), track and field (b,g), yoga (g); coed interscholastic: badminton, crew, cross-country running, rowing, tennis, track and field; coed intramural: aerobics, backpacking, badminton, bicycling, billiards, broomball, canoeing/kayaking, climbing, cooperative games, cross-country running, fitness, fitness walking, floor hockey, golf, hiking/backpacking, ice hockey, ice skating, indoor soccer, jogging, kayaking, mountain biking, outdoor activities, outdoor education, physical fitness, physical training, rock climbing, running, skiing (cross-country), skiing (downhill), snowboarding, snowshoeing, squash, street hockey, strength & conditioning, tennis, track and field, ultimate Frisbee, volleyball, walking, wall climbing, weight training. 4 PE instructors.

Computers Computers are regularly used in all classes. Computer network features include on-campus library services, Internet access, wireless campus network, Internet filtering or blocking technology, Website for each academic course, informative, interactive online community for parents, teachers, and students. Campus intranet and student e-mail accounts are available to students. Students grades are available online. The school has a published electronic and media policy.

Contact Mrs. Elizabeth Kitchen, Associate Director of Admission. 506-848-0866. Fax: 506-848-0851. E-mail: kitchene@rns.cc. Web site: www.rns.cc.

ROTTERDAM INTERNATIONAL SECONDARY SCHOOL, WOLFERT VAN BORSELEN

Bentincklaan 294
Rotterdam 3039 KK, Netherlands
Head of School: Ms. Jane Forrest

General Information Coeducational day college-preparatory, bilingual studies, and languages school. Grades 6–12. Founded: 1988. Setting: urban. 2-hectare campus. 1 building on campus. Approved or accredited by European Council of International Schools, International Baccalaureate Organization, New England Association of Schools and Colleges, and state department of education. Language of instruction: English. Total enrollment: 193. Upper school average class size: 15. Upper school faculty-student ratio: 1:10. There are 190 required school days per year for Upper School students. Upper School students typically attend 5 days per week. The average school day consists of 6 hours.

Upper School Student Profile Grade 6: 18 students (12 boys, 6 girls); Grade 7: 20 students (8 boys, 12 girls); Grade 8: 23 students (13 boys, 10 girls); Grade 9: 29 students (21 boys, 8 girls); Grade 10: 27 students (16 boys, 11 girls); Grade 11: 30 students (14 boys, 16 girls); Grade 12: 46 students (24 boys, 22 girls).

Faculty School total: 32. In upper school: 8 men, 18 women; 16 have advanced degrees.

Special Academic Programs International Baccalaureate program; ESL.

College Admission Counseling 31 students graduated in 2010; 20 went to college. Other: 1 entered military service, 10 had other specific plans.

Student Life Upper grades have student council. Discipline rests primarily with faculty.

Tuition and Aid Day student tuition: €5800–€7500. Tuition installment plan (monthly payment plans, eight yearly payments).

Admissions Admissions testing required. Deadline for receipt of application materials: none. Application fee required: €250. On-campus interview required.

Athletics Coed Interscholastic: basketball, soccer; coed intramural: baseball, basketball, bicycling, rowing, soccer, tai chi, track and field, volleyball. 4 PE instructors.

Computers Computers are regularly used in all academic classes. Computer network features include online commercial services, Internet access. Student e-mail accounts are available to students. Students grades are available online. The school has a published electronic and media policy.

Contact Alexa Nijpels, Admissions Officer. 31-10 890 7745. Fax: 31-10 8907755. E-mail: info.riss@wolfert.nl. Web site: www.wolfert.nl/riss/.

ROUTT HIGH SCHOOL

500 East College
Jacksonville, Illinois 62650
Head of School: Mr. Gale Thoroman

General Information Coeducational day college-preparatory, arts, business, and religious studies school, affiliated with Roman Catholic Church; primarily serves students with learning disabilities and individuals with Attention Deficit Disorder. Grades 9–12. Founded: 1902. Setting: small town. Nearest major city is Springfield. 3-acre campus. 1 building on campus. Approved or accredited by North Central Association of Colleges and Schools and Illinois Department of Education. Total enrollment: 131. Upper school average class size: 15. Upper school faculty-student ratio: 1:8. There are 176 required school days per year for Upper School students. Upper School students typically attend 5 days per week. The average school day consists of 6 hours and 30 minutes.

Upper School Student Profile Grade 9: 33 students (16 boys, 17 girls); Grade 10: 36 students (20 boys, 16 girls); Grade 11: 33 students (19 boys, 14 girls); Grade 12: 29 students (17 boys, 12 girls). 75% of students are Roman Catholic.

Faculty School total: 18. In upper school: 5 men, 13 women; 4 have advanced degrees.

Subjects Offered Advanced computer applications, Advanced Placement courses, algebra, American history-AP, American literature-AP, band, biology, calculus, Catholic belief and practice, chemistry, composition, drama, earth science, economics-AP, English, English literature-AP, environmental science, French, geography, geometry, government, health, history of the Catholic Church, Life of Christ, physical education, physics, psychology, public speaking, sociology, Spanish, U.S. history-AP, world history, world religions.

Graduation Requirements 15 community service hours per year (60 total).

Special Academic Programs 2 Advanced Placement exams for which test preparation is offered; honors section; study at local college for college credit; remedial reading and/or remedial writing; remedial math.

College Admission Counseling 32 students graduated in 2009; 31 went to college, including Southern Illinois University Edwardsville; Western Illinois University. Other: 1 went to work. Median composite ACT: 20. 16% scored over 26 on composite ACT.

Student Life Upper grades have uniform requirement, student council, honor system. Discipline rests primarily with faculty. Attendance at religious services is required.

Tuition and Aid Day student tuition: $3700. Tuition installment plan (FACTS Tuition Payment Plan). Tuition reduction for siblings, merit scholarship grants, need-based scholarship grants available. In 2009–10, 100% of upper-school students received aid; total upper-school merit-scholarship money awarded: $3500.

Admissions Traditional secondary-level entrance grade is 9. ACT-Explore required. Deadline for receipt of application materials: none. No application fee required. Interview required.

Athletics Interscholastic: baseball (boys), basketball (b,g), cheering (g), dance team (g), football (b), golf (b), softball (g), swimming and diving (b,g), track and field (b,g), volleyball (g); intramural: pom squad (g); coed intramural: bocce, cooperative games. 1 PE instructor, 10 coaches.

Computers Computers are regularly used in computer applications, desktop publishing, journalism, keyboarding, photojournalism, Web site design, word processing, yearbook classes. Computer network features include Internet access, Internet filtering or blocking technology. The school has a published electronic and media policy.

Contact Mr. Dude Wildrick, Counselor. 217-243-5323. Fax: 217-243-3138. E-mail: dwildrick@routtcatholic.com. Web site: www.routtcatholic.com.

ROWLAND HALL

843 South Lincoln Street
Salt Lake City, Utah 84102
Head of School: Mr. Alan C. Sparrow

General Information Coeducational day college-preparatory school. Grades PK–12. Founded: 1867. Setting: urban. 4-acre campus. 1 building on campus. Approved or accredited by National Association of Episcopal Schools, Northwest Accreditation Commission, Northwest Association of Schools and Colleges, Pacific Northwest Association of Independent Schools, The College Board, and Utah Department of Education. Member of National Association of Independent Schools. Endowment: $4 million. Total enrollment: 985. Upper school average class size: 16. Upper school faculty-student ratio: 1:8. There are 170 required school days per year for Upper School students. Upper School students typically attend 5 days per week. The average school day consists of 5 hours and 16 minutes.

Upper School Student Profile Grade 9: 76 students (42 boys, 34 girls); Grade 10: 79 students (43 boys, 36 girls); Grade 11: 67 students (27 boys, 40 girls); Grade 12: 64 students (35 boys, 29 girls).

Faculty School total: 38. In upper school: 19 men, 19 women; 28 have advanced degrees.

Subjects Offered Adolescent issues, algebra, biology, biology-AP, calculus, calculus-AP, ceramics, chemistry, chemistry-AP, Chinese, chorus, computer graphics, creative writing, dance, debate, drama, English, English language and composition-AP, English literature and composition-AP, environmental science, ethics, European history-AP, filmmaking, French, French language-AP, French literature-AP, geometry, graphic arts, graphic design, history, human development, intro to computers, jazz band, Latin, Latin-AP, math applications, modern European history-AP, newspaper, orchestra, photography, physical education, physics, physics-AP, political science, pre-calculus, psychology-AP, Spanish, Spanish-AP, speech and debate, statistics-AP, studio art, studio art-AP, theater, trigonometry, U.S. history, U.S. history-AP, Web site design, weight training, Western civilization, world cultures, world religions, yearbook.

Graduation Requirements American history, arts and fine arts (art, music, dance, drama), biology, chemistry, English, ethics, foreign language, health education, mathematics, physical education (includes health), science, social studies (includes history), world religions.

Special Academic Programs 17 Advanced Placement exams for which test preparation is offered; honors section; independent study.

College Admission Counseling 61 students graduated in 2010; 60 went to college, including Scripps College; University of Redlands; University of Utah; Wake Forest University; Westminster College. Other: 1 had other specific plans. Mean SAT critical reading: 653, mean SAT math: 641, mean SAT writing: 645, mean composite ACT: 28. 71% scored over 600 on SAT critical reading, 73% scored over 600 on SAT math, 67% scored over 600 on SAT writing, 73% scored over 26 on composite ACT.

Student Life Upper grades have specified standards of dress, student council, honor system. Discipline rests equally with students and faculty.

Summer Programs Enrichment, advancement, sports, art/fine arts, computer instruction programs offered; session focuses on advancement and elective courses; held on campus; accepts boys and girls; open to students from other schools. 60 students usually enrolled. 2011 schedule: June 20 to July 29. Application deadline: none.

Tuition and Aid Day student tuition: $16,340. Tuition installment plan (monthly payment plans, individually arranged payment plans, 2-installment plan). Merit scholarship grants, need-based scholarship grants, diversity scholarship grants available. In 2010–11, 21% of upper-school students received aid; total upper-school merit-scholarship money awarded: $49,500. Total amount of financial aid awarded in 2010–11: $344,700.

Admissions Traditional secondary-level entrance grade is 9. For fall 2010, 49 students applied for upper-level admission, 33 were accepted, 30 enrolled. ACT-Explore, ERB CTP IV, ISEE, TOEFL or writing sample required. Deadline for receipt of application materials: March 1. Application fee required: $50. Interview recommended.

Athletics Interscholastic: baseball (boys), basketball (b,g), golf (b,g), skiing (downhill) (b,g), soccer (b,g), softball (g), swimming and diving (b,g), tennis (b,g), volleyball (g); intramural: alpine skiing (b,g), skiing (downhill) (b,g); coed interscholastic: cross-country running, dance, modern dance, physical fitness, physical training, ropes courses, strength & conditioning; coed intramural: climbing, deck hockey, hiking/backpacking, mountain biking, outdoor activities, outdoor education, rock climbing, skiing (cross-country), snowboarding, swimming and diving, telemark skiing, weight training, yoga. 6 PE instructors, 12 coaches, 2 athletic trainers.

Computers Computers are regularly used in desktop publishing, graphic design, yearbook classes. Computer network features include on-campus library services, Internet access, wireless campus network, Internet filtering or blocking technology, all students have their own laptop computer. Campus intranet, student e-mail accounts, and computer access in designated common areas are available to students. Students grades are available online. The school has a published electronic and media policy.

Contact Karen Hyde, Director of Admission. 801-924-5940. Fax: 801-355-0474. E-mail: karenhyde@rowlandhall.org. Web site: www.rowlandhall.org.

THE ROXBURY LATIN SCHOOL

101 St. Theresa Avenue
West Roxbury, Massachusetts 02132
Head of School: Mr. Kerry Paul Brennan

General Information Boys' day college-preparatory school. Grades 7–12. Founded: 1645. Setting: urban. Nearest major city is Boston. 117-acre campus. 10 buildings on campus. Approved or accredited by Association of Independent Schools in New England, Headmasters' Conference, and New England Association of Schools and Colleges. Member of National Association of Independent Schools and Secondary School Admission Test Board. Endowment: $100 million. Total enrollment: 296. Upper school average class size: 14. Upper school faculty-student ratio: 1:8. There are 176 required school days per year for Upper School students. Upper School students typically attend 5 days per week. The average school day consists of 6 hours and 30 minutes.

Upper School Student Profile Grade 7: 45 students (45 boys); Grade 8: 43 students (43 boys); Grade 9: 52 students (52 boys); Grade 10: 53 students (53 boys); Grade 11: 52 students (52 boys); Grade 12: 51 students (51 boys).

Faculty School total: 38. In upper school: 33 men, 5 women; 31 have advanced degrees.

Subjects Offered Advanced chemistry, advanced math, advanced studio art-AP, algebra, American Civil War, American government, American history, American literature, analytic geometry, Ancient Greek, ancient history, ancient world history, art, art history, art history-AP, arts, biology, calculus, calculus-AP, chemistry, classical Greek literature, classical language, college counseling, college placement, computer science, computer science-AP, creative writing, drama, earth science, economics, economics-AP, English, English literature, European history, expository writing, fine arts, French, French literature-AP, geometry, government/civics, grammar, Greek, history, history-AP, Latin, Latin-AP, life science, macro/microeconomics-AP, mathematics, mathematics-AP, Middle East, music, music theory-AP, personal development, photography, physical education, physical science, physics, science, senior project, Spanish, statistics-AP, studio art, studio art-AP, theater, trigonometry, U.S. government and politics-AP, U.S. history-AP, Western civilization, world history, writing.

Graduation Requirements Arts, arts and fine arts (art, music, dance, drama), computer science, English, foreign language, Latin, mathematics, physical education (includes health), science, social studies (includes history), U.S. history, independent senior project.

Special Academic Programs Advanced Placement exam preparation; honors section; independent study; academic accommodation for the gifted, the musically talented, and the artistically talented.

College Admission Counseling 50 students graduated in 2010; all went to college, including Boston College; Boston University; College of the Holy Cross; Dartmouth College; Georgetown University; Harvard University. Median SAT critical reading: 760, median SAT math: 750, median SAT writing: 740, median combined SAT: 2250. 98% scored over 600 on SAT critical reading, 100% scored over 600 on SAT math, 98% scored over 600 on SAT writing, 100% scored over 1800 on combined SAT.

Student Life Upper grades have specified standards of dress, student council, honor system. Discipline rests equally with students and faculty.

Summer Programs Enrichment, sports, computer instruction programs offered; held on campus; accepts boys and girls; open to students from other schools.

Tuition and Aid Day student tuition: $20,800. Tuition installment plan (Insured Tuition Payment Plan, Key Tuition Payment Plan, 2-payment plan). Need-based scholarship grants available. In 2010–11, 39% of upper-school students received aid. Total amount of financial aid awarded in 2010–11: $1,775,370.

Admissions Traditional secondary-level entrance grade is 7. For fall 2010, 446 students applied for upper-level admission, 71 were accepted, 59 enrolled. ISEE or SSAT required. Deadline for receipt of application materials: January 7. No application fee required. On-campus interview required.

Athletics Interscholastic: baseball, basketball, cross-country running, football, ice hockey, lacrosse, soccer, tennis, track and field, wrestling. 1 PE instructor, 11 coaches, 1 athletic trainer.

Computers Computers are regularly used in all academic, desktop publishing, literary magazine, newspaper, yearbook classes. Computer network features include on-campus library services, online commercial services, Internet access, Internet filtering or blocking technology. Campus intranet, student e-mail accounts, and computer access in designated common areas are available to students. The school has a published electronic and media policy.

Contact Ms. Lindsay Schuyler, Assistant Director of Admission. 617-325-4920. Fax: 617-325-3585. E-mail: admission@roxburylatin.org. Web site: www.roxburylatin.org.

ROYAL CANADIAN COLLEGE

8610 Ash Street
Vancouver, British Columbia V6P 3M2, Canada
Head of School: Mr. Howard H. Jiang

General Information Coeducational day college-preparatory and general academic school. Grades 8–12. Founded: 1989. Setting: suburban. 1-acre campus. 1 building on campus. Approved or accredited by British Columbia Department of Education. Language of instruction: English. Total enrollment: 54. Upper school average class size: 20. Upper school faculty-student ratio: 1:15. There are 197 required school days per year for Upper School students. Upper School students typically attend 5 days per week. The average school day consists of 5 hours.

Upper School Student Profile Grade 9: 3 students (2 boys, 1 girl); Grade 10: 10 students (6 boys, 4 girls); Grade 11: 13 students (9 boys, 4 girls); Grade 12: 28 students (18 boys, 10 girls).

Faculty School total: 5. In upper school: 5 men.

Subjects Offered 20th century world history, accounting, applied skills, biology, calculus, Canadian geography, Canadian history, career planning, chemistry, communications, computer science, computer science-AP, drama, economics, English, ESL, fine arts, general science, history, information technology, Mandarin, mathematics, physical education, physics, social sciences, world history, writing.

Graduation Requirements Applied skills, arts and fine arts (art, music, dance, drama), career and personal planning, language arts, mathematics, science, social studies (includes history).

Special Academic Programs ESL (12 students enrolled).

College Admission Counseling 25 students graduated in 2010; 24 went to college, including McGill University; McMaster University; Simon Fraser University; The University of British Columbia; University of Toronto. Other: 1 had other specific plans.

Royal Canadian College

Student Life Upper grades have student council, honor system. Discipline rests primarily with faculty.

Summer Programs ESL programs offered; session focuses on learning survival English conversational skills, and Canadian cultural experience; held on campus; accepts boys and girls; open to students from other schools. 30 students usually enrolled. 2011 schedule: July 4 to August 26. Application deadline: May 31.

Tuition and Aid Day student tuition: CAN$13,500. Merit scholarship grants available. Total upper-school merit-scholarship money awarded for 2010–11: CAN$10,000.

Admissions Traditional secondary-level entrance grade is 11. For fall 2010, 18 students applied for upper-level admission, 17 were accepted, 17 enrolled. English language required. Deadline for receipt of application materials: none. Application fee required: CAN$200. Interview recommended.

Athletics Intramural: badminton (boys, girls), baseball (b,g), basketball (b,g), soccer (b,g), ultimate Frisbee (b,g); coed intramural: badminton, baseball, soccer, ultimate Frisbee. 1 PE instructor.

Computers Computers are regularly used in accounting, career exploration, English, information technology, programming, science, social studies classes. Computer network features include Internet access, wireless campus network, Internet filtering or blocking technology. Computer access in designated common areas is available to students.

Contact Mr. Jeffry Yip, Senior Administrator. 604-738-2221. Fax: 604-738-2282. E-mail: info@royalcanadiancollege.com. Web site: www.royalcanadiancollege.com.

ROYCEMORE SCHOOL

640 Lincoln Street
Evanston, Illinois 60201
Head of School: Mr. Joseph A. Becker

General Information Coeducational day college-preparatory and arts school. Grades PK–12. Founded: 1915. Setting: suburban. Nearest major city is Chicago. 1-acre campus. 1 building on campus. Approved or accredited by Independent Schools Association of the Central States and Illinois Department of Education. Member of National Association of Independent Schools. Endowment: $1 million. Total enrollment: 262. Upper school average class size: 9. Upper school faculty-student ratio: 1:5. There are 165 required school days per year for Upper School students. Upper School students typically attend 5 days per week. The average school day consists of 7 hours.

Upper School Student Profile Grade 9: 14 students (7 boys, 7 girls); Grade 10: 19 students (11 boys, 8 girls); Grade 11: 33 students (18 boys, 15 girls); Grade 12: 27 students (18 boys, 9 girls).

Faculty School total: 37. In upper school: 5 men, 15 women; 14 have advanced degrees.

Subjects Offered African-American literature, algebra, American literature, art, biology, biology-AP, calculus-AP, chemistry, choir, comedy, composition, drawing, English language and composition-AP, English literature, environmental science, European history-AP, French, French-AP, geometry, government/civics, human development, independent study, international relations, introduction to theater, literature-AP, microeconomics, modern European history, music composition, music history, music theory, music theory-AP, mythology, painting, physical education, physics, physics-AP, pottery, public speaking, sculpture, society, politics and law, sociology, Spanish, Spanish-AP, studio art-AP, trigonometry, U.S. history, U.S. history-AP, world history, world literature, world religions, yearbook.

Graduation Requirements Arts and fine arts (art, music, dance, drama), English, foreign language, mathematics, physical education (includes health), science, social studies (includes history), participation in a 2-week January short-term project each year.

Special Academic Programs 10 Advanced Placement exams for which test preparation is offered; accelerated programs; independent study; study at local college for college credit.

College Admission Counseling 16 students graduated in 2010; all went to college, including Columbia University; DePaul University; Purdue University; The George Washington University; University of Illinois at Urbana–Champaign. Median SAT critical reading: 560, median SAT math: 650, median SAT writing: 620, median combined SAT: 1830, median composite ACT: 24. 44% scored over 600 on SAT critical reading, 67% scored over 600 on SAT math, 56% scored over 600 on SAT writing, 56% scored over 1800 on combined SAT, 46% scored over 26 on composite ACT.

Student Life Upper grades have specified standards of dress, student council, honor system. Discipline rests primarily with faculty.

Tuition and Aid Day student tuition: $22,810. Tuition installment plan (individually arranged payment plans, semiannual payment plan, 9-month payment plan). Merit scholarship grants, need-based scholarship grants, discounts for children of Northwestern University and NorthShore University, HealthSystem employees available. In 2010–11, 57% of upper-school students received aid; total upper-school merit-scholarship money awarded: $123,000. Total amount of financial aid awarded in 2010–11: $620,400.

Admissions Traditional secondary-level entrance grade is 9. For fall 2010, 28 students applied for upper-level admission, 20 were accepted, 15 enrolled. Any standardized test or writing sample required. Deadline for receipt of application materials: none. Application fee required: $75. Interview required.

Athletics Interscholastic: basketball (boys, girls), volleyball (g); intramural: softball (b), strength & conditioning (b), volleyball (b); coed interscholastic: soccer; coed intramural: gymnastics, table tennis. 3 PE instructors, 2 coaches.

Computers Computers are regularly used in all academic classes. Computer network features include on-campus library services, Internet access, wireless campus network. The school has a published electronic and media policy.

Contact Ms. Jessica Acee, Director of Admissions. 847-866-6055. Fax: 847-866-6545. E-mail: jacee@roycemoreschool.org. Web site: www.roycemoreschool.org.

RUDOLF STEINER SCHOOL

15 East 78th Street
New York, New York 10075
Head of School: Mr. Josh Eisen

General Information Coeducational day college-preparatory and arts school. Grades PK–12. Founded: 1928. Setting: urban. 2 buildings on campus. Approved or accredited by Association of Waldorf Schools of North America, National Independent Private Schools Association, New York State Association of Independent Schools, and New York Department of Education. Member of National Association of Independent Schools. Endowment: $1 million. Total enrollment: 320. Upper school average class size: 22. Upper school faculty-student ratio: 1:4.

Upper School Student Profile Grade 9: 25 students (14 boys, 11 girls); Grade 10: 19 students (11 boys, 8 girls); Grade 11: 25 students (16 boys, 9 girls); Grade 12: 17 students (6 boys, 11 girls).

Faculty School total: 60. In upper school: 8 men, 14 women; 10 have advanced degrees.

Subjects Offered African drumming, African history, algebra, American literature, anatomy, ancient history, art history, Asian history, atomic theory, biology, bookbinding, botany, British literature, calculus, calligraphy, carpentry, chamber groups, chemistry, chorus, classical Greek literature, computer programming, creative writing, drama, drama workshop, drawing, earth science, electronics, environmental science, epic literature, eurythmy, expository writing, fine arts, French, genetics, geology, geometry, German, grammar, history of architecture, history of computing, history of drama, history of mathematics, history of music, inorganic chemistry, jazz band, Latin American history, logarithms, logic, medieval history, medieval literature, modern European history, Native American history, oil painting, optics, orchestra, organic chemistry, philosophy, physical education, physics, poetry, projective geometry, Russian literature, SAT preparation, sculpture, Spanish, speech, U.S. history, water color painting, weaving, word processing, world history, world literature, zoology.

Graduation Requirements Arts and fine arts (art, music, dance, drama), computer science, English, foreign language, mathematics, physical education (includes health), science, senior internship, social sciences, social studies (includes history), community service program requirements, fine art and music are part of the required curriculum. Community service is required.

Special Academic Programs Independent study; term-away projects; study abroad.

College Admission Counseling 16 students graduated in 2009; all went to college, including Hunter College of the City University of New York; New York University; Smith College; Vassar College.

Student Life Upper grades have specified standards of dress, student council. Discipline rests primarily with faculty.

Tuition and Aid Day student tuition: $30,350. Tuition installment plan (Academic Management Services Plan, monthly payment plans, individually arranged payment plans, tuition assistance). Need-based scholarship grants available. In 2009–10, 40% of upper-school students received aid.

Admissions Traditional secondary-level entrance grade is 9. ISEE required. Deadline for receipt of application materials: January 30. Application fee required: $55. On-campus interview required.

Athletics Interscholastic: basketball (boys, girls), softball (b,g), volleyball (g); coed interscholastic: cross-country running, soccer, track and field; coed intramural: aerobics, climbing, fencing, hiking/backpacking, independent competitive sports, Newcombe ball, outdoor adventure, outdoor education, outdoor recreation, outdoors, ropes courses, tai chi, yoga. 3 PE instructors, 4 coaches.

Computers Computers are regularly used in English, history, mathematics, science classes. Computer network features include on-campus library services, Internet access.

Contact Julia Hays, Director of Upper School Admissions. 212-879-1101 Ext. 340. Fax: 212-794-1554. E-mail: jhays@steiner.edu. Web site: www.steiner.edu.

RUMSEY HALL SCHOOL

Washington Depot, Connecticut
See Junior Boarding Schools section.

RUNDLE COLLEGE

4411 Manitoba Road SE
Calgary, Alberta T2G 4B9, Canada
Head of School: Mtro. David Hauk

General Information Coeducational day college-preparatory, arts, business, bilingual studies, and technology school. Grades PK–12. Founded: 1985. Setting:

suburban. 5-acre campus. 1 building on campus. Approved or accredited by Association of Independent Schools and Colleges of Alberta and Alberta Department of Education. Language of instruction: English. Total enrollment: 783. Upper school average class size: 14. Upper school faculty-student ratio: 1:14. There are 187 required school days per year for Upper School students. Upper School students typically attend 5 days per week. The average school day consists of 5 hours and 36 minutes.

Upper School Student Profile Grade 6: 56 students (26 boys, 30 girls); Grade 7: 84 students (46 boys, 38 girls); Grade 8: 84 students (35 boys, 49 girls); Grade 9: 84 students (46 boys, 38 girls); Grade 10: 83 students (43 boys, 40 girls); Grade 11: 82 students (43 boys, 39 girls); Grade 12: 80 students (36 boys, 44 girls).

Faculty School total: 70. In upper school: 11 men, 14 women; 4 have advanced degrees.

Subjects Offered Accounting, art, band, biology, calculus, chemistry, computer science, drama, English, French, general science, mathematics, physical education, physics, science, social studies, Spanish, theater.

Graduation Requirements Career and personal planning, English, mathematics, physical education (includes health), science, social sciences.

Special Academic Programs Honors section; study abroad.

College Admission Counseling 80 students graduated in 2010; 78 went to college, including The University of British Columbia; The University of Western Ontario; University of Alberta; University of Calgary; University of Victoria; University of Waterloo. Other: 2 had other specific plans.

Student Life Upper grades have uniform requirement, student council, honor system. Discipline rests primarily with faculty.

Tuition and Aid Day student tuition: CAN$12,000. Tuition installment plan (monthly payment plans). Bursaries, merit scholarship grants available. In 2010–11, 1% of upper-school students received aid; total upper-school merit-scholarship money awarded: CAN$24,000. Total amount of financial aid awarded in 2010–11: CAN$24,000.

Admissions Traditional secondary-level entrance grade is 10. For fall 2010, 50 students applied for upper-level admission, 25 were accepted, 20 enrolled. Achievement tests and SSAT or WISC III required. Deadline for receipt of application materials: none. Application fee required: CAN$100. On-campus interview required.

Athletics Interscholastic: badminton (boys, girls), basketball (b,g), cross-country running (b,g), curling (b,g), dance squad (b,g), flag football (b,g), floor hockey (b,g), football (b), golf (b,g), rugby (b,g), soccer (b,g), track and field (b,g), volleyball (b,g), wrestling (b,g); intramural: aerobics (g), badminton (b,g), dance (g), football (b); coed interscholastic: badminton, softball; coed intramural: badminton, baseball, basketball, cross-country running, flag football, football, lacrosse, outdoor recreation, skiing (downhill), soccer, table tennis, track and field, volleyball, weight lifting, wrestling. 4 PE instructors.

Computers Computers are regularly used in all classes. Computer network features include Internet access, wireless campus network, Web page hosting, multimedia productions, streaming video student news. Student e-mail accounts are available to students. The school has a published electronic and media policy.

Contact Lynn Moriarity, Director of Admissions. 403-291-3866 Ext. 106. Fax: 403-291-5458. E-mail: moriarity@rundle.ab.ca. Web site: www.rundle.ab.ca.

RUTGERS PREPARATORY SCHOOL

1345 Easton Avenue
Somerset, New Jersey 08873
Head of School: Dr. Steven A. Loy

General Information Coeducational day college-preparatory and arts school. Grades PK–12. Founded: 1766. Setting: suburban. Nearest major city is New York, NY. 37-acre campus. 8 buildings on campus. Approved or accredited by Middle States Association of Colleges and Schools and New Jersey Association of Independent Schools. Member of National Association of Independent Schools and Secondary School Admission Test Board. Endowment: $6 million. Total enrollment: 702. Upper school average class size: 14. Upper school faculty-student ratio: 1:6.

Upper School Student Profile Grade 9: 85 students (44 boys, 41 girls); Grade 10: 87 students (53 boys, 34 girls); Grade 11: 74 students (38 boys, 36 girls); Grade 12: 89 students (43 boys, 46 girls).

Faculty School total: 105. In upper school: 29 men, 31 women; 42 have advanced degrees.

Subjects Offered Algebra, American history, American literature, architecture, art, art history, astronomy, biology, calculus, ceramics, chemistry, classics, community service, comparative religion, computer programming, computer science, creative writing, discrete mathematics, drama, driver education, economics, English, English literature, environmental science, European history, fine arts, foundations of civilization, French, geometry, government/civics, health, history, Japanese, Latin, literature, mathematics, media, multimedia, music, photography, physical education, physical science, physics, poetry, psychology, psychology-AP, science, Shakespeare, social studies, Spanish, statistics, theater, word processing, world history, writing.

Graduation Requirements Arts and fine arts (art, music, dance, drama), computer science, English, foreign language, mathematics, physical education (includes health), science, social studies (includes history). Community service is required.

Special Academic Programs Advanced Placement exam preparation; honors section; independent study; term-away projects; academic accommodation for the gifted, the musically talented, and the artistically talented.

College Admission Counseling 89 students graduated in 2009; all went to college, including American University; Brown University; Rutgers, The State University of New Jersey, Rutgers College; Syracuse University; The George Washington University; University of Pennsylvania. Mean SAT critical reading: 624, mean SAT math: 632, mean SAT writing: 640. 60.7% scored over 600 on SAT critical reading, 64% scored over 600 on SAT math, 65% scored over 600 on SAT writing.

Student Life Upper grades have specified standards of dress, student council, honor system. Discipline rests primarily with faculty.

Tuition and Aid Day student tuition: $24,900. Tuition installment plan (Key Tuition Payment Plan, individually arranged payment plans, Tuition Management Systems). Need-based scholarship grants, need-based financial aid, Key Education Resources available. In 2009–10, 20% of upper-school students received aid. Total amount of financial aid awarded in 2009–10: $1,011,793.

Admissions Traditional secondary-level entrance grade is 9. For fall 2009, 129 students applied for upper-level admission, 76 were accepted, 46 enrolled. Iowa Tests of Basic Skills and SSAT required. Deadline for receipt of application materials: none. Application fee required: $75. On-campus interview required.

Athletics Interscholastic: baseball (boys), basketball (b,g), lacrosse (b,g); intramural: dance team (g); coed interscholastic: cross-country running, golf. 6 PE instructors, 8 coaches, 1 athletic trainer.

Computers Computers are regularly used in English, foreign language, history, mathematics, music, science classes. Computer network features include on-campus library services, online commercial services, Internet access, wireless campus network, Internet filtering or blocking technology, laptops.

Contact Audrey Forte, Admission Assistant. 732-545-5600 Ext. 261. Fax: 732-214-1819. E-mail: forte@rutgersprep.org. Web site: www.rutgersprep.org.

RYE COUNTRY DAY SCHOOL

Cedar Street
Rye, New York 10580-2034
Head of School: Mr. Scott A. Nelson

General Information Coeducational day college-preparatory, arts, and technology school. Grades PK–12. Founded: 1869. Setting: suburban. Nearest major city is New York. 30-acre campus. 8 buildings on campus. Approved or accredited by New York State Association of Independent Schools and New York Department of Education. Member of National Association of Independent Schools and Secondary School Admission Test Board. Endowment: $23 million. Total enrollment: 876. Upper school average class size: 13. Upper school faculty-student ratio: 1:7. There are 165 required school days per year for Upper School students. Upper School students typically attend 5 days per week. The average school day consists of 6 hours and 50 minutes.

Upper School Student Profile Grade 9: 95 students (52 boys, 43 girls); Grade 10: 94 students (47 boys, 47 girls); Grade 11: 99 students (48 boys, 51 girls); Grade 12: 97 students (53 boys, 44 girls).

Faculty School total: 130. In upper school: 27 men, 31 women; 49 have advanced degrees.

Subjects Offered 20th century history, algebra, American history, American history-AP, American literature, American literature-AP, art, art history, art history-AP, art-AP, astronomy, biology, biology-AP, calculus, calculus-AP, ceramics, chemistry, chemistry-AP, chorus, classics, computer music, computer programming, computer science-AP, computer-aided design, CPR, creative writing, dance, drama, driver education, economics, English, English literature, English literature-AP, English-AP, environmental science, environmental science-AP, European history, European history-AP, expository writing, fencing, fine arts, forensics, French, French-AP, geometry, government, government and politics-AP, government-AP, Greek, health, history, honors English, honors geometry, independent study, instrumental music, interdisciplinary studies, jazz band, Latin, Latin-AP, Mandarin, mathematics, mechanical drawing, modern European history-AP, music, music theory-AP, oceanography, philosophy, photography, physical education, physics, physics-AP, psychology, psychology-AP, science, social studies, Spanish, Spanish-AP, speech, squash, statistics-AP, studio art-AP, The 20th Century, the Sixties, theater, theater arts, trigonometry, U.S. government and politics-AP, U.S. history, U.S. history-AP, U.S. literature, weight training, wind ensemble, world civilizations, writing.

Graduation Requirements Arts and fine arts (art, music, dance, drama), English, foreign language, life management skills, mathematics, physical education (includes health), science, social studies (includes history).

Special Academic Programs 26 Advanced Placement exams for which test preparation is offered; honors section; independent study; academic accommodation for the gifted; special instructional classes for deaf students.

College Admission Counseling 97 students graduated in 2010; all went to college, including Northwestern University; University of Pennsylvania; University of Richmond; Vanderbilt University; Washington University in St. Louis; Yale University. Mean SAT critical reading: 671, mean SAT math: 688, mean SAT writing: 680, mean combined SAT: 2039.

Student Life Upper grades have student council. Discipline rests primarily with faculty.

Summer Programs Remediation, enrichment, advancement, ESL, sports, art/fine arts, computer instruction programs offered; session focuses on remediation; held on campus; accepts boys and girls; open to students from other schools. 200 students usually enrolled. 2011 schedule: June 27 to August 5. Application deadline: June 1.

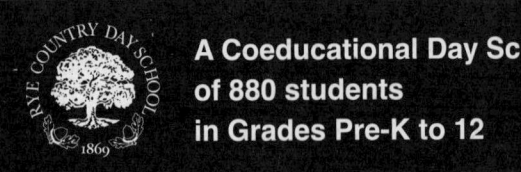

A Coeducational Day School
of 880 students
in Grades Pre-K to 12

Rye Country Day School

RCDS students enjoy the benefits of:

- A challenging, age-appropriate curriculum

- Advanced Placement in 23 subject areas with outstanding results

- A state-of-the-art technology department and a laptop program in Grades 7 - 12

- A competitive, interscholastic athletic program offering 65 teams for girls and boys in 18 sports

- A strong performing arts program

- College counseling that provides individual attention resulting in a highly selective placement history

**Rye Country Day School
Cedar Street
Rye, New York 10580**

914.925.4513
www.RyeCountryDay.org

Tuition and Aid Day student tuition: $31,500. Tuition installment plan (monthly payment plans, individually arranged payment plans). Need-based scholarship grants available. In 2010–11, 19% of upper-school students received aid. Total amount of financial aid awarded in 2010–11: $2,034,603.

Admissions Traditional secondary-level entrance grade is 9. For fall 2010, 188 students applied for upper-level admission, 48 were accepted, 29 enrolled. ISEE or SSAT required. Deadline for receipt of application materials: December 15. Application fee required: $60. On-campus interview required.

Athletics Interscholastic: baseball (boys), basketball (b,g), cross-country running (b,g), fencing (b,g), field hockey (g), football (b), golf (b,g), ice hockey (b,g), lacrosse (b,g), sailing (b,g), soccer (b,g), softball (g), squash (b,g), tennis (b,g), wrestling (b); intramural: basketball (b), fitness (b,g), physical fitness (b,g), physical training (b,g), squash (b,g), strength & conditioning (b,g), tennis (b,g), ultimate Frisbee (b), weight training (b,g), wrestling (b); coed intramural: aerobics/dance, cross-country running, dance, fitness, ice skating, modern dance, running, squash, yoga. 2 PE instructors, 14 coaches, 2 athletic trainers.

Computers Computers are regularly used in art, classics, English, foreign language, history, mathematics, music, photography, publishing, science, technology, yearbook classes. Computer network features include on-campus library services, online commercial services, Internet access, wireless campus network, Internet filtering or blocking technology, student and faculty schedules online. Campus intranet and student e-mail accounts are available to students. Students grades are available online. The school has a published electronic and media policy.

Contact Mr. Matthew J.M. Suzuki, Director of Admissions. 914-925-4513. Fax: 914-921-2147. E-mail: matt_suzuki@ryecountryday.org. Web site: www. ryecountryday.org.

See Display on this page and Close-Up on page 828.

SACRAMENTO ADVENTIST ACADEMY
5601 Winding Way
Carmichael, California 95608-1298
Head of School: Bettesue Constanzo

General Information Coeducational day college-preparatory, general academic, arts, business, vocational, religious studies, bilingual studies, and technology school, affiliated with Seventh-day Adventist Church. Grades K–12. Founded: 1957. Setting: suburban. Nearest major city is Sacramento. 36-acre campus. 5 buildings on campus. Approved or accredited by Board of Regents, General Conference of Seventh-day Adventists, National Council for Private School Accreditation, Western Association of Schools and Colleges, and California Department of Education. Total enrollment: 272. Upper school average class size: 29. Upper school faculty-student ratio: 1:12. There are 180 required school days per year for Upper School students. Upper School students typically attend 5 days per week. The average school day consists of 7 hours and 15 minutes.

Upper School Student Profile 96% of students are Seventh-day Adventists.

Faculty School total: 25. In upper school: 8 men, 4 women; 4 have advanced degrees.

Subjects Offered Accounting, advanced math, Advanced Placement courses, algebra, art, band, Bible, biology, biology-AP, business technology, calculus-AP, chemistry, choir, computer applications, computer education, conceptual physics, concert band, consumer mathematics, driver education, economics, English, English composition, English language and composition-AP, geometry, graphic design, handbells, health, health education, keyboarding, life skills, microcomputer technology applications, photography, physical education, physics, public speaking, religion, softball, Spanish, Spanish-AP, speech, technical skills, U.S. government, U.S. history, word processing, world history, world history-AP, World War I.

Graduation Requirements Arts and fine arts (art, music, dance, drama), biology, computer applications, economics, English, keyboarding, life skills, mathematics, physical education (includes health), religion (includes Bible studies and theology), science, U.S. government, U.S. history, 100 hours of documented work experience, 25 hours of documented community service per year of attendance.

Special Academic Programs 4 Advanced Placement exams for which test preparation is offered; honors section; accelerated programs; study at local college for college credit; remedial math.

College Admission Counseling 27 students graduated in 2009; 25 went to college, including American River College; La Sierra University; Pacific Union College; Sierra College; Walla Walla University. Other: 2 went to work. Mean SAT critical reading: 559, mean SAT math: 566, mean composite ACT: 23. 22% scored over 600 on SAT critical reading, 44% scored over 600 on SAT math, 45% scored over 26 on composite ACT.

Student Life Upper grades have specified standards of dress, student council. Discipline rests primarily with faculty.

Tuition and Aid Day student tuition: $5010–$9100. Tuition installment plan (monthly payment plans, individually arranged payment plans). Tuition reduction for siblings, paying campus jobs, academy day scholarships available. In 2009–10, 5% of upper-school students received aid. Total amount of financial aid awarded in 2009–10: $10,000.

Admissions Traditional secondary-level entrance grade is 9. Deadline for receipt of application materials: none. Application fee required: $25. Interview required.

Athletics Interscholastic: baseball (girls), basketball (b,g), flag football (b,g), golf (b), softball (b,g), volleyball (g). 1 PE instructor, 1 coach.

Computers Computers are regularly used in accounting, business applications, English, history, keyboarding, religion, word processing classes. Computer network features include on-campus library services, online commercial services, Internet access.

Contact Mrs. Sheri Miller, Registrar/Guidance Counselor. 916-481-2300 Ext. 102. Fax: 916-481-7426. E-mail: smiller@sacaa.org. Web site: www.sacaa.org.

SACRAMENTO COUNTRY DAY SCHOOL

2636 Latham Drive
Sacramento, California 95864-7198
Head of School: Stephen T. Repsher

General Information Coeducational day college-preparatory, arts, and technology school. Grades PK–12. Founded: 1964. Setting: suburban. 12-acre campus. 8 buildings on campus. Approved or accredited by California Association of Independent Schools and Western Association of Schools and Colleges. Member of National Association of Independent Schools. Total enrollment: 471. Upper school average class size: 12. Upper school faculty-student ratio: 1:9. The average school day consists of 7 hours and 25 minutes.

Upper School Student Profile Grade 9: 46 students (24 boys, 22 girls); Grade 10: 32 students (18 boys, 14 girls); Grade 11: 39 students (18 boys, 21 girls); Grade 12: 37 students (15 boys, 22 girls).

Faculty School total: 110. In upper school: 18 men, 10 women; 19 have advanced degrees.

Subjects Offered Acting, algebra, American history, American literature, ancient history, ancient/medieval philosophy, art, art history, art history-AP, art-AP, band, biology, biology-AP, British literature, calculus, calculus-AP, ceramics, chamber groups, chemistry, chemistry-AP, community service, computer skills, computer technologies, concert band, creative writing, digital imaging, digital music, drama, drama performance, drawing, earth science, economics, English, English literature, European history, fine arts, French, French-AP, geography, geometry, government/civics, grammar, history, international relations, jazz band, journalism, language and composition, Latin, Latin-AP, mathematics, newspaper, nutrition, orchestra, physical education, physics, physics-AP, physiology, pre-calculus, public speaking, science, social studies, Spanish, Spanish-AP, speech, studio art, studio art-AP, technology/design, theater, trigonometry, U.S. history, U.S. history-AP, world history, world literature, writing.

Graduation Requirements Arts and fine arts (art, music, dance, drama), computer science, electives, English, foreign language, history, mathematics, physical education (includes health), science, 40-hour senior project. Community service is required.

Special Academic Programs Advanced Placement exam preparation; independent study; study at local college for college credit.

College Admission Counseling 42 students graduated in 2009; 41 went to college, including California State University, Chico; Saint Mary's College of California; Stanford University; University of California, Santa Cruz; University of Chicago; University of Puget Sound. Other: 1 had other specific plans. Median SAT critical reading: 620, median SAT math: 638, median SAT writing: 644.

Student Life Upper grades have specified standards of dress, student council, honor system. Discipline rests primarily with faculty.

Tuition and Aid Day student tuition: $18,700. Tuition installment plan (Insured Tuition Payment Plan, monthly payment plans, individually arranged payment plans). Need-based scholarship grants available. In 2009–10, 29% of upper-school students received aid. Total amount of financial aid awarded in 2009–10: $499,100.

Admissions Traditional secondary-level entrance grade is 9. For fall 2009, 25 students applied for upper-level admission, 12 were accepted, 9 enrolled. ERB, Otis-Lennon Mental Ability Test and writing sample required. Deadline for receipt of application materials: none. Application fee required: $25. Interview required.

Athletics Interscholastic: baseball (boys), basketball (b,g), cross-country running (b,g), flag football (b), soccer (b,g), softball (g), swimming and diving (b,g), track and field (b,g), volleyball (b,g); coed interscholastic: golf, skiing (downhill), tennis, wrestling. 3 PE instructors, 14 coaches.

Computers Computer network features include on-campus library services, online commercial services, Internet access, Internet filtering or blocking technology. Campus intranet and student e-mail accounts are available to students. The school has a published electronic and media policy.

Contact Lonna Bloedau, Director of Admission. 916-481-8811. Fax: 916-481-6016. E-mail: lbloedau@saccds.org. Web site: www.saccds.org.

SACRAMENTO WALDORF SCHOOL

3750 Bannister Road
Fair Oaks, California 95628
Head of School: Elizabeth Beaven

General Information Coeducational day college-preparatory, general academic, and arts school. Grades PK–12. Founded: 1959. Setting: suburban. Nearest major city is Sacramento. 22-acre campus. 8 buildings on campus. Approved or accredited by Association of Waldorf Schools of North America and Western Association of Schools and Colleges. Endowment: $50,000. Total enrollment: 422. Upper school average class size: 15. Upper school faculty-student ratio: 1:7. There are 170 required school

days per year for Upper School students. Upper School students typically attend 5 days per week. The average school day consists of 6 hours and 30 minutes.

Upper School Student Profile Grade 9: 47 students (20 boys, 27 girls); Grade 10: 32 students (17 boys, 15 girls); Grade 11: 38 students (14 boys, 24 girls); Grade 12: 42 students (17 boys, 25 girls).

Faculty School total: 53. In upper school: 13 men, 14 women; 9 have advanced degrees.

Subjects Offered 20th century American writers, 20th century history, 20th century world history, 3-dimensional art, 3-dimensional design, acting, advanced math, aesthetics, algebra, American government, American history, American literature, anatomy, animal husbandry, applied arts, applied music, architectural drawing, architecture, art, art history, arts, astronomy, band, biology, bookbinding, bookmaking, botany, British literature, calculus, calligraphy, chemistry, choir, choral music, chorus, classical Greek literature, community service, computer education, computer literacy, concert choir, crafts, creative arts, creative thinking, drama, drama performance, drama workshop, dramatic arts, drawing, electives, English, English composition, English literature, ensembles, European civilization, European history, European literature, eurythmy, expressive arts, fabric arts, fiber arts, fine arts, gardening, general math, general science, geology, geometry, German, government/civics, Greek drama, health, honors English, human sexuality, literature, mathematics, medieval history, medieval literature, medieval/Renaissance history, music, music appreciation, music performance, musical productions, orchestra, parent/child development, parenting, participation in sports, performing arts, physical education, physical science, physics, physiology, play production, pottery, pre-calculus, printmaking, Russian literature, science, sculpture, senior career experience, senior project, sex education, sexuality, Shakespeare, Shakespearean histories, social sciences, social studies, Spanish, strings, student publications, studio art, theater, theater arts, theater design and production, theater production, theory of knowledge, trigonometry, U.S. literature, visual and performing arts, visual arts, vocal ensemble, vocal jazz, vocal music, wood lab, woodworking, world arts, world civilizations, world cultures, world geography, world history, world literature, writing, writing workshop, yearbook, zoology.

Graduation Requirements Aesthetics, arts and fine arts (art, music, dance, drama), computer literacy, English, foreign language, mathematics, physical education (includes health), science, senior project, social sciences, social studies (includes history). Community service is required.

Special Academic Programs Honors section; independent study; term-away projects; study abroad.

College Admission Counseling 40 students graduated in 2009; 37 went to college, including Occidental College; Saint Mary's College of California; University of California, Berkeley; University of Puget Sound; University of Redlands. Other: 3 had other specific plans. Median SAT critical reading: 590, median SAT math: 580, median SAT writing: 590, median combined SAT: 1680. 40% scored over 600 on SAT critical reading, 40% scored over 600 on SAT math, 40% scored over 600 on SAT writing, 20% scored over 1800 on combined SAT.

Student Life Upper grades have specified standards of dress, student council, honor system. Discipline rests equally with students and faculty.

Tuition and Aid Day student tuition: $8280–$12,435. Tuition installment plan (Insured Tuition Payment Plan, monthly payment plans, semiannual and annual payment plans). Tuition reduction for siblings, need-based scholarship grants available. In 2009–10, 56% of upper-school students received aid. Total amount of financial aid awarded in 2009–10: $180,474.

Admissions Traditional secondary-level entrance grade is 9. For fall 2009, 61 students applied for upper-level admission, 55 were accepted, 47 enrolled. Math Placement Exam or TOEFL required. Deadline for receipt of application materials: none. Application fee required: $50. Interview required.

Athletics Interscholastic: baseball (boys), basketball (b,g), golf (b), running (b,g), soccer (b,g), volleyball (g); coed interscholastic: aerobics/Nautilus, ball hockey, climbing, combined training, cooperative games, dance, fitness, flag football, floor hockey, Frisbee, kickball, outdoor activities, physical fitness, physical training, pillo polo, touch football, track and field, ultimate Frisbee, winter soccer, yoga. 1 PE instructor, 8 coaches.

Computers Computers are regularly used in college planning, independent study, introduction to technology, mathematics, photography, Web site design, word processing, yearbook classes. Computer network features include Internet access, wireless campus network, Internet filtering or blocking technology, online college and career searches. Campus intranet and computer access in designated common areas are available to students. The school has a published electronic and media policy.

Contact Sharon Caraccio, High School Coordinator. 916-860-2525. Fax: 916-961-3970. E-mail: scaraccio@sacwaldorf.org. Web site: www.sacwaldorf.org.

SACRED HEART ACADEMY

3175 Lexington Road
Louisville, Kentucky 40206
Head of School: Dr. Beverly McAuliffe, EdD

General Information Girls' day college-preparatory, arts, religious studies, and technology school, affiliated with Roman Catholic Church. Grades 9–12. Founded: 1877. Setting: suburban. 46-acre campus. 2 buildings on campus. Approved or accredited by Southern Association of Colleges and Schools and Kentucky Department of Education. Upper school average class size: 21. Upper school faculty-student ratio: 1:15.

Sacred Heart Academy

Upper School Student Profile 87% of students are Roman Catholic.

Faculty School total: 87. In upper school: 9 men, 78 women; 48 have advanced degrees.

Subjects Offered Algebra, American history, American literature, anatomy, art, art history, Bible studies, biology, business, business law, calculus, ceramics, chemistry, computer graphics, computer programming, computer science, creative writing, drama, economics, English, English literature, environmental science, ethics, European history, French, geography, geometry, German, government/civics, grammar, health, history, home economics, journalism, Latin, marketing, mathematics, music, nutrition, physical education, physics, physiology, psychology, religion, science, social studies, sociology, Spanish, speech, statistics, theater, theology, trigonometry, video, world history, world literature, writing.

Graduation Requirements Computer science, English, foreign language, mathematics, physical education (includes health), religion (includes Bible studies and theology), science, social studies (includes history).

Special Academic Programs Advanced Placement exam preparation; honors section; independent study; study at local college for college credit; academic accommodation for the gifted, the musically talented, and the artistically talented.

College Admission Counseling Colleges students went to include Bellarmine University; Miami University; Saint Louis University; University of Kentucky; University of Louisville; Xavier University.

Student Life Upper grades have uniform requirement, student council. Discipline rests primarily with faculty. Attendance at religious services is required.

Tuition and Aid Day student tuition: $5035. Merit scholarship grants, need-based scholarship grants, paying campus jobs available. In 2010–11, 86% of upper-school students received aid; total upper-school merit-scholarship money awarded: $10,500.

Admissions High School Placement Test required. Deadline for receipt of application materials: none. No application fee required. On-campus interview required.

Athletics Interscholastic: basketball, cross-country running, diving, field hockey, golf, soccer, softball, swimming and diving, tennis, track and field, volleyball; intramural: basketball, volleyball. 1 PE instructor, 14 coaches, 1 athletic trainer.

Computers Computers are regularly used in English, mathematics classes. Computer network features include on-campus library services, Internet access, Internet filtering or blocking technology, America Online. Student e-mail accounts and computer access in designated common areas are available to students. Students grades are available online.

Contact Dean of Studies. 502-897-6097. Fax: 502-896-3935. Web site: www. sacredheartschools.org.

SACRED HEART/GRIFFIN HIGH SCHOOL

1200 West Washington
Springfield, Illinois 62702-4794
Head of School: Sr. Katherine O'Connor, OP

General Information Coeducational day college-preparatory, arts, business, vocational, religious studies, and technology school, affiliated with Roman Catholic Church. Grades 9–12. Founded: 1895. Setting: urban. 13-acre campus. 2 buildings on campus. Approved or accredited by North Central Association of Colleges and Schools and Illinois Department of Education. Endowment: $8. Total enrollment: 793. Upper school average class size: 20. Upper school faculty-student ratio: 1:17. There are 181 required school days per year for Upper School students. Upper School students typically attend 5 days per week. The average school day consists of 6 hours and 30 minutes.

Upper School Student Profile Grade 9: 183 students (100 boys, 83 girls). 92% of students are Roman Catholic.

Faculty School total: 60. In upper school: 22 men, 30 women; 24 have advanced degrees.

Subjects Offered Advanced biology.

Graduation Requirements 80 hours of service to community or approved organizations.

Special Academic Programs 8 Advanced Placement exams for which test preparation is offered; honors section; domestic exchange program; academic accommodation for the gifted, the musically talented, and the artistically talented.

College Admission Counseling 214 students graduated in 2009; 208 went to college. Other: 2 entered military service, 4 had other specific plans. Median SAT critical reading: 583, median SAT math: 615, median SAT writing: 596, median composite ACT: 24.

Student Life Upper grades have specified standards of dress, student council, honor system. Discipline rests primarily with faculty. Attendance at religious services is required.

Tuition and Aid Day student tuition: $6375. Tuition installment plan (FACTS Tuition Payment Plan, individually arranged payment plans). Tuition reduction for siblings, merit scholarship grants, need-based scholarship grants available. In 2009–10, 28% of upper-school students received aid; total upper-school merit-scholarship money awarded: $11,000. Total amount of financial aid awarded in 2009–10: $475,000.

Admissions Traditional secondary-level entrance grade is 9. For fall 2009, 220 students applied for upper-level admission, 220 were accepted, 214 enrolled. Explore required. Deadline for receipt of application materials: none. Application fee required: $150. Interview required.

Athletics Interscholastic: aquatics (boys, girls), baseball (b), basketball (b,g), cheering (g), cross-country running (b,g), diving (b,g), football (b), golf (b,g), hockey (b), pom squad (g), softball (g), tennis (b,g), track and field (b,g), volleyball (g). 1 PE instructor, 3 coaches, 1 athletic trainer.

Computers Computers are regularly used in all academic classes. Computer resources include on-campus library services, Internet access, wireless campus network, Internet filtering or blocking technology. Students grades are available online. The school has a published electronic and media policy.

Contact Peggy Egizii, Marketing Coordinator. 217-787-9732. Fax: 217-726-9791. E-mail: egizii@shg.org. Web site: www.shg.org.

SACRED HEART SCHOOL OF HALIFAX

5820 Spring Garden Road
Halifax, Nova Scotia B3H 1X8, Canada
Head of School: Ms. Patricia Donnelly

General Information Coeducational day college-preparatory and religious studies school, affiliated with Roman Catholic Church. Grades K–12. Founded: 1849. Setting: urban. 1 building on campus. Approved or accredited by Canadian Association of Independent Schools, Canadian Educational Standards Institute, and Nova Scotia Department of Education. Language of instruction: English. Total enrollment: 485. Upper school average class size: 18. Upper school faculty-student ratio: 1:15. There are 175 required school days per year for Upper School students. Upper School students typically attend 5 days per week. The average school day consists of 7 hours.

Upper School Student Profile Grade 7: 60 students (18 boys, 42 girls); Grade 8: 55 students (17 boys, 38 girls); Grade 9: 54 students (22 boys, 32 girls); Grade 10: 38 students (11 boys, 27 girls); Grade 11: 37 students (7 boys, 30 girls); Grade 12: 41 students (10 boys, 31 girls). 60% of students are Roman Catholic.

Faculty School total: 65. In upper school: 1 man, 23 women; 11 have advanced degrees.

Subjects Offered 20th century history, 20th century world history, algebra, art, Bible studies, biology, calculus, Canadian history, chemistry, creative writing, earth science, economics, English, English literature, environmental science, European history, expository writing, French, geography, geometry, government/civics, grammar, health, history, mathematics, music, physical education, physics, religion, science, social studies, sociology, Spanish, theater, trigonometry, world history, writing.

Graduation Requirements Arts and fine arts (art, music, dance, drama), English, foreign language, history, mathematics, physical education (includes health), religion (includes Bible studies and theology), science. Community service is required.

Special Academic Programs 8 Advanced Placement exams for which test preparation is offered; honors section; domestic exchange program (with Network of Sacred Heart Schools); study abroad; ESL (19 students enrolled).

College Admission Counseling 25 students graduated in 2010; all went to college, including Carleton University; Dalhousie University; Mount Allison University; St. Francis Xavier University; University of Ottawa.

Student Life Upper grades have uniform requirement, student council, honor system. Discipline rests primarily with faculty. Attendance at religious services is required.

Summer Programs Remediation, enrichment programs offered; session focuses on French remediation, debate; held on campus; accepts boys and girls; open to students from other schools. 15 students usually enrolled. Application deadline: none.

Tuition and Aid Day student tuition: CAN$11,771. Tuition installment plan (monthly payment plans, individually arranged payment plans). Tuition reduction for siblings, bursaries, merit scholarship grants, need-based scholarship grants available. In 2010–11, 12% of upper-school students received aid; total upper-school merit-scholarship money awarded: CAN$106,000. Total amount of financial aid awarded in 2010–11: CAN$138,000.

Admissions Traditional secondary-level entrance grade is 7. For fall 2010, 53 students applied for upper-level admission, 52 were accepted, 50 enrolled. Otis-Lennon School Ability Test and school's own test required. Deadline for receipt of application materials: none. Application fee required: CAN$100. On-campus interview required.

Athletics Interscholastic: aquatics (girls), badminton (b,g), basketball (b,g), cross-country running (b,g), field hockey (g), ice hockey (b), soccer (b,g), swimming and diving (b,g), tennis (g), volleyball (g); intramural: alpine skiing (b,g), badminton (b,g), basketball (b,g), cross-country running (b,g), curling (g), fitness walking (g), jogging (b,g), running (b,g), skiing (downhill) (b,g), soccer (b,g), swimming and diving (b), tennis (g), track and field (g), volleyball (g). 3 PE instructors.

Computers Computer network features include on-campus library services, Internet access, wireless campus network, Internet filtering or blocking technology. Campus intranet and student e-mail accounts are available to students. The school has a published electronic and media policy.

Contact Pauline Mary Scott, Principal, Sacred Heart High School. 902-422-4459 Ext. 209. Fax: 902-423-7691. E-mail: pscott@shsh.ca. Web site: www. sacredheartschool.ns.ca.

SADDLEBACK VALLEY CHRISTIAN SCHOOL

26333 Oso Road
San Juan Capistrano, California 92675
Head of School: Mr. Edward Carney

General Information Coeducational day college-preparatory, general academic, arts, religious studies, and technology school, affiliated with Christian faith. Grades PK–12. Founded: 1997. Setting: suburban. Nearest major city is Irvine/Anaheim. 69-acre campus. 8 buildings on campus. Approved or accredited by Association of Christian Schools International, Western Association of Schools and Colleges, and California Department of Education. Total enrollment: 816. Upper school average class size: 20. Upper school faculty-student ratio: 1:12. There are 180 required school days per year for Upper School students. Upper School students typically attend 5 days per week. The average school day consists of 6 hours and 35 minutes.

Upper School Student Profile Grade 9: 84 students (40 boys, 44 girls); Grade 10: 79 students (40 boys, 39 girls); Grade 11: 67 students (37 boys, 30 girls); Grade 12: 72 students (35 boys, 37 girls). 75% of students are Christian faith.

Faculty School total: 74. In upper school: 9 men, 28 women; 9 have advanced degrees.

Subjects Offered 1½ elective credits, algebra, American history, American history-AP, American literature, American sign language, anatomy and physiology, applied arts, art, art history-AP, ASB Leadership, athletic training, Bible, Bible as literature, biology, biology-AP, British literature, business mathematics, calculus-AP, chemistry, computers, concert choir, debate, drama, English language and composition-AP, English literature and composition-AP, environmental science, ESL, geography, geometry, government and politics-AP, history, honors English, music, musical theater, oceanography, psychology-AP, public speaking, religious studies, science, senior project, Spanish, Spanish language-AP, speech and debate, sports, statistics-AP, studio art-AP, trigonometry, U.S. government and politics, U.S. government and politics-AP, U.S. history, U.S. history, U.S. history-AP, visual and performing arts, world history, world literature, world religions, yearbook.

Graduation Requirements Algebra, American history, American literature, anatomy and physiology, art, Bible, biology, British literature, earth science, English, English literature, foreign language, geometry, history, life science, physical education (includes health), physical science, science, senior project, Spanish, speech, trigonometry, U.S. history, visual arts, world history, Senior Project required for seniors to graduate.

Special Academic Programs 11 Advanced Placement exams for which test preparation is offered; honors section; independent study; study at local college for college credit; study abroad; remedial reading and/or remedial writing; remedial math; programs in English, mathematics, general development for dyslexic students; special instructional classes for students with learning disabilities; ESL (24 students enrolled).

College Admission Counseling 76 students graduated in 2010; 68 went to college, including Azusa Pacific University; Biola University; California Polytechnic State University, San Luis Obispo; Point Loma Nazarene University; University of California, Los Angeles. Other: 6 went to work, 2 entered military service. Median SAT critical reading: 540, median SAT math: 540, median SAT writing: 540, median combined SAT: 1620, median composite ACT: 22. 32% scored over 600 on SAT critical reading, 21% scored over 600 on SAT math, 32% scored over 600 on SAT writing, 26% scored over 1800 on combined SAT, 27% scored over 26 on composite ACT.

Student Life Upper grades have uniform requirement, student council, honor system. Discipline rests primarily with faculty. Attendance at religious services is required.

Summer Programs Remediation programs offered; session focuses on Make-up of school work; held on campus; accepts boys and girls; not open to students from other schools. 10 students usually enrolled. 2011 schedule: June 20 to July 31. Application deadline: June 5.

Tuition and Aid Day student tuition: $7900. Tuition installment plan (monthly payment plans). Tuition reduction for siblings, merit scholarship grants, need-based scholarship grants available. In 2010–11, 25% of upper-school students received aid; total upper-school merit-scholarship money awarded: $175,000. Total amount of financial aid awarded in 2010–11: $175,000.

Admissions Traditional secondary-level entrance grade is 9. For fall 2010, 65 students applied for upper-level admission, 65 were accepted, 60 enrolled. Placement test required. Deadline for receipt of application materials: none. Application fee required: $200. Interview required.

Athletics Interscholastic: baseball (boys), basketball (b,g), cheering (g), cross-country running (b,g), football (b), golf (b,g), soccer (b,g), softball (g), swimming and diving (b,g), tennis (g), track and field (b,g), volleyball (b,g); intramural: equestrian sports (g); coed interscholastic: dance team. 4 PE instructors, 10 coaches, 3 athletic trainers.

Computers Computers are regularly used in computer applications classes. Computer network features include Internet access, Internet filtering or blocking technology. Student e-mail accounts are available to students. Students grades are available online. The school has a published electronic and media policy.

Contact Mrs. Denise Karlsen, Registrar. 949-443-4050. Fax: 949-443-3941 Ext. 1201. E-mail: denisek@svcschools.org. Web site: www.svcschools.org.

SADDLEBROOK PREPARATORY SCHOOL

5700 Saddlebrook Way
Wesley Chapel, Florida 33543
Head of School: Mr. Larry W. Robison

General Information Coeducational boarding and day college-preparatory school. Boarding grades 6–12, day grades 3–12. Founded: 1993. Setting: suburban. Nearest major city is Tampa. Students are housed in single-sex dormitories. 50-acre campus. 8 buildings on campus. Approved or accredited by Florida Council of Independent Schools, Southern Association of Colleges and Schools, and Florida Department of Education. Total enrollment: 89. Upper school average class size: 11. Upper school faculty-student ratio: 1:11. There are 175 required school days per year for Upper School students. Upper School students typically attend 5 days per week. The average school day consists of 7 hours and 15 minutes.

Upper School Student Profile Grade 9: 12 students (6 boys, 6 girls); Grade 10: 15 students (12 boys, 3 girls); Grade 11: 22 students (16 boys, 6 girls); Grade 12: 14 students (9 boys, 5 girls); Postgraduate: 5 students (4 boys, 1 girl). 61% of students are boarding students. 7% are state residents. 16 states are represented in upper school student body. 55% are international students. International students from Germany, India, Mexico, Russian Federation, Switzerland, and Turkey; 13 other countries represented in student body.

Faculty School total: 12. In upper school: 6 men, 3 women; 3 have advanced degrees; 2 reside on campus.

Subjects Offered Algebra, American government, American history, biology, calculus, calculus-AP, chemistry, economics, English, geometry, marine biology, physical science, physics, pre-algebra, pre-calculus, psychology, SAT preparation, Spanish, world geography, world history.

Graduation Requirements American history, English, mathematics, physical education (includes health), science, social studies (includes history).

Special Academic Programs 3 Advanced Placement exams for which test preparation is offered; honors section; ESL (9 students enrolled).

College Admission Counseling 19 students graduated in 2010; 15 went to college, including Lafayette College; Lehigh University; New York University; The University of Alabama; University of Mary Washington; Washington University in St. Louis. Other: 4 entered a postgraduate year.

Student Life Upper grades have uniform requirement, student council, honor system. Discipline rests primarily with faculty.

Summer Programs Remediation, advancement, ESL programs offered; session focuses on academics; held on campus; accepts boys and girls; open to students from other schools. 10 students usually enrolled. 2011 schedule: June 8 to August 2. Application deadline: May 25.

Tuition and Aid Day student tuition: $16,135; 7-day tuition and room/board: $32,015. Tuition installment plan (individually arranged payment plans). Tuition reduction for siblings available.

Admissions For fall 2010, 32 students applied for upper-level admission, 32 were accepted, 29 enrolled. Deadline for receipt of application materials: none. Application fee required: $50. Interview recommended.

Athletics Interscholastic: golf (boys, girls). 25 coaches, 3 athletic trainers.

Computers Computers are regularly used in English, foreign language, history, mathematics, science classes. Computer network features include on-campus library services, online commercial services, Internet access, wireless campus network, Internet filtering or blocking technology, Edline, Homework Hero. Student e-mail accounts and computer access in designated common areas are available to students. Students grades are available online. The school has a published electronic and media policy.

Contact Ms. Donna Claggett, Administrative Manager. 813-907-4525. Fax: 813-991-4713. E-mail: dclaggett@saddlebrookresort.com. Web site: www.saddlebrookprep.com.

SADDLE RIVER DAY SCHOOL

147 Chestnut Ridge Road
Saddle River, New Jersey 07458
Head of School: Eileen F. Lambert

General Information Coeducational day college-preparatory, arts, bilingual studies, and technology school. Grades K–12. Founded: 1957. Setting: suburban. Nearest major city is New York, NY. 26-acre campus. 3 buildings on campus. Approved or accredited by Middle States Association of Colleges and Schools, New Jersey Association of Independent Schools, and New Jersey Department of Education. Member of National Association of Independent Schools and Secondary School Admission Test Board. Endowment: $5 million. Total enrollment: 276. Upper school average class size: 14. Upper school faculty-student ratio: 1:7. There are 160 required school days per year for Upper School students. Upper School students typically attend 5 days per week. The average school day consists of 7 hours.

Upper School Student Profile Grade 9: 32 students (14 boys, 18 girls); Grade 10: 36 students (19 boys, 17 girls); Grade 11: 27 students (16 boys, 11 girls); Grade 12: 46 students (23 boys, 23 girls).

Faculty School total: 56. In upper school: 16 men, 25 women; 21 have advanced degrees.

Subjects Offered Advanced Placement courses, algebra, American history, American literature, anatomy, art, astronomy, bell choir, biology, calculus, chemistry,

computer programming, computer science, concert choir, creative writing, drama, driver education, earth science, economics, English, English literature, European history, finance, fine arts, French, geography, geometry, government/civics, grammar, history, Latin, mathematics, music, physical education, physics, psychology, science, social sciences, social studies, Spanish, theater, trigonometry, world history, writing.
Graduation Requirements Arts and fine arts (art, music, dance, drama), computer science, English, foreign language, mathematics, physical education (includes health), science, social sciences, social studies (includes history).
Special Academic Programs 12 Advanced Placement exams for which test preparation is offered; honors section; term-away projects; study abroad; academic accommodation for the gifted, the musically talented, and the artistically talented.
College Admission Counseling 30 students graduated in 2009; 28 went to college, including Boston University; Brandeis University; Lafayette College; Rutgers, The State University of New Jersey, New Brunswick; University of Chicago. Other: 2 had other specific plans. Median SAT critical reading: 560, median SAT math: 590, median SAT writing: 580.
Student Life Upper grades have specified standards of dress, student council, honor system. Discipline rests primarily with faculty.
Tuition and Aid Day student tuition: $26,328. Tuition installment plan (The Tuition Plan, Insured Tuition Payment Plan, monthly payment plans). Tuition reduction for siblings, need-based scholarship grants available. In 2009–10, 20% of upper-school students received aid. Total amount of financial aid awarded in 2009–10: $887,238.
Admissions Traditional secondary-level entrance grade is 9. For fall 2009, 78 students applied for upper-level admission, 48 were accepted, 19 enrolled. ISEE, placement test, SSAT or writing sample required. Deadline for receipt of application materials: February 1. Application fee required: $50. On-campus interview required.
Athletics Interscholastic: baseball (boys), basketball (b,g), cross-country running (b,g), golf (b), soccer (b,g), softball (g), tennis (b,g), track and field (b,g), volleyball (g), winter (indoor) track (b,g); intramural: tennis (b,g); coed intramural: fitness, fly fishing, Frisbee, lacrosse, skiing (downhill), snowboarding, weight training. 3 PE instructors, 15 coaches.
Computers Computers are regularly used in English, foreign language, mathematics, science, social studies classes. Computer network features include on-campus library services, online commercial services, Internet access, wireless campus network.
Contact Kris Sweeny, Assistant to the Director of Admissions. 201-327-4050 Ext. 1105. Fax: 201-327-6161. E-mail: ksweeny@saddleriverday.org. Web site: www. saddleriverday.org.

SAGE HILL SCHOOL

20402 Newport Coast Drive
Newport Coast, California 92657-0300
Head of School: Mr. Gordon McNeill

General Information Coeducational day college-preparatory and arts school. Grades 9–12. Founded: 2000. Setting: suburban. Nearest major city is Newport Beach. 30-acre campus. 6 buildings on campus. Approved or accredited by California Association of Independent Schools, Western Association of Schools and Colleges, and California Department of Education. Endowment: $8 million. Total enrollment: 429. Upper school average class size: 15. Upper school faculty-student ratio: 1:9. There are 160 required school days per year for Upper School students. Upper School students typically attend 5 days per week. The average school day consists of 7 hours.
Upper School Student Profile Grade 9: 108 students (52 boys, 56 girls); Grade 10: 112 students (46 boys, 66 girls); Grade 11: 95 students (47 boys, 48 girls); Grade 12: 114 students (63 boys, 51 girls).
Faculty School total: 46. In upper school: 26 men, 20 women; 26 have advanced degrees.
Subjects Offered Algebra, art, art history, art history-AP, art-AP, biology, biology-AP, calculus, calculus-AP, chemistry, chemistry-AP, Chinese, computer science-AP, dance, dance performance, digital art, economics, English, English-AP, environmental science-AP, European history, European history-AP, forensics, French, French language-AP, geometry, Latin, marine science, music, music theory-AP, physical science, physics-AP, pre-calculus, Spanish, Spanish-AP, statistics, statistics-AP, studio art-AP, theater, U.S. history, U.S. history-AP, United States government-AP.
Graduation Requirements Arts, English, history, languages, mathematics, physical education (includes health), science.
Special Academic Programs 18 Advanced Placement exams for which test preparation is offered; honors section; independent study; academic accommodation for the gifted, the musically talented, and the artistically talented.
College Admission Counseling 112 students graduated in 2010; 111 went to college, including Boston University; Brown University; Loyola Marymount University; New York University; Stanford University; University of California, Los Angeles. Other: 1 had other specific plans. Mean combined SAT: 1939.
Student Life Upper grades have specified standards of dress, student council, honor system. Discipline rests equally with students and faculty.
Summer Programs Remediation, enrichment, advancement, sports, art/fine arts programs offered; session focuses on academics; held on campus; accepts boys and girls; open to students from other schools. 200 students usually enrolled. 2011 schedule: June to July.
Tuition and Aid Day student tuition: $27,750. Tuition installment plan (Insured Tuition Payment Plan, monthly payment plans). Need-based scholarship grants

available. In 2010–11, 17% of upper-school students received aid. Total amount of financial aid awarded in 2010–11: $1,684,890.
Admissions Traditional secondary-level entrance grade is 9. For fall 2010, 229 students applied for upper-level admission, 168 were accepted, 124 enrolled. ISEE required. Deadline for receipt of application materials: February 15. Application fee required: $100. On-campus interview required.
Athletics Interscholastic: baseball (boys), basketball (b,g), cross-country running (b,g), diving (b,g), football (b), golf (b,g), lacrosse (b,g), soccer (b,g), softball (g), swimming and diving (b,g), tennis (b,g), track and field (b,g), volleyball (b,g), water polo (b). 3 PE instructors, 34 coaches, 1 athletic trainer.
Computers Computers are regularly used in computer applications, digital applications, video film production classes. Computer network features include on-campus library services, online commercial services, Internet access, wireless campus network, Internet filtering or blocking technology. Student e-mail accounts and computer access in designated common areas are available to students. Students grades are available online. The school has a published electronic and media policy.
Contact Ms. Elaine Mijalis-Kahn, Director of Admission and Financial Aid. 949-219-1337. Fax: 949-219-1399. E-mail: mijaliskahne@sagehillschool.org. Web site: www.sagehillschool.org.

SAGE RIDGE SCHOOL

2515 Crossbow Court
Reno, Nevada 89511
Head of School: Mr. Colburn Shindell III

General Information Coeducational day college-preparatory, arts, and technology school. Grades 5–12. Founded: 1997. Setting: suburban. 44-acre campus. 2 buildings on campus. Approved or accredited by Accreditation Commission of the Texas Association of Baptist Schools, Pacific Northwest Association of Independent Schools, and Nevada Department of Education. Total enrollment: 227. Upper school average class size: 14. Upper school faculty-student ratio: 1:8. There are 180 required school days per year for Upper School students. Upper School students typically attend 5 days per week. The average school day consists of 7 hours and 10 minutes.
Upper School Student Profile Grade 9: 28 students (15 boys, 13 girls); Grade 10: 19 students (11 boys, 8 girls); Grade 11: 23 students (10 boys, 13 girls); Grade 12: 21 students (11 boys, 10 girls).
Faculty School total: 29. In upper school: 12 men, 5 women; 11 have advanced degrees.
Subjects Offered Advanced chemistry, algebra, American history-AP, American literature, American literature-AP, analytic geometry, anatomy and physiology, ancient world history, art history, biology, biology-AP, British literature, British literature-AP, calculus, calculus-AP, ceramics, chemistry, choir, classical language, college counseling, conceptual physics, creative writing, debate, drama performance, electives, English language and composition-AP, English language-AP, English literature and composition-AP, English literature-AP, European history, European literature, foreign language, geometry, honors algebra, honors English, lab science, language-AP, Latin, Latin-AP, medieval history, modern European history, music history, music performance, music theory, outdoor education, philosophy, physical education, physical fitness, physics, playwriting and directing, poetry, pre-algebra, pre-calculus, probability and statistics, public speaking, senior internship, senior seminar, senior thesis, Spanish, Spanish language-AP, Spanish literature, Spanish literature-AP, Spanish-AP, statistics, studio art, studio art-AP, theater, theater arts, theater history, theory of knowledge, trigonometry, U.S. government and politics-AP, U.S. history, U.S. history-AP, Western literature, world history.
Graduation Requirements 20th century world history, algebra, American history, American literature, analytic geometry, ancient world history, art history, biology, British literature, chemistry, conceptual physics, English composition, European history, foreign language, history of music, modern European history, music, outdoor education, participation in sports, pre-calculus, public speaking, science, senior internship, senior thesis, speech, theater history, trigonometry, U.S. history, 15 hours of community service per year, senior thesis and senior internship, two mini-semester seminars per year.
Special Academic Programs 16 Advanced Placement exams for which test preparation is offered; honors section; independent study; academic accommodation for the gifted.
College Admission Counseling 15 students graduated in 2010; all went to college, including Brown University; Kenyon College; New York University; University of Southern California; Vanderbilt University; Yale University. Mean SAT critical reading: 592, mean SAT math: 640, mean SAT writing: 602, mean combined SAT: 1833, mean composite ACT: 26.
Student Life Upper grades have uniform requirement, student council, honor system. Discipline rests equally with students and faculty.
Summer Programs Enrichment, art/fine arts programs offered; session focuses on enrichment for middle school students; held on campus; accepts boys and girls; open to students from other schools. 150 students usually enrolled. 2011 schedule: July 12 to July 30.
Tuition and Aid Day student tuition: $17,000–$17,500. Tuition installment plan (Insured Tuition Payment Plan, FACTS Tuition Payment Plan). Need-based scholarship grants available. In 2010–11, 13% of upper-school students received aid. Total amount of financial aid awarded in 2010–11: $176,225.

Admissions Traditional secondary-level entrance grade is 9. For fall 2010, 18 students applied for upper-level admission, 11 were accepted, 8 enrolled. ERB required. Deadline for receipt of application materials: none. Application fee required: $50. Interview required.

Athletics Interscholastic: alpine skiing (boys, girls), basketball (b), cross-country running (b,g), golf (b), skiing (downhill) (b,g), tennis (b,g), track and field (b,g), volleyball (g), wrestling (b,g); intramural: alpine skiing (b,g), basketball (b,g), cross-country running (b,g), golf (b,g), skiing (downhill) (b,g), track and field (b,g), volleyball (g); coed intramural: bicycling, Frisbee, lacrosse, outdoor education, ropes courses, soccer. 2 PE instructors, 12 coaches.

Computers Computers are regularly used in art, classics, college planning, current events, English, foreign language, history, humanities, independent study, Latin, literary magazine, mathematics, newspaper, publications, SAT preparation, science, senior seminar, social sciences, social studies, Spanish, speech, word processing, writing, yearbook classes. Computer network features include on-campus library services, online commercial services, Internet access, wireless campus network, Internet filtering or blocking technology. Student e-mail accounts are available to students. Students grades are available online.

Contact Ms. Carol Murphy, Director of Admission. 775-852-6222 Ext. 503. Fax: 775-852-6228. E-mail: cmurphy@sageridge.org. Web site: www.sageridge.org.

ST. AGNES ACADEMY
9000 Bellaire Boulevard
Houston, Texas 77036
Head of School: Sr. Jane Meyer

General Information Girls' day college-preparatory, arts, business, religious studies, and technology school, affiliated with Roman Catholic Church. Grades 9–12. Founded: 1906. Setting: urban. 33-acre campus. 3 buildings on campus. Approved or accredited by Southern Association of Colleges and Schools, Texas Education Agency, and Texas Department of Education. Endowment: $6 million. Total enrollment: 864. Upper school average class size: 22. Upper school faculty-student ratio: 1:15. There are 180 required school days per year for Upper School students. Upper School students typically attend 5 days per week. The average school day consists of 6 hours and 5 minutes.

Upper School Student Profile Grade 9: 219 students (219 girls); Grade 10: 219 students (219 girls); Grade 11: 214 students (214 girls); Grade 12: 211 students (211 girls). 78% of students are Roman Catholic.

Faculty School total: 80. In upper school: 18 men, 62 women; 51 have advanced degrees.

Subjects Offered Accounting, acting, algebra, American history, American literature, art, art history, biology, business law, business skills, calculus, chemistry, community service, computer programming, computer science, creative writing, dance, drama, economics, English, English literature, European history, fine arts, French, geology, geometry, government/civics, health, history, integrated physics, journalism, keyboarding, Latin, marine biology, mathematics, music, philosophy, photography, physical education, physics, physiology, psychology, religion, science, social sciences, social studies, Spanish, speech, theater, theology, trigonometry, video film production, world history, world literature.

Graduation Requirements Arts and fine arts (art, music, dance, drama), computer science, electives, English, foreign language, mathematics, physical education (includes health), religion (includes Bible studies and theology), science, social sciences, social studies (includes history), speech, 100 hours of community service.

Special Academic Programs Advanced Placement exam preparation; honors section; independent study.

College Admission Counseling 212 students graduated in 2010; all went to college, including Louisiana State University and Agricultural and Mechanical College; St. Edward's University; Texas A&M University; The University of Texas at Austin; The University of Texas at San Antonio. Mean SAT critical reading: 620, mean SAT math: 620, mean composite ACT: 26. 56% scored over 600 on SAT critical reading, 58% scored over 600 on SAT math, 50% scored over 26 on composite ACT.

Student Life Upper grades have uniform requirement, student council, honor system. Discipline rests primarily with faculty. Attendance at religious services is required.

Summer Programs Remediation, art/fine arts, computer instruction programs offered; session focuses on remediation and elective credit; held on campus; accepts girls; not open to students from other schools. 100 students usually enrolled.

Tuition and Aid Day student tuition: $11,700. Tuition installment plan (plans arranged through local bank). Merit scholarship grants, need-based scholarship grants available. In 2010–11, 30% of upper-school students received aid; total upper-school merit-scholarship money awarded: $24,000. Total amount of financial aid awarded in 2010–11: $450,000.

Admissions Traditional secondary-level entrance grade is 9. For fall 2010, 490 students applied for upper-level admission, 315 were accepted, 219 enrolled. ISEE required. Deadline for receipt of application materials: January 15. Application fee required: $50. On-campus interview required.

Athletics Interscholastic: aquatics, basketball, cheering, cross-country running, dance team, diving, golf, lacrosse, soccer, softball, swimming and diving, tennis, track and field, volleyball, water polo, winter soccer; intramural: badminton, floor hockey, volleyball. 4 PE instructors, 6 coaches, 1 athletic trainer.

Computers Computers are regularly used in all classes. Computer network features include on-campus library services, online commercial services, Internet access,

wireless campus network, Internet filtering or blocking technology. Campus intranet and student e-mail accounts are available to students. Students grades are available online. The school has a published electronic and media policy.

Contact Deborah Whalen, Director of Admission. 713-219-5400. Fax: 713-219-5499. E-mail: dwhalen@st-agnes.org. Web site: www.st-agnes.org.

SAINT AGNES BOYS HIGH SCHOOL
555 West End Avenue
New York, New York 10024
Head of School: Robert J. Conte

General Information Boys' day college-preparatory and religious studies school, affiliated with Roman Catholic Church. Grades 9–12. Founded: 1892. Setting: urban. 1 building on campus. Approved or accredited by Middle States Association of Colleges and Schools, New York State Board of Regents, New York State University, and New York Department of Education. Language of instruction: Spanish. Upper school average class size: 25. Upper school faculty-student ratio: 1:16. There are 180 required school days per year for Upper School students. Upper School students typically attend 5 days per week. The average school day consists of 6 hours and 6 minutes.

Upper School Student Profile Grade 9: 95 students (95 boys); Grade 10: 90 students (90 boys); Grade 11: 90 students (90 boys); Grade 12: 75 students (75 boys). 85% of students are Roman Catholic.

Faculty School total: 25. In upper school: 18 men, 7 women; 20 have advanced degrees.

Special Academic Programs Advanced Placement exam preparation; honors section.

College Admission Counseling 92 students graduated in 2009; 90 went to college, including Hunter College of the City University of New York; Manhattan College; St. John's University; State University of New York at Binghamton. Other: 1 went to work, 1 entered military service. Mean SAT critical reading: 450, mean SAT math: 450.

Student Life Upper grades have specified standards of dress. Discipline rests primarily with faculty. Attendance at religious services is required.

Tuition and Aid Day student tuition: $5350. Tuition installment plan (monthly payment plans). Need-based scholarship grants available. In 2009–10, 60% of upper-school students received aid.

Admissions Traditional secondary-level entrance grade is 9. For fall 2009, 390 students applied for upper-level admission, 280 were accepted, 100 enrolled. Cooperative Entrance Exam (McGraw-Hill) required. Deadline for receipt of application materials: none. No application fee required. Interview recommended.

Athletics Interscholastic: baseball, basketball, bowling, cross-country running, soccer; intramural: basketball, floor hockey, table tennis, volleyball. 1 PE instructor, 5 coaches.

Computers Computer network features include on-campus library services, Internet access. The school has a published electronic and media policy.

Contact Principal. 212-873-9100. Fax: 212-873-9292. Web site: www.staghs.org.

ST. ALBANS SCHOOL
Mount Saint Alban
Washington, District of Columbia 20016
Head of School: Mr. Vance Wilson

General Information Boys' boarding and day college-preparatory school, affiliated with Episcopal Church. Boarding grades 9–12, day grades 4–12. Founded: 1909. Setting: urban. Students are housed in single-sex dormitories. 54-acre campus. 7 buildings on campus. Approved or accredited by Association of Independent Maryland Schools, Association of Independent Schools of Greater Washington, The Association of Boarding Schools, and District of Columbia Department of Education. Member of National Association of Independent Schools and Secondary School Admission Test Board. Endowment: $38.5 million. Total enrollment: 583. Upper school average class size: 13. Upper school faculty-student ratio: 1:7.

Upper School Student Profile Grade 9: 80 students (80 boys); Grade 10: 82 students (82 boys); Grade 11: 79 students (79 boys); Grade 12: 82 students (82 boys). 4% of students are boarding students. 5 states are represented in upper school student body. 2% are international students. International students from Bulgaria, China, Ireland, Mexico, Republic of Korea, and Ukraine; 5 other countries represented in student body. 20% of students are members of Episcopal Church.

Faculty School total: 90. In upper school: 51 men, 18 women; 43 have advanced degrees; 6 reside on campus.

Subjects Offered Advanced Placement courses, algebra, American history, American literature, art, art history, Bible studies, biology, calculus, ceramics, chemistry, Chinese, community service, computer math, computer programming, computer science, creative writing, dance, drama, earth science, economics, English, English literature, ethics, European history, expository writing, fine arts, French, geography, geometry, government/civics, Greek, history, Japanese, Latin, marine biology, mathematics, music, photography, physical education, physics, religion, science, social studies, Spanish, speech, theater.

St. Albans School

Graduation Requirements American history, ancient history, arts and fine arts (art, music, dance, drama), English, ethics, foreign language, mathematics, physical education (includes health), science, participation in athletic program. Community service is required.

Special Academic Programs Advanced Placement exam preparation; honors section; independent study; term-away projects.

College Admission Counseling Colleges students went to include Amherst College; Bowdoin College; Georgetown University; Harvard University; The College of William and Mary; University of Michigan.

Student Life Upper grades have specified standards of dress, student council, honor system. Discipline rests equally with students and faculty. Attendance at religious services is required.

Summer Programs Remediation, enrichment, advancement, ESL, sports, art/fine arts, rigorous outdoor training, computer instruction programs offered; session focuses on academics and day camp; held on campus; accepts boys and girls; open to students from other schools. 1,500 students usually enrolled. 2011 schedule: June 7 to August 21. Application deadline: none.

Tuition and Aid Day student tuition: $34,465; 7-day tuition and room/board: $48,753. Tuition installment plan (Insured Tuition Payment Plan, monthly payment plans, individually arranged payment plans). Need-based scholarship grants, need-based loans available. In 2010–11, 25% of upper-school students received aid. Total amount of financial aid awarded in 2010–11: $2,131,478.

Admissions Traditional secondary-level entrance grade is 9. For fall 2010, 159 students applied for upper-level admission, 44 were accepted, 25 enrolled. ISEE or SSAT required. Deadline for receipt of application materials: January 15. Application fee required: $80. Interview required.

Athletics Interscholastic: aquatics, baseball, basketball, canoeing/kayaking, climbing, crew, cross-country running, diving, football, golf, ice hockey, independent competitive sports, indoor soccer, indoor track, indoor track & field, kayaking, lacrosse, rappelling, rock climbing, soccer, swimming and diving, tennis, track and field, wall climbing, weight training, winter (indoor) track, winter soccer, wrestling; intramural: aquatics, basketball, combined training, dance, fitness, indoor soccer, outdoor activities, physical training, tennis, track and field, yoga. 5 coaches, 2 athletic trainers.

Computers Computers are regularly used in mathematics, programming, science classes. Computer network features include on-campus library services, online commercial services, Internet access, wireless campus network. Campus intranet and student e-mail accounts are available to students. The school has a published electronic and media policy.

Contact Mr. Kyle Slatery, Admissions and Financial Aid Coordinator. 202-537-6440. Fax: 202-537-2225. E-mail: kslatery@cathedral.org. Web site: www.stalbansschool.org/.

ST. ANDREW'S COLLEGE

15800 Yonge Street
Aurora, Ontario L4G 3H7, Canada
Head of School: Mr. Kevin R. McHenry

General Information Boys' boarding and day college-preparatory, arts, business, and technology school. Grades 6–12. Founded: 1899. Setting: small town. Nearest major city is Toronto, Canada. Students are housed in single-sex dormitories. 110-acre campus. 24 buildings on campus. Approved or accredited by Canadian Association of Independent Schools, Canadian Educational Standards Institute, Conference of Independent Schools of Ontario, The Association of Boarding Schools, and Ontario Department of Education. Affiliate member of National Association of Independent Schools; member of Secondary School Admission Test Board. Language of instruction: English. Endowment: CAN$21.3 million. Total enrollment: 580. Upper school average class size: 17. Upper school faculty-student ratio: 1:9. Upper School students typically attend 5 days per week. The average school day consists of 5 hours and 20 minutes.

Upper School Student Profile Grade 9: 83 students (83 boys); Grade 10: 115 students (115 boys); Grade 11: 120 students (120 boys); Grade 12: 126 students (126 boys). 60% of students are boarding students. 80% are province residents. 8 provinces are represented in upper school student body. 20% are international students. International students from China, Hong Kong, Jamaica, Mexico, Republic of Korea, and Taiwan; 20 other countries represented in student body.

Faculty School total: 64. In upper school: 43 men, 8 women; 14 have advanced degrees; 24 reside on campus.

Subjects Offered Accounting, Advanced Placement courses, algebra, American history, art, biology, business, calculus, chemistry, communications, community service, computer science, creative writing, drama, economics, English, English literature, environmental science, fine arts, French, geography, geometry, health, history, mathematics, music, physical education, physics, physiology, science, social sciences, social studies, sociology, Spanish, statistics, world history, world religions.

Graduation Requirements Arts, arts and fine arts (art, music, dance, drama), business, careers, civics, computer science, dance, drama, English, foreign language, French, geography, health education, history, mathematics, physical education (includes health), science, science and technology, social sciences. Community service is required.

Special Academic Programs 9 Advanced Placement exams for which test preparation is offered; honors section; accelerated programs; independent study; term-away projects; study abroad; ESL (16 students enrolled).

College Admission Counseling 99 students graduated in 2010; all went to college, including McGill University; Queen's University at Kingston; The University of Western Ontario; University of Toronto; University of Waterloo. Median SAT critical reading: 539, median SAT math: 631, median SAT writing: 577, median combined SAT: 1747.

Student Life Upper grades have uniform requirement, student council, honor system. Discipline rests equally with students and faculty. Attendance at religious services is required.

Summer Programs ESL, sports, art/fine arts programs offered; session focuses on Scottish music (piping and drumming), sports/arts camps, leadership camps, academics; held on campus; accepts boys and girls; open to students from other schools. 1,200 students usually enrolled. 2011 schedule: June 20 to August 12. Application deadline: none.

Tuition and Aid Day student tuition: CAN$26,960; 5-day tuition and room/board: CAN$43,335; 7-day tuition and room/board: CAN$43,335. Tuition installment plan (monthly payment plans, one-time payment, three installments plan). Bursaries, merit scholarship grants, need-based scholarship grants available. In 2010–11, 20% of upper-school students received aid; total upper-school merit-scholarship money awarded: CAN$166,500. Total amount of financial aid awarded in 2010–11: CAN$170,000.

Admissions Traditional secondary-level entrance grade is 9. For fall 2010, 181 students applied for upper-level admission, 135 were accepted, 102 enrolled. CAT, SLEP, SSAT or TOEFL required. Deadline for receipt of application materials: none. Application fee required: CAN$150. Interview required.

Athletics Interscholastic: alpine skiing, aquatics, badminton, baseball, basketball, biathlon, cricket, cross-country running, curling, fencing, football, golf, ice hockey, indoor track, indoor track & field, lacrosse, marksmanship, nordic skiing, rugby, running, skiing (cross-country), skiing (downhill), soccer, softball, squash, swimming and diving, table tennis, tennis, track and field, triathlon, volleyball, winter (indoor) track; intramural: aquatics, archery, backpacking, badminton, ball hockey, baseball, basketball, canoeing/kayaking, climbing, cooperative games, cross-country running, curling, fencing, fitness, flag football, floor hockey, football, Frisbee, golf, hiking/backpacking, ice hockey, ice skating, jogging, lacrosse, marksmanship, mountain biking, nordic skiing, outdoor activities, outdoor education, outdoor skills, physical fitness, rock climbing, ropes courses, running, scuba diving, self defense, skiing (cross-country), skiing (downhill), snowboarding, soccer, softball, squash, strength & conditioning, swimming and diving, table tennis, tennis, touch football, track and field, triathlon, ultimate Frisbee, volleyball, wall climbing, water polo, weight training, wilderness survival. 7 athletic trainers.

Computers Computers are regularly used in all academic classes. Computer network features include on-campus library services, online commercial services, Internet access, wireless campus network, Internet filtering or blocking technology. The school has a published electronic and media policy.

Contact Mrs. Natascia Stewart, Admission Associate. 905-727-3178 Ext. 303. Fax: 905-727-9032. E-mail: admission@sac.on.ca. Web site: www.sac.on.ca.

ST. ANDREW'S EPISCOPAL SCHOOL

8804 Postoak Road
Potomac, Maryland 20854
Head of School: Chap. Robert Kosasky

General Information Coeducational day college-preparatory school, affiliated with Episcopal Church. Grades PS–12. Founded: 1978. Setting: suburban. Nearest major city is Washington, DC. 19-acre campus. 5 buildings on campus. Approved or accredited by Association of Independent Maryland Schools, Association of Independent Schools of Greater Washington, Middle States Association of Colleges and Schools, and National Association of Episcopal Schools. Member of National Association of Independent Schools and Secondary School Admission Test Board. Endowment: $3.2 million. Total enrollment: 527. Upper school average class size: 13. Upper school faculty-student ratio: 1:6. There are 172 required school days per year for Upper School students. Upper School students typically attend 5 days per week. The average school day consists of 6 hours and 40 minutes.

Upper School Student Profile Grade 6: 28 students (24 boys, 4 girls); Grade 7: 30 students (19 boys, 11 girls); Grade 8: 46 students (24 boys, 22 girls); Grade 9: 84 students (53 boys, 31 girls); Grade 10: 80 students (43 boys, 37 girls); Grade 11: 75 students (39 boys, 36 girls); Grade 12: 97 students (58 boys, 39 girls). 20% of students are members of Episcopal Church.

Faculty School total: 82. In upper school: 23 men, 28 women; 37 have advanced degrees.

Subjects Offered 20th century history, 3-dimensional art, 3-dimensional design, acting, Advanced Placement courses, advanced studio art-AP, algebra, American history, American literature, art, art history, art history-AP, art-AP, athletics, band, Bible, biology, biology-AP, British literature, calculus, calculus-AP, ceramics, chemistry, chorus, civics, college counseling, composition-AP, computer animation, computer art, computer graphics, computer science, creative writing, dance, digital photography, drama, dramatic arts, earth science, English, English literature, English literature and composition-AP, English-AP, ethics, European history, fine arts, French, French language-AP, French literature-AP, geography, geometry, global studies,

French language-AP, French literature-AP, geography, geometry, global studies, government/civics, guitar, health, history, instrumental music, jazz band, journalism, Latin, Latin American studies, Latin-AP, mathematics, modern European history, music, musical theater, newspaper, orchestra, organic biochemistry, painting, photography, physical education, physical science, physics, physics-AP, pre-algebra, pre-calculus, public speaking, religion, robotics, science, service learning/internship, Spanish, Spanish language-AP, Spanish literature-AP, Spanish-AP, sports, stage design, statistics, student publications, studio art, studio art-AP, theater, theater design and production, theology, trigonometry, U.S. history, U.S. history-AP, video, visual and performing arts, vocal music, world cultures, world history, world religions, writing, yearbook.

Graduation Requirements English, foreign language, history, mathematics, performing arts, physical education (includes health), religion (includes Bible studies and theology), science, senior thesis, visual arts. Community service is required.

Special Academic Programs Advanced Placement exam preparation; independent study.

College Admission Counseling 82 students graduated in 2009; 81 went to college, including Bucknell University; The Colorado College; University of Maryland, College Park; University of Virginia; Wake Forest University; Washington University in St. Louis. Other: 1 had other specific plans.

Student Life Upper grades have specified standards of dress, student council, honor system. Discipline rests primarily with faculty. Attendance at religious services is required.

Tuition and Aid Day student tuition: $31,130. Tuition installment plan (Key Tuition Payment Plan, FACTS Tuition Payment Plan, monthly payment plans). Need-based scholarship grants, AchieverLoans (Key Education Resources) available. In 2009–10, 21% of upper-school students received aid. Total amount of financial aid awarded in 2009–10: $1,242,330.

Admissions Traditional secondary-level entrance grade is 9. ISEE or SSAT required. Deadline for receipt of application materials: February 1. Application fee required: $50. On-campus interview required.

Athletics Interscholastic: baseball (boys), basketball (b,g), cross-country running (b,g), lacrosse (b,g), soccer (b,g), softball (g), tennis (b,g), volleyball (g); coed interscholastic: equestrian sports, golf, track and field, wrestling; coed intramural: dance, fitness, physical fitness, weight training. 12 coaches, 1 athletic trainer.

Computers Computers are regularly used in English, foreign language, graphic arts, history, journalism, mathematics, music, science classes. Computer network features include on-campus library services, online commercial services, Internet access, wireless campus network, Internet filtering or blocking technology. Campus intranet and student e-mail accounts are available to students. Students grades are available online. The school has a published electronic and media policy.

Contact Mrs. Aileen Moodie, Admission Coordinator. 301-983-5200 Ext. 236. Fax: 301-983-4620. E-mail: admission@saes.org. Web site: www.saes.org.

ST. ANDREW'S ON THE MARSH SCHOOL

601 Penn Waller Road
Savannah, Georgia 31410
Head of School: Mr. Gil Webb

General Information Coeducational day college-preparatory, arts, and bilingual studies school. Grades PK–12. Founded: 1947. Setting: suburban. 28-acre campus. 5 buildings on campus. Approved or accredited by Georgia Independent School Association, South Carolina Independent School Association, Southern Association of Colleges and Schools, Southern Association of Independent Schools, and Georgia Department of Education. Member of National Association of Independent Schools. Endowment: $150,000. Total enrollment: 469. Upper school average class size: 16. Upper school faculty-student ratio: 1:9.

Upper School Student Profile Grade 9: 42 students (25 boys, 17 girls); Grade 10: 28 students (13 boys, 15 girls); Grade 11: 45 students (26 boys, 19 girls); Grade 12: 38 students (22 boys, 16 girls).

Faculty School total: 72. In upper school: 11 men, 14 women; 13 have advanced degrees.

Subjects Offered Algebra, American history, American literature, anatomy, art, art history, biology, calculus, chemistry, classical studies, community service, computer programming, computer science, creative writing, drama, earth science, economics, English, English literature, environmental science, European history, fine arts, geography, geometry, government/civics, health, history, mathematics, music, physical education, physics, psychology, science, social studies, Spanish, theater, trigonometry, Web site design, world history.

Graduation Requirements Arts and fine arts (art, music, dance, drama), computer science, English, foreign language, mathematics, physical education (includes health), science, social studies (includes history), senior work project. Community service is required.

Special Academic Programs International Baccalaureate program; Advanced Placement exam preparation; honors section; accelerated programs; independent study; study at local college for college credit; study abroad.

College Admission Counseling 50 students graduated in 2009; all went to college, including Auburn University; Georgia Institute of Technology; Georgia Southern University; Savannah College of Art and Design; University of Georgia; University of South Carolina. Median SAT critical reading: 541, median SAT math: 547, median SAT writing: 535.

Student Life Upper grades have specified standards of dress, student council, honor system. Discipline rests equally with students and faculty.

Tuition and Aid Day student tuition: $10,220. Tuition installment plan (monthly payment plans, individually arranged payment plans). Need-based scholarship grants, need-based grants available. In 2009–10, 25% of upper-school students received aid. Total amount of financial aid awarded in 2009–10: $150,000.

Admissions Traditional secondary-level entrance grade is 9. For fall 2009, 25 students applied for upper-level admission, 20 were accepted, 16 enrolled. Admissions testing, ERB, Iowa Tests of Basic Skills, Stanford Achievement Test or TOEFL or SLEP required. Deadline for receipt of application materials: none. Application fee required: $100. Interview required.

Athletics Interscholastic: baseball (boys), basketball (b,g), cheering (g), cross-country running (b,g), football (b), golf (b,g), physical fitness (b,g), soccer (b,g), softball (g), strength & conditioning (b,g), swimming and diving (g), tennis (b,g), track and field (b,g), volleyball (g), weight lifting (b,g), weight training (b,g); intramural: basketball (b,g), soccer (b,g), softball (g), volleyball (b,g), weight lifting (b,g), weight training (b,g); coed interscholastic: cheering, cross-country running, physical fitness, weight lifting, weight training. 4 PE instructors, 2 coaches, 1 athletic trainer.

Computers Computers are regularly used in history, research skills, science, Spanish, yearbook classes. Computer network features include on-campus library services, Internet access, Internet filtering or blocking technology. The school has a published electronic and media policy.

Contact Mrs. Beth G. Aldrich, Director of Admissions. 912-897-4941 Ext. 303. Fax: 912-897-4943. E-mail: Aldrichb@saintschool.com. Web site: www.saintschool.com.

ST. ANDREW'S PRIORY SCHOOL

224 Queen Emma Square
Honolulu, Hawaii 96813
Head of School: Ms. Sandra J. Theunick

General Information Girls' day college-preparatory, arts, and technology school, affiliated with Episcopal Church. Grades K–12. Founded: 1867. Setting: urban. 3-acre campus. 7 buildings on campus. Approved or accredited by National Association of Episcopal Schools, The College Board, The Hawaii Council of Private Schools, Western Association of Schools and Colleges, and Hawaii Department of Education. Member of National Association of Independent Schools and Secondary School Admission Test Board. Endowment: $3.2 million. Total enrollment: 401. Upper school average class size: 12. Upper school faculty-student ratio: 1:8. There are 175 required school days per year for Upper School students. Upper School students typically attend 5 days per week. The average school day consists of 7 hours and 15 minutes.

Upper School Student Profile Grade 6: 37 students (37 girls); Grade 7: 30 students (30 girls); Grade 8: 29 students (29 girls); Grade 9: 34 students (34 girls); Grade 10: 43 students (43 girls); Grade 11: 26 students (26 girls); Grade 12: 44 students (44 girls). 15% of students are members of Episcopal Church.

Faculty School total: 55. In upper school: 13 men, 25 women; 27 have advanced degrees.

Subjects Offered Algebra, American government, American history, American literature, ancient history, applied arts, applied music, art, art history, Asian studies, Bible studies, biology, biology-AP, British literature, British literature-AP, calculus, calculus-AP, ceramics, chemistry, chemistry-AP, choir, college counseling, college placement, community service, competitive science projects, computer art, computer education, computer graphics, computer literacy, computer multimedia, computer programming, computer science, computer technology certification, creative writing, drama, economics, economics and history, English, English literature, English literature-AP, ESL, European history, expository writing, fine arts, French, geography, geometry, government/civics, grammar, guidance, handbells, Hawaiian history, Hawaiian language, health, history, honors U.S. history, humanities, Japanese, journalism, Latin, leadership, life skills, mathematics, mechanical drawing, medieval history, microbiology, modern world history, music, Pacific Island studies, photography, physical education, physics, physics-AP, physiology, Polynesian dance, pre-algebra, pre-calculus, psychology, religion, science, science research, social sciences, social studies, sociology, Spanish, Spanish-AP, speech, speech communications, theater, theology, trigonometry, U.S. history-AP, United States government-AP, video and animation, visual and performing arts, wind ensemble, women's studies, world civilizations, world history, world literature, world wide web design, writing workshop, yearbook.

Graduation Requirements Advanced Placement courses, arts and fine arts (art, music, dance, drama), computer science, English, foreign language, Hawaiian history, humanities, mathematics, physical education (includes health), religion (includes Bible studies and theology), science, science research, social sciences, social studies (includes history), speech, technological applications. Community service is required.

Special Academic Programs 8 Advanced Placement exams for which test preparation is offered; honors section; independent study; study at local college for college credit; academic accommodation for the musically talented and the artistically talented; ESL (5 students enrolled).

College Admission Counseling 62 students graduated in 2010; all went to college, including Barnard College; Brown University; University of Hawaii at Manoa; University of San Francisco.

Student Life Upper grades have uniform requirement, student council, honor system. Discipline rests primarily with faculty. Attendance at religious services is required.

Summer Programs Remediation, enrichment, advancement, ESL, sports, art/fine arts, rigorous outdoor training, computer instruction programs offered; session focuses on academics, arts, sports; held on campus; accepts boys and girls; open to students from other schools. 500 students usually enrolled. 2011 schedule: June 13 to July 22. Application deadline: March.

Tuition and Aid Day student tuition: $14,500. Tuition installment plan (FACTS Tuition Payment Plan, monthly payment plans, individually arranged payment plans). Tuition reduction for siblings, merit scholarship grants, need-based scholarship grants available. In 2010–11, 32% of upper-school students received aid; total upper-school merit-scholarship money awarded: $166,750. Total amount of financial aid awarded in 2010–11: $512,990.

Admissions Traditional secondary-level entrance grade is 9. PSAT or SAT for applicants to grade 11 and 12 or SSAT required. Deadline for receipt of application materials: none. Application fee required: $50. On-campus interview required.

Athletics Interscholastic: basketball, bowling, canoeing/kayaking, cheering, cross-country running, dance team, diving, drill team, golf, gymnastics, martial arts, ocean paddling, sailing, soccer, softball, swimming and diving, tennis, track and field, volleyball, water polo, wrestling; intramural: aerobics/dance, badminton, dance squad, drill team, fitness, flag football, jogging, outdoor activities, outdoor adventure, physical fitness, ropes courses, self defense, strength & conditioning, tai chi, weight training, windsurfing. 4 PE instructors, 18 coaches.

Computers Computers are regularly used in animation, art, college planning, English, ESL, foreign language, graphic design, history, humanities, independent study, library, literary magazine, mathematics, media arts, music, newspaper, photojournalism, psychology, religion, science, speech, technology, writing, yearbook classes. Computer network features include on-campus library services, online commercial services, Internet access, wireless campus network, Internet filtering or blocking technology. Campus intranet and student e-mail accounts are available to students. Students grades are available online. The school has a published electronic and media policy.

Contact Sue Ann Wargo, Director of Admissions. 808-532-2418. Fax: 808-531-8426. E-mail: sawargo@priory.net. Web site: www.priory.net.

ST. ANDREW'S REGIONAL HIGH SCHOOL
880 Mckenzie Avenue
Victoria, British Columbia V8X 3G5, Canada
Head of School: Mr. Andrew Keleher

General Information Coeducational day college-preparatory, general academic, and religious studies school, affiliated with Roman Catholic Church. Grades 8–12. Founded: 1983. Setting: urban. 2-acre campus. 1 building on campus. Approved or accredited by British Columbia Department of Education. Language of instruction: English. Upper school average class size: 24. Upper school faculty-student ratio: 1:14. There are 178 required school days per year for Upper School students. Upper School students typically attend 5 days per week. The average school day consists of 5 hours.

Upper School Student Profile 65% of students are Roman Catholic.

Faculty School total: 37. In upper school: 16 men, 15 women; 11 have advanced degrees.

Subjects Offered English literature and composition-AP, religious education, yoga.

Graduation Requirements Religious studies.

Special Academic Programs 1 Advanced Placement exam for which test preparation is offered; honors section.

College Admission Counseling 103 students graduated in 2010.

Student Life Upper grades have uniform requirement, student council, honor system. Discipline rests primarily with faculty. Attendance at religious services is required.

Tuition and Aid Tuition reduction for siblings, bursaries available.

Admissions Deadline for receipt of application materials: February 28. Application fee required: CAN$50. Interview required.

Athletics Interscholastic: badminton (boys, girls), basketball (b,g), bicycling (b,g), cross-country running (b,g), rowing (b,g), running (b,g), soccer (b,g), track and field (b,g), volleyball (b,g); intramural: basketball (b), soccer (b,g); coed interscholastic: aquatics; coed intramural: dance team, indoor hockey, physical fitness.

Computers Computer resources include on-campus library services, Internet access, Internet filtering or blocking technology. The school has a published electronic and media policy.

Contact Diane Chimich, Vice Principal. 250-479-1414. Fax: 250-479-5356. Web site: www.standrewshigh.ca/.

ST. ANDREW'S SCHOOL
350 Noxontown Road
Middletown, Delaware 19709
Head of School: Daniel T. Roach

General Information Coeducational boarding college-preparatory, arts, and religious studies school, affiliated with Episcopal Church. Grades 9–12. Founded: 1929. Setting: small town. Nearest major city is Wilmington. Students are housed in single-sex dormitories. 2,200-acre campus. 15 buildings on campus. Approved or accredited by Middle States Association of Colleges and Schools, National Association of Episcopal Schools, The Association of Boarding Schools, The College Board, and Delaware Department of Education. Member of National Association of Independent Schools and Secondary School Admission Test Board. Endowment: $165 million. Total enrollment: 290. Upper school average class size: 11. Upper school faculty-student ratio: 1:5.

Upper School Student Profile Grade 9: 60 students (31 boys, 29 girls); Grade 10: 75 students (41 boys, 34 girls); Grade 11: 84 students (44 boys, 40 girls); Grade 12: 71 students (37 boys, 34 girls). 100% of students are boarding students. 14% are state residents. 26 states are represented in upper school student body. 13% are international students. International students from Bermuda, Canada, China, Germany, India, and Republic of Korea; 7 other countries represented in student body. 30% of students are members of Episcopal Church.

Faculty School total: 71. In upper school: 36 men, 33 women; 54 have advanced degrees; 67 reside on campus.

Subjects Offered 20th century world history, acting, advanced chemistry, advanced math, algebra, American history, American literature, art, art history, art history-AP, Asian history, biology, calculus, calculus-AP, ceramics, chemistry, Chinese, choir, choral music, college counseling, comparative religion, computer literacy, computer programming, concert choir, creative writing, digital music, drama, drawing, driver education, East Asian history, English, English literature, English literature-AP, environmental science, ethics, European history, European history-AP, film, film studies, fine arts, French, French literature-AP, geometry, Greek, history, honors geometry, improvisation, Islamic history, Latin, Latin-AP, mathematics, Middle Eastern history, modern European history, music, music theory, organic chemistry, painting, philosophy, photography, physics, physics-AP, poetry, pottery, psychology, religion, religious studies, science, science research, Spanish, Spanish literature-AP, speech, statistics-AP, theater, trigonometry, U.S. history, Western religions.

Graduation Requirements Arts and fine arts (art, music, dance, drama), English, foreign language, history, mathematics, religion (includes Bible studies and theology), science.

Special Academic Programs Honors section; independent study; academic accommodation for the gifted, the musically talented, and the artistically talented.

College Admission Counseling 75 students graduated in 2010; 68 went to college, including Davidson College; Duke University; Middlebury College; University of Delaware; University of Virginia; Williams College. Other: 7 had other specific plans. Mean SAT critical reading: 656, mean SAT math: 651.

Student Life Upper grades have specified standards of dress, student council, honor system. Discipline rests equally with students and faculty. Attendance at religious services is required.

Tuition and Aid 7-day tuition and room/board: $44,250. Tuition installment plan (Key Tuition Payment Plan, monthly payment plans). Need-based scholarship grants available. In 2010–11, 46% of upper-school students received aid. Total amount of financial aid awarded in 2010–11: $4,300,000.

Admissions Traditional secondary-level entrance grade is 9. For fall 2010, 450 students applied for upper-level admission, 125 were accepted, 77 enrolled. ISEE, SSAT or TOEFL required. Deadline for receipt of application materials: January 15. Application fee required: $50. On-campus interview required.

Athletics Interscholastic: aquatics (boys, girls), baseball (b), basketball (b,g), crew (b,g), cross-country running (b,g), field hockey (g), football (b), lacrosse (b,g), rowing (b,g), soccer (b,g), squash (b,g), swimming and diving (b,g), tennis (b,g), volleyball (g), wrestling (b); coed intramural: aerobics, aerobics/dance, canoeing/kayaking, dance, fencing, fishing, fitness, Frisbee, indoor soccer, kayaking, outdoors, paddle tennis, physical training, rowing, sailboarding, sailing, weight lifting, weight training, windsurfing, yoga. 1 athletic trainer.

Computers Computers are regularly used in English, foreign language, history, mathematics, science classes. Computer network features include on-campus library services, online commercial services, Internet access, Internet filtering or blocking technology. Campus intranet, student e-mail accounts, and computer access in designated common areas are available to students. The school has a published electronic and media policy.

Contact Louisa H. Zendt, Director of Admission. 302-285-4230. Fax: 302-378-7120. E-mail: lzendt@standrews-de.org. Web site: www.standrews-de.org.

SAINT ANDREW'S SCHOOL
3900 Jog Road
Boca Raton, Florida 33434
Head of School: Dr. Ann Marie Krejcarek

General Information Coeducational boarding and day college-preparatory school, affiliated with Episcopal Church. Boarding grades 9–12, day grades JK–12. Founded: 1961. Setting: suburban. Nearest major city is West Palm Beach. Students are housed in single-sex dormitories. 80-acre campus. 18 buildings on campus. Approved or accredited by Florida Council of Independent Schools, The Association of Boarding Schools, and Florida Department of Education. Member of National Association of Independent Schools and Secondary School Admission Test Board. Endowment: $10 million. Total enrollment: 1,303. Upper school average class size: 15. Upper school faculty-student ratio: 1:9. Upper School students typically attend 5 days per week. The average school day consists of 7 hours and 30 minutes.

Upper School Student Profile Grade 9: 142 students (76 boys, 66 girls); Grade 10: 152 students (75 boys, 77 girls); Grade 11: 153 students (87 boys, 66 girls); Grade 12: 144 students (77 boys, 67 girls). 17% of students are boarding students. 82% are state residents. 11 states are represented in upper school student body. 12% are international students. International students from Bahamas, China, Germany,

Jamaica, Japan, and Republic of Korea; 17 other countries represented in student body. 15% of students are members of Episcopal Church.

Faculty School total: 210. In upper school: 55 men, 75 women; 80 have advanced degrees; 35 reside on campus.

Subjects Offered Advanced studio art-AP, algebra, American history, American literature, American studies, anatomy, archaeology, art, art history, Bible studies, biology, biology-AP, calculus, calculus-AP, chemistry, chemistry-AP, Chinese, community service, computer math, computer programming, computer science, computer science-AP, creative writing, drafting, drama, earth science, ecology, economics, English, English literature, English-AP, environmental science, ethics, European history, expository writing, fine arts, French, French-AP, geography, geometry, German, German-AP, government/civics, grammar, history, journalism, Latin, marine biology, mathematics, music, photography, physical education, physics, physics-AP, pre-calculus, psychology, science, social studies, Spanish, Spanish-AP, speech, statistics, theater, theology, trigonometry, U.S. history-AP, world history, world history-AP, world literature, writing.

Graduation Requirements Arts and fine arts (art, music, dance, drama), computer science, English, foreign language, mathematics, physical education (includes health), religion (includes Bible studies and theology), science, social studies (includes history), speech, visual and performing arts, participation in sports, community service hours. Community service is required.

Special Academic Programs 21 Advanced Placement exams for which test preparation is offered; honors section; academic accommodation for the gifted; ESL (20 students enrolled).

College Admission Counseling 151 students graduated in 2009; 148 went to college, including Florida State University; The George Washington University; University of Central Florida; University of Florida; University of Miami; Vanderbilt University. Mean SAT critical reading: 608, mean SAT math: 624, mean SAT writing: 616, mean combined SAT: 1848, mean composite ACT: 27. 50% scored over 600 on SAT critical reading, 60% scored over 600 on SAT math, 57% scored over 600 on SAT writing, 59% scored over 1800 on combined SAT, 58% scored over 26 on composite ACT.

Student Life Upper grades have specified standards of dress, student council, honor system. Discipline rests primarily with faculty. Attendance at religious services is required.

Tuition and Aid Day student tuition: $22,720; 7-day tuition and room/board: $40,300. Tuition installment plan (Insured Tuition Payment Plan, FACTS Tuition Payment Plan, monthly payment plans, individually arranged payment plans). Need-based scholarship grants available. In 2009–10, 15% of upper-school students received aid. Total amount of financial aid awarded in 2009–10: $2,600,000.

Admissions Traditional secondary-level entrance grade is 9. For fall 2009, 214 students applied for upper-level admission, 161 were accepted, 101 enrolled. SSAT and TOEFL or SLEP required. Deadline for receipt of application materials: February 1. Application fee required: $75. Interview required.

Athletics Interscholastic: baseball (boys), basketball (b,g), cheering (g), cross-country running (b,g), danceline (g), diving (b,g), football (b), golf (b,g), lacrosse (b,g), soccer (b,g), softball (g), swimming and diving (b,g), tennis (b,g), track and field (b,g), volleyball (g), water polo (b,g), wrestling (b); intramural: weight lifting (b,g); coed interscholastic: bowling, water polo. 48 coaches.

Computers Computers are regularly used in college planning, English, foreign language, history, mathematics, science classes. Computer network features include on-campus library services, online commercial services, Internet access, wireless campus network, Internet filtering or blocking technology. Computer access in designated common areas is available to students. Students grades are available online. The school has a published electronic and media policy.

Contact Kilian J. Forgus, Associate Headmaster for Enrollment and Strategic Planning. 561-210-2000. Fax: 561-210-2027. E-mail: admission@saintandrews.net. Web site: www.saintandrews.net.

ST. ANDREW'S SCHOOL

63 Federal Road
Barrington, Rhode Island 02806
Head of School: Mr. John D. Martin

General Information Coeducational boarding and day college-preparatory and arts school. Boarding grades 9–12, day grades 3–12. Founded: 1893. Setting: suburban. Nearest major city is Providence. Students are housed in single-sex dormitories. 100-acre campus. 33 buildings on campus. Approved or accredited by Massachusetts Department of Education, National Association of Episcopal Schools, New England Association of Schools and Colleges, Rhode Island State Certified Resource Progam, The Association of Boarding Schools, and Rhode Island Department of Education. Member of National Association of Independent Schools and Secondary School Admission Test Board. Endowment: $17 million. Total enrollment: 213. Upper school average class size: 9. Upper school faculty-student ratio: 1:4. There are 150 required school days per year for Upper School students. Upper School students typically attend 5 days per week. The average school day consists of 8 hours.

Upper School Student Profile Grade 9: 39 students (27 boys, 12 girls); Grade 10: 44 students (30 boys, 14 girls); Grade 11: 39 students (25 boys, 14 girls); Grade 12: 40 students (25 boys, 15 girls). 37% of students are boarding students. 54% are state residents. 6 states are represented in upper school student body. 22% are international students. International students from China, India, Republic of Korea, Senegal, and Taiwan.

Faculty School total: 49. In upper school: 20 men, 20 women; 24 have advanced degrees; 22 reside on campus.

Subjects Offered Addiction, Advanced Placement courses, algebra, American history, American literature, ancient history, art, astronomy, biology, calculus,

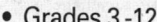

St. Andrew's School

calculus-AP, ceramics, chemistry, chorus, college counseling, computer applications, computer graphics, computer science, consumer mathematics, contemporary issues, creative writing, digital applications, digital photography, drawing, English, environmental science, ESL, ethics, European history, film history, fine arts, French, geometry, graphic arts, graphic design, history of music, human anatomy, literature, mathematics, oceanography, oral communications, photography, physical education, physics, physics-AP, portfolio art, pre-calculus, probability and statistics, remedial study skills, SAT preparation, science, social studies, Spanish, statistics-AP, study skills, theater, theater arts, TOEFL preparation, trigonometry, word processing, yearbook.

Graduation Requirements Arts and fine arts (art, music, dance, drama), English, mathematics, physical education (includes health), science, social studies (includes history), community service.

Special Academic Programs Advanced Placement exam preparation; honors section; independent study; remedial reading and/or remedial writing; programs in English for dyslexic students; special instructional classes for students with mild language-based learning disabilities, students with attention/organizational issues (ADHD); ESL (12 students enrolled).

College Admission Counseling 46 students graduated in 2010; all went to college, including Brandeis University; Emory University; Mitchell College; Mount Ida College; New York University; Rollins College. Median SAT critical reading: 480, median SAT math: 470, median SAT writing: 470, median combined SAT: 1420. 8% scored over 600 on SAT critical reading, 29% scored over 600 on SAT math, 17% scored over 600 on SAT writing, 14% scored over 1800 on combined SAT.

Student Life Upper grades have specified standards of dress, student council. Discipline rests primarily with faculty.

Summer Programs Remediation, enrichment, advancement, ESL, sports, art/fine arts, rigorous outdoor training, computer instruction programs offered; session focuses on skills development; held on campus; accepts boys and girls; open to students from other schools. 1,200 students usually enrolled. 2011 schedule: June 28 to August 13. Application deadline: June 21.

Tuition and Aid Day student tuition: $28,300; 7-day tuition and room/board: $42,900. Tuition installment plan (Key Tuition Payment Plan). Need-based scholarship grants, need-based loans, paying campus jobs available. In 2010–11, 47% of upper-school students received aid. Total amount of financial aid awarded in 2010–11: $1,657,175.

Admissions Traditional secondary-level entrance grade is 9. For fall 2010, 381 students applied for upper-level admission, 139 were accepted, 67 enrolled. Any standardized test required. Deadline for receipt of application materials: January 15. Application fee required: $50. Interview required.

Athletics Interscholastic: basketball (boys, girls), cross-country running (b), golf (b), lacrosse (b,g), soccer (b,g), tennis (b,g); coed interscholastic: soccer; coed intramural: badminton, ball hockey, basketball, bicycling, bocce, cooperative games, croquet, fitness, fitness walking, flag football, floor hockey, Frisbee, horseshoes, jogging, physical fitness, project adventure, ropes courses, running, soccer, strength & conditioning, tennis, touch football, ultimate Frisbee, walking, weight lifting, weight training, yoga. 1 PE instructor, 20 coaches, 1 athletic trainer.

Computers Computers are regularly used in all academic, computer applications, library skills, multimedia, photography, SAT preparation, yearbook classes. Computer network features include on-campus library services, Internet access, wireless campus network, Internet filtering or blocking technology, NetClassroom is available for parents and students. Campus intranet, student e-mail accounts, and computer access in designated common areas are available to students. Students grades are available online. The school has a published electronic and media policy.

Contact Mary Bishop, Administrative Assistant to Admissions. 401-246-1230 Ext. 3025. Fax: 401-246-0510. E-mail: mbishop@standrews-ri.org. Web site: www.standrews-ri.org.

See Display on page 543 and Close-Up on page 830.

ST. ANN'S ACADEMY
205 Columbia Street
Kamloops, British Columbia V2C 2S7, Canada
Head of School: Mr. Shawn Chisholm
General Information Coeducational day college-preparatory, general academic, arts, and religious studies school, affiliated with Roman Catholic Church. Grades K–12. Founded: 1880. Setting: urban. Nearest major city is Vancouver, Canada. 10-acre campus. 3 buildings on campus. Approved or accredited by Canadian Association of Independent Schools, Christian Brothers Association, North Central Association of Colleges and Schools, and British Columbia Department of Education. Language of instruction: English. Total enrollment: 528. Upper school average class size: 24. Upper school faculty-student ratio: 1:24. There are 181 required school days per year for Upper School students. Upper School students typically attend 5 days per week. The average school day consists of 5 hours.
Upper School Student Profile 80% of students are Roman Catholic.
Faculty School total: 33. In upper school: 11 men, 7 women; 6 have advanced degrees.
Subjects Offered All academic.
Special Academic Programs Independent study; remedial reading and/or remedial writing; remedial math; ESL (11 students enrolled).

College Admission Counseling 72 students graduated in 2010; 64 went to college, including The University of British Columbia. Other: 7 went to work, 1 had other specific plans.
Student Life Upper grades have specified standards of dress, student council, honor system. Discipline rests primarily with faculty. Attendance at religious services is required.
Tuition and Aid Day student tuition: CAN$9000. Tuition reduction for siblings, merit scholarship grants available. In 2010–11, 12% of upper-school students received aid; total upper-school merit-scholarship money awarded: CAN$3000. Total amount of financial aid awarded in 2010–11: CAN$30,000.
Admissions For fall 2010, 26 students applied for upper-level admission, 19 were accepted, 19 enrolled. English Composition Test for ESL students required. Deadline for receipt of application materials: none. No application fee required. Interview required.
Athletics Interscholastic: badminton (boys, girls), basketball (b,g), bicycling (b,g), bowling (g), cross-country running (b,g), flag football (b,g), football (b,g), golf (b,g), rugby (g), snowboarding (b,g), soccer (b,g), track and field (b,g), volleyball (b,g); intramural: track and field (b,g); coed interscholastic: aquatics. 3 PE instructors, 5 coaches.
Computers Computers are regularly used in mathematics classes. Computer network features include on-campus library services, online commercial services, Internet access, Internet filtering or blocking technology. The school has a published electronic and media policy.
Contact Mr. Shawn Chisholm, Principal. 250-372-5452 Ext. 222. Fax: 250-372-5257. E-mail: principal@stannsacademy.bc.ca.

ST. ANSELM'S ABBEY SCHOOL
4501 South Dakota Avenue NE
Washington, District of Columbia 20017
Head of School: Mr. Louis Silvano
General Information Boys' day college-preparatory school, affiliated with Roman Catholic Church. Grades 6–12. Founded: 1942. Setting: urban. 40-acre campus. 3 buildings on campus. Approved or accredited by Association of Independent Maryland Schools, Association of Independent Schools of Greater Washington, Middle States Association of Colleges and Schools, and National Catholic Education Association. Member of National Association of Independent Schools. Endowment: $2.3 million. Total enrollment: 238. Upper school average class size: 12. Upper school faculty-student ratio: 1:5. There are 180 required school days per year for Upper School students. Upper School students typically attend 5 days per week. The average school day consists of 7 hours.
Upper School Student Profile Grade 9: 44 students (44 boys); Grade 10: 32 students (32 boys); Grade 11: 34 students (34 boys); Grade 12: 32 students (32 boys). 60% of students are Roman Catholic.
Faculty School total: 51. In upper school: 30 men, 10 women; 31 have advanced degrees.
Subjects Offered Advanced Placement courses, advanced studio art-AP, algebra, American history, American history-AP, American literature, American literature-AP, anatomy, Ancient Greek, ancient world history, anthropology, applied music, Arabic, art, art history, art history-AP, athletic training, athletics, band, bell choir, Bible studies, biology, botany, British literature-AP, calculus, calculus-AP, career planning, career/college preparation, Catholic belief and practice, ceramics, chemistry, chemistry-AP, choir, choral music, church history, classical Greek literature, classical language, classical music, college counseling, college placement, comparative government and politics, comparative government and politics-AP, composition-AP, computer education, computer graphics, computer math, computer programming, computer science, creative drama, debate, drama, earth science, economics, economics-AP, English, English language and composition-AP, English language-AP, English literature, English literature and composition-AP, English literature-AP, English-AP, English/composition-AP, environmental science, environmental science-AP, environmental studies, ethics, European history, European history-AP, expository writing, fencing, fine arts, foreign language, forensics, French, French as a second language, French language-AP, French literature-AP, French-AP, geography, geology, geometry, government and politics-AP, government-AP, government/civics, grammar, Greek, history, history of music, history of science, history of the Catholic Church, history-AP, instrumental music, journalism, language-AP, Latin, Latin-AP, literature and composition-AP, macro/microeconomics-AP, mathematics, mathematics-AP, medieval history, medieval literature, medieval/Renaissance history, model United Nations, modern European history, modern languages, modern politics, modern Western civilization, modern world history, music, music appreciation, music history, music performance, music theory-AP, music-AP, Native American studies, Navajo, non-Western societies, opera, oral communications, oral expression, orchestra, organizational studies, performing arts, philosophy, physical education, physical fitness, physics, physics-AP, play production, pre-calculus, religion, religious education, religious studies, robotics, Roman civilization, Roman culture, science, Shakespeare, social issues, social studies, Spanish, Spanish language-AP, Spanish literature-AP, Spanish-AP, speech, speech and debate, speech and oral interpretations, speech communications, statistics, statistics-AP, studio art-AP, theater, theology, trigonometry, U.S. government and politics-AP, United States government-AP, vocal music, weightlifting, world history, world history-AP, world literature, writing.

Graduation Requirements Arts and fine arts (art, music, dance, drama), English, foreign language, mathematics, physical education (includes health), religion (includes Bible studies and theology), science, social studies (includes history), community service for 11th and 12th grade.

Special Academic Programs Advanced Placement exam preparation; academic accommodation for the gifted.

College Admission Counseling 39 students graduated in 2009; all went to college, including Boston College; Georgetown University; New York University; The College of William and Mary; University of Maryland, College Park; University of Notre Dame. Median SAT critical reading: 657, median SAT math: 667, median SAT writing: 619, median combined SAT: 1943. 100% scored over 600 on SAT critical reading, 100% scored over 600 on SAT math, 100% scored over 600 on SAT writing, 100% scored over 1800 on combined SAT.

Student Life Upper grades have specified standards of dress, student council. Discipline rests primarily with faculty. Attendance at religious services is required.

Tuition and Aid Day student tuition: $19,990. Tuition installment plan (monthly payment plans, individually arranged payment plans, two payments (one prior to each semester), 10-month (June-March)). Need-based scholarship grants, Archdiocese of Washington financial aid program, Washington Scholarship Fund, Latino Student Fund available. In 2009–10, 28% of upper-school students received aid. Total amount of financial aid awarded in 2009–10: $700,000.

Admissions Traditional secondary-level entrance grade is 9. For fall 2009, 45 students applied for upper-level admission, 20 were accepted, 12 enrolled. Admissions testing and OLSAT and SCAT required. Deadline for receipt of application materials: none. Application fee required: $50. On-campus interview required.

Athletics Interscholastic: baseball, basketball, cross-country running, fencing, golf, soccer, tennis, track and field, wrestling; intramural: baseball, basketball, bicycling, fitness, flag football, football, jogging, kickball, outdoor activities, physical fitness, physical training, strength & conditioning, weight lifting, weight training. 3 PE instructors, 8 coaches.

Computers Computers are regularly used in all academic, art, Christian doctrine, classics, college planning, computer applications, creative writing, design, desktop publishing, drawing and design, economics, engineering, English, ethics, French, geography, graphic design, graphics, health, history, humanities, Latin, library, literary magazine, mathematics, music, news writing, newspaper, philosophy, photography, reading, religion, science, social sciences, Spanish, speech, study skills, theater, theology, Web site design, writing, yearbook classes. Computer network features include on-campus library services, online commercial services, Internet access, Internet filtering or blocking technology. Computer access in designated common areas is available to students. Students grades are available online. The school has a published electronic and media policy.

Contact Mrs. E.V. Downey, Director of Admissions. 202-269-2379. Fax: 202-269-2373. E-mail: admissions@saintanselms.org. Web site: www.saintanselms.org.

ST. ANTHONY CATHOLIC HIGH SCHOOL

3200 McCullough Avenue
San Antonio, Texas 78212-3099

Head of School: Mr. Rene Escobedo

General Information Coeducational boarding and day college-preparatory, arts, business, religious studies, bilingual studies, and technology school, affiliated with Roman Catholic Church. Grades 9–12. Founded: 1905. Setting: urban. Students are housed in single-sex by floor dormitories. 14-acre campus. 3 buildings on campus. Approved or accredited by National Catholic Education Association, Southern Association of Colleges and Schools, Texas Education Agency, and The College Board. Total enrollment: 453. Upper school average class size: 23. Upper school faculty-student ratio: 1:22. There are 180 required school days per year for Upper School students. Upper School students typically attend 5 days per week. The average school day consists of 7 hours.

Upper School Student Profile Grade 9: 110 students (65 boys, 45 girls); Grade 10: 121 students (76 boys, 45 girls); Grade 11: 115 students (65 boys, 50 girls); Grade 12: 105 students (67 boys, 38 girls). 7% of students are boarding students. 95% are state residents. 5 states are represented in upper school student body. 6% are international students. International students from China, Hong Kong, Japan, Mexico, Republic of Korea, and Spain; 3 other countries represented in student body. 85% of students are Roman Catholic.

Faculty School total: 34. In upper school: 17 men, 17 women; 21 have advanced degrees.

Subjects Offered Acting, advanced biology, advanced chemistry, advanced math, Advanced Placement courses, algebra, anatomy and physiology, aquatics, art, Bible studies, biology, calculus, Catholic belief and practice, chemistry, choir, computer graphics, computer literacy, economics, English, English literature, environmental science, ESL, French, geometry, government, graphic arts, graphic design, health, history, Japanese, jazz band, keyboarding, language, Latin, mathematical modeling, photography, photojournalism, physical education, physics, physics-AP, pre-calculus, psychology, robotics, sexuality, sociology, Spanish, Spanish-AP, speech, technical writing, theater, theology, trigonometry, typing, U.S. government, U.S. history, U.S. literature, world history, world religions, writing, yearbook.

Graduation Requirements Arts and fine arts (art, music, dance, drama), computer applications, economics, English, foreign language, government, mathematics,

physical education (includes health), religion (includes Bible studies and theology), science, speech, U.S. history, word processing, world history.

Special Academic Programs Advanced Placement exam preparation; study at local college for college credit; study abroad; academic accommodation for the gifted; ESL (15 students enrolled).

College Admission Counseling 113 students graduated in 2010; 111 went to college, including Texas A&M University; Texas State University–San Marcos; The University of Texas at Austin; Trinity University; United States Air Force Academy; University of the Incarnate Word. Other: 2 entered military service.

Student Life Upper grades have uniform requirement, student council, honor system. Discipline rests primarily with faculty. Attendance at religious services is required.

Summer Programs Remediation, enrichment, advancement, ESL, sports programs offered; session focuses on enrichment/advancement; held on campus; accepts boys and girls; open to students from other schools. 200 students usually enrolled. 2011 schedule: June to July.

Tuition and Aid Day student tuition: $5400; 5-day tuition and room/board: $14,000; 7-day tuition and room/board: $14,000. Tuition installment plan (monthly payment plans). Tuition reduction for siblings, need-based scholarship grants available. In 2010–11, 35% of upper-school students received aid. Total amount of financial aid awarded in 2010–11: $95,000.

Admissions Traditional secondary-level entrance grade is 9. For fall 2010, 207 students applied for upper-level admission, 150 were accepted, 110 enrolled. High School Placement Test required. Deadline for receipt of application materials: none. No application fee required. Interview required.

Athletics Interscholastic: baseball (boys), basketball (b,g), cheering (g), dance (g), dance team (g), football (b), lacrosse (b), soccer (b,g), softball (g), swimming and diving (b,g), tennis (b,g), volleyball (g), wrestling (b); coed interscholastic: cross-country running, golf, track and field. 3 PE instructors, 15 coaches, 2 athletic trainers.

Computers Computers are regularly used in all classes. Computer network features include on-campus library services, Internet access, Internet filtering or blocking technology. Students grades are available online. The school has a published electronic and media policy.

Contact Mr. Paul Alexander, Director of Enrollment. 210-832-5632. Fax: 210-832-5633. E-mail: sachs@uiwtx.edu. Web site: www.sachs.org.

SAINT ANTHONY HIGH SCHOOL

304 East Roadway Avenue
Effingham, Illinois 62401

Head of School: Mr. Ron Niebrugge

General Information Coeducational day college-preparatory, arts, business, religious studies, bilingual studies, and technology school, affiliated with Roman Catholic Church. Grades 9–12. Setting: small town. Nearest major city is St. Louis, MO. 1 building on campus. Approved or accredited by Illinois Department of Education. Total enrollment: 190. Upper school average class size: 20. Upper school faculty-student ratio: 1:10. Upper School students typically attend 5 days per week.

Upper School Student Profile Grade 9: 36 students (20 boys, 16 girls); Grade 10: 51 students (23 boys, 28 girls); Grade 11: 49 students (31 boys, 18 girls); Grade 12: 54 students (33 boys, 21 girls). 97% of students are Roman Catholic.

Faculty School total: 24. In upper school: 8 men, 14 women; 8 have advanced degrees.

Subjects Offered Accounting, advanced math, algebra, American government, anatomy, art appreciation, band, biology, British literature, calculus-AP, career exploration, Catholic belief and practice, ceramics, chemistry, chorus, communications, composition, computer applications, conceptual physics, concert band, consumer education, criminal justice, current events, drawing, earth science, English literature, English-AP, environmental science, finite math, forensics, general math, geography, geometry, health, microbiology, music appreciation, physical education, physical science, physics, pre-algebra, psychology, publications, Spanish, statistics-AP, U.S. history, world history, world wide web design.

Graduation Requirements American government, arts and fine arts (art, music, dance, drama), computer science, consumer education, English, mathematics, physical education (includes health), religion (includes Bible studies and theology), science, social sciences, speech, U.S. history, world history.

Special Academic Programs International Baccalaureate program; 3 Advanced Placement exams for which test preparation is offered; independent study; study at local college for college credit; remedial math; special instructional classes for deaf students.

College Admission Counseling 55 students graduated in 2010; 53 went to college, including Eastern Illinois University; Southern Illinois University Edwardsville; University of Illinois at Urbana–Champaign. Other: 1 went to work, 1 entered military service. Median composite ACT: 24.

Student Life Upper grades have specified standards of dress, student council. Discipline rests primarily with faculty. Attendance at religious services is required.

Tuition and Aid Tuition installment plan (monthly payment plans). Need-based scholarship grants available.

Admissions Traditional secondary-level entrance grade is 9. No application fee required.

Saint Anthony High School

Athletics Interscholastic: baseball (boys), basketball (b,g), cheering (g), dance team (g), golf (b,g), soccer (b,g), softball (g), tennis (b,g), track and field (b,g), volleyball (g), wrestling (b); coed interscholastic: cross-country running. 3 PE instructors, 19 coaches.

Computers Computers are regularly used in drafting, publications, yearbook classes. Computer network features include on-campus library services, Internet access, Internet filtering or blocking technology. Student e-mail accounts are available to students. The school has a published electronic and media policy.

Contact Mr. Ron Niebrugge, Principal. 217-342-6969. Fax: 217-342-6997. E-mail: rniebrugge@stanthony.com. Web site: www.stanthony.com.

SAINT ANTHONY'S HIGH SCHOOL

275 Wolf Hill Road
South Huntington, New York 11747-1394
Head of School: Br. Gary Cregan, OSF

General Information Coeducational day college-preparatory school, affiliated with Roman Catholic Church. Grades 9–12. Founded: 1933. Setting: suburban. Nearest major city is Huntington. 30-acre campus. 1 building on campus. Approved or accredited by Middle States Association of Colleges and Schools, New York State Board of Regents, and New York Department of Education. Total enrollment: 2,523. Upper school average class size: 35. Upper school faculty-student ratio: 1:30. There are 169 required school days per year for Upper School students. Upper School students typically attend 5 days per week. The average school day consists of 6 hours and 15 minutes.

Upper School Student Profile Grade 9: 664 students (370 boys, 294 girls); Grade 10: 679 students (352 boys, 327 girls); Grade 11: 622 students (329 boys, 293 girls); Grade 12: 558 students (282 boys, 276 girls). 90% of students are Roman Catholic.

Faculty School total: 122. In upper school: 44 men, 78 women; 87 have advanced degrees.

Subjects Offered Accounting, Advanced Placement courses, algebra, American history, American literature, architecture, art, arts, band, biology, business law, calculus, ceramics, chemistry, chorus, computer science, creative writing, drama, drawing, earth science, economics, English, English literature, fine arts, French, government/civics, health, humanities, jazz, keyboarding, Latin, literature, marine science, mathematics, music, music theory, oceanography, orchestra, painting, philosophy, physical education, physics, political science, printmaking, public speaking, religion, science, social studies, sociology, Spanish, theater, Western civilization, world affairs.

Graduation Requirements Arts and fine arts (art, music, dance, drama), English, foreign language, mathematics, physical education (includes health), religion (includes Bible studies and theology), science, social studies (includes history).

Special Academic Programs Advanced Placement exam preparation; study at local college for college credit.

College Admission Counseling 546 students graduated in 2009; 542 went to college, including Hofstra University; Sacred Heart University; Siena College; St. John's University; Stony Brook University, State University of New York; The University of Scranton. Other: 4 entered military service.

Student Life Upper grades have uniform requirement, student council. Discipline rests primarily with faculty. Attendance at religious services is required.

Tuition and Aid Day student tuition: $7500. Tuition installment plan (monthly payment plans).

Admissions Traditional secondary-level entrance grade is 9. For fall 2009, 2,019 students applied for upper-level admission, 664 enrolled. Catholic High School Entrance Examination required. Deadline for receipt of application materials: none. Application fee required: $35.

Athletics Interscholastic: badminton (girls), baseball (b), basketball (b,g), bowling (b,g), cheering (g), cross-country running (b,g), danceline (g), diving (b,g), football (b), golf (b,g), ice hockey (b), indoor track & field (b,g), lacrosse (b,g), soccer (b,g), softball (g), swimming and diving (b,g), tennis (b,g), track and field (b,g), volleyball (b,g), winter (indoor) track (b,g), wrestling (b); intramural: baseball (b), basketball (b,g), dance squad (g), strength & conditioning (b,g); coed interscholastic: crew; coed intramural: equestrian sports. 8 PE instructors, 167 coaches, 2 athletic trainers.

Computers Computer resources include Internet access. The school has a published electronic and media policy.

Contact Br. Ferdinand Vogrin, OSF, Director of Admissions. 631-271-2020 Ext. 213. Fax: 631-351-1507. Web site: www.stanthonyshs.org.

ST. ANTHONY'S JUNIOR-SENIOR HIGH SCHOOL

1618 Lower Main Street
Wailuku, Hawaii 96793
Head of School: Mrs. Patricia Rickard

General Information Coeducational day college-preparatory, general academic, arts, religious studies, and technology school, affiliated with Roman Catholic Church. Grades 7–12. Founded: 1848. Setting: small town. 15-acre campus. 13 buildings on campus. Approved or accredited by National Catholic Education Association, Western Association of Schools and Colleges, and Hawaii Department of Education. Endowment: $216,177. Total enrollment: 153. Upper school average class size: 22. Upper school faculty-student ratio: 1:10. There are 179 required school days per year

for Upper School students. Upper School students typically attend 5 days per week. The average school day consists of 6 hours and 45 minutes.

Upper School Student Profile Grade 9: 32 students (22 boys, 10 girls); Grade 10: 22 students (10 boys, 12 girls); Grade 11: 26 students (11 boys, 15 girls); Grade 12: 35 students (22 boys, 13 girls). 65% of students are Roman Catholic.

Faculty School total: 19. In upper school: 8 men, 11 women; 8 have advanced degrees.

Subjects Offered Advanced math, American government, American history, American history-AP, American literature, American literature-AP, anatomy and physiology, applied arts, art, athletic training, athletics, baseball, basic skills, basketball, Bible, Bible as literature, Bible studies, biology, biology-AP, bowling, British literature, British literature (honors), British literature-AP, business, calculus, calculus-AP, campus ministry, chemistry, chemistry-AP, college counseling, college planning, computer education, computer graphics, computer literacy, computer skills, computer technologies, computer technology certification, computer tools, computer-aided design, computers, creative arts, dance, drama, drama performance, drama workshop, dramatic arts, drawing, drawing and design, driver education, electives, English, English language and composition-AP, English language-AP, English literature, English literature and composition-AP, English literature-AP, English-AP, English/composition-AP, environmental science, environmental science-AP, foreign language, health, keyboarding, mathematics, music, physical education, Polynesian dance, pre-algebra, pre-calculus, religion, religious studies, SAT preparation, SAT/ACT preparation, science, social studies, Spanish language-AP, sports medicine, standard curriculum, technology, U.S. government and politics-AP, U.S. history-AP, world geography, writing, writing, yearbook, zoology.

Graduation Requirements Art, English, languages, mathematics, physical education (includes health), religion (includes Bible studies and theology), science, social studies (includes history), technology.

Special Academic Programs Advanced Placement exam preparation; study at local college for college credit.

College Admission Counseling 39 students graduated in 2010; 38 went to college, including Fordham University; Pacific Lutheran University; University of San Diego; University of San Francisco; University of Washington; Vanguard University of Southern California. Other: 1 entered military service. 50% scored over 600 on SAT critical reading, 50% scored over 600 on SAT math, 50% scored over 600 on SAT writing, 50% scored over 1800 on combined SAT, 50% scored over 26 on composite ACT.

Student Life Upper grades have uniform requirement, student council. Discipline rests primarily with faculty. Attendance at religious services is required.

Summer Programs Remediation, enrichment programs offered; session focuses on remediation; held on campus; accepts boys and girls; open to students from other schools. 100 students usually enrolled. 2011 schedule: June 13 to July 15. Application deadline: June 1.

Tuition and Aid Day student tuition: $9400–$9800. Tuition installment plan (FACTS Tuition Payment Plan). Merit scholarship grants, need-based scholarship grants, need-based loans available. In 2010–11, 30% of upper-school students received aid.

Admissions Traditional secondary-level entrance grade is 9. For fall 2010, 40 students applied for upper-level admission, 36 were accepted, 36 enrolled. Achievement tests or Educational Development Series required. Deadline for receipt of application materials: none. Application fee required: $300. Interview required.

Athletics Interscholastic: aquatics (boys, girls), baseball (b), basketball (b), bowling (b,g), canoeing/kayaking (b,g), cross-country running (b,g), curling (b,g), drill team (b,g), golf (b,g), judo (b,g), ocean paddling (b,g), paddling (b,g), racquetball (b,g), riflery (b,g), running (b,g), soccer (b,g), softball (g), strength & conditioning (b,g), surfing (b,g), swimming and diving (g), tennis (b,g), touch football (b,g), track and field (b,g), volleyball (g), weight lifting (b,g), weight training (b,g), wrestling (b,g); intramural: basketball (b,g), flag football (b,g); coed interscholastic: cheering, flag football, paddling, racquetball; coed intramural: flag football. 2 PE instructors, 36 coaches, 1 athletic trainer.

Computers Computers are regularly used in construction classes. Computer network features include on-campus library services, Internet access, Internet filtering or blocking technology. Student e-mail accounts and computer access in designated common areas are available to students. Students grades are available online. The school has a published electronic and media policy.

Contact Mrs. Cindy Martin, Guidance/College Counselor. 808-244-4190 Ext. 224. Fax: 808-242-8081. E-mail: cmartin@sasmaui.org. Web site: www.sasmaui.org.

ST. AUGUSTINE HIGH SCHOOL

3266 Nutmeg Street
San Diego, California 92104-5199
Head of School: James Walter Horne

General Information Boys' day college-preparatory and religious studies school, affiliated with Roman Catholic Church. Grades 9–12. Founded: 1922. Setting: urban. 6-acre campus. 10 buildings on campus. Approved or accredited by National Catholic Education Association, Western Association of Schools and Colleges, and Western Catholic Education Association. Endowment: $1 million. Total enrollment: 700. Upper school average class size: 28. Upper school faculty-student ratio: 1:28. Upper School students typically attend 5 days per week.

Upper School Student Profile Grade 9: 190 students (190 boys); Grade 10: 180 students (180 boys); Grade 11: 170 students (170 boys); Grade 12: 160 students (160 boys). 95% of students are Roman Catholic.

Faculty School total: 45. In upper school: 34 men, 11 women; 30 have advanced degrees.

Subjects Offered Algebra, American history, American literature, anatomy, art, art history, arts, Bible studies, biology, calculus, chemistry, computer science, driver education, economics, economics-AP, English, English literature, English-AP, ethics, fine arts, French, geometry, government/civics, grammar, health, history, Latin, mathematics, music, philosophy, physical education, physics, physiology, psychology, religion, science, social studies, Spanish, speech, theology, trigonometry, world history, world literature, writing.

Graduation Requirements Arts and fine arts (art, music, dance, drama), English, foreign language, mathematics, physical education (includes health), religion (includes Bible studies and theology), science, social studies (includes history), speech, 100 hours of Christian service over four years.

Special Academic Programs Advanced Placement exam preparation; honors section; academic accommodation for the gifted; remedial reading and/or remedial writing; remedial math; programs in English, mathematics, general development for dyslexic students.

College Admission Counseling 166 students graduated in 2009; 165 went to college, including Gonzaga University; San Diego State University; University of California, Los Angeles; University of California, San Diego; University of Notre Dame; University of San Diego. 45% scored over 600 on SAT critical reading, 45% scored over 600 on SAT math, 45% scored over 600 on SAT writing, 55% scored over 26 on composite ACT.

Student Life Upper grades have specified standards of dress, student council, honor system. Discipline rests primarily with faculty. Attendance at religious services is required.

Tuition and Aid Day student tuition: $11,950. Tuition installment plan (monthly payment plans, quarterly and annual payment plans). Merit scholarship grants, need-based scholarship grants, paying campus jobs available. In 2009–10, 30% of upper-school students received aid.

Admissions For fall 2009, 340 students applied for upper-level admission, 200 were accepted, 190 enrolled. High School Placement Test required. Deadline for receipt of application materials: January 23. Application fee required: $50. Interview required.

Athletics Interscholastic: baseball, basketball, bicycling, cross-country running, football, golf, mountain biking, soccer, street hockey, surfing, swimming and diving, tennis, track and field, volleyball, wrestling; intramural: basketball, flag football, volleyball. 5 PE instructors, 26 coaches, 1 athletic trainer.

Computers Computers are regularly used in foreign language, mathematics, science, Web site design, writing classes. Computer resources include on-campus library services, online commercial services, Internet access, wireless campus network, Internet filtering or blocking technology, online databases, remote access. Campus intranet and computer access in designated common areas are available to students. The school has a published electronic and media policy.

Contact Jeannie Oliwa, Registrar. 619-282-2184 Ext. 5512. Fax: 619-282-1203. E-mail: joliwa@sahs.org. Web site: www.sahs.org.

ST. AUGUSTINE HIGH SCHOOL

1300 Galveston
Laredo, Texas 78040
Head of School: Mrs. Olga P. Gentry

General Information Coeducational day college-preparatory and religious studies school, affiliated with Roman Catholic Church. Grades 9–12. Founded: 1927. Setting: urban. Nearest major city is San Antonio. 3-acre campus. 6 buildings on campus. Approved or accredited by National Catholic Education Association, Texas Catholic Conference, Texas Education Agency, and Texas Department of Education. Endowment: $1.6 million. Total enrollment: 598. Upper school average class size: 22. Upper school faculty-student ratio: 1:20. There are 180 required school days per year for Upper School students. Upper School students typically attend 5 days per week. The average school day consists of 8 hours and 6 minutes.

Upper School Student Profile Grade 9: 93 students (45 boys, 48 girls); Grade 10: 124 students (63 boys, 61 girls); Grade 11: 97 students (43 boys, 54 girls); Grade 12: 122 students (51 boys, 71 girls). 94% of students are Roman Catholic.

Faculty School total: 32. In upper school: 11 men, 18 women; 10 have advanced degrees.

Subjects Offered Accounting, algebra, American history, art, art appreciation, biology, calculus, chemistry, Christian scripture, church history, computer applications, computer literacy, computer programming, creative writing, critical writing, drawing, economics, English, geography, geometry, government, health, language arts, mathematics, novels, painting, physical education, physics, pre-calculus, psychology, reading, religion, science, social justice, social studies, Spanish, speech, technical writing, theater arts, world history, world religions, yearbook.

Graduation Requirements Arts and fine arts (art, music, dance, drama), computer science, English, foreign language, mathematics, physical education (includes health), religion (includes Bible studies and theology), science, social studies (includes history), 100 hours of community service.

Special Academic Programs Advanced Placement exam preparation; study at local college for college credit.

College Admission Counseling 126 students graduated in 2009; 122 went to college, including St. Mary's University; Texas A&M International University; Texas A&M University; The University of Texas at Austin; The University of Texas at San Antonio; University of the Incarnate Word. Other: 1 entered military service, 3 entered a postgraduate year. Mean SAT critical reading: 486, mean SAT math: 465, mean composite ACT: 20.

Student Life Upper grades have uniform requirement, student council, honor system. Discipline rests primarily with faculty. Attendance at religious services is required.

Tuition and Aid Day student tuition: $4350. Tuition installment plan (monthly payment plans). Tuition reduction for siblings, need-based scholarship grants available. In 2009–10, 12% of upper-school students received aid. Total amount of financial aid awarded in 2009–10: $86,000.

Admissions Traditional secondary-level entrance grade is 9. For fall 2009, 40 students applied for upper-level admission, 38 were accepted, 34 enrolled. High School Placement Test required. Deadline for receipt of application materials: March 15. Application fee required: $150. On-campus interview required.

Athletics Interscholastic: baseball (boys), basketball (b,g), cheering (g), cross-country running (b,g), dance team (g), golf (b,g), softball (g), tennis (b,g), track and field (b,g); coed interscholastic: tennis, track and field. 2 PE instructors, 6 coaches.

Computers Computers are regularly used in accounting, art, English, history, mathematics, science, Web site design classes. Computer network features include on-campus library services, Internet access. The school has a published electronic and media policy.

Contact Mrs. Linda Solano, Administrative Assistant. 956-724-8131 Ext. 1003. Fax: 956-724-8770. E-mail: solano@st-augustine.org. Web site: www.st-augustine.org.

SAINT AUGUSTINE PREPARATORY SCHOOL

611 Cedar Avenue
PO Box 279
Richland, New Jersey 08350
Head of School: Rev. Francis J. Horn, OSA

General Information Boys' day college-preparatory and religious studies school, affiliated with Roman Catholic Church. Grades 9–12. Founded: 1959. Setting: rural. Nearest major city is Vineland. 120-acre campus. 4 buildings on campus. Approved or accredited by Middle States Association of Colleges and Schools, National Catholic Education Association, and New Jersey Department of Education. Endowment: $250,000. Total enrollment: 681. Upper school average class size: 17. Upper school faculty-student ratio: 1:13. There are 180 required school days per year for Upper School students. Upper School students typically attend 5 days per week. The average school day consists of 6 hours and 8 minutes.

Upper School Student Profile Grade 9: 169 students (169 boys); Grade 10: 183 students (183 boys); Grade 11: 152 students (152 boys); Grade 12: 177 students (177 boys). 79% of students are Roman Catholic.

Faculty School total: 57. In upper school: 45 men, 12 women; 20 have advanced degrees.

Subjects Offered 20th century history, accounting, Advanced Placement courses, advanced studio art-AP, algebra, American literature, anatomy and physiology, ancient world history, art, band, Bible, biology, biology-AP, British literature, British literature (honors), calculus, calculus-AP, Catholic belief and practice, chemistry, chemistry-AP, choir, Christian and Hebrew scripture, Christian doctrine, Christian ethics, church history, classical language, college counseling, college planning, community service, comparative religion, computer applications, computer programming, computer science, computer-aided design, concert choir, constitutional law, culinary arts, drama, drama performance, driver education, engineering, English, English composition, English literature, English literature-AP, environmental education, ethics and responsibility, European history, European history-AP, finance, French, geometry, grammar, guitar, history, history of the Catholic Church, history-AP, honors algebra, honors English, honors geometry, honors U.S. history, independent study, Italian, jazz band, jazz ensemble, lab science, language-AP, Latin, marine biology, mathematics-AP, model United Nations, moral theology, music theory, music theory-AP, peer ministry, philosophy, physical education, physics, physics-AP, political science, pre-calculus, psychology, psychology-AP, religion, religious studies, SAT preparation, scripture, service learning/internship, social skills, sociology, Spanish, Spanish language-AP, Spanish literature-AP, Spanish-AP, statistics-AP, studio art, travel, U.S. history AP, vocal music, world cultures, world religions, writing.

Graduation Requirements Electives, English, foreign language, lab science, mathematics, religion (includes Bible studies and theology), service learning/internship, U.S. history, world cultures, social service project—approximately 100 hours, retreat experiences, third semester experiences.

Special Academic Programs 13 Advanced Placement exams for which test preparation is offered; honors section; independent study; study at local college for college credit; study abroad; programs in general development for dyslexic students.

College Admission Counseling 150 students graduated in 2010; all went to college, including Drexel University; High Point University; La Salle University; Loyola University Maryland; New York University; Saint Joseph's University. Mean SAT critical reading: 545, mean SAT math: 581, mean SAT writing: 552, mean combined SAT: 1678.

Student Life Upper grades have uniform requirement, student council, honor system. Discipline rests primarily with faculty. Attendance at religious services is required.

Saint Augustine Preparatory School

Summer Programs Enrichment, advancement, sports, art/fine arts, rigorous outdoor training, computer instruction programs offered; session focuses on academic enrichment, community relations, sports camps; held on campus; accepts boys and girls; open to students from other schools. 656 students usually enrolled. 2011 schedule: June 20 to August 5. Application deadline: May 15.

Tuition and Aid Day student tuition: $12,950. Tuition installment plan (FACTS Tuition Payment Plan, monthly payment plans, individually arranged payment plans, credit card payment; discount for pre-payment). Merit scholarship grants, need-based scholarship grants available. In 2010–11, 30% of upper-school students received aid; total upper-school merit-scholarship money awarded: $75,000. Total amount of financial aid awarded in 2010–11: $1,000,000.

Admissions Traditional secondary-level entrance grade is 9. For fall 2010, 283 students applied for upper-level admission, 246 were accepted, 169 enrolled. School's own exam required. Deadline for receipt of application materials: January 30. Application fee required: $75. On-campus interview recommended.

Athletics Interscholastic: baseball, basketball, bowling, crew, cross-country running, fencing, football, golf, ice hockey, indoor track, lacrosse, rowing, rugby, sailing, soccer, swimming and diving, tennis, track and field, volleyball, winter (indoor) track, wrestling; intramural: basketball, ultimate Frisbee, weight training. 2 PE instructors, 11 coaches, 1 athletic trainer.

Computers Computers are regularly used in all academic, art, career education, design classes. Computer network features include on-campus library services, online commercial services, Internet access, wireless campus network, Internet filtering or blocking technology, syllabus, current grades, and assignments available online for all courses. Computer access in designated common areas is available to students. Students grades are available online. The school has a published electronic and media policy.

Contact Mrs. Linda Pine, Director of Admissions. 856-697-2600 Ext. 112. Fax: 856-697-8389. E-mail: mrs.pine@hermits.com. Web site: www.hermits.com.

SAINT BASIL ACADEMY

711 Fox Chase Road
Jenkintown, Pennsylvania 19046
Head of School: Sr. Carla Hernandez

General Information Girls' day college-preparatory, arts, business, religious studies, bilingual studies, and technology school, affiliated with Roman Catholic Church. Grades 9–12. Founded: 1931. Setting: suburban. Nearest major city is Philadelphia. 28-acre campus. 1 building on campus. Approved or accredited by Middle States Association of Colleges and Schools and Pennsylvania Department of Education. Endowment: $500,000. Total enrollment: 365. Upper school average class size: 24. Upper school faculty-student ratio: 1:12. There are 180 required school days per year for Upper School students. Upper School students typically attend 5 days per week. The average school day consists of 6 hours and 30 minutes.

Upper School Student Profile Grade 9: 89 students (89 girls); Grade 10: 79 students (79 girls); Grade 11: 95 students (95 girls); Grade 12: 102 students (102 girls). 96% of students are Roman Catholic.

Faculty School total: 34. In upper school: 5 men, 25 women; 22 have advanced degrees.

Subjects Offered Accounting, advanced biology, algebra, American history, American history-AP, American literature, anatomy, art, band, biology, British literature, business, calculus-AP, chemistry, Christian and Hebrew scripture, computer applications, concert choir, creative writing, desktop publishing, digital applications, economics, English, English language-AP, English literature, English literature-AP, ensembles, environmental science, European history, fine arts, French, French literature-AP, geometry, German, government/civics, guitar, health, Hebrew scripture, history, honors algebra, honors English, honors geometry, Italian, journalism, keyboarding, Latin, mathematics, music, physical education, physics, pre-calculus, probability and statistics, psychology, religion, religious studies, SAT preparation, science, Shakespeare, social studies, sociology, Spanish, Spanish literature-AP, Spanish-AP, statistics, trigonometry, U.S. government and politics-AP, U.S. history, U.S. history-AP, Ukrainian, world cultures, world history.

Graduation Requirements Arts and fine arts (art, music, dance, drama), English, foreign language, keyboarding, mathematics, physical education (includes health), religion (includes Bible studies and theology), science, social studies (includes history). Community service is required.

Special Academic Programs Advanced Placement exam preparation; honors section; study at local college for college credit.

College Admission Counseling 102 students graduated in 2010; 100 went to college, including Drexel University; La Salle University; Penn State University Park; Saint Joseph's University; Temple University; West Chester University of Pennsylvania. Other: 2 had other specific plans. Mean SAT critical reading: 566, mean SAT math: 531, mean SAT writing: 586, mean combined SAT: 1683, mean composite ACT: 21.

Student Life Upper grades have uniform requirement, student council, honor system. Discipline rests primarily with faculty. Attendance at religious services is required.

Summer Programs Enrichment, sports programs offered; session focuses on sports camps, enrichment programs; held on campus; accepts girls; open to students from other schools. 50 students usually enrolled. 2011 schedule: June 15 to June 30. Application deadline: May 31.

Tuition and Aid Tuition installment plan (monthly payment plans, 2-installments (pay 1/2 tuition July 15, 1/2 tuition November 15), first installment (due July 15 (3 months), 7 installments (pay Oct. 15-April 15)). Tuition reduction for siblings, merit scholarship grants, need-based scholarship grants, Ellis Grant for children of single parents living in Philadelphia, BLOCS scholarships and foundations available. In 2010–11, 19% of upper-school students received aid; total upper-school merit-scholarship money awarded: $209,150. Total amount of financial aid awarded in 2010–11: $273,700.

Admissions Traditional secondary-level entrance grade is 9. For fall 2010, 185 students applied for upper-level admission, 89 enrolled. High School Placement Test required. Deadline for receipt of application materials: October 26. Application fee required: $40.

Athletics Interscholastic: basketball, cheering, cross-country running, field hockey, indoor track, lacrosse, soccer, softball, tennis, track and field, volleyball, winter (indoor) track. 1 PE instructor, 25 coaches.

Computers Computers are regularly used in accounting, computer applications, creative writing, desktop publishing, digital applications, economics, journalism, keyboarding, science classes. Computer network features include Internet access, wireless campus network, Internet filtering or blocking technology, student accessible server storage space, on-campus and Web-based library services (catalog and book request). Student e-mail accounts are available to students. The school has a published electronic and media policy.

Contact Mrs. Maureen Walsh, Director of Admissions. 215-885-6952. Fax: 215-885-0395. E-mail: mwalsh@stbasilacademy.org. Web site: www.stbasilacademy.org.

ST. BENEDICT AT AUBURNDALE

8250 Varnavas Drive
Cordova, Tennessee 38016
Head of School: Mr. George D. Valadie

General Information Coeducational day college-preparatory, arts, business, religious studies, bilingual studies, and technology school, affiliated with Roman Catholic Church. Grades 9–12. Founded: 1966. Setting: suburban. Nearest major city is Memphis. 40-acre campus. 1 building on campus. Approved or accredited by National Catholic Education Association, Southern Association of Colleges and Schools, Tennessee Association of Independent Schools, and Tennessee Department of Education. Endowment: $100,000. Total enrollment: 982. Upper school average class size: 26. Upper school faculty-student ratio: 1:15. There are 186 required school days per year for Upper School students. Upper School students typically attend 5 days per week. The average school day consists of 7 hours and 15 minutes.

Upper School Student Profile Grade 9: 254 students (110 boys, 144 girls); Grade 10: 255 students (125 boys, 130 girls); Grade 11: 245 students (110 boys, 135 girls); Grade 12: 228 students (102 boys, 126 girls). 85% of students are Roman Catholic.

Faculty School total: 65. In upper school: 15 men, 50 women; 40 have advanced degrees.

Subjects Offered Accounting, algebra, American government, American history, American history-AP, American literature-AP, anatomy and physiology, applied music, art, art appreciation, art education, art history, art-AP, astronomy, band, biology, calculus, calculus-AP, Catholic belief and practice, chemistry, choir, choral music, choreography, chorus, church history, cinematography, clayworking, comparative religion, composition-AP, computer graphics, computer multimedia, computers, creative writing, dance, digital art, digital photography, drama, drama performance, drawing, driver education, ecology, economics, economics-AP, English, English language-AP, English literature-AP, English-AP, English/composition-AP, etymology, European history, film, filmmaking, fine arts, first aid, fitness, forensics, French, French-AP, general business, geometry, German, government, government-AP, graphic arts, graphic design, health and wellness, health education, history, history of the Catholic Church, history-AP, honors algebra, honors English, honors geometry, honors U.S. history, human anatomy, human biology, instrumental music, internship, jazz band, jazz dance, journalism, keyboarding, lab/keyboard, Latin, literature-AP, macroeconomics-AP, marketing, modern history, music appreciation, music history, music theory, newspaper, performing arts, personal finance, photography, physical education, physical science, physics, play production, pre-algebra, pre-calculus, psychology, religion, set design, sociology, Spanish, Spanish-AP, speech, sports conditioning, stage design, statistics-AP, student publications, U.S. government and politics-AP, U.S. history-AP, world geography, world history, yearbook.

Graduation Requirements Arts and fine arts (art, music, dance, drama), economics, English, foreign language, government, mathematics, physical education (includes health), religion (includes Bible studies and theology), science, social studies (includes history), technology, theology.

Special Academic Programs 10 Advanced Placement exams for which test preparation is offered; study at local college for college credit; academic accommodation for the gifted, the musically talented, and the artistically talented; remedial reading and/or remedial writing; remedial math; programs in English, mathematics, general development for dyslexic students; special instructional classes for students with diagnosed learning disabilities and Attention Deficit Disorder.

College Admission Counseling 239 students graduated in 2010; 238 went to college, including Christian Brothers University; Middle Tennessee State University; Mississippi State University; The University of Alabama; The University of Tennessee; University of Memphis. Other: 1 entered military service. Mean SAT critical reading:

570, mean SAT math: 560, mean composite ACT: 24. 38% scored over 600 on SAT critical reading, 37% scored over 600 on SAT math, 30% scored over 26 on composite ACT.

Student Life Upper grades have uniform requirement, student council, honor system. Discipline rests primarily with faculty. Attendance at religious services is required.

Summer Programs Remediation, enrichment programs offered; session focuses on enrichment for math and language; held on campus; accepts boys and girls; not open to students from other schools. 30 students usually enrolled. 2011 schedule: July 5 to July 29. Application deadline: none.

Tuition and Aid Day student tuition: $7750. Tuition installment plan (FACTS Tuition Payment Plan, monthly payment plans, individually arranged payment plans). Merit scholarship grants, need-based scholarship grants available. In 2010–11, 4% of upper-school students received aid; total upper-school merit-scholarship money awarded: $30,000. Total amount of financial aid awarded in 2010–11: $35,000.

Admissions Traditional secondary-level entrance grade is 9. For fall 2010, 287 students applied for upper-level admission, 280 were accepted, 273 enrolled. High School Placement Test required. Deadline for receipt of application materials: none. Application fee required: $50. Interview required.

Athletics Interscholastic: baseball (boys), basketball (b,g), bowling (b,g), cheering (g), cross-country running (b,g), dance (g), dance squad (g), dance team (g), football (b), Frisbee (b,g), golf (b,g), lacrosse (b,g), pom squad (g), soccer (b,g), softball (g), strength & conditioning (b), swimming and diving (b,g), tennis (b,g), track and field (b,g), volleyball (g), weight lifting (b), weight training (b), wrestling (b); coed intramural: Frisbee. 4 PE instructors, 17 coaches, 1 athletic trainer.

Computers Computers are regularly used in all academic, art, business, commercial art, current events, dance, design, desktop publishing, economics, French, graphic arts, graphic design, health, history, journalism, lab/keyboard, Latin, mathematics, music, newspaper, photography, psychology, publications, religion, science, social sciences, social studies, Spanish, speech, study skills, technology, theater, theater arts, theology, Web site design, writing, yearbook classes. Computer network features include on-campus library services, Internet access, wireless campus network, Internet filtering or blocking technology. Students grades are available online. The school has a published electronic and media policy.

Contact Mrs. Ann O'Leary, Director of Admissions. 901-260-2875. Fax: 901-260-2850. E-mail: olearya@sbaeagles.org. Web site: www.sbaeagles.org.

SAINT BENEDICT HIGH SCHOOL

3900 North Leavitt Street
Chicago, Illinois 60618
Head of School: Mr. Sante Iacovelli

General Information Coeducational day college-preparatory, arts, business, religious studies, bilingual studies, and technology school, affiliated with Roman Catholic Church. Grades 9–12. Founded: 1950. Setting: urban. 3 buildings on campus. Approved or accredited by National Catholic Education Association, North Central Association of Colleges and Schools, The College Board, and Illinois Department of Education. Total enrollment: 250. Upper school average class size: 12. Upper school faculty-student ratio: 1:12.

Upper School Student Profile Grade 9: 61 students (34 boys, 27 girls); Grade 10: 62 students (32 boys, 30 girls); Grade 11: 62 students (28 boys, 34 girls); Grade 12: 65 students (35 boys, 30 girls); Postgraduate: 250 students (129 boys, 121 girls). 80% of students are Roman Catholic.

Faculty School total: 26. In upper school: 12 men, 14 women; 18 have advanced degrees.

Subjects Offered Advanced chemistry, advanced computer applications, advanced math, Advanced Placement courses, advanced studio art-AP, algebra, American government, American history, American history-AP, American literature, American literature-AP, analytic geometry, anatomy and physiology, applied arts, applied music, art, art appreciation, art history, audio visual/media, biology, British literature, British literature (honors), British literature-AP, business applications, calculus-AP, career planning, chemistry, chorus, Christian doctrine, Christian ethics, Christian scripture, computer education, computer multimedia, computer skills, consumer economics, CPR, drama, drama performance, English language-AP, English literature-AP, environmental science, European history-AP, general science, geometry, government, health, honors algebra, honors English, honors geometry, honors U.S. history, honors world history, human anatomy, human biology, intro to computers, keyboarding, lab science, library assistant, literature, mathematics, mathematics-AP, modern European history-AP, multimedia, music, newspaper, novels, oil painting, painting, physics, psychology, SAT/ACT preparation, social justice, social studies, Spanish, Spanish language-AP, Spanish-AP, speech, theology, U.S. government, U.S. history, weight-lifting, world geography, world history, world religions, writing, yearbook.

Graduation Requirements Arts and fine arts (art, music, dance, drama), computer applications, English, foreign language, keyboarding, mathematics, physical education (includes health), science, social studies (includes history), theology, U.S. constitutional history, U.S. government, service hours.

Special Academic Programs Advanced Placement exam preparation; honors section; study at local college for college credit; academic accommodation for the gifted and the artistically talented; remedial reading and/or remedial writing.

College Admission Counseling 52 students graduated in 2009; all went to college, including DePaul University; Illinois State University; Loyola University Chicago; Northeastern Illinois University; University of Illinois at Chicago; University of Illinois at Urbana–Champaign.

Student Life Upper grades have uniform requirement, student council, honor system. Discipline rests primarily with faculty. Attendance at religious services is required.

Tuition and Aid Day student tuition: $8150. Tuition installment plan (monthly payment plans). Merit scholarship grants, need-based scholarship grants, paying campus jobs available. In 2009–10, 50% of upper-school students received aid; total upper-school merit-scholarship money awarded: $25,000. Total amount of financial aid awarded in 2009–10: $130,000.

Admissions Traditional secondary-level entrance grade is 9. ACT-Explore required. Deadline for receipt of application materials: none. No application fee required. Interview required.

Athletics Interscholastic: baseball (boys), basketball (b,g), bowling (b,g), cheering (g), cross-country running (b,g), flag football (b), golf (b,g), physical fitness (b,g), soccer (b,g), softball (g), tennis (b,g), track and field (b,g), volleyball (b,g); intramural: dance (b,g), fencing (b); coed interscholastic: bowling; coed intramural: aerobics/dance, bowling, dance, Frisbee, outdoor adventure, outdoor recreation, skiing (downhill), strength & conditioning, weight lifting, weight training. 1 PE instructor, 12 coaches, 1 athletic trainer.

Computers Computers are regularly used in all academic classes. Computer network features include on-campus library services, online commercial services, Internet access, wireless campus network, Internet filtering or blocking technology. Campus intranet, student e-mail accounts, and computer access in designated common areas are available to students. Students grades are available online. The school has a published electronic and media policy.

Contact Mr. Kevin Walsh, Director of Admissions and Marketing. 773-539-0066 Ext. 314. Fax: 773-279-0690. E-mail: kwalsh@stbenedict.com. Web site: www.sbhs.stbenedict.com.

ST. BENEDICT'S PREPARATORY SCHOOL

520 Dr. Martin Luther King, Jr. Boulevard
Newark, New Jersey 07102-1314
Head of School: Rev. Edwin D. Leahy, OSB

General Information Boys' day college-preparatory school, affiliated with Roman Catholic Church. Grades 7–12. Founded: 1868. Setting: urban. 12-acre campus. 15 buildings on campus. Approved or accredited by Middle States Association of Colleges and Schools, New Jersey Association of Independent Schools, and New Jersey Department of Education. Endowment: $28 million. Total enrollment: 561. Upper school average class size: 20. Upper school faculty-student ratio: 1:11. Upper School students typically attend 5 days per week. The average school day consists of 6 hours.

Upper School Student Profile Grade 9: 132 students (132 boys); Grade 10: 118 students (118 boys); Grade 11: 116 students (116 boys); Grade 12: 109 students (109 boys). 40% of students are Roman Catholic.

Faculty School total: 55. In upper school: 44 men, 8 women; 40 have advanced degrees.

Subjects Offered Algebra, American history, American literature, architecture, art, astronomy, Bible studies, biology, Black history, calculus, chemistry, computer science, creative writing, drama, economics, English, English literature, ESL, European history, French, geometry, health, Hispanic literature, history, Latin, mathematics, mechanical drawing, music, physical education, physics, religion, social studies, sociology, Spanish, theater, trigonometry, world history.

Graduation Requirements English, foreign language, mathematics, physical education (includes health), religion (includes Bible studies and theology), science, social studies (includes history), spring projects, summer phase courses.

Special Academic Programs Term-away projects; domestic exchange program (with The Network Program Schools); remedial reading and/or remedial writing; remedial math; ESL (20 students enrolled).

College Admission Counseling 119 students graduated in 2010; 115 went to college, including Boston College; College of the Holy Cross; Rutgers, The State University of New Jersey, Newark; Saint John's University; Saint Peter's College; University of Notre Dame. Other: 2 went to work, 2 entered military service. Mean SAT critical reading: 468, mean SAT math: 492, mean SAT writing: 476, mean combined SAT: 1436.

Student Life Upper grades have uniform requirement, student council, honor system. Discipline rests equally with students and faculty. Attendance at religious services is required.

Summer Programs Remediation, enrichment, ESL, art/fine arts, computer instruction programs offered; session focuses on enrichment or remedial academic courses as appropriate; held on campus; accepts boys; not open to students from other schools. 550 students usually enrolled. 2011 schedule: July 26 to August 27.

Tuition and Aid Day student tuition: $8250; 5-day tuition and room/board: $13,250. Tuition installment plan (FACTS Tuition Payment Plan). Need-based scholarship grants available. In 2010–11, 75% of upper-school students received aid. Total amount of financial aid awarded in 2010–11: $1,833,000.

Admissions For fall 2010, 365 students applied for upper-level admission, 281 were accepted, 175 enrolled. Deadline for receipt of application materials: December 31. No application fee required. On-campus interview required.

Athletics Interscholastic: baseball, basketball, cross-country running, fencing, golf, indoor track & field, soccer, swimming and diving, tennis, track and field, water polo, winter (indoor) track, wrestling; intramural: basketball, flag football, floor hockey, hiking/backpacking, life saving, outdoor adventure, outdoor skills, physical training, soccer, swimming and diving, weight lifting. 2 PE instructors, 20 coaches.
Computers Computers are regularly used in English, information technology, journalism, science classes. Computer network features include on-campus library services, online commercial services, Internet access, wireless campus network, Internet filtering or blocking technology. Student e-mail accounts are available to students. The school has a published electronic and media policy.
Contact Ms. Doris Lamourt, Admissions Administrative Assistant. 973-792-5744. Fax: 973-792-5706. E-mail: DLamourt@sbp.org. Web site: www.sbp.org.

ST. BERNARD'S CATHOLIC SCHOOL
222 Dollison Street
Eureka, California 95501
Head of School: Mr. David Sharp
General Information Coeducational boarding and day college-preparatory and religious studies school, affiliated with Roman Catholic Church. Boarding grades 9–12, day grades PK–12. Founded: 1954. Setting: small town. Nearest major city is San Francisco. 5-acre campus. 4 buildings on campus. Approved or accredited by National Catholic Education Association, Western Association of Schools and Colleges, Western Catholic Education Association, and California Department of Education. Endowment: $63,000. Total enrollment: 300. Upper school average class size: 20. Upper school faculty-student ratio: 1:12. There are 162 required school days per year for Upper School students. Upper School students typically attend 5 days per week. The average school day consists of 6 hours.
Upper School Student Profile 35% of students are Roman Catholic.
Faculty School total: 20. In upper school: 9 men, 11 women; 5 have advanced degrees.
Subjects Offered Arts, community service, English, fine arts, mathematics, physical education, religion, science, social studies.
Graduation Requirements Arts and fine arts (art, music, dance, drama), English, foreign language, mathematics, physical education (includes health), science, social studies (includes history), theology, Follow the University of California requirements, 250 units. Community service is required.
Special Academic Programs Advanced Placement exam preparation; honors section; remedial reading and/or remedial writing; remedial math; special instructional classes for students with learning disabilities.
College Admission Counseling 55 students graduated in 2010; 52 went to college, including College of the Redwoods; Humboldt State University; Pacific University; Sonoma State University; University of California, San Diego; University of San Francisco. Other: 1 entered military service, 2 had other specific plans.
Student Life Upper grades have specified standards of dress, student council. Discipline rests equally with students and faculty. Attendance at religious services is required.
Summer Programs Remediation programs offered; session focuses on Make up; held on campus; accepts boys and girls; open to students from other schools. 10 students usually enrolled. 2011 schedule: June 16 to July 23. Application deadline: June 6.
Tuition and Aid Day student tuition: $6300. Tuition installment plan (SMART Tuition Payment Plan, 3% reduction if paid in full by July 10). Tuition reduction for siblings, merit scholarship grants, need-based scholarship grants, paying campus jobs available. In 2010–11, 47% of upper-school students received aid; total upper-school merit-scholarship money awarded: $2500. Total amount of financial aid awarded in 2010–11: $75,000.
Admissions Traditional secondary-level entrance grade is 9. Admissions testing required. Deadline for receipt of application materials: none. Application fee required: $40. Interview required.
Athletics Interscholastic: baseball (boys), basketball (b,g), football (b), soccer (b,g), softball (g), tennis (b,g), volleyball (g), wrestling (b); intramural: cheering (g); coed interscholastic: golf, track and field. 1 PE instructor, 15 coaches, 1 athletic trainer.
Computers Computers are regularly used in graphic design, yearbook classes. Computer network features include on-campus library services, Internet access, wireless campus network, Internet filtering or blocking technology. Students grades are available online. The school has a published electronic and media policy.
Contact Mrs. Shirley Sobol, Domestic Admissions. 707-444-9431. Fax: 707-443-4723. E-mail: sobol@saintbernards.us. Web site: www.saintbernards.us/.

ST. BRENDAN HIGH SCHOOL
2950 Southwest 87th Avenue
Miami, Florida 33165-3295
Head of School: Br. Felix Elardo
General Information Coeducational day college-preparatory, general academic, arts, business, religious studies, bilingual studies, and technology school, affiliated with Roman Catholic Church. Grades 9–12. Founded: 1975. Setting: urban. 34-acre campus. 3 buildings on campus. Approved or accredited by Southern Association of Colleges and Schools and Florida Department of Education. Total enrollment: 1,181.

Upper school average class size: 28. Upper school faculty-student ratio: 1:15. There are 180 required school days per year for Upper School students. Upper School students typically attend 5 days per week. The average school day consists of 6 hours and 45 minutes.
Upper School Student Profile Grade 9: 316 students (59 boys, 257 girls); Grade 10: 299 students (73 boys, 226 girls); Grade 11: 297 students (83 boys, 214 girls); Grade 12: 269 students (78 boys, 191 girls). 98% of students are Roman Catholic.
Faculty School total: 95. In upper school: 27 men, 68 women; 50 have advanced degrees.
Graduation Requirements Students must complete 100 community service hours in their four years of high school.
Special Academic Programs 10 Advanced Placement exams for which test preparation is offered; honors section; study at local college for college credit; academic accommodation for the gifted; remedial reading and/or remedial writing.
College Admission Counseling 284 students graduated in 2010; 282 went to college, including Florida International University; Florida State University; Miami Dade College; University of Florida; University of Miami. Other: 2 entered military service. Mean combined SAT: 960, mean composite ACT: 20.
Student Life Upper grades have uniform requirement, student council, honor system. Discipline rests primarily with faculty. Attendance at religious services is required.
Summer Programs Remediation, advancement, computer instruction programs offered; held on campus; accepts boys and girls; open to students from other schools. 100 students usually enrolled.
Tuition and Aid Guaranteed tuition plan. Tuition installment plan (FACTS Tuition Payment Plan, monthly payment plans). Need-based scholarship grants, paying campus jobs available. In 2010–11, 15% of upper-school students received aid.
Admissions Traditional secondary-level entrance grade is 9. For fall 2010, 550 students applied for upper-level admission, 400 were accepted, 400 enrolled. Catholic High School Entrance Examination or placement test required. Deadline for receipt of application materials: January 21. Application fee required: $50.
Athletics Interscholastic: baseball (boys, girls), basketball (b,g), cheering (g), cross-country running (b,g), dance team (g), soccer (b,g), softball (g), swimming and diving (b,g), tennis (b,g), track and field (b,g), volleyball (g). 3 PE instructors, 17 coaches.
Computers Computers are regularly used in business, computer applications, graphic design, remedial study skills, research skills, science, speech, Web site design, word processing, yearbook classes. Computer network features include on-campus library services, Internet access, wireless campus network, Internet filtering or blocking technology. Computer access in designated common areas is available to students. Students grades are available online. The school has a published electronic and media policy.
Contact Candice Barket, Director of Admissions. 305-223-5181 Ext. 578. Fax: 305-220-7434. E-mail: cbarket@stbhs.org. Web site: www.stbhs.org.

ST. CATHERINE'S ACADEMY
Anaheim, California
See Junior Boarding Schools section.

ST. CATHERINE'S SCHOOL
6001 Grove Avenue
Richmond, Virginia 23226
Head of School: Laura J. Fuller
General Information Girls' day college-preparatory school, affiliated with Episcopal Church. Grades JK–12. Founded: 1890. Setting: suburban. Nearest major city is Washington, DC. 17-acre campus. 22 buildings on campus. Approved or accredited by Virginia Association of Independent Schools and Virginia Department of Education. Member of National Association of Independent Schools and Secondary School Admission Test Board. Endowment: $535 million. Total enrollment: 909. Upper school average class size: 16.
Upper School Student Profile Grade 9: 78 students (78 girls); Grade 10: 76 students (76 girls); Grade 11: 65 students (65 girls); Grade 12: 59 students (59 girls). 46% of students are members of Episcopal Church.
Faculty School total: 127. In upper school: 18 men, 27 women; 34 have advanced degrees.
Subjects Offered Acting, adolescent issues, advanced chemistry, advanced computer applications, advanced math, African-American literature, algebra, American government, American history, American history-AP, American literature, ancient history, architecture, art, art and culture, art history, art history-AP, band, Bible, biology, British literature-AP, calculus, calculus-AP, ceramics, chamber groups, chemistry, chemistry-AP, Chinese, choir, choral music, choreography, chorus, comparative government and politics-AP, comparative religion, computer applications, computer math, computer programming, computer science, computer science-AP, constitutional law, creative writing, dance, dance performance, desktop publishing, drama, driver education, economics, economics-AP, English, English language and composition-AP, English literature, English literature and composition-AP, environmental science, environmental science-AP, ethics, ethics and responsibility, European history, expository writing, film and literature, fine arts, French, French language-AP, French literature-AP, gender issues, geography, geometry, government and

politics-AP, government/civics, grammar, Greek, guitar, health and wellness, health education, history, history of jazz, honors algebra, honors English, honors geometry, independent study, Latin, Latin-AP, macro/microeconomics-AP, mathematics, modern dance, moral and social development, moral theology, music, music history, music theory, music theory-AP, orchestra, painting, performing arts, philosophy, photography, physical education, physical fitness, physics, physics-AP, playwriting and directing, portfolio art, post-calculus, pre-calculus, printmaking, regional literature, religion, rhetoric, robotics, science, sculpture, short story, social studies, Southern literature, Spanish, Spanish language-AP, Spanish literature, Spanish literature-AP, speech, speech communications, statistics, statistics-AP, theater, theater arts, theology, trigonometry, U.S. government and politics-AP, Vietnam, world cultures, world geography, world history, world literature, writing.

Graduation Requirements Arts and fine arts (art, music, dance, drama), computer science, English, foreign language, mathematics, physical education (includes health), religion (includes Bible studies and theology), science, social sciences, social studies (includes history), Community Service reuirement.

Special Academic Programs Advanced Placement exam preparation; honors section; independent study; term-away projects; study abroad.

College Admission Counseling 60 students graduated in 2010; all went to college, including James Madison University; The College of William and Mary; Tulane University; University of Virginia; Vanderbilt University; Virginia Polytechnic Institute and State University. Median SAT math: 640, median SAT writing: 660, median combined SAT: 1930, median composite ACT: 26. Mean SAT critical reading: 636. 72% scored over 600 on SAT critical reading, 66.7% scored over 600 on SAT math, 82.5% scored over 600 on SAT writing, 77.2% scored over 1800 on combined SAT, 60% scored over 26 on composite ACT.

Student Life Upper grades have specified standards of dress, student council, honor system. Discipline rests equally with students and faculty. Attendance at religious services is required.

Summer Programs Enrichment, advancement, sports, art/fine arts programs offered; session focuses on creative arts program and sports camps; held both on and off campus; held at James River (rafting) outdoor adventures; accepts boys and girls; open to students from other schools. 1,200 students usually enrolled. 2011 schedule: June 6 to August 8. Application deadline: March 1.

Tuition and Aid Day student tuition: $15,400-$20,340. Tuition installment plan (monthly payment plans, Tuition Management Systems Plan). Need-based scholarship grants available. In 2010–11, 13% of upper-school students received aid. Total amount of financial aid awarded in 2010–11: $448,800.

Admissions Traditional secondary-level entrance grade is 9. SSAT, TOEFL and TOEFL or SLEP required. Deadline for receipt of application materials: none. Application fee required: $50. Interview required.

Athletics Interscholastic: basketball, cross-country running, diving, field hockey, golf, indoor track, indoor track & field, lacrosse, soccer, softball, squash, swimming and diving, tennis, track and field, volleyball, winter (indoor) track; intramural: aerobics, aerobics/dance, aerobics/Nautilus, aquatics, ballet, basketball, canoeing/ kayaking, climbing, dance, equestrian sports, field hockey, golf, lacrosse, martial arts, modern dance, physical fitness, physical training, soccer, softball, strength & conditioning, swimming and diving, tennis, track and field, volleyball, weight lifting, weight training, wilderness, yoga; coed interscholastic: indoor track & field, track and field; coed intramural: aerobics/dance, backpacking, ballet, canoeing/kayaking, climbing, dance, modern dance, outdoor adventure, wilderness. 3 PE instructors, 50 coaches, 2 athletic trainers.

Computers Computers are regularly used in all classes. Computer network features include on-campus library services, online commercial services, Internet access, wireless campus network. Campus intranet and student e-mail accounts are available to students. Students grades are available online. The school has a published electronic and media policy.

Contact Jennifer Cullinan, Director of Admissions. 804-288-2804. Fax: 804-285-8169. E-mail: jcullinan@st.catherines.org. Web site: www.st.catherines.org.

ST. CECILIA ACADEMY
4210 Harding Road
Nashville, Tennessee 37205
Head of School: Sr. Mary Thomas, OP

General Information Girls' day college preparatory, arts, religious studies, and technology school, affiliated with Roman Catholic Church. Grades 9–12. Founded: 1860. Setting: suburban. 83-acre campus. 6 buildings on campus. Approved or accredited by National Catholic Education Association, Southern Association of Colleges and Schools, Southern Association of Independent Schools, Tennessee Association of Independent Schools, The College Board, and Tennessee Department of Education. Total enrollment: 257. Upper school average class size: 14. Upper school faculty-student ratio: 1:9. There are 180 required school days per year for Upper School students. Upper School students typically attend 5 days per week. The average school day consists of 7 hours.

Upper School Student Profile Grade 9: 59 students (59 girls); Grade 10: 71 students (71 girls); Grade 11: 71 students (71 girls); Grade 12: 56 students (56 girls). 70% of students are Roman Catholic.

Faculty School total: 32. In upper school: 4 men, 28 women; 21 have advanced degrees.

Subjects Offered Algebra, American history-AP, American literature, anatomy and physiology, biology, biology-AP, British literature, calculus, calculus-AP, Catholic belief and practice, chamber groups, chemistry, chemistry-AP, chorus, church history, computer programming, computer science, current events, dance, drawing, economics, economics and history, English literature, English-AP, ethics, European civilization, European history, European history-AP, fine arts, French, French language-AP, geometry, German, German-AP, government, government/civics, Internet research, journalism, Latin, microcomputer technology applications, moral theology, music, music appreciation, music theory, natural history, photography, physical education, physics, physics-AP, religion, scripture, Spanish language-AP, Spanish-AP, speech, studio art-AP, tap dance, theology, trigonometry, U.S. history, U.S. history-AP, visual and performing arts, visual arts, world history, yearbook.

Graduation Requirements Arts and fine arts (art, music, dance, drama), computer science, English, foreign language, history, mathematics, physical education (includes health), religion (includes Bible studies and theology), science.

Special Academic Programs Advanced Placement exam preparation; honors section; study at local college for college credit; academic accommodation for the gifted, the musically talented, and the artistically talented.

College Admission Counseling 53 students graduated in 2010; all went to college. Mean SAT critical reading: 601, mean SAT math: 540, mean SAT writing: 601, mean composite ACT: 26.

Student Life Upper grades have uniform requirement, student council, honor system. Discipline rests primarily with faculty. Attendance at religious services is required.

Summer Programs Computer instruction programs offered; session focuses on course fulfillment; held on campus; accepts girls; not open to students from other schools. 20 students usually enrolled. 2011 schedule: June to July.

Tuition and Aid Day student tuition: $14,200. Tuition installment plan (Tuition Management Systems Plan). Need-based scholarship grants available. In 2010–11, 42% of upper-school students received aid. Total amount of financial aid awarded in 2010–11: $650,000.

Admissions Traditional secondary-level entrance grade is 9. For fall 2010, 117 students applied for upper-level admission, 90 were accepted, 60 enrolled. High School Placement Test and ISEE required. Deadline for receipt of application materials: January 10. Application fee required: $60. Interview required.

Athletics Interscholastic: aquatics, basketball, bowling, cross-country running, diving, golf, running, soccer, softball, swimming and diving, tennis, track and field, volleyball; intramural: dance, dance team, independent competitive sports, lacrosse, modern dance, physical training, self defense, strength & conditioning, weight lifting, weight training. 1 PE instructor, 16 coaches, 1 athletic trainer.

Computers Computers are regularly used in art, English, foreign language, history, journalism, mathematics, newspaper, publications, science, Spanish, writing classes. Computer network features include on-campus library services, online commercial services, Internet access, Internet filtering or blocking technology. Students grades are available online. The school has a published electronic and media policy.

Contact Mrs. Betty Bader, Director of Admissions. 615-298-4525 Ext. 377. Fax: 615-783-0561. E-mail: admissions@stcecilia.edu. Web site: www.stcecilia.edu.

SAINT CECILIA HIGH SCHOOL
521 North Kansas Avenue
Hastings, Nebraska 68901-7594
Head of School: Rev. Fr. Troy J. Schweiger

General Information Coeducational day and distance learning college-preparatory, arts, business, vocational, religious studies, and technology school, affiliated with Roman Catholic Church. Grades 6–12. Distance learning grades 11–12. Founded: 1912. Setting: small town. Nearest major city is Lincoln. 1-acre campus. 2 buildings on campus. Approved or accredited by National Catholic Education Association, North Central Association of Colleges and Schools, and Nebraska Department of Education. Endowment: $1 million. Total enrollment: 262. Upper school average class size: 20. Upper school faculty-student ratio: 1:5. There are 178 required school days per year for Upper School students. Upper School students typically attend 5 days per week. The average school day consists of 6 hours and 16 minutes.

Upper School Student Profile Grade 9: 36 students (20 boys, 16 girls); Grade 10: 38 students (17 boys, 21 girls); Grade 11: 43 students (17 boys, 26 girls); Grade 12: 43 students (27 boys, 16 girls). 98% of students are Roman Catholic.

Faculty School total: 32. In upper school: 12 men, 20 women; 15 have advanced degrees.

Subjects Offered Accounting, aerospace education, algebra, American history, American literature-AP, art history, automated accounting, band, Basic programming, biology, business law, business mathematics, calculus-AP, career education, Catholic belief and practice, chemistry, chorus, computer applications, computer programming, computer technology certification, computer-aided design, consumer economics, drafting, drawing, driver education, economics, English, environmental science, ESL, family and consumer science, fashion, fine arts, foods, geometry, health, history of the Catholic Church, instrumental music, interior design, Internet, introduction to technology, jazz band, language arts, library skills, Life of Christ, marketing, music, musical productions, newspaper, painting, peace and justice, physical education, physics, play production, portfolio art, pre-calculus, probability and statistics, psychology, religion, science, science project, sculpture, social sciences, social studies, sociology, Spanish, Spanish literature, speech, statistics, textiles, theater arts, TOEFL preparation, trigonometry, U.S. government, video film production, vocational arts, weight training, world history, yearbook.

Graduation Requirements Algebra, American government, American history, American literature, arts and fine arts (art, music, dance, drama), British literature, career education, computer skills, economics, English, foreign language, mathematics, physical education (includes health), practical arts, religion (includes Bible studies and theology), science, social studies (includes history), speech, vocational arts, vocational-technical courses, 50-60 volunteer service hours.

Special Academic Programs 1 Advanced Placement exam for which test preparation is offered; honors section; independent study; study at local college for college credit; remedial reading and/or remedial writing; remedial math; special instructional classes for students with learning disabilities and Attention Deficit Disorder; ESL (24 students enrolled).

College Admission Counseling 44 students graduated in 2010; 43 went to college, including Benedictine College; Creighton University; Doane College; University of Nebraska–Lincoln; University of Nebraska at Kearney; University of Nebraska at Omaha. Other: 1 went to work. Median SAT critical reading: 550, median SAT math: 650, median SAT writing: 420, median combined SAT: 1200, median composite ACT: 22. 1% scored over 600 on SAT math, 18% scored over 26 on composite ACT.

Student Life Upper grades have uniform requirement, student council, honor system. Discipline rests primarily with faculty. Attendance at religious services is required.

Summer Programs Sports programs offered; session focuses on driver's education; held on campus; accepts boys and girls; open to students from other schools. 22 students usually enrolled. 2011 schedule: May 29 to July 25. Application deadline: April 1.

Tuition and Aid Day student tuition: $1375. Guaranteed tuition plan. Tuition installment plan (monthly payment plans, individually arranged payment plans, automatic bank draft). Tuition reduction for siblings, merit scholarship grants, scrip participation program, tuition assistance with parish pastors, parish pastor will pay or match family contribution to reach the total tuition available. In 2010–11, 16% of upper-school students received aid; total upper-school merit-scholarship money awarded: $8000. Total amount of financial aid awarded in 2010–11: $8000.

Admissions ACT, ACT-Explore, English proficiency, PSAT, Terra Nova-CTB, TOEFL or writing sample required. Deadline for receipt of application materials: none. No application fee required. Interview required.

Athletics Interscholastic: aerobics/dance (girls), basketball (b,g), bowling (b,g), cheering (g), dance (g), dance team (g), drill team (g), football (b), golf (b,g), running (b,g), tennis (g), volleyball (g), wrestling (b); intramural: dance team (g), drill team (g), power lifting (b); coed interscholastic: track and field; coed intramural: badminton, bowling, juggling, jump rope, life saving, physical fitness, physical training, weight lifting, weight training. 2 PE instructors, 2 athletic trainers.

Computers Computers are regularly used in accounting, business, career education, career exploration, career technology, Christian doctrine, college planning, computer applications, desktop publishing, ESL, drafting, drawing and design, English, ESL, foreign language, graphic design, graphics, health, journalism, keyboarding, mathematics, media production, music, newspaper, reading, science, Spanish, speech, video film production, vocational-technical courses, Web site design, word processing, writing, writing, yearbook classes. Computer network features include on-campus library services, online commercial services, Internet access, wireless campus network, Internet filtering or blocking technology, SmartBoards. Student e-mail accounts and computer access in designated common areas are available to students. Students grades are available online. The school has a published electronic and media policy.

Contact Mrs. Marie K. Butler, Assistant Super/Curriculum Director. 402-462-2105. Fax: 402-462-2106. E-mail: mbutler@esu9.org. Web site: www.hastingscatholicschools.org.

ST. CHRISTOPHER'S SCHOOL

711 St. Christopher's Road
Richmond, Virginia 23226
Head of School: Mr. Charles M. Stillwell

General Information Boys' day college-preparatory school, affiliated with Episcopal Church. Grades JK–12. Founded: 1911. Setting: suburban. 46-acre campus. 9 buildings on campus. Approved or accredited by National Association of Episcopal Schools and Virginia Association of Independent Schools. Member of National Association of Independent Schools and Secondary School Admission Test Board. Endowment: $61.6 million. Total enrollment: 952. Upper school average class size: 15. Upper school faculty-student ratio: 1:6. Upper School students typically attend 5 days per week. The average school day consists of 7 hours and 30 minutes.

Upper School Student Profile Grade 9: 64 students (64 boys); Grade 10: 68 students (68 boys); Grade 11: 76 students (76 boys); Grade 12: 73 students (73 boys). 45% of students are members of Episcopal Church.

Faculty School total: 148. In upper school: 31 men, 16 women; 32 have advanced degrees.

Subjects Offered Algebra, American history, American literature, ancient history, architecture, art, art history, astronomy, Bible studies, biology, calculus, ceramics, chemistry, Chinese, community service, computer math, computer programming, computer science, creative thinking, creative writing, dance, drama, driver education, ecology, economics, English, English literature, environmental science, ethics,

European history, expository writing, fine arts, French, geography, geology, geometry, government/civics, grammar, Greek, health, history, industrial arts, journalism, Latin, mathematics, music, philosophy, photography, physics, public speaking, religion, science, social studies, Spanish, speech, statistics, theater, theology, trigonometry, typing, woodworking, writing.

Graduation Requirements 1½ elective credits, algebra, American history, American literature, ancient history, arts and fine arts (art, music, dance, drama), biology, British literature, chemistry, church history, computer science, English, English literature, European history, foreign language, geometry, physical education (includes health), physics, public speaking, religion (includes Bible studies and theology), speech, U.S. history. Community service is required.

Special Academic Programs 20 Advanced Placement exams for which test preparation is offered; honors section; independent study; academic accommodation for the gifted, the musically talented, and the artistically talented.

College Admission Counseling 80 students graduated in 2010; 79 went to college, including The College of William and Mary; University of Virginia; Virginia Military Institute; Virginia Polytechnic Institute and State University; Washington and Lee University. Other: 1 had other specific plans.

Student Life Upper grades have specified standards of dress, student council, honor system. Discipline rests equally with students and faculty. Attendance at religious services is required.

Summer Programs Advancement programs offered; session focuses on enrichment, sports, day camp, leadership; held on campus; accepts boys and girls; open to students from other schools. 750 students usually enrolled. 2011 schedule: June 20 to July 29. Application deadline: none.

Tuition and Aid Day student tuition: $20,820. Tuition installment plan (Academic Management Services Plan, Tuition Refund Plan). Merit scholarship grants, need-based scholarship grants available. In 2010–11, 25% of upper-school students received aid; total upper-school merit-scholarship money awarded: $3000. Total amount of financial aid awarded in 2010–11: $783,200.

Admissions Traditional secondary-level entrance grade is 9. For fall 2010, 56 students applied for upper-level admission, 36 were accepted, 18 enrolled. SSAT and writing sample required. Deadline for receipt of application materials: none. Application fee required: $50. On-campus interview recommended.

Athletics Interscholastic: baseball, basketball, cross-country running, diving, football, golf, indoor soccer, indoor track & field, lacrosse, sailing, soccer, squash, strength & conditioning, swimming and diving, tennis, track and field, weight lifting, weight training, winter (indoor) track, wrestling; coed interscholastic: canoeing/kayaking, climbing, dance, martial arts, outdoor adventure, rappelling. 5 coaches, 2 athletic trainers.

Computers Computers are regularly used in computer applications, desktop publishing, digital applications, English, foreign language, health, history, journalism, literary magazine, mathematics, music, photography, publications, science classes. Computer network features include on-campus library services, online commercial services, Internet access, wireless campus network, Internet filtering or blocking technology. Student e-mail accounts and computer access in designated common areas are available to students. Students grades are available online. The school has a published electronic and media policy.

Contact Cary C. Mauck, Director of Admissions. 804-282-3185 Ext. 2388. Fax: 804-673-6632. E-mail: mauckc@stcva.org. Web site: www.stchristophers.com.

ST. CLEMENT SCHOOL

88 Main St
Ottawa, Ontario K1S 1C2, Canada
Head of School: Mrs. Beryl Devine

General Information Coeducational day college-preparatory school, affiliated with Roman Catholic Church. Grades 7–12. Founded: 1996. Setting: urban. Approved or accredited by Ontario Department of Education. Language of instruction: English. Total enrollment: 37. Upper school average class size: 9. Upper school faculty-student ratio: 1:3. There are 181 required school days per year for Upper School students. Upper School students typically attend 5 days per week. The average school day consists of 6 hours.

Upper School Student Profile Grade 7: 6 students (3 boys, 3 girls); Grade 8: 6 students (4 boys, 2 girls); Grade 9: 4 students (4 boys); Grade 10: 9 students (3 boys, 6 girls); Grade 11: 7 students (2 boys, 5 girls); Grade 12: 5 students (4 boys, 1 girl). 100% of students are Roman Catholic.

Faculty School total: 15. In upper school: 7 men, 4 women; 9 have advanced degrees.

Subjects Offered Advanced math, algebra, arts and crafts, calculus, Canadian geography, Canadian history, Catholic belief and practice, chemistry, choir, church history, English literature and composition-AP, French, French as a second language, geometry, Greek, history, Latin, mathematics, music history, music theory, physical education, science, world history.

Graduation Requirements Biology, calculus, chemistry, church history, English, French, French as a second language, Greek, Latin, mathematics, music history, music theory, physics, religion (includes Bible studies and theology).

Special Academic Programs Honors section; ESL.

College Admission Counseling 4 students graduated in 2010; all went to college.

Student Life Upper grades have uniform requirement, honor system. Discipline rests primarily with faculty. Attendance at religious services is required.

Tuition and Aid Day student tuition: CAN$3700. Tuition installment plan (full payment in advance, 5-month payment plan). Tuition reduction for siblings available.
Admissions Traditional secondary-level entrance grade is 9. Canadian Standardized Test required. Deadline for receipt of application materials: April 1. No application fee required. On-campus interview required.
Athletics Coed Intramural: fitness, Frisbee, independent competitive sports, paddle tennis, physical training, running, soccer, tennis, touch football, track and field, volleyball. 2 PE instructors.
Computers Computer resources include Internet access, word processing, encyclopedia.
Contact Mrs. Beryl Devine, Headmistress. 613-236-7231. Fax: 613-236-9159. E-mail: stclementschool@bellnet.ca.

ST. CLEMENT'S SCHOOL

21 St. Clements Avenue
Toronto, Ontario M4R 1G8, Canada
Head of School: Ms. Martha Perry
General Information Girls' day college-preparatory, arts, business, and technology school, affiliated with Anglican Church of Canada. Grades 1–12. Founded: 1901. Setting: urban. 1 building on campus. Approved or accredited by Canadian Association of Independent Schools, Canadian Educational Standards Institute, Conference of Independent Schools of Ontario, and Ontario Department of Education. Affiliate member of National Association of Independent Schools; member of Secondary School Admission Test Board. Language of instruction: English. Total enrollment: 455. Upper school average class size: 16. Upper school faculty-student ratio: 1:7. Upper School students typically attend 5 days per week.
Upper School Student Profile Grade 10: 60 students (60 girls); Grade 11: 60 students (60 girls); Grade 12: 60 students (60 girls).
Faculty School total: 62. In upper school: 7 men, 43 women; 20 have advanced degrees.
Subjects Offered Accounting, Advanced Placement courses, algebra, Ancient Greek, ancient world history, art, art history-AP, art-AP, band, biology, biology-AP, business, business studies, calculus, calculus-AP, Canadian geography, Canadian history, Canadian law, Canadian literature, career and personal planning, career education, character education, chemistry, chemistry-AP, civics, classics, college admission preparation, communication arts, computer science, creative writing, dance, data processing, design, drama, economics, economics-AP, English, English language-AP, English literature, English literature and composition-AP, environmental science, environmental science-AP, European history, European history-AP, exercise science, film studies, fine arts, finite math, French, French-AP, geography, geometry, grammar, graphic design, guidance, health, history, history-AP, human geography—AP, instrumental music, interdisciplinary studies, jazz ensemble, keyboarding, kinesiology, language and composition, language arts, Latin, Latin-AP, law, leadership and service, library, macro/microeconomics-AP, Mandarin, mathematics, modern Western civilization, music, music theory-AP, musical theater, philosophy, photography, physical education, physics, physics-AP, physiology, religion, science, social sciences, social studies, Spanish, Spanish-AP, statistics-AP, studio art-AP, theater, trigonometry, U.S. history-AP, Western civilization, world history, world issues, writing workshop.
Graduation Requirements Arts, business skills (includes word processing), career/college preparation, civics, computer science, English, foreign language, geography, history, mathematics, physical education (includes health), science, social studies (includes history).
Special Academic Programs 20 Advanced Placement exams for which test preparation is offered; independent study; academic accommodation for the gifted.
College Admission Counseling 63 students graduated in 2010; all went to college, including Dalhousie University; McGill University; Queen's University at Kingston; The University of British Columbia; The University of Western Ontario; University of Toronto.
Student Life Upper grades have uniform requirement, student council, honor system. Discipline rests equally with students and faculty. Attendance at religious services is required.
Summer Programs Advancement, art/fine arts programs offered; session focuses on cooperative program and summer school credit courses; held both on and off campus; held at Europe; accepts boys and girls; open to students from other schools. 15 students usually enrolled. 2011 schedule: June 20 to July 22. Application deadline: May.
Tuition and Aid Day student tuition: CAN$23,100. Tuition installment plan (monthly payment plans, individually arranged payment plans). Bursaries, merit scholarship grants, need-based scholarship grants available. In 2010–11, 7% of upper-school students received aid.
Admissions SSAT required. Deadline for receipt of application materials: December 10. Application fee required: CAN$125. Interview required.
Athletics Interscholastic: alpine skiing, badminton, basketball, cross-country running, dance, dance team, equestrian sports, field hockey, hockey, ice hockey, nordic skiing, running, skiing (downhill), soccer, softball, swimming and diving, tennis, track and field, volleyball; intramural: aerobics, aerobics/dance, backpacking, badminton, basketball, bocce, canoeing/kayaking, cooperative games, cross-country running, dance, dance team, field hockey, fitness, floor hockey, hiking/backpacking, indoor soccer, jogging, life saving, outdoor education, paddle tennis, running, soccer, softball, swimming and diving, table tennis, tennis, track and field, ultimate Frisbee, volleyball, wilderness survival, yoga. 5 PE instructors, 12 coaches.

Computers Computers are regularly used in all academic classes. Computer network features include on-campus library services, online commercial services, Internet access, wireless campus network, Internet filtering or blocking technology. Campus intranet, student e-mail accounts, and computer access in designated common areas are available to students. The school has a published electronic and media policy.
Contact Ms. Elena Holeton, Director of Admissions. 416-483-4414 Ext. 2227. Fax: 416-483-8242. E-mail: elena.holeton@scs.on.ca. Web site: www.scs.on.ca.

ST. CROIX COUNTRY DAY SCHOOL

RR #1, Box 6199
Kingshill, Virgin Islands 00850-9807
Head of School: Mr. William D. Sinfield
General Information Coeducational day college-preparatory and technology school. Grades N–12. Founded: 1964. Setting: rural. Nearest major city is Christiansted, U.S. Virgin Islands. 25-acre campus. 6 buildings on campus. Approved or accredited by Middle States Association of Colleges and Schools and Virgin Islands Department of Education. Member of National Association of Independent Schools. Endowment: $574,000. Total enrollment: 460. Upper school average class size: 14. Upper school faculty-student ratio: 1:12. Upper School students typically attend 5 days per week. The average school day consists of 7 hours.
Upper School Student Profile Grade 9: 37 students (19 boys, 18 girls); Grade 10: 40 students (21 boys, 19 girls); Grade 11: 47 students (22 boys, 25 girls); Grade 12: 42 students (20 boys, 22 girls).
Faculty School total: 51. In upper school: 6 men, 17 women; 11 have advanced degrees.
Subjects Offered Algebra, American history, American literature, art, art history, arts, band, biology, calculus, ceramics, chemistry, chorus, community service, computer programming, computer science, creative writing, current events, dance, drama, earth science, ecology, economics, electronics, English, English literature, film, fine arts, French, geometry, government/civics, health, history, journalism, keyboarding, marine biology, mathematics, music, Native American studies, photography, physical education, physical science, physics, pre-calculus, psychology, public speaking, science, social studies, sociology, Spanish, statistics, swimming, theater, trigonometry, world history.
Graduation Requirements Arts and fine arts (art, music, dance, drama), computer science, English, foreign language, mathematics, physical education (includes health), science, social studies (includes history), swimming, typing. Community service is required.
Special Academic Programs Advanced Placement exam preparation.
College Admission Counseling 42 students graduated in 2010; all went to college, including Michigan Technological University; University of Pennsylvania; University of Pittsburgh; Vassar College. Median SAT critical reading: 520, median SAT math: 540, median composite ACT: 22. 35% scored over 600 on SAT critical reading, 25% scored over 600 on SAT math, 19% scored over 26 on composite ACT.
Student Life Upper grades have specified standards of dress, student council, honor system. Discipline rests primarily with faculty.
Tuition and Aid Day student tuition: $12,650. Tuition installment plan (monthly payment plans, individually arranged payment plans, semiannual and annual payment plans). Merit scholarship grants, need-based scholarship grants available. In 2010–11, 33% of upper-school students received aid; total upper-school merit-scholarship money awarded: $42,500. Total amount of financial aid awarded in 2010–11: $265,550.
Admissions Traditional secondary-level entrance grade is 9. For fall 2010, 45 students applied for upper-level admission, 30 were accepted, 19 enrolled. Essay and Test of Achievement and Proficiency required. Deadline for receipt of application materials: none. Application fee required: $150. On-campus interview required.
Athletics Interscholastic: baseball (boys), basketball (b,g), football (b), softball (g), tennis (b,g), volleyball (b,g); intramural: volleyball (b,g); coed interscholastic: aerobics, aquatics, basketball, cross-country running, sailing, soccer; coed intramural: basketball, soccer, ultimate Frisbee. 1 PE instructor, 15 coaches.
Computers Computers are regularly used in mathematics, music, science, yearbook classes. Computer network features include on-campus library services, online commercial services, Internet access. The school has a published electronic and media policy.
Contact Mrs. Alma V. Castro-Nieves, Registrar. 340-778-1974 Ext. 2108. Fax: 340-779-3331. E-mail: anieves@stxcountryday.com. Web site: www.stxcountryday.com.

ST. CROIX SCHOOLS

1200 Oakdale Avenue
West St. Paul, Minnesota 55118
Head of School: Dr. Gene Pfeifer
General Information Coeducational boarding and day college-preparatory, general academic, arts, business, vocational, religious studies, bilingual studies, technology, and ESL school, affiliated with Wisconsin Evangelical Lutheran Synod, Christian faith. Grades 6–12. Founded: 1958. Setting: suburban. Nearest major city is St. Paul. Students are housed in single-sex dormitories. 30-acre campus. 3 buildings on campus. Approved or accredited by Minnesota Non-Public School Accrediting Association and

Minnesota Department of Education. Endowment: $1.6 million. Total enrollment: 460. Upper school average class size: 22. Upper school faculty-student ratio: 1:15. There are 176 required school days per year for Upper School students. Upper School students typically attend 5 days per week. The average school day consists of 5 hours and 30 minutes.

Upper School Student Profile Grade 6: 11 students (5 boys, 6 girls); Grade 7: 9 students (4 boys, 5 girls); Grade 8: 10 students (6 boys, 4 girls); Grade 9: 100 students (49 boys, 51 girls); Grade 10: 98 students (51 boys, 47 girls); Grade 11: 117 students (59 boys, 58 girls); Grade 12: 105 students (50 boys, 55 girls). 30% of students are boarding students. 74% are state residents. 7 states are represented in upper school student body. 20% are international students. International students from China, Japan, Republic of Korea, Taiwan, Thailand, and Viet Nam; 4 other countries represented in student body. 70% of students are Wisconsin Evangelical Lutheran Synod, Christian.

Faculty School total: 32. In upper school: 19 men, 10 women; 16 have advanced degrees; 4 reside on campus.

Subjects Offered Accounting, advanced math, Advanced Placement courses, algebra, American history, American literature, art, band, Bible studies, biology, biology-AP, business skills, calculus, chemistry, choir, chorus, computer programming, computer science, drama, economics, English, English literature, environmental science, general science, geography, geology, geometry, German, home economics, keyboarding, Latin, literature, Mandarin, mathematics, music, physical education, physics, pre-algebra, reading, religion, science, social sciences, social studies, Spanish, speech, trigonometry, world history, writing.

Graduation Requirements Algebra, arts and fine arts (art, music, dance, drama), biology, chemistry, English, English composition, English literature, foreign language, geometry, government, grammar, literature, physical education (includes health), physics, religion (includes Bible studies and theology), science, social studies (includes history), speech, world geography.

Special Academic Programs 11 Advanced Placement exams for which test preparation is offered; honors section; independent study; academic accommodation for the gifted, the musically talented, and the artistically talented; remedial reading and/or remedial writing; remedial math; programs in English for dyslexic students; special instructional classes for students with learning disabilities; ESL (30 students enrolled).

College Admission Counseling 105 students graduated in 2010; 102 went to college, including Bethany Lutheran College; Martin Luther College; Minnesota State University Mankato; University of Minnesota, Twin Cities Campus; University of Wisconsin–Madison. Other: 1 went to work, 2 entered military service.

Student Life Upper grades have specified standards of dress, student council, honor system. Discipline rests equally with students and faculty.

Summer Programs ESL, sports programs offered; session focuses on ESL and activities, and a variety of sports camps; held on campus; accepts boys and girls; open to students from other schools. 80 students usually enrolled. 2011 schedule: July 11 to July 29. Application deadline: June 1.

Tuition and Aid 7-day tuition and room/board: $24,300. Tuition installment plan (SMART Tuition Payment Plan). Merit scholarship grants, need-based scholarship grants available. In 2010–11, 35% of upper-school students received aid; total upper-school merit-scholarship money awarded: $28,000. Total amount of financial aid awarded in 2010–11: $412,000.

Admissions Traditional secondary-level entrance grade is 9. For fall 2010, 133 students applied for upper-level admission, 111 were accepted, 100 enrolled. Secondary Level English Proficiency or writing sample required. Deadline for receipt of application materials: none. Application fee required: $100. Interview recommended.

Athletics Interscholastic: baseball (boys), basketball (b,g), bowling (b,g), cheering (g), cross-country running (b,g), dance team (g), football (b), golf (b,g), hockey (b,g), ice hockey (b,g), softball (g), swimming and diving (b,g), tennis (b,g), track and field (b,g), volleyball (g), wrestling (b); intramural: basketball (b,g); coed intramural: alpine skiing, ball hockey, basketball, bowling, cheering, cross-country running, dance team, flag football, floor hockey, Frisbee, jogging, juggling, kickball, physical fitness, physical training, power lifting, skiing (downhill), snowboarding, softball, swimming and diving, table tennis, tennis, track and field, ultimate Frisbee, volleyball, weight lifting, weight training, whiffle ball. 3 PE instructors, 7 coaches, 2 athletic trainers.

Computers Computers are regularly used in accounting, computer applications, desktop publishing, economics, keyboarding, media production, yearbook classes. Computer network features include on-campus library services, online commercial services, Internet access, wireless campus network, Internet filtering or blocking technology. Computer access in designated common areas is available to students. Students grades are available online. The school has a published electronic and media policy.

Contact Mr. Jeff Lemke, Admissions Director. 651-455-1521. Fax: 651-451-3968. E-mail: international@stcroixschools.org. Web site: www.stcroixschools.org.

ST. DAVID'S SCHOOL
3400 White Oak Road
Raleigh, North Carolina 27609
Head of School: Mr. Kevin J. Lockerbie

General Information Coeducational day college-preparatory, arts, religious studies, and technology school, affiliated with Episcopal Church, Christian faith. Grades K–12. Founded: 1972. Setting: suburban. 15-acre campus. 7 buildings on campus.

Approved or accredited by National Association of Episcopal Schools, North Carolina Association of Independent Schools, Southern Association of Colleges and Schools, Southern Association of Independent Schools, and North Carolina Department of Education. Member of Secondary School Admission Test Board. Endowment: $1.6 million. Total enrollment: 611. Upper school average class size: 12. Upper school faculty-student ratio: 1:7. There are 180 required school days per year for Upper School students. Upper School students typically attend 5 days per week. The average school day consists of 7 hours and 15 minutes.

Upper School Student Profile Grade 9: 55 students (25 boys, 30 girls); Grade 10: 50 students (27 boys, 23 girls); Grade 11: 46 students (29 boys, 17 girls); Grade 12: 44 students (30 boys, 14 girls).

Faculty School total: 69. In upper school: 17 men, 14 women; 24 have advanced degrees.

Subjects Offered Algebra, American history, American literature, art, Bible, biology, biology-AP, calculus, calculus-AP, ceramics, chemistry, chemistry-AP, choir, composition, computer programming, computer-aided design, drama, drawing, earth science, English, English literature, English literature-AP, English/composition-AP, European history, European history-AP, French, French language-AP, geography, geometry, Greek, Latin, Latin-AP, mathematics, media production, music theory-AP, philosophy, physical education, physical science, physics, physics-AP, psychology-AP, public speaking, robotics, science, social studies, Spanish, Spanish-AP, statistics-AP, studio art, studio art-AP, theater, U.S. history-AP, Web site design, wind ensemble, world history, world literature.

Graduation Requirements English, foreign language, mathematics, physical education (includes health), religion (includes Bible studies and theology), science, social studies (includes history), 80 hours of community service, Senior Seminar.

Special Academic Programs Advanced Placement exam preparation; honors section; independent study.

College Admission Counseling 60 students graduated in 2010; all went to college, including Appalachian State University; Elon University; North Carolina State University; The University of North Carolina at Chapel Hill; Vanderbilt University; Wake Forest University. Mean SAT critical reading: 600, mean SAT math: 589, mean SAT writing: 599, mean combined SAT: 1788, mean composite ACT: 25.

Student Life Upper grades have specified standards of dress, student council, honor system. Discipline rests equally with students and faculty. Attendance at religious services is required.

Summer Programs Enrichment, advancement, sports, art/fine arts, computer instruction programs offered; held on campus; accepts boys and girls; open to students from other schools. 170 students usually enrolled. 2011 schedule: June 6 to August 5. Application deadline: April 15.

Tuition and Aid Day student tuition: $15,900. Tuition installment plan (Insured Tuition Payment Plan, monthly payment plans, 10-month payment plan). Need-based scholarship grants available.

Admissions Traditional secondary-level entrance grade is 9. For fall 2010, 35 students applied for upper-level admission, 31 were accepted, 23 enrolled. ISEE and writing sample required. Deadline for receipt of application materials: February 21. Application fee required: $75. On-campus interview required.

Athletics Interscholastic: baseball (boys, girls), basketball (b,g), cheering (g), cross-country running (b,g), football (b), indoor track & field (b,g), lacrosse (b), soccer (b,g), softball (g), tennis (b,g), track and field (b,g), volleyball (g), winter (indoor) track (b,g), wrestling (b); intramural: basketball (b,g), soccer (b,g); coed interscholastic: golf, swimming and diving. 5 PE instructors, 5 coaches, 1 athletic trainer.

Computers Computers are regularly used in all academic classes. Computer network features include on-campus library services, Internet access. Computer access in designated common areas is available to students. Students grades are available online. The school has a published electronic and media policy.

Contact Mrs. Teresa Wilson, Director of Admissions. 919-782-3331 Ext. 230. Fax: 919-232-5053. E-mail: twilson@sdsw.org. Web site: www.sdsw.org.

SAINT DOMINIC ACADEMY
Bishop Joseph OSB Boulevard
121 Gracelawn Road
Auburn, Maine 04210
Head of School: Mr. Donald Fournier

General Information Coeducational day and distance learning college-preparatory, arts, business, and religious studies school, affiliated with Roman Catholic Church. Grades 9–12. Distance learning grades 11–12. Founded: 1941. Setting: suburban. 70-acre campus. 1 building on campus. Approved or accredited by Maine Department of Education. Total enrollment: 598. Upper school average class size: 17. Upper school faculty-student ratio: 1:12. There are 175 required school days per year for Upper School students. Upper School students typically attend 5 days per week. The average school day consists of 6 hours and 15 minutes.

Upper School Student Profile Grade 7: 34 students (19 boys, 15 girls); Grade 8: 43 students (18 boys, 25 girls); Grade 9: 50 students (30 boys, 20 girls); Grade 10: 58 students (28 boys, 30 girls); Grade 11: 78 students (41 boys, 37 girls); Grade 12: 56 students (29 boys, 27 girls). 70% of students are Roman Catholic.

Faculty School total: 25. In upper school: 10 men, 15 women.

Special Academic Programs International Baccalaureate program; Advanced Placement exam preparation; honors section; independent study.

College Admission Counseling 53 students graduated in 2010; 50 went to college. Other: 2 went to work, 1 entered military service. Median SAT critical reading: 542, median SAT math: 534, median SAT writing: 524, median combined SAT: 1600.
Student Life Upper grades have specified standards of dress, student council, honor system. Discipline rests primarily with faculty. Attendance at religious services is required.
Summer Programs Enrichment, sports, art/fine arts, computer instruction programs offered; session focuses on recreational fun, sports, activities; held both on and off campus; held at various locations; accepts boys and girls; open to students from other schools. 150 students usually enrolled. 2011 schedule: June 15 to August 5.
Tuition and Aid Day student tuition: $9075. Tuition installment plan (FACTS Tuition Payment Plan). Merit scholarship grants, need-based scholarship grants available. In 2010–11, 33% of upper-school students received aid.
Admissions Traditional secondary-level entrance grade is 9. Scholastic Testing Service High School Placement Test required. Deadline for receipt of application materials: none. Application fee required: $50. On-campus interview required.
Athletics Interscholastic: baseball (boys), basketball (b,g), field hockey (g), hockey (b,g), indoor hockey (b,g), soccer (b,g), softball (g), tennis (b,g); coed interscholastic: aquatics, cheering, cross-country running, dance team, golf, swimming and diving, track and field. 1 PE instructor, 30 coaches.
Computers Computer network features include on-campus library services, online commercial services, Internet access, Internet filtering or blocking technology. Campus intranet, student e-mail accounts, and computer access in designated common areas are available to students. Students grades are available online. The school has a published electronic and media policy.
Contact Mr. James Boulet, Director of Admissions. 207-782-6911 Ext. 2110. Fax: 207-795-6439. E-mail: james.boulet@portlanddiocese.org. Web site: www.st-dominic.net.

SAINT DOMINIC ACADEMY

2572 Kennedy Boulevard
Jersey City, New Jersey 07304
Head of School: Deborah Egan
General Information Girls' day college-preparatory, arts, business, religious studies, and technology school, affiliated with Roman Catholic Church. Grades 9–12. Founded: 1878. Setting: urban. Nearest major city is New York, NY. 2-acre campus. 1 building on campus. Approved or accredited by Middle States Association of Colleges and Schools, National Catholic Education Association, and New Jersey Association of Independent Schools. Endowment: $83,213. Total enrollment: 451. Upper school average class size: 24. Upper school faculty-student ratio: 1:12. There are 180 required school days per year for Upper School students. Upper School students typically attend 5 days per week. The average school day consists of 6 hours and 5 minutes.
Upper School Student Profile Grade 9: 77 students (77 girls); Grade 10: 114 students (114 girls); Grade 11: 132 students (132 girls); Grade 12: 128 students (128 girls). 74% of students are Roman Catholic.
Faculty School total: 44. In upper school: 11 men, 32 women; 24 have advanced degrees.
Subjects Offered Accounting, advanced chemistry, algebra, American history, American literature, anatomy, art, art appreciation, art history, art history-AP, Bible studies, biology, business, business applications, business education, business skills, calculus, calculus-AP, chemistry, Chinese, collage and assemblage, college counseling, college placement, college writing, computer applications, computer education, computer literacy, computer math, computer processing, computer programming, computer science, CPR, creative writing, critical thinking, critical writing, drama, driver education, economics, English, English language and composition-AP, English literature, European history, fine arts, French, French language-AP, geometry, government/civics, health, history, history-AP, International Baccalaureate courses, Italian, keyboarding, Latin, mathematics, music, music performance, music theory, peer counseling, peer ministry, physical education, physics, physiology, psychology, psychology-AP, religion, science, social studies, sociology, Spanish, Spanish language-AP, theater, theology, trigonometry, women in literature, women's studies, world history, world literature, writing.
Graduation Requirements Arts and fine arts (art, music, dance, drama), business skills (includes word processing), computer science, English, foreign language, mathematics, physical education (includes health), religion (includes Bible studies and theology), science, social studies (includes history), 40 hours of community service, term paper.
Special Academic Programs International Baccalaureate program; Advanced Placement exam preparation; honors section; study at local college for college credit; remedial reading and/or remedial writing; remedial math.
College Admission Counseling 137 students graduated in 2009; 133 went to college, including Montclair State University; New Jersey City University; New York University; Rutgers, The State University of New Jersey, New Brunswick; Saint Peter's College; Seton Hall University. Other: 3 went to work, 1 had other specific plans. Median SAT critical reading: 480, median SAT math: 460, median SAT writing: 500. Mean composite ACT: 20. 14.4% scored over 600 on SAT critical reading, 9.1% scored over 600 on SAT math, 15.9% scored over 600 on SAT writing, 10.6% scored over 1800 on combined SAT, 7.5% scored over 26 on composite ACT.

Student Life Upper grades have uniform requirement, student council, honor system. Discipline rests primarily with faculty. Attendance at religious services is required.
Tuition and Aid Day student tuition: $7100. Tuition installment plan (SMART Tuition Payment Plan, monthly payment plans, individually arranged payment plans, quarterly payment plan, semiannual payment plan, prepayment plan). Tuition reduction for siblings, merit scholarship grants, need-based scholarship grants, paying campus jobs available. In 2009–10, 20% of upper-school students received aid; total upper-school merit-scholarship money awarded: $86,000. Total amount of financial aid awarded in 2009–10: $107,000.
Admissions Traditional secondary-level entrance grade is 9. For fall 2009, 324 students applied for upper-level admission, 285 were accepted, 77 enrolled. Cooperative Entrance Exam (McGraw-Hill) required. Deadline for receipt of application materials: December 5. Application fee required: $40.
Athletics Interscholastic: basketball (girls), cross-country running (g), dance team (g), diving (g), indoor track & field (g), outdoor activities (g), soccer (g), softball (g), swimming and diving (g), tennis (g), track and field (g); intramural: volleyball (g). 3 PE instructors, 18 coaches.
Computers Computers are regularly used in accounting, art, basic skills, business applications, business education, business skills, business studies, career education, career exploration, career technology, creative writing, economics, introduction to technology, keyboarding, programming classes. Computer network features include on-campus library services, Internet access, Internet filtering or blocking technology. Campus intranet and student e-mail accounts are available to students. Students grades are available online. The school has a published electronic and media policy.
Contact Ms. Barbara Vergel, Director of Admissions. 201-434-5938 Ext. 31. Fax: 201-434-2603. E-mail: bvergel@stdominicacad.com. Web site: www.stdominicacad.com.

ST. DOMINIC'S INTERNATIONAL SCHOOL, PORTUGAL

Rua Maria Brown
Outeiro de Polima
Sao Domingos de Rana 2785-816, Portugal
Head of School: Mr. Robert Clarence
General Information Coeducational day college-preparatory and general academic school, affiliated with Christian faith, Roman Catholic Church. Grades 1–13. Founded: 1974. Setting: suburban. Nearest major city is Lisbon, Portugal. 5-acre campus. 5 buildings on campus. Approved or accredited by European Council of International Schools, International Baccalaureate Organization, and New England Association of Schools and Colleges. Language of instruction: English. Endowment: €8 million. Total enrollment: 689. Upper school average class size: 18. Upper school faculty-student ratio: 1:6. There are 180 required school days per year for Upper School students. Upper School students typically attend 5 days per week. The average school day consists of 5 hours and 40 minutes.
Upper School Student Profile Grade 6: 49 students (28 boys, 21 girls); Grade 7: 61 students (35 boys, 26 girls); Grade 8: 49 students (32 boys, 17 girls); Grade 9: 53 students (19 boys, 34 girls); Grade 10: 52 students (28 boys, 24 girls); Grade 11: 57 students (31 boys, 26 girls); Grade 12: 47 students (26 boys, 21 girls); Grade 13: 52 students (27 boys, 25 girls). 60% of students are Christian faith, Roman Catholic.
Faculty School total: 77. In upper school: 18 men, 31 women; 20 have advanced degrees.
Graduation Requirements Arts, humanities, languages, mathematics, science.
Special Academic Programs International Baccalaureate program; academic accommodation for the gifted, the musically talented, and the artistically talented; remedial reading and/or remedial writing; remedial math; programs in English, mathematics, general development for dyslexic students; ESL (27 students enrolled).
College Admission Counseling 39 students graduated in 2009.
Student Life Upper grades have uniform requirement, student council, honor system. Discipline rests equally with students and faculty.
Tuition and Aid Day student tuition: 13,981 Estonian kroner–18,369 Estonian kroner. Merit scholarship grants available. In 2009–10, 1% of upper-school students received aid; total upper-school merit-scholarship money awarded: €36,738.
Admissions Traditional secondary-level entrance grade is 12. For fall 2009, 3 students applied for upper-level admission, 3 were accepted, 3 enrolled. Math and English placement tests required. Deadline for receipt of application materials: none. No application fee required.
Athletics Interscholastic: badminton (boys, girls), basketball (b,g), fitness (b,g), floor hockey (b,g), football (b,g), gymnastics (b,g), independent competitive sports (b,g), judo (b,g), martial arts (b,g), outdoor adventure (b,g), physical training (b,g), soccer (b,g), table tennis (b,g), tennis (b,g), track and field (b,g), volleyball (b,g); intramural: badminton (b,g), basketball (b,g), dance (b,g), fitness (b,g), floor hockey (b,g), football (b,g), gymnastics (b,g), independent competitive sports (b,g), judo (b,g), martial arts (b,g), modern dance (b,g), outdoor adventure (b,g), outdoor education (b,g), physical training (b,g), soccer (b,g), table tennis (b,g), tennis (b,g), track and field (b,g), volleyball (b,g), yoga (b,g). 4 PE instructors.
Computers Computers are regularly used in all academic classes. Computer network features include on-campus library services, Internet access, wireless campus network. Computer access in designated common areas is available to students. The school has a published electronic and media policy.

St. Dominic's International School, Portugal

Contact Admissions. 351-214440434. Fax: 351-214443072. E-mail: school@dominics-int.org. Web site: www.dominics-int.org.

ST. EDMUND HIGH SCHOOL
351 West Magnolia Street
Eunice, Louisiana 70535-0000
Head of School: Mrs. Elizabeth Christ
General Information Coeducational day college-preparatory, business, religious studies, and technology school, affiliated with Roman Catholic Church. Grades K–12. Founded: 1911. Setting: small town. Nearest major city is Lafayette. 4-acre campus. 4 buildings on campus. Approved or accredited by Southern Association of Colleges and Schools and Louisiana Department of Education. Endowment: $1 million. Total enrollment: 588. Upper school average class size: 24. Upper school faculty-student ratio: 1:10. There are 180 required school days per year for Upper School students. Upper School students typically attend 5 days per week. The average school day consists of 6 hours.
Upper School Student Profile Grade 6: 55 students (24 boys, 31 girls); Grade 7: 37 students (23 boys, 14 girls); Grade 8: 46 students (21 boys, 25 girls); Grade 9: 41 students (16 boys, 25 girls); Grade 10: 39 students (20 boys, 19 girls); Grade 11: 44 students (25 boys, 19 girls); Grade 12: 32 students (15 boys, 17 girls). 90% of students are Roman Catholic.
Faculty School total: 22. In upper school: 6 men, 13 women; 4 have advanced degrees.
Special Academic Programs Honors section; study at local college for college credit.
College Admission Counseling 49 students graduated in 2009; 48 went to college, including Louisiana State University and Agricultural and Mechanical College; Louisiana State University at Eunice; Louisiana Tech University; Northwestern State University of Louisiana; University of Louisiana at Lafayette. Other: 1 went to work. 30% scored over 26 on composite ACT.
Student Life Upper grades have uniform requirement, student council, honor system. Discipline rests primarily with faculty. Attendance at religious services is required.
Tuition and Aid Tuition installment plan (monthly payment plans, individually arranged payment plans). Tuition reduction for siblings, need-based scholarship grants available. In 2009–10, 5% of upper-school students received aid.
Admissions Stanford 9 required. Deadline for receipt of application materials: January 22. No application fee required. On-campus interview recommended.
Athletics Interscholastic: baseball (boys, girls), basketball (b,g), cheering (g), cross-country running (g), dance team (g), football (b), golf (b), physical fitness (b,g), pom squad (g), running (b,g), self defense (g), softball (g), tennis (b,g), track and field (b,g); intramural: badminton (b,g), cheering (g), dance team (g), fitness walking (g), flag football (b,g), jogging (b,g), jump rope (b,g), pom squad (g), running (b,g), softball (g), tennis (b,g), track and field (b,g), volleyball (b,g), walking (b,g), weight lifting (b,g), weight training (b,g). 7 PE instructors, 7 coaches.
Computers Computer network features include on-campus library services, Internet access, wireless campus network, Internet filtering or blocking technology. Campus intranet and computer access in designated common areas are available to students. Students grades are available online. The school has a published electronic and media policy.
Contact Mr. James Wallett, Assistant Principal. 337-457-5988. Fax: 337-457-5989. E-mail: jwallet@stedmund.com.

SAINT EDMUND HIGH SCHOOL
2474 Ocean Avenue
Brooklyn, New York 11229
Head of School: Mr. John P. Lorenzetti
General Information Coeducational day college-preparatory, arts, business, religious studies, and technology school, affiliated with Roman Catholic Church. Grades 9–12. Founded: 1932. Setting: urban. Nearest major city is New York. 1 building on campus. Approved or accredited by International Baccalaureate Organization, Middle States Association of Colleges and Schools, and New York State Board of Regents. Upper school average class size: 30. Upper school faculty-student ratio: 1:15. There are 180 required school days per year for Upper School students. Upper School students typically attend 5 days per week. The average school day consists of 6 hours.
Upper School Student Profile 95% of students are Roman Catholic.
Faculty School total: 52. In upper school: 20 men, 32 women; 34 have advanced degrees.
Subjects Offered 3-dimensional design, accounting, advanced biology, advanced chemistry, advanced computer applications, advanced math, Advanced Placement courses, advanced studio art-AP, African American studies, algebra, American history-AP, analysis and differential calculus, anthropology, applied music, architecture, art, art-AP, Asian studies, athletic training, Basic programming, Bible studies, biology, biology-AP, broadcast journalism, business law, calculus-AP, chemistry, chemistry-AP, chorus, Christian education, computer education, computer graphics, computer programming, computer science, consumer mathematics, CPR, dance, desktop publishing, discrete mathematics, drawing, driver education, earth science, economics, English, English composition, English literature, English literature and composition-AP, environmental science, ethics, European history, European

history-AP, film studies, forensics, French, geometry, global studies, government, government and politics-AP, history, history of the Americas, history of the Catholic Church, honors algebra, honors geometry, instruments, International Baccalaureate courses, intro to computers, Irish literature, jazz, jazz band, Life of Christ, mathematics-AP, music, poetry, pre-calculus, science, Spanish-AP, sports, studio art-AP, U.S. government and politics-AP, U.S. history-AP, Web authoring, Web site design, weight fitness, women's literature, world religions, world wide web design, World-Wide-Web publishing.
Special Academic Programs International Baccalaureate program; Advanced Placement exam preparation; honors section; study at local college for college credit; academic accommodation for the artistically talented; remedial reading and/or remedial writing; remedial math; programs in English for dyslexic students.
College Admission Counseling 170 students graduated in 2009; 160 went to college, including City College of the City University of New York; St. Francis College; St. John's University; State University of New York at Binghamton.
Student Life Upper grades have uniform requirement, student council. Discipline rests primarily with faculty. Attendance at religious services is required.
Tuition and Aid Day student tuition: $7500. Tuition installment plan (monthly payment plans, individually arranged payment plans). Tuition reduction for siblings, merit scholarship grants, need-based scholarship grants available. In 2009–10, 5% of upper-school students received aid; total upper-school merit-scholarship money awarded: $50,000. Total amount of financial aid awarded in 2009–10: $66,000.
Admissions Cooperative Entrance Exam (McGraw-Hill) required. Application fee required: $500.
Athletics Interscholastic: baseball (boys, girls), basketball (b,g), bowling (b), cheering (g), cross-country running (b,g), handball (b), hockey (b), ice hockey (b), rugby (b), soccer (b,g), swimming and diving (b,g), volleyball (g), wrestling (b); coed intramural: volleyball. 3 PE instructors, 20 coaches.
Computers Computers are regularly used in accounting, business, business studies, computer applications, desktop publishing, English, foreign language, history, literary magazine, mathematics, media, newspaper, religion, science, technology, Web site design, yearbook classes. Computer network features include on-campus library services, online commercial services, Internet access, wireless campus network, Internet filtering or blocking technology. Campus intranet and computer access in designated common areas are available to students. Students grades are available online. The school has a published electronic and media policy.
Contact Deacon Ron Rizzuto, Director of Admissions. 718-743-6100 Ext. 42. Fax: 718-743-5243. E-mail: rrizzuto@stedmundprep.org. Web site: www.stedmundprep.org.

SAINT EDWARD'S SCHOOL
1895 Saint Edward's Drive
Vero Beach, Florida 32963
Head of School: Mr. Michael J. Mersky
General Information Coeducational day college-preparatory, technology, and Advanced Placement school, affiliated with Episcopal Church. Grades PK–12. Founded: 1965. Setting: suburban. Nearest major city is West Palm Beach. 33-acre campus. 12 buildings on campus. Approved or accredited by Florida Council of Independent Schools, National Association of Episcopal Schools, Southern Association of Colleges and Schools, and The College Board. Member of National Association of Independent Schools and Secondary School Admission Test Board. Endowment: $3.1 million. Total enrollment: 541. Upper school average class size: 14. Upper school faculty-student ratio: 1:8. There are 172 required school days per year for Upper School students. Upper School students typically attend 5 days per week. The average school day consists of 5 hours and 45 minutes.
Upper School Student Profile Grade 9: 53 students (23 boys, 30 girls); Grade 10: 46 students (19 boys, 27 girls); Grade 11: 67 students (32 boys, 35 girls); Grade 12: 62 students (34 boys, 28 girls). 15% of students are members of Episcopal Church.
Faculty School total: 63. In upper school: 13 men, 20 women; 20 have advanced degrees.
Subjects Offered Advanced Placement courses, algebra, American history, American literature, anatomy and physiology, art, band, biology, biology-AP, calculus, calculus-AP, chemistry, chemistry-AP, Chinese, choir, choral music, chorus, Christian ethics, computer science-AP, concert band, concert choir, contemporary issues, contemporary studies, drama, economics, economics-AP, English, English as a foreign language, English language and composition-AP, English literature and composition-AP, ethics, fine arts, French, French language-AP, geometry, global studies, government, government-AP, graphic design, health and wellness, honors algebra, honors English, honors geometry, human geography—AP, instrumental music, Internet research, Mandarin, marine biology, mathematics, model United Nations, modern European history-AP, music, music theory-AP, performing arts, physical education, physical fitness, physics, physics-AP, pre-calculus, psychology, religion, science, senior internship, senior project, social sciences, social studies, sociology, Spanish, Spanish language-AP, statistics-AP, theater arts, U.S. government and politics-AP, U.S. history-AP, white-water trips, world history, world history-AP.
Graduation Requirements Arts and fine arts (art, music, dance, drama), English, foreign language, mathematics, physical education (includes health), religion (includes Bible studies and theology), science, social sciences, social studies (includes history), 20 hours of community service each year of high school.

Special Academic Programs Advanced Placement exam preparation; honors section; independent study; study at local college for college credit; study abroad; academic accommodation for the gifted, the musically talented, and the artistically talented; ESL (10 students enrolled).

College Admission Counseling 82 students graduated in 2010; all went to college, including Florida State University; Northeastern University; Trinity College; University of Miami; University of North Florida. Mean SAT critical reading: 586, mean SAT math: 597, mean SAT writing: 580, mean combined SAT: 1763, mean composite ACT: 25. 45% scored over 600 on SAT critical reading, 49% scored over 600 on SAT math, 40% scored over 600 on SAT writing, 43% scored over 1800 on combined SAT, 49% scored over 26 on composite ACT.

Student Life Upper grades have specified standards of dress, student council, honor system. Discipline rests primarily with faculty. Attendance at religious services is required.

Summer Programs Remediation, enrichment, sports, art/fine arts, computer instruction programs offered; session focuses on enrichment, water activities, sports, study skills; held both on and off campus; held at Waterfront Indian River Lagoon; accepts boys and girls; open to students from other schools. 870 students usually enrolled. 2011 schedule: June 6 to August 12. Application deadline: June 1.

Tuition and Aid Day student tuition: $8600–$23,000. Tuition installment plan (FACTS Tuition Payment Plan, 1-, 2-, and 10-payment plans). Merit scholarship grants, need-based scholarship grants available. In 2010–11, 33% of upper-school students received aid; total upper-school merit-scholarship money awarded: $24,000. Total amount of financial aid awarded in 2010–11: $1,183,206.

Admissions Traditional secondary-level entrance grade is 9. For fall 2010, 33 students applied for upper-level admission, 22 were accepted, 18 enrolled. ACT, PSAT, SAT or SSAT required. Deadline for receipt of application materials: February 15. Application fee required: $50. Interview recommended.

Athletics Interscholastic: baseball (boys), basketball (b,g), cheering (g), crew (b,g), cross-country running (b,g), football (b), golf (b,g), independent competitive sports (b,g), lacrosse (b,g), soccer (b,g), swimming and diving (b,g), tennis (b,g), volleyball (g), weight lifting (b,g); intramural: baseball (b), basketball (b,g), cheering (g), cross-country running (b,g), flagball (b), football (b), golf (b,g), lacrosse (b,g), physical fitness (b,g), sailing (b,g), soccer (b,g), tennis (b,g), volleyball (g); coed interscholastic: aquatics, swimming and diving; coed intramural: aquatics, outdoor education, physical fitness, soccer, softball. 4 PE instructors, 14 coaches, 1 athletic trainer.

Computers Computers are regularly used in all academic classes. Computer network features include on-campus library services, online commercial services, Internet access, wireless campus network, Internet filtering or blocking technology, Issuance of tablet technology to all students in grades 6-12, Electonic submission of homework, class assignments and homework available online. Campus intranet and student e-mail accounts are available to students. Students grades are available online. The school has a published electronic and media policy.

Contact Ms. Peggy Anderson, Director of Admission. 772-492-2364. Fax: 772-231-2427. E-mail: panderson@steds.org. Web site: www.steds.org.

SAINT ELIZABETH HIGH SCHOOL

1530 34th Avenue
Oakland, California 94601

Head of School: Sr. Mary Liam Brock, OP

General Information Coeducational day college-preparatory, arts, and religious studies school, affiliated with Roman Catholic Church. Grades 9–12. Founded: 1921. Setting: urban. Nearest major city is Berkeley. 2-acre campus. 1 building on campus. Approved or accredited by National Catholic Education Association, Western Association of Schools and Colleges, and California Department of Education. Endowment: $520,000. Total enrollment: 165. Upper school average class size: 16. Upper school faculty-student ratio: 1:15. There are 180 required school days per year for Upper School students. Upper School students typically attend 5 days per week. The average school day consists of 6 hours and 48 minutes.

Upper School Student Profile Grade 9: 46 students (27 boys, 19 girls); Grade 10: 38 students (21 boys, 17 girls); Grade 11: 44 students (21 boys, 23 girls); Grade 12: 37 students (18 boys, 19 girls). 67% of students are Roman Catholic.

Faculty School total: 21. In upper school: 10 men, 11 women; 14 have advanced degrees.

Subjects Offered Advanced math, algebra, American literature, American literature-AP, anatomy and physiology, art and culture, biology, business mathematics, calculus-AP, Catholic belief and practice, chemistry, Christian and Hebrew scripture, Christian testament, civics, composition, computer applications, computer graphics, computer literacy, creative writing, drawing and design, economics, economics and history, English, English literature and composition-AP, geometry, journalism, learning strategies, moral and social development, physical education, physical science, physics, pre-algebra, pre-calculus, psychology, social justice, Spanish, Spanish language-AP, Spanish literature-AP, speech, speech communications, trigonometry, U.S. history, world cultures, world geography, world history, world religions.

Graduation Requirements Arts and fine arts (art, music, dance, drama), electives, English, foreign language, mathematics, physical education (includes health), religious studies, science, social sciences, 100 hours of community service.

Special Academic Programs 3 Advanced Placement exams for which test preparation is offered; honors section; remedial reading and/or remedial writing; remedial

math; programs in English, mathematics for dyslexic students; special instructional classes for students with learning disabilities, Attention Deficit Disorder, dyslexia, and emotional and behavioral problems.

College Admission Counseling 72 students graduated in 2010; 70 went to college, including California State University, East Bay; San Francisco State University; San Jose State University; University of California, Berkeley. Other: 2 went to work.

Student Life Upper grades have specified standards of dress, honor system. Discipline rests primarily with faculty. Attendance at religious services is required.

Summer Programs Remediation programs offered; session focuses on academics; held on campus; accepts boys and girls; not open to students from other schools. 25 students usually enrolled. 2011 schedule: June 16 to July 15. Application deadline: June 1.

Tuition and Aid Day student tuition: $10,700. Tuition reduction for siblings, merit scholarship grants, need-based scholarship grants available. In 2010–11, 88% of upper-school students received aid; total upper-school merit-scholarship money awarded: $52,000. Total amount of financial aid awarded in 2010–11: $970,000.

Admissions Traditional secondary-level entrance grade is 9. For fall 2010, 83 students applied for upper-level admission, 68 were accepted, 46 enrolled. High School Placement Test required. Deadline for receipt of application materials: none. Application fee required: $75. Interview required.

Athletics Interscholastic: baseball (boys), basketball (b,g), football (b), soccer (b,g), softball (g), track and field (b,g), volleyball (b,g). 1 PE instructor, 5 coaches.

Computers Computer network features include on-campus library services, Internet access, wireless campus network, Internet filtering or blocking technology. Students grades are available online. The school has a published electronic and media policy.

Contact Lisseth Aguilar, Secretary. 510-532-8947. Fax: 510-532-9754. E-mail: laguilar@stliz-hs.org. Web site: www.stliz-hs.org.

ST. FRANCIS DE SALES HIGH SCHOOL

2323 West Bancroft Street
Toledo, Ohio 43607

Head of School: Mr. Eric J. Smola

General Information Boys' day college-preparatory, religious studies, AP courses, and community service school, affiliated with Roman Catholic Church. Grades 9–12. Founded: 1955. Setting: urban. Nearest major city is Cleveland. 25-acre campus. 1 building on campus. Approved or accredited by Ohio Catholic Schools Accreditation Association (OCSAA) and Ohio Department of Education. Endowment: $7 million. Total enrollment: 604. Upper school average class size: 24. Upper school faculty-student ratio: 1:14. There are 180 required school days per year for Upper School students. Upper School students typically attend 5 days per week. The average school day consists of 6 hours and 30 minutes.

Upper School Student Profile Grade 9: 175 students (175 boys); Grade 10: 142 students (142 boys); Grade 11: 151 students (151 boys); Grade 12: 136 students (136 boys). 73% of students are Roman Catholic.

Faculty School total: 52. In upper school: 41 men, 11 women; 29 have advanced degrees.

Subjects Offered Advanced Placement courses, advanced studio art-AP, algebra, American history, American history-AP, American literature, American literature-AP, anatomy, animation, art, biology, biology-AP, British literature, calculus, calculus-AP, ceramics, chemistry, chemistry-AP, Chinese, chorus, church history, community service, computer programming, computer science, creative writing, criminal justice, drawing, economics, English literature, English-AP, environmental science, expository writing, French, French-AP, geometry, German, German-AP, government/civics, grammar, graphic design, health, Latin, Latin-AP, macroeconomics-AP, math analysis, mathematics, microeconomics-AP, military history, music, New Testament, physical education, physical science, physics, physics-AP, pre-algebra, pre-calculus, psychology, psychology-AP, public speaking, science, social justice, social studies, Spanish, Spanish-AP, statistics, theology, trigonometry, U.S. government, U.S. government and politics-AP, U.S. history-AP, Web site design, world geography, world history, yearbook.

Graduation Requirements Art, computer science, English, foreign language, mathematics, physical education, religion (includes Bible studies and theology), science, social studies (includes history), participation in religious retreats 4 of 4 years. Community service is required.

Special Academic Programs Advanced Placement exam preparation; honors section; study at local college for college credit.

College Admission Counseling 139 students graduated in 2010; 137 went to college, including Bowling Green State University; Ohio University; The University of Toledo; University of Cincinnati; University of Dayton. Other: 2 entered military service. Mean SAT critical reading: 549, mean SAT math: 582, mean SAT writing: 527, mean composite ACT: 24.

Student Life Upper grades have specified standards of dress, student council. Discipline rests primarily with faculty. Attendance at religious services is required.

Summer Programs Enrichment programs offered; session focuses on mathematics, English, reading; held on campus; accepts boys; not open to students from other schools. 100 students usually enrolled. 2011 schedule: June 13 to July 1. Application deadline: June 1.

Tuition and Aid Day student tuition: $8950. Tuition installment plan (monthly payment plans, quarterly payment plan). Tuition reduction for siblings, merit scholarship grants, need-based scholarship grants, paying campus jobs available. In

2010–11, 66% of upper-school students received aid; total upper-school merit-scholarship money awarded: $436,659. Total amount of financial aid awarded in 2010–11: $1,669,600.

Admissions Traditional secondary-level entrance grade is 9. For fall 2010, 234 students applied for upper-level admission, 204 were accepted, 179 enrolled. STS required. Deadline for receipt of application materials: none. No application fee required. On-campus interview required.

Athletics Interscholastic: baseball, basketball, bowling, crew, cross-country running, diving, football, golf, ice hockey, lacrosse, soccer, swimming and diving, tennis, track and field, water polo, winter (indoor) track, wrestling; intramural: basketball, football. 22 coaches, 1 athletic trainer.

Computers Computers are regularly used in animation, art, desktop publishing, English, mathematics, science, Web site design classes. Computer network features include Internet access, Internet filtering or blocking technology. Student e-mail accounts and computer access in designated common areas are available to students. Students grades are available online. The school has a published electronic and media policy.

Contact Mrs. Jacqueline VanDemark, Administrative Assistant. 419-531-1618. Fax: 419-531-9740. E-mail: jvandemark@sfstoledo.org. Web site: www.sfstoledo.org.

SAINT FRANCIS GIRLS HIGH SCHOOL

5900 Elvas Avenue
Sacramento, California 95819
Head of School: Mrs. Marion L. Bishop

General Information Girls' day college-preparatory, arts, and religious studies school, affiliated with Roman Catholic Church. Grades 9–12. Founded: 1940. Setting: urban. 11 buildings on campus. Approved or accredited by Western Association of Schools and Colleges, Western Catholic Education Association, and California Department of Education. Total enrollment: 1,139. Upper school average class size: 24. Upper school faculty-student ratio: 1:15. Upper School students typically attend 5 days per week.

Upper School Student Profile Grade 9: 299 students (299 girls); Grade 10: 277 students (277 girls); Grade 11: 279 students (279 girls); Grade 12: 284 students (284 girls). 73% of students are Roman Catholic.

Faculty School total: 77. In upper school: 20 men, 57 women; 59 have advanced degrees.

Subjects Offered Acting, advanced biology, advanced chemistry, advanced computer applications, advanced math, Advanced Placement courses, advanced studio art-AP, algebra, American government, American history, American history-AP, American literature, anatomy and physiology, art, art history-AP, biology, biology-AP, biotechnology, calculus, calculus-AP, chemistry, chemistry-AP, choir, Christian ethics, church history, civics, computer education, computer multimedia, computer science-AP, dance, drawing, economics, English literature and composition-AP, equality and freedom, ethics, film and literature, fitness, French, French literature-AP, French-AP, geography, geometry, health, Hebrew scripture, integrated science, Italian, jazz, Latin, model United Nations, orchestra, painting, philosophy, physics, prayer/spirituality, pre-calculus, robotics, sculpture, self-defense, Spanish, Spanish language-AP, Spanish literature-AP, speech, statistics, studio art-AP, U.S. government and politics-AP, U.S. history, U.S. history-AP, world history, world religions, yearbook, yoga.

Special Academic Programs 13 Advanced Placement exams for which test preparation is offered; honors section.

College Admission Counseling 262 students graduated in 2010; 260 went to college, including California Polytechnic State University, San Luis Obispo; California State University, Chico; California State University, Sacramento; Saint Mary's College of California; San Francisco State University; University of Oregon. Other: 2 had other specific plans. Mean SAT critical reading: 566, mean SAT math: 543, mean SAT writing: 588, mean composite ACT: 24.

Student Life Upper grades have uniform requirement, student council, honor system. Discipline rests primarily with faculty. Attendance at religious services is required.

Summer Programs Enrichment, advancement, sports, art/fine arts programs offered; held on campus; accepts boys and girls; open to students from other schools. 750 students usually enrolled.

Tuition and Aid Day student tuition: $11,100. Tuition installment plan (monthly payment plans). Need-based scholarship grants available. In 2010–11, 15% of upper-school students received aid. Total amount of financial aid awarded in 2010–11: $1,000,000.

Admissions Traditional secondary-level entrance grade is 9. CTBS (or similar from their school) required. Deadline for receipt of application materials: January 28. No application fee required. Interview required.

Athletics Interscholastic: basketball, cheering, cross-country running, golf, lacrosse, soccer, softball, swimming and diving, tennis, track and field, volleyball, water polo. 4 PE instructors, 45 coaches, 2 athletic trainers.

Computers Computer resources include on-campus library services, Internet access, wireless campus network, Internet filtering or blocking technology. Student e-mail accounts and computer access in designated common areas are available to students. Students grades are available online. The school has a published electronic and media policy.

Contact Mrs. Moira O'Brien, Director of Admissions. 916-727-5095. E-mail: mobrien@stfrancishs.org. Web site: www.stfrancishs.org.

SAINT FRANCIS HIGH SCHOOL

200 Foothill Boulevard
La Canada Flintridge, California 91011
Head of School: Mr. Thomas G. Moran

General Information Boys' day college-preparatory and religious studies school, affiliated with Roman Catholic Church. Grades 9–12. Founded: 1946. Setting: suburban. Nearest major city is Los Angeles. 19-acre campus. 5 buildings on campus. Approved or accredited by Western Association of Schools and Colleges and Western Catholic Education Association. Total enrollment: 671. Upper school average class size: 28. Upper school faculty-student ratio: 1:15. There are 182 required school days per year for Upper School students. Upper School students typically attend 5 days per week. The average school day consists of 6 hours.

Upper School Student Profile Grade 9: 180 students (180 boys); Grade 10: 156 students (156 boys); Grade 11: 169 students (169 boys); Grade 12: 166 students (166 boys). 71% of students are Roman Catholic.

Faculty School total: 48. In upper school: 38 men, 10 women; 20 have advanced degrees.

Subjects Offered Advanced Placement courses, English, fine arts, foreign language, health, history, mathematics, physical education, religion, science, social sciences, technology.

Graduation Requirements Arts and fine arts (art, music, dance, drama), English, foreign language, mathematics, physical education (includes health), religion (includes Bible studies and theology), science, social sciences, technology, Christian service hours, retreat each year of attendance. Community service is required.

Special Academic Programs Advanced Placement exam preparation; honors section.

College Admission Counseling 162 students graduated in 2010; 158 went to college, including California State University, Northridge; Loyola Marymount University; Occidental College; University of California, Los Angeles; University of California, Riverside; University of Oregon. Other: 1 went to work, 1 entered military service, 2 had other specific plans. Mean SAT critical reading: 561, mean SAT math: 557, mean SAT writing: 538, mean composite ACT: 23.

Student Life Upper grades have specified standards of dress, student council. Discipline rests primarily with faculty. Attendance at religious services is required.

Summer Programs Remediation, enrichment, sports programs offered; session focuses on remediation and enrichment; held on campus; accepts boys and girls; open to students from other schools. 450 students usually enrolled. 2011 schedule: June 20 to July 22. Application deadline: June 13.

Tuition and Aid Day student tuition: $11,200. Tuition installment plan (monthly payment plans). Merit scholarship grants, need-based scholarship grants available. In 2010–11, 20% of upper-school students received aid; total upper-school merit-scholarship money awarded: $35,000. Total amount of financial aid awarded in 2010–11: $420,000.

Admissions Traditional secondary-level entrance grade is 9. For fall 2010, 402 students applied for upper-level admission, 220 were accepted, 180 enrolled. High School Placement Test required. Deadline for receipt of application materials: January 30. Application fee required: $75. On-campus interview required.

Athletics Interscholastic: baseball, basketball, cross-country running, football, golf, soccer, tennis, track and field, volleyball. 3 PE instructors, 14 coaches, 1 athletic trainer.

Computers Computers are regularly used in all academic, yearbook classes. Computer network features include on-campus library services, Internet access, wireless campus network, Internet filtering or blocking technology. Students grades are available online. The school has a published electronic and media policy.

Contact Ms. Stephanie Vasquez, Registrar. 818-790-0325 Ext. 502. Fax: 818-790-5542. E-mail: vasquezs@sfhs.net. Web site: www.sfhs.net.

SAINT FRANCIS HIGH SCHOOL

1885 Miramonte Avenue
Mountain View, California 94040
Head of School: Mr. Kevin Makley

General Information Coeducational day college-preparatory, arts, religious studies, and technology school, affiliated with Roman Catholic Church, Advent Christian Church. Grades 9–12. Founded: 1954. Setting: suburban. Nearest major city is San Jose. 25-acre campus. 10 buildings on campus. Approved or accredited by Western Association of Schools and Colleges and California Department of Education. Total enrollment: 1,666. Upper school average class size: 29. Upper school faculty-student ratio: 1:29. There are 180 required school days per year for Upper School students. Upper School students typically attend 5 days per week. The average school day consists of 6 hours and 30 minutes.

Upper School Student Profile Grade 9: 450 students (225 boys, 225 girls); Grade 10: 421 students (209 boys, 212 girls); Grade 11: 397 students (196 boys, 201 girls); Grade 12: 399 students (193 boys, 206 girls). 70% of students are Roman Catholic, Advent Christian Church.

Faculty School total: 103. In upper school: 56 men, 47 women; 63 have advanced degrees.

Subjects Offered 20th century American writers, 3-dimensional design, accounting, algebra, American literature, analytic geometry, anatomy and physiology, Arabic studies, band, biology, biology-AP, British literature, British literature (honors), business, calculus-AP, chemistry, chemistry-AP, Christianity, computer graphics, computer literacy, computer programming, computer science, computer science-AP, concert band, concert choir, contemporary issues, contemporary problems, creative writing, design, drama, drawing, economics, electronic music, English, English literature-AP, film and literature, French, French-AP, geography, geometry, German, German-AP, global science, graphics, health science, human biology, information technology, Irish literature, jazz band, jazz ensemble, journalism, music, oil painting, philosophy, physical education, physical science, pre-calculus, printmaking, psychology, religious studies, science fiction, short story, social justice, Spanish, Spanish-AP, speech, speech communications, statistics, symphonic band, technical drawing, technology, trigonometry, typing, U.S. government, U.S. government and politics-AP, U.S. history, U.S. history-AP, water color painting, word processing, world history, world religions.

Graduation Requirements Computer literacy, English, foreign language, human biology, mathematics, physical education (includes health), religious studies, science, social studies (includes history).

Special Academic Programs Advanced Placement exam preparation; honors section; study at local college for college credit.

College Admission Counseling 398 students graduated in 2009; all went to college, including Loyola Marymount University; Stanford University; University of California, Berkeley; University of California, Los Angeles; University of Southern California. Mean SAT critical reading: 699, mean SAT math: 706, mean SAT writing: 713.

Student Life Upper grades have specified standards of dress, student council. Discipline rests primarily with faculty. Attendance at religious services is required.

Tuition and Aid Day student tuition: $12,700. Tuition installment plan (monthly payment plans, individually arranged payment plans). Need-based scholarship grants, paying campus jobs available. In 2009–10, 18% of upper-school students received aid. Total amount of financial aid awarded in 2009–10: $1,200,000.

Admissions Traditional secondary-level entrance grade is 9. For fall 2009, 1,235 students applied for upper-level admission, 650 were accepted, 476 enrolled. High School Placement Test required. Deadline for receipt of application materials: December 16. Application fee required: $65. On-campus interview required.

Athletics Interscholastic: aquatics (boys, girls), baseball (b,g), basketball (b,g), cheering (g), cross-country running (b,g), dance squad (g), diving (b,g), drill team (b,g), field hockey (g), football (b), golf (b,g), gymnastics (g), lacrosse (b,g), soccer (b,g), softball (g), strength & conditioning (b,g), swimming and diving (b,g), track and field (b,g), volleyball (b,g), water polo (b,g), wrestling (b); intramural: cooperative games (b,g), crew (g), dance (b,g), dance squad (b,g), flag football (b,g), floor hockey (b,g), indoor soccer (b,g), jogging (b,g), physical fitness (b,g), rugby (b,g), soccer (b,g), softball (b,g), strength & conditioning (b,g), swimming and diving (b,g), table tennis (b,g), touch football (b,g), track and field (b,g), ultimate Frisbee (b,g), volleyball (b,g), weight lifting (b,g); coed interscholastic: cheering; coed intramural: basketball, cooperative games, dance, dance squad, Frisbee. 6 PE instructors, 51 coaches, 1 athletic trainer.

Computers Computers are regularly used in creative writing, current events, digital applications, graphic arts, graphic design, photography, publications classes. Computer network features include on-campus library services, Internet access, wireless campus network, Internet filtering or blocking technology. Campus intranet, student e-mail accounts, and computer access in designated common areas are available to students. Students grades are available online.

Contact Mr. Michael Speckman, Director of Admissions. 650-968-1213 Ext. 213. Fax: 650-968-1706. E-mail: mikespeckman@sfhs.com. Web site: www.sfhs.com.

ST. FRANCIS HIGH SCHOOL
233 West Broadway
Louisville, Kentucky 40202
Head of School: Ms. Alexandra Schreiber Thurstone
General Information Coeducational day college-preparatory and arts school. Grades 9–12. Founded: 1976. Setting: urban. 2-acre campus. 1 building on campus. Approved or accredited by Independent Schools Association of the Central States and Kentucky Department of Education. Member of National Association of Independent Schools. Endowment: $1 million. Total enrollment: 126. Upper school average class size: 11. Upper school faculty-student ratio: 1:7. There are 174 required school days per year for Upper School students. Upper School students typically attend 5 days per week. The average school day consists of 7 hours.

Upper School Student Profile Grade 9: 21 students (10 boys, 11 girls); Grade 10: 32 students (13 boys, 19 girls); Grade 11: 41 students (24 boys, 17 girls); Grade 12: 32 students (18 boys, 14 girls).

Faculty School total: 18. In upper school: 12 men, 6 women; 15 have advanced degrees.

Subjects Offered African studies, algebra, American history, ancient history, ancient world history, art, biology, biology-AP, business, calculus, calculus-AP, chemistry, chemistry-AP, Chinese, Chinese history, civil rights, community service, creative writing, drama, drawing, English, English literature, English literature-AP, environmental science, environmental science-AP, European history, European history-AP, film studies, filmmaking, fine arts, finite math, French, French language-AP, French literature-AP, French-AP, gender and religion, gender issues, geometry, health, history-AP, journalism, law, medieval history, modern civilization, photography, physical education, physics, physics-AP, playwriting, pre-calculus, senior project,

Spanish, Spanish language-AP, Spanish literature-AP, Spanish-AP, statistics, statistics-AP, The 20th Century, U.S. history-AP, video film production, world history, writing, zoology.

Graduation Requirements Arts and fine arts (art, music, dance, drama), English, foreign language, history, mathematics, physical education (includes health), science, senior project (year-long research project on a topic of student's choice). Community service is required.

Special Academic Programs Advanced Placement exam preparation; independent study; study abroad; academic accommodation for the gifted and the artistically talented.

College Admission Counseling 34 students graduated in 2009; 33 went to college. Other: 1 entered military service.

Student Life Upper grades have student council. Discipline rests equally with students and faculty.

Tuition and Aid Day student tuition: $16,500. Tuition installment plan (Insured Tuition Payment Plan, FACTS Tuition Payment Plan, monthly payment plans). Merit scholarship grants, need-based scholarship grants, tuition remission for children of faculty and staff available. In 2009–10, 48% of upper-school students received aid; total upper-school merit-scholarship money awarded: $44,710. Total amount of financial aid awarded in 2009–10: $615,000.

Admissions Traditional secondary-level entrance grade is 9. For fall 2009, 47 students applied for upper-level admission, 42 were accepted, 39 enrolled. Deadline for receipt of application materials: January 15. Application fee required: $50. On-campus interview required.

Athletics Interscholastic: basketball (boys, girls), field hockey (g), lacrosse (b), running (b,g), tennis (b,g), track and field (b,g), volleyball (g); intramural: indoor hockey (g), indoor soccer (b); coed interscholastic: indoor track & field, soccer; coed intramural: dance team, fitness, physical fitness, physical training, power lifting, racquetball, rowing, ultimate Frisbee, wall climbing, wallyball, weight lifting, weight training, yoga. 1 PE instructor, 12 coaches.

Computers Computers are regularly used in English, French, history, mathematics, science, Spanish classes. Computer network features include Internet access, wireless campus network, word processing, publishing, and Web page programs. Student e-mail accounts and computer access in designated common areas are available to students. The school has a published electronic and media policy.

Contact Ms. Annie Murphy, Director of Admissions, Marketing and Financial Aid. 502-736-1009. Fax: 502-736-1049. E-mail: murphy@stfrancishighschool.com. Web site: www.stfrancishighschool.com.

ST. FRANCIS SCHOOL
13440 Cogburn Road
Alpharetta, Georgia 30004
Head of School: Mr. Drew Buccellato
General Information Coeducational day college-preparatory, arts, and technology school. Grades K–12. Founded: 1976. Setting: suburban. Nearest major city is Atlanta. 43-acre campus. 5 buildings on campus. Approved or accredited by Georgia Accrediting Commission, Georgia Independent School Association, Southern Association of Colleges and Schools, and Southern Association of Independent Schools. Endowment: $2 million. Total enrollment: 827. Upper school average class size: 14. Upper school faculty-student ratio: 1:14. The average school day consists of 6 hours and 30 minutes.

Upper School Student Profile Grade 9: 73 students (53 boys, 20 girls); Grade 10: 79 students (41 boys, 38 girls); Grade 11: 70 students (39 boys, 31 girls); Grade 12: 65 students (38 boys, 27 girls).

Faculty School total: 52. In upper school: 18 men, 34 women; 22 have advanced degrees.

Subjects Offered Algebra, American literature, art-AP, biology, British literature, calculus, character education, cheerleading, chemistry, chorus, college counseling, computer processing, computer programming, drama, drawing, economics, English, English literature-AP, English-AP, geography, geometry, government, graphic design, health, history-AP, honors algebra, honors English, honors geometry, honors U.S. history, honors world history, instrumental music, journalism, keyboarding, Latin, mathematics, newspaper, painting, physical education, physical science, physics, play production, psychology, public speaking, SAT preparation, science, social studies, Spanish, studio art, study skills, trigonometry, U.S. government, U.S. government and politics-AP, U.S. history, U.S. history-AP, word processing, world history, writing, yearbook.

Graduation Requirements Arts and fine arts (art, music, dance, drama), electives, English, foreign language, mathematics, physical education (includes health), science, social studies (includes history), technology, writing, community service hours.

Special Academic Programs Honors section; study at local college for college credit; remedial reading and/or remedial writing; remedial math; special instructional classes for students with learning disabilities and Attention Deficit Disorder.

College Admission Counseling 82 students graduated in 2009; they went to Georgia College & State University; Kennesaw State University; The University of Alabama; University of Georgia.

Student Life Upper grades have uniform requirement, student council, honor system. Discipline rests primarily with faculty.

Tuition and Aid Day student tuition: $16,900. Tuition installment plan (FACTS Tuition Payment Plan). Tuition reduction for siblings, need-based scholarship grants available. In 2009–10, 4% of upper-school students received aid. Total amount of financial aid awarded in 2009–10: $80,000.

Admissions Traditional secondary-level entrance grade is 9. For fall 2009, 75 students applied for upper-level admission, 47 were accepted, 39 enrolled. School placement exam required. Deadline for receipt of application materials: none. Application fee required: $100. On-campus interview required.

Athletics Interscholastic: baseball (boys), basketball (b,g), cheering (g), equestrian sports (g), football (b), golf (b,g), physical fitness (b,g), soccer (b,g), softball (g), swimming and diving (b,g), volleyball (g), wrestling (b); intramural: equestrian sports (g), horseback riding (g); coed interscholastic: cross-country running, swimming and diving, tennis, track and field, weight lifting. 3 PE instructors, 6 coaches, 1 athletic trainer.

Computers Computers are regularly used in English, graphic design, journalism, keyboarding, newspaper, research skills, science, typing, word processing, writing, yearbook classes. Computer network features include on-campus library services, Internet access, Internet filtering or blocking technology. Students grades are available online. The school has a published electronic and media policy.

Contact Mr. Brandon Bryan, Assistant Admissions Director. 678-339-9989 Ext. 33. Fax: 678-339-0473. E-mail: bbryan@stfranschool.com. Web site: www.saintfrancischools.com.

SAINT FRANCIS SCHOOL

2707 Pamoa Road
Honolulu, Hawaii 96822
Head of School: Sr. Joan of Arc Souza

General Information Coeducational day college-preparatory, arts, religious studies, bilingual studies, technology, and ESL school, affiliated with Roman Catholic Church. Boys grades K–10, girls grades K–12. Founded: 1924. Setting: suburban. 11-acre campus. 9 buildings on campus. Approved or accredited by Western Association of Schools and Colleges, Western Catholic Education Association, and Hawaii Department of Education. Total enrollment: 412. Upper school average class size: 20. Upper school faculty-student ratio: 1:20. There are 176 required school days per year for Upper School students. Upper School students typically attend 5 days per week. The average school day consists of 6 hours and 30 minutes.

Upper School Student Profile Grade 6: 16 students (6 boys, 10 girls); Grade 7: 23 students (9 boys, 14 girls); Grade 8: 39 students (13 boys, 26 girls); Grade 9: 71 students (29 boys, 42 girls); Grade 10: 80 students (20 boys, 60 girls); Grade 11: 59 students (59 girls); Grade 12: 41 students (41 girls). 80% of students are Roman Catholic.

Faculty School total: 46. In upper school: 10 men, 17 women; 23 have advanced degrees.

Subjects Offered Algebra, American history, American literature, American sign language, ancient history, art, Asian history, band, Bible studies, biology, biology-AP, calculus-AP, Catholic belief and practice, ceramics, chemistry, choir, chorus, cinematography, college admission preparation, college counseling, college planning, community service, computer literacy, computer technologies, creative writing, earth science, English, English language and composition-AP, English literature, English literature and composition-AP, environmental science, ESL, European history, fine arts, geography, geometry, government-AP, government/civics, grammar, health, history, humanities, Japanese, Japanese as Second Language, journalism, keyboarding, mathematics, medieval/Renaissance history, music, newspaper, NJROTC, oral communications, physical education, physical science, physics, pre-algebra, pre-calculus, psychology, religion, SAT preparation, science, social studies, Spanish, Spanish language-AP, speech, theater, TOEFL preparation, trigonometry, U.S. history-AP, world history, world literature, world religions, writing, yearbook.

Graduation Requirements Algebra, American history, American literature, arts and fine arts (art, music, dance, drama), biology, chemistry, computer applications, computer skills, English, foreign language, humanities, keyboarding, mathematics, physical education (includes health), religion (includes Bible studies and theology), science, social studies (includes history), U.S. history, 100 hours of community service. Community service is required.

Special Academic Programs 7 Advanced Placement exams for which test preparation is offered; honors section; independent study; study at local college for college credit; special instructional classes for deaf students; ESL (13 students enrolled).

College Admission Counseling 56 students graduated in 2010; 53 went to college, including Chaminade University of Honolulu; Hawai'i Pacific University; Seattle University; Southern Oregon University; University of Hawaii at Manoa; University of Oregon. Other: 3 went to work.

Student Life Upper grades have uniform requirement, student council, honor system. Discipline rests primarily with faculty. Attendance at religious services is required.

Summer Programs Remediation, enrichment, advancement, ESL, computer instruction programs offered; session focuses on enrichment and advancement; held on campus; accepts boys and girls; open to students from other schools. 150 students usually enrolled. 2011 schedule: June 8 to July 7. Application deadline: May 20.

Tuition and Aid Day student tuition: $8600. Tuition installment plan (FACTS Tuition Payment Plan, monthly payment plans, individually arranged payment plans, semi-annual payment plan). Tuition reduction for siblings, merit scholarship grants, need-based scholarship grants, alumni scholarships, Support A Student Scholarships, Alverna Scholarships available. In 2010–11, 25% of upper-school students received

aid; total upper-school merit-scholarship money awarded: $26,000. Total amount of financial aid awarded in 2010–11: $194,000.

Admissions Traditional secondary-level entrance grade is 9. For fall 2010, 291 students applied for upper-level admission, 227 were accepted, 137 enrolled. School placement exam or SSAT required. Deadline for receipt of application materials: none. Application fee required: $40. Interview required.

Athletics Interscholastic: archery (girls), baseball (b), basketball (b,g), bowling (g), canoeing/kayaking (g), cheering (g), diving (g), football (b), ocean paddling (g), paddling (g), riflery (b,g), running (g), soccer (g), softball (g), swimming and diving (b,g), tennis (b,g), track and field (b,g), volleyball (g), water polo (g), wrestling (b,g); coed interscholastic: cross-country running, golf, indoor track & field, JROTC drill, weight training. 2 PE instructors, 36 coaches, 1 athletic trainer.

Computers Computers are regularly used in art, English, foreign language, mathematics, music, newspaper, religion, science, social studies, yearbook classes. Computer network features include on-campus library services, Internet access, wireless campus network, Internet filtering or blocking technology. Computer access in designated common areas is available to students. Students grades are available online. The school has a published electronic and media policy.

Contact Karen Curry, Director of Admissions. 808-988-4111 Ext. 712. Fax: 808-988-5497. E-mail: kcurry@stfrancis-oahu.org. Web site: www.stfrancis-oahu.org.

ST. GEORGE'S INDEPENDENT SCHOOL

1880 Wolf River Road
Collierville, Tennessee 38017
Head of School: Mr. William W. Taylor

General Information Coeducational day college-preparatory school, affiliated with Christian faith. Grades PK–12. Founded: 1959. Setting: suburban. Nearest major city is Memphis. 250-acre campus. 5 buildings on campus. Approved or accredited by Southern Association of Colleges and Schools and Southern Association of Independent Schools. Endowment: $2.2 million. Total enrollment: 1,189. Upper school average class size: 20. Upper school faculty-student ratio: 1:7. There are 175 required school days per year for Upper School students. Upper School students typically attend 5 days per week. The average school day consists of 7 hours and 18 minutes.

Upper School Student Profile Grade 9: 87 students (44 boys, 43 girls); Grade 10: 91 students (46 boys, 45 girls); Grade 11: 100 students (44 boys, 56 girls); Grade 12: 89 students (45 boys, 44 girls).

Faculty School total: 126. In upper school: 21 men, 22 women; 31 have advanced degrees.

Subjects Offered Algebra, American literature, astronomy, band, biology, biology-AP, calculus, calculus-AP, chemistry, chemistry-AP, chorus, composition-AP, computer programming, drama, drawing, English, English language and composition-AP, English language-AP, English literature and composition-AP, environmental science, European history-AP, European literature, film, French, French language-AP, geometry, global studies, government, government/civics, honors algebra, honors geometry, human anatomy, independent study, journalism, Latin, Latin-AP, painting, photography, physics, physics-AP, pottery, pre-calculus, printmaking, psychology, religion, short story, social justice, Southern literature, Spanish, Spanish language-AP, statistics-AP, theater, trigonometry, U.S. history, U.S. history-AP, visual arts, weightlifting, wellness, world history, world history-AP.

Graduation Requirements Art, electives, English, history, independent study, language, mathematics, religion (includes Bible studies and theology), science, wellness, senior independent study, senior Global Challenge.

Special Academic Programs Advanced Placement exam preparation; honors section; independent study.

College Admission Counseling 82 students graduated in 2010; 80 went to college, including Mississippi State University; The University of Alabama; The University of Tennessee; University of Arkansas; University of Mississippi; Vanderbilt University. Other: 1 entered military service, 1 had other specific plans. Mean SAT critical reading: 596, mean SAT math: 581, mean SAT writing: 581, mean combined SAT: 1758, mean composite ACT: 27.

Student Life Upper grades have specified standards of dress, student council, honor system. Discipline rests equally with students and faculty. Attendance at religious services is required.

Summer Programs Remediation, enrichment, advancement, sports, art/fine arts, computer instruction programs offered; session focuses on enrichment; held on campus; accepts boys and girls; open to students from other schools. 2011 schedule: June to August. Application deadline: June.

Tuition and Aid Day student tuition: $14,657. Need-based scholarship grants available.

Admissions Traditional secondary-level entrance grade is 9. For fall 2010, 16 students applied for upper-level admission, 16 were accepted, 16 enrolled. Admissions testing or ISEE required. Deadline for receipt of application materials: none. Application fee required: $50. Interview required.

Athletics Interscholastic: baseball (boys), basketball (b,g), cheering (g), cross-country running (b,g), football (b), golf (b,g), lacrosse (b,g), pom squad (g), soccer (b,g), softball (g), tennis (b,g), track and field (b,g), volleyball (g), wrestling (b); coed interscholastic: swimming and diving. 5 PE instructors, 3 coaches, 2 athletic trainers.

Computers Computers are regularly used in all classes. Computer network features include on-campus library services, Internet access, wireless campus network, Internet

filtering or blocking technology. Campus intranet, student e-mail accounts, and computer access in designated common areas are available to students. Students grades are available online. The school has a published electronic and media policy.
Contact Mrs. Julie Loftin, Director of Admissions. 901-457-2150. Fax: 901-457-2152. E-mail: jloftin@sgis.org. Web site: www.sgis.org.

ST. GEORGE'S SCHOOL

372 Purgatory Road
Middletown, Rhode Island 02842-5984
Head of School: Eric F. Peterson

General Information Coeducational boarding and day college-preparatory, arts, religious studies, technology, and marine sciences school, affiliated with Episcopal Church. Grades 9–12. Founded: 1896. Setting: suburban. Nearest major city is Providence. Students are housed in single-sex dormitories. 150-acre campus. 47 buildings on campus. Approved or accredited by Association of Independent Schools in New England, National Association of Episcopal Schools, New England Association of Schools and Colleges, The Association of Boarding Schools, and Rhode Island Department of Education. Member of National Association of Independent Schools and Secondary School Admission Test Board. Endowment: $92.8 million. Total enrollment: 367. Upper school average class size: 11. Upper school faculty-student ratio: 1:6. Upper School students typically attend 6 days per week. The average school day consists of 6 hours and 50 minutes.
Upper School Student Profile Grade 9: 75 students (36 boys, 39 girls); Grade 10: 99 students (54 boys, 45 girls); Grade 11: 97 students (41 boys, 56 girls); Grade 12: 93 students (41 boys, 52 girls). 80% of students are boarding students. 34% are state residents. 27 states are represented in upper school student body. 15% are international students. International students from Bermuda, China, Republic of Korea, and Thailand; 13 other countries represented in student body.
Faculty School total: 68. In upper school: 39 men, 29 women; 53 have advanced degrees; 56 reside on campus.
Subjects Offered 3-dimensional art, 3-dimensional design, acting, advanced biology, advanced chemistry, advanced computer applications, advanced math, Advanced Placement courses, advanced studio art-AP, African American history, African American studies, algebra, American history, American history-AP, American literature, American literature-AP, American studies, analytic geometry, architectural drawing, architecture, art, art history, art-AP, Asian studies, Bible, Bible as literature, Bible studies, biology, biology-AP, calculus, calculus-AP, ceramics, chemistry, chemistry-AP, Chinese, computer graphics, computer math, computer programming, computer science, computer science-AP, creative writing, dance, DNA, drama, dramatic arts, drawing, ecology, economics, economics-AP, English, English language and composition-AP, English literature, English literature-AP, environmental science, environmental science-AP, ethics, European history, European history-AP, expository writing, fine arts, French, French language-AP, geometry, global studies, government/civics, grammar, health, history, journalism, Latin, Latin-AP, law, logic, macro/microeconomics-AP, Mandarin, marine biology, mathematics, microbiology, music, music theory-AP, navigation, oceanography, philosophy, photography, physics, physics-AP, psychology, public speaking, religion, robotics, science, sculpture, social studies, Spanish, Spanish language-AP, Spanish literature-AP, statistics, studio art-AP, theater, theology, trigonometry, U.S. government and politics-AP, veterinary science, world history, world history-AP, world literature, writing.
Graduation Requirements Arts and fine arts (art, music, dance, drama), computer science, English, foreign language, mathematics, physical education (includes health), religion (includes Bible studies and theology), science, social studies (includes history).
Special Academic Programs Advanced Placement exam preparation; honors section; independent study; term-away projects; study abroad; academic accommodation for the gifted, the musically talented, and the artistically talented.
College Admission Counseling 89 students graduated in 2010; all went to college, including Cornell University; Hamilton College; Lehigh University; The Colorado College; The George Washington University; Trinity College. Mean SAT critical reading: 626, mean SAT math: 651, mean SAT writing: 628, mean combined SAT: 1905.
Student Life Upper grades have specified standards of dress, student council, honor system. Discipline rests primarily with faculty. Attendance at religious services is required.
Tuition and Aid Day student tuition: $31,000; 7-day tuition and room/board: $45,000. Tuition installment plan (Insured Tuition Payment Plan, Academic Management Services Plan, Key Tuition Payment Plan, monthly payment plans, individually arranged payment plans). Need-based scholarship grants, need-based loans, middle-income loans available. In 2010–11, 30% of upper-school students received aid.
Admissions Traditional secondary-level entrance grade is 9. For fall 2010, 676 students applied for upper-level admission, 235 were accepted, 111 enrolled. ISEE, PSAT, SSAT or TOEFL required. Deadline for receipt of application materials: February 1. Application fee required: $50. Interview required.
Athletics Interscholastic: baseball (boys), basketball (b,g), cross-country running (b,g), field hockey (g), football (b), hockey (b,g), ice hockey (b,g), lacrosse (b,g), sailing (b,g), soccer (b,g), softball (g), squash (b,g), swimming and diving (b,g), tennis (b,g), track and field (b,g); coed interscholastic: dance, sailing; coed intramural:

aerobics/dance, dance, modern dance, mountain biking, Nautilus, soccer, softball, squash, strength & conditioning. 2 coaches, 3 athletic trainers.
Computers Computers are regularly used in art, English, foreign language, history, mathematics, music, religion, science, theater classes. Computer network features include on-campus library services, online commercial services, Internet access, wireless campus network, Internet filtering or blocking technology, scanners, digital cameras, and access to printers. Campus intranet, student e-mail accounts, and computer access in designated common areas are available to students. Students grades are available online. The school has a published electronic and media policy.
Contact James A. Hamilton, Director of Admission. 401-842-6600. Fax: 401-842-6696. E-mail: admission@stgeorges.edu. Web site: www.stgeorges.edu.

SAINT GEORGE'S SCHOOL

2929 West Waikiki Road
Spokane, Washington 99208
Head of School: Mo Copeland

General Information Coeducational day college-preparatory, arts, and technology school. Grades K–12. Founded: 1955. Setting: suburban. 120-acre campus. 10 buildings on campus. Approved or accredited by Northwest Association of Schools and Colleges, Pacific Northwest Association of Independent Schools, and Washington Department of Education. Member of National Association of Independent Schools. Endowment: $3 million. Total enrollment: 381. Upper school average class size: 15. Upper school faculty-student ratio: 1:7. There are 174 required school days per year for Upper School students. Upper School students typically attend 5 days per week. The average school day consists of 5 hours and 45 minutes.
Upper School Student Profile Grade 9: 30 students (15 boys, 15 girls); Grade 10: 31 students (17 boys, 14 girls); Grade 11: 32 students (22 boys, 10 girls); Grade 12: 45 students (24 boys, 21 girls).
Faculty School total: 44. In upper school: 13 men, 7 women; 12 have advanced degrees.
Subjects Offered Algebra, American history, American literature, art, biology, calculus, ceramics, chemistry, community service, computer science, creative writing, drama, earth science, ecology, economics, English, English literature, environmental science, European history, fine arts, French, geography, geometry, grammar, health, history, humanities, journalism, Mandarin, mathematics, music, photography, physical education, physical science, physics, science, social studies, Spanish, theater, trigonometry, world history, writing.
Graduation Requirements Arts and fine arts (art, music, dance, drama), computer science, English, foreign language, history, mathematics, physical education (includes health), science. Community service is required.
Special Academic Programs Advanced Placement exam preparation; honors section; study at local college for college credit.
College Admission Counseling 28 students graduated in 2009; all went to college, including Duke University; Macalester College; Princeton University; Rensselaer Polytechnic Institute; Vanderbilt University; Western Washington University. Mean SAT critical reading: 624, mean SAT math: 634, mean SAT writing: 616, mean combined SAT: 1874.
Student Life Upper grades have student council, honor system. Discipline rests equally with students and faculty.
Tuition and Aid Day student tuition: $16,710. Tuition installment plan (Insured Tuition Payment Plan, monthly payment plans, individually arranged payment plans). Merit scholarship grants, need-based scholarship grants available. In 2009–10, 26% of upper-school students received aid; total upper-school merit-scholarship money awarded: $8356. Total amount of financial aid awarded in 2009–10: $370,751.
Admissions Traditional secondary-level entrance grade is 9. For fall 2009, 23 students applied for upper-level admission, 16 were accepted, 9 enrolled. School's own test or TOEFL required. Deadline for receipt of application materials: none. Application fee required: $50. On-campus interview required.
Athletics Interscholastic: baseball (boys), basketball (b,g), cross-country running (b,g), soccer (b), softball (g), tennis (b,g), track and field (b,g), volleyball (g); coed interscholastic: rock climbing. 4 PE instructors, 10 coaches.
Computers Computers are regularly used in all academic classes. Computer network features include on-campus library services, Internet access. Computer access in designated common areas is available to students. Students grades are available online. The school has a published electronic and media policy.
Contact Debra Duvoisin, Director of Admissions. 509-466-1636 Ext. 304. Fax: 509-467-3258. E-mail: debbie.duvoisin@sgs.org. Web site: www.sgs.org.

ST. GEORGE'S SCHOOL

4175 West 29th Avenue
Vancouver, British Columbia V6S 1V1, Canada
Head of School: Dr. Tom Matthews

General Information Boys' boarding and day college-preparatory, arts, bilingual studies, and technology school. Boarding grades 7–12, day grades 1–12. Founded: 1930. Setting: suburban. Students are housed in single-sex dormitories. 27-acre campus. 2 buildings on campus. Approved or accredited by Canadian Association of Independent Schools, The Association of Boarding Schools, and British Columbia Department of Education. Affiliate member of National Association of Independent

St. George's School

Schools; member of Secondary School Admission Test Board. Language of instruction: English. Total enrollment: 1,157. Upper school average class size: 19. Upper school faculty-student ratio: 1:10.

Upper School Student Profile Grade 8: 144 students (144 boys); Grade 9: 149 students (149 boys); Grade 10: 157 students (157 boys); Grade 11: 156 students (156 boys); Grade 12: 155 students (155 boys). 18% of students are boarding students. 91% are province residents. 9 provinces are represented in upper school student body. 9% are international students. International students from Germany, Hong Kong, Mexico, Republic of Korea, Taiwan, and United States; 4 other countries represented in student body.

Faculty School total: 130. In upper school: 63 men, 23 women; 35 have advanced degrees; 9 reside on campus.

Subjects Offered Advanced chemistry, advanced computer applications, advanced math, algebra, analysis and differential calculus, applied arts, applied music, applied skills, architecture, art, art history, art history-AP, biology, biology-AP, business, business skills, calculus, calculus-AP, Canadian geography, Canadian history, Canadian literature, career and personal planning, ceramics, chemistry, chemistry-AP, comparative government and politics-AP, computer graphics, computer programming, computer programming-AP, computer science, computer science-AP, creative writing, critical thinking, debate, drama, drama performance, dramatic arts, earth science, economics, economics-AP, English, English literature, English literature-AP, environmental science, European history, expository writing, film, fine arts, French, French-AP, geography, geology, geometry, German, German-AP, government/civics, grammar, history, industrial arts, introduction to theater, Japanese, journalism, Latin, Latin-AP, law, library, Mandarin, mathematics, mathematics-AP, music, music-AP, performing arts, photography, physical education, physical fitness, physics, physics-AP, psychology, psychology-AP, science, social studies, society, politics and law, Spanish, Spanish-AP, speech and debate, studio art, studio art-AP, technical theater, theater, trigonometry, typing, U.S. history-AP, United States government-AP, Western civilization, world history, world literature, writing.

Graduation Requirements Arts and fine arts (art, music, dance, drama), business skills (includes word processing), English, foreign language, mathematics, physical education (includes health), science, social studies (includes history).

Special Academic Programs Advanced Placement exam preparation; honors section; remedial reading and/or remedial writing.

College Admission Counseling 155 students graduated in 2010; 152 went to college, including McGill University; Queen's University at Kingston; The University of British Columbia; The University of Western Ontario; University of Toronto; University of Victoria.

Student Life Upper grades have uniform requirement, student council, honor system. Discipline rests primarily with faculty.

Summer Programs Advancement, ESL, sports, art/fine arts, computer instruction programs offered; session focuses on recreation and enrichment; held both on and off campus; held at other schools in area (outdoor education); accepts boys and girls; open to students from other schools. 1,000 students usually enrolled. 2011 schedule: July 2 to August 15. Application deadline: none.

Tuition and Aid Day student tuition: CAN$15,355–CAN$46,000; 7-day tuition and room/board: CAN$37,470–CAN$46,000. Tuition installment plan (monthly payment plans, individually arranged payment plans, term payment plan, one-time payment plan). Tuition reduction for siblings, bursaries, merit scholarship grants, need-based scholarship grants available. In 2010–11, 12% of upper-school students received aid; total upper-school merit-scholarship money awarded: CAN$75,000. Total amount of financial aid awarded in 2010–11: CAN$800,000.

Admissions Traditional secondary-level entrance grade is 8. For fall 2010, 250 students applied for upper-level admission, 90 were accepted, 50 enrolled. School's own exam and SSAT required. Deadline for receipt of application materials: February 10. Application fee required: CAN$200. Interview required.

Athletics Interscholastic: badminton, basketball, cricket, cross-country running, field hockey, golf, ice hockey, rowing, rugby, soccer, swimming and diving, tennis, track and field, triathlon, volleyball, water polo; intramural: badminton, ball hockey, basketball, bicycling, canoeing/kayaking, cross-country running, flag football, floor hockey, ice hockey, martial arts, outdoor education, outdoor recreation, physical fitness, rugby, running, sailing, skiing (downhill), soccer, softball, squash, swimming and diving, table tennis, tennis, track and field, ultimate Frisbee, volleyball, water polo, weight lifting. 4 PE instructors, 8 coaches.

Computers Computers are regularly used in desktop publishing, history, information technology, mathematics, media, publications, science, technology classes. Computer network features include on-campus library services, online commercial services, Internet access. The school has a published electronic and media policy.

Contact Mr. Lindsay Thierry, Director of Admissions and Residential Life. 604-221-3881. Fax: 604-224-5820. E-mail: lthierry@stgeorges.bc.ca. Web site: www.stgeorges.bc.ca.

ST. GEORGE'S SCHOOL IN SWITZERLAND

Chemin de St. Georges 19
Clarens/Montreux 1815, Switzerland
Head of School: Mr. Ilya Eigenbrot

General Information Girls' boarding and coeducational day college-preparatory and general academic school. Boarding girls grades 6–12, day boys grades K–12, day girls grades K–12. Founded: 1927. Setting: small town. Nearest major city is Lausanne, Switzerland. Students are housed in single-sex by floor dormitories. 4-hectare campus. 2 buildings on campus. Member of European Council of International Schools. Language of instruction: English. Total enrollment: 399. Upper school average class size: 15. Upper school faculty-student ratio: 1:7.

Upper School Student Profile 32% of students are boarding students. 32% are international students. International students from United Kingdom; 25 other countries represented in student body.

Faculty School total: 31. In upper school: 13 men, 18 women; 18 have advanced degrees; 3 reside on campus.

Subjects Offered Algebra, art, art history, biology, business, calculus, chemistry, computer programming, computer science, creative writing, drama, economics, English, English literature, ESL, European history, foreign language, French, geography, geometry, German, history, Italian, mathematics, music, physical education, physics, psychology, science, social sciences, Spanish, theater, trigonometry, typing, word processing, world history.

Graduation Requirements English, foreign language, mathematics, physical education (includes health), science, social sciences, TOEFL score of 550/213 or C or better in GCSE English.

Special Academic Programs International Baccalaureate program; remedial reading and/or remedial writing; remedial math; ESL.

College Admission Counseling 20 students graduated in 2009; all went to college, including Johnson & Wales University; Long Beach City College; Lynn University; Penn State University Park; San Diego State University; The George Washington University.

Student Life Upper grades have uniform requirement, student council. Discipline rests primarily with faculty.

Tuition and Aid Tuition reduction for siblings, bursaries, merit scholarship grants available.

Admissions Deadline for receipt of application materials: none. Application fee required: 1000 Swiss francs. On-campus interview recommended.

Athletics Interscholastic: basketball (boys, girls), climbing (b,g), cross-country running (b,g), equestrian sports (g), indoor hockey (b,g), skiing (downhill) (b,g); intramural: aerobics/dance (g), basketball (b,g), netball (b,g), rounders (b,g), skiing (downhill) (b,g); coed interscholastic: alpine skiing, aquatics, archery, backpacking, bowling, cricket, cross-country running, fencing, field hockey, football, gymnastics, indoor hockey, indoor track & field, jogging, outdoor activities, rounders, tennis, volleyball; coed intramural: badminton, basketball, cross-country running, field hockey, indoor hockey, skiing (downhill). 3 PE instructors, 3 coaches.

Computers Computers are regularly used in business, typing classes. Computer resources include on-campus library services, Internet access, wireless campus network, Internet filtering or blocking technology. Student e-mail accounts are available to students.

Contact Ms. V. Perbos-Parsons, Head of Admissions. 41-21-9643411. Fax: 41-21-9644932. E-mail: admissions@st-georges.ch. Web site: www.st-georges.ch.

ST. GEORGE'S SCHOOL OF MONTREAL

3100 The Boulevard
Montreal, Quebec H3Y 1R9, Canada
Head of School: Mr. James A. Officer

General Information Coeducational day college-preparatory, arts, bilingual studies, and technology school. Grades K–11. Founded: 1930. Setting: urban. 2-acre campus. 1 building on campus. Approved or accredited by Canadian Association of Independent Schools, Quebec Association of Independent Schools, and Quebec Department of Education. Affiliate member of National Association of Independent Schools. Languages of instruction: English and French. Total enrollment: 445. Upper school average class size: 17. Upper school faculty-student ratio: 1:17. There are 200 required school days per year for Upper School students. Upper School students typically attend 5 days per week. The average school day consists of 7 hours.

Upper School Student Profile Grade 7: 40 students (28 boys, 12 girls); Grade 8: 49 students (28 boys, 21 girls); Grade 9: 39 students (23 boys, 16 girls); Grade 10: 66 students (31 boys, 35 girls); Grade 11: 61 students (44 boys, 17 girls).

Faculty School total: 42. In upper school: 19 men, 23 women; 18 have advanced degrees.

Subjects Offered Advanced chemistry, advanced math, Advanced Placement courses, algebra, art, art history, art-AP, biology, biology-AP, calculus, Canadian history, chemistry, civics, computer art, computer math, computer programming, computer science, creative writing, dance, debate, drama, earth science, ecology, economics, English, English literature, English-AP, environmental science, expository writing, film, fine arts, French, French as a second language, French studies, French-AP, general math, general science, geography, government/civics, Internet research, leadership, library research, mathematics, media, moral and social development, moral reasoning, music, music appreciation, musical productions, newspaper, outdoor education, performing arts, physical education, physics, pre-calculus, psychology, science, science project, set design, social studies, theater, writing.

Graduation Requirements Economics, English, French as a second language, mathematics, physical education (includes health), science, social studies (includes history).

Special Academic Programs Advanced Placement exam preparation; honors section; independent study; academic accommodation for the gifted, the musically talented, and the artistically talented; remedial reading and/or remedial writing;

remedial math; programs in English, mathematics, general development for dyslexic students; special instructional classes for deaf students; ESL (6 students enrolled).

College Admission Counseling 56 students graduated in 2010; all went to college.

Student Life Upper grades have specified standards of dress, student council. Discipline rests primarily with faculty.

Admissions Traditional secondary-level entrance grade is 7. For fall 2010, 24 students applied for upper-level admission, 24 were accepted, 24 enrolled. Academic Profile Tests, admissions testing, school's own exam or SSAT required. Deadline for receipt of application materials: none. Application fee required: CAN$125. Interview required.

Athletics Interscholastic: badminton (boys, girls), basketball (b,g), flag football (g), hockey (g), ice hockey (g), indoor track & field (b,g), rugby (g); intramural: basketball (b,g); coed interscholastic: aquatics, cross-country running, dance, Frisbee, independent competitive sports, soccer, track and field; coed intramural: aerobics, alpine skiing, aquatics, backpacking, badminton, ball hockey, baseball, basketball, bicycling, canoeing/kayaking, climbing, cooperative games, Cosom hockey, cross-country running, curling, fencing, fitness, fitness walking, flag football, floor hockey, freestyle skiing, Frisbee, golf, ice hockey, ice skating, independent competitive sports, indoor hockey, indoor soccer, indoor track & field, jogging, life saving, outdoor education, rock climbing, scuba diving, self defense, skiing (cross-country), soccer, squash, track and field, wall climbing, yoga. 3 PE instructors, 5 coaches.

Computers Computers are regularly used in all academic classes. Campus intranet and student e-mail accounts are available to students.

Contact Ms. Kathay Carson, Director of High School Admissions. 514-904-0542. Fax: 514-933-3621. E-mail: kathay.carson@stgeorges.qc.ca. Web site: www.stgeorges.qc.ca.

SAINT GERTRUDE HIGH SCHOOL

3215 Stuart Avenue
Richmond, Virginia 23221
Head of School: Mrs. Susan Walker

General Information Girls' day college-preparatory and religious studies school, affiliated with Roman Catholic Church. Grades 9–12. Founded: 1922. Setting: urban. Nearest major city is Washington, DC. 1 building on campus. Approved or accredited by National Independent Private Schools Association and Southern Association of Colleges and Schools. Member of National Association of Independent Schools. Total enrollment: 283. Upper school average class size: 15. Upper school faculty-student ratio: 1:9.

Upper School Student Profile Grade 9: 75 students (75 girls); Grade 10: 68 students (68 girls); Grade 11: 67 students (67 girls); Grade 12: 73 students (73 girls). 67% of students are Roman Catholic.

Faculty School total: 29. In upper school: 3 men, 26 women; 26 have advanced degrees.

Subjects Offered Advanced Placement courses, algebra, American history, American history-AP, American literature, American literature-AP, anatomy, art, bell choir, Bible studies, biology, calculus, calculus-AP, ceramics, chemistry, chemistry-AP, chorus, church history, community service, computer science, drama, drawing, driver education, English, English language and composition-AP, English language-AP, English literature, English literature and composition-AP, environmental science, European history, expository writing, fine arts, French, geometry, government and politics-AP, government/civics, grammar, history, honors algebra, honors English, honors world history, humanities, keyboarding, Latin, mathematics, media, music, painting, physical education, physics, physics-AP, pre-calculus, probability and statistics, psychology, religion, science, social sciences, social studies, sociology, Spanish, Spanish literature, studio art-AP, theater, theology, trigonometry, U.S. government and politics-AP, world history, world literature, writing, yearbook.

Graduation Requirements Arts and fine arts (art, music, dance, drama), computer science, English, keyboarding, mathematics, physical education (includes health), religion (includes Bible studies and theology), science, social sciences, social studies (includes history). Community service is required.

Special Academic Programs Advanced Placement exam preparation; honors section.

College Admission Counseling 66 students graduated in 2009; all went to college, including James Madison University; The College of William and Mary; University of Richmond; University of Virginia; Virginia Commonwealth University; Virginia Polytechnic Institute and State University.

Student Life Upper grades have uniform requirement, student council, honor system. Discipline rests primarily with faculty. Attendance at religious services is required.

Tuition and Aid Day student tuition: $11,600. Tuition installment plan (FACTS Tuition Payment Plan). Tuition reduction for siblings, merit scholarship grants, need-based scholarship grants available. In 2009–10, 22% of upper-school students received aid; total upper-school merit-scholarship money awarded: $20,200.

Admissions Traditional secondary-level entrance grade is 9. For fall 2009, 140 students applied for upper-level admission, 100 were accepted, 75 enrolled. ACT-Explore, admissions testing, latest standardized score from previous school and Otis-Lennon School Ability Test required. Deadline for receipt of application materials: January 31. Application fee required: $50. On-campus interview required.

Athletics Interscholastic: basketball, cross-country running, diving, field hockey, golf, indoor track, lacrosse, soccer, softball, swimming and diving, tennis, track and field, volleyball. 1 PE instructor, 14 coaches, 1 athletic trainer.

Computers Computers are regularly used in all academic classes. Computer network features include on-campus library services, Internet access, wireless campus network. Student e-mail accounts and computer access in designated common areas are available to students. The school has a published electronic and media policy.

Contact Maureen Williams, Director of Admission and Marketing. 804-358-9885 Ext. 341. Fax: 804-353-8929. E-mail: mwilliams@saintgertrude.org. Web site: www.saintgertrude.org.

ST. GREGORY COLLEGE PREPARATORY SCHOOL

3231 North Craycroft Road
Tucson, Arizona 85712
Head of School: Mr. Jonathan Martin

General Information Coeducational day college-preparatory and arts school. Grades 6–PG. Founded: 1980. Setting: suburban. 40-acre campus. 9 buildings on campus. Approved or accredited by Independent Schools Association of the Southwest, The College Board, and Arizona Department of Education. Member of National Association of Independent Schools and Secondary School Admission Test Board. Total enrollment: 290. Upper school average class size: 16. Upper school faculty-student ratio: 1:9. Upper School students typically attend 5 days per week. The average school day consists of 7 hours and 30 minutes.

Upper School Student Profile Grade 9: 54 students (29 boys, 25 girls); Grade 10: 51 students (27 boys, 24 girls); Grade 11: 27 students (14 boys, 13 girls); Grade 12: 35 students (15 boys, 20 girls).

Faculty School total: 33. In upper school: 10 men, 11 women; 15 have advanced degrees.

Subjects Offered Advanced studio art-AP, algebra, American history, American literature, anatomy and physiology, ancient world history, art, art history, band, biology, biology-AP, calculus, ceramics, chemistry, chemistry-AP, choir, chorus, college counseling, college placement, community service, comparative government and politics-AP, computer programming, creative writing, drama, earth science, ecology, economics, English, English literature, English-AP, ethics, European history, European history-AP, expository writing, fine arts, finite math, French, French language-AP, French-AP, geography, geology, geometry, government and politics-AP, government/civics, government/civics-AP, grammar, history, history of drama, history of music, humanities, independent study, jazz band, journalism, Latin, Latin-AP, literature, marine biology, mathematics, music, music theory, music theory-AP, newspaper, photography, physical education, physical science, physics, pre-calculus, religion, SAT preparation, science, social studies, Spanish, Spanish language-AP, Spanish-AP, speech, stage design, stagecraft, studio art-AP, theater, trigonometry, U.S. government and politics-AP, U.S. history-AP, world history, writing.

Graduation Requirements Arts and fine arts (art, music, dance, drama), English, foreign language, history, humanities, mathematics, science, senior internships. Community service is required.

Special Academic Programs Advanced Placement exam preparation; honors section; accelerated programs; independent study; term-away projects; study at local college for college credit; academic accommodation for the gifted, the musically talented, and the artistically talented.

College Admission Counseling 39 students graduated in 2010; 38 went to college, including Cornell University; Stanford University; The University of Arizona; University of Pennsylvania; University of Southern California. Other: 1 had other specific plans. Mean SAT critical reading: 573, mean SAT math: 590, mean composite ACT: 26.

Student Life Upper grades have specified standards of dress, student council, honor system. Discipline rests primarily with faculty.

Tuition and Aid Day student tuition: $14,750–$15,750. Tuition installment plan (Insured Tuition Payment Plan, monthly payment plans, 2- and 10-payment plans). Need-based scholarship grants available. In 2010–11, 44% of upper-school students received aid. Total amount of financial aid awarded in 2010–11: $774,648.

Admissions Traditional secondary-level entrance grade is 9. For fall 2010, 58 students applied for upper-level admission, 47 were accepted, 35 enrolled. CTBS (or similar from their school) and writing sample required. Deadline for receipt of application materials: none. Application fee required: $45. Interview recommended.

Athletics Interscholastic: baseball (boys), basketball (b,g), golf (b,g), soccer (b,g), softball (g), swimming and diving (b,g), tennis (b,g), volleyball (b,g); intramural: touch football (b); coed interscholastic: cross-country running, hiking/backpacking, outdoor education, ropes courses, strength & conditioning; coed intramural: basketball, cooperative games, cross-country running, dance, flag football, football, hiking/backpacking, outdoor education, outdoor recreation, outdoor skills, physical training, ropes courses, strength & conditioning, volleyball, weight training, yoga. 2 PE instructors, 12 coaches, 1 athletic trainer.

Computers Computers are regularly used in English, foreign language, history, journalism, mathematics, newspaper, photography, science classes. Computer network features include on-campus library services, online commercial services, Internet access, wireless campus network, Internet filtering or blocking technology. Campus intranet, student e-mail accounts, and computer access in designated common areas are available to students. Students grades are available online. The school has a published electronic and media policy.

Contact Director of Admissions. 520-327-6395 Ext. 209. Fax: 520-327-8276. E-mail: admissions@stgregoryschool.org. Web site: www.stgregoryschool.org.

ST. IGNATIUS COLLEGE PREPARATORY

2001 37th Avenue
San Francisco, California 94116
Head of School: Mr. Patrick Ruff

General Information Coeducational day college-preparatory, arts, religious studies, and technology school, affiliated with Roman Catholic Church. Grades 9–12. Founded: 1855. Setting: urban. 11-acre campus. 8 buildings on campus. Approved or accredited by Jesuit Secondary Education Association and Western Association of Schools and Colleges. Endowment: $45 million. Total enrollment: 1,442. Upper school average class size: 25. Upper school faculty-student ratio: 1:14. Upper School students typically attend 5 days per week. The average school day consists of 6 hours.

Upper School Student Profile 76% of students are Roman Catholic.

Faculty School total: 120. In upper school: 57 men, 46 women; 89 have advanced degrees.

Subjects Offered Algebra, American history, American literature, architecture, art, arts, Bible studies, biology, business, calculus, chemistry, computer programming, computer science, creative writing, dance, drama, driver education, earth science, economics, English, English literature, ethics, European history, expository writing, fine arts, French, geography, geometry, German, government/civics, grammar, health, history, journalism, Latin, mathematics, music, philosophy, physical education, physics, physiology, psychology, religion, science, social sciences, social studies, Spanish, speech, theater, theology, trigonometry, world history, world literature, writing.

Graduation Requirements Arts and fine arts (art, music, dance, drama), English, foreign language, mathematics, physical education (includes health), religion (includes Bible studies and theology), science, social sciences, social studies (includes history), 100 hours of supervised community service.

Special Academic Programs Advanced Placement exam preparation.

College Admission Counseling Colleges students went to include Santa Clara University; University of California, Berkeley; University of California, Davis; University of California, Los Angeles; University of California, San Diego.

Student Life Upper grades have specified standards of dress, student council. Discipline rests primarily with faculty. Attendance at religious services is required.

Tuition and Aid Day student tuition: $15,210. Tuition installment plan (monthly payment plans). Need-based scholarship grants available. In 2009–10, 20% of upper-school students received aid. Total amount of financial aid awarded in 2009–10: $1,800,000.

Admissions Traditional secondary-level entrance grade is 9. For fall 2009, 1,300 students applied for upper-level admission, 400 were accepted, 360 enrolled. High School Placement Test required. Deadline for receipt of application materials: November 17. Application fee required: $85.

Athletics Interscholastic: baseball (boys), basketball (b,g), crew (b,g), cross-country running (b,g), diving (b,g), field hockey (g), football (b), golf (b,g), lacrosse (b,g), rowing (b,g), soccer (b,g), softball (g), swimming and diving (b,g), tennis (b,g), track and field (b,g), volleyball (b,g), water polo (b,g); intramural: basketball (b,g), bicycling (b,g), football (b); coed interscholastic: golf, rowing, track and field; coed intramural: bicycling, bowling, cheering, flag football, yoga. 4 PE instructors, 100 coaches, 2 athletic trainers.

Computers Computers are regularly used in Bible studies, business applications, career exploration, college planning, creative writing, economics, English, ethics, foreign language, French, French as a second language, geography, graphic design, historical foundations for arts, history, independent study, journalism, keyboarding, Latin, mathematics, psychology, publishing, reading, religious studies, social sciences, word processing, writing, yearbook classes. Computer network features include on-campus library services, online commercial services, Internet access, wireless campus network, Internet filtering or blocking technology. Campus intranet and student e-mail accounts are available to students. Students grades are available online.

Contact Laura M. Scully, Admissions Associate. 415-731-7500 Ext. 400. E-mail: admissions@siprep.org. Web site: www.siprep.org.

SAINT JAMES SCHOOL

6010 Vaughn Road
Montgomery, Alabama 36116
Head of School: Mrs. Melba Richardson

General Information Coeducational day college-preparatory, arts, and technology school. Grades PK–12. Founded: 1955. Setting: suburban. 80-acre campus. 9 buildings on campus. Approved or accredited by Southern Association of Colleges and Schools, Southern Association of Independent Schools, and The College Board. Endowment: $1.7 million. Total enrollment: 998. Upper school average class size: 20. Upper school faculty-student ratio: 1:20. There are 175 required school days per year for Upper School students. Upper School students typically attend 5 days per week. The average school day consists of 7 hours and 30 minutes.

Upper School Student Profile Grade 9: 80 students (35 boys, 45 girls); Grade 10: 85 students (46 boys, 39 girls); Grade 11: 81 students (34 boys, 47 girls); Grade 12: 65 students (30 boys, 35 girls).

Faculty School total: 100. In upper school: 11 men, 26 women; 21 have advanced degrees.

Subjects Offered Advanced computer applications, advanced studio art-AP, algebra, American government, American history, American history-AP, American literature, American literature-AP, anatomy, art, art history-AP, art-AP, athletics, band, Basic programming, biology, biology-AP, British literature, British literature-AP, calculus, calculus-AP, chemistry, chemistry-AP, choir, choral music, chorus, community service, computer applications, computer information systems, computer multimedia, computer processing, computer programming, computer science, concert band, concert choir, creative writing, critical thinking, debate, drama, drama performance, dramatic arts, earth science, economics, economics-AP, English, English literature, English literature and composition-AP, English literature-AP, English-AP, environmental science, European history-AP, fine arts, foreign language, forensics, French, French language-AP, geography, geometry, government/civics, government/civics-AP, grammar, interpersonal skills, jazz band, journalism, keyboarding, Latin, Latin-AP, library assistant, marching band, mathematics, music, music theater, musical productions, newspaper, performing arts, personal development, philosophy, photography, physical education, physics, physiology, pre-algebra, psychology, publications, science, social studies, Spanish, Spanish-AP, speech, speech and debate, statistics, studio art-AP, technical theater, The 20th Century, theater, theater arts, theater design and production, theater production, trigonometry, U.S. government, U.S. government and politics-AP, U.S. history, U.S. history-AP, visual arts, vocal music, world affairs, world history, world literature, world religions, writing, yearbook.

Graduation Requirements Biology, biology-AP, chemistry, chemistry-AP, computer science, concert band, critical thinking, debate, dramatic arts, English, English literature, English literature-AP, foreign language, mathematics, physical education (includes health), physical fitness, science, social studies (includes history), fine arts and community service (for honors diplomas).

Special Academic Programs 12 Advanced Placement exams for which test preparation is offered; independent study; academic accommodation for the gifted and the artistically talented; remedial reading and/or remedial writing; ESL.

College Admission Counseling 80 students graduated in 2009; all went to college, including Auburn University; Auburn University Montgomery; Birmingham-Southern College; Samford University; The University of Alabama; The University of Alabama at Birmingham. Mean SAT critical reading: 578, mean SAT math: 572, mean SAT writing: 573, mean composite ACT: 24.

Student Life Upper grades have uniform requirement, student council, honor system. Discipline rests primarily with faculty.

Tuition and Aid Day student tuition: $5273–$9383. Tuition installment plan (Insured Tuition Payment Plan, monthly payment plans, individually arranged payment plans). Tuition reduction for siblings, merit scholarship grants, need-based scholarship grants, need-based tuition reduction through SSS available. In 2009–10, 3% of upper-school students received aid; total upper-school merit-scholarship money awarded: $20,000. Total amount of financial aid awarded in 2009–10: $40,700.

Admissions Traditional secondary-level entrance grade is 9. For fall 2009, 20 students applied for upper-level admission, 18 were accepted, 14 enrolled. ERB Reading and Math, Otis-Lennon School Ability Test, Wechsler Intelligence Scale for Children III or writing sample required. Deadline for receipt of application materials: none. Application fee required: $75. On-campus interview recommended.

Athletics Interscholastic: baseball (boys), basketball (b,g), cheering (g), cross-country running (b,g), dance team (g), football (b), golf (b,g), indoor track & field (b,g), power lifting (b), soccer (b,g), softball (g), strength & conditioning (b,g), swimming and diving (b,g), tennis (b,g), track and field (b,g), volleyball (g), weight lifting (b), weight training (b,g), wrestling (b); coed intramural: physical fitness. 6 PE instructors, 10 coaches.

Computers Computers are regularly used in all academic classes. Computer network features include on-campus library services, online commercial services, Internet access. Students grades are available online. The school has a published electronic and media policy.

Contact Mrs. Aimee B. Steineker, Director of Admissions. 334-273-3000. Fax: 334-274-9097. E-mail: asteineker@stjweb.org. Web site: www.stjweb.org.

SAINT JAMES SCHOOL

17641 College Road
St. James, Maryland 21781-9999
Head of School: Rev. Dr. D. Stuart Dunnan

General Information Coeducational boarding and day college-preparatory school, affiliated with Episcopal Church. Grades 8–12. Founded: 1842. Setting: rural. Nearest major city is Washington, DC. Students are housed in single-sex dormitories. 1,000-acre campus. 36 buildings on campus. Approved or accredited by Association of Independent Maryland Schools, Association of Independent Schools of Greater Washington, Middle States Association of Colleges and Schools, National Association of Episcopal Schools, The Association of Boarding Schools, and Maryland Department of Education. Member of National Association of Independent Schools and Secondary School Admission Test Board. Endowment: $21 million. Total enrollment: 232. Upper school average class size: 12. Upper school faculty-student ratio: 1:7. There are 173 required school days per year for Upper School students. Upper School students typically attend 5 days per week. The average school day consists of 6 hours and 30 minutes.

Upper School Student Profile Grade 8: 28 students (19 boys, 9 girls); Grade 9: 44 students (23 boys, 21 girls); Grade 10: 51 students (29 boys, 22 girls); Grade 11: 55 students (34 boys, 21 girls); Grade 12: 54 students (32 boys, 22 girls). 75% of students are boarding students. 55% are state residents. 13 states are represented in upper school

student body. 13% are international students. International students from Bermuda, China, Hong Kong, Japan, Republic of Korea, and Uganda; 7 other countries represented in student body. 38% of students are members of Episcopal Church.
Faculty School total: 31. In upper school: 17 men, 14 women; 16 have advanced degrees; 29 reside on campus.
Subjects Offered Algebra, American history-AP, American literature, ancient history, art, art history, art-AP, biology-AP, calculus-AP, chemistry, chemistry-AP, choir, community service, economics, English, English literature, environmental science, European history-AP, fine arts, French-AP, geography, geometry, government-AP, keyboarding, Latin-AP, mathematics, modern European history, music, music history, physical science, physics, physics-AP, political science, science, Spanish-AP, theology, voice, world literature, writing workshop.
Graduation Requirements Arts and fine arts (art, music, dance, drama), English, foreign language, history, mathematics, science. Community service is required.
Special Academic Programs 14 Advanced Placement exams for which test preparation is offered; honors section; academic accommodation for the musically talented.
College Admission Counseling 38 students graduated in 2009; all went to college, including Cornell University; Davidson College; Sewanee: The University of the South; The George Washington University; University of Maryland, College Park; University of Virginia.
Student Life Upper grades have specified standards of dress, student council, honor system. Discipline rests equally with students and faculty. Attendance at religious services is required.
Tuition and Aid Day student tuition: $22,900; 7-day tuition and room/board: $34,600. Tuition installment plan (FACTS Tuition Payment Plan, individually arranged payment plans, Sallie Mae). Need-based scholarship grants available. In 2009–10, 33% of upper-school students received aid. Total amount of financial aid awarded in 2009–10: $1,267,000.
Admissions Traditional secondary-level entrance grade is 9. For fall 2009, 228 students applied for upper-level admission, 119 were accepted, 73 enrolled. PSAT or SAT, SSAT or TOEFL required. Deadline for receipt of application materials: January 31. Application fee required: $50. Interview required.
Athletics Interscholastic: baseball (boys), basketball (b,g), cross-country running (b), field hockey (g), football (b), golf (b), lacrosse (b,g), soccer (b,g), softball (g), tennis (b,g), volleyball (g), wrestling (b); intramural: aerobics/dance (g), ballet (g), dance (g), fencing (b,g), modern dance (g), weight training (b,g); coed intramural: alpine skiing, indoor soccer, martial arts, skiing (downhill), strength & conditioning. 2 coaches, 1 athletic trainer.
Computers Computers are regularly used in all academic classes. Computer network features include on-campus library services, online commercial services, Internet access, wireless campus network, Internet filtering or blocking technology. Student e-mail accounts are available to students. The school has a published electronic and media policy.
Contact Lawrence J. Jensen, Director of Admissions. 301-733-9330. Fax: 301-739-1310. E-mail: admissions@stjames.edu. Web site: www.stjames.edu.

SAINT JOHN BOSCO HIGH SCHOOL

13460 Bellflower Boulevard
Bellflower, California 90706
Head of School: Fr. Joseph Nguyen
General Information Boys' day college-preparatory and religious studies school, affiliated with Roman Catholic Church. Grades 9–12. Founded: 1940. Setting: suburban. Nearest major city is Los Angeles. 35-acre campus. 5 buildings on campus. Approved or accredited by Western Association of Schools and Colleges and California Department of Education. Total enrollment: 821. Upper school average class size: 30. Upper school faculty-student ratio: 1:15. There are 170 required school days per year for Upper School students. Upper School students typically attend 5 days per week. The average school day consists of 6 hours and 30 minutes.
Upper School Student Profile Grade 9: 210 students (210 boys); Grade 10: 182 students (182 boys); Grade 11: 223 students (223 boys); Grade 12: 206 students (206 boys). 95% of students are Roman Catholic.
Faculty School total: 53. In upper school: 39 men, 14 women; 25 have advanced degrees.
Subjects Offered Advanced computer applications, algebra, American history, American literature, American literature-AP, art history, art history-AP, Bible studies, biology, biology-AP, British literature, business, business law, calculus-AP, chemistry, civics, computer applications, cultural geography, desktop publishing, drama, drawing, economics, English language and composition-AP, English literature and composition-AP, English literature-AP, French, French language-AP, geometry, government and politics-AP, government-AP, health, history-AP, instrumental music, journalism, modern world history, moral theology, music appreciation, music theory, oceanography, painting, physical education, physical science, physics, pre-calculus, psychology, religious studies, social justice, Spanish, Spanish language-AP, Spanish literature-AP, trigonometry, U.S. government and politics-AP, U.S. history, U.S. history-AP, Web site design, world history, world history-AP, world literature, world religions.

Graduation Requirements Arts and fine arts (art, music, dance, drama), computer science, English, foreign language, mathematics, physical education (includes health), religion (includes Bible studies and theology), science, social studies (includes history).
Special Academic Programs 12 Advanced Placement exams for which test preparation is offered.
College Admission Counseling 248 students graduated in 2009; 247 went to college, including California State University, Fullerton; California State University, Long Beach; Long Beach City College; University of California, Riverside; University of California, Santa Barbara. Other: 1 had other specific plans. Mean SAT critical reading: 490, mean SAT math: 500, mean SAT writing: 470, mean combined SAT: 1460, mean composite ACT: 22.
Student Life Upper grades have specified standards of dress, student council. Discipline rests primarily with faculty. Attendance at religious services is required.
Tuition and Aid Day student tuition: $8600. Need-based scholarship grants available. In 2009–10, 20% of upper-school students received aid. Total amount of financial aid awarded in 2009–10: $200,000.
Admissions Traditional secondary-level entrance grade is 9. For fall 2009, 370 students applied for upper-level admission, 280 were accepted, 210 enrolled. STS required. Deadline for receipt of application materials: February 1. Application fee required: $50.
Athletics Interscholastic: baseball, basketball, cross-country running, football, golf, lacrosse, soccer, swimming and diving, tennis, track and field, volleyball, water polo, wrestling; intramural: flag football, football, soccer, softball, touch football. 3 PE instructors, 1 athletic trainer.
Computers Computers are regularly used in computer applications, desktop publishing, graphic design classes. Computer network features include on-campus library services, online commercial services, Internet access, wireless campus network, Internet filtering or blocking technology. Computer access in designated common areas is available to students. Students grades are available online. The school has a published electronic and media policy.
Contact Mr. Ernie Antonelli, Admissions Director. 562-920-1734 Ext. 232. Fax: 562-867-2408. E-mail: eantonel@bosco.org. Web site: www.bosco.org.

ST. JOHNSBURY ACADEMY

PO Box 906
1000 Main Street
St. Johnsbury, Vermont 05819
Head of School: Mr. Thomas W. Lovett
General Information Coeducational boarding and day college-preparatory, general academic, arts, business, vocational, bilingual studies, and technology school; primarily serves students with learning disabilities, individuals with Attention Deficit Disorder, and dyslexic students. Grades 9–PG. Founded: 1842. Setting: small town. Nearest major city is Boston, MA. Students are housed in single-sex dormitories. 50-acre campus. 28 buildings on campus. Approved or accredited by Independent Schools of Northern New England, New England Association of Schools and Colleges, The Association of Boarding Schools, and Vermont Department of Education. Member of National Association of Independent Schools and Secondary School Admission Test Board. Endowment: $13 million. Total enrollment: 958. Upper school average class size: 12. Upper school faculty-student ratio: 1:9. There are 175 required school days per year for Upper School students. Upper School students typically attend 5 days per week. The average school day consists of 6 hours and 30 minutes.
Upper School Student Profile Grade 9: 179 students (103 boys, 76 girls); Grade 10: 237 students (141 boys, 96 girls); Grade 11: 276 students (150 boys, 126 girls); Grade 12: 265 students (128 boys, 137 girls); Postgraduate: 1 student (1 boy). 24% of students are boarding students. 70% are state residents. 15 states are represented in upper school student body. 20% are international students. International students from Bermuda, Germany, Hong Kong, Republic of Korea, Spain, and Taiwan; 19 other countries represented in student body.
Faculty School total: 129. In upper school: 70 men, 59 women; 90 have advanced degrees; 20 reside on campus.
Subjects Offered Accounting, acting, Advanced Placement courses, advanced studio art-AP, advanced TOEFL/grammar, algebra, American government, American history, American history-AP, American literature, analysis, anatomy and physiology, ancient world history, architectural drawing, architecture, art, astronomy, audio visual/media, auto mechanics, automated accounting, band, basic skills, biology, biology-AP, British literature, business, business communications, business skills, calculus-AP, career education, career experience, carpentry, chemistry, chemistry-AP, Chinese, chorus, civics, college writing, Coming of Age in the 20th Century, composition-AP, computer math, computer programming, computer science-AP, concert band, construction, CPR, culinary arts, dance, dance performance, desktop publishing, developmental math, digital art, directing, discrete mathematics, drafting, drama, drama performance, drama workshop, dramatic arts, drawing and design, driver education, earth science, economics, electronics, engineering, English, English language and composition-AP, English literature, English literature and composition-AP, environmental education, environmental science, environmental science-AP, ESL, European history, European history-AP, expository writing, fashion, film studies, forest resources, forestry, French, French language-AP, French literature-AP, French-AP, geometry, government,

government-AP, government/civics, guitar, health, health education, history, industrial arts, introduction to theater, Japanese, jazz band, journalism, keyboarding, land management, Latin, linear algebra, mathematics, mechanical drawing, media production, modern European history-AP, music, music appreciation, music theory, navigation, newspaper, nutrition, oil painting, photography, physical education, physics, physics-AP, playwriting and directing, portfolio art, pottery, pre-algebra, pre-calculus, pre-vocational education, probability and statistics, psychology, psychology-AP, reading/study skills, Russian, science, sculpture, small engine repair, social sciences, social studies, sociology, Spanish, Spanish literature, sports medicine, sports science, stagecraft, statistics-AP, studio art-AP, study skills, technical education, technical writing, technology, theater, theater design and production, TOEFL preparation, trigonometry, U.S. government and politics-AP, U.S. history-AP, video communication, video film production, visual and performing arts, vocal ensemble, Web site design, welding, wilderness education, wind ensemble, wind instruments, woodworking, word processing, world civilizations, world history, world literature, yearbook.

Graduation Requirements English, health education, humanities, keyboarding, mathematics, physical education (includes health), science, social studies (includes history), Senior Capstone Project.

Special Academic Programs 21 Advanced Placement exams for which test preparation is offered; honors section; term-away projects; academic accommodation for the gifted and the artistically talented; remedial reading and/or remedial writing; remedial math; programs in English, mathematics, general development for dyslexic students; ESL (90 students enrolled).

College Admission Counseling 244 students graduated in 2009; 215 went to college, including Northeastern University; Rochester Institute of Technology; University of New Hampshire; University of Vermont; University of Wisconsin–Madison; Washington University in St. Louis. Other: 27 went to work, 2 entered military service. Mean SAT critical reading: 511, mean SAT math: 533, mean SAT writing: 509. 27% scored over 600 on SAT critical reading, 37% scored over 600 on SAT math, 25% scored over 600 on SAT writing.

Student Life Upper grades have specified standards of dress, student council, honor system. Discipline rests primarily with faculty.

Tuition and Aid Day student tuition: $13,470; 7-day tuition and room/board: $39,900. Tuition installment plan (individually arranged payment plans, two payments (August 1 and November 25)). Need-based scholarship grants available. In 2009–10, 11% of upper-school students received aid. Total amount of financial aid awarded in 2009–10: $1,021,995.

Admissions Traditional secondary-level entrance grade is 9. For fall 2009, 521 students applied for upper-level admission, 392 were accepted, 317 enrolled. Deadline for receipt of application materials: none. Application fee required: $20. Interview recommended.

Athletics Interscholastic: alpine skiing (boys, girls), baseball (b), basketball (b,g), cross-country running (b,g), field hockey (g), football (b), golf (b,g), gymnastics (g), ice hockey (b), lacrosse (b,g), nordic skiing (b,g), skiing (cross-country) (b,g), skiing (downhill) (b,g), soccer (b,g), softball (g), tennis (b,g), track and field (b,g), ultimate Frisbee (b,g), wrestling (b); intramural: ice hockey (g), volleyball (b,g); coed interscholastic: cheering, indoor track & field, ultimate Frisbee; coed intramural: aerobics/dance, badminton, basketball, bowling, canoeing/kayaking, cricket, dance, fencing, fishing, flag football, floor hockey, hiking/backpacking, hockey, indoor track, martial arts, mountain biking, outdoor adventure, paddle tennis, swimming and diving, ultimate Frisbee, volleyball, weight lifting, wilderness. 3 PE instructors, 10 coaches, 1 athletic trainer.

Computers Computers are regularly used in business education, career education, computer applications, desktop publishing, drafting, English, foreign language, journalism, keyboarding, mathematics, newspaper, publications, science, senior seminar, technical drawing, technology, video film production, Web site design, yearbook classes. Computer network features include on-campus library services, online commercial services, Internet access, wireless campus network, Internet filtering or blocking technology. Computer access in designated common areas is available to students. The school has a published electronic and media policy.

Contact Mrs. MaryAnn Gessner, Director of Admissions. 802-751-2130. Fax: 802-748-5463. E-mail: mgessner@stjacademy.org. Web site: www.stjohnsburyacademy.org.

ST. JOHN'S CATHOLIC PREP

889 Butterfly Lane
Frederick, Maryland 21703
Head of School: Dr. Jack Campbell
General Information Coeducational day college-preparatory school, affiliated with Roman Catholic Church. Grades 9–12. Founded: 1829. Setting: suburban. Nearest major city is Baltimore. 31-acre campus. 9 buildings on campus. Approved or accredited by Association of Independent Maryland Schools and Maryland Department of Education. Total enrollment: 258. Upper school average class size: 15. Upper school faculty-student ratio: 1:10.
Upper School Student Profile Grade 9: 61 students (26 boys, 35 girls); Grade 10: 89 students (39 boys, 50 girls); Grade 11: 54 students (30 boys, 24 girls); Grade 12: 54 students (24 boys, 30 girls). 75% of students are Roman Catholic.
Faculty School total: 26. In upper school: 10 men, 15 women.

Special Academic Programs Advanced Placement exam preparation; honors section; study at local college for college credit; ESL (5 students enrolled).
College Admission Counseling 54 students graduated in 2009; all went to college, including University of Maryland, College Park. Median SAT critical reading: 602, median SAT math: 596, median SAT writing: 576.
Student Life Upper grades have uniform requirement, honor system. Discipline rests primarily with faculty. Attendance at religious services is required.
Tuition and Aid Day student tuition: $11,900. Tuition installment plan (FACTS Tuition Payment Plan). Tuition reduction for siblings, merit scholarship grants, need-based scholarship grants available. In 2009–10, 33% of upper-school students received aid; total upper-school merit-scholarship money awarded: $20,000. Total amount of financial aid awarded in 2009–10: $250,000.
Admissions Traditional secondary-level entrance grade is 9. For fall 2009, 126 students applied for upper-level admission, 123 were accepted, 61 enrolled. High School Placement Test (closed version) from Scholastic Testing Service required. Deadline for receipt of application materials: none. Application fee required: $95. On-campus interview required.
Athletics Interscholastic: baseball (boys), basketball (b,g), cheering (g), cross-country running (b,g), football (b), golf (b,g), lacrosse (b,g), soccer (b,g), softball (g), swimming and diving (b,g), tennis (b,g), volleyball (g), wrestling (b); coed interscholastic: indoor track & field, track and field; coed intramural: equestrian sports, horseback riding, indoor hockey, skiing (downhill), snowboarding, strength & conditioning, weight training. 2 PE instructors, 14 coaches, 1 athletic trainer.
Computers Computer network features include on-campus library services, Internet access. Student e-mail accounts are available to students.
Contact Mr. Michael W. Schultz, Director of Enrollment Management. 301-662-4210 Ext. 121. Fax: 301-662-5166. E-mail: mschultz@saintjohnsprep.org. Web site: www.saintjohnsprep.org.

ST. JOHNS COUNTRY DAY SCHOOL

3100 Doctors Lake Drive
Orange Park, Florida 32073
Head of School: Mr. Gregory L. Foster
General Information Coeducational day college-preparatory, arts, religious studies, and technology school. Grades PK–12. Founded: 1953. Setting: suburban. Nearest major city is Jacksonville. 26-acre campus. 11 buildings on campus. Approved or accredited by Florida Council of Independent Schools, Southern Association of Colleges and Schools, and Florida Department of Education. Member of National Association of Independent Schools. Endowment: $4 million. Total enrollment: 733. Upper school average class size: 17. Upper school faculty-student ratio: 1:10. There are 180 required school days per year for Upper School students. Upper School students typically attend 5 days per week. The average school day consists of 6 hours.
Upper School Student Profile Grade 9: 55 students (25 boys, 30 girls); Grade 10: 55 students (23 boys, 32 girls); Grade 11: 52 students (24 boys, 28 girls); Grade 12: 52 students (25 boys, 27 girls).
Faculty School total: 85. In upper school: 13 men, 25 women; 34 have advanced degrees.
Subjects Offered Algebra, American history, American literature, anatomy, art, art history, biology, calculus, ceramics, chemistry, computer programming, computer science, creative writing, drama, drawing, earth science, economics, English, English literature, ethics, European history, fine arts, French, geometry, government/civics, grammar, health, history, Holocaust studies, journalism, Latin, marine biology, mathematics, music, oceanography, painting, physical education, physics, psychology, religion, science, social studies, sociology, Spanish, speech, statistics, theater, trigonometry, world history, world literature, writing.
Graduation Requirements Arts and fine arts (art, music, dance, drama), computer science, English, ethics, foreign language, government, history, lab science, mathematics, physical education (includes health), senior practicum.
Special Academic Programs Advanced Placement exam preparation; honors section; independent study; study at local college for college credit; academic accommodation for the gifted, the musically talented, and the artistically talented.
College Admission Counseling 43 students graduated in 2009; all went to college, including Florida State University; The University of Alabama; University of Central Florida; University of Florida; University of North Florida. Median SAT critical reading: 550, median SAT math: 590, median SAT writing: 570, median composite ACT: 26. 27% scored over 600 on SAT critical reading, 32% scored over 600 on SAT math, 34% scored over 26 on composite ACT.
Student Life Upper grades have specified standards of dress, student council, honor system. Discipline rests primarily with faculty.
Tuition and Aid Day student tuition: $14,000. Tuition installment plan (monthly payment plans, individually arranged payment plans). Need-based scholarship grants available. In 2009–10, 12% of upper-school students received aid. Total amount of financial aid awarded in 2009–10: $157,100.
Admissions Traditional secondary-level entrance grade is 9. For fall 2009, 19 students applied for upper-level admission, 15 were accepted, 11 enrolled. CTP III, ERB, independent norms and school's own exam required. Deadline for receipt of application materials: none. Application fee required: $150. Interview required.
Athletics Interscholastic: baseball (boys), basketball (b,g), cheering (g), crew (b,g), cross-country running (b,g), football (b), golf (b,g), rowing (b,g), soccer (b,g), softball (g), swimming and diving (b,g), tennis (b,g), track and field (b,g), volleyball (g);

intramural: aerobics/dance (g), dance squad (g); coed interscholastic: aquatics; coed intramural: aquatics, cooperative games, cross-country running, fitness, fitness walking, flag football, floor hockey, golf, gymnastics, independent competitive sports, indoor soccer, jogging, jump rope, kickball, life saving, Nautilus, Newcombe ball, outdoor activities, outdoor adventure, outdoor education, outdoor recreation, paddle tennis, physical fitness, racquetball, roller blading, running, soccer, softball, speedball, street hockey, strength & conditioning, swimming and diving, table tennis, team handball, tennis, touch football, track and field, triathlon, volleyball, walking, water polo, water volleyball, weight lifting, weight training, whiffle ball, winter soccer. 7 PE instructors, 22 coaches.

Computers Computers are regularly used in English, foreign language, mathematics, music, science, social studies classes. Computer network features include on-campus library services, online commercial services, Internet access, wireless campus network, Internet filtering or blocking technology. Student e-mail accounts are available to students. The school has a published electronic and media policy.

Contact Mrs. Amy Weaver, Director of Admissions. 904-264-9572. Fax: 904-264-0375. E-mail: aweaver@sjcds.net. Web site: www.sjcds.net.

ST. JOHN'S INTERNATIONAL

#300—1885 West Broadway
Vancouver, British Columbia V6J 1Y5, Canada
Head of School: Mr. Rick Shelly

General Information Coeducational day college-preparatory and sciences school. Grades 10–12. Founded: 1988. Setting: urban. 1 building on campus. Approved or accredited by British Columbia Department of Education. Language of instruction: English. Upper school average class size: 10. Upper school faculty-student ratio: 1:12. There are 225 required school days per year for Upper School students. Upper School students typically attend 5 days per week. The average school day consists of 6 hours.

Upper School Student Profile Grade 10: 34 students (22 boys, 12 girls); Grade 11: 32 students (19 boys, 13 girls); Grade 12: 17 students (12 boys, 5 girls).

Faculty School total: 7. In upper school: 7 men; all have advanced degrees.

Graduation Requirements Arabic studies, general science, language, math applications, physical education (includes health).

Special Academic Programs ESL (30 students enrolled).

College Admission Counseling 28 students graduated in 2009; 23 went to college, including Queen's University at Kingston; University of Hawaii at Manoa; York University. Other: 1 went to work, 2 entered a postgraduate year, 1 had other specific plans.

Student Life Upper grades have specified standards of dress, honor system. Discipline rests primarily with faculty.

Tuition and Aid Day student tuition: CAN$14,400.

Admissions Traditional secondary-level entrance grade is 10. For fall 2009, 40 students applied for upper-level admission, 35 were accepted, 30 enrolled. English for Non-native Speakers or English language required. Deadline for receipt of application materials: none. Application fee required: CAN$200.

Athletics 1 PE instructor.

Computers Computers are regularly used in art classes. Computer resources include Internet access, open lab for assignments.

Contact Admissions Officer. 604-683-4572. Fax: 604-683-4579. E-mail: general@stjohnsis.com. Web site: www.stjohnsis.com.

ST. JOHN'S NORTHWESTERN MILITARY ACADEMY

1101 Genesee Street
Delafield, Wisconsin 53018-1498
Head of School: Mr. Jack H. Albert Jr.

General Information Boys' boarding and day college-preparatory, arts, business, and military school, affiliated with Episcopal Church; primarily serves underachievers. Boarding grades 7–PG, day grades 6–PG. Founded: 1884. Setting: small town. Nearest major city is Milwaukee. Students are housed in single-sex dormitories. 110-acre campus. 15 buildings on campus. Approved or accredited by Independent Schools Association of the Central States, Midwest Association of Boarding Schools, National Association of Episcopal Schools, North Central Association of Colleges and Schools, The Association of Boarding Schools, and Wisconsin Department of Education. Member of National Association of Independent Schools and Secondary School Admission Test Board. Endowment: $6.5 million. Total enrollment: 300. Upper school average class size: 12. Upper school faculty-student ratio: 1:12.

Upper School Student Profile Grade 9: 56 students (56 boys); Grade 10: 63 students (63 boys); Grade 11: 51 students (51 boys); Grade 12: 55 students (55 boys); Postgraduate: 14 students (14 boys). 98% of students are boarding students. 22% are state residents. 22 states are represented in upper school student body. 28% are international students. International students from Canada, China, Mexico, Nicaragua, Republic of Korea, and Thailand; 6 other countries represented in student body. 4% of students are members of Episcopal Church.

Faculty School total: 40. In upper school: 34 men, 6 women; 16 have advanced degrees; 12 reside on campus.

Subjects Offered Advanced math, algebra, American government, American literature, art, aviation, band, biology, British literature, calculus, ceramics, chemistry, choir, Christianity, computer programming, computer science, current events, drama, driver education, earth science, economics, English, entrepreneurship, environmental science, ESL, geography, geometry, German, government/civics, grammar, health, history, honors English, honors U.S. history, journalism, JROTC, mathematics, music, physical science, physics, psychology, reading, science, social studies, sociology, Spanish, statistics, strings, trigonometry, U.S. history, world geography, world history, world literature.

Graduation Requirements Advanced math, algebra, American government, American literature, arts and fine arts (art, music, dance, drama), biology, British literature, chemistry, computer science, electives, foreign language, geometry, introduction to literature, JROTC, physical science, U.S. history, world history, world literature. Community service is required.

Special Academic Programs Honors section; independent study; study at local college for college credit; ESL (10 students enrolled).

College Admission Counseling 56 students graduated in 2010; all went to college, including DePaul University; Embry-Riddle Aeronautical University; Marquette University; Purdue University; University of Illinois at Urbana–Champaign; University of Wisconsin–Madison.

Student Life Upper grades have uniform requirement, student council, honor system. Discipline rests primarily with faculty. Attendance at religious services is required.

Summer Programs Remediation, enrichment, advancement, ESL, computer instruction programs offered; session focuses on academics; held on campus; accepts boys; open to students from other schools.

Tuition and Aid 7-day tuition and room/board: $31,000. Tuition installment plan (Key Tuition Payment Plan, FACTS Tuition Payment Plan, TeriPlease Tuition Payment Plans). Tuition reduction for siblings, merit scholarship grants, need-based scholarship grants, tuition remission for children of employees, endowed scholarships, alumni scholarships available. In 2010–11, 29% of upper-school students received aid; total upper-school merit-scholarship money awarded: $113,500. Total amount of financial aid awarded in 2010–11: $950,000.

Admissions Traditional secondary-level entrance grade is 9. For fall 2010, 430 students applied for upper-level admission, 236 were accepted, 125 enrolled. Kuhlmann-Anderson, SSAT or TOEFL required. Deadline for receipt of application materials: none. Application fee required: $100. On-campus interview required.

Athletics Interscholastic: archery, baseball, basketball, cross-country running, equestrian sports, football, golf, hockey, ice hockey, lacrosse, scuba diving; intramural: billiards, fishing, handball. 2 PE instructors.

Computers Computers are regularly used in all academic classes. Computer network features include on-campus library services, Internet access, Internet filtering or blocking technology. Campus intranet and student e-mail accounts are available to students. Students grades are available online. The school has a published electronic and media policy.

Contact Duane E. Rutherford, Director of Enrollment Services. 262-646-7122. Fax: 262-646-7128. E-mail: admissions@sjnma.org. Web site: www.sjnma.org.

ST. JOHN'S PREPARATORY SCHOOL

72 Spring Street
Danvers, Massachusetts 01923
Head of School: Dr. Albert J. Shannon, PhD

General Information Boys' day college-preparatory, arts, religious studies, and technology school, affiliated with Roman Catholic Church. Grades 9–12. Founded: 1907. Setting: suburban. Nearest major city is Boston. 175-acre campus. 9 buildings on campus. Approved or accredited by National Catholic Education Association and New England Association of Schools and Colleges. Endowment: $7 million. Total enrollment: 1,248. Upper school average class size: 19. Upper school faculty-student ratio: 1:11. There are 161 required school days per year for Upper School students. Upper School students typically attend 5 days per week. The average school day consists of 6 hours and 10 minutes.

Upper School Student Profile Grade 9: 312 students (312 boys); Grade 10: 312 students (312 boys); Grade 11: 312 students (312 boys); Grade 12: 312 students (312 boys). 60% of students are Roman Catholic.

Faculty School total: 111. In upper school: 69 men, 42 women; 74 have advanced degrees.

Subjects Offered Accounting, acting, algebra, American history, American history-AP, American literature, anatomy and physiology, art, biology, biology-AP, business, calculus, calculus-AP, ceramics, chemistry, chemistry-AP, Chinese, chorus, computer programming, computer science, computer science-AP, desktop publishing, drama, driver education, economics, economics-AP, English, English literature, English-AP, environmental science, environmental studies, ethics, European history, European history-AP, geometry, German, German-AP, government/civics, Latin, Latin-AP, mathematics, music, neuroscience, physical education, physics, physics-AP, religion, robotics, science, sculpture, social studies, society, politics and law, Spanish, Spanish-AP, statistics, statistics-AP, studio art, technology, trigonometry, U.S. government and politics-AP, U.S. history-AP, world history, world religions.

Graduation Requirements Arts and fine arts (art, music, dance, drama), English, foreign language, mathematics, physical education (includes health), religion (includes Bible studies and theology), science, social studies (includes history).

Special Academic Programs Advanced Placement exam preparation; honors section; independent study; study abroad; academic accommodation for the gifted, the musically talented, and the artistically talented.

College Admission Counseling 306 students graduated in 2010; 299 went to college, including Boston College; Boston University; Northeastern University; Providence College; University of Massachusetts Amherst; Villanova University. Other: 1 entered military service, 4 entered a postgraduate year, 2 had other specific plans. Mean SAT critical reading: 600, mean SAT math: 610, mean SAT writing: 600.

Student Life Upper grades have specified standards of dress, student council. Discipline rests primarily with faculty. Attendance at religious services is required.

Summer Programs Enrichment, sports, art/fine arts, computer instruction programs offered; session focuses on academic enrichment, study skills, arts, and fitness; held on campus; accepts boys and girls; open to students from other schools.

Tuition and Aid Day student tuition: $18,150. Tuition installment plan (monthly payment plans). Need-based scholarship grants available. In 2010–11, 28% of upper-school students received aid. Total amount of financial aid awarded in 2010–11: $2,800,000.

Admissions Traditional secondary-level entrance grade is 9. SSAT or STS, Diocese Test required. Deadline for receipt of application materials: December 15. No application fee required.

Athletics Interscholastic: alpine skiing, baseball, basketball, cross-country running, fencing, football, Frisbee, golf, hockey, ice hockey, indoor track, lacrosse, rugby, sailing, skiing (downhill), soccer, swimming and diving, tennis, track and field, ultimate Frisbee, volleyball, water polo, winter (indoor) track, wrestling; intramural: baseball, basketball, bicycling, bocce, bowling, boxing, climbing, combined training, cooperative games, crew, flag football, floor hockey, Frisbee, golf, ice hockey, martial arts, mountain biking, Nautilus, physical fitness, rowing, sailing, skiing (downhill), snowboarding, strength & conditioning, surfing, table tennis, tennis, touch football, ultimate Frisbee, volleyball, weight lifting, weight training, whiffle ball. 2 PE instructors, 57 coaches, 2 athletic trainers.

Computers Computers are regularly used in all academic, career exploration, college planning, research skills classes. Computer network features include on-campus library services, Internet access, wireless campus network, Internet filtering or blocking technology, student access to 300 computer workstations. Student e-mail accounts are available to students. Students grades are available online. The school has a published electronic and media policy.

Contact Ms. Maureen Ward, Admissions Assistant. 978-624-1301. Fax: 978-624-1315. E-mail: mward@stjohnsprep.org. Web site: www.stjohnsprep.org.

SAINT JOHN'S PREPARATORY SCHOOL

Box 4000
1857 Watertower Road
Collegeville, Minnesota 56321
Head of School: Fr. Timothy Backous, OSB

General Information Coeducational boarding and day college-preparatory, arts, religious studies, bilingual studies, and theatre school, affiliated with Roman Catholic Church. Boarding grades 9–PG, day grades 7–PG. Founded: 1857. Setting: rural. Nearest major city is St. Cloud. Students are housed in single-sex dormitories. 2,700-acre campus. 23 buildings on campus. Approved or accredited by Independent Schools Association of the Central States, Midwest Association of Boarding Schools, The Association of Boarding Schools, and Minnesota Department of Education. Member of National Association of Independent Schools. Endowment: $6.9 million. Total enrollment: 321. Upper school average class size: 16. Upper school faculty-student ratio: 1:10. There are 172 required school days per year for Upper School students. Upper School students typically attend 5 days per week. The average school day consists of 5 hours and 35 minutes.

Upper School Student Profile Grade 9: 49 students (23 boys, 26 girls); Grade 10: 66 students (35 boys, 31 girls); Grade 11: 65 students (35 boys, 30 girls); Grade 12: 71 students (41 boys, 30 girls); Postgraduate: 2 students (1 boy, 1 girl). 36% of students are boarding students. 61% are state residents. 7 states are represented in upper school student body. 25% are international students. International students from Austria, China, Japan, Republic of Korea, Taiwan, and Thailand; 12 other countries represented in student body. 50% of students are Roman Catholic.

Faculty School total: 34. In upper school: 18 men, 16 women; 27 have advanced degrees.

Subjects Offered 3-dimensional design, advanced chemistry, Advanced Placement courses, algebra, American history, American literature, art, art history, band, Bible studies, biology, biology-AP, British literature, calculus, ceramics, chemistry, Chinese, choir, civics, conceptual physics, creative writing, current events, drawing, driver education, earth science, economics, English, English literature, English-AP, environmental science-AP, ESL, European history, fine arts, geometry, German, government/civics, health, history, mathematics, music, orchestra, photography, physical education, physics, pre-calculus, religion, science, social studies, Spanish, speech, statistics, theology, trigonometry, world history, world literature, writing.

Special Academic Programs Advanced Placement exam preparation; honors section; independent study; term-away projects; study at local college for college credit; study abroad; academic accommodation for the gifted, the musically talented, and the artistically talented; ESL (27 students enrolled).

College Admission Counseling 62 students graduated in 2009; 59 went to college, including College of Saint Benedict; St. John's University; University of Illinois at Urbana–Champaign; University of Minnesota, Twin Cities Campus; University of Portland. Other: 2 went to work, 1 had other specific plans. Mean SAT critical reading: 657, mean SAT math: 617, mean SAT writing: 603, mean combined SAT: 1877, mean composite ACT: 26.

Student Life Upper grades have specified standards of dress, student council, honor system. Discipline rests primarily with faculty. Attendance at religious services is required.

Tuition and Aid Day student tuition: $13,245; 5-day tuition and room/board: $26,782; 7-day tuition and room/board: $30,070. Tuition installment plan (monthly payment plans, individually arranged payment plans, semester payment plan). Merit scholarship grants, need-based scholarship grants, paying campus jobs available. In 2009–10, 38% of upper-school students received aid; total upper-school merit-scholarship money awarded: $29,900. Total amount of financial aid awarded in 2009–10: $817,102.

Admissions Traditional secondary-level entrance grade is 9. For fall 2009, 140 students applied for upper-level admission, 97 were accepted, 77 enrolled. Differential Aptitude Test required. Deadline for receipt of application materials: none. Application fee required: $25. Interview required.

Athletics Interscholastic: alpine skiing (boys, girls), aquatics (g), baseball (b), basketball (b,g), cross-country running (b,g), diving (g), football (b), gymnastics (g), ice hockey (b,g), indoor track & field (b,g), nordic skiing (b,g), soccer (b,g), softball (g), swimming and diving (g), tennis (b,g), track and field (b,g); intramural: aerobics (g), aerobics/dance (g), dance (g), figure skating (g), golf (b,g), ice skating (g); coed intramural: bicycling, canoeing/kayaking, cross-country running, fitness, fitness walking, flag football, floor hockey, Frisbee, indoor soccer, mountain biking, nordic skiing, physical fitness, physical training, racquetball, rock climbing, roller blading, skiing (cross-country), skiing (downhill), soccer, strength & conditioning, swimming and diving, ultimate Frisbee, volleyball, walking, wall climbing, wallyball, weight lifting, weight training, winter (indoor) track, winter walking, yoga. 1 PE instructor, 21 coaches.

Computers Computers are regularly used in English, mathematics, science classes. Computer network features include on-campus library services, Internet access, Internet filtering or blocking technology. Student e-mail accounts and computer access in designated common areas are available to students. Students grades are available online. The school has a published electronic and media policy.

Contact Jennine Klosterman, Director of Admissions. 320-363-3321. Fax: 320-363-3322. E-mail: jklosterman@csbsju.edu. Web site: www.sjprep.net.

ST. JOHN'S-RAVENSCOURT SCHOOL

400 South Drive
Winnipeg, Manitoba R3T 3K5, Canada
Head of School: Dr. Stephen Johnson

General Information Coeducational boarding and day college-preparatory school. Boarding grades 8–12, day grades K–12. Founded: 1820. Setting: suburban. Students are housed in single-sex dormitories. 23-acre campus. 6 buildings on campus. Approved or accredited by Canadian Association of Independent Schools, Canadian Educational Standards Institute, The Association of Boarding Schools, and Manitoba Department of Education. Language of instruction: English. Endowment: CAN$8.3 million. Total enrollment: 836. Upper school average class size: 20. Upper school faculty-student ratio: 1:9. There are 172 required school days per year for Upper School students. Upper School students typically attend 5 days per week. The average school day consists of 5 hours and 30 minutes.

Upper School Student Profile Grade 9: 87 students (53 boys, 34 girls); Grade 10: 91 students (48 boys, 43 girls); Grade 11: 102 students (55 boys, 47 girls); Grade 12: 94 students (62 boys, 32 girls). 4% of students are boarding students. 97% are province residents. 3 provinces are represented in upper school student body. 2% are international students. International students from China, Democratic People's Republic of Korea, Germany, Hong Kong, Japan, and Taiwan; 2 other countries represented in student body.

Faculty School total: 78. In upper school: 25 men, 23 women; 13 have advanced degrees; 4 reside on campus.

Subjects Offered Advanced Placement courses, algebra, American history, animation, art, biology, biology-AP, calculus, calculus-AP, Canadian geography, Canadian history, chemistry, chemistry-AP, computer science, debate, drama, driver education, economics, English, English literature, European history, European history-AP, French, French-AP, geography, geometry, history, information technology, law, linear algebra, mathematics, music, physical education, physics, physics-AP, pre-calculus, psychology, psychology-AP, science, social studies, Spanish, theater, visual arts, Web site design, world issues.

Graduation Requirements Canadian geography, Canadian history, computer science, English, French, geography, history, mathematics, physical education (includes health), pre-calculus, science, social sciences.

Special Academic Programs Advanced Placement exam preparation; honors section; independent study; study at local college for college credit; ESL (27 students enrolled).

College Admission Counseling 83 students graduated in 2010; all went to college, including McGill University; Queen's University at Kingston; The University of British Columbia; The University of Western Ontario; University of Manitoba; University of Toronto.

Student Life Upper grades have uniform requirement, student council, honor system. Discipline rests equally with students and faculty.

Tuition and Aid Day student tuition: CAN$15,660; 7-day tuition and room/board: CAN$30,790–CAN$40,740. Tuition installment plan (monthly payment plans, individually arranged payment plans). Bursaries, merit scholarship grants available. In 2010–11, 21% of upper-school students received aid; total upper-school merit-scholarship money awarded: CAN$95,000. Total amount of financial aid awarded in 2010–11: CAN$262,250.

Admissions Traditional secondary-level entrance grade is 9. For fall 2010, 72 students applied for upper-level admission, 47 were accepted, 39 enrolled. Otis-Lennon School Ability Test, school's own exam or TOEFL or SLEP required. Deadline for receipt of application materials: none. Application fee required: CAN$125. Interview recommended.

Athletics Interscholastic: aerobics (boys, girls), badminton (b,g), basketball (b,g), cross-country running (b,g), Frisbee (b,g), golf (b), hockey (b,g), ice hockey (b,g), indoor track (b,g), indoor track & field (b,g), lacrosse (b,g), rugby (b,g), soccer (b,g), track and field (b,g), ultimate Frisbee (b,g), volleyball (b,g); intramural: badminton (b,g), basketball (b,g), cross-country running (b,g), dance (b,g), hockey (b,g), rock climbing (b,g), rugby (b,g), self defense (g), soccer (b,g), strength & conditioning (b,g), ultimate Frisbee (b,g), volleyball (g), wall climbing (b,g), weight training (b,g), yoga (b,g); coed interscholastic: badminton, Frisbee, physical fitness, running, skiing (cross-country), softball, speedball, ultimate Frisbee, water polo; coed intramural: badminton, flag football, floor hockey, rock climbing, running, skiing (cross-country), ultimate Frisbee. 6 PE instructors.

Computers Computers are regularly used in business skills, career exploration, college planning, creative writing, English, history, library skills, newspaper, science, social studies, yearbook classes. Computer network features include on-campus library services, Internet access, wireless campus network, Internet filtering or blocking technology, EBSCO. Campus intranet and student e-mail accounts are available to students. The school has a published electronic and media policy.

Contact Mrs. Lisa Kachulak-Babey, Director of Admissions and Communications. 204-477-2400. Fax: 204-477-2429. E-mail: admissions@sjr.mb.ca. Web site: www.sjr.mb.ca.

ST. JOSEPH ACADEMY

155 State Road 207
St. Augustine, Florida 32084

Head of School: Mr. Michael H. Heubeck

General Information Coeducational day college-preparatory, arts, religious studies, and technology school, affiliated with Roman Catholic Church. Grades 9–12. Founded: 1866. Setting: suburban. 33-acre campus. 13 buildings on campus. Approved or accredited by National Council for Nonpublic Schools, Southern Association of Colleges and Schools, and Florida Department of Education. Total enrollment: 270. Upper school average class size: 15. Upper school faculty-student ratio: 1:13. There are 184 required school days per year for Upper School students. Upper School students typically attend 5 days per week. The average school day consists of 5 hours and 6 minutes.

Upper School Student Profile Grade 9: 76 students (36 boys, 40 girls); Grade 10: 61 students (30 boys, 31 girls); Grade 11: 63 students (30 boys, 33 girls); Grade 12: 70 students (32 boys, 38 girls). 84% of students are Roman Catholic.

Faculty School total: 27. In upper school: 12 men, 12 women, 10 have advanced degrees.

Subjects Offered Advanced computer applications, advanced math, Advanced Placement courses, advanced studio art-AP, algebra, American government, American history, American sign language, anatomy and physiology, ancient world history, applied arts, art, art history, Bible studies, biology, calculus-AP, career education, career exploration, career planning, Catholic belief and practice, chemistry, Christianity, church history, clayworking, college counseling, college placement, college planning, community service, computer applications, computer education, computer skills, costumes and make-up, creative drama, drama, drama performance, drama workshop, drawing, English, English composition, English language-AP, environmental science, government, history of the Catholic Church, honors algebra, honors English, honors geometry, honors U.S. history, honors world history, integrated mathematics, Internet research, keyboarding, life management skills, marine biology, Microsoft, moral theology, peer ministry, personal fitness, physical education, physics, play production, playwriting and directing, portfolio art, pottery, pre-algebra, pre-calculus, psychology, religious education, senior career experience, Shakespeare, Spanish, Spanish language-AP, Spanish literature-AP, theology, U.S. history, weight training.

Graduation Requirements Advanced Placement courses, career/college preparation, Catholic belief and practice, college writing, computer literacy, dramatic arts, economics, English, environmental science, foreign language, government, mathematics, physical education (includes health), religion (includes Bible studies and theology), social studies (includes history), theology.

Special Academic Programs Advanced Placement exam preparation; study at local college for college credit; academic accommodation for the gifted and the artistically talented; special instructional classes for students with Attention Deficit Disorder.

College Admission Counseling 80 students graduated in 2010; all went to college, including University of Central Florida; University of Florida; University of North Florida.

Student Life Upper grades have uniform requirement, student council, honor system. Discipline rests primarily with faculty. Attendance at religious services is required.

Summer Programs Sports programs offered; session focuses on football conditioning, weight training, basketball clinics and tournaments; held on campus; accepts boys and girls; not open to students from other schools. 92 students usually enrolled. 2011 schedule: June 1 to July 30.

Tuition and Aid Day student tuition: $7300–$9780. Tuition installment plan (FACTS Tuition Payment Plan). Need-based scholarship grants available. In 2010–11, 36% of upper-school students received aid. Total amount of financial aid awarded in 2010–11: $128,480.

Admissions Traditional secondary-level entrance grade is 9. For fall 2010, 86 students applied for upper-level admission, 78 were accepted, 78 enrolled. ACT-Explore, any standardized test, Gates MacGinite Reading Tests, Iowa Tests of Basic Skills, Iowa Tests of Basic Skills-Grades 7-8, Archdiocese HSEPT-Grade 9, PSAT or SAT required. Deadline for receipt of application materials: none. Application fee required: $730. Interview required.

Athletics Interscholastic: baseball (boys), basketball (b,g), cross-country running (b,g), flag football (g), football (b), golf (b), physical fitness (b,g), physical training (b,g), soccer (b,g), softball (g), swimming and diving (b,g), tennis (b,g), track and field (b,g), volleyball (g), weight training (b), winter soccer (b,g), wrestling (b). 1 PE instructor, 2 coaches, 2 athletic trainers.

Computers Computer network features include on-campus library services, Internet access, Internet filtering or blocking technology. Students grades are available online. The school has a published electronic and media policy.

Contact Mr. Patrick M. Keane, Director of Admissions. 904-824-0431 Ext. 305. Fax: 904-824-4412. E-mail: admissions@sjaweb.org. Web site: www.sjaweb.org.

SAINT JOSEPH ACADEMY HIGH SCHOOL

3430 Rocky River Drive
Cleveland, Ohio 44111

Head of School: Dr. Jim Cantwell

General Information Girls' day college-preparatory, technology, pre-engineering, and Mandarin school, affiliated with Roman Catholic Church. Grades 9–12. Founded: 1890. Setting: urban. 44-acre campus. 2 buildings on campus. Approved or accredited by North Central Association of Colleges and Schools, Ohio Catholic Schools Accreditation Association (OCSAA), and Ohio Department of Education. Endowment: $3.5 million. Total enrollment: 650. Upper school average class size: 23. Upper school faculty-student ratio: 1:12. The average school day consists of 7 hours.

Upper School Student Profile Grade 9: 166 students (166 girls); Grade 10: 170 students (170 girls); Grade 11: 169 students (169 girls); Grade 12: 145 students (145 girls). 90% of students are Roman Catholic.

Faculty School total: 63. In upper school: 15 men, 48 women; 38 have advanced degrees.

Graduation Requirements 4 credits of Theology.

Special Academic Programs 7 Advanced Placement exams for which test preparation is offered; honors section; independent study; study abroad.

College Admission Counseling 145 students graduated in 2010; 138 went to college, including Cleveland State University; John Carroll University; Kent State University; Miami University; Ohio University; University of Dayton. Other: 7 went to work. Mean SAT critical reading: 540, mean SAT math: 521, mean SAT writing: 528, mean combined SAT: 1589, mean composite ACT: 23.

Student Life Upper grades have uniform requirement, student council, honor system. Discipline rests primarily with faculty. Attendance at religious services is required.

Tuition and Aid Day student tuition: $9575. Tuition installment plan (monthly payment plans). Merit scholarship grants, need-based scholarship grants, need-based loans, paying campus jobs available. In 2010–11, 60% of upper-school students received aid; total upper-school merit-scholarship money awarded: $130,000. Total amount of financial aid awarded in 2010–11: $850,000.

Admissions Traditional secondary-level entrance grade is 9. For fall 2010, 200 students applied for upper-level admission, 195 were accepted, 175 enrolled. ACT-Explore required. Deadline for receipt of application materials: January 28. No application fee required. Interview required.

Athletics Interscholastic: basketball, cheering, cross-country running, diving, golf, rugby, soccer, softball, swimming and diving, tennis, track and field, volleyball; intramural: alpine skiing, dance team, physical fitness, strength & conditioning. 2 PE instructors, 14 coaches.

Computers Computer network features include on-campus library services, Internet access, wireless campus network, Internet filtering or blocking technology. Student e-mail accounts and computer access in designated common areas are available to students. Students grades are available online. The school has a published electronic and media policy.

Contact Ms. Diane Marie Kanney, Director of Admissions. 216-251-4868 Ext. 220. Fax: 216-251-5809. E-mail: admissions@sja1890.org. Web site: www.sja1890.org.

SAINT JOSEPH CENTRAL CATHOLIC HIGH SCHOOL

702 Croghan Street
Fremont, Ohio 43420
Head of School: Mr. Michael Gabel
General Information Coeducational day college-preparatory, arts, business, religious studies, bilingual studies, and technology school, affiliated with Roman Catholic Church. Grades 9–12. Founded: 1893. Setting: small town. Nearest major city is Toledo. 5-acre campus. 1 building on campus. Approved or accredited by National Catholic Education Association and Ohio Department of Education. Endowment: $540,000. Total enrollment: 224. Upper school average class size: 20. Upper school faculty-student ratio: 1:15. There are 180 required school days per year for Upper School students. Upper School students typically attend 5 days per week. The average school day consists of 6 hours and 15 minutes.
Upper School Student Profile Grade 9: 46 students (24 boys, 22 girls); Grade 10: 53 students (26 boys, 27 girls); Grade 11: 69 students (38 boys, 31 girls); Grade 12: 55 students (23 boys, 32 girls). 93% of students are Romah Catholic.
Faculty School total: 19. In upper school: 7 men, 12 women; 7 have advanced degrees.
Subjects Offered Advanced computer applications, advanced math, advanced TOEFL/grammar, American history, American literature, art, band, biology, biology-AP, bookkeeping, calculus, Catholic belief and practice, chemistry, choir, desktop publishing, drama, earth science, English, environmental science, family and consumer science, French, general business, graphic design, health education, honors English, human biology, integrated mathematics, philosophy, physical education, physics, probability and statistics, programming, psychology, public speaking, reading/study skills, religion, senior project, social justice, social studies, Spanish, yearbook.
Graduation Requirements Computer literacy, English, government, humanities, mathematics, physical education (includes health), religion (includes Bible studies and theology), science, social studies (includes history), citizenship.
Special Academic Programs Advanced Placement exam preparation; honors section; study at local college for college credit; remedial reading and/or remedial writing; remedial math.
College Admission Counseling 62 students graduated in 2009; 60 went to college, including Bowling Green State University; Eastern Michigan University; Kent State University; Ohio University; The Ohio State University; The University of Toledo. Other: 2 went to work.
Student Life Upper grades have uniform requirement, student council, honor system. Discipline rests primarily with faculty. Attendance at religious services is required.
Tuition and Aid Day student tuition: $4050. Tuition reduction for siblings, merit scholarship grants, need-based scholarship grants available. In 2009–10, 20% of upper-school students received aid; total upper-school merit-scholarship money awarded: $2000. Total amount of financial aid awarded in 2009–10: $20,000.
Admissions Traditional secondary-level entrance grade is 9. High School Placement Test required. Deadline for receipt of application materials: none. Application fee required: $100.
Athletics Interscholastic: baseball (boys), basketball (b), bowling (b,g), cheering (g), cross-country running (b,g), football (b), golf (b), soccer (b,g), softball (g), swimming and diving (b,g), tennis (b,g), track and field (b,g), volleyball (g), wrestling (b); intramural: indoor track & field (b,g); coed intramural: basketball. 1 PE instructor, 10 coaches.
Computers Computers are regularly used in computer applications, desktop publishing, graphic design, Spanish, yearbook classes. Computer network features include Internet access, wireless campus network. Student e-mail accounts are available to students. Students grades are available online.
Contact Mrs. Susan Kusmer, Office Manager. 419-332-9947. Fax: 419-332-4945. E-mail: skusmer@fremontstjoe.org. Web site: www.fremontstjoe.org.

ST. JOSEPH HIGH SCHOOL

4120 Bradley Road
Santa Maria, California 93455
Head of School: Mr. Joseph Thomas Myers
General Information Coeducational day college-preparatory, arts, religious studies, and technology school, affiliated with Roman Catholic Church. Grades 9–12. Founded: 1964. Setting: suburban. 15-acre campus. 8 buildings on campus. Approved or accredited by National Catholic Education Association, Western Association of Schools and Colleges, and Western Catholic Education Association. Endowment: $3.6 million. Total enrollment: 561. Upper school average class size: 25. Upper school faculty-student ratio: 1:19. There are 180 required school days per year for Upper School students. Upper School students typically attend 5 days per week. The average school day consists of 5 hours and 45 minutes.
Upper School Student Profile Grade 9: 139 students (64 boys, 75 girls); Grade 10: 159 students (77 boys, 82 girls); Grade 11: 118 students (55 boys, 63 girls); Grade 12: 190 students (91 boys, 99 girls). 66% of students are Roman Catholic.
Faculty School total: 36. In upper school: 15 men, 21 women; 16 have advanced degrees.
Subjects Offered Art, biology, biology-AP, computer literacy, economics, English literature, English literature-AP, ethics, European history-AP, French, general science,

grammar, Hebrew scripture, keyboarding, language and composition, marine science, New Testament, painting, peace and justice, physical science, physics, pre-algebra, psychology, remedial study skills, scripture, sculpture, sociology, Spanish, Spanish language-AP, speech, U.S. government, U.S. history, U.S. history-AP, U.S. literature, weight training, Western civilization.
Graduation Requirements Arts and fine arts (art, music, dance, drama), Catholic belief and practice, Christian and Hebrew scripture, Christian doctrine, Christian ethics, church history, civics, communication arts, composition, computer skills, economics, English, English literature, ethics, foreign language, health, history, human biology, introduction to literature, keyboarding, language structure, life science, literature, mathematics, religion (includes Bible studies and theology), science, U.S. government, Western civilization, world geography.
Special Academic Programs Remedial reading and/or remedial writing; remedial math.
College Admission Counseling 132 students graduated in 2010; all went to college, including California Polytechnic State University, San Luis Obispo; Loyola Marymount University; Santa Clara University; University of California, Santa Barbara. Mean SAT critical reading: 532, mean SAT math: 533, mean SAT writing: 538. 22% scored over 600 on SAT critical reading, 28% scored over 600 on SAT math, 22% scored over 600 on SAT writing.
Student Life Upper grades have specified standards of dress, student council. Discipline rests primarily with faculty. Attendance at religious services is required.
Summer Programs Remediation, advancement, sports programs offered; held on campus; accepts boys and girls; not open to students from other schools. 400 students usually enrolled. 2011 schedule: June 20 to July 22. Application deadline: June 20.
Tuition and Aid Day student tuition: $7350. Tuition installment plan (monthly payment plans). Tuition reduction for siblings, merit scholarship grants, need-based scholarship grants, paying campus jobs available. In 2010–11, 30% of upper-school students received aid; total upper-school merit-scholarship money awarded: $12,000. Total amount of financial aid awarded in 2010–11: $310,000.
Admissions Traditional secondary-level entrance grade is 9. For fall 2010, 158 students applied for upper-level admission, 154 were accepted, 139 enrolled. High School Placement Test required. Deadline for receipt of application materials: February 5. Application fee required: $50.
Athletics Interscholastic: baseball (boys), basketball (b,g), cross-country running (b,g), football (b), golf (b,g), soccer (b,g), softball (g), swimming and diving (b,g), tennis (b,g), track and field (b,g), volleyball (b,g), water polo (b,g); intramural: dance team (g), flag football (g); coed interscholastic: cheering, wrestling; coed intramural: basketball. 3 PE instructors, 35 coaches, 1 athletic trainer.
Computers Computers are regularly used in computer applications, economics, English, history, keyboarding, mathematics, religion, Spanish, theology, yearbook classes. Computer network features include on-campus library services, online commercial services, Internet access, wireless campus network, Internet filtering or blocking technology. Computer access in designated common areas is available to students. Students grades are available online. The school has a published electronic and media policy.
Contact Joanne Poloni, Director of Admissions. 805-937-2038 Ext. 114. Fax: 805-937-4248. E-mail: poloni@sjhsknights.com. Web site: www.sjhsknights.com.

SAINT JOSEPH HIGH SCHOOL

10900 West Cermak Road
Westchester, Illinois 60154-4299
Head of School: Ms. Donna Kiel
General Information Coeducational day college-preparatory, arts, business, vocational, religious studies, bilingual studies, and technology school, affiliated with Roman Catholic Church. Grades 9–12. Founded: 1960. Setting: suburban. Nearest major city is Chicago. 21-acre campus. 2 buildings on campus. Approved or accredited by Christian Brothers Association, North Central Association of Colleges and Schools, and Illinois Department of Education. Total enrollment: 671. Upper school average class size: 20. Upper school faculty-student ratio: 1:17. There are 180 required school days per year for Upper School students. Upper School students typically attend 5 days per week. The average school day consists of 6 hours and 45 minutes.
Upper School Student Profile Grade 9: 159 students (90 boys, 69 girls); Grade 10: 165 students (97 boys, 68 girls); Grade 11: 164 students (100 boys, 64 girls); Grade 12: 183 students (106 boys, 77 girls). 60% of students are Roman Catholic.
Faculty School total: 68. In upper school: 34 men, 33 women; 25 have advanced degrees.
Subjects Offered Accounting, ACT preparation, acting, advanced studio art-AP, algebra, American foreign policy, American history, anatomy and physiology, art, band, biology, business law, calculus, calculus-AP, ceramics, chemistry, Christian ethics, computer applications, computer graphics, computer programming, computer science-AP, computer-aided design, concert band, concert choir, consumer economics, creative writing, current events, digital photography, economics, English, English-AP, environmental science, European history-AP, film studies, fine arts, French, geography, geometry, graphic arts, health, human biology, internship, Italian, jazz band, journalism, Mandarin, marching band, marketing, men's studies, moral and social development, music appreciation, peace and justice, peer ministry, photography, physical education, physics, physics-AP, pre-algebra, pre-calculus, reading, reading/ study skills, sociology, Spanish, Spanish-AP, speech, sports conditioning, sports

medicine, studio art, studio art-AP, theater production, U.S. history, Web site design, women spirituality and faith, world cultures, world religions.

Graduation Requirements Arts and fine arts (art, music, dance, drama), computer applications, economics, English, foreign language, mathematics, physical education (includes health), religion (includes Bible studies and theology), science, social studies (includes history), each student must complete 40 community service hours.

Special Academic Programs 7 Advanced Placement exams for which test preparation is offered; honors section; study at local college for college credit; academic accommodation for the gifted, the musically talented, and the artistically talented; remedial reading and/or remedial writing; remedial math.

College Admission Counseling 193 students graduated in 2010; 186 went to college, including DePaul University; Illinois State University; Lewis University; Loyola University Chicago; Northern Illinois University; University of Illinois at Urbana–Champaign. Other: 7 went to work. Median composite ACT: 22. 14% scored over 26 on composite ACT.

Student Life Upper grades have uniform requirement, student council, honor system. Discipline rests primarily with faculty. Attendance at religious services is required.

Summer Programs Remediation, enrichment, advancement, sports, art/fine arts, computer instruction programs offered; session focuses on remediation; held on campus; accepts boys and girls; open to students from other schools. 200 students usually enrolled. 2011 schedule: June 15 to July 25. Application deadline: May 31.

Tuition and Aid Day student tuition: $8400. Tuition installment plan (monthly payment plans, individually arranged payment plans, based on parents income special arrangements are made with income tax return). Tuition reduction for siblings, merit scholarship grants, need-based scholarship grants, paying campus jobs available. In 2010–11, 57% of upper-school students received aid; total upper-school merit-scholarship money awarded: $95,000. Total amount of financial aid awarded in 2010–11: $600,000.

Admissions Traditional secondary-level entrance grade is 9. For fall 2010, 187 students applied for upper-level admission, 187 were accepted, 159 enrolled. Explore required. Deadline for receipt of application materials: none. Application fee required: $300. Interview required.

Athletics Interscholastic: aerobics/dance (girls), baseball (b), basketball (b,g), bowling (b,g), boxing (b), cheering (g), cross-country running (b,g), dance team (g), football (b), golf (b,g), hockey (g), soccer (b,g), softball (g), strength & conditioning (b,g), tennis (b,g), track and field (b,g), volleyball (b,g), wrestling (b). 30 coaches, 1 athletic trainer.

Computers Computers are regularly used in business applications, computer applications, current events, desktop publishing, drafting, economics, English, French, geography, graphic arts, graphic design, health, history, journalism, mathematics, music, newspaper, photography, reading, religion, science, social studies, Spanish, speech, technology, theater arts, writing, yearbook classes. Computer network features include on-campus library services, online commercial services, Internet access, wireless campus network, Internet filtering or blocking technology, all students have a laptop computer with wireless access to the Internet, anywhere on campus. Campus intranet and student e-mail accounts are available to students. Students grades are available online. The school has a published electronic and media policy.

Contact Ms. Tricia Devereux, Co-Director of Admissions. 708-562-4433 Ext. 253. Fax: 708-562-4459. E-mail: tdevereux@stjoeshs.org.

SAINT JOSEPH HIGH SCHOOL
328 Vine Street
Hammonton, New Jersey 08037
Head of School: Mrs. Lynn Domenico

General Information Coeducational day college-preparatory, arts, religious studies, technology, and global studies/distance learning school, affiliated with Roman Catholic Church. Grades 9–12. Founded: 1939. Setting: small town. Nearest major city is Philadelphia, PA. 7-acre campus. 2 buildings on campus. Approved or accredited by Middle States Association of Colleges and Schools and New Jersey Department of Education. Total enrollment: 520. Upper school average class size: 25. Upper school faculty-student ratio: 1:17. There are 180 required school days per year for Upper School students. Upper School students typically attend 5 days per week. The average school day consists of 5 hours and 30 minutes.

Upper School Student Profile Grade 9: 143 students (74 boys, 69 girls); Grade 10: 142 students (69 boys, 73 girls); Grade 11: 135 students (78 boys, 57 girls); Grade 12: 100 students (54 boys, 46 girls). 90% of students are Roman Catholic.

Faculty School total: 35. In upper school: 14 men, 16 women; 10 have advanced degrees.

Subjects Offered Advanced Placement courses, algebra, American history, American history-AP, American literature-AP, anatomy and physiology, biology, biology-AP, British literature, British literature (honors), business technology, calculus, calculus-AP, chemistry, chemistry-AP, Christian doctrine, Christian scripture, church history, community service, composition-AP, computer applications, creative writing, desktop publishing, earth science, economics, English, English composition, English language and composition-AP, English literature and composition-AP, environmental science, European history, French, geometry, health education, history, honors algebra, honors English, honors geometry, honors U.S. history, honors world history, lab science, physical education, physical science, physics, pre-calculus, psychology, religion, Spanish, U.S. history, U.S. history-AP, world cultures, world history.

Graduation Requirements 20th century history, algebra, American history, American literature, biology, British literature, chemistry, church history, computer education, driver education, English, English literature, European history, geometry, health, history of the Catholic Church, lab science, languages, mathematics, religious education, science, social studies (includes history), theology, U.S. history, world cultures. Community service is required.

Special Academic Programs Academic accommodation for the gifted; remedial reading and/or remedial writing; programs in English, mathematics, general development for dyslexic students.

College Admission Counseling 121 students graduated in 2010; 98 went to college, including Penn State University Park; Widener University. Other: 10 went to work, 5 entered military service, 5 entered a postgraduate year, 3 had other specific plans. Median SAT critical reading: 500, median SAT math: 490, median SAT writing: 450, median combined SAT: 1440. 4% scored over 600 on SAT critical reading, 11% scored over 600 on SAT math, 3% scored over 600 on SAT writing, 1% scored over 1800 on combined SAT.

Student Life Upper grades have uniform requirement, student council, honor system. Discipline rests primarily with faculty. Attendance at religious services is required.

Summer Programs Remediation, enrichment programs offered; session focuses on jump starting the high school experience and enhancing the school year; held on campus; accepts boys and girls; open to students from other schools. 120 students usually enrolled. 2011 schedule: July 10 to August 18. Application deadline: June 1.

Tuition and Aid Day student tuition: $7400. Tuition installment plan (SMART Tuition Payment Plan). Tuition reduction for siblings, merit scholarship grants, need-based scholarship grants available. In 2010–11, 20% of upper-school students received aid; total upper-school merit-scholarship money awarded: $10,000. Total amount of financial aid awarded in 2010–11: $50,000.

Admissions Traditional secondary-level entrance grade is 9. For fall 2010, 400 students applied for upper-level admission, 160 were accepted, 147 enrolled. Admissions testing, any standardized test, CAT, Catholic High School Entrance Examination, CTBS, Stanford Achievement Test, any other standardized test, Iowa Tests of Basic Skills, Stanford Achievement Test, STS Examination or Terra Nova-CTB required. Deadline for receipt of application materials: none. Application fee required: $200. Interview recommended.

Athletics Interscholastic: baseball (boys, girls), basketball (b,g), bowling (b,g), cheering (b,g), cross-country running (b,g), dance (g), field hockey (g), football (b), golf (b,g), gymnastics (g), ice hockey (b), ice skating (g), indoor track (b,g), indoor track & field (b,g), lacrosse (b,g), physical training (b,g), power lifting (b), soccer (b,g), softball (g), swimming and diving (g), track and field (b,g), volleyball (g), weight lifting (b,g), weight training (b,g), winter (indoor) track (b,g), wrestling (b); coed interscholastic: bowling; coed intramural: bowling, snowboarding, weight training. 3 PE instructors, 43 coaches, 1 athletic trainer.

Computers Computers are regularly used in business applications, desktop publishing classes. Computer network features include on-campus library services, Internet access, wireless campus network, Internet filtering or blocking technology. Campus intranet and student e-mail accounts are available to students. Students grades are available online. The school has a published electronic and media policy.

Contact Mrs. Rhonda Bianchini, Director of Advancement. 609-561-8700 Ext. 5. Fax: 609-561-8701. E-mail: rbianchini@stjoek12.org. Web site: www.stjoek12.org.

SAINT JOSEPH HIGH SCHOOL
2401 69th Street
Kenosha, Wisconsin 53143
Head of School: Mr. Edward Kovochich

General Information Coeducational day college-preparatory, general academic, arts, religious studies, and technology school, affiliated with Roman Catholic Church. Grades 6–12. Founded: 1957. Setting: suburban. Nearest major city is Milwaukee. 1 building on campus. Approved or accredited by North Central Association of Colleges and Schools and Wisconsin Department of Education. Endowment: $100,000. Total enrollment: 654. Upper school average class size: 20. Upper school faculty-student ratio: 1:20. There are 180 required school days per year for Upper School students. Upper School students typically attend 5 days per week. The average school day consists of 7 hours.

Upper School Student Profile Grade 6: 40 students (19 boys, 21 girls); Grade 7: 45 students (27 boys, 18 girls); Grade 8: 70 students (33 boys, 37 girls); Grade 9: 85 students (42 boys, 43 girls); Grade 10: 82 students (39 boys, 43 girls); Grade 11: 72 students (44 boys, 28 girls); Grade 12: 53 students (26 boys, 27 girls). 80% of students are Roman Catholic.

Faculty School total: 34. In upper school: 11 men, 19 women; 12 have advanced degrees.

Subjects Offered Algebra, American government, anatomy and physiology, architecture, art, band, biology, biology-AP, calculus-AP, ceramics, chemistry, chemistry-AP, choir, Christian scripture, computer applications, computers, consumer mathematics, creative writing, critical writing, drafting, drama, drawing, economics, English, English-AP, film, French, geometry, health, Hebrew scripture, Italian, journalism, keyboarding, mathematics, microeconomics-AP, newspaper, photography, physical education, physical science, physics-AP, pre-algebra, pre-calculus, psychology, reading/study skills, science, social studies, Spanish, speech, statistics, studio art, theater, theology, trigonometry, U.S. history, world history, world religions, yearbook.

Saint Joseph High School

Graduation Requirements Arts and fine arts (art, music, dance, drama), computers, electives, English, mathematics, physical education (includes health), religion (includes Bible studies and theology), science, social studies (includes history).

Special Academic Programs Advanced Placement exam preparation; honors section; study at local college for college credit.

College Admission Counseling 79 students graduated in 2010; 75 went to college, including Marquette University; University of Wisconsin–Madison; University of Wisconsin–Milwaukee. Other: 4 went to work. Mean composite ACT: 23. 25% scored over 26 on composite ACT.

Student Life Upper grades have specified standards of dress, student council, honor system. Discipline rests primarily with faculty. Attendance at religious services is required.

Tuition and Aid Day student tuition: $6650–$7150. Tuition installment plan (monthly payment plans, individually arranged payment plans, Tuition Management Systems). Tuition reduction for siblings, merit scholarship grants, need-based scholarship grants available. In 2010–11, 50% of upper-school students received aid; total upper-school merit-scholarship money awarded: $45,000. Total amount of financial aid awarded in 2010–11: $150,000.

Admissions Traditional secondary-level entrance grade is 9. For fall 2010, 110 students applied for upper-level admission, 105 were accepted, 89 enrolled. ACT-Explore or admissions testing required. Deadline for receipt of application materials: none. Application fee required: $100.

Athletics Interscholastic: baseball (boys), basketball (b,g), cheering (b,g), cross-country running (b,g), football (b), golf (b,g), soccer (b,g), softball (g), tennis (b,g), track and field (b,g), volleyball (g), wrestling (b); coed intramural: bowling, weight lifting, weight training. 2 PE instructors, 15 coaches, 1 athletic trainer.

Computers Computers are regularly used in all classes. Computer network features include Internet access, wireless campus network, Internet filtering or blocking technology. Campus intranet is available to students. Students grades are available online.

Contact Mrs. Wanda Jaraczewski, Director of Admissions. 262-654-8651 Ext. 104. Fax: 262-654-1615. E-mail: wjaraczewski@kenoshastjoseph.com. Web site: www.kenoshastjoseph.com.

SAINT JOSEPH JUNIOR-SENIOR HIGH SCHOOL

1000 Ululani Street
Hilo, Hawaii 96720
Head of School: Ms. Victoria Torcolini

General Information Coeducational day college-preparatory, arts, religious studies, and technology school, affiliated with Roman Catholic Church. Grades 7–12. Founded: 1948. Setting: urban. 14-acre campus. 3 buildings on campus. Approved or accredited by The Hawaii Council of Private Schools, Western Association of Schools and Colleges, Western Catholic Education Association, and Hawaii Department of Education. Total enrollment: 193. Upper school average class size: 18. Upper school faculty-student ratio: 1:12. There are 176 required school days per year for Upper School students. Upper School students typically attend 5 days per week. The average school day consists of 5 hours and 25 minutes.

Upper School Student Profile 55% of students are Roman Catholic.

Faculty School total: 32. In upper school: 8 men, 9 women; 6 have advanced degrees.

Subjects Offered Algebra, American history, American literature, art, astronomy, biology, calculus, chemistry, computer science, creative writing, drama, earth science, economics, English, English literature, ethics, European history, expository writing, fine arts, geometry, government/civics, history, Japanese, marine biology, mathematics, music, physical education, physics, physiology, psychology, religion, science, social studies, sociology, Spanish, speech, theater, theology, trigonometry, typing, world history, world literature, yearbook.

Graduation Requirements Arts and fine arts (art, music, dance, drama), English, foreign language, mathematics, physical education (includes health), religion (includes Bible studies and theology), science, social studies (includes history).

Special Academic Programs Advanced Placement exam preparation; honors section; independent study; study at local college for college credit; academic accommodation for the gifted; remedial math; ESL (12 students enrolled).

College Admission Counseling 48 students graduated in 2010; 46 went to college, including Chaminade University of Honolulu; University of Hawaii at Hilo; University of Hawaii at Manoa. Other: 2 entered military service. Median SAT critical reading: 510, median SAT math: 489, median composite ACT: 21.

Student Life Upper grades have uniform requirement, student council, honor system. Discipline rests primarily with faculty. Attendance at religious services is required.

Summer Programs Enrichment, sports, art/fine arts, computer instruction programs offered; session focuses on SAT/ACT preparation, enrichment; held on campus; accepts boys and girls; open to students from other schools. 140 students usually enrolled. 2011 schedule: June 12 to July 21. Application deadline: May 15.

Tuition and Aid Day student tuition: $7500. Guaranteed tuition plan. Tuition installment plan (individually arranged payment plans). Tuition reduction for siblings, need-based scholarship grants, paying campus jobs available. In 2010–11, 23% of upper-school students received aid. Total amount of financial aid awarded in 2010–11: $225,000.

Admissions For fall 2010, 43 students applied for upper-level admission, 36 were accepted. 3-R Achievement Test and English proficiency required. Deadline for receipt of application materials: none. Application fee required: $25. Interview required.

Athletics Interscholastic: baseball (boys), basketball (b,g), bowling (b,g), cheering (g), cross-country running (b,g), paddling (b,g), riflery (b,g), soccer (b,g), swimming and diving (b,g), tennis (b,g), volleyball (b,g); coed interscholastic: paddling. 2 PE instructors.

Computers Computers are regularly used in business education, college planning, creative writing, data processing, desktop publishing, ESL, keyboarding, lab/keyboard, library, mathematics, newspaper, publications, technology, typing, word processing, yearbook classes. Computer network features include on-campus library services, Internet access, State of Hawaii's College and Career Information Delivery System. Students grades are available online.

Contact Mrs. Marilyn Pakele, Registrar. 808-935-4936 Ext. 226. Fax: 808-969-9019. Web site: www.sjhshilo.org.

SAINT JOSEPH REGIONAL HIGH SCHOOL

40 Chestnut Ridge Road
Montvale, New Jersey 07645
Head of School: Mr. Barry Donnelly

General Information Boys' day college-preparatory school, affiliated with Roman Catholic Church. Grades 9–12. Founded: 1962. Setting: suburban. Nearest major city is New York, NY. 33-acre campus. 1 building on campus. Approved or accredited by Middle States Association of Colleges and Schools and New Jersey Department of Education. Total enrollment: 501. Upper school average class size: 23. Upper school faculty-student ratio: 1:14.

Upper School Student Profile Grade 9: 142 students (142 boys); Grade 10: 131 students (131 boys); Grade 11: 112 students (112 boys); Grade 12: 116 students (116 boys).

Faculty School total: 35. In upper school: 27 men, 8 women; 21 have advanced degrees.

Subjects Offered Accounting, advanced chemistry, advanced math, Advanced Placement courses, algebra, American government, American history, American history-AP, American literature, anatomy, art, art appreciation, Bible studies, biology, biology-AP, British literature, calculus, calculus-AP, Catholic belief and practice, chemistry, chemistry-AP, Christian doctrine, church history, computer applications, computer science, driver education, economics, English, English-AP, European history-AP, French, geography, geometry, health education, honors algebra, honors English, honors geometry, honors U.S. history, honors world history, keyboarding, Latin, law, New Testament, physical education, physics, physics-AP, pre-calculus, psychology, religion, science, social studies, Spanish, Spanish-AP, studio art, The 20th Century, theology, U.S. government, U.S. history, U.S. history-AP, Western civilization, word processing, world cultures, world geography, world history.

Special Academic Programs Advanced Placement exam preparation; honors section; study at local college for college credit.

College Admission Counseling 116 students graduated in 2009; all went to college, including Fairfield University; Iona College; Penn State University Park; Rutgers, The State University of New Jersey, New Brunswick; The University of Scranton.

Student Life Upper grades have specified standards of dress, student council, honor system. Discipline rests primarily with faculty. Attendance at religious services is required.

Tuition and Aid Day student tuition: $10,600. Tuition installment plan (FACTS Tuition Payment Plan). Tuition reduction for siblings, merit scholarship grants, need-based scholarship grants, need-based loans available.

Admissions Traditional secondary-level entrance grade is 9. Cooperative Entrance Exam (McGraw-Hill) required. Deadline for receipt of application materials: none. No application fee required. Interview required.

Athletics Interscholastic: baseball, basketball, bowling, cross-country running, football, golf, ice hockey, indoor track & field, lacrosse, physical fitness, running, soccer, tennis, track and field, weight lifting, weight training, winter (indoor) track, wrestling.

Computers Computers are regularly used in all classes. Computer network features include Internet access, wireless campus network, Internet filtering or blocking technology. Campus intranet is available to students. The school has a published electronic and media policy.

Contact Mr. Michael J. Doherty, Director of Admissions. 201-391-3300 Ext. 41. Fax: 201-391-8073. E-mail: mdoherty@saintjosephregional.org. Web site: www.saintjosephregional.org.

ST. JOSEPH'S ACADEMY

3015 Broussard Street
Baton Rouge, Louisiana 70808
Head of School: Mrs. Linda Fryoux Harvison

General Information Girls' day college-preparatory, arts, religious studies, and technology school, affiliated with Roman Catholic Church. Grades 9–12. Founded: 1868. Setting: urban. 14-acre campus. 6 buildings on campus. Approved or accredited by National Catholic Education Association, Southern Association of Colleges and

Schools, Southern Association of Independent Schools, and Louisiana Department of Education. Endowment: $3.6 million. Total enrollment: 952. Upper school average class size: 23. Upper school faculty-student ratio: 1:13. There are 178 required school days per year for Upper School students. Upper School students typically attend 5 days per week. The average school day consists of 7 hours and 15 minutes.

Upper School Student Profile Grade 9: 255 students (255 girls); Grade 10: 250 students (250 girls); Grade 11: 223 students (223 girls); Grade 12: 224 students (224 girls). 96% of students are Roman Catholic.

Faculty School total: 74. In upper school: 8 men, 66 women; 37 have advanced degrees.

Subjects Offered Accounting, acting, advanced chemistry, advanced computer applications, advanced math, Advanced Placement courses, algebra, American history, American history-AP, American literature, American literature-AP, analysis, analysis and differential calculus, art, art appreciation, band, Basic programming, biology, biology-AP, business law, calculus-AP, campus ministry, Catholic belief and practice, chemistry, child development, choir, choral music, chorus, Christian and Hebrew scripture, church history, civics, civics/free enterprise, computer applications, computer information systems, computer multimedia, computer programming, computer technologies, computer technology certification, CPR, critical studies in film, dance, desktop publishing, drama, drama performance, economics, English, English literature-AP, English-AP, entrepreneurship, environmental science, European history-AP, family and consumer science, film and literature, fine arts, foreign language, French, French as a second language, geometry, grammar, health, health and safety, health education, Hebrew scripture, honors algebra, honors English, honors geometry, human sexuality, independent study, information technology, Latin, marching band, media arts, media production, music, novels, physical education, physical fitness, physics, poetry, pre-calculus, public speaking, religion, research, Shakespeare, social justice, Spanish, speech, speech communications, technology, the Web, transition mathematics, U.S. history, U.S. history-AP, U.S. literature, visual arts, vocal ensemble, vocal music, Web authoring, Web site design, world history-AP.

Graduation Requirements Advanced math, algebra, American history, arts and fine arts (art, music, dance, drama), biology, chemistry, civics, computer applications, English, foreign language, geometry, physical education (includes health), physical science, physics, religion (includes Bible studies and theology), world history, service hours.

Special Academic Programs Advanced Placement exam preparation; honors section; independent study; study at local college for college credit.

College Admission Counseling 212 students graduated in 2010; 211 went to college, including Auburn University; Louisiana State University and Agricultural and Mechanical College; Louisiana Tech University; Loyola University New Orleans; University of Louisiana at Lafayette; University of Mississippi. Other: 1 went to work. 69% scored over 26 on composite ACT.

Student Life Upper grades have uniform requirement, student council, honor system. Discipline rests primarily with faculty. Attendance at religious services is required.

Summer Programs Computer instruction programs offered; session focuses on computer orientation for incoming 9th grade students; held on campus; accepts girls; not open to students from other schools. 254 students usually enrolled. 2011 schedule: June 1 to June 30. Application deadline: March 16.

Tuition and Aid Day student tuition: $9185. Tuition installment plan (monthly debit plan). Need-based scholarship grants available. In 2010–11, 6% of upper-school students received aid. Total amount of financial aid awarded in 2010–11: $274,500.

Admissions Traditional secondary-level entrance grade is 9. For fall 2010, 302 students applied for upper-level admission, 272 were accepted, 255 enrolled. ACT-Explore required. Deadline for receipt of application materials: November 19. Application fee required: $45. On-campus interview required.

Athletics Interscholastic: basketball, bowling, cheering, cross-country running, dance squad, golf, gymnastics, indoor track, modern dance, physical fitness, physical training, rodeo, running, soccer, softball, strength & conditioning, swimming and diving, tennis, track and field, triathlon, volleyball, weight training, winter (indoor) track; coed intramural: volleyball. 5 PE instructors, 9 coaches, 1 athletic trainer.

Computers Computers are regularly used in all classes. Computer network features include on-campus library services, online commercial services, Internet access, wireless campus network, Internet filtering or blocking technology, administrative software/grading/scheduling. Student e-mail accounts are available to students. Students grades are available online. The school has a published electronic and media policy.

Contact Mrs. Kathy Meares, Assistant Principal of Records. 225-388-2213. Fax: 225-344-5714. E-mail: mearesk@sjabr.org. Web site: www.sjabr.org.

ST. JOSEPH'S ACADEMY

2307 South Lindberg Boulevard
St. Louis, Missouri 63131
Head of School: Sr. Michaela Zahner, CSJ

General Information Girls' day college-preparatory, arts, business, religious studies, bilingual studies, technology, and military school, affiliated with Roman Catholic Church. Grades 9–12. Founded: 1840. Setting: suburban. 36-acre campus. 3 buildings on campus. Approved or accredited by North Central Association of Colleges and Schools and Missouri Department of Education. Endowment: $1 million. Upper school average class size: 24. Upper school faculty-student ratio: 1:11. There

are 175 required school days per year for Upper School students. Upper School students typically attend 5 days per week. The average school day consists of 7 hours.

Upper School Student Profile 98% of students are Roman Catholic.

Faculty School total: 60. In upper school: 7 men, 52 women; 58 have advanced degrees.

Subjects Offered Accounting, algebra, American government, American history, astronomy, biology, business law, calculus, chemistry, child development, computer applications, consumer education, cultural geography, death and loss, environmental science-AP, global science, honors algebra, honors U.S. history, human anatomy, humanities, keyboarding, life issues, math analysis, Microsoft, nutrition, physical education, physics, politics, prayer/spirituality, probability and statistics, psychology, sociology, theology, trigonometry, wellness, world history, world religions, zoology.

Graduation Requirements Arts and fine arts (art, music, dance, drama), English, foreign language, lab science, mathematics, physical education (includes health), practical arts, social studies (includes history), theology, 90 hours of community service in the senior year.

Special Academic Programs 9 Advanced Placement exams for which test preparation is offered; study at local college for college credit.

College Admission Counseling 156 students graduated in 2009; 155 went to college, including Indiana University–Purdue University Fort Wayne; Northwestern University; Saint Louis University; University of Dayton; University of Missouri; University of Notre Dame. Other: 1 had other specific plans. Median composite ACT: 25.

Student Life Upper grades have uniform requirement, student council, honor system. Discipline rests equally with students and faculty. Attendance at religious services is required.

Tuition and Aid Day student tuition: $6100. Tuition installment plan (FACTS Tuition Payment Plan). Paying campus jobs available. In 2009–10, 5% of upper-school students received aid. Total amount of financial aid awarded in 2009–10: $260,000.

Admissions Traditional secondary-level entrance grade is 9. For fall 2009, 200 students applied for upper-level admission, 170 were accepted, 170 enrolled. Deadline for receipt of application materials: December 5. No application fee required.

Athletics Interscholastic: basketball, crew, cross-country running, diving, field hockey, golf, lacrosse, racquetball, running, soccer, softball, swimming and diving, tennis, track and field, volleyball. 2 PE instructors, 10 coaches, 1 athletic trainer.

Computers Computers are regularly used in art classes. Computer network features include on-campus library services, Internet access, wireless campus network, Internet filtering or blocking technology. Campus intranet and student e-mail accounts are available to students. Students grades are available online. The school has a published electronic and media policy.

Contact Sr. Carol Gerondale, CSJ, Director of Admissions. 314-965-7205 Ext. 233. Fax: 314-965-9114. E-mail: cgerondale@stjosephacademy.org. Web site: www.stjosephacademy.org.

ST. JOSEPH'S CATHOLIC SCHOOL

100 St. Joseph's Drive
Greenville, South Carolina 29607
Head of School: Mr. Keith F. Kiser

General Information Coeducational day college-preparatory school, affiliated with Roman Catholic Church. Grades 6–12. Founded: 1993. Setting: suburban. 36-acre campus. 3 buildings on campus. Approved or accredited by South Carolina Independent School Association and South Carolina Department of Education. Total enrollment: 594. Upper school average class size: 19. Upper school faculty-student ratio: 1:12. Upper School students typically attend 5 days per week. The average school day consists of 7 hours and 10 minutes.

Upper School Student Profile Grade 9: 107 students (51 boys, 56 girls); Grade 10: 91 students (46 boys, 45 girls); Grade 11: 72 students (34 boys, 38 girls); Grade 12: 77 students (32 boys, 45 girls). 78% of students are Roman Catholic.

Faculty School total: 49. In upper school: 15 men, 22 women; 18 have advanced degrees.

Subjects Offered Algebra, American history, American literature, art, arts appreciation, bell choir, biology, biology-AP, calculus-AP, chemistry, chemistry-AP, chorus, Christian doctrine, Christian ethics, church history, composition, computer applications, computer graphics, dance, drama workshop, drawing, economics, economics-AP, English literature and composition-AP, English-AP, ensembles, European history, European history-AP, European literature, exercise science, film studies, fine arts, forensics, French, geometry, government, government-AP, honors algebra, honors English, honors geometry, human movement and its application to health, Latin, literature, medieval/Renaissance history, moral theology, newspaper, personal money management, physical education, physics, physics-AP, pre-calculus, science fiction, Shakespeare, Spanish, Spanish-AP, speech, statistics-AP, strings, theater arts, theater production, U.S. history, U.S. history-AP, yearbook.

Graduation Requirements 65 hours of community service.

Special Academic Programs Advanced Placement exam preparation; honors section.

College Admission Counseling 63 students graduated in 2010; all went to college, including Clemson University; College of Charleston; Furman University; University of Notre Dame; University of South Carolina. Median SAT critical reading: 614, median SAT math: 608, median SAT writing: 609, median combined SAT: 1831, median composite ACT: 27.

St. Joseph's Catholic School

Student Life Upper grades have uniform requirement, student council, honor system. Discipline rests primarily with faculty. Attendance at religious services is required.
Summer Programs Sports, art/fine arts programs offered; held on campus; accepts boys and girls; open to students from other schools.
Tuition and Aid Day student tuition: $8790. Tuition installment plan (monthly payment plans, yearly payment plan, semiannual payment plan). Tuition reduction for siblings, merit scholarship grants, need-based scholarship grants, tuition reduction for staff available. In 2010–11, 38% of upper-school students received aid; total upper-school merit-scholarship money awarded: $34,800. Total amount of financial aid awarded in 2010–11: $292,033.
Admissions Traditional secondary-level entrance grade is 9. For fall 2010, 57 students applied for upper-level admission, 50 were accepted, 40 enrolled. High School Placement Test (closed version) from Scholastic Testing Service required. Deadline for receipt of application materials: May 31. Application fee required: $125. On-campus interview required.
Athletics Interscholastic: baseball (boys), basketball (b,g), cheering (g), cross-country running (b,g), football (b), golf (b), soccer (b,g), softball (g), swimming and diving (b,g), tennis (b,g), volleyball (g), wrestling (b); intramural: basketball (b,g), flag football (b), Frisbee (b,g), soccer (b,g), volleyball (g); coed interscholastic: golf; coed intramural: dance, weight training.
Computers Computers are regularly used in computer applications, graphic design, keyboarding, programming, yearbook classes. Computer network features include Internet access.
Contact Mrs. Barbara L. McGrath, Director of Admissions. 864-234-9009 Ext. 104. Fax: 864-234-5516. E-mail: bmcgrath@sjcatholicschool.org. Web site: www.sjcatholicschool.org.

SAINT JOSEPH'S HIGH SCHOOL
145 Plainfield Avenue
Metuchen, New Jersey 08840
Head of School: Mr. John A. Anderson '70
General Information Boys' day college-preparatory, arts, religious studies, and technology school, affiliated with Roman Catholic Church, United Church of Canada. Grades 9–12. Founded: 1961. Setting: suburban. Nearest major city is New York, NY. 68-acre campus. 8 buildings on campus. Approved or accredited by Middle States Association of Colleges and Schools, National Catholic Education Association, and New Jersey Department of Education. Endowment: $2 million. Total enrollment: 810. Upper school average class size: 21. Upper school faculty-student ratio: 1:16. There are 170 required school days per year for Upper School students. Upper School students typically attend 5 days per week. The average school day consists of 6 hours and 12 minutes.
Upper School Student Profile Grade 9: 225 students (225 boys); Grade 10: 195 students (195 boys); Grade 11: 195 students (195 boys); Grade 12: 195 students (195 boys). 75% of students are Roman Catholic, United Church of Canada.
Faculty School total: 75. In upper school: 44 men, 31 women; 58 have advanced degrees.
Subjects Offered Accounting, acting, Advanced Placement courses, algebra, American Civil War, American government, American history, American literature, art, arts, astronomy, biology, biology-AP, calculus, calculus-AP, campus ministry, career education, Catholic belief and practice, chemistry, chemistry-AP, Christian ethics, Christian scripture, Christian studies, Christianity, church history, computer animation, computer applications, computer programming, computer science, computer science-AP, desktop publishing, discrete mathematics, driver education, English, English literature, English-AP, European history, European history-AP, French, French as a second language, French-AP, geometry, German, German literature, guitar, health, history, journalism, lab science, Latin, mathematics, mathematics-AP, meteorology, music, personal finance, photo shop, photography, physical education, physics, physics-AP, pre-calculus, public speaking, religion, social studies, Spanish, Spanish-AP, technical drawing, theology, U.S. government and politics-AP, U.S. history-AP, Web site design, world history, world literature, writing.
Graduation Requirements Arts and fine arts (art, music, dance, drama), career education, computer science, English, foreign language, lab science, mathematics, physical education (includes health), religion (includes Bible studies and theology), science, social studies (includes history). Community service is required.
Special Academic Programs 33 Advanced Placement exams for which test preparation is offered; honors section; independent study; study at local college for college credit; academic accommodation for the gifted.
College Admission Counseling 197 students graduated in 2010; 194 went to college, including Kean University; Ramapo College of New Jersey; Rutgers, The State University of New Jersey, Rutgers College; Syracuse University; The University of Scranton. Other: 3 entered military service. Mean SAT critical reading: 554, mean SAT math: 571, mean SAT writing: 544.
Student Life Upper grades have specified standards of dress, student council, honor system. Discipline rests primarily with faculty. Attendance at religious services is required.
Summer Programs Remediation, enrichment, advancement, sports, computer instruction programs offered; session focuses on remediation and enrichment; held on campus; accepts boys and girls; open to students from other schools. 205 students usually enrolled. 2011 schedule: June to July. Application deadline: June.

Tuition and Aid Day student tuition: $10,900. Tuition installment plan (FACTS Tuition Payment Plan, monthly payment plans, individually arranged payment plans). Merit scholarship grants, need-based scholarship grants available. In 2010–11, 10% of upper-school students received aid; total upper-school merit-scholarship money awarded: $150,000. Total amount of financial aid awarded in 2010–11: $250,000.
Admissions Traditional secondary-level entrance grade is 9. For fall 2010, 400 students applied for upper-level admission, 280 were accepted, 225 enrolled. High School Placement Test required. Deadline for receipt of application materials: none. No application fee required. On-campus interview recommended.
Athletics Interscholastic: baseball, basketball, bowling, cross-country running, football, golf, ice hockey, indoor track & field, lacrosse, soccer, swimming and diving, tennis, track and field, volleyball, winter (indoor) track; intramural: crew, flag football, Frisbee, skiing (downhill), snowboarding, strength & conditioning, ultimate Frisbee, volleyball, weight lifting, weight training. 3 PE instructors, 41 coaches, 1 athletic trainer.
Computers Computers are regularly used in animation, computer applications, desktop publishing, desktop publishing, ESL, drawing and design, graphic design, graphics, journalism, lab/keyboard, mathematics, news writing, newspaper, photography, publications, publishing, science, technical drawing, technology, Web site design, word processing, yearbook classes. Computer network features include on-campus library services, online commercial services, Internet access, Internet filtering or blocking technology. Students grades are available online. The school has a published electronic and media policy.
Contact Mr. Thomas Bacsik '06, Admissions Director. 732-549-7600 Ext. 221. Fax: 732-549-0282. E-mail: admissions@stjoes.org. Web site: www.stjoes.org.

ST. JOSEPH'S PREPARATORY SCHOOL
1733 Girard Avenue
Philadelphia, Pennsylvania 19130
Head of School: Rev. George W. Bur, SJ
General Information Boys' day college-preparatory, arts, and religious studies school, affiliated with Roman Catholic Church. Grades 9–12. Founded: 1851. Setting: urban. 7-acre campus. 3 buildings on campus. Approved or accredited by Jesuit Secondary Education Association, Middle States Association of Colleges and Schools, National Catholic Education Association, and Pennsylvania Department of Education. Member of National Association of Independent Schools. Endowment: $9 million. Total enrollment: 987. Upper school average class size: 22. Upper school faculty-student ratio: 1:16. Upper School students typically attend 5 days per week. The average school day consists of 6 hours.
Upper School Student Profile Grade 9: 275 students (275 boys); Grade 10: 254 students (254 boys); Grade 11: 236 students (236 boys); Grade 12: 222 students (222 boys). 95% of students are Roman Catholic.
Faculty School total: 75. In upper school: 60 men, 15 women; 65 have advanced degrees.
Subjects Offered Algebra, American history, American literature, anatomy, archaeology, art, biology, business, calculus, chemistry, classics, computer math, computer programming, computer science, driver education, earth science, economics, English, English literature, environmental science, ethics, European history, fine arts, French, geometry, German, government/civics, Greek, history, Latin, Mandarin, marine biology, mathematics, photography, physical education, physics, physiology, religion, science, social sciences, social studies, Spanish, speech, trigonometry, world history, world literature.
Graduation Requirements Arts and fine arts (art, music, dance, drama), classics, computer science, English, foreign language, mathematics, physical education (includes health), religion (includes Bible studies and theology), science, social sciences, social studies (includes history), Christian service hours in junior and senior year.
Special Academic Programs 17 Advanced Placement exams for which test preparation is offered; honors section; accelerated programs; independent study; study at local college for college credit; study abroad; academic accommodation for the gifted, the musically talented, and the artistically talented.
College Admission Counseling 235 students graduated in 2010; 234 went to college, including Fordham University; Georgetown University; Penn State University Park; Saint Joseph's University; Temple University; University of Pennsylvania. Other: 1 entered a postgraduate year. Mean SAT critical reading: 604, mean SAT math: 620, mean SAT writing: 617, mean combined SAT: 1841. 55% scored over 600 on SAT critical reading, 55% scored over 600 on SAT math, 55% scored over 600 on SAT writing, 55% scored over 1800 on combined SAT.
Student Life Upper grades have specified standards of dress, student council. Discipline rests primarily with faculty. Attendance at religious services is required.
Summer Programs Remediation, enrichment, art/fine arts programs offered; session focuses on pre-8th grade enrichment; held on campus; accepts boys and girls; open to students from other schools. 500 students usually enrolled. 2011 schedule: June 27 to July 27. Application deadline: none.
Tuition and Aid Day student tuition: $17,300. Tuition installment plan (monthly payment plans). Tuition reduction for siblings, merit scholarship grants, need-based scholarship grants, need-based loans, middle-income loans, paying campus jobs available. In 2010–11, 35% of upper-school students received aid; total upper-school merit-scholarship money awarded: $500,000. Total amount of financial aid awarded in 2010–11: $2,000,000.

Admissions Traditional secondary-level entrance grade is 9. For fall 2010, 645 students applied for upper-level admission, 310 were accepted, 275 enrolled. 3-R Achievement Test, High School Placement Test or High School Placement Test (closed version) from Scholastic Testing Service required. Deadline for receipt of application materials: November 12. Application fee required: $75. On-campus interview recommended.

Athletics Interscholastic: baseball, basketball, bowling, crew, cross-country running, football, Frisbee, golf, ice hockey, indoor track & field, lacrosse, rowing, rugby, soccer, squash, swimming and diving, tennis, track and field, ultimate Frisbee, winter (indoor) track, wrestling; intramural: basketball, flag football, juggling, martial arts, table tennis, volleyball, water polo. 35 coaches, 1 athletic trainer.

Computers Computers are regularly used in English, mathematics, science classes. Computer network features include on-campus library services, online commercial services, Internet access, wireless campus network, Internet filtering or blocking technology. Student e-mail accounts and computer access in designated common areas are available to students. Students grades are available online. The school has a published electronic and media policy.

Contact Jason M. Zazyczny, Director of Admission. 215-978-1958. Fax: 215-978-1920. E-mail: jzazyczny@sjprep.org. Web site: www.sjprep.org.

ST. JUDE'S SCHOOL

888 Trillium Drive

Kitchener, Ontario N2R 1K4, Canada

Head of School: Mr. Frederick T. Gore

General Information Coeducational day college-preparatory, arts, and bright learning disabled school; primarily serves underachievers. Grades 1–12. Founded: 1982. Setting: small town. Nearest major city is Toronto, Canada. 10-acre campus. 1 building on campus. Approved or accredited by Ontario Ministry of Education and Ontario Department of Education. Language of instruction: English. Total enrollment: 30. Upper school average class size: 6. Upper school faculty-student ratio: 1:6. There are 200 required school days per year for Upper School students. Upper School students typically attend 5 days per week. The average school day consists of 7 hours.

Upper School Student Profile Grade 6: 3 students (2 boys, 1 girl); Grade 7: 5 students (3 boys, 2 girls); Grade 8: 5 students (3 boys, 2 girls); Grade 9: 7 students (4 boys, 3 girls); Grade 10: 2 students (2 boys); Grade 11: 1 student (1 boy).

Faculty School total: 6. In upper school: 3 men, 3 women; 3 have advanced degrees.

Subjects Offered 20th century history, 20th century physics, 20th century world history, accounting, acting, adolescent issues, advanced chemistry, advanced math, algebra, analytic geometry, ancient history, ancient world history, ancient/medieval philosophy, anthropology, applied arts, art, art appreciation, art education, art history, basic skills, biology, bookkeeping, business education, business law, business mathematics, business studies, calculus, Canadian history, Canadian law, Canadian literature, career and personal planning, career education, chemistry, civics, college counseling, communication skills, computer literacy, computer science, computer skills, computer studies, discrete mathematics, dramatic arts, drawing and design, earth and space science, ecology, ecology, environmental systems, economics, economics and history, English, English literature, environmental studies, ESL, family studies, fencing, finite math, French as a second language, general science, geography, health, health education, history, honors algebra, honors English, honors geometry, independent study, intro to computers, keyboarding, law, law studies, marketing, media studies, modern Western civilization, modern world history, philosophy, physical education, physical fitness, physics-AP, remedial study skills, remedial/makeup course work, science, science and technology, society, politics and law, sociology, Spanish, study skills, visual arts, Western philosophy, world issues.

Graduation Requirements Ontario requirements.

Special Academic Programs Remedial reading and/or remedial writing; remedial math; programs in English, mathematics, general development for dyslexic students; special instructional classes for students with learning disabilities, Attention Deficit Disorder, and dyslexia; ESL (2 students enrolled).

College Admission Counseling 5 students graduated in 2010; all went to college, including University of Waterloo; Wilfrid Laurier University.

Student Life Upper grades have uniform requirement, student council, honor system. Discipline rests primarily with faculty.

Summer Programs Session focuses on English and math; held on campus; accepts boys and girls; open to students from other schools. 15 students usually enrolled. 2011 schedule: July 1 to July 30. Application deadline: June 1.

Tuition and Aid Day student tuition: CAN$16,900. Tuition installment plan (monthly payment plans, individually arranged payment plans).

Admissions For fall 2010, 5 students applied for upper-level admission, 5 were accepted, 5 enrolled. Academic Profile Tests, achievement tests and Woodcock-Johnson Educational Evaluation, WISC III required. Deadline for receipt of application materials: none. No application fee required. Interview required.

Athletics Interscholastic: synchronized swimming (girls); coed interscholastic: basketball, bowling, cross-country running, fencing, golf; coed intramural: badminton, ball hockey, baseball, basketball, bowling, cross-country running, curling, fencing, fitness, floor hockey, golf, martial arts. 2 PE instructors.

Computers Computers are regularly used in all classes. Computer network features include Internet access, Internet filtering or blocking technology.

Contact Frederick T. Gore, Director of Education. 519-888-0807. Fax: 519-888-0316. E-mail: director@stjudes.com. Web site: www.stjudes.com.

ST. LAWRENCE SEMINARY

301 Church Street

Mount Calvary, Wisconsin 53057

Head of School: Fr. Dennis Druggan, OFMCAP

General Information Boys' boarding college-preparatory and religious studies school, affiliated with Roman Catholic Church. Grades 9–12. Founded: 1860. Setting: rural. Nearest major city is Milwaukee. Students are housed in single-sex dormitories. 150-acre campus. 11 buildings on campus. Approved or accredited by National Catholic Education Association, North Central Association of Colleges and Schools, and Wisconsin Department of Education. Total enrollment: 200. Upper school average class size: 17. Upper school faculty-student ratio: 1:10. The average school day consists of 7 hours and 25 minutes.

Upper School Student Profile Grade 9: 47 students (47 boys); Grade 10: 55 students (55 boys); Grade 11: 52 students (52 boys); Grade 12: 47 students (47 boys). 100% of students are boarding students. 30% are state residents. 16 states are represented in upper school student body. 14% are international students. International students from India, Mali, Philippines, Republic of Korea, Saudi Arabia, and Viet Nam; 4 other countries represented in student body. 100% of students are Roman Catholic.

Faculty School total: 26. In upper school: 19 men, 6 women; 10 have advanced degrees; 7 reside on campus.

Subjects Offered Accounting, algebra, American history, American literature, art, biology, business, business law, calculus, chemistry, classical studies, computer science, English, English literature, fine arts, geometry, German, government/civics, health, health and wellness, humanities, industrial arts, lab/keyboard, Latin, literary genres, mathematics, mechanical drawing, music, physical education, physics, psychology, religion, science, socioeconomic problems, Spanish, theology, trigonometry, world history, world literature.

Graduation Requirements Arts and fine arts (art, music, dance, drama), business skills (includes word processing), computer science, English, foreign language, health education, humanities, mathematics, physical education (includes health), religion (includes Bible studies and theology), science, social studies (includes history), study skills, Ministry hours.

Special Academic Programs Study at local college for college credit.

College Admission Counseling 46 students graduated in 2009; 45 went to college, including Marquette University; Saint Xavier University; University of Chicago; University of Dallas; University of Minnesota, Duluth; University of Wisconsin–Madison. Other: 1 entered military service. Median SAT critical reading: 550, median SAT math: 600, median SAT writing: 540, median combined SAT: 1630, median composite ACT: 23. 10% scored over 600 on SAT critical reading, 50% scored over 600 on SAT math, 20% scored over 600 on SAT writing, 30% scored over 1800 on combined SAT, 23% scored over 26 on composite ACT.

Student Life Upper grades have specified standards of dress, student council, honor system. Discipline rests primarily with faculty. Attendance at religious services is required.

Tuition and Aid 7-day tuition and room/board: $9000. Tuition installment plan (monthly payment plans, individually arranged payment plans). Need-based scholarship grants available. In 2009–10, 73% of upper-school students received aid. Total amount of financial aid awarded in 2009–10: $778,110.

Admissions Traditional secondary-level entrance grade is 9. For fall 2009, 77 students applied for upper-level admission, 65 were accepted, 57 enrolled. 3-R Achievement Test and any standardized test required. Deadline for receipt of application materials: May 31. Application fee required: $25. Interview recommended.

Athletics Interscholastic: baseball, basketball, cross-country running, soccer, tennis, track and field, wrestling; intramural: basketball, billiards, bowling, floor hockey, Frisbee, handball, kickball, outdoor activities, outdoor recreation, physical fitness, physical training, racquetball, skiing (downhill), softball, table tennis, tennis, volleyball, wallyball, weight lifting, winter soccer. 3 PE instructors, 8 coaches, 1 athletic trainer.

Computers Computers are regularly used in accounting, business education, classics, creative writing, drafting, economics, English, keyboarding, mathematics, psychology, science, typing, writing, yearbook classes. Computer network features include on-campus library services, Internet access, Internet filtering or blocking technology. Campus intranet, student e-mail accounts, and computer access in designated common areas are available to students. The school has a published electronic and media policy.

Contact Ms. Mary Patricia Voell, Director of Admissions. 920-753-7522. Fax: 920-753-7507. E-mail: mvoell@stlawrence.edu. Web site: www.stlawrence.edu.

SAINT LOUIS PRIORY SCHOOL

500 South Mason Road

St. Louis, Missouri 63141

Head of School: Rev. Michael Brunner, OSB

General Information Boys' day college-preparatory and religious studies school, affiliated with Roman Catholic Church. Grades 7–12. Founded: 1955. Setting: suburban. 150-acre campus. 9 buildings on campus. Approved or accredited by Independent Schools Association of the Central States. Member of National Association of Independent Schools and Educational Records Bureau. Endowment: $20 million. Total enrollment: 424. Upper school average class size: 17. Upper school faculty-student ratio: 1:8. There are 166 required school days per year for Upper School students. Upper School students typically attend 5 days per week. The average school day consists of 7 hours and 1 minutes.

Upper School Student Profile Grade 9: 67 students (67 boys); Grade 10: 64 students (64 boys); Grade 11: 68 students (68 boys); Grade 12: 59 students (59 boys). 85% of students are Roman Catholic.

Faculty School total: 57. In upper school: 43 men, 14 women; 44 have advanced degrees.

Subjects Offered Advanced biology, Advanced Placement courses, algebra, American history, American literature, ancient world history, art, art history, astronomy, baseball, basketball, Bible studies, biology, biology-AP, calculus, calculus-AP, calligraphy, Catholic belief and practice, chemistry, chemistry-AP, Chinese literature, Chinese studies, Christian doctrine, Civil War, civil war history, classical civilization, community service, comparative government and politics-AP, computer applications, computer math, computer programming, computer programming-AP, computer science, creative writing, critical studies in film, drama, dramatic arts, earth science, ecology, ecology, environmental systems, economics, English, English literature, environmental science, environmental science-AP, ethics, European history, European history-AP, expository writing, fine arts, foreign language, French, French language-AP, general science, geography, geometry, government/civics, grammar, Greek, health, history, history-AP, honors geometry, integrated science, Japanese studies, Latin, mathematics, media arts, media communications, medieval/Renaissance history, modern European history-AP, moral theology, music, music theory, music theory-AP, peace and justice, philosophy, photography, physical education, physics, poetry, pre-calculus, probability and statistics, psychology, religion, science, senior seminar, sexuality, Shakespeare, social justice, social studies, Spanish, Spanish language-AP, speech, sports, stained glass, statistics-AP, studio art, theater, theater arts, theology, track and field, trigonometry, U.S. government and politics-AP, U.S. history-AP, visual arts, vocal music, women in literature, world history, world literature, world religions, wrestling, writing.

Graduation Requirements Arts and fine arts (art, music, dance, drama), classical language, computer science, English, foreign language, mathematics, physical education (includes health), religion (includes Bible studies and theology), science, senior thesis, social studies (includes history), service projects, sports requirements (every season of every year).

Special Academic Programs 16 Advanced Placement exams for which test preparation is offered; honors section; independent study; study at local college for college credit; academic accommodation for the gifted.

College Admission Counseling 62 students graduated in 2009; all went to college, including Boston College; Marquette University; University of Missouri; University of Notre Dame; Vanderbilt University; Washington University in St. Louis. Mean SAT critical reading: 641, mean SAT math: 660, mean SAT writing: 636, mean combined SAT: 1937, mean composite ACT: 30. 71% scored over 600 on SAT critical reading, 75% scored over 600 on SAT math, 70% scored over 600 on SAT writing, 87% scored over 26 on composite ACT.

Student Life Upper grades have specified standards of dress, student council, honor system. Discipline rests primarily with faculty. Attendance at religious services is required.

Tuition and Aid Day student tuition: $17,280. Tuition installment plan (FACTS Tuition Payment Plan, monthly payment plans, individually arranged payment plans). Need-based scholarship grants available. In 2009–10, 25% of upper-school students received aid. Total amount of financial aid awarded in 2009–10: $1,100,000.

Admissions ISEE required. Deadline for receipt of application materials: January 22. Application fee required: $40. Interview required.

Athletics Interscholastic: baseball, basketball, cross-country running, football, Frisbee, golf, ice hockey, rugby, soccer, strength & conditioning, tennis, track and field, ultimate Frisbee; intramural: cross-country running, football, Frisbee, indoor soccer, jogging, physical fitness, racquetball, soccer, softball, strength & conditioning, tennis, track and field, weight training. 2 coaches, 1 athletic trainer.

Computers Computers are regularly used in all academic, English, foreign language, mathematics, science classes. Computer network features include on-campus library services, online commercial services, Internet access, wireless campus network, Internet filtering or blocking technology. Campus intranet and student e-mail accounts are available to students. Students grades are available online. The school has a published electronic and media policy.

Contact Rev. Deacon Thomas O. Mulvihill Jr., Director of Admission. 314-434-3690 Ext. 151. Fax: 314-576-7088. E-mail: tmulvihill@priory.org. Web site: www.priory.org/.

SAINT LOUIS UNIVERSITY HIGH SCHOOL

4970 Oakland Avenue
St. Louis, Missouri 63110
Head of School: Mr. David J. Laughlin

General Information college-preparatory school, affiliated with Roman Catholic Church (Jesuit order). Founded: 1818. Setting: urban. 34-acre campus. 2 buildings on campus. Approved or accredited by Jesuit Secondary Education Association, North Central Association of Colleges and Schools, and Missouri Department of Education. Upper school average class size: 21. Upper school faculty-student ratio: 1:12. There

are 167 required school days per year for Upper School students. Upper School students typically attend 5 days per week. The average school day consists of 7 hours and 10 minutes.

Upper School Student Profile 94% of students are Roman Catholic Church (Jesuit order).

Faculty School total: 90. In upper school: 70 men, 20 women; 86 have advanced degrees.

Special Academic Programs 20 Advanced Placement exams for which test preparation is offered; honors section; study abroad.

College Admission Counseling 260 students graduated in 2009; all went to college, including Loyola University New Orleans; Saint Louis University; Truman State University; University of Dayton; University of Missouri; University of Notre Dame. Median SAT critical reading: 660, median SAT math: 680, median SAT writing: 640, median combined SAT: 1990, median composite ACT: 30. 70.5% scored over 600 on SAT critical reading, 83.2% scored over 600 on SAT math, 65.3% scored over 600 on SAT writing, 80% scored over 1800 on combined SAT, 83.2% scored over 26 on composite ACT.

Student Life Upper grades have specified standards of dress, student council, honor system. Discipline rests primarily with faculty. Attendance at religious services is required.

Tuition and Aid Day student tuition: $11,750. Tuition installment plan (FACTS Tuition Payment Plan, individually arranged payment plans, quarterly, semi-annually). Need-based scholarship grants available. In 2009–10, 25% of upper-school students received aid. Total amount of financial aid awarded in 2009–10: $1,625,000.

Admissions Traditional secondary-level entrance grade is 9. For fall 2009, 320 students applied for upper-level admission, 280 were accepted, 277 enrolled. Deadline for receipt of application materials: November. No application fee required. Interview required.

Athletics Interscholastic: baseball (boys), basketball (b), cross-country running (b), diving (b), football (b), golf (b), ice hockey (b), lacrosse (b), racquetball (b), riflery (b), rugby (b), soccer (b), swimming and diving (b), tennis (b), track and field (b), volleyball (b), water polo (b), wrestling (b); intramural: bicycling (b), billiards (b), Circus (b), climbing (b), outdoor adventure (b), table tennis (b), ultimate Frisbee (b).

Computers Computer resources include on-campus library services, online commercial services, Internet access, wireless campus network, Internet filtering or blocking technology. Campus intranet, student e-mail accounts, and computer access in designated common areas are available to students. Students grades are available online.

Contact Mr. Craig Hannick, Director of Admission and Financial Aid. 314-531-0330 Ext. 298. E-mail: channick@sluh.org. Web site: www.sluh.org.

SAINT LUCY'S PRIORY HIGH SCHOOL

655 West Sierra Madre Avenue
Glendora, California 91741-1997
Head of School: Sr. Monica Collins, OSB

General Information Girls' day college-preparatory, arts, religious studies, and technology school, affiliated with Roman Catholic Church. Grades 9–12. Founded: 1962. Setting: suburban. Nearest major city is Pasadena. 14-acre campus. 4 buildings on campus. Approved or accredited by European Council of International Schools, The College Board, Western Association of Schools and Colleges, Western Catholic Education Association, and California Department of Education. Endowment: $2 million. Total enrollment: 696. Upper school average class size: 20. Upper school faculty-student ratio: 1:20. There are 182 required school days per year for Upper School students. Upper School students typically attend 5 days per week. The average school day consists of 6 hours and 45 minutes.

Upper School Student Profile Grade 9: 165 students (165 girls); Grade 10: 187 students (187 girls); Grade 11: 170 students (170 girls); Grade 12: 174 students (174 girls). 80% of students are Roman Catholic.

Faculty School total: 38. In upper school: 6 men, 31 women; 15 have advanced degrees.

Subjects Offered Adolescent issues, advanced math, algebra, art, art appreciation, ASB Leadership, athletics, Bible studies, biology, biology-AP, calculus, calculus-AP, calligraphy, chemistry, child development, Christian ethics, Christian scripture, church history, commercial art, computer art, creative dance, creative writing, dance, drama, drawing, early childhood, economics, English, English language and composition-AP, English literature, English literature-AP, ethics, European history-AP, film studies, French, geometry, health, health education, Hebrew scripture, journalism, kinesiology, library assistant, literary magazine, mechanical drawing, media arts, meditation, modern European history-AP, moral and social development, moral theology, musical productions, painting, physical education, physical science, physics, physiology, psychology, religion, sculpture, sewing, Spanish, Spanish-AP, theater production, trigonometry, U.S. government, U.S. government and politics-AP, U.S. history, U.S. history-AP, voice, world history, yearbook.

Graduation Requirements Arts and fine arts (art, music, dance, drama), English, foreign language, mathematics, physical education (includes health), religion (includes Bible studies and theology), science, social sciences, social studies (includes history).

Special Academic Programs Advanced Placement exam preparation; honors section.

College Admission Counseling 195 students graduated in 2010; all went to college, including Azusa Pacific University; California State Polytechnic University, Pomona; Loyola Marymount University; Mount St. Mary's College; University of California, Irvine; University of California, Riverside. Mean SAT critical reading: 564, mean SAT math: 532, mean SAT writing: 562, mean composite ACT: 25. 40% scored over 600 on SAT critical reading, 20% scored over 600 on SAT math, 35% scored over 600 on SAT writing, 46% scored over 26 on composite ACT.

Student Life Upper grades have uniform requirement, student council. Discipline rests equally with students and faculty. Attendance at religious services is required.

Summer Programs Remediation programs offered; session focuses on remediation; held on campus; accepts girls; not open to students from other schools. 115 students usually enrolled. 2011 schedule: June 20 to July 15. Application deadline: June 1.

Tuition and Aid Day student tuition: $7100. Tuition installment plan (monthly payment plans, individually arranged payment plans, quarterly payment plan). Tuition reduction for siblings, merit scholarship grants, need-based scholarship grants available. In 2010–11, 5% of upper-school students received aid; total upper-school merit-scholarship money awarded: $15,000. Total amount of financial aid awarded in 2010–11: $90,000.

Admissions STS required. Deadline for receipt of application materials: January 21. Application fee required: $75. On-campus interview required.

Athletics Interscholastic: basketball, cross-country running, drill team, soccer, softball, swimming and diving, tennis, track and field, volleyball, water polo; intramural: badminton, basketball, cheering, dance squad, dance team, physical fitness, soccer, softball. 2 PE instructors, 36 coaches, 1 athletic trainer.

Computers Computers are regularly used in art, drawing and design, English, graphic arts, history, journalism, literary magazine, mathematics, media production, music, psychology, science, yearbook classes. Computer resources include Internet access, wireless campus network, Internet filtering or blocking technology. Campus intranet and computer access in designated common areas are available to students. Students grades are available online.

Contact Mrs. Irma Esparza, Secretary. 626-335-3322. Fax: 626-335-4373. Web site: www.stlucys.com.

ST. MARGARET'S EPISCOPAL SCHOOL

31641 La Novia Avenue
San Juan Capistrano, California 92675
Head of School: Mr. Marcus D. Hurlbut

General Information Coeducational day college-preparatory, arts, religious studies, and technology school, affiliated with Episcopal Church. Grades PS–12. Founded: 1979. Setting: suburban. Nearest major city is Los Angeles/San Diego. 21-acre campus. 6 buildings on campus. Approved or accredited by California Association of Independent Schools, National Association of Episcopal Schools, Western Association of Schools and Colleges, and California Department of Education. Member of National Association of Independent Schools. Endowment: $2.4 million. Total enrollment: 1,228. Upper school average class size: 14. Upper school faculty-student ratio: 1:7. There are 176 required school days per year for Upper School students. Upper School students typically attend 5 days per week. The average school day consists of 7 hours and 15 minutes.

Upper School Student Profile Grade 9: 105 students (57 boys, 48 girls); Grade 10: 114 students (52 boys, 62 girls); Grade 11: 108 students (50 boys, 58 girls); Grade 12: 104 students (51 boys, 53 girls). 13% of students are members of Episcopal Church.

Faculty School total: 62. In upper school: 20 men, 21 women; 23 have advanced degrees.

Subjects Offered Algebra, American history, American literature, anatomy and physiology, anthropology, art, art history, art history-AP, art-AP, astronomy, Bible studies, biology, biology-AP, calculus, calculus-AP, chemistry, chemistry-AP, Chinese, community service, computer math, computer programming, computer science, computer science-AP, creative writing, drama, economics, English, English language and composition-AP, English language-AP, English literature, English literature and composition-AP, environmental science, environmental science-AP, ethics, European history, expository writing, fine arts, French, French language-AP, French literature-AP, French-AP, geography, geometry, government-AP, government/civics, history, history-AP, human development, Japanese, Japanese literature, journalism, Latin, Latin-AP, marine science, mathematics, music, music theory-AP, philosophy, physical education, physics, physics-AP, religion, science, social sciences, social studies, Spanish, Spanish language-AP, Spanish literature-AP, Spanish-AP, speech, statistics-AP, theater, trigonometry, world history, world history-AP, world literature, world religions, writing.

Graduation Requirements Arts and fine arts (art, music, dance, drama), computer science, English, foreign language, mathematics, physical education (includes health), religion (includes Bible studies and theology), science, social sciences, social studies (includes history). Community service is required.

Special Academic Programs Advanced Placement exam preparation; honors section; independent study; academic accommodation for the gifted, the musically talented, and the artistically talented.

College Admission Counseling 96 students graduated in 2010; all went to college, including New York University; Northwestern University; Pitzer College; University of California, Berkeley; University of Southern California; University of Washington.

Mean SAT critical reading: 610, mean SAT math: 621, mean SAT writing: 638, mean combined SAT: 1869, mean composite ACT: 27.

Student Life Upper grades have specified standards of dress, student council, honor system. Discipline rests equally with students and faculty. Attendance at religious services is required.

Summer Programs Enrichment, advancement, sports, art/fine arts programs offered; session focuses on academic enrichment; held on campus; accepts boys and girls; open to students from other schools. 217 students usually enrolled. 2011 schedule: June 28 to August 6.

Tuition and Aid Day student tuition: $22,100. Tuition installment plan (monthly payment plans). Need-based scholarship grants available. In 2010–11, 26% of upper-school students received aid. Total amount of financial aid awarded in 2010–11: $1,929,690.

Admissions Traditional secondary-level entrance grade is 9. For fall 2010, 62 students applied for upper-level admission, 54 were accepted, 42 enrolled. ISEE required. Deadline for receipt of application materials: February 1. Application fee required: $75. Interview required.

Athletics Interscholastic: aquatics (boys, girls), basketball (b,g), cheering (g), cross-country running (b,g), equestrian sports (b,g), football (b), golf (b,g), lacrosse (b,g), soccer (b,g), swimming and diving (b,g), tennis (b,g), track and field (b,g), volleyball (b,g); coed interscholastic: baseball. 1 PE instructor, 7 coaches, 1 athletic trainer.

Computers Computers are regularly used in English, foreign language, history, mathematics, science, technology classes. Computer network features include on-campus library services, Internet access, wireless campus network, Internet filtering or blocking technology. Campus intranet, student e-mail accounts, and computer access in designated common areas are available to students. Students grades are available online. The school has a published electronic and media policy.

Contact Mrs. Phoebe F. Larson, Director of Admission and Financial Aid. 949-661-0108 Ext. 251. Fax: 949-240-1748. E-mail: phoebe.larson@smes.org. Web site: www.smes.org.

ST. MARGARET'S SCHOOL

444 Water Lane
PO Box 158
Tappahannock, Virginia 22560
Head of School: Margaret R. Broad

General Information Girls' boarding and day college-preparatory, arts, and religious studies school, affiliated with Episcopal Church. Grades 8–12. Founded: 1921. Setting: small town. Nearest major city is Richmond. Students are housed in single-sex dormitories. 51-acre campus. 9 buildings on campus. Approved or accredited by Southern Association of Colleges and Schools, Virginia Association of Independent Schools, and Virginia Department of Education. Member of National Association of Independent Schools and Secondary School Admission Test Board. Endowment: $5.7 million. Total enrollment: 123. Upper school average class size: 8. Upper school faculty-student ratio: 1:6.

Upper School Student Profile Grade 8: 11 students (11 girls); Grade 9: 24 students (24 girls); Grade 10: 31 students (31 girls); Grade 11: 24 students (24 girls); Grade 12: 33 students (33 girls). 80% of students are boarding students. 39% are state residents. 13 states are represented in upper school student body. 28% are international students. International students from China, Japan, Mexico, Republic of Korea, and Viet Nam; 5 other countries represented in student body. 25% are members of Episcopal Church.

Faculty School total: 34. In upper school: 8 men, 22 women; 16 have advanced degrees; 30 reside on campus.

Subjects Offered Algebra, American literature, anatomy and physiology, ancient history, art, art history, biology, biology-AP, British literature, calculus, calculus-AP, ceramics, chemistry, chorus, community service, computer science, conceptual physics, creative writing, drama, driver education, ecology, English, English-AP, ESL, European history, finance, fine arts, French, French-AP, geography, geometry, government/civics, health, history, history-AP, illustration, journalism, Latin, leadership, mathematics, music, music history, painting, photography, physical education, physics, piano, pre-algebra, religion, science, social studies, Spanish, U.S. government, world history, world literature, writing.

Graduation Requirements Arts and fine arts (art, music, dance, drama), computer science, English, foreign language, history, mathematics, physical education (includes health), religion (includes Bible studies and theology), science. Community service is required.

Special Academic Programs Advanced Placement exam preparation; honors section; independent study; study abroad; ESL (29 students enrolled).

College Admission Counseling 33 students graduated in 2010; 32 went to college, including Longwood University; Michigan State University; Randolph-Macon College; Rhode Island School of Design; University of Richmond. Other: 1 had other specific plans. Mean SAT critical reading: 533, mean SAT math: 573, mean SAT writing: 563, mean combined SAT: 1669.

Student Life Upper grades have uniform requirement, student council, honor system. Discipline rests equally with students and faculty. Attendance at religious services is required.

Tuition and Aid Day student tuition: $16,800; 7-day tuition and room/board: $43,200. Tuition installment plan (monthly payment plans, Pay in Full, 10-Month Plan). Need-based scholarship grants available. In 2010–11, 37% of upper-school students received aid. Total amount of financial aid awarded in 2010–11: $949,000.
Admissions Traditional secondary-level entrance grade is 9. For fall 2010, 86 students applied for upper-level admission, 75 were accepted, 46 enrolled. SSAT required. Deadline for receipt of application materials: none. Application fee required: $40. On-campus interview required.
Athletics Interscholastic: basketball, crew, cross-country running, field hockey, golf, indoor track & field, lacrosse, soccer, softball, swimming and diving, tennis, volleyball; intramural: ballet, canoeing/kayaking, crew, dance, fitness, fitness walking, horseback riding, kayaking, modern dance, outdoor activities, strength & conditioning, tennis, ultimate Frisbee, walking, weight training, yoga. 1 PE instructor, 7 coaches, 1 athletic trainer.
Computers Computers are regularly used in English, foreign language, history, journalism, science, yearbook classes. Computer network features include on-campus library services, online commercial services, Internet access, wireless campus network, Internet filtering or blocking technology. Campus intranet, student e-mail accounts, and computer access in designated common areas are available to students. The school has a published electronic and media policy.
Contact Kimberly McDowell, Assistant Head, External Affairs/Director of Admission. 804-443-3357. Fax: 804-443-6781. E-mail: admit@sms.com. Web site: www.sms.org.

ST. MARGARET'S SCHOOL
1080 Lucas Avenue
Victoria, British Columbia V8X 3P7, Canada
Head of School: Linda McGregor
General Information Girls' boarding and day college-preparatory, general academic, arts, technology, and ESL school. Boarding grades 7–12, day grades JK–12. Founded: 1908. Setting: suburban. Students are housed in single-sex dormitories. 22-acre campus. 10 buildings on campus. Approved or accredited by Standards in Excellence And Learning (SEAL), The Association of Boarding Schools, and British Columbia Department of Education. Language of instruction: English. Total enrollment: 346. Upper school average class size: 18. Upper school faculty-student ratio: 1:8.
Upper School Student Profile 30% of students are boarding students. 70% are province residents. 6 provinces are represented in upper school student body. 30% are international students. International students from China, Hong Kong, Japan, Mexico, Republic of Korea, and Taiwan; 6 other countries represented in student body.
Faculty School total: 38. In upper school: 7 men, 30 women; 12 have advanced degrees.
Subjects Offered Advanced Placement courses, algebra, applied skills, art, biology, calculus, Canadian geography, Canadian history, career and personal planning, chemistry, Chinese, choir, communications, comparative civilizations, computer science, creative writing, dance, drama, English, English literature, ESL, fine arts, French, geography, history, information technology, Japanese, journalism, law, leadership, Mandarin, mathematics, music, music appreciation, outdoor education, performing arts, photography, physical education, physics, science, social studies, Spanish, theater, Western civilization, writing.
Graduation Requirements Applied skills, arts and fine arts (art, music, dance, drama), English, foreign language, mathematics, science, social studies (includes history).
Special Academic Programs Advanced Placement exam preparation; ESL (38 students enrolled).
College Admission Counseling 44 students graduated in 2009; 42 went to college, including McGill University; Simon Fraser University; The University of British Columbia; University of Toronto; University of Victoria; University of Waterloo. Other: 2 had other specific plans.
Student Life Upper grades have uniform requirement, student council. Discipline rests primarily with faculty.
Tuition and Aid Day student tuition: CAN$6054–CAN$16,301; 7-day tuition and room/board: CAN$31,831–CAN$39,411. Tuition installment plan (Insured Tuition Payment Plan, monthly payment plans). Tuition reduction for siblings, bursaries, merit scholarship grants, need-based scholarship grants available. In 2009–10, 17% of upper-school students received aid; total upper-school merit-scholarship money awarded: CAN$30,000. Total amount of financial aid awarded in 2009–10: CAN$70,000.
Admissions Traditional secondary-level entrance grade is 7. For fall 2009, 115 students applied for upper-level admission, 97 were accepted, 92 enrolled. School's own exam required. Deadline for receipt of application materials: none. Application fee required. Interview required.
Athletics Interscholastic: aerobics/dance, aquatics, badminton, basketball, cross-country running, dance, field hockey, fitness, rowing, running, soccer, swimming and diving, synchronized swimming, track and field, volleyball; intramural: aerobics, aerobics/dance, alpine skiing, aquatics, backpacking, badminton, baseball, basketball, bicycling, canoeing/kayaking, climbing, cooperative games, cross-country running, dance, equestrian sports, field hockey, figure skating, fitness, floor hockey, Frisbee, golf, gymnastics, hiking/backpacking, horseback riding, ice skating, indoor soccer, jogging, jump rope, kayaking, martial arts, modern dance, mountain biking, ocean

paddling, outdoor activities, paddle tennis, physical fitness, rock climbing, ropes courses, rugby, running, sailing, skiing (cross-country), skiing (downhill), snow-boarding, soccer, softball, squash, strength & conditioning, surfing, swimming and diving, table tennis, tennis, track and field, ultimate Frisbee, volleyball, wallyball, weight training, wilderness, wilderness survival, yoga. 4 PE instructors, 3 coaches, 1 athletic trainer.
Computers Computers are regularly used in career exploration, English, ESL, foreign language, French, history, journalism, mathematics, science classes. Computer network features include Internet access, wireless campus network, Internet filtering or blocking technology. Student e-mail accounts and computer access in designated common areas are available to students.
Contact Mrs. Kathy Charleson, Director of Admissions. 250-479-7171. Fax: 250-479-8976. E-mail: stmarg@stmarg.ca. Web site: www.stmarg.ca.

ST. MARK'S HIGH SCHOOL
2501 Pike Creek Road
Wilmington, Delaware 19808
Head of School: Mark J. Freund
General Information Coeducational day college-preparatory, arts, business, religious studies, and technology school, affiliated with Roman Catholic Church. Grades 9–12. Founded: 1969. Setting: suburban. Nearest major city is Philadelphia, PA. 50-acre campus. 3 buildings on campus. Approved or accredited by Middle States Association of Colleges and Schools, National Catholic Education Association, and Delaware Department of Education. Endowment: $3 million. Total enrollment: 1,360. Upper school average class size: 24. Upper school faculty-student ratio: 1:15. Upper School students typically attend 5 days per week.
Upper School Student Profile Grade 9: 293 students (147 boys, 146 girls); Grade 10: 313 students (155 boys, 158 girls); Grade 11: 360 students (170 boys, 190 girls); Grade 12: 380 students (180 boys, 200 girls). 80% of students are Roman Catholic.
Faculty School total: 110. In upper school: 40 men, 70 women; 60 have advanced degrees.
Subjects Offered Advanced Placement courses, art, business, computer science, drama, driver education, English, family and consumer science, fine arts, French, general science, German, history, Italian, mathematics, media, music, physical education, reading, religion, science, social studies, Spanish, theater.
Graduation Requirements Arts and fine arts (art, music, dance, drama), English, health education, mathematics, physical education (includes health), religion (includes Bible studies and theology), science, social studies (includes history).
Special Academic Programs Advanced Placement exam preparation; honors section; study at local college for college credit; study abroad; academic accommodation for the gifted; remedial reading and/or remedial writing; special instructional classes for students with learning challenges.
College Admission Counseling 380 students graduated in 2009; 360 went to college, including Penn State University Park; Saint Joseph's University; Towson University; University of Delaware; University of Maryland, College Park; York College of Pennsylvania. Mean SAT critical reading: 585, mean SAT math: 575. 33% scored over 600 on SAT critical reading, 33% scored over 600 on SAT math.
Student Life Upper grades have uniform requirement, student council. Discipline rests primarily with faculty. Attendance at religious services is required.
Tuition and Aid Day student tuition: $9200. Tuition installment plan (monthly payment plans). Merit scholarship grants, need-based scholarship grants, full academic scholarships for gifted students available. In 2009–10, 30% of upper-school students received aid; total upper-school merit-scholarship money awarded: $250,000. Total amount of financial aid awarded in 2009–10: $800,000.
Admissions Traditional secondary-level entrance grade is 9. For fall 2009, 420 students applied for upper-level admission, 395 were accepted, 303 enrolled. High School Placement Test or STS required. Deadline for receipt of application materials: none. Application fee required: $60.
Athletics Interscholastic: baseball (boys), basketball (b,g), crew (b,g), cross-country running (b,g), diving (b,g), field hockey (g), football (b), ice hockey (b), indoor track & field (b,g), lacrosse (b,g), soccer (b,g), softball (g), swimming and diving (b,g), tennis (b,g), track and field (b,g), volleyball (b), wrestling (b); coed interscholastic: golf, indoor hockey. 4 PE instructors, 10 coaches, 1 athletic trainer.
Computers Computers are regularly used in all academic classes. Computer network features include on-campus library services, online commercial services, Internet access, wireless campus network, Internet filtering or blocking technology, Power-School system for parents to monitor child's progress. Campus intranet and student e-mail accounts are available to students. Students grades are available online. The school has a published electronic and media policy.
Contact Thomas J. Lemon, Director of Admissions. 302-757-8723. Fax: 302-738-5132. E-mail: tlemon@stmarkshs.net. Web site: www.stmarkshs.net.

SAINT MARK'S SCHOOL
25 Marlborough Road
Southborough, Massachusetts 01772
Head of School: Mr. John Warren
General Information Coeducational boarding and day college-preparatory, arts, religious studies, technology, and classics, math school, affiliated with Episcopal

Church. Grades 9–12. Founded: 1865. Setting: suburban. Nearest major city is Boston. Students are housed in single-sex dormitories. 250-acre campus. 15 buildings on campus. Approved or accredited by New England Association of Schools and Colleges and Massachusetts Department of Education. Member of National Association of Independent Schools and Secondary School Admission Test Board. Endowment: $108 million. Total enrollment: 340. Upper school average class size: 12. Upper school faculty-student ratio: 1:5. There are 160 required school days per year for Upper School students. Upper School students typically attend 6 days per week. The average school day consists of 5 hours and 40 minutes.

Upper School Student Profile Grade 9: 73 students (41 boys, 32 girls); Grade 10: 88 students (45 boys, 43 girls); Grade 11: 86 students (47 boys, 39 girls); Grade 12: 93 students (53 boys, 40 girls). 78% of students are boarding students. 58% are state residents. 17 states are represented in upper school student body. 18% are international students. International students from Canada, China, Japan, Republic of Korea, Saudi Arabia, and Taiwan; 10 other countries represented in student body. 30% of students are members of Episcopal Church.

Faculty School total: 75. In upper school: 41 men, 34 women; 52 have advanced degrees; all reside on campus.

Subjects Offered 20th century history, Advanced Placement courses, algebra, American history, American literature, art, art history, biology, calculus, ceramics, chemistry, civil war history, computer math, computer science, computer science-AP, computer skills, computer studies, constitutional history of U.S., creative writing, DNA, drama, drama workshop, earth science, Eastern religion and philosophy, English, English literature, environmental science, ethics, European history, expository writing, fine arts, French, geography, geometry, German, government/civics, Greek, history, Latin, Latin-AP, logic, mathematics, music, music history, music theory, music theory-AP, music-AP, photography, physics, physiology, psychology, religion, science, social studies, Spanish, Spanish language-AP, Spanish literature, Spanish literature-AP, statistics, studio art, studio art-AP, theater, trigonometry, world history, world literature.

Graduation Requirements Arts and fine arts (art, music, dance, drama), English, foreign language, mathematics, religion (includes Bible studies and theology), science, social studies (includes history).

Special Academic Programs 23 Advanced Placement exams for which test preparation is offered; honors section; independent study; term-away projects; study abroad; academic accommodation for the gifted, the musically talented, and the artistically talented.

College Admission Counseling 86 students graduated in 2010; all went to college, including Colby College; Georgetown University; Massachusetts Institute of Technology; Tufts University; University of Pennsylvania; Villanova University. Median SAT critical reading: 635, median SAT math: 680, median SAT writing: 655, median combined SAT: 1970.

Student Life Upper grades have specified standards of dress, student council, honor system. Discipline rests equally with students and faculty. Attendance at religious services is required.

Tuition and Aid Day student tuition: $36,000; 7-day tuition and room/board: $45,100. Tuition installment plan (Key Tuition Payment Plan, monthly payment plans). Need-based scholarship grants available. In 2010–11, 28% of upper-school students received aid. Total amount of financial aid awarded in 2010–11: $3,500,000.

Admissions Traditional secondary-level entrance grade is 9. For fall 2010, 654 students applied for upper-level admission, 252 were accepted, 106 enrolled. SSAT and TOEFL required. Deadline for receipt of application materials: January 31. Application fee required: $50. Interview required.

Athletics Interscholastic: baseball (boys), basketball (b,g), crew (b,g), cross-country running (b,g), field hockey (g), Fives (b), football (b), golf (b,g), ice hockey (b,g), lacrosse (b,g), soccer (b,g), softball (g), squash (b,g), tennis (b,g), volleyball (g), wrestling (b); intramural: aerobics/dance (g), volleyball (b,g), weight lifting (b,g); coed interscholastic: dance; coed intramural: aerobics, aerobics/Nautilus, billiards, outdoor activities, yoga. 15 coaches, 2 athletic trainers.

Computers Computers are regularly used in English, foreign language, mathematics, science classes. Computer network features include on-campus library services, Internet access, wireless campus network, Internet filtering or blocking technology. Student e-mail accounts and computer access in designated common areas are available to students. The school has a published electronic and media policy.

Contact Anne E. Behnke, Director of Admission. 508-786-6000. Fax: 508-786-6120. E-mail: annebehnke@stmarksschool.org. Web site: www.stmarksschool.org.

ST. MARK'S SCHOOL OF TEXAS

10600 Preston Road
Dallas, Texas 75230-4000
Head of School: Mr. Arnold E. Holtberg

General Information Boys' day college-preparatory, arts, technology, and advanced placement school. Grades 1–12. Founded: 1906. Setting: urban. 40-acre campus. 13 buildings on campus. Approved or accredited by Independent Schools Association of the Southwest. Member of National Association of Independent Schools. Endowment: $90.3 million. Total enrollment: 854. Upper school average class size: 14. Upper school faculty-student ratio: 1:8. There are 175 required school days per year for Upper School students. Upper School students typically attend 5 days per week. The average school day consists of 7 hours and 55 minutes.

Upper School Student Profile Grade 9: 97 students (97 boys); Grade 10: 94 students (94 boys); Grade 11: 93 students (93 boys); Grade 12: 83 students (83 boys).

Faculty School total: 105. In upper school: 41 men, 18 women; 51 have advanced degrees.

HELPING BOYS BECOME GOOD MEN

For more than a century, St. Mark's School of Texas has provided boys with exceptional educational opportunities.

In every aspect of their lives, St. Mark's students are challenged to live out the School's motto: "Courage and Honor." Our goal is to prepare young men for responsible lives of service and leadership.

St. Mark's School of Texas does not discriminate in the administration of its admission and education policies on the basis of race, color, religion, sexual orientation, or national or ethnic origin.

St. Mark's School of Texas
10600 Preston Road
Dallas, Texas 75230-4047
www.smtexas.org
214.436.8700

St. Mark's School of Texas

Subjects Offered 3-dimensional art, acting, algebra, American history-AP, ancient world history, art, art history, astronomy, Basic programming, biology, biology-AP, calculus, calculus-AP, ceramics, chemistry, chemistry-AP, Chinese, choir, community service, computer programming, computer science, computer science-AP, concert band, creative writing, digital art, digital photography, DNA, DNA science lab, drama, drama workshop, economics, economics-AP, English, English literature and composition-AP, English literature-AP, environmental science-AP, European history, European history-AP, fine arts, geology, geometry, German-AP, history, honors English, honors geometry, independent study, Japanese, journalism, Latin, Latin-AP, macroeconomics-AP, mathematics, microeconomics-AP, modern European history-AP, modern world history, music, photography, physical education, physics, physics-AP, pottery, psychology, science, senior project, Spanish, Spanish language-AP, Spanish literature-AP, statistics-AP, studio art-AP, theater, trigonometry, U.S. history, video film production, woodworking, world history, world religions.

Graduation Requirements Arts and fine arts (art, music, dance, drama), English, foreign language, mathematics, physical education (includes health), science, social studies (includes history), senior exhibition. Community service is required.

Special Academic Programs Advanced Placement exam preparation; honors section; independent study; term-away projects; academic accommodation for the gifted.

College Admission Counseling 94 students graduated in 2010; all went to college, including Dartmouth College; Princeton University; Southern Methodist University; The University of Texas at Austin; University of Missouri; University of Southern California. Median SAT critical reading: 690, median SAT math: 750, median SAT writing: 700, median composite ACT: 33. 91% scored over 600 on SAT critical reading, 94% scored over 600 on SAT math, 85% scored over 600 on SAT writing, 98% scored over 26 on composite ACT.

Student Life Upper grades have uniform requirement, student council, honor system. Discipline rests primarily with faculty. Attendance at religious services is required.

Tuition and Aid Day student tuition: $23,020–$24,503. Tuition installment plan (Insured Tuition Payment Plan, financial aid student monthly payment plan). Need-based scholarship grants, tuition remission for sons of faculty and staff, need-based middle-income financial aid available. In 2010–11, 18% of upper-school students received aid. Total amount of financial aid awarded in 2010–11: $1,188,359.

Admissions Traditional secondary-level entrance grade is 9. For fall 2010, 88 students applied for upper-level admission, 18 were accepted, 15 enrolled. ISEE required. Deadline for receipt of application materials: January 10. Application fee required: $125. Interview required.

Athletics Interscholastic: backpacking, baseball, basketball, cheering, climbing, crew, cross-country running, diving, fencing, football, golf, hiking/backpacking, hockey, ice hockey, lacrosse, outdoor education, outdoor skills, physical fitness, physical training, soccer, strength & conditioning, swimming and diving, tennis, track and field, volleyball, wall climbing, water polo, weight training, wilderness, winter soccer, wrestling; intramural: basketball, bicycling, cooperative games, cross-country running, fitness, flag football, floor hockey, jump rope, kickball, lacrosse, physical fitness, physical training, soccer, softball, swimming and diving, table tennis, team handball, tennis, track and field, volleyball, water polo, weight training, winter soccer, wrestling. 8 PE instructors, 9 coaches, 2 athletic trainers.

Computers Computers are regularly used in English, foreign language, humanities, mathematics, science classes. Computer network features include on-campus library services, online commercial services, Internet access, wireless campus network, Internet filtering or blocking technology. Student e-mail accounts are available to students. The school has a published electronic and media policy.

Contact Mr. David P. Baker, Director of Admission and Financial Aid. 214-346-8700. Fax: 214-346-8701. E-mail: admission@smtexas.org. Web site: www.smtexas.org.

See Display on page 579 and Close-Up on page 832.

ST. MARTIN'S EPISCOPAL SCHOOL

225 Green Acres Road
Metairie, Louisiana 70003
Head of School: Rev. Walter J. Baer

General Information Coeducational day college-preparatory school, affiliated with Episcopal Church. Grades PK–12. Founded: 1947. Setting: suburban. Nearest major city is New Orleans. 18-acre campus. 13 buildings on campus. Approved or accredited by Independent Schools Association of the Southwest, National Association of Episcopal Schools, Southern Association of Colleges and Schools, Southwest Association of Episcopal Schools, The College Board, and Louisiana Department of Education. Member of National Association of Independent Schools. Endowment: $5.4 million. Total enrollment: 510. Upper school average class size: 17. Upper school faculty-student ratio: 1:8. There are 178 required school days per year for Upper School students. Upper School students typically attend 5 days per week. The average school day consists of 5 hours and 30 minutes.

Upper School Student Profile Grade 9: 67 students (38 boys, 29 girls); Grade 10: 58 students (32 boys, 26 girls); Grade 11: 54 students (33 boys, 21 girls); Grade 12: 42 students (19 boys, 23 girls). 13.5% of students are members of Episcopal Church.

Faculty School total: 62. In upper school: 12 men, 18 women; 16 have advanced degrees.

Subjects Offered Advanced chemistry, advanced math, Advanced Placement courses, advanced studio art-AP, algebra, American history, American history-AP, American literature, American literature-AP, art, art history, band, baseball, basketball, bell choir, Bible studies, biology, biology-AP, calculus, calculus-AP, career education internship, career/college preparation, ceramics, cheerleading, chemistry, chemistry-AP, Chinese studies, chorus, civics, college counseling, community garden, community service, computer literacy, creative writing, digital photography, drama, earth science, economics, economics and history, economics-AP, English, English language and composition-AP, English literature, English literature and composition-AP, English literature-AP, environmental science, ethics, European history-AP, film studies, fine arts, French, French-AP, geography, geology, geometry, grammar, history-AP, honors algebra, honors English, honors geometry, humanities, internship, journalism, lab science, Latin, Latin-AP, life management skills, life skills, literary magazine, Mandarin, mathematics, Middle East, music, music appreciation, musical productions, newspaper, philosophy, physical education, physics, pre algebra, publications, religion, SAT preparation, science, scripture, senior internship, social studies, softball, Southern literature, Spanish, Spanish-AP, speech, statistics-AP, student government, studio art, studio art-AP, swimming, tennis, theater, theology, track and field, trigonometry, U.S. history-AP, volleyball, world history, world literature, world religions, writing.

Graduation Requirements Arts and fine arts (art, music, dance, drama), electives, English, foreign language, life skills, mathematics, physical education (includes health), religion (includes Bible studies and theology), science, senior internship, social studies (includes history), senior intern program, 50 hours of community service.

Special Academic Programs 10 Advanced Placement exams for which test preparation is offered; honors section; independent study.

College Admission Counseling 61 students graduated in 2010; 59 went to college, including Eckerd College; Georgetown University; Louisiana State University and Agricultural and Mechanical College; Loyola University New Orleans; Trinity University; Washington and Lee University. Other: 1 went to work, 1 had other specific plans. Median SAT critical reading: 570, median SAT math: 580, median SAT writing: 570, median combined SAT: 1700, median composite ACT: 26. 43.3% scored over 600 on SAT critical reading, 41.7% scored over 600 on SAT math, 40% scored over 600 on SAT writing, 41.7% scored over 1800 on combined SAT, 41.7% scored over 26 on composite ACT.

Student Life Upper grades have specified standards of dress, student council, honor system. Discipline rests primarily with faculty. Attendance at religious services is required.

Summer Programs Remediation, enrichment, advancement, sports, art/fine arts, computer instruction programs offered; session focuses on academics, athletics, creative arts, and enrichment; held on campus; accepts boys and girls; open to students from other schools. 477 students usually enrolled. 2011 schedule: June 1 to August 7. Application deadline: May 15.

Tuition and Aid Day student tuition: $17,220. Tuition installment plan (local bank-arranged plan). Merit scholarship grants, need-based scholarship grants available. In 2010–11, 25% of upper-school students received aid; total upper-school merit-scholarship money awarded: $119,250. Total amount of financial aid awarded in 2010–11: $442,370.

Admissions Traditional secondary-level entrance grade is 9. For fall 2010, 61 students applied for upper-level admission, 56 were accepted, 29 enrolled. CTP, ISEE, WISC III or other aptitude measures; standardized achievement test or writing sample required. Deadline for receipt of application materials: none. Application fee required: $50. On-campus interview required.

Athletics Interscholastic: baseball (boys), basketball (b,g), cheering (b,g), cross-country running (b,g), flag football (b), football (b), golf (b,g), running (b,g), soccer (b,g), softball (g), swimming and diving (b,g), tennis (b,g), track and field (b,g), volleyball (g); intramural: basketball (b,g), cheering (b,g), cross-country running (b,g), golf (b,g), ropes courses (b,g), running (b,g), soccer (b,g), swimming and diving (b,g), tennis (b,g), track and field (b,g), volleyball (g); coed interscholastic: cheering, football; coed intramural: cheering. 4 PE instructors, 5 coaches, 1 athletic trainer.

Computers Computers are regularly used in all academic classes. Computer network features include on-campus library services, online commercial services, Internet access, wireless campus network, Internet filtering or blocking technology, VPN for teachers, staff and students. Campus intranet, student e-mail accounts, and computer access in designated common areas are available to students. Students grades are available online. The school has a published electronic and media policy.

Contact Mary White, Assistant Director of Admission. 504-736-9918. Fax: 504-736-8802. E-mail: mary.white@stmsaints.com. Web site: www.stmsaints.com.

SAINT MARY HIGH SCHOOL

64 Chestnut Street
Rutherford, New Jersey 07070
Head of School: Roy Corso

General Information Coeducational day college-preparatory, religious studies, bilingual studies, and technology school, affiliated with Roman Catholic Church; primarily serves students with learning disabilities, individuals with Attention Deficit Disorder, individuals with emotional and behavioral problems, and dyslexic students. Grades 9–12. Founded: 1929. Setting: suburban. Nearest major city is New York, NY. 2-acre campus. 2 buildings on campus. Approved or accredited by Middle States

Association of Colleges and Schools and New Jersey Department of Education. Upper school average class size: 17. Upper school faculty-student ratio: 1:11.

Upper School Student Profile Grade 9: 86 students (43 boys, 43 girls); Grade 10: 80 students (40 boys, 40 girls); Grade 11: 90 students (45 boys, 45 girls); Grade 12: 90 students (45 boys, 45 girls). 90% of students are Roman Catholic.

Faculty School total: 30. In upper school: 14 men, 16 women; 15 have advanced degrees.

Special Academic Programs International Baccalaureate program; Advanced Placement exam preparation; independent study.

College Admission Counseling 92 students graduated in 2009; 91 went to college, including Montclair State University; Rutgers, The State University of New Jersey, New Brunswick; Saint Joseph's University. Other: 1 went to work.

Student Life Upper grades have uniform requirement, student council, honor system. Discipline rests equally with students and faculty. Attendance at religious services is required.

Tuition and Aid Day student tuition: $7000. Tuition reduction for siblings, merit scholarship grants, need-based scholarship grants, middle-income loans available.

Admissions Traditional secondary-level entrance grade is 9. For fall 2009, 300 students applied for upper-level admission, 100 were accepted, 70 enrolled. Cooperative Entrance Exam (McGraw-Hill) required. Deadline for receipt of application materials: none. Application fee required.

Athletics Interscholastic: baseball (boys), basketball (b,g), cheering (g), football (b), soccer (b,g), softball (g), volleyball (b), wrestling (g); coed interscholastic: bowling, cross-country running, track and field. 2 PE instructors, 8 coaches, 1 athletic trainer.

Computers Computers are regularly used in business applications, computer applications, desktop publishing, English, graphic design, history, information technology, keyboarding, library, multimedia, newspaper, programming, science, technology, typing, video film production, Web site design, yearbook classes. Computer network features include on-campus library services, online commercial services, Internet access, wireless campus network, Internet filtering or blocking technology. Campus intranet, student e-mail accounts, and computer access in designated common areas are available to students. The school has a published electronic and media policy.

Contact Mr. Chris Sweet, Director of Admissions. 201-933-5220 Ext. 251. Fax: 201-933-0834. E-mail: csweet@stmaryhs.org. Web site: www.stmaryhs.org.

SAINT MARY'S COLLEGE HIGH SCHOOL

1294 Albina Avenue
Peralta Park
Berkeley, California 94706

Head of School: Peter Imperial

General Information Coeducational day college-preparatory school, affiliated with Roman Catholic Church. Grades 9–12. Founded: 1863. Setting: urban. Nearest major city is Oakland. 13-acre campus. 9 buildings on campus. Approved or accredited by National Catholic Education Association, Western Association of Schools and Colleges, and Western Catholic Education Association. Endowment: $3.6 million. Total enrollment: 625. Upper school average class size: 28. Upper school faculty-student ratio: 1:16. There are 180 required school days per year for Upper School students. Upper School students typically attend 5 days per week. The average school day consists of 5 hours and 50 minutes.

Upper School Student Profile Grade 9: 168 students (90 boys, 78 girls); Grade 10: 156 students (72 boys, 84 girls); Grade 11: 154 students (74 boys, 80 girls); Grade 12: 147 students (64 boys, 83 girls). 55% of students are Roman Catholic.

Faculty School total: 44. In upper school: 27 men, 17 women; 27 have advanced degrees.

Subjects Offered Algebra, American history, American literature, art, band, biology, biology-AP, calculus-AP, chemistry, chorus, conceptual physics, concert band, dance, diversity studies, economics, English, English language and composition-AP, English literature, English literature and composition-AP, finite math, forensics, French, French language-AP, geometry, government-AP, government/civics, graphic design, health education, jazz band, math analysis, mathematics, philosophy, photography, physical education, physics, physics-AP, psychology, religion, scripture, Spanish, Spanish language-AP, sports medicine, studio art-AP, theater, trigonometry, U.S. government and politics-AP, U.S. history-AP, world history, world history-AP, world religions, world religions, yearbook.

Graduation Requirements Electives, English, foreign language, health and wellness, lab science, mathematics, physical education (includes health), religious studies, U.S. history, visual and performing arts, world history, service learning, enrichment week mini-course (once a year).

Special Academic Programs 13 Advanced Placement exams for which test preparation is offered; honors section.

College Admission Counseling 141 students graduated in 2010; 139 went to college, including Saint Mary's College of California; San Diego State University; San Francisco State University; University of California, Berkeley; University of California, Riverside; University of California, Santa Cruz. Other: 2 had other specific plans.

Student Life Upper grades have specified standards of dress, student council. Discipline rests primarily with faculty. Attendance at religious services is required.

Summer Programs Remediation programs offered; held on campus; accepts boys and girls; not open to students from other schools. 45 students usually enrolled.

Tuition and Aid Day student tuition: $15,500. Tuition installment plan (monthly payment plans). Merit scholarship grants, need-based scholarship grants available. In 2010–11, 39% of upper-school students received aid; total upper-school merit-scholarship money awarded: $10,000. Total amount of financial aid awarded in 2010–11: $1,900,000.

Admissions Traditional secondary-level entrance grade is 9. For fall 2010, 397 students applied for upper-level admission, 310 were accepted, 175 enrolled. High School Placement Test and writing sample required. Deadline for receipt of application materials: January 5. Application fee required: $85. Interview required.

Athletics Interscholastic: baseball (boys), basketball (b,g), cross-country running (b,g), football (b), golf (b,g), lacrosse (b), soccer (b,g), softball (g); coed interscholastic: cheering, diving, swimming and diving; coed intramural: basketball. 1 PE instructor, 1 athletic trainer.

Computers Computers are regularly used in all academic, art, college planning, graphic arts, yearbook classes. Computer network features include on-campus library services, online commercial services, Internet access, wireless campus network, Internet filtering or blocking technology. Student e-mail accounts are available to students. Students grades are available online. The school has a published electronic and media policy.

Contact Lawrence Puck, Director of Admissions. 510-559-6235. Fax: 510-559-6277. E-mail: lpuck@stmchs.org. Web site: www.saintmaryschs.org.

ST. MARY'S DOMINICAN HIGH SCHOOL

7701 Walmsley Avenue
New Orleans, Louisiana 70125-0000

Head of School: Dr. Cynthia A. Thomas, EdD

General Information Girls' day college-preparatory school, affiliated with Roman Catholic Church. Grades 8–12. Founded: 1860. Setting: urban. 3 buildings on campus. Approved or accredited by Southern Association of Colleges and Schools and Louisiana Department of Education. Total enrollment: 919. Upper school average class size: 25. Upper school faculty-student ratio: 1:13.

Faculty School total: 67.

Special Academic Programs Advanced Placement exam preparation; honors section.

College Admission Counseling 176 students graduated in 2009.

Student Life Upper grades have uniform requirement, student council, honor system. Discipline rests primarily with faculty. Attendance at religious services is required.

Tuition and Aid Merit scholarship grants, need-based scholarship grants, paying campus jobs available.

Admissions Traditional secondary-level entrance grade is 8. High School Placement Test required. No application fee required. On-campus interview required.

Athletics Interscholastic: basketball (girls), bowling (g), cheering (g), dance squad (g), dance team (g), danceline (g), golf (g), gymnastics (g), indoor track (g), indoor track & field (g), soccer (g), softball (g), swimming and diving (g), tennis (g), track and field (g), volleyball (g); intramural: flag football (g), kickball (g). 4 PE instructors, 18 coaches, 1 athletic trainer.

Computers Computer network features include on-campus library services, Internet access, Internet filtering or blocking technology. The school has a published electronic and media policy.

Contact Mrs. Cathy Rice, Director of Admissions. 504-865-9401. E-mail: admissions@stmarysdominican.org.

ST. MARY'S EPISCOPAL SCHOOL

60 Perkins Extended
Memphis, Tennessee 38117-3199

Head of School: Ms. Marlene R. Shaw

General Information Girls' day college-preparatory, arts, religious studies, technology, and global issues school, affiliated with Episcopal Church. Grades PK–12. Founded: 1847. Setting: urban. 25-acre campus. 8 buildings on campus. Approved or accredited by National Association of Episcopal Schools, Southern Association of Colleges and Schools, Southern Association of Independent Schools, Tennessee Association of Independent Schools, The College Board, and Tennessee Department of Education. Member of National Association of Independent Schools. Endowment: $14.9 million. Total enrollment: 858. Upper school average class size: 13. Upper school faculty-student ratio: 1:13. There are 175 required school days per year for Upper School students. Upper School students typically attend 5 days per week. The average school day consists of 6 hours and 40 minutes.

Upper School Student Profile Grade 9: 65 students (65 girls); Grade 10: 65 students (65 girls); Grade 11: 62 students (62 girls); Grade 12: 60 students (60 girls). 15% of students are members of Episcopal Church.

Faculty School total: 105. In upper school: 7 men, 26 women; 26 have advanced degrees.

Subjects Offered Algebra, anatomy and physiology, art history, art history-AP, biology, biology-AP, calculus, calculus-AP, chamber groups, chemistry, chemistry-AP, choir, comparative religion, economics, English, English language and composition-AP, English literature and composition-AP, ethics, French, French-AP,

St. Mary's Episcopal School

geometry, global issues, guitar, health, humanities, instrumental music, Latin, Latin-AP, microbiology, music theory-AP, performing arts, physical education, physics, physics-AP, pre-calculus, psychology, religion, robotics, Spanish, Spanish-AP, speech, studio art, studio art-AP, technology, theater, U.S. government, U.S. history, U.S. history-AP, wind ensemble, world history, world history-AP.

Graduation Requirements 1½ elective credits, algebra, arts and fine arts (art, music, dance, drama), biology, calculus, chemistry, English, English language-AP, English literature-AP, foreign language, geometry, physical education (includes health), physics, pre-calculus, religion (includes Bible studies and theology), social studies (includes history), U.S. history, world history.

Special Academic Programs 15 Advanced Placement exams for which test preparation is offered; honors section; independent study; academic accommodation for the gifted, the musically talented, and the artistically talented.

College Admission Counseling 55 students graduated in 2010; all went to college, including Emory University; New York University; The University of Tennessee; University of Georgia; Vanderbilt University; Washington University in St. Louis. Median SAT critical reading: 660, median SAT math: 660, median combined SAT: 1960, median composite ACT: 29. 58% scored over 600 on SAT critical reading, 40% scored over 600 on SAT math, 64% scored over 600 on SAT writing, 73% scored over 1800 on combined SAT, 73% scored over 26 on composite ACT.

Student Life Upper grades have specified standards of dress, student council, honor system. Discipline rests equally with students and faculty. Attendance at religious services is required.

Summer Programs Enrichment, sports, art/fine arts programs offered; session focuses on summer enrichment; held on campus; accepts boys and girls; open to students from other schools. 200 students usually enrolled. 2011 schedule: June 1 to July 30. Application deadline: none.

Tuition and Aid Day student tuition: $16,225. Tuition installment plan (monthly payment plans, credit card payment). Need-based scholarship grants, discounts for children of faculty, staff, and clergy available. In 2010–11, 17% of upper-school students received aid. Total amount of financial aid awarded in 2010–11: $268,076.

Admissions Traditional secondary-level entrance grade is 9. For fall 2010, 29 students applied for upper-level admission, 21 were accepted, 18 enrolled. ISEE and writing sample required. Deadline for receipt of application materials: none. Application fee required: $75. On-campus interview required.

Athletics Interscholastic: basketball, bowling, cross-country running, dance team, golf, lacrosse, soccer, softball, swimming and diving, tennis, track and field, volleyball. 1 PE instructor, 7 coaches, 1 athletic trainer.

Computers Computers are regularly used in all academic, career exploration, college planning, creative writing, library, literary magazine, music, newspaper, research skills, SAT preparation, speech, theater arts, yearbook classes. Computer network features include on-campus library services, Internet access, wireless campus network, Internet filtering or blocking technology, online database services for research available at school and at home. Campus intranet and computer access in designated common areas are available to students. Students grades are available online. The school has a published electronic and media policy.

Contact Ms. Nicole Hernandez, Director of Admission and Financial Aid. 901-537-1405. Fax: 901-685-1098. E-mail: nhernandez@stmarysschool.org. Web site: www.stmarysschool.org.

SAINT MARY'S HALL
9401 Starcrest Drive
San Antonio, Texas 78217
Head of School: Mr. Bob Windham

General Information Coeducational day college-preparatory and arts school. Grades PK–12. Founded: 1879. Setting: suburban. 60-acre campus. 13 buildings on campus. Approved or accredited by Independent Schools Association of the Southwest. Member of National Association of Independent Schools and Secondary School Admission Test Board. Endowment: $31.7 million. Total enrollment: 988. Upper school average class size: 13. Upper school faculty-student ratio: 1:6. There are 173 required school days per year for Upper School students. Upper School students typically attend 5 days per week. The average school day consists of 7 hours and 10 minutes.

Upper School Student Profile Grade 9: 102 students (44 boys, 58 girls); Grade 10: 94 students (47 boys, 47 girls); Grade 11: 92 students (39 boys, 53 girls); Grade 12: 79 students (36 boys, 43 girls).

Faculty School total: 102. In upper school: 30 men, 30 women; 34 have advanced degrees.

Subjects Offered 3-dimensional art, Advanced Placement courses, algebra, American history-AP, American literature, anatomy and physiology, art, art history, art history-AP, art-AP, athletic training, ballet, baseball, basketball, biology, biology-AP, British literature, calculus, calculus-AP, cell biology, ceramics, chemistry, chemistry-AP, choir, college counseling, composition, computer science, computer science-AP, concert choir, creative writing, dance, digital photography, directing, drama, drawing, drawing and design, economics, economics-AP, English language and composition-AP, English literature and composition-AP, environmental science-AP, European history, European history-AP, fitness, French, French language-AP, genetics, geology, geometry, golf, government/civics, great books, guitar, health, human geography—AP, Japanese, jazz band, Latin, Latin-AP, literary

magazine, marine biology, model United Nations, music theory, painting, photography, physical education, physics, physics-AP, piano, pre-calculus, religious studies, science research, sculpture, set design, softball, Spanish, Spanish language-AP, Spanish literature-AP, speech, statistics-AP, swimming, technical theater, tennis, track and field, U.S. history, voice, volleyball, Web site design, world geography, world history, world literature, world religions, yearbook, zoology.

Graduation Requirements Arts and fine arts (art, music, dance, drama), athletics, electives, English, foreign language, mathematics, physical education (includes health), science, social studies (includes history), 40 hours of community service.

Special Academic Programs 25 Advanced Placement exams for which test preparation is offered; honors section; independent study; study abroad.

College Admission Counseling 84 students graduated in 2010; all went to college, including Loyola University New Orleans; Southern Methodist University; Texas Tech University; The University of Texas at Austin; Tulane University; University of Vermont. Median SAT critical reading: 640, median SAT math: 627, median SAT writing: 642, median composite ACT: 27.

Student Life Upper grades have uniform requirement, student council, honor system. Discipline rests primarily with faculty. Attendance at religious services is required.

Summer Programs Enrichment, sports, art/fine arts, computer instruction programs offered; held on campus; accepts boys and girls; open to students from other schools. 837 students usually enrolled. 2011 schedule: June 1 to August 5. Application deadline: May 13.

Tuition and Aid Day student tuition: $19,650. Tuition installment plan (monthly payment plans, individually arranged payment plans, full-year payment plan, 2-payment plan). Merit scholarship grants, need-based scholarship grants available. In 2010–11, 42% of upper-school students received aid; total upper-school merit-scholarship money awarded: $397,250. Total amount of financial aid awarded in 2010–11: $583,800.

Admissions Traditional secondary-level entrance grade is 9. For fall 2010, 139 students applied for upper-level admission, 104 were accepted, 48 enrolled. ISEE required. Deadline for receipt of application materials: November 19. Application fee required: $50. Interview required.

Athletics Interscholastic: ballet (boys, girls), baseball (b), basketball (b,g), dance (b,g), field hockey (g), fitness (b,g), golf (b,g), independent competitive sports (b,g), lacrosse (b), soccer (b,g), softball (g), volleyball (b,g); coed interscholastic: cross-country running, physical fitness, physical training, strength & conditioning, tennis, track and field, weight training. 14 coaches, 2 athletic trainers.

Computers Computers are regularly used in media arts classes. Computer network features include on-campus library services, Internet access, wireless campus network, Internet filtering or blocking technology, SmartBoards. Student e-mail accounts are available to students. Students grades are available online. The school has a published electronic and media policy.

Contact Mrs. Julie Hellmund, Director of Admission. 210-483-9234. Fax: 210-655-5211. E-mail: jhellmund@smhall.org. Web site: www.smhall.org.

SAINT MARY'S HIGH SCHOOL
2525 North Third Street
Phoenix, Arizona 85004
Head of School: Mrs. Suzanne M. Fessler

General Information Coeducational day college-preparatory, general academic, arts, and religious studies school, affiliated with Roman Catholic Church. Grades 9–12. Founded: 1917. Setting: urban. 6-acre campus. 5 buildings on campus. Approved or accredited by North Central Association of Colleges and Schools, Western Catholic Education Association, and Arizona Department of Education. Endowment: $1 million. Total enrollment: 601. Upper school average class size: 27. Upper school faculty-student ratio: 1:17. There are 180 required school days per year for Upper School students. Upper School students typically attend 5 days per week. The average school day consists of 6 hours and 45 minutes.

Upper School Student Profile Grade 9: 135 students (55 boys, 80 girls); Grade 10: 160 students (80 boys, 80 girls); Grade 11: 138 students (83 boys, 55 girls); Grade 12: 168 students (90 boys, 78 girls). 71% of students are Roman Catholic.

Faculty School total: 35. In upper school: 16 men, 19 women; 29 have advanced degrees.

Subjects Offered Advanced Placement courses, algebra, American government, American history, American history-AP, American literature, art, band, biology, British literature, British literature (honors), calculus-AP, Catholic belief and practice, chemistry, chorus, Christian and Hebrew scripture, composition, computer graphics, conceptual physics, dance, drama, economics, electives, English, English composition, English language and composition-AP, English literature, English literature and composition-AP, fine arts, foreign language, French, geometry, health, history, history of the Catholic Church, honors algebra, honors English, honors geometry, honors U.S. history, intro to computers, journalism, Life of Christ, personal finance, physical education, physical science, physics, prayer/spirituality, pre-algebra, pre-calculus, religious education, remedial study skills, social studies, Spanish, Spanish language-AP, standard curriculum, state government, state history, theology, trigonometry, U.S. government and politics-AP, world geography, world history, world religions, yearbook.

Graduation Requirements Advanced math, algebra, American government, American history, American literature, anatomy and physiology, arts and fine arts (art, music, dance, drama), biology, British literature, Catholic belief and practice, chemistry, Christian and Hebrew scripture, composition, economics, electives, English, foreign language, geometry, health education, history of the Catholic Church, language and composition, physical education (includes health), physics, pre-calculus, theology, trigonometry, world history, world literature, 90 hours of Christian community service.

Special Academic Programs 6 Advanced Placement exams for which test preparation is offered; honors section; study at local college for college credit; remedial reading and/or remedial writing; remedial math; ESL (10 students enrolled).

College Admission Counseling 172 students graduated in 2010; 167 went to college, including Arizona State University; Grand Canyon University; Northern Arizona University; The University of Arizona. Other: 3 entered military service, 2 had other specific plans. Median composite ACT: 21. Mean SAT critical reading: 475, mean SAT math: 463, mean SAT writing: 469. 10% scored over 600 on SAT critical reading, 10% scored over 600 on SAT math, 6% scored over 600 on SAT writing, 11% scored over 26 on composite ACT.

Student Life Upper grades have uniform requirement, student council. Discipline rests primarily with faculty. Attendance at religious services is required.

Summer Programs Remediation, enrichment, advancement, sports, art/fine arts programs offered; session focuses on high school preparation for incoming freshmen; held on campus; accepts boys and girls; not open to students from other schools. 200 students usually enrolled. 2011 schedule: June 2 to July 12. Application deadline: May 13.

Tuition and Aid Day student tuition: $8300–$10,700. Tuition installment plan (FACTS Tuition Payment Plan, monthly payment plans, individually arranged payment plans, quarterly and semester payment plans). Need-based scholarship grants, paying campus jobs available. In 2010–11, 70% of upper-school students received aid. Total amount of financial aid awarded in 2010–11: $1,500,000.

Admissions Traditional secondary-level entrance grade is 9. For fall 2010, 150 students applied for upper-level admission, 145 were accepted, 135 enrolled. High School Placement Test required. Deadline for receipt of application materials: none. Application fee required: $300. On-campus interview required.

Athletics Interscholastic: baseball (boys), basketball (b,g), cheering (g), football (b), golf (b,g), physical fitness (b,g), soccer (b,g), softball (g), strength & conditioning (b,g), tennis (b,g), volleyball (b,g), weight training (b,g), winter soccer (b,g); intramural: dance (g); coed interscholastic: cross-country running, physical fitness, strength & conditioning, swimming and diving, track and field, weight training; coed intramural: bowling. 4 PE instructors, 20 coaches, 1 athletic trainer.

Computers Computers are regularly used in computer applications, graphics, journalism, newspaper, Web site design, yearbook classes. Computer resources include on-campus library services, Internet access, Internet filtering or blocking technology. Students grades are available online. The school has a published electronic and media policy.

Contact Mrs. Linda Schmaltz, Office Manager. 602-251-2500. Fax: 602-251-2595. E-mail: lschmaltz@smknights.org. Web site: www.smknights.org.

ST. MARY'S HIGH SCHOOL

2501 East Yampa Street
Colorado Springs, Colorado 80909
Head of School: Mr. John McCord

General Information Coeducational day college-preparatory and religious studies school, affiliated with Roman Catholic Church. Grades 9–12. Founded: 1885. Setting: urban. 5-acre campus. 4 buildings on campus. Approved or accredited by National Catholic Education Association, North Central Association of Colleges and Schools, and Colorado Department of Education. Total enrollment: 389. Upper school average class size: 17. Upper school faculty-student ratio: 1:11. Upper School students typically attend 5 days per week.

Upper School Student Profile Grade 9: 78 students (37 boys, 41 girls); Grade 10: 99 students (45 boys, 54 girls); Grade 11: 90 students (39 boys, 51 girls); Grade 12: 95 students (41 boys, 54 girls). 70% of students are Roman Catholic.

Faculty School total: 31. In upper school: 16 men, 15 women; 16 have advanced degrees.

Subjects Offered 3-dimensional art, advanced biology, advanced chemistry, advanced computer applications, advanced math, Advanced Placement courses, advanced studio art-AP, algebra, American government, American history, American history-AP, American literature, anatomy and physiology, art, Basic programming, biology, business, calculus, calculus-AP, ceramics, choir, Christian studies, computer applications, computer programming, computer studies, contemporary history, drama, earth science, ecology, economics, English, English-AP, finance, French, geometry, health.

Graduation Requirements Biology, computer applications, English, foreign language, geometry, mathematics, physical education (includes health), religious studies, science, social studies (includes history), speech, world geography, community service-150 hours over 4 years, theology.

Special Academic Programs Advanced Placement exam preparation; honors section; independent study.

College Admission Counseling 93 students graduated in 2009; 83 went to college, including Colorado School of Mines; Colorado State University; Gonzaga University; University of Colorado at Boulder; University of Northern Colorado. Other: 5 went to work.

Student Life Upper grades have specified standards of dress, student council. Discipline rests primarily with faculty. Attendance at religious services is required.

Tuition and Aid Day student tuition: $7200. Tuition installment plan (SMART Tuition Payment Plan). Merit scholarship grants, need-based scholarship grants available. In 2009–10, 30% of upper-school students received aid; total upper-school merit-scholarship money awarded: $10,000. Total amount of financial aid awarded in 2009–10: $250,000.

Admissions Traditional secondary-level entrance grade is 9. For fall 2009, 93 students applied for upper-level admission, 83 were accepted, 83 enrolled. High School Placement Test (closed version) from Scholastic Testing Service required. Deadline for receipt of application materials: February 15. Application fee required: $400. Interview required.

Athletics Interscholastic: baseball (boys), basketball (b,g), cheering (b,g), cross-country running (b,g), football (b), golf (b,g), lacrosse (b), soccer (b,g), softball (g), swimming and diving (g), tennis (g), track and field (b,g), volleyball (g), wrestling (b). 2 PE instructors, 25 coaches, 2 athletic trainers.

Computers Computers are regularly used in computer applications classes. Computer network features include Internet filtering or blocking technology. Campus intranet is available to students. Students grades are available online.

Contact Mrs. Robyn Cross, Director of Admissions. 719-635-7540 Ext. 16. Fax: 719-471-7623. E-mail: rcross@smhscs.org. Web site: www.smhscs.org.

SAINT MARY'S HIGH SCHOOL

113 Duke of Gloucester Street
Annapolis, Maryland 21401
Head of School: Mr. Richard Bayhan

General Information Coeducational day college-preparatory, arts, religious studies, bilingual studies, and technology school, affiliated with Roman Catholic Church. Grades 9–12. Founded: 1946. Setting: small town. 5-acre campus. 3 buildings on campus. Approved or accredited by Maryland Department of Education. Total enrollment: 490. Upper school average class size: 25. Upper school faculty-student ratio: 1:15. Upper School students typically attend 5 days per week.

Upper School Student Profile 80% of students are Roman Catholic.

Faculty School total: 41. In upper school: 17 men, 24 women; 32 have advanced degrees.

Subjects Offered Accounting, algebra, American government, American literature, art, art history, art history-AP, biology, biology-AP, British literature, calculus-AP, Catholic belief and practice, chemistry, chemistry-AP, Christian scripture, Christianity, cinematography, computer applications, creative writing, current events, drama, economics, environmental science, European history-AP, fiction, French, geography, geometry, health, integrated mathematics, interdisciplinary studies, Irish literature, Latin, literature and composition-AP, math analysis, mathematics, mechanical drawing, microbiology, musical theater, peace and justice, physical education, physical science, physics, physics-AP, pre-calculus, psychology, public speaking, relationships, religion, religion and culture, senior project, Shakespeare, social justice, sociology, Spanish, sports conditioning, studio art, trigonometry, U.S. government and politics-AP, U.S. history, U.S. history-AP, weight training, world arts, world history, world literature, writing, zoology.

Graduation Requirements Arts and fine arts (art, music, dance, drama), computers, English, foreign language, mathematics, physical education (includes health), religion (includes Bible studies and theology), science, social studies (includes history).

Special Academic Programs Advanced Placement exam preparation; honors section; study at local college for college credit; study abroad; academic accommodation for the gifted.

College Admission Counseling 135 students graduated in 2010; all went to college, including United States Naval Academy; University of Maryland, College Park; Washington College. Mean combined SAT: 1670. 50% scored over 1800 on combined SAT.

Student Life Upper grades have uniform requirement, student council, honor system. Discipline rests primarily with faculty. Attendance at religious services is required.

Tuition and Aid Day student tuition: $12,710. Tuition installment plan (monthly payment plans). Merit scholarship grants, need-based scholarship grants available. In 2010–11, 25% of upper-school students received aid; total upper-school merit-scholarship money awarded: $30,000. Total amount of financial aid awarded in 2010–11: $250,000.

Admissions Traditional secondary-level entrance grade is 9. For fall 2010, 265 students applied for upper-level admission, 175 were accepted, 128 enrolled. High School Placement Test required. Deadline for receipt of application materials: January 7. Application fee required: $75.

Athletics Interscholastic: baseball (boys), basketball (b,g), cross-country running (b,g), dance team (g), field hockey (g), football (b), golf (b,g), lacrosse (b,g), soccer (b,g), swimming and diving (b,g), tennis (b,g), track and field (b,g), volleyball (g), wrestling (b); intramural: crew (g); coed interscholastic: weight training; coed intramural: dance team, fishing, Frisbee, sailing, yoga. 2 PE instructors, 56 coaches, 1 athletic trainer.

Computers Computers are regularly used in all classes. Computer network features include on-campus library services, online commercial services, Internet access, wireless campus network. The school has a published electronic and media policy.

Saint Mary's High School

Contact Mrs. Chrissie Chomo, Director of Admissions. 410-990-4236. Fax: 410-269-7843. E-mail: cchomo@stmarysannapolis.org. Web site: www.stmarysannapolis.org.

ST. MARY'S PREPARATORY SCHOOL

3535 Indian Trail
Orchard Lake, Michigan 48324
Head of School: James Glowacki

General Information Boys' boarding and day college-preparatory school, affiliated with Roman Catholic Church. Grades 9–12. Founded: 1885. Setting: suburban. Nearest major city is Detroit. Students are housed in single-sex dormitories. 80-acre campus. 12 buildings on campus. Approved or accredited by Michigan Association of Non-Public Schools and Michigan Department of Education. Total enrollment: 480. Upper school average class size: 18. Upper school faculty-student ratio: 1:10. There are 185 required school days per year for Upper School students. Upper School students typically attend 5 days per week. The average school day consists of 7 hours.

Upper School Student Profile Grade 9: 106 students (106 boys); Grade 10: 110 students (110 boys); Grade 11: 140 students (140 boys); Grade 12: 117 students (117 boys). 15% of students are boarding students. 80% are state residents. 5 states are represented in upper school student body. 15% are international students. International students from Brazil, China, Japan, Poland, Republic of Korea, and Taiwan. 80% of students are Roman Catholic.

Faculty School total: 58. In upper school: 43 men, 15 women; 16 have advanced degrees; 6 reside on campus.

Subjects Offered Algebra, American history, American literature, art, band, Bible studies, biology, business, business skills, calculus, chemistry, Chinese, computer programming, computer science, creative writing, drafting, driver education, earth science, ecology, economics, English, English literature, expository writing, fine arts, French, geometry, government/civics, grammar, health, history, journalism, law, mathematics, music technology, mythology, physical education, physics, Polish, psychology, religion, robotics, science, social sciences, social studies, Spanish, speech, theology, trigonometry, world history, writing.

Graduation Requirements Arts and fine arts (art, music, dance, drama), business skills (includes word processing), computer science, English, foreign language, mathematics, physical education (includes health), religion (includes Bible studies and theology), science, social sciences, social studies (includes history).

Special Academic Programs Advanced Placement exam preparation; honors section; study at local college for college credit; academic accommodation for the musically talented and the artistically talented; programs in general development for dyslexic students; special instructional classes for students with learning disabilities, Attention Deficit Disorder, and dyslexia; ESL (40 students enrolled).

College Admission Counseling 136 students graduated in 2010; 130 went to college, including Michigan State University; Oakland University; University of Detroit Mercy; University of Michigan; Wayne State University; Western Michigan University. Other: 1 entered a postgraduate year. Median SAT critical reading: 503, median SAT math: 600, median SAT writing: 510, median combined SAT: 1613, median composite ACT: 25. 5% scored over 600 on SAT critical reading, 15% scored over 600 on SAT math, 40% scored over 26 on composite ACT.

Student Life Upper grades have specified standards of dress, student council, honor system. Discipline rests primarily with faculty. Attendance at religious services is required.

Summer Programs Remediation, sports programs offered; session focuses on football, basketball, and lacrosse; held on campus; accepts boys and girls; open to students from other schools. 400 students usually enrolled. 2011 schedule: June to August. Application deadline: June.

Tuition and Aid Day student tuition: $9800; 5-day tuition and room/board: $20,000; 7-day tuition and room/board: $22,000. Tuition installment plan (FACTS Tuition Payment Plan, individually arranged payment plans). Tuition reduction for siblings, merit scholarship grants, need-based scholarship grants available. In 2010–11, 80% of upper-school students received aid.

Admissions Traditional secondary-level entrance grade is 9. For fall 2010, 250 students applied for upper-level admission, 180 were accepted, 130 enrolled. STS and TOEFL required. Deadline for receipt of application materials: none. Application fee required: $35. Interview recommended.

Athletics Interscholastic: alpine skiing, baseball, basketball, crew, cross-country running, football, freestyle skiing, golf, hockey, ice hockey, indoor track, indoor track & field, jogging, lacrosse, rowing, skiing (downhill), soccer, track and field, wrestling; intramural: aerobics/Nautilus, aquatics, basketball, bicycling, billiards, bowling, broomball, fitness, Frisbee, golf, hockey, ice hockey, ice skating, indoor hockey, indoor soccer, indoor track, jogging, lacrosse, mountain biking, Nautilus, physical fitness, physical training, rowing, running, skiing (downhill), snowboarding, soccer, strength & conditioning, swimming and diving, table tennis, tennis, weight lifting, weight training, whiffle ball. 2 PE instructors, 25 coaches, 3 athletic trainers.

Computers Computers are regularly used in desktop publishing, drafting, engineering, yearbook classes. Computer network features include on-campus library services, Internet access, Internet filtering or blocking technology. Campus intranet and student e-mail accounts are available to students. Students grades are available online.

Contact Candace Knight, Dean of Admissions. 248-683-0514. Fax: 248-683-1740. E-mail: cknight@stmarysprep.com. Web site: www.stmarysprep.com/.

SAINT MARY'S SCHOOL

900 Hillsborough Street
Raleigh, North Carolina 27603-1689
Head of School: Ms. Theo W. Coonrod

General Information Girls' boarding and day college-preparatory, arts, religious studies, and technology school, affiliated with Episcopal Church. Grades 9–12. Founded: 1842. Setting: urban. Students are housed in single-sex dormitories. 23-acre campus. 26 buildings on campus. Approved or accredited by National Association of Episcopal Schools, North Carolina Association of Independent Schools, Southern Association of Colleges and Schools, Southern Association of Independent Schools, and The Association of Boarding Schools. Member of National Association of Independent Schools and Secondary School Admission Test Board. Total enrollment: 274. Upper school average class size: 10. Upper school faculty-student ratio: 1:8. The average school day consists of 7 hours.

Upper School Student Profile Grade 9: 53 students (53 girls); Grade 10: 57 students (57 girls); Grade 11: 76 students (76 girls); Grade 12: 88 students (88 girls). 45% of students are boarding students. 78% are state residents. 12 states are represented in upper school student body. 9% are international students. International students from Cayman Islands, China, Panama, Republic of Korea, Switzerland, and United Kingdom. 20% of students are members of Episcopal Church.

Faculty School total: 40. In upper school: 10 men, 30 women; 30 have advanced degrees; 39 reside on campus.

Subjects Offered 3-dimensional art, acting, advanced chemistry, advanced math, Advanced Placement courses, algebra, American government, American history, American history-AP, American literature, anatomy, art, astronomy, athletics, ballet, biology, biology-AP, calculus, calculus-AP, ceramics, chemistry, chemistry-AP, choir, choral music, computer science, dance, drama, drama performance, drawing, drawing and design, earth science, ecology, English, English literature, English literature-AP, European history, French, French language-AP, geometry, government, government-AP, government/civics, honors English, honors geometry, honors U.S. history, honors world history, Latin, Latin-AP, mathematics, philosophy, physical education, physics, physics-AP, piano, psychology-AP, religion, senior project, Spanish, Spanish language-AP, speech, U.S. government and politics-AP, U.S. history, U.S. history-AP, Western civilization, world literature, yearbook, yoga.

Graduation Requirements Algebra, arts and fine arts (art, music, dance, drama), biology, electives, English, foreign language, geometry, government, physical education (includes health), physical science, religion (includes Bible studies and theology), social sciences, U.S. history, Western civilization.

Special Academic Programs Advanced Placement exam preparation; honors section; independent study; study at local college for college credit.

College Admission Counseling 67 students graduated in 2010; all went to college, including Clemson University; Elon University; North Carolina State University; The University of North Carolina at Chapel Hill; University of Georgia; University of South Carolina.

Student Life Upper grades have specified standards of dress, student council, honor system. Discipline rests equally with students and faculty. Attendance at religious services is required.

Summer Programs Enrichment, sports, art/fine arts, computer instruction programs offered; held on campus; accepts girls; open to students from other schools.

Tuition and Aid Day student tuition: $17,540; 7-day tuition and room/board: $37,630. Tuition installment plan (FACTS Tuition Payment Plan, monthly payment plans). Need-based scholarship grants available. In 2010–11, 39% of upper-school students received aid. Total amount of financial aid awarded in 2010–11: $1,133,000.

Admissions Traditional secondary-level entrance grade is 9. ISEE or SSAT required. Deadline for receipt of application materials: none. Application fee required: $100. Interview required.

Athletics Interscholastic: basketball, cross-country running, field hockey, golf, lacrosse, soccer, softball, swimming and diving, tennis, track and field, volleyball; intramural: ballet, dance, dance team, modern dance. 2 PE instructors, 32 coaches, 1 athletic trainer.

Computers Computers are regularly used in dance, English, foreign language, history, introduction to technology, mathematics, newspaper, publications, science, senior seminar, writing, yearbook classes. Computer network features include on-campus library services, online commercial services, Internet access, wireless campus network, Internet filtering or blocking technology. Student e-mail accounts are available to students. Students grades are available online. The school has a published electronic and media policy.

Contact Ms. Carol DeWitt, Admission Assistant. 800-948-2557. Fax: 919-424-4122. E-mail: cdewitt@sms.edu. Web site: www.sms.edu.

ST. MARY'S SCHOOL

816 Black Oak Drive
Medford, Oregon 97504-8504
Head of School: Mr. Frank Phillips

General Information Coeducational boarding and day college-preparatory, arts, and religious studies school, affiliated with Roman Catholic Church. Boarding grades 9–12, day grades 6–12. Founded: 1865. Setting: small town. Nearest major city is Eugene. Students are housed in single-sex by floor dormitories. 23-acre campus. 9 buildings on campus. Approved or accredited by National Catholic Education

Association, Northwest Association of Schools and Colleges, Pacific Northwest Association of Independent Schools, and Oregon Department of Education. Member of National Association of Independent Schools. Total enrollment: 448. Upper school average class size: 18. Upper school faculty-student ratio: 1:11. There are 180 required school days per year for Upper School students. Upper School students typically attend 5 days per week. The average school day consists of 7 hours and 15 minutes.

Upper School Student Profile Grade 9: 69 students (34 boys, 35 girls); Grade 10: 82 students (47 boys, 35 girls); Grade 11: 81 students (37 boys, 44 girls); Grade 12: 78 students (32 boys, 46 girls). 8% of students are boarding students. 92% are state residents. 2 states are represented in upper school student body. 8% are international students. International students from China, Israel, Mexico, and Republic of Korea; 4 other countries represented in student body. 35% of students are Roman Catholic.

Faculty School total: 48. In upper school: 22 men, 26 women; 21 have advanced degrees; 2 reside on campus.

Subjects Offered Adolescent issues, Advanced Placement courses, algebra, American history, American history-AP, American literature, ancient history, art, art history-AP, biology, biology-AP, calculus-AP, chamber groups, chemistry, chemistry-AP, chorus, community service, computer programming-AP, computer science, creative writing, drama, earth science, economics-AP, English, English-AP, environmental science-AP, ESL, ethics, European history, European history-AP, expository writing, fine arts, general science, geometry, German, government/civics, government/civics-AP, grammar, health, history, human geography—AP, instrumental music, jazz band, Latin, Latin-AP, mathematics, music theory-AP, physical education, physics, physics-AP, religion, science, social sciences, social studies, Spanish, Spanish-AP, speech, studio art-AP, theater, trigonometry, world history, world literature, writing.

Graduation Requirements Arts and fine arts (art, music, dance, drama), electives, English, foreign language, mathematics, physical education (includes health), religion (includes Bible studies and theology), science, social sciences, social studies (includes history), 100 hours of community service (25 each year in upper school).

Special Academic Programs 18 Advanced Placement exams for which test preparation is offered; independent study; study at local college for college credit; academic accommodation for the gifted, the musically talented, and the artistically talented; ESL (35 students enrolled).

College Admission Counseling 63 students graduated in 2010; 62 went to college, including Oregon State University; Portland State University; Santa Clara University; University of Oregon; University of Portland; University of San Diego. Other: 1 had other specific plans. Mean SAT critical reading: 598, mean SAT math: 586, mean SAT writing: 597, mean combined SAT: 1781.

Student Life Upper grades have specified standards of dress, student council, honor system. Discipline rests equally with students and faculty. Attendance at religious services is required.

Summer Programs Remediation, enrichment, advancement, sports, art/fine arts, computer instruction programs offered; session focuses on enrichment and SAT prep; held on campus; accepts boys and girls; open to students from other schools. 196 students usually enrolled. 2011 schedule: July 1 to August 27. Application deadline: none.

Tuition and Aid Day student tuition: $11,200. Tuition installment plan (monthly payment plans, semiannual and annual payment plans). Need-based scholarship grants available. In 2010–11, 47% of upper-school students received aid. Total amount of financial aid awarded in 2010–11: $650,000.

Admissions Traditional secondary-level entrance grade is 9. For fall 2010, 127 students applied for upper-level admission, 116 were accepted, 95 enrolled. Deadline for receipt of application materials: February 15. Application fee required: $50. Interview required.

Athletics Interscholastic: baseball (boys), basketball (b,g), combined training (b,g), cross-country running (b,g), football (b), golf (b,g), independent competitive sports (b,g), soccer (b,g), softball (g), tennis (b,g), track and field (b,g), volleyball (g); intramural: alpine skiing (b,g), canoeing/kayaking (b,g), dance team (g), equestrian sports (b,g), flag football (g), hiking/backpacking (b,g); coed interscholastic: martial arts; coed intramural: backpacking, fitness, floor hockey, outdoor adventure, skiing (cross-country), strength & conditioning, tennis, weight lifting. 2 PE instructors.

Computers Computers are regularly used in English, history, mathematics, science, speech classes. Computer network features include on-campus library services, online commercial services, Internet access, wireless campus network, Internet filtering or blocking technology, access to homework, daily bulletins and teachers via e-mail, Wifi. Campus intranet and computer access in designated common areas are available to students. Students grades are available online. The school has a published electronic and media policy.

Contact Rebecca Naumes, Director of Admissions. 541-773-7877. Fax: 541-772-8973. E-mail: admissions@smschool.us. Web site: www.smschool.us.

SAINT MAUR INTERNATIONAL SCHOOL

83 Yamate-cho, Naka-ku
Yokohama 231-8654, Japan
Head of School: Jeanette K. Thomas

General Information Coeducational day college-preparatory, general academic, arts, technology, and science school, affiliated with Roman Catholic Church. Grades PK–12. Founded: 1872. Setting: urban. 1-hectare campus. 7 buildings on campus. Approved or accredited by East Asia Regional Council of Schools, European Council of International Schools, International Baccalaureate Organization, Ministry of Education, Japan, and New England Association of Schools and Colleges. Language of instruction: English. Total enrollment: 434. Upper school average class size: 15. Upper school faculty-student ratio: 1:5. There are 175 required school days per year for Upper School students. Upper School students typically attend 5 days per week. The average school day consists of 5 hours and 30 minutes.

Upper School Student Profile Grade 6: 34 students (13 boys, 21 girls); Grade 7: 39 students (14 boys, 25 girls); Grade 8: 33 students (13 boys, 20 girls); Grade 9: 25 students (11 boys, 14 girls); Grade 10: 28 students (12 boys, 16 girls); Grade 11: 30 students (10 boys, 20 girls); Grade 12: 39 students (19 boys, 20 girls). 23% of students are Roman Catholic.

Faculty School total: 63. In upper school: 17 men, 22 women; 22 have advanced degrees.

Subjects Offered 20th century history, art, Asian studies, biology, chemistry, Chinese history, computer science, drama, drama performance, economics, economics-AP, English, fine arts, French, geography, information technology, Japanese, Japanese history, mathematics, music, music performance, physical education, physics, psychology, religious education, religious studies, science, social studies, Spanish, TOEFL preparation, visual arts, world history.

Graduation Requirements Arts and fine arts (art, music, dance, drama), English, foreign language, mathematics, physical education (includes health), religion (includes Bible studies and theology), science, social studies (includes history), graduation requirements for IB diploma differ.

Special Academic Programs International Baccalaureate program; 11 Advanced Placement exams for which test preparation is offered; independent study; academic accommodation for the gifted, the musically talented, and the artistically talented; ESL (18 students enrolled).

College Admission Counseling 32 students graduated in 2010; 29 went to college, including International Christian University; Northeastern University; Smith College; Washington University in St. Louis. Other: 1 had other specific plans. Median combined SAT: 1620. Mean SAT critical reading: 477, mean SAT math: 615, mean SAT writing: 543. 29% scored over 1800 on combined SAT.

Student Life Upper grades have uniform requirement, student council. Discipline rests primarily with faculty. Attendance at religious services is required.

Summer Programs Enrichment, advancement, ESL, sports, art/fine arts, computer instruction programs offered; session focuses on TOEFL and SAT preparation; held both on and off campus; held at various off-campus locations; accepts boys and girls; open to students from other schools. 60 students usually enrolled. 2011 schedule: June 13 to July 1. Application deadline: May 15.

Tuition and Aid Day student tuition: ¥1,990,000.

Admissions For fall 2010, 31 students applied for upper-level admission, 25 were accepted, 20 enrolled. School's own test required. Deadline for receipt of application materials: none. Application fee required: ¥20,000. On-campus interview required.

Athletics Interscholastic: baseball (boys), basketball (b,g), cross-country running (b,g), soccer (b,g), volleyball (g); intramural: soccer (b); coed intramural: hiking/backpacking, tennis. 2 PE instructors.

Computers Computers are regularly used in computer applications, economics, English, foreign language, French, geography, information technology, mathematics, media, music, SAT preparation, science, social studies, Spanish classes. Computer network features include on-campus library services, Internet access, wireless campus network, Internet filtering or blocking technology. Campus intranet and computer access in designated common areas are available to students. Students grades are available online. The school has a published electronic and media policy.

Contact Jeanette K. Thomas, School Head. 81-(0) 45-641-5751. Fax: 81-(0) 45-641-6688. E-mail: jthomas@stmaur.ac.jp. Web site: www.stmaur.ac.jp.

ST. MICHAEL'S COLLEGE SCHOOL

1515 Bathurst Street
Toronto, Ontario M5P 3H4, Canada
Head of School: Fr. Joseph Redican, CSB

General Information Boys' day college-preparatory and religious studies school, affiliated with Roman Catholic Church. Grades 7–12. Founded: 1852. Setting: urban. 10-acre campus. 2 buildings on campus. Approved or accredited by Ontario Department of Education. Language of instruction: English. Total enrollment: 1,072. Upper school average class size: 24. Upper school faculty-student ratio: 1:16. There are 184 required school days per year for Upper School students. Upper School students typically attend 5 days per week. The average school day consists of 6 hours.

Upper School Student Profile Grade 7: 88 students (88 boys); Grade 8: 125 students (125 boys); Grade 9: 231 students (231 boys); Grade 10: 234 students (234 boys); Grade 11: 198 students (198 boys); Grade 12: 198 students (198 boys). 95% of students are Roman Catholic.

Faculty School total: 73. In upper school: 59 men, 13 women; 20 have advanced degrees.

Subjects Offered Advanced Placement courses, all academic, American history, anatomy and physiology, ancient history, art, biology, calculus, calculus-AP, Canadian geography, Canadian history, Canadian law, Canadian literature, career and personal planning, career education, chemistry, civics, computer multimedia, economics, English, English composition, English literature, finite math, French, functions, geography, history, Italian, Latin, leadership, mathematics, media arts, modern Western civilization, outdoor education, physical education, religion, science, Spanish, theology, world religions.

Special Academic Programs Advanced Placement exam preparation.

College Admission Counseling 201 students graduated in 2010; all went to college, including Queen's University at Kingston; The University of Western Ontario; University of Guelph; University of Toronto; University of Waterloo; York University.

Student Life Upper grades have uniform requirement, student council, honor system. Discipline rests primarily with faculty. Attendance at religious services is required.

Tuition and Aid Day student tuition: CAN$16,050. Tuition installment plan (monthly payment plans, individually arranged payment plans, all up front-$300 discount, three monthly installments (March, June, August)-$100 discount). Bursaries, merit scholarship grants, need-based scholarship grants available. In 2010–11, 16% of upper-school students received aid; total upper-school merit-scholarship money awarded: CAN$105,000. Total amount of financial aid awarded in 2010–11: CAN$1,700,000.

Admissions Traditional secondary-level entrance grade is 9. For fall 2010, 261 students applied for upper-level admission, 185 were accepted, 142 enrolled. SSAT required. Deadline for receipt of application materials: none. Application fee required: CAN$100.

Athletics Interscholastic: alpine skiing, aquatics, archery, badminton, baseball, basketball, cross-country running, football, golf, ice hockey, lacrosse, mountain biking, skiing (downhill), snowboarding, soccer, softball, swimming and diving, tennis, track and field, volleyball; intramural: archery, badminton, basketball, flag football, outdoor education, power lifting.

Computers Computers are regularly used in media arts classes. Computer resources include on-campus library services, Internet access, Internet filtering or blocking technology. The school has a published electronic and media policy.

Contact Ms. Marilyn Furgiuele, Admissions Assistant. 416-653-3180 Ext. 438. Fax: 416-653-7704. E-mail: furgiuele@smcs.toronto.on.ca. Web site: www.stmichaelscollegeschool.com.

ST. MICHAEL'S PREPARATORY SCHOOL OF THE NORBERTINE FATHERS

19292 El Toro Road

Silverado, California 92676-9710

Head of School: Rev. Gabriel D. Stack, OPRAEM

General Information Boys' boarding college-preparatory and religious studies school, affiliated with Roman Catholic Church. Grades 9–12. Founded: 1961. Setting: suburban. Nearest major city is Los Angeles. Students are housed in single-sex dormitories. 35-acre campus. 2 buildings on campus. Approved or accredited by National Catholic Education Association, Western Association of Schools and Colleges, and California Department of Education. Total enrollment: 64. Upper school average class size: 6. Upper school faculty-student ratio: 1:3. Upper School students typically attend 5 days per week. The average school day consists of 7 hours.

Upper School Student Profile Grade 9: 17 students (17 boys); Grade 10: 14 students (14 boys); Grade 11: 19 students (19 boys); Grade 12: 14 students (14 boys). 100% of students are boarding students. 90% are state residents. 4 states are represented in upper school student body. 4% are international students. International students from Mexico and Republic of Korea; 2 other countries represented in student body. 98% of students are Roman Catholic.

Faculty School total: 20. In upper school: 18 men, 2 women; 18 have advanced degrees; 13 reside on campus.

Subjects Offered Algebra, American history, American history-AP, American literature, ancient history, art history, Bible studies, biology, calculus-AP, chemistry, chorus, economics, economics-AP, English, English literature, ethics, fine arts, geography, geometry, government-AP, government/civics, Greek, health, history, Latin, Latin-AP, mathematics, philosophy, physical education, physical science, physics, pre-calculus, religion, science, social studies, Spanish, Spanish-AP, theology, trigonometry, world literature.

Graduation Requirements Arts and fine arts (art, music, dance, drama), English, foreign language, mathematics, physical education (includes health), religion (includes Bible studies and theology), science, social studies (includes history), Senior Matura.

Special Academic Programs Advanced Placement exam preparation; honors section; independent study; ESL (1 student enrolled).

College Admission Counseling 11 students graduated in 2010; all went to college, including California State Polytechnic University, Pomona; California State University, Fullerton; California State University, Long Beach; Thomas Aquinas College; University of California, Davis; University of Notre Dame. Mean SAT critical reading: 514, mean SAT math: 530.

Student Life Upper grades have uniform requirement, student council, honor system. Discipline rests equally with students and faculty. Attendance at religious services is required.

Tuition and Aid 5-day tuition and room/board: $17,900. Tuition installment plan (FACTS Tuition Payment Plan, monthly payment plans, individually arranged payment plans). Need-based scholarship grants available. Total amount of financial aid awarded in 2010–11: $350,000.

Admissions Traditional secondary-level entrance grade is 9. High School Placement Test required. Deadline for receipt of application materials: June 30. Application fee required: $100. Interview required.

Athletics Interscholastic: baseball, cross-country running, football, soccer; intramural: basketball, field hockey, outdoor activities, swimming and diving, table tennis, volleyball, weight lifting. 1 PE instructor, 2 coaches.

Computers Computers are regularly used in English, mathematics, science classes. Computer resources include on-campus library services, Internet access, Internet filtering or blocking technology. Computer access in designated common areas is available to students. Students grades are available online.

Contact Mrs. Pamela M. Christian, School Secretary. 949-858-0222 Ext. 237. Fax: 949-858-7365. E-mail: admissions@stmichaelsprep.org. Web site: www.stmichaelsprep.org.

ST. MICHAELS UNIVERSITY SCHOOL

3400 Richmond Road

Victoria, British Columbia V8P 4P5, Canada

Head of School: Robert T. Snowden

General Information Coeducational boarding and day college-preparatory and arts school, affiliated with Church of England (Anglican). Boarding grades 8–12, day grades K–12. Founded: 1906. Setting: suburban. Students are housed in coed dormitories. 20-acre campus. 12 buildings on campus. Approved or accredited by Canadian Association of Independent Schools, Canadian Educational Standards Institute, Pacific Northwest Association of Independent Schools, The Association of Boarding Schools, and British Columbia Department of Education. Language of instruction: English. Endowment: CAN$5 million. Total enrollment: 934. Upper school average class size: 20. Upper school faculty-student ratio: 1:10.

Upper School Student Profile Grade 9: 142 students (54 boys, 88 girls); Grade 10: 145 students (78 boys, 67 girls); Grade 11: 158 students (93 boys, 65 girls); Grade 12: 169 students (76 boys, 93 girls). 42% of students are boarding students. 78% are province residents. 9 provinces are represented in upper school student body. 20% are international students. International students from China, Germany, Mexico, Republic of Korea, Taiwan, and United States; 16 other countries represented in student body. 15% of students are members of Church of England (Anglican).

Faculty School total: 87. In upper school: 40 men, 20 women; 23 have advanced degrees; 15 reside on campus.

Subjects Offered Advanced Placement courses, algebra, art, art history, biology, calculus, career and personal planning, chemistry, computer programming, computer science, creative writing, drama, earth science, economics, English, English literature, environmental science, ESL, European history, fine arts, French, geography, geology, geometry, history, Japanese, mathematics, music, physical education, physics, science, social studies, Spanish, theater, trigonometry.

Graduation Requirements Arts and fine arts (art, music, dance, drama), career and personal planning, computer science, English, foreign language, mathematics, physical education (includes health), science, social studies (includes history), 30 hours of work experience.

Special Academic Programs Advanced Placement exam preparation; honors section; accelerated programs; term-away projects; study abroad; ESL (40 students enrolled).

College Admission Counseling 160 students graduated in 2010; all went to college, including McGill University; Queen's University at Kingston; Simon Fraser University; The University of British Columbia; University of Toronto; University of Victoria. Mean SAT critical reading: 574, mean SAT math: 653.

Student Life Upper grades have uniform requirement, student council, honor system. Discipline rests primarily with faculty. Attendance at religious services is required.

Summer Programs Enrichment, advancement, ESL, sports, art/fine arts, computer instruction programs offered; session focuses on ESL; held both on and off campus; held at locations in local community; accepts boys and girls; open to students from other schools. 80 students usually enrolled. 2011 schedule: July to August.

Tuition and Aid Day student tuition: CAN$10,460–CAN$13,000; 7-day tuition and room/board: CAN$28,650–CAN$45,240. Tuition installment plan (Insured Tuition Payment Plan, monthly payment plans, 2-payment plan). Tuition reduction for siblings, bursaries, merit scholarship grants, need-based scholarship grants available. In 2010–11, 10% of upper-school students received aid; total upper-school merit-scholarship money awarded: CAN$100,000. Total amount of financial aid awarded in 2010–11: CAN$620,000.

Admissions Traditional secondary-level entrance grade is 9. For fall 2010, 381 students applied for upper-level admission, 260 were accepted, 210 enrolled. Naglieri Nonverbal School Ability Test, OLSAT, Stanford Achievement Test, SLEP, SSAT, Stanford Achievement Test, Otis-Lennon School Ability Test, Stanford Achievement Test, Otis-Lennon School Ability Test, school's own exam or writing sample required. Deadline for receipt of application materials: none. Application fee required: CAN$250. On-campus interview required.

Athletics Interscholastic: badminton (boys, girls), basketball (b,g), bicycling (b,g), crew (b,g), cricket (b,g), cross-country running (b,g), field hockey (g), rowing (b,g), rugby (b), running (b,g), soccer (b,g), squash (b,g), swimming and diving (b,g), tennis (b,g), track and field (b,g), volleyball (b,g); intramural: aerobics/dance (g), rugby (b,g), squash (b,g), strength & conditioning (b,g), volleyball (b,g); coed interscholastic: badminton, golf, rowing, running, squash; coed intramural: aerobics, aerobics/dance, aerobics/Nautilus, alpine skiing, aquatics, backpacking, badminton, ball hockey,

basketball, bowling, canoeing/kayaking, climbing, cricket, cross-country running, dance, dance team, equestrian sports, fitness, floor hockey, fly fishing, hiking/backpacking, ice skating, indoor soccer, kayaking, martial arts, mountain biking, Nautilus, outdoor activities, outdoor education, outdoor skills, physical training, rock climbing, sailing, skiing (downhill), snowboarding, soccer, softball, squash, strength & conditioning, swimming and diving, triathlon, ultimate Frisbee, volleyball, wall climbing, weight lifting, weight training, yoga. 5 PE instructors.
Computers Computers are regularly used in English, foreign language, humanities, library, mathematics, science, social sciences, writing, yearbook classes. Computer network features include on-campus library services, Internet access.
Contact Ms. Maurine McKay, Admissions Assistant. 250-370-6170. Fax: 250-519-7502. E-mail: admissions@smus.bc.ca. Web site: www.smus.bc.ca.

SAINT MONICA'S HIGH SCHOOL
1030 Lincoln Boulevard
Santa Monica, California 90403-4096
Head of School: Mr. Thom Gasper
General Information Coeducational day college-preparatory, arts, and religious studies school, affiliated with Roman Catholic Church. Grades 9–12. Founded: 1937. Setting: urban. Nearest major city is Los Angeles. 5-acre campus. 4 buildings on campus. Approved or accredited by National Catholic Education Association, Western Association of Schools and Colleges, and California Department of Education. Total enrollment: 602. Upper school average class size: 25. Upper school faculty-student ratio: 1:14.
Upper School Student Profile 73% of students are Roman Catholic.
Faculty School total: 46. In upper school: 22 men, 24 women; 20 have advanced degrees.
Subjects Offered Accounting, acting, Advanced Placement courses, algebra, American history, American history-AP, applied music, art, arts, Bible studies, calculus, calculus-AP, campus ministry, ceramics, chemistry, chorus, college counseling, community service, drama, driver education, economics, English, English-AP, European history-AP, film, fine arts, French, geometry, government/civics, graphic arts, health, Japanese, keyboarding, marine biology, mathematics, physical education, physics, psychology, reading, religion, science, social studies, Spanish, Spanish language-AP, theater, trigonometry, U.S. government and politics-AP, U.S. history-AP, world history, yearbook.
Graduation Requirements Arts and fine arts (art, music, dance, drama), English, foreign language, mathematics, physical education (includes health), religion (includes Bible studies and theology), science, social studies (includes history). Community service is required.
Special Academic Programs Advanced Placement exam preparation; honors section; study at local college for college credit; remedial reading and/or remedial writing; remedial math.
College Admission Counseling 121 students graduated in 2009; all went to college.
Student Life Upper grades have uniform requirement, student council, honor system. Discipline rests primarily with faculty. Attendance at religious services is required.
Tuition and Aid Day student tuition: $7500. Tuition installment plan (monthly payment plans, individually arranged payment plans). Merit scholarship grants, need-based scholarship grants available. In 2009–10, 24% of upper-school students received aid.
Admissions Traditional secondary-level entrance grade is 9. High School Placement Test (closed version) from Scholastic Testing Service required. Deadline for receipt of application materials: January 16. Application fee required: $70. On-campus interview required.
Athletics Interscholastic: baseball (boys), basketball (b,g), cheering (g), cross-country running (b,g), dance squad (b,g), football (b), golf (b,g), soccer (b,g), softball (g), tennis (b,g), track and field (b,g), volleyball (b,g); coed interscholastic: bowling, surfing. 2 PE instructors, 12 coaches, 1 athletic trainer.
Computers Computers are regularly used in all academic classes. Computer network features include on-campus library services, online commercial services, Internet access. Computer access in designated common areas is available to students. Students grades are available online. The school has a published electronic and media policy.
Contact Ms. Therese Charkut, Director of Admissions. 310-394-3701 Ext. 448. Fax: 310-458-1353. E-mail: tcharkut@stmonicahs.net. Web site: www.stmonicahs.org

ST. PATRICK CATHOLIC HIGH SCHOOL
18300 St. Patrick Road
Biloxi, Mississippi 39532
Head of School: Mr. Bobby Trosclair
General Information Coeducational day college-preparatory and religious studies school, affiliated with Roman Catholic Church. Grades 7–12. Founded: 2007. Setting: suburban. 32-acre campus. 7 buildings on campus. Approved or accredited by Southern Association of Colleges and Schools and Mississippi Department of Education. Endowment: $400,000. Total enrollment: 491. Upper school average class size: 20. Upper school faculty-student ratio: 1:15. There are 180 required school days per year for Upper School students. Upper School students typically attend 5 days per week. The average school day consists of 6 hours and 45 minutes.

Upper School Student Profile Grade 7: 103 students (53 boys, 50 girls); Grade 8: 81 students (44 boys, 37 girls); Grade 9: 87 students (43 boys, 44 girls); Grade 10: 75 students (38 boys, 37 girls); Grade 11: 74 students (37 boys, 37 girls); Grade 12: 72 students (30 boys, 42 girls). 80% of students are Roman Catholic.
Faculty School total: 32. In upper school: 14 men, 18 women; 18 have advanced degrees.
Subjects Offered Accounting, advanced chemistry, advanced computer applications, advanced math, Advanced Placement courses, algebra, American government, American history, American literature, analytic geometry, anatomy and physiology, art, athletics, band, baseball, Basic programming, basketball, biology, British literature, business applications, business law, calculus, calculus-AP, campus ministry, Catholic belief and practice, cheerleading, chemistry, chemistry-AP, choral music, Christian and Hebrew scripture, church history, civics, college counseling, college placement, college planning, composition-AP, computer applications, creative writing, desktop publishing, drama, driver education, earth science, economics, English, English literature and composition-AP, environmental science, French, geometry, global studies, health, introduction to theater, journalism, keyboarding, law, Life of Christ, marching band, marine biology, marine science, oral communications, physical education, physical science, pre-algebra, pre-calculus, probability and statistics, psychology, softball, Spanish, track and field, trigonometry, U.S. government, U.S. history, U.S. history-AP, volleyball, Web site design, weight fitness, weight training, weightlifting, wood processing, world geography, world history, yearbook.
Graduation Requirements Algebra, American history, American literature, art, biology, British literature, cell biology, chemistry, computer applications, English literature, foreign language, physical education (includes health), state history, U.S. government, U.S. history, world geography, world history, world literature.
Special Academic Programs Advanced Placement exam preparation; study at local college for college credit; remedial reading and/or remedial writing.
College Admission Counseling 87 students graduated in 2010; 86 went to college, including Louisiana State University and Agricultural and Mechanical College; Millsaps College; Mississippi State University; University of Mississippi; University of South Alabama; University of Southern Mississippi. Other: 1 went to work. Mean SAT critical reading: 592, mean SAT math: 596, mean SAT writing: 576, mean composite ACT: 22. 40% scored over 600 on SAT critical reading, 20% scored over 600 on SAT math, 40% scored over 600 on SAT writing, 32% scored over 26 on composite ACT.
Student Life Upper grades have uniform requirement, student council, honor system. Discipline rests primarily with faculty. Attendance at religious services is required.
Tuition and Aid Day student tuition: $5500. Tuition installment plan (monthly payments through local bank). Tuition reduction for siblings, need-based scholarship grants available. In 2010–11, 4% of upper-school students received aid.
Admissions Traditional secondary-level entrance grade is 7. For fall 2010, 328 students applied for upper-level admission, 311 were accepted, 308 enrolled. Deadline for receipt of application materials: none. No application fee required. Interview required.
Athletics Interscholastic: baseball (boys), basketball (b,g), cheering (g), cross-country running (b,g), dance team (g), football (b), golf (b,g), power lifting (b,g), soccer (b,g), softball (g), swimming and diving (b,g), tennis (b,g), track and field (b,g), volleyball (g), weight lifting (b,g), weight training (b,g); intramural: bicycling (b,g); coed intramural: sailing. 3 PE instructors, 18 coaches, 1 athletic trainer.
Computers Computers are regularly used in accounting, business applications, business education, computer applications, desktop publishing, mathematics, newspaper, Web site design, word processing, yearbook classes. Computer network features include on-campus library services, Internet access, Internet filtering or blocking technology. Campus intranet and computer access in designated common areas are available to students. Students grades are available online.
Contact Renee McDaniel, Vice Principal. 228-702-0500. Fax: 228-702-0511. E-mail: rmcdaniel@stpatrickhighschool.net. Web site: www.stpatrickhighschool.net.

SAINT PATRICK HIGH SCHOOL
5900 West Belmont Avenue
Chicago, Illinois 60634
Head of School: Br. Konrad Diebold
General Information Boys' day college-preparatory, arts, and religious studies school, affiliated with Roman Catholic Church. Grades 9–12. Founded: 1861. Setting: urban. 1 building on campus. Approved or accredited by Christian Brothers Association, North Central Association of Colleges and Schools, and Illinois Department of Education. Endowment: $5.8 million. Total enrollment: 844. Upper school average class size: 24. Upper school faculty-student ratio: 1:17. There are 178 required school days per year for Upper School students. Upper School students typically attend 5 days per week. The average school day consists of 6 hours and 40 minutes.
Upper School Student Profile Grade 9: 242 students (242 boys); Grade 10: 197 students (197 boys); Grade 11: 205 students (205 boys); Grade 12: 200 students (200 boys). 75% of students are Roman Catholic.
Faculty School total: 67. In upper school: 44 men, 19 women; 43 have advanced degrees.
Subjects Offered Accounting, algebra, American history, American literature, anatomy, art, art history, biology, broadcasting, business, business skills, calculus,

Saint Patrick High School

chemistry, Chinese, chorus, computer graphics, computer science, creative writing, culinary arts, drama, driver education, ecology, economics, English, English literature, ESL, ethics, European history, fine arts, French, geography, geometry, German, government/civics, grammar, health, history, journalism, keyboarding, mathematics, music, physical education, physics, psychology, religion, science, social sciences, social studies, sociology, Spanish, speech, theater, trigonometry, word processing, world history, writing.

Graduation Requirements Arts and fine arts (art, music, dance, drama), business skills (includes word processing), computer science, English, mathematics, physical education (includes health), religion (includes Bible studies and theology), science, service learning/internship, social sciences, social studies (includes history), participation in a retreat program. Community service is required.

Special Academic Programs Advanced Placement exam preparation; honors section; study at local college for college credit; remedial reading and/or remedial writing; remedial math; ESL.

College Admission Counseling 205 students graduated in 2010; 197 went to college, including DePaul University; Lewis University; Northeastern Illinois University; Northern Illinois University; University of Illinois at Chicago; University of Illinois at Urbana–Champaign. Other: 4 went to work, 3 entered military service, 1 had other specific plans. Mean composite ACT: 22. 28% scored over 26 on composite ACT.

Student Life Upper grades have specified standards of dress, student council, honor system. Discipline rests primarily with faculty. Attendance at religious services is required.

Summer Programs Remediation, enrichment, sports, art/fine arts, computer instruction programs offered; session focuses on remediation; held on campus; accepts boys and girls; open to students from other schools. 225 students usually enrolled. 2011 schedule: June 20 to August 12. Application deadline: June 15.

Tuition and Aid Day student tuition: $8590. Tuition installment plan (monthly payment plans, quarterly payment plan). Need-based scholarship grants available. In 2010–11, 33% of upper-school students received aid. Total amount of financial aid awarded in 2010–11: $970,000.

Admissions Traditional secondary-level entrance grade is 9. For fall 2010, 312 students applied for upper-level admission, 308 were accepted, 242 enrolled. ACT-Explore or any standardized test required. Deadline for receipt of application materials: none. No application fee required. On-campus interview required.

Athletics Interscholastic: baseball, basketball, bowling, cross-country running, diving, fishing, football, golf, hockey, soccer, swimming and diving, tennis, track and field, volleyball, water polo, wrestling; intramural: basketball, football, volleyball. 4 PE instructors, 25 coaches, 1 athletic trainer.

Computers Computers are regularly used in business, English, foreign language, geography, graphic arts, graphic design, graphics, history, information technology, introduction to technology, library skills, mathematics, media arts, media production, media services, newspaper, photojournalism, religion, remedial study skills, research skills, science, typing, word processing, yearbook classes. Computer network features include on-campus library services, online commercial services, Internet access, Internet filtering or blocking technology. Students grades are available online. The school has a published electronic and media policy.

Contact Christopher Perez, Director of Curriculum. 773-282-8844 Ext. 228. Fax: 773-282-2361. E-mail: cperez@stpatrick.org. Web site: www.stpatrick.org.

SAINT PATRICK—SAINT VINCENT HIGH SCHOOL

1500 Benicia Road
Vallejo, California 94591
Head of School: Ms. Mary Ellen Ryan

General Information Coeducational day college-preparatory, arts, business, religious studies, and technology school, affiliated with Roman Catholic Church. Grades 9–12. Founded: 1870. Setting: suburban. 31-acre campus. 8 buildings on campus. Approved or accredited by Western Association of Schools and Colleges, Western Catholic Education Association, and California Department of Education. Total enrollment: 558. Upper school average class size: 30. Upper school faculty-student ratio: 1:30. There are 180 required school days per year for Upper School students. Upper School students typically attend 5 days per week. The average school day consists of 6 hours and 15 minutes.

Upper School Student Profile Grade 9: 129 students (77 boys, 52 girls); Grade 10: 139 students (65 boys, 74 girls); Grade 11: 143 students (68 boys, 75 girls); Grade 12: 145 students (64 boys, 81 girls). 80% of students are Roman Catholic.

Faculty School total: 40. In upper school: 19 men, 21 women; 23 have advanced degrees.

Subjects Offered Algebra, art, biology, calculus-AP, campus ministry, Catholic belief and practice, chemistry, chemistry-AP, choir, civics, college counseling, college planning, computer multimedia, concert bell choir, concert choir, economics, English, English-AP, environmental science, environmental studies, ethnic studies, film appreciation, French, French language-AP, geometry, health, history-AP, honors English, honors world history, human biology, keyboarding, leadership, organic chemistry, physical education, physics, psychology, religion, science, Spanish, Spanish language-AP, statistics, statistics-AP, studio art-AP, theater arts, U.S. history, vocal jazz, world history.

Graduation Requirements English, foreign language, mathematics, physical education (includes health), religion (includes Bible studies and theology), science, social studies (includes history), Christian service.

Special Academic Programs Advanced Placement exam preparation; honors section; academic accommodation for the gifted; remedial math.

College Admission Counseling 143 students graduated in 2010; 140 went to college, including California State University, Sacramento; San Francisco State University; University of California, Berkeley; University of California, Irvine; University of California, Santa Barbara. Other: 2 entered military service, 1 had other specific plans.

Student Life Upper grades have specified standards of dress, student council, honor system. Discipline rests primarily with faculty. Attendance at religious services is required.

Summer Programs Remediation, enrichment, sports, art/fine arts programs offered; session focuses on enrichment; held on campus; accepts boys and girls; open to students from other schools. 489 students usually enrolled. 2011 schedule: June 14 to July 23. Application deadline: June 4.

Tuition and Aid Day student tuition: $10,475. Tuition installment plan (FACTS Tuition Payment Plan). Tuition reduction for siblings, need-based scholarship grants available. In 2010–11, 23% of upper-school students received aid. Total amount of financial aid awarded in 2010–11: $377,600.

Admissions Traditional secondary-level entrance grade is 9. For fall 2010, 179 students applied for upper-level admission, 165 were accepted, 131 enrolled. High School Placement Test required. Deadline for receipt of application materials: none. Application fee required: $40. Interview required.

Athletics Interscholastic: baseball (boys), basketball (b,g), cross-country running (b,g), golf (b,g), soccer (b,g), softball (g), swimming and diving (b,g), tennis (b,g), track and field (b,g), volleyball (b,g), water polo (b,g), wrestling (b,g); coed interscholastic: cheering, football, yoga. 3 PE instructors, 67 coaches, 1 athletic trainer.

Computers Computers are regularly used in business education, business studies, career education, career exploration, college planning, computer applications, desktop publishing, drawing and design, economics, English, foreign language, graphic arts, graphic design, history, library, library skills, mathematics, psychology, religious studies, science, social studies, Spanish, theater arts, theology, Web site design, word processing, yearbook classes. Computer network features include on-campus library services, Internet access, wireless campus network, Internet filtering or blocking technology. Student e-mail accounts are available to students. Students grades are available online. The school has a published electronic and media policy.

Contact Mrs. Sheila Williams, Director of Admissions. 707-644-4425 Ext. 448. Fax: 707-644-4770. E-mail: s.williams@spsv.org. Web site: spsv.org.

ST. PATRICK'S REGIONAL SECONDARY

115 East 11th Avenue
Vancouver, British Columbia V5T 2C1, Canada
Head of School: Mr. John V. Bevacqua

General Information Coeducational day college-preparatory, general academic, arts, business, religious studies, and technology school, affiliated with Roman Catholic Church. Grades 8–12. Founded: 1923. Setting: urban. 2 buildings on campus. Approved or accredited by British Columbia Department of Education. Language of instruction: English. Total enrollment: 500. Upper school average class size: 25. The average school day consists of 6 hours.

Upper School Student Profile 97% of students are Roman Catholic.

Faculty School total: 35. In upper school: 15 men, 15 women; 5 have advanced degrees.

Special Academic Programs Advanced Placement exam preparation; ESL (15 students enrolled).

College Admission Counseling 100 students graduated in 2010; all went to college, including University of Alaska Fairbanks.

Student Life Upper grades have uniform requirement. Attendance at religious services is required.

Tuition and Aid Tuition installment plan (monthly payment plans).

Admissions Application fee required: CAN$100. Interview required.

Athletics Interscholastic: basketball (boys, girls), soccer (b,g), track and field (b,g), volleyball (g), wrestling (b,g); coed intramural: badminton. 5 PE instructors, 5 coaches.

Contact Mr. John V. Bevacqua, Principal. 604-874-6422. Fax: 604-874-5176. E-mail: administration@stpats.bc.ca. Web site: www.stpats.bc.ca.

ST. PAUL ACADEMY AND SUMMIT SCHOOL

1712 Randolph Avenue
St. Paul, Minnesota 55105
Head of School: Bryn S. Roberts

General Information Coeducational day college-preparatory school. Grades K–12. Founded: 1900. Setting: urban. 32-acre campus. 4 buildings on campus. Approved or accredited by Independent Schools Association of the Central States and Minnesota Department of Education. Member of National Association of Independent Schools. Endowment: $31.1 million. Total enrollment: 855. Upper school average class size: 14. Upper school faculty-student ratio: 1:7.

Upper School Student Profile Grade 9: 99 students (49 boys, 50 girls); Grade 10: 92 students (46 boys, 46 girls); Grade 11: 82 students (34 boys, 48 girls); Grade 12: 87 students (47 boys, 40 girls).

Faculty School total: 104. In upper school: 18 men, 20 women; 32 have advanced degrees.

Subjects Offered Algebra, American literature, art, biology, calculus, ceramics, chemistry, Chinese, creative writing, current events, debate, drama, earth science, economics, English, English literature, European history, expository writing, fine arts, French, geometry, German, journalism, law and the legal system, marine biology, mathematics, multicultural studies, music, music theory, newspaper, photography, physical education, physics, psychology, science, senior project, Shakespeare, social psychology, social studies, sociology, space and physical sciences, Spanish, trigonometry, world history, world literature, world religions, yearbook.

Graduation Requirements Arts and fine arts (art, music, dance, drama), English, foreign language, mathematics, physical education (includes health), science, social studies (includes history), participation in athletics, month-long senior project, senior speech.

Special Academic Programs Honors section; independent study; term-away projects; study abroad.

College Admission Counseling 93 students graduated in 2010; all went to college, including St. Olaf College; The George Washington University; Tufts University; University of Minnesota, Twin Cities Campus; University of Wisconsin–Madison; Washington University in St. Louis. Median SAT critical reading: 640, median SAT math: 660, median SAT writing: 640, median combined SAT: 1940, median composite ACT: 30. 68% scored over 600 on SAT critical reading, 79% scored over 600 on SAT math, 77% scored over 600 on SAT writing, 73% scored over 1800 on combined SAT, 89% scored over 26 on composite ACT.

Student Life Upper grades have specified standards of dress, student council. Discipline rests equally with students and faculty.

Tuition and Aid Day student tuition: $22,040–$24,180. Tuition installment plan (Insured Tuition Payment Plan, monthly payment plans). Need-based scholarship grants available. In 2010–11, 22% of upper-school students received aid. Total amount of financial aid awarded in 2010–11: $1,154,740.

Admissions Traditional secondary-level entrance grade is 9. For fall 2010, 52 students applied for upper-level admission, 34 were accepted, 21 enrolled. SSAT, ERB, PSAT, SAT, PLAN or ACT or writing sample required. Deadline for receipt of application materials: February 1. Application fee required: $75. Interview required.

Athletics Interscholastic: alpine skiing (boys, girls), baseball (b), basketball (b,g), cross-country running (b,g), dance (g), dance team (g), diving (b,g), fencing (b,g), football (b), golf (b,g), ice hockey (b,g), skiing (cross-country) (b,g), skiing (downhill) (b,g), soccer (b,g), softball (g), swimming and diving (b,g), tennis (b,g); intramural: outdoor adventure (b,g); coed interscholastic: lacrosse, strength & conditioning, track and field; coed intramural: hiking/backpacking, physical fitness, snowboarding, table tennis. 3 PE instructors, 101 coaches, 1 athletic trainer.

Computers Computers are regularly used in all academic classes. Computer network features include on-campus library services, online commercial services, Internet access, wireless campus network, Internet filtering or blocking technology, laptop program (beginning in grade 7). Student e-mail accounts and computer access in designated common areas are available to students. The school has a published electronic and media policy.

Contact Mrs. Heather Cameron Ploen, Director of Admission and Financial Aid. 651-698-2451. Fax: 651-698-6787. E-mail: hploen@spa.edu. Web site: www.spa.edu.

SAINT PAUL LUTHERAN HIGH SCHOOL

205 South Main Street
PO Box 719
Concordia, Missouri 64020
Head of School: Rev. Paul M. Mehl

General Information Coeducational boarding and day college-preparatory, general academic, arts, and religious studies school, affiliated with Lutheran Church–Missouri Synod. Grades 9–12. Founded: 1883. Setting: small town. Nearest major city is Kansas City. Students are housed in single-sex dormitories. 50-acre campus. 9 buildings on campus. Approved or accredited by Lutheran School Accreditation Commission, Midwest Association of Boarding Schools, North Central Association of Colleges and Schools, and Missouri Department of Education. Endowment: $2.5 million. Total enrollment: 189. Upper school average class size: 20. Upper school faculty-student ratio: 1:9. There are 173 required school days per year for Upper School students. Upper School students typically attend 5 days per week. The average school day consists of 6 hours and 1 minutes.

Upper School Student Profile Grade 9: 40 students (24 boys, 16 girls); Grade 10: 29 students (14 boys, 15 girls); Grade 11: 72 students (31 boys, 41 girls); Grade 12: 48 students (24 boys, 24 girls). 43% are state residents. 15 states are represented in upper school student body. 40% are international students. 60% of students are Lutheran Church–Missouri Synod.

Faculty School total: 21. In upper school: 12 men, 9 women; 18 have advanced degrees; 9 reside on campus.

Subjects Offered Accounting, ADL skills, advanced biology, algebra, American history, American literature, analytic geometry, art, athletic training, band, Bible studies, biology, business law, calculus, ceramics, chemistry, child development, chorus, Christian doctrine, church history, community service, comparative religion, composition, computer science, concert choir, creative writing, current events, drama, drawing, economics, English, English literature, ESL, family studies, freshman

seminar, general science, geography, geometry, German, government/civics, health, human anatomy, music appreciation, music theory, novels, painting, physical education, physical science, physics, poetry, pre-algebra, psychology, religion, Shakespeare, sociology, Spanish, speech, statistics, theology, trigonometry, world history, world literature, writing.

Graduation Requirements Arts and fine arts (art, music, dance, drama), computer science, English, foreign language, mathematics, physical education (includes health), practical arts, religion (includes Bible studies and theology), science, social studies (includes history), 3.0 grade point average on a 4.0 scale for college preparatory students, above (national) average score on ACT or SAT. Community service is required.

Special Academic Programs International Baccalaureate program; independent study; study at local college for college credit.

College Admission Counseling 35 students graduated in 2009; 31 went to college, including Concordia University; Rockhurst University; University of Central Missouri; University of Missouri. Other: 2 went to work, 2 entered a postgraduate year. Median SAT critical reading: 450, median SAT math: 650, median SAT writing: 490, median combined SAT: 1590, median composite ACT: 24. 15% scored over 600 on SAT critical reading, 66% scored over 600 on SAT math, 14% scored over 600 on SAT writing, 26% scored over 1800 on combined SAT, 40% scored over 26 on composite ACT.

Student Life Upper grades have specified standards of dress, student council, honor system. Discipline rests primarily with faculty. Attendance at religious services is required.

Tuition and Aid Day student tuition: $8000; 7-day tuition and room/board: $12,375. Guaranteed tuition plan. Tuition installment plan (monthly payment plans, individually arranged payment plans, lump sum payment discount plan). Tuition reduction for siblings, need-based scholarship grants, paying campus jobs, LCMS Grants for church vocation students, early bird tuition grants available. In 2009–10, 54% of upper-school students received aid. Total amount of financial aid awarded in 2009–10: $273,555.

Admissions Traditional secondary-level entrance grade is 9. For fall 2009, 106 students applied for upper-level admission, 105 were accepted, 96 enrolled. School placement exam and SLEP for foreign students required. Deadline for receipt of application materials: none. Application fee required: $100. On-campus interview recommended.

Athletics Interscholastic: baseball (boys), basketball (b,g), cheering (g), cross-country running (b,g), football (b), golf (b,g), soccer (b,g), softball (g), track and field (b,g), volleyball (g); intramural: baseball (b), basketball (b,g), dance team (g), football (b), golf (b,g), jogging (b,g), roller blading (b,g), running (b,g), soccer (b,g), softball (g), strength & conditioning (b,g), tennis (b,g), volleyball (b,g), weight lifting (b,g); coed interscholastic: cross-country running, track and field; coed intramural: jogging, roller blading, running, soccer, table tennis, ultimate Frisbee. 2 PE instructors, 1 coach.

Computers Computers are regularly used in Christian doctrine, creative writing, data processing, English, freshman foundations, history, keyboarding, lab/keyboard, library skills, religious studies, speech, study skills, word processing, writing, writing classes. Computer resources include Internet access, wireless campus network. Students grades are available online. The school has a published electronic and media policy.

Contact Mr. Bill Lemmons, Director of Recruitment. 660-463-2238 Ext. 232. Fax: 660-463-7621. E-mail: blemmons@splhs.org. Web site: www.splhs.org.

ST. PAUL PREPARATORY SCHOOL

380 Jackson Street
Suite 100
Saint Paul, Minnesota 55101
Head of School: Dr. Frank Tarsitano

General Information Coeducational boarding and day college-preparatory, arts, business, bilingual studies, and liberal arts school. Grades 9–12. Founded: 2002. Setting: urban. Nearest major city is St. Paul. Students are housed in host family homes. 2-acre campus. 1 building on campus. Approved or accredited by National Association of Episcopal Schools, North Central Association of Colleges and Schools, and Minnesota Department of Education. Languages of instruction: Spanish, French, and Mandarin. Total enrollment: 145. Upper school average class size: 17. Upper school faculty-student ratio: 1:11. There are 175 required school days per year for Upper School students. Upper School students typically attend 5 days per week. The average school day consists of 6 hours and 30 minutes.

Upper School Student Profile 15% are state residents. 1 state is represented in upper school student body. 85% are international students.

Faculty School total: 13. In upper school: 6 men, 7 women; 12 have advanced degrees.

Subjects Offered Algebra, American government, American history, art, art history, biology, calculus, chemistry, Chinese, communications, computer science, earth science, ESL, French, geometry, German, Italian, life science, literature, modern European history, music, physical fitness, physical science, physics, pre-calculus, Russian, Spanish, theater, trigonometry, world civilizations, world cultures, writing, writing workshop.

Special Academic Programs 7 Advanced Placement exams for which test preparation is offered; honors section; accelerated programs; independent study; study at local college for college credit; study abroad; academic accommodation for the gifted, the musically talented, and the artistically talented; ESL (45 students enrolled).

College Admission Counseling 64 students graduated in 2009; 58 went to college, including Gustavus Adolphus College; Hamline University; University of St. Thomas. Other: 6 had other specific plans.

Student Life Upper grades have specified standards of dress, student council, honor system. Discipline rests equally with students and faculty.

Tuition and Aid Day student tuition: $9000; 7-day tuition and room/board: $21,500. Tuition installment plan (monthly payment plans). Tuition reduction for siblings, merit scholarship grants, paying campus jobs available.

Admissions Traditional secondary-level entrance grade is 11. For fall 2009, 155 students applied for upper-level admission, 151 were accepted, 145 enrolled. Iowa Tests of Basic Skills, Stanford Achievement Test or TOEFL or SLEP required. Deadline for receipt of application materials: none. No application fee required. Interview required.

Athletics Interscholastic: basketball (boys, girls), soccer (b,g). 1 PE instructor, 2 coaches.

Computers Computers are regularly used in creative writing, desktop publishing, English, ESL, foreign language, information technology, mathematics, science, social sciences, writing, yearbook classes. Computer network features include Internet access, Internet filtering or blocking technology. Computer access in designated common areas is available to students. Students grades are available online. The school has a published electronic and media policy.

Contact Jennifer Bratulich, Director of Admissions. 651-288-4610. Fax: 651-288-4616. E-mail: jbratulich@stpaulprep.org. Web site: www.stpaulprep.org.

ST. PAUL'S EPISCOPAL SCHOOL

161 Dogwood Lane
Mobile, Alabama 36608
Head of School: Mr. F. Martin Lester Jr.

General Information Coeducational day college-preparatory, arts, technology, and honors, Advanced Placement school, affiliated with Episcopal Church. Grades PK–12. Founded: 1947. Setting: suburban. 32-acre campus. 10 buildings on campus. Approved or accredited by National Association of Episcopal Schools, Southern Association of Colleges and Schools, Southern Association of Independent Schools, and Alabama Department of Education. Member of National Association of Independent Schools and Secondary School Admission Test Board. Endowment: $1.6 million. Total enrollment: 1,405. Upper school average class size: 20. Upper school faculty-student ratio: 1:12. There are 177 required school days per year for Upper School students. Upper School students typically attend 5 days per week. The average school day consists of 6 hours and 10 minutes.

Upper School Student Profile Grade 9: 92 students (44 boys, 48 girls); Grade 10: 133 students (69 boys, 64 girls); Grade 11: 132 students (80 boys, 52 girls); Grade 12: 138 students (71 boys, 67 girls).

Faculty School total: 143. In upper school: 21 men, 35 women; 35 have advanced degrees.

Subjects Offered Advanced biology, advanced chemistry, advanced math, Advanced Placement courses, advanced studio art-AP, algebra, American history, American literature, anatomy and physiology, art, arts, band, biology, biology-AP, calculus, calculus-AP, chemistry, chemistry-AP, choir, choral music, civics, composition, computer science, concert choir, digital photography, drama, driver education, economics, economics-AP, English, English literature, English-AP, environmental science, environmental science-AP, European history, European history-AP, fine arts, foreign language, French, French-AP, geometry, government-AP, government/civics, grammar, history, history-AP, honors algebra, honors English, honors geometry, human anatomy, instrumental music, journalism, Latin, marching band, marine biology, mathematics, music, oil painting, painting, photography, physical education, physics, physics-AP, pre-algebra, pre-calculus, public service, Spanish, speech, theater, theater arts, trigonometry, U.S. history-AP, weight training, world history, yearbook.

Graduation Requirements Arts and fine arts (art, music, dance, drama), electives, English, foreign language, history, mathematics, science, 4 years of English, mathematics, social studies, and science, 2 year minimum foreign language, 60 hours of community service. Community service is required.

Special Academic Programs Advanced Placement exam preparation; honors section; study at local college for college credit; special instructional classes for students with diagnosed learning disabilities.

College Admission Counseling 137 students graduated in 2010; 136 went to college, including Auburn University; Birmingham-Southern College; The University of Alabama; Tulane University; University of Mississippi; University of South Alabama. Other: 1 entered military service.

Student Life Upper grades have uniform requirement, student council, honor system. Discipline rests primarily with faculty. Attendance at religious services is required.

Summer Programs Remediation, enrichment, advancement, sports, art/fine arts, computer instruction programs offered; session focuses on enrichment; held both on and off campus; held at Trip abroad; accepts boys and girls; open to students from other schools. 2011 schedule: June 1 to August 1. Application deadline: none.

Tuition and Aid Tuition installment plan (Insured Tuition Payment Plan, monthly payment plans, individually arranged payment plans, semiannual payment plan). Need-based scholarship grants available. Total amount of financial aid awarded in 2010–11: $353,000.

Admissions Traditional secondary-level entrance grade is 9. For fall 2010, 24 students applied for upper-level admission, 22 were accepted, 18 enrolled. ERB CTP IV or Otis-Lennon and 2 sections of ERB required. Deadline for receipt of application materials: none. Application fee required. Interview required.

Athletics Interscholastic: baseball (boys), basketball (b,g), cheering (g), cross-country running (b,g), diving (b,g), football (b), golf (b,g), indoor track & field (b,g), soccer (b,g), softball (g), strength & conditioning (b,g), swimming and diving (b,g), tennis (b,g), track and field (b,g), volleyball (g), weight training (b), winter (indoor) track (b,g); intramural: basketball (b,g), soccer (b,g), volleyball (g), weight training (b); coed interscholastic: fencing. 6 PE instructors, 13 coaches, 4 athletic trainers.

Computers Computers are regularly used in economics, English, foreign language, history, independent study, journalism, keyboarding, mathematics, newspaper, publications, science, Spanish, writing, yearbook classes. Computer network features include on-campus library services, online commercial services, Internet access, wireless campus network, Internet filtering or blocking technology. Campus intranet, student e-mail accounts, and computer access in designated common areas are available to students. Students grades are available online. The school has a published electronic and media policy.

Contact Ms. Julie L. Taylor, Advancement/Admissions Director. 251-461-2129. Fax: 251-342-1844. E-mail: jtaylor@stpaulsmobile.net. Web site: www.stpaulsmobile.net.

ST. PAUL'S HIGH SCHOOL

2200 Grant Avenue
Winnipeg, Manitoba R3P 0P8, Canada
Head of School: Fr. Alan Fogarty, SJ

General Information Boys' day college-preparatory, arts, religious studies, and technology school, affiliated with Roman Catholic Church. Grades 9–12. Founded: 1926. Setting: suburban. 18-acre campus. 5 buildings on campus. Approved or accredited by Jesuit Secondary Education Association and Manitoba Department of Education. Language of instruction: English. Endowment: CAN$5.5 million. Total enrollment: 585. Upper school average class size: 26. Upper school faculty-student ratio: 1:14. There are 193 required school days per year for Upper School students. Upper School students typically attend 5 days per week. The average school day consists of 5 hours and 50 minutes.

Upper School Student Profile Grade 9: 152 students (152 boys); Grade 10: 143 students (143 boys); Grade 11: 153 students (153 boys); Grade 12: 137 students (137 boys). 68% of students are Roman Catholic.

Faculty School total: 44. In upper school: 37 men, 7 women; 14 have advanced degrees.

Subjects Offered Algebra, American history, art, biology, calculus, chemistry, classics, computer science, current events, economics, English, ethics, French, geography, geometry, history, law, mathematics, media, multimedia, multimedia design, music, physical education, physics, political science, psychology, religion, science, social studies, speech, theology, world wide web design.

Graduation Requirements English, mathematics, physical education (includes health), religion (includes Bible studies and theology), science, social studies (includes history), completion of Christian service program.

Special Academic Programs Advanced Placement exam preparation; honors section; remedial math.

College Admission Counseling 143 students graduated in 2010; 133 went to college, including McGill University; Queen's University at Kingston; The University of British Columbia; The University of Winnipeg; University of Manitoba; University of Toronto. Other: 3 went to work, 7 had other specific plans.

Student Life Upper grades have specified standards of dress, student council, honor system. Discipline rests primarily with faculty. Attendance at religious services is required.

Summer Programs Sports programs offered; session focuses on sport skills and relationship building; held on campus; accepts boys; open to students from other schools. 80 students usually enrolled. 2011 schedule: August 21 to September 4.

Tuition and Aid Day student tuition: CAN$6450. Tuition installment plan (Insured Tuition Payment Plan, monthly payment plans, individually arranged payment plans). Bursaries, need-based loans available. In 2010–11, 13% of upper-school students received aid. Total amount of financial aid awarded in 2010–11: CAN$275,000.

Admissions Traditional secondary-level entrance grade is 9. For fall 2010, 305 students applied for upper-level admission, 168 were accepted, 160 enrolled. Achievement tests and STS required. Deadline for receipt of application materials: February 6. Application fee required: CAN$75. On-campus interview required.

Athletics Interscholastic: badminton, basketball, cross-country running, curling, football, golf, ice hockey, indoor track, indoor track & field, rugby, soccer, track and field, volleyball, wrestling; intramural: badminton, basketball, curling, flag football, golf, physical fitness, physical training, skiing (downhill), strength & conditioning, table tennis, volleyball, weight training. 4 PE instructors, 1 athletic trainer.

Computers Computers are regularly used in French, French as a second language, geography, mathematics, multimedia, religious studies, science, Web site design classes. Computer network features include on-campus library services, online commercial services, Internet access, Internet filtering or blocking technology. Campus intranet, student e-mail accounts, and computer access in designated common areas are available to students. Students grades are available online. The school has a published electronic and media policy.

Contact Mr. Tom Lussier, Principal. 204-831-2300. Fax: 204-831-2340. E-mail: tlussier@stpauls.mb.ca. Web site: www.stpauls.mb.ca.

ST. PAUL'S SCHOOL

11152 Falls Road
PO Box 8100
Brooklandville, Maryland 21022-8100
Head of School: Mr. Thomas J. Reid

General Information Coeducational day (girls' only in lower grades) college-preparatory school, affiliated with Episcopal Church. Boys grades K–12, girls grades K–4. Founded: 1849. Setting: suburban. Nearest major city is Baltimore. 95-acre campus. 23 buildings on campus. Approved or accredited by Association of Independent Maryland Schools and Maryland Department of Education. Member of National Association of Independent Schools. Endowment: $24.7 million. Total enrollment: 828. Upper school average class size: 17. Upper school faculty-student ratio: 1:9.

Faculty School total: 90.

Subjects Offered Acting, algebra, American history, American literature, anatomy, art, art history, biology, biology-AP, calculus, calculus-AP, chemistry, community service, design, drama, drawing, economics, English, ethics, forensics, French, French-AP, geometry, German, German-AP, International Baccalaureate courses, Japanese, mathematics, model United Nations, music, painting, photography, physical education, physics, physics-AP, psychology, religion, Spanish, Spanish-AP, statistics, statistics-AP, theater, trigonometry, world history, world literature.

Graduation Requirements Arts and fine arts (art, music, dance, drama), English, foreign language, mathematics, physical education (includes health), religion (includes Bible studies and theology), science, social sciences, social studies (includes history). Community service is required.

Special Academic Programs International Baccalaureate program; Advanced Placement exam preparation; honors section; independent study; term-away projects; study abroad; academic accommodation for the gifted; programs in general development for dyslexic students.

College Admission Counseling 77 students graduated in 2009; all went to college, including Elon University; The University of North Carolina Wilmington; Tulane University; University of Colorado at Boulder.

Student Life Upper grades have specified standards of dress, student council, honor system. Discipline rests equally with students and faculty. Attendance at religious services is required.

Tuition and Aid Day student tuition: $19,750. Tuition installment plan (Key Tuition Payment Plan). Need-based scholarship grants available. In 2009–10, 30% of upper-school students received aid. Total amount of financial aid awarded in 2009–10: $1,175,000.

Admissions Traditional secondary-level entrance grade is 9. For fall 2009, 108 students applied for upper-level admission, 81 were accepted, 37 enrolled. CTP III, ERB, ISEE or SSAT required. Deadline for receipt of application materials: January 15. Application fee required: $50. On-campus interview required.

Athletics Interscholastic: baseball (boys), basketball (b), crew (b), cross-country running (b), football (b), golf (b), ice hockey (b), independent competitive sports (b), lacrosse (b), soccer (b), squash (b), swimming and diving (b), tennis (b), volleyball (b), wrestling (b); intramural: bicycling (b), combined training (b), Frisbee (b), mountain biking (b), outdoor activities (b), physical fitness (b), physical training (b), ropes courses (b), running (b), soccer (b), strength & conditioning (b), ultimate Frisbee (b), weight training (b). 3 PE instructors, 3 coaches, 2 athletic trainers.

Computers Computers are regularly used in all classes. Computer network features include on-campus library services, online commercial services, Internet access, wireless campus network, Internet filtering or blocking technology. Student e-mail accounts are available to students. The school has a published electronic and media policy.

Contact Ms. Amy Hall Furlong, Director of Admissions. 410-821-3034. Fax: 410-427-0380. E-mail: admissions@stpaulsschool.org. Web site: www. stpaulsschool.org.

ST. PAUL'S SCHOOL

325 Pleasant Street
Concord, New Hampshire 03301-2591
Head of School: Mr. William R. Matthews Jr.

General Information Coeducational boarding college-preparatory and arts school, affiliated with Episcopal Church. Grades 9–12. Founded: 1856. Setting: suburban. Students are housed in single-sex dormitories. 2,000-acre campus. 75 buildings on campus. Approved or accredited by Association of Independent Schools in New England, National Association of Episcopal Schools, New England Association of Schools and Colleges, The Association of Boarding Schools, and New Hampshire Department of Education. Member of National Association of Independent Schools and Secondary School Admission Test Board. Endowment: $346 million. Total

enrollment: 535. Upper school average class size: 11. Upper school faculty-student ratio: 1:5. Upper School students typically attend 5 days per week. The average school day consists of 6 hours.

Upper School Student Profile Grade 9: 109 students (49 boys, 60 girls); Grade 10: 149 students (78 boys, 71 girls); Grade 11: 144 students (73 boys, 71 girls); Grade 12: 133 students (63 boys, 70 girls). 100% of students are boarding students. 11% are state residents. 30 states are represented in upper school student body. 17% are international students. International students from Canada, China, Democratic People's Republic of Korea, Hong Kong, Japan, and United Kingdom; 14 other countries represented in student body. 33% of students are members of Episcopal Church.

Faculty School total: 102. In upper school: 46 men, 33 women; 76 have advanced degrees; all reside on campus.

Subjects Offered 3-dimensional design, algebra, American history, American literature, applied arts, applied music, architecture, art, art history, astronomy, ballet, biology, calculus, ceramics, chemistry, Chinese, classical civilization, classical Greek literature, classical language, computer math, computer programming, computer science, creative writing, drama, driver education, ecology, English, English literature, environmental science, ethics, European history, fine arts, French, geometry, German, government/civics, grammar, Greek, health, history, humanities, independent study, instrumental music, Japanese, Latin, mathematics, music, photography, physical education, physics, religion, robotics, science, social studies, Spanish, speech, statistics, theater, trigonometry, writing.

Graduation Requirements Art, athletics, humanities, language, mathematics, music, religion (includes Bible studies and theology), science, residential life. Community service is required.

Special Academic Programs 9 Advanced Placement exams for which test preparation is offered; honors section; accelerated programs; independent study; term-away projects; study abroad; academic accommodation for the gifted, the musically talented, and the artistically talented.

College Admission Counseling 134 students graduated in 2009; all went to college, including Columbia University; Dartmouth College; Georgetown University; Harvard University; Tufts University; Yale University. Median SAT critical reading: 683, median SAT math: 683, median SAT writing: 681.

Student Life Upper grades have specified standards of dress, student council, honor system. Discipline rests primarily with faculty.

Tuition and Aid 7-day tuition and room/board: $42,900. Tuition installment plan (Academic Management Services Plan, monthly payment plans). Need-based scholarship grants, tuition remission for children of faculty and staff available. In 2009–10, 36% of upper-school students received aid. Total amount of financial aid awarded in 2009–10: $7,200,000.

Admissions Traditional secondary-level entrance grade is 9. For fall 2009, 1,226 students applied for upper-level admission, 236 were accepted, 173 enrolled. SSAT required. Deadline for receipt of application materials: January 15. Application fee required: $50. Interview required.

Athletics Interscholastic: alpine skiing (boys, girls), baseball (b), basketball (b,g), crew (b,g), cross-country running (b,g), field hockey (g), football (b), ice hockey (b,g), lacrosse (b,g), rowing (b,g), skiing (cross-country) (b,g), skiing (downhill) (b,g), soccer (b,g), softball (g), squash (b,g), tennis (b,g), track and field (b,g), volleyball (g), wrestling (b); intramural: crew (b,g), ice hockey (b,g), rowing (b,g), soccer (b,g); coed interscholastic: ballet; coed intramural: aerobics, aerobics/Nautilus, alpine skiing, backpacking, baseball, basketball, crew, equestrian sports, fitness, fly fishing, horseback riding, ice hockey, physical fitness, rowing, skeet shooting, skiing (cross-country), skiing (downhill), snowboarding, soccer, squash, tai chi, tennis, weight training, wrestling. 2 coaches, 2 athletic trainers.

Computers Computers are regularly used in English, foreign language, humanities, mathematics, science classes. Computer network features include on-campus library services, online commercial services, Internet access, wireless campus network, Internet filtering or blocking technology. Campus intranet, student e-mail accounts, and computer access in designated common areas are available to students. Students grades are available online. The school has a published electronic and media policy.

Contact Ms. Holly Foote, Office Manager. 603-229-4700. Fax: 603-229-4771. E-mail: admissions@sps.edu. Web site: www.sps.edu.

ST. PAUL'S SCHOOL FOR GIRLS

11232 Falls Road
Brooklandville, Maryland 21022
Head of School: Dr. Monica M. Gillespie

General Information Girls' day college-preparatory, arts, religious studies, technology, and AP and honors, leadership school, affiliated with Episcopal Church. Grades 5–12. Founded: 1959. Setting: suburban. Nearest major city is Baltimore. 38-acre campus. 4 buildings on campus. Approved or accredited by Association of Independent Maryland Schools, National Association of Episcopal Schools, and Maryland Department of Education. Member of National Association of Independent Schools. Endowment: $6.9 million. Total enrollment: 444. Upper school average class size: 15. Upper school faculty-student ratio: 1:6. There are 170 required school days per year for Upper School students. Upper School students typically attend 5 days per week. The average school day consists of 7 hours.

Upper School Student Profile Grade 9: 65 students (65 girls); Grade 10: 74 students (74 girls); Grade 11: 60 students (60 girls); Grade 12: 70 students (70 girls).

St. Paul's School for Girls

Faculty School total: 71. In upper school: 14 men, 36 women; 37 have advanced degrees.

Subjects Offered Algebra, American history, American literature, anatomy, ancient history, art, biology, biology-AP, biotechnology, calculus, calculus-AP, chemistry, chemistry-AP, Chinese, chorus, community service, computer science, dance, drama, economics, economics-AP, English, English language and composition-AP, English literature and composition-AP, English-AP, environmental science, environmental science-AP, ethics, fine arts, forensics, French, French-AP, genetics, geography, geometry, German, German-AP, health, history, Japanese, journalism, leadership and service, literary magazine, literature, mathematics, mechanics, medieval history, modern history, music, newspaper, optics, photography, physical education, physics, physics-AP, physiology, pre-calculus, programming, psychology-AP, religion, research skills, science, senior project, social studies, Spanish, Spanish language-AP, speech, statistics, studio art-AP, theater, trigonometry, U.S. history-AP, world cultures, world history.

Graduation Requirements Arts and fine arts (art, music, dance, drama), English, foreign language, mathematics, physical education (includes health), religion (includes Bible studies and theology), science, social studies (includes history), senior work project, senior speech. Community service is required.

Special Academic Programs 17 Advanced Placement exams for which test preparation is offered; honors section; independent study; term-away projects; domestic exchange program; study abroad; academic accommodation for the gifted, the musically talented, and the artistically talented.

College Admission Counseling 71 students graduated in 2009; all went to college, including Bucknell University; Franklin & Marshall College; James Madison University; The College of William and Mary; University of Maryland, College Park; University of Virginia.

Student Life Upper grades have uniform requirement, student council, honor system. Discipline rests equally with students and faculty. Attendance at religious services is required.

Tuition and Aid Day student tuition: $22,300. Tuition installment plan (Key Tuition Payment Plan, monthly payment plans). Merit scholarship grants, need-based scholarship grants, paying campus jobs available. In 2009–10, 26% of upper-school students received aid; total upper-school merit-scholarship money awarded: $22,300. Total amount of financial aid awarded in 2009–10: $1,427,445.

Admissions Traditional secondary-level entrance grade is 9. ISEE required. Deadline for receipt of application materials: January 8. Application fee required: $50. On-campus interview required.

Athletics Interscholastic: aerobics/dance, aquatics, badminton, ballet, basketball, crew, cross-country running, dance, field hockey, golf, indoor soccer, lacrosse, modern dance, physical fitness, rowing, soccer, softball, squash, swimming and diving, tennis, volleyball; coed intramural: sailing. 2 PE instructors, 12 coaches, 1 athletic trainer.

Computers Computers are regularly used in college planning, creative writing, current events, English, French, geography, history, introduction to technology, journalism, language development, library science, literary magazine, mathematics, newspaper, photography, psychology, religious studies, research skills, SAT preparation, science, Spanish, study skills, technology, yearbook classes. Computer network features include on-campus library services, online commercial services, Internet access, wireless campus network, Internet filtering or blocking technology, Moodle, Senior Systems, 200 free tablets. Campus intranet, student e-mail accounts, and computer access in designated common areas are available to students. The school has a published electronic and media policy.

Contact Debbie Awalt, Assistant Director of Admission. 443-632-1002. Fax: 410-828-7238. E-mail: dwalt@spsfg.org. Web site: www.spsfg.org.

ST. PETER'S PREPARATORY SCHOOL

144 Grand Street
Jersey City, New Jersey 07302
Head of School: Rev. Robert E. Reiser, SJ

General Information Boys' day college-preparatory, arts, technology, and music school, affiliated with Roman Catholic Church. Grades 9–12. Founded: 1872. Setting: urban. Nearest major city is New York, NY. 7-acre campus. 8 buildings on campus. Approved or accredited by Jesuit Secondary Education Association, Middle States Association of Colleges and Schools, and New Jersey Department of Education. Endowment: $17 million. Total enrollment: 905. Upper school average class size: 22. Upper school faculty-student ratio: 1:12. There are 170 required school days per year for Upper School students. Upper School students typically attend 5 days per week. The average school day consists of 5 hours and 30 minutes.

Upper School Student Profile Grade 9: 259 students (259 boys); Grade 10: 236 students (236 boys); Grade 11: 189 students (189 boys); Grade 12: 221 students (221 boys). 80% of students are Roman Catholic.

Faculty School total: 79. In upper school: 53 men, 25 women; 45 have advanced degrees.

Subjects Offered Advanced Placement courses, algebra, American history, American history-AP, American legal systems, American literature, Ancient Greek, art, art history, Bible studies, biology, biology-AP, calculus, calculus-AP, ceramics, chemistry, chemistry-AP, choral music, Christian ethics, community service, computer programming, computer science, computer science-AP, concert band, creative writing, drawing, English, English language-AP, English literature, English literature-AP, European history, French, geometry, German, health, history, human anatomy, Italian, jazz band, Latin, Latin-AP, mathematics, music, music theory, physical education, physics, religion, sculpture, social justice, Spanish, Spanish language-AP, Spanish literature-AP, statistics-AP, studio art, theology, trigonometry, Web site design, world civilizations, world history, world literature, writing.

Graduation Requirements Algebra, American history, American literature, ancient world history, art, Basic programming, biology, British literature, chemistry, computer education, English, geometry, Latin, modern languages, music, physical education (includes health), physics, religion (includes Bible studies and theology), U.S. history, world civilizations, 20 hours of community service in freshman and sophomore years, 60 hours in the third (junior) year.

Special Academic Programs International Baccalaureate program; 12 Advanced Placement exams for which test preparation is offered; honors section; study at local college for college credit; study abroad.

College Admission Counseling 216 students graduated in 2010; 212 went to college, including College of the Holy Cross; Loyola University Maryland; Rutgers, The State University of New Jersey, Rutgers College; Saint Joseph's University; Saint Peter's College; The College of New Jersey. Other: 2 went to work, 1 entered military service, 1 entered a postgraduate year. Median SAT critical reading: 570, median SAT math: 590. Mean SAT writing: 567, mean combined SAT: 1700. 42% scored over 600 on SAT critical reading, 48% scored over 600 on SAT math, 50% scored over 600 on SAT writing, 50% scored over 1800 on combined SAT.

Student Life Upper grades have specified standards of dress, student council, honor system. Discipline rests primarily with faculty.

Summer Programs Remediation, enrichment, sports, art/fine arts programs offered; session focuses on make-up course work for failed classes and enrichment for students trying to advance their studies; held on campus; accepts boys and girls; open to students from other schools. 150 students usually enrolled. 2011 schedule: June 27 to July 29. Application deadline: June 17.

Tuition and Aid Day student tuition: $10,120. Tuition installment plan (SMART Tuition Payment Plan, monthly payment plans). Merit scholarship grants, need-based scholarship grants, paying campus jobs available. In 2010–11, 48% of upper-school students received aid; total upper-school merit-scholarship money awarded: $450,000. Total amount of financial aid awarded in 2010–11: $950,000.

Admissions Traditional secondary-level entrance grade is 9. For fall 2010, 825 students applied for upper-level admission, 445 were accepted, 260 enrolled. Cooperative Entrance Exam (McGraw-Hill) or SSAT required. Deadline for receipt of application materials: November 16. No application fee required.

Athletics Interscholastic: baseball, basketball, bowling, crew, cross-country running, diving, fencing, football, golf, ice hockey, indoor track, indoor track & field, lacrosse, rugby, soccer, swimming and diving, tennis, track and field, volleyball, winter (indoor) track, wrestling; intramural: basketball, flag football, Frisbee, handball, indoor soccer, outdoor recreation, team handball, touch football, ultimate Frisbee, weight lifting, whiffle ball. 4 PE instructors, 23 coaches, 1 athletic trainer.

Computers Computers are regularly used in all academic classes. Computer network features include on-campus library services, online commercial services, Internet access, wireless campus network, Internet filtering or blocking technology. Campus intranet and student e-mail accounts are available to students. Students grades are available online. The school has a published electronic and media policy.

Contact Mr. John T. Irvine, Director of Admissions. 201-547-6389. Fax: 201-547-2341. E-mail: Irvinej@spprep.org. Web site: www.spprep.org.

ST. PIUS X CATHOLIC HIGH SCHOOL

2674 Johnson Road NE
Atlanta, Georgia 30345
Head of School: Mr. Steve Spellman

General Information Coeducational day college-preparatory school, affiliated with Roman Catholic Church. Grades 9–12. Founded: 1958. Setting: suburban. 25-acre campus. 8 buildings on campus. Approved or accredited by National Catholic Education Association, Southern Association of Colleges and Schools, The College Board, and Georgia Department of Education. Member of Secondary School Admission Test Board. Total enrollment: 1,075. Upper school average class size: 21. Upper school faculty-student ratio: 1:12. There are 180 required school days per year for Upper School students.

Upper School Student Profile Grade 9: 295 students (148 boys, 147 girls); Grade 10: 260 students (130 boys, 130 girls); Grade 11: 260 students (130 boys, 130 girls); Grade 12: 260 students (130 boys, 130 girls). 82% of students are Roman Catholic.

Faculty School total: 95. In upper school: 47 men, 48 women; 62 have advanced degrees.

Subjects Offered Accounting, algebra, American history, American literature, anatomy, art, band, biology, business, business law, calculus, ceramics, chemistry, chorus, computer programming, computer science, creative writing, current events, dance, drama, driver education, economics, English, English literature, European history, expository writing, French, geography, geometry, German, government/civics, health, history, instrumental music, journalism, Latin, mathematics, music, physical education, physical science, physics, physiology, psychology, religion, science, social studies, sociology, Spanish, speech, statistics, theater, trigonometry, word processing, world history, world literature.

Graduation Requirements American history, computer science, English, foreign language, mathematics, physical education (includes health), religion (includes Bible studies and theology), science, social studies (includes history).

Special Academic Programs 20 Advanced Placement exams for which test preparation is offered; honors section; special instructional classes for students with learning disabilities and Attention Deficit Disorder.

College Admission Counseling 266 students graduated in 2010; 264 went to college, including Emory University; Furman University; Georgia Institute of Technology; Georgia State University; University of Georgia; University of Notre Dame. Other: 2 had other specific plans. 60% scored over 600 on SAT critical reading, 60% scored over 600 on SAT math, 50% scored over 26 on composite ACT.

Student Life Upper grades have uniform requirement, student council, honor system. Discipline rests equally with students and faculty. Attendance at religious services is required.

Tuition and Aid Day student tuition: $10,800. Tuition installment plan (FACTS Tuition Payment Plan, monthly payment plans). Tuition reduction for siblings, need-based scholarship grants, paying campus jobs available. In 2010–11, 18% of upper-school students received aid. Total amount of financial aid awarded in 2010–11: $400,000.

Admissions Traditional secondary-level entrance grade is 9. For fall 2010, 500 students applied for upper-level admission, 340 were accepted, 308 enrolled. SSAT required. Deadline for receipt of application materials: February 1. Application fee required: $100.

Athletics Interscholastic: baseball (boys), basketball (b,g), cheering (b,g), cross-country running (b,g), dance (b), dance squad (g), dance team (g), diving (b,g), drill team (g), football (b), golf (b,g), lacrosse (b,g), soccer (b,g), softball (g), strength & conditioning (b,g), swimming and diving (b,g), tennis (b,g), track and field (b,g), volleyball (g), water polo (b,g), weight training (b,g), wrestling (b); coed interscholastic: sailing, water polo. 4 PE instructors, 33 coaches, 1 athletic trainer.

Computers Computers are regularly used in science, Web site design classes. Computer network features include on-campus library services, online commercial services, Internet access, Internet filtering or blocking technology. Campus intranet and student e-mail accounts are available to students. Students grades are available online. The school has a published electronic and media policy.

Contact Terry Sides, Coordinator of Admissions. 404-636-0323 Ext. 291. Fax: 404-636-2118. E-mail: tsides@spx.org. Web site: www.spx.org.

ST. PIUS X HIGH SCHOOL
5301 St. Joseph Drive NW
Albuquerque, New Mexico 87120
Head of School: Mrs. Barbara M. Rothweiler

General Information Coeducational day college-preparatory and religious studies school, affiliated with Roman Catholic Church. Grades 9–12. Founded: 1956. Setting: urban. 57-acre campus. 6 buildings on campus. Approved or accredited by North Central Association of Colleges and Schools and New Mexico Department of Education. Endowment: $3 million. Total enrollment: 884. Upper school average class size: 22. Upper school faculty-student ratio: 1:16. There are 180 required school days per year for Upper School students. Upper School students typically attend 5 days per week. The average school day consists of 7 hours.

Upper School Student Profile Grade 9: 235 students (124 boys, 111 girls); Grade 10: 213 students (112 boys, 101 girls); Grade 11: 206 students (98 boys, 108 girls); Grade 12: 230 students (99 boys, 131 girls). 95% of students are Roman Catholic.

Faculty School total: 66. In upper school: 32 men, 34 women; 49 have advanced degrees.

Subjects Offered 20th century American writers, 20th century history, 20th century physics, 3-dimensional art, accounting, acting, algebra, American government, American history, American history-AP, American literature, American literature-AP, anatomy, anatomy and physiology, applied arts, applied music, art, art and culture, art appreciation, art history-AP, astronomy, band, Bible, biology, biology-AP, business law, calculus, calculus-AP, campus ministry, chemistry, child development, choir, chorus, church history, community service, comparative religion, computer art, computer literacy, computer programming, conceptual physics, concert band, creative writing, culinary arts, debate, drafting, drama, drawing, economics, English language-AP, English literature-AP, environmental science-AP, French, geometry, government, government-AP, health, history of the Catholic Church, honors algebra, honors geometry, human anatomy, independent living, jazz ensemble, math analysis, mechanical drawing, model United Nations, moral theology, music appreciation, newspaper, orchestra, painting, peer ministry, photography, physical education, physics, play production, pre-calculus, printmaking, probability and statistics, psychology, set design, social justice, softball, Spanish, Spanish language-AP, sports medicine, statistics-AP, studio art, study skills, swimming, theology, trigonometry, U.S. government and politics-AP, weight training, world geography, world history, writing, yearbook.

Graduation Requirements Algebra, American government, American history, American literature, art, biology, computer skills, English, foreign language, geometry, history, language and composition, literature, music, physical education (includes health), physical science, science, theology, world history.

Special Academic Programs Advanced Placement exam preparation; honors section; remedial reading and/or remedial writing.

College Admission Counseling 239 students graduated in 2009; 220 went to college, including New Mexico State University; University of New Mexico. Other: 5 entered military service. Mean composite ACT: 23.

Student Life Upper grades have uniform requirement, student council, honor system. Discipline rests primarily with faculty. Attendance at religious services is required.

Tuition and Aid Day student tuition: $9375. Tuition installment plan (FACTS Tuition Payment Plan). Tuition reduction for siblings, merit scholarship grants, need-based scholarship grants available. In 2009–10, 20% of upper-school students received aid; total upper-school merit-scholarship money awarded: $30,000. Total amount of financial aid awarded in 2009–10: $250,000.

Admissions Traditional secondary-level entrance grade is 9. For fall 2009, 435 students applied for upper-level admission, 330 were accepted, 289 enrolled. High School Placement Test (closed version) from Scholastic Testing Service required. Deadline for receipt of application materials: none. No application fee required.

Athletics Interscholastic: aerobics/dance (girls), baseball (b), basketball (b,g), cheering (g), cross-country running (b,g), drill team (g), football (b), ice hockey (b), physical fitness (b,g), soccer (b,g), softball (g), swimming and diving (b,g), tennis (b,g), track and field (b,g), volleyball (g), weight lifting (b,g), weight training (b,g), wrestling (b); intramural: basketball (b,g), flag football (b,g), soccer (b,g); coed interscholastic: diving, golf; coed intramural: softball, table tennis. 3 PE instructors, 1 athletic trainer.

Computers Computers are regularly used in graphic arts, journalism, newspaper, writing, yearbook classes. Computer network features include on-campus library services, online commercial services, Internet access, Internet filtering or blocking technology. Students grades are available online. The school has a published electronic and media policy.

Contact Mrs. Barbara Ducaj, Assistant Principal, Academics. 505-831-8443. Fax: 505-831-8413. E-mail: bducaj@spx.k12.nm.us.

ST. PIUS X HIGH SCHOOL
811 West Donovan
Houston, Texas 77091-5699
Head of School: Sr. Donna M. Pollard, OP

General Information Coeducational day college-preparatory, arts, business, religious studies, and technology school, affiliated with Roman Catholic Church. Grades 9–12. Founded: 1956. Setting: urban. 26-acre campus. 1 building on campus. Approved or accredited by Southern Association of Colleges and Schools, Texas Catholic Conference, Texas Education Agency, The College Board, and Texas Department of Education. Endowment: $2.6 million. Total enrollment: 689. Upper school average class size: 22. Upper school faculty-student ratio: 1:12. There are 180 required school days per year for Upper School students. Upper School students typically attend 5 days per week. The average school day consists of 7 hours.

Upper School Student Profile Grade 9: 170 students (92 boys, 78 girls); Grade 10: 171 students (93 boys, 78 girls); Grade 11: 187 students (105 boys, 82 girls); Grade 12: 161 students (82 boys, 79 girls). 71% of students are Roman Catholic.

Faculty School total: 57. In upper school: 21 men, 36 women; 40 have advanced degrees.

Subjects Offered Advanced chemistry, advanced computer applications, advanced math, Advanced Placement courses, advanced studio art-AP, algebra, American history-AP, American literature, American literature-AP, anatomy and physiology, art, band, biology, biology-AP, business law, calculus, calculus-AP, campus ministry, Catholic belief and practice, chemistry, choir, chorus, Christian ethics, church history, college counseling, community service, computer applications, computer multimedia, computer programming, computer science-AP, cultural geography, dance, death and loss, desktop publishing, earth and space science, economics, English language-AP, English literature-AP, environmental science, film history, fine arts, foreign language, French, geography, geometry, graphic design, health, history of the Catholic Church, honors geometry, honors world history, introduction to theater, Italian, jewelry making, language arts, Latin, Latin-AP, library assistant, marching band, moral and social development, moral theology, musical productions, painting, philosophy, photography, physical education, physics, psychology, reading/study skills, SAT/ACT preparation, Shakespeare, social justice, sociology, Spanish, Spanish language-AP, Spanish-AP, speech, speech communications, stagecraft, student government, student publications, technical theater, theology, U.S. government, U.S. government and politics-AP, U.S. history, U.S. history-AP, Web site design, world history, world religions, yearbook.

Graduation Requirements Advanced math, algebra, American government, American history, ancient world history, art, biology, chemistry, communications, economics, electives, English, geometry, government, health, integrated physics, physical education (includes health), physics, theology, 2 years of foreign language or reading development, Christian Service Learning-100 hours of community service, 4 years of theology.

Special Academic Programs 10 Advanced Placement exams for which test preparation is offered; honors section; study at local college for college credit; remedial reading and/or remedial writing; remedial math; programs in English, mathematics, general development for dyslexic students.

College Admission Counseling 155 students graduated in 2010; all went to college, including St. Edward's University; Texas A&M University; Texas Christian University; Texas Tech University; The University of Texas at San Antonio; University of Houston. Mean SAT critical reading: 545, mean SAT math: 540, mean composite ACT: 22. 27% scored over 600 on SAT critical reading, 26% scored over 600 on SAT math, 19% scored over 26 on composite ACT.

St. Pius X High School

Student Life Upper grades have uniform requirement, student council, honor system. Discipline rests primarily with faculty. Attendance at religious services is required.

Summer Programs Enrichment, sports, art/fine arts, computer instruction programs offered; held on campus; accepts boys and girls; not open to students from other schools. 100 students usually enrolled. 2011 schedule: June 6 to July 30. Application deadline: May 1.

Tuition and Aid Day student tuition: $10,100. Tuition installment plan (monthly payment plans, individually arranged payment plans). Tuition reduction for siblings, merit scholarship grants, need-based scholarship grants available. In 2010–11, 28% of upper-school students received aid; total upper-school merit-scholarship money awarded: $21,000. Total amount of financial aid awarded in 2010–11: $704,665.

Admissions Traditional secondary-level entrance grade is 9. For fall 2010, 264 students applied for upper-level admission, 230 were accepted, 186 enrolled. Catholic High School Entrance Examination required. Deadline for receipt of application materials: January 15. Application fee required: $50. Interview required.

Athletics Interscholastic: baseball (boys), basketball (b,g), cheering (g), cross-country running (b,g), dance squad (g), dance team (b,g), drill team (g), football (b), golf (b,g), soccer (b,g), softball (g), swimming and diving (b,g), tennis (b,g), track and field (b,g), volleyball (g). 3 PE instructors, 6 coaches, 1 athletic trainer.

Computers Computers are regularly used in art, career exploration, career technology, desktop publishing, drawing and design, graphic design, journalism, mathematics, multimedia, news writing, newspaper, publications, technology, video film production, yearbook classes. Computer network features include on-campus library services, Internet access, wireless campus network, Internet filtering or blocking technology, faculty Web pages for courses. Student e-mail accounts and computer access in designated common areas are available to students. Students grades are available online. The school has a published electronic and media policy.

Contact Ms. Susie Kramer, Admissions Director. 713-579-7507. Fax: 713-692-5725. E-mail: kramers@stpiusx.org. Web site: www.stpiusx.org.

ST. SCHOLASTICA ACADEMY

7416 North Ridge Boulevard
Chicago, Illinois 60645-1998
Head of School: Mr. Ronald Hoover

General Information Girls' day college-preparatory, arts, and religious studies school, affiliated with Roman Catholic Church. Grades 9–12. Founded: 1865. Setting: urban. 14-acre campus. 1 building on campus. Approved or accredited by International Baccalaureate Organization, National Catholic Education Association, North Central Association of Colleges and Schools, and Illinois Department of Education. Endowment: $3.9 million. Total enrollment: 250. Upper school average class size: 14. Upper school faculty-student ratio: 1:9.

Upper School Student Profile Grade 9: 65 students (65 girls); Grade 10: 50 students (50 girls); Grade 11: 65 students (65 girls); Grade 12: 70 students (70 girls). 60% of students are Roman Catholic.

Faculty School total: 28. In upper school: 5 men, 23 women; 21 have advanced degrees.

Subjects Offered 20th century world history, algebra, American history, American literature, anatomy and physiology, art, arts appreciation, biology, British literature, calculus, ceramics, chemistry, chorus, Christian and Hebrew scripture, consumer economics, consumer education, creative writing, desktop publishing, drama performance, dramatic arts, drawing, English literature, fine arts, French, geometry, graphic arts, graphic design, health, honors algebra, honors English, honors geometry, honors U.S. history, honors world history, information technology, International Baccalaureate courses, journalism, language arts, Latin, music, painting, peace and justice, philosophy, photography, physical education, physics, pre-calculus, psychology, service learning/internship, Spanish, speech, student publications, theater arts, theology, theory of knowledge, trigonometry, word processing, world cultures, world geography, world history, world literature.

Graduation Requirements Algebra, American literature, arts and fine arts (art, music, dance, drama), biology, British literature, chemistry, electives, foreign language, geography, geometry, health, introduction to literature, keyboarding, speech, theology, U.S. history, world literature.

Special Academic Programs International Baccalaureate program; Advanced Placement exam preparation; honors section; remedial reading and/or remedial writing; remedial math.

College Admission Counseling 77 students graduated in 2009; all went to college, including Benedictine College; DePaul University; Loyola University Chicago; Northeastern Illinois University; University of Illinois at Chicago; University of Illinois at Urbana–Champaign.

Student Life Upper grades have uniform requirement, student council. Discipline rests primarily with faculty. Attendance at religious services is required.

Tuition and Aid Day student tuition: $9600. Tuition installment plan (FACTS Tuition Payment Plan). Tuition reduction for siblings, merit scholarship grants, need-based scholarship grants available. In 2009–10, 50% of upper-school students received aid; total upper-school merit-scholarship money awarded: $76,800. Total amount of financial aid awarded in 2009–10: $509,000.

Admissions Traditional secondary-level entrance grade is 9. For fall 2009, 135 students applied for upper-level admission, 129 were accepted, 60 enrolled. STS required. Deadline for receipt of application materials: none. No application fee required.

Athletics Interscholastic: basketball, bowling, cross-country running, indoor track & field, soccer, softball, tennis, track and field, volleyball; intramural: dance. 1 PE instructor, 6 coaches.

Computers Computers are regularly used in English, foreign language, graphic design, journalism, keyboarding, library skills, literary magazine, mathematics, science, social sciences, theology, word processing, writing, yearbook classes. Computer network features include on-campus library services, online commercial services, Internet access, wireless campus network, wireless Internet access. Computer access in designated common areas is available to students. Students grades are available online. The school has a published electronic and media policy.

Contact Ms. Emily Paulus, Director of Pre-Admissions. 773-764-5715 Ext. 356. Fax: 773-764-0304. E-mail: epaulus@scholastica.us. Web site: www.scholastica.us.

ST. SEBASTIAN'S SCHOOL

1191 Greendale Avenue
Needham, Massachusetts 02492
Head of School: Mr. William L. Burke III

General Information Boys' day college-preparatory school, affiliated with Roman Catholic Church. Grades 7–12. Founded: 1941. Setting: suburban. Nearest major city is Boston. 25-acre campus. 5 buildings on campus. Approved or accredited by New England Association of Schools and Colleges and Massachusetts Department of Education. Member of National Association of Independent Schools and Secondary School Admission Test Board. Endowment: $10.4 million. Total enrollment: 355. Upper school average class size: 11. Upper school faculty-student ratio: 1:7.

Upper School Student Profile Grade 9: 66 students (66 boys); Grade 10: 62 students (62 boys); Grade 11: 63 students (63 boys); Grade 12: 66 students (66 boys). 80% of students are Roman Catholic.

Faculty School total: 61. In upper school: 48 men, 13 women; 35 have advanced degrees.

Subjects Offered Algebra, American history, American literature, art, art history, biology, calculus, chemistry, computer science, drama, economics, English, English literature, ethics, European history, fine arts, geography, geometry, government/civics, Greek, history, Latin, mathematics, music, philosophy, photography, physical education, physics, religion, science, social studies, Spanish, speech, theater, trigonometry, world history, world literature, writing.

Graduation Requirements Arts and fine arts (art, music, dance, drama), English, foreign language, mathematics, physical education (includes health), religion (includes Bible studies and theology), science, social studies (includes history), senior service, chapel speaking program.

Special Academic Programs Advanced Placement exam preparation; honors section; independent study; academic accommodation for the gifted, the musically talented, and the artistically talented.

College Admission Counseling 61 students graduated in 2010; all went to college, including College of the Holy Cross; Hobart and William Smith Colleges; Loyola University Maryland; Stonehill College; University of Richmond; Villanova University. Median SAT critical reading: 640, median SAT math: 640.

Student Life Upper grades have specified standards of dress, student council, honor system. Discipline rests primarily with faculty. Attendance at religious services is required.

Tuition and Aid Day student tuition: $31,550. Tuition installment plan (Academic Management Services Plan, Key Tuition Payment Plan). Need-based scholarship grants, need-based loans available. In 2010–11, 26% of upper-school students received aid. Total amount of financial aid awarded in 2010–11: $1,750,000.

Admissions Traditional secondary-level entrance grade is 9. For fall 2010, 100 students applied for upper-level admission, 34 were accepted, 17 enrolled. ISEE or SSAT required. Deadline for receipt of application materials: January 15. Application fee required: $40. On-campus interview required.

Athletics Interscholastic: baseball, basketball, cross-country running, football, golf, ice hockey, lacrosse, sailing, skiing (downhill), soccer, squash, swimming and diving, tennis; intramural: strength & conditioning, ultimate Frisbee, weight lifting, whiffle ball, wrestling. 1 athletic trainer.

Computers Computers are regularly used in English, foreign language, mathematics, science, social studies, writing classes. Computer network features include on-campus library services, Internet access, wireless campus network, Internet filtering or blocking technology. Campus intranet is available to students. The school has a published electronic and media policy.

Contact Mrs. Deborah Sewall, Assistant to Dean of Admissions. 781-449-5200 Ext. 125. Fax: 781-449-5630. E-mail: admissions@stsebs.org. Web site: www. saintsebastiansschool.org.

SAINTS PETER AND PAUL HIGH SCHOOL

900 High Street
Easton, Maryland 21601
Head of School: Mr. James Edward Nemeth

General Information Coeducational day college-preparatory school, affiliated with Roman Catholic Church. Grades 9–12. Founded: 1958. Setting: small town. Nearest major city is Baltimore. 4-acre campus. 4 buildings on campus. Approved or accredited by Middle States Association of Colleges and Schools, National Catholic

Education Association, and Maryland Department of Education. Total enrollment: 206. Upper school average class size: 15. Upper school faculty-student ratio: 1:9. There are 178 required school days per year for Upper School students. Upper School students typically attend 5 days per week. The average school day consists of 6 hours and 30 minutes.

Upper School Student Profile Grade 9: 52 students (31 boys, 21 girls); Grade 10: 52 students (26 boys, 26 girls); Grade 11: 54 students (36 boys, 18 girls); Grade 12: 47 students (27 boys, 20 girls). 70% of students are Roman Catholic.

Faculty School total: 23. In upper school: 12 men, 11 women; 13 have advanced degrees.

Subjects Offered Advanced computer applications, algebra, American government, American literature, anatomy and physiology, art and culture, biology, biology-AP, British literature, British literature (honors), calculus, calculus-AP, campus ministry, Catholic belief and practice, chemistry, chemistry-AP, Christian and Hebrew scripture, Christian ethics, Christianity, church history, computer multimedia, computer programming, computer science, conceptual physics, creative writing, drama, earth science, economics, English literature and composition-AP, environmental science, French, geography, geometry, health and wellness, Hebrew scripture, honors algebra, honors English, honors geometry, honors U.S. history, honors world history, Microsoft, moral theology, music appreciation, music theory, philosophy, physical education, physics, pre-calculus, probability and statistics, Spanish, speech, studio art-AP, theology, U.S. government and politics-AP, U.S. history, U.S. history-AP, Web site design, world history, yearbook.

Graduation Requirements Algebra, American literature, arts and fine arts (art, music, dance, drama), biology, British literature, Catholic belief and practice, chemistry, Christian and Hebrew scripture, Christianity, computer applications, computer science, English, foreign language, geometry, history of the Catholic Church, mathematics, moral theology, physical education (includes health), physics, social justice, U.S. government, U.S. history, world history.

Special Academic Programs 7 Advanced Placement exams for which test preparation is offered; honors section; independent study.

College Admission Counseling 34 students graduated in 2010; 32 went to college, including Loyola University Maryland; Salisbury University; Towson University; University of Maryland, College Park; Washington College. Other: 2 went to work. Median SAT critical reading: 490, median SAT math: 490, median SAT writing: 490. 12% scored over 600 on SAT critical reading, 9% scored over 600 on SAT math, 12% scored over 600 on SAT writing.

Student Life Upper grades have uniform requirement. Discipline rests primarily with faculty. Attendance at religious services is required.

Tuition and Aid Day student tuition: $10,000. Tuition installment plan (FACTS Tuition Payment Plan). Tuition reduction for siblings, need-based scholarship grants, parish subsidies available. In 2010–11, 3% of upper-school students received aid. Total amount of financial aid awarded in 2010–11: $8500.

Admissions Traditional secondary-level entrance grade is 9. For fall 2010, 58 students applied for upper-level admission, 57 were accepted, 52 enrolled. Diocesan Entrance Exam required. Deadline for receipt of application materials: none. Application fee required: $50. On-campus interview required.

Athletics Interscholastic: baseball (boys), basketball (b,g), cross-country running (b,g), field hockey (g), golf (b), ice hockey (b), lacrosse (b,g), soccer (b,g), softball (g), swimming and diving (b,g), tennis (b,g). 1 PE instructor, 23 coaches.

Computers Computers are regularly used in all academic classes. Computer network features include on-campus library services, Internet access, wireless campus network, Internet filtering or blocking technology. Students grades are available online. The school has a published electronic and media policy.

Contact Mrs. Carolyn Smith Hayman, Administrative Assistant. 410-822-2275 Ext. 150. Fax: 410-822-1767. E-mail: chayman@ssppeaston.org. Web site: www.ssppeaston.org.

ST. STANISLAUS COLLEGE
304 South Beach Boulevard
Bay St. Louis, Mississippi 39520
Head of School: Br. Bernard Couvillion, SC

General Information Boys' boarding and day college-preparatory, general academic, religious studies, and ESL school, affiliated with Roman Catholic Church. Grades 7–PG. Founded: 1854. Setting: small town. Nearest major city is New Orleans, LA. Students are housed in single-sex dormitories. 54-acre campus. 8 buildings on campus. Approved or accredited by National Catholic Education Association, Southern Association of Colleges and Schools, Southern Association of Independent Schools, and Mississippi Department of Education. Member of Secondary School Admission Test Board. Endowment: $7 million. Total enrollment: 381. Upper school average class size: 20. Upper school faculty-student ratio: 1:23. There are 180 required school days per year for Upper School students. Upper School students typically attend 5 days per week. The average school day consists of 6 hours and 23 minutes.

Upper School Student Profile Grade 9: 63 students (63 boys); Grade 10: 56 students (56 boys); Grade 11: 62 students (62 boys); Grade 12: 87 students (87 boys); Postgraduate: 1 student (1 boy). 22% of students are boarding students. 1% are state residents. 6 states are represented in upper school student body. 17% are international students. International students from China, India, Mexico, Republic of Korea, Thailand, and Viet Nam; 2 other countries represented in student body. 70% of students are Roman Catholic.

Faculty School total: 42. In upper school: 28 men, 14 women; 21 have advanced degrees; 13 reside on campus.

Subjects Offered Accounting, ACT preparation, advanced biology, advanced chemistry, advanced computer applications, advanced math, Advanced Placement courses, algebra, American history, American history-AP, American literature, anatomy, art, astronomy, biology, biology-AP, British literature-AP, business, business education, business law, calculus, calculus-AP, campus ministry, ceramics, chemistry, chemistry-AP, choir, chorus, computer programming, computer science, computer science-AP, creative writing, desktop publishing, drama, economics, economics and history, English, English language and composition-AP, English literature, English literature and composition-AP, environmental science, ESL, European history-AP, finance, French, French as a second language, genetics, geography, geology, geometry, government, government/civics, grammar, guidance, health, health education, history, journalism, law, marine biology, marine science, mathematics, music, music performance, physical education, physics, physics-AP, pre-calculus, psychology, psychology-AP, religion, science, scuba diving, short story, social sciences, social studies, sociology, Spanish, speech, swimming, symphonic band, theater, theater arts, theology, track and field, trigonometry, typing, U.S. history-AP, world history, world literature.

Graduation Requirements Arts and fine arts (art, music, dance, drama), computer science, English, foreign language, mathematics, physical education (includes health), religion (includes Bible studies and theology), science, social sciences, social studies (includes history), service hours are required.

Special Academic Programs 8 Advanced Placement exams for which test preparation is offered; honors section; remedial reading and/or remedial writing; remedial math; programs in English, mathematics, general development for dyslexic students; special instructional classes for students with Attention Deficit Disorder; ESL (10 students enrolled).

College Admission Counseling 77 students graduated in 2010; all went to college, including Louisiana State University and Agricultural and Mechanical College; Mississippi State University; University of Mississippi; University of New Orleans; University of South Alabama; University of Southern Mississippi. Median SAT critical reading: 520, median SAT math: 620, median SAT writing: 570, median composite ACT: 21. 40% scored over 600 on SAT critical reading, 50% scored over 600 on SAT math, 35% scored over 600 on SAT writing, 22% scored over 1800 on combined SAT, 17% scored over 26 on composite ACT.

Student Life Upper grades have uniform requirement, student council. Discipline rests primarily with faculty. Attendance at religious services is required.

Summer Programs ESL programs offered; session focuses on outdoor summer camp and ESL, cultural summer camp; held both on and off campus; held at Mississippi, Louisiana, and Florida; accepts boys and girls; open to students from other schools. 180 students usually enrolled. 2011 schedule: June 13 to July 20. Application deadline: none.

Tuition and Aid Day student tuition: $5570; 7-day tuition and room/board: $20,655. Tuition installment plan (monthly payment plans, individually arranged payment plans). Need-based scholarship grants, need-based loans, paying campus jobs available.

Admissions Traditional secondary-level entrance grade is 9. Deadline for receipt of application materials: none. Application fee required: $100. On-campus interview recommended.

Athletics Interscholastic: baseball, basketball, cross-country running, football, golf, power lifting, sailing, soccer, swimming and diving, tennis, track and field; intramural: baseball, basketball, billiards, cheering, fishing, flag football, floor hockey, football, hiking/backpacking, jogging, outdoor activities, outdoor adventure, outdoor education, outdoor recreation, outdoor skills, outdoors, physical fitness, physical training, power lifting, scuba diving, swimming and diving, table tennis, tennis, touch football, volleyball, water polo, water skiing, weight lifting, weight training. 5 PE instructors, 16 coaches, 1 athletic trainer.

Computers Computers are regularly used in accounting, English, mathematics, religion, SAT preparation, science, Spanish classes. Computer network features include on-campus library services, online commercial services, Internet access, wireless campus network, Internet filtering or blocking technology. Campus intranet and computer access in designated common areas are available to students. Students grades are available online.

Contact Mr. John Thibodeaux, Director of Admissions. 228-467-9057 Ext. 226. Fax: 228-466-2972. E-mail: admissions@ststan.com. Web site: www.ststan.com.

ST. STEPHEN'S & ST. AGNES SCHOOL
1000 St. Stephen's Road
Alexandria, Virginia 22304
Head of School: Mrs. Joan G. Ogilvy Holden

General Information Coeducational day college-preparatory, arts, religious studies, and technology school, affiliated with Episcopal Church. Grades JK–12. Founded: 1924. Setting: suburban. Nearest major city is Washington, DC. 35-acre campus. 5 buildings on campus. Approved or accredited by Association of Independent Schools of Greater Washington, National Association of Episcopal Schools, and Virginia Association of Independent Schools. Member of National Association of Independent Schools and Secondary School Admission Test Board. Endowment: $19.6 million. Total enrollment: 1,123. Upper school average class size: 14. Upper school faculty-student ratio: 1:9. There are 170 required school days per year for Upper

St. Stephen's & St. Agnes School

School students. Upper School students typically attend 5 days per week. The average school day consists of 7 hours and 10 minutes.

Upper School Student Profile Grade 9: 122 students (67 boys, 55 girls); Grade 10: 119 students (58 boys, 61 girls); Grade 11: 105 students (53 boys, 52 girls); Grade 12: 105 students (60 boys, 45 girls). 25% of students are members of Episcopal Church.

Faculty School total: 133. In upper school: 20 men, 31 women; 33 have advanced degrees.

Subjects Offered 1½ elective credits, Advanced Placement courses, algebra, American history, American literature, art, art history, art history-AP, bioethics, biology, biology-AP, calculus, calculus-AP, ceramics, chemistry, chemistry-AP, Christian education, Christian ethics, Christian scripture, Christian testament, comparative government and politics-AP, concert choir, directing, drama, drawing, economics, English, English-AP, ensembles, environmental science-AP, ethics, European history, European history-AP, forensics, French, French language-AP, geometry, government/civics-AP, history, honors English, honors geometry, honors U.S. history, honors world history, instrumental music, jazz ensemble, Latin, Latin-AP, macro/microeconomics-AP, Mandarin, mathematics, medieval history, medieval/Renaissance history, microeconomics-AP, music, music theory-AP, newspaper, painting, physical education, physics, physics-AP, playwriting and directing, precalculus, psychology-AP, religion, sculpture, senior project, Spanish, Spanish language-AP, Spanish literature-AP, sports, sports medicine, statistics-AP, studio art, studio art-AP, technical theater, theater, theater arts, trigonometry, U.S. history-AP, world history, writing, yearbook, yoga.

Graduation Requirements Arts and fine arts (art, music, dance, drama), English, family studies, foreign language, history, mathematics, physical education (includes health), religion (includes Bible studies and theology), science, technological applications, senior year independent off-campus project, 40 hours of community service.

Special Academic Programs 22 Advanced Placement exams for which test preparation is offered; honors section; independent study; term-away projects; study abroad; academic accommodation for the gifted, the musically talented, and the artistically talented.

College Admission Counseling 112 students graduated in 2010; all went to college, including Columbia University; Georgetown University; The College of William and Mary; The University of North Carolina at Chapel Hill; University of Pennsylvania; University of Virginia. Mean SAT critical reading: 616, mean SAT math: 631, mean SAT writing: 619, mean combined SAT: 1866.

Student Life Upper grades have specified standards of dress, student council, honor system. Discipline rests equally with students and faculty. Attendance at religious services is required.

Summer Programs Enrichment, advancement, art/fine arts, computer instruction programs offered; session focuses on enrichment; held both on and off campus; held at Chesapeake Bay, DC, VA and MD area; accepts boys and girls; open to students from other schools. 1,750 students usually enrolled. 2011 schedule: June 20 to August 19. Application deadline: none.

Tuition and Aid Day student tuition: $28,444. Tuition installment plan (FACTS Tuition Payment Plan). Need-based scholarship grants available. In 2010–11, 25% of upper-school students received aid. Total amount of financial aid awarded in 2010–11: $2,074,475.

Admissions Traditional secondary-level entrance grade is 9. ISEE or SSAT required. Deadline for receipt of application materials: January 15. Application fee required: $70. Interview required.

Athletics Interscholastic: baseball (boys), basketball (b,g), field hockey (g), football (b), ice hockey (b), lacrosse (b,g), soccer (b,g), softball (g), swimming and diving (b,g), tennis (b,g), track and field (b,g), volleyball (g), winter soccer (g), wrestling (b); intramural: dance team (g), independent competitive sports (b,g); coed interscholastic: cross-country running, diving, golf, winter (indoor) track; coed intramural: basketball, fitness, independent competitive sports, jogging, physical fitness, physical training, strength & conditioning, weight lifting, weight training, yoga. 6 PE instructors, 14 coaches, 2 athletic trainers.

Computers Computers are regularly used in all academic classes. Computer network features include on-campus library services, online commercial services, Internet access, wireless campus network, Internet filtering or blocking technology, computer labs for foreign language, math, technology, library, newspaper, physics, and chemistry, homework assignments posted online, mobile wireless laptop cart (180 laptops), computers available in study hall and library. Campus intranet and computer access in designated common areas are available to students. Students grades are available online. The school has a published electronic and media policy.

Contact Mr. Jon Kunz, Director of Admission, Grades 6-12. 703-212-2706. Fax: 703-212-2788. E-mail: jkunz@sssas.org. Web site: www.sssas.org.

SAINT STEPHEN'S EPISCOPAL SCHOOL

315 41st Street West
Bradenton, Florida 34209
Head of School: Janet S. Pullen

General Information Coeducational day college-preparatory, arts, religious studies, and marine science school, affiliated with Episcopal Church. Grades PK–12. Founded: 1970. Setting: small town. Nearest major city is Tampa. 35-acre campus. 3 buildings on campus. Approved or accredited by Florida Council of Independent Schools,

National Association of Episcopal Schools, Southern Association of Colleges and Schools, and Southern Association of Independent Schools. Member of National Association of Independent Schools. Endowment: $958,000. Total enrollment: 646. Upper school average class size: 16. Upper school faculty-student ratio: 1:10. There are 177 required school days per year for Upper School students. Upper School students typically attend 5 days per week. The average school day consists of 7 hours.

Upper School Student Profile Grade 9: 68 students (35 boys, 33 girls); Grade 10: 71 students (38 boys, 33 girls); Grade 11: 56 students (31 boys, 25 girls); Grade 12: 66 students (31 boys, 35 girls). 15% of students are members of Episcopal Church.

Faculty School total: 85. In upper school: 7 men, 15 women; 20 have advanced degrees.

Subjects Offered 3-dimensional art, Advanced Placement courses, advanced studio art-AP, algebra, American government, American history, American history-AP, American literature, art, art history, art history-AP, art-AP, astronomy, band, biology, biology-AP, British literature, broadcast journalism, calculus, calculus-AP, ceramics, chemistry, chemistry-AP, choir, chorus, community service, comparative religion, composition, composition-AP, computer programming, computer programming-AP, computer science, computer science-AP, conceptual physics, debate, digital art, digital photography, discrete mathematics, drama, economics, English, English language and composition-AP, English language-AP, English literature, English literature and composition-AP, English literature-AP, English-AP, environmental science-AP, European history, European history-AP, French, French language-AP, geometry, graphic design, humanities, international relations, journalism, Latin, Latin-AP, marine biology, marine science, music, newspaper, organic chemistry, painting, photography, physical education, physics, physics-AP, portfolio art, pre-calculus, probability and statistics, psychology, public speaking, science research, Spanish, Spanish language-AP, speech and debate, studio art, studio art-AP, trigonometry, U.S. history, U.S. history-AP, weight training, Western civilization, world history, world history-AP.

Graduation Requirements Arts and fine arts (art, music, dance, drama), electives, English, foreign language, mathematics, physical education (includes health), science, social studies (includes history), senior speech. Community service is required.

Special Academic Programs 17 Advanced Placement exams for which test preparation is offered; honors section.

College Admission Counseling 52 students graduated in 2010; 51 went to college, including Florida State University; University of Central Florida; University of Florida; University of Miami; University of South Florida. Other: 1 had other specific plans. Mean SAT critical reading: 570, mean SAT math: 614, mean SAT writing: 579, mean composite ACT: 25. 39% scored over 600 on SAT critical reading, 56% scored over 600 on SAT math, 36% scored over 600 on SAT writing, 38% scored over 26 on composite ACT.

Student Life Upper grades have specified standards of dress, student council, honor system. Discipline rests primarily with faculty. Attendance at religious services is required.

Summer Programs Enrichment, advancement, sports, art/fine arts, computer instruction programs offered; session focuses on academic enrichment and sports; held on campus; accepts boys and girls; open to students from other schools. 500 students usually enrolled. 2011 schedule: June 13 to August 12. Application deadline: June 1.

Tuition and Aid Day student tuition: $16,000. Tuition installment plan (monthly payment plans). Need-based scholarship grants available. In 2010–11, 85% of upper-school students received aid. Total amount of financial aid awarded in 2010–11: $249,000.

Admissions Traditional secondary-level entrance grade is 9. For fall 2010, 48 students applied for upper-level admission, 35 were accepted, 22 enrolled. School's own exam required. Deadline for receipt of application materials: none. Application fee required: $200. Interview recommended.

Athletics Interscholastic: aerobics/dance (girls), aquatics (b,g), baseball (b), basketball (b,g), cheering (g), cross-country running (b,g), dance (g), dance team (g), diving (b,g), football (b), golf (b,g), independent competitive sports (b,g), soccer (b,g), softball (g), swimming and diving (b,g), tennis (b,g), track and field (b,g), volleyball (g), winter soccer (b,g), wrestling (b); intramural: aerobics/dance (g), ballet (g), basketball (b,g), cheering (g), cross-country running (b,g), dance (g), fitness (b,g), horseback riding (b,g), jogging (b,g), lacrosse (b,g), physical fitness (b,g), physical training (b,g), running (b,g), soccer (b,g), softball (b,g), strength & conditioning (b,g), tennis (b,g), track and field (b,g), volleyball (b,g), weight training (b,g), wrestling (b); coed intramural: kayaking, yoga. 8 PE instructors, 14 coaches, 1 athletic trainer.

Computers Computers are regularly used in art, computer applications, foreign language, journalism, library, mathematics, media, science, social sciences, word processing, writing, yearbook classes. Computer network features include on-campus library services, online commercial services, Internet access, wireless campus network, Internet filtering or blocking technology, Microsoft Office. Computer access in designated common areas is available to students. Students grades are available online. The school has a published electronic and media policy.

Contact Linda G. Lutz, Director of Admissions. 941-746-2121 Ext. 568. Fax: 941-345-1237. E-mail: llutz@saintstephens.org. Web site: www.saintstephens.org.

ST. STEPHEN'S EPISCOPAL SCHOOL

6500 St. Stephen's Drive
Austin, Texas 78746

Head of School: Mr. Robert Kirkpatrick

General Information Coeducational boarding and day college-preparatory and theater school, affiliated with Episcopal Church. Boarding grades 8–12, day grades 6–12. Founded: 1950. Setting: suburban. Students are housed in single-sex dormitories. 370-acre campus. 40 buildings on campus. Approved or accredited by Independent Schools Association of the Southwest, National Association of Episcopal Schools, Texas Education Agency, The Association of Boarding Schools, and Texas Department of Education. Member of National Association of Independent Schools. Endowment: $8.2 million. Total enrollment: 668. Upper school average class size: 17. Upper school faculty-student ratio: 1:8. There are 165 required school days per year for Upper School students. Upper School students typically attend 5 days per week. The average school day consists of 6 hours and 58 minutes.

Upper School Student Profile Grade 9: 109 students (52 boys, 57 girls); Grade 10: 132 students (64 boys, 68 girls); Grade 11: 108 students (61 boys, 47 girls); Grade 12: 113 students (68 boys, 45 girls). 33% of students are boarding students. 81% are state residents. 5 states are represented in upper school student body. 18% are international students. International students from China, Mexico, Republic of Korea, Saudi Arabia, Taiwan, and Thailand; 12 other countries represented in student body. 18% of students are members of Episcopal Church.

Faculty School total: 98. In upper school: 42 men, 43 women; 48 have advanced degrees; 36 reside on campus.

Subjects Offered 3-dimensional design, acting, algebra, American history, American history-AP, anthropology, art, art history, art history-AP, astrophysics, ballet, band, biology, biology-AP, calculus, calculus-AP, ceramics, chamber groups, chemistry, chemistry-AP, Chinese, choreography, classics, computer applications, computer math, computer science, computer studies, creative writing, directing, drama, English, English literature, environmental science, European history, European history-AP, fine arts, French, French-AP, geology, geometry, government/civics, history, jazz band, Latin, mathematics, music, music theory-AP, musical theater, photography, physical education, physics, physics-AP, play/screen writing, pre-calculus, psychology, public policy issues and action, public speaking, religion, science, social studies, Spanish, Spanish-AP, statistics-AP, studio art-AP, theater arts, theology, video, world history, world literature.

Graduation Requirements Arts and fine arts (art, music, dance, drama), electives, English, foreign language, mathematics, physical education (includes health), religion (includes Bible studies and theology), science, social studies (includes history), community service requirement in middle and upper schools.

Special Academic Programs Advanced Placement exam preparation; honors section; independent study; study abroad; ESL (23 students enrolled).

College Admission Counseling 111 students graduated in 2010; all went to college, including Georgetown University; Rhodes College; The George Washington University; The University of Texas at Austin; Trinity University. Mean SAT critical reading: 636, mean SAT math: 662, mean SAT writing: 641, mean combined SAT: 1939.

Student Life Upper grades have specified standards of dress, student council. Discipline rests equally with students and faculty. Attendance at religious services is required.

Summer Programs Sports, art/fine arts programs offered; session focuses on soccer, tennis, travel abroad, foreign language/culture, fine arts, community service; held both on and off campus; held at locations in Europe, El Salvador, Nicaragua, Costa Rica, American wilderness areas; accepts boys and girls; open to students from other schools. 120 students usually enrolled. 2011 schedule: June 1 to July 31. Application deadline: none.

Tuition and Aid Day student tuition: $20,870; 7-day tuition and room/board: $36,700. Tuition installment plan (individually arranged payment plans). Merit scholarship grants, need-based scholarship grants, partial tuition remission for children of faculty and staff available. In 2010–11, 15% of upper-school students received aid; total upper-school merit-scholarship money awarded: $30,000. Total amount of financial aid awarded in 2010–11: $1,900,000.

Admissions Traditional secondary-level entrance grade is 9. For fall 2010, 284 students applied for upper-level admission, 151 were accepted, 86 enrolled. ISEE or SSAT required. Deadline for receipt of application materials: February 1. Application fee required: $50. Interview required.

Athletics Interscholastic: baseball (boys), basketball (b,g), cheering (g), crew (b,g), cross-country running (b,g), dance (g), field hockey (g), football (b), golf (b,g), lacrosse (b,g), soccer (b,g), softball (g), swimming and diving (b,g), tennis (b,g), track and field (b,g), volleyball (g), winter soccer (b,g); intramural: bicycling (b,g), climbing (b,g), combined training (b,g), dance (b,g), fitness (b,g), hiking/backpacking (b,g), modern dance (b,g), mountain biking (b,g), mountaineering (b,g), outdoor adventure (b,g), outdoor education (b,g), physical fitness (b,g), rock climbing (b,g), ropes courses (b,g), strength & conditioning (b,g), surfing (b,g), triathlon (b,g), weight training (b,g). 2 PE instructors, 7 coaches, 1 athletic trainer.

Computers Computer network features include on-campus library services, online commercial services, Internet access, wireless campus network, Internet filtering or blocking technology, online schedules, syllabi, homework, examples, and links to information sources. Student e-mail accounts and computer access in designated common areas are available to students. Students grades are available online.

Contact Lawrence Sampleton, Director of Admission. 512-327-1213 Ext. 210. Fax: 512-327-6771. E-mail: admission@sstx.org. Web site: www.sstx.org.

ST. STEPHEN'S SCHOOL, ROME

Via Aventina 3
Rome 00153, Italy

Head of School: Ms. Lesley Jane Murphy

General Information Coeducational boarding and day college-preparatory, arts, and bilingual studies school. Grades 9–PG. Founded: 1964. Setting: urban. Students are housed in single-sex by floor dormitories. 2-acre campus. 2 buildings on campus. Approved or accredited by European Council of International Schools, International Baccalaureate Organization, New England Association of Schools and Colleges, and US Department of State. Affiliate member of National Association of Independent Schools. Language of instruction: English. Endowment: €691,771. Total enrollment: 251. Upper school average class size: 13. Upper school faculty-student ratio: 1:7. There are 176 required school days per year for Upper School students. Upper School students typically attend 5 days per week. The average school day consists of 7 hours.

Upper School Student Profile Grade 9: 54 students (24 boys, 30 girls); Grade 10: 55 students (26 boys, 29 girls); Grade 11: 69 students (26 boys, 43 girls); Grade 12: 73 students (37 boys, 36 girls). 15% of students are boarding students. 67% are international students. International students from Germany, India, Netherlands, Sweden, United Kingdom, and United States; 25 other countries represented in student body.

Faculty School total: 44. In upper school: 11 men, 33 women; 29 have advanced degrees; 6 reside on campus.

Subjects Offered Algebra, American literature, art, art history, biology, calculus, chemistry, chorus, classical studies, dance, drama, economics, English, English literature, European history, French, geometry, health, Islamic studies, Italian, Latin, music appreciation, physical education, physics, pre-calculus, Roman civilization, sculpture, theory of knowledge, trigonometry, U.S. history, world literature.

Graduation Requirements Arts and fine arts (art, music, dance, drama), English, foreign language, mathematics, physical education (includes health), science, social studies (includes history), senior essay, computer proficiency examination.

Special Academic Programs International Baccalaureate program; 10 Advanced Placement exams for which test preparation is offered; domestic exchange program (with Buckingham Browne & Nichols School, Friends Seminary, Choate Rosemary Hall); ESL (14 students enrolled).

College Admission Counseling 55 students graduated in 2009; 49 went to college, including Boston University; Gustavus Adolphus College; New York University; St. John's University; Tufts University; University of Wisconsin–Madison. Other: 1 entered military service, 5 had other specific plans. Mean SAT critical reading: 593, mean SAT math: 550, mean SAT writing: 571, mean combined SAT: 1715, mean composite ACT: 21.

Student Life Upper grades have student council. Discipline rests equally with students and faculty.

Tuition and Aid Day student tuition: €20,400–€20,800; 7-day tuition and room/board: €31,600–€32,000. Tuition installment plan (individually arranged payment plans). Tuition reduction for siblings, need-based scholarship grants available. In 2009–10, 20% of upper-school students received aid. Total amount of financial aid awarded in 2009–10: €387,000.

Admissions Traditional secondary-level entrance grade is 9. For fall 2009, 153 students applied for upper-level admission, 125 were accepted, 95 enrolled. School's own exam required. Deadline for receipt of application materials: February 19. Application fee required: €100. Interview recommended.

Athletics Interscholastic: basketball (boys, girls), soccer (b,g), volleyball (b,g); intramural: basketball (b,g), dance (b,g), soccer (b,g), tennis (b,g), track and field (b,g), volleyball (b,g); coed interscholastic: tennis, track and field; coed intramural: dance, martial arts, tennis, track and field, volleyball. 4 coaches.

Computers Computers are regularly used in English, foreign language, mathematics, science, social studies classes. Computer network features include on-campus library services, Internet access, wireless campus network, Internet filtering or blocking technology. Campus intranet, student e-mail accounts, and computer access in designated common areas are available to students. Students grades are available online. The school has a published electronic and media policy.

Contact Ms. Alex Perniciaro, Admissions Coordinator. 39-06-575-0605. Fax: 39-06-574-1941. E-mail: ststephens@ststephens-rome.com. Web site: www.ststephens-rome.com.

SAINT TERESA'S ACADEMY

5600 Main Street
Kansas City, Missouri 64113

Head of School: Mrs. Nan Tiehen Bone

General Information Girls' day college-preparatory school, affiliated with Roman Catholic Church. Grades 9–12. Founded: 1866. Setting: urban. 20-acre campus. 3 buildings on campus. Approved or accredited by National Catholic Education Association, North Central Association of Colleges and Schools, and Missouri Department of Education. Endowment: $150,000. Total enrollment: 533. Upper

Saint Teresa's Academy

school average class size: 21. Upper school faculty-student ratio: 1:12. Upper School students typically attend 5 days per week. The average school day consists of 6 hours and 40 minutes.

Upper School Student Profile Grade 9: 140 students (140 girls); Grade 10: 139 students (139 girls); Grade 11: 124 students (124 girls); Grade 12: 130 students (130 girls). 87% of students are Roman Catholic.

Faculty School total: 47. In upper school: 9 men, 38 women; 31 have advanced degrees.

Subjects Offered Advanced chemistry, advanced math, algebra, American government, American history, American literature, analysis, anatomy and physiology, art, athletics, basketball, biology, biology-AP, botany, British literature, calculus, career/college preparation, chamber groups, chemistry, chemistry-AP, choir, chorus, computer graphics, computer programming, computer science-AP, current events, dance, directing, drama, drawing, ecology, English, English language and composition-AP, English language-AP, English literature, European history-AP, fiber arts, fitness, foreign language, forensics, French, French language-AP, French-AP, freshman seminar, geometry, golf, graphic design, health, independent study, journalism, keyboarding, language arts, Latin, Latin History, music-AP, newspaper, painting, physical education, portfolio art, psychology, Shakespeare, social issues, social studies, sociology, softball, Spanish, Spanish language-AP, Spanish-AP, speech, sports conditioning, sports performance development, stagecraft, swimming, tennis, theater, theology and the arts, track and field, trigonometry, U.S. government, U.S. government and politics-AP, U.S. history, volleyball, Western civilization, women spirituality and faith, world geography, world religions, writing, yearbook.

Graduation Requirements Arts and fine arts (art, music, dance, drama), computer science, electives, English, foreign language, mathematics, physical education (includes health), science, social studies (includes history), theology. Community service is required.

Special Academic Programs Advanced Placement exam preparation; honors section; study at local college for college credit.

College Admission Counseling 131 students graduated in 2009; 129 went to college, including Kansas State University; Saint Louis University; The University of Kansas; University of Missouri; University of Notre Dame. Other: 2 had other specific plans. Mean SAT critical reading: 600, mean SAT math: 580, mean SAT writing: 610, mean combined SAT: 1780, mean composite ACT: 26.

Student Life Upper grades have uniform requirement. Discipline rests primarily with faculty. Attendance at religious services is required.

Tuition and Aid Day student tuition: $9300. Tuition installment plan (SMART Tuition Payment Plan). Tuition reduction for siblings, merit scholarship grants, need-based scholarship grants available. In 2009–10, 17% of upper-school students received aid; total upper-school merit-scholarship money awarded: $125,000. Total amount of financial aid awarded in 2009–10: $137,000.

Admissions Traditional secondary-level entrance grade is 9. For fall 2009, 174 students applied for upper-level admission, 165 were accepted, 140 enrolled. Placement test required. Deadline for receipt of application materials: February 28. No application fee required.

Athletics Interscholastic: aerobics/dance, basketball, cross-country running, diving, drill team, golf, soccer, softball, swimming and diving, tennis, track and field, volleyball; intramural: aerobics/dance, badminton, fitness, fitness walking, jogging, lacrosse, physical fitness, physical training, running, strength & conditioning, table tennis, volleyball, walking, weight lifting, weight training. 2 PE instructors, 25 coaches, 1 athletic trainer.

Computers Computers are regularly used in business education, creative writing, graphics, journalism, library, newspaper, photography, research skills, science, writing, yearbook classes. Computer network features include on-campus library services, Internet access, wireless campus network, Internet filtering or blocking technology. Campus intranet is available to students. The school has a published electronic and media policy.

Contact Mrs. Roseann Hudnall, Admissions Director. 816-501-0011 Ext. 135. Fax: 816-523-0232. E-mail: rhudnall@stteresasacademy.org. Web site: www.stteresasacademy.org.

SAINT THOMAS ACADEMY

949 Mendota Heights Road
Mendota Heights, Minnesota 55120
Head of School: Thomas B. Mich, PhD

General Information Boys' day college-preparatory and military school, affiliated with Roman Catholic Church. Grades 7–12. Founded: 1885. Setting: suburban. Nearest major city is St. Paul. 72-acre campus. 3 buildings on campus. Approved or accredited by Independent Schools Association of the Central States. Endowment: $17.1 million. Total enrollment: 669. Upper school average class size: 17. Upper school faculty-student ratio: 1:10. There are 175 required school days per year for Upper School students. Upper School students typically attend 5 days per week. The average school day consists of 6 hours and 40 minutes.

Upper School Student Profile Grade 7: 55 students (55 boys); Grade 8: 80 students (80 boys); Grade 9: 130 students (130 boys); Grade 10: 146 students (146 boys); Grade 11: 126 students (126 boys); Grade 12: 132 students (132 boys). 75% of students are Roman Catholic.

Faculty School total: 65. In upper school: 27 men, 24 women; 44 have advanced degrees.

Subjects Offered Advanced Placement courses, algebra, American history, American literature, art, art history, band, biology, calculus, campus ministry, chemistry, Chinese, computer science, creative writing, earth science, economics, English, English literature, environmental studies, European history, fine arts, French, geometry, government/civics, health, history, JROTC, Latin, mathematics, military science, music, physical education, physics, psychology, religion, science, social studies, Spanish, trigonometry, world history, world literature, writing.

Graduation Requirements Arts and fine arts (art, music, dance, drama), English, foreign language, health education, JROTC or LEAD (Leadership Education and Development), mathematics, physical education (includes health), religion (includes Bible studies and theology), science, social studies (includes history), U.S. history, world history, 100 hours of community service in 12th grade.

Special Academic Programs 11 Advanced Placement exams for which test preparation is offered; honors section; independent study; study at local college for college credit.

College Admission Counseling 133 students graduated in 2010; 131 went to college, including Saint John's University; St. Olaf College; University of Minnesota, Twin Cities Campus; University of Notre Dame; University of St. Thomas; University of Wisconsin–Madison. Other: 2 had other specific plans. Mean SAT critical reading: 646, mean SAT math: 655, mean SAT writing: 641, mean composite ACT: 27.

Student Life Upper grades have uniform requirement, student council, honor system. Discipline rests primarily with faculty. Attendance at religious services is required.

Summer Programs Enrichment programs offered; session focuses on study and organizational strategies, time management, test preparation and orientation; held on campus; accepts boys; not open to students from other schools. 12 students usually enrolled. 2011 schedule: July 5 to August 5. Application deadline: May 13.

Tuition and Aid Day student tuition: $16,600. Tuition installment plan (monthly payment plans, individually arranged payment plans, quarterly payment plan). Merit scholarship grants, need-based scholarship grants available. In 2010–11, 39% of upper-school students received aid; total upper-school merit-scholarship money awarded: $49,500. Total amount of financial aid awarded in 2010–11: $2,100,000.

Admissions Traditional secondary-level entrance grade is 9. For fall 2010, 297 students applied for upper-level admission, 221 were accepted, 151 enrolled. Cognitive Abilities Test required. Deadline for receipt of application materials: January 11. No application fee required. On-campus interview recommended.

Athletics Interscholastic: alpine skiing, baseball, basketball, cross-country running, drill team, fitness, football, golf, hockey, ice hockey, JROTC drill, lacrosse, marksmanship, nordic skiing, outdoor skills, physical fitness, riflery, skiing (cross-country), skiing (downhill), soccer, swimming and diving, tennis, track and field, wrestling; intramural: basketball, bowling, football, hockey, physical training, strength & conditioning, table tennis, weight lifting, weight training. 3 PE instructors, 1 athletic trainer.

Computers Computers are regularly used in all academic, art, foreign language, music classes. Computer network features include on-campus library services, online commercial services, Internet access, wireless campus network, Internet filtering or blocking technology. Students grades are available online. The school has a published electronic and media policy.

Contact Peggy Mansur, Admissions Assistant. 651-683-1515. Fax: 651-683-1576. E-mail: pmansur@cadets.com. Web site: www.cadets.com.

SAINT THOMAS AQUINAS HIGH SCHOOL

11411 Pflumm Road
Overland Park, Kansas 66215-4816
Head of School: Dr. William P. Ford

General Information Coeducational day college-preparatory, religious studies, and technology school, affiliated with Roman Catholic Church. Grades 9–12. Founded: 1988. Setting: suburban. Nearest major city is Kansas City, MO. 44-acre campus. 2 buildings on campus. Approved or accredited by National Catholic Education Association, North Central Association of Colleges and Schools, and Kansas Department of Education. Total enrollment: 1,001. Upper school average class size: 25. Upper school faculty-student ratio: 1:15. There are 180 required school days per year for Upper School students. Upper School students typically attend 5 days per week. The average school day consists of 7 hours.

Upper School Student Profile Grade 9: 235 students (110 boys, 125 girls); Grade 10: 251 students (113 boys, 138 girls); Grade 11: 255 students (114 boys, 141 girls); Grade 12: 260 students (126 boys, 134 girls). 97% of students are Roman Catholic.

Faculty School total: 68. In upper school: 30 men, 38 women; 58 have advanced degrees.

Graduation Requirements Arts and fine arts (art, music, dance, drama), computer technologies, electives, English, Latin, mathematics, modern languages, physical education (includes health), science, social studies (includes history), speech, theology, service (one fourth credit each of 4 years).

Special Academic Programs Advanced Placement exam preparation; honors section; study at local college for college credit; academic accommodation for the gifted; remedial reading and/or remedial writing; remedial math.

College Admission Counseling 278 students graduated in 2010; 276 went to college, including Benedictine College; Johnson County Community College; Kansas State University; Saint Louis University; The University of Kansas; University of Notre Dame. Other: 2 entered military service. Mean SAT critical reading: 610, mean SAT math: 618, mean SAT writing: 615, mean composite ACT: 25.

Student Life Upper grades have uniform requirement, student council. Discipline rests primarily with faculty. Attendance at religious services is required.
Summer Programs Remediation, advancement, sports programs offered; session focuses on sports camps and selected academic coursework; held on campus; accepts boys and girls; open to students from other schools.
Tuition and Aid Day student tuition: $7250–$8250. Tuition installment plan (SMART Tuition Payment Plan). Need-based scholarship grants available.
Admissions Traditional secondary-level entrance grade is 9. ACT-Explore required. Deadline for receipt of application materials: none. Application fee required: $125. Interview required.
Athletics Interscholastic: baseball (boys), basketball (b,g), bowling (b,g), cross-country running (b,g), dance team (g), diving (b,g), football (b), golf (b,g), soccer (b,g), softball (g), swimming and diving (b,g), tennis (b,g), track and field (b,g), volleyball (g), wrestling (b); coed interscholastic: cheering; coed intramural: table tennis, ultimate Frisbee. 3 PE instructors, 1 athletic trainer.
Computers Computers are regularly used in all academic, computer applications, desktop publishing, programming, video film production, Web site design classes. Computer network features include on-campus library services, Internet access, wireless campus network, computer labs and laptop carts. Student e-mail accounts are available to students. Students grades are available online. The school has a published electronic and media policy.
Contact Mrs. Diane Pyle, Director of Admissions. 913-319-2423. Fax: 913-345-2319. E-mail: dpyle@stasaints.net. Web site: www.stasaints.net.

ST. THOMAS AQUINAS HIGH SCHOOL
197 Dover Point Road
Dover, New Hampshire 03820
Head of School: Mr. Kevin Collins
General Information Coeducational day college-preparatory and religious studies school, affiliated with Roman Catholic Church. Grades 9–12. Founded: 1960. Setting: small town. Nearest major city is Boston, MA. 11-acre campus. 2 buildings on campus. Approved or accredited by New England Association of Schools and Colleges and New Hampshire Department of Education. Total enrollment: 664. Upper school average class size: 18. Upper school faculty-student ratio: 1:14. There are 185 required school days per year for Upper School students. Upper School students typically attend 5 days per week. The average school day consists of 6 hours and 25 minutes.
Upper School Student Profile Grade 9: 150 students (68 boys, 82 girls); Grade 10: 169 students (82 boys, 87 girls); Grade 11: 168 students (100 boys, 68 girls); Grade 12: 177 students (85 boys, 92 girls).
Faculty School total: 49. In upper school: 21 men, 28 women; 25 have advanced degrees.
Subjects Offered Algebra, anatomy and physiology, biology, biology-AP, calculus, calculus-AP, chemistry, chorus, Christian ethics, concert band, contemporary studies, drawing, economics, English, environmental science-AP, finite math, French, geography, geometry, honors algebra, honors English, honors geometry, humanities, introduction to technology, Latin, marine biology, math applications, media arts, music appreciation, music theory, painting, physics, prayer/spirituality, pre-calculus, psychology, science, scripture, sculpture, social justice, sociology, Spanish, statistics-AP, studio art, theology, trigonometry, U.S. government and politics-AP, U.S. history, U.S. history-AP, wellness, Western civilization, world religions.
Graduation Requirements Arts and fine arts (art, music, dance, drama), Christian ethics, electives, English, foreign language, freshman seminar, mathematics, prayer/spirituality, science, scripture, social justice, social studies (includes history), theology, world religions, 40 hour community service requirement.
Special Academic Programs Advanced Placement exam preparation; honors section.
College Admission Counseling 157 students graduated in 2010; 150 went to college, including Keene State College; University of New Hampshire; University of Vermont; Villanova University. Other: 2 entered a postgraduate year, 5 had other specific plans. Mean SAT critical reading: 571, mean SAT math: 561, mean SAT writing: 569.
Student Life Upper grades have specified standards of dress, student council. Discipline rests primarily with faculty. Attendance at religious services is required.
Tuition and Aid Day student tuition: $9735. Tuition installment plan (annual, semiannual, and 10-month payment plans). Need-based scholarship grants available.
Admissions Traditional secondary-level entrance grade is 9. Scholastic Testing Service High School Placement Test required. Deadline for receipt of application materials: December 31. Application fee required: $40.
Athletics Interscholastic: baseball (boys), basketball (b,g), cross-country running (b,g), field hockey (g), football (b), golf (b,g), ice hockey (b,g), lacrosse (b,g), skiing (downhill) (b,g), soccer (b,g), softball (g), swimming and diving (b,g), tennis (b,g), track and field (b,g), volleyball (g), winter (indoor) track (b,g), wrestling (b); intramural: dance team (g). 51 coaches, 1 athletic trainer.
Computers Computers are regularly used in introduction to technology, media arts classes. Computer network features include on-campus library services, Internet access, wireless campus network. Student e-mail accounts and computer access in designated common areas are available to students. Students grades are available online.
Contact Mrs. Patricia Krupsky, Director of Admissions. 603-742-3206. Fax: 603-749-7822. E-mail: pkrupsky@stalux.org. Web site: www.stalux.org.

ST. THOMAS CHOIR SCHOOL
New York, New York
See Junior Boarding Schools section.

ST. THOMAS HIGH SCHOOL
4500 Memorial Drive
Houston, Texas 77007-7332
Head of School: Rev. Patrick Fulton, CSB
General Information Boys' day college-preparatory and religious studies school, affiliated with Roman Catholic Church. Grades 9–12. Founded: 1900. Setting: urban. 37-acre campus. 6 buildings on campus. Approved or accredited by Southern Association of Colleges and Schools, Texas Catholic Conference, Texas Education Agency, and Texas Department of Education. Endowment: $10.5 million. Total enrollment: 709. Upper school average class size: 16. Upper school faculty-student ratio: 1:14. There are 185 required school days per year for Upper School students. Upper School students typically attend 5 days per week. The average school day consists of 7 hours and 20 minutes.
Upper School Student Profile Grade 9: 201 students (201 boys); Grade 10: 171 students (171 boys); Grade 11: 179 students (179 boys); Grade 12: 158 students (158 boys). 75% of students are Roman Catholic.
Faculty School total: 52. In upper school: 36 men, 16 women; 31 have advanced degrees.
Subjects Offered Algebra, American government, American history, American history-AP, American literature, ancient history, art, arts, Basic programming, Bible studies, bioethics, biology, biology-AP, British literature, calculus, calculus-AP, ceramics, chemistry, chemistry-AP, civics/free enterprise, classical civilization, college counseling, comparative government and politics-AP, computer applications, computer information systems, computer programming, computer studies, creative writing, critical thinking, critical writing, decision making skills, desktop publishing, digital photography, drama, drawing, ecology, environmental systems, economics, economics-AP, English, English language-AP, English literature, English literature-AP, environmental education, environmental science, ethics, European history, fine arts, forensics, French, geography, geology, geometry, government and politics-AP, government/civics, grammar, guidance, health, health education, history of the Catholic Church, Holocaust studies, instrumental music, jazz band, journalism, Latin, marine biology, mathematics, military history, oceanography, oral communications, orchestra, painting, photography, physical education, physics, physics-AP, pre-calculus, programming, public speaking, publications, religion, social studies, Spanish, Spanish language-AP, speech, student government, student publications, theater, theology, trigonometry, U.S. government and politics-AP, world history, world literature.
Graduation Requirements Arts and fine arts (art, music, dance, drama), computer applications, English, foreign language, mathematics, physical education (includes health), religion (includes Bible studies and theology), science, social studies (includes history).
Special Academic Programs 10 Advanced Placement exams for which test preparation is offered; honors section.
College Admission Counseling 174 students graduated in 2010; 172 went to college, including Baylor University; Texas A&M University; Texas Tech University; The University of Texas at Austin; University of Houston; University of Notre Dame. Other: 2 entered military service. Mean composite ACT: 26.
Student Life Upper grades have specified standards of dress, student council. Discipline rests primarily with faculty. Attendance at religious services is required.
Tuition and Aid Day student tuition: $11,700. Tuition installment plan (monthly payment plans). Merit scholarship grants, need-based scholarship grants, middle-income loans available. In 2010–11, 32% of upper-school students received aid; total upper-school merit-scholarship money awarded: $200,000. Total amount of financial aid awarded in 2010–11: $1,150,000.
Admissions Traditional secondary level entrance grade is 9. For fall 2010, 457 students applied for upper-level admission, 257 were accepted, 206 enrolled. High School Placement Test required. Deadline for receipt of application materials: January 15. Application fee required: $50.
Athletics Interscholastic: baseball, basketball, cross-country running, football, golf, roller hockey, soccer; intramural: basketball, bowling, flag football, Frisbee, rugby. 2 PE instructors, 2 coaches, 1 athletic trainer.
Computers Computers are regularly used in data processing, desktop publishing, multimedia, newspaper, photography, programming, publications, word processing classes. Computer network features include on-campus library services, Internet access, Internet filtering or blocking technology. Computer access in designated common areas is available to students. Students grades are available online. The school has a published electronic and media policy.
Contact Ms. Christine Westman, Assistant Principal. 713-864-6348. Fax: 713-864-5750. E-mail: chris.westman@sths.org. Web site: www.sths.org.

SAINT THOMAS MORE CATHOLIC HIGH SCHOOL

450 East Farrel Road
Lafayette, Louisiana 70508
Head of School: Mrs. Audrey C. Menard

General Information Coeducational day college-preparatory, arts, business, religious studies, bilingual studies, and technology school, affiliated with Roman Catholic Church. Grades 9–12. Founded: 1982. Setting: suburban. Nearest major city is Baton Rouge. 45-acre campus. 1 building on campus. Approved or accredited by Southern Association of Colleges and Schools and Louisiana Department of Education. Endowment: $1.6 million. Total enrollment: 1,029. Upper school average class size: 25. Upper school faculty-student ratio: 1:25. There are 180 required school days per year for Upper School students. Upper School students typically attend 5 days per week. The average school day consists of 7 hours and 4 minutes.

Upper School Student Profile Grade 9: 276 students (129 boys, 147 girls); Grade 10: 262 students (138 boys, 124 girls); Grade 11: 272 students (135 boys, 137 girls); Grade 12: 219 students (108 boys, 111 girls). 89% of students are Roman Catholic.

Faculty School total: 90. In upper school: 27 men, 47 women; 23 have advanced degrees.

Subjects Offered Accounting, advanced chemistry, advanced math, Advanced Placement courses, advanced studio art-AP, algebra, American history, American history-AP, applied music, art, athletics, band, biology, business, calculus-AP, campus ministry, chemistry, chorus, civics/free enterprise, communication skills, computer science, creative writing, debate, desktop publishing, drama, economics, economics and history, English, English literature-AP, English-AP, environmental science, film studies, fine arts, first aid, fitness, French, geography, geometry, health, history, honors algebra, honors English, honors U.S. history, honors world history, independent study, keyboarding, kinesiology, mathematics, newspaper, photography, physical education, physical fitness, physical science, physics, play production, pre-calculus, psychology, public speaking, publications, reading, religion, science, social studies, Spanish, speech and debate, studio art-AP, study skills, theology, trigonometry, U.S. history-AP, Web site design, weight training, word processing, world history, yearbook.

Graduation Requirements Arts and fine arts (art, music, dance, drama), business applications, English, French, keyboarding, mathematics, physical education (includes health), religion (includes Bible studies and theology), science, social studies (includes history), Spanish, world history.

Special Academic Programs 8 Advanced Placement exams for which test preparation is offered; honors section; independent study; study at local college for college credit; academic accommodation for the gifted; remedial reading and/or remedial writing; remedial math.

College Admission Counseling 269 students graduated in 2010; 255 went to college, including Louisiana State University and Agricultural and Mechanical College; University of Louisiana at Lafayette. Other: 2 entered military service, 3 had other specific plans.

Student Life Upper grades have uniform requirement, student council, honor system. Discipline rests primarily with faculty. Attendance at religious services is required.

Summer Programs Enrichment, sports, art/fine arts, computer instruction programs offered; session focuses on enrichment and athletics; held both on and off campus; held at area businesses; accepts boys and girls; open to students from other schools. 500 students usually enrolled. 2011 schedule: June 1 to August 5. Application deadline: none.

Tuition and Aid Day student tuition: $6070. Tuition installment plan (monthly payment plans). Merit scholarship grants, need-based scholarship grants, paying campus jobs available. In 2010–11, 20% of upper-school students received aid; total upper-school merit-scholarship money awarded: $500. Total amount of financial aid awarded in 2010–11: $130,000.

Admissions Traditional secondary-level entrance grade is 9. For fall 2010, 1,052 students applied for upper-level admission, 1,040 were accepted, 1,035 enrolled. Achievement tests and ACT-Explore required. Deadline for receipt of application materials: January 19. Application fee required: $350.

Athletics Interscholastic: aquatics (boys, girls), baseball (b), basketball (b,g), bowling (b,g), cheering (g), cross-country running (b,g), dance squad (g), dance team (g), floor hockey (b), football (b), golf (b,g), physical training (b,g), power lifting (b), soccer (b,g), softball (g), strength & conditioning (b,g), tennis (b,g), track and field (b,g), volleyball (g), weight lifting (b,g), weight training (b,g), wrestling (b); intramural: flag football (b,g), indoor hockey (b), lacrosse (b); coed interscholastic: Special Olympics. 4 PE instructors, 3 coaches, 1 athletic trainer.

Computers Computers are regularly used in business applications, desktop publishing, English, foreign language, history, keyboarding, lab/keyboard, library, literary magazine, mathematics, newspaper, publications, reading, remedial study skills, science, word processing, yearbook classes. Computer network features include on-campus library services, online commercial services, Internet access, wireless campus network, Internet filtering or blocking technology, computer access in the library before and after school and during lunch. Campus intranet, student e-mail accounts, and computer access in designated common areas are available to students. Students grades are available online. The school has a published electronic and media policy.

Contact Ms. Melanie O. Lauer '96, Director of Admissions. 337-988-7779. Fax: 337-988-2911. E-mail: melanielauer@stmcougars.com. Web site: www.stmcougars.com.

ST. TIMOTHY'S SCHOOL

8400 Greenspring Avenue
Stevenson, Maryland 21153
Head of School: Randy S. Stevens

General Information Girls' boarding and day college-preparatory, arts, Cambridge (UK) General Certificate of Secondary Education, and IB (International Baccalaureate diploma program) school, affiliated with Episcopal Church. Grades 9–12. Founded: 1882. Setting: rural. Nearest major city is Baltimore. Students are housed in single-sex dormitories. 145-acre campus. 23 buildings on campus. Approved or accredited by Association of Independent Maryland Schools, International Baccalaureate Organization, Middle States Association of Colleges and Schools, National Association of Episcopal Schools, The Association of Boarding Schools, and Maryland Department of Education. Member of National Association of Independent Schools and Secondary School Admission Test Board. Endowment: $10 million. Total enrollment: 150. Upper school average class size: 10. Upper school faculty-student ratio: 1:5. Upper School students typically attend 5 days per week.

Upper School Student Profile Grade 9: 27 students (27 girls); Grade 10: 38 students (38 girls); Grade 11: 40 students (40 girls); Grade 12: 45 students (45 girls). 70% of students are boarding students. 40% are state residents. 16 states are represented in upper school student body. 30% are international students. International students from Bahamas, China, Germany, Mexico, Republic of Korea, and Spain; 12 other countries represented in student body.

Faculty School total: 38. In upper school: 12 men, 18 women; 21 have advanced degrees; 29 reside on campus.

Subjects Offered Algebra, American literature, art, art history, biology, British literature, calculus, chemistry, Chinese, comparative politics, creative writing, dance, drama, drama performance, drama workshop, economics, English, English composition, English literature, ESL, ethics, European history, fine arts, foreign language, French, geometry, history, International Baccalaureate courses, Latin, Mandarin, mathematics, modern dance, music, music theory, photography, physics, piano, religion, science, Spanish, U.S. history, world history, world literature, writing.

Graduation Requirements Arts and fine arts (art, music, dance, drama), English, foreign language, history, mathematics, physical education (includes health), religion (includes Bible studies and theology), science, extended essay, Community, Action and Service (CAS). Community service is required.

Special Academic Programs International Baccalaureate program; honors section; independent study; ESL (12 students enrolled).

College Admission Counseling 39 students graduated in 2010; all went to college, including Amherst College; Duke University; University of Colorado at Boulder; University of Maryland, College Park; Wake Forest University.

Student Life Upper grades have uniform requirement, student council, honor system. Discipline rests equally with students and faculty. Attendance at religious services is required.

Summer Programs Enrichment, ESL programs offered; session focuses on leadership and intensive language; held on campus; accepts boys and girls; open to students from other schools. 2011 schedule: July 1 to July 28. Application deadline: May 1.

Tuition and Aid Day student tuition: $25,750; 5-day tuition and room/board: $44,300; 7-day tuition and room/board: $44,300. Tuition installment plan (FACTS Tuition Payment Plan). Merit scholarship grants, need-based scholarship grants, need-based loans available. In 2010–11, 45% of upper-school students received aid; total upper-school merit-scholarship money awarded: $75,000. Total amount of financial aid awarded in 2010–11: $1,750,000.

Admissions Traditional secondary-level entrance grade is 9. For fall 2010, 187 students applied for upper-level admission, 84 were accepted, 52 enrolled. ISEE, SLEP for foreign students, SSAT or TOEFL required. Deadline for receipt of application materials: February 1. Application fee required: $50. Interview required.

Athletics Interscholastic: badminton, basketball, dressage, equestrian sports, field hockey, golf, horseback riding, ice hockey, indoor soccer, lacrosse, soccer, softball, squash, swimming and diving, tennis, volleyball; intramural: ballet, cross-country running, dance, dance squad, equestrian sports, horseback riding, modern dance, outdoor adventure, weight training, yoga. 2 coaches, 1 athletic trainer.

Computers Computers are regularly used in art, college planning, economics, English, mathematics, publications, SAT preparation, science, yearbook classes. Computer network features include on-campus library services, online commercial services, Internet access, wireless campus network, Internet filtering or blocking technology. Student e-mail accounts are available to students. The school has a published electronic and media policy.

Contact Deborah Haskins, Associate Head for Enrollment Management. 410-486-7401. Fax: 410-486-1167. E-mail: dhaskins@stt.org. Web site: www.stt.org.

SAINT URSULA ACADEMY

4025 Indian Road
Toledo, Ohio 43606
Head of School: Sr. Mary Kay Homan, OP

General Information Girls' day college-preparatory, arts, business, religious studies, bilingual studies, technology, and physical education school, affiliated with Roman Catholic Church. Grades 9–12. Founded: 1854. Setting: suburban. 16-acre campus. 1 building on campus. Approved or accredited by North Central Association of Colleges and Schools, Ohio Catholic Schools Accreditation Association (OCSAA), and Ohio Department of Education. Total enrollment: 511. Upper school average class size: 16. Upper school faculty-student ratio: 1:16. There are 180 required school days per year for Upper School students. Upper School students typically attend 5 days per week. The average school day consists of 7 hours and 20 minutes.

Upper School Student Profile Grade 8: 1 student (1 girl); Grade 9: 134 students (134 girls); Grade 10: 118 students (118 girls); Grade 11: 133 students (133 girls); Grade 12: 125 students (125 girls). 75% of students are Roman Catholic.

Faculty School total: 45. In upper school: 6 men, 38 women; 32 have advanced degrees.

Subjects Offered 3-dimensional art, accounting, Advanced Placement courses, advanced studio art-AP, algebra, American government, American history, American history-AP, American literature, anatomy, anatomy and physiology, art, art-AP, ballet, biology, British literature, British literature-AP, business law, calculus-AP, career exploration, Catholic belief and practice, ceramics, chemistry, chemistry-AP, choral music, choreography, chorus, church history, comparative government and politics-AP, comparative religion, composition-AP, computer applications, computer graphics, concert choir, dance, digital photography, drama, drawing, economics, electives, engineering, English language and composition-AP, English literature and composition-AP, fashion, female experience in America, film history, foreign language, French language-AP, geometry, government, government and politics-AP, graphic arts, health, history of the Catholic Church, honors algebra, honors English, honors geometry, honors world history, human geography—AP, instrumental music, Latin, Latin-AP, literature, literature and composition-AP, Mandarin, marketing, mathematics-AP, microeconomics, music, music theory-AP, New Testament, orchestra, painting, personal finance, photography, physical education, physics, physiology, pre-calculus, printmaking, probability and statistics, psychology, psychology-AP, religion and culture, religious education, sculpture, single survival, social psychology, Spanish, Spanish language-AP, speech, statistics, statistics-AP, student publications, studio art-AP, symphonic band, theology, trigonometry, U.S. government and politics, U.S. government and politics-AP, U.S. history, U.S. history-AP, U.S. literature, United States government-AP, vocal music, women's health, women's studies, yearbook.

Graduation Requirements Arts and fine arts (art, music, dance, drama), computers, English, foreign language, health, mathematics, physical education (includes health), science, social studies (includes history), theology, Community Service, Career Exploration Experience.

Special Academic Programs 13 Advanced Placement exams for which test preparation is offered; honors section; study at local college for college credit.

College Admission Counseling 144 students graduated in 2010; all went to college, including Miami University; The Ohio State University; University of Dayton; University of Michigan. Mean SAT critical reading: 570, mean SAT math: 572, mean SAT writing: 569, mean composite ACT: 24. 42% scored over 600 on SAT critical reading, 44% scored over 600 on SAT math, 35% scored over 600 on SAT writing.

Student Life Upper grades have uniform requirement, student council. Discipline rests primarily with faculty. Attendance at religious services is required.

Summer Programs Enrichment, advancement, sports, art/fine arts, computer instruction programs offered; session focuses on athletics and academics; held both on and off campus; held at golf course; accepts girls; open to students from other schools. 300 students usually enrolled. 2011 schedule: June 6 to July 29. Application deadline: June 1.

Tuition and Aid Day student tuition: $8900. Tuition installment plan (SMART Tuition Payment Plan). Tuition reduction for siblings, merit scholarship grants, need-based scholarship grants, paying campus jobs available. In 2010–11, 65% of upper-school students received aid.

Admissions Traditional secondary-level entrance grade is 9. For fall 2010, 160 students applied for upper-level admission, 151 were accepted, 121 enrolled. High School Placement Test required. Deadline for receipt of application materials: none. No application fee required.

Athletics Interscholastic: aerobics/dance, basketball, bowling, broomball, cheering, crew, cross-country running, dance team, diving, equestrian sports, fencing, golf, gymnastics, horseback riding, independent competitive sports, lacrosse, modern dance, physical fitness, physical training, rowing, soccer, softball, swimming and diving, tennis, track and field, volleyball, water polo, weight training; intramural: badminton, cooperative games, volleyball. 1 PE instructor, 32 coaches, 1 athletic trainer.

Computers Computers are regularly used in accounting, computer applications, graphic arts, newspaper, Web site design, yearbook classes. Computer network features include on-campus library services, Internet access, wireless campus network, Internet filtering or blocking technology. Campus intranet, student e-mail accounts, and computer access in designated common areas are available to students. Students grades are available online. The school has a published electronic and media policy.

Contact Mrs. Kimberly Sofo, Principal. 419-329-2279. Fax: 419-531-4575. E-mail: ksofo@toledosua.org. Web site: www.toledosua.org.

SAINT VIATOR HIGH SCHOOL

1213 East Oakton Street
Arlington Heights, Illinois 60004
Head of School: Rev. Robert M. Egan, CSV

General Information Coeducational day college-preparatory, arts, religious studies, bilingual studies, and technology school, affiliated with Roman Catholic Church.

Grades 9–12. Founded: 1961. Setting: suburban. Nearest major city is Chicago. 1 building on campus. Approved or accredited by North Central Association of Colleges and Schools and Illinois Department of Education. Upper school average class size: 25. Upper school faculty-student ratio: 1:18.

Faculty School total: 69. In upper school: 27 men, 42 women; 51 have advanced degrees.

Graduation Requirements 25 hours of Christian Service each year (100 total hours).

College Admission Counseling 265 students graduated in 2010; 261 went to college, including DePaul University; Dominican University; Illinois State University; Indiana University Bloomington; Loyola University Chicago; Marquette University. Other: 4 had other specific plans. Mean composite ACT: 25.

Student Life Upper grades have specified standards of dress, student council, honor system. Discipline rests primarily with faculty. Attendance at religious services is required.

Summer Programs Enrichment, advancement, sports, art/fine arts, computer instruction programs offered; held on campus; accepts boys and girls; not open to students from other schools. 2011 schedule: June 13 to July 29.

Tuition and Aid Day student tuition: $10,500. Tuition installment plan (monthly payment plans). Need-based scholarship grants available. In 2010–11, 26% of upper-school students received aid. Total amount of financial aid awarded in 2010–11: $1,100,000.

Admissions Traditional secondary-level entrance grade is 9. ETS high school placement exam required. Application fee required: $400.

Athletics Interscholastic: baseball (boys), basketball (b,g), cheering (g), cross-country running (b,g), football (b), golf (b,g), ice hockey (b), lacrosse (b), pom squad (g), soccer (b,g), softball (g), swimming and diving (b,g), tennis (b,g), track and field (b,g), volleyball (b,g), water polo (b,g), wrestling (b); coed intramural: outdoor adventure. 3 PE instructors, 87 coaches, 1 athletic trainer.

Computers Computer network features include Internet access, faculty Web pages. Students grades are available online.

Contact Mrs. Eileen Manno, Principal. 847-392-4050 Ext. 229. Fax: 847-392-8305. E-mail: emanno@saintviator.com. Web site: www.saintviator.com.

ST. VINCENT PALLOTTI HIGH SCHOOL

113 St. Mary's Place
Laurel, Maryland 20707
Head of School: Mr. Stephen J. Edmonds

General Information Coeducational day college-preparatory and religious studies school, affiliated with Roman Catholic Church. Grades 9–12. Founded: 1921. Setting: suburban. Nearest major city is Washington, DC. 6-acre campus. 5 buildings on campus. Approved or accredited by Association of Independent Maryland Schools, The College Board, and Maryland Department of Education. Total enrollment: 500. Upper school average class size: 18. Upper school faculty-student ratio: 1:18.

Upper School Student Profile Grade 9: 100 students (55 boys, 45 girls); Grade 10: 120 students (60 boys, 60 girls); Grade 11: 150 students (70 boys, 80 girls); Grade 12: 136 students (70 boys, 66 girls). 70% of students are Roman Catholic.

Faculty School total: 60.

Graduation Requirements 80 hours of community service.

Special Academic Programs Advanced Placement exam preparation; honors section; independent study; study at local college for college credit; academic accommodation for the musically talented; programs in English, mathematics, general development for dyslexic students; special instructional classes for deaf students, blind students.

College Admission Counseling 139 students graduated in 2010; 136 went to college, including Mount St. Mary's University; Shepherd University; Towson University; University of Maryland, College Park; West Virginia University; York College of Pennsylvania. Other: 1 went to work, 2 entered military service. Mean SAT critical reading: 560, mean SAT math: 580, mean SAT writing: 570.

Student Life Upper grades have uniform requirement, student council, honor system. Discipline rests primarily with faculty. Attendance at religious services is required.

Summer Programs Remediation, enrichment, sports programs offered; held on campus; accepts boys and girls; open to students from other schools. 2011 schedule: June 22 to August 15. Application deadline: April.

Tuition and Aid Day student tuition: $11,595. Tuition installment plan (FACTS Tuition Payment Plan). Tuition reduction for siblings, merit scholarship grants, need-based scholarship grants available. Total amount of financial aid awarded in 2010–11: $400,000.

Admissions Traditional secondary-level entrance grade is 9. For fall 2010, 325 students applied for upper-level admission, 250 were accepted, 105 enrolled. Archdiocese of Washington Entrance Exam required. Deadline for receipt of application materials: December 15. Application fee required: $100. On-campus interview required.

Athletics Interscholastic: baseball (boys), basketball (b,g), dance squad (g), field hockey (g), football (b), lacrosse (b,g), pom squad (g), soccer (b,g), softball (g), volleyball (g), wrestling (b); coed interscholastic: cheering, cross-country running, dance, golf, tennis; coed intramural: mountain biking, skiing (downhill), snowboarding. 1 PE instructor, 30 coaches, 1 athletic trainer.

Computers Computer network features include on-campus library services, Internet access, wireless campus network, Internet filtering or blocking technology. Campus intranet and student e-mail accounts are available to students. Students grades are available online. The school has a published electronic and media policy.

Contact Mrs. Kelly Hawse, Director of Admissions. 301-725-3228 Ext. 202. Fax: 301-776-4343. E-mail: khawse@pallottihs.org. Web site: www.pallottihs.org.

See Display below and Close-Up on page 834.

SAINT VINCENT-SAINT MARY HIGH SCHOOL

15 North Maple Street
Akron, Ohio 44303-2394
Head of School: Mr. David V. Rathz

General Information Coeducational day college-preparatory school, affiliated with Roman Catholic Church. Grades 9–12. Founded: 1972. Setting: urban. 10-acre campus. 3 buildings on campus. Approved or accredited by North Central Association of Colleges and Schools, Ohio Catholic Schools Accreditation Association (OCSAA), and Ohio Department of Education. Endowment: $8 million. Total enrollment: 686. Upper school average class size: 23. Upper school faculty-student ratio: 1:14. There are 180 required school days per year for Upper School students. Upper School students typically attend 5 days per week. The average school day consists of 7 hours.

Upper School Student Profile Grade 9: 180 students (95 boys, 85 girls); Grade 10: 170 students (82 boys, 88 girls); Grade 11: 188 students (98 boys, 90 girls); Grade 12: 148 students (73 boys, 75 girls). 80% of students are Roman Catholic.

Faculty School total: 49. In upper school: 19 men, 30 women; 35 have advanced degrees.

Graduation Requirements 98 Christian service hours.

Special Academic Programs Advanced Placement exam preparation; honors section; study at local college for college credit.

College Admission Counseling 155 students graduated in 2009; 154 went to college, including Kent State University; Ohio University; The Ohio State University; The University of Akron; University of Dayton. Other: 1 went to work.

Student Life Upper grades have specified standards of dress, student council, honor system. Discipline rests primarily with faculty. Attendance at religious services is required.

Tuition and Aid Tuition installment plan (FACTS Tuition Payment Plan, monthly payment plans). Tuition reduction for siblings, merit scholarship grants, need-based scholarship grants available. In 2009–10, 49% of upper-school students received aid.

Admissions Traditional secondary-level entrance grade is 9. For fall 2009, 1,068 students applied for upper-level admission, 904 were accepted, 680 enrolled. High School Placement Test (closed version) from Scholastic Testing Service required. Deadline for receipt of application materials: none. No application fee required. Interview recommended.

Athletics Interscholastic: baseball (boys), basketball (b,g), bowling (b,g), cross-country running (b,g), football (b), golf (b,g), soccer (b,g), softball (g), swimming and diving (g), tennis (b,g), track and field (b,g), volleyball (b,g), winter (indoor) track (b,g), wrestling (b); coed interscholastic: cheering; coed intramural: skiing (downhill), table tennis, weight training.

Computers Computers are regularly used in all academic classes. Computer network features include on-campus library services, online commercial services, Internet access, wireless campus network, Internet filtering or blocking technology, homework assignments available online. Student e-mail accounts are available to students. Students grades are available online. The school has a published electronic and media policy.

Contact Mrs. Joanne Wiseman, Director of Admissions. 330-253-9113 Ext. 115. Fax: 330-996-0020. E-mail: jwiseman@stvm.com. Web site: www.stvm.com.

SAINT XAVIER HIGH SCHOOL

1609 Poplar Level Road
Louisville, Kentucky 40217
Head of School: Dr. Perry Sangalli

General Information Boys' day college-preparatory, arts, business, religious studies, bilingual studies, and technology school, affiliated with Roman Catholic Church. Grades 9–12. Founded: 1864. Setting: suburban. 72-acre campus. 7 buildings on campus. Approved or accredited by Southern Association of Colleges and Schools and Kentucky Department of Education. Endowment: $10 million. Total enrollment: 1,455. Upper school average class size: 22. Upper school faculty-student ratio: 1:12.

Upper School Student Profile Grade 9: 390 students (390 boys); Grade 10: 362 students (362 boys); Grade 11: 317 students (317 boys); Grade 12: 342 students (342 boys). 75% of students are Roman Catholic.

Faculty School total: 117. In upper school: 93 men, 24 women; 99 have advanced degrees.

Subjects Offered Accounting, acting, Advanced Placement courses, algebra, American government, anatomy and physiology, band, biology, business law, ceramics, chemistry, chorus, computer applications, computer programming, computer-aided design, creative writing, desktop publishing, drafting, economics, English, environmental science, fitness, French, geometry, German, global issues, health, humanities, journalism, keyboarding, mathematics, mechanical drawing,

music, music history, music theory, philosophy, photography, physical education, physics, probability and statistics, psychology, reading, sculpture, sociology, Spanish, speech, theology, trigonometry, U.S. history, world civilizations, world geography, yearbook.

Graduation Requirements Arts and fine arts (art, music, dance, drama), electives, English, foreign language, mathematics, physical education (includes health), science, social studies (includes history), theology, U.S. history.

Special Academic Programs Advanced Placement exam preparation; honors section; study at local college for college credit; academic accommodation for the gifted, the musically talented, and the artistically talented; remedial reading and/or remedial writing; remedial math; programs in English, mathematics, general development for dyslexic students; special instructional classes for students with Attention Deficit Disorder, Attention Deficit Hyperactivity Disorder, dyslexia, central auditory processing disorder.

College Admission Counseling Colleges students went to include Bellarmine University; Saint Louis University; University of Dayton; University of Kentucky; University of Louisville; Xavier University.

Student Life Upper grades have specified standards of dress, student council, honor system. Discipline rests primarily with faculty. Attendance at religious services is required.

Admissions Traditional secondary-level entrance grade is 9. For fall 2009, 475 students applied for upper-level admission, 475 were accepted, 381 enrolled. STS required. Deadline for receipt of application materials: none. Application fee required: $100. On-campus interview recommended.

Athletics Interscholastic: aquatics, baseball, basketball, bowling, cheering, cross-country running, diving, fishing, football, golf, ice hockey, indoor track, indoor track & field, lacrosse, power lifting, running, soccer, strength & conditioning, swimming and diving, tennis, track and field, volleyball, water polo, weight lifting, weight training, wrestling; intramural: alpine skiing, backpacking, basketball, bicycling, billiards, bowling, cooperative games, fishing, flag football, fly fishing, football, Frisbee, golf, ice hockey, kayaking, kickball, mountain biking, outdoor activities, outdoor adventure, outdoor education, outdoor recreation, scuba diving, skiing (downhill), snowboarding, soccer, table tennis, tennis, touch football, ultimate Frisbee, weight training. 3 PE instructors, 63 coaches, 1 athletic trainer.

Computers Computers are regularly used in all classes. Computer network features include on-campus library services, online commercial services, Internet access, Internet filtering or blocking technology. Students grades are available online.

Contact Br. Edwards Driscoll, CFX, Principal. 502-637-4712. Fax: 502-634-2171. E-mail: edriscoll@saintx.com. Web site: www.saintx.com.

SAINT XAVIER HIGH SCHOOL

600 North Bend Road
Cincinnati, Ohio 45224
Head of School: Rev. Timothy A. Howe, SJ

General Information Boys' day college-preparatory, arts, religious studies, technology, and service learning school, affiliated with Roman Catholic Church. Grades 9–12. Founded: 1831. Setting: suburban. 100-acre campus. 1 building on campus. Approved or accredited by Jesuit Secondary Education Association, North Central Association of Colleges and Schools, Ohio Catholic Schools Accreditation Association (OCSAA), and Ohio Department of Education. Endowment: $27 million. Upper school average class size: 28. Upper school faculty-student ratio: 1:15.

Upper School Student Profile 81% of students are Roman Catholic.

Faculty School total: 100. In upper school: 72 men, 28 women; 88 have advanced degrees.

Subjects Offered Arts, biology, chemistry, Chinese, computer science, English, fine arts, French, German, Greek, health, Latin, mathematics, physical education, physics, religion, science, social studies, Spanish.

Graduation Requirements Arts and fine arts (art, music, dance, drama), computer science, English, foreign language, forensics, mathematics, physical education (includes health), religion (includes Bible studies and theology), science, social studies (includes history).

Special Academic Programs Advanced Placement exam preparation; independent study; term-away projects; study at local college for college credit.

College Admission Counseling 361 students graduated in 2009; all went to college, including Miami University; Saint Louis University; The Ohio State University; University of Cincinnati; University of Notre Dame; Xavier University. Median SAT critical reading: 630, median SAT math: 640, median composite ACT: 27. 64% scored over 600 on SAT critical reading, 72% scored over 600 on SAT math, 60% scored over 26 on composite ACT.

Student Life Upper grades have specified standards of dress, student council. Discipline rests primarily with faculty. Attendance at religious services is required.

Tuition and Aid Day student tuition: $10,675. Merit scholarship grants, need-based scholarship grants, paying campus jobs available. In 2009–10, 28% of upper-school students received aid. Total amount of financial aid awarded in 2009–10: $2,300,000.

Admissions Traditional secondary-level entrance grade is 9. For fall 2009, 880 students applied for upper-level admission, 450 were accepted, 395 enrolled. High School Placement Test required. Deadline for receipt of application materials: December 1. Application fee required: $25.

Athletics Interscholastic: baseball, basketball, bowling, crew, cross-country running, diving, football, golf, ice hockey, lacrosse, soccer, swimming and diving, tennis, track

and field, volleyball, wrestling; intramural: basketball, football, golf, soccer, table tennis, tennis, volleyball. 3 PE instructors, 2 athletic trainers.

Computers Computers are regularly used in art, design, drawing and design, foreign language, graphic arts, graphic design, graphics, keyboarding, lab/keyboard, language development, library, programming, research skills, science classes. Computer network features include on-campus library services, online commercial services, Internet access, wireless campus network, Internet filtering or blocking technology. Campus intranet, student e-mail accounts, and computer access in designated common areas are available to students. Students grades are available online. The school has a published electronic and media policy.

Contact Mr. Roderick D. Hinton, Director of Admissions. 513-761-7815 Ext. 106. Fax: 513-761-3811. E-mail: rhinton@stxavier.org. Web site: www.stxavier.org.

SALEM ACADEMY

500 Salem Avenue
Winston-Salem, North Carolina 27108-0578
Head of School: Mr. Karl Sjolund

General Information Girls' boarding and day college-preparatory and arts school, affiliated with Moravian Church. Grades 9–12. Founded: 1772. Setting: urban. Students are housed in single-sex dormitories. 60-acre campus. 4 buildings on campus. Approved or accredited by North Carolina Association of Independent Schools, Southern Association of Colleges and Schools, The Association of Boarding Schools, and North Carolina Department of Education. Member of National Association of Independent Schools and Secondary School Admission Test Board. Endowment: $7 million. Total enrollment: 161. Upper school average class size: 10. Upper school faculty-student ratio: 1:7. The average school day consists of 7 hours and 30 minutes.

Upper School Student Profile Grade 9: 26 students (26 girls); Grade 10: 50 students (50 girls); Grade 11: 42 students (42 girls); Grade 12: 43 students (43 girls). 60% of students are boarding students. 70% are state residents. 12 states are represented in upper school student body. 21% are international students. International students from Bulgaria, China, Democratic People's Republic of Korea, Germany, and Taiwan. 4% of students are Moravian.

Faculty School total: 24. In upper school: 3 men, 21 women; 13 have advanced degrees; 3 reside on campus.

Subjects Offered Algebra, American history, art, biology, calculus, chemistry, dance, drama, economics, English, European history, fine arts, French, geometry, government/civics, Latin, mathematics, music, physical education, physics, precalculus, psychology, religion, science, social sciences, social studies, Spanish, theater, trigonometry, world history.

Graduation Requirements Arts and fine arts (art, music, dance, drama), English, foreign language, mathematics, physical education (includes health), religion (includes Bible studies and theology), science, social sciences, social studies (includes history), completion of January term.

Special Academic Programs 9 Advanced Placement exams for which test preparation is offered; honors section; term-away projects; study at local college for college credit; study abroad; ESL (8 students enrolled).

College Admission Counseling 44 students graduated in 2009; all went to college, including James Madison University; North Carolina State University; The University of North Carolina at Chapel Hill; The University of North Carolina at Greensboro; Wake Forest University. Mean SAT critical reading: 618, mean SAT math: 627, mean SAT writing: 631, mean combined SAT: 1876.

Student Life Upper grades have specified standards of dress, student council, honor system. Discipline rests equally with students and faculty.

Tuition and Aid Day student tuition: $17,805; 7-day tuition and room/board: $35,405. Tuition installment plan (Key Tuition Payment Plan, monthly payment plans). Merit scholarship grants, need-based scholarship grants available. In 2009–10, 45% of upper-school students received aid; total upper-school merit-scholarship money awarded: $123,100. Total amount of financial aid awarded in 2009–10: $1,033,794.

Admissions Traditional secondary-level entrance grade is 9. For fall 2009, 160 students applied for upper-level admission, 85 were accepted, 65 enrolled. ACT, PSAT, SAT, SSAT or TOEFL required. Deadline for receipt of application materials: none. Application fee required: $50. Interview required.

Athletics Interscholastic: basketball, cross-country running, field hockey, golf, soccer, softball, swimming and diving, tennis, track and field, volleyball; intramural: aerobics/dance, archery, badminton, dance, fitness, flag football, floor hockey, golf, horseback riding, indoor hockey, indoor soccer, self defense. 2 PE instructors, 15 coaches, 1 athletic trainer.

Computers Computers are regularly used in all academic classes. Computer network features include on-campus library services, online commercial services, Internet access, wireless campus network. Student e-mail accounts are available to students. Students grades are available online.

Contact C. Lucia Uldrick, Director of Admissions. 336-721-2643. Fax: 336-917-5340. E-mail: academy@salem.edu. Web site: www.salemacademy.com.

SALEM ACADEMY

942 Lancaster Drive NE
Salem, Oregon 97301

Head of School: Ken Friesen, EdD

General Information Coeducational day college-preparatory, general academic, arts, vocational, religious studies, bilingual studies, and technology school, affiliated with Protestant Church. Grades K–12. Founded: 1945. Setting: suburban. 34-acre campus. 6 buildings on campus. Approved or accredited by Association of Christian Schools International, Northwest Association of Schools and Colleges, and Oregon Department of Education. Total enrollment: 608. Upper school average class size: 20. Upper school faculty-student ratio: 1:9. Upper School students typically attend 5 days per week. The average school day consists of 7 hours and 15 minutes.

Upper School Student Profile 90% of students are Protestant.

Faculty School total: 48. In upper school: 16 men, 15 women; 4 have advanced degrees.

Subjects Offered Advanced chemistry, Advanced Placement courses, algebra, American history, American literature, anatomy and physiology, art, athletics, auto mechanics, baseball, Bible, Bible studies, biology, business, calculus, ceramics, cheerleading, chemistry, choir, college counseling, college writing, computer programming, computer science, drama, drama performance, economics, English, English literature, English literature and composition-AP, English literature-AP, ESL, foods, geography, geometry, government/civics, grammar, health, history, history-AP, home economics, honors English, industrial arts, Japanese, jazz ensemble, mathematics, music, physical education, physical science, physics, psychology, religion, SAT preparation, science, shop, social sciences, social studies, softball, Spanish, speech, track and field, typing, U.S. history-AP, vocal music, volleyball, weight training, woodworking, world history, world literature, writing.

Graduation Requirements English, foreign language, mathematics, physical education (includes health), religion (includes Bible studies and theology), science, social sciences, social studies (includes history), one credit in biblical studies for each year attended, 40 hours of community service (high school).

Special Academic Programs Advanced Placement exam preparation; honors section; independent study; study at local college for college credit; academic accommodation for the musically talented and the artistically talented; ESL (23 students enrolled).

College Admission Counseling 58 students graduated in 2010; 55 went to college, including Chemeketa Community College; Corban University; George Fox University; Oregon State University; Seattle Pacific University; University of Oregon. Other: 3 went to work.

Student Life Upper grades have specified standards of dress, student council. Discipline rests primarily with faculty.

Tuition and Aid Tuition reduction for siblings, need-based scholarship grants available.

Admissions Traditional secondary-level entrance grade is 9. Math Placement Exam, Reading for Understanding, school's own exam and writing sample required. Deadline for receipt of application materials: none. Application fee required: $50. On-campus interview required.

Athletics Interscholastic: baseball (boys), basketball (b,g), cheering (g), cross-country running (b,g), football (b), golf (b), softball (g), track and field (b,g), volleyball (g); coed interscholastic: equestrian sports; coed intramural: racquetball. 2 PE instructors.

Computers Computers are regularly used in yearbook classes. Computer network features include on-campus library services, Internet access, wireless campus network. The school has a published electronic and media policy.

Contact Mr. Shannon deVries, Dean of Students. 503-378-1211. Fax: 503-375-3265. E-mail: sdevries@salemacademy.org. Web site: www.salemacademy.org.

SALEM BAPTIST CHRISTIAN SCHOOL

429 South Broad Street
Winston-Salem, North Carolina 27101

Head of School: Ms. Martha Drake

General Information Coeducational day college-preparatory school, affiliated with Baptist Church. Grades P3–12. Founded: 1950. Setting: urban. 6-acre campus. 13 buildings on campus. Approved or accredited by Association of Christian Schools International, Southern Association of Colleges and Schools, and North Carolina Department of Education. Total enrollment: 391. Upper school average class size: 17. Upper school faculty-student ratio: 1:10.

Upper School Student Profile 50% of students are Baptist.

Faculty School total: 35. In upper school: 5 men, 5 women; 3 have advanced degrees.

Subjects Offered Advanced computer applications, advanced math, Advanced Placement courses, algebra, American government, American history, American history-AP, American literature, anatomy and physiology, ancient world history, art, art history, band, Bible, biology, biology-AP, business mathematics, calculus-AP, campus ministry, chemistry, choir, Christian doctrine, church history, civics, computer applications, consumer mathematics, drama, earth science, economics, English composition, English literature, English literature-AP, European history, fine arts, geography, geometry, government, honors algebra, honors English, honors geometry,

honors U.S. history, honors world history, Life of Christ, music, personal money management, psychology, theater, U.S. history, U.S. history-AP, world history, world wide web design.

Special Academic Programs Advanced Placement exam preparation; honors section; study at local college for college credit; academic accommodation for the gifted.

College Admission Counseling 26 students graduated in 2010; 24 went to college, including Cedarville University; North Carolina State University; The University of North Carolina at Charlotte; The University of North Carolina at Greensboro. Other: 1 went to work, 1 entered military service.

Student Life Upper grades have specified standards of dress, student council, honor system. Discipline rests primarily with faculty.

Admissions Traditional secondary-level entrance grade is 9. Application fee required: $125. Interview required.

Athletics Interscholastic: baseball (boys), basketball (b,g), cheering (g), golf (b,g), soccer (b,g), swimming and diving (g), track and field (b,g), volleyball (g). 1 PE instructor, 8 coaches.

Computers Computer network features include on-campus library services, Internet access, Internet filtering or blocking technology. Students grades are available online.

Contact 336-725-6113. Fax: 336-725-8455. Web site: www.mysbcs.com.

SALESIAN HIGH SCHOOL

2851 Salesian Avenue
Richmond, California 94804

Head of School: Mr. Timothy J. Chambers

General Information Coeducational day college-preparatory, arts, and religious studies school, affiliated with Roman Catholic Church. Grades 9–12. Founded: 1960. Setting: urban. Nearest major city is San Francisco. 25-acre campus. 3 buildings on campus. Approved or accredited by National Catholic Education Association, Western Association of Schools and Colleges, Western Catholic Education Association, and California Department of Education. Endowment: $100,000. Total enrollment: 524. Upper school average class size: 27. Upper school faculty-student ratio: 1:22. There are 178 required school days per year for Upper School students. Upper School students typically attend 5 days per week. The average school day consists of 6 hours and 50 minutes.

Upper School Student Profile Grade 9: 125 students (71 boys, 54 girls); Grade 10: 141 students (63 boys, 78 girls); Grade 11: 150 students (68 boys, 82 girls); Grade 12: 108 students (52 boys, 56 girls). 55% of students are Roman Catholic.

Faculty School total: 42. In upper school: 22 men, 20 women.

Subjects Offered 20th century history, advanced math, advanced studio art-AP, algebra, American history-AP, American legal systems, American literature, American literature-AP, anatomy, ancient world history, art, art history, art history-AP, biology, calculus, calculus-AP, Catholic belief and practice, Christian scripture, Christianity, classical language, computer literacy, drama, dramatic arts, economics, English, English composition, English language and composition-AP, English literature, English literature-AP, English-AP, environmental science, French, French language-AP, French-AP, geometry, government, government/civics, health and wellness, history of the Catholic Church, history-AP, honors U.S. history, mathematics, mathematics-AP, performing arts, physical education, physics, pre-algebra, pre-calculus, psychology, religion, SAT preparation, science, Spanish, Spanish language-AP, Spanish-AP, U.S. government, U.S. history, visual and performing arts, world history, world religions.

Graduation Requirements Arts and fine arts (art, music, dance, drama), English, foreign language, mathematics, physical education (includes health), religion (includes Bible studies and theology), science, social sciences, 20 hours of Christian service per year.

Special Academic Programs 8 Advanced Placement exams for which test preparation is offered; honors section; remedial reading and/or remedial writing.

College Admission Counseling 140 students graduated in 2010; 138 went to college, including San Francisco State University; University of California, Berkeley; University of California, Davis; University of California, Santa Cruz. Other: 2 went to work.

Student Life Upper grades have uniform requirement, student council. Discipline rests primarily with faculty. Attendance at religious services is required.

Summer Programs Remediation, enrichment, advancement, sports, art/fine arts, computer instruction programs offered; session focuses on enrichment, remediation and recruitment of 6, 7, and 8th grade students; held on campus; accepts boys and girls; open to students from other schools. 280 students usually enrolled. 2011 schedule: June 20 to July 29. Application deadline: June 17.

Tuition and Aid Day student tuition: $12,000. Tuition installment plan (SMART Tuition Payment Plan). Merit scholarship grants, need-based scholarship grants available. In 2010–11, 40% of upper-school students received aid; total upper-school merit-scholarship money awarded: $50,000. Total amount of financial aid awarded in 2010–11: $1,250,000.

Admissions Traditional secondary-level entrance grade is 9. For fall 2010, 300 students applied for upper-level admission, 160 were accepted, 125 enrolled. High School Placement Test, High School Placement Test (closed version) from Scholastic Testing Service and Standardized Diocesan Test required. Deadline for receipt of application materials: December 18. Application fee required: $75. On-campus interview required.

Athletics Interscholastic: baseball (boys), basketball (b,g), cheering (g), cross-country running (b,g), football (b), physical training (b), soccer (b,g), softball (g), swimming and diving (b,g), volleyball (b,g), weight training (b), winter soccer (b,g); intramural: basketball (b,g), football (b), roller hockey (b), weight training (b); coed interscholastic: golf, track and field. 1 PE instructor, 25 coaches.

Computers Computers are regularly used in computer applications, history, library, yearbook classes. Computer network features include on-campus library services, Internet access, wireless campus network, Internet filtering or blocking technology. Student e-mail accounts and computer access in designated common areas are available to students. Students grades are available online. The school has a published electronic and media policy.

Contact Mrs. Connie Decuir, Director of Admissions. 510-234-4433 Ext. 1128. Fax: 510-236-4636. E-mail: cdecuir@salesian.com. Web site: www.salesian.com.

SALESIAN HIGH SCHOOL
148 Main Street
New Rochelle, New York 10801
Head of School: Mr. John P. Flaherty

General Information Boys' day college-preparatory, general academic, arts, religious studies, technology, and American studies school, affiliated with Roman Catholic Church. Grades 9–12. Founded: 1920. Setting: suburban. Nearest major city is New York. 19-acre campus. 4 buildings on campus. Approved or accredited by Middle States Association of Colleges and Schools and New York Department of Education. Endowment: $500,000. Total enrollment: 500. Upper school average class size: 25. Upper school faculty-student ratio: 1:14.

Upper School Student Profile 80% of students are Roman Catholic.

Faculty School total: 37. In upper school: 28 men, 9 women; 28 have advanced degrees.

Subjects Offered Algebra, American history, American history-AP, American literature, art, arts, Bible studies, biology, British literature, business, calculus, chemistry, community service, computer math, computer science, creative writing, driver education, earth science, economics, English, English literature, environmental science, ethics, European history, fine arts, geography, geometry, government/civics, grammar, health, history, Italian, law, mathematics, music, physical education, physics, physiology, psychology, religion, science, social studies, sociology, Spanish, theology, trigonometry, world affairs, world history, world literature, writing.

Graduation Requirements Arts and fine arts (art, music, dance, drama), computer science, English, foreign language, mathematics, physical education (includes health), religion (includes Bible studies and theology), science, social studies (includes history). Community service is required.

Special Academic Programs Advanced Placement exam preparation; honors section; study at local college for college credit.

College Admission Counseling 107 students graduated in 2009; 87 went to college.

Student Life Upper grades have uniform requirement, student council, honor system. Discipline rests equally with students and faculty. Attendance at religious services is required.

Tuition and Aid Day student tuition: $5675. Tuition installment plan (FACTS Tuition Payment Plan). Tuition reduction for siblings, merit scholarship grants available. Total amount of financial aid awarded in 2009–10: $100,000.

Admissions Traditional secondary-level entrance grade is 9. School's own test required. Deadline for receipt of application materials: none. No application fee required. On-campus interview required.

Athletics Interscholastic: baseball, basketball, bowling, cross-country running, golf, indoor track, soccer, tennis, track and field, volleyball, winter (indoor) track, wrestling; intramural: backpacking, baseball, basketball, bowling, flag football, floor hockey, football, hiking/backpacking, martial arts, physical fitness, softball, track and field, volleyball, weight training. 2 PE instructors, 6 coaches.

Computers Computers are regularly used in drafting, yearbook classes. Computer network features include on-campus library services, Internet access, Internet filtering or blocking technology.

Contact Sr. Barbara Wright, Assistant Principal. 914-632-0248. Fax: 914-632-1362. E-mail: bwright@salesianhigh.com. Web site: www.salesianhigh.org.

SALESIANUM SCHOOL
1801 North Broom Street
Wilmington, Delaware 19802-3891
Head of School: Rev. J. Christian Beretta, OSFS

General Information Boys' day college-preparatory school, affiliated with Roman Catholic Church. Grades 9–12. Founded: 1903. Setting: suburban. 22-acre campus. 1 building on campus. Approved or accredited by Middle States Association of Colleges and Schools and Delaware Department of Education. Total enrollment: 1,027. Upper school average class size: 20. Upper school faculty-student ratio: 1:12.

Upper School Student Profile Grade 9: 256 students (256 boys); Grade 10: 246 students (246 boys); Grade 11: 263 students (263 boys); Grade 12: 262 students (262 boys). 88% of students are Roman Catholic.

Faculty School total: 92. In upper school: 67 men, 25 women; 53 have advanced degrees.

Subjects Offered Algebra, American history, American history-AP, American literature, anatomy, architecture, art, art-AP, band, biology, biology-AP, business, business law, calculus, calculus-AP, career/college preparation, chemistry, chemistry-AP, chorus, community service, computer applications, computer programming, computer science, computer science-AP, drafting, driver education, ecology, economics, English, English literature, English-AP, ensembles, environmental science-AP, European history-AP, fine arts, foreign policy, French, French-AP, geometry, German-AP, government/civics, health, journalism, Latin, law, literature, marketing, mathematics, physical education, physics, physics-AP, pre-calculus, psychology, psychology-AP, religion, science, social sciences, social studies, Spanish, Spanish-AP, statistics, statistics-AP, television, trigonometry, U.S. government and politics-AP, video, Western literature, world affairs, world history, world literature.

Graduation Requirements Arts and fine arts (art, music, dance, drama), college planning, computer science, driver education, electives, English, foreign language, mathematics, physical education (includes health), religion (includes Bible studies and theology), science, social sciences, social studies (includes history). Community service is required.

Special Academic Programs Advanced Placement exam preparation; honors section; independent study; study at local college for college credit; domestic exchange program (with Ursuline Academy, Padua Academy); academic accommodation for the gifted; remedial reading and/or remedial writing; remedial math.

College Admission Counseling 242 students graduated in 2010; 238 went to college, including Penn State University Park; Saint Joseph's University; University of Delaware; Villanova University; Virginia Polytechnic Institute and State University. Other: 3 went to work, 1 entered military service. Mean SAT critical reading: 573, mean SAT math: 589, mean SAT writing: 559, mean combined SAT: 1721. 32% scored over 600 on SAT critical reading, 41% scored over 600 on SAT math, 27% scored over 600 on SAT writing.

Student Life Upper grades have specified standards of dress, student council. Discipline rests primarily with faculty. Attendance at religious services is required.

Summer Programs Enrichment, computer instruction programs offered; session focuses on freshman transition and technology; held on campus; accepts boys; not open to students from other schools.

Tuition and Aid Day student tuition: $11,475. Tuition installment plan (Insured Tuition Payment Plan, monthly payment plans, semester payment plan, annual payment plan, monthly payment plan). Merit scholarship grants, need-based scholarship grants, paying campus jobs available. In 2010–11, 18% of upper-school students received aid; total upper-school merit-scholarship money awarded: $315,000. Total amount of financial aid awarded in 2010–11: $500,000.

Admissions Traditional secondary-level entrance grade is 9. Scholastic Testing Service High School Placement Test required. Deadline for receipt of application materials: December 1. Application fee required: $55.

Athletics Interscholastic: baseball, basketball, cross-country running, diving, football, golf, ice hockey, lacrosse, soccer, swimming and diving, tennis, track and field, volleyball, wrestling; intramural: basketball, bowling, flag football, Frisbee, lacrosse, roller hockey, rowing, skateboarding, tennis, ultimate Frisbee, weight lifting. 4 PE instructors, 58 coaches, 1 athletic trainer.

Computers Computers are regularly used in architecture, college planning, drafting, English, foreign language, mathematics, science, social studies, yearbook classes. Computer network features include on-campus library services, online commercial services, Internet access, wireless campus network, Internet filtering or blocking technology. Campus intranet and computer access in designated common areas are available to students. Students grades are available online.

Contact Mrs. Barbara Palena, Administrative Assistant to the Admissions Office. 302-654-2495 Ext. 148. Fax: 302-654-7767. E-mail: bpalena@salesianum.org. Web site: www.salesianum.org.

SALPOINTE CATHOLIC HIGH SCHOOL
1545 East Copper Street
Tucson, Arizona 85719-3199
Head of School: Fr. Bob C. Carroll, OCARM

General Information Coeducational day college-preparatory, arts, and religious studies school, affiliated with Roman Catholic Church. Grades 9–12. Founded: 1950. Setting: urban. 40-acre campus. 10 buildings on campus. Approved or accredited by National Catholic Education Association, North Carolina Department of Exceptional Children, North Central Association of Colleges and Schools, Western Catholic Education Association, and Arizona Department of Education. Endowment: $3.5 million. Total enrollment: 1,158. Upper school average class size: 24. Upper school faculty-student ratio: 1:14.

Upper School Student Profile 75% of students are Roman Catholic.

Faculty School total: 83. In upper school: 35 men, 48 women; 43 have advanced degrees.

Subjects Offered Algebra, American history, American literature, art, art history, Bible studies, biology, business, calculus, ceramics, chemistry, computer programming, computer science, creative writing, drama, driver education, economics, English, English literature, ethics, European history, expository writing, French, geography, geometry, government/civics, grammar, history, history of ideas, home economics, journalism, Latin, logic, mathematics, music, philosophy, photography, physical education, physics, psychology, religion, science, social studies, Spanish, speech, theater, theology, trigonometry, typing, world history, world literature, writing.

Salpointe Catholic High School

Graduation Requirements English, humanities, mathematics, modern languages, religion (includes Bible studies and theology), science, social studies (includes history).

Special Academic Programs Advanced Placement exam preparation; honors section; study at local college for college credit; remedial reading and/or remedial writing; remedial math; programs in English, mathematics, general development for dyslexic students.

College Admission Counseling 275 students graduated in 2009; they went to Arizona State University; Gonzaga University; Northern Arizona University; Pima Community College; The University of Arizona. Other: 1 entered military service, 1 entered a postgraduate year, 3 had other specific plans. Median SAT critical reading: 534, median SAT math: 529, median SAT writing: 534, median composite ACT: 23.

Student Life Upper grades have specified standards of dress, student council, honor system. Discipline rests equally with students and faculty. Attendance at religious services is required.

Tuition and Aid Day student tuition: $6180–$7135. Tuition installment plan (monthly payment plans, individually arranged payment plans). Tuition reduction for siblings, merit scholarship grants, need-based scholarship grants, USS Education Loan Program available. In 2009–10, 23% of upper-school students received aid; total upper-school merit-scholarship money awarded: $8000. Total amount of financial aid awarded in 2009–10: $1,000,000.

Admissions Traditional secondary-level entrance grade is 9. High School Placement Test required. Deadline for receipt of application materials: none. Application fee required: $45. On-campus interview required.

Athletics Interscholastic: aerobics/dance (girls), baseball (b), basketball (b,g), cross-country running (b,g), dance team (g), diving (b,g), football (b), golf (b,g), soccer (b,g), softball (g), swimming and diving (b,g), tennis (b,g), track and field (b,g), volleyball (b,g), weight lifting (b,g), wrestling (b); intramural: bicycling (b,g), ice hockey (b), lacrosse (b); coed interscholastic: cheering; coed intramural: basketball, bowling, outdoor adventure, ultimate Frisbee, volleyball. 2 PE instructors, 75 coaches, 2 athletic trainers.

Computers Computers are regularly used in English, mathematics, science classes. Computer network features include on-campus library services, Internet access, Internet filtering or blocking technology. Students grades are available online. The school has a published electronic and media policy.

Contact Ms. Meg Gossmann, Admissions Coordinator. 520-547-4460. Fax: 520-327-8477. E-mail: mgossmann@salpointe.org. Web site: www.salpointe.org.

SALT LAKE LUTHERAN HIGH SCHOOL

4020 South 900 East
Salt Lake City, Utah 84124-1169

Head of School: Mr. Charles Gebhardt

General Information Coeducational day and distance learning college-preparatory, general academic, and religious studies school, affiliated with Lutheran Church. Grades 9–12. Distance learning grades 11–12. Founded: 1984. Setting: urban. 3-acre campus. 1 building on campus. Approved or accredited by National Lutheran School Accreditation, Northwest Accreditation Commission, Northwest Association of Schools and Colleges, and Utah Department of Education. Total enrollment: 58. Upper school average class size: 13. Upper school faculty-student ratio: 1:7. There are 180 required school days per year for Upper School students. Upper School students typically attend 5 days per week. The average school day consists of 6 hours and 45 minutes.

Upper School Student Profile Grade 9: 10 students (5 boys, 5 girls); Grade 10: 12 students (10 boys, 2 girls); Grade 11: 13 students (6 boys, 7 girls); Grade 12: 23 students (12 boys, 11 girls). 40% of students are Lutheran.

Faculty School total: 10. In upper school: 4 men, 6 women; 7 have advanced degrees.

Subjects Offered Advanced biology, advanced chemistry, advanced computer applications, advanced math, Advanced Placement courses, algebra, American history, American literature, art, band, bell choir, Bible studies, biology, calculus, chemistry, chorus, computer science, drama, English, general science, geography, geometry, government/civics, health, journalism, keyboarding, literature, mathematics, novels, physical education, physics, psychology, religion, science, social sciences, sociology, Spanish, speech, vocal music, word processing, world history, world literature.

Graduation Requirements Arts and fine arts (art, music, dance, drama), business skills (includes word processing), computer science, English, mathematics, physical education (includes health), religion (includes Bible studies and theology), science, social sciences.

Special Academic Programs Honors section; accelerated programs; independent study; academic accommodation for the gifted; remedial reading and/or remedial writing.

College Admission Counseling 22 students graduated in 2010; all went to college, including Boise State University; Concordia College; Southern Utah University; University of Utah; Utah State University; Westminster College. Median composite ACT: 24. 23% scored over 26 on composite ACT.

Student Life Upper grades have specified standards of dress, student council, honor system. Discipline rests equally with students and faculty. Attendance at religious services is required.

Summer Programs Sports programs offered; session focuses on fundamentals and fun; held on campus; accepts boys and girls; open to students from other schools. 50 students usually enrolled. 2011 schedule: July 1 to August 15. Application deadline: June 1.

Tuition and Aid Day student tuition: $8300. Tuition installment plan (monthly payment plans). Tuition reduction for siblings, merit scholarship grants, need-based scholarship grants available. In 2010–11, 60% of upper-school students received aid; total upper-school merit-scholarship money awarded: $4000. Total amount of financial aid awarded in 2010–11: $99,000.

Admissions Traditional secondary-level entrance grade is 9. For fall 2010, 65 students applied for upper-level admission, 58 were accepted, 58 enrolled. School placement exam, SLEP for foreign students, TOEFL or SLEP or writing sample required. Deadline for receipt of application materials: none. Application fee required: $50. Interview required.

Athletics Interscholastic: baseball (boys), basketball (b,g), cross-country running (b,g), golf (b,g), soccer (b,g), swimming and diving (b,g), track and field (b,g), volleyball (g); coed interscholastic: cross-country running, golf, swimming and diving, track and field; coed intramural: badminton, basketball, cross-country running, fencing, golf, outdoors, physical fitness, physical training, soccer, track and field, volleyball, weight training. 3 coaches.

Computers Computers are regularly used in history, writing, yearbook classes. Computer network features include on-campus library services, Internet access.

Contact Mr. Charles Gebhardt, Principal/Executive Director. 801-266-6676. Fax: 801-266-1953. E-mail: charles.gebhardt@lhs-slc.org. Web site: www.lhs-slc.org.

SALTUS GRAMMAR SCHOOL

PO Box HM 2224
Hamilton HM JX, Bermuda

Head of School: Mr. E. G. (Ted) Staunton

General Information Coeducational day college-preparatory, general academic, arts, business, and technology school, affiliated with Church of England (Anglican). Grades K–12. Founded: 1888. Setting: suburban. 6 buildings on campus. Approved or accredited by Canadian Educational Standards Institute. Affiliate member of National Association of Independent Schools. Language of instruction: English. Endowment: 5 million Bermuda dollars. Total enrollment: 1,015. Upper school average class size: 18. Upper school faculty-student ratio: 1:13. There are 195 required school days per year for Upper School students. Upper School students typically attend 5 days per week. The average school day consists of 5 hours and 30 minutes.

Upper School Student Profile Grade 9: 60 students (33 boys, 27 girls); Grade 10: 60 students (41 boys, 19 girls); Grade 11: 49 students (25 boys, 24 girls); Grade 12: 69 students (34 boys, 35 girls).

Faculty School total: 95. In upper school: 18 men, 18 women; 20 have advanced degrees.

Subjects Offered Advanced Placement courses, American history, art, art history, biology, business, chemistry, computer programming, computer science, design, drama, earth science, economics, electronics, English, English literature, environmental science, European history, French, geography, health, history, mathematics, music, photography, physical education, physics, psychology, social studies, sociology, Spanish, speech, statistics, theater, trigonometry, world history.

Graduation Requirements English, mathematics.

Special Academic Programs 17 Advanced Placement exams for which test preparation is offered.

College Admission Counseling 60 students graduated in 2010; 58 went to college, including Dalhousie University; McGill University; New York University; Queen's University at Kingston; The University of Western Ontario; University of Guelph. Other: 1 went to work, 1 had other specific plans.

Student Life Upper grades have uniform requirement, student council. Discipline rests primarily with faculty.

Tuition and Aid Day student tuition: 16,945 Bermuda dollars. Tuition installment plan (monthly payment plans, One Payment Plan, two payment plan). Bursaries, merit scholarship grants, need-based scholarship grants available. In 2010–11, 15% of upper-school students received aid; total upper-school merit-scholarship money awarded: 100,000 Bermuda dollars. Total amount of financial aid awarded in 2010–11: 32,500,000 Bermuda dollars.

Admissions Traditional secondary-level entrance grade is 11. Grade equivalent tests required. Deadline for receipt of application materials: none. Application fee required: 50 Bermuda dollars. On-campus interview required.

Athletics Interscholastic: badminton (boys, girls), basketball (b,g), cricket (b), cross-country running (b,g), field hockey (g), golf (b), netball (g), rugby (b), running (b,g), soccer (b,g), softball (b,g), swimming and diving (b,g), track and field (b,g), volleyball (b,g); intramural: badminton (b,g), basketball (b,g), cricket (b), cross-country running (b,g), field hockey (b,g), golf (b), gymnastics (b,g), indoor soccer (b,g), lacrosse (b,g), netball (g), rugby (b), running (b,g), soccer (b,g), softball (b,g), squash (b,g), swimming and diving (b,g), table tennis (b,g), tennis (b,g), track and field (b,g), volleyball (b,g), wall climbing (b,g); coed interscholastic: badminton, basketball, field hockey, running, swimming and diving, water polo; coed intramural: badminton, field hockey, gymnastics, running, swimming and diving, table tennis, water polo. 5 PE instructors.

Computers Computers are regularly used in all classes. Computer network features include on-campus library services, Internet access, wireless campus network, Internet

filtering or blocking technology. Campus intranet and student e-mail accounts are available to students. The school has a published electronic and media policy.
Contact Mr. Malcolm J. Durrant, Deputy Headmaster. 441-292-6177. Fax: 441-295-4977. E-mail: mdurrant@saltus.bm. Web site: www.saltus.bm.

THE SAMUEL SCHECK HILLEL COMMUNITY DAY SCHOOL

19000 25th Avenue
North Miami Beach, Florida 33180
Head of School: Dr. Adam Holden

General Information Coeducational day and distance learning college-preparatory, religious studies, and bilingual studies school, affiliated with Jewish faith; primarily serves students with learning disabilities and dyslexic students. Grades PK–12. Distance learning grades 9–12. Founded: 1970. Setting: suburban. 3 buildings on campus. Approved or accredited by Southern Association of Colleges and Schools and Florida Department of Education. Total enrollment: 882. Upper school average class size: 20. Upper school faculty-student ratio: 1:15. There are 180 required school days per year for Upper School students. Upper School students typically attend 5 days per week.
Upper School Student Profile 100% of students are Jewish.
Faculty School total: 250.
Subjects Offered Studio art, studio art-AP, tennis, the Web, theater, track and field, U.S. government, U.S. government and politics-AP, U.S. history-AP, United States government-AP, Web site design, world history, world history-AP.
Graduation Requirements Jewish studies.
Special Academic Programs International Baccalaureate program; Advanced Placement exam preparation; honors section; study at local college for college credit; academic accommodation for the gifted and the artistically talented; remedial reading and/or remedial writing; remedial math; programs in English for dyslexic students; ESL (15 students enrolled).
College Admission Counseling 88 students graduated in 2009; all went to college, including Florida International University; Florida State University; University of Central Florida; University of Florida; University of Maryland, Baltimore County; University of Miami. Mean SAT critical reading: 577, mean SAT math: 612, mean SAT writing: 574, mean composite ACT: 24.
Student Life Upper grades have uniform requirement, student council, honor system. Discipline rests primarily with faculty. Attendance at religious services is required.
Tuition and Aid Day student tuition: $20,100. Tuition installment plan (FACTS Tuition Payment Plan, Tuition Management Systems). Merit scholarship grants, need-based scholarship grants available. In 2009–10, 25% of upper-school students received aid; total upper-school merit-scholarship money awarded: $75,000.
Admissions Traditional secondary-level entrance grade is 9. SSAT required. Deadline for receipt of application materials: February 15. Application fee required: $200. Interview required.
Athletics Interscholastic: baseball (boys), basketball (b,g), crew (b,g), cross-country running (b,g), fencing (b,g), flag football (b), football (b), golf (b), soccer (b,g), softball (g), tennis (b,g), volleyball (g); coed interscholastic: crew, cross-country running, fencing, tennis. 10 PE instructors.
Computers Computer network features include Internet access, Internet filtering or blocking technology. Campus intranet, student e-mail accounts, and computer access in designated common areas are available to students. Students grades are available online.
Contact Mrs. Betty Salinas, Director of Admissions. 305-931-2831 Ext. 173. Fax: 305-932-7463. E-mail: salinas@hillel-nmb.net. Web site: www.hillel-nmb.org/.

SANDIA PREPARATORY SCHOOL

532 Osuna Road NE
Albuquerque, New Mexico 87113
Head of School: B. Stephen Albert

General Information Coeducational day college-preparatory and arts school. Grades 6–12. Founded: 1966. Setting: suburban. 27-acre campus. 13 buildings on campus. Approved or accredited by Independent Schools Association of the Southwest and New Mexico Department of Education. Member of National Association of Independent Schools. Endowment: $4 million. Total enrollment: 659. Upper school average class size: 17. Upper school faculty-student ratio: 1:10. There are 180 required school days per year for Upper School students. The average school day consists of 7 hours and 30 minutes.
Upper School Student Profile Grade 9: 92 students (44 boys, 48 girls); Grade 10: 90 students (38 boys, 52 girls); Grade 11: 86 students (42 boys, 44 girls); Grade 12: 101 students (58 boys, 43 girls).
Faculty School total: 74. In upper school: 40 men, 33 women; 47 have advanced degrees.
Subjects Offered 20th century American writers, 3-dimensional art, adolescent issues, advanced biology, advanced chemistry, advanced computer applications, advanced math, algebra, American history, American literature, American politics in film, anatomy and physiology, ancient world history, art, astronomy, band, biology, calculus, ceramics, chemistry, chorus, computer programming, computer science, creative writing, drawing, earth science, ecology, environmental systems, economics,

English, English literature, environmental science, film, film history, filmmaking, fine arts, foreign language, French, French as a second language, geology, geometry, global issues, grammar, guitar, healthful living, history, jazz band, journalism, language arts, library skills, life science, mathematics, media communications, modern world history, music, newspaper, orchestra, outdoor education, painting, performing arts, personal development, philosophy, photography, physical education, physics, pottery, pre-algebra, pre-calculus, science, Shakespearean histories, social studies, Spanish, state history, statistics, technical theater, technology, theater, trigonometry, women in world history, world history, world literature, World War I, World War II, yearbook.
Graduation Requirements Arts and fine arts (art, music, dance, drama), electives, English, foreign language, mathematics, physical education (includes health), science, social studies (includes history), completion of a one-month volunteer Senior Experience in a professional, academic or volunteer area of interest during May of the Senior year.
Special Academic Programs Independent study; study at local college for college credit; study abroad; academic accommodation for the gifted.
College Admission Counseling 91 students graduated in 2010; all went to college, including Carnegie Mellon University; Duke University; Knox College; Lake Forest Academy; Trinity University; University of New Mexico. Median SAT critical reading: 660, median SAT math: 610, median composite ACT: 27. 65% scored over 600 on SAT critical reading, 59% scored over 600 on SAT math, 60% scored over 26 on composite ACT.
Student Life Upper grades have specified standards of dress, student council. Discipline rests primarily with faculty.
Summer Programs Enrichment, sports, art/fine arts, computer instruction programs offered; session focuses on summer enrichment; held on campus; accepts boys and girls; open to students from other schools. 350 students usually enrolled. 2011 schedule: June 1 to July 18. Application deadline: May 1.
Tuition and Aid Day student tuition: $16,400. Tuition installment plan (FACTS Tuition Payment Plan). Need-based scholarship grants available. In 2010–11, 20% of upper-school students received aid. Total amount of financial aid awarded in 2010–11: $950,000.
Admissions Traditional secondary-level entrance grade is 9. For fall 2010, 332 students applied for upper-level admission, 275 were accepted, 136 enrolled. Deadline for receipt of application materials: February 6. Application fee required: $40. On-campus interview required.
Athletics Interscholastic: baseball (boys), basketball (b,g), cross-country running (b,g), dance squad (g), golf (b,g), soccer (b,g), softball (g), swimming and diving (b,g), table tennis (b), tennis (b,g), track and field (b,g), volleyball (g); intramural: basketball (b,g), self defense (g); coed interscholastic: archery, dance, kickball; coed intramural: backpacking, bocce, canoeing/kayaking, climbing, Frisbee, hiking/backpacking, kayaking, lacrosse, modern dance, nordic skiing, ocean paddling, outdoor adventure, outdoor education, outdoor skills, rock climbing, yoga. 5 PE instructors, 40 coaches, 1 athletic trainer.
Computers Computers are regularly used in art, college planning, graphic arts, history, information technology, journalism, library skills, literacy, mathematics, multimedia, newspaper, photography, publications, science, study skills, technology, typing, word processing, yearbook classes. Computer network features include on-campus library services, online commercial services, Internet access, Internet filtering or blocking technology, individual student accounts, productivity software. Students grades are available online. The school has a published electronic and media policy.
Contact Ester Tomelloso, Director of Admissions. 505-338-3000. Fax: 505-338-3099. E-mail: etomelloso@sandiaprep.org. Web site: www.sandiaprep.org.

SAN DIEGO ACADEMY

2800 East 4th Street
National City, California 91950-3097
Head of School: Mr. Mervin Kesler

General Information Coeducational day college-preparatory school, affiliated with Seventh-day Adventist Church. Grades K–12. Founded: 1899. Setting: suburban. Nearest major city is San Diego. 4 buildings on campus. Approved or accredited by Western Association of Schools and Colleges and California Department of Education. Upper school average class size: 25. Upper school faculty-student ratio: 1:12. There are 180 required school days per year for Upper School students. Upper School students typically attend 5 days per week. The average school day consists of 7 hours and 15 minutes.
Upper School Student Profile 80% of students are Seventh-day Adventists.
Faculty School total: 20. In upper school: 5 men, 6 women; 6 have advanced degrees.
College Admission Counseling 24 students graduated in 2009; all went to college, including La Sierra University.
Student Life Upper grades have specified standards of dress. Discipline rests primarily with faculty. Attendance at religious services is required.
Admissions Traditional secondary-level entrance grade is 9. Deadline for receipt of application materials: none. No application fee required. Interview required.
Athletics Interscholastic: basketball (boys, girls), flag football (b), volleyball (g).
Computers The school has a published electronic and media policy.
Contact Mrs. Mary Mendoza, Administrative Assistant. 619-267-9550 Ext. 153. E-mail: school@sdacademy.com. Web site: www.sdacademy.com.

SAN DOMENICO SCHOOL

1500 Butterfield Road
San Anselmo, California 94960
Head of School: Dr. Mathew Heersche

General Information Girls' boarding and coeducational day college-preparatory, arts, religious studies, music, and theater arts, dance school, affiliated with Roman Catholic Church. Boarding girls grades 9–12, day boys grades PK–8, day girls grades PK–12. Founded: 1850. Setting: suburban. Nearest major city is San Francisco. Students are housed in single-sex dormitories. 515-acre campus. 4 buildings on campus. Approved or accredited by California Association of Independent Schools, Western Association of Schools and Colleges, and Western Catholic Education Association. Member of National Association of Independent Schools. Endowment: $7.1 million. Total enrollment: 525. Upper school average class size: 12. Upper school faculty-student ratio: 1:8. Upper School students typically attend 5 days per week. The average school day consists of 7 hours and 5 minutes.

Upper School Student Profile Grade 9: 20 students (20 girls); Grade 10: 31 students (31 girls); Grade 11: 30 students (30 girls); Grade 12: 41 students (41 girls). 57% of students are boarding students. 68% are state residents. 2 states are represented in upper school student body. 32% are international students. International students from China, Hong Kong, Republic of Korea, Taiwan, Thailand, and Viet Nam; 5 other countries represented in student body. 30% of students are Roman Catholic.

Faculty School total: 33. In upper school: 5 men, 24 women; 7 reside on campus.

Subjects Offered Acting, algebra, American history, American literature, art, art history, biology, biology-AP, calculus, ceramics, chemistry, community service, drama, English, English literature, environmental science, ESL, ethics, European history, expository writing, fine arts, French, freshman foundations, geometry, government/civics, grammar, history, mathematics, modern world history, music, music composition, music theater, music theory, musical productions, musicianship, photography, physical education, physics, religion, science, social studies, sociology, Spanish, studio art-AP, theater, theology, trigonometry, world history, world literature.

Graduation Requirements Arts and fine arts (art, music, dance, drama), English, foreign language, health, mathematics, physical education (includes health), religion (includes Bible studies and theology), science, social studies (includes history). Community service is required.

Special Academic Programs Advanced Placement exam preparation; honors section; independent study; academic accommodation for the musically talented; ESL (10 students enrolled).

College Admission Counseling 40 students graduated in 2009; all went to college, including Boston University; Loyola Marymount University; Seattle University; University of California, Berkeley; University of California, Santa Cruz; University of Illinois at Urbana–Champaign. Mean SAT critical reading: 584, mean SAT math: 606, mean SAT writing: 592, mean combined SAT: 1782, mean composite ACT: 29.

Student Life Upper grades have specified standards of dress, student council, honor system. Discipline rests primarily with faculty. Attendance at religious services is required.

Tuition and Aid Day student tuition: $27,950; 5-day tuition and room/board: $40,450; 7-day tuition and room/board: $40,450. Tuition installment plan (Insured Tuition Payment Plan, monthly payment plans). Need-based scholarship grants available. In 2009–10, 30% of upper-school students received aid. Total amount of financial aid awarded in 2009–10: $1,000,000.

Admissions Traditional secondary-level entrance grade is 9. For fall 2009, 59 students applied for upper-level admission, 47 were accepted, 20 enrolled. High School Placement Test, ISEE or SSAT required. Deadline for receipt of application materials: January 14. Application fee required: $100. Interview required.

Athletics Interscholastic: badminton, basketball, cross-country running, soccer, volleyball; intramural: dance, equestrian sports, horseback riding, modern dance. 1 PE instructor, 5 coaches.

Computers Computers are regularly used in freshman foundations, mathematics, science, social studies, yearbook classes. Computer network features include on-campus library services, online commercial services, Internet access, wireless campus network, Internet filtering or blocking technology. Student e-mail accounts are available to students. Students grades are available online. The school has a published electronic and media policy.

Contact Ms. Risa Oganesoff Heersche, Director of Upper School Admissions/ International Student Relations. 415-258-1905 Ext. 1124. Fax: 415-258-1906. E-mail: rheersche@sandomenico.org. Web site: www.sandomenico.org/.

SANDY SPRING FRIENDS SCHOOL

16923 Norwood Road
Sandy Spring, Maryland 20860
Head of School: Thomas R. Gibian

General Information Coeducational boarding and day college-preparatory, arts, and ESL school, affiliated with Society of Friends. Boarding grades 9–12, day grades PK–12. Founded: 1961. Setting: suburban. Nearest major city is Washington, DC. Students are housed in single-sex by floor dormitories. 140-acre campus. 15 buildings on campus. Approved or accredited by Association of Independent Maryland Schools, Association of Independent Schools of Greater Washington, Friends Council on Education, The Association of Boarding Schools, and Maryland Department of Education. Member of National Association of Independent Schools and Secondary School Admission Test Board. Endowment: $1 million. Total enrollment: 571. Upper school average class size: 15. Upper school faculty-student ratio: 1:8. There are 171

required school days per year for Upper School students. Upper School students typically attend 5 days per week. The average school day consists of 7 hours and 30 minutes.

Upper School Student Profile Grade 9: 53 students (24 boys, 29 girls); Grade 10: 58 students (32 boys, 26 girls); Grade 11: 76 students (39 boys, 37 girls); Grade 12: 79 students (39 boys, 40 girls). 11% of students are boarding students. 82% are state residents. 7 states are represented in upper school student body. 8% are international students. International students from China, Ethiopia, Republic of Korea, Taiwan, Thailand, and Viet Nam; 2 other countries represented in student body. 11% of students are members of Society of Friends.

Faculty School total: 74. In upper school: 15 men, 17 women; 19 have advanced degrees; 17 reside on campus.

Subjects Offered Algebra, American history, American literature, art, biology, British literature-AP, calculus, calculus-AP, ceramics, chemistry, chemistry-AP, choral music, creative writing, cultural geography, dance, dance performance, desktop publishing, drama, drawing, English, English as a foreign language, English literature and composition-AP, English literature-AP, environmental science-AP, ESL, ESL, French, French language-AP, geology, geometry, grammar, history, mathematics, music, music theory-AP, Native American history, painting, photography, physical education, physics, poetry, Quakerism and ethics, Russian literature, science, Spanish, Spanish language-AP, statistics-AP, trigonometry, U.S. history-AP, weaving, Western civilization, world literature.

Graduation Requirements Art, English, foreign language, history, mathematics, physical education (includes health), religion (includes Bible studies and theology), science. Community service is required.

Special Academic Programs 9 Advanced Placement exams for which test preparation is offered; independent study; ESL (25 students enrolled).

College Admission Counseling 67 students graduated in 2010; 66 went to college, including Bowdoin College; Connecticut College; Guilford College; Haverford College; New York University; University of Maryland, College Park. Other: 1 had other specific plans. Median SAT critical reading: 620, median SAT math: 610, median SAT writing: 620, median combined SAT: 1850, median composite ACT: 27.

Student Life Upper grades have specified standards of dress, student council, honor system. Discipline rests equally with students and faculty. Attendance at religious services is required.

Summer Programs Enrichment, ESL, sports, art/fine arts programs offered; session focuses on recreational and enrichment; held on campus; accepts boys and girls; open to students from other schools. 400 students usually enrolled. 2011 schedule: June 21 to August 21. Application deadline: May 1.

Tuition and Aid Day student tuition: $26,860; 5-day tuition and room/board: $38,400; 7-day tuition and room/board: $47,100. Tuition installment plan (Insured Tuition Payment Plan, individually arranged payment plans, The Tuition Management Plan). Need-based scholarship grants available. In 2010–11, 26% of upper-school students received aid. Total amount of financial aid awarded in 2010–11: $1,172,144.

Admissions Traditional secondary-level entrance grade is 9. For fall 2010, 190 students applied for upper-level admission, 106 were accepted, 57 enrolled. SSAT or TOEFL or SLEP required. Deadline for receipt of application materials: January 15. Application fee required: $75. Interview required.

Athletics Interscholastic: baseball (boys), basketball (b,g), cross-country running (b,g), lacrosse (b,g), soccer (b,g), softball (g), tennis (b,g), volleyball (g); coed interscholastic: cooperative games, modern dance, track and field; coed intramural: dance, flag football, Frisbee, outdoor education, physical fitness, physical training, table tennis, track and field, ultimate Frisbee, walking, weight lifting, yoga. 5 PE instructors, 3 coaches, 1 athletic trainer.

Computers Computers are regularly used in all academic classes. Computer network features include on-campus library services, Internet access. Student e-mail accounts and computer access in designated common areas are available to students.

Contact Kent Beck, Director of Upper School Admissions. 301-774-7455 Ext. 203. Fax: 301-924-1115. E-mail: kent.beck@ssfs.org. Web site: www.ssfs.org.

See Display on page 608 and Close-Up on page 836.

SANFORD SCHOOL

6900 Lancaster Pike
PO Box 888
Hockessin, Delaware 19707-0888
Head of School: Douglas MacKelcan

General Information Coeducational day college-preparatory school. Grades PK–12. Founded: 1930. Setting: suburban. Nearest major city is Wilmington. 100-acre campus. 6 buildings on campus. Approved or accredited by Middle States Association of Colleges and Schools and Delaware Department of Education. Member of National Association of Independent Schools and Secondary School Admission Test Board. Total enrollment: 572. Upper school average class size: 14. Upper school faculty-student ratio: 1:10. There are 162 required school days per year for Upper School students. Upper School students typically attend 5 days per week. The average school day consists of 5 hours and 15 minutes.

Upper School Student Profile Grade 9: 46 students (21 boys, 25 girls); Grade 10: 61 students (31 boys, 30 girls); Grade 11: 60 students (27 boys, 33 girls); Grade 12: 54 students (20 boys, 34 girls).

Faculty School total: 85. In upper school: 11 men, 21 women; 20 have advanced degrees.

Subjects Offered Algebra, American literature, anatomy and physiology, art, biology, biology-AP, calculus-AP, ceramics, chemistry, chemistry-AP, choir, Civil War, collage and assemblage, computer art, computer graphics, computer science-AP, concert band, drawing, driver education, ecology, ecology, environmental systems, economics, engineering, English, English language-AP, English literature, English literature-AP, environmental science-AP, fine arts, French, French-AP, functions, geometry, German, German-AP, graphic design, health, history, jazz band, Latin, Latin-AP, mathematics, music, music appreciation, painting, photography, physics, physics-AP, pre-calculus, printmaking, psychology, social studies, Spanish, Spanish-AP, statistics, statistics-AP, studio art-AP, technology, trigonometry, U.S. history, U.S. history-AP, video film production, visual arts, vocal ensemble, voice, world civilizations, world history, world history-AP, world literature, writing, yearbook.

Graduation Requirements Arts and fine arts (art, music, dance, drama), athletics, computer science, electives, English, foreign language, health, lab science, mathematics, music, social sciences, 2-week senior project/internship in May.

Special Academic Programs Advanced Placement exam preparation; honors section.

College Admission Counseling 60 students graduated in 2010; all went to college, including Cornell University; Elon University; Gettysburg College; Lynchburg College; Syracuse University; University of Delaware.

Student Life Upper grades have specified standards of dress, student council, honor system. Discipline rests equally with students and faculty.

Summer Programs Remediation, enrichment, advancement, art/fine arts, computer instruction programs offered; session focuses on enrichment; held on campus; accepts boys and girls; open to students from other schools. 2011 schedule: June 27 to August 5. Application deadline: none.

Tuition and Aid Day student tuition: $22,000. Tuition installment plan (Tuition Management System (TMS)). Need-based scholarship grants available. In 2010–11, 44% of upper-school students received aid. Total amount of financial aid awarded in 2010–11: $1,306,600.

Admissions Traditional secondary-level entrance grade is 9. For fall 2010, 77 students applied for upper-level admission, 63 were accepted, 29 enrolled. ERB CTP IV, ISEE or SSAT required. Deadline for receipt of application materials: January 7. Application fee required: $40. On-campus interview required.

Athletics Interscholastic: baseball (boys), basketball (b,g), cross-country running (b,g), field hockey (g), lacrosse (b,g), soccer (b,g), swimming and diving (b,g), tennis (b,g), volleyball (g), wrestling (b); coed interscholastic: golf, indoor track; coed intramural: physical fitness. 27 coaches, 1 athletic trainer.

Computers Computers are regularly used in art, computer applications, English, foreign language, history, mathematics, newspaper, science, yearbook classes. Computer network features include on-campus library services, online commercial services, Internet access, Internet filtering or blocking technology. Campus intranet and student e-mail accounts are available to students. The school has a published electronic and media policy.

Contact Ceil Baum, Admission Administrative Assistant. 302-239-5263 Ext. 265. Fax: 302-239-1912. E-mail: admission@sanfordschool.org. Web site: www.sanfordschool.org.

SAN FRANCISCO WALDORF SCHOOL

470 West Portal Avenue
San Francisco, California 94127
Head of School: Dan Ingoglia

General Information Coeducational day college-preparatory, arts, and music school. Grades 9–12. Founded: 1997. Setting: urban. 1-acre campus. 1 building on campus. Approved or accredited by Association of Waldorf Schools of North America, Western Association of Schools and Colleges, and California Department of Education. Total enrollment: 143. Upper school average class size: 15. Upper school faculty-student ratio: 1:15. There are 168 required school days per year for Upper School students. Upper School students typically attend 5 days per week. The average school day consists of 7 hours and 25 minutes.

Upper School Student Profile Grade 9: 33 students (14 boys, 19 girls); Grade 10: 40 students (22 boys, 18 girls); Grade 11: 43 students (24 boys, 19 girls); Grade 12: 27 students (12 boys, 15 girls).

Faculty School total: 34. In upper school: 14 men, 20 women; 17 have advanced degrees.

Subjects Offered 20th century American writers, 20th century history, 20th century world history, acting, adolescent issues, advanced chemistry, advanced computer applications, advanced math, African American history, African studies, algebra, American Civil War, American government, American history, American literature, anatomy and physiology, ancient world history, Arabic studies, architecture, art, art history, arts and crafts, Asian studies, astronomy, athletic training, backpacking, basketball, biochemistry, biology, bookbinding, botany, calculus, cell biology, chemistry, choir, choral music, civics, composition, computer skills, computer studies, contemporary art, CPR, drama, drawing, earth science, ecology, environmental systems, economics, economics and history, English, English composition, environmental science, eurythmy, fabric arts, fencing, fiber arts, film, fine arts, fitness, genetics, geometry, German, German literature, government, grammar, Greek culture,

San Francisco Waldorf School

guitar, Harlem Renaissance, health education, HTML design, human anatomy, human biology, inorganic chemistry, internship, introduction to technology, jazz band, lab science, Latin American studies, mechanics, medieval history, medieval/Renaissance history, metalworking, Middle Eastern history, modern history, modern politics, modern world history, music, music history, nature writers, optics, orchestra, organic chemistry, outdoor education, painting, performing arts, personal fitness, photography, physical education, physical fitness, physics, play production, poetry, political economy, pottery, pre-algebra, pre-calculus, printmaking, robotics, Russian literature, sculpture, senior composition, senior internship, senior project, senior seminar, set design, sewing, Spanish, sports conditioning, stagecraft, stained glass, state government, stone carving, studio art, theater arts, theater design and production, trigonometry, U.S. history, video film production, vocal ensemble, volleyball, weaving, weight training, wilderness education, wilderness experience, world civilizations, world geography, world history, world issues, zoology.

Graduation Requirements African studies, algebra, American government, American history, anatomy, Ancient Greek, ancient world history, art, art history, Asian studies, astronomy, botany, chemistry, classical Greek literature, comparative religion, creative writing, drama, drawing, economics, economics and history, English, English composition, environmental science, eurythmy, foreign language, geography, geometry, Greek culture, health, health education, history of architecture, history of music, independent study, internship, Islamic studies, Latin American studies, metalworking, meteorology, minority studies, modern politics, music, music history, optics, painting, physical education (includes health), physics, pottery, pre-calculus, projective geometry, reading/study skills, Roman civilization, science, senior project, social skills, state history, studio art, theater arts, U.S. history, weaving, world governments, writing, independent senior project.

Special Academic Programs Honors section; independent study; study abroad; remedial math; ESL (6 students enrolled).

College Admission Counseling 38 students graduated in 2009; 34 went to college, including Lewis & Clark College; Oberlin College; Reed College; Sarah Lawrence College; Smith College; University of California, Berkeley. Other: 2 went to work, 2 had other specific plans. Mean SAT critical reading: 581, mean SAT math: 528, mean SAT writing: 585. 77% scored over 600 on SAT critical reading, 62% scored over 600 on SAT math, 77% scored over 600 on SAT writing.

Student Life Upper grades have specified standards of dress, student council, honor system. Discipline rests primarily with faculty.

Tuition and Aid Day student tuition: $27,500. Tuition installment plan (SMART Tuition Payment Plan). Tuition reduction for siblings, need-based scholarship grants available. In 2009–10, 53% of upper-school students received aid.

Admissions Traditional secondary-level entrance grade is 9. Deadline for receipt of application materials: January 15. Application fee required: $75. Interview required.

Athletics Interscholastic: baseball (boys), basketball (b,g), sailing (b,g), soccer (b,g), volleyball (g); coed interscholastic: badminton, strength & conditioning; coed intramural: backpacking, canoeing/kayaking, climbing, dance, fencing, flag football, floor hockey, golf, hiking/backpacking, outdoor activities, outdoor education, rock climbing, tennis, ultimate Frisbee. 4 PE instructors, 14 coaches.

Computers Computers are regularly used in data processing, independent study, introduction to technology, library skills, mathematics, music, photography, science, video film production, Web site design, yearbook classes. Computer network features include on-campus library services, online commercial services, Internet access, wireless campus network. Student e-mail accounts are available to students. The school has a published electronic and media policy.

Contact Lisa Barry, Director of Admission. 415-431-2736 Ext. 139. Fax: 415-431-1712. E-mail: lbarry@sfwaldorf.org. Web site: www.sfwaldorfhighschool.org.

SAN MARCOS BAPTIST ACADEMY

2801 Ranch Road Twelve
San Marcos, Texas 78666-9406
Head of School: Dr. John H. Garrison

General Information Coeducational boarding and day college-preparatory, general academic, arts, business, religious studies, technology, learning skills, and ESL school, affiliated with Baptist Church. Grades 7–12. Founded: 1907. Setting: small town. Nearest major city is Austin. Students are housed in single-sex dormitories. 220-acre campus. 8 buildings on campus. Approved or accredited by Accreditation Commission of the Texas Association of Baptist Schools, Southern Association of Colleges and Schools, Texas Education Agency, The Association of Boarding Schools, and Texas Department of Education. Member of National Association of Independent Schools. Endowment: $5 million. Total enrollment: 271. Upper school average class size: 12. Upper school faculty-student ratio: 1:5. There are 180 required school days per year for Upper School students. Upper School students typically attend 5 days per week. The average school day consists of 6 hours.

Upper School Student Profile Grade 7: 28 students (18 boys, 10 girls); Grade 8: 24 students (13 boys, 11 girls); Grade 9: 40 students (26 boys, 14 girls); Grade 10: 50 students (36 boys, 14 girls); Grade 11: 77 students (48 boys, 29 girls); Grade 12: 52 students (29 boys, 23 girls). 63% of students are boarding students. 63% are state residents. 6 states are represented in upper school student body. 33% are international students. International students from Angola, China, Mexico, Nigeria, Republic of Korea, and Taiwan; 5 other countries represented in student body. 15% of students are Baptist.

Faculty School total: 41. In upper school: 19 men, 22 women; 19 have advanced degrees; 3 reside on campus.

Subjects Offered Advanced math, Advanced Placement courses, algebra, American government, American history, American literature, analysis and differential calculus, analytic geometry, anatomy and physiology, ancient world history, applied arts, applied music, art, athletic training, athletics, band, baseball, Basic programming, basketball, Bible, Bible studies, biology, biology-AP, British literature, British literature (honors), British literature-AP, business applications, calculus, calculus-AP, career/college preparation, character education, cheerleading, chemistry, choir, Christian scripture, Christian testament, Christianity, civics, civics/free enterprise, clayworking, college admission preparation, college counseling, college planning, communication skills, community service, comparative religion, computer applications, computer information systems, computer programming, computer science, computers, concert band, concert choir, contemporary art, critical thinking, desktop publishing, digital photography, drama, drama performance, drama workshop, dramatic arts, drawing, driver education, earth and space science, earth science, economics, economics and history, English, English as a foreign language, English composition, English literature, English literature and composition-AP, English literature-AP, English-AP, ESL, family and consumer science, fine arts, foreign language, French, geography, geometry, golf, government/civics, grammar, guidance, health, health education, history, history of the Americas, honors algebra, honors geometry, honors U.S. history, honors world history, HTML design, human anatomy, human biology, instrumental music, instruments, intro to computers, introduction to theater, jazz band, journalism, JROTC, JROTC or LEAD (Leadership Education and Development), keyboarding, language and composition, language arts, leadership, leadership education training, learning strategies, library, library skills, library studies, Life of Christ, life skills, literature, literature and composition-AP, literature-AP, logic, mathematical modeling, mathematics, mathematics-AP, military science, music, music appreciation, music performance, music theory, musical productions, musical theater, musicianship, New Testament, news writing, newspaper, novels, painting, participation in sports, personal and social education, personal fitness, personal growth, photography, photojournalism, physical education, physical fitness, physical science, physics, piano, play production, pottery, prayer/spirituality, pre-calculus, psychology, public speaking, reading, reading/study skills, religion, religious education, remedial study skills, research skills, SAT preparation, SAT/ACT preparation, science, social skills, social studies, society and culture, sociology, softball, Spanish, speech, speech and debate, speech communications, sports, sports conditioning, sports performance development, sports team management, state government, state history, stock market, student government, student publications, study skills, swimming, tennis, Texas history, theater, theater arts, theater production, theology, TOEFL preparation, track and field, U.S. government, U.S. government and politics, U.S. history, U.S. literature, visual arts, vocal ensemble, vocal jazz, vocal music, voice, voice and diction, voice ensemble, volleyball, Web authoring, Web site design, weight training, weightlifting, Western civilization, world civilizations, world cultures, world geography, world history, world issues, world literature, world religions, world religions, world studies, world wide web design, World-Wide-Web publishing, yearbook.

Graduation Requirements Arts and fine arts (art, music, dance, drama), computer science, economics, electives, English, foreign language, JROTC or LEAD (Leadership Education and Development), mathematics, physical education (includes health), religion (includes Bible studies and theology), science, social studies (includes history), speech.

Special Academic Programs Advanced Placement exam preparation; honors section; accelerated programs; independent study; study at local college for college credit; academic accommodation for the gifted, the musically talented, and the artistically talented; remedial reading and/or remedial writing; remedial math; programs in English, mathematics, general development for dyslexic students; special instructional classes for deaf students, students with Section 504 learning disabilities, Attention Deficit Disorder, and dyslexia; ESL (51 students enrolled).

College Admission Counseling 54 students graduated in 2010; 52 went to college, including Baylor University; Syracuse University; Texas State University–San Marcos; Texas Tech University; The University of Texas at Austin; University of Illinois at Urbana–Champaign. Other: 2 went to work. Mean SAT critical reading: 461, mean SAT math: 547, mean SAT writing: 447, mean combined SAT: 1455. 5% scored over 600 on SAT critical reading, 42% scored over 600 on SAT math, 2% scored over 600 on SAT writing, 15% scored over 1800 on combined SAT.

Student Life Upper grades have uniform requirement, student council, honor system. Discipline rests primarily with faculty. Attendance at religious services is required.

Tuition and Aid Day student tuition: $7867; 7-day tuition and room/board: $26,530. Guaranteed tuition plan. Tuition installment plan (monthly payment plans, individually arranged payment plans). Need-based scholarship grants available. In 2010–11, 21% of upper-school students received aid. Total amount of financial aid awarded in 2010–11: $306,200.

Admissions Traditional secondary-level entrance grade is 9. For fall 2010, 161 students applied for upper-level admission, 143 were accepted, 125 enrolled. Deadline for receipt of application materials: none. Application fee required: $100. Interview required.

Athletics Interscholastic: baseball (boys), basketball (b,g), cross-country running (b,g), flag football (b), football (b), golf (b,g), JROTC drill (b,g), power lifting (b,g), softball (g), swimming and diving (b,g), tennis (b,g), track and field (b,g), volleyball (g), weight lifting (b,g); coed interscholastic: cheering, drill team, equestrian sports, marksmanship, soccer, winter soccer; coed intramural: billiards, fitness walking, Frisbee, horseback riding, soccer, table tennis, weight lifting, weight training, winter soccer. 11 coaches, 1 athletic trainer.

Computers Computers are regularly used in computer applications, desktop publishing, information technology, keyboarding, newspaper, photojournalism, technology, typing, Web site design, yearbook classes. Computer network features include on-campus library services, Internet access, wireless campus network, Internet filtering or blocking technology. Student e-mail accounts are available to students. Students grades are available online. The school has a published electronic and media policy.

Contact Mr. Jeffrey D. Baergen, Director of Admissions. 800-428-5120. Fax: 512-753-8031. E-mail: admissions@smba.org. Web site: www.smabears.org.

SANTA CATALINA SCHOOL

1500 Mark Thomas Drive
Monterey, California 93940-5291
Head of School: Sr. Claire Barone

General Information Girls' boarding and day college-preparatory and liberal arts school, affiliated with Roman Catholic Church. Grades 9–12. Founded: 1950. Setting: small town. Nearest major city is San Francisco. Students are housed in single-sex dormitories. 36-acre campus. 21 buildings on campus. Approved or accredited by California Association of Independent Schools, The Association of Boarding Schools, Western Association of Schools and Colleges, and California Department of Education. Member of National Association of Independent Schools and Secondary School Admission Test Board. Endowment: $24 million. Total enrollment: 252. Upper school average class size: 12. Upper school faculty-student ratio: 1:8. There are 166 required school days per year for Upper School students. Upper School students typically attend 5 days per week. The average school day consists of 5 hours and 25 minutes.

Upper School Student Profile Grade 9: 82 students (82 girls); Grade 10: 58 students (58 girls); Grade 11: 50 students (50 girls); Grade 12: 61 students (61 girls). 46% of students are boarding students. 80% are state residents. 14 states are represented in upper school student body. 12% are international students. International students from Canada, China, Democratic People's Republic of Korea, Mexico, Taiwan, and Thailand; 4 other countries represented in student body. 40% of students are Roman Catholic.

Faculty School total: 35. In upper school: 15 men, 18 women; 27 have advanced degrees; 25 reside on campus.

Subjects Offered Algebra, American literature, art, art history-AP, ballet, biology, biology-AP, calculus, calculus-AP, ceramics, chemistry, chemistry-AP, Chinese, choir, college counseling, conceptual physics, creative writing, dance, digital art, drama, drama performance, economics-AP, English, English language-AP, English literature, English literature-AP, ensembles, environmental science-AP, European history, European history-AP, fine arts, French, French language-AP, French literature-AP, geometry, health, honors algebra, honors English, honors geometry, jazz dance, Latin, Latin-AP, marine science, music, music theory-AP, peace and justice, philosophy, photography, physical education, physics, physics-AP, pre-calculus, psychology, Spanish, Spanish language-AP, Spanish literature-AP, statistics, studio art, studio art-AP, theater, theology, trigonometry, U.S. history, U.S. history-AP, women spirituality and faith, world history, world issues, world literature, world religions.

Graduation Requirements Arts, English, foreign language, history, lab science, mathematics, physical education (includes health), religious studies.

Special Academic Programs 18 Advanced Placement exams for which test preparation is offered; honors section; academic accommodation for the gifted, the musically talented, and the artistically talented.

College Admission Counseling 63 students graduated in 2010; all went to college, including Santa Clara University; University of California, Berkeley; University of California, Los Angeles; University of California, Santa Barbara; University of Redlands; University of San Diego. Mean SAT critical reading: 576, mean SAT math: 563, mean SAT writing: 593.

Student Life Upper grades have uniform requirement, student council. Discipline rests equally with students and faculty. Attendance at religious services is required.

Tuition and Aid Day student tuition: $27,500; 7-day tuition and room/board: $42,500. Tuition installment plan (monthly payment plans, Tuition Management Systems). Merit scholarship grants, need-based scholarship grants, need-based loans available. In 2010–11, 40% of upper-school students received aid; total upper-school merit-scholarship money awarded: $9200. Total amount of financial aid awarded in 2010–11: $1,776,950.

Admissions Traditional secondary-level entrance grade is 9. For fall 2010, 208 students applied for upper-level admission, 152 were accepted, 99 enrolled. ISEE, SSAT or TOEFL required. Deadline for receipt of application materials: February 1. Application fee required: $75. Interview required.

Athletics Interscholastic: basketball, cross-country running, diving, equestrian sports, field hockey, golf, lacrosse, soccer, softball, swimming and diving, tennis, track and field, volleyball, water polo; intramural: ballet, canoeing/kayaking, dance, fencing, fitness, horseback riding, kayaking, modern dance, outdoor activities, physical fitness, rafting, rock climbing, self defense, strength & conditioning, surfing, ultimate Frisbee, weight training, yoga. 3 PE instructors, 26 coaches.

Computers Computers are regularly used in English, foreign language, media arts, science classes. Computer network features include on-campus library services,

Internet access, wireless campus network, Internet filtering or blocking technology. Campus intranet, student e-mail accounts, and computer access in designated common areas are available to students. The school has a published electronic and media policy.

Contact Mrs. Jamie Buffington Browne '85, Director of Admission. 831-655-9356. Fax: 831-655-7535. E-mail: jamie_brown@santacatalina.org. Web site: www.santacatalina.org.

SANTA FE PREPARATORY SCHOOL

1101 Camino Cruz Blanca
Santa Fe, New Mexico 87505
Head of School: Mr. James W. Leonard

General Information Coeducational day college-preparatory, arts, and community service school. Grades 7–12. Founded: 1961. Setting: suburban. 13-acre campus. 4 buildings on campus. Approved or accredited by Independent Schools Association of the Southwest and New Mexico Department of Education. Member of National Association of Independent Schools. Endowment: $4.3 million. Total enrollment: 323. Upper school average class size: 13. Upper school faculty-student ratio: 1:10. There are 171 required school days per year for Upper School students. Upper School students typically attend 5 days per week. The average school day consists of 6 hours and 25 minutes.

Upper School Student Profile Grade 7: 45 students (22 boys, 23 girls); Grade 8: 70 students (30 boys, 40 girls); Grade 9: 50 students (31 boys, 19 girls); Grade 10: 59 students (23 boys, 36 girls); Grade 11: 51 students (29 boys, 22 girls); Grade 12: 48 students (25 boys, 23 girls).

Faculty School total: 47. In upper school: 24 men, 23 women; 21 have advanced degrees.

Subjects Offered Acting, advanced chemistry, advanced computer applications, advanced math, algebra, American Civil War, American culture, American democracy, American government, American history, American history-AP, American literature, analytic geometry, art, art appreciation, art history, art history-AP, arts, athletics, basketball, biology, calculus, calculus-AP, ceramics, chemistry, chemistry-AP, chorus, clayworking, college counseling, community service, computer applications, computer graphics, computer literacy, computer programming, computer science, conceptual physics, creative writing, drama, drama performance, dramatic arts, driver education, earth science, English, English literature, European history, fine arts, French, geography, geometry, health, history, humanities, journalism, keyboarding, Latin, mathematics, music, photography, physical education, physics, psychology, science, social studies, Spanish, theater, trigonometry, world history, world literature, writing.

Graduation Requirements Arts and fine arts (art, music, dance, drama), computer science, English, foreign language, humanities, mathematics, music appreciation, physical education (includes health), science, social studies (includes history), senior seminar program. Community service is required.

Special Academic Programs 5 Advanced Placement exams for which test preparation is offered; honors section; independent study; study at local college for college credit; study abroad.

College Admission Counseling 52 students graduated in 2010; 51 went to college, including Lewis & Clark College; Middlebury College; The Colorado College; University of Colorado at Boulder; University of Denver; University of New Mexico. Other: 1 went to work. Mean SAT critical reading: 626, mean SAT math: 596, mean SAT writing: 636, mean combined SAT: 1857, mean composite ACT: 27. 56% scored over 600 on SAT critical reading, 49% scored over 600 on SAT math, 60% scored over 600 on SAT writing, 64% scored over 1800 on combined SAT, 50% scored over 26 on composite ACT.

Student Life Upper grades have specified standards of dress, student council. Discipline rests equally with students and faculty.

Tuition and Aid Day student tuition: $17,820. Tuition installment plan (individually arranged payment plans, Tuition Management Systems Plan). Need-based scholarship grants, tuition remission for faculty available. In 2010–11, 26% of upper-school students received aid. Total amount of financial aid awarded in 2010–11: $781,128.

Admissions Traditional secondary-level entrance grade is 9. For fall 2010, 27 students applied for upper-level admission, 23 were accepted, 14 enrolled. Placement test required. Deadline for receipt of application materials: none. Application fee required: $55. On-campus interview required.

Athletics Interscholastic: baseball (boys), basketball (b,g), cross-country running (b,g), diving (b,g), lacrosse (b,g), soccer (b,g), softball (g), swimming and diving (b,g), tennis (b,g), track and field (b,g), volleyball (g); intramural: basketball (b,g), cross-country running (b,g), football (b,g), soccer (b,g), tennis (b,g), track and field (b,g), volleyball (g); coed interscholastic: aerobics/dance, dance team; coed intramural: basketball, bowling, skiing (downhill), swimming and diving. 1 PE instructor, 16 coaches, 1 athletic trainer.

Computers Computers are regularly used in current events, English, French, freshman foundations, geography, graphic arts, history, humanities, journalism, library, literary magazine, mathematics, newspaper, photography, photojournalism, science, social sciences, writing, yearbook classes. Computer network features include on-campus library services, Internet access, wireless campus network, Internet filtering or blocking technology. Campus intranet, student e-mail accounts, and computer access in designated common areas are available to students. The school has a published electronic and media policy.

Contact Marta M. Miskolczy, Director of Admissions. 505-982-1829 Ext. 1212. Fax: 505-982-2897. E-mail: admissions@sfprep.org. Web site: www.santafeprep.org.

SANTA MARGARITA CATHOLIC HIGH SCHOOL

22062 Antonio Parkway
Rancho Santa Margarita, California 92688
Head of School: Mr. Ray Dunne

General Information Coeducational day college-preparatory, arts, religious studies, technology, International Baccalaureate, and Auxiliary Studies Program school, affiliated with Roman Catholic Church. Grades 9–12. Founded: 1987. Setting: suburban. Nearest major city is Mission Viejo. 42-acre campus. 15 buildings on campus. Approved or accredited by Western Association of Schools and Colleges, Western Catholic Education Association, and California Department of Education. Total enrollment: 1,580. Upper school average class size: 25. Upper school faculty-student ratio: 1:16. There are 180 required school days per year for Upper School students. Upper School students typically attend 5 days per week. The average school day consists of 7 hours.

Upper School Student Profile Grade 9: 394 students (209 boys, 185 girls); Grade 10: 384 students (189 boys, 195 girls); Grade 11: 389 students (190 boys, 199 girls); Grade 12: 413 students (189 boys, 224 girls). 65% of students are Roman Catholic.

Faculty School total: 114. In upper school: 59 men, 55 women; 59 have advanced degrees.

Subjects Offered 20th century world history, advanced chemistry, advanced math, Advanced Placement courses, aerobics, algebra, American Civil War, American government, American history, American history-AP, American legal systems, anatomy, anatomy and physiology, Ancient Greek, ancient history, ancient world history, art, art and culture, art appreciation, art education, art history, art history-AP, art-AP, ASB Leadership, athletic training, athletics, ballet, ballet technique, band, baseball, Basic programming, basketball, bell choir, Bible studies, biology, biology-AP, British history, British literature, British literature (honors), British literature-AP, broadcast journalism, broadcasting, business, business applications, business communications, business education, business law, business mathematics, business skills, business studies, business technology, calculus, calculus-AP, campus ministry, career/college preparation, Catholic belief and practice, cell biology, ceramics, chamber groups, cheerleading, chemistry, chemistry-AP, Chinese, Chinese history, Chinese literature, Chinese studies, choir, choral music, choreography, chorus, Christian and Hebrew scripture, Christian doctrine, Christian education, Christian ethics, Christian scripture, Christian studies, Christian testament, Christianity, church history, cinematography, civics, civil war history, classical Greek literature, classical language, classical music, classical studies, community service, comparative government and politics, comparative government and politics-AP, comparative political systems-AP, comparative politics, comparative religion, computer education, computer graphics, computer information systems, computer literacy, computer math, computer programming, computer science, computer science-AP, computers, concert band, concert bell choir, concert choir, CPR, creative arts, creative dance, creative drama, creative thinking, creative writing, cultural geography, current events, current history, dance, dance performance, design, developmental language skills, developmental math, digital photography, drama, drama performance, drama workshop, dramatic arts, drawing, drawing and design, earth science, East Asian history, East European studies, Eastern religion and philosophy, Eastern world civilizations, economics, economics and history, economics-AP, electives, English, English composition, English literature, English literature and composition-AP, English literature-AP, English-AP, English/composition-AP, environmental geography, environmental science, environmental science-AP, ethics, ethics and responsibility, European civilization, European history, European history-AP, European literature, film, film and literature, film appreciation, film history, film studies, finance, fine arts, forensics, French, French language-AP, French literature-AP, French studies, French-AP, geography, geology, geometry, geometry with art applications, German-AP, government and politics-AP, government-AP, government/civics, government/civics-AP, Greek, Greek culture, guitar, handbells, health, health and safety, health and wellness, health education, health science, history, history of dance, history of religion, history of the Americas, history of the Catholic Church, history-AP, Holocaust, Holocaust and other genocides, Holocaust legacy, Holocaust seminar, Holocaust studies, honors algebra, honors English, honors geometry, honors U.S. history, honors world history, human biology, instrumental music, International Baccalaureate courses, international relations, jazz, jazz band, jazz dance, jazz ensemble, journalism, language and composition, language arts, language-AP, languages, Latin, Latin-AP, law, literacy, literature and composition-AP, literature-AP, macro/microeconomics-AP, macroeconomics-AP, marching band, marine biology, mathematics, mathematics-AP, microeconomics-AP, model United Nations, music, music appreciation, music history, music performance, music theater, musical productions, news writing, newspaper, nutrition, orchestra, painting, personal fitness, philosophy, photography, photojournalism, physical education, physical science, physics, physics-AP, physiology, play production, playwriting and directing, poetry, political science, politics, pre-algebra, pre-calculus, probability, probability and statistics, psychology, psychology-AP, public speaking, reading/study skills, religion, religion and culture, religious education, religious studies, remedial/makeup course work, SAT preparation, SAT/ACT preparation, science, social sciences, social studies, sociology, softball, Spanish, Spanish language-AP, Spanish literature, Spanish literature-AP, Spanish-AP, speech, speech and debate, speech and oral interpretations, speech communications, sports, sports conditioning, statistics, statistics-AP, student government, student publications, studio art, studio art-AP, swimming, tap dance, television, The 20th Century, the Presidency, theater production, theology and the arts, theory of knowledge, trigonometry, U.S. constitutional history, U.S. government, U.S. government and politics, U.S. government and politics-AP, U.S. history, U.S. history-AP, United States government-AP, video, Vietnam, Vietnam history, Vietnam War, vocal ensemble, vocal jazz, vocal music, volleyball, water color painting, water polo, weight training, weightlifting, wind ensemble, wind instruments, world governments, world history, world history-AP, world issues, world literature, world religions, World War I, World War II, wrestling, writing, writing, yearbook.

Graduation Requirements Arts and fine arts (art, music, dance, drama), business skills (includes word processing), computer science, English, foreign language, mathematics, physical education (includes health), religion (includes Bible studies and theology), science, social sciences, social studies (includes history). Community service is required.

Special Academic Programs International Baccalaureate program; 17 Advanced Placement exams for which test preparation is offered; honors section; independent study; study at local college for college credit; academic accommodation for the gifted, the musically talented, and the artistically talented; remedial reading and/or remedial writing; remedial math; programs in English, mathematics, general development for dyslexic students; special instructional classes for deaf students, blind students, students with learning disabilities, Attention Deficit Disorder, and dyslexia.

College Admission Counseling 376 students graduated in 2009; 373 went to college, including Harvard University; Loyola Marymount University; Santa Clara University; University of Notre Dame; University of San Diego; University of Southern California. Other: 1 entered military service, 2 had other specific plans. Mean SAT critical reading: 555, mean SAT math: 561, mean SAT writing: 563, mean combined SAT: 1679, mean composite ACT: 25.

Student Life Upper grades have uniform requirement, student council, honor system. Discipline rests primarily with faculty. Attendance at religious services is required.

Tuition and Aid Day student tuition: $10,000. Tuition installment plan (monthly payment plans). Tuition reduction for siblings, need-based scholarship grants available. In 2009–10, 23% of upper-school students received aid. Total amount of financial aid awarded in 2009–10: $675,000.

Admissions Traditional secondary-level entrance grade is 9. For fall 2009, 530 students applied for upper-level admission, 450 were accepted, 395 enrolled. High School Placement Test required. Deadline for receipt of application materials: none. Application fee required: $50.

Athletics Interscholastic: aerobics/dance (girls), aquatics (b,g), ballet (g), baseball (b), basketball (b,g), cheering (g), cross-country running (b,g), dance (g), dance squad (g), dance team (g), diving (b,g), dressage (b,g), drill team (g), equestrian sports (b,g), football (b), golf (b,g), hockey (b), ice hockey (b), in-line hockey (b), lacrosse (b,g), modern dance (g), roller hockey (b), running (b,g), soccer (b,g), softball (g), surfing (b,g), swimming and diving (b,g), tennis (b,g), track and field (b,g), volleyball (b,g), water polo (b,g), wrestling (b); intramural: aerobics (g), aerobics/Nautilus (g), ballet (g), fitness (b,g), flag football (b), jogging (b,g), physical fitness (b,g), physical training (b,g), power lifting (b), running (b,g), self defense (b,g), touch football (b), walking (g), weight lifting (b,g), weight training (b,g), yoga (g); coed intramural: bowling, Frisbee, Special Olympics, table tennis, ultimate Frisbee. 4 PE instructors, 40 coaches, 2 athletic trainers.

Computers Computers are regularly used in all academic classes. Computer network features include on-campus library services, online commercial services, Internet access, wireless campus network, Internet filtering or blocking technology, ISIS Program, Aeries. Campus intranet is available to students. Students grades are available online. The school has a published electronic and media policy.

Contact Mr. Ron Blanc, Admissions Director. 949-766-6076. Fax: 949-766-6005. E-mail: admissions@smhs.org. Web site: www.smhs.org.

SANTIAM CHRISTIAN SCHOOL

7220 Northeast Arnold Avenue
Corvallis, Oregon 97330-9498
Head of School: Mr. Stan Baker

General Information Coeducational day college-preparatory, arts, business, vocational, religious studies, bilingual studies, and technology school, affiliated with Christian faith. Grades PS–12. Founded: 1978. Setting: small town. Nearest major city is Salem. 18-acre campus. 14 buildings on campus. Approved or accredited by Association of Christian Schools International, Northwest Accreditation Commission, Northwest Association of Schools and Colleges, and Oregon Department of Education. Total enrollment: 723. Upper school average class size: 22. Upper school faculty-student ratio: 1:17. There are 170 required school days per year for Upper School students. Upper School students typically attend 5 days per week. The average school day consists of 6 hours and 8 minutes.

Upper School Student Profile Grade 9: 64 students (34 boys, 30 girls); Grade 10: 58 students (36 boys, 22 girls); Grade 11: 71 students (36 boys, 35 girls); Grade 12: 76 students (38 boys, 38 girls). 95% of students are Christian faith.

Faculty School total: 41. In upper school: 17 men, 13 women; 12 have advanced degrees.

Subjects Offered 20th century American writers, 20th century physics, 20th century world history, 3-dimensional art, 3-dimensional design, acting, advanced computer applications, advanced math, advanced studio art-AP, algebra, American biography,

American Civil War, American culture, American democracy, American foreign policy, American literature, anatomy and physiology, ancient world history, animal science, art, art appreciation, band, Bible studies, biology, body human, British history, business applications, calculus, career and personal planning, career education, carpentry, character education, chemistry, child development, choir, choral music, Christian doctrine, Christian education, Christian ethics, Christian testament, Christianity, church history, civics, Civil War, college counseling, college writing, comparative government and politics, computer applications, computer education, computer graphics, computer programming, concert band, concert choir, drama, drama performance, drawing, early childhood, earth science, economics, English, English composition, English literature, ethics, family living, fine arts, first aid, fitness, food and nutrition, foods, French, general math, general science, geography, geometry, global studies, government, grammar, graphic arts, guidance, health and wellness, health education, human anatomy, instrumental music, Internet, intro to computers, introduction to literature, journalism, keyboarding, language arts, leadership, library, Life of Christ, literature, marine biology, marketing, mathematics, moral and social development, music, music appreciation, music composition, music performance, occupational education, oral expression, physics, play production, playwriting and directing, poetry, pre-algebra, pre-calculus, public speaking, science, sewing, Spanish, speech, stage design, studio art-AP, theater, theater arts, theater production, U.S. government, U.S. history, vocal music, Western civilization, woodworking, world history, world literature, writing.

Graduation Requirements Arts and fine arts (art, music, dance, drama), computer science, English, health, mathematics, physical education (includes health), religion (includes Bible studies and theology), science, social sciences, social studies (includes history).

Special Academic Programs 3 Advanced Placement exams for which test preparation is offered; honors section; independent study; study at local college for college credit.

College Admission Counseling 71 students graduated in 2009; 67 went to college, including George Fox University; Linn-Benton Community College; Oregon State University; University of Oregon; Western Oregon University. Other: 1 went to work, 2 entered military service, 1 had other specific plans. Mean SAT critical reading: 561, mean SAT math: 531, mean SAT writing: 540, mean combined SAT: 1632.

Student Life Upper grades have specified standards of dress, student council. Discipline rests primarily with faculty. Attendance at religious services is required.

Tuition and Aid Day student tuition: $5140. Tuition installment plan (monthly payment plans, individually arranged payment plans, prepayment discount plan). Tuition reduction for siblings, need-based scholarship grants, paying campus jobs available. Total amount of financial aid awarded in 2009–10: $130,000.

Admissions Traditional secondary-level entrance grade is 9. For fall 2009, 90 students applied for upper-level admission, 75 were accepted, 70 enrolled. Deadline for receipt of application materials: none. Application fee required: $35. Interview required.

Athletics Interscholastic: baseball (boys), basketball (b,g), cheering (g), cross-country running (b,g), equestrian sports (g), football (b), golf (b,g), soccer (b,g), softball (g), track and field (b,g), volleyball (g), wrestling (b). 3 PE instructors, 3 coaches.

Computers Computers are regularly used in career education, computer applications, keyboarding, photography, yearbook classes. Computer network features include on-campus library services, Internet access, Internet filtering or blocking technology. Student e-mail accounts are available to students. Students grades are available online.

Contact Mrs. Sami Beam, Registrar. 541-745-5524 Ext. 203. Fax: 541-745-6338. E-mail: beams@santiam.org. Web site: www.santiamchristian.org.

SAVANNAH CHRISTIAN PREPARATORY SCHOOL

PO Box 2848
Savannah, Georgia 31402-2848
Head of School: Mr. Roger L. Yancey

General Information Coeducational day college-preparatory school, affiliated with Christian faith. Grades PK–12. Founded: 1951. Setting: suburban. 236-acre campus. 6 buildings on campus. Approved or accredited by Georgia Independent School Association, Southern Association of Colleges and Schools, and Georgia Department of Education. Endowment: $1.1 million. Total enrollment: 1,407. Upper school average class size: 23. Upper school faculty-student ratio: 1:14. There are 180 required school days per year for Upper School students. Upper School students typically attend 5 days per week. The average school day consists of 6 hours and 35 minutes.

Upper School Student Profile Grade 9: 129 students (68 boys, 61 girls); Grade 10: 118 students (61 boys, 57 girls); Grade 11: 126 students (75 boys, 51 girls); Grade 12: 104 students (42 boys, 62 girls). 95% of students are Christian faith.

Faculty School total: 125. In upper school: 10 men, 25 women; 26 have advanced degrees.

Subjects Offered 20th century history, accounting, algebra, American Civil War, American history, American history-AP, art, astronomy, band, Bible, biology, botany, business law, calculus-AP, chemistry, chemistry-AP, chorus, Christian ethics, computer applications, computer-aided design, creative writing, design, drama, driver education, earth science, ecology, economics, English, English-AP, European history-AP, French, geometry, government/civics, graphic arts, health, marine biology, mathematics, mechanical drawing, music appreciation, physical education, physics,

probability and statistics, psychology, science, social studies, sociology, Spanish, speech, technical theater, theater, trigonometry, typing, world history, yearbook.

Graduation Requirements Accounting, algebra, biology, chemistry, economics, English, foreign language, geometry, mathematics, physical education (includes health), religion (includes Bible studies and theology), science, social studies (includes history).

Special Academic Programs Advanced Placement exam preparation; honors section; study at local college for college credit.

College Admission Counseling 108 students graduated in 2009; 107 went to college, including Armstrong Atlantic State University; Georgia College & State University; Georgia Southern University; University of Georgia; University of South Carolina; Valdosta State University. Other: 1 entered military service. Mean SAT critical reading: 545, mean SAT math: 551, mean SAT writing: 545, mean combined SAT: 1641, mean composite ACT: 24.

Student Life Upper grades have uniform requirement, student council, honor system. Discipline rests primarily with faculty.

Tuition and Aid Day student tuition: $7098. Tuition installment plan (monthly payment plans). Tuition reduction for siblings, merit scholarship grants, need-based scholarship grants available. In 2009–10, 15% of upper-school students received aid; total upper-school merit-scholarship money awarded: $100,000. Total amount of financial aid awarded in 2009–10: $110,000.

Admissions Traditional secondary-level entrance grade is 9. For fall 2009, 61 students applied for upper-level admission, 58 were accepted, 58 enrolled. Stanford Achievement Test and writing sample required. Deadline for receipt of application materials: January 31. Application fee required: $175. On-campus interview required.

Athletics Interscholastic: baseball (boys), basketball (b,g), cheering (g), cross-country running (b,g), dance team (g), football (b), golf (b,g), soccer (b,g), softball (g), tennis (b,g), track and field (b,g), volleyball (g); coed intramural: sailing. 3 PE instructors, 3 coaches, 1 athletic trainer.

Computers Computers are regularly used in accounting, business applications, computer applications, English, graphic arts, history, science, word processing, yearbook classes. Computer network features include on-campus library services, Internet access, wireless campus network, Internet filtering or blocking technology. Computer access in designated common areas is available to students. Students grades are available online. The school has a published electronic and media policy.

Contact Mrs. Debbie Fairbanks, Director of Admissions. 912-234-1653 Ext. 106. Fax: 912-234-0491. E-mail: dfairbanks@savcps.com. Web site: www.savcps.com.

THE SAVANNAH COUNTRY DAY SCHOOL

824 Stillwood Drive
Savannah, Georgia 31419-2643
Head of School: Mrs. Marcia Hull

General Information Coeducational day college-preparatory, arts, and technology school. Grades PK–12. Founded: 1955. Setting: suburban. 65-acre campus. 11 buildings on campus. Approved or accredited by Georgia Independent School Association, Southern Association of Colleges and Schools, and Southern Association of Independent Schools. Member of National Association of Independent Schools. Endowment: $32.2 million. Total enrollment: 910. Upper school average class size: 16. Upper school faculty-student ratio: 1:8. Upper School students typically attend 5 days per week. The average school day consists of 7 hours.

Upper School Student Profile Grade 9: 51 students (25 boys, 26 girls); Grade 10: 58 students (25 boys, 33 girls); Grade 11: 73 students (41 boys, 32 girls); Grade 12: 68 students (33 boys, 35 girls).

Faculty School total: 81. In upper school: 15 men, 19 women; 24 have advanced degrees.

Subjects Offered Advanced Placement courses, algebra, American history, American literature, analysis and differential calculus, anatomy and physiology, art, art history, biology, biology-AP, British literature-AP, calculus, calculus-AP, ceramics, chemistry, chemistry-AP, chorus, composition, computer education, computer science, dance, drama, drama performance, economics and history, English, English literature, English-AP, environmental science, environmental science-AP, European history, European history-AP, fine arts, French, geometry, government-AP, government/civics, guidance, health, honors algebra, honors English, honors geometry, honors U.S. history, honors world history, independent study, instrumental music, intro to computers, jazz band, language-AP, Latin, Latin-AP, music, photography, physical education, physics, physics-AP, pre-calculus, public speaking, Spanish, Spanish language-AP, statistics, studio art-AP, theater, U.S. history-AP, world history, world history-AP, yearbook.

Graduation Requirements Arts and fine arts (art, music, dance, drama), English, foreign language, health education, history, mathematics, physical education (includes health), science, speech.

Special Academic Programs Advanced Placement exam preparation; honors section; independent study; study at local college for college credit.

College Admission Counseling 79 students graduated in 2009; all went to college, including Clemson University; Savannah College of Art and Design; The University of Alabama at Birmingham; University of Georgia; University of South Carolina. Mean SAT critical reading: 680, mean SAT math: 660, mean SAT writing: 660, mean combined SAT: 2000.

Student Life Upper grades have uniform requirement, student council, honor system. Discipline rests equally with students and faculty.

The Savannah Country Day School

Tuition and Aid Day student tuition: $16,400. Tuition installment plan (Insured Tuition Payment Plan, FACTS Tuition Payment Plan, monthly payment plans, individually arranged payment plans). Merit scholarship grants, need-based scholarship grants available. In 2009–10, 4% of upper-school students received aid; total upper-school merit-scholarship money awarded: $2000. Total amount of financial aid awarded in 2009–10: $364,400.

Admissions Traditional secondary-level entrance grade is 9. For fall 2009, 8 students applied for upper-level admission, 4 were accepted, 4 enrolled. ERB Reading and Math, Math Placement Exam, Otis-Lennon Mental Ability Test or writing sample required. Deadline for receipt of application materials: none. Application fee required: $175. Interview required.

Athletics Interscholastic: baseball (boys), basketball (b,g), cheering (g), crew (b,g), cross-country running (b,g), football (b), golf (b,g), soccer (b,g), softball (g), tennis (b,g), track and field (b,g), volleyball (g), wrestling (b); intramural: basketball (b,g), bocce (b,g), cheering (g), climbing (b,g), cross-country running (b,g), dance (b,g), in-line hockey (b), outdoor adventure (b,g), outdoor education (b,g), physical training (b,g), power lifting (b,g), project adventure (b,g), ropes courses (b,g), strength & conditioning (b,g), track and field (b,g), volleyball (g), water polo (g), weight lifting (b,g), weight training (b,g). 1 coach, 2 athletic trainers.

Computers Computers are regularly used in college planning, creative writing, English, foreign language, history, library skills, mathematics, publications, publishing, research skills, SAT preparation, science, yearbook classes. Computer network features include on-campus library services, online commercial services, Internet access, wireless campus network, Internet filtering or blocking technology. Campus intranet and student e-mail accounts are available to students. The school has a published electronic and media policy.

Contact Mrs. Josceline Reardon, Assistant Director of Admissions and Financial Aid. 912-961-8807. Fax: 912-920-7800. E-mail: reardon@savcds.org. Web site: www.savcds.org.

SAYRE SCHOOL
194 North Limestone Street
Lexington, Kentucky 40507
Head of School: Mr. Clayton G. Chambliss

General Information Coeducational day college-preparatory, arts, and technology school. Grades PK–12. Founded: 1854. Setting: urban. 60-acre campus. 10 buildings on campus. Approved or accredited by Independent Schools Association of the Central States and Kentucky Department of Education. Member of National Association of Independent Schools and Secondary School Admission Test Board. Endowment: $64 million. Total enrollment: 563. Upper school average class size: 14. Upper school faculty-student ratio: 1:9. There are 179 required school days per year for Upper School students. Upper School students typically attend 5 days per week. The average school day consists of 6 hours and 15 minutes.

Upper School Student Profile Grade 9: 40 students (16 boys, 24 girls); Grade 10: 49 students (22 boys, 27 girls); Grade 11: 61 students (30 boys, 31 girls); Grade 12: 72 students (32 boys, 40 girls).

Faculty School total: 32. In upper school: 12 men, 16 women; 22 have advanced degrees.

Subjects Offered Algebra, American history, American literature, art, art history, biology, calculus, chemistry, community service, computer science, creative writing, drama, earth science, English, English literature, fine arts, French, geometry, government/civics, health, history, journalism, mathematics, music, photography, physical education, physics, public speaking, science, social studies, Spanish, speech, statistics, theater, U.S. constitutional history, world history, writing.

Graduation Requirements Arts and fine arts (art, music, dance, drama), computer science, creative writing, English, foreign language, mathematics, physical education (includes health), public speaking, science, social studies (includes history), senior project internship. Community service is required.

Special Academic Programs 13 Advanced Placement exams for which test preparation is offered; honors section; independent study; term-away projects; study at local college for college credit; academic accommodation for the gifted and the artistically talented.

College Admission Counseling 61 students graduated in 2010; all went to college, including Centre College; Miami University; University of Georgia; University of Kentucky; Vanderbilt University. Median SAT critical reading: 570, median SAT math: 580, median SAT writing: 580, median combined SAT: 1760, median composite ACT: 25. 38% scored over 600 on SAT critical reading, 42% scored over 600 on SAT math, 44% scored over 600 on SAT writing, 41% scored over 1800 on combined SAT, 41% scored over 26 on composite ACT.

Student Life Upper grades have specified standards of dress, student council, honor system. Discipline rests equally with students and faculty.

Tuition and Aid Day student tuition: $16,000–$19,000. Tuition installment plan (Insured Tuition Payment Plan, monthly payment plans, individually arranged payment plans). Need-based scholarship grants available. In 2010–11, 21% of upper-school students received aid. Total amount of financial aid awarded in 2010–11: $510,000.

Admissions Traditional secondary-level entrance grade is 9. For fall 2010, 39 students applied for upper-level admission, 33 were accepted, 27 enrolled. Admissions testing, Math Placement Exam, PSAT and SAT for applicants to grade 11 and 12,

school's own exam or writing sample required. Deadline for receipt of application materials: none. Application fee required: $75. On-campus interview required.

Athletics Interscholastic: baseball (boys), basketball (b,g), cheering (g), diving (b,g), golf (b,g), lacrosse (b), physical fitness (b), physical training (b,g), soccer (b,g), softball (g), swimming and diving (b,g), tennis (b,g); coed interscholastic: cross-country running. 5 PE instructors, 4 coaches, 1 athletic trainer.

Computers Computers are regularly used in English, foreign language, history, mathematics, music, science classes. Computer network features include on-campus library services, online commercial services, Internet access, wireless campus network, Internet filtering or blocking technology. Student e-mail accounts are available to students. Students grades are available online. The school has a published electronic and media policy.

Contact Mr. John W. Hackworth, Director of Admission. 859-254-1361 Ext. 207. Fax: 859-254-5627. E-mail: jwhackworth@sayreschool.org. Web site: www.sayreschool.org.

SCARBOROUGH CHRISTIAN SCHOOL
Signet Christian School (changed school name)
95 Jonesville Crescent
North York, Ontario M4A 1H2, Canada
Head of School: Mr. Martin D. Sandford

General Information Coeducational day college-preparatory and business school, affiliated with Christian faith. Grades JK–12. Founded: 1975. Setting: urban. Nearest major city is Toronto, Canada. 1-acre campus. 1 building on campus. Approved or accredited by Association of Christian Schools International and Ontario Department of Education. Language of instruction: English. Total enrollment: 78. Upper school average class size: 12. Upper school faculty-student ratio: 1:7. There are 178 required school days per year for Upper School students. Upper School students typically attend 5 days per week. The average school day consists of 6 hours and 30 minutes.

Upper School Student Profile Grade 9: 13 students (4 boys, 9 girls); Grade 10: 6 students (2 boys, 4 girls); Grade 11: 9 students (5 boys, 4 girls); Grade 12: 21 students (9 boys, 12 girls). 50% of students are Christian.

Faculty School total: 15. In upper school: 3 men, 4 women.

Subjects Offered Biology, business studies, calculus, Canadian geography, Canadian history, career education, chemistry, civics, English, ESL, French as a second language, math analysis, math applications, physics, science, visual arts.

Graduation Requirements English, Ontario Ministry of Education requirements.

Special Academic Programs Independent study; ESL (4 students enrolled).

Student Life Upper grades have uniform requirement, student council. Discipline rests primarily with faculty. Attendance at religious services is required.

Tuition and Aid Day student tuition: CAN$6120. Tuition installment plan (individually arranged payment plans). Tuition reduction for siblings available. In 2010–11, 20% of upper-school students received aid.

Admissions Traditional secondary-level entrance grade is 9. SLEP required. Deadline for receipt of application materials: none. No application fee required.

Athletics Coed Intramural: basketball, bowling, cross-country running, ice skating, skiing (downhill), snowboarding, soccer, track and field.

Computers Computers are regularly used in English, mathematics, technology classes. Computer network features include Internet access.

Contact Admissions. 416-750-7515. Fax: 416-750-7720. E-mail: scs@titan.tcn.net. Web site: www.signetschool.ca.

SCATTERGOOD FRIENDS SCHOOL
1951 Delta Avenue
West Branch, Iowa 52358-8507
Head of School: Ms. Ginny Winsor

General Information Coeducational boarding and day college-preparatory and arts school, affiliated with Society of Friends. Boarding grades 9–PG, day grades 9–12. Founded: 1890. Setting: rural. Nearest major city is Iowa City. Students are housed in single-sex dormitories. 120-acre campus. 15 buildings on campus. Approved or accredited by Friends Council on Education, Independent Schools Association of the Central States, Midwest Association of Boarding Schools, The Association of Boarding Schools, and Iowa Department of Education. Member of National Association of Independent Schools. Endowment: $3.5 million. Total enrollment: 45. Upper school average class size: 10. Upper school faculty-student ratio: 1:2.

Upper School Student Profile Grade 9: 9 students (5 boys, 4 girls); Grade 10: 14 students (10 boys, 4 girls); Grade 11: 15 students (7 boys, 8 girls); Grade 12: 12 students (5 boys, 7 girls); Postgraduate: 1 student (1 girl). 100% of students are boarding students. 37% are state residents. 11 states are represented in upper school student body. 26% are international students. International students from China, Ethiopia, India, Mexico, Republic of Korea, and Rwanda. 14% of students are members of Society of Friends.

Faculty School total: 24. In upper school: 13 men, 11 women; 5 have advanced degrees; 21 reside on campus.

Subjects Offered 3-dimensional art, advanced TOEFL/grammar, agriculture, algebra, alternative physical education, American government, American history, art, biology, calculus, career/college preparation, ceramics, chemistry, choreography, college admission preparation, community service, conflict resolution, creative writing, critical thinking, dance, dance performance, digital art, drama, drama performance, drawing and design, ecology, environmental systems, electronic music, environmental science, ESL, ethics, expository writing, fencing, fine arts, gardening, geometry, glassblowing, government/civics, grammar, history, horticulture, independent study, industrial arts, Internet research, library research, martial arts, mathematics, organic gardening, physics, portfolio writing, pottery, Quakerism and ethics, religion, research seminar, SAT/ACT preparation, science, senior seminar, set design, social studies, Spanish, stained glass, studio art, swimming, U.S. history, wilderness education, woodworking, writing workshop, yearbook, yoga.

Graduation Requirements Algebra, American literature, art, biology, chemistry, English, foreign language, geometry, government, history, humanities, junior and senior seminars, physical education (includes health), physics, portfolio writing, Quakerism and ethics, SAT/ACT preparation, U.S. history, world history, world literature, 30 hours of community service per year in attendance, 20-page senior research paper with a thesis defense presentation, acceptance at 4-year college or university.

Special Academic Programs Honors section; accelerated programs; independent study; term-away projects; study abroad; ESL (15 students enrolled).

College Admission Counseling 12 students graduated in 2009; 7 went to college, including Cornell College; Earlham College; Fort Lewis College; The University of Iowa. Other: 4 went to work, 1 had other specific plans. Mean SAT critical reading: 570, mean SAT math: 578, mean SAT writing: 540, mean combined SAT: 1688, mean composite ACT: 24.

Student Life Upper grades have specified standards of dress, student council. Discipline rests equally with students and faculty. Attendance at religious services is required.

Tuition and Aid Day student tuition: $14,500; 5-day tuition and room/board: $22,500; 7-day tuition and room/board: $23,650. Tuition installment plan (Academic Management Services Plan, monthly payment plans, individually arranged payment plans). Merit scholarship grants, need-based scholarship grants, paying campus jobs, scholarships for Quaker students available. In 2009–10, 76% of upper-school students received aid; total upper-school merit-scholarship money awarded: $1000. Total amount of financial aid awarded in 2009–10: $534,000.

Admissions Traditional secondary-level entrance grade is 9. For fall 2009, 29 students applied for upper-level admission, 26 were accepted, 22 enrolled. Deadline for receipt of application materials: none. Application fee required: $50. Interview required.

Athletics Coed Interscholastic: basketball, fencing, indoor soccer, soccer; coed intramural: aquatics, archery, backpacking, ball hockey, bicycling, canoeing/kayaking, combined training, cooperative games, dance, fitness, hiking/backpacking, in-line hockey, jogging, juggling, martial arts, modern dance, physical fitness, roller hockey, running, skateboarding, strength & conditioning, swimming and diving, ultimate Frisbee, volleyball, yoga.

Computers Computers are regularly used in all classes. Computer network features include online commercial services, Internet access, wireless campus network, Internet filtering or blocking technology, laptop computers for each student. Campus intranet, student e-mail accounts, and computer access in designated common areas are available to students. The school has a published electronic and media policy.

Contact Glenn Singer, Director of Admissions. 319-643-7628. Fax: 319-643-7638. E-mail: admissions@scattergood.org. Web site: www.scattergood.org.

SCECGS REDLANDS

272 Military Road
Cremorne 2090, Australia
Head of School: Dr. Peter Lennox

General Information Coeducational day college-preparatory school, affiliated with Church of England (Anglican). Grades PK–12. Founded: 1884. Setting: suburban. Nearest major city is Sydney, Australia. 14-acre campus. 11 buildings on campus. Approved or accredited by New South Wales Department of School Education. Language of instruction: English. Total enrollment: 1,500. Upper school average class size: 20.

Upper School Student Profile 60% of students are members of Church of England (Anglican).

Faculty School total: 111.

Subjects Offered Ancient history, art, ballet, biology, business studies, chemistry, computer math, computer science, computer studies, creative arts, dance, drama, economics, English, ESL, French, geography, geology, German, government/civics, Greek, health, history, industrial arts, information processing, information technology, Japanese, JROTC, language, Latin, Mandarin, mathematics, modern history, music, personal development, photography, physical education, physics, religion, science, social studies, software design, speech, textiles, theater, visual arts.

Graduation Requirements English, foreign language, mathematics, physical education (includes health), religion (includes Bible studies and theology), science, social studies (includes history).

Special Academic Programs International Baccalaureate program; honors section; accelerated programs; independent study; remedial reading and/or remedial writing; remedial math; programs in English, mathematics, general development for dyslexic students; special instructional classes for students with learning disabilities; ESL.

College Admission Counseling 173 students graduated in 2010; 136 went to college, including Macquarie University; University of New South Wales.

Student Life Upper grades have uniform requirement, student council, honor system. Discipline rests equally with students and faculty. Attendance at religious services is required.

Tuition and Aid Day student tuition: 16,780 Australian dollars–22,560 Australian dollars. Merit scholarship grants available.

Admissions For fall 2010, 364 students applied for upper-level admission, 119 were accepted. Deadline for receipt of application materials: none. Application fee required. On-campus interview recommended.

Athletics Interscholastic: basketball (boys, girls), crew (b), cricket (b), cross-country running (b,g), diving (b), golf (b), riflery (b), rugby (b), soccer (b,g), squash (b), swimming and diving (b,g), tennis (b,g), track and field (b); intramural: badminton (b,g), basketball (b,g), crew (b), cricket (b), cross-country running (b,g), diving (b), equestrian sports (b,g), riflery (b), rugby (b), sailing (b,g), soccer (b,g), softball (b,g), squash (b), swimming and diving (b,g), tennis (b,g), touch football (b), track and field (b), water polo (b,g).

Computers Computer resources include on-campus library services, wireless campus network. Student e-mail accounts are available to students.

Contact Ms. Terese Kielt, Registrar. 61-2-9968-9890. Fax: 61-2-9909-3228. E-mail: registrar@redlands.nsw.edu.au. Web site: www.redlands.nsw.edu.au.

SCHLARMAN HIGH SCHOOL

2112 North Vemilion
Danville, Illinois 61832
Head of School: Adm. Robert A. Rice

General Information Coeducational day college-preparatory, arts, business, religious studies, and technology school, affiliated with Roman Catholic Church. Grades 9–12. Founded: 1945. Setting: small town. 15-acre campus. 1 building on campus. Approved or accredited by North Central Association of Colleges and Schools and Illinois Department of Education. Endowment: $1 million. Total enrollment: 180. Upper school average class size: 18. Upper school faculty-student ratio: 1:17. There are 174 required school days per year for Upper School students. Upper School students typically attend 5 days per week. The average school day consists of 7 hours.

Upper School Student Profile Grade 9: 35 students (20 boys, 15 girls); Grade 10: 48 students (33 boys, 15 girls); Grade 11: 51 students (26 boys, 25 girls); Grade 12: 46 students (20 boys, 26 girls). 70% of students are Roman Catholic.

Faculty School total: 22. In upper school: 8 men, 14 women; 9 have advanced degrees.

Special Academic Programs Advanced Placement exam preparation; honors section; independent study; study at local college for college credit.

College Admission Counseling 38 students graduated in 2009; 37 went to college, including University of Illinois at Urbana–Champaign. Other: 1 entered military service. Mean composite ACT: 25.

Student Life Upper grades have specified standards of dress, student council. Discipline rests primarily with faculty. Attendance at religious services is required.

Tuition and Aid Day student tuition: $5280. Tuition installment plan (FACTS Tuition Payment Plan). Tuition reduction for siblings, need-based scholarship grants available. In 2009–10, 35% of upper-school students received aid. Total amount of financial aid awarded in 2009–10: $120,000.

Admissions Traditional secondary-level entrance grade is 9. For fall 2009, 180 students applied for upper-level admission, 180 were accepted, 180 enrolled. Deadline for receipt of application materials: none. No application fee required. Interview recommended.

Athletics Interscholastic: aerobics/dance (girls), baseball (b), basketball (b), cheering (g), cross-country running (b,g), dance squad (g), dance team (g), diving (b,g), football (b), golf (b), indoor track (b,g), indoor track & field (b,g), soccer (b), softball (g), swimming and diving (b,g), tennis (b,g), track and field (b,g), volleyball (g), wrestling (b). 2 PE instructors, 20 coaches.

Computers Computer network features include wireless campus network, Internet filtering or blocking technology. Student e-mail accounts are available to students. Students grades are available online. The school has a published electronic and media policy.

Contact Adm. Robert A. Rice, Principal. 217-442-2725. Fax: 217-442-0293. E-mail: brice@schlarman.com.

SCHOLAR'S HALL PREPARATORY SCHOOL

888 Trillium Drive
Kitchener, Ontario N2R 1K4, Canada
Head of School: Dr. Frederick T. Gore

General Information Coeducational day college-preparatory, general academic, arts, and business school. Grades JK–12. Founded: 1997. Setting: small town. Nearest major city is Toronto, Canada. 10-acre campus. 1 building on campus. Approved or accredited by Ontario Department of Education. Language of instruction: English. Total enrollment: 105. Upper school faculty-student ratio: 1:10. There are 200 required school days per year for Upper School students. Upper School students typically attend 5 days per week. The average school day consists of 7 hours.

Upper School Student Profile Grade 6: 10 students (5 boys, 5 girls); Grade 7: 10 students (5 boys, 5 girls); Grade 8: 10 students (5 boys, 5 girls); Grade 9: 10 students

(5 boys, 5 girls); Grade 10: 10 students (5 boys, 5 girls); Grade 11: 10 students (5 boys, 5 girls); Grade 12: 10 students (5 boys, 5 girls).

Faculty School total: 10. In upper school: 5 men, 5 women.

Special Academic Programs ESL (20 students enrolled).

College Admission Counseling 5 students graduated in 2010; all went to college, including The University of Western Ontario; University of Waterloo; Wilfrid Laurier University.

Student Life Upper grades have uniform requirement, student council, honor system. Discipline rests primarily with faculty.

Summer Programs Remediation, advancement, ESL programs offered; session focuses on acdemic; held on campus; accepts boys and girls; open to students from other schools. 100 students usually enrolled. 2011 schedule: July 1 to August 30. Application deadline: May 30.

Tuition and Aid Day student tuition: CAN$10,900. Guaranteed tuition plan. Tuition installment plan (The Tuition Plan, monthly payment plans, individually arranged payment plans). Tuition reduction for siblings, bursaries available. In 2010–11, 10% of upper-school students received aid. Total amount of financial aid awarded in 2010–11: CAN$20,000.

Admissions Traditional secondary-level entrance grade is 9. Woodcock-Johnson Educational Evaluation, WISC III required. Deadline for receipt of application materials: June 1. No application fee required. Interview required.

Athletics Coed Interscholastic: badminton, ball hockey, baseball, basketball, cross-country running, fencing, fitness, fitness walking, flag football, floor hockey, Frisbee, golf, independent competitive sports, martial arts, outdoor activities, outdoor education, physical fitness, self defense, soccer, softball, table tennis, volleyball; coed intramural: badminton, ball hockey, baseball, basketball, bowling, cross-country running, fencing, fitness, fitness walking, flag football, floor hockey, Frisbee, golf, martial arts, outdoor activities, outdoor education, physical fitness, self defense, soccer, softball, table tennis, volleyball. 2 PE instructors.

Computers Computers are regularly used in all classes. Computer network features include Internet access, wireless campus network, Internet filtering or blocking technology. Campus intranet is available to students. The school has a published electronic and media policy.

Contact 519-888-6620. Fax: 519-884-0316. Web site: http://www.scholarshall.com.

SCHOOL FOR YOUNG PERFORMERS

175 West 92nd Street
Suite 1D
New York, New York 10025
Head of School: Ms. Alison Pitt

General Information Coeducational day college-preparatory, general academic, and arts school. Grades K–12. Founded: 1995. Setting: urban. Approved or accredited by New York Department of Education. Upper school average class size: 1. Upper school faculty-student ratio: 1:1.

Faculty School total: 45. In upper school: 15 have advanced degrees.

Graduation Requirements Electives, English, history, mathematics, science, foreign language requirement.

Special Academic Programs Advanced Placement exam preparation; honors section; accelerated programs; independent study; term-away projects; study abroad; academic accommodation for the gifted, the musically talented, and the artistically talented; remedial reading and/or remedial writing; remedial math; programs in English, mathematics, general development for dyslexic students; special instructional classes for deaf students, blind students; ESL.

College Admission Counseling Colleges students went to include Columbia College; Harvard University; New York University; University of California, Los Angeles.

Student Life Upper grades have honor system. Discipline rests equally with students and faculty.

Tuition and Aid Day student tuition: $6000. Tuition installment plan (semester payment plan). Tuition reduction for siblings, need-based scholarship grants available.

Admissions Deadline for receipt of application materials: none. No application fee required. Interview recommended.

Computers Computers are regularly used in all classes.

Contact Ms. Alison Pitt, Head of School. 212-663-3921. Fax: 914-666-3810. E-mail: alison@schoolforyoungperformers.org.
Web site: www.schoolforyoungperformers.org.

SCHOOL OF THE HOLY CHILD

2225 Westchester Avenue
Rye, New York 10580
Head of School: Ann F. Sullivan

General Information Girls' day college-preparatory school, affiliated with Roman Catholic Church. Grades 5–12. Founded: 1904. Setting: suburban. Nearest major city is White Plains. 17-acre campus. 2 buildings on campus. Approved or accredited by New York State Association of Independent Schools, The College Board, and New York Department of Education. Member of National Association of Independent Schools and Secondary School Admission Test Board. Endowment: $3 million. Total

enrollment: 345. Upper school average class size: 14. Upper school faculty-student ratio: 1:7. Upper School students typically attend 5 days per week. The average school day consists of 7 hours.

Upper School Student Profile Grade 9: 58 students (58 girls); Grade 10: 70 students (70 girls); Grade 11: 59 students (59 girls); Grade 12: 63 students (63 girls). 85% of students are Roman Catholic.

Faculty School total: 53. In upper school: 6 men, 36 women; 36 have advanced degrees.

Subjects Offered Algebra, American history, American literature, anatomy, art, art history, art history-AP, arts, arts and crafts, astronomy, Bible studies, bioethics, biology, biology-AP, calculus, ceramics, chamber groups, chemistry, chorus, community service, computer programming, computer science, creative writing, dance, design, drama, drawing, driver education, economics, English, English literature, ethics, European history, expository writing, film, fine arts, French, French-AP, geometry, government/civics, grammar, health, history, illustration, Latin, Mandarin, mathematics, music, music theory-AP, physical education, physics, psychology, religion, science, Shakespeare, social studies, Spanish, Spanish-AP, speech, statistics, studio art-AP, theater, trigonometry, world history, writing.

Graduation Requirements Arts and fine arts (art, music, dance, drama), English, foreign language, independent study, mathematics, physical education (includes health), religion (includes Bible studies and theology), science, social studies (includes history), senior internship project, life skills for 9th and 10th grades, guidance for 11th and 12th grades, 100 hours of community service.

Special Academic Programs Advanced Placement exam preparation; honors section; independent study; term-away projects; domestic exchange program; study abroad.

College Admission Counseling 62 students graduated in 2010; all went to college, including Boston College; Georgetown University; Lehigh University; The Johns Hopkins University; University of Chicago; Villanova University.

Student Life Upper grades have uniform requirement, student council. Discipline rests primarily with faculty. Attendance at religious services is required.

Summer Programs Enrichment, sports, art/fine arts programs offered; session focuses on performing and fine arts immersion and sports camps; held on campus; accepts boys and girls; open to students from other schools. 120 students usually enrolled. 2011 schedule: June 1 to August 31.

Tuition and Aid Day student tuition: $26,000–$27,000. Tuition installment plan (Key Tuition Payment Plan, monthly payment plans). Merit scholarship grants, need-based scholarship grants, need-based loans, merit-based scholarships/grants (9th grade only) available. In 2010–11, 23% of upper-school students received aid.

Admissions Traditional secondary-level entrance grade is 9. Catholic High School Entrance Examination, ISEE or SSAT required. Deadline for receipt of application materials: January 4. Application fee required: $50. On-campus interview required.

Athletics Interscholastic: basketball, cross-country running, field hockey, golf, indoor track & field, lacrosse, soccer, softball, squash, swimming and diving, tennis, track and field, volleyball, winter (indoor) track; intramural: basketball, dance, dance squad, dance team, fitness, fitness walking, modern dance, volleyball, winter (indoor) track. 2 PE instructors, 37 coaches, 1 athletic trainer.

Computers Computers are regularly used in all academic classes. Computer network features include on-campus library services, online commercial services, Internet access, wireless campus network, Internet filtering or blocking technology. Campus intranet, student e-mail accounts, and computer access in designated common areas are available to students. The school has a published electronic and media policy.

Contact Admission Office. 914-967-5622 Ext. 227. Fax: 914-967-6476. E-mail: admission@holychildrye.org. Web site: www.holychildrye.org.

SCICORE ACADEMY

410 Princeton-Hightstown Road
Princeton Junction, New Jersey 08550
Head of School: Arthur T. Poulos, PhD

General Information Coeducational day college-preparatory school. Grades K–12. Founded: 2002. Setting: suburban. Nearest major city is Trenton. 5-acre campus. 1 building on campus. Approved or accredited by Middle States Association of Colleges and Schools. Total enrollment: 98. Upper school average class size: 13. Upper school faculty-student ratio: 1:7. There are 170 required school days per year for Upper School students. Upper School students typically attend 5 days per week. The average school day consists of 6 hours and 30 minutes.

Faculty School total: 17. In upper school: 9 men, 5 women; 6 have advanced degrees.

Subjects Offered 3-dimensional design, advanced chemistry, advanced math, algebra, American government, American history, American literature, anatomy and physiology, art, Basic programming, biotechnology, British literature, calculus, Chinese, choir, drafting, drama, electronics, English composition, French, German, history of science, Italian, Japanese, lab science, logic, rhetoric, and debate, metalworking, microcomputer technology applications, moral reasoning, music appreciation, optics, physics, pre-calculus, programming, public speaking, SAT preparation, science project, senior project, Spanish, speech and debate, U.S. history, Western civilization, world literature.

Graduation Requirements Algebra, American government, American history, American literature, biology, British literature, chemistry, civics, computer programming, English composition, geometry, lab science, Latin, logic, rhetoric, and debate, physical education (includes health), physics, programming, SAT preparation, science project, U.S. history, Western civilization, world literature.

Special Academic Programs 3 Advanced Placement exams for which test preparation is offered; honors section; independent study; academic accommodation for the gifted and the artistically talented; ESL (4 students enrolled).

College Admission Counseling 9 students graduated in 2009; all went to college, including Messiah College; New Jersey Institute of Technology; Rensselaer Polytechnic Institute; Syracuse University.

Student Life Upper grades have specified standards of dress, honor system. Discipline rests primarily with faculty.

Tuition and Aid Day student tuition: $8440. Tuition reduction for siblings available.

Admissions Traditional secondary-level entrance grade is 9. Admissions testing required. Deadline for receipt of application materials: none. No application fee required. Interview required.

Athletics Coed Interscholastic: cross-country running, soccer; coed intramural: cross-country running. 2 PE instructors, 1 coach.

Computers Computers are regularly used in English, foreign language, French, programming, science, Spanish, yearbook classes. Computer resources include Internet access, wireless campus network. Computer access in designated common areas is available to students.

Contact Mrs. Danette N. Poulos, Vice Principal. 609-448-8950. Fax: 609-448-8952. E-mail: atpoulos@scicore.org. Web site: www.scicore.org/.

SCOTTSDALE CHRISTIAN ACADEMY

14400 North Tatum Boulevard
Phoenix, Arizona 85032
Head of School: Mr. Tim Hillen

General Information Coeducational day college-preparatory and religious studies school, affiliated with Christian faith. Grades PK–12. Founded: 1968. Setting: suburban. 15-acre campus. 6 buildings on campus. Approved or accredited by Association of Christian Schools International and North Central Association of Colleges and Schools. Total enrollment: 934. Upper school average class size: 25. Upper school faculty-student ratio: 1:25. There are 180 required school days per year for Upper School students. Upper School students typically attend 5 days per week. The average school day consists of 6 hours and 30 minutes.

Upper School Student Profile 99% of students are Christian.

Faculty School total: 30. In upper school: 14 men, 14 women.

Subjects Offered Advanced Placement courses, algebra, American history, American history-AP, American literature, American sign language, anatomy, art, Bible studies, biology, biology-AP, calculus, chemistry, creative writing, drama, economics, English, English-AP, fine arts, French, geography, geometry, government/civics, graphic design, guitar, history, honors geometry, honors U.S. history, mathematics, music, physical education, physical science, physics, physics-AP, religion, science, social studies, Spanish, speech, trigonometry, world history.

Graduation Requirements American government, American history, ancient world history, arts and fine arts (art, music, dance, drama), Bible, biology, chemistry, Christian ethics, economics, English, foreign language, government, mathematics, physical education (includes health), religion (includes Bible studies and theology), science, social sciences, social studies (includes history), speech, U.S. history, world history.

Special Academic Programs Advanced Placement exam preparation; honors section; independent study; study at local college for college credit.

College Admission Counseling 75 students graduated in 2010; 74 went to college, including Arizona State University; Baylor University; Grand Canyon University; Paradise Valley Community College; Southwestern College; The University of Arizona. Other: 1 entered military service.

Student Life Upper grades have specified standards of dress, student council. Discipline rests primarily with faculty. Attendance at religious services is required.

Summer Programs Sports, art/fine arts programs offered; session focuses on Camps; held on campus; accepts boys and girls; not open to students from other schools.

Tuition and Aid Day student tuition: $10,000. Tuition installment plan (Academic Management Services Plan). Need-based scholarship grants available.

Admissions Deadline for receipt of application materials: none. Application fee required: $100. On-campus interview required.

Athletics Interscholastic: baseball (boys), basketball (b,g), cheering (g), cross-country running (b,g), football (b), golf (b,g), soccer (b,g), softball (g), swimming and diving (b,g), tennis (b,g), track and field (b,g), volleyball (g), winter soccer (b); intramural: weight lifting (b); coed intramural: martial arts. 3 PE instructors, 10 coaches.

Computers Computer resources include on-campus library services, Internet access, wireless campus network, Internet filtering or blocking technology, EXPAN. Student e-mail accounts are available to students. Students grades are available online. The school has a published electronic and media policy.

Contact Joan Rockwell, Admissions. 602-992-5100. Fax: 602-992-0575. E-mail: jrockwell@scottsdalechristian.org. Web site: www.scottsdalechristian.org.

SCOTUS CENTRAL CATHOLIC HIGH SCHOOL

1554 18th Avenue
Columbus, Nebraska 68601-5132
Head of School: Mr. Wayne Morfeld

General Information Coeducational day college-preparatory, arts, business, religious studies, and technology school, affiliated with Roman Catholic Church. Grades 7–12. Founded: 1884. Setting: rural. Nearest major city is Omaha. 1-acre campus. 1 building on campus. Approved or accredited by National Catholic Education Association, North Central Association of Colleges and Schools, and Nebraska Department of Education. Endowment: $65 million. Total enrollment: 369. Upper school average class size: 20. Upper school faculty-student ratio: 1:12.

Upper School Student Profile Grade 9: 70 students (29 boys, 41 girls); Grade 10: 71 students (38 boys, 33 girls); Grade 11: 47 students (20 boys, 27 girls); Grade 12: 53 students (24 boys, 29 girls). 97% of students are Roman Catholic.

Faculty School total: 27. In upper school: 10 men, 17 women; 9 have advanced degrees.

Subjects Offered Accounting, advanced math, Advanced Placement courses, algebra, American history, art, Bible studies, biology, bookkeeping, calculus, campus ministry, career/college preparation, character education, chemistry, choir, computer applications, CPR, digital applications, drama, earth science, economics, English, family and consumer science, guidance, jazz band, keyboarding, life skills, modern world history, personal fitness, physical science, physics, physiology, pottery, psychology, sociology, Spanish, speech, speech and debate, textiles, theater, vocal ensemble, volleyball, yearbook.

Special Academic Programs Advanced Placement exam preparation; study at local college for college credit.

College Admission Counseling 54 students graduated in 2010; all went to college, including Creighton University; University of Nebraska–Lincoln; University of Nebraska at Kearney; University of Nebraska at Omaha. Median composite ACT: 25. 38% scored over 26 on composite ACT.

Student Life Upper grades have uniform requirement, student council. Discipline rests equally with students and faculty. Attendance at religious services is required.

Tuition and Aid Day student tuition: $2115–$2215. Tuition installment plan (monthly payment plans). Need-based scholarship grants available. In 2010–11, 23% of upper-school students received aid. Total amount of financial aid awarded in 2010–11: $81,087.

Admissions Traditional secondary-level entrance grade is 9. Deadline for receipt of application materials: none. No application fee required.

Athletics Interscholastic: baseball (boys), basketball (b,g), cross-country running (b,g), football (b), golf (b,g), soccer (b,g), softball (g), swimming and diving (b,g), tennis (b,g), track and field (b,g), volleyball (g), wrestling (b); coed interscholastic: weight training. 3 PE instructors, 15 coaches, 2 athletic trainers.

Computers Computers are regularly used in business, newspaper, Web site design, word processing, yearbook classes. Computer network features include Internet access, Internet filtering or blocking technology. Student e-mail accounts are available to students. Students grades are available online. The school has a published electronic and media policy.

Contact Mrs. Pamela K. Weir, 7-12 Guidance Counselor. 402-564-7165. Fax: 402-564-6004. E-mail: pweir@esu7.org. Web site: www.scotuscc.org.

SEABURY HALL

480 Olinda Road
Makawao, Hawaii 96768-9399
Head of School: Mr. Joseph J. Schmidt

General Information Coeducational day college-preparatory, arts, and technology school, affiliated with Episcopal Church. Grades 6–12. Founded: 1964. Setting: rural. Nearest major city is Kahului. 55-acre campus. 8 buildings on campus. Approved or accredited by Western Association of Schools and Colleges. Member of National Association of Independent Schools and Secondary School Admission Test Board. Endowment: $17.1 million. Total enrollment: 449. Upper school average class size: 18. Upper school faculty-student ratio: 1:11. There are 175 required school days per year for Upper School students. Upper School students typically attend 5 days per week. The average school day consists of 7 hours and 30 minutes.

Upper School Student Profile Grade 9: 85 students (34 boys, 51 girls); Grade 10: 84 students (37 boys, 47 girls); Grade 11: 74 students (35 boys, 39 girls); Grade 12: 72 students (38 boys, 34 girls). 5% of students are members of Episcopal Church.

Faculty School total: 53. In upper school: 23 men, 15 women; 23 have advanced degrees.

Subjects Offered Acting, algebra, American history, American literature, art, band, biology, biology-AP, calculus-AP, ceramics, chemistry, chorus, community service, comparative religion, computer programming, dance, drawing, economics, English, English literature, ethics, European history-AP, expository writing, fine arts, geometry, global studies, government, history, Japanese, keyboarding, mathematics, mythology, painting, philosophy, physical education, physical science, physics, physics-AP, political science, pre-algebra, pre-calculus, religion, science, set design, social studies, Spanish, Spanish-AP, speech, studio art-AP, yearbook.

Seabury Hall

Graduation Requirements Arts and fine arts (art, music, dance, drama), English, foreign language, mathematics, physical education (includes health), religion (includes Bible studies and theology), science, social studies (includes history), speech. Community service is required.

Special Academic Programs 13 Advanced Placement exams for which test preparation is offered; honors section; independent study; academic accommodation for the gifted.

College Admission Counseling 69 students graduated in 2010; all went to college, including Gonzaga University; Humboldt State University; Massachusetts Institute of Technology; Santa Clara University; University of Colorado at Boulder; University of Hawaii at Manoa. Mean SAT critical reading: 580, mean SAT math: 570, mean SAT writing: 590, mean combined SAT: 1740, mean composite ACT: 25.

Student Life Upper grades have specified standards of dress, student council, honor system. Discipline rests primarily with faculty.

Summer Programs Enrichment, sports, art/fine arts programs offered; session focuses on enrichment; held on campus; accepts boys and girls; open to students from other schools. 200 students usually enrolled. 2011 schedule: June 13 to July 8. Application deadline: June 13.

Tuition and Aid Day student tuition: $16,500. Tuition installment plan (FACTS Tuition Payment Plan). Need-based scholarship grants available. In 2010–11, 38% of upper-school students received aid. Total amount of financial aid awarded in 2010–11: $847,100.

Admissions Traditional secondary-level entrance grade is 9. For fall 2010, 98 students applied for upper-level admission, 73 were accepted, 54 enrolled. ERB CTP III, ISEE or SSAT required. Deadline for receipt of application materials: February 19. Application fee required: $55. Interview required.

Athletics Interscholastic: basketball (boys, girls), cross-country running (b,g), dance (g), golf (b,g), paddling (b,g), physical fitness (b,g), soccer (b,g), swimming and diving (b,g), tennis (b,g), track and field (b,g), volleyball (b,g); intramural: basketball (b,g), dance (g), fitness (b,g), strength & conditioning (b,g); coed interscholastic: baseball, dance, paddling, physical fitness; coed intramural: ballet, baseball, cross-country running, dance, fitness, track and field, volleyball. 4 PE instructors, 12 coaches, 1 athletic trainer.

Computers Computers are regularly used in art, economics, English, foreign language, history, journalism, mathematics, newspaper, science, speech, yearbook classes. Computer network features include on-campus library services, online commercial services, Internet access, wireless campus network, Internet filtering or blocking technology. Campus intranet, student e-mail accounts, and computer access in designated common areas are available to students. Students grades are available online. The school has a published electronic and media policy.

Contact Elaine V. Nelson, Director of Admissions. 808-572-0807. Fax: 808-572-2042. E-mail: enelson@seaburyhall.org. Web site: www.seaburyhall.org.

SEATTLE ACADEMY OF ARTS AND SCIENCES

1201 East Union Street
Seattle, Washington 98122
Head of School: Joe Puggelli

General Information Coeducational day college-preparatory, arts, and technology school. Grades 6–12. Founded: 1983. Setting: urban. 3-acre campus. 5 buildings on campus. Approved or accredited by Northwest Accreditation Commission, Northwest Association of Schools and Colleges, Pacific Northwest Association of Independent Schools, and Washington Department of Education. Member of National Association of Independent Schools. Endowment: $800,000. Total enrollment: 619. Upper school average class size: 18. Upper school faculty-student ratio: 1:9. There are 174 required school days per year for Upper School students. Upper School students typically attend 5 days per week. The average school day consists of 6 hours and 45 minutes.

Upper School Student Profile Grade 9: 105 students (56 boys, 49 girls); Grade 10: 108 students (57 boys, 51 girls); Grade 11: 86 students (31 boys, 55 girls); Grade 12: 75 students (37 boys, 38 girls).

Faculty School total: 87. In upper school: 44 men, 43 women; 72 have advanced degrees.

Subjects Offered Acting, advanced chemistry, algebra, American history, American literature, Asian studies, biology, biotechnology, calculus, chemistry, choir, civics, community service, dance, debate, drawing, economics, English, French, geometry, health, history, humanities, independent study, instrumental music, lab science, literature, Mandarin, marine science, math analysis, musical productions, painting, physical education, physics, printmaking, sculpture, Spanish, speech, stagecraft, statistics, visual arts, vocal music, world literature, yearbook.

Graduation Requirements Arts and fine arts (art, music, dance, drama), English, foreign language, mathematics, physical education (includes health), science, social studies (includes history). Community service is required.

Special Academic Programs Honors section; independent study; term-away projects; study abroad; academic accommodation for the gifted, the musically talented, and the artistically talented; remedial reading and/or remedial writing; remedial math; programs in English, mathematics, general development for dyslexic students.

College Admission Counseling 87 students graduated in 2010; 84 went to college, including Brown University; Stanford University; The Colorado College; University of Oregon; University of Washington; Willamette University. Other: 3 had other specific plans. Mean SAT critical reading: 642, mean SAT math: 603, mean SAT writing: 619, mean combined SAT: 1864, mean composite ACT: 26. 75% scored over

600 on SAT critical reading, 57% scored over 600 on SAT math, 61% scored over 600 on SAT writing, 64% scored over 1800 on combined SAT, 60% scored over 26 on composite ACT.

Student Life Upper grades have student council, honor system. Discipline rests equally with students and faculty.

Summer Programs Enrichment, sports, art/fine arts programs offered; held both on and off campus; held at Outdoor Trips to Various National and International Locations; accepts boys and girls; open to students from other schools. 100 students usually enrolled. 2011 schedule: June 20 to August 12.

Tuition and Aid Day student tuition: $24,990. Tuition installment plan (Academic Management Services Plan, monthly payment plans). Need-based scholarship grants available. In 2010–11, 20% of upper-school students received aid.

Admissions Traditional secondary-level entrance grade is 9. ISEE required. Deadline for receipt of application materials: January 13. Application fee required: $50. Interview required.

Athletics Interscholastic: basketball (boys, girls), cross-country running (b,g), golf (b,g), soccer (b,g), tennis (b,g), track and field (b,g), ultimate Frisbee (b,g), volleyball (g); intramural: fly fishing (b); coed interscholastic: dance, dance squad, dance team, Frisbee; coed intramural: bowling, in-line skating, outdoor activities, paint ball, roller blading, roller skating, skateboarding, skiing (downhill), snowboarding, squash. 5 PE instructors, 30 coaches, 2 athletic trainers.

Computers Computers are regularly used in all academic, English, foreign language, graphic design, history, mathematics, newspaper, science, speech, study skills, theater arts, video film production, yearbook classes. Computer network features include on-campus library services, online commercial services, Internet access, wireless campus network, Internet filtering or blocking technology. Student e-mail accounts are available to students. The school has a published electronic and media policy.

Contact Jim Rupp, Admission Director. 206-324-7227. Fax: 206-323-6618. E-mail: jrupp@seattleacademy.org. Web site: www.seattleacademy.org.

SEATTLE CHRISTIAN SCHOOLS

18301 Military Road South
Seattle, Washington 98188
Head of School: Ms. Gloria Hunter

General Information Coeducational day college-preparatory, general academic, and religious studies school, affiliated with Christian faith. Grades K–12. Founded: 1946. Setting: suburban. 13-acre campus. 1 building on campus. Approved or accredited by Association of Christian Schools International and Washington Department of Education. Endowment: $933,181. Total enrollment: 567. Upper school average class size: 16. Upper school faculty-student ratio: 1:12. There are 180 required school days per year for Upper School students. Upper School students typically attend 5 days per week. The average school day consists of 7 hours.

Upper School Student Profile Grade 9: 48 students (24 boys, 24 girls); Grade 10: 59 students (28 boys, 31 girls); Grade 11: 62 students (31 boys, 31 girls); Grade 12: 50 students (23 boys, 27 girls). 100% of students are Christian faith.

Faculty School total: 25. In upper school: 11 men, 10 women; 16 have advanced degrees.

Subjects Offered Algebra, American literature, anatomy and physiology, art, band, Bible, biology, business mathematics, calculus, calculus-AP, chemistry, Christian education, Christian studies, civics, desktop publishing, English-AP, ensembles, geometry, Greek, health, language arts, Latin, Life of Christ, math analysis, multimedia, music, Pacific Northwest seminar, physical education, physics, psychology, Spanish, theater arts, U.S. history, U.S. history-AP, weight training, world history, world literature, yearbook.

Graduation Requirements Algebra, arts and fine arts (art, music, dance, drama), Bible, biology, chemistry, civics, foreign language, geometry, language arts, Life of Christ, mathematics, occupational education, Pacific Northwest seminar, physical education (includes health), physics, science, U.S. history, world history, UTT-Understanding the Times, Acts and Paul and Life of Christ, Bible Survey.

Special Academic Programs 3 Advanced Placement exams for which test preparation is offered; honors section; independent study; study at local college for college credit; remedial reading and/or remedial writing; programs in English for dyslexic students.

College Admission Counseling 60 students graduated in 2010; 57 went to college, including Bellevue College; Highline Community College; Seattle Pacific University; Seattle University; University of Washington; Western Washington University. Other: 1 went to work, 2 entered military service. Median SAT critical reading: 575, median SAT math: 530, median SAT writing: 590, median combined SAT: 1720, median composite ACT: 23. 37% scored over 600 on SAT critical reading, 43% scored over 600 on SAT math, 41% scored over 600 on SAT writing, 40.5% scored over 1800 on combined SAT, 13% scored over 26 on composite ACT.

Student Life Upper grades have specified standards of dress, student council, honor system. Discipline rests primarily with faculty. Attendance at religious services is required.

Tuition and Aid Day student tuition: $8760. Tuition installment plan (FACTS Tuition Payment Plan, monthly payment plans). Tuition reduction for siblings, need-based scholarship grants available. In 2010–11, 9% of upper-school students received aid. Total amount of financial aid awarded in 2010–11: $85,394.

Admissions Traditional secondary-level entrance grade is 9. For fall 2010, 13 students applied for upper-level admission, 13 were accepted, 11 enrolled. Admissions testing required. Deadline for receipt of application materials: none. Application fee required: $75. On-campus interview required.

Athletics Interscholastic: baseball (boys), basketball (b,g), cheering (g), cross-country running (b,g), golf (b,g), soccer (b,g), softball (g), track and field (b,g), volleyball (g); coed interscholastic: cross-country running, track and field; coed intramural: archery, badminton, baseball, basketball, field hockey, fitness, floor hockey, juggling, lacrosse, softball, strength & conditioning, touch football, weight training. 1 PE instructor.

Computers Computers are regularly used in art, library, mathematics, multimedia, reading, science, social studies, Web site design, yearbook classes. Computer network features include on-campus library services, Internet access, Internet filtering or blocking technology, accelerated reading and math program. Computer access in designated common areas is available to students. Students grades are available online. The school has a published electronic and media policy.

Contact Fran Hubeek, Admissions Coordinator. 206-246-8241 Ext. 1301. Fax: 206-246-9066. E-mail: admissions@seattlechristian.org. Web site: www.seattlechristian.org.

SECOND BAPTIST SCHOOL

6410 Woodway Drive
Houston, Texas 77057
Head of School: Dr. Jeff Williams

General Information Coeducational day college-preparatory and religious studies school, affiliated with Baptist Church. Grades PK–12. Founded: 1946. Setting: suburban. 42-acre campus. 4 buildings on campus. Approved or accredited by Southern Association of Colleges and Schools, Southern Association of Independent Schools, and Texas Department of Education. Upper school average class size: 13.

Upper School Student Profile 65% of students are Baptist.

Faculty In upper school: 49 have advanced degrees.

Subjects Offered 3-dimensional art, Advanced Placement courses, algebra, American literature, anatomy and physiology, art, art-AP, band, Bible, biology, biology-AP, British literature, British literature-AP, broadcasting, calculus, calculus-AP, chemistry, chemistry-AP, choir, computer programming, computer programming-AP, computer science, computer science-AP, concert band, concert choir, debate, desktop publishing, drama, economics, English, English-AP, European history-AP, French, French language-AP, French literature-AP, geometry, government, health, honors algebra, honors geometry, jazz ensemble, journalism, Latin, marching band, music theory-AP, photography, physical education, physics, physics-AP, pre-calculus, Spanish, Spanish language-AP, Spanish literature-AP, speech, statistics-AP, U.S. history, U.S. history-AP, world geography, world history.

Graduation Requirements Arts and fine arts (art, music, dance, drama), Bible, computer science, economics, electives, English, foreign language, government, mathematics, physical education (includes health), science, social studies (includes history), speech.

Special Academic Programs Advanced Placement exam preparation; honors section; accelerated programs; independent study; term-away projects; study at local college for college credit; study abroad.

College Admission Counseling 81 students graduated in 2010; all went to college.

Student Life Upper grades have specified standards of dress, student council. Discipline rests primarily with faculty. Attendance at religious services is required.

Tuition and Aid Day student tuition: $13,116. Tuition installment plan (monthly payment plans). Merit scholarship grants, need-based scholarship grants available. In 2010–11, 20% of upper-school students received aid.

Admissions ISEE and writing sample required. Deadline for receipt of application materials: none. Application fee required: $100. Interview required.

Athletics Interscholastic: baseball (boys), basketball (b,g), cross-country running (b,g), diving (b,g), drill team (g), fitness (b,g), football (b), golf (b,g); coed interscholastic: cheering. 9 PE instructors, 37 coaches, 2 athletic trainers.

Computers Computers are regularly used in all academic classes. Computer network features include on-campus library services, online commercial services, Internet access, wireless campus network, Internet filtering or blocking technology, science student interactive programs and computer-based labs. The school has a published electronic and media policy.

Contact Mrs. Andrea Prothro, Director of Admissions. 713-365-2314. Fax: 713-365-2445. E-mail: aprothro@secondbaptistschool.org. Web site: www.secondbaptistschool.org.

SEISEN INTERNATIONAL SCHOOL

12-15 Yoga 1-chome, Setagaya-ku
Tokyo 158-0097, Japan
Head of School: Sr. Concesa Martin

General Information Coeducational day (boys' only in lower grades) college-preparatory school, affiliated with Roman Catholic Church. Boys grade K, girls grades K–12. Founded: 1962. Setting: urban. 1-hectare campus. 3 buildings on campus. Approved or accredited by Department of Defense Dependents Schools, East Asia Regional Council of Schools, European Council of International Schools, International Baccalaureate Organization, Ministry of Education, Japan, National Catholic Education Association, and New England Association of Schools and Colleges.

Seisen International School

Member of Secondary School Admission Test Board. Language of instruction: English. Total enrollment: 680. Upper school average class size: 21. Upper school faculty-student ratio: 1:3. There are 177 required school days per year for Upper School students. Upper School students typically attend 5 days per week. The average school day consists of 6 hours.

Upper School Student Profile Grade 9: 43 students (43 girls); Grade 10: 35 students (35 girls); Grade 11: 44 students (44 girls); Grade 12: 38 students (38 girls). 20% of students are Roman Catholic.

Faculty School total: 87. In upper school: 12 men, 36 women; 27 have advanced degrees.

Subjects Offered 3-dimensional art, advanced math, art, bell choir, biology, business, career planning, chemistry, choir, college planning, computer graphics, computers, drama, English, environmental studies, ESL, French, geography, geometry, German, health education, history, honors algebra, honors geometry, information technology, International Baccalaureate courses, Japanese, journalism, Korean, library, math methods, mathematics, model United Nations, music, music composition, music performance, painting, performing arts, personal and social education, physical education, physics, pottery, psychology, religion, science, social sciences, social studies, Spanish, speech, theory of knowledge, trigonometry, visual arts, world history, yearbook.

Graduation Requirements Electives, English, foreign language, mathematics, physical education (includes health), religion (includes Bible studies and theology), science, social studies (includes history).

Special Academic Programs International Baccalaureate program; honors section; independent study; remedial reading and/or remedial writing; remedial math; ESL (19 students enrolled).

College Admission Counseling 40 students graduated in 2010; all went to college, including International Christian University; Northeastern University; Penn State University Park; Sophia Universtiy; University of Southern California; University of Virginia. Mean SAT critical reading: 540, mean SAT math: 630, mean SAT writing: 562, mean combined SAT: 1732. 29% scored over 600 on SAT critical reading, 86% scored over 600 on SAT math, 41% scored over 600 on SAT writing, 52% scored over 1800 on combined SAT.

Student Life Upper grades have uniform requirement, student council, honor system. Discipline rests primarily with faculty.

Summer Programs Remediation, ESL programs offered; session focuses on high school remedial work only; held on campus; accepts girls; not open to students from other schools. 20 students usually enrolled. 2011 schedule: June 13 to July 1. Application deadline: May 1.

Tuition and Aid Day student tuition: ¥1,940,000. Tuition installment plan (monthly payment plans, individually arranged payment plans). Tuition reduction for siblings, need-based scholarship grants available. In 2010–11, 0% of upper-school students received aid. Total amount of financial aid awarded in 2010–11: ¥1,222,000.

Admissions Traditional secondary-level entrance grade is 9. For fall 2010, 24 students applied for upper-level admission, 19 were accepted, 12 enrolled. Admissions testing, mathematics proficiency exam, Reading for Understanding or writing sample required. Deadline for receipt of application materials: none. Application fee required: ¥20,000. On-campus interview required.

Athletics Interscholastic: basketball, cross-country running, running, soccer, swimming and diving, tennis, track and field, volleyball; intramural: badminton, outdoor activities, running, soccer, table tennis, tennis, winter soccer. 2 PE instructors, 1 coach.

Computers Computers are regularly used in art, business studies, career education, college planning, English, foreign language, graphic design, history, information technology, journalism, mathematics, music, psychology, science, study skills, writing, yearbook classes. Computer network features include on-campus library services, online commercial services, Internet access, wireless campus network, Internet filtering or blocking technology. Campus intranet and computer access in designated common areas are available to students.

Contact Sr. Concesa Martin, School Head. 81-3-3704-2661. Fax: 81-3-3701-1033. E-mail: sisinfo@seisen.com. Web site: www.seisen.com.

See Display on page 619 and Close-Up on page 838.

SELWYN HOUSE SCHOOL

95 chemin Côte St-Antoine
Westmount, Quebec H3Y 2H8, Canada

Head of School: Mr. Hal Hannaford

General Information Boys' day college-preparatory, bilingual studies, and technology school. Grades K–11. Founded: 1908. Setting: urban. Nearest major city is Montreal, Canada. 2-acre campus. 3 buildings on campus. Approved or accredited by International Coalition of Boys Schools, National Institute of Independent Schools, Quebec Association of Independent Schools, and Quebec Department of Education, Standards in Excellence And Learning (SEAL). Affiliate member of National Association of Independent Schools; member of Secondary School Admission Test Board. Languages of instruction: English and French. Endowment: CAN$8.1 million. Total enrollment: 546. Upper school average class size: 15. Upper school faculty-student ratio: 1:8.

Upper School Student Profile Grade 9: 54 students (54 boys); Grade 10: 66 students (66 boys); Grade 11: 64 students (64 boys).

Faculty School total: 66. In upper school: 21 men, 14 women; 12 have advanced degrees.

Subjects Offered Art, biology, calculus, Canadian history, chemistry, computer multimedia, computer programming, computer science, creative writing, current events, debate, digital art, drama, drawing, economics, English, English literature, environmental science, French, geography, golf, history, jazz band, jazz ensemble, law, leadership, mathematics, model United Nations, music, outdoor education, photography, physical education, physics, public speaking, publishing, robotics, social justice, Spanish, U.S. history, world history, world issues, yearbook.

Graduation Requirements English, French, history, mathematics, physical science.

Special Academic Programs 4 Advanced Placement exams for which test preparation is offered; honors section.

College Admission Counseling 61 students graduated in 2010; all went to college, including Choate Rosemary Hall; Kent School; Phillips Exeter Academy; St. Paul's School; The Hotchkiss School.

Student Life Upper grades have uniform requirement, student council, honor system. Discipline rests primarily with faculty.

Summer Programs Sports programs offered; session focuses on football, basketball, hockey and cycling camps; held both on and off campus; held at sixteen rented facilities along with two on-site gyms, fitness centre, and combatives room; accepts boys and girls; open to students from other schools. 2011 schedule: June 21 to August 27. Application deadline: May 1.

Tuition and Aid Day student tuition: CAN$18,225. Guaranteed tuition plan. Tuition installment plan (monthly payment plans, individually arranged payment plans, 2- and 4-installment plans, credit card payments). Bursaries, merit scholarship grants, need-based scholarship grants, three-year merit-based scholarship to a new Grade 9 student, staff tuition discount, some 50 percent bursaries available for students who qualify for financial assistance available. In 2010–11, 16% of upper-school students received aid; total upper-school merit-scholarship money awarded: CAN$33,000. Total amount of financial aid awarded in 2010–11: CAN$145,830.

Admissions For fall 2010, 16 students applied for upper-level admission, 13 were accepted, 8 enrolled. English, French, and math proficiency required. Deadline for receipt of application materials: October 22. Application fee required: CAN$75. Interview required.

Athletics Interscholastic: badminton, ball hockey, baseball, basketball, cross-country running, curling, fitness, football, golf, ice hockey, rock climbing, rowing, rugby, skiing (cross-country), soccer, tennis, track and field, wrestling; intramural: badminton, ball hockey, fitness, golf, ice hockey, rowing, rugby, skiing (cross-country), soccer, tennis, track and field, weight lifting. 7 PE instructors, 7 coaches, 1 athletic trainer.

Computers Computers are regularly used in all classes. Computer network features include on-campus library services, online commercial services, Internet access, wireless campus network, Internet filtering or blocking technology, one-to-one laptop program for grades 7 to 11, course conferences, Lon Capa—online tutorial for grades 9 to 11 math and science students. Student e-mail accounts are available to students. Students grades are available online. The school has a published electronic and media policy.

Contact Ms. Nathalie Gervais, Director of Admission. 514-931-2775. Fax: 514-932-8776. E-mail: admission@selwyn.ca. Web site: www.selwyn.ca.

SEOUL FOREIGN SCHOOL

55 Yonhi-Dong
Sodaemun-Gu
Seoul 120-113, Republic of Korea

Head of School: Dr. John Engstrom

General Information Coeducational day college-preparatory and International Baccalaureate school, affiliated with Christian faith. Grades PK–12. Founded: 1912. Setting: urban. 25-acre campus. 8 buildings on campus. Approved or accredited by International Baccalaureate Organization and Western Association of Schools and Colleges. Affiliate member of National Association of Independent Schools; member of European Council of International Schools. Language of instruction: English. Endowment: $3.5 million. Total enrollment: 1,414. Upper school average class size: 18. Upper school faculty-student ratio: 1:10.

Upper School Student Profile Grade 9: 116 students (60 boys, 56 girls); Grade 10: 106 students (46 boys, 60 girls); Grade 11: 110 students (59 boys, 51 girls); Grade 12: 101 students (55 boys, 46 girls). 80% of students are Christian faith.

Faculty School total: 162. In upper school: 18 men, 32 women; 41 have advanced degrees.

Subjects Offered 3-dimensional art, algebra, American history, art, art history, Bible studies, biology, business, calculus, chemistry, computer science, creative writing, drama, economics, English, ESL, European history, expository writing, French, health, integrated mathematics, International Baccalaureate courses, international relations, Korean, Korean culture, mathematics, music, philosophy, photography, physical education, physics, psychology, religion, Spanish, speech, theory of knowledge, world history, world literature.

Graduation Requirements Arts and fine arts (art, music, dance, drama), biology, computers, English, foreign language, Korean culture, mathematics, physical education (includes health), physical science, religion (includes Bible studies and theology), social studies (includes history).

Special Academic Programs International Baccalaureate program; 1 Advanced Placement exam for which test preparation is offered; honors section; academic accommodation for the gifted, the musically talented, and the artistically talented; ESL (15 students enrolled).

College Admission Counseling 110 students graduated in 2010; 104 went to college, including Babson College; Boston University; Carnegie Mellon University; New York University; Northwestern University; Tufts University. Other: 6 had other specific plans. Mean SAT critical reading: 610, mean SAT math: 670, mean SAT writing: 640.

Student Life Upper grades have specified standards of dress, student council, honor system. Discipline rests primarily with faculty.

Summer Programs Remediation, enrichment, advancement programs offered; held on campus; accepts boys and girls; not open to students from other schools. 2011 schedule: June 13 to August 5.

Tuition and Aid Day student tuition: $24,600. Tuition installment plan (individually arranged payment plans, 2-payment plan with final payment due in January). Need-based scholarship grants available. In 2010–11, 12% of upper-school students received aid. Total amount of financial aid awarded in 2010–11: $395,000.

Admissions Traditional secondary-level entrance grade is 9. For fall 2010, 90 students applied for upper-level admission, 47 were accepted, 45 enrolled. Deadline for receipt of application materials: none. Application fee required: $250. On-campus interview required.

Athletics Interscholastic: basketball (boys, girls), cross-country running (b,g), dance team (g), soccer (b,g), swimming and diving (b,g), tennis (b,g), volleyball (b,g); coed interscholastic: aerobics/dance, badminton, cheering; coed intramural: badminton, lacrosse, weight lifting. 2 PE instructors.

Computers Computers are regularly used in English, history, mathematics, music, science classes. Computer network features include on-campus library services, Internet access, wireless campus network, Internet filtering or blocking technology.

Contact Mrs. Nicole Oakes, Admissions Director. 822-330-3100 Ext. 121. Fax: 822-335-2045. E-mail: admissions@seoulforeign.org. Web site: www.seoulforeign.org.

SETON CATHOLIC CENTRAL HIGH SCHOOL

70 Seminary Avenue
Binghamton, New York 13905
Head of School: Miss Kathleen M. Dwyer

General Information Coeducational day college-preparatory, arts, business, vocational, religious studies, technology, and cybersecurity school, affiliated with Roman Catholic Church. Grades 9–12. Founded: 1963. Setting: suburban. Nearest major city is Syracuse. 4-acre campus. 1 building on campus. Approved or accredited by Middle States Association of Colleges and Schools, National Catholic Education Association, New York State Board of Regents, The College Board, and New York Department of Education. Total enrollment: 330. Upper school average class size: 23. Upper school faculty-student ratio: 1:23. There are 200 required school days per year for Upper School students. Upper School students typically attend 5 days per week. The average school day consists of 6 hours and 45 minutes.

Upper School Student Profile 90% of students are Roman Catholic.

Faculty School total: 35. In upper school: 19 men, 13 women; 27 have advanced degrees.

Subjects Offered 3-dimensional design, accounting, advanced computer applications, Advanced Placement courses, advertising design, algebra, alternative physical education, American government, American history-AP, American legal systems, American literature, American literature-AP, ancient world history, applied music, architectural drawing, art-AP, band, Bible, biology, biology-AP, business, business law, business mathematics, calculus, calculus-AP, chemistry, chemistry-AP, chorus, Christian scripture, church history, comparative religion, computer applications, computer programming, computer programming-AP, creative drama, criminal justice, dramatic arts, economics, English, English language and composition-AP, English literature and composition-AP, entrepreneurship, environmental science, ethical decision making, ethics and responsibility, European history-AP, food and nutrition, foreign language, forensics, French, government/civics, guitar, health, honors English, honors geometry, instrumental music, integrated mathematics, keyboarding, Latin, Latin-AP, law and the legal system, literature and composition-AP, math applications, mathematics-AP, music theater, music theory, performing arts, photography, physical education, physics, physics-AP, pre-algebra, religion, social psychology, Spanish, Spanish-AP, studio art-AP, theater arts, theology, U.S. history, U.S. history-AP, wood processing, work-study, world history-AP, world religions.

Graduation Requirements Arts and fine arts (art, music, dance, drama), English, foreign language, mathematics, physical education (includes health), science, social studies (includes history), theology.

Special Academic Programs 18 Advanced Placement exams for which test preparation is offered; honors section; study at local college for college credit; academic accommodation for the gifted and the artistically talented; remedial reading and/or remedial writing; remedial math.

College Admission Counseling 108 students graduated in 2010; 107 went to college, including Le Moyne College; Marywood University; State University of New York at Binghamton; The University of Scranton; Villanova University. Other: 1 entered military service. Mean SAT critical reading: 561, mean SAT math: 587, mean SAT writing: 561.

Student Life Upper grades have specified standards of dress, student council, honor system. Discipline rests primarily with faculty.

Summer Programs Enrichment, sports programs offered; held on campus; accepts boys and girls; open to students from other schools. 200 students usually enrolled.

Tuition and Aid Tuition installment plan (monthly payment plans). Tuition reduction for siblings, merit scholarship grants, need-based scholarship grants, middle-income loans available. In 2010–11, 40% of upper-school students received aid. Total amount of financial aid awarded in 2010–11: $200,000.

Admissions Traditional secondary-level entrance grade is 9. High School Placement Test required. Deadline for receipt of application materials: none. Application fee required: $100. Interview required.

Athletics Interscholastic: baseball (boys), basketball (b,g), cross-country running (b,g), field hockey (g), football (b), ice hockey (b), indoor track & field (b,g), lacrosse (b,g), soccer (b,g), softball (g), swimming and diving (b,g), tennis (b,g), track and field (b,g), winter (indoor) track (b,g); intramural: snowboarding (b,g), strength & conditioning (b,g), weight training (b,g); coed interscholastic: cheering, golf; coed intramural: alpine skiing. 2 PE instructors, 25 coaches, 1 athletic trainer.

Computers Computers are regularly used in business applications, computer applications, desktop publishing, economics, English, foreign language, history, keyboarding, Latin, mathematics, science, social studies, Spanish, technology, yearbook classes. Computer network features include on-campus library services, online commercial services, Internet access, wireless campus network, Internet filtering or blocking technology. Computer access in designated common areas is available to students. The school has a published electronic and media policy.

Contact Guidance Office. 607-723-5307. Fax: 607-723-4811. E-mail: secathb@syrdiocese.org. Web site: www.setoncchs.com.

SETON CATHOLIC HIGH SCHOOL

1150 North Dobson Road
Chandler, Arizona 85224
Head of School: Patricia L. Collins

General Information Coeducational day college-preparatory, arts, religious studies, bilingual studies, technology, and dual enrollment with Seton Hill Univ. in specific classes school, affiliated with Roman Catholic Church. Grades 9–12. Founded: 1954. Setting: suburban. Nearest major city is Phoenix. 30-acre campus. 10 buildings on campus. Approved or accredited by North Central Association of Colleges and Schools, Western Catholic Education Association, and Arizona Department of Education. Endowment: $342,000. Total enrollment: 541. Upper school average class size: 22. Upper school faculty-student ratio: 1:13. There are 182 required school days per year for Upper School students. Upper School students typically attend 5 days per week. The average school day consists of 5 hours and 30 minutes.

Upper School Student Profile Grade 9: 152 students (81 boys, 71 girls); Grade 10: 142 students (68 boys, 74 girls); Grade 11: 113 students (60 boys, 53 girls); Grade 12: 118 students (61 boys, 57 girls). 92% of students are Roman Catholic.

Faculty School total: 42. In upper school: 19 men, 23 women; 29 have advanced degrees.

Subjects Offered Aerobics, algebra, American government, American history, anatomy, art, athletic training, Basic programming, biology, biology-AP, calculus, chemistry, chemistry-AP, choir, Christian and Hebrew scripture, Christian scripture, church history, computer applications, dance, drama, drawing, economics, English, English-AP, European history-AP, fitness, foreign language, French, geometry, government, guitar, health, honors English, honors geometry, honors U.S. history, keyboarding, Latin, Latin-AP, personal fitness, photography, physics, pre-calculus, psychology, reading/study skills, religion, scripture, social justice, Spanish, Spanish-AP, study skills, television, theology, U.S. government, U.S. history, video film production, weight training, world history, world religions, yearbook.

Graduation Requirements Arts and fine arts (art, music, dance, drama), computer applications, computer literacy, English, foreign language, mathematics, physical education (includes health), religion (includes Bible studies and theology), science, social studies (includes history), study skills.

Special Academic Programs Advanced Placement exam preparation; honors section.

College Admission Counseling 139 students graduated in 2010; all went to college, including Arizona State University; Northern Arizona University; The University of Arizona. Mean SAT critical reading: 553, mean SAT math: 559, mean SAT writing: 537, mean composite ACT: 24. 26% scored over 600 on SAT critical reading, 31% scored over 600 on SAT math, 20% scored over 600 on SAT writing.

Student Life Upper grades have uniform requirement, student council, honor system. Discipline rests primarily with faculty. Attendance at religious services is required.

Summer Programs Remediation, sports programs offered; session focuses on Academic support for incoming students & athletic camps; held on campus; accepts boys and girls; open to students from other schools. 60 students usually enrolled. 2011 schedule: June 1 to June 30. Application deadline: May 30.

Tuition and Aid Day student tuition: $11,050. Tuition installment plan (FACTS Tuition Payment Plan, monthly payment plans). Merit scholarship grants, need-based scholarship grants, Catholic Tuition Organization of Diocese of Phoenix available. In 2010–11, 34% of upper-school students received aid; total upper-school merit-scholarship money awarded: $44,000. Total amount of financial aid awarded in 2010–11: $705,000.

Admissions Traditional secondary-level entrance grade is 9. For fall 2010, 249 students applied for upper-level admission, 185 were accepted, 152 enrolled. Catholic High School Entrance Examination or Scholastic Testing Service High School Placement Test required. Deadline for receipt of application materials: none. Application fee required: $75. Interview required.

Athletics Interscholastic: baseball (boys), basketball (b,g), cross-country running (b,g), diving (b,g), football (b), golf (b,g), soccer (b,g), swimming and diving (b,g), tennis (b,g), track and field (b,g), volleyball (g), wrestling (b); coed interscholastic: aerobics/dance, cheering, dance, football, physical fitness, strength & conditioning, weight training. 2 PE instructors, 1 athletic trainer.

Computers Computers are regularly used in all academic, religious studies, yearbook classes. Computer network features include on-campus library services, Internet access, Internet filtering or blocking technology, Turnitin®. Student e-mail accounts are available to students. Students grades are available online. The school has a published electronic and media policy.

Contact Mr. Chris Moore, Director of Admissions. 480-963-1900 Ext. 2008. Fax: 480-963-1974. E-mail: cmoore@setonchs.org. Web site: www.setoncatholic.org.

SETON HALL PREPARATORY SCHOOL

120 Northfield Avenue
West Orange, New Jersey 07052
Head of School: Rev. Msgr. Michael Kelly

General Information Boys' day college-preparatory and religious studies school, affiliated with Roman Catholic Church. Grades 9–12. Founded: 1856. Setting: suburban. Nearest major city is Newark. 50-acre campus. 2 buildings on campus. Approved or accredited by Middle States Association of Colleges and Schools. Endowment: $12 million. Total enrollment: 940. Upper school average class size: 19. Upper school faculty-student ratio: 1:12. There are 160 required school days per year for Upper School students. Upper School students typically attend 5 days per week. The average school day consists of 6 hours.

Upper School Student Profile Grade 9: 255 students (255 boys); Grade 10: 240 students (240 boys); Grade 11: 225 students (225 boys); Grade 12: 220 students (220 boys). 81% of students are Roman Catholic.

Faculty School total: 78. In upper school: 64 men, 14 women; 74 have advanced degrees.

Subjects Offered Algebra, American literature, band, Bible studies, biology, biology-AP, calculus, calculus-AP, Catholic belief and practice, chemistry, chemistry-AP, church history, classical studies, computer programming, computer science, computer science-AP, creative writing, drawing, driver education, ecology, economics, English, English language and composition-AP, English language-AP, English literature, English literature and composition-AP, English literature-AP, English-AP, environmental science, environmental science-AP, epic literature, film, French, geometry, global studies, health, honors algebra, honors English, honors geometry, honors U.S. history, honors world history, human geography—AP, Italian, Latin, Latin-AP, leadership, literature, macro/microeconomics-AP, mathematics, modern European history, modern European history-AP, music, music history, music theory, music theory-AP, organic chemistry, physical education, physics, science, Spanish, Spanish language-AP, Spanish-AP, speech, statistics-AP, studio art-AP, theater arts, theology, U.S. history, U.S. history-AP, video film production, world history.

Graduation Requirements Arts and fine arts (art, music, dance, drama), English, foreign language, mathematics, physical education (includes health), religion (includes Bible studies and theology), science, social studies (includes history). Community service is required.

Special Academic Programs Advanced Placement exam preparation; honors section; independent study; academic accommodation for the gifted, the musically talented, and the artistically talented; programs in English, mathematics for dyslexic students.

College Admission Counseling 232 students graduated in 2009; 230 went to college, including New Jersey Institute of Technology; Penn State University Park; Rutgers, The State University of New Jersey, Rutgers College; Seton Hall University; The University of Scranton; Villanova University. Other: 1 went to work, 1 entered military service. Median SAT critical reading: 566, median SAT math: 579, median SAT writing: 571, median combined SAT: 1716. 43% scored over 600 on SAT critical reading, 41% scored over 600 on SAT math, 35% scored over 600 on SAT writing, 37% scored over 1800 on combined SAT.

Student Life Upper grades have specified standards of dress, student council. Discipline rests primarily with faculty. Attendance at religious services is required.

Tuition and Aid Day student tuition: $11,750. Tuition installment plan (monthly payment plans, monthly payment plan or tuition-in-full for a $150 discount). Merit scholarship grants, need-based scholarship grants available. In 2009–10, 40% of upper-school students received aid; total upper-school merit-scholarship money awarded: $490,000. Total amount of financial aid awarded in 2009–10: $1,010,000.

Admissions Traditional secondary-level entrance grade is 9. For fall 2009, 608 students applied for upper-level admission, 411 were accepted, 255 enrolled. SHP Entrance Test required. Deadline for receipt of application materials: January 2. Application fee required: $45.

Athletics Interscholastic: baseball (boys), basketball (b), bowling (b), cross-country running (b), football (b), golf (b), ice hockey (b), indoor track (b), lacrosse (b), riflery (b), soccer (b), swimming and diving (b), tennis (b), track and field (b), wrestling (b);

intramural: basketball (b), bocce (b), skiing (downhill) (b), volleyball (b), weight lifting (b). 4 PE instructors, 45 coaches, 1 athletic trainer.

Computers Computers are regularly used in art, economics, English, history, mathematics, music, science, Spanish, speech, theater arts classes. Computer network features include on-campus library services, online commercial services, Internet access, wireless campus network, Internet filtering or blocking technology, interlibrary loan program, online newspaper, magazine, and encyclopedia services. Campus intranet, student e-mail accounts, and computer access in designated common areas are available to students. The school has a published electronic and media policy.

Contact Mrs. Rosemary Shannon, Assistant to the Director of Admission. 973-325-6640. Fax: 973-325-7619. E-mail: rshannon@shp.org. Web site: www.shp.org.

SETON KEOUGH HIGH SCHOOL

1201 Caton Avenue
Baltimore, Maryland 21227
Head of School: Mr. Dennis Meehan

General Information Girls' day college-preparatory, arts, business, religious studies, and technology school, affiliated with Roman Catholic Church. Grades 9–12. Founded: 1988. Setting: urban. 33-acre campus. 1 building on campus. Approved or accredited by Middle States Association of Colleges and Schools, National Catholic Education Association, and Maryland Department of Education. Total enrollment: 500. Upper school average class size: 20. Upper school faculty-student ratio: 1:12. There are 175 required school days per year for Upper School students. Upper School students typically attend 5 days per week. The average school day consists of 6 hours and 40 minutes.

Upper School Student Profile Grade 9: 131 students (131 girls); Grade 10: 126 students (126 girls); Grade 11: 122 students (122 girls); Grade 12: 121 students (121 girls). 88% of students are Roman Catholic.

Faculty School total: 51. In upper school: 6 men, 42 women; 39 have advanced degrees.

Special Academic Programs Advanced Placement exam preparation; honors section; study at local college for college credit.

Student Life Upper grades have uniform requirement, student council, honor system. Discipline rests primarily with faculty. Attendance at religious services is required.

Tuition and Aid Tuition installment plan (monthly payment plans). Tuition reduction for siblings, merit scholarship grants, need-based scholarship grants available.

Admissions Traditional secondary-level entrance grade is 9. High School Placement Test (closed version) from Scholastic Testing Service required. Deadline for receipt of application materials: January 8. Application fee required. Interview required.

Athletics Interscholastic: ball hockey, basketball, cross-country running, field hockey, indoor track, lacrosse, soccer, softball, tennis, volleyball.

Computers Computers are regularly used in accounting, business, computer applications, engineering, introduction to technology, technology, yearbook classes. Computer network features include Internet access, wireless campus network, Internet filtering or blocking technology. Campus intranet and computer access in designated common areas are available to students. Students grades are available online. The school has a published electronic and media policy.

Contact Ms. Danielle Moran, Director of Admissions. 410-646-4444 Ext. 1222. Fax: 443-573 0107. E-mail: dmoran@setonkeough.com. Web site: www. setonkeough.com.

THE SEVEN HILLS SCHOOL

5400 Red Bank Road
Cincinnati, Ohio 45227
Head of School: Mr. Christopher P. Garten

General Information Coeducational day college-preparatory, arts, and technology school. Grades PK–12. Founded: 1974. Setting: suburban. 35-acre campus. 16 buildings on campus. Approved or accredited by Independent Schools Association of the Central States. Member of National Association of Independent Schools and Secondary School Admission Test Board. Endowment: $19.2 million. Total enrollment: 966. Upper school average class size: 15. Upper school faculty-student ratio: 1:9. There are 171 required school days per year for Upper School students. Upper School students typically attend 5 days per week. The average school day consists of 7 hours and 5 minutes.

Upper School Student Profile Grade 9: 59 students (28 boys, 31 girls); Grade 10: 77 students (38 boys, 39 girls); Grade 11: 60 students (28 boys, 32 girls); Grade 12: 70 students (31 boys, 39 girls).

Faculty School total: 138. In upper school: 20 men, 25 women; 40 have advanced degrees.

Subjects Offered Acting, advanced computer applications, Advanced Placement courses, algebra, American history, American literature, ancient history, art, art history, biology, British literature, calculus, ceramics, chemistry, computer programming, computer science, economics, English, European history, fine arts, French, geometry, journalism, Latin, linear algebra, Mandarin, medieval/Renaissance history, modern political theory, music, physical education, physics, pre-calculus, psychology, Spanish, speech, theater, world history, world literature, writing.

Graduation Requirements Algebra, arts and fine arts (art, music, dance, drama), biology, chemistry, computer science, English, foreign language, geometry, performing arts, physical education (includes health), physics, U.S. history, U.S. literature, completion of a personal challenge project, successfully pass writing competency exam, 30 hours of community service.

Special Academic Programs 16 Advanced Placement exams for which test preparation is offered; honors section; independent study; term-away projects; academic accommodation for the gifted.

College Admission Counseling 79 students graduated in 2010; all went to college, including Duke University; Massachusetts Institute of Technology; Miami University; Northwestern University; Tufts University; Washington University in St. Louis. Median SAT critical reading: 640, median SAT math: 670, median SAT writing: 655. 74% scored over 600 on SAT critical reading, 87% scored over 600 on SAT math, 84% scored over 600 on SAT writing.

Student Life Upper grades have specified standards of dress, student council. Discipline rests primarily with faculty.

Summer Programs Enrichment programs offered; session focuses on SAT review, sports clinics, and acting workshop; held on campus; accepts boys and girls; open to students from other schools. 400 students usually enrolled. 2011 schedule: June 14 to August 13. Application deadline: none.

Tuition and Aid Day student tuition: $19,350–$19,850. Tuition installment plan (monthly payment plans, individually arranged payment plans). Merit scholarship grants, need-based scholarship grants available. In 2010–11, 16% of upper-school students received aid; total upper-school merit-scholarship money awarded: $84,000. Total amount of financial aid awarded in 2010–11: $500,000.

Admissions Traditional secondary-level entrance grade is 9. For fall 2010, 39 students applied for upper-level admission, 28 were accepted, 14 enrolled. ISEE required. Deadline for receipt of application materials: December 3. Application fee required: $50. On-campus interview required.

Athletics Interscholastic: baseball (boys), basketball (b,g), cheering (g), cross-country running (b,g), golf (b), gymnastics (g), lacrosse (b,g), soccer (b,g), softball (g), swimming and diving (b,g), tennis (b,g), volleyball (g); coed interscholastic: track and field. 3 PE instructors, 9 coaches.

Computers Computers are regularly used in foreign language, mathematics, science classes. Computer network features include on-campus library services, online commercial services, Internet access, wireless campus network.

Contact Mrs. Janet S. Hill, Director of Admission and Financial Aid. 513-271-9027. Fax: 513-271-2471. E-mail: janet.hill@7hills.org. Web site: www.7hills.org.

SEVERN SCHOOL

201 Water Street
Severna Park, Maryland 21146
Head of School: Douglas H. Lagarde

General Information Coeducational day college-preparatory, arts, and technology school. Grades 6–12, Founded: 1914. Setting: suburban. Nearest major city is Annapolis. 19-acre campus. 8 buildings on campus. Approved or accredited by Association of Independent Maryland Schools, Middle States Association of Colleges and Schools, and Maryland Department of Education. Member of National Association of Independent Schools and Secondary School Admission Test Board. Endowment: $6 million. Total enrollment: 582. Upper school average class size: 15. Upper school faculty-student ratio: 1:8. There are 175 required school days per year for Upper School students. Upper School students typically attend 5 days per week. The average school day consists of 6 hours and 35 minutes.

Upper School Student Profile Grade 9: 99 students (43 boys, 56 girls); Grade 10: 105 students (47 boys, 58 girls); Grade 11: 94 students (51 boys, 43 girls); Grade 12: 89 students (48 boys, 41 girls).

Faculty School total: 81. In upper school: 27 men, 30 women; 38 have advanced degrees.

Subjects Offered Algebra, American history, American literature, art, biology, calculus, ceramics, chemistry, community service, computer programming, computer science, CPR, creative writing, dance, desktop publishing, digital art, digital imaging, digital photography, discrete mathematics, drama, drama performance, dramatic arts, drawing, drawing and design, earth science, ecology, economics, economics-AP, English, English literature, environmental science, environmental systems, European civilization, European history, European history-AP, expository writing, fine arts, forensics, French, French language-AP, French literature-AP, geometry, government/civics, grammar, graphic arts, health, history, journalism, Latin, marine biology, mathematics, multimedia, music, photography, physical education, physics, psychology, science, social studies, Spanish, speech, theater, trigonometry, world history, world literature, writing.

Graduation Requirements Arts and fine arts (art, music, dance, drama), computer science, CPR, English, foreign language, mathematics, physical education (includes health), science, social studies (includes history). Community service is required.

Special Academic Programs Advanced Placement exam preparation; honors section; independent study; study abroad; academic accommodation for the gifted, the musically talented, and the artistically talented.

College Admission Counseling 100 students graduated in 2010; all went to college, including Bowdoin College; Bucknell University; Connecticut College; University of Colorado at Boulder; University of Maryland, College Park; University of South Carolina. 46% scored over 600 on SAT critical reading, 55% scored over 600 on SAT math, 58% scored over 600 on SAT writing, 56% scored over 1800 on combined SAT, 33% scored over 26 on composite ACT.

Student Life Upper grades have uniform requirement, student council, honor system. Discipline rests primarily with faculty.

Summer Programs Remediation, enrichment, advancement, sports, art/fine arts, computer instruction programs offered; session focuses on advanced math, day camp, and sports camps; held both on and off campus; held at SPY Swimming Pool; accepts boys and girls; open to students from other schools. 250 students usually enrolled. 2011 schedule: June 23 to August 1.

Tuition and Aid Day student tuition: $21,550. Tuition installment plan (Academic Management Services Plan). Need-based scholarship grants available. In 2010–11, 22% of upper-school students received aid. Total amount of financial aid awarded in 2010–11: $1,500,000.

Admissions Traditional secondary-level entrance grade is 9. For fall 2010, 105 students applied for upper-level admission, 55 were accepted, 44 enrolled. ISEE required. Deadline for receipt of application materials: February 1. Application fee required: $55. On-campus interview required.

Athletics Interscholastic: baseball (boys), basketball (b,g), combined training (b,g), dance team (g), field hockey (g), football (b), lacrosse (b,g), soccer (b,g), tennis (b,g); coed interscholastic: cross-country running, dance, diving, golf, sailing, strength & conditioning, swimming and diving, track and field, weight training; coed intramural: aerobics/dance, ice hockey, outdoor adventure, paint ball, table tennis. 56 coaches, 2 athletic trainers.

Computers Computers are regularly used in all academic classes. Computer network features include on-campus library services, online commercial services, Internet access, Internet filtering or blocking technology. Campus intranet, student e-mail accounts, and computer access in designated common areas are available to students. Students grades are available online. The school has a published electronic and media policy.

Contact Ellen Murray, Associate Director of Admissions. 410-647-7701 Ext. 2266. Fax: 410-544-9451. E-mail: e.murray@severnschool.com. Web site: www.severnschool.com.

SEWICKLEY ACADEMY

315 Academy Avenue
Sewickley, Pennsylvania 15143
Head of School: Mr. Kolia J. O'Connor

General Information Coeducational day college-preparatory, arts, and technology school. Grades PK–12. Founded: 1838. Setting: suburban. Nearest major city is Pittsburgh. 30-acre campus. 10 buildings on campus. Approved or accredited by Middle States Association of Colleges and Schools, National Independent Private Schools Association, Pennsylvania Association of Independent Schools, and Pennsylvania Department of Education. Member of National Association of Independent Schools. Endowment: $27.8 million. Total enrollment: 733. Upper school average class size: 15. Upper school faculty-student ratio: 1:8. There are 167 required school days per year for Upper School students. Upper School students typically attend 5 days per week. The average school day consists of 7 hours.

Upper School Student Profile Grade 9: 82 students (47 boys, 35 girls); Grade 10: 62 students (36 boys, 26 girls); Grade 11: 78 students (38 boys, 40 girls); Grade 12: 72 students (37 boys, 35 girls).

Faculty School total: 106. In upper school: 28 men, 28 women; 32 have advanced degrees.

Subjects Offered Advanced chemistry, advanced studio art-AP, African studies, algebra, American history, American history-AP, American literature, American literature-AP, art, art-AP, astronomy, band, biology, biology-AP, calculus, calculus-AP, ceramics, chemistry, chemistry-AP, choral music, chorus, clayworking, computer applications, computer art, computer programming, computer science, computer science-AP, concert band, concert choir, contemporary issues, creative writing, dance, dance performance, digital art, drama, drama performance, drama workshop, drawing, driver education, economics, English, English literature, environmental science, ethics, European history, European history-AP, expository writing, fine arts, French, French language-AP, French literature-AP, geometry, German, German-AP, government/civics, health, health education, history, Italian, keyboarding, Mandarin, music, musical theater, performing arts, photography, physical education, physics, physics-AP, pre-calculus, psychology, psychology-AP, senior project, Spanish, Spanish literature, Spanish-AP, speech and debate, statistics, statistics AP, studio art, theater, trigonometry, U.S. history-AP, U.S. literature, Vietnam War, world history, world literature, writing.

Graduation Requirements Arts and fine arts (art, music, dance, drama), English, foreign language, health education, mathematics, physical education (includes health), science, social studies (includes history), U.S. history, world cultures, world studies. Community service is required.

Special Academic Programs Advanced Placement exam preparation; honors section; independent study; term-away projects; study at local college for college credit; study abroad.

College Admission Counseling 79 students graduated in 2010; all went to college, including Boston University; Carnegie Mellon University; Colgate University; Harvard University; Penn State University Park; University of Richmond.

Student Life Upper grades have specified standards of dress, student council, honor system. Discipline rests equally with students and faculty.

Summer Programs Enrichment, advancement, sports, art/fine arts programs offered; session focuses on academics, athletics, and musical theater; held on campus; accepts boys and girls; open to students from other schools. 150 students usually enrolled. 2011 schedule: June 11 to August 10. Application deadline: none.

Tuition and Aid Day student tuition: $21,275. Tuition installment plan (monthly payment plans). Need-based scholarship grants available. In 2010–11, 20% of upper-school students received aid. Total amount of financial aid awarded in 2010–11: $600,000.

Admissions Traditional secondary-level entrance grade is 9. For fall 2010, 64 students applied for upper-level admission, 40 were accepted, 28 enrolled. ISEE required. Deadline for receipt of application materials: February 4. Application fee required: $50. Interview required.

Athletics Interscholastic: baseball (boys), basketball (b,g), golf (b,g), hockey (b), ice hockey (b), lacrosse (b,g), physical fitness (b,g), soccer (b,g), softball (g), tennis (b,g); coed interscholastic: bowling, cross-country running, diving, field hockey, physical fitness, swimming and diving, track and field. 5 PE instructors, 5 coaches, 1 athletic trainer.

Computers Computers are regularly used in all academic classes. Computer network features include on-campus library services, online commercial services, Internet access, wireless campus network, Internet filtering or blocking technology. Campus intranet, student e-mail accounts, and computer access in designated common areas are available to students. The school has a published electronic and media policy.

Contact Ms. Wendy Berns, Admission Assistant. 412-741-2235. Fax: 412-741-1411. E-mail: wberns@sewickley.org. Web site: www.sewickley.org.

SHADES MOUNTAIN CHRISTIAN SCHOOL
2290 Old Tyler Road
Hoover, Alabama 35226
Head of School: Mr. Laird Crump
General Information Coeducational day college-preparatory and Biblical studies school, affiliated with Christian faith. Grades K–12. Founded: 1974. Setting: suburban. Nearest major city is Birmingham. 30-acre campus. 3 buildings on campus. Approved or accredited by Association of Christian Schools International, Southern Association of Colleges and Schools, and Alabama Department of Education. Total enrollment: 408. Upper school average class size: 20. Upper school faculty-student ratio: 1:10. There are 180 required school days per year for Upper School students. Upper School students typically attend 5 days per week. The average school day consists of 6 hours and 50 minutes.
Upper School Student Profile Grade 9: 33 students (17 boys, 16 girls); Grade 10: 38 students (22 boys, 16 girls); Grade 11: 24 students (14 boys, 10 girls); Grade 12: 24 students (9 boys, 15 girls). 50% of students are Christian faith.
Faculty School total: 36. In upper school: 9 men, 9 women; 7 have advanced degrees.
Subjects Offered Advanced chemistry, advanced math, algebra, American government, American literature, anatomy and physiology, ancient world history, art, band, Bible studies, business applications, calculus-AP, character education, chemistry, choir, choral music, Christian doctrine, Christian education, Christian ethics, Christian scripture, Christian studies, Christianity, civics, competitive science projects, composition, composition-AP, computer applications, computer literacy, consumer economics, CPR, creative thinking, creative writing, decision making skills, driver education, earth and space science, economics, English, English composition, English language and composition-AP, English literature, ensembles, ethics and responsibility, finance, first aid, general science, geography, geometry, government/civics, guitar, instruments, jazz band, junior and senior seminars, keyboarding, leadership, Life of Christ, marching band, math applications, math methods, math review, mathematics, mathematics-AP, music appreciation, mythology, news writing, personal finance, philosophy, physical education, physical science, physics, pre-algebra, pre-calculus, psychology, reading/study skills, relationships, religion, research and reference, research skills, rhetoric, science, science project, science research, social sciences, social skills, social studies, Spanish, sports medicine, technology, trigonometry, typing, U.S. government and politics, U.S. history, values and decisions, world history, yearbook.
Graduation Requirements American history, Bible, computers, economics, English, foreign language, government, mathematics, philosophy, physical education (includes health), science, world history.
Special Academic Programs 2 Advanced Placement exams for which test preparation is offered; honors section; independent study; programs in English, mathematics, general development for dyslexic students; special instructional classes for students with learning disabilities.
College Admission Counseling 34 students graduated in 2010; 30 went to college, including Auburn University; Samford University; The University of Alabama; The University of Alabama at Birmingham; University of Montevallo. Other: 3 went to work, 1 entered military service. Mean composite ACT: 22. 21% scored over 26 on composite ACT.
Student Life Upper grades have specified standards of dress, student council, honor system. Discipline rests primarily with faculty. Attendance at religious services is required.
Tuition and Aid Day student tuition: $6000. Tuition installment plan (monthly payment plans, individually arranged payment plans). Tuition reduction for siblings, need-based scholarship grants available. In 2010–11, 15% of upper-school students received aid. Total amount of financial aid awarded in 2010–11: $13,000.
Admissions Any standardized test required. Deadline for receipt of application materials: none. Application fee required: $500. Interview required.

Athletics Interscholastic: baseball (boys), basketball (b,g), cheering (g), cross-country running (b,g), football (b), golf (b,g), independent competitive sports (b,g), physical fitness (b,g), physical training (b,g), soccer (b,g), softball (g), strength & conditioning (b,g), swimming and diving (b,g), tennis (b,g), volleyball (g), wrestling (b). 2 PE instructors, 2 coaches, 1 athletic trainer.
Computers Computers are regularly used in keyboarding classes. Computer resources include on-campus library services, Internet access, Internet filtering or blocking technology. Students grades are available online. The school has a published electronic and media policy.
Contact Mrs. Beth Buyck, School Secretary. 205-978-6001. Fax: 205-978-9120. E-mail: bethbuyck@smcs.org.

SHADY SIDE ACADEMY
423 Fox Chapel Road
Pittsburgh, Pennsylvania 15238
Head of School: Mr. Thomas Cangiano
General Information Coeducational boarding and day college-preparatory school. Boarding grades 9–12, day grades PK–12. Founded: 1883. Setting: suburban. Students are housed in single-sex dormitories. 130-acre campus. 26 buildings on campus. Approved or accredited by Middle States Association of Colleges and Schools, Pennsylvania Association of Independent Schools, The Association of Boarding Schools, and Pennsylvania Department of Education. Member of National Association of Independent Schools. Endowment: $42.1 million. Total enrollment: 931. Upper school average class size: 13. Upper school faculty-student ratio: 1:8. There are 172 required school days per year for Upper School students. Upper School students typically attend 5 days per week.
Upper School Student Profile Grade 9: 120 students (60 boys, 60 girls); Grade 10: 119 students (70 boys, 49 girls); Grade 11: 129 students (78 boys, 51 girls); Grade 12: 118 students (56 boys, 62 girls). 10% of students are boarding students. 99% are state residents. 2 states are represented in upper school student body.
Faculty School total: 115. In upper school: 28 men, 32 women; 32 have advanced degrees; 17 reside on campus.
Subjects Offered Advanced Placement courses, algebra, American history, American literature, architectural drawing, architecture, art, art history, biology, calculus, calculus-AP, ceramics, chemistry, Chinese, Chinese history, computer graphics, computer math, computer programming, computer science, computer science-AP, creative writing, drama, driver education, economics, English, English literature, ethics, European history, expository writing, fine arts, fractal geometry, French, French-AP, gender issues, geography, geometry, German, German-AP, health, history, Latin, linear algebra, logic, mathematics, music, music technology, musical theater, philosophy, photography, physical education, physics, religion and culture, science, social studies, Spanish, Spanish-AP, speech, statistics, studio art, technical theater, trigonometry, world history, world literature, writing.
Graduation Requirements Arts and fine arts (art, music, dance, drama), athletics, computer science, English, foreign language, mathematics, physical education (includes health), science, social studies (includes history), participation in five seasons of athletics.
Special Academic Programs 6 Advanced Placement exams for which test preparation is offered; honors section; accelerated programs; independent study; term-away projects; study at local college for college credit; study abroad; academic accommodation for the gifted, the musically talented, and the artistically talented.
College Admission Counseling 124 students graduated in 2010; 123 went to college, including Boston University; Carnegie Mellon University; Penn State University Park; The George Washington University; University of Michigan; University of Pittsburgh. Other: 1 entered a postgraduate year. Median SAT critical reading: 610, median SAT math: 650, median SAT writing: 630, median combined SAT: 1870, median composite ACT: 27. 52.3% scored over 600 on SAT critical reading, 69.7% scored over 600 on SAT math, 71.6% scored over 600 on SAT writing, 62.4% scored over 1800 on combined SAT, 60.9% scored over 26 on composite ACT.
Student Life Upper grades have specified standards of dress, student council. Discipline rests primarily with faculty.
Summer Programs Remediation, enrichment, advancement, sports, art/fine arts, computer instruction programs offered; session focuses on academic and non-academic enrichment; held on campus; accepts boys and girls; open to students from other schools. 1,100 students usually enrolled. 2011 schedule: June 21 to July 30. Application deadline: none.
Tuition and Aid Day student tuition: $24,750; 5-day tuition and room/board: $34,700. Tuition installment plan (monthly payment plans, Tuition Refund Plan available through Dewar's). Tuition reduction for siblings, merit scholarship grants, need-based scholarship grants, merit-base scholarships for boarding students, FAME awards, partial tuition remission for children of full-time employees available. In 2010–11, 19% of upper-school students received aid; total upper-school merit-scholarship money awarded: $80,000. Total amount of financial aid awarded in 2010–11: $1,533,500.
Admissions Traditional secondary-level entrance grade is 9. For fall 2010, 129 students applied for upper-level admission, 103 were accepted, 69 enrolled. ISEE, SSAT or TOEFL required. Deadline for receipt of application materials: January 31. Application fee required: $50. On-campus interview required.
Athletics Interscholastic: baseball (boys), basketball (b,g), crew (g), cross-country running (b,g), field hockey (g), football (b), golf (b,g), ice hockey (b,g), lacrosse (b,g),

soccer (b,g), softball (g), squash (b,g), swimming and diving (b,g), tennis (b,g), track and field (b,g), wrestling (b); intramural: cheering (g); coed intramural: aerobics/dance, backpacking, badminton, bowling, cricket, ultimate Frisbee, weight lifting. 1 PE instructor, 47 coaches, 2 athletic trainers.

Computers Computers are regularly used in all classes. Computer network features include on-campus library services, online commercial services, Internet access, Internet filtering or blocking technology. Student e-mail accounts and computer access in designated common areas are available to students. The school has a published electronic and media policy.

Contact Ms. Katherine H. Mihm, Director of Enrollment Management and Marketing. 412-968-3179. Fax: 412-968-3213. E-mail: kmihm@ shadysideacademy.org. Web site: www.shadysideacademy.org.

SHANNON FOREST CHRISTIAN SCHOOL

829 Garlington Road
Greenville, South Carolina 29615
Head of School: Mr. Bob Collins

General Information Coeducational day college-preparatory, arts, religious studies, and technology school, affiliated with Presbyterian Church. Grades PK–12. Founded: 1968. Setting: small town. 50-acre campus. 7 buildings on campus. Approved or accredited by Association of Christian Schools International and Southern Association of Colleges and Schools. Endowment: $200,000. Total enrollment: 445. Upper school average class size: 17. Upper school faculty-student ratio: 1:17. There are 180 required school days per year for Upper School students. The average school day consists of 7 hours.

Upper School Student Profile Grade 6: 27 students (21 boys, 6 girls); Grade 7: 38 students (23 boys, 15 girls); Grade 8: 47 students (19 boys, 28 girls); Grade 9: 35 students (15 boys, 20 girls); Grade 10: 30 students (13 boys, 17 girls); Grade 11: 29 students (13 boys, 16 girls); Grade 12: 29 students (11 boys, 18 girls). 3% of students are Presbyterian.

Faculty School total: 49. In upper school: 7 men, 20 women; 16 have advanced degrees.

Subjects Offered Algebra, American literature, art, Bible, Bible studies, biology, biology-AP, calculus, calculus-AP, career/college preparation, chemistry, choir, college planning, computer science, drama, economics, English, English literature-AP, English-AP, European history-AP, French, geometry, government, health, journalism, keyboarding, literature, music, physical education, physical science, physics, pre-algebra, pre-calculus, psychology, SAT preparation, sociology, Spanish, theater arts, U.S. history, U.S. history-AP, world geography, world history, yearbook.

Graduation Requirements Computer science, English, foreign language, mathematics, physical education (includes health), religion (includes Bible studies and theology), SAT preparation, science, social sciences, social studies (includes history), annual attendance at two fine arts programs (grades 9—12), 30 hours of community service per year.

Special Academic Programs Advanced Placement exam preparation; honors section; programs in English, mathematics, general development for dyslexic students; special instructional classes for students with emotional/behavioral problems, learning disabilities, Attention Deficit Hyperactivity Disorder.

College Admission Counseling 29 students graduated in 2010; all went to college, including Anderson University; Clemson University; Furman University; Presbyterian College; University of South Carolina; Wofford College.

Student Life Upper grades have uniform requirement, student council, honor system. Discipline rests primarily with faculty. Attendance at religious services is required.

Summer Programs Enrichment, sports, art/fine arts, computer instruction programs offered; held on campus; accepts boys and girls; not open to students from other schools. 150 students usually enrolled. 2011 schedule: June 1 to August 1. Application deadline: June 1.

Tuition and Aid Day student tuition: $7200. Tuition installment plan (FACTS Tuition Payment Plan). Need-based scholarship grants, Scholar loans available. In 2010–11, 19% of upper-school students received aid. Total amount of financial aid awarded in 2010–11: $15,000.

Admissions Traditional secondary-level entrance grade is 7. For fall 2010, 80 students applied for upper-level admission, 51 were accepted, 40 enrolled. Stanford Achievement Test required. Deadline for receipt of application materials: none. Application fee required: $100. Interview required.

Athletics Interscholastic: baseball (boys), basketball (b,g), cheering (g), cross-country running (b,g), golf (b,g), soccer (b,g), softball (g), swimming and diving (b,g), tennis (b,g), volleyball (g); intramural: baseball (b), flag football (b,g), soccer (b,g), tennis (b,g). 3 PE instructors, 18 coaches, 1 athletic trainer.

Computers Computers are regularly used in English, journalism, keyboarding, yearbook classes. Computer network features include on-campus library services, online commercial services, Internet access, wireless campus network, Internet filtering or blocking technology. Campus intranet is available to students. Students grades are available online. The school has a published electronic and media policy.

Contact Mrs. Lynn Pittman, Admissions Coordinator. 864-414-1308. Fax: 864-281-9372. E-mail: lpittman@shannonforest.com. Web site: www.shannonforest.com.

SHATTUCK-ST. MARY'S SCHOOL

1000 Shumway Avenue
PO Box 218
Faribault, Minnesota 55021
Head of School: Nicholas J.B. Stoneman

General Information Coeducational boarding and day college-preparatory, arts, and BioScience, STEM Education school, affiliated with Episcopal Church. Grades 6–PG. Founded: 1858. Setting: small town. Nearest major city is Minneapolis/St. Paul. Students are housed in single-sex dormitories. 250-acre campus. 10 buildings on campus. Approved or accredited by Independent Schools Association of the Central States, Midwest Association of Boarding Schools, National Association of Episcopal Schools, The Association of Boarding Schools, and Minnesota Department of Education. Member of National Association of Independent Schools and Secondary School Admission Test Board. Total enrollment: 438. Upper school average class size: 12. Upper school faculty-student ratio: 1:9. There are 167 required school days per year for Upper School students. The average school day consists of 7 hours.

Upper School Student Profile Grade 9: 63 students (41 boys, 22 girls); Grade 10: 102 students (69 boys, 33 girls); Grade 11: 124 students (74 boys, 50 girls); Grade 12: 105 students (60 boys, 45 girls); Postgraduate: 4 students (1 boy, 3 girls). 72% of students are boarding students. 25% are state residents. 39 states are represented in upper school student body. 32% are international students. International students from Canada, China, Japan, Republic of Korea, Sweden, and Taiwan; 14 other countries represented in student body.

Faculty In upper school: 25 men, 30 women; 60 reside on campus.

Subjects Offered 20th century world history, Advanced Placement courses, advanced studio art-AP, advanced TOEFL/grammar, algebra, American Civil War, American history, American history-AP, American literature, American sign language, anatomy and physiology, art, art history, astronomy, ballet, band, Bible studies, bioethics, biology, British literature, calculus, calculus-AP, ceramics, chamber groups, chemistry, chemistry-AP, choir, choral music, community service, composition, dance, digital photography, drama, drawing, economics, English, English language and composition-AP, English literature, English literature and composition-AP, environmental science-AP, ESL, ethics, European civilization, European history, European history-AP, expository writing, field ecology, film studies, fine arts, French, French language-AP, geography, geometry, government/civics, grammar, Greek, high adventure outdoor program, history, human anatomy, Latin, Latin American history, Mandarin, mathematics, microbiology, Middle Eastern history, music, Native American history, oil painting, orchestra, painting, physics, physics-AP, piano, pottery, pre-algebra, pre-calculus, psychology, psychology-AP, public speaking, religion, robotics, Roman civilization, science, social studies, South African history, Spanish, Spanish-AP, speech, statistics, statistics-AP, theater, trigonometry, U.S. history-AP, world geography, world history, world history-AP, writing.

Graduation Requirements Arts and fine arts (art, music, dance, drama), English, foreign language, mathematics, religion (includes Bible studies and theology), science, social studies (includes history), 20 hours of community service per year.

Special Academic Programs 14 Advanced Placement exams for which test preparation is offered; honors section; independent study; academic accommodation for the gifted and the musically talented; remedial reading and/or remedial writing; remedial math; programs in English, mathematics, general development for dyslexic students; ESL (85 students enrolled).

College Admission Counseling 104 students graduated in 2010; 100 went to college, including Butler University; Cornell University; University of Illinois at Urbana–Champaign; University of Minnesota, Twin Cities Campus; University of Rochester; University of Wisconsin–Madison. Other: 2 entered a postgraduate year, 2 had other specific plans.

Student Life Upper grades have specified standards of dress, student council. Discipline rests primarily with faculty. Attendance at religious services is required.

Summer Programs ESL, sports, art/fine arts programs offered; session focuses on challenging, diversified instruction in the arts and athletics; ESL summer program; held on campus; accepts boys and girls; open to students from other schools.

Tuition and Aid Day student tuition: $24,950; 7-day tuition and room/board: $38,450. Tuition installment plan (Insured Tuition Payment Plan, monthly payment plans). Merit scholarship grants, need-based scholarship grants, Performing arts scholarship, Headmasters Scholarship available. In 2010–11, 44% of upper-school students received aid. Total amount of financial aid awarded in 2010–11: $3,900,000.

Admissions Traditional secondary-level entrance grade is 9. For fall 2010, 388 students applied for upper-level admission, 247 were accepted, 157 enrolled. SLEP, SSAT or TOEFL required. Deadline for receipt of application materials: none. Application fee required: $50. Interview required.

Athletics Interscholastic: baseball (boys), basketball (b,g), fencing (b,g), golf (b,g), ice hockey (b,g), indoor hockey (b,g), indoor soccer (b,g), lacrosse (b,g), soccer (b,g), tennis (b,g), track and field (b,g), volleyball (b,g); intramural: drill team (b,g), weight training (b,g); coed interscholastic: figure skating, soccer; coed intramural: aerobics/dance, badminton, basketball, dance, dance team, Frisbee, ice skating, jogging, martial arts, outdoor activities, outdoor recreation, ropes courses, strength & conditioning, table tennis, ultimate Frisbee. 29 coaches, 3 athletic trainers.

Computers Computers are regularly used in animation, college planning, creative writing, English, ESL, foreign language, history, independent study, mathematics, photography, SAT preparation, science, senior seminar, speech, writing, writing, yearbook classes. Computer network features include on-campus library services,

Internet access, wireless campus network, Internet filtering or blocking technology. Campus intranet, student e-mail accounts, and computer access in designated common areas are available to students. Students grades are available online. The school has a published electronic and media policy.

Contact Amy D. Wolf, Director of Admissions and Communications. 800-421-2724. Fax: 507-333-1661. E-mail: awolf@s-sm.org. Web site: www.s-sm.org.

SHAWE MEMORIAL JUNIOR/SENIOR HIGH SCHOOL

201 West State Street
Madison, Indiana 47250-2899
Head of School: Mr. Philip J. Kahn

General Information Coeducational day college-preparatory and religious studies school, affiliated with Roman Catholic Church. Grades 7–12. Founded: 1954. Setting: small town. 30-acre campus. 1 building on campus. Approved or accredited by North Central Association of Colleges and Schools and Indiana Department of Education. Endowment: $2. Total enrollment: 408. Upper school average class size: 13. Upper school faculty-student ratio: 1:10. There are 180 required school days per year for Upper School students. Upper School students typically attend 5 days per week. The average school day consists of 8 hours and 15 minutes.

Upper School Student Profile Grade 7: 23 students (9 boys, 14 girls); Grade 8: 28 students (13 boys, 15 girls); Grade 9: 20 students (8 boys, 12 girls); Grade 10: 44 students (23 boys, 21 girls); Grade 11: 21 students (12 boys, 9 girls); Grade 12: 27 students (14 boys, 13 girls). 70% of students are Roman Catholic.

Faculty School total: 18. In upper school: 3 men, 15 women; 10 have advanced degrees; 10 reside on campus.

Graduation Requirements No.

Special Academic Programs International Baccalaureate program; Advanced Placement exam preparation; honors section; independent study; study at local college for college credit; academic accommodation for the gifted; remedial reading and/or remedial writing; special instructional classes for deaf students, some special needs students can be accommodated on an individual basis.

College Admission Counseling 22 students graduated in 2010; all went to college, including Indiana University Bloomington.

Student Life Upper grades have specified standards of dress, student council. Discipline rests primarily with faculty. Attendance at religious services is required.

Tuition and Aid Day student tuition: $3600. Tuition installment plan (The Tuition Plan, FACTS Tuition Payment Plan, individually arranged payment plans, multiple options). Tuition reduction for siblings, need-based scholarship grants available. In 2010–11, 20% of upper-school students received aid. Total amount of financial aid awarded in 2010–11: $200,000.

Admissions Traditional secondary-level entrance grade is 9. For fall 2010, 23 students applied for upper-level admission, 19 were accepted, 19 enrolled. Deadline for receipt of application materials: none. Application fee required: $100. Interview required.

Athletics Interscholastic: archery (boys), baseball (b), basketball (b,g), cheering (g), cross-country running (b,g), fencing (b), golf (b,g), soccer (b,g), softball (g), tennis (b,g), track and field (b,g), volleyball (g). 2 PE instructors, 10 coaches, 1 athletic trainer.

Computers Computer network features include on-campus library services, Internet access, wireless campus network, Internet filtering or blocking technology. Campus intranet is available to students. Students grades are available online.

Contact Mr. Philip J. Kahn, President. 812-273-5835 Ext. 245. Fax: 812-273-8975. E-mail: poppresident@popeace.org.

SHAWNIGAN LAKE SCHOOL

1975 Renfrew Road
Postal Bag 2000
Shawnigan Lake, British Columbia V0R 2W1, Canada
Head of School: Mr. David Robertson

General Information Coeducational boarding and day college-preparatory, fine arts, athletics, leadership, citizenship, and entrepreneurship, and language studies school, affiliated with Anglican Church of Canada. Grades 8–12. Founded: 1916. Setting: rural. Nearest major city is Victoria, Canada. Students are housed in single-sex dormitories. 300-acre campus. 30 buildings on campus. Approved or accredited by British Columbia Independent Schools Association, Standards in Excellence And Learning (SEAL), The Association of Boarding Schools, Western Boarding Schools Association, and British Columbia Department of Education. Affiliate member of National Association of Independent Schools. Languages of instruction: English and French. Endowment: CAN$8 million. Total enrollment: 446. Upper school average class size: 14. Upper school faculty-student ratio: 1:9.

Upper School Student Profile Grade 8: 42 students (24 boys, 18 girls); Grade 9: 53 students (28 boys, 25 girls); Grade 10: 108 students (59 boys, 49 girls); Grade 11: 117 students (63 boys, 54 girls); Grade 12: 123 students (69 boys, 54 girls). 90% of students are boarding students. 64% are province residents. 14 provinces are represented in upper school student body. 23% are international students. International students from Democratic People's Republic of Korea, Germany, Hong Kong, Mexico, Taiwan, and United States; 14 other countries represented in student body.

Faculty School total: 79. In upper school: 52 men, 25 women; 22 have advanced degrees; 31 reside on campus.

Subjects Offered Advanced Placement courses, advanced studio art-AP, algebra, art, art history, art history-AP, biology, biology-AP, business skills, calculus, calculus-AP, career and personal planning, chemistry, chemistry-AP, computer science, computer science-AP, creative writing, earth science, economics, English, English language and composition-AP, English literature, English literature and composition-AP, English-AP, environmental science, European history-AP, expository writing, fine arts, French, French language-AP, French literature-AP, French-AP, geography, geometry, health, history, human geography—AP, industrial arts, mathematics, media studies, music, physical education, physics, physics-AP, religion, science, social studies, Spanish, sports science, study skills, trigonometry, U.S. history-AP, writing.

Graduation Requirements Arts and fine arts (art, music, dance, drama), career and personal planning, English, foreign language, mathematics, physical education (includes health), science, social studies (includes history).

Special Academic Programs Advanced Placement exam preparation; honors section; academic accommodation for the gifted; remedial reading and/or remedial writing; remedial math; special instructional classes for students with learning disabilities.

College Admission Counseling 105 students graduated in 2009; 96 went to college, including McGill University; Queen's University at Kingston; The University of British Columbia; The University of Western Ontario; University of Alberta; University of Victoria. Other: 6 went to work, 1 entered military service, 2 had other specific plans.

Student Life Upper grades have uniform requirement, student council, honor system. Discipline rests equally with students and faculty. Attendance at religious services is required.

Tuition and Aid Day student tuition: CAN$18,400; 7-day tuition and room/board: CAN$34,000–CAN$45,000. Tuition installment plan (Insured Tuition Payment Plan, individually arranged payment plans). Tuition reduction for siblings, bursaries, merit scholarship grants available. In 2009–10, 25% of upper-school students received aid; total upper-school merit-scholarship money awarded: CAN$300,000. Total amount of financial aid awarded in 2009–10: CAN$1,230,767.

Admissions Traditional secondary-level entrance grade is 10. For fall 2009, 372 students applied for upper-level admission, 160 were accepted, 145 enrolled. English entrance exam, Math Placement Exam, Otis-Lennon School Ability Test and school's own exam required. Deadline for receipt of application materials: none. Application fee required: CAN$200. Interview required.

Athletics Interscholastic: basketball (boys, girls), crew (b,g), cross-country running (b,g), field hockey (g), hockey (b), ice hockey (b), rowing (b,g), rugby (b,g), soccer (b), squash (b), tennis (b,g), volleyball (g), winter soccer (b); intramural: alpine skiing (b,g), ballet (g), basketball (b,g), crew (b,g), field hockey (g), golf (b,g), rowing (b,g), rugby (b,g), soccer (b), squash (b,g), strength & conditioning (b,g), tennis (b,g), volleyball (g), weight training (b,g); coed interscholastic: hockey, ice hockey, track and field; coed intramural: aerobics, aerobics/dance, alpine skiing, aquatics, backpacking, badminton, canoeing/kayaking, climbing, cross-country running, dance, fitness, golf, hiking/backpacking, jogging, kayaking, modern dance, nordic skiing, ocean paddling, outdoor activities, outdoor adventure, outdoor education, outdoor recreation, outdoor skills, outdoors, physical fitness, riflery, running, swimming and diving, track and field, wilderness survival, yoga. 4 PE instructors, 20 coaches, 2 athletic trainers.

Computers Computers are regularly used in animation, art, business, computer applications, creative writing, design, drawing and design, English, foreign language, graphic arts, history, library, mathematics, photography, research skills, science, social studies, video film production, yearbook classes. Computer network features include on-campus library services, online commercial services, Internet access, Internet filtering or blocking technology. Campus intranet and student e-mail accounts are available to students. Students grades are available online. The school has a published electronic and media policy.

Contact Ms. Margot Allen, Associate Director of Admission. 250-743-6207. Fax: 250-743-6280. E-mail: admissions@shawnigan.ca. Web site: www.sls.bc.ca.

SHELTON SCHOOL AND EVALUATION CENTER

Dallas, Texas
See Special Needs Schools section.

SHENANDOAH VALLEY ACADEMY

234 West Lee Highway
New Market, Virginia 22844
Head of School: Mr. Spencer Hannah

General Information Coeducational boarding and day college-preparatory, general academic, business, vocational, religious studies, bilingual studies, and technology school, affiliated with Seventh-day Adventist Church. Grades 9–12. Founded: 1908. Setting: rural. Nearest major city is Harrisonburg. Students are housed in single-sex dormitories. 380-acre campus. 15 buildings on campus. Approved or accredited by Southern Association of Colleges and Schools and Virginia Department of Education. Total enrollment: 221. Upper school average class size: 30. Upper school faculty-student ratio: 1:14.

Upper School Student Profile Grade 9: 58 students (32 boys, 26 girls); Grade 10: 57 students (23 boys, 34 girls); Grade 11: 60 students (28 boys, 32 girls); Grade 12: 46 students (21 boys, 25 girls). 81% of students are boarding students. 47% are state residents. 12 states are represented in upper school student body. 10% are international students. International students from Angola, Brazil, Colombia, Peru, Republic of Korea, and United Kingdom. 80% of students are Seventh-day Adventists.

Faculty School total: 16. In upper school: 9 men, 7 women; 10 have advanced degrees; 2 reside on campus.

Subjects Offered Accounting, algebra, anatomy and physiology, art, band, basketball, biology, business education, calculus-AP, chemistry, choir, Christianity, computer applications, concert choir, drama, driver education, English, English-AP, foreign language, general science, geometry, government/civics, health, honors English, mathematics, music, orchestra, organ, physical education, physics, piano, pre-calculus, religion, social studies, softball, Spanish, strings, swimming, symphonic band, tennis, U.S. government, U.S. history, U.S. history-AP, voice, volleyball, welding, world history.

Graduation Requirements American government, American history, American literature, applied arts, arts and fine arts (art, music, dance, drama), biology, British literature, chemistry, computer applications, consumer education, English, European history, geometry, health and wellness, personal finance, physical education (includes health), Spanish, world geography, world history, one year of religion for each year in school.

Special Academic Programs Advanced Placement exam preparation; honors section; term-away projects; study at local college for college credit; academic accommodation for the gifted, the musically talented, and the artistically talented; remedial reading and/or remedial writing; remedial math; programs in English, mathematics, general development for dyslexic students; ESL (10 students enrolled).

College Admission Counseling 39 students graduated in 2009; 36 went to college, including Andrews University; Southern Adventist University; Southwestern Adventist University. Other: 2 went to work, 1 entered military service.

Student Life Upper grades have specified standards of dress, student council, honor system. Discipline rests primarily with faculty. Attendance at religious services is required.

Tuition and Aid Day student tuition: $9850; 7-day tuition and room/board: $6550. Tuition installment plan (FACTS Tuition Payment Plan). Merit scholarship grants, need-based scholarship grants, paying campus jobs available. In 2009–10, 70% of upper-school students received aid; total upper-school merit-scholarship money awarded: $50,000.

Admissions Traditional secondary-level entrance grade is 9. TOEFL required. Deadline for receipt of application materials: August 17. Application fee required: $50. Interview recommended.

Athletics Interscholastic: baseball (boys), basketball (b,g), soccer (b,g), softball (g), volleyball (g); intramural: softball (b,g); coed interscholastic: gymnastics; coed intramural: aerobics/Nautilus, backpacking, basketball, field hockey, flag football, floor hockey, indoor hockey, life saving, paddle tennis, physical fitness, skiing (downhill), snowboarding, soccer, volleyball. 1 PE instructor, 1 coach.

Computers Computers are regularly used in accounting, art, Bible studies, business education, career education, career exploration, history, library skills, newspaper, psychology, religion, research skills, SAT preparation, science, Spanish, word processing, writing, yearbook classes. Computer network features include on-campus library services, Internet access, Internet filtering or blocking technology. Student e-mail accounts and computer access in designated common areas are available to students. Students grades are available online. The school has a published electronic and media policy.

Contact Mrs. Wendy Dean, Director of Admissions. 540-740-2206. Fax: 540-740-3336. E-mail: wendy.dean@sva-va.org. Web site: www.shenandoahvalleyacademy.org.

SHERIDAN ACADEMY

4948 Kootenai Street
Boise, Idaho 83705
Head of School: Greg P. Norton

General Information Coeducational day college-preparatory, general academic, business, vocational, and bilingual studies school. Grades 1–12. Founded: 1995. Setting: small town. 1-acre campus. 1 building on campus. Approved or accredited by Northwest Accreditation Commission. Total enrollment: 19. Upper school average class size: 12. Upper school faculty-student ratio: 1:10. There are 180 required school days per year for Upper School students. Upper School students typically attend 5 days per week.

Upper School Student Profile Grade 9: 6 students (5 boys, 1 girl); Grade 10: 2 students (1 boy, 1 girl); Grade 11: 3 students (1 boy, 2 girls); Grade 12: 4 students (3 boys, 1 girl).

Faculty School total: 3. In upper school: 1 man, 2 women; all have advanced degrees.

Subjects Offered Art, computers, economics, English, government, history, humanities, literature, mathematics, physical education, reading, science, Spanish-AP.

Graduation Requirements Economics, English, government, history, humanities, mathematics, reading, science, speech.

Special Academic Programs Accelerated programs; independent study; term-away projects; academic accommodation for the gifted; remedial reading and/or remedial

writing; remedial math; programs in English, general development for dyslexic students; special instructional classes for students with Attention Deficit Disorder.

College Admission Counseling 3 students graduated in 2010; all went to college, including Boise State University.

Student Life Upper grades have specified standards of dress, honor system. Discipline rests primarily with faculty.

Summer Programs Remediation, enrichment, advancement, computer instruction programs offered; session focuses on remediation; held on campus; accepts boys and girls; open to students from other schools. 2011 schedule: June 6 to August 1.

Tuition and Aid Day student tuition: $4500. Tuition installment plan (monthly payment plans, individually arranged payment plans). Tuition reduction for siblings, merit scholarship grants available.

Admissions Traditional secondary-level entrance grade is 9. For fall 2010, 10 students applied for upper-level admission, 10 were accepted. Deadline for receipt of application materials: none. Application fee required: $100. Interview required.

Athletics Coed Interscholastic: baseball, basketball, fishing, fly fishing, jogging, kickball, mountain biking, skateboarding, snowboarding, softball, touch football, walking, winter soccer, winter walking.

Computers Computer resources include Internet access.

Contact 208-331-2044. Fax: 208-331-7724.

THE SHIPLEY SCHOOL

814 Yarrow Street
Bryn Mawr, Pennsylvania 19010-3525
Head of School: Dr. Steven S. Piltch

General Information Coeducational day college-preparatory school. Grades PK–12. Founded: 1894. Setting: suburban. Nearest major city is Philadelphia. 36-acre campus. 4 buildings on campus. Approved or accredited by Middle States Association of Colleges and Schools and Pennsylvania Association of Independent Schools. Member of National Association of Independent Schools and Secondary School Admission Test Board. Endowment: $14 million. Total enrollment: 835. Upper school average class size: 15. Upper school faculty-student ratio: 1:7. There are 167 required school days per year for Upper School students. Upper School students typically attend 5 days per week. The average school day consists of 7 hours and 30 minutes.

Upper School Student Profile Grade 9: 72 students (39 boys, 33 girls); Grade 10: 84 students (42 boys, 42 girls); Grade 11: 89 students (42 boys, 47 girls); Grade 12: 85 students (46 boys, 39 girls).

Faculty School total: 125. In upper school: 26 men, 38 women; 44 have advanced degrees.

Subjects Offered Advanced Placement courses, advanced studio art-AP, algebra, American history, American literature, ancient world history, art, art history, athletic training, athletics, band, bioethics, biology, calculus, chamber groups, chemistry, chorus, classical language, college admission preparation, college counseling, conceptual physics, concert bell choir, CPR, drama, drama performance, dramatic arts, ecology, environmental systems, economics, economics and history, English, English literature, European history, film studies, fine arts, forensics, French, geometry, global issues, global studies, grammar, health, health and wellness, health education, Homeric Greek, honors English, honors geometry, honors U.S. history, honors world history, independent study, introduction to theater, jazz band, Latin, leadership, library skills, Mandarin, mathematics, medieval history, Middle East, model United Nations, music, music theory, musical productions, orchestra, performing arts, philosophy, photography, physical education, physical fitness, physics, pre-calculus, research skills, science, senior project, senior seminar, service learning/internship, Shakespeare, Spanish, speech and debate, statistics, student publications, studio art-AP, theater, theater arts, urban studies, wind ensemble, world history, world literature.

Graduation Requirements English, foreign language, mathematics, performing arts, physical education (includes health), research skills, science, senior project, senior seminar, social studies (includes history), studio art, 40 hours of community service/service learning.

Special Academic Programs 2 Advanced Placement exams for which test preparation is offered; honors section; accelerated programs; independent study; term-away projects; study abroad; academic accommodation for the gifted.

College Admission Counseling 85 students graduated in 2010; all went to college, including Boston University; New York University; Syracuse University; The George Washington University; University of Pennsylvania; University of Southern California. Mean SAT critical reading: 633, mean SAT math: 647, mean SAT writing: 645, mean combined SAT: 1850. 64% scored over 1800 on combined SAT.

Student Life Upper grades have specified standards of dress, student council, honor system. Discipline rests equally with students and faculty.

Summer Programs Sports programs offered; session focuses on sports; held on campus; accepts boys and girls; open to students from other schools. 29 students usually enrolled. 2011 schedule: June 20 to July 29.

Tuition and Aid Day student tuition: $28,995. Tuition installment plan (monthly payment plans). Need-based scholarship grants available. In 2010–11, 26% of upper-school students received aid. Total amount of financial aid awarded in 2010–11: $2,097,925.

Admissions Traditional secondary-level entrance grade is 9. For fall 2010, 305 students applied for upper-level admission, 244 were accepted, 136 enrolled. ISEE, SSAT or WISC-R or WISC-III required. Deadline for receipt of application materials: January 13. Application fee required: $60. On-campus interview required.

Athletics Interscholastic: baseball (boys), basketball (b,g), crew (b,g), cross-country running (b,g), field hockey (g), independent competitive sports (b,g), lacrosse (b,g), rowing (b,g), soccer (b,g), softball (g), squash (b,g), tennis (b,g), volleyball (g), weight training (b,g); intramural: aerobics (b,g), aerobics/Nautilus (b,g), dance (g), modern dance (g), Nautilus (b,g); coed interscholastic: diving, golf, independent competitive sports, swimming and diving, weight training; coed intramural: aerobics, aerobics/ Nautilus, fitness, Nautilus, physical fitness, yoga. 6 PE instructors, 51 coaches, 2 athletic trainers.

Computers Computers are regularly used in graphic design, research skills, writing classes. Computer network features include on-campus library services, online commercial services, Internet access, wireless campus network, Internet filtering or blocking technology, all progress, midterm, and final reports are online. Campus intranet, student e-mail accounts, and computer access in designated common areas are available to students. Students grades are available online. The school has a published electronic and media policy.

Contact Mrs. Zoe Marshall, Assistant to the Director of Admissions. 610-525-4300 Ext. 4118. Fax: 610-525-5082. E-mail: zmarshall@shipleyschool.org. Web site: www.shipleyschool.org.

See Display on this page and Close-Up on page 840.

SHOORE CENTRE FOR LEARNING

Toronto, Ontario, Canada
See Special Needs Schools section.

SHORECREST PREPARATORY SCHOOL

5101 First Street NE
Saint Petersburg, Florida 33703
Head of School: Mr. Michael A. Murphy

General Information Coeducational day college-preparatory and arts school. Grades PK–12. Founded: 1923. Setting: suburban. Nearest major city is Tampa. 28-acre campus. 3 buildings on campus. Approved or accredited by Florida Council of Independent Schools, Southern Association of Colleges and Schools, Southern Association of Independent Schools, The College Board, and Florida Department of Education. Member of National Association of Independent Schools and Secondary School Admission Test Board. Endowment: $1.5 million. Total enrollment: 968. Upper school average class size: 15. Upper school faculty-student ratio: 1:12. There are 175 required school days per year for Upper School students. Upper School students typically attend 5 days per week. The average school day consists of 6 hours and 45 minutes.

Upper School Student Profile Grade 9: 69 students (41 boys, 28 girls); Grade 10: 68 students (39 boys, 29 girls); Grade 11: 71 students (31 boys, 40 girls); Grade 12: 76 students (32 boys, 44 girls).

Faculty School total: 97. In upper school: 21 men, 14 women; 24 have advanced degrees.

Subjects Offered 3-dimensional design, algebra, American literature, anatomy and physiology, ancient history, art, art history, art history-AP, band, biology, biology-AP, calculus, calculus-AP, chemistry, chemistry-AP, computer graphics, computer music, computer science, computer science-AP, conceptual physics, contemporary issues, creative writing, dance, digital imaging, drama, drawing and design, economics, economics-AP, English, English language-AP, English literature-AP, European history, European history-AP, film history, fine arts, fitness, French, French language-AP, French literature-AP, geometry, guitar, health, history of ideas, history of rock and roll, human geography—AP, humanities, journalism, Latin, Latin-AP, macroeconomics-AP, marine biology, music, music theory-AP, musical productions, musical theater, photography, physical education, physics, physics-AP, play/screen writing, political science, portfolio art, pre-calculus, probability and statistics, psychology, psychology-AP, social studies, Spanish, Spanish language-AP, studio art-AP, theater, trigonometry, U.S. history, U.S. history-AP, video film production, Web site design, weight training, Western civilization, world civilizations, world history, world history-AP, world literature, world religions, world wide web design, writing, yearbook.

Graduation Requirements Arts and fine arts (art, music, dance, drama), English, foreign language, health education, mathematics, science, social studies (includes history).

Special Academic Programs 22 Advanced Placement exams for which test preparation is offered; honors section; independent study; academic accommodation for the gifted.

College Admission Counseling 55 students graduated in 2009; all went to college, including Florida State University; Harvard University; Princeton University; Southern Methodist University; University of Colorado at Boulder; University of Miami. Mean SAT critical reading: 610, mean SAT math: 604, mean SAT writing: 596, mean combined SAT: 1810, mean composite ACT: 26.

Student Life Upper grades have specified standards of dress, student council, honor system. Discipline rests primarily with faculty.

Tuition and Aid Day student tuition: $17,115. Tuition installment plan (monthly payment plans, semiannual payment plan). Need-based scholarship grants available. In 2009–10, 5% of upper-school students received aid. Total amount of financial aid awarded in 2009–10: $232,175.

Admissions Traditional secondary-level entrance grade is 9. For fall 2009, 41 students applied for upper-level admission, 31 were accepted, 19 enrolled. ERB, ISEE, PSAT or SAT, school's own test or SSAT required. Deadline for receipt of application materials: none. Application fee required: $75. On-campus interview required.

Athletics Interscholastic: baseball (boys), basketball (b,g), cheering (g), cross-country running (b,g), diving (b,g), football (b), golf (b,g), soccer (b,g), softball (g), swimming and diving (b,g), tennis (b,g), track and field (b,g), volleyball (g); coed interscholastic: sailing. 4 PE instructors, 28 coaches, 1 athletic trainer.

Computers Computers are regularly used in all academic classes. Computer network features include on-campus library services, online commercial services, Internet access, wireless campus network, Internet filtering or blocking technology. Campus intranet, student e-mail accounts, and computer access in designated common areas are available to students. Students grades are available online. The school has a published electronic and media policy.

Contact Mrs. Diana Craig, Director of Admissions. 727-456-7511. Fax: 727-527-4191. E-mail: admissions@shorecrest.org. Web site: www.shorecrest.org.

SHORELINE CHRISTIAN

2400 Northeast 147th Street
Shoreline, Washington 98155
Head of School: Mr. Timothy E. Visser

General Information Coeducational day college-preparatory and general academic school, affiliated with Christian faith. Grades PS–12. Founded: 1952. Setting: suburban. Nearest major city is Seattle. 7-acre campus. 2 buildings on campus. Approved or accredited by Christian Schools International, Northwest Accreditation Commission, Northwest Association of Schools and Colleges, and Washington Department of Education. Endowment: $291,000. Total enrollment: 222. Upper school average class size: 20. Upper school faculty-student ratio: 1:7.

Upper School Student Profile Grade 9: 16 students (11 boys, 5 girls); Grade 10: 25 students (11 boys, 14 girls); Grade 11: 14 students (12 boys, 2 girls); Grade 12: 21 students (14 boys, 7 girls). 100% of students are Christian faith.

Faculty School total: 28. In upper school: 8 men, 6 women; 8 have advanced degrees.

Subjects Offered 20th century history, advanced computer applications, advanced math, Advanced Placement courses, algebra, American history, American literature, art, band, Bible, biology, British literature, calculus, chemistry, choir, Christian doctrine, college writing, composition, computer applications, consumer education, creative writing, current events, current history, drama, drawing, English, film, film appreciation, geometry, global studies, government, health, human anatomy, jazz band, keyboarding, life science, life skills, literature, media, music appreciation, physical education, physical science, physics, psychology, sculpture, sociology, Spanish, speech, study skills, Washington State and Northwest History, weight training, Western civilization, world literature, world religions, yearbook.

Graduation Requirements American government, American literature, Bible, British literature, college writing, composition, electives, English, foreign language, global issues, keyboarding, life skills, mathematics, occupational education, physical education (includes health), science, social sciences, speech, U.S. history, Washington State and Northwest History, Western civilization, world literature.

Special Academic Programs Independent study; study at local college for college credit; remedial reading and/or remedial writing.

College Admission Counseling 21 students graduated in 2010; 20 went to college, including Azusa Pacific University; Calvin College; Dordt College; Seattle Pacific University; University of Washington; Western Washington University. Other: 1 went to work. Median SAT critical reading: 520, median SAT math: 540, median SAT writing: 560, median composite ACT: 26. 80% scored over 26 on composite ACT.

Student Life Upper grades have specified standards of dress, student council. Discipline rests primarily with faculty. Attendance at religious services is required.

Tuition and Aid Day student tuition: $9650–$10,050. Tuition installment plan (monthly payment plans, individually arranged payment plans, prepaid cash tuition discount, quarterly or semi-annual payment plans). Tuition reduction for siblings, need-based scholarship grants, discount for qualifying Pastor families available. In 2010–11, 18% of upper-school students received aid. Total amount of financial aid awarded in 2010–11: $41,869.

Admissions Traditional secondary-level entrance grade is 9. For fall 2010, 14 students applied for upper-level admission, 6 were accepted, 6 enrolled. Deadline for receipt of application materials: none. Application fee required: $100. Interview required.

Athletics Interscholastic: baseball (boys), basketball (b,g), soccer (b), softball (g), volleyball (g); coed interscholastic: cheering, golf, soccer, track and field. 1 PE instructor.

Computers Computers are regularly used in all academic, art, library, media, music, occupational education, research skills, yearbook classes. Computer network features include on-campus library services, Internet access. Students grades are available online.

Contact Mrs. Laurie Dykstra, Director of Development. 206-364-7777 Ext. 308. Fax: 206-364-0349. E-mail: ldykstra@shorelinechristian.org. Web site: www.shorelinechristian.org.

SKY RANCH FOR BOYS, INC.

Sky Ranch, South Dakota
See Special Needs Schools section.

SMITH SCHOOL

New York, New York
See Special Needs Schools section.

SOLOMON COLLEGE

#228, 10621 100th Avenue
Edmonton, Alberta T5J 0B3, Canada
Head of School: Ms. Ping Ping Lee

General Information Coeducational day and distance learning college-preparatory and general academic school. Grades 10–12. Distance learning grades 10–12. Founded: 1994. Setting: urban. 1 building on campus. Approved or accredited by Association of Independent Schools and Colleges of Alberta and Alberta Department of Education. Language of instruction: English. Total enrollment: 15. Upper school average class size: 10. Upper school faculty-student ratio: 1:10. There are 225 required school days per year for Upper School students. Upper School students typically attend 5 days per week. The average school day consists of 4 hours and 30 minutes.

Upper School Student Profile Grade 11: 1 student (1 boy); Grade 12: 14 students (7 boys, 7 girls).

Faculty School total: 5. In upper school: 2 men, 3 women; 2 have advanced degrees.

Subjects Offered Biology, calculus, career and personal planning, chemistry, Chinese, computer information systems, computer skills, computer technologies, English literature, ESL, keyboarding, mathematics, physics, social studies.

Special Academic Programs ESL (80 students enrolled).

College Admission Counseling 20 students graduated in 2010; 12 went to college, including University of Alberta; University of Calgary; University of Lethbridge.

Student Life Discipline rests equally with students and faculty.

Tuition and Aid Day student tuition: CAN$5800.

Admissions Traditional secondary-level entrance grade is 10. For fall 2010, 15 students applied for upper-level admission, 15 were accepted, 15 enrolled. Placement test required. Deadline for receipt of application materials: August 1. Application fee required: CAN$200.

Computers Computer network features include Internet access, wireless campus network, Internet filtering or blocking technology. Campus intranet is available to students.

Contact Mr. Sunny Ip, Registrar. 780-431-1516. Fax: 780-431-1644. E-mail: admin@solomoncollege.ca.

SONOMA ACADEMY

2500 Farmers Lane
Santa Rosa, California 95404
Head of School: Janet Durgin

General Information Coeducational day college-preparatory, arts, and technology school. Grades 9–12. Founded: 1999. 34-acre campus. 3 buildings on campus. Approved or accredited by National Independent Private Schools Association, Western Association of Schools and Colleges, and California Department of Education. Total enrollment: 231. Upper school average class size: 15. Upper school faculty-student ratio: 1:12. The average school day consists of 7 hours.

Faculty School total: 24. In upper school: 9 men, 15 women; 19 have advanced degrees.

Special Academic Programs 7 Advanced Placement exams for which test preparation is offered; honors section; independent study; study abroad.

College Admission Counseling 49 students graduated in 2010.

Student Life Upper grades have student council. Discipline rests equally with students and faculty.

Tuition and Aid Tuition installment plan (Insured Tuition Payment Plan, monthly payment plans). Need-based scholarship grants available. In 2010–11, 50% of upper-school students received aid.

Admissions Traditional secondary-level entrance grade is 9. SSAT required. Deadline for receipt of application materials: January 13. Application fee required: $85. Interview required.

Athletics Interscholastic: basketball (boys, girls), cross-country running (b,g), lacrosse (b,g), soccer (b,g), track and field (b,g), volleyball (g); coed intramural: aerobics/dance, ballet, baseball, combined training, dance, fencing, fitness, flag football, Frisbee, kickball, martial arts, physical fitness, physical training, softball, strength & conditioning, tai chi, weight training, whiffle ball, yoga. 9 coaches.

Computers Computers are regularly used in all classes. Computer network features include on-campus library services, online commercial services, Internet access, wireless campus network, Internet filtering or blocking technology. Campus intranet and student e-mail accounts are available to students. The school has a published electronic and media policy.

Sonoma Academy

Contact Sandy Stack, Director of Enrollment & Marketing. 707-545-1770. Fax: 707-636-2474. E-mail: sandy.stack@sonomaacademy.org. Web site: http://www.sonomaacademy.org/.

SORENSON'S RANCH SCHOOL

Koosharem, Utah
See Special Needs Schools section.

SOUNDVIEW PREPARATORY SCHOOL

370 Underhill Avenue
Yorktown Heights, New York 10598
Head of School: W. Glyn Hearn
General Information Coeducational day college-preparatory, arts, and technology school. Grades 6–PG. Founded: 1989. Setting: suburban. Nearest major city is New York. 13-acre campus. 7 buildings on campus. Approved or accredited by New York State Association of Independent Schools and New York Department of Education. Total enrollment: 75. Upper school average class size: 7. Upper school faculty-student ratio: 1:5. Upper School students typically attend 5 days per week. The average school day consists of 6 hours and 13 minutes.
Upper School Student Profile Grade 9: 12 students (4 boys, 8 girls); Grade 10: 14 students (7 boys, 7 girls); Grade 11: 15 students (10 boys, 5 girls); Grade 12: 23 students (18 boys, 5 girls).
Faculty School total: 16. In upper school: 1 man, 12 women; 12 have advanced degrees.
Subjects Offered Advanced Placement courses, algebra, American history, American literature, anatomy and physiology, art, biology, calculus, chemistry, computer literacy, creative writing, drama, earth science, English, English literature, European history-AP, French, geometry, grammar, health, Italian, Latin, mathematics, philosophy, physical education, physics, psychology, science, sculpture, social studies, Spanish, U.S. government, U.S. history-AP, world history.
Graduation Requirements Art, electives, English, foreign language, health, history, mathematics, physical education (includes health), science.
Special Academic Programs Advanced Placement exam preparation; honors section; accelerated programs; independent study; academic accommodation for the gifted and the artistically talented; special instructional classes for students needing wheelchair accessibility.
College Admission Counseling 6 students graduated in 2010; all went to college, including Barnard College; Dickinson College; Drew University; Muhlenberg

College; Pace University; Rhode Island School of Design. Median SAT critical reading: 595, median SAT math: 560, median SAT writing: 523, median composite ACT: 24.
Student Life Discipline rests primarily with faculty.
Tuition and Aid Day student tuition: $31,100–$32,200. Need-based scholarship grants available. In 2010–11, 28% of upper-school students received aid. Total amount of financial aid awarded in 2010–11: $470,000.
Admissions Traditional secondary-level entrance grade is 9. For fall 2010, 52 students applied for upper-level admission, 26 were accepted, 24 enrolled. ERB (CTP-Verbal, Quantitative) or ERB Mathematics required. Deadline for receipt of application materials: none. Application fee required: $50. On-campus interview required.
Athletics Interscholastic: basketball (girls); coed interscholastic: basketball, soccer, tennis, ultimate Frisbee; coed intramural: cheering, sailing, skiing (downhill), volleyball. 1 PE instructor, 1 coach.
Computers Computers are regularly used in all academic classes. Computer network features include Internet access, wireless campus network, Internet filtering or blocking technology. Campus intranet and student e-mail accounts are available to students. The school has a published electronic and media policy.
Contact Mary E. Ivanyi, Assistant Head. 914-962-2780. Fax: 914-302-2769. E-mail: mivanyi@soundviewprep.org. Web site: www.soundviewprep.org.

See Display below and Close-Up on page 842.

SOUTHERN ONTARIO COLLEGE

430 York Boulevard
Hamilton, Ontario L8R 3K8, Canada
Head of School: Susan J. Woods
General Information Coeducational day college-preparatory school. Grades 9–12. Founded: 1980. Setting: urban. 1 building on campus. Approved or accredited by Ontario Ministry of Education and Ontario Department of Education. Language of instruction: English. Upper school average class size: 20. Upper school faculty-student ratio: 1:15. Upper School students typically attend 5 days per week.
Faculty School total: 7. In upper school: 5 men, 2 women; 3 have advanced degrees.
Special Academic Programs ESL (15 students enrolled).
College Admission Counseling 50 students graduated in 2010; 5 went to college, including Penn State University Park. Other: 45 entered a postgraduate year.
Student Life Upper grades have uniform requirement, honor system. Discipline rests primarily with faculty.
Tuition and Aid Guaranteed tuition plan.
Admissions Application fee required: CAN$150.

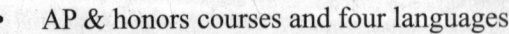

Computers Computers are regularly used in accounting, career education, computer applications classes. Computer resources include Internet access, wireless campus network, Internet filtering or blocking technology.

Contact Mr. Robert Glaister, Admissions Officer. 905-546-1501. Fax: 905-546-5415. E-mail: admin@mysoc.ca. Web site: www.mysoc.ca.

SOUTHFIELD CHRISTIAN HIGH SCHOOL

28650 Lahser Road
Southfield, Michigan 48034-2099
Head of School: Mrs. Margie Baldwin

General Information Coeducational day college-preparatory, arts, religious studies, and technology school, affiliated with Christian faith, Evangelical faith. Grades K–12. Founded: 1970. Setting: suburban. Nearest major city is Detroit. 28-acre campus. 1 building on campus. Approved or accredited by Association of Christian Schools International, Independent Schools Association of the Central States, North Central Association of Colleges and Schools, and Michigan Department of Education. Endowment: $1.5 million. Total enrollment: 489. Upper school average class size: 22. Upper school faculty-student ratio: 1:20. There are 175 required school days per year for Upper School students. Upper School students typically attend 5 days per week. The average school day consists of 6 hours and 30 minutes.

Upper School Student Profile Grade 9: 41 students (18 boys, 23 girls); Grade 10: 42 students (18 boys, 24 girls); Grade 11: 42 students (20 boys, 22 girls); Grade 12: 53 students (26 boys, 27 girls). 100% of students are Christian faith, members of Evangelical faith.

Faculty School total: 20. In upper school: 10 men, 10 women; 18 have advanced degrees.

Subjects Offered Accounting, Advanced Placement courses, algebra, American government, American history, American history-AP, American literature, American literature-AP, ancient world history, art, band, Bible, biology, biology-AP, British literature, calculus-AP, chemistry, chemistry-AP, choir, chorus, communication arts, composition-AP, computer applications, computer programming, conceptual physics, creative writing, drawing and design, economics, English language-AP, English literature and composition-AP, film and literature, French, geography, geometry, government, graphic design, health, instrumental music, Life of Christ, literature and composition-AP, Middle Eastern history, New Testament, organic chemistry, photography, physical education, physics-AP, pre-calculus, probability and statistics, Russian history, senior project, Spanish, speech and debate, U.S. history, vocal music, Web site design, world studies, yearbook.

Special Academic Programs Advanced Placement exam preparation; honors section; independent study.

College Admission Counseling 54 students graduated in 2010; all went to college, including Grand Valley State University; Hope College; Michigan State University; Oakland University; University of Michigan; Wheaton College. Median SAT critical reading: 612, median SAT math: 589, median composite ACT: 25. 62% scored over 600 on SAT critical reading, 42% scored over 600 on SAT math, 46% scored over 26 on composite ACT.

Student Life Upper grades have uniform requirement, student council. Discipline rests primarily with faculty. Attendance at religious services is required.

Summer Programs Rigorous outdoor training programs offered; session focuses on physical education; held on campus; accepts boys and girls; not open to students from other schools. 10 students usually enrolled. 2011 schedule: June 13 to July 1. Application deadline: May 1.

Tuition and Aid Day student tuition: $8100. Tuition installment plan (FACTS Tuition Payment Plan). Tuition reduction for siblings, need-based scholarship grants available. In 2010–11, 5% of upper-school students received aid. Total amount of financial aid awarded in 2010–11: $191,000.

Admissions Traditional secondary-level entrance grade is 9. For fall 2010, 30 students applied for upper-level admission, 20 were accepted, 10 enrolled. Any standardized test required. Deadline for receipt of application materials: none. No application fee required. On-campus interview required.

Athletics Interscholastic: baseball (boys), cheering (g), football (b), softball (g), volleyball (g); coed interscholastic: basketball, cross-country running, golf, soccer, track and field; coed intramural: archery, backpacking, badminton, bicycling, flag football, floor hockey, Frisbee, skiing (cross-country), weight lifting. 1 PE instructor, 1 athletic trainer.

Computers Computers are regularly used in accounting, art, commercial art, computer applications, creative writing, drawing and design, graphic arts, graphic design, independent study, media production, programming, publishing, Web site design, writing, yearbook classes. Computer network features include on-campus library services, Internet access, wireless campus network, Internet filtering or blocking technology. Students grades are available online. The school has a published electronic and media policy.

Contact Mrs. Sue Hoffenbacher, High School Principal. 248-357-3660 Ext. 247. Fax: 248-357-5271. E-mail: shoffenbacher@southfieldchristian.org. Web site: www.southfieldchristian.org.

SOUTH KENT SCHOOL

40 Bulls Bridge Road
South Kent, Connecticut 06785
Head of School: Mr. Andrew J. Vadnais

General Information Boys' boarding and day college-preparatory, arts, and technology school, affiliated with Episcopal Church. Grades 9–PG. Founded: 1923. Setting: rural. Nearest major city is New York, NY. Students are housed in single-sex dormitories. 320-acre campus. 30 buildings on campus. Approved or accredited by National Association of Episcopal Schools, New England Association of Schools and Colleges, The Association of Boarding Schools, and Connecticut Department of Education. Member of National Association of Independent Schools and Secondary School Admission Test Board. Endowment: $4 million. Total enrollment: 163. Upper school average class size: 7. Upper school faculty-student ratio: 1:5. Upper School students typically attend 6 days per week. The average school day consists of 6 hours.

Upper School Student Profile Grade 9: 13 students (13 boys); Grade 10: 33 students (33 boys); Grade 11: 40 students (40 boys); Grade 12: 54 students (54 boys); Postgraduate: 23 students (23 boys). 83% of students are boarding students. 28% are state residents. 17 states are represented in upper school student body. 38% are international students. International students from Brazil, Canada, China, Japan, Republic of Korea, and Taiwan; 10 other countries represented in student body. 35% of students are members of Episcopal Church.

Faculty School total: 34. In upper school: 23 men, 11 women; 11 have advanced degrees; 25 reside on campus.

Subjects Offered Advanced biology, Advanced Placement courses, advanced studio art-AP, algebra, American history, American literature, art, biology, calculus, calculus-AP, chemistry, creative writing, digital applications, driver education, ecology, economics-AP, English, English language and composition-AP, English literature, entrepreneurship, environmental science, environmental studies, ESL, European history, expository writing, finance, fine arts, French, French-AP, functions, geography, geometry, government and politics-AP, grammar, history, Latin, marketing, mathematics, Native American history, photography, physics, physiology, pre-calculus, psychology, psychology-AP, robotics, science, Spanish, Spanish-AP, statistics, statistics-AP, trigonometry, U.S. history-AP, world history, writing.

Graduation Requirements Art, English, foreign language, lab science, mathematics, U.S. history.

Special Academic Programs Advanced Placement exam preparation; honors section; independent study; ESL (35 students enrolled).

College Admission Counseling 56 students graduated in 2010; 54 went to college, including Charleston Southern University; Clemson University; Hobart and William Smith Colleges; Lafayette College; Northeastern University; Purdue University. Other: 2 entered a postgraduate year. Median SAT critical reading: 520, median SAT math: 500. 18% scored over 600 on SAT critical reading, 24% scored over 600 on SAT math.

Student Life Upper grades have specified standards of dress, student council, honor system. Discipline rests primarily with faculty. Attendance at religious services is required.

Summer Programs ESL programs offered; held on campus; accepts boys; open to students from other schools. 15 students usually enrolled. 2011 schedule: August to September. Application deadline: May.

Tuition and Aid Day student tuition: $26,000; 7-day tuition and room/board: $43,000. Tuition installment plan (The Tuition Plan, Insured Tuition Payment Plan, monthly payment plans). Merit scholarship grants, need-based scholarship grants available. In 2010–11, 40% of upper-school students received aid. Total amount of financial aid awarded in 2010–11: $1,900,000.

Admissions Traditional secondary-level entrance grade is 9. For fall 2010, 190 students applied for upper-level admission, 139 were accepted, 90 enrolled. SSAT and writing sample required. Deadline for receipt of application materials: none. Application fee required: $50. Interview required.

Athletics Interscholastic: baseball, basketball, crew, cross-country running, golf, ice hockey, lacrosse, ropes courses, soccer, tennis; intramural: alpine skiing, baseball, basketball, bicycling, canoeing/kayaking, climbing, crew, golf, hiking/backpacking, ice hockey, outdoor activities, skiing (cross-country), skiing (downhill), snowboarding, soccer, strength & conditioning, ultimate Frisbee, wall climbing, weight lifting, weight training. 28 coaches, 2 athletic trainers.

Computers Computers are regularly used in art classes. Computer network features include on-campus library services, online commercial services, Internet access, wireless campus network, Internet filtering or blocking technology. Student e-mail accounts are available to students. The school has a published electronic and media policy.

Contact Mr. Richard A. Brande, Director of Enrollment and Financial Aid. 860-927-3539 Ext. 202. Fax: 888-803-0140. E-mail: brander@southkentschool.org. Web site: www.southkentschool.org.

SOUTHWEST CHRISTIAN SCHOOL, INC.

7001 Benbrook Lake Drive
Fort Worth, Texas 76132
Head of School: Dr. Penny Armstrong

General Information Coeducational day college-preparatory, arts, religious studies, and technology school, affiliated with Christian faith. Grades PK–12. Founded: 1969.

Southwest Christian School, Inc.

Setting: suburban. 24-acre campus. 3 buildings on campus. Approved or accredited by Association of Christian Schools International, Southern Association of Colleges and Schools, Texas Education Agency, and Texas Department of Education. Total enrollment: 929. Upper school average class size: 16. Upper school faculty-student ratio: 1:11. There are 176 required school days per year for Upper School students. Upper School students typically attend 5 days per week. The average school day consists of 7 hours.

Upper School Student Profile Grade 7: 59 students (24 boys, 35 girls); Grade 8: 76 students (35 boys, 41 girls); Grade 9: 83 students (42 boys, 41 girls); Grade 10: 71 students (34 boys, 37 girls); Grade 11: 80 students (29 boys, 51 girls); Grade 12: 80 students (39 boys, 41 girls).

Faculty School total: 45. In upper school: 12 men, 33 women; 20 have advanced degrees.

Subjects Offered 1½ elective credits, advanced math, algebra, American government, American literature, American literature-AP, anatomy and physiology, art, Bible studies, biology, biology-AP, British literature, British literature-AP, calculus, calculus-AP, chemistry, chemistry-AP, choir, drama, English, English literature-AP, English-AP, foreign language, French, geometry, government, history, honors algebra, honors English, honors geometry, honors U.S. history, honors world history, journalism, keyboarding, lab science, leadership, literature and composition-AP, physics, physics-AP, pre-algebra, pre-calculus, psychology, SAT preparation, Spanish, speech, technology, U.S. history, U.S. history-AP, Web site design.

Graduation Requirements 4 years of Bible courses.

Special Academic Programs Advanced Placement exam preparation; honors section; accelerated programs; study at local college for college credit; study abroad; academic accommodation for the gifted.

College Admission Counseling 81 students graduated in 2010; 79 went to college, including Abilene Christian University; Baylor University; Texas A&M University; Texas Christian University; University of North Texas. Other: 1 went to work, 1 entered military service. Median SAT critical reading: 533, median SAT math: 530, median SAT writing: 530, median combined SAT: 1595, median composite ACT: 24. 31% scored over 600 on SAT critical reading, 20% scored over 600 on SAT math, 18% scored over 600 on SAT writing, 15% scored over 1800 on combined SAT, 31% scored over 26 on composite ACT.

Student Life Upper grades have uniform requirement, student council, honor system. Discipline rests primarily with faculty. Attendance at religious services is required.

Summer Programs Enrichment, sports, art/fine arts, computer instruction programs offered; session focuses on enrichment, athletics; held on campus; accepts boys and girls; open to students from other schools. 2011 schedule: June to June. Application deadline: June.

Tuition and Aid Day student tuition: $11,050–$11,500. Tuition installment plan (FACTS Tuition Payment Plan). Need-based scholarship grants available. In 2010–11, 20% of upper-school students received aid. Total amount of financial aid awarded in 2010–11: $455,000.

Admissions Traditional secondary-level entrance grade is 9. For fall 2010, 106 students applied for upper-level admission, 99 were accepted, 62 enrolled. Stanford 9 required. Deadline for receipt of application materials: March 30. No application fee required. Interview required.

Athletics Interscholastic: aerobics/dance (girls), baseball (b), basketball (b,g), cheering (g), cross-country running (b,g), dance team (g), equestrian sports (b,g), football (b), golf (b,g), soccer (b,g), softball (g), track and field (b,g), volleyball (g), wrestling (b); intramural: physical training (b,g); coed interscholastic: aquatics, equestrian sports, paint ball, rodeo; coed intramural: aquatics, fitness, strength & conditioning, weight training. 2 PE instructors, 12 coaches, 1 athletic trainer.

Computers Computers are regularly used in all academic classes. Computer network features include on-campus library services, online commercial services, Internet access, wireless campus network, Internet filtering or blocking technology, computer carts for classroom use. Student e-mail accounts and computer access in designated common areas are available to students. Students grades are available online. The school has a published electronic and media policy.

Contact Mrs. Libby Madison, Prep Campus Admissions Associate. 817-294-9596 Ext. 252. Fax: 817-292-3644. E-mail: lmadison@southwestchristian.org. Web site: www.southwestchristian.org.

SOUTHWESTERN ACADEMY

Beaver Creek Ranch Campus
Rimrock, Arizona 86335
Head of School: Mr. Kenneth Veronda

General Information Coeducational boarding and day college-preparatory and general academic school. Grades 9–PG. Founded: 1963. Setting: rural. Nearest major city is Sedona. Students are housed in single-sex dormitories. 180-acre campus. 24 buildings on campus. Approved or accredited by Arizona Association of Independent Schools, The Association of Boarding Schools, and Arizona Department of Education. Endowment: $9.2 million. Total enrollment: 32. Upper school average class size: 6.

Upper school faculty-student ratio: 1:3. Upper School students typically attend 5 days per week. The average school day consists of 8 hours.

Upper School Student Profile Grade 9: 7 students (3 boys, 4 girls); Grade 10: 5 students (3 boys, 2 girls); Grade 11: 12 students (5 boys, 7 girls); Grade 12: 5 students (3 boys, 2 girls); Postgraduate: 3 students (2 boys, 1 girl). 100% of students are boarding students. 3% are state residents. 5 states are represented in upper school student body. 53% are international students. International students from China, Japan, Republic of Korea, Serbia and Montenegro, Taiwan, and Thailand; 3 other countries represented in student body.

Faculty School total: 12. In upper school: 5 men, 7 women; 4 have advanced degrees; 7 reside on campus.

Subjects Offered Advanced math, Advanced Placement courses, algebra, American history, American literature, American literature-AP, art, art appreciation, art history, astronomy, biology, biology-AP, British literature, calculus, chemistry, earth science, ecology, economics, English, English composition, environmental education, environmental science, environmental studies, ESL, fashion, fine arts, general math, geometry, health, integrated science, Latin, math review, mathematics, music, music appreciation, outdoor education, physics, pre-algebra, Spanish, studio art, U.S. government, world cultures, yearbook.

Graduation Requirements Algebra, American government, American history, American literature, British literature, computer literacy, economics, electives, English, foreign language, geometry, lab science, mathematics, physical education (includes health), visual and performing arts, world cultures. Community service is required.

Special Academic Programs Advanced Placement exam preparation; honors section; accelerated programs; independent study; term-away projects; study at local college for college credit; ESL (6 students enrolled).

College Admission Counseling 8 students graduated in 2010; all went to college, including Arizona State University; California State University, Long Beach; Pacific Lutheran University; Trent University. Median SAT critical reading: 450, median SAT math: 600, median SAT writing: 550.

Student Life Upper grades have specified standards of dress, student council, honor system. Discipline rests primarily with faculty.

Summer Programs Remediation, enrichment, advancement, ESL, art/fine arts, rigorous outdoor training programs offered; session focuses on academics and outdoor/environmental education; held on campus; accepts boys and girls; open to students from other schools. 30 students usually enrolled. 2011 schedule: June 21 to August 13. Application deadline: none.

Tuition and Aid Day student tuition: $14,900; 7-day tuition and room/board: $30,700. Tuition installment plan (monthly payment plans, individually arranged payment plans). Need-based scholarship grants available. In 2010–11, 43% of upper-school students received aid. Total amount of financial aid awarded in 2010–11: $392,300.

Admissions Traditional secondary-level entrance grade is 9. For fall 2010, 33 students applied for upper-level admission, 24 were accepted, 11 enrolled. Deadline for receipt of application materials: none. Application fee required: $100. Interview recommended.

Athletics Interscholastic: basketball (boys, girls), volleyball (g); coed interscholastic: golf, soccer; coed intramural: alpine skiing, archery, backpacking, ballet, baseball, basketball, bicycling, billiards, climbing, cross-country running, equestrian sports, fishing, fitness, golf, hiking/backpacking, horseback riding, horseshoes, ice skating, mountain biking, outdoor activities, outdoor adventure, outdoor education, outdoor recreation, outdoor skills, paint ball, rock climbing, ropes courses, skiing (cross-country), skiing (downhill), snowboarding, soccer, softball, swimming and diving, table tennis, tennis, track and field, volleyball. 1 PE instructor, 2 coaches.

Computers Computers are regularly used in all classes. Computer network features include on-campus library services, Internet access, wireless campus network, Internet filtering or blocking technology. Student e-mail accounts and computer access in designated common areas are available to students.

Contact Office of Admissions. 626-799-5010 Ext. 5. Fax: 626-799-0407. E-mail: bthomas@southwesternacademy.edu. Web site: www.southwesternacademy.edu.

See Display on page 632 and Close-Up on page 844.

SOUTHWESTERN ACADEMY
2800 Monterey Road
San Marino, California 91108
Head of School: Kenneth R. Veronda

General Information Coeducational boarding and day college-preparatory, general academic, arts, and ESL school. Grades 6–PG. Founded: 1924. Setting: suburban. Nearest major city is Pasadena. Students are housed in single-sex dormitories. 8-acre campus. 9 buildings on campus. Approved or accredited by The Association of Boarding Schools, Western Association of Schools and Colleges, and California Department of Education. Member of Secondary School Admission Test Board. Endowment: $15 million. Total enrollment: 139. Upper school average class size: 12.

Southwestern Academy

Upper school faculty-student ratio: 1:6. Upper School students typically attend 5 days per week. The average school day consists of 8 hours.

Upper School Student Profile Grade 9: 19 students (13 boys, 6 girls); Grade 10: 29 students (18 boys, 11 girls); Grade 11: 44 students (29 boys, 15 girls); Grade 12: 48 students (32 boys, 16 girls); Postgraduate: 1 student (1 girl). 72% of students are boarding students. 29% are state residents. 7 states are represented in upper school student body. 55% are international students. International students from China, Hong Kong, Japan, Republic of Korea, Taiwan, and Viet Nam; 10 other countries represented in student body.

Faculty School total: 29. In upper school: 12 men, 11 women; 12 have advanced degrees; 10 reside on campus.

Subjects Offered Algebra, American history, American literature, animation, art, art history, audio visual/media, biology, calculus, calculus-AP, chemistry, college counseling, creative writing, drama, earth science, economics, English, English literature, ESL, European history, expository writing, fashion, fine arts, geography, geology, geometry, government/civics, grammar, health, history, journalism, mathematics, music, photography, physical education, physics, psychology, science, social sciences, social studies, Spanish, speech, world cultures, world history, world literature, writing.

Graduation Requirements Algebra, American government, American history, American literature, British literature, computer literacy, economics, electives, English, foreign language, geometry, lab science, mathematics, physical education (includes health), visual and performing arts, world cultures, 100 hours of community service. Community service is required.

Special Academic Programs Advanced Placement exam preparation; honors section; accelerated programs; independent study; study at local college for college credit; ESL (27 students enrolled).

College Admission Counseling 30 students graduated in 2010; all went to college, including Occidental College; Pepperdine University; University of California, Irvine; University of California, Los Angeles; University of California, San Diego; University of La Verne.

Student Life Upper grades have specified standards of dress, student council, honor system. Discipline rests primarily with faculty.

Summer Programs Remediation, enrichment, advancement, ESL, art/fine arts, computer instruction programs offered; session focuses on academics; held on campus; accepts boys and girls; open to students from other schools. 60 students usually enrolled. 2011 schedule: June 14 to September 17. Application deadline: none.

Tuition and Aid Day student tuition: $14,900; 7-day tuition and room/board: $30,700. Tuition installment plan (monthly payment plans, individually arranged payment plans). Need-based scholarship grants available. In 2010–11, 20% of upper-school students received aid. Total amount of financial aid awarded in 2010–11: $750,000.

Admissions Traditional secondary-level entrance grade is 9. For fall 2010, 189 students applied for upper-level admission, 94 were accepted, 68 enrolled. Deadline for receipt of application materials: none. Application fee required: $100. Interview recommended.

Athletics Interscholastic: baseball (boys), basketball (b,g), track and field (b,g), volleyball (b,g); intramural: baseball (b), basketball (b,g), track and field (b,g), volleyball (b,g); coed interscholastic: baseball, bowling, climbing, cross-country running, fishing, horseback riding, soccer, tennis; coed intramural: archery, backpacking, baseball, bicycling, bowling, climbing, cross-country running, fishing, golf, hiking/backpacking, horseback riding, outdoor activities, physical fitness, skiing (downhill), snowboarding, soccer, table tennis, tennis, weight training. 2 PE instructors, 4 coaches, 1 athletic trainer.

Computers Computers are regularly used in art, English, ESL, foreign language, history, mathematics, music, science, yearbook classes. Computer network features include on-campus library services, online commercial services, Internet access, wireless campus network, Internet filtering or blocking technology. Student e-mail accounts and computer access in designated common areas are available to students. The school has a published electronic and media policy.

Contact Ms. Maia Moore, Assistant Director. 626-799-5010 Ext. 1204. Fax: 626-799-0407. E-mail: admissions@southwesternacademy.edu. Web site: www.SouthwesternAcademy.edu.

See Display on page 633 and Close-Up on page 846.

SPARHAWK SCHOOL

18 Maple Street
Salisbury, Massachusetts 01952
Head of School: Louise Stilphen

General Information Coeducational day college-preparatory, arts, and humanities school. Grades K–12. Founded: 1994. Setting: small town. Nearest major city is Boston. 7-acre campus. 1 building on campus. Approved or accredited by Massachusetts Department of Education. Candidate for accreditation by New England Association of Schools and Colleges. Total enrollment: 176. Upper school average class size: 10. Upper school faculty-student ratio: 1:6. There are 181 required school days per year for Upper School students. Upper School students typically attend 5 days per week. The average school day consists of 7 hours and 15 minutes.

Upper School Student Profile Grade 6: 8 students (5 boys, 3 girls); Grade 7: 10 students (5 boys, 5 girls); Grade 8: 10 students (4 boys, 6 girls); Grade 9: 18 students

(8 boys, 10 girls); Grade 10: 13 students (3 boys, 10 girls); Grade 11: 21 students (13 boys, 8 girls); Grade 12: 22 students (13 boys, 9 girls).

Faculty School total: 14. In upper school: 5 men, 9 women; 9 have advanced degrees.

Subjects Offered Algebra, Ancient Greek, art, biology, calculus, career/college preparation, ceramics, chemistry, choral music, college admission preparation, community service, conceptual physics, creative arts, creative thinking, creative writing, critical thinking, dance, debate, drama, earth science, ecology, environmental science, ethics and responsibility, fencing, fine arts, forensics, French, geology, geometry, global issues, global studies, grammar, great issues, history, humanities, independent study, integrated arts, interdisciplinary studies, internship, Italian, lab science, Latin, literature, methods of research, music, performing arts, personal development, philosophy, physics, poetry, pre-calculus, SAT preparation, science, senior project, senior seminar, service learning/internship, social sciences, Spanish, studio art, technology, theater arts, trigonometry, world history, writing.

Graduation Requirements Algebra, college admission preparation, creative arts, critical thinking, geometry, global studies, history, humanities, interdisciplinary studies, lab science, languages, literature, mathematics, personal development, philosophy, research, SAT preparation, senior seminar, synthesis projects, graduation portfolio, graduation by exhibition. Community service is required.

Special Academic Programs Honors section; independent study; term-away projects; study abroad; academic accommodation for the gifted, the musically talented, and the artistically talented.

College Admission Counseling 11 students graduated in 2009; all went to college, including Bard College; Bennington College; Bentley University; Brandeis University; Ithaca College; Lesley University. Mean SAT critical reading: 611, mean SAT math: 550, mean SAT writing: 580, mean combined SAT: 1741. 50% scored over 600 on SAT critical reading, 33% scored over 600 on SAT math, 17% scored over 600 on SAT writing, 33% scored over 1800 on combined SAT.

Student Life Upper grades have student council, honor system. Discipline rests equally with students and faculty.

Tuition and Aid Day student tuition: $18,500. Tuition installment plan (monthly payment plans, Sallie Mae TuitionPay, Salem Five Cents Tuition Plan). Need-based scholarship grants, need-based loans available. In 2009–10, 32% of upper-school students received aid. Total amount of financial aid awarded in 2009–10: $248,548.

Admissions Traditional secondary-level entrance grade is 9. For fall 2009, 60 students applied for upper-level admission, 40 were accepted, 35 enrolled. SSAT required. Deadline for receipt of application materials: none. Application fee required: $40. Interview required.

Athletics Coed Interscholastic: cross-country running; coed intramural: cross-country running, Frisbee, running, skiing (downhill), snowboarding, tennis, volleyball. 2 coaches.

Computers Computers are regularly used in all classes. Computer network features include on-campus library services, Internet access, wireless campus network. Campus intranet and student e-mail accounts are available to students. Students grades are available online. The school has a published electronic and media policy.

Contact Ms. Jane Fantry, Admissions Assistant. 978-388-5354. Fax: 978-499-4303. E-mail: admissions@sparhawkschool.com. Web site: www.sparhawkschool.com/home.html.

SPARTANBURG DAY SCHOOL

1701 Skylyn Drive
Spartanburg, South Carolina 29307
Head of School: Mr. Christopher A. Dorrance

General Information Coeducational day college-preparatory and arts school. Grades PK–12. Founded: 1957. Setting: suburban. Nearest major city is Charlotte, NC. 52-acre campus. 9 buildings on campus. Approved or accredited by Southern Association of Colleges and Schools and Southern Association of Independent Schools. Member of National Association of Independent Schools. Endowment: $4.1 million. Total enrollment: 487. Upper school average class size: 12. Upper school faculty-student ratio: 1:9. There are 175 required school days per year for Upper School students. Upper School students typically attend 5 days per week. The average school day consists of 8 hours.

Upper School Student Profile Grade 9: 42 students (27 boys, 15 girls); Grade 10: 29 students (11 boys, 18 girls); Grade 11: 38 students (23 boys, 15 girls); Grade 12: 32 students (16 boys, 16 girls).

Faculty School total: 67. In upper school: 9 men, 10 women; 15 have advanced degrees.

Subjects Offered Advanced chemistry, advanced math, algebra, American government, American history, American history-AP, American literature, applied music, art, art history-AP, arts appreciation, band, biochemistry, biology, biology-AP, calculus, calculus-AP, career/college preparation, character education, chemistry, chemistry-AP, chorus, college counseling, college placement, college writing, community service, computer education, concert band, creative drama, creative writing, critical thinking, critical writing, cultural arts, debate, drama performance, drawing, drawing and design, earth science, English, English composition, English literature, English literature-AP, European history, fine arts, French, French language-AP, geometry, government/civics, history, jazz band, keyboarding, Latin, Latin-AP, mathematics, modern European history-AP, music, music theory, philosophy, physics, physics-AP, science, Spanish, Spanish language-AP, speech, statistics, statistics-AP, studio art-AP, trigonometry, U.S. government and politics-AP, world history.

Graduation Requirements Algebra, arts and fine arts (art, music, dance, drama), biology, chemistry, English, foreign language, geometry, ancient or European history, one additional lab science, participation in one sport per year.

Special Academic Programs Advanced Placement exam preparation; honors section; independent study; study at local college for college credit; academic accommodation for the gifted and the artistically talented; programs in English, mathematics, general development for dyslexic students.

College Admission Counseling 32 students graduated in 2010; all went to college, including Clemson University; College of Charleston; Furman University; University of Georgia. Mean SAT critical reading: 585, mean SAT math: 604, mean SAT writing: 607. 59% scored over 600 on SAT critical reading, 46% scored over 600 on SAT math.

Student Life Upper grades have specified standards of dress, student council, honor system. Discipline rests primarily with faculty.

Summer Programs Enrichment, sports, art/fine arts, computer instruction programs offered; session focuses on enrichment; held on campus; accepts boys and girls; open to students from other schools. 10 students usually enrolled. 2011 schedule: June 4 to August 4. Application deadline: May 1.

Tuition and Aid Day student tuition: $13,548. Tuition installment plan (monthly payment plans, tuition insurance). Merit scholarship grants, need-based scholarship grants, tuition reduction for children of faculty and staff, tuition reduction for children of benefit-receiving employees of Wofford College, Converse College, UCSUpstate available. In 2010–11, 26% of upper-school students received aid; total upper-school merit-scholarship money awarded: $45,810. Total amount of financial aid awarded in 2010–11: $182,000.

Admissions Traditional secondary-level entrance grade is 9. For fall 2010, 35 students applied for upper-level admission, 26 were accepted, 15 enrolled. ERB, Kaufman Test of Educational Achievement, Metropolitan Test, ITBS, Otis-Lennon School Ability Test, Stanford Achievement Test or writing sample required. Deadline for receipt of application materials: none. Application fee required: $50. On-campus interview recommended.

Athletics Interscholastic: aquatics (boys, girls), baseball (b), basketball (b,g), cheering (g), lacrosse (b), soccer (b,g), swimming and diving (b,g), tennis (b,g), volleyball (g); coed interscholastic: cooperative games, cross-country running, golf, martial arts, physical fitness, track and field, weight training. 4 PE instructors, 8 coaches, 1 athletic trainer.

Computers Computers are regularly used in art, English, history, mathematics classes. Computer network features include on-campus library services, Internet access, wireless campus network, Internet filtering or blocking technology, multimedia presentation stations. Student e-mail accounts are available to students. The school has a published electronic and media policy.

Contact Mrs. Susan J. Jeffords, Director of Admissions. 864-327-0802. Fax: 864-948-0026. E-mail: susan.jeffords@sdsgriffin.org. Web site: www.spartanburgdayschool.org.

THE SPENCE SCHOOL

22 East 91st Street
New York, New York 10128-0657
Head of School: Ellanor N. (Bodie) Brizendine

General Information Girls' day college-preparatory school. Grades K–12. Founded: 1892. Setting: urban. 1 building on campus. Approved or accredited by New York State Association of Independent Schools. Member of National Association of Independent Schools and Secondary School Admission Test Board. Endowment: $72.8 million. Total enrollment: 690. Upper school average class size: 14. Upper school faculty-student ratio: 1:10. There are 159 required school days per year for Upper School students. Upper School students typically attend 5 days per week. The average school day consists of 6 hours.

Upper School Student Profile Grade 9: 60 students (60 girls); Grade 10: 59 students (59 girls); Grade 11: 47 students (47 girls); Grade 12: 54 students (54 girls).

Faculty School total: 124. In upper school: 24 men, 85 women; 77 have advanced degrees.

Subjects Offered Acting, advanced math, African literature, African-American literature, algebra, American literature, art, art history, art-AP, Asian literature, astronomy, biology, calculus, ceramics, chemistry, Chinese history, computer science, critical writing, design, drama, dramatic arts, earth science, English, European history, exercise science, fiber arts, French, geometry, health, history, Indian studies, Japanese history, Latin, Latin American history, Latin American literature, Latin American studies, Mandarin, mathematics, Middle East, music, music composition, non-Western literature, novels, painting, performing arts, photo shop, photography, physical education, physics, poetry, pre-algebra, robotics, science, sculpture, Shakespeare, Spanish, Spanish literature, speech, statistics, technology, theater production, U.S. history, visual and performing arts, women's studies, world religions, world studies.

Graduation Requirements Advanced math, algebra, American literature, art, biology, chemistry, computer science, dance, drama, English, European history, foreign language, geometry, history, music, non-Western societies, physical education (includes health), physics, pre-algebra, science, Shakespeare, speech, technology, U.S. history, visual and performing arts, world religions, world studies.

Special Academic Programs 1 Advanced Placement exam for which test preparation is offered; independent study; term-away projects; study abroad.

College Admission Counseling 56 students graduated in 2010; all went to college, including Duke University; Harvard University; Middlebury College; University of Chicago; University of Pennsylvania; Yale University. Median SAT critical reading: 700, median SAT math: 710, median SAT writing: 740.

Student Life Upper grades have uniform requirement, student council. Discipline rests primarily with faculty.

Tuition and Aid Day student tuition: $36,200. Tuition installment plan (Academic Management Services Plan). Need-based scholarship grants, prepGATE loans, Academic Management Services Private Loans available. In 2010–11, 28% of upper-school students received aid. Total amount of financial aid awarded in 2010–11: $1,870,795.

Admissions Traditional secondary-level entrance grade is 9. For fall 2010, 114 students applied for upper-level admission, 47 were accepted, 17 enrolled. ERB, ISEE and school's own test required. Deadline for receipt of application materials: December 1. Application fee required: $65. On-campus interview required.

Athletics Interscholastic: badminton, basketball, cross-country running, field hockey, lacrosse, soccer, softball, squash, swimming and diving, tennis, track and field, volleyball; intramural: fencing. 8 PE instructors, 18 coaches, 2 athletic trainers.

Computers Computers are regularly used in basic skills, design, independent study, library, library skills, literary magazine, mathematics, news writing, newspaper, programming, publications, research skills, yearbook classes. Computer network features include on-campus library services, online commercial services, Internet access, wireless campus network, Internet filtering or blocking technology. Campus intranet, student e-mail accounts, and computer access in designated common areas are available to students. The school has a published electronic and media policy.

Contact Susan Parker, Director of Admissions. 212-710-8140. Fax: 212-289-6025. E-mail: sparker@spenceschool.org. Web site: www.spenceschool.org.

SPRINGSIDE SCHOOL

8000 Cherokee Street
Philadelphia, Pennsylvania 19118
Head of School: Dr. Priscilla Sands

General Information Girls' day college-preparatory, arts, technology, science, and math school. Grades PK–12. Founded: 1879. Setting: suburban. 30-acre campus. 1 building on campus. Approved or accredited by Pennsylvania Association of Independent Schools and Pennsylvania Department of Education. Member of National Association of Independent Schools and Secondary School Admission Test Board. Endowment: $16 million. Total enrollment: 655. Upper school average class size: 16. Upper school faculty-student ratio: 1:7. There are 174 required school days per year for Upper School students. Upper School students typically attend 5 days per week. The average school day consists of 7 hours and 30 minutes.

Upper School Student Profile Grade 9: 62 students (62 girls); Grade 10: 54 students (54 girls); Grade 11: 70 students (70 girls); Grade 12: 53 students (53 girls).

Faculty School total: 94. In upper school: 8 men, 22 women; 23 have advanced degrees.

Subjects Offered Adolescent issues, Advanced Placement courses, African studies, algebra, American history, American literature, architecture, art, art history, biology, biology-AP, botany, calculus, calculus-AP, chemistry, choral music, community service, comparative government and politics-AP, computer math, computer programming, computer science, creative writing, dance, dance performance, drama, earth science, economics, English, English literature, English-AP, environmental science, European history, European history-AP, expository writing, fine arts, forensics, French, French language-AP, geology, geometry, handbells, jazz ensemble, Latin, Latin-AP, logic, mathematics, Middle Eastern history, music, orchestra, photography, physical education, physics, physics-AP, physiology, science, Shakespeare, social studies, Spanish, Spanish-AP, speech, statistics, statistics-AP, theater, trigonometry, U.S. government and politics-AP, world history-AP, writing, yearbook, yoga.

Graduation Requirements Arts and fine arts (art, music, dance, drama), computer science, English, foreign language, history, mathematics, music, physical education (includes health), science. Community service is required.

Special Academic Programs Advanced Placement exam preparation; honors section; independent study; term-away projects; study abroad.

College Admission Counseling 50 students graduated in 2010; all went to college, including Smith College; University of Pennsylvania. Mean SAT critical reading: 587, mean SAT math: 608, mean SAT writing: 592, mean composite ACT: 26.

Student Life Upper grades have uniform requirement, student council, honor system. Discipline rests equally with students and faculty.

Summer Programs Remediation, enrichment, sports, art/fine arts, computer instruction programs offered; held on campus; accepts boys and girls; open to students from other schools. 180 students usually enrolled. 2011 schedule: June 14 to August 21.

Tuition and Aid Day student tuition: $25,850. Tuition installment plan (monthly payment plans, Higher Education Service, Inc) Merit scholarship grants, need-based scholarship grants available. In 2010–11, 36% of upper-school students received aid; total upper-school merit-scholarship money awarded: $5000. Total amount of financial aid awarded in 2010–11: $1,329,700.

Springside School

Admissions Traditional secondary-level entrance grade is 9. For fall 2010, 77 students applied for upper-level admission, 38 were accepted, 23 enrolled. SSAT required. Deadline for receipt of application materials: January 15. Application fee required: $50. On-campus interview required.

Athletics Interscholastic: basketball, crew, cross-country running, field hockey, golf, independent competitive sports, indoor track, lacrosse, soccer, softball, squash, swimming and diving, tennis, track and field, volleyball; intramural: aerobics, aerobics/dance, badminton, ballet, basketball, dance, fitness, fitness walking, flag football, Frisbee, golf, martial arts, outdoor activities, physical fitness, physical training, power lifting, ropes courses, soccer, softball, ultimate Frisbee, volleyball, weight training, yoga. 4 PE instructors, 6 coaches, 1 athletic trainer.

Computers Computers are regularly used in all academic classes. Computer network features include on-campus library services, online commercial services, Internet access, wireless campus network, Internet filtering or blocking technology. Student e-mail accounts and computer access in designated common areas are available to students. The school has a published electronic and media policy.

Contact Ms. Murielle Telemaque, Admissions Office Manager. 215-247-7007. Fax: 215-247-8628. E-mail: mtelemaque@springside.org. Web site: www.springside.org.

SQUAW VALLEY ACADEMY

235 Squaw Valley Road
Olympic Valley, California 96146
Head of School: Mr. Donald Rees

General Information Coeducational boarding and day college-preparatory and arts school. Grades 8–12. Founded: 1978. Setting: rural. Nearest major city is Reno, NV. Students are housed in dormitories. 3-acre campus. 4 buildings on campus. Approved or accredited by Western Association of Schools and Colleges. Total enrollment: 74. Upper school average class size: 9. Upper school faculty-student ratio: 1:7. Upper School students typically attend 5 days per week. The average school day consists of 8 hours.

Faculty School total: 12. In upper school: 9 men, 3 women; 6 have advanced degrees.

Subjects Offered Addiction, advanced biology, advanced chemistry, advanced math, Advanced Placement courses, advanced TOEFL/grammar, algebra, American democracy, American government, American history, American history-AP, American literature, American literature-AP, anatomy, applied arts, applied music, art, art education, art history, backpacking, band, biology, biology-AP, calculus, calculus-AP, ceramics, chemistry, civics, college admission preparation, college counseling, college placement, college planning, college writing, computer science, computers, creative writing, drama, English, English literature, environmental science, expository writing, fine arts, French, geography, geometry, government/civics, grammar, health, history, history-AP, instruments, Internet, Internet research, jazz, language-AP, linear algebra, literature-AP, martial arts, mathematics, mathematics-AP, music, music appreciation, music history, music performance, music theory, novels, outdoor education, photography, physical education, physics, physics-AP, pre-calculus, psychology, publications, research and reference, SAT preparation, SAT/ACT preparation, science, social sciences, social studies, Spanish, Spanish-AP, student government, student publications, studio art, surfing, swimming, TOEFL preparation, travel, trigonometry, typing, video, visual and performing arts, weight fitness, world history, world history-AP, writing, yearbook, yoga.

Graduation Requirements Arts and fine arts (art, music, dance, drama), English, foreign language, mathematics, outdoor education, physical education (includes health), science, social sciences, social studies (includes history), participation in skiing and snowboarding.

Special Academic Programs 9 Advanced Placement exams for which test preparation is offered; honors section; accelerated programs; independent study; academic accommodation for the gifted, the musically talented, and the artistically talented; programs in English, mathematics for dyslexic students; special instructional classes for students with ADD and dyslexia; ESL (15 students enrolled).

College Admission Counseling 17 students graduated in 2010; all went to college, including Case Western Reserve University; Michigan State University; Penn State University Park; University of California, Santa Cruz; University of Colorado at Boulder; University of Oregon. Median SAT critical reading: 410, median SAT math: 550, median SAT writing: 445, median combined SAT: 1405. 20% scored over 600 on SAT critical reading, 40% scored over 600 on SAT math, 20% scored over 600 on SAT writing, 20% scored over 1800 on combined SAT.

Student Life Upper grades have uniform requirement, student council, honor system. Discipline rests primarily with faculty.

Summer Programs Remediation, enrichment, advancement, ESL, sports, art/fine arts programs offered; session focuses on academics and mountain sports; held both on and off campus; held at Lake Tahoe; accepts boys and girls; open to students from other schools. 25 students usually enrolled. 2011 schedule: July 10 to August 19. Application deadline: none.

Tuition and Aid Day student tuition: $17,010; 7-day tuition and room/board: $40,165. Tuition installment plan (individually arranged payment plans). Tuition reduction for siblings, need-based scholarship grants available.

Admissions Traditional secondary-level entrance grade is 10. Math Placement Exam and writing sample required. Deadline for receipt of application materials: none. Application fee required: $100. Interview required.

Athletics Interscholastic: alpine skiing (boys, girls), freestyle skiing (b,g), golf (b,g), skiing (downhill) (b,g), snowboarding (b,g); intramural: aerobics (b,g), aerobics/ Nautilus (b,g), alpine skiing (b,g), aquatics (b,g), backpacking (b,g), badminton (b,g), bicycling (b,g), billiards (b,g), blading (b,g), bowling (b,g), canoeing/kayaking (b,g), climbing (b,g), combined training (b,g), croquet (b,g), cross-country running (b,g), fishing (b,g), fitness (b,g), fitness walking (b,g), flag football (b,g), fly fishing (b,g), freestyle skiing (b,g), Frisbee (b,g), golf (b,g), hiking/backpacking (b,g), horseback riding (b,g), ice skating (b,g), jogging (b,g), kayaking (b,g), martial arts (b,g), mountain biking (b,g), mountaineering (b,g), nordic skiing (b,g), outdoor activities (b,g), outdoor adventure (b,g), outdoor education (b,g), outdoor recreation (b,g), outdoor skills (b,g), outdoors (b,g), paddling (b,g), paint ball (b,g), physical fitness (b,g), physical training (b,g), rafting (b,g), rock climbing (b,g), ropes courses (b,g), running (b,g), self defense (b,g), skateboarding (b,g), skiing (cross-country) (b,g), skiing (downhill) (b,g), snowboarding (b,g), snowshoeing (b,g), strength & conditioning (b,g), swimming and diving (b,g), table tennis (b,g), tai chi (b,g), telemark skiing (b,g), tennis (b,g), ultimate Frisbee (b,g), volleyball (b,g), walking (b,g), wall climbing (b,g), weight lifting (b,g), weight training (b,g), yoga (b,g); coed interscholastic: alpine skiing, freestyle skiing, golf, skiing (downhill), snowboarding, soccer; coed intramural: aerobics, aerobics/Nautilus, alpine skiing, aquatics, backpacking, badminton, baseball, bicycling, billiards, blading, bowling, canoeing/kayaking, climbing, combined training, croquet, cross-country running, fishing, fitness, fitness walking, flag football, fly fishing, freestyle skiing, Frisbee, golf, hiking/backpacking, horseback riding, ice skating, jogging, kayaking, martial arts, mountain biking, mountaineering, nordic skiing, outdoor activities, outdoor adventure, outdoor education, outdoor recreation, outdoor skills, outdoors, paddling, paint ball, physical fitness, physical training, rafting, rock climbing, ropes courses, running, self defense, skateboarding, skiing (cross-country), skiing (downhill), snowboarding, snowshoeing, soccer, softball, strength & conditioning, swimming and diving, table tennis, tai chi, telemark skiing, tennis, ultimate Frisbee, volleyball, walking, wall climbing, weight lifting, weight training, yoga.

Computers Computers are regularly used in all academic classes. Computer network features include on-campus library services, online commercial services, Internet access, wireless campus network, Internet filtering or blocking technology. Computer access in designated common areas is available to students.

Contact Adrienne Forbes, M.Ed., Admissions Director. 530-583-9393 Ext. 105. Fax: 530-581-1111. E-mail: enroll@sva.org. Web site: www.sva.org.

STANBRIDGE ACADEMY

San Mateo, California
See Special Needs Schools section.

STANSTEAD COLLEGE

450 Dufferin Street
Stanstead, Quebec J0B 3E0, Canada
Head of School: Mr. Michael Wolfe

General Information Coeducational boarding and day college-preparatory and bilingual studies school, affiliated with Christian faith. Grades 7–12. Founded: 1872. Setting: rural. Nearest major city is Montreal, Canada. Students are housed in single-sex dormitories. 720-acre campus. 10 buildings on campus. Approved or accredited by New England Association of Schools and Colleges, Quebec Association of Independent Schools, Standards in Excellence And Learning (SEAL), and Quebec Department of Education. Affiliate member of National Association of Independent Schools. Language of instruction: English. Endowment: CAN$5 million. Total enrollment: 187. Upper school average class size: 12. Upper school faculty-student ratio: 1:8.

Upper School Student Profile Grade 10: 43 students (24 boys, 19 girls); Grade 11: 54 students (31 boys, 23 girls); Grade 12: 31 students (21 boys, 10 girls). 75% of students are boarding students. 45% are province residents. 10 provinces are represented in upper school student body. 38% are international students. International students from China, Germany, Mexico, Republic of Korea, Taiwan, and United States; 10 other countries represented in student body.

Faculty School total: 30. In upper school: 16 men, 14 women; 7 have advanced degrees; 17 reside on campus.

Subjects Offered Algebra, art, biology, calculus, career planning, chemistry, computer programming, computer science, drama, ecology, economics, English, English literature, environmental science, ESL, ethics, French, geography, geometry, history, home economics, mathematics, music, philosophy, physics, political science, psychology, science, social studies, sociology, Spanish, statistics, technology, theater, trigonometry, world history.

Graduation Requirements English, foreign language, mathematics, science, social studies (includes history).

Special Academic Programs Advanced Placement exam preparation; honors section; independent study; study abroad; special instructional classes for students with mild learning disorders; ESL (7 students enrolled).

College Admission Counseling 48 students graduated in 2009; 47 went to college, including Harvard University; Queen's University at Kingston; Stanford University; University of Ottawa; University of Toronto; University of Vermont. Other: 1 entered a postgraduate year.

Student Life Upper grades have uniform requirement, student council, honor system. Discipline rests primarily with faculty.

Tuition and Aid Day student tuition: CAN$18,700; 7-day tuition and room/board: CAN$40,400. Tuition installment plan (monthly payment plans, monthly or term payment plans). Tuition reduction for siblings, merit scholarship grants, need-based scholarship grants, need-based loans available. In 2009–10, 35% of upper-school students received aid; total upper-school merit-scholarship money awarded: CAN$800,000. Total amount of financial aid awarded in 2009–10: CAN$800,000.
Admissions Traditional secondary-level entrance grade is 10. For fall 2009, 130 students applied for upper-level admission, 121 were accepted, 93 enrolled. OLSAT, Stanford Achievement Test or SSAT required. Deadline for receipt of application materials: none. Application fee required: CAN$100. Interview required.
Athletics Interscholastic: basketball (boys, girls), football (b), ice hockey (b,g), rugby (b,g), soccer (b,g), squash (b,g), swimming and diving (b,g), tennis (b,g), track and field (b,g); coed interscholastic: aquatics, cross-country running, golf, skiing (cross-country); coed intramural: aerobics, alpine skiing, backpacking, badminton, basketball, broomball, canoeing/kayaking, curling, dance, equestrian sports, figure skating, fitness, hiking/backpacking, horseback riding, kayaking, life saving, martial arts, nordic skiing, outdoor activities, outdoor education, outdoor recreation, outdoor skills, physical fitness, scuba diving, skiing (cross-country), skiing (downhill), snowboarding, softball, swimming and diving, track and field, volleyball, walking, water polo, weight training. 3 PE instructors, 2 coaches, 1 athletic trainer.
Computers Computers are regularly used in English, mathematics, science classes. Computer network features include on-campus library services, Internet access, wireless campus network, Internet filtering or blocking technology. Student e-mail accounts are available to students. The school has a published electronic and media policy.
Contact Joanne Tracy Carruthers, Director of Admissions. 819-876-2223. Fax: 819-876-5891. E-mail: admissions@stansteadcollege.com. Web site: www.stansteadcollege.com.

THE STANWICH SCHOOL

257 Stanwich Road
Greenwich, Connecticut 06830
Head of School: Mrs. Patricia G. Young
General Information Coeducational day college-preparatory, arts, and technology school. Grades PK–12. Founded: 1998. Approved or accredited by European Council of International Schools and Connecticut Department of Education. Total enrollment: 407. Upper school faculty-student ratio: 1:10. The average school day consists of 8 hours and 30 minutes.
Upper School Student Profile Grade 7: 40 students (24 boys, 16 girls); Grade 8: 50 students (24 boys, 26 girls); Grade 9: 19 students (10 boys, 9 girls).
Faculty School total: 100. In upper school: 5 men, 2 women; 7 have advanced degrees.
Special Academic Programs International Baccalaureate program; 12 Advanced Placement exams for which test preparation is offered; honors section; accelerated programs; independent study; study abroad; academic accommodation for the gifted.
Tuition and Aid Day student tuition: $21,000–$30,000. Tuition installment plan (Insured Tuition Payment Plan, monthly payment plans). Merit scholarship grants, need-based scholarship grants available. Total upper-school merit-scholarship money awarded for 2010–11: $30,000.
Admissions Traditional secondary-level entrance grade is 7. For fall 2010, 36 students applied for upper-level admission, 23 were accepted, 12 enrolled. ISEE required. Deadline for receipt of application materials: January 15. Application fee required: $75. Interview required.
Athletics Interscholastic: baseball (boys), basketball (b), field hockey (g), football (b); intramural: softball (g); coed interscholastic: tennis; coed intramural: dance, fitness, flag football, golf, ice hockey, physical fitness, running.
Computers Computers are regularly used in all classes. Computer network features include on-campus library services, Internet access, wireless campus network, Internet filtering or blocking technology. Student e-mail accounts are available to students. Students grades are available online. The school has a published electronic and media policy.
Contact Ms. May Rawls, Director of Admissions, Grades 4-12. 203-542-0055. Fax: 203-869-4641. E-mail: mrawls@stanwichschool.org. Web site: http://www.stanwichschool.org/.

STARKVILLE ACADEMY

505 Academy Road
Starkville, Mississippi 39759
Head of School: Mr. John "Doc" Stephens
General Information Coeducational day college-preparatory, arts, and technology school. Grades K4–12. Founded: 1970. Setting: small town. Nearest major city is Jackson. 30-acre campus. 5 buildings on campus. Approved or accredited by Mississippi Private School Association, Southern Association of Colleges and Schools, and Southern Association of Independent Schools. Total enrollment: 795. Upper school average class size: 23. Upper school faculty-student ratio: 1:14.

Upper School Student Profile Grade 7: 64 students (32 boys, 32 girls); Grade 8: 67 students (31 boys, 36 girls); Grade 9: 55 students (28 boys, 27 girls); Grade 10: 63 students (31 boys, 32 girls); Grade 11: 40 students (24 boys, 16 girls); Grade 12: 62 students (30 boys, 32 girls).
Faculty School total: 26. In upper school: 9 men, 17 women.
Subjects Offered Advanced chemistry, advanced math, Advanced Placement courses, algebra, American government, American history, anatomy and physiology, art, athletics, baseball, basketball, biology, business mathematics, calculus-AP, cheerleading, chemistry, chemistry-AP, chorus, computer literacy, computer programming, desktop publishing, driver education, earth science, English, environmental science, ethics, foreign language, geography, geometry, government, government/civics, health, honors English, jazz ensemble, library assistant, musical productions, physical science, physics-AP, pre-algebra, public speaking, publications, softball, Spanish, speech, state government, U.S. government, U.S. history, weight-lifting, world geography, world history, yearbook.
Graduation Requirements Computers, English, foreign language, history, mathematics, science, students must take the ACT.
Special Academic Programs Advanced Placement exam preparation; honors section.
College Admission Counseling 60 students graduated in 2009; 59 went to college, including Mississippi State University; University of Mississippi; University of Southern Mississippi. Other: 1 entered military service. Median composite ACT: 22. 20% scored over 26 on composite ACT.
Student Life Upper grades have specified standards of dress, student council. Discipline rests primarily with faculty.
Tuition and Aid Day student tuition: $2910. Tuition installment plan (monthly payment plans). Tuition reduction for siblings available.
Admissions Traditional secondary-level entrance grade is 9. For fall 2009, 30 students applied for upper-level admission, 30 were accepted, 30 enrolled. Admissions testing required. Deadline for receipt of application materials: none. Application fee required: $300. Interview required.
Athletics Interscholastic: baseball (boys, girls), basketball (b,g), cheering (g), cross-country running (b,g), dance team (g), football (b), golf (b,g), soccer (b,g), softball (g), swimming and diving (b,g), tennis (b,g), track and field (b,g); intramural: strength & conditioning (b,g), weight lifting (b). 1 PE instructor, 10 coaches, 1 athletic trainer.
Computers Computers are regularly used in all academic classes. Computer network features include on-campus library services, Internet access. Students grades are available online.
Contact Mrs. Julie MacGown, Secretary. 662-323-7814 Ext. 101. Fax: 662-323-5480. E-mail: jmacgown@starkvilleacademy.org.

STATEN ISLAND ACADEMY

715 Todt Hill Road
Staten Island, New York 10304
Head of School: Mrs. Diane J. Hulse
General Information Coeducational day college-preparatory, arts, and technology school. Grades PK–12. Founded: 1886. Setting: suburban. Nearest major city is New York. 12-acre campus. 7 buildings on campus. Approved or accredited by Middle States Association of Colleges and Schools and New York State Association of Independent Schools. Member of National Association of Independent Schools. Endowment: $4 million. Total enrollment: 400. Upper school average class size: 17. Upper school faculty-student ratio: 1:10. Upper School students typically attend 5 days per week. The average school day consists of 6 hours and 30 minutes.
Upper School Student Profile Grade 9: 42 students (22 boys, 20 girls); Grade 10: 32 students (16 boys, 16 girls); Grade 11: 33 students (16 boys, 17 girls); Grade 12: 37 students (20 boys, 17 girls).
Faculty School total: 58. In upper school: 15 men, 31 women; 35 have advanced degrees.
Subjects Offered Algebra, American history, American literature, anatomy, art, art history, astronomy, biology, calculus, ceramics, chemistry, community service, computer science, creative writing, dance, drama, economics, English, English literature, European history, expository writing, fine arts, French, geometry, grammar, health, human relations, journalism, Latin, law, mathematics, meteorology, music, oceanography, photography, physical education, physical science, physics, psychology, public speaking, robotics, science, social sciences, social studies, Spanish, speech, statistics, theater, trigonometry, visual and performing arts, Web site design, world history, writing.
Graduation Requirements 3-dimensional art, arts and fine arts (art, music, dance, drama), computer science, English, foreign language, human relations, mathematics, physical education (includes health), public speaking, science, science and technology, social sciences, social studies (includes history), senior year internship program. Community service is required.
Special Academic Programs Advanced Placement exam preparation; honors section; independent study; study at local college for college credit; study abroad; academic accommodation for the gifted, the musically talented, and the artistically talented.
College Admission Counseling 37 students graduated in 2009; all went to college, including Cornell University; Dartmouth College; Drew University; New York

University; University of Pennsylvania. Mean SAT critical reading: 612, mean SAT math: 637, mean SAT writing: 627, mean combined SAT: 1876.

Student Life Upper grades have uniform requirement, student council. Discipline rests primarily with faculty.

Tuition and Aid Day student tuition: $20,850–$27,550. Tuition installment plan (monthly payment plans, SML Tuition Plan). Need-based scholarship grants available. In 2009–10, 26% of upper-school students received aid. Total amount of financial aid awarded in 2009–10: $1,000,000.

Admissions Traditional secondary-level entrance grade is 9. For fall 2009, 110 students applied for upper-level admission, 80 were accepted, 20 enrolled. ERB or ISEE required. Deadline for receipt of application materials: January 15. Application fee required: $50. On-campus interview required.

Athletics Interscholastic: baseball (boys), basketball (b,g), lacrosse (g), soccer (b,g), softball (g), tennis (b,g), volleyball (b,g); intramural: baseball (b,g); coed interscholastic: cheering, cross-country running, dance, golf; coed intramural: physical fitness, swimming and diving. 7 PE instructors, 19 coaches.

Computers Computers are regularly used in art, data processing, English, graphic design, independent study, journalism, keyboarding, library, mathematics, newspaper, publications, research skills, SAT preparation, science, social sciences, word processing, writing, yearbook classes. Computer network features include on-campus library services, online commercial services, Internet access, wireless campus network. Campus intranet and student e-mail accounts are available to students. The school has a published electronic and media policy.

Contact Mrs. Linda Shuffman, Director of Admission. 718-303-7803. Fax: 718-979-7641. E-mail: lshuffman@statenislandacademy.org. Web site: www.statenislandacademy.org.

STEPHEN T. BADIN HIGH SCHOOL

571 New London Road
Hamilton, Ohio 45013
Head of School: Mr. Frank Margello

General Information Coeducational day college-preparatory, general academic, arts, business, vocational, and religious studies school, affiliated with Roman Catholic Church. Grades 9–12. Founded: 1966. Setting: urban. Nearest major city is Cincinnati. 22-acre campus. 2 buildings on campus. Approved or accredited by National Catholic Education Association, North Central Association of Colleges and Schools, Ohio Catholic Schools Accreditation Association (OCSAA), and Ohio Department of Education. Endowment: $120,000. Total enrollment: 449. Upper school average class size: 24. Upper school faculty-student ratio: 1:17. There are 181 required school days per year for Upper School students. Upper School students typically attend 5 days per week. The average school day consists of 6 hours and 55 minutes.

Upper School Student Profile Grade 9: 118 students (63 boys, 55 girls); Grade 10: 110 students (65 boys, 45 girls); Grade 11: 105 students (53 boys, 52 girls); Grade 12: 116 students (56 boys, 60 girls). 92% of students are Roman Catholic.

Faculty School total: 32. In upper school: 18 men, 14 women; 19 have advanced degrees.

Subjects Offered Accounting, algebra, American history, American literature, art, band, biology, British literature, calculus, calculus-AP, chemistry, chorus, computer programming, computer resources, computer science, consumer economics, consumer mathematics, drawing and design, economics, English, English literature, English-AP, French, geometry, government/AP, government/civics, grammar, history, integrated science, intro to computers, journalism, Latin, marketing, mathematics, music, music theory, physical education, physical science, physics, physiology, pre-calculus, publications, religion, science, senior science survey, social studies, Spanish, trigonometry, Web site design, Western literature, word processing, world history.

Graduation Requirements Computer science, English, mathematics, physical education (includes health), religion (includes Bible studies and theology), science, social studies (includes history), 10 hours of community service per year.

Special Academic Programs 8 Advanced Placement exams for which test preparation is offered; honors section; study at local college for college credit; study abroad; remedial reading and/or remedial writing; remedial math.

College Admission Counseling 124 students graduated in 2010; 119 went to college, including College of Mount St. Joseph; Miami University; The Ohio State University; University of Cincinnati; Wright State University; Xavier University. Other: 4 went to work, 1 entered military service. Median SAT critical reading: 518, median SAT math: 529, median SAT writing: 522, median combined SAT: 1569, median composite ACT: 23. 19% scored over 600 on SAT critical reading, 21% scored over 600 on SAT math, 18% scored over 600 on SAT writing, 27% scored over 1800 on combined SAT, 31% scored over 26 on composite ACT.

Student Life Upper grades have uniform requirement, student council. Discipline rests primarily with faculty. Attendance at religious services is required.

Tuition and Aid Day student tuition: $7500. Tuition installment plan (monthly payment plans, individually arranged payment plans, quarterly payment plan). Merit scholarship grants, need-based scholarship grants, paying campus jobs available. In 2010–11, 32% of upper-school students received aid; total upper-school merit-scholarship money awarded: $23,000. Total amount of financial aid awarded in 2010–11: $2,950,000.

Admissions Traditional secondary-level entrance grade is 9. Deadline for receipt of application materials: none. No application fee required. On-campus interview recommended.

Athletics Interscholastic: aquatics (boys, girls), baseball (b), basketball (b,g), bowling (b,g), cheering (g), diving (b,g), football (b), golf (b,g), gymnastics (g), hockey (b), soccer (b,g), softball (g), swimming and diving (b,g), tennis (g), volleyball (b,g); coed interscholastic: fishing. 2 PE instructors, 35 coaches, 1 athletic trainer.

Computers Computers are regularly used in drawing and design, mathematics, music, science, Web site design classes. Computer network features include on-campus library services, Internet access, Internet filtering or blocking technology, scanners, travelling laptops, digital cameras. Students grades are available online.

Contact Mrs. Angie Gray, Director of Recruitment. 513-863-3993 Ext. 145. Fax: 513-785-2844. E-mail: agray@mail.badinhs.org. Web site: www.stephen-t-badin.cnd.pvt.k12.oh.us.

STERNE SCHOOL

San Francisco, California
See Special Needs Schools section.

STEVENSON SCHOOL

3152 Forest Lake Road
Pebble Beach, California 93953
Head of School: Mr. Joseph E. Wandke

General Information Coeducational boarding and day college-preparatory, arts, and technology school. Boarding grades 9–12, day grades K–12. Founded: 1952. Setting: suburban. Nearest major city is San Francisco. Students are housed in single-sex by floor dormitories. 70-acre campus. 22 buildings on campus. Approved or accredited by Western Association of Schools and Colleges and California Department of Education. Member of National Association of Independent Schools and Secondary School Admission Test Board. Endowment: $21 million. Total enrollment: 730. Upper school average class size: 14. Upper school faculty-student ratio: 1:10. Upper School students typically attend 5 days per week. The average school day consists of 6 hours.

Upper School Student Profile Grade 9: 114 students (58 boys, 56 girls); Grade 10: 126 students (64 boys, 62 girls); Grade 11: 139 students (73 boys, 66 girls); Grade 12: 152 students (80 boys, 72 girls). 50% of students are boarding students. 71% are state residents. 16 states are represented in upper school student body. 20% are international students. International students from China, Hong Kong, Republic of Korea, Singapore, Taiwan, and Thailand; 10 other countries represented in student body.

Faculty School total: 65. In upper school: 37 men, 17 women; 36 have advanced degrees; 28 reside on campus.

Subjects Offered 3-dimensional art, advanced chemistry, Advanced Placement courses, algebra, American history, American literature, American literature-AP, architecture, art, art history, art-AP, biology, biology-AP, broadcasting, calculus, calculus-AP, ceramics, chemistry, chemistry-AP, computer programming, computer science, concert band, creative writing, dance, dance performance, drama, drama performance, drama workshop, dramatic arts, drawing, drawing and design, driver education, economics, economics-AP, English, English literature, English-AP, environmental science, environmental science-AP, ethics, European civilization, European history, expository writing, fine arts, French, French-AP, geometry, German-AP, government/civics, grammar, history of ideas, history-AP, honors algebra, honors English, honors geometry, honors U.S. history, Japanese, jazz, jazz band, jazz ensemble, jazz theory, journalism, Latin, Latin-AP, macroeconomics-AP, marine biology, mathematics, mathematics-AP, microbiology, music, musical productions, musical theater, ornithology, photography, physical education, physics, physics-AP, portfolio art, pre-calculus, psychology, science, social studies, Spanish, Spanish-AP, speech, stage design, stagecraft, studio art-AP, tap dance, theater, trigonometry, U.S. history-AP, visual and performing arts, visual arts, vocal ensemble, wilderness education, wilderness experience, wind ensemble, world cultures, world history, world literature, world studies, writing, yearbook.

Graduation Requirements Arts and fine arts (art, music, dance, drama), English, foreign language, mathematics, physical education (includes health), science, social studies (includes history).

Special Academic Programs Advanced Placement exam preparation; honors section; independent study; term-away projects; study abroad.

College Admission Counseling 128 students graduated in 2010; 127 went to college, including Boston University; New York University; University of California, Davis; University of California, Los Angeles; University of Oregon; University of Pennsylvania. Median SAT critical reading: 600, median SAT math: 630, median SAT writing: 600, median combined SAT: 1840, median composite ACT: 25. 52% scored over 600 on SAT critical reading, 60% scored over 600 on SAT math, 52% scored over 600 on SAT writing, 58% scored over 1800 on combined SAT, 50% scored over 26 on composite ACT.

Student Life Upper grades have specified standards of dress, student council, honor system. Discipline rests equally with students and faculty.

Summer Programs Enrichment programs offered; held on campus; accepts boys and girls; open to students from other schools. 140 students usually enrolled. 2011 schedule: June 28 to July 30. Application deadline: none.

Tuition and Aid Day student tuition: $28,300; 7-day tuition and room/board: $46,600. Tuition installment plan (Insured Tuition Payment Plan). Need-based scholarship grants available. In 2010–11, 21% of upper-school students received aid. Total amount of financial aid awarded in 2010–11: $2,600,000.

Admissions Traditional secondary-level entrance grade is 9. For fall 2010, 459 students applied for upper-level admission, 220 were accepted, 136 enrolled. SSAT required. Deadline for receipt of application materials: February 15. Application fee required: $75. Interview required.

Athletics Interscholastic: baseball (boys), basketball (b,g), cross-country running (b,g), diving (b,g), field hockey (g), football (b), golf (b,g), lacrosse (b,g), sailing (b,g), soccer (b,g), softball (g), swimming and diving (b,g), tennis (b,g), track and field (b,g), volleyball (g), water polo (b,g); intramural: dance (b,g), golf (b,g), horseback riding (b,g), kayaking (b,g), modern dance (b,g), mountaineering (b,g), outdoor education (b,g), outdoors (b,g), power lifting (b,g), rock climbing (b,g), strength & conditioning (b,g), table tennis (b,g), weight lifting (b,g), wilderness (b,g), yoga (b,g); coed interscholastic: sailing; coed intramural: basketball, bicycling, climbing, dance, equestrian sports, fencing, horseback riding, kayaking, modern dance, mountaineering, outdoor education, outdoors, rock climbing, sailing, softball, strength & conditioning, table tennis, weight lifting, wilderness, yoga. 22 coaches.

Computers Computers are regularly used in all classes. Computer network features include on-campus library services, online commercial services, Internet access, wireless campus network, Internet filtering or blocking technology. Campus intranet and student e-mail accounts are available to students. Students grades are available online. The school has a published electronic and media policy.

Contact Mr. Thomas W. Sheppard, Director of Admission. 831-625-8309. Fax: 831-625-5208. E-mail: info@stevensonschool.org. Web site: www. stevensonschool.org.

STONELEIGH–BURNHAM SCHOOL
574 Bernardston Road
Greenfield, Massachusetts 01301
Head of School: Sally Mixsell

General Information Girls' boarding and day college-preparatory and arts school. Grades 7–PG. Founded: 1869. Setting: small town. Nearest major city is Boston. Students are housed in single-sex dormitories. 100-acre campus. 7 buildings on campus. Approved or accredited by Association of Independent Schools in New England, New England Association of Schools and Colleges, The Association of Boarding Schools, and Massachusetts Department of Education. Member of National Association of Independent Schools. Endowment: $2.8 million. Total enrollment: 140. Upper school average class size: 10. Upper school faculty-student ratio: 1:6. Upper School students typically attend 5 days per week. The average school day consists of 7 hours and 30 minutes.

Upper School Student Profile Grade 7: 16 students (16 girls); Grade 8: 16 students (16 girls); Grade 9: 24 students (24 girls); Grade 10: 28 students (28 girls); Grade 11: 31 students (31 girls); Grade 12: 25 students (25 girls). 71% of students are boarding students. 35% are state residents. 12 states are represented in upper school student body. 38% are international students. International students from China, Japan, Mexico, Republic of Korea, Rwanda, and Taiwan; 7 other countries represented in student body.

Faculty School total: 33. In upper school: 9 men, 24 women; 24 have advanced degrees; 16 reside on campus.

Subjects Offered Acting, Advanced Placement courses, algebra, American history, anatomy, art, astronomy, band, biology, biology-AP, botany, calculus, calculus-AP, ceramics, chemistry, Chinese, conceptual physics, dance, desktop publishing, drama, drawing, ecology, English, English-AP, environmental science-AP, equine science, ESL, ethical decision making, European history, European history-AP, fine arts, French, French-AP, gender issues, geometry, graphic arts, health, history, mathematics, music, music theory, nutrition, photography, physics, poetry, political science, psychology, public speaking, science, senior seminar, social studies, Spanish, Spanish-AP, sports medicine, theater, U.S. history-AP, values and decisions, water color painting, weaving, Web site design, yearbook.

Graduation Requirements Art, arts and fine arts (art, music, dance, drama), English, foreign language, history, mathematics, physical education (includes health), science, U.S. history.

Special Academic Programs Advanced Placement exam preparation; honors section; independent study; ESL (9 students enrolled).

College Admission Counseling 27 students graduated in 2010; all went to college, including Georgetown University; Hamilton College; Mount Holyoke College; Smith College; The George Washington University; Tufts University.

Student Life Upper grades have specified standards of dress, student council, honor system. Discipline rests equally with students and faculty.

Summer Programs Enrichment, ESL, sports, art/fine arts programs offered; session focuses on debate, softball, dance, riding, soccer, academic (math and English); held on campus; accepts girls; open to students from other schools. 210 students usually enrolled. 2011 schedule: June to August. Application deadline: none.

Tuition and Aid Day student tuition: $28,890; 7-day tuition and room/board: $46,180. Tuition installment plan (monthly payment plans). Merit scholarship grants, need-based scholarship grants available. In 2010–11, 22% of upper-school students received aid; total upper-school merit-scholarship money awarded: $20,000. Total amount of financial aid awarded in 2010–11: $904,000.

Admissions Traditional secondary-level entrance grade is 9. For fall 2010, 210 students applied for upper-level admission, 100 were accepted, 60 enrolled. ISEE, SAT, SSAT or TOEFL or SLEP required. Deadline for receipt of application materials: February 15. Application fee required: $50. Interview required.

Athletics Interscholastic: aerobics/dance, ballet, basketball, cross-country running, dance, dressage, equestrian sports, horseback riding, lacrosse, modern dance, soccer, softball, tennis, volleyball; intramural: alpine skiing, fitness, golf, ice skating, skiing (downhill), snowboarding, strength & conditioning. 1 PE instructor, 1 athletic trainer.

Computers Computers are regularly used in all classes. Computer network features include on-campus library services, Internet access, wireless campus network, Internet filtering or blocking technology. Campus intranet, student e-mail accounts, and computer access in designated common areas are available to students. The school has a published electronic and media policy.

Contact Laura Lavallee, Associate Director of Admissions. 413-774-2711 Ext. 257. Fax: 413-772-2602. E-mail: admissions@sbschool.org. Web site: www.sbschool.org.

STONE MOUNTAIN SCHOOL
Black Mountain, North Carolina
See Special Needs Schools section.

THE STONY BROOK SCHOOL
1 Chapman Parkway
Stony Brook, New York 11790
Head of School: Mr. Robert E. Gustafson Jr.

General Information Coeducational boarding and day college-preparatory, arts, and religious studies school, affiliated with Christian faith. Grades 7–12. Founded: 1922. Setting: suburban. Nearest major city is New York. Students are housed in single-sex dormitories. 55-acre campus. 15 buildings on campus. Approved or accredited by Council of Accreditation and School Improvement, Middle States Association of Colleges and Schools, New York State Association of Independent Schools, New York State Board of Regents, The Association of Boarding Schools, and New York Department of Education. Member of National Association of Independent Schools and Secondary School Admission Test Board. Endowment: $10.3 million. Total enrollment: 315. Upper school average class size: 13. Upper school faculty-student ratio: 1:8.

Upper School Student Profile Grade 9: 63 students (39 boys, 24 girls); Grade 10: 51 students (26 boys, 25 girls); Grade 11: 75 students (37 boys, 38 girls); Grade 12: 63 students (31 boys, 32 girls). 60% of students are boarding students. 63% are state residents. 12 states are represented in upper school student body. 20% are international students. International students from Bermuda, Germany, Jamaica, Republic of Korea, Saudi Arabia, and Taiwan; 12 other countries represented in student body.

Faculty School total: 48. In upper school: 24 men, 18 women; 28 have advanced degrees; 39 reside on campus.

Subjects Offered Algebra, American history, American history-AP, ancient history, art, art-AP, Bible, Bible studies, biology, biology-AP, calculus, calculus-AP, ceramics, chamber groups, character education, chemistry, chemistry-AP, chorus, comparative government and politics, concert choir, creative writing, drawing, English, English literature, English-AP, environmental science-AP, ESL, European history, European history-AP, expository writing, fine arts, French, French-AP, general science, geometry, health, history, humanities, instrumental music, instruments, intro to computers, Islamic studies, jazz, jazz band, Jewish studies, Latin, Latin-AP, marine science, mathematics, modern European history, music, orchestra, painting, photography, physical education, physical science, physics, physics-AP, piano, political science, pre-algebra, pre-calculus, psychology, psychology-AP, science, social studies, Spanish, Spanish-AP, statistics-AP, studio art-AP, study skills, theater arts, U.S. government and politics-AP, U.S. history, U.S. history-AP, visual arts, world history, writing.

Graduation Requirements Algebra, arts and fine arts (art, music, dance, drama), Bible, biology, English, European history, foreign language, geometry, Islamic studies, Jewish studies, mathematics, physical education (includes health), science, social studies (includes history), U.S. history.

Special Academic Programs Advanced Placement exam preparation; honors section; independent study; study at local college for college credit; ESL (26 students enrolled).

College Admission Counseling 63 students graduated in 2009; all went to college, including Gordon College; New York University; Rutgers, The State University of New Jersey, New Brunswick; St. John's University; Stony Brook University, State University of New York; University of Pennsylvania. Mean SAT critical reading: 579, mean SAT math: 598, mean SAT writing: 595, mean combined SAT: 1772.

Student Life Upper grades have specified standards of dress, student council, honor system. Discipline rests equally with students and faculty. Attendance at religious services is required.

Tuition and Aid Day student tuition: $22,200; 7-day tuition and room/board: $37,300. Tuition installment plan (monthly payment plans, Tuition Management Systems). Need-based scholarship grants available. In 2009–10, 30% of upper-school students received aid.

Admissions Traditional secondary-level entrance grade is 9. SSAT required. Deadline for receipt of application materials: none. Application fee required. Interview required.

Athletics Interscholastic: baseball (boys), basketball (b,g), cross-country running (b,g), football (b), soccer (b,g), softball (g), tennis (b,g), track and field (b,g), volleyball (g), wrestling (b); intramural: football (b), weight lifting (b,g); coed interscholastic: golf, sailing; coed intramural: flag football, physical fitness. 6 coaches.

Computers Computers are regularly used in Bible studies, English, foreign language, history, mathematics, science classes. Computer network features include Internet access, Internet filtering or blocking technology. Campus intranet and student e-mail accounts are available to students. Students grades are available online. The school has a published electronic and media policy.

Contact Mr. Joseph R. Austin, Director of Admissions. 631-751-1800 Ext. 1. Fax: 631-751-4211. E-mail: admissions@stonybrookschool.org. Web site: www.stonybrookschool.org.

STORM KING SCHOOL

314 Mountain Road
Cornwall-on-Hudson, New York 12520-1899
Head of School: Mrs. Helen S. Chinitz

General Information Coeducational boarding and day college-preparatory and arts school. Grades 8–12. Founded: 1867. Setting: small town. Nearest major city is New York. Students are housed in single-sex dormitories. 55-acre campus. 24 buildings on campus. Approved or accredited by Middle States Association of Colleges and Schools, New York State Association of Independent Schools, The Association of Boarding Schools, and New York Department of Education. Member of National Association of Independent Schools and Secondary School Admission Test Board. Endowment: $1 million. Total enrollment: 140. Upper school average class size: 12. Upper school faculty-student ratio: 1:6. There are 165 required school days per year for Upper School students. Upper School students typically attend 5 days per week. The average school day consists of 9 hours.

Upper School Student Profile Grade 9: 20 students (12 boys, 8 girls); Grade 10: 39 students (23 boys, 16 girls); Grade 11: 35 students (17 boys, 18 girls); Grade 12: 39 students (21 boys, 18 girls). 74% of students are boarding students. 34% are state residents. 9 states are represented in upper school student body. 45% are international students. International students from China, Republic of Korea, Spain, and Taiwan; 9 other countries represented in student body.

Faculty School total: 33. In upper school: 17 men, 16 women; 22 have advanced degrees; 17 reside on campus.

Subjects Offered Acting, Advanced Placement courses, advanced TOEFL/grammar, algebra, American history, American sign language, art, biology, calculus, calculus-AP, ceramics, chemistry, choral music, college counseling, community service, creative writing, dance, drama, drawing, economics, English, English literature, English literature-AP, environmental science, ESL, fine arts, foreign language, geometry, government/civics, guitar, health, history, Mandarin, mathematics, mechanical drawing, music, painting, performing arts, photography, physical education, physics, piano, playwriting, psychology, SAT preparation, science, social studies, Spanish, stagecraft, studio art-AP, theater, world history, writing.

Graduation Requirements English, foreign language, health, Internet, mathematics, performing arts, physical education (includes health), public speaking, science, social studies (includes history), visual arts. Community service is required.

Special Academic Programs Advanced Placement exam preparation; academic accommodation for the musically talented and the artistically talented; remedial reading and/or remedial writing; programs in English, mathematics, general development for dyslexic students; ESL (44 students enrolled).

College Admission Counseling 32 students graduated in 2009; 31 went to college, including State University of New York at New Paltz; Stevens Institute of Technology; University of Michigan. Other: 1 had other specific plans. Median SAT critical reading: 380, median SAT math: 580, median SAT writing: 400. Mean composite ACT: 21.

Student Life Upper grades have specified standards of dress, student council, honor system. Discipline rests equally with students and faculty.

Tuition and Aid Day student tuition: $19,950; 7-day tuition and room/board: $36,950. Tuition installment plan (individually arranged payment plans). Tuition reduction for siblings, merit scholarship grants, need-based scholarship grants available. In 2009–10, 28% of upper-school students received aid; total upper-school merit-scholarship money awarded: $65,000. Total amount of financial aid awarded in 2009–10: $392,800.

Admissions Traditional secondary-level entrance grade is 9. For fall 2009, 180 students applied for upper-level admission, 138 were accepted, 64 enrolled. Admissions testing and TOEFL or SLEP required. Deadline for receipt of application materials: none. Application fee required: $85. Interview required.

Athletics Interscholastic: basketball (boys, girls), lacrosse (b), soccer (b,g), softball (g), volleyball (b,g); coed interscholastic: cross-country running, freestyle skiing, Frisbee, golf, jogging, skiing (downhill), snowboarding, tennis, ultimate Frisbee; coed intramural: aerobics/dance, aerobics/Nautilus, alpine skiing, backpacking, ballet, bicycling, billiards, blading, bocce, bowling, canoeing/kayaking, cheering, climbing, dance, fitness, fitness walking, flag football, freestyle skiing, golf, hiking/backpacking, ice skating, jogging, martial arts, modern dance, mountain biking, Nautilus, outdoor adventure, paddle tennis, paint ball, physical fitness, power lifting,

rafting, rock climbing, ropes courses, running, skiing (cross-country), skiing (downhill), snowboarding, strength & conditioning, table tennis, tai chi, tennis, touch football, track and field, ultimate Frisbee, volleyball, weight lifting, wilderness, yoga. 2 coaches.

Computers Computers are regularly used in drawing and design, yearbook classes. Computer network features include on-campus library services, online commercial services, Internet access, wireless campus network, Parent/student/teacher communication portal. Student e-mail accounts and computer access in designated common areas are available to students. Students grades are available online. The school has a published electronic and media policy.

Contact Mrs. Joanna Evans, Associate Director of Admissions. 845-534-9860 Ext. 236. Fax: 845-534-4128. E-mail: admissions@sks.org. Web site: www.sks.org.

STRAKE JESUIT COLLEGE PREPARATORY

8900 Bellaire Boulevard
Houston, Texas 77036
Head of School: Fr. Dan Lahart, SJ

General Information Boys' day college-preparatory school, affiliated with Roman Catholic Church (Jesuit order). Grades 9–12. Founded: 1960. Setting: suburban. 44-acre campus. 21 buildings on campus. Approved or accredited by Jesuit Secondary Education Association, Southern Association of Colleges and Schools, Texas Catholic Conference, Texas Education Agency, and Texas Department of Education. Endowment: $8 million. Total enrollment: 895. Upper school average class size: 25. Upper school faculty-student ratio: 1:11. There are 180 required school days per year for Upper School students. Upper School students typically attend 5 days per week. The average school day consists of 7 hours.

Upper School Student Profile Grade 9: 235 students (235 boys); Grade 10: 240 students (240 boys); Grade 11: 211 students (211 boys); Grade 12: 209 students (209 boys). 74% of students are Roman Catholic Church (Jesuit order).

Faculty School total: 81. In upper school: 61 men, 20 women; 26 have advanced degrees.

Subjects Offered Accounting, algebra, American history, American literature, art, art history, band, biology, broadcasting, calculus, chemistry, chorus, community service, computer science, debate, drama, drawing, economics, English, English literature, French, geography, geometry, government/civics, health, journalism, Latin, mathematics, music, music theory, oceanography, orchestra, painting, physical education, physical science, physics, physiology, pre-calculus, reading, religion, science, social studies, Spanish, speech, television, theater, theology, trigonometry, video, word processing, world history, world literature.

Graduation Requirements Arts and fine arts (art, music, dance, drama), business skills (includes word processing), computer science, English, foreign language, geography, health, mathematics, physical education (includes health), religion (includes Bible studies and theology), science, social studies (includes history), speech. Community service is required.

Special Academic Programs Advanced Placement exam preparation; honors section; study at local college for college credit.

College Admission Counseling 218 students graduated in 2010; 216 went to college, including Baylor University; Louisiana State University in Shreveport; Texas A&M University; Texas Christian University; The University of Texas at Austin; The University of Texas at San Antonio. Other: 2 had other specific plans. Median SAT critical reading: 630, median SAT math: 650, median SAT writing: 630, median combined SAT: 1900, median composite ACT: 28. 62% scored over 600 on SAT critical reading, 72% scored over 600 on SAT math, 65% scored over 600 on SAT writing, 71% scored over 1800 on combined SAT, 67% scored over 26 on composite ACT.

Student Life Upper grades have specified standards of dress, student council, honor system. Discipline rests primarily with faculty. Attendance at religious services is required.

Summer Programs Remediation, enrichment, sports programs offered; held on campus; accepts boys and girls; open to students from other schools.

Tuition and Aid Day student tuition: $14,450. Tuition installment plan (monthly payment plans). Need-based scholarship grants available. In 2010–11, 14% of upper-school students received aid. Total amount of financial aid awarded in 2010–11: $1,350,000.

Admissions Traditional secondary-level entrance grade is 9. For fall 2010, 552 students applied for upper-level admission, 351 were accepted, 235 enrolled. High School Placement Test (closed version) from Scholastic Testing Service required. Deadline for receipt of application materials: January 15. Application fee required: $50.

Athletics Interscholastic: baseball, basketball, cross-country running, football, golf, lacrosse, rugby, soccer, swimming and diving, tennis, track and field, water polo, wrestling. 4 PE instructors, 33 coaches, 2 athletic trainers.

Computers Computer network features include on-campus library services, online commercial services, Internet access. Student e-mail accounts are available to students. Students grades are available online. The school has a published electronic and media policy.

Contact Mrs. Patti McNeil, Assistant to the Director of Admissions. 713-490-8113. Fax: 713-272-4300. E-mail: pledesma@strakejesuit.org. Web site: www.strakejesuit.org.

STRATFORD ACADEMY

6010 Peake Road
Macon, Georgia 31220-3903
Head of School: Dr. Robert E. Veto
General Information college-preparatory, arts, and technology school. Founded: 1960. Setting: suburban. Nearest major city is Atlanta. 70-acre campus. 3 buildings on campus. Approved or accredited by Georgia Independent School Association, Southern Association of Colleges and Schools, Southern Association of Independent Schools, and Georgia Department of Education. Member of National Association of Independent Schools. Endowment: $1 million. Total enrollment: 948. Upper school average class size: 17. Upper school faculty-student ratio: 1:13. There are 180 required school days per year for Upper School students. Upper School students typically attend 5 days per week. The average school day consists of 6 hours.
Faculty School total: 89. In upper school: 25 men, 22 women; 25 have advanced degrees.
Subjects Offered Advanced Placement courses, algebra, American history, American literature, anatomy, art, art history, art-AP, athletics, baseball, basketball, biology, biology-AP, calculus, calculus-AP, chemistry, chemistry-AP, community service, comparative government and politics-AP, computer programming, computer science, creative writing, drama, drama performance, driver education, earth science, economics, English, English literature, English literature-AP, English-AP, European history, European history-AP, expository writing, French, French-AP, geography, geometry, government/civics, grammar, history, history-AP, humanities, journalism, keyboarding, Latin, Latin-AP, madrigals, mathematics, mathematics-AP, music, physical education, physical science, physics, pre-calculus, science, social sciences, social studies, sociology, Spanish, Spanish-AP, speech, theater, trigonometry, U.S. government and politics-AP, water color painting, world history, world literature, writing.
Graduation Requirements English, foreign language, math applications, mathematics, science, senior seminar, social sciences, social studies (includes history). Community service is required.
Special Academic Programs Advanced Placement exam preparation; independent study; special instructional classes for students with learning disabilities, Attention Deficit Disorder, and dyslexia.
College Admission Counseling 72 students graduated in 2010; all went to college, including Auburn University; Georgia Institute of Technology; Georgia Southern University; Harvard University; University of Georgia; University of Mississippi.
Student Life Upper grades have uniform requirement, student council, honor system. Discipline rests primarily with faculty.
Tuition and Aid Day student tuition: $11,910. Tuition installment plan (Insured Tuition Payment Plan, monthly payment plans, individually arranged payment plans). Merit scholarship grants, need-based scholarship grants available. Total upper-school merit-scholarship money awarded for 2010–11: $11,910.
Admissions Traditional secondary-level entrance grade is 9. ERB required. Deadline for receipt of application materials: none. Application fee required: $50. On-campus interview required.
Athletics Interscholastic: aerobics (girls), aquatics (b,g), baseball (b), basketball (b,g), cheering (g), cross-country running (b,g), dance team (g), drill team (g), football (b), physical training (b,g), soccer (b,g), tennis (b,g), wrestling (b), yoga (g); coed interscholastic: badminton, golf. 8 PE instructors, 6 coaches, 1 athletic trainer.
Computers Computers are regularly used in art, creative writing, English, French, graphics, information technology, Spanish classes. Computer network features include on-campus library services, Internet access, wireless campus network. Computer access in designated common areas is available to students. The school has a published electronic and media policy.
Contact Ms. Marilyn Holton-Walker, Registrar/Admissions Assistant. 478-477-8073 Ext. 205. Fax: 478-477-0299. E-mail: marilyn.walker@stratford.org. Web site: www.stratford.org.

STRATHCONA-TWEEDSMUIR SCHOOL

RR 2
Okotoks, Alberta T1S 1A2, Canada
Head of School: Mr. William Jones
General Information Coeducational day college-preparatory, arts, and technology school. Grades 1–12. Founded: 1905. Setting: rural. Nearest major city is Calgary, Canada. 160-acre campus. 1 building on campus. Approved or accredited by International Baccalaureate Organization, Standards in Excellence And Learning (SEAL), and Alberta Department of Education. Affiliate member of National Association of Independent Schools. Language of instruction: English. Endowment: CAN$5 million. Total enrollment: 670. Upper school average class size: 20. Upper school faculty-student ratio: 1:20. Upper School students typically attend 5 days per week. The average school day consists of 6 hours and 30 minutes.
Upper School Student Profile Grade 6: 44 students (18 boys, 26 girls); Grade 7: 63 students (27 boys, 36 girls); Grade 8: 71 students (41 boys, 30 girls); Grade 9: 74 students (44 boys, 30 girls); Grade 10: 70 students (31 boys, 39 girls); Grade 11: 84 students (35 boys, 49 girls); Grade 12: 83 students (40 boys, 43 girls).
Faculty School total: 80. In upper school: 24 men, 27 women; 15 have advanced degrees.

Subjects Offered Art, band, biology, calculus, chemistry, computer science, drama, English, fine arts, French, Latin, mathematics, music, outdoor education, physical education, physics, science, social sciences, social studies, Spanish, theater.
Graduation Requirements Arts and fine arts (art, music, dance, drama), business skills (includes word processing), English, foreign language, mathematics, physical education (includes health), science, social sciences, social studies (includes history).
Special Academic Programs International Baccalaureate program; term-away projects.
College Admission Counseling 73 students graduated in 2009; all went to college, including Acadia University; Queen's University at Kingston; The University of British Columbia; The University of Western Ontario; University of Calgary; University of Victoria.
Student Life Upper grades have uniform requirement, student council, honor system. Discipline rests primarily with faculty.
Tuition and Aid Day student tuition: CAN$13,530–CAN$16,140. Tuition installment plan (monthly payment plans). Bursaries, need-based scholarship grants available. In 2009–10, 2% of upper-school students received aid. Total amount of financial aid awarded in 2009–10: CAN$37,250.
Admissions CTBS, OLSAT, Henmon-Nelson or SSAT required. Deadline for receipt of application materials: none. Application fee required: CAN$100. Interview required.
Athletics Interscholastic: badminton (boys, girls), basketball (b,g), canoeing/kayaking (b,g), cross-country running (b,g), fencing (b,g), field hockey (g), golf (b,g), hiking/backpacking (b,g), jump rope (b,g), nordic skiing (b,g), outdoor activities (b,g), outdoor education (b,g), rugby (b), soccer (g), telemark skiing (b,g), track and field (b,g), triathlon (b,g), volleyball (b,g), wall climbing (b,g); coed interscholastic: alpine skiing, backpacking, badminton, bicycling, canoeing/kayaking, climbing, cross-country running, hiking/backpacking, jump rope, mountain biking, mountaineering, nordic skiing, outdoor activities, outdoor education; coed intramural: basketball, volleyball. 10 PE instructors, 38 coaches, 2 athletic trainers.
Computers Computers are regularly used in all classes. Computer network features include on-campus library services, online commercial services, Internet access, wireless campus network, Internet filtering or blocking technology. Student e-mail accounts are available to students. Students grades are available online. The school has a published electronic and media policy.
Contact Mr. Bruce Mutch, Director of Admissions. 403-938-8303. Fax: 403-938-4492. E-mail: mutchb@sts.ab.ca. Web site: www.sts.ab.ca.

STRATTON MOUNTAIN SCHOOL

World Cup Circle
Stratton Mountain, Vermont 05155
Head of School: Christopher G. Kaltsas
General Information Coeducational boarding and day college-preparatory, arts, bilingual studies, and technology school. Grades 7–PG. Founded: 1972. Setting: rural. Nearest major city is Albany, NY. Students are housed in single-sex by floor dormitories. 12-acre campus. 7 buildings on campus. Approved or accredited by New England Association of Schools and Colleges and Vermont Department of Education. Member of National Association of Independent Schools. Endowment: $2.4 million. Total enrollment: 120. Upper school average class size: 10. Upper school faculty-student ratio: 1:6. There are 170 required school days per year for Upper School students. Upper School students typically attend 5 days per week. The average school day consists of 5 hours.
Upper School Student Profile Grade 9: 21 students (11 boys, 10 girls); Grade 10: 23 students (11 boys, 12 girls); Grade 11: 19 students (10 boys, 9 girls); Grade 12: 25 students (14 boys, 11 girls); Postgraduate: 4 students (4 boys). 59% of students are boarding students. 46% are state residents. 22 states are represented in upper school student body. 6% are international students. International students from Argentina, Australia, Canada, Italy, Japan, and New Zealand.
Faculty School total: 23. In upper school: 9 men, 9 women; 7 have advanced degrees; 17 reside on campus.
Subjects Offered Algebra, American history, American literature, art, biology, calculus, chemistry, computer science, English, English literature, environmental science, French, geography, geometry, grammar, health, history, journalism, mathematics, nutrition, physical education, physics, science, social studies, Spanish, world history.
Graduation Requirements Arts and fine arts (art, music, dance, drama), computer education, English, foreign language, health education, mathematics, science, social studies (includes history), superior competence in winter sports (skiing/snowboarding). Community service is required.
Special Academic Programs Independent study; ESL (3 students enrolled).
College Admission Counseling 29 students graduated in 2010; 24 went to college, including Dartmouth College; Middlebury College; St. Lawrence University; University of Colorado at Boulder; University of New Hampshire; University of Vermont. Other: 2 went to work, 3 entered a postgraduate year. Mean SAT critical reading: 580, mean SAT math: 570, mean SAT writing: 600, mean combined SAT: 1750. 32% scored over 600 on SAT critical reading, 21% scored over 600 on SAT math, 47% scored over 600 on SAT writing, 42% scored over 1800 on combined SAT.
Student Life Upper grades have specified standards of dress, student council, honor system. Discipline rests primarily with faculty.

Stratton Mountain School

Tuition and Aid Day student tuition: $30,250; 7-day tuition and room/board: $41,500. Tuition installment plan (choice of one or two tuition installments plus advance deposit). Need-based scholarship grants, need-based loans available. In 2010–11, 44% of upper-school students received aid. Total amount of financial aid awarded in 2010–11: $737,000.

Admissions Traditional secondary-level entrance grade is 9. For fall 2010, 71 students applied for upper-level admission, 51 were accepted, 44 enrolled. Mathematics proficiency exam required. Deadline for receipt of application materials: March 15. Application fee required: $100. On-campus interview required.

Athletics Interscholastic: alpine skiing (boys, girls), bicycling (b,g), cross-country running (b,g), freestyle skiing (b,g), golf (b,g), lacrosse (b,g), nordic skiing (b,g), skiing (cross-country) (b,g), skiing (downhill) (b,g), snowboarding (b,g), soccer (b,g), tennis (b,g); intramural: strength & conditioning (b,g), tennis (b,g), yoga (b,g); coed intramural: skateboarding, tennis, yoga. 24 coaches, 1 athletic trainer.

Computers Computers are regularly used in computer applications, graphic design, mathematics, media production, research skills, science, Web site design, yearbook classes. Computer network features include on-campus library services, online commercial services, Internet access, Internet filtering or blocking technology. Student e-mail accounts are available to students. The school has a published electronic and media policy.

Contact Mrs. Kate Nolan Joyce, Director of Admissions. 802-856-1124. Fax: 802-297-0020. E-mail: knolan@gosms.org. Web site: www.gosms.org.

STUART COUNTRY DAY SCHOOL OF THE SACRED HEART

1200 Stuart Road
Princeton, New Jersey 08540-1219
Head of School: Frances de la Chapelle, RSCJ

General Information Coeducational day (boys' only in lower grades) college-preparatory, arts, religious studies, and technology school, affiliated with Roman Catholic Church. Boys grade PS, girls grades PS–12. Founded: 1963. Setting: suburban. 55-acre campus. 1 building on campus. Approved or accredited by Middle States Association of Colleges and Schools, Network of Sacred Heart Schools, New Jersey Association of Independent Schools, and New Jersey Department of Education. Member of National Association of Independent Schools and Secondary School Admission Test Board. Endowment: $8.5 million. Total enrollment: 491. Upper school average class size: 12. Upper school faculty-student ratio: 1:12. There are 161 required school days per year for Upper School students. Upper School students typically attend 5 days per week. The average school day consists of 6 hours.

Upper School Student Profile Grade 9: 36 students (36 girls); Grade 10: 35 students (35 girls); Grade 11: 30 students (30 girls); Grade 12: 33 students (33 girls). 50% of students are Roman Catholic.

Faculty School total: 123. In upper school: 3 men, 39 women; 14 have advanced degrees.

Subjects Offered African studies, algebra, American culture, American literature, anatomy, art, art history, Bible studies, biology, biology-AP, calculus, calculus-AP, ceramics, chemistry, college counseling, communications, community service, computer programming, computer science, conceptual physics, creative writing, dance, drama, drawing and design, economics, English, English literature, English-AP, environmental science, environmental science-AP, ethics, European history, European history-AP, expository writing, film, fine arts, French, French-AP, geometry, government/civics, handbells, health education, independent study, Latin, Latin-AP, mathematics, music, music history, music theory, philosophy, photography, physical education, physical fitness, physics, physics-AP, physiology, portfolio art, pre-calculus, probability and statistics, religion, religious studies, science, senior project, social studies, Spanish, Spanish-AP, speech, stagecraft, studio art, studio art-AP, theater, theology, trigonometry, U.S. history, U.S. history-AP, visual arts, vocal ensemble, world cultures, world literature, world religions, writing.

Graduation Requirements Arts and fine arts (art, music, dance, drama), computer science, English, foreign language, history, lab science, mathematics, physical education (includes health), religious studies, 50 hours of community service per year for each year of high school.

Special Academic Programs Advanced Placement exam preparation; honors section; accelerated programs; independent study; term-away projects; study at local college for college credit; study abroad.

College Admission Counseling 40 students graduated in 2009; all went to college, including Cornell University; Georgetown University; Princeton University; Villanova University; Yale University. Mean composite ACT: 28. 76% scored over 26 on composite ACT.

Student Life Upper grades have specified standards of dress, student council, honor system. Discipline rests equally with students and faculty. Attendance at religious services is required.

Tuition and Aid Day student tuition: $28,040. Tuition installment plan (Academic Management Services Plan). Merit scholarship grants, need-based scholarship grants, prepGATE loans available. In 2009–10, 21% of upper-school students received aid; total upper-school merit-scholarship money awarded: $63,000. Total amount of financial aid awarded in 2009–10: $895,000.

Admissions Traditional secondary-level entrance grade is 9. For fall 2009, 51 students applied for upper-level admission, 33 were accepted, 15 enrolled. SSAT

required. Deadline for receipt of application materials: January 30. Application fee required: $75. On-campus interview required.

Athletics Interscholastic: aerobics/dance, basketball, cross-country running, dance, field hockey, fitness, golf, independent competitive sports, lacrosse, squash, tennis, track and field; intramural: basketball, dance, fitness. 2 PE instructors, 16 coaches, 1 athletic trainer.

Computers Computers are regularly used in all academic classes. Computer network features include on-campus library services, Internet access, wireless campus network, Internet filtering or blocking technology. Student e-mail accounts and computer access in designated common areas are available to students. Students grades are available online. The school has a published electronic and media policy.

Contact Stephanie Lupero, Director of Admissions. 609-921-2330 Ext. 235. Fax: 609-497-0784. E-mail: slupero@stuartschool.org. Web site: www.stuartschool.org.

STUART HALL

235 West Frederick Street
PO Box 210
Staunton, Virginia 24401
Head of School: Mr. Mark H. Eastham

General Information Girls' boarding and coeducational day college-preparatory and arts school, affiliated with Episcopal Church. Boarding girls grades 8–12, day boys grades PK–12, day girls grades PK–12. Founded: 1844. Setting: small town. Nearest major city is Richmond. Students are housed in single-sex dormitories. 8-acre campus. 6 buildings on campus. Approved or accredited by National Association of Episcopal Schools, Virginia Association of Independent Schools, and Virginia Department of Education. Member of National Association of Independent Schools and Secondary School Admission Test Board. Endowment: $900,000. Total enrollment: 289. Upper school average class size: 10. Upper school faculty-student ratio: 1:12. There are 172 required school days per year for Upper School students. Upper School students typically attend 5 days per week. The average school day consists of 6 hours and 20 minutes.

Upper School Student Profile Grade 9: 17 students (4 boys, 13 girls); Grade 10: 26 students (9 boys, 17 girls); Grade 11: 27 students (5 boys, 22 girls); Grade 12: 35 students (12 boys, 23 girls). 30% of students are boarding students. 82% are state residents. 9 states are represented in upper school student body. 17% are international students. International students from China, Republic of Korea, and Rwanda; 5 other countries represented in student body. 25% of students are members of Episcopal Church.

Faculty School total: 40. In upper school: 12 men, 12 women; 16 have advanced degrees; 4 reside on campus.

Subjects Offered Algebra, American literature, ancient world history, applied arts, applied music, art appreciation, art history, biology, biology-AP, British literature, calculus-AP, career education, career/college preparation, ceramics, chamber groups, chemistry, chemistry-AP, choir, choral music, chorus, civics, college counseling, composition, creative writing, drama, drama performance, dramatic arts, English, English composition, English language and composition-AP, English literature-AP, English-AP, environmental science, environmental science-AP, ESL, fine arts, French, French language-AP, geometry, grammar, guitar, health education, history of drama, history of music, history-AP, honors algebra, honors English, honors geometry, honors world history, instrumental music, lab science, language and composition, learning lab, mathematics, modern world history, music, music composition, music history, music performance, music theater, music theory, philosophy, photography, physical education, physical fitness, physics, piano, playwriting and directing, portfolio art, pre-algebra, pre-calculus, probability and statistics, religion, SAT preparation, science, social studies, Spanish, Spanish language-AP, Spanish-AP, stage and body movement, stage design, strings, student government, student publications, study skills, theater, theater arts, theater history, theater production, trigonometry, U.S. government, U.S. government and politics-AP, U.S. history, U.S. history-AP, visual and performing arts, visual arts, vocal ensemble, vocal music, voice, voice ensemble, world geography, world history, world history-AP, world literature, yearbook.

Graduation Requirements Arts and fine arts (art, music, dance, drama), English, foreign language, mathematics, philosophy, physical education (includes health), religion (includes Bible studies and theology), SAT preparation, science, social studies (includes history).

Special Academic Programs Advanced Placement exam preparation; honors section; study at local college for college credit; academic accommodation for the gifted, the musically talented, and the artistically talented; ESL (10 students enrolled).

College Admission Counseling 26 students graduated in 2009; all went to college, including Brandeis University; New England Conservatory of Music; Roanoke College; University of Virginia; Virginia Military Institute; Virginia Polytechnic Institute and State University. Mean SAT critical reading: 577, mean SAT math: 567, mean SAT writing: 561.

Student Life Upper grades have specified standards of dress, student council, honor system. Discipline rests equally with students and faculty.

Tuition and Aid Day student tuition: $12,140; 5-day tuition and room/board: $35,445; 7-day tuition and room/board: $38,555. Tuition installment plan (Academic Management Services Plan, monthly payment plans, individually arranged payment plans). Need-based scholarship grants available. In 2009–10, 33% of upper-school students received aid. Total amount of financial aid awarded in 2009–10: $767,425.

Admissions Traditional secondary-level entrance grade is 10. For fall 2009, 60 students applied for upper-level admission, 30 were accepted, 17 enrolled. TOEFL or SLEP required. Deadline for receipt of application materials: none. Application fee required: $45. Interview required.

Athletics Interscholastic: basketball (boys, girls), cheering (g), golf (b,g), horseback riding (b,g), jogging (b,g), lacrosse (b,g), soccer (b,g), swimming and diving (b,g), tennis (b,g), track and field (b,g), volleyball (g); intramural: cheering (g), skiing (downhill) (b,g), snowboarding (b,g); coed interscholastic: cross-country running, lacrosse, running, soccer; coed intramural: golf. 2 PE instructors, 9 coaches.

Computers Computers are regularly used in all classes. Computer network features include on-campus library services, Internet access, wireless campus network, Internet filtering or blocking technology. Student e-mail accounts and computer access in designated common areas are available to students. The school has a published electronic and media policy.

Contact Mrs. Mia Kivlighan, Associate Director of Enrollment Management. 888-306-8926. Fax: 540-886-2275. E-mail: mkivlighan@stuart-hall.org. Web site: www.stuart-hall.org.

STU'ATE LELUM SECONDARY SCHOOL

Box 730
Ladysmith, British Columbia V9G1A5, Canada
Head of School: Len Merriman

General Information Coeducational day college-preparatory, general academic, and vocational school. Grades 8–12. Founded: 1985. Setting: small town. Nearest major city is Nanaimo, Canada. 10-acre campus. 5 buildings on campus. Approved or accredited by British Columbia Department of Education. Language of instruction: English. Upper school average class size: 20. Upper school faculty-student ratio: 1:15. There are 120 required school days per year for Upper School students. Upper School students typically attend 5 days per week. The average school day consists of 5 hours.

Faculty School total: 8. In upper school: 3 men, 4 women; 1 has an advanced degree.

Subjects Offered Advanced biology, biology.

Graduation Requirements 1968.

Student Life Upper grades have student council, honor system. Discipline rests primarily with faculty.

Admissions CAT 2 required. Deadline for receipt of application materials: none. No application fee required. Interview required.

Contact Bev Knight, Student Services Coordinator. 250-245-3522. Fax: 250-245-8263. E-mail: bev.knight@cfnation.com. Web site: www.stuatelelum.com.

SUBIACO ACADEMY

405 North Subiaco Avenue
Subiaco, Arkansas 72865
Head of School: Mr. Michael Burke

General Information Boys' boarding and day college-preparatory, arts, religious studies, bilingual studies, technology, and art and performing art school, affiliated with Roman Catholic Church. Grades 7–12. Founded: 1887. Setting: small town. Nearest major city is Little Rock. Students are housed in single-sex dormitories. 100-acre campus. 10 buildings on campus. Approved or accredited by Headmasters' Conference, Independent Schools Association of the Central States, Midwest Association of Boarding Schools, National Catholic Education Association, North Central Association of Colleges and Schools, The Association of Boarding Schools, and Arkansas Department of Education. Member of National Association of Independent Schools. Endowment: $3.5 million. Total enrollment: 172. Upper school average class size: 12. Upper school faculty-student ratio: 1:10. There are 180 required school days per year for Upper School students. Upper School students typically attend 5 days per week. The average school day consists of 7 hours and 30 minutes.

Upper School Student Profile Grade 8: 16 students (16 boys); Grade 9: 37 students (37 boys); Grade 10: 40 students (40 boys); Grade 11: 41 students (41 boys); Grade 12: 38 students (38 boys). 24% of students are boarding students. 40% are state residents. 16 states are represented in upper school student body. 24% are international students. International students from China, Mexico, Netherlands Antilles, Republic of Korea, Russian Federation, and Spain. 70% of students are Roman Catholic.

Faculty School total: 24. In upper school: 16 men, 8 women; 2 reside on campus.

Subjects Offered Algebra, American history, American history-AP, American literature, anthropology, art, art-AP, band, biology, biology AP, calculus, calculus-AP, chemistry, chemistry-AP, choral music, chorus, Christian and Hebrew scripture, Christian doctrine, Christian education, Christian scripture, Christian studies, Christian testament, church history, communications, computer art, computer science, drama, drama workshop, driver education, earth and space science, earth science, economics, English, English literature, English literature and composition-AP, English-AP, European history, finance, fine arts, geography, geometry, government/civics, international relations, jazz ensemble, journalism, Latin, Latin-AP, mathematics-AP, music, physical education, physics, piano, psychology, religion, sociology, Spanish, Spanish language-AP, speech, statistics-AP, Western civilization, world history.

Graduation Requirements Arts and fine arts (art, music, dance, drama), computer science, English, foreign language, mathematics, physical education (includes health), religion (includes Bible studies and theology), science, social studies (includes

history), Western civilization, a student must complete at least two (2) years at Subiaco Academy to graduate. Community service is required.

Special Academic Programs 9 Advanced Placement exams for which test preparation is offered; honors section; academic accommodation for the gifted, the musically talented, and the artistically talented; ESL (15 students enrolled).

College Admission Counseling 37 students graduated in 2009; all went to college, including Arkansas State University—Jonesboro; Texas A&M University–Commerce; The University of Texas at Austin; University of Arkansas.

Student Life Upper grades have uniform requirement, student council. Discipline rests primarily with faculty. Attendance at religious services is required.

Tuition and Aid Day student tuition: $5600; 5-day tuition and room/board: $17,100; 7-day tuition and room/board: $18,500. Tuition installment plan (monthly payment plans, individually arranged payment plans). Need-based scholarship grants, paying campus jobs available. In 2009–10, 35% of upper-school students received aid.

Admissions Traditional secondary-level entrance grade is 10. SSAT or TOEFL or SLEP required. Deadline for receipt of application materials: July 1. Application fee required: $50. Interview required.

Athletics Interscholastic: baseball, basketball, cross-country running, football, golf, soccer; intramural: archery, backpacking, baseball, basketball, bicycling, billiards, blading, bowling, canoeing/kayaking, cheering, climbing, cross-country running, diving, fishing, fitness, fly fishing, football, Frisbee, golf, handball, hiking/backpacking, horseshoes, in-line skating, indoor soccer, jogging, kayaking, marksmanship, outdoor activities, physical fitness, physical training, power lifting, riflery, rock climbing, roller blading, running, skateboarding, skeet shooting, skiing (downhill), soccer, softball, strength & conditioning. 1 PE instructor, 12 coaches.

Computers Computers are regularly used in art, Christian doctrine, commercial art, creative writing, desktop publishing, digital applications, drawing and design, economics, English, geography, graphic arts, history, journalism, keyboarding, literary magazine, mathematics, news writing, newspaper, photography, photojournalism, publications, religion, religious studies, SAT preparation, science, Spanish, stock market, video film production, word processing, writing, yearbook classes. Computer network features include Internet access, wireless campus network, Internet filtering or blocking technology. Computer access in designated common areas is available to students. Students grades are available online. The school has a published electronic and media policy.

Contact Ms. Evelyn Bauer, Assistant Director of Admissions. 800-364-7824. Fax: 479-934-1033. E-mail: ebauer@subi.org. Web site: www.subi.org.

THE SUDBURY VALLEY SCHOOL

2 Winch Street
Framingham, Massachusetts 01701
Head of School: Michael Sadofsky

General Information Coeducational day college-preparatory and general academic school. Grades PS–12. Founded: 1968. Setting: suburban. Nearest major city is Boston. 10-acre campus. 2 buildings on campus. Approved or accredited by Massachusetts Department of Education. Total enrollment: 160. Upper school faculty-student ratio: 1:16. There are 180 required school days per year for Upper School students. Upper School students typically attend 5 days per week. The average school day consists of 6 hours.

Faculty School total: 9. In upper school: 4 men, 5 women; 3 have advanced degrees.

Subjects Offered Algebra, American history, American literature, anatomy, anthropology, archaeology, art, art history, Bible studies, biology, botany, business, calculus, ceramics, chemistry, computer programming, computer science, creative writing, dance, drama, economics, English, English literature, ethics, European history, expository writing, French, geography, geometry, German, government/civics, grammar, Hebrew, history, history of ideas, history of science, home economics, Latin, mathematics, music, philosophy, photography, physical education, physics, physiology, psychology, religion, social studies, Spanish, speech, theater, trigonometry, typing, world history, world literature, writing.

Graduation Requirements Students must successfully defend the thesis that they have taken responsibility for preparing themselves to be an effective adult in the community.

Special Academic Programs Independent study.

College Admission Counseling 15 students graduated in 2010; 9 went to college. Other: 3 went to work, 3 had other specific plans.

Student Life Upper grades have student council, honor system. Discipline rests equally with students and faculty.

Tuition and Aid Day student tuition: $7000.

Admissions Deadline for receipt of application materials: none. Application fee required: $30. On-campus interview required.

Computers Computer network features include on-campus library services, Internet access. Student e-mail accounts are available to students. The school has a published electronic and media policy.

Contact Hanna Greenberg, Admissions Clerk. 508-877-3030. Fax: 508-788-0674. E-mail: office@sudval.org. Web site: www.sudval.org.

Suffield Academy

SUFFIELD ACADEMY
185 North Main Street
Suffield, Connecticut 06078
Head of School: Charles Cahn III

General Information Coeducational boarding and day college-preparatory, arts, technology, and leadership school. Grades 9–PG. Founded: 1833. Setting: small town. Nearest major city is Hartford. Students are housed in single-sex dormitories. 340-acre campus. 49 buildings on campus. Approved or accredited by Connecticut Association of Independent Schools, New England Association of Schools and Colleges, and The Association of Boarding Schools. Member of National Association of Independent Schools and Secondary School Admission Test Board. Endowment: $29 million. Total enrollment: 412. Upper school average class size: 10. Upper school faculty-student ratio: 1:5. There are 180 required school days per year for Upper School students. Upper School students typically attend 6 days per week. The average school day consists of 5 hours and 35 minutes.

Upper School Student Profile Grade 9: 59 students (30 boys, 29 girls); Grade 10: 112 students (53 boys, 59 girls); Grade 11: 124 students (77 boys, 47 girls); Grade 12: 117 students (66 boys, 51 girls); Postgraduate: 12 students (12 boys). 66% of students are boarding students. 36% are state residents. 15 states are represented in upper school student body. 21% are international students. International students from Bermuda, China, Italy, Republic of Korea, Spain, and Thailand; 27 other countries represented in student body.

Faculty School total: 82. In upper school: 40 men, 28 women; 51 have advanced degrees; 65 reside on campus.

Subjects Offered Acting, Advanced Placement courses, algebra, American history, American literature, anatomy and physiology, archaeology, art, art history, biology, biology-AP, calculus, calculus-AP, ceramics, chemistry, chemistry-AP, Chinese, computer math, computer programming, computer science, constitutional law, dance, drama, economics, economics-AP, English, English literature, English-AP, environmental science, ESL, ethics, European history, expository writing, fine arts, French, French-AP, geometry, government-AP, government/civics, grammar, health, history, jazz band, leadership, mathematics, mechanical drawing, music, music theory, news writing, philosophy, photography, physical education, physics, physics-AP, probability and statistics, religion, science, senior seminar, short story, social studies, sociology, Spanish, Spanish-AP, statistics, statistics-AP, technology, theater, theater arts, trigonometry, U.S. history, U.S. history-AP, visual and performing arts, visual arts, voice ensemble, wilderness education, wind ensemble, wind instruments, woodworking, world history, writing.

Graduation Requirements Arts and fine arts (art, music, dance, drama), English, foreign language, leadership, mathematics, physical education (includes health), religion (includes Bible studies and theology), science, social studies (includes history), technology portfolio.

Special Academic Programs 17 Advanced Placement exams for which test preparation is offered; honors section; independent study; academic accommodation for the gifted, the musically talented, and the artistically talented; ESL (12 students enrolled).

College Admission Counseling 117 students graduated in 2010; all went to college, including Amherst College; Bates College; Boston University; Union College; Wheaton College. Mean SAT critical reading: 553, mean SAT math: 577, mean SAT writing: 554, mean combined SAT: 1684, mean composite ACT: 24. 27% scored over 600 on SAT critical reading, 43% scored over 600 on SAT math, 30% scored over 600 on SAT writing, 33% scored over 1800 on combined SAT, 52% scored over 26 on composite ACT.

Student Life Upper grades have specified standards of dress, student council, honor system. Discipline rests primarily with faculty.

Summer Programs Enrichment, ESL, art/fine arts, computer instruction programs offered; session focuses on academics; held on campus; accepts boys and girls; open to students from other schools. 125 students usually enrolled. 2011 schedule: June 26 to July 29. Application deadline: June 1.

Tuition and Aid Day student tuition: $31,550; 7-day tuition and room/board: $44,500. Tuition installment plan (monthly payment plans). Need-based scholarship grants, tuition remission for children of faculty and staff who meet years of service requirement available. In 2010–11, 33% of upper-school students received aid. Total amount of financial aid awarded in 2010–11: $3,500,000.

Admissions Traditional secondary-level entrance grade is 9. For fall 2010, 828 students applied for upper-level admission, 314 were accepted, 133 enrolled. PSAT or SAT, SSAT or TOEFL required. Deadline for receipt of application materials: January 15. Application fee required: $50. Interview required.

Athletics Interscholastic: aquatics (boys, girls), baseball (b), basketball (b,g), cross-country running (b,g), field hockey (g), football (b), lacrosse (b,g), soccer (b,g), softball (g), squash (b,g), swimming and diving (b,g), tennis (b,g), track and field (b,g), volleyball (g), water polo (b,g); coed interscholastic: alpine skiing, backpacking, canoeing/kayaking, climbing, dance, diving, fitness, golf, outdoors, riflery, rock climbing, ropes courses, skiing (downhill), snowboarding, wrestling; coed intramural: rock climbing, ropes courses, weight lifting. 3 coaches, 2 athletic trainers.

Computers Computers are regularly used in architecture, art, English, foreign language, history, mathematics, science classes. Computer network features include on-campus library services, online commercial services, Internet access, wireless campus network. Student e-mail accounts are available to students. The school has a published electronic and media policy.

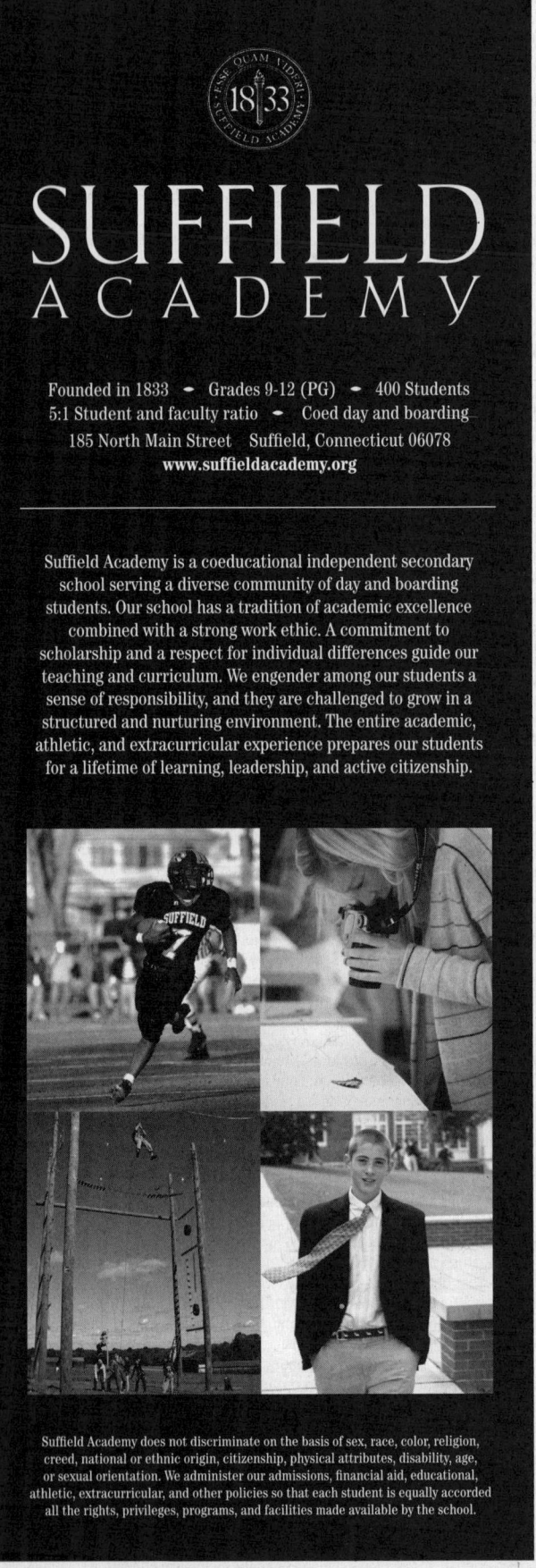

SUFFIELD ACADEMY

Founded in 1833 ♦ Grades 9-12 (PG) ♦ 400 Students
5:1 Student and faculty ratio ♦ Coed day and boarding
185 North Main Street   Suffield, Connecticut 06078
www.suffieldacademy.org

Suffield Academy is a coeducational independent secondary school serving a diverse community of day and boarding students. Our school has a tradition of academic excellence combined with a strong work ethic. A commitment to scholarship and a respect for individual differences guide our teaching and curriculum. We engender among our students a sense of responsibility, and they are challenged to grow in a structured and nurturing environment. The entire academic, athletic, and extracurricular experience prepares our students for a lifetime of learning, leadership, and active citizenship.

Contact Terry Breault, Director of Admissions and Financial Aid. 860-386-4440. Fax: 860-668-2966. E-mail: saadmit@suffieldacademy.org. Web site: www. suffieldacademy.org.

See Display on page 644 and Close-Up on page 848.

SUMMERFIELD WALDORF SCHOOL

655 Willowside Road
Santa Rosa, California 95401
Head of School: Ms. Renate Lundberg
General Information Coeducational day college-preparatory, arts, and Waldorf curriculum school. Grades 1–12. Founded: 1974. Setting: rural. 38-acre campus. 8 buildings on campus. Approved or accredited by Association of Waldorf Schools of North America, Western Association of Schools and Colleges, and California Department of Education. Total enrollment: 390. Upper school average class size: 28. Upper school faculty-student ratio: 1:7. Upper School students typically attend 5 days per week. The average school day consists of 7 hours.
Upper School Student Profile Grade 9: 29 students (8 boys, 21 girls); Grade 10: 28 students (13 boys, 15 girls); Grade 11: 19 students (9 boys, 10 girls); Grade 12: 19 students (6 boys, 13 girls).
Faculty School total: 23. In upper school: 11 men, 12 women; all have advanced degrees.
Subjects Offered Advanced chemistry, arts, history, humanities, literature, mathematics, music, science.
Graduation Requirements Humanities, Senior Thesis Project.
Special Academic Programs Honors section; study abroad.
College Admission Counseling 24 students graduated in 2010; 21 went to college, including Bard College; Rhode Island School of Design; University of California, Berkeley; University of California, San Diego; University of California, Santa Cruz; University of Colorado at Boulder. Other: 2 went to work, 1 entered a postgraduate year.
Student Life Upper grades have specified standards of dress, student council. Discipline rests primarily with faculty.
Tuition and Aid Day student tuition: $15,900. Tuition installment plan (FACTS Tuition Payment Plan, monthly payment plans). Tuition reduction for siblings, need-based scholarship grants available. In 2010–11, 40% of upper-school students received aid.
Admissions Traditional secondary-level entrance grade is 9. For fall 2010, 34 students applied for upper-level admission, 30 were accepted, 30 enrolled. Deadline for receipt of application materials: January 14. Application fee required: $75. On-campus interview required.
Athletics Interscholastic: baseball (boys), basketball (b,g), soccer (b,g); intramural: volleyball (b,g); coed interscholastic: tennis. 2 PE instructors, 5 coaches.
Computers The school has a published electronic and media policy.
Contact Ms. Sallie Miller, Admissions Director. 707-575-7194 Ext. 102. Fax: 707-575-3217. E-mail: sallie@summerfieldwaldof.org. Web site: www. summerfieldwaldorf.org.

THE SUMMIT COUNTRY DAY SCHOOL

2161 Grandin Road
Cincinnati, Ohio 45208-3300
Head of School: Dr. Jerry Jellig
General Information Coeducational day college-preparatory school, affiliated with Roman Catholic Church. Grades PK–12. Founded: 1890. Setting: suburban. 24-acre campus. 2 buildings on campus. Approved or accredited by Independent Schools Association of the Central States, Ohio Association of Independent Schools, The College Board, and Ohio Department of Education. Member of Secondary School Admission Test Board. Endowment: $11 million. Total enrollment: 1,094. Upper school average class size: 16. Upper school faculty-student ratio: 1:9. There are 187 required school days per year for Upper School students. Upper School students typically attend 5 days per week. The average school day consists of 6 hours and 30 minutes.
Upper School Student Profile Grade 9: 103 students (48 boys, 55 girls); Grade 10: 98 students (41 boys, 57 girls); Grade 11: 100 students (56 boys, 44 girls); Grade 12: 88 students (52 boys, 36 girls). 60% of students are Roman Catholic.
Faculty School total: 136. In upper school: 14 men, 23 women; 31 have advanced degrees.
Subjects Offered 1968, Advanced Placement courses, algebra, American history, American history-AP, American literature, anatomy and physiology, archaeology, area studies, art, Basic programming, Bible studies, biology, biology-AP, business, business law, calculus, calculus-AP, ceramics, chemistry, chemistry-AP, chorus, college admission preparation, college placement, community service, computer applications, computer programming, computer science, computer science-AP, concert choir, creative writing, critical studies in film, critical thinking, drama, earth science, economics, English, English literature, English-AP, environmental science, European history, European history-AP, expository writing, fine arts, French, French-AP, geometry, government-AP, government/civics, grammar, graphic design, health, history, history of science, history-AP, Holocaust studies, language-AP, Latin, Latin-AP, leadership, leadership and service, leadership education training, literary

magazine, mathematics, music, music theory-AP, music-AP, philosophy, physical education, physics, physics-AP, pre-calculus, psychology, psychology-AP, public speaking, religion, religious studies, science, senior career experience, service learning/internship, social studies, Spanish, Spanish language-AP, Spanish-AP, speech, speech communications, statistics-AP, student government, studio art, studio art-AP, study skills, theater, theology, trigonometry, U.S. government and politics-AP, world history, world history-AP, world literature, world religions, writing.
Graduation Requirements Arts and fine arts (art, music, dance, drama), computer applications, computer science, English, foreign language, mathematics, physical education (includes health), religion (includes Bible studies and theology), science, social sciences, social studies (includes history), speech communications, junior year leadership course (one semester), junior year speech course, 40 hours of Christian service, senior search (2-week field experience in career of interest area).
Special Academic Programs 19 Advanced Placement exams for which test preparation is offered; honors section; independent study; study abroad; academic accommodation for the gifted.
College Admission Counseling 94 students graduated in 2009; all went to college, including Boston University; Miami University; The Ohio State University; Washington University in St. Louis; Xavier University. Median SAT critical reading: 631, median SAT math: 609, median composite ACT: 28.
Student Life Upper grades have uniform requirement, student council, honor system. Discipline rests equally with students and faculty. Attendance at religious services is required.
Tuition and Aid Day student tuition: $1700–$17,500. Tuition installment plan (monthly payment plans, individually arranged payment plans). Merit scholarship grants, need-based scholarship grants available. In 2009–10, 50% of upper-school students received aid.
Admissions Traditional secondary-level entrance grade is 9. For fall 2009, 80 students applied for upper-level admission, 72 were accepted, 47 enrolled. High School Placement Test or ISEE required. Deadline for receipt of application materials: December 18. Application fee required: $50. On-campus interview recommended.
Athletics Interscholastic: baseball (boys, girls), basketball (b,g), bowling (b,g), cheering (g), cross-country running (b,g), diving (b,g), field hockey (g), football (b), golf (b,g), lacrosse (b), soccer (b,g), softball (g), swimming and diving (b,g), tennis (b,g), track and field (b,g), volleyball (g), wrestling (b); intramural: dance team (g); coed interscholastic: weight lifting. 52 coaches, 1 athletic trainer.
Computers Computers are regularly used in all classes. Computer network features include on-campus library services, online commercial services, Internet access, wireless campus network, Internet filtering or blocking technology, mobile laptop computer lab, Basmati Grades, Blackboard, Sketchpad, 8 full-text databases including Big Chalk, World Book, Children's Lit, SIRS, Biography Resource Center, Wilson Web, INFOhio, JSTOR. Campus intranet, student e-mail accounts, and computer access in designated common areas are available to students. Students grades are available online. The school has a published electronic and media policy.
Contact Mrs. Kelley Schiess, Director of Admission. 513-871-4700 Ext. 207. Fax: 513-533-5350. E-mail: schiess_k@summitcds.org. Web site: www.summitcds.org.

SUMMIT PREPARATORY SCHOOL

Kalispell, Montana
See Special Needs Schools section.

SUNHAWK ADOLESCENT RECOVERY CENTER

St. George, Utah
See Special Needs Schools section.

SUNRISE ACADEMY

Hurricane, Utah
See Special Needs Schools section.

TABOR ACADEMY

66 Spring Street
Marion, Massachusetts 02738
Head of School: Mr. Jay S. Stroud
General Information Coeducational boarding and day college-preparatory and arts school. Grades 9–12. Founded: 1876. Setting: suburban. Nearest major city is Boston. Students are housed in single-sex dormitories. 85-acre campus. 42 buildings on campus. Approved or accredited by Association of Independent Schools in New England, New England Association of Schools and Colleges, and The Association of Boarding Schools. Member of National Association of Independent Schools and Secondary School Admission Test Board. Endowment: $32.8 million. Total enrollment: 500. Upper school average class size: 12. Upper school faculty-student ratio: 1:6. There are 159 required school days per year for Upper School students. Upper School students typically attend 5 days per week. The average school day consists of 7 hours.
Upper School Student Profile Grade 9: 84 students (45 boys, 39 girls); Grade 10: 150 students (88 boys, 62 girls); Grade 11: 131 students (73 boys, 58 girls); Grade

12: 135 students (75 boys, 60 girls). 69% of students are boarding students. 63% are state residents. 22 states are represented in upper school student body. 15% are international students. International students from Bermuda, China, Hong Kong, Republic of Korea, Taiwan, and Thailand; 11 other countries represented in student body.

Faculty School total: 86. In upper school: 52 men, 34 women; 55 have advanced degrees; 59 reside on campus.

Subjects Offered Algebra, American history, American literature, ancient history, architecture, art, art history, astronomy, biology, calculus, celestial navigation, ceramics, chemistry, creative writing, drama, ecology, economics, English, English literature, European history, fine arts, French, freshman foundations, geology, geometry, German, Greek, health, history, Latin, maritime history, mathematics, meteorology, microbiology, music, navigation, oceanography, photography, physics, physiology, science, social sciences, social studies, Spanish, speech, statistics, theater, trigonometry, world history, world literature.

Graduation Requirements Algebra, arts and fine arts (art, music, dance, drama), biology, English, foreign language, geometry, mathematics, science, social sciences, social studies (includes history).

Special Academic Programs Advanced Placement exam preparation; honors section; independent study; term-away projects; academic accommodation for the gifted, the musically talented, and the artistically talented; ESL (12 students enrolled).

College Admission Counseling 145 students graduated in 2010; all went to college, including Boston College; Boston University; University of Colorado at Boulder. Mean SAT critical reading: 600, mean SAT math: 620, mean SAT writing: 592, mean combined SAT: 1812.

Student Life Upper grades have specified standards of dress, student council, honor system. Discipline rests equally with students and faculty.

Summer Programs Enrichment programs offered; session focuses on Summer Camp; held on campus; accepts boys and girls; open to students from other schools. 500 students usually enrolled. 2011 schedule: June 26 to August 7. Application deadline: none.

Tuition and Aid Day student tuition: $32,700; 7-day tuition and room/board: $45,700. Tuition installment plan (Academic Management Services Plan, Key Tuition Payment Plan, monthly payment plans, Tuition Management Systems Plan). Need-based scholarship grants available. In 2010–11, 32% of upper-school students received aid. Total amount of financial aid awarded in 2010–11: $3,500,000.

Admissions Traditional secondary-level entrance grade is 9. For fall 2010, 692 students applied for upper-level admission, 436 were accepted, 160 enrolled. ISEE, PSAT or SSAT required. Deadline for receipt of application materials: January 31. Application fee required: $50. Interview required.

Athletics Interscholastic: baseball (boys), basketball (b,g), crew (b,g), cross-country running (b,g), field hockey (g), football (b), ice hockey (b,g), lacrosse (b,g), sailing (b,g), soccer (b,g), softball (g), squash (b,g), tennis (b,g), track and field (b,g), wrestling (b); intramural: crew (b,g), ice hockey (g), squash (b,g), tennis (b,g); coed interscholastic: dance, dance team, golf; coed intramural: aerobics, canoeing/kayaking, combined training, dance, fitness, Frisbee, kayaking, physical training, sailing, strength & conditioning, weight training. 2 athletic trainers.

Computers Computers are regularly used in English, foreign language, history, literary magazine, mathematics, newspaper, photography, publications, science, yearbook classes. Computer network features include on-campus library services, online commercial services, Internet access, wireless campus network, Internet filtering or blocking technology, digital media labs. Campus intranet, student e-mail accounts, and computer access in designated common areas are available to students. The school has a published electronic and media policy.

Contact Leslie Geil, Admissions Assistant. 508-291-8300. Fax: 508-291-8301. E-mail: admissions@taboracademy.org. Web site: www.taboracademy.org.

TAIPEI AMERICAN SCHOOL

800 Chung Shan North Road, Section 6
Taipei 11152, Taiwan
Head of School: Dr. Sharon Hennessy

General Information Coeducational day college-preparatory school. Grades PK–12. Founded: 1949. Setting: urban. 15-acre campus. 4 buildings on campus. Approved or accredited by International Baccalaureate Organization, US Department of State, and Western Association of Schools and Colleges. Affiliate member of National Association of Independent Schools; member of European Council of International Schools. Language of instruction: English. Endowment: $29 million. Total enrollment: 2,163. Upper school average class size: 17. Upper school faculty-student ratio: 1:11. There are 180 required school days per year for Upper School students. Upper School students typically attend 5 days per week. The average school day consists of 6 hours and 20 minutes.

Upper School Student Profile Grade 9: 208 students (93 boys, 115 girls); Grade 10: 231 students (118 boys, 113 girls); Grade 11: 223 students (95 boys, 128 girls); Grade 12: 205 students (103 boys, 102 girls).

Faculty School total: 240. In upper school: 55 men, 50 women; 82 have advanced degrees.

Subjects Offered Advanced math, Advanced Placement courses, advanced studio art-AP, algebra, American literature, art history, Asian studies, biology, business, calculus, ceramics, chemistry, chemistry-AP, Chinese, choir, computer science, computer science-AP, contemporary history, current history, dance, digital photog-

raphy, drawing, earth science, English, English language-AP, English literature-AP, environmental science-AP, European history-AP, expository writing, fitness, French, French-AP, geography, geometry, health, International Baccalaureate courses, Japanese, jazz ensemble, journalism, linear algebra, macro/microeconomics-AP, macroeconomics-AP, microeconomics-AP, music theory-AP, orchestra, physical education, physics, physics-AP, pre-algebra, pre-calculus, psychology, research seminar, rhetoric, Spanish, Spanish-AP, statistics-AP, theater, theory of knowledge, trigonometry, U.S. history, U.S. history-AP, video film production, visual arts, wind ensemble, world cultures, world history, world literature, yearbook.

Graduation Requirements English, mathematics, modern languages, physical education (includes health), science, social studies (includes history), visual and performing arts.

Special Academic Programs International Baccalaureate program; 24 Advanced Placement exams for which test preparation is offered; honors section.

College Admission Counseling 219 students graduated in 2010; 217 went to college, including McGill University; New York University; University of Illinois at Urbana–Champaign; University of Southern California; University of Washington; Washington University in St. Louis. Other: 2 had other specific plans. Mean SAT critical reading: 619, mean SAT math: 704, mean SAT writing: 632, mean combined SAT: 1955.

Student Life Upper grades have specified standards of dress, student council, honor system. Discipline rests primarily with faculty.

Summer Programs Remediation, enrichment, advancement programs offered; session focuses on internships, advancement, and make-up courses; held on campus; accepts boys and girls; open to students from other schools. 80 students usually enrolled. 2011 schedule: June 6 to July 1. Application deadline: May 30.

Tuition and Aid Day student tuition: 499,400 Taiwan dollars.

Admissions Traditional secondary-level entrance grade is 9. For fall 2010, 153 students applied for upper-level admission, 89 were accepted, 70 enrolled. California Achievement Test, English for Non-native Speakers, ERB CTP IV, ISEE, latest standardized score from previous school, PSAT, SAT, SSAT or Stanford Achievement Test required. Deadline for receipt of application materials: none. Application fee required: 10,000 Taiwan dollars.

Athletics Interscholastic: badminton (boys, girls), basketball (b,g), cross-country running (b,g), dance (b,g), rugby (b,g), soccer (b,g), softball (b,g), swimming and diving (b,g), tennis (b,g), track and field (b,g), volleyball (b,g); intramural: swimming and diving (b,g). 6 PE instructors.

Computers Computers are regularly used in all academic classes. Computer network features include on-campus library services, online commercial services, Internet access, wireless campus network, NetClassroom is being piloted this year. Campus intranet and student e-mail accounts are available to students. The school has a published electronic and media policy.

Contact Dr. Winnie Tang, Admissions Officer. 886-2-2873-9900 Ext. 328. Fax: 886-2-2873-1641. E-mail: admissions@tas.edu.tw. Web site: www.tas.edu.tw.

TALLULAH FALLS SCHOOL

PO Box 249
Tallulah Falls, Georgia 30573
Head of School: Mr. Larry Peevy

General Information Coeducational boarding and day college-preparatory school, affiliated with Christian faith. Boarding grades 7–12, day grades 6–12. Founded: 1909. Setting: rural. Nearest major city is Atlanta. Students are housed in single-sex dormitories. 500-acre campus. 16 buildings on campus. Approved or accredited by Georgia Independent School Association, Southern Association of Colleges and Schools, and The Association of Boarding Schools. Member of NAFSA: Association of International Educators. Endowment: $26 million. Total enrollment: 175. Upper school average class size: 12. Upper school faculty-student ratio: 1:10. Upper School students typically attend 5 days per week. The average school day consists of 7 hours and 15 minutes.

Upper School Student Profile 67% of students are boarding students. 80% are state residents. 9 states are represented in upper school student body. 15% are international students. International students from China, Germany, Hong Kong, Japan, Republic of Korea, and Viet Nam; 2 other countries represented in student body.

Faculty School total: 27. In upper school: 7 men, 11 women; 12 have advanced degrees; 3 reside on campus.

Subjects Offered Advanced chemistry, advanced math, Advanced Placement courses, algebra, American culture, American government, American history, American literature, American literature-AP, anatomy, animation, art, arts appreciation, athletics, biology, calculus, chemistry, chorus, computer animation, computer applications, computer education, computer graphics, computer information systems, computer literacy, computer multimedia, computer processing, computer programming, computer science, computer studies, computer technologies, computer-aided design, creative writing, dance, earth science, English literature, English literature and composition-AP, French, geometry, government/civics, health, history, home economics, industrial arts, journalism, keyboarding, mathematics, music, physical education, physical science, physics, physiology, Spanish, technology, trigonometry, world literature.

Graduation Requirements Algebra, American government, American literature, biology, British literature, chemistry, computer science, English, foreign language, geometry, government, mathematics, physical education (includes health), physical fitness, physical science, physics, political science, pre-calculus, science, social sciences, social studies (includes history).

Special Academic Programs Advanced Placement exam preparation; honors section; independent study; study at local college for college credit; ESL (20 students enrolled).

College Admission Counseling 28 students graduated in 2009; all went to college, including Georgia State University; Mercer University; North Georgia College & State University; University of Georgia. Median SAT critical reading: 520, median SAT math: 530. 40% scored over 600 on SAT critical reading, 50% scored over 600 on SAT math.

Student Life Upper grades have uniform requirement, student council, honor system. Discipline rests primarily with faculty. Attendance at religious services is required.

Tuition and Aid Day student tuition: $9000; 5-day tuition and room/board: $15,000; 7-day tuition and room/board: $20,000–$22,000. Tuition installment plan (monthly payment plans, individually arranged payment plans). Tuition reduction for siblings, merit scholarship grants, need-based scholarship grants available. In 2009–10, 65% of upper-school students received aid. Total amount of financial aid awarded in 2009–10: $1,500,000.

Admissions Traditional secondary-level entrance grade is 9. TOEFL required. Deadline for receipt of application materials: February 15. Application fee required: $30. Interview required.

Athletics Interscholastic: aerobics/dance (boys, girls), basketball (b,g), cheering (g), cross-country running (b,g), soccer (b), tennis (b,g), track and field (b,g), volleyball (g); intramural: dance (b,g); coed interscholastic: baseball, fishing, golf, running; coed intramural: backpacking, bicycling, canoeing/kayaking, climbing, fishing, fitness, flag football, hiking/backpacking, kayaking, martial arts, mountain biking, outdoor activities, paint ball, physical fitness, ropes courses, skiing (downhill), table tennis, track and field, volleyball, weight lifting, weight training. 2 PE instructors, 8 coaches, 1 athletic trainer.

Computers Computers are regularly used in career exploration, college planning, commercial art, economics, English, graphic design, history, mathematics, SAT preparation, science, social studies, yearbook classes. Computer network features include on-campus library services, online commercial services, Internet access, wireless campus network, Internet filtering or blocking technology, students are issued laptops to be used during the school year. Student e-mail accounts and computer access in designated common areas are available to students. Students grades are available online. The school has a published electronic and media policy.

Contact Mrs. Lindsey Goss, Admissions Counselor. 706-754-0400. Fax: 706-754-5757. E-mail: admissions@tallulahfalls.org. Web site: www.tallulahfalls.org.

TAMPA PREPARATORY SCHOOL

727 West Cass Street
Tampa, Florida 33606
Head of School: Mr. Kevin M. Plummer

General Information Coeducational day college-preparatory, arts, and technology school. Grades 6–12. Founded: 1974. Setting: urban. 12-acre campus. 3 buildings on campus. Approved or accredited by Association of Independent Schools of Florida, Southern Association of Colleges and Schools, and Florida Department of Education. Member of National Association of Independent Schools and Secondary School Admission Test Board. Endowment: $2.5 million. Total enrollment: 576. Upper school average class size: 18. Upper school faculty-student ratio: 1:10. There are 180 required school days per year for Upper School students. Upper School students typically attend 5 days per week. The average school day consists of 7 hours and 10 minutes.

Upper School Student Profile Grade 6: 44 students (25 boys, 19 girls); Grade 7: 62 students (29 boys, 33 girls); Grade 8: 67 students (33 boys, 34 girls); Grade 9: 98 students (61 boys, 37 girls); Grade 10: 102 students (53 boys, 49 girls); Grade 11: 118 students (51 boys, 67 girls); Grade 12: 102 students (44 boys, 58 girls).

Faculty School total: 66. In upper school: 28 men, 38 women; 31 have advanced degrees.

Subjects Offered Anatomy, art history, astronomy, computer math, ethics, physiology, religion, science, trigonometry, world affairs, world literature.

Graduation Requirements Algebra, arts and fine arts (art, music, dance, drama), English, foreign language, geometry, history, physical education (includes health), pre-calculus, science.

Special Academic Programs 19 Advanced Placement exams for which test preparation is offered; honors section; accelerated programs; independent study; term-away projects; academic accommodation for the gifted, the musically talented, and the artistically talented.

College Admission Counseling Colleges students went to include Emory University; Florida State University; Southern Methodist University; University of Central Florida; University of Florida; University of Pennsylvania.

Student Life Upper grades have specified standards of dress, student council, honor system. Discipline rests equally with students and faculty.

Tuition and Aid Day student tuition: $17,050. Guaranteed tuition plan. Tuition installment plan (FACTS Tuition Payment Plan, individually arranged payment plans). Merit scholarship grants, need-based scholarship grants available. In 2009–10, 16% of upper-school students received aid; total upper-school merit-scholarship money awarded: $90,500. Total amount of financial aid awarded in 2009–10: $650,000.

Admissions Traditional secondary-level entrance grade is 9. For fall 2009, 212 students applied for upper-level admission, 180 were accepted, 139 enrolled. Deadline for receipt of application materials: February 15. Application fee required: $75. On-campus interview required.

Athletics Interscholastic: baseball (boys), basketball (b,g), crew (b,g), cross-country running (b,g), dance team (g), diving (b,g), golf (b,g), lacrosse (b,g), rowing (b,g), running (b,g), soccer (b,g), softball (g), swimming and diving (b,g), tennis (b,g), track and field (b,g), volleyball (b,g); intramural: dance team (g), physical fitness (b,g), racquetball (b,g); coed interscholastic: aquatics, bowling, wrestling; coed intramural: badminton, dance, fitness, flag football, modern dance, physical training, scuba diving, strength & conditioning, table tennis, weight training. 4 PE instructors, 57 coaches, 2 athletic trainers.

Computers Computers are regularly used in creative writing, economics, graphic design, introduction to technology, journalism, mathematics, science, word processing, yearbook classes. Computer network features include on-campus library services, online commercial services, Internet access, wireless campus network, Internet filtering or blocking technology. Students grades are available online. The school has a published electronic and media policy.

Contact Mrs. Linda Y Quinn, Admissions Assistant. 813-251-8481 Ext. 4011. Fax: 813-254-2106. E-mail: lquinn@tampaprep.org. Web site: www.tampaprep.org.

TANDEM FRIENDS SCHOOL

279 Tandem Lane
Charlottesville, Virginia 22902
Head of School: Paul B. Perkinson

General Information Coeducational day college-preparatory and arts school, affiliated with Society of Friends. Grades 5–12. Founded: 1970. Setting: small town. Nearest major city is Richmond. 23-acre campus. 7 buildings on campus. Approved or accredited by Friends Council on Education and Virginia Association of Independent Schools. Member of National Association of Independent Schools. Total enrollment: 205. Upper school average class size: 12. Upper school faculty-student ratio: 1:6. There are 180 required school days per year for Upper School students. Upper School students typically attend 5 days per week. The average school day consists of 7 hours.

Upper School Student Profile Grade 9: 27 students (11 boys, 16 girls); Grade 10: 29 students (13 boys, 16 girls); Grade 11: 32 students (19 boys, 13 girls); Grade 12: 36 students (19 boys, 17 girls). 3% of students are members of Society of Friends.

Faculty School total: 34. In upper school: 15 men, 17 women; 20 have advanced degrees.

Subjects Offered Algebra, American literature, anatomy, art, bioethics, biology, biology-AP, calculus, calculus-AP, ceramics, chemistry, chemistry-AP, college counseling, computer applications, creative writing, cultural geography, discrete mathematics, drama, economics, economics and history, English, English-AP, environmental science-AP, expository writing, fine arts, French, French-AP, geometry, health and wellness, jazz ensemble, Latin, Latin-AP, marine biology, media studies, modern world history, music, musical productions, performing arts, photo shop, photography, physics, Quakerism and ethics, senior project, Spanish, Spanish-AP, statistics, statistics-AP, student government, student publications, studio art, theater, trigonometry, U.S. government, U.S. history, U.S. history-AP, weaving, world history, world literature, writing, yearbook.

Graduation Requirements Arts and fine arts (art, music, dance, drama), computer science, English, foreign language, government/civics, history, mathematics, science, senior year independent experiential learning project. Community service is required.

Special Academic Programs Advanced Placement exam preparation; independent study; academic accommodation for the gifted; remedial reading and/or remedial writing; remedial math.

College Admission Counseling 19 students graduated in 2010; 17 went to college, including James Madison University; The College of William and Mary; University of Virginia; Virginia Commonwealth University. Other: 2 had other specific plans. Median SAT critical reading: 654, median SAT math: 586, median combined SAT: 1256, median composite ACT: 26.

Student Life Upper grades have student council, honor system. Discipline rests equally with students and faculty. Attendance at religious services is required.

Tuition and Aid Day student tuition: $16,245. Tuition installment plan (Insured Tuition Payment Plan, monthly payment plans, individually arranged payment plans). Need-based scholarship grants, tuition remission for children of full-time faculty available. In 2010–11, 24% of upper-school students received aid.

Admissions Traditional secondary-level entrance grade is 9. For fall 2010, 19 students applied for upper-level admission, 14 were accepted, 14 enrolled. Woodcock-Johnson and writing sample required. Deadline for receipt of application materials: none. Application fee required: $50. Interview required.

Athletics Interscholastic: basketball (boys, girls), field hockey (g), lacrosse (b,g), soccer (b,g), volleyball (g); coed interscholastic: cross-country running, fencing, golf, mountain biking, tennis; coed intramural: fencing. 2 PE instructors, 15 coaches.

Computers Computers are regularly used in all academic classes. Computer network features include on-campus library services, online commercial services, Internet access, wireless campus network, Internet filtering or blocking technology, virtual classroom. Student e-mail accounts and computer access in designated common areas are available to students. Students grades are available online. The school has a published electronic and media policy.

Tandem Friends School

Contact   Louise DeCamp Cole, Director of Admissions. 434-951-9314. Fax: 434-296-1886. E-mail: lcole@tandemfs.org. Web site: www.tandemfs.org.

TAPPLY BINET COLLEGE

245 Garner Road West
Ancaster, Ontario L9G 3K9, Canada
Head of School: Ms. Sue Davidson

General Information Coeducational day college-preparatory and general academic school. Grades 7–12. Founded: 1997. Setting: small town. Nearest major city is Hamilton, Canada. 1-acre campus. 1 building on campus. Approved or accredited by Ontario Department of Education. Language of instruction: English. Total enrollment: 17. Upper school average class size: 5. Upper school faculty-student ratio: 1:3.

Upper School Student Profile Grade 9: 2 students (1 boy, 1 girl); Grade 10: 3 students (2 boys, 1 girl); Grade 11: 2 students (1 boy, 1 girl); Grade 12: 10 students (7 boys, 3 girls).

Faculty School total: 5. In upper school: 2 men, 3 women; 2 have advanced degrees.

College Admission Counseling Colleges students went to include Brock University; Wilfrid Laurier University.

Student Life Upper grades have uniform requirement, student council, honor system. Discipline rests primarily with faculty.

Admissions Battery of testing done through outside agency required. Deadline for receipt of application materials: none. No application fee required.

Athletics Coed Interscholastic: aerobics/Nautilus. 1 PE instructor.

Contact Ms. Sue Davidson, Principal. 905-648-2737. Fax: 905-648-8762. E-mail: tapply@bellnet.ca. Web site: www.tapplybinetcollege.com.

TASIS THE AMERICAN SCHOOL IN ENGLAND

Coldharbour Lane
Thorpe, Surrey TW20 8TE, United Kingdom
Head of School: Mr. Lyle D. Rigg

General Information Coeducational boarding and day college-preparatory and arts school. Boarding grades 9–13, day grades N–13. Founded: 1976. Setting: rural. Nearest major city is London, United Kingdom. Students are housed in single-sex dormitories. 43-acre campus. 24 buildings on campus. Approved or accredited by European Council of International Schools, International Baccalaureate Organization, New England Association of Schools and Colleges, Office for Standards in Education (OFSTED), The Association of Boarding Schools, and state department of education. Affiliate member of National Association of Independent Schools; member of Secondary School Admission Test Board. Language of instruction: English. Total enrollment: 700. Upper school average class size: 15. Upper school faculty-student ratio: 1:7. Upper School students typically attend 5 days per week. The average school day consists of 5 hours and 50 minutes.

Upper School Student Profile Grade 9: 65 students (35 boys, 30 girls); Grade 10: 100 students (55 boys, 45 girls); Grade 11: 110 students (50 boys, 60 girls); Grade 12: 95 students (40 boys, 55 girls). 47% of students are boarding students. 44% are international students. International students from China, Germany, Republic of Korea, Russian Federation, Spain, and United States; 46 other countries represented in student body.

Faculty School total: 108. In upper school: 24 men, 27 women; 34 have advanced degrees; 19 reside on campus.

Subjects Offered 20th century history, acting, algebra, American history, American history-AP, American literature, ancient history, art, art history, art history-AP, biology, biology-AP, calculus-AP, ceramics, chemistry, chemistry-AP, choir, computer graphics, computer science, computer science-AP, drawing, earth science, economics, economics-AP, English, English language and composition-AP, English literature, English literature and composition-AP, ensembles, environmental science, environmental science-AP, ESL, European history, European history-AP, fine arts, French, French-AP, geometry, German, government and politics-AP, health and wellness, humanities, international affairs, international relations, journalism, keyboarding, Latin, mathematics, music theory, music theory-AP, painting, photography, physical education, physical science, physics, physics-AP, pre-calculus, printmaking, sculpture, senior humanities, Shakespeare, Spanish, Spanish-AP, statistics-AP, theater arts, theory of knowledge, visual arts, Web site design, Western civilization, world history, yearbook.

Graduation Requirements Arts and fine arts (art, music, dance, drama), computer science, English, foreign language, health, history, lab science, mathematics, physical education (includes health), senior humanities, sports. Community service is required.

Special Academic Programs International Baccalaureate program; Advanced Placement exam preparation; independent study; academic accommodation for the gifted; remedial reading and/or remedial writing; ESL (75 students enrolled).

College Admission Counseling 80 students graduated in 2009; 79 went to college. Other: 1 had other specific plans.

Student Life Upper grades have uniform requirement, student council. Discipline rests primarily with faculty.

Tuition and Aid Day student tuition: £18,100; 7-day tuition and room/board: £29,150. Tuition installment plan (monthly payment plans, individually arranged payment plans). Merit scholarship grants, need-based scholarship grants available.

Admissions TOEFL or SLEP required. Deadline for receipt of application materials: none. Application fee required: £125. Interview recommended.

Athletics Interscholastic: baseball (boys), basketball (b,g), cross-country running (b,g), rugby (b), soccer (b,g), softball (g), tennis (b,g), volleyball (b,g); intramural: aerobics (g), aerobics/dance (g), badminton (b,g), ballet (g), cricket (b,g), dance (g), dance team (g), field hockey (b,g), fitness (b,g), floor hockey (b,g), gymnastics (b,g), handball (b,g), indoor soccer (b,g), jump rope (b,g), lacrosse (b,g), modern dance (b,g), outdoor activities (b,g), outdoor adventure (b,g), physical fitness (b,g), physical training (b,g), rhythmic gymnastics (b,g), rugby (b), running (b,g), scooter football (b,g), soccer (b,g), softball (b,g), strength & conditioning (b,g), team handball (b,g), weight training (b,g), winter soccer (b,g); coed interscholastic: cheering, golf; coed intramural: basketball, bicycling, golf, gymnastics, handball, horseback riding, indoor soccer, lacrosse, martial arts, outdoor activities, outdoor adventure, squash, strength & conditioning, swimming and diving, table tennis, team handball, tennis, track and field, volleyball, weight training, winter soccer. 5 PE instructors, 12 coaches, 1 athletic trainer.

Computers Computers are regularly used in all academic classes. Computer network features include on-campus library services, online commercial services, Internet access, wireless campus network, Internet filtering or blocking technology. Campus intranet, student e-mail accounts, and computer access in designated common areas are available to students. The school has a published electronic and media policy.

Contact Mrs. Bronwyn Thorburn-Riseley, Director of Admissions. 44-1932-565252. Fax: 44-1932-564644. E-mail: ukadmissions@tasisengland.org. Web site: www.tasis.com/England/.

TASIS, THE AMERICAN SCHOOL IN SWITZERLAND

Via Collina d'Oro
Montagnola-Lugano CH-6926, Switzerland
Head of School: Mr. Michael Ulku-Steiner

General Information Coeducational boarding and day college-preparatory, arts, and sports school. Boarding grades 7–PG, day grades 1–PG. Founded: 1956. Setting: small town. Nearest major city is Lugano, Switzerland. Students are housed in single-sex dormitories. 9-acre campus. 19 buildings on campus. Approved or accredited by European Council of International Schools, New England Association of Schools and Colleges, and Swiss Federation of Private Schools. Affiliate member of National Association of Independent Schools; member of Secondary School Admission Test Board. Language of instruction: English. Total enrollment: 599. Upper school average class size: 13. Upper school faculty-student ratio: 1:5. Upper School students typically attend 5 days per week.

Upper School Student Profile Grade 7: 37 students (22 boys, 15 girls); Grade 8: 21 students (9 boys, 12 girls); Grade 9: 51 students (28 boys, 23 girls); Grade 10: 99 students (44 boys, 55 girls); Grade 11: 118 students (47 boys, 71 girls); Grade 12: 68 students (23 boys, 45 girls); Postgraduate: 2 students (1 boy, 1 girl). 80% of students are boarding students. 82% are international students. International students from Brazil, Germany, Italy, and United States; 47 other countries represented in student body.

Faculty In upper school: 30 men, 39 women; 39 have advanced degrees; 32 reside on campus.

Subjects Offered Advanced Placement courses, algebra, American history, American literature, ancient history, art, art history, art history-AP, biology, biology-AP, calculus, calculus-AP, ceramics, chemistry, chemistry-AP, digital photography, drama, economics, economics-AP, English, English language and composition-AP, English literature, English literature and composition-AP, environmental science, ESL, European history, European history-AP, fine arts, French, French language-AP, geography, geometry, German-AP, graphic design, health, history, international relations, Italian, mathematics, medieval/Renaissance history, music, photography, physical education, physics, science, social studies, Spanish, Spanish language-AP, theater, theory of knowledge, U.S. government, U.S. history-AP, world cultures, world history, world literature.

Graduation Requirements Arts, English, European history, foreign language, mathematics, science, senior humanities, sports, U.S. history. Community service is required.

Special Academic Programs International Baccalaureate program; Advanced Placement exam preparation; honors section; ESL (205 students enrolled).

College Admission Counseling 82 students graduated in 2010; 80 went to college, including Pace University; The American University of Paris; The George Washington University. Other: 2 entered a postgraduate year. Median SAT critical reading: 570, median SAT math: 570. 30% scored over 600 on SAT critical reading, 22% scored over 600 on SAT math.

Student Life Upper grades have specified standards of dress, student council, honor system. Discipline rests equally with students and faculty.

Summer Programs ESL, sports, art/fine arts programs offered; session focuses on languages, sports, and arts; held both on and off campus; held at TASIS Lugano Campus and Chateau d'Oex; accepts boys and girls; open to students from other schools. 650 students usually enrolled. 2011 schedule: June 25 to August 13. Application deadline: none.

Tuition and Aid Day student tuition: 41,800 Swiss francs; 7-day tuition and room/board: 68,300 Swiss francs. Tuition installment plan (individually arranged payment plans). Need-based scholarship grants available. In 2010–11, 15% of upper-school students received aid.

Admissions Traditional secondary-level entrance grade is 11. For fall 2010, 235 students applied for upper-level admission, 188 were accepted, 153 enrolled. TOEFL or SLEP required. Deadline for receipt of application materials: none. Application fee required: 300 Swiss francs. Interview recommended.

Athletics Interscholastic: basketball (boys, girls), golf (b), rugby (b), soccer (b,g), swimming and diving (b,g), tennis (b,g), track and field (b,g), volleyball (b,g); intramural: basketball (b,g), rugby (b); coed interscholastic: softball, swimming and diving, track and field; coed intramural: aerobics, aerobics/dance, aerobics/Nautilus, basketball, climbing, combined training, cross-country running, dance, fitness, flag football, floor hockey, golf, horseback riding, indoor soccer, jogging, lacrosse, martial arts, modern dance, physical fitness, physical training, rock climbing, running, sailing, soccer, softball, squash, strength & conditioning, swimming and diving, tennis, ultimate Frisbee, volleyball, weight lifting, weight training. 2 PE instructors.

Computers Computers are regularly used in art, English, ESL, foreign language, history, photography, science classes. Computer network features include on-campus library services, Internet access, wireless campus network, Internet filtering or blocking technology. Student e-mail accounts are available to students. Students grades are available online. The school has a published electronic and media policy. **Contact** William E. Eichner, Director of Admissions. 41-91-960-5151. Fax: 41-91-993-2979. E-mail: admissions@tasis.ch. Web site: www.tasis.com.

See Display below and Close-Up on page 850.

THE TATNALL SCHOOL

1501 Barley Mill Road
Wilmington, Delaware 19807
Head of School: Eric G. Ruoss

General Information Coeducational day college-preparatory school. Grades N–12. Founded: 1930. Setting: suburban. 110-acre campus. 5 buildings on campus. Approved or accredited by Middle States Association of Colleges and Schools and Delaware Department of Education. Member of National Association of Independent Schools. Endowment: $17 million. Total enrollment: 640. Upper school average class size: 15. Upper school faculty-student ratio: 1:6.

Upper School Student Profile Grade 9: 54 students (27 boys, 27 girls); Grade 10: 64 students (33 boys, 31 girls); Grade 11: 64 students (34 boys, 30 girls); Grade 12: 72 students (38 boys, 34 girls).

Faculty School total: 101. In upper school: 17 men, 23 women; 33 have advanced degrees.

Subjects Offered 20th century American writers, 20th century world history, 3-dimensional art, 3-dimensional design, acting, advanced chemistry, advanced computer applications, advanced math, Advanced Placement courses, advanced studio art-AP, African-American literature, algebra, American Civil War, American government, American history, American history-AP, American literature, analysis and differential calculus, anatomy, art, athletic training, athletics, baseball, biology, biology-AP, botany, calculus, calculus-AP, ceramics, chemistry, chemistry-AP, college counseling, community service, computer programming, computer science, concert band, concert choir, drama, driver education, ecology, economics, English, English literature, English literature-AP, environmental science, environmental science-AP, European history, European history-AP, film, fine arts, French, French language-AP, geometry, health, history, Holocaust, Latin, Latin-AP, literature and composition-AP, marine biology, mathematics, modern European history-AP, music, newspaper, physical education, physics, physics-AP, psychology, psychology-AP, science, service learning/internship, social studies, Spanish, Spanish-AP, statistics, statistics-AP, theater, theater arts, theater production, trigonometry, U.S. history-AP, video, Vietnam War, world history, world literature, writing, yearbook.

Graduation Requirements Arts and fine arts (art, music, dance, drama), computer literacy, English, foreign language, mathematics, physical education (includes health), science, social studies (includes history). Community service is required.

Special Academic Programs Advanced Placement exam preparation; honors section; accelerated programs; independent study; term-away projects; study abroad; academic accommodation for the gifted, the musically talented, and the artistically talented.

College Admission Counseling 70 students graduated in 2009; all went to college, including Loyola University Maryland; Lynn University; University of Colorado at Boulder; University of Delaware; Villanova University; Yale University. Mean SAT critical reading: 580, mean SAT math: 593, mean SAT writing: 594.

Student Life Upper grades have specified standards of dress, student council. Discipline rests primarily with faculty.

Tuition and Aid Day student tuition: $22,100. Tuition installment plan (Key Tuition Payment Plan). Need-based scholarship grants, need-based loans available. In 2009–10, 30% of upper-school students received aid. Total amount of financial aid awarded in 2009–10: $1,081,270.

Admissions Traditional secondary-level entrance grade is 9. For fall 2009, 76 students applied for upper-level admission, 44 were accepted, 20 enrolled. ERB CTP IV required. Deadline for receipt of application materials: January 16. Application fee required: $40. On-campus interview required.

The Tatnall School

Athletics Interscholastic: baseball (boys), basketball (b,g), cheering (g), cross-country running (b,g), field hockey (g), football (b), ice hockey (b), indoor track & field (b,g), lacrosse (b,g), soccer (b,g), swimming and diving (b,g), tennis (b,g), track and field (b,g), volleyball (g), winter (indoor) track (b,g), wrestling (b); coed interscholastic: golf; coed intramural: ultimate Frisbee. 2 PE instructors, 1 athletic trainer.

Computers Computers are regularly used in all classes. Computer network features include on-campus library services, online commercial services, Internet access, wireless campus network, Internet filtering or blocking technology. The school has a published electronic and media policy.

Contact Sharon A. Vandiver, Admissions Coordinator. 302-892-4285. Fax: 302-892-4387. E-mail: vandiver@tatnall.org. Web site: www.tatnall.org.

TELLURIDE MOUNTAIN SCHOOL

200 San Miguel River Drive
Telluride, Colorado 81435

Head of School: Mr. James E. Loan

General Information Coeducational day college-preparatory, arts, technology, and music, visual and dramatic arts school. Grades PK–12. Founded: 1989. Setting: small town. Nearest major city is Denver. 1 building on campus. Approved or accredited by Association of Colorado Independent Schools. Upper school average class size: 8.

Upper School Student Profile Grade 9: 6 students (4 boys, 2 girls); Grade 10: 2 students (2 girls); Grade 11: 2 students (2 girls).

Subjects Offered Algebra, alternative physical education, American Civil War, American history, American literature, ancient world history, applied music, art, backpacking, biology, calculus, character education, chemistry, civil rights, college admission preparation, college counseling, college planning, community service, computer education, computer literacy, computer multimedia, computer music, CPR, creative writing, critical thinking, critical writing, digital music, drama, dramatic arts, English composition, English literature, environmental education, European history, film studies, geography, geology, geometry, grammar, guitar, history, history of rock and roll, instrumental music, Internet research, keyboarding, Latin American literature, leadership, leadership and service, music, music performance, music technology, outdoor education, painting, portfolio writing, pre-algebra, pre-calculus, public speaking, reading/study skills, Spanish, Spanish literature, studio art, trigonometry, video film production, visual arts, white-water trips, wilderness education, world history.

Graduation Requirements Algebra, biology, chemistry, college admission preparation, college counseling, dramatic arts, English, English composition, English literature, geometry, grammar, history, music, physics, pre-calculus, Spanish, trigonometry, U.S. history, visual arts, wilderness education, world history.

Special Academic Programs Study abroad.

College Admission Counseling 3 students graduated in 2010; 2 went to college. Other: 1 had other specific plans.

Student Life Upper grades have specified standards of dress.

Tuition and Aid Day student tuition: $17,250. Tuition installment plan (monthly payment plans, individually arranged payment plans). Need-based scholarship grants available. In 2010–11, 30% of upper-school students received aid.

Admissions Traditional secondary-level entrance grade is 9. Deadline for receipt of application materials: none. Application fee required: $50. Interview required.

Athletics Interscholastic: alpine skiing (boys, girls), freestyle skiing (b,g), hockey (b), ice hockey (b), lacrosse (b), skiing (cross-country) (b,g), skiing (downhill) (b,g), snowboarding (b,g), soccer (b); coed interscholastic: nordic skiing; coed intramural: alpine skiing, backpacking, canoeing/kayaking, climbing, cooperative games, fly fishing, hiking/backpacking, kayaking, mountaineering, outdoor activities, rappelling, rock climbing, snowshoeing, telemark skiing, wilderness. 1 PE instructor, 5 coaches.

Computers Computers are regularly used in all classes. Computer network features include Internet access, wireless campus network. Campus intranet, student e-mail accounts, and computer access in designated common areas are available to students. The school has a published electronic and media policy.

Contact Mrs. Robin Hope, Program Coordinator. 970-728-1969. Fax: 970-369-4412. E-mail: rhope@telluridemtnschool.org. Web site: www.telluridemtnschool.org/.

THE TENNEY SCHOOL

2055 South Gessner
Houston, Texas 77063

Head of School: Mr. Michael E. Tenney

General Information Coeducational day college-preparatory and general academic school. Grades 6–12. Founded: 1973. Setting: suburban. 1-acre campus. 1 building on campus. Approved or accredited by Southern Association of Colleges and Schools and Texas Department of Education. Total enrollment: 65. Upper school average class size: 1. Upper school faculty-student ratio: 1:2. There are 170 required school days per year for Upper School students. Upper School students typically attend 5 days per week. The average school day consists of 5 hours and 30 minutes.

Upper School Student Profile Grade 6: 2 students (2 girls); Grade 7: 6 students (3 boys, 3 girls); Grade 8: 3 students (2 boys, 1 girl); Grade 9: 14 students (8 boys, 6 girls); Grade 10: 15 students (10 boys, 5 girls); Grade 11: 14 students (7 boys, 7 girls); Grade 12: 11 students (5 boys, 6 girls).

Faculty School total: 26. In upper school: 1 man, 22 women; 13 have advanced degrees.

Subjects Offered Accounting, algebra, American history, American literature, biology, British literature, business law, calculus, chemistry, computer programming, computer studies, creative writing, economics, English, fine arts, geometry, government, health, independent study, journalism, keyboarding, mathematics, microcomputer technology applications, physical education, physical science, physics, pre-calculus, psychology, science, social studies, sociology, Spanish, studio art, theater arts, world geography, world history, world literature, yearbook.

Graduation Requirements American government, American history.

Special Academic Programs Advanced Placement exam preparation; honors section; academic accommodation for the gifted, the musically talented, and the artistically talented; remedial reading and/or remedial writing; remedial math; special instructional classes for deaf students; ESL (13 students enrolled).

College Admission Counseling 10 students graduated in 2010; 9 went to college, including Houston Baptist University; Texas A&M University; The University of Texas at Austin; University of Houston. Other: 1 entered a postgraduate year.

Student Life Upper grades have specified standards of dress. Discipline rests primarily with faculty.

Summer Programs Remediation, enrichment, advancement, computer instruction programs offered; session focuses on academic course work; held on campus; accepts boys and girls; open to students from other schools. 45 students usually enrolled. 2011 schedule: June 9 to July 1. Application deadline: May 28.

Tuition and Aid Day student tuition: $22,000.

Admissions Traditional secondary-level entrance grade is 9. For fall 2010, 35 students applied for upper-level admission, 26 were accepted, 25 enrolled. Scholastic Achievement Test required. Deadline for receipt of application materials: none. No application fee required. On-campus interview required.

Athletics 1 PE instructor.

Computers Computers are regularly used in computer applications, creative writing, desktop publishing, English, foreign language, journalism, keyboarding, speech, word processing, yearbook classes. Computer network features include on-campus library services, Internet access, wireless campus network, Internet filtering or blocking technology. Computer access in designated common areas is available to students.

Contact Michael E. Tenney, Director. 713-783-6990. Fax: 713-783-0786. E-mail: mtenney@tenneyschool.com. Web site: www.tenneyschool.com.

TEURLINGS CATHOLIC HIGH SCHOOL

139 Teurlings Drive
Lafayette, Louisiana 70501-3832

Head of School: Mr. Michael Harrison Boyer

General Information Coeducational day and distance learning college-preparatory and religious studies school, affiliated with Roman Catholic Church. Grades 9–12. Distance learning grades 10–12. Founded: 1955. Setting: urban. Nearest major city is Baton Rouge. 25-acre campus. 13 buildings on campus. Approved or accredited by National Catholic Education Association, Southern Association of Colleges and Schools, and Louisiana Department of Education. Endowment: $140,000. Total enrollment: 658. Upper school average class size: 21. Upper school faculty-student ratio: 1:21. There are 179 required school days per year for Upper School students. Upper School students typically attend 5 days per week. The average school day consists of 6 hours and 50 minutes.

Upper School Student Profile Grade 9: 161 students (78 boys, 83 girls); Grade 10: 179 students (91 boys, 88 girls); Grade 11: 165 students (86 boys, 79 girls); Grade 12: 153 students (69 boys, 84 girls). 93% of students are Roman Catholic.

Faculty School total: 44. In upper school: 13 men, 31 women; 13 have advanced degrees.

Subjects Offered 20th century history, accounting, acting, advanced chemistry, advanced computer applications, advanced math, algebra, American history, American literature, anatomy and physiology, art, biology, business applications, business law, calculus, campus ministry, chemistry, choral music, civics/free enterprise, computer science, drama, earth science, English, entrepreneurship, environmental science, fine arts, food and nutrition, French, geography, geometry, health, honors algebra, honors English, honors geometry, honors U.S. history, honors world history, interpersonal skills, keyboarding, Latin, music, newspaper, physical education, physical science, physics, psychology, public speaking, publications, Spanish, speech, sports medicine, theology, Web site design, world history.

Graduation Requirements Advanced math, algebra, American history, American literature, biology, chemistry, civics, civics/free enterprise, computer applications, computer literacy, electives, English, geometry, literature, physical education (includes health), physical science, public speaking, theology, world geography, world history.

Special Academic Programs Honors section; study at local college for college credit.

College Admission Counseling 166 students graduated in 2010; 158 went to college, including Centenary College of Louisiana; Louisiana State University and Agricultural and Mechanical College; Louisiana State University at Eunice; Northwestern

State University of Louisiana; Spring Hill College; University of Louisiana at Lafayette. Other: 2 went to work, 3 entered military service, 3 had other specific plans. Median composite ACT: 21. 12% scored over 26 on composite ACT.

Student Life Upper grades have uniform requirement, student council. Discipline rests equally with students and faculty. Attendance at religious services is required.

Tuition and Aid Day student tuition: $5200. Tuition installment plan (monthly payment plans). Need-based scholarship grants, paying campus jobs available. In 2010–11, 5% of upper-school students received aid. Total amount of financial aid awarded in 2010–11: $84,000.

Admissions Traditional secondary-level entrance grade is 9. For fall 2010, 202 students applied for upper-level admission, 181 were accepted, 151 enrolled. ACT, ACT-Explore, any standardized test, Explore or Stanford Achievement Test required. Deadline for receipt of application materials: January 28. No application fee required.

Athletics Interscholastic: baseball (boys), basketball (b,g), bowling (b,g), cheering (b,g), cross-country running (b,g), dance team (g), football (b), golf (b,g), gymnastics (b), indoor track & field (b,g), soccer (b,g), softball (g), strength & conditioning (b,g), swimming and diving (b,g), tennis (b,g), track and field (b,g), volleyball (g), winter (indoor) track (b,g), wrestling (b); intramural: cheering (g); coed interscholastic: archery, riflery, skeet shooting, trap and skeet. 3 coaches.

Computers Computer network features include on-campus library services, Internet access, wireless campus network, Internet filtering or blocking technology. Student e-mail accounts and computer access in designated common areas are available to students. Students grades are available online. The school has a published electronic and media policy.

Contact Mrs. Kathy Dodson, Administrative Secretary. 337-235-5711 Ext. 101. Fax: 337-234-8057. E-mail: kdodson@tchs.net. Web site: www.tchs.net.

TEXAS NEURONREHAB CENTER

Austin, Texas
See Special Needs Schools section.

THE THACHER SCHOOL

5025 Thacher Road
Ojai, California 93023
Head of School: Michael K. Mulligan

General Information Coeducational boarding and day college-preparatory, arts, and technology school. Grades 9–12. Founded: 1889. Setting: small town. Nearest major city is Santa Barbara. Students are housed in single-sex dormitories. 450-acre campus. 89 buildings on campus. Approved or accredited by California Association of Independent Schools, The Association of Boarding Schools, Western Association of Schools and Colleges, and California Department of Education. Member of National Association of Independent Schools and Secondary School Admission Test Board. Endowment: $106 million. Total enrollment: 249. Upper school average class size: 11. Upper school faculty-student ratio: 1:5.

Upper School Student Profile Grade 9: 54 students (28 boys, 26 girls); Grade 10: 69 students (34 boys, 35 girls); Grade 11: 62 students (29 boys, 33 girls); Grade 12: 64 students (31 boys, 33 girls). 90% of students are boarding students. 58% are state residents. 25 states are represented in upper school student body. 10% are international students. International students from Australia, Canada, Hong Kong, Japan, Saudi Arabia, and Taiwan; 5 other countries represented in student body.

Faculty School total: 46. In upper school: 22 men, 20 women; 37 have advanced degrees; 42 reside on campus.

Subjects Offered 3-dimensional art, ACT preparation, acting, advanced chemistry, advanced math, Advanced Placement courses, advanced studio art-AP, algebra, American history, American history-AP, American literature, art, art history, art history-AP, astronomy, biology, biology-AP, calculus, calculus-AP, ceramics, chemistry, chemistry-AP, Chinese, computer math, computer science, computer science-AP, conceptual physics, creative writing, dance, drama, ecology, economics, economics and history, electronic music, English, English literature, English literature-AP, English/composition-AP, environmental science, environmental science-AP, European history, European history-AP, film, fine arts, French, French language-AP, French literature-AP, geography, geometry, health, history, journalism, Latin, logic, marine biology, mathematics, music, music theory-AP, philosophy, photography, physical education, physics, physics-AP, psychology, religion, science, social studies, Spanish, Spanish language-AP, Spanish literature-AP, statistics, studio art-AP, theater, trigonometry, U.S. history-AP, world history, world literature, writing.

Graduation Requirements Arts and fine arts (art, music, dance, drama), English, foreign language, mathematics, physical education (includes health), science, social studies (includes history), senior exhibition program (students choose an academic topic of interest and study it for one year, culminating in a school-wide presentation).

Special Academic Programs Advanced Placement exam preparation; honors section; independent study; study abroad; academic accommodation for the gifted, the musically talented, and the artistically talented.

College Admission Counseling 63 students graduated in 2010; all went to college, including Brown University; Columbia College; Dartmouth College; Stanford University; The Colorado College; University of California, Berkeley. Mean SAT critical reading: 650, mean SAT math: 620, mean SAT writing: 650, mean combined SAT: 1950.

Student Life Upper grades have specified standards of dress, student council, honor system. Discipline rests equally with students and faculty.

Tuition and Aid Day student tuition: $29,500; 7-day tuition and room/board: $44,500. Tuition installment plan (Key Tuition Payment Plan, monthly payment plans). Need-based scholarship grants available. In 2010–11, 32% of upper-school students received aid. Total amount of financial aid awarded in 2010–11: $1,965,000.

Admissions Traditional secondary-level entrance grade is 9. For fall 2010, 410 students applied for upper-level admission, 82 were accepted, 65 enrolled. ISEE, PSAT or SSAT required. Deadline for receipt of application materials: January 15. Application fee required: $75. Interview required.

Athletics Interscholastic: baseball (boys), basketball (b,g), cross-country running (b,g), dance (b,g), football (b), lacrosse (b,g), soccer (b,g), tennis (b,g), track and field (b,g), volleyball (g); intramural: backpacking (b,g), ballet (g), bicycling (b,g), canoeing/kayaking (b,g), climbing (b,g), dance (b,g), horseback riding (b,g), outdoor activities (b,g), weight training (b,g), wilderness (b,g), wilderness survival (b,g), yoga (b,g); coed interscholastic: dance, equestrian sports; coed intramural: backpacking, bicycling, bowling, canoeing/kayaking, climbing, dance, equestrian sports, fencing, golf, handball, hiking/backpacking, horseback riding, modern dance, outdoor activities, pistol, polo, Polocrosse, riflery, rock climbing, rodeo, skiing (downhill), surfing, trap and skeet, ultimate Frisbee, wall climbing, weight lifting, yoga. 4 coaches.

Computers Computers are regularly used in English, foreign language, history, mathematics, science classes. Computer network features include on-campus library services, online commercial services, Internet access, wireless campus network, Internet filtering or blocking technology. Campus intranet and student e-mail accounts are available to students. Students grades are available online. The school has a published electronic and media policy.

Contact Mr. William P. McMahon, Director of Admission. 805-640-3210. Fax: 805-640-9377. E-mail: admission@thacher.org. Web site: www.thacher.org.

THOMAS JEFFERSON SCHOOL

4100 South Lindbergh Boulevard
St. Louis, Missouri 63127
Head of School: Mr. William C. Rowe

General Information Coeducational boarding and day college-preparatory and Classical education school. Grades 7–PG. Founded: 1946. Setting: suburban. Students are housed in single-sex dormitories. 20-acre campus. 12 buildings on campus. Approved or accredited by Independent Schools Association of the Central States, Midwest Association of Boarding Schools, and The Association of Boarding Schools. Member of National Association of Independent Schools and Secondary School Admission Test Board. Endowment: $1.5 million. Total enrollment: 89. Upper school average class size: 14. Upper school faculty-student ratio: 1:6. There are 130 required school days per year for Upper School students. Upper School students typically attend 5 days per week. The average school day consists of 8 hours and 30 minutes.

Upper School Student Profile Grade 9: 19 students (11 boys, 8 girls); Grade 10: 17 students (10 boys, 7 girls); Grade 11: 17 students (8 boys, 9 girls); Grade 12: 19 students (5 boys, 14 girls). 63% of students are boarding students. 47% are state residents. 7 states are represented in upper school student body. 33% are international students. International students from Canada, China, Japan, Poland, and Republic of Korea.

Faculty School total: 18. In upper school: 6 men, 7 women; 8 have advanced degrees; 7 reside on campus.

Subjects Offered Advanced Placement courses, algebra, American history-AP, ancient history, ancient world history, art, art history, biology, biology-AP, calculus, calculus-AP, ceramics, chemistry, chemistry-AP, dance, earth science, English, English language-AP, English literature-AP, ESL, fine arts, French, geography, geometry, government and politics-AP, government/civics, Greek, history, Homeric Greek, Italian, Latin, life science, mathematics, music, physical science, physics, physics-AP, science, social studies, trigonometry, U.S. history-AP, world history, world history-AP.

Graduation Requirements Arts and fine arts (art, music, dance, drama), English, foreign language, mathematics, science, social studies (includes history). Community service is required.

Special Academic Programs 10 Advanced Placement exams for which test preparation is offered; honors section; academic accommodation for the gifted; ESL (17 students enrolled).

College Admission Counseling 13 students graduated in 2010; all went to college, including Boston University; Case Western Reserve University; The Johns Hopkins University. Median SAT critical reading: 710, median SAT math: 690, median SAT writing: 700, median combined SAT: 2100.

Student Life Upper grades have specified standards of dress, student council, honor system. Discipline rests equally with students and faculty.

Summer Programs ESL programs offered; held on campus; accepts boys and girls; open to students from other schools. 24 students usually enrolled. 2011 schedule: July 1 to July 29. Application deadline: April 1.

Tuition and Aid Day student tuition: $21,200; 5-day tuition and room/board: $34,000; 7-day tuition and room/board: $36,500. Tuition installment plan (monthly payment plans, individually arranged payment plans, Sallie Mae TuitionPay). Merit scholarship grants, need-based scholarship grants, paying campus jobs available. In

2010–11, 39% of upper-school students received aid; total upper-school merit-scholarship money awarded: $10,000. Total amount of financial aid awarded in 2010–11: $507,000.

Admissions Traditional secondary-level entrance grade is 9. For fall 2010, 63 students applied for upper-level admission, 17 were accepted, 15 enrolled. SSAT or TOEFL or SLEP required. Deadline for receipt of application materials: February 15. Application fee required: $40. Interview required.

Athletics Interscholastic: basketball (boys, girls), soccer (b,g), volleyball (b,g); intramural: basketball (b,g), soccer (b,g), volleyball (b,g); coed interscholastic: soccer; coed intramural: dance, fitness, physical fitness, tennis, weight training, yoga.

Computers Computers are regularly used in foreign language, mathematics, science, yearbook classes. Computer network features include Internet access, wireless campus network, Internet filtering or blocking technology. Campus intranet, student e-mail accounts, and computer access in designated common areas are available to students. The school has a published electronic and media policy.

Contact Mrs. Jane Roth, Co-Director of Admissions. 314-843-4151 Ext. 133. Fax: 314-843-3527. E-mail: admissions@tjs.org. Web site: www.tjs.org.

See Display below and Close-Up on page 852.

TIDEWATER ACADEMY

217 Church Street
Post Office Box 1000
Wakefield, Virginia 23888
Head of School: Mr. Rodney L. Taylor

General Information Coeducational day college-preparatory, arts, religious studies, and technology school. Grades PK–12. Founded: 1964. Setting: rural. Nearest major city is Richmond. 10-acre campus. 4 buildings on campus. Approved or accredited by Virginia Association of Independent Schools. Total enrollment: 198. Upper school average class size: 15. Upper school faculty-student ratio: 1:15. There are 180 required school days per year for Upper School students. Upper School students typically attend 5 days per week. The average school day consists of 6 hours and 50 minutes.

Upper School Student Profile Grade 6: 11 students (6 boys, 5 girls); Grade 7: 17 students (11 boys, 6 girls); Grade 8: 12 students (6 boys, 6 girls); Grade 9: 12 students (5 boys, 7 girls); Grade 10: 10 students (6 boys, 4 girls); Grade 11: 16 students (11 boys, 5 girls); Grade 12: 24 students (12 boys, 12 girls).

Faculty School total: 25. In upper school: 4 men, 9 women; 2 have advanced degrees.

Subjects Offered Algebra, American history, American literature, art, arts, biology, calculus, chemistry, computer applications, creative writing, driver education, earth science, English, English literature, English-AP, fine arts, geography, geometry, government/civics, grammar, health, history, journalism, life skills, mathematics, music, physical education, science, social sciences, social studies, Spanish, world history, world literature, writing.

Graduation Requirements Arts and fine arts (art, music, dance, drama), business skills (includes word processing), computer science, English, foreign language, mathematics, physical education (includes health), science, social sciences, social studies (includes history).

Special Academic Programs 5 Advanced Placement exams for which test preparation is offered; honors section; independent study.

College Admission Counseling 22 students graduated in 2010; 20 went to college, including James Madison University; Radford University; Randolph-Macon College; Virginia Polytechnic Institute and State University. Other: 1 went to work, 1 entered military service. Median SAT critical reading: 516, median SAT math: 501. 5% scored over 600 on SAT critical reading.

Student Life Upper grades have specified standards of dress, student council, honor system. Discipline rests primarily with faculty.

Tuition and Aid Day student tuition: $6250. Tuition installment plan (FACTS Tuition Payment Plan, monthly payment plans, individually arranged payment plans). Need-based scholarship grants available. In 2010–11, 35% of upper-school students received aid. Total amount of financial aid awarded in 2010–11: $125,000.

Admissions Traditional secondary-level entrance grade is 11. For fall 2010, 10 students applied for upper-level admission, 6 were accepted, 6 enrolled. Any standardized test required. Deadline for receipt of application materials: none. Application fee required: $25. On-campus interview required.

Athletics Interscholastic: baseball (boys), basketball (b,g), cheering (g), football (b), softball (g), tennis (b,g), volleyball (g). 2 PE instructors, 2 coaches.

Computers Computers are regularly used in yearbook classes. Computer resources include on-campus library services, Internet access, wireless campus network.

Contact Robyn Croft, Admissions Counselor. 757-899-5401. Fax: 757-899-2521. E-mail: r_croft@tidewateracademy-pvt-va.us. Web site: www.tawarriors.org.

TILTON SCHOOL

30 School Street
Tilton, New Hampshire 03276
Head of School: James R. Clements

General Information Coeducational boarding and day college-preparatory school. Grades 9–PG. Founded: 1845. Setting: small town. Nearest major city is Concord. Students are housed in single-sex dormitories. 150-acre campus. 30 buildings on campus. Approved or accredited by Association of Independent Schools in New England, Independent Schools of Northern New England, New England Association of Schools and Colleges, The Association of Boarding Schools, and New Hampshire

Department of Education. Member of National Association of Independent Schools and Secondary School Admission Test Board. Endowment: $14.6 million. Total enrollment: 250. Upper school average class size: 11. Upper school faculty-student ratio: 1:6. There are 187 required school days per year for Upper School students. Upper School students typically attend 6 days per week. The average school day consists of 7 hours.

Upper School Student Profile Grade 9: 41 students (24 boys, 17 girls); Grade 10: 50 students (31 boys, 19 girls); Grade 11: 80 students (51 boys, 29 girls); Grade 12: 64 students (44 boys, 20 girls); Postgraduate: 15 students (11 boys, 4 girls). 76% of students are boarding students. 35% are state residents. 23 states are represented in upper school student body. 20% are international students. International students from Canada, China, Germany, Republic of Korea, Spain, and Taiwan; 8 other countries represented in student body.

Faculty School total: 44. In upper school: 28 men, 16 women; 18 have advanced degrees; 40 reside on campus.

Subjects Offered Advanced chemistry, advanced math, advanced studio art-AP, algebra, American history, American literature, anatomy and physiology, art, band, biology, biology-AP, calculus, calculus-AP, chemistry, chemistry-AP, chorus, clay-working, college counseling, community service, computer graphics, criminal justice, debate, drama, drawing, ecology, economics, English, English language and composition-AP, English literature-AP, ESL, European history-AP, forensics, French, French-AP, functions, geology, geometry, honors algebra, honors English, honors geometry, independent study, integrated mathematics, integrated science, leadership, marine ecology, music, music appreciation, music theory, musical productions, newspaper, painting, photography, physics, physics-AP, politics, pre-calculus, psychology-AP, SAT preparation, sociology, Spanish, Spanish-AP, statistics, studio art, studio art-AP, theater, trigonometry, wilderness education, world cultures, world literature, world religions, yearbook.

Graduation Requirements American history, arts and fine arts (art, music, dance, drama), English, foreign language, history, lab science, mathematics, science, annual participation in Plus/5 (including activities in art and culture, athletics, community service, leadership, and outdoor experience).

Special Academic Programs 11 Advanced Placement exams for which test preparation is offered; honors section; independent study; ESL (16 students enrolled).

College Admission Counseling 104 students graduated in 2009; 100 went to college, including Bates College; Rollins College; Stonehill College; University of Connecticut; University of New Hampshire; University of Rhode Island. Other: 2 went to work, 2 entered military service. Mean SAT critical reading: 520, mean SAT math: 536, mean SAT writing: 522, mean combined SAT: 1578.

Student Life Upper grades have specified standards of dress, student council, honor system. Discipline rests primarily with faculty.

Tuition and Aid Day student tuition: $24,500; 7-day tuition and room/board: $42,500. Tuition installment plan (FACTS Tuition Payment Plan, individually arranged payment plans). Merit scholarship grants, need-based scholarship grants, need-based loans available. In 2009–10, 49% of upper-school students received aid; total upper-school merit-scholarship money awarded: $379,000. Total amount of financial aid awarded in 2009–10: $2,034,450.

Admissions Traditional secondary-level entrance grade is 9. For fall 2009, 483 students applied for upper-level admission, 314 were accepted, 108 enrolled. PSAT or SAT for applicants to grade 11 and 12, SLEP for foreign students, SSAT or writing sample required. Deadline for receipt of application materials: February 1. Application fee required: $50. Interview required.

Athletics Interscholastic: baseball (boys), basketball (b,g), field hockey (g), football (b), ice hockey (b,g), lacrosse (b,g), soccer (b,g), softball (g), tennis (b,g); coed interscholastic: alpine skiing, cross-country running, golf, mountain biking, skiing (downhill), snowboarding, weight lifting, weight training, wrestling; coed intramural: canoeing/kayaking, hiking/backpacking, outdoor activities, outdoor education, outdoor skills, rock climbing, squash, strength & conditioning, wall climbing, weight training, wilderness survival. 1 athletic trainer.

Computers Computers are regularly used in English, foreign language, graphic arts, history, mathematics, newspaper, science, yearbook classes. Computer network features include on-campus library services, online commercial services, Internet access, wireless campus network, Internet filtering or blocking technology, USB Ports, Smart Media Readers. Campus intranet, student e-mail accounts, and computer access in designated common areas are available to students. The school has a published electronic and media policy.

Contact Beth A. Skoglund, Director of Admissions. 603-286-1733. Fax: 603-286-1705. E-mail: bskoglund@tiltonschool.org. Web site: www.tiltonschool.org.

See Display on this page and Close-Up on page 854.

TIMOTHY CHRISTIAN HIGH SCHOOL

1061 South Prospect Avenue
Elmhurst, Illinois 60126
Head of School: Mr. Clyde Rinsema
General Information Coeducational day college-preparatory, general academic, arts, business, vocational, religious studies, and technology school, affiliated with Christian faith. Grades K–12. Founded: 1911. Setting: suburban. Nearest major city is Chicago. 26-acre campus. 1 building on campus. Approved or accredited by Christian Schools International, North Central Association of Colleges and Schools,

and Illinois Department of Education. Endowment: $4 million. Total enrollment: 1,074. Upper school average class size: 13. Upper school faculty-student ratio: 1:13. Upper School students typically attend 5 days per week. The average school day consists of 6 hours and 45 minutes.

Upper School Student Profile Grade 6: 78 students (40 boys, 38 girls); Grade 7: 81 students (39 boys, 42 girls); Grade 8: 84 students (44 boys, 40 girls); Grade 9: 91 students (39 boys, 52 girls); Grade 10: 102 students (57 boys, 45 girls); Grade 11: 103 students (41 boys, 62 girls); Grade 12: 100 students (48 boys, 52 girls). 100% of students are Christian.

Faculty School total: 30. In upper school: 18 men, 12 women; 25 have advanced degrees.

Subjects Offered Advanced math, algebra, American literature, anatomy and physiology, art, band, Bible, biology, British literature, business studies, calculus-AP, ceramics, chemistry, child development, choir, Christian doctrine, Christian ethics, church history, communication skills, community service, computer applications, computer art, computer graphics, computer-aided design, concert choir, desktop publishing, drafting, drawing and design, economics, electives, English, English literature-AP, expository writing, food and nutrition, French, geometry, German, health, home economics, honors algebra, honors geometry, human anatomy, independent living, industrial arts, industrial technology, instrumental music, interior design, jazz ensemble, media arts, music, music appreciation, music theory, New Testament, oral communications, orchestra, parent/child development, photography, physical education, physics, physics-AP, pre-calculus, psychology, sewing, Spanish, trigonometry, U.S. government, U.S. history, U.S. history-AP, United States government-AP, Western civilization, world cultures, world literature.

Graduation Requirements Computer processing, English, mathematics, music, physical education (includes health), religious studies, science, social studies (includes history), senior service retreat at end of 12th grade, service requirement in grades 9-11 (10 hours per year).

Special Academic Programs 6 Advanced Placement exams for which test preparation is offered; honors section; remedial reading and/or remedial writing.

College Admission Counseling 99 students graduated in 2010; 93 went to college, including Azusa Pacific University; Calvin College; Hope College; Trinity Christian College; University of Chicago. Other: 3 went to work, 3 had other specific plans. Mean composite ACT: 24. 60% scored over 26 on composite ACT.

Student Life Upper grades have specified standards of dress, student council, honor system. Discipline rests primarily with faculty. Attendance at religious services is required.

Summer Programs Sports, art/fine arts programs offered; session focuses on athletics; held on campus; accepts boys and girls; open to students from other schools. 136 students usually enrolled. 2011 schedule: June 6 to July 31. Application deadline: May 31.

Tuition and Aid Day student tuition: $8130; 7-day tuition and room/board: $13,060. Tuition installment plan (FACTS Tuition Payment Plan, FACTS is required unless paying the total tuition at once). Need-based scholarship grants, some financial assistance based on need is available, through the school foundation available. In 2010–11, 10% of upper-school students received aid. Total amount of financial aid awarded in 2010–11: $65,225.

Admissions Traditional secondary-level entrance grade is 9. For fall 2010, 61 students applied for upper-level admission, 49 were accepted, 42 enrolled. Scholastic Testing Service High School Placement Test, school's own exam or SLEP for foreign students required. Deadline for receipt of application materials: none. Application fee required: $50. On-campus interview required.

Athletics Interscholastic: baseball (boys), basketball (b,g), cross-country running (b,g), pom squad (g), soccer (b,g), softball (g), tennis (b,g), track and field (b,g), volleyball (g); intramural: basketball (b), flag football (b,g); coed interscholastic: cheering, golf; coed intramural: volleyball. 2 PE instructors, 1 athletic trainer.

Computers Computers are regularly used in art, computer applications, English, graphic design, industrial technology, keyboarding, science, writing classes. Computer network features include on-campus library services, Internet access, wireless campus network, Internet filtering or blocking technology. Student e-mail accounts are available to students. Students grades are available online. The school has a published electronic and media policy.

Contact Mr. Rudi Gesch, Marketing Director. 630-782-4043. Fax: 630-833-9238. E-mail: gesch@timothychristian.com. Web site: www.timothychristian.com.

TIMOTHY CHRISTIAN SCHOOL

2008 Ethel Road
Piscataway, New Jersey 08854
Head of School: Mr. Mark A. Stanton

General Information Coeducational day college-preparatory, arts, business, religious studies, and technology school, affiliated with Christian faith. Grades K–12. Founded: 1949. Setting: suburban. Nearest major city is Newark. 25-acre campus. 7 buildings on campus. Approved or accredited by Association of Christian Schools International and Middle States Association of Colleges and Schools. Endowment: $76,000. Total enrollment: 552. Upper school average class size: 18. Upper school faculty-student ratio: 1:11. There are 175 required school days per year for Upper School students. Upper School students typically attend 5 days per week. The average school day consists of 6 hours and 30 minutes.

Upper School Student Profile Grade 9: 48 students (22 boys, 26 girls); Grade 10: 52 students (25 boys, 27 girls); Grade 11: 57 students (20 boys, 37 girls); Grade 12: 63 students (31 boys, 32 girls). 100% of students are Christian faith.

Faculty School total: 62. In upper school: 16 men, 17 women; 15 have advanced degrees.

Subjects Offered Accounting, acting, advanced chemistry, advanced computer applications, advanced math, Advanced Placement courses, algebra, American history, American literature, art, band, Bible, Bible studies, biology, British literature, calculus-AP, chamber groups, chemistry, computer applications, computer programming, computer science, computer science-AP, concert choir, creative writing, critical thinking, debate, earth science, English, English language-AP, French, home economics, journalism, keyboarding, music, music theory, physics, pre-algebra, pre-calculus, programming, psychology, Spanish, technical theater, theater arts, trigonometry, woodworking, yearbook.

Graduation Requirements Algebra, American literature, Bible, Bible studies, biology, British literature, chemistry, composition, earth science, geometry, health, introduction to literature, physical education (includes health), trigonometry, U.S. history, world history, world literature, Worldview Studies.

Special Academic Programs Honors section; independent study; programs in English, mathematics, general development for dyslexic students.

College Admission Counseling 65 students graduated in 2009; 63 went to college, including Gordon College; Liberty University; Messiah College; Rutgers, The State University of New Jersey, New Brunswick; Virginia Polytechnic Institute and State University; Wheaton College. Other: 2 went to work. Median SAT critical reading: 556, median SAT math: 524.

Student Life Upper grades have uniform requirement, student council, honor system. Discipline rests primarily with faculty. Attendance at religious services is required.

Tuition and Aid Day student tuition: $8950. Tuition installment plan (SMART Tuition Payment Plan). Tuition reduction for siblings, need-based scholarship grants available. In 2009–10, 14% of upper-school students received aid. Total amount of financial aid awarded in 2009–10: $60,000.

Admissions Traditional secondary-level entrance grade is 9. For fall 2009, 22 students applied for upper-level admission, 19 were accepted, 19 enrolled. CAT required. Deadline for receipt of application materials: none. Application fee required: $60. On-campus interview required.

Athletics Interscholastic: baseball (boys), basketball (b,g), cheering (g); cross-country running (b,g), golf (b,g), soccer (b,g), softball (g), track and field (b,g), volleyball (g). 4 PE instructors, 25 coaches.

Computers Computers are regularly used in foreign language, yearbook classes. Computer network features include on-campus library services, Internet access, Internet filtering or blocking technology.

Contact Mrs. Merrijane Gottshall, Admissions Secretary. 732-985-0300 Ext. 613. Fax: 732-985-8008. E-mail: mgottshall@timothychristian.org. Web site: www.timothychristian.org.

TMI—THE EPISCOPAL SCHOOL OF TEXAS

20955 West Tejas Trail
San Antonio, Texas 78257
Head of School: Dr. James A. Freeman

General Information Coeducational boarding and day college-preparatory, arts, and religious studies school, affiliated with Episcopal Church, Christian faith. Boarding grades 9–12, day grades 6–12. Founded: 1893. Setting: suburban. Students are housed in single-sex dormitories. 80-acre campus. 17 buildings on campus. Approved or accredited by Independent Schools Association of the Southwest, National Association of Episcopal Schools, Southwest Association of Episcopal Schools, The Association of Boarding Schools, and Texas Department of Education. Total enrollment: 428. Upper school average class size: 15. Upper school faculty-student ratio: 1:15. There are 168 required school days per year for Upper School students. Upper School students typically attend 5 days per week. The average school day consists of 6 hours and 10 minutes.

Upper School Student Profile Grade 9: 77 students (44 boys, 33 girls); Grade 10: 78 students (54 boys, 24 girls); Grade 11: 67 students (43 boys, 24 girls); Grade 12: 58 students (34 boys, 24 girls). 17% of students are boarding students. 96% are state residents. 5 states are represented in upper school student body. 3% are international students. International students from China, Mexico, Panama, Republic of Korea, and Viet Nam; 2 other countries represented in student body. 83% of students are members of Episcopal Church, Christian.

Faculty School total: 60. In upper school: 26 men, 16 women; 26 have advanced degrees; 13 reside on campus.

Subjects Offered 20th century history, acting, Advanced Placement courses, advanced studio art-AP, algebra, American Civil War, American history, American literature, anatomy and physiology, astronomy, athletics, biology, British literature, calculus, ceramics, chemistry, choir, computer programming, conceptual physics, earth science, economics, English, English literature, environmental science, fine arts, geometry, government, Greek, history, JROTC, Latin, meteorology, military history, philosophy, photography, physics, playwriting, religion, Spanish, statistics, studio art, theater arts, theater design and production, world history, writing.

Graduation Requirements Arts and fine arts (art, music, dance, drama), electives, English, foreign language, history, mathematics, philosophy, physical education (includes health), religion (includes Bible studies and theology), science, students must pass the Assessment of Basic English Skills, senior chapel talk, community service requirement.

Special Academic Programs Advanced Placement exam preparation; honors section; independent study.

College Admission Counseling 62 students graduated in 2010; all went to college, including Baylor University; Harvard University; Rice University; Southern Methodist University; Texas A&M University; Texas Christian University. Median SAT critical reading: 600, median SAT math: 590, median SAT writing: 610, median combined SAT: 1800.

Student Life Upper grades have uniform requirement, student council, honor system. Discipline rests equally with students and faculty. Attendance at religious services is required.

Summer Programs Enrichment, advancement, sports programs offered; session focuses on academics and enrichment; held on campus; accepts boys and girls; open to students from other schools. 30 students usually enrolled. 2011 schedule: June 8 to July 17. Application deadline: May 28.

Tuition and Aid Day student tuition: $17,995; 5-day tuition and room/board: $32,495; 7-day tuition and room/board: $36,740. Tuition installment plan (Academic Management Services Plan, FACTS Tuition Payment Plan, monthly payment plans). Merit scholarship grants, need-based scholarship grants, tuition remission for children of faculty available. In 2010–11, 25% of upper-school students received aid; total upper-school merit-scholarship money awarded: $55,000. Total amount of financial aid awarded in 2010–11: $555,500.

Admissions Traditional secondary-level entrance grade is 9. For fall 2010, 75 students applied for upper-level admission, 71 were accepted, 60 enrolled. ISEE required. Deadline for receipt of application materials: January 15. Application fee required: $75. Interview required.

Athletics Interscholastic: baseball (boys), basketball (b,g), cheering (g), cross-country running (b,g), diving (b,g), fitness (b,g), football (b), golf (b,g), lacrosse (b,g), soccer (b,g), softball (g), strength & conditioning (b,g), swimming and diving (b,g), tennis (b,g), track and field (b,g), volleyball (g), weight training (b,g); coed interscholastic: JROTC drill, marksmanship, physical training, riflery, strength & conditioning. 10 coaches, 1 athletic trainer.

Computers Computers are regularly used in journalism, language development, literary magazine, newspaper, programming, science, yearbook classes. Computer network features include on-campus library services, online commercial services, Internet access, Internet filtering or blocking technology. Campus intranet, student e-mail accounts, and computer access in designated common areas are available to students. Students grades are available online. The school has a published electronic and media policy.

Contact Mr. Aaron Hawkins, Associate Director. 210-564-6152. Fax: 210-698-0715. E-mail: a.hawkins@tmi-sa.org. Web site: www.tmi-sa.org.

TORONTO DISTRICT CHRISTIAN HIGH SCHOOL

377 Woodbridge Avenue
Woodbridge, Ontario L4L 2V7, Canada
Head of School: Ren Siebenga

General Information Coeducational day college-preparatory, general academic, arts, business, religious studies, bilingual studies, and technology school, affiliated with Christian faith, Christian faith. Grades 9–12. Founded: 1963. Setting: urban. Nearest major city is Toronto, Canada. 16-acre campus. 1 building on campus. Approved or accredited by Association of Christian Schools International, Christian Schools International, Ontario Ministry of Education, and Ontario Department of Education. Language of instruction: English. Endowment: CAN$100,000. Total enrollment: 430. Upper school average class size: 22. Upper school faculty-student ratio: 1:14. The average school day consists of 5 hours and 20 minutes.

Upper School Student Profile Grade 9: 94 students (46 boys, 48 girls); Grade 10: 100 students (51 boys, 49 girls); Grade 11: 121 students (57 boys, 64 girls); Grade 12: 122 students (59 boys, 63 girls). 99% of students are Christian faith, Christian.

Faculty School total: 33. In upper school: 21 men, 12 women; 8 have advanced degrees.

Subjects Offered 20th century history, advanced math, ancient history, art, athletic training, Bible, biology, bookkeeping, business applications, business education, business mathematics, business technology, cabinet making, calculus, Canadian geography, Canadian history, career and personal planning, chemistry, choir, civics, computer applications, computer multimedia, computer programming, concert band, creative writing, discrete mathematics, dramatic arts, economics, English, English literature, environmental studies, ESL, family living, family studies, French, geography, global issues, guitar, health, history, industrial arts, keyboarding, law, media studies, modern Western civilization, music, philosophy, physical education, physics, remedial study skills, science, social justice, theater arts, video film production, visual arts, Western civilization, world issues, world religions.

Graduation Requirements Ontario Ministry of Education requirements.

Special Academic Programs Honors section; term-away projects; study abroad; remedial reading and/or remedial writing; remedial math; programs in English, mathematics, general development for dyslexic students; ESL (21 students enrolled).

College Admission Counseling 109 students graduated in 2010; 87 went to college, including McMaster University; Redeemer University College; University of Guelph; University of Toronto; University of Waterloo; York University. Other: 10 went to work, 12 had other specific plans.

Student Life Upper grades have specified standards of dress, student council, honor system. Discipline rests equally with students and faculty.

Summer Programs Sports programs offered; session focuses on entry-level sports for incoming grade 9 students; held on campus; accepts boys and girls; not open to students from other schools. 24 students usually enrolled.

Tuition and Aid Day student tuition: CAN$9250–CAN$12,020. Tuition installment plan (monthly payment plans, individually arranged payment plans). Tuition reduction for siblings, need-based scholarship grants available.

Admissions Traditional secondary-level entrance grade is 9. Deadline for receipt of application materials: none. Application fee required: CAN$400. On-campus interview required.

Athletics Interscholastic: badminton (boys, girls), basketball (b,g), hockey (b), soccer (b,g), volleyball (b,g), water badminton (b); intramural: badminton (b,g), water badminton (b); coed interscholastic: badminton, cross-country running, track and field, ultimate Frisbee; coed intramural: badminton, ice hockey. 5 PE instructors, 5 coaches.

Computers Computers are regularly used in accounting, all academic, business applications, programming, technology, video film production, yearbook classes. Computer network features include on-campus library services, Internet access, wireless campus network, Internet filtering or blocking technology. Campus intranet, student e-mail accounts, and computer access in designated common areas are available to students. Students grades are available online. The school has a published electronic and media policy.

Contact Mr. Tim Bentum, Vice Principal, Students and Admissions. 905-851-1772 Ext. 202. Fax: 905-851-9992. E-mail: bentum@tdchristian.ca. Web site: www.tdchristian.ca.

TORONTO WALDORF SCHOOL

9100 Bathurst Street
Thornhill, Ontario L4J 8C7, Canada
Head of School: Ms. Michele Andrews

General Information Coeducational day college-preparatory, general academic, arts, business, vocational, bilingual studies, and technology school; primarily serves underachievers. Grades JK–12. Founded: 1968. Setting: suburban. Nearest major city is Toronto, Canada. 25-acre campus. 2 buildings on campus. Approved or accredited by Association of Waldorf Schools of North America, Standards in Excellence And Learning (SEAL), and Ontario Department of Education. Language of instruction: English. Endowment: CAN$200,000. Total enrollment: 294. Upper school average class size: 20. Upper school faculty-student ratio: 1:5.

Upper School Student Profile Grade 9: 29 students (14 boys, 15 girls); Grade 10: 25 students (12 boys, 13 girls); Grade 11: 23 students (10 boys, 13 girls); Grade 12: 18 students (7 boys, 11 girls).

Faculty School total: 55. In upper school: 8 men, 12 women; 10 have advanced degrees.

Subjects Offered Acting, advanced computer applications, algebra, American history, ancient history, art, art history, astronomy, atomic theory, biochemistry, botany, business mathematics, business studies, Canadian geography, Canadian history, careers, chemistry, choir, civics, clayworking, composition, computer science, crafts, drama, drama performance, drawing, English composition, English literature, ESL, eurythmy, evolution, family studies, French, gardening, genetics, geography, geology, geometry, German, grammar, health, history, history of architecture, history of drama, history of music, human anatomy, inorganic chemistry, literature, mathematics, mechanics, medieval/Renaissance history, meteorology, microbiology, modeling, modern history, music, mythology, novels, nutrition, optics, orchestra, organic chemistry, painting, performing arts, philosophy, physical education, physics, physiology, practical arts, reading, Shakespeare, trigonometry, visual arts, water color painting, woodworking, writing, zoology.

Special Academic Programs Term-away projects; study abroad; ESL (10 students enrolled).

College Admission Counseling 30 students graduated in 2009; 25 went to college.

Student Life Upper grades have specified standards of dress, student council. Discipline rests primarily with faculty.

Tuition and Aid Day student tuition: CAN$16,200. Tuition installment plan (monthly payment plans). Bursaries, need-based scholarship grants available.

Admissions For fall 2009, 25 students applied for upper-level admission, 15 were accepted, 10 enrolled. Deadline for receipt of application materials: none. Application fee required: CAN$100. On-campus interview required.

Athletics Intramural: badminton (boys, girls), basketball (b,g), cross-country running (b,g), mountain biking (b,g); coed interscholastic: artistic gym, badminton, basketball, canoeing/kayaking, Circus, cooperative games, cross-country running, fitness, indoor track & field, juggling, outdoor adventure, outdoor education, physical fitness, physical training, rhythmic gymnastics, running, skiing (cross-country), skiing (downhill), strength & conditioning, track and field, unicycling, wallyball, wilderness survival, wildernessways, yoga. 2 PE instructors, 2 coaches.

Computers Computers are regularly used in yearbook classes. Computer resources include Internet access, Internet filtering or blocking technology.

Toronto Waldorf School

Contact Ms. Aileen Stewart, Admissions Coordinator. 905-881-1611 Ext. 314. Fax: 905-881-6710. E-mail: astewart@torontowaldorfschool.com. Web site: www. torontowaldorfschool.com.

TOWER HILL SCHOOL
2813 West 17th Street
Wilmington, Delaware 19806
Head of School: Dr. Christopher D. Wheeler

General Information Coeducational day college-preparatory, arts, and technology school. Grades PS–12. Founded: 1919. Setting: suburban. Nearest major city is Philadelphia, PA. 44-acre campus. 4 buildings on campus. Approved or accredited by Middle States Association of Colleges and Schools and Delaware Department of Education. Member of National Association of Independent Schools and Secondary School Admission Test Board. Endowment: $27 million. Total enrollment: 756. Upper school average class size: 14. Upper school faculty-student ratio: 1:8. There are 162 required school days per year for Upper School students. Upper School students typically attend 5 days per week. The average school day consists of 7 hours.

Upper School Student Profile Grade 9: 60 students (36 boys, 24 girls); Grade 10: 54 students (31 boys, 23 girls); Grade 11: 53 students (23 boys, 30 girls); Grade 12: 55 students (25 boys, 30 girls).

Faculty School total: 97. In upper school: 17 men, 9 women; 22 have advanced degrees.

Subjects Offered Acting, advanced biology, advanced chemistry, advanced computer applications, advanced math, advanced studio art-AP, algebra, American history, American literature, art, art history, band, biology, British literature, calculus, chemistry, China/Japan history, chorus, classical Greek literature, community service, computer science, creative writing, current events, DNA, drama, drawing, driver education, English, English literature, ethics, European history, film, fine arts, French, geometry, historical research, history, human anatomy, jazz band, Latin, mathematics, music, music theory, organic chemistry, painting, photography, physical science, physics, poetry, pre-calculus, psychology, Russian literature, science, Shakespeare, Spanish, Spanish literature, strings, theater, theater design and production, U.S. constitutional history, Vietnam War, Web authoring, woodworking, world history, writing.

Graduation Requirements Arts and fine arts (art, music, dance, drama), athletics, English, foreign language, mathematics, science, social studies (includes history). Community service is required.

Special Academic Programs Advanced Placement exam preparation; honors section; independent study; academic accommodation for the gifted, the musically talented, and the artistically talented.

College Admission Counseling 48 students graduated in 2010; all went to college, including Columbia University; Georgetown University; Tufts University; University of Delaware; Wake Forest University; Yale University. Mean SAT critical reading: 633, mean SAT math: 661, mean SAT writing: 643. 75% scored over 600 on SAT critical reading, 81% scored over 600 on SAT math, 66% scored over 600 on SAT writing.

Student Life Upper grades have specified standards of dress, student council, honor system. Discipline rests equally with students and faculty.

Summer Programs Enrichment, advancement, sports programs offered; held on campus; accepts boys and girls; open to students from other schools. 60 students usually enrolled. 2011 schedule: June 13 to August 12. Application deadline: May 1.

Tuition and Aid Day student tuition: $23,710. Tuition installment plan (Key Tuition Payment Plan, monthly payment plans, individually arranged payment plans). Need-based scholarship grants available. In 2010–11, 19% of upper-school students received aid. Total amount of financial aid awarded in 2010–11: $790,844.

Admissions Traditional secondary-level entrance grade is 9. For fall 2010, 57 students applied for upper-level admission, 39 were accepted, 15 enrolled. ERB CTP IV, PSAT or SAT for applicants to grade 11 and 12, SSAT or writing sample required. Deadline for receipt of application materials: January 7. Application fee required: $40. On-campus interview required.

Athletics Interscholastic: baseball (boys), basketball (b,g), cross-country running (b,g), field hockey (g), football (b), indoor track (b,g), lacrosse (b,g), soccer (b,g), swimming and diving (b,g), tennis (b,g), track and field (b,g), volleyball (g), winter (indoor) track (b,g), wrestling (b); intramural: fitness (g), self defense (g), yoga (g); coed interscholastic: golf; coed intramural: aerobics/Nautilus, strength & conditioning, weight lifting. 21 coaches, 2 athletic trainers.

Computers Computers are regularly used in all academic classes. Computer network features include on-campus library services, Internet access, wireless campus network, Internet filtering or blocking technology. Student e-mail accounts and computer access in designated common areas are available to students. Students grades are available online. The school has a published electronic and media policy.

Contact Mr. William R. Ushler, Associate Director of Admission. 302-657-8350. Fax: 302-657-8377. E-mail: wushler@towerhill.org. Web site: www.towerhill.org.

TOWN CENTRE PRIVATE HIGH SCHOOL
155 Clayton Drive
Markham, Ontario L3R 7P3, Canada
Head of School: Mr. Patrick McCarthy

General Information Coeducational day college-preparatory school. Grades PS–12. Founded: 1986. Setting: suburban. Nearest major city is Toronto, Canada. 5-acre campus. 1 building on campus. Approved or accredited by Ontario Ministry of Education and Ontario Department of Education. Language of instruction: English. Upper school average class size: 15. Upper school faculty-student ratio: 1:15. There are 178 required school days per year for Upper School students. Upper School students typically attend 5 days per week. The average school day consists of 5 hours and 20 minutes.

Upper School Student Profile Grade 9: 42 students (22 boys, 20 girls); Grade 10: 41 students (18 boys, 23 girls); Grade 11: 57 students (27 boys, 30 girls); Grade 12: 45 students (23 boys, 22 girls).

Faculty School total: 17. In upper school: 11 men, 6 women; 6 have advanced degrees.

Subjects Offered Accounting, advanced chemistry, advanced computer applications, advanced math, Advanced Placement courses, algebra, anthropology, art, band, biology, biology-AP, business, business applications, business studies, calculus, calculus-AP, Canadian geography, Canadian history, Canadian law, career education, chemistry, civics, computer information systems, computer programming, discrete mathematics, economics, English, English as a foreign language, English-AP, ESL, family living, French, geography, health education, health science, history, history-AP, keyboarding, macroeconomics-AP, microeconomics-AP, music, music theory, physics, religion, science, sociology, statistics-AP, visual arts, world religions.

Graduation Requirements Arts, Canadian geography, Canadian history, English, French, mathematics, physical education (includes health), science, technology/design, Ontario Secondary School's Literacy Test, 40 hours community service.

Special Academic Programs 7 Advanced Placement exams for which test preparation is offered; ESL (27 students enrolled).

College Admission Counseling 57 students graduated in 2010; all went to college, including McMaster University; The University of Western Ontario; University of Guelph; University of Toronto; University of Waterloo; York University.

Student Life Upper grades have uniform requirement, student council, honor system. Discipline rests primarily with faculty.

Summer Programs Remediation, enrichment programs offered; session focuses on academic upgrading; held on campus; accepts boys and girls; open to students from other schools. 30 students usually enrolled. 2011 schedule: July 5 to July 29. Application deadline: none.

Tuition and Aid Day student tuition: CAN$13,400. Tuition installment plan (monthly payment plans, individually arranged payment plans, 2 installments and full payment). Tuition reduction for siblings available.

Admissions Traditional secondary-level entrance grade is 9. For fall 2010, 23 students applied for upper-level admission, 17 were accepted, 16 enrolled. High School Placement Test required. Deadline for receipt of application materials: none. Application fee required: CAN$200. Interview recommended.

Athletics Interscholastic: badminton (boys, girls), ball hockey (b,g), basketball (b,g), flag football (b), floor hockey (b,g), soccer (b,g), volleyball (b,g); intramural: ball hockey (b), ballet (g), basketball (b,g), soccer (b,g), volleyball (b,g); coed interscholastic: cooperative games, golf, physical fitness, softball, ultimate Frisbee; coed intramural: archery, badminton, ball hockey, baseball, bowling, cricket, cross-country running, fitness, flag football, floor hockey, golf, softball, table tennis, tennis, ultimate Frisbee. 2 PE instructors.

Computers Computers are regularly used in accounting, business, computer applications, information technology, mathematics classes. Computer network features include Internet access, Internet filtering or blocking technology. The school has a published electronic and media policy.

Contact Ms. Patricia Ego, Admissions. 905-470-1200. Fax: 905-470-1721. E-mail: pat.ego@tcphs.com. Web site: www.tcphs.com.

TRADITIONAL LEARNING ACADEMY
1189 Rochester Avenue
Coquitlam, British Columbia V3K 2X3, Canada
Head of School: Mr. Martin Charles Postgate Dale

General Information Coeducational day college-preparatory and general academic school, affiliated with Roman Catholic Church. Grades K–12. Founded: 1991. Setting: suburban. Nearest major city is Vancouver, Canada. 4-acre campus. 1 building on campus. Approved or accredited by home study and British Columbia Department of Education. Language of instruction: English. Total enrollment: 200. Upper school average class size: 12. Upper school faculty-student ratio: 1:10. The average school day consists of 5 hours and 15 minutes.

Upper School Student Profile Grade 8: 13 students (2 boys, 11 girls); Grade 9: 9 students (4 boys, 5 girls); Grade 10: 12 students (4 boys, 8 girls); Grade 11: 8 students (5 boys, 3 girls); Grade 12: 15 students (6 boys, 9 girls). 85% of students are Roman Catholic.

Faculty School total: 17. In upper school: 6 men, 4 women; 2 have advanced degrees.

Subjects Offered Art, choral music, English literature, French, grammar, history, Latin, mathematics, physical education, religion, science, social studies.

College Admission Counseling 5 students graduated in 2009; 3 went to college, including California State University, San Bernardino; Simon Fraser University; The University of British Columbia; Trinity Western University. Other: 2 went to work. Mean SAT critical reading: 800, mean SAT math: 720. 100% scored over 600 on SAT critical reading, 100% scored over 600 on SAT math.

Student Life Upper grades have uniform requirement, honor system. Discipline rests equally with students and faculty. Attendance at religious services is required.

Tuition and Aid Day student tuition: CAN$3500. Tuition installment plan (monthly payment plans, individually arranged payment plans). Tuition reduction for siblings, need-based scholarship grants available. In 2009–10, 10% of upper-school students received aid. Total amount of financial aid awarded in 2009–10: CAN$15,000.

Admissions Traditional secondary-level entrance grade is 8. For fall 2009, 5 students applied for upper-level admission, 3 were accepted, 2 enrolled. English entrance exam required. Deadline for receipt of application materials: none. Application fee required: CAN$50. On-campus interview required.

Athletics Interscholastic: basketball (boys, girls), floor hockey (b), soccer (b,g), softball (b,g), track and field (b,g), volleyball (b,g); intramural: basketball (b,g), floor hockey (b), volleyball (g); coed interscholastic: curling, Frisbee, ultimate Frisbee; coed intramural: alpine skiing, badminton, canoeing/kayaking, dance, hiking/backpacking, kayaking, tennis. 1 PE instructor.

Computers Computers are regularly used in career education classes. Computer resources include Internet access, Internet filtering or blocking technology.

Contact Mrs. Rina Caan, Secretary. 604-931-7265. Fax: 604-931-3432. E-mail: tlaoffice@traditionallearning.com. Web site: www.traditionallearning.com.

TRAFALGAR CASTLE SCHOOL

401 Reynolds Street
Whitby, Ontario L1N 3W9, Canada
Head of School: Mr. Adam de Pencier

General Information Girls' boarding and day college-preparatory, arts, business, and technology school. Boarding grades 7–12, day grades 5–12. Founded: 1874. Setting: small town. Nearest major city is Toronto, Canada. Students are housed in single-sex dormitories. 28-acre campus. 2 buildings on campus. Approved or accredited by Canadian Association of Independent Schools, Canadian Educational Standards Institute, Conference of Independent Schools of Ontario, Ontario Ministry of Education, The Association of Boarding Schools, and Ontario Department of Education. Language of instruction: English. Endowment: CAN$153,000. Total enrollment: 189. Upper school average class size: 15. Upper school faculty-student ratio: 1:9. There are 170 required school days per year for Upper School students. Upper School students typically attend 5 days per week. The average school day consists of 7 hours and 30 minutes.

Upper School Student Profile Grade 9: 27 students (27 girls); Grade 10: 28 students (28 girls); Grade 11: 25 students (25 girls); Grade 12: 34 students (34 girls). 24% of students are boarding students. 80% are province residents. 3 provinces are represented in upper school student body. 20% are international students. International students from Bahamas, China, Egypt, Hong Kong, Mexico, and Republic of Korea; 4 other countries represented in student body.

Faculty School total: 27. In upper school: 4 men, 23 women; 6 have advanced degrees; 5 reside on campus.

Subjects Offered Algebra, art, art history, biology, business skills, calculus, chemistry, computer math, computer science, creative writing, drama, earth science, economics, English, English literature, environmental science, ESL, European history, fine arts, French, geography, geometry, grammar, law, mathematics, music, photography, physical education, physics, science, social studies, world history, world literature, writing.

Graduation Requirements Arts and fine arts (art, music, dance, drama), business skills (includes word processing), computer science, English, foreign language, mathematics, physical education (includes health), science, social studies (includes history).

Special Academic Programs Advanced Placement exam preparation; honors section; term-away projects; domestic exchange program (with Sedbergh School); special instructional classes for students with slight learning disabilities; ESL (17 students enrolled).

College Admission Counseling 37 students graduated in 2010; all went to college, including McGill University; Queen's University at Kingston; The University of Western Ontario; University of Toronto; University of Waterloo; Wilfrid Laurier University.

Student Life Upper grades have uniform requirement, student council. Discipline rests primarily with faculty.

Tuition and Aid Day student tuition: CAN$18,700–CAN$20,750; 5-day tuition and room/board: CAN$36,000; 7-day tuition and room/board: CAN$39,000–CAN$43,000. Tuition installment plan (monthly payment plans, individually arranged payment plans, early payment discounts). Tuition reduction for siblings, bursaries, merit scholarship grants, need-based scholarship grants available. In 2010–11, 3% of upper-school students received aid; total upper-school merit-scholarship money awarded: CAN$16,000. Total amount of financial aid awarded in 2010–11: CAN$43,000.

Admissions Traditional secondary-level entrance grade is 9. For fall 2010, 75 students applied for upper-level admission, 70 were accepted, 64 enrolled. Cognitive

Abilities Test required. Deadline for receipt of application materials: none. Application fee required: CAN$2500. Interview required.

Athletics Interscholastic: badminton, baseball, basketball, cross-country running, field hockey, gymnastics, ice hockey, independent competitive sports, soccer, softball, swimming and diving, synchronized swimming, tennis, track and field, volleyball; intramural: badminton, baseball, basketball, cross-country running, dance team, field hockey, fitness, fitness walking, gymnastics, ice hockey, outdoor activities, outdoor adventure, outdoor education, physical fitness, ropes courses, running, skiing (cross-country), skiing (downhill), snowboarding, soccer, softball, swimming and diving, synchronized swimming, tennis, track and field, volleyball, yoga. 3 PE instructors.

Computers Computers are regularly used in all academic classes. Computer network features include on-campus library services, Internet access, wireless campus network, Internet filtering or blocking technology. Campus intranet and student e-mail accounts are available to students. Students grades are available online. The school has a published electronic and media policy.

Contact Irene Talent, Admissions Officer. 905-668-3358 Ext. 227. Fax: 905-668-4136. E-mail: talenti@castle-ed.com. Web site: www.castle-ed.com.

TRIDENT ACADEMY

Mt. Pleasant, South Carolina
See Special Needs Schools section.

TRINITY CHRISTIAN ACADEMY

10 Windy City Road
Jackson, Tennessee 38305
Head of School: Dr. Sam Botta

General Information Coeducational day college-preparatory school. Grades K4–12. Founded: 1986. Setting: small town. Nearest major city is Memphis. 30-acre campus. 1 building on campus. Approved or accredited by Association of Christian Schools International, Southern Association of Colleges and Schools, and Tennessee Department of Education. Total enrollment: 752. Upper school average class size: 22. Upper school faculty-student ratio: 1:9. There are 176 required school days per year for Upper School students. Upper School students typically attend 5 days per week. The average school day consists of 5 hours and 20 minutes.

Faculty School total: 48. In upper school: 6 men, 11 women; 6 have advanced degrees.

Subjects Offered Algebra, art, Bible studies, biology, biology-AP, British literature, British literature (honors), calculus-AP, chemistry, choir, computers, drama, economics, English, etymology, fine arts, geography, geometry, government, physical science, physics, physics-AP, pre-calculus, U.S. history, U.S. history-AP, wellness, world history, yearbook.

Graduation Requirements Arts and fine arts (art, music, dance, drama), Bible, computers, English, foreign language, history, mathematics, science, wellness.

College Admission Counseling 37 students graduated in 2010; all went to college, including Jackson State Community College; Mary Baldwin College; Mississippi College; The University of Tennessee; The University of Tennessee at Martin; Union University. Median composite ACT: 24.

Student Life Upper grades have uniform requirement, student council, honor system. Discipline rests primarily with faculty. Attendance at religious services is required.

Tuition and Aid Day student tuition: $7190. Tuition installment plan (monthly payment plans). Need-based scholarship grants available.

Admissions Traditional secondary-level entrance grade is 9. SAT required. Deadline for receipt of application materials: none. Application fee required: $200. On-campus interview required.

Athletics Interscholastic: baseball (girls), basketball (b,g), cheering (b), cross-country running (b,g), football (g), golf (g), softball (b), tennis (b,g), track and field (b,g), volleyball (b); coed interscholastic: soccer. 2 PE instructors, 6 coaches.

Computers Computer resources include Internet access, Internet filtering or blocking technology. Students grades are available online.

Contact Mrs. Andrea Moody, Admissions Director. 731-668-8500 Ext. 107. Fax: 731-668-3232. E-mail: amoody@tcalions.com. Web site: www.tcalions.com.

TRINITY CHRISTIAN ACADEMY

17001 Addison Road
Addison, Texas 75001-5096
Head of School: Mr. David Delph

General Information Coeducational day college-preparatory, arts, religious studies, bilingual studies, and technology school, affiliated with Christian faith. Grades K–12. Founded: 1970. Setting: suburban. Nearest major city is Dallas. 40-acre campus. 1 building on campus. Approved or accredited by Association of Christian Schools International, Christian Schools International, Southern Association of Colleges and Schools, The College Board, and Texas Department of Education. Endowment: $8.2 million. Total enrollment: 1,515. Upper school average class size: 18. Upper school faculty-student ratio: 1:10. There are 175 required school days per year for Upper School students. Upper School students typically attend 5 days per week. The average school day consists of 7 hours.

Trinity Christian Academy

Upper School Student Profile Grade 9: 120 students (60 boys, 60 girls); Grade 10: 120 students (60 boys, 60 girls); Grade 11: 120 students (60 boys, 60 girls); Grade 12: 120 students (60 boys, 60 girls). 100% of students are Christian faith.

Faculty School total: 130. In upper school: 15 men, 35 women; 31 have advanced degrees.

Subjects Offered Advanced biology, advanced computer applications, advanced math, Advanced Placement courses, advanced studio art-AP, algebra, American government, American history, American history-AP, American literature, American literature-AP, anatomy and physiology, art, athletics, Bible, Bible studies, biology, biology-AP, calculus, calculus-AP, chemistry, community service, computer animation, computer applications, computer art, computer graphics, computer information systems, computer literacy, computer multimedia, computer programming, computer science, computer science-AP, desktop publishing, digital art, digital photography, drama, drama performance, drawing, economics, economics-AP, English, English language and composition-AP, English literature, European history, European history-AP, European literature, expository writing, fine arts, French, French-AP, geography, geometry, government, government-AP, government/civics, health, history, history of ideas, history-AP, honors algebra, honors English, honors geometry, honors world history, keyboarding, Latin, literature and composition-AP, mathematics, music, painting, performing arts, photography, physical education, physics, printmaking, psychology, religion, science, social sciences, social studies, Spanish, Spanish-AP, speech, speech communications, studio art-AP, theater, theater arts, trigonometry, U.S. government and politics-AP, vocal music, Web site design, world history, world literature.

Graduation Requirements Arts and fine arts (art, music, dance, drama), Bible, economics, English, foreign language, government, mathematics, physical education (includes health), science, social sciences, social studies (includes history), speech communications, technology. Community service is required.

Special Academic Programs 11 Advanced Placement exams for which test preparation is offered; honors section; independent study; study abroad.

College Admission Counseling 118 students graduated in 2009; all went to college, including Baylor University; Pepperdine University; Texas A&M University; The University of Texas at Austin; Wake Forest University; Wheaton College. Mean SAT critical reading: 600, mean SAT math: 622, mean SAT writing: 598, mean combined SAT: 1820, mean composite ACT: 26.

Student Life Upper grades have uniform requirement, student council, honor system. Discipline rests equally with students and faculty. Attendance at religious services is required.

Tuition and Aid Day student tuition: $14,140–$15,170. Tuition installment plan (monthly payment plans). Need-based scholarship grants available. In 2009–10, 5% of upper-school students received aid. Total amount of financial aid awarded in 2009–10: $190,000.

Admissions Traditional secondary-level entrance grade is 9. For fall 2009, 58 students applied for upper-level admission, 44 were accepted, 29 enrolled. ISEE and Stanford Achievement Test required. Deadline for receipt of application materials: February 1. Application fee required: $100. On-campus interview required.

Athletics Interscholastic: baseball (boys), basketball (b,g), cheering (g), drill team (g), football (b), golf (b,g), running (b,g), soccer (b,g), softball (g), strength & conditioning (b,g), volleyball (g), weight lifting (b), weight training (b), winter soccer (b,g), wrestling (b); coed interscholastic: cross-country running, swimming and diving, tennis, track and field. 2 PE instructors, 39 coaches, 1 athletic trainer.

Computers Computers are regularly used in animation, art, Bible studies, career exploration, college planning, desktop publishing, digital applications, English, foreign language, mathematics, multimedia, photojournalism, publications, science, technology, video film production, Web site design, word processing, yearbook classes. Computer network features include on-campus library services, Internet access, Internet filtering or blocking technology. Computer access in designated common areas is available to students. Students grades are available online. The school has a published electronic and media policy.

Contact Mary Helen Noland, Admission Director. 972-931-8325. Fax: 972-931-8923. E-mail: mhnoland@trinitychristian.org. Web site: www.trinitychristian.org.

TRINITY COLLEGE SCHOOL

55 Deblaquire Street North
Port Hope, Ontario L1A 4K7, Canada

Head of School: Mr. Stuart K.C. Grainger

General Information Coeducational boarding and day college-preparatory school, affiliated with Church of England (Anglican). Boarding grades 9–12, day grades 5–12. Founded: 1865. Setting: small town. Nearest major city is Toronto, Canada. Students are housed in single-sex dormitories. 100-acre campus. 15 buildings on campus. Approved or accredited by Canadian Association of Independent Schools, Canadian Educational Standards Institute, Conference of Independent Schools of Ontario, The Association of Boarding Schools, and Ontario Department of Education. Affiliate member of National Association of Independent Schools; member of Secondary School Admission Test Board. Language of instruction: English. Endowment: CAN$24 million. Total enrollment: 590. Upper school average class size: 16. Upper school faculty-student ratio: 1:8. There are 165 required school days per year for Upper School students. Upper School students typically attend 5 days per week.

Upper School Student Profile Grade 9: 96 students (52 boys, 44 girls); Grade 10: 106 students (53 boys, 53 girls); Grade 11: 158 students (80 boys, 78 girls); Grade 12: 150 students (87 boys, 63 girls). 60% of students are boarding students. 61% are province residents. 8 provinces are represented in upper school student body. 33% are international students. International students from Bahamas, Bermuda, China, Germany, Mexico, and Republic of Korea; 23 other countries represented in student body. 30% of students are members of Church of England (Anglican).

Faculty School total: 86. In upper school: 37 men, 29 women; 17 have advanced degrees; 11 reside on campus.

Subjects Offered Algebra, art, art history-AP, astronomy, biology, biology-AP, calculus, calculus-AP, Canadian geography, Canadian history, career education, career/college preparation, chemistry, chemistry-AP, civics, classical civilization, classics, community service, computer programming, computer science, creative writing, dramatic arts, earth science, economics, English, English literature, English-AP, environmental science, environmental studies, ESL, European history, fine arts, finite math, French, French-AP, general science, geography, geometry, German, guidance, health, history, independent study, Latin, law, mathematics, modern Western civilization, music, philosophy, physical education, physics, physics-AP, political science, science, social sciences, social studies, Spanish.

Graduation Requirements Arts and fine arts (art, music, dance, drama), Canadian geography, Canadian history, civics, English, French, guidance, mathematics, physical education (includes health), science, social sciences, technology, minimum 40 hours of community service.

Special Academic Programs Advanced Placement exam preparation; independent study; term-away projects; study abroad; ESL (15 students enrolled).

College Admission Counseling 144 students graduated in 2010; all went to college, including Dalhousie University; McGill University; Queen's University at Kingston; The University of Western Ontario; University of Guelph; University of Toronto. 25.5% scored over 600 on SAT critical reading, 30% scored over 600 on SAT math, 23% scored over 600 on SAT writing, 30% scored over 1800 on combined SAT.

Student Life Upper grades have uniform requirement, student council, honor system. Discipline rests primarily with faculty. Attendance at religious services is required.

Summer Programs Advancement, art/fine arts, computer instruction programs offered; session focuses on advancement through cultural enrichment; held off campus; held at England; accepts boys and girls; open to students from other schools. 30 students usually enrolled. 2011 schedule: July 3 to July 25. Application deadline: April 12.

Tuition and Aid Day student tuition: CAN$26,490; 5-day tuition and room/board: CAN$45,250–CAN$45,750; 7-day tuition and room/board: CAN$47,300–CAN$47,800. Tuition installment plan (monthly payment plans, quarterly payment plan). Bursaries, need-based scholarship grants available. In 2010–11, 26% of upper-school students received aid. Total amount of financial aid awarded in 2010–11: CAN$1,000,000.

Admissions Traditional secondary-level entrance grade is 9. For fall 2010, 500 students applied for upper-level admission, 338 were accepted, 256 enrolled. CCAT, SSAT, ERB, PSAT, SAT, PLAN or ACT or TOEFL required. Deadline for receipt of application materials: none. Application fee required: CAN$200. Interview required.

Athletics Interscholastic: baseball (boys), basketball (b,g), cricket (b), field hockey (g), football (b), ice hockey (b,g), rugby (b,g), soccer (b,g), softball (g), squash (b,g), tennis (b,g), volleyball (b,g); coed interscholastic: badminton, cross-country running, dressage, equestrian sports, golf, nordic skiing, outdoor education, rowing, skiing (cross-country), swimming and diving, track and field; coed intramural: aerobics, aerobics/dance, alpine skiing, badminton, basketball, bicycling, cricket, cross-country running, dance, equestrian sports, fitness, golf, horseback riding, ice hockey, jogging, mountain biking, paddling, skiing (downhill), snowboarding, soccer, softball, squash, strength & conditioning, swimming and diving, table tennis, tennis, water polo, weight lifting, weight training, yoga. 4 PE instructors, 5 coaches, 2 athletic trainers.

Computers Computers are regularly used in career education, college planning, English, ESL, foreign language, French, geography, history, humanities, independent study, information technology, mathematics, music, science, technology classes. Computer network features include on-campus library services, Internet access, wireless campus network. Student e-mail accounts are available to students.

Contact Ms. Kathryn A. LaBranche, Director of Admissions. 905-885-3209. Fax: 905-885-7444. E-mail: admissions@tcs.on.ca. Web site: www.tcs.on.ca.

TRINITY EPISCOPAL SCHOOL

3850 Pittaway Drive
Richmond, Virginia 23235

Head of School: Dr. Thomas G. Aycock

General Information Coeducational day college-preparatory, arts, and International Baccalaureate school, affiliated with Episcopal Church. Grades 8–12. Founded: 1972. Setting: suburban. 40-acre campus. 6 buildings on campus. Approved or accredited by National Association of Episcopal Schools, Virginia Association of Independent Schools, and Virginia Department of Education. Member of National Association of Independent Schools. Endowment: $150,000. Total enrollment: 414. Upper school average class size: 13. Upper school faculty-student ratio: 1:10. There are 180 required school days per year for Upper School students. Upper School students typically attend 5 days per week.

Upper School Student Profile Grade 8: 24 students (14 boys, 10 girls); Grade 9: 93 students (47 boys, 46 girls); Grade 10: 101 students (50 boys, 51 girls); Grade 11: 98 students (52 boys, 46 girls); Grade 12: 98 students (63 boys, 35 girls).

Faculty School total: 51. In upper school: 26 men, 25 women; 30 have advanced degrees.

Subjects Offered 20th century history, 20th century world history, 3-dimensional art, Advanced Placement courses, advanced studio art-AP, algebra, American government, American history, American history-AP, American literature, American politics in film, anatomy, art, astronomy, band, Bible studies, biology, biology-AP, calculus, calculus-AP, chemistry, chemistry-AP, chorus, computer graphics, computer programming, computer science, concert band, concert choir, creative writing, digital music, drama, driver education, earth science, economics, English, English literature, English-AP, environmental science, European history, European history-AP, foreign policy, French, French-AP, geography, geology, geometry, German, German-AP, government-AP, government/civics, International Baccalaureate courses, jazz band, keyboarding, Latin, math analysis, mathematics, music, physics, physics-AP, pre-calculus, religion, science, social sciences, social studies, Southern literature, Spanish, studio art-AP, theater, theology, theory of knowledge, trigonometry, U.S. government and politics-AP, U.S. history-AP, Web site design, word processing, world history, world literature, world religions, writing.

Graduation Requirements Arts and fine arts (art, music, dance, drama), computer science, English, foreign language, mathematics, religion (includes Bible studies and theology), science, social sciences, social studies (includes history). Community service is required.

Special Academic Programs International Baccalaureate program; 13 Advanced Placement exams for which test preparation is offered; honors section; independent study; academic accommodation for the gifted, the musically talented, and the artistically talented.

College Admission Counseling 112 students graduated in 2009; 107 went to college, including James Madison University; The College of William and Mary; University of South Carolina; University of Virginia; Virginia Polytechnic Institute and State University. Other: 5 had other specific plans.

Student Life Upper grades have specified standards of dress, student council, honor system. Discipline rests equally with students and faculty. Attendance at religious services is required.

Tuition and Aid Day student tuition: $16,880. Tuition installment plan (Key Tuition Payment Plan, monthly payment plans). Merit scholarship grants, need-based scholarship grants available. In 2009–10, 24% of upper-school students received aid; total upper-school merit-scholarship money awarded: $1350. Total amount of financial aid awarded in 2009–10: $915,000.

Admissions Traditional secondary-level entrance grade is 9. For fall 2009, 209 students applied for upper-level admission, 193 were accepted, 112 enrolled. English entrance exam, Math Placement Exam and Otis-Lennon School Ability Test required. Deadline for receipt of application materials: February 26. Application fee required: $50. On-campus interview required.

Athletics Interscholastic: baseball (boys), basketball (b,g), cross-country running (b,g), field hockey (g), football (b), indoor soccer (b,g), lacrosse (b,g), soccer (b,g), softball (g), tennis (b,g), track and field (b,g), volleyball (b,g), winter soccer (b,g); coed interscholastic: aquatics, crew, diving, golf, indoor track, rowing, running, swimming and diving, winter (indoor) track; coed intramural: aerobics/dance, canoeing/kayaking, climbing, dance, fitness, physical fitness, physical training, rock climbing, scuba diving, strength & conditioning, wall climbing, weight training, yoga. 1 PE instructor, 14 coaches, 2 athletic trainers.

Computers Computer resources include on-campus library services, online commercial services, Internet access, wireless campus network. The school has a published electronic and media policy.

Contact Mrs. Emily H. McLeod, Director of Admission. 804-327-3156. Fax: 804-272-4652. E-mail: emilymcleod@trinityes.org. Web site: www.trinityes.org.

TRINITY HIGH SCHOOL

7574 West Division Street
River Forest, Illinois 60305
Head of School: Dr. Antonia C. Bouillette

General Information Girls' day college-preparatory, arts, and religious studies school, affiliated with Roman Catholic Church. Grades 9–12. Founded: 1918. Setting: suburban. Nearest major city is Chicago. 1-acre campus. 2 buildings on campus. Approved or accredited by International Baccalaureate Organization, National Catholic Education Association, North Central Association of Colleges and Schools, The College Board, and Illinois Department of Education. Endowment: $2 million. Total enrollment: 547. Upper school average class size: 20. Upper school faculty-student ratio: 1:14.

Upper School Student Profile Grade 9: 147 students (147 girls); Grade 10: 154 students (154 girls); Grade 11: 114 students (114 girls); Grade 12: 132 students (132 girls). 80% of students are Roman Catholic.

Faculty School total: 40. In upper school: 3 men, 37 women; 28 have advanced degrees.

Subjects Offered Algebra, British literature, choir, comparative religion, computer art, computer graphics, creative dance, creative drama, dance, desktop publishing, digital art, ecology, environmental systems, economics, English, environmental science, European history, film studies, French, geometry, government, graphic design, health, honors algebra, honors English, honors geometry, honors U.S. history, honors world history, integrated mathematics, Italian, keyboarding, math methods, moral theology, newspaper, painting, physical education, physics, pre-calculus,

pre-college orientation, probability and statistics, psychology, religious studies, scripture, Spanish, speech, speech and debate, theater, theology, theory of knowledge, U.S. government, U.S. government and politics, U.S. history, vocal music, women in society, word processing, world civilizations, world geography, world governments, world history, world religions, world studies, yearbook.

Graduation Requirements Algebra, American literature, arts and fine arts (art, music, dance, drama), biology, British literature, Catholic belief and practice, chemistry, Christian ethics, Christian scripture, church history, computer applications, English composition, foreign language, geometry, health education, keyboarding, physical education (includes health), speech, theology, U.S. history, world history, world literature, world religions, world studies.

Special Academic Programs International Baccalaureate program; honors section; independent study; academic accommodation for the gifted.

College Admission Counseling 108 students graduated in 2009; all went to college, including DePaul University; Dominican University; Illinois State University; Loyola University Chicago; University of Chicago; University of Illinois at Urbana–Champaign. Median composite ACT: 23. 19% scored over 26 on composite ACT.

Student Life Upper grades have uniform requirement, student council. Discipline rests primarily with faculty. Attendance at religious services is required.

Tuition and Aid Day student tuition: $8650. Tuition installment plan (FACTS Tuition Payment Plan, monthly payment plans, individually arranged payment plans). Tuition reduction for siblings, merit scholarship grants, need-based scholarship grants, paying campus jobs available. In 2009–10, 30% of upper-school students received aid; total upper-school merit-scholarship money awarded: $28,900. Total amount of financial aid awarded in 2009–10: $372,500.

Admissions Traditional secondary-level entrance grade is 9. For fall 2009, 235 students applied for upper-level admission, 215 were accepted, 163 enrolled. ACT-Explore or High School Placement Test required. Deadline for receipt of application materials: none. No application fee required. On-campus interview recommended.

Athletics Interscholastic: basketball, bowling, cross-country running, golf, soccer, softball, swimming and diving, tennis, track and field, volleyball, water polo. 2 PE instructors, 35 coaches, 1 athletic trainer.

Computers Computers are regularly used in all classes. Computer network features include on-campus library services, online commercial services, Internet access, wireless campus network, Internet filtering or blocking technology, Edline. Campus intranet and computer access in designated common areas are available to students. Students grades are available online. The school has a published electronic and media policy.

Contact Miss Deborah Murphy, Assistant Principal. 708-771-8383. Fax: 708-488-2014. E-mail: dmurphy@trinityhs.org. Web site: www.trinityhs.org.

TRINITY HIGH SCHOOL

4011 Shelbyville Road
Louisville, Kentucky 40207-9427
Head of School: Robert J. Mullen, EdD

General Information Boys' day college-preparatory, arts, business, religious studies, and technology school, affiliated with Roman Catholic Church. Grades 9–12. Founded: 1953. Setting: suburban. 110-acre campus. 11 buildings on campus. Approved or accredited by National Catholic Education Association, Southern Association of Colleges and Schools, and Kentucky Department of Education. Endowment: $10 million. Total enrollment: 1,333. Upper school average class size: 21. Upper school faculty-student ratio: 1:13. There are 175 required school days per year for Upper School students. Upper School students typically attend 5 days per week. The average school day consists of 6 hours and 45 minutes.

Upper School Student Profile Grade 9: 365 students (365 boys); Grade 10: 350 students (350 boys); Grade 11: 326 students (326 boys); Grade 12: 292 students (292 boys). 84% of students are Roman Catholic.

Faculty School total: 118. In upper school: 88 men, 30 women; 110 have advanced degrees.

Subjects Offered 20th century history, 3-dimensional art, accounting, acting, adolescent issues, advanced chemistry, advanced computer applications, advanced math, Advanced Placement courses, advanced studio art-AP, algebra, American Civil War, American democracy, American foreign policy, American government, American history, American history AP, American literature, American literature-AP, analysis and differential calculus, analysis of data, anatomy and physiology, ancient history, ancient world history, applied arts, applied music, art, art and culture, art appreciation, art education, art history, art-AP, arts, arts appreciation, athletic training, athletics, band, banking, Basic programming, Bible as literature, biology, biology-AP, broadcasting, business, business education, business law, business mathematics, business studies, business technology, calculus, calculus-AP, campus ministry, career exploration, career planning, career/college preparation, cell biology, character education, cheerleading, chemistry, chemistry-AP, choir, choral music, chorus, Christian doctrine, Christian ethics, Christian scripture, church history, cinematography, civics, Civil War, classical civilization, classical Greek literature, classical music, college admission preparation, college awareness, college counseling, college placement, college planning, communication arts, communication skills, community service, comparative cultures, comparative government and politics, composition-AP, computer animation, computer applications, computer art, computer education, computer graphics, computer information systems, computer literacy, computer math, computer multimedia, computer music, computer processing, computer programming, computer science, computer skills, computer studies, computer technologies, computer technology certification, computer tools, computers, concert band, concert choir, conflict resolution, constitutional law, contemporary art, CPR, creative writing, critical studies in film, critical thinking, critical writing, data analysis, data processing, death and loss, decision making skills, developmental math, digital photography, DNA research, drama, drama performance, drawing, drawing and design, earth and space science, earth science, ecology, economics, economics and history, economics-AP, English, English language and composition-AP, English literature, English-AP, environmental studies, European civilization, European history, evolution, family living, fencing, film, film studies, finite math, first aid, forensics, French, general science, geography, geometry, German, health, health science, Hebrew scripture, Holocaust studies, HTML design, humanities, independent study, information technology, instrumental music, integrated mathematics, interdisciplinary studies, Internet, jazz band, journalism, keyboarding, language arts, leadership and service, literature, literature-AP, martial arts, mathematics, modern civilization, moral and social development, multimedia design, music performance, musical theater, New Testament, news writing, newspaper, oil painting, painting, peace and justice, philosophy, photography, photojournalism, physical education, physical fitness, physical science, physics, physics-AP, post-calculus, pottery, pre-algebra, pre-calculus, probability and statistics, programming, psychology, public speaking, religion, religious studies, Roman civilization, Romantic period literature, Russian history, SAT/ACT preparation, science, sculpture, senior seminar, social justice, social psychology, social sciences, social studies, sociology, software design, space and physical sciences, Spanish, Spanish literature, Spanish-AP, speech and debate, sports medicine, sports nutrition, stage design, stained glass, statistics, student government, student publications, technology, trigonometry, U.S. government and politics-AP, U.S. history-AP, video film production, Web site design, weight training, Western civilization, work-study, world civilizations, world history, world history-AP, yearbook.

Graduation Requirements Communication arts, English, foreign language, humanities, lab science, mathematics, physical education (includes health), religion (includes Bible studies and theology), science, social studies (includes history), several elective offerings. Community service is required.

Special Academic Programs Advanced Placement exam preparation; honors section; independent study; study at local college for college credit; study abroad; academic accommodation for the gifted, the musically talented, and the artistically talented; remedial reading and/or remedial writing; remedial math; programs in English, mathematics, general development for dyslexic students; special instructional classes for deaf students, blind students.

College Admission Counseling 361 students graduated in 2010; 355 went to college, including Bellarmine University; Eastern Kentucky University; Indiana University Bloomington; University of Dayton; University of Kentucky; University of Louisville. Other: 6 had other specific plans. Mean combined SAT: 1854, mean composite ACT: 23.

Student Life Upper grades have specified standards of dress, student council, honor system. Discipline rests primarily with faculty. Attendance at religious services is required.

Summer Programs Remediation, enrichment, advancement, sports, art/fine arts, computer instruction programs offered; session focuses on academic advancement and enrichment/sports camps; held on campus; accepts boys; not open to students from other schools. 1,000 students usually enrolled. 2011 schedule: June 1 to August 3. Application deadline: May 15.

Tuition and Aid Day student tuition: $10,300. Guaranteed tuition plan. Tuition installment plan (monthly payment plans, individually arranged payment plans, Tuition Management Systems). Merit scholarship grants, need-based scholarship grants, paying campus jobs available. In 2010–11, 40% of upper-school students received aid. Total amount of financial aid awarded in 2010–11: $1,300,000.

Admissions Traditional secondary-level entrance grade is 9. High School Placement Test required. Deadline for receipt of application materials: none. Application fee required: $75. Interview required.

Athletics Interscholastic: archery, baseball, basketball, bicycling, bowling, cheering, crew, cross-country running, diving, football, golf, hockey, ice hockey, lacrosse, power lifting, rugby, soccer, swimming and diving, tennis, track and field, volleyball, weight lifting, wrestling; intramural: alpine skiing, basketball, bocce, climbing, cricket, fencing, fishing, flag football, freestyle skiing, Frisbee, golf, hiking/backpacking, indoor soccer, kickball, life saving, martial arts, mountain biking, paddle tennis, rock climbing, skiing (downhill), snowboarding, soccer, softball, strength & conditioning, table tennis, ultimate Frisbee, volleyball, water polo, weight lifting, weight training; coed intramural: bowling. 5 PE instructors, 30 coaches, 3 athletic trainers.

Computers Computers are regularly used in all classes. Computer network features include on-campus library services, online commercial services, Internet access, wireless campus network, Internet filtering or blocking technology. Campus intranet, student e-mail accounts, and computer access in designated common areas are available to students. Students grades are available online. The school has a published electronic and media policy.

Contact Mr. Joseph M. Porter Jr., Vice President for Advancement. 502-736-2119. Fax: 502-899-2052. E-mail: porter@thsrock.net. Web site: www.trinityrocks.com.

TRINITY HIGH SCHOOL
581 Bridge Street
Manchester, New Hampshire 03104
Head of School: Mr. Denis Mailloux

General Information Coeducational day college-preparatory, arts, religious studies, and technology school, affiliated with Roman Catholic Church. Grades 9–12. Founded: 1886. Setting: urban. Nearest major city is Boston, MA. 5-acre campus. 2 buildings on campus. Approved or accredited by New England Association of Schools and Colleges and New Hampshire Department of Education. Total enrollment: 428. Upper school average class size: 15. Upper school faculty-student ratio: 1:14. There are 180 required school days per year for Upper School students. Upper School students typically attend 5 days per week. The average school day consists of 6 hours and 30 minutes.

Upper School Student Profile Grade 9: 126 students (62 boys, 64 girls); Grade 10: 102 students (51 boys, 51 girls); Grade 11: 95 students (59 boys, 36 girls); Grade 12: 105 students (50 boys, 55 girls). 80% of students are Roman Catholic.

Faculty School total: 35. In upper school: 17 men, 18 women; 20 have advanced degrees.

Subjects Offered 3-dimensional art, advanced biology, advanced math, Advanced Placement courses, algebra, American government, American history, American history-AP, American literature, analysis, anatomy and physiology, art, Bible studies, biology, calculus, calculus-AP, chemistry, computer science, driver education, English, English literature, English-AP, ethics, French, geometry, grammar, health, history, human development, journalism, Latin, mathematics, physical education, physics, psychology, religion, science, social studies, sociology, Spanish, theology, trigonometry, U.S. history-AP, world history, world literature.

Special Academic Programs 6 Advanced Placement exams for which test preparation is offered; honors section; study at local college for college credit.

College Admission Counseling 95 students graduated in 2010; all went to college, including Saint Anselm College; University of New Hampshire; Worcester Polytechnic Institute. Mean SAT critical reading: 550, mean SAT math: 559, mean SAT writing: 557. 29% scored over 600 on SAT critical reading, 36% scored over 600 on SAT math, 32% scored over 600 on SAT writing.

Student Life Upper grades have specified standards of dress, student council, honor system. Discipline rests primarily with faculty. Attendance at religious services is required.

Tuition and Aid Day student tuition: $8605. Tuition installment plan (FACTS Tuition Payment Plan). Need-based scholarship grants available. In 2010–11, 10% of upper-school students received aid.

Admissions Traditional secondary-level entrance grade is 9. STS required. Deadline for receipt of application materials: none. Application fee required: $50. On-campus interview recommended.

Athletics Interscholastic: baseball (boys), basketball (b,g), cheering (g), cross-country running (b,g), football (b), gymnastics (g), hockey (b), ice hockey (b), indoor track & field (b,g), lacrosse (b), skiing (cross-country) (b,g), skiing (downhill) (b,g), soccer (b,g), softball (g), swimming and diving (b,g), tennis (b,g), volleyball (g), winter (indoor) track (b,g), wrestling (b); coed interscholastic: alpine skiing, golf, track and field; coed intramural: gymnastics. 1 PE instructor, 25 coaches, 1 athletic trainer.

Computers Computers are regularly used in English, journalism, science, social sciences, yearbook classes. Computer resources include Internet access, Internet filtering or blocking technology. Students grades are available online.

Contact Mr. Patrick Smith, Admissions Director. 603-668-2910 Ext. 18. Fax: 603-668-2913. E-mail: psmith@trinity-hs.org. Web site: www.trinity-hs.org.

TRINITY HIGH SCHOOL
12425 Granger Road
Garfield Heights, Ohio 44125
Head of School: Ms. Carla Fritsch

General Information Coeducational day college-preparatory, arts, business, religious studies, technology, technical, and medical school, affiliated with Roman Catholic Church. Grades 9–12. Founded: 1926. Setting: suburban. Nearest major city is Cleveland. 26-acre campus. 3 buildings on campus. Approved or accredited by National Catholic Education Association, North Central Association of Colleges and Schools, Ohio Catholic Schools Accreditation Association (OCSAA), and Ohio Department of Education. Total enrollment: 365. Upper school average class size: 17. Upper school faculty-student ratio: 1:10. There are 199 required school days per year for Upper School students. Upper School students typically attend 5 days per week. The average school day consists of 7 hours.

Upper School Student Profile Grade 9: 91 students (43 boys, 48 girls); Grade 10: 92 students (50 boys, 42 girls); Grade 11: 82 students (39 boys, 43 girls); Grade 12: 100 students (62 boys, 38 girls). 89% of students are Roman Catholic.

Faculty School total: 37. In upper school: 16 men, 21 women; 18 have advanced degrees.

Subjects Offered 3-dimensional art, accounting, advanced biology, advanced chemistry, advanced computer applications, advanced math, Advanced Placement courses, advanced studio art-AP, algebra, American government, American history, American history-AP, American literature, analysis and differential calculus, anatomy and physiology, animation, art, athletics, automated accounting, band, Bible, Bible studies, biology, bookkeeping, British literature, British literature (honors), business applications, business skills, business technology, calculus-AP, campus ministry, career and personal planning, career education, career education internship, career experience, career exploration, career planning, career/college preparation, Catholic belief and practice, ceramics, chemistry, choir, Christian and Hebrew scripture, Christian doctrine, Christian ethics, Christian scripture, Christian testament, church history, college admission preparation, college awareness, college counseling, college placement, college planning, college writing, communication skills, community service, comparative religion, competitive science projects, computer animation, computer applications, computer art, computer education, computer graphics, computer information systems, computer multimedia, computer technologies, computer technology certification, computer-aided design, concert band, concert choir, consumer economics, creative writing, critical thinking, critical writing, culinary arts, digital applications, drama performance, drawing and design, earth science, economics and history, electives, English, English literature and composition-AP, environmental science, ethics, European history, food and nutrition, foods, foreign language, four units of summer reading, geometry, global studies, government-AP, graphic arts, graphic design, graphics, guidance, health education, honors algebra, honors English, honors geometry, human anatomy, human biology, instrumental music, integrated mathematics, Internet research, internship, lab science, library, life issues, Life of Christ, marching band, marine biology, Microsoft, moral theology, musical theater, neuroscience, oral communications, participation in sports, peace and justice, peer ministry, personal finance, photo shop, physical education, physics, play production, portfolio art, prayer/spirituality, pre-algebra, pre-calculus, psychology, public speaking, SAT/ACT preparation, speech, sports, studio art-AP, study skills, symphonic band, theology, U.S. government and politics-AP, video, video and animation, vocal ensemble, Web site design, wind ensemble, word processing, world history, yearbook.

Graduation Requirements Arts and fine arts (art, music, dance, drama), electives, English, government, human relations, mathematics, physical education (includes health), science, social studies (includes history), theology, Western civilization, service hours, internship.

Special Academic Programs Advanced Placement exam preparation; honors section; independent study; academic accommodation for the gifted and the artistically talented; remedial math; programs in English, mathematics, general development for dyslexic students.

College Admission Counseling 87 students graduated in 2009; 81 went to college, including Baldwin-Wallace College; Bowling Green State University; Cleveland State University; John Carroll University; Kent State University; The University of Akron. Other: 6 had other specific plans. Median SAT critical reading: 500, median SAT math:

520, median SAT writing: 520, median combined SAT: 1540, median composite ACT: 20. 13% scored over 600 on SAT critical reading, 26% scored over 600 on SAT math, 16% scored over 600 on SAT writing, 15% scored over 1800 on combined SAT, 15% scored over 26 on composite ACT.

Student Life Upper grades have uniform requirement, student council. Discipline rests primarily with faculty. Attendance at religious services is required.

Tuition and Aid Day student tuition: $8800. Tuition installment plan (individually arranged payment plans, private bank loans). Tuition reduction for siblings, need-based scholarship grants, middle-income loans, private bank loans available. In 2009–10, 25% of upper-school students received aid. Total amount of financial aid awarded in 2009–10: $356,000.

Admissions Traditional secondary-level entrance grade is 9. For fall 2009, 105 students applied for upper-level admission, 100 were accepted, 91 enrolled. Scholastic Testing Service High School Placement Test required. Deadline for receipt of application materials: none. Application fee required: $20. On-campus interview required.

Athletics Interscholastic: baseball (boys), basketball (b,g), cheering (g), cross-country running (b,g), danceline (g), football (b), ice hockey (b), soccer (g), softball (g), track and field (b,g), volleyball (g), wrestling (b); intramural: danceline (g); coed interscholastic: golf, indoor track & field; coed intramural: skiing (downhill), snowboarding. 1 PE instructor, 34 coaches, 1 athletic trainer.

Computers Computers are regularly used in all academic classes. Computer network features include on-campus library services, online commercial services, Internet access, wireless campus network, Internet filtering or blocking technology, Citrix, network printing, personal storage on network, weekly email grade reports, electronic newsletters, remote access, school website, online homework tracking system. Computer access in designated common areas is available to students. Students grades are available online. The school has a published electronic and media policy.

Contact Sr. Dian Majsterek, Administrative Assistant, Admissions and Marketing. 216-581-1644 Ext. 113. Fax: 216-581-9348. E-mail: SisterDian@ths.org. Web site: www.ths.org.

TRINITY-PAWLING SCHOOL

700 Route 22
Pawling, New York 12564
Head of School: Mr. Archibald A. Smith III
General Information Boys' boarding and day college-preparatory, arts, religious studies, technology, and ESL school, affiliated with Episcopal Church. Boarding

"A commitment to Character"

A College Preparatory School for Boys
Boarding students grades 9-12 & PG
Day students grades 7-12

700 Route 22 • Pawling, NY 12564 • phone: 845-855-4825 fax: 845-855-4827
www.trinitypawling.org

Trinity-Pawling School

grades 9–PG, day grades 7–PG. Founded: 1907. Setting: small town. Nearest major city is New York. Students are housed in single-sex dormitories. 140-acre campus. 23 buildings on campus. Approved or accredited by New York State Association of Independent Schools, New York State Board of Regents, and The Association of Boarding Schools. Member of National Association of Independent Schools and Secondary School Admission Test Board. Endowment: $32 million. Total enrollment: 300. Upper school average class size: 12. Upper school faculty-student ratio: 1:8. There are 186 required school days per year for Upper School students. Upper School students typically attend 6 days per week. The average school day consists of 6 hours and 30 minutes.

Upper School Student Profile Grade 9: 40 students (40 boys); Grade 10: 68 students (68 boys); Grade 11: 75 students (75 boys); Grade 12: 82 students (82 boys); Postgraduate: 15 students (15 boys). 80% of students are boarding students. 20% are state residents. 38 states are represented in upper school student body. 25% are international students. International students from Canada, China, Hong Kong, Republic of Korea, Saudi Arabia, and Spain; 12 other countries represented in student body. 20% of students are members of Episcopal Church.

Faculty School total: 53. In upper school: 36 men, 15 women; 40 have advanced degrees; 50 reside on campus.

Subjects Offered Advanced Placement courses, advanced studio art-AP, algebra, American government, American history, American legal systems, American literature, American studies, anatomy, anatomy and physiology, architectural drawing, art, art history, art history-AP, Asian history, Asian studies, astronomy, Bible, biology, biology-AP, calculus, calculus-AP, ceramics, chemistry, chemistry-AP, choir, chorus, Christian ethics, civil rights, composition-AP, computer applications, computer information systems, computer math, computer music, computer programming, computer science, computer science-AP, computer technologies, constitutional history of U.S., data analysis, drafting, drama, drama performance, earth science, East Asian history, ecology, economics, economics-AP, English, English language-AP, English literature, English literature-AP, English-AP, English/composition-AP, environmental science, environmental science-AP, environmental studies, ESL, ethics, European history, European history-AP, fine arts, French, French language-AP, French studies, geology, geometry, government, government and politics-AP, government/civics, grammar, health science, history, honors algebra, honors English, honors geometry, honors U.S. history, honors world history, human anatomy, keyboarding, Latin, Latin American literature, Latin-AP, law and the legal system, literature, literature and composition-AP, Mandarin, mathematics, mechanical drawing, model United Nations, music, philosophy, photography, physical education, physics, physics-AP, physiology, political science, pre-calculus, probability and statistics, psychology, public speaking, reading/study skills, religion, religious education, religious studies, SAT preparation, science, Shakespeare, social justice, social sciences, social studies, Spanish, Spanish language-AP, Spanish literature-AP, statistics-AP, studio art, studio art-AP, study skills, theater, theology, trigonometry, U.S. government and politics, U.S. history, U.S. history-AP, Vietnam War, word processing, world history, writing, yearbook.

Graduation Requirements Arts and fine arts (art, music, dance, drama), English, foreign language, mathematics, physical education (includes health), religion (includes Bible studies and theology), science, social studies (includes history).

Special Academic Programs 17 Advanced Placement exams for which test preparation is offered; honors section; remedial reading and/or remedial writing; programs in English for dyslexic students; ESL (25 students enrolled).

College Admission Counseling 94 students graduated in 2010; all went to college, including Boston University; Cornell University; Hobart and William Smith Colleges; Rensselaer Polytechnic Institute; Syracuse University; The Johns Hopkins University. Mean SAT critical reading: 580, mean SAT math: 570.

Student Life Upper grades have specified standards of dress, student council, honor system. Discipline rests equally with students and faculty. Attendance at religious services is required.

Tuition and Aid Day student tuition: $32,000; 7-day tuition and room/board: $45,000. Tuition installment plan (Insured Tuition Payment Plan, Academic Management Services Plan, individually arranged payment plans, Payment plans arranged directly with the school business office.). Need-based scholarship grants, need-based loans available. In 2010–11, 35% of upper-school students received aid. Total amount of financial aid awarded in 2010–11: $3,000,000.

Admissions Traditional secondary-level entrance grade is 9. For fall 2010, 350 students applied for upper-level admission, 265 were accepted, 106 enrolled. PSAT or SAT, SSAT, TOEFL, Wechsler Intelligence Scale for Children III or WISC-R required. Deadline for receipt of application materials: February 1. Application fee required: $50. On-campus interview required.

Athletics Interscholastic: alpine skiing, baseball, basketball, cross-country running, football, golf, hockey, ice hockey, lacrosse, ropes courses, skiing (downhill), soccer, squash, strength & conditioning, tennis, track and field, weight lifting, weight training, wrestling; intramural: alpine skiing, basketball, bicycling, climbing, fishing, fitness, floor hockey, fly fishing, Frisbee, golf, hiking/backpacking, ice skating, mountain biking, outdoor education, outdoor recreation, physical training, rock climbing, running, skiing (downhill), snowboarding, soccer, softball, squash, strength & conditioning, tennis, trap and skeet, ultimate Frisbee, wall climbing, weight lifting. 30 coaches, 2 athletic trainers.

Computers Computers are regularly used in English, history, mathematics, remedial study skills, science classes. Computer network features include on-campus library services, online commercial services, Internet access, wireless campus network,

Internet filtering or blocking technology. Campus intranet, student e-mail accounts, and computer access in designated common areas are available to students. Students grades are available online. The school has a published electronic and media policy.
Contact Mr. MacGregor Robinson, Assistant Headmaster for External Affairs. 845-855-4825. Fax: 845-855-4827. E-mail: grobinson@trinitypawling.org. Web site: www.trinitypawling.org.

See Display on page 661 and Close-Up on page 856.

TRINITY PREPARATORY SCHOOL

5700 Trinity Prep Lane
Winter Park, Florida 32792
Head of School: Craig S. Maughan

General Information Coeducational day college-preparatory, arts, and technology school, affiliated with Episcopal Church. Grades 6–12. Founded: 1966. Setting: suburban. Nearest major city is Orlando. 100-acre campus. 12 buildings on campus. Approved or accredited by Florida Council of Independent Schools, National Association of Episcopal Schools, The College Board, and Florida Department of Education. Member of National Association of Independent Schools and Secondary School Admission Test Board. Endowment: $7.3 million. Total enrollment: 834. Upper school average class size: 17. Upper school faculty-student ratio: 1:12. There are 175 required school days per year for Upper School students. Upper School students typically attend 5 days per week. The average school day consists of 5 hours and 45 minutes.

Upper School Student Profile Grade 6: 90 students (46 boys, 44 girls); Grade 7: 124 students (70 boys, 54 girls); Grade 8: 128 students (67 boys, 61 girls); Grade 9: 133 students (66 boys, 67 girls); Grade 10: 124 students (73 boys, 51 girls); Grade 11: 118 students (65 boys, 53 girls); Grade 12: 117 students (55 boys, 62 girls). 11% of students are members of Episcopal Church.

Faculty School total: 78. In upper school: 16 men, 21 women; 25 have advanced degrees.

Subjects Offered 20th century American writers, 20th century world history, 3-dimensional art, advanced math, Advanced Placement courses, advanced studio art-AP, algebra, American history, American literature, anatomy, animal science, art, athletic training, audio visual/media, band, Basic programming, Bible, biology, biology-AP, calculus, calculus-AP, character education, chemistry, chemistry-AP, civics, comparative religion, computer graphics, computer multimedia, computer processing, computer programming, computer programming-AP, concert band, concert choir, creative writing, critical studies in film, drama, economics, economics-AP, English, English language and composition-AP, English literature, English literature and composition-AP, environmental science, environmental science-AP, ethics, European history, European history-AP, fine arts, forensics, French, French language-AP, French literature-AP, geography, geometry, government and politics-AP, health, honors algebra, honors English, honors geometry, journalism, Latin, Latin-AP, life management skills, mathematics, music, music theory-AP, newspaper, painting, photography, physical education, physics, physics-AP, portfolio art, pottery, pre-algebra, pre-calculus, probability and statistics, psychology, psychology-AP, science, sculpture, social studies, Spanish, Spanish language-AP, Spanish literature-AP, speech, strings, studio art-AP, theater, trigonometry, U.S. government and politics-AP, U.S. history-AP, weight training, world history, world wide web design, writing, yearbook.

Graduation Requirements Arts and fine arts (art, music, dance, drama), computer science, electives, English, foreign language, life management skills, mathematics, physical education (includes health), science, social sciences.

Special Academic Programs 25 Advanced Placement exams for which test preparation is offered; honors section; independent study; study at local college for college credit; academic accommodation for the gifted, the musically talented, and the artistically talented.

College Admission Counseling 109 students graduated in 2010; all went to college, including Auburn University; Duke University; Florida State University; University of Central Florida; University of Florida; Yale University. Mean SAT critical reading: 633, mean SAT math: 653, mean SAT writing: 637, mean combined SAT: 1922, mean composite ACT: 28. 62% scored over 600 on SAT critical reading, 76% scored over 600 on SAT math, 66% scored over 600 on SAT writing, 66% scored over 1800 on combined SAT, 71% scored over 26 on composite ACT.

Student Life Upper grades have specified standards of dress, student council, honor system. Discipline rests primarily with faculty. Attendance at religious services is required.

Summer Programs Remediation, enrichment, advancement, sports, art/fine arts, computer instruction programs offered; session focuses on enrichment; held on campus; accepts boys and girls; open to students from other schools. 300 students usually enrolled. 2011 schedule: June 14 to August 8. Application deadline: none.

Tuition and Aid Day student tuition: $16,200. Tuition installment plan (Insured Tuition Payment Plan, FACTS Tuition Payment Plan, monthly payment plans, semiannual and annual payment plans). Need-based scholarship grants, middle-income loans available. In 2010–11, 22% of upper-school students received aid. Total amount of financial aid awarded in 2010–11: $1,130,580.

Admissions Traditional secondary-level entrance grade is 9. For fall 2010, 78 students applied for upper-level admission, 54 were accepted, 34 enrolled. CTP, ISEE,

PSAT, SAT or SSAT required. Deadline for receipt of application materials: February 12. Application fee required: $50. Interview required.

Athletics Interscholastic: baseball (boys), basketball (b,g), bowling (b,g), cheering (g), cross-country running (b,g), diving (b,g), flag football (b), football (b), golf (b,g), lacrosse (b), physical fitness (b,g), soccer (b,g), softball (g), strength & conditioning (b,g), swimming and diving (b,g), tennis (b,g), track and field (b,g), volleyball (g), weight lifting (b,g), weight training (b,g); intramural: ropes courses (b,g), sailing (b,g), strength & conditioning (b,g). 5 PE instructors, 48 coaches, 1 athletic trainer.

Computers Computers are regularly used in all classes. Computer network features include on-campus library services, online commercial services, Internet access, wireless campus network, Internet filtering or blocking technology. Student e-mail accounts and computer access in designated common areas are available to students. Students grades are available online. The school has a published electronic and media policy.

Contact Sherryn M. Hay, Director of Admission. 321-282-2523. Fax: 407-671-6935. E-mail: hays@trinityprep.org. Web site: www.trinityprep.org.

TRINITY SCHOOL
139 West 91st Street
New York, New York 10024
Head of School: Allman John

General Information Coeducational day college-preparatory school, affiliated with Episcopal Church. Grades K–12. Founded: 1709. Setting: urban. 1 building on campus. Approved or accredited by National Association of Private Schools for Exceptional Children, New York State Association of Independent Schools, and New York Department of Education. Member of National Association of Independent Schools. Endowment: $50 million. Total enrollment: 990. Upper school average class size: 16. Upper school faculty-student ratio: 1:7. Upper School students typically attend 5 days per week.

Upper School Student Profile Grade 9: 110 students (55 boys, 55 girls); Grade 10: 110 students (55 boys, 55 girls); Grade 11: 110 students (55 boys, 55 girls); Grade 12: 110 students (55 boys, 55 girls). 15% of students are members of Episcopal Church.

Faculty School total: 163. In upper school: 50 men, 43 women; 72 have advanced degrees.

Subjects Offered Algebra, American history, American literature, art, art history, biology, calculus, ceramics, chemistry, computer math, computer programming, computer science, creative writing, dance, drama, driver education, economics, English, English literature, environmental science, ethics, European history, expository writing, fine arts, French, geometry, German, government/civics, Greek, history, Latin, marine biology, mathematics, music, photography, physical education, physics, psychology, religion, science, social studies, Spanish, speech, statistics, theater, trigonometry.

Graduation Requirements Arts and fine arts (art, music, dance, drama), English, foreign language, mathematics, physical education (includes health), religion (includes Bible studies and theology), science, social studies (includes history).

Special Academic Programs Advanced Placement exam preparation; honors section; independent study.

College Admission Counseling 110 students graduated in 2010; all went to college, including Brown University; Columbia College; Harvard University; Princeton University; University of Pennsylvania.

Student Life Upper grades have specified standards of dress, student council. Discipline rests equally with students and faculty.

Tuition and Aid Day student tuition: $36,120. Middle-income loans, need-based grants available. In 2010–11, 20% of upper-school students received aid. Total amount of financial aid awarded in 2010–11: $2,500,000.

Admissions Traditional secondary-level entrance grade is 9. For fall 2010, 400 students applied for upper-level admission, 90 were accepted, 55 enrolled. SSAT required. Deadline for receipt of application materials: January 15. Application fee required: $60. On-campus interview required.

Athletics Interscholastic: baseball (boys), basketball (b,g), golf (b,g), indoor track & field (b,g), lacrosse (b,g), soccer (b,g), softball (g), tennis (b,g), track and field (b,g), volleyball (g), winter (indoor) track (b,g), wrestling (b); coed interscholastic: cross-country running, swimming and diving, water polo. 16 PE instructors, 45 coaches, 1 athletic trainer.

Computers Computers are regularly used in art, mathematics, science classes. Computer network features include on-campus library services, Internet access. The school has a published electronic and media policy.

Contact Hannah Trooboff McCollum, Associate Director of Admission. 212-932-6823. Fax: 212-932-6812 Ext. 6819. E-mail: hannah.mccollum@trinityschoolnyc.org. Web site: www.trinityschoolnyc.org.

TRINITY SCHOOL AT GREENLAWN
107 South Greenlawn Avenue
South Bend, Indiana 46617
Head of School: Mr. John A. Lee

General Information Coeducational day college-preparatory, general academic, and Classical curriculum school, affiliated with Protestant faith, Roman Catholic Church.

Grades 7–12. Founded: 1981. Setting: suburban. 4-acre campus. 3 buildings on campus. Approved or accredited by Independent Schools Association of the Central States and Indiana Department of Education. Upper school average class size: 15. Upper school faculty-student ratio: 1:7. Upper School students typically attend 5 days per week. The average school day consists of 5 hours.

Upper School Student Profile 90% of students are Protestant, Roman Catholic.

Faculty School total: 23. In upper school: 10 men, 13 women; 12 have advanced degrees.

Subjects Offered Acting, advanced biology, advanced chemistry, advanced math, algebra, American history, American literature, analysis and differential calculus, anatomy, ancient history, applied arts, applied music, art, art history, Bible as literature, biology, British history, British literature, calculus, calligraphy, Catholic belief and practice, chemistry, choral music, Christian and Hebrew scripture, Christian doctrine, classical Greek literature.

College Admission Counseling 26 students graduated in 2010; 25 went to college, including Indiana University Bloomington; Purdue University; Saint Mary's College; University of Notre Dame. Other: 1 went to work. Mean SAT critical reading: 646, mean SAT math: 600, mean SAT writing: 646, mean combined SAT: 1892.

Student Life Upper grades have uniform requirement. Discipline rests primarily with faculty.

Tuition and Aid Day student tuition: $9100. Tuition installment plan (individually arranged payment plans). Need-based scholarship grants available. In 2010–11, 40% of upper-school students received aid.

Admissions Deadline for receipt of application materials: none. Application fee required: $50. Interview required.

Athletics Interscholastic: basketball (boys, girls), soccer (b,g), volleyball (g); coed intramural: golf.

Computers Computer access in designated common areas is available to students. The school has a published electronic and media policy.

Contact Ms. Gina Massa, Director of Community Relations. 574-850-7168. E-mail: gmassa@trinityschools.org. Web site: www.trinitygreenlawn.org.

TRINITY SCHOOL OF MIDLAND
3500 West Wadley Avenue
Midland, Texas 79707
Head of School: Mr. Geoffrey Butler

General Information Coeducational day college-preparatory, arts, bilingual studies, and technology school, affiliated with Episcopal Church. Grades PK–12. Founded: 1958. Setting: suburban. 25-acre campus. 1 building on campus. Approved or accredited by Independent Schools Association of the Southwest, Texas Education Agency, and Texas Department of Education. Member of National Association of Independent Schools. Endowment: $3.3 million. Total enrollment: 503. Upper school average class size: 15. Upper school faculty-student ratio: 1:8. There are 180 required school days per year for Upper School students. Upper School students typically attend 5 days per week. The average school day consists of 8 hours.

Upper School Student Profile Grade 9: 53 students (25 boys, 28 girls); Grade 10: 39 students (19 boys, 20 girls); Grade 11: 39 students (16 boys, 23 girls); Grade 12: 23 students (10 boys, 13 girls). 10% of students are members of Episcopal Church.

Faculty School total: 67. In upper school: 12 men, 13 women; 13 have advanced degrees.

Subjects Offered 3-dimensional art, advanced computer applications, algebra, American history, American literature, anatomy and physiology, art, art history, band, biology, British literature, British literature (honors), calculus, calculus-AP, chemistry, chemistry-AP, choir, college counseling, computer applications, computer graphics, computer science-AP, English language and composition-AP, English literature, English literature-AP, foreign language, French, French-AP, geometry, health, honors algebra, honors English, honors geometry, honors U.S. history, honors world history, instrumental music, jazz band, Latin, Latin-AP, modern European history, modern European history-AP, musical theater, photography, physical education, physics, pre-calculus, senior seminar, Spanish, Spanish-AP, strings, studio art, studio art-AP, U.S. government, U.S. government and politics-AP, world history, world history-AP, world religions, yearbook.

Graduation Requirements Algebra, American government, American history, American literature, biology, chemistry, computer applications, English, English literature, foreign language, geometry, modern European history, physical education (includes health), physics, senior seminar, world history, service hours.

Special Academic Programs 14 Advanced Placement exams for which test preparation is offered; honors section; independent study; study at local college for college credit; study abroad; academic accommodation for the musically talented.

College Admission Counseling 41 students graduated in 2009; all went to college, including Texas A&M University; Texas Christian University; Texas Tech University; The University of Texas at Austin. Mean SAT critical reading: 613, mean SAT math: 632. 49% scored over 600 on SAT critical reading, 64% scored over 600 on SAT math.

Student Life Upper grades have specified standards of dress, student council, honor system. Discipline rests equally with students and faculty. Attendance at religious services is required.

Tuition and Aid Day student tuition: $14,300. Tuition installment plan (monthly payment plans). Tuition reduction for siblings, merit scholarship grants, need-based scholarship grants available. In 2009–10, 20% of upper-school students received aid;

total upper-school merit-scholarship money awarded: $40,000. Total amount of financial aid awarded in 2009–10: $128,000.

Admissions Traditional secondary-level entrance grade is 9. For fall 2009, 15 students applied for upper-level admission, 12 were accepted, 9 enrolled. Otis-Lennon School Ability Test and writing sample required. Deadline for receipt of application materials: none. Application fee required: $75.

Athletics Interscholastic: baseball (boys), basketball (b,g), cheering (g), cross-country running (b,g), football (b), golf (b,g), swimming and diving (b,g), tennis (b,g), track and field (b,g), volleyball (g); intramural: fitness (b,g), floor hockey (b,g), physical fitness (b,g), weight training (b,g); coed intramural: bowling, field hockey, kickball, soccer, table tennis, wall climbing. 8 coaches, 1 athletic trainer.

Computers Computers are regularly used in all academic, graphics, yearbook classes. Computer network features include on-campus library services, Internet access, wireless campus network, Internet filtering or blocking technology. The school has a published electronic and media policy.

Contact Mrs. Adrianne Clifton, Director of Admissions. 432-697-3281 Ext. 202. Fax: 432-697-7403. E-mail: a_clifton@trinitymidland.org. Web site: www.trinitymidland.org.

TRINITY SCHOOL OF TEXAS

215 Teague Street
Longview, Texas 75601
Head of School: Mr. Richard L. Beard

General Information Coeducational day and distance learning college-preparatory, arts, religious studies, and technology school, affiliated with Episcopal Church. Grades PK–12. Distance learning grades 10–12. Founded: 1957. Setting: small town. Nearest major city is Dallas. 14-acre campus. 4 buildings on campus. Approved or accredited by National Association of Episcopal Schools, Southern Association of Colleges and Schools, Southwest Association of Episcopal Schools, Texas Education Agency, and Texas Department of Education. Endowment: $315,000. Total enrollment: 326. Upper school average class size: 12. Upper school faculty-student ratio: 1:8. There are 174 required school days per year for Upper School students. Upper School students typically attend 5 days per week. The average school day consists of 6 hours and 20 minutes.

Upper School Student Profile Grade 9: 12 students (5 boys, 7 girls); Grade 10: 14 students (5 boys, 9 girls); Grade 11: 21 students (11 boys, 10 girls); Grade 12: 17 students (10 boys, 7 girls). 11% of students are members of Episcopal Church.

Faculty School total: 38. In upper school: 3 men, 13 women; 3 have advanced degrees.

Subjects Offered Advanced studio art-AP, algebra, American history, art, astronomy, athletics, biology, biology-AP, calculus, calculus-AP, Central and Eastern European history, character education, chemistry, chemistry-AP, choir, choral music, college admission preparation, college writing, community service, computer applications, computer literacy, conflict resolution, creative writing, desktop publishing, digital photography, drama performance, earth science, economics, English-AP, environmental science, environmental studies, European history-AP, geography, geometry, government, government/civics, grammar, health, junior and senior seminars, keyboarding, language and composition, language arts, leadership and service, library, life science, literature and composition-AP, mathematics, modern European history, modern Western civilization, modern world history, music, music performance, mythology, newspaper, participation in sports, personal finance, photography, photojournalism, physical education, physical fitness, physical science, physics, pre-algebra, pre-calculus, probability and statistics, psychology, psychology-AP, religious studies, research seminar, research skills, SAT preparation, SAT/ACT preparation, sociology, Spanish, Spanish language-AP, sports, statistics, strings, student publications, studio art, Texas history, U.S. government, U.S. history, world geography, world history, world religions, yearbook.

Graduation Requirements Arts and fine arts (art, music, dance, drama), computers, English, government/civics, languages, mathematics, physical education (includes health), science, social sciences, speech, theology, na.

Special Academic Programs Advanced Placement exam preparation; accelerated programs; independent study; term-away projects; study at local college for college credit; study abroad; academic accommodation for the gifted, the musically talented, and the artistically talented; programs in English, mathematics for dyslexic students.

College Admission Counseling 16 students graduated in 2010; all went to college, including LeTourneau University; Morehouse College; Northeastern University; Texas A&M University; The University of Texas at Arlington; The University of Texas at Austin. Median SAT critical reading: 530, median SAT math: 620, median SAT writing: 535, median combined SAT: 1690, median composite ACT: 23. 18% scored over 600 on SAT critical reading, 23% scored over 600 on SAT math, 13% scored over 600 on SAT writing, 42% scored over 26 on composite ACT.

Student Life Upper grades have specified standards of dress, student council, honor system. Discipline rests primarily with faculty. Attendance at religious services is required.

Summer Programs Remediation, enrichment, advancement, sports, art/fine arts, computer instruction programs offered; session focuses on Our programs focus upon broad, age-appropriate opportunities for child development.; held both on and off campus; held at a wide variety of excursions related to weekly themes; accepts boys and girls; open to students from other schools. 47 students usually enrolled. 2011 schedule: May 31 to July 29. Application deadline: April 15.

Tuition and Aid Day student tuition: $7897. Tuition installment plan (FACTS Tuition Payment Plan, monthly payment plans, individually arranged payment plans, semester payment plan). Merit scholarship grants, need-based scholarship grants available. In 2010–11, 12% of upper-school students received aid; total upper-school merit-scholarship money awarded: $74,497. Total amount of financial aid awarded in 2010–11: $99,875.

Admissions Traditional secondary-level entrance grade is 9. For fall 2010, 12 students applied for upper-level admission, 12 were accepted, 12 enrolled. Otis-Lennon, Stanford Achievement Test, PSAT or SAT for applicants to grade 11 and 12, Woodcock-Johnson Revised Achievement Test and writing sample required. Deadline for receipt of application materials: none. Application fee required: $850. On-campus interview required.

Athletics Interscholastic: baseball (boys), basketball (b,g), cheering (g), football (b), golf (b,g), physical fitness (b), power lifting (b), tennis (b,g), track and field (b,g), volleyball (g); intramural: football (b), physical fitness (b,g), tennis (b,g), volleyball (g); coed interscholastic: soccer; coed intramural: soccer, track and field, weight training. 2 PE instructors, 4 coaches.

Computers Computers are regularly used in college planning, computer applications, creative writing, English, geography, history, journalism, keyboarding, library, mathematics, newspaper, photography, photojournalism, psychology, publications, publishing, research skills, SAT preparation, science, senior seminar, Spanish, technology, writing, yearbook classes. Computer network features include on-campus library services, online commercial services, Internet access, Internet filtering or blocking technology. The school has a published electronic and media policy.

Contact Mrs. Toni Brothers, Director of Admission. 903-753-0612 Ext. 236. Fax: 903-753-4812. E-mail: tbrothers@trinityschooloftexas.com. Web site: www.trinityschooloftexas.com.

TRINITY VALLEY SCHOOL

7500 Dutch Branch Road
Fort Worth, Texas 76132
Head of School: Dr. Gary Krahn

General Information Coeducational day college-preparatory school. Grades K–12. Founded: 1959. Setting: urban. 75-acre campus. 7 buildings on campus. Approved or accredited by Independent Schools Association of the Southwest, Texas Education Agency, and Texas Department of Education. Member of National Association of Independent Schools. Endowment: $18 million. Total enrollment: 970. Upper school average class size: 16. Upper school faculty-student ratio: 1:9. There are 170 required school days per year for Upper School students. Upper School students typically attend 5 days per week. The average school day consists of 7 hours.

Upper School Student Profile Grade 9: 77 students (31 boys, 46 girls); Grade 10: 90 students (43 boys, 47 girls); Grade 11: 88 students (39 boys, 49 girls); Grade 12: 86 students (38 boys, 48 girls).

Faculty School total: 95. In upper school: 18 men, 17 women; 34 have advanced degrees.

Subjects Offered Algebra, American history, American history-AP, ancient history, art, Asian history, biology, biology-AP, British history, calculus, calculus-AP, ceramics, chemistry, chemistry-AP, Chinese, choir, computer science, computer science-AP, constitutional law, creative writing, debate, drama, economics, economics-AP, English, English language-AP, English literature-AP, French, French-AP, geometry, government-AP, government/civics, humanities, Latin, Latin-AP, leadership, medieval/Renaissance history, music theory, photography, physical education, physics, physics-AP, psychology-AP, Spanish, Spanish-AP, speech, statistics, statistics-AP, video film production, writing workshop, yearbook.

Graduation Requirements Algebra, American government, American history, arts and fine arts (art, music, dance, drama), biology, chemistry, economics, English, foreign language, geometry, physical education (includes health), physics, pre-calculus, Western civilization, students must complete 60 hours of community service in the U.S. Community service is required.

Special Academic Programs 22 Advanced Placement exams for which test preparation is offered; honors section; academic accommodation for the gifted, the musically talented, and the artistically talented.

College Admission Counseling 86 students graduated in 2009; all went to college, including Baylor University; Southern Methodist University; Texas A&M University; Texas Christian University; University of Georgia; University of Oklahoma.

Student Life Upper grades have uniform requirement, student council, honor system. Discipline rests equally with students and faculty.

Tuition and Aid Day student tuition: $15,815. Tuition installment plan (monthly payment plans). Need-based scholarship grants, loans from bank associated with school available. In 2009–10, 11% of upper-school students received aid. Total amount of financial aid awarded in 2009–10: $424,977.

Admissions Traditional secondary-level entrance grade is 9. For fall 2009, 30 students applied for upper-level admission, 22 were accepted, 13 enrolled. CTP or ISEE required. Deadline for receipt of application materials: March 6. Application fee required: $75. Interview recommended.

Athletics Interscholastic: baseball (boys), basketball (b,g), cross-country running (b,g), field hockey (g), football (b), golf (b,g), soccer (b,g), softball (g), tennis (b,g), track and field (b,g), volleyball (b,g). 10 PE instructors, 2 athletic trainers.

Computers Computers are regularly used in all academic classes. Computer network features include on-campus library services, online commercial services, Internet access, Internet filtering or blocking technology. Campus intranet, student e-mail accounts, and computer access in designated common areas are available to students. Students grades are available online. The school has a published electronic and media policy.

Contact Judith Kinser, Director of Admissions and Financial Aid. 817-321-0116. Fax: 817-321-0105. E-mail: kinserj@trinityvalleyschool.org. Web site: www. trinityvalleyschool.org.

TURNING WINDS ACADEMIC INSTITUTE
Bonners Ferry, Idaho
See Special Needs Schools section.

TUSCALOOSA ACADEMY
420 Rice Valley Road North
Tuscaloosa, Alabama 35406
Head of School: Dr. Jeffrey Mitchell, PhD
General Information Coeducational day college-preparatory, arts, bilingual studies, technology, and ESL school. Grades PK–12. Founded: 1967. Setting: suburban. Nearest major city is Birmingham. 35-acre campus. 2 buildings on campus. Approved or accredited by Southern Association of Colleges and Schools and Southern Association of Independent Schools. Total enrollment: 366. Upper school average class size: 15. Upper school faculty-student ratio: 1:15. There are 176 required school days per year for Upper School students. Upper School students typically attend 5 days per week. The average school day consists of 6 hours and 55 minutes.
Upper School Student Profile Grade 6: 32 students (20 boys, 12 girls); Grade 7: 26 students (14 boys, 12 girls); Grade 8: 26 students (11 boys, 15 girls); Grade 9: 29 students (12 boys, 17 girls); Grade 10: 32 students (18 boys, 14 girls); Grade 11: 25 students (13 boys, 12 girls); Grade 12: 30 students (14 boys, 16 girls).
Faculty School total: 47. In upper school: 10 men, 18 women; 11 have advanced degrees.
Subjects Offered ACT preparation, advanced math, Advanced Placement courses, algebra, American government, American history, American history-AP, American literature, American literature-AP, anatomy, art, art history, art-AP, baseball, basketball, biology, biology-AP, calculus, calculus-AP, cheerleading, chemistry, chemistry-AP, choir, choral music, chorus, college counseling, computer programming, computer science, computer studies, creative writing, drama, earth science, economics, English, English literature, English-AP, English/composition-AP, European history, expository writing, fine arts, French, French language-AP, French-AP, geography, geometry, government/civics, grammar, health, history, history-AP, journalism, Latin, Latin-AP, mathematics, mathematics-AP, music, physical education, psychology, psychology-AP, SAT preparation, SAT/ACT preparation, science, social studies, sociology, Spanish, Spanish language-AP, Spanish-AP, speech, sports conditioning, studio art, studio art-AP, theater, track and field, trigonometry, U.S. history-AP, world history.
Graduation Requirements Algebra, American government, American history, arts and fine arts (art, music, dance, drama), biology, computer science, English, foreign language, geometry, mathematics, modern European history, physical education (includes health), physical science, pre-calculus, science, social studies (includes history), speech, U.S. history, 80 community service hours.
Special Academic Programs Advanced Placement exam preparation; honors section; independent study; study at local college for college credit; academic accommodation for the gifted; ESL (34 students enrolled).
College Admission Counseling 31 students graduated in 2010; all went to college, including Auburn University; Birmingham-Southern College; Shelton State Community College; The University of Alabama; University of Mississippi. Mean composite ACT: 25. 45% scored over 26 on composite ACT.
Student Life Upper grades have specified standards of dress, student council, honor system. Discipline rests primarily with faculty.
Summer Programs Enrichment, sports, art/fine arts, computer instruction programs offered; session focuses on enrichment and sports; held on campus; accepts boys and girls; open to students from other schools. 150 students usually enrolled. 2011 schedule: June 1 to July 30. Application deadline: none.
Tuition and Aid Day student tuition: $7334–$8792. Guaranteed tuition plan. Tuition installment plan (Insured Tuition Payment Plan, monthly payment plans, semester payment plan, annual payment plan). Tuition reduction for siblings, merit scholarship grants, need-based scholarship grants available. In 2010–11, 10% of upper-school students received aid; total upper-school merit-scholarship money awarded: $27,000. Total amount of financial aid awarded in 2010–11: $160,000.
Admissions Traditional secondary-level entrance grade is 9. For fall 2010, 38 students applied for upper-level admission, 30 were accepted, 21 enrolled. Achievement/Aptitude/Writing and Scholastic Achievement Test required. Deadline for receipt of application materials: none. Application fee required: $75. Interview required.
Athletics Interscholastic: baseball (boys), basketball (b,g), cheering (g), cross-country running (b,g), dance team (g), football (b), golf (b,g), softball (g), strength & conditioning (b), tennis (b,g), track and field (b,g), volleyball (g), weight training (b); coed interscholastic: soccer. 2 PE instructors, 10 coaches, 6 athletic trainers.

Computers Computers are regularly used in journalism, keyboarding, yearbook classes. Computer network features include on-campus library services, online commercial services, Internet access, wireless campus network, Internet filtering or blocking technology, laptop program. Campus intranet, student e-mail accounts, and computer access in designated common areas are available to students. Students grades are available online. The school has a published electronic and media policy.
Contact Anne D. Huffaker, Director of Admission. 205-758-4462 Ext. 202. Fax: 205-758-4418. E-mail: ahuffaker@tuscaloosaacademy.org. Web site: www. tuscaloosaacademy.org or www.WhyTa.org.

TYLER STREET CHRISTIAN ACADEMY
915 West 9th Street
Dallas, Texas 75208
Head of School: Dr. Karen J. Egger, PhD
General Information Coeducational day college-preparatory, general academic, arts, religious studies, and technology school, affiliated with Christian faith. Grades P3–12. Founded: 1972. Setting: urban. 5-acre campus. 2 buildings on campus. Approved or accredited by Association of Christian Schools International, Southern Association of Colleges and Schools, Texas Education Agency, Texas Private School Accreditation Commission, and Texas Department of Education. Endowment: $120,000. Total enrollment: 198. Upper school average class size: 10. Upper school faculty-student ratio: 1:8. There are 176 required school days per year for Upper School students. Upper School students typically attend 5 days per week. The average school day consists of 7 hours and 20 minutes.
Upper School Student Profile Grade 6: 9 students (8 boys, 1 girl); Grade 7: 24 students (16 boys, 8 girls); Grade 8: 18 students (9 boys, 9 girls); Grade 9: 32 students (14 boys, 18 girls); Grade 10: 12 students (8 boys, 4 girls); Grade 11: 10 students (4 boys, 6 girls); Grade 12: 12 students (7 boys, 5 girls). 82% of students are Christian faith.
Faculty School total: 31. In upper school: 5 men, 7 women; 5 have advanced degrees.
Subjects Offered Advanced Placement courses, algebra, American government, American history, art, art appreciation, art history, band, bell choir, Bible studies, biology, British literature, British literature (honors), calculus, calculus-AP, chemistry, choir, college counseling, community service, composition, computer applications, computer literacy, concert band, CPR, economics, English literature, family living, freshman seminar, geometry, grammar, guidance, health, Holocaust studies, honors algebra, honors English, honors geometry, keyboarding, lab science, literature, physical education, physical science, physics, pre-calculus, Spanish, speech communications, student government, U.S. literature, world geography, world history, world literature, yearbook.
Graduation Requirements Algebra, American government, arts and fine arts (art, music, dance, drama), Bible, biology, calculus, chemistry, computer science, economics, English, geometry, physical education (includes health), physical science, physics, Spanish, speech communications, U.S. history, world geography, world history.
Special Academic Programs 1 Advanced Placement exam for which test preparation is offered; honors section; independent study; study at local college for college credit.
College Admission Counseling 12 students graduated in 2010; all went to college, including Baylor University; Rice University; Texas A&M University; Texas Tech University; The University of Texas at Arlington; University of North Texas. Mean SAT critical reading: 564, mean SAT math: 506, mean composite ACT: 25. 43% scored over 600 on SAT critical reading, 15% scored over 600 on SAT math, 28% scored over 600 on SAT writing, 15% scored over 1800 on combined SAT, 9% scored over 26 on composite ACT.
Student Life Upper grades have uniform requirement, student council, honor system. Discipline rests primarily with faculty. Attendance at religious services is required.
Tuition and Aid Day student tuition: $6390. Tuition installment plan (FACTS Tuition Payment Plan). Merit scholarship grants, need-based scholarship grants available. In 2010–11, 45% of upper-school students received aid; total upper-school merit-scholarship money awarded: $2500. Total amount of financial aid awarded in 2010–11: $146,000.
Admissions Traditional secondary-level entrance grade is 9. For fall 2010, 51 students applied for upper level admission, 49 were accepted, 34 enrolled. Admissions testing, English entrance exam, mathematics proficiency exam and writing sample required. Deadline for receipt of application materials: none. Application fee required: $50. On-campus interview required.
Athletics Interscholastic: basketball (boys, girls), cheering (g), football (b), life saving (b), modern dance (g), strength & conditioning (b,g), track and field (b,g), volleyball (g). 1 PE instructor, 3 coaches.
Computers Computers are regularly used in business applications, computer applications, desktop publishing, introduction to technology, library, word processing, yearbook classes. Computer network features include on-campus library services, Internet access, Internet filtering or blocking technology, on-campus library services for Accelerated Reader Program. Computer access in designated common areas is available to students. Students grades are available online. The school has a published electronic and media policy.
Contact Mrs. Perla Gonzalez, Registrar. 214-941-9717 Ext. 200. Fax: 214-941-0324. E-mail: perlagonzalez@tsca.org. Web site: www.tsca.org.

UNITED MENNONITE EDUCATIONAL INSTITUTE

614 Mersea Road 6, RR 5
Leamington, Ontario N8H 3V8, Canada
Head of School: Mr. Victor Winter

General Information Coeducational day college-preparatory, arts, and religious studies school, affiliated with Mennonite Church USA. Grades 9–12. Founded: 1945. Setting: rural. Nearest major city is Windsor, Canada. 12-acre campus. 3 buildings on campus. Approved or accredited by Ontario Department of Education. Language of instruction: English. Total enrollment: 80. Upper school average class size: 18. Upper school faculty-student ratio: 1:15.

Upper School Student Profile 65% of students are Mennonite Church USA.

Faculty School total: 10. In upper school: 5 men, 5 women; 1 has an advanced degree.

Subjects Offered 20th century physics, advanced chemistry, advanced math, algebra, American history, ancient world history, art, Bible, biology, business studies, career exploration, chemistry, choir, choral music, Christian ethics, church history, civics, communication arts, computer applications, computer studies, computer technologies, English, environmental geography, family studies, film and new technologies, foreign language, French as a second language, German, instrumental music, introduction to theater, mathematics, orchestra, parenting, religious studies, society challenge and change, theater arts.

Graduation Requirements Arts, Canadian geography, Canadian history, careers, civics, English, French, mathematics, physical education (includes health), science.

College Admission Counseling 19 students graduated in 2009; 16 went to college. Other: 2 went to work, 1 had other specific plans.

Student Life Upper grades have specified standards of dress, student council. Discipline rests equally with students and faculty. Attendance at religious services is required.

Tuition and Aid Day student tuition: CAN$5300. Tuition installment plan (monthly payment plans). Tuition reduction for siblings, need-based scholarship grants, need-based loans available. In 2009–10, 5% of upper-school students received aid. Total amount of financial aid awarded in 2009–10: CAN$4000.

Admissions Traditional secondary-level entrance grade is 9. For fall 2009, 19 students applied for upper-level admission, 19 were accepted, 19 enrolled. Deadline for receipt of application materials: none. No application fee required.

Athletics Interscholastic: badminton (boys, girls), baseball (b,g), basketball (b,g), cross-country running (b,g), floor hockey (b,g), golf (b), softball (g), volleyball (b,g); intramural: badminton (b,g), baseball (b,g), basketball (b,g), bicycling (b), football (b), indoor soccer (b,g), volleyball (b,g); coed intramural: skiing (downhill), ultimate Frisbee. 1 PE instructor.

Computers Computers are regularly used in all classes. Computer network features include on-campus library services, Internet access, Internet filtering or blocking technology.

Contact Mr. Victor J. Winter, Principal. 519-326 7448. Fax: 519-326-0278. E-mail: umeiadmi@mnsi.net. Web site: www.umei.on.ca.

UNITED NATIONS INTERNATIONAL SCHOOL

24-50 Franklin Roosevelt Drive
New York, New York 10010-4046
Head of School: Mr. George Dymond

General Information Coeducational day college-preparatory, arts, technology, English as Second Language and Eight Mother Tongue programs, and International Baccalaureate, Eight 3rd Language Programs school. Grades K–12. Founded: 1947. Setting: urban. 3-acre campus. 1 building on campus. Approved or accredited by European Council of International Schools, International Baccalaureate Organization, New York State Association of Independent Schools, New York State Board of Regents, and New York Department of Education. Member of National Association of Independent Schools. Endowment: $13.3 million. Total enrollment: 1,542. Upper school average class size: 20. Upper school faculty-student ratio: 1:3. There are 172 required school days per year for Upper School students. Upper School students typically attend 5 days per week. The average school day consists of 6 hours and 40 minutes.

Upper School Student Profile Grade 9: 123 students (58 boys, 65 girls); Grade 10: 105 students (51 boys, 54 girls); Grade 11: 114 students (57 boys, 57 girls); Grade 12: 125 students (63 boys, 62 girls).

Faculty School total: 221. In upper school: 64 men, 82 women; 44 have advanced degrees.

Subjects Offered 3-dimensional art, algebra, American history, American literature, American studies, anthropology, Arabic, art, biology, calculus, chemistry, Chinese, community service, computer applications, computer science, creative writing, drama, economics, English, English literature, ESL, European history, expository writing, film, film studies, fine arts, French, geometry, German, history, humanities, Italian, Japanese, journalism, languages, library, mathematics, media production, modern languages, music, philosophy, photography, physical education, physics, psychology, Russian, science, social sciences, social studies, Spanish, theater arts, theory of knowledge, United Nations and international issues, video, video and animation, video communication, video film production, world history, world literature, writing.

Graduation Requirements Art, electives, English, health and wellness, humanities, mathematics, modern languages, music, physical education (includes health), science,

United Nations and international issues, International Baccalaureate, Theory of Knowledge, extended essay, Creative Aesthetic Service, individual project. Community service is required.

Special Academic Programs International Baccalaureate program; independent study; academic accommodation for the gifted, the musically talented, and the artistically talented; ESL (137 students enrolled).

College Admission Counseling 126 students graduated in 2010; 121 went to college, including Cornell University; McGill University; New York University; The University of North Carolina at Chapel Hill; University of Michigan; University of Toronto. Other: 1 entered military service, 4 had other specific plans. Median SAT critical reading: 600, median SAT math: 600, median SAT writing: 610, median combined SAT: 1808, median composite ACT: 25. 55% scored over 600 on SAT critical reading, 55% scored over 600 on SAT math, 65% scored over 600 on SAT writing, 58% scored over 1800 on combined SAT.

Student Life Upper grades have specified standards of dress, student council. Discipline rests primarily with faculty.

Summer Programs Enrichment, ESL, sports, art/fine arts, computer instruction programs offered; session focuses on recreational program for 4 to 14 years old students; held on campus; accepts boys and girls; open to students from other schools. 300 students usually enrolled. 2011 schedule: June 29 to July 29. Application deadline: April 30.

Tuition and Aid Day student tuition: $24,900–$25,450. Tuition installment plan (Tuition Management System (formerly Key Tuition Plan)). Bursaries available. In 2010–11, 7% of upper-school students received aid. Total amount of financial aid awarded in 2010–11: $286,290.

Admissions Traditional secondary-level entrance grade is 9. For fall 2010, 75 students applied for upper-level admission, 46 were accepted, 36 enrolled. ISEE, PSAT and SAT for applicants to grade 11 and 12 or SSAT required. Deadline for receipt of application materials: November 15. Application fee required: $75. On-campus interview required.

Athletics Interscholastic: baseball (boys), basketball (b,g), indoor track (b,g), indoor track & field (b,g), soccer (b,g), softball (g), track and field (b,g), volleyball (b,g); intramural: volleyball (b,g); coed interscholastic: swimming and diving; coed intramural: aerobics, aerobics/dance, aerobics/Nautilus, aquatics, badminton, ball hockey, basketball, canoeing/kayaking, climbing, cooperative games, dance, fitness, flag football, floor hockey, gymnastics, hiking/backpacking, independent competitive sports, indoor hockey, indoor soccer, indoor track, indoor track & field, jogging, jump rope, life saving, martial arts, modern dance, outdoor activities, physical fitness, physical training, rock climbing, ropes courses, rounders, running, soccer, softball, strength & conditioning, swimming and diving, table tennis, team handball, tennis, touch football, track and field, volleyball, wall climbing, weight training. 10 PE instructors, 26 coaches.

Computers Computers are regularly used in all academic, animation, art, basic skills, career education, career exploration, career technology, classics, college planning, computer applications, creative writing, current events, data processing, desktop publishing, desktop publishing, ESL, digital applications, drawing and design, economics, English, ESL, foreign language, French, French as a second language, graphic arts, graphic design, graphics, health, history, humanities, independent study, information technology, introduction to technology, journalism, keyboarding, lab/keyboard, learning cognition, library, library science, library skills, life skills, literacy, literary magazine, mathematics, media, media arts, media production, media services, multimedia, music, music technology, news writing, newspaper, philosophy, photography, photojournalism, programming, publications, publishing, research skills, science, social sciences, social studies, Spanish, study skills, technology, theater, theater arts, video film production, Web site design, writing, yearbook classes. Computer network features include on-campus library services, online commercial services, Internet access, wireless campus network, Internet filtering or blocking technology, media lab, TV studio, web portal, film production, digital video streaming, digital video editing. Campus intranet, student e-mail accounts, and computer access in designated common areas are available to students. Students grades are available online.

Contact Admissions Office. 212-584-3071. Fax: 212-685-5023. E-mail: admissions@unis.org. Web site: www.unis.org.

THE UNITED WORLD COLLEGE—USA

PO Box 248
Montezuma, New Mexico 87731
Head of School: Lisa A. H. Darling

General Information Coeducational boarding college-preparatory, arts, bilingual studies, wilderness, search and rescue, conflict resolution, and service, science, humanities school. Grades 11–12. Founded: 1982. Setting: small town. Nearest major city is Santa Fe. Students are housed in single-sex dormitories. 320-acre campus. 20 buildings on campus. Approved or accredited by Independent Schools Association of the Southwest, International Baccalaureate Organization, and New Mexico Department of Education. Languages of instruction: English, Spanish, and French. Endowment: $91 million. Total enrollment: 206. Upper school average class size: 8. Upper school faculty-student ratio: 1:8. There are 245 required school days per year for Upper School students. Upper School students typically attend 5 days per week. The average school day consists of 6 hours and 30 minutes.

Upper School Student Profile Grade 11: 106 students (52 boys, 54 girls); Grade 12: 100 students (50 boys, 50 girls), 100% of students are boarding students. 37 states are represented in upper school student body. 78% are international students. International students from Canada, Germany, Hong Kong, Mexico, Spain, and Venezuela; 75 other countries represented in student body.

Faculty School total: 28. In upper school: 15 men, 13 women; 22 have advanced degrees; 22 reside on campus.

Subjects Offered Anthropology, art, biology, calculus, chemistry, community service, conflict resolution, economics, English, English literature, environmental geography, environmental science, environmental studies, environmental systems, ESL, fine arts, French, German, history, information technology, International Baccalaureate courses, mathematics, music, physics, science, social sciences, social studies, Spanish, theater arts, theory of knowledge, world history, world literature, world religions.

Graduation Requirements American history, arts and fine arts (art, music, dance, drama), biology, calculus, chemistry, comparative religion, economics, English literature, environmental geography, environmental systems, European history, foreign language, French, French as a second language, geography, German, German literature, global issues, global studies, history of the Americas, International Baccalaureate courses, literature, math methods, mathematics, music, music theory, organic chemistry, peace studies, physics, post-calculus, pre-algebra, pre-calculus, research, science, senior thesis, social justice, social sciences, Spanish, Spanish literature, statistics, studio art, theater, theater arts, theory of knowledge, visual arts, wilderness education, wilderness experience, world religions, extended essay, independent research, theory of knowledge. Community service is required.

Special Academic Programs International Baccalaureate program; honors section; independent study; academic accommodation for the musically talented and the artistically talented; ESL (43 students enrolled).

College Admission Counseling 100 students graduated in 2010; 94 went to college, including Brown University; Dartmouth College; Earlham College; Harvard University; Princeton University; Trinity College. Other: 3 entered military service, 3 entered a postgraduate year. 25% scored over 600 on SAT critical reading, 75% scored over 600 on SAT math, 95% scored over 26 on composite ACT.

Student Life Upper grades have student council, honor system. Discipline rests equally with students and faculty.

Tuition and Aid 7-day tuition and room/board: $18,000. Guaranteed tuition plan. Tuition installment plan (all accepted U.S. students are awarded full merit scholarships, need-based aid available to all other students). Merit scholarship grants, need-based scholarship grants, full tuition merit scholarships awarded to all admitted U.S. citizens available. In 2010–11, 90% of upper-school students received aid; total upper-school merit-scholarship money awarded: $2,800,000. Total amount of financial aid awarded in 2010–11: $2,800,000.

Admissions Traditional secondary-level entrance grade is 11. For fall 2010, 483 students applied for upper-level admission, 50 were accepted, 50 enrolled. ACT, PSAT or SAT or PSAT, SAT, or ACT for applicants to grade 11 and 12 required. Deadline for receipt of application materials: January 10. No application fee required. Interview required.

Athletics Coed Intramural: aerobics, aerobics/dance, aerobics/Nautilus, alpine skiing, aquatics, backpacking, badminton, ballet, baseball, basketball, bicycling, billiards, canoeing/kayaking, climbing, combined training, cooperative games, cricket, cross-country running, dance, fitness, Frisbee, hiking/backpacking, jogging, modern dance, mountaineering, nordic skiing, outdoor activities, physical training, racquetball, ropes courses, running, sailing, skiing (cross-country), skiing (downhill), snowboarding, snowshoeing, soccer, softball, squash, strength & conditioning, swimming and diving, table tennis, tennis, volleyball, walking, weight lifting, weight training, wilderness, wilderness survival, yoga. 1 PE instructor, 12 athletic trainers.

Computers Computers are regularly used in art, English, ESL, foreign language, mathematics, music, science classes. Computer network features include on-campus library services, Internet access, wireless campus network, Internet filtering or blocking technology. Campus intranet, student e-mail accounts, and computer access in designated common areas are available to students. Students grades are available online.

Contact Tim Smith, Director of Admissions. 505-454-4201. Fax: 505-454-4294. E-mail: tim.smith@uwc-usa.org. Web site: www.uwc-usa.org.

UNIVERSITY CHRISTIAN PREPARATORY SCHOOL

4800 Mooringsport Road
Shreveport, Louisiana 71107
Head of School: Ms. Beryl Cowthran

General Information Coeducational day college-preparatory, general academic, arts, religious studies, and technology school, affiliated with Christian faith. Grades K–12. Founded: 1970. Setting: urban. Nearest major city is Bossier City. 25-acre campus. 14 buildings on campus. Approved or accredited by European Council of International Schools, Southern Association of Colleges and Schools, and Louisiana Department of Education. Total enrollment: 59. Upper school average class size: 14. Upper school faculty-student ratio: 1:14. There are 178 required school days per year for Upper School students. Upper School students typically attend 5 days per week. The average school day consists of 7 hours.

Upper School Student Profile Grade 9: 5 students (3 boys, 2 girls); Grade 10: 1 student (1 boy); Grade 11: 5 students (5 boys); Grade 12: 8 students (6 boys, 2 girls). 98% of students are Christian faith.

Faculty School total: 12. In upper school: 2 men, 4 women; 1 has an advanced degree.

Subjects Offered Algebra, American history, art, Bible, biology, business mathematics, chemistry, civics/free enterprise, computer applications, computer literacy, general math, general science, geography, geometry, health, Internet research, language arts, mathematics, physical education, physical science, reading, reading/study skills, student teaching, world geography, world history, yearbook.

Graduation Requirements Advanced math, algebra, American history, American literature, Bible, biology, chemistry, civics/free enterprise, computer applications, earth and space science, electives, foreign language, geometry, grammar, language arts, life science, literature, physical education (includes health), physical science, world geography, world history.

College Admission Counseling 13 students graduated in 2010; 11 went to college, including Louisiana State University in Shreveport. Other: 1 went to work, 1 entered military service.

Student Life Upper grades have uniform requirement, student council, honor system. Discipline rests primarily with faculty. Attendance at religious services is required.

Tuition and Aid Day student tuition: $4500. Tuition installment plan (individually arranged payment plans). Tuition reduction for siblings, need-based scholarship grants available. In 2010–11, 13% of upper-school students received aid.

Admissions Traditional secondary-level entrance grade is 9. For fall 2010, 7 students applied for upper-level admission, 4 were accepted, 4 enrolled. Deadline for receipt of application materials: none. No application fee required. Interview recommended.

Athletics Interscholastic: basketball (boys, girls); intramural: basketball (b,g), weight training (b,g).

Computers Computers are regularly used in library, yearbook classes. Computer network features include Internet access. Computer access in designated common areas is available to students.

Contact Mrs. Catherine Johnson, Office Manager. 318-221-2697. Fax: 318-221-2790. Web site: www.universitychristianprep.com.

UNIVERSITY LAKE SCHOOL

4024 Nagawicka Road
Hartland, Wisconsin 53029
Head of School: Mr. Bradley F. Ashley

General Information Coeducational day college-preparatory, arts, and technology school. Grades PK–12. Founded: 1956. Setting: small town. Nearest major city is Milwaukee. 180-acre campus. 4 buildings on campus. Approved or accredited by Independent Schools Association of the Central States. Member of National Association of Independent Schools. Endowment: $2.4 million. Total enrollment: 312. Upper school average class size: 12. Upper school faculty-student ratio: 1:9.

Upper School Student Profile Grade 8: 27 students (15 boys, 12 girls); Grade 9: 16 students (10 boys, 6 girls); Grade 10: 13 students (5 boys, 8 girls); Grade 11: 24 students (10 boys, 14 girls); Grade 12: 25 students (9 boys, 16 girls).

Faculty School total: 48. In upper school: 9 men, 5 women; 11 have advanced degrees.

Subjects Offered Algebra, American history, American literature, art, biology, calculus, chemistry, cinematography, computer science, creative writing, design, drama, English, English literature, environmental science, fine arts, French, geometry, government/civics, journalism, mathematics, music, photography, physical education, physics, science, social studies, Spanish, speech, statistics, theater, video film production, Web site design, world history, world literature, writing.

Graduation Requirements Art, arts and fine arts (art, music, dance, drama), computer science, English, foreign language, literature, mathematics, physical education (includes health), science, social studies (includes history), speech.

Special Academic Programs Advanced Placement exam preparation; honors section; independent study; study at local college for college credit; academic accommodation for the gifted, the musically talented, and the artistically talented; remedial reading and/or remedial writing; remedial math; programs in English for dyslexic students; special instructional classes for blind students.

College Admission Counseling 24 students graduated in 2009; 23 went to college, including Dartmouth College; University of Wisconsin–Madison. Other: 1 had other specific plans. Median SAT critical reading: 535, median SAT math: 550, median composite ACT: 26.

Student Life Upper grades have specified standards of dress, student council, honor system. Discipline rests equally with students and faculty.

Tuition and Aid Day student tuition: $14,200. Tuition installment plan (Insured Tuition Payment Plan, FACTS Tuition Payment Plan, monthly payment plans). Merit scholarship grants, need-based scholarship grants available. In 2009–10, 25% of upper-school students received aid; total upper-school merit-scholarship money awarded: $42,000. Total amount of financial aid awarded in 2009–10: $120,000.

Admissions Traditional secondary-level entrance grade is 9. For fall 2009, 10 students applied for upper-level admission, 10 were accepted, 9 enrolled. Admissions testing, Kuhlmann-Anderson and Kulhmann-Anderson Level G (for grades 7-9) or Level H (for grades 10-12) required. Deadline for receipt of application materials: none. Application fee required: $25. On-campus interview recommended.

Athletics Interscholastic: basketball (boys, girls), field hockey (g), skiing (downhill) (b,g), soccer (b,g), tennis (b,g), volleyball (g); coed interscholastic: alpine skiing, cross-country running, golf, ice hockey; coed intramural: alpine skiing, aquatics, volleyball, wall climbing. 2 PE instructors, 7 coaches.

Computers Computers are regularly used in all academic classes. Computer network features include on-campus library services, Internet access, wireless campus network, Internet filtering or blocking technology, one-to-one notebook computing program. Campus intranet and student e-mail accounts are available to students. Students grades are available online. The school has a published electronic and media policy.

Contact Mrs. Angela Wenger, Director of Admissions. 262-367-6011 Ext. 1455. Fax: 262-367-3146. E-mail: awenger@universitylake.org. Web site: www. universitylake.org.

UNIVERSITY OF CHICAGO LABORATORY SCHOOLS
1362 East 59th Street
Chicago, Illinois 60637
Head of School: Dr. David W. Magill

General Information Coeducational day college-preparatory school. Grades N–12. Founded: 1896. Setting: urban. 11-acre campus. 3 buildings on campus. Approved or accredited by Independent Schools Association of the Central States, North Central Association of Colleges and Schools, and Illinois Department of Education. Member of National Association of Independent Schools. Endowment: $15.5 million. Total enrollment: 1,801. Upper school average class size: 16. Upper school faculty-student ratio: 1:10. There are 170 required school days per year for Upper School students. Upper School students typically attend 5 days per week. The average school day consists of 7 hours.

Upper School Student Profile Grade 9: 125 students (57 boys, 68 girls); Grade 10: 130 students (51 boys, 79 girls); Grade 11: 124 students (55 boys, 69 girls); Grade 12: 120 students (68 boys, 52 girls).

Faculty School total: 215. In upper school: 32 men, 34 women; 60 have advanced degrees.

Subjects Offered Acting, advanced biology, advanced chemistry, African-American history, algebra, American history, art, art history, art history-AP, biology, calculus, calculus-AP, chemistry, Chinese, community service, computer science, creative writing, drama, drawing, driver education, English, English literature, European history, European history-AP, expository writing, fine arts, French, French-AP, geometry, German, German-AP, government/civics, history, Holocaust, jazz band, journalism, Latin, Mandarin, mathematics, modern European history, music, music theory-AP, orchestra, painting, photography, photojournalism, physical education, physics, play production, post-calculus, science, sculpture, social studies, Spanish, Spanish language-AP, Spanish-AP, statistics, statistics-AP, studio art, theater, trigonometry, Web site design, Western civilization, world history, writing, yearbook.

Graduation Requirements Arts and fine arts (art, music, dance, drama), computer science, English, foreign language, mathematics, music, physical education (includes health), science, social studies (includes history). Community service is required.

Special Academic Programs 8 Advanced Placement exams for which test preparation is offered; accelerated programs; independent study; study at local college for college credit.

College Admission Counseling 117 students graduated in 2010; 116 went to college, including Carleton College; Northwestern University; University of Chicago; University of Illinois at Urbana–Champaign; University of Michigan; Yale University. Other: 1 had other specific plans. Median SAT critical reading: 681, median SAT math: 675, median SAT writing: 668, median combined SAT: 2024, median composite ACT: 30. 78% scored over 600 on SAT critical reading, 75% scored over 600 on SAT math, 78% scored over 600 on SAT writing, 82% scored over 1800 on combined SAT, 81% scored over 26 on composite ACT.

Student Life Upper grades have student council. Discipline rests primarily with faculty.

Summer Programs Enrichment, advancement, sports programs offered; session focuses on advancement of placement in courses; held on campus; accepts boys and girls; open to students from other schools. 100 students usually enrolled. 2011 schedule: June 20 to July 29. Application deadline: May 15.

Tuition and Aid Day student tuition: $23,928. Tuition installment plan (monthly payment plans, quarterly payment plan). Need-based scholarship grants available. In 2010–11, 19% of upper-school students received aid. Total amount of financial aid awarded in 2010–11: $1,043,106.

Admissions Traditional secondary-level entrance grade is 9. For fall 2010, 166 students applied for upper-level admission, 57 were accepted, 33 enrolled. ISEE required. Deadline for receipt of application materials: December 1. Application fee required: $75. On-campus interview required.

Athletics Interscholastic: baseball (boys), basketball (b,g), cross-country running (b,g), indoor track & field (b,g), soccer (b,g), swimming and diving (b,g), tennis (b,g), track and field (b,g), volleyball (g), winter (indoor) track (b,g); intramural: dance squad (g), weight training (b,g); coed interscholastic: cross-country running, fencing, flag football, golf; coed intramural: life saving. 12 PE instructors, 31 coaches, 1 athletic trainer.

Computers Computers are regularly used in mathematics, music, newspaper, science, yearbook classes. Computer network features include on-campus library services, Internet access, wireless campus network. Student e-mail accounts are available to students. The school has a published electronic and media policy.

Contact Irene Reed, Executive Director of Admissions and Financial Aid. 773-702-9451. Fax: 773-702-7455. E-mail: ireed@ucls.uchicago.edu. Web site: www. ucls.uchicago.edu/.

UNIVERSITY OF DETROIT JESUIT HIGH SCHOOL AND ACADEMY
8400 South Cambridge Avenue
Detroit, Michigan 48221
Head of School: Mr. Anthony Trudel

General Information Boys' day college-preparatory, arts, religious studies, and technology school, affiliated with Roman Catholic Church (Jesuit order). Grades 7–12. Founded: 1877. Setting: urban. 14-acre campus. 1 building on campus. Approved or accredited by Jesuit Secondary Education Association, Michigan Association of Non-Public Schools, North Central Association of Colleges and Schools, and Michigan Department of Education. Endowment: $15 million. Total enrollment: 858. Upper school average class size: 22. Upper school faculty-student ratio: 1:14. There are 183 required school days per year for Upper School students. Upper School students typically attend 5 days per week. The average school day consists of 6 hours and 45 minutes.

Upper School Student Profile Grade 9: 238 students (238 boys); Grade 10: 163 students (163 boys); Grade 11: 166 students (166 boys); Grade 12: 178 students (178 boys). 72% of students are Roman Catholic Church (Jesuit order).

Faculty School total: 52. In upper school: 37 men, 15 women; 34 have advanced degrees.

Subjects Offered Acting, African-American history, algebra, American history, American history-AP, American literature, anatomy, art, Bible studies, biochemistry, biology, biology-AP, calculus, calculus-AP, ceramics, chemistry, chemistry-AP, Chinese, Christian and Hebrew scripture, Christian doctrine, Christian education, Christian ethics, Christian studies, Christian testament, church history, comparative religion, computer applications, computer programming, computer-aided design, drawing, earth science, economics, English, English literature, English literature-AP, English-AP, environmental science, ethics, European history, expository writing, French, geography, geometry, government-AP, government/civics, history, history of the Catholic Church, history-AP, Latin, Latin-AP, Mandarin, mathematics, music, physical education, physical science, physics, physics-AP, psychology, public speaking, religion, science, social studies, sociology, Spanish, Spanish-AP, speech, theology, trigonometry, U.S. government and politics-AP, U.S. history, U.S. history-AP, world history, world literature, writing.

Graduation Requirements Arts and fine arts (art, music, dance, drama), business skills (includes word processing), English, foreign language, mathematics, physical education (includes health), public speaking, religion (includes Bible studies and theology), science, social studies (includes history), senior Community Service program.

Special Academic Programs Advanced Placement exam preparation; honors section; independent study; study at local college for college credit.

College Admission Counseling 141 students graduated in 2010; all went to college, including Loyola University Chicago; Michigan State University; University of Dayton; University of Michigan; University of Notre Dame; Wayne State University. Mean SAT critical reading: 605, mean SAT math: 608, mean SAT writing: 597, mean combined SAT: 1810, mean composite ACT: 25.

Student Life Upper grades have specified standards of dress, student council. Discipline rests primarily with faculty. Attendance at religious services is required.

Summer Programs Remediation, art/fine arts, computer instruction programs offered; held on campus; accepts boys; not open to students from other schools. 50 students usually enrolled. 2011 schedule: June 20 to July 22.

Tuition and Aid Day student tuition: $10,270. Tuition installment plan (FACTS Tuition Payment Plan). Merit scholarship grants, need-based scholarship grants available. In 2010–11, 45% of upper-school students received aid; total upper-school merit-scholarship money awarded: $250,000. Total amount of financial aid awarded in 2010–11: $1,550,000.

Admissions Traditional secondary-level entrance grade is 9. For fall 2010, 500 students applied for upper-level admission, 375 were accepted, 238 enrolled. Scholastic Testing Service High School Placement Test or STS—Educational Development Series required. Deadline for receipt of application materials: none. No application fee required. On-campus interview recommended.

Athletics Interscholastic: baseball, basketball, bowling, cross-country running, diving, football, golf, ice hockey, lacrosse, skiing (downhill), soccer, swimming and diving, tennis, track and field, wrestling; intramural: basketball, bowling, flag football, football, Frisbee, soccer, touch football. 2 PE instructors, 15 coaches, 2 athletic trainers.

Computers Computers are regularly used in all academic, art, history, mathematics, science, speech classes. Computer network features include on-campus library services, online commercial services, Internet access, wireless campus network, Internet filtering or blocking technology. Student e-mail accounts are available to students. Students grades are available online. The school has a published electronic and media policy.

Contact Mr. Atif Lodhi, Director of Admissions. 313-862-5400 Ext. 2380. Fax: 313-862-3299. E-mail: atif.lodhi@uofdjesuit.org. Web site: www.uofdjesuit.org/.

UNIVERSITY PREP

8000 25th Avenue NE
Seattle, Washington 98115
Head of School: Erica L. Hamlin

General Information Coeducational day college-preparatory, arts, bilingual studies, technology, and global education school. Grades 6–12. Founded: 1976. Setting: urban. 6-acre campus. 5 buildings on campus. Approved or accredited by Northwest Association of Schools and Colleges, Pacific Northwest Association of Independent Schools, and Washington Department of Education. Member of National Association of Independent Schools. Endowment: $5.3 million. Total enrollment: 501. Upper school average class size: 16. Upper school faculty-student ratio: 1:9. There are 169 required school days per year for Upper School students. Upper School students typically attend 5 days per week. The average school day consists of 6 hours and 50 minutes.

Upper School Student Profile Grade 9: 83 students (45 boys, 38 girls); Grade 10: 68 students (32 boys, 36 girls); Grade 11: 68 students (37 boys, 31 girls); Grade 12: 70 students (33 boys, 37 girls).

Faculty School total: 62. In upper school: 24 men, 29 women; 45 have advanced degrees.

Subjects Offered 3-dimensional art, advanced chemistry, advanced math, African drumming, African-American studies, algebra, American government, American history, American literature, applied arts, applied music, art, art and culture, art history, Asian literature, Asian studies, astronomy, athletics, audio visual/media, band, biology, British literature, calculus, career and personal planning, career planning, career/college preparation, chemistry, Chinese, Chinese studies, choir, chorus, civil rights, classical civilization, college counseling, college placement, college planning, community service, comparative government and politics, comparative religion, composition, computer art, computer literacy, computer science, conceptual physics, creative dance, creative drama, creative writing, critical thinking, critical writing, dance, decision making skills, democracy in America, design, digital art, digital photography, diversity studies, drafting, drama, drama performance, dramatic arts, drawing, ecology, economics, electives, English, English composition, English literature, ensembles, environmental education, environmental science, environmental studies, ethnic studies, European history, expository writing, film studies, fine arts, fitness, foreign language, French, freshman seminar, geography, geometry, global studies, golf, government, government/civics, graphic design, health, history, history of religion, independent study, information technology, introduction to technology, Japanese, Japanese history, Japanese studies, jazz ensemble, journalism, languages, Latin American studies, library, life skills, literary magazine, mathematics, media, medieval/Renaissance history, minority studies, multicultural studies, music, music performance, music theory, orchestra, Pacific Northwest seminar, painting, performing arts, personal fitness, philosophy, photography, physical education, physical fitness, physics, play production, play/screen writing, poetry, political science, politics, programming, psychology, public policy, publishing, research, Russian studies, science, senior thesis, social justice, Spanish, stagecraft, statistics, student publications, theater, theater arts, theater design and production, trigonometry, vocal ensemble, weight training, weightlifting, wilderness education, wilderness experience, women in society, world literature, yearbook.

Graduation Requirements American history, arts and fine arts (art, music, dance, drama), biology, chemistry, English, foreign language, life skills, mathematics, Pacific Northwest seminar, physical education (includes health), physics, science, senior thesis, social studies (includes history). Community service is required.

Special Academic Programs Advanced Placement exam preparation; independent study; term-away projects; study abroad; programs in English, mathematics, general development for dyslexic students; special instructional classes for college-bound students with high intellectual potential who have diagnosed specific learning disability.

College Admission Counseling 66 students graduated in 2010; all went to college, including Emory University; Santa Clara University; University of Pennsylvania; University of Redlands; University of Washington. Median SAT critical reading: 630, median SAT math: 635, median SAT writing: 635, median combined SAT: 1875, median composite ACT: 26. 68% scored over 600 on SAT critical reading, 66% scored over 600 on SAT math, 66% scored over 600 on SAT writing, 76% scored over 1800 on combined SAT, 68% scored over 26 on composite ACT.

Student Life Upper grades have student council, honor system. Discipline rests equally with students and faculty.

Tuition and Aid Day student tuition: $25,410. Tuition installment plan (Insured Tuition Payment Plan, Key Tuition Payment Plan, monthly payment plans, individually arranged payment plans, Dewar Tuition Refund Plan). Need-based scholarship grants available. In 2010–11, 23% of upper-school students received aid. Total amount of financial aid awarded in 2010–11: $1,238,663.

Admissions Traditional secondary-level entrance grade is 9. For fall 2010, 145 students applied for upper-level admission, 50 were accepted, 25 enrolled. ISEE required. Deadline for receipt of application materials: January 13. Application fee required: $70. On-campus interview required.

Athletics Interscholastic: baseball (boys), basketball (b,g), cross-country running (b,g), flag football (b), Frisbee (b,g), soccer (b,g), softball (g), tennis (b,g), track and field (b,g), volleyball (g); intramural: golf (b,g), ultimate Frisbee (b,g); coed interscholastic: ultimate Frisbee; coed intramural: aerobics, aerobics/dance, backpacking, dance, fitness, hiking/backpacking, modern dance, outdoor activities, outdoor adventure, outdoor education, outdoor skills, outdoors, rock climbing, skiing (downhill), snowboarding, strength & conditioning, ultimate Frisbee, wall climbing, weight training, wilderness, yoga. 5 PE instructors, 65 coaches.

Computers Computers are regularly used in English, foreign language, history, information technology, journalism, library, mathematics, media, music, photography, publications, science, technology, yearbook classes. Computer network features include on-campus library services, online commercial services, Internet access, wireless campus network, Internet filtering or blocking technology. Campus intranet, student e-mail accounts, and computer access in designated common areas are available to students. Students grades are available online. The school has a published electronic and media policy.

Contact Melaine Taylor, Associate Director of Admission. 206-523-6407. Fax: 206-525-5320. E-mail: admissionoffice@universityprep.org. Web site: www. universityprep.org.

UNIVERSITY SCHOOL

2785 SOM Center Road
Hunting Valley, Ohio 44022
Head of School: Mr. Stephen S. Murray

General Information Boys' day college-preparatory, arts, business, bilingual studies, and technology school. Grades K–12. Founded: 1890. Setting: suburban. Nearest major city is Cleveland. 220-acre campus. 1 building on campus. Approved or accredited by Independent Schools Association of the Central States, Ohio Association of Independent Schools, and Ohio Department of Education. Member of National Association of Independent Schools. Endowment: $54.7 million. Total enrollment: 880. Upper school average class size: 14. Upper school faculty-student ratio: 1:7. Upper School students typically attend 5 days per week. The average school day consists of 7 hours and 15 minutes.

Upper School Student Profile Grade 9: 99 students (99 boys); Grade 10: 108 students (108 boys); Grade 11: 109 students (109 boys); Grade 12: 101 students (101 boys).

Faculty School total: 66. In upper school: 52 men, 14 women; 53 have advanced degrees.

Subjects Offered Advanced math, algebra, American history, American literature, art, art history, biology, calculus, ceramics, chemistry, Chinese, computer animation, computer graphics, computer programming, computer science, computer-aided design, CPR, digital photography, drama, earth science, ecology, economics, engineering, English, English language-AP, English literature, English literature-AP, environmental science, ethics, European history, filmmaking, fine arts, French, geometry, government/civics, Greek, health, history, history-AP, Latin, mathematics, mathematics-AP, music, orchestra, philosophy, photography, physical education, physics, psychology, science, social studies, Spanish, theater, trigonometry, woodworking, world history, writing.

Graduation Requirements Arts and fine arts (art, music, dance, drama), English, foreign language, history, mathematics, physical education (includes health), science.

Special Academic Programs Advanced Placement exam preparation; honors section; independent study; term-away projects; study at local college for college credit; study abroad; academic accommodation for the gifted, the musically talented, and the artistically talented.

College Admission Counseling 102 students graduated in 2009; all went to college, including Brown University; Case Western Reserve University; Colgate University; Duke University; Kenyon College; The George Washington University. Median SAT critical reading: 620, median SAT math: 670, median SAT writing: 630, median combined SAT: 1885, median composite ACT: 28. 86% scored over 600 on SAT critical reading, 63% scored over 600 on SAT math, 75% scored over 600 on SAT writing, 72% scored over 1800 on combined SAT, 61% scored over 26 on composite ACT.

Student Life Upper grades have specified standards of dress, student council, honor system. Discipline rests equally with students and faculty.

Tuition and Aid Day student tuition: $21,200–$23,100. Tuition installment plan (Academic Management Services Plan, Key Tuition Payment Plan). Need-based scholarship grants available. In 2009–10, 37% of upper-school students received aid. Total amount of financial aid awarded in 2009–10: $2,236,365.

Admissions Traditional secondary-level entrance grade is 9. For fall 2009, 87 students applied for upper-level admission, 72 were accepted, 37 enrolled. ISEE required. Deadline for receipt of application materials: none. No application fee required. On-campus interview required.

Athletics Interscholastic: baseball, basketball, cross-country running, football, golf, ice hockey, lacrosse, soccer, squash, swimming and diving, tennis, track and field, wrestling; intramural: alpine skiing, skiing (downhill), soccer, swimming and diving, tennis, volleyball. 5 coaches, 1 athletic trainer.

Computers Computers are regularly used in animation, art, business education, classics, drafting, drawing and design, economics, engineering, foreign language, graphics, journalism, literary magazine, music technology, newspaper, photography, science, yearbook classes. Computer network features include on-campus library services, Internet access, wireless campus network, Internet filtering or blocking technology. Campus intranet, student e-mail accounts, and computer access in designated common areas are available to students. Students grades are available online. The school has a published electronic and media policy.

Contact Mr. Sean Grosz, Director of Enrollment Planning/Director of Admission, Grades 9-12. 216-831-2200 Ext. 7335. Fax: 216-292-7810. E-mail: sgrosz@us.edu. Web site: www.us.edu.

UNIVERSITY SCHOOL OF JACKSON

232/240 McClellan Road
Jackson, Tennessee 38305
Head of School: Clay Lilienstern

General Information Coeducational day college-preparatory, arts, and technology school. Grades PK–12. Founded: 1970. Setting: suburban. 140-acre campus. 3 buildings on campus. Approved or accredited by Southern Association of Colleges and Schools and Tennessee Department of Education. Member of National Association of Independent Schools. Endowment: $85,000. Total enrollment: 1,232. Upper school average class size: 20. Upper school faculty-student ratio: 1:13. There are 180 required school days per year for Upper School students. Upper School students typically attend 5 days per week. The average school day consists of 7 hours and 5 minutes.

Upper School Student Profile Grade 9: 68 students (35 boys, 33 girls); Grade 10: 91 students (51 boys, 40 girls); Grade 11: 105 students (60 boys, 45 girls); Grade 12: 84 students (44 boys, 40 girls).

Faculty School total: 95. In upper school: 12 men, 22 women; 25 have advanced degrees.

Subjects Offered 3-dimensional art, 3-dimensional design, accounting, advanced chemistry, advanced math, Advanced Placement courses, algebra, American history, American history-AP, anatomy and physiology, art, biology, biology-AP, calculus, calculus-AP, chemistry, chemistry-AP, chorus, community service, computer applications, computer programming, computer science, creative writing, current events, dramatic arts, ecology, ecology, environmental systems, economics, English, English language-AP, English literature-AP, environmental science-AP, European history-AP, fine arts, French, geography, geology, geometry, government/civics, honors algebra, honors English, honors geometry, humanities, keyboarding, mathematics, music theory, music theory-AP, performing arts, physical education, physical science, physics, pre-calculus, psychology, science, social studies, Spanish, Spanish language-AP, speech and debate, trigonometry, U.S. history, U.S. history-AP, vocal ensemble, world history, world religions, yearbook.

Graduation Requirements Arts and fine arts (art, music, dance, drama), computer science, English, foreign language, mathematics, science, social studies (includes history), 50 hours of community service.

Special Academic Programs Advanced Placement exam preparation; honors section; academic accommodation for the gifted, the musically talented, and the artistically talented; ESL (10 students enrolled).

College Admission Counseling 82 students graduated in 2010; 80 went to college, including Middle Tennessee State University; Mississippi State University; Tennessee Technological University; The University of Tennessee; Union University; University of Mississippi. Other: 2 had other specific plans. Median SAT critical reading: 540, median SAT math: 560, median SAT writing: 540, median combined SAT: 1640, median composite ACT: 23. 31% scored over 600 on SAT critical reading, 38% scored over 600 on SAT math, 24% scored over 600 on SAT writing, 24% scored over 1800 on combined SAT, 30% scored over 26 on composite ACT.

Student Life Upper grades have uniform requirement, student council, honor system. Discipline rests equally with students and faculty.

Summer Programs Remediation, enrichment, sports, art/fine arts, computer instruction programs offered; session focuses on enrichment and remediation; held on campus; accepts boys and girls; open to students from other schools. 500 students usually enrolled. 2011 schedule: June 1 to July 31. Application deadline: none.

Tuition and Aid Day student tuition: $5650–$7475. Tuition installment plan (monthly payment plans, quarterly payment plan). Tuition reduction for siblings, need-based financial aid available. In 2010–11, 3% of upper-school students received aid. Total amount of financial aid awarded in 2010–11: $130,000.

Admissions Traditional secondary-level entrance grade is 9. For fall 2010, 37 students applied for upper-level admission, 32 were accepted, 27 enrolled. Math Placement Exam, Otis-Lennon School Ability Test, SCAT and writing sample required. Deadline for receipt of application materials: none. Application fee required: $50. On-campus interview required.

Athletics Interscholastic: baseball (boys), basketball (b,g), cheering (g), cross-country running (b,g), football (b), golf (b,g), soccer (b,g), softball (g), tennis (b,g), track and field (b,g), volleyball (g), weight lifting (b,g), weight training (b,g); intramural: bowling (b,g), in-line hockey (b); coed interscholastic: trap and skeet; coed intramural: bowling. 2 coaches.

Computers Computers are regularly used in art, English, foreign language, history, journalism, keyboarding, music, science, technology, theater arts, word processing, writing, yearbook classes. Computer network features include on-campus library services, online commercial services, Internet access. Students grades are available online. The school has a published electronic and media policy.

Contact Kay Shearin, Director of Admissions. 731-660-1692. Fax: 731-668-6910. E-mail: kshearin@usjbruins.org. Web site: www.usjbruins.org.

UNIVERSITY SCHOOL OF MILWAUKEE

2100 West Fairy Chasm Road
Milwaukee, Wisconsin 53217
Head of School: Ward J. Ghory, EdD

General Information Coeducational day college-preparatory, arts, and technology school. Grades PK–12. Founded: 1851. Setting: suburban. 131-acre campus. 2 buildings on campus. Approved or accredited by Independent Schools Association of the Central States and Wisconsin Department of Education. Member of National Association of Independent Schools and Secondary School Admission Test Board. Endowment: $42 million. Total enrollment: 1,058. Upper school average class size: 15. Upper school faculty-student ratio: 1:9. There are 178 required school days per year for Upper School students. Upper School students typically attend 5 days per week. The average school day consists of 6 hours and 45 minutes.

Upper School Student Profile Grade 9: 94 students (51 boys, 43 girls); Grade 10: 79 students (40 boys, 39 girls); Grade 11: 92 students (41 boys, 51 girls); Grade 12: 92 students (56 boys, 36 girls).

Faculty School total: 112. In upper school: 19 men, 17 women; 29 have advanced degrees.

Subjects Offered Algebra, American history, American literature, art, art history, band, biology, calculus, chemistry, computer programming, computer science, concert choir, discrete mathematics, drama, drawing, economics, English, English literature, European history, expository writing, French, geometry, health, Latin, mathematics, music, orchestra, painting, photography, physical education, physics, printmaking, psychology, SAT/ACT preparation, sculpture, Spanish, statistics, theater, U.S. history, world history, world literature.

Graduation Requirements Arts and fine arts (art, music, dance, drama), English, foreign language, history, mathematics, physical education (includes health), science, 40 hours of community service.

Special Academic Programs Advanced Placement exam preparation; honors section; independent study; study at local college for college credit.

College Admission Counseling 89 students graduated in 2010; 88 went to college, including Miami University; Southern Methodist University; University of Richmond; University of Wisconsin–Madison; Wake Forest University; Washington University in St. Louis. Other: 1 had other specific plans. Median SAT critical reading: 700, median SAT math: 700, median SAT writing: 730, median combined SAT: 2150, median composite ACT: 29. 96% scored over 600 on SAT critical reading, 96% scored over 600 on SAT math, 91% scored over 600 on SAT writing, 96% scored over 1800 on combined SAT, 76% scored over 26 on composite ACT.

Student Life Upper grades have specified standards of dress, student council, honor system. Discipline rests equally with students and faculty.

Summer Programs Enrichment, sports, art/fine arts, computer instruction programs offered; session focuses on reading, writing, math, science, sports, visual arts, music, drama, and computer enrichment/instruction; held on campus; accepts boys and girls; open to students from other schools. 1,500 students usually enrolled. 2011 schedule: June 13 to August 19. Application deadline: none.

Tuition and Aid Day student tuition: $19,761. Tuition installment plan (FACTS Tuition Payment Plan, monthly payment plans). Need-based scholarship grants available. In 2010–11, 24% of upper-school students received aid. Total amount of financial aid awarded in 2010–11: $884,100.

Admissions Traditional secondary-level entrance grade is 9. For fall 2010, 54 students applied for upper-level admission, 38 were accepted, 28 enrolled. ERB Achievement Test required. Deadline for receipt of application materials: none. Application fee required: $50. Interview required.

Athletics Interscholastic: baseball (boys), basketball (b,g), cross-country running (b,g), dance team (g), diving (b,g), field hockey (g), football (b), golf (b), ice hockey (b,g), lacrosse (b), skiing (downhill) (b,g), soccer (b,g), swimming and diving (b,g), tennis (b,g), track and field (b,g), volleyball (g). 1 PE instructor, 52 coaches, 2 athletic trainers.

Computers Computers are regularly used in college planning, creative writing, English, foreign language, history, journalism, mathematics, science, yearbook classes. Computer network features include on-campus library services, online commercial services, Internet access, wireless campus network, Internet filtering or blocking technology. Student e-mail accounts are available to students. Students grades are available online. The school has a published electronic and media policy.

Contact Kathleen Friedman, Director of Admissions. 414-540-3321. Fax: 414-352-8076. E-mail: kfriedman@usmk12.org. Web site: www.usmk12.org.

UNIVERSITY SCHOOL OF NASHVILLE

2000 Edgehill Avenue
Nashville, Tennessee 37212-2198
Head of School: Mr. Vincent W. Durnan

General Information Coeducational day college-preparatory, arts, and technology school. Grades K–12. Founded: 1915. Setting: urban. 7-acre campus. 4 buildings on campus. Approved or accredited by Southern Association of Colleges and Schools. Member of National Association of Independent Schools. Endowment: $1.7 million. Total enrollment: 1,008. Upper school average class size: 15. Upper school faculty-student ratio: 1:12.

Upper School Student Profile Grade 9: 93 students (50 boys, 43 girls); Grade 10: 84 students (43 boys, 41 girls); Grade 11: 99 students (47 boys, 52 girls); Grade 12: 82 students (42 boys, 40 girls).

Faculty School total: 110. In upper school: 22 men, 34 women; 37 have advanced degrees.

Subjects Offered 3-dimensional art, acting, algebra, American history, American literature, analysis and differential calculus, ancient world history, art history, art history-AP, astronomy, band, biology, biology-AP, British literature, calculus, calculus-AP, ceramics, chemistry, chemistry-AP, college planning, community service, comparative religion, computer multimedia, computer programming, computer tools, concert choir, contemporary issues in science, creative dance, creative writing, dance, debate, desktop publishing, drama, drawing, economics, English, English composition, English literature, English literature-AP, environmental science, ethics, filmmaking, French, French-AP, functions, geology, geometry, government and politics-AP, government/civics, Harlem Renaissance, history, history-AP, jazz band, journalism, Latin, Latin-AP, literary magazine, modern dance, music appreciation, music theory, newspaper, painting, peer counseling, performing arts, photography, physical education, physics, pre-calculus, psychology, science research, sculpture, social issues, Spanish, Spanish language-AP, sports nutrition, statistics, statistics-AP, studio art, theater, theater arts, theater production, trigonometry, U.S. history-AP, visual literacy, Western civilization, wilderness education, world history, yearbook.

Graduation Requirements Algebra, American history, American literature, ancient world history, arts and fine arts (art, music, dance, drama), biology, British literature, chemistry, English, foreign language, geometry, history, physical education (includes health), physics, Western civilization.

Special Academic Programs Advanced Placement exam preparation; honors section; independent study; term-away projects; study at local college for college credit; academic accommodation for the gifted, the musically talented, and the artistically talented; ESL (4 students enrolled).

College Admission Counseling 87 students graduated in 2009; 86 went to college, including Indiana University Bloomington; Kenyon College; The George Washington University; The University of Tennessee; Vanderbilt University; Washington University in St. Louis. Other: 1 had other specific plans. Mean SAT critical reading: 670, mean SAT math: 667. 46% scored over 600 on SAT critical reading, 44% scored over 600 on SAT math.

Student Life Upper grades have specified standards of dress, student council, honor system. Discipline rests equally with students and faculty.

Tuition and Aid Day student tuition: $14,325. Tuition installment plan (Insured Tuition Payment Plan, monthly payment plans). Need-based scholarship grants available. In 2009–10, 7% of upper-school students received aid. Total amount of financial aid awarded in 2009–10: $204,075.

Admissions Traditional secondary-level entrance grade is 9. For fall 2009, 101 students applied for upper-level admission, 40 were accepted, 24 enrolled. Deadline for receipt of application materials: none. Application fee required: $50. Interview required.

Athletics Interscholastic: baseball (boys), basketball (b,g), cross-country running (b,g), golf (b,g), lacrosse (b,g), soccer (b,g), softball (g), swimming and diving (b,g), tennis (b,g), track and field (b,g), volleyball (g), weight training (b,g); coed interscholastic: ultimate Frisbee; coed intramural: backpacking, canoeing/kayaking, climbing, fitness walking, Frisbee, hiking/backpacking. 7 PE instructors, 2 coaches, 1 athletic trainer.

Computers Computers are regularly used in all classes. Computer network features include on-campus library services, online commercial services, Internet access.

Contact Ms. Juliet Douglas, Director of Admissions and Financial Aid. 615-327-3812. Fax: 615-321-0889. E-mail: jdouglas@usn.org. Web site: www.usn.org.

UNIVERSITY SCHOOL OF NOVA SOUTHEASTERN UNIVERSITY

3375 SW 75 Avenue
Lower School Building
Fort Lauderdale, Florida 33314
Head of School: Dr. Jerome S. Chermak

General Information Coeducational day college-preparatory school. Grades PK–12. Founded: 1970. Setting: suburban. 300-acre campus. 4 buildings on campus. Approved or accredited by Association of Independent Schools of Florida, Florida Council of Independent Schools, Southern Association of Colleges and Schools, and Florida Department of Education. Member of National Association of Independent Schools. Endowment: $750,000. Total enrollment: 1,902. Upper school average class size: 20. Upper school faculty-student ratio: 1:11. There are 176 required school days per year for Upper School students. Upper School students typically attend 5 days per week. The average school day consists of 6 hours.

Upper School Student Profile Grade 9: 174 students (95 boys, 79 girls); Grade 10: 176 students (92 boys, 84 girls); Grade 11: 162 students (86 boys, 76 girls); Grade 12: 168 students (91 boys, 77 girls).

Faculty School total: 181. In upper school: 26 men, 35 women; 43 have advanced degrees.

Subjects Offered Advanced Placement courses, advanced studio art-AP, algebra, American government, American history, American literature, anatomy, art, band, biology, calculus, ceramics, chemistry, chorus, community service, computer programming, computer science, concert choir, creative writing, debate, directing, drawing and design, economics, English, English literature, environmental science, expository writing, fine arts, forensics, French, geometry, grammar, guitar, Internet, journalism, keyboarding, Latin, media production, music, music appreciation, music theory, orchestra, performing arts, personal fitness, physical education, physics, portfolio art, pre-calculus, psychology, public speaking, Spanish, speech, theater, trigonometry, video film production, world geography, world history, world literature, writing.

Graduation Requirements Art, computer science, electives, English, expository writing, foreign language, health education, journalism, mathematics, music, personal fitness, physical education (includes health), public speaking, science, social studies (includes history), speech and debate. Community service is required.

Special Academic Programs Advanced Placement exam preparation; honors section; accelerated programs; independent study; term-away projects; study at local college for college credit; academic accommodation for the gifted, the musically talented, and the artistically talented; remedial reading and/or remedial writing.

College Admission Counseling 148 students graduated in 2010; all went to college, including Boston University; Florida State University; University of Central Florida; University of Florida; University of Miami; University of Pennsylvania.

Student Life Upper grades have uniform requirement, student council. Discipline rests primarily with faculty.

Summer Programs Remediation, enrichment, advancement, sports, art/fine arts programs offered; session focuses on sports, arts, and academics; held on campus; accepts boys and girls; open to students from other schools. 400 students usually enrolled. 2011 schedule: June 4 to August 11. Application deadline: none.

Tuition and Aid Day student tuition: $18,900. Tuition installment plan (Key Tuition Payment Plan). Tuition reduction for siblings, need-based scholarship grants available. In 2010–11, 15% of upper-school students received aid. Total amount of financial aid awarded in 2010–11: $1,500,000.

Admissions Traditional secondary-level entrance grade is 9. For fall 2010, 168 students applied for upper-level admission, 106 were accepted, 71 enrolled. SSAT required. Deadline for receipt of application materials: none. Application fee required: $100. On-campus interview required.

Athletics Interscholastic: baseball (boys), basketball (b,g), cheering (g), crew (b,g), cross-country running (b,g), dance team (g), diving (b,g), football (b), golf (b,g), ice hockey (b), lacrosse (g), roller hockey (b), soccer (b,g), softball (g), swimming and diving (b,g), tennis (b,g), track and field (b,g), volleyball (b,g), wrestling (b); coed interscholastic: dance. 3 PE instructors, 43 coaches, 1 athletic trainer.

Computers Computers are regularly used in all classes. Computer network features include on-campus library services, Internet access, wireless campus network, Internet filtering or blocking technology. Student e-mail accounts and computer access in designated common areas are available to students. Students grades are available online. The school has a published electronic and media policy.

Contact Ms. Allison Musso, Coordinator of Admissions. 954-262-4405. Fax: 954-262-3691. E-mail: amusso@nova.edu. Web site: www.uschool.nova.edu.

UPPER CANADA COLLEGE

200 Lonsdale Road
Toronto, Ontario M4V 1W6, Canada
Head of School: Dr. Jim Power

General Information Boys' boarding and day college-preparatory, arts, bilingual studies, and technology school. Boarding grades 8–13, day grades K–13. Founded: 1829. Setting: urban. Students are housed in single-sex dormitories. 40-acre campus. 15 buildings on campus. Approved or accredited by The Association of Boarding Schools and Ontario Department of Education. Affiliate member of National Association of Independent Schools; member of Secondary School Admission Test Board. Language of instruction: English. Total enrollment: 1,154. Upper school average class size: 19. Upper school faculty-student ratio: 1:11. Upper School students typically attend 5 days per week. The average school day consists of 6 hours and 30 minutes.

Upper School Student Profile 8% of students are boarding students. 90% are province residents. 9 provinces are represented in upper school student body. 10% are international students. International students from Germany, Hong Kong, Mexico, Saudi Arabia, United Arab Emirates, and United States; 21 other countries represented in student body.

Faculty School total: 143. In upper school: 52 men, 23 women; 29 have advanced degrees; 17 reside on campus.

Subjects Offered Algebra, American history, art, athletics, biology, calculus, career and personal planning, chemistry, Chinese, civics, community service, computer programming, computer science, creative writing, digital art, drama, economics, English, English literature, environmental science, European history, expository writing, film, fine arts, French, geography, geometry, German, health, history, Latin, mathematics, music, physical education, physics, science, social sciences, social studies, Spanish, theater, theater arts, theory of knowledge, trigonometry, visual arts, world history, writing.

Graduation Requirements English, foreign language, mathematics, science, social sciences. Community service is required.

Special Academic Programs International Baccalaureate program; honors section; term-away projects.

Upper Canada College

College Admission Counseling 150 students graduated in 2009; 143 went to college, including Columbia University; Cornell University; McGill University; Queen's University at Kingston; The University of Western Ontario; University of Toronto. Other: 7 had other specific plans.

Student Life Upper grades have uniform requirement, student council, honor system. Discipline rests primarily with faculty.

Tuition and Aid Day student tuition: CAN$26,020; 7-day tuition and room/board: CAN$45,915–CAN$47,915. Tuition installment plan (Insured Tuition Payment Plan, monthly payment plans, term payment plan, full-payment discount plan). Need-based scholarship grants, need-based financial assistance available. In 2009–10, 7% of upper-school students received aid.

Admissions Traditional secondary-level entrance grade is 9. SAT or SSAT required. Deadline for receipt of application materials: none. Application fee required: CAN$200. Interview required.

Athletics Interscholastic: badminton, baseball, basketball, crew, cricket, cross-country running, football, golf, hockey, ice hockey, indoor hockey, lacrosse, outdoor education, rowing, rugby, running, skiing (cross-country), skiing (downhill), soccer, softball, squash, swimming and diving, tennis, volleyball; intramural: badminton, baseball, basketball, bicycling, canoeing/kayaking, climbing, combined training, cooperative games, fencing, flag football, floor hockey, Frisbee, hiking/backpacking, hockey, ice hockey, in-line hockey, indoor hockey, kayaking, life saving, martial arts, mountain biking, outdoor activities, outdoor adventure, physical fitness, physical training, power lifting, rock climbing, ropes courses, soccer, softball, strength & conditioning, ultimate Frisbee, volleyball, weight training, wilderness.

Computers Computers are regularly used in art, geography, library, music, science, video film production classes. Computer network features include on-campus library services, online commercial services, Internet access, Internet filtering or blocking technology. Campus intranet, student e-mail accounts, and computer access in designated common areas are available to students. The school has a published electronic and media policy.

Contact Tricia Rankin, Coordinator, Upper School Admission. 416-488-1125 Ext. 2221. Fax: 416-484-8618. E-mail: trankin@ucc.on.ca. Web site: www.ucc.on.ca.

UPPER COLUMBIA ACADEMY

3025 East Spangle-Waverly Road
Spangle, Washington 99031-9799
Head of School: Troy Patzer, EdD

General Information Coeducational boarding and day college-preparatory, general academic, arts, vocational, religious studies, and technology school, affiliated with Seventh-day Adventist Church. Grades 9–12. Founded: 1945. Setting: rural. Nearest major city is Spokane. Students are housed in single-sex dormitories. 350-acre campus. 10 buildings on campus. Approved or accredited by Board of Regents, General Conference of Seventh-day Adventists, Northwest Association of Schools and Colleges, and Washington Department of Education. Total enrollment: 268. Upper school average class size: 20. Upper school faculty-student ratio: 1:15. There are 185 required school days per year for Upper School students. Upper School students typically attend 5 days per week. The average school day consists of 6 hours and 15 minutes.

Upper School Student Profile Grade 9: 39 students (19 boys, 20 girls); Grade 10: 44 students (23 boys, 21 girls); Grade 11: 87 students (41 boys, 46 girls); Grade 12: 97 students (47 boys, 50 girls). 77% of students are boarding students. 60% are state residents. 14 states are represented in upper school student body. 5% are international students. International students from Canada, Republic of Korea, and Taiwan; 1 other country represented in student body. 95% of students are Seventh-day Adventists.

Faculty School total: 18. In upper school: 11 men, 7 women; 17 have advanced degrees; all reside on campus.

Subjects Offered Accounting, aerobics, algebra, art, auto mechanics, Bible studies, biology, calculus, calculus-AP, chemistry, child development, computer literacy, computer-aided design, desktop publishing, driver education, English, English language and composition-AP, English literature, geography, geometry, interior design, journalism, keyboarding, physical education, physical science, physics, pre-calculus, Spanish, speech, U.S. history.

Graduation Requirements Art, business skills (includes word processing), computer science, English, mathematics, physical education (includes health), religion (includes Bible studies and theology), science, social sciences, social studies (includes history). Community service is required.

Special Academic Programs Advanced Placement exam preparation.

College Admission Counseling 99 students graduated in 2009; 80 went to college, including Andrews University; Pacific Union College; Southern Adventist University; Walla Walla University. Other: 16 went to work, 2 entered military service.

Student Life Upper grades have specified standards of dress, student council. Discipline rests primarily with faculty. Attendance at religious services is required.

Tuition and Aid Day student tuition: $8040; 7-day tuition and room/board: $14,375. Tuition installment plan (monthly payment plans, individually arranged payment plans). Tuition reduction for siblings, merit scholarship grants, need-based scholarship grants, paying campus jobs available. In 2009–10, 41% of upper-school students received aid; total upper-school merit-scholarship money awarded: $5000. Total amount of financial aid awarded in 2009–10: $450,000.

Admissions Deadline for receipt of application materials: none. Application fee required: $25. Interview recommended.

Athletics Interscholastic: basketball (boys, girls), flag football (b,g); intramural: baseball (b,g), basketball (b,g), flag football (b,g); coed interscholastic: alpine skiing, archery, backpacking, badminton, canoeing/kayaking, golf, gymnastics; coed intramural: baseball, gymnastics, hiking/backpacking. 1 PE instructor, 3 coaches.

Computers Computers are regularly used in business education, English, history, keyboarding, mathematics classes. Campus intranet, student e-mail accounts, and computer access in designated common areas are available to students. The school has a published electronic and media policy.

Contact Florence Lacey, Registrar. 509-245-3627. Fax: 509-245-3643. E-mail: fmlacey@ucaa.org. Web site: www.ucaa.org.

URSULINE ACADEMY

85 Lowder Street
Dedham, Massachusetts 02026-4299
Head of School: Ms. Rosann Whiting

General Information Girls' day college-preparatory school, affiliated with Roman Catholic Church. Grades 7–12. Founded: 1946. Setting: suburban. Nearest major city is Boston. 28-acre campus. 3 buildings on campus. Approved or accredited by Association of Independent Schools in New England, National Catholic Education Association, New England Association of Schools and Colleges, The College Board, and Massachusetts Department of Education. Member of National Association of Independent Schools. Total enrollment: 397. Upper school average class size: 18. Upper school faculty-student ratio: 1:9. Upper School students typically attend 5 days per week. The average school day consists of 5 hours and 45 minutes.

Upper School Student Profile Grade 7: 56 students (56 girls); Grade 8: 63 students (63 girls); Grade 9: 73 students (73 girls); Grade 10: 68 students (68 girls); Grade 11: 74 students (74 girls); Grade 12: 63 students (63 girls). 88% of students are Roman Catholic.

Faculty School total: 38. In upper school: 6 men, 31 women; 34 have advanced degrees.

Subjects Offered Algebra, American history, American literature, anatomy and physiology, art, art history, biology, biology-AP, British literature (honors), calculus, calculus-AP, chemistry, chemistry-AP, communication arts, computer studies, English, English literature, English-AP, French, geography, geometry, government/civics, grammar, history, Latin, life science, mathematics, modern European history-AP, music, physical education, physical science, physics, pre-algebra, pre-calculus, psychology, public speaking, social studies, Spanish, Spanish language-AP, studio art, study skills, theology, trigonometry, U.S. history, U.S. history-AP, world history, world literature.

Graduation Requirements Arts and fine arts (art, music, dance, drama), computer science, English, foreign language, mathematics, physical education (includes health), public speaking, religion (includes Bible studies and theology), science, social studies (includes history), study skills, senior year community service field project.

Special Academic Programs 7 Advanced Placement exams for which test preparation is offered; honors section.

College Admission Counseling 62 students graduated in 2010; all went to college, including Boston College; Boston University; College of the Holy Cross; Harvard University; Quinnipiac University; Wake Forest University. Mean SAT critical reading: 626, mean SAT math: 595, mean SAT writing: 631, mean combined SAT: 1853.

Student Life Upper grades have uniform requirement, student council, honor system. Discipline rests primarily with faculty. Attendance at religious services is required.

Tuition and Aid Day student tuition: $13,000. Tuition installment plan (Insured Tuition Payment Plan, FACTS Tuition Payment Plan, monthly payment plans, individually arranged payment plans, semester, quarterly and monthly payment plans). Need-based scholarship grants available. In 2010–11, 15% of upper-school students received aid.

Admissions Traditional secondary-level entrance grade is 9. Archdiocese of Boston or STS or school's own exam required. Deadline for receipt of application materials: December 15. Application fee required: $30.

Athletics Interscholastic: alpine skiing, basketball, cross-country running, diving, field hockey, golf, ice hockey, lacrosse, soccer, softball, swimming and diving, tennis, track and field, volleyball, winter (indoor) track; intramural: dance, golf, skiing (downhill), tennis. 2 PE instructors, 26 coaches.

Computers Computers are regularly used in all classes. Computer network features include on-campus library services, Internet access, Internet filtering or blocking technology. Campus intranet, student e-mail accounts, and computer access in designated common areas are available to students. Students grades are available online. The school has a published electronic and media policy.

Contact Catherine Spencer, Director of Admissions. 781-326-6161 Ext. 107. Fax: 781-329-3926. E-mail: admissions@ursulineacademy.net. Web site: www. ursulineacademy.net.

THE URSULINE ACADEMY OF DALLAS

4900 Walnut Hill Lane
Dallas, Texas 75229
Head of School: Ms. Elizabeth Bourgeois

General Information Girls' day college-preparatory, arts, religious studies, and technology school, affiliated with Roman Catholic Church. Grades 9–12. Founded: 1874. Setting: urban. 26-acre campus. 5 buildings on campus. Approved or accredited by Independent Schools Association of the Southwest, National Catholic Education Association, Texas Catholic Conference, The College Board, and Texas Department of Education. Total enrollment: 800. Upper school average class size: 18. Upper school faculty-student ratio: 1:10.

Upper School Student Profile Grade 9: 200 students (200 girls); Grade 10: 200 students (200 girls); Grade 11: 200 students (200 girls); Grade 12: 200 students (200 girls). 85% of students are Roman Catholic.

Faculty School total: 91. In upper school: 15 men, 76 women; 68 have advanced degrees.

Subjects Offered 20th century history, Advanced Placement courses, algebra, anatomy, anatomy and physiology, Arabic, band, biology, bookbinding, calculus, ceramics, chemistry, choir, Christian and Hebrew scripture, community service, comparative government and politics, comparative religion, computer programming, computer science, concert choir, creative writing, current events, dance, design, digital imaging, digital photography, discrete mathematics, drama, drawing, economics, English literature, environmental science, ethics, European history, fitness, French, geography, geology, geometry, government, government/civics, graphic design, health and wellness, journalism, Latin, Latin American literature, Mandarin, newspaper, oceanography, orchestra, painting, peer ministry, photography, physical education, physics, pre-calculus, printmaking, psychology, social justice, Spanish, speech, statistics, theater, theology, U.S. history, U.S. literature, Web authoring, Western civilization, world history, world literature, yearbook.

Graduation Requirements Arts and fine arts (art, music, dance, drama), computer science, English, foreign language, mathematics, physical education (includes health), religion (includes Bible studies and theology), science, social studies (includes history), speech. Community service is required.

Special Academic Programs Advanced Placement exam preparation; honors section; independent study.

College Admission Counseling 191 students graduated in 2010; all went to college, including Louisiana State University and Agricultural and Mechanical College; Southern Methodist University; Texas A&M University; Texas Christian University; The University of Texas at Austin; University of Oklahoma. Mean SAT critical reading: 614, mean SAT math: 608, mean SAT writing: 619, mean combined SAT: 1841, mean composite ACT: 28.

Student Life Upper grades have uniform requirement, student council, honor system. Discipline rests equally with students and faculty. Attendance at religious services is required.

Summer Programs Remediation, advancement, art/fine arts, computer instruction programs offered; session focuses on remediation and advancement; held on campus; accepts girls; not open to students from other schools. 200 students usually enrolled. 2011 schedule: June 8 to July 1. Application deadline: January 7.

Tuition and Aid Day student tuition: $14,975. Tuition installment plan (individually arranged payment plans, annual, semi-annual, and monthly (by bank draft) payment plans). Merit scholarship grants, need-based scholarship grants available. In 2010–11, 23% of upper-school students received aid. Total amount of financial aid awarded in 2010–11: $851,300.

Admissions Traditional secondary-level entrance grade is 9. For fall 2010, 411 students applied for upper-level admission, 215 enrolled. ISEE required. Deadline for receipt of application materials: January 7. Application fee required: $60. Interview required.

Athletics Interscholastic: basketball, cheering, crew, cross-country running, diving, drill team, golf, lacrosse, soccer, softball, swimming and diving, tennis, track and field, volleyball; intramural: crew, drill team. 3 PE instructors, 15 coaches, 1 athletic trainer.

Computers Computers are regularly used in all classes. Computer network features include on-campus library services, online commercial services, Internet access, wireless campus network. Campus intranet and student e-mail accounts are available to students. Students grades are available online.

Contact Mrs. Mary Campise, Assistant Director of Admission. 469-232-1839. Fax: 469-232-1836. E-mail: mcampise@ursulinedallas.org. Web site: www.ursulinedallas.org.

URSULINE HIGH SCHOOL

90 Ursuline Road
Santa Rosa, California 95403
Head of School: Ms. Julie Carver

General Information Girls' day college-preparatory, arts, business, religious studies, and technology school, affiliated with Roman Catholic Church. Grades 9–12. Founded: 1880. Setting: suburban. 51-acre campus. 5 buildings on campus. Approved or accredited by Western Association of Schools and Colleges, Western Catholic Education Association, and California Department of Education. Endowment: $800,000. Total enrollment: 281. Upper school average class size: 20. Upper school faculty-student ratio: 1:18. There are 180 required school days per year for Upper

School students. Upper School students typically attend 5 days per week. The average school day consists of 6 hours and 30 minutes.

Upper School Student Profile Grade 9: 78 students (78 girls); Grade 10: 75 students (75 girls); Grade 11: 70 students (70 girls); Grade 12: 58 students (58 girls). 65% of students are Roman Catholic.

Faculty School total: 32. In upper school: 6 men, 26 women; 20 have advanced degrees.

Subjects Offered 20th century world history, algebra, art, ASB Leadership, biology, biology-AP, calculus, calculus-AP, chemistry, choir, Christian and Hebrew scripture, computers, conceptual physics, creative writing, cultural geography, dance, design, desktop publishing, drama, dramatic arts, drawing, economics, English, English literature-AP, ensembles, ethics, film, fine arts, French, geometry, health, honors English, journalism, Latin, literature-AP, photography, physical education, physical science, physics-AP, pre-algebra, pre-calculus, psychology, public speaking, social justice, Spanish, Spanish language-AP, studio art-AP, trigonometry, U.S. government, U.S. history-AP, water color painting, world history, world religions, yearbook.

Graduation Requirements Bible studies, biology, Christian ethics, church history, cultural geography, economics, English, foreign language, government, mathematics, physical education (includes health), physical science, public speaking, social justice, visual and performing arts, world history, world religions, 25 hours of student service per year, cumulative 2.0 GPA (8 semesters).

Special Academic Programs Advanced Placement exam preparation; honors section; study at local college for college credit.

College Admission Counseling 80 students graduated in 2010; all went to college, including Loyola Marymount University; Sonoma State University; The University of Arizona; University of California, Davis; University of California, Santa Barbara.

Student Life Upper grades have uniform requirement, student council, honor system. Discipline rests primarily with faculty. Attendance at religious services is required.

Summer Programs Remediation, enrichment, advancement programs offered; session focuses on enrichment, advancement, math make-up courses; held on campus; accepts girls; not open to students from other schools. 80 students usually enrolled. 2011 schedule: June 13 to July 15. Application deadline: May 22.

Tuition and Aid Day student tuition: $12,560. Tuition installment plan (monthly payment plans, semiannual and annual payment plans). Merit scholarship grants, need-based scholarship grants available. In 2010–11, 31% of upper-school students received aid; total upper-school merit-scholarship money awarded: $30,000. Total amount of financial aid awarded in 2010–11: $510,000.

Admissions Traditional secondary-level entrance grade is 9. For fall 2010, 112 students applied for upper-level admission, 110 were accepted, 90 enrolled. STS Examination required. Deadline for receipt of application materials: none. Application fee required: $75. On-campus interview required.

Athletics Interscholastic: basketball, cross-country running, diving, golf, lacrosse, soccer, softball, swimming and diving, tennis, track and field, volleyball, water polo. 2 PE instructors, 27 coaches.

Computers Computers are regularly used in business applications, computer applications, media, Web site design, yearbook classes. Computer network features include on-campus library services, online commercial services, Internet access, Internet filtering or blocking technology, Bridges, Atomic Learning, Family Connection by Naviance, Blackboard, MyAccess. Campus intranet and computer access in designated common areas are available to students. The school has a published electronic and media policy.

Contact Ms. Lisa Ormond, Admissions Director. 707-524-1133. Fax: 707-542-0131. E-mail: lormond@ursulinehs.org. Web site: www.ursulinehs.org.

VACAVILLE CHRISTIAN SCHOOLS

1117 Davis Street
Vacaville, California 95687
Head of School: Mr. Paul Harrell

General Information Coeducational day college-preparatory, general academic, arts, business, religious studies, and technology school, affiliated with Christian faith, Christian faith. Grades K–12. Founded: 1975. Setting: suburban. Nearest major city is Sacramento. 24-acre campus. 11 buildings on campus. Approved or accredited by Association of Christian Schools International, Western Association of Schools and Colleges, and California Department of Education. Total enrollment: 1,358. Upper school average class size: 25. Upper school faculty-student ratio: 1:20. There are 176 required school days per year for Upper School students. Upper School students typically attend 5 days per week. The average school day consists of 7 hours.

Upper School Student Profile Grade 6: 82 students (33 boys, 49 girls); Grade 7: 91 students (47 boys, 44 girls); Grade 8: 92 students (45 boys, 47 girls); Grade 9: 84 students (40 boys, 44 girls); Grade 10: 70 students (33 boys, 37 girls); Grade 11: 75 students (34 boys, 41 girls); Grade 12: 77 students (39 boys, 38 girls). 80% of students are Christian, Christian faith.

Faculty School total: 56. In upper school: 12 men, 12 women; 6 have advanced degrees.

Subjects Offered Algebra, American literature, art, band, Bible, biology, British literature, British literature (honors), broadcasting, calculus-AP, chemistry, choir, college planning, computer applications, computer graphics, conceptual physics, consumer mathematics, digital photography, drama, economics, economics-AP, English, English literature, food and nutrition, French, geometry, government, government-AP, graphic arts, health, honors U.S. history, honors world history, instrumental music, jazz band, journalism, Life of Christ, life skills, media production, Microsoft, New Testament, newspaper, participation in sports, performing arts, physical education, physics, physics-AP, pre-calculus, psychology, psychology-AP, radio broadcasting, Spanish, speech, sports, student government, study skills, symphonic band, U.S. government, U.S. government and politics-AP, U.S. history, Web site design, weight training, world history, yearbook.

Graduation Requirements Algebra, arts and fine arts (art, music, dance, drama), Bible, biology, British literature, chemistry, conceptual physics, economics, electives, English, foreign language, geometry, government, physical education (includes health), practical arts, U.S. history, world history, 104 community service hours.

Special Academic Programs Advanced Placement exam preparation; honors section.

College Admission Counseling 88 students graduated in 2009; 50 went to college, including California Polytechnic State University, San Luis Obispo; California State University, Sacramento; San Diego State University; Sonoma State University; University of California, Davis; Vanguard University of Southern California. Other: 3 entered military service. Median SAT critical reading: 540, median SAT math: 585, median SAT writing: 560, median combined SAT: 1805. 22% scored over 600 on SAT critical reading, 19% scored over 600 on SAT math, 22% scored over 600 on SAT writing.

Student Life Upper grades have specified standards of dress, student council, honor system. Discipline rests primarily with faculty. Attendance at religious services is required.

Tuition and Aid Day student tuition: $6359. Tuition installment plan (monthly payment plans). Tuition reduction for siblings, merit scholarship grants, need-based scholarship grants available. In 2009–10, 5% of upper-school students received aid. Total amount of financial aid awarded in 2009–10: $43,000.

Admissions Traditional secondary-level entrance grade is 9. For fall 2009, 125 students applied for upper-level admission, 94 were accepted, 94 enrolled. Stanford 9 required. Deadline for receipt of application materials: none. Application fee required: $270. Interview required.

Athletics Interscholastic: baseball (boys), basketball (b,g), football (b), golf (b), wrestling (b,g); intramural: flag football (b,g), physical fitness (b,g); coed interscholastic: bowling, cheering, cross-country running, golf; coed intramural: physical training. 3 PE instructors.

Computers Computers are regularly used in graphic arts, graphic design, journalism, media production, newspaper, Web site design, yearbook classes. Computer network features include on-campus library services, Internet access, Internet filtering or blocking technology. Students grades are available online. The school has a published electronic and media policy.

Contact Mrs. Faith Rodgers, Communications Director. 707-446-1776 Ext. 2102. Fax: 707-446-1514. E-mail: admissions@go-vcs.com. Web site: www.go-vcs.com.

VAIL MOUNTAIN SCHOOL

3000 Booth Falls Road
Vail, Colorado 81657
Head of School: Peter M. Abuisi

General Information Coeducational day college-preparatory school. Grades K–12. Founded: 1962. Setting: small town. Nearest major city is Denver. 9-acre campus. 2 buildings on campus. Approved or accredited by Association of Colorado Independent Schools, National Independent Private Schools Association, and Colorado Department of Education. Member of National Association of Independent Schools. Endowment: $1.5 million. Total enrollment: 349. Upper school average class size: 16. Upper school faculty-student ratio: 1:8. There are 175 required school days per year for Upper School students. Upper School students typically attend 5 days per week. The average school day consists of 7 hours.

Upper School Student Profile Grade 9: 36 students (16 boys, 20 girls); Grade 10: 25 students (12 boys, 13 girls); Grade 11: 24 students (15 boys, 9 girls); Grade 12: 21 students (9 boys, 12 girls).

Faculty School total: 37. In upper school: 10 have advanced degrees.

Subjects Offered Advanced Placement courses, algebra, American history, American literature, art, arts, biology, calculus, chemistry, computer math, computer science, creative writing, drama, earth science, English, English literature, environmental science, ethics, European history, expository writing, fine arts, geography, geometry, government/civics, grammar, history, Latin, Latin American literature, mathematics, photography, physical education, physics, poetry, psychology, science, Shakespeare, social sciences, social studies, Spanish, theater, trigonometry, world history, writing.

Graduation Requirements Arts and fine arts (art, music, dance, drama), English, foreign language, mathematics, physical education (includes health), psychology, science, social sciences, social studies (includes history), Spanish, acceptance into a four-year college or university.

Special Academic Programs 8 Advanced Placement exams for which test preparation is offered; ESL (6 students enrolled).

College Admission Counseling 22 students graduated in 2010; all went to college, including Cornell University; University of Colorado at Boulder; University of Southern California; Washington University in St. Louis.

Student Life Upper grades have specified standards of dress, honor system. Discipline rests primarily with faculty.

Summer Programs Remediation, enrichment, advancement, sports, art/fine arts programs offered; session focuses on math and English enrichment for Hispanic students; held on campus; accepts boys and girls; open to students from other schools. 75 students usually enrolled. 2011 schedule: June 15 to July 31.

Tuition and Aid Day student tuition: $18,500. Tuition installment plan (monthly payment plans, individually arranged payment plans). Need-based scholarship grants, need-based loans available. In 2010–11, 33% of upper-school students received aid. Total amount of financial aid awarded in 2010–11: $390,000.

Admissions Traditional secondary-level entrance grade is 9. For fall 2010, 18 students applied for upper-level admission, 10 were accepted, 7 enrolled. Any standardized test required. Deadline for receipt of application materials: January 28. Application fee required: $50. Interview required.

Athletics Interscholastic: alpine skiing (boys, girls), freestyle skiing (b,g), golf (b,g), nordic skiing (b,g), skiing (cross-country) (b,g), skiing (downhill) (b,g), soccer (b,g), tennis (g); intramural: backpacking (b,g), basketball (b,g), dance team (g), ice hockey (b), independent competitive sports (b,g), indoor soccer (b,g), jogging (b,g), outdoor activities (b,g), outdoor adventure (b,g), outdoor education (b,g), physical fitness (b,g), physical training (b,g), rock climbing (b,g), skiing (cross-country) (b,g), skiing (downhill) (b,g), strength & conditioning (b,g), telemark skiing (b,g), volleyball (g), weight lifting (b,g); coed interscholastic: freestyle skiing, nordic skiing, snowboarding; coed intramural: backpacking, basketball, canoeing/kayaking, climbing, fishing, fitness, Fives, fly fishing, Frisbee, hiking/backpacking, indoor soccer, jogging, jump rope, kayaking, mountain biking, mountaineering, outdoor activities, outdoor adventure, outdoor education, physical fitness, physical training, rafting, rock climbing, ropes courses, running, snowboarding, snowshoeing, strength & conditioning, telemark skiing, touch football, ultimate Frisbee, weight lifting, wilderness survival, yoga. 1 PE instructor, 15 coaches, 1 athletic trainer.

Computers Computers are regularly used in all academic, art, basic skills, college planning, computer applications, creative writing, desktop publishing, English, ethics, foreign language, graphic arts, history, humanities, independent study, introduction to technology, keyboarding, library, library skills, music technology, photography, reading, research skills, senior seminar, social sciences, social studies, Spanish, study skills, technology, Web site design, word processing, writing, writing, yearbook classes. Computer network features include on-campus library services, online commercial services, Internet access, wireless campus network, Internet filtering or blocking technology. Campus intranet and student e-mail accounts are available to students. Students grades are available online. The school has a published electronic and media policy.

Contact Mr. Jeremy Thelen, Director of Admission. 970-477-7164. Fax: 970-476-3860. E-mail: admissions@vms.edu. Web site: www.vms.edu.

VALLE CATHOLIC HIGH SCHOOL

40 North Fourth Street
Ste. Genevieve, Missouri 63670
Head of School: Ms. Sara C. Menard

General Information Coeducational day college-preparatory, arts, business, vocational, religious studies, and technology school, affiliated with Roman Catholic Church. Grades 9–12. Founded: 1837. Setting: small town. Nearest major city is St. Louis. 3-acre campus. 3 buildings on campus. Approved or accredited by North Central Association of Colleges and Schools and Missouri Department of Education. Endowment: $2 million. Total enrollment: 132. Upper school average class size: 15. Upper school faculty-student ratio: 1:9. There are 171 required school days per year for Upper School students. Upper School students typically attend 5 days per week. The average school day consists of 5 hours and 50 minutes.

Upper School Student Profile Grade 9: 39 students (15 boys, 24 girls); Grade 10: 26 students (10 boys, 16 girls); Grade 11: 28 students (14 boys, 14 girls); Grade 12: 33 students (18 boys, 15 girls). 98% of students are Roman Catholic.

Faculty School total: 15. In upper school: 6 men, 9 women; 7 have advanced degrees.

Subjects Offered 20th century American writers, accounting, advanced chemistry, advanced computer applications, advanced math, algebra, American democracy, American history, American literature, analysis and differential calculus, anatomy and physiology, architectural drawing, art, art history, arts, band, biology, British literature, business, business applications, business communications, business law, business mathematics, business skills, business studies, calculus, calculus-AP, Catholic belief and practice, chemistry-AP, Christian and Hebrew scripture, Christian scripture, church history, civics, civics/free enterprise, classics, communications, comparative religion, composition, computer applications, computer multimedia, computer science, computer skills, concert band, consumer economics, consumer education, consumer law, consumer mathematics, drafting, drama, drama performance, dramatic arts, drawing, earth science, ecology, environmental systems, economics, economics and history, English, entrepreneurship, environmental science, environmental systems, foreign language, freshman seminar, geography, geometry, history of the Catholic Church, honors algebra, honors English, honors U.S. history, human anatomy, journalism, keyboarding, marching band, math analysis, mathematics, media communications, moral theology, novels, orchestra, painting, peace and justice, physical education, physics, practical arts, psychology, religion, science, social studies, sociology, Spanish, technical drawing, U.S. government, values and decisions, visual arts, Western civilization, yearbook.

Graduation Requirements Advanced math, algebra, American history, American literature, biology, Catholic belief and practice, chemistry, Christian and Hebrew scripture, civics, English, English composition, ethical decision making, foreign language, geometry, government/civics, history of the Catholic Church, mathematics, physical education (includes health), practical arts, religion (includes Bible studies and theology), science, senior composition, social justice, social studies (includes history), Spanish, 80 hours of community service.

Special Academic Programs 1 Advanced Placement exam for which test preparation is offered; honors section; study at local college for college credit; academic accommodation for the gifted and the artistically talented; remedial reading and/or remedial writing; remedial math.

College Admission Counseling 34 students graduated in 2010; 30 went to college, including Missouri State University; Saint Louis University; Southeast Missouri State University; Truman State University; University of Missouri. Other: 3 went to work, 1 had other specific plans. Mean SAT critical reading: 720, mean SAT math: 780, mean composite ACT: 24. 100% scored over 600 on SAT critical reading, 100% scored over 600 on SAT math, 26% scored over 26 on composite ACT.

Student Life Upper grades have uniform requirement, student council, honor system. Discipline rests primarily with faculty. Attendance at religious services is required.

Summer Programs Remediation, enrichment, advancement programs offered; session focuses on advancement and remediation/make-up; held on campus; accepts boys and girls; not open to students from other schools. 5 students usually enrolled. 2011 schedule: June 3 to July 31.

Tuition and Aid Day student tuition: $4500. Tuition installment plan (The Tuition Plan, monthly payment plans, individually arranged payment plans, tuition assistance through the St. Louis Archdiocese and Scholarships available through the School). Tuition reduction for siblings, merit scholarship grants, need-based scholarship grants, tuition relief funds available from St. Louis Archdiocese available. In 2010–11, 20% of upper-school students received aid; total upper-school merit-scholarship money awarded: $10,000. Total amount of financial aid awarded in 2010–11: $165,000.

Admissions Traditional secondary-level entrance grade is 9. For fall 2010, 5 students applied for upper-level admission, 5 were accepted, 3 enrolled. Any standardized test, school placement exam and writing sample required. Deadline for receipt of application materials: none. Application fee required: $25. Interview recommended.

Athletics Interscholastic: baseball (boys), basketball (b,g), dance team (g), drill team (g), football (b), track and field (b,g), volleyball (g), weight training (b); coed interscholastic: cheering, cross-country running, golf, physical training, strength & conditioning, weight lifting. 1 PE instructor.

Computers Computers are regularly used in accounting, business, career exploration, classics, college planning, economics, English, foreign language, geography, history, humanities, journalism, mathematics, psychology, religion, science, Spanish, writing, yearbook classes. Computer network features include Internet access, Internet filtering or blocking technology. Student e-mail accounts and computer access in designated common areas are available to students. The school has a published electronic and media policy.

Contact Ms. Sara C. Menard, Principal. 573-883-7496 Ext. 241. Fax: 573-883-9142. E-mail: menards@valleschools.org. Web site: www.valleschools.org.

VALLEY CATHOLIC HIGH SCHOOL

4275 Southwest 148th Avenue
Beaverton, Oregon 97007
Head of School: Mr. Ross Thomas

General Information college-preparatory, arts, and religious studies school, affiliated with Roman Catholic Church. Founded: 1902. Setting: suburban. Nearest major city is Portland. 15-acre campus. 4 buildings on campus. Approved or accredited by Northwest Accreditation Commission and Oregon Department of Education. Total enrollment: 457. Upper school average class size: 19. Upper school faculty-student ratio: 1:12. There are 175 required school days per year for Upper School students. Upper School students typically attend 5 days per week. The average school day consists of 6 hours.

Upper School Student Profile Grade 9: 59 students (27 boys, 32 girls); Grade 10: 92 students (39 boys, 53 girls); Grade 11: 84 students (40 boys, 44 girls); Grade 12: 98 students (42 boys, 56 girls). 94% are state residents. 1 state is represented in upper school student body. 6% are international students. 70% of students are Roman Catholic.

Faculty School total: 32. In upper school: 16 men, 16 women; 24 have advanced degrees.

Subjects Offered Advanced Placement courses, algebra, American history, American literature, anthropology, art, band, Bible studies, biology, biology-AP, calculus, chemistry, choir, composition, computer applications, computer-aided design, drama, English, English literature, English literature-AP, English-AP, expository writing, French, geometry, government, health, Japanese, journalism, orchestra, physical education, physics, physiology, poetry, pre-calculus, psychology, scripture, sociology, Spanish, Vietnam, Vietnam War, world history, world literature, world religions, World War II.

Graduation Requirements Arts and fine arts (art, music, dance, drama), computer science, electives, English, foreign language, mathematics, physical education (includes health), religion (includes Bible studies and theology), science, social studies (includes history).

Special Academic Programs Advanced Placement exam preparation; honors section; accelerated programs; ESL (10 students enrolled).

College Admission Counseling 86 students graduated in 2009; 81 went to college, including Oregon State University; Portland State University; University of Oregon; University of Portland; Western Oregon University. Other: 5 went to work. Mean SAT critical reading: 569, mean SAT math: 554, mean SAT writing: 540.

Student Life Upper grades have specified standards of dress, student council, honor system. Discipline rests primarily with faculty. Attendance at religious services is required.

Tuition and Aid Day student tuition: $9350. Tuition installment plan (monthly payment plans). Tuition reduction for siblings, merit scholarship grants, need-based scholarship grants available. In 2009–10, 20% of upper-school students received aid. Total amount of financial aid awarded in 2009–10: $300,000.

Admissions Traditional secondary-level entrance grade is 9. For fall 2009, 140 students applied for upper-level admission, 125 were accepted, 60 enrolled. STS required. Deadline for receipt of application materials: January 15. Application fee required: $50.

Athletics Interscholastic: baseball (boys), basketball (b,g), cross-country running (b,g), dance team (g), football (b), golf (b,g), soccer (b,g), softball (g), swimming and diving (b,g), tennis (b,g), track and field (b,g), volleyball (g); coed interscholastic: equestrian sports; coed intramural: outdoor activities, outdoor education, rock climbing. 3 PE instructors, 24 coaches, 1 athletic trainer.

Computers Computers are regularly used in computer applications, media, newspaper, science, yearbook classes. Computer network features include on-campus library services, Internet access, Internet filtering or blocking technology. Campus intranet and student e-mail accounts are available to students. Students grades are available online. The school has a published electronic and media policy.

Contact Mrs. Claudia Thomas, Director of Admissions. 503-644-3745. Fax: 503-646-4054. E-mail: cthomas@valleycatholic.org. Web site: www.valleycatholic.org.

VALLEY CHRISTIAN SCHOOL

100 Skyway Drive
San Jose, California 95111
Head of School: Dr. Clifford Daugherty

General Information Coeducational day and distance learning college-preparatory, arts, religious studies, technology, Conservatory of the Arts, and Institute for Applied Math & Sciences school, affiliated with Christian faith. Grades K–12. Distance learning grades 8–12. Founded: 1960. Setting: suburban. 53-acre campus. 4 buildings on campus. Approved or accredited by Association of Christian Schools International, Western Association of Schools and Colleges, and California Department of Education. Total enrollment: 2,266. Upper school average class size: 28. Upper school faculty-student ratio: 1:17. There are 174 required school days per year for Upper School students. Upper School students typically attend 5 days per week. The average school day consists of 6 hours and 45 minutes.

Upper School Student Profile Grade 6: 144 students (69 boys, 75 girls); Grade 7: 199 students (104 boys, 95 girls); Grade 8: 221 students (105 boys, 116 girls); Grade 9: 321 students (175 boys, 146 girls); Grade 10: 314 students (170 boys, 144 girls); Grade 11: 333 students (169 boys, 164 girls); Grade 12: 288 students (154 boys, 134 girls). 85% of students are Christian.

Faculty School total: 139. In upper school: 28 men, 50 women; 23 have advanced degrees.

Subjects Offered 20th century American writers, acting, advanced chemistry, advanced computer applications, advanced math, Advanced Placement courses, advanced studio art-AP, algebra, American history, American literature, American sign language, anatomy and physiology, ancient world history, applied music, art, audio visual/media, Basic programming, Bible, Bible studies, biology, biology-AP, British literature-AP, broadcasting, calculus-AP, career and personal planning, cheerleading, chemistry, chemistry-AP, Chinese, choir, choral music, choreography, Christian doctrine, Christian ethics, Christian scripture, Christian studies, college admission preparation, college counseling, college planning, comparative political systems-AP, composition-AP, computer art, computer literacy, computer music, computer science-AP, concert choir, consumer mathematics, critical studies in film, dance, dance performance, digital art, drama, drama performance, dramatic arts, English, English language and composition-AP, English literature-AP, European history-AP, film-making, finite math, foreign language, French, French studies, geometry, global studies, government, grammar, health education, health science, history, history of music, honors English, honors U.S. history, honors world history, HTML design, instrumental music, introduction to theater, Japanese, Japanese as Second Language, jazz band, jazz dance, jazz ensemble, journalism, keyboarding, Latin, leadership, leadership and service, literature and composition-AP, macro/microeconomics-AP, Mandarin, marching band, mathematics, mathematics-AP, Microsoft, music theater, music theory-AP, musical productions, musical theater, photo shop, photojournalism, physical science, physics, physics-AP, play/screen writing, pre-algebra, pre-calculus, radio broadcasting, SAT preparation, sign language, Spanish, Spanish-AP, stage design, statistics, statistics-AP, student government, studio art-AP, symphonic band, tap dance, technical theater, telecommunications, theater arts, theater production, trigonometry, typing, U.S. government, U.S. government and politics-AP, U.S. history, U.S. history-AP, video film production, vocal ensemble, weight training, wind ensemble, world history, yearbook.

Graduation Requirements American government, arts and fine arts (art, music, dance, drama), biology, Christian and Hebrew scripture, Christian doctrine, Christian studies, computers, economics, English, English composition, English literature, global studies, mathematics, physical education (includes health), science, technology, U.S. government, U.S. history, world geography, world history.

Special Academic Programs 22 Advanced Placement exams for which test preparation is offered; honors section; programs in English, mathematics, general development for dyslexic students.

College Admission Counseling 280 students graduated in 2009; 274 went to college, including Azusa Pacific University; California Polytechnic State University, San Luis Obispo; California State University, Chico; San Jose State University; University of California, Berkeley; University of California, Davis. Other: 4 went to work, 2 entered military service. Median SAT critical reading: 540, median SAT math: 530, median SAT writing: 590, median combined SAT: 1660. 35% scored over 600 on SAT critical reading, 38% scored over 600 on SAT math, 32% scored over 600 on SAT writing, 31% scored over 1800 on combined SAT.

Student Life Upper grades have specified standards of dress, student council, honor system. Discipline rests primarily with faculty.

Tuition and Aid Day student tuition: $13,100. Tuition installment plan (FACTS Tuition Payment Plan). Tuition reduction for siblings, need-based scholarship grants available. In 2009–10, 20% of upper-school students received aid. Total amount of financial aid awarded in 2009–10: $1,250,000.

Admissions Traditional secondary-level entrance grade is 9. For fall 2009, 272 students applied for upper-level admission, 180 were accepted, 140 enrolled. Admissions testing, essay, Iowa Subtests, mathematics proficiency exam, school's own test or TOEFL or SLEP required. Deadline for receipt of application materials: none. Application fee required: $70. Interview required.

Athletics Interscholastic: aquatics (boys, girls), baseball (b), basketball (b,g), cheering (b,g), cross-country running (b,g), dance squad (b,g), dance team (b), diving (b,g), football (b), golf (b,g), ice hockey (b,g), rugby (b), soccer (b,g), softball (g), swimming and diving (b,g), tennis (b,g), track and field (b,g), volleyball (b,g), water polo (b,g), wrestling (b); intramural: weight training (b,g). 3 PE instructors, 23 coaches, 2 athletic trainers.

Computers Computers are regularly used in Bible studies, computer applications, digital applications, foreign language, graphic arts, graphic design, journalism, keyboarding, lab/keyboard, library, mathematics, media arts, music, music technology, news writing, newspaper, photography, photojournalism, science, technology, typing, video film production, Web site design, word processing, yearbook classes. Computer network features include on-campus library services, Internet access, wireless campus network, Internet filtering or blocking technology, ten online classes, through two online learning labs. Campus intranet and computer access in designated common areas are available to students. Students grades are available online. The school has a published electronic and media policy.

Contact Alana James, High School Admissions Coordinator. 408-513-2512. Fax: 408-513-2517. E-mail: ajames@vcs.net. Web site: www.vcs.net.

VALLEY CHRISTIAN SCHOOL

2526 Sunset Lane
Missoula, Montana 59804

Head of School: Mrs. Sally Baier

General Information Coeducational day and distance learning college-preparatory, general academic, business, religious studies, and bilingual studies school, affiliated with Christian faith. Grades K–12. Distance learning grades 7–12. Founded: 1978. Setting: small town. Nearest major city is Spokane, WA. 5-acre campus. 2 buildings on campus. Approved or accredited by Montana Department of Education. Total enrollment: 211. Upper school average class size: 18. Upper school faculty-student ratio: 1:8. Upper School students typically attend 5 days per week.

Upper School Student Profile Grade 9: 25 students (13 boys, 12 girls); Grade 10: 15 students (9 boys, 6 girls); Grade 11: 31 students (16 boys, 15 girls); Grade 12: 23 students (16 boys, 7 girls). 100% of students are Christian faith.

Faculty School total: 23. In upper school: 6 men, 8 women; 5 have advanced degrees.

Subjects Offered Accounting, algebra, American history, American literature, art, arts, band, Bible studies, biology, biology-AP, business, business skills, chemistry, chorus, computer science, economics, English, English literature, environmental science, fine arts, geometry, German, government/civics, health, keyboarding, literature, mathematics, physical education, physics, science, social studies, Spanish, world history.

Special Academic Programs Advanced Placement exam preparation; honors section.

College Admission Counseling 27 students graduated in 2009; 24 went to college, including Montana State University; University of Nebraska at Kearney; University of Richmond. Other: 2 went to work, 1 entered military service.

Student Life Upper grades have specified standards of dress, student council, honor system. Discipline rests primarily with faculty. Attendance at religious services is required.

Tuition and Aid Day student tuition: $4975. Tuition installment plan (FACTS Tuition Payment Plan, monthly payment plans, individually arranged payment plans). Tuition reduction for siblings, need-based scholarship grants, paying campus jobs available.

Admissions Traditional secondary-level entrance grade is 9. For fall 2009, 10 students applied for upper-level admission, 10 were accepted, 10 enrolled. Deadline for receipt of application materials: none. Application fee required: $100. Interview required.

Athletics Interscholastic: basketball (boys, girls), independent competitive sports (b,g), soccer (b), tennis (b,g), track and field (b,g), volleyball (g). 1 PE instructor, 10 coaches.

Computers Computers are regularly used in accounting, foreign language, information technology, journalism, library skills, multimedia classes. Computer network features include Internet access, Internet filtering or blocking technology. Campus intranet and computer access in designated common areas are available to students. Students grades are available online. The school has a published electronic and media policy.

Contact Janelle Taberna, Office Manager. 406-549-0482 Ext. 230. Fax: 406-549-5047. E-mail: Janelle.Taberna@valleychristian.org. Web site: www.valleychristian.org.

VALLEY FORGE MILITARY ACADEMY & COLLEGE

1001 Eagle Road
Wayne, Pennsylvania 19087-3695

Head of School: Mr. Charles A. McGeorge

General Information Boys' boarding and day college-preparatory, arts, business, religious studies, bilingual studies, technology, music, and military school. Boarding grades 7–PG, day grades 7–12. Founded: 1928. Setting: suburban. Nearest major city is Philadelphia. Students are housed in single-sex dormitories. 120-acre campus. 83 buildings on campus. Approved or accredited by Middle States Association of Colleges and Schools, The Association of Boarding Schools, and Pennsylvania Department of Education. Member of National Association of Independent Schools and Secondary School Admission Test Board. Endowment: $12 million. Total enrollment: 248. Upper school average class size: 12. Upper school faculty-student ratio: 1:11. There are 175 required school days per year for Upper School students. Upper School students typically attend 5 days per week. The average school day consists of 5 hours and 50 minutes.

Upper School Student Profile Grade 9: 34 students (34 boys); Grade 10: 37 students (37 boys); Grade 11: 74 students (74 boys); Grade 12: 59 students (59 boys); Postgraduate: 23 students (23 boys). 100% of students are boarding students. 30% are state residents. 35 states are represented in upper school student body. 15% are international students. International students from China, Egypt, Mexico, Republic of Korea, Russian Federation, and Saudi Arabia; 29 other countries represented in student body.

Faculty School total: 30. In upper school: 16 men, 12 women; 18 have advanced degrees; 14 reside on campus.

Subjects Offered ACT preparation, algebra, American government, American history-AP, anatomy and physiology, ancient world history, applied music, art, biology, calculus, chemistry, Chinese, computer programming, creative writing, driver education, earth science, English, English literature and composition-AP, ESL, ESL, European history, French, French studies, geometry, government/civics, health, health education, honors geometry, honors U.S. history, instrumental music, Latin, mathematics, modern world history, music, music theory, physical education, physics, physics-AP, pre-algebra, Russian, social sciences, sociology, Spanish, speech, statistics-AP, TOEFL preparation, U.S. government, U.S. history, U.S. history-AP, world history, world religions, world religions.

Special Academic Programs Advanced Placement exam preparation; honors section; independent study; study at local college for college credit; study abroad; academic accommodation for the musically talented and the artistically talented; remedial reading and/or remedial writing; remedial math; ESL (24 students enrolled).

College Admission Counseling 73 students graduated in 2009; 65 went to college, including Drexel University; George Mason University; Penn State University Park; United States Military Academy; United States Naval Academy; University of Chicago. Other: 3 went to work, 1 entered a postgraduate year, 4 had other specific plans. Median SAT critical reading: 500, median SAT math: 530, median SAT writing: 450, median combined SAT: 1440. 28% scored over 600 on SAT critical reading, 38% scored over 600 on SAT math, 16% scored over 600 on SAT writing, 16% scored over 1800 on combined SAT.

Student Life Upper grades have uniform requirement, student council, honor system. Discipline rests equally with students and faculty. Attendance at religious services is required.

Tuition and Aid Day student tuition: $21,400; 5-day tuition and room/board: $35,890; 7-day tuition and room/board: $35,890. Tuition installment plan (monthly payment plans, individually arranged payment plans, HES). Tuition reduction for siblings, merit scholarship grants, need-based scholarship grants available. In 2009–10, 73% of upper-school students received aid; total upper-school merit-scholarship money awarded: $2,230,907. Total amount of financial aid awarded in 2009–10: $2,230,907.

Admissions Traditional secondary-level entrance grade is 11. For fall 2009, 339 students applied for upper-level admission, 204 were accepted, 105 enrolled. TOEFL or SLEP required. Deadline for receipt of application materials: none. Application fee required: $100. Interview required.

Athletics Interscholastic: baseball, basketball, climbing, cross-country running, dressage, drill team, equestrian sports, fitness, football, golf, horseback riding, indoor track, judo, lacrosse, marksmanship, outdoor activities, outdoor recreation, paint ball, physical fitness, physical training, soccer, swimming and diving, weight lifting, weight training, wrestling; intramural: blading, boxing, fencing, hockey, indoor soccer, life saving, martial arts, physical training, rugby, scuba diving, soccer. 3 PE instructors, 12 coaches, 2 athletic trainers.

Computers Computers are regularly used in all classes. Computer network features include on-campus library services, Internet access, wireless campus network, Internet filtering or blocking technology, Blackboard. Campus intranet, student e-mail accounts, and computer access in designated common areas are available to students. Students grades are available online. The school has a published electronic and media policy.

Contact Capt. Gerald Hale, Dean of Enrollment Management. 610-989-1300. Fax: 610-688-1545. E-mail: admissions@vfmac.edu. Web site: www.vfmac.edu.

See Display below and Close-Up on page 858.

VALLEY LUTHERAN HIGH SCHOOL

5199 North 7th Avenue
Phoenix, Arizona 85013-2043
Head of School: Mr. Robert Koehne
General Information Coeducational day college-preparatory, arts, religious studies, and technology school, affiliated with Lutheran Church–Missouri Synod. Grades 9–12. Founded: 1981. Setting: urban. 10-acre campus. 4 buildings on campus. Approved or accredited by National Lutheran School Accreditation, North Central Association of Colleges and Schools, and Arizona Department of Education. Total enrollment: 190. Upper school average class size: 15. Upper school faculty-student ratio: 1:12. There are 180 required school days per year for Upper School students. Upper School students typically attend 5 days per week. The average school day consists of 6 hours and 45 minutes.
Upper School Student Profile Grade 9: 40 students (20 boys, 20 girls); Grade 10: 54 students (35 boys, 19 girls); Grade 11: 44 students (24 boys, 20 girls); Grade 12: 52 students (27 boys, 25 girls). 56% of students are Lutheran Church–Missouri Synod.
Faculty School total: 17. In upper school: 9 men, 8 women; 7 have advanced degrees.
Subjects Offered Algebra.
Special Academic Programs 3 Advanced Placement exams for which test preparation is offered; honors section; term-away projects; academic accommodation for the gifted and the musically talented; remedial math; special instructional classes for deaf students.
College Admission Counseling 44 students graduated in 2010; 43 went to college, including Arizona State University; Azusa Pacific University; Baylor University; Grand Canyon University; Northern Arizona University; The University of Arizona.

Other: 1 entered military service. Median SAT critical reading: 540, median SAT math: 540, median SAT writing: 520, median combined SAT: 1575, median composite ACT: 24. 18% scored over 600 on SAT critical reading, 25% scored over 600 on SAT math, 18% scored over 600 on SAT writing, 20% scored over 1800 on combined SAT, 43% scored over 26 on composite ACT.
Student Life Upper grades have specified standards of dress, student council, honor system. Discipline rests primarily with faculty. Attendance at religious services is required.
Tuition and Aid Day student tuition: $8250. Tuition installment plan (monthly payment plans, individually arranged payment plans, Vanco Services online payments). Merit scholarship grants, need-based scholarship grants, association grants, Christian worker discounts available. In 2010–11, 30% of upper-school students received aid. Total amount of financial aid awarded in 2010–11: $166,770.
Admissions Traditional secondary-level entrance grade is 9. For fall 2010, 70 students applied for upper-level admission, 66 were accepted, 60 enrolled. High School Placement Test and school's own test required. Deadline for receipt of application materials: none. Application fee required: $50. On-campus interview required.
Athletics Interscholastic: baseball (boys), basketball (b,g), cheering (g), football (b), pom squad (g), power lifting (b,g), softball (g), track and field (b,g), volleyball (g), wrestling (b); coed interscholastic: cross-country running, golf, power lifting, running, soccer, strength & conditioning, tennis, weight training. 13 coaches.
Computers Computers are regularly used in computer applications, desktop publishing, photography, Web site design, word processing, yearbook classes. Computer network features include Internet access, Internet filtering or blocking technology. Students grades are available online. The school has a published electronic and media policy.
Contact Mrs. Kelly Abram, Admissions Director. 602-230-1600 Ext. 118. Fax: 602-230-1602. E-mail: kabram@vlhs.org. Web site: www.vlhs.org/.

VALLEY LUTHERAN HIGH SCHOOL

3560 McCarty Road
Saginaw, Michigan 48603
Head of School: Dr. John M. Brandt
General Information Coeducational day college-preparatory, arts, and religious studies school, affiliated with Lutheran Church–Missouri Synod. Grades 9–12. Founded: 1977. Setting: suburban. Nearest major city is Detroit. 50-acre campus. 1 building on campus. Approved or accredited by Lutheran School Accreditation Commission, Michigan Association of Non-Public Schools, North Central Asso-

ciation of Colleges and Schools, and Michigan Department of Education. Endowment: $1.2 million. Total enrollment: 361. Upper school average class size: 22. Upper school faculty-student ratio: 1:17. There are 180 required school days per year for Upper School students. Upper School students typically attend 5 days per week. The average school day consists of 7 hours and 5 minutes.

Upper School Student Profile Grade 9: 109 students (54 boys, 55 girls); Grade 10: 88 students (37 boys, 51 girls); Grade 11: 85 students (37 boys, 48 girls); Grade 12: 90 students (43 boys, 47 girls). 75% of students are Lutheran Church–Missouri Synod.

Faculty School total: 25. In upper school: 13 men, 12 women; 19 have advanced degrees.

Subjects Offered Accounting, algebra, American history, American literature, art, band, Bible studies, biology, business, calculus-AP, chemistry, chorus, composition, computer graphics, computer programming, drama, economics, English, ethics, fine arts, French, general science, geography, geometry, government/civics, health, keyboarding, Latin, mathematics, physical education, physics, pre-algebra, pre-calculus, psychology, reading, religion, science, social studies, Spanish, speech, word processing, world history, world literature, writing.

Graduation Requirements Arts and fine arts (art, music, dance, drama), English, mathematics, physical education (includes health), religion (includes Bible studies and theology), science, social studies (includes history).

Special Academic Programs Advanced Placement exam preparation; honors section.

College Admission Counseling 83 students graduated in 2009; 81 went to college, including Central Michigan University; Concordia University; Delta College; Grand Valley State University; Saginaw Valley State University. Other: 1 went to work, 1 entered military service. Median composite ACT: 23. 14% scored over 26 on composite ACT.

Student Life Upper grades have specified standards of dress, student council. Discipline rests primarily with faculty. Attendance at religious services is required.

Tuition and Aid Day student tuition: $4400–$5700. Tuition installment plan (monthly payment plans). Need-based scholarship grants available. In 2009–10, 30% of upper-school students received aid. Total amount of financial aid awarded in 2009–10: $150,000.

Admissions Traditional secondary-level entrance grade is 9. For fall 2009, 109 students applied for upper-level admission, 105 were accepted, 102 enrolled. Deadline for receipt of application materials: none. Application fee required: $200. Interview recommended.

Athletics Interscholastic: baseball (boys), basketball (b,g), cross-country running (b,g), football (b), golf (b), pom squad (g); coed interscholastic: pom squad. 2 PE instructors.

Computers Computers are regularly used in art, English, history classes. Computer network features include Internet access, Internet filtering or blocking technology. Students grades are available online.

Contact Mr. Randy Rogers, Guidance Director. 989-790-1676. Fax: 989-790-1680. E-mail: rrogers@vlhs.com. Web site: www.vlhs.com.

THE VALLEY SCHOOL

2474 South Ballenger Highway
Flint, Michigan 48507
Head of School: Kaye C. Panchula

General Information Coeducational day college-preparatory and arts school. Grades PK–12. Founded: 1970. Setting: urban. 1-acre campus. 1 building on campus. Approved or accredited by Independent Schools Association of the Central States. Total enrollment: 47. Upper school average class size: 14. Upper school faculty-student ratio: 1:8. There are 180 required school days per year for Upper School students. Upper School students typically attend 5 days per week. The average school day consists of 5 hours and 30 minutes.

Upper School Student Profile Grade 9: 4 students (3 boys, 1 girl); Grade 10: 2 students (2 girls); Grade 11: 6 students (3 boys, 3 girls); Grade 12: 1 student (1 boy).

Faculty School total: 12. In upper school: 4 men, 3 women; 3 have advanced degrees.

Subjects Offered Algebra, American history, American literature, art, art history, biology, ceramics, chemistry, current events, earth science, English, English literature, European history, expository writing, fine arts, geometry, government/civics, grammar, history, mathematics, music, physical education, physics, probability and statistics, SAT/ACT preparation, science, social sciences, Spanish, trigonometry, world cultures, world history, world literature, writing.

Graduation Requirements Arts and fine arts (art, music, dance, drama), English, foreign language, mathematics, physical education (includes health), science, social sciences, social studies (includes history), senior project off campus.

Special Academic Programs Honors section; independent study; term-away projects; study at local college for college credit; academic accommodation for the gifted and the artistically talented.

College Admission Counseling 5 students graduated in 2009; all went to college, including University of Michigan. Mean composite ACT: 25. 29% scored over 26 on composite ACT.

Student Life Upper grades have student council. Discipline rests equally with students and faculty.

Tuition and Aid Day student tuition: $9399. Tuition installment plan (FACTS Tuition Payment Plan). Tuition reduction for siblings, merit scholarship grants, need-based scholarship grants available. In 2009–10, 30% of upper-school students received aid;

total upper-school merit-scholarship money awarded: $50,000. Total amount of financial aid awarded in 2009–10: $74,992.

Admissions Traditional secondary-level entrance grade is 9. For fall 2009, 1 student applied for upper-level admission, 1 was accepted, 1 enrolled. School's own exam required. Deadline for receipt of application materials: none. No application fee required. On-campus interview required.

Athletics Interscholastic: basketball (boys, girls). 1 PE instructor, 2 coaches.

Computers Computers are regularly used in English, mathematics, science, social sciences classes. Computer resources include Internet access, wireless campus network.

Contact Minka Owens, Director of Admissions. 810-767-4004. Fax: 810-767-0841. E-mail: email@valleyschool.org. Web site: www.valleyschool.org.

VALLEY VIEW SCHOOL

North Brookfield, Massachusetts
See Special Needs Schools section.

VALWOOD SCHOOL

4380 US Highway 41 North
Hahira, Georgia 31632
Head of School: Cobb Atkinson

General Information Coeducational day college-preparatory school. Grades PK–12. Founded: 1969. Setting: rural. Nearest major city is Jacksonville, FL. 45-acre campus. 7 buildings on campus. Approved or accredited by Georgia Accrediting Commission, Georgia Independent School Association, Southern Association of Colleges and Schools, and Southern Association of Independent Schools. Member of National Association of Independent Schools and Secondary School Admission Test Board. Upper school average class size: 15. Upper school faculty-student ratio: 1:6. There are 180 required school days per year for Upper School students.

Upper School Student Profile Grade 9: 24 students (16 boys, 8 girls); Grade 10: 33 students (17 boys, 16 girls); Grade 11: 20 students (5 boys, 15 girls); Grade 12: 18 students (12 boys, 6 girls).

Faculty School total: 45. In upper school: 6 men, 9 women; 6 have advanced degrees.

Subjects Offered Algebra, American history, anatomy and physiology, art, biology, business skills, calculus, calculus-AP, chemistry, chemistry-AP, composition, drama, economics, English, English language-AP, English literature-AP, fitness, French, French-AP, geography, geometry, global issues, government/civics, health, honors algebra, honors English, honors geometry, instruments, Latin, literature, mathematics, model United Nations, music, music appreciation, physical education, physical science, physics, physics-AP, pre-calculus, psychology, science, senior project, Spanish, speech, strings, technology, trigonometry, U.S. history, U.S. history-AP, world history, world history-AP, yearbook.

Graduation Requirements Arts and fine arts (art, music, dance, drama), composition, computer science, English, foreign language, mathematics, physical education (includes health), science, social sciences, social studies (includes history), speech, technology, 20 hours of community service annually.

Special Academic Programs 9 Advanced Placement exams for which test preparation is offered; honors section; independent study; academic accommodation for the gifted and the musically talented.

College Admission Counseling 31 students graduated in 2009; all went to college, including Auburn University; Georgia Institute of Technology; University of Georgia; University of Mississippi; Valdosta State University; Wake Forest University. Median SAT critical reading: 570, median SAT math: 540, median SAT writing: 550, median combined SAT: 1490, median composite ACT: 24. 48% scored over 600 on SAT critical reading, 19% scored over 600 on SAT math, 33% scored over 600 on SAT writing, 29% scored over 1800 on combined SAT, 33% scored over 26 on composite ACT.

Student Life Upper grades have specified standards of dress, student council, honor system. Discipline rests equally with students and faculty.

Tuition and Aid Day student tuition: $8460. Tuition installment plan (monthly payment plans). Tuition reduction for siblings, merit scholarship grants, need-based scholarship grants available.

Admissions Traditional secondary-level entrance grade is 9. ACT, admissions testing, Explore, latest standardized score from previous school, PSAT or SAT, Stanford Achievement Test or writing sample required. Deadline for receipt of application materials: none. Application fee required: $50. Interview required.

Athletics Interscholastic: baseball (boys), basketball (b,g), cheering (g), cross-country running (b,g), football (b), golf (b,g), soccer (b,g), softball (g), tennis (b,g), track and field (b,g), wrestling (b). 1 PE instructor, 3 coaches, 1 athletic trainer.

Computers Computers are regularly used in creative writing, mathematics, science, technology, writing classes. Computer network features include on-campus library services, Internet access, wireless campus network, Internet filtering or blocking technology. Student e-mail accounts are available to students. Students grades are available online.

Contact Ginger D. Holley, Director of Admission. 229-242-8491. Fax: 229-245-7894. E-mail: gholley@valwood.org. Web site: www.valwood.org.

VANDEBILT CATHOLIC HIGH SCHOOL

209 South Hollywood Road
Houma, Louisiana 70360
Head of School: Mr. David T. Keife

General Information Coeducational day college-preparatory, arts, business, religious studies, and technology school, affiliated with Roman Catholic Church; primarily serves individuals with Attention Deficit Disorder and dyslexic students. Grades 8–12. Founded: 1965. Setting: suburban. Nearest major city is New Orleans. 29-acre campus. 8 buildings on campus. Approved or accredited by Southern Association of Colleges and Schools and Louisiana Department of Education. Endowment: $620,000. Total enrollment: 921. Upper school average class size: 25. Upper school faculty-student ratio: 1:25.

Upper School Student Profile Grade 8: 198 students (95 boys, 103 girls); Grade 9: 201 students (98 boys, 103 girls); Grade 10: 173 students (90 boys, 83 girls); Grade 11: 199 students (97 boys, 102 girls); Grade 12: 150 students (61 boys, 89 girls). 85% of students are Roman Catholic.

Faculty School total: 63. In upper school: 25 men, 38 women; 20 have advanced degrees.

Subjects Offered 20th century world history, 3-dimensional art, accounting, advanced chemistry, advanced math, algebra, American history, art, band, biology, bookkeeping, business education, calculus, chemistry, choir, civics, computer applications, computer science, driver education, earth science, English, English literature, French, general business, geography, history of music, honors algebra, honors English, honors geometry, honors U.S. history, keyboarding, Latin, leadership, mathematics, media, music appreciation, physical education, physical science, physics, pre-algebra, reading, reading/study skills, religion, Spanish, speech, world history.

Graduation Requirements Algebra, American history, athletics, biology, chemistry, civics, civics/free enterprise, computer applications, English, geometry, physical education (includes health), religion (includes Bible studies and theology), science, social studies (includes history).

Special Academic Programs Programs in English, mathematics for dyslexic students; special instructional classes for students with Attention Deficit Disorder and dyslexia.

College Admission Counseling 166 students graduated in 2009; 165 went to college, including Louisiana State University and Agricultural and Mechanical College; Louisiana Tech University; Loyola University New Orleans; Nicholls State University; Tulane University; University of Louisiana at Lafayette. Other: 1 went to work. Mean composite ACT: 23. 40% scored over 26 on composite ACT.

Student Life Upper grades have uniform requirement, student council. Discipline rests primarily with faculty. Attendance at religious services is required.

Tuition and Aid Day student tuition: $5635. Tuition installment plan (monthly payment plans). Merit scholarship grants, need-based scholarship grants, middle-income loans available. In 2009–10, 10% of upper-school students received aid; total upper-school merit-scholarship money awarded: $20,000. Total amount of financial aid awarded in 2009–10: $95,000.

Admissions Traditional secondary-level entrance grade is 8. For fall 2009, 895 students applied for upper-level admission, 894 were accepted, 894 enrolled. Deadline for receipt of application materials: none. No application fee required. On-campus interview required.

Athletics Interscholastic: baseball (boys), basketball (b,g), bowling (b), cheering (g), cross-country running (b,g), dance squad (g), football (b), golf (b), gymnastics (b,g), power lifting (b), soccer (b,g), tennis (b,g), track and field (b,g), weight training (b,g). 5 PE instructors, 15 coaches.

Computers Computers are regularly used in accounting, aerospace science, all academic, animation, architecture, art, aviation, basic skills, Bible studies, business, business applications, business education, business skills, business studies, cabinet making, career education, career exploration, career technology, Christian doctrine, classics, college planning, commercial art, computer applications, construction, creative writing, current events, dance, data processing, design, desktop publishing, desktop publishing, ESL, digital applications, drafting, drawing and design, economics, engineering, English, ESL, ethics, foreign language, French, French as a second language, freshman foundations, geography, graphic design, graphics, health, historical foundations for arts, history, human geography—AP, humanities, independent study, industrial technology, information technology, introduction to technology, journalism, JROTC, lab/keyboard, language development, Latin, learning cognition, library, library science, library skills, life skills, literacy, literary magazine, mathematics, media, media arts, media production, media services, mentorship program, multimedia, music, music technology, news writing, newspaper, NJROTC, occupational education, philosophy, photography, photojournalism, programming, psychology, publications, publishing, reading, religion, religious studies, remedial study skills, research skills, SAT preparation, science, senior seminar, social sciences, social studies, Spanish, speech, stock market, study skills, technical drawing, technology, theater, theater arts, theology, typing, video film production, vocational-technical courses, Web site design, wilderness education, woodworking, word processing, writing, writing classes. Computer network features include on-campus library services, Internet access, Internet filtering or blocking technology. Computer access in designated common areas is available to students. Students grades are available online. The school has a published electronic and media policy.

Contact Mr. Quinn Moreaux, Assistant Principal. 985-876-2551. Fax: 985-868-9774. E-mail: qmoreaux@htdiocese.org. Web site: www.vandebiltcatholic.org.

THE VANGUARD SCHOOL

Lake Wales, Florida
See Special Needs Schools section.

VENTA PREPARATORY SCHOOL

2013 Old Carp Road
Ottawa, Ontario K0A 1L0, Canada
Head of School: Ms. Marilyn Mansfield

General Information Coeducational boarding and day college-preparatory, arts, and music school. Grades 1–10. Founded: 1981. Setting: small town. Students are housed in single-sex by floor dormitories. 50-acre campus. 8 buildings on campus. Approved or accredited by Ontario Department of Education. Language of instruction: English. Total enrollment: 96. Upper school average class size: 12. Upper school faculty-student ratio: 1:6. Upper School students typically attend 5 days per week.

Upper School Student Profile Grade 8: 13 students (7 boys, 6 girls); Grade 9: 8 students (4 boys, 4 girls); Grade 10: 7 students (5 boys, 2 girls). 40% of students are boarding students. 90% are province residents. 5 provinces are represented in upper school student body. International students from Bermuda, China, Hong Kong, Mexico, and United States.

Faculty School total: 18. In upper school: 6 men, 12 women; 3 have advanced degrees; 6 reside on campus.

Special Academic Programs Independent study; academic accommodation for the gifted; remedial reading and/or remedial writing; remedial math; programs in English, mathematics, general development for dyslexic students.

Student Life Upper grades have uniform requirement, honor system. Discipline rests primarily with faculty.

Tuition and Aid Day student tuition: CAN$17,070–CAN$18,585; 5-day tuition and room/board: CAN$24,290; 7-day tuition and room/board: CAN$25,680. Tuition installment plan (monthly payment plans, individually arranged payment plans). Tuition reduction for siblings, merit scholarship grants available.

Admissions Traditional secondary-level entrance grade is 9. Psychoeducational evaluation required. Deadline for receipt of application materials: none. Application fee required: CAN$75. On-campus interview required.

Athletics Coed Intramural: ball hockey, baseball, basketball, canoeing/kayaking, fitness, ice hockey, jogging, outdoor recreation. 4 PE instructors.

Computers Computers are regularly used in current events, geography, keyboarding, mathematics, research skills, science, Web site design classes. Computer network features include Internet access, wireless campus network, Internet filtering or blocking technology. The school has a published electronic and media policy.

Contact Mr. Cory Awde, Director of Marketing and Admissions. 613-839-2175 Ext. 240. Fax: 613-839-1956. E-mail: info@ventaprep.com. Web site: www.ventapreparatoryschool.com.

VERDALA INTERNATIONAL SCHOOL

Fort Pembroke
Pembroke PBK1641, Malta
Head of School: Mr. Nollaig Mac an Bhaird

General Information Coeducational boarding and day college-preparatory and general academic school. Boarding grades 9–12, day grades PK–12. Founded: 1977. Setting: suburban. Nearest major city is Valletta, Malta. Students are housed in host family homes. 6-acre campus. 6 buildings on campus. Approved or accredited by International Baccalaureate Organization and Middle States Association of Colleges and Schools. Member of European Council of International Schools. Language of instruction: English. Endowment: €91,000. Total enrollment: 310. Upper school average class size: 15. Upper school faculty-student ratio: 1:7. There are 176 required school days per year for Upper School students. Upper School students typically attend 5 days per week. The average school day consists of 5 hours and 30 minutes.

Upper School Student Profile Grade 9: 28 students (15 boys, 13 girls); Grade 10: 31 students (14 boys, 17 girls); Grade 11: 33 students (16 boys, 17 girls); Grade 12: 27 students (11 boys, 16 girls). 12% of students are boarding students. 90% are international students. International students from Germany, Russian Federation, Sweden, United Kingdom, and United States; 32 other countries represented in student body.

Faculty School total: 48. In upper school: 5 men, 18 women; 7 have advanced degrees.

Subjects Offered Algebra, art, art history, biology, calculus, chemistry, computer science, drama, English, English literature, fine arts, French, geography, geometry, grammar, health, history, Italian, mathematics, music, physical education, physics, psychology, science, social studies, Spanish, theory of knowledge, trigonometry, world history, world literature, writing.

Graduation Requirements Arts and fine arts (art, music, dance, drama), computer science, English, foreign language, mathematics, physical education (includes health), science, social studies (includes history).

Special Academic Programs International Baccalaureate program; ESL (52 students enrolled).

College Admission Counseling 28 students graduated in 2010; 25 went to college. Other: 3 went to work. Median SAT critical reading: 500, median SAT math: 640, median SAT writing: 520.

Verdala International School

Student Life Upper grades have specified standards of dress, student council, honor system. Discipline rests primarily with faculty.

Tuition and Aid Day student tuition: €6780; 7-day tuition and room/board: €7260. Tuition installment plan (monthly payment plans, individually arranged payment plans). Tuition reduction for siblings, need-based scholarship grants available. In 2010–11, 64% of upper-school students received aid. Total amount of financial aid awarded in 2010–11: $18,750.

Admissions Traditional secondary-level entrance grade is 9. Academic Profile Tests required. Deadline for receipt of application materials: none. No application fee required. On-campus interview required.

Athletics Interscholastic: basketball (boys), volleyball (b,g); intramural: physical fitness (b,g), soccer (b,g), swimming and diving (b,g), track and field (b,g); coed intramural: physical fitness, swimming and diving. 2 coaches, 1 athletic trainer.

Computers Computer resources include on-campus library services, online commercial services, Internet access. Computer access in designated common areas is available to students.

Contact Mrs. Daphne Baldacchino, Secretary. 356-21375133. Fax: 356-21372387. E-mail: vis1@verdala.org. Web site: www.verdala.org.

VERDE VALLEY SCHOOL

3511 Verde Valley School Road
Sedona, Arizona 86351
Head of School: Mr. Paul Domingue

General Information Coeducational boarding and day college-preparatory and International Baccalaureate Programme school. Grades 9–12. Founded: 1948. Setting: rural. Nearest major city is Phoenix. Students are housed in single-sex dormitories. 160-acre campus. 20 buildings on campus. Approved or accredited by International Baccalaureate Organization, Ohio Association of Independent Schools, and Arizona Department of Education. Candidate for accreditation by Independent Schools Association of the Southwest and North Central Association of Colleges and Schools. Member of National Association of Independent Schools and Secondary School Admission Test Board. Endowment: $2 million. Total enrollment: 123. Upper school average class size: 9. Upper school faculty-student ratio: 1:6. There are 170 required school days per year for Upper School students. Upper School students typically attend 5 days per week. The average school day consists of 7 hours and 30 minutes.

Upper School Student Profile Grade 9: 25 students (15 boys, 10 girls); Grade 10: 24 students (10 boys, 14 girls); Grade 11: 44 students (19 boys, 25 girls); Grade 12: 28 students (13 boys, 15 girls). 78% of students are boarding students. 36% are state residents. 9 states are represented in upper school student body. 46% are international students. International students from China, Germany, Republic of Korea, Russian Federation, Rwanda, and Viet Nam; 8 other countries represented in student body.

Faculty School total: 24. In upper school: 16 men, 8 women; 13 have advanced degrees; 22 reside on campus.

Subjects Offered Algebra, American history, American literature, anthropology, art, art and culture, art history, biology, calculus, ceramics, chemistry, creative writing, dance, drama, drawing, earth science, ecology, English, English literature, environmental science, ESL, European history, expository writing, fine arts, geography, geometry, grammar, history, journalism, mathematics, music, Native American studies, painting, photography, physical education, physics, poetry, science, social studies, Spanish, theater, trigonometry, world history.

Graduation Requirements Arts and fine arts (art, music, dance, drama), English, foreign language, mathematics, science, social studies (includes history), participation in annual Project Period and Field Trip program, meet requirements of International Baccalaureate Programme.

Special Academic Programs International Baccalaureate program; independent study; academic accommodation for the gifted, the musically talented, and the artistically talented; ESL (8 students enrolled).

College Admission Counseling 23 students graduated in 2009; 16 went to college, including Columbia College; Northern Arizona University; Rochester Institute of Technology; Smith College; Stanford University; University of Colorado at Boulder. Other: 6 entered a postgraduate year, 1 had other specific plans. Mean SAT critical reading: 538, mean SAT math: 601, mean SAT writing: 546, mean combined SAT: 1685, mean composite ACT: 24.

Student Life Upper grades have student council. Discipline rests equally with students and faculty.

Tuition and Aid Day student tuition: $21,500; 5-day tuition and room/board: $39,900; 7-day tuition and room/board: $39,900. Tuition installment plan (FACTS Tuition Payment Plan, monthly payment plans). Need-based scholarship grants, need- and merit-based program available. In 2009–10, 56% of upper-school students received aid. Total amount of financial aid awarded in 2009–10: $1,906,600.

Admissions Traditional secondary-level entrance grade is 9. For fall 2009, 110 students applied for upper-level admission, 70 were accepted, 44 enrolled. SLEP for foreign students, SSAT or TOEFL required. Deadline for receipt of application materials: none. Application fee required: $75. Interview required.

Athletics Interscholastic: basketball (boys, girls), golf (b,g), soccer (b,g); coed interscholastic: bicycling, horseback riding; coed intramural: aerobics/dance, aerobics/Nautilus, aquatics, archery, backpacking, bicycling, canoeing/kayaking, climbing, cross-country running, dressage, equestrian sports, fencing, fitness, fitness walking, golf, hiking/backpacking, horseback riding, jogging, kayaking, martial arts, modern dance, mountain biking, mountaineering, Nautilus, outdoor activities, physical fitness, rappelling, rock climbing, ropes courses, running, skiing (cross-country), skiing (downhill), snowboarding, strength & conditioning, swimming and diving, table tennis, tai chi, tennis, walking, wall climbing, wilderness, yoga.

Computers Computers are regularly used in English, mathematics, science classes. Computer network features include on-campus library services, Internet access, wireless campus network, Internet filtering or blocking technology. Student e-mail accounts are available to students. The school has a published electronic and media policy.

Contact Ms. Erin Fanelli, Assistant Director of Admission. 928-284-2272 Ext. 31. Fax: 928-284-0432. E-mail: admission@vvsaz.org. Web site: www.vvsaz.org.

VIANNEY HIGH SCHOOL

1311 South Kirkwood Road
St. Louis, Missouri 63122
Head of School: Mr. Lawrence D. Keller

General Information Boys' day college-preparatory, arts, business, religious studies, and technology school, affiliated with Roman Catholic Church. Grades 9–12. Founded: 1960. Setting: suburban. 37-acre campus. 6 buildings on campus. Approved or accredited by National Catholic Education Association, North Central Association of Colleges and Schools, and The College Board. Total enrollment: 622. Upper school average class size: 22. Upper school faculty-student ratio: 1:12. There are 165 required school days per year for Upper School students. Upper School students typically attend 5 days per week. The average school day consists of 6 hours and 5 minutes.

Upper School Student Profile Grade 9: 178 students (178 boys); Grade 10: 150 students (150 boys); Grade 11: 150 students (150 boys); Grade 12: 144 students (144 boys). 98% of students are Roman Catholic.

Faculty School total: 50. In upper school: 42 men, 8 women; 49 have advanced degrees.

Subjects Offered Accounting, advanced chemistry, Advanced Placement courses, algebra, American government, American history, American literature, analysis, analytic geometry, architectural drawing, art, art education, art history, arts appreciation, athletic training, band, British literature (honors), business law, business mathematics, calculus, calculus-AP, Catholic belief and practice, chemistry, Christian and Hebrew scripture, Christian ethics, Christian studies, college writing, communication skills, composition, computer applications, computer programming, computer skills, constitutional history of U.S., consumer education, current events, drama, economics, English composition, English literature, European history, expository writing, foreign language, fractal geometry, French, geometry, German, German literature, government, health and wellness, honors algebra, honors English, honors geometry, honors U.S. history, journalism, keyboarding, leadership, mythology, probability and statistics, publications, research skills, scripture, sex education, Shakespeare, Spanish, Spanish literature, sports conditioning, stage design, stagecraft, technical drawing, technology, technology/design, the Web, theater arts, theater design and production, theater history, trigonometry, U.S. government, U.S. history, U.S. literature, Web site design, weight training, world civilizations, world history, writing.

Graduation Requirements American history, American literature, arts and fine arts (art, music, dance, drama), biology, English, English composition, foreign language, government/civics, history, keyboarding, mathematics, physical education (includes health), physical fitness, religious studies, science, social issues, 100 hours of community service.

Special Academic Programs 3 Advanced Placement exams for which test preparation is offered; honors section; study at local college for college credit; special instructional classes for students with learning disabilities, Attention Deficit Disorder, dyslexia, emotional and behavioral problems.

College Admission Counseling 133 students graduated in 2010; 130 went to college, including Missouri State University; Saint Louis University; Southeast Missouri State University; St. Louis Community College at Meramec; University of Missouri. Other: 2 went to work, 1 entered military service. Median composite ACT: 23. 25% scored over 26 on composite ACT.

Student Life Upper grades have specified standards of dress, student council, honor system. Discipline rests equally with students and faculty. Attendance at religious services is required.

Summer Programs Sports programs offered; session focuses on reinforcing athletic skills; held on campus; accepts boys and girls; open to students from other schools. 1,100 students usually enrolled. 2011 schedule: June 7 to July 30. Application deadline: May 28.

Tuition and Aid Day student tuition: $10,350. Tuition installment plan (The Tuition Plan, FACTS Tuition Payment Plan, monthly payment plans, individually arranged payment plans). Tuition reduction for siblings, merit scholarship grants, need-based scholarship grants, paying campus jobs available. In 2010–11, 27% of upper-school students received aid; total upper-school merit-scholarship money awarded: $135,127. Total amount of financial aid awarded in 2010–11: $316,127.

Admissions Traditional secondary-level entrance grade is 9. For fall 2010, 187 students applied for upper-level admission, 184 were accepted, 178 enrolled. High School Placement Test (closed version) from Scholastic Testing Service required. Deadline for receipt of application materials: none. No application fee required. On-campus interview required.

Athletics Interscholastic: aquatics, baseball, basketball, cross-country running, diving, football, golf, ice hockey, lacrosse, racquetball, roller hockey, soccer, swimming and diving, tennis, track and field, volleyball, wrestling; intramural: bowling, flag football, paint ball, Special Olympics, touch football, 3 PE instructors, 40 coaches, 1 athletic trainer.

Computers Computers are regularly used in all academic, architecture, computer applications, creative writing, drafting, journalism, yearbook classes. Computer network features include on-campus library services, online commercial services, Internet access, wireless campus network, Internet filtering or blocking technology. Campus intranet, student e-mail accounts, and computer access in designated common areas are available to students. Students grades are available online. The school has a published electronic and media policy.

Contact Mr. Terry Cochran, Director of Admissions. 314-965-4853 Ext. 142. Fax: 314-965-1950. E-mail: tcochran@vianney.com. Web site: www.vianney.com.

VICKSBURG CATHOLIC SCHOOL

1900 Grove Street
Vicksburg, Mississippi 39183
Head of School: Mrs. Michele Connelly

General Information Coeducational day college-preparatory and religious studies school, affiliated with Roman Catholic Church. Grades PK–12. Founded 1860. Setting: urban. Nearest major city is Jackson. 8-acre campus. 3 buildings on campus. Approved or accredited by National Catholic Education Association, Southern Association of Colleges and Schools, and Mississippi Department of Education. Endowment: $350,000. Total enrollment: 577. Upper school average class size: 16. Upper school faculty-student ratio: 1:11. There are 180 required school days per year for Upper School students. Upper School students typically attend 5 days per week. The average school day consists of 5 hours and 50 minutes.

Upper School Student Profile Grade 7: 45 students (30 boys, 15 girls); Grade 8: 53 students (26 boys, 27 girls); Grade 9: 47 students (30 boys, 17 girls); Grade 10: 36 students (18 boys, 18 girls); Grade 11: 39 students (21 boys, 18 girls); Grade 12: 37 students (18 boys, 19 girls). 50% of students are Roman Catholic.

Faculty School total: 49. In upper school: 11 men, 14 women; 6 have advanced degrees.

Subjects Offered Accounting, algebra, American government, American history, anatomy, anatomy and physiology, art, band, biology, biology-AP, calculus-AP, ceramics, chemistry, chemistry-AP, choir, computer applications, creative writing, desktop publishing, drama, earth science, economics, English, English language and composition-AP, environmental science, foreign language, geography, geology, geometry, global studies, government and politics-AP, health, honors algebra, honors English, honors geometry, humanities, keyboarding, law, learning lab, minority studies, music, physical education, physics, physics-AP, pre-algebra, pre-calculus, psychology, public speaking, sociology, Spanish, state history, theology, trigonometry, U.S. government, U.S. history, world geography, world history, yearbook.

Graduation Requirements Algebra, American government, American history, biology, computer skills, economics, English, geography, geometry, government, health, history, lab science, law, physical education (includes health), Spanish, theology, U.S. government, U.S. history, world history, Mississippi state requirements.

Special Academic Programs 6 Advanced Placement exams for which test preparation is offered; honors section; special instructional classes for students with learning disabilities, Attention Deficit Disorder, dyslexia, emotional and behavioral problems.

College Admission Counseling 31 students graduated in 2010; 30 went to college, including Hinds Community College; Louisiana State University and Agricultural and Mechanical College; Mississippi State University; University of Mississippi; University of Southern Mississippi. Other: 1 went to work. Median composite ACT: 22. 22% scored over 26 on composite ACT.

Student Life Upper grades have uniform requirement, student council, honor system. Discipline rests primarily with faculty. Attendance at religious services is required.

Tuition and Aid Day student tuition: $5600. Tuition installment plan (monthly payment plans, bank draft). Tuition reduction for siblings, need-based scholarship grants available. In 2010–11, 2% of upper-school students received aid. Total amount of financial aid awarded in 2010–11: $79,000.

Admissions Traditional secondary-level entrance grade is 7. For fall 2010, 20 students applied for upper-level admission, 20 were accepted, 20 enrolled. Deadline for receipt of application materials: none. Application fee required: $50. Interview required.

Athletics Interscholastic: baseball (boys), basketball (b,g), cheering (g), cross-country running (b,g), dance squad (g), football (b), golf (b), power lifting (b), soccer (b,g), softball (g), swimming and diving (b,g), tennis (b,g), track and field (b,g), weight lifting (b); coed interscholastic: swimming and diving, tennis. 2 PE instructors, 4 coaches.

Computers Computers are regularly used in accounting, desktop publishing, keyboarding classes. Computer network features include on-campus library services, online commercial services, Internet access, Internet filtering or blocking technology. Students grades are available online. The school has a published electronic and media policy.

Contact Mrs. Patricia Rabalais, Registrar. 601-636-2256 Ext. 16. Fax: 601-631-0430. E-mail: patricia.rabalais@vicksburgcatholic.org. Web site: www.vicksburgcatholic.org.

VICTORY CHRISTIAN SCHOOL

7700 South Lewis Avenue
Tulsa, Oklahoma 74136
Head of School: Dr. Dennis Demuth

General Information Coeducational day college-preparatory, arts, religious studies, and technology school, affiliated with Christian faith, Evangelical faith. Grades K–12. Founded: 1979. Setting: suburban. 35-acre campus. 3 buildings on campus. Approved or accredited by North Central Association of Colleges and Schools and Oklahoma Department of Education. Total enrollment: 1,211. Upper school average class size: 20. Upper school faculty-student ratio: 1:20. There are 175 required school days per year for Upper School students. The average school day consists of 6 hours.

Upper School Student Profile 75% of students are Christian faith, members of Evangelical faith.

Faculty School total: 71. In upper school: 12 men, 14 women; 10 have advanced degrees.

Subjects Offered Algebra, American history, anatomy, art, art-AP, band, Bible studies, biology, calculus-AP, chemistry, chorus, computer science, drama, English, English literature-AP, fine arts, geometry, government/civics, music, physical education, physical science, physics, physiology, religion, social studies, Spanish, speech, trigonometry, typing, word processing, world history.

Graduation Requirements Arts and fine arts (art, music, dance, drama), computer science, English, foreign language, mathematics, physical education (includes health), religion (includes Bible studies and theology), science, social studies (includes history).

Special Academic Programs Study at local college for college credit; academic accommodation for the gifted, the musically talented, and the artistically talented.

College Admission Counseling 94 students graduated in 2009; 79 went to college. Other: 8 went to work, 2 entered military service, 5 had other specific plans. Mean composite ACT: 22.

Student Life Upper grades have specified standards of dress, student council, honor system. Discipline rests primarily with faculty.

Tuition and Aid Day student tuition: $3900. Tuition installment plan (monthly payment plans, individually arranged payment plans, semester and annual payment plans). Tuition reduction for siblings, tuition reduction for children of faculty available.

Admissions Traditional secondary-level entrance grade is 9. For fall 2009, 96 students applied for upper-level admission, 90 were accepted, 88 enrolled. Achievement tests required. Deadline for receipt of application materials: none. Application fee required. Interview required.

Athletics Interscholastic: baseball (boys), basketball (b,g), cheering (g), cross-country running (b,g), football (b), golf (b,g), soccer (b,g), softball (g), track and field (b,g), volleyball (g); coed interscholastic: bowling, drill team, jogging; coed intramural: jogging. 2 PE instructors.

Computers Computers are regularly used in English, mathematics, science classes. Computer network features include on-campus library services, Internet access, Internet filtering or blocking technology. Student e-mail accounts and computer access in designated common areas are available to students.

Contact Mrs. Sherrill Whipple, Registrar. 918-491-7721. Web site: www.vcstulsa.org.

VILLA DUCHESNE AND OAK HILL SCHOOL

801 South Spoede Road
St. Louis, Missouri 63131
Head of School: Sr. Lucie Nordmann, RSCJ

General Information Coeducational day college-preparatory, arts, religious studies, and technology school, affiliated with Roman Catholic Church. Boys grades JK–6, girls grades JK–12. Founded: 1929. Setting: suburban. 60-acre campus. 2 buildings on campus. Approved or accredited by Independent Schools Association of the Central States, National Catholic Education Association, Network of Sacred Heart Schools, North Central Association of Colleges and Schools, and Missouri Department of Education. Total enrollment: 710. Upper school average class size: 15. Upper school faculty-student ratio: 1:9. There are 173 required school days per year for Upper School students.

Upper School Student Profile 90% of students are Roman Catholic.

Faculty School total: 131. In upper school: 15 men, 42 women; 36 have advanced degrees.

Subjects Offered American government, American literature, American literature-AP, anatomy and physiology, art, biology, biology-AP, British literature, calculus, calculus-AP, campus ministry, ceramics, chemistry, chorus, civics, computers, creative writing, discrete mathematics, drawing, economics, English, European history, European history-AP, Far Eastern history, French, geography, geometry, health, integrated physics, math analysis, Middle East, music, newspaper, painting, personal development, physical education, physics, pre-algebra, pre-calculus, print-making, psychology, public speaking, religion, scripture, sculpture, social justice, Spanish, studio art, studio art-AP, theater arts, U.S. history, U.S. history-AP, Western civilization, women's studies, world literature, yearbook.

Graduation Requirements Students must perform community service to graduate.

Special Academic Programs International Baccalaureate program; 11 Advanced Placement exams for which test preparation is offered; honors section; independent study; term-away projects; study at local college for college credit; domestic exchange program (with Network of Sacred Heart Schools); study abroad; remedial reading and/or remedial writing; remedial math.

College Admission Counseling 76 students graduated in 2010; all went to college, including Loyola University Chicago; Saint Louis University; University of Dayton; University of Missouri. Mean combined SAT: 1823, mean composite ACT: 27.

Student Life Upper grades have uniform requirement, student council, honor system. Discipline rests primarily with faculty. Attendance at religious services is required.

Summer Programs Enrichment, advancement, sports, art/fine arts, computer instruction programs offered; session focuses on enrichment and college preparation; held on campus; accepts boys and girls; open to students from other schools. 150 students usually enrolled. 2011 schedule: June 6 to June 24. Application deadline: May 30.

Tuition and Aid Day student tuition: $16,775. Tuition installment plan (monthly payment plans, individually arranged payment plans, 8-month plan, trimester plan, or full-payment plan). Tuition reduction for siblings, merit scholarship grants, need-based scholarship grants available. In 2010–11, 15% of upper-school students received aid. Total amount of financial aid awarded in 2010–11: $1,000,000.

Admissions Traditional secondary-level entrance grade is 9. Deadline for receipt of application materials: November 16. Application fee required: $40. On-campus interview required.

Athletics Interscholastic: basketball (girls), cross-country running (g), diving (g), field hockey (g), golf (g), lacrosse (g), racquetball (g), soccer (g), softball (g), swimming and diving (g), tennis (g), track and field (g), volleyball (g). 7 PE instructors, 34 coaches, 1 athletic trainer.

Computers Computers are regularly used in all academic classes. Computer network features include on-campus library services, online commercial services, Internet access, wireless campus network, Internet filtering or blocking technology, students in grades 7 to 12 have personal HP tablet PCs. Campus intranet, student e-mail accounts, and computer access in designated common areas are available to students. Students grades are available online. The school has a published electronic and media policy.

Contact Mrs. Elaine Brooks, Admissions Assistant. 314-810-3566. Fax: 314-432-0199. E-mail: ebrooks@vdoh.org. Web site: www.vdoh.org.

VILLAGE CHRISTIAN SCHOOLS

8930 Village Avenue
Sun Valley, California 91352

Head of School: Mr. Tom Konjoyan

General Information Coeducational day college-preparatory, general academic, arts, religious studies, and technology school, affiliated with Christian faith. Grades K–12. Founded: 1949. Setting: suburban. Nearest major city is Los Angeles. 110-acre campus. 7 buildings on campus. Approved or accredited by Association of Christian Schools International, Western Association of Schools and Colleges, and California Department of Education. Total enrollment: 1,091. Upper school average class size: 25. Upper school faculty-student ratio: 1:25. There are 169 required school days per year for Upper School students. Upper School students typically attend 5 days per week. The average school day consists of 6 hours and 30 minutes.

Upper School Student Profile 75% of students are Christian faith.

Faculty School total: 87. In upper school: 20 men, 15 women; 10 have advanced degrees.

Subjects Offered Algebra, American history-AP, American literature, anatomy, art, ASB Leadership, band, Bible studies, biology, biology-AP, British literature, calculus-AP, career education, careers, ceramics, chemistry, choir, choral music, church history, clayworking, computer graphics, computer literacy, drama, earth science, economics, English, English language and composition-AP, English literature and composition-AP, English-AP, environmental science-AP, geometry, health education, history-AP, honors English, jazz band, leadership, library assistant, Life of Christ, marching band, mathematics, music theory-AP, painting, physical education, physics, physiology, pre-calculus, Spanish, Spanish language-AP, Spanish literature-AP, statistics, statistics-AP, strings, theater arts, trigonometry, U.S. government, U.S. government and politics-AP, U.S. history, world history, world religions, yearbook.

Graduation Requirements Arts and fine arts (art, music, dance, drama), computer science, English, foreign language, mathematics, physical education (includes health), religion (includes Bible studies and theology), science, social sciences, social studies (includes history).

Special Academic Programs Advanced Placement exam preparation; honors section; study at local college for college credit.

College Admission Counseling 127 students graduated in 2010; 125 went to college, including Azusa Pacific University; California State University, Northridge; San Diego State University; University of California, Irvine; University of California, Los Angeles; University of Southern California. Other: 1 went to work, 1 entered military service. Mean SAT critical reading: 597, mean SAT math: 582.

Student Life Upper grades have uniform requirement, student council. Discipline rests equally with students and faculty.

Summer Programs Remediation, enrichment, advancement, sports, art/fine arts, computer instruction programs offered; session focuses on academic advancement and

remediation; held on campus; accepts boys and girls; open to students from other schools. 590 students usually enrolled. 2011 schedule: June 21 to July 30. Application deadline: June 1.

Tuition and Aid Day student tuition: $9500. Tuition installment plan (monthly payment plans, individually arranged payment plans). Tuition reduction for siblings, merit scholarship grants, need-based scholarship grants, short-term emergency help for continuing families, fine arts scholarships to current students available.

Admissions Traditional secondary-level entrance grade is 9. Deadline for receipt of application materials: February 1. Application fee required: $100. On-campus interview required.

Athletics Interscholastic: baseball (boys), basketball (b,g), cheering (g), cross-country running (b,g), dance team (g), football (b), physical fitness (b,g), physical training (b,g), soccer (b,g), softball (g), tennis (b,g), track and field (b,g), volleyball (b,g); intramural: basketball (b,g), cross-country running (b,g), physical fitness (b,g), physical training (b,g); coed interscholastic: equestrian sports, golf; coed intramural: equestrian sports. 6 PE instructors, 15 coaches, 1 athletic trainer.

Computers Computers are regularly used in English, graphic arts, history, mathematics, science, Spanish, technology, yearbook classes. Computer network features include on-campus library services, online commercial services, Internet access, Internet filtering or blocking technology. Student e-mail accounts and computer access in designated common areas are available to students. The school has a published electronic and media policy.

Contact Co-Director sof Admissions. 818-767-8382. Fax: 818-768-2006. E-mail: admissions@villagechristian.org. Web site: www.villagechristian.org.

VILLA JOSEPH MARIE HIGH SCHOOL

1180 Holland Road
Holland, Pennsylvania 18966

Head of School: Mrs. Mary T. Michel

General Information Girls' day college-preparatory, arts, religious studies, and drama school, affiliated with Roman Catholic Church. Grades 9–12. Founded: 1932. Setting: suburban. Nearest major city is Philadelphia. 55-acre campus. 3 buildings on campus. Approved or accredited by Middle States Association of Colleges and Schools and Pennsylvania Department of Education. Total enrollment: 381. Upper school average class size: 15. Upper school faculty-student ratio: 1:14. Upper School students typically attend 5 days per week. The average school day consists of 6 hours and 45 minutes.

Upper School Student Profile Grade 9: 95 students (95 girls); Grade 10: 93 students (93 girls); Grade 11: 106 students (106 girls); Grade 12: 88 students (88 girls). 98% of students are Roman Catholic.

Faculty School total: 37. In upper school: 9 men, 28 women; 30 have advanced degrees.

Subjects Offered Algebra, American government, American history, American history-AP, anatomy and physiology, ancient history, art, art appreciation, biology, biology-AP, business mathematics, calculus-AP, chemistry, chemistry-AP, chorus, conceptual physics, dance, drama, earth science, English, English literature-AP, environmental science, environmental science-AP, European history-AP, film and literature, forensics, French, geometry, health, Latin, music, physical education, physics, physics-AP, pre-calculus, psychology, psychology-AP, sociology, Spanish, speech, studio art, theology, trigonometry, world history, writing.

Graduation Requirements Arts and fine arts (art, music, dance, drama), English, foreign language, mathematics, physical education (includes health), religion (includes Bible studies and theology), science, social sciences, social studies (includes history), service hours requirement.

Special Academic Programs 13 Advanced Placement exams for which test preparation is offered; honors section; independent study; study at local college for college credit; academic accommodation for the gifted, the musically talented, and the artistically talented.

College Admission Counseling 88 students graduated in 2010; all went to college, including Loyola University Maryland; Penn State University Park; Saint Joseph's University; The University of Scranton; Villanova University. Mean SAT critical reading: 580, mean SAT math: 555, mean SAT writing: 603.

Student Life Upper grades have uniform requirement, student council, honor system. Discipline rests primarily with faculty. Attendance at religious services is required.

Summer Programs Enrichment, sports programs offered; session focuses on enrichment; held on campus; accepts girls; open to students from other schools. 45 students usually enrolled.

Tuition and Aid Day student tuition: $10,650. Tuition installment plan (monthly payment plans). Tuition reduction for siblings, merit scholarship grants, need-based scholarship grants available. Total upper-school merit-scholarship money awarded for 2010–11: $160,000.

Admissions Traditional secondary-level entrance grade is 9. For fall 2010, 200 students applied for upper-level admission, 125 were accepted, 95 enrolled. High School Placement Test required. Deadline for receipt of application materials: November 12. Application fee required: $55. On-campus interview required.

Athletics Interscholastic: basketball, cheering, cross-country running, field hockey, golf, indoor track, lacrosse, soccer, softball, tennis, track and field, volleyball, winter (indoor) track. 1 PE instructor, 14 coaches, 1 athletic trainer.

Computers Computers are regularly used in art, English, foreign language, history, library, literary magazine, mathematics, religion, science, yearbook classes. Computer network features include on-campus library services, online commercial services, Internet access, wireless campus network, Internet filtering or blocking technology. Computer access in designated common areas is available to students. Students grades are available online. The school has a published electronic and media policy.

Contact Mrs. Maureen Cleary, Director of Institutional Advancement. 215-357-8810 Ext. 124. Fax: 215-357-9410. E-mail: mclea@vjmhs.org. Web site: www.vjmhs.org.

VILLA MARIA ACADEMY

2403 West Eighth Street
Erie, Pennsylvania 16505-4492
Head of School: Fr. Scott Jabo

General Information Coeducational day college-preparatory school, affiliated with Roman Catholic Church. Boys grades 11–12, girls grades 9–12. Founded: 1892. Setting: suburban. 4 buildings on campus. Approved or accredited by Middle States Association of Colleges and Schools and National Catholic Education Association. Total enrollment: 303. Upper school average class size: 20. Upper school faculty-student ratio: 1:12. There are 180 required school days per year for Upper School students. Upper School students typically attend 5 days per week. The average school day consists of 6 hours.

Upper School Student Profile Grade 9: 78 students (78 girls); Grade 10: 81 students (81 girls); Grade 11: 66 students (8 boys, 58 girls); Grade 12: 78 students (9 boys, 69 girls). 87% of students are Roman Catholic.

Faculty School total: 26. In upper school: 7 men, 19 women; 12 have advanced degrees.

Subjects Offered 3-dimensional art, advanced math, Advanced Placement courses, algebra, American history, American history-AP, aquatics, art, arts, athletics, audio visual/media, biology, ceramics, community service, computer science, English, fine arts, geometry, graphic arts, health, keyboarding, Latin, mathematics, newspaper, photography, physical education, physical fitness, physics, practical arts, psychology, psychology-AP, religious education, SAT preparation, science, senior project, social studies, Spanish, speech, student government, theology, U.S. history, U.S. history-AP, word processing, world history, yearbook.

Graduation Requirements Arts and fine arts (art, music, dance, drama), English, foreign language, mathematics, physical education (includes health), religion (includes Bible studies and theology), science, social studies (includes history). Community service is required.

Special Academic Programs 7 Advanced Placement exams for which test preparation is offered; honors section; accelerated programs; independent study; study at local college for college credit.

College Admission Counseling 61 students graduated in 2010; 59 went to college, including Edinboro University of Pennsylvania; Gannon University; Mercyhurst College; Penn State Erie, The Behrend College; Penn State University Park; University of Pittsburgh. Other: 1 went to work, 1 entered military service.

Student Life Upper grades have uniform requirement, student council, honor system. Discipline rests primarily with faculty.

Tuition and Aid Day student tuition: $6915–$7240. Tuition installment plan (FACTS Tuition Payment Plan). Tuition reduction for siblings, merit scholarship grants, need-based scholarship grants available. In 2010–11, 42% of upper-school students received aid; total upper-school merit-scholarship money awarded: $64,735. Total amount of financial aid awarded in 2010–11: $270,628.

Admissions Traditional secondary-level entrance grade is 9. For fall 2010, 160 students applied for upper-level admission, 136 were accepted, 78 enrolled. Placement test required. Deadline for receipt of application materials: none. No application fee required.

Athletics Interscholastic: basketball (girls), bowling (g), cheering (g), golf (b,g), lacrosse (g), soccer (g), softball (g), swimming and diving (g), tennis (b,g), volleyball (g), water polo (g); coed interscholastic: cross-country running, track and field. 1 PE instructor.

Computers Computers are regularly used in all academic classes. Computer network features include on-campus library services, online commercial services, Internet access, wireless campus network, Internet filtering or blocking technology. Campus intranet, student e-mail accounts, and computer access in designated common areas are available to students. Students grades are available online. The school has a published electronic and media policy.

Contact Mrs. Kathy Roach, Director of Admissions. 814-838-2061 Ext. 3239. Fax: 814-836-0881. E-mail: kroach@villamaria.com. Web site: www.villamaria.com.

VILLA MARIA ACADEMY

370 Old Lincoln Highway
Malvern, Pennsylvania 19355
Head of School: Sr. Marita Carmel McCarthy, IHM

General Information Girls' day college-preparatory, arts, religious studies, and technology school, affiliated with Roman Catholic Church. Grades 9–12. Founded: 1872. Setting: suburban. Nearest major city is Philadelphia. 28-acre campus. 4 buildings on campus. Approved or accredited by Middle States Association of Colleges and Schools, The College Board, and Pennsylvania Department of Education. Total enrollment: 442. Upper school average class size: 15. Upper school faculty-student ratio: 1:9. There are 172 required school days per year for Upper

School students. Upper School students typically attend 5 days per week. The average school day consists of 6 hours and 30 minutes.

Upper School Student Profile Grade 9: 107 students (107 girls); Grade 10: 117 students (117 girls); Grade 11: 107 students (107 girls); Grade 12: 111 students (111 girls). 95% of students are Roman Catholic.

Faculty School total: 51. In upper school: 9 men, 40 women; 39 have advanced degrees.

Subjects Offered Accounting, advanced chemistry, advanced math, algebra, American government, American literature, analysis, art, Bible, biology, biology-AP, British literature, British literature (honors), calculus, calculus-AP, Catholic belief and practice, chemistry, chemistry-AP, choral music, church history, college counseling, computer applications, computer literacy, discrete mathematics, drama, driver education, English, English composition, English language-AP, English literature, English literature-AP, environmental science, European history, European history-AP, first aid, French, French-AP, geography, geometry, government-AP, grammar, guidance, health education, history of the Catholic Church, honors algebra, honors English, honors geometry, honors U.S. history, honors world history, information design technology, keyboarding, Latin, library skills, literary magazine, modern European history, modern European history-AP, music performance, music theory, music-AP, orchestra, physical education, physics, physics-AP, piano, religious studies, social studies, Spanish, Spanish language-AP, statistics, statistics-AP, studio art, studio art-AP, trigonometry, U.S. history, U.S. history-AP, vocal ensemble, voice, Western civilization, world issues.

Graduation Requirements Catholic belief and practice, college admission preparation, computer applications, English, foreign language, keyboarding, mathematics, physical education (includes health), science, social studies (includes history), theology.

College Admission Counseling 109 students graduated in 2009; 104 went to college, including Penn State University Park; Saint Joseph's University; University of Delaware; University of Pittsburgh; Villanova University. Other: 1 went to work, 3 entered military service. Mean SAT critical reading: 600, mean SAT math: 600.

Student Life Upper grades have uniform requirement, student council, honor system. Discipline rests equally with students and faculty. Attendance at religious services is required.

Tuition and Aid Day student tuition: $13,700. Tuition installment plan (monthly payment plans). Tuition reduction for siblings, merit scholarship grants, need-based scholarship grants available. In 2009–10, 48% of upper-school students received aid; total upper-school merit-scholarship money awarded: $241,100. Total amount of financial aid awarded in 2009–10: $599,500.

Admissions Traditional secondary-level entrance grade is 9. For fall 2009, 239 students applied for upper-level admission, 187 were accepted, 107 enrolled. Deadline for receipt of application materials: December 8. Application fee required: $50. On-campus interview required.

Athletics Interscholastic: basketball, cross-country running, dance team, field hockey, golf, indoor track, indoor track & field, lacrosse, soccer, softball, swimming and diving, tennis, track and field, volleyball, winter (indoor) track, yoga. 2 PE instructors, 12 coaches, 1 athletic trainer.

Computers Computers are regularly used in accounting, art, Bible studies, Christian doctrine, college planning, economics, English, French, geography, health, history, humanities, Latin, library skills, mathematics, music, publications, religious studies, science, social studies, Spanish, theology, writing, yearbook classes. Computer network features include on-campus library services, online commercial services, Internet access, wireless campus network, Internet filtering or blocking technology. Campus intranet, student e-mail accounts, and computer access in designated common areas are available to students. Students grades are available online. The school has a published electronic and media policy.

Contact Mrs. Mary Kay D. Napoli, Director of Admissions. 610-644-2551 Ext. 1020. Fax: 610-644-2866. E-mail: mknapoli@vmahs.org. Web site: www.vmahs.org.

VILLA VICTORIA ACADEMY

376 West Upper Ferry Road
Ewing, New Jersey 08628
Head of School: Sr. Lillian Harrington, MPF

General Information Girls' day college-preparatory, arts, religious studies, and technology school, affiliated with Roman Catholic Church. Grades PK–12. Founded: 1933. Setting: suburban. Nearest major city is Trenton. 44-acre campus. 7 buildings on campus. Approved or accredited by Middle States Association of Colleges and Schools, National Catholic Education Association, New Jersey Association of Independent Schools, and New Jersey Department of Education. Member of Secondary School Admission Test Board. Endowment: $375,000. Total enrollment: 190. Upper school average class size: 12. Upper school faculty-student ratio: 1:8. There are 180 required school days per year for Upper School students. Upper School students typically attend 5 days per week. The average school day consists of 6 hours.

Upper School Student Profile Grade 7: 7 students (7 girls); Grade 8: 16 students (16 girls); Grade 9: 21 students (21 girls); Grade 10: 21 students (21 girls); Grade 11: 17 students (17 girls); Grade 12: 11 students (11 girls). 79% of students are Roman Catholic.

Faculty School total: 24. In upper school: 5 men, 17 women; 15 have advanced degrees.

Villa Victoria Academy

Subjects Offered Algebra, American literature, art, art history, art-AP, Bible studies, biology, calculus, calculus-AP, campus ministry, Catholic belief and practice, ceramics, chemistry, chemistry-AP, Chinese studies, choral music, chorus, college planning, community service, computer science, creative writing, drama, earth science, English, English literature, English-AP, European history, fine arts, French, geography, geometry, health, history, humanities, mathematics, multimedia, music, peer ministry, personal development, photography, physical education, physics, religion, SAT preparation, science, social studies, Spanish, Spanish-AP, theater, trigonometry, world history, world literature.

Graduation Requirements American literature, art history, arts and fine arts (art, music, dance, drama), biology, British literature, chemistry, computer science, English, foreign language, mathematics, physical education (includes health), physics, religion (includes Bible studies and theology), SAT/ACT preparation, science, social studies (includes history), world cultures, world literature, interdisciplinary humanities. Community service is required.

Special Academic Programs Advanced Placement exam preparation; honors section; independent study; academic accommodation for the gifted, the musically talented, and the artistically talented.

College Admission Counseling 28 students graduated in 2009; all went to college, including New York University; Northwestern University; Rutgers, The State University of New Jersey, Newark; The George Washington University; University of Pennsylvania; Yale University. Median combined SAT: 1814.

Student Life Upper grades have uniform requirement, student council, honor system. Discipline rests primarily with faculty. Attendance at religious services is required.

Tuition and Aid Day student tuition: $10,550. Tuition installment plan (FACTS Tuition Payment Plan, individually arranged payment plans, 2-payment plan). Merit scholarship grants, need-based scholarship grants available. In 2009–10, 25% of upper-school students received aid; total upper-school merit-scholarship money awarded: $50,000. Total amount of financial aid awarded in 2009–10: $175,000.

Admissions School placement exam or SSAT required. Deadline for receipt of application materials: December 10. Application fee required: $50. On-campus interview required.

Athletics Interscholastic: basketball, cross-country running, soccer, softball, tennis, track and field; intramural: dance, outdoor activities, outdoor education, walking. 1 PE instructor, 4 coaches.

Computers Computers are regularly used in art, English, foreign language, history, mathematics, music, SAT preparation, science, theater classes. Computer network features include on-campus library services, Internet access, wireless campus network, Internet filtering or blocking technology. Students grades are available online. The school has a published electronic and media policy.

Contact Mrs. Karen M. ODonnell, Director of Advancement. 609-882-1700 Ext. 19. Fax: 609-882-8421. E-mail: kodonnell@villavictoria.org. Web site: www.villavictoria.org.

VILLA WALSH ACADEMY

455 Western Avenue
Morristown, New Jersey 07960
Head of School: Sr. Patricia Pompa

General Information Girls' day college-preparatory, arts, religious studies, and technology school, affiliated with Roman Catholic Church. Grades 7–12. Founded: 1967. Setting: suburban. Nearest major city is New York, NY. 130-acre campus. 3 buildings on campus. Approved or accredited by Middle States Association of Colleges and Schools, National Catholic Education Association, New Jersey Association of Independent Schools, and New Jersey Department of Education. Endowment: $5 million. Total enrollment: 254. Upper school average class size: 12. Upper school faculty-student ratio: 1:8. There are 176 required school days per year for Upper School students. Upper School students typically attend 5 days per week. The average school day consists of 6 hours and 30 minutes.

Upper School Student Profile Grade 7: 15 students (15 girls); Grade 8: 15 students (15 girls); Grade 9: 59 students (59 girls); Grade 10: 54 students (54 girls); Grade 11: 54 students (54 girls); Grade 12: 57 students (57 girls). 90% of students are Roman Catholic.

Faculty School total: 35. In upper school: 3 men, 32 women; 20 have advanced degrees.

Subjects Offered Advanced Placement courses, algebra, American history, American literature, anatomy and physiology, art, Bible as literature, biology, biology-AP, British literature, British literature (honors), calculus, calculus-AP, career/college preparation, chemistry, chemistry-AP, choral music, chorus, church history, college admission preparation, computer applications, computer graphics, computer literacy, computer processing, computer programming, computer science, computer skills, CPR, creative writing, desktop publishing, driver education, economics, economics and history, English, English language and composition-AP, English literature, ethics, European civilization, family living, finite math, first aid, French, French language-AP, French-AP, geometry, health education, honors English, honors geometry, honors U.S. history, Italian, keyboarding, life science, mathematics, modern European history, modern European history-AP, moral theology, philosophy, physical education, physics, physics-AP, pre-algebra, pre-calculus, psychology, psychology-AP, religion, Spanish, Spanish-AP, statistics-AP, studio art, theology, U.S. government and politics, U.S. history, U.S. history-AP, voice ensemble, Web site design, world history, world literature.

Graduation Requirements Arts and fine arts (art, music, dance, drama), English, foreign language, mathematics, physical education (includes health), science, social studies (includes history), theology.

Special Academic Programs Advanced Placement exam preparation; honors section; independent study; academic accommodation for the gifted, the musically talented, and the artistically talented.

College Admission Counseling 57 students graduated in 2010; all went to college, including Bucknell University; Case Western Reserve University; Georgetown University; Princeton University; University of Notre Dame; Villanova University. Mean SAT critical reading: 660, mean SAT math: 650, mean SAT writing: 690, mean combined SAT: 2000, mean composite ACT: 28. 78% scored over 600 on SAT critical reading, 85% scored over 600 on SAT math, 90% scored over 600 on SAT writing, 80% scored over 1800 on combined SAT, 80% scored over 26 on composite ACT.

Student Life Upper grades have uniform requirement, student council, honor system. Discipline rests primarily with faculty. Attendance at religious services is required.

Tuition and Aid Day student tuition: $16,900. Tuition installment plan (Insured Tuition Payment Plan, Key Tuition Payment Plan, individually arranged payment plans). Merit scholarship grants, need-based scholarship grants available. In 2010–11, 12% of upper-school students received aid; total upper-school merit-scholarship money awarded: $10,000. Total amount of financial aid awarded in 2010–11: $140,000.

Admissions Traditional secondary-level entrance grade is 9. For fall 2010, 180 students applied for upper-level admission, 70 were accepted, 62 enrolled. Math, reading, and mental ability tests required. Deadline for receipt of application materials: none. Application fee required: $50. On-campus interview required.

Athletics Interscholastic: basketball, cross-country running, indoor track, lacrosse, soccer, softball, swimming and diving, tennis, track and field, volleyball, winter (indoor) track. 1 PE instructor, 26 coaches, 2 athletic trainers.

Computers Computers are regularly used in college planning, desktop publishing, independent study, keyboarding, library science, mathematics, newspaper, programming, SAT preparation, science, technology, Web site design, word processing, yearbook classes. Computer network features include on-campus library services, Internet access, wireless campus network, Internet filtering or blocking technology. The school has a published electronic and media policy.

Contact Sr. Doris Lavinthal, Director. 973-538-3680 Ext. 175. Fax: 973-538-6733. E-mail: lavinthald@aol.com. Web site: www.villawalsh.org.

VIRGINIA BEACH FRIENDS SCHOOL

1537 Laskin Road
Virginia Beach, Virginia 23451
Head of School: Mr. Edward B. Hollinger

General Information Coeducational day college-preparatory, arts, religious studies, and technology school, affiliated with Society of Friends. Grades PK–12. Founded: 1955. Setting: suburban. 11-acre campus. 4 buildings on campus. Approved or accredited by Friends Council on Education, Virginia Association of Independent Schools, and Virginia Department of Education. Endowment: $109,000. Total enrollment: 210. Upper school average class size: 12. Upper school faculty-student ratio: 1:5.

Upper School Student Profile Grade 9: 17 students (10 boys, 7 girls); Grade 10: 13 students (7 boys, 6 girls); Grade 11: 11 students (6 boys, 5 girls); Grade 12: 14 students (9 boys, 5 girls). 5% of students are members of Society of Friends.

Faculty School total: 45. In upper school: 2 men, 9 women; 4 have advanced degrees.

Subjects Offered 3-dimensional design, Advanced Placement courses, American government, Arabic, art education, art history, arts appreciation, Asian literature, athletics, audio visual/media, Basic programming, basketball, Bible as literature, biology, British literature, Buddhism, calculus, calculus-AP, ceramics, chemistry, Chinese, college admission preparation, college counseling, college placement, college planning, community service, computer applications, computer art, computer graphics, computer literacy, computer multimedia, computer programming, computer programming-AP, computer skills, computer technologies, computer tools, computers, conflict resolution, contemporary art, desktop publishing, digital art, drawing, drawing and design, electives, English composition, English language and composition-AP, English literature, English literature and composition-AP, English-AP, English/composition-AP, environmental education, environmental science, environmental science-AP, environmental studies, film and literature, filmmaking, fitness, foreign language, general science, geometry, government, grammar, graphic arts, graphic design, graphics, guidance, history of the Americas, introduction to technology, Japanese, jewelry making, Jewish studies, journalism, junior and senior seminars, keyboarding, Korean literature, lab science, language and composition, language arts, language-AP, Latin, Latin-AP, leadership, leatherworking, library, library skills, literature seminar, literature-AP, math applications, mathematics, mathematics-AP, media arts, media communications, media literacy, media services, media studies, modern world history, multicultural literature, multicultural studies, multimedia, multimedia design, music appreciation, music composition, neuroanatomy, neuroscience, non-Western literature, non-Western societies, North American literature, oceanography, oil painting, organic chemistry, participation in sports, peace and justice, peace studies, photography, photojournalism, physical education, physical fitness, physical science, physics, physics-AP, portfolio art, pre-algebra, pre-calculus, probability and statistics, programming, psychology, psychology-AP, reading, reading/study skills, religion and culture, SAT preparation, science and technology, science project, sculpture, senior composition, senior internship, senior project, sex education, Shakespeare, Shakespearean histories, short story, Spanish, sports, sports conditioning, sports psychology, stained glass, statistics, student government, student publications, student teaching, studio art, study skills, substance abuse, technical arts, technology, technology/design, telecommunications, telecommunications and the Internet, travel, U.S. and Virginia government, U.S. and Virginia history, U.S. constitutional history, U.S. government, U.S. government and politics, U.S. history, values and decisions, video, video and animation, video communication, Web authoring, Web site design, weight fitness, weight training, Western civilization, Western literature, Western religions, woodworking, world civilizations, world cultures, world geography, world governments, world history, world history-AP, world issues, world literature, world religions, world religions, world studies, world wide web design, World-Wide-Web publishing, writing, writing workshop, yearbook, youth culture.

Graduation Requirements Peace studies, physical education (includes health), practical arts, Quakerism and ethics, science, senior internship, senior project, U.S. history, Quaker Studies. Community service is required.

Special Academic Programs Advanced Placement exam preparation; honors section; accelerated programs; independent study; term-away projects; academic accommodation for the gifted, the musically talented, and the artistically talented.

College Admission Counseling 12 students graduated in 2009; 11 went to college, including Old Dominion University; Virginia Wesleyan College. Other: 1 went to work. Median SAT critical reading: 600, median SAT math: 550, median composite ACT: 22.

Student Life Upper grades have specified standards of dress, student council, honor system. Discipline rests equally with students and faculty. Attendance at religious services is required.

Tuition and Aid Day student tuition: $11,300. Tuition installment plan (Insured Tuition Payment Plan, monthly payment plans, individually arranged payment plans, Layaway Plans, Balloon Payment Plans, extended payment plans). Merit scholarship grants, need-based scholarship grants available. In 2009–10, 25% of upper-school students received aid; total upper-school merit-scholarship money awarded: $10,000. Total amount of financial aid awarded in 2009–10: $45,000.

Admissions Traditional secondary-level entrance grade is 9. For fall 2009, 22 students applied for upper-level admission, 21 were accepted, 16 enrolled. Achievement tests or admissions testing required. Deadline for receipt of application materials: none. Application fee required: $25. Interview required.

Athletics Interscholastic: basketball (boys, girls), lacrosse (b), volleyball (g); coed interscholastic: independent competitive sports, soccer, softball; coed intramural: cross-country running, fitness, hiking/backpacking, indoor soccer, physical fitness. 2 PE instructors, 8 coaches.

Computers Computers are regularly used in all academic, animation, architecture, art, commercial art, design, drawing and design, media arts, multimedia, newspaper, photography, photojournalism, publishing, technology, video film production, Web site design, yearbook classes. Computer network features include on-campus library services, online commercial services, Internet access. The school has a published electronic and media policy.

Contact Ms. Jacquie Whitt, Director of Admissions. 757-428-7534 Ext. 104. Fax: 757-428-7511. E-mail: tjacquie@friends-school.org. Web site: www.friends-school.org.

VISITATION ACADEMY OF ST. LOUIS COUNTY

3020 North Ballas Road
St. Louis, Missouri 63131
Head of School: Mrs. Rosalie Henry

General Information Coeducational day (boys' only in lower grades) college-preparatory, arts, and technology school, affiliated with Roman Catholic Church. Boys grade PK, girls grades PK–12. Founded: 1833. Setting: suburban. 30-acre campus. 1 building on campus. Approved or accredited by Independent Schools Association of the Central States, National Catholic Education Association, North Central Association of Colleges and Schools, and Missouri Department of Education. Member of National Association of Independent Schools. Endowment: $7 million. Total enrollment: 633. Upper school average class size: 18. Upper school faculty-student ratio: 1:9. Upper School students typically attend 5 days per week. The average school day consists of 6 hours and 30 minutes.

Upper School Student Profile Grade 7: 70 students (70 girls); Grade 8: 76 students (76 girls); Grade 9: 98 students (98 girls); Grade 10: 62 students (62 girls); Grade 11: 72 students (72 girls); Grade 12: 90 students (90 girls). 85% of students are Roman Catholic.

Faculty School total: 53. In upper school: 9 men, 44 women; 31 have advanced degrees.

Subjects Offered Algebra, American history, American literature, anatomy, art, art history, Bible studies, biology, calculus, ceramics, chemistry, computer art, computer math, computer programming, computer science, creative writing, drama, earth science, economics, English, English literature, European history, expository writing, fine arts, French, geography, geometry, government/civics, grammar, health, history, journalism, keyboarding, Latin, mathematics, music, photography, physical education, physical science, physics, psychology, science, social studies, Spanish, speech, theater, theology, trigonometry, world literature.

Graduation Requirements Arts and fine arts (art, music, dance, drama), computers, electives, English, foreign language, mathematics, physical education (includes health), science, social studies (includes history), theology, 120 hours of community service.

Special Academic Programs 12 Advanced Placement exams for which test preparation is offered; honors section; independent study; study at local college for college credit.

College Admission Counseling 70 students graduated in 2010; all went to college, including Rhodes College; Saint Louis University; University of Missouri; University of Notre Dame; Washington University in St. Louis. Median SAT critical reading: 640, median SAT math: 620, median SAT writing: 635, median composite ACT: 29.

Student Life Upper grades have uniform requirement, student council. Discipline rests primarily with faculty. Attendance at religious services is required.

Summer Programs Sports programs offered; session focuses on sports camps; held on campus; accepts girls; open to students from other schools. 100 students usually enrolled.

Tuition and Aid Day student tuition: $14,885. Tuition installment plan (FACTS Tuition Payment Plan). Need-based scholarship grants available. In 2010–11, 10% of upper-school students received aid.

Admissions Traditional secondary-level entrance grade is 7. For fall 2010, 100 students applied for upper-level admission, 95 were accepted, 66 enrolled. SSAT required. Deadline for receipt of application materials: January 21. Application fee required: $75. On-campus interview required.

Athletics Interscholastic: basketball, cheering, cross-country running, diving, field hockey, golf, lacrosse, racquetball, soccer, softball, swimming and diving, tennis, volleyball; intramural: basketball, dance, field hockey, soccer, softball, volleyball. 4 PE instructors, 17 coaches, 1 athletic trainer.

Computers Computers are regularly used in art, English, foreign language, history, mathematics, science, theology classes. Computer network features include on-campus library services, Internet access, wireless campus network, Internet filtering or blocking technology. Campus intranet and student e-mail accounts are available to students. Students grades are available online. The school has a published electronic and media policy.

Contact Mrs. Ashley Giljum, Director of Admission. 314-625-9102. Fax: 314-432-7210. E-mail: agiljum@visitationacademy.org. Web site: www.visitationacademy.org.

WAKEFIELD SCHOOL

4439 Old Tavern Road
PO Box 107
The Plains, Virginia 20198
Head of School: Mr. Peter A. Quinn

General Information Coeducational day college-preparatory and arts school. Grades PS–12. Founded: 1972. Setting: rural. Nearest major city is Washington, DC. 65-acre campus. 6 buildings on campus. Approved or accredited by Association of Independent Schools of Greater Washington, Virginia Association of Independent Schools, and Virginia Department of Education. Total enrollment: 461. Upper school average class size: 14. Upper school faculty-student ratio: 1:14. There are 180 required school days per year for Upper School students. Upper School students typically attend 5 days per week. The average school day consists of 7 hours.

Upper School Student Profile Grade 9: 42 students (14 boys, 28 girls); Grade 10: 45 students (26 boys, 19 girls); Grade 11: 35 students (17 boys, 18 girls); Grade 12: 29 students (11 boys, 18 girls).

Faculty School total: 84. In upper school: 15 men, 13 women; 13 have advanced degrees.

Subjects Offered Acting, Advanced Placement courses, algebra, American government, American history-AP, American literature, art, art history, bell choir, biology, biology-AP, British history, British literature, calculus, calculus-AP, chemistry, chemistry-AP, chorus, classical language, composition, computer applications, computer programming, conservation, drama, dramatic arts, earth science, Eastern world civilizations, ecology, English language and composition-AP, English literature and composition-AP, environmental science, environmental science-AP, European history-AP, French, French language-AP, geometry, geopolitics, government and politics-AP, government/civics, Latin, Latin AP, model United Nations, music, music composition, music history, music theory, music theory-AP, physical fitness, physics, physics-AP, political science, psychology, publications, Spanish, Spanish language-AP, statistics, statistics-AP, studio art, studio art-AP, U.S. history, world civilizations.

Graduation Requirements Advanced math, algebra, American history, American literature, arts, biology, British literature, chemistry, computer literacy, English, geometry, government/civics, grammar, language, physical education (includes health), pre-calculus, world civilizations, 2 interdisciplinary compositions, 2 thesis and portfolio projects, including senior thesis.

Special Academic Programs 11 Advanced Placement exams for which test preparation is offered; honors section; independent study.

College Admission Counseling 33 students graduated in 2009; all went to college, including University of Mary Washington; University of Virginia; Virginia Polytechnic Institute and State University. Mean SAT critical reading: 628, mean SAT math: 591, mean SAT writing: 609, mean combined SAT: 1828.

Student Life Upper grades have uniform requirement, student council, honor system. Discipline rests equally with students and faculty.

Tuition and Aid Day student tuition: $9600–$19,500. Tuition installment plan (FACTS Tuition Payment Plan, monthly payment plans, The Tuition Refund Plan). Need-based scholarship grants available. In 2009–10, 18% of upper-school students received aid. Total amount of financial aid awarded in 2009–10: $1,000,000.

Admissions Traditional secondary-level entrance grade is 9. Admissions testing or SSAT required. Deadline for receipt of application materials: none. Application fee required: $60. Interview required.

Athletics Interscholastic: basketball (boys, girls), field hockey (g), lacrosse (b,g), soccer (b,g), squash (b), strength & conditioning (b,g), tennis (b,g), volleyball (g); intramural: field hockey (g), fitness (b,g), lacrosse (b,g), outdoor activities (b,g), soccer (b,g), squash (b), strength & conditioning (b,g), tennis (b,g), volleyball (g), weight training (b,g); coed interscholastic: aquatics, cross-country running, fitness, golf, physical fitness, squash, swimming and diving; coed intramural: aquatics, cross-country running, squash, swimming and diving. 4 PE instructors, 3 coaches.

Computers Computers are regularly used in computer applications, English, independent study, publications, writing, yearbook classes. Computer network features include on-campus library services, online commercial services, Internet access, wireless campus network, Internet filtering or blocking technology, new Science and Technology building opened in January 2007, student center login/password protected portal for students on new website. Campus intranet, student e-mail accounts, and computer access in designated common areas are available to students. Students grades are available online. The school has a published electronic and media policy. **Contact** Office of Admissions. 540-253-7600. Fax: 540-253-5492. E-mail: admissions@wakefieldschool.org. Web site: www.wakefieldschool.org.

WALDORF HIGH SCHOOL OF MASSACHUSETTS BAY

160 Lexington Street
Belmont, Massachusetts 02478
Head of School: Mara D. White

General Information Coeducational day college-preparatory and arts school. Grades 9–12. Founded: 1996. Setting: suburban. Nearest major city is Boston. 1 building on campus. Approved or accredited by Association of Waldorf Schools of North America, New England Association of Schools and Colleges, and Massachusetts Department of Education. Total enrollment: 50. Upper school average class size: 12. Upper school faculty-student ratio: 1:4. There are 165 required school days per year for Upper School students. Upper School students typically attend 5 days per week. The average school day consists of 6 hours and 30 minutes.

Upper School Student Profile Grade 9: 8 students (5 boys, 3 girls); Grade 10: 15 students (6 boys, 9 girls); Grade 11: 14 students (3 boys, 11 girls); Grade 12: 13 students (10 boys, 3 girls).

Faculty School total: 12. In upper school: 6 men, 6 women; 7 have advanced degrees.

Subjects Offered Algebra, American history, American literature, American studies, analysis and differential calculus, anatomy and physiology, ancient history, ancient world history, art, art history, astronomy, athletics, Bible as literature, biology, bookbinding, botany, calculus, chamber groups, chemistry, child development, chorus, classical Greek literature, college admission preparation, college counseling, college placement, community service, computer applications, computer resources, creative writing, current events, drama, drama performance, earth science, electives, English, English literature, epic literature, European history, expository writing, fine arts, fitness, geography, geometry, global studies, grammar, history of architecture, history of music, Internet research, jazz ensemble, mathematics, medieval/Renaissance history, model United Nations, modern history, music, Native American history, orchestra, painting, physical education, physics, play production, poetry, projective geometry, Russian literature, SAT preparation, senior internship, senior seminar, Spanish, theory of knowledge, trigonometry, U.S. government, woodworking, world history, world literature, writing, yearbook, zoology.

Graduation Requirements Algebra, arts and fine arts (art, music, dance, drama), chemistry, English, English literature, foreign language, geometry, global studies, mathematics, music, performing arts, physical education (includes health), physics, practical arts, science, social studies (includes history). Community service is required.

Special Academic Programs Honors section; independent study; term-away projects; study abroad.

College Admission Counseling 14 students graduated in 2010; 8 went to college, including Boston University; Connecticut College; Oberlin College; University of California, Santa Barbara; Wheaton College. Other: 6 went to work.

Student Life Upper grades have specified standards of dress, student council. Discipline rests primarily with faculty.

Tuition and Aid Day student tuition: $22,900. Tuition installment plan (Insured Tuition Payment Plan, monthly payment plans, individually arranged payment plans). Tuition reduction for siblings, merit scholarship grants, need-based scholarship grants available. In 2010–11, 44% of upper-school students received aid; total upper-school merit-scholarship money awarded: $29,648. Total amount of financial aid awarded in 2010–11: $263,200.

Admissions Traditional secondary-level entrance grade is 9. For fall 2010, 20 students applied for upper-level admission, 19 were accepted, 13 enrolled. Essay, grade equivalent tests or math and English placement tests required. Deadline for receipt of application materials: none. Application fee required: $50. Interview required.

Athletics Interscholastic: basketball (boys, girls), soccer (b,g); coed intramural: running. 1 PE instructor, 3 coaches.

Computers Computers are regularly used in college planning, creative writing, current events, independent study, mathematics, research skills, SAT preparation, Spanish, yearbook classes. Computer network features include Internet access, Internet filtering or blocking technology. Computer access in designated common areas is available to students. The school has a published electronic and media policy. **Contact** Susan Morris, Enrollment Coordinator. 617-489-6600 Ext. 11. Fax: 617-489-6619. E-mail: s.morris@waldorfhighschool.org. Web site: www. waldorfhighschool.org.

THE WALDORF SCHOOL OF SARATOGA SPRINGS

122 Regent Street
Saratoga Springs, New York 12866
Head of School: Ms. Katherine Scharff

General Information Coeducational day college-preparatory, general academic, and arts school. Grades PK–12. Founded: 1981. Setting: suburban. 5-acre campus. 1 building on campus. Approved or accredited by Association of Waldorf Schools of North America, California Association of Independent Schools, and New York Department of Education. Total enrollment: 233. Upper school average class size: 13. Upper school faculty-student ratio: 1:3. There are 170 required school days per year for Upper School students. Upper School students typically attend 5 days per week. The average school day consists of 6 hours and 20 minutes.

Upper School Student Profile Grade 9: 11 students (5 boys, 6 girls); Grade 10: 10 students (8 boys, 2 girls); Grade 11: 12 students (2 boys, 10 girls); Grade 12: 14 students (8 boys, 6 girls).

Faculty School total: 24. In upper school: 6 men, 9 women; 7 have advanced degrees.

Graduation Requirements Art, chemistry, earth science, English, eurythmy, foreign language, history, life science, mathematics, music, physical education (includes health), physics, juniors must complete an internship program, seniors must complete a senior project.

Special Academic Programs Study abroad.

College Admission Counseling 13 students graduated in 2009; 11 went to college, including Drexel University; Eugene Lang College The New School for Liberal Arts; Massachusetts Institute of Technology; Rhode Island School of Design; University at Albany, State University of New York; Wesleyan University. Other: 2 had other specific plans.

Student Life Upper grades have specified standards of dress, honor system. Discipline rests primarily with faculty.

Tuition and Aid Day student tuition: $12,800. Tuition installment plan (monthly payment plans). Tuition reduction for siblings, need-based scholarship grants available. In 2009–10, 30% of upper-school students received aid.

Admissions Traditional secondary-level entrance grade is 9. Non-standardized placement tests required. Deadline for receipt of application materials: none. No application fee required. Interview required.

Athletics Interscholastic: cross-country running (boys, girls). 2 PE instructors.

Computers The school has a published electronic and media policy. **Contact** Ms. Anne Maguire, Enrollment Director. 518-587-2224. Fax: 518-581-1466. E-mail: admissions@waldorfsaratoga.org. Web site: www.waldorfsaratoga.org/.

THE WALKER SCHOOL

700 Cobb Parkway North
Marietta, Georgia 30062
Head of School: Donald B. Robertson

General Information Coeducational day college-preparatory, arts, bilingual studies, and technology school. Grades PK–12. Founded: 1957. Setting: suburban. Nearest major city is Atlanta. 45-acre campus. 7 buildings on campus. Approved or accredited by Southern Association of Colleges and Schools, Southern Association of Independent Schools, and Georgia Department of Education. Member of National Association of Independent Schools and Secondary School Admission Test Board. Endowment: $1.9 million. Total enrollment: 1,039. Upper school average class size: 14. Upper school faculty-student ratio: 1:14. There are 178 required school days per year for Upper School students. Upper School students typically attend 5 days per week. The average school day consists of 7 hours.

Upper School Student Profile Grade 9: 79 students (40 boys, 39 girls); Grade 10: 101 students (49 boys, 52 girls); Grade 11: 89 students (40 boys, 49 girls); Grade 12: 80 students (39 boys, 41 girls).

Faculty School total: 135. In upper school: 27 men, 15 women; 42 have advanced degrees.

Subjects Offered Acting, advanced chemistry, advanced computer applications, algebra, American history, American literature, anatomy, art, art education, art history, art-AP, astronomy, athletics, band, Bible, biology, biology-AP, botany, calculus, calculus-AP, ceramics, chemistry, chemistry-AP, computer programming, computer science, computer science-AP, computer technologies, creative writing, dance, drama, driver education, economics, economics-AP, English, English-AP, environmental science-AP, ethics, European history, expository writing, film history, fine arts, fitness, French, French language-AP, French literature-AP, genetics, geometry, German, German-AP, government and politics-AP, government-AP, government/civics, grammar, history, history-AP, Latin, Latin-AP, literature and composition-AP, mathematics, music, musical theater, newspaper, orchestra, personal finance, physical education, physics, physics-AP, play production, psychology, public speaking, science, social studies, Spanish, Spanish-AP, statistics, statistics-AP, trigonometry, U.S. history-AP, Web site design, world history, world history-AP, world literature, writing, zoology.

Graduation Requirements Advanced Placement courses, American government, arts and fine arts (art, music, dance, drama), computer science, economics, English, English composition, English literature, foreign language, mathematics, physical education (includes health), science, social studies (includes history).

Special Academic Programs 25 Advanced Placement exams for which test preparation is offered; honors section; independent study; study abroad; academic accommodation for the gifted and the artistically talented.

College Admission Counseling 101 students graduated in 2010; all went to college, including Auburn University; Furman University; Georgia Institute of Technology; University of Georgia; Vanderbilt University; Virginia Polytechnic Institute and State University. Median SAT critical reading: 600, median SAT math: 640, median SAT writing: 590, median combined SAT: 1810, median composite ACT: 27. 43% scored over 600 on SAT critical reading, 64% scored over 600 on SAT math, 47% scored over 600 on SAT writing, 59% scored over 1800 on combined SAT.

Student Life Upper grades have specified standards of dress, student council, honor system. Discipline rests equally with students and faculty.

Summer Programs Enrichment programs offered; session focuses on prep for school for new students; held on campus; accepts boys and girls; open to students from other schools. 60 students usually enrolled. 2011 schedule: June 15 to August 10.

Tuition and Aid Day student tuition: $17,110. Tuition installment plan (monthly payment plans, school's own payment plan). Need-based scholarship grants available. In 2010–11, 15% of upper-school students received aid. Total amount of financial aid awarded in 2010–11: $1,000,000.

Admissions Traditional secondary-level entrance grade is 9. For fall 2010, 55 students applied for upper-level admission, 45 were accepted, 23 enrolled. Otis-Lennon School Ability Test, SSAT or WISC III or Stanford Achievement Test required. Deadline for receipt of application materials: February 21. Application fee required: $75. On-campus interview required.

Athletics Interscholastic: aquatics (boys, girls), baseball (b), basketball (b,g), cheering (g), dance (g), dance squad (g), dance team (g), football (b), golf (b,g), physical training (b,g), soccer (b,g), softball (g), swimming and diving (b,g), tennis (b,g), track and field (b,g), volleyball (g), wrestling (b); intramural: aerobics (g), bowling (b,g), flag football (g), golf (b,g), strength & conditioning (b,g), weight training (b,g); coed interscholastic: cricket, cross-country running, dance, diving, fitness, golf, swimming and diving; coed intramural: bowling, cricket, fencing, fishing, fly fishing, golf, rugby. 8 PE instructors, 9 coaches, 2 athletic trainers.

Computers Computers are regularly used in art, drawing and design, English, foreign language, history, information technology, introduction to technology, literary magazine, mathematics, news writing, newspaper, science, writing classes. Computer network features include on-campus library services, online commercial services, Internet access, wireless campus network, Internet filtering or blocking technology. Student e-mail accounts are available to students. Students grades are available online. The school has a published electronic and media policy.

Contact Patricia H. Mozley, Director of Admission. 678-581-6921. Fax: 770-514-8122. E-mail: patty.mozley@thewalkerschool.org. Web site: www.thewalkerschool.org.

WALNUT HILL SCHOOL

12 Highland Street
Natick, Massachusetts 01760-2199
Head of School: Dr. Joseph A. Keefe

General Information Coeducational boarding and day college-preparatory and arts school. Grades 9–PG. Founded: 1893. Setting: suburban. Nearest major city is Boston. Students are housed in single-sex dormitories. 30-acre campus. 19 buildings on campus. Approved or accredited by New England Association of Schools and Colleges and Massachusetts Department of Education. Member of National Association of Independent Schools and Secondary School Admission Test Board. Endowment: $12 million. Total enrollment: 298. Upper school average class size: 14. Upper school faculty-student ratio: 1:6.

Upper School Student Profile Grade 9: 43 students (15 boys, 28 girls); Grade 10: 71 students (19 boys, 52 girls); Grade 11: 86 students (27 boys, 59 girls); Grade 12: 98 students (36 boys, 62 girls). 80% of students are boarding students. 31% are state residents. 32 states are represented in upper school student body. 32% are international students. International students from Brazil, Canada, China, Japan, Republic of Korea, and Taiwan; 11 other countries represented in student body.

Faculty School total: 51. In upper school: 24 men, 27 women; 47 have advanced degrees; 20 reside on campus.

Subjects Offered 20th century world history, 3-dimensional art, acting, advanced chemistry, advanced math, algebra, American history, American literature, art history, arts, ballet, ballet technique, biology, calculus, ceramics, chemistry, choral music,

choreography, chorus, classical music, college counseling, community service, creative writing, dance, directing, drama, drawing, English, English literature, environmental science, ESL, fine arts, French, geometry, health, history, history of dance, jazz dance, mathematics, modern dance, music history, music theory, musical theater, musical theater dance, opera, orchestra, painting, photography, physics, piano, poetry, pre-calculus, research seminar, science, sculpture, set design, Shakespeare, social studies, Spanish, stage design, technical theater, theater, theater design and production, theater production, U.S. history, visual and performing arts, visual arts, vocal music, voice, voice ensemble, world history, writing.

Graduation Requirements Arts, English, foreign language, mathematics, science, social studies (includes history), U.S. history, completion of arts portfolio, body of writing, or participation in performing arts ensembles and/or solo recital.

Special Academic Programs Advanced Placement exam preparation; honors section; independent study; academic accommodation for the gifted, the musically talented, and the artistically talented; ESL (35 students enrolled).

College Admission Counseling 98 students graduated in 2009; all went to college, including McGill University; New England Conservatory of Music; Rhode Island School of Design; Rice University; Smith College; The Boston Conservatory. Median SAT critical reading: 590, median SAT math: 580, median SAT writing: 580, median composite ACT: 26.

Student Life Upper grades have student council. Discipline rests equally with students and faculty.

Tuition and Aid Day student tuition: $32,800; 7-day tuition and room/board: $42,840. Tuition installment plan (Insured Tuition Payment Plan, Academic Management Services Plan, monthly payment plans). Need-based scholarship grants available. In 2009–10, 52% of upper-school students received aid. Total amount of financial aid awarded in 2009–10: $2,900,000.

Admissions Traditional secondary-level entrance grade is 10. For fall 2009, 407 students applied for upper-level admission, 178 were accepted, 119 enrolled. Any standardized test, audition, TOEFL or SLEP or writing sample required. Deadline for receipt of application materials: February 1. Application fee required: $65. Interview recommended.

Athletics Intramural: self defense (girls); coed intramural: aerobics, aerobics/dance, ballet, dance, fitness, modern dance, outdoor activities, physical fitness, physical training, self defense, yoga. 3 athletic trainers.

Computers Computer network features include on-campus library services, Internet access, wireless campus network, Internet filtering or blocking technology. Campus intranet, student e-mail accounts, and computer access in designated common areas are available to students. The school has a published electronic and media policy.

Contact Lorie K. Komlyn '88, JD, Dean for Admission and Placement. 508-650-5020. Fax: 508-655-3726. E-mail: admissions@walnuthillarts.org. Web site: www.walnuthillarts.org.

WARING SCHOOL

35 Standley Street
Beverly, Massachusetts 01915
Head of School: Mr. Peter L. Smick

General Information Coeducational day college-preparatory school. Grades 6–12. Founded: 1972. Setting: suburban. Nearest major city is Boston. 32-acre campus. 6 buildings on campus. Approved or accredited by Association of Independent Schools in New England and New England Association of Schools and Colleges. Endowment: $4 million. Total enrollment: 150. Upper school average class size: 14. Upper school faculty-student ratio: 1:8. There are 170 required school days per year for Upper School students. Upper School students typically attend 5 days per week. The average school day consists of 9 hours.

Upper School Student Profile Grade 6: 13 students (5 boys, 8 girls); Grade 7: 17 students (8 boys, 9 girls); Grade 8: 24 students (11 boys, 13 girls); Grade 9: 27 students (12 boys, 15 girls); Grade 10: 27 students (16 boys, 11 girls); Grade 11: 20 students (7 boys, 13 girls); Grade 12: 22 students (9 boys, 13 girls).

Faculty School total: 45. In upper school: 15 men, 15 women; 17 have advanced degrees.

Subjects Offered Adolescent issues, advanced biology, advanced math, Advanced Placement courses, African studies, algebra, American studies, athletics, biology, calculus, chemistry, chorus, college counseling, drama, drawing, earth science, European history, European literature, fine arts, French, French language-AP, functions, graphic design, great books, music appreciation, music performance, music theory, photography, physics, statistics, theater, theater arts, trigonometry, writing, yearbook.

Graduation Requirements Advanced math, algebra, arts and fine arts (art, music, dance, drama), biology, chemistry, drawing, English, foreign language, French, geometry, history, literature, mathematics, music, physical education (includes health), physics, science, social sciences, writing, musical performance.

Special Academic Programs 2 Advanced Placement exams for which test preparation is offered; honors section; independent study; term-away projects; study abroad; academic accommodation for the gifted, the musically talented, and the artistically talented.

College Admission Counseling 24 students graduated in 2010; all went to college, including Ithaca College; Kenyon College; New York University; University of Massachusetts Amherst; University of Southern California; Wesleyan University. Median SAT critical reading: 680, median SAT math: 610, median SAT writing: 680.

Waring School

Mean combined SAT: 1960. 83% scored over 600 on SAT critical reading, 63% scored over 600 on SAT math, 88% scored over 600 on SAT writing, 75% scored over 1800 on combined SAT.

Student Life Upper grades have specified standards of dress, honor system. Discipline rests primarily with faculty.

Summer Programs Art/fine arts programs offered; session focuses on arts camp & music camp; held on campus; accepts boys and girls; open to students from other schools. 115 students usually enrolled. 2011 schedule: July 6 to August 15. Application deadline: February 1.

Tuition and Aid Day student tuition: $24,557. Tuition installment plan (Insured Tuition Payment Plan, monthly payment plans, TMS). Need-based scholarship grants available. In 2010–11, 32% of upper-school students received aid. Total amount of financial aid awarded in 2010–11: $541,926.

Admissions Traditional secondary-level entrance grade is 9. For fall 2010, 25 students applied for upper-level admission, 13 were accepted, 8 enrolled. Deadline for receipt of application materials: January 20. Application fee required: $50. On-campus interview required.

Athletics Interscholastic: basketball (boys, girls), lacrosse (b,g), soccer (b,g); coed interscholastic: cross-country running; coed intramural: basketball, dance, fitness, lacrosse, mountain biking, physical fitness, running, soccer, yoga. 11 coaches.

Computers Computers are regularly used in all academic, literary magazine, mathematics, music, publications, science, writing, yearbook classes. Computer network features include on-campus library services, Internet access, wireless campus network, Internet filtering or blocking technology. Computer access in designated common areas is available to students. The school has a published electronic and media policy.

Contact Ms. Dorothy Wang, Assistant Head of School and Director of Admissions. 978-927-8793 Ext. 226. Fax: 978-921-2107. E-mail: dwang@waringschool.org. Web site: www.waringschool.org.

WASATCH ACADEMY

120 South 100 West

Mt. Pleasant, Utah 84647

Head of School: Mr. Joseph Loftin

General Information Coeducational boarding and day college-preparatory, arts, bilingual studies, technology, and debate school. Grades 8–12. Founded: 1875. Setting: small town. Nearest major city is Provo. Students are housed in single-sex dormitories. 30-acre campus. 19 buildings on campus. Approved or accredited by European Council of International Schools, Northwest Association of Schools and Colleges, Pacific Northwest Association of Independent Schools, The Association of Boarding Schools, and Utah Department of Education. Member of National Association of Independent Schools. Endowment: $1 million. Total enrollment: 250. Upper school average class size: 13. Upper school faculty-student ratio: 1:10.

Upper School Student Profile Grade 9: 29 students (18 boys, 11 girls); Grade 10: 68 students (36 boys, 32 girls); Grade 11: 75 students (40 boys, 35 girls); Grade 12: 77 students (40 boys, 37 girls); Postgraduate: 1 student (1 boy). 98% of students are boarding students. 19% are state residents. 24 states are represented in upper school student body. 45% are international students. International students from China, Germany, Mali, Republic of Korea, Taiwan, and Viet Nam; 30 other countries represented in student body.

Faculty School total: 53. In upper school: 25 men, 26 women; 19 have advanced degrees; 48 reside on campus.

Subjects Offered Acting, advanced studio art-AP, advanced TOEFL/grammar, algebra, anatomy, ballet, biology, biology-AP, calculus-AP, ceramics, chemistry, chemistry-AP, choir, college counseling, college placement, comedy, community garden, community service, dance, design, drama, drawing, drawing and design, driver education, earth science, electronic music, English, English-AP, equine science, ESL, European history-AP, fencing, film, filmmaking, fine arts, forensics, French, geography, geology, global issues, golf, guitar, honors algebra, honors English, honors U.S. history, Japanese, jewelry making, Latin, learning strategies, math applications, music, music theory, outdoor education, painting, performing arts, philosophy, photography, physical education, physical science, physics, piano, play production, pottery, pre-calculus, reading, SAT/ACT preparation, Spanish, Spanish-AP, speech and debate, stained glass, statistics-AP, study skills, theater, TOEFL preparation, U.S. history, U.S. history-AP, weightlifting, Western civilization, woodworking, world religions, yoga.

Graduation Requirements Arts and fine arts (art, music, dance, drama), computer literacy, English, foreign language, mathematics, physical education (includes health), science, social sciences, social studies (includes history), U.S. history, outdoor, cultural, community service, and recreational requirements.

Special Academic Programs Advanced Placement exam preparation; honors section; accelerated programs; independent study; study at local college for college credit; programs in English, mathematics, general development for dyslexic students; ESL (29 students enrolled).

College Admission Counseling 69 students graduated in 2010; 66 went to college, including Boston University; Lewis & Clark College; University of California, Berkeley; University of Pennsylvania; University of San Diego; University of Utah. Other: 1 went to work, 1 entered a postgraduate year, 1 had other specific plans.

Median SAT critical reading: 500, median SAT math: 480, median composite ACT: 22. 13% scored over 600 on SAT critical reading, 9% scored over 600 on SAT math, 27% scored over 26 on composite ACT.

Student Life Upper grades have specified standards of dress, student council, honor system. Discipline rests primarily with faculty.

Summer Programs Remediation, enrichment, advancement, ESL programs offered; session focuses on boarding program transition; held on campus; accepts boys and girls; open to students from other schools. 25 students usually enrolled. 2011 schedule: June 26 to August 6. Application deadline: May 15.

Tuition and Aid Day student tuition: $23,500; 5-day tuition and room/board: $38,400; 7-day tuition and room/board: $41,400. Tuition installment plan (Key Tuition Payment Plan, monthly payment plans, individually arranged payment plans). Merit scholarship grants, need-based scholarship grants, need-based loans available. In 2010–11, 40% of upper-school students received aid; total upper-school merit-scholarship money awarded: $55,000. Total amount of financial aid awarded in 2010–11: $600,000.

Admissions Traditional secondary-level entrance grade is 11. For fall 2010, 304 students applied for upper-level admission, 283 were accepted, 250 enrolled. ACT, ISEE, SSAT, Stanford Achievement Test or TOEFL or SLEP required. Deadline for receipt of application materials: none. Application fee required: $75. Interview required.

Athletics Interscholastic: alpine skiing (boys, girls), baseball (b), basketball (b,g), climbing (b,g), cross-country running (b,g), dance (b,g), dressage (b,g), equestrian sports (b,g), fencing (b,g), golf (b,g), horseback riding (b,g), outdoor activities (b,g), outdoor education (b,g), paint ball (b,g), physical training (b,g), rodeo (b,g), running (b,g), skiing (cross-country) (b,g), skiing (downhill) (b,g), snowboarding (b,g), snowshoeing (b,g), soccer (b,g), tennis (b,g), track and field (b,g), volleyball (g), weight training (b,g); intramural: dance (g), skiing (downhill) (b,g), soccer (b,g), table tennis (b,g); coed interscholastic: aerobics/dance, archery, backpacking, ballet, bicycling, canoeing/kayaking, cheering, climbing, combined training, cross-country running, dance, dressage, equestrian sports, fencing, fishing, fly fishing, golf, hiking/backpacking, horseback riding, kayaking, life saving, martial arts, modern dance, mountain biking, nordic skiing, outdoor activities, paint ball, physical training, rock climbing, rodeo, running, ski jumping, skiing (cross-country), skiing (downhill), snowboarding, snowshoeing, swimming and diving, table tennis, telemark skiing, tennis, track and field, weight training, yoga; coed intramural: aerobics/dance, aquatics, archery, backpacking, badminton, ballet, bicycling, billiards, blading, bowling, canoeing/kayaking, climbing, combined training, cooperative games, dance team, equestrian sports, fishing, fitness, flag football, fly fishing, freestyle skiing, Frisbee, golf, hiking/backpacking, horseback riding, horseshoes, jogging, lacrosse, life saving, modern dance, mountain biking, nordic skiing, outdoor activities, paint ball, physical training, power lifting, rafting, rappelling, rock climbing, running, skateboarding, skiing (downhill), snowshoeing, swimming and diving, table tennis, telemark skiing, ultimate Frisbee, volleyball, weight lifting, weight training, yoga. 2 coaches, 1 athletic trainer.

Computers Computers are regularly used in all academic classes. Computer network features include on-campus library services, online commercial services, Internet access, wireless campus network, Internet filtering or blocking technology. Campus intranet and student e-mail accounts are available to students. Students grades are available online.

Contact Mrs. Carol Reeve, Director of Admissions. 435-462-1415. Fax: 435-462-1450. E-mail: carolreeve@wasatchacademy.org. Web site: www.wasatchacademy.org.

WASHINGTON ACADEMY

66 Cutler Road, PO Box 190

East Machias, Maine 04630

Head of School: Judson McBrine

General Information Coeducational boarding and day college-preparatory, general academic, arts, business, and vocational school. Grades 9–12. Founded: 1792. Setting: small town. Nearest major city is Bangor. Students are housed in single-sex dormitories and host family homes. 65-acre campus. 10 buildings on campus. Approved or accredited by Independent Schools of Northern New England, New England Association of Schools and Colleges, and Maine Department of Education. Endowment: $1.2 million. Total enrollment: 414. Upper school average class size: 16. Upper school faculty-student ratio: 1:11. There are 175 required school days per year for Upper School students. Upper School students typically attend 5 days per week. The average school day consists of 6 hours and 24 minutes.

Upper School Student Profile Grade 9: 97 students (53 boys, 44 girls); Grade 10: 107 students (59 boys, 48 girls); Grade 11: 89 students (47 boys, 42 girls); Grade 12: 121 students (67 boys, 54 girls). 19% of students are boarding students. 81% are state residents. 4 states are represented in upper school student body. 19% are international students. International students from Bermuda, China, Jamaica, Republic of Korea, Spain, and Viet Nam; 10 other countries represented in student body.

Faculty School total: 38. In upper school: 15 men, 23 women; 17 have advanced degrees; 15 reside on campus.

Subjects Offered Accounting, Advanced Placement courses, algebra, American culture, American history-AP, art, art-AP, band, basic language skills, Basic programming, biology, biology-AP, boat building, calculus, calculus-AP, career education internship, carpentry, chemistry, Chinese, Chinese history, chorus, computer-aided design, consumer mathematics, creative writing, digital photography, drafting, drama, ecology, English, English-AP, environmental science, environmental systems, ESL, ESL, field ecology, film, film studies, foreign language, French, geography, geometry, government/civics, guitar, honors algebra, HTML design, industrial technology, jazz band, Latin, Latin-AP, literature, marine studies, mathematics, Microsoft, music, music technology, outdoor education, photography, physical education, physical science, physics, pre-calculus, psychology, sociology, Spanish, Spanish-AP, speech, technical drawing, theater, TOEFL preparation, U.S. history, U.S. history-AP, video, video film production, vocational-technical courses, welding, woodworking, world history.

Graduation Requirements Arts and fine arts (art, music, dance, drama), English, mathematics, physical education (includes health), science, social studies (includes history), one credit of advisor/advisee.

Special Academic Programs Advanced Placement exam preparation; study at local college for college credit; remedial reading and/or remedial writing; remedial math; programs in general development for dyslexic students; special instructional classes for students with learning disabilities; ESL (78 students enrolled).

College Admission Counseling 94 students graduated in 2009; 73 went to college, including Husson University; Maine Maritime Academy; University of Maine. Other: 10 went to work, 3 entered military service, 4 had other specific plans. Mean SAT critical reading: 451, mean SAT math: 452, mean SAT writing: 458. 8% scored over 600 on SAT critical reading, 9% scored over 600 on SAT math, 8% scored over 600 on SAT writing.

Student Life Upper grades have specified standards of dress, student council. Discipline rests primarily with faculty.

Tuition and Aid Day student tuition: $12,000; 7-day tuition and room/board: $35,000. Tuition installment plan (Insured Tuition Payment Plan). Need-based scholarship grants available. In 2009–10, 12% of upper-school students received aid. Total amount of financial aid awarded in 2009–10: $515,561.

Admissions Traditional secondary-level entrance grade is 9. SLEP or TOEFL required. Deadline for receipt of application materials: none. Application fee required: $50. Interview recommended.

Athletics Interscholastic: baseball (boys), basketball (b,g), cross-country running (b,g), football (b), golf (b,g), soccer (b,g), softball (g), swimming and diving (b,g), tennis (b,g), volleyball (g), wrestling (b,g); intramural: basketball (b,g), indoor soccer (b,g); coed interscholastic: cheering; coed intramural: bowling, fencing, outdoor activities, sailing, skiing (cross-country), skiing (downhill), snowboarding, table tennis. 3 PE instructors, 30 coaches.

Computers Computers are regularly used in photography, video film production classes. Computer network features include on-campus library services, online commercial services, Internet access, wireless campus network, Internet filtering or blocking technology. Students grades are available online. The school has a published electronic and media policy.

Contact Kim Gardner, Admissions Coordinator. 207-255-8301 Ext. 207. Fax: 207-255-8303. E-mail: admissions@washingtonacademy.org. Web site: www.washingtonacademy.org.

See Display below and Close-Up on page 860.

WASHINGTON INTERNATIONAL SCHOOL

3100 Macomb Street NW
Washington, District of Columbia 20008
Head of School: Clayton W. Lewis

General Information Coeducational day college-preparatory, bilingual studies, and International Baccalaureate school. Grades PK–12. Founded: 1966. Setting: urban. 6-acre campus. 8 buildings on campus. Approved or accredited by Association of Independent Schools of Greater Washington, European Council of International Schools, International Baccalaureate Organization, Middle States Association of Colleges and Schools, and District of Columbia Department of Education. Member of National Association of Independent Schools and Secondary School Admission Test Board. Languages of instruction: English, Spanish, and French. Endowment: $1.2 million. Total enrollment: 901. Upper school average class size: 15. Upper school faculty-student ratio: 1:7.

Upper School Student Profile Grade 9: 59 students (24 boys, 35 girls); Grade 10: 63 students (36 boys, 27 girls); Grade 11: 64 students (33 boys, 31 girls); Grade 12: 68 students (27 boys, 41 girls).

Faculty School total: 107. In upper school: 15 men, 27 women; 21 have advanced degrees.

Subjects Offered Advanced chemistry, advanced math, art, arts, biology, calculus, chemistry, chorus, community service, comparative government and politics, contemporary history, drama, Dutch, economics, English, English literature, environmental science, ESL, fine arts, French, geography, history, information technology, integrated mathematics, International Baccalaureate courses, Italian, Japanese, literature seminar, music, musical productions, physical education, physics, science, social sciences, Spanish, theater, theory of knowledge, world history.

Graduation Requirements Algebra, arts and fine arts (art, music, dance, drama), biology, chemistry, computer science, English, foreign language, geography, geometry, physical education (includes health), physics, trigonometry, world history, world literature, IB program. Community service is required.

Special Academic Programs International Baccalaureate program; ESL (10 students enrolled).

College Admission Counseling 62 students graduated in 2009; all went to college, including Columbia College; McGill University; New York University; University of Virginia. Mean SAT math: 646, mean SAT writing: 610.

Student Life Upper grades have specified standards of dress, student council, honor system. Discipline rests primarily with faculty.

Tuition and Aid Day student tuition: $28,465. Tuition installment plan (Key Tuition Payment Plan, monthly payment plans, 2-payment plan). Need-based scholarship grants available. In 2009–10, 14% of upper-school students received aid. Total amount of financial aid awarded in 2009–10: $56,483.

Admissions Traditional secondary-level entrance grade is 9. For fall 2009, 63 students applied for upper-level admission, 32 were accepted, 17 enrolled. School's own exam required. Deadline for receipt of application materials: January 10. Application fee required: $50. On-campus interview required.

Athletics Interscholastic: baseball (boys), basketball (b,g), soccer (b,g), softball (g), tennis (b,g), track and field (b,g), volleyball (g); coed interscholastic: cross-country running, golf; coed intramural: equestrian sports. 3 PE instructors, 2 coaches.

Computers Computers are regularly used in all classes. Computer network features include on-campus library services, online commercial services, Internet access, wireless campus network, Internet filtering or blocking technology. Campus intranet and student e-mail accounts are available to students. The school has a published electronic and media policy.

Contact Ms. Schulman Ama, Associate Director for Middle and Upper School Admissions. 202-243-1815. Fax: 202-243-1807. E-mail: schulman@wis.edu. Web site: www.wis.edu.

THE WATERFORD SCHOOL
1480 East 9400 South
Sandy, Utah 84093
Head of School: Mrs. Nancy M. Heuston
General Information Coeducational day college-preparatory, arts, technology, and visual arts, music, photography, dance, and theater school. Grades PK–12. Founded: 1981. Setting: suburban. Nearest major city is Salt Lake City. 50-acre campus. 10 buildings on campus. Approved or accredited by Northwest Association of Schools and Colleges, Pacific Northwest Association of Independent Schools, and Utah Department of Education. Member of National Association of Independent Schools. Total enrollment: 900. Upper school average class size: 16. Upper school faculty-student ratio: 1:5.

Upper School Student Profile Grade 9: 57 students (24 boys, 33 girls); Grade 10: 59 students (29 boys, 30 girls); Grade 11: 62 students (27 boys, 35 girls); Grade 12: 54 students (25 boys, 29 girls).

Faculty School total: 137. In upper school: 46 men, 37 women; 64 have advanced degrees.

Subjects Offered 20th century history, 3-dimensional design, acting, advanced math, Advanced Placement courses, aerobics, algebra, American history, American history-AP, American literature, art, Asian history, baseball, basketball, biology, biology-AP, British literature, calculus, calculus-AP, ceramics, chemistry, chemistry-AP, chorus, computer applications, computer art, computer graphics, computer programming, computer science, computer science-AP, creative writing, debate, drama, drama performance, drama workshop, drawing, ecology, economics, English-AP, European history, European history-AP, French, French-AP, geology, geometry, German, German-AP, Japanese, jazz ensemble, Latin, Latin American literature, music history, music performance, music theater, newspaper, outdoor education, painting, philosophy, photography, physical education, physics, physics-AP, pre-calculus, probability and statistics, psychology, sculpture, Spanish, Spanish-AP, statistics-AP, strings, studio art-AP, trigonometry, voice ensemble, volleyball, weight training, wind ensemble, world literature, writing workshop, yearbook, zoology.

Graduation Requirements 20th century world history, algebra, American history, American literature, biology, British literature, calculus, chemistry, computer science, English, European history, foreign language, geometry, music performance, physics, pre-calculus, trigonometry, visual arts, world history, writing workshop, six terms of physical education or participation on athletic teams.

Special Academic Programs Advanced Placement exam preparation; honors section; independent study; term-away projects; academic accommodation for the gifted, the musically talented, and the artistically talented.

College Admission Counseling 74 students graduated in 2010; all went to college. Mean SAT critical reading: 591, mean SAT math: 598, mean SAT writing: 576, mean combined SAT: 1765, mean composite ACT: 26.

Student Life Upper grades have uniform requirement, student council, honor system. Discipline rests equally with students and faculty.

Summer Programs Enrichment, advancement, sports, art/fine arts, computer instruction programs offered; session focuses on enrichment and advancement; held both on and off campus; held at various locations in Utah and abroad; accepts boys and girls; not open to students from other schools. 100 students usually enrolled. 2011 schedule: June 10 to August 10. Application deadline: March 15.

Tuition and Aid Day student tuition: $17,975. Guaranteed tuition plan. Tuition installment plan (Insured Tuition Payment Plan, monthly payment plans). Tuition reduction for siblings, need-based scholarship grants available. In 2010–11, 10% of upper-school students received aid.

Admissions Traditional secondary-level entrance grade is 9. For fall 2010, 46 students applied for upper-level admission, 31 were accepted, 25 enrolled. ERB CTP IV required. Deadline for receipt of application materials: none. Application fee required: $35. On-campus interview required.

Athletics Interscholastic: basketball (boys, girls), crew (b,g), cross-country running (b,g), golf (b,g), lacrosse (b,g), soccer (b,g), tennis (b,g), volleyball (g); intramural: indoor soccer (b,g); coed interscholastic: alpine skiing, ballet, dance, Frisbee, outdoor education, racquetball, skiing (downhill); coed intramural: aerobics, alpine skiing, backpacking, climbing, crew, mountain biking, nordic skiing, outdoor recreation, rock climbing, wall climbing, weight training. 7 PE instructors, 6 coaches.

Computers Computers are regularly used in animation, college planning, graphic design, library, literary magazine, newspaper, photography, publications, yearbook classes. Computer network features include on-campus library services, Internet access.

Contact Mr. Todd Winters, Director of Admissions. 801-816-2213. Fax: 801-572-1787. E-mail: toddwinters@waterfordschool.org. Web site: www.waterfordschool.org.

WATKINSON SCHOOL
180 Bloomfield Avenue
Hartford, Connecticut 06105
Head of School: Mr. John W. Bracker
General Information Coeducational day college-preparatory, arts, technology, and athletics, global studies school. Grades 6–PG. Founded: 1881. Setting: suburban. 40-acre campus. 6 buildings on campus. Approved or accredited by Association of Independent Schools in New England, Connecticut Association of Independent Schools, New England Association of Schools and Colleges, and Connecticut Department of Education. Member of National Association of Independent Schools and Secondary School Admission Test Board. Endowment: $2.9 million. Total enrollment: 245. Upper school average class size: 11. Upper school faculty-student ratio: 1:6. There are 164 required school days per year for Upper School students. Upper School students typically attend 5 days per week. The average school day consists of 7 hours and 30 minutes.

Upper School Student Profile Grade 9: 46 students (28 boys, 18 girls); Grade 10: 31 students (14 boys, 17 girls); Grade 11: 41 students (25 boys, 16 girls); Grade 12: 44 students (23 boys, 21 girls).

Faculty School total: 50. In upper school: 12 men, 23 women; 20 have advanced degrees.

Subjects Offered African history, algebra, American history, American literature, American sign language, anatomy, ancient world history, art, Asian history, biology, calculus, ceramics, chemistry, creative writing, dance, drama, drawing, earth science, English, English literature, environmental science, environmental studies, European history, expository writing, fine arts, forensics, French, geography, geometry, health, history, internship, life skills, mathematics, modern European history, painting, photography, physics, pottery, science, social studies, Spanish, theater, U.S. history, world history, world literature, writing.

Graduation Requirements Arts and fine arts (art, music, dance, drama), English, foreign language, health and wellness, mathematics, science, social studies (includes history), technology.

Special Academic Programs Independent study; term-away projects; study at local college for college credit; academic accommodation for the gifted, the musically talented, and the artistically talented; remedial reading and/or remedial writing; remedial math; programs in English, mathematics, general development for dyslexic students; ESL (3 students enrolled).

College Admission Counseling 56 students graduated in 2010; 53 went to college, including American University; Brandeis University; Roger Williams University; Sacred Heart University; Syracuse University; University of Connecticut. Other: 2 went to work. Median SAT critical reading: 570, median SAT math: 560, median SAT writing: 550, median combined SAT: 1650, median composite ACT: 25. 42% scored over 600 on SAT critical reading, 40% scored over 600 on SAT math, 32% scored over 600 on SAT writing, 36% scored over 1800 on combined SAT, 38% scored over 26 on composite ACT.

Student Life Upper grades have specified standards of dress, student council. Discipline rests equally with students and faculty.

Summer Programs Remediation, enrichment programs offered; session focuses on academics; held on campus; accepts boys and girls; open to students from other schools. 25 students usually enrolled. 2011 schedule: June 26 to August 8. Application deadline: none.

Tuition and Aid Day student tuition: $31,100. Tuition installment plan (Insured Tuition Payment Plan, Sallie Mae). Need-based scholarship grants available. In 2010–11, 39% of upper-school students received aid. Total amount of financial aid awarded in 2010–11: $1,261,540.

Admissions Traditional secondary-level entrance grade is 9. For fall 2010, 70 students applied for upper-level admission, 44 were accepted, 30 enrolled. ISEE or SSAT required. Deadline for receipt of application materials: February 1. Application fee required: $50. On-campus interview required.

Athletics Interscholastic: baseball (boys), basketball (b,g), crew (b,g), cross-country running (b,g), lacrosse (b,g), soccer (b,g), softball (g), tennis (b,g), volleyball (g); coed interscholastic: crew, cross-country running, tennis, ultimate Frisbee; coed intramural: alpine skiing, ballet, Circus, climbing, combined training, dance, fencing, fitness, juggling, martial arts, outdoor activities, outdoor adventure, physical fitness, physical training, skiing (downhill), snowboarding, street hockey, strength & conditioning, tennis, ultimate Frisbee, volleyball, weight lifting, yoga. 9 coaches, 1 athletic trainer.

Computers Computers are regularly used in computer applications, desktop publishing classes. Computer network features include on-campus library services, online commercial services, Internet access, wireless campus network, Internet filtering or blocking technology. Campus intranet, student e-mail accounts, and computer access in designated common areas are available to students. The school has a published electronic and media policy.

Contact Mrs. Cathy Batson, Admissions Office Assistant. 860-236-5618 Ext. 136. Fax: 860-233-8295. E-mail: cathy_batson@watkinson.org. Web site: www.watkinson.org.

THE WAVERLY SCHOOL

67 West Bellevue Drive
Pasadena, California 91105
Head of School: Ms. Heidi Johnson

General Information Coeducational day college-preparatory and arts school. Grades PK–12. Founded: 1993. Setting: urban. Nearest major city is Los Angeles. 1-acre campus. 7 buildings on campus. Approved or accredited by Western Association of Schools and Colleges. Total enrollment: 327. Upper school average class size: 12. Upper school faculty-student ratio: 1:8.

Upper School Student Profile Grade 9: 33 students (18 boys, 15 girls); Grade 10: 17 students (9 boys, 8 girls); Grade 11: 21 students (11 boys, 10 girls); Grade 12: 22 students (12 boys, 10 girls).

Faculty School total: 49. In upper school: 5 men, 9 women; 9 have advanced degrees.

Subjects Offered 20th century history, algebra, American history-AP, American literature, ancient history, art, biology, biology-AP, calculus-AP, chemistry, college counseling, composition, contemporary issues, creative writing, English composition, English language-AP, English-AP, environmental science-AP, environmental studies, ethics, European history-AP, European literature, filmmaking, French-AP, geometry, history, modern civilization, performing arts, physical science, physics-AP, physiology, pre-calculus, Spanish-AP, statistics, world religions, yearbook.

Graduation Requirements Algebra, American history, American literature, ancient history, art, biology, chemistry, foreign language, geometry, performing arts, physical science, world history. Community service is required.

Special Academic Programs Advanced Placement exam preparation; independent study.

College Admission Counseling 17 students graduated in 2009; all went to college, including Occidental College; Pitzer College; Trinity College; University of California, Berkeley; University of California, Santa Barbara; University of California, Santa Cruz. Median SAT critical reading: 640, median SAT math: 610. 57% scored over 600 on SAT critical reading, 71% scored over 600 on SAT math.

Student Life Upper grades have student council, honor system. Discipline rests primarily with faculty.

Tuition and Aid Day student tuition: $18,220. Tuition installment plan (monthly payment plans). Need-based scholarship grants available. In 2009–10, 8% of upper-school students received aid. Total amount of financial aid awarded in 2009–10: $17,000.

Admissions Traditional secondary-level entrance grade is 9. For fall 2009, 30 students applied for upper-level admission, 15 were accepted, 10 enrolled. Non-standardized placement tests required. Deadline for receipt of application materials: February 1. Application fee required: $100. On-campus interview required.

Athletics Interscholastic: baseball (boys), basketball (b,g), cross-country running (b,g); intramural: cooperative games (b,g); coed interscholastic: equestrian sports, flag football, golf; coed intramural: basketball, cooperative games, fencing, fitness. 2 PE instructors, 10 coaches.

Computers Computers are regularly used in science classes.

Contact Jennifer Dakin, Admissions Director. 626-792-5940. Fax: 626-683-5460. E-mail: Jennifer@thewaverlyschool.org. Web site: www.thewaverlyschool.org.

WAYNE COUNTRY DAY SCHOOL

480 Country Day Road
Goldsboro, North Carolina 27530
Head of School: Mr. Todd Anderson

General Information Coeducational day college-preparatory school. Grades PK–12. Founded: 1968. Setting: rural. Nearest major city is Raleigh. 40-acre campus. 5 buildings on campus. Approved or accredited by Southern Association of Colleges and Schools and North Carolina Department of Education. Total enrollment: 253. Upper school average class size: 19. Upper school faculty-student ratio: 1:15. Upper School students typically attend 5 days per week.

Upper School Student Profile Grade 7: 13 students (5 boys, 8 girls); Grade 8: 14 students (9 boys, 5 girls); Grade 9: 31 students (16 boys, 15 girls); Grade 10: 21 students (15 boys, 6 girls); Grade 11: 23 students (9 boys, 14 girls); Grade 12: 19 students (13 boys, 6 girls).

Faculty School total: 36. In upper school: 5 men, 15 women; 6 have advanced degrees.

Subjects Offered Algebra, art, athletics, baseball, basketball, biology, biology-AP, calculus, calculus-AP, cheerleading, chemistry, choir, civics, college counseling, composition, composition-AP, computers, creative writing, critical writing, earth science, ecology, electives, English, English composition, English language and composition-AP, English language-AP, English literature, English literature and composition-AP, English literature-AP, English-AP, environmental science, film and literature, film history, geography, geometry, health, honors English, honors geometry, honors U.S. history, honors world history, keyboarding, life science, marine biology, multimedia design, music, music theory-AP, North Carolina history, photography, physical education, physical science, physics, pre-algebra, pre-calculus, Spanish, studio art, study skills, theater, theater production, U.S. history, U.S. history-AP, weightlifting, Western civilization, world history, world history-AP, yearbook.

Graduation Requirements Arts and fine arts (art, music, dance, drama), composition, computer science, English, foreign language, mathematics, physical education (includes health), science, social studies (includes history). Community service is required.

Special Academic Programs Advanced Placement exam preparation; honors section; independent study; academic accommodation for the gifted.

College Admission Counseling 17 students graduated in 2009; all went to college, including Davidson College; East Carolina University; North Carolina State University; The University of North Carolina at Chapel Hill; The University of North Carolina Wilmington; University of Southern California.

Student Life Upper grades have specified standards of dress, student council, honor system. Discipline rests equally with students and faculty.

Tuition and Aid Day student tuition: $7900. Guaranteed tuition plan. Need-based scholarship grants available. In 2009–10, 30% of upper-school students received aid.

Admissions Traditional secondary-level entrance grade is 9. Admissions testing required. Deadline for receipt of application materials: none. Application fee required: $60. Interview required.

Athletics Interscholastic: baseball (boys), basketball (b,g), field hockey (g), soccer (b,g), tennis (b,g), volleyball (g), weight training (b,g); coed interscholastic: golf, strength & conditioning, swimming and diving, weight training; coed intramural: soccer. 3 PE instructors, 5 coaches.

Computers Computers are regularly used in English, foreign language, history, science classes. Computer network features include online commercial services, Internet access. The school has a published electronic and media policy.

Contact Ms. Elidia M. Eason, Director of Admissions. 919-736-1045 Ext. 233. Fax: 919-583-9493. E-mail: wcdsadmissions@waynecountryday.com. Web site: www.waynecountryday.com.

WAYNFLETE SCHOOL

360 Spring Street
Portland, Maine 04102
Head of School: Dr. Mark Segar

General Information Coeducational day college-preparatory school. Grades PK–12. Founded: 1898. Setting: urban. Nearest major city is Boston, MA. 37-acre campus. 11 buildings on campus. Approved or accredited by Association of Independent Schools in New England, Independent Schools of Northern New England, New England Association of Schools and Colleges, The College Board, and Maine Department of Education. Member of National Association of Independent Schools. Endowment: $15 million. Total enrollment: 553. Upper school average class size: 13. Upper school faculty-student ratio: 1:12. There are 170 required school days per year for Upper School students. Upper School students typically attend 5 days per week. The average school day consists of 7 hours and 15 minutes.

Upper School Student Profile Grade 9: 63 students (28 boys, 35 girls); Grade 10: 59 students (26 boys, 33 girls); Grade 11: 57 students (28 boys, 29 girls); Grade 12: 61 students (30 boys, 31 girls).

Faculty School total: 77. In upper school: 20 men, 26 women; 29 have advanced degrees.

Subjects Offered African literature, algebra, American history, American literature, art history, biology, calculus, ceramics, chemistry, computer science, creative writing, dance, drama, English, English literature, ethics, European history, expository writing, film, fine arts, French, geometry, government/civics, grammar, health, Latin, Mandarin, marine biology, mathematics, music, physical education, physics, psychology, social studies, Spanish, studio art, theater, trigonometry, world history, world literature, writing.

Graduation Requirements Arts, biology, English, foreign language, geometry, history, mathematics, performing arts, science, sports, U.S. history. Community service is required.

Special Academic Programs Independent study; term-away projects; study abroad.

College Admission Counseling 57 students graduated in 2010; all went to college, including Bates College; Bowdoin College; Connecticut College; Hampshire College; The Colorado College; Wheaton College. Median SAT critical reading: 600, median SAT math: 570, median SAT writing: 610, median combined SAT: 1695, median composite ACT: 26. 53% scored over 600 on SAT critical reading, 44% scored over 600 on SAT math, 60% scored over 600 on SAT writing, 55% scored over 1800 on combined SAT, 59% scored over 26 on composite ACT.

Student Life Upper grades have student council. Discipline rests primarily with faculty.

Summer Programs Enrichment, sports, art/fine arts programs offered; session focuses on Sports, Performing Arts, and Sustainable Ocean Studies; held both on and off campus; held at Fore River Fields, Portland, ME and Casco Bay, Darling Marine Center, Damariscotta River; accepts boys and girls; open to students from other schools. 175 students usually enrolled. 2011 schedule: June 14 to July 29. Application deadline: June 1.

Tuition and Aid Day student tuition: $23,460. Tuition installment plan (Insured Tuition Payment Plan, monthly payment plans). Need-based scholarship grants available. In 2010–11, 31% of upper-school students received aid. Total amount of financial aid awarded in 2010–11: $1,181,749.

Admissions Traditional secondary-level entrance grade is 9. For fall 2010, 62 students applied for upper-level admission, 31 were accepted, 21 enrolled. Writing sample required. Deadline for receipt of application materials: February 10. Application fee required: $40. Interview required.

Athletics Interscholastic: baseball (boys), basketball (b,g), cross-country running (b,g), field hockey (g), golf (b,g), lacrosse (b,g), skiing (cross-country) (b,g), soccer (b,g), tennis (b,g); intramural: backpacking (b,g); coed interscholastic: crew, nordic skiing, rowing, swimming and diving, track and field; coed intramural: dance, fitness walking, modern dance, physical fitness, sailing, swimming and diving, tennis, weight lifting, weight training, yoga. 4 PE instructors, 20 coaches, 1 athletic trainer.

Computers Computers are regularly used in all academic classes. Computer network features include on-campus library services, online commercial services, Internet access, wireless campus network, Internet filtering or blocking technology, academic data bases, including JSTOR, MARVEL, Infotrac, Noodle Tools, and URSUS. Student e-mail accounts and computer access in designated common areas are available to students.

Contact Admission Office. 207-774-5721 Ext. 224. Fax: 207-772-4782. E-mail: admissionoffice@waynflete.org. Web site: www.waynflete.org.

THE WEBB SCHOOL

319 Webb Road East
PO Box 488
Bell Buckle, Tennessee 37020
Head of School: Mr. Ray Broadhead

General Information Coeducational boarding and day college-preparatory, arts, technology, and wilderness leadership school. Boarding grades 7–12, day grades 6–12. Founded: 1870. Setting: rural. Nearest major city is Nashville. Students are housed in single-sex dormitories. 145-acre campus. 17 buildings on campus. Approved or accredited by Southern Association of Colleges and Schools, Southern Association of Independent Schools, Tennessee Association of Independent Schools, The Association of Boarding Schools, and Tennessee Department of Education. Member of National Association of Independent Schools and Secondary School Admission Test Board. Endowment: $22 million. Total enrollment: 310. Upper school average class size: 12. Upper school faculty-student ratio: 1:7. There are 175 required school days per year for Upper School students. Upper School students typically attend 5 days per week. The average school day consists of 6 hours and 30 minutes.

Upper School Student Profile Grade 9: 55 students (29 boys, 26 girls); Grade 10: 63 students (33 boys, 30 girls); Grade 11: 64 students (28 boys, 36 girls); Grade 12: 48 students (25 boys, 23 girls); Postgraduate: 1 student (1 boy). 33% of students are boarding students. 81% are state residents. 10 states are represented in upper school student body. 12% are international students. International students from Brazil, China, Jamaica, Republic of Korea, Taiwan, and Viet Nam; 2 other countries represented in student body.

Faculty School total: 45. In upper school: 20 men, 23 women; 23 have advanced degrees; 17 reside on campus.

Subjects Offered Advanced Placement courses, algebra, American Civil War, American government, American history, American literature, American literature-AP, anatomy, art, art appreciation, art education, art history, arts appreciation, biology, calculus, calculus-AP, ceramics, chemistry, chemistry-AP, choir, chorus, computer programming, computer science, creative writing, drama, driver education, earth science, ecology, economics, economics-AP, English, English literature, English-AP, ESL, ESL, ethical decision making, ethics, European history, fine arts, French, geography, geometry, German, government/civics, grammar, health, history, history of rock and roll, history-AP, honors algebra, honors English, honors geometry, honors U.S. history, journalism, Latin, mathematics, modern European history-AP, music, music appreciation, music history, music performance, music theory, outdoor education, physical education, physics, physics-AP, physiology, piano, poetry, pre-algebra, pre-calculus, psychology, religion, Russian history, science, senior composition, Shakespeare, social sciences, social studies, Spanish, speech, speech communications, statistics, statistics-AP, technology, theater, theater arts, trigonometry, U.S. history, U.S. history-AP, Western civilization, wilderness education, world cultures, world geography, world history, world literature.

Graduation Requirements American government, American history, arts and fine arts (art, music, dance, drama), computer science, economics, English, ethics, foreign language, mathematics, physical education (includes health), science, senior thesis, social sciences, social studies (includes history), speech, Public Exhibition Program-declamation, oration, performance piece, original creative work.

Special Academic Programs 10 Advanced Placement exams for which test preparation is offered; honors section; independent study; study abroad; academic accommodation for the gifted; programs in English, general development for dyslexic students; special instructional classes for deaf students; ESL (18 students enrolled).

College Admission Counseling 56 students graduated in 2010; all went to college, including Georgetown University; Sewanee: The University of the South; The Johns Hopkins University; Vanderbilt University; Wake Forest University; Yale University. Mean SAT critical reading: 561, mean SAT math: 593, mean SAT writing: 568, mean combined SAT: 1722, mean composite ACT: 26.

Student Life Upper grades have uniform requirement, student council, honor system. Discipline rests equally with students and faculty.

Tuition and Aid Day student tuition: $15,700; 5-day tuition and room/board: $28,100; 7-day tuition and room/board: $36,900. Tuition installment plan (monthly payment plans, individually arranged payment plans). Merit scholarship grants, need-based scholarship grants available. In 2010–11, 41% of upper-school students received aid; total upper-school merit-scholarship money awarded: $258,000. Total amount of financial aid awarded in 2010–11: $1,100,000.

Admissions Traditional secondary-level entrance grade is 9. For fall 2010, 150 students applied for upper-level admission, 115 were accepted, 53 enrolled. ISEE, SSAT or TOEFL or SLEP required. Deadline for receipt of application materials: March 1. Application fee required: $50. Interview required.

Athletics Interscholastic: baseball (boys), basketball (b,g), cross-country running (b,g), golf (b,g), lacrosse (b,g), soccer (b,g), volleyball (g); intramural: aerobics (g), aerobics/Nautilus (b,g); coed interscholastic: marksmanship, running, trap and skeet; coed intramural: aerobics/Nautilus, aquatics, backpacking, badminton, ballet, bowling, canoeing/kayaking, climbing, combined training, fishing, fitness, fitness walking, fly fishing, Frisbee, hiking/backpacking, horseback riding, kayaking, mountain biking, outdoor activities, physical fitness, physical training, rock climbing, ropes courses, skeet shooting, table tennis, ultimate Frisbee, weight lifting, weight training, wilderness survival. 1 PE instructor, 17 coaches, 1 athletic trainer.

Computers Computers are regularly used in computer applications, English, foreign language, history, mathematics, science, writing classes. Computer network features include on-campus library services, online commercial services, Internet access, wireless campus network, Internet filtering or blocking technology. Campus intranet, student e-mail accounts, and computer access in designated common areas are available to students. Students grades are available online. The school has a published electronic and media policy.

Contact Mrs. Julie Harris, Director of Admissions. 931-389-6003. Fax: 931-389-6657. E-mail: admissions@webbschool.com. Web site: www.thewebbschool.com.

WEBB SCHOOL OF KNOXVILLE

9800 Webb School Drive
Knoxville, Tennessee 37923-3399
Head of School: Mr. Scott L. Hutchinson

General Information Coeducational day college-preparatory, arts, religious studies, and technology school. Grades K–12. Founded: 1955. Setting: urban. Nearest major city is Chattanooga. 108-acre campus. 6 buildings on campus. Approved or accredited by Southern Association of Colleges and Schools, Southern Association of Independent Schools, and Tennessee Department of Education. Member of National Association of Independent Schools and Secondary School Admission Test Board. Endowment: $5.3 million. Total enrollment: 1,040. Upper school average class size: 15. Upper school faculty-student ratio: 1:10. There are 175 required school days per year for Upper School students. Upper School students typically attend 5 days per week. The average school day consists of 8 hours and 5 minutes.

Upper School Student Profile Grade 9: 127 students (67 boys, 60 girls); Grade 10: 107 students (48 boys, 59 girls); Grade 11: 122 students (58 boys, 64 girls); Grade 12: 108 students (60 boys, 48 girls).

Faculty School total: 102. In upper school: 19 men, 26 women; 36 have advanced degrees.

Subjects Offered 20th century world history, 3-dimensional design, advanced math, algebra, American sign language, anatomy and physiology, anthropology, art history-AP, astronomy, biology, biology-AP, calculus, calculus-AP, ceramics, chamber groups, chemistry, chemistry-AP, civil war history, computer science-AP, concert choir, creative writing, digital imaging, drama, dramatic arts, drawing, economics, English, English composition, English language and composition-AP, English literature, English literature and composition-AP, English-AP, environmental science-AP, film, French, French-AP, freshman foundations, geometry, German, German-AP, government and politics-AP, handbells, history of music, honors algebra, honors English, honors geometry, honors world history, independent study, journalism, Latin, Latin-AP, Mandarin, modern European history-AP, modern world history, music theory-AP, painting, photography, physics, physics-AP, pre-calculus, printmaking, probability and statistics, psychology, psychology-AP, science research, Shakespeare, Spanish, Spanish-AP, speech communications, stage design, strings, studio art-AP, theater arts, U.S. government and politics, U.S. government and politics-AP, U.S. history, U.S. history-AP, video film production, wind ensemble, world history, world history-AP, world religions, yearbook.

Graduation Requirements Algebra, American history, arts and fine arts (art, music, dance, drama), biology, chemistry, electives, English, foreign language, freshman foundations, geometry, mathematics, physical education (includes health), public service, science, world history, world religions, public speaking (two chapel talks), 25 hours of community service per year.

Special Academic Programs 22 Advanced Placement exams for which test preparation is offered; honors section; independent study; study abroad; remedial reading and/or remedial writing; remedial math.

College Admission Counseling 118 students graduated in 2010; 117 went to college, including Belmont University; New York University; The University of Alabama at Birmingham; The University of Tennessee; University of Mississippi; University of Virginia. Mean SAT critical reading: 612, mean SAT math: 597, mean SAT writing: 602, mean composite ACT: 27. 75% scored over 600 on SAT critical reading, 75% scored over 600 on SAT math, 75% scored over 600 on SAT writing, 60% scored over 26 on composite ACT.

Student Life Upper grades have uniform requirement, student council, honor system. Discipline rests equally with students and faculty.

Summer Programs Remediation, enrichment, advancement, sports, art/fine arts programs offered; session focuses on camp and sports-oriented fun; held on campus; accepts boys and girls; open to students from other schools. 1,389 students usually enrolled. 2011 schedule: June 6 to August 5. Application deadline: June 6.

Tuition and Aid Day student tuition: $15,300. Tuition installment plan (monthly payment plans, individually arranged payment plans, Tuition Payments can also be paid in two installments-last calendar day in July and November). Need-based scholarship grants available. In 2010–11, 14% of upper-school students received aid. Total amount of financial aid awarded in 2010–11: $670,132.

Admissions Traditional secondary-level entrance grade is 9. For fall 2010, 52 students applied for upper-level admission, 39 were accepted, 32 enrolled. ISEE required. Deadline for receipt of application materials: January 10. Application fee required: $50. On-campus interview required.

Athletics Interscholastic: baseball (boys), basketball (b,g), bowling (b,g), cheering (g), climbing (b,g), cross-country running (b,g), field hockey (g), football (b), golf (b,g), lacrosse (b), soccer (b,g), softball (g), swimming and diving (b,g), tennis (b,g), track and field (b,g), volleyball (g), wrestling (b); coed interscholastic: sailing; coed intramural: weight training. 26 coaches, 1 athletic trainer.

Computers Computers are regularly used in art, English, foreign language, graphic design, history, journalism, mathematics, music, science, technology, yearbook classes. Computer network features include on-campus library services, Internet access, wireless campus network, Internet filtering or blocking technology. Student e-mail accounts are available to students. Students grades are available online. The school has a published electronic and media policy.

Contact Mrs. Christy Widener, Admissions Administrative Assistant. 865-291-3830. Fax: 865-291-1532. E-mail: christy_widener@webbschool.org. Web site: www.webbschool.org.

THE WEBB SCHOOLS

1175 West Baseline Road
Claremont, California 91711
Head of School: Mrs. Susan A. Nelson

General Information Coeducational boarding and day college-preparatory school. Grades 9–12. Founded: 1922. Setting: suburban. Nearest major city is Pasadena. Students are housed in single-sex dormitories. 70-acre campus. 57 buildings on campus. Approved or accredited by California Association of Independent Schools, The Association of Boarding Schools, Western Association of Schools and Colleges, and California Department of Education. Member of National Association of Independent Schools and Secondary School Admission Test Board. Endowment: $20 million. Total enrollment: 370. Upper school average class size: 16. Upper school faculty-student ratio: 1:7.

Upper School Student Profile Grade 9: 73 students (35 boys, 38 girls); Grade 10: 111 students (57 boys, 54 girls); Grade 11: 94 students (52 boys, 42 girls); Grade 12: 92 students (47 boys, 45 girls). 61% of students are boarding students. 64% are state residents. 13 states are represented in upper school student body. 16% are international students. International students from China, Democratic People's Republic of Korea, Germany, Hong Kong, Kazakhstan, and Nigeria; 22 other countries represented in student body.

Faculty School total: 56. In upper school: 31 men, 25 women; 42 have advanced degrees; 44 reside on campus.

Subjects Offered Algebra, American history, American literature, art, biology, biology-AP, calculus-AP, chemistry, chemistry-AP, chorus, composition-AP, computer math, computer science, discrete mathematics, drama, economics, English, English language and composition-AP, English literature, English literature and composition-AP, environmental science, European history, European history-AP, fine arts, French, French language-AP, French literature-AP, geometry, government/civics, history, leadership, literature, modern European history-AP, museum science, music, orchestra, paleontology, physical education, physical science, physics, physics-AP, poetry, pre-calculus, psychology, SAT preparation, science, social studies, Spanish, Spanish language-AP, Spanish literature-AP, speech, statistics-AP, technology, theater, trigonometry, U.S. history-AP, world history, world history-AP, writing, yearbook.

Graduation Requirements Arts and fine arts (art, music, dance, drama), computer science, English, foreign language, mathematics, physical education (includes health), science, social studies (includes history).

Special Academic Programs Advanced Placement exam preparation; honors section; study at local college for college credit; academic accommodation for the gifted.

College Admission Counseling 97 students graduated in 2009; all went to college, including Harvard University; Stanford University; The Johns Hopkins University; University of Pennsylvania; University of Southern California. Mean combined SAT: 1920.

Student Life Upper grades have specified standards of dress, student council, honor system. Discipline rests equally with students and faculty.

Tuition and Aid Day student tuition: $32,240; 7-day tuition and room/board: $45,330. Tuition installment plan (Insured Tuition Payment Plan, monthly payment plans). Need-based scholarship grants, AchieverLoans (Key Education Resources) available. In 2009–10, 30% of upper-school students received aid. Total amount of financial aid awarded in 2009–10: $25,500.

Admissions Traditional secondary-level entrance grade is 9. For fall 2009, 327 students applied for upper-level admission, 160 were accepted, 109 enrolled. ISEE or SSAT required. Deadline for receipt of application materials: January 30. Application fee required: $75. On-campus interview required.

Athletics Interscholastic: baseball (boys), basketball (b,g), cross-country running (b,g), diving (b,g), football (b), golf (b,g), independent competitive sports (b,g), soccer (b,g), softball (g), swimming and diving (b,g), tennis (b,g), track and field (b,g), volleyball (g), water polo (b,g), winter soccer (b), wrestling (b); intramural: physical fitness (g), weight lifting (b); coed intramural: backpacking, climbing, dance, fitness, fitness walking, Frisbee, hiking/backpacking, outdoor activities, physical fitness, rock climbing, strength & conditioning, surfing, ultimate Frisbee. 12 coaches, 1 athletic trainer.

Computers Computers are regularly used in English, foreign language, graphic design, health, history, mathematics, science classes. Computer network features include on-campus library services, Internet access, Internet filtering or blocking technology. Student e-mail accounts are available to students. The school has a published electronic and media policy.

Contact Mr. Leo G. Marshall, Director of Admission and Financial Aid. 909-482-5214. Fax: 909-445-8269. E-mail: admissions@webb.org. Web site: www.webb.org/admission.

THE WEBER SCHOOL

6751 Roswell Road
Sandy Springs, Georgia 30328
Head of School: Simcha Pearl

General Information Coeducational day college-preparatory, religious studies, and bilingual studies school, affiliated with Jewish faith. Grades 9–12. Founded: 1997. Setting: suburban. Nearest major city is Atlanta. 20-acre campus. 2 buildings on campus. Approved or accredited by Georgia Independent School Association, Southern Association of Colleges and Schools, Southern Association of Independent Schools, The College Board, and Georgia Department of Education. Languages of instruction: English and Hebrew. Total enrollment: 220. Upper school average class size: 16. Upper school faculty-student ratio: 1:8.

Upper School Student Profile 100% of students are Jewish.

Faculty School total: 38. In upper school: 12 men, 26 women; 35 have advanced degrees.

Subjects Offered Advanced chemistry, advanced computer applications, advanced math, Advanced Placement courses, algebra, American government, American history, American history-AP, American literature, American literature-AP, ancient history, art, Bible, Bible studies, biology, biology-AP, British literature, British literature (honors), calculus, calculus-AP, chemistry, chemistry-AP, choir, college admission preparation, college awareness, college counseling, college placement, college planning, composition, composition-AP, computer applications, computer multimedia, critical thinking, digital photography, drama, economics, electives, English, English language and composition-AP, English language-AP, English literature, English literature and composition-AP, literature-AP, environmental science, European history, European history-AP, evolution, experiential education, fine arts, geometry, Hebrew, Hebrew scripture, history, history-AP, Holocaust, honors algebra, honors English, honors geometry, honors U.S. history, honors world history, integrated arts, jazz ensemble, Jewish history, Jewish studies, Judaic studies, Latin, literature, literature and composition-AP, literature-AP, mathematics, modern European history, multimedia, peer counseling, physics, physics-AP, pre-calculus, Rabbinic literature, Spanish, Spanish-AP, student government, studio art, Talmud, U.S. history, U.S. history-AP.

Special Academic Programs 10 Advanced Placement exams for which test preparation is offered; honors section; independent study; study at local college for college credit; study abroad.

College Admission Counseling 36 students graduated in 2009; all went to college, including Columbia University; Cornell College; Tulane University; University of Georgia; University of Maryland, College Park; University of Pennsylvania. Median SAT critical reading: 612, median SAT math: 624, median SAT writing: 639, median combined SAT: 1875.

The Weber School

Student Life Upper grades have specified standards of dress, student council. Discipline rests primarily with faculty. Attendance at religious services is required.
Tuition and Aid Day student tuition: $19,855. Tuition installment plan (FACTS Tuition Payment Plan, individually arranged payment plans, Supplemental Tuition Assistance). Need-based scholarship grants available. In 2009–10, 30% of upper-school students received aid.
Admissions Traditional secondary-level entrance grade is 9. For fall 2009, 82 students applied for upper-level admission, 78 were accepted, 61 enrolled. PSAT and SAT for applicants to grade 11 and 12 or SSAT required. Deadline for receipt of application materials: February 26. Application fee required: $75. On-campus interview required.
Athletics Interscholastic: baseball (boys), basketball (b,g), soccer (b,g), volleyball (g), wrestling (b); coed interscholastic: cross-country running, golf, tennis, track and field. 14 coaches, 1 athletic trainer.
Computers Computers are regularly used in all academic classes. Computer network features include on-campus library services, online commercial services, Internet access, wireless campus network, Internet filtering or blocking technology, wireless lab, learning center. Student e-mail accounts and computer access in designated common areas are available to students. Students grades are available online. The school has a published electronic and media policy.
Contact Rise Arkin, Director of Admissions. 404-917-2500 Ext. 117. Fax: 404-917-2501. E-mail: risearkin@weberschool.org. Web site: www.weberschool.org.

THE WEDIKO SCHOOL AND TREATMENT PROGRAM

Windsor, New Hampshire
See Special Needs Schools section.

THE WELLINGTON SCHOOL

3650 Reed Road
Columbus, Ohio 43220
Head of School: Mr. Robert D. Brisk
General Information Coeducational day college-preparatory, arts, and bilingual studies school. Grades PK–12. Founded: 1982. Setting: suburban. 21-acre campus. 1 building on campus. Approved or accredited by Independent Schools Association of the Central States, Ohio Association of Independent Schools, and Ohio Department of Education. Member of National Association of Independent Schools. Total enrollment: 621. Upper school average class size: 15. Upper school faculty-student ratio: 1:12. Upper School students typically attend 5 days per week. The average school day consists of 7 hours.
Upper School Student Profile Grade 9: 45 students (25 boys, 20 girls); Grade 10: 56 students (24 boys, 32 girls); Grade 11: 48 students (25 boys, 23 girls); Grade 12: 48 students (29 boys, 19 girls).
Faculty School total: 56. In upper school: 15 men, 16 women; 24 have advanced degrees.
Subjects Offered Algebra, art and culture, band, biology, biology-AP, calculus-AP, ceramics, chemistry, chemistry-AP, choir, chorus, computer graphics, creative arts, drama, drawing, earth and space science, economics, English, English-AP, European history-AP, film, finite math, French, French-AP, geometry, government, issues of the 90's, journalism, Latin, Latin-AP, mathematics, modern history, music appreciation, music theory-AP, painting, photography, physical education, physics, printmaking, Spanish, Spanish-AP, speech, strings, studio art-AP, U.S. history, U.S. history-AP, visual arts, voice, Western civilization, word processing, writing, yearbook.
Graduation Requirements 3-dimensional art, arts and fine arts (art, music, dance, drama), English, foreign language, government, lab science, mathematics, physical education (includes health), science, social sciences, social studies (includes history), speech, senior independent project. Community service is required.
Special Academic Programs Advanced Placement exam preparation; honors section; accelerated programs; independent study; study at local college for college credit; study abroad; academic accommodation for the gifted, the musically talented, and the artistically talented; ESL.
College Admission Counseling 49 students graduated in 2010; all went to college, including Elon University; Georgetown University; Miami University; The Ohio State University.
Student Life Upper grades have specified standards of dress, student council. Discipline rests equally with students and faculty.
Summer Programs Enrichment, advancement, sports, art/fine arts programs offered; session focuses on enrichment/active learning; held on campus; accepts boys and girls; open to students from other schools. 50 students usually enrolled. 2011 schedule: June 11 to August 17. Application deadline: none.
Tuition and Aid Day student tuition: $17,825–$18,575. Tuition installment plan (Key Tuition Payment Plan, monthly payment plans, individually arranged payment plans, 2-, 6-, and 10-month payment plans). Merit scholarship grants, need-based scholarship grants, need-based loans available.
Admissions Traditional secondary-level entrance grade is 9. Admissions testing or ERB required. Deadline for receipt of application materials: none. Application fee required: $50. On-campus interview required.

Athletics Interscholastic: baseball (boys), basketball (b,g), diving (b,g), fencing (b,g), golf (b,g), lacrosse (b,g), soccer (b,g), softball (g), tennis (b,g); intramural: basketball (b,g), independent competitive sports (g), lacrosse (g); coed interscholastic: fencing, swimming and diving; coed intramural: canoeing/kayaking, climbing, flag football, martial arts. 2 PE instructors, 15 coaches, 1 athletic trainer.
Computers Computers are regularly used in English, foreign language, library, mathematics, music, newspaper, research skills, science, senior seminar, theater arts, typing, yearbook classes. Computer network features include on-campus library services, online commercial services, Internet access, wireless campus network, Internet filtering or blocking technology, SmartBoards. Campus intranet, student e-mail accounts, and computer access in designated common areas are available to students. Students grades are available online. The school has a published electronic and media policy.
Contact Ms. Lynne Steger, Assistant Director of Admission. 614-324-1647. Fax: 614-442-3286. E-mail: steger@wellington.org. Web site: www.wellington.org.

THE WELL SCHOOL

360 Middle Hancock Road
Peterborough, New Hampshire 03458
Head of School: Lee Garland
General Information Coeducational day college-preparatory, arts, and business school. Grades PK–12. Founded: 1967. Setting: rural. Nearest major city is Keene. 70-acre campus. 4 buildings on campus. Approved or accredited by New Hampshire Department of Education. Total enrollment: 134. Upper school average class size: 15.
Faculty School total: 20. In upper school: 2 men, 9 women.
Special Academic Programs Independent study; term-away projects; study abroad.
Student Life Upper grades have honor system. Discipline rests primarily with faculty.
Tuition and Aid Tuition installment plan (individually arranged payment plans).
Admissions Traditional secondary-level entrance grade is 9. Deadline for receipt of application materials: none. Application fee required: $99. Interview required.
Contact Deborah Schultz, Admissions Associate. 603-924-6908 Ext. 27. Fax: 603-924-2141. E-mail: lgarland@wellschool.org. Web site: www.wellschool.org.

WELLSPRING FOUNDATION

Bethlehem, Connecticut
See Special Needs Schools section.

WELLSPRINGS FRIENDS SCHOOL

3590 West 18th Avenue
Eugene, Oregon 97402
Head of School: Dennis Hoerner
General Information Coeducational day college-preparatory and general academic school, affiliated with Society of Friends; primarily serves underachievers. Grades 9–12. Founded: 1994. Setting: small town. Nearest major city is Portland. 4-acre campus. 2 buildings on campus. Approved or accredited by Northwest Association of Schools and Colleges and Oregon Department of Education. Endowment: $8,000. Total enrollment: 60. Upper school average class size: 10. Upper school faculty-student ratio: 1:8. The average school day consists of 6 hours.
Upper School Student Profile Grade 9: 7 students (7 girls); Grade 10: 12 students (5 boys, 7 girls); Grade 11: 24 students (13 boys, 11 girls); Grade 12: 18 students (7 boys, 11 girls); Grade 13: 1 student (1 girl).
Faculty School total: 10. In upper school: 5 men, 5 women; 4 have advanced degrees.
Subjects Offered 20th century world history, advanced math, algebra, creative writing, English, film, finance, fine arts, geometry, German, government, human sexuality, life science, personal finance, physical education, physical science, poetry, pre-algebra, reading, Spanish, U.S. history.
Graduation Requirements English, foreign language, mathematics, science, social studies (includes history). Community service is required.
Special Academic Programs Independent study; remedial reading and/or remedial writing; remedial math.
College Admission Counseling 21 students graduated in 2010; 8 went to college, including Lane Community College; University of Oregon. Other: 6 went to work, 2 entered military service, 5 had other specific plans.
Student Life Upper grades have student council. Discipline rests equally with students and faculty.
Tuition and Aid Day student tuition: $6000. Tuition installment plan (monthly payment plans, individually arranged payment plans). Need-based scholarship grants available.
Admissions Traditional secondary-level entrance grade is 9. For fall 2010, 15 students applied for upper-level admission, 15 were accepted, 14 enrolled. Deadline for receipt of application materials: none. No application fee required. Interview required.
Athletics Coed Intramural: basketball, bocce, football, Frisbee, hiking/backpacking, physical fitness, skateboarding, table tennis, yoga. 1 PE instructor.

Computers Computers are regularly used in career education, career exploration, music, writing, yearbook classes. Computer network features include Internet access, wireless campus network.

Contact Office Manager. 541-686-1223. Fax: 541-687-1493. E-mail: info@ wellspringsfriends.org. Web site: www.wellspringsfriends.org.

WENTWORTH MILITARY ACADEMY AND JUNIOR COLLEGE

1880 Washington Avenue
Lexington, Missouri 64067-1799
Head of School: Col. William Sellers

General Information Coeducational boarding and day college-preparatory, general academic, arts, business, technology, and military school. Grades 9–12. Founded: 1880. Setting: small town. Nearest major city is Kansas City. Students are housed in coed-by-floor dorms. 137-acre campus. 9 buildings on campus. Approved or accredited by North Central Association of Colleges and Schools and Missouri Department of Education. Endowment: $30 million. Total enrollment: 140. Upper school average class size: 12. Upper school faculty-student ratio: 1:10.

Upper School Student Profile Grade 9: 30 students (20 boys, 10 girls); Grade 10: 37 students (30 boys, 7 girls); Grade 11: 45 students (31 boys, 14 girls); Grade 12: 28 students (22 boys, 6 girls). 99% of students are boarding students. 25% are state residents. 30 states are represented in upper school student body. 10% are international students. International students from China, Guatemala, Mexico, Nicaragua, Oman, and Republic of Korea; 6 other countries represented in student body.

Faculty School total: 27. In upper school: 6 men, 5 women; 10 have advanced degrees; 5 reside on campus.

Subjects Offered ACT preparation, algebra, American history, American literature, art, biology, business, calculus, chemistry, computer science, economics, English, ESL, fine arts, geography, geometry, German, government/civics, health, journalism, JROTC, mathematics, music, physical education, physics, science, Spanish, speech, trigonometry, typing, world history.

Graduation Requirements Arts and fine arts (art, music, dance, drama), computer science, English, foreign language, JROTC, mathematics, physical education (includes health), science, social studies (includes history), community service (hours vary by grade level).

Special Academic Programs Honors section; study at local college for college credit; academic accommodation for the gifted and the musically talented; remedial reading and/or remedial writing; remedial math; special instructional classes for students with Attention Deficit Disorder; ESL (5 students enrolled).

College Admission Counseling 25 students graduated in 2009; all went to college, including Kansas State University; The University of Kansas; United States Air Force Academy; University of Central Missouri; University of Missouri; University of Missouri–St. Louis. Mean combined SAT: 1110, mean composite ACT: 24.

Student Life Upper grades have uniform requirement, student council, honor system. Discipline rests equally with students and faculty.

Tuition and Aid 7-day tuition and room/board: $29,750. Guaranteed tuition plan. Tuition installment plan (individually arranged payment plans, monthly payment plans using ACH withdrawals). Tuition reduction for siblings, merit scholarship grants, need-based scholarship grants available. In 2009–10, 45% of upper-school students received aid; total upper-school merit-scholarship money awarded: $100,000.

Admissions Traditional secondary-level entrance grade is 10. For fall 2009, 350 students applied for upper-level admission, 160 were accepted, 140 enrolled. Admissions testing required. Deadline for receipt of application materials: none. Application fee required: $100. Interview recommended.

Athletics Interscholastic: football (boys), soccer (b), volleyball (g); intramural: archery (b,g); coed interscholastic: aquatics, archery, baseball, basketball, canoeing/ kayaking, cross-country running, dance squad, drill team, fitness, flag football, Frisbee, golf, indoor track, indoor track & field, JROTC drill, marksmanship, physical fitness, physical training, riflery, running, swimming and diving, tennis, track and field, winter (indoor) track, wrestling; coed intramural: aerobics/Nautilus, aquatics, baseball, basketball, bowling, cheering, climbing, cross-country running, diving, equestrian sports, fishing, fitness, flag football, horseback riding, jogging, outdoor activities, outdoor adventure, outdoor education, outdoor recreation, outdoor skills, outdoors, paint ball, physical fitness, physical training, racquetball, rappelling, riflery, rock climbing, running, scuba diving, soccer, strength & conditioning, swimming and diving, touch football, water polo, wilderness survival, wrestling. 4 PE instructors, 4 coaches.

Computers Computers are regularly used in career exploration, college planning, mathematics, media, media arts, SAT preparation, science, technology, typing, Web site design, writing, yearbook classes. Computer network features include Internet access, wireless campus network, Internet filtering or blocking technology. Campus intranet and student e-mail accounts are available to students. The school has a published electronic and media policy.

Contact Maj. Gloria Ryun, Director of High School Admissions. 660-259-2221 Ext. 1214. Fax: 660-259-2677. E-mail: admissions@wma.edu. Web site: www.wma.edu.

WESLEYAN ACADEMY

PO Box 1489
Guaynabo, Puerto Rico 00970-1489
Head of School: Mrs. Nívea E. Dávila

General Information Coeducational day college-preparatory school, affiliated with Wesleyan Church. Grades PK–12. Founded: 1955. Setting: urban. Nearest major city is San Juan. 6-acre campus. 1 building on campus. Approved or accredited by Association of Christian Schools International, Middle States Association of Colleges and Schools, and Puerto Rico Department of Education. Total enrollment: 922. Upper school average class size: 25. Upper school faculty-student ratio: 1:23. There are 180 required school days per year for Upper School students. Upper School students typically attend 6 days per week. The average school day consists of 6 hours and 15 minutes.

Upper School Student Profile Grade 7: 75 students (42 boys, 33 girls); Grade 8: 56 students (24 boys, 32 girls); Grade 9: 60 students (27 boys, 33 girls); Grade 10: 64 students (35 boys, 29 girls); Grade 11: 58 students (28 boys, 30 girls); Grade 12: 35 students (20 boys, 15 girls). 50% of students are members of Wesleyan Church.

Faculty School total: 72. In upper school: 10 men, 12 women; 4 have advanced degrees.

Subjects Offered Accounting, algebra, American history, anatomy and physiology, art, Bible, biology, calculus, career and personal planning, choir, college planning, computer skills, critical writing, English, general math, general science, geography, geometry, global studies, golf, guidance, handbells, health, history, Internet, intro to computers, keyboarding, lab science, library, mathematics, music, music appreciation, personal development, poetry, pre-algebra, pre-calculus, pre-college orientation, Puerto Rican history, science, social sciences, Spanish, swimming, trigonometry, U.S. government, volleyball, world affairs, world history, yearbook.

Graduation Requirements American government, American history, Bible, computer science, electives, English, foreign language, mathematics, physical education (includes health), science, social sciences, social studies (includes history), Spanish, 30 hours of community service.

Special Academic Programs Advanced Placement exam preparation; honors section; independent study.

College Admission Counseling 35 students graduated in 2010; all went to college, including Abilene Christian University; University of Puerto Rico, Cayey University College; University of Puerto Rico, Río Piedras. Mean SAT critical reading: 487, mean SAT math: 458, mean SAT writing: 471, mean combined SAT: 1416. 11% scored over 600 on SAT critical reading, 6% scored over 600 on SAT writing.

Student Life Upper grades have uniform requirement, student council, honor system. Discipline rests primarily with faculty.

Summer Programs Remediation, enrichment, advancement programs offered; session focuses on remediation and enrichment classes; held on campus; accepts boys and girls; open to students from other schools. 100 students usually enrolled. 2011 schedule: June 2 to June 29. Application deadline: May 31.

Tuition and Aid Day student tuition: $6700. Guaranteed tuition plan. Tuition installment plan (monthly payment plans, full-payment discount plan, semester payment plan). Need-based scholarship grants, need-based financial aid available. In 2010–11, 2% of upper-school students received aid. Total amount of financial aid awarded in 2010–11: $10,000.

Admissions For fall 2010, 80 students applied for upper-level admission, 45 were accepted, 45 enrolled. Academic Profile Tests, admissions testing, mathematics proficiency exam and Metropolitan Achievement Test required. Deadline for receipt of application materials: none. Application fee required: $100. On-campus interview required.

Athletics Interscholastic: basketball (boys, girls), cross-country running (b), golf (b), indoor soccer (b,g), soccer (b,g), swimming and diving (b,g), track and field (b,g), volleyball (b,g); intramural: basketball (b,g), cross-country running (b), indoor soccer (b,g), soccer (b,g), track and field (b,g), volleyball (b,g); coed interscholastic: tennis. 3 PE instructors, 3 coaches.

Computers Computers are regularly used in all academic classes. Computer network features include on-campus library services, Internet access, Internet filtering or blocking technology. Computer access in designated common areas is available to students. The school has a published electronic and media policy.

Contact Mrs. Mae Ling Cardona, Admissions Clerk. 787-720-8959 Ext. 237. Fax: 787-790-0730. E-mail: mcardona@wesleyanacademy.org. Web site: www.wesleyanacademy.org.

WESLEYAN SCHOOL

5405 Spalding Drive
Norcross, Georgia 30092
Head of School: Mr. Zach Young

General Information Coeducational day college-preparatory, arts, religious studies, and technology school, affiliated with Christian faith. Grades K–12. Founded: 1963. Setting: suburban. Nearest major city is Atlanta. 75-acre campus. 9 buildings on campus. Approved or accredited by Southern Association of Colleges and Schools, Southern Association of Independent Schools, and Georgia Department of Education. Endowment: $8.1 million. Total enrollment: 1,091. Upper school average class size: 16. Upper school faculty-student ratio: 1:14. There are 180 required school days per year for Upper School students.

Wesleyan School

Upper School Student Profile Grade 9: 114 students (54 boys, 60 girls); Grade 10: 109 students (55 boys, 54 girls); Grade 11: 100 students (60 boys, 40 girls); Grade 12: 106 students (51 boys, 55 girls).
Faculty School total: 135. In upper school: 33 men, 30 women; 48 have advanced degrees.
Subjects Offered 20th century history, 20th century world history, 3-dimensional art, acting, advanced chemistry, advanced computer applications, advanced math, algebra, American government, American literature, art, art history-AP, band, Basic programming, Bible, biology, biology-AP, British literature, British literature (honors), calculus, calculus-AP, chemistry, chemistry-AP, choral music, chorus, Christian doctrine, Christian education, Christian ethics, Christian studies, computer science-AP, economics, English literature and composition-AP, English literature-AP, environmental science, European history-AP, French, geometry, government, health and wellness, Latin, literary genres, modern world history, New Testament, photography, physical education, physics, pre-calculus, public speaking, Spanish, Spanish language-AP, studio art-AP, theater, U.S. history, U.S. history-AP, vocal ensemble, weight training, word processing, world literature.
Graduation Requirements Algebra, American history, American literature, analysis, arts and fine arts (art, music, dance, drama), Bible, biology, British literature, chemistry, economics, environmental science, foreign language, geometry, government, modern world history, physical education (includes health), physics, pre-calculus, statistics, world literature, writing.
Special Academic Programs Advanced Placement exam preparation; honors section.
College Admission Counseling 91 students graduated in 2009; all went to college, including Auburn University; Georgia Institute of Technology; Rhodes College; Samford University; The University of Alabama; University of Georgia. Mean SAT critical reading: 607, mean SAT math: 615, mean SAT writing: 605. 51% scored over 600 on SAT critical reading, 59% scored over 600 on SAT math, 44% scored over 600 on SAT writing, 51% scored over 1800 on combined SAT, 36% scored over 26 on composite ACT.
Student Life Upper grades have uniform requirement, student council, honor system. Discipline rests equally with students and faculty. Attendance at religious services is required.
Tuition and Aid Day student tuition: $17,530. Tuition installment plan (Insured Tuition Payment Plan). Need-based scholarship grants available. In 2009–10, 8% of upper-school students received aid. Total amount of financial aid awarded in 2009–10: $376,000.
Admissions Traditional secondary-level entrance grade is 9. For fall 2009, 78 students applied for upper-level admission, 40 were accepted, 32 enrolled. PSAT, SSAT and writing sample required. Deadline for receipt of application materials: February 17. Application fee required: $75. Interview required.
Athletics Interscholastic: baseball (boys, girls), basketball (b,g), cross-country running (b,g), diving (b,g), football (b), golf (b,g), lacrosse (b,g), soccer (b,g), softball (g), swimming and diving (b,g), tennis (b,g), track and field (b,g), volleyball (g), wrestling (b); intramural: cheering (g); coed intramural: bowling, Frisbee, water polo. 1 PE instructor, 1 athletic trainer.
Computers Computers are regularly used in all classes. Computer network features include on-campus library services, Internet access, wireless campus network, Internet filtering or blocking technology. Student e-mail accounts are available to students. Students grades are available online. The school has a published electronic and media policy.
Contact Ms. Sylvia Pryor, Admissions Assistant. 770-448-7640 Ext. 2267. Fax: 770-448-3699. E-mail: spryor@wesleyanschool.org. Web site: www.wesleyanschool.org.

WESTBURY CHRISTIAN SCHOOL

10420 Hillcroft
Houston, Texas 77096
Head of School: Mr. Greg J. Glenn
General Information Coeducational day college-preparatory, arts, business, and religious studies school, affiliated with Church of Christ. Grades PK–12. Founded: 1975. Setting: urban. 13-acre campus. 1 building on campus. Approved or accredited by National Christian School Association, Southern Association of Colleges and Schools, Texas Education Agency, Texas Private School Accreditation Commission, The College Board, and Texas Department of Education. Endowment: $300,000. Total enrollment: 518. Upper school average class size: 22. Upper school faculty-student ratio: 1:10. There are 180 required school days per year for Upper School students. Upper School students typically attend 5 days per week. The average school day consists of 7 hours and 45 minutes.
Upper School Student Profile Grade 9: 44 students (28 boys, 16 girls); Grade 10: 51 students (26 boys, 25 girls); Grade 11: 59 students (28 boys, 31 girls); Grade 12: 75 students (44 boys, 31 girls). 18% of students are members of Church of Christ.
Faculty School total: 56. In upper school: 20 men, 11 women; 9 have advanced degrees.
Subjects Offered Accounting, algebra, anatomy and physiology, art, athletics, band, basketball, Bible, biology, biology-AP, business, calculus-AP, cheerleading, chemistry, chemistry-AP, community service, computer applications, drama, economics, English, English language and composition-AP, English literature and composition-AP, entrepreneurship, geography, geometry, government,

government-AP, health, human geography—AP, macro/microeconomics-AP, marketing, photography, physical education, physical science, physics, pre-calculus, psychology-AP, Spanish, speech, statistics-AP, studio art-AP, U.S. history, U.S. history-AP, vocal music, weight training, world history, world history-AP, yearbook.
Graduation Requirements Arts and fine arts (art, music, dance, drama), Bible, electives, English, foreign language, geometry, mathematics, physical education (includes health), science, social studies (includes history), speech, continuous participation in student activities programs, community service each semester.
Special Academic Programs 15 Advanced Placement exams for which test preparation is offered; independent study.
College Admission Counseling 78 students graduated in 2010; 77 went to college, including Harding University; Houston Baptist University; Houston Community College System; Texas A&M University; The University of Texas at Austin; University of Houston. Other: 1 entered a postgraduate year. Mean SAT critical reading: 481, mean SAT math: 520, mean SAT writing: 479, mean combined SAT: 1480, mean composite ACT: 22. 11% scored over 600 on SAT critical reading, 22% scored over 600 on SAT math, 10% scored over 600 on SAT writing, 13% scored over 1800 on combined SAT, 7% scored over 26 on composite ACT.
Student Life Upper grades have uniform requirement, student council, honor system. Discipline rests primarily with faculty.
Summer Programs Sports programs offered; session focuses on week-long basketball, football & volleyball instruction camps; held on campus; accepts boys and girls; open to students from other schools. 150 students usually enrolled. 2011 schedule: June 6 to June 24. Application deadline: none.
Tuition and Aid Day student tuition: $9020. Tuition installment plan (FACTS Tuition Payment Plan, tuition discount if entire year paid by enrollment date). Tuition reduction for siblings, merit scholarship grants, need-based scholarship grants available. In 2010–11, 16% of upper-school students received aid; total upper-school merit-scholarship money awarded: $9000. Total amount of financial aid awarded in 2010–11: $185,000.
Admissions Traditional secondary-level entrance grade is 9. For fall 2010, 84 students applied for upper-level admission, 70 were accepted, 58 enrolled. ISEE, Otis-Lennon School Ability Test, SLEP for foreign students or Stanford Achievement Test required. Deadline for receipt of application materials: none. Application fee required: $75. Interview required.
Athletics Interscholastic: baseball (boys), basketball (b,g), cheering (g), cross-country running (b,g), football (b), golf (b,g), soccer (b,g), softball (g), strength & conditioning (b,g), swimming and diving (b,g), tennis (b,g), track and field (b,g), volleyball (g); intramural: weight training (b). 1 PE instructor, 5 coaches.
Computers Computers are regularly used in all academic classes. Computer network features include on-campus library services, online commercial services, Internet access, Internet filtering or blocking technology. Students grades are available online. The school has a published electronic and media policy.
Contact Mrs. Phylis Frye, Director of Admissions. 713-551-8100 Ext. 1018. Fax: 713-551-8117. E-mail: admissions@westburychristian.org. Web site: www.westburychristian.org.

WEST CATHOLIC HIGH SCHOOL

1801 Bristol Avenue NW
Grand Rapids, Michigan 49504
Head of School: Mr. Tom Maj
General Information Coeducational day college-preparatory and religious studies school, affiliated with Roman Catholic Church. Grades 9–12. Founded: 1962. Setting: urban. 20-acre campus. 1 building on campus. Approved or accredited by National Catholic Education Association, North Central Association of Colleges and Schools, and Michigan Department of Education. Endowment: $1 million. Total enrollment: 544. Upper school average class size: 25. Upper school faculty-student ratio: 1:25. There are 180 required school days per year for Upper School students. Upper School students typically attend 5 days per week. The average school day consists of 6 hours.
Upper School Student Profile Grade 9: 121 students (72 boys, 49 girls); Grade 10: 127 students (65 boys, 62 girls); Grade 11: 152 students (81 boys, 71 girls); Grade 12: 140 students (73 boys, 67 girls). 95% of students are Roman Catholic.
Faculty School total: 29. In upper school: 12 men, 17 women; 20 have advanced degrees.
Subjects Offered 20th century world history, acting, advanced chemistry, advanced computer applications, advanced math, American government, American literature, anatomy, art, band, Basic programming, biology, biology-AP, calculus, calculus-AP, career planning, chemistry, chemistry-AP, choir, Christian doctrine, composition, composition-AP, computer applications, computer programming, concert band, desktop publishing, drama, drawing, earth science, economics, economics-AP, English, English language and composition-AP, English literature, English literature and composition-AP, English literature-AP, environmental science, family living, French, general math, geometry, government, government and politics-AP, government-AP, government/civics, history, history of the Catholic Church, honors algebra, honors English, honors geometry, honors world history, human anatomy, intro to computers, jazz band, journalism, marching band, physics, pre-algebra, pre-calculus, psychology, sexuality, social justice, sociology, Spanish, U.S. government and politics-AP, U.S. history, Web site design, world history, yearbook.

Graduation Requirements Economics, electives, English composition, foreign language, government, health, mathematics, religion (includes Bible studies and theology), science, social studies (includes history), U.S. history, visual arts.

Special Academic Programs Advanced Placement exam preparation; honors section; study at local college for college credit.

College Admission Counseling 133 students graduated in 2010; 129 went to college, including Central Michigan University; Grand Valley State University; Michigan State University; University of Michigan; Western Michigan University. Other: 2 went to work, 2 entered military service. Mean SAT critical reading: 650, mean SAT math: 660, mean SAT writing: 610, mean combined SAT: 1920, mean composite ACT: 23. 50% scored over 600 on SAT critical reading, 50% scored over 600 on SAT math, 50% scored over 600 on SAT writing, 50% scored over 1800 on combined SAT, 25% scored over 26 on composite ACT.

Student Life Upper grades have uniform requirement, student council, honor system. Discipline rests primarily with faculty. Attendance at religious services is required.

Summer Programs Sports programs offered; session focuses on sports enrichment; held on campus; accepts boys and girls; not open to students from other schools. 100 students usually enrolled. 2011 schedule: June 13 to August 20. Application deadline: June 3.

Tuition and Aid Day student tuition: $7625. Tuition installment plan (Tuition Management Systems). Need-based scholarship grants available. In 2010–11, 25% of upper-school students received aid.

Admissions Traditional secondary-level entrance grade is 9. High School Placement Test, Iowa Tests of Basic Skills and Math Placement Exam required. Deadline for receipt of application materials: February 1. Application fee required: $150. Interview required.

Athletics Interscholastic: baseball (boys), basketball (b,g), bowling (b,g), cheering (g), cross-country running (b,g), diving (b,g), football (b), golf (b,g), gymnastics (g), hockey (b), ice hockey (b), pom squad (g), skiing (downhill) (b,g), soccer (b,g), softball (g), swimming and diving (b,g), tennis (b,g), track and field (b,g), volleyball (g), weight lifting (b), weight training (b), wrestling (b); intramural: basketball (b,g). 1 PE instructor, 66 coaches, 1 athletic trainer.

Computers Computers are regularly used in all academic classes. Computer network features include Internet access, Internet filtering or blocking technology. Student e-mail accounts and computer access in designated common areas are available to students. Students grades are available online. The school has a published electronic and media policy.

Contact Mrs. Lauri Ford, Guidance Secretary. 616-233-5909. Fax: 616-453-4320. E-mail: lauriford@grcss.org. Web site: www.grwestcatholic.org.

WESTCHESTER COUNTRY DAY SCHOOL

2045 North Old Greensboro Road
High Point, North Carolina 27265
Head of School: Mr. Cobb Atkinson

General Information Coeducational day college-preparatory, arts, bilingual studies, and technology school. Grades K–12. Founded: 1967. Setting: rural. 53-acre campus. 6 buildings on campus. Approved or accredited by North Carolina Association of Independent Schools, Southern Association of Colleges and Schools, and Southern Association of Independent Schools. Member of National Association of Independent Schools. Endowment: $2.5 million. Total enrollment: 419. Upper school average class size: 16. Upper school faculty-student ratio: 1:7. There are 173 required school days per year for Upper School students. Upper School students typically attend 5 days per week. The average school day consists of 5 hours and 45 minutes.

Upper School Student Profile Grade 9: 44 students (28 boys, 16 girls); Grade 10: 40 students (16 boys, 24 girls); Grade 11: 35 students (25 boys, 10 girls); Grade 12: 41 students (26 boys, 15 girls).

Faculty School total: 57. In upper school: 6 men, 17 women; 13 have advanced degrees.

Subjects Offered Advanced Placement courses, advanced studio art-AP, algebra, American history, American literature, art, art history-AP, art-AP, biology, biology-AP, British literature, calculus, chemistry, chemistry-AP, community service, computer science, creative writing, earth science, economics, English, English literature, environmental science, European history, fine arts, French, geography, geometry, government/civics, grammar, health, history, Mandarin, mathematics, music, physical education, physics, probability and statistics, science, social studies, Spanish, speech, statistics-AP, theater, Web site design, world history, world literature, writing.

Graduation Requirements Arts and fine arts (art, music, dance, drama), civics, English, foreign language, mathematics, physical education (includes health), science, social studies (includes history), community service project, senior speech.

Special Academic Programs 12 Advanced Placement exams for which test preparation is offered; honors section; independent study.

College Admission Counseling 28 students graduated in 2010; all went to college, including Appalachian State University; College of Charleston; North Carolina State University; The University of North Carolina at Chapel Hill; The University of North Carolina at Charlotte; The University of North Carolina Wilmington. Median SAT critical reading: 605, median SAT math: 625, median SAT writing: 580.

Student Life Upper grades have specified standards of dress, student council, honor system. Discipline rests primarily with faculty.

Summer Programs Enrichment, sports, art/fine arts, computer instruction programs offered; session focuses on academics, sports, hobby-related; held on campus; accepts

boys and girls; open to students from other schools. 300 students usually enrolled. 2011 schedule: June 15 to August 14. Application deadline: none.

Tuition and Aid Day student tuition: $13,125. Tuition installment plan (FACTS Tuition Payment Plan, monthly payment plans). Need-based scholarship grants available. In 2010–11, 13% of upper-school students received aid. Total amount of financial aid awarded in 2010–11: $474,125.

Admissions Traditional secondary-level entrance grade is 9. For fall 2010, 29 students applied for upper-level admission, 21 were accepted, 19 enrolled. Brigance Test of Basic Skills, ERB CTP IV, Metropolitan Achievement Test, Wide Range Achievement Test or Woodcock-Johnson Revised Achievement Test required. Deadline for receipt of application materials: none. Application fee required: $75. On-campus interview recommended.

Athletics Interscholastic: baseball (boys), basketball (b,g), cheering (g), dance (g), dance team (g), soccer (b,g), softball (g), tennis (b,g), volleyball (g); coed interscholastic: aquatics, cross-country running, golf, physical fitness, swimming and diving, track and field. 4 PE instructors, 23 coaches.

Computers Computers are regularly used in English, foreign language, history, library science, mathematics, science, Web site design, yearbook classes. Computer network features include on-campus library services, Internet access, wireless campus network, Internet filtering or blocking technology. Student e-mail accounts and computer access in designated common areas are available to students. Students grades are available online. The school has a published electronic and media policy.

Contact Mrs. Kerie Beth Scott, Director of Admissions. 336-822-4005. Fax: 336-869-6685. E-mail: keriebeth.scott@westchestercds.org. Web site: www.westchestercds.org.

WESTERN CHRISTIAN SCHOOLS

100 W 9th Street
Upland, California 91786
Head of School: Robert Yovino

General Information Coeducational day college-preparatory, arts, and religious studies school, affiliated with Christian faith. Grades 9–12. Founded: 1920. Setting: suburban. Nearest major city is Los Angeles. 8 buildings on campus. Approved or accredited by Association of Christian Schools International, Western Association of Schools and Colleges, and California Department of Education. Member of European Council of International Schools. Total enrollment: 475. Upper school average class size: 17. Upper school faculty-student ratio: 1:17. There are 175 required school days per year for Upper School students. Upper School students typically attend 5 days per week. The average school day consists of 6 hours and 50 minutes.

Upper School Student Profile 75% of students are Christian.

Faculty School total: 27. In upper school: 12 men, 15 women.

Subjects Offered Advanced Placement courses, aerobics, algebra, American history, anatomy, art, band, Bible studies, biology, biology-AP, calculus, calculus-AP, ceramics, chemistry, chorus, computer science, consumer mathematics, creative writing, drama, economics, English, English-AP, environmental science-AP, ESL, film, French, French-AP, geography, geometry, government-AP, government/civics, health, journalism, math analysis, mathematics, physical education, physics, physiology, psychology, sociology, Spanish, Spanish-AP, speech and debate, theater, world history.

Special Academic Programs 7 Advanced Placement exams for which test preparation is offered.

College Admission Counseling 132 students graduated in 2010; 82 went to college, including Azusa Pacific University; California State Polytechnic University, Pomona; California State University, Fullerton; University of California, Irvine; University of California, Los Angeles; University of Southern California.

Student Life Upper grades have uniform requirement. Discipline rests primarily with faculty.

Summer Programs Remediation, enrichment, ESL programs offered; held on campus; accepts boys and girls; open to students from other schools. 75 students usually enrolled. 2011 schedule: June 20 to July 30. Application deadline: June 15.

Tuition and Aid Financial aid available to upper-school students. In 2010–11, 50% of upper-school students received aid. Total amount of financial aid awarded in 2010–11: $150,000.

Admissions School's own test required. Deadline for receipt of application materials: none. No application fee required. On-campus interview required.

Athletics Interscholastic: baseball (boys), basketball (b,g), cheering (g), cross-country running (b,g), football (b), soccer (b,g), softball (g), track and field (b,g), volleyball (g); coed interscholastic: golf. 2 PE instructors, 9 coaches.

Contact John Attwood, Vice Principal. 909-920-5858. Fax: 909-985-3449.

WESTERN MENNONITE SCHOOL

9045 Wallace Road NW
Salem, Oregon 97304-9716
Head of School: Darrel Camp

General Information Coeducational boarding and day college-preparatory, general academic, and religious studies school, affiliated with Mennonite Church USA. Boarding grades 9–12, day grades 6–12. Founded: 1945. Setting: rural. Students are housed in single-sex dormitories. 45-acre campus. 10 buildings on campus. Approved or accredited by Mennonite Education Agency, Mennonite Schools Council, Northwest Association of Schools and Colleges, and Oregon Department of Education. Total enrollment: 251. Upper school average class size: 16. Upper school faculty-student ratio: 1:14. There are 173 required school days per year for Upper School students. Upper School students typically attend 5 days per week. The average school day consists of 5 hours and 25 minutes.

Upper School Student Profile Grade 6: 27 students (9 boys, 18 girls); Grade 7: 23 students (13 boys, 10 girls); Grade 8: 39 students (24 boys, 15 girls); Grade 9: 40 students (20 boys, 20 girls); Grade 10: 31 students (17 boys, 14 girls); Grade 11: 50 students (24 boys, 26 girls); Grade 12: 39 students (16 boys, 23 girls). 12% of students are boarding students. 85% are state residents. 3 states are represented in upper school student body. 12% are international students. International students from China, Germany, Hong Kong, Japan, Republic of Korea, and Taiwan; 7 other countries represented in student body. 18% of students are Mennonite Church USA.

Faculty School total: 26. In upper school: 12 men, 14 women; 8 have advanced degrees; 10 reside on campus.

Subjects Offered Accounting, advanced math, algebra, anatomy and physiology, art, Bible studies, biology, calculus, career and personal planning, career education, chemistry, choral music, Christian education, Christian scripture, church history, computer applications, computer programming, drawing and design, economics, English, English composition, English literature, general math, geography, geometry, government, health education, human anatomy, instrumental music, intro to computers, keyboarding, mathematics, music, music performance, novels, physical education, physical fitness, physical science, physics, pre-algebra, pre-calculus, psychology, religious education, religious studies, research, science, Spanish, U.S. government, U.S. history, U.S. literature, woodworking, yearbook.

Graduation Requirements Algebra, applied arts, Bible studies, biology, career education, chemistry, choir, economics, English, English literature, geometry, global studies, music, physical education (includes health), Spanish, U.S. government, U.S. history, U.S. literature, world geography, Mini-Term-one week of co-curricular activity at end of academic year (sophomore through senior year).

Special Academic Programs Independent study; term-away projects; study at local college for college credit.

College Admission Counseling 42 students graduated in 2010; 38 went to college, including Chemeketa Community College; Corban University; Eastern Mennonite University; Oregon State University; Seattle Pacific University; Western Oregon University. Median SAT math: 520, median composite ACT: 27. 11% scored over 600 on SAT math, 50% scored over 26 on composite ACT.

Student Life Upper grades have specified standards of dress, student council, honor system. Discipline rests primarily with faculty. Attendance at religious services is required.

Summer Programs Sports programs offered; session focuses on soccer, volleyball, basketball; held on campus; accepts boys and girls; open to students from other schools. 25 students usually enrolled. 2011 schedule: June to August. Application deadline: June.

Tuition and Aid Day student tuition: $7700; 5-day tuition and room/board: $11,748; 7-day tuition and room/board: $13,431. Tuition installment plan (monthly payment plans, individually arranged payment plans). Tuition reduction for siblings, merit scholarship grants, need-based scholarship grants, paying campus jobs available. In 2010–11, 41% of upper-school students received aid.

Admissions Traditional secondary-level entrance grade is 9. Deadline for receipt of application materials: none. Application fee required: $50. Interview recommended.

Athletics Interscholastic: baseball (boys, girls), basketball (b,g), cross-country running (b), soccer (b,g), volleyball (g); coed intramural: softball. 5 PE instructors, 8 coaches.

Computers Computers are regularly used in independent study, introduction to technology, keyboarding, yearbook classes. Computer network features include on-campus library services, online commercial services, Internet access, wireless campus network, Internet filtering or blocking technology. Campus intranet, student e-mail accounts, and computer access in designated common areas are available to students. Students grades are available online. The school has a published electronic and media policy.

Contact Mrs. Cheryl Mayo, Admissions Coordinator. 503-363-2000 Ext. 121. Fax: 503-370-9455. E-mail: cmayo@westernmennoniteschool.org. Web site: www.westernmennoniteschool.org.

WESTERN RESERVE ACADEMY

115 College Street
Hudson, Ohio 44236
Head of School: Christopher D. Burner

General Information Coeducational boarding and day college-preparatory and arts school. Grades 9–PG. Founded: 1826. Setting: small town. Nearest major city is Cleveland. Students are housed in single-sex dormitories. 190-acre campus. 49 buildings on campus. Approved or accredited by Independent Schools Association of the Central States, Midwest Association of Boarding Schools, North Central Association of Colleges and Schools, Ohio Association of Independent Schools, The Association of Boarding Schools, and Ohio Department of Education. Member of National Association of Independent Schools and Secondary School Admission Test Board. Endowment: $97.7 million. Total enrollment: 389. Upper school average class size: 12. Upper school faculty-student ratio: 1:6. There are 182 required school days per year for Upper School students. Upper School students typically attend 6 days per week. The average school day consists of 7 hours and 15 minutes.

Upper School Student Profile Grade 9: 84 students (40 boys, 44 girls); Grade 10: 115 students (62 boys, 53 girls); Grade 11: 100 students (61 boys, 39 girls); Grade 12: 90 students (39 boys, 51 girls). 68% of students are state residents. 20 states are represented in upper school student body. 18% are international students. International students from Canada, China, Germany, Republic of Korea, Saudi Arabia, and Taiwan; 10 other countries represented in student body.

Faculty School total: 64. In upper school: 39 men, 25 women; 53 have advanced degrees; 58 reside on campus.

Subjects Offered Algebra, American history, American literature, architecture, art, art history, astronomy, band, biology, calculus, ceramics, chemistry, chorus, computer programming, creative writing, dance, drafting, drama, economics, engineering, English, English literature, environmental science, European history, fine arts, French, geometry, German, health, history, humanities, independent study, industrial arts, Latin, Mandarin, mathematics, mechanical drawing, music, music history, music theory, orchestra, photography, physical education, physics, science, social studies, Spanish, speech, statistics, theater, trigonometry, world history, zoology.

Graduation Requirements Arts and fine arts (art, music, dance, drama), English, foreign language, history, mathematics, physical education (includes health), science, senior seminar, senior thesis.

Special Academic Programs 19 Advanced Placement exams for which test preparation is offered; honors section; independent study; study at local college for college credit; study abroad; academic accommodation for the gifted, the musically talented, and the artistically talented.

College Admission Counseling 110 students graduated in 2010; all went to college, including Boston College; Case Western Reserve University; Cornell University; Dartmouth College; New York University; The Ohio State University.

Student Life Upper grades have specified standards of dress, student council. Discipline rests equally with students and faculty.

Summer Programs Enrichment, ESL, sports programs offered; held on campus; accepts boys and girls; open to students from other schools. 2011 schedule: June 15 to July 15. Application deadline: April 15.

Tuition and Aid Day student tuition: $28,900; 7-day tuition and room/board: $40,700. Tuition installment plan (The Tuition Plan, Insured Tuition Payment Plan, Key Tuition Payment Plan, monthly payment plans, individually arranged payment plans). Merit scholarship grants, need-based scholarship grants, need-based loans available. In 2010–11, 34% of upper-school students received aid. Total amount of financial aid awarded in 2010–11: $3,600,000.

Admissions Traditional secondary-level entrance grade is 9. For fall 2010, 364 students applied for upper-level admission, 229 were accepted, 154 enrolled. ISEE, SSAT or TOEFL required. Deadline for receipt of application materials: January 15. Application fee required: $50. Interview required.

Athletics Interscholastic: baseball (boys), basketball (b,g), cross-country running (b,g), diving (b,g), field hockey (g), football (b), golf (b), ice hockey (b), lacrosse (b,g), soccer (b,g), softball (g), swimming and diving (b,g), tennis (b,g), track and field (b,g), volleyball (g), wrestling (b); intramural: basketball (b); coed interscholastic: marksmanship, riflery; coed intramural: aerobics, aerobics/dance, aerobics/Nautilus, backpacking, bicycling, dance, fitness, hiking/backpacking, jogging, martial arts, modern dance, Nautilus, outdoor recreation, paddle tennis, physical fitness, physical training, running, skeet shooting, skiing (downhill), snowboarding, soccer, strength & conditioning, weight lifting, weight training, winter (indoor) track, yoga. 1 coach, 2 athletic trainers.

Computers Computers are regularly used in architecture, drawing and design, economics, engineering, English, foreign language, history, mathematics, science, technical drawing classes. Computer network features include on-campus library services, online commercial services, Internet access, wireless campus network, Internet filtering or blocking technology. Campus intranet and student e-mail accounts are available to students. The school has a published electronic and media policy.

Contact Mrs. Anne F. Sheppard, Dean of Admission and Financial Aid. 330-650-9717. Fax: 330-650-5858. E-mail: admission@wra.net. Web site: www.wra.net.

See Display on page 698 and Close-Up on page 862.

WESTGATE MENNONITE COLLEGIATE

86 West Gate
Winnipeg, Manitoba R3C 2E1, Canada
Head of School: Mr. Bob Hummelt

General Information Coeducational day college-preparatory, general academic, arts, religious studies, technology, and music, German, and French school, affiliated with Mennonite Church USA. Grades 7–12. Founded: 1958. Setting: urban. 3-acre campus. 1 building on campus. Approved or accredited by Manitoba Department of Education. Language of instruction: English. Total enrollment: 322. Upper school average class size: 25. Upper school faculty-student ratio: 1:15.

Upper School Student Profile Grade 10: 62 students (26 boys, 36 girls); Grade 11: 59 students (26 boys, 33 girls); Grade 12: 51 students (31 boys, 20 girls). 55% of students are Mennonite Church USA.

Faculty School total: 27. In upper school: 15 men, 11 women; 5 have advanced degrees.

Special Academic Programs Advanced Placement exam preparation; independent study; term-away projects.

College Admission Counseling 50 students graduated in 2009; 45 went to college, including The University of Winnipeg; University of Manitoba. Other: 2 went to work, 3 had other specific plans.

Student Life Upper grades have specified standards of dress, student council. Discipline rests primarily with faculty. Attendance at religious services is required.

Tuition and Aid Day student tuition: CAN$4800. Tuition installment plan (monthly payment plans, individually arranged payment plans). Tuition reduction for siblings, bursaries, merit scholarship grants, need-based scholarship grants available. In 2009–10, 10% of upper-school students received aid; total upper-school merit-scholarship money awarded: CAN$5000. Total amount of financial aid awarded in 2009–10: CAN$36,000.

Admissions Traditional secondary-level entrance grade is 10. Deadline for receipt of application materials: March 10. Application fee required: CAN$50. Interview required.

Athletics Interscholastic: badminton (boys, girls), baseball (b,g), basketball (b,g), bowling (b,g), cheering (b,g), cross-country running (b,g), curling (b,g), floor hockey (b,g), golf (b,g), gymnastics (b,g), outdoor education (b,g), outdoor skills (b,g), rock climbing (b,g), running (b,g), soccer (b,g), strength & conditioning (b,g), volleyball (b,g); intramural: aerobics/dance (b,g), backpacking (b,g), badminton (b,g), basketball (b,g), bicycling (b,g), broomball (b,g), canoeing/kayaking (b,g), cross-country running (b,g), curling (b,g), field hockey (b,g), floor hockey (b,g), football (b,g), golf (b,g), gymnastics (b,g), hiking/backpacking (b,g), ice hockey (b,g), ice skating (b,g), outdoor education (b,g), paddle tennis (b,g), racquetball (b,g), rock climbing (b,g), running (b,g), soccer (b,g), strength & conditioning (b,g), swimming and diving (b,g), volleyball (b,g), wall climbing (b,g); coed interscholastic: badminton, baseball, basketball, bowling, cheering, cross-country running, curling, floor hockey, golf, gymnastics, outdoor education, outdoor skills, rock climbing, running, soccer, strength & conditioning, ultimate Frisbee, volleyball; coed intramural: aerobics/dance, backpacking, badminton, basketball, bicycling, broomball, canoeing/kayaking, cross-country running, curling, field hockey, floor hockey, football, golf, gymnastics, hiking/backpacking, ice hockey, ice skating, outdoor education, paddle tennis, racquetball, rock climbing, running, soccer, strength & conditioning, swimming and diving, volleyball, wall climbing. 3 PE instructors, 7 coaches, 4 athletic trainers.

Computers Computer network features include on-campus library services, online commercial services, Internet access. The school has a published electronic and media policy.

Contact Mr. Bob Hummelt, Principal. 204-775-7111 Ext. 202. Fax: 204-786-1651. E-mail: westgate@westgatemennonite.ca. Web site: www.westgatemennonite.ca.

WEST ISLAND COLLEGE

7410 Blackfoot Trail SE
Calgary, Alberta T2H IM5, Canada
Head of School: Ms. Carol Grant-Watt

General Information Coeducational day college-preparatory, arts, business, bilingual studies, technology, and advanced placement school. Grades 7–12. Founded: 1982. Setting: urban. 18-acre campus. 2 buildings on campus. Approved or accredited by Canadian Association of Independent Schools and Alberta Department of Education. Languages of instruction: English, Spanish, and French. Total enrollment: 464. Upper school average class size: 18. Upper school faculty-student ratio: 1:17. There are 185 required school days per year for Upper School students. Upper School students typically attend 5 days per week. The average school day consists of 6 hours and 12 minutes.

Upper School Student Profile Grade 10: 71 students (34 boys, 37 girls); Grade 11: 69 students (39 boys, 30 girls); Grade 12: 67 students (35 boys, 32 girls).

Faculty School total: 44. In upper school: 20 men, 20 women; 15 have advanced degrees.

Subjects Offered Advanced Placement courses, anthropology, art, arts, biology, business, chemistry, choral music, communications, debate, drama, English, European history, experiential education, French, French studies, health, information processing, information technology, leadership, literature, mathematics, modern languages, music, outdoor education, philosophy, physical education, physics, political thought, politics, psychology, public speaking, science, social sciences, social studies, sociology, Spanish, standard curriculum, study skills, world geography, world history, world religions.

Graduation Requirements Alberta education requirements.

Special Academic Programs 10 Advanced Placement exams for which test preparation is offered; honors section; independent study; study abroad; academic accommodation for the gifted.

College Admission Counseling 62 students graduated in 2010; all went to college, including McGill University; Queen's University at Kingston; The University of British Columbia; University of Alberta; University of Calgary; University of Victoria.

Student Life Upper grades have uniform requirement, student council, honor system. Discipline rests equally with students and faculty.

Summer Programs Enrichment, advancement, sports, computer instruction programs offered; session focuses on study skills and academic preparedness; held both on and off campus; held at various public parks in the city; accepts boys and girls; not open to students from other schools. 55 students usually enrolled. 2011 schedule: August 15 to August 19. Application deadline: March 31.

Tuition and Aid Day student tuition: CAN$11,935. Tuition installment plan (monthly payment plans).

West Island College

Admissions Traditional secondary-level entrance grade is 10. For fall 2010, 30 students applied for upper-level admission, 16 were accepted, 16 enrolled. 3-R Achievement Test, CCAT, CTBS, OLSAT, Gates MacGinite Reading Tests and Otis-Lennon IQ Test required. Deadline for receipt of application materials: none. Application fee required: CAN$100. Interview required.

Athletics Interscholastic: basketball (boys, girls), field hockey (g), rugby (b), volleyball (b,g); intramural: aquatics (b,g), basketball (b,g), floor hockey (b,g), volleyball (b,g); coed interscholastic: badminton, climbing, cross-country running, soccer; coed intramural: alpine skiing, backpacking, badminton, bicycling, bowling, canoeing/kayaking, climbing, cross-country running, curling, dance, fitness, golf, hiking/backpacking, kayaking, mountaineering, nordic skiing, outdoor activities, physical fitness, physical training, rock climbing, sailing, skiing (cross-country), skiing (downhill), snowboarding, soccer, swimming and diving, touch football, wilderness survival, wildernessways. 4 PE instructors, 10 coaches, 2 athletic trainers.

Computers Computers are regularly used in business, career education, career exploration, career technology, economics, English, French, independent study, mathematics, media arts, media production, multimedia, science, social studies, technology, word processing classes. Computer network features include on-campus library services, online commercial services, Internet access, wireless campus network, Internet filtering or blocking technology. Campus intranet and student e-mail accounts are available to students. The school has a published electronic and media policy.

Contact Ms. Nicole Bernard, Director of Admissions. 403-444-0023. Fax: 403-444-2820. E-mail: admissions@westislandcollege.ab.ca. Web site: www.westislandcollege.ab.ca.

WESTMARK SCHOOL

Encino, California
See Special Needs Schools section.

WEST MEMPHIS CHRISTIAN HIGH SCHOOL

1101 North Missouri
West Memphis, Arkansas 72301
Head of School: Dr. Loretta Dale

General Information Coeducational day college-preparatory school, affiliated with Church of Christ, Christian faith. Grades 7–12. Founded: 1970. Setting: small town. Nearest major city is Memphis, TN. 1 building on campus. Approved or accredited by Mississippi Private School Association and Arkansas Department of Education. Candidate for accreditation by North Central Association of Colleges and Schools. Total enrollment: 208. Upper school average class size: 20. Upper school faculty-student ratio: 1:12. There are 180 required school days per year for Upper School students. Upper School students typically attend 5 days per week. The average school day consists of 6 hours and 8 minutes.

Upper School Student Profile Grade 7: 19 students (10 boys, 9 girls); Grade 8: 21 students (13 boys, 8 girls); Grade 9: 21 students (12 boys, 9 girls); Grade 10: 31 students (25 boys, 6 girls); Grade 11: 18 students (7 boys, 11 girls); Grade 12: 17 students (11 boys, 6 girls). 80% of students are members of Church of Christ, Christian faith.

Faculty School total: 20. In upper school: 10 men, 10 women; 10 have advanced degrees.

College Admission Counseling 19 students graduated in 2010; all went to college, including Arkansas State University—Jonesboro; Harding University; University of Arkansas; University of Memphis. Mean composite ACT: 23.

Student Life Upper grades have specified standards of dress, student council, honor system. Discipline rests primarily with faculty. Attendance at religious services is required.

Admissions No application fee required.

Athletics 3 PE instructors, 4 coaches.

Contact Mary Anne Pike, Director of Admissions. 870-400-4000. Fax: 870-735-0570. E-mail: mpike@wmcs.com. Web site: www.wmcs.com.

WESTMINSTER CATAWBA CHRISTIAN

2650 India Hook Road
Rock Hill, South Carolina 29732
Head of School: Mr. Ray Casey

General Information Coeducational day college-preparatory, arts, and religious studies school, affiliated with Presbyterian Church in America. Grades PK–12. Founded: 1993. Setting: suburban. Nearest major city is Charlotte, NC. 22-acre campus. 8 buildings on campus. Approved or accredited by Association of Christian Schools International, Southern Association of Colleges and Schools, and South Carolina Department of Education. Endowment: $200,000. Total enrollment: 575. Upper school average class size: 22. There are 180 required school days per year for Upper School students. Upper School students typically attend 5 days per week. The average school day consists of 7 hours and 10 minutes.

Upper School Student Profile Grade 7: 40 students (20 boys, 20 girls); Grade 8: 57 students (29 boys, 28 girls); Grade 9: 50 students (26 boys, 24 girls); Grade 10: 35 students (12 boys, 23 girls); Grade 11: 39 students (22 boys, 17 girls); Grade 12: 46 students (23 boys, 23 girls). 35% of students are Presbyterian Church in America.

Faculty School total: 102. In upper school: 5 men, 21 women; 16 have advanced degrees.

Subjects Offered ACT preparation, advanced computer applications, Advanced Placement courses, advanced studio art-AP, algebra, American literature-AP, art, art-AP, Bible studies, biology, biology-AP, British literature-AP, calculus, calculus-AP, career planning, career/college preparation, chemistry, choir, Christian ethics, Christian scripture, Christian studies, Christian testament, Christianity, college counseling, college placement, college planning, college writing, computer skills, concert band, drama, economics, English, English language-AP, English literature-AP, fine arts, foreign language, geography, geometry, government, human anatomy, keyboarding, Latin, library research, Life of Christ, physical education, physical science, physics, U.S. history, world history.

Graduation Requirements Arts and fine arts (art, music, dance, drama), Bible, English, foreign language, mathematics, physical education (includes health), science, social studies (includes history), 60 hours of community service. Community service is required.

Special Academic Programs Advanced Placement exam preparation; honors section; study at local college for college credit.

College Admission Counseling 35 students graduated in 2009; 34 went to college, including Clemson University; College of Charleston; University of South Carolina; York Technical College. Other: 1 entered military service. Mean SAT critical reading: 560, mean SAT math: 517, mean SAT writing: 575, mean combined SAT: 1652, mean composite ACT: 24.

Student Life Upper grades have specified standards of dress, student council, honor system. Discipline rests primarily with faculty. Attendance at religious services is required.

Tuition and Aid Day student tuition: $6015–$6355. Tuition installment plan (FACTS Tuition Payment Plan, monthly payment plans). Tuition reduction for siblings, need-based scholarship grants available.

Admissions School's own test and WRAT required. Deadline for receipt of application materials: none. Application fee required: $50. Interview required.

Athletics Interscholastic: baseball (boys), basketball (b,g), cheering (b,g), cross-country running (b,g), football (b), golf (b,g), soccer (b,g), softball (g), swimming and diving (b,g), tennis (b,g), volleyball (g). 2 PE instructors, 10 coaches.

Computers Computers are regularly used in all classes. Computer network features include on-campus library services, Internet access, wireless campus network, Internet filtering or blocking technology. Campus intranet is available to students. Students grades are available online. The school has a published electronic and media policy.

Contact Mrs. Patty Limerick, Admissions Coordinator. 803-366-6703. Fax: 803-325-8191. E-mail: plimerick@wccs.org. Web site: www.wccs.org.

WESTMINSTER CHRISTIAN ACADEMY

237 Johns Road
Huntsville, Alabama 35806
Head of School: Mr. Craig L. Bouvier

General Information Coeducational day college-preparatory, general academic, arts, religious studies, and technology school, affiliated with Presbyterian Church in America. Grades K–12. Founded: 1964. Setting: suburban. Nearest major city is Birmingham. 42-acre campus. 5 buildings on campus. Approved or accredited by Christian Schools International, Southern Association of Colleges and Schools, and Alabama Department of Education. Member of Secondary School Admission Test Board. Endowment: $3.9 million. Total enrollment: 675. Upper school average class size: 16. Upper school faculty-student ratio: 1:16. There are 180 required school days per year for Upper School students. Upper School students typically attend 5 days per week. The average school day consists of 7 hours and 20 minutes.

Upper School Student Profile Grade 6: 62 students (35 boys, 27 girls); Grade 7: 56 students (24 boys, 32 girls); Grade 8: 60 students (27 boys, 33 girls); Grade 9: 67 students (40 boys, 27 girls); Grade 10: 65 students (39 boys, 26 girls); Grade 11: 44 students (17 boys, 27 girls); Grade 12: 53 students (28 boys, 25 girls). 15% of students are Presbyterian Church in America.

Faculty School total: 56. In upper school: 11 men, 18 women; 16 have advanced degrees.

Subjects Offered Advanced computer applications, algebra, American history, American history-AP, art, band, Bible studies, biology, botany, business mathematics, business skills, calculus, calculus-AP, chemistry, choir, civics, computer programming, computer programming-AP, concert choir, consumer mathematics, CPR, drama, drama performance, economics-AP, English, English-AP, ensembles, environmental science, first aid, fitness, French, geography, geometry, government, government-AP, health education, home economics, interior design, journalism, keyboarding, Latin, modern dance, painting, photography, physical education, physical science, physics, physiology, pre-calculus, psychology, Spanish, Web site design, world history, yearbook.

Graduation Requirements Arts and fine arts (art, music, dance, drama), computer applications, electives, English, foreign language, mathematics, physical education (includes health), religion (includes Bible studies and theology), science, social studies (includes history).

Special Academic Programs Advanced Placement exam preparation; honors section; independent study; study at local college for college credit; academic accommodation for the gifted, the musically talented, and the artistically talented; remedial reading and/or remedial writing; remedial math.

College Admission Counseling 57 students graduated in 2010; 54 went to college, including Auburn University; Calhoun Community College; Covenant College; The University of Alabama; The University of Alabama in Huntsville; University of North Alabama. Other: 3 had other specific plans. 35% scored over 600 on SAT critical reading, 50% scored over 600 on SAT math.

Student Life Upper grades have specified standards of dress, student council. Discipline rests primarily with faculty. Attendance at religious services is required.

Tuition and Aid Day student tuition: $7196. Guaranteed tuition plan. Tuition installment plan (monthly payment plans, individually arranged payment plans). Tuition reduction for siblings, need-based scholarship grants, free tuition for children of faculty available. In 2010–11, 15% of upper-school students received aid. Total amount of financial aid awarded in 2010–11: $200,000.

Admissions Any standardized test, school's own test or writing sample required. Deadline for receipt of application materials: none. Application fee required: $50. Interview required.

Athletics Interscholastic: baseball (boys), basketball (b,g), cheering (g), cross-country running (b,g), football (b), golf (b,g), physical training (b,g), soccer (b,g), softball (g), swimming and diving (b,g), track and field (b,g), volleyball (g), weight training (b,g), wrestling (b); intramural: physical fitness (b,g), physical training (b,g), strength & conditioning (b,g), weight training (b,g); coed interscholastic: cheering; coed intramural: weight training. 6 coaches, 1 athletic trainer.

Computers Computers are regularly used in all academic classes. Computer network features include on-campus library services, Internet access, wireless campus network, Internet filtering or blocking technology. Student e-mail accounts and computer access in designated common areas are available to students. Students grades are available online. The school has a published electronic and media policy.

Contact Mrs. Leslie Parker, Admissions Director. 256-705-8216. Fax: 256-705-8001. E-mail: leslie.parker@wca-hsv.org. Web site: www.wca-hsv.org.

WESTMINSTER CHRISTIAN ACADEMY

186 Westminster Drive
Opelousas, Louisiana 70570
Head of School: Mrs. Merida Brooks

General Information Coeducational day college-preparatory, arts, religious studies, bilingual studies, and technology school, affiliated with Protestant-Evangelical faith, Christian faith. Grades PK–12. Founded: 1978. Setting: rural. Nearest major city is Lafayette. 30-acre campus. 6 buildings on campus. Approved or accredited by Louisiana Department of Education. Endowment: $170,044. Total enrollment: 1,042. Upper school average class size: 23. Upper school faculty-student ratio: 1:13. There are 175 required school days per year for Upper School students. Upper School students typically attend 5 days per week. The average school day consists of 7 hours.

Upper School Student Profile Grade 6: 61 students (27 boys, 34 girls); Grade 7: 74 students (35 boys, 39 girls); Grade 8: 72 students (32 boys, 40 girls); Grade 9: 61 students (25 boys, 36 girls); Grade 10: 58 students (26 boys, 32 girls); Grade 11: 58 students (32 boys, 26 girls); Grade 12: 49 students (35 boys, 14 girls). 95% of students are Protestant-Evangelical faith, Christian faith.

Faculty School total: 66. In upper school: 13 men, 12 women; 5 have advanced degrees.

Subjects Offered Advanced math, algebra, American history, art, biology, calculus, calculus-AP, ceramics, chemistry, chemistry-AP, civics, concert choir, creative writing, drama, economics, English, English-AP, fine arts, French, geometry, guitar, history-AP, Latin, music, physics, religion, Spanish, world history, yearbook.

Graduation Requirements Arts and fine arts (art, music, dance, drama), computer literacy, English, foreign language, mathematics, physical education (includes health), religion (includes Bible studies and theology), science, social studies (includes history).

Special Academic Programs Advanced Placement exam preparation; honors section; accelerated programs; special instructional classes for students with mild learning disabilities and Attention Deficit Disorder.

College Admission Counseling 47 students graduated in 2010; 46 went to college, including Louisiana State University and Agricultural and Mechanical College; Louisiana Tech University; Loyola University New Orleans, Olivet Nazarene University; University of Louisiana at Lafayette. Other: 1 entered military service. Mean composite ACT: 26.

Student Life Upper grades have uniform requirement, student council. Discipline rests primarily with faculty. Attendance at religious services is required.

Summer Programs Sports programs offered; session focuses on Training for football; held on campus; accepts boys; not open to students from other schools. 85 students usually enrolled. 2011 schedule: July 31.

Tuition and Aid Day student tuition: $5235. Guaranteed tuition plan. Tuition installment plan (FACTS Tuition Payment Plan, monthly payment plans, annual and biannual payment plans). Need-based scholarship grants, pastor discounts available. In 2010–11, 10% of upper-school students received aid. Total amount of financial aid awarded in 2010–11: $36,981.

Admissions Traditional secondary-level entrance grade is 9. School's own exam and Stanford Achievement Test required. Deadline for receipt of application materials: none. Application fee required: $100. On-campus interview required.

Athletics Interscholastic: baseball (boys), basketball (b,g), cheering (g), football (b), golf (b), hiking/backpacking (b,g), soccer (b), softball (g), swimming and diving (b,g), tennis (b,g), track and field (b,g), volleyball (g).

Computers Computers are regularly used in literacy classes. Computer network features include on-campus library services, Internet access. Student e-mail accounts are available to students. Students grades are available online.

Contact Mrs. Michelle Nezat, Admissions Director. 337-948-4623 Ext. 123. Fax: 337-948-4090. E-mail: mnezat@wcala.org. Web site: www.wcala.org.

WESTMINSTER CHRISTIAN SCHOOL

6855 Southwest 152nd Street
Palmetto Bay, Florida 33157
Head of School: Mr. A. J. West

General Information Coeducational day and distance learning college-preparatory, arts, and religious studies school, affiliated with Christian faith. Grades PK–12. Distance learning grades 9–12. Founded: 1961. Setting: suburban. Nearest major city is Miami. 26-acre campus. 9 buildings on campus. Approved or accredited by Christian Schools of Florida, Florida Council of Independent Schools, Southern Association of Colleges and Schools, and Florida Department of Education. Endowment: $2.2 million. Total enrollment: 1,054. Upper school average class size: 17. Upper school faculty-student ratio: 1:11. There are 173 required school days per year for Upper School students. Upper School students typically attend 5 days per week. The average school day consists of 7 hours.

Upper School Student Profile Grade 9: 104 students (40 boys, 64 girls); Grade 10: 102 students (50 boys, 52 girls); Grade 11: 114 students (55 boys, 59 girls); Grade 12: 107 students (57 boys, 50 girls). 100% of students are Christian.

Faculty School total: 104. In upper school: 20 men, 24 women; 25 have advanced degrees.

Subjects Offered Advanced Placement courses, algebra, American history, American literature, anatomy, art, Bible studies, biology, biology-AP, business law, business skills, calculus, ceramics, chemistry, chemistry-AP, community service, computer programming, computer science, creative writing, drama, economics, English, English literature, fine arts, French, French-AP, general science, geometry, government-AP, government/civics, grammar, health, history, macroeconomics-AP, marine biology, mathematics, music, musical theater, organic chemistry, photography, physical education, physics, physiology, psychology, religion, SAT preparation, science, scripture, sculpture, sex education, social studies, sociology, softball, Spanish, Spanish language-AP, Spanish-AP, speech, sports, statistics-AP, strings, study skills, swimming, theater, track and field, trigonometry, typing, U.S. government, U.S. government and politics-AP, U.S. history, U.S. history-AP, vocal ensemble, volleyball, weightlifting, wind ensemble, world history, world literature, wrestling, writing, yearbook.

Graduation Requirements Arts and fine arts (art, music, dance, drama), Bible, computer science, electives, English, foreign language, health science, lab science, mathematics, physical education (includes health), science, social studies (includes history), speech. Community service is required.

Special Academic Programs 13 Advanced Placement exams for which test preparation is offered; honors section; accelerated programs; independent study; academic accommodation for the gifted, the musically talented, and the artistically talented; programs in English, mathematics for dyslexic students.

College Admission Counseling 117 students graduated in 2009; all went to college, including Florida Gulf Coast University; Florida International University; Florida State University; Miami Dade College; University of Central Florida; University of Miami. Mean SAT critical reading: 552, mean SAT math: 539, mean SAT writing: 559, mean combined SAT: 1651, mean composite ACT: 24. 15% scored over 600 on SAT critical reading, 10% scored over 600 on SAT math, 10% scored over 600 on SAT writing, 10% scored over 1800 on combined SAT, 15% scored over 26 on composite ACT.

Student Life Upper grades have uniform requirement, student council, honor system. Discipline rests primarily with faculty. Attendance at religious services is required.

Tuition and Aid Day student tuition: $15,570. Tuition installment plan (monthly payment plans, individually arranged payment plans, semiannual and annual payment plans). Need-based scholarship grants available. In 2009–10, 10% of upper-school students received aid. Total amount of financial aid awarded in 2009–10: $750,000.

Admissions Traditional secondary-level entrance grade is 9. For fall 2009, 121 students applied for upper-level admission, 66 were accepted, 56 enrolled. Iowa Tests of Basic Skills and writing sample required. Deadline for receipt of application materials: February 1. Application fee required: $125. On-campus interview required.

Athletics Interscholastic: baseball (boys), basketball (b,g), cheering (g), cross-country running (b,g), football (b), golf (b,g), soccer (b,g), softball (g), swimming and diving (b,g), tennis (b,g), track and field (b,g), volleyball (b,g), wrestling (b). 8 PE instructors, 75 coaches, 2 athletic trainers.

Computers Computers are regularly used in accounting, art, Bible studies, business applications, career exploration, college planning, computer applications, creative writing, economics, English, foreign language, keyboarding, mathematics, music, photography, programming, science, word processing, writing, writing, yearbook classes. Computer network features include on-campus library services, online commercial services, Internet access, wireless campus network, Internet filtering or blocking technology. Campus intranet is available to students. Students grades are available online. The school has a published electronic and media policy.

Westminster Christian School

Contact Ms. Caroline H. Stone, Director of Admission. 305-233-2030 Ext. 1246. Fax: 305-253-9623. E-mail: cstone@wcsmiami.org. Web site: www.wcsmiami.org.

WESTMINSTER SCHOOL

995 Hopmeadow Street
Simsbury, Connecticut 06070
Head of School: Mr. W. Graham Cole Jr.

General Information Coeducational boarding and day college-preparatory, arts, and technology school. Grades 9–PG. Founded: 1888. Setting: suburban. Nearest major city is Hartford. Students are housed in single-sex dormitories. 230-acre campus. 38 buildings on campus. Approved or accredited by Connecticut Association of Independent Schools, New England Association of Schools and Colleges, The Association of Boarding Schools, and Connecticut Department of Education. Member of National Association of Independent Schools and Secondary School Admission Test Board. Endowment: $68 million. Total enrollment: 392. Upper school average class size: 12. Upper school faculty-student ratio: 1:7. There are 185 required school days per year for Upper School students. Upper School students typically attend 6 days per week. The average school day consists of 6 hours and 30 minutes.

Upper School Student Profile Grade 9: 68 students (38 boys, 30 girls); Grade 10: 104 students (55 boys, 49 girls); Grade 11: 107 students (57 boys, 50 girls); Grade 12: 104 students (64 boys, 40 girls); Postgraduate: 9 students (9 boys). 67% of students are boarding students. 51% are state residents. 26 states are represented in upper school student body. 12% are international students. International students from Bermuda, Canada, China, Hong Kong, Mexico, and Republic of Korea; 15 other countries represented in student body.

Faculty School total: 59. In upper school: 33 men, 26 women; 48 have advanced degrees; 49 reside on campus.

Subjects Offered Acting, advanced chemistry, advanced computer applications, advanced math, Advanced Placement courses, advanced studio art-AP, African American history, algebra, American history, American history-AP, American literature, American literature-AP, anatomy and physiology, Ancient Greek, architecture, art, art history, art history-AP, art-AP, Asian history, astronomy, athletics, band, biology, biology-AP, calculus, calculus-AP, character education, chemistry, chemistry-AP, Chinese, choir, choral music, comparative government and politics-AP, computer programming, computer science-AP, creative writing, dance, discrete mathematics, drama, drama workshop, drawing, drawing and design, driver education, ecology, economics, economics-AP, English, English literature, English-AP, English/ composition-AP, environmental science-AP, ethics, ethics and responsibility, European history, European history-AP, female experience in America, fine arts, French, French language-AP, French literature-AP, geology, geometry, graphic design, health, history, honors algebra, honors English, honors geometry, illustration, Latin, Latin-AP, literature and composition-AP, macro/microeconomics-AP, mathematics, mathematics-AP, mechanical drawing, modern European history-AP, music, music appreciation, music composition, music theory-AP, musical theater, Native American history, painting, philosophy, photography, physics, physics-AP, pre-calculus, probability and statistics, SAT preparation, SAT/ACT preparation, science, set design, social studies, Spanish, Spanish language-AP, Spanish literature, Spanish literature-AP, stagecraft, statistics, statistics-AP, studio art-AP, theater, trigonometry, U.S. history-AP, world history, writing.

Graduation Requirements Arts, English, foreign language, history, mathematics, science.

Special Academic Programs 23 Advanced Placement exams for which test preparation is offered; honors section; independent study; term-away projects; study abroad.

College Admission Counseling 100 students graduated in 2009; all went to college, including Boston College; Columbia College; Trinity College; University of Vermont; Yale University. Median SAT critical reading: 600, median SAT math: 640, median SAT writing: 625, median combined SAT: 1865.

Student Life Upper grades have specified standards of dress, student council. Discipline rests primarily with faculty.

Tuition and Aid Day student tuition: $31,700; 7-day tuition and room/board: $42,900. Tuition installment plan (Academic Management Services Plan). Need-based scholarship grants available. In 2009–10, 30% of upper-school students received aid. Total amount of financial aid awarded in 2009–10: $3,540,000.

Admissions Traditional secondary-level entrance grade is 9. For fall 2009, 887 students applied for upper-level admission, 277 were accepted, 128 enrolled. PSAT and SAT for applicants to grade 11 and 12 or TOEFL required. Deadline for receipt of application materials: January 15. Application fee required: $75. On-campus interview required.

Athletics Interscholastic: baseball (boys), basketball (b,g), cross-country running (b,g), diving (b,g), field hockey (g), football (b), golf (b,g), hockey (b,g), ice hockey (b,g), lacrosse (b,g), soccer (b,g), softball (g), swimming and diving (b,g), squash (b,g), tennis (b,g), track and field (b,g); intramural: strength & conditioning (b,g); coed interscholastic: dance, martial arts, modern dance; coed intramural: aerobics/dance, ballet, bowling, canoeing/kayaking, dance, fly fishing, freestyle skiing, ice skating, modern dance, mountain biking, outdoor activities, rugby, skiing (cross-country), skiing (downhill), table tennis, unicycling. 2 athletic trainers.

Computers Computers are regularly used in English, foreign language, history, mathematics, science classes. Computer network features include on-campus library services, online commercial services, Internet access, wireless campus network,

Internet filtering or blocking technology. Campus intranet, student e-mail accounts, and computer access in designated common areas are available to students. The school has a published electronic and media policy.

Contact Mr. Jon C. Deveaux, Director of Admissions. 860-408-3060. Fax: 860-408-3042. E-mail: admit@westminster-school.org. Web site: www.westminster-school.org.

WESTMINSTER SCHOOLS OF AUGUSTA

3067 Wheeler Road
Augusta, Georgia 30909
Head of School: Mr. Stephen D. O'Neil

General Information Coeducational day college-preparatory, arts, religious studies, and music, debate and drama school, affiliated with Presbyterian Church in America. Grades PK–12. Founded: 1972. Setting: suburban. 30-acre campus. 7 buildings on campus. Approved or accredited by Georgia Independent School Association, Southern Association of Colleges and Schools, and Southern Association of Independent Schools. Member of National Association of Independent Schools. Endowment: $290,000. Total enrollment: 536. Upper school average class size: 14. Upper school faculty-student ratio: 1:8. There are 180 required school days per year for Upper School students. Upper School students typically attend 5 days per week. The average school day consists of 7 hours and 30 minutes.

Upper School Student Profile Grade 6: 28 students (19 boys, 9 girls); Grade 7: 39 students (22 boys, 17 girls); Grade 8: 40 students (29 boys, 11 girls); Grade 9: 52 students (23 boys, 29 girls); Grade 10: 36 students (16 boys, 20 girls); Grade 11: 33 students (17 boys, 16 girls); Grade 12: 32 students (16 boys, 16 girls). 40% of students are Presbyterian Church in America.

Faculty School total: 54. In upper school: 18 men, 14 women; 26 have advanced degrees.

Subjects Offered Algebra, analysis and differential calculus, analysis of data, analytic geometry, anatomy and physiology, Ancient Greek, art, arts, band, Bible studies, biology, biology-AP, British literature (honors), calculus, calculus-AP, chemistry, chemistry-AP, choir, chorus, Christian scripture, classical Greek literature, community service, computer programming, computer skills, computers, concert band, concert choir, drama, drama performance, dramatic arts, earth science, economics, English, English language and composition-AP, English language-AP, English literature, English literature and composition-AP, English literature-AP, European history, family living, French, French language-AP, French-AP, geography, geometry, government/civics, Greek, guidance, health, health education, history, history-AP, honors algebra, honors English, honors geometry, honors U.S. history, keyboarding, lab science, Latin, Latin-AP, mathematics, modern European history, modern European history-AP, modern history, modern world history, music, physical education, physical science, physics, physics-AP, pre-algebra, pre-calculus, psychology, religion, SAT preparation, science, social studies, Spanish, Spanish language-AP, Spanish-AP, speech, statistics-AP, studio art, study skills, swimming, trigonometry, U.S. government and politics-AP, U.S. history, U.S. history-AP, U.S. literature, United States government-AP, weight training, word processing, world history, world literature, writing, yearbook.

Graduation Requirements Arts and fine arts (art, music, dance, drama), electives, English, foreign language, mathematics, physical education (includes health), religion (includes Bible studies and theology), science, social studies (includes history).

Special Academic Programs Advanced Placement exam preparation; honors section; academic accommodation for the gifted; programs in general development for dyslexic students.

College Admission Counseling 38 students graduated in 2009; all went to college, including Augusta State University; Clemson University; Covenant College; Samford University; University of Georgia; University of South Carolina. Median SAT critical reading: 631, median SAT math: 633, median SAT writing: 637. 59% scored over 600 on SAT critical reading, 68% scored over 600 on SAT math, 62% scored over 600 on SAT writing.

Student Life Upper grades have specified standards of dress, honor system. Discipline rests primarily with faculty.

Tuition and Aid Day student tuition: $10,524. Tuition installment plan (monthly payment plans). Tuition reduction for siblings, need-based scholarship grants available. In 2009–10, 20% of upper-school students received aid. Total amount of financial aid awarded in 2009–10: $250,000.

Admissions Traditional secondary-level entrance grade is 9. For fall 2009, 23 students applied for upper-level admission, 20 were accepted, 19 enrolled. ERB-verbal abilities, reading comprehension, quantitative abilities (level F, form 1), mathematics proficiency exam and writing sample required. Deadline for receipt of application materials: none. Application fee required: $75. On-campus interview required.

Athletics Interscholastic: baseball (boys), basketball (b,g), cheering (g), cross-country running (b,g), golf (b), soccer (b,g), swimming and diving (b,g), tennis (b,g), track and field (b,g), volleyball (g). 3 PE instructors, 4 coaches, 1 athletic trainer.

Computers Computers are regularly used in college planning, keyboarding, programming, SAT preparation, technology, yearbook classes. Computer network features include Internet access, Internet filtering or blocking technology. Campus intranet, student e-mail accounts, and computer access in designated common areas are available to students. Students grades are available online. The school has a published electronic and media policy.

Contact Mrs. Aimee C. Lynch, Director of Admissions. 706-731-5260 Ext. 2220. Fax: 706-261-7786. E-mail: alynch@wsa.net. Web site: www.wsa.net.

WEST NOTTINGHAM ACADEMY
1079 Firetower Road
Colora, Maryland 21917-1599
Head of School: Dr. D. John Watson, PhD

General Information Coeducational boarding and day college-preparatory, arts, and ESL school. Grades 9–PG. Founded: 1744. Setting: rural. Nearest major city is Baltimore. Students are housed in single-sex dormitories. 120-acre campus. 12 buildings on campus. Approved or accredited by Association of Independent Maryland Schools, Middle States Association of Colleges and Schools, National Commission of Accreditation of Special Education Services, The Association of Boarding Schools, and Maryland Department of Education. Member of National Association of Independent Schools and Secondary School Admission Test Board. Total enrollment: 117. Upper school average class size: 10. Upper school faculty-student ratio: 1:6. There are 170 required school days per year for Upper School students. Upper School students typically attend 5 days per week. The average school day consists of 7 hours.

Upper School Student Profile Grade 9: 14 students (8 boys, 6 girls); Grade 10: 25 students (15 boys, 10 girls); Grade 11: 36 students (21 boys, 15 girls); Grade 12: 37 students (19 boys, 18 girls). 61% of students are boarding students. 22% are state residents. 9 states are represented in upper school student body. 26% are international students. International students from China, Japan, Republic of Korea, Russian Federation, Taiwan, and Thailand; 7 other countries represented in student body.

Faculty School total: 28. In upper school: 13 men, 10 women; 16 have advanced degrees; 23 reside on campus.

Subjects Offered Advanced chemistry, advanced math, advanced TOEFL/grammar, African-American history, algebra, American literature, anatomy, ancient world history, applied arts, art, art history, Asian history, astronomy, basic language skills, biology, biology-AP, body human, British literature, British literature (honors), calculus, calculus-AP, ceramics, chemistry, chemistry-AP, clayworking, college counseling, comparative religion, computer education, drama, drama performance, drawing, earth science, English, English literature, English literature-AP, English-AP, environmental science, equestrian sports, ESL, ethics, ethics and responsibility, European history, European history-AP, fine arts, French, French-AP, geography, geometry, government/civics, guitar, health, history, history-AP, honors algebra, honors English, honors geometry, honors U.S. history, human anatomy, human biology, humanities, independent study, instrumental music, journalism, Latin, marketing, mathematics, modern European history, modern European history-AP, multicultural studies, music, music appreciation, photography, physical education, physics, physics-AP, physiology, piano, play production, pottery, pre-calculus, psychology, religion, SAT preparation, science, senior humanities, senior project, senior thesis, social studies, Spanish, Spanish-AP, sports, stage design, student government, student publications, studio art, studio art-AP, U.S. history, U.S. history-AP, visual and performing arts, voice, voice ensemble, weight training, wellness, world history, world literature, world religions, wrestling, writing, yearbook.

Graduation Requirements Senior research paper.

Special Academic Programs Advanced Placement exam preparation; honors section; independent study; study at local college for college credit; academic accommodation for the gifted, the musically talented, and the artistically talented; remedial reading and/or remedial writing; remedial math; programs in English, mathematics, general development for dyslexic students; ESL (10 students enrolled).

College Admission Counseling 26 students graduated in 2009; all went to college, including Arizona State University; Kansas State University; New York University; Wellesley College.

Student Life Upper grades have specified standards of dress, student council. Discipline rests primarily with faculty.

Tuition and Aid Day student tuition: $19,350; 7-day tuition and room/board: $37,100. Tuition installment plan (monthly payment plans, individually arranged payment plans). Need-based scholarship grants available. In 2009–10, 35% of upper-school students received aid. Total amount of financial aid awarded in 2009–10: $721,000.

Admissions Traditional secondary-level entrance grade is 9. For fall 2009, 184 students applied for upper-level admission, 91 were accepted, 45 enrolled. ISEE, SSAT, TOEFL or TOEFL or SLEP required. Deadline for receipt of application materials: none. Application fee required: $50. On-campus interview required.

Athletics Interscholastic: baseball (boys), basketball (b,g), cheering (g), cross-country running (b,g), field hockey (g), football (b), golf (b,g), lacrosse (b), soccer (b,g), tennis (b,g), track and field (b,g), volleyball (g), wrestling (b); intramural: bicycling (b); coed interscholastic: cross-country running, power lifting, tennis, track and field, weight training; coed intramural: equestrian sports, horseback riding, strength & conditioning, weight training. 2 coaches, 1 athletic trainer.

Computers Computers are regularly used in computer applications, introduction to technology, mathematics, SAT preparation, science classes. Computer network features include on-campus library services, Internet access, wireless campus network, Internet filtering or blocking technology. Campus intranet and student e-mail accounts are available to students. The school has a published electronic and media policy.

Contact Mr. Jesse Wilson Roberts, IV, Director of Admission. 410-658-5556 Ext. 9224. Fax: 410-658-9264. E-mail: admissions@wna.org. Web site: www.wna.org.

WESTOVER SCHOOL
1237 Whittemore Road
Middlebury, Connecticut 06762
Head of School: Mrs. Ann S. Pollina

General Information Girls' boarding and day college-preparatory, arts, technology, and mathematics and science school. Grades 9–12. Founded: 1909. Setting: small town. Nearest major city is New York, NY. Students are housed in single-sex dormitories. 145-acre campus. 11 buildings on campus. Approved or accredited by Association of Independent Schools in New England, Connecticut Association of Independent Schools, New England Association of Schools and Colleges, The Association of Boarding Schools, and Connecticut Department of Education. Member of National Association of Independent Schools and Secondary School Admission Test Board. Endowment: $38 million. Total enrollment: 210. Upper school average class size: 11. Upper school faculty-student ratio: 1:8. There are 183 required school days per year for Upper School students. Upper School students typically attend 6 days per week. The average school day consists of 6 hours.

Upper School Student Profile Grade 9: 52 students (52 girls); Grade 10: 48 students (48 girls); Grade 11: 62 students (62 girls); Grade 12: 48 students (48 girls). 62% of students are boarding students. 56% are state residents. 16 states are represented in upper school student body. 18% are international students. International students from Bahamas, China, Japan, Netherlands, Republic of Korea, and Russian Federation; 11 other countries represented in student body.

Faculty School total: 37. In upper school: 13 men, 24 women; 29 have advanced degrees; 20 reside on campus.

Subjects Offered Advanced chemistry, Advanced Placement courses, African-American studies, algebra, American history, American history-AP, American literature, art, art history, art-AP, astronomy, ballet technique, bell choir, biology, biology-AP, calculus, calculus-AP, ceramics, chemistry, clayworking, community service, computer literacy, computer science, computer science-AP, creative writing, dance, drama, drawing, English, English language and composition-AP, English literature, environmental science, ESL, etymology, European history, European history-AP, filmmaking, fine arts, French, French-AP, geography, geometry, grammar, health and wellness, journalism, Latin, mathematics, model United Nations, music, music theory-AP, musical productions, painting, performing arts, photo shop, photography, physics, physics-AP, poetry, politics, portfolio art, pre-calculus, religion, robotics, science, sculpture, Shakespeare, short story, social studies, Spanish, Spanish-AP, speech, studio art-AP, theater, trigonometry, wilderness education, women's studies, world history, writing.

Graduation Requirements Art, athletics, English, foreign language, general science, mathematics, science, summer reading. Community service is required.

Special Academic Programs 15 Advanced Placement exams for which test preparation is offered; honors section; independent study; term-away projects; study abroad; academic accommodation for the gifted, the musically talented, and the artistically talented; special instructional classes for deaf students; ESL (5 students enrolled).

College Admission Counseling 50 students graduated in 2010; all went to college, including Dartmouth College; Massachusetts Institute of Technology; Middlebury College; Mount Holyoke College; Worcester Polytechnic Institute. Median composite ACT: 27. Mean SAT critical reading: 597, mean SAT math: 594, mean SAT writing: 621. 61% scored over 600 on SAT critical reading, 59% scored over 600 on SAT math, 64% scored over 600 on SAT writing, 54% scored over 1800 on combined SAT, 56% scored over 26 on composite ACT.

Student Life Upper grades have specified standards of dress, student council, honor system. Discipline rests equally with students and faculty.

Tuition and Aid Day student tuition: $30,800; 7-day tuition and room/board: $43,400. Tuition installment plan (The Tuition Plan, Insured Tuition Payment Plan, FACTS Tuition Payment Plan). Need-based scholarship grants, need-based loans, middle-income loans available. In 2010–11, 46% of upper-school students received aid. Total amount of financial aid awarded in 2010–11: $2,446,400.

Admissions Traditional secondary-level entrance grade is 9. For fall 2010, 245 students applied for upper-level admission, 108 were accepted, 63 enrolled. SSAT or TOEFL required. Deadline for receipt of application materials: February 1. Application fee required: $50. On-campus interview required.

Athletics Interscholastic: basketball, cross-country running, field hockey, golf, independent competitive sports, lacrosse, outdoor activities, soccer, softball, squash, tennis, volleyball; intramural: aerobics, aerobics/dance, alpine skiing, backpacking, ballet, canoeing/kayaking, climbing, dance, fitness, fitness walking, Frisbee, hiking/backpacking, jogging, kayaking, modern dance, outdoor activities, outdoor education, outdoor skills, outdoors, paddle tennis, physical fitness, physical training, rappelling, rock climbing, running, self defense, skiing (downhill), snowboarding, strength & conditioning, tennis, ultimate Frisbee, walking, wall climbing, weight lifting, weight training, wilderness, yoga. 2 PE instructors, 10 coaches, 1 athletic trainer.

Computers Computers are regularly used in all academic classes. Computer network features include on-campus library services, online commercial services, Internet access, wireless campus network, Internet filtering or blocking technology. Campus intranet, student e-mail accounts, and computer access in designated common areas are available to students. Students grades are available online. The school has a published electronic and media policy.

Contact Mrs. Laura Volovski, Director of Admission. 203-577-4521. Fax: 203-577-4588. E-mail: admission@westoverschool.org. Web site: www.westoverschool.org.

WESTRIDGE SCHOOL
324 Madeline Drive
Pasadena, California 91105-3399
Head of School: Ms. Elizabeth J. McGregor
General Information Girls' day college-preparatory, arts, and technology school. Grades 4–12. Founded: 1913. Setting: suburban. Nearest major city is Los Angeles. 10-acre campus. 11 buildings on campus. Approved or accredited by California Association of Independent Schools, National Independent Private Schools Association, The College Board, Western Association of Schools and Colleges, and California Department of Education. Member of National Association of Independent Schools. Endowment: $15 million. Total enrollment: 495. Upper school average class size: 14. Upper school faculty-student ratio: 1:6. Upper School students typically attend 5 days per week. The average school day consists of 6 hours and 30 minutes.
Upper School Student Profile Grade 9: 77 students (77 girls); Grade 10: 69 students (69 girls); Grade 11: 71 students (71 girls); Grade 12: 65 students (65 girls).
Faculty School total: 67. In upper school: 12 men, 25 women; 27 have advanced degrees.
Subjects Offered Acting, Advanced Placement courses, algebra, American history, American literature, art, art history, biology, calculus, cell biology, ceramics, chemistry, Chinese, chorus, classical language, college counseling, computer applications, computer graphics, computer science, creative writing, dance, directing, drama, earth science, English, English literature, environmental science, European history, fine arts, French, geometry, government/civics, history, Latin, life science, Mandarin, mathematics, modern languages, music, orchestra, photography, physical education, physical science, physics, physiology, pre-calculus, science, Spanish, Spanish literature, statistics, studio art, theater, trigonometry, video, visual and performing arts, visual arts, world history, world literature.
Graduation Requirements Art, college counseling, cultural arts, English, foreign language, history, mathematics, music, physical education (includes health), science, senior project, statistics. Community service is required.
Special Academic Programs Advanced Placement exam preparation; honors section; independent study.
College Admission Counseling 74 students graduated in 2010; all went to college, including Cornell University; New York University; Princeton University; University of California, Santa Cruz; University of Chicago; University of Southern California. Median SAT critical reading: 670, median SAT math: 630, median SAT writing: 685, median combined SAT: 1980. Mean composite ACT: 27.
Student Life Upper grades have uniform requirement, student council. Discipline rests primarily with faculty.
Summer Programs Art/fine arts programs offered; session focuses on Performing Arts; held on campus; accepts girls; open to students from other schools. 40 students usually enrolled. 2011 schedule: June 20 to July 22. Application deadline: May 27.
Tuition and Aid Day student tuition: $27,850. Tuition installment plan (monthly payment plans, full payment, two payment plan, 10-month tuition payment). Need-based scholarship grants available. In 2010–11, 31% of upper-school students received aid. Total amount of financial aid awarded in 2010–11: $1,452,200.
Admissions Traditional secondary-level entrance grade is 9. For fall 2010, 91 students applied for upper-level admission, 64 were accepted, 26 enrolled. ISEE, school's own exam or writing sample required. Deadline for receipt of application materials: February 1. Application fee required: $85. On-campus interview required.
Athletics Interscholastic: aerobics/dance, basketball, cross-country running, dance, diving, fencing, golf, lacrosse, martial arts, modern dance, physical fitness, soccer, softball, swimming and diving, tennis, track and field, volleyball, water polo, yoga. 4 PE instructors, 22 coaches, 1 athletic trainer.
Computers Computers are regularly used in art, English, foreign language, history, mathematics, science classes. Computer network features include on-campus library services, online commercial services, Internet access, wireless campus network, Internet filtering or blocking technology, course Web sites, Remote access to email and files, school Internet portal/website. Student e-mail accounts are available to students. The school has a published electronic and media policy.
Contact Ms. Helen V. Hopper, Director of Admissions. 626-799-1153 Ext. 213. Fax: 626-799-7068. E-mail: hhopper@westridge.org. Web site: www.westridge.org.

WEST SOUND ACADEMY
16571 Creative Drive NE
Poulsbo, Washington 98370
Head of School: Joe Kennedy
General Information Coeducational boarding and day college-preparatory, arts, and International Baccalaureate school. Boarding grades 9–12, day grades 7–12. Founded: 1998. Setting: rural. Nearest major city is Seattle. Students are housed in coed dormitories. 20-acre campus. 4 buildings on campus. Approved or accredited by Northwest Accreditation Commission, Pacific Northwest Association of Independent Schools, and Washington Department of Education. Total enrollment: 96. Upper school average class size: 11. Upper school faculty-student ratio: 1:7. There are 178 required school days per year for Upper School students. Upper School students typically attend 5 days per week. The average school day consists of 6 hours and 15 minutes.
Upper School Student Profile Grade 9: 12 students (5 boys, 7 girls); Grade 10: 19 students (10 boys, 9 girls); Grade 11: 14 students (9 boys, 5 girls); Grade 12: 13 students (7 boys, 6 girls). 9% of students are boarding students. 72% are state residents. 2 states are represented in upper school student body. 26% are international students. International students from China, Egypt, Germany, India, Philippines, and Ukraine; 1 other country represented in student body.
Faculty School total: 19. In upper school: 5 men, 9 women; 10 have advanced degrees.
Subjects Offered Advanced biology, advanced chemistry, advanced math, algebra, American history, analytic geometry, ancient world history, art, biology, calculus, chemistry, college counseling, computer technologies, contemporary issues, culinary arts, dance, debate, drawing, electives, English, filmmaking, fitness, four units of summer reading, French, geometry, guitar, history, International Baccalaureate courses, linear algebra, literary magazine, logarithms, Mandarin, marine biology, model United Nations, music, music performance, non-Western literature, non-Western societies, outdoor education, painting, photography, physics, poetry, portfolio art, portfolio writing, SAT preparation, senior thesis, Spanish, sports, studio art, technology, U.S. history, Washington State and Northwest History, Western civilization, Western literature, wilderness experience, world history, yearbook.
Graduation Requirements Biology, English, foreign language, history, International Baccalaureate courses, mathematics, senior thesis, service learning/internship, theory of knowledge, visual arts, West Sound Academy has a 4-1-4 academic calendar. Students are required to complete a, Jan-Term courses are month-long short courses of intense study in a variety of subjects outside the usual curriculum., Fall and Spring trips to varied locations teach leadership, environmental ethics, and technical skills.
Special Academic Programs International Baccalaureate program; 5 Advanced Placement exams for which test preparation is offered; independent study; term-away projects; ESL.
College Admission Counseling 11 students graduated in 2010; 10 went to college, including Lawrence University; Marlboro College; Skidmore College; The Colorado College. Other: 1 entered a postgraduate year. Median SAT critical reading: 560, median SAT math: 545, median SAT writing: 540, median combined SAT: 1645. 37.5% scored over 600 on SAT critical reading, 25% scored over 600 on SAT math, 25% scored over 600 on SAT writing, 13% scored over 1800 on combined SAT, 50% scored over 26 on composite ACT.
Student Life Upper grades have specified standards of dress, student council, honor system. Discipline rests primarily with faculty.
Summer Programs ESL programs offered; session focuses on ESL for international students; held both on and off campus; held at International students stay in Murphy International House, West Sound Academy's off-campus dormitory., The program includes both on-campus classes and off-campus field trips to various places of interest, and Examples: Seattle, Mount Rainier, Olympic National Park, Mt St Helens; accepts boys and girls; open to students from other schools. 15 students usually enrolled. 2011 schedule: July 11 to August 12. Application deadline: March 1.
Tuition and Aid Day student tuition: $15,805; 7-day tuition and room/board: $32,905. Tuition installment plan (Insured Tuition Payment Plan). Merit scholarship grants, need-based scholarship grants available. In 2010–11, 58% of upper-school students received aid; total upper-school merit-scholarship money awarded: $79,313. Total amount of financial aid awarded in 2010–11: $225,027.
Admissions Traditional secondary-level entrance grade is 9. For fall 2010, 35 students applied for upper-level admission, 24 were accepted, 21 enrolled. TOEFL or SLEP required. Deadline for receipt of application materials: none. Application fee required: $60. Interview required.
Athletics Coed Intramural: hiking/backpacking, kayaking, outdoor education, rock climbing, soccer. 1 PE instructor.
Computers Computers are regularly used in all classes. Computer network features include on-campus library services, Internet access, wireless campus network. Student e-mail accounts are available to students. The school has a published electronic and media policy.
Contact Jim Kolv, Director of Admissions. 360-598-5954. Fax: 360-598-5494. E-mail: lgsellman@westsoundacademy.org. Web site: www.westsoundacademy.org/.

WESTTOWN SCHOOL
975 Westtown Road
West Chester, Pennsylvania 19382-5700
Head of School: John W. Baird
General Information Coeducational boarding and day college-preparatory, arts, and religious studies school, affiliated with Society of Friends. Boarding grades 9–12, day grades PK–10. Founded: 1799. Setting: suburban. Nearest major city is Philadelphia. Students are housed in single-sex by floor dormitories and single-sex dormitories. 600-acre campus. 38 buildings on campus. Approved or accredited by Middle States Association of Colleges and Schools, Pennsylvania Association of Independent Schools, and Pennsylvania Department of Education. Member of National Association of Independent Schools and Secondary School Admission Test Board. Endowment: $57 million. Total enrollment: 762. Upper school average class size: 15. Upper school faculty-student ratio: 1:6. The average school day consists of 9 hours and 20 minutes.

Upper School Student Profile Grade 9: 72 students (28 boys, 44 girls); Grade 10: 104 students (56 boys, 48 girls); Grade 11: 104 students (58 boys, 46 girls); Grade 12: 113 students (50 boys, 63 girls). 77% of students are boarding students. 59% are state residents. 21 states are represented in upper school student body. 16% are international students. International students from China, Germany, Hong Kong, Nigeria, Republic of Korea, and Thailand; 12 other countries represented in student body. 15% of students are members of Society of Friends.

Faculty School total: 112. In upper school: 32 men, 34 women; 50 have advanced degrees; 58 reside on campus.

Subjects Offered 3-dimensional art, ACT preparation, advanced biology, advanced chemistry, advanced math, African dance, algebra, American culture, American foreign policy, American history, American literature, Ancient Greek, ancient history, Arabic, art, Asian history, astronomy, astrophysics, ballet, band, baseball, basketball, Bible, Bible studies, biology, botany, British literature, calculus, Chinese, choir, choral music, chorus, Christian and Hebrew scripture, classical language, classical studies, comparative religion, computer applications, concert band, concert choir, crafts, creative dance, creative writing, dance, dance performance, drama, drama performance, drama workshop, drawing, drawing and design, earth science, Eastern religion and philosophy, ecology, ecology, environmental systems, electives, English, English as a foreign language, English composition, English literature, environmental science, environmental studies, ESL, European history, film and literature, folk art, foreign language, foreign policy, fractal geometry, French, functions, geometry, German, graphic design, Greek, Holocaust and other genocides, honors algebra, honors geometry, honors U.S. history, honors world history, Italian, Japanese, jazz, jazz band, jazz dance, jazz ensemble, lab science, language, Latin, Latin American history, leadership, library research, linear algebra, literature, literature seminar, Mandarin, mathematics, model United Nations, modern dance, music, music composition, music performance, music theater, musical theater, mythology, nature writers, non-Western literature, peace and justice, physics, piano, play production, playwriting and directing, pre-algebra, pre-calculus, Quakerism and ethics, religion, robotics, SAT preparation, science, senior project, senior seminar, Shakespeare, Spanish, Spanish literature, stage design, statistics, student government, student publications, studio art, swimming, tap dance, tennis, theater, theater design and production, theater history, theater production, trigonometry, U.S. history, U.S. literature, visual and performing arts, visual arts, vocal ensemble, vocal music, water color painting, weight fitness, Western civilization, Western literature, Western religions, woodworking, work-study, world history, world literature, world religions, wrestling, writing, writing workshop, yearbook.

Graduation Requirements Arts and fine arts (art, music, dance, drama), English, foreign language, mathematics, physical education (includes health), religion (includes Bible studies and theology), religious studies, science, senior project, social sciences.

Special Academic Programs Advanced Placement exam preparation; honors section; independent study; study abroad; academic accommodation for the gifted, the musically talented, and the artistically talented; remedial math; ESL (18 students enrolled).

College Admission Counseling 89 students graduated in 2009; all went to college, including American University; Earlham College; Haverford College; New York University; The George Washington University; University of Pennsylvania.

Student Life Upper grades have specified standards of dress, student council. Discipline rests equally with students and faculty. Attendance at religious services is required.

Admissions Traditional secondary-level entrance grade is 9. For fall 2009, 296 students applied for upper-level admission, 172 were accepted, 71 enrolled. ISEE, SSAT or TOEFL required. Deadline for receipt of application materials: none. Application fee required: $50. On-campus interview required.

Athletics Interscholastic: baseball (boys), basketball (b,g), cross-country running (b,g), field hockey (g), independent competitive sports (b,g), lacrosse (b,g), soccer (b,g); coed interscholastic: dance team, golf, independent competitive sports, indoor track, indoor track & field; coed intramural: aquatics, ballet, basketball, canoeing/kayaking, combined training, dance, fitness, hiking/backpacking, indoor soccer, life saving, modern dance, outdoor activities, physical fitness, physical training, ropes courses, running. 18 coaches, 1 athletic trainer.

Computers Computers are regularly used in all academic, animation, art, career exploration, college planning, current events, desktop publishing, digital applications, graphic arts, introduction to technology, library, library skills, literary magazine, newspaper, publications, research skills, theater, yearbook classes. Computer network features include on-campus library services, online commercial services, Internet access, wireless campus network, Internet filtering or blocking technology. Campus intranet, student e-mail accounts, and computer access in designated common areas are available to students. Students grades are available online. The school has a published electronic and media policy.

Contact Nathan Bohn, Director of Admissions. 610-399-7900. Fax: 610-399-7909. E-mail: admissions@westtown.edu. Web site: www.westtown.edu.

WEST VALLEY CHRISTIAN CHURCH SCHOOLS
22450 Sherman Way
West Hills, California 91307
Head of School: Dr. Robert Lozano

General Information Coeducational day college-preparatory and religious studies school, affiliated with Christian faith, Christian Church (Disciples of Christ). Grades K–12. Founded: 1978. Setting: suburban. Nearest major city is Los Angeles. 5-acre campus. 6 buildings on campus. Approved or accredited by Association of Christian Schools International, Western Association of Schools and Colleges, and California Department of Education. Total enrollment: 204. Upper school average class size: 25. Upper school faculty-student ratio: 1:15. There are 179 required school days per year for Upper School students. Upper School students typically attend 5 days per week. The average school day consists of 6 hours and 15 minutes.

Upper School Student Profile Grade 6: 14 students (5 boys, 9 girls); Grade 7: 21 students (14 boys, 7 girls); Grade 8: 18 students (6 boys, 12 girls); Grade 9: 9 students (4 boys, 5 girls); Grade 10: 15 students (8 boys, 7 girls); Grade 11: 13 students (6 boys, 7 girls); Grade 12: 26 students (11 boys, 15 girls). 60% of students are Christian, Christian Church (Disciples of Christ).

Faculty School total: 13. In upper school: 6 men, 7 women; 4 have advanced degrees.

Subjects Offered Bible, English, fine arts, history, mathematics, physical education, science, Spanish, technical arts.

Graduation Requirements Arts and fine arts (art, music, dance, drama), career and personal planning, economics, English, government, health, history, mathematics, physical education (includes health), religion (includes Bible studies and theology), science, Spanish.

Special Academic Programs Advanced Placement exam preparation; honors section; study at local college for college credit; academic accommodation for the gifted; remedial math.

College Admission Counseling 11 students graduated in 2010; all went to college, including Azusa Pacific University; Biola University; California State University, Northridge; The University of Arizona; University of California, Riverside; Westmont College. Mean SAT critical reading: 480, mean SAT math: 490, mean SAT writing: 490, mean composite ACT: 21.

Student Life Upper grades have uniform requirement, student council, honor system. Discipline rests primarily with faculty. Attendance at religious services is required.

Tuition and Aid Day student tuition: $8260. Tuition installment plan (monthly payment plans, individually arranged payment plans). Tuition reduction for siblings, need-based scholarship grants available. In 2010–11, 45% of upper-school students received aid. Total amount of financial aid awarded in 2010–11: $150,000.

Admissions Traditional secondary-level entrance grade is 9. For fall 2010, 20 students applied for upper-level admission, 19 were accepted, 19 enrolled. BASIS or TAP required. Deadline for receipt of application materials: none. Application fee required: $150. Interview recommended.

Athletics Interscholastic: basketball (boys, girls), flag football (b), football (b), physical fitness (b,g), track and field (b,g), volleyball (b,g); coed interscholastic: cross-country running; coed intramural: martial arts, outdoor education. 2 PE instructors, 4 coaches.

Computers Computers are regularly used in word processing, yearbook classes. Computer resources include on-campus library services, Internet access. Students grades are available online.

Contact Lisa Kabelitz, School Secretary. 818-884-4710 Ext. 221. Fax: 818-884-4749. Web site: www.westvalleychristianschool.com.

WHEATON ACADEMY
900 Prince Crossing Road
West Chicago, Illinois 60185
Head of School: Dr. Gene Frost

General Information Coeducational day college-preparatory and religious studies school, affiliated with Christian faith. Grades 9–12. Founded: 1853. Setting: suburban. Nearest major city is Chicago. 43-acre campus. 8 buildings on campus. Approved or accredited by Association of Christian Schools International, North Central Association of Colleges and Schools, and Illinois Department of Education. Total enrollment: 645. Upper school average class size: 21. Upper school faculty-student ratio: 1:15. There are 175 required school days per year for Upper School students. Upper School students typically attend 5 days per week. The average school day consists of 7 hours.

Upper School Student Profile Grade 9: 153 students (72 boys, 81 girls); Grade 10: 150 students (71 boys, 79 girls); Grade 11: 178 students (85 boys, 93 girls); Grade 12: 164 students (79 boys, 85 girls). 99% of students are Christian faith.

Faculty School total: 46. In upper school: 25 men, 21 women; 33 have advanced degrees.

Subjects Offered 20th century history, ACT preparation, algebra, art, arts and crafts, band, Bible, Bible studies, biology, biology-AP, British literature, business, business applications, calculus, calculus-AP, ceramics, chemistry, chemistry-AP, child development, choir, Christian doctrine, Christian education, classics, comparative government and politics-AP, computer art, computer education, computer graphics, computer multimedia, computer processing, computer programming-AP, computer science, concert choir, consumer economics, creative writing, debate, desktop publishing, drama, drama workshop, drawing, driver education, earth science, economics, English, English language and composition-AP, English literature, English literature and composition-AP, environmental science, European history, European history-AP, family living, fiber arts, fine arts, foods, French, French language-AP, freshman seminar, geology, geometry, government/civics, graphic design, Greek, health, health and wellness, history, honors English, honors geometry, honors U.S. history, industrial arts, internship, journalism, keyboarding, leadership, literature, mathematics, multimedia design, music, music theory-AP, novels, orchestra, personal growth, physical education, physics, physics-AP, portfolio art, pre-algebra, psychology, publications, science, social sciences, social studies, sociology, Spanish, Spanish language-AP, speech, statistics, student publications, theater, theology, trigonometry, U.S. government, U.S. government and politics-AP, U.S. history, U.S. history AP, U.S. literature, world history, world literature, writing.

Graduation Requirements Arts and fine arts (art, music, dance, drama), English, mathematics, physical education (includes health), religion (includes Bible studies and theology), science, social sciences, social studies (includes history), Winterim (3-week period during January allowing students to take two classes beyond the typical curriculum).

Special Academic Programs 14 Advanced Placement exams for which test preparation is offered; honors section; independent study; term-away projects; study at local college for college credit; academic accommodation for the gifted, the musically talented, and the artistically talented; remedial reading and/or remedial writing; remedial math; special instructional classes for students with learning disabilities.

College Admission Counseling 163 students graduated in 2010; 154 went to college, including Calvin College; Taylor University; University of Illinois at Urbana–Champaign; Wheaton College. Other: 3 went to work, 6 had other specific plans. Median composite ACT: 25. 45% scored over 26 on composite ACT.

Student Life Upper grades have specified standards of dress, honor system. Discipline rests primarily with faculty. Attendance at religious services is required.

Summer Programs Advancement, sports, art/fine arts, computer instruction programs offered; held on campus; accepts boys and girls; open to students from other schools. 65 students usually enrolled. 2011 schedule: June 6 to June 24.

Tuition and Aid Day student tuition: $12,500. Tuition installment plan (monthly payment plans, semester payment plan). Tuition reduction for siblings, merit scholarship grants, need-based scholarship grants, paying campus jobs available. In 2010–11, 30% of upper-school students received aid; total upper-school merit-scholarship money awarded: $15,000. Total amount of financial aid awarded in 2010–11: $540,000.

Admissions Traditional secondary-level entrance grade is 9. ACT-Explore or placement test required. Deadline for receipt of application materials: none. Application fee required: $50. On-campus interview required.

Athletics Interscholastic: baseball (boys), basketball (b,g), cheering (g), cross-country running (b,g), dance team (g), football (b), golf (b,g), ice hockey (b), pom squad (g), soccer (b,g), softball (g), tennis (b,g), track and field (b,g), volleyball (b,g); intramural: aerobics (g), flagball (g), ice hockey (b), wilderness survival (b); coed interscholastic: modern dance, physical training, running; coed intramural: climbing, floor hockey, hiking/backpacking, outdoor education, outdoor skills, power lifting, project adventure, rock climbing, skiing (cross-country), strength & conditioning, wall climbing, weight lifting, weight training. 2 PE instructors, 6 coaches.

Computers Computers are regularly used in Bible studies, graphic design, independent study, mathematics, multimedia, writing, yearbook classes. Computer network features include on-campus library services, online commercial services, Internet access, Internet filtering or blocking technology. Student e-mail accounts are available to students. Students grades are available online.

Contact Ms. Rachel Swanson, Admissions Assistant. 630-562-7500 Ext. 7501. Fax: 630-231-0842. E-mail: rswanson@wheatonacademy.org. Web site: www.wheatonacademy.org.

THE WHEELER SCHOOL

216 Hope Street
Providence, Rhode Island 02906
Head of School: Dan Miller, PhD

General Information Coeducational day college-preparatory, arts, Community Action Program (service-based learning), and AERIE Program (individual academic enrichment grades 9-12) school. Grades N–12. Founded: 1889. Setting: urban. 5-acre campus. 8 buildings on campus. Approved or accredited by Association of Independent Schools in New England, New England Association of Schools and Colleges, and Rhode Island Department of Education. Member of National Association of Independent Schools. Endowment: $11 million. Total enrollment: 787. Upper school average class size: 15. Upper school faculty-student ratio: 1:9. There are 165 required school days per year for Upper School students. Upper School students typically attend 5 days per week. The average school day consists of 6 hours and 25 minutes.

Upper School Student Profile Grade 9: 82 students (45 boys, 37 girls); Grade 10: 78 students (37 boys, 41 girls); Grade 11: 66 students (33 boys, 33 girls); Grade 12: 96 students (48 boys, 48 girls).

Faculty School total: 130. In upper school: 21 men, 36 women; 42 have advanced degrees.

Subjects Offered 20th century world history, acting, Advanced Placement courses, advanced studio art-AP, algebra, American history, anatomy, art, art history, biology, biology-AP, biotechnology, Black history, business skills, calculus, calculus-AP,

ceramics, chemistry, Chinese, Chinese studies, choral music, civil rights, computer programming, computer science, contemporary issues, dance, drama, drawing, economics, engineering, English, English literature, English-AP, environmental science, environmental science-AP, European history, fine arts, forensics, French, geometry, guitar, Japanese, jazz ensemble, kinesiology, Latin, Latin American history, Latin American studies, mathematics, Middle Eastern history, music, nutrition, photography, physical education, physics, physiology, pre-calculus, printmaking, psychology, research, science, sculpture, social studies, Spanish, statistics, theater, trigonometry, Western civilization.

Graduation Requirements Arts and fine arts (art, music, dance, drama), English, foreign language, history, mathematics, performing arts, physical education (includes health), science, community service, Unity and Diversity curriculum.

Special Academic Programs 17 Advanced Placement exams for which test preparation is offered; honors section; accelerated programs; independent study; term-away projects; study at local college for college credit; study abroad; academic accommodation for the gifted; programs in general development for dyslexic students.

College Admission Counseling 81 students graduated in 2010; 80 went to college, including Boston University; Harvard University; The George Washington University; University of Pennsylvania; University of Rhode Island; Yale University. Other: 1 entered a postgraduate year. Mean SAT critical reading: 630, mean SAT math: 640, mean SAT writing: 630, mean combined SAT: 1900, mean composite ACT: 27. 57% scored over 600 on SAT critical reading, 61% scored over 600 on SAT math, 61% scored over 600 on SAT writing, 61% scored over 1800 on combined SAT, 57% scored over 26 on composite ACT.

Student Life Upper grades have specified standards of dress, student council. Discipline rests equally with students and faculty.

Summer Programs Session focuses on Jazz Camp; held on campus; accepts boys and girls; open to students from other schools.

Tuition and Aid Day student tuition: $26,265. Tuition installment plan (Insured Tuition Payment Plan, Key Tuition Payment Plan, monthly payment plans). Need-based scholarship grants available. In 2010–11, 23% of upper-school students received aid. Total amount of financial aid awarded in 2010–11: $1,158,146.

Admissions Traditional secondary-level entrance grade is 9. For fall 2010, 96 students applied for upper-level admission, 75 were accepted, 38 enrolled. ISEE or SSAT required. Deadline for receipt of application materials: January 31. Application fee required: $60. On-campus interview required.

Athletics Interscholastic: baseball (boys), basketball (b,g), cross-country running (b,g), field hockey (g), football (b), ice hockey (b,g), lacrosse (b,g), soccer (b,g), softball (g), tennis (b,g), track and field (b,g), winter (indoor) track (b,g); intramural: weight training (g); coed interscholastic: golf, squash. 6 PE instructors, 23 coaches, 1 athletic trainer.

Computers Computers are regularly used in health, mathematics, science, Spanish classes. Computer network features include on-campus library services, online commercial services, Internet access, wireless campus network. Student e-mail accounts are available to students. The school has a published electronic and media policy.

Contact Jeanette Epstein, Director of Admission. 401-421-8100. Fax: 401-751-7674. E-mail: jeanetteepstein@wheelerschool.org. Web site: www.wheelerschool.org.

WHITEFIELD ACADEMY

7711 Fegenbush Lane
Louisville, Kentucky 40228

General Information Coeducational day college-preparatory, arts, religious studies, and technology school, affiliated with Baptist Church. Grades PS–12. Founded: 1976. Setting: suburban. 30-acre campus. 2 buildings on campus. Approved or accredited by Association of Christian Schools International, CITA (Commission on International and Trans-Regional Accreditation), Council of Accreditation and School Improvement, Southern Association of Colleges and Schools, and Kentucky Department of Education. Total enrollment: 726. Upper school average class size: 20. Upper school faculty-student ratio: 1:20. There are 179 required school days per year for Upper School students. Upper School students typically attend 5 days per week. The average school day consists of 6 hours and 25 minutes.

Upper School Student Profile Grade 9: 56 students (23 boys, 33 girls); Grade 10: 56 students (25 boys, 31 girls); Grade 11: 46 students (22 boys, 24 girls); Grade 12: 54 students (29 boys, 25 girls). 45% of students are Baptist.

Faculty School total: 60. In upper school: 8 men, 9 women; 11 have advanced degrees.

Subjects Offered Adolescent issues, advanced math, algebra, anatomy, anatomy and physiology, art, arts, band, Bible studies, biology, calculus, calculus-AP, chemistry, choir, choral music, chorus, Christian education, Christian studies, college placement, college planning, college writing, communication skills, composition, computer applications, computer education, computers, current events, drama, drama performance, economics, English, English composition, English literature, English literature-AP, foreign language, geometry, history, honors English, library, mathematics, music, political science, pre-calculus, reading, SAT/ACT preparation, science, science project, sex education, social sciences, Spanish, speech and debate, student government, student publications, U.S. history, U.S. history-AP.

Graduation Requirements Algebra, arts and fine arts (art, music, dance, drama), Bible, biology, chemistry, economics, electives, English, foreign language, geometry, physical education (includes health), physical science, physics, political science, U.S. history, world civilizations.

Special Academic Programs Advanced Placement exam preparation; honors section; independent study; academic accommodation for the gifted.

College Admission Counseling 53 students graduated in 2010; 51 went to college, including Bellarmine University; Eastern Kentucky University; Jefferson Community and Technical College; University of Kentucky; University of Louisville; Western Kentucky University. Other: 1 went to work, 1 entered military service. Median composite ACT: 23. 31% scored over 26 on composite ACT.

Student Life Upper grades have uniform requirement, student council, honor system. Discipline rests primarily with faculty. Attendance at religious services is required.

Tuition and Aid Day student tuition: $6200. Tuition installment plan (FACTS Tuition Payment Plan, annual payment in full plan). Tuition reduction for siblings, need-based scholarship grants available. In 2010–11, 10% of upper-school students received aid. Total amount of financial aid awarded in 2010–11: $40,498.

Admissions Traditional secondary-level entrance grade is 9. For fall 2010, 14 students applied for upper-level admission, 14 were accepted, 14 enrolled. Stanford Achievement Test required. Deadline for receipt of application materials: none. Application fee required: $350. On-campus interview required.

Athletics Interscholastic: aquatics (boys, girls), baseball (b), basketball (b,g), cheering (b,g), cross-country running (b,g), golf (b,g), soccer (b,g), softball (g), swimming and diving (b,g), tennis (b,g), track and field (b,g), volleyball (g); intramural: aerobics (g), fitness (b,g), physical fitness (b,g), weight lifting (b,g). 2 PE instructors.

Computers Computers are regularly used in all academic classes. Computer network features include on-campus library services, Internet access, wireless campus network, Internet filtering or blocking technology. Computer access in designated common areas is available to students. Students grades are available online. The school has a published electronic and media policy.

Contact Mrs. Diane Fow, Director of Admissions. 502-231-6261. Fax: 502-239-3144. E-mail: dfow@whitefield.org.

THE WHITE MOUNTAIN SCHOOL

371 West Farm Road
Bethlehem, New Hampshire 03574
Head of School: Tim Breen, PhD

General Information Coeducational boarding and day college-preparatory, arts, and sustainability studies school, affiliated with Episcopal Church. Grades 9–PG. Founded: 1886. Setting: rural. Nearest major city is Concord. Students are housed in single-sex dormitories. 250-acre campus. 13 buildings on campus. Approved or accredited by Association for Experiential Education, National Association of Episcopal Schools, New England Association of Schools and Colleges, The Association of Boarding Schools, and New Hampshire Department of Education. Member of National Association of Independent Schools and Secondary School Admission Test Board. Endowment: $1.5 million. Total enrollment: 99. Upper school average class size: 9. Upper school faculty-student ratio: 1:5. Upper School students typically attend 5 days per week. The average school day consists of 5 hours and 45 minutes.

Upper School Student Profile 85% of students are boarding students. 25% are state residents. 22 states are represented in upper school student body. 30% are international students. International students from China, Ethiopia, Kenya, Republic of Korea, Ukraine, and Zambia; 5 other countries represented in student body. 5% of students are members of Episcopal Church.

Faculty School total: 28. In upper school: 15 men, 13 women; 15 have advanced degrees; 24 reside on campus.

Subjects Offered Algebra, American literature, American studies, anatomy and physiology, biology, calculus, Caribbean history, ceramics, chemistry, Chinese history, college counseling, community garden, community service, creative writing, drawing and design, earth science, economics, English, environmental education, environmental science, environmental studies, ESL, ethics, French, geometry, health, human development, independent study, Japanese history, jazz theory, learning strategies, literature, Middle Eastern history, music history, painting, philosophy, photography, physics, pre-calculus, printmaking, senior project, social justice, Spanish, studio art, theater arts, theater production, U.S. history, Vietnam, world history, writing.

Graduation Requirements Algebra, American history, arts and fine arts (art, music, dance, drama), English, geometry, health, literature, non-Western societies, physical science, theology, Western civilization, writing, field courses, sustainability studies, community service. Community service is required.

Special Academic Programs 4 Advanced Placement exams for which test preparation is offered; honors section; independent study; term-away projects; academic accommodation for the gifted, the musically talented, and the artistically talented; programs in English, mathematics, general development for dyslexic students; special instructional classes for students with dysgraphia and other learning differences; ESL (19 students enrolled).

College Admission Counseling 27 students graduated in 2010; all went to college, including Fort Lewis College; St. Lawrence University; The College of Wooster; University of Vermont; Warren Wilson College; Western State College of Colorado. 10% scored over 600 on SAT critical reading, 24% scored over 600 on SAT math.

Student Life Upper grades have specified standards of dress, student council, honor system. Discipline rests primarily with faculty.

Summer Programs Sports programs offered; session focuses on whitewater kayaking, rock climbing, and hiking; held both on and off campus; held at local rivers and open water and White Mountain National Forest; accepts boys and girls; open to students from other schools. 40 students usually enrolled. 2011 schedule: June 15 to July 30.

Tuition and Aid Day student tuition: $22,100; 7-day tuition and room/board: $43,600. Tuition installment plan (Insured Tuition Payment Plan, Academic Management Services Plan, 2-payment plan). Merit scholarship grants, need-based scholarship grants available. In 2010–11, 47% of upper-school students received aid. Total amount of financial aid awarded in 2010–11: $1,412,000.

Admissions For fall 2010, 126 students applied for upper-level admission, 65 were accepted, 39 enrolled. TOEFL or SLEP, WISC III or other aptitude measures; standardized achievement test or writing sample required. Deadline for receipt of application materials: February 1. Application fee required: $50. Interview required.

Athletics Interscholastic: basketball (boys), lacrosse (b,g), soccer (b,g); intramural: dance (g); coed interscholastic: climbing, freestyle skiing, mountain biking, rock climbing; coed intramural: aerobics/Nautilus, alpine skiing, backpacking, bicycling, canoeing/kayaking, climbing, combined training, fitness, freestyle skiing, Frisbee, hiking/backpacking, kayaking, martial arts, mountain biking, mountaineering, Nautilus, nordic skiing, outdoor activities, outdoor adventure, outdoor education, outdoor recreation, outdoor skills, outdoors, paddling, physical fitness, physical training, rappelling, rock climbing, running, skiing (cross-country), skiing (downhill), snowboarding, snowshoeing, strength & conditioning, telemark skiing, tennis, ultimate Frisbee, wall climbing, wilderness, wilderness survival, yoga. 1 athletic trainer.

Computers Computers are regularly used in college planning, foreign language, library skills, mathematics, media arts, science, yearbook classes. Computer network features include on-campus library services, online commercial services, Internet access, wireless campus network, Internet filtering or blocking technology. Student e-mail accounts and computer access in designated common areas are available to students. The school has a published electronic and media policy.

Contact Beth Towle, Director of Admission. 603-444-2928 Ext. 19. Fax: 603-444-5568. E-mail: beth.towle@whitemountain.org. Web site: www.whitemountain.org.

WICHITA COLLEGIATE SCHOOL

9115 East 13th Street
Wichita, Kansas 67206
Head of School: Mr. Chris Ashbrook

General Information Coeducational day college-preparatory, arts, and technology school. Grades PS–12. Founded: 1963. Setting: urban. 42-acre campus. 1 building on campus. Approved or accredited by Independent Schools Association of the Southwest. Member of National Association of Independent Schools. Endowment: $3.5 million. Total enrollment: 1,036. Upper school average class size: 10. Upper school faculty-student ratio: 1:10.

Upper School Student Profile Grade 9: 75 students (38 boys, 37 girls); Grade 10: 69 students (43 boys, 26 girls); Grade 11: 63 students (30 boys, 33 girls); Grade 12: 63 students (31 boys, 32 girls).

Faculty School total: 99. In upper school: 14 men, 12 women; 12 have advanced degrees.

Subjects Offered Advanced Placement courses, algebra, American history, American history-AP, American literature, art, biology, biology-AP, calculus, calculus-AP, chemistry, chemistry-AP, computer programming, computer science, computer science-AP, drama, economics, economics-AP, English, English literature, English-AP, European history, fine arts, French, French-AP, geometry, global studies, government-AP, government/civics, history, humanities, journalism, Latin, Latin-AP, macroeconomics-AP, mathematics, medieval/Renaissance history, music, photography, physical education, physics, physics-AP, science, social studies, Spanish, Spanish-AP, statistics, statistics-AP, theater, trigonometry, U.S. history-AP, United States government-AP, video, video film production, world history, world literature, writing, yearbook.

Graduation Requirements Arts and fine arts (art, music, dance, drama), computer science, economics, English, foreign language, humanities, mathematics, physical education (includes health), science, social studies (includes history).

Special Academic Programs 18 Advanced Placement exams for which test preparation is offered; study at local college for college credit; academic accommodation for the gifted.

College Admission Counseling 49 students graduated in 2009; all went to college, including Baylor University; Kansas State University; Oklahoma State University; The University of Kansas; University of Tulsa; Vanderbilt University. Median SAT critical reading: 610, median SAT math: 610, median SAT writing: 600, median combined SAT: 1820, median composite ACT: 27. 51% scored over 600 on SAT critical reading, 61% scored over 600 on SAT math, 50% scored over 600 on SAT writing, 52% scored over 1800 on combined SAT, 57% scored over 26 on composite ACT.

Student Life Upper grades have specified standards of dress, student council, honor system. Discipline rests primarily with faculty.

Tuition and Aid Day student tuition: $12,950. Tuition installment plan (monthly payment plans, individually arranged payment plans, 3-payment plan). Need-based scholarship grants available. In 2009–10, 22% of upper-school students received aid. Total amount of financial aid awarded in 2009–10: $444,533.

Admissions Traditional secondary-level entrance grade is 9. For fall 2009, 34 students applied for upper-level admission, 32 were accepted, 27 enrolled. Otis-Lennon, Stanford Achievement Test and Stanford Achievement Test, Otis-Lennon School Ability Test required. Deadline for receipt of application materials: none. Application fee required: $35. Interview recommended.

Athletics Interscholastic: baseball (boys), basketball (b,g), cheering (b,g), cross-country running (b,g), dance team (g), football (b), golf (b), softball (g), strength & conditioning (b,g), tennis (b,g), track and field (b,g), volleyball (g); coed interscholastic: bowling, cross-country running, swimming and diving, track and field. 2 PE instructors, 16 coaches, 1 athletic trainer.

Computers Computers are regularly used in video film production classes. Computer network features include on-campus library services, Internet access. Students grades are available online. The school has a published electronic and media policy.

Contact Ms. Susie Steed, Director of Admission and Communication. 316-771-2203. Fax: 316-634-0598. E-mail: ssteed@wcsks.com. Web site: www.wcsks.com.

WILBRAHAM & MONSON ACADEMY

423 Main Street
Wilbraham, Massachusetts 01095
Head of School: Rodney LaBrecque

General Information Coeducational boarding and day college-preparatory, arts, business, and technology school. Boarding grades 9–PG, day grades 6–PG. Founded: 1804. Setting: suburban. Nearest major city is Springfield. Students are housed in single-sex by floor dormitories and single-sex dormitories. 300-acre campus. 24 buildings on campus. Approved or accredited by Association of Independent Schools in New England, New England Association of Schools and Colleges, and The Association of Boarding Schools. Member of National Association of Independent Schools and Secondary School Admission Test Board. Endowment: $5 million. Total enrollment: 362. Upper school average class size: 12. Upper school faculty-student ratio: 1:7. Upper School students typically attend 5 days per week.

Upper School Student Profile Grade 9: 59 students (32 boys, 27 girls); Grade 10: 63 students (35 boys, 28 girls); Grade 11: 80 students (45 boys, 35 girls); Grade 12: 84 students (50 boys, 34 girls); Postgraduate: 15 students (14 boys, 1 girl). 53% of students are boarding students. 73% are state residents. 11 states are represented in upper school student body. 30% are international students. International students from China, Germany, Japan, Republic of Korea, Taiwan, and Thailand; 16 other countries represented in student body.

Faculty School total: 52. In upper school: 25 men, 22 women; 28 have advanced degrees; 41 reside on campus.

Subjects Offered Advanced Placement courses, algebra, American history, American literature, art, art history, biology, biology-AP, bookmaking, calculus, calculus-AP, ceramics, chemistry, chemistry-AP, college admission preparation, computer programming, computer science, computer-aided design, conceptual physics, creative writing, critical studies in film, decision making skills, desktop publishing, drama, driver education, economics, economics-AP, English, English literature, English-AP, entrepreneurship, environmental science, environmental science-AP, ESL, ethical decision making, European history, European history-AP, finance, fine arts, French, French-AP, geometry, global studies, honors algebra, honors geometry, honors U.S. history, honors world history, humanities, instrumental music, instruments, Internet research, Irish literature, Latin, Latin-AP, leadership, Mandarin, mathematics, modern European history, modern European history-AP, music-AP, painting, performing arts, personal finance, photography, physical education, physics, play/screen writing, poetry, pre-algebra, pre-calculus, pre-college orientation, probability and statistics, public speaking, research and reference, SAT preparation, science, sculpture, Shakespeare, short story, social studies, sociology, Spanish, Spanish-AP, statistics-AP, studio art, studio art-AP, the Web, theater, U.S. history, U.S. history-AP, Vietnam War, visual arts, vocal ensemble, Web site design, world history, world literature, writing, writing workshop.

Graduation Requirements Algebra, American history, arts and fine arts (art, music, dance, drama), English, foreign language, geometry, lab science, physical education (includes health).

Special Academic Programs Advanced Placement exam preparation; honors section; independent study; academic accommodation for the musically talented and the artistically talented; ESL (8 students enrolled).

College Admission Counseling 84 students graduated in 2009; 83 went to college, including Boston University; Bryant University; Connecticut College; Princeton University; Smith College; University of Massachusetts Amherst. Other: 1 entered military service. Mean SAT critical reading: 528, mean SAT math: 606, mean SAT writing: 532, mean combined SAT: 1666.

Student Life Upper grades have specified standards of dress, student council, honor system. Discipline rests equally with students and faculty.

Tuition and Aid Day student tuition: $28,300; 7-day tuition and room/board: $42,625. Tuition installment plan (The Tuition Plan, Academic Management Services Plan, monthly payment plans, Tuition Management Systems Plan, Key Bank). Tuition reduction for siblings, need-based scholarship grants, need-based loans available. In 2009–10, 40% of upper-school students received aid.

Admissions Traditional secondary-level entrance grade is 9. For fall 2009, 514 students applied for upper-level admission, 315 were accepted, 132 enrolled. Deadline for receipt of application materials: February 1. Application fee required: $75. Interview required.

Athletics Interscholastic: baseball (boys), basketball (b,g), cross-country running (b,g), field hockey (g), football (b), independent competitive sports (b,g), lacrosse (b,g), soccer (b,g), softball (g), swimming and diving (b,g), tennis (b,g), track and field (b,g), volleyball (g), wrestling (b); intramural: basketball (b,g); coed interscholastic: alpine skiing, dance, golf, independent competitive sports, modern dance, riflery, skiing (downhill), water polo, winter (indoor) track; coed intramural: aerobics, aerobics/dance, aerobics/Nautilus, backpacking, canoeing/kayaking, climbing, fitness, hiking/backpacking, jogging, kayaking, life saving, outdoor adventure, physical fitness, physical training, rock climbing, running, snowboarding, strength & conditioning, tai chi, tennis, weight lifting, weight training, yoga. 1 PE instructor, 11 coaches, 1 athletic trainer.

Computers Computers are regularly used in architecture, art, college planning, drawing and design, English, graphic design, library skills, literary magazine, mathematics, music, newspaper, research skills, science, Web site design, yearbook classes. Computer network features include on-campus library services, online commercial services, Internet access, wireless campus network, Internet filtering or blocking technology. Campus intranet and student e-mail accounts are available to students. Students grades are available online. The school has a published electronic and media policy.

Contact Ms. Bonnie R. Tetrault, Administrative Assistant, Admission. 413-596-6811 Ext. 107. Fax: 413-599-1749. E-mail: btetrault@wma.us. Web site: www.wma.us.

WILLIAM PENN CHARTER SCHOOL

3000 West School House Lane
Philadelphia, Pennsylvania 19144
Head of School: Darryl J. Ford

General Information Coeducational day college-preparatory school, affiliated with Society of Friends. Grades PK–12. Founded: 1689. Setting: urban. 44-acre campus. 8 buildings on campus. Approved or accredited by Middle States Association of Colleges and Schools. Member of National Association of Independent Schools. Endowment: $52 million. Total enrollment: 960. Upper school average class size: 16. Upper school faculty-student ratio: 1:9. There are 181 required school days per year for Upper School students. Upper School students typically attend 5 days per week. The average school day consists of 6 hours.

Upper School Student Profile Grade 9: 119 students (70 boys, 49 girls); Grade 10: 94 students (47 boys, 47 girls); Grade 11: 110 students (63 boys, 47 girls); Grade 12: 113 students (57 boys, 56 girls). 3% of students are members of Society of Friends.

Faculty School total: 134. In upper school: 36 men, 37 women; 57 have advanced degrees.

Subjects Offered Algebra, American history, American literature, architectural drawing, art, art history-AP, Asian studies, band, Bible studies, bioethics, biology, biology-AP, botany, British literature, calculus, calculus-AP, calligraphy, ceramics, chemistry, chemistry-AP, choral music, chorus, college counseling, computer math, computer programming, computer science, creative writing, design, drama, drawing, earth science, Eastern religion and philosophy, ecology, economics, electronic music, English, English literature, environmental science, environmental science-AP, ethics, European history, European history-AP, film, filmmaking, fine arts, French, French-AP, genetics, geology, geometry, government and politics-AP, health, Hebrew scripture, history, history of rock and roll, history of science, human anatomy, independent study, Irish literature, jazz band, junior and senior seminars, Latin, learning cognition, learning strategies, marine biology, mathematics, Middle East, model United Nations, modern European history-AP, music, music performance, oceanography, organic chemistry, painting, peace and justice, photography, physical education, physics, physics-AP, pottery, pre-calculus, public speaking, Quakerism and ethics, religion, science, sculpture, senior project, service learning/internship, Shakespeare, social studies, Spanish, Spanish-AP, speech, statistics-AP, symphonic band, theater, theater arts, theater design and production, theater production, trigonometry, U.S. history-AP, United States government-AP, video, visual and performing arts, world history, world literature, world religions, writing.

Graduation Requirements Computer science, English, foreign language, mathematics, music, physical education (includes health), religious studies, science, social studies (includes history), theater, visual arts.

Special Academic Programs 14 Advanced Placement exams for which test preparation is offered; honors section; independent study; study at local college for college credit; academic accommodation for the gifted, the musically talented, and the artistically talented.

College Admission Counseling 90 students graduated in 2009; all went to college, including Boston College; Lehigh University; The George Washington University; University of Pennsylvania; University of Vermont; University of Virginia. Mean SAT critical reading: 628, mean SAT math: 631, mean SAT writing: 632, mean combined SAT: 1891, mean composite ACT: 27. 58% scored over 600 on SAT critical reading, 60% scored over 600 on SAT math, 57% scored over 600 on SAT writing, 59% scored over 1800 on combined SAT, 50% scored over 26 on composite ACT.

Student Life Upper grades have specified standards of dress, student council, honor system. Discipline rests equally with students and faculty. Attendance at religious services is required.

Tuition and Aid Day student tuition: $23,220. Tuition installment plan (Academic Management Services Plan, Key Tuition Payment Plan, Sallie Mae TuitionPay). Need-based scholarship grants available. In 2009–10, 35% of upper-school students received aid. Total amount of financial aid awarded in 2009–10: $2,561,830.

Admissions Traditional secondary-level entrance grade is 9. For fall 2009, 246 students applied for upper-level admission, 105 were accepted, 47 enrolled. ISEE or SSAT required. Deadline for receipt of application materials: none. Application fee required: $30. On-campus interview required.

Athletics Interscholastic: aquatics (boys, girls), baseball (b), basketball (b,g), cross-country running (b,g), diving (b,g), field hockey (g), football (b), golf (b,g), lacrosse (b,g), soccer (b,g), softball (g), squash (b,g), swimming and diving (b,g), tennis (b,g), track and field (b,g), water polo (b,g), wrestling (b); intramural: basketball (b,g); coed intramural: ultimate Frisbee. 10 PE instructors, 46 coaches, 2 athletic trainers.

Computers Computer network features include on-campus library services, online commercial services, Internet access, wireless campus network, Internet filtering or blocking technology. Campus intranet, student e-mail accounts, and computer access in designated common areas are available to students. The school has a published electronic and media policy.

Contact Stephen A. Bonnie, Director of Admissions. 215-844-3460. Fax: 215-843-3939. E-mail: sbonnie@penncharter.com. Web site: www.penncharter.com.

THE WILLIAMS SCHOOL

182 Mohegan Avenue
New London, Connecticut 06320-4110
Head of School: Mark Fader

General Information Coeducational day college-preparatory school. Grades 7–12. Founded: 1891. Setting: suburban. 25-acre campus. 2 buildings on campus. Approved or accredited by Connecticut Association of Independent Schools, New England Association of Schools and Colleges, and Connecticut Department of Education. Member of National Association of Independent Schools and Secondary School Admission Test Board. Endowment: $4 million. Total enrollment: 271. Upper school average class size: 13. Upper school faculty-student ratio: 1:6. There are 165 required school days per year for Upper School students. Upper School students typically attend 5 days per week. The average school day consists of 6 hours.

Upper School Student Profile Grade 9: 54 students (26 boys, 28 girls); Grade 10: 52 students (24 boys, 28 girls); Grade 11: 68 students (32 boys, 36 girls); Grade 12: 49 students (28 boys, 21 girls).

Faculty School total: 36. In upper school: 19 men, 17 women; 29 have advanced degrees.

Subjects Offered Algebra, American history, art, band, biology, biology-AP, calculus, calculus-AP, chemistry, chemistry-AP, chorus, computer science, dance, digital art, drama, economics, English, English literature, English-AP, environmental science, European history, expository writing, fine arts, French, French-AP, geography, geometry, Greek, history, jazz, journalism, Latin-AP, mathematics, modern European history, music, music composition, music history, music theory, music theory-AP, physical education, physics, physics-AP, pre-calculus, science, social studies, Spanish, Spanish-AP, theater, trigonometry, world history, world literature.

Graduation Requirements Arts and fine arts (art, music, dance, drama), classical language, English, foreign language, mathematics, physical education (includes health), science, senior project, social studies (includes history), at least one year of Latin, four years of math in Upper School.

Special Academic Programs 10 Advanced Placement exams for which test preparation is offered; honors section; independent study; study at local college for college credit; study abroad; academic accommodation for the gifted, the musically talented, and the artistically talented.

College Admission Counseling 58 students graduated in 2010; 57 went to college, including Boston University; Connecticut College; Fairfield University; Muhlenberg College; University of Vermont; Vassar College. Other: 1 went to work. Mean SAT critical reading: 623, mean SAT math: 612, mean SAT writing: 610, mean combined SAT: 1845, mean composite ACT: 29. 62% scored over 600 on SAT critical reading, 4% scored over 600 on SAT math, 59% scored over 600 on SAT writing, 63% scored over 1800 on combined SAT, 60% scored over 26 on composite ACT.

Student Life Upper grades have specified standards of dress, student council. Discipline rests primarily with faculty.

Summer Programs Sports programs offered; session focuses on lacrosse and field hockey; held on campus; accepts boys and girls; open to students from other schools. 160 students usually enrolled. 2011 schedule: June 21 to August 20. Application deadline: June 15.

Tuition and Aid Day student tuition: $24,885. Tuition installment plan (Insured Tuition Payment Plan, FACTS Tuition Payment Plan, monthly payment plans, individually arranged payment plans). Need-based scholarship grants available. In 2010–11, 40% of upper-school students received aid. Total amount of financial aid awarded in 2010–11: $1,270,680.

Admissions Traditional secondary-level entrance grade is 9. For fall 2010, 93 students applied for upper-level admission, 82 were accepted, 38 enrolled. SSAT required. Deadline for receipt of application materials: February 1. Application fee required: $50. On-campus interview required.

Athletics Interscholastic: baseball (boys), basketball (b,g), cross-country running (b,g), field hockey (g), lacrosse (b,g), sailing (b,g), soccer (b,g), softball (g), squash (b,g), swimming and diving (b,g), tennis (b,g); intramural: dance (b,g), dance team (b,g), fencing (b,g), fitness (b,g), yoga (b); coed interscholastic: cross-country running, golf, sailing, swimming and diving; coed intramural: basketball, dance, dance team, fencing, fitness, golf, modern dance, weight training. 2 PE instructors, 7 coaches, 1 athletic trainer.

Computers Computers are regularly used in mathematics classes. Computer network features include on-campus library services, online commercial services, Internet access, wireless campus network, Internet filtering or blocking technology. Campus intranet, student e-mail accounts, and computer access in designated common areas are available to students. The school has a published electronic and media policy.

Contact Julie Way, Associate Director of Admission. 860-439-2756. Fax: 860-439-2796. E-mail: jway@williamsschool.org. Web site: www.williamsschool.org.

THE WILLISTON NORTHAMPTON SCHOOL

19 Payson Avenue
Easthampton, Massachusetts 01027
Head of School: Mr. Robert W. Hill

General Information Coeducational boarding and day college-preparatory school. Boarding grades 9–PG, day grades 7–12. Founded: 1841. Setting: small town. Nearest major city is Northampton. Students are housed in single-sex dormitories. 125-acre campus. 57 buildings on campus. Approved or accredited by Association of Independent Schools in New England, New England Association of Schools and Colleges, and The Association of Boarding Schools. Member of National Association of Independent Schools and Secondary School Admission Test Board. Endowment: $36 million. Total enrollment: 529. Upper school average class size: 13. Upper school faculty-student ratio: 1:7. There are 160 required school days per year for Upper School students. Upper School students typically attend 5 days per week. The average school day consists of 8 hours and 30 minutes.

Upper School Student Profile Grade 9: 83 students (43 boys, 40 girls); Grade 10: 102 students (53 boys, 49 girls); Grade 11: 114 students (54 boys, 60 girls); Grade 12: 130 students (64 boys, 66 girls); Postgraduate: 12 students (12 boys). 64% of students are boarding students. 50% are state residents. 22 states are represented in upper school student body. 16% are international students. International students from Bermuda, China, Hong Kong, Japan, Republic of Korea, and Taiwan; 23 other countries represented in student body.

Faculty School total: 90. In upper school: 41 men, 40 women; 60 have advanced degrees; 59 reside on campus.

Subjects Offered African-American history, algebra, American history, American literature, anatomy and physiology, animal behavior, art, art history, astronomy, biology, biology-AP, calculus, calculus-AP, chemistry, chemistry-AP, China/Japan history, Chinese, choral music, choreography, Christian and Hebrew scripture, comparative government and politics-AP, comparative politics, computer math, computer programming, computer science, computer science-AP, constitutional law, creative writing, dance, discrete mathematics, drama, economics, economics and history, economics-AP, English, English language-AP, English literature, English literature-AP, environmental science, ESL, ethics, European history, expository writing, fine arts, French, French language-AP, French literature-AP, French-AP, genetics, geometry, global studies, government/civics, health, history, history of jazz, honors algebra, honors English, honors geometry, Islamic studies, Latin, Latin American history, Latin-AP, mathematics, music, music theory, organic biochemistry, organic chemistry, philosophy, photography, photojournalism, physics, physics-AP, play production, playwriting, poetry, psychology, psychology-AP, religion, religion and culture, Russian history, science, sculpture, social studies, Spanish, Spanish language-AP, Spanish literature-AP, statistics-AP, theater, theology, trigonometry, U.S. history-AP, world history, world literature, writing workshop.

Graduation Requirements Arts and fine arts (art, music, dance, drama), English, foreign language, history, mathematics, philosophy, religion (includes Bible studies and theology), science, participation in the athletic program.

Special Academic Programs 18 Advanced Placement exams for which test preparation is offered; honors section; independent study; term-away projects; study abroad; academic accommodation for the gifted, the musically talented, and the artistically talented; special instructional classes for deaf students; ESL (12 students enrolled).

College Admission Counseling 130 students graduated in 2010; all went to college, including Bates College; Boston College; Boston University; Colby College; Connecticut College; University of Vermont. Mean SAT critical reading: 580, mean SAT math: 608, mean SAT writing: 589, mean combined SAT: 1777. 42% scored over 600 on SAT critical reading, 47% scored over 600 on SAT math, 43% scored over 600 on SAT writing.

Student Life Upper grades have specified standards of dress, student council, honor system. Discipline rests equally with students and faculty.

Summer Programs Sports, art/fine arts programs offered; session focuses on sports camps and summer theater; held on campus; accepts boys and girls; open to students from other schools. 2011 schedule: June 19 to August 19.

Tuition and Aid Day student tuition: $33,000; 7-day tuition and room/board: $46,600. Tuition installment plan (Academic Management Services Plan, monthly payment plans). Need-based scholarship grants, need-based loans available. In 2010–11, 46% of upper-school students received aid. Total amount of financial aid awarded in 2010–11: $5,855,400.

The Williston Northampton School

Admissions Traditional secondary-level entrance grade is 9. For fall 2010, 621 students applied for upper-level admission, 274 were accepted, 118 enrolled. ACT, ISEE, PSAT or SAT for applicants to grade 11 and 12, SSAT or TOEFL required. Deadline for receipt of application materials: February 1. Application fee required: $50. Interview required.

Athletics Interscholastic: alpine skiing (boys, girls), baseball (b), basketball (b,g), crew (b,g), cross-country running (b,g), field hockey (g), football (b), golf (b,g), ice hockey (b,g), lacrosse (b,g), soccer (b,g), softball (g), squash (b,g), swimming and diving (b,g), tennis (b,g), track and field (b,g), volleyball (g), water polo (b,g), wrestling (b); intramural: self defense (g); coed interscholastic: dance, diving; coed intramural: aerobics, aerobics/dance, dance, dance team, equestrian sports, fitness, Frisbee, horseback riding, judo, martial arts, modern dance, mountain biking, snowboarding, weight lifting, weight training, yoga. 1 PE instructor, 5 coaches, 2 athletic trainers.

Computers Computers are regularly used in college planning, geography, graphic design, history, library, mathematics, newspaper, photography, photojournalism, programming, science, yearbook classes. Computer network features include on-campus library services, online commercial services, Internet access, wireless campus network, Internet filtering or blocking technology. Campus intranet, student e-mail accounts, and computer access in designated common areas are available to students. The school has a published electronic and media policy.

Contact Ms. Caitlin E. Church, Assistant Director of Admission. 413-529-3401. Fax: 413-527-9494. E-mail: admission@williston.com. Web site: www.williston.com.

See Display below and Close-Up on page 864.

WILLOW HILL SCHOOL

Sudbury, Massachusetts
See Special Needs Schools section.

THE WILLOWS ACADEMY

1012 Thacker Street
Des Plaines, Illinois 60016
Head of School: Mary J. Keenley

General Information Girls' day college-preparatory, arts, religious studies, and technology school, affiliated with Roman Catholic Church. Grades 6–12. Founded: 1974. Setting: suburban. Nearest major city is Chicago. 4-acre campus. 1 building on campus. Approved or accredited by Illinois Department of Education. Total enrollment: 210. Upper school average class size: 18. Upper school faculty-student ratio: 1:10. Upper School students typically attend 5 days per week. The average school day consists of 6 hours and 30 minutes.

Upper School Student Profile Grade 9: 43 students (43 girls); Grade 10: 36 students (36 girls); Grade 11: 28 students (28 girls); Grade 12: 36 students (36 girls). 85% of students are Roman Catholic.

Faculty School total: 35. In upper school: 1 man, 23 women; 15 have advanced degrees.

Subjects Offered Algebra, American history, American literature, art, biology, calculus, chemistry, choir, choral music, computer graphics, computer programming, computer science, economics, English, English literature, ethics, European history, fine arts, four units of summer reading, French, geography, geometry, government/civics, grammar, health, history, instrumental music, Latin, mathematics, music, music history, music theory, musical productions, philosophy, physical education, physics, pre-calculus, science, social studies, Spanish, statistics, theology, visual arts, vocal music, world history, world literature, writing.

Graduation Requirements Arts and fine arts (art, music, dance, drama), English, foreign language, four units of summer reading, mathematics, physical education (includes health), religion (includes Bible studies and theology), science, social studies (includes history), 40 hours of service work per year.

Special Academic Programs Advanced Placement exam preparation; honors section.

College Admission Counseling 46 students graduated in 2009; all went to college, including Marquette University; Northwestern University; Purdue University; University of Dallas; University of Illinois at Urbana–Champaign; University of Notre Dame. Mean SAT critical reading: 613, mean SAT math: 600, mean SAT writing: 611, mean composite ACT: 25.

Student Life Upper grades have uniform requirement, student council, honor system. Discipline rests primarily with faculty.

Tuition and Aid Day student tuition: $12,300. Tuition installment plan (Insured Tuition Payment Plan, monthly payment plans, quarterly, semiannual, and annual payment plans). Tuition reduction for siblings, need-based scholarship grants available. In 2009–10, 30% of upper-school students received aid.

Admissions Traditional secondary-level entrance grade is 9. For fall 2009, 26 students applied for upper-level admission, 26 were accepted, 23 enrolled. Any standardized test, ISEE or school's own exam required. Deadline for receipt of application materials: none. Application fee required: $50. On-campus interview required.

Athletics Interscholastic: basketball, cross-country running, dance team, golf, soccer, softball, swimming and diving, tennis, volleyball. 1 PE instructor, 8 coaches.

Computers Computers are regularly used in mathematics, science classes. Computer network features include Internet access. Students grades are available online.

Contact Stephanie Sheffield, Director of Admissions, 847-824-6927. Fax: 847-824-7089. E-mail: sheffield@willowsacademy.org. Web site: www.willowsacademy.org.

WILLOW WOOD SCHOOL

55 Scarsdale Road
Don Mills, Ontario M3B 2R3, Canada
Head of School: Ms. Joy Kurtz

General Information Coeducational day college-preparatory, general academic, arts, technology, and sports school. Grades 1–12. Founded: 1980. Setting: suburban. Nearest major city is Toronto, Canada. 3-acre campus. 1 building on campus. Approved or accredited by Ontario Ministry of Education and Ontario Department of Education. Languages of instruction: English, Spanish, and French. Total enrollment: 191. Upper school average class size: 16. Upper school faculty-student ratio: 1:7. There are 185 required school days per year for Upper School students. Upper School students typically attend 5 days per week. The average school day consists of 7 hours and 15 minutes.

Upper School Student Profile Grade 9: 23 students (17 boys, 6 girls); Grade 10: 25 students (21 boys, 4 girls); Grade 11: 26 students (16 boys, 10 girls); Grade 12: 31 students (27 boys, 4 girls).

Faculty School total: 35. In upper school: 9 men, 7 women; 4 have advanced degrees.

Subjects Offered 20th century world history, accounting, advanced chemistry, advanced math, algebra, ancient world history, applied arts, art, art history, biology, business applications, business mathematics, calculus, Canadian geography, Canadian history, Canadian law, Canadian literature, career and personal planning, careers, chemistry, civics, computer applications, computer graphics, computer information systems, computer literacy, computer multimedia, computer science, creative writing, data processing, dramatic arts, economics, English, English composition, English literature, environmental science, ESL, family studies, finite math, French, geography, geometry, global issues, guidance, health education, history, independent study, keyboarding, learning strategies, mathematics, media studies, medieval history, modern Western civilization, philosophy, photography, physical education, physics, politics, psychology, reading/study skills, remedial/makeup course work, research skills, science and technology, skills for success, social skills, society challenge and change, society, politics and law, Spanish, study skills, The 20th Century, visual arts, world religions, yearbook.

Graduation Requirements Arts, business, Canadian geography, Canadian history, career education, civics, electives, English, French, history, mathematics, physical education (includes health), science, social sciences, Provincial Literacy Test requirement, community service hours.

Special Academic Programs Accelerated programs; independent study; study abroad; academic accommodation for the gifted and the artistically talented; remedial reading and/or remedial writing; remedial math; programs in English, mathematics, general development for dyslexic students; special instructional classes for students with learning disabilities and Attention Deficit Disorder; ESL (14 students enrolled).

College Admission Counseling 22 students graduated in 2010; all went to college, including Brock University; McMaster University; University of Guelph; University of Toronto; University of Waterloo; York University.

Student Life Upper grades have uniform requirement, student council, honor system. Discipline rests primarily with faculty.

Summer Programs Remediation, enrichment, advancement, ESL, computer instruction programs offered; session focuses on acquiring secondary school credits; held on campus; accepts boys and girls; open to students from other schools. 40 students usually enrolled. 2011 schedule: July 4 to August 5. Application deadline: June 1.

Tuition and Aid Day student tuition: CAN$16,200. Tuition installment plan (individually arranged payment plans, 10% due upon acceptance; balance divided into three equal payments due June 1, October 1, December 1). Tuition reduction for siblings available.

Admissions Traditional secondary-level entrance grade is 9. For fall 2010, 22 students applied for upper-level admission, 18 were accepted, 18 enrolled. Achievement/Aptitude/Writing, Canada Quick Individual Educational Test, CTBS, Stanford Achievement Test, any other standardized test, non-standardized placement tests, school's own test or writing sample required. Deadline for receipt of application materials: none. No application fee required. On-campus interview required.

Athletics Interscholastic: badminton (boys, girls), ball hockey (b,g), basketball (b,g), cooperative games (b,g), croquet (b,g), flag football (b,g), floor hockey (b,g), hockey (b), track and field (b,g), volleyball (b,g); intramural: ball hockey (b,g), basketball (b,g), cooperative games (b,g), flag football (b,g), floor hockey (b,g), indoor hockey (b,g), track and field (b,g); coed interscholastic: badminton, ball hockey, baseball, bowling, cross-country running, curling, fitness walking, Frisbee, golf, hockey, ice hockey, indoor soccer, jogging, outdoor education, outdoor recreation, physical fitness, physical training, running, soccer, softball, table tennis, ultimate Frisbee, walking; coed intramural: aerobics, badminton, ball hockey, baseball, bowling, fitness, fitness walking, hockey, ice hockey, indoor soccer, jogging, outdoor education, outdoor recreation, physical fitness, physical training, running, soccer, softball, strength & conditioning, table tennis, ultimate Frisbee, volleyball, walking. 2 PE instructors, 1 athletic trainer.

Computers Computers are regularly used in accounting, business applications, career exploration, college planning, creative writing, data processing, English, ESL,

geography, graphic arts, independent study, learning cognition, publishing, remedial study skills, typing, Web site design, writing, yearbook classes. Computer network features include on-campus library services, online commercial services, Internet access, wireless campus network, Internet filtering or blocking technology. Computer access in designated common areas is available to students. Students grades are available online. The school has a published electronic and media policy.

Contact Ms. Joy Kurtz, Director. 416-444-7644. Fax: 416-444-1801. E-mail: joykurtz@willowwoodschool.ca. Web site: www.willowwoodschool.ca.

WILMINGTON CHRISTIAN SCHOOL

825 Loveville Road
Hockessin, Delaware 19707
Head of School: Mr. William F. Stevens Jr.

General Information Coeducational day college-preparatory, arts, religious studies, and technology school, affiliated with Protestant faith. Grades PK–12. Founded: 1946. Setting: suburban. Nearest major city is Wilmington. 15-acre campus. 1 building on campus. Approved or accredited by Association of Christian Schools International, Middle States Association of Colleges and Schools, and Delaware Department of Education. Endowment: $400,000. Total enrollment: 457. Upper school average class size: 25. Upper school faculty-student ratio: 1:15. There are 177 required school days per year for Upper School students. Upper School students typically attend 5 days per week. The average school day consists of 6 hours and 40 minutes.

Upper School Student Profile Grade 9: 46 students (22 boys, 24 girls); Grade 10: 38 students (15 boys, 23 girls); Grade 11: 54 students (25 boys, 29 girls); Grade 12: 40 students (17 boys, 23 girls). 98% of students are Protestant.

Faculty School total: 51. In upper school: 7 men, 16 women; 9 have advanced degrees.

Subjects Offered Accounting, advanced math, algebra, American history, American history-AP, American minority experience, anatomy and physiology, art, band, biology, calculus, calculus-AP, chemistry, chorus, Christian doctrine, Christian ethics, church history, civics, computer applications, consumer mathematics, creative writing, democracy in America, driver education, ecology, economics, English, geometry, German, health; honors algebra, honors English, honors geometry, information processing, journalism, lab science, library assistant, marine biology, modern history, music theory, novels, physical education, physical science, physics, pre-calculus, Spanish, speech, study skills, trigonometry, world civilizations, world religions, yearbook.

Graduation Requirements Bible studies, English, foreign language, health education, mathematics, physical education (includes health), science, social studies (includes history), 40 hours of community service.

Special Academic Programs Advanced Placement exam preparation; honors section; study at local college for college credit; remedial reading and/or remedial writing; remedial math.

College Admission Counseling 35 students graduated in 2009; 33 went to college, including Drexel University; Eastern University; Gordon College; Liberty University; Messiah College; University of Delaware. Other: 2 went to work. Mean SAT critical reading: 591, mean SAT math: 628, mean SAT writing: 620, mean combined SAT: 1839.

Student Life Upper grades have uniform requirement, student council, honor system. Discipline rests primarily with faculty. Attendance at religious services is required.

Tuition and Aid Day student tuition: $10,750. Tuition installment plan (STEP Plan) (monthly deduction from a checking account). Tuition reduction for siblings, need-based scholarship grants available. In 2009–10, 46% of upper-school students received aid. Total amount of financial aid awarded in 2009–10: $142,500.

Admissions Traditional secondary-level entrance grade is 9. For fall 2009, 19 students applied for upper-level admission, 13 were accepted, 13 enrolled. Stanford Achievement Test required. Deadline for receipt of application materials: August 1. Application fee required: $250. On-campus interview required.

Athletics Interscholastic: baseball (boys), basketball (b,g), cheering (g), field hockey (g), lacrosse (b), soccer (b,g), softball (g), volleyball (g), wrestling (b); coed interscholastic: cross-country running, golf, running. 2 PE instructors, 16 coaches, 1 athletic trainer.

Computers Computers are regularly used in accounting, business education, data processing, information technology, newspaper, yearbook classes. Computer network features include on-campus library services, Internet access. The school has a published electronic and media policy.

Contact Mrs. Kim Connell, Admissions/Headmaster's Assistant. 302-239-2121 Ext. 3205. Fax: 302-239-2778. E-mail: kconnell@wilmingtonchristian.org. Web site: www.wilmingtonchristian.org.

WILMINGTON FRIENDS SCHOOL

101 School Road
Wilmington, Delaware 19803
Head of School: Bryan K. Garman

General Information Coeducational day college-preparatory school, affiliated with Society of Friends. Grades PS–12. Founded: 1748. Setting: suburban. Nearest major city is Philadelphia, PA. 57-acre campus. 4 buildings on campus. Approved or accredited by Friends Council on Education, International Baccalaureate Organization, Middle States Association of Colleges and Schools, and Delaware Department of Education. Member of National Association of Independent Schools. Endowment: $15.6 million. Total enrollment: 781. Upper school average class size: 16. Upper school faculty-student ratio: 1:9. There are 169 required school days per year for Upper School students. Upper School students typically attend 5 days per week. The average school day consists of 7 hours.

Upper School Student Profile Grade 9: 63 students (34 boys, 29 girls); Grade 10: 63 students (25 boys, 38 girls); Grade 11: 70 students (27 boys, 43 girls); Grade 12: 56 students (29 boys, 27 girls). 5% of students are members of Society of Friends.

Faculty School total: 97. In upper school: 13 men, 13 women; 23 have advanced degrees.

Subjects Offered 3-dimensional art, advanced chemistry, algebra, American history, art, art history, biology, calculus, chemistry, community service, computer art, drama, driver education, earth science, economics, English, environmental science, ethics, European history, French, geometry, global science, history, history of the Americas, improvisation, independent study, integrated mathematics, Internet, jazz ensemble, journalism, mathematics, media studies, music, music theory, physical education, physics, pre-calculus, Quakerism and ethics, religion, science, social sciences, Spanish, studio art, theater, theater arts, Web site design, wellness, wind ensemble, world history.

Graduation Requirements Computer science, English, foreign language, mathematics, participation in sports, performing arts, religion (includes Bible studies and theology), science, service learning/internship, social sciences, visual arts, wellness, 50 hours of community service (single organization) before senior year.

Special Academic Programs International Baccalaureate program; 2 Advanced Placement exams for which test preparation is offered; honors section; independent study; term-away projects; study abroad; academic accommodation for the gifted, the musically talented, and the artistically talented.

College Admission Counseling 71 students graduated in 2009; 69 went to college, including Swarthmore College; Tulane University; University of Delaware. Other: 2 had other specific plans. Mean SAT critical reading: 630, mean SAT math: 631, mean SAT writing: 633, mean combined SAT: 1893, mean composite ACT: 23.

Student Life Upper grades have specified standards of dress, student council. Discipline rests primarily with faculty. Attendance at religious services is required.

Tuition and Aid Day student tuition: $20,875. Tuition installment plan (Key Tuition Payment Plan, Tuition Management Systems (purchased Key Tuition Plan)). Need-based scholarship grants available. In 2009-10, 26% of upper-school students received aid. Total amount of financial aid awarded in 2009-10: $831,580.

Admissions Traditional secondary-level entrance grade is 9. For fall 2009, 60 students applied for upper-level admission, 32 were accepted, 15 enrolled. CTP and ERB required. Deadline for receipt of application materials: none. Application fee required: $40. On-campus interview required.

Athletics Interscholastic: baseball (boys), basketball (b,g), cross-country running (b,g), field hockey (g), football (b), lacrosse (b,g), soccer (b,g), swimming and diving (b,g), tennis (b,g), volleyball (g), wrestling (b); coed intramural: aerobics/Nautilus. 3 PE instructors, 30 coaches, 1 athletic trainer.

Computers Computers are regularly used in art, English, library skills, literary magazine, mathematics, music, newspaper, science, social studies, Spanish, yearbook classes. Computer network features include on-campus library services, Internet access, document storage, backup, and security, off-campus library services (catalog and book request), Blackbaud's Netcommunity and Netclassroom. The school has a published electronic and media policy.

Contact Ms. Kathleen Hopkins, Director of Admissions and Financial Aid. 302-576-2930. Fax: 302-576-2939. E-mail: khopkins@wilmingtonfriends.org. Web site: www.wilmingtonfriends.org.

WILSON HALL
520 Wilson Hall Road
Sumter, South Carolina 29150
Head of School: Mr. Frederick B. Moulton

General Information Coeducational day college-preparatory, arts, and technology school. Grades PS-12. Founded: 1966. Setting: small town. Nearest major city is Columbia. 17-acre campus. 6 buildings on campus. Approved or accredited by South Carolina Independent School Association, Southern Association of Colleges and Schools, Southern Association of Independent Schools, and South Carolina Department of Education. Endowment: $280,000. Total enrollment: 837. Upper school average class size: 20. Upper school faculty-student ratio: 1:13. There are 180 required school days per year for Upper School students. Upper School students typically attend 5 days per week. The average school day consists of 6 hours and 20 minutes.

Upper School Student Profile Grade 8: 68 students (38 boys, 30 girls); Grade 9: 63 students (42 boys, 21 girls); Grade 10: 74 students (37 boys, 37 girls); Grade 11: 53 students (27 boys, 26 girls); Grade 12: 60 students (34 boys, 26 girls).

Faculty School total: 80. In upper school: 15 men, 27 women; 21 have advanced degrees.

Subjects Offered 3-dimensional design, algebra, anatomy, biology-AP, calculus-AP, chemistry-AP, computer applications, computer programming, computer programming-AP, drawing, economics, English, English language-AP, English literature-AP, environmental science, European history-AP, French, French language-AP, government, government-AP, journalism, Latin, Latin-AP, multimedia,

music theory-AP, philosophy, physical education, physical science, physics-AP, pottery, Spanish, Spanish language-AP, studio art-AP, trigonometry, U.S. history-AP, world history.

Graduation Requirements Arts and fine arts (art, music, dance, drama), business skills (includes word processing), computer science, English, foreign language, mathematics, physical education (includes health), science, social studies (includes history), acceptance into four-year college or university, 20 hours community service.

Special Academic Programs Advanced Placement exam preparation; honors section.

College Admission Counseling 48 students graduated in 2010; all went to college, including Clemson University; College of Charleston; Duke University; The Citadel, The Military College of South Carolina; University of South Carolina; University of Virginia. Median SAT critical reading: 580, median SAT math: 580.

Student Life Upper grades have specified standards of dress, honor system. Discipline rests primarily with faculty.

Summer Programs Enrichment, sports, art/fine arts, computer instruction programs offered; session focuses on enrichment; held on campus; accepts boys and girls; not open to students from other schools. 100 students usually enrolled. 2011 schedule: June 1 to July 15. Application deadline: May 20.

Tuition and Aid Day student tuition: $5175-$5695. Tuition installment plan (monthly payment plans). Need-based scholarship grants available. In 2010-11, 8% of upper-school students received aid. Total amount of financial aid awarded in 2010-11: $115,000.

Admissions Traditional secondary-level entrance grade is 9. For fall 2010, 153 students applied for upper-level admission, 110 were accepted, 106 enrolled. ACT, CTBS, OLSAT, Iowa Tests of Basic Skills, PSAT and SAT for applicants to grade 11 and 12, school's own test or Stanford Achievement Test, Otis-Lennon School Ability Test required. Deadline for receipt of application materials: none. Application fee required: $150. Interview recommended.

Athletics Interscholastic: baseball (boys), basketball (b,g), bowling (b), cheering (g), cross-country running (b,g), equestrian sports (g), fly fishing (b), football (b), golf (b,g), Nautilus (b,g), riflery (b), skeet shooting (b), softball (g), strength & conditioning (b,g), swimming and diving (b,g), tennis (b,g), track and field (b,g), trap and skeet (b), volleyball (g), wrestling (b); intramural: table tennis (b), weight lifting (b,g), weight training (b,g); coed interscholastic: bowling, climbing, equestrian sports, fly fishing, hiking/backpacking, mountain biking, outdoor adventure, outdoor education, paint ball, riflery, skeet shooting, soccer; coed intramural: outdoor adventure, rafting, rock climbing, ropes courses, table tennis. 4 PE instructors, 12 coaches.

Computers Computers are regularly used in English, journalism, literary magazine, technology, yearbook classes. Computer network features include on-campus library services, online commercial services, Internet access, Internet filtering or blocking technology. The school has a published electronic and media policy.

Contact Sean Hoskins, Director of Admissions and Public Relations. 803-469-3475 Ext. 107. Fax: 803-469-3477. E-mail: sean_hoskins@hotmail.com. Web site: www.wilsonhall.org.

WINCHESTER THURSTON SCHOOL
555 Morewood Avenue
Pittsburgh, Pennsylvania 15213-2899
Head of School: Mr. Gary J. Niels

General Information Coeducational day college-preparatory and arts school. Grades PK-12. Founded: 1887. Setting: urban. 5-acre campus. 2 buildings on campus. Approved or accredited by Middle States Association of Colleges and Schools, Pennsylvania Association of Independent Schools, The College Board, and Pennsylvania Department of Education. Member of National Association of Independent Schools. Endowment: $9 million. Upper school average class size: 15. Upper school faculty-student ratio: 1:8. There are 170 required school days per year for Upper School students. Upper School students typically attend 5 days per week. The average school day consists of 6 hours and 50 minutes.

Upper School Student Profile Grade 6: 43 students (26 boys, 17 girls); Grade 7: 38 students (22 boys, 16 girls); Grade 8: 41 students (22 boys, 19 girls); Grade 9: 66 students (41 boys, 25 girls); Grade 10: 57 students (25 boys, 32 girls); Grade 11: 56 students (33 boys, 23 girls); Grade 12: 63 students (38 boys, 25 girls).

Faculty School total: 91. In upper school: 16 men, 16 women; 16 have advanced degrees.

Subjects Offered Algebra, American history, American history-AP, American literature, animal behavior, art, art history, biology, biology-AP, calculus, calculus-AP, ceramics, chemistry, Chinese, choir, chorus, classics, composition-AP, computer programming, computer science, computer science-AP, creative writing, dance, drama, drawing, economics, economics-AP, English, English literature, English literature-AP, English-AP, European history, European history-AP, expository writing, filmmaking, French, French-AP, geometry, government/civics, health, history, journalism, Latin, Latin-AP, mathematics, music, music theory, philosophy, photography, physical education, physics, physics-AP, psychology, SAT preparation, science, social studies, Spanish, Spanish-AP, speech, statistics-AP, visual arts, world history, world literature, writing, yearbook.

Graduation Requirements Arts and fine arts (art, music, dance, drama), computer science, English, foreign language, mathematics, physical education (includes health), science, social studies (includes history), speech.

Special Academic Programs Advanced Placement exam preparation; independent study; term-away projects; study at local college for college credit; study abroad; academic accommodation for the gifted, the musically talented, and the artistically talented; ESL (2 students enrolled).

College Admission Counseling 43 students graduated in 2010; 42 went to college, including Boston College; Boston University; Carnegie Mellon University; Lehigh University; University of Pennsylvania; University of Pittsburgh. Other: 1 entered a postgraduate year. Mean SAT critical reading: 633, mean SAT math: 611, mean SAT writing: 640, mean combined SAT: 1884, mean composite ACT: 26. 49% scored over 600 on SAT critical reading, 42% scored over 600 on SAT math, 46% scored over 600 on SAT writing, 66% scored over 1800 on combined SAT, 67% scored over 26 on composite ACT.

Student Life Upper grades have specified standards of dress, student council. Discipline rests equally with students and faculty.

Summer Programs Enrichment, sports, art/fine arts programs offered; session focuses on adventure and play, sports and physical fitness, creative arts, and academics; held on campus; accepts boys and girls; open to students from other schools. 500 students usually enrolled. 2011 schedule: June 22 to July 31. Application deadline: May 15.

Tuition and Aid Day student tuition: $21,950–$23,950. Tuition installment plan (monthly payment plans). Need-based scholarship grants available. In 2010–11, 38% of upper-school students received aid. Total amount of financial aid awarded in 2010–11: $1,249,000.

Admissions Traditional secondary-level entrance grade is 9. For fall 2010, 76 students applied for upper-level admission, 60 were accepted, 30 enrolled. ISEE or TOEFL or SLEP required. Deadline for receipt of application materials: December 10. Application fee required: $50. Interview required.

Athletics Interscholastic: basketball (boys, girls), drill team (g), field hockey (g), lacrosse (b,g), rowing (b,g), running (b,g), tennis (b,g); intramural: squash (b); coed interscholastic: crew, cross-country running, fencing, golf, soccer, squash, track and field; coed intramural: basketball, dance, Frisbee, independent competitive sports, outdoor activities, physical fitness, physical training, soccer, strength & conditioning, ultimate Frisbee, weight training, winter soccer, yoga. 4 PE instructors, 24 coaches, 1 athletic trainer.

Computers Computers are regularly used in art, college planning, computer applications, creative writing, English, foreign language, history, library, mathematics, music, photography, science, senior seminar, social studies, writing, writing, yearbook classes. Computer network features include on-campus library services, online commercial services, Internet access, wireless campus network, Internet filtering or blocking technology. Campus intranet, student e-mail accounts, and computer access in designated common areas are available to students. Students grades are available online. The school has a published electronic and media policy.

Contact Mr. Scot Lorenzi, Associate Director of Admission. 412-578-3738. Fax: 412-578-7504. E-mail: lorenzis@winchesterthurston.org. Web site: www.winchesterthurston.org.

WINDERMERE PREPARATORY SCHOOL

6189 Winter Garden-Vineland Road
Windermere, Florida 34786
Head of School: Mrs. Donna Montague-Russell

General Information Boys' boarding and coeducational day college-preparatory, arts, and technology school. Boarding boys grades 9–12, day boys grades PK–12, day girls grades PK–12. Founded: 2000. Setting: small town. Nearest major city is Orlando. Students are housed in single-sex dormitories. 48-acre campus. 3 buildings on campus. Approved or accredited by Association of Independent Schools of Florida, European Council of International Schools, Florida Council of Independent Schools, International Baccalaureate Organization, National Independent Private Schools Association, Southern Association of Colleges and Schools, Southern Association of Independent Schools, and Florida Department of Education. Total enrollment: 969. Upper school average class size: 18. Upper school faculty-student ratio: 1:11. There are 180 required school days per year for Upper School students. Upper School students typically attend 5 days per week. The average school day consists of 7 hours and 15 minutes.

Upper School Student Profile Grade 9: 76 students (38 boys, 38 girls); Grade 10: 72 students (35 boys, 37 girls); Grade 11: 75 students (36 boys, 39 girls); Grade 12: 51 students (23 boys, 28 girls). 9% of students are boarding students. 91% are state residents. 9% are international students. International students from Austria, Canada, China, Germany, Switzerland, and Turkey; 8 other countries represented in student body.

Faculty School total: 103. In upper school: 11 men, 30 women; 23 have advanced degrees; 3 reside on campus.

Subjects Offered 20th century history, 3-dimensional art, acting, Advanced Placement courses, algebra, American government, American history, American literature, art, biology, biology-AP, business, calculus, calculus-AP, ceramics, chemistry, chemistry-AP, choir, chorus, composition-AP, creative writing, dance, dance performance, drama, drama performance, economics, economics-AP, electives, engineering, English, English composition, English language and composition-AP, English literature, English literature and composition-AP, environmental science, ethics, film, forensics, French, geometry, graphic design, honors algebra, honors English, honors U.S. history, honors world history, Latin, music, music theory,

personal fitness, physical education, physics, physics-AP, pre-calculus, psychology, psychology-AP, Spanish, speech and debate, theory of knowledge, world history, world history-AP, world literature, yearbook.

Graduation Requirements Arts and fine arts (art, music, dance, drama), electives, English, foreign language, history, mathematics, performing arts, physical fitness, science, 6 additional elective credits. Community service is required.

Special Academic Programs International Baccalaureate program; 11 Advanced Placement exams for which test preparation is offered; honors section; independent study; academic accommodation for the musically talented and the artistically talented.

College Admission Counseling 18 students graduated in 2010; all went to college, including Boston College; Elon University; Rollins College; University of Central Florida; University of Florida; University of North Florida. Median SAT critical reading: 578, median SAT math: 592, median SAT writing: 563.

Student Life Upper grades have uniform requirement, student council, honor system. Discipline rests primarily with faculty.

Summer Programs Enrichment, sports, art/fine arts programs offered; session focuses on enrichment, academics, and athletics; held on campus; accepts boys and girls; open to students from other schools. 200 students usually enrolled. 2011 schedule: June to August. Application deadline: May.

Tuition and Aid Day student tuition: $14,025; 7-day tuition and room/board: $38,950. Tuition installment plan (monthly payment plans). Need-based scholarship grants available. In 2010–11, 9% of upper-school students received aid. Total amount of financial aid awarded in 2010–11: $126,672.

Admissions Traditional secondary-level entrance grade is 9. For fall 2010, 67 students applied for upper-level admission, 52 were accepted, 52 enrolled. Achievement tests or SSAT, ERB, PSAT, SAT, PLAN or ACT required. Deadline for receipt of application materials: none. Application fee required: $100. Interview recommended.

Athletics Interscholastic: ballet (girls), baseball (b), basketball (b,g), cheering (g), dance (g), dance team (g), golf (b,g), lacrosse (b), modern dance (g), physical fitness (b,g), physical training (b,g), soccer (b,g), softball (g), strength & conditioning (g), swimming and diving (b), tennis (b,g), track and field (b,g), volleyball (g), weight training (g); coed interscholastic: crew, cross-country running, equestrian sports, track and field; coed intramural: flag football, golf. 6 PE instructors, 14 coaches.

Computers Computers are regularly used in all academic classes. Computer network features include on-campus library services, Internet access, wireless campus network, Internet filtering or blocking technology. Student e-mail accounts are available to students. Students grades are available online. The school has a published electronic and media policy.

Contact Mrs. Carol Riggs, Director of Admissions. 407-905-7737. Fax: 407-905-7710. E-mail: carol.riggs@windermereprep.com. Web site: www.windermereprep.com.

THE WINDSOR SCHOOL

Administration Building
136-23 Sanford Avenue
Flushing, New York 11355
Head of School: Mr. James Seery

General Information Coeducational day college-preparatory and arts school. Grades 6–PG. Founded: 1968. Setting: urban. Nearest major city is New York. 2-acre campus. 3 buildings on campus. Approved or accredited by Middle States Association of Colleges and Schools, New York Department of Education, New York State Association of Independent Schools, New York State Board of Regents, The College Board, and US Department of State. Total enrollment: 160. Upper school average class size: 12. Upper school faculty-student ratio: 1:14. There are 185 required school days per year for Upper School students. Upper School students typically attend 5 days per week. The average school day consists of 6 hours.

Upper School Student Profile Grade 8: 12 students (6 boys, 6 girls); Grade 9: 14 students (8 boys, 6 girls); Grade 10: 26 students (16 boys, 10 girls); Grade 11: 48 students (27 boys, 21 girls); Grade 12: 60 students (33 boys, 27 girls).

Faculty School total: 12. In upper school: 7 men, 5 women; all have advanced degrees.

Subjects Offered Advanced Placement courses, algebra, American history, American literature, art, basic skills, biology, business, business applications, calculus, ceramics, chemistry, computer programming, computer science, computer skills, computer studies, creative writing, driver education, economics, English, English literature, environmental science, ESL, European history, fine arts, French, geometry, government/civics, grammar, health, marketing, mathematics, music, physical education, physics, pre-calculus, psychology, science, social sciences, social studies, Spanish, trigonometry, world affairs, world history.

Graduation Requirements Arts and fine arts (art, music, dance, drama), English, foreign language, mathematics, physical education (includes health), science, social sciences, social studies (includes history).

Special Academic Programs Advanced Placement exam preparation; honors section; accelerated programs; independent study; academic accommodation for the gifted, the musically talented, and the artistically talented; remedial reading and/or remedial writing; remedial math; ESL (38 students enrolled).

The Windsor School

College Admission Counseling 34 students graduated in 2010; 32 went to college, including Adelphi University; Cornell University; Queens College of the City University of New York; St. John's University; State University of New York at Binghamton. Other: 2 went to work. Median SAT critical reading: 440, median SAT math: 550, median SAT writing: 460. 10% scored over 600 on SAT critical reading, 23% scored over 600 on SAT math, 10% scored over 600 on SAT writing.

Student Life Upper grades have specified standards of dress. Discipline rests primarily with faculty.

Summer Programs Remediation, enrichment, advancement, ESL, art/fine arts, computer instruction programs offered; session focuses on advancement, enrichment, remediation; held on campus; accepts boys and girls; open to students from other schools. 600 students usually enrolled. 2011 schedule: July 1 to August 18. Application deadline: June 30.

Tuition and Aid Day student tuition: $19,600. Tuition installment plan (individually arranged payment plans). Financial aid available to upper-school students. In 2010–11, 10% of upper-school students received aid. Total amount of financial aid awarded in 2010–11: $30,000.

Admissions Traditional secondary-level entrance grade is 9. For fall 2010, 63 students applied for upper-level admission, 58 were accepted, 52 enrolled. School's own exam required. Deadline for receipt of application materials: none. No application fee required. On-campus interview required.

Athletics Interscholastic: basketball (boys, girls), soccer (b,g), softball (b,g); intramural: aerobics (b,g), basketball (b,g), cooperative games (b,g), fitness (b,g), jump rope (g), physical fitness (b,g), soccer (b,g), softball (b,g), tennis (b,g), volleyball (b,g); coed interscholastic: basketball, soccer, softball; coed intramural: basketball, fitness, jump rope, physical fitness, soccer, softball, table tennis, tennis, volleyball. 2 PE instructors, 2 coaches.

Computers Computers are regularly used in art, business applications, mathematics, research skills, typing, yearbook classes. Computer resources include Internet access.

Contact Dr. Philip A. Stewart, Director of Admissions. 718-359-8300. Fax: 718-359-1876. E-mail: admin@thewindsorschool.com. Web site: www.windsorschool.com.

WINDWARD SCHOOL

11350 Palms Boulevard
Los Angeles, California 90066
Head of School: Tom Gilder

General Information Coeducational day college-preparatory school. Grades 7–12. Founded: 1971. Setting: urban. 9-acre campus. 11 buildings on campus. Approved or accredited by California Association of Independent Schools and Western Association of Schools and Colleges. Member of National Association of Independent Schools. Total enrollment: 525. Upper school average class size: 16. Upper school faculty-student ratio: 1:7. The average school day consists of 7 hours.

Upper School Student Profile Grade 9: 94 students (46 boys, 48 girls); Grade 10: 91 students (48 boys, 43 girls); Grade 11: 91 students (43 boys, 48 girls); Grade 12: 89 students (44 boys, 45 girls).

Faculty School total: 65. In upper school: 32 men, 27 women; 37 have advanced degrees.

Subjects Offered Algebra, American history, American literature, art, art history, biology, calculus, ceramics, chemistry, Chinese, chorus, computer science, creative writing, dance, drama, English, English literature, environmental science, European history, fine arts, French, geometry, government/civics, health, history, Japanese, journalism, Latin, marine biology, mathematics, music, photography, physical education, physiology, science, social studies, Spanish, theater, trigonometry, world history.

Graduation Requirements Arts and fine arts (art, music, dance, drama), English, foreign language, mathematics, physical education (includes health), science, social studies (includes history).

Special Academic Programs 16 Advanced Placement exams for which test preparation is offered; honors section; independent study; study at local college for college credit.

College Admission Counseling 71 students graduated in 2010; all went to college, including Columbia University; Massachusetts Institute of Technology; New York University; Tufts University; University of California, Berkeley; Williams College. Mean SAT critical reading: 646, mean SAT math: 633, mean SAT writing: 658, mean combined SAT: 1937.

Student Life Upper grades have specified standards of dress, student council, honor system. Discipline rests primarily with faculty.

Summer Programs Sports programs offered; session focuses on skill development and team play; held on campus; accepts boys and girls; open to students from other schools. 75 students usually enrolled. 2011 schedule: June 20 to August 20.

Tuition and Aid Day student tuition: $30,243. Tuition installment plan (Key Tuition Payment Plan, monthly payment plans). Need-based scholarship grants, need-based loans available. In 2010–11, 17% of upper-school students received aid. Total amount of financial aid awarded in 2010–11: $1,461,345.

Admissions Traditional secondary-level entrance grade is 9. For fall 2010, 138 students applied for upper-level admission, 24 were accepted, 17 enrolled. ISEE required. Deadline for receipt of application materials: December 15. Application fee required: $100. On-campus interview required.

WINDWARD SCHOOL

responsible

caring

well informed

ethical

prepared

A dynamic education.

Athletics Interscholastic: baseball (boys), basketball (b,g), football (b); coed interscholastic: cross-country running, flag football. 5 PE instructors, 13 coaches, 2 athletic trainers.

Computers Computers are regularly used in art, English, history, mathematics, science classes. Computer network features include on-campus library services, online commercial services, Internet access, wireless campus network, Internet filtering or blocking technology. Student e-mail accounts are available to students. The school has a published electronic and media policy.

Contact Sharon Pearline, Director of Admissions. 310-391-7127. Fax: 310-397-5655. Web site: www.windwardschool.org.

See Display on page 714 and Close-Up on page 866.

THE WINSOR SCHOOL

103 Pilgrim Road
Boston, Massachusetts 02215
Head of School: Mrs. Rachel Friis Stettler

General Information Girls' day college-preparatory school. Grades 5–12. Founded: 1886. Setting: urban. 8-acre campus. 2 buildings on campus. Approved or accredited by Association of Independent Schools in New England, New England Association of Schools and Colleges, and Massachusetts Department of Education. Member of National Association of Independent Schools. Endowment: $54.6 million. Total enrollment: 436. Upper school average class size: 13. Upper school faculty-student ratio: 1:5. There are 160 required school days per year for Upper School students. Upper School students typically attend 5 days per week. The average school day consists of 6 hours and 30 minutes.

Upper School Student Profile Grade 9: 70 students (70 girls); Grade 10: 61 students (61 girls); Grade 11: 52 students (52 girls); Grade 12: 54 students (54 girls).

Faculty School total: 66. In upper school: 12 men, 34 women; 39 have advanced degrees.

Subjects Offered Acting, advanced studio art-AP, African history, African literature, algebra, architecture, art, art history, astronomy, biology, calculus, ceramics, chemistry, Chinese, Chinese history, Chinese literature, contemporary history, creative writing, digital art, drama, engineering, English, environmental science, expository writing, fine arts, French, geometry, health, Islamic history, Latin, Latin American history, literature, macroeconomics-AP, marine biology, Middle Eastern history, music, photography, physical education, physics, pre-calculus, psychology, Russian history, sculpture, Spanish, statistics, theater, U.S. history, U.S. literature.

Graduation Requirements Algebra, art, biology, English, European history, French, geometry, Latin, physical education (includes health), Spanish, U.S. history.

Special Academic Programs 10 Advanced Placement exams for which test preparation is offered; honors section.

College Admission Counseling 52 students graduated in 2010; all went to college, including Dartmouth College; Harvard University; New York University; Princeton University; Stanford University; Yale University. Median SAT critical reading: 710, median SAT math: 700, median SAT writing: 760, median combined SAT: 2170, median composite ACT: 30.

Student Life Upper grades have specified standards of dress, student council, honor system. Discipline rests primarily with faculty.

Tuition and Aid Day student tuition: $34,025. Tuition installment plan (Tuition Management Systems). Need-based scholarship grants available. In 2010–11, 24% of upper-school students received aid. Total amount of financial aid awarded in 2010–11: $1,490,140.

Admissions Traditional secondary-level entrance grade is 9. For fall 2010, 101 students applied for upper-level admission, 20 were accepted, 16 enrolled. ISEE or SSAT required. Deadline for receipt of application materials: December 17. Application fee required: $45. On-campus interview required.

Athletics Interscholastic: basketball, crew, cross-country running, field hockey, ice hockey, lacrosse, sailing, soccer, softball, squash, swimming and diving, tennis, track and field. 3 PE instructors, 3 coaches, 1 athletic trainer.

Computers Computers are regularly used in photography, programming, Web site design classes. Computer network features include on-campus library services, Internet access, wireless campus network, Internet filtering or blocking technology. Student e-mail accounts are available to students. The school has a published electronic and media policy.

Contact Mrs. Pamela Parks McLaurin, Director of Admission. 617-735-9503. Fax: 617-912-1381. Web site: www.winsor.edu/.

See Display below and Close-Up on page 868.

WINSTON PREPARATORY SCHOOL

New York, New York
See Special Needs Schools section.

THE WINSOR SCHOOL

What's different when it's all girls? Everything.

Explore all that Winsor means to academically motivated and promising girls in grades 5-12. Our reputation as a top day school has drawn Boston-area families for 125 years. They want the world for their daughters. So do *we*.

Winsor teachers expect the best from every girl. They know girls learn best when they listen actively, think critically and voice their own ideas. To learn more about our urban day school, call 617 735-9503 or visit us online.

THE WINSOR SCHOOL *Pilgrim Road, Boston, Massachusetts 02215* www.winsor.edu/admission

THE WINSTON SCHOOL SAN ANTONIO

San Antonio, Texas
See Special Needs Schools section.

WISCONSIN ACADEMY

N2355 DuBorg Road
Columbus, Wisconsin 53925
Head of School: Mr. Marshall W. Bowers
General Information Coeducational boarding and day college-preparatory, general academic, and religious studies school, affiliated with Seventh-day Adventist Church. Grades 9–12. Founded: 1950. Setting: rural. Nearest major city is Madison. Students are housed in single-sex dormitories. 50-acre campus. 7 buildings on campus. Approved or accredited by Association of American Schools in South America, Board of Regents, General Conference of Seventh-day Adventists, North Central Association of Colleges and Schools, and Wisconsin Department of Education. Endowment: $100,000. Total enrollment: 98. Upper school average class size: 30. Upper school faculty-student ratio: 1:6. There are 176 required school days per year for Upper School students. Upper School students typically attend 5 days per week. The average school day consists of 6 hours.
Upper School Student Profile Grade 9: 25 students (10 boys, 15 girls); Grade 10: 16 students (8 boys, 8 girls); Grade 11: 24 students (11 boys, 13 girls); Grade 12: 33 students (17 boys, 16 girls). 80% of students are boarding students. 88% are state residents. 5 states are represented in upper school student body. 6% are international students. 85% of students are Seventh-day Adventists.
Faculty School total: 15. In upper school: 9 men, 5 women; 5 have advanced degrees; all reside on campus.
Subjects Offered Advanced math, algebra, American government, American history, American literature, anatomy and physiology, art, bell choir, Bible, biology, chemistry, choir, chorus, composition, computer applications, computer graphics, computer literacy, driver education, economics, English, English-AP, general math, geography, geometry, guitar, gymnastics, handbells, health, home economics, keyboarding, newspaper, photo shop, physical education, physical science, physics, piano, pre-algebra, pre-calculus, religion, Spanish, work-study.
Graduation Requirements Algebra, American government, American history, American literature, Bible, biology, computer literacy, computer skills, English, foreign language, geometry, lab/keyboard, physical education (includes health), science, social studies (includes history), U.S. government.
College Admission Counseling 25 students graduated in 2009; 19 went to college, including Andrews University; Southern Adventist University. Other: 6 went to work.
Student Life Upper grades have specified standards of dress, student council, honor system. Discipline rests primarily with faculty. Attendance at religious services is required.
Tuition and Aid Day student tuition: $8710; 7-day tuition and room/board: $13,885. Tuition installment plan (monthly payment plans, individually arranged payment plans). Tuition reduction for siblings, need-based scholarship grants, paying campus jobs available. In 2009–10, 55% of upper-school students received aid. Total amount of financial aid awarded in 2009–10: $150,000.
Admissions Traditional secondary-level entrance grade is 9. For fall 2009, 102 students applied for upper-level admission, 102 were accepted, 98 enrolled. Iowa Test, CTBS, or TAP or TOEFL required. Deadline for receipt of application materials: none. No application fee required. Interview recommended.
Athletics Intramural: basketball (boys, girls), flag football (b,g), flagball (b,g), floor hockey (b,g), soccer (b,g), softball (b,g), volleyball (b,g); coed intramural: volleyball. 1 PE instructor.
Computers Computers are regularly used in all academic classes. Computer resources include on-campus library services, Internet access, Internet filtering or blocking technology. Student e-mail accounts are available to students. Students grades are available online. The school has a published electronic and media policy.
Contact Mrs. Stephanie Gottfried, Registrar. 920-623-3300 Ext. 13. Fax: 920-623-3318. E-mail: registrar@wisacad.org. Web site: www.wisacad.org.

THE WOODHALL SCHOOL

PO Box 550
58 Harrison Lane
Bethlehem, Connecticut 06751
Head of School: Matthew C. Woodhall
General Information Boys' boarding and day college-preparatory, arts, and ESL school. Grades 9–PG. Founded: 1983. Setting: rural. Nearest major city is Waterbury. Students are housed in single-sex dormitories. 38-acre campus. 5 buildings on campus. Approved or accredited by Association of Independent Schools in New England, Connecticut Association of Independent Schools, New England Association of Schools and Colleges, and Connecticut Department of Education. Member of National Association of Independent Schools. Endowment: $120,000. Total enrollment: 38. Upper school average class size: 4. Upper school faculty-student ratio: 1:4. There are 184 required school days per year for Upper School students. Upper School students typically attend 6 days per week.

Upper School Student Profile Grade 9: 6 students (6 boys); Grade 10: 10 students (10 boys); Grade 11: 15 students (15 boys); Grade 12: 8 students (8 boys). 100% of students are boarding students. 12% are state residents. 22 states are represented in upper school student body. International students from Switzerland.
Faculty School total: 16. In upper school: 14 men, 2 women; 12 have advanced degrees; 11 reside on campus.
Subjects Offered Algebra, American history, anatomy, art, biology, calculus, chemistry, comparative government and politics, drama, English, environmental science, geometry, Greek, language and composition, Latin, physics, pre-calculus, Spanish, world civilizations.
Graduation Requirements Arts and fine arts (art, music, dance, drama), communication skills, English, foreign language, mathematics, physical education (includes health), science, social studies (includes history).
Special Academic Programs Advanced Placement exam preparation; independent study; special instructional classes for students with Attention Deficit Disorder and non-verbal learning disabilities; ESL.
College Admission Counseling 14 students graduated in 2010; all went to college, including Guilford College; Ithaca College; Keene State College; Lynchburg College; Northeastern University; University of Vermont. Median SAT critical reading: 652, median SAT math: 500, median SAT writing: 569, median combined SAT: 574.
Student Life Upper grades have specified standards of dress, student council, honor system. Discipline rests primarily with faculty.
Tuition and Aid Day student tuition: $43,680; 7-day tuition and room/board: $57,200. Tuition installment plan (individually arranged payment plans).
Admissions Traditional secondary-level entrance grade is 10. Deadline for receipt of application materials: none. Application fee required: $100. On-campus interview required.
Athletics Interscholastic: basketball, cross-country running, lacrosse, soccer; intramural: alpine skiing, basketball, bicycling, bowling, canoeing/kayaking, cross-country running, fishing, fitness, fitness walking, Frisbee, hiking/backpacking, ice skating, jogging, lacrosse, mountain biking, outdoor activities, outdoor education, outdoor recreation, physical fitness, physical training, rafting, running, skiing (cross-country), skiing (downhill), snowboarding, soccer, street hockey, strength & conditioning, table tennis, volleyball, walking, wall climbing, weight lifting, winter walking.
Computers Computers are regularly used in art, English, foreign language, history, mathematics, science, social sciences classes. Computer resources include Internet access. The school has a published electronic and media policy.
Contact Matthew C. Woodhall, Head of School. 203-266-7788. Fax: 203-266-5896. E-mail: mwoodhall@woodhallschool.org. Web site: www.woodhallschool.org.

WOODLYNDE SCHOOL

445 Upper Gulph Road
Strafford, Pennsylvania 19087
Head of School: Christopher M. Fulco, EdD
General Information Coeducational day college-preparatory, arts, and technology school; primarily serves individuals with Attention Deficit Disorder, dyslexic students, and language-based learning disabilities. Grades 1–12. Founded: 1976. Setting: suburban. Nearest major city is Philadelphia. 8-acre campus. 2 buildings on campus. Approved or accredited by Pennsylvania Association of Independent Schools and Pennsylvania Department of Education. Member of National Association of Independent Schools. Endowment: $559,699. Total enrollment: 262. Upper school average class size: 10. Upper school faculty-student ratio: 1:5. There are 168 required school days per year for Upper School students. Upper School students typically attend 5 days per week. The average school day consists of 6 hours and 55 minutes.
Upper School Student Profile Grade 6: 24 students (16 boys, 8 girls); Grade 7: 21 students (13 boys, 8 girls); Grade 8: 35 students (18 boys, 17 girls); Grade 9: 22 students (12 boys, 10 girls); Grade 10: 22 students (12 boys, 10 girls); Grade 11: 26 students (14 boys, 12 girls); Grade 12: 28 students (20 boys, 8 girls).
Faculty School total: 62. In upper school: 11 men, 10 women; 7 have advanced degrees.
Subjects Offered Algebra, American history, American literature, art, art-AP, arts, biology, chemistry, creative writing, earth science, English, English literature, English-AP, European history, fine arts, French, geometry, government/civics, health, history, journalism, mathematics, music, photography, physical education, physics, political science, psychology, science, social studies, Spanish, studio art, world history, world literature, writing.
Graduation Requirements Arts and fine arts (art, music, dance, drama), English, foreign language, mathematics, physical education (includes health), science, social studies (includes history), community service, senior project, senior speech.
Special Academic Programs Honors section; remedial reading and/or remedial writing.
College Admission Counseling 29 students graduated in 2010; 28 went to college, including Johnson & Wales University; Penn State University Park. Other: 1 went to work.
Student Life Upper grades have specified standards of dress, student council. Discipline rests primarily with faculty.
Summer Programs Remediation, enrichment, advancement, sports, art/fine arts programs offered; session focuses on mathematics and reading enrichment; held on campus; accepts boys and girls; open to students from other schools. 75 students usually enrolled. 2011 schedule: June 20 to July 22. Application deadline: May 30.

Tuition and Aid Day student tuition: $28,300. Tuition installment plan (FACTS Tuition Payment Plan). Need-based scholarship grants available. In 2010–11, 35% of upper-school students received aid. Total amount of financial aid awarded in 2010–11: $525,475.

Admissions Traditional secondary-level entrance grade is 9. For fall 2010, 19 students applied for upper-level admission, 10 were accepted, 6 enrolled. Individual IQ required. Deadline for receipt of application materials: none. Application fee required: $100. On-campus interview required.

Athletics Interscholastic: basketball (boys, girls), lacrosse (b,g), soccer (b,g), softball (g), tennis (b,g), volleyball (g); coed interscholastic: cross-country running. 4 PE instructors, 10 coaches, 1 athletic trainer.

Computers Computers are regularly used in all academic, art, creative writing, drawing and design, English, foreign language, French, graphic arts, graphic design, history, music, newspaper, publications, social studies, Spanish, study skills, technology, word processing, writing, yearbook classes. Computer network features include on-campus library services, Internet access, wireless campus network, Internet filtering or blocking technology. Student e-mail accounts are available to students. The school has a published electronic and media policy.

Contact Karen Duffy, Assistant Director of Admissions. 610-687-9660 Ext. 534. Fax: 610-293-6680. E-mail: duffy@woodlynde.org. Web site: www.woodlynde.org.

WOODSIDE INTERNATIONAL SCHOOL

1555 Irving Street
San Francisco, California 94122-1908
Head of School: Mr. John S. Edwards

General Information Coeducational day college-preparatory and arts school. Grades 6–12. Founded: 1976. Setting: urban. 2 buildings on campus. Approved or accredited by Western Association of Schools and Colleges and California Department of Education. Total enrollment: 85. Upper school average class size: 16. Upper school faculty-student ratio: 1:5.

Faculty School total: 19. In upper school: 11 men, 8 women; 7 have advanced degrees.

Subjects Offered Anatomy and physiology, art, art history, biology, calculus, calculus-AP, chemistry, chemistry-AP, civics, community service, creative writing, current events, economics, English, English as a foreign language, ESL, film appreciation, French, general science, geography, guitar, health, high adventure outdoor program, Japanese, Mandarin, music, music performance, music theory, parenting, philosophy, photography, physical education, physics, physics-AP, portfolio art, pre-calculus, Russian, science, Spanish, U.S. history, work experience, world history, writing.

Graduation Requirements Arts and fine arts (art, music, dance, drama), current events, English, foreign language, mathematics, parenting, philosophy, physical education (includes health), science, social studies (includes history). Community service is required.

Special Academic Programs Advanced Placement exam preparation; honors section; accelerated programs; independent study; academic accommodation for the gifted, the musically talented, and the artistically talented; ESL (20 students enrolled).

College Admission Counseling 25 students graduated in 2009; 23 went to college, including Academy of Art University; California State University; City College of San Francisco; San Francisco State University; University of California System; University of San Francisco. Other: 1 went to work, 1 entered military service.

Student Life Discipline rests primarily with faculty.

Tuition and Aid Day student tuition: $19,800. Tuition installment plan (Key Tuition Payment Plan, monthly payment plans, individually arranged payment plans). Tuition reduction for siblings, need-based scholarship grants, need-based loans, middle-income loans, prepGATE loans available.

Admissions Any standardized test required. Deadline for receipt of application materials: none. Application fee required: $50. On-campus interview required.

Athletics Coed Intramural: basketball, martial arts, outdoor adventure, soccer. 3 PE instructors.

Computers Computer network features include Internet access, wireless campus network, online weekly homework assignments. Computer access in designated common areas is available to students.

Contact Ms. Janet McClelland, Admissions Counselor. 415-564-1063. Fax: 415-564-2511. E-mail: jmcclelland@wissf.com. Web site: www.wissf.com.

WOODSIDE PRIORY SCHOOL

302 Portola Road
Founders Hall
Portola Valley, California 94028
Head of School: Mr. Tim Molak

General Information Coeducational boarding and day college-preparatory, arts, religious studies, and technology school, affiliated with Roman Catholic Church. Boarding grades 9–12, day grades 6–12. Founded: 1957. Setting: suburban. Nearest major city is San Francisco. Students are housed in single-sex dormitories. 50-acre campus. 25 buildings on campus. Approved or accredited by California Association of Independent Schools, National Catholic Education Association, The Association of Boarding Schools, The College Board, Western Association of Schools and Colleges,

Western Catholic Education Association, and California Department of Education. Member of National Association of Independent Schools and Secondary School Admission Test Board. Endowment: $10 million. Total enrollment: 352. Upper school average class size: 18. Upper school faculty-student ratio: 1:9. There are 175 required school days per year for Upper School students. Upper School students typically attend 5 days per week. The average school day consists of 6 hours and 30 minutes.

Upper School Student Profile Grade 9: 74 students (44 boys, 30 girls); Grade 10: 68 students (33 boys, 35 girls); Grade 11: 70 students (36 boys, 34 girls); Grade 12: 58 students (30 boys, 28 girls). 17% of students are boarding students. 100% are state residents. 4 states are represented in upper school student body. 12% are international students. International students from China, Hungary, Philippines, Republic of Korea, Taiwan, and Viet Nam; 10 other countries represented in student body. 40% of students are Roman Catholic.

Faculty School total: 70. In upper school: 28 men, 27 women; 48 have advanced degrees; 30 reside on campus.

Subjects Offered 20th century physics, 3-dimensional art, acting, advanced chemistry, advanced computer applications, advanced math, Advanced Placement courses, advanced studio art-AP, algebra, American democracy, American government, American history, American literature, analysis and differential calculus, animation, architecture, art, art history, art-AP, ASB Leadership, astronomy, Basic programming, biology, biology-AP, British literature, calculus, calculus-AP, ceramics, chemistry, chemistry-AP, choir, choral music, Christian and Hebrew scripture, church history, classics, college admission preparation, college counseling, community garden, community service, comparative cultures, computer applications, computer art, computer graphics, computer math, computer programming, computer science, computer science-AP, computer technologies, computers, constitutional history of U.S., contemporary issues, creative arts, creative writing, desktop publishing, drama, drama performance, earth and space science, earth science, ecology, economics, economics-AP, English, English composition, English literature, English literature-AP, English-AP, environmental science-AP, ethics, European history, European history-AP, expository writing, fine arts, French, French-AP, geography, geometry, government/civics, grammar, health and wellness, history of ideas, honors English, humanities, Japanese, journalism, keyboarding, Latin, life science, mathematics, music, music appreciation, music performance, peer counseling, personal fitness, philosophy, photography, physical education, physics, physics-AP, play production, portfolio art, pre-algebra, pre-calculus, probability and statistics, psychology, religion, science, social sciences, social studies, sociology, Spanish, Spanish language-AP, Spanish literature-AP, speech, studio art-AP, theater, theology, trigonometry, typing, U.S. history-AP, world history, world literature, writing.

Graduation Requirements Algebra, arts and fine arts (art, music, dance, drama), biology, British literature, calculus, chemistry, Christian and Hebrew scripture, comparative religion, computer science, earth science, English, environmental science, expository writing, foreign language, geometry, mathematics, physical education (includes health), physics, science, social sciences, social studies (includes history), theology. Community service is required.

Special Academic Programs 20 Advanced Placement exams for which test preparation is offered; honors section; independent study; academic accommodation for the gifted, the musically talented, and the artistically talented.

College Admission Counseling 65 students graduated in 2009; all went to college, including Princeton University; Santa Clara University; Stanford University; University of California, Berkeley; University of California, Los Angeles; Yale University. Median SAT critical reading: 628, median SAT math: 640, median SAT writing: 621. 35% scored over 600 on SAT critical reading, 44% scored over 600 on SAT math, 39% scored over 600 on SAT writing.

Student Life Upper grades have specified standards of dress, student council, honor system. Discipline rests equally with students and faculty.

Tuition and Aid Day student tuition: $31,700; 7-day tuition and room/board: $45,400. Tuition installment plan (monthly payment plans, individually arranged payment plans). Need-based scholarship grants available. In 2009–10, 21% of upper-school students received aid. Total amount of financial aid awarded in 2009–10: $1,650,000.

Admissions Traditional secondary-level entrance grade is 9. For fall 2009, 277 students applied for upper-level admission, 137 were accepted, 73 enrolled. High School Placement Test (closed version) from Scholastic Testing Service, ISEE, PSAT or SAT for applicants to grade 11 and 12, SLEP for foreign students, SSAT, TOEFL or writing sample required. Deadline for receipt of application materials: January 15. Application fee required: $75. On-campus interview required.

Athletics Interscholastic: baseball (boys), basketball (b,g), cross-country running (b,g), flag football (b), football (b), golf (b,g), soccer (b,g), softball (g), swimming and diving (g), track and field (b,g), volleyball (g), water polo (b); intramural: alpine skiing (b,g); coed interscholastic: cross-country running, dance, golf, outdoor education, tennis; coed intramural: alpine skiing, bowling, canoeing/kayaking, cross-country running, fitness, ropes courses. 4 PE instructors, 10 coaches, 1 athletic trainer.

Computers Computers are regularly used in all academic, animation, art, college planning, drafting, library, literary magazine, media arts, research skills, senior seminar, study skills, technology, yearbook classes. Computer network features include on-campus library services, online commercial services, Internet access, wireless campus network, Internet filtering or blocking technology. Campus intranet and student e-mail accounts are available to students. Students grades are available online. The school has a published electronic and media policy.

Woodside Priory School

Contact Mr. Al D. Zappelli, Dean of Admissions and Financial Aid. 650-851-8223 Ext. 101. Fax: 650-851-2839. E-mail: azappelli@PrioryCA.org. Web site: www. PrioryCA.org.

WOODSTOCK SCHOOL

Landour
Mussoorie
Uttarakhand 248 179, India
Head of School: Dr. David Laurenson

General Information Cocducational boarding and day college-preparatory, music, and science school, affiliated with Christian faith. Boarding grades 3–12, day grades N–12. Founded: 1854. Setting: rural. Nearest major city is New Delhi, India. Students are housed in single-sex dormitories. 290-acre campus. 7 buildings on campus. Approved or accredited by CITA (Commission on International and Trans-Regional Accreditation) and Middle States Association of Colleges and Schools. Member of European Council of International Schools. Language of instruction: English. Total enrollment: 522. Upper school average class size: 17. Upper school faculty-student ratio: 1:17. There are 180 required school days per year for Upper School students. Upper School students typically attend 5 days per week. The average school day consists of 6 hours and 30 minutes.

Upper School Student Profile Grade 7: 44 students (28 boys, 16 girls); Grade 8: 55 students (32 boys, 23 girls); Grade 9: 73 students (36 boys, 37 girls); Grade 10: 76 students (39 boys, 37 girls); Grade 11: 90 students (49 boys, 41 girls); Grade 12: 81 students (37 boys, 44 girls). 93% of students are boarding students. 63% are international students. International students from Bhutan, Democratic People's Republic of Korea, Japan, Nepal, Thailand, and United States; 21 other countries represented in student body. 47% of students are Christian.

Faculty School total: 70. In upper school: 18 men, 16 women; 17 have advanced degrees; all reside on campus.

Subjects Offered Algebra, American history, American history-AP, American literature, American studies, art, art history, Asian studies, Bible, Bible studies, biology, biology-AP, calculus, calculus-AP, ceramics, chemistry, chemistry-AP, choir, choral music, Christianity, community service, comparative religion, computer science, concert band, drama, economics, English, English language-AP, English literature, English-AP, environmental science, environmental science-AP, ethics, European history, fine arts, French, French-AP, geometry, government, government and politics-AP, health education, Hindi, Indian studies, jazz band, journalism, macro/microeconomics-AP, macroeconomics-AP, mathematics, mathematics-AP, microeconomics-AP, music, philosophy, physical education, physics, physics-AP, religion, science, social studies, theater, trigonometry, U.S. government and politics-AP, vocal music, world history, world history-AP, world literature, world religions, writing, yearbook.

Graduation Requirements Arts and fine arts (art, music, dance, drama), Christian studies, computer literacy, English, foreign language, mathematics, physical education (includes health), science, social studies (includes history). Community service is required.

Special Academic Programs 17 Advanced Placement exams for which test preparation is offered; independent study; study abroad; academic accommodation for the gifted, the musically talented, and the artistically talented; ESL (23 students enrolled).

College Admission Counseling 62 students graduated in 2010; 60 went to college, including Bard College; Columbia University; Mercyhurst College; Middlebury College; Northeastern University; Stanford University. Other: 2 had other specific plans. Median SAT critical reading: 566, median SAT math: 630, median SAT writing: 590, median combined SAT: 1810, median composite ACT: 27. 37% scored over 600 on SAT critical reading, 60% scored over 600 on SAT math, 48% scored over 600 on SAT writing, 56% scored over 1800 on combined SAT, 33% scored over 26 on composite ACT.

Student Life Upper grades have specified standards of dress, student council, honor system. Discipline rests equally with students and faculty. Attendance at religious services is required.

Tuition and Aid Day student tuition: $17,400; 7-day tuition and room/board: $17,400. Tuition installment plan (individually arranged payment plans). Need-based scholarship grants available. In 2010–11, 20% of upper-school students received aid.

Admissions Traditional secondary-level entrance grade is 11. For fall 2010, 310 students applied for upper-level admission, 74 were accepted, 68 enrolled. Any standardized test or TOEFL or SLEP required. Deadline for receipt of application materials: none. Application fee required: $80. Interview recommended.

Athletics Interscholastic: basketball (boys, girls), cricket (b), cross-country running (b,g), field hockey (b,g), soccer (b,g), strength & conditioning (b,g), swimming and diving (b,g), track and field (b,g); intramural: aerobics/dance (g), backpacking (b,g), badminton (b,g), basketball (b,g), climbing (b,g), cricket (b), cross-country running (b,g), field hockey (b,g), gymnastics (b,g), hiking/backpacking (b,g), hockey (b,g), outdoor activities (b,g), outdoor education (b,g), physical fitness (b,g), physical training (b,g), rock climbing (b,g), running (b,g), soccer (b,g), squash (b,g), strength & conditioning (b,g), swimming and diving (b,g), table tennis (b,g), tennis (b,g), track and field (b,g), volleyball (b,g), walking (b,g), wall climbing (b,g), weight training (b,g), wilderness survival (b,g); coed intramural: backpacking, hiking/backpacking, outdoor education, physical fitness, physical training, rock climbing. 4 PE instructors.

Computers Computers are regularly used in all academic classes. Computer network features include on-campus library services, Internet access, wireless campus network, Internet filtering or blocking technology. Campus intranet, student e-mail accounts, and computer access in designated common areas are available to students. Students grades are available online. The school has a published electronic and media policy. **Contact** Ms. Kirsten Bradby, Director of Admissions. 91-135-661-5104. Fax: 91-135-263-0897. E-mail: admissions@woodstock.ac.in. Web site: www.woodstock.ac.in.

WOODWARD ACADEMY

1662 Rugby Avenue
College Park, Georgia 30337
Head of School: Mr. Stuart Gulley, PhD

General Information Coeducational day college-preparatory and arts school. Grades PK–12. Founded: 1900. Setting: suburban. Nearest major city is Atlanta. 90-acre campus. 50 buildings on campus. Approved or accredited by Georgia Independent School Association, Southern Association of Colleges and Schools, and Georgia Department of Education. Member of National Association of Independent Schools and Secondary School Admission Test Board. Endowment: $94 million. Total enrollment: 2,729. Upper school average class size: 17.

Faculty School total: 384. In upper school: 45 men, 68 women; 85 have advanced degrees.

Subjects Offered 20th century world history, 3-dimensional art, 3-dimensional design, acting, Advanced Placement courses, algebra, American government, American history, American history-AP, anatomy and physiology, art, astronomy, audio visual/media, band, biology, biology-AP, calculus, calculus-AP, ceramics, chemistry, chemistry-AP, choir, choral music, chorus, comparative religion, computer education, computer programming, computer programming-AP, computer science, computer science-AP, concert band, contemporary history, contemporary issues, creative writing, dance, debate, digital music, drama, drama performance, drawing, drawing and design, earth science, ecology, economics, economics and history, economics-AP, English, English language and composition-AP, English literature, English literature and composition-AP, English-AP, environmental science, environmental science-AP, European history, European history-AP, fine arts, French, French language-AP, French-AP, geography, geometry, government and politics-AP, government/civics, grammar, health, history, history-AP, honors English, honors geometry, honors U.S. history, honors world history, independent study, Japanese, jewelry making, journalism, Latin, literature and composition-AP, marching band, marine ecology, mathematics, meteorology, microeconomics-AP, Middle East, modern European history-AP, multicultural literature, music, oceanography, performing arts, personal fitness, photography, physical education, physics, physics-AP, pre-calculus, probability and statistics, science, social studies, Spanish, Spanish language-AP, Spanish-AP, speech communications, statistics, statistics-AP, television, the Sixties, theater, trigonometry, U.S. government and politics, U.S. government and politics-AP, U.S. history, U.S. history-AP, video, voice ensemble, world history, world literature, world religions, yearbook.

Graduation Requirements Arts and fine arts (art, music, dance, drama), computer science, English, foreign language, mathematics, physical education (includes health), religion (includes Bible studies and theology), science, social studies (includes history).

Special Academic Programs Advanced Placement exam preparation; honors section; independent study.

College Admission Counseling 254 students graduated in 2010; all went to college, including Auburn University; Georgia Institute of Technology; Georgia Southern University; The University of Alabama; University of Georgia.

Student Life Upper grades have uniform requirement, student council, honor system. Discipline rests primarily with faculty.

Tuition and Aid Day student tuition: $20,675. Tuition installment plan (Your Tuition Solution—Springstone Financial). Need-based scholarship grants available. In 2010–11, 9% of upper-school students received aid. Total amount of financial aid awarded in 2010–11: $1,006,220.

Admissions Traditional secondary-level entrance grade is 9. SSAT required. Deadline for receipt of application materials: March 1. Application fee required: $75. On-campus interview required.

Athletics Interscholastic: baseball (boys), basketball (b,g), cheering (g), cross-country running (b,g), diving (b,g), football (b), golf (b,g), lacrosse (b,g), soccer (b,g), softball (g), swimming and diving (b,g), tennis (b,g), track and field (b,g), volleyball (g); intramural: basketball (b,g), cheering (g), football (b), soccer (b,g), softball (g), swimming and diving (b,g), tennis (b,g), track and field (b,g), volleyball (g); coed interscholastic: Frisbee, power lifting, ultimate Frisbee, weight lifting; coed intramural: fencing, horseback riding. 4 PE instructors, 34 coaches, 1 athletic trainer.

Computers Computers are regularly used in creative writing, English, foreign language, graphic design, journalism, literary magazine, mathematics, media production, newspaper, science, yearbook classes. Computer network features include on-campus library services, online commercial services, Internet access. Student e-mail accounts are available to students. Students grades are available online. **Contact** Russell L. Slider, Vice President/Dean of Admissions. 404-765-4001. Fax: 404-765-4009. E-mail: rusty.slider@woodward.edu. Web site: www.woodward.edu.

THE WOODWARD SCHOOL

1102 Hancock Street
Quincy, Massachusetts 02169
Head of School: Thomas L. Wesner, JD

General Information Girls' day college-preparatory, arts, and technology school. Grades 6–12. Founded: 1869. Setting: urban. Nearest major city is Boston. 1-acre campus. 1 building on campus. Approved or accredited by Association of Independent Schools in New England, New England Association of Schools and Colleges, and Massachusetts Department of Education. Endowment: $231,000. Total enrollment: 150. Upper school average class size: 15. Upper school faculty-student ratio: 1:8. There are 160 required school days per year for Upper School students. Upper School students typically attend 5 days per week. The average school day consists of 6 hours and 35 minutes.

Upper School Student Profile Grade 6: 15 students (15 girls); Grade 7: 15 students (15 girls); Grade 8: 20 students (20 girls); Grade 9: 25 students (25 girls); Grade 10: 25 students (25 girls); Grade 11: 25 students (25 girls); Grade 12: 25 students (25 girls).

Faculty School total: 24. In upper school: 6 men, 18 women; 12 have advanced degrees.

Subjects Offered Advanced computer applications, algebra, American history, American literature, anatomy, art, arts, biology, calculus, calculus-AP, chemistry, classical studies, classics, community service, computer graphics, computer science, constitutional law, drama, ecology, English, English language and composition-AP, environmental science, filmmaking, fine arts, French, health and wellness, health science, language arts, Latin, Latin-AP, law and the legal system, literature, literature and composition-AP, mathematics, media studies, physics, physics-AP, physiology, political science, portfolio art, pre-algebra, psychology, science, social sciences, social studies, Spanish, theater arts, U.S. government, U.S. history, Web authoring, Web site design, world history, world literature, World War II, writing.

Graduation Requirements Arts and fine arts (art, music, dance, drama), computer science, English, foreign language, mathematics, science, social studies (includes history). Community service is required.

Special Academic Programs Advanced Placement exam preparation; honors section; independent study; study at local college for college credit; academic accommodation for the artistically talented; ESL (8 students enrolled).

College Admission Counseling 22 students graduated in 2009; all went to college, including Boston College; Boston University; College of the Holy Cross; Stonehill College; University of Massachusetts Amherst.

Student Life Upper grades have specified standards of dress, student council, honor system. Discipline rests primarily with faculty.

Tuition and Aid Day student tuition: $10,250. Tuition installment plan (individually arranged payment plans, Tuition Management Systems). Tuition reduction for siblings, merit scholarship grants, need-based scholarship grants, prepGate K-12 Education Loan, AchieverLoans (Key Education Resources) available. In 2009–10, 35% of upper-school students received aid; total upper-school merit-scholarship money awarded: $9250. Total amount of financial aid awarded in 2009–10: $187,146.

Admissions Traditional secondary-level entrance grade is 9. For fall 2009, 66 students applied for upper-level admission, 52 were accepted, 39 enrolled. School's own exam and writing sample required. Deadline for receipt of application materials: none. Application fee required: $40. On-campus interview required.

Athletics Interscholastic: basketball, lacrosse, soccer, softball, track and field. 1 PE instructor, 6 coaches, 1 athletic trainer.

Computers Computers are regularly used in all academic, desktop publishing, digital applications, English, history, mathematics, photography, science, technology, video film production, Web site design, yearbook classes. Computer network features include on-campus library services, Internet access, wireless campus network, Internet filtering or blocking technology. Computer access in designated common areas is available to students. The school has a published electronic and media policy.

Contact Barbara A. Segadelli, Director of Admissions. 617-773-5610. Fax: 617-770-1551. E-mail: bsegadelli@thewoodwardschool.org. Web site: www.thewoodwardschool.org.

WORCESTER ACADEMY

81 Providence Street
Worcester, Massachusetts 01604
Head of School: Dexter P. Morse

General Information Coeducational boarding and day college-preparatory, arts, technology, and ESL school. Boarding grades 9–PG, day grades 6–12. Founded: 1834. Setting: urban. Nearest major city is Boston. Students are housed in single-sex dormitories. 60-acre campus. 14 buildings on campus. Approved or accredited by Association of Independent Schools in New England, New England Association of Schools and Colleges, and The Association of Boarding Schools. Member of National Association of Independent Schools and Secondary School Admission Test Board. Endowment: $22 million. Total enrollment: 651. Upper school average class size: 13. Upper school faculty-student ratio: 1:8. There are 160 required school days per year for Upper School students. Upper School students typically attend 5 days per week. The average school day consists of 6 hours and 45 minutes.

Upper School Student Profile Grade 6: 30 students (19 boys, 11 girls); Grade 7: 59 students (37 boys, 22 girls); Grade 8: 71 students (31 boys, 40 girls); Grade 9: 94 students (47 boys, 47 girls); Grade 10: 128 students (63 boys, 65 girls); Grade 11: 115 students (58 boys, 57 girls); Grade 12: 127 students (70 boys, 57 girls); Postgraduate: 27 students (26 boys, 1 girl). 33% of students are boarding students. 72% are state residents. 15 states are represented in upper school student body. 20% are international students. International students from China, Hong Kong, Japan, Republic of Korea, Taiwan, and Viet Nam; 15 other countries represented in student body.

Faculty School total: 113. In upper school: 58 men, 45 women; 61 have advanced degrees; 27 reside on campus.

Subjects Offered Acting, advanced studio art-AP, algebra, American history, American history-AP, American literature, American studies, anatomy, Ancient Greek, architecture, art, art-AP, band, biology, biology-AP, British literature, calculus, calculus-AP, ceramics, chemistry, chemistry-AP, Chinese, choral music, chorus, computer programming, computer science-AP, contemporary issues, creative writing, directing, economics, English, English language-AP, English literature, English literature-AP, English-AP, environmental science, environmental studies, ESL, ESL, ethics, European history, European history-AP, French, geography, geometry, government-AP, health, history, Holocaust studies, honors English, honors world history, human anatomy, journalism, Latin, mathematics, music, music theory, physical education, physics, post-calculus, pre-algebra, pre-calculus, sculpture, Spanish, statistics, studio art-AP, U.S. government and politics-AP, U.S. history-AP, world history, world history-AP, world religions, World War II.

Graduation Requirements Algebra, American literature, arts and fine arts (art, music, dance, drama), biology, chemistry, English, foreign language, geometry, health and wellness, mathematics, physical education (includes health), social sciences, U.S. history, world literature, writing, senior projects, community service.

Special Academic Programs 16 Advanced Placement exams for which test preparation is offered; honors section; independent study; ESL (8 students enrolled).

College Admission Counseling 148 students graduated in 2010; all went to college, including Boston College; Bowdoin College; College of the Holy Cross; Emory University; University of Illinois at Urbana–Champaign; Worcester Polytechnic Institute. Mean SAT critical reading: 560, mean SAT math: 620, mean composite ACT: 26. 35% scored over 600 on SAT critical reading, 40% scored over 600 on SAT math, 50% scored over 26 on composite ACT.

Student Life Upper grades have specified standards of dress, student council, honor system. Discipline rests equally with students and faculty.

Summer Programs ESL programs offered; session focuses on English preparation, TOEFL and SAT preparation; held on campus; accepts boys and girls; open to students from other schools. 20 students usually enrolled. 2011 schedule: August 7 to August 28.

Tuition and Aid Day student tuition: $26,610; 5-day tuition and room/board: $40,060; 7-day tuition and room/board: $47,070. Tuition installment plan (Academic Management Services Plan). Need-based scholarship grants, paying campus jobs available. In 2010–11, 36% of upper-school students received aid. Total amount of financial aid awarded in 2010–11: $4,400,000.

Admissions Traditional secondary-level entrance grade is 9. For fall 2010, 428 students applied for upper-level admission, 229 were accepted, 117 enrolled. ACT, ISEE, PSAT or SAT for applicants to grade 11 and 12, SSAT or TOEFL required. Deadline for receipt of application materials: January 15. Application fee required: $50. Interview required.

Athletics Interscholastic: baseball (boys), basketball (b,g), cross-country running (b,g), field hockey (g), football (b), ice hockey (b,g), lacrosse (g), skiing (downhill) (b,g), soccer (b,g), softball (g), tennis (b,g), track and field (b,g), volleyball (g), wrestling (b); coed interscholastic: crew, golf, swimming and diving; coed intramural: aerobics/dance, dance team, paddle tennis. 3 PE instructors, 5 coaches, 3 athletic trainers.

Computers Computers are regularly used in all academic, art, college planning, library, media arts, music, theater arts, video film production, yearbook classes. Computer network features include on-campus library services, online commercial services, Internet access, wireless campus network, Internet filtering or blocking technology. Campus intranet, student e-mail accounts, and computer access in designated common areas are available to students. Students grades are available online. The school has a published electronic and media policy.

Contact Gregory Cappello, Director of Admission. 508-754-5302 Ext. 199. Fax: 508-752-2382. E-mail: gregory.cappello@worcesteracademy.org. Web site: www.worcesteracademy.org.

WORCESTER PREPARATORY SCHOOL

508 South Main Street
PO Box 1006
Berlin, Maryland 21811
Head of School: Dr. Barry W. Tull

General Information Coeducational day college-preparatory, arts, and technology school. Grades PK–12. Founded: 1970. Setting: small town. Nearest major city is Ocean City. 45-acre campus. 7 buildings on campus. Approved or accredited by Association of Independent Maryland Schools, Middle States Association of Colleges and Schools, and Maryland Department of Education. Member of National Association of Independent Schools. Total enrollment: 548. Upper school average class size: 14. Upper school faculty-student ratio: 1:9. There are 173 required school days per year for Upper School students. Upper School students typically attend 5 days per week. The average school day consists of 6 hours and 30 minutes.

Upper School Student Profile Grade 9: 53 students (26 boys, 27 girls); Grade 10: 52 students (29 boys, 23 girls); Grade 11: 59 students (25 boys, 34 girls); Grade 12: 39 students (23 boys, 16 girls).

Faculty School total: 62. In upper school: 14 men, 21 women; 28 have advanced degrees.

Subjects Offered Advanced Placement courses, algebra, American history, American literature, art, art history, biology, biology-AP, calculus, calculus-AP, chemistry, chemistry-AP, computer programming, computer science, creative writing, dance, drama, earth science, economics, English, English literature, English literature and composition-AP, English-AP, European history, fine arts, French, geography, geometry, government/civics, Latin, literature and composition-AP, literature-AP, mathematics, military history, music, music theory, physical education, physics, physics-AP, psychology, SAT preparation, science, social sciences, social studies, Spanish, speech, statistics, technological applications, technology/design, theater, typing, U.S. history-AP, vocal music, world history, world history-AP, world literature, writing.

Graduation Requirements Art appreciation, arts and fine arts (art, music, dance, drama), computer science, English, foreign language, mathematics, music appreciation, physical education (includes health), science, social sciences.

Special Academic Programs 8 Advanced Placement exams for which test preparation is offered; honors section; independent study; academic accommodation for the gifted.

College Admission Counseling 49 students graduated in 2010; all went to college, including American University; Carnegie Mellon University; College of Charleston; United States Naval Academy; University of Delaware; University of Maryland, College Park.

Student Life Upper grades have uniform requirement, student council, honor system. Discipline rests primarily with faculty.

Tuition and Aid Day student tuition: $11,150. Tuition installment plan (Key Tuition Payment Plan, monthly payment plans, individually arranged payment plans). Need-based scholarship grants available. In 2010–11, 1% of upper-school students received aid.

Admissions Traditional secondary-level entrance grade is 9. For fall 2010, 16 students applied for upper-level admission, 11 were accepted, 8 enrolled. Achievement/Aptitude/Writing and writing sample required. Deadline for receipt of application materials: none. Application fee required: $50. On-campus interview required.

Athletics Interscholastic: basketball (boys, girls), field hockey (g), lacrosse (b,g), soccer (b,g), tennis (b,g), weight training (b,g), winter soccer (b,g); intramural: basketball (b,g), dance (b,g), dance squad (b,g), flag football (b,g), soccer (b,g); coed interscholastic: cheering, golf, tennis; coed intramural: dance, dance squad. 3 PE instructors, 3 coaches, 1 athletic trainer.

Computers Computers are regularly used in all classes. Computer network features include on-campus library services, online commercial services, Internet access, wireless campus network, Internet filtering or blocking technology. Campus intranet, student e-mail accounts, and computer access in designated common areas are available to students. The school has a published electronic and media policy.

Contact Lisa B. Cook, Director of Admissions. 410-641-3575. Fax: 410-641-3586. E-mail: lcook@worcesterprep.org. Web site: www.worcesterprep.org.

WYOMING SEMINARY

201 North Sprague Avenue
Kingston, Pennsylvania 18704-3593
Head of School: Dr. Kip P. Nygren

General Information Coeducational boarding and day college-preparatory school, affiliated with United Methodist Church. Boarding grades 9–PG, day grades PK–PG. Founded: 1844. Setting: suburban. Nearest major city is Wilkes-Barre. Students are housed in single-sex dormitories. 22-acre campus. 12 buildings on campus. Approved or accredited by Middle States Association of Colleges and Schools, Pennsylvania Association of Independent Schools, The Association of Boarding Schools, The College Board, and Pennsylvania Department of Education. Member of National Association of Independent Schools and Secondary School Admission Test Board. Endowment: $39 million. Total enrollment: 771. Upper school average class size: 14. Upper school faculty-student ratio: 1:10. There are 170 required school days per year for Upper School students. Upper School students typically attend 5 days per week. The average school day consists of 7 hours.

Upper School Student Profile Grade 9: 84 students (45 boys, 39 girls); Grade 10: 96 students (47 boys, 49 girls); Grade 11: 116 students (64 boys, 52 girls); Grade 12: 112 students (54 boys, 58 girls); Postgraduate: 19 students (18 boys, 1 girl). 45% of students are boarding students. 50% are state residents. 16 states are represented in upper school student body. 20% are international students. International students from China, Germany, Japan, Republic of Korea, Thailand, and Viet Nam; 15 other countries represented in student body. 10% of students are United Methodist Church.

Faculty School total: 124. In upper school: 37 men, 25 women; 35 have advanced degrees; 30 reside on campus.

Subjects Offered 20th century world history, 3-dimensional design, advanced computer applications, African American history, African history, algebra, alternative physical education, American Civil War, American history, American literature, analysis, analysis and differential calculus, analytic geometry, anatomy and physiology, ancient world history, animal behavior, art, art appreciation, art history, art

history-AP, astronomy, Bible studies, biology, biology-AP, botany, British literature, calculus, calculus-AP, ceramics, chemistry, chemistry-AP, choral music, civil rights, college admission preparation, college counseling, community service, computer education, computer graphics, computer programming, computer science, conceptual physics, creative writing, critical writing, dance, discrete mathematics, drama, drawing and design, ecology, economics, economics and history, English, English literature, environmental science, environmental science-AP, ESL, European history, European history-AP, expository writing, fine arts, forensics, French, French-AP, geometry, health education, history, history of music, honors geometry, independent study, Judaic studies, Latin, Latin-AP, marine biology, mathematics, microeconomics, music, music theory, music theory-AP, philosophy, photography, physical education, physics, poetry, pre-calculus, printmaking, psychology, psychology-AP, public speaking, religion, Russian, Russian literature, science, science research, Shakespeare, social studies, sociology, Spanish, Spanish-AP, statistics, statistics-AP, studio art-AP, theater, trigonometry, U.S. government and politics-AP, U.S. history-AP, women in literature, world civilizations, world geography, world history, world literature, world religions, World War II, zoology.

Graduation Requirements Art history, Bible as literature, biology, computer science, English, foreign language, health education, mathematics, music history, physical education (includes health), public speaking, science, social studies (includes history), U.S. history, world civilizations, 40 hours of community service, extracurricular participation.

Special Academic Programs 25 Advanced Placement exams for which test preparation is offered; honors section; independent study; term-away projects; study at local college for college credit; study abroad; ESL (37 students enrolled).

College Admission Counseling 128 students graduated in 2010; 127 went to college, including Boston College; Boston University; Bucknell University; Drexel University; Fordham University; New York University. Other: 1 entered a postgraduate year. Mean SAT critical reading: 568, mean SAT math: 597, mean SAT writing: 571, mean combined SAT: 1736, mean composite ACT: 25.

Student Life Upper grades have specified standards of dress, student council, honor system. Discipline rests equally with students and faculty.

Summer Programs Enrichment, advancement, ESL, art/fine arts, computer instruction programs offered; session focuses on performing arts and ESL; held on campus; accepts boys and girls; open to students from other schools. 500 students usually enrolled. 2011 schedule: June 27 to August 21. Application deadline: June 9.

Tuition and Aid Day student tuition: $20,500; 7-day tuition and room/board: $40,550. Tuition installment plan (FACTS Tuition Payment Plan, monthly payment plans). Merit scholarship grants, need-based scholarship grants, need-based loans, prepGATE loans available. In 2010–11, 50% of upper-school students received aid; total upper-school merit-scholarship money awarded: $400,000. Total amount of financial aid awarded in 2010–11: $6,000,000.

Admissions Traditional secondary-level entrance grade is 9. For fall 2010, 346 students applied for upper-level admission, 199 were accepted, 118 enrolled. ACT, PSAT or SAT for applicants to grade 11 and 12, SSAT or TOEFL or SLEP required. Deadline for receipt of application materials: none. Application fee required: $75. Interview required.

Athletics Interscholastic: baseball (boys), basketball (b,g), cross-country running (b,g), diving (b,g), field hockey (g), football (b), ice hockey (b,g), lacrosse (b,g), soccer (b,g), softball (g), swimming and diving (b,g), tennis (b,g), wrestling (b); intramural: paint ball (b), power lifting (b); coed interscholastic: golf, strength & conditioning; coed intramural: alpine skiing, backpacking, badminton, ballet, bowling, combined training, dance, fencing, fitness, flag football, Frisbee, martial arts, modern dance, Nautilus, outdoor activities, outdoor recreation, physical training, skiing (downhill), tai chi, wall climbing, yoga. 2 PE instructors, 4 coaches, 2 athletic trainers.

Computers Computers are regularly used in art, English, foreign language, history, mathematics, music, science classes. Computer network features include on-campus library services, online commercial services, Internet access, wireless campus network, Internet filtering or blocking technology. Campus intranet, student e-mail accounts, and computer access in designated common areas are available to students. The school has a published electronic and media policy.

Contact Mr. David R. Damico, Director of Admission. 570-270-2160. Fax: 570-270-2191. E-mail: admission@wyomingseminary.org. Web site: www.wyomingseminary.org.

XAVERIAN BROTHERS HIGH SCHOOL

800 Clapboardtree Street
Westwood, Massachusetts 02090-1799
Head of School: Br. Daniel E. Skala, CFX

General Information Boys' day college-preparatory, arts, religious studies, and technology school, affiliated with Roman Catholic Church. Grades 9–12. Founded: 1963. Setting: suburban. Nearest major city is Boston. 35-acre campus. 1 building on campus. Approved or accredited by Association of Independent Schools in New England and New England Association of Schools and Colleges. Endowment: $27 million. Total enrollment: 915. Upper school average class size: 22. Upper school faculty-student ratio: 1:22. There are 165 required school days per year for Upper School students. Upper School students typically attend 5 days per week. The average school day consists of 6 hours and 15 minutes.

Upper School Student Profile Grade 9: 238 students (238 boys); Grade 10: 244 students (244 boys); Grade 11: 219 students (219 boys); Grade 12: 214 students (214 boys). 85% of students are Roman Catholic.

Faculty School total: 87. In upper school: 72 men, 15 women; 65 have advanced degrees.

Subjects Offered Algebra, American history, American history-AP, American literature, art, biology, biology-AP, business, calculus, calculus-AP, chemistry, chemistry-AP, computer applications, computer math, computer programming, computer science, creative writing, driver education, economics, English, English literature, English-AP, European history, French, French-AP, government/civics, history, law, marine biology, mathematics, modern European history-AP, music, oceanography, physical education, physics, physics-AP, psychology, science, social sciences, social studies, Spanish, Spanish-AP, studio art-AP, theology, world history.

Graduation Requirements Arts and fine arts (art, music, dance, drama), computer science, English, foreign language, mathematics, physical education (includes health), religion (includes Bible studies and theology), science, social studies (includes history).

Special Academic Programs International Baccalaureate program; Advanced Placement exam preparation; honors section; term-away projects; academic accommodation for the gifted, the musically talented, and the artistically talented; remedial reading and/or remedial writing; remedial math; special instructional classes for deaf students, blind students.

College Admission Counseling 240 students graduated in 2009; 236 went to college, including Fairfield University; Northeastern University; Providence College; Quinnipiac University; Saint Michael's College; Villanova University. Other: 1 went to work, 1 entered military service, 1 entered a postgraduate year, 1 had other specific plans. Median SAT critical reading: 591, median SAT math: 608, median SAT writing: 587. 49% scored over 600 on SAT critical reading, 56% scored over 600 on SAT math, 43% scored over 600 on SAT writing.

Student Life Upper grades have specified standards of dress, student council, honor system. Discipline rests primarily with faculty. Attendance at religious services is required.

Tuition and Aid Day student tuition: $13,500. Tuition installment plan (monthly payment plans, individually arranged payment plans, The Tuition Solution). Merit scholarship grants, need-based scholarship grants available. In 2009–10, 40% of upper-school students received aid; total upper-school merit-scholarship money awarded: $510,000. Total amount of financial aid awarded in 2009–10: $1,500,000.

Admissions Traditional secondary-level entrance grade is 9. For fall 2009, 600 students applied for upper-level admission, 500 were accepted, 245 enrolled. Archdiocese of Boston High School entrance exam provided by STS required. Deadline for receipt of application materials: December 31. No application fee required. Interview recommended.

Athletics Interscholastic: alpine skiing, baseball, basketball, cross-country running, diving, football, golf, ice hockey, lacrosse, power lifting, rugby, skiing (downhill), soccer, strength & conditioning, swimming and diving, tennis, track and field, ultimate Frisbee, volleyball, weight training, winter (indoor) track, wrestling; intramural: baseball, basketball, bicycling, billiards, bowling, floor hockey, football, Frisbee, golf, handball, racquetball, skiing (downhill), snowboarding, strength & conditioning, touch football, weight training. 2 PE instructors, 100 coaches, 2 athletic trainers.

Computers Computers are regularly used in business, mathematics, music, science classes. Computer network features include on-campus library services, online commercial services, Internet access, wireless campus network, Internet filtering or blocking technology, common desktop applications: MS Office and Adobe Creative Suite, printing, access to digital and video cameras for music/video production. Campus intranet and computer access in designated common areas are available to students. Students grades are available online. The school has a published electronic and media policy.

Contact Mr. Tim McDonough, Director of Admissions. 781-326-6392. Fax: 781-320-0458. E-mail: tmcdonough@xbhs.com. Web site: www.xbhs.com.

XAVIER COLLEGE PREPARATORY

4710 North Fifth Street
Phoenix, Arizona 85012

Head of School: Sr. Joan Fitzgerald, BVM

General Information Girls' day college preparatory, arts, religious studies, technology, and Great Books, Advanced Placement, dual college enrollment school, affiliated with Roman Catholic Church. Grades 9–12. Founded: 1943. Setting: urban. 20-acre campus. 7 buildings on campus. Approved or accredited by National Catholic Education Association, North Central Association of Colleges and Schools, Western Catholic Education Association, and Arizona Department of Education. Endowment: $1.2 million. Total enrollment: 1,178. Upper school average class size: 24. Upper school faculty-student ratio: 1:22. There are 181 required school days per year for Upper School students. Upper School students typically attend 5 days per week. The average school day consists of 5 hours.

Upper School Student Profile Grade 9: 292 students (292 girls); Grade 10: 316 students (316 girls); Grade 11: 291 students (291 girls); Grade 12: 279 students (279 girls). 75% of students are Roman Catholic.

Faculty School total: 95. In upper school: 20 men, 75 women; 70 have advanced degrees.

Subjects Offered Accounting, advanced biology, advanced chemistry, advanced computer applications, Advanced Placement courses, advanced studio art-AP, algebra, American government, American history, American history-AP, American literature, analysis and differential calculus, anatomy and physiology, architecture, art, art history, astronomy, athletic training, audition methods, band, bell choir, biology, biology-AP, calculus, calculus-AP, ceramics, cheerleading, chemistry, chemistry-AP, child development, Chinese, choir, community service, computer programming-AP, computer science, computer studies, concert choir, contemporary issues, culinary arts, dance, dance performance, digital photography, drama, economics, English, English language-AP, English literature, English literature-AP, environmental science-AP, ethics, European history-AP, family and consumer science, film studies, fine arts, French, French language-AP, geography, geometry, graphic design, great books, guitar, jazz band, Latin, Latin-AP, music, music theory-AP, musical theater, New Testament, newspaper, philosophy, physical education, physics, physics-AP, precalculus, psychology, sociology, Spanish, Spanish language-AP, Spanish literature-AP, sports medicine, stagecraft, statistics-AP, student government, theology, trigonometry, U.S. government and politics-AP, visual arts, weight training, world history-AP, world literature.

Graduation Requirements American literature, arts and fine arts (art, music, dance, drama), computer science, English, foreign language, mathematics, physical education (includes health), religion (includes Bible studies and theology), science, social studies (includes history), AZ history and free enterprise independent study, summer reading program, 50 hours of community service.

Special Academic Programs Advanced Placement exam preparation; honors section; independent study; study at local college for college credit; academic accommodation for the gifted and the artistically talented.

College Admission Counseling 288 students graduated in 2009; all went to college, including Arizona State University; New York University; Northern Arizona University; The University of Arizona; University of Colorado at Boulder; University of San Diego. Median composite ACT: 25.

Student Life Upper grades have uniform requirement, student council, honor system. Discipline rests primarily with faculty. Attendance at religious services is required.

Tuition and Aid Day student tuition: $10,269–$13,257. Tuition installment plan (monthly payment plans, semester payment plan). Need-based scholarship grants, reduced tuition rate for Catholic families registered in Catholic parishes of the Diocese of Phoenix available. In 2009–10, 30% of upper-school students received aid. Total amount of financial aid awarded in 2009–10: $1,200,000.

Admissions Traditional secondary-level entrance grade is 9. For fall 2009, 498 students applied for upper-level admission, 350 were accepted, 320 enrolled. High School Placement Test required. Deadline for receipt of application materials: January 29. Application fee required: $50.

Athletics Interscholastic: aerobics/dance, badminton, basketball, cheering, crew, cross-country running, dance team, danceline, diving, golf, ice hockey, lacrosse, pom squad, rowing, soccer, softball, swimming and diving, tennis, track and field, volleyball, winter soccer; intramural: basketball, crew, dance, fencing, fitness, floor hockey, modern dance, strength & conditioning, weight training; coed interscholastic: hockey; coed intramural: badminton, basketball, flag football, soccer, softball, tennis, volleyball. 4 PE instructors, 21 coaches, 2 athletic trainers.

Computers Computers are regularly used in all classes. Computer network features include on-campus library services, online commercial services, Internet access, Internet filtering or blocking technology, Blackboard Learning Systems, Blackbaud NetClassroom. Computer access in designated common areas is available to students. Students grades are available online. The school has a published electronic and media policy.

Contact Mrs. Paula Petrowski, Director of Admissions. 602-277-3772 Ext. 3104. Fax: 602-240-3175. E-mail: ppetrowski@xcp.org. Web site: www.xcp.org.

XAVIER UNIVERSITY PREPARATORY SCHOOL

5116 Magazine Street
New Orleans, Louisiana 70115-1699

Head of School: Mrs. Carolyn Oubre

General Information Girls' day college-preparatory, arts, religious studies, technology, honors, and Advanced Placement school, affiliated with Roman Catholic Church. Grades 7–12. Founded: 1915. Setting: urban. 2-acre campus. 4 buildings on campus. Approved or accredited by National Catholic Education Association, Southern Association of Colleges and Schools, Southern Association of Independent Schools, and Louisiana Department of Education. Total enrollment: 269. Upper school average class size: 20. Upper school faculty-student ratio: 1:9. There are 176 required school days per year for Upper School students. Upper School students typically attend 5 days per week. The average school day consists of 6 hours.

Upper School Student Profile Grade 7: 8 students (8 girls); Grade 8: 30 students (30 girls); Grade 9: 50 students (50 girls); Grade 10: 68 students (68 girls); Grade 11: 51 students (51 girls); Grade 12: 62 students (62 girls). 60% of students are Roman Catholic.

Faculty School total: 24. In upper school: 4 men, 19 women; 9 have advanced degrees.

Subjects Offered ACT preparation, African American studies, algebra, American history, art, art appreciation, art history, band, Bible, biology, British literature, British literature (honors), calculus, chemistry, chorus, civics, computer applications, computer literacy, conceptual physics, concert band, drama, drama performance, drawing,

drawing and design, driver education, earth science, English, English literature, French, geometry, health and wellness, health education, history, honors algebra, honors English, honors geometry, honors U.S. history, honors world history, Latin, moral theology, music, music appreciation, New Testament, newspaper, psychology, religion, SAT/ACT preparation, science, sculpture, senior thesis, Shakespeare, Spanish, speech, studio art, technical theater, theater arts, U.S. history, U.S. literature, world geography, world history.

Graduation Requirements Advanced math, algebra, American history, American literature, biology, calculus, chemistry, civics, computer applications, computer literacy, English, foreign language, French, Latin, Spanish, U.S. history, U.S. literature, completion of a Senior Thesis.

Special Academic Programs Honors section; independent study; study at local college for college credit; academic accommodation for the musically talented and the artistically talented.

College Admission Counseling 69 students graduated in 2009; 68 went to college, including Dillard University; Loyola University New Orleans; University of New Orleans; Xavier University of Louisiana. Other: 1 entered military service. 16% scored over 600 on SAT critical reading, 10% scored over 600 on SAT math, 16% scored over 600 on SAT writing, 10% scored over 1800 on combined SAT, 10% scored over 26 on composite ACT.

Student Life Upper grades have uniform requirement, student council, honor system. Discipline rests primarily with faculty. Attendance at religious services is required.

Tuition and Aid Day student tuition: $5670. Tuition installment plan (The Tuition Plan, monthly payment plans). Tuition reduction for siblings, merit scholarship grants, middle-income loans, paying campus jobs available. In 2009–10, 1% of upper-school students received aid; total upper-school merit-scholarship money awarded: $17,000. Total amount of financial aid awarded in 2009–10: $20,000.

Admissions Traditional secondary-level entrance grade is 9. For fall 2009, 131 students applied for upper-level admission, 92 were accepted, 61 enrolled. Iowa Tests of Basic Skills-Grades 7-8, Archdiocese HSEPT-Grade 9 required. Deadline for receipt of application materials: none. Application fee required: $20. On-campus interview required.

Athletics Interscholastic: baseball, basketball, cross-country running, softball, track and field, volleyball; intramural: cheering, dance team, golf. 1 PE instructor, 4 coaches.

Computers Computers are regularly used in computer applications, foreign language, publications, SAT preparation, study skills, yearbook classes. Computer network features include on-campus library services, Internet access, wireless campus network, Internet filtering or blocking technology. Computer access in designated common areas is available to students. Students grades are available online. The school has a published electronic and media policy.

Contact Mrs. Tiffany Neville Cambre, Director of Admissions and Student Activities. 504-899-6061 Ext. 324. Fax: 504-899-0547. E-mail: tcambre@xavierprep.com. Web site: www.xavierprep.com.

YANG ACADEMY

111 Central Avenue
Gaithersburg, Maryland 20877
Head of School: Mrs. Zenia Yang

General Information Coeducational day college-preparatory, arts, bilingual studies, and mathematics, science school. Grades K–12. Founded: 2005. Setting: suburban. Nearest major city is Washington, DC. 4-acre campus. 1 building on campus. Approved or accredited by Maryland Department of Education. Total enrollment: 5. Upper school average class size: 1. Upper school faculty-student ratio: 1:1. There are 175 required school days per year for Upper School students. Upper School students typically attend 5 days per week. The average school day consists of 6 hours.

Upper School Student Profile Grade 10: 1 student (1 girl).

Faculty School total: 5. In upper school: 1 man, 4 women; 4 have advanced degrees.

Subjects Offered Advanced Placement courses, art, college counseling, computer programming, English, entrepreneurship, foreign language, independent study, mathematics, music, physical education, research, science, social studies.

Graduation Requirements English, foreign language, mathematics, science, social studies (includes history). Community service is required.

Special Academic Programs 5 Advanced Placement exams for which test preparation is offered; honors section; accelerated programs; independent study; term-away projects; study abroad; academic accommodation for the gifted, the musically talented, and the artistically talented.

Student Life Upper grades have honor system. Discipline rests equally with students and faculty.

Tuition and Aid Day student tuition: $10,000. Tuition installment plan (monthly payment plans, individually arranged payment plans). Tuition reduction for siblings available.

Admissions Traditional secondary-level entrance grade is 9. Admissions testing required. Deadline for receipt of application materials: none. Application fee required: $25. On-campus interview required.

Computers Computers are regularly used in programming, research skills classes.

Contact Mrs. Zenia Yang, Head of School. 301-294-0811. Fax: 301-294-0820. E-mail: ya@yangacademy.com. Web site: http://www.yangacademy.com.

YESHIVA HIGH SCHOOL

7135 North Carpenter Road
Skokie, Illinois 60077
Head of School: Rabbi Moshe Wender

General Information Boys' boarding and day college-preparatory, religious studies, and technology school, affiliated with Jewish faith. Grades 9–12. Founded: 1922. Setting: suburban. Nearest major city is Chicago. Students are housed in single-sex dormitories. 11-acre campus. 2 buildings on campus. Approved or accredited by North Central Association of Colleges and Schools and Illinois Department of Education. Language of instruction: Hebrew. Total enrollment: 130. Upper school average class size: 13. Upper school faculty-student ratio: 1:13. There are 197 required school days per year for Upper School students. Upper School students typically attend 5 days per week.

Upper School Student Profile Grade 9: 35 students (35 boys); Grade 10: 35 students (35 boys); Grade 11: 36 students (36 boys); Grade 12: 24 students (24 boys). 33% of students are boarding students. 68% are state residents. 13 states are represented in upper school student body. International students from Canada and Mexico. 100% of students are Jewish.

Faculty School total: 34. In upper school: 34 men; 15 have advanced degrees; 1 resides on campus.

Subjects Offered Bible, computers, economics, English, Hebrew, Jewish history, mathematics, physical education, science, social studies, Talmud.

Special Academic Programs 7 Advanced Placement exams for which test preparation is offered; honors section; independent study; academic accommodation for the gifted; remedial reading and/or remedial writing; remedial math.

College Admission Counseling 25 students graduated in 2009; all went to college, including Loyola University Chicago; Northwestern University; University of Illinois at Chicago; Yeshiva University. Mean SAT critical reading: 600, mean SAT math: 610, mean composite ACT: 27.

Student Life Upper grades have specified standards of dress, student council. Discipline rests primarily with faculty. Attendance at religious services is required.

Tuition and Aid 7-day tuition and room/board: $15,315. Tuition installment plan (monthly payment plans, individually arranged payment plans). Need-based loans available. In 2009–10, 60% of upper-school students received aid.

Admissions Traditional secondary-level entrance grade is 9. For fall 2009, 55 students applied for upper-level admission, 39 were accepted, 24 enrolled. ACT-Explore, admissions testing or any standardized test required. Deadline for receipt of application materials: none. Application fee required. On-campus interview required.

Athletics Interscholastic: basketball, physical training; intramural: aerobics, basketball, fitness, flag football, football, martial arts, soccer, softball. 1 PE instructor, 4 coaches.

Computers Computers are regularly used in stock market classes. Computer network features include on-campus library services, Internet access.

Contact Rabbi Joshua Zisook, Director of Admissions. 847-982-2500. Fax: 847-677-6381. E-mail: zisook@htc.edu.

YOKOHAMA INTERNATIONAL SCHOOL

258 Yamate-cho, Naka-ku
Yokohama 231-0862, Japan
Head of School: Mr. James MacDonald

General Information Coeducational day college-preparatory, arts, bilingual studies, and technology school. Grades N–12. Founded: 1924. Setting: urban. 3-acre campus. 8 buildings on campus. Approved or accredited by European Council of International Schools, International Baccalaureate Organization, and New England Association of Schools and Colleges. Language of instruction: English. Total enrollment: 670. Upper school average class size: 16. Upper school faculty-student ratio: 1:8. There are 174 required school days per year for Upper School students. Upper School students typically attend 5 days per week. The average school day consists of 7 hours.

Upper School Student Profile Grade 6: 50 students (30 boys, 20 girls); Grade 7: 54 students (29 boys, 25 girls); Grade 8: 56 students (33 boys, 23 girls); Grade 9: 58 students (34 boys, 24 girls); Grade 10: 62 students (22 boys, 40 girls); Grade 11: 57 students (26 boys, 31 girls); Grade 12: 61 students (29 boys, 32 girls).

Faculty School total: 90. In upper school: 30 men, 20 women; 23 have advanced degrees.

Subjects Offered Advanced chemistry, advanced math, art, band, biology, ceramics, chemistry, choir, computer programming, drama, Dutch, economics, English, English literature, environmental science, French, geography, German, information technology, International Baccalaureate courses, Japanese, mathematics, modern languages, music composition, music theory, physical education, physics, Spanish, studio art, theater, theater arts, theory of knowledge, world history, world literature.

Graduation Requirements Arts, English, foreign language, information technology, mathematics, physical education (includes health), science, senior thesis, social studies (includes history), theory of knowledge, 50 hours of community service.

Special Academic Programs International Baccalaureate program; ESL.

College Admission Counseling 59 students graduated in 2010; 54 went to college, including New York University; The University of British Columbia; University of Toronto. Other: 5 had other specific plans. Mean SAT critical reading: 550, mean SAT math: 586, mean SAT writing: 556.

Student Life Upper grades have specified standards of dress, student council. Discipline rests primarily with faculty.

Summer Programs Remediation, enrichment, sports programs offered; session focuses on English, mathematics, and basketball; held on campus; accepts boys and girls; open to students from other schools. 30 students usually enrolled. 2011 schedule: June to July. Application deadline: May.

Tuition and Aid Day student tuition: ¥2,250,000. Tuition installment plan (individually arranged payment plans).

Admissions Traditional secondary-level entrance grade is 9. For fall 2010, 50 students applied for upper-level admission, 24 were accepted, 18 enrolled. School's own test required. Deadline for receipt of application materials: none. Application fee required: ¥20,000. Interview recommended.

Athletics Interscholastic: baseball (boys), basketball (b,g), cross-country running (b,g), field hockey (g), soccer (b,g), track and field (b,g), volleyball (g); coed interscholastic: tennis; coed intramural: backpacking, ball hockey, bicycling, canoeing/kayaking, diving, floor hockey, gymnastics, hiking/backpacking, kayaking, netball, outdoor education, skateboarding, skiing (downhill), yoga. 4 PE instructors.

Computers Computers are regularly used in all academic classes. Computer network features include on-campus library services, online commercial services, Internet access, wireless campus network, Internet filtering or blocking technology. Campus intranet, student e-mail accounts, and computer access in designated common areas are available to students. Students grades are available online. The school has a published electronic and media policy.

Contact Ms. Susan Chen, Administrative Officer. 81-45-622-0084. Fax: 81-45-621-0379. E-mail: admissions@yis.ac.jp. Web site: www.yis.ac.jp.

YORK CATHOLIC HIGH SCHOOL

601 East Springettsbury Avenue
York, Pennsylvania 17403
Head of School: Mr. George E. Andrews Jr.

General Information Coeducational day college-preparatory and general academic school, affiliated with Roman Catholic Church. Grades 7–12. Founded: 1927. Setting: suburban. 19-acre campus. 1 building on campus. Approved or accredited by Middle States Association of Colleges and Schools, National Catholic Education Association, and Pennsylvania Department of Education. Total enrollment: 656. Upper school average class size: 21.

Upper School Student Profile Grade 7: 90 students (45 boys, 45 girls); Grade 8: 103 students (43 boys, 60 girls); Grade 9: 116 students (55 boys, 61 girls); Grade 10: 127 students (57 boys, 70 girls); Grade 11: 101 students (56 boys, 45 girls); Grade 12: 123 students (58 boys, 65 girls). 89% of students are Roman Catholic.

College Admission Counseling 110 students graduated in 2010; 104 went to college. Other: 6 entered military service. Median SAT critical reading: 542, median SAT math: 521, median SAT writing: 538, median combined SAT: 1601.

Student Life Upper grades have uniform requirement, student council, honor system. Discipline rests primarily with faculty. Attendance at religious services is required.

Tuition and Aid Tuition installment plan (SMART Tuition Payment Plan). Tuition reduction for siblings, need-based scholarship grants available. In 2010–11, 26% of upper-school students received aid.

Admissions Deadline for receipt of application materials: none. No application fee required. Interview required.

Athletics Interscholastic: baseball (boys), basketball (b,g), cross-country running (b,g), diving (b,g), football (b), golf (b,g), lacrosse (b,g), running (b,g), soccer (b,g), softball (g), swimming and diving (b,g), tennis (b,g), track and field (b,g), volleyball (g), wrestling (b); intramural: strength & conditioning (b); coed intramural: bowling, ice hockey, skiing (downhill), table tennis.

Computers Computer resources include on-campus library services, Internet access, Internet filtering or blocking technology. Campus intranet is available to students. Students grades are available online.

Contact Ms. Heather Hoffman, Director of Admissions. 717-846-8871 Ext. 20. Fax: 717-843-4588. E-mail: hhoffman@yorkcatholic.org. Web site: www.yorkcatholic.org.

YORK COUNTRY DAY SCHOOL

1071 Regents Glen Boulevard
York, Pennsylvania 17403
Head of School: Nathaniel W. Coffman

General Information Coeducational day college-preparatory, arts, and bilingual studies school. Grades PS–12. Founded: 1953. Setting: suburban. Nearest major city is Baltimore, MD. 15-acre campus. 1 building on campus. Approved or accredited by Middle States Association of Colleges and Schools, Pennsylvania Association of Independent Schools, and Pennsylvania Department of Education. Member of National Association of Independent Schools. Endowment: $1.3 million. Total enrollment: 206. Upper school average class size: 12. Upper school faculty-student ratio: 1:4. There are 170 required school days per year for Upper School students. Upper School students typically attend 5 days per week. The average school day consists of 7 hours and 30 minutes.

Upper School Student Profile Grade 9: 13 students (5 boys, 8 girls); Grade 10: 14 students (10 boys, 4 girls); Grade 11: 17 students (8 boys, 9 girls); Grade 12: 13 students (8 boys, 5 girls).

Faculty School total: 42. In upper school: 8 men, 11 women; 12 have advanced degrees.

Subjects Offered Advanced Placement courses, algebra, American history, American history-AP, American literature, art, art history, biochemistry, biology, biology-AP, calculus, calculus-AP, chemistry, chemistry-AP, choral music, community service, computer programming, computer science, creative writing, drama, English, English literature, English literature-AP, European history, fine arts, French, French-AP, geography, geometry, government/civics, health, history, Latin, literature, mathematics, music, physical education, physics, psychology, public speaking, science, social studies, Spanish, Spanish language-AP, studio art-AP, theater, world history, world history-AP.

Graduation Requirements Arts and fine arts (art, music, dance, drama), English, foreign language, history, independent study, mathematics, physical education (includes health), public speaking, science, visual arts, independent study (3 semesters) through our Magnet Program, two semester classes. Community service is required.

Special Academic Programs Advanced Placement exam preparation; honors section; independent study; term-away projects; study at local college for college credit; study abroad; academic accommodation for the gifted, the musically talented, and the artistically talented; remedial reading and/or remedial writing.

College Admission Counseling 11 students graduated in 2010; all went to college, including James Madison University; Swarthmore College; University of Denver; University of Pittsburgh; York College of Pennsylvania. Median SAT critical reading: 540, median SAT math: 510.

Student Life Upper grades have specified standards of dress, student council, honor system. Discipline rests equally with students and faculty.

Summer Programs Sports, art/fine arts programs offered; session focuses on Provide sports, arts, crafts and swimming; held off campus; held at York College of Pennsylvania; accepts boys and girls; open to students from other schools. 35 students usually enrolled. 2011 schedule: June 20 to July 31. Application deadline: June 15.

Tuition and Aid Day student tuition: $16,200. Tuition installment plan (Insured Tuition Payment Plan, monthly payment plans, semester payment plan). Need-based scholarship grants available. In 2010–11, 40% of upper-school students received aid. Total amount of financial aid awarded in 2010–11: $292,100.

Admissions Traditional secondary-level entrance grade is 9. 3-R Achievement Test, Academic Profile Tests, California Achievement Test, ISEE, Otis-Lennon Ability or Stanford Achievement Test or PSAT and SAT for applicants to grade 11 and 12 required. Deadline for receipt of application materials: none. Application fee required: $35. On-campus interview required.

Athletics Interscholastic: baseball (boys), basketball (b,g), bowling (b,g), cross-country running (b,g), field hockey (g), football (b), golf (b,g), soccer (b,g), softball (g), swimming and diving (b,g), tennis (b,g), volleyball (g), wrestling (b); intramural: basketball (b,g), soccer (b,g); coed intramural: soccer. 2 PE instructors, 6 coaches.

Computers Computers are regularly used in all academic classes. Computer network features include on-campus library services, online commercial services, Internet access, Internet filtering or blocking technology. Student e-mail accounts are available to students.

Contact Ms. Alison C. Greer, Director of Admission and Communication. 717-843-9805. Fax: 717-815-6769. E-mail: agreer@ycds.org. Web site: www.ycds.org.

YORK PREPARATORY SCHOOL

40 West 68th Street
New York, New York 10023-6092
Head of School: Ronald P. Stewart

General Information Coeducational day college-preparatory, arts, technology, music (practical and theory), and drama school. Grades 6–12. Founded: 1969. Setting: urban. 1 building on campus. Approved or accredited by Middle States Association of Colleges and Schools and National Independent Private Schools Association. Total enrollment: 351. Upper school average class size: 15. Upper school faculty-student ratio: 1:6. There are 158 required school days per year for Upper School students. Upper School students typically attend 5 days per week. The average school day consists of 6 hours and 30 minutes.

Upper School Student Profile Grade 6: 23 students (13 boys, 10 girls); Grade 7: 33 students (20 boys, 13 girls); Grade 8: 50 students (29 boys, 21 girls); Grade 9: 62 students (35 boys, 27 girls); Grade 10: 63 students (32 boys, 31 girls); Grade 11: 57 students (34 boys, 23 girls); Grade 12: 63 students (36 boys, 27 girls).

Faculty School total: 62. In upper school: 23 men, 39 women; 50 have advanced degrees.

Subjects Offered 20th century history, 20th century world history, 3-dimensional art, advanced chemistry, advanced computer applications, Advanced Placement courses, advanced studio art-AP, algebra, American history, American history-AP, American literature, anatomy, animation, anthropology, art, art appreciation, astronomy, biology, calculus, calculus-AP, ceramics, chemistry, chemistry-AP, community service, comparative religion, computer math, computer programming, computer science, computer skills, concert band, creative writing, current events, drama, drama performance, driver education, earth science, economics, English, English literature, English-AP,

"An Intimate Place to Learn in the Heart of a Great City"

York Preparatory School

40 West 68ᵗʰ Street - New York, NY 10023

With **39 clubs** and **24 sports teams**
for **350 students**,
there is something for everyone at York Prep.

York Prep
is a coeducational college preparatory school
serving students from grades 6-12.

For more information, contact our
Admissions Office
at admissions@yorkprep.org or
212-362-0400

www.yorkprep.org

environmental science, ethics, European history, expository writing, filmmaking, fine arts, French, genetics, geography, geology, geometry, government/civics, grammar, health education, Holocaust studies, law, literary magazine, mathematics, music, music history, philosophy, photography, physical education, physics, physiology, political science, politics, pre-calculus, psychology, reading/study skills, research skills, SAT preparation, science, science project, social studies, Spanish, statistics, theater, trigonometry, typing, world history, world literature, writing, zoology.

Graduation Requirements Arts and fine arts (art, music, dance, drama), English, foreign language, mathematics, physical education (includes health), science, social studies (includes history), 100 hours of community service. Community service is required.

Special Academic Programs Advanced Placement exam preparation; honors section; accelerated programs; independent study; study at local college for college credit; academic accommodation for the gifted, the musically talented, and the artistically talented; programs in English, mathematics, general development for dyslexic students; special instructional classes for students with mild learning issues (extra tutoring program); ESL (2 students enrolled).

College Admission Counseling 63 students graduated in 2010; all went to college, including Cornell University; Hobart and William Smith Colleges; New York University; Syracuse University; University of Vermont; Vassar College.

Student Life Upper grades have specified standards of dress, student council, honor system. Discipline rests primarily with faculty.

Summer Programs Remediation, advancement programs offered; held on campus; accepts boys and girls; not open to students from other schools. 30 students usually enrolled. 2011 schedule: June 15 to July 31. Application deadline: none.

Tuition and Aid Day student tuition: $34,800–$35,400. Tuition installment plan (Insured Tuition Payment Plan, monthly payment plans, individually arranged payment plans). Tuition reduction for siblings, bursaries, merit scholarship grants, need-based scholarship grants available. In 2010–11, 20% of upper-school students received aid. Total amount of financial aid awarded in 2010–11: $750,000.

Admissions Traditional secondary-level entrance grade is 9. ISEE required. Deadline for receipt of application materials: January 15. Application fee required: $50. On-campus interview required.

Athletics Interscholastic: baseball (boys), basketball (b,g), cross-country running (b,g), softball (b,g), volleyball (b,g); intramural: dance squad (g), volleyball (b,g); coed interscholastic: basketball, cross-country running, fencing, golf, hockey, soccer, tennis, track and field; coed intramural: aerobics, aerobics/dance, aquatics, backpacking, basketball, billiards, bowling, cross-country running, dance, equestrian sports, fencing, Frisbee, golf, horseback riding, judo, lacrosse, roller hockey, skiing (downhill), soccer, softball, swimming and diving, ultimate Frisbee, yoga. 4 PE instructors, 6 coaches, 3 athletic trainers.

Computers Computers are regularly used in all academic classes. Computer network features include on-campus library services, online commercial services, Internet access, wireless campus network, Internet filtering or blocking technology, T1 Internet connection in every class. Students grades are available online. The school has a published electronic and media policy.

Contact Jacqueline Leber, Director of Admissions. 212-362-0400 Ext. 127. Fax: 212-362-7424. E-mail: jleber@yorkprep.org. Web site: www.yorkprep.org.

See Display on this page and Close-Up on page 870.

YORK SCHOOL

9501 York Road
Monterey, California 93940
Head of School: Chuck Harmon

General Information Coeducational day college-preparatory, arts, bilingual studies, and technology school, affiliated with Episcopal Church. Grades 8–12. Founded: 1959. Setting: suburban. Nearest major city is San Jose. 25-acre campus. 6 buildings on campus. Approved or accredited by California Association of Independent Schools, National Association of Episcopal Schools, Western Association of Schools and Colleges, and California Department of Education. Member of National Association of Independent Schools. Endowment: $4.6 million. Total enrollment: 230. Upper school average class size: 14. Upper school faculty-student ratio: 1:9. Upper School students typically attend 5 days per week. The average school day consists of 7 hours.

Upper School Student Profile Grade 8: 21 students (8 boys, 13 girls); Grade 9: 59 students (30 boys, 29 girls); Grade 10: 45 students (18 boys, 27 girls); Grade 11: 51 students (27 boys, 24 girls); Grade 12: 54 students (30 boys, 24 girls).

Faculty School total: 31. In upper school: 17 men, 14 women; 24 have advanced degrees.

Subjects Offered Advanced studio art-AP, algebra, American history-AP, anatomy, ancient history, art, art history, Asian history, band, biology, biology-AP, calculus, calculus-AP, chemistry, chemistry-AP, choir, community service, computer science, creative writing, digital art, drama, English, English-AP, environmental science, film, fine arts, French, French language-AP, geometry, Greek, jazz, Latin, Latin-AP, marine biology, mathematics, music, music theory-AP, orchestra, painting, philosophy, photography, physical education, physical science, physics, physics-AP, physiology, pre-calculus, psychology-AP, science, social studies, Spanish, Spanish language-AP, studio art, U.S. history, U.S. history-AP, world history, yearbook.

Graduation Requirements Arts and fine arts (art, music, dance, drama), computer science, English, foreign language, mathematics, physical education (includes health), science, social studies (includes history), Ensemble Participation. Community service is required.

Special Academic Programs Advanced Placement exam preparation; honors section.

College Admission Counseling 45 students graduated in 2010; all went to college, including New York University; Santa Clara University; University of California, Berkeley; University of California, Davis; University of California, Santa Barbara; University of Pennsylvania. Mean SAT critical reading: 683, mean SAT math: 661, mean SAT writing: 656, mean combined SAT: 2000.

Student Life Upper grades have specified standards of dress, student council, honor system. Discipline rests primarily with faculty.

Tuition and Aid Day student tuition: $24,995. Tuition installment plan (individually arranged payment plans, 2 Payments, 10 Payments). Need-based scholarship grants, need-based loans available. In 2010–11, 44% of upper-school students received aid. Total amount of financial aid awarded in 2010–11: $1,367,560.

Admissions Traditional secondary-level entrance grade is 9. For fall 2010, 133 students applied for upper-level admission. Admissions testing and McGraw-Hill, ETS (short-form) ability, in-house writing sample and math test required. Deadline for receipt of application materials: February 15. Application fee required: $75. Interview required.

Athletics Interscholastic: basketball (boys, girls), cross-country running (b,g), diving (b,g), field hockey (g), golf (b,g), soccer (b,g), softball (g), swimming and diving (b,g), tennis (b,g), volleyball (g); coed interscholastic: lacrosse; coed intramural: badminton, basketball, fitness walking, independent competitive sports, jogging, soccer, ultimate Frisbee, walking, weight training, yoga. 18 coaches.

Computers Computers are regularly used in computer applications, technology, yearbook classes. Computer network features include on-campus library services, Internet access, wireless campus network. The school has a published electronic and media policy.

Contact Rachel Gaudoin, Admission Associate. 831-372-7338 Ext. 116. Fax: 831-372-8055. E-mail: rachel@york.org. Web site: www.york.org.

ACADEMY OF OUR LADY OF MERCY, LAURALTON HALL

Milford, Connecticut

Type: Girls college-preparatory day school
Grades: 9–12
Enrollment: 437
Head of School: Antoinette Iadarola, Ph.D., President

THE ACADEMY

The Academy of Our Lady of Mercy, Lauralton Hall, is a Catholic college-preparatory high school, founded in 1905 by the Sisters of Mercy. The oldest independent Catholic college preparatory school for young women in Connecticut, it is over 100 years old—a major milestone for any school and even more significant for a Catholic girls' school. A member of the National Coalition of Girls' Schools, Lauralton Hall is accredited by the New England Association of Schools and Colleges and the Connecticut Department of Education. The Lauralton day school experience prepares girls to become competent, confident, and compassionate women, giving of themselves—especially to those in need. Students are challenged to succeed academically.

Lauralton Hall is one of a select group of Catholic girls' schools that has remained true to its original mission, which is to foster a community atmosphere enriched by the Mercy tradition and to educate young women to pursue knowledge, recognize truth, and respond to the needs of others. This empowers young women to excel in any endeavor, to find their own voices, and to be bearers of mercy for others. Since Lauralton believes character formation is as essential as academic achievement, the core values of a Mercy education play an integral role in a Lauralton Hall education: compassion and service, educational excellence, concern for women and women's issues, global vision and responsibility, spiritual growth and development, and collaboration.

Lauralton attracts more than 400 students from over thirty communities. Centrally located in historic downtown Milford and within walking distance of the train station, students come by train, car, or bus, seeking the same rigorous preparation for college as the more than 6,000 alumnae who have passed through Lauralton's halls for over 100 years. The student body is composed of young women from diverse socioeconomic, religious, and ethnic backgrounds.

ACADEMIC PROGRAMS

The well-rounded Lauralton Hall curriculum fully prepares students for college study, with demanding honors and Advanced Placement classes offered in all academic disciplines. As an added dimension, the formation of character is valued as highly as intellectual achievement. In keeping with the tradition of the Sisters of Mercy, students are constantly challenged to think of others and to reach out to those in need. They are expected to become Renaissance women for the twenty-first century—articulate and poised, confident and compassionate, gracious in their strength, at home in their own times, respectful of the past, and fully prepared to embrace the future.

Lauralton strives to develop clear, independent thinkers who appreciate knowledge and the learning process. The school offers a solid and well-balanced college-preparatory curriculum, which emphasizes a mastery of analytical and critical thinking skills, problem solving, and the ability to communicate ideas effectively. Challenging and demanding college-preparatory, honors, and Advanced Placement courses are offered. Courses are also available through the UConn Early College Experience (ECE), a concurrent enrollment program that allows motivated high school students to take UConn courses at their high schools for both high school and college credit. Every course taken through the UConn ECE is equivalent to the same course at the University of Connecticut. Established in 1955, the UConn ECE is the nation's longest running concurrent enrollment program and is nationally accredited by the National Alliance of Concurrent Enrollment Partnerships (NACEP).

Lauralton Hall offers Advanced Placement (AP) courses in biology, calculus, chemistry, English language and composition, English literature and composition, European history, French, Latin, physics, Spanish, and United States history. UConn ECE courses are offered in biology, English literature and composition, European history, finite mathematics, French, fundamentals of music, and U.S. history.

In order to graduate, a minimum of 25 credits must be earned, which must include six major subject areas (English, world languages, history, mathematics, science, and religion), a fine arts course, physical education, and 75 hours of community service. The average class size is about 18 students.

FACULTY AND ADVISERS

There are 37 faculty members, 7 administrators, and 4 guidance counselors. About 80 percent of the faculty members hold advanced degrees. There is also 1 Sister of Mercy on staff as well as 2 Sisters of Mercy on the Board of Trustees and other Sisters of Mercy volunteers.

COLLEGE ADMISSION COUNSELING

Guidance seminars and individual conferences are an integral, ongoing part of each student's schedule during her four years. The counselors guide students in making appropriate college choices and help students with the application process.

All 104 members of Lauralton's class of 2010 pursued higher education after graduating. Sixty-nine percent of the class of 2010 were honor students; merit-based scholarships awarded to the class of 2010 totaled over $7 million.

In recent years, Lauralton Hall graduates have attended top-tier institutions such as Brown, Carnegie Mellon, College of the Holy Cross, Columbia, Dartmouth, Georgetown, Harvard, Vassar, the United States Military Academy, the United States Naval Academy, the United States Coast Guard Academy, the University of Pennsylvania, and Worcester Polytechnic, to name a few.

STUDENT BODY AND CONDUCT

More than 430 young women from thirty-five Connecticut towns attend Lauralton Hall. The students are from diverse socioeconomic, religious, and ethnic backgrounds; about 80 percent are Catholic, and 17 percent are members of minority groups. Students are expected to abide by the codes of conduct found in the school's Student/Parent Handbook of Standards and Expectations.

ACADEMIC FACILITIES

The beautiful 30-acre campus is centered around a Victorian Gothic mansion built in 1864. The mansion and its property were purchased by the Sisters of Mercy in 1905 for use as a school. The administrative building, known as Mercy Hall, and the St. Joseph school building were added to provide classrooms, offices, an auditorium, a library/media center, and the school chapel. The school also has a music building, a gym/fitness center, three new state-of-the-art science labs, and recently renovated art rooms.

ATHLETICS

At Lauralton Hall, students have the opportunity to participate in many different interscholastic athletics and are required to take physical education classes. "We've got the spirit!" summarizes what student athletes at Lauralton Hall experience: the joy of competition, pride in school and personal accomplishments, and the ability to win or lose with heads held high. Lauralton Hall athletes are expected to play fair; enjoy honest competition; and demonstrate sportsmanship, dedication, and compassion for one another, opponents, officials, and spectators. The school is a member of the Connecticut Interscholastic Athletic Conference (CIAC) and the South West Conference (SWC). There are fifteen varsity sports: basketball, cheerleading, cross-country, field hockey, golf, gymnastics, indoor track, lacrosse, skiing, soccer, softball, swimming and diving, tennis, track and field, and volleyball. The school also has an ice hockey club. The campus has its own playing fields and a gym, which houses a basketball court as well as a fully equipped fitness center.

EXTRACURRICULAR OPPORTUNITIES

Students may participate in academic teams, clubs, social activities, community service, and cultural trips. With more than thirty clubs and organizations to choose from, there is something to fit the interest of every young woman. Extracurricular activities include a fall musical, a spring play, a Christmas concert, art club, field trips, youth and government, environmental club, percussion ensemble, Shakespeare club, student literary publications, class retreats, student council, honor societies, and more. Mixers/dances are also permitted and encouraged to provide students the opportunity for social development. Helping others is an integral part of a Mercy School education. Therefore, students are required to give of themselves by doing 75 hours of community service.

DAILY LIFE

Classes begin at 8 a.m. with the Teacher Advisory period and end at 2:16 p.m., Monday through Friday. Sports and activities are offered after school.

SUMMER PROGRAMS

Lauralton Hall offers summer sports and enrichment programs for girls and boys. A qualified adult staff guides children through a week of learning and fun in a safe environment. Open to students ages 6 and up, these high-quality, educational, fun workshops offer participants an opportunity to experience community and engage in diverse activities on the beautiful Lauralton Hall campus at various times and dates from the end of June through August, depending on the workshop.

Enrichment programs include a variety of offerings in art, sports, science, dance, cooking, and more. Recent sessions have included STEM Gems, Raging Robotics, Ecology Crusaders, Cooking 101, Art Adventure, Fun Adventures, Creative Dance Lab, Dance—hip hop/jazz/mod hop, soccer, basketball, baseball, field hockey, and cheerleading.

COSTS AND FINANCIAL AID

Tuition for 2010–11 is $14,250. There is a $250 activity/technology fee, in addition to the cost of books and uniform. There is also a $100 athletics fee per sport per athlete. Financial aid and scholarships are available. About 28 percent of students receive financial aid.

ADMISSIONS INFORMATION

Interested parents and prospective students, including transfer students, may request information by contacting Mrs. Kathleen O. Shine, Director of Admissions and Financial Aid at 203-877-2786, Ext. 125 or kshine@lauraltonhall.org. Information can also be accessed on the school Web site, www.lauraltonhall.org. Prospective students are also welcome to spend a day at the school.

APPLICATION TIMETABLE

Inquiries are welcome anytime. Applications should be submitted online by November 15, but they are accepted later, space permitting. The application fee is $60. The application fee for transfer students is $75.

ADMISSIONS CORRESPONDENCE

Admissions Office
Academy of Our Lady of Mercy, Lauralton Hall
200 High Street
Milford, Connecticut 06460
Phone: 203-877-2786 Ext. 125
Fax: 203-876-9760
E-mail: admission@lauraltonhall.org
Web site: http://www.lauraltonhall.org

AMERICAN HERITAGE SCHOOL

Plantation and Delray Beach, Florida

Type: Coeducational, day, independent, nonsectarian
Grades: PK-3–grade 12
Enrollment: 2,400, Plantation campus; 1,011, Boca/Delray campus
Head of School: William Laurie, President and Founder

THE SCHOOL

American Heritage School's mission is to graduate students who are prepared in mind, body, and spirit to meet the requirements of the colleges of their choice. To this end, the School strives to offer a challenging college preparatory curriculum, opportunities for leadership, and superior programs in the arts and athletics. American Heritage is committed to providing a safe and nurturing environment for learning so that children of average to gifted intelligence may achieve their full potential to be intelligent, creative, and contributing members of society. Students receive a well-rounded education that provides opportunities for leadership and character building and extensive opportunities for growth in the arts, athletics, and new technology.

ACADEMIC PROGRAMS

The curriculum for the preprimary child is developmental and age appropriate at each level. Daily language, speech, and auditory development activities help children to listen, understand, speak, and learn effectively. The program seeks to maximize the academic potential of each child, while fostering a positive self-image and providing the skills necessary for the next level of education.

The Lower School is committed to developing a student's basic skills, helping the student master content areas, and maintaining the student's enthusiasm for learning. Students learn the fundamentals of reading, process writing, mathematics, and English through a logical progressive sequence, and they learn social studies, handwriting, spelling, science, and health, with an emphasis on the development of good study skills. In math and reading, students are grouped according to ability. Enrichment classes in computer education, art, media center, music, Spanish, Chinese, physical education, and investigative science lab are offered. Field trips, special projects and events, and assemblies supplement the work introduced in class.

Math, reading, grammar, literature, social studies, and science are the core subjects of the junior high curriculum, where critical-thinking skills become increasingly important. Writing skills are emphasized, helping students become literate and articulate thinkers and writers. Enrichment courses are an important part of the junior high curriculum, with courses rotated on a nine-week basis. Honors classes are available in all core subject areas.

At the high school level, emphasis is placed on college preparation and on higher-level thinking skills. Students are challenged by required research and speech and writing assignments in all subject areas. An extensive variety of classes in all areas of the fine arts is available. A selection of electives—from marine biology to Advanced Placement Chinese to stagecraft—rounds out the students' schedules, allowing them to explore other interests and talents. In addition to traditional lecture and discussion, teachers supplement the text curriculum with activities, projects, and field trips that make subjects more relevant and meaningful to the students.

Honors and Advanced Placement (AP) courses are available to qualified students. Students may gain college credit as a benefit of the successful completion of AP courses, which include American government, American history, biology, calculus, chemistry, economics, English language, English literature, environmental studies, European history, French, music theory, physics, psychology, Spanish, and world history.

American Heritage School offers unique pre-medical, prelaw, and pre-engineering programs to qualified high school students. The programs challenge those ninth- through twelfth-grade students who have an interest in these fields of study and encourage students to consider these areas as potential career choices. The many course offerings are most often taught by working professionals in each area. In addition to course work for both programs, there are required internships that match students with professionals in their area of study.

In 2010, the school had 31 National Merit Scholarship Semifinalists and was the top-ranked private school at the National Mu Alpha Theta (mathematics honor society) annual conference.

Through the international program, in addition to an international student's regular academic classes, one to two hours of English language instruction is provided daily. Living with an American family produces more opportunity for language development and practice.

FACULTY AND ADVISERS

The students at American Heritage are served by 187 teachers, counselors, and administrators at the Plantation location and 106 teachers, counselors, and administrators at the Delray campus. Sixty-five percent hold master's or doctoral degrees. Teachers actively seek out both school-year and summer workshops to attend, and they return with creative ideas for their teaching. Faculty turnover is minimal. The faculty is also committed to the Heritage philosophy of developing good character and self-esteem as well as the reinforcement of traditional values in students. Teachers maintain close communication with parents regarding their child's progress, with frequent written progress reports, phone calls, and scheduled conference days. The school provides a Web-based service, Edline, on which students and parents can access information ranging from general school, club, and sports topics to specific content for individual classes. Classes are small, with a 17:1 student-teacher ratio.

COLLEGE ADMISSION COUNSELING

At American Heritage, the goal is to send seniors to colleges that match their goals and expectations for college life. There are 6 full-time guidance counselors in the high school, including a Director of College Placement and a Scholarship Specialist.

The college placement process begins in seventh grade with academic advising about curriculum and course selection and continues through high school with college-preparation advising. The counselors keep abreast of current admissions trends through attendance at national and local conferences and frequent contact with college admissions representatives.

The preparation for college intensifies as students in grades 9 through 12 follow a program designed to help them score well on the SATs. The program includes SAT prep mini-exercises in their English and math classes. In tenth grade and above, students may take an intensive daily SAT prep class taught on campus during the regular school day.

At this level, academic counseling gives consideration to graduation requirements and course selection, study skills and time management, leadership and club involvement, and referral to mentoring or professional tutoring, if needed. College advising is offered in the classroom on topics such as standardized test taking, the college application process, resume and essay writing, and searching for colleges and majors. The School reviews all college applications sent, writes letters of recommendation, finds scholarships for students, prepares students for college interviews, invites college admission representatives to campus, hosts a college fair, and proctors AP exams. A guidance resource room with catalogs, videos, and guidebooks is available for students and parents.

Virtually all graduates continue their educations and are admitted to the nation's finest colleges and universities. In recent years, graduates have been admitted to such schools as Boston College, Colgate, Columbia, Cornell, Duke, Harvard, Georgetown, MIT, NYU, Pepperdine, Princeton, Rutgers, Tufts, Wake Forest, West Point, Yale, and the Universities of Connecticut, Maryland, Pennsylvania, and Southern California.

STUDENT BODY AND CONDUCT

In the Lower School, the PK-3 classes enroll about 16 students; PK-4, 17; Kindergarten, 18; grades 1 and 2, 21; grades 3 and 4, 22; and grades 5 and 6, 23. In preschool through grade six, each class has a teacher and a full-time assistant. Grades 7 through 12 in the Upper School average 17 students.

The Plantation campus has 2,400 students, with 1,170 in the Lower School and 1,230 in the Upper School. The Boca/Delray student population totals 1,011, with 348 students in the Lower School and 663 in the Upper School. The School's day population is culturally diverse, with students representing forty-three countries from around the world.

ACADEMIC FACILITIES

The Plantation campus includes a fully equipped science lab, ten state-of-the-art computer rooms, and a $25-million Center for the Arts that houses a state-of-the-art 800-seat theater, a black-box theater, spacious art studios, a graphic design lab, choral and band rooms, and individual practice rooms. There are two new library/media centers, one that services the Lower School and another that meets all the technological requirements of students in the Upper School. Heritage has an excellent physical education center that includes an Olympic-sized swimming and diving facility, a gymnasium, six tennis courts, a track, four modern locker rooms, a weight-training room, and acres of well-maintained athletic fields.

The American Heritage Boca/Delray campus provides four state-of-the-art iMac computer labs, fully equipped science labs, art studios, a college guidance computer lab, a library/media center and research lab, a new $20 million center for the arts, an Olympic-sized swimming pool with eight racing lanes, a 2,600-square-foot teaching pool, a 25,000-square-foot gymnasium/auditorium, six lighted tennis courts, a football and soccer field, fully equipped weight training room, locker rooms, two well-equipped playgrounds, acres of well-maintained baseball and softball fields, practice fields for soccer and football, and beautifully landscaped grounds and courtyards.

ATHLETICS

The athletic program is an important part of the sense of community that has developed at Heritage. Parents, teachers, administrators, and students develop a special kind of camaraderie while cheering on the Patriot teams. Awards evenings are held for athletes and parents at the conclusion of each season. Heritage offers a complete competitive sports program. A "no-cut" policy allows every student who wants to participate an opportunity to play on the Patriot team of his or her choice. Coaches provide high-quality instruction in all sports. Sportsmanship, team-work, recognition of effort, and thorough training and preparation are the goals toward which the School works every day. Each year, a number of student-athletes receive financial help for their college education based on their athletic ability and their performance. More importantly, however, for those who do not have the ability—or maybe the desire—to participate at the collegiate level, athletic opportunities offer a very enjoyable and memorable experience, with accomplishments and relationships that last a lifetime. American Heritage competes as a member of the Florida High School Activities Association, and the athletics programs are consistently ranked in the top ten in the state of Florida.

EXTRACURRICULAR OPPORTUNITIES

The extensive activities offered at Heritage serve several purposes. Primarily, they assist in the growth and development of students, but they also provide opportunities for leadership and excellence, which are increasingly required for college admission. Among the activities and clubs offered to high school students are the National Honor Society; Student Council; Spanish/French Honor Society; Premed, Prelaw, and Pre-engineering Clubs; the Modern Language Club; Mu Alpha Theta (math club); SADD; the computer club; yearbook; the student newspaper; thespians; marching band; orchestra; jazz band; and chorus. Lower School students can take after-school classes in art, dance, instrumental music, karate, cooking,

computers, and other areas of interest. Students may also participate in Student Council, Junior Thespians, or Math Superstars.

American Heritage School provides an outstanding fine arts program to students in PK-3 through grade 12. The Center for the Arts is a beautiful, specially designed facility that enhances the arts program. Students participating in art, music, and drama programs have won awards at local, state, and national levels of competition in recent years. This recognition includes the Florida Vocal Association (superior ratings for choir, solo, and ensemble), Florida Orchestra Association (superior ratings for solo and ensemble/guitar and strings), American Choral Directors Award, and National Scholastic Art Competition (gold and silver medals).

Many students participate in enrichment and leadership programs offered in Broward County, including the National Conference for Community and Justice, Leadership Broward, Boys and Girls Clubs, Silver Knights, and the Institute for Math and Computer Science. Nationally, students have participated in Hugh O'Brian Youth Foundation, Freedoms Foundation, Presidential Classroom, and Global Young Leaders Conference. In addition, American Heritage School is home to two nonprofit organizations: Mosaic Theatre, an organization committed to promoting the dramatic arts, where students are able to work alongside professional actors, and the Center for the Arts Scholarship Foundation, a fund-raising organization that awards scholarships to talented students in the arts.

SUMMER PROGRAMS

American Heritage has provided summer fun for young campers since 1981. Summer camp provides activities that help build confidence and self-esteem. Campers enjoy the challenges and rewards of teamwork as they work and play. Through the numerous activities that are offered, campers continue to develop the socialization skills begun in school. Campers enjoy good relationships with the high school and college counselors, who serve as role models for them. American Heritage Day Camp sessions are available for students 13 years old and under.

For students who have failed a credit course in high school or have been required by their current school to attend summer school in order to pass to the next grade level, summer school is a necessity. However, many others can benefit from American Heritage's summer academic program, including preschoolers who need readiness skills to succeed in kindergarten or first grade; elementary and junior high students who need practice and development of basic skills in math, reading, and language arts; any students who perform one or two years below grade level; students for whom English is a second language; high school students who want to advance themselves academically by earning extra credits during the summer; and high school students who will soon take the SAT or ACT tests for

college admission. More information can be obtained by contacting the American Heritage School.

COSTS AND FINANCIAL AID

In 2010–11, tuition and fees total between $16,781 for preschoolers and $21,121 for twelfth-grade students. An international program is available at additional cost for the academic school year—August through May—and includes tuition, housing, three meals a day, books, uniforms, and 2 hours a day of English language.

American Heritage offers financial aid to parents who qualify.

ADMISSIONS INFORMATION

Enrollment at American Heritage School is limited to students who are above average to gifted in intelligence and who are working at or above grade level. Math, reading, vocabulary, and IQ tests are administered and are used to determine if the student has the background and basic skills necessary to be successful. The results of these entrance exams are discussed with the parents at a conference following the testing. I-20 visas are granted to international students who are accepted. Details are available from the Director of Admissions. Students are admitted without regard to race, creed, or national origin.

For acceptance into American Heritage's international program, families must supply complete academic records from the age of 12, translated into English; two teacher letters of recommendation, translated into English; copies of the student's passport; and a completed American Heritage School application form. The American Heritage Admissions Committee reviews the student's records and determines suitable placement. Full tuition for the school year is due upon acceptance. After tuition has been received, the School issues an I-20 form, which must be taken to the U.S. Embassy in the student's country to obtain a student visa.

APPLICATION TIMETABLE

First-semester classes begin in mid-August. For information regarding specific deadlines, students should contact American Heritage School's Plantation campus.

ADMISSIONS CORRESPONDENCE

Attn: Admissions
American Heritage School
12200 West Broward Boulevard
Plantation, Florida 33325

Phone: 954-472-0022
E-mail: admissions@ahschool.com
Web site: http://www.ahschool.com

American Heritage School Boca/Delray
6200 Linton Boulevard
Delray Beach, Florida 33484

Phone: 561-495-7272
E-mail: admissions@mailhost.ahschoolbd.com
Web site: http://www.ahschool.com

THE BALDWIN SCHOOL

Bryn Mawr, Pennsylvania

Type: Girls' day college-preparatory school
Grades: PK–12: Lower School, PK–5; Middle School, 6–8; Upper School, 9–12
Enrollment: School total: 556
Head of School: Sally M. Powell

THE SCHOOL

Baldwin is an independent school for thinking girls, where the joy of intellectual rigor in academics, aesthetic accomplishment in the arts, and collegial competition in athletics form confident women living balanced lives—women who know their own minds and use them in community and the larger world. The School facility is impressive and welcoming—century-old cherry trees frame the spires, wide stone steps lead to open front doors—offering an education for today's world in a traditional setting. The hallways echo with animated classroom conversation and the laughter of girls walking back from the playing field. The students are thoughtful, embrace curiosity, and have boundless imagination, much like the women and men who have built Baldwin. By design, the School is filled with energy and hums with the joy of exploration, the anticipation of learning, and the pride of achievement.

Founded in 1888 by Florence Baldwin to prepare girls for admission to Bryn Mawr College, Baldwin expanded rapidly from its opening class of 13. It now enrolls 556 girls. Baldwin celebrated its centennial in 1988. The School had boarding students for much of its history, but in 1972 the decision was made to phase out the boarding program. Today, day students come from throughout the Philadelphia area, including Montgomery, Chester, and Delaware counties in Pennsylvania and New Jersey and Delaware as well. The School is located 11 miles west of Philadelphia in the Main Line community of Bryn Mawr (population 8,400). Bryn Mawr College and Haverford College are within walking distance. Nearby bus and rail services provide access to the historic, cultural, and recreational resources of Philadelphia.

The Baldwin School is a nonprofit institution governed by a 30-member, self-perpetuating Board of Trustees, which meets five times a year. An active Alumnae Association maintains contact with the more than 4,400 graduates and plays a direct role in fund-raising and school events. The School has an endowment of $7 million. Annual Giving raised $901,802 last year.

The Baldwin School is accredited by the Middle States Association of Colleges and Schools and the Pennsylvania Association of Private Academic Schools. It is a member of the National Association of Independent Schools, the Association of Delaware Valley Independent Schools, the Secondary School Admission Test Board, and the Pennsylvania Association of Independent Schools.

ACADEMIC PROGRAMS

Students are expected to take 5 units of credit each year in addition to physical education. Graduation requirements include 4 units of English; 3 units of one foreign language or 2 units each of two languages; 3 units of history, 1 unit each of U.S. history, ancient history, and medieval history; 3 units of mathematics; 3 units of science; 2 units of fine arts; 1 trimester course each of speech, health, and human development; and 5 units of electives.

Among the Upper School courses offered are English I–IV and a variety of English electives; Latin I–III, Virgil, AP Latin, AP French I–V, and AP Spanish I–V; modern European history, economics, and comparative world issues; algebra I, algebra and consumer mathematics, geometry, algebra II and trigonometry, calculus, and topics in advanced mathematics; environmental science, biology I–II, chemistry I–II, and physics I–II; and art I–IV, art history, ceramics, design, architecture, photography, jewelry I–IV, theater I–III, instrumental ensemble, and chorus and handbell choir. Honors courses and independent study are available in several subjects. Baldwin also has a partnership with the Notre-Dame de Mongre School in France and the Perse School in England.

Technology is strongly supported. Students have access to more than 200 computers on campus, laptops are available for students to sign out to take home, and mobile computer labs are available for use in individual classrooms.

The average class size at Baldwin is 14, with an overall student-faculty ratio of about 7:1. Students who need extra work are recommended for either the math or writing labs, which provide supplemental work. In addition, the math lab provides enrichment for those with exceptional ability.

FACULTY AND ADVISERS

Faculty members include 74 full-time teachers and 15 part-time teachers, 79 women and 10 men. They hold eighty-nine baccalaureate and sixty-seven advanced degrees from such institutions as Curtis Institute of Music, Emory, Johns Hopkins, Pennsylvania Academy of the Fine Arts, the Sorbonne, University of Pennsylvania, and Yale. Faculty turnover is low.

Sally Powell was appointed as the seventh head of Baldwin in 2006. A native of Great Britain, she was educated in England at the Perse School for Girls and at Cambridge University where she received both her bachelor's and master's degrees. Prior to coming to Baldwin, Mrs. Powell worked at the Dwight-Englewood School in Englewood, New Jersey.

Beyond their dedication to teaching in their discipline, the Baldwin faculty members are known for their extraordinary commitment to the individual development of each girl. Many faculty members serve as advisers to individual students (with approximately 10 advisees each), grade advisers, or club advisers. Every adult in the Baldwin community is seen as a role model for the students, and faculty members are supported by the school counselor and the administration in their roles outside the classroom.

COLLEGE ADMISSION COUNSELING

The college placement process at Baldwin begins in the junior year with a College Night for students and their parents. Each girl and her parents meet with the College Adviser to define individual goals, realistic choices, and special interests as they pertain to the college admission process. There is a full-time Director of College Counseling and a part-time College Counselor.

The class of 2010 had average SAT scores of 600–720 verbal, 630–720 math, and 630–730 writing with 5 National Merit Semifinalists, and 5 National Merit Commended Students and 2 Outstanding Participants in the National Achievement Scholarship Program for Black Americans. Among the college choices for the class of 2010 were Cornell, Harvard, Princeton, Stanford, Yale, and the Universities of Chicago and Pennsylvania.

STUDENT BODY AND CONDUCT

In 2010–11, the School enrolled 556 girls in prekindergarten through grade 12 as follows: 10 in prekindergarten, 23 in kindergarten, 27 in grade 1, 28 in grade 2, 42 in grade 3, 45 in grade 4, 43 in grade 5, 48 in grade 6, 43 in grade 7, 49 in grade 8, 54 in grade 9, 44 in grade 10, 37 in grade 11, and 58 in grade 12. Students represented a variety of ethnic, religious, socioeconomic, cultural, and racial backgrounds. Of the total school population, 35 percent were students of color.

At Baldwin, all members of the school community are responsible for knowing the rules governing behavior, academics, and honesty. Minor infractions incur detentions (depending on the severity of the infraction), while more serious violations are heard by the Discipline Committee, which is made up of the Head of the School, the Director of the Upper School, 3 faculty members, and 4 grade-12 student senators.

ACADEMIC FACILITIES

The Baldwin campus is located on 25 acres. The Residence (1896) houses administrative offices, a reception area, an assembly room, the dining room, the kitchen, the Music Wing, the Middle School music room, an extensive arts facility (1984–86), an Early Childhood Center (1998), and a bookstore. A former resort hotel designed by Frank Furness and featuring distinctive Victorian architecture, the Residence is listed on the National Register of Historic Places. The Schoolhouse (1925, renovated 1998) contains Upper and Middle School classrooms, the library, and offices for the Head of the School as well as the Middle and Upper School directors. The Science Building (1961), expanded and renovated in 1995, provides a variety of science laboratories. A new Athletic Center was opened in November 2008. Additional school facilities include the Mrs. Cornelius Otis Skinner Dramatic Workshop, and Krumrine House (the residence of the Head of the School). The School-owned plant is valued at $31 million.

The Baldwin Library is an integral part of each student's educational experience. The librarians at Baldwin are trained teachers who work to develop in each student the ability to locate and utilize all types of print and nonprint materials, to instill an appreciation of the different kinds of literature and media, and to help each student on her way to becoming a lifelong, independent library user. The Baldwin libraries have 30,000 volumes, online database searching through the Access Pennsylvania network, and membership in the local PREP consortium for resource sharing.

ATHLETICS

At Baldwin, team sports and physical education classes provide an important opportunity for students to compete in interschool and interclass competitive settings. Girls may choose each season between playing a team sport or joining a physical education class. In many sports, teams are fielded at varsity, junior varsity, and third-team levels so that girls of every level of athletic ability may participate. Baldwin competes in a girls' interscholastic league with Agnes Irwin, Episcopal Academy, Notre Dame, Germantown Academy, Springside, and Penn Charter. Teams are fielded in basketball, crew, cross-country, dance, diving, field hockey, golf, lacrosse, soccer, softball, squash, swimming, tennis, volleyball, and winter track. Athletic facilities include one outdoor and two indoor swimming pools, three fields, five tennis courts, four international squash courts, a dance studio, a raised three-lane interior running track, a two-level fitness center, and two gymnasiums.

EXTRACURRICULAR OPPORTUNITIES

Student organizations, clubs, and activities form an important part of the Baldwin experience. Most Baldwin students participate in at least one extracurricular activity; many are involved in more. The four organizations are Student Senate, Class Officers, the Athletic Association Board, and Service League. Clubs include Lamplighters (student tour guides), Model Congress, Model U.N, Mock Trial, Peer Counseling, SADD, the Maskers (drama), Chorus, B-Flats (a cappella group), *Roman Candle* (literary magazine), *The Hourglass* (newspaper), *The Prism* (yearbook), Debate Club, Amnesty International, Ecology Club, Fashion Club, Black Students' Union, French Club, G.L.I. (Girls Learn International), and Asian Students Alliance.

There is also a wide range of activities and traditions that punctuate the year. These include dances, a Book Fair, Pumpkin Sale, Father-Daughter Phillies Game, Athletic Association Halloween Party, IX Banner Assembly, Ring Day, Middle School Ski Trip, Café Internationale, Service Day, Annual Student Art Show, Marching-In Dinner, Senior Project Presentations, Alumnae Luncheon for Seniors, and Class Night.

Because of Baldwin's proximity to Philadelphia, to historic sites in Pennsylvania, and to New York City, clubs and classes frequently take part in field trips.

All of these activities constitute a vital part of the Baldwin education. Girls learn to lead as well as to be intelligent, committed members of a group. Through events sponsored by its groups, the School reaches out to the community beyond the School itself.

DAILY LIFE

The school day begins at 8:15, when students meet with advisers in homeroom to hear the daily announcements. Class periods vary in length from 42 to 75 minutes. Monday through Thursday, classes are over at 3:30; Friday classes end at 2:45. Students in grades 9 and 10 must attend study hall during a free period, while students in grades 11 and 12 have choices to make regarding free time. Girls may bring their own lunch or purchase a hot meal, salad, sandwich, or soup in the dining room. Baldwin has adopted a two-week rotating schedule that allows for club and class meetings during the school day and provides for lengthened periods for laboratory classes. There are no bells and no passing time.

Built into the weekly schedule are assemblies, a full period for meeting with advisers, and time for assignments to math or writing lab.

COSTS AND FINANCIAL AID

Tuition in grades 9–12 for the academic year 2010–11 ranged from $27,000 to $28,000. Expenses such as lunch, books, lab fees, uniforms, and optional music lessons were billed separately. A tuition insurance plan is available.

For 2010–11, Baldwin awarded approximately $1.9 million in financial aid to 25 percent of the students, representing 14 percent of the tuition revenue. The number of students awarded financial aid was 128, and the average grant was $15,026. All aid is allocated according to the need analysis procedures of the School and Student Service office in Princeton, New Jersey. Renewal of all financial aid is made annually after the Financial Aid Committee has reviewed the most recent Parents' Financial Statement, tax forms, and student record for each family seeking continued assistance. Baldwin values diversity in its student body and seeks to make its education available to academically talented girls regardless of parental income level. Baldwin is committed to a policy of nondiscrimination and anti-harassment in all aspects of its members' actions and relationships on any basis, including, but not limited to, race, religion, ancestry, color, age, gender, sexual orientation, familial status, disability, veteran status, or national origin.

ADMISSIONS INFORMATION

Each year, Baldwin admits students to grades from PK–12. The School seeks girls with demonstrated academic motivation and achievement who love to learn. Individual talents and diversity of background and interests are also valued. Students are admitted on the basis of a written application, standardized test scores (WPPSI-III for prekindergarten and kindergarten, WISC-IV for grades 1–5, and SSAT or ISEE for grades 6–12), a personal interview and school visit, previous school records, two recommendations, a letter to the Head of the School, and the results of an English Placement Test (grades 6–12). Although Baldwin does not use any cutoff score on standardized tests, the Admissions Committee looks for a pattern of strong achievement in the school records. Motivation is also carefully assessed, as are the student's contributions to the previous school. There is a $50 application fee.

APPLICATION TIMETABLE

Admission inquiries should be made in the fall preceding the September of desired enrollment. Initially, parents should make an appointment to meet with the Director of Admissions and tour the School. After this visit, the application should be filed, testing should be scheduled, and the candidate should plan to come to Baldwin to visit classes. The admission deadline is February 1 for grades 2–12 and January 8 for PK, kindergarten, and grade 1. March 1 is the parents' reply date once a student has been accepted. The Baldwin admissions team strongly encourages applicants to grades 2–12 to complete their applications by early January, prior to the February 1 deadline.

ADMISSIONS CORRESPONDENCE

Sarah J. Goebel
Director of Admissions and Financial Aid
The Baldwin School
701 West Montgomery Avenue
Bryn Mawr, Pennsylvania 19010

Phone: 610-525-2700
Web site: http://www.baldwinschool.org/

BARRIE SCHOOL
Silver Spring, Maryland

Type: Co-educational, independent college-preparatory day school
Grades: PK–12: Primary, age 2–6; Lower Elementary, Grades 1–3; Upper Elementary, Grades 4 and 5; Middle School, Grades 6–8; Upper School, Grades 9–12
Enrollment: School total: Approximately 300
Head of School: Charles H. Abelmann

THE SCHOOL

The student-centered, teacher-guided interdisciplinary education at Barrie School promotes the academic, athletic, artistic, and social growth of each student. Barrie's Montessori Lower, dynamic Middle, and college-focused Upper Schools form a welcoming community that emphasizes hands-on learning experiences and respect for self, others, and the environment. Barrie empowers students to develop confidence, independent thinking, and teamwork essential for world citizenship.

Since its founding in 1932, Barrie has maintained a commitment to multiculturalism and diversity. Faculty and staff members at Barrie School believe that all individuals possess an innate curiosity about the world and that the best education is one that transforms curiosity into passionate intellectual pursuit.

Barrie School values a safe and nurturing environment and a curriculum that challenges students to reach beyond their grasp. The School believes that education is a journey that responds to the needs of students as they develop from concrete, multisensory learners into abstract thinkers with an increased capacity for critical analysis and sophisticated communication. Barrie believes that education should strike a balance between theoretical and practical learning, and it aims to instill in its students a continuing desire to strive for personal excellence in a complex and ever-changing world.

Barrie's 45-acre campus provides space for learning, play, and exploration. Whether taking water samples at the pond, running on the cross-country course, or quietly reading near the fireplace, the campus is a lively place.

ACADEMIC PROGRAMS

The Lower School curriculum, based on the philosophy and methodology of Dr. Maria Montessori, is designed to engage children in thoughtful pursuits and to encourage a lifelong love of learning. Students experience concepts and develop skills at each level of understanding. The School challenges students by establishing high standards for thoughtful work. Each classroom is a structured environment, and teachers provide a consistent approach, which assists in the development of orderly thought. Hands-on materials are sequenced, and activities are organized into curricular areas by degree of difficulty. Within this framework, each child develops at his or her own pace. Respect for self, others, and the environment is a fundamental theme and forms the cornerstone of all relationships. Guided choice and freedom with responsibility, based upon self-discipline and developmental needs, are also important aspects at Barrie.

The Middle School academic program provides opportunities for students to begin to understand themselves as learners, independent thinkers, and resourceful problem-solvers. While academic expectations for middle school students are high, careful attention is given to the intellectual, social, and emotional needs of developing 11 to 14 year olds. Curiosity and confidence, engagement, and energy define the middle school experience.

The Upper School offers a rigorous academic and broad-based learning program that prepares students for college and life in the twenty-first century. In their core, elective, and AP classes, students are taught to interact collaboratively and think critically, and they learn to access and analyze information in a wide range of media and disciplines. Students grapple with the complexities of global citizenship and develop an appreciation for cultural diversity. Extension Days and Extended Study Week are an integral part of the curriculum and carry learning beyond the classroom. Internships and Community Service enable students to design and participate in meaningful life experiences.

Students must take a minimum of 6 credits per year. Most graduates exceed this minimum. Graduation requirements include the following: humanities (8 credits), mathematics (3 credits), science (3 credits), modern language (3 credits), fine or performing arts (2.5 credits), physical education (1 credit: two of three seasons or one semester per year), and health (0.5 credit). Most college-bound seniors are advised to take a fourth year of mathematics.

Student-specific modifications to these requirements for transfer students must be approved by the School. Credits earned by transfer students at other educational institutions may be accepted by Barrie but will not appear on Barrie's transcripts. Summer school courses are not accepted as replacements for Barrie's required courses, nor do they earn credit, unless approved by Barrie School. Approval must be gained prior to the end of the fourth marking period preceding the summer course. Credits earned at summer school do not appear on Barrie's transcripts.

In addition, Barrie students are given extensive opportunities to cultivate an appreciation for the arts. The curriculum offers students a variety of creative pursuits, including visual arts, music, dance, and drama. Small classes and enthusiastic teachers encourage students to explore the creative arts. New talents are revealed, skills and techniques are developed, and gifted artists flourish.

In the Performing Arts program, an integration of music, dance, and story-telling in the Lower School leads to specialized drama and music classes in Middle and Upper School. Classes and performances are held in the School's black box theater and music rooms. In the Visual Arts program, students in the Lower School embark upon a lifelong journey of creating art for self-expression and discovery. The Middle and Upper School art programs refine technique and expand horizons.

FACULTY AND ADVISERS

Faculty and staff members at Barrie School are interesting, highly educated, and talented professionals. They model lifelong learning through the pursuit of both professional development and personal interests. Most faculty members hold advanced degrees; Lower School teachers are certified Montessori-trained educators. Barrie's teachers are also scientists, artists, playwrights, and athletes in their own right.

Barrie values its low student-to-faculty ratio. Teachers guide students' learning experiences, including their academic, social, athletic, and artistic development. The faculty appreciates students as individuals and creates opportunities for each student to succeed.

COLLEGE ADMISSION COUNSELING

Barrie focuses on helping students plan their journey after graduation. Barrie students apply to a wide range of colleges and universities. Beginning in January of the junior year, students research colleges, visit a local university as a group, and identify more specific criteria for choosing a college.

The college counselor meets with parents and students to help determine the best fit for each student to allow them to continue growing as lifelong learners. The School helps students write resumes, personal statements, and essays and guides them through the application process. Education, travel, and work options are all examined in the context of "life beyond Barrie."

In the past four years, Barrie School graduates have matriculated to such schools as Arcadia, Art Institute of Boston at Lesley, Babson, Bard, Boston College, Boston University, Brown, Carnegie Mellon, Catholic University, Denison, DePaul, Dickinson, Franklin & Marshall, Gettysburg, Hampshire, Hofstra, Ithaca, James Madison, Kenyon, Maryland Institute College of Art, McGill, Mount Holyoke, NYU, Ohio Wesleyan, Penn State, Princeton, Rensselaer Polytechnic, Rhode Island School of Design, Sarah Lawrence, Savannah College of Art and Design, SUNY Binghamton, Towson, Virginia Tech, Washington (St. Louis), and the Universities of Arizona, Delaware, Illinois at Chicago, Pennsylvania, Pittsburgh, Richmond, and Vermont.

STUDENT BODY AND CONDUCT

Barrie serves approximately 300 students from age 2 through Grade 12. Barrie is a lively, welcoming place where students fit in and find best friends. Students feel safe to be themselves, engage with others, and try new things.

There are no school uniforms; however the School expects students to adhere to Barrie's dress code guidelines.

ACADEMIC FACILITIES

Classes take place in a variety of buildings—from charming one-story structures that border the wooded campus and outdoor play areas to newer modular spaces in the Middle and Upper School.

In Middle and Upper School, students walk between classroom buildings organized by subject area—languages, humanities, mathematics, and science. The Barrie Center houses one of two gymnasia, the Black Box theater, and locker, fitness, and training rooms. The Commons building offers classroom spaces and open central areas with fireplaces where the School community frequently gathers.

In Lower School, students enjoy classrooms all situated close to their "specialists" spaces—the Strauss Gymnasium and the Language, Art, and Music Rooms.

The Lower School maintains two libraries of approximately 4,500 volumes each supplemented by an ever-growing video collection as well as a number of magazine subscriptions. Databases are also available for student use. One of the libraries serves the students and teachers in the Upper Elementary division and is centrally located in their classroom building for easy access by independent researchers. The other library, a bright and airy facility, serves the students and teachers in the Primary and Lower Elementary divisions and provides a meeting space when needed.

The Middle and Upper School libraries are decentralized and consist of a number of classroom-based satellite libraries stocked with materials that support classroom curricula. In the Middle School, these are located in humanities classrooms and are supplemented by materials for recreational reading. The Upper School houses the bulk of its fiction collection in a specially designated reading room. The Middle and Upper Schools also provide students and teachers with online and print subscriptions for student use.

Arts facilities include a black box theater, art studios, and music rooms.

Wireless technology connects Barrie's campus to the world.

ATHLETICS

Barrie's athletic program and coaches place a strong emphasis on participation, perseverance, and skill development. While competition is an important aspect of sports at Barrie, teamwork and sportsmanship are highly valued. Athletic facilities include two gymnasia, a playing field, a wooded cross-country course, and an equestrian riding and jumping facility.

The Lower School physical education program is designed to inspire and encourage an active lifestyle. Students are exposed to a wide variety of games that help to develop balance, coordination, and endurance.

The Middle and Upper Schools field interscholastic teams in baseball, basketball, cross-country, equestrian, golf, lacrosse, soccer, tennis, track and field, volleyball, and wrestling.

The Upper School Athletic program competes in the Potomac Valley Athletic Conference (PVAC), Capital Area Lacrosse League (CALL), Maryland Independent School Athletic League (MISAL), and the Interschool Horse Show Series (IHSS).

EXTRACURRICULAR OPPORTUNITIES

Because Barrie's students have wide-ranging interests and potentials, the School offers numerous activities outside of the classroom. Connection and meaningful involvement are central to student experiences. Leadership opportunities and service to others help to shape the Barrie student. Whether organizing games on the playground, hosting a student diversity conference, or planning a Poetry Slam, Barrie students initiate activities and take leadership roles. Service to others can manifest itself in helping a friend tie a shoe, volunteering at an animal shelter, or working on environmental sustainability in Panama.

In the Upper School, a Clubs and Committees period is a regularly scheduled part of the school week, and students are required to participate. Students may form a new club with a requisite number of student members, faculty member sponsorship, and division head approval.

DAILY LIFE

The Lower School (Primary – Grade 3) attends from 9 a.m. to 3:15 p.m.; Upper Elementary (Grades 4 and 5) hours are 8:30 a.m. to 3:15 p.m.; and Middle and Upper School (Grades 6–12) students attend from 8:10 a.m. to 3:30 p.m.

SUMMER PROGRAMS

Barrie School's Day Camp program provides an appealing mix of traditional camp activities and present-day favorites. The core program includes on-site swimming, riding ponies, sports, nature, arts and crafts, dance, music, creative dramatics, and canoeing. Campers in Middle Camp and Upper Camp are also offered archery, ceramics, cooperative games, flagpole, karate, and optional overnight campouts. Campers in Upper Camp are scheduled for daylong field trips about once every two weeks.

Additional resources and staff are provided to 4- and 5-year-old campers who have their own homeroom space, or base camp. Rooms are furnished and equipped with age-appropriate activities that can be used during free periods. The rooms also share an outdoor, fenced playground for Lower Camper use only. Each Lower Camp group is supervised not only by a team of counselors, but also a Lower Camp Specialist, a fully trained educator.

Specialty Camp programs combine a half day of activity in a specific interest area and a half day of Regular Camp activity. Specialty activity is normally scheduled for the morning, unless an additional group is formed due to high interest in the program. Campers enjoy all of the Regular Camp programs the other half of the day, but they do not participate in instructional swims. Annual Specialty Camp programs include Karate Kids, The Naturalists, Riding Camp, Summer Sports, Summer Stage, Summer Studio, Digital Video Arts, and the Camper/Counselor-in-Training Program.

COSTS AND FINANCIAL AID

For the 2010–11 academic year, tuition was as follows: Grades 9 through 12, $24,565; Grades 6–8, $22,265; Grades 1–5, $19,265; Full-Day 2/3 and Primary, $17,085; and Half-Day 2/3 and 3-Year-Old Primary, $11,985.

Barrie School offers tuition assistance based on financial need to current and incoming families. The goal of the School's financial aid program is two-fold: to provide deserving students the opportunity for a Barrie education that may otherwise be unobtainable and to foster the School's commitment to maintaining a student body that reflects economic diversity. Barrie School offers tuition assistance to current and incoming families based on financial need, the number of applicants, and availability of funds.

No type of merit aid is awarded as all financial aid awards are based on demonstrated financial need. In order to financially assist as many families as possible, the school grants awards based on a percentage of full need. Each year, the School awards aid to approximately 12–15 percent of the student body. In the 2010–11 academic year, Barrie awarded over $1,000,000.

ADMISSIONS INFORMATION

Prospective families should begin the admissions process by calling the Admission Office at 301-576-2800 and scheduling an Admission Tour. A view book, application materials, and other necessary forms are sent to prospective families upon inquiry.

Barrie School does not discriminate on the basis of race, color, sex, creed, national or ethnic origin, physical disabilities, or sexual orientation; in the administration of its admissions, hiring and educational policies, financial aid programs, athletic and other school administered programs.

APPLICATION TIMETABLE

Applications are accepted during the fall of the year prior to entry. The deadline is January 15 for first-round admission decisions. Admission files must be complete by February 1 for first-round consideration.

ADMISSIONS CORRESPONDENCE

Admissions Office
Barrie School
13500 Layhill Road
Silver Spring, Maryland 20906

Phone: 301-576-2800
Fax: 301-576-2803
Web site: http://www.barrie.org
http://www.barrie.org/admission/request-information/index.aspx

BAYLOR SCHOOL

Chattanooga, Tennessee

Type: Coeducational day (6–12) and boarding (9–12) college-preparatory school
Grades: 6–12: Lower School, 6–8; Upper School, 9–12
Enrollment: School total: 1,053; Upper School: 733
Head of School: Mr. Scott Wilson, Headmaster

THE SCHOOL

Founded in 1893, Baylor School's mission is to foster in students the desire and ability to make a positive difference in the world. The admission office actively seeks students who bring different geographic, economic, social, ethnic, and racial backgrounds to the school community. At Baylor—as in the real world—both girls and boys occupy leadership positions and participate fully in the life of the school. And all students benefit from the global and cultural perspectives that the boarding students bring.

In addition to an excellent academic program, great care has been applied over the years to maintain and preserve the 670 acres of land and the turn-of-the century buildings that overlook the Tennessee River gorge. Classes are spread out among various academic buildings that are all within walking distance. Each element of the campus is beautiful, safe, and functional. Together, they are nothing less than spectacular.

The scenic backdrop for Baylor's campus is the dynamic city of Chattanooga, a midsized city (population of 312,000 in Hamilton County) that has become a model for urban revitalization. Chattanooga residents enjoy abundant recreational and cultural opportunities, and the city is an invaluable educational resource for Baylor students and faculty members.

Baylor is accredited by the Southern Association of Colleges and Schools. It holds membership in the Educational Records Bureau, the Mid-South Association of Independent Schools, the National Association of Independent Schools, the Southern Association of Independent Schools, the Southeastern Association of Boarding Schools, the College Board, and the National Association of College Admission Counselors. The School is eligible for participation in the Morehead Scholarship program, the Jefferson Scholars program, the Boston University Trustee Scholarships program, and the Emory University Awards.

ACADEMIC PROGRAMS

A recent survey of day and boarding alums from the last four decades revealed that the primary reason for attending Baylor was academic quality. Baylor's small classes, innovative curriculum, and individualized attention from teachers and advisers are all designed to help each student thrive in the classroom. At Baylor, students quickly find peers who value academic achievement and are surrounded by faculty members who are committed to helping them reach their full academic potential.

The idea of learning outside of the traditional classroom is deeply entrenched at Baylor (and the envy of many schools). Baylor's outdoor education program (Walkabout) leads students through the Grand Canyon, up the Himalayas, and down Costa Rica's Pacuare River; and art students have the opportunity to live and study in Florence, Italy.

Closer to home, students can work in the school's organic garden or tutor inner city children each afternoon.

Graduation requirements include at least 4 years of English, 3 years of mathematics, 3 years of science, 3 years of social studies, 2 years of one foreign language, and 1 year of fine arts. College counseling is part of the curriculum in grades 9–12. A total of 22 credits are needed to graduate. In addition to these required courses, Baylor offers an extensive selection of electives, including creative writing, digital design, film history and criticism, visual literacy, drawing, painting, curricular theater, forensics, current world topics, Eastern religions, ethics, astronomy, pottery, and vocal and instrumental music.

In addition, students can choose from college-level AP courses in nineteen subjects, including English (language and literature), Latin, French, German, Spanish, American history, European history, U.S. government and politics, calculus (AB and BC levels), biology, chemistry, physics, and studio art. More than 80 percent of Baylor students who take the AP exams qualify for college credit or waivers.

All students have an adviser. Extra-help sessions are also built into the daily schedule, so students can receive immediate attention if they are experiencing difficulty. The Writing Center is open daily and on certain evenings, and the library is open seven days a week and at night. Baylor's English as a Foreign Language (EFL) program plays a vital role in the success of the school's international students. New students attend proctored day study hall with access to the study skills director and peer tutors until the end of the first grading period, at which time their study needs are reevaluated. All boarding students are expected to study nightly, and quiet is maintained in the dorms by student proctors and residential faculty members.

FACULTY AND ADVISERS

More than 70 percent of Baylor faculty members hold advanced degrees from such schools as Boston University, Cornell, Duke, Emory, Harvard, Notre Dame, and Vanderbilt (including many with Ph.D. degrees). Teachers also serve as advisers, regularly interacting closely with students in all aspects of their school life.

COLLEGE ADMISSION COUNSELING

Baylor has a comprehensive college counseling program beginning in the ninth grade. Individual sessions with students and their parents, SAT prep classes, college visits, and contact with college admission officers who visit Baylor on a regular basis are all an integral part of the college counseling process.

In the past four years, Baylor students have been offered more than $40 million in merit scholarships for excellence in academics, fine arts,

leadership, community service, and athletics. Colleges that have accepted Baylor graduates recently include Amherst, Brown, Columbia, Cornell, Dartmouth, Davidson, Duke, Emory, Furman, Georgetown, Harvard, Northwestern, MIT, Princeton, Rhodes, Sewanee, Stanford, Tulane, the U.S. Air Force Academy, the U.S. Military Academy, the U.S. Naval Academy, Vanderbilt, Williams, Yale, and the Universities of Alabama, Georgia, North Carolina, Tennessee, and Virginia.

STUDENT BODY AND CONDUCT

Baylor is one of the few college-preparatory schools in the United States that emphasizes instruction in leadership. The Leadership Baylor Program was launched in 2005 with the goal of reaching out to all students to help them discover and develop their unique leadership skills. Beginning in the ninth grade and continuing through their senior year, students are required to take a quarter-long Leadership Baylor course.

Baylor was one of the first secondary schools to establish an Honor Code, and to this day it remains central to the Baylor experience. At the beginning of each school year, students sign a pledge indicating that they will not lie, cheat, steal, or plagiarize. This community of trust is fostered by students who conduct themselves with integrity and expect the same from their peers. An elected student Honor Council investigates alleged honor offenses and suggests appropriate punishments to the administration.

ACADEMIC FACILITIES

The academic and residential facilities at Baylor comprise a physical plant worth $110 million. An extensive library renovation provides students with a twenty-first century state-of-the-art academic center. Other noteworthy additions to Baylor's academic facilities include a $5-million fine arts complex consisting of three separate buildings for music, studio arts, and performing arts. The $6.5-million Weeks Science building provides state-of-the-art technology and science classrooms, and all Baylor classrooms are equipped with projectors connected to computers. All teachers have course Web sites, and many use the Moodle course management system.

BOARDING AND GENERAL FACILITIES

Eight dormitories house boarding students and resident faculty members. Most dormitory rooms house 2 people, although there are some single rooms. Internet access, laundry facilities, and television lounges are available in all dorms, as are a centrally located refrigerator, microwave oven, and soft drink machine. Student proctors aid the resident adult in keeping order in the dorms. Baylor's newest dorm is LEED certified.

The student center is a popular place, complete with large-screen television, pool tables, comfy couches and a snack bar—a cozy gathering spot complete with Starbucks coffee, smoothies, burgers, and snacks.

At least one nurse is on duty in the health center 24 hours a day, seven days a week. The school also maintains a close relationship with several local doctors, and the nurse in the health center arranges for any necessary medical attention.

ATHLETICS

Sports Illustrated magazine recently named Baylor's athletic program the top program in Tennessee and among the top 25 in the country. Central to its athletic philosophy are the lessons learned through teamwork and good sportsmanship. In addition, the school strives to instill in students the lifelong enjoyment that comes from an active lifestyle.

Baylor fields seventy-four teams in seventeen sports, thirteen of which are sanctioned by the state athletic association. These teams include baseball, basketball, bowling, cross-country, football, golf, lacrosse, soccer, softball, tennis, track and field, volleyball, and wrestling. Teams also compete interscholastically in cheerleading, crew, dance, diving, fencing, and swimming.

Baylor's athletic facilities include two gyms and a field house complex containing basketball courts and a basketball arena, volleyball courts, a cardio room, and wrestling facility. This complex also contains the only indoor 50-meter pool within a 130-mile radius and a new fitness center with state-of-the-art equipment and training for elite athletes.

Baylor's campus provides ample space for a football stadium with artificial turf; a seven-lane track; baseball, softball, lacrosse, and soccer fields; football practice fields; a cross-country course; outdoor and indoor tennis courts; and an outdoor pool. A golf short game practice center features six stations, a chipping green with bunkering, and a putting green. Crew team members also enjoy Baylor's proximity to the Tennessee River, launching their boats directly from a campus dock.

EXTRACURRICULAR OPPORTUNITIES

Basic to Baylor's philosophy of educating the whole person is the belief that students should participate in a variety of activities. To that end, almost sixty clubs and activities are offered each year. Students are active in community service projects, religious fellowship groups, and environmental awareness through school clubs and afternoon activities. Four publications are produced every year by Baylor students and students may also run for student government and dorm leadership positions.

DAILY LIFE

Students are expected to enroll in five academic classes, unless they carry several AP courses or hold an elected office. One period of a student's schedule is devoted to lunch and one to free time for study or intramural recreation. Students are required to participate in either an athletic activity or other activities, such as community service, each afternoon following the academic day. Breakfast is served each morning and dinner is served in the evening, followed by evening study hall and quiet hours.

WEEKEND LIFE

Boarding students are allowed day, overnight, and weekend leaves starting on Friday night and ending Sunday evening. Typically, students go shopping, eat at one of the many nearby restaurants, attend Baylor athletic events, go to the movies, or visit the homes of day school friends. School-sponsored activities are planned each weekend by a full-time staff member and typically include trips to shopping malls, nearby attractions, restaurants, movie theaters, concerts, and sporting events as well as on-campus activities. The Student Center is also a hub of activity during the week and on weekends, providing an inviting place for games, movies, and relaxation.

In addition, Baylor's Walkabout outdoor program schedules at least two trips each weekend, providing an opportunity for students to become proficient at rock climbing, hiking, camping, canoeing, rafting, kayaking, and many other outdoor activities.

Students are encouraged (and transportation is provided each week) to attend worship services at area churches and congregations.

COSTS AND FINANCIAL AID

Baylor's 2010–11 tuition and comprehensive fees are $19,536 for day students and $39,790 for boarding students. The school subscribes to the School and Student Service for Financial Aid, and awards are made on the basis of need. In 2010, Baylor awarded $3.5 million in need-based financial aid. A merit-based scholarship is available on a competitive basis for qualified ninth-grade boarding students.

ADMISSIONS INFORMATION

Baylor seeks boys and girls of high moral character who are willing to compete in a rigorous college-preparatory curriculum. Students are accepted in grades 6 through 11. Transcripts, recommendations, a personal interview and visit, Secondary School Admission Test scores, and an application fee complete the application. Baylor School does not discriminate on the basis of color, race, religion, or national or ethnic origin.

APPLICATION TIMETABLE

Inquiries are welcome at any time, and required campus tours and interviews are available by appointment year-round. Baylor operates under a rolling admission policy, with the review of completed files beginning in January and continuing until all available spaces are filled. The application fee is $75; for international applicants, the fee is $100. Office hours are 8 a.m. to 4 p.m., Monday through Friday. Prospective students are encouraged to visit while school is in session to experience a regular day of classes and activities.

ADMISSIONS CORRESPONDENCE

Bill Murdock
Director of Admissions
Baylor School
171 Baylor School Road
Chattanooga, Tennessee 37405
Phone: 423-267-8505
Fax: 423-757-2525
E-mail: bill_murdock@baylorschool.org
        admission@baylorschool.org
Web site: http://www.baylorschool.org

THE BEEKMAN SCHOOL
AND THE TUTORING SCHOOL

New York, New York

THE
BEEKMAN
SCHOOL

Type: Coeducational day college-preparatory and general academic school
Grades: 9–12, postgraduate year
Enrollment: 80
Head of School: George Higgins, Headmaster

THE SCHOOL

The Beekman School/The Tutoring School of New York was founded by George Matthew in 1925. The School was organized to offer a college-preparatory curriculum with the advantage of highly individualized instruction. Since each student has different abilities, learning issues, or goals, teaching is geared to the needs of the individual student. Thus, classes are limited to a maximum of 10 students in The Beekman School and a maximum of 3 students in The Tutoring School.

In addition to having small classes, The Beekman School combines a traditional academic education with a flexible yet structured approach. For instance, some students are eager to complete high school in less than four years for reasons that range from having been retained in a grade earlier in their education to feeling a natural desire to move ahead to college. If there appears (to all concerned) to be a readiness to accomplish this, the School proceeds with a program that will achieve this goal. This is done by adding one or two extra classes to the student's schedule and/or through attendance in the summer session.

In order for students to move effectively at their own pace, the School provides them with the proper level of classes in as many subjects as seems appropriate. Some students require more support to facilitate their learning in the state-mandated academic curriculum. Teachers have several periods free each day to meet with students, and there are supervised study halls each period throughout the day until 5 p.m. In addition, all homework assignments are posted on the School's Web site daily. Upon request, tutors are available through The Tutoring School.

The Tutoring School is a program within The Beekman School. This program specializes in educating students who require private or semiprivate classes. The Tutoring School teaches college-level courses as well as standard courses. Its mission is to provide a supportive environment in which students can realize their academic potential and achieve their educational goals. Generally, incoming students follow The Beekman School's college-preparatory curriculum and receive credit from The Beekman School. However, if necessary, The Tutoring School can follow any school's course syllabus, and course credit is granted by that school upon successful completion of all course work. After-school or home tutoring is available for midterm and final-exam preparation, SAT preparation, or academic support in any subject. In addition, The Tutoring School can arrange at-home schooling, if necessary.

The Beekman School is registered by the Board of Regents of the State of New York and is a member of the College Entrance Examination Board and the Educational Records Bureau.

ACADEMIC PROGRAMS

The requirements of the Board of Regents of the State of New York form the core of the college-preparatory curriculum at The Beekman School and The Tutoring School. It is strongly advised, however, that students exceed these requirements, especially in the areas of mathematics, the sciences, and humanities. In addition to the requirements, The Beekman School faculty has developed many interesting and challenging elective courses from which students may choose. Some of these are psychology, bioethics, ecology, computer animation, creative writing, modern politics, filmmaking, darkroom photography, Eastern and Western philosophy, poetry, and art. Students also participate in after-school activities, such as the literary magazine, yearbook projects, and the School's volunteer program. Students can elect to study music, music theory, voice, various musical instruments, or composition at the Turtle Bay Music School, which is a 2-block walk from The Beekman School. If 6 or more students wish to form a particular course, the administration will offer the course at The Beekman School. If 1 to 3 students wish to take a particular course, it will be offered through The Tutoring School. Otherwise, students are encouraged to take specialized elective courses at various institutions throughout the city.

If students take an elective course off campus, they must complete 48 course hours to earn a semester credit and 96 course hours to earn a full-year credit. For the college-bound student, the suggested academic high school program consists of the following courses: 4 years of English, 4 years of history (including a senior-year program that consists of a semester of U.S. government and a semester of economics), 3 years of mathematics (through algebra II/trigonometry), 3 years of science (including 1 year of a lab science), 3 years of a foreign language, 1 year of art or music, several elective courses, and 1 semester of health education and computer science.

The grading system of the School is A to D (passing) and F (failing). Sixty percent is the minimum passing grade. Midway through each quarter, an interim progress report is mailed home to any student who is earning below 70 percent in any course. Weekly updates by phone can be arranged so that parents always know the academic status of their child.

Because of the independent nature and small size of the School community, the scheduling of classes and the number of classes in which a student enrolls are flexible. Students can begin their day with the first, second, or third period. For the same reasons of independence and adaptability, the School also tries to accommodate any reasonable requests of the students for additional courses. Similarly, tutoring for study and organizational skills and remediation courses in English and math are offered through The Tutoring School.

FACULTY AND ADVISERS

There are 14 full-time members of The Beekman School faculty.

The current Headmaster, George Higgins, has been at the School since 1980, first as a teacher, then as Assistant Headmaster, before serving the School as Headmaster.

All faculty members have graduate degrees or are enrolled in a graduate degree program. In addition to teaching, faculty members also act as advisers to small groups of students. Faculty advisers review progress reports with students and hold meetings periodically to listen to student concerns and discuss upcoming events. Parent conferences are held as frequently as they are needed or requested. Twice during the school year, parents are invited to the School to attend open-house evenings, at which time they can discuss their child's progress with the teachers. When necessary, the Headmaster or classroom teacher calls parents to keep them informed of their child's homework and general behavior.

The School's offices are open to the students almost all day, every day. Students feel welcome to visit the Headmaster to talk, complain, laugh, or ask questions.

COLLEGE ADMISSION COUNSELING

Each year, approximately 95 percent of the graduating class attends college. The aim of the School's college guidance program is to find the right college for each graduating senior. Major considerations include how competitive an environment the student wants, what area of study the student is leaning toward, what size of school would be conducive to success, and where the student would like to live (i.e., city, suburb, East Coast, West Coast). In the past five years, graduates of the School have been accepted at the following colleges and universities: Bard, Boston University, Columbia, Harvard, Ithaca, NYU, Sarah Lawrence, School of Visual Arts, Smith, SUNY at Purchase, and the University of Colorado, to name a few. The Beekman School's staff and faculty members make every effort to examine not just where a student will likely be admitted but where that student will learn, grow, and feel successful for the next four years.

The senior class numbers approximately 25 students. Each student is carefully guided through the college application process, as are his or her parents. A Parents' College Evening, hosted by the School's college guidance counselor, is held each fall for the parents of seniors. It is always an informative evening for parents; the guest speaker is an administrator from the admissions office of a nearby university, who is also there to answer questions. The college guidance counselor schedules several individual appointments with all seniors in order to help them navigate the college application process.

STUDENT BODY AND CONDUCT

Each year, The Beekman School begins the fall term with approximately 70 students. Its rolling admissions policy means that the School adds members to the student body until it reaches its maximum enrollment of 80 students. The enrollment is generally evenly divided between boys and girls. All students are from the immediate tristate area of Connecticut, New Jersey, and New York and its suburbs. The success of The Beekman School's philosophy is proven by the distance students gladly travel in order to be in a school where the enrollment and class size are small, the faculty is supportive and caring, and the education is challenging yet can be paced according to the student's abilities and needs.

There is a School code of behavior that has been shaped by the students and teachers of the School. The main tenet of the code is based on the Golden Rule—"Do unto others as you would have others do unto you." The small, intimate environment makes any type of behavior problem untenable; if the code of the School is violated, there is always an appropriate response. There have been no serious discipline or behavior issues at the School; Beekman students respect their school and its philosophy and recognize the need for tolerance, compassion, and respect in this global community.

ACADEMIC FACILITIES

The School is located in an East Side Manhattan town house. There are eight classrooms; a small library; a state-of-the-art laboratory for biology, chemistry, and physics; a darkroom; a computer lab updated with the latest technology; a study hall equipped with computers; a beautifully landscaped garden; and a student lounge where students can eat lunch and socialize. Rapid Internet access is available throughout the School. Each administrator and teacher has an e-mail address, so parents and students can easily communicate with staff members.

ATHLETICS

The Beekman School meets the New York State requirements for physical education by providing a gym program at a nearby athletic facility. Students may participate in the School's program or design their own program; for example, they may wish to attend their neighborhood gym while being supervised by a private trainer, or they may decide to take dance lessons, karate lessons, or other lessons. Students must exercise for 2 hours each week. In the School's program, an instructor is provided, and students begin the year with aerobics and weight training. Activities in the gym program vary throughout the year and include swimming, volleyball, basketball, cardiovascular exercise, and track. If a student is seriously involved in an intramural activity outside the School, such as soccer or tennis, he or she may be excused from the School's sports program.

EXTRACURRICULAR OPPORTUNITIES

The School's Manhattan location gives it the opportunity to use New York City and its immediate environs as an extension of the classroom. Groups from the School attend plays, films, operas, and dance performances and visit various museums, exhibitions, historical sites, and other points of interest in and around Manhattan and as far away as Philadelphia.

Any student who wants to work on the yearbook or school literary magazine is welcome to do so, and about one third of the student body participates in

one way or another. Additional after-school activities include the drama club, photography club, and film club. Upperclassmen can also take part in a community volunteer program if the desire and maturity are present.

DAILY LIFE

Students' schedules reflect their individual needs. The school day begins at 8:45 a.m. and continues until 3:50 p.m. When possible, students who have a long commuting distance are scheduled to begin classes at 9:30 or 10:15. Students with professional programs outside of school can have classes arranged for mornings or afternoons. Supervised study halls are provided throughout the day from 8:45 a.m. to 5 p.m. Lunch periods are scheduled throughout the day on a staggered basis.

SUMMER PROGRAMS

The Beekman School is in session almost year-round. In June, when the academic year is over, the School begins a three-week mini-session of intensive work for students who want or need private tutoring in a specific subject area, who need to make up work in a course for which they received an incomplete, or who exceeded the School's attendance policy (sixteen absences are allowed in a year course, and eight are allowed in a semester course).

Following the mini-session, The Beekman School operates a six-week summer session, which is attended by the School's students and by students from boarding and other private day schools who wish to accelerate in any major academic course, enrich their knowledge of a particular subject, or repeat a course. Each summer class is 2 hours long; there are four classes each day, and the program lasts for twenty-four days. The Beekman School's summer session is approved by the New York State Education Department.

COSTS AND FINANCIAL AID

The annual tuition is $30,000, which is divided into four payments. In addition, an activity fee and an administrative fee ($250 each) are charged. All twelfth-grade students pay a senior fee of $500.

The tuition for the mini-session depends upon the individual's length of study. The tuition for the six-week summer session is $2000 per 2-hour course.

If a student wishes to take a course in The Tutoring School (average student-teacher ratio is 2:1), tuition is $8000 for each yearlong course and

$4300 for each semester course. Activity and administration fees are included. Currently, there is no financial aid.

ADMISSIONS INFORMATION

It is a reflection of the School's philosophy that it does not use admissions tests as a means to determine a prospective student's eligibility to attend the School. The Headmaster or Director meets with each prospective student and his or her parents in an intensive interview so that all may better understand each other. Together, they try to assess whether the School would be a good match for the student. Previous school transcripts and records of testing are reviewed but are not solely used to determine a course of study. Prospective students are also welcome to observe for a half or full day so they can gain a clearer understanding of the style of the School. Informal evaluations in math and English may be administered to determine the best course placement for various students.

APPLICATION TIMETABLE

Since there are several different types of secondary schools offering many different programs, it is advisable that interviews take place during the early spring of the year prior to entry. Selecting a school in which to study and socialize is an important process, and students and their families should take the time to look closely at several schools before coming to a final decision. Occasionally, students choose a school that is not a good fit for them. Because Beekman has a rolling admissions policy, even if the traditional day program is filled, students can begin their day in the afternoon and take classes into the late afternoon or early evening. These courses are usually semiprivate and cost more than the regular Beekman tuition. The School believes that a successful secondary education is of vital importance to all young adults; its goal is to make the School available to any student who wishes to actively participate in his or her education.

ADMISSIONS CORRESPONDENCE

George Higgins, Headmaster
The Beekman School
220 East 50th Street
New York, New York 10022

Phone: 212-755-6666
Fax: 212-888-6085
E-mail: georgeh@beekmanschool.org
Web site: http://www.beekmanschool.org

BERKELEY PREPARATORY SCHOOL

Tampa, Florida

Type: Coeducational independent college-preparatory day school
Grades: PK–12: Lower Division, Prekindergarten–5; Middle Division, 6–8; Upper Division, 9–12
Enrollment: School total: approximately 1,200; Lower Division: 400; Middle Division: 300; Upper Division: 500
Head of School: Joseph A. Merluzzi, Headmaster

THE SCHOOL

The Latin words *Disciplina, Diligentia,* and *Integritas* in Berkeley's motto describe the School's mission to nurture students' intellectual, emotional, spiritual, and physical development so they can achieve their highest human potential. Episcopal in heritage, Berkeley was founded in 1960 and opened for grades 7–12 the following year. Kindergarten through grade 6 were added in 1967, and prekindergarten began in 1988. Berkeley's purpose is to enable its students to achieve academic excellence in preparation for higher education and to instill in students a strong sense of morality, ethics, and social responsibility.

Berkeley is located on an 80-acre campus in the suburban Town 'N Country area of Tampa, a location that attracts students from Hillsborough, Pinellas, Pasco, Polk, Citrus, and Hernando Counties and throughout the greater Tampa Bay area. Private bus transportation is available.

Berkeley is incorporated as a nonprofit institution and is governed by a 31-member Board of Trustees that includes alumni, parents of current students, and parents of alumni. The presidents of the Alumni Association and Parents' Club are also members of the board.

ACADEMIC PROGRAMS

The school year runs from the end of August to the first week of June and includes Thanksgiving, Christmas, and spring vacations. The curriculum naturally varies within each division.

In the Lower Division, the program seeks to provide appropriate, challenging learning experiences in a safe environment that reflects the academic, social, moral, and ethical values the School espouses in its philosophy. Curricular emphasis is on core subjects of reading and mathematics. An interdisciplinary approach is used in world language and social studies, and manipulatives are used extensively in the science and mathematics programs. Each student also receives instruction in library skills and computers.

Academic requirements in the Middle Division, where classes average 16 to 20 students, are English, English expressions, mathematics, history, foreign language, science, computers, physical education, art, drama, and music. All students in grades 6 and 7 take Latin and a choice of French, Spanish, or Chinese. Continuing grade 8 students have the option of Latin, French, Spanish, or Chinese. Every class meets five days a week and has one weekly

scheduled makeup period. Extra help is available from teachers, and grades are sent to parents four times a year.

The Upper Division program, with average classes of 15 to 18 students meeting five days a week, requires students to take four or five credit courses a year, in addition to fine arts and physical education requirements. To graduate, a student must complete 22 credits, including 4 in English and 3 each in mathematics, history, science, and foreign language. Students must also complete one year of personal fitness/health and an additional year of physical education, two years of fine arts, and two electives. In addition, Berkeley students are required to take a semester of religious studies each year and complete 76 hours of community service. More than twenty Advanced Placement courses are offered.

FACULTY AND ADVISERS

There are more than 175 full-time faculty members and administrators. They hold baccalaureate, more than seventy-five graduate, and several doctoral degrees. Headmaster Joseph A. Merluzzi, who joined Berkeley in 1987, received his bachelor's degree from Western Connecticut State University and his master's degree in mathematics from Fairfield University. He came to Berkeley from the Cranbrook Kingswood School in Michigan.

In addition to teaching responsibilities, faculty members are involved in Berkeley's cocurricular programs as coaches and student activity advisers. In the Upper Division, 3 teach part-time and serve as academic grade advisers for students in ninth and tenth grades, and 3 full-time college counselors assist students in grades 11 and 12 with academic advising and the college process. Berkeley faculty members receive support for professional development opportunities, and a number have been recipients of National Endowment for the Humanities grants.

COLLEGE ADMISSION COUNSELING

Traditionally, Berkeley's entire graduating class goes on to attend college. Although Berkeley does not rank its students, more than 125 colleges visit the School each year to recruit its graduates. The mean SAT scores for the class of 2010 were 612 critical reading, 622 writing, and 631 math. Berkeley's college counseling department works to assist students and their families in selecting colleges that best suit their academic, financial, and social needs.

Recent graduates are attending Boston College, Brown, Cornell, Dartmouth, Duke, Emory, Georgetown, Harvard, Northwestern, Notre Dame, NYU, Princeton, Stanford, Vanderbilt, Villanova, Yale, and the Universities of Florida, Miami, Michigan, North Carolina, Pennsylvania, and Virginia. Scholarship offers totaling more than $6 million were made to the class of 2010, and 12 percent of the graduates committed to pursuing athletic competition at the collegiate level.

STUDENT BODY AND CONDUCT

In all divisions, Berkeley students are expected to maintain high standards. Mature conduct and use of manners are expected, and an honor code outlines students' responsibilities. In exchange, students are entrusted with certain privileges, such as direct access to the administration and the opportunity to initiate School-sponsored clubs. Students wear uniforms to class.

ACADEMIC FACILITIES

The 80-acre campus is located in the Town 'N Country suburb of Tampa. It consists of classrooms, a fine arts wing, a science wing, two libraries, technology labs, general convocation rooms, physical education fields, a 19,000-square-foot student center, a prekindergarten wing, and administrative offices for the Lower, Middle, and Upper Divisions.

The arts program was enhanced in 1997 with the addition of a 634-seat performing arts center that also includes a gallery for visual arts displays, a flex studio for both dance recitals and small drama productions, dressing rooms, and an orchestra pit.

ATHLETICS

Varsity sports for boys include baseball, basketball, crew, cross-country, diving, football, golf, lacrosse, soccer, swimming, tennis, track, weight lifting, and wrestling. Girls compete in basketball, crew, cross-country, diving, golf, soccer, softball, swimming, tennis, track, volleyball, and weight lifting. The campus has several playing fields. Upper Division teams are members of the Bay Conference, while Middle and Lower Division teams compete in the Florida West Coast League and the Youth Sports League.

Athletes use two gymnasiums, a wrestling/gymnastics room, a weight-lifting room, a rock-climbing wall, a stadium (for track meets and football and soccer games), baseball and softball diamonds, tennis courts, a ropes course, and a junior Olympic swimming pool.

Seasonal sports award banquets and a homecoming football game are scheduled annually.

EXTRACURRICULAR OPPORTUNITIES

In addition to its broad-based commitment to student organizations and clubs and its community service requirements, Berkeley offers its students a vast array of outside-the-classroom possibilities. Berkeley's Pipe and Drum Corps continues to make a significant impact in the community by performing at several special events, including the Boston St. Patrick's Day Parade and Walt Disney World. Student artwork is accepted each year into the prestigious Scarfone Gallery Art Show, and several students receive gold key awards each year from the Alliance for Young Artists and Writers. An after-school Lower Division Chess Club attracts close to 50 students from kindergarten through fifth grade. Middle and Upper Division students, as well as many faculty members, participate in several international experiences, with trips to Australia, China, Costa Rica, France, Italy, Paris, Belize, Switzerland, and Spain.

DAILY LIFE

Students in prekindergarten through grade 5 attend classes from 8 a.m. to 3:10 p.m. Middle and Upper Division students also begin at 8 and end at 3:20. Teachers are available to assist students and offer extra help during activity periods, which are scheduled into each class day. Supervised study halls are also scheduled for some students.

SUMMER PROGRAMS

A six-week summer academic program for prekindergarten through grade 12 students is offered. Tuition ranges from $900 to $2100.

COSTS AND FINANCIAL AID

The tuition schedule for 2010–11 is as follows: $15,840 for prekindergarten–grade 5, $17,650 for grades 6–8, and $18,940 for grades 9–12. Tuition is payable in eight installments and must be paid in full by January 1. Tuition payments do not cover costs of uniforms, supplies, transportation, special event admission fees, or other expenses incurred in the ordinary course of student activities at Berkeley.

Berkeley makes all admission decisions without regard to financial status. Financial aid in the form of partial-tuition scholarships is available for families who demonstrate need. The School and Student Service for Financial Aid (SSS) guidelines are used in determining need. Berkeley may not be able to accommodate all financial aid applicants in a given year, but once a student is awarded aid, the aid continues until graduation as long as the student remains in good standing and demonstrates need. An SSS form, available from the admissions office, must be submitted annually, and Berkeley's financial aid committee determines all awards by mid-March.

Berkeley also has twenty-one named scholarships, eleven full scholarships, and ten partial scholarships that are available to students.

ADMISSIONS INFORMATION

In considering applicants, Berkeley evaluates a student's talent, academic skills, personal interests, motivation to learn, and desire to attend. Special consideration is given to qualified applicants who are children of faculty members or alumni or who have siblings currently attending Berkeley.

Lower Division candidates visit age-appropriate classrooms and are evaluated for placement by Berkeley teachers. Middle and Upper Division candidates are required to take the Secondary School Admissions Test (SSAT) and should register for a November, December, or January test date. Entering juniors and seniors may submit PSAT, SAT, PLAN, or ACT scores in place of sitting for the SSAT.

The admission process is selective and is based on information gathered from the application form, interviews, the candidate's record, admission tests, and teacher recommendations.

Berkeley admits students of any race, color, sex, religion, and national or ethnic origin and does not discriminate on the basis of any category protected by law in the administration of its educational policies, admission policies, and scholarship, financial aid, athletic, and other School-administered programs.

APPLICATION TIMETABLE

Applications should be submitted by the fall one year prior to the student's entrance into Berkeley. Applications are considered in the order received and decisions are made in early March. Parents are notified of their child's status as soon as possible thereafter. All applications after the initial selection process are considered on a space-available basis.

Berkeley welcomes inquiries from families throughout the year. However, because of the competitive nature of the admission process, families are encouraged to visit the campus as early as possible to become familiar with the School, its programs, and its admission procedure.

ADMISSIONS CORRESPONDENCE

Janie McIlvaine
Director of Admissions
Berkeley Preparatory School
4811 Kelly Road
Tampa, Florida 33615

Phone: 813-885-1673
Fax: 813-886-6933
E-mail: mcilvjan@berkeleyprep.org
Web site: http://www.berkeleyprep.org/
admissions

BERKSHIRE SCHOOL

Sheffield, Massachusetts

Type: Coeducational boarding and day college-preparatory school
Grades: 9–12 (Forms III–VI), postgraduate year
Enrollment: 394
Head of School: Michael J. Maher

THE SCHOOL

Berkshire School is a coed college preparatory boarding school offering rigorous academics. Pioneering programs—such as Math/Science Research, Sustainability and Resource Management, Chinese language, and Aviation Science (including flight training and FAA Ground School certification)—are available along with advanced sections and AP offerings in all disciplines. With a range of artistic and athletic offerings, a state-of-the-art academic building, brand new facilities for music and dance, and national recognition for its efforts in environmental conservation, Berkshire is an extraordinary setting in which students are encouraged to learn, in the words of the school motto, "Not just for school, but for life."

In 1907, Mr. and Mrs. Seaver B. Buck, graduates of Harvard and Smith respectively, rented the building of Glenny Farm at the foot of Mt. Everett and founded Berkshire School. For thirty-five years, the Bucks devoted themselves to educating young men to the values of academic excellence, physical vigor, and high personal standards. In 1969, this commitment to excellence was extended to include girls.

Situated at the base of Mt. Everett, the second-highest mountain in Massachusetts, Berkshire's campus spans 500 acres. It is a 75-minute drive to both Albany International Airport and Hartford's Bradley International Airport, and just over 2 hours from Boston and New York City.

Berkshire School is incorporated as a not-for-profit institution, governed by a 28-member self-perpetuating Board of Trustees. The School has an $85-million endowment. Annual operating expenses exceed $25 million. Annual Giving in 2009–10 exceeded $2.77 million. The Berkshire Chapter of the Cum Laude Society was established in 1942.

Berkshire School is accredited by the New England Association of Schools and Colleges and holds memberships in the Independent School Association of Massachusetts, the National Association of Independent Schools, the College Entrance Examination Board, the National Association for College Admission Counseling, the Secondary School Admission Test Board, and the Association of Boarding Schools.

ACADEMIC PROGRAMS

Berkshire's academic program is firmly rooted in a college-preparatory curriculum that features advanced and AP courses across all disciplines. In addition, unique opportunities to excel in math/science research, student-directed independent study, and electives in science, history, and fine arts allow students to pursue advanced study at Berkshire. As creative and agile problem solvers, strong critical thinkers, persuasive communicators, and active global citizens, Berkshire's students are equipped with the skills required to excel in the twenty-first century. The School's balance between academic rigor and possibility allows students to flourish as independent learners, community members, and professionals.

Believing that the best preparation for college is the acquisition of knowledge from a variety of disciplines, Berkshire requires the following credits:

4 years of English; 3 years each of mathematics, a foreign language, and history; 2 years of science; and 1 year of the visual or performing arts. All departments provide for accelerated sections, and students are placed at a level commensurate with their skills and talent. Many students take one or more of the sixteen Advanced Placement courses offered.

Most students carry five courses. The average number of students in a class is 12, and the student-teacher ratio is 7:1. The academic year is divided into two semesters, each culminating with an assessment period. Students receive grades, teacher comments, and adviser letters twice each semester. Berkshire uses a traditional letter-grading system of A–F (D is passing).

In 2007, Berkshire introduced its advanced math/science research course in which students use the strong foundation of knowledge acquired in the regular Berkshire curriculum as a springboard for beyond-the-curriculum projects in areas of cutting-edge research and other fields. Students intern with a professional scientist to conduct research in facilities located in the nearby Hartford, Connecticut and Albany, New York areas. Students work closely with their mentor in the field of their choice for 4 to 8 hours a week. The course culminates with a critical review paper and a research paper, both in scientific format.

FACULTY AND ADVISERS

The Berkshire teaching faculty numbers 58, 47 of whom live on campus. Thirty-one teachers hold a master's degree and 4 hold doctorates. Faculty members contribute to both the academic and personal development of each student. The small size of the Berkshire community permits faculty members to become involved in students' lives outside, as well as inside, the classroom. Each student is paired with a faculty adviser who provides guidance, monitors academic progress, and serves as a liaison with the student's family. Berkshire also retains the services of 4 pediatricians, a nurse practitioner, 4 registered nurses, and 2 certified athletic trainers.

Michael J. Maher was named Berkshire's fifteenth head of school in the spring of 2004. He holds a bachelor's degree in political science from the University of Vermont and a master's degree in liberal studies from Wesleyan University. Mr. Maher is in his seventh year at Berkshire; previously he held positions as administrator, teacher, and hockey coach. He and his wife, Jean, an associate director of admission and a member of the Foreign Language Department, have 3 children, 2 of whom attend Berkshire.

COLLEGE ADMISSION COUNSELING

College counseling at Berkshire is the responsibility of 3 full-time and 2 part-time professionals who assist students and their parents in the search for an appropriate college or university. The formal process begins in the Fifth Form, with individual conferences with the college counselors, and the opportunity to meet with some of the approximately 100 college admissions representatives who visit the campus. In February, Fifth Formers and their parents attend a two-day seminar on the college admission process.

Admission strategies are discussed and specific institutions are identified for each student's consideration. During the summer, students are encouraged to visit colleges and write the first draft of their college application essay. The application process is generally completed by winter vacation in the Sixth Form year.

Members of the classes of 2008, 2009, and 2010 enrolled at a variety of four-year colleges or universities, including Bard, Bates, Berkeley, Boston College, Boston University, Bowdoin, Brown, Carnegie Mellon, Colby, Colgate, Cornell, Dartmouth, Denison, Dickinson, Emory, Johns Hopkins, Kenyon, Lehigh, Middlebury, MIT, NYU, Northeastern, Northwestern, SMU, St. Lawrence, Syracuse, Union, Villanova, Williams, and the Universities of Connecticut, Maine, Massachusetts, Michigan, New Hampshire, Wisconsin, and Vermont

STUDENT BODY AND CONDUCT

In the 2010–11 academic year, there were 352 boarders and 42 day students; with 3 students studying abroad in the first semester. The student body is drawn from twenty-five states and twenty-four countries.

Students contribute directly to the life of the school community through involvement in the Student Government, the Prefect Program, dormitory life, and various clubs and activities. Participation gives students a positive growth experience supporting the School motto of learning "not just for school, but for life." The rules at Berkshire are simple and straightforward and are consistent with the values and ideals of the School. They are designed to help students live orderly lives within an environment of mutual trust and respect.

ACADEMIC FACILITIES

Berkshire Hall, the primary academic facility built in 1930 and the centerpiece of the campus, reopened in the fall of 2008 after a full renovation. It now features larger classrooms with state-of-the-art technology, new administrative offices, a two-story atrium, and a Great Room for student study and special functions. A new music center opened in the fall of 2010, featuring two specially designed classrooms to meet the needs of the instrumental, choral, and chamber music programs. The center has five practice rooms, plenty of spacious storage cabinets for instruments, a recording studio, and storage and office space for the music program. A new dance studio also opened in the fall of 2010 as part of the existing gymnasium. Godman House is home to several darkrooms and a digital art and electronic music studio, and deWindt Dormitory houses a visual arts studio. In 2009, the School opened its Center for Writing and Critical Thinking, which is home to a nightly writing tutoring program. The center also hosts faculty forums and 4 visiting writers each year.

The Geier Library contains approximately 43,000 volumes in open stacks, an extensive reference collection in both print and electronic format, numerous periodicals, and a fine audiovisual collection. The library has wireless Internet access, as well as twenty computers with Internet access and an online card catalog for student use. ProQuest

Direct, the Expanded Academic Index ASAP, the *New York Times* full text (1994 to present), and the current ninety days' full text of 150 Northeastern newspapers, including the *Wall Street Journal* online, keep the library fully up-to-date on breaking information.

At the Dixon Observatory, computer synchronized telescopes make it possible to view and photograph objects in the solar system and beyond. Given the combination of equipment, software, and location, Berkshire's observatory is among the best in New England.

BOARDING AND GENERAL FACILITIES
Berkshire has ten residential houses, including two girls' dormitories that were completed in the fall of 2002. Three faculty families, many with small children, generally reside in each house along with a prefect—Sixth Formers whose primary responsibility is to assist dorm parents with daily routines, such as study hall and room inspection. Dorm rooms all have Internet access and private phone lines. There is a common room in each house, where students may relax or study. Benson Commons, the school center, features a dining hall capable of seating the entire School, a post office, the School bookstore, the Student Life office, the Center for Writing and Critical Thinking, and recreational spaces.

ATHLETICS
Berkshire enjoys a proud tradition of athletic excellence. The School provides competition in twenty-seven interscholastic sports, including baseball, basketball, crew, cross-country running, field hockey, football, golf, ice hockey, lacrosse, mountain biking, skiing, soccer, softball, squash, tennis, track and field, and volleyball. Students may also participate in the Ritt Kellogg Mountain Program, a program that utilizes Berkshire's natural environment and its proximity to the Appalachian Trail to present athletic challenges, teach leadership, and foster environmental responsibility.

In January 2009 the 117,000-square-foot Jackman L. Stewart Athletic Center opened. The facility offers two ice rinks (one Olympic-size), fourteen locker rooms, seating for 800 spectators, a 34-machine fitness center and athletic training rooms. It can also be used for indoor tennis and can accommodate all-school functions. A second athletic center features full-size courts for basketball and volleyball, four international squash courts, a climbing wall, and a dance studio. Other facilities include the new Thomas H. Young Field for baseball, new softball fields, an all-weather track, a lighted football field, and two synthetic-turf fields. A new twelve-court tennis facility was completed in the fall of 2010.

EXTRACURRICULAR OPPORTUNITIES
Berkshire offers students a variety of opportunities to express their talents and passions. Students publish a newspaper, a yearbook, and a literary magazine that features student writing, art, and photography. The Ritt Kellogg Mountain Program offers backcountry skills, boatbuilding, fly fishing, hiking, kayaking, rock climbing, and winter mountaineering.

There are a number of active clubs, including the Drama Club, the International Club, the Investment Club, the Maple Syrup Program, the Philanthropy Society, and a Student Activities Committee.

Berkshire's student-run FM radio station, WBSL, operates with a power of 250 watts and is capable of reaching 10,000 listeners. Berkshire is one of the few secondary schools to hold membership in the Intercollegiate Broadcasting System and the only one affiliated with both the Associated Press wire service and its radio service.

Berkshire students pursue the arts in the classroom and in extracurricular activities. The theater program offers two plays in the fall and spring as well as a winter musical. There are three choral groups: Ursa Major, an all-school chorus; Ursa Minor, a girls' a cappella group; and Greensleeves, an all male chorus. There are two music groups: a jazz band and a chamber music ensemble. Students can also take private voice and instrumental lessons. Each season the Berkshire community looks forward to various performances, such as dance and music recitals, a jazz café, and poetry readings. Visual arts include painting, drawing, sculpture, digital art, photography, and ceramics. Students display their work in galleries in the Student Center and in Berkshire Hall.

DAILY LIFE
The first of the six class periods in a school day begins at 8 a.m., and the final class concludes at 2:45 p.m., except on Wednesday and Saturday, when the last class ends by 11:35 a.m. Berkshire follows a rotating schedule in which classes meet at different times each day.

Athletics, outdoor experiences, and art activities occupy the afternoon. Clubs often meet after dinner, before the 2-hour supervised study period that begins at 8 p.m.

WEEKEND LIFE
Weekend activities are planned by a Director of Student Activities and include first-run movies, dances with live bands, and other dances hosted by DJs. There are trips to local amusement parks and theaters as well as shopping trips to Hartford and Albany. In addition, students and faculty members journey to New York and Boston to visit museums, attend theater and music productions, or take in professional sports events.

COSTS AND FINANCIAL AID
For the 2010–11 academic year, tuition is $42,900 for boarding students and $35,900 for day students. For most students, $100 a month is sufficient personal spending money. Ten percent of the tuition is paid upon enrollment, 50 percent is payable on July 1, and 40 percent is payable on November 30. Various tuition payment plans are available.

Financial aid is awarded on the basis of need to about 30 percent of the student body. The total financial aid spent in 2010–11 was $3.9 million. The School and Student Service (SSS) Parents Financial Statement and a 1040 form are required.

ADMISSIONS INFORMATION
Berkshire adheres to the principle that in diversity there is strength and, therefore, actively seeks students from a broad range of geographic, ethnic, religious, and socioeconomic backgrounds. Admission is most frequent in the Third and Fourth Forms, and the School enrolls a small number of postgraduates each year.

In order to assess the student's academic record, potential, character, and contributions to his or her school, Berkshire requires a personal interview, a transcript, test scores, and recommendations from English and mathematics teachers, along with the actual application. Candidates should have their Secondary School Admission Test (SSAT) scores forwarded to Berkshire School (school code 1612).

APPLICATION TIMETABLE
Interested families are encouraged to visit the campus in the fall or winter preceding the September in which admission is desired. Visits are arranged according to the academic schedule, Monday through Friday, from 8 a.m. to 2 p.m. and Saturday from 8 to 10:45 a.m. January 15 is the deadline for submitting applications; late applications are accepted as long as space is anticipated. Berkshire adheres to the standard notification date of March 10 and the families' reply date of April 10. Depending on availability, late applications are processed on a rolling basis. Applications for admission are available online at the School's Web site: http://www.berkshireschool.org.

ADMISSIONS CORRESPONDENCE
Andrew Bogardus, Director of Admission
Berkshire School
245 North Undermountain Road
Sheffield, Massachusetts 01257

Phone: 413-229-1003
Fax: 413-229-1016
E-mail: admission@berkshireschool.org
Web site: http://www.berkshireschool.org

BESANT HILL SCHOOL

Ojai, California

Type: Coeducational boarding and day college-preparatory school with a focus on divergent thinking, creativity, and environmental sustainability
Grades: 9–12
Enrollment: 105
Head of School: Mr. Paul Amadio

THE SCHOOL

Founded in 1946 by Aldous Huxley, J. Krishnamurti, Guido Ferrando, and Rosalind Rajagopal on 520 acres in the resort town of Ojai, California, this residential school community offers a vigorous college-preparatory curriculum with a cornerstone of creative expression, sustainability, and divergent thinking. Besant Hill offers thirty-three art electives, competitive athletics, travel and experiential education programs, small classes, and a 4:1 student-teacher ratio.

The School was envisioned as an educational community that would provide an atmosphere where students could develop and discover both their intellectual and creative potential and where they would learn "how to think not what to think™." This philosophy is still the core of the School today.

In addition to its fine arts and athletic programs, Besant Hill School has an academic program that integrates best practice teaching techniques and universal design. This cutting-edge program prepares students for a lifetime of learning as well as a foundation for their professional career. The School has recently added SmartBoards in 100 percent of its classrooms, making the Socratic method of teaching it uses even more accessible to many styles of learners.

Besant Hill School holds membership in the California Association of Independent Schools, the National Association of Independent Schools, and Western Boarding Schools Association. The School is accredited by the Western Association of Schools and Colleges.

ACADEMIC PROGRAMS

The Academic Dean is responsible for the academic life of the School. The curriculum is absolutely and without exception college preparatory. Courses of study follow the University of California (UC) system and can also be determined by the individual student's future plans and interests. The average load is five academic solids, an elective, and an art.

Class size averages 10 students. Independent study is available for especially well-motivated students, and Advanced Placement courses are offered in calculus, English, government, physics, and Spanish.

Besant Hill has two academic semesters, and evaluations are sent to parents four times a year. An evening study hall is required.

Graduation requirements are as follows: English, 4 years; Science, 3 years (including 1 year of biology and 1 year of chemistry); Foreign language, 2 years of the same language; Math, 3 years (through algebra II); Social Science, 3 years (including world cultures and American (U.S.) history); Arts, 2 years (visual, theater, music) with at least 1 year of the same art; Fitness, 4 years; and Electives, at least 3 (one must be senior capstone).

English as a second language (ESL) is also offered. This program works to improve the development of English and oral and listening comprehension skills. Concentration on vocabulary expansion, improved pronunciation, and use of idioms aid the students in understanding and participating in class. The full-year course, which requires an additional fee, is two or three periods a day and can include ESL classes in science, social studies, U.S. history, and TOEFL preparation.

FACULTY AND ADVISERS

There are 35 teachers and administrators on the Besant Hill staff. Twenty-one faculty members and administrators reside on campus, and all faculty and staff members are involved in the life of the community beyond the classroom. Of the 25 full-time teachers, half have advanced degrees, 2 of whom hold their doctorates.

COLLEGE ADMISSION COUNSELING

All students take a college-preparatory curriculum and begin their testing program with the Preliminary SAT (PSAT) in the fall of the sophomore year. They take the PSAT again as juniors, in preparation for the SAT, which they take later that same year and then again as seniors. The SAT Subject Tests are administered to those juniors and seniors for whom it is appropriate.

The School receives annual visits from college representatives. The Director of College Counseling is on campus and begins working with students in their sophomore year. In 2010, colleges or universities accepted all of the graduates. Recent graduates are attending colleges such as Bard, Beloit, Berklee School of Music, Bowdoin, Cal Arts, Chicago Institute of the Arts, Columbia, Mills, NYU, University of Washington, and various campuses of the California State University and University of California systems.

STUDENT BODY AND CONDUCT

Of the 105 students attending Besant Hill School this year, one fifth are day students and four fifths are residential. Besant Hill School seeks to instill in students a lifelong love of learning. This goal is reflected in the School motto "Aun Aprendo" ("I am still learning"). The community sets reasonable limits for its members. Elected students participate in a Disciplinary Advisory Committee, along with faculty members and administrators. The School disciplinary system works on a basis of minors and majors. Students may have occasional work crew hours or more serious disciplinary action, depending on the offense.

ACADEMIC FACILITIES

There are twelve buildings on campus. Networked computer stations are available in several buildings. Most of the campus has wireless access. The School houses a science lab, photography lab, new art studio, theater, recording studio, ceramics studio, and digital media lab. The renowned Zalk Theater houses both the drama and music departments. The School has also recently added four soundproof music practice rooms.

BOARDING AND GENERAL FACILITIES

The Besant Hill School campus offers boarding facilities for both boys and girls. The residents are housed 2 to a room in bedrooms that contain study and storage facilities for each student. Dorm parents live in each wing of the dormitories and supervise the boarding students with the help of student prefects. Other facilities include a modern dining hall, tennis courts, volleyball courts, a baseball field, basketball courts, and a soccer field.

ATHLETICS

Team experience and personal challenges through athletics are a valuable part of any education and are made available to every student. The School competes interscholastically in baseball, basketball, cross-country, soccer, and volleyball. Boys varsity basketball is the School's most competitive athletic program, and the team has won back-to-back Southern California Section titles.

EXTRACURRICULAR OPPORTUNITIES

The School's proximity to both the coast and the mountains provides students with a wide range of recreational activities, from surfing to rock climbing. Students can also take advantage of museums, movies, concerts, plays, skating, shopping, and bowling.

DAILY LIFE

Boarding students are responsible for cleaning their rooms and performing assigned crew jobs. Breakfast is served from 7 to 8 a.m. Academic classes are until 2:45 p.m. In the afternoon, fitness and athletics classes are offered. Dinner is at 6 p.m., followed by evening study hall.

WEEKEND LIFE

Weekends give students a chance to relax, catch up on their studies, or partake in planned activities by the Residential Life Director. Weekend trips to Los Angeles, Santa Barbara, and Ventura are frequent.

Students who have parental permission may leave the campus on open weekends, provided they are in good standing with the School.

COSTS AND FINANCIAL AID

The cost of tuition, room, and board for the 2010–11 academic year was $41,990. Day student tuition was $21,990. A book and activity fee of $2600 is required to cover the costs of books, trips, and other expenses. The ESL fee for first-year students is $7000. Participation in the School's instructional support program is $7200.

Approximately 20 percent of the School's income is given annually in scholarship and financial aid. Information on aid availability can be obtained from the Admissions Office.

ADMISSIONS INFORMATION

Students are selected on the basis of character and academic promise. Personal interviews and references are used to identify those students who are most likely to benefit from the Besant Hill School experience. Consequently, a visit to the School is strongly urged for each applicant. Acceptance is based upon records, recommendations, and a personal interview.

APPLICATION TIMETABLE

Candidates should schedule an interview with a member of the Besant Hill School admissions team, schedule a class visit, go on a tour of the School, and begin working on the Besant Hill School application for admission by fall 2011. Students should also begin requesting recommendations, transcripts, and school reports from their current school. The financial aid deadline is January 15, and the application deadline is February 22. Admissions decisions should be mailed by March 10, and new student contracts are due by April 10. Applications received after February 22 are reviewed and acted upon on a space-available basis as soon as the candidate's file is complete. After April 10, remaining spaces will be filled through a rolling admissions policy.

ADMISSIONS CORRESPONDENCE

Randy Bertin
Besant Hill School
P.O. Box 850
Ojai, California 93024
Phone: 805-646-4343 Ext. 422
        800-900-0487 (toll-free)
Fax: 805-646-4371
E-mail: rbertin@besanthillschool.org
Web site: http://www.besanthillschool.org

BLAIR ACADEMY
Blairstown, New Jersey

Type: Coeducational boarding and day college-preparatory school
Grades: 9–12, postgraduate year
Enrollment: 455
Head of School: T. Chandler Hardwick III

THE SCHOOL

In its 163rd year, Blair Academy continues to offer a superior college-preparatory program while holding firmly to its tradition of being a community fully focused on the development of each individual student. In this environment, students learn to advocate for themselves, become service-minded, and develop the leadership skills necessary for success in college and beyond. Students balance their academic responsibilities with extensive opportunities to develop in drama, music, competitive athletics, and numerous extracurricular activities. The balance between high academic and personal expectations, and a willingness to provide individual focus are among Blair's greatest strengths.

Situated on 423 hilltop acres adjacent to the village of Blairstown in one of New Jersey's most scenic counties, Blair is just 10 minutes from the Appalachian Trail and the Delaware Water Gap, only 60 miles from New York City, and 2 hours from Philadelphia.

Blair maintains an enrollment of 450 students on average, large enough to support a broad program of studies, activities, and athletics, yet small enough so that everyone can receive individualized instruction and ample attention. The average class size is 11 students, and the dual advisory system also makes for close relationships between students and faculty members.

A Board of Trustees directs the school, and alumni are well represented on the Board. The school's endowment is estimated at approximately $56 million. Blair received $4.4 million in capital gifts for 2009–10 and the Blair Fund raised $2.47 million.

Blair Academy is accredited by the Middle States Association of Colleges and Schools. Its memberships include the Cum Laude Society, New Jersey Association of Independent Schools, National Association of Independent Schools, The Association of Boarding Schools, Council for Advancement and Support of Education, and Secondary School Admission Test Board.

ACADEMIC PROGRAMS

With twenty-one Advanced Placement (AP) courses and a wide range of electives such as Roman history, Mandarin Chinese, marine biology, ethical philosophy, architecture, and video production, Blair students enhance their potential and awaken new interests with the guidance of committed teachers. The talented and diverse faculty brings enthusiasm, passion, and global perspective to lessons. Caring and committed to each individual student, the faculty members serve as housemasters, advisers, coaches, and friends while laying the necessary foundation for academic success at Blair and beyond.

Blair has a notable fine and performing arts program that is integral to its well-rounded curriculum. From introductory-level to advanced, art courses encourage students to think and express themselves creatively through various mediums, including canvas, dance, music, theater, film, graphic design, and ceramics. In the spring of 2009, the Blair wind symphony and string ensemble joined to form the first-ever Blair Academy Orchestra, a momentous occasion for the music program. With vocal and instrumental performance tours across Eastern Europe, musicians and vocalists at Blair are able to explore international travel while performing at some of Europe's most historic concert venues.

History teacher Quint Clarke, affectionately known as Q, has taken students to such faraway places as Vietnam, Beijing, and many locations in Africa. A trip to Kenya he conducted several years ago as a community service effort was so successful and meaningful that it has now become Q's annual summer destination. Other faculty members have also taken students on trips abroad, most recently to Spain, Tunisia, France, and China. Spring break offers an opportunity to travel to countries like Russia, France, and Greece, while Long Winter Weekend allows marine science students to expand upon their classroom studies in the Cayman Islands.

FACULTY AND ADVISERS

For the 2010–11 academic year, Blair employs 79 full-time faculty members and administrators, more than half of whom hold graduate degrees. Ninety-two percent of faculty members and administrators live on campus, many as houseparents in the dormitories. They also serve as coaches, academic monitors, and advisers. Faculty members have high expectations for their students and seek to provide individual focus in addition to the rigorous and challenging academic program. This allows each student to cultivate positive relationships with many adults in the Blair community. Through a dual advisory system, faculty advisers and academic monitors guide Blair students' personal growth. Blair is further set apart by allowing each student to choose his or her own adviser, which helps the student develop a strong sense of independence, responsibility, and confidence in engaging the world around them.

T. Chandler Hardwick III was appointed the Academy's fifteenth Headmaster in 1989. A graduate of the University of North Carolina (B.A., 1975) and Middlebury College (M.A., 1983), Mr. Hardwick previously taught English and was Senior Dean at the Taft School, as well as the Director of the Taft Summer School.

COLLEGE ADMISSION COUNSELING

College counselors begin working with students and their families during the winter term of their junior year. Each student is required to have at least five private meetings with a college counselor to map out their college search and application process. Counselors communicate regularly with parents to keep them informed and involved. Parents of juniors are invited to spend a day on campus for an informational introduction to the Blair College Counseling Office and process; in 2010 the guest speaker was Diane McKoy, Senior Associate Director of Admission at Columbia University in New York. In addition, Blair hosts on-campus visits from representatives of at least seventy colleges and universities each year. One-hundred percent of students from the class of 2010 went on to attend competitive universities and colleges.

Blair works with each individual student to craft an academic program that emphasizes areas of strength while fulfilling the expectations of competitive college admissions. Students from recent graduating classes are attending colleges and universities such as Brown, Columbia, Cornell, Davidson, Georgetown, Harvard, Middlebury, NYU, Princeton, Stanford, U.S. Military Academy, U.S. Naval Academy, Williams, Yale, and the Universities of Pennsylvania and Virginia.

STUDENT BODY AND CONDUCT

Blair attempts to maintain a geographically, ethnically, and socioeconomically diverse student body. For 2010–11, Blair welcomes students from twenty-two states and twenty-one countries, including Zimbabwe, Hong Kong, Spain, South Africa, and Thailand. The composition of the 2010–11 student body is as follows: senior class and postgraduate year, 80 boys, 59 girls; junior class, 67 boys, 57 girls; sophomore class, 68 boys, 50 girls; and freshman class, 41 boys, 33 girls. Of the total enrollment of 455, there are 116 day and 339 boarding students.

ACADEMIC FACILITIES

At the center of the campus are the four major classroom buildings: Clinton Hall, Bogle Hall, Timken Library, and Armstrong-Hipkins Center for the Arts. Bogle Hall, dedicated in 1989, provides laboratories and classrooms for the math and science departments and includes a state-of-the-art computer laboratory and a 150-seat auditorium. Armstrong-Hipkins Center for the Arts was dedicated in 1997 and includes DuBois auditorium, which seats 500 people. The renovated Timken Library, which includes classrooms and a computer center, opened in 1998 and houses over 20,000 volumes. The library also subscribes to several excellent databases. These are recognized academic sites with information that has been collected and reviewed specifically for student use.

BOARDING AND GENERAL FACILITIES

The newest additions to the Blair campus were completed in 2009. Several additions were made to the exterior sports facilities including a new turf field, ten new tennis courts, an improved all-weather track, stadium seating to accompany the turf field, and a tennis house. A new interior athletic space houses seven squash courts, a weight-lifting center, a fitness center, three basketball courts, a six-lane swimming pool, wrestling rooms, and ample locker space for students and coaches. The bookstore, canteen, and college counseling suite moved to the activities portion of the new building. Both the athletic facility and student activities center have quickly become an integral part of campus life and complement Blair's existing facilities.

There is an ongoing initiative to improve the physical campus as part of Blair's Ever Always campaign. Summer 2010 saw changes to central campus, where only pedestrian traffic is allowed now as part of a plan to develop a parklike setting for recreation and study through improvements to the campus infrastructure and landscaping.

Ten dormitories house boarding students. The housemaster and other dorm faculty members play a unique role in residential life. They help create a community and ensure that students adapt to dorm life and school. They make sure the dorm offers an atmosphere conducive to study but also provides a social liveliness that builds dorm spirit. In addition to having a housemaster and dorm parents, each underclass dormitory unit has in-residence senior prefects, who are selected by the faculty for their leadership ability and commitment to Blair. Prefects devote their senior year to living with the younger students in order to help them make a smooth transition to Blair, all the while balancing their own college applications, varsity athletics, and demanding course schedules of honors and AP courses.

ATHLETICS

Blair's philosophy is that physical education is beneficial and important; hence all students participate in a program of athletics or supervised recreational sports. Blair fields twenty-eight competitive varsity teams in baseball, basketball, crew, cross-country, field hockey, football, golf, ice hockey, lacrosse, skiing, soccer, softball, squash, swimming, tennis, wrestling, and winter and spring track. Because participation is key to Blair's sports program, most teams field varsity and thirds-level competitive units.

EXTRACURRICULAR OPPORTUNITIES

Blair students are also offered numerous learning opportunities outside of the classroom, ranging from weekly lectures as part of the Society of Skeptics, to travel abroad with faculty and peers. The Society of Skeptics, the longest continuously running high school lecture series in the country (now in its thirty-third year), was an outgrowth of the Blair International Society, begun in 1962, and has served as a forum for the discussion and debate of important national and international issues. For more than three decades, under the tutelage of Dr. Martin Miller, the weekly lecture series has featured a wide variety of speakers who are engaging, accomplished in their respective fields, and often controversial.

The Nevett Bartow Series brings to campus some twenty programs each year. The mission of the Bartow Series is to expand the artistic experiences of Blair students by bringing professional performers from far and wide to the Blair stage, including such offerings as Rockapella, Solid Brass, Loudon Wainwright III, the Cincinnati Boychoir, the David Grisman Quintet, Tom Chapin, Judy Collins, Arlo Guthrie, and visiting lecturers. Trips are arranged to the theater, concerts, opera, ballet, and museums in New York City.

Among popular campus organizations are the Blair Academy Singers, the Blair Academy Players, the String Orchestra, the Wind Symphony and Jazz Ensemble, the Community Service and Environmental Clubs, Model United Nations, and the Investment Club. The outdoor-skills group takes full advantage of Blair's proximity to the Delaware Water Gap and the Appalachian Trail, while the Ski Club utilizes the Pocono Mountains for daily skiing excursions. Students write for the school newspaper, *The Blair Breeze,* compose the yearbook, and publish a literary magazine each year. Service-oriented organizations, such as the Blue and White Key, encourage students to become engaged and active citizens within the Blair community.

DAILY LIFE

Classes are 55 minutes long and meet four times during a six-day week. Four days per week, classes end at 3 p.m. Wednesday and Saturday are shortened days, with afternoons dedicated to athletic competitions and extended theater practices.

Afternoons are devoted to athletics practices and games, play rehearsals, recreational sports, or activities. Family-style dinner, a formal dining room meal, is held two to three days per week for boarding students. Each dormitory, including senior dorms, has monitored evening study hours from 8 to 10 p.m. Students who have earned study privileges (known as honor nights) can be in their rooms, the library, the canteen computer labs; or receive tutoring from an individual faculty member during these hours. Most importantly, faculty members do not disappear into their apartments at the end of the school day but instead are present around campus as mentors, friends, and houseparents.

WEEKEND LIFE

Weekends might be a little less structured than weekdays, but that doesn't mean students are any less active. The campus bustles with activity on the weekends. Every Saturday evening, there is a community-focused event, such as dances, game night, athletic competitions, open-mic night, and student theater productions. In addition, the Residential Life Office sponsors numerous local off-campus trips (movies, mall trips, hikes) as well as other low-key entertainment events (B.I.G. events, volleyball tournaments, scavenger hunts) throughout the weekends. Highlights include International Weekend, the midwinter formal, Super Sunday, and Peddie Week. Closed weekends during examinations and the first two weeks of September require all boarding students to remain on campus. Otherwise, students are allowed to take weekends away from campus according to a scale based on their grade in school.

COSTS AND FINANCIAL AID

Tuition for 2010–11 is $45,700 for boarders and $32,500 for day students. Additional deposits or fees are charged for the use of certain equipment, private music lessons, and extra medical services.

Financial aid is awarded on the basis of demonstrated financial need and proven personal and academic merit in accordance with procedures established by the School and Student Service for Financial Aid. Approximately $4 million in aid was distributed to 32 percent of the student body for the 2010–11 academic year.

ADMISSIONS INFORMATION

Blair is interested in students who seek the satisfaction of personal achievement through an experience that is both broad and challenging. Blair students are determined to make the most of their secondary school years and to prepare for college and beyond by being active participants in an engaging environment. Academic preparation is only part of being ready for college; Blair also emphasizes social responsibility, involvement, and leadership. Students take on such roles as team captains, dormitory prefects, or members of class council, which play an important part in shaping the Blair experience for those around them. They share in school planning and decision-making, and serve with faculty members on committees involving residential life, discipline, academic honor, multiculturalism, health, and student activities. Each student leader has an opportunity to influence the direction of Blair and impact the experiences of his or her classmates—skills that he or she will carry beyond Blair.

Blair enrolls students in grades 9–11 each year and also admits a limited number of high school graduates who wish to pursue a postgraduate year of study.

In addition to a personal interview, several written components complete the formal application. To complement the school transcript and teachers' recommendations, Blair requests results from a standardized test: the SSAT or ISEE for grades 9–10; and the PSAT, SAT, or ACT for eleventh-grade entry and postgraduates. Application forms must be accompanied by a nonrefundable fee of $50 ($125 for international applicants). The application deadline is February 1.

APPLICATION TIMETABLE

The initial inquiry is welcome at any time. The Admission Office is open for interviews and tours by appointment on weekdays and Saturdays. Applicants who complete the admissions process prior to February 1 are notified of the decision on March 10.

ADMISSIONS CORRESPONDENCE

Ryan M. Pagotto, Dean of Admissions
Blair Academy
P.O. Box 600
Blairstown, New Jersey 07825-0600

Phone: 908-362-2024
  800-462-5247 (toll-free)
Fax: 908-362-7975
E-mail: admissions@blair.edu
Web site: http://www.blair.edu

BRENTWOOD COLLEGE SCHOOL

Mill Bay, British Columbia, Canada

Type: Coeducational boarding and day university-preparatory school
Grades: 9–12
Enrolment: 441
Head of School: Andrea M. Pennells

THE SCHOOL

Founded in 1923, Brentwood College School is a coeducational university-preparatory boarding school (grades 9–12) with a limited number of day students. Brentwood's 47-acre oceanfront campus is located close to the village of Mill Bay, 30 miles north of Victoria and 10 miles south of Duncan. Superb modern facilities for academics, athletics, and the arts, with comfortable accommodation in a pristine Vancouver Island setting, provide a remarkable boarding school environment; the proximity of Victoria provides access to numerous cultural and recreational opportunities.

While academics take priority, the Brentwood curriculum is uniquely scheduled to facilitate full student participation in diverse athletic and arts programmes. At Brentwood, there is no narrow view of education, and the School's philosophical goals are grounded in current research. Opportunities also abound for social time with friends, special events, and leadership through service. Every student has the chance to shine, each in his or her own way, and Brentwood celebrates the confidence with which graduates pursue their varied paths. For a more comprehensive overview, students should visit Brentwood's Web site (http://www.brentwood.bc.ca).

Registered as a nonprofit association under the British Columbia Societies Act, Brentwood is guided by a Board of Governors (18 members), many of whom are alumni. The full board meets three times annually, while the Executive, Finance, and Building committees meet more frequently.

Brentwood College School is a member of the Canadian Association of Independent Schools, the Independent Schools Association of British Columbia, the Western Boarding School Association, the Association of Boarding Schools, the Boarding School Review, and the Secondary School Admission Test Board.

ACADEMIC PROGRAMS

Brentwood encourages all students to achieve their personal best in the classroom in pursuit of academic excellence. Teachers' expectations are high. SMARTBoard technology supports traditional teaching to promote critical thinking; both have a place and purpose. Strong teacher-student relationships are forged through favourable class sizes and access to teachers for extra help. The average class size is 16.

The academic year, which begins in early September and ends in late June, is divided into three terms, with major vacations at Christmas (three weeks) and Spring Break (two weeks).

Each student meets regularly with a designated faculty member, who acts as an advisor for academic guidance and counselling. Academic progress is discussed with students monthly, and academic reports, showing both percentage grades and comments, are sent to parents at the end of each term.

The Brentwood curriculum includes 18 Advanced Placement courses at the first-year university level in art history, biology, chemistry, comparative government and politics, computer science, environmental science, human geography, physics, economics, English language and literature, French, Spanish, psychology, calculus, music theory, and studio arts; this allows greater flexibility and individual choice for senior students. With a strong focus on English, mathematics, science, history, and modern languages, Brentwood has also developed unique programmes in entrepreneurship, marketing, environmental science, and global studies.

The development of skills in the arts is an important aspect of a Brentwood education. Courses offered include drawing and painting, pottery, sculpture, photography and film, drafting and design, concert choir, vocal jazz, pops orchestra, jazz band, rock band, drama, dance, musical theatre, public speaking, and debating. Every student must enrol in at least two of these courses, and some pursue as many as four. Their decisions may vary from year to year as they develop a general background of experience. Specialization is possible, particularly for students seriously interested in careers in the arts, leading to the development of the portfolios necessary to support applications to postsecondary institutions.

FACULTY AND ADVISERS

Andrea M. Pennells, Head of School, holds a Master of Arts degree from the University of Edinburgh and a Master of Education degree from the University of British Columbia. Prior to her appointment as Head, she served at Brentwood for eighteen years in successive roles as a teacher of English and English literature, Houseparent, Head of the English Department, Director of Arts, and Assistant Head of School.

The full-time faculty consists of 41 teachers (24 men and 17 women), 23 of whom live on campus. They hold forty-seven baccalaureate degrees and twelve master's degrees, representing study at major universities in Canada, the United States, England, Ireland, Scotland, New Zealand, Australia, and France. Twenty-three part-time instructors teach visual and performing arts, and additional part-time instructors assist in coaching major sports.

COLLEGE ADMISSION COUNSELING

It is expected that all students wish to pursue postsecondary studies. University counsellors provide comprehensive advice on all major schools in North America and Europe while supervising all aspects of the application process, including registration for SATs and application for university scholarships. Brentwood's track record in postsecondary planning speaks for itself: graduates receive admission offers from the finest institutions across the globe, many with entrance scholarships. For

the complete list of the universities Brentwood graduates are attending, students can visit the School's Web site at http://www.brentwood.bc.ca.

STUDENT BODY AND CONDUCT

Brentwood is home away from home for 187 boarding boys, 181 boarding girls, and 73 day students. Although more than thirty-two countries are typically represented on campus, most Brentonians hail from Canada and the American Pacific Northwest. A significant number are expatriate Canadians whose parents work overseas. Brentwood students are expected to demonstrate the characteristics that are fundamental to an orderly, wholesome school community: self-discipline, humour, mutual respect, humility, and consideration for others.

ACADEMIC FACILITIES

All School facilities are located on a 47-acre oceanfront campus. The Academic Centre is a modern three-story facility with SMARTBoard-equipped classrooms, an expanded library, administrative and counselling offices, an art gallery, and exhibition spaces. The classrooms are designed to form distinct teaching areas and include six fully appointed science laboratories, two computer instruction centres, an audiovisual language laboratory, and separate studios for pottery, sculpture, photography, painting, and drawing. A raked lecture theatre, which is equipped for mixed-media presentations, also serves as a recital room and recording facility. A 28,000-square-foot performing arts centre with a 431-seat theatre, dance studio, media arts room, lighting and audio control room, music facilities, centre for business, and other supporting amenities is the focal point of Brentwood's performance programmes.

BOARDING AND GENERAL FACILITIES

Campus residential facilities include four Houses for boys and four for girls, all designed to accommodate 2 students per room. Each House has a recreation room, a snack kitchen, a lounge, and computer facilities. While there are washing machines in each residence, full services are provided in a central laundry facility. All residences have faculty advisors serving as houseparents, counsellors, and tutors. All meals are served in the new Crooks Dining Hall, an oceanfront dining room and student services centre. Crooks is a warm, welcoming, West Coast-style facility which is student friendly and built to LEED Gold standards. For students, it is a one-stop social experience and campus heart, where they eat; relax; socialize; buy school supplies; drop-off and pick-up laundry, uniforms, and sports clothing; have meetings, dances, coffee houses, and special events; and meet parents and faculty in a supervised setting. They can also learn important business skills in the Center for Business and Entrepreneurship located on the lower level.

Brentwood's Health Centre contains three examination rooms and a six-bed dormitory and isolation room in each of the boys' and girls' wings. The School doctor is regularly on call, full-time nursing service is provided, and a physiotherapist is on site on sports afternoons. Access is available to laboratory facilities in Mill Bay and hospitals in Duncan and Victoria. By arrangement, regular and specialized dental needs can be accommodated.

ATHLETICS

Brentonians value physical fitness, teamwork, and sportsmanship—and they love to compete. Through team and individual sports and outdoor pursuits, Brentwood students develop commitment, endurance, resilience, confidence, and teamwork. Brentwood is proud to offer twenty-one sports options, including, but not limited to: rowing (crew), rugby, basketball, field hockey, volleyball, tennis, ice hockey, soccer, squash, cross-country, golf, sailing, kayaking, and hiking. Most of these options are available at different skill levels, from introductory to advanced. In grades 9 and 10, students are encouraged to develop a wide range of skills. Senior students may elect to specialize as training and competition become more intense.

For its size, Brentwood has produced a remarkable number of international athletes, including 23 Olympians, among them gold medalist Malcolm Howard and silver medalists Scott Frandson and Dave Calder. Athletic facilities include a world-class boathouse (crew), an indoor rowing tank, seven sports fields, eight tennis courts, an outdoor basketball court, and a modern sportsplex with a gymnasium, weight rooms, and squash courts. These facilities are augmented by a sheltered oceanfront and the spectacular natural environment of Vancouver Island, British Columbia.

EXTRACURRICULAR OPPORTUNITIES

Through leadership roles, members of the grade 12 class are responsible for many aspects of daily School life. Seniors are expected to mentor younger members of the School and support the faculty in administering the daily routine. In addition, a Student Activities Council, representative of each grade level, consults and works with faculty sponsors to plan social events and special outings and to promote student involvement in community and global charities.

Parents are encouraged to visit the School at any time. Traditionally, they are loyal supporters at sports events and attend concerts and performances (Brentwood features seventeen nights of public performances), the Annual Brentwood Rowing Regatta, the Graduation Dinner and Dance, and the Closing Day Ceremonies.

DAILY LIFE

Academic classes are held between 8:15 a.m. and 1:15 p.m.; sports and arts programmes are offered on alternate afternoons in hour-long periods. Students are expected to make a minimum 2-hour commitment to their sports and arts.

A quiet, supervised study session, or "prep," is held in the residences from 7:30 to 9:30 p.m. This study time, while adequate for junior students, may need to be increased by senior students to meet their academic demands.

There is also a full School assembly at least once a week.

WEEKEND LIFE

On-campus activities include dances, concerts, showcase games, theme-based Open Houses hosted by the various residences, and other special weekend activities. Students find endless ways to relax and have fun on campus. Weekend ski trips to Mt. Washington are scheduled each Sunday during the ski season. In addition, students participate in School-sponsored excursions to Victoria for music, theatre, and other cultural events and occasionally for a meal, a movie, and some shopping.

In each of the three terms, a midterm break of five days provides most students with an opportunity to return home to visit family. In addition, Sunday leave and weekend leave may be obtained by request from the Houseparent.

COSTS AND FINANCIAL AID

The Board of Governors meets every spring to determine the upcoming year's school fees. For the 2010–11 academic year, fees are as follows. For Canadian students entering all grades, tuition and boarding fees are Can$36,000. For American students entering all grades, the fees are Can$40,000; for residents of other countries, the fees are Can$46,500, payable at the time acceptance is confirmed. Canadian-based parents may elect to pay the annual fee in full before the beginning of the first term or in three installments in advance of each term. Day student tuition is Can$18,800. There is a 5 percent reduction on aggregate annual fees for siblings during their joint enrolment. Tuition insurance is required, the premium for which is waived should the entire annual fee be paid in advance. Parents are responsible for transportation costs between the student's home and the School. Arrangements for such travel, including transportation to and from the airport, are provided by the School's travel office.

Scholarship awards, based on academic standing and performance on Brentwood's scholarship examinations, are only available to new Canadian grade 9 and 10 boarding students. Financial assistance grants are needs based and are available to all new Canadian students.

ADMISSIONS INFORMATION

Students capable of succeeding in a university-preparatory programme are best suited to the School's course of studies. Admission, however, is based not only on an applicant's academic potential, but also on his or her character and willingness to participate actively in the athletics and arts programmes. In addition to taking the required entrance examination and having an admissions interview, candidates must submit previous school records and an academic and personal recommendation. Brentwood can make arrangements for the entrance test to be taken at the student's present school should distance make a campus visit impractical. The School also accepts SSAT results instead of the Brentwood entrance test. Students should visit http://www.ssat.org for online test registration and information. Students must request that SSAT test scores be sent directly to Brentwood College School by the test board, so they should designate Brentwood (#1816) as a score recipient when they register.

APPLICATION TIMETABLE

It is recommended that prospective students apply one year prior to admission. At the time of application, a $2500 registration fee and deposit are required, $1500 of which is applied to the first year's fees if the application is successful. The registration fee and deposit are refunded in full should Brentwood be unable to offer the student a place or should the applicant's family decline the offer of a place at the School.

ADMISSIONS CORRESPONDENCE

Mr. Clayton Johnston, Director of Admissions
Brentwood College School
2735 Mount Baker Road
Mill Bay, British Columbia V0R 2P1
Canada
Phone: 250-743-5521
Fax: 250-743-2911
E-mail: admissions@brentwood.bc.ca
Web site: http://www.brentwood.bc.ca

BUXTON SCHOOL

Williamstown, Massachusetts

Type: Coeducational college-preparatory boarding and day school
Grades: 9–12
Enrollment: 90
Head of School: C. William Bennett and Peter Smith, Co-Directors

THE SCHOOL

In 1928, Ellen Geer Sangster founded Buxton School as a coeducational day school in Short Hills, New Jersey. In 1947, she moved the high school to her family estate in Williamstown, Massachusetts, and formed it anew as a boarding school.

From the beginning, Buxton has been a progressive school, one devoted to innovation and change. Today, that devotion remains steadfast. At Buxton, students' pursuits help them develop the clear vision they need to comprehend the world they live in and to define their future lives. Each student's bridge to the larger world is the informed, skilled, confident self that he or she develops while at Buxton.

Buxton places great importance on the composition and character of its student body. Foremost, a young person must want to be at Buxton. In addition, Buxton seeks to enroll students who have the intelligence, motivation, creativity, and intellectual curiosity to succeed there. Prior to coming to Buxton, students have experienced positive relationships with adults as well as peers. Buxton students take a responsible and ambitious role in shaping their own lives and wish to make significant and mature social contributions. They are conscious of the importance of being useful and contributory, of serving as an asset to others, and of aiding in others' efforts to enrich the life of the group. One of the first tasks Buxton students encounter is that of developing and maintaining a sound, compassionate, stimulating environment for oneself and for the entire group.

Buxton promotes personal growth and cultivates students' abilities to understand and manage their lives. Presenting a way of life that students can come to understand and manage is of primary importance. The student body is diverse; life at the School is flexible, noninstitutional, and open to change. Opportunities often arise for collective deliberation of life's most pressing challenges. A Buxton education reflects the fundamental premise that a mature individual must be morally and actively committed, each in his or her own way, to the creation and betterment of a healthy society.

The 150-acre campus of Buxton overlooks historic Williamstown, which is located approximately 170 miles north of New York City and 150 miles west of Boston. Williams College, the Clark Art Institute, and the Massachusetts Museum of Contemporary Art (MASS MoCA) are nearby and are all exceptional resources for Buxton students.

Buxton is a nonprofit, nonsectarian institution governed by a 24-member self-perpetuating Board of Trustees. The board includes the Co-Directors, Associate Director, faculty members, alumni, parents of students and alumni, and friends of the School.

The physical plant at Buxton is valued at $6 million. The operating budget is $4 million annually. The current endowment is $1.7 million, and the Annual Fund for 2009–10 raised $220,133.

Buxton is accredited by the New England Association of Schools and Colleges and is approved by the Massachusetts Department of Education. It is a member of the Secondary School Admission Test Board, The Association of Boarding Schools, the Association of Independent Schools of New England, the National Association of Independent Schools, and the Small Boarding School Association as well as other professional organizations.

ACADEMIC PROGRAMS

Academic courses, activities, and community life are all essential parts of a Buxton education. Each offers the opportunity for unique and vital growth; therefore, each is of educational significance.

Buxton's academic curriculum is broad and demanding, offering an unusual combination of traditional subjects, courses in the arts, and electives in subjects that are usually only encountered at the college level. Students collaborate with teachers to design their course programs. Although they are advised to design a course schedule that will prepare them for higher education, students have considerable freedom of choice about what courses they take and when they take them.

Sixteen credits are required for graduation. Students must take 4 years of English and 1 year of American history. They are also counseled to complete a minimum of 3 years of mathematics, 2 years of social science, 2 years of laboratory science, and at least 2 years of a foreign language (French, Spanish, and Indonesian are offered), although 3 years are strongly recommended. Students are also encouraged to pursue courses in the arts—studio art; ceramics; black-and-white and digital photography; video production; music theory, composition, and performance; and beginning and advanced drama.

Buxton offers a range of elective courses—those offered recently include writing workshops, Shakespeare, Twentieth-Century Literature, The Practice of Poetry, Coming of Age, Traditional Taoism and Western Literature, Advanced European Studies, Media Literacy, Cultural Anthropology, Film History, Sound and Music in the Twentieth Century, Rights and the Law, Contemporary Social and Political Movements, Africa, Topics in Religion and Politics, Radio and the Social Documentary, History of Dissent in the United States, Calculus II, Marine Science, Geology, Astronomy, Psychology, Kinesiology and Sociology of Sports, Environmental Studies, Behavioral and Chemical Addiction Studies, Chemistry of Photography, Sculpture: Metal Fabrication, and Book Arts.

Students in their junior year are invited to participate in a year-long research project that culminates in a substantial scholarly paper as well as a creative project that grows out of their research. Topics in recent years have included a history of the Israeli/Palestinian conflict, the invention of the steam engine, the worldwide problem of human trafficking, the history and tradition of the Japanese tea ceremony, cowboy history and lore, and an exploration of the life and work of the film and theater director Elia Kazan.

Buxton divides its academic year into two semesters. The School has a 5:1 student-teacher ratio, and class size averages 9 students. Faculty-supervised study periods are held daily during class hours and for 2 hours in the evening. Students may be required to attend.

Each year in March, the whole School travels to a major North American city. Atlanta, Chicago, Havana, Mexico City, New Orleans, Philadelphia, San Juan, Toronto, Washington, D.C., and three cities in Nicaragua are among those visited in recent years. This event is of central importance in the school year, and students are involved in all aspects of planning and executing the weeklong trip. Social, economic, and political issues are the focus of project groups, and the entire Buxton community takes part in the All-School Play or other performances, which are presented several times during the trip. Upon returning to Buxton, students share their project experiences with the School and archive their reports.

FACULTY AND ADVISERS

There are 21 faculty members—12 men and 9 women. Four hold master's degrees. Thirteen live on campus. C. William Bennett, Director of the School since 1983, is a graduate of Williams College and has been at Buxton since 1969. In 2008, Peter Smith became Co-Director with Mr. Bennett. Mr. Smith graduated from Buxton in 1974, is a graduate of Clark University, and has been working at Buxton since 1984.

Most teaching families and teachers live at the School, interweaving their daily lives with those of the Buxton community. Along with teaching in the classroom, faculty members have advisory, leadership, administrative, and caretaking responsibilities. As advisers, faculty members are in regular contact with parents.

Compassionate adult action and reaction form the foundation of education at Buxton. Teachers seek to motivate students to engage in sincere intellectual commitment and self-evaluation. The adults are available and open to young people and are concerned with their growth in academic disciplines as well as in every other respect. Buxton faculty and staff members react to young people knowledgeably, deeply, and personally. Developing honest and caring friendships between Buxton adults and students is an educational goal in itself.

COLLEGE ADMISSION COUNSELING

Buxton faculty members counsel students as they form their college plans. Students are assigned faculty advisers in the spring of their junior year. The advisers guide students in making appropriate college choices and help students with the application process.

In recent years, Buxton graduates have attended Amherst, Bard, Bennington, Berklee College of Music, Carleton, Cornell, Emory, Hampshire, Lewis and Clark, Middlebury, Mount Holyoke, Oberlin, Reed, St. John's, Sarah Lawrence, Skidmore, Smith, Swarthmore, Wellesley, and Williams.

STUDENT BODY AND CONDUCT

Enrollment at Buxton averages 90 students, with an equal number of boys and girls. In 2010–11, twelve states and the countries of Bermuda, Bolivia, China,

Ecuador, Mexico, the Republic of Korea, Rwanda, and Switzerland are represented among the student population.

ACADEMIC FACILITIES
The campus contains four classroom buildings (one housing science labs and a computer lab), a library with Internet-access computers and extra Ethernet ports for students' portable computers, an art studio, a ceramics studio, a darkroom, a music classroom and practice rooms, and a theater. Designated campus areas are equipped for wireless Internet access. A new music and fine arts complex is scheduled to be completed in early 2011.

BOARDING AND GENERAL FACILITIES
In addition to the academic facilities, there are a number of other buildings on campus. The Main House contains a girls' dormitory, the School dining room, and administrative offices. The Gate House serves as an additional girls' dormitory; the boys' dormitory is a converted barn. The School has additional buildings for administrative offices and for faculty and staff housing. Williamstown Medical Associates provides medical services to students.

ATHLETICS
At Buxton, competitive and recreational sports programs do not merely fulfill physical education requirements; they also expose students to the challenges inherent in disciplined physical activity and different kinds of team play. Students acquire personal confidence and a sense of mastery as well as leadership skills through participation in these activities.

Competitive sports are not mandatory, but regular outdoor activity is expected of everyone. Interscholastic soccer and basketball take place on a scheduled and supervised basis. Other activities include yoga classes, biking, hiking, horseback riding, indoor soccer, intramural basketball, martial arts, running, skating, skiing and snowboarding at a local area, sledding, softball, spring soccer, table tennis, tennis, and Ultimate (Frisbee).

The campus has its own playing fields, a basketball court, a weight room, three ponds for ice skating, and a hill for sledding and skiing. Hiking trips are scheduled when there is student interest. Riding lessons can be arranged.

EXTRACURRICULAR OPPORTUNITIES
In keeping with the Buxton philosophy that all aspects of School life are valuable to the education of a student, activities play a prominent role. Students of every degree of interest and ability are urged to take part and are counted on to support the efforts of each other as co-participant, audience, or encouraging friend. All of Buxton's activities, which include art, music, drama, dance, drumming, and creative writing, are designed to foster personal expression and commitment

through a combination of self-discipline, patient practice, interpersonal skill, and astute observation of life. The art studio has an extensive array of two- and three-dimensional media. Painting, drawing, figure drawing, printmaking, book arts, sculpture, metal fabrication, work with fabric or found objects, mixed media, ceramics, and black-and-white and digital photography are available. Chorus, chamber orchestra, and chamber ensembles are offered at Buxton as music activities. Drama includes acting, working on technical crews, and costuming. The dance and drumming program at Buxton focuses on West African and Afro-Caribbean traditional influences. Students also have the chance to study Balinese dance and drumming in the summer program in Bali. Each year, seniors raise funds for and produce the School yearbook, which they present as a gift to the Buxton community.

An essential part of a Buxton education is Work Program, which takes place on Tuesday afternoons and Saturday mornings. At these times, students engage in tasks such as forestry work and gardening, construction projects, office work, and cooking. Administered by volunteer students and faculty members, Work Program requires a great deal of planning, budgeting, and managing. What is done and who does it are always changing, but it is a consistent, direct challenge to everyone that Work Program can and must fill a major part of Buxton's nonprofessional needs.

The annual Fall and Spring Arts Festivals offer students' families the opportunity to share in Buxton life. Over the three days of these events, the School presents performances by the chorus, chamber orchestra, and chamber ensembles; performances of student composers' work; drama productions; and readings of students' creative writing. The School also exhibits new student artwork. Independent and joint science projects are often presented on these weekends as well. In addition, there is ample time for parent-faculty conferences.

The proximity of Williams College is particularly significant, as it provides a source of stimulation and example as well as the opportunity to occasionally attend lectures and events and use the college library. Bordering the Buxton campus is the Clark Art Institute, one of the finest small art museums in the country.

DAILY LIFE
Each day, students clean their rooms and complete minor housekeeping tasks around the School. Classes begin at 8 a.m. and are held until 3 p.m., five days a week. Sports and activities are offered from 3 to 5 p.m. Students attend study hall, study on their own, or participate in rehearsals or other activities from 7 to 9 p.m. Meals are family-style, with student waiters; students attend lunch at 12:30 and dinner at 6 in the School dining room.

WEEKEND LIFE
Weekends at Buxton are considered just as important as weekdays. Students plan and organize Friday night activities, which include outdoor sports and games, dances, swimming, and theme events. On Saturday mornings, everyone in the School participates in Work Program. Students are free to go into Williamstown to buy necessities or attend a movie or cultural event on Saturday afternoons and evenings. All Saturday meals are planned and prepared by students. Sundays begin with brunch and typically are devoted to academic work. Sunday evenings feature a formal dinner and arts events or presentations concerning social issues. Students remain at Buxton on weekends except for a designated Home Weekend each semester.

Students who wish to do so may attend religious services locally.

COSTS AND FINANCIAL AID
Tuition and fees for 2010–11 are $43,500 for boarding students and $27,500 for day students. This included room and board and academic study, plus basic materials for courses, lab fees, field trips, tickets to approved cultural events, athletics (including ski passes), and programs and activities held on campus. Books, all-school trip fees, laundry fees, some art supplies, weekly allowance, and travel are the family's responsibility.

Buxton is committed to maintaining the diversity of its student body. Approximately 47 percent receive need-based financial aid; $1.2 million was awarded for 2010–11.

ADMISSIONS INFORMATION
Buxton admits students into grades 9 through 11. Interested parents and prospective students may request an information packet by calling or writing the Admissions Office or through the School Web site. An on-campus interview is required, and the student's most recent SSAT or TOEFL scores should accompany the application.

APPLICATION TIMETABLE
Inquiries are welcome any time. Applications are due February 1, although they are accepted later if space is available. The application fee is $50 for U.S. students and $100 for international students.

ADMISSIONS CORRESPONDENCE
Admissions Office
Buxton School
291 South Street
Williamstown, Massachusetts 01267
Phone: 413-458-3919
Fax: 413-458-9428
E-mail: Admissions@BuxtonSchool.org
Web site: http://www.BuxtonSchool.org

CAMPBELL HALL (EPISCOPAL)

North Hollywood, California

Type: Coeducational day college-preparatory school
Grades: K–12: Lower School, K–6; Middle School, 7–8; Upper School, 9–12
Enrollment: School total: 1,085; Upper School: 533
Head of School: The Reverend Canon Julian Bull, Headmaster

THE SCHOOL

Campbell Hall is an independent, K–12, coeducational, nonprofit day school affiliated with the Episcopal Church. It offers college-preparatory academic training within the perspective of the Judeo-Christian tradition. Campbell Hall was founded in 1944 by the Reverend Alexander K. Campbell as a school dedicated not only to the finest in academic education but also to the discovery of the values of a religious heritage. Campbell Hall enrolls students in kindergarten through the twelfth grade.

The school's 15-acre campus is located in a residential suburb 10 miles north of Los Angeles. Students take advantage of the school's proximity to museums, missions, historic sites, science centers, and universities.

The basic structure and operation of the school and the formulation of educational and other school policies are guided by a 20-member Board of Directors. The board is composed of community leaders, alumni, and parents of students at Campbell Hall. The Headmaster has traditionally served as a liaison between the board and the various segments of the school community.

The school's advancement programs include annual and capital campaigns.

Campbell Hall is accredited by the Western Association of Schools and Colleges and the California Association of Independent Schools. It holds memberships in the National Association of Independent Schools, National Association of Episcopal Schools, Episcopal Diocesan Commission on Schools, Educational Records Bureau, National Association of College Admission Counselors, Council for Advancement and Support of Education, College Board, Council for Religion in Independent Schools, and Cum Laude Society.

ACADEMIC PROGRAMS

Students at the high school must complete 7½ units in the humanities, including 4 units of the English component, 3 units of the history component, and ½ unit of senior seminar. Other requirements for graduation include 3 units of mathematics, 3 of foreign language, 3 of laboratory sciences, 2 years of physical education, 1 year of a visual or performing art, ½ year of art history, and ½ year of music history. In addition to the required courses, students must complete at least 3½ additional units chosen from electives, such as music theory, creative writing, economics, ethics, physiology, poetry, computer programming, philosophy, psychology, and visual and performing arts. In addition, students must complete 20 hours of community service each year.

A number of special academic options attract qualified students. Twenty-one Advanced Placement courses and sixteen honors courses are offered and include calculus, probability and statistics, English, French, Japanese, Spanish, European history, U.S. history, American government, geography, biology, chemistry, physics, music theory, psychology, economics, and computer science. In addition, qualified seniors may take college-level courses through the Talented High School Student Program of the California State University at Northridge, through local community colleges, and through the UCLA High School Scholars' Program.

Classes range in size from 8 or fewer students in advanced courses to 19 in some of the required courses.

The school's grading system uses percentages: 100–90 is an A; 89–80 is a B; 79–70 is a C; 69–60 is a D, and no credit is given for a grade below 59. Report cards, which are issued twice each semester, include evaluations of work habits and cooperation. At the midpoint of each quarter, students who are in academic difficulty in one or more courses are notified, as are their parents.

Each semester, students who earn all A's in all classes are eligible for the Headmaster's List; students who earn a 3.6 academic average qualify for the Honor Roll. On the basis of course history and semester grades, students may qualify for recognition by the California Scholarship Federation, and academically outstanding juniors and seniors are eligible for membership in the Cum Laude Society.

FACULTY AND ADVISERS

There are 110 full-time faculty members (71 women and 39 men); 57 hold master's degrees, and 7 have doctorates. Faculty members are encouraged to attend seminars and conferences in their fields. In addition to giving academic and social guidance to individual students, faculty advisers work closely with class officers to ensure unity and success in various class projects and social activities.

The Reverend Canon Julian Bull was appointed Headmaster in 2003. He is a graduate of Dartmouth (B.A., 1982), Boston College (M.A., 1988), and received his M.Div. from Virginia Theological Seminary in 2007. Mr. Bull was formerly Head of School at Trinity Episcopal in New Orleans, Louisiana.

COLLEGE ADMISSION COUNSELING

In October, all sophomores and juniors take the PSAT. Throughout their high school years, students receive extensive college counseling through group workshops and in-depth individual conferences with the college counseling staff members. High school families are invited to the annual Senior College Night at which the college admissions process is delineated and college-financing strategies are explained. During the fall semester, juniors and seniors have the opportunity to hear presentations from a nationwide selection of college admission officers who visit Campbell Hall. One hundred percent of Campbell Hall graduates are accepted to four-year colleges or universities. They are drawn to a broad range of schools, and in recent years have enrolled at Berklee College of Music, Berkeley, Carnegie Mellon, Claremont McKenna, Columbia, Cornell, Duke, Emory, Georgetown, Grinnell College, Middlebury, NYU, Northwestern, Rhode Island School of Design, Rice, Scripps, UCLA, USC, Spelman, Stanford, Swarthmore, Tufts, the U.S. Air Force Academy, Vassar, Washington (St. Louis), Wesleyan, Whitman, and the Universities of Chicago, Michigan, and Pennsylvania.

STUDENT BODY AND CONDUCT

Of the 533 boys and girls in the Upper School (grades 9–12), 134 are in the ninth grade, 136 in the tenth, 135 in the eleventh, and 128 in the twelfth. Most students live in the suburban areas of Los Angeles.

Because Campbell Hall is concerned with the formation of character traits and values that reflect a sense of responsibility as well as a concern for the needs of others, misconduct is subject to disciplinary action. Violation of school rules and regulations may result in suspension or expulsion.

ACADEMIC FACILITIES

Campus academic facilities include classroom complexes, a math-science building, seven science labs, four computer labs, the Fine Arts Building, and a theater. A 22,000-square-foot library and academic center serves as the hub for technological resources. The campus is equipped with wireless access and every classroom has computers available, including four laptop carts, networked overhead projectors, and SmartBoards. Every student and faculty member has a school-managed e-mail account. The Internet is available as are research tools on CD-ROM. The school library subscribes to a number of online databases. The new Arts and Education Center is under construction on the Campbell Hall campus. This 111,000-square-foot project includes three two-story connected buildings, a multilevel subterranean parking garage, twenty-four state-of-the-art classrooms, an art gallery, a faculty resource center, outdoor learning spaces, terraces, and gardens, with extensive use of multimedia throughout. Designed by Gensler, an architectural firm renowned for its expertise in education design and innovative sustainability practices, the project is slated to be LEED certified at completion.

ATHLETICS

There are two basic components to the athletics program. First, required physical education courses provide basic and advanced instruction for sports that are in season; and second, Campbell Hall is a member of the California Interscholastic Federation (Gold Coast Athletic Association) and field teams in baseball, basketball, cheerleading, cross-country, 11-man tackle football, equestrian, golf, soccer, softball, tennis, track and field, and volleyball.

The school has two well-equipped gymnasiums, a baseball diamond, an artificial turf football and soccer field, a softball field, and five outdoor basketball/volleyball courts.

EXTRACURRICULAR OPPORTUNITIES

The students have an active student government with elected officers representing each division of the student body. Among the student-planned events are dances; homecoming; the Winter Formal; and the Halloween, Christmas, and Valentine's Day celebrations. The year's social schedule culminates in a spring prom, planned by the junior class to honor the senior class.

There are also many curricular field trips and about sixty special interest groups, such as the Speech and Debate Team, Highlanders, the Cultural Awareness Club, the Spirit Club,

Thespians, the Creative Writing Club, Amnesty International, Junior Statesmen of America, GSA, the Community Service Committee, and the High School Academic Honor Board.

DAILY LIFE

Monday through Thursday, there are four 80-minute academic classes that meet between 8:15 and 3:30. On Friday, each class meets for 75 minutes, between 8:15 and 2:20. Each Monday through Thursday, 40 minutes are devoted to chapel (every Monday and Thursday), advisee group meetings, or clubs. There is a 45-minute lunch break. Interspersed among the academic courses are electives that provide enrichment in the fine arts (painting, drawing, ceramics, sculpture, and photography), the performing arts (chorus, instrumental music, drama, stagecraft, and dance), sports (physical education and team sports), robotics, and computer programming. Yearbook, newspaper, and journalism are also available as curricular classes.

SUMMER PROGRAMS

The school offers a full complement of summer programs for students in kindergarten through grade 12, including summer school courses, a creative arts camp, and sports camps. Additional information may be obtained by calling or e-mailing the Summer Programs Director.

COSTS AND FINANCIAL AID

Tuition for 2010–11, including fees, is $22,200 to $27,270. Tuition payments may be made annually, biannually or, at an additional charge to cover interest costs, in ten monthly installments. Students may either bring their own lunches to school or purchase them at the student store or from a caterer at the school at lunchtime. There is a dress code. Bus service is available from some parts of town.

Financial aid is available and is awarded on the basis of family need. Continuing students

have priority for renewal. In 2010–11, 25 percent of Middle and Upper School students received financial aid.

ADMISSIONS INFORMATION

The school seeks students who are able to benefit from a rigorous college-preparatory curriculum and who will contribute to extracurricular as well as other community activities. The school does not discriminate against applicants on the basis of race, religion, or national or ethnic origin. Campbell Hall is a diverse school community. Students of color make up 32.7 percent of the student body, and a variety of different faiths and family structures are also represented.

An entrance examination is required, as are recommendations from 2 teachers, a transcript from the school in which the applicant is currently enrolled, and an interview.

APPLICATION TIMETABLE

The Admissions Office is open from 8 a.m. to 4 p.m., Monday through Friday, to answer inquiries and to arrange interviews and campus visits. Applicants should file an application, accompanied by a $100 fee, by January 28 of the year entrance is desired. Most applications are submitted by December of the year preceding the desired entrance. Applicants take the Independent School Entrance Examination.

The school makes most decisions concerning new admissions by March. Parents are expected to reply to an offer of acceptance within two weeks and to pay a $2000 registration fee, which is credited toward the first semester's tuition.

ADMISSIONS CORRESPONDENCE

Alice Fleming, Director of Admissions
George White, Associate Director
Campbell Hall
4533 Laurel Canyon Boulevard
P.O. Box 4036
North Hollywood, California 91617-9985
Phone: 818-980-7280
Web site: http://www.campbellhall.org

CANTERBURY SCHOOL

Ft. Myers, Florida

Type: Coeducational, day, college-preparatory
Grades: Prekindergarten–12: Lower School, Pre-K–3; Intermediate School, 4–6; Middle School, 7–8; Upper School, 9–12
Enrollment: 615; Upper School, 203
Head of School: Anthony J. Paulus

THE SCHOOL

Founded in 1964, the Canterbury School sits on 33 acres located on College Parkway between U.S. 41 and McGregor Boulevard. The School is dedicated to academic excellence within a caring and supportive community, preparing students of ability, promise, and diverse backgrounds for selective colleges. Canterbury's motto, "Education, character, leadership, service," defines the focus of the School's program and underscores all that its students do in and out of the classroom.

There are four divisions—Lower (grades prekindergarten–3), Intermediate (grades 4–6), Middle (grades 7–8), and Upper (grades 9–12). At all levels, the academic program emphasizes individual growth, skill development, a high caliber of instruction, collaboration, and high standards. Canterbury provides all students with an opportunity to challenge themselves and take risks in an atmosphere of mutual respect and partnership among students, parents, and teachers. Canterbury's integrated, innovative curriculum emphasizes group and individual study of the liberal arts, in addition to experiential learning and community service opportunities.

The Canterbury School is accredited by the Southern Association of Independent Schools (SAIS), Southern Association of Colleges and Schools/Council on Accreditation and School Improvement (SACS/CASI), Florida Council of Independent Schools (FCIS), the College Board, and the Florida Kindergarten Council (FKC).

ACADEMIC PROGRAMS

All students pursue a demanding schedule of college-preparatory classes for four years in the Upper School, earning a minimum of 26 credits to graduate. Students play an active role in their course of study, and juniors and seniors may pursue advanced work in areas of significant interest or expertise. Although Honors and Advanced Placement courses, as well as independent studies, give students extra challenges, even the standard-level courses thoroughly prepare students for college work. Offering a rigorous and rewarding liberal arts curriculum, the Upper School program is rich in math,

science, modern and classical languages, music, visual arts, social sciences, foreign language, and drama, with a special emphasis on writing, research, and the discourse of ideas. Study strategies, self-discipline, academic responsibility, and fluency in technology are underscored in each content area. Students learn academic honesty, competitive fair play, and good citizenship through a respected honor code. Students master key skills that will serve them well in their college careers as they actively participate in intellectual inquiry, analysis, and evaluation.

Middle School students take one course in each of the major disciplines every year—English, mathematics, science, social studies, and foreign language—and classes in the arts and in physical education/health, as well as other electives.

Canterbury's Intermediate School offers instruction in a math, science, and technology triad, as well as the "Writing Across the Curriculum" initiative, which links critical thinking and written expression in every curriculum area. Lower School celebrates childhood in an age-appropriate, developmental learning environment for students in prekindergarten through third grade; a balance between hard work and fun creates an environment where children are encouraged to take risks and assume personal responsibility for their learning as they embark upon their learning journey.

FACULTY AND ADVISERS

There are 80 faculty members, 38 of whom teach in the Upper School. Canterbury's talented and dedicated faculty seeks to inspire young minds through a rigorous and rewarding curriculum. Passionate about ideas and mentoring, instructors understand how students learn most effectively. Teaching is more than facts, figures, and formulas—it's a way of life. Canterbury's teachers personalize their approach to meet individual student needs. Small class sizes allow one-on-one time for personal attention, challenging and supporting students as they stretch their minds and their opportunities.

COLLEGE ADMISSION COUNSELING

College preparation is a primary focus of Canterbury's curriculum, so students receive the highly personalized direction and encouragement they need to choose the undergraduate institution with the right fit. An experienced college counselor guides juniors and seniors, as well as their families, through the process—helping them gain a comprehensive understanding of college acceptance practices. The result? An ongoing tradition of a 100 percent college-acceptance rate among Canterbury graduates. Recent graduates have been accepted to such distinguished institutions as Carnegie Mellon, Dartmouth, Georgetown, Harvard, and Princeton.

STUDENT BODY AND CONDUCT

About 615 students are enrolled in grades prekindergarten–12. They come from diverse backgrounds, but the majority live in Fort Myers and the surrounding area.

ACADEMIC FACILITIES

The Canterbury School Libraries offer instruction, materials, and technology to promote the skills of information literacy and fluency, the love of reading, and the joy of intellectual discovery. By providing resources for both academic and recreational reading needs, the libraries help students develop research competencies for college and facilitate lifelong learning. The libraries also provide space for individual reflection and creation, as well as a forum for the sharing of ideas within the Canterbury community. The Ellenberg Library (grades 6-12) has established several special collections, in addition to the familiar biography, fiction, nonfiction, periodical, reference, and story collections. The Hilliard Library serves students from pre-K through fifth grade and their teachers. The library collection, of both print and nonprint resources, includes books, videotapes, magazines, Internet access, professional resources, and online subscription databases.

The Lower and Intermediate schools have dedicated art and music classrooms, science laboratories, computer labs and classrooms. They share a library. The Middle and Upper schools share a library, a language listening lab, and music and art classrooms, but they have separate science laboratories, computer labs, classrooms, and commons areas. The entire school shares the dining hall, a gymnasium and a sports center, an outdoor marine biology touch tank and classroom, and the Performing Arts Center.

ATHLETICS

At Canterbury, the life of the mind is complemented by a strong athletic program. Canterbury School fields teams in soccer, basketball, baseball, six-man football, volleyball, swimming, tennis, golf, cross-country, track and field, and lacrosse. Students are encouraged to become involved with athletics; around 85 percent of all Middle and Upper School students participate in interscholastic sports. Canterbury School is a member of the Florida High School Athletic Association (FHSAA) and is accredited by the Southern Association of Schools and Colleges (SACS). The Middle School belongs to the Suncoast Middle School League.

EXTRACURRICULAR OPPORTUNITIES

Clubs and organizations play key roles in student life. Students can choose from more than twenty active clubs on campus, including yearbook, newspaper, chess, mock trial, and Model UN, which meet regularly throughout the year. Students can also participate in a variety of local, state, national, and international scholastic competitions.

DAILY LIFE

Students spend their days in class, followed by after-school activities ranging from community service, student government, and athletics to clubs and study groups.

SUMMER PROGRAMS

Summer academic programs are available to students of all ages. Students can brush up their math, writing, or Spanish skills or take SAT-prep courses. Canterbury provides a recommended summer reading list for prekindergarten to fifth grade students so that they can begin, continue, and support the process of developing comprehension and analytical skills. Students in grades 6–12 receive a required summer reading list to support their academic course selection for the following year.

COSTS AND FINANCIAL AID

Upper School students pay $17,760 plus fees per academic year. Tuition is $13,920 for prekindergarten and kindergarten, $15,395 for grades 1–3, $16,610 for grades 4–6, and $17,200 for Middle School. Fees are additional. In 2010–11, Canterbury provided more than $1.25 million in financial assistance to 22 percent of the student body, with awards ranging from 20 percent to 95 percent of tuition.

Tuition payments include both a nonrefundable deposit and the remaining tuition balance. The nonrefundable 20 percent deposit is due upon enrollment and must accompany the student's enrollment contract. On July 1, another 30 percent of tuition is due, and the remaining 50 percent is due October 1. With this plan, tuition

refund insurance is optional. Payment plan options are presented in the addendum to the enrollment contract.

ADMISSIONS INFORMATION

As a college-preparatory school with high academic standards, Canterbury seeks students of demonstrated abilities with potential for intellectual growth. Boys and girls entering prekindergarten through grade eleven are invited to apply, beginning the fall prior to the school year they wish to attend. Applications can be submitted online or by mail and must include the $75 application fee.

Applicants are first evaluated by testing, using the ERB, CTP 4 Test, or the SSAT in grades 3–11. Next, candidates' files are forwarded to the Admission Committee, which assesses each application based on the student's past academic achievement, performance on the admission test, a written essay, personal recommendations, and an interview with the division head and director of admission.

APPLICATION TIMETABLE

Open houses are scheduled October through April; attendees must reserve a space by contacting the admission office. Applications are accepted continually.

ADMISSIONS CORRESPONDENCE

Julie Peters, Director of Admissions
Canterbury School
8141 College Parkway
Fort Myers, Florida 33919
Phone: 239-415-8945
Fax: 239-481-8339
E-mail: jpeters@canterburyfortmyers.org
Web site: http://www.canterburyfortmyers.org/

CHATHAM HALL

Chatham, Virginia

Type: Girls' boarding and day college-preparatory school
Grades: 9–12
Enrollment: 129
Head of School: Gary J. Fountain, Rector

THE SCHOOL

Since its founding 1894, Chatham Hall, an independent, all-girls boarding and day high school in Chatham, Virginia, has earned a national and international reputation for its broad, strong college-preparatory program and its global educational community. At the center of the School is its honor code and strong Episcopal heritage. Its alumnae have earned positions of prominence in politics, business, education, medicine, engineering, and the arts, and include renowned painter Georgia O'Keeffe and Pulitzer Prize-winning poet Claudia Emerson.

Chatham Hall's unique programming includes annual service trips to South Africa and its Leader in Residence Program, which brings world leaders to campus to meet with students. Recent leaders in residence have included Jane Goodall, well-known anthropologist and primatologist; the late Benazir Bhutto, Prime Minister of Pakistan; Ellen Johnson-Sirleaf, the current and first female President of Liberia; and Nancy Brinker, founder of Race for the Cure.

Chatham Hall benefits from its proximity to educational and cultural centers in Raleigh, Durham, Chapel Hill, and Greensboro, North Carolina; and Charlottesville, Lynchburg, and Roanoke, Virginia. Located in the Piedmont section of Virginia, its 362-acre campus has rolling countryside with woods, streams, and pasturelands.

Chatham Hall is governed by a national, self-perpetuating Board of Trustees. The school's recorded endowment is valued at $20 million, and the average gift to the school is one of the highest among girls' schools.

Accredited by the Southern Association of Colleges and Schools and the National Association of Independent Schools, Chatham Hall holds memberships in the National Association of Principals of Schools for Girls, the National Association of College Admission Counselors, the National Coalition of Girls' Schools, the Secondary School Admission Test Board, the Council for the Advancement and Support of Education, and the Virginia Association of Independent Schools.

ACADEMIC PROGRAMS

The school's curriculum emphasizes analytical reasoning, expressive abilities, character and vision, and physical vigor. To graduate from Chatham Hall, students must complete their senior year at the school and fulfill the following minimum distribution requirements: 4 years of English, 3 years of mathematics, 3 years of history (1 of which must be U.S. history), 3 years of one foreign language, 3 years of lab science (2 of which must be biology and chemistry), 1 year of fine or performing arts, 1 trimester of religion, and 1 trimester of ethics. In addition, students must participate in the physical fitness program each trimester. A total of 20 credits are required.

Advanced Placement courses are offered in each department, and students may apply to the Discovery Challenge independent-study program. Electives include such courses as DNA Science and Veterinary Science.

Classes meet five days per week for 45-, 60-, and 75-minute periods. The average class size is 8 students, and the overall student-teacher ratio is approximately 7:1. Typically, students carry five to six academic courses each trimester. Grading is on a scale of A to F with pluses and minuses. Grade reports with teacher comments are sent home at the middle and end of each trimester. Parents also have regular communication with the student's adviser.

FACULTY AND ADVISERS

The faculty consists of 33 teaching members. Sixty-two percent have advanced degrees. Nearly all faculty members live on campus, and each serves as an adviser to a small group of girls, meeting with each girl individually and helping her to define and realize her goals for the year and for the future.

Dr. Gary Fountain is Chatham Hall's ninth rector in its 110-year history. He received an A.B. degree from Brown University, a Master of Arts in Religion from Yale Divinity School, and a Ph.D. from the Department of English and American Literature at Boston University. Prior to coming to Chatham Hal, Fountain was an associate professor of English and Director of English Teacher Education at Ithaca College in New York. He also has served in faculty or administration positions at Saint Joseph's College, Miss Porter's School, and Ethel Walker School.

COLLEGE PLACEMENT

Chatham Hall is a college-preparatory school; as such, students prepare for college from the moment they enter Chatham Hall. Students begin working formally with the school's college counselor early in their Chatham Hall experience and meet frequently with her throughout the process. Recently, Chatham Hall graduates have attended such schools as Colgate, Cornell, Dartmouth, Duke, Georgetown, Johns Hopkins, Stanford, Swarthmore, Wellesley, and the Universities of North Carolina and Virginia.

STUDENT BODY AND CONDUCT

Chatham Hall is one of the few girls' schools in which more than 80 percent of the students are seven-day boarders. In 2009–10, the student body consisted of 129 girls from twenty-two states and twelve other countries.

The entire Chatham Hall community upholds the Honor Code as the foundation upon which the school is built. In matters of daily living, Chatham Hall students also depend on a clear statement of citizenship, known as the Purple and Golden Rule. Chatham Hall does not subscribe to a demerit system. Rather, Chatham Hall students value a system of implicit understandings over explicit and restrictive rules. The school believes in each girl's innate ability to make good choices and to lead herself according to her conscience. Under the Purple and Golden Rule, each girl is responsible for her actions and accepts the consequences of them, and she embraces the concept of White Flag—respect for people and property. The Purple and Golden Rule establishes a framework by which each girl governs herself and her peers throughout the school year. As a custodian of these principles, she sets an example for others and counsels others when they are not living up to these principles.

ACADEMIC FACILITIES

The Chatham Hall Intranet connects the school community electronically. Each dorm room has two data ports and two phone ports. Each classroom and office is also networked. A full-time Director of Instructional Technology works with faculty members on integrating technology into their curricula. Pruden Hall contains offices, formal sitting rooms, two dormitory floors, a nine-bed Health Care Center, and a darkroom facility. Dabney Hall contains eleven classrooms; a computer lab; two dormitory floors; a day student room; and a student center, including a kitchen, a viewing room, mail boxes, the bookstore, and a fitness center. The Shaw Science and Technology building has four state-of-the-art laboratory classrooms, a sophisticated technology classroom, a seminar room, and a wireless computer network. The Holt Language Building has four foreign language classrooms. Boasting award-winning architecture, the Edmund and Lucy Lee Library contains 30,000 holdings, is fully computerized, and allows students online access to virtually every resource in the country through VLIN, Dialog, OCLC, and Internet connections. The Whitner Dance/Art Studio has large, flexible spaces that are well equipped for modern dance and ballet; for painting, pottery, sculpture, and weaving; and for drama in the black box theater. Willis Hall contains two large classrooms and the Advancement Office.

The School has also recently completed construction of the Van Voorhis Lecture Hall. This new lecture hall makes it possible for the entire Chatham Hall community and guests to gather on campus to hear lectures by some of the world's greatest leaders, thinkers and artists. The new 3,788-square-foot lecture hall accommodates an audience of up to 350 people.

Chatham Hall's dining facility, Yardley Hall, received a massive renovation during the summer of 2008. In addition to a state-of-the-art, open-air kitchen, the dining hall has been refurbished with new tables, chairs, and carpeting. The sleek yet comfortable design and layout is a perfect setting for Chatham's community meals.

BOARDING AND GENERAL FACILITIES

Students live on one of four dormitory floors located in Pruden and Dabney. They generally share a room, but some may live in a single. Houseparents live on each floor, as do members of the Student Council. Both dormitories have phone and Internet access and individual heating/air conditioning units in each room. St. Mary's Chapel is a focal point of the school, hosting three weekly services, Senior Chapel Talks, choir rehearsals, and piano and voice lessons. Chatham Hall's forty-stall riding facility features the Mars Riding Arena, a 125-foot by 250-foot indoor riding facility that is among the best on the East Coast. The physical plant is valued at $25.2 million.

ATHLETICS

Physical fitness is a vital part of the Chatham Hall experience. All students participate in athletics each trimester. The school supports varsity teams in basketball, cross-country, field hockey, riding, soccer, swimming, tennis, and volleyball. Chatham Hall's Riding Program offers hunt seat riding and features a competitive, varsity show team that participates in AA shows in USEF Zone 3.

The recently renovated and air-conditioned gymnasium serves as both an athletic facility for basketball and volleyball and as a recreation and performance space for mixers, aerobics, and dance. The school also has three playing fields and six all-weather tennis courts. Riding facilities include forty stalls, a 125-foot by 250-foot indoor arena, a 275-foot by 175-foot show arena, a permanent hunter trial course, three large schooling and teaching fields, and extensive trails.

EXTRACURRICULAR OPPORTUNITIES

Chatham Hall students belong to more than thirty organizations representing a wide range of interests, including FOCUS; various art, language, and riding clubs; the environmental club; and numerous student publications. All students and faculty are members of one of the branches of the Service League: Community Life, School Life, or Church Life.

Students have performance and academic instruction opportunities in theater, dance, and music. The Sherwood Dramatic Club performs two major productions a year. Panache, Chatham Hall's modern dance ensemble, performs on and off campus several times a year. Singers have a variety of performance opportunities to perform in St. Mary's Choir, the Chamber Choir, and Sextet.

DAILY LIFE

Classes begin at 8 a.m. and end at 3:30 p.m. Afternoons are devoted to athletics. Required chapel services are held three times each week. The community gathers in the Well in Pruden on Monday and Thursday mornings for an all-school assembly. The school eats meals together; most meals are buffet-style. There are three seated meals each week: lunch on Wednesday and Thursday and dinner on Monday. Students sit with faculty advisers. Clubs generally meet after dinner. There are required study hours from 7:30 to 9:30 on school nights. Students may study in their rooms, the library, special group study rooms, or one of the computer labs. Room bell in the dormitories is at 10:25 p.m.

WEEKEND LIFE

Chatham Hall is a seven-day boarding school, and offers a variety of fun and enriching activities both on and off campus. Taking advantage of the school's location, Chatham Hall students spend weekends attending concerts and theater and art shows in nearby cities, enjoying a wide variety of outdoor activities such as skiing and hiking, or going out to dinner and movies with friends. Chatham Hall also arranges large trips to Washington D.C. and Baltimore for cultural and shopping excursions. Chatham Hall participates in the Boarding Schools Social Activities Committee (BSSAC), which coordinates mixers and other events with boarding schools throughout Virginia.

COSTS AND FINANCIAL AID

The comprehensive fee for boarders is $39,000, which includes tuition, room, and board. The fee for day students is $16,500. Books, transportation, private music lessons, English as a second language, swimming, and riding carry additional charges.

Chatham Hall is committed to bringing qualified girls to the school. To this end, the school offers financial aid grants to families who demonstrate need under the guidelines of the School and Student Service for Financial Aid.

ADMISSIONS INFORMATION

Chatham Hall admits young women whose character and integrity, academic and intellectual promise, motivation, and enthusiasm for participating in the life of the school will predictably make them successful members of the school community.

APPLICATION TIMETABLE

Chatham Hall's application deadline is February 1. After that date, students are admitted on a rolling basis. Candidates should plan to visit the school early in the process for an interview and tour and to spend the night in a dorm. In addition to completing the application forms, candidates must also submit standardized test scores, such as those from the Secondary School Admission Test (SSAT).

ADMISSIONS CORRESPONDENCE

Vicki Wright
Director of Admission and Financial Aid
Chatham Hall
800 Chatham Hall Circle
Chatham, Virginia 24531

Phone: 434-432-2941
Fax: 434-432-2405
E-mail: admission@chathamhall.com
Web site: http://www.chathamhall.org

CHOATE ROSEMARY HALL

Wallingford, Connecticut

Type: Coeducational boarding and day college-preparatory school
Grades: 9–12, postgraduate year (Forms III–VI): Third Form, 9; Fourth Form, 10; Fifth Form, 11; Sixth Form, 12, postgraduate year
Enrollment: 831 on campus; 19 abroad
Head of School: Edward J. Shanahan, Ph.D., Headmaster

THE SCHOOL

Choate Rosemary Hall's rigorous academic program, through its small classes, both challenges and supports its students. This approach is the root of the school's reputation for academic excellence. At Choate, talented students and teachers from diverse backgrounds live and learn together creatively. Community spirit builds from this richness of difference in persons, cultures, and traditions to prepare students to assume leadership positions in today's global community.

The school's hope for its graduates is that they go forth from a community that valued each of them for particular talents and enthusiasms, affirmed the importance of personal integrity and a sense of self-worth, inspired and nourished joy in learning and love of truth, and provided the intellectual stimulation that generates independent thought, confident expression, and worthwhile commitments. Ideally, graduates will embody the five principles that both historically and currently capture the essence of Choate Rosemary Hall: academic excellence, character, community, physical and spiritual well-being, and giving back.

Choate Rosemary Hall was established through the merger of Rosemary Hall, a girls' school founded by Caroline Ruutz-Rees in 1890 in Wallingford, Connecticut, and The Choate School, a boys' school founded by Judge William Gardner Choate in 1896 in the same town. In 1971, the trustees of each school announced their coordination, and, in 1974, the two boards joined to form The Choate Rosemary Hall Foundation, Inc. Since 1977, the school has functioned as a single coeducational institution. The 458-acre campus is 12 miles north of New Haven, 20 miles south of Hartford, and a 2-hour drive from Boston and New York City.

The School is governed by a Board of Trustees, most of whose 26 members are alumni. The endowment is currently valued at $240 million.

Choate Rosemary Hall is accredited by the New England Association of Schools and Colleges. It holds memberships in the National Association of Independent Schools, the Connecticut Association of Independent Schools, A Better Chance, the Secondary School Admission Test Board, and the School Scholarship Service.

ACADEMIC PROGRAMS

A student's schedule for the three-term academic year is planned individually. The student chooses from more than 240 courses with the help of the academic adviser, the Dean, and college counselors. Course levels are chosen according to academic preparedness, ability, and talent in an academic area, not necessarily by age or grade level.

Students are expected to carry 15 course credits per year or five courses per term. To receive a diploma, a four-year student must have a total of 60 course credits, including 4 years of English (one course each term at Choate); algebra I, geometry, algebra II, and 14 terms in secondary school of a quantitative course; 1 year of a laboratory course in physical science, either physics or chemistry; and 1 year of a laboratory course in biology; 1 year of world history, 1 year of U.S. history, 1 term of philosophy or religion, and 1 term in contemporary global studies; 3 years (through the 300 or 350 level) of a diploma language, namely Arabic, Chinese, French, Latin, or Spanish; 3 terms of athletics or 2 terms of athletics and 1 term of an alternate activity per term; and 3 terms of arts from two areas: music, visual arts, or theater.

Each of the six academic departments offers courses that prepare students for Advanced Placement work. Special features are a nationally ranked economics team; a science research program encompassing university-based lab experience; an arts concentration program; full integration of technology into the academic curriculum; a two-term creative writing seminar for qualified seniors; and the Capstone Program, an opportunity for talented seniors to explore an area of the curriculum in depth.

A number of opportunities are available for study abroad during the academic year, including immersion programs in China, France, and Spain; term-long study in Rome; and summer programs in China, France, and Spain.

The average class size is 12. Students are graded six times a year on an A–F scale; D– is the lowest passing grade. Written comments by teachers and advisers are sent home at the end of each trimester.

FACULTY AND ADVISERS

There are 62 men and 45 women on the teaching faculty, 74 percent of whom hold advanced degrees. Each serves as academic, athletic, and personal adviser to 8 to 10 students. Most also coach and are involved in extracurricular pursuits. Choate Rosemary Hall supports the same breadth in its faculty members as in its students.

Edward J. Shanahan (St. Joseph's College, 1965; M.A., Fordham University, 1968; Ph.D., University of Wisconsin, 1982), Headmaster, came to the school in 1991 after nine years as Dean of the College at Dartmouth.

COLLEGE ADMISSION COUNSELING

College counseling is facilitated by a director and 5 associates and generally begins in the winter for the Fourth Form, when students receive assistance in registering for Subject Tests. The counselors work closely with students, conduct interviews with them and their parents, accompany them to college fairs, and help them prepare for formal interviews with college representatives, 200 of whom visit the campus each year. In the winter, juniors attend mock interviews held by college admissions officials who visit the school, and their parents are invited to the campus for a weekend of programs with the College Counseling Office and various university admission officers about the process of applying to college.

From 2006 through 2010, the most popular college choices included Georgetown (52), NYU (41), Yale (34), Wesleyan (30), Boston University (28), George Washington (27), Columbia (26), Boston College, Cornell, Tufts (24), Dartmouth (23), Brown, University of Pennsylvania (22), Princeton, Trinity (21), and Harvard (20).

STUDENT BODY AND CONDUCT

In 2010–11, the school had 625 boarders and 225 day students from forty states and forty-five countries.

The Student Council, which is composed of elected members of each form, provides a forum in which students can address school-related topics and plans, and it conducts and oversees social events and community matters.

Students are expected to follow school rules. Violations of the basic honor code or major school rules, or the accumulation of a number of violations of other rules, generally lead to suspension or dismissal. Rule violations are investigated by the Judicial Committee—a committee of elected students, deans, and an appointed faculty member—which makes recommendations to the Dean of Students.

ACADEMIC FACILITIES

Most campus academic facilities are the result of generous gifts from alumni and parents. The Carl C. Icahn Center for Science (1989), a $14-million, three-story building designed by I. M. Pei, includes twenty-two classrooms and laboratories, a 150-seat auditorium, and a conservatory. Another I. M. Pei building, the Paul Mellon Arts Center (1971), houses two theaters, a recital hall, music classrooms and practice rooms, art studios, dance and film facilities, offices, and an art gallery. All academic buildings and meeting spaces are part of Choate's wireless network.

The Andrew Mellon Library, which opened in 1926, was renovated in 2003 to integrate technological innovations with traditional library resources. The collection includes more than 114,000 titles, a Web-accessible catalog and reference collection, a wireless network, more than 120 magazine subscriptions, English- and foreign-language newspapers, and thousands of reels of microfilm, videos, DVDs, and sound recordings. Additional electronic resources include a wide variety of databases and indexes that are also available via MEL—the virtual branch of the Mellon Library. Special collections include those pertaining to Adlai Stevenson ('18) and John F. Kennedy ('35), along with the Rare Book, Thomas Hardy, and the Haffenreffer Autograph Collections and the school's extensive archives.

The Paul Mellon Humanities Center houses a computer center and a digital video production studio. Other facilities provide a total of forty-three classrooms as well as several computer centers with 120 fully networked workstations. All student rooms have wireless access to the Internet.

BOARDING AND GENERAL FACILITIES

Resident faculty members, their families, and Sixth Form house prefects live and work with small groups of students in residential settings that house as few as 7 students or as many as 75. Larger dormitories are divided into smaller sections, with 1 faculty member advising approximately 8–10 students to ensure feelings of community and warmth. Some students live in double rooms; others choose singles. Trained student peer counselors are an intrinsic part of the support system for students. Two new dormitories that house 80 students and eight faculty families opened in fall 2008.

The Pratt Health Center is open all day every day. Registered nurses are on duty 24 hours a day; the school physician lives on campus and is always on call.

The Student Activities Center houses the School Store and Post Office and has a cyber café, games, large-screen TVs, and spaces for parties and dances.

ATHLETICS

There is an appropriate level of athletics for every student. Some athletes come from very competitive programs and want to hone their skills with dedicated coaches and a serious sports program. Other students take advantage of the breadth of offerings and begin a new sport at the introductory level. The physical education and athletic program emphasizes acquiring lifetime skills, shaping positive attitudes about oneself as an individual and as a contributing member of a team, and developing a sense of honesty and fair play. All students participate in class-day or after-school sports each term.

There are eighty-one varsity, JV, and third-level interscholastic teams in most sports, as well as intramural teams. The program also includes all major sports and such activities as scuba, CPR, weight training, and fitness and conditioning.

The Johnson Athletic Center includes three basketball courts, three volleyball courts, ten international squash courts, a wrestling room, team weight rooms, and a suspended 1/10-mile track. The Edward A. Fox ('54) Fitness Pavillion contains a fully equipped fitness center, a sports medicine suite, and a dance studio as well as the school's Athletics Hall of Fame. There are twenty-two outdoor tennis courts at the Hunt Tennis Center; thirteen athletic fields; a cross-country course; hockey arena; boathouse; a 25-meter, eight-lane swimming pool; and the Bruce ('45) and Lueza Gelb Track. Shanahan Field, a multifield athletic complex, opened in 2010. Students also use a nearby golf course and a riding stable.

EXTRACURRICULAR OPPORTUNITIES

The School has more than sixty extracurricular activities, clubs, and organizations through which students may pursue special interests that range from astrophysics to conservation and from various publications to debating. Because each group requires club officers, leadership positions abound. Students are required to commit 30 hours to community service. The school's proximity to major cities provides access to cultural events, museums, and exhibits.

DAILY LIFE

Classes are held five days per week and on five Saturdays. They are scheduled in seven 50-minute periods between 8 a.m. and 2:50 p.m. four days per week; on Wednesdays and academic Saturdays, classes are held in four 50-minute periods and the academic day ends at 12:30. The afternoon sports program follows. Late afternoon provides time for study or extracurricular activities, and dinner is served between 5:15 and 7:15 p.m.

Students return to their dorm by 7:30 for a 1½-hour study time but may sign out to use the library or other academic facilities. There is a break from 9 to 9:45, with final dorm check-in at 9:30. There is a second study period from 9:45 to 10:30 p.m.

WEEKEND LIFE

Weekend social and recreational events and activities, in addition to those already scheduled at the Arts Center or by student organizations, are planned for all students. Every weekend there are dances, movies, and excursions to New York, Boston, or other nearby towns and cities. There are such seasonal activities as Harvest Fest and Spring Fest, and shuttle vans provide transportation to local ski areas, shopping, theaters, and sports venues.

SUMMER PROGRAMS

The five-week residential summer session is designed primarily for students who are seeking enrichment in skills-oriented courses that are not offered in their home schools. Summer Programs include The Writing Project, John F. Kennedy ('35) Institute in Government, English Language Institute, Academic Enrichment, and math and science workshops. Also offered are enrichment programs for middle school students, including a mathematics/science institute for girls who have completed grades 6–8 and the Writing Workshop. Classroom work is supplemented by such activities as lecture series, field trips, and sports. About 600 boys and girls attend.

The School also sponsors study trips to China, France, and Spain. Requests for information should be sent to Choate Summer Programs, 333 Christian Street, Wallingford, Connecticut 06492.

COSTS AND FINANCIAL AID

For 2010–11, the total cost for a boarder is $45,905 and for a day student, $35,105. Books are extra. An optional laundry service is available at an additional cost. Financial aid and loans are available for students whose families qualify. Decisions are mailed March 10. In 2010–11, 33 percent of the students received financial aid totaling $8.5 million, with the average award amounting to 70 percent of tuition.

Choate Rosemary Hall seeks students of diverse geographic, economic, social, ethnic, and racial backgrounds. The SSAT is required of applicants for grades 9 and 10 and should be taken in December if possible. The median score for ninth and tenth graders is at the 85th percentile. Most entering students test between the 80th and 99th percentiles. The PSAT/SAT is required for candidates for grades 11 and 12 and postgraduates. The TOEFL is suggested for those whose native language is not English. Applicants should be motivated achievers in their schools.

For September 2010 entry, there were 1,761 final applications. The 2010–11 total enrollment of 850 included 262 new on-campus students. Students are accepted at all levels.

APPLICATION TIMETABLE

Students may submit the Pre-Interview Information Form online at http://www.choate.edu/applying. A personal interview is required, preferably in the fall prior to the year of proposed enrollment. A final application—also submitted online—including recommendations, a transcript, and a $60 nonrefundable fee must be completed by January 10.

The Admission Office schedules appointments from 9 to 2, Monday through Friday, and 9 to noon on selected Saturdays.

The Admission Committee reviews a student's records, recommendations from teachers and the principal, test results, extracurricular interests, and interview. If all materials have been completed by January 10, applicants are notified of the decision on March 10.

ADMISSIONS CORRESPONDENCE

Raymond M. Diffley III
Director of Admission
Choate Rosemary Hall
333 Christian Street
Wallingford, Connecticut 06492-3800

Phone: 203-697-2239
Fax: 203-697-2629
E-mail: admission@choate.edu
Web site: http://www.choate.edu

CHRIST SCHOOL

Arden, North Carolina

Type: Boys' boarding and day college-preparatory school
Grades: 8–12
Enrollment: 243
Head of School: Paul M. Krieger, Headmaster

THE SCHOOL

Founded in 1900 and located just south of Asheville, North Carolina, Christ School is located on a beautiful 500-acre suburban mountain campus. The school is home to 243 students; 165 live on campus and 77 are day students. They come from nineteen states and nine other countries, including Germany, China, Canada, South Korea, Lithuania, Hong Kong, and Jamaica.

A traditional college preparatory boarding school for boys, Christ School's focus and offerings center on providing opportunities for boys to simply become a more mature expression of who they are intended to be.

Comfortable, genuine, quality minus pretense—these are ways in which the school is often described. A student sums it up in this way: "Christ School is not a coat and tie school; it's a necktie and shorts school." In short, Christ School is a place where solid academic programming can coexist alongside solid athletic and extracurricular programming—one does not come at the expense of the other.

ACADEMIC PROGRAMS

Preparing boys academically for college is Christ School's primary objective. The curriculum is designed to provide students with a firm foundation in both the academic subjects and the study skills they will need in college. The School's curriculum also stresses the knowledge and skills that will enable a student to become an informed and intelligent citizen of his community. The School has always believed that these objectives can best be fulfilled through a concentration in the traditional arts and sciences.

Small classes and individual attention are the keys to a boy's academic development. A structured program of independent and supervised study enables a student to better achieve his potential.

Requirements for graduation include the completion of 21 credits: English (4); mathematics (4); science (3); history (3); foreign language—Latin, French, or Spanish (2); fine arts (1); religious studies (0.5); computers (0.5); and electives (3). Electives include Advanced Placement courses in the arts, computer programming, English, foreign languages, history, mathematics, and science. General elective courses include choir, economics, government, history of Vietnam, journalism, marine biology, music of Western civilization, music prac-

ticum, music theory and composition, studio art I and II, and theater.

Most students carry a course load of five academic subjects, independent or supervised study, and a choice of extracurricular activities.

The average class size is 10–12 students; the student-faculty ratio is 5:1. Students are placed in classes on the basis of their achievement levels, their interests, and the requirements for graduation.

Christ School's Learning Resource Program offers academic support in English, math, and study skills within the context of a rigorous college-preparatory curriculum. The program serves those who can meet the challenges of a full academic schedule while benefiting from the program's supportive techniques.

FACULTY AND ADVISERS

The faculty consists of 43 full-time members, 23 with advanced degrees. Twenty-eight reside on campus.

Paul M. Krieger was appointed the twelfth Headmaster of Christ School in 2003. He had previously served as the school's Principal since August 2000. Before coming to Christ School, he served as Head of the Middle School at Montgomery Academy in Chester Springs, Pennsylvania. Following an extensive career in marketing, much of which was spent in the Eastern Mediterranean and the Middle East, he chose to leave the business field in 1989 for education. At the Hill School, in Pottstown, Pennsylvania, he served as Assistant Director of Development and Alumni Affairs and Assistant Director of Admissions, was Founder and Director of the Hill Sports Camp, and held the Knobloch Chair in Economics, teaching Advanced Placement courses. Mr. Krieger has a Bachelor of Arts degree from Gettysburg College and a Master of Education Leadership from Immaculata College.

The School seeks teachers who are dedicated to the academic, social, and spiritual well-being of students and who share the common interest in self-improvement that sets boys upon the path to maturity and manhood. A student's progress throughout his years at Christ School is monitored closely by the faculty. Each boy has an adviser for guidance, mentorship, and support in his academic and personal life at the School.

A strong relationship between the student and adviser is formed through formal and informal meetings and frequent gatherings for meals and recreation. In addition, each new

student is matched with an outstanding upper-classman as a Big Brother to further help the adjustment to boarding school life.

COLLEGE ADMISSION COUNSELING

In a student's sophomore, junior, and senior years, the Dean and College Counselor work with the student and his family to assist him in securing admission to the college most suited to his needs. In addition, college representatives visit the campus in the fall and winter to discuss college admission requirements and procedures with students.

Christ School graduated 38 seniors in 2008, all of whom were accepted at four-year colleges and universities. The School administered sixty Advanced Placement exams.

Graduates have been accepted at a variety of colleges and universities. Among them are the Air Force Academy, Art Institute of Boston, Brown, Clemson, Columbia, Duke, Elon, Furman, George Washington, Georgia Tech, Harvard, Macalester, Morehouse, Northeastern, Presbyterian, Rensselaer, SMU, Stanford, Wake Forest, Washington and Lee, Wheaton, William and Mary, Wofford, the University of North Carolina at Chapel Hill, and the University of the South.

STUDENT BODY AND CONDUCT

Christ School has a boarding student population of 166 boarders and 77 day students. Nineteen states and nine other countries are represented among the student body, and boys come from various religious and socioeconomic backgrounds.

The responsibility for student life and conduct at Christ School is largely in the hands of the students themselves. A student council, composed of prefects appointed by the Headmaster and members elected by the various forms, makes recommendations to the Headmaster regarding discipline and other aspects of School life. Sixth Formers (twelfth graders) guide and help supervise various activities, such as house life and the self-help work program.

ACADEMIC FACILITIES

The academic facilities are housed mainly in Wetmore Hall, which contains classrooms, four science labs, a computer lab, and a music room. The Information and Media Center houses the main reading and research room, with a state-of-the-art computer center that links an in-house service with the Internet global community. The Pingree Fine Arts Auditorium was dedicated in 1992.

BOARDING AND GENERAL FACILITIES

Christ School students reside in five houses and typically, two boys are assigned to a room. Each house is supervised by prefects and proctors under the direction of a dorm parent. All houses are fully equipped with computer networking capabilities. Students in grades 8 and 9 live separately from students in grades 10 through 12. A student center includes a game room, lounge, fireplace, snack shop, barbershop, bookstore, and forty-seat theater/TV room. Renovations of St. Joseph's chapel, which was built in 1907, were completed in 2006.

ATHLETICS

Physical development, sportsmanship, cooperation, and self-esteem are all fostered by organized athletics. The various levels in all team sports allow each boy to choose those activities that best meet his interests and competence.

On the School grounds are six hardsurfaced tennis courts, a football field, a baseball field, three soccer fields, an all-weather track, a challenging 5K cross-country course, and a 3-acre lake that is used for kayaking, canoeing, fishing, and swimming. Indoor athletics facilities are housed in a modern field house containing a basketball court and three full-sized practice courts. The remodeled Memorial Gymnasium contains a wrestling gym, three racquetball courts, a new weight room, a training room, an equipment room, four locker rooms, and offices for coaches.

The School fields interscholastic teams in football, cross-country, soccer, basketball, wrestling, swimming, lacrosse, baseball, tennis, golf, and track. In lieu of athletics, students have the option to participate in the theater program, debate, an intramural program, or the outdoor program. An outdoor education program provides instruction and trips in white-water canoeing, climbing, hiking, camping, mountain biking, and initiatives on a low-ropes course. The outdoor program is available as an alternative to team sports.

EXTRACURRICULAR OPPORTUNITIES

Daily periods are set aside for extracurricular activities. On weekends, a wide range of planned activities is available for students to explore other interests.

For students who are learning to play musical instruments, private lessons in guitar, drums, keyboards, and other instruments can be arranged. The School yearbook and literary magazine provide opportunities for creative writing, photography, and art. The student newspaper is produced using the latest computer technology and appears on the School Web site. A theater program produces three plays a year, enabling students to express their talents in acting, set designing, and stage managing. The art studio contains tools and equipment for extracurricular painting, woodworking, drawing, and ceramics.

Because of the School's proximity to various winter resorts, there are many opportunities for Christ School students to ski on designated ski days and weekends.

WEEKEND LIFE

Weekends offer a less structured environment that allows participation in sports, planned activities, and free time to pursue a wide variety of interests. Christ School has a student activities director to coordinate weekend and coeducational activities. Weekends provide opportunities for interscholastic athletics; white-water rafting; taking in a concert or a movie; trips to cultural events in Asheville, Atlanta, Charlotte, and Knoxville; attending professional and collegiate sporting events; shopping; dances; and course work.

COSTS AND FINANCIAL AID

For the 2010–11 school year, tuition and room and board are $39,030 for boarders and $19,825 for day students. In addition, a weekly allowance can be arranged through the school bookstore to cover additional expenses for each individual student. Tuition insurance and tuition payment plans are available.

Financial aid and merit scholarships are available to qualified students. For the 2010–11 school year, the School will award $1.8 million in aid and scholarships.

ADMISSIONS INFORMATION

Christ School accepts students in grades 8–11. Admission policies are based on academic ability and personal qualifications. The School seeks students who can realize their full potential in a school that emphasizes the value of structure, community, and personal responsibility. Of paramount importance is the ability of each potential student to fit into and contribute to a small, caring community.

The School requires prospective candidates to schedule a campus visit, and submit teacher recommendations, a transcript, and application essays. The SSAT is required.

Campus visits include a tour of the campus and a personal interview with the admission office, as well as time with the Headmaster.

A small number of students are accepted for the second semester, which begins in January. The School encourages families to set up a campus visit in the fall.

APPLICATION TIMETABLE

For boarding students, the nonbinding, early action application deadline is December 15, and decisions are mailed on January 1. The regular application deadline for boarders is February 15, and decisions are mailed on March 1. For day students, the application deadline is February 15, with decisions mailed on March 1. After March 1, admissions are made on a rolling basis. There are very limited openings after June 1.

ADMISSIONS CORRESPONDENCE

Morgan B. Scoville
Director of Admission
Christ School
500 Christ School Road
Arden, North Carolina 28704
Phone: 828-684-6232 Ext. 106
        800-422-3212 (toll-free)
Fax: 828-209-0003
E-mail: admission@christschool.org
Web site: http://www.christschool.org

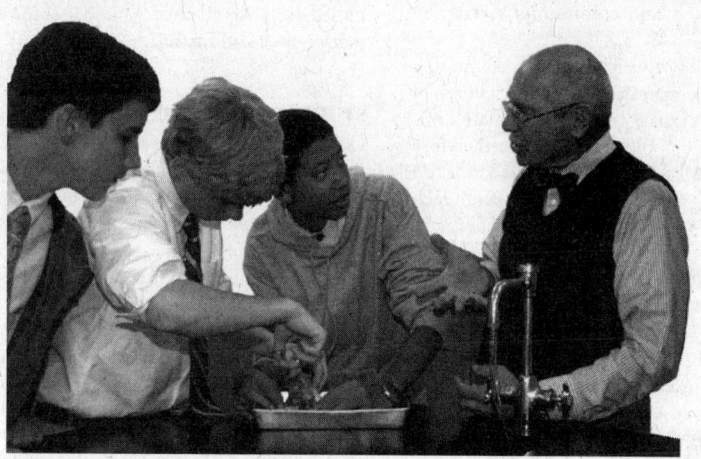

COLUMBUS SCHOOL FOR GIRLS

Columbus, Ohio

Type: All girls' college-preparatory day school
Grades: Program for Young Children (age 3–K); Lower School (1–5); Middle School (6–8); Upper School (9–12)
Enrollment: School total: 615; Preschool–Middle School: 393; Upper School: 222
Head of School: Elizabeth (Liza) Lee, Head of School

THE SCHOOL

Columbus School for Girls (CGS) was founded in 1898 by Mary Bole Scott and Florence Kelley. The School is a college-preparatory day school serving central Ohio students from age 3 through Form XII. The exceptional education offered at CSG is based upon its fundamental values of separate education for women, challenging preparation for college, supportive relationships, diversity, and excellence in all endeavors.

Columbus School for Girls is governed by a Board of Trustees and is accredited by the Independent School Association of the Central States.

The School is an active member of the National Association of Independent Schools, Ohio Association of Independent Schools, the National Coalition of Girls' Schools, Cum Laude Society, the College Board, and the National Association for College Admission Counseling.

ACADEMIC PROGRAMS

Columbus School for Girls prides itself on small class sizes. The student-faculty ratio is 9:1 with random class groupings. All study time is supervised in a classroom or library.

Grading is completed quarterly with the following grade scale: 98–100 (A+), 92–97 (A), 90–91 (A-), 88–89 (B+), 82–87 (B), 80–81 (B-), 78–79 (C+), 72–77 (C), 70–71 (C-), 68–69 (D+), 62–67 (D), 60–61 (D-), and below 60 (F).

In order to graduate, a student must complete a minimum of 21 credits including the following requirements: English, 4; mathematics, 4; history, 3; science, 3; modern and classical language, 3; fine arts, 1.5; physical education, 0.5; computer, 0.25; public speaking, 0.25; electives, 2; and community service, 60 hours.

Courses are not weighted when computing grade point average. Because of the admission standards, class ranks are not representative of a normal student population and are therefore not available. All students are required to take a minimum of five full-credit courses each semester and may take up to six full-credit courses.

In aggregate, during the 2009–10 school year, 175 Advanced Placement (AP) exams were taken by 98 Upper School students at CSG. Some of the AP courses offered include: biology; calculus AB; calculus BC; chemistry; computer science AB; English language/composition; English literature; European history; French language; German language; government and politics: United States; gov-ernment and politics: comparative; Latin: Vergil; physics C: mechanics; psychology; language; studio art: drawing, or 2-D and 3-D design.

FACULTY AND ADVISERS

Columbus School for Girls is led by Elizabeth (Liza) Lee, Head of School. She was previously head of the Hockaday School for fourteen years and interim head at Trinity Episcopal School. Mrs. Lee holds a Bachelor of Arts, magna cum laude from Mount Holyoke College and a Master of Arts from Columbia University.

The exceptional faculty at CSG includes 92 teaching faculty with 65 percent holding advanced degrees, both master's and doctoral. Faculty members also serve as coaches, club advisers, and academic mentors.

COLLEGE ADMISSION COUNSELING

Columbus School for Girls has a top-ranked college counseling program available to its Upper School students. Two full-time counselors and an assistant help guide students and parents through the college selection and admission process. One hundred percent of the young women who graduated in the class of 2010 were accepted to and are attending colleges and universities. A complete list of acceptances is available on the School Web site at http://www.columbusschoolforgirls.org.

Students in the class of 2010 scored the following mean results on their SAT tests: critical reading, 620; mathematics, 621; and writing, 638. The ACT composite score was a mean of 28. Students had the following mean results on the SAT subject tests: biology–molecular, 676; chemistry, 633; literature, 670; math I, 667; and math II, 679.

STUDENT BODY AND CONDUCT

Columbus School for Girls enrolled 615 students for the 2010–11 school year. International enrollment is 1 percent, with a growing interest. Student diversity is as follows: 76 percent white, 7 percent African-American, 6 percent Asian, 1 percent Latino, and 10 percent other/multiracial.

The Upper School student body consists of 53 students in grade 9, 59 students in grade 10, 48 students in grade 11, and 62 students in grade 12. The student body is led by Student Council officers. Each student signs the Honor Code, which is supported by the selected Honor Council members.

ACADEMIC FACILITIES

The main campus of Columbus School for Girls is located in Bexley, Ohio, a suburb of Columbus. The facility is situated on 8 acres and includes four academic divisions. The academic building includes two libraries, math and writing centers, an arena theater, three art studios, a photography lab, weight room, swimming pool, two gymnasiums, technology complexes, and six science laboratories. The Program for Young Children is in a separate academic building but joins the larger community often.

ATHLETICS

Interscholastic sports begin in grade 3. Organized team sports begin in grade 6. Fall sports include cross-country, field hockey, golf, soccer, tennis, and volleyball. Winter sports include basketball and swimming and diving. Spring sports include lacrosse and track and field.

Kirk Campus, a 70-acre athletic complex, includes a track, field hockey and lacrosse fields, two soccer fields, eight tennis courts, nature trails, and a retreat house.

EXTRACURRICULAR OPPORTUNITIES

The young women at Columbus School for Girls have many extracurricular opportunities to broaden their experiences in the arts, engineering, service, and leadership. Some of the special interest clubs and activities available include the Ambassador Society, Thespian Society, service clubs, Political Club, Tae Kwon Do Club Team, Young Adult Fiction Club, and the Jewish Cultural Club.

A play or a musical is produced each spring and fall for both the Middle School and the Upper School. Middle School students in grade 6 also have a long-standing tradition of performing *The Second Shepherds' Play* annually.

Instrumental and vocal ensembles available to students include strings starting in third grade, band starting in fifth grade, Concert Choir starting in fourth grade, and The Grace Notes starting in Upper School.

Engineering is introduced to all girls in Lower School. CGS has one of the only all-female robotics teams in the nation. Lego League is offered in Lower School, F.I.R.S.T. LEGO League robotics team in Middle School, and F.I.R.S.T. robotics team is open to all Upper School students.

DAILY LIFE

The Columbus School for Girls campus comes alive at 7:30 a.m. with the arrival of students from a 40-mile radius of Columbus. The School has a staggered start time and a staggered end time to ensure the safety of all students. The oldest students start the school day at 8 a.m. and end at 3:30 p.m. Before-care and after-hour care is available to students starting at 7:30 a.m. and ending at 6 p.m.

Students in all divisions follow a block schedule, allowing 80 minutes in each academic class every other day, totaling four periods per day, plus music and lunch.

SUMMER PROGRAMS

Summer is a busy time at Columbus School for Girls. Two summer program sessions, each with three-week schedules, are offered to students age 3 through grade 11. Programming includes classes for academic credit, enrichment, review, and recreational opportunities. One-week intensive sport camps are offered for many sports.

COSTS AND FINANCIAL AID

The annual cost of an education at Columbus School for Girls varies by grade. The Parents and Children Together class (PACT) meets one day a week at a cost of $1545. Half-day students in the preschool are charged $10,600 for tuition and lunch. The tuition range for kindergarten through grade 5 is $17,300 to $17,700. The Middle School tuition range is $18,100 to $18,600, and the Upper School range is $19,000 to $19,700.

A deposit of $1500 is required of all students. Tuition can be paid with a single payment in August, or two payments with 60 percent of tuition paid by August 1 and the remaining 40 percent by January 1. Another option is monthly payments, contracted with and paid directly to Tuition Management Systems. The CGS business office at sends all statements electronically to families.

All financial aid is need-based with the majority of grants awarded to students in grades 6–12. Currently 22 percent of the student body receives financial aid with a grant amount averaging $9565. Financial aid paperwork is due the first week of March and award letters are mailed by April 15. Families applying for financial aid are asked to pay a $500 deposit to hold their daughter's place in the class.

ADMISSIONS INFORMATION

Completed applications may be submitted anytime. To be considered for first-round decisions, the application must be received and all other steps completed by February 11, 2011. The Admission Committee reviews the applicant's file when the following have been completed and the required paperwork received: application and $50 application fee; official transcript, including standardized scores, and past and current grades; recommendation from the student's homeroom teacher or mathematics and language arts teachers mailed directly to CSG; personal parent visit with an Admission Director after September 1; classroom visit for students entering grades 2–12; and copy of birth certificate.

Admission testing/screening is required of all applicants. Students who are age 3 through grade 1 must complete small group screenings. Scheduling begins in November.

Applicants for grades 2–4 must complete an individual screening and classroom visit. Students entering grade 4 will be administered the Educational Record Bureau, Comprehensive Testing Program, fourth edition (ERB, CPT IV). Appointments begin in October.

Applicants in grades 5–12 must complete the Independent School Entrance Examination (ISEE). Test dates and registration are available at http://www.iseetest.org. Scheduling begins in October.

Ninety-two new students were enrolled for the 2010–11 year with a 60 percent acceptance rate. The majority of new students are accepted in transition years going into sixth and ninth grades.

APPLICATION TIMETABLE

Inquiries are welcome anytime throughout the year. Admission open house dates are November 7 and January 13 for prospective students and their families. Student visitations are scheduled one day a month or on an individual basis as needed.

To be considered for admission in the first round of decisions for the 2011–12 school year, all paperwork, a $50 application fee, assessments, and required visits must be completed by February 11, 2011. After this date, applicants will be considered on a rolling basis, depending on available openings. Decision letters will be mailed March 1 and parents have ten days to return a signed contract with deposit. The Admission Committee takes into consideration whether the applicant has family members who are currently enrolled or who have attended CGS in the past.

ADMISSIONS CORRESPONDENCE

Betsy Gugle, Director of Admission and
    Financial Aid
Columbus School for Girls
56 South Columbia Avenue
Columbus, Ohio 43209

Phone: 614-252-0781 Ext. 104
Fax: 614-252-0571
E-mail: bgugle@columbusschoolforgirls.org
Web site: http://www.columbusschoolforgirls.org

CONVENT OF THE SACRED HEART

Greenwich, Connecticut

Type: Independent, Catholic day school for girls
Grades: P–12: Lower School, Preschool–4; Middle School, 5–8; Upper School, 9–12
Enrollment: School total: 777; Upper School: 290
Head of School: Pamela Juan Hayes, Head of School

THE SCHOOL

Convent of the Sacred Heart is situated on a beautiful 110-acre wooded campus in Greenwich, Connecticut. Greenwich is a suburban town located about 30 miles from New York City and 40 minutes from New Haven. An independent Catholic school for girls in preschool through grade 12, Sacred Heart was first established in New York City in 1848 and moved to Greenwich in 1945. Convent of the Sacred Heart is one of twenty-one Sacred Heart schools in the United States and part of an international network of schools that includes more than 200 schools in twenty-eight countries around the world.

A Sacred Heart education provides a strong academic foundation appropriate to each student's individual talents and abilities within an environment that fosters the development of her spiritual life and a strong sense of personal values. True to its international heritage, the school welcomes students and faculty members of diverse backgrounds and faiths, so that each student will grow in her understanding of different cultures and peoples. Graduates are prepared to become leaders with broad intellectual and spiritual horizons.

Convent of the Sacred Heart is a nonprofit institution governed by a 26-member Board of Trustees, which is responsible to the Society of the Sacred Heart for the implementation of the society's educational philosophy. Parents, religious, alumnae, and educators serve on the board. Sacred Heart benefits from the active involvement and strong support of its parent and alumnae organizations.

The school is accredited by the New England Association of Schools and Colleges and approved by the Connecticut State Board of Education. It is a member of the National Association of Independent Schools, the Connecticut Association of Independent Schools, the National Coalition of Girls' Schools, and the Network of Sacred Heart Schools in the United States.

ACADEMIC PROGRAMS

Sacred Heart is committed to the development of each student's intellectual, physical, spiritual, and emotional well-being. The academic program in the Upper School provides a rigorous educational foundation that enables students to become independent and creative thinkers. Students are active participants in the learning process, expanding their experience through exploration, inquiry, and discovery. Students analyze, critique, evaluate, and make important connections with the concepts they learn.

Sacred Heart's academic program is comprehensive, rigorous, and flexible. Serious study is emphasized, and the development of essential academic skills necessary for success in college and life is encouraged. College-preparatory, honors, and advanced-placement courses are offered throughout the core curriculum, which includes mathematics, science, English, history and social sciences, world languages, theology, and the arts. A student is afforded opportunities for exploration of her own talents and interests through special projects, study abroad, summer programs, and independent study. Emphasizing the connection between the disciplines is critical to learning at Sacred Heart. Faculty

collaboration helps students in discovering and understanding the relevance of all subject areas and the importance of their learning in relationship to society and their daily lives.

A student's schedule for the three-term academic year is planned individually. The student plans her course of study with the support of her academic adviser and the Academic Dean. Course levels are chosen according to academic readiness, ability, and talent in an academic area. Each student typically takes between 6 and 8 credits per school year in a combination of required courses and electives.

Graduation requirements are based on the expectations of highly selective colleges and universities; all of Sacred Heart's graduates choose to attend college. To receive a diploma, students must complete a minimum of 25 credits, although all students complete more than this minimum number. The requirements include 4 credits of English, 4 credits in theology, 3 credits in history, 3 credits in mathematics, 3 credits in a world language, 3 credits in science, and 2 elective credits, at least 1 of which must be in the arts. Students must also complete 2 years of physical education and a 2-year health education requirement.

All academic disciplines employ the computer as a tool for writing, research, analysis, and presentation, including the use of multimedia presentations, spreadsheets and databases for organization and analysis, and desktop publishing. The program also addresses the possibilities and responsibilities associated with the use of technology in today's society. All students in grades 7–12 use laptop computers in the classroom and anywhere else they study or work.

FACULTY AND ADVISERS

High expectations and positive role models are important to the success of girls and young women. A student-faculty ratio of 7:1 and an average class size of approximately 13 students ensure the teachers know every student. Assured of the faculty's support, students are motivated to take risks through which confidence and self-discipline develop. Individual teaching styles are complemented by a common commitment to the goals and criteria of a Sacred Heart education.

Convent of the Sacred Heart has 112 faculty members, with 40 full-time and 9 part-time members teaching in the Upper School. Each serves as a personal and academic adviser to about 8 advisees. Many serve as club advisers and coaches as well. Students meet with their advisers regularly during a special advisory period. They also meet informally with faculty members at daily assemblies and weekly chapel services.

Teachers regularly participate in workshops, summer study, curriculum development, travel, and research. Approximately 82 percent of the faculty members hold advanced degrees, including 9 who have doctoral degrees. The full-time faculty has an average of sixteen years of teaching experience.

COLLEGE ADMISSION COUNSELING

The College Guidance Department at Sacred Heart believes in the importance of an individualized

college process and works hard to find the best match possible for each student. An informational parent meeting in the sophomore year helps to set this tone. The Directors of College Guidance also assist sophomores with course selection, review PSAT scores, and help their student advisees plan schedules for appropriate SAT Subject Tests.

In junior year, students and parents meet with the Directors of College Guidance to identify goals and discuss expectations about college plans. The college search process is explained at an evening winter program, which features college representatives and the college counselors. Juniors also attend guidance classes that explore issues surrounding the college selection process, including identifying prospective colleges, the campus visit and interview, the college essay, and financial aid and scholarships. Students have access to a variety of college search resources, including guidebooks, Internet search engines, and an internal software program. Students are also encouraged to take advantage of opportunities to meet with the many college representatives who visit Sacred Heart in the fall.

During the senior year, each student and her parents examine the more specific details of the application process: deadlines, the submission of standardized test scores, the college essay, resumes, and financial aid. In the school's 162-year history, Sacred Heart graduates have attended many of the nation's finest colleges and universities. Recent graduates are currently attending schools such as Boston College, Brown, Georgetown, Harvard, Holy Cross, Johns Hopkins, Notre Dame, Stanford, Wellesley, Yale, and the University of Pennsylvania.

STUDENT BODY AND CONDUCT

There are 777 students enrolled in preschool through grade 12, with 290 students enrolled in the Upper School. Students join the high school from more than sixty-seven different communities, coming from public, private, and parochial schools in Connecticut and New York State. The student body includes a diversity of ethnic, socioeconomic, and religious backgrounds that allows for a dynamic community with a wide range of interests, talents, and passions.

School policies and practices foster the acceptance of responsibility, self-discipline, respect for the self and others, and caring for the school and wider community. The student government, student/faculty disciplinary board, and the administration work together to establish and enforce policies and minimal rules that govern the school community.

ACADEMIC FACILITIES

Overlooking Long Island Sound, the campus consists of modern classrooms, science laboratories, an observatory, playgrounds, synthetic-turf fields, a media center, a theater, a chapel, a broadcast journalism studio, a gymnasium, a fitness room, a swimming pool, and a dance studio.

The media center holds a collection of 22,000 books, CD-ROM resources, online databases and encyclopedias, videos, and Internet access.

A 29,000-square-foot science center has state-of-the-art science laboratories for all three divisions, including the Upper School's Science Research

Program, in addition to space for the Upper School art studio, special space for drama and music, classrooms, and offices. On campus, there is a freestanding state-of-the-art observatory, which offers students interested in astronomy the opportunity for viewings of the night sky through a computerized, 16-inch telescope with 800x magnification. In addition, outside the observatory there is a pad with ten 8-inch telescopes.

The broadcast journalism studio consists of control, editing, and recording rooms. Students learn how to operate camera, audio, lighting, and editing equipment to tell their stories. This state-of-the-art space provides students with the opportunity to practice media literacy in a meaningful, hands-on fashion.

Students studying art, environmental science, and ecology make frequent use of the school's acres of woods, trails, fields, and a working vegetable garden. The campus is further enlivened by traditions and events unique to Convent of the Sacred Heart.

ATHLETICS
The energy of the Sacred Heart community extends beyond the walls of the school buildings. The indoor competition swimming pool, tennis courts, and the synthetic and grass playing fields outside are showcases for girls accepting challenges, testing limits, and cooperating with teammates. Sacred Heart provides a full schedule of varsity, junior varsity, and thirds sports, including basketball, crew, cross-country, field hockey, golf, lacrosse, soccer, softball, squash, swimming and diving, tennis, and volleyball. The teams are supported with the very best facilities and equipment, including two synthetic-turf fields. Convent of the Sacred Heart is a member of the twelve-school Fairchester League and the New England Preparatory School Athletic Council (NEPSAC). A certified athletic trainer services both the Middle and Upper School student-athletes.

The physical education program is designed to develop skills for a healthy and active life. Opportunities are provided for competition, excellence, and fun in a variety of activities for all students.

EXTRACURRICULAR OPPORTUNITIES
A wide range of clubs, committees, and activities provide opportunities for students to contribute to the school community, pursue their interests, and develop leadership and team skills. Students produce major theatrical productions, govern the student body through extensive collaboration with student-elected representatives, and publish their own language newspapers, school newspaper, and literary magazine. Students win awards through their participation in the Forensics/Speech and Debate Club and the Model United Nations Club. Sacred Heart students participate in local, regional, and national competitions with their peers from other schools. These programs are designed to promote self-expression, intellectual challenge, and individual leadership opportunities.

Music, dramatic readings, and gallery art shows are an important part of the Upper School experience. Diverse curricular offerings in visual arts, theater, music, and dance provide opportunities for interdisciplinary study, and core academic classes often collaborate on thematic projects with the arts departments.

Recognizing that one's own creative development emerges from exposure to the creativity of others, Sacred Heart emphasizes a balance between performance and appreciation. Guest artists, performers, and lecturers regularly visit the school. Proximity to New York City creates opportunities to investigate unlimited cultural resources, while student exhibitions and performances showcase the talents cultivated in the school's classes and studios.

The Community Service Program is also an integral part of the Upper School experience at Sacred Heart. Using age-appropriate tools, students study a wide range of issues, including racism, poverty, housing, and education. Analysis of social injustices helps the students recognize that they can use their talents to be agents of change in the world. The Community Service Program explores domestic and global issues and includes guest speakers, individual yearly projects, service trips, and retreats. While service is required for Upper School students, most exceed the graduation requirement of 100 hours with extra volunteer work. The Barat Foundation is a student-run philanthropic organization that awards grants to community nonprofits and teaches financial literacy to students.

The Sacred Heart Exchange Program allows students to experience different cultures in the United States and around the world. Upper School students may complete an academic exchange of two to ten weeks at another Sacred Heart school. Convent of the Sacred Heart also welcomes exchange students to its campus. Recently, Sacred Heart students have studied in California, Chicago, Houston, Miami, New Orleans, and Seattle and abroad in England, France, Spain, Australia, Chile, Mexico, and Nova Scotia. Upon graduating, students are given an international Sacred Heart Passport listing the Sacred Heart schools throughout the world where they are always welcome.

DAILY LIFE
The first academic period begins at 8:25 a.m. The school day includes an advisory period, assembly periods, and time for many activities and club meetings. The day concludes at 3:25 p.m. Sports and a variety of activities occur after school. Students may buy or bring their lunch. A hot lunch is provided for a yearly fee.

SUMMER PROGRAMS
Sacred Heart hosts an annual Summer Outreach Program for 250 boys and girls in grades 2 through 9 from low-income families. The academic program is augmented with extracurricular activities, including team sports, swimming lessons, and hands-on experience with a vegetable garden. The

Summer Science Academy is for girls who show interest and promise in science and math entering grades 6 through 9 from low-income families. The five-week program includes traditional classroom experiences as well as guided scientific activities, independent investigations, and field trips.

As part of the Summer Outreach, the Summer Humanities Academy, which began in 2002, accepts girls entering grades 7 and 8 and offers a curriculum focused on writing, literature, and art. Students refined their writing skills, enhanced their reading and analytical skills, and had hands-on experiences that allowed them to understand the distinction between and the union of art and craft. Students used computers to create a literary magazine. Artists-in-residence offered workshops in writing, dance, and music. In addition, students received swimming instruction and participated in the farm program.

COSTS AND FINANCIAL AID
An education at Sacred Heart is an investment that provides many important and valuable opportunities. Tuition for 2010–11 is $32,200 for grades 9–12. The Financial Aid Committee is committed to helping families find ways to make an education at Convent of the Sacred Heart affordable. The Financial Aid Committee works with families to determine personalized need-based assistance and financial planning. Applying for financial aid has no bearing on admission to Convent of the Sacred Heart.

ADMISSIONS INFORMATION
Sacred Heart admits students without regard to race, religion, nationality, or ethnic origin. Applicants are considered on the basis of their school records, teacher recommendations, admission test scores, class visit, and personal interview. Entrance exams are administered at the school in November and January and at other local independent schools throughout the fall.

Families are encouraged to attend the Saturday Open House event (on November 6, 2010) or Thursday morning Tour Day programs (October, November, December, and January). On October 28, 2010, Sacred Heart also hosts an evening Upper School Open House for students interested in grades 9–12. Individual tours and interviews are also available.

APPLICATION TIMETABLE
All application materials and visits must be completed by February 1. Decision letters are mailed by March 1. Applications for financial aid with supporting documentation are due by February 15.

ADMISSIONS CORRESPONDENCE
Catherine Machir, Director of Admission and
    Financial Aid
Convent of the Sacred Heart
1177 King Street
Greenwich, Connecticut 06831
Phone: 203-532-3534
Fax: 203-532-3301
E-mail: admission@cshgreenwich.org
Web site: http://www.cshgreenwich.org

CRANBROOK SCHOOLS

Bloomfield Hills, Michigan

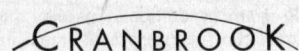

Type: Coeducational day and boarding college-preparatory school
Grades: PK–12: Brookside Lower School, Prekindergarten–5; Cranbrook Kingswood Middle School, 6–8; Cranbrook Kingswood Upper School, 9–12
Enrollment: School total: 1,655; Upper School: 797; Middle School: 343; Lower School: 515
Head of School: Arlyce M. Seibert, Director of Schools

THE SCHOOL

First established in 1922, Cranbrook Schools seek to prepare young men and women from diverse backgrounds to develop intellectually, morally, and physically; to move into higher education with competence and confidence; and to appreciate the arts. The Schools also strive to instill in their students a strong sense of social responsibility and the ability to contribute in an increasingly complex world.

Its founders, George and Ellen Scripps Booth, believed that "a life without beauty is only half lived." Critics have called the 315-acre Cranbrook campus "a masterpiece of American architecture." The buildings, gardens, and fountains were designed by Finnish architect, Eliel Saarinen, and offer students an exquisite environment in which to live and learn.

The Schools are a division of Cranbrook Educational Community, which also includes Cranbrook Institute of Science (a natural history and science museum serving Michigan and the Great Lakes region) and Cranbrook Academy of Art, known worldwide for its prestigious graduate programs in fine arts and architecture as well as its Art Museum. The entire complex has been designated a National Historic Landmark.

Cranbrook offers a comprehensive college-preparatory education that commences with Brookside (PK–5), continues in Cranbrook Kingswood Middle School (6–8, separate programs for boys and girls), and culminates in the opportunity and possibility that is provided by graduation from Cranbrook Kingswood Upper School (day and boarding, 9–12).

Bloomfield Hills is a residential suburb (population 3,985) approximately 25 minutes northwest of Detroit and 5 minutes from Birmingham.

A nonprofit corporation, Cranbrook is directed by a 21-member, self-perpetuating Board of Trustees, which meets four times a year. The corporation has a $215 million endowment.

Cranbrook Kingswood is accredited by the Independent Schools Association of the Central States. It is a member of the National Association of Independent Schools.

ACADEMIC PROGRAMS

The school year, from September to early June, is divided into semesters. Classes, which enroll an average of 16 students each, meet five days a week. Eight academic periods are scheduled daily. All boarding students participate in supervised evening study hours from Sunday through Thursday. Grades are sent to parents quarterly, written evaluations are given semiannually, and progress reports for new students are issued in October.

Promotion from one class level to another is contingent upon faculty recommendations and is necessary for graduation. Each student is expected to take five academic classes each semester, along with a class chosen from the fine arts, performing arts, or computer departments. In order to graduate,

students must complete the following minimum unit requirements: English, 4; mathematics, 4; foreign language, 2; social science/history, 2½; science, 3; religion/philosophy, 1; and performing or fine arts, 1. (One unit is the equivalent of a full-year course.)

In addition to sixty-eight full-year courses, Cranbrook Kingswood Upper School offers seventy-six semester courses, including anatomy, astronomy, Eastern religious traditions, ethics, genetics, geology, heroes in British literature and film, human geography, principles of macroeconomics, principles of psychology, and Russia and Eastern Europe. An extensive fine and performing arts program includes basic design, drawing, painting, sculpture, metalsmithing, ceramics, weaving, photography, dance, concert band, symphony orchestra, madrigals, jazz band, mastersingers, concert choir, acting, speech, and stagecraft.

Sixteen Advanced Placement (AP) courses are available in English, foreign languages, mathematics, and social sciences. Honors courses and directed-study programs are also offered for qualified students. ESL is offered for international students who demonstrate a strong academic record and a high intermediate level of English proficiency.

The Tennessee Wilderness Expedition (modeled on Outward Bound) is available to tenth graders each March. Seniors can participate in Senior May (off-campus internships) during the spring term.

Students are graded on an A–E scale, although some elective courses are pass/fail. Students must maintain a minimum C- average to avoid academic probation. Classes are generally grouped by ability within grade level. The student-teacher ratio is 8:1.

FACULTY AND ADVISERS

More than 70 percent of the 95 full-time Cranbrook Kingswood Upper School faculty members reside on campus; 51 are men and 44 are women; 85 percent of the Upper School faculty members hold master's degrees or Ph.D.'s in the subject area that they teach. The average tenure of a Cranbrook Schools teacher is more than fourteen years.

In selecting its faculty, Cranbrook Kingswood seeks men and women with educational and intellectual curiosity. Faculty members are encouraged to explore special interests and talents that extend beyond their academic discipline. They are continually involved in professional advancement programs—course work, conferences, and workshops, the cost of which Cranbrook Kingswood largely underwrites. All faculty members are involved in some type of extracurricular activity, and each is an adviser to an average of 8 students, helping them in all aspects of school life from course selection to peer relationships.

Arlyce M. Seibert was appointed Vice President of Cranbrook Educational Community and the Director of Schools in 1996. Mrs. Seibert joined the

Upper School in 1970 and has served in many capacities in her thirty-nine years with the Schools.

COLLEGE ADMISSION COUNSELING

Four full-time counselors help students select colleges, and representatives from more than 140 colleges visit Cranbrook Kingswood each year. The selection process begins in the junior year, involving both students and parents.

Among Cranbrook Kingswood's 2010 graduates, the mean SAT scores were 633 critical reading, 665 math, and 641 writing. A total of 194 graduates are attending such colleges and universities as Amherst, Brown, Carnegie Mellon, Columbia, Cornell, Dartmouth, Duke, Georgetown, Harvard, Johns Hopkins, MIT, Oberlin, Princeton, Williams, Yale, and the Universities of Chicago, Michigan, and Pennsylvania.

STUDENT BODY AND CONDUCT

The 2010–11 Upper School was composed of 149 boarding boys, 261 day boys, 102 boarding girls, and 285 day girls, distributed as follows: 186 in the ninth grade, 201 in tenth, 192 in eleventh, and 218 in twelfth. Twenty-four states and twenty countries were represented. Twenty-eight percent of students identified themselves as members of minority groups, and international students made up 11 percent of the student body.

Cranbrook Kingswood's disciplinary system is designed to be educative, not punitive. Honest conduct, regular attendance, punctual completion of assignments, and thoughtful adherence to school policies and rules are the minimum commitments expected of students. A Discipline Committee, consisting of faculty members, the deans, and elected students, assumes responsibility in matters of conduct. Major offenses may result in dismissal.

Students participate in several committees that help to shape life at Cranbrook Schools, such as the Conduct Review Board, the Dormitory Council, the Athletic Committee, the Diversity Committee, the Student Leadership Task Force, and the President's Council.

ACADEMIC FACILITIES

Students have the advantage of full access to two educational campuses. Kingswood's world-famous, Saarinen-designed building is a single continuous unit that includes a library with 23,500 volumes, a gymnasium, and six separate art studios. A girls' middle school is under construction and is scheduled to open in 2011.

Cranbrook's classrooms are located around a quadrangle in Lindquist Hall (1927) and Hoey Hall (1927). Other facilities that compose the quadrangle complex are a library with more than 21,500 volumes, a dining hall, boys' dormitories, and a student center. A recently renovated performing arts center and the Gordon Science Center are located adjacent to the quadrangle.

Students take shuttle buses from one campus to another according to their class schedules. Students also have access to the museums and other resources at the Cranbrook Institute of Science and the Cranbrook Art Museum.

BOARDING AND GENERAL FACILITIES

Cranbrook Kingswood maintains single-sex boarding facilities. The campus buildings are linked by a fiber-optic network and provide telephone, computer, and video access in each dormitory room, classroom, lab, and faculty and student work area. The campus is equipped with more than ninety SmartBoards.

The Kingswood dormitory for girls, adjacent to Kingswood Lake, houses 102 girls. Most live in suites that contain two single or double bedrooms with adjoining bath. The dormitory has two lounges with televisions, stereo equipment, and a piano. Two kitchenettes and laundry facilities are available, in addition to a four-lane bowling alley.

At the Cranbrook campus, there are single rooms for 158 boys, who are divided according to their grade. The student activity center has a dance floor, a snack bar, a performance space, recently renovated kitchen, and a small theater for videotape recording and viewing.

Many Cranbrook Kingswood faculty members live in the dormitories with their families. Others live in faculty homes clustered throughout the grounds. Resident Advisers (senior students) live on each floor and act as confidants and helpmates to their fellow boarders.

ATHLETICS

Cranbrook Kingswood Upper School provides the opportunity for participation in eighteen interscholastic sports, including baseball, basketball, cross-country, crew, fencing, field hockey, football, golf, ice hockey, lacrosse, skiing, soccer, softball, swimming, tennis, track, volleyball, and wrestling. Recent state championships include boys' and girls' tennis, girls' golf, boys' lacrosse, and boys' and girls' hockey. Among the intramural and noncompetitive athletic activities are martial arts, modern dance, rock climbing, strength and fitness, and walking for fitness.

Athletics facilities include a football stadium, a track, fifteen outdoor tennis courts, a dance studio, an indoor ice arena, three gymnasiums, and numerous playing fields. The School's award-winning natatorium was designed by a Cranbrook graduate.

EXTRACURRICULAR OPPORTUNITIES

Cranbrook Kingswood offers thirty-nine student organizations, including Model UN, forensics, ethnic clubs, dramatics, community service, and publications including a newspaper and an arts and literary publication. Other clubs meet to discuss topics as varied as politics and racial diversity.

The cultural and educational events on campus include the exhibitions, lectures, films, and concerts offered through the science and art museums, highlighted by regular planetarium and laser shows, a world-class collection of modern American and European paintings, and traveling exhibits. The spacious grounds, wooded areas, lakes and indoor and outdoor theaters provide a serene setting for cross-country skiing, biking, jogging, swimming, and canoeing, as well as the Cranbrook Music Festival, the American Artists Series, the Cranbrook Kingswood Film Program, the Symposium Series, and the Cranbrook Retreat for Writers and Artists.

DAILY LIFE

The school day is divided into eight 45-minute classes between 8 a.m. and 3:20 p.m., including lunch, Monday through Friday. After-school activities such as class meetings, extra-help sessions, and athletics follow. Dinner for boarders begins at 5:30 weekdays, followed by a study period from 8 to 10 p.m.

WEEKEND LIFE

Boarding students have an unusual opportunity to take part in urban and rural activities on the weekends. Although students may go home some weekends with parental permission, there are weekends during the year when all boarding students must stay on the campus for special activities. Shuttle buses drive students to nearby Birmingham for shopping and entertainment, and groups can go to places such as Detroit and Ann Arbor for professional sporting events and cultural activities. There are frequent weekend camping, hiking, rock climbing, and skiing trips during the year. On-campus activities include dances, concerts, exhibits, lectures, sporting events, and recent movies at the student center.

SUMMER PROGRAMS

The Cranbrook Educational Community conducts several summer programs for day and boarding students and the community at large. These include day camps, a theater school, a soccer clinic, a filmmaking seminar, a compensatory educational program for youngsters from low-income families, a jazz ensemble, and ice hockey, lacrosse, and tennis camps.

COSTS AND FINANCIAL AID

The 2010–11 fees are $36,450 for boarding students and $26,450 for day students. Other expenses are for books ($500) and a room deposit fee ($200). A tuition-payment plan, health insurance plan, and tuition insurance are offered.

In 2010–11, 30 percent of the Upper School students received some amount of tuition aid, some as much as 50 percent of day or boarding tuition. Aid is based on financial need, following procedures established by the School and Student Service for Financial Aid.

ADMISSIONS INFORMATION

Cranbrook admits day students in preschool through grade 12 and boarding students in grades 9 through 12. The Schools accept students without regard to race, religion, national origin, sex, or handicap. Admission is based on recommendations, past performance, a personal interview, a writing sample, and results of the SSAT or other standardized examinations. Recommended grades for entrance are all A's or A's and B's.

APPLICATION TIMETABLE

An initial inquiry is welcome at any time. Campus tours and interviews are arranged on weekdays through the admissions office. Notification of acceptance begins in February. The application fee is $50.

ADMISSIONS CORRESPONDENCE

Drew Miller
Dean of Admission and Financial Aid
Cranbrook Schools
39221 Woodward Avenue
P.O. Box 801
Bloomfield Hills, Michigan 48303-0801

Phone: 248-645-3610
Fax: 248-645-3025
E-mail: admission@cranbrook.edu
Web site: http://www.schools.cranbrook.edu

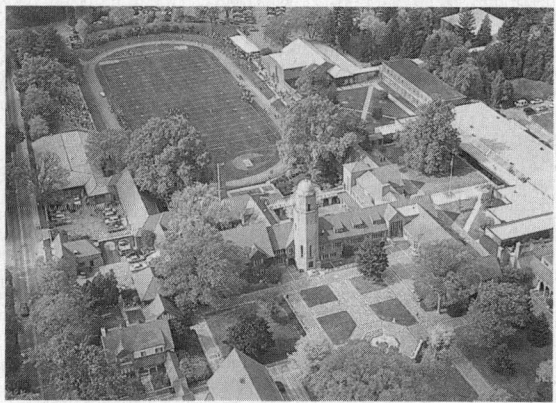

CUSHING ACADEMY

Ashburnham, Massachusetts

Type: Coeducational boarding and day college-preparatory school
Grades: 9–12, postgraduate year
Enrollment: 445
Head of School: Dr. James Tracy, Ph.D., M.B.A.

THE SCHOOL

Cushing Academy, founded in 1865, opened as a coeducational boarding school with funds provided by Thomas Parkman Cushing. Since its founding, Cushing Academy has prepared boys and girls in grades 9 through 12 and postgraduate to be contributing members of colleges and universities and of the modern world. Students live and learn with students from over thirty countries and twenty-eight states in a quiet, safe, and supportive community 1 hour west of Boston. At Cushing Academy, students are prepared for the technological, political, artistic, environmental, scientific, cultural, and ethical issues already present in their lives—the big questions of this new century that frame their academics, athletics, activities, and life on campus. Cushing builds students' global awareness, helps them to fulfill their aspirations, and enables them to learn the skills they will need to succeed throughout their lives.

Cushing's 162-acre campus lies in the small, rural town of Ashburnham in north-central Massachusetts, 55 miles west of Boston and 10 miles south of the New Hampshire border. Proximity to Boston permits extensive use of the city's cultural, entertainment, and commercial resources.

The Academy is governed by an 18-member Board of Trustees, 6 of whom are alumni. The operating budget for 2010–11 is $24 million, and the endowment is estimated at $22.6 million. Total voluntary support received in 2009–10 exceeded $5 million.

Cushing is accredited by the New England Association of Schools and Colleges. The Academy is a member of the National Association of Independent Schools, the Association of Independent Schools in New England, the Secondary School Admission Test Board, and the Cum Laude Society.

ACADEMIC PROGRAMS

The hub of Cushing's academic program is the Cushing Institute for 21st Century Leadership, founded in 2007. Designed to help high-school students understand the world of today and tomorrow at their academic level, the Institute brings current issues into every classroom, drives curriculum, facilitates global travel experiences, and brings a range of speakers to campus—including the twice-yearly Oxford-Cushing Panel Discussions—in order to deliver the world to Cushing students. The Institute also provides leadership and entrepreneurial opportunities on campus and coordinates internships and the Cushing Scholars, an enrichment program for students selected on the basis of intellectual, athletic, and artistic promise, as well as leadership potential.

The Academy offers more than 150 full-year courses and seminars, including ten laboratory courses and fifteen advanced-level courses. Advanced independent study programs may be arranged through the Dean of Academics.

Typically, Cushing Academy students carry five major courses every trimester, in addition to a required elective in the visual or performing arts. To satisfy Cushing's diploma requirements, students must earn a minimum of 18 credits distributed as follows: English, 4; mathematics, 4; foreign language, 2; history and social science, 2; science, 2; and fine arts, ⅓ per year at Cushing. The remaining requirements may be filled by choosing from numerous electives, including ethics, creative writing, ecology, marine biology, economics, comparative religions, global diplomacy, and leadership.

All teachers are available in their classrooms during a daily extra-help period. Informal tutoring may also take place after dinner or during free time.

The Academy offers a structured academic support program staffed by 6 educational specialists who work with students on a variety of strategies to assist them with their studies. Students who enroll in the academic support program, either through the admissions process or who are identified as needing additional support after they arrive at Cushing, take one or more courses with the academic support specialists, concurrent with their other classes, for an additional fee. With students from thirty countries, Cushing also has a thriving international community. Students entering Cushing in need of English as a second language enroll in the ESL program for one or more years and then transition into the standard academic offerings.

The academic year is divided into three terms of twelve, ten, and nine weeks in length. Cumulative final exams are given at the end of fall and spring terms in all academic courses. Evaluations are sent home six times each year. Letters warning of academic difficulty are written at the discretion of the Academic Dean.

Cushing uses a letter grading system that follows a 4.0 scale; 1.2 is passing, 3.3–3.6 is honors, and 3.7 and above is high honors. Class placement is determined by demonstrated ability and past performance in each subject area. The average class size is 12 students. The student-teacher ratio is approximately 8:1. On weeknights from 8 to 10 p.m., students work quietly in their rooms during supervised study hall.

FACULTY AND ADVISERS

In 2010–11, the faculty and administration consisted of 92 full-time teachers and administrators—45 women and 47 men, of whom 52 had master's degrees, and 7 had earned their Ph.D.'s. Seventy percent of faculty members live on campus, and all faculty members are involved in the daily life of students beyond the classroom experience. Each teacher is responsible for the academic, social, extracurricular, and dorm life for 5 to 7 student advisees.

The Headmaster, Dr. James Tracy, joined the Cushing community in 2006. He received an M.A. from the University of Massachusetts, a Ph.D. from Stanford University, and an M.B.A. from Boston University.

COLLEGE ADMISSION COUNSELING

Staffed by 5 experienced professionals, the Cushing Academy College Counseling Office is a resource available to all students and parents. The counseling process begins when a student enters the school, at which time a comprehensive College Counseling Guide is presented to each student and his or her parents. Cushing believes in engaging the students at all levels and that the college advising process should focus on each student's particular needs, aspirations, and abilities. The goal is to provide students and parents with information that will help all to feel knowledgeable, confident, and organized as they move through this exciting time.

Group meetings are held regularly for each of the various grade levels on such topics as summer activities, college research, campus visits, athletic recruitment, interviews, financial aid, applications, and standardized tests. Workshops for parents are presented during family weekends in the fall and spring. During the winter and spring trimesters, juniors meet individually with a member of the college counseling staff to establish a prospective list of colleges. The following fall, a new round of group meetings and individual interviews take place to aid the seniors in completing their applications to universities of responsible choice.

Standardized tests, including the SAT and the ACT, are administered on-site at Cushing throughout the year, beginning with the PSAT in October. Individual tutoring and group test preparation is available for an additional fee.

The College Counseling Office utilizes Naviance, a Web-based counseling tool and database that aids the students and the office in the research process as well as in the organization and management of the application process. In addition, a library of college counseling books, course catalogs, viewbooks, DVDs, and other college materials are available in the College Counseling Office.

Recent college enrollments include Boston College, Boston University, Bowdoin, Brown, Cornell, College of the Holy Cross, Dartmouth, George Washington, Hofstra, Parsons School of Design, Purdue, Syracuse, University of Virginia, Vanderbilt, and Wellesley. Admissions representatives from over eighty colleges and universities visit the Cushing Academy campus each fall to meet with the students and college counseling staff.

STUDENT BODY AND CONDUCT

The 2010–11 student body consists of 41 boys and 24 girls in the freshman class; 67 boys and 40 girls in the sophomore class; 71 boys and 69 girls in the junior class; 70 boys and 40 girls in the senior class; and 20 boys and 3 girls in the postgraduate class.

Of these 445 students, 374 were boarders. Students were predominantly from Massachusetts (136) and other parts of New England (59), as well as from New Jersey (16), New York (11), Florida (11), and Georgia (7), and Texas (7). Twenty-eight states and Puerto Rico, as well as thirty countries, ranging from Indonesia to Germany, were represented. Of the total enrollment, 8 percent were African American.

Students play an active role in school governance through their participation in the school's thriving student organizations, such as student proctors, class officers, student-faculty senate, and tour guides, and through participation in the school's discipline committee process. Through these and other organizations, students influence decision making at the school and serve as leaders for the community.

ACADEMIC FACILITIES

At the center of Cushing's campus is the Main Building, which houses classrooms, offices, and Cowell Chapel where members of the community gather for all-school meetings and performing arts productions. Also in the Main Building is the Fisher-Watkins Library, which was transformed in 2009 to a primarily digital learning center. In addition to its collection of e-readers and online data sources, the library features collaborative instruction space, large-screen monitors for viewing interactive data and news feeds from around the world, quiet study carrels, and a cyber café. The Joseph R. Curry Academic Center houses mathematics, the sciences, and the performing arts. This state-of-the-art facility of more than 56,000 square feet includes instructional laboratories, studios, student project rooms, and seminar space. The English Building houses seven newly renovated classrooms. The Emily Fisher Landau Center for Visual Arts has both studio and gallery space for students to create and display professional-quality work in a variety of media, including fused and stained glass, silver, ceramics, photography, painting, and sculpture. Cushing Academy students have been invited to display their works in galleries in Santa Fe, New York, and Oxford University.

The Cushing Network, a campuswide wireless computer network, may be accessed throughout the school, including all classrooms and dormitory rooms. CushNet and MyCushing, the school's intranet systems, allow students to send e-mail, join bulletin-board discussions for classes, communicate with teachers and friends, follow campus happenings, monitor homework and submit assignments. Parents and guardians of Cushing students may log in to a separate portal where they may access their students' course syllabi, school news items, calendars, and events. SmartBoard technology is available in all classrooms.

BOARDING AND GENERAL FACILITIES
The Academy houses more than 350 students in seven dormitories and six student-faculty houses that vary in capacity from 3 to 81 students each. Almost all rooms are doubles, and returning students select rooms through a room-draw system that favors seniority. New students are assigned rooms by the Co-Directors of Admission and the Student Life Office. The ratio of faculty to students in the dormitories is generally 1:12.

Cushing's dining commons houses a student center on the lower level, which includes a recreational area, snack bar, bookstore, and post office. Formal family-style dinners are served once a month.

ATHLETICS
In the belief that physical fitness and agility enrich both the individual and the community, Cushing's renowned athletic program is designed to involve everyone in physical endeavors. There are boys' interscholastic teams in baseball, basketball, cross-country, football, golf, ice hockey, lacrosse, skiing, soccer, tennis, and track; girls compete in basketball, cross-country, field hockey, ice hockey, lacrosse, skiing, soccer, softball, tennis, track, and volleyball. Organized recreational sports include aerobics, dance, figure skating, horseback riding, skiing, snowboarding, tennis, and weight lifting.

The Heslin Gymnasium contains four locker rooms, the John Biggs Jr. Memorial Fitness Center, a training room, and a basketball/volleyball court. There are also six playing fields and six tennis courts. In addition to year-round ice skating, the Theodore Iorio Ice Arena offers boys' and girls' locker rooms, workout facilities, a multipurpose function room, and a snack bar. Cushing's Athletic Leadership Program further challenges student-athletes who wish to take their drive beyond the playing fields through workshops, guest speakers, and off campus opportunities.

EXTRACURRICULAR OPPORTUNITIES
In addition to their commitments in the classroom and on the playing fields, Cushing students take advantage of the many opportunities to join or start up clubs and to organize campus events. Always based on student interest, clubs in recent years have included Open Doors, International Club, Environmental Club, Cushing Academy Music Association, Literary Magazine, Radio Station, Mock Trial, Model United Nations, and Book Club. Students are also involved in coordinating campus events.

Cushing's proximity to Boston enables students to have access to the city's resources—museums, sporting events, shopping, theater— and regular trips to take advantage of these opportunities are scheduled throughout the year. Students interested in exploring opportunities in business, the arts, law, or other fields can also pursue internships with Boston-area professionals.

DAILY LIFE
The Monday-through-Friday schedule, which begins with classes at 8 a.m., provides time for an extra-help period, activities, and athletics before evening study hall at 8 p.m. Lights-out is at 10:30 p.m. for underclassmen and 11 for seniors and postgraduates. Classes are 40 minutes long on Mondays and Fridays and 55 minutes long on Tuesdays, Wednesdays, and Thursdays. Courses, activities, and athletics are all centrally scheduled to avoid unnecessary conflicts. On weekdays, the hours from 3 to 5 p.m. are reserved for athletics, arts, and activities; interscholastic competitions occur on Wednesday, Friday (occasionally), and Saturday.

WEEKEND LIFE
On a typical weekend at the Academy, students enjoy many off-campus trips with faculty chaperones. Movies are shown on campus each weekend, while dances and concerts are often scheduled in the evening. Students are permitted to spend a limited number of weekends off campus, but on any given weekend 70 to 75 percent of the boarding population chooses to remain at school. One weekend each month is designated an on-campus weekend, meaning students remain at Cushing to enjoy performances, sporting events, and special activities as a community.

SUMMER PROGRAMS
During the five-week summer session, Cushing offers a unique boarding school experience for girls and boys ages 12–18 from throughout the United States and around the world. The program features Prep for Success for middle school students, regular and advanced college-preparatory courses for high school students, intensive art, and extensive English as a second language instruction. Each program is combined with interesting artistic and athletic electives as well as exciting excursions throughout New England. For further information, students should contact Margaret Lee, Director of Summer Programs at mlee@cushing.org or 978-827-7700.

COSTS AND FINANCIAL AID
Tuition and required fees for 2010–11 were $44,600 for boarding students and $32,300 for day students. There are optional fees for skiing, music lessons, and fine arts materials. A $4460 nonrefundable enrollment deposit ($3220 for day students) is credited toward the balance due; half of the remaining total is due on July 1 and the balance on December 1.

In 2010–11, 26 percent of the student body received $3.2 million in financial aid. Funds are awarded on the basis of need as demonstrated by established criteria of the School and Student Service for Financial Aid. Financial aid is renewed annually, subject to continued need and availability of funds.

ADMISSIONS INFORMATION
Cushing Academy seeks students who are interested in taking an active role in promoting their own academic and social growth. Cushing values strong character, motivation, diversity, and strength in extracurricular activities. Candidates are evaluated based on school performance, SSAT, PSAT, SAT, ACT, TOEFL, or other tests, and a personal interview. If travel is too difficult, international applicants may request a video interview via Skype.

APPLICATION TIMETABLE
Initial inquiries are welcome at any time. Application materials are available online and are provided, along with the school's viewbook, upon request. Interviews and campus tours are scheduled Monday through Friday and some Saturdays.

Completed applications should be submitted, along with the $50 nonrefundable application fee ($100 for international students), by February 1. Applications may be submitted after February 1, and will be acted on after March 10, subject to the availability of spaces in the classes. Decisions are mailed out on March 10 for students submitting applications by the deadline and for others on a rolling basis as space permits.

ADMISSIONS CORRESPONDENCE
Deborah Gustafson, Co-Director of Admission
Adam Payne, Co-Director of Admission
Cushing Academy
39 School Street
P.O. Box 8000
Ashburnham, Massachusetts 01430

Phone: 978-827-7300
Fax: 978-827-6253
E-mail: admission@cushing.org
Web site: http://www.cushing.org

DEERFIELD ACADEMY
Deerfield, Massachusetts

Type: Coeducational boarding and day college-preparatory school
Grades: 9–12, postgraduate year
Enrollment: 630
Head of School: Dr. Margarita O'Byrne Curtis

THE SCHOOL

Since its founding in 1797, Deerfield Academy has provided a unique and challenging opportunity for young people. Deerfield Academy is a vibrant learning community nurturing high standards of scholarship, citizenship, and personal responsibility. Through a demanding liberal arts curriculum, extensive cocurricular program, and supportive residential environment, Deerfield encourages each student to develop an inquisitive and creative mind, sound body, strong moral character, and commitment to service. The setting of the campus, which is rich in tradition and beauty, inspires reflection, study and play, the cultivation of friendships, and the growth of a defining community spirit.

The school's 280-acre campus is located in the center of Historic Deerfield, a restored Colonial village in western Massachusetts, 90 miles from Boston and 55 miles from Hartford. Only 20 minutes south is the five-college area that includes Amherst, Smith, Mount Holyoke, and Hampshire Colleges and the University of Massachusetts, providing rich cultural and intellectual resources.

A 28-member Board of Trustees is the Academy's governing body. The endowment is valued at approximately $315 million. In 2009–10, operating expenses totaled $48.6 million, capital gifts amounted to $14.6 million, and Annual Giving was $5.6 million, with 49 percent of the 9,238 alumni participating.

Deerfield is accredited by the New England Association of Schools and Colleges. It is a member of the National Association of Independent Schools, the Independent School Association of Massachusetts, and the Secondary School Admission Test Board.

ACADEMIC PROGRAMS

Deerfield's curriculum is designed to enable its students to assume active and intelligent roles in the world community. Courses and teaching methods are aimed at developing logical and imaginative thinking, systematic approaches to problem solving, clear and correct expression in writing and speech, and the confidence to pursue creatively one's interests and talents. Students take five courses per trimester. Their schedules are planned individually in consultation with advisers and the Academic Dean.

Graduation requirements include English, 4 years; mathematics, 3 years; foreign language, 3 years of a language (Arabic, Chinese, French, Greek, Latin, or Spanish); history, 2 years (including 1 year of U.S. history); laboratory science, 2 years; fine arts, two terms; and philosophy and religious studies, one term. All sophomores take a one-term course in health issues. In addition, all new students take a required course in library skills. Honors and Advanced Placement (AP) courses are offered in nineteen subject areas. Last year, 289 students sat for 640 AP exams. Ninety percent of the tests received qualifying scores of 3 or better. Independent study is offered in all departments.

During the spring term, seniors may engage in off-campus alternate-studies projects, ranging from working in a local hospital to serving as an intern for a member of Congress. Juniors may spend half of their year at the Maine Coast Semester, which combines regular classes with studies of environmental issues; at the Mountain School in Vermont; or at a boarding school in South Africa, Botswana, or Kenya. Sophomores and juniors may spend a semester at the Island School on Eleuthera in the Bahamas. The Swiss Semester in Zermatt is a program that gives sophomores an opportunity to study geology, European history, and foreign language at the foot of the Matterhorn. Deerfield participates in the School Year Abroad program in China, France, Italy, Japan, Spain, and Vietnam, which is available for juniors and seniors. Students may also choose from many exchange programs, including programs in Australia, Hong Kong, Jordan, and New Zealand. Summer opportunities are available in China, the Dominican Republic, France, Greece, Italy, Spain, and Uruguay.

The average class size is 12. The overall faculty-student ratio is 1:6. Placement in AP courses, honors sections, and accelerated courses is based upon preparedness, ability, and interest. All students have study hours Sunday through Thursday evenings.

The school year is divided into three 11-week terms. Grades are sent at the end of each term and at midterm. In the fall and spring, the student's academic adviser prepares a formal written report, commenting extensively on the student's academic performance, attitude, work habits, dormitory life, and participation in athletics and cocurricular activities and as a citizen of the school.

Grading is based on a numerical scale of 0 to 100; 60 is passing. The honor roll is made up of students with minimum averages of 87, and the high honor roll recognizes students with averages of 93 and above. Students in academic difficulty are reviewed by the Academic Standing Committee at the end of each term. Teachers are available during evenings, weekends, and free periods to assist students individually. Students can also get help from the Study Skills Coordinator.

FACULTY AND ADVISERS

The high quality of Deerfield's faculty is the school's greatest endowment. The faculty consists of 114 members (50 women and 64 men); 74 percent hold advanced degrees. Ninety percent reside on campus or live in the village of Deerfield. All faculty members act as advisers to students, coach sports, head tables in the dining hall, and serve on various committees. Teachers receive summer grants and time away from the Academy for advanced study, travel, and exchange teaching.

Dr. Margarita O'Byrne Curtis was appointed Head of School in July 2006. She earned her B.A. from Tulane, her B.S. from Mankato State, and a Ph.D. in Romance languages and literature from Harvard.

COLLEGE ADMISSION COUNSELING

College advising is coordinated by 4 college advisers. Beginning in their junior year, all students attend small-group discussions that help them make informed decisions about college. In mid-winter, every junior is assigned to an individual college adviser, who further develops, with parental consultation, a list of prospective colleges. In the fall of the senior year, college advisers assist students in narrowing their college choices and in making the most effective presentation of their strengths. During the fall, representatives of approximately 150 colleges visit the Academy for presentations and interviews.

Normally, sophomores and juniors take the PSAT in October. Juniors take the SAT in January; SAT Subject Tests in December, May, and June; and Advanced Placement (AP) tests in May. Seniors, whenever advisable, take the SAT in the fall and additional AP tests later in the year. The midrange of SAT scores for the class of 2010 was 620–700 critical reading, 620–720 math, and 620–720 writing.

Of the 193 graduates in 2010, 183 are attending college; 10 students deferred admission to college for a year. Colleges attended by 5 or more students are: Georgetown (16); Harvard (10); Dartmouth (7); Brown, Williams, and Yale (6 each); and Bowdoin, Colby, Middlebury, Princeton, and Richmond (5 each).

STUDENT BODY AND CONDUCT

In fall 2010, Deerfield enrolled 630 students: 312 girls and 318 boys. There were 86 boarders and 11 day students in the ninth grade, 147 boarders and 17 day students in the tenth grade, 155 boarders and 26 day students in the eleventh grade, and 168 boarders and 20 day students in the twelfth grade (including 20 postgraduates). Recognizing that diversity enriches the school, the Academy seeks to foster an appreciation of difference. To that end, international students make up 14 percent of the student body, and those from minority groups make up 25 percent. Deerfield students come from thirty-eight states and twenty-four countries.

In all communities, a healthy tension exists between the need for individuality and the need for common values and standards. A community's shared values define the place, giving it a distinct sense of itself. In all facets of school life, Deerfield strives to teach that honesty, tolerance, compassion, and responsibility are essential to the well-being of the individual, the school, and society. Deerfield Academy is a residential community in which students learn to conduct themselves according to high standards of citizenship. Expectations for students

www.facebook.com/sec.schools

are clear, and the response to misbehavior is timely and as supportive as possible of the students involved.

ACADEMIC FACILITIES

Deerfield's campus has eighty-one buildings. The Frank L. Boyden Library has a collection of more than 85,000 books, periodicals, and films. Most of the library's collection is accessible via a fully integrated online catalog. The Koch Center, a new, state-of-the-art 80,000-square-foot center for science, mathematics, and technology, includes a new planetarium; thirty classroom and laboratory spaces, including dedicated spaces for independent research; a 225-seat auditorium; the Star Terrace; and a central atrium.

The Memorial Building contains the main auditorium, Hilson Gallery, Russell Gallery, art studios, a black-box theater, a dance facility, and music recital and practice rooms.

BOARDING AND GENERAL FACILITIES

There are eighteen dormitories. Faculty members live in apartments attached to each dorm corridor and maintain a close, supportive relationship with students. Two senior proctors also live on the freshman and sophomore corridors. Eighty-five percent of the boarding students have single rooms.

The fifteen-bed health center, Dewey House, is staffed full-time by a physician and registered nurses.

ATHLETICS

Participation in sports—at the student's level of ability—is the athletic program's central focus. The Academy fields interscholastic teams in baseball, basketball, crew, cross-country, cycling, diving, field hockey, football, golf, ice hockey, lacrosse, skiing, soccer, softball, squash, swimming, tennis, track, volleyball, water polo, and wrestling. Supervised recreational activities include aerobics, cycling, dance, skiing, squash, strength training, tennis, and an outdoor skills program.

Deerfield's gymnasium complex contains three basketball courts; a wrestling arena; an indoor hockey rink; a new 5,500-square-foot fitness center with state-of-the-art cardiovascular and weight lifting equipment, trainer's room, and locker rooms; the Dewey Squash Center, a 16,000-square-foot facility housing ten international squash courts and tournament seating; and the largest preparatory school natatorium in New England, which includes an indoor, eight-lane, 25-yard pool with a separate diving well. Ninety acres of playing fields include three football fields, twelve soccer/lacrosse fields, three field hockey fields, eighteen tennis courts, a major-league-quality baseball field, a softball field, paddle tennis courts, a new boathouse and crew facility, and a new eight-lane track. Two synthetic turf fields were added in the summer of 2008.

EXTRACURRICULAR OPPORTUNITIES

Deerfield students and faculty members are extraordinarily productive in the performing and visual arts. Musical groups include wind ensemble, chamber music, string orchestra, jazz ensemble, brass choir, madrigal singers, a cappella groups, and the Academy Chorus. Many opportunities exist for acting as well. In addition to the three major theater productions each year, plays and scenes are also performed by advanced acting classes. Students who

are interested in dance may explore modern, jazz, and ballet, with the opportunity to perform all three terms.

Cocurricular organizations include Peer Counselors, the Diversity Task Force, Amnesty International, and debate, photography, and political clubs. Outing groups offer opportunities to ski, rock climb, and bike on weekends. Publications include an award-winning campus newspaper, the yearbook, and literary publications.

Students provide service as tutors, dormitory proctors, tour guides, and waiters in the dining hall. Students serve responsibly on various standing and ad hoc administrative committees and play an especially important role on the disciplinary committee. Students are also involved in various community service projects. The Community Service program encourages Deerfield students and faculty members to broaden their perspectives by sharing with and learning from people of different ages, abilities, cultures, and economic backgrounds. Ongoing projects include mentoring at nearby schools, volunteering in shelters and day-care centers, tutoring, organic farming and on-campus recycling, visiting nursing homes, and sponsoring Red Cross blood drives. Some students also serve as Big Brothers or Big Sisters to local youth. In addition, each sophomore also participates in Deerfield Perspectives, an on-campus service program.

DAILY LIFE

Students normally take five courses each term, and each course meets four times per week. The length of a class period ranges from 45 to 70 minutes. Classes begin at 8:30 and end at 3, except on Wednesday, when classes end at 12:45 and are followed by interscholastic athletics and cocurricular activities. Classes do not meet on Saturdays. One morning a week, students and faculty members gather together for a school meeting, and students and faculty members attend seven family-style meals per week. All sports and drama activities take place after classes. Clubs and cocurricular groups meet between dinner and study hours or on weekends.

Students study in their dormitory rooms between 7:45 and 9:45 p.m., Sunday through Thursday. They may also study in the library, perform laboratory experiments, or seek help from a faculty member or the student tutoring service. During the school week, the curfew for freshmen and sophomores is 7:45; for juniors and seniors, it is 9:45.

WEEKEND LIFE

In addition to athletic events on Saturday afternoon, there are films, theatrical productions, and musical performances. Social activities, sponsored by the Student Activities Committee and chaperoned by faculty members, include coffeehouses, talent shows, concerts, and dances. Deerfield's rural setting and extensive athletic facilities are ideal for recreational hiking, rock climbing, skiing, swimming, ice skating, and other activities.

The Academy Events Committee plans and sponsors events throughout the school year. The Robert Crow Lecture Series brings to the Academy leaders in politics, government, education, science, and journalism. Students attend concerts and film series. Art exhibitions and numerous dramatic productions provide recognition for promising young

artists, photographers, and actors. Students also have access to cultural programs in the five-college area.

Freshmen may take two weekends off campus in the fall term and three each in the winter and spring terms; sophomores may take two weekends in fall, three in winter, and an unlimited number in spring; juniors and seniors in good standing may take unlimited weekends. On weekends, the curfew for freshmen and sophomores is at 10:30 p.m. on Friday and 11 on Saturday. For juniors and seniors, Friday curfew is at 11; Saturday curfew is at 11:30.

COSTS AND FINANCIAL AID

For 2010–11, the cost for boarding students is $43,800; for day students, it is $31,400. Additional fees include $1975 for books, infirmary, and technology. Parents are asked to maintain a drawing account of $75 for their child's personal expenses. Tuition is payable in two installments—on August 1 and December 1. A $2500 deposit (credited to the August tuition bill) is due within four weeks of the student's acceptance by Deerfield.

Deerfield awards financial aid to 35 percent of its students. Financial aid totals $6.6 million for the current academic year; grants, based on demonstrated need and procedures established by the School and Student Service for Financial Aid, range from $2500 to full tuition.

ADMISSIONS INFORMATION

Deerfield maintains rigorous academic standards and seeks a diverse student body—geographic, socioeconomic, and racial. Selection is based upon academic ability and performance, character and maturity, and promise as a positive community citizen. The Admission Committee closely examines candidates' teacher and school recommendations and personal essays.

The SSAT or ISEE is required of applicants for grades 9 and 10 and should be taken during an applicant's current academic year. The SSAT, ISEE, or PSAT is required for eleventh-grade applicants, and the PSAT, SAT or ACT is required for twelfth-grade and postgraduate candidates. The TOEFL may be taken in place of the aforementioned tests by students for whom English is not their first language.

Deerfield Academy does not discriminate on the basis of race, color, creed, handicap, sexual orientation, or national or ethnic origin in its admission policies or financial aid program.

APPLICATION TIMETABLE

Applicants normally visit the Academy in the year prior to the proposed date of entrance. Campus tours and interviews are conducted from 8:30 to 2:20 on Monday, Tuesday, Thursday, and Friday; from 8:15 to noon on Wednesday; and at 9, 10, and 11 on Saturday. Weekdays are preferable, since there are no Saturday classes. The completed application—including teacher recommendations, the school transcript, and essays—should be submitted no later than January 15. Applicants receive notification of the admission decision on March 10. The candidate reply date is April 11, 2011

ADMISSIONS CORRESPONDENCE

Patricia L. Gimbel
Dean of Admission and Financial Aid
Deerfield Academy
Deerfield, Massachusetts 01342
Phone: 413-774-1400
E-mail: admission@deerfield.edu
Web site: http://www.deerfield.edu

DELBARTON SCHOOL

Morristown, New Jersey

Type: Boys' day college-preparatory school
Grades: 7–12: Middle School, 7–8; Upper School, 9–12
Enrollment: School total: 548; Upper School: 482
Head of School: Br. Paul Diveny, O.S.B., Headmaster

THE SCHOOL

Delbarton School was established in 1939 by the Benedictine monks of Saint Mary's Abbey as an independent boarding and day school. Now a day school, Delbarton is located on a 200-acre woodland campus 3 miles west of historic Morristown and 30 miles west of New York City. Adjacent to the campus is Jockey Hollow, a national historic park.

Delbarton School seeks to enroll boys of good character who have demonstrated scholastic achievement and the capacity for further growth. The faculty strives to support each boy's efforts toward intellectual development and to reinforce his commitment to help build a community of responsible individuals. The faculty encourages each boy to become an independent seeker of information, not a passive recipient, and to assume responsibility for gaining both knowledge and judgment that will strengthen his contribution to the life of the School and his later contribution to society. While the School offers much, it also seeks boys who are willing to give much and who are eager to understand as well as to be understood.

The School is governed by the 9-member Board of Trustees of the Order of Saint Benedict of New Jersey, located at Saint Mary's Abbey in Morristown. Delbarton's 2010–11 annual operating expenses totaled $18.1 million. It has an endowment of $19.1 million. This includes annual fund-raising support from 45 percent of the alumni.

Delbarton School is accredited by the Middle States Association of Colleges and Schools and approved by the Department of Education of the State of New Jersey. It is a member of the National Association of Independent Schools, the New Jersey Association of Independent Schools, the Council for Advancement and Support of Education, the National Catholic Educational Association, and the New Jersey State Interscholastic Athletic Association.

ACADEMIC PROGRAMS

The academic program in the Upper School is college preparatory. The course of study offers preparation in all major academic subjects and a number of electives. The studies are intended to help a boy shape a thought and a sentence, speak clearly about ideas and effectively about feelings, and suspend judgment until all the facts are known. Course work, on the whole, is intensive and involves about 20 hours of outside preparation each week. The curriculum contains both a core of required subjects that are fundamental to a liberal education and various elective courses that are designed to meet the individual interests of the boys. Instruction is given in all areas that are necessary for gaining admission to liberal arts or technical institutions of higher learning.

The school year is divided into three academic terms. In each term, every boy must take five major courses, physical education, and religious studies. The specific departmental requirements in grades 9 through 12 are English (4 years), mathematics (4 years), foreign language (3 years), science (3 years), history (3 years), religious studies (2 terms in each of 4 years), physical education and health (4 years), fine arts (1 major course, 1 term of art, and 1 term of music), and computer technology (2 terms). For qualified boys in the junior and senior years, all departments offer Advanced Placement courses, and it is also possible in certain instances to pursue work through independent study or to study at neighboring colleges.

The grading system uses 4 to 0 (failing) designations with pluses and minuses. Advisory reports are sent to parents in the middle of each term as well as at the end of the three terms. Parents are also contacted when a student has received an academic warning or is placed on probation. The average class size is 15, and the student-teacher ratio is about 7:1, which fosters close student-faculty relations.

FACULTY AND ADVISERS

In 2010–11 the faculty consisted of 12 Benedictine monks and 71 lay teachers. All are full-time members, with 49 holding advanced degrees.

Br. Paul Diveny, O.S.B., became Headmaster in July 2007. Br. Paul received his B.A. from the Catholic University of America in 1975; his diploma in Monastic Studies from the Pontificio Ateneo Sant'Anselmo in Rome, Italy in 1982; and his M.A. in German from Middlebury College in 1987. He has served the School previously as a teacher of Latin, German, ancient history, and religious studies, and as Assistant Headmaster.

The teaching tradition of the School has called upon faculty members to serve as coaches, counselors, or administrators. A genuine interest in the development of people leads the faculty to be involved in many student activities. Every boy is assigned to a guidance counselor, who advises in the selection of courses that meet School and college requirements as well as personal interests. Individual conferences are regularly arranged to discuss academic and personal development. The counselor also contacts the boy's parents when it seems advisable.

COLLEGE ADMISSION COUNSELING

Preparation for college begins when a boy enters Delbarton. The PSAT is given to everyone in the tenth and eleventh grades. Guidance for admission to college is directed by the senior class counselor. This process generally begins in the fall of the junior year, when the junior class counselor meets with each boy to help clarify his goals and interests. Many college admissions officers visit the School annually for conferences. Every effort is made to direct each boy toward an institution that will challenge his abilities and satisfy his interests.

The mean SAT critical reading and math score for the class of 2010 was 1330. More than 25 percent of the young men in the classes of 2007, 2008, 2009, and 2010 have been named National Merit Scholars, Semifinalists, or Commended Students. In addition, 85 percent of the members of the class of 2010 were enrolled in at least one AP course.

All of the graduates of the classes of 2007, 2008, 2009, and 2010 went on to college, with 5 or more attending such schools as Boston College, Columbia, Cornell, Dartmouth, Duke, Georgetown, Harvard, Holy Cross, Johns Hopkins, Middlebury, Notre Dame, Princeton, Villanova, Williams, Yale, and the Universities of Pennsylvania and Virginia.

STUDENT BODY AND CONDUCT

The 2010–11 Upper School student body consisted of 130 ninth graders, 120 tenth graders, 119 eleventh graders, and 112 twelfth graders. The Middle School has 32 seventh and 34 eighth graders. All of the students are from New Jersey, particularly the counties of Morris, Essex, Somerset, Union, Bergen, Hunterdon, Passaic, and Sussex.

Regulations, academic and social, are relatively few. The School eschews the manipulative, the coercive, the negative, or the merely punitive approach to discipline. The basic understanding underlying the School's regulations is that each boy, entering with others in a common educational enterprise, shares responsibility with his fellow students and with faculty members for developing and maintaining standards that contribute to the welfare of the entire School community. Moreover, shared responsibility is essential to the growth of the community; at the same time, much of an individual boy's growth, the increase in his capacity for self-renewal, his sense of belonging, and his sense of identity spring from his eagerness and willingness to contribute to the life of the School. Each class has a moderator, who is available for advice and assistance. The moderator works closely with the boys, assisting them in their progress.

ACADEMIC FACILITIES

The physical facilities include two classroom buildings, a fine arts center, a science pavilion, a greenhouse, the church, and the dining hall. Academic facilities include thirty-four classrooms, six science laboratories, art and music studios, a language laboratory, and a library of more than 20,000 volumes. The five computer laboratories consist of 250 workstations in a networked system. Also, the music department provides twelve personal computers for the advanced study of music and composition.

ATHLETICS

Sports at the School are an integral part of student life. The School holds the traditional belief that much can be learned about cooperation, competition, and character through participating in sports. Almost 80 percent of the boys participate on one or more interscholastic athletics teams. Varsity sports offered in the fall term are football, soccer, and cross-country; in the winter term, basketball, wrestling, track, hockey, squash, bowling, and swimming (in an off-campus pool); and in the spring, baseball, track, lacrosse, tennis, and golf. In most of these sports, there are junior varsity, freshman, and Middle School teams. Some intramural sports are available, depending upon interest, every year.

The facilities consist of two gymnasiums, eight athletics fields, six tennis courts, and an outdoor pool for swimming during warm weather. Students who join the golf team are able to play at nearby golf clubs.

EXTRACURRICULAR OPPORTUNITIES

The School provides opportunities for individual development outside the classroom as well as within. The faculty encourages the boys to express their intellectual, cultural, social, and recreational interests through a variety of activities and events. For example, fine arts at Delbarton are available both within and outside the curriculum. Studio hours accommodate boys after school, and students visit galleries and museums. In the music department, vocal and instrumental instruction is available. Performing ensembles include an orchestra, band, and chorus and smaller vocal and instrumental ensembles. Under the aegis of the Abbey Players, drama productions are staged three times a year, involving boys in a wide variety of experiences.

Other activities include Deaneries (student support groups promoting School unity and spirit), the *Courier* (the School newspaper), the *Archway* (the yearbook), *Schola Cantorum* (a vocal ensemble), the Abbey Orchestra, and the Model UN, Mock Trial, Speech and Debate, Junior Statesmen, Art, History, Chess, Cycling, Stock Exchange, and Future Business Leaders clubs. In addition, faculty moderators of the Ski Club regularly organize and chaperone trips during School vacations.

To expose students to other cultures and to enhance their understanding of the world, faculty members have organized trips to Europe, Africa, and Latin America. The Campus Ministry office is active in sponsoring several outreach programs that lead boys to an awareness of the needs of others and the means to answer calls for help. The outreach programs include community soup kitchens, Big Brothers of America, Adopt a Grandparent, Basketball Clinic for exceptional children, and a program in which volunteers travel to Appalachia during break to contribute various services to the poor of that area.

Students' imagination and initiative are also given opportunities for expression through Student Council committees and assemblies. The students are also offered School-sponsored trips to cultural and recreational events at area colleges and in nearby cities.

DAILY LIFE

Classes begin at 8:15 a.m. and end at 2:34 p.m. The average number of classes per day for each student is six. Two classes are an hour long, while the remainder are 40 minutes each. The School operates on a six-day cycle, and each class meets five days per cycle. Physical education classes are held during the school day. After classes, students are involved in athletics and the arts. Clubs and organizations also meet after school, while many meet at night.

COSTS AND FINANCIAL AID

Charges at Delbarton for the 2010–11 academic year are $26,975. These are comprehensive fees that include a daily hot lunch as well as library and athletics fees. The only other major expenses are the bookstore bill and transportation, the cost of which varies. Optional expenses may arise for such items as the yearbook, music lessons, or trips.

Because of the School's endowment and generous alumni and parent support, a financial aid program enables many boys to attend the School. All awards are based on financial need, as determined by the criteria set by the School and Student Service for Financial Aid. No academic or athletics scholarships are awarded. Financial aid is granted to boys in grades 7 through 12. This year, the School was able to grant $1.4 million to students.

ADMISSIONS INFORMATION

Delbarton School selects students whose academic achievement and personal promise indicate that they are likely to become positive members of the community. The object of the admissions procedure is for the School and prospective student to learn as much as possible about each other. Admission is based on the candidate's overall qualifications, without regard to race, color, religion, or national or ethnic origin.

The typical applicant takes one of the four entrance tests administered by the School in October, November, and December. Candidates are considered on the basis of their transcript, recommendations, test results, and personal interview in addition to the formal application. In 2010–11, 343 students were tested for entrance in grades 7 and 9; of these, 144 were accepted. Eighty-six percent of the students who were accepted for the seventh grade were enrolled; 91 percent of those accepted for the ninth grade were enrolled. Delbarton does not admit postgraduate students or students who are entering the twelfth grade.

APPLICATION TIMETABLE

The School welcomes inquiries at any time during the year. Students who apply are invited to spend a day at Delbarton attending classes with a School host. Interested applicants should arrange this day visit through the Admissions Office. Tours of the campus are generally given in conjunction with interviews, from 9 a.m. to noon on Saturdays in the fall, or by special arrangement. The formal application for admission must be accompanied by a nonrefundable fee of $65. Application fee waivers are available upon request.

It is advisable to initiate the admissions process in the early fall. Acceptance notifications for applicants to grades 7 and 9 are made by the end of January. Applicants to all remaining grades, as well as students placed in a waitpool, are given acceptance notification as late as June. Parents are expected to reply to acceptances two to three weeks after notification. A refundable deposit is also required. Application for financial aid should be made as early as possible; the committee hopes to notify financial aid applicants by the middle of March.

ADMISSIONS CORRESPONDENCE

Dr. David Donovan
Dean of Admissions
Delbarton School
Morristown, New Jersey 07960

Phone: 973-538-3231 Ext. 3019
Fax: 973-538-8836
E-mail: admissions@delbarton.org
Web site: http://www.delbarton.org/admissions

THE DERRYFIELD SCHOOL

Manchester, New Hampshire

Type: Coeducational, college-preparatory day school
Grades: Grades 6–12
Enrollment: Total: 381; Middle School: 133; Upper School: 248
Head of School: Craig N. Sellers, Head of School

THE SCHOOL

The Derryfield School, an independent, coeducational, college-preparatory day school, was founded by local citizens in 1964 to provide an outstanding secondary education for students who want to live at home.

Derryfield inspires bright, motivated young people to be their best, and provides them with the skills and experiences needed to be valued, dynamic, confident, and purposeful members of any community.

The School is governed by a 20-member Board of Trustees and, in addition to tuition, is supported financially through annual giving and an endowment fund of more than $4.4 million.

Derryfield is accredited by the New England Association of Schools and Colleges and is a member of the National Association of Independent Schools (NAIS), the Association of Independent Schools of New England (AISNE), and the Independent Schools Association of Northern New England (ISANNE).

ACADEMIC PROGRAMS

Derryfield's challenging academic program combines a seriousness of purpose with a sense of spirit. A core college-preparatory curriculum is enhanced by more than seventy elective classes and independent learning opportunities.

Students entering Derryfield in the Middle School participate in a curriculum that provides a firm background in skills and basic discipline areas in preparation for Upper School courses. All students in grades 6, 7, and 8 take English, mathematics, science, history, and a foreign language. In addition, all Middle School students participate in drama, music, wellness, physical education, and art.

Students entering the Upper School (grades 9–12) plan their course of study in the context of graduation requirements, college plans, and interests. A total of 18 academic credits is required with the following departmental distribution: 4 credits in English, 2 credits in history, 3 credits in mathematics, 3 credits in a world language, 2⅓ credits in science, 1 credit in fine arts, and participation in either the alternative sports program or a team sport two seasons per year. Each student carries a minimum of five courses each term. The academic year consists of three terms.

The Independent Senior Project is an option for seniors during the final six weeks of the spring term. The project allows students to explore their interests and to gain practical experience outside of the classroom.

FACULTY AND ADVISERS

The Derryfield faculty consists of 48 members (21 men and 27 women). Master's degrees are held by 23 members and Ph.D.'s are held by 2 members. Sixteen faculty members have taught at Derryfield for ten or more years, and annual faculty turnover is low. The student-faculty ratio is 8:1.

Faculty members are hired on the basis of a high level of expertise in their academic areas as well as enthusiasm to contribute to the overall success of their students and the School. In addition to their classroom obligations, faculty members advise approximately 8 students, coach Derryfield's athletic and academic teams, advise student activities, and make themselves available to counsel students in other areas of student life.

COLLEGE ADMISSION COUNSELING

A dedicated college counselor begins working with students in February of their junior year. College counseling is an active process that includes group seminars and individual meetings with students and their families. More than 50 college representatives visit Derryfield each year.

The average SAT scores for the class of 2009 were 622 in critical reading, 617 in math, and 616 in the writing section. Sixty-five students graduated in 2010, with 100 percent of the class going to college. A sampling of the colleges and universities currently attended by 2 or more Derryfield graduates includes Bates, Boston College, Brandeis, Carnegie Mellon, Colby, Emory, George Washington, Hamilton, Harvard, Holy Cross, Lehigh, Middlebury, Rensselaer Polytechnic, Smith, Trinity, Tufts, Tulane, Vassar, Wellesley, Wesleyan, and the Universities of California, New Hampshire, Pennsylvania, and Vermont.

STUDENT BODY AND CONDUCT

Of the 381 students enrolled at The Derryfield School, 133 students attend the Middle School program and 248 students attend the Upper School program. Students come from forty local communities.

Violations of School rules are handled by the Discipline Committee, which consists of elected students and faculty members who evaluate discipline issues and make recommendations to the Head of School.

ACADEMIC FACILITIES

Derryfield's academic facilities include classroom buildings with five fully equipped science laboratories, a technology center with workstations and laptops, a 95-seat multimedia lyceum, a 17,000-volume library with a large subscription database, two art studios, an art gallery, and a 400-seat performing arts center. Outdoor classroom facilities include several miles of cross-country trails, high and low ropes courses, and many acres of woods. A turf field, a full-sized gymnasium, weight-training area, and trainer's room are also valuable learning sites for courses in physical education and health and wellness.

ATHLETICS

"A healthy mind in a healthy body" defined the Greek ideal and is the concept at the core of Derryfield's physical education, health and wellness, and athletics philosophy.

All Middle Schoolers (grades 6–8) take physical education and health and wellness. Seventh and eighth graders also have competitive athletic requirements. Offerings include baseball, basketball, cross-country running, field hockey, lacrosse, Nordic and alpine skiing, soccer, softball, and tennis.

In the Upper School (grades 9–12), two levels of competitive sports teams (junior varsity and varsity), as well as some alternative physical activities (e.g., yoga, weight training) are offered. Upper School athletics include baseball, basketball, crew, cross-country running, field hockey, golf, lacrosse, Nordic and alpine skiing, soccer, softball, and tennis. The School also honors areas of physical interest that it does not offer on site; students may request that an independent physical activity be a replacement for one of the two required seasons.

Derryfield is a member of the New Hampshire Interscholastic Athletic Association, participating in Division III and IV, according to sport. Derryfield currently has the most athletic offerings of any Division IV school in New Hampshire and has garnered more than twenty-five state championships in the last ten years.

EXTRACURRICULAR OPPORTUNITIES

Derryfield's commitment to the arts is evident. High school students perform two large-scale drama productions each year, while seventh and eighth graders take part in their own musical. Each sixth grade drama class produces its own junior musical. Instrumental ensembles that include classical, jazz, and orchestral instruments are active in both the Middle and Upper School. There are vocal groups in both schools, and Upper School students may audition for a select chorus. All musicians participate in two concerts per year and frequently in talent shows and assemblies. Students are encouraged to audition for the New Hampshire All-State Chorus and Band. Visual art students regularly submit materials to the New Hampshire Student Artist Awards and the Boston Globe Scholastic Art Awards, and help organize displays of their own work in Derryfield's art gallery openings.

In each of the two schools, Middle and Upper, students participate in more than a dozen student-organized clubs. Choices include School Council, Conservation Club, Art Club, Gay/Straight Alliance, Cartooning Club, Robotics Club, and Chinese Culture Club, among others. Derryfield also offers competitive clubs, including the math and debate teams, Granite State Challenge, and Model United Nations. Students publish newspapers, literary magazines, and a yearbook.

Field trips, organized through classes or clubs, include regular visits to New York City, Boston, and Manchester museums, theaters, courtrooms, and outdoor areas of interest. Each year, different faculty members lead groups of students on cultural or service-learning outings. Recent trips have been led to Europe, the Dominican Republic, and the Galapagos Islands.

In its dedication to local and global communities, Derryfield's Key Club actively partners with more than a dozen organizations, including the New Hampshire Food Bank, Heifer International, New Horizons Soup Kitchen, Boys and Girls Club, and local immigrant relocation programs.

Breakthrough Manchester, a year-round, tuition-free academic program, is also an important part of The Derryfield School. Breakthrough offers motivated students from Manchester's public elementary schools the opportunity to learn from outstanding high school and college students. Several Derryfield faculty members work as mentor teachers, while a large number of Derryfield students teach for Breakthrough.

Traditional Derryfield events and celebrations include Founders' Day, Winter Carnival, Grandparents' Day, Head's Holiday, Country Fair, Moose Revue talent show, and the Prom.

DAILY LIFE

Because Derryfield students come from approximately forty different surrounding towns, the School itself becomes a hub for learning, playing, serving, and socializing.

A full Derryfield School day begins at 7:55 a.m. and ends between 2:45 and 3:20 p.m. Departure times vary, depending on grade, a student's level of involvement in extracurricular activities or desire to obtain extra help from a teacher, use the library, or attend study hall.

Homeroom gatherings occur two mornings per week, and advisories meet three times per week. The Tuesday and Friday class schedules allow time for an activities period, during which clubs meet. A 30-minute all-school assembly takes place each Monday morning. The class schedule is a seven-period, seven-"day," rotating schedule.

SUMMER PROGRAMS

Derryfield offers several summer camps, including tennis and two drama camps.

COSTS AND FINANCIAL AID

Tuition and fees for 2010–11 were $25,200. In addition to the Financial Aid Program, which offers direct grants, the School offers installment payment options.

The Financial Aid Program is designed to make a Derryfield education accessible to qualified students who could not otherwise afford the cost of attending. On average, Derryfield provides financial assistance to 24 percent of the student body, with awards that vary from 5 to 95 percent of tuition. Derryfield awards nearly $1.5 million in financial aid grants annually.

The Merit Scholarship Program is designed to recognize students who demonstrate qualities that will add meaning and vitality to Derryfield's core values or are distinguished by a commitment to purposeful involvement in both the local and global community. Awards of up to $15,000 are made annually.

ADMISSIONS INFORMATION

The Admission Committee considers applications from students entering grades 6 through 12. Although the largest number of students enters in grades 6, 7, and 9, spaces are often available in other grades as well.

Applicants are required to complete an on-campus interview and a written application. The SSAT is required for all applications to grades 6 through 9. Applicants to grade 10, 11, and 12 have the option to submit their PSAT or SAT scores.

APPLICATION TIMETABLE

The priority deadline for applications is February 1. Tours and interviews are offered through the Admission Office. There is a $50 preliminary application fee for applicants.

Notification of acceptance is mailed on March 10, and families are expected to reply by April 10.

ADMISSIONS CORRESPONDENCE

Admission Office
The Derryfield School
2108 River Road
Manchester, New Hampshire 03104-1396

Phone: 603-669-4524
Fax: 603-641-9521
E-mail: admission@derryfield.org
Web site: http://www.derryfield.org

ECOLE D'HUMANITÉ

Hasliberg-Goldern, Switzerland

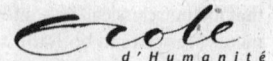

Type: Coeducational, international, college-preparatory, boarding school
Grades: Ungraded, ages 12–19 in American program, 12–Matura in Swiss/German Program
Enrollment: 130 (45 in American Program)

THE SCHOOL

The Ecole d'Humanité is located in Hasliberg Goldern, Switzerland, just off the rail line between Interlaken and Lucerne. Surrounded by the awe-inspiring peaks of the Bernese Oberland, this international village for living, learning, and growing is home to students and teachers from some twenty-five different countries. The stunning natural setting provides both a wholesome learning environment and exceptional opportunities for hiking, skiing, climbing, and other outdoor activities.

The school was founded in Germany by Edith Geheeb-Cassirer and Paul Geheeb, early leaders in the progressive education movement of the late nineteenth and early twentieth centuries. Very radical for its day, their coeducational boarding school involved students in new forms of learning. During the Nazi era, the Geheebs emigrated to Switzerland rather than compromise their educational principles. In 1946, the school was moved to its present location in the Swiss Alps. The philosophy of the Ecole d'Humanité continues to emphasize education of the person as a whole—a balance between artistic, athletic, and rigorous academic programs.

The Ecole d'Humanité strives to realize a simple, environmentally responsible lifestyle. By strictly limiting both material and electronic consumerism, the school attempts to create a space where students can engage directly and honestly with other people, with its common cultural heritage, and with the natural world, and where they are free to discover and explore their own unique strengths and passions.

The Ecole d'Humanité offers both Swiss and American academic programs. The American Program leads to a High School Diploma and includes preparation for the College Board SAT exams, for which the Ecole is an official testing center. Students can also prepare for exams leading to the AP International Diploma (APID) and entrance to universities around the world.

The Ecole d'Humanité is an international boarding school that has been legally registered with and recognized by the education department of the Canton of Berne, Switzerland since 1946, and is accredited by the North Central Association Commission on Accreditation and School Improvement (NCA CASI).

ACADEMIC PROGRAMS

The academic program at the Ecole d'Humanité aims to promote meaningful understanding rather than surface knowledge. Students take the same three classes for a full trimester every morning from Monday through Saturday. They select their own courses with the help of faculty advisors, balancing university requirements, career plans and their personal preferences. Having only three academic subjects at a time enables the classes to explore topics in more depth than in traditional school systems.

Small classes (student-teacher ratio is 5:1) allow for individualized instruction and demand active participation. Students are not "marked" with grades, but instead receive extensive feedback from their teachers based on their papers, tests, quizzes, and oral presentations. They assess their own work in regular written reflections that help them come to see their education as primarily their own responsibility.

The Ecole d'Humanité offers full preparation for exams leading to the Advanced Placement International Diploma (APID). These exams qualify students for entrance to universities not only throughout the Unites States, but also in many European countries and around the world. The College Board grants the APID to students at international schools who have earned a U.S. High School Diploma and have, in addition, received passing scores on five AP exams in a constellation, ensuring breadth and depth of study as well as a global perspective. AP courses at the Ecole are open to all interested students. Students can choose to take any number of APs—or none at all—according to their own particular strengths, interests, and ambitions.

Why APs rather than the IB? The Ecole carefully considered offering the IB and was impressed by its many merits. In its view, however, the APs offer a more flexible and less bureaucratic program, one that is better suited to the Ecole's philosophical underpinnings and to the size of the school. APs are recognized in more than forty countries, including Switzerland, Germany, Austria, and the United Kingdom and have been determined to be the right choice for this globally oriented school.

Under normal circumstances a graduating student will have completed 20 course credits, including 4 years of English, 3–4 years of mathematics, 2–3 years of science, 2 years of history or social science, and 3 years of a foreign language. He or she will also have written two Source Themes—extensive research papers on topics of the student's choice. In addition, most students will have completed several electives. Arts, sports, and music courses are required throughout each student's academic career. Extended hiking trips every fall and spring, an annual project week, and regular community service round out the program.

FACULTY AND ADVISERS

Forty full-time teachers and teacher/administrators and 5 part-time teachers live on campus. Additional teachers are engaged part-time as needed for instruction of specialty courses such as musical instruments, ski touring, and mountain climbing. The teachers also serve as "family heads" and as academic advisers, conferring with students about their individual goals, counseling them as they choose their courses, and following their progress throughout their time at the school. Teachers are passionate about both academic and nonacademic pursuits, and so offer sports, music, arts, and crafts courses as well as courses in their academic disciplines.

Ashley Curtis is the director of the American Program and co-director of the school. He served as a teacher at the Ecole from 1988 to 2003, returning in 2009 to direct the school. Ashley has also taught at schools in Massachusetts and in Italy. He earned B.A. and M.A.R. degrees at Yale University.

COLLEGE ADMISSION COUNSELING

The Dean of Academics meets with juniors to review college aspirations and to plan a college-visiting tour, using catalogs and online resources. Each senior meets weekly with a college adviser to complete college applications. The Ecole is an official College Board Testing Center, and students take the SAT and SAT Subject tests, as well as any AP exams they have chosen, right on campus. American colleges and other colleges around the world readily accept students who have had a thorough U.S. high school education combined with the experience of living abroad. Recent graduates of the American Program have attended a wide array of colleges and universities, including Bard, Bennington, Boston Conservatory, Brown, Colorado College, Dartmouth, Hampshire, NYU, Oberlin, Reed, Sarah Lawrence, the Universities of Chicago and Michigan, and the Universities of Southampton, Richmond, and Bristol in England.

STUDENT BODY AND CONDUCT

The student body for 2010–11 totals 130—71 boys and 59 girls. Seven are day students. Approximately 50 percent of the students come from Switzerland and the rest from twenty-four other countries. About 20 percent of the student body is non-Caucasian; 25 percent of students receive financial assistance.

Although this is a school with a demanding academic program, it is also a living community. Students at the Ecole take charge of such important tasks as organizing weekend activities, delivering firewood, taking care of the donkeys, and running the library and the fire brigade. Some are active in the Student Council or involved in peer counseling. Everyone participates in the weekly school meeting, which is chaired by a student. Here students can address both individual and community concerns, learning to find their own voices within a public forum.

ACADEMIC FACILITIES

Twelve buildings are used for academic purposes. Besides regular classrooms, they house three science laboratories; a workshop each for wood, stone-carving, pottery, metal, silver smithy, and studio art; a flexible performance space/assembly hall;

seven instrumental practice rooms; a computer room; a kitchen for general use; and an audiovisual room. The library houses more than 22,000 volumes in German and English, and French.

BOARDING AND GENERAL FACILITIES
All students live in family groups that are usually composed of 2 faculty members and about 8 boys and girls. Most students have one roommate. Each family lives together in one of the school houses and eats together in the common dining room. Wednesday evening is Family Evening, and the family members spend it together as a group—playing games, cooking a meal, working on a project, or just talking.

Teachers take particular interest in the students in their family and are concerned with their total development on a day-to-day basis, assuming such parental roles as planning birthday celebrations and offering counsel when problems arise. After their first year, students are able to choose the family and the house they wish to live in.

These family groups foster more open relationships among young people and between staff members and students. Living with a mixed group including both sexes and various cultures helps everyone to see beyond the stereotypes and appreciate individual differences. The mixture of older and younger children is also an important aspect of the family atmosphere.

A trained professional assists the family heads in administering to common illnesses and ailments. A physician visits the school regularly and is available for consultation in the next village. Trained professionals in psychology are available to consult with students as needed or to make special arrangements outside the school.

ATHLETICS
The Alps provide a stunning natural setting for outdoor sports, which include hiking, skiing, rock climbing, ski touring, and, occasionally, mountain biking and kayaking. In winter, students have the opportunity to ski or snowboard almost every day at the Meiringen-Hasliberg ski area, which extends right down to the school. The school also offers team sports such as basketball, soccer, and volleyball. Students and faculty members often organize intramural competitions on weekends. The school has its own playing field and basketball and volleyball courts as well as access to the local gymnasium. A swimming pool is located in a nearby village.

Twice a year, in the fall and spring trimesters, the entire school sets out in small groups on four- and six-day hikes into the mountains of Switzerland and Italy.

EXTRACURRICULAR OPPORTUNITIES
To balance the intensive academic program in the morning, students devote their afternoons to the arts, sports, and practical work, selecting from some eighty possible courses. Blacksmithing, skiing or snowboarding, woodworking, painting, pottery, rock-climbing, the annual Shakespeare production, French theater, classical, jazz, folk, and pop music ensembles, instrumental and voice lessons, gardening, and animal husbandry are just a few of the fields students can choose to explore and then concentrate on in their afternoons. In the middle of the fall trimester, an "Intensive Week" allows students to devote an entire week, morning and afternoon, to a single project. Student theater as well as musical and dance performances are presented throughout the year.

DAILY LIFE
Wake-up is at 6:30 a.m., with breakfast at 7:05. All meals are eaten in family groups in the common dining hall, with a Service Group of students serving the meal and washing up after. The first morning course begins at 8:05 a.m., and the last morning course ends at 12:30 p.m. The nonacademic courses take place Monday through Thursday between 2:30 and 6:15, following lunch and siesta. After dinner, there is free time until the evening Quiet Hour. Family Evening is on Wednesday. The school gathers for a community meeting on Friday afternoon and singing on Saturday morning.

WEEKEND LIFE
The weekend officially lasts from Saturday at midday until Sunday dinner. Students and teachers alike organize activities for the weekend, including sports events, coffeehouses, films, and biweekly disco and folk-dance evenings. Students and/or teachers present an "Andacht" on Sunday evenings, which is generally a reflection on ethical, philosophical, or social issues. Older students may visit the nearby town, and all are free to explore the surrounding natural wonders. In winter, many students spend at least part of the weekend skiing or snowboarding.

COSTS AND FINANCIAL AID
Tuition is quoted in Swiss francs, and, for those paying in other currencies, is dependent on the current exchange rate. The tuition for the academic year 2010–11 is CHF 44,000. Tuition is payable in one payment, three payments (one per term), or ten installments (monthly). The Scholarship Committee reviews applications for financial aid.

ADMISSIONS INFORMATION
The Admissions Committee seeks students who are eager to challenge themselves academically, to discover and develop their own individual passions, and to participate in a simple and ecologically sound community life without the distractions of excessive electronic entertainment. All applicants who live in or near Switzerland must visit the school for an interview and tour that offer the opportunity to meet students and faculty members. Applicants who live farther away can request an interview by phone or with someone familiar with the school in their area. The American program requires two letters of recommendation and school records.

APPLICATION TIMETABLE
Applications are accepted on a rolling basis. Applications received by May 15 have the best chance of acceptance. An American student who is enrolling at the school must obtain a student visa, which can take up to eight weeks for processing by the Swiss Embassy.

ADMISSIONS CORRESPONDENCE
Ecole d'Humanité
CH-6085 Hasliberg-Goldern
Switzerland

Phone: +41-33-972-92-92
Fax: +41-33-972-92-11
E-mail: admissions@ecole.ch
Web site: http://www.ecole.ch

EMMA WILLARD SCHOOL

Troy, New York

Type: Girls' boarding and day college-preparatory school
Grades: 9–12, postgraduate year
Enrollment: 317
Head of School: Trudy E. Hall

THE SCHOOL

In 1814, Emma Hart Willard founded the school that now bears her name, making it the oldest institution for the higher education of young women in the United States. Her belief in women's intellectual capabilities, a radical idea for the time, is the cornerstone of a curriculum that has challenged Emma Willard students for nearly 200 years.

The exceptionally beautiful 137-acre campus has forty-three buildings. Emma Willard School is located on the edge of the city of Troy, 7 miles from Albany, at the crossroads of the Berkshires, the Adirondacks, and the Catskills.

The 31-member Board of Trustees includes 16 alumnae, 4 parents, and 1 faculty member. An operating budget of $18 million is supported in part through a $78.5-million endowment and Annual Giving that exceeds $1.8 million.

Emma Willard School (EWS) is accredited by the New York State Association of Independent Schools and by the New York State Board of Regents. It is a member of the National Association of Independent Schools, the New York State Association of Independent Schools, the Cum Laude Society, and the National Coalition of Girls Schools.

ACADEMIC PROGRAMS

The Emma Willard curriculum develops those abilities and qualities of mind that are essential to the successful woman. The rigorous college-preparatory curriculum ensures a strong foundation in all major academic areas in addition to extensive exposure to the arts. Emma Willard celebrates leadership, rewards successes, offers appropriate support, and reminds girls of the limitless possibilities the world presents an educated woman.

Each student's faculty adviser helps her plan her courses in coordination with the Director of College Counseling and the Dean of Curriculum and Programs. Graduation requirements include a minimum of 4 years of English; 3 years of mathematics, history, and foreign language; 2 years of lab science (including biology and chemistry); and 2 years of visual and performing arts. All students are required to participate in the service program and the Emma Willard seminar program, as well as in physical education.

The School offers more than 130 courses, including Advanced Placement (AP) preparation in all academic departments, including arts and computer science. A student who wishes to study subjects beyond the curriculum offerings may arrange individualized tutorials with faculty supervision.

All underclass women are assigned to a daily supervised study hall during the fall term; students in good academic standing are excused from this study hall at the end of the term. There is a 2-hour evening study period Sunday through Thursday for all boarding students all year. Students may be assigned by their advisers to a supervised evening study hall. The library is open 15 hours a day, seven days a week. At least one professional librarian is on duty 66 hours a week.

Emma Willard students may take courses for credit at nearby universities. In addition, the School is a member of the National Network of Complementary Schools, which offers students an opportunity to pursue special programs on an exchange basis. Practicum, Emma Willard's independent study program, provides opportunities to earn credit and explore a career interest through hands-on experience in many industries, organizations, and professions. Recent Practicum projects have focused on broadcasting, publishing, microbiology, veterinary medicine, law, environmental engineering, photojournalism, advertising, government, and architecture. Vacation trips abroad, as well as work with Habitat for Humanity, are undertaken by students with faculty chaperones each year; groups have traveled to Austria, Belize, England, Ethiopia, France, Germany, Greece, Ireland, Italy, Russia, and Spain.

The grading system uses letter grades with plus and minus notations. A few courses are graded Credit/No Credit. Grades and comments are issued to parents and students at midterm and at the end of each semester.

FACULTY AND ADVISERS

The faculty numbers 53 (40 full-time and 13 part-time); 77 percent are women and 23 percent are men. The student-faculty ratio is 6:1. Many faculty members reside on campus. Faculty members, administrators, and residence staff members hold forty-four advanced degrees, including Ph.D.'s, J.D.'s, and master's degrees, earned at such colleges and universities as Amherst, Boston College, Boston University, Brown, Bryn Mawr, Columbia, Dartmouth, Duke, Fairleigh Dickinson, Harvard, Macalester, Manhattanville, Massachusetts College of Liberal Arts, Middlebury, Mount Holyoke, Northeastern, NYU, Oxford, Princeton, Rensselaer, Russell Sage, Smith, St. Lawrence, Saint Rose, SUNY at Albany, Swarthmore, UCLA, Vassar, Wellesley, Wesleyan, Williams, and Yale.

Trudy E. Hall was appointed Head of School in 1999. She holds a B.S. from St. Lawrence University, an M.Ed. from Harvard University, and an M.A.L.S. from Duke University.

In selecting its teachers, Emma Willard looks for adults who are dedicated to enriching the lives of young people in and out of the classroom. The School has a full-time Director of Faculty Development. Faculty development grants are available to those who wish to pursue advanced degrees or enrich their current areas of study and to those who wish to develop new courses. Sabbaticals and travel funds are available to all faculty members. Most dormitory staff members are full-time residence personnel and do not teach. All faculty members act as advisers to 4–6 students each. Faculty members chaperone weekend activities, sit on School committees, and advise student organizations. Annual faculty turnover is typically less than 10 percent.

COLLEGE ADMISSION COUNSELING

Formal college counseling begins in the junior year. The director of college counseling supervises all college placement testing (the PSAT, the SAT, and Subject Tests), coordinates visits to Emma Willard by college admissions officers, assists students in planning college visits, and writes a comprehensive recommendation for each senior, based on the student's academic record and teachers' written evaluations.

Seventy-four students in the class of 2010 have enrolled in colleges and universities, including Amherst, Barnard, Boston University, Brandeis, Bryn Mawr, Connecticut College, Cornell, Dartmouth, Duke, Hamilton, Hobart and William Smith, Hollins, Kentucky Wesleyan, Lewis & Clark, Middlebury, Mount Holyoke, NYU, Oberlin, Rice, Rollins, Smith, Trinity, Tufts, Vassar, Wellesley, Williams, and the Universities of Chicago, Pennsylvania, Pittsburgh, Toronto, and Vermont. The average SAT scores for the class of 2010 were 1908: 633 (critical reading), 620 (math), and 655 (writing).

STUDENT BODY AND CONDUCT

In 2010–11, Emma Willard has 202 boarding and 115 day students, as follows: grade 9, 68; grade 10, 79; grade 11, 87; and grade 12, 83. Students come from twenty states and thirty other countries; 17 percent are students of color.

The School seeks to enroll girls who are responsible and mature enough not to require rigid structure, but all are expected to abide by the fundamental rules that govern major issues of discipline.

Uniforms are not required, but students are expected to meet standards of neatness and cleanliness in dress code during the academic day or in the dormitories. Dress for plays, concerts, and academic convocations is more formal.

ACADEMIC FACILITIES

The oldest buildings, of Tudor Gothic design, include the Alumnae Chapel and Slocum Hall, which contains classrooms, offices, Kiggins Hall, the main auditorium, a lab theater, and a dance studio. The Hunter Science Center, an addition to Weaver Hall, opened in 1996. Hunter includes computer equipment integrated with revolutionary fractal laboratories. Completing the main quadrangle is the art, music, and library complex designed by Edward Larabee Barnes and constructed from 1967 to 1971. Other campus buildings house an additional auditorium and dance studio, ten music practice rooms, twenty-one grand pianos, six science laboratories, an audiovisual center, two photography darkrooms, a microcomputer center, and a weaving studio.

The William Moore Dietel Library holds more than 35,000 volumes in addition to a growing collection of e-books, and 77 periodical subscriptions. Eighteen online databases with full text augment the journal collection. The collection also includes hundreds of CDs, a sizable art and architecture slide collection, and the School archives, which include nineteenth-century photographs and manuscripts and some medieval manuscripts.

BOARDING AND GENERAL FACILITIES

Students reside in three connected dormitories, Sage, Hypen, and Kellas. Sophomores, juniors, and seniors live together on various halls; ninth grade students live together on the same hall. There are single rooms, doubles, and suites. Professional residential faculty members supervise student life in the dormitories. A team of faculty affiliates, student proctors, and peer educators shares in dormitory responsibilities. Day students are assigned to residence halls to facilitate their integration into the residential program.

In 2004, the School embarked on a $32-million "adaptive reuse" project of the first and garden levels of the residence halls to create new community spaces. The design included a new state-of-the-art dining hall, student center, student study lounge, e-café, admissions suite, and student services offices. The project was completed in fall 2007. Other campus buildings include a variety of on-campus faculty residences.

ATHLETICS

Emma Willard encourages students to combine lifetime sports with competition; students can fulfill the physical activities requirement through team sports, individual sports, or dance. Emma Willard teams compete in a league with other local schools, both public and private, in basketball, crew, cross-country, field hockey, lacrosse, soccer, softball, swimming, tennis, track, and volleyball. Recreational activities include cross-country skiing, dance, skating, swimming, tennis, volleyball, weight conditioning, and yoga. In addition to the Mott Gymnasium, which includes two indoor tennis courts and full facilities for basketball, volleyball, and fitness training, facilities include six outdoor tennis courts, three large playing fields, and an all-weather 400-meter track. In 1998, the Helen S. Cheel Aquatics and Fitness Center opened with a competition-size swimming pool and state-of-the-art fitness equipment.

EXTRACURRICULAR OPPORTUNITIES

The Serving and Shaping Her World Speakers Series and the 175th Anniversary Speakers Series bring prominent individuals to campus for lectures, classroom interaction, and residencies. Speakers have included Poet Laureate Billy Collins; mathematician and author Edward Burger; ABC news correspondent Lynn Sherr; science writer Margaret Wertheim; Pulitzer Prize–winning authors Nicholas Kristof and Sheryl WuDunn; artist, slam poet, and filmmaker Kip Fulbeck; and award-winning novelist Tobias Wolff. The EWS arts calendar features an impressive array of renowned chamber groups, dance companies, artists, and exhibitions.

The surrounding region offers performances at the historic Troy Music Hall, the Saratoga Performing Arts Center, and Tanglewood; events at the Empire State Performing Arts Center in Albany; ethnic festivals; sports events; theater; and activities at nearby colleges and universities. The School sponsors a world-class chamber music series and all students are required to attend at least two cultural events each term.

Among the many clubs and organizations are the Outing Club, Slavery No More, Student Organization for Animal Rights, EMMA Green (environmental group), Quiz Team, Fair Trade, Foreign and American Student Organization, Black and Hispanic Awareness, Phila (charitable service club), and various singing groups. There are also three student publications: *Triangle,* the arts and literary magazine; *The Clock,* the School newspaper; and *Gargoyle,* the yearbook. Through Interact, girls may serve the community in volunteer projects such as Big Brothers/Big Sisters. Traditions include the opening-of-school Academic Convocation, fall and spring senior dinners, holiday Eventide, Revels, the surprise holiday Principal's Play Day, May Day, and the Flame Ceremony.

DAILY LIFE

Classes are held Monday through Friday from 8 to 3:30, in time blocks of 50-minute and 75-minute periods. On Wednesdays, students and teachers gather to participate in schoolwide academic activities, such as the service program and the Serving and Shaping Her World Speakers Series. A mid-morning all-school meeting is held three times a week. Team sports, choir, some dance classes, and drama rehearsals meet after 3:30. Dinner is served from 5:30 to 7 p.m., and quiet study hours are 7:30 to 9:30. All students must be on their floor by 10:30 and in their rooms by 11 p.m.

WEEKEND LIFE

An extensive weekend activities program is developed and coordinated by a full-time staff member of Student Affairs. The Emma Willard campus is at the crossroads of New England, the Adirondacks, the Catskills, and the Berkshires. This location gives students an exciting array of cultural and recreational venues. Weekend activities include sports events, dances with boys' schools, dinner in the Capital District, movies on and off campus, and trips to Boston, New York, and Montreal. Generally, 75 to 80 percent of the boarders remain on campus during the weekend, and day students are encouraged to participate in weekend activities. Transportation to area events and places of worship is provided upon request.

COSTS AND FINANCIAL AID

Tuition, room, and board in 2010–11 are $41,500. Day student tuition is $26,400. A SmartCard fee of $600 for boarding students in grades 9–11 ($650 for seniors) and $400 for day students in grades 9–11 ($450 for seniors) covers testing, field trips, and other class-related expenses. A technology fee of $350 per year is required to cover all technology services, including the use of the computer and access to all of the services available over the wired and wireless networks. Emma Willard requires all new students in grades 9 and 10 to have a laptop computer.

Families purchase text books directly from the School's online vendor. The average cost of books per year is $500. Special-fee courses include private music lessons, ballet, skiing, and horseback riding. A $1500 deposit is required to confirm enrollment; School fees are billed in July and December, and families may elect to pay 60 percent in August, with the remainder due in January. Families who wish to make monthly tuition payments may do so through the School's ten-month installment plan.

The School is committed to maintaining the diversity of its student body and allocated more than $3.8 million in financial aid to 53 percent of the student body during 2010–11. Aid is awarded on the basis of academic promise and family financial need, as determined by the parents' financial statement of the School and Student Service for Financial Aid. Applications for financial aid must be submitted by February 1. As long as a student is in good standing and family circumstances warrant continued assistance, grants are renewed from year to year.

ADMISSIONS INFORMATION

Emma Willard seeks students of above-average to superior academic ability who are self-motivated, responsible, interested in learning, and involved in activities outside the classroom. All candidates for admission must submit an application, a personal essay, transcripts, three recommendations, and the results of the SSAT. Students for whom English is not their first language should submit the results of the TOEFL in lieu of the SSAT. An interview is strongly encouraged. Applicants for the postgraduate year should submit SAT scores.

APPLICATION TIMETABLE

Initial inquiries are welcome at any time. Campus visits include tours for parents and daughters, interviews, a class visit, and frequently a meal. On weekdays, office hours are 8 a.m. to 4:30 p.m. Appointments may be made at any time of year, but October through April visits are strongly recommended. Open house programs are scheduled in the fall.

The application fee of $50 ($100 for international students) is nonrefundable. The application deadline is February 1. Prospective students and their parents are notified of the Admission Committee's decision in March. Applications received after that time are accepted on a space-available basis.

ADMISSIONS CORRESPONDENCE

Director of Admissions
Emma Willard School
285 Pawling Avenue
Troy, New York 12180

Phone: 518-833-1320
Fax: 518-833-1805
E-mail: admissions@emmawillard.org
Web site: http://www.emmawillard.org

FOUNTAIN VALLEY SCHOOL OF COLORADO

Colorado Springs, Colorado

Type: Coeducational boarding and day college-preparatory school
Grades: 9–12
Enrollment: 261
Head of School: Craig W. Larimer Jr. '69, Headmaster

THE SCHOOL

Fountain Valley School of Colorado (FVS) was established in 1930 and was opened the following year led by a group of visionary men and women who were philanthropists, statesmen, scientists, entrepreneurs, and educators. Many had personal and professional ties to the East; all shared the conviction that the Eastern independent school tradition of academic excellence, progressive ideals, self-reliance, and intellectual curiosity would thrive in the expansiveness of the Rocky Mountain West. John Dewey, the notable American educational reformer, was on the first Board of Trustees, and his grandson graduated with the class of 1940.

The School's mission remains unchanged: FVS is dedicated to providing a rigorous college-preparatory curriculum in academics, athletics, and the arts. The community endeavors to foster a lifelong love of challenge and learning in an environment of diversity and mutual respect and to prepare adolescents to become individuals who are open-minded, curious, courageous, self-reliant, and compassionate.

The School is situated at the base of Pikes Peak on the former Bradley Ranch on 1,100 acres of rolling prairie in southeastern Colorado Springs. The School's 40-acre Mountain Campus is located 115 miles west of the main campus, in the San Isabel National Forest.

Fountain Valley School of Colorado is a nonprofit corporation governed by a 23-member Board of Trustees, 18 of whom are alumni. The School's endowment is valued at more than $23 million. In 2009–10, annual giving was $1.2 million. More than 2,600 alumni maintain contact with FVS, and many are actively involved. In June 2005, more than 600 alumni returned to campus to celebrate the School's seventy-fifth anniversary. In 2003, FVS completed a $24-million capital campaign, the largest in Colorado independent-school history.

FVS is accredited by the Colorado State Board of Education and the Association of Colorado Independent Schools and holds memberships in the National Association of Independent Schools, the Secondary School Admission Test Board, the College Board, the Association of Boarding Schools, the Western Boarding School Association, the Council for Advancement and Support of Education, the Colorado High School Activities Association, and the Cum Laude Society.

ACADEMIC PROGRAMS

Fountain Valley's academic program is rigorous and comprehensive, offering honors and Advanced Placement courses in all disciplines and providing a flexible approach to placing students in courses appropriate to their abilities. More than 70 courses were offered by seven departments in the 2009–10 year.

The school year is divided into two semesters; major semester courses receive ½ credit. Twenty credits in major courses are required for graduation (most seniors graduate with more than 22 credits), with the following minimum departmental expectations: 4 credits of English; completion of the third-year level of one foreign language (French, Mandarin Chinese, or Spanish); 3 credits of high school mathematics, with the minimum successful completion of algebra II; 3 credits of science (including 1 credit of biology); 3½ credits of history (including 1 credit of Western civilization, 1 credit of global studies, 1 credit of U.S. history and 1 credit of senior history elective); 1 credit

of visual and performing arts; ½ credit of computer skills; ½ credit of human development; and 4 credits of physical education. Most students take one minor and five major courses per semester. In addition, English as a second language (ESL) is offered at the intermediate and advanced levels. Qualified seniors, with the approval of the Curriculum Committee, design Independent Study Projects to supplement their advanced studies. All seniors participate in the Senior Seminar, a weeklong service project culminating their FVS education. Freshmen are required to take the Freshman Transitions class, which seeks to help students adjust to life at FVS, and Freshman Arts, a yearlong introduction to all the arts.

The Western Immersion Program (WIP) is a signature interdisciplinary program for all FVS sophomores. Weaving together the disciplines of literature, history, science, and art, WIP explores how the Western landscape shaped the people, history, and culture of the region. Sophomores also take Career Development.

The student-teacher ratio is 6:1, and the average class size is 12 students. The small classes allow for personal attention and provide an intimate learning environment characterized by mutual respect and active participation.

Grades (letters A through E) are given at midterm and at the conclusion of each semester. Written comments are provided for each course at the fall midterm for all new students and at the end of the term for all students.

FACULTY AND ADVISERS

FVS has a 47 member teaching faculty, with 36 teaching full-time. Seventy percent of faculty members hold advanced degrees; 27 live on campus, with 9 in residence halls; 34 are advisers; and 28 are coaches.

Fountain Valley's seventh headmaster, Craig W. Larimer Jr. '69, assumed the leadership of the School in 2007. He graduated from Pomona College and earned his M.A. from Johns Hopkins School of Advanced International Studies. Prior to his appointment as headmaster, Larimer served for five years as president of the FVS Board of Trustees, where he coauthored the School's current Strategic Plan. Professionally, he worked for twenty-two years in international capital markets with the First National Bank of Chicago and Bank One. Larimer began his career in government, where he served in the U.S. Treasury Department's office at the U.S. Embassy in London as well as the Office of International Monetary Affairs in Washington, D.C.

Because all faculty members share responsibility for the residential and cocurricular programs at the School, Fountain Valley seeks to recruit teachers with personal idealism, a genuine respect for students, and high professional competence. An endowment and annually budgeted funds ensure continued faculty professional development.

COLLEGE ADMISSION COUNSELING

Students begin to prepare for college in their first year at Fountain Valley through course choice and careful planning with the Academic Dean. College counseling starts in the sophomore year. Sessions are planned to help students understand the complexities of the college application process and learn about the range of colleges offering programs in which they are interested.

Each fall, Fountain Valley holds a college fair to give juniors and seniors an opportunity to talk with representatives from approximately 150 colleges and universities. Students gather firsthand information from the Director of College Counseling, college Web sites and other college Internet resources, an extensive library of college catalogs and media, and a workbook designed to help them with the college application process.

FVS has a detailed section on its own Web site devoted to college counseling. The section includes information on college programs, summer programs and scholarships, financial aid, and detailed Web listings to help the college-bound student.

The Director of College Counseling begins working with individual students and small groups during the junior year, while other staff members work with sophomores. She creates an individual list of college possibilities for each junior tailored to their expressed interests and needs. She continues to work closely with each senior in refining his or her college plans.

The classes of 2008 through 2010 had an SAT range of scores (middle 50 percent) of critical reading, 500–663; math, 540–680; and writing, 500–650. From 2006 through 2010, FVS graduates were admitted to 308 four-year colleges and universities.

STUDENT BODY AND CONDUCT

In 2010–11 the School's enrollment is 174 boarding students and 87 day students from twenty-seven states and nineteen countries.

The School works to create and maintain an environment for learning in which goodwill and mutual trust exist among all members of the campus community. At the same time, it adheres to the belief that every strong community must have a clear set of standards and defined values for all its members to uphold. If a student is found to be involved in a serious disciplinary matter, the case is heard by an honor council composed of elected student representatives and faculty members. The council considers all facets of each case and recommends a course of action to the Headmaster.

A Community Council chaired by the president of the student body provides a forum in which any members of the School community can make recommendations regarding the operation of the School.

ACADEMIC FACILITIES

The majority of classes are conducted in the Froelicher Academic Building, which includes a state-of-the-art science annex and two computer labs (with both PCs and Macintosh computers). There are also clusters of computers in other parts of campus that students can use, including in the library and the Learning Center.

The William Thayer Tutt Art Center (Art Barn) houses art, jewelry, and ceramics studios; an art gallery; a photo laboratory; and production rooms for the School's publications. The John B. Hawley, Jr. Library has forty-one study carrels, two seminar rooms, and a film editing and projection room. The library has an online catalog of more than 25,000 volumes and a collection of periodicals on microfilm.

The FVS Learning Center offers important education support for students, parents, and teachers. Students who need help with study skills, personal organization, time management, or test anxiety can meet with a trained staff member individually or in small groups.

Students who need continued, regular support for their learning issues can be enrolled by their parents in the Learning Assistance Program. There is an additional charge for the program; enrollment is limited.

BOARDING AND GENERAL FACILITIES
Fountain Valley School's four residence halls include ten individual houses where 174 students and 13 houseparent families live. Spacious double and triple bedrooms, common rooms, a kitchen, dining area, bathrooms, laundry facilities, and a computer lab are laid out in floor plans unique to each house.

The Hacienda, Fountain Valley's original ranch house, has dining facilities for 300, private dining rooms for meetings, and a living room for meetings and quiet conversation. The dining room was renovated in 2008 to provide a better atmosphere and a wider selection of menu choices for students and faculty. The Chase Stone Infirmary is a recently renovated ten-bed facility with a nurse on call at all times.

The Frautschi Campus Center was completed in 1990 and has a student-operated snack bar, a campus bookstore, a post office, lounge and recreation facilities, a faculty lounge, a multimedia viewing room, and a meeting space.

The Lewis Perry Jr. Chapel, currently being expanded to accommodate the School's increased student population, houses weekly All-School meetings, concerts, and other regular activities. The Performing Arts Center contains a small black-box type theater that houses the School's three yearly productions.

ATHLETICS
Fountain Valley believes strongly in the value of sports for building physical fitness, self-confidence, and character. Most students fulfill their requirement by participating in a variety of interscholastic sports, including basketball, climbing, cross-country, golf, ice hockey, lacrosse, soccer, tennis, track, and volleyball for boys and basketball, climbing, cross-country, field hockey, lacrosse, soccer, swimming, tennis, track, and volleyball for girls.

Students may also earn physical education credit for horseback riding, skiing, snowboarding, and outdoor education. The School provides suitable levels of competition for students of varying abilities. FVS offers a comprehensive horsemanship program that provides diverse training in both English and Western riding. Riding facilities include the largest outdoor arena in the Colorado Springs area, a covered arena, a barn, stables, and more than 1,000 acres of open prairie. In 2007 and 2010, the English riding team earned the hunt seat national title at the Interscholastic Equestrian Association championships. A new state-of-

the-art indoor riding facility that includes stables, tack rooms, offices, and classroom space opened in 2008.

The Penrose Sports Center includes a gymnasium, two squash courts, a newly renovated strength and conditioning facility, and a five-lane, 25-yard indoor swimming pool. FVS athletic fields are some of the finest in Colorado for soccer, field hockey, and lacrosse. Also, the School's first-ever outdoor track opened in 2008. Nine tennis courts and a climbing wall complete the facilities.

EXTRACURRICULAR OPPORTUNITIES
Extracurricular activities vary from season to season. Students can perform in three major drama productions annually, including a winter musical. Guest speakers and artists regularly visit the campus for formal presentations and lectures. There are three student publications (newspaper, poetry book, and yearbook) and about twenty student activity clubs.

Special annual events include gymkhanas in which a riding team from Fountain Valley competes with teams from local riding clubs, Earth Day, Mountain Bike Weekend, Ski Weekend, Stupid Night Out, and Unity Day.

During Interim, traditional classes are suspended, and students participate in a variety of on- and off-campus programs. Recent Interims have included learning about French culture while in Paris, discovering southern culture and the blues in Memphis, kayaking in Georgia, and connecting with American musical theater in New York. Freshman Interim introduces students to the central premise of Interim—learning by doing. Organized in small groups, Freshman Interim focuses on the history of Colorado by exploring subjects such as ranching, Colorado wildlife, Native American heritage, Hispanic heritage, and pioneer heritage.

DAILY LIFE
Classes meet five days per week in six 50-minute sessions between 8 and 3. Afternoon activities (athletics or theater) are scheduled from 3:15 to 5:30. One period each week is used for student-adviser and All-School meetings. Students and teachers generally have at least one free period daily.

Dinner is at 5:30, and study hours run from 7 to 8:30 p.m. and 9 to 10 p.m. All boarding students are expected to observe study hours, although seniors in good academic standing may be excused in the spring of their senior year.

Day students are expected to be on campus before their first commitment and to remain until 5:30 p.m. on weekdays. Day students may stay overnight in a residence hall with permission from the houseparent and the student's parents.

WEEKEND LIFE
Weekends are time for relaxation and taking advantage of campus resources and a host of opportunities in the surrounding mountain region.

Student and faculty teams sponsor recreational activities throughout the weekend. Events include mountain climbing, skiing, and pack trips, often based at the Mountain Campus; excursions to Colorado Springs and Denver for movies, theater, concerts, dinner, and shopping; and dances, barbecues, movies, and athletics on campus.

Students with parental permission may request a weekend away from the campus. Many students visit friends or relatives or are invited to another student's home.

COSTS AND FINANCIAL AID
In 2010–11, tuition was $42,000 for boarding students; the cost (including all meals and bus transportation) for day students was $22,800. A book fee of $1060 covers textbooks, art supplies, lab fees, and one yearbook.

Interim, a required weeklong experiential learning opportunity, varies in cost according to the student's choice of trip. There are also fees for optional activities such as music lessons, horseback riding, and horse boarding. Tuition insurance and a tuition payment plan are available.

In 2009–10, 36 percent of students received approximately $1.8 million in merit- and need-based financial aid. Fountain Valley School adheres to the principles of good practice in its need-based aid distribution as part of the National Association of Independent Schools. All first-round applicants for ninth and tenth grade are considered for merit scholarships through the School's Summit Scholarship program.

ADMISSIONS INFORMATION
Students are admitted without regard to race, religion, or nationality. Fountain Valley School of Colorado seeks students who have the potential to benefit from a rigorous academic program and contribute to the School community. Students are admitted in grades 9 through 11 (in some cases grade 12) on the basis of previous school records, three academic recommendations, results of the Secondary School Admission Test (SSAT), an essay, and a personal interview.

APPLICATION TIMETABLE
Fountain Valley subscribes to the March 10 notification date endorsed by the SSAT Board. The application deadline is February 1. Applications are processed after that date if openings remain. The application fee is $50 for applicants residing in the United States and $100 for applicants living outside the United States.

ADMISSIONS CORRESPONDENCE
Randy Roach
Director of Admission and Financial Aid
Fountain Valley School of Colorado
6155 Fountain Valley School Road
Colorado Springs, Colorado 80911

Phone: 719-390-7035 Ext. 251
Fax: 719-390-7762
E-mail: admission@fvs.edu
Web site: http://www.fvs.edu

GEORGE STEVENS ACADEMY

Blue Hill, Maine

Type: Coeducational boarding and day college-preparatory school
Grades: 9–12
Enrollment: 300
Head of School: Bayard Brokaw, Head of School (interim)

THE SCHOOL

George Stevens Academy (GSA) was founded in 1803 as Blue Hill Academy. The first students, men and women from nearby towns, were taught by a preceptor and 2 teachers, and their courses of study included Greek, Latin, and navigation. The Academy flourished under the guardianship of the Congregational Church, but in 1832, George Stevens, the first non-Congregationalist to become a member of the Board of Trustees, offered money and land to the Academy on the condition that it become an equal-opportunity institution. When the Board refused, he donated 150 acres of land to build another school, the George Stevens Academy. In 1943, the two schools finally merged into Blue Hill–George Stevens Academy.

Today, GSA consists of 20 acres, including administrative buildings and athletic fields, plus another 500 acres for future development. The mission of the Academy is to create a caring and dynamic community that educates and encourages students to reach their highest potential through a wide array of challenging academic and extracurricular programs. It is committed to academic excellence, creative thinking, and artistic expression and offers diverse opportunities for self-discovery that enable and require students to make responsible choices. The governing body includes the Head of School, the Assistant Head of School, the Academic Dean, the Dean of Students, and a 20-person Board of Trustees, on which many GSA alumni sit.

Academically, students from GSA rank among the best in the state, with many graduates attending the top universities and colleges in the U.S. In music, the Jazz Band and the Jazz Combo have won state championships for the past seven years, bringing home six first-place trophies and six MVP awards. For more than eighteen years, the Jazz Band placed in the top three spots at the State Competition. GSA's Jazz Combo, Musiquarium, won fourth place at the 2005 Berklee College of Music Jazz Festival in Boston. In athletics, the boys' tennis team won the Eastern Maine Championships in 2010 and 2008, and the girls' team won the same championship in 2009. In 2006, the girls' soccer team won the Eastern Maine Championship. The baseball and softball teams won the Eastern Maine Championship in 2010, and the girls' basketball team won that title in 2009. That same year, one of the girls scored her 1,000th point as a GSA basketball player. In 2009, the golf team (coed) qualified for the State Team Championship.

GSA is accredited by the New England Association of Schools and Colleges (NEAS&C) and the Maine Department of Educational and Cultural Services. GSA is also a member of the College Board, the Secondary School Admission Test Board (SSATB), and the Independent Schools Association of Northern New England.

ACADEMIC PROGRAMS

The academic year is divided into two semesters: September through December and January through June. In order to graduate, students must earn a total of 22 academic credits, including 4 English credits, 3 math credits, 3 science credits, 3 social science credits, 1 physical education credit, 1 fine arts credit, ½ credit in health, and 6½ elective credits. All students are required to carry a minimum of 5 credits each semester. Juniors and seniors may also participate in a two-week Independent Study and Internship Program. Seniors must fulfill a senior debate requirement in order to graduate. Every June, seniors debate one another on a wide range of topics, from current events to legal issues. Public speaking, research, cooperation with partners and team members, synthesizing an informed argument, and self-expression are important elements of the debate process. The debate is a logical culmination of the high school language arts experience and gives students an opportunity to study, in depth, a topic of their choice.

In order to accommodate different learning styles and abilities, GSA offers a varied curriculum at three different levels: skills, college-prep (CP4), and honors. Seven AP courses are also available. Honors and AP courses challenge students to pursue subjects deeply, intensively, and rigorously. The foreign language program includes French, Spanish, and Latin. Some of the more unique courses at GSA are human geography, earthworks, boat building, marine science, Maine environment, forensics, jazz, chamber music for strings, photography, psychology, lab geometry, and advanced applications of finite math. A state-certified special education teacher is available to support students with special needs who are taking the majority of their courses in regular classes.

GSA offers a comprehensive ESL program for international students at three levels: beginner, intermediate, and advanced. Students are tested prior to placement in one of the levels. ESL courses focus on developing conversational and writing skills as well as the language necessary for regular subject classes. Special emphasis is also placed on preparing students for the TOEFL exam and entry into U.S. colleges and universities.

An Alternative Course Contract (ACC) provides an opportunity for a student to take a course not offered in the regular curriculum. A student, in consultation with the Office of Student Services and a member of the GSA faculty, may design the curriculum and write a course proposal that includes a description of the course, goals, and objectives and the amount of credit to be earned. An Alternative Course Contract may be taken on a pass/fail basis or for a numerical grade. Alternative Course Contracts are usually taken in addition to the required 5 academic credits. The Head of School must pre-approve all Alternative Course Contracts.

FACULTY AND ADVISERS

There are 31 teachers at the Academy; more than half of the instructors have advanced degrees. The faculty is composed almost equally of men and women. GSA faculty members are skilled, caring educators who are actively involved in students' lives. Each full-time faculty member serves as an adviser for up to 15 students to assist them in their academic, social, and emotional development. They help students set educational goals and develop the skills necessary to accomplish them. In addition, advisers assist students through the college-admission process, including the coordination of college aptitude tests and the various aspects of applying to college. Faculty members are also involved in advising student clubs and coaching athletics.

Bayard Brokaw has a B.A. in history and political science from Bowdoin College and an M.A. in international studies from Denver University. Mr. Brokaw joined the GSA faculty in 2002, serving first as Dean of Students and more recently, as Academic Dean. Prior to coming to GSA, he was Director of the Bay School in Blue Hill. Between 1992 and 1996 he helped establish and direct Souhegan High School in Amherst, Massachusetts.

COLLEGE ADMISSION COUNSELING

The Office of Student Services meets with students on an individual and group basis to discuss and map out students' future plans, explore and refine individual goals, and organize a time-management system for the college application process. There is a dedicated college counselor specifically for international students who guides students through the college selection and application process. This counselor also helps arrange for students to take the SAT, ACT, or TOEFL exams. The Academy hosts a number of college admissions representatives and financial aid workshops every year. About 81 percent of students who graduate from the Academy attend postsecondary institutions. Within Maine, recent graduates have attended Bates, Bowdoin, Colby, and the Universities of Maine and Southern Maine. Recent graduates are attending such colleges and universities as Berklee College of Music, Cornell, Dartmouth, Harvard, NYU, Penn State, RPI, Smith, Stanford, Yale, the University of Virginia, and the U.S. Naval Academy.

STUDENT BODY AND CONDUCT

In the 2010–11 academic year, the Academy has enrolled a total of 300 students: 142 boys and 157 girls. In grade 9, there are 37 boys and 24 girls; grade 10, 42 boys and 36 girls; grade 11, 29 boys and 47 girls; and grade 12, 34 boys and 50 girls. The majority of students come from Blue Hill and the surrounding towns. The socioeconomic range is wide; students have parents in occupations ranging from lobstermen and mill workers to lawyers and doctors. In fall 2010, GSA admitted 33 international students from China, Japan, Germany, Korea, Thailand, and Vietnam.

Students participate in the management of the school through the Student Council, which provides leadership, school service, a forum for student voice, and channels for student involvement. Students' rights and responsibilities are outlined in the school handbook, and both students and faculty members are expected to maintain an atmosphere of respect and encouragement for learning, take responsibility for their actions, foster a safe and caring atmosphere, use courteous and appropriate language, abide by the highest standards of honesty, and remain chemically free. GSA's administrators and faculty members are responsible for discipline.

ACADEMIC FACILITIES

GSA's campus is located in the heart of Blue Hill and currently consists of four main buildings plus two residence halls. The Academy's library contains a collection of more than 8,000 items for research and recreational reading. Materials are offered in a variety of formats, including books, magazines, microfiche, videotapes, and CD-ROMs. The library also includes seven computers with Internet access. There are thirty laptops in two mobile units for student use as well as sixteen computers in the campus computer lab. In addition, the school has fifty netbooks for student use. The entire campus is wireless, and every teacher has an in-class computer. Students also have access to the Blue Hill Library, which has more than 39,000 items, and the MERI Center for Marine Studies.

BOARDING AND GENERAL FACILITIES

GSA has two residential options for international students: home stay and boarding. The Host Family Program provides international students with the opportunity to live with a family in the community. Students become a member of that family for the school year and may spend time with their host family after school, on weekends, and during vacations. This offers students the chance to practice English intensively while experiencing life in an American household. GSA also has one recently renovated and one new residence hall. The girls' residence houses 8 students, and the boys' dormitory holds 16. Each building also houses full-time dorm parents who provide constant supervision for the students. GSA's residential facilities are a reflection of the school's overall aim to provide students with a comfortable environment in a warm, caring community.

ATHLETICS

GSA participates in twelve interscholastic sports throughout the year, including baseball, basketball, golf, indoor and outdoor track, sailing, soccer, tennis, and wrestling. Games and practice times take place after school during the week and sometimes in the morning on weekends. In order to play, students must be enrolled in five full-credit courses at the Academy and maintain good academic standing. Other requirements include a parents consent form, a yearly physical examination, an emergency medical card completed and on file in the Athletic Office, and attendance at a preseason meeting. In addition to a newly renovated gymnasium, GSA also has extensive athletic fields where teams play baseball, soccer, and softball.

EXTRACURRICULAR OPPORTUNITIES

There are more than twenty-five clubs and activities for students at GSA. Some of the clubs include Amnesty International, Chess Team, Drama Club, Environmental Action Club, French Club, International Cooking Club, Jazz Band, Jazz Combo, Literary Magazine, Math Team, Model United Nations, National Honor Society, Outing Club, Spanish Club, Student Council, and Yearbook.

GSA sponsors an annual Arts Festival, a five-day event that celebrates arts in all its forms and allows students to show parents and friends their special accomplishments. Every year, students can take part in three days of studio-based learning at Haystack Mountain School of Crafts, which attracts some of the finest craftspeople in the nation. The Academy also offers numerous opportunities to participate in sports, performing arts, community service, and other interests.

DAILY LIFE

The school day begins at 8 a.m. and ends at 2:35 p.m., with a 15-minute break at 9:20 and a 45-minute lunch beginning at 12:15. The Academy runs on an eight-period schedule. Each eight-period cycle lasts two days. Each day is divided into four periods, which are 75 minutes in length. Students may spend one of these periods in a study hall, and juniors and seniors may have the opportunity to explore an academic or vocational interest through a self-designed, two-week course of study. Residential students are required to participate in activities from 3 to 4:30. These might include sports, yoga, painting, volunteering, or working with young children. Dinner is from 5:15 until 6, and from 7 to 8:30, there is a mandatory study hall in the library. This is an opportunity for students to work with tutors or each other on their homework.

WEEKEND LIFE

Students can spend their weekends in the Blue Hill Peninsula, which is known for its traditional, coastal fishing and boatbuilding history. More recently, it has become a haven for writers, painters, sculptors, and musicians. The village of Blue Hill offers shops, art galleries, pottery studios, and restaurants. Throughout the year, there are opportunities to attend or participate in classical, jazz, steel drum, and choral concerts. The Blue Hill Library hosts Friday movie nights. Students can walk along the beach, hike up Blue Hill Mountain, go canoeing and kayaking, take a bike ride through blueberry fields, kick a soccer ball in the park, and browse local shops and bookstores. In the winter, there are plenty of chances for ice-skating, cross-country skiing, and downhill skiing. Chaperoned weekend trips may include shopping, movies, or bowling in nearby Ellsworth or Bangor; visits to Acadia National Park and Bar Harbor; whale watching; and cultural visits to Portland and Boston. Blue Hill is an hour's drive from Acadia National Park or the Camden Snow Bowl, 3 hours from Portland or Sugarloaf Mountain, and 5 hours from Boston.

COSTS AND FINANCIAL AID

The Academy admits almost any student from Blue Hill or a neighboring town that does not have its own high school as well as international students and students from nonsupporting towns who are open to new challenges and experiences. The homestay tuition of $35,000 per year includes tuition, the stipend for host families, book rental, and most regular school activities. The boarding tuition is also $35,000 and includes tuition, room and board, book rental, and most regular school activities. Participation in the English as a second language course costs $1500 per semester. Students requiring health insurance must pay $800 per year, and all students are required to pay a $1000 general deposit for emergency expenses.

ADMISSIONS INFORMATION

George Stevens Academy admits students of any race, religion, gender, national origin, or sexual orientation to the rights, privileges, programs, and activities available to students at the school. GSA does not discriminate in the administration of its educational policies, admissions policies, or any other programs administered by the school. Admission is based on the candidate's transcript, application essay, recommendations, and, when possible, PSAT, SSAT, TOEFL, or SLEP scores. GSA's Admissions Committee carefully screens all applicants to determine their level of maturity, academic competency, and ability to function successfully in the GSA community.

APPLICATION TIMETABLE

A $50 nonrefundable processing fee is required at the time of application. A campus visit and interview are highly recommended for all applicants. Telephone interviews are arranged for candidates who are unable to visit. GSA has a rolling admissions policy, which means that applications are accepted throughout the school year and summer. However, candidates are encouraged to complete the application process by March 1. An admissions decision is made within three weeks of receipt of the application.

ADMISSIONS CORRESPONDENCE

Sheryl Stearns
Director of International Student Program
George Stevens Academy
23 Union Street
Blue Hill, Maine 04614

Phone: 207-374-2808 Ext. 134
Fax: 207-374-2982
E-mail: s.stearns@georgestevens.org
Web site: http://www.georgestevensacademy.org

GRIGGS INTERNATIONAL ACADEMY

Silver Spring, Maryland

Type: Christian distance education school
Grades: Preschool–Grade 12
Enrollment: 1,878
Head of School: Dr. Donald R. Sahly, President

THE SCHOOL

At the beginning of the twentieth century, correspondence education was increasing in popularity within the United States. An educator by the name of Frederick Griggs envisioned educating people around the world. Within the context of the Seventh-day Adventist school system, his vision took shape in 1909 with the establishment of the Fireside Correspondence School. The goal was to provide the benefits of an education to those who were unable to attend traditional schools. Within two years, the Fireside Correspondence School offered eleven secondary and nine college courses. By 1916, its students represented nearly every state and province in the United States and Canada, as well as ten other countries. The Fireside Correspondence School was later renamed Home Study Institute (HSI); the name was subsequently changed to Home Study International.

In 1990, the HSI Board of Directors assigned names to its three academic divisions; thus, Home Study Elementary School, Home Study High School, and Griggs University became part of HSI's terminology. In 1991, Griggs University began offering college degrees.

In recent years, the home-school movement has exploded, but the term "home school" has taken on special meaning for school districts and families who design their own school programs. Pressure from overseas affiliations drove the HSI Board of Directors to reexamine the school's name and determine something that better reflected the mission and operation of HSI. In 2005, the board voted to change the name of the Preschool–Grade 12 division to Griggs International Academy (GIA).

Since 1909, more than a quarter of a million people have studied with Griggs University and Griggs International Academy. Griggs plays a unique and vital role in the educational development of students of all ages in all parts of the world. People from all walks of life have discovered that the quiet conditions of private correspondence and online study help develop self-reliance, independent thinking, and responsibility. From its humble beginnings in a one-room office, Griggs has grown into a worldwide school that maintains high scholastic standards and utilizes the services of qualified professionals in all phases of its operation, yet Griggs maintains a personal touch in its student-teacher relationships.

In addition, GIA also helps fill in the educational gaps in private traditional schools with programs such as the Alternative Program for Learning Enrichment (APLE), which helps small private schools augment their course offerings.

Griggs International Academy is regionally accredited by the Southern Association of Colleges and Schools (SACS) Commissions on Elementary, Middle, and Secondary Schools and the Middle States Association of Colleges and Schools (MSA) Commission on Elementary Schools. Griggs is also accredited by the Commission on International and Trans-Regional Accreditation (CITA), the Accrediting Commission of the Distance Education and Training Council (DETC), and the Accrediting Association of Seventh-day Adventist Schools, Colleges, and Universities (AAA). GIA is approved as a nonpublic school by the State of Maryland.

ACADEMIC PROGRAMS

GIA offers both a basic high school diploma and a college-preparatory diploma. The basic diploma requires 21 Carnegie units, which must include 4 units of English, 3 units of math, 3 units of social studies (one of which must be American history), 2 units of science, and 4 units of Bible study (students may be excused from the Bible requirement if their personal convictions and familial belief systems so dictate). One half-credit is given toward a Griggs diploma for a student who has taken driver's education.

The college-preparatory diploma requires 24 units, including those listed for the basic diploma plus an additional unit in science and 2 units of a language.

Each Griggs International Academy course comes equipped with a "teacher on paper"—the course study guide. The study guide includes all learning objectives, instructional sections, reading assignments, supplemental information, self-diagnostic tools, and lessons/submissions. The student also receives a full set of supplies, including a textbook and, sometimes, cassettes, CDs, lab equipment, and reading supplements. Experienced teachers are assigned to each course to provide positive, individual interaction with students. Students may be given phone numbers or e-mail addresses for the teachers of individual courses.

For most courses, two examinations are required each semester—a midterm and a semester examination. All examinations must be supervised by a school or community official (such as a teacher or registrar) or by a responsible adult who is not related to the student. If a student is enrolled in another school while taking GIA courses, the examinations should be taken under the direction of that school's registrar or testing department. Final grades are issued as A, B, C, D, or F. At the high school level, pluses and minuses (e.g., B+ and B–) are also used.

Because GIA's high school program offers year-round registration and self-paced instruction, students may adapt their class schedules to meet learning needs. The structure of the instructional materials engenders self-discipline and motivation as well as academic excellence.

Since July 2003, Griggs International Academy has been offering high school courses online. Available courses are listed on the Griggs Web site.

FACULTY AND ADVISERS

The writers for GIA courses are exceptional professionals in their specialties, and most hold degrees at the master's or doctoral level. The courses are intellectually stimulating and designed to foster academic excellence. Griggs has 1 full-time and 62 part-time faculty members. In addition, 18 full-time nonteaching professionals provide assistance to students and teachers. Of Griggs' 63 teachers (25 women and 38 men), 45 have advanced degrees.

Dr. Alayne Thorpe, the vice president for education, has been with Griggs International Academy since 1980. Dr. Thorpe has taught in the Maryland state public school system and at the University of Maryland. She has served as a master teacher, a curriculum supervisor, and a writing consultant. Dr. Thorpe holds a Ph.D. from the University of Maryland.

Faculty members are chosen on the basis of their expertise in their disciplines and their ability to counsel, advise, and instruct an international, multicultural student body.

COLLEGE ADMISSION COUNSELING

Graduates of GIA attend colleges and universities throughout the world. The Advisory Teacher, the Registrar, the Assistant Registrar, and the Vice President for Education provide guidance counseling and college placement information to all interested students.

STUDENT BODY AND CONDUCT

Griggs International Academy's elementary and high school enrollment is approximately 2,000 students in grades kindergarten through 12. Because Griggs is not limited to a traditional school year, enrollment figures may shift slightly from month to month as new students enroll and others finish their programs. Griggs also provides opportunities for supplementing and augmenting programs for students attending traditional secondary schools.

In 2009–10, the GIA student body consisted of students from every state in the United States as well as thirty other countries.

DAILY LIFE

GIA students progress at their own speed. This allows most students to finish the study portion of their day early. The rest of the day is available to reinforce what is being learned or to expand upon one's studies. The student is not held back by a classroom of other students who learn at various levels.

Full-time Griggs students can enjoy intramural sports groups and have extra time to use the library, museums, and other learning centers near their homes.

On average, full-time students spend 4 to 5 hours a day on their studies.

COSTS AND FINANCIAL AID

GIA offers two options (grades K–8)—the Accredited Plan and the Non-Accredited Plan.

The Accredited Plan is state approved and includes tuition, textbooks and study guides, daily lesson plans, exams, teacher assistance, grading services, record keeping, report cards, and transcript services. The 2009–10 prices for core subjects for one full year, and a $10 enrollment fee, were preschool, $77; kindergarten, $499; grade 1, $974; grade 2, $955; grade 3, $944; grade 4, $979; grade 5, $1001; and grade 6, $1036.

The junior high program (grades 7 and 8) allows for more immediate interaction between parent and student. The prices for the four core courses, including shipping and an $80 enrollment fee, were $1008 for grade 7 and $1010 for grade 8 in 2009–10.

The 2009–10 high school tuition prices were $205 per semester per course plus the cost of supplies, an $80 enrollment fee, and shipping. An additional technology fee of $35 per semester applies for all online courses.

The Non-Accredited Plan (K–8 only) is for those who do not choose to use Griggs International Academy's teaching, grading, advising, or record-keeping services. However, this plan does offer guides/activity sheets/tests (no answer keys for tests) and placement advising for the student if necessary. Prices for the Non-Accredited Plan are substantially lower. Financial aid is not available. All prices are subject to change July 1 of each year. For the 2009–10 school year, costs were preschool, $79; kindergarten, $333; grade 1, $613; grade 2, $624; grade 3, $606; grade 4, $671; grade 5, $647; and grade 6, $701.

ADMISSIONS INFORMATION

Griggs accepts applications for admission at any time. Applications/enrollments can now be completed online through the Griggs Web site.

ADMISSIONS CORRESPONDENCE

Joan Wilson, Director of Admissions/ Registrar
Griggs International Academy
12501 Old Columbia Pike
Silver Spring, Maryland 20904
Phone: 301-680-6570
800-782-4769 (toll-free; enrollment inquiries only)
E-mail: enrollmentservices@griggs.edu
Web site: http://www.griggs.edu

GROTON SCHOOL

Groton, Massachusetts

Type: Coeducational boarding and day college-preparatory school
Grades: 8–12: Lower School, Forms II and III; Upper School, Forms IV–VI
Enrollment: School total: 372; Upper School: 272
Head of School: Richard B. Commons, Headmaster

THE SCHOOL

Groton was founded in 1884 by the Reverend Endicott Peabody as a school whose aims were the intellectual, moral, and physical development of its students in preparation not only for college but also for "the active work of life." While the means of achieving these aims have changed, the aims themselves continue to govern a Groton education, and many of the original practices of the School have become valued traditions.

While Groton does not hold as its exclusive goal the preparation of students for college, it does offer a curriculum that prepares students for the most demanding of college environments. Groton is by design a small school, enabling the School community to gather together daily and to develop close personal relationships. As students adjust to life at Groton, they come to appreciate less the emblems of success and more the personal qualities of peers and faculty members. A notable characteristic of Groton is the expectation of leadership. All students are expected to grow into positions of leadership in the School, and, traditionally, every member of the Sixth Form has been a prefect of the School, with particular responsibilities in almost every aspect of School life.

The School is 40 miles northwest of Boston and a little more than a mile from the town of Groton. Its location permits the students the freedom of country life along with the accessibility of Boston and its museums, plays, concerts, and sports events. The 390-acre campus includes fields and woodlands as well as the academic buildings and dormitories that are grouped around the lawn of the Circle.

A not-for-profit corporation, Groton is governed by a 26-member Board of Trustees. The endowment is currently valued at more than $265 million and is supplemented by an Annual Fund that totaled more than $2.8 million last year. This generous support comes from parents, friends, and an alumni body of more than 3,500.

Groton is accredited by the New England Association of Schools and Colleges and is affiliated with the National Association of Independent Schools, the Independent School Association of Massachusetts, the Council for Religion in Independent Schools, and the Secondary School Admission Test Board.

ACADEMIC PROGRAMS

The Groton curriculum is predicated on the belief that certain qualities are of major importance: to be able to reason carefully and logically and to think imaginatively and sensitively, to have a command of precise and articulate communication, to be able to compute accurately and reason quantitatively, to have a grasp of scientific approaches to problem solving, to be able to identify and develop creative talents, and to acquire an understanding of the cultural, social, scientific, and political background of Western and non-Western civilizations. Students in the Second, Third, and Fourth Forms are, therefore, introduced to a wide variety of courses that draw on interests and capabilities that might otherwise be unchallenged. Older students have choices among elective courses, independent studies, off-campus projects, and concentrations in specific areas of interest.

Minimum graduation requirements include a Lower School and an Upper School science course; English, through expository writing in the Sixth Form year; mathematics, through trigonometry; American history and European history; biblical studies and ethics; a Lower and an Upper School arts course; and three years through the end of Fifth Form in either French, Greek, Latin, or Spanish. Students joining Groton in eighth or ninth grade take two years of Latin in addition to their modern language.

At Groton, an average class contains between 10 and 14 students. The mathematics and language courses are sectioned on the basis of interest and ability, and Advanced Placement courses are offered in every discipline. The minimum course load for Upper Schoolers is 5 credits each term; most students take 6 or 6½. The grading system is numerical, with 60 being a passing grade and 85 or above, honors. Grades, along with teachers' comments and a letter from the faculty adviser, are sent home three times a year.

FACULTY AND ADVISERS

The Groton teaching faculty consists of 63 full- and part-time members (25 women and 38 men). The Headmaster, who was appointed in 2003, is a graduate of the University of Virginia and Stanford University (M.A.) and holds an M.A. from Middlebury College's Bread Loaf School of English.

In selecting its faculty, Groton looks for individuals who are excited by their subject, who enjoy working with adolescents, who involve themselves in the nonacademic life of a residential school, and who have lively interests of their own. Every faculty member at Groton fills a variety of roles, taking on responsibilities in the classroom, in the dormitory, on the athletics field, in various activities, and as an adviser to students. An adviser assumes a major role in communication with the parents and is the resident expert on his or her advisees. Faculty benefits at Groton include financial support for continuing education and a ten-year sabbatical program.

COLLEGE ADMISSION COUNSELING

College advising is the responsibility of 3 members of the faculty, who assist students and their families in determining what kind of environment and options the students are seeking for their college years. The median SAT scores for the class of 2010 were 690 on the critical reading, 690 on the mathematics, and 710 on the writing sections. The 83 members of the class of 2010 are attending sixty different colleges and universities. The most popular are Georgetown (4), Trinity College (4), Colby (3), Harvard (3), and Yale (2).

STUDENT BODY AND CONDUCT

In 2010–11, Groton's enrollment totals 372. There are 192 boys and 180 girls; 316 are boarders and 56 are day students. Students from thirty states and eleven other countries enrolled. The student body represents diversity in both geographic and socioeconomic backgrounds.

At Groton, the breaking of major School rules (lying, cheating, stealing, or using or possessing drugs or alcohol) is a serious matter and may lead to dismissal. Disciplinary action is not taken, however, without the advice of the Discipline Committee (composed of students and faculty members), which considers all circumstances. Beyond rules and regulations, the School expects all its students to offer both courtesy and respect to other students and to teachers, staff members, and their families. This expectation is one of the most important characteristics of Groton.

ACADEMIC FACILITIES

The academic heart of the School is the Schoolhouse, where most of the classrooms, the science laboratories, the woodworking shop, music rehearsal studios and performance halls, and administrative offices are found. Adjacent to the Schoolhouse is the Dillon Center for the Visual Arts, which houses ceramics, painting, sculpture, and drawing studios as well as multimedia and gallery space. The library contains approximately 60,000 volumes; 150 periodical subscriptions, including publications in French, German, and Spanish; and a rare-book collection. It also provides access to 75,000 e-books and full-text articles from several thousand journals, magazines, and newspapers through electronic resources. Local, national, and international newspapers are received daily. The library's microfilm, microfiche, and CD-ROM material and ProQuest and other Internet databases are used for periodical research.

BOARDING AND GENERAL FACILITIES

Groton houses its 316 boarding students in seventeen dormitories, all of which have been completely renovated in the last ten years. The Upper School dormitories have single, double, and some triple rooms and house from 14 to 23 students each, with a faculty member or faculty family living in the dormitory. Each dormitory's common room, which comprises a large and comfortable living room and kitchenette, adjoins the faculty residence. Student rooms are equipped with voice and intranet hookups. Use of the Internet is available in dorm rooms and common room spaces as well as in public computer space. A wireless laptop program was initiated in 2003. There is a central dining hall where faculty members and students sit down together for dinner three times a week. Other meals are more informal and are served buffet-style. Adjacent to the dining hall is the School Center, which has a snack bar, a dance floor, the student radio station, a game room, and a television-viewing room.

ATHLETICS

Sports are an essential part of the curriculum at Groton, and the School follows an "athletics for all" philosophy. It holds that, through sports, much can be learned about cooperation, competition, and character and that every student, regardless of ability, should have the opportunity to participate. Groton fields interscholastic teams in baseball, basketball, crew, cross-country running, field hockey, football, ice hockey, lacrosse, soccer, squash, and tennis.

Intramural and recreational sports include canoeing, figure skating, fives, recreational and cross-country skiing, running, soccer, softball, squash, swimming, tennis, and weight training.

Not far from the buildings on the Circle are the School's eight playing fields and Athletic Center. In 1998, the School completed the construction of a new Athletic Center, which houses twelve international squash courts, twelve outdoor and eight indoor tennis courts, three basketball courts, an indoor track, two hockey rinks, an indoor pool, a dance studio, and a fitness center as well as locker rooms and a training facility for athletic rehabilitation. The Bingham Boathouse is on the Nashua River, which flows by the campus on its western boundary.

EXTRACURRICULAR OPPORTUNITIES
A lecture series brings to Groton on numerous occasions speakers of distinction in politics, government, science, art, education, and other fields. There is also a concert series that brings to the campus various individuals and groups with special talents in the performing arts. In addition, proximity to Boston and Cambridge provides opportunities to attend concerts, lectures, plays, and sports events.

An elected Student Congress represents all Forms and dormitories, and students serve on the Discipline Committee, the Student Activities Committee, and a number of other student-faculty committees. Sixth Formers assume major responsibilities in the dormitories, the dining hall, the library, the School Center, and the work program, through which all students share responsibility for cleaning and other routine chores on campus. Students do volunteer work in the local public schools, at a local day care center and institution for retarded children, and in a nearby regional hospital, among others. Other activities include bell ringing, chess, orchestra, jazz band, choral and instrumental groups, dramatics, debating, a minority awareness society, literary magazines, a newspaper, a student vestry, and the yearbook.

DAILY LIFE
Classes at Groton meet six days a week and are 45- or 75-minute periods, with a shortened day on Wednesday and Saturday. Four days a week, the School gathers for a morning chapel service, whose centerpiece is a chapel talk given by a student and at other times by the Chaplain, the Headmaster, a member of the faculty, or a visiting speaker. While no attempt is made to indoctrinate students in any particular religious faith, the School does maintain that religious faith is as important to human life as other areas of concern.

Athletics are scheduled at the end of the class day and before dinner time. The evening hours are for study, with Second, Third, and Fourth Formers having a supervised study period. All students check in at their dormitories by 10 p.m.

WEEKEND LIFE
Weekend activities at Groton are planned by a student-faculty Social Activities Committee. In addition to interscholastic sports, these activities include coffeehouse entertainment, regular Saturday night dances, and special events such as casino night, games, and dorm competitions. Saturday afternoon and Sunday are also times for excursions to Boston or to the mountains. Each term includes a long weekend (Friday noon to Monday evening), and, if desired, a student may take two additional weekend leaves in each of the three terms. Day students participate fully in the life at Groton, whether on weekends or in evening activities during the week.

COSTS AND FINANCIAL AID
Tuition at Groton for 2010–11 is $48,895 for boarders and $37,020 for day students. This fee covers instruction, residence, routine infirmary care, athletics, use of laboratories and studios, and admission to all athletic events, plays, lectures, and concerts held at the School. Additional costs that are not included are personal expenses, such as laundry, books, rental of sports equipment, and travel. The charges for the year are due and payable in two equal installments in August and January. Monthly payment plans, tuition-refund insurance, and accident and sickness insurance are available.

The School aims to accept students on their own qualifications, without regard to their families' financial situation. Accordingly, no student should be deterred from applying out of concern for the family's ability to pay. Financial aid grants are based on the guidelines established by the School and Student Service for Financial Aid. In 2010–11, approximately 37 percent of the students received aid that totaled more than $4.7 million.

ADMISSIONS INFORMATION
Groton accepts applications for Forms II–V (eighth through eleventh grades). Though it would be difficult to define admission policies in quantifiable terms, the School clearly favors students with plentiful spirit, significant academic ability, a willingness to participate fully in the School community, outstanding special talents, and interesting backgrounds.

Applicants must submit a school record, a writing sample, three recommendations, and the results of the SSAT. In addition, all candidates are expected to have a personal interview with a member of the admission staff or a representative of the School. Approximately 15 percent of applicants are offered admission.

APPLICATION TIMETABLE
The initial inquiry and a candidate profile and application fee of $50 ($100 for international students) are welcome at any time. Visits to the campus should be made during the months of September through January prior to the anticipated year of entrance. Appointments should be made by e-mail, mail or, preferably, telephone well in advance of the intended visit. The Admission Office schedules visits that begin between 8:45 a.m. and 2 p.m. on weekdays and between 8 and 10:40 a.m. on Saturdays. Because applications should be completed by January 15, the SSAT should be taken in October, November, December, or January. With the exception of late applicants (those whose applications are completed after January 15), all applicants are mailed notification letters on March 10, and are expected to reply by April 10.

ADMISSIONS CORRESPONDENCE
Mr. Ian Gracey
Director of Admission
Groton School
P.O. Box 991
Groton, Massachusetts 01450

Phone: 978-448-7510
Fax: 978-448-9623
E-mail: admission_office@groton.org
Web site: http://www.groton.org

THE HARKER SCHOOL

San Jose, California

HARKER®
Est. 1893 · K-12 College Prep

Type: Coeducational day college-preparatory school
Grades: K–12: Lower School, Kindergarten–5; Middle School, 6–8; Upper School, 9–12
Enrollment: School total: 1,762; Lower School: 592; Middle School: 475; Upper School: 695
Head of School: Christopher Nikoloff

THE SCHOOL

The origins of The Harker School belong in the city of Palo Alto where two schools, Manzanita Hall and Miss Harker's School, were established in 1893 to provide incoming Stanford University students with the finest college-preparatory education available.

Harker's three campuses are located minutes from each other in the heart of California's famed Silicon Valley. The campuses are well maintained, beautifully landscaped, and secured with an emphasis on student safety. The Upper School campus is 16 acres, the Middle School campus is 40 acres, and the Lower School campus is 10 acres. The Harker Upper School opened in 1998 and graduated its first senior class in 2002.

Harker's suburban San Jose location attracts day students from surrounding communities, such as Los Gatos, Saratoga, Cupertino, Los Altos, and Fremont.

Harker operates as a nonprofit organization, governed by a board of directors composed of business leaders, educators, and parents. With strong support from parent volunteers, the School's Annual Fund raised more than $1 million during the 2009–10 school year. Funds are used to enhance programs such as computer science and fine arts.

Harker is accredited by the Western Association of Schools and Colleges and is a member of the California Association of Independent Schools.

ACADEMIC PROGRAMS

The Harker School is a coeducational day school for students in kindergarten through grade 12. Harker students are highly motivated, creative young people who come from families with strong commitments to educational values. The exceptional faculty, caring and qualified support staff, and modern, safe campuses give students a definite advantage in becoming top achievers. For example, students consistently score among the highest percentiles in nationally normed achievement tests. Each year, an impressive number of seventh-grade students qualify for academic recognition as Johns Hopkins University Scholars by scoring above 500 on the SAT. Small class sizes, with an average of 16 students, enable teachers to form flexible ability groupings so that children's needs are constantly evaluated and met.

The Upper School curriculum offers a full array of academic courses, from introductory-level to Advanced Placement and honors-level courses in every discipline, from sciences and math to English, foreign language, and the fine arts. The Upper School offers a complete athletic program for boys and girls as well as a full extracurricular program, including yearbook, performing arts, newspaper, and debate.

The use of technology in teaching is an important facet of the academic program, and every student takes a semester of technology as a graduation requirement. A unique aspect of the program is Harker's requirement that every student have Internet access at home. The Internet is utilized for academic research through the Harker Library's online periodical databases and access to faculty help after school hours. Grades 6–12 are also required to have a personal laptop that is linked to the School's wireless network. A Middle School laptop program was implemented in fall 2007.

Graduation requirements include 4 years of English, third-year proficiency in a foreign language (French, Spanish, Japanese, or Latin), 3 years of science (physics, chemistry, and biology), 3 years of mathematics (with a strong recommendation to take 4 years), 3 years of history, 2 years of physical education, 1 year of fine arts, and 1 semester of computer science.

The Lower and Middle Schools' solid curriculum in both the core subjects of math and language arts and the enriching opportunities with specialists in science, expository writing, Spanish, French, Japanese, computer science, physical education, art, music, dance, and drama provides a solid foundation for the Upper School academic program.

The Lower School's full-day program allows all students ample time for learning through games, dancing, and other physical activities. Harker kindergarteners have access to teaching specialists and campus resources such as extensively equipped computer science labs and the library. In grades 1–5 the curriculum is strongly academic. In keeping with the School's commitment to treat each child as an individual, students who show special promise have ample opportunity to go beyond the standard curriculum through Harker's advanced placement grouping. Study-travel trips to Marin Headlands and California's Gold Country add field experience to the academic science offerings.

Harker's Middle School program offers students a safe and trusting atmosphere in which to grow through the challenging times of early adolescence. Special courses aid students in gaining a sense of self-worth, dealing with anxiety, understanding the risks of substance abuse, and learning about other major health issues. Student performances, field trips, art exhibitions, and assembly presentations enliven the School atmosphere. Study-travel trips to Yosemite, the Grand Canyon, and Washington, D.C., are meaningful Middle School experiences.

FACULTY AND ADVISERS

The Harker faculty is composed of 186 professionals, 117 of whom hold advanced degrees. Christopher Nikoloff, Head of School, earned his B.A. in English literature and his M.A.T. in education at Boston University. Faculty members serve as advisers to students on a daily basis. Many participate in after-school athletics as well as academic and arts enrichment activities. Continuing education is facilitated with monthly meetings and individual incentives for professional growth. Harker seeks highly qualified candidates who reflect the School's commitment to academic excellence and diversity.

COLLEGE ADMISSION COUNSELING

Harker is a college-preparatory school whose rigorous curriculum prepares students for top universities. Four college counselors provide extensive guidance to students and parents in the junior and senior years regarding preparation for college admission. Over the four years of high school, there are parent workshops, family interviews, individual student interviews, classes for students, visits from college representatives, and special speakers from college admission offices.

STUDENT BODY AND CONDUCT

During the 2010–11 academic year, there are 1,762 students enrolled in kindergarten through grade 12. The student body reflects the dynamic and diverse Bay Area population, and the international programs further prepare the students as global citizens.

Harker Lower and Middle School students are required to wear uniforms. Upper School students adhere to a dress code. Students are expected to comply with rules defined in the *Student/Parent Handbook*. Good citizenship, along with academic and athletic achievement, is frequently rewarded. Discipline rests primarily with the faculty.

With leadership from its Student Council, the entire School communicates its views on codes and policies and works on community service projects. Students participate in a variety of leadership opportunities, spirit commission, and service volunteer programs.

ACADEMIC FACILITIES

Harker's strong sense of community ties three campuses into one school, while allowing children close contact with their peers. The Lower, Middle, and Upper School campuses are within 3 miles of each other. Modern, extensively equipped facilities such as computer and science labs and art and dance studios provide enhanced learning opportunities for students at all grade levels. A new state-of-the-art Science and Technology Center opened in 2008.

The library system has 44,900 items among the three campuses. Each campus has its own library facility, staffed by full-time professional librarians, and equipped with an array of quality print and digital resources. With over 80 subscription databases, students have 24/7 access to materials from Gale, ProQuest, EBSCO, Oxford University Press, JSTOR, Project MUSE, LexisNexis, and others. Librarians and instructional technologists team with classroom teachers to select appropriate technology tools to support twenty-first-century learning.

Harker has extensive student support services. The full-time staff includes licensed school counselors, college counselors, registered school nurses, certified lifeguards, and a professional chef.

ATHLETICS

Students of all ability levels are encouraged to participate in the School's extensive athletics program. Baseball, basketball, cross-country, football, golf, soccer, softball, tennis, track, and volleyball are popular Upper School sports. Combined athletic facilities include two competition-sized pools, eight tennis courts, three wood-floored gymnasiums, a new lighted football/soccer field with synthetic turf, and expansive playing fields.

EXTRACURRICULAR OPPORTUNITIES

While the basic goal is to prepare students for future schooling by introducing them to a large body of knowledge, the focus on academics is balanced with numerous opportunities for personal development, including school spirit, sports and arts activities, and community service projects. Students take an active role in their school community, including planning school dances and rallies and participation in more than forty clubs. Harker's proximity to San Francisco makes frequent field trips to major cultural attractions and performances possible for students at all grade levels.

DAILY LIFE

Students can arrive on campus as early as 7 a.m. The school day begins and ends at staggered times between 8 a.m. and 3:30 p.m. The campus closes at 6 p.m. Supervised after-school recreation and athletics programs are available to all students at no additional cost. A professional chef supervises food service on all campuses, providing nutritious lunch selections of hot meals, fresh fruits, salad bars, and vegetarian options.

SUMMER PROGRAMS

Harker Summer Programs offers an intriguing variety of activities for boys and girls ages 4½ to 18. For students in grades K–8, day camp choices offer academic enrichment combined with sports, recreation, and computer science for a total of eight weeks. Field trips to local natural and cultural attractions such as Santa Cruz beaches, local redwood forests, and San Francisco are a popular aspect of the program. Harker's Summer Institute for students in grades 9–12 runs for 6 weeks during the summer. Students attend academic credit courses to hone existing skills or learn new topics. Offerings have included the Summer Conservatory program of music, theater, and dance; Speech and Debate Camp; rigorous math and science courses; and an enrichment courses in expository writing, Spanish, and PSAT/SAT. Annual enrollment is approximately 1,300. Enrollment in Harker's academic program is not required. Harker Summer Programs is accredited by the American Camping Association and the Western Association of Independent Camps. Further information can be obtained by contacting Summer Programs Director Kelly Espinosa at the Harker School office.

COSTS AND FINANCIAL AID

For the 2010–11 school year, tuition ranges from $23,794 to $35,372. An $1100 to $1200 lunch fee is added to tuition for Middle and Upper Schools. Estimated extra costs are as follows: $400 to $550 plus lunch fee for Lower School and $700 to $850 for Middle and Upper School students. A nonrefundable $700 new Lower and Middle School student fee and an enrollment deposit of $2500 for students are due within seven days of acceptance. Financial aid based on need is available.

ADMISSIONS INFORMATION

Harker seeks a diversified student body that reflects a range of backgrounds, aptitudes, and interests.

Students performing at average to above-average levels are considered for acceptance. Student motivation and the ability to adjust comfortably to a close-knit and congenial educational community are also important factors. The specific criteria used in admissions are entrance exams, school records, character evaluations by a teacher or principal, and extracurricular experiences.

APPLICATION TIMETABLE

An initial inquiry is welcome at any time, and students should visit the Web site for School and application information. Potential students and their families are encouraged to attend an open house or schedule a visit because there is no better way to appreciate Harker's warmth and vitality. A visit may be arranged by contacting the School offices, which are open from 8 a.m. to 5 p.m.

ADMISSIONS CORRESPONDENCE

Ms. Nan Nielsen
Director of Admission and Financial Aid
The Harker School, Saratoga Campus

Lower School (K–5)
4300 Bucknall Road
San Jose, California 95130

Phone: 408-871-4600
Fax: 408-871-4320

Middle School (6–8)
3800 Blackford Avenue
San Jose, California 95117

Phone: 408-248-2510
Fax: 408-248-2502

Upper School (9–12)
500 Saratoga Avenue
San Jose, California 95129

Phone: 408-249-2510
Fax: 408-984-2325
E-mail: admissions@harker.org
Web site: http://www.harker.org

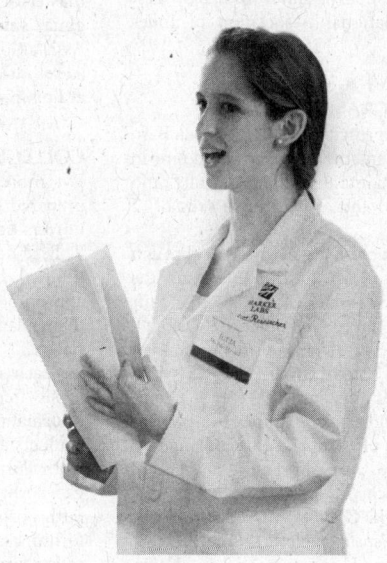

THE HILL SCHOOL

Pottstown, Pennsylvania

The Hill School

Type: Coeducational boarding and day college-preparatory school
Grades: 9–PG (Forms III–VI)
Enrollment: 500
Head of School: David R. Dougherty, Headmaster

THE SCHOOL

The Hill School was founded in 1851 by Matthew Meigs, and the Meigs family was instrumental in guiding the course of the School for three generations. In 1920, ownership was transferred to the alumni, who now operate the School as a not-for-profit institution through a 28-member Board of Trustees. In 1998, the School began admitting young women and became a coeducational institution.

The Hill School continues to emphasize both structure and guidance in the quest for academic excellence. The School's mission is to prepare students well for college, careers, and life. The Hill also strives to instill an awareness of accountability for all decisions and to teach those standards of personal conduct that are expected throughout life.

The Hill's 200-acre campus in Pottstown is located 37 miles northwest of Philadelphia and 15 miles from Valley Forge National Park. Because of its Middle Atlantic location, students at The Hill can take advantage of a balanced climate, including warm autumn weather and a winter season that makes possible such activities as skiing in the nearby Pocono Mountains.

The School's endowment is approximately $103 million. The amount of Annual Giving for 2009–10 was more than $2 million, with approximately 30 percent of the living alumni participating.

The Hill School is accredited by the Middle States Association of Colleges and Schools and is a member of the Secondary School Admission Test Board and the National Association of Independent Schools.

ACADEMIC PROGRAMS

The Hill School's principal academic goal is to instill in each student the capacity and desire to learn. The School maintains a student-faculty ratio of approximately 7:1 and an average class size of 12 students.

Sixteen academic credits in grades 9 through 12 are required to earn a diploma, and the distribution of courses includes no fewer than four in English (4 years), three in mathematics (algebra I, geometry, and algebra II), three in one foreign language (or two in each of two languages), two in history, two in laboratory science (biology, chemistry, or physics), and a course in the arts as well as one in theology or philosophy. Foreign language offerings include 6 years of Latin, 5 years of Spanish and French, and 4 years of Chinese, German, and Greek. Courses offered within the Department of History include world history, European history, and U.S. history; U.S. Civil War, World War II, and Vietnam history; Islamic, Latin American, and Native American civilizations; economics; and other electives. Department of Mathematics offerings include algebra I and II, geometry, pre-calculus, functions and discrete math, cal-

culus, graph theory, and advanced topics. Science courses include 2 years of biology, 2 years of chemistry, 2 years of physics, and 2 years of computer science as well as environmental science, astronomy, human physiology, kinesiology, and psychology. Twenty-two Advanced Placement (AP) courses are offered; in 2009, 149 students took 308 AP exams.

Academic reports are sent home at the conclusion of each of the three terms. Comments from instructors, the dorm parent, and the academic adviser are mailed to parents after the fall and spring terms. Students have seven-day-a-week access to the teaching faculty, nearly all of whom live on campus; many faculty members live in the residence halls as dormitory parents. The School library is open 12 hours each school day as well as weekends.

FACULTY AND ADVISERS

The Hill has 68 teaching faculty members. Seventy percent hold or are working toward advanced degrees. Nearly all reside in dormitories serving as dorm parents or live in homes on campus with their families.

David R. Dougherty was appointed Headmaster in 1993. He received a B.A. in English from Washington and Lee University in 1968. He earned an M.A. in English from Georgetown University and a master's in literature from Middlebury College's Bread Loaf School of English at Lincoln College, Oxford. Prior to becoming The Hill's tenth Headmaster, Mr. Dougherty had been Headmaster of North Cross School in Roanoke, Virginia, since 1987. From 1982 to 1987, he was Assistant Headmaster of Episcopal High School in Alexandria, Virginia. He began his teaching career at Episcopal High School in 1968.

COLLEGE ADMISSION COUNSELING

For more than 155 years, the Hill School has prepared students for outstanding colleges and universities throughout the United States. The College Advising Office, staffed by 5 individuals, is devoted exclusively to helping students select appropriate colleges and universities and to helping them plan and prepare college admission materials.

Each year, more than 100 college and university representatives visit The Hill to present information about their institutions. Interested students are invited to attend these sessions, and Sixth Form students may schedule formal interviews with college representatives. During the Fifth Form year, students participate in a college forum class, which addresses the college application process. Topics covered include decision making, career interest identification, essay writing, interview techniques, methods of quality assessment, and SAT practice tests.

A complete range of standardized tests is administered on campus, including SAT and SAT

Subject Tests, ACT, Advanced Placement, and TOEFL; students generally take those exams at regular intervals during the Fifth and Sixth Form years. The middle 50 percent ranges on the SAT for the class of 2010 were 560–670 critical reading, 570–680 math, and 580–690 writing.

Recent graduates are attending such colleges and universities as Amherst, Brown, Bowdoin, Bucknell, Colgate, Cornell, Dickinson, George Washington, Georgetown, Harvard, Princeton, Tufts, the United States Naval Academy, Wellesley, William and Mary, Yale, and the Universities of Pennsylvania, Richmond, St. Andrews (Scotland), and the South.

STUDENT BODY AND CONDUCT

In the Third Form, there are 51 boarding and 42 day students; in the Fourth Form, there are 70 boarding and 41 day students; in the Fifth Form, there are 93 boarding and 35 day students; in the Sixth Form, there are 150 students; and in the PG class, there are 18 students. Students come from twenty-seven states and twenty-one other countries. Sixty-nine percent of the students come from Middle Atlantic states, with the rest of the students coming in equal measure from New England, the Southeast, and Midwestern and Western states. Thirty-four percent of Hill's student body is multicultural.

In 1997, the Hill School students and faculty members adopted a student-initiated Honor Code to promote an environment of mutual trust and respect and to uphold the School's principles of trust, honor, and integrity in all intellectual, athletic, and social pursuits. Most disciplinary matters are handled by either the Discipline Committee or Honor Council, depending on the nature of the offense. Both groups consist of students and faculty members who have been chosen by their peers.

ACADEMIC FACILITIES

The Hill School's fifty-five academic buildings include the 40,000-volume John P. Ryan Library, the Alumni Chapel, Harry Elkins Widener Memorial Science Building, Theodore N. Danforth Computer Center, the 31,000-square-foot Center for the Arts, the $12-million Academic and Student Center, and the McIlvain Multimedia Learning Classroom, a state-of-the-art, twenty-four-computer digital language lab.

BOARDING AND GENERAL FACILITIES

The Hill School's eleven major dormitory structures are divided into residential units that most often house 12 students and one faculty family. Housing has been designed for 2 students per dormitory room. Two selected Sixth Form prefects, who share some supervisory responsibilities with the residential faculty family, live on each dormitory corridor. New students are assigned roommates by the Residential Life and Admission

Offices; in subsequent years, however, roommate selections are made by each student. There is a formal dining room where students and faculty families enjoy seated family-style and buffet meals.

The Student Health Service is staffed by full-time registered nurses and 2 physicians who are on call around the clock.

ATHLETICS

Athletics are an integral part of The Hill's educational offering. A program of twenty-nine sports enables each student to compete and develop expertise in the sports of their choice.

The athletic facilities at The Hill include a 34,000-square-foot field house and seven squash courts, a gymnasium complex, four basketball courts, a six-lane swimming pool, and a fitness center that includes twenty cardiovascular machines, Body Masters strength training equipment, and free weights. Additional structures include a brand-new 92-foot by 200-foot collegiate-sized indoor ice-hockey arena and a wrestling room. The Hill shares an eighteen-hole golf course and owns eleven tennis courts and 90 acres of playing fields for baseball, cross-country, field hockey, football, lacrosse, and soccer.

EXTRACURRICULAR OPPORTUNITIES

Students at The Hill are involved in many pursuits that take them well beyond the classroom and frequently beyond the campus itself. The students publish a newspaper, a literary magazine, and a yearbook. Students fulfill a community service requirement, which includes a written reflection, and also initiate a variety of community-wide service projects. For students interested in music, there are several instrumental and vocal groups, including the Hilltones and Hilltrebles (a cappella groups), jazz band, orchestra, men's glee club, women's chorus, and more. Other student organizations include the Hill Athletic Association, Student Government Association, Ellis Theatre Guild, and numerous clubs that reflect special interests.

The Hill School Humanities Fund provides students with tickets and transportation to hear the Philadelphia Orchestra and makes possible other cultural excursions as well. In addition, numerous on-campus lectures, concerts, plays, and exhibits are scheduled to stimulate and enrich students' cultural life.

DAILY LIFE

Classes are held six days a week, with a mid-morning chapel service on Monday and Thursday. A full academic day is divided into eight 40-minute periods, beginning at 8:25 a.m. and ending at 3:30 p.m. Wednesday and Saturday classes meet in the morning only. Athletic practice takes place between 3:45 and 5:45 p.m. Additional help with faculty members can be scheduled during free periods and in the evening. Student organizations meet after dinner. Evening study hours are supervised by faculty members and prefects.

Every Hill student "gives back" to the School by completing specifically assigned jobs within the School community several times each week for approximately 40 minutes each session.

WEEKEND LIFE

The Student Activities Office organizes weekend activities for Hill students. Off-campus activities include trips to movie theaters and malls, sporting events, amusement parks, outdoor activities (skiing, snow tubing, paintball), and excursions to Baltimore, Philadelphia, the Jersey shore, New York City, and Washington, D.C. Special on-campus events include concerts, dances, karaoke night, outdoor movie nights, the International Food Fair, and Spring Fling, where student participate in schoolwide volleyball competitions and rock climbing, listen to live bands, and more.

COSTS AND FINANCIAL AID

The annual charge for boarding students in 2010–11 is $45,500. This fee covers instruction, board, room, concerts, lectures, movies, athletic contests, services of the School physician and nurses at daily dispensaries, and athletic equipment on an issue basis. It also includes subscriptions for the newspaper and the literary magazine. There is an optional laundry service for an additional fee.

The day student tuition in 2010–11 is $31,500, which includes lunch for every day except Sunday. All day students are required to board for one year.

Financial aid is awarded to students whose parents are unable to meet the full cost of tuition. Aid is granted without regard to race, color, or ethnic origin. Financial aid grants are based on the guidelines established by the School and Student Service for Financial Aid. Grants are renewed annually; parents must submit the School and Student Service for Financial Aid form each year. About 40 percent of students receive financial aid. Applications for financial aid should be submitted by December 15.

ADMISSIONS INFORMATION

The Hill School seeks to enroll students who show academic promise, intellectual curiosity, and strong character. The School encourages applications from students who demonstrate involvement in the arts, athletics, and community service. The following credentials are required for admission: a formal application; a writing sample; a transcript of grades; results from the SSAT, PSAT, or SAT; a letter of recommendation from the school counselor and English and mathematics teachers; and an interview.

APPLICATION TIMETABLE

During the year preceding the applicant's proposed entrance, a formal application for admission should be filed, accompanied by a nonrefundable application fee of $50 ($100 for international students). January 31 is the deadline for consideration in the first round; late applications are considered on a space-available basis.

Families are encouraged to visit The Hill during the school term to meet members of the faculty and student body. An appointment should be made in advance.

ADMISSIONS CORRESPONDENCE

Thomas Eccleston IV, '87
Assistant Headmaster for Admission and External Affairs
The Hill School
717 East High Street
Pottstown, Pennsylvania 19464

Phone: 610-326-1000
Fax: 610-705-1753
E-mail: admission@thehill.org
Web site: http://www.thehill.org

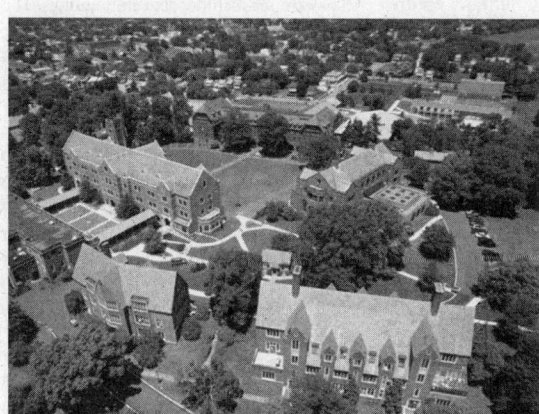

THE HOCKADAY SCHOOL

Dallas, Texas

Type: Girls' day college-preparatory (Prekindergarten to grade 12) and boarding (grades 8–12) school
Grades: Prekindergarten–12: Lower School, Prekindergarten–4; Middle School, 5–8; Upper School, 9–12 (Forms I–IV)
Enrollment: School total: 1,087
Head of School: Jeanne P. Whitman, Eugene McDermott Headmistress

THE SCHOOL

The Hockaday School, founded in 1913, provides a nationally recognized college-preparatory education for bright girls of strong potential who may be expected to assume positions of responsibility and leadership in a rapidly changing world. Ela Hockaday dedicated herself to giving each girl a foundation for living based on scholarship, character, courtesy, and athletics—the traditional Four Cornerstones that remain the dominant influence in the School's educational philosophy.

Hockaday's campus encompasses almost 100 acres of open fields and wooded creeks in residential northwest Dallas. The School's contemporary architectural setting features an academic quadrangle built to provide views of exterior gardens and landscaped terraces. The science center and Clements Lecture Hall opened in 1983, the Ashley Priddy Lower School Building in 1984, the Biggs Dining Room and Whittenburg Dining Terrace in 1985, the Fine Arts Wing in 1987, the Lower School addition in 2001, the Liza Lee Academic Research Center in 2002, the renovated Middle and Upper Schools in 2005, and the renovated Clements Lecture Hall in 2007.

A Board of Trustees is the governing body. The School's endowment is more than $100 million, and the operating income is supplemented by Annual Fund giving of more than $2 million. The Alumnae Association, with more than 7,000 graduates and former students, contributes significantly to the ongoing programs of the School.

The Hockaday School is accredited by the Independent Schools Association of the Southwest. It holds membership in the National Association of Independent Schools, the National Association of Principals of Schools for Girls, the College Board, the National Association for College Admission Counseling, the Educational Records Bureau, the National Coalition of Girls' Schools, and the Secondary School Admission Test Board.

ACADEMIC PROGRAMS

Students are exposed to a rigorous academic curriculum that offers core educational subjects as well as unique offerings in technology, the arts, and leadership and personal development. Graduation requirements (in years) include English, 4; mathematics, 3; history, 2.5; foreign language, 2; laboratory science, 3; fine arts, 1.5; physical education and health, 4; and academic electives from any department, 2, plus basic proficiency in computer usage. Hockaday offers 121 courses, including many honors courses. Advanced Placement courses are offered in eighteen subjects, including English, modern European history, U.S. history, AB and BC calculus, statistics, physics, chemistry, biology, studio art, Latin, French, Spanish, computer science, and economics. For some selected courses, Hockaday has a cooperative program with St. Mark's School of Texas, a boys' school in Dallas. Private lessons are available in cello, flute, guitar, piano, violin, and voice.

A one-year English as a second language (ESL) program is offered to students on intermediate and advanced levels. Intensive language training in writing, reading, listening, and speaking skills is the focus of the program. Students may continue at Hockaday after the first year, following acceptance into the regular academic program. International students with intermediate or advanced English proficiency may study at Hockaday. Along with these special classes, students may study math, science, fine arts, and other courses in the mainstream curriculum. First-year students travel to Washington, D.C., and the Texas Hill Country.

Class sizes average 15 students, with an overall student-teacher ratio of 10:1.

The grading system in grades 7–12 uses A to F designations with pluses and minuses. Reports are sent to parents at the end of each quarter period. High achievement in the Upper School is recognized by inclusion on the Headmistress's List and by initiation into a number of honor societies, including the Cum Laude Society.

Each student receives careful counseling throughout her Hockaday career. Academic counseling begins even in the admissions process and continues under the supervision of the counseling office, which coordinates the faculty adviser system and general counseling program. Each student has an interested, concerned faculty adviser to assist her with academic or personal matters on a daily basis.

FACULTY AND ADVISERS

The Hockaday faculty is represented by accomplished individuals, most of whom have advanced degrees, with 6 holding Ph.D.'s.

Hockaday's teachers are chosen for depth of knowledge in their fields of specialization, personal integrity, and the ability to facilitate the progress of individual students. Many are successful writers, lecturers, artists, musicians, photographers, or composers; many regularly assist colleagues in other schools by giving workshops and lectures. Summer study grants are awarded to faculty members to encourage both research and professional development.

Ms. Jeanne P. Whitman, the Eugene McDermott Headmistress, is a magna cum laude graduate of Wake Forest University. She earned her master's degree in English from the University of Virginia and a second master's degree in business from Wake Forest University.

COLLEGE ADMISSION COUNSELING

The college counselors work directly with Upper School students in their college planning. Each student participates with her parents in conferences with the counselor concerning applications and final selection.

In 2009, SAT scores ranged from 610 to 740 in critical reading, 630 to 730 in math, and 630 to 730 in writing. The class of 2010 had 16 National Merit Finalists, 16 National Merit Semifinalists, 21 National Merit Commended Students, 2 National Achievement Finalists, 2 National Achievement Scholars, 2 National Achievement Outstanding Participants, and 2 National Hispanic Honorable Mention Finalists. There are 117 Hockaday students from the classes of 2009 through 2011 who have been recognized as AP Scholars, 10 of whom qualified for the National AP Scholar Award. Hockaday alumnae are Hesburgh-Yusko Scholars (Notre Dame), Jefferson-Echols Scholars (Virginia), Marshall Scholars, Morehead-Cain Scholars (UNC-CH), a Rhodes Scholar, and Truman Scholars. They have received the Michael C. Rockefeller Memorial Fellowship at Harvard and have been named to the Gates Millennium Scholars Program. Traditionally, 100 percent of Hockaday graduates attend four-year colleges or universities. The 123 members of the class of 2010 were admitted to 193 institutions, including Brown, Carnegie Mellon, Claremont McKenna, Duke, George Washington, Harvard, McGill (Canada), Middlebury, Northwestern, Oxford (England), Princeton, SMU, Stanford, Vanderbilt, Wake Forest, Washington (St. Louis), Yale, and the Universities of Chicago and Texas at Austin, among others.

STUDENT BODY AND CONDUCT

The student body is composed of 1,087 girls (85 of whom board) from eight states and twelve countries outside of the United States. Thirty-seven percent of the girls are members of minority groups.

The Upper School Student Council and the Honor Council exert strong, active, and responsible leadership in student affairs. In addition to planning activities, allocating funds, and serving as a forum for student concerns, these councils promote and exemplify the School's written Honor Code.

Students are expected to abide by the guidelines set forth in the Upper School manual. Disciplinary measures rest primarily with the Head of the Upper School and the Headmistress.

ACADEMIC FACILITIES

The campus includes sixteen buildings. The Liza Lee Academic Research Center is 52,000-square-feet and hosts two expansive libraries, several computer labs, breakout rooms, and a versatile hall that doubles as a lecture facility and audiovisual theater. In the academic area are classrooms; laboratories for languages, computers, and reading; and a study center. The campus is fully wireless, and Middle and Upper School classrooms are equipped with SmartBoard technology for use in conjunction with students' laptops, required for every girl in grades 6–12. The Fine Arts facilities include a 600-seat auditorium, instrumental and voice studios, practice rooms, a painting studio, ceramics facilities with outdoor kilns, a photography laboratory, printmaking facilities, and an electronic music studio. The Science Center contains a recently renovated lecture hall, study lounges, classrooms, ten major laboratories, a computer lab, and a greenhouse. The Wellness Center includes the 5,000-square-foot Hill Family Fitness Center, an 1,800-square-foot aerobics room with state-of-the-art aerobic and resistance equipment, and athletic training facilities fully equipped for the treatment of sports-related injuries.

BOARDING AND GENERAL FACILITIES

Accommodations for boarding students are comfortable dormitories, updated study areas, and lounges. Girls of similar grades are normally housed on a separate hall, each with its own lounge, kitchen, large-screen plasma television, DVR, and laundry room. The dormitories are wireless and all laptops are equipped with Skype. An additional common lounge is also updated with a large-screen television, kitchen, and fireplace, and overlooks an outdoor swimming pool and tennis courts. Rooms are shared by two students, and each hall contains a small suite for the adult counselor in charge. The dormitories are closed for Thanksgiving, Christmas, and spring vacations.

An infirmary is located on the ground floor of the dormitory area, with a registered nurse on duty at all times and the School doctor on call. Campus security is maintained 24 hours a day.

The Wellness Center features an aerobics center, a fitness testing area, a trainer's facility, and the Hill Fitness Center, a 5,000-square-foot facility offering aerobic, resistance, and circuit training equipment.

ATHLETICS

Athletic facilities include two gymnasiums housing basketball courts (convertible to volleyball and indoor tennis courts), a climbing wall, two racquetball courts, a swimming pool, and a dance studio. On the grounds are six athletic fields, a softball complex, an all-weather track, a tennis center with ten courts and seating for 90, and 100 acres of open space. Interscholastic sports include basketball, crew, cross-country, fencing, field hockey, golf, lacrosse, soccer, softball, swimming and diving, tennis, track, and volleyball.

EXTRACURRICULAR OPPORTUNITIES

The Hockaday educational experience includes far more than just the classroom. There is a vast range of extracurricular opportunities for students to take part in: more than fifty student clubs, community service projects that impact the world beyond the campus, class bonding trips that build lifelong friendships, world-renowned speakers who expand students' perspectives, talent showcases at the Coffeehouse, and more.

To encourage student creativity, the Upper School sponsors a literary and journalistic magazine, a newspaper, and the Hockaday yearbook. These publications are edited by students with the guidance of faculty advisers. The literary magazine, *Vibrato*, won a Gold Crown Award from Columbia Scholastic Press Association (CSPA) and was named All American with four marks of distinction by the National Scholastic Press Association (NSPA). *Vibrato* has won top distinctions in ten of the last eleven years. Hockaday's student newspaper, *The Fourcast*, was awarded a Silver Medal by CSPA, and ranked First Class with three marks of distinction by the NSPA. The yearbook, *Cornerstones*, was featured in a full-page treatment in the 2010 edition of Taylor Publishing's *Yearbook Yearbook*. All three of Hockaday's scholastic press publications were featured in the NSPA's *Best of the High School Press*.

Service to the School and its surrounding community is an important part of a girl's life at Hockaday. Each Upper School student is required to contribute a minimum of 15 volunteer hours per year in service to the wider community.

DAILY LIFE

Upper School classes begin at 8 a.m. and end at 3:45 p.m. Monday through Friday. The daily schedule provides time for academic help sessions and club meetings.

Varsity sports meet after the close of the regular school day. Residence students have a 2-hour required study time, Sunday through Thursday nights.

WEEKEND LIFE

Off-campus activities each weekend enable residence students to take advantage of the many cultural and recreational resources in the Dallas–Fort Worth area. Faculty members are frequently involved in boarding activities, as are families of the Hockaday Parents Association, who sponsor girls who are new to Hockaday and include them in family activities. Each residence student is matched with a local Dallas family through the Host Family Program. The host families offer local support for the girls and encourage their participation in social activities outside of school.

SUMMER PROGRAMS

A six-week coed academic summer session is offered for day and boarding students. Students may attend three- or six-week sessions beginning in June and July. Summer boarding is limited to girls ages 12–17. Programs in language immersion, math and science enrichment, computers, sports, SAT preparation, study skills, English, creative writing, and arts/theater are offered. Academic courses focus on enrichment opportunities. English as a second language, an international program lasting three weeks, begins in July. Information on the summer session is available in late spring. Applications are accepted until all spaces are filled, although students are encouraged to apply early to ensure their preferred course selection.

COSTS AND FINANCIAL AID

In 2010–11, tuition for Upper School day students averaged $23,000. For resident students, costs were approximately $42,000 for tuition, room, and board. Additional expenses for both day and resident students include, among others, those for books and uniforms. A deposit of $1000 is due with the signed enrollment contract, and the balance of tuition and fees is due by July 1 prior to entrance in August. Partial payment for room and board for resident students is also made at this time. The room and board balance for resident students is payable by December 1 following entrance in August.

The Hockaday Financial Aid Program offers assistance based on financial need. Parents of all applicants for financial aid must provide financial information as required by the Financial Aid Committee. Close to $3 million was awarded to students in 2010–11. Details of the programs are available from the Admission Office.

ADMISSIONS INFORMATION

Applicants to Hockaday's Upper School are considered on the basis of their previous academic records, results of aptitude and achievement testing, teacher and head of school evaluations, and, in most cases, a personal interview. There is no discrimination because of race, creed, or nationality. Because the School requires a student to attend the School for at least two years to be eligible for graduation, new students are not normally admitted to the senior class. In order to qualify for admission and have a successful experience at Hockaday, a girl needs to possess a strong potential and desire to learn.

APPLICATION TIMETABLE

Initial inquiries are welcome at any time, and applications are received continuously. There is a nonrefundable application fee for both day-student and boarding-student applications. Entrance tests are scheduled in December, January, and February and periodically throughout the spring and summer. Campus tours are available at convenient times during the year. Notification of the admission decision is made approximately six weeks after the testing. Parents are expected to reply to an offer of admission within two weeks.

ADMISSIONS CORRESPONDENCE

Jen Liggitt, Director of Admission
The Hockaday School
11600 Welch Road
Dallas, Texas 75229-2999

Phone: 214-363-6311
Fax: 214-265-1649
E-mail: admissions@mail.hockaday.org
Web site: http://www.hockaday.org

HOOSAC SCHOOL

Hoosick, New York

Type: Coeducational boarding college-preparatory school
Grades: 8–12, postgraduate year
Enrollment: 113
Head of School: Richard J. Lomuscio, Headmaster

THE SCHOOL

Hoosac is an independent coeducational boarding school. Founded in 1889, the School still follows many of the traditions for which it is well known—for example, the nation's first student work program, in which students participate in the maintenance of their environment, and the Boar's Head and Yule Log Christmas Celebration, in which Burgess Meredith ('26) performed as a student.

Hoosac School is well suited to students who are academically motivated and are seeking a small-school environment. Hoosac also serves those who have not lived up to their potential in larger school settings, students with mild learning differences, and students who have talent but have received poor training through the years.

Hoosick is a rural community located 30 miles northeast of Albany, New York; 7 miles west of Bennington, Vermont; and 13 miles northwest of Williamstown, Massachusetts. The name of the town, like that of the School, is one of several spellings of a Native American word meaning "Place of the Owl."

Hoosac's setting amid 350 acres of fields and woods at the head of the Taconic Valley allows for a variety of outdoor activities, and the proximity of Williams College and Rensselaer Polytechnic Institute and the larger centers of Albany and Troy provide access to a wide range of cultural and educational opportunities.

Hoosac follows the Episcopal tradition in the short chapel services offered several times a week.

The School is operated by the Headmaster for an independent, self-perpetuating Board of Trustees. The plant is valued at $15 million.

Hoosac is accredited by the Middle States Association of Colleges and Schools and chartered by the New York State Board of Regents. It is a member of the National Association of Independent Schools, the Secondary School Admission Test Board, the National Association of Episcopal Schools, and the New York State Association of Independent Schools.

ACADEMIC PROGRAMS

The student-faculty ratio of 5:1 ensures that classes are kept small and that students receive a great deal of individual attention. One-to-one tutorials, independent study, and Advanced Placement courses are all available.

The curriculum consists of English I–IV, French I–II, ancient and modern European history, global studies, U.S. history, early American history, algebra I and II, geometry, precalculus, biology, chemistry, physics, psychology, earth science, computer literacy, art, photography, drama, music, film appreciation, criminology, fashion design, dance, and health. Advanced Placement courses are offered in calculus, U.S. history, and English.

In addition, the Oasis Program provides individual instruction to students with mild learning problems, relying on tutorials to establish healthy patterns of self-reliance.

Graduation requirements include the following: 4 years of English, 3 of science, 3 of mathematics, 3 of history and social studies (including 1 of U.S. history), 2 of a foreign language, 1 of a lab science, 1 of health, 1 of ethics, 1 of computers, and 1 trimester each of music, drama, and art. A two-year ESL program is available for international students.

Hoosac uses "Mastery Teaching." The concept of mastery education is older than the one-room schoolhouse where it was practiced; only the name is new. Mastery is an approach commonly used in every walk of life except formal education. For example, a person who wants to learn how to play tennis would not say, "I have 40 minutes to learn to serve. If I cannot do it in this time, I will never play tennis." Learning to serve a tennis ball well may take time. Therefore, a person would keep practicing until he or she mastered it. As in tennis, many things in life require time and repetition to learn. Given enough time and exposure, most people can master most things. Given enough exposure and support, students can learn almost anything.

Mastery uses testing as part of the instructional process. Each test reveals what a student does not know. On the basis of this, he or she is redirected and retaught in the weak areas. Each test, therefore, is a review of a student's knowledge for the purpose of reteaching. For example, a student takes a test, which is corrected and returned in class. The student is then retaught the information that they did not understand and tested again. Students also get extra help outside of class.

Mastery is an old and proven technique. It is used all over the United States, and it is a successful approach for most students. It allows the student to develop self-confidence and self-reliance.

FACULTY AND ADVISERS

Hoosac's Headmaster is Richard J. Lomuscio. Mr. Lomuscio is a graduate of NYU. He has been a newspaper editor and taught in both public and private schools. Mr. Lomuscio has served Hoosac for thirty-five years in many capacities—teacher of math, French, science, history, and English; housemaster; coach; college counselor; Director of Athletics; Director of Studies; Dean; and Headmaster.

The faculty numbers 24, of whom 8 are women. Faculty members live on campus. They and their families participate fully in all activities.

The School's adviser system is one more example of the individual attention given to students. The system provides the structure and support students need to be successful. A faculty member is responsible for up to 8 advisees, whom he or she sees at least twice a week—once in a private meeting and once in a group meeting.

Advisers receive biweekly reports on each student from the student's teachers so that any changes or problems that arise can be handled quickly. Parents also play a significant role in this system; they can monitor their child's progress by keeping in close contact with his or her adviser.

COLLEGE ADMISSION COUNSELING

College counseling, supervised by the Headmaster, begins in the junior year, and students visit colleges during the summer and fall. Admissions officers from many colleges and universities visit Hoosac.

In the last several years, graduates have been accepted to Bennington, Boston College, Boston University, Bowdoin, Clarkson, Connecticut College, Drexel, Hamilton, Hartwick, Manhattanville, Northeastern, NYU, Penn State, Rensselaer, St. Lawrence, Syracuse, Trinity (Hartford), Vassar, Vanderbilt, Washington and Jefferson, Wheaton, and the Universities of Hartford, New Hampshire, Southern California, and Vermont.

STUDENT BODY AND CONDUCT

Hoosac enrolls 113 boarding boys and girls. Most students come from the northeastern United States; others are from Georgia, Virginia, Pennsylvania, Idaho, California, Texas, and Florida and from several other countries.

Students are represented in school affairs through a traditional prefect system and play major leadership roles in important areas of school life. The kitchen and dining hall are supervised by student stewards. All class bells are rung by a student bell ringer, and the coaches are helped by student assistants. The work program is supervised by student proctors, as are the dormitory facilities. The faculty and administration offer careful guidance in order to strengthen the lessons of leadership and responsibility.

Minor infractions of Hoosac's rules and regulations result in an obligation to donate work for the benefit of the School community; more serious infractions of the regulations can result in suspension, and very serious cases can lead to dismissal.

ACADEMIC FACILITIES

Tibbits Hall, built in 1828 and remodeled in 1860, is a freestone Gothic castle containing offices, classrooms, a dormitory, and faculty apartments. Wood Hall contains the School's library, a faculty apartment, and a dormitory area. Crosby Arts Center provides facilities for theater, art, music, and dance.

Other buildings include Memorial Dining Hall (1963), which houses a spacious dining area and student lounge as well as classrooms. Blake Hall (1969) is the science building and includes classrooms, laboratories, a darkroom, a lecture hall,

www.facebook.com/sec.schools

and an observatory equipped with two telescopes. A new theater for the performing arts was recently added to Blake.

BOARDING AND GENERAL FACILITIES

Lewisohn and Dudley houses are small dormitories. Whitcomb Hall houses the chapel, a dormitory, and a faculty residence.

Pitt Mason Hall (1967) is the largest of the dormitories, housing 30 students; it includes apartments for three faculty families. Lavino House (1969) also serves as a dormitory. The Edith McCullough House (1990) holds 8 students and a faculty family, as does Cannon House, built in 1970.

About half the dormitory rooms are doubles and the rest are singles. At least one faculty family lives in every dormitory.

ATHLETICS

Every student is required to participate in athletics or an athletics alternative during the afternoon. The School fields teams at the varsity level in soccer, ice hockey, lacrosse, basketball, tennis, baseball, and volleyball and offers skiing and flag football as intramural sports. Modern dance and fitness classes are also available. Hoosac's teams participate in league competition.

Campus sports facilities include three soccer fields, one baseball diamond, a skating pond, 6 miles of cross-country running and skiing trails, and tennis courts. Students can also fish in nearby trout streams and hike and camp in Tibbits Forest. The School's sports complex includes a gymnasium, a locker and shower area, and a swimming pool. Hoosac has a ski slope on campus as well.

EXTRACURRICULAR OPPORTUNITIES

Because the student body is small, individual interests and casual groups, rather than formal clubs, are emphasized. Extracurricular activities include student publications, academic clubs, music, and art. The students present theatrical productions and participate annually in the century-old Boar's Head and Yule Log Christmas Celebration.

The Student Activities Committee works with a faculty member to provide weekend opportunities. Informal organized activities include hiking, camping, horseback riding, fishing, skiing, and skating. Traditional events for the School community include two Parents' Weekends. There is a banquet with a speaker every Friday evening.

A driver's education course is offered, as is a Red Cross lifeguarding course.

DAILY LIFE

Breakfast is served at 7:20 a.m. Chapel is at 8, followed by a Schoolwide meeting. Classes run from 8:30 to 2:55; there is a break at noon for a family-style sit-down lunch. Sports take place in the afternoon after classes. Dinner is at 6, followed each evening by a required study period. Lights-out is at 10:30.

Classes meet six days a week for 40 minutes each period; Wednesday and Saturday are half days to leave time for special activities, athletic competition, and free time.

WEEKEND LIFE

Dances, concerts, lectures, and other special activities are planned with local schools, such as Emma Willard, Stoneleigh-Burnham, Miss Hall's, and Doane Stuart. On Saturday evenings, students go to movies or the mall in Pittsfield, Albany, and Saratoga or at the School or participate in other leisure-time activities. They may also attend musical, theatrical, and educational programs at local colleges, particularly Williams and Rensselaer in Troy.

Following brunch on Sunday, students explore the woodlands, climb, hike, fish, or ski on campus or at nearby resort areas. One long weekend is scheduled during each trimester, and students may take additional weekend leaves.

COSTS AND FINANCIAL AID

Boarding tuition for 2010–11 is $35,000; day tuition is $16,000. Students enrolled in the ESL program paid an additional fee of $3500. Students enrolled in the OASIS program paid an additional fee of $7500. Books and laundry totaled an additional $1300.

Hoosac, which subscribes to the School and Student Service for Financial Aid, grants financial aid on the basis of demonstrated need. Approximately 30 percent of the students receive aid totaling more than $500,000 per year.

ADMISSIONS INFORMATION

New students are accepted at all grade levels on the basis of previous academic records and a personal interview. The first step for interested students and their families is to request a catalog and application and schedule a visit to the campus.

APPLICATION TIMETABLE

Candidates are encouraged to apply by March 15, although applications are considered at any time during the year as long as there are spaces available.

ADMISSIONS CORRESPONDENCE

Dean S. Foster, Assistant Headmaster
Hoosac School
Hoosick, New York 12089

Phone: 800-822-0159 (toll-free)
Fax: 518-686-3370
E-mail: info@hoosac.com
Web site: http://www.hoosac.com

IDYLLWILD ARTS ACADEMY

Idyllwild, California

Type: Coeducational boarding and day college-preparatory school emphasizing the performing and visual arts
Grades: 9–12, postgraduate year
Enrollment: 275
Head of School: William M. Lowman, President

THE SCHOOL

The Idyllwild Arts Academy is a boarding and day academy offering preprofessional arts training and academic preparation for colleges and conservatories to boys and girls in grades 9 through 12 and to those taking a postgraduate year.

Dr. Max Krone and Beatrice Krone founded the Idyllwild Arts Foundation in 1946 and established the Academy as a summer program in 1950. The summer program opened for 100 students that year. The summer program, which reached an enrollment of more than 1,300 children and adults, was the Academy's focus for much of its history.

The Idyllwild Arts Academy seeks to prepare students for further education, for advanced arts studies, and for adult life as contributing, productive members of society. The Academy believes in an education of high quality that places demands on both faculty members and students, who in turn must be committed to the good of the school community.

The Academy is situated on 205 acres at an elevation of more than 5,000 feet in the San Jacinto Mountains. Strawberry Creek borders the campus, which is surrounded by more than 20,000 acres of protected forest and parkland. The village of Idyllwild, a community of 2,500 year-round residents, is a center for wilderness enthusiasts, who use the hundreds of miles of trails for hiking and mountain biking and the nearby lakes and creeks for boating and fishing. Idyllwild is about 100 miles from San Diego and 125 miles from Los Angeles. Its location near the junction of Routes 74 and 243 makes it accessible from all directions over freeway and highway routes. Motels, inns, campgrounds, and bed-and-breakfast facilities are available for visitors.

The Idyllwild Arts Foundation, which administers the Academy, is a nonprofit corporation governed by a 50-member self-perpetuating Board of Trustees. The trustees elect 18 of their members to a Board of Governors, which meets four times a year to conduct the foundation's affairs.

The Idyllwild Arts Academy is accredited by the Western Association of Schools and Colleges and is a member of the Secondary School Admission Test Board, Western Boarding Schools, NAFSA: Association of International Educators, the Network of Performing and Visual Arts Schools, the National Association of Independent Schools, California Association of Independent Schools, and the Federation of American and International Schools.

ACADEMIC PROGRAMS

In order to stimulate young people intellectually and to advance their knowledge in all areas, the Arts Academy provides an exciting and challenging academic program. In accordance with the thesis that artistically inclined young people tend to learn best by experiencing and doing rather than by simply reading or listening to information, the Academy's program of studies is designed to motivate students to think for themselves and to use disciplined inquiry to explore concepts in the various domains of knowledge.

Upon graduation, Arts Academy students have met or exceeded the admission requirements of the University of California System and are prepared to enter selective colleges, universities, and conservatories across the nation. Students must complete 17 academic units in addition to their arts curriculum. The academic units must include 4 units of English, 3 of mathematics, 2 of foreign language, 2 of laboratory sciences, 3 of social studies, 2 of physical education, and 1 of academic electives. In addition, students must meet the Academy's requirement for computer literacy. Postgraduates engage in a one-year intensive program in academics and the arts.

Students choose a major and plan individual schedules with faculty members and the Dean of the Arts and Dean of Academics. Placement in arts courses is by level of ability and experience; students then advance according to their performance. Areas of study include creative writing, music (including classical and jazz), dance, acting, theatrical production and design, musical theater, moving pictures, interdisciplinary arts, and the visual arts. Each program incorporates courses in four categories: theory, history, and fundamentals of the form; creation, production, presentation, or performance; specialized master classes and private instruction; and field trips to arts communities of southern California to observe professionals at work.

Among the regular courses offered are tap, ballet, modern dance, pointe, jazz, men's class, pas de deux, and dance composition; music fundamentals, introduction to music literature, ear training/sight singing, music theory, music history, voice class, chamber music, orchestra, class piano, piano proficiency, accompaniment, and repertoire class; acting, voice and diction, musical theater, technical theater, drama history and literature, movement, playwriting, directing, and stage design; drawing and painting, art history, ceramics, sculpture, design and aesthetics, computer graphics illustration, and photography; and creative writing I and II, individual critique, and visiting artist workshops.

The academic year is divided into two semesters. Teachers are available to provide extra help in both the academic and the arts programs. Grades are issued and sent to parents four times a year.

FACULTY AND ADVISERS

William M. Lowman, a graduate of the University of Redlands (A.B.), is President of both the Arts Academy and the Idyllwild Arts Foundation. A recipient of the Nevada Governor's Arts Award, Mr. Lowman founded the Nevada School for the Arts.

The full-time faculty, including administrators who teach, numbers 39 members. All have distinguished themselves as teachers and professional artists. They hold baccalaureate and graduate degrees from such institutions as California Institute of the Arts, Catawba, DePaul, Harvard, Juilliard, New England Conservatory of Music, Oberlin, Royal College of Music (London), San Francisco Conservatory of Music, Stanford, UCLA, USC, Yale, and the Universities of California, Santa Cruz; New Mexico; and Texas at Austin. Private instructors are appointed on a part-time or short-term basis to meet special needs. Prominent performing artists are scheduled to be in residence at various times during the academic year to conduct master classes and give performance examples.

COLLEGE ADMISSION COUNSELING

College guidance for students is provided by their advisers and one full-time college counselor. Students take the SAT and ACT and receive coaching on auditions and portfolio presentation.

More than 95 percent of Arts Academy graduates have gone on to attend a wide range of colleges and conservatories, including Art Center College of Design, Berkeley, Boston Conservatory, California Institute of the Arts, Carnegie Mellon, Cornish College of the Arts, Curtis Institute, Harvard, Indiana University, Juilliard, New England Conservatory, NYU (Tisch School of the Arts, Steinhardt School of Education, Gallatin School of Individualized Study, College of General Studies, and the College of Arts and Science), Oberlin College Conservatory of Music, Peabody Conservatory of Music, Rice, Sarah Lawrence, Stanford, UCLA, USC, Yale, and the Universities of California at San Diego and Santa Cruz, Hartford (Hartt School of Music), and Michigan.

Other graduates of the Arts Academy have gone directly to positions with institutions such as the San Francisco Ballet, BalletMet, and Circle Repertory Company.

STUDENT BODY AND CONDUCT

In 2009–10, the Academy enrolled 167 girls and 108 boys. The student body represents thirty states and twenty-two other countries.

The Dean of Students is responsible for students' residential life. The Judicial Committee, comprising 2 faculty members, 1 dorm parent, and 3 students, works in cooperation with the Dean of Students to oversee the rules and regulations instituted by the Academy. There is no formal dress code.

ACADEMIC FACILITIES

The campus of the Idyllwild Arts Academy is designed to be in harmony with its forested surroundings. Lecture halls, science laboratories, classrooms, art and dance studios, and three theaters are among the many campus facilities that enable Arts Academy students to live, study, practice, and perform in this special high school environment. The Bruce Ryan soundstage opened in 2002 for students in the moving pictures (film and video) major. Nelson Hall, a dining facility, opened in May 2006.

The Max and Bee Krone Library, a state-of-the-art multimedia center, opened in 2000. It includes a museum, a 6,000-volume music library, 6,564 books, and a computer graphics lab.

The Idyllwild Arts Foundation Theater, seating 300 people, is ideal for concerts, recitals, and mainstage plays.

Three dance facilities, complete with barres, mirrors, and resilient flooring, are in constant use throughout the year.

Music facilities include excellent recital and performance areas as well as practice rooms and several studios for ensemble rehearsals.

Studios for painting and drawing, design, sculpture, and photography are located near the center of the campus. A large ceramics studio has separate facilities for throwing on the wheel and hand building. A variety of kilns, including raku, Anagama, salt, gas, and wood, are available for student use.

Parks Exhibition Center, which opened in 2002, provides a spacious, well-lighted facility where students, faculty members, and guest exhibitors show their work.

BOARDING AND GENERAL FACILITIES
For most of the nine-month academic year, the dormitories are home to the Academy's boarding students. They share double rooms in four modern, comfortable dormitories supervised by faculty members and dorm parents. The close-knit family atmosphere provides a strong base of support for the artistic, academic, and social life of the students.

A registered nurse is available at all times, and a physician in Idyllwild is on call. Emergency medical care is available at nearby hospitals.

ATHLETICS
Owing to the type of curriculum offered at the Arts Academy, the physical education program tends to be more creative than typical standardized course offerings. Physical education courses are intended to inspire a lifelong commitment to fitness.

Although students are required to complete 2 years of physical education, including one semester of health education, it is recommended that they take a physical education course each semester they are enrolled.

Health education serves to promote knowledge of nutrition and weight control as well as an understanding of stress in work and recreation, substance abuse, family issues, sexuality and relationships, and values in the decision-making process.

Idyllwild's current Physical Education facility includes a swimming pool, small gym with Universal weights and cardio equipment, tennis court, and playing field.

EXTRACURRICULAR OPPORTUNITIES
Extracurricular activities are planned by the student government and Student Services personnel. All students and faculty members are invited to make suggestions for these activities. Students sometimes go off campus for skiing, skating, and rock climbing and for trips to concerts, art museums, dance performances, theater productions, conferences, sports events, and beaches. Students who sign up for an off-campus trip are charged according to the cost of that particular event, including the costs of transportation, food consumed away from school, and entrance fees/tickets.

Students are also encouraged to become involved in Peer Ears, a student counseling group; and student publications, including the yearbook and *Parallax,* a literary and visual art publication.

DAILY LIFE
Academic classes begin at 8 a.m. and are held Monday through Saturday mornings. Arts classes are held in the afternoons, Monday through Friday, until dinner at 6:30. Evenings are set aside for rehearsals, study halls, and studio time.

WEEKEND LIFE
On weekend field trips, students enjoy the outstanding cultural attractions of Los Angeles and San Diego—museums, theaters, art galleries, and concert halls—and the many world-famous recreational areas nearby, including Disneyland, Knott's Berry Farm, Magic Mountain, Sea World, and the San Diego Zoo. In addition, southern California offers a wide variety of world-class sports attractions. The Arts Academy seeks to offer its students both the renewing serenity of the mountains and the bright lights and cultural stimulation of the city—the best of two worlds.

SUMMER PROGRAMS
The Summer Arts Program offers a wide variety of courses ranging in length from a weekend to two weeks for students of all ages. These include a Children's Arts Center, Creative Writing and Poetry (for junior high and high school students and adults), Native American arts, and comprehensive offerings in dance, music, theater and musical theater, and the visual arts. Steven Fraider is the Vice President and Director of the Summer Program.

COSTS AND FINANCIAL AID
For the 2010–11 school year, boarding tuition was $49,875 and day tuition was $33,385. The Academy subscribes to the School and Student Service for Financial Aid and awards more than $4.5 million in financial aid annually on the basis of talent and financial need. A tuition payment plan is available.

ADMISSIONS INFORMATION
The Idyllwild Arts Academy seeks dedicated, motivated, and talented students. Students are admitted in grades 9 through 12 and for a postgraduate year on the basis of academic transcripts, recommendations, a personal interview, and a demonstration of potential in the performing or visual arts through audition or portfolio.

APPLICATION TIMETABLE
Application deadlines begin February 1, and applicants are accepted until quotas are filled in each major. Students may be admitted at midyear, if space is available. The priority deadline for financial aid is February 1. The application fee is $50 for U.S. citizens and $100 for international applicants.

ADMISSIONS CORRESPONDENCE
Marek Pramuka, Dean of Admission and
    Financial Aid
Academy Admission Office
Idyllwild Arts Academy
52500 Temecula Road
P.O. Box 38
Idyllwild, California 92549-0038
Phone: 951-659-2171 Ext. 2223
Fax: 951-659-3168
E-mail: admission@idyllwildarts.org
Web site: http://www.idyllwildarts.org

INTERNATIONAL SCHOOL OF BERNE

Guemligen, Switzerland

International School of Berne

Type: Coeducational college-preparatory day school
Grades: Prekindergarten (Early Learning Centre, 3–5 year olds), Elementary School: K–grade 5, Secondary School: grade 6–12
Enrollment: 246 (Early Learning Centre 22, Elementary School 72, Secondary School 152)
Head of School: Kevin Page, Director

THE SCHOOL

The International School of Berne (ISBerne) was founded in 1961 by representatives of the American Embassy and General Motors in Berne to provide an education in English for their children. The School will be celebrating its fiftieth anniversary in 2011–12.

Today the International School of Berne is a coeducational day school serving the diplomatic and international business communities in the cantons of Berne, Fribourg, and Neuchatel. ISBerne provides an international education in English to approximately 250 students representing over 40 nationalities.

The School is a creative learning community of students, staff, and parents, characterized by its commitment to quality education, a strong international outlook, and respect for self and others.

ISBerne was first accredited in 1984, and reaccredited in 1994 and 2004 by the Council of International Schools (CIS) and the New England Association of Schools and Colleges (NEASC). As an International Baccalaureate (I.B.) World School, it is authorized to offer all three I.B. Programmes.

ISBerne is located in Guemligen, a suburb 5 kilometres from the centre of Berne. It is easily accessible by public transport and by motorway.

ACADEMIC PROGRAMS

ISBerne is as one of only 152 schools worldwide authorized to offer all three I.B. programmes: the Primary Years Programme (PYP), ages 3–11, in the Early Learning Centre (ELC) and the Elementary School; and the Middle Years Programme (MYP) ages 11–16 and Diploma Programme (DP) ages 16–19, in the Secondary School. The I.B. programmes, taught in over 3,000 schools worldwide, ensure a smooth and easy transfer for students to and from schools anywhere in the world. The I.B. diploma is recognized around the world as a premier university entrance qualification. In the I.B. exams, ISBerne students regularly attain results above the world average.

The curriculum follows a philosophy of education based on the principles of educating the whole person; of promoting international understanding; of education through a broad, balanced curriculum; and of respect for and tolerance of cultural diversity.

The elementary and middle school offerings include English, French, German, music, visual arts, theatre arts, the sciences, humanities, mathematics, and PE. Grade 5 students complete the PYP with an exhibition and the MYP is completed with a personal project in grade 10.

The I.B. DP in grades 11 and 12 is a comprehensive and rigorous two-year curriculum to prepare students for university entrance. I.B. DP students study three courses at the higher level and three at the standard level. ISBerne currently offers the following I.B. DP courses at both levels: English, French, German A (group 1); English, French, German B (group 2); economics, geography, history (group 3); chemistry, physics, biology (group 4); mathematics/mathematical studies (group 5); theatre, visual arts (group 6). Students must choose one subject each from groups 1 to 5, thus ensuring breadth of experience in languages, social studies, the experimental sciences, and mathematics. The sixth subject may be an arts subject chosen from group 6, or the student may choose another subject from groups 1 to 4.

In addition, the DP has three core requirements that are included to broaden the educational experience and challenge students to apply their knowledge and understanding: an extended essay; Theory of Knowledge; and creativity, action, and service. The extended essay requires students to engage in independent research and produce a 4,000-word essay on the in-depth study of a question relating to one of the subjects they are studying. Theory of Knowledge is a course designed to encourage each student to reflect on the nature of knowledge by critically examining different ways of knowing (perception, emotion, language, and reason), and different areas of knowledge (scientific, artistic, mathematical, and historical). The creativity, action, and service requirement ensures that students actively learn from the experience of doing real tasks beyond the classroom. Students can combine all three components or do activities related to each one of them separately.

The School offers a learning support program and college guidance, as well as an English as an additional language (EAL) program for non-English speakers.

The school year runs from August to June and is divided into two semesters, with attainment marks being awarded at the end of each semester. Students are assessed using the International Baccalaureate grade scale, 7 (high)–1 (low). The School's testing program includes the International Schools Achievement Tests in grades 3, 5, 7, and 9; the PSAT; SSAT; and SAT.

FACULTY AND ADVISERS

ISBerne has a highly qualified international teaching faculty consisting of 42 members, 28 of whom are in the Secondary School. Nineteen of the Secondary School faculty members hold advanced degrees (master's or above). Several faculty members serve as examiners, curriculum developers, and workshop leaders for the I.B.

ISBerne offers continuous in-house and external professional development opportunities to faculty members. The School has developed an ongoing relationship with Harvard Project Zero, focusing on teaching for understanding and intellectual character.

COLLEGE ADMISSION COUNSELING

The School offers a college guidance service to assist students with the application process.

ISBerne's SAT score averages for August 2009–June 2010 (11 students) were critical reading, 571; math, 647; and writing, 581. Seven students took a total of sixteen SAT subject tests and had an average score of 634. ISBerne does not offer SAT preparation courses.

Graduating classes average about 20 students per year and ninety percent go on to attend institutions of higher learning around the world. In the last three years, ISBerne graduates have been admitted to the following schools in Europe: Cambridge, Imperial College, Kings College, Royal Holloway, and the Universities of Berne, Glasgow, Warwick, and Webster. Those bound for North America attend four-year colleges and universities, including Brown, George Mason, McGill, McMaster, Northeastern, Queens, Quest, Simon Fraser, Syracuse, and York, and the Universities of British Columbia, Rochester, Toronto, and Waterloo, as well as schools in the University of California system.

STUDENT BODY AND CONDUCT

Approximately 250 students ages 3–19 from over forty nationalities study at ISBerne; 152 of those students (87 boys, 65 girls) are in Secondary School. There is an average of 21 students per grade level in Secondary School and the student-teacher ratio is 5:1. The largest nationalities represented at ISBerne are U.S. (16 percent), British (9 percent), German (8.5 percent), Swiss (8 percent), and Indian (7 percent).

There are student councils for both the Elementary School and the Secondary School, which foster student involvement in curriculum, rules, privileges and discipline. Expectations for student conduct at school and in the wider community are based upon respect. Rules are detailed in *The Parent Student Handbook* and include provisions for attendance, participation in school activities, and an electronic use agreement.

ACADEMIC FACILITIES
The School sections, ELC, Elementary, and Secondary, are on three sites, all within 200 meters of one another. Specialist areas include a gymnasium, two ICT (information and communications technology) labs, three science labs, two art rooms, two libraries, a theatre arts rehearsal area, and music rooms. A well-organized playground and a sports field are also provided. Extensive use of local facilities for athletics, sports tournaments, and theatre and music productions complements the School's programs.

ATHLETICS
Sports include basketball, volleyball, soccer, unihockey (floorball), swimming, and track and field. In winter the PE curriculum offers an ice skating program for kindergarten and grade 1, and a skiing/snowboarding program for grades 2–12 which includes seven days with professional snow sport instructors. Sports teams regularly participate in Swiss Group of International Schools (SGIS) sports tournaments.

EXTRACURRICULAR OPPORTUNITIES
ISBerne offers a broad range of extracurricular activities to complement and develop existing curricula aims and objectives. Students have access to activities that cannot normally be offered within the framework of the curriculum and provide them with challenging, new experiences to enrich their time at ISBerne.

There are activities to meet students' differing interests, such as a theatre club, Model United Nations, student councils, eco club, languages, art club, board games, and more.

DAILY LIFE
In Secondary School the day is divided into three 2-hour teaching blocks. Registration commences at 8:30 and classes begin at 8:40. Blocks run from 8:40 to 10:40 (two 60-minute lessons) and 11 to 1 (two 60-minute lessons) with a 20-minute morning recess between them. Lunch recess is from 1–1:50 (grades 9–12) or 1–2 (grades 6–8). There is another teaching block in the afternoon from 1:50 to 3:50 (two 60-minute lessons for grades 9–12) or 2 to 3:40 (two 50-minute lessons for grades 6–8). The school day ends at 3:40 for grades 6–8, and 3:50 for grades 9–12.

COSTS AND FINANCIAL AID
Annual tuition rates for the 2010–11 school year are as follows: grades 6–8, CHF 26,820; and grades 9–12, CHF 30,140. There is an application fee of CHF 250 and a one-time capital fund fee of CHF 3,500 payable upon entry. Not included in the fees are I.B. examination fees, sports trips/tournaments, PSAT/SSAT fees, PE clothes, optional curriculum-enriching trips (e.g. creativity, action, and service; Model UN; language trips, etc.), and the book and locker deposit of CHF 300. For a complete overview of fees please refer to http://www.isberne.ch/admissions/financial-regulations.

ADMISSIONS INFORMATION
The School has a nonselective open admissions policy, and applicants will be accepted for admission unless there is reason to believe that this would not be in the best interest of the applicant or the School. ISBerne welcomes applications from students who have demonstrated academic and social skills, a sound character, reliability, and an eagerness to learn. Admission to the International School of Berne is based upon the potential of the applicant to benefit from the educational services provided and the capacity of the School to meet the educational needs of the applicant.

A personal interview is requested, and all grade 6–10 applicants are asked to take entrance tests in English and mathematics. ISBerne does not normally admit students to grade 12 unless they are transferring from an International Baccalaureate school and can demonstrate reasonable compatibility between courses undertaken at their previous school and ISBerne's I.B. Diploma Programme. Final decisions on admissions require the approval of the Director.

Specific details of the complete admission process and the documents required are available online at http://www.isberne.ch/admissions/application-process.

APPLICATION TIMETABLE
Entry to ISBerne is possible year-round. All admissions are subject to availability; students may be wait-listed if their designated grade level is full. Therefore it is recommended that applications be made as early as possible.

ADMISSIONS CORRESPONDENCE
Admissions
International School of Berne
Mattenstrasse 3
3073 Guemligen
Switzerland
Phone: +41-31-951-23-58
Fax: +41-31-951-17-10
E-mail: office@isberne.ch
Web site: http://www.isberne.com

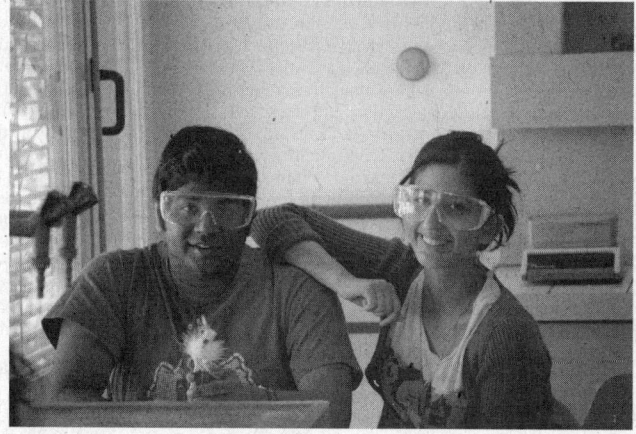

THE LAWRENCEVILLE SCHOOL

Lawrenceville, New Jersey

Type: Coeducational boarding and day college-preparatory school
Grades: 9–PG (Forms II–V): Lower School, Form II; Circle/Crescent Level, Forms III–IV; Fifth Form
Enrollment: 815
Head of School: Elizabeth A. Duffy, Head Master

THE SCHOOL

The Lawrenceville School was established in 1810 as an academy by the pastor of the village church, whose elders had sons to educate. By 1885, the physical plant was greatly enlarged, the present House system adopted, and the enrollment expanded. Lawrenceville, a small historic town, is 55 miles from New York City and 40 miles from Philadelphia.

In 1987, Lawrenceville became coeducational, enrolling girls at all grade levels. Girls account for 45 percent of the student population.

The mission of the Lawrenceville School is to inspire and educate promising young people from diverse backgrounds for responsible leadership, personal fulfillment, and enthusiastic participation in the world. Through its unique House system, collaborative Harkness approach to teaching and learning, close mentoring relationships, and extensive cocurricular opportunities, Lawrenceville helps students develop high standards of character and scholarship, a passion for learning, an appreciation for diversity, a global perspective, and strong commitments to personal, community, and environmental responsibility.

Lawrenceville is accredited by the Middle States Association of Colleges and Schools and is a member of the Secondary School Admission Test Board, the National Association of Independent Schools, the New Jersey Association of Independent Schools, and the Council for Religion in Independent Schools.

ACADEMIC PROGRAMS

In fall 2006, after an eighteen-month curriculum review, the School adopted new graduation requirements. These requirements are designed to ensure that students at the School receive a strong foundation in all disciplines during their first two years that can be built upon in the upper forms. They also meet NCAA standards and are aligned with the standard requirements for college admissions, which will simplify academic advising.

The requirements for entering Second Formers are: arts, 3 terms; English, 9 terms; history, 6 terms; humanities–English, 3 terms; humanities–cultural studies, 3 terms; interdisciplinary, 2 terms (at the advanced level); language through unit 9 (foundational level–through unit 6)*; mathematics through advanced algebra or precalculus (foundational level–through math 3)*; religion, 2 terms; and science, 9 terms (foundational level–6 terms)*. Students are also required to give at least 40 hours of community service before they graduate. (*Students may opt to finish their course work in one of these disciplines at the foundational level with approval.)

Individual participation is encouraged in small classroom sections with an average of 12 students. Classes are grouped randomly and are taught around a large oval table called the Harkness Table. Evening study periods, held in the houses, are supervised by the Housemaster, the Assistant Housemaster, or an Associate Housemaster.

Students with a particular interest in exploring new fields or in testing themselves against the challenge of a job may apply for independent study, off-campus projects, School Year Abroad (Europe or China), or the Lawrenceville international program. Recent destinations include China, the Dominican Republic, Mexico, Japan, France, Peru, Nicaragua, Ghana, the Galapagos, Great Britain, South Africa, and Tanzania. Driver's education is also available.

Lawrenceville uses a letter grading system (A–F) in which D– is passing and B+ qualifies for honors.

The school year is divided into three 10-week terms. Full reports are sent home at the end of each term, with interim reports at midterm. The full reports include comments and grades from each of a student's teachers indicating his or her accomplishments, efforts, and attitudes. Less formal progress reports are also written by teachers throughout the term as needed. Students in academic difficulty are placed on academic review, which entails close supervision and additional communication with parents.

FACULTY AND ADVISERS

There are 139 full-time faculty members, of whom 85 hold master's degrees and 19 hold doctorates. Most reside on the campus, and many serve as residential housemasters, coaches, and club advisers. All are active in advising and counseling students.

Elizabeth A. Duffy was appointed the twelfth Head Master of the Lawrenceville School in 2003. Ms. Duffy graduated magna cum laude from Princeton University in 1988 with an A.B. in molecular biology. In 1993, she received an M.B.A. from the Graduate School of Business at Stanford University and an A.M. in administration and policy analysis from the School of Education there. She has spent her entire career working with educators at all levels.

COLLEGE ADMISSION COUNSELING

The goal of the College Counseling Office is to educate students and families about the nuances of college admissions, advise students about a range of interesting college options that best suit their individual needs, and support and encourage students as they complete the application process.

Lawrenceville's experienced college counselors provide timely advice to families and help students present their abilities, talents, and experiences to the colleges in the most appropriate manner. Families and students receive information through newsletters, classwide meetings, and parent weekend programming. They also have access to a detailed Blackboard-based college counseling program via the Web, which gives them unlimited access to relevant topics on college admission and links to important sources of information and support, as well as overall advice on selecting and applying to college. These resources are designed to ensure that students and their families are well prepared to embrace the college counseling process when students are officially assigned to individual counselors in the middle of their Fourth Form year. Over the course of their junior and senior years, all students engage in a series of college-related standardized testing, a self-reflective process, college visits, on-campus college fairs, visits and/or interviews with more than 150 colleges, and individual meetings with college counselors to discuss their goals and aspirations.

The class of 2010's median SAT scores were: 676 critical reading, 697 math, and 687 writing. Between 2007 and 2009, the twenty colleges most attended by Lawrenceville students were: Princeton, 36; Pennsylvania, 29; Georgetown, 27; NYU, 24; Columbia, 23; Yale, 19; Stanford, 18; Johns Hopkins, 16; Trinity, 16; George Washington, 15; Cornell, 14; Middlebury, 13; Vanderbilt, 12; Virginia, 12; Barnard, 11; Duke, 11; USC, 11; Boston College, 10; Dartmouth, 10; and Brown, 9.

STUDENT BODY AND CONDUCT

For 2010–11, there are 815 students: boarding 553, day 262; male 433, and female 382. Students come from thirty-two states and thirty-two countries.

Lawrenceville expects its students to achieve good records and develop self-control, systematic study habits, and a clear sense of responsibility. The School has a high regard for energy, initiative, a positive attitude, and active cooperation. Students accepting this premise have no trouble following the basic regulations.

The School separates disciplinary action into three categories. They are, in decreasing order of severity, the breaking of a rule for which dismissal from school is a possible consequence, general misbehavior deemed inappropriate by the School community, and house-related offenses that reflect a lack of cooperation in the day-to-day working of the house. A student-faculty committee makes recommendations to the Head Master in regard to disciplinary action for offenses in the first category.

The student body elects 5 governing officers from among students in the Fifth Form, and each house elects its own Student Council.

ACADEMIC FACILITIES

There are thirty-nine major buildings on Lawrenceville's 700-acre campus, including the Bunn Library (with space for 100,000 volumes), which opened in 1996. The Bunn Library offers sophisticated computer research facilities, a state-of-the-art electronic classroom, and greatly expanded study areas. A 56,000-square-foot science building opened in spring 1998, a visual arts center opened in fall 1998, a history center reopened in fall 1999, and a music center opened in fall 2000.

Lawrenceville's computer network links all academic and administrative buildings. All Lawrenceville students have network ports in their dorm rooms.

BOARDING AND GENERAL FACILITIES

Lawrenceville's most distinguishing feature is its House System. In each of the twenty houses, the housemaster maintains close contact with the residents. House athletics teams compete intramurally, and house identity is maintained through separate dining rooms in the Dining Center for the underformers. This distinctive system provides a small social environment in which each student's contribution is important and measurable.

Services in Edith Memorial Chapel are nondenominational. The Al Rashid Health and Wellness Center has a full-time resident physician and an around-the-clock nursing staff.

ATHLETICS

Because many physical, social, and moral values can be instilled through the disciplines and demands of team sports, competitive athletics at both the interscholastic and house levels are the core of the physical education program. There are interscholastic teams in baseball, basketball, crew, cross-country, fencing, field hockey, football, golf, ice hockey, lacrosse, soccer, softball, squash, swimming, tennis, track and field (indoor and outdoor), volleyball, water polo, and wrestling. Dance, karate, outdoor programs, and yoga add to the physical fitness offerings at Lawrenceville. An extensive lifetime sports program is offered, as are a variety of intramural sports among the houses, including 8-man tackle football for boys' Circle Houses.

Athletic facilities include the Al Rashid Strength and Conditioning Center, Lavino Field House (three basketball, tennis, and volleyball courts; 200-meter banked indoor track; indoor ice hockey rink; wrestling and fitness rooms; indoor competition pool; ten international squash courts), a nine-hole golf course, a ¼-mile outdoor track, twelve tennis courts, a state-of-the-art ropes course (built by an expert in outdoor experiential education and considered one of the best of its kind on the East Coast), two softball and two baseball diamonds, two TurfField artificial playing surfaces with lights, fourteen other natural grass athletic fields, and a crew boathouse.

EXTRACURRICULAR OPPORTUNITIES

Lawrenceville offers students numerous opportunities for extracurricular activities. Students can choose from more than 100 organizations in debating, drama, music (the Lawrenceville Orchestra, the Lawrenceville Chorus, Jazz Ensemble, and Lawrentians), art, history, religion, science, language, photography, and video. The largest single student enterprise is the Periwig Club, whose dramas, comedies, and musicals attract more than a third of the students. Publications include *The Lawrence,* the *Lit,* and the *Olla Pod* (yearbook). Exhibits occur throughout the year. Several lecture programs bring to the campus authoritative speakers and artists from many fields. Student clubs have their own guest lecturers.

There is a required Community Service Program, in which students may serve as tutors, elementary school study center supervisors, directors of sports, and group activity counselors. The School sponsors organized educational and cultural trips to New York City and Washington, D.C.

Annual events include Parents' Weekend in the fall, Parents' Winter Gathering, and Alumni Weekend in the spring.

DAILY LIFE

Lawrenceville classes are generally 55 minutes per session—science classes and advanced classes in other disciplines also have one double period each week. Classes meet for half days on Wednesdays and Saturdays. Students engage in sports in the afternoon; most clubs and groups meet in the evening. Students take lunch at their adviser's table on Mondays.

WEEKEND LIFE

The School's location provides numerous opportunities for social, cultural, and entertainment activities. Regular weekends begin after the last class on Saturday. Students may go out for dinner with responsible adults. Drama and musical performances are often held on weekends, as are major sports events, mixers, and dances. Day students are welcome at all of these.

COSTS AND FINANCIAL AID

The annual charges for 2010–11 are $46,475 for boarding students and $38,050 for day students.

Through the generosity of alumni, friends, and foundations, approximately $9.1 million in funds are available to provide financial assistance to qualified students. Currently, 29 percent of the student body receives assistance. Awards are made on the basis of character, ability, past performance, and future promise. Amounts are based solely on need, range from $1000 to the full annual cost, and are determined by procedures established by the School and Student Service for Financial Aid.

ADMISSIONS INFORMATION

All students who enter must be able to meet the academic standards. Lawrenceville also looks for students who possess the potential to become vitally interested members of the student body—students who make individual contributions.

Selection is based on all-around qualifications without regard to race, creed, or national origin. Character, seriousness of purpose, and future promise as well as past performance, the recommendation of a headmaster or principal, and the results of the SSAT are all taken into consideration by the Admission Committee.

For fall 2010, there were 1,929 formal applications for grades 9 through 12, of which 244 enrolled. Thirty-one percent were from public schools, 39 percent from private schools, 18 percent from international schools, and 12 percent from church-related schools.

Required for admission is the formal application, which includes a written essay, a transcript of the applicant's school record, and a letter of recommendation from the head of the current school, plus three reference letters, SSAT or ISEE and/or TOEFL scores, and an on-campus interview.

APPLICATION TIMETABLE

Campus interviews are conducted throughout the week from 9 to 2 Monday, Tuesday, Thursday, and Friday. Applicants can also interview on Wednesdays between 9 and 10:30 and on Saturdays from 8:30 to10:30. Interviews are not conducted on Saturday during the summer months.

The application deadline is January 31 for boarding students and January 14 for day students, at which time three teacher recommendations, student transcripts, SSAT scores, and the head-of-school recommendation must be submitted. All campus interviews should also be completed by this date.

The notification date is March 10, and parents reply by April 10.

ADMISSIONS CORRESPONDENCE

Dean of Admission
The Lawrenceville School
2500 Main Street
P.O. Box 6008
Lawrenceville, New Jersey 08648
Phone: 609-895-2030
    800-735-2030 (toll-free outside New Jersey)
Fax: 609-895-2217
E-mail: admissions@lawrenceville.org
Web site: http://www.lawrenceville.org

LEYSIN AMERICAN SCHOOL IN SWITZERLAND

Leysin, Switzerland

Type: Coeducational boarding college-preparatory school
Grades: 8–12, postgraduate year
Enrollment: 380
Head of School: Dr. K. Steven Ott, Chairman of the Board; Dr. Marc-Frédéric Ott, Head of School; Mr. Stephen Dexter, Dean of Faculty and Academic Affairs

THE SCHOOL

As an international university-preparatory high school committed to excellence, the Leysin American School in Switzerland (LAS) educates students to respect people of other cultures and to be responsible, productive, and ethical citizens with the skills to think creatively, reason critically, and communicate effectively. This is achieved because students live in a family-like global community with high standards. LAS offers both an International Baccalaureate (I.B.) program and a U.S. high school curriculum. LAS teachers are highly qualified, dedicated international educators.

The School is located in Leysin, an alpine resort above Lake Geneva. About 90 minutes from the Geneva International Airport, Leysin is easily accessible by car or train. The magnificent beauty, serenity, and healthy environment of Leysin are enhanced by the cultural wealth of Europe and unlimited opportunities for outdoor enjoyment.

LAS strives to foster a harmonious community of young people who represent more than fifty-five nationalities. By living and learning together, students develop into "citizens of the world" with an appreciation for other cultures and languages. LAS provides a challenging college-preparatory program within a supportive framework. Many students take I.B. certificate courses; a limited number pursue the International Baccalaureate Diploma. Virtually all students continue their studies in excellent universities in the U.S., Canada, Europe, and Asia.

The Leysin American School was founded in 1960 by Mr. and Mrs. Fred C. Ott and graduated its first class in 1961. It was solely owned and operated by the Ott family until June 2005. Today, the Foundation for the Advancement of International Education is the majority owner of the Leysin American School, but the School continues under the family's leadership. It is governed by a 5-person Foundation Board under the chairmanship of Dr. K. Steven Ott.

A new program, focused on grades 8 and 9, began in the 2009–10 school year. Following in the existing boarding school structure, teachers who work with the younger students will also be living in dormitories, as well as working with them after classes for their extracurricular activities. This curriculum includes a Life Skills/Advisory class, which consists of 10–13 students who are the same age but of different nationalities.

LAS is accredited by the Council of International Schools, the Middle States Association of Colleges and Schools, and the Department of Swiss Private Education. LAS holds membership in the Swiss Group of International Schools, Advanced Placement, the College Board, and the International Baccalaureate organization. In 1999, LAS became the first high school worldwide to be certified ISO 9001 by the Swiss Association of Quality and Management Systems (SQS).

ACADEMIC PROGRAMS

The school year is divided into two semesters. The first extends from late August to mid-December and the second from January to early June. The grading system is based upon a standard A to F, 4-point scale. LAS was the first school outside of the United States to provide PowerSchool Internet access to parents interested in communicating directly with teachers, administrators, and students. PowerSchool provides real-time information for students and parents and includes complete grade access, attendance records, discipline and health information, financial accounts, and the daily School bulletin.

Students follow a demanding college-preparatory curriculum, including International Baccalaureate study. AP calculus AB and BC are also offered.

The college-preparatory curriculum meets admission requirements for colleges and universities in the U.S. and Canada. The high school diploma is granted on the basis of the following criteria: a minimum of two semesters of LAS residency, including the two semesters of the final year, and completion of a minimum of 24 credits, which include 4 credits in English, 3 in social studies, 3 in modern languages, 3 in sciences, 3 in mathematics, 2 in creative arts, 1 in senior humanities, 1 in physical education, 1 in computer studies, and 3 electives. ESL students must earn 7 ESL course credits, which thus fulfills the English and modern languages requirements.

The International Baccalaureate, a challenging program that is open to qualified students, can be followed during the last two years of high school. Students take courses leading to external exams in six areas (three higher level and three standard level); enroll in the Theory of Knowledge (TOK) course; write an extended essay; and participate in creativity, action, and service requirements. The I.B. Diploma is recognized by universities throughout the world and, in some cases, allows up to one year of advanced standing in U.S. universities. I.B. graduates are also awarded the U.S. high school diploma.

All students are encouraged to take a full range of courses to enrich their education. LAS offers electives such as visual arts, band, choir, drama, photography, private piano lessons, yearbook, additional modern languages, social studies electives, and computer science studies. The average class size is 14 students. The academic staff–student ratio is 1:7. Students take seven courses per semester.

The annual educational travel program includes two cultural excursions that are designed to acquaint students with the history and culture of Switzerland and major European cities. The students travel in small groups to various regions and submit a cultural report.

FACULTY AND ADVISERS

LAS has 75 faculty members and administrators. Ninety percent are from countries whose native language is English, and more than 70 percent hold advanced degrees. The School is firmly committed to its *in loco parentis* philosophy. Faculty members reside on campus, taking on a strong parenting role for the students. They share in dormitory and study-period supervision, sponsor sports and recreational activities, and supervise excursions.

Faculty members also serve as sponsors for Faculty Families, which play an important role in providing a caring, family-oriented environment for students. Two faculty members "adopt" 10–15 students of different nationalities and ages and serve as personal/academic advisers, guiding students through all aspects of boarding school life. Families meet regularly during the week and join in activities and excursions on weekends.

Dr. K. Steven Ott was appointed Executive Director of the School in 1982, and Chairman of the Board in 2008. He served in numerous capacities at LAS from 1970 to 1977, at which point he was appointed professor and charged with curriculum development at the newly founded King Faisal University in Saudi Arabia. He earned his B.S., M.S., and Ph.D. degrees at Stanford University.

Dr. Marc Frédéric Ott was appointed Director of External Relations in 2005, Associate Executive Director in 2007, and Head of School in 2008. He earned his master's degree in teaching business, economics, and accounting at the University of St. Gallen, Switzerland. He holds a doctorate in education (Ed.D.) from Teachers College, Columbia University.

COLLEGE ADMISSION COUNSELING

A full-time college counselor and 2 assistant counselors give advice and guidance to students as they prepare for admission to universities. Current college materials and online resources are available in the College Counseling Office. Students have many opportunities to meet college admissions officers from American and European campuses. On average, 35 school representatives visit LAS each year.

LAS is a regional testing center for the SAT and SAT Subject Tests and ACT tests. TOEFL examinations are taken online and are organized through the School's English as a second language department. Graduating students continue their education in leading U.S. and Canadian universities such as Bates, Boston University, Cornell, Dartmouth, Duke, Harvard, McGill, Stanford, U.S. Air Force Academy, and Yale.

International placements include the Federal Institute of Technology (Switzerland), Cambridge and King's College (England), Keio University (Tokyo), and the Universities of Bremen (Germany), Durham (England), and St. Andrew's (Scotland).

STUDENT BODY AND CONDUCT

In 2009–10, 385 students were enrolled from sixty-one countries. Just under 30 percent were U.S. passport holders, many of whom had families living abroad. Some of the other countries represented included Brazil, Germany, Japan, Kazakhstan, Mexico, Mongolia, Norway, Russia, Saudi Arabia, Spain, and Taiwan. Approximately one third of the student body was enrolled in LAS's English as a second language program.

The LAS publications explain community standards and behavioral expectations. LAS fosters a sense of responsibility for the School community and the individual, with honesty, respect, and fairness as key concepts. Both on and off campus, LAS is a non-smoking school at all times. LAS has a zero-tolerance policy on drug use and related activities and imposes testing.

ACADEMIC FACILITIES

The LAS campus offers excellent facilities in every academic area. There are two main academic complexes and seven additional residential halls.

The Belle Époque Complex was inaugurated in 2010 as the new home for the I.B. program. This campus is now a premier I.B. facility with the completion of a two-year, 25-million Swiss franc renovation of the Leysin Grand Hotel, a former sanatorium and hotel built in 1892. The new facility has 25 classrooms, administrative offices, dining facilities, a new academic center, Art Loft, science labs, I.B. literature library, and performance spaces.

The Savoy Complex has thirty classrooms, administrative offices, and an Information and Technology Center that includes a teaching lab and an additional lab of thirty computers. There is a modern and spacious library with 20,000 volumes, a CD-ROM online data bank, and Internet access. The Savoy also houses the dining room; health center; Visual Arts Center, which includes a darkroom for photography; a ceramics studio; and a beautiful painting studio with terraces overlooking the Rhone Valley. There is also a modern theater (The Black Box), a music room with recording technology, and two new art galleries. Athletic facilities, next to the Savoy, feature a gymnasium, a squash court, a fitness center, and a dance studio.

The Beau Site houses the Science Center, with four labs and a lecture hall. The Admissions Office and the primary reception area are located in Beau Site. Students can relax in the student center (the Red Frog), and dance in the Valley View multipurpose hall, which is frequently the LAS Disco. The Vermont Complex, which is located directly between the Savoy and the Beau Site, includes a bookstore, activities and travel offices, and the math chalet with six classrooms.

The Beau Réveil facility, which was renovated in 2005, houses the six classes of the modern languages department, offices, and a computer language lab. The language lab features twenty computers with networked online Auralog TeLL me More® language software in French, German, and ESL.

Beginning in 2007, LAS began a green project to upgrade the heating facilities in all campus dormitories. The 500,000 Swiss franc project includes installing solar panels on all dormitories supported by clean-burning natural gas boilers. Two of the seven planned buildings have already been completed.

BOARDING AND GENERAL FACILITIES
The LAS campus blends into the friendly, picturesque village of Leysin. From every building there is a spectacular view of the Alps.

Residence halls are the key to the well being and positive functioning of the School community. Students and teachers have rooms and apartments, respectively, in electronic-key-controlled-entry residence halls. The newly installed key system ensures a secure environment. The constant adult presence of teachers and their families creates a homelike atmosphere. Students have comfortable rooms, sharing them with 1 or 2 roommates of different nationalities. Every room has a private toilet and shower. Students enjoy wireless Internet access from anywhere on campus and have their own personal LAS cell phone. Every dormitory has recreation/TV rooms, community kitchens, and laundry facilities.

ATHLETICS
Sports and physical education are an integral part of the balanced program, which is designed to develop lifelong skills and to promote health and vitality, teamwork, and school spirit. During the fall and spring terms, students devote at least one afternoon per week to instructional sports. Team sports include basketball, cross-country, soccer, swimming, tennis, and volleyball. Individual sports include aerobics, hiking, horseback riding, ice skating, mountain biking, rock climbing, swimming, and weight lifting.

LAS uses its own gymnasium as well as two local sports centers. Facilities include a full-size skating rink, 25-meter indoor swimming pool, gymnasium, indoor and outdoor tennis courts, soccer field, indoor squash courts, two indoor climbing walls, fitness center, exercise room, and cross-country running track.

Beginning in January, students enjoy two afternoons a week during the winter term participating in winter sports in and around the alpine village of Leysin. Skiing and snowboarding, as well as ice skating and snowshoeing, are offered. The ski resorts of Leysin and Les Mosses, which are connected by a short bus link, offer unlimited access to 110 kilometers of downhill trails. In addition, there are more than 20 kilometers of cross-country trails right at LAS's front door. Professionally trained members of the Swiss Ski School provide lessons.

EXTRACURRICULAR OPPORTUNITIES
LAS provides many leadership opportunities through Student Council, National Honor Society, Model UN, and dormitory/student life committees. There are several groups that are active in global awareness projects, including Habitat for Humanity. Students attend concerts, visit museums, go to plays, and enjoy festivals, fairs, and special events.

Three major LAS-sponsored excursions introduce Europe's wealth of culture and history. The September Weekend is a three-day outing organized by Faculty Families. Swiss Cultural Excursions acquaint students with the host country, with small groups traveling to a variety of destinations. Seniors and postgraduate (PG) students participate in a separate trip to Rome, Florence, or Venice as part of their Theory of Knowledge course. The five-day European Cultural Excursions introduce the historic and cultural richness of neighboring countries. Typical destinations are Budapest, Istanbul, Munich, Paris, Prague, Salzburg, and Vienna. Students may join one of the humanitarian trips to Hungary, Poland, and Romania. Seniors have the choice of a humanitarian trip or a special senior trip, with typical destinations of Madrid and Kiev.

DAILY LIFE
Classes are held five days a week from 8 a.m. to 3:30 p.m., followed by sports and activities or free time. Faculty Families meet once a week within the school day. There is one weekly assembly for all students and faculty members. Monitored study time is held in the students' rooms from 7:30 to 10, Sunday through Thursday evenings. The library, computer labs, and music and art studios are open throughout the day.

WEEKEND LIFE
Weekends offer many options, including sports tournaments; trips to Lausanne, Geneva, and other nearby cities; Faculty Family excursions; and special outings. There are regular hiking and biking trips sponsored by the faculty. Students may go to the village after classes and on weekends. Friday and Saturday evenings, students may attend the local cinema, School-sponsored dances, sports events, or cultural activities.

SUMMER PROGRAMS
Summer in Switzerland (SIS) is LAS's well-established summer academic enrichment, recreation, and travel program. Boys and girls from more than forty-five countries participate in one of three programs: Alpine Adventure for ages 8–12, Alpine Exploration for ages 13–15, and Alpine Challenge for ages 16–19. All three programs offer challenging academic/language courses, a choice of excursions, creative arts, and exciting sports—all in the spectacular setting of the Swiss Alps.

SIS provides courses that are appropriate to the age group served, including French (in native French-speaking Leysin), Spanish, English literature, math, computer studies, and SAT/ACT preparation. Stu-dents may be able to earn high school credit in certain subjects, including French, English, and math.

The creative arts program offers theater, music, and art. The theater program schedules two productions in one 3-week session. Musicians and visual artists develop individual skills in their chosen instrument or discipline.

In the mornings, students attend classes, while the afternoons are devoted to sports activities and excursions. Choices include tennis, soccer, skating, paragliding, and alpine activities such as climbing, hiking, and rafting. Weekend excursions permit students to explore cities such as Geneva, Lausanne, Lucerne, Zermatt, and Montreux, as well as Paris and Milan for the Alpine Challenge participants.

SIS also offers three specialized programs for 13- to 19-year-olds. Theatre International enables students to focus on their theatrical skills and credits in an international setting. The intensive Outdoor Leadership Adventure program allows students to explore the beauty of the Swiss Alps while learning to lead others and work as part of a close-knit group. The SAT-prep program allows students to prepare for the SAT and ACT in an intensive three-week program sponsored by StudyWorks, Inc.

There are two 3-week sessions, beginning in late June and ending in early August. Optional faculty-supervised weeklong excursions within Switzerland or to another European destination, such as England, France, Italy, Spain, or Germany, are also offered for Alpine Exploration and Alpine Challenge students.

COSTS AND FINANCIAL AID
In 2010–11, enrollment, tuition, room, and board fees are SF 74,500 for the full school year. Fees cover all regular instruction and laboratory fees, book charges, dormitory facilities, full board, LAS health plan (accident and health insurances and use of health center), residence permit, three major LAS-sponsored excursions, weekend activities, social events, spring prom, and a sports/ski pass with ski/snowboard lessons.

Parents establish a personal account for disbursement of weekly pocket money and extra expenses. Financial aid is available. Families living or transferring overseas and receiving educational allowances from their employers may apply for the LAS Corporate Plan based on company policy.

ADMISSIONS INFORMATION
Students who demonstrate good character and academic potential may apply for admission. LAS requires a school transcript, three recommendations, personal essay, and completed application form. An interview is recommended. Applicants are notified without delay regarding acceptance status. LAS encourages prospective students to visit the campus.

APPLICATION TIMETABLE
LAS encourages candidates to apply between late fall and early spring but accepts applications on a rolling admissions basis beginning in January before the school year begins, space permitting.

ADMISSIONS CORRESPONDENCE
Admissions Office
Leysin American School
CH-1854 Leysin
Switzerland

Phone: 41-24-493-3777 (Swiss)
603-431-7654 (United States)
888-642-4142 (toll-free within the U.S.)
Fax: 41-24-494-1585 (Swiss)
E-mail: admissions@las.ch
Web site: http://www.las.ch

LYNDON INSTITUTE

Lyndon Center, Vermont

Type: College-preparatory and general academic coeducational day and boarding school
Grades: 9–12
Enrollment: 608
Head of School: Richard D. Hilton, Headmaster

THE SCHOOL

Lyndon Institute (LI) was founded in 1867 in the tradition of the New England academy. The Institute still shows the effects of the shaping hand of T. N. Vail, founder of AT&T, who served as president of LI in the early 1900s and was responsible for considerable growth in its programs and facilities.

An accomplished faculty that includes published authors, noted artists, college faculty members, and others active in their professional fields provides a challenging, comprehensive educational program in a picturesque Vermont village setting. Lyndon students enjoy personal attention from the faculty members, genuine respect for their individuality and unique talents, a truly inclusive environment, and outstanding preparation for their choices of colleges and careers.

Lyndon Institute consists of three campuses on 150 acres centered on the village green of historic Lyndon Center, Vermont. It is a safe, supportive community of exceptional beauty.

LI is located 10 miles north of St. Johnsbury on Interstate 91. Boston and Hartford are 3–4 hours away by car. Burlington, Vermont, and Montreal are only 2 hours from the campus. Airline service to Burlington; Manchester, New Hampshire; or Boston, Massachusetts, provides easy access. Burke Mountain Ski Area is 7 miles away.

The school's operating budget is $10.1 million; parents, friends, and an active alumni group raise about $250,000 in annual support. The endowment is $8 million.

Lyndon Institute is accredited by the New England Association of Schools and Colleges and approved by the Vermont Department of Education. Memberships include the Independent School Association of Northern New England, the Vermont Independent School Association, the Secondary School Admission Test Board, and The Association of Boarding Schools.

ACADEMIC PROGRAMS

Lyndon Institute is a comprehensive secondary school offering college-preparatory and fine arts programs of study as well as business, information, and technical education areas. Twenty-two credits are required for graduation, with the following distribution: English, 4 credits; social studies, 3 credits; mathematics, 3 credits; science, 3 credits; fine arts, 1 credit; health and physical education, 2½ credits; and electives, 4½ credits.

Other course offerings include French, 4 years; Japanese, 4 years; Latin, 4 years; Spanish, 4 years; band and chorus, 4 years; art and theater, 4 years; advanced math, 2 years; algebra, 2 years; geometry, 1 year; Calculus, 2 years; biology, 2 years; chemistry, 2 years; physics, 2 years; computer science, 7 courses; technology, 14 courses; drafting, 5 courses, including computer-aided design; word processing, 3 courses; and office technology, 3 courses. Honors courses are offered in American literature,

English literature, algebra 1 and 2, geometry, world geography, U.S. history, contemporary U.S. history, world civilizations, biology, chemistry, physics, and advanced art. LI offers Advanced Placement courses in English composition, English literature, chemistry, physics, environmental science, European history, U.S. history, calculus A/B and B/C, and studio art in both drawing and design.

The fine and performing arts program allows students to take a series of courses within the fine arts concentration, which includes concert band, jazz band, improvisation, music theory, chorus, select chorus, art, art 4, advanced art, book arts, painting, printmaking, design, 2-D and 3-D art, photography, dance, jazz dance, lyrical ballet, four years of acting, and theater production.

Classes are grouped on the basis of ability. The student-teacher ratio is 10:1, with an average class size of 18. The grading system ranges from A to F and is calculated on a 4-point scale: A, 4.0; B, 3.0; C, 2.0; D, 1.0; and F, 0.0. The academic year is divided into two semesters consisting of two quarters each. Exchange trips are available during vacation times, and many opportunities for class travel are offered throughout the year.

FACULTY AND ADVISERS

There are 61 full-time and part-time faculty members at Lyndon Institute. Thirty-one percent have earned a master's degree or higher.

Richard D. Hilton was appointed Headmaster in 1999. He holds a B.A. in English from Notre Dame and a master's degree from Villanova.

COLLEGE ADMISSION COUNSELING

College planning is accomplished through individual and small-group counseling beginning in the freshman year. Two full-time counselors work in concert with students and families to develop postsecondary plans. In a student's junior year, counselors from the Student Services Office help with coordinating college applications and essay writing.

Representatives from more than thirty colleges visit Lyndon Institute annually. LI cosponsors the Northeast Kingdom College Night program each spring with representatives from more than 100 colleges and universities in attendance.

Last year, 86 percent of LI graduates pursued postsecondary options. Recent graduates have attended Boston College, Boston University, Brown, Clarkson, Cornell, Dartmouth, Harvard, McGill, Middlebury, Northeastern, Purdue, Rensselaer, Smith, St. Lawrence, and the Universities of Illinois, Maine, Massachusetts, Michigan, New Hampshire, Vermont, and Washington.

STUDENT BODY AND CONDUCT

The total enrollment is 608 students, who come from the surrounding communities in Vermont and New Hampshire and from countries around

the globe. The school implemented a boarding program in 2003–04, which had 95 students in grades 9–12 in the 2009–10 school year. Countries represented in the international program in the last five years include Afghanistan, China, Germany, Japan, Kazakhstan, Korea, Mexico, Pakistan, Spain, Sweden, and Taiwan.

The Code of Conduct is established by the faculty members, the administration, and the Board of Trustees and is based on common courtesy, mutual respect, and socially acceptable behavior.

ACADEMIC FACILITIES

Lyndon Institute comprises three campuses. The Darling Campus consists of the Main Building, containing ten classrooms, four science labs, a small performing arts space, administrative offices, and a multilevel media center; Pierce Hall, containing seven classrooms, a computer lab, and a 250-seat cafeteria; Alumni Wing, which houses a 550-seat gymnasium and a 650-seat auditorium; and Lewis Field.

The Harris Campus consists of five main buildings, including the school's health center, and Sanborn Hall, which provides locker rooms, athletic training facilities, and a full-size auxiliary gymnasium.

The Vail Campus comprises eleven buildings, eight of which house technology classrooms, laboratories, and workshops, including a fully networked computer-aided design (CAD) lab and drafting studio, a newly dedicated art center (2003), and four residence dormitories.

BOARDING AND GENERAL FACILITIES

Seven dorms make up the housing for boarding students at Lyndon Institute, including a new dormitory for 20 students. The dormitories can accomodate 106 students in single or double rooms, as well as 15 resident dorm parents.

ATHLETICS

In the 2009–10 school year, roughly 45 percent of the student body participated in the fall sports program. Lyndon Institute is involved in 15 interscholastic sports and students can use the multiple game and practice fields; the Fenton Chester Ice Arena, which is adjacent to the school; and Burke Mountain Ski Area, just 7 miles from campus. The golf team practices at nearby St. Johnsbury Country Club's championship golf course. In the last five years, LI teams have won state championships in baseball, cross-country running, golf, Nordic skiing, softball, and track.

EXTRACURRICULAR OPPORTUNITIES

Student clubs and organizations include Student Council, National Honor Society, Future Business Leaders of America, and USA Skills/Vocational Industrial Clubs of America. Students may join the jazz ensemble; choral and drama groups; French,

Latin, and Spanish clubs; the forensics team, and the scholars bowl team. The award-winning art and literature magazine, *Janus*; the *Viking Voice*, LI's student newspaper; *Cynosure*, the yearbook; and the Writers Workshop offer students writing, editing, and desktop publishing opportunities.

The French and Spanish clubs organize trips abroad in alternating years. Students can take advantage of the cultural events and concerts at LSC, the Catamount Film and Arts Center in St. Johnsbury, and the Hopkins Center at Dartmouth College. The Music, Dance, and Art Departments offer students opportunities to work and perform with guest artists-in-residence. In addition to dances, plays, concerts, and athletics events, Spirit Week and Winter Carnival are two schoolwide events that engage the entire student body. Kingdom Trails offers a network of trails in the region for mountain biking in the summer and fall, and cross-country skiing and snowshoeing in the winter. Numerous field trips throughout Vermont, New England, and Canada are offered throughout the year.

DAILY LIFE

Classes begin each day at 7:55 a.m. and end at 2:45 p.m. There are eight class periods of 47 minutes each. Faculty members remain in their classrooms until 3 p.m. to assist students. Activities are scheduled at 3 p.m. or later to allow students additional time to meet with faculty members as needed. The library is open from 7:30 a.m. to 4:30 p.m.

WEEKEND LIFE

Weekends in the Northeast Kingdom are always an adventure. Many interscholastic events take place on Saturday. Trips are scheduled to nearby ski areas and to the urban centers of Burlington; Hanover, New Hampshire; and Montreal. Catamount Film and Arts Center in St. Johnsbury frequently hosts special events or series in the area, some of which are scheduled at LI and Lyndon State College. Students in good standing and with advance permission have the option to spend the weekend with a host family in the area or to travel home.

SUMMER PROGRAMS

Lyndon Institute sponsors day camps for football, basketball, and soccer in late July and August, and it sponsors camps for dance and theater in July.

COSTS AND FINANCIAL AID

Tuition for boarding students for 2011–12 is $39,600. A deposit of $2000 is due by May 31 to reserve a place. The Institute works with parents to arrange alternative payment schedules when needed.

Financial aid is based on need as determined by the School's Financial Aid Committee.

ADMISSIONS INFORMATION

Acceptance to Lyndon Institute is based on academic performance and potential, school citizenship, and motivation. The SSAT is required for domestic students. The TOEFL or SLEP is required for international students whose native language is not English. A minimum score of 50 on the SLEP is necessary for acceptance.

Lyndon Institute admits students of any race, color, or national or ethnic origin to all the rights, privileges, programs, and activities generally accorded or made available to students at the school. LI does not discriminate on the basis of race, color, or national or ethnic origin in the administration of its educational policies, admission policies, scholarships, and loan programs or athletics and other school-administered programs.

APPLICATION TIMETABLE

Inquiries are welcome at any time. An interview is strongly suggested. Interviews and tours are scheduled between 10 a.m. and 2 p.m., Monday through Friday. Weekend appointments are available by special arrangement. Admissions decisions are made on a rolling basis. Since the boarding program is limited in enrollment, early application (by March 31) is recommended.

ADMISSIONS CORRESPONDENCE

Mary B. Thomas
Assistant Head for Admissions
Lyndon Institute
P.O. Box 127
Lyndon Center, Vermont 05850-0127

Phone: 802-626-5232
Fax: 802-626-6138
E-mail: admissions@lyndon.institute.org
Web site: http://www.lyndoninstitute.org

MAINE CENTRAL INSTITUTE

Pittsfield, Maine

Type: Coeducational traditional boarding and day college-preparatory and comprehensive curriculum
Grades: 9–12, postgraduate year
Enrollment: 480
Head of School: Christopher Hopkins

THE SCHOOL

Founded in 1866 by Free Will Baptists, Maine Central Institute (MCI) retains the inventive spirit and philosophy of its founders but no longer has a formal affiliation with the church. During the school's pioneer years, MCI served as a feeder school to Bates College in nearby Lewiston, Maine. Although adhering to upstanding and traditional educational values, MCI is progressive and broadminded, pledging to provide a comprehensive college-preparatory education to a multicultural student body diverse in talents, abilities, and interests.

MCI regards each student as an individual with individual needs and aspirations. In keeping with its belief in individuality, MCI strives to foster an overall environment of mutual respect, cooperation, and tolerance among all of its members and with the surrounding community. In a safe and caring atmosphere, students are encouraged to develop a moral and social consciousness, self-esteem, and social responsibility and to become globally aware, lifelong learners.

The rural town of Pittsfield (population 4,500) is nestled in between the Atlantic Ocean and the mountains of western Maine. The region of central Maine provides prime opportunities for hiking, skiing, biking, fishing, skating, and snowmobiling. The campus is within walking distance of local eateries, recreational parks, shopping, hiking trials, and a movie theater.

Maine Central Institute is accredited by the New England Association of Schools and Colleges and approved by the State of Maine Department of Education. MCI is also a member of the College Board and the National Association of Independent Schools.

ACADEMIC PROGRAMS

MCI offers a rigorous comprehensive curriculum to accommodate various learning styles and academic abilities. MCI fosters the intellectual curiosities of its student body by offering accelerated and advanced placement courses in all core subject areas.

For grades 9–12, 20 credits are required for graduation. Students must successfully complete units in English (4), mathematics (4), social studies (3, including U.S. history), science (4), physical education (1), fine arts (1), computer science (½), and health (½). Students are required to take the equivalent of at least 5 units

each semester. MCI also offers a postgraduate academic year with college prep and, more specifically, SAT prep.

MCI's math and science programs exceed national standards and utilize state-of-the-art technology and academic facilities. Students in MCI's well-known humanities program understand the culture of an era through a study of its history, literature, and art. The Institute has an award-winning music program.

The foreign language program includes four levels of French and Spanish. In 2009, MCI added a Chinese Mandarin program to the foreign languages, which is taught by an exchange teacher from China. In addition to the traditional offerings, students may take courses in psychology, music composition, the Internet, sociology, child development, computer-assisted drawing, personal finance, vocational subjects, WMCI, and philosophy.

MCI offers a structured ESL program for the international student who is planning for a university education. Students receive individual testing before placement at one of three levels of ESL. The extensive ESL program includes American history for international students and carefully structured math classes that focus on the development of math language skills. MCI also offers a four-week summer program for ESL.

FACULTY AND ADVISERS

The 2010–11 faculty consists of 42 full-time members. More than a quarter of the faculty and staff members reside on campus, while the rest live in nearby towns such as Newport, Waterville, and Bangor.

Faculty members are selected on the basis of three main criteria. They must possess a strong subject-matter background, the ability to relate to students, and an educational philosophy consistent with that of the institution and its mission. Faculty members are also expected to become actively involved in coaching, supervising dormitories, advising, counseling, and student affairs.

COLLEGE ADMISSION COUNSELING

A guidance team of 4 professionals is available for students. Counselors are responsible primarily for helping students with postsecondary placement and academic program planning. Approximately 75 college admissions representatives visit MCI's campus annually. Career counseling is also an integral part of the guidance department. Financial aid workshops for seniors,

postgraduates, and their parents are offered. Preparation for the SAT and ACT is offered within the math and English curricula.

MCI has a strong history of placing students in postsecondary school. Schools attended by recent graduates include Bates, Boston University, Colby, Cornell, Emerson, Emory, George Mason, Gettysburg, Hofstra, Husson, Maine Maritime Academy, Michigan State, Muhlenberg, Northeastern, Syracuse, Tufts, Worcester Polytechnic, and the Universities of Connecticut, Maine, New England, New Hampshire, and Rhode Island.

STUDENT BODY AND CONDUCT

The 2010–11 enrollment of 480 includes day and boarding students. Students come to MCI from eleven states and seventeen countries.

Students at MCI are expected to be good citizens and are held responsible for their behavior. The rules that provide the structure for the school community are written in the student handbook. Disciplinary issues are the responsibility of the administration, the faculty, and the residence hall staff.

ACADEMIC FACILITIES

There are seventeen buildings housed on the 23-acre campus. Visitors are greeted upon entrance with the stoic simplicity of the campus with its brick-front buildings and the historic bell tower of Founder's Hall.

The Math and Science Center is a 23,000-square-foot recent addition to MCI, including fourteen instructional spaces, two computer classrooms, and a botany area. More than 210 computers are available for student use campuswide, many of which have Internet and e-mail access. The 12,000-volume Powell Memorial Library has a computerized card catalogue as well as Internet access. The Pittsfield Public Library is also available for school use.

BOARDING AND GENERAL FACILITIES

Boarding students reside in single-sex residence halls on campus, supervised by resident faculty and staff members. Each residence hall has its own recreation room and laundry facilities. MCI celebrated the opening in fall 2007 of an Honors Dormitory, converted from a home owned by the school to reward the highest-achieving residential students. Construction of the Donna Leavitt Furman Student Center was a second notable addition to the MCI campus in 2007. It is home to the dining hall, student lounge, and garden sitting area, including a performance stage, food court, garden benches, and game room.

Weymouth Hall houses the Student Services Center, consisting of the student union, snack machines, the Wellness Center, and the school bookstore.

MCI offers a unique Host Family Program. Participating students are paired with a family from the community that makes the student a part of its family for the school year. Students may spend time with their host family on weekends, after school, and during vacations, if so desired.

ATHLETICS
MCI believes that athletics not only provide a wholesome outlet for youthful energies but also help students apply and further develop their skills in various sports. The school strives to furnish opportunities for participation by students of all abilities by offering JV, varsity, and club-level sports. MCI also provides an opportunity for postgraduate basketball, and many alumni have gone on to play in the NCAA Division 1 and 9 and also in the NBA.

There are seventeen sports teams for boys and girls, including baseball, basketball, cheering, field hockey, football, golf, rifle, skiing, soccer, softball, tennis, track, and wrestling.

Wright Gymnasium and Parks Gymnasium are multiple-use athletic facilities, and each contains a weight room and locker facilities. Located on the main campus are a football field, a practice field, a ¼-mile track, two tennis courts, and a rifle range. Manson Park has fields for soccer, field hockey, baseball, and softball as well as three tennis courts. The school has the use of a local golf course and ski areas for competitive teams and recreation.

EXTRACURRICULAR OPPORTUNITIES
MCI students may choose from among more than thirty campus organizations, which represent some of the following interests: drama production; foreign languages and travel to places such as Spain, England, and Russia;

chess; hiking; weight lifting; Future Problem Solvers; Key Club, which is the school's community service organization; computer science; and public speaking. Students may participate in Student Council; MCI's strong, award-winning music program includes concert band, concert choir, chamber choir, vocal jazz ensemble, instrumental jazz ensemble, jazz combo, percussion ensemble, and pep band; and the Math Team and the Science Olympiad, which compete locally and statewide.

Bossov Ballet Theatre offers MCI students a unique opportunity to study classical ballet as part of the academic curriculum. Ballet classes are taught by Andrei Bossov, a world-renowned teacher who previously taught at the Vaganova Academy in Saint Petersburg, Russia. The program consists of a preprofessional-level syllabus that prepares students for a professional ballet career.

DAILY LIFE
The school day begins at 7:40 and ends at 2:36, with a 42-minute lunch break beginning at 11:30. Classes run from Monday through Friday, with dinner served from 5 to 6:30 p.m.

Sunday through Thursday, there is a mandatory supervised study hall from 7 to 8:30 p.m. for all boarding students.

WEEKEND LIFE
Supervised weekend activities include trips to Canada, Boston, the nearby capital of Augusta, the city of Portland, historic ports, lighthouses and coastal towns along the Atlantic shoreline, and cultural and athletic events both on and off campus. Activities such as whale watching, white-water rafting, and skiing at Sugarloaf Resort are also offered. With parental permission, students are allowed to go home on weekends or visit the home of their host family.

COSTS AND FINANCIAL AID
The 2010–11 tuition, room, and board are $38,000 for boarding students, and tuition is $10,000 for private day students. The cost for ESL support is $2500 for the first class and

$1500 for each additional class. The nonrefundable deposit of $3000 is due within two weeks of an offer of admission. A variety of payment plans are available.

Financial aid is awarded on a need basis, determined by information shown on the Parents' Confidential Statement and any additional financial information that is requested.

ADMISSIONS INFORMATION
MCI's Admissions Committee screens all applicants to determine their compatibility with MCI's philosophy that students should assume a mature responsibility for their own education. No entrance tests are required, but an on-campus interview with each student and his or her parents is strongly recommended. School transcripts and results of standardized tests are used to determine academic ability and appropriate academic placement in classes in accordance with the student's individual needs, abilities, and interests.

Maine Central Institute does not discriminate on the basis of race, sex, age, sexual preference, disability, religion, or national or ethnic origin in the administration of its educational and admission policies, financial aid programs, and athletic or other school-administered programs and activities.

APPLICATION TIMETABLE
Inquiries and applications are welcome at any time; however, applying by June 1 is recommended. Visits may be scheduled at any time during the year but are most effective when school is in session. Tours and interviews can be arranged by calling the Admissions Office, which is open Monday through Friday from 8 to 4:30. A nonrefundable application fee of $50 is required.

ADMISSIONS CORRESPONDENCE
Clint M. Williams, Director of Admission
Maine Central Institute
295 Main Street
Pittsfield, Maine 04967

Phone: 207-487-2282
Fax: 207-487-3512
E-mail: cwilliams@mci-school.org
Web site: http://www.mci-school.org

MARYMOUNT SCHOOL OF NEW YORK

New York, New York

Type: Girls' independent college-preparatory Catholic day school
Grades: N–12: Lower School, Nursery–3; Middle School, 4–7; Upper School, 8–12
Enrollment: School total: 613; Upper School: 240
Head of School: Concepcion R. Alvar

THE SCHOOL

Marymount School of New York is an independent Catholic day school that educates girls in a tradition of academic excellence and moral values. The School promotes in each student a respect for her own unique abilities and provides a foundation for exploring and acting on questions of integrity and ethical decision-making. Founded by Mother Joseph Butler in 1926 as part of a worldwide network of schools directed by the Religious of the Sacred Heart of Mary, Marymount remains faithful to its mission "to educate young women who question, risk, and grow; young women who care, serve, and lead; young women prepared to challenge, shape, and change the world." Committed to its Catholic heritage, the School welcomes and values the religious diversity of its student body and seeks to give all students a deeper understanding of the role of the spiritual in life. The School also has an active social service program and integrates social justice and human rights into the curriculum.

Marymount occupies three adjoining landmark Beaux Arts mansions, located on Fifth Avenue's historic Museum Mile, and a fourth mansion at 2 East 82nd Street. The School has recently expanded to include an additional facility with 42,000-square-feet of space on East 97th Street. The Metropolitan Museum of Art and Central Park, both located directly across the street from the School, provide resources that are integral to the School's academic and extracurricular programs. Middle School art classes meet once a week in studios at the Museum. As part of the Class IX humanities curriculum, and in AP Art History, Upper School students visit the Museum as often as twice a week. Central Park is used for science and physical education classes as well as extracurricular activities. Other city sites, such as the United Nations, the Tenement Museum, Ellis Island, the New York Zoological Society, the American Museum of Natural History, the Rose Planetarium, the Frick and Guggenheim Museums, and El Museo Del Barrio are also frequent extensions of the classroom for students in Classes K through XII.

Since 1969, the School has been independently incorporated under the direction of a 30-member Board of Trustees made up of parents, alumnae, educators, and members of the founding order. The School benefits from a strong Parents' Association; an active Alumnae Association; the involvement of parents, alumnae, and student volunteers; and a successful Annual Giving Program.

Marymount is accredited by the New York State Association of Independent Schools (NYSAIS). The School holds membership in the National Association of Independent Schools (NAIS), NYSAIS, the Independent Schools Admissions Association of Greater New York, the National Catholic Education Association, the National Coalition of Girls' Schools (NCGS), and the Educational Records Bureau.

ACADEMIC PROGRAMS

Emphasizing classic disciplines and scientific inquiry, the challenging college-preparatory curriculum provides students with the skills necessary to succeed in competitive colleges and in life beyond the classroom. Through its rigorous academic program and its focus on the education of young women, Marymount seeks to instill in its students self-confidence, leadership ability, a risk-taking spirit, and a love of learning.

Technology is part of the DNA of the School. The commitment to twenty-first century learning and the STEM initiative (science, technology, engineering, and mathematics for girls) is reflected in its curriculum, which fully integrates information and communication technologies into all subject areas. Students have access to wired and wireless desktop and laptop computers as well as other mobile computing devices throughout the School. Upper School students and staff members have individual e-mail accounts and use computers and other mobile computing devices to carry out research, create presentations, publish work, communicate, and demonstrate ideas and concepts. Students learn a wide variety of authoring tools to create and publish digital media. Using Moodle, podcasts, blogs, and other interactive media, students extend discussions and collaborations beyond the classroom. Using Web-based tools and video-conferencing, students collaborate on projects with other Marymount Schools and with students and researchers from around the globe.

Marymount's position at the forefront of educational technology relies on more than the investment in laptops, SmartBoards, software, and networks. To maintain its cutting-edge program, recognized for excellence by NAIS and NCGS, the School offers two weeks of technology seminars every summer, in addition to workshops during the school year for the faculty and other NAIS-school faculty members.

High school graduation requirements include satisfactory completion of 4 years of English, 3 years of history, 3 years of math, 3 years of laboratory science, 3 years of a world language, 4 years of religious studies, 4 years of physical education, 1 year of studio art, 1 year of computer science, 6 semesters of health/guidance, and 1 semester of speech. These requirements are structured to provide a broad, solid base of knowledge while sharpening problem-solving and research skills and promoting critical and creative thinking.

The School offers honors and Advanced Placement courses as well as electives such as AP art history, economics, classical Greek, music history, history of theater, two AP studio art courses, African studies, Latin American studies, Middle Eastern studies, history of modern China, and programming languages. In senior English, students choose from seminars that cover topics from Shakespeare's history plays to modern Irish literature to the literature of African American and Asian American women writers. Most students elect to take a fourth year of math; advanced offerings include AP calculus, AP statistics, and finite math. Fourth-year science courses include AP biology, AP chemistry, AP physics C, and atmospheric science. The science program connects with and utilizes the research of numerous institutions, including the New York Academy of Sciences and Princeton University, as well as participating in the STEM Internship Program and the STEM Research Program.

While the School is a leader in science and technological education, Marymount is also committed to the study of humanities. All Class IX students take part in the Integrated Humanities Program, an interdisciplinary curriculum that focuses on history, literature, art history, and world religions in the study of ancient civilizations. Classes are held at the Metropolitan Museum of Art at least once a week. The program includes a performance-based World Civilizations

Festival and collaborative research projects in history and art history. Seniors must submit a writing portfolio of selected work from their last three years of high school.

The Visual Arts Department offers studio art, AP 2-D design, and AP drawing. The performing arts program includes a school chorus, a chamber choir, courses in music history and the history of theater, speech classes, and a rich extracurricular program in forensics and dramatic arts.

The Religious Studies Program includes comparative religions, Hebrew Scriptures, the New Testament, social justice, and ethics. With a focus on moral and ethical decision making, students analyze systemic social issues and immerse themselves in the community through numerous service projects, as well as the Youth and Philanthropy Initiative. The Catholic-Jewish Initiative provides students with a deeper understanding of the Judeo-Christian tradition. This program includes Holocaust studies and a trip to the National Holocaust Museum in Washington, D.C.

During the last four weeks of the academic year, seniors participate in an off-campus internship to gain significant exposure to a career of interest. Students have interned at hospitals, research laboratories, law firms, financial organizations, theaters, schools, nonprofit organizations, and corporations. They also attend a career day, with visiting alumnae as guest speakers. A financial literacy curriculum helps prepare graduates for the financial challenges of college and life.

As members of a worldwide network of schools, students may opt to spend the second semester of their sophomore year at a Marymount International School in London or Rome. Annual concert and study tours and service trips extend the curriculum. Recent study tours have included the mathematics and culture of ancient Greece, the ecology of the Galapagos Islands, the theater and literature of Shakespeare's London and Stratford-upon-Avon, and the music, language, and culture of Italy, France, and Spain. Recent School-sponsored service trips have brought students to work with disabled orphans in Jamaica, rebuild homes in New Orleans, and promote justice for trafficked women in New York City. The Marymount Singers enjoys an annual concert tour in Europe every spring. They have performed in churches and concert halls in Italy, France, Austria, the Czech Republic, Ireland, Portugal, and Spain.

Upper School students are formally evaluated four times a year, using an A–F grading system. The evaluation process includes written reports and parent/student/teacher conferences.

The Middle School curriculum welcomes the diverse interests of young adolescents and is structured to channel their energy and natural love of learning. The integrated core curriculum gradually increases in the degree of departmentalization at each grade level, and challenging learning activities and flexible groupings in main subject areas ensure that the students achieve their full potential. In Class IV, students are introduced to French, Latin, and Spanish; in Class V, students choose to pursue a three-year sequence in one of these languages. The Middle School years culminate in a study tour to France and Spain; the integration of language, mathematics, social studies, science, architecture, religious studies, and art makes the study tour a rich intellectual experience as well as accentuating the relevance of the students' classroom study to the world at large. All students enjoy regular visits to the Metropolitan Museum of Art, including weekly studio art classes. Technology enhances all aspects of the curriculum, and each student has a laptop at school.

Twice weekly speech classes prepare the girls for dramatic presentations reflective of their social studies and literature curriculum: *Revolutionary Voices, Greek Mythology*, and scenes from *The Canterbury Tales* and *A Midsummer Night's Dream*. Uptown Broadway, an extracurricular option offered each semester, allows the students to participate in a full-scale musical production. The entire Middle School celebrates music and voice at their annual spring concert.

The Lower School provides child-centered, creative learning within a challenging, structured environment. The Lower School curriculum focuses on the acquisition of foundational skills, often through an interdisciplinary approach. Programs engage students in the exciting process of learning about themselves, their surroundings, and the larger world. A hands-on science program, an emphasis on technology integration, a study of robotics in Class III, a popular Lower School chorus, and an extensive after-school program are some highlights of the Lower School.

FACULTY AND ADVISERS
There are 99 full-time and 2 part-time faculty members, allowing for a 6:1 student-teacher ratio. Seventy-two percent of the faculty members hold master's degrees, and 11 percent hold doctoral degrees. In Nursery through Class I, each class has a head teacher and at least one assistant teacher. Classes II and III have two co-head teachers in each classroom. In the Middle School, students make the transition from having homeroom teachers to having advisers. In Classes IV and V, each class has two homeroom teachers. In Classes V–XII, each student has a homeroom teacher and an adviser, usually one of her teachers, who follows her academic progress and provides guidance and support. Technologists, learning resource specialists, a school nurse, artists-in-residence, a school counselor, and a school psychologist work with students throughout the School.

Concepcion R. Alvar was appointed Headmistress in 2004 after serving thirteen years as the Director of Admissions and three years as a head teacher. She also served as the Director and Supervisor of Marymount Summer for sixteen years. Mrs. Alvar holds a B.S. from Maryknoll College (Philippines) and an M.A. from Columbia University, Teachers College.

COLLEGE ADMISSION COUNSELING
Under the guidance of the Director of College Counseling, Marymount's formal college counseling program begins during the junior year. In the second semester, two College Nights are held for students and parents. Individual counseling throughout the semester directs each student to those colleges that best match her achievements and interests. Students participate in weekly guidance classes to learn about general requirements for college admission, the application process, and standardized tests. During the fall of their senior year, students continue the weekly sessions, focusing on essay writing, admissions interviews, and financial aid applications.

Graduates from recent classes are attending the following colleges and universities: Amherst, Barnard, Boston College, Boston University, Bowdoin, Brown, Columbia, Cooper Union, Connecticut, Cornell, Dartmouth, Davidson, Duke, Fairfield, Fordham, George Washington, Georgetown, Harvard, Holy Cross, Kenyon, Middlebury, NYU, Oberlin, Princeton, Skidmore, Smith, Stanford, Trinity, Tufts, Vanderbilt, Villanova, Wake Forest, Wellesley, Wesleyan, Wheaton, Williams, Yale, and the Universities of Notre Dame, Pennsylvania, St. Andrew's (Scotland), and Virginia.

STUDENT BODY AND CONDUCT
Marymount's enrollment is 613 students in Nursery through Class XII, with 240 girls in the Upper School. Most students reside in the five boroughs of New York City; however, Upper School students also commute from Long Island, New Jersey, and Westchester County. Students wear uniforms, except on special days; participate in athletic and extracurricular activities; and attend weekly chapel services, all-school masses, and annual class retreats.

Marymount encourages the students to be active participants in their own education and in the life of the School community. Students seek out leadership and volunteer opportunities, serving as advocates for one another through peer mentoring, retreat teams, and the Big Sister/Little Sister program. Student government and campus ministry provide social and service opportunities that enable students to broaden their perspectives, develop their capacity for leadership, sharpen their public-speaking skills, and form lasting friendships.

Teachers and administrators encourage each student to respect herself and others and to be responsible members of the community. While there are relatively few rules, those that exist are consistently enforced to promote freedom and growth for the individual and the entire School community.

ACADEMIC FACILITIES
The Beaux Arts mansions provide spacious rooms for the Nursery–Class XII educational program. Facilities include wired and wireless classrooms with Smart-Boards, a networked library complex, five state-of-the-art science laboratories, two computer centers, a math laboratory, an art suite, a chapel, a language lab, an auditorium, a courtyard playground, two gymnasiums, and the Middle School multipurpose Commons.

ATHLETICS
The athletic program promotes good health, physical fitness, coordination, skill development, confidence, and a spirit of competition and collaboration through its physical education classes, the electives program for Classes X–XII, and individual and team sports.

Marymount provides a full schedule for varsity and junior varsity sports, as well as Middle School teams at the V/VI and VII/VIII class levels. In the Middle School, students stay two days per week for an after-school sports program. The junior varsity and varsity teams compete within the Athletic Association of Independent Schools League (AAIS) in badminton, basketball, cross-country, fencing, field hockey, lacrosse, soccer, softball, swimming, tennis, track and field, and volleyball.

In addition to its gymnasiums, Marymount uses the facilities of nearby Catholic schools, the Harlem Armory, Riverbank State Park, and Roberto Clemente State Park. Central Park, Randall's Island, and Van Cortland Park are preferred sites for field sports. Tennisport, Riverbank State Park, and Flushing Meadows are competitive sites for the tennis and swim teams. Additional athletic facilities are used throughout New York City.

EXTRACURRICULAR OPPORTUNITIES
A wide range of clubs and activities complement the academic program and provide students with the opportunity to contribute to the School community, pursue their individual interests, and develop communication, cooperation, and leadership skills. Upper School activities and clubs offered include Amnesty International, art club, book club, campus ministry, chamber choir, cultural awareness, digital photography, science and the environment club, film club, finance club, forensics team, Mathletes, Marymount Singers, Marymount Players, Mock Trial (2006 state champions, 2009 NYC finalists), Model United Nations, National Honor Society, philosophy club, set design/tech crew, student government, and women in action. Student publications include a yearbook (*Marifia*), a newspaper (*Joritan*), and an award-winning literary/arts journal (*Muse*). A wide range of Friday noontime clubs in the Middle School includes Student Council; Italian, Latin, and French clubs; altar servers; handbells; environmental science; art; drama; handwork; and the literary magazine, *Chez Nous*.

Each year, the Upper School presents two dramatic productions, including a musical; organizes either a Bias Awareness Day or Harambee Celebration during Black History Month; sponsors an Art Festival Week; and participates in numerous community service projects, local and national competitions, and conferences with other schools.

The Vincent A. Lisanti Speakers Series brings people of stature and high achievement to the School, including former poet laureate Billy Collins, athlete Tegla Laroupe, author Jhumpa Lahiri, bioethicist Ronald Green, nanotechnologist Dr. Susan Arney, African American painter Philomena Williamson, feminist Gloria Steinem, Sr. Helen Prejean, author of *Dead Man Walking*, and Sheryl WuDunn, coauthor of *Half the Sky*. The Maggie Murray Fund supports a series of writing-related events to enrich the students' literary experiences and has given students the opportunity to attend conversations with such celebrated writers as Toni Morrison and Chinua Achebe.

Students have the opportunity to interact with boys from neighboring schools through exchange days, dramatic productions, community service projects, walka-thons, dances, and other student-run social activities.

DAILY LIFE
Upper School classes are held from 8:20 a.m. to 3:30 p.m. on Monday, Tuesday, and Thursday. To accommodate electives, extracurricular activities, and team sports, classes end at 2:45 p.m. on Wednesdays and Fridays. Class periods are each 45 minutes in length and typically meet nine out of ten days in a two-week cycle, with a double period each week in each course. Students meet daily with their advisory group, gather with the entire Upper School every Friday for assembly, and frequently meet individually with their classroom teachers. After classes have ended, most students remain for sports, extracurricular activities, and/or independent study.

COSTS AND FINANCIAL AID
The tuition for the 2010–11 academic year ranges from $20,500 for Nursery to $35,400 for Class XII. In February, parents are required to make a deposit of $5000, which is credited toward the November tuition. The Key Education Resources Payment Plan is available.

Nearly $3 million in financial aid was awarded in 2010–11 to students of outstanding academic promise after establishing need through School and Student Services. Over 22 percent of Marymount students receive financial aid.

ADMISSIONS INFORMATION
As a college-preparatory school, Marymount aims to enroll young women of academic promise and sound character who are seeking a challenging educational environment and multiple opportunities for learning outside the classroom. Educational Records Bureau tests, school records, and interviews are used in selecting students.

The School admits students of any race, color, and national or ethnic origin to all the rights, privileges, programs, and activities generally accorded or made available to students at the School and does not discriminate on these bases in the administration of its educational policies, admissions policies, scholarship or loan programs, or athletic or other School-administered programs.

APPLICATION TIMETABLE
Interested students are encouraged to contact the Admissions Office as early as possible in the fall for admission the following year. The application deadline is November 30, but may be changed at the discretion of the Director of Admissions. Notification of admissions decisions is sent during February and March, according to the dates established by the Independent School Admissions Association of Greater New York.

ADMISSIONS CORRESPONDENCE
Lillian Issa
Deputy Head/Director of Admissions
Marymount School of New York
1026 Fifth Avenue
New York, New York 10028

Phone: 212-744-4486
Fax: 212-744-0163 (general)
212-744-0716 (admissions)
E-mail: admissions@marymountnyc.org
Web site: http://www.marymountnyc.org

MILTON ACADEMY

Milton, Massachusetts

Type: Coeducational boarding and day college-preparatory school
Grades: K–12: (Lower School: K–8; Upper School: 9–12)
Enrollment: School total: 980; Upper School: 675
Head of School: Todd Bland

THE SCHOOL

The Academy received its charter in 1798 under the Massachusetts land-grant policy. It bequeathed to the school a responsibility to "open the way for all the people to a higher order of education than the common schools can supply." Milton's motto, "Dare to be true," not only states a core value, it describes Milton's culture. Milton fosters intellectual inquiry and encourages initiative and the open exchange of ideas. Teaching and learning at Milton are active processes that recognize the intelligence, talents, and potential of each member of the Academy.

For more than 200 years, Milton has developed confident, independent thinkers in an intimate, friendly setting where students and faculty members understand that the life of the mind is the pulse of the school. A gifted and dedicated faculty motivates a diverse student body, providing students with the structure to learn and the support to take risks. The faculty's teaching expertise and passion for scholarship generates extraordinary growth in students who learn to expect the most of themselves. The Milton community connects purposefully with world issues. Students graduate with a clear sense of themselves, their world, and how to contribute.

From Milton Academy's suburban 125-acre campus, 8 miles south of Boston in the town of Milton (population 26,000), students and faculty members access the vast cultural resources of Boston and Cambridge. Minutes from campus is the Blue Hills Reservation, 6,000 wooded acres of hiking trails and ski slopes.

Milton Academy is a nonprofit organization with a self-perpetuating Board of Trustees. Its endowment is $167 million (as of June 1, 2010).

Milton Academy is accredited by the New England Association of Schools and Colleges and holds memberships in the National Association of Independent Schools, the Cum Laude Society, and the Association of Independent Schools in New England.

ACADEMIC PROGRAMS

Milton students and faculty members are motivated participants in the world of ideas, concepts, and values. Milton's curriculum provides rigorous preparation for college and includes more than 182 courses in nine academic departments. For students entering Milton in the ninth grade, a minimum of 18 credits are required for graduation. This includes 4 years of English, 2 years of history (including U.S. and modern world history), 2 years of science, 1 year of an arts course, and successful completion of algebra II, geometry, and a level III foreign language course. Noncredit requirements include current events/public speaking, physical education, a ninth-grade arts course (music/drama/visual arts), and a four-year affective education curriculum that includes health, values, social awareness, and senior transitions.

Electives are offered in all academic areas. Examples of electives include computer programming, comparative government, performing literature, Spanish film and social change, advanced architecture, philosophy and literature, choreography, film and video production, psychology, engineering, nuclear physics, issues in environmental science, creative writing, music theory, observational astronomy, and marine biology. Students may petition to take independent study courses, and Advanced Placement courses leading to college credit are offered in most subject areas.

In January, seniors submit a proposal for a five-week spring independent project, on or off campus. Senior projects give students the opportunity to pursue in-depth interests stemming from their work at Milton.

The typical class size is 14 students, and the overall student-teacher ratio is 5:1. Nightly 2-hour study periods in the houses are supervised for boarding students.

Faculty members are available for individual help throughout the day and in the houses at night. Students seeking assistance with assignments or help with specific skills, organization, and/or time management visit the Academic Skills Center, which is staffed throughout the day.

The school year, which is divided into two semesters, runs from early September to early June with an examination period at the end of January. Students typically take five courses per semester. Students earn letter grades from E (failure) through A+, and comments prepared by each student's teachers and adviser are sent to parents three times a year in November, February, and June.

All academic buildings and residential houses are part of a campuswide computer network. MiltONline, the Academy's e-mail and conferencing system, allows students to join conference discussions for many classes and extracurricular activities, communicate with faculty members and friends, and submit assignments. Students have access to the Milton Intranet as well as the Internet.

Class II students (eleventh graders) may apply to spend either the fall or spring semester at the Mountain School Program of Milton Academy (an interdisciplinary academic program set on a working 300-acre farm in Vermont); at CITYterm at the Master's School in Dobbs Ferry, New York; or at the Maine Coast Semester at Chewonki. Through School Year Abroad, Milton provides opportunities in Spain, France, Italy, and China. Milton also offers six- to eight-week exchange programs with schools in Spain, France, and China.

FACULTY AND ADVISERS

The deep commitment of a learned and experienced group of teachers is Milton's greatest treasure. Teaching in Classes IV-I (grades 9–12) are 127 full-time faculty members, 78 percent of whom hold advanced degrees (Ph.D. and master's degrees). Eighty percent of faculty members live on campus.

In addition to teaching, faculty members also serve as house parents and coaches, as well as advisers to student clubs, organizations, publications, and activities. Each faculty member is an adviser to a group of 6 to 8 students and supports the students' emotional, social, and academic well-being at Milton.

COLLEGE ADMISSION COUNSELING

Four college counselors work one-on-one with students, beginning in their Class II (eleventh grade) year, in a highly personal and effective approach toward the college admissions process.

For the graduating classes of 2008, 2009, and 2010, the top college enrollments were Harvard (25), Brown (24), Tufts (16), Georgetown (15), Boston College (14), Columbia (13), Cornell (13), George Washington (13), Wesleyan (12), and Yale (12).

STUDENT BODY AND CONDUCT

Of the 675 students in the Upper School, 50 percent are boys and 50 percent are girls; 50 percent are boarding students and 50 percent are day students. Forty-two percent of Milton's enrolled students are students of color. Ten percent of the Upper School students are international, coming from eighteen countries across the globe. Thirty-two percent of Milton students receive financial aid, and the average grants account for 75 percent of tuition.

All Upper School students from Classes IV-I (grades 9–12) participate in the Self-Governing Association, led by 2 elected student representatives, 1 senior girl and 1 senior boy. Elected class representatives serve with faculty members on the Discipline Committee, which recommends to the Head of School appropriate responses when infractions of major school rules occur. Rules at Milton Academy foster the cohesion and morale of the community and enhance education by upholding standards of conduct developed by generations of students and faculty members.

ACADEMIC FACILITIES

Among the prominent buildings on the Milton campus are three primarily academic buildings: Warren Hall (English), Wigglesworth Hall (history), and Ware Hall (math and foreign languages); the Kellner Performing Arts Center, with a 350-seat teaching theater, a studio theater, dressing rooms, scene shop, practice rooms, orchestral rehearsal room, dance studio, and speech/debate room; the Athletic and Convocation Center, with a hockey rink, a fitness center, three basketball courts, and an indoor track; the Williams Squash Courts; the Ayer Observatory; and Apthorp Chapel. The new Pritzker Science Center, which opened in 2010, integrates classroom areas with laboratory tables and equipment, to create an environment that allows students to work collaboratively and move seamlessly between discussion and hands-on lab work.

Cox Library contains more than 46,000 volumes, more than 150 periodicals with back issues on microfilm, and a newspaper collection dating back to 1704. It also provides CD-ROM sources, Internet access and online search capabilities. Within Cox Library is one of several computer laboratories.

BOARDING AND GENERAL FACILITIES

Milton Academy students live in one of eight single-sex houses ranging in size from 31 to 48 students; four for boys and four for girls. Single rooms house one third of the students, while the other two thirds of the students reside in double rooms. Milton houses include all four classes as well as faculty members' families. Students spend all their Milton years in one house, experiencing a family-at-school context for developing close relationships with valued

f www.facebook.com/sec.schools

adults, learning about responsibility to the community, taking leadership roles with peers, and sharing social and cultural traditions. All rooms are networked, and each student has an e-mail account, a telephone line, and voicemail. School computers are available for student use in the house common rooms.

The Health and Counseling Center and the Academic Skills Center, as well as house parents in each residential house, class deans, and the office of the school chaplain, are available to meet students' needs.

ATHLETICS

Milton believes that teamwork, sportsmanship, and the pursuit of excellence are important values and that regular vigorous exercise is a foundation of good health. Milton offers a comprehensive athletic program that includes physical education classes and a range of intramural and interscholastic sports geared to the needs and interests of every student.

The school's offerings in interscholastic sports are Alpine skiing, baseball, basketball, cross-country, field hockey, football, golf, ice hockey, lacrosse, sailing, soccer, softball, squash, swimming and diving, tennis, track, volleyball, and wrestling.

Intramural offerings include the outdoor program, pilates, soccer, squash, strength and conditioning, tennis, Ultimate (Frisbee), and yoga.

Sports facilities include four athletic buildings, an ice hockey rink and fitness center, two indoor climbing walls, twelve playing fields, seventeen tennis courts, seven international squash courts, an all-weather track, a cross-country course, and a ropes course.

EXTRACURRICULAR OPPORTUNITIES

The breadth of extracurricular opportunities means that every student finds a niche—a comfortable place to develop new skills, take on leadership, show commitment, make friends, and have fun. Clubs and organizations include cultural groups such as the Asian Society, Latino Association, Onyx, and Common Ground (an umbrella organization for the various groups); the Arts Board; Dance Workshop; the Outdoor Club; the Chinese, French, and Spanish clubs; the debate, math, and speech teams; and Students for Gender Equality. There are eleven student publications, among them *The Asian, La Voz,*

MAGUS/MABUS, Mille Tonnes, Milton Measure, Milton Paper, and the yearbook. Music programs include the chamber singers, the gospel choir, the glee club, the orchestra, improvisational jazz combos, and five a cappella groups. The performing arts are an important part of the extracurricular offerings at Milton. Main stage theater productions, studio theater productions, play readings, and speech and debate team are a few of the available opportunities. Milton stages ten major theater productions each year, including a Class IV (ninth grade) play, student directed one-act plays, a dance concert, and a biennial musical. Service opportunities include the audiovisual crew, community service, Lorax (environmental group), Orange and Blue Key (admission tour guides and leaders), and the Public Issues Board.

DAILY LIFE

The academic day runs from 8 a.m. to 2:55 p.m., except on Wednesday, when classes end at 1:15 p.m. There are no classes on Saturday or Sunday. Cafeteria-style lunch is served from 11 a.m. to 1:30 p.m., and students eat during a free period within that time. The students' activities period is from 3 to 3:30 p.m. Athletics and extracurricular activities take place from 3:30 to 5:30 p.m. Family-style dinner is at 6 p.m., and the evening study period runs from 7:30 to 9:30 p.m. Lights-out time depends on the grade level of each student.

WEEKEND LIFE

Interscholastic games are held on Wednesday, Friday, and Saturday afternoons. Social activities on Friday and Saturday evenings are planned by the Student Activities Association. Day students join boarders every weekend for events such as dances with live or recorded music, classic and new films, concerts, plays, drama readings, dormitory open houses, and trips to professional sports events, arts events, or local museums.

Prior to leaving campus, students must check their plans with house parents, who must approve their whereabouts and any overnight plans.

SUMMER PROGRAMS

Milton Academy's summer programs develop, schedule, and supervise a wide range of offerings that connect with the school's mission. These programs include professional development opportunities for teachers, academic and recreational activities for students, and corporate and community-related events. In addition to hosting many outside programs, the Academy runs Sports Plus and Milton Academy Summer Hockey camps, as well as E-Cast Computer/Science School, all for students, along with the Cultural Diversity Institute and the Boarding Staff Conference for teachers from across the country.

COSTS AND FINANCIAL AID

For the 2010–11 academic year, tuition is $43,975 for boarding students and $36,100 for day students.

Milton seeks to enroll the most qualified applicants regardless of their financial circumstances. To that end, more than $7.65 million in financial aid will be provided to students in the 2010–11 school year. All financial aid at Milton is awarded on the basis of need. In addition to the program of direct grants, the school offers installment payment options and two low-interest loan programs.

ADMISSIONS INFORMATION

Milton Academy seeks students who are able, energetic, intellectually curious, and have strong values and a willingness to grow. Applicants must submit the Secondary School Admission Test (SSAT) scores (students applying for eleventh grade may submit PSAT or SAT scores if applicable). All applicants must also submit a preliminary application, school transcript, teacher recommendations, parental statement, and two essays. An interview, on or off campus, is also required.

APPLICATION TIMETABLE

The deadline for applying is January 15. Notification letters are sent out March 10; the reply date is April 10. There is a $50 application fee for U.S. applicants and a $100 fee for international applicants.

ADMISSIONS CORRESPONDENCE

Paul Rebuck, Dean of Admission
Milton Academy
170 Centre Street
Milton, Massachusetts 02186

Phone: 617-898-2227
Fax: 617-898-1701
E-mail: admissions@milton.edu
Web site: http://www.milton.edu

MISS PORTER'S SCHOOL

Farmington, Connecticut

Type: Girls' boarding and day college-preparatory school
Grades: 9–12
Enrollment: 322
Head of School: Dr. Katherine Gladstone Windsor

THE SCHOOL

Located in the center of Farmington, Connecticut, Porter's is a college-preparatory boarding and day school for girls in grades 9 through 12. Founded in 1843 by lifelong scholar and educator, Sarah Porter, the School's innovative, rigorous, well-rounded approach to education prepares girls to expand their minds and grow into socially engaged, confident young women. With 322 students hailing from twenty-three states and twenty-seven countries, Porter's provides a diverse high school experience that helps young women become local and global leaders of the future.

A respected leader in preparing young women for college, Porter's demanding curriculum, collaborative environment, and supportive community distinguishes it as one of the nation's finest boarding schools. Porter's mission statement sets high expectations for students: "We challenge our students to become informed, bold, resourceful, and ethical global citizens. We expect our graduates to shape a changing world."

The teaching faculty serves as educators, advisers, coaches, and mentors—developing close relationships with their students as they accept this challenge. All graduates earn acceptance into four-year colleges and universities.

Porter's location allows students to enjoy the charm of Farmington, while providing easy access to Hartford, New York, and Boston for social, cultural, and academic events. The picturesque, 50-acre campus is close to village stores and within a short walk of the Farmington River.

The School's governing board is composed of 33 trustees, both men and women, 23 of whom are alumnae. The Annual Fund Program provides 13 percent of the operating budget each year.

Porter's is accredited by the New England Association of Schools and Colleges. It is a member of the National Coalition of Girls' Schools, the Association of Boarding Schools, the Connecticut Association of Independent Schools, the National Association of Independent Schools, the Council for Advancement and Support of Education, and the Cum Laude Society.

ACADEMIC PROGRAMS

Porter's academic program prepares girls for college and beyond by emphasizing oral and written communication, critical thinking, research skills, and leadership development through the rigorous study of mathematics, foreign languages, science, history, English, and visual and performing arts.

During the fall and spring semesters, 110 courses are offered. To graduate, each student must have a total of 36 semester units, including 8 units of English, 6 units of a foreign language, 5 units of history, 6 units of math, 6 units of science, 2 units in the arts (visual art, music, theater, dance, art history, or photography), 1 unit in computers, and a ½ unit in ethical leadership. Students also must complete 20 hours of community service and 80 hours of an experiential education project (often an internship). They must participate in one of a variety of team sports offered for a minimum of two seasons, and in athletics-based classes during the other seasons.

Advanced Placement examination preparation is available in art history, biology, calculus AB, calculus BC, chemistry, Chinese language and culture, computer science A, English language and composition, English literature and composition, environ-

mental science, European history, French language, Latin: Vergil, music theory, physics B, Spanish language, Spanish literature, statistics, studio art: drawing, and U.S. history.

Porter's average class size is 11 students. Honors courses are available for exceptional students. All ninth grade boarding students attend a required study hall each evening, while upper class boarding students observe quiet hours from 7:30 to 9:30 p.m. Grades, based on the letter system, and comments are provided four times a year. Adviser and house faculty comments are mailed at the end of each semester.

Qualified students may participate in independent projects and are encouraged to investigate career opportunities in carefully selected internships across the country. Juniors may choose to spend either their fall or their spring semester in the Maine Coast Semester or the Rocky Mountain Semester, or they may elect to participate in the School Year Abroad in France, Spain, China, or Italy.

FACULTY AND ADVISERS

Katherine Gladstone Windsor began as Head of School on July 1, 2008 and brings to Porter's a passion for education, a belief in the importance of educating girls for leadership, and a wide-range of experience with independent schools.

Prior to her tenure at Miss Porter's School, Dr. Windsor served as the head of The Sage School in Foxboro, Massachusetts, an elementary and middle school for gifted and talented students. She earned her Doctor of Education degree from the University of Pennsylvania and was a Klingenstein Visiting Fellow at Columbia University. Her undergraduate and graduate studies were completed at the University of Rochester and the College of Notre Dame. An active member of the Connecticut Association of Independent Schools Board of Trustees, National Association of Principals of Schools for Girls leadership program faculty, the Center for the Study of Boys' and Girls' Lives board of directors, and the Visionary Heads Group, Dr. Windsor is a frequent lecturer on single-sex education, most recently presenting "Educating Young Women to Lead: Outsmarting the Stereotypes" for the National Association of Independent Schools. Dr. Windsor lives on campus with her husband, Jonas, and their two sons. For Dr. Windsor's complete biography, please visit http://www.porters.org/headofschool.

There are 57 teaching faculty members. Of these, 63 percent have advanced degrees. The School seeks teachers who are committed both to their own academic discipline and to the intellectual and personal development of young women. Faculty members participate fully in boarding school life, also serving as student advisers, coaches, and club advisers. House directors supervise dormitories, getting to know students individually and serving as parental influences. Each student has her own adviser, who helps her manage her academic program and is in frequent contact with her parents as well as with her teachers, coaches, and house director.

Summer sabbaticals for study and travel are available to faculty members who have served at the School for at least seven years. Assistance also is offered in financing graduate study.

COLLEGE PLACEMENT

The Director and Assistant Director of College Counseling help students plan their educational futures. Responsibility for handling college applications falls ultimately on the student, but the School offers strong support and counsels parents and students from the beginning to the end of the process. Beginning in February of the students' junior year, the college counselors meet with the students in small groups. They also confer with girls individually, helping each to understand her unique situation. When each girl leaves for spring vacation, she takes with her a recommended college list and is urged to visit at least one campus during that break.

Before June, students usually have decided on which colleges to visit during the summer. A comprehensive letter is sent to parents outlining each girl's choices, with assessments by the college counselor of the student's chances for admission. During the fall, more than 120 college representatives visit the School to meet with interested girls. During Family Weekend in October, the college counselor holds individual conferences with parents of boarding seniors. Local parents of day students may schedule an appointment at any time.

For the class of 2010, the middle 50 percent of SAT scores were 560–700 on the critical reading portion, 560–670 on the mathematics portion, and 590–710 on the writing component. In 2010, students took 248 Advanced Placement tests. Thirty-three percent of the students achieved a score of 5, 37 percent achieved a score of 4, and 90 percent achieved a score of 3 or higher.

The class of 2010 had 85 graduates. The majority of graduates elected liberal arts programs, but a small number selected specialized curricula—fine arts, architecture, engineering, and business. Brown, Cornell, Georgetown, George Washington, Johns Hopkins, Princeton, Smith, Stanford, and the U.S. Military Academy at West Point are just a few examples of the colleges and universities Porter's graduates currently are attending.

STUDENT BODY AND CONDUCT

In 2010–11, the student distribution by grade is grade 9, 66; grade 10, 78; grade 11, 89; and grade 12, 89. The current total of 322 students includes 198 boarding students and 124 day students from twenty-three states and twenty-seven countries.

The goal of developing self-discipline and concern for others underlies student conduct rules. Each girl is expected to abide by School rules and adhere to the following Honor Code: As a student and member of the Miss Porter's School community, I promise to uphold the tradition of honesty and fairness that this community has taught since 1843. I will be truthful. I will be respectful of others, their property, and their opinions. I promise to foster these values in the community.

An important facet of the School's structure is the student government. The Student Council serves as the judiciary board in cases of rule infractions. When rules are broken, judicial decisions are made by the council and are subject to review by the head of school.

ACADEMIC FACILITIES

History and English classes meet in the Hamilton Building. The Ann Whitney Olin Center for the Arts and Sciences houses classrooms with state-of-the-art equipment and technology for the instruction of math, science, and computer technology, including Mac and PC labs. Art studios for photography, ceramics, painting, sculpture, printmaking, and jewelry making and a computer lab for graphic design are also located in Olin. Theater classes convene in the Barbara Lang Hacker '29 Theater. Dance classes are held in the recently renovated Gaines Dance Barn. Music classes meet in the KLG. The M. Burch Tracy Ford Library offers a number of amenities to support education and research, including a 22,100-volume general collection, 2,175-volume art history library, fully wired classroom computers, conference rooms, and tranquil study spaces. Interlibrary loan networking supports the research curriculum. The Leila Dilworth Jones '44 Memorial holds a state-of-the-art language laboratory and classrooms for foreign language instruction.

BOARDING AND GENERAL FACILITIES
Nine dormitories, most of which were formerly private homes, are supervised by house directors. House directors are usually couples with children, and they provide students a real sense of parental influence and family life. In five of the dormitories, students from grades 9 through 11 live together; two dormitories are reserved for ninth graders, and two are reserved for seniors.

The dining room and administrative offices are located in Main, which also houses the Daisy Café, a student gathering place. The Ivy–The Shop at Miss Porter's School is Porter's on-campus store. The Colgate Health Center is staffed 24 hours a day by registered nurses. A physician makes regular visits and is on call 24 hours a day.

ATHLETICS
Porter's believes in maintaining a healthy balance between intellectual activity and physical exercise; each student participates daily on a team or in a sports class. Porter's belongs to the highly competitive Founders League. Interscholastic sports are badminton, basketball, crew, cross-country, equestrian, field hockey, golf, lacrosse, skiing, soccer, softball, squash, swimming and diving, tennis, track and field, Ultimate (Frisbee), and volleyball. An extensive number of playing fields and seven DecoTurf tennis courts are available. An athletics/recreation center contains two gyms, an indoor track, a climbing wall, a fitness center, and basketball and volleyball courts. An additional athletic facility with an eight-lane pool and eight international squash courts opened in September 2007. A new boathouse for crew is located on the Farmington River. Equestrian and skiing participants use nearby facilities.

EXTRACURRICULAR OPPORTUNITIES
Endowments bring concerts, speakers, drama productions, and poets to the campus. There are many weekend activities both on and off the campus. Membership in campus clubs is open to any student who wishes to participate; most students belong to at least one extracurricular group. Among the organizations are *Salmagundy* (student newspaper), *Daeges Eage* (yearbook), *Chautauqua* (expository writing), *Haggis Baggis* (creative writing), Archives (school history), several singing groups, debate Team, Concordia (social service), Model UN, dance workshop, Players/Mandolin Performance Troupe, and Watu Wazuri (multicultural organization). Theater, dance, vocal, and instrumental performances are staged several times a year. Annual events include Family Weekend, Grandparents' Day, Reunion Weekend, and graduation.

DAILY LIFE
Classes, held Monday through Friday, begin at 7:45, following breakfast. Each class is 50 minutes long. Lunch is served from 11:30 to 1:30. Sports begin at 3:45. Morning meetings are held two times a week, and the entire School community gathers regularly for assemblies and convocations. Club meetings take place during Clubs Period once a week and before or after the 5:30 dinner hour. Study hours begin at 7:30 and end at 9:30. Students may study in the dormitories, in the library, or in monitored study halls.

WEEKEND LIFE
Each weekend, a variety of activities are offered, ranging from dances, movies, and trips to plays, special dinners, and concerts. During closed weekends, students remain on the campus, except for day trips. On open weekends, girls may, with permission from home, leave school for the weekend, but many girls remain at school and participate in the wide variety of activities. Day students are encouraged to take part in all weekend activities. About half of a semester's weekends are open.

Coeducational events are held frequently on campus and at other schools, including concerts, dances, and community service activities. Churches and synagogues are located nearby.

COSTS AND FINANCIAL AID
The cost of tuition, room, and board in 2010–11 is $45,100. Day student tuition is $35,450. A health center fee and an activities fee are additional charges for both day students and boarders. Books and private music or athletic lessons are extra.

For the 2010–11 school year, financial aid totaling $3.9 million was awarded to approximately 40 percent of the students. Scholarship aid is given on the basis of merit and need. Financial aid decisions are announced at the time of the admission decisions and are renewable each year if the student demonstrates continued need and meets academic standards.

ADMISSIONS INFORMATION
Admission is based on school records, aptitude and achievement, character, citizenship, and potential. A personal interview is required. The Secondary School Admission Test (SSAT) or ISEE should be taken in November, December, or January preceding the September in which a student wishes to enter. International students must also take the TOEFL if English is not their first language. Students may apply for entrance in grade 9, 10, 11, or 12. The School encourages able students to apply, without regard to race, color, creed, national or ethnic origin, or socioeconomic background.

APPLICATION TIMETABLE
Applicants are urged to contact the Admission Office to arrange for a tour, class visit, and interview. The office is open Monday through Friday from 8:30 to 4:30. Most interviews and tours take place in the fall, but they may be scheduled year-round. The application, including recommendations, SSAT scores, and a $50 nonrefundable fee ($100 for international applicants), must be completed by January 15. Candidates are notified by March 10 of the admission committee's decision, and families must reply by April 10. If openings are available after April 10, interested families are encouraged to complete the application process.

ADMISSIONS CORRESPONDENCE
Liz Schmitt
Office of Admission
Miss Porter's School
Farmington, Connecticut 06032
Phone: 860-409-3530 (admission)
       860-409-3500 (general)
Fax: 860-409-3531
E-mail: admission@missporters.org
Web site: http://www.porters.org

MORAVIAN ACADEMY

Bethlehem, Pennsylvania

Type: Day college-preparatory school
Grades: PK–12: Lower School, Prekindergarten–5; Middle School, 6–8; Upper School, 9–12
Enrollment: School total: 764; Upper School: 287
Head of School: George N. King Jr., Headmaster

THE SCHOOL

Moravian Academy (MA) traces its origin back to 1742 and the Moravians who settled Bethlehem. Guided by the wisdom of John Amos Comenius, Moravian bishop and renowned educator, the Moravian Church established schools in every community in which it settled. Moravian Academy became incorporated in 1971 when Moravian Seminary for Girls and Moravian Preparatory School were merged. The school has two campuses: the Lower–Middle School campus in the historic downtown area of Bethlehem and the Upper School campus on a 120-acre estate 6 miles to the east.

For more than 268 years, Moravian Academy has encouraged sound innovations to meet contemporary challenges while recognizing the permanence of basic human values. The school seeks to promote young people's full development in mind, body, and spirit by fostering a love for learning, respect for others, joy in participation and service, and skill in decision making. Preparation for college occurs in an atmosphere characterized by an appreciation for the individual.

Moravian Academy is governed by a Board of Trustees. Six members are representatives of the Moravian Church. The school is valued at $32.2 million, of which $10.3 million is endowment. In 2009–10, Annual Giving was $437,196, and operating expenses were $14.6 million.

Moravian Academy is accredited by the Middle States Association of Colleges and Schools and the Pennsylvania Association of Independent Schools. The school is a member of the National Association of Independent Schools, the Association of Delaware Valley Independent Schools, the College Board, the Council for Spiritual and Ethical Education, the School and Student Service for Financial Aid, and the Secondary School Admission Test Board.

Moravian Academy does not discriminate on the basis of race, nationality, sex, sexual orientation, religious affiliation, or ethnic origin in the administration of its educational and admission policies, financial aid awards, and athletic or other school-administered programs. Applicants who are disabled (or applicants' family members who are disabled) and require any type of accommodation during the application process, or at any other time, are encouraged to identify themselves and indicate what type of accommodation is needed.

ACADEMIC PROGRAMS

Students are required to carry five major courses per year. Minimum graduation requirements include English, 4 credits; mathematics, 3 credits; lab sciences, 3 credits; global language, 3 credits; social studies, 3 credits; fine arts, 2 credits; and physical education and health. All students must successfully complete a semester course in world religions or ethics. Community service is an integral part of the curriculum. Electives are offered in many areas, such as fine and performing arts, sciences, English, math, history, and global language. Moravian Academy offers Advanced Placement courses, numerous honors courses, and honors independent study. The Academy also participates in a high school scholars program that enables highly qualified students to take college courses at no cost. The overall student-faculty ratio is about 9:1, with classes ranging from 10 to 18 students.

Grades in most courses are A–F; D is a passing grade. However, a C- is required to advance to the next level in math and global languages. Reports are sent to parents, and parent-conference opportunities are scheduled in the fall semester. Faculty and staff members are available for additional conferences whenever necessary. Examinations are held at the end of each seventeen-week semester in all major subjects. In the senior year, final examinations are given in May to allow seniors time for a two-week Post Term Experience before graduation.

FACULTY AND ADVISERS

The Upper School has 37 full-time and 4 part-time faculty members. Ninety-two percent of the full-time Upper School faculty members have advanced degrees. Several faculty members have degrees in counseling in addition to other subjects, and the entire faculty shares in counseling through the Faculty Advisor Program.

George N. King Jr. was appointed Headmaster in 2007. He previously served as the Head of the Wooster School in Danbury, Connecticut. Mr. King received his B.A. from Murray State University and his M.A. from the New England Conservatory of Music.

COLLEGE ADMISSION COUNSELING

The Director of Academic Counseling begins group work in college guidance in the eleventh grade. Tenth graders take the PSAT as practice and repeat it the following year. College Night is held annually for juniors and their parents. Juniors meet weekly in small groups for college counseling during the second semester and have an individual family conference in the spring. They take the PSAT, SAT Reasoning Test, and SAT Subject Tests. Some students also elect to take the ACT in their junior or senior year. Seniors meet twice weekly in small groups during the first semester for additional guidance and are guided through the college application process. They take the SAT Reasoning Test and Subject Tests again, if necessary. In recent years, approximately 85 to 90 percent of the junior and senior classes take at least one Advanced Placement course and earn a score of 3 or higher.

Average SAT scores of 2010 graduates were 655 critical reading, 676 math, and 653 writing. Graduates of 2010 are attending Barnard, Bucknell, Carnegie Mellon, Columbia, Cornell, Dartmouth, Duke, Emory, Georgetown, Notre Dame, Princeton, Tufts, USC, Vanderbilt, Wake Forest, Wellesley, and the Universities of New York and Pennsylvania. Some students participate in travel abroad or Rotary international exchange programs before attending college.

STUDENT BODY AND CONDUCT

The Upper School has 287 students in 2010–11. The school understands the value of diversity in the educational setting. In all divisions, students and faculty members from a variety of ethnic, cultural, religious, and socioeconomic backgrounds carry on this commitment. Through classroom activities, nondenominational chapel services discussing many faiths, and active engagement with each other, students at Moravian Academy are encouraged to appreciate one another's individuality.

Students enjoy the small classes and the opportunity for participation in sports and other activities. Students are expected to wear clothing that is neat and appropriate for school. Denim is not permitted during the school day, and a school uniform is required for members of performing groups. Students participate actively in a Student Council. Serious matters of discipline come before a faculty-student discipline committee.

ACADEMIC FACILITIES

Snyder House, Walter Hall, and the Heath Science Complex hold the classrooms, studios, and laboratories (chemistry, physics, biology, and computer). In September 2007, the Academy dedicated the new Van S. Merle-Smith Woodworking Studio. All of the library's resources are integrated with the instructional program to intensify and individualize the educational experience. Technology plays an important role in enhancing learning and students get hands-on experience with the latest equipment in classrooms and labs. There are dedicated computer labs, additional computers in the library, portable wireless labs, and a computer in every classroom. SmartBoards are used in all divisions to enhance the learning process. The Couch Fine Arts Center houses the studio arts department. A 350-seat auditorium enhances the music and theater programs. Students can also use the resources and facilities of the seven colleges and universities in the area.

ATHLETICS
A strong athletics program meets the guidelines of the school's philosophy that a person must be nurtured in body, as well as in mind and spirit, and that respect for others and participation are important goals. A large gymnasium, eight athletics fields, and six tennis courts provide the school with facilities for varsity and junior varsity teams in boys' lacrosse and baseball; girls' field hockey; boys' and girls' basketball, cross-country, soccer, swimming, and tennis; coeducational golf; and a girls' varsity softball team. Students also have the opportunity to participate in football, track, and wrestling in co-operative programs with a local school. A gymnasium that includes a weight room complements the physical education facilities in Walter Hall. An outdoor recreational pool is available for special student functions as well as the Academy's summer day camp program for younger children.

All students have the chance to take part in team sports—and many of them do. In any given athletic season, more than one third of the Upper School student body participates in after-school athletics at the Academy.

In addition to the on-campus programs, students may take advantage of the golf courses in the Lehigh Valley, along with an indoor rock-climbing facility, a bicycle velodrome, and indoor stables. Many students belong to the Academy's ski club, which offers weekly ski excursions to local ski areas over five consecutive Fridays during the winter.

EXTRACURRICULAR OPPORTUNITIES
Moravian Academy's activity program provides opportunities for varied interests and talents. Included are service projects, outdoor education, International Club, *Legacy* (yearbook), *The Moravian Star* (newspaper), *Green Ponderer* (literary magazine), Model Congress, Model UN, PJAS, Scholastic Scrimmage, and a variety of activities that change in response to student interests. A fine arts series combines music, art, drama, and dance. In addition, the Academy's outdoor education program offers a variety of off-campus experiences. The annual Country Fair gives students an opportunity to work with the Parents' Association to create a family fun day for the school and Lehigh Valley community. Rooted in Moravian tradition, a strong appreciation of music has continued. There are several student musical groups, including chorale, MA Chamber Singers, a cappella group, handbell choirs, and instrumental ensembles. A highlight of the year is the Christmas Vespers Service.

DAILY LIFE
A typical school day begins at 8 a.m., and classes run until 3:15 p.m. on Monday, Tuesday, Wednesday, and Friday. On Thursday, classes conclude at 2:45. The average length of class periods is about 40 minutes. Students usually take six classes a day.

A weekly nondenominational chapel service is held on Thursday mornings. On Monday, Tuesday, Wednesday, and Friday, there is a period for class, school, or advisory meetings.

COSTS AND FINANCIAL AID
Tuition for 2010–11 is $21,570. There is an additional dining fee for students. An initial deposit of $1000 is required upon acceptance, and the remainder of the fee is to be paid in two installments, unless other arrangements are made. An additional fee for tuition insurance is recommended for all new students.

Financial aid is available. Moravian Academy uses the services of the School and Student Service for Financial Aid by NAIS. Aid is awarded on the basis of demonstrated financial need. Aid is received by approximately 20 percent of Upper School students.

ADMISSIONS INFORMATION
Students are admitted in grades 9–11. Each applicant is carefully considered. Students who demonstrate an ability and willingness to handle a rigorous academic program as well as such qualities as intellectual curiosity, responsibility, creativity, and cooperation, are encouraged to apply. Scores on tests administered by the school are also used in the admission process. In addition, school records, recommendations, and a personal interview are required. Admissions are usually completed by May, but there are sometimes openings available after that time.

APPLICATION TIMETABLE
Inquiries are welcome at any time. The Admission Office makes arrangements for tours and classroom visits during the school week. If necessary, other arrangements for tours can be made. The application fee is $65. Test dates are scheduled on specified Saturday mornings from January through March. Notifications are sent after February 15, and families are asked to respond within two weeks.

ADMISSIONS CORRESPONDENCE
Daniel J. Axford
Director of Admissions, Upper School
Moravian Academy
4313 Green Pond Road
Bethlehem, Pennsylvania 18020
Phone: 610-691-1600
Web site: http://www.moravianacademy.org

MUNICH INTERNATIONAL SCHOOL

Starnberg, Germany

Type: Coeducational day college-preparatory school
Grades: PK–12: Junior School, Early Childhood (ages 4 and 5)–grade 4; Middle School, grades 5–8; Senior School, grades 9–12
Enrollment: School total: 1,217; Junior School: 420, Middle School: 380, Senior School: 417
Head of School: Simon Taylor

THE SCHOOL

Munich International School (MIS) is a non-profit coeducational primary and secondary day school that serves students from early childhood (ages 4 and 5) through grade 12, with English as the language of instruction. A total of 1,217 students who represent about fifty countries and nationalities attend MIS. Students are accepted without regard to race, creed, nationality, or religion. The 26-acre MIS campus lies in an environmentally protected area of woodlands and farmland near scenic Lake Starnberg, some 20 kilometres (12 miles) south of Munich. School buses serve the cities of Munich and Starnberg and the surrounding region.

Founded in 1966, the School serves the international community in and around Munich, Germany, as well as those from the local community who wish to take advantage of the unique MIS educational experience. As an exemplary English language International Baccalaureate (I.B.) World School, MIS inspires students to be interculturally aware and achieve their potential within a stimulating and caring learning environment. The curriculum follows the frameworks of the I.B. Primary Years Programme (IBPYP) and the I.B. Middle Years Programme (IBMYP), which culminate in the final two years with the International Baccalaureate Diploma (IBDP) or the American high school diploma.

MIS regards the acquisition of knowledge, concepts, and skills as essential. They are seen as part of a broad and significant process of personal development toward independence, understanding, and tolerance. Learning is a lifelong process, and students are encouraged to cultivate a respect for learning and the ability and wisdom to use it well. Furthermore, since the School is an international and multicultural community, it seeks to develop in young people an active and lasting commitment to international cooperation.

All parents whose children attend MIS constitute the membership of the MIS Association, a tax-exempt, nonprofit organisation that elects a Board of Directors from its membership to operate the School in accordance with its Articles of Association.

Munich International School is fully accredited by the Council of International Schools (CIS) and the New England Association of Schools and Colleges (NEASC) and is approved by the German and Bavarian Educational Authorities.

ACADEMIC PROGRAMME

The academic programme throughout the School covers English language and literature, mathematics, humanities (including history, business and management, economics, geography, and social studies), sciences (including biology, chemistry, and physics), foreign languages, computer science, the fine arts, and film studies.

In the belief that students best benefit from the experience of living in Germany if they are able to communicate effectively and take part in local culture, MIS offers German language instruction to all students in early childhood classes through grade 12. Furthermore, comprehensive instruction in English as a second language (ESL) is offered to students who come to MIS with minimal or no English language skills. In the Senior School, however, English language competence is required for admission.

The School programme is designed so that all students have the opportunity to pursue studies in the fine arts (art, music, drama, and film studies) and computing, athletic, and recreational skills.

The Junior School (early childhood–grade 4) follows the curriculum of the IBPYP, which emphasises an inquiry-based approach to learning across all core academic subjects. The children are taught in self-contained classes in a nurturing environment. The early childhood classes prepare the students for successful entry into grade 1.

The Middle School (grades 5–8) provides a caring, stable environment with a balance of challenging academic studies and opportunities for curricular and extracurricular skill development. The curriculum conforms to the frameworks of the IBMYP in grades 6, 7, and 8. The IBMYP is also part of the curriculum in grades 9 and 10. Studies emphasise the development of skills that involve moral reasoning, aesthetic judgement, and the use of scientific method. The Middle School is committed to providing students with the knowledge, learning strategies, and study skills necessary for the demanding Senior School programme. Food technology and ethics are introduced in grade 6, and French and Spanish are offered as electives from grade 6 onwards. Additional programmes that focus on health, design and technology, social skills, and the importance of the environment are also provided.

The academic programme of the Senior School (grades 9–12) is designed to prepare students for higher education. The guidance counselor especially encourages career planning to make students aware of the education and skills necessary to pursue lifetime goals. The academic programme culminates in grades 11 and 12, with studies leading to a full International Baccalaureate Diploma or an American high school diploma.

FACULTY AND ADVISERS

At MIS, more than 160 teachers from twenty-three nations are part of this broad international experience, coming from such countries as Australia, Canada, France, Germany, Great Britain, Hungary, Ireland, the Netherlands, New Zealand, Sri Lanka, and the United States. The faculty members are fully qualified; many have taught overseas and hold advanced degrees.

COLLEGE ADMISSION COUNSELING

Students have the opportunity to prepare and sit for the American PSAT, SAT, and ACT—tests normally needed for U.S. college entrance. About 90 percent of MIS graduates continue their education at universities and colleges in the world, including Columbia, Duke, the London School of Economics and Political Science, Middlebury, Politecnico Milano (Italy), Sciences Po (France), Tokyo Institute of Technology, Universita Bocconi (Italy), University of Munich, and the University of St. Andrews (Scotland), to cite some recent examples.

STUDENT BODY AND CONDUCT

The strong MIS community of students, teachers, and parents works together. MIS teachers and administrators understand the uncertainties and complexities that accompany a student's transition from one country to another and from one school to another, as well as the normal challenges of growing up. A coordinated support system across the School consists of homeroom teachers, grade coordinators, year coordinators, year advisers, IBPYP/IBMYP/IB coordinators, and guidance counselors.

ACADEMIC FACILITIES

The Junior School is housed in a modern facility, with spacious, light-filled classrooms that radiate from a central multipurpose activity area. There are rooms for computing, German, ESL, learning support, art, and music classes as well as a large, well-equipped library. The Health Office and the School cafeteria, which serves hot meals, are also located in this building.

The Middle School is also located in a modern building. The architectural concept maximizes the use of windows, allowing students to feel close to the natural beauty of the campus. In addition to the spacious classrooms, there are two science laboratories, and a multipurpose auditorium as well as rooms for ESL, academic support, music, and food technology.

The Senior School combines a new building and a traditional Bavarian-style building. Multipurpose classrooms are enhanced by five science laboratories, music and computer rooms, a library, a student lounge, and a performing arts center.

Stately Schloss Buchhof, an original manor house of the area that dates back to 1875, has been renovated to house the Middle and Senior School fine arts departments as well as the administrative offices of the School.

ATHLETICS

Sports activities, which play an important role at MIS, are conducted for all ages after school and during weekends. Soccer, skiing, volleyball, basketball, track and field, tennis, cross-country, and softball are the main sports offered. Tennis courts, several sports fields, and a well-equipped triple gymnasium are available on campus.

The School competes in several ISST tournaments and participates in local leagues and events under the auspices of a School-sponsored sports club. Middle and Senior School teams represent MIS at various international school competitions across Europe.

EXTRACURRICULAR OPPORTUNITIES

In order to take advantage of the experience of living in Germany and Europe, there is a wide range of half- or full-day field trips at all school levels. There are overnight trips for the Middle and Senior School, when teachers and students travel both within Germany and beyond for educational and cultural experiences.

Students may select from a variety of activities in the fine arts, ranging from painting, drawing, and ceramics to handicrafts, drama, and dance. There are several School choirs, bands, and an orchestra. Private instrumental instruction is available. A number of student drama productions are performed throughout the year. Senior and Middle School students participate in the International School Theatre Festival, the Speech and Debate Team, and several international school tournaments. Students in grades 11 and 12 have a weekly period set aside for recreational sports and service activities. They may take part in the Business@ School and Model United Nations programmes.

Each year, a group of 8 to 10 students travels to Tanzania to visit project sites funded by donations from the MIS community. The travelling students present their findings at special assemblies held in each division of the School.

An active Parent-Teacher Organisation (PTO) operates as a voluntary support group for the School and fellow parents. The PTO organises a wide range of activities throughout the year, including a Ski Swap, Winterfest, and, in the spring, Frühlingsfest.

DAILY LIFE

The school year begins at the end of August and ends in late June. It is interspersed with short vacations, usually a week at the end of October, two weeks at Christmas, a Ski Week, and two weeks for Spring Break.

The school day starts at 9:10 a.m.; it ends at 3:15 p.m. for Junior School students and at 4 p.m. for Middle and Senior School students. Buses organised by the School and serving most areas in and around Munich provide transportation for nearly 80 percent of the students.

SUMMER PROGRAMMES

A two-week daytime sports programme at the beginning of July includes a week of camping in the Dolomite Mountains in northern Italy.

COSTS AND FINANCIAL AID

In the school year 2010–11, tuition is €12,900–€13,050 for pre-reception–grade 5, €14,720–€15,110 for grades 6–8, and €16,210 for grades 9–12. There is also an entrance fee of €4800 per child upon initial admission and an additional €1500 per child in each of the following two school years.

ADMISSIONS INFORMATION

Applicants are advised that the School does not have the facilities to serve the educational needs of students who have mental, emotional, or physical handicaps or severe learning disabilities. The School does not have boarding facilities.

APPLICATION TIMETABLE

Interested students are required to submit a completed MIS application packet. Following submission of all required documentation, applicants are screened. Based on the School's judgment of the suitability of the educational programme for the prospective student and on space availability, applicants are admitted throughout the year. Earliest acceptance of application material is six months prior to attendance and/or January of that particular year. A nonrefundable application fee is paid in advance of admission decisions being made.

ADMISSIONS CORRESPONDENCE

Admissions Office
Munich International School
Schloss Buchhof
D-82319 Starnberg
Germany
Phone: 49-8151-366-120
Fax: 49-8151-366-129
E-mail: admissions@mis-munich.de
Web site: http://www.mis-munich.de

THE NEWMAN SCHOOL

Boston, Massachusetts

Type: Coeducational day college-preparatory school
Grades: 9–12
Enrollment: 250
Head of School: J. Harry Lynch, Headmaster

THE SCHOOL

The Newman School provides a diverse student body with a college-preparatory, liberal arts education based on Judeo-Christian values, intellectual rigor, and trust, guided by the spirit and philosophy of John Henry Cardinal Newman. Located in the heart of Boston's historic Back Bay district, the Newman School, near Copley Square and the Prudential Center, is convenient to railroad stations, bus terminals, and MBTA stations. Newman's motto "let heart speak to heart" establishes the tone for each day, encouraging students to form mature and stimulating relationships with teachers and peers and to recognize their individual gifts.

The Newman School, which was named in honor of John Henry Cardinal Newman, was founded in 1945 by Dr. J. Harry Lynch to provide a year of college-preparatory work. Since then, the Newman School has grown into a four-year high school. Classes are offered in fall, winter, and summer sessions, enabling students to attend the School year-round, if desired. Intensive instruction for international students is also available.

Newman is incorporated as a not-for-profit organization and directed by a self-perpetuating 10-member Board of Trustees, which meets quarterly and includes several alumni.

The Newman School is approved by the Boston School Committee and the Department of Education of the Commonwealth of Massachusetts and is accredited by the New England Association of Schools and Colleges. The School holds membership in the Association of Independent Schools of New England (AISNE), the National Association of Secondary School Principals, the Massachusetts Secondary School Principals Association, the National Association of College Admission Counselors, and the Secondary School Admission Test Board. It is approved by the U.S. Immigration and Naturalization Service for the teaching of international students.

ACADEMIC PROGRAMS

The Newman School is recognized by the International Baccalaureate Organization as a World School, offering the International Baccalaureate (I.B.) Diploma Programme in the eleventh and twelfth grades. Freshmen and sophomores pursue a course of pre-I.B. studies in language, mathematics, English literature and composition, and lab science leading to I.B. studies in the junior and senior years.

Transfer credit may be accepted for high school work completed in other schools; however, diploma candidates must take a minimum of 6 credits at Newman. To graduate, a student must complete 22 credits as follows: 4 English, 3 social studies (including U.S. history), 4 mathematics, 3 laboratory science, 2 foreign language, 1 fine/applied arts, 1 computer science, and 4 electives.

The International Student Adviser and the School's Guidance Department aid students from other countries who are preparing for entrance to American colleges and universities. Intermediate and advanced English courses for international students are offered in an intensive program of six classes per day for sixteen weeks in the fall and spring semesters and ten weeks in the summer session. Special attention is given to preparing for the Test of English as a Foreign Language and for College Board tests.

FACULTY AND ADVISERS

J. Harry Lynch, the Headmaster, is a graduate of the College of the Holy Cross (B.A., 1974) and Northeastern University (M.B.A., 1976). He has been Headmaster of Newman since 1985.

The faculty includes 22 full-time teachers and 2 part-time teachers. These 9 men and 13 women hold twenty-two baccalaureate degrees, thirteen master's degrees, and one doctorate.

Members of the faculty are available each day to give students extra help with their course work.

COLLEGE ADMISSION COUNSELING

The College and Career Reference Area provides students with information regarding college admissions and the employment outlook in various fields.

An average graduating class has approximately 65 students, of whom more than 95 percent attend four-year colleges and universities. Recent graduates from Newman have been accepted to the following four-year colleges and universities, among others: American, Assumption, Babson, Bates, Boston College, Boston University, California Institute of Technology, Clark, Columbia, Emerson, Fairfield, Georgetown, Grinnell, Harvard, Holy Cross, McGill, MIT, NYU, Oberlin, Regis, St. Anselm, Smith, Stonehill, Tufts, Tulane, the U.S. Air Force Academy, Vassar, Wellesley, Wheaton, Worcester Polytechnic, and the Universities of Connecticut, Delaware, Maryland, Massachusetts, Miami, New Hampshire, and Rhode Island.

STUDENT BODY AND CONDUCT

The Newman School enrolls approximately 250 day students ranging from 14 to 19 years of age. About 50 of them are out-of-town residents who are temporarily living in Boston. Current and recent students have come from California, Connecticut, Florida, Illinois, Massachusetts, New Hampshire, New Jersey, New York, Ohio, Austria, France, Germany, Greece, India, Iran, Ireland, Italy, Japan, Korea, the People's Republic of China, Poland, Russia, Saudi Arabia, Thailand, Spain, Vietnam, the West Indies, and several Central and South American countries.

Admission to and continuance in the Newman School is to be regarded as a privilege and not a right; the Board of Trustees requires the withdrawal of any student for disciplinary or scholastic reasons that it deems sufficiently grave to warrant such action. The board is the final judge in matters of admission and retention of students. Each student has the responsibility of being thoroughly informed at all times concerning the regulations and requirements of Newman; these are outlined in the School brochure and student handbook.

ACADEMIC FACILITIES

The School plant consists of two nineteenth-century town houses located on Marlborough Street that contain libraries, laboratories, classrooms, and offices. Both buildings are wireless-network accessible. The School

www.facebook.com/sec.schools

does not maintain boarding facilities but does assist out-of-town students in finding homestay families.

ATHLETICS

The School competes interscholastically with other independent schools in sports such as boys' and girls' basketball and soccer, girls' softball, and boys' baseball and cross-country. Intramural sports, which include competitive cheerleading, crew, flag football, rugby, sailing, and tennis, are available according to student interest but may not be available each term.

EXTRACURRICULAR OPPORTUNITIES

Extracurricular activities that are available each year include a yearbook and a newspaper (247). There are drama, dance, student government, community services, peer leadership, robotics, photography, film, recreation and outing, and science clubs, as well as chorus, ensembles, and bands that perform throughout the year. Other activities may be organized based on student interest. The School has sponsored study-abroad as well as student exchange programs with Spain, Italy, and Colombia.

DAILY LIFE

The academic year is divided into semesters and each semester has four marking periods. At the end of each quarter, grade reports are mailed home. Academic alerts are mailed any time when faculty members observe poor performance by a student. Semesters begin in September and January and a ten-week session begins in June. The school day starts at 8:10 and ends by 3. Classes are held five days a week; to permit completion of a year's work in one fall or spring session, many courses meet for two periods each day.

The summer session incorporates the same amount of work in extended class periods. Thus, summer students may earn a full year's credit for courses not previously taken.

SUMMER PROGRAMS

Newman students may continue their studies during the summer session, receiving academic credit for regular high school courses. In addition, refresher and makeup courses are offered for students from other schools who need to correct deficiencies. International students may attend the Newman School's summer program to work on their English skills and to experience many aspects of American culture within the city of Boston.

COSTS AND FINANCIAL AID

Day tuition is estimated at $14,500 to $24,500 for the 2010–11 school year, depending on the individual schedule. Additional expenses include books (approximately $300 per semester). Estimated living expenses for out-of-town students are $10,600 for the 2010–11 school year.

Entering ninth graders may be given scholarships, depending on the result of the entrance examinations. The School awarded $75,000 in scholarship aid for 2010–11. Financial aid is also available.

ADMISSIONS INFORMATION

Applicants are accepted for enrollment in September, January, and June. Transcripts of any previous high school work, a personal interview, and a character reference letter from the previous school are all part of the requirements to determine acceptance. Applicants must also take a placement test that is administered at the School.

It has always been the policy of the Newman School to admit students without distinction as to race, color, creed, sex, age, ethnic background, or national origin.

APPLICATION TIMETABLE

Candidates for admission should file an application on the required form at the earliest feasible date preceding the session in which they wish to enroll. There is a $40 application fee for American students and a $300 application and processing fee for international students.

ADMISSIONS CORRESPONDENCE

Mrs. Patricia Lynch, Ph.D.
Director of Admissions
The Newman School
247 Marlborough Street
Boston, Massachusetts 02116

Phone: 617-267-4530
Fax: 617-267-7070
E-mail: @newmanboston.org
Web site: http://www.newmanboston.org

NORTHWOOD SCHOOL

Lake Placid, New York

Type: Independent, coeducational, college-preparatory boarding and day school
Grades: 9–12, postgraduate
Enrollment: 180
Head of School: Edward M. Good

THE SCHOOL

Founded in 1905, Northwood is located in the heart of the Adirondack Mountains in Lake Placid, a small village that twice hosted the Winter Olympics (1932 and 1980). It is also the home of the Lake Placid Center for the Arts; consequently, the area offers unique outdoor, athletic, and cultural opportunities. The School is 2 hours from Montreal, Ontario, Canada; Albany, New York; and Burlington, Vermont. The 85-acre campus is nestled in the heart of the village and at the base of Cobble Mountain. The Adirondack Mountains surround the village and are a beautiful backdrop for the School.

Northwood is dedicated to sound scholarship in a diverse environment. It endeavors to stimulate intellectual curiosity in its students and encourages them to learn for themselves through the guidance of its faculty and the examples set by all in the Northwood community. In addition to its academic rigor, the School also stresses responsibility to self and community, asking students to discuss and establish core values, respect different perspectives, and contribute to both the School and its surroundings through various student activities and required community services.

Northwood has a wide variety of athletic opportunities, in both competitive team sports and intense outdoor experiences. All students are asked to challenge themselves and display their talents through concerts and theater productions, presentation of darkroom and studio work in art shows and the annual Artsfest, and writing for the School newspaper and literary magazine. Informed by their active lives, Northwood students are independent young men and women who are prepared to lead and achieve in college.

Northwood School is accredited by the New York State Association of Independent Schools (NYSAIS) and the New York State Board of Regents.

ACADEMIC PROGRAMS

Graduation requirements include 19½ units in the following areas: English (4 years), social science (3 years), U.S. history (1 year), science (3 years), mathematics (3 years), language (2 years), fine arts (1 year), and health (½ year). The required number of courses per year is five.

Advanced Placement courses include biology, calculus, English literature, English language, and U.S. history.

Honors courses include algebra II, biology, chemistry, English III, physics, precalculus, and U.S. history.

Elective courses include art exploration, art history, anthropology, ceramics, constitutional law, drama, drawing and painting I and II, economics, ethics, fiber arts, geology, government, Great Issues, instrumental ensemble, Irish history, photography, political geography, psychology, sculpture, and steel drums.

The average class size is 9, and the overall student-teacher ratio is 6:1. In the evening, students who struggle with a particular course are assigned supervised study hall. Study hall conditions are in effect for room study Monday through Thursday evenings from 7 to 9 p.m. Ample time is given to all students for laboratory work and library study. Lectures and workshops are scheduled on a regular basis with nearby colleges (St. Lawrence and Middlebury, for example). Trips are scheduled to museums and art centers in Ottawa, Ontario, and other cities near the School.

Many opportunities are available for trips to other countries, especially for the language department. The English as a second language (ESL) program is designed for nonnative English speakers.

The grading system is based on letter grades from A to F. Academic reports go home to parents and to advisers four times per year.

FACULTY AND ADVISERS

There are 30 full-time faculty members, 20 of whom reside on campus. Thirteen of the 30 faculty members have master's degrees. Mr. Edward M. Good, the Headmaster, comes from thirty years of experience in education. He holds a bachelor's degree from Bowdoin, a master's degree from Brown, and a CAGS from the University of Massachusetts. Mr. Good has been at Northwood since 1996. He teaches one current events course. Faculty turnover is very low at Northwood. Faculty members serve as advisers to students, with whom they meet periodically. The adviser communicates any problems to the parents.

COLLEGE ADMISSION COUNSELING

The Director of College Guidance is Jeffrey Edwards. Mr. Edwards works with each senior on a regular basis until the student is accepted by a college or university. He assists students and parents with the college application process. Three other faculty members also assist with the college application process. The average verbal SAT score is 553, and the average math SAT score is 582.

Of last year's 54 graduates, 95 percent were accepted and enrolled at four-year colleges or universities. Last year, Northwood seniors chose to attend schools such as Babson, Boston College, Clarkson, Cornell, Hamilton College, Hobart and William Smith, Lehigh, Middlebury, Queens, and St. Lawrence.

STUDENT BODY AND CONDUCT

Northwood has 180 students. Of these, 144 are boarders and 36 are day students. The boy-to-girl ratio is 2:1. Thirty percent of the student population is international, coming from countries such as Canada, China, Colombia, England, Finland, Korea, Norway, Russia, Scotland, Spain, and Vietnam.

ACADEMIC FACILITIES

Northwood has twelve classrooms, a lecture hall, a fine arts studio, four science laboratories, a theater, and a library. The library is student friendly and provides many resources for both academic and personal growth.

The fine arts department has been renovated to provide a photography studio, a fiber arts room, and first-rate painting and drawing facilities as well as a pottery studio. The dining room, kitchen, and administrative offices were remodeled in the summer of 2002.

BOARDING AND GENERAL FACILITIES

Residential facilities include one main-building dormitory for boys, separated on three floors. A girls' dorm is located away from the main building.

The Student Center is complete with pool tables and video games, as well as vending machines and a separate television lounge. The bookstore and student mailboxes are also located in the student lounge area.

A state-of-the-art fitness center has been built, complete with all new fitness/weight machines, an indoor climbing wall, and a racquetball/squash court.

Four outdoor tennis courts, three soccer/lacrosse fields, and an outdoor adventure cabin and lean-to make up the outside facilities for athletics. Northwood also has two indoor tennis courts to complete the on-campus facilities. The School uses the Olympic Center for all figure skating and hockey practices and home games.

ATHLETICS

True to the credo on its seal, "Power Through Health and Knowledge," Northwood has a wide variety of athletics opportunities in both competitive team sports and intense outdoor experiences through the Outdoor Adventure Program. A full-time athletics trainer resides on campus.

Girls' sports include Alpine/Nordic skiing, crew, cycling, figure skating, freestyle skiing, golf, ice hockey, lacrosse, soccer, and tennis. Boys' sports include Alpine/Nordic skiing, crew, cycling, freestyle skiing, golf, ice hockey, lacrosse, soccer, and tennis. Coed athletics offerings include canoeing, conditioning, four-season camping, hiking, kayaking, orienteering, rock/ice climbing, telemarking/backcountry skiing, and wilderness first aid.

Northwood also has access to other Olympic facilities for sports such as bobsledding, luge, ski jumping, and speed skating.

EXTRACURRICULAR OPPORTUNITIES

There are various extracurricular activities at Northwood. The yearbook is created mostly by upperclass students. The literary magazine focuses on publishing student works and entering literary accomplishments in local writing competitions. The newly formed student-faculty steel drums band performs both on campus and for the community. Trips to nearby cities for cultural or sporting events are frequent. Students are encouraged to join one of the many on-campus clubs or groups, such as the French club or the food committee.

Learning at Northwood School happens in many ways and on many levels. One of the most significant lessons students learn is their responsibility to the greater community. Over the years, students have adopted many service projects as expressions of this sense of responsibility. They run blood drives for the Red Cross, maintain several miles of cross-country ski and hiking trails, and organize annual fundraisers for the Myelin Project and breast cancer research. Students work one-on-one as athletes' assistants for the Special Olympics winter events, and they offer a certified group of search-and-rescue volunteers to help the New York State forest rangers.

Northwood School's faculty members and students are ever mindful of their obligation to serve beyond the boundaries of their campus.

DAILY LIFE
Breakfast starts at 6:50 a.m. and finishes at 7:20. Students attend class from 7:45 until 2:30 p.m., Monday through Friday. A two-week rotating academic schedule incorporates a work program, daily School meeting, and lunch within the 40-minute class periods. Friday evenings are often used for outside presentations and lectures.

Sports and activities meet each afternoon from 3 to 4:30 p.m. After dinner there is a supervised 2-hour study hall.

During the winter schedule, classes, which normally take place after lunch, are moved to 4:15 p.m. to allow skiers and other winter athletes to train at appropriate times.

WEEKEND LIFE
Weekends are full of diverse events. There are trips to Montreal for hockey or baseball games and trips to nearby colleges, such as Middlebury College or St. Lawrence University. The movie theater, bowling alley, and Main Street shopping in town or in nearby cities are popular weekend activities. Friday evenings often include on-campus activities and visiting musical groups as well as talent night and trivia night. A weekend might also include an overnight camping trip or snowshoeing to a cabin in the woods. Students and faculty members together enjoy planning weekend events at Northwood.

SUMMER PROGRAMS
The Northwood School campus is home to the Lake Placid Soccer Center, the Can/Am Hockey camp, and various cultural programs that make Lake Placid their home in the summer.

COSTS AND FINANCIAL AID
The 2010–11 tuition for boarding students is $42,500. Day student tuition is $24,000. There is an additional fee of $1000 for international students and $2000 for those needing ESL.

Fifty percent of Northwood School students receive financial assistance.

ADMISSIONS INFORMATION
Northwood School accepts students on a rolling admissions basis. Upon receipt of the application and all required admissions material, the admissions committee meets to discuss acceptance. Admission to Northwood School is based upon evaluation of the applicant's academic record and aptitude test results received from his or her present school. Each candidate is required to take the Secondary School Admission Test, which is published by the Educational Testing Service, Princeton, New Jersey, and is administered numerous times each year at various centers. Northwood may designate other testing according to need. A short essay exercise is required of all candidates who visit the campus.

APPLICATION TIMETABLE
Persons interested can call, write, or visit the School's Web site for information. The Web site has much information and pictures of the facilities and students. Prospective students can download an application or apply online from the admissions page of the Web site.

ADMISSIONS CORRESPONDENCE
Timothy Weaver
Director of Admissions and Financial Aid
Northwood School
92 Northwood Road
P.O. Box 1070
Lake Placid, New York 12946
Phone: 518-523-3357
E-mail: admissions@northwoodschool.com
Web site: http://www.northwoodschool.com

OAK KNOLL SCHOOL OF THE HOLY CHILD

Summit, New Jersey

Type: Girls' day college-preparatory religious school (girls only Upper School 7–12; coeducational in Lower School); a member of the Holy Child Network of Schools

Grades: K–12: Lower School, K–6; Upper School, 7–12

Enrollment: School total: 544; Upper School: 314

Head of School: Timothy J. Saburn

THE SCHOOL

Oak Knoll School of the Holy Child, founded in 1924, is an independent Roman Catholic day school for boys and girls in grades K–6 and for young women only in grades 7–12. Located on an 11-acre campus in Summit, New Jersey, the School enjoys the cultural and historic resources of the metropolitan New York area. An additional 14 acres in nearby Chatham Township, New Jersey, was recently developed into state-of-the-art athletic fields.

Operated by the Sisters of the Holy Child Jesus, Oak Knoll helps each student develop to his or her fullest potential in an environment that fosters the growth of the whole child. The curriculum is designed to engage students' interests and challenge their abilities. The School aims to infuse young people not only with knowledge but also with the spiritual, aesthetic, and moral values that will prepare them for a life of achievement, service, and fulfillment.

Oak Knoll is governed by a 20-member Board of Trustees. The 2010–11 operating budget is $17.6 million, and the 2009–10 Annual Giving campaign raised $1,137,000. The School's endowment is approximately $8.5 million.

Oak Knoll is accredited by the Middle States Association of Colleges and Schools and the New Jersey State Department of Education. It is a member of the National Association of Independent Schools, the Holy Child Network of Schools, the National Coalition of Girls Schools, the New Jersey Association of Independent Schools, the School Consortium of New Jersey, the Secondary School Admission Test Board, the Educational Records Bureau, CSEE, NAPSG, NCEA, NACAC, NJACAC, and the Cum Laude Society.

ACADEMIC PROGRAMS

Graduation requirements include 4 years of English and theology; 3 years of mathematics, laboratory science, foreign language, and history (including 2 years of world history and 1 year of U.S. history); and physical education. Three additional elective courses are required from offerings in computer science, mathematics, science, social studies, and studio art. Yearlong courses carry 3 academic credits; 82 credits are required for graduation. A cycle program, which includes art, music, computer, and dance, is required for grades 9 and 10.

An accelerated program in mathematics begins in the seventh grade. In addition, an honors option is available in most subjects, and there are Advanced Placement studies in biology, calculus AB, calculus BC, chemistry, computer science, English language, English literature, European history, French, physics, Spanish, studio art, U.S. history, and world history, for a total of fourteen. Given the intensity of AP courses, students apply for these courses and must sit for the AP exams.

The program of studies lists nearly 100 courses for grades 7–12. Latin is a requirement in grades 7 and 8 and a course offering in grades 9, 11, and 12. Italian I/II Honors is offered as college-level course for seniors who excel in languages. The widest variety of electives is open to juniors and seniors. Engineering Science Honors—The Infinity Project is an innovative course that allows students to learn how engineers create, design, and test the technologies and devices of the twenty-first century using their math, science, and technology skills. The Senior Capstone Project was introduced in spring 2010. At the end of April, each senior is allowed five weeks to independently explore an area of interest in academic, creative, career, or service-oriented fields. Students work in collaboration with a professor, specialist, or manager in an internship position.

Report cards with letter grades are issued after each trimester, and exams are scheduled at the end of the year.

Each year, the School inducts students into the Cum Laude Society as well as the French, Spanish, and Science honor societies. The Latin honor society was added in fall 2010. Oak Knoll is a wireless campus and students have individual tablet laptops in grades 9 through 12. Grades 7 and 8 have individual laptops available for each class.

The average class size is 15 students. With a 1:8 faculty-student ratio, the School is noted for what its Middle States Association's evaluation cited as "the personal devotion of the administration and faculty to the students. This pleasant rapport among the members of the School community and the evident responsiveness on the part of the students are perfectly in accord with the School's concept of the importance of the individual, the formation of Christian community, and the development of a sense of service to the larger world community."

FACULTY AND ADVISERS

The Upper School faculty has 52 full-time teachers and 1 part-time teacher. Sixty-three percent of the faculty members have advanced degrees.

Faculty members serve as homeroom teachers, advisers, and moderators for a variety of extracurricular activities, clubs, and student organizations.

Timothy J. Saburn, the Head of School, was appointed by the Board of Trustees in 2005. He holds a Bachelor of Arts from St. Lawrence University, was a Klingenstein Summer Fellow within Columbia University's Teachers College, and received an Ed.M. in administration, planning, and social policy from Harvard University.

COLLEGE ADMISSION COUNSELING

College guidance begins in the sophomore year under the direction of the College Counselor. In the tenth grade, students take the PSAT/NMSQT for the first time. Students attend college fairs in the metropolitan New York area, and college admissions representatives visit the School. Each September, the junior class takes a three-day college trip to the Boston, Philadelphia, Virginia, or Washington, D.C., area; the trip includes visiting numerous colleges, attending information sessions, and touring the campuses. A PSAT prep course is offered to the entire junior class on five fall weekends. The PSAT is administered to the sophomore and junior classes. One hundred percent of graduates enter four-year colleges or universities.

In the College Counseling Office, two counselors work directly with the senior and junior classes in weekly guidance classes as well as in individual meetings with both the student and her parents or guardians. Guidance classes are held for grades 7 through 12 and focus on academic and social issues, personal and group values, community building, course selection, and individual college planning. In addition to the college counselors, two Deans, a guidance counselor, and a consulting psychologist all work together to support the students in their academic pursuits and to support the guidance and college programs.

Oak Knoll graduates are accepted at highly competitive colleges and universities. The 63 members of the class of 2010 are now attending numerous institutions, including Boston College, Bucknell, Cornell, Dartmouth, Duke, Fordham, Georgetown, Holy Cross, Lafayette, Loyola Maryland, Middlebury, MIT, NYU, Notre Dame, Princeton, Santa Clara, Vanderbilt, Villanova, and the Universities of Michigan, North Carolina (Chapel Hill), Pennsylvania, and Richmond.

STUDENT BODY AND CONDUCT

The Upper School enrolls 314 girls in grades 7–12, drawing its diverse student body from nearly seventy communities in the suburban Summit area.

A Code of Conduct outlines the rules and regulations of the School, which are designed to facilitate the partnership of faculty members and students in a community. It is the responsibility of each student to think of others, to respect their rights, and to manifest behavior that results from inner convictions and a high regard for truth, honesty, and integrity. A Conduct Review Committee made up of administrators, teachers, and students advises the two Deans in cases of major disciplinary infractions.

The dress code requires the wearing of a school uniform while on campus.

ACADEMIC FACILITIES

Oak Knoll is situated on a wooded hill in a residential suburban neighborhood. Grace Hall provides administrative and faculty offices, six classrooms, a chapel, and a creative arts center with media, music, and art studios and a photography darkroom.

Connelly Hall includes a library, a performing arts center, a dining hall, three science laboratories, nine classrooms, a computer center, a senior class lounge, a publications room, and faculty and administrative offices.

The Tisdall Hall complex houses the gymnasium; the weight training room; the dance studio; the offices of the school nurse, athletic director, athletic trainer, and the physical education staff; and two classrooms.

The Hope Memorial Library offers computerized information services and a book collection of 11,000 volumes. Additional materials are available through an interlibrary loan system.

ATHLETICS

Oak Knoll School of the Holy Child is committed to a strong athletic program that balances physical fitness with a personal commitment to good sportsmanship, which is reflected in gym classes, on the playing fields, and in individual competition. Team spirit in competitive play teaches skills in cooperative effort, and lifelong lessons are learned in victory and defeat. Involvement in the extracurricular sports program is optional.

Oak Knoll athletic memberships for 2010–11 include the Union County Conference, the Union County Interscholastic Athletic Conference (UCIAC, county level), the New Jersey State Interscholastic Athletic Association (NJSIAA, state level), the New Jersey Independent School Athletic Association (NJISAA, preps), the New Jersey Catholic Track Conference (NJCTC), the North Jersey Girls Golf League (NJGGL), the North Jersey Girls Lacrosse League (NJGILL), and the Essex-Union Field Hockey League. Oak Knoll's 14 acres of athletic fields and its field house are located a short distance away in Chatham Township. A newly renovated turf field was recently completed in Summit.

Young women in grades 9–12 compete on twenty teams at the varsity and junior varsity level. Fall sports are cross-country, field hockey, soccer, tennis, and volleyball. The winter season offers basketball, fencing, winter track, and swimming. In spring, girls compete on golf, lacrosse, outdoor track and field, and softball teams. For the 2009–10 school year, championships include: field hockey, Union County Conference (UCC); tennis, UCC–Valley Division; lacrosse, UCC, NJSIAA Sectional, and NJSIAA Group I; track, 4 x 400 m relay, UCC.

Students in grades 7 and 8 experience interscholastic competition in cross-country, soccer, and field hockey in the fall; basketball in the winter; and lacrosse and softball in the spring. Spring tennis, as a noncompetitive program, is also offered. Oak Knoll also competes annually in the cross-country and tennis events sponsored through the New Jersey Middle School Consortium.

EXTRACURRICULAR OPPORTUNITIES

Student activities and organizations appeal to a variety of interests and talents. An active Student Council provides leadership opportunities and directs the life of the School in five areas: academic, athletic, campus ministry, creative arts, and social. Student fund-raising for particular charities is also done through the Student Council each year. Students publish a yearbook, newspaper, a newsletter in both French and Spanish, and an award-winning literary magazine, in addition to the writers' roundtables. In the creative arts, students can join the Jesters (a drama group), the Dancers, the Ensemble (and other various choral music groups), a Chamber Orchestra, and the photography club.

Other extracurricular activities include Mock Trial, Junior Great Books, Senior Peer Leaders and Peer Mentors, forensics, "Operation Smile," Junior Statesmen, book and film clubs, tour guides, the competitions of the New Jersey Science and Math Leagues, The Society of Black Scholars, and Shades. Seventh and eighth graders actively participate in the New Jersey Middle School Consortium.

"Culture Vultures" draws students interested in experiencing opera, ballet, Broadway musicals, drama, and concerts in both New Jersey and New York. There is an annual musical theater production and dance concert. The Concert Choirs are featured in the Christmas and Spring Concerts.

An integral part of Holy Child education is its emphasis on service to others. Students in grades 7–12 keep service portfolios. All students participate in annual service days, during which the entire School travels to a variety of sites to volunteer. Service projects organized by the School include Bridges runs, tutoring programs for inner-city children, Operation Smile, and a clowning ministry that visits hospitals and makes monthly trips to a regional food bank. Ongoing outreach programs support a variety of local and national charities.

DAILY LIFE

The School runs on a six-day-cycle schedule, with the day beginning at 8:10 a.m. and ending at 3:05 p.m.; classes are 45-minute periods.

Oak Knoll students arrive at school via various methods. Many students utilize New Jersey Transit buses and trains. Oak Knoll provides a shuttle bus that runs to and from the Summit train station—both in the morning and after school—for a fee. Many families carpool. Oak Knoll offers private transportation routes in New Jersey's Bergen, Essex, Morris, and Union counties for a fee.

Hot/cold lunch is served daily in the School dining hall and is included in the tuition.

COSTS AND FINANCIAL AID

Tuition for the 2010–11 academic year is $30,800 for grades 7–12. Included in the tuition is the cost of a hot lunch program. There are additional expenses for a laptop, books, uniforms, and transportation for contracted van service. Some suburban school districts provide bus service to Oak Knoll; others provide reimbursement for part of the transportation cost. A contract with a tuition deposit is due by early March. Monthly payments can be arranged through Key Tuition Payment Plans.

Financial aid is available. Families apply through TADS. For the 2010–11 school year, tuition grants of approximately $1.3 million were awarded; the grants ranged from $1000 to $25,000.

ADMISSIONS INFORMATION

Oak Knoll Upper School seeks young women of promise, those who are achievement oriented, and those who have the potential to succeed in a challenging college-preparatory program. The School does not discriminate on the basis of race, creed, or national origin in the administration of its educational policies, financial aid program, or athletic or other School-administered programs.

Seventh and ninth grades are the primary entry grades for the Upper School. Applicants for grades 7 and 9 are required to take the ISEE test, which is administered at Oak Knoll on two test dates, one in November and one in December. Transcripts of report cards and standardized test records and two current teacher recommendations must be forwarded from the sending school. Applicants are also asked to bring a graded paper with them at the time of their visit. An application, $50 fee, an interview at Oak Knoll, and a day spent visiting classes are also required. Applications for eighth and tenth grades may be accepted on a limited basis. Openings in these grades, if any, are based on attrition.

APPLICATION TIMETABLE

Inquiries are always welcome. Open Houses usually occur in October and November. Interviews and visiting days run from November through January. An early application date of December 8, 2010 assists families whose search is focused on Catholic schools with earlier notification dates. The January 26 deadline for the entire admissions process remains in place. These decisions are mailed approximately the third week of February. After this date, applications and visits are handled on a rolling-admission basis. Interviews and visits are conducted by appointment only. Admissions office hours are 8 a.m. to 5 p.m. during the academic year or 9 a.m. to 4 p.m., Monday through Thursday, during the summer.

ADMISSIONS CORRESPONDENCE

Suzanne Kimm Lewis, Admissions Director
Oak Knoll School of the Holy Child
44 Blackburn Road
Summit, New Jersey 07901

Phone: 908-522-8109
Fax: 908-277-1838
E-mail: admissions@oakknoll.org
Web site: http://www.oakknoll.org

THE PENNINGTON SCHOOL

Pennington, New Jersey

Type: Coeducational day and boarding college-preparatory school
Grades: 6–12: Middle School, 6–8; Upper School, 9–12
Enrollment: School total: 485; Middle School, 95; Upper School: 390
Head of School: Stephanie G. Townsend, Head of School

THE SCHOOL

The Pennington School is an independent coeducational school for students in grades 6 through 12, with both day and boarding programs. The curriculum is college preparatory, with an emphasis on fostering the development of the whole student through academics, athletics, community service, and the creative and performing arts. There are also specialized programs within the curriculum for international students and for students with learning differences. Founded in 1838, Pennington values both tradition and innovation, applying the values gleaned from centuries of learning along with the most up-to-date knowledge, to a rapidly changing world. The School's faculty members focus not only on what they can teach the students but also on what the varied perspectives of the student body can impart to the overall educational experience.

The 54-acre campus is strategically located in a suburban setting just 60 miles from New York City, 40 miles from Philadelphia, and within 8 miles of Trenton and Princeton. This makes it convenient for cultural and educational field trips.

The governing body is a 36-member Board of Trustees. Pennington's endowment currently stands at $27 million.

The Pennington School is accredited by the Middle States Association of Colleges and Schools and approved by the New Jersey State Department of Education. It is a member of the National Association of Independent Schools, the New Jersey Association of Independent Schools, and the Secondary School Admission Test Board. Pennington is affiliated with the University Senate and the Board of Higher Education and Ministry of the United Methodist Church.

ACADEMIC PROGRAMS

Pennington's objectives are to offer a challenging academic program and to nurture the moral development of its students, helping them to acquire the kind of stable maturity that contributes to success in college and in life.

Middle School students concentrate on five major subject areas: math, English, social studies, science, and foreign language. All students rotate through a series of exploratory courses during the year, including art/drama, music, health, technology, writing workshop, and ethics.

Students in the Upper School usually take six classes per day. The minimum number of credits necessary for graduation is 20. Requirements include the following: English, 4; mathematics, 3; history, 3; science, 3; foreign language, 2; religion, 1; art, 1; health, 1; technology, ½; and public speaking, ¼. Honors and Advanced Placement courses are offered in all disciplines.

The student-teacher ratio is 9:1, and the average class size is 13, with a maximum of 18 students in any one class. A 2-hour evening study period for

boarders is supervised. The School library is open during the day and for 3 hours each evening.

The School uses the semester system, but, with midterm evaluations, there are four marking periods. Parent-teacher-student conferences are held twice a year. Individual conferences are arranged as required.

Official grades are issued at the conclusion of each semester. Pennington uses a letter grading system in which D– (60) is the passing grade and C– (70) the minimum grade for a course to count toward graduation requirements.

The Pennington School has two unique programs: a Center for Learning, a program designed for academically talented students with language-based learning disabilities, and a comprehensive English as a second language (ESL) program.

FACULTY AND ADVISERS

The faculty consists of 100 men and women, about half of whom live on campus. The faculty holds thirty-five baccalaureate, sixty master's, and four doctoral degrees. Faculty members serve as advisers for 6 to 8 students. Other counseling is available from trained counselors. Teachers also serve as hall parents, providing the basis for yet another kind of close relationship.

Stephanie (Penny) Townsend, appointed Head of School in 2006, earned her bachelor's degree from the University of Connecticut and her master's degree from Middlebury College. Before coming to Pennington, she taught Spanish at Northfield Mount Hermon School in Massachusetts and at the Taft School in Connecticut. Most recently, Townsend served as the Dean of Faculty at the Taft School.

COLLEGE ADMISSION COUNSELING

College counseling is the responsibility of trained counselors who coordinate all aspects of the college planning and placement process, including the taking of PSAT, SAT, TOEFL, and Advanced Placement tests. Representatives from almost 200 colleges visit Pennington to meet with students. Juniors and seniors meet individually with their college counselors and attend a College Ahead Program, during which a panel of returning graduates share their college experiences. Juniors attend special college programs, including two spring on-campus college fairs.

Among the schools graduates of the class of 2009 are attending are American, Boston College, Boston University, Brown, Bucknell, Columbia, Emory, Georgetown, Hofstra, Lehigh, Muhlenberg, Parsons School of Design, Rutgers, Syracuse, Villanova, and the University of Pennsylvania.

STUDENT BODY AND CONDUCT

Of Pennington's 485 students, 95 are in the Middle School and 390 are in the Upper School; 360 are day students, and 125 are boarding students. The ratio of girls to boys in the Upper School is

approximately 4:5. Students represent nine states and come from several countries, including Canada, China, Germany, Great Britain, France, Italy, Ivory Coast, Jamaica, Kenya, Romania, Russia, South Africa, South Korea, Spain, Taiwan, Thailand, and Uzbekistan. Twenty percent of the students belong to minority groups.

There is a Student Council, elected by the student body, and a Boarding Council. Students are expected to follow the rules defined in the *Student Handbook*. Violations may be dealt with by the Behavior Review Board, which is made up of students and faculty members.

During class hours, Upper School boys must wear dress shirts and ties, slacks, and dress shoes; girls must wear dresses, or slacks or skirts with blouses or sweaters. Middle School students wear Pennington polo shirts and khakis. Monday dinner and certain programs call for jackets and ties for boys and dresses or skirts and blouses for girls. The dress code permits jeans, T-shirts, and sneakers to be worn by students after class hours and on weekends but not during class time.

ACADEMIC FACILITIES

The centers of academic activities are Stainton Hall, a classroom/administration building; the Campus Center, containing art and music studios, a theater, foreign language classrooms, and the Student Center; Meckler Library, which contains the academic book collection, online databases, and the Computer Center; and Old Main, which houses classrooms and five residence halls.

BOARDING AND GENERAL FACILITIES

There are two additional dormitories containing another five residence halls: Becher Hall, a one-story residence with ten student rooms and two faculty apartments, and Buck Hall, containing four halls with double rooms and private bathrooms. There are eight faculty apartments in this building. The School has an attractive dining facility and a health center, with 2 registered nurses in residence. Boarding facilities close for the Christmas and spring holidays and for Thanksgiving, so all students must leave the campus during those vacation periods.

ATHLETICS

The Pennington School believes that the lessons learned through athletics involvement are valuable ones. Thus, every student is expected to participate in a team or individual sport that fits his or her own ability level. Although Pennington's athletics teams are very successful and frequently win state championships, the emphasis is on participation, collective effort, sportsmanship, and personal growth. All students must participate in at least one sport per year. Boarders must take three terms of activities. When boarding students are not involved in a sport, they must be involved in other extracurricular activities.

The sports available for boys and girls in grades 9 to 12 are basketball, cheerleading, cross-country, golf, lacrosse, soccer, swimming, tennis, track and field, and club water polo. In addition, field hockey and softball are available for girls, and baseball, football, and ice hockey are offered for boys.

In addition to a gymnasium/swimming pool complex, Pennington has five tennis courts, 30 acres of playing fields, an all-weather-surface track, and a lighted turf field lined for lacrosse, soccer, and football.

EXTRACURRICULAR OPPORTUNITIES

Life at Pennington is more than classrooms, laboratories, and the library, essential as these are. Opportunities exist for participation in a wide range of extracurricular activities.

Apart from the athletics program, there are many clubs and organizations that students may join. These include three drama productions a year, the Pennington Singers, Mock Trial, Peer Leadership, National Honor Society, Photography Club, International Club, International Thespian Society, Model United Nations, Pennington Sports News, Brazilian Ju-Jitsu, Youth Service Fellowship, Campus Guides, United People of Many Colors, jazz ensemble, chamber ensemble, Junior Proctors, foreign language clubs, and staffs of the yearbook, newspaper, and literary annual, which contains creative writing of students and faculty members. All students are encouraged to do community service during the year. Students do volunteer work for hospitals and charitable organizations in Pennington, Princeton, and Trenton.

A student activities program provides for social events such as dances, ski trips, movies, theater presentations, and visits to area places of interest.

Life at Pennington also includes a weekly chapel service.

DAILY LIFE

The day's activities begin at 8 a.m. and conclude at 2:45. There is an activities period on Fridays and a bimonthly assembly on Wednesdays. There are two lunch periods. A half-hour extra help conference period follows the class day. Sports practice takes place from 3:15 to 5:15, and dinner follows at 5:30. A monitored study period for boarders from 7:30 to 9:30 completes the day. Lights are out at 10:30 p.m. on weekdays.

WEEKEND LIFE

Day students and boarders are encouraged to participate in weekend activities. These include functions on campus as well as trips off campus to attend plays, museums, festivals, and professional sports contests. The library, swimming pool, and gymnasium are open on weekends. Transportation is also provided to shopping centers, where students may shop, eat, or see a movie.

COSTS AND FINANCIAL AID

The 2009–10 charges were $27,300 for day students, $40,600 for boarding students, $12,250–$15,450 for the Center for Learning classes, and $2500 for each ESL course. Additional costs are a book deposit of $500 or $600, and an activity fee of $145 or $275. There are special fees for private music lessons and tutoring. An allowance of $15 to $25 per week is recommended for spending money for residential students.

When an enrollment contract is signed, a nonrefundable deposit of 10 percent of tuition for day students and boarders is required to hold a space for the student; it is applied toward the year's tuition. The remainder of the tuition may be paid in installments of one half on August 1 and the remaining half on November 1, or tuition may be paid through a ten-month payment plan. Enrollment in school tuition insurance is required.

Financial aid is based on demonstrated need, except for two competitive merit scholarships.

Parents applying for aid must submit the required paperwork and forms through TADS. Financial aid is granted on an annual basis. Twenty-five percent of the students received financial aid for the 2009–10 school year.

ADMISSIONS INFORMATION

Pennington seeks students who have strong academic ability, as demonstrated on the SSAT, good character, and a record of good citizenship. Approximately 37 percent of the applicants are accepted for admission.

The School does not discriminate on the basis of race, color, religion, gender, or national or ethnic origin in the administration of its admission or educational policies or the financial aid, athletic, or other School-administered programs.

APPLICATION TIMETABLE

Students should begin the application process for Pennington early in the fall. The School uses a March 10 notification date, an April 10 reply date, and then rolling admissions as space is available. Students who wish to be considered in March should have all materials and the $50 application fee submitted and the interview completed by February 1. The Admission Office is open throughout the year for interviews and tours of the campus from 8:30 to 2, Monday through Friday, by appointment.

ADMISSIONS CORRESPONDENCE

Mark Saunders
Director of Admissions and Financial Aid
The Pennington School
Pennington, New Jersey 08534

Phone: 609-737-6128
Fax: 609-730-1405
E-mail: admiss@pennington.org
Web site: http://www.pennington.org

POMFRET SCHOOL

Pomfret, Connecticut

Type: Coeducational boarding and day college-preparatory school
Grades: 9–12 (Forms III–VI) and PG
Enrollment: 352
Head of School: Bradford Hastings '68, Headmaster

THE SCHOOL

Founded in 1894, Pomfret School is an independent coeducational college-preparatory boarding and day school for students in grades 9 through 12 and postgraduates. Set on a stunning 500-acre campus in northeastern Connecticut and brought to life by an exceptional faculty, Pomfret offers a rich and rewarding experience for students from various cultural and socioeconomic backgrounds.

Pomfret's campus is an oasis, with boutique shopping, movie theaters, malls, and Connecticut's premier antique district all close by. The School is just 50 minutes from Providence, 50 minutes from Hartford, a little over an hour from Boston, and 3 hours from New York City. Interesting and challenging academics (thirty-seven AP and honors courses and independent projects offered in all disciplines) combined with competitive athletics and exciting opportunities in the creative arts continue the 117-year tradition of educational excellence that defines Pomfret School. In addition to its excellent academic programs, Pomfret is particularly well-known for its strong community atmosphere, a rigorous and engaging education, a commitment to service beyond self, and numerous opportunities for personal growth in academic, athletic, artistic, and residential settings.

The School is governed by a Board of Trustees, most of whose 26 active members are alumni, current parents, or parents of alumni. The physical plant is valued at $100 million, and the endowment is in excess of $40 million. In 2009–10, more than $1.8 million was donated to the Annual Giving fund; 86 percent of current parents participated.

Pomfret School is accredited by the New England Association of Schools and Colleges and is approved by the Connecticut State Department of Education. Its memberships include the Connecticut Association of Independent Schools, the Headmasters' Association, the National Association of Independent Schools, the Secondary School Admission Test Board, A Better Chance (ABC), and the Cum Laude Society.

ACADEMIC PROGRAMS

Pomfret School offers a traditional college-preparatory curriculum that stresses the fundamentals. Emphasis is placed on reading, writing, math, foreign languages, science, history, and computer competence. The minimum academic requirements for graduation include 4 years of English, 3 years of mathematics through the junior year and through algebra II, a foreign language through the third level, 3 years of history, 3 years of science (physics, chemistry, and biology, taken in that sequence), 1 trimester of religion, and 1 trimester of social issues. The school year is divided into trimesters, with exams in November and June.

Pomfret School recognizes the value of imaginative and creative development and offers a particularly strong arts program. Students are required to enroll in an art course in two of three terms each year they attend Pomfret. Creative arts courses are offered in music, theater, painting, sculpture, film, dance, creative writing, photography, painting, drawing, and digital arts. The religion requirement may be met through such electives as Faith and Imagination and World Religions. Pomfret encourages its students to participate in community service. Options include tutoring, assisting youth groups, hospital projects, blood drives, and environmental activities.

The average class size is 11 students, and the faculty-student ratio is 1:6. The grading system uses letter grades of A to E. Grades are given twice during each trimester, and teacher comments accompany grades three times per year. A faculty adviser works closely with a group of 5 to 7 students.

FACULTY AND ADVISERS

There are 82 faculty members (46 men and 36 women), 58 of whom teach; 65 are full-time, 42 have earned master's degrees, and 4 hold doctorates. Most faculty members have advisees and live on the campus. The average length of teaching experience is eleven years.

Pomfret employs teachers who engender enthusiasm for learning. The job of any faculty member goes beyond the classroom to include coaching, advising, and running a dormitory. Pomfret believes it is at the forefront in providing for the professional growth of its faculty members.

Bradford Hastings became Headmaster in 1993, after serving as Assistant Headmaster at Deerfield Academy. He is a graduate of Pomfret and was on the faculty from 1972 to 1978. Mr. Hastings served on Pomfret's Board of Trustees from 1985 to 1992. His master's degree in education is from Harvard University.

COLLEGE ADMISSION COUNSELING

College placement starts with college counseling, a process that begins at Pomfret during the sophomore year and continues as a refining and defining process until graduation. At all times, it is thought of as an effort that fosters individual social maturity, academic growth, and a deeper commitment to School activities.

All juniors take the PSAT in the fall and the SAT and SAT Subject Tests in the winter and spring.

A complete portrait of each individual's life at Pomfret—social, academic, and extracurricular—and a personal understanding of each student's aspirations enable the college counseling office to provide very close personal attention.

STUDENT BODY AND CONDUCT

Pomfret currently has 268 boarding and 84 day students. There are 54 in the Third Form (grade 9), 95 in the Fourth Form (grade 10), 94 in the Fifth Form (grade 11), and 109 in the Sixth Form (grade 12). The students come from twenty-six states and thirteen countries. Twelve percent of students classify themselves as members of minority groups.

Participation in the student government enables students to assume active leadership roles within the School. A president (a Sixth Former) chairs the government, which is made up of elected representatives from each Form and from the faculty.

Students at Pomfret are expected to follow the School rules outlined in the student handbook. Any infraction of these rules leads to an appearance before the Discipline Committee, which is composed of both students and faculty members and is chaired by the Dean of Students. The committee makes recommendations on discipline to the Headmaster.

ACADEMIC FACILITIES

The School is located on 500 acres, which consist of thirteen playing fields, two turf fields, rolling hills, and woodlands. The principal school buildings are grouped in the middle of the campus. The athletic and student center, which opened in 2004, houses a two-floor student center, study room, snack bar, student radio station, student publications office, and bookstore. It also includes eight international-size squash courts, a wrestling room, a fitness center, locker rooms, an athletic trainer's facility, a trophy room, and offices for the Athletic Director and Director of Student Activities. In addition to the new athletic and student center, Pomfret recently opened a new ice-hockey rink, boathouse, and outdoor tennis center.

The School House contains history and foreign language classrooms, administrative offices, and the recently renovated music center. It is flanked on one side by four brick dormitories and on the other by Hard Auditorium, the center for dramatic and musical productions.

Nearby is the Monell Science Building, with laboratories for biology, chemistry, and physics as well as lecture rooms furnished with video equipment. The Centennial Building (1996) houses all mathematics and English classes as well as two- and three-dimensional art studios, metal and wood shops, and a 125-seat state-of-the-art theater.

The du Pont Library completes the current academic buildings. Along with its 22,000 volumes and the Technology Center, the library provides students with Internet access, a fully automated catalog and circulation system, and more than a dozen online subscription databases that cover a broad spectrum of disciplines with full-text and print capability. In addition, materials from outside the library are available through interlibrary loan.

Other nearby buildings include a dance studio and the Main House, which contains the dining hall, mail room, and health center, which is staffed by 3 registered nurses. The School physician is at the health center in the mornings. Clark Memorial Chapel also occupies a central location on campus.

BOARDING AND GENERAL FACILITIES

Pomfret students are housed in ten dormitories on campus. Four converted homes, four large brick dormitories, Pyne Hall, and Robinson House serve as student residences. A wireless campus connects all Pomfret dormitory rooms, classrooms, faculty apartments, and offices, permitting computer and telephone networking throughout the campus as well as access to e-mail and the Internet in each dorm room. Most students are assigned to double rooms, though some returning students can choose to live in single rooms. All dorms are supervised by live-in faculty dorm parents, each of whom supervises between 7 and 14 students on his or her floor.

ATHLETICS

Athletics at Pomfret are an integral part of the educational experience, and all students are expected to participate each season at the level that is most challenging to them. Coaching responsibilities are shared by most faculty members. In addition, the School employs an athletics trainer.

The goal of the athletics program is to field competitive teams that exhibit discipline, the desire to excel, and pride in themselves and the School.

A varied interscholastic program is offered throughout the academic year. It includes cross-country, field hockey, football, soccer, and volleyball in the fall; basketball, ice hockey, squash, and wrestling in the winter; and baseball, crew, golf, lacrosse, softball, and tennis in the spring. In addition, aerobics, community service, dance, drama, and outdoor education are offered as athletic alternatives.

Pomfret has a fully equipped, 3,000-square-foot fitness center. Under faculty supervision, students are able to supplement their work on the playing field with a complete resistance training or aerobic program.

Students may opt to undertake an independent project for a given season rather than engage in sports.

EXTRACURRICULAR OPPORTUNITIES

Pomfret encourages student participation in a wide range of extracurricular activities. The *Pontefract* (newspaper), *Griffin* (yearbook), and *Manuscripts* (magazine) enjoy good student leadership and participation. An active theater program presents three plays and numerous theater projects each year, including musical productions (staged each winter). Auditions are open to students, faculty members, and local artists.

DAILY LIFE

Classes are held in 50-minute periods with two 80-minute periods scheduled on Monday, Tuesday, Thursday, and Friday. Classes run from 8 to 3:15. Sports practices are scheduled in the afternoons from 3:45 to 5:45. The class day ends at 12:25 p.m. on Wednesdays and at 11:30 a.m. on Saturdays. Evening study hours are 8 to 10 p.m., Sunday through Friday. Students study in their rooms. Lights-out is at 10:30 for Third and Fourth Formers and Fifth and Sixth Formers are expected to be in their rooms at 11.

The academic year, which is divided into trimesters, begins in early September and ends in early June, with vacations scheduled for one week at Thanksgiving, two weeks at Christmas, and two weeks in March.

WEEKEND LIFE

Most students prefer to remain at school on the weekends to enjoy time with friends and take advantage of the scheduled activities. On Saturday afternoons, there are interscholastic athletics contests. Students appreciate the local area, which combines rural beauty with elegant shopping and café dining. They also enjoy Sunday trips to Boston, Vermont ski slopes, and area shopping malls and movie theaters. Indoor and outdoor movie nights, concerts, dances, and other special events on campus at Pomfret School are always popular.

The student lounge, tuck shop, indoor tennis courts, squash courts, and gymnasium are open and available seven days a week. On Sundays, students are invited but not required to attend a chapel service or a local church service. Brunch is served at 10. The weekend officially ends on Sunday before dinner. There are regular study hours on Sunday evening in preparation for Monday classes.

COSTS AND FINANCIAL AID

In 2010–11, tuition is $46,500 for boarding students and $29,000 for day students. Costs for textbooks, stationery, athletics equipment, laundry, and dry cleaning are charged separately through a student debit account. For families who qualify, $3.4 million in need-based financial aid is available.

ADMISSIONS INFORMATION

Pomfret seeks students whose past achievement indicates that they could benefit from and contribute to life at the School. Pomfret gives prime consideration to those applicants who possess academic ability, interest in the arts and/or athletics, and a willingness to become involved in and supportive of the Pomfret School community.

Each applicant must submit an application, come to Pomfret for an interview, and take the SSAT by January 15. Notification to prospective students is made on March 10.

Pomfret School admits students of any race, color, creed, handicap, gender, sexual orientation, or national origin to all the rights, privileges, programs, and activities generally accorded or made available to students at the School. The School does not discriminate on the basis of race, color, religion, disability, gender, sexual orientation, age, marital status, national origin, or any other status protected by law in the administration of its educational or admissions policies, financial aid, or other programs.

APPLICATION TIMETABLE

Initial inquiries are welcome at any time, and tours and interviews can be arranged by calling the Admissions Office. Office hours are 8 to 4 Monday through Friday and 8 to noon on Saturdays with classes. School catalogs and applications can be obtained from the Admissions Office or on the Web site at http://www.pomfretschool.org.

Pomfret adheres to the Parents' Reply Date of April 10. Thus, a place that has been offered on March 10 is reserved until April 10. Late applications (those to which it is not possible to reply by March 10) are accepted and acted upon as soon as possible and as enrollment permits.

ADMISSIONS CORRESPONDENCE

Rachel Tilney
Director of Admissions and Financial Aid
Pomfret School
398 Pomfret Street
P.O. Box 128
Pomfret, Connecticut 06258-0128

Phone: 860-963-6120
Fax: 860-963-2042
E-mail: admission@pomfretschool.org
Web site: http://www.pomfretschool.org

RANNEY SCHOOL
Tinton Falls, New Jersey

Type: Coeducational college-preparatory day school
Grades: BG (3 years old)–grade 12: Lower School, BG–Grade 5; Middle School, Grades 6–8; Upper School, Grades 9–12
Enrollment: School total: 807
Head of School: Lawrence S. Sykoff, Ed.D.

THE SCHOOL

Ranney School was founded in 1960 by Russell G. Ranney for the purpose of fostering high academic achievement. A former Associate Director of the New York University Reading Institute, Mr. Ranney was a firm believer in the three R's. A 16-member Board of Trustees, plus the Head of School, supervises the School's operation on its campus of more than 60 acres in a residential neighborhood located approximately 45 miles south of New York City.

The purpose of Ranney School is to prepare its students for college and to encourage them to become independent and self-reliant young adults. The School believes a well-prepared student is one who is inquisitive, knows how to acquire knowledge, and exercises sound judgment and common sense in all matters.

The Board of Trustees is the School's governing body. During 2009–10, annual giving totaled $385,000; annual operating expenses average $19 million.

Ranney School alumni number approximately 1,555; an Alumni Council oversees alumni activities.

Ranney School is accredited by the Middle States Association of Colleges and Schools. The School maintains active membership in the National Association of Independent Schools (NAIS), the New Jersey Association of Independent Schools (NJAIS), the Council for Advancement and Support of Education (CASE), the Educational Records Bureau (ERB), and the National Association for College Admission Counseling (NACAC).

ACADEMIC PROGRAMS

The Lower School (Beginners (age 3) through grade 5) curriculum is designed to stimulate a child's natural love of learning. Goals are set forth in a program consistent with the early stages of child development. The primary goal is to maximize the growth of each individual. The curriculum remains rooted in the development of language arts. Course time is allotted to vocabulary building, spelling, grammar usage, reading, and the development of writing skills. Strong programs in mathematics, science, social studies, instrumental music, and computer education complement these courses. Students are also introduced to studies in the fine arts, music, and foreign languages. Aquatics and physical education complete the course of study. Teaching strategies include cooperative learning, interdisciplinary arrangements, and individual attention.

The Middle School (grades 6 through 8) curriculum is designed to provide a special community in which students can grow, learn about themselves, develop personal and group values, and prepare for the challenges of higher learning, particularly within the Ranney Upper School. The comprehensive English and mathematics programs initiated in the Lower School continue through the middle years, along with additional concentrations in science, history, and foreign languages, including a foundation in Latin. Courses in computer fundamentals, art, music, drama, word processing, physical education, and aquatics are part of the total curriculum. To provide flexibility in instruction, some classes in math, history, and foreign languages are arranged to cover the curriculum over a two-year period.

The Upper School (grades 9 through 12) graduation requirements include a minimum of 20 academic credits, plus 4 units in health and physical education. All students are expected to take 5 full credits of course work each year. Specific requirements include English (4 credits), foreign language (3 credits), history (3 credits, 1 of which must be American history), mathematics (3 credits), science (2 credits with lab, including biology and either chemistry or physics), art (1 credit), and physical education (4 credits). In addition to required courses, a number of single-semester and full-year electives are available to sophomores, juniors, and seniors. The Upper School curriculum also offers many honors and college-level Advanced Placement (AP) courses. Nineteen AP units are available to students who are capable of accelerated study.

Ranney utilizes the letter grade system (A through F). The school year consists of two semesters and four marking periods, with grades and written evaluations being sent home at the end of the first and third marking periods. Report cards with grades only are sent at the end of each semester. Midterm exams are given in January and final exams in June.

FACULTY AND ADVISERS

There are 94 full-time faculty members, plus 2 part-time instructors. Forty faculty members have master's degrees or higher. Each Middle and Upper School faculty member serves as an adviser to an average of 6 to 8 students. Ranney faculty members are accomplished and recognized professionals whose contributions to the growth and status of their calling often extend outside the School community.

Dr. Lawrence S. Sykoff was appointed Headmaster in June 1993. He holds degrees from the University of San Diego (Ed.D. and M.Ed.) and Baruch College of Business Administration of the City University of New York (B.B.A.).

COLLEGE ADMISSION COUNSELING

The College Guidance Office assists in planning family visits to colleges. It schedules visits with college admission representatives, many of whom visit Ranney each year to interview prospective students. Juniors attend various college fairs to gather information about colleges throughout the country.

Early in the sophomore year, students take the PSATs. In the junior year, group and individual meetings with students and parents are held to assist in the college selection process. During the summer prior to their senior year, students meet with the Director of College Guidance to formulate a list of college choices and devise a plan of action for the senior year. As the application process reaches its peak in the fall of that year, students receive individual help and encouragement. All seniors receive assistance from the Director of College Guidance in writing college essays and preparing their final applications.

The mean SAT scores for 2010 graduates were 620 critical reading, 630 writing, and 600 math.

The senior class of 2010 achieved 100 percent college acceptance at schools such as Barnard, Columbia, Duke, Emory, Lehigh, and NYU.

STUDENT BODY AND CONDUCT

The 2010–11 student body consisted of 807 students, as follows: 174 boys and 175 girls in the Lower School, 117 boys and 110 girls in the Middle School, and 111 boys and 120 girls in the Upper School.

Ranney's families represent many different countries, including China, India, Japan, and Russia. The School sponsors an International Week of Celebration each year in all three divisions.

A Judicial Board handles routine disciplinary issues in the Upper School. The board consists of 2 faculty members and 2 students and is chaired by the Dean of Students. Recommendations are given to the Principal and the Headmaster for review and decision.

ACADEMIC FACILITIES

The Lower School is composed of three buildings and has its own computer lab, science lab, and library. Each classroom is equipped with two computers, and all computers are connected to the network and the Internet. The Middle School and Upper School are housed in Ranney's modern and high-tech academic complex. The facility offers thirty-three classrooms, state-of-the-art biology and chemistry laboratories, a foreign language laboratory, a college guidance center, a modern library, student assembly areas, 300 computers, and a unique Distance Learning Center. The entire building is wired for the Internet. In addition, the Middle and Upper Schools have their own dining hall.

ATHLETICS

Ranney School encourages students to participate in sports and views athletics as an important part of the educational program. All students are eligible to participate regardless of ability. The middle and upper divisions field teams in soccer, cross-country, tennis, basketball, swimming, baseball, softball, golf, and lacrosse. Ranney competes against other accredited public and private schools in the area and maintains active membership in the New Jersey Prep Conference and the New Jersey State Interscholastic Athletic Association. Interscholastic competition begins in the sixth grade. The School has two gymnasiums, a 25-meter indoor swimming pool, new tennis courts, two baseball fields, and brand-new athletic facilities, including a synthetic turf field and a state-of-the-art track. In addition there is a new fitness center with a certified athletic trainer on duty.

EXTRACURRICULAR OPPORTUNITIES

The Lower School offers a variety of extracurricular and after-school activities for grades 2 through 5, including computers, art instruction, creative writing, chorus, band, cooking, swimming, and other sports.

Both the Middle and Upper Schools have a broad selection of student organizations in which to participate. Both schools have a student council, foreign language clubs, and excellent forensics teams. Students in grades 6 through 9 are eligible to join the Science Olympiad Team, which travels to Rider University for participation in the New Jersey State Science Olympiad.

The Upper School has an active chapter of the National Honor Society. Students can also participate in Mock Trial, math, chess, and academic bowl teams. Chorus and drama clubs offer students an opportunity to perform for friends, parents, and peers. Publications include *Horizons* (the School's award-winning yearbook), *The Torch*, and *RSVP (Ranney School Verse & Prose)*, which showcases the talents of Ranney's young artists and authors.

Throughout the year, the Ranney School Fine Arts Department and Thespian Troupe present art exhibitions, music recitals, and two major drama productions. Traditional events include Spirit Day/Homecoming, International Week, Halloween Parade, Grandparents' Thanksgiving Feast, Parents' Day Tea, and Lower, Middle, and Upper School Carnivals (fund-raisers). Field trips, both inter-state and intrastate, offer cultural exposure outside the Ranney campus for students in the middle and upper divisions.

DAILY LIFE

The typical school day consists of six 45-minute academic periods and one 60-minute period, with a 10-minute break between second and third periods, plus a lunch period. Assemblies are held throughout the year. Each week, grades 6–12 meet with their advisers for approximately 20 minutes during an adviser period. School begins at 8:25 a.m. and ends at 3:25 p.m. The cafeteria serves hot and cold lunches. Bus transportation is available to most students.

SUMMER PROGRAMS

Students can enroll for two through six weeks to take enhancement and/or credit courses in several academic subject areas. Most courses are taught by Ranney School faculty members. In addition, an eight-, six-, or four-week summer day camp program is available for boys and girls ages 3 through 13. Ranney-in-the-Summer is fully accredited by the American Camping Association.

COSTS AND FINANCIAL AID

Tuition for 2010–11 ranges from $10,550 to $24,410. Extras include books (Lower School: $150–$550; Middle School: $400–$650; Upper School: $600–$900) and transportation ($4000–$4500). Parents of students in grades pre-K through 12 are required to purchase a $1000 bond, which is redeemed when the child either graduates or leaves Ranney School.

Ranney School is committed to awarding financial aid to those students who demonstrate a financial need. Families who feel that a need for assistance exists are encouraged to apply. The Financial Aid Committee of the Board of Trustees bases financial aid decisions on the formula provided by the School and Student Service for Financial Aid (SSS) in Princeton, New Jersey. The Financial Aid Committee diligently reviews each application in order to distribute available funds equitably. All applications are held in strict confidence. Each student applying for aid must be in good standing in all aspects of student life. Parents must complete the SSS financial aid form annually and should send it to Princeton as early as possible. Inquiries should be directed to the Associate Head for Admissions and Marketing.

Parents can arrange to pay the tuition over a ten-month period through Tuition Management Services. An enrollment deposit must be paid directly to the School upon registration.

ADMISSIONS INFORMATION

Standardized placement tests are administered on an individual or small-group basis. Transferring students should forward a completed application and appropriate school records to the Admission Office prior to the scheduled date of the placement exam. All candidates must complete an interview with appropriate members of the Admission Committee. Ranney School does not discriminate on the basis of sex, race, religion, ethnic origin, or disabilities in the administration of its education, hiring, and admission policies; financial aid program; and athletic or other School-administered programs.

APPLICATION TIMETABLE

Ranney School does not stipulate a formal application deadline, but it strongly recommends that parents contact the Admission Office during the fall to enroll for the next academic year. There is a $75 application fee.

ADMISSIONS CORRESPONDENCE

Heather Rudisi, Associate Head for Admissions and Marketing
Ranney School
235 Hope Road
Tinton Falls, New Jersey 07724

Phone: 732-542-4777 Ext. 1107
Fax: 732-460-1078
E-mail: hrudisi@ranneyschool.com
Web site: http://www.ranneyschool.org

RYE COUNTRY DAY SCHOOL

Rye, New York

Type: Coeducational day college-preparatory school
Grades: P–12: Lower School, Prekindergarten–4; Middle School, 5–8; Upper School, 9–12
Enrollment: School total: 876; Upper School: 385
Head of School: Scott A. Nelson, Headmaster

THE SCHOOL

Founded in 1869, Rye Country Day School (RCDS) is entering its 141st year. Reflecting and reaffirming the School's purposes, the mission statement states, "Rye Country Day School is a coeducational, college-preparatory school dedicated to providing students from Pre-Kindergarten through Grade Twelve with an excellent education using both traditional and innovative approaches. In a nurturing and supportive environment, we offer a challenging program that stimulates individuals to achieve their maximum potential through academic, athletic, creative, and social endeavors. We are actively committed to diversity. We expect and promote moral responsibility, and strive to develop strength of character within a respectful school community. Our goal is to foster a lifelong passion for learning, understanding, and service in an ever-changing world."

The 26-acre campus is located in Rye at the junction of routes I-95 and I-287, one block from the train station. The School's location, 25 miles from Manhattan, provides easy access to both New York City and to a suburban setting with ample playing fields and open spaces. Through frequent field trips, internships, and community service projects, the School takes considerable advantage of the cultural opportunities in the New York metropolitan area.

A nonprofit, nonsectarian institution, Rye Country Day is governed by a 26-member Board of Trustees that includes parents and alumni. The annual operating budget is $24.5 million, and the physical plant assets have a book value in excess of $54 million. Annual gifts from parents, alumni, and friends amount to more than $5.7 million. The endowment of the School is valued at more than $21 million.

Rye Country Day School is accredited by the Middle States Association of Colleges and Schools and the New York State Association of Independent Schools and is chartered and registered by the New York State Board of Regents. It is a member of the National Association of Independent Schools, the New York State Association of Independent Schools, the Educational Records Bureau, the College Board, and the National Association for College Admission Counseling.

ACADEMIC PROGRAMS

Leading to the college-preparatory program of the Upper School, the program in the Middle School (grades 5–8) emphasizes the development of skills and the acquisition of information needed for success at the secondary school level by exposing students to a wide range of opportunities. The academic program is fully departmentalized. Spanish or French is offered to all students in grades 2–5. Starting in grade 6 students may choose Latin or Mandarin Chinese or continue with Spanish or French. The math, foreign language, and writing programs lead directly into the Upper School curriculum. Programs in art, music (vocal and instrumental), computer use, and dramatics are offered in all grades. Students in kindergarten through grade 6 are scheduled for sports for 45 to 75 minutes daily, and a full interscholastic sports program is available to both boys and girls in grades 7 and 8, and in the Upper School.

Sixteen courses are required for Upper School graduation, including 4 years of English, 3 years of mathematics, 3 years of one foreign language, 2 years of science, and 2 years of history. Students entering the School by grade 9 must complete ½ unit in art and music survey, and ½ unit in the arts. Seniors must successfully complete an off-campus June-term community service program. In addition, seniors must satisfactorily complete 1 unit in the senior humanities seminar. Students are expected to carry five academic courses per year.

Full-year courses in English include English 9, 10, and 11; major American writers; English and American literature; and creative and expository writing. Required mathematics courses are algebra I, algebra II, trigonometry, and geometry. Regular course work extends through calculus BC, and tutorials are available for more advanced students. Yearlong courses in science are environmental science, biology, chemistry, and physics. Science courses are laboratory based. The computer department offers beginning and advanced programming, software applications courses, desktop publishing, and independent study opportunities.

The modern language department offers five years of Mandarin Chinese, French, and Spanish, and the classics department teaches five years of Latin. History courses include world civilizations, U.S. history, government, and modern European history. Semester electives in the humanities include philosophy, psychology, government, and economics.

In the arts, full-year courses in studio art, art history, and music theory are available. Participation in the Concert Choir and Wind Ensemble earns students full academic credit. Semester courses in drawing, printmaking, sculpture, graphic design, ceramics, and photography are available. The drama department offers electives in technique, history, oral presentation, technical theater, and dance.

Advanced Placement courses leading to the AP examinations are offered in biology, psychology, environmental science, chemistry, physics, statistics, calculus, English, government, U.S. and modern European history, French, Spanish, Latin, music theory, art, and computer science. Honors sections are scheduled in tenth- and eleventh-grade English, math, physics, biology, and chemistry, and in foreign languages at all levels. Independent study is available in grades 11 and 12 in all disciplines.

The student-teacher ratio is 8:1, and the average class size in the Upper School is 12. Extra help is provided for students as needed.

The year is divided into two semesters. Examinations are given in March. Grades are scaled from A to F and are given four times a year. Written comments accompany grades at the end of each quarter.

Academic classes travel to New York City and other areas to supplement classroom work. Although not a graduation requirement, all students are involved in community service programs. Semester class projects as well as individual experiences involve work with local charities and schools, YMCA, Midnight Run, United Cerebral Palsy, Big Brother-Big Sister, Doctors Without Borders, AmeriCares, and numerous local organizations.

Students in grades 7–12 are required to have laptop computers. The campus supports wireless Internet connection and provides appropriate filters for student and faculty educational use. A technology department supports and updates the network and assists students with software and hardware issues. Students receiving financial aid awards receive new laptop computers from the school which are replaced every three years.

FACULTY AND ADVISERS

The Upper School faculty consists of 65 full-time teachers—35 men and 30 women, the large majority of whom hold at least one advanced degree. The average length of service is eight years, and annual faculty turnover averages fewer than 6 teachers.

Scott A. Nelson became Headmaster in 1993. He holds a B.A. from Brown University and an M.A. from Fordham University. Prior to his appointment at Rye, he served as Upper School Director both at the Marlborough School in Los Angeles and at the Hackley School in Tarrytown, New York. Mr. Nelson and his family reside on campus.

Nearly all faculty members in the Middle and Upper Schools serve as advisers for 5 to 12 students each. In addition to helping students select courses, faculty advisers monitor the students' progress in all areas of school life and provide ongoing support. The advisers also meet with students' parents at various times throughout the year.

Rye Country Day seeks faculty members who are effective teachers in their field and who, by virtue of their sincere interest in the students' overall well-being, will further the broad goals of the School's philosophy. The School supports the continuing education of its faculty through grants and summer sabbaticals totaling more than $330,000 a year.

COLLEGE ADMISSION COUNSELING

The college selection process is supervised by a full-time Director of College Counseling and an Associate Director. Advising is done in groups and on an individual basis, with the staff meeting with

www.facebook.com/sec.schools

both students and their families. More than 100 college representatives visit the campus each year.

The 97 graduates of the class of 2010 enrolled in fifty-four colleges and universities, including Barnard, Bowdoin, Brown, Caltech, Chicago, Colgate, Columbia, Dartmouth, Davidson, Duke, Georgetown, Michigan, Middlebury, MIT, Northwestern, Notre Dame, Pennsylvania, St. Andrew's (U.K.), Stanford, Texas, Tufts, Vanderbilt, Vassar, Wake Forest, Washington (St. Louis), Washington and Lee, Wesleyan, Williams, and Yale.

STUDENT BODY AND CONDUCT
The Upper School enrollment for 2010–11 totaled 385: 200 boys and 185 girls. There were 95 students in grade 9, 94 in grade 10, 99 in grade 11, and 97 in grade 12. Members of minority groups represented 28 percent of the student body in grades 5–12. Students came from more than forty different school districts in Westchester and Fairfield Counties as well as New York City. Students holding citizenship in fourteen countries are enrolled.

While School regulations are few, the School consciously and directly emphasizes a cooperative, responsible, and healthy community life. The Student Council plays a major role in administering School organizations and activities. Minor disciplinary problems are handled by the Division Principal or Grade Level Dean; more serious matters in the Upper School may be brought before the Disciplinary Committee. There is student representation on the Academic Affairs and other major committees.

ACADEMIC FACILITIES
Academic facilities at Rye Country Day School include the Main Building (1927) and Main Building Addition (2002), with separate areas for kindergarten through grade 4, grades 5 and 6, and grades 7 and 8. The Lower and Middle School divisions have separate art, computer, and science facilities.

The Upper School is housed in the Pinkham Building (1964), which was completely renovated in 2010. The new 14,000-square-foot addition includes a 140-seat auditorium, a college counseling center, faculty offices, classrooms, and three science labs.

There are two libraries on campus—the Lower School Library (2002) and the Klingenstein Library (1984), which serves the Middle and Upper School divisions. The Klingenstein Library contains more than 25,000 volumes with fully automated circulation and collection management technology. Resources include significant periodical and reference materials that are available via direct online services and the Internet, CD-ROM, and substantial videotape collection.

The school has invested in technology infrastructure and classroom SmartBoards in all three divisions. Laptop computers, which are required for all students in grades 7 through 12, are used extensively throughout the curriculum. Access to the RCDS network and Internet is via a campuswide wireless network. In total, there are 650 networked computers on campus.

The performing arts programs are housed in the Dunn Performing Arts Center (1990), which includes a 400-seat theater-auditorium and classroom spaces for vocal music, instrumental music, and a dance studio. There also are five music practice rooms which adjunct faculty use for private music lessons.

ATHLETICS
Rye Country Day's athletic program offers seventy-two interscholastic teams for students in grades 7 through 12. Varsity competition includes boys' and girls' teams in soccer, cross-country, basketball, ice hockey, fencing, squash, tennis, golf, and lacrosse, as well as football, field hockey, wrestling, baseball, softball, and coed sailing. Approximately 70 percent of the students participate in at least one team sport.

The physical education department offers classes in aerobics, CPR, ice skating, kickboxing, squash, tennis, weight training, yoga, and dance.

Athletic facilities include the LaGrange Field House (1972) with its indoor ice rink/tennis courts; the Nelson Athletic Center (2000), which houses a two-court gymnasium, four squash courts, four locker rooms, and an athletic training facility; and a state-of-the-art fitness center. Between 2007 and 2009, the School installed four artificial turf fields, making it the premier outdoor athletic facility in the area.

EXTRACURRICULAR OPPORTUNITIES
More than thirty-five extracurricular activities are available. Students can choose vocal music (Concert Choir, Madrigal Singers, and solfeggio classes) and instrumental music (Wind Ensemble, Concert Band, and Jazz Band). Many of these offerings have curricular status. The performance groups give local concerts and occasionally travel to perform at schools and universities here and abroad. In addition, 10 professional instructors offer private instrumental and voice lessons during and after the school day. The drama department presents major productions three times a year. Recent productions have included *The Laramie Project*, *South Pacific*, *Dark of the Moon*, *The Mystery of Edwin Drood*, *Macbeth*, *The Pajama Game*, *The Arabian Nights*, *Anything Goes*, *Alice in Wonderland*, *Urinetown*, *Museum*, and *Bye Bye Birdie*.

Student publications include a yearbook, newspaper, literary magazine, graphic arts and photography magazines, and a public affairs journal, each of which is composed using student publications desktop publishing facilities. The School's Web site (http://www.ryecountryday.org) is an ever-changing location for student- and staff-provided information on and perspectives of the School. Students participate in Model Congress programs on campus and at other schools and colleges. The School has a dynamic community service program that embodies the RCDS motto: "Not for self, but for service." Students also participate in many other activities and School organizations, including foreign language, mock trial, debate, theater, sports, and computer clubs.

DAILY LIFE
Beginning each day at 8:05, the Upper School utilizes a six-day schedule cycle. Most courses meet five of the six days, with one or two longer, 70-minute periods per cycle. The day includes an activity/meeting period and two lunch periods as well as seven class periods. Class periods end at 2:50, and team sport practices and games begin at 3:30. Breakfast and lunch may be purchased in the school dining room; seniors may have lunch off campus. Study halls are required for grade 9.

SUMMER PROGRAMS
The Rye Country Day Summer School enrolls approximately 200 students—grades 6 to postgraduate—in remedial, enrichment, and advanced-standing courses. Some courses prepare students for the New York State Regents exams that may be taken at the local public schools. The program is six weeks long and runs on a five-period schedule from 8 a.m. to noon, Monday through Friday. Tuition averages $1200 per course. A brochure is available after April 1 from the Director of the Summer School or on the School's Web site.

In addition to the Summer School, Rye conducts a summer program, ACTION, for students in grades 6–8 from nearby Westchester communities. Fifty students from minority groups enroll in a four-week program that emphasizes academic enrichment in the areas including writing, math, leadership, and computer use.

COSTS AND FINANCIAL AID
Tuition for grade 9 for 2010–11 is $31,500. Additional charges are made for textbooks, lunches, sports, field trips, and private music lessons, as appropriate.

Tuition aid is available on a need basis. For 2010–11, 124 students received a total of more than $3.3 million in aid. All aid applications are processed through the School and Student Service for Financial Aid.

ADMISSIONS INFORMATION
Students are accepted in all grades. In 2010–11, 17 new students enrolled in the ninth grade, 10 in the tenth grade, and 1 in the eleventh grade. Academic readiness is a prerequisite; a diversity of skills and interests, as well as general academic aptitude, is eagerly sought. The School seeks and enrolls students of all backgrounds; a diverse student body is an important part of the School's educational environment.

Required in the admissions process are the results of the Educational Records Bureau's ISEE or the Secondary School Admission Test (SSAT); the student's school record; and school and faculty recommendations. A visit to the campus and an interview are also required.

APPLICATION TIMETABLE
Inquiries are welcome throughout the year. Interviews and tours of the campus begin in late September. To be considered in initial admissions decisions, applicants must fully complete the Application by December 15. All other parts of the Application Folder (transcripts, testing, recommendation forms, interview, etc.) are due by January 15. Candidates whose Application Folders are complete by that date are notified by approximately February 15. Applications received after December 15 are evaluated on a rolling basis.

ADMISSIONS CORRESPONDENCE
Matthew J. M. Suzuki, Director of Admissions
Rye Country Day School
Cedar Street
Rye, New York 10580-2034
Phone: 914-925-4513
Fax: 914-921-2147
E-mail: matt_suzuki@ryecountryday.org
Web site: http://www.ryecountryday.org

ST. ANDREW'S SCHOOL

Barrington, Rhode Island

Type: Coeducational boarding and day college-preparatory school
Grades: 3–12: Lower School, 3–5; Middle School, 6–8; Upper School and Boarding, 9–12
Enrollment: School total: 213; Upper School: 162
Head of School: John D. Martin

THE SCHOOL

St. Andrew's School is a coeducational boarding and day school for students in grades 3–12, with the boarding program starting in the ninth grade. The School is located on a 100-acre campus in Barrington (population 16,000), a suburban community 10 miles southeast of Providence on Narragansett Bay. The campus contains open space and woodlands. Its proximity to Providence and Newport, as well as Boston, offers a wide variety of cultural opportunities for students.

St. Andrew's School was founded in 1893 by Rev. William Merrick Chapin as a school for homeless boys. From these simple beginnings through its years as a working farm school to its present role as a coeducational boarding and day college preparatory school, St. Andrew's steadfastly maintains the same sense of purpose and concern for the individual. The curriculum is designed primarily to prepare students for college, with emphasis on helping them to develop stronger academic skills, study habits, and self-esteem.

St. Andrew's is designated a School of Distinction by the nationally recognized All Kinds of Minds institute. Every St. Andrew's teacher is trained to teach using a multisensory approach for the different ways students may learn. St. Andrew's students find that when they get to college, they are well prepared to handle the course work because they have a true understanding of how they learn and an awareness of the tools they need to achieve their best.

St. Andrew's School is a nonsectarian, nonprofit corporation. A Board of Trustees governs the School; this 21-member board meets five times a year. The School's physical plant is valued at approximately $23 million. The School's endowment is currently valued at more than $17 million.

St. Andrew's is accredited by the New England Association of Schools and Colleges. It is a member of the National Association of Independent Schools, the Association of Independent Schools in New England, the Association of Boarding Schools, and the Independent Schools Association of Rhode Island.

ACADEMIC PROGRAMS

St. Andrew's School believes that every student can find success in the classroom. With a 5:1 student-teacher ratio, the average class size at St. Andrew's is 10 students. Small classes, along with twice-daily adviser meetings, help to ensure that no student is overlooked. The homelike community, nurturing environment, and hands-on approach to learning and teaching help maintain close student-teacher relationships.

To graduate from the Upper School, a student must complete 26 credits: 24 academic credits and 2 credits in physical education. Students are expected to take course work in English, math, science, social studies, and physical education each year. Preparation in a foreign language is also highly recommended. Students may only have one study hall in their schedule. Seniors must pass the equivalent of five full-credit courses in order to graduate. Specific minimum requirements for Upper School students are 4 credits in English, 3 credits in social studies

(including 1 in U.S. history), 3 credits in mathematics, 3 credits in science (including 2 in a lab science), 2 credits in physical education, 1 credit in art, and 10 elective credits. An English as a Second Language (ESL) Program is provided for international students. The School's computer network, which is available to all students, provides Internet access from all classrooms, dorm rooms, and offices.

The School's Learning Services program (certified by the State of Rhode Island and Providence Plantations) for students who have been identified with language-based learning differences or attentional challenges is taught by certified learning support teachers. All students enrolled in a program receive instruction and support to enable academic success in the School's college-preparatory course of study. An Individual Education Plan is designed and updated annually with input from the student, family, and each teacher. This plan identifies both the skills and support to be provided throughout the year to guide learning success. Individualized programs are available to support the advancement of reading, writing, speech and language, and study skills (e.g., materials management, test preparation, focus and homework strategies, time management, organization, and planning).

St. Andrew's School is one of the first schools selected by All Kinds of Minds, a national nonprofit organization based in North Carolina, to receive its School of Distinction designation. This prestigious award recognizes schools around the world that have embraced the organization's vision that when schools teach to how minds are wired to learn, every student can find success in school and life.

The school year runs on a semester basis. Students are evaluated frequently by their teachers so that each student's progress is monitored closely throughout the year. Each advisee meets twice a day with his or her adviser to discuss issues pertaining to the student's academic progress and his or her involvement in the School community. Advisers communicate with families every three weeks by phone or e-mail.

FACULTY AND ADVISERS

The faculty numbers 48, with 20 men and 28 women. Twenty reside with their families on campus and seven of them serve as dorm parents. All full-time faculty members serve as advisers. John D. Martin was appointed Head of School on July 1, 1996, and has an extensive background in independent schools, including teaching and administrative positions at Sewickley Academy, Peddie School, and Tabor Academy. He holds a Master of Divinity degree from Yale University, a Master of Education degree from American International College, and a Bachelor of Arts degree from Tufts University.

COLLEGE ADMISSION COUNSELING

All of St. Andrew's graduates enter four-year colleges, two-year colleges, post-graduate programs, or technical schools upon graduation each year. Goal setting, short- and long-term planning, and informal discussions about careers and postsecondary plans are ongoing between students and advisers from the moment a student enters the Upper School. Formal

college counseling begins in the eleventh grade. The college counselor works with students and their parents to assist in determining the best steps for each student. The advisers and other faculty members assist the college counselor in assessing each student's options. PSATs are given in the fall of sophomore year and again at the start of junior year. SATs should be taken during the junior and senior years. College representatives visit the campus throughout the year to meet with interested students.

St. Andrew's graduates have matriculated to the following colleges and universities in the last three years: Boston College, Bryant, Emmanuel, Emory, George Washington, Iona, Ithaca, New England College, Parsons School of Design, Providence, Purdue, Randolph-Macon, Rhode Island College, Roger Williams, Savannah College of Art and Design, Simmons, Syracuse, and the Universities of Illinois, Louisville, Maine, Massachusetts, Minnesota, Rhode Island, Vermont, and Wisconsin.

STUDENT BODY AND CONDUCT

The School enrolls both boarding and day students. Approximately one third of the Upper School population boards. Approximately 25 percent of the School's population is enrolled in the Lower and Middle Schools, and less than 40 percent of the School's population participates in the Resource/Focus Programs.

Over the years, St. Andrew's School has attracted boarding students from all corners of the United States and other countries, including China, France, Germany, India, Israel, Jamaica, Japan, Senegal, South Korea, and Taiwan.

Each student is required to read the *Parent and Student Handbook*, which defines expectations for students within the community. Difficulties, if they arise, are handled according to degree; minor issues are handled by teachers and dorm parents, while major offenses are handled by the Director of Student Life in conjunction with a joint student-faculty disciplinary committee. Faculty advisers play a major role in working with students to help them understand the expectations of them as members of the community.

ACADEMIC FACILITIES

Stone Academic Center (1988) houses fifteen classrooms, a newly renovated resource wing with five classrooms for instruction, a computer lab, academic offices, and a faculty workroom. It is also the site of a new library, which features study carrels, meeting rooms, and computer workstations. Hardy Hall (1898) was renovated in 2008 and houses the Middle School (6–8) and new Lower School (3–5). The classrooms are designed for interactive learning in groups of 5 to 12 students. The George M. Sage Gymnasium (2001) and the Karl P. Jones Gymnasium (1965) each house a full-size gymnasium and locker room facilities. The Annie Lee Steele Adams Memorial Student Service Center (1997) houses the Health Center, classrooms, and additional office space. The David A. Brown '52 Science Center houses four science labs, two regular classrooms, and the office of the Director of College Counseling. The

Norman E. and Dorothy R. McCulloch Center for the Arts (2004) houses a 287-seat theater, two visual art classrooms, a ceramics lab, a music classroom, music practice rooms, a black-box/theater classroom, a computer graphics lab, storage, and theater scene shop.

BOARDING AND GENERAL FACILITIES
Upper School girls live in Cady House (1969) and Coleman House (circa 1795). Upper School boys live in Bill's House (1970) and Perry Hall (1927). Students are assigned to single or double rooms. Each dormitory is supervised by faculty dorm parents, who are aided by the Director of Student Life. Each dorm has a common room, laundry facilities, access to a kitchen area, and ample storage space. Gardiner Hall (1926) houses the Herbert W. Spink Dining Room and the Headmaster's Dining Room. McVickar Hall (1913) contains the Admissions office, the Headmaster's office, the Development and Communications department, and reception area. Peck Hall (circa 1895) contains the Business office. Clark Hall (1899) houses the Student Center, offering students space for entertainment and relaxation. The second floor provides faculty housing.

Coleman House and the Rectory, the Headmaster's house, are late-eighteenth-century buildings that were acquired by the School from two local estates. Both buildings are said to have been stops for travelers on the Underground Railroad. The Rectory has a "hidden" back staircase and room.

ATHLETICS
Upper School students participate in athletics at the completion of each class day. St. Andrew's fields varsity teams in boys' and girls' basketball, cross-country, golf, lacrosse, soccer, and tennis. Intramural sports programs are also offered and include fitness training, weight training, yoga, biking, lawn games, and Project Adventure Ropes Course. St. Andrew's also offers an extensive health and fitness center that comprises separate cardio and weight-training facilities.

EXTRACURRICULAR OPPORTUNITIES
The School's proximity to Providence, Newport, and Boston provides a myriad of cultural and recreational activities. Students may take advantage of museums, movies, concerts, plays, rock climbing, skating, bowling, skiing, and professional and collegiate sporting events. Among the on-campus extracurricular activities are theater, photography, debate club, and yearbook. The St. Andrew's Parent Association (SAPA) organizes a wide variety of social activities for students throughout the year, from dances to laser tag to paintball to barbecues.

DAILY LIFE
Boarding students generally rise at about 7 a.m. and are responsible for making their beds, cleaning their rooms, and performing other assorted dorm chores. Breakfast is served at 7:30 and is a favorite gathering time for day and boarding students alike. Students assemble for Morning Meeting at 8 and then meet in their advising groups. Classes begin at 8:30. Adviser meetings are held again at the end of the day. Activities and athletics begin at 3 p.m. and run until approximately 4. Students may leave the campus between athletics and dinner if they are in good standing in the community. Dinner is at 5:30, and evening study hall is from 7:30 to 9:30. All study halls are proctored by faculty members, who are able to provide extra academic assistance if needed. During study hall, the library is open for those students who need to conduct research.

The Student Center is open on weekdays from 11 a.m. to 1 p.m., all day Saturday, and at other times depending on scheduled special activities.

WEEKEND LIFE
Weekend activities are planned by the Director of Student Life and the Coordinator of Weekend Activities, with student and faculty input. Students choose from an array of on- and off-campus activities, including sporting events, concerts, movies, plays, hayrides, open gymnasium, bicycle riding, skiing, attending performances by special guests on campus, dances, skating, festivals and fairs, hiking, and shopping. Visits to nearby cities and other places of interest are also offered. Boarders may leave for the weekend, with parental permission, either to go home or to visit a day student's family. Each weekend, about 75 percent of the boarding community remains on campus.

COSTS AND FINANCIAL AID
Tuition for a boarder in 2010–11 is $42,900; for a day student, it is $28,300. Additional costs for the Resource and Focus Programs are $9900. The yearly book fee is about $425. Parents of a boarding student should plan to set up an account in the on-campus bank for weekly allowance needs. The amount varies from family to family and student to student.

Approximately 47 percent of students received financial aid for the 2010–11 academic year, with more than $2 million offered in grants and loans. Financial aid is based solely on need. St. Andrew's School is affiliated with School and Student Services by NAIS in Randolph, Massachusetts for financial aid and works in conjunction with this organization to provide an objective and fair basis for awarding financial aid. All required information is due to the School by February 12. Final awards are determined by the School's Financial Aid Committee.

ADMISSIONS INFORMATION
In order to assess the match between student and school and to plan an appropriate academic program, the School requires a tour, a personal interview, an application with a fee of $50 ($100 for international students), a school transcript covering the last three years, three teacher recommendations, and standardized test scores. For applicants to the Resource Program, an educational evaluation and a psychological evaluation (both within eighteen months of potential enrollment) and a current Individualized Education Plan (if applicable) are required. A student applying to the Focus Program must establish a history of attention difficulties and supply the School with a medical diagnosis from a physician and appropriate testing results. International students must also submit results from an SLEP or TOEFL evaluation.

APPLICATION TIMETABLE
Parents and prospective students are encouraged to contact the Admissions Office for information during the fall semester. Because the School considers a visit to the campus and a personal interview with the candidate to be such a critical part of the admissions process, it asks that all families call for an appointment. It is best to visit the School during the fall if considering enrollment for the following September, although the School welcomes campus visitors throughout the year.

St. Andrew's School does not discriminate on the basis of race, creed, gender, or handicap in the administration of policies, practices, and procedures.

Applications are due by January 31. Students are notified of acceptance by March 11, and the School holds a place for accepted students until April 10. Depending on available space, rolling admission may be offered thereafter. A nonrefundable deposit of $1000 is due when students agree to attend and is credited toward tuition.

ADMISSIONS CORRESPONDENCE
R. Scott Telford
Director of Admissions
St. Andrew's School
63 Federal Road
Barrington, Rhode Island 02806

Phone: 401-246-1230
Fax: 401-246-0510
E-mail: inquiry@standrews-ri.org
Web site: http://www.standrews-ri.org

ST. MARK'S SCHOOL OF TEXAS
Dallas, Texas

Type: Boys' day college-preparatory school
Grades: 1–12: Lower School, 1–4; Middle School, 5–8; Upper School, 9–12
Enrollment: School total: 854; Upper School: 367
Head of School: Arnold E. Holtberg, Headmaster

THE SCHOOL

St. Mark's is the descendant of three former Dallas boys' schools: Terrill School (1906–1944), Texas Country Day School (1933–1950), and Cathedral School (1944–1950). St. Mark's was organized in 1950 on the Preston Road campus of Texas Country Day School (TCD) when the Cathedral School merged with TCD. The campus is located on 43 acres in the residential area of North Dallas.

St. Mark's college-preparatory program fosters intellectual, academic, and artistic excellence in young men by offering a broad range of intellectual, artistic, and athletic opportunities for its students. Challenging studies in the sciences, arts, and humanities form the basis of a St. Mark's education. Teachers work to instill an enthusiasm for learning, encourage independent and critical judgment, and demonstrate the methods for making sound inquiries and for effective communications. St. Mark's aims to prepare young men for lives of leadership and responsibility.

St. Mark's Lower School (grades 1–4) is housed in a single building and has approximately 25 faculty members. The program offers diverse learning activities, including academic instruction in Spanish language and culture, language arts, mathematics, science, and social studies; regular instruction in the arts (visual arts, music, creative dramatics); and a developmental physical education program that teaches fundamental skills at a level geared to the age and abilities of the child.

St. Mark's School of Texas is accredited by the Independent Schools Association of the Southwest. Its memberships include the National Association of Independent Schools, the Cum Laude Society, the International Boys' School Coalition, and the College Board.

ACADEMIC PROGRAMS

The academic program in the Upper School is designed to satisfy the most exacting requirements for admission to colleges and universities across the country, but it is more broadly defined by the School and the faculty as preparation for personal independence, enlightenment, and maturity.

There are required courses, Advanced Placement courses, and many electives available. Graduation requirements are 4 years of English, 3 years of a foreign language, 3 years of mathematics, 4 years of physical education or athletics, 3 years of social studies, 3 years of a laboratory science, 1 year in fine arts, a senior exhibition, and 15 hours of community service each Upper School year. Each student takes five classes per year, and some students, with the permission of the Head of the Upper School, may take more.

The individual teaching sections average about 14 students. In most classes, the students are randomly grouped; the notable exceptions are in honors and Advanced Placement courses.

The School operates on a trimester system. Grade reports are given three times a year and are made available to the parents with written comments. Interim reports are also written to help ensure adequate reporting to the parents. Parents are encouraged to communicate at any time with their son's adviser. Only final grades in Upper School classes are recorded for transcript purposes.

FACULTY AND ADVISERS

For the academic year 2010–11, the non-administrative faculty consisted of 98 full-time members; 72 hold master's degrees, and 6 have earned doctoral degrees.

The Headmaster, Arnold E. Holtberg, graduated cum laude from Princeton University in 1970 with a baccalaureate degree in sociology. He also received an M.A. degree in pastoral care and counseling in 1976 from the Lutheran Theological Seminary in Philadelphia, Pennsylvania.

The School seeks to employ faculty members who are willing to participate fully in the many areas of school life. The School compensates teachers in the top 10 percent of independent schools nationally and supports fourteen endowed teaching positions.

COLLEGE ADMISSION COUNSELING

The Director of College Counseling and staff members coordinate college planning and counseling. All Upper School students are encouraged to attend the College Pre-

views, held in September, and are welcome to utilize the college office. Several required college conferences are scheduled with students and parents, beginning in the junior year. The SAT mean scores for the class of 2011 were critical reading, 673; math, 713; and writing, 662.

St. Mark's graduates attend major universities throughout the country. Ten or more students in the Classes of 2006–2010 have enrolled at Dartmouth, Georgetown, Harvard, Northwestern, Princeton, Rice, Southern Methodist, Stanford, Vanderbilt, Washington (St. Louis), Yale, and the Universities of Pennsylvania, Southern California, and Texas at Austin.

STUDENT BODY AND CONDUCT

In 2010–11, there were 97 boys in grade 9, 94 in grade 10, 93 in grade 11, and 83 in grade 12. Since St. Mark's is a day school, almost all of the boys come from the Dallas area. Approximately 39 percent of the boys are students of color.

While the rules that govern the School are published by the School, these rules or guidelines provide only a part of the criteria that determine student behavior. Students are also encouraged to take responsibility for their own actions, with the guidance of the faculty and class sponsors. A faculty- and student-led Discipline Council deals with some disciplinary problems.

Each boy has a faculty adviser who is available for personal counseling and advice and is responsible for reporting to the parents and the School on the student's overall performance.

ACADEMIC FACILITIES

Among the campus buildings are Centennial Hall and the Hoffman Center, both new facilities for fall 2008; the Green-McDermott Science and Mathematics Center; the Cecil and Ida Green Library; Nearburg Hall; the H. Ben Decherd Center for the Arts; the St. Mark's Chapel; Thomas O. Hicks Family Athletic Center; Mullen Family Fitness Center; Wirt Davis Hall; the A. Earl Cullum, Jr., Alumni Commons; and the Athletic Center, which includes the Morris G. Spencer Gymnasium and the Ralph B. Rogers Natatorium. The Cecil and

Ida Green Library houses 56,000 volumes and a state-of-the-art computer laboratory for research and Internet access, which includes online subscription databases. Three professional librarians and a technical assistant staff the library. The School has an integrated campuswide technology network that includes video projection systems in more than 90 percent of the classrooms and numerous labs and access to extensive advanced information systems.

ATHLETICS
Every boy at St. Mark's is required to participate daily in some form of athletics. Upper School boys may select either the physical education program or one of the sports teams.

In physical education, the School is concerned with students' neuromuscular and cardiovascular development, as well as their development of an appreciation of physical fitness, through the specialty classes and intramural program.

The School provides many levels of interscholastic team sports to fit the needs of each student. There are sixteen different sports that are available to Middle and Upper School students, including baseball, basketball, crew, cross-country, cheerleading, fencing, football, golf, lacrosse, soccer, swimming, tennis, track and field, volleyball, water polo, and wrestling. For the 2009–10 school year, St. Mark's was awarded the Athletic Director's trophy for the best overall boys' athletic program in the Southwest Preparatory Conference.

EXTRACURRICULAR OPPORTUNITIES
Students at St. Mark's are encouraged to do more than excel in their academic subjects. Boys have the opportunity to participate in speech and debate, the Student Council, the mathematics team, the robotics team, the School's yearbook and newspaper, drama activities, the environmental club, the letterman's club, the Cum Laude Society, the Lion and Sword Society, the tutorial program, the astronomy club, the School's literary magazine, and many other activities.

DAILY LIFE
The school day begins at 8 a.m. for all boys and ends at 3:55 p.m. for grades 9–12. Most of the classes, except science and fine arts, last 45 minutes. Sports and extracurricular activities for grades 9–12 are from 4 to 6 p.m.

COSTS AND FINANCIAL AID
In 2010–11, tuition, including textbooks and supplies, lunches, and fees, was $24,503 for grade 9, $23,020 for grades 10 and 11, and $23,766 for grade 12. At the time of enrollment, a deposit of $1000 is due with the signed enrollment contract, and the balance of the tuition is due by July 1 prior to entrance in August.

The awarding of financial aid is based upon the student's financial need. Approximately 19 percent of the students receive financial aid. Parents are expected to furnish all of the financial information, as requested by the financial aid committee. Specific details are available from the Office of Admission.

ADMISSIONS INFORMATION
Applicants receive information about the School upon request or at the School's Web site at http://www.smtexas.org. Parents are asked to file an application, obtain a teacher's recommendation, and send a transcript of the applicant's prior work. Applicants take general aptitude, reading comprehension, vocabulary, and mathematics tests. A writing sample and on-campus interviews are also required. The application fee is $50 for grade 1 and $125 for grades 2–12.

APPLICATION TIMETABLE
Inquiries are welcome at any time. Group tours and individual tours are recommended. Applications should be submitted by December for grade 1 and by November for grades 2 through 4. Applications for grades 5 through 12 are due in January. Testing and interviewing are completed in February, and decision letters are mailed in mid-March.

ADMISSIONS CORRESPONDENCE
David Baker
Director of Admission
St. Mark's School of Texas
10600 Preston Road
Dallas, Texas 75230-4000

Phone: 214-346-8700
Fax: 214-346-8701
E-mail: admission@smtexas.org
Web site: http://www.smtexas.org

ST. VINCENT PALLOTTI HIGH SCHOOL

Laurel, Maryland

Type: Independent, coeducational, college-preparatory, Catholic secondary school
Grades: 9–12
Enrollment: School total: 500
Head of School: Stephen Edmonds, President/Principal

THE SCHOOL

An independent, coeducational, college-preparatory, Catholic secondary school, St. Vincent Pallotti High School offers young men and women the best of both worlds for their education. It is large enough to boast a wide-ranging curriculum, cutting-edge technology, spiritually enriching retreats and service opportunities, a diverse selection of extracurricular activities, and twenty-one interscholastic sports teams. Yet, Pallotti is small enough that each student is able to be treated as an individual, possessing unique talents and abilities. Pallotti is a place where young people can receive the nurturing they need and the freedom to spread their wings.

Following in the footsteps of the School's patron saint, St. Vincent, Pallotti strives to meet the needs of each student and compels them to work to reach their fullest potential. Through extensive course offerings at various levels—College Preparatory, Honors, Advanced Placement (AP), and Learning Center—students are challenged to excel at the highest levels possible. Pallotti equips each student with the tools necessary to continue to grow after graduation—the tools to pursue higher education and to continue to build knowledge and to better serve God and the world around them. In fact, 100 percent of Pallotti students complete a minimum of 80 hours of community service.

St. Vincent Pallotti High School is the oldest Catholic coeducational high school in the Archdiocese of Washington D.C. It is accredited by the Middle States Association and the Association of Independent Maryland Schools.

ACADEMIC PROGRAMS

Students must complete the following college-preparatory curriculum requirements for graduation: English (4 credits), Religion (4 credits), Social Studies (3 credits; must include world history, U.S. history, and American government), Foreign Language (3 credits), Math (4 credits; must include algebra I, geometry, and algebra II), Science (3 credits; must include conceptual physics, biology, and chemistry), Health/Physical Education 1 credit), Technology (½ credit), Fine Arts (½ credit), and four electives.

Honors classes are available in English, Foreign Language, Information and Technology, Mathematics, Religion, Science, Social Studies, and Visual and Performing Arts. Advanced Placement (AP) courses are available in English (English and English Language), Science (Biology, Chemistry, and Environmental Science), and Social Studies (European History and U.S. History).

The Learning Center at St. Vincent Pallotti High School strives to accommodate the needs of students who have been diagnosed with a mild to moderate learning disability. The majority of participants have a diagnosis of ADHD and/or a specific learning disability; however, staff members have worked with students who have other disabilities that impact their learning, including Asperger's syndrome, Tourette's syndrome, and various physical disabilities.

St. Vincent Pallotti High School has been developing its Technology in the Classroom Program for more than eight years and officially launched the student program in August 2009. The teacher program was launched in 2007. Students learn how to use the available technological tools to broaden their learning horizons, including using Web 2.0 tools and the Internet effectively and responsibly, and are prepared for the workplace of tomorrow. The program teaches students how to use the numerous research tools available on the Web and gives students the confidence to conduct research on their own. Organizational and study skills—from organizing lecture notes to completing homework and submitting it electronically—are taught using school-provided software on the notebook computers, which each student purchases and uses throughout the school day and at home.

FACULTY AND ADVISERS

It is through Pallotti's challenging and diverse curriculum that students develop into independent, self-motivated, socially conscious young adults who are prepared to enter college as critical thinkers. The 35 faculty members captivate students and impart a thirst for knowledge, accountability, and responsibility.

COLLEGE ADMISSION COUNSELING

The full Pallotti curriculum (academics, enrichment activities, and athletics) equips students with the knowledge, confidence, study skills, and habits necessary for college success. In its college counseling, the School is committed to assisting and guiding students in this important planning for future educational challenges.

The college selection process at Pallotti offers each student a rich opportunity to take the lead, make reasoned and informed decisions, advocate effectively for themselves, and to exercise organizational skills in following a schedule and meeting deadlines. The School is eager to work alongside each student to advise and support them.

Each junior and senior meets individually with one of the counselors to help identify his or her needs, talents, and interests; to discover what colleges and universities will nurture and develop these; and to discuss the selection and application process. The School also provides other opportunities including special parent "college nights" that provide information on school choice, the application process, and financial aid.

In the past two years, Pallotti graduates have been accepted to such colleges and universities as American, Boston University, Bucknell, Catholic University, College of William and Mary, Drexel, Duke, Elon, Fairmont State, George Mason, George Washington, Goucher, Hofstra, Jacksonville, James Madison, Lafayette, Marshall, Mount St. Mary's, North Carolina State, Purdue, Providence, Rutgers, Virginia Commonwealth, Virginia Tech, Wake Forest, and the Universities of Delaware, Illinois, Maryland, South Carolina, Virginia, and West Virginia.

STUDENT BODY AND CONDUCT

Pallotti has approximately 125 students in each grade. The average size class is 19 students.

Each student must wear the uniform for the required season. Compliance with the dress code begins before entering the building and continues until the end of the school day. Students who violate the dress/appearance code will be subject to disciplinary action.

As a Catholic school, which holds Jesus Christ as the ideal for human behavior, Pallotti High School sets before its students as their code of conduct the teachings of Jesus contained in the gospel. Realizing that all people are called to live as Jesus did, the Pallotti approach to student discipline strives to teach students Christian virtues. Thus it is expected that students will also show respect for self and others, charity, honesty and responsibility.

It is also expected that Pallotti students will exhibit concern and charity in their dealings with other members of the Pallotti community and its guests. Students are to respect the dignity and rights of other persons and property, with an unceasing watchfulness to avoid inflicting harm or suffering upon another. Each

www.facebook.com/sec.schools

student is expected to develop and maintain a high standard of personal integrity and honor and to observe the regulations of the school.

ACADEMIC FACILITIES

Pallotti has 4 academic buildings on campus. Three of the four buildings are used for the fine and performing arts program. The School is 100 percent wireless, with one-to-one laptop technology.

ATHLETICS

Participation in one of the School's twenty-one interscholastic sports teams offers the student-athletes at Pallotti not only the chance to develop their physical well-being but also the opportunity to learn invaluable life lessons. The "Panthers" participate in the Maryland Inter-scholastic Athletic Association (MIAA) and the Interscholastic Athletic Association of Maryland (IAAM).

Varsity sports include men's baseball, basketball, cross-country, football, golf, lacrosse, soccer, swimming, tennis, and wrestling and women's basketball, cheerleading, cross-country, field hockey, lacrosse, poms, soccer, softball, swimming, tennis, and volleyball.

In keeping with Pallotti's mission statement, the athletic program provides students with the core values and helps them strive to develop their God-given abilities. It is through athletics that they learn to develop teamwork, sportsmanship, and self-esteem. The School's athletic teams stress excellence in the classroom as well as on the field of play.

EXTRACURRICULAR OPPORTUNITIES

A wide variety of co-curricular enrichment activities are offered at Pallotti High School to supplement the varied academic curriculum. Committed to educating the whole person and developing well-rounded individuals, the School strongly encourages all students to become an active part of the school community by participating in one or more activities. It is Pallotti's belief that through the exploration of extracurricular activities as well as the visual and performing arts, students will grow in character and depth of thinking. Through these activities,

students become more well-rounded individuals and are able to contribute to society in a variety of enriching ways. It is hoped that each student will take the initiative to actively participate and strive toward personal accomplishment.

More than twenty activities and clubs are offered at Pallotti, including Campus Ministry, Chess Club, Environmental club, French Honor Society, International Cuisine, Library Club, Mentors, Mountain Biking Club, National Honors Society, PAWS for Pallotti, Ski Club, Spanish Honor Society, and more.

DAILY LIFE

The school day runs from 7:45 a.m. to 2:30 p.m. The school day is eight periods, seven for classes and one period for lunch. Each class is 45 minutes long. Lunch is catered by Three Brothers Pizza, offering students a selection of hot and cold food items.

COSTS AND FINANCIAL AID

Tuition for 2010–11 is $12,585 for grades 9–12. There are additional expenses for such items as books, uniforms, textbooks, and lunches. Payment plans are available.

Financial aid is available for students in grades 9–12 and is based upon the family's documented need, which is determined each year by the School and Student Service for Financial Aid (SSS) in Princeton, New Jersey. Parents who wish to apply for aid should request the SSS form from the Pallotti Business Office and send it directly to Princeton by January 12 and to Pallotti High School by January 26.

Academic scholarships are available for all entering freshmen. Applicants whose academic record, standardized test scores, recommendations, and applications indicate superior performance may be named Pallotti Scholars and receive one of several $3000 scholarship grant annually. No additional application is required.

Pallotti offers three $2000 band scholarships to entering freshmen. Auditions and application (online at http://www.pallottihs.org/admissions/BandScholarship.pdf) are required.

Prospective families should call the Office of Admissions for more information.

ADMISSIONS INFORMATION

Each year, the St. Vincent Pallotti High School Admissions Committee seeks to enroll a diverse group of talented, highly motivated students who wish to succeed in a challenging college-preparatory program, while contributing to the spirit and community of the school. The experience offered at Pallotti is unlike that offered by any other neighboring private Catholic secondary school.

Testing and interviewing play critical roles in the admissions process. The committee gives great consideration to educational performance, teacher recommendations, personal characteristics, and special talents or circumstances that warrant the admission of students who are likely to contribute to the vitality of the Pallotti community.

Pallotti High School encourages and welcomes applications without regard to race, color, religion, or national origin, and does not discriminate in its education policies, financial aid programs, or other school-administered extracurricular activities.

APPLICATION TIMETABLE

Due to the overwhelming number of applicants and the increasing demand for financial aid, Pallotti High School encourages students to apply as early as possible in the fall of their eighth-grade year and to submit their financial aid applications with their admissions application. U.S. citizens are required to pay a $100 application fee; international students must pay a $150 application fee. Pallotti offers rolling admissions and early admissions. The Early Admissions application deadline is December 15. Decision letters are mailed on February 25.

ADMISSIONS CORRESPONDENCE

Kelly Hawse, Director of Admissions
St. Vincent Pallotti High School
113 St. Marys Place
Laurel, Maryland 20707

Phone: 301-725-3228
Fax: 301-776-4343
E-mail: admissions@pallottihs.org
Web site: http://www.pallottihs.org

SANDY SPRING FRIENDS SCHOOL

Sandy Spring, Maryland

Type: Coeducational day and five- and seven-day boarding college-preparatory school
Grades: PK –12: Lower School, PK–5; Middle School 6–8; Upper School 9–12
Enrollment: School total: 572; Lower School: 157; Middle School: 149; Upper School: 265
Head of School: Thomas R. Gibian

THE SCHOOL

Sandy Spring Friends School (SSFS) was founded by Brook Moore in 1961 under the care of the Sandy Spring Monthly Meeting of Friends. The School provides a college-preparatory liberal arts curriculum for students of varying ethnic, economic, and religious backgrounds. It is situated on a 140-acre campus that contains woodlands, a pond and stream, walking and biking paths, playing fields, and one of the largest aerial ropes courses in the United States, the Adventure Park of Sandy Spring. Sandy Spring is in Montgomery County and is located approximately 35 minutes from both Washington, D.C., and Baltimore.

As a Quaker school, Sandy Spring Friends School shares the Quaker philosophy for the unique worth of the individual. Qualities of sensitivity, inventiveness, persistence, and humor are valued, along with intellectual traits. The School's goal is to help each student develop a sense of personal integrity while growing academically and learning to be a responsible member of the community. The School offers a diverse liberal arts curriculum, with courses ranging from college-preparatory to Advanced Placement courses. Performing and fine arts courses and athletics are an important part of the curriculum.

The 24-member Board of Trustees includes appointments by the Baltimore Yearly Meeting, the Sandy Spring Monthly Meeting, and Sandy Spring Friends School. The 2010–11 budget exceeds $14 million, with a growing endowment program that began in 1989.

The School is accredited by the Association of Independent Maryland Schools and approved by the State of Maryland Department of Education. It is a member of the National Association of Independent Schools, the Association of Independent Maryland Schools, the Association of Independent Schools of Greater Washington, the Association of Boarding Schools, the Friends Council on Education, the Secondary School Admission Test Board, the Education Records Bureau, A Better Chance, the National Association for College Admission Counseling, the Black Student Fund, the Potomac and Chesapeake Association of College Admissions Counselors, and the College Board.

ACADEMIC PROGRAMS

The curriculum at Sandy Spring Friends School is intended to prepare students not only for college but also for being valuable citizens of the world. It focuses on Quaker values, academic excellence, and personal growth in an environment that values personal responsibility. The school year, from early September to early June, includes Thanksgiving, winter, and spring vacations. A typical daily schedule includes six academic periods, jobs, lunch, an electives period, and sports. The school day is from 8 to 3:20, with sports and activities after school. Boarding students are required to attend dinner at 6 and study hall from 7:30 to 9:30 p.m. The average class size is 14, with a faculty-student ratio of 1:8.

Meeting for Worship is required once a month for Lower School children and once a week for Middle and Upper School students.

The required academic load for an Upper School student is six courses. To graduate, students must earn 24 credits, including English, 4; foreign language, 3; history, 3 (including United States history); mathematics, 3; science, 3; fine arts, 3; and electives, 3. Additional requirements are participating in a physical activity two times per year, passing a semester course on Quakerism, and community service. Advanced Placement courses are available in English, Spanish, French, history, math, art, and science. The ESL program is open to students in grades 9–12; currently, 61 students are enrolled.

Intersession week in March gives Upper School students an opportunity to participate in off-campus activities that supplement the standard curriculum. Projects have included trips to countries such as Belize, Brazil, France, Greece, Italy, Korea, Senegal, and Turkey after intensive study; community service projects in Georgia, Maryland, New York, North Carolina, Tennessee, Virginia, and Washington, D.C.; intensive arts workshops in modern dance, improvisational theater, spinning and weaving, and other arts; and numerous opportunities for outdoor exploration by foot, bike, and boat.

The Upper School operates on a semester schedule, and the grading systems vary by division according to the developmental needs of the students in the age group. The Lower School works within the framework of parent and teacher conferences with extensive comments; the Middle and Upper Schools use letter grades, with additional comments and parent-teacher conferences as appropriate.

FACULTY AND ADVISERS

There are 66 full-time and 7 part-time teachers and administrators who teach. Seventeen live on campus, 6 with their families. Twenty-eight faculty members hold advanced degrees.

Tom Gibian, the seventh Head of School, came to Sandy Spring Friends School in July, 2010 after ten years as CEO, managing director, and founding partner of Emerging Capital Partners, the largest fund manager working across the African continent. Prior to returning to the Washington D.C. area, he was Executive Director in the Asia-Pacific region of Goldman Sachs (Asia) Limited from 1992 to 1995, having joined Goldman Sachs in 1987 as vice president. Throughout his career, he has focused on staying true to his Quaker values and using them in the business world. He has served on both the Sandy Spring Friends School and the Sidwell School Boards, and has dedicated his volunteer efforts to the governance of Quaker schools.

Mr. Gibian grew up in Sandy Spring, Maryland, and is a member of Sandy Spring Monthly Meeting. He received a bachelor's degree with honors from the College of Wooster in Ohio, and an M.B.A. in finance from the University of Pennsylvania's Wharton School of Business. As a college senior, his independent study project at College of Wooster was entitled "Dissent and Experimentation in American Schools, 1900–1960." He taught at Wooster High School and received a secondary school teaching certificate. After college he was a community organizer and, later, an administrator in a local anti-poverty agency.

Sandy Spring faculty members share a variety of nonacademic duties, including supervising student activities, proctoring the dorms, and advising students. The School encourages and supports faculty members in the pursuit of educational interests by providing funding and by supporting a professional development committee of the School.

Middle and Upper School students have a strong adviser-advisee relationship that is based on developing a mutual trust and respect. It provides parents with a personal contact when they have questions or concerns about their child's progress.

COLLEGE ADMISSION COUNSELING

Active college planning begins in the junior year with individual meetings with the College Guidance Director to discuss the general admissions process and to identify colleges of interest. Parents and students attend College Night Programs that include information regarding common admission and application for financial aid procedures. Also, many college representatives make personal visits to the School each year. The School's goal is to match the student with the right school.

One hundred percent of the students in the class of 2010 were accepted to college. They are attending institutions such as American, Bowdoin, Boston Conservatory, Dartmouth, Dickinson, Earlham, Emerson, Georgia Tech, Haverford, Johns Hopkins, Penn State, St. Mary's (Maryland), Tufts, Xavier, and the Universities of Delaware, Maryland, Pittsburgh, St. Andrews (U.K.), Vermont, Virginia, and Washington.

STUDENT BODY AND CONDUCT

In 2010–11, the Upper School enrolled 266 students, 139 boys and 127 girls, as follows: 52 in grade 9, 63 in grade 10, 75 in grade 11, and 76 in grade 12. The boarding program enrolled 61 students from the mid-Atlantic region and eight countries. Nine percent are members of the Religious Society of Friends, and 40 percent are students of color. International students represent 17 percent of the Upper School student body.

The Torch Committee, the student government organization, includes day and boarding students as well as faculty and administration representatives. The committee, operating by consensus, considers student concerns and makes recommendations to faculty committees and to the administration. A student member of Torch is invited to attend faculty and business meetings and meetings of the Board of Trustees.

ACADEMIC FACILITIES
The School's physical plant, which is valued at more than $41 million, includes a science center; a Lower School building and a Middle School building; a dormitory and dining hall; three major classroom buildings and an administration building; a performing arts center with a fine arts wing; an athletic complex; and Yarnall Hall, a $1.75-million resource center that houses a 20,000-volume library, a gymnasium, and an observatory. Computers are integrated into many aspects of the curriculum. Every division of the School is equipped with its own computer lab, and every classroom includes at least one computer and is wired for network and Internet access. The School's library includes computers for online research through the public library system, subscription to online reference tools, and the Internet. A fiber-optic backbone connects the network, and a T1 line connects the Internet and e-mail accounts to students and faculty members. All faculty members and students use Moodle (a course management software).

BOARDING AND GENERAL FACILITIES
All of the boarding students live with their roommates in one 2-story dormitory. Boys and girls each have a separate floor. Community life for boarders includes regular dorm meetings (with decisions reached by consensus), committee-style sponsored activities, family-style dinners with resident staff members, and visits to the homes of day student friends. The dorm staff members (6 adults for 61 boarders in 2010–11) all reside in either apartments or town houses located near the Westview dormitory.

The School nurse assists with the appropriate care for students who may become ill. The School's infirmary is open during the school day.

ATHLETICS
Sandy Spring Friends School is a member of the Potomac Valley Athletic Conference. The Middle and Upper School teams compete in the following interscholastic sports: baseball, basketball, cross-country, golf, lacrosse, soccer, softball, tennis, track and field, and volleyball. Other activities include weight lifting and outdoor exploration.

The athletic facilities include a new complex with a 9,000-square-foot gymnasium, a fully equipped fitness center, and state-of-the-art training and locker room facilities. The 140-acre campus includes four soccer and lacrosse fields and a 5-kilometer cross-country course.

EXTRACURRICULAR OPPORTUNITIES
Getting involved is made easy at Sandy Spring Friends by a weekly activities period that allows students to participate in clubs such as Amnesty International (now in its tenth year at SSFS), the Multicultural Club, the International Student Club, the Open Door Club, the ski club (eight weeks of Friday-night skiing plus other trips), the chess club, and the outdoor exploration club. The yearbook and the award-winning literary magazine are also popular activities for students.

The Community Service Program at Sandy Spring Friends School seeks to respond to the needs of others and enrich the School community and the lives of its members. Every student at the School completes community service hours as a requirement for graduation. The service programs are diverse and allow for individual interests to be pursued.

DAILY LIFE
Breakfast for the boarding community begins at 7. Classes begin at 8 and end at 3:20. Advisory and tutorial periods occur once a week, Meeting for Worship occurs once each week, and a "jobs" period is scheduled daily for dorm students. Lunch is served cafeteria-style daily.

Athletics take place between 3:30 and 5:30, and dinner is served family-style at 6. Dorm meetings or activity groups frequently meet before the study hours, which begin nightly at 7:30, Sunday through Thursday.

WEEKEND LIFE
Weekends at the School are relaxed. Activities, which are frequently designed by both students and faculty members, have included adventures such as day trips into Washington, D.C., for a museum visit, a march on the Mall, lunch at Planet Hollywood and a show at the Kennedy Center, or shopping in Georgetown. In addition, the students have visited Baltimore's Inner Harbor, Harper's Ferry, and various hot spots around the School. While boarding students are not required to stay at the School on weekends, all students can choose the weekend activities in which they wish to participate (day students and five-day boarders are charged an appropriate fee for the off-campus activities). One third of the weekends during the school year include on-campus activities such as School dances; student performances in theater, music, and modern dance; art shows; and special concerts and symposiums in the areas of science and the arts.

COSTS AND FINANCIAL AID
In 2010–11, tuition ranged from $19,900 to $21,900 in the Lower School, $24,260 in the Middle School, and $26,860 in the Upper School. Boarding tuition was $38,400 for five days and $47,100 for seven days. A hot lunch is provided beginning in the first grade. Additional costs include an incidental account for the School store, student allowances, laboratory fees, and art supplies.

Sandy Spring Friends School offers financial aid on the basis of need. The financial aid decisions for applications submitted by January 15 are made by mid-March for the following year. Thirty-three percent of the students received financial aid for the 2010–11 school year. The average award was $30,250 for boarders and $14,750 for day students in the Upper School.

ADMISSIONS INFORMATION
Sandy Spring Friends School actively seeks a diverse, curious, and enthusiastic community of students. The student body is diverse in race, creed, and economic and social background. The admissions process allows prospective students and their families to become familiar with as many aspects of the School as possible. New students enter at all grade levels as space permits.

APPLICATION TIMETABLE
Inquiries are welcome at any time. The Admissions Office is open from 8 a.m. to 4:30 p.m., Monday through Friday. Application forms are due by January 15. The application process must be completed by February 1 to ensure first-round consideration. Applications received after January 15 are reviewed as space permits.

ADMISSIONS CORRESPONDENCE
Kent Beck, Upper School Admissions
Sandy Spring Friends School
16923 Norwood Road
Sandy Spring, Maryland 20860-1199

Phone: 301-774-7455 Ext. 203
Fax: 301-924-1115
E-mail: admissions@ssfs.org
Web site: http://www.ssfs.org

SEISEN INTERNATIONAL SCHOOL

Tokyo, Japan

Type: Girls' Catholic college-preparatory day school with a coeducational Montessori Kindergarten
Grades: K–12: Montessori Kindergarten; Elementary School, 1–6; Middle School, 7–8; High School, 9–12
Enrollment: School total: 680; High School: 162
Head of School: Sr. Concesa Martin, School Head

THE SCHOOL

Seisen International School began in 1949 as a kindergarten with only 4 American children. When the School moved to Gotanda in 1962, it enrolled 70 students and started a first-grade program as well. By 1970, the School included nine grades; in 1973, when Seisen moved to its present location, its curriculum was extended to grade 12. The School has an enrollment of approximately 700 students representing more than fifty nationalities.

Seisen is operated by the Handmaids of the Sacred Heart of Jesus under the auspices of the Seisen Jogakuin Educational Foundation. The order was founded in 1877 by St. Rafaela Maria Porras to dedicate its efforts to educational activities. As a Catholic school with a Christian atmosphere in which students of all races, nationalities, and creeds can thrive, Seisen has high expectations for the students' character development, particularly in respect, compassion, and international understanding.

Seisen offers a Montessori kindergarten, which is designed to take full advantage of young children's self-motivation and their sensitivity to their environment. In this program, the teacher observes each child's interests and needs and offers the stimulation and guidance that will enable him or her to experience the excitement of learning by choice. The Montessori equipment helps in the development of concentration, coordination, good working habits, and basic skills according to each child's capacities and in a noncompetitive atmosphere.

Seisen's Elementary School strives to create a Christian environment that welcomes and respects children of all nationalities and faiths. Seisen, an authorized International Baccalaureate (I.B.) Primary Years Programme (P.Y.P.) school, follows the PYP model in elementary school, grades 1–6. The P.Y.P. is a transdisciplinary program of international education designed to foster the development of the whole child and encourage students to be inquirers and critical thinkers.

P.Y.P. focuses on the development of the whole child, touching hearts and minds. In addition to academics, P.Y.P. encompasses social, physical, emotional, and cultural aspects of learning. P.Y.P. strives to give children a strong foundation in all the major areas of knowledge: social studies, science, language, the arts, math, and personal, social, and physical education. The heart of the P.Y.P. program is grounded in the use of inquiry to foster knowledge and skills. Teachers and students work together in a P.Y.P. classroom to create an environment that encourages the inquiry process. The goal is to enable students to gain essential knowledge and skills and to engage in responsible action.

The High School program prepares young women to face the challenges of a global society with excellent academic preparation, a strong program of athletics, advanced preparation in the visual and performing arts, and an emphasis on community service. From the time the I.B. Diploma Programme was adopted at Seisen in 1988, Seisen students have consistently scored higher than the worldwide I.B. mean each year.

Seisen is accredited by the New England Association of Schools and Colleges, the Council of International Schools, and the Japanese Ministry of Education. The School is also a member of the Japan Council of Overseas Schools, the Kanto Plain Association of Secondary School Principals, and the East Asia Regional Council of Overseas Schools.

The School is located in Tokyo's largest residential area, Setagaya-ku. It is easily accessible from downtown Tokyo and surrounding cities by public transportation. Seisen also operates ten school buses, which cover different routes throughout Tokyo.

ACADEMIC PROGRAMS

Seisen requires that students earn 22 credits in grades 9 through 12. Graduation requirements are as follows: English, 4 credits; social sciences, 4 credits; mathematics, 3 credits; science, 3 credits; foreign language, 3 credits; religion, 2 credits; physical education, 1 credit; and academic electives, 2 credits. Academic electives in high school include art, music, math, history, foreign language, and an introduction to Montessori teachings. Other electives are yearbook, journalism, survival Japanese, computer graphics, choir, drama, 2-D art, and pottery. In grades 9 and 10, students are required to take a performing/visual arts block, drama, music, pottery, or 2-D art. The Personal Social Health Education course is also a requirement at the ninth and tenth grade levels. Special instruction in English as a second language is available.

Class size varies according to subject. The grading system uses letter grades (A to F) for all subjects. Reports are sent to parents at the end of each quarter.

Students are grouped heterogeneously, except in mathematics, in which there are regular, honors, and accelerated groups. The average course load is five or six classes in academic subjects and one elective. The library is open during the school day and before and after school.

To fully serve the needs of a university-bound, international student body, Seisen offers a program of studies in grades 11 and 12 that can culminate in either a full International Baccalaureate diploma or certificates in individual subjects. These attainments are recognized for admission by over 2,000 universities in more than seventy countries, including many American colleges that accept the I.B. for advanced standing. The I.B. diploma is considered equivalent to most European university entrance requirements.

The following are administered in the School: PSAT/NMSQT, SAT and SAT Subject Tests, selected IGCSE, the Iowa Test of Basic Skills, and the Iowa Test of Educational Development.

FACULTY AND ADVISERS

The faculty consists of 70 full-time members, of whom 54 are women. Approximately 50 percent of the faculty members hold a master's degree or higher.

The administration and faculty members endeavor to educate the students in academic areas and to foster their spiritual and emotional growth. Teachers are involved in counseling and advising students. The personal counselor helps students with life strategies, and teachers assist through the homeroom and teacher-adviser system.

COLLEGE ADMISSION COUNSELING

The college advisers help students in college selection and career orientation. Many college representatives visit the School each year, and some Seisen graduates return to give juniors and seniors information about various colleges.

During the junior year, all students take the PSAT and SAT. The SAT middle 50 percent range of scores for last year's graduates was 540 for verbal, 630 for mathematics, and 562 for writing.

Virtually all Seisen graduates move on to higher education. A representative list of schools in which Seisen graduates have been matriculated in the past three years includes Barnard, Boston University, Central St. Martins College of Art and Design, Clark, Columbia, Cornell, Denison, Durham (UK), Duke, Elon, George Washington, ICU (Tokyo), Kingston, Lewis & Clark, London School of Economics, McGill, NYU, Parsons, Pepperdine, School of the Art

Institute of Chicago, Stanford, Sophia (Tokyo), Temple, UCLA, USC, Waseda (Tokyo), Wesleyan, York, and the Universities of British Columbia; California, San Diego; California, Santa Barbara; Glasgow; Hawaii at Manoa; Kansas; Miami (Florida); Pennsylvania; Toronto; Virginia; and Washington (Seattle).

STUDENT BODY AND CONDUCT

The 2010–11 student body includes 43 in the ninth grade, 37 in the tenth, 44 in the eleventh, and 38 in the twelfth. The largest percentages of students are from the United States, Korea, the United Kingdom, India, and Japan, but nationalities from all over the world are represented.

ACADEMIC FACILITIES

In addition to classrooms, the School has a chapel, three science laboratories, a computer center, a music room, two art rooms, a media center, a gymnasium, two tennis courts, playgrounds, and a cafeteria.

The School's libraries have a collection of more than 20,000 volumes of books and subscribe to fifty periodicals and two newspapers. The High School library houses a multimedia center, two color printers, ten computer workstations, and twenty laptops. Students are able to access the library homepage as well as various online references and databases from outside the School.

ATHLETICS

In addition to the physical education program, Seisen offers badminton, basketball, cross-country, futsal, soccer, swimming, tennis, track and field, and volleyball. Basketball, tennis, and volleyball are offered at varsity and junior varsity levels.

EXTRACURRICULAR OPPORTUNITIES

As a member of the Kanto Plain Association of Secondary School Principals, Seisen is active in various competitions (debate, speech, Brain Bowl, Math Field Day). There are vocal and instrumental groups and a drama club. Other organizations and activities include the National Honor Society, the Student Council, student publications, Alleluia Club, Bell Choir, Booster Club, Model United Nations (MUN), social service groups, and the Girls' Athletic Association (GAA).

Seisen After School Activities (SASA), which are offered to elementary school students, include sports, art, computer graphics, music, dance, cooking, sewing, science, and language classes.

DAILY LIFE

Students have eight 40-minute classes, which include study halls and activity periods. The School cafeteria serves hot lunches, but students may choose to bring their own lunch from home. Classes begin at 8:20 a.m. and end at 3:20 p.m. There are no Saturday classes. Students are encouraged to participate in competitive sports and other activities after school.

SUMMER PROGRAMS

A three-week program of remedial studies is offered in June. Enrichment programs and sports are offered on a limited basis.

COSTS AND FINANCIAL AID

School fees are quoted in Japanese yen. For the 2010–11 school year, the High School tuition is 1.94 million yen. Transportation and lunches are available for additional costs. A registration fee of 300,000 yen and a land and building development fee of 400,000 yen are payable when a student registers.

ADMISSIONS INFORMATION

Seisen International School serves the needs of diplomatic, business, and professional families of the international community. It also provides education for Japanese children who have lived abroad and wish to continue their education in English.

A completed application form and Confidential Counselor Recommendation, transcripts from the school(s) previously attended, and payment of the application fee are required of all applicants in the initial process of admission. An interview with the principal or the School Head of Seisen International School and an entrance examination are required in the final phase of the admission process.

APPLICATION TIMETABLE

Applications are welcome at any time. Parents and prospective students are encouraged to visit the School.

ADMISSIONS CORRESPONDENCE

Sr. Concesa Martin, School Head
Seisen International School
12-15, Yoga 1-chome
Setagaya-ku
Tokyo
Japan 158-0097

Phone: 81-3-3704-2661
Fax: 81-3-3701-1033
E-mail: sisadmissions@seisen.com
Web site: http://www.seisen.com

THE SHIPLEY SCHOOL

Bryn Mawr, Pennsylvania

Type: Coeducational, day, college-preparatory school
Grades: P–12: Lower School, Prekindergarten–5; Middle School, 6–8; Upper School, 9–12
Enrollment: School total: 835; Upper School: 330
Head of School: Dr. Steven Piltch

THE SCHOOL

The Shipley School, a coeducational, college preparatory day school, was founded in 1894 by the Misses Hannah, Elizabeth, and Katherine Shipley to prepare girls for Bryn Mawr College. In 1972 the School began to admit boys and now has roughly equal numbers of boys and girls.

The Upper and Lower Schools are located on landscaped campuses (36 acres) one block apart near the SEPTA railroad station and directly opposite the Bryn Mawr College campus. Bryn Mawr is a suburban community 10 miles west of Philadelphia, and Shipley is one of the closest schools to the SEPTA trains.

While Shipley places the greatest emphasis on education of the mind and academic excellence, it is also concerned with the moral and emotional needs of its students and is dedicated to developing in each one a love of learning and a compassionate participation in the world. Through a strong college-preparatory curriculum in the humanities and sciences, the School encourages curiosity, creativity, and respect for intellectual effort. Shipley upholds and promotes moral integrity, a sense of personal achievement and worth, and concern for others at school and in the larger community.

A nonprofit institution, Shipley is governed by a 29-member Board of Trustees, which includes parents, past parents, alumni, and friends of the School involved in industry, the professions, and education. An active Alumni Association represents the more than 5,200 living graduates.

The School plant is valued at $60.4 million. The School endowment is estimated at $14 million.

The Shipley School is accredited by the Pennsylvania Association of Private Academic Schools and the Middle States Association of Colleges and Schools and is a member of the Secondary School Admission Test Board, the National Association of Independent Schools, the Pennsylvania Association of Independent Schools, and the Delaware Valley Association of Independent Schools.

ACADEMIC PROGRAMS

To graduate, a student must complete at least 16 credits in grades 9–12, including 4 years of English; 3 years of mathematics, through algebra II as a minimum; 3 years of a world language; 2 years of history, including U.S. history; and 2 years of science. Most graduates have many more credits than the minimum. Students in grade 9 are also required to take performing arts and visual arts, and all Upper School students must participate in sports or physical education, take a seminar in health, and perform 40 hours of community service.

Yearlong courses include English, French, history, Latin, mathematics, music, philosophy, science, Spanish, and studio art. An Advanced Placement-level course is available in studio art (drawing and 2-D design). Other courses have honors-level sections. Major electives include American studies, film studies, global studies, macroeconomics, and a new social impact minor elective course that combines study with service learning.

The school year is divided into semesters, and most students carry five subjects per term. Most classes are homogeneously grouped, particularly mathematics and foreign languages. There are 15 or 16 students in an average class. Students in grades 9–10 attend supervised study halls during free periods. The overall student-teacher ratio is 7:1.

In grades 6 through 12, grades are discussed with the student by his or her academic adviser and then sent to parents four times a year. Reports have letter grades with comments written by individual faculty members. Extra help is often available from faculty members.

Independent service projects are required of seniors after the completion of their final exams in mid-May.

During spring and summer vacations, various departments offer study-travel trips, some with homestays. In the past few years, students have traveled to France, Panama, and Italy. They have also participated in The Mountain School, Rocky Mountain Semester, and the Island School term-away programs.

FACULTY AND ADVISERS

The Upper School faculty consists of 64 teachers (58 full-time and 6 part-time), including 26 men and 38 women. Nine administrators who teach are part of the faculty as well. Forty-four percent of Upper School teachers hold advanced degrees.

The Head of School, Dr. Steven Piltch, was appointed in 1992. A graduate of Williams College, Dr. Piltch has received two master's degrees in education from Harvard University, one in counseling and consulting psychology, and the other in secondary and middle school administration. In 1991, he received a Doctor of Education degree from Harvard in administration, planning, and social policy.

All members of the faculty and administration are active in advising and counseling students. Many of them coach. Through the School's robust professional development program, faculty members are supported in continuing their education.

Two nurses are on duty at the health centers, a physician is on call, and 3 consultants are at the School several days per week.

COLLEGE ADMISSION COUNSELING

Beginning in the eleventh grade, 2 college guidance counselors and an assistant work closely with students, helping them individually throughout the college-selection process. The counselors also meet once a week with small groups of their advisees during both their junior and senior years. College admissions officers from across the country come to the School each fall to conduct interviews, and students are assisted in making plans to visit colleges themselves. Virtually all graduates attend four-year colleges and universities. A representative list of institutions attended includes Amherst, Bates, Bowdoin, Brown, Bucknell, Carnegie Mellon, Columbia, Cornell, Dickinson, Drexel, Duke, Franklin and Marshall, George Washington, Hamilton, Harvard, Haverford, Lehigh, Middlebury, Muhlenberg, NYU, Penn State, Princeton, Rhode Island School of Design, Syracuse, Trinity (Connecticut), Tufts, Villanova, Wesleyan, Williams, Yale, and the Universities of Colorado, Delaware, Michigan, Pennsylvania, Pittsburgh, Vermont, Virginia, and Wisconsin.

STUDENT BODY AND CONDUCT

There are 330 students in grades 9 through 12, with 169 boys and 161 girls.

Students come from fifty-five towns and cities in the greater Philadelphia area. Members of minority groups represent 19 percent of the total enrollment.

The Shipley School Student Government consists of the Executive Council, which discusses and implements decisions; and the Judicial Board, which handles all serious disciplinary matters. In addition, there is an Athletic Association, an Arts Association, a Students' Organization for Service, and a Community Life Organization.

ACADEMIC FACILITIES

Two wings of the main Upper School building house classrooms, the Snyder Science Center, art studios, music rooms, the library, the gymnasium, and regularly upgraded computer facilities, college counseling offices, and student and faculty lounges. Administrative offices, the dining rooms, and the kitchen are also housed in the main building. The Middle School was built in 1994 and the new Lower School opened in 2001; another Lower School gym was added in 2002. The School added two new turf fields in 2006.

ATHLETICS

All students are members of the Athletic Association and are members of the Blue or Green teams, which reflect the school colors. Shipley believes that important physical, social, and moral values are learned through the experience of team sports and a rigorous physical education program; and that these are vital to the successful development of the whole student. Cross-country, crew, field hockey, soccer, lacrosse, tennis, baseball, golf, and softball are the fall and spring varsity activities. In winter, basketball, squash, swimming, and volleyball are options. Games are scheduled with schools in suburban Philadelphia. Shipley is a member of the Friends Schools League.

The Yarnall Gymnasium has two basketball courts with stands; the same area converts easily for volleyball, badminton, gymnastics, and indoor tennis. On the lower level, there are coaches' offices, locker rooms, and a fitness center. Some games and practices also take place in the new Lower School Gym.

www.facebook.com/sec.schools

The Fuller fields on campus include a separate lacrosse field and a softball field, adjacent to six tennis courts. Three additional athletics fields, 2 miles away, are reached by bus. Three of the School's fields have recently been converted to safer, synthetic turf.

EXTRACURRICULAR OPPORTUNITIES

Shipley offers students a variety of extracurricular activities, such as *The Beacon,* the school newspaper; *Tempora Praeterita,* the yearbook; and *The Compass,* the literary and art magazine; selective singing groups, the Madrigals and Madriguys; the Upper School Choir; instrumental and jazz ensembles; the School orchestra; Model UN; Students United for Racial Equality (SURE); Amnesty International; and Sprouts, an award-winning horticultural group. Other activities, which vary from year to year, include Arabic Club, Chess Club, Green Gators Environmental Club, the Science Underground, World Affairs, and others. Students also volunteer to help the Admissions Office, tutor inner-city children, rehabilitate urban housing, and work in local hospitals and nursing homes through the Students' Organization for Service (SOS). Participation in the community service program is required, including a service project at the end of the senior year.

Annual events include parents' evenings and barbecues, "Shipley Today" open houses for parents of prospective students, Alumni Weekend, award-winning fall plays and spring musicals, and annual academic, character, and sports award assemblies. The Social Committee plans many on-campus activities and organizes exchange events with nearby schools. Dances and other social events, including Super Saturday, an annual charity fund-raiser, are scheduled on weekends. In addition, students can be in downtown Philadelphia in 20 minutes, where they can attend cultural and recreational events.

DAILY LIFE

Classes are 45 or 80 minutes long and run from 8:30 a.m. to 3:15 p.m. A hot meal and salad bar are available for lunch daily. Prepaid school lunches are required in the Middle and Upper Schools. There are six academic periods per day. The day includes "office hours," when all students are free to meet with teachers individually. Most students have at least one free period (a study hall for grades 9 and 10) every day.

SUMMER PROGRAMS

Shipley also hosts a Summer Enrichment Camp for boys and girls ages 6–14, with a focus on sports and the arts, a reading program, cooking classes, and sports clinics in soccer, lacrosse, and basketball. Last year the school initiated a multi-sport camp for students in grades 5–9. Shipley and the Young Scholars Fund of Philadelphia cosponsor a transitional program for urban youth in July every summer. This program is for students who have completed grade 7 or 8 and are interested in applying to independent school for grade 9. It involves four weeks of classes in English, Mandarin, mathematics, and science, and is taught by Shipley teachers.

COSTS AND FINANCIAL AID

The 2010–11 tuition for Upper School students is $28,995. Other expenses (books, lab fees, testing, athletic fees, and trips) vary from $500 to $1000, not including lunches. The lunches cost $795 per year. Tuition insurance and a tuition payment plan are offered.

More than 26 percent of students receive need-based financial aid. Grants are made possible through the generosity of certain foundations, endowment income, and the Annual Giving campaign and are determined by procedures established by the School and Student Service for Financial Aid. Recipients are chosen for their ability, character, past performance, and promise. Awards range from $1000 to $26,000 and total more than $3.5 million per year. All families are expected to contribute to their children's educational expenses. The Centennial Scholarship Exam, given each January, provides endowed scholarships to incoming ninth graders based on need and merit (as judged by the exam). Winners receive more than 100 percent of demonstrated financial need for four years.

ADMISSIONS INFORMATION

Shipley seeks responsible, self-directed students of above-average to superior ability who enjoy learning. New students are admitted at all grade levels. An interview, the School's placement testing, and reports from previous schools are required of all applicants. Students must also submit results of the SSAT, the ISEE, or the Wechsler Intelligence Scale for Children (WISC–IV). For entrance to the Upper School in the 2010–11 academic year, there were 108 applicants. Of these, 81 were accepted, and 29 new students enrolled.

APPLICATION TIMETABLE

Shipley seeks applicants who will thrive in Shipley's challenging learning environment and make positive contributions to the School. The admissions process is designed to give families opportunities to become familiar with Shipley and to help the School get to know the child and the family. Applications are welcome for admission to all grades, prekindergarten through grade 12, for the 2011–12 school year.

Students who complete all parts of the admissions process by December 10, 2010, will receive early notification of an admissions decision before winter break and will have an enrollment deadline of March 1, 2011. Students who complete all parts of the admissions process by January 13, 2011 will receive an admissions decision before February 1, 2011. The enrollment deadline is March 1, 2011. Students who complete all parts of the admissions process after January 13, 2011 will receive an admissions decision within two weeks of the completion of their application. The enrollment deadline will be determined at the time of notification.

The Admissions Office is open year-round. Campus interviews and tours may be scheduled throughout the week during the school year from 8:30 to 4:30.

ADMISSIONS CORRESPONDENCE

Dorothy Bond Maddock, Director of Admissions
The Shipley School
814 Yarrow Street
Bryn Mawr, Pennsylvania 19010-3598

Phone: 610-525-4300 Ext. 4120
Fax: 610-525-5082
E-mail: admit@shipleyschool.org
Web site: http://www.shipleyschool.org

SOUNDVIEW PREPARATORY SCHOOL

Yorktown Heights, New York

Type: Coeducational day college-preparatory school
Grades: Middle School, 6–8; Upper School, 9–12
Enrollment: Total, 75; Middle School, 11; Upper School, 64
Head of School: W. Glyn Hearn, Headmaster

THE SCHOOL

Soundview Preparatory School, a coeducational, college-preparatory school for grades 6 through 12, was founded in 1989 on the belief that the best environment for students is one where classes are small, teachers know the learning style and interests of each student, and an atmosphere of mutual trust prevails. At Soundview, students and teachers work in close collaboration in classes with an average size of 7 students.

The School's mission is to provide a college-preparatory education in a supportive and non-competitive environment that requires rigorous application to academics, instills respect for ethical values, and fosters self-confidence by helping each student feel recognized and valued. Soundview empowers students to develop their potential and reach their own goals in a setting that promotes respect for others and a sense of community.

Soundview Prep opened its doors with 13 students in the spring of 1989. In the spring of 1998, having outgrown its original quarters in Pocantico Hills, New York, the School moved to a larger facility in Mount Kisco, New York. On January 14, 2008, Soundview moved to its first permanent home, a 13.8-acre campus in Yorktown Heights, New York. New York City, only an hour away, provides a wealth of cultural opportunities for Soundview students to explore on class trips.

The School is governed by a 10-member Board of Trustees. The current operating budget is $2.1 million. In 2009–10, Soundview raised a gross total amount of $244,746 through the Annual Fund and fund-raising events, and from parents, alumni families, grandparents, friends, foundations, and corporations.

Soundview is chartered by the New York State Board of Regents and is accredited by the New York State Association of Independent Schools. The School is a member of the National Association of Independent Schools, the Education Records Bureau, and the Council for Advancement and Support of Education.

ACADEMIC PROGRAMS

Soundview provides a rigorous academic program to ensure that students not only develop the skills and acquire the knowledge needed for college work but also have the opportunity to pursue their own personal goals.

The academic day is carefully structured but informal, with nurture a crucial ingredient. Soundview's student-teacher ratio of 5:1 guarantees that students are monitored closely and receive the support they need. At the same time, the School provides advanced courses for students who wish to go beyond the high school level or take a subject that is not usually offered, allowing students to soar academically and truly develop their potential.

The Middle School curriculum is designed to establish a foundation of knowledge and skills in each academic discipline, strong comprehension

and communication skills, good work habits and study skills, confidence in using technology, and creativity in the arts.

The Upper School curriculum provides a traditional college-preparatory education in academics and the arts. In addition to the core subjects—English, history, math, and science—Soundview offers four languages (Latin, French, Spanish, and Italian), studio art, and electives such as history of philosophy, drama, forensics, psychology, government, creative writing, journalism, environmental science, and a three-year individual science research project.

AP courses are made available according to students' abilities and interests. Recently, AP courses have been offered in calculus, biology, physics, U.S. history, European history, government, art, French, and Spanish.

Academic requirements for graduation are 4 years each of English and history, 3 years each of math and science, 3 years of one foreign language or 2 years each of two different languages, 1 year of art, and ½ year of health.

Computer technology at Soundview is integrated into the curriculum. Teachers post assignments on the School's Web site, and students upload completed work into teachers' folders. The School is wired for wireless technology and has a well-equipped computer lab.

The School's annual two-week trips abroad (to Argentina, Russia, China, and Italy over the last few years) offer students experience with other cultures.

The school year is divided into two semesters, with letter grades sent out at the end of each. Individual conferences with parents, students, faculty members, and the Headmaster are arranged throughout the year.

Students take the Educational Records Bureau (ERB) standardized tests every year for use by the School in monitoring each student's progress.

FACULTY AND ADVISERS

The faculty consists of 16 teachers (13 women and 3 men); the majority hold advanced degrees. Three teachers are part-time; the rest, full-time. Turnover is low, with an average of one or two replacements per year.

Each teacher serves as adviser to up to 5 students. Most faculty members supervise a club or publication or coach an athletic team.

W. Glyn Hearn has served as Headmaster since the School was founded in 1989. He obtained his B.A. in English at the University of Texas at Austin and his M.A. in American literature at Texas Tech University. He spent twelve years at the Awty International School of Houston, Texas, where he served as Principal of the Lower, Middle, and Upper Schools and Head of the American Section, before becoming Assistant Headmaster and then Headmaster of the American Renaissance School in Westchester County in 1987.

COLLEGE ADMISSION COUNSELING

College placement at Soundview is directed by Carol Gill, president of Carol Gill Associates and one of the nation's leading college counseling experts. The process starts early on, when eighth, ninth, and tenth graders plan and refine a course sequence that is appropriate for a competitive college. In the junior year, students and their parents begin meeting with Ms. Gill to discuss the college application process, develop lists of colleges, and plan college visits. The meetings continue through the senior year to complete applications.

Because of the School's small size, the faculty and staff members know each student well and are able to assist students in selecting colleges that are the right match for them. The Headmaster writes a personal recommendation for each senior.

College acceptances in recent years include Allegheny, Bard, Barnard, Bates, Brandeis, Brown, Carnegie Mellon, Clark, College of Wooster, Columbia, Dickinson, Drew, Earlham, Franklin & Marshall, Gettysburg, Hampshire, Hartwick, Hobart and William Smith, Manhattanville, Maryland Institute College of Art, Muhlenberg, Northeastern, NYU, Oberlin, Rhode Island School of Design, Roger Williams, Sarah Lawrence, SUNY, Susquehanna, Vassar, Williams, and the Universities of Maine and Vermont.

STUDENT BODY AND CONDUCT

Soundview reflects the diversity—ethnic, religious, and economic—of American society. The 44 boys and 31 girls come from Westchester, Fairfield, and Rockland Counties and New York City. Approximately 15 percent of the student body are members of minority groups.

Respect for ethical values such as kindness, honesty, and respect for others are paramount at Soundview, where individual responsibility and a sense of community are stressed.

The School's disciplinary structure is informal, since it is based on the assumption that students attending the School desire to be there and are therefore willing to adhere to a code of conduct that demonstrates awareness that the community is based upon a shared sense of purpose and commitment. Despite the cordiality of its atmosphere, Soundview has high expectations of personal conduct. The result of this policy is a remarkably cooperative, considerate group of students who value each other and who appreciate their teachers.

Attire appropriate for a school is expected of all students, although there is no formal dress code.

ACADEMIC FACILITIES

Soundview's campus consists of 13.8 rustic acres with a historic main house, numerous outbuildings, a large pond, meadows, and woods, all in the heart of the village of Yorktown Heights, New York. The main house, the former Underhill mansion built by Yorktown's leading family in the nineteenth century, contains classrooms, administrative offices, the computer lab, and meeting rooms. A large barn houses the science lab, art studios, additional classrooms, and a cafeteria-meeting hall, while a third building is home to the Middle School. A fourth building provides another large meeting space, while a small former chapel is used seasonally for drama rehearsals. Woodland paths and footbridges lead across streams and around the property.

ATHLETICS

Physical education and sports at Soundview offer students the opportunity to develop leadership and teamwork skills as well as to excel in individual sports. Students participate on coed soccer, coed basketball, girls' basketball, and Ultimate Frisbee teams that compete against other independent schools in the Hudson Valley region. Depending upon student interest in a given year, other sports, such as tennis, softball, and baseball are also offered. Any student who wishes to play is accepted, regardless of ability.

The Ski and Snowboard Club offers opportunities for noncompetitive sports. For physical education, students play intramural sports, work out on exercise equipment, and participate in the Outdoors Club, clearing trails and planting gardens on school property.

Soundview's home gym is the Solaris Sports Club in Yorktown Heights, a state-of-the-art multisport center just blocks from the School. The facility includes tennis courts, a large indoor basketball court, and exercise equipment.

EXTRACURRICULAR OPPORTUNITIES

Soundview offers a wide range of clubs and activities, with additional choices added each year by students themselves.

Drama is important at Soundview. Students perform at School functions, attend plays on Broadway, and meet backstage with theater professionals. The Language Club sponsors schoolwide activities and organizes trips at home and an annual trip abroad. The Community Service Club works on such projects as collecting food for local food banks.

Other activities students are likely to sign up for include yearbook, literary magazine, student newspaper, mock trials, Film Club, Chess Club, Politics Club, Ski and Snowboarding Club, Tech Club, and Arts and Music Club.

Major annual functions at Soundview include the Back-to-School Picnic; the Spring Gala, a dinner and fund-raiser for the Soundview community; the Talent Show, which involves every student in the School; Texas Day, a lighthearted event featuring a barbecue, games, and spoofs on the Headmaster's home state; and the Graduation Dinner, an evening for Soundview parents to honor the graduating class.

DAILY LIFE

The school day begins at 8:10 with Morning Meeting, when the entire student body, faculty, and staff assemble to hear announcements about ongoing activities, listen to presentations by clubs, and discuss the day's national and international news. The Headmaster encourages students to express their views and helps them to assess events that are unfolding in the world around them.

Classes begin at 8:25 and end at 3:25. There are eight academic periods plus lunch.

SUMMER PROGRAMS

Soundview offers a small summer school on an as-needed basis, with classes that vary each year. A typical offering includes English, writing, math, history, a science, and a language. Students have

the opportunity to work one-on-one with a teacher or in small classes to skip ahead in a given subject or fulfill a requirement.

COSTS AND FINANCIAL AID

Tuition and fees for 2010–11 were $32,600 for Middle School and $33,700 for Upper School. Fees include gym, books, art and lab fees, ERB exams, and literary publications.

In 2009–10, the School provided a total of $436,000 in financial aid to approximately 30 percent of the student body.

ADMISSIONS INFORMATION

Soundview operates on a rolling admissions policy, with students accepted throughout the year in all grades except twelfth. Families of prospective students meet with the Admissions Director, after which the student spends a day at the School. The SSAT is not required, but portions of the ERB standardized examination are administered (unless the applicant provides the School with sufficient, current test data).

Students of all backgrounds are welcomed. The academic program is demanding, but the School's small size allows it to work with each individual student in order to develop strategies for success.

APPLICATION TIMETABLE

Soundview accepts applications on a rolling basis throughout the year. The application fee is $50.

ADMISSIONS CORRESPONDENCE

Mary E. Ivanyi
Director of Admissions and Assistant Head
Soundview Preparatory School
370 Underhill Road
Yorktown Heights, New York 10598

Phone: 914-962-2780
E-mail: info@soundviewprep.org
Web site: http://www.soundviewprep.org

SOUTHWESTERN ACADEMY

Beaver Creek Ranch, Arizona

Type: Coeducational boarding and day college-preparatory and general academic school
Grades: 9–12, postgraduate year
Enrollment: 45
Head of School: Kenneth R. Veronda, Headmaster

THE SCHOOL

Southwestern Academy offers achievement-based, departmentalized, and supportively structured classes limited to 9 to 12 students. Small classes allow for individualized attention in a noncompetitive environment. Southwestern was founded by Maurice Veronda in 1924 as a college-preparatory program "for capable students who could do better" in small, supportive classes. While maintaining that commitment, Southwestern Academy includes U.S. and international students with strong academic abilities who are eager to learn and strengthen English-language skills as well as pursue a general scholastic program in a small, supportive school structure. Southwestern Academy is accredited by the Western Association of Schools and Colleges (WASC).

Southwestern Academy offers students the opportunity to study at either of two distinctly different and beautiful campuses. The Arizona campus, which is known as Beaver Creek Ranch, is located deep in a red-rock canyon in northern Arizona. The San Marino, California, campus is situated in a historic orange grove area near Pasadena. Students may attend either campus and, if space permits, may divide the academic year between the two.

The Beaver Creek campus is a 180-acre ranch located 100 miles north of Phoenix, 12 miles from the resort community of Sedona, and 45 miles south of Flagstaff. The San Marino campus occupies 8 acres in a residential suburb 10 miles from downtown Los Angeles and immediately south of Pasadena, home to the renowned Tournament of Roses Parade. Although the program and philosophies are the same at both campuses, each offers a very different learning environment. Students studying at the Beaver Creek Ranch campus enjoy a living and learning environment that takes full advantage of the rich cultural, scenic, and environmentally significant region. Students at the California campus draw on the offerings of the urban setting.

A mix of U.S. and international students from several countries offers a unique blend of cultural, social, and educational opportunities for all. Every effort is made to enroll a well-balanced student body that represents the rich ethnic diversity of U.S. citizens and students from around the world. The student body consists of college-bound students who prefer a small, personalized education; above-average students who have the potential to become excellent academic achievers in the right learning environment; and average students who, with a supportive structure, can achieve academic success.

Southwestern Academy is incorporated as a not-for-profit organization. Operating expenses are approximately $4.2 million per annum and are met by tuition (92 percent) and grants and annual giving (8 percent). The Academy has no indebtedness.

ACADEMIC PROGRAMS

Middle school students are placed in classes based on individual achievement levels. High school classes are divided by grade level, and students are assigned based on ability and achievement.

High school graduation requirements are based on University of California requirements and include completion of a minimum of 200 academic credits plus 40 credit hours of physical education. The academic term is mid-September through mid-June, with a summer quarter offered at both campuses. Requirements include 4 years of English, 3 years of mathematics, 2 years of a foreign language, 2 years of laboratory sciences, and 1 year each of U.S. history and world cultures, plus one semester of U.S. government and economics and 2 years of visual/performing arts. Proficiency exams in English, mathematics, and computer literacy, as well as community service hours, are also required for graduation.

A typical semester of course work includes six classes plus physical education. Advanced Placement classes are available in English, history, language, math, and science. Review and remedial classes are made available to students who need additional instruction. International students are offered three levels of classes in English as a second language (ESL), including an introductory class, to prepare them to enter and succeed in other academic areas.

Teachers are available daily during a midafternoon study period to work individually with students and meet with parents. There is no extra charge for this tutoring. Boarding students are required to attend a monitored evening study hall, where additional teacher assistance is available.

Student achievement is recognized with a grading system that ranges from A to F. Progress letters are sent monthly to parents and report cards are sent quarterly. The minimum college-recommending grade upon completion of academic requirements is C.

Students studying at the Beaver Creek Ranch campus attend classes on a block schedule, Monday through Thursday. Each Friday, students participate in educational, project-oriented, and assignment-based field trips. Experiential learning allows students to apply knowledge from the classroom. It also supports an integrated academic element that links core subject areas in a practical, applied manner, promoting understanding and retention of key concepts.

FACULTY AND ADVISERS

Headmaster Kenneth Veronda was born at the San Marino campus that his father founded. Mr. Veronda attended classes at Southwestern, graduated, and completed undergraduate and graduate work in American history and foreign relations at Stanford University. The majority of 31 faculty members, 9 in Arizona and 22 in California, hold advanced degrees in their subject areas. Each teacher serves as a faculty adviser to a few students and meets with them individually throughout the school year. On-campus college and career counselors are also available to meet with and assist students in making post–high school graduation plans.

COLLEGE ADMISSION COUNSELING

The college counselors closely monitor the advisement and placement needs of each student. Beginning in the ninth grade, every effort is made to assist students in researching a variety of colleges and universities that match their interests and academic achievement levels. Students are provided a college planning handbook that offers helpful hints and suggestions regarding college application processes.

A variety of college representatives are invited annually to visit each campus and meet with students.

Approximately 35 students graduate each year from Southwestern Academy. Almost all enter a U.S. college or university. Some choose to attend a local two-year community college before transferring to a four-year college or university. In recent years, Southwestern Academy graduates have been accepted to the following schools: American; Arizona State; Art Center College of Design; Azusa Pacific; Boston University; Brown; Butler; California State, Fullerton, Monterey Bay, and Northridge; California State Polytechnic, Pomona; Columbia; Hampton; Howard; Loyola; Marymount; Menlo College; Mills; Occidental; Oregon State; Parsons; Penn State; Pepperdine; Pitzer; Temple; USC, Whittier; Woodbury; Wooster; Xavier; and the Universities of California, La Verne, Nevada, New Orleans, the Pacific, San Diego, San Francisco, and Washington (Seattle).

ACADEMIC FACILITIES

At the Beaver Creek Ranch campus, newly renovated classrooms, a learning resource center, and the dormitories blend into the picturesque setting. The campus also includes recreation rooms, a gymnasium, several large activity fields, and an indoor, solar-heated swimming pool.

The San Marino campus includes seven buildings encircling a large multisport athletic field. Lincoln Hall, the main academic building, houses morning assembly and study hall, ten classrooms, science and computer labs, and the library. Pioneer Hall includes several classrooms, a kitchen, dining rooms, and business offices. A separate building is home to large music and art studios and an additional science classroom and lab.

BOARDING AND GENERAL FACILITIES

The Beaver Creek Ranch Campus offers dorm rooms that accommodate 1 to 4 people. Meals are served in the dining room and sometimes in the charming courtyard. Picnics are also popular. A lounge with a huge fireplace is a favorite spot for students to watch movies and DirectTV®.

Seven stone cottages are home to faculty and staff members and sometimes upperclassmen and are set along the trout-filled Beaver Creek. Two fishing ponds, pastures, prehistoric Indian caves, and a favorite swimming hole in the creek are found on campus. Even in this remote, rugged environment, students can e-mail friends and surf the Internet, thanks to the T-1 wireless connectivity.

Four dormitory halls are located on the San Marino campus. Each is designed to accommodate up to 20 boys in double and single rooms. Two off-campus dormitories (located within a mile) house a total of 32 girls. Dorm parents live in apartments adjoining each hall.

ATHLETICS

Gyms and playing fields are available to all students at both campuses, where sports opportunities exist for physical education requirements and recreation. As a member of federated leagues in Arizona and California, Southwestern Academy fields teams at both campuses in all major sports except tackle football. Athletic events are held in late afternoon following the regular school day.

EXTRACURRICULAR OPPORTUNITIES

At the Beaver Creek Ranch campus, students can learn to ride and care for horses or swing on a rope over the creek—and drop in for a swim! The indoor pool is heated for those who prefer warmer water. The campus offers a full program of sports, including golf, and a full range of art classes. Wildlife, including mule deer, bighorn sheep, and javelina, can be seen on hikes. Other recreation opportunities include camping, hiking, mountain biking, fishing, and backpacking.

Southwestern offers a wide range of co-curricular and extracurricular activities and opportunities, including art, drama, music, journalism, student government, and student clubs. Current clubs include chess, Interact, International, the Southwestern Arts Society, Southwestern Environmental Associates, and tennis. Frequent class trips to southern California and northern Arizona places of interest, such as tide pools, museums, archaeological sites, art galleries, and live theater, are great learning experiences for students at both campuses.

DAILY LIFE

Boarding students begin each school day with a breakfast buffet at 7:30 a.m.. Following breakfast, day and boarding students meet for a required assembly at 8:10, with classes following from 8:30 to 2:45. Required study halls and optional clubs and athletic events are held between 2:50 and 4:30 p.m.. Dinner is served at 6 and is followed by a monitored study hall lasting until 8. Lights out is at 10:30 for middle school students and 11 for those in high school.

SUMMER PROGRAMS

Summer school sessions are offered at both campuses. Both offer intensive yet enjoyable individualized classes in English and other subjects, plus educational and recreational trips to interesting places in northern Arizona and southern California.

Summer sessions at Beaver Creek Ranch combine review and enrichment courses with experiential learning and high-adventure activities in classwork, camp-type activities, and travel in northern Arizona. ESL is offered at the Beaver Creek campus during the summer.

The summer program in San Marino is an excellent opportunity for domestic students to catch up, if needed, or to move ahead academically in order to take more advanced courses before graduation. For non-English-speaking international students, the summer session can provide an entire semester of the appropriate ESL level necessary to successfully complete a college-preparatory curriculum.

COSTS AND FINANCIAL AID

Tuition for a 2010–11 U.S. boarding student is $30,700. International student tuition is $36,750. The cost for a day student (U.S. citizens and permanent residents only) is $14,900. An incidental account containing $2000 for boarding students or $1000 for day students is required of all students to cover expenses such as books, school supplies, physical education uniforms, and discretionary spending money. Payment is due in advance unless other arrangements are made with the business office.

Financial aid is awarded based on financial need. More than $730,000 was awarded in 2010–11.

ADMISSIONS INFORMATION

Southwestern Academy admits students of any race, color, national and ethnic origin, creed, or sex. A completed application packet is required, followed by a personal on-campus interview with students and parents. A daylong visit to classes (and an overnight for prospective boarding students) is strongly encouraged for prospective students already living in the United States. Interviews with prospective international students and parents are scheduled by the international admissions director and do not require a campus visit.

Each campus offers exceptional learning opportunities. Prospective students are encouraged to seriously consider both campuses and apply to the one that seems better suited to them.

Admission materials and other information can be downloaded from the Southwestern Academy Web site. It can also be obtained by contacting the Office of Admissions.

APPLICATION TIMETABLE

Admission offers are made throughout the year, as space permits. Appointments are required for interviews and campus tours at both locations. The admissions office for both campus locations is located in San Marino. Students should write or call the San Marino office for information on either campus.

ADMISSIONS CORRESPONDENCE

Office of Admissions
Southwestern Academy
2800 Monterey Road
San Marino, California 91108
Phone: 626-799-5010 Ext. 5
Fax: 626-799-0407
E-mail: admissions@southwesternacademy.edu
Web site: http://www.southwesternacademy.edu

SOUTHWESTERN ACADEMY

San Marino, California

Type: Coeducational boarding and day college-preparatory and general academic school
Grades: 6–12, postgraduate year
Enrollment: 140
Head of School: Kenneth R. Veronda, Headmaster

THE SCHOOL

Southwestern Academy offers achievement-based, departmentalized, and supportively structured classes limited to 9 to 12 students. Small classes allow for individualized attention in a noncompetitive environment. Southwestern was founded by Maurice Veronda in 1924 as a college-preparatory program "for capable students who could do better" in small, supportive classes. While maintaining that commitment, Southwestern Academy includes U.S. and international students with strong academic abilities who are eager to learn and strengthen English-language skills as well as pursue a general scholastic program in a small, supportive school structure. Southwestern Academy is accredited by the Western Association of Schools and Colleges (WASC).

Southwestern Academy offers students the opportunity to study at either of two distinctly different and beautiful campuses. The San Marino, California, campus is situated in a historic orange grove area near Pasadena. The Arizona campus, which is known as Beaver Creek Ranch, is located deep in a red-rock canyon in northern Arizona. Students may attend either campus and, if space permits, may divide the academic year between the two.

The San Marino campus occupies 8 acres in a residential suburb 10 miles from downtown Los Angeles and immediately south of Pasadena, home to the renowned Tournament of Roses Parade. The Beaver Creek campus is a 180-acre ranch located 100 miles north of Phoenix, 12 miles from the resort community of Sedona, and 45 miles south of Flagstaff. Although the program and philosophies are the same at both campuses, each offers a very different learning environment. Students at the California campus draw on the offerings of the urban setting. Students studying at the Beaver Creek Ranch campus enjoy a living and learning environment that takes full advantage of the rich cultural, scenic, and environmentally significant region.

A mix of U.S. and international students from several countries offers a unique blend of cultural, social, and educational opportunities for all. Every effort is made to enroll a well-balanced student body that represents the rich ethnic diversity of U.S. citizens and students from around the world. The student body consists of college-bound students who prefer a small, personalized education; above-average students who have the potential to become excellent academic achievers in the right learning environment; and average students who, with a supportive structure, can achieve academic success.

Southwestern Academy is incorporated as a not-for-profit organization. Operating expenses are approximately $4.2 million per annum and are met by tuition (92 percent) and grants and annual giving (8 percent). The Academy has no indebtedness.

ACADEMIC PROGRAMS

Middle school students are placed in classes based on individual achievement levels. High school classes are divided by grade level, and students are assigned based on ability and achievement.

High school graduation requirements are based on University of California requirements and include completion of a minimum of 200 academic credits plus 40 credit hours of physical education. The academic term is mid-September through mid-June, with a summer quarter offered at both campuses. Requirements include 4 years of English, 3 years of mathematics, 2 years of a foreign language, 2 years of laboratory sciences, and 1 year each of U.S. history and world cultures, plus one semester of U.S. government and economics and 2 years of visual/performing arts. Proficiency exams in English, mathematics, and computer literacy, as well as community service hours, are also required for graduation.

A typical semester of course work includes six classes plus physical education. Advanced Placement classes are available in English, history, language, math, and science. Review and remedial classes are made available to students who need additional instruction. International students are offered three levels of classes in English as a second language (ESL), including an introductory class, to prepare them to enter and succeed in other academic areas.

Teachers are available daily during a midafternoon study period to work individually with students and meet with parents. There is no extra charge for this tutoring. Boarding students are required to attend a monitored evening study hall, where additional teacher assistance is available.

Student achievement is recognized with a grading system that ranges from A to F. Progress letters are sent monthly to parents and report cards are sent quarterly. The minimum college-recommending grade upon completion of academic requirements is C.

While studying at the Beaver Creek Ranch campus, students attend classes on a block schedule, Monday through Thursday. Each Friday, students participate in educational, project-oriented, and assignment-based field trips. Experiential learning allows students to apply knowledge from the classroom. It also supports an integrated academic element that links core subject areas in a practical, applied manner, promoting understanding and retention of key concepts.

FACULTY AND ADVISERS

Headmaster Kenneth Veronda was born at the San Marino campus that his father founded. Mr. Veronda attended classes at Southwestern, graduated, and completed undergraduate and graduate work in American history and foreign relations at Stanford University. The majority of 31 faculty members, 22 in California and 9 in Arizona, hold advanced degrees in their subject areas. Each

teacher serves as a faculty adviser to a few students and meets with them individually throughout the school year. On-campus college and career counselors are also available to meet with and assist students in making post–high school graduation plans.

COLLEGE ADMISSION COUNSELING

The college counselors closely monitor the advisement and placement needs of each student. Beginning in the ninth grade, every effort is made to assist students in researching a variety of colleges and universities that match their interests and academic achievement levels. Students are provided a college planning handbook that offers helpful hints and suggestions regarding college application processes. A variety of college representatives are invited annually to visit each campus and meet with students.

Approximately 35 students graduate each year from Southwestern Academy. Almost all enter a U.S. college or university. Some choose to attend a local two-year community college before transferring to a four-year college or university. In recent years, Southwestern Academy graduates have been accepted to the following schools: American; Arizona State; Art Center College of Design; Azusa Pacific; Boston University; Brown; Butler; California State, Fullerton, Monterey Bay, and Northridge; California State Polytechnic, Pomona; Columbia; Hampton; Howard; Loyola; Marymount; Menlo College; Mills; Occidental; Oregon State; Parsons; Penn State; Pepperdine; Pitzer; Temple; USC, Whittier; Woodbury; Wooster; Xavier; and the Universities of California, La Verne, Nevada, New Orleans, the Pacific, San Diego, San Francisco, and Washington (Seattle).

ACADEMIC FACILITIES

The San Marino campus includes seven buildings encircling a large multisport athletic field. Lincoln Hall, the main academic building, houses morning assembly and study hall, ten classrooms, science and computer labs, and the library. Pioneer Hall includes several classrooms, a kitchen, dining rooms, and business offices. A separate building is home to large music and art studios and an additional science classroom and lab.

Newly renovated classrooms, a learning resource center, and the dormitories blend into the picturesque setting along Beaver Creek.

BOARDING AND GENERAL FACILITIES

Four dormitory halls are located on the San Marino campus. Each is designed to accommodate up to 20 boys in double and single rooms. Two off-campus dormitories (located within a mile) house a total of 32 girls. Dorm parents live in apartments adjoining each hall.

At Beaver Creek, seven stone cottages encircle the main campus area and provide faculty/staff housing. Four recently renovated residence halls accommodate up to 56 students. The Beaver Creek

Ranch campus includes recreation rooms, a gymnasium, several large activity fields, and an indoor, solar-heated swimming pool.

ATHLETICS

Gyms and playing fields are available to all students at both campuses, where sports opportunities exist for physical education requirements and recreation. As a member of federated leagues in California and Arizona, Southwestern Academy fields teams at both campuses in all major sports except tackle football. Athletic events are held in late afternoon, following the regular school day.

EXTRACURRICULAR OPPORTUNITIES

Southwestern offers a wide range of cocurricular and extracurricular activities and opportunities, including art, drama, music, journalism, student government, and student clubs. Current clubs include chess, Interact, International, the Southwestern Arts Society, Southwestern Environmental Associates, and tennis. Frequent class trips to southern California and northern Arizona places of interest, such as tide pools, museums, archaeological sites, art galleries, and live theater, are great learning experiences for students at both campuses.

DAILY LIFE

Boarding students begin each school day with a breakfast buffet at 7:30. Following breakfast, day and boarding students meet for a required assembly at 8:10, with classes following from 8:30 to 2:45. Required study halls and optional clubs and athletic events are held between 2:50 and 4:30. Dinner is served at 6 and is followed by a monitored study hall lasting until 8. Lights out is at 10:30 for middle school students and 11 for high schoolers.

WEEKEND LIFE

Students in good standing may leave the campus, with permission, during any weekend. Many students take advantage of the planned activities that are arranged for them, including theater performances, shopping at the malls and Old Town Pasadena, barbecues, beach parties, and movies. Visits are planned to Disneyland, Magic Mountain, and Big Surf, and the other attractions of the two-state areas are a part of the social program at Southwestern Academy. Day students are welcome to attend all weekend activities if space permits.

SUMMER PROGRAMS

Summer school sessions are offered at both campuses. Both offer intensive yet enjoyable individualized classes in English and other subjects, plus educational and recreational trips to interesting places in southern California and northern Arizona.

The summer program in San Marino is an excellent opportunity for domestic students to catch up, if needed, or to move ahead academically in order to take more advanced courses before graduation. For non-English-speaking international students, the summer session can provide an entire semester of the appropriate ESL level necessary to successfully complete a college-preparatory curriculum.

Summer sessions at Beaver Creek Ranch combine review and enrichment courses with experiential learning and high-adventure activities in classwork, camp-type activities, and travel in northern Arizona. ESL is offered at the Beaver Creek campus during the summer.

COSTS AND FINANCIAL AID

Tuition for the 2010–11 U.S. boarding student is $30,700. International student tuition is $36,750. The cost for a day student (U.S. citizens and permanent residents only) is $14,900. An incidental account containing $2000 for boarding students or $1000 for day students is required of all students to cover expenses such as books, school supplies, physical education uniforms, and discretionary spending money. Payment is due in advance unless other arrangements are made with the business office.

Financial aid is awarded based on financial need. More than $730,000 was awarded in 2010–11.

ADMISSIONS INFORMATION

Southwestern Academy admits students of any race, color, national and ethnic origin, creed, or sex. A completed application packet is required, followed by a personal on-campus interview with students and parents. A daylong visit to classes (and an overnight for prospective boarding students) is strongly encouraged for prospective students already living in the United States. Interviews with prospective international students and parents are scheduled by the international admissions director and do not require a campus visit.

Each campus offers exceptional learning opportunities. Prospective students are encouraged to seriously consider both campuses and apply to the one that seems better suited to them.

Admission materials and other information can be downloaded from the Southwestern Academy Web site. It can also be obtained by contacting the Office of Admissions.

APPLICATION TIMETABLE

Admission offers are made throughout the year, as space permits. Appointments are required for interviews and campus tours at both locations. The admissions office for both campus locations is located in San Marino. Students should write or call the San Marino office for information on either campus.

ADMISSIONS CORRESPONDENCE

Office of Admissions
Southwestern Academy
2800 Monterey Road
San Marino, California 91108

Phone: 626-799-5010 Ext. 5
Fax: 626-799-0407
E-mail: admissions@southwesternacademy.edu
Web site: http://www.southwesternacademy.edu

SUFFIELD ACADEMY

Suffield, Connecticut

Type: Coeducational boarding and day college-preparatory school
Grades: 9–12, postgraduate year
Enrollment: 400
Head of School: Charles Cahn III, Headmaster

THE SCHOOL

Challenge, structure, support, and a strong sense of community characterize Suffield Academy. A rigorous college-preparatory program in academics is supported by an extensive emphasis on leadership training. Beautiful new facilities for academics, athletics, and the arts support each student's education. The school has a tradition of academic and athletic excellence and a deep sense of community spirit.

Founded as the Connecticut Literary Institution in 1833, the school became coeducational in 1843 and provided a traditional education for 100 years as both a private academy and the town's only public high school. It took the name of Suffield Academy in 1916 and after World War II became a fully independent boarding and day school for boys. In 1974, Suffield Academy returned to coeducation.

Suffield's strength lies in the personal concern and support shown for each student. The school emphasizes small classes and a structured academic program. In this setting, faculty members encourage students to take an active role in their education and to seek creative insights and solutions.

Each student is challenged intellectually, ethically, and physically to make the best use of his or her talents while developing a sound system of personal and social values.

The Academy's beautiful 350-acre campus is located in the historic residential town of Suffield, Connecticut, a community of 15,000 people located in a region that offers excellent opportunities for bicycling and hiking. Concerts, museums, theaters, and other city offerings are easily accessible in Springfield, Massachusetts, 10 miles north of Suffield, and Hartford, Connecticut, 17 miles to the south. New York is 135 miles to the south, and Boston is 90 miles to the northeast. Bradley International Airport is 5 miles from the campus.

A nonprofit institution, Suffield is governed by a self-perpetuating 30-member Board of Trustees. It has an endowment of $32 million. The School has raised over $55 million since 2002 and the annual budget is more than $17 million.

Suffield is accredited by the New England Association of Schools and Colleges. It is a member of or is affiliated with each of the following organizations: the Connecticut Association of Independent Schools, the National Association of Independent Schools, the Cum Laude Society, American Secondary Schools for International Students and Teachers (ASSIST), the Secondary School Admission Test Board, A Better Chance, the Council for Advancement and Support of Education, Hartford Area Boarding Schools, the Hartford Youth Scholars Foundation, the SPHERE Consortium, and the WALKS Foundation.

ACADEMIC PROGRAMS

Suffield offers a college-preparatory curriculum that is grounded in the liberal arts. The academic program stresses acquiring the fundamental skills and knowledge needed to succeed in a variety of academic disciplines and in college. With careful guidance, students select a program of study designed to meet special interests and needs.

The school year is divided into three terms. Classes are held six days a week but end at noon on Wednesday and at 11 a.m. on Saturday, when athletics contests are scheduled in the afternoon. Classes average 10 students, and each class meets four times per week (two 45-minute periods and two extended 70-minute periods). Teachers are available for extra help on an individual basis. Students also have the support of faculty advisers and a walk-in counseling office. The student-faculty ratio is 7:1.

The Suffield Leadership program is a distinguishing characteristic of the school. The program is required for all students and emphasizes seven core elements which each student is exposed to in direct ways: (1) personal mastery, (2) moral foundation, (3) goal-setting, (4) communication skills, (5) problem-solving, (6) self-awareness, and (7) inspiring and mobilizing others. The overarching goal is to help students build the skills and habits that lend themselves to effective leadership. The program is housed in a beautiful academic building (Centurion Hall) and also makes use of the Courtney Robinson '88 Outdoor Leadership Center. This facility, located on 40 acres, houses an indoor climbing wall and outdoor high ropes course.

Students may choose from course offerings in the visual arts (painting, sculpture, woodworking, architecture, computer graphics, and more) or the performing arts (instrument ensembles, choral groups, dance, and private instruction in voice or instrument) to satisfy the requirement of a year's study in the arts. Artists wishing to pursue these areas in an in-depth fashion will also have this opportunity at Suffield, as a gifted faculty and extensive facilities are dedicated to the arts.

The Academic Support Office provides resources for students who have different learning styles or challenges, as shown by their prior academic evaluation. The Director of Academic Support meets regularly with each student to create strategies that will sharpen their focus and strengthen their academic performance in the classroom. The Director also works with faculty members to communicate specific student needs so that Academy teachers are better able to meet the needs of students who have a broad range of learning styles.

Freshmen and sophomores carry five or six full-credit courses; juniors and seniors carry four, five, or six. To graduate, a student must demonstrate computer literacy and complete a total of 20⅓ credits, including 4 credits in English; 4 in leadership classes; 3 in mathematics; 2 in history, including 1 in U.S. history and 1 in area studies; 2 in language studies; 2 in science, including 1 in a laboratory science; 2 in technology portfolios; 1 in the arts; ⅓ in religion; and the balance in electives.

All major departments offer honors-level courses. Advanced Placement courses are offered in computer science, English, foreign languages, history, math, and science. Interest in a course may lead to individual work with a teacher. In the senior year, students may select an independent study project for credit.

Grades, based on a minimum passing grade of D-, are recorded every five weeks. Effort also plays a significant part in the grading system. Academic reports from teachers (including grade, effort rating, and detailed comments), along with an evaluation from the adviser, are sent to parents at the end of each term and at the first midterm.

Ample time is provided for uninterrupted study, both during the day and in the evening. All boarding students study in their rooms, in the library, or in the computer lab in the evening from 8 to 10. Unsatisfactory effort necessitates attendance at supervised study halls during the day and evening until the student's effort improves.

FACULTY AND ADVISERS

There are 85 dedicated men and women on the faculty at Suffield Academy, over 60 of whom have or are working toward graduate degrees. Faculty members and their families live on campus and all serve as advisers, coaches, dormitory parents, activity supervisors, and trip leaders. They engage in training programs and workshops as well as graduate programs leading to advanced degrees and professional expertise in their academic discipline.

Charles Cahn III is in his seventh year as Headmaster. He has been a leader at Suffield for sixteen years. Mr. Cahn is a respected, dynamic person with great enthusiasm for Suffield Academy. He is widely admired in the independent school community and is a tremendous asset for Suffield. Prior to being appointed headmaster in 2003, Mr. Cahn served as an English teacher, varsity lacrosse coach, dorm parent, director of admissions, dean of faculty, and associate headmaster. He is familiar with all aspects of the school. A native of Baltimore, Maryland, Mr. Cahn is a graduate of Gilman School, the University of Michigan, and Wesleyan University. His wife, Hillary Rockwell Cahn ('88) teaches photography and coaches Suffield's alpine ski team. They live on the Suffield campus with their 2 children.

Suffield is above all a caring school, and its faculty members reflect this attitude. All faculty members serve as advisers, with an average advisee group of 5 students. Students select their advisers, meet with them on a regular basis, and confer with them when needed. Two traditional annual events, Parents' Day in the fall and Spring Parents' Weekend, feature parental conferences with teachers and advisers that enable parents to share the results of their son's or daughter's experience at Suffield. Advisers are available to meet with parents and teachers as needed concerning a student's progress.

COLLEGE ADMISSION COUNSELING

Suffield's College Counseling Office provides a comprehensive program. This is one of the school's main focal points. The office is well staffed and offers proactive and hands-on college search assistance for students and parents. Preparatory testing begins in the sophomore year, and all students take part in College 101 during the junior year. This six-week course provides an overview of several important areas: the college counseling process at Suffield, options for standardized test preparation and the differences between the SAT and the ACT, shaping a college list, writing effective application essays, building a resume, and preparing for campus visits. Representatives of more than 100 colleges visit the school annually, and students are encouraged to visit colleges.

In 2010, graduates enrolled in over eighty colleges and universities, including Amherst, Brown, Columbia, Cornell, Georgetown, Middlebury, NYU, Swarthmore, Vanderbilt, and Williams.

STUDENT BODY AND CONDUCT

The student community of 2010–11 had an enrollment of 410 students; 155 were boarding boys, 125 were boarding girls, 60 were day boys, and 70 were day girls. Students came from twenty states and twenty-six other countries. A wealth of understanding and enrichment is fostered through this diversity of cultural backgrounds.

Although all students are encouraged to become constructively involved in the extracurricular life of the school, class representatives contribute to the decision-making process through participation in the Student Council and Discipline Committee. Cooperation and consideration of the rights of others are important factors in the decision-making process of each student. Each student holds at least one leadership position as part of the school's four-year leadership program.

The School Work Program and off-campus Community Service Program are vital parts of Suffield Academy life, promoting pride in the school and respect for other people. Everyone in the Suffield community performs a daily job that contributes to the general well-being of the school. A number of seniors and faculty members oversee this program.

ACADEMIC FACILITIES

The school occupies over twenty major buildings, including Centurion Hall, the main classroom building that houses courses for leadership, math, and history. Memorial Building is where English and language courses are held; this facility also houses the technology center and Academic Support Office. There is a dedicated science building with several labs, and a beautiful, historic library. The Jeanice H. Seaverns Performing Arts Center and Guttag Music Center include a 200-seat theater, an art gallery, a set design studio and scene shop, a recording studio, practice rooms, and space for Suffield's dance and choral programs. The Emily Hall Tremaine Visual Arts Center features a multipurpose art studio, ceramics studio, graphics lab, photography lab, library office, and gallery. Nondenominational chapel services are held once a week in the town's Second Baptist Church. The new wellness center opened in fall

2007, and renovations in the music and performing arts center were completed in winter 2008.

BOARDING AND GENERAL FACILITIES

Twelve dormitories provide double rooms for 280 students. All dorm rooms are wired for both telephone and Internet use. Five new cottage-style dorms opened in September 1998. The newest dorm, Rockwell Hall, opened in 2008. It also houses a state-of-the-art Health Center. Fuller and Spencer Halls are larger dormitories housing 46 and 50 students, respectively. There are also four homes, each shared by between 6 and 12 students. All dormitories have faculty residents, including families, and student proctors.

The downstairs part of Brewster Hall contains the school dining room, the kitchen, and the student union with lounge, TV room, game room, snack area, bookstore, and post office. Other buildings are the Fuller Hall administration building and the historic Gay Mansion, the official residence of the Headmaster.

ATHLETICS

With more than thirty-five interscholastic teams, as well as various other athletics options, all students participate in sports on a level of competition that matches individual experience and ability. Athletics at Suffield stress good sportsmanship, acquisition of skills, and leadership development. The new Tisch Fieldhouse, opened in 2009, is a gorgeous, 30,000-square-foot facility housing two multipurpose courts, a squash center, and a new athletic training facility. It complements Sherman Perry Gymnasium, which has a newly renovated fitness center and wrestling room, a riflery range, and a classic wood basketball court. The campus includes a football field, five soccer fields, two baseball diamonds and a softball diamond, ten tennis courts, a hockey field, three lacrosse fields, a sand volleyball pit, and an all-weather track. Facilities for skiing and golf are available nearby. Fitness programs, outdoor programs, team management, volunteer service, or play production may be undertaken in lieu of interscholastic sports. A new synthetic turf field was constructed in 2008.

EXTRACURRICULAR OPPORTUNITIES

Suffield believes that every student should become constructively involved in the life of the school outside of the classroom. In addition to weekly chapel and a varied program of assemblies, both required, the school sponsors visiting artists and professionals who share experiences with the student body that often provoke new interests.

Students may choose from more than twenty-five activities, including concert and theater series, bicycling, bands, the yearbook, drama productions, the school newspaper, photography, chess, horseback riding, community service, and computers. Suffield Outdoor Leadership Opportunities (S.O.L.O.) maintains an active program, including rock-climbing, caving, backpacking, hiking, canoeing, camping, and other seasonal activities. The school opened an outdoor leadership center in 2000 with a rock-climbing wall and high and low ropes courses. Suffield's location gives students access to plays, concerts, and museums in two major cities.

DAILY LIFE

Classes begin at 8 a.m. and conclude at 3:05 p.m. on Monday, Tuesday, Thursday, and Friday. Athletics follow the end of the academic day. Only morning classes are scheduled on Wednesday and

Saturday; the afternoons are reserved for interscholastic athletics contests. Most clubs meet after dinner.

WEEKEND LIFE

The Student Union was expanded, redesigned, and renovated in 1992. The Weekend Activities and Film committees, as well as the Student Union Board of Governors, use this facility as the center of social life at the school.

On-campus weekend activities include dances, live entertainment, films, plays, and special events, such as Chill on the Hill and Luau. Off-campus options include movies, ski and shopping trips, indoor tennis, and activities sponsored by the Weekend Committee.

Boarding students in good standing may, with parental permission, take an unlimited number of weekends. Rapport between day and boarding students is close, with day students sharing campus activities and many boarding students visiting day students' homes on weekends.

COSTS AND FINANCIAL AID

Charges for 2010–11 are $44,500 for boarders and $31,550 for day students. Additional expenses include books and supplies ($400–$600), spending money ($20/week), laundry, and travel. The required, subsidized computer purchase ranges in cost from $750 to $1800.

For 2010–11, 146 scholarships with a total value of almost $3.5 million have been awarded.

ADMISSIONS INFORMATION

The Admissions Committee seeks students who are committed to serious study and who have a sense of purpose, a good previous record both academically and personally, and supportive recommendations from persons who know the student well. Admissions requirements include the application form with a written essay; an academic transcript from the current school; letters of recommendation from the student's guidance counselor or placement officer, English and mathematics teachers, and a third teacher of the student's choice; and SSAT, SAT, PSAT, or WISC results. TOEFL is required from students for whom English is not their spoken language.

APPLICATION TIMETABLE

When classes are in session, campus interviews and tours are conducted daily from 8 a.m. to 2 p.m., (8 to 10 a.m. on Wednesday and Saturday). Prospective students are encouraged to visit the campus. Visits can also be arranged at times when school is not in session by contacting the Admissions Office.

Applications are due January 15 and should be accompanied by a $50 fee for domestic applicants; and a $100 fee for international applicants. The mailing of acceptances is March 10, and students are asked to reply by April 10.

ADMISSIONS CORRESPONDENCE

Terry Breault
Director of Admissions and Financial Aid
Suffield Academy
185 North Main Street
Suffield, Connecticut 06078

Phone: 860-386-4440
Fax: 860-668-2966
E-mail: saadmit@suffieldacademy.org
Web site: http://www.suffieldacademy.org

TASIS THE AMERICAN SCHOOL IN SWITZERLAND

Montagnola-Lugano, Switzerland

TASIS

Type: Coeducational boarding and day college-preparatory school
Grades: Pre-K–12, PG: Elementary School, pre-K–6; Middle School, 7–8; High School, 9–12, postgraduate year
Enrollment: School total: 600; High School: 341; Middle School: 59; Elementary School: 200
Head of School: Michael Ulku-Steiner, Headmaster

THE SCHOOL

TASIS The American School in Switzerland was founded in 1956 by Mrs. M. Crist Fleming to offer a strong American college-preparatory education in a European setting. TASIS was the first American boarding school established in Europe. Over time, it has become a school for students from more than fifty countries seeking an American independent school experience. The International Baccalaureate (I.B.) Program is also offered within this setting.

The objective of the School is to foster both a vital enthusiasm for learning and habits that are essential to a full realization of each student's moral and intellectual potential. The curriculum gives special emphasis to the achievements of the Western heritage, many elements of which are easily accessible from the School's location. By providing an international dimension to education, the School stresses the need for young people to mature with confidence and competence in an increasingly interrelated world.

The beautiful campus is in the village of Montagnola, overlooking the city and the lake of Lugano, nestled among the southernmost of the Swiss Alps in the Italian-speaking canton of Ticino. Ideally situated in the heart of Europe, the School makes the most of its location by introducing students to European cultures and languages through extensive travel programs.

The TASIS Foundation, a not-for-profit Swiss foundation, owns the School. The TASIS Foundation also has a school near London and offers summer programs in England, Spain, and Italy as well as Switzerland. Alumni provide enthusiastic support for the School's activities and participate in annual reunions and other special events.

TASIS is accredited by the Council of International Schools (CIS) and the New England Association of Schools and Colleges (NEASC) and is a member of the National Association of Independent Schools and the Swiss Group of International Schools.

ACADEMIC PROGRAMS

The minimum requirements for graduation from the high school college-preparatory program are 4 years of English, 3 years of history (including European and U.S. history), a third-year proficiency in a modern foreign language, 3 years of mathematics (through algebra II), 3 years of laboratory science (including physical and biological sciences), and 1 year of fine arts, plus senior humanities, sports/physical education, and community service requirements. Students must satisfactorily complete a minimum of 19 credits. Students are required to enroll in a minimum of five full-credit courses per year or the equivalent. A normal course load for students consists of six courses.

TASIS offers an extensive English as an additional language program that focuses on oral and written academic English skills and competence in a high school curriculum leading to the TASIS college-preparatory diploma.

TASIS offers a diverse and challenging curriculum, including the Advanced Placement Program (AP), the International Baccalaureate (I.B.) Diploma Programme, and a wide range of required and elective courses. In 2009, 59 students took ninety AP exams in ten subject areas; 21 percent of the scores were 4 or above and 7 percent earned the top score of 5. Students may also select I.B. courses and can earn subject-specific certificates or the full diploma. In 2009, 57 students took 305 I.B. exams; 82 percent of the scores were 4 or above, 56 percent were 5 or above, and 26 percent were 6 or above.

The average class size is 12; the teacher-student ratio is 1:6. The student's day is fully structured, including time for academics, sports and activities, meals and socializing, and supervised evening study hours. The grading system uses A to F for performance and assigns effort grades of 1 to 5, reflecting students' attitudes and application to their work. The academic year is divided into two semesters and grades and comment reports are e-mailed to parents five times a year.

The postgraduate year presents an additional opportunity to high school graduates who wish to spend an interim year in Europe before going on to college. Each postgraduate student can design a tailor-made course of study with the assistance and approval of the Academic Dean that enables him or her to explore and develop new interests, strengthen academic weaknesses, or concentrate in areas of strength or particular interest. It includes a course-related Academic Travel program.

FACULTY AND ADVISERS

The faculty represents one of the School's strongest assets. Its members are a group of dedicated professionals who are enthusiastic about working with young people. The TASIS faculty includes 91 full-time teaching administrators and faculty members, of whom 51 are women and 40 are men. Seventy-two percent of the faculty members have advanced degrees. Thirty-two faculty members live on campus; the rest live nearby and participate in most campus activities. In addition to teaching, faculty members act as advisers, sports coaches, trip chaperones, and dormitory residents and help to create a warm, family-like atmosphere.

COLLEGE ADMISSION COUNSELING

The School employs 4 full-time college counselors, who meet with students individually and in groups during their junior and senior years. The college counseling office maintains a reference library of university catalogs from around the world so that students can familiarize themselves with the wide variety of opportunities that are open to them. As a counseling resource, the School provides a small computer lab for college research. Many college admissions officers from universities in the U.S. and Europe visit the School and speak to students. TASIS is an official testing center for the PSAT, SAT, SAT Subject Tests, ACT, TOEFL, and all AP and I.B. examinations.

Recent graduates attend such institutions as Edinburgh, Reading, and Nottingham Universities in the U.K. and Boston University, Colorado College, George Washington, Notre Dame, Stanford, and Tufts in the United States.

STUDENT BODY AND CONDUCT

The total student enrollment of 600 consists of 200 Elementary day students, 280 Middle and High School boarding students, and 117 Middle and High School day students. They come from more than forty countries; 20 percent are American.

Each student is honor bound to abide by the rules, as defined in the TASIS *Student Handbook.* The School employs a variety of counseling, disciplinary, and administrative responses to rules violations, determined on a case-by-case basis. The School administration and Conduct Review Board handle more serious offenses. All responses take into account the seriousness of the offense, the number of previous offenses, any mitigating circumstances, and the student's record as a member of the TASIS community.

Students at TASIS bear a serious responsibility to conduct themselves not only in a way that does credit to them, to their School, and to their country of origin, but also in a way that is consistent with the high standards set by the citizens of the European countries they visit. For this reason, TASIS has established reasonable but definitive standards of behavior, attitude, and appearance for all of its students. The School reserves the right to ask any student to withdraw for failure to maintain these standards.

ACADEMIC FACILITIES

The historic and architecturally interesting seventeenth century Villa De Nobili was the original building of the School and houses the dining hall and dormitories. An extension houses the administration and the School's science laboratories. Hadsall House contains classrooms and dormitories. Villa Monticello contains modern classrooms, a computer center, and a computer-based language lab. Beside Villa Monticello is the 22,000-volume M. Crist Fleming Library. Villa Aurora contains classrooms and a large rehearsal space. The fine arts department is housed in Ca'Gioia. Classes are also held in the dormitories of Belvedere and Villa Del Sole. The Coach House has classrooms and photography studios. The School's Palestra houses a sports complex containing a gymnasium, a fitness center, a dance studio, locker rooms, a student lounge with a café, and music rooms. The School recently completed the John E. Palmer Cultural Center, which includes a state-of-the-art theater, and Fiammetta, which houses classrooms. Lanterna is the newest building, which includes classrooms and the health center. The newly renovated Casa Al Focolare houses Elementary School students from prekindergarten to the second grade.

BOARDING AND GENERAL FACILITIES

The campus includes ten dormitories, each of which houses from 6 to 43 students. Dormitories are located in Villa De Nobili, Villa Monticello, Hadsall House, Villa Del Sole, Balmelli, Giani, Belvedere, and Lanterna. All dormitories are supervised, and some faculty members live in the dormitories. Rooms accommodate from 2 to 4 students each. Although School facilities are closed during the winter and spring vacations, optional faculty-chaperoned trips are offered for students who are unable to return home.

Two recreation centers and a snack bar serve as focal points for student social activities. Three fully qualified nurses are in residence.

ATHLETICS

Students are required to participate in either a varsity sport three days a week or recreational sports after classes. Sports available include soccer, basketball, fitness training, mountain biking, volleyball, rugby, tennis, track and field, squash, swimming, rock climbing, and aerobics. Horseback riding and tennis are available at an extra cost. On weekends, students often go on hiking and mountain-climbing trips in the Swiss Alps during the fall and spring and go skiing during the winter. During Ski Week in Crans-Montana (High School) or Verbier (Middle School), every student takes lessons in downhill or cross-country skiing or snowboarding. The Fleming Cup ski race and a faculty versus students hockey game are held during the Crans-Montana week.

Varsity sports give students the opportunity to compete against many schools in Switzerland and other countries and to take part in tournaments sponsored by the Swiss Group of International Schools. Varsity sports include soccer, volleyball, basketball, tennis, and track and field. Students also have the opportunity to enroll in the AC Milan soccer program, run by the coaches of the renowned Italian soccer team AC Milan.

Facilities include a playing field, a gym, and an outdoor basketball/volleyball area. The newly constructed Palestra sports complex includes a gymnasium with seating for up to 400 spectators, a dance studio, a fitness center, changing rooms, and a student lounge with a café.

EXTRACURRICULAR OPPORTUNITIES

The School's location in central Europe offers an enviable range of cultural opportunities. Trips to concerts, art galleries, and museums in Lugano, Locarno, and Milan extend education beyond the classroom. All students participate in the the Academic Travel program, a four-day, faculty-chaperoned trip in the fall and a seven-day, faculty-chaperoned trip in the spring to such cities as Athens, Barcelona, Florence, Madrid, Munich, Nice, Paris, Prague, Rome, Venice, and Vienna.

On-campus activities include drama productions, choral and instrumental music, Model Congress, Environmental Club, Student Council, yearbook, and the Student Weekend Activities Team (SWAT). The Service Learning program focuses on the TASIS community, the local community, the inter-school community, and the global community. Opportunities include peer tutoring, volunteering at a local domestic violence shelter, participating in Model

UN, and work with Habitat for Humanity. TASIS also offers an annual summer service trip to Africa. Special annual social events include Family Weekend, dinner dances at the beginning of the academic year and at Christmas, prom, and the spring arts festival, along with a special graduation banquet and ceremony for seniors.

DAILY LIFE

Classes start at 8 a.m. and follow a rotating schedule. Classes meet from 50 to 65 minutes. There are weekly all-School assemblies, and students meet with their advisers every day. Sports and activities take place after school until 5:30 p.m. Meals are served buffet-style except for Wednesday evenings, when students share a formal dinner with their adviser group. Evening study is from 7 until 10.

WEEKEND LIFE

Both day and boarding students are encouraged to participate in organized events on weekends, including mountain-climbing and camping trips to scenic areas in Switzerland, shopping trips to open-air markets in northern Italy, and sightseeing excursions to Zurich, Milan, Venice, or Florence. On-campus events include talent shows, open-mic coffeehouse afternoons, films, and discotheque dances.

On weekends, students have Lugano town privileges if they have no School commitments and are in good academic and social standing. All excursions beyond Lugano are chaperoned by a member of the faculty, except those for seniors and some juniors, who, with parental permission, enjoy the privilege of independent travel in groups of 2 or more.

SUMMER PROGRAMS

Lugano: The TASIS Summer Program offers three- and four-week sessions of intensive French, Italian, and English as an additional language (EAL) for beginner, intermediate, and advanced levels of instruction for students aged 14–18. Art history, drawing and painting, and digital photography are also offered. Approximately 350 students attend annually, a small number of whom are TASIS academic-year students seeking credit or enrichment. The experienced staff includes instructors drawn from TASIS and other schools, along with visiting faculty members and counselors from the U.S. and throughout the world. Adventure sports, social activities, and excursions are parts of the program. Students also have the opportunity to participate in the AC Milan Junior Soccer Camp, under the supervision of the team's coaches. TASIS also offers two sessions of summer language programs in French, Italian, and EAL for younger students. The Château des Enfants Program serves children aged 4–10 and offers instruction in EAL, Italian, and French. The Middle School Program includes 11–13-year-olds and offers EAL and French courses. Both programs include exciting excursions, sports, and activities, along with the chance to make friends from around the world.

Chateau d'Oex: The TASIS French Language Program, which is located in the French-speaking canton of Vaud, offers a five-week full-academic-credit course along with various sports and activities for students aged 14–18 who wish to improve their French language skills. The Middle School Program at Château d'Oex offers French and EAL study for 11–13-year-olds along with an exciting activities program focused on improving language fluency.

COSTS AND FINANCIAL AID

The all-inclusive tuition fee for boarding students is CHF 68,300 for the 2010–11 academic year, with an enrollment deposit of CHF 3000. This includes all fees that are necessary for attendance: room, board, tuition, eleven days of academic travel, Ski Week, all textbooks, laundry, activities, and most lab fees. A monthly personal allowance of CHF 250–300 is recommended. Seventy percent of the tuition is due by July 1 and the remainder by November 15.

Students may apply for financial aid, which is granted on the basis of merit, need, and the student's ability to contribute to the School community.

ADMISSIONS INFORMATION

All applicants are considered on the basis of previous academic records, three teachers' evaluations, a personal statement, and a parental statement. The SSAT is recommended, and the SLEP test is required for students whose native language is not English. TASIS does not discriminate on the basis of race, color, nationality, or ethnic origin in its admissions policies and practices.

Application for entrance is recommended only for those students with sufficient academic interest and motivation to benefit from the program. The School accepts students from prekindergarten to grade 12 and at the postgraduate level.

APPLICATION TIMETABLE

TASIS has a rolling admissions policy and considers applications throughout the year. Applicants are encouraged to make an appointment to visit the campus. Within ten days of receipt of a completed application, the CHF 300 application fee, an official transcript from the previous school, and three teachers' evaluations, the Admissions Committee notifies the parents of its decision.

ADMISSIONS CORRESPONDENCE

Mr. William E. Eichner, Director of Admissions
TASIS The American School in Switzerland
CH-6926 Montagnola-Lugano
Switzerland

Phone: 41-91-960-5151
Fax: 41-91-993-2979
E-mail: admissions@tasis.ch
Web site: http://www.tasis.com

or

The TASIS Schools
1640 Wisconsin Avenue, NW
Washington, D.C. 20007

Phone: 202-965-5800
Fax: 202-965-5816
E-mail: usadmissions@tasis.com

THOMAS JEFFERSON SCHOOL

St. Louis, Missouri

Type: Coeducational boarding and day college-preparatory school
Grades: 7–12
Enrollment: 89
Head of School: William C. Rowe

THE SCHOOL

Thomas Jefferson School was founded in 1946. It has received national attention for its academic excellence and its teacher-trustee system, the two guiding ideas of the founders. It became coeducational in 1971. The campus is a 20-acre estate in Sunset Hills, a suburb 15 miles southwest of downtown St. Louis.

The School's mission is to give its students the strongest possible academic background through a classical education. Within a nurturing community, students develop a responsibility for their own learning and a desire to lift up the world with beauty and intellect. Many of the School's distinctive features, such as the daily schedule, are outgrowths of this mission.

The School is unique in its business organization. A majority of the members of its Board of Trustees must be teachers in the School; moreover, no one may teach full-time for more than five years without becoming a trustee. The Headmaster and the other teacher-trustees make up the administration of the School, with the exception of the Director of Development, who is not a faculty member. This structure gives teachers a greater stake in the School and a breadth of experience that produces better teaching.

Thomas Jefferson School is a member of the National Association of Independent Schools, the Association of Boarding Schools, the Independent Schools Association of the Central States, Midwest Boarding Schools, the School and Student Service for Financial Aid, and the Educational Records Bureau.

ACADEMIC PROGRAMS

Thomas Jefferson offers a challenging approach to learning, with the emphasis on the student's own efforts. Classes are short, and the teachers seldom lecture; instead, all students are called on to answer questions and generate discussion. During afternoon and evening study time, the students have a good deal of freedom in choosing when and where to do their homework, with help readily available from faculty members.

Seventh and eighth graders take English, mathematics, science, social studies, and Latin. In the ninth through twelfth grades, students take 4 years of English; 4 years of mathematics through calculus; 2 years of Greek (ninth and tenth grades); 2 years of Italian or French (tenth and eleventh); at least 3 years of science, including an AP course; and at least 2 years of history, including AP American history. Electives include additional language, science, and history courses. Advanced Placement exams are a standard part of the courses in American history, government and politics, calculus, biology, advanced French, junior and senior English, physics, and chemistry. The faculty members also help students work toward AP exams in Latin, computer science, and studio art.

The English curriculum gives students intensive training in grammar, vocabulary, and writing skills. They also read and discuss a great deal of literature, including recognized classics (Shakespeare, the Bible, and epics), time-tested authors (Austen, Dickens, Dostoyevsky, Fitzgerald, Manzoni, Melville, and Shaw), and more recent major authors, such as Amy Tan, Ralph Ellison, and Chaim Potok.

A special feature is the study of classical Greek, which contributes to intellectual development (including concrete benefits such as enhanced vocabulary) and cultural background. This subject, in which the School is a national leader, continues to stir curiosity and ambition. A number of graduates continue to study it in college; others do so independently or later in life.

The average class size is 14, and the overall student-teacher ratio is 6:1. During the day, teachers are accessible to everyone and are ready to help; one teacher is on duty each evening and visits the students' rooms to assist with homework. Younger new students and those having academic difficulty are placed in afternoon or evening study halls.

The grading system uses letter grades of A, B, C, D, and E. An average of B– is Honors; an average of A– is High Honors. To remain in good standing, a student must have no more than one D in any marking period; students in their first year, however, are allowed extra time to adjust. One-hour examinations are given at the end of the first and third quarters (October and April), and 2- to 3-hour examinations are given at midyear and at the end of the year. Following each exam period, a student's adviser sends the parents a letter discussing the student's progress and giving the latest grades and teachers' comments.

The unusually long winter and spring vacations (about one month each) give students an opportunity to unwind, spend time with their families, and do independent work for extra credit.

FACULTY AND ADVISERS

The faculty consists of 7 women and 6 men, including the Head of School. Faculty members hold thirteen baccalaureate degrees, nine master's degrees, one law degree, and one Ph.D.

William C. Rowe became the third Head of School in the summer of 2000, succeeding Lawrence Morgan. Mr. Rowe attended Thomas Jefferson School and Wesleyan University (A.B., 1967) and holds a master's degree from Washington University.

All faculty members are expected to continue educating themselves by regular reading, both within and outside the subject areas they teach. They meet periodically to report on their reading and to discuss it.

Currently, 5 of the 13 faculty members live on the campus, along with 2 resident assistants and one staff member. Each teacher, whether resident or not, has several duties besides teaching, such as athletics

supervision, evening study help, and advising students. Teachers meet with each of their advisees regularly to check the student's grades and to keep in touch with his or her personal development.

COLLEGE ADMISSION COUNSELING

The Headmaster visits a number of colleges each year; he and other faculty members help students decide where to apply. Guidance is provided throughout the application process, and great care is taken in writing recommendations.

In sixty-four years, the School has had 576 graduates; all have gone to college—most to well-known, selective institutions. Among the colleges and universities attended by Thomas Jefferson graduates in the past eight years are Boston University (6), Brown (2), Caltech (2), Carnegie Mellon (1), Carleton (1), Claremont-McKenna (2), Columbia (2), Duke (3), Emory (3), Harvard (1), Haverford (4), Johns Hopkins (4), Lake Forest (2), Northwestern (6), Pitzer (2), Pomona (3), Reed (3), Rensselaer (2), Rhodes (4), Smith (2), Stanford (1), Swarthmore (2), Vanderbilt (3), Washington (St. Louis) (7), Wesleyan (3), and the Universities of Missouri (5) and Chicago (3).

Ten-year medians for the SAT are 710 critical reading and 670 math.

STUDENT BODY AND CONDUCT

In 2010–11, the School has 89 students (53 boarding, 36 day). Most students come from the region between the Appalachians and the Great Plains. Approximately one third are international students from various countries (ESL instruction is available, although knowledge of English is required for admission). Most grades have girls and boys in about equal numbers.

A Student Council, whose members are elected twice a year, brings student concerns before the faculty and helps maintain a healthy, studious atmosphere. Collectively, the council has one vote in faculty meetings on any decision concerning student life.

Demerits are given for misconduct, lateness, and other routine matters; a student who receives too many demerits in one week has to do chores around the campus on Saturday. Students may appeal any demerits, even those given by the Head of School, before a Student Appeals Court.

ACADEMIC FACILITIES

The Main Building, a former residence, provides a comfortable, homelike setting for classes and meals; it also contains faculty and administrative offices, the library, computer terminals, and an art gallery. Sayers Hall, next to the Main Building, provides science laboratories, classrooms, and a library/computer annex. In 2008, the School opened a new art facility and built an addition onto the gymnasium.

BOARDING AND GENERAL FACILITIES

Boarders live in the Gables—a smaller building from the original estate—and in five modern one-story houses, built in 1960, plus one additional, similar house added in 1994. Each house has four double rooms; each room has an outside entrance, a private bath, large windows, wall-to-wall carpeting, and air conditioning. The houses were designed to provide quiet, privacy, and independence. Normally, 2 boarding students share a room with 2 day students. All dorm rooms provide phone and Internet access.

ATHLETICS

Thomas Jefferson School athletics are meant to help students relax, stay healthy and in good condition, and study better. Outdoor sports include intramural tennis (five courts), varsity soccer, and fitness; indoor sports are volleyball and basketball, both varsity and JV. Athletics are required on Monday, Tuesday, Thursday, and Friday afternoons. Teams compete with other local schools in basketball, soccer, and volleyball.

EXTRACURRICULAR OPPORTUNITIES

St. Louis has a wealth of resources in art, music, and theater, as well as an excellent zoo, a science museum, and a world-renowned botanical garden. The faculty members keep the students informed about opportunities around town and help provide them with transportation and tickets whenever possible. Teachers often take groups of students on informal weekend field trips. In recent years, groups have gone to the Ozarks for camping, to the Mississippi River to see bald eagles, and to many symphony concerts, ballets, and plays. Students also attend movies, sports events, and concerts.

Volunteer service is a required part of the program, and the School helps students find opportunities for service. All students must plan and complete a required amount of voluntary community service before they graduate. Students are encouraged to pursue their own interests, such as music lessons, and the School helps make arrangements. A piano is available. Over the years, students have initiated and sustained major activities, such as the School yearbook, a student newspaper, mock trial, and the all-school play.

DAILY LIFE

A school day begins with breakfast at 7:45. Eight 35-minute class periods (and lunch) take place between 8:30 and 1:10. In grades 11 and 12, students take four classes and in grades 7 through 10, they take five. Classes meet daily, but AP classes, which have longer assignments, may meet only four days a week. After lunch, a student may have a science lab, a language lab, or other supplementary academic work. Then they have an hour of athletics, perhaps a meeting with their adviser or study help from another teacher, and some independent time in which they are expected to start their homework for the next day. Dinner is at 5:45, and evenings are devoted to study. On Wednesday and Friday afternoons, there are fine-arts classes in such subjects as drawing, photography, ceramics, and art and music appreciation, and students may leave the campus for nearby shopping centers. Day students are on campus from about 8:30 to 5.

WEEKEND LIFE

Weekends are leisure time. As long as students are in good standing academically, they have considerable freedom and may leave the campus for movies, shopping, dates, and overnights. Older students may keep cars on campus at the discretion of the faculty, and a school driver provides transportation for students as well. The sports facilities are available for weekend use. Dances are organized periodically by the Student Council.

SUMMER PROGRAMS

The School organizes summer trips to Europe for students in grades 10–12, often led by the Head of School or other experienced faculty members. Students in grades 7–9 may participate in a weeklong trip to London in the spring.

COSTS AND FINANCIAL AID

Charges for 2010–11 are $36,500 for full boarding, $34,000 for weekday boarding, and $21,200 for day students. This includes room plus all meals for boarders and all lunches for day students. Approximately $2000 covers books, school supplies, and other expenses related to School activities. Optional off-campus activities such as music lessons (and the necessary transportation) cost extra.

A $2000 deposit, nonrefundable but credited to tuition, is required when a student enrolls. The balance of the tuition is paid through Sallie Mae's TuitionPay program.

Financial aid is available, based on a family's need. About 40 percent of the student body currently receives some financial aid; the total amount awarded is more than $625,000. An applicant's family must file a statement with the School and Student Service, and this information is used in judging need. Many middle-income families receive some assistance.

ADMISSIONS INFORMATION

The School looks for signs of native intelligence, liveliness, energy, ambition, and curiosity. Strong grades and test scores are important considerations but not always the deciding ones. A candidate should submit the results of the Secondary School Admission Test (SSAT); international students submit the results of the SLEP or TOEFL. About 40 percent of those who complete the application process are accepted.

APPLICATION TIMETABLE

Inquiries and applications are welcome at any time, but the School has three rounds of admissions: early decision applicants submit their materials by mid-December and receive an answer in early January; regular decision applicants submit their materials by mid-February and receive an answer in early March; after April, applications for any remaining openings are considered as they are received. As part of the application process, prospective students usually spend a day at the School visiting classes, having lunch, and spending time with the admissions staff to ask questions and have an interview. There is a $40 fee for domestic applications, and a $100 fee for international applications.

ADMISSIONS CORRESPONDENCE

Jane Roth and Ken Colston, Co-Directors of Admissions
Thomas Jefferson School
4100 South Lindbergh Boulevard
St. Louis, Missouri 63127

Phone: 314-843-4151
Fax: 314-843-3527
E-mail: admissions@tjs.org
Web site: http://www.tjs.org

TILTON SCHOOL

Tilton, New Hampshire

Type: Coeducational boarding and day college-preparatory
Grades: 9–12, postgraduate year
Enrollment: 256
Head of School: James R. Clements

THE SCHOOL

Tilton School challenges students to embrace and navigate a world marked by diversity and change. Through the quality of human relationships, Tilton School's faculty cultivates in its students the curiosity, the skills, the knowledge and understanding, the character, and the integrity requisite for the passionate pursuit of lifelong personal success and service.

Tilton School values education—the active pursuit of knowledge and the growth of intellectual curiosity. The rigorous academic program is designed to prepare graduates to be successful college students and contributing members of society. Various pathways to learning are supported; the acquisition of genuine understanding is the goal. Tilton is committed to the principle that all students can excel. Through a broad range of learning experiences, students discover the power of their potential by developing problem-solving skills and self confidence while becoming independent and critical thinkers.

A nonprofit corporation, Tilton is governed by the Head of School and a 24-member Board of Trustees. Annual expenses of $8.8 million are met through tuition, endowment, and annual giving. The endowment currently totals $15.2 million. More than 5,200 living alumni have a beneficial impact on fund raising, with pledges and gifts to the School of more than $1.7 million annually for both annual and restricted purposes.

Tilton School is accredited by the New England Association of Schools and Colleges and is a member of the National Association of Independent Schools, the Independent Schools Association of Northern New England, the Cum Laude Society, the National Honor Society, the Secondary School Admission Test Board, and the Council for Religion in Independent Schools.

ACADEMIC PROGRAMS

Tilton's academic program offers a traditional college-preparatory curriculum framed within a twenty-first century skills-based program, supporting the student's intellectual maturation and encouraging the development of academic and personal competencies. The School seeks to produce students who have a genuine interest in intellectual pursuits, to teach students self-discipline, and to reinforce in students the sound moral and ethical judgment that are needed to successfully navigate the complex and changing world of the twenty-first century.

The school year is divided into two semesters. During each term, students at Tilton take a minimum of five full-credit courses. Required credits include English, mathematics, world language, fine arts, laboratory science, and social science (history), for a total of 18.

Interdisciplinary standards in the five essential domains of critical thinking, communication, creativity, community, and character are the cornerstones of the curriculum.

The program of study for ninth grade students is a team-taught integrated program (F.I.R.S.T.—foundation, integrity, respect, service, team) emphasizing a strong academic foundation and supportive intellectual, personal, and social development.

Additional grade-level programs are designed from grade 10 through grades 11, 12, and the postgraduate (PG) year to support student growth and development in a purposefully designed program. At the end of the tenth grade year, and prior to graduation, all students must provide evidence of learning that meets benchmark curriculum standards through participation in performance assessment programs, the Gateway Program (grade 10), and the Capstone Project (graduating class).

The average class size is 12 students, and the student-teacher ratio is 6:1. Evening study hall is supervised. Evening study hours are designed to allow for availability of resources and a quiet, uninterrupted study atmosphere where reinforcement of learned skills can be emphasized under direct supervision by faculty members. Academic focus is the primary purpose of evening study hall, which provides a balance of structure and self-directed study.

At Tilton School, student learning is assessed by measuring demonstrated performance of learned skills and knowledge against specific standards developed for grade levels, departments, and specific courses that have been structured within the school's twenty-first century skills-curriculum framework, with reference to national and state standards for specific academic disciplines. Within this system, letter grades mean the following; A = significantly exceeds the standard; B = exceeds the standard; C = meets the standard; D = does not yet meet the standard.

The Learning Center serves approximately 30 percent of the students, complementing their regular academic instruction by identifying individual needs and helping to devise strategies that enable them to achieve academic success. The center provides specialized instructional support for students whose academic progress is limited by deficiencies in basic skills or study habits, or by distinct learning-style differences. A 2:1 SAT tutorial is also offered through the center.

The English as a Second Language Program serves students who need intermediate and advanced English language support skills.

FACULTY AND ADVISERS

Tilton's faculty consists of 42 members. All of the faculty members hold bachelor's degrees, and there are fifteen advanced degrees, including two Ph.D.'s. Most members of the faculty and administration live on campus with their families.

Faculty members must have not only a high level of expertise in their academic areas but also an enthusiastic commitment to students' interests and student life. In addition to dormitory and afternoon coaching and activity duties, most faculty members have 6 to 8 student advisees. The adviser is responsible for monitoring academic progress and for counseling in other areas of school life.

James R. Clements, appointed Head of School in 1998, is a graduate of the University of New Hampshire (B.A., 1972; M.B.A., 1998). Prior to joining Tilton, Mr. Clements spent twenty-one years at the Chapel Hill–Chauncy Hall School in Waltham, Massachusetts, most recently as Head of School from 1993–98.

COLLEGE ADMISSION COUNSELING

Three full-time counselors guide students in the selection of colleges and coordinate the application process, beginning in the junior year. College admissions officers visit the School each year to talk with groups of students or to interview individual students.

Members of the classes of 2006–10 were accepted at numerous colleges and universities, including Bates, Bowdoin, Boston University, Carnegie Mellon, Clarkson, Colby, Cornell, Denison, Hobart and William Smith, Holy Cross, Lake Forest, Middlebury, Notre Dame, Syracuse, Trinity, Tufts, Union, Vassar, Wesleyan, and the Universities of Massachusetts, New Hampshire, and Vermont.

STUDENT BODY AND CONDUCT

In 2010–11, Tilton enrolled 256 students—75 percent are boarders and 25 percent are day students. There are 165 boys and 91 girls. Tilton students represent many racial, religious, and socioeconomic backgrounds; twenty-two states are represented, with approximately 60 percent of the students coming from New England, 20 percent from other parts of the United States, and 20 percent from twenty-one other countries.

Expectations at Tilton are high and are thoroughly communicated. Although the immediate goal of School rules and regulations is to promote order, mutual respect, and academic excellence, this structure serves, in the long range, to prepare students for productive and responsible roles in a changing society. At Tilton, there is a basic faith in young people. Guided by the attitude that students can learn and want to learn, faculty members are eager to inspire commitment, pride, and responsibility in their students.

ACADEMIC FACILITIES

Plimpton Hall and the academic building create the academic quad on the West side of campus. Plimpton Hall houses ten classrooms for English, social science, and English as a second language (ESL), the Center for Leadership room, the computer center, admissions, college counseling, the business office, and the school store. The academic building is home to three state-of-the-art science classrooms/labs, three math classrooms, four world language classrooms, a world language lab, the ninth grade seminar room, a solarium, the Learning Center, and the Davis Lecture Hall that seats 100. All classrooms include wireless access and electronic interactive whiteboards.

Two music classrooms, two practice rooms and the art gallery are contained in the lower level of the chapel. The Helene Grant Daly Art Center provides excellent facilities for art classes, including ceramics, graphic arts, studio art, printmaking, sculpture, silk-screening, and photography. The Lucien Hunt Memorial Library contains approximately 17,500 volumes, including subscriptions to numerous periodicals, newspapers, encyclopedias, and an online periodical index. The library features ten computers; several Kindles, iPods, and iPads; reading and conference rooms; and extensive facilities for research. Drama and musical productions are performed in the Rome Theater in Hamilton Hall.

The Tilton campus is connected by a fiber-optic backbone that supports the School's intranet and access to the Internet. All classrooms and dormitories are connected to the network via a combination of wired and wireless networks. All students have their own account, accessible through a password. The network supports both Windows and MAC OS environments. The world language lab is a state-of-the-art digital lab with twenty-four workstations. There is also a student computer lab, two laptop carts with twenty-one laptops, and iPads available for classroom use. The Daly Art Center has both iMacs and computers for graphic arts and photography instruction.

BOARDING AND GENERAL FACILITIES
Nine dormitories, each housing 18 to 48 students and 1 to 4 faculty members and their families, are located on campus. Students live in double or single rooms. Returning students may state their preference for room assignments.

The new Maloney Hall is a 15,000-square-foot dormitory housing 20 students and includes three faculty apartments. Highlights of the new facility include a two-story common room, a group study room, suite-style rooms (two double rooms that share a common bathroom), a recreation room, a laundry area, and storage space.

The school store, MARC Student Center, and the snack bar are open at various times of the day and evening. There is a six-bed health center operated by LRGH (Lakes Region General Hospital), with a resident nurse and a doctor on call.

ATHLETICS
The School believes that people of all ages perform best when they are active and healthy and that organized sports promote physical development, physical courage, self-discipline, and a sense of team spirit. All students must participate in an afternoon activity. Students must play at least one sport each year to fulfill their annual athletic requirement.

Boys' sports include baseball, basketball, football, ice hockey, lacrosse, soccer, tennis, and wrestling. Girls' sports are basketball, field hockey, ice hockey, lacrosse, soccer, softball, and tennis. Coed sports include Alpine skiing, cross-country running, golf, mountain biking, and snowboarding.

Facilities include 25 acres of outstanding playing fields, 3 miles of cross-country trails, three tennis courts, a gymnasium, a field house with an indoor ice rink, and an outdoor swimming pool. The golf team uses a nearby eighteen-hole course.

EXTRACURRICULAR OPPORTUNITIES
Tilton's +5 Program, distinctive among independent secondary schools, requires that all students involve themselves in five areas of nonacademic campus life: art and culture, team athletics, outdoor experiences, community service, and leadership roles. These learning experiences enhance self-confidence and self-esteem.

By structuring extracurricular activities, the School broadens students' interests, enables them to develop skills that enhance their self-worth, and provides enjoyment during their free time. Faculty members' commitment to excellence and their guidance encourage and reassure students who may be doubtful of their abilities. As a result, strong relationships develop, and students and teachers work together more effectively in the classroom.

Offerings in art and culture include drama, musical theater, tech crew, ceramics, graphic arts, studio art, photography, music studio, drum line, and chorus.

Throughout the school year, there are opportunities to participate in outdoor trips for canoeing, mountain biking, Alpine skiing, fishing, rock climbing, hiking, snowshoeing, or cross-country skiing.

Community service opportunities are available both on campus and in the Tilton community. This division of the +5 Program encourages students to commit themselves to helping others. Other projects include helping at a soup kitchen; reading to patients at the New Hampshire Veterans' Home; tutoring local children; raising funds for UNICEF, Oxfam, and Toys for Tots; and teaching in a learn-to-skate program for young children.

Leadership may be the most important of the five areas. Experience as an admissions ambassador, dorm proctor, work-program supervisor, Student Council officer, editor, or team captain offers a rigorous challenge.

Movies, plays, lectures, and concerts are regular events on campus, while trips to museums and theaters in Boston are regular off-campus activities.

DAILY LIFE
Class periods are approximately 45 minutes long, with each class meeting once a week for a double period. Mid-morning each day, there is a meeting either with advisee groups, special committees, or the entire School at School Meeting, which is held two times per week. Conference period and campus service programs are also part of student life. The conference period is an opportunity to meet teachers for extra help or to make an appointment to meet a teacher later in the evening for more extensive work.

After classes, everyone participates in after-school programs. Wednesday and Saturday schedules are half days, which allows time for athletic competitions and program activities.

WEEKEND LIFE
Faculty and staff teams plan all weekend activities with student support. Saturday events include sports competitions, movies, dances, concerts, and trips to shopping areas and movie theaters. The gym, field house, student center, and art center are periodically open both Saturday and Sunday. Sunday is for scheduled activities, both on and off the campus. Day students are invited to participate and are active in weekend life.

COSTS AND FINANCIAL AID
For 2010–11, tuition, room, and board cost $43,775; tuition for day students is $25,235. Additional expenses, such as those for books and laundry, range from $600 to $1000. Private music or voice lessons, skiing, snowboarding, learning center sessions, and ESL classes are charged separately. Tuition may be paid in full in mid-July, or families can take advantage of one of Tilton's payment plan options.

Forty percent of the students receive financial aid in the form of direct grants and/or loans. For 2010–11, more than $2 million in aid was granted. Applications for aid, which should be made before February 15, are reviewed separately from admission decisions.

ADMISSIONS INFORMATION
The Admissions Committee seeks to admit students who will benefit from and contribute to Tilton and those of diverse backgrounds and individual personal strengths. Students with various academic abilities who seek to challenge themselves and take advantage of Tilton's programs within and outside the classroom are excellent candidates for admission. Candidates for the ninth and tenth grades should take the SSAT and have the results sent to Tilton. Eleventh and twelfth graders and postgraduates should take the PSAT or SAT. Additional application requirements for admission include the student's school transcript and current teacher recommendations. All prospective students are expected to visit the School and interview with the Admissions Office. Students may enter at all grade levels; entry in the eleventh or twelfth grade or the postgraduate year is more competitive.

APPLICATION TIMETABLE
Initial inquiries are welcome at any time but are recommended before the late spring prior to the year in which admission is sought. Ideally, applications (accompanied by a $50 application fee or $100 international application fee) should be filed by February 1. The Admissions Office is open for interviews on weekdays and on selected Saturday mornings. It is best to plan a visit while school is in session.

Admissions decisions for applications received by February 1 are made on March 10. After March 10 decisions are made on a rolling basis. The School adheres to the Parents' Reply Date of April 10. A nonrefundable deposit is required to hold a place at Tilton and is applied to tuition for the year.

ADMISSIONS CORRESPONDENCE
Beth Skoglund
Director of Admissions
Tilton School
Tilton, New Hampshire 03276

Phone: 603-286-1733
Fax: 603-286-1705
E-mail: admissions@tiltonschool.org
Web site: http://www.tiltonschool.org

TRINITY–PAWLING SCHOOL

Pawling, New York

Type: Boys' boarding (9–PG) and day (7–PG) college-preparatory school
Grades: 7–12, postgraduate year
Enrollment: 310
Head of School: Archibald A. Smith III, Headmaster

THE SCHOOL

The Pawling School was founded in 1907 by Dr. Frederick Gamage. In 1946, it was renamed Trinity-Pawling School in recognition of its ties with Trinity School of New York City. In 1978, Trinity-Pawling School became a separate educational and corporate entity. Trinity-Pawling's Episcopal background is reflected in daily chapel services and course offerings in religion, ethics, and psychology. On weekends, boarding students attend services in the School chapel, at a Roman Catholic church, or at a synagogue.

The School is located 68 miles north of New York City along the Connecticut border; regular train service is available from Grand Central Station to Pawling (population 5,000). The campus, set on 140 acres of rolling hills, is just over an hour's drive from New York's major airports. On vacations, the School transports students to and from the airports and train stations.

It is Trinity-Pawling's belief that an appreciation of one's own worth can best be discovered by experiencing the worth of others, by understanding the value of one's relationship with others, and by acquiring a sense of self-confidence that comes through living and working competently at the level of one's own potential. Trinity-Pawling respects and recognizes the differences in individuals and the different processes required to achieve their educational potential.

The School is governed by a self-perpetuating 26-member Board of Trustees. The School raises more than $1 million in Annual Giving, in part from its more than 4,000 alumni. The School's endowment exceeds $29 million, and its operating budget for 2010–11 is more than $10 million.

Trinity-Pawling is accredited by the New York State Association of Independent Schools and chartered by the New York State Board of Regents. It is a member of the National Association of Independent Schools, the Secondary School Admission Test Board, the New York State Association of Independent Schools (NYSAIS), and the National Association of Episcopal Schools.

ACADEMIC PROGRAMS

To graduate from Trinity-Pawling, a student must obtain a minimum of 112 credits. A full-year course is worth 6 credits, and a term course (trimester) is worth 2 credits. If a student enters after grade 9, his school record is evaluated and translated into Trinity-Pawling's system.

The total number of required credits is 102, distributed as follows: 24 credits in English; 18 credits in mathematics; 18 credits in a laboratory science; 18 credits in social studies; 12 credits in a foreign language; 6 credits in fine, performing, or manual arts (music, art, drafting, or drama); 4 credits in religion or philosophy; and 2 credits in health. Elective courses must be taken to make up the additional 10 credits. Advanced Placement courses are offered in English, U.S. history, European history,

chemistry, physics, biology, mathematics, computer science, Latin, French, and Spanish. No credit is given for physical education courses since they are required by New York State law.

Students carry a minimum of five courses per term. Evening study periods, held in student residences, are supervised by dorm masters. Students with academic difficulty have a formally supervised study hall. Teachers are available to give students extra help at any time that is agreeable to both. Reports are posted online for parents three times per term. Trinity-Pawling uses a number grading system (0–100) in which 60 is passing, 80 qualifies for honors, and 85 qualifies for high honors.

In addition to academic grades, the School utilizes a unique effort system to rank students based on overall effort in many aspects of School life, including academics, athletics, clubs, and dormitory life. A student's privileges are then tied to his overall effort ranking. This program is designed to work in conjunction with the School's philosophy of encouraging each student to work toward his own personal potential.

The Language Program, open to a maximum of 40 students, is initiated in the ninth and tenth grades. A modification of the Orton-Gillingham method, it strives to retrain students with developmental dyslexia. First-year students work in pairs with tutors. In addition, they take a skills-oriented language arts course. Phonetics, sequencing ideas, handwriting, memorization, and other language skills are emphasized. The second-year student is placed in an analytical writing class in addition to a skills-level English class. All students in the program also take basic history, mathematics, and science courses. The program's goal is to enable students to complete Trinity-Pawling's regular college-preparatory curriculum. Students in the program are not required to take a foreign language but may elect to do so.

FACULTY AND ADVISERS

There are 55 full-time members of the faculty, all of whom reside on the campus. Members of the teaching faculty hold fifty-five baccalaureate and thirty-five graduate degrees. All participate in counseling and advising students. The School actively supports advanced study for its teachers during summers and other holidays.

Archibald A. Smith III was appointed Headmaster in 1990, after having served at Trinity-Pawling as a chemistry teacher, Director of College Placement, and Assistant Headmaster at various times since 1975. He is a graduate of St. John's School in Houston, Texas; Trinity College (Hartford) (B.S., 1972); and Wesleyan University (M.S., 1980). His career also includes teaching at the Northwood School in Lake Placid, New York. Mr. Smith is the past president of the New York State Association of Independent Schools and a member of the Accreditation Council of NYSAIS. He is a trustee of Dutchess Day School, a trustee of

the International Boys School Coalition, a trustee of the Parents' League of New York, and is a member of the Headmasters Association.

COLLEGE ADMISSION COUNSELING

Trinity-Pawling's Director of College Counseling works closely with other administrators and faculty members to advise and aid students and their families with college placement. Individual meetings and group workshops are held on a regular basis, and more than 80 college representatives visit the campus each fall for presentations and interviews. More than 95 percent of the class of 2010 gained admission to their first- or second-choice college.

All of the 2010 graduates earned college or university acceptances. Among those they attend are Boston University, Case Western, Colby, Colgate, Cornell, Clemson, Emory Oxford, George Washington, Georgetown, Hobart and William Smith, Johns Hopkins, Kenyon, Lehigh, Maryland, Northwestern, Rice, Sacred Heart, Salve Regina, Syracuse, Trinity, and Wesleyan.

STUDENT BODY AND CONDUCT

Boarding students number 240, and day students number 70. Students come from twenty-nine states and thirteen countries. Students from minority groups make up 18 percent of the total enrollment. Students who choose Trinity-Pawling tend to desire a reasonably structured community that is dedicated to individual growth. A strong academic program in harmony with fine athletics and activities programs brings the School together. The School seeks students who want to actively pursue their academic and social development in a caring atmosphere.

Major violations of community rules are handled by a Faculty-Student Disciplinary Committee, which makes recommendations to the Headmaster. Less serious breaches are handled by the Dean of Students and others.

The Student-Faculty Senate is composed of School prefects and elected student and faculty representatives. The senate works to develop self-government, plans School activities, and fosters a bond between the students and the faculty. It consists of six committees, each with a responsibility for specific areas of School life.

ACADEMIC FACILITIES

The Dann Building (1964) and the Science and Technology Center (2002) house classrooms and science and computer labs. The Art Building, completed in 2004, houses the fine arts, theater, and music programs. This building contains a theater that is used for student productions, lectures, and visiting professional performances. The library features an online catalog, more than 28,000 volumes, and available computers. It is located in the historic Cluett Building, which also contains administrative offices and the student center.

BOARDING AND GENERAL FACILITIES

Students reside in single or double rooms in eighteen dormitory units located in eight buildings, including Starr Hall (1984), Starr East (1987), and Cluett (renovated 1995). Each is under the supervision of 1 or more faculty members aided by senior proctors. Students are allowed to choose roommates, and, whenever possible, housing choice is granted. Students are grouped in housing units according to grade level. A student's dorm master is usually his adviser, so a strong personal relationship often develops. Trinity-Pawling stresses the value of close student-faculty relationships.

Students enjoy a School store and snack bar that are open daily. The Scully Dining Hall was completed in 2009. Medical services are provided by the Health Center, staffed by a resident nurse and a doctor who makes daily visits. Several hospitals serve the area. Trinity-Pawling is within walking distance of the village of Pawling.

ATHLETICS

Trinity-Pawling is a member of the New England Private School Athletic Conference and the Founders League, which affords it the opportunity to play schools in New England, such as Avon, Choate, Hotchkiss, Kent, Loomis Chaffee, Salisbury, Taft, and Westminster. Because the School believes that athletics and physical development are key ingredients in a student's growth, all students are required to participate in the program during the school year. Three or four levels of teams are formed in each interscholastic sport, including baseball, basketball, cross-country, football, golf, hockey, lacrosse, soccer, squash, tennis, track and field, and wrestling. Also offered at both the interscholastic and intramural levels are running, skiing, and weight training.

The Carleton Gymnasium contains a 50-foot by 90-foot basketball court with two cross courts for practice. The lower floor and wing contain weight-training rooms, five international squash courts, and locker rooms. There are also six soccer fields, a new football field, baseball fields, an all-weather track, twelve tennis courts, three lacrosse fields, ponds for skating and fishing, the McGraw wrestling pavilion, and the enclosed Tirrell Hockey Rink, which underwent a $1 million renovation in 2007.

EXTRACURRICULAR OPPORTUNITIES

Each student is encouraged to participate in one or more of the twenty-four activities offered on the campus. These activities are often initiated and directed by the students with the guidance of an interested faculty adviser. Among the offerings are the student newspaper, Model United Nations, the Minority Student Union, the yearbook, the choir, the photography club, the dramatic club, the chess club, the computer club, the fishing club, foreign language clubs, jazz groups, and the outing club. Trinity-Pawling encourages student initiative in starting new activities.

The School sponsors regular trips to nearby areas of educational and cultural interest, including museums and theaters in New York City. Annual events include Parents' Weekend, Junior Parents' Weekend, and several alumni functions. The concert series, offering five concerts annually, brings a rich variety of musical talent to the campus during the school year.

Each student participates in the work program that emphasizes the School's policy of self-responsibility and economy of operation. Boys assist with parts of the routine maintenance work throughout the buildings and on the grounds.

DAILY LIFE

At 8 a.m., four mornings a week, a brief community chapel service is held for all students. Classes are scheduled from 8:20 until 2:40 four days a week and until noon on Wednesdays and Saturdays. Wednesday and Saturday afternoons are reserved for interscholastic sports events. Athletic practices take place in the afternoon, while most extracurricular activities are scheduled in the evening. Lunches are generally served cafeteria-style, dinners sit-down family-style. Students are required to study from 7:30 to 9:30 in their rooms, the library, or the study hall, depending upon their academic status.

WEEKEND LIFE

Dances, plays, concerts, trips to New York City, and informal activities are planned for weekends. The Student-Faculty Senate organizes and plans many of the weekend activities. Social activities are also arranged with girls' schools in the area. Weekend leaves from the School are based upon a group rating, which encompasses a student's record in academic effort and achievement, general citizenship, and dormitory life. In general, as the group rating increases, so do the amount and nature of privileges. Students are evaluated twice per term.

COSTS AND FINANCIAL AID

Charges for 2010–11 are $45,000 for boarding students, $32,000 for day students in ninth through twelfth grade, and $22,000 for day students in seventh and eighth grade. Extra expenses total approximately $2000 per year. The Language Program is an additional $5100–$7300 per year, depending on the grade. A tuition payment plan and tuition insurance are available.

Thirty-five percent of the students receive a total of over $3 million in financial aid each year. Trinity-Pawling subscribes to the School and Student Service for Financial Aid and grants aid on the basis of need.

ADMISSIONS INFORMATION

Trinity-Pawling seeks the well-rounded student who will both gain from and give to the School. New students are accepted in all grades; a limited number are accepted for the postgraduate year. Selection is based upon all-around qualifications without regard to race, color, creed, or national origin. Candidates must submit a complete transcript plus two or three teachers' recommendations, have a personal interview at the School, and take the SSAT. Candidates for the Language Retraining Program are asked to have completed a Wechsler Test (WISC-R).

In 2010, there were 344 applicants, of whom 260 were accepted and 100 enrolled.

APPLICATION TIMETABLE

Initial inquiries are welcome at any time. Campus tours and interviews (allow 1½–2 hours) can be arranged by appointment, Monday through Friday, 8:30–1:30, and on Saturday, 8:30–11. All candidates must have an interview. The completed forms must be accompanied by a nonrefundable fee of $40 ($100 for international students).

Fall is the usual time for applying, and notification of acceptance begins in early March. Parents are expected to reply to acceptances one month after notification.

ADMISSIONS CORRESPONDENCE

MacGregor Robinson
Director of Admission
Trinity-Pawling School
Pawling, New York 12564

Phone: 845-855-4825
Fax: 845-855-4827
E-mail: pmccracken@trinitypawling.org
Web site: http://www.trinitypawling.org

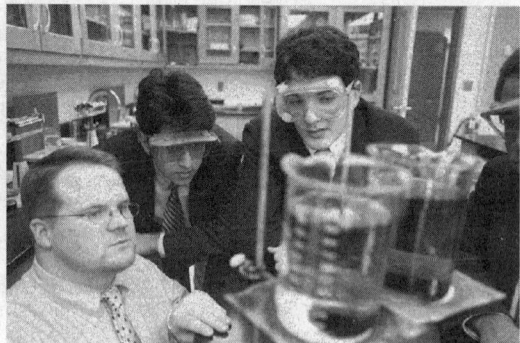

VALLEY FORGE MILITARY ACADEMY & COLLEGE

Wayne, Pennsylvania

Type: Boys' college-preparatory and coeducational transfer college military boarding school
Grades: 7–PG: Middle School, 7–8; Upper School, 9–PG
Enrollment: 565
Head of School: Col. David R. Gray, Ph.D., USA (Ret.), President

THE SCHOOL

The 100-acre campus of Valley Forge Military Academy includes a boys' boarding preparatory high school and a coeducational transfer college, located 15 miles west of Philadelphia. The mission of Valley Forge is to educate individuals to be fully prepared to meet their responsibilities, alert in mind, sound in body, and considerate of others and to have a high sense of duty, honor, loyalty, and courage. Valley Forge fosters these goals through a comprehensive system that is built on the five cornerstones of academic excellence, character development, personal motivation, physical development, and leadership.

The Academy is accredited by the Middle States Association of Colleges and Schools. It holds memberships in the Association of Military Colleges and Schools of the United States, the Council for Religion in Independent Schools, the Boarding School Headmasters' Association, the International Boys School Coalition (IBSC), and the National Association of Independent Schools. The U.S. Department of the Army designates Valley Forge as an honor unit with distinction.

ACADEMIC PROGRAMS

Valley Forge seeks to educate and develop students for college entrance, career success, and responsible citizenship. A challenging curriculum, dedicated faculty members, small classes, individual attention, and faculty-supervised evening study hall provide cadets with an environment conducive to attaining academic success. The acquisition of knowledge, the development of skills, and the shaping of attitudes are emphasized to enable cadets to excel academically and to inspire them to pursue education throughout life.

The school year extends from late August to early June and is divided into two semesters; each has two marking periods. At the end of each marking period, grades are sent to parents. Unsatisfactory grades result in special afternoon help and extra study hall, with biweekly evaluations forwarded to parents. Evening study hall is required of all students. Cadets are placed in one of three college-preparatory curricula—honors, intermediate, or standard—according to aptitude level or achievement. The grading system uses A to F with pluses and minuses. Class periods (eight per day) normally cover 45 minutes each, with double periods for laboratory courses. Twenty and a half credits are required for graduation, distributed as follows: English, 4; mathematics, 4; social studies, 3 (1 of which must be U.S. history); foreign language, 2; science, 2; laboratory science, 1; and electives, 4.5.

The average Academy class size is 13; the student-teacher ratio is approximately 10:1. Opportunities for independent study, off-campus field trips, and enrollment in courses at Valley Forge Military College are available to eligible cadets.

FACULTY AND ADVISERS

There are 52 full-time and 13 part-time teachers at the Academy. Thirty-one members hold master's degrees; currently, 2 have doctorates.

Col. David R. Gray, USA (ret.), is a 1980 Distinguished Military Graduate of Western Illinois University where he majored in history. He is a graduate of the Infantry Officer Basic and Advanced Courses, the Command and General Staff College, the Armed Forces Staff College (JPME II), and the U.S. Army War College. He has earned a master's degree in strategic studies from the U.S. Army War College and master's and doctorate degrees in military history from Ohio State University. He has published articles in several professional journals including *Parameters, Military Review, Army History,* and *Army Magazine.*

Experienced teachers, dedicated to educating young men, are selected primarily for their professional ability and concern for young people. Faculty members perform additional duties as athletic coaches, study hall supervisors, and advisers for extracurricular activities. Ongoing professional development is strongly encouraged.

COLLEGE ADMISSION COUNSELING

The Guidance Department has 4 full-time counselors and gives continual assistance and counseling to each cadet. The department follows each cadet's academic progress and keeps in close contact with parents. College orientation and parent involvement begin during the second semester of the junior year and continue throughout the cadet's residence. College orientation sessions cover college selection, nomination to service academies, financial aid, the Army ROTC program, and contacts with college placement representatives. College test requirements are reviewed, and cadets are counseled in college application preparation and interview procedures. Ninety-nine percent of the class of 2010 went on to college, with the greatest representation at Embry-Riddle, Holy Cross, Penn State, Purdue, the U.S. Air Force Academy, the U.S. Naval Academy, and Villanova.

STUDENT BODY AND CONDUCT

The 2009–10 Upper School student body was composed of 350 boarding cadets. The student body is diverse, and this year cadets came from thirty-three states and thirty-one countries. Eight percent were African American, 11 percent were Hispanic, 13 percent were Asian/Pacific Islanders, and 13 percent were international students.

The military structure of Valley Forge provides extraordinary opportunities for students to develop and exercise their leadership abilities in a safe environment. The Valley Forge experience is designed to foster the development of individual responsibility, self-discipline, and sound leadership skills by providing opportunities for the practical application of leadership theories in positions of increasing responsibility.

The Corps of Cadets is a self-administering body organized in eight company units along military lines, with a cadet officer and noncommissioned officer organization for cadet control and administration. Cadet leadership and positive peer encouragement within this structured setting result in a brotherhood and camaraderie among cadets. Through their student representatives, cadets cooperate with the administration in enforcing regulations regarding student conduct. A Student Advisory Council represents the cadets in the school administration. The Dean's Council meets regularly to discuss aspects of academic life.

Character development and personal motivation are integral parts of the Valley Forge experience. The character development program includes weekly chapel and vesper services and monthly character development seminars that are facilitated by peer/faculty teams. Valley Forge emphasizes time-proven standards of conduct, ethical behavior, integrity, spiritual values, and service to community and country. It also motivates young men to strive for excellence, both as individuals and as members of an organization, in all areas of endeavor. Motivation is encouraged through positive competition, recognition, loyalty, teamwork, organizational pride, and the establishment of personal goals.

ACADEMIC FACILITIES

Shannon Hall is the principal academic building. In addition to classrooms, it includes biology, chemistry, and physics laboratories; a computer complex; and the military science department. The Friedman Auditorium, adjacent to Shannon Hall, serves as a large study hall, a conference and instructional center, and a center for SAT and other testing procedures. The May H. Baker Library provides more than 70,000 books, 500 video titles, more than 60 periodical subscriptions, and more than 30 subscriptions to online research resources. To integrate library resources into the curriculum, the library faculty collaborates with the classroom faculty in implementing information literacy instruction in two fully networked computer classrooms and two seminar rooms. The educational psychologists of the Cadet Achievement Center, housed in the library, counsel and advise cadets concerning learning and personal issues.

A fiber-optic, Internet-capable network connects all classrooms, laboratories, and library and dormitory rooms on the campus.

BOARDING AND GENERAL FACILITIES

Cadets are housed by their military companies in individual dormitories, 2 cadets to a room, under the supervision of adult Tactical Officers and their cadet leaders. Cadets eat together in the Regimental Mess. The Health Center has a resident physician and a 24-hour staff; special consultants are always available. The Alumni Chapel of St. Cornelius the Centurion seats 1,500. The service is nondenominational but Christian in format, and services are available for all faiths. Mellon Hall provides a parents' reception room, a ballroom, piano and instrument practice rooms, a photography laboratory, a 10-point rifle and pistol range, and meeting rooms. Other facilities include the student center, the cadet laundry, the tailor shop, and the Cadet Store. Price Athletic Center and Trainer Hall house three full-size and six intermediate-size basketball courts, a five-lane swimming pool, locker rooms, weight rooms, meeting rooms, administrative offices, and the L. Maitland Blank Hall of Fame. Also on campus are six athletic fields, nine outdoor tennis courts, an outdoor Olympic-size swimming pool, the cavalry stables, and the Mellon Polo Pavilion.

ATHLETICS

Athletics and physical well-being are important elements in a Valley Forge education. The aim of the program is to develop all-around fitness, alertness, character, esprit de corps, leadership, courage, competitive spirit, and genuine desire for physical and mental achievement. There is competition at three levels: varsity, junior varsity, and intramural. To have every cadet on a team is the constant goal. Sports opportunities include baseball, basketball, cross-country, equestrian jumping, football, golf, lacrosse, rugby, soccer, swimming, tennis, track, and wrestling.

Valley Forge has a strong athletic tradition. Since 1986, the VFMA&C football program has sent more than 140 cadets to Division I schools on full football scholarships. Seven VF alumni currently play in the NFL. One alumnus currently plays for a major league baseball team. In 2003, the equestrian show jumping team participated in the Junior Olympics.

EXTRACURRICULAR OPPORTUNITIES

Clubs, honor societies, publications, intramurals, the Regimental Choir, the Anthony Wayne Legion Guard, and some thirty-five other organizations (forensic, literary, language, science, and Boy Scouts, to name a few) attract about 75 percent of the Corps. Publications include the *Legionnaire* (the newspaper) and *Crossed Sabres* (the yearbook).

Outside lecturers visit the Academy regularly. The band and choir travel widely and have performed at the Kennedy Center, Carnegie Hall, Westminster Abbey, Lincoln Center, and the White House and have participated in inaugural events for several U.S. presidents. Various cadet units assist local communities in parades, community events, and horse shows. Cadets participate in various public service activities in the surrounding communities; several cadet groups pay regular visits during the year to local children's homes, centers for the disabled, and nursing homes. Important traditional events are Parents' and Grandparents' Weekend, Regimental Mounted Parades, Dunaway Oratorical Contest, and frequent band and choir concerts.

DAILY LIFE

Classes (45 minutes each) are held five days a week from 7:30 a.m. to 3:30 p.m. The average number of classes per student is six in an eight-period day. An extra instruction period is available after the last class period. Athletics and other activities are held between 3 and 5:45 p.m. daily. Evening study hours extend from 7:30 to 9:30 p.m. Taps sounds at 10 p.m. Monday afternoon is reserved for drill, company meetings, and special activities, such as the ropes course and rappelling.

WEEKEND LIFE

Special or afternoon leaves as well as overnight and weekend privileges may be earned. Ample opportunities exist for cadets to take advantage of the cultural and entertainment opportunities in the Philadelphia area. Cadets desiring to stay at school can use all facilities and attend movies on Friday and Saturday nights in the student center. The cadets frequently enjoy mixers, formal dances, plays, band concerts, special sports events, and polo matches with students from neighboring schools. All events are chaperoned by faculty members.

Gold and Silver Star cadets are those who have earned academic achievement. They are granted trips into town on Wednesday afternoons and evenings. On Friday, Saturday, and Sunday, those not restricted for academic or other reasons may visit town after their last duty until early evening. Periodically during the year, weekend leaves are authorized for the entire corps; other times there are special weekend leaves for Gold and Silver Star honor students. The leaves help reinforce positive peer pressure to excel in both academics and leadership tasks. Following chapel and Regimental Parade on Sunday, cadets may leave the grounds on special dinner leave with their parents or other authorized adults.

SUMMER PROGRAMS

A four-week residential summer camp is available for young men ages 8–16. A day camp is available for young men and women ages 6–16. These programs provide them with the very best in recreational and educational opportunities.

COSTS AND FINANCIAL AID

The annual charge for 2010–11 is $38,290. This charge includes tuition, room and board, uniforms, and all other fees. There is an optional charge for private music lessons, developmental reading, and driver's education. Health center stays for each period of more than 24 hours' duration are also an additional expense. A nonrefundable application fee of $100 is required with an application. At the time of acceptance, a $500 validation fee is required.

In 2009–10, approximately 40 percent of the students received financial aid totaling more than $1 million. Merit-based scholarships are offered for academic excellence and performance in athletics, the band, and the choir. Through the generosity of many friends of Valley Forge, some special and endowed scholarships, with varying need and/or merit-based criteria, are available.

ADMISSIONS INFORMATION

Admission is based on academic aptitude as measured by the Otis-Lennon Mental Ability Test and/or the SSAT, information pertaining to grade level, personal character and scholastic references, and the recommendation of the Admissions Counselor based on a personal interview with the applicant. Applicants must present evidence of being capable of meeting the demands of a college-preparatory curriculum.

The admission policies of Valley Forge Military Academy & College are nondiscriminatory with respect to race, color, creed, and national or ethnic origin and are in compliance with federal laws.

APPLICATION TIMETABLE

Inquiries are always welcome. Those seeking further information are invited to attend periodic Sunday Campus Visitations; everyone is encouraged to contact the admissions office to make an appointment to visit the campus. New cadets are enrolled in late August, and limited openings also exist for January, or midyear, entry. While there is no application deadline, it is recommended that applications be submitted three months before the desired entry date.

ADMISSIONS CORRESPONDENCE

Dean of Admissions
Valley Forge Military Academy & College
Wayne, Pennsylvania 19087-3695

Phone: 610-989-1490
        866-923-VFMA (toll-free)
Fax: 610-688-1545
E-mail: admissions@vfmac.edu
Web site: http://academy.vfmac.edu

WASHINGTON ACADEMY

East Machias, Maine

Since 1792
Washington
Academy

Type: Coeducational boarding and day college-preparatory school; business studies and vocational training available
Grades: 9–12, PG
Enrollment: 430
Head of School: Judson L. McBrine III, Head of School

THE SCHOOL

As one of the oldest academies in Maine, Washington Academy (WA) has been meeting the educational needs of students in grades 9–12 since the school's charter was signed by John Hancock in 1792.

Originally a feeder school for Bowdoin College in the early 1900s, the Academy has maintained an emphasis on academics and success for the individual. Taking into account each student's differences, the Academy strives to create opportunities that equip students socially and intellectually for their future endeavors. The curriculum is geared toward college preparation, but it is also flexible enough for the student who seeks a quality education that includes business and technology education and vocational studies. Emphasis is placed on the performing and visual arts, math and sciences, and involvement in the community.

The Academy's 65-acre campus is located in a safe, rural community in coastal Downeast Maine. The location enhances the nurturing environment created by a low student-teacher ratio, individualized attention, and a welcoming community. Just 2 miles from the Atlantic Ocean, the area also provides excellent recreational opportunities, including kayaking, sailing, fishing, hiking, and nature walks.

The school is governed by a 15-member, self-perpetuating Board of Trustees. An active Alumni Association supports the school's Development Office in annual giving and alumni relations. Washington Academy is accredited by the New England Association of Schools and Colleges and approved by the Maine Department of Education.

ACADEMIC PROGRAMS

The Academy offers a challenging and comprehensive curriculum to meet the needs of students of varying academic abilities. Courses range from training opportunities in boat building to Advanced Placement and Honors courses in many disciplines. More than 100 courses are offered, with class sizes ranging from 2 to 20. The average class size is 16 and the student-teacher ratio is 11:1.

Twenty-three (23) credits are required for graduation. Required credits include 4 credits in English; 3 credits in science, including 1 credit in biology or coastal studies/environmental science and 1 credit in chemistry or physical science; 3 credits in math; 3 credits in social studies, including 1 credit in U.S. history, ½ in government and ½ in introduction to social science; ½ credit in health; 1 credit in physical education; 1 credit in fine arts; and 1 credit in adviser/advisee. Fifteen hours of community service per year, with a minimum of 5 hours per semester, are also required.

Students are given latitude in selecting electives, which include many fine arts courses, such as advanced digital photography, music composition, and concert chorus. Other electives include eight Advanced Placement courses, foreign languages (Spanish, French, Chinese, and Latin), coastal ecology, and internships, including an exploratory course in health occupations at a local hospital. With a four-by-four block schedule, students must carry at least three subjects per semester or six for two semesters.

For the Academy's English Language Learners, the curriculum includes English as a second language (ESL). Students are provided with beginning, intermediate, and advanced ESL, as well as courses in American culture and history and science. International students are integrated into classes within the regular curriculum. A one-on-one personal learning lab is available to students needing help with standard curriculum courses, as well as support labs in English and math. The Academy operates a TOEFL test center on campus which is available for testing throughout the year

The Academy operates on a two-semester system. Reports with grades and comments are sent to parents every four weeks. Student grade reports are available online at any time. Attendance and discipline records may also be viewed by parents.

FACULTY AND ADVISERS

The staff consists of 39 full-time instructors and 27 administrators and support personnel. Faculty members are available after school and during prep periods for academic assistance. The faculty provides co-curricular activities during and after school.

The Academy operates an adviser/advisee program that mentors students through their four years of high school. Each faculty member oversees a group of 9 to 14 students from the time they are freshmen through graduation. Groups meet daily to monitor student progress, discuss concerns, and facilitate character development and career planning. New students are paired with a peer proctor during their first few weeks at the Academy.

Judson L. McBrine III, a graduate of the University of Maine (B.S., 1990) and University of Maine Graduate School (M.Ed., 1996), was appointed Head of School in 1997. In 2006, he received his Certificate of Advanced Studies in educational leadership. Mr. McBrine had formerly been the Assistant Head of School at Washington Academy, as well as a history, health, and physical education teacher in a number of Maine schools. In 2007, McBrine was named the state of Maine's Principal of the Year. He is married to Paula McBrine, and they have two sons, Jacob and Landon.

COLLEGE ADMISSION COUNSELING

The Guidance Office assists students in preparing for their postsecondary education and career objectives. A full-time college placement counselor who assists the guidance counselors in researching colleges, admissions and financial aid applications, and scholarship opportunities joined the staff in 2004. Visits by college representatives to the Academy are open to interested juniors and seniors. New England Association for College Admission Counseling college admission fairs take place every other year at the Academy and every year locally.

In recent years, on average, 85 percent of the graduating class has applied and been accepted to colleges or universities. Recent graduates have been accepted at American, Bates, Bowdoin, Boston University, Bryant, Cornell, Dartmouth, Ithaca, Maine Maritime Academy, Middlebury, MIT, Roger Williams, Vassar, Worcester Polytechnic Institute, and the University of Maine.

STUDENT BODY AND CONDUCT

The student enrollment at Washington Academy for 2010–11 is 430. Of these students, 340 are day students and 90 are residential boarding students. The residential students represent sixteen different countries, including Bermuda, Bosnia, China, Germany, Jamaica, Korea, Mexico, Nigeria, Philippines, Russia, Spain, Taiwan, Ukraine, United Arab Emirates (UAE), the United States, and Vietnam.

Disciplinary problems are handled by the Dean of Students, in cooperation with the Head of School, and in accordance with established policies. Policies are clearly defined in the *Student Handbook*. School policies emphasize the acceptance of responsibility, personal integrity, and zero tolerance for harassment.

ACADEMIC FACILITIES

The Academy is located on a 65-acre campus with ten buildings. Four of the buildings serve as the academic facilities. The original Academy Building, built in 1823 and renovated most recently in 1994, houses foreign languages, special education, and mathematics. The Alumni Building is the main facility for administrative offices and classrooms. Renovated in the early 1970s and again in 1994, the building is also home to three science labs, an art studio, cafeteria, and the Larson Library.

The library holds 10,000 volumes and is fully automated. Using the library's seven computers and services provided by the University of Maine System, students may access a suite of shared databases and journal articles.

The Gardner Gymnasium has two courts with tiered seating and a seating capacity of 1,100. It also contains music classrooms, practice rooms, and a computer lab for music composition. Gardner Gym hosts volleyball and basketball games, assemblies, concerts and music programs, the junior prom, graduation, and other special events. An Arts and Music Center was completed in the summer of 2010 and consists of four new classrooms, a Student Center, a music performance room, and a new art room. In addition, a new Health & Wellness Center was created in the Gardner Gymnasium.

The Industrial Technology Building houses the Marine Trades Program, Industrial Arts, and Diesel Engines classes. The facility has computerized numerical cutting equipment, a professional paint booth, fiberglass boat building resources, and a CAD/drafting lab.

The Academy's computer resources include a campuswide network with both wired and wireless capabilities. Students are encouraged to bring their own laptops. For students who do not have their own laptops, the library houses desktops as well as twenty laptops for student use. Desktop computers are also located in the study hall for access during study periods and within individual classrooms. For classroom use led by a teacher, the Academy hosts a nineteen-station technology lab for digital media technology, a ten-station marine trades drafting lab, a ten-station remedial math lab, and fifteen laptops available for classroom use in the Old Academy building.

Students and parents alike particularly appreciate the Academy's student management system. Grades, attendance, and discipline are all entered in daily and are immediately available over a secure network to both students and parents with Internet access. For those parents without Internet access, the Academy still provides traditional progress reports and report cards.

During fall 2008, a new Point of Sale system (POS) school lunch program was implemented. This POS is a Web-based application that allows parents to view lunch balances and detailed records of a student's purchases within the past thirty days, and parents can use a credit card to place money into the school account if they prefer not sending in cash or checks.

BOARDING AND GENERAL FACILITIES

Washington Academy currently operates four boarding facilities. The newest dormitory opened in December 2006 and houses 48 boys. The Larson dormitory houses up to 12 boys, with 2 students in each room. The Edwin and Linnie Cates dormitory, with its recent sixteen-bed addition, has the capacity to house 32 girls. The Clifford House is an honors dorm for qualifying seniors. Wireless Internet and cable access is available in all rooms. The Academy employs dorm parents to supervise the facilities. There are dorm parents living in each dorm with 24-hour supervision on the weekends. All dorm parents are residential faculty members and teach two to four classes per semester in addition to their residential responsibilities. Breakfast, lunch, and dinner are provided each day at the school cafeteria. Weekend and after-school activities are coordinated, including transportation, by the Director of Residential Life and her 3 staff members.

The Academy also operates an active Host Home Placement Program for both boys and girls. Families in the program have been carefully screened and matched with incoming students.

ATHLETICS

The Academy promotes sports and activities as an integral part of the educational process. Team sports include baseball, basketball, cheerleading, cross-country, football, golf, soccer, softball, swimming, tennis, track and field, volleyball, and wrestling. The Academy competes with both private and public schools in the area. The Academy has competed in many eastern Maine and state championships, winning both the boys' state soccer and basketball championships in the last two years. Due to the rural setting, the community is very involved in the Academy's athletic program. The amount of support and pride from fans is tremendous and has been more evident with the addition of a lighted soccer field in 2006, allowing for more community attendance during evening hours.

Athletic fields occupy the rear portion of the campus and consist of soccer, baseball, and softball fields. A new practice field is under construction along with a regulation 5K cross-country trail and four new tennis courts. The Academy's wooded cross-country trail covers blueberry fields and ascends a notoriously difficult hill. Outdoor basketball courts are located behind the rear parking lot.

EXTRACURRICULAR OPPORTUNITIES

Students are encouraged to get involved in clubs and activities and to start their own groups that can benefit the overall student body. The Academy offers more than thirty clubs, including, but not limited to, National Honor Society, Robotics, Student Council, Model United Nations, Yearbook Committee, JMG Career Association, chess, yoga, ski outings, and a championship math team.

The *Silver Quill* (literary magazine) and the yearbook provide opportunities for artistic and written self-expression.

The WA Players, the Academy's theater troupe, produces a fall show for the community and competes in spring competitions, often placing within the top three to five in the state. Musicians are given opportunities to learn and demonstrate musical talents through jazz band, pep band, choruses, all-state auditions, music festivals, steel drum band, and guitar class.

DAILY LIFE

The Academy's daily schedule consists of a semester block or four-period day. All courses are for a single semester and run for 80 minutes, with the exception of Advanced Placement courses and music which run for 40 minutes and for the full year. The school day runs from 7:45 until 2:14. No classes are held on weekends and holidays.

Washington Academy's After School Enrichment Program offers fun, structured activities between 3 and 5:30 for all residential boarding students and day students who wish to participate. Each quarter, students sign up for the programs that interest them most. Students often learn a new skill in these classes, such as Latin dancing or how to play the dulcimer. Some involve volunteering in the community or even cheering on the school's athletic teams. All provide a fun way to unwind after school, make new friends, and stay productive through the afternoon.

In addition to participating in these classes, students document what they learn through their choice of a journal or presentation, giving them more opportunities to practice their all-important English skills.

WEEKEND LIFE

Boarding students are provided with many supervised weekend activities. Weekend trips to Bar Harbor, Acadia National Park (1 hour away); Boston (6 hours away); and Canada (½ hour away) provide access to cultural and recreational events. Skiing, whale watching, and hiking on the bold coast are all within walking and driving distances. Residential students are provided with memberships to the local University's Life Long Learning Center (3 miles away), which includes an Olympic size pool, a weight room, racquetball courts, a gym, and cardiovascular equipment. Karate, dance, music, and horseback lessons are all available within a short driving distance of the school.

On-campus activities often include athletic competitions, concerts, plays, and special events, such as the winter arts festival and Junior Prom.

COSTS AND FINANCIAL AID

The cost of tuition, room, and board for the 2011–12 school year is $32,650. Costs for English as a Second Language depend on the student's English proficiency and are $2500 for the University Prep Program, $4500 for the Integrated Transitional Language Program, and $6000 for the Individualized Immersion Program. A nonrefundable enrollment deposit of $3000 is due within thirty days of acceptance. Most parents set up accounts for weekly spending and extra expenses through a local bank or bank card.

Scholarships are based upon academic achievement, extracurricular involvement, and financial need. The Scholarship Committee determines financial awards. All submitted information is confidential.

ADMISSIONS INFORMATION

Washington Academy seeks students who are likely to both benefit from and positively contribute to the school and its student body. Entrance tests are not required; however TOEFL or SLEP scores are required for international students to determine placement for ESL courses. Admission decisions are made by an Admissions Committee after reviewing information on the candidate's academic ability, achievements, and other interests.

Washington Academy does not discriminate on the basis of race, religion, sex, national origin, or disability. The school is committed to ensuring all enrolled students are provided with equal social and academic opportunity.

APPLICATION TIMETABLE

The Admissions Office accepts applications throughout the year but strongly encourages fall applicants to send all forms and supporting documents to the Admissions Office by April 1. Parents are notified of the committee's decision on a rolling basis. The school encourages both campus interviews and visits at anytime (by appointment). The school is open from 7:30 a.m. until 4 p.m. Students may make an initial inquiry of the school through an online inquiry and application form. There is a $50 application fee.

ADMISSIONS CORRESPONDENCE

Robin Moloff-Gautier
Admissions Director
Washington Academy
66 Cutler Road
P.O. Box 190
East Machias, Maine 04630

Phone: 207-255-8301 Ext. 209
Fax: 207-255-8303
E-mail: admissions@washingtonacademy.org
Web site: http://www.washingtonacademy.org

WESTERN RESERVE ACADEMY

Hudson, Ohio

Type: Coeducational, boarding and day, college-preparatory
Grades: 9–12, postgraduate year
Enrollment: 390
Head of School: Christopher D. Burner, Head of School

THE SCHOOL

Founded in 1826 as a preparatory school for Western Reserve College, Western Reserve Academy (WRA) inherited its present campus in Hudson when the college moved to Cleveland in 1882 to eventually become Case Western Reserve University. In 1916, the Academy was greatly aided by a handsome endowment given by James W. Ellsworth. The school's endowment ranks among the top boarding/day, independent secondary schools in the United States.

Reserve is a traditional college-preparatory school that is committed to maintaining academic excellence and to offering its students a well-rounded program so that they may develop into interesting, knowledgeable, and sensitive adults. The academic part of the day is not overly structured, but an atmosphere of academic seriousness prevails. Close relationships among the adults and students are an essential and natural part of daily life.

Hudson lies between Cleveland (30 minutes away) and Akron (25 minutes away), just off the Ohio Turnpike (U.S. 80). The main part of the Western Reserve Academy campus is located one block from downtown Hudson, but most of its 190 acres extend into the surrounding countryside. Thus, outdoor activities are as much a part of life at WRA as are those kinds of activities associated with major urban areas. Concerts (classical and otherwise), drama, art museums, outdoor activities, and cinema are a functional part of a student's life at the school.

Western Reserve Academy is governed by a board of 30 trustees who supervise the school's $97.7-million endowment. The annual budget of more than $15.5 million is fortified by the interest from that endowment as well as by funds from an Annual Giving Program. Parent organizations such as the Dad's Club and the Pioneer Women are actively involved in campus events as well. Approximately $3.6 million is allocated for financial aid, providing an opportunity for students who otherwise would be unable to attend.

Western Reserve Academy is accredited by the Independent Schools Association of the Central States. It is a member of the National Association of Independent Schools, the Secondary School Admission Test Board, the School and Student Service for Financial Aid, the Committee on Boarding Schools, the Midwest Boarding Schools, the Association of Boarding Schools, and the Ohio Association of Independent Schools.

ACADEMIC PROGRAMS

Western Reserve Academy offers a spirited four-year academic program of the highest caliber; students typically find it challenging. Structured beginning-level courses prepare younger students for what lies ahead in their final two years: opportunities to take advanced work in computer programming and Advanced Placement (AP) courses in English, Latin, French, Spanish, German, U.S. history, European history, art history, biology, physics, chemistry, computer science, statistics, calculus, and economics, as well as the opportunity to take several courses for college credit through a special School College Articulation Program (SCAP) in conjunction with Kenyon College. Each student graduates with at least 21 credits, which are earned in the following configuration: 4 credits of English, 3 of mathematics, 3 of a foreign language, 3 of a lab science, 3 of history (including U.S. history), 1 of fine arts and a Senior Seminar, and ½ each of health and ethics and athletics, with the remaining credits in electives.

For upperclass students, the AP and SCAP courses may be supplemented by independent study. Upperclass students may also participate in the School Year Abroad program.

On the average, students take approximately 5 credits per year, in schedules arranged with their faculty advisers. The classes are small, with an average size of 12, although classes for advanced-level courses are typically smaller in size. There are no formal opportunities for remedial studies in any academic discipline.

To a great extent, students determine the use of their free periods during the academic day on an individual basis; there are no supervised study halls except during the evenings. At that time, students typically study in their dormitory rooms, although they may study in the library or in open classrooms or labs, depending on their specific needs.

Advisers work closely with students and parents to determine academic programs, daily schedules, preparation for final exams, and the need for extra help.

FACULTY AND ADVISERS

Western Reserve Academy has 69 full- and part-time faculty members, of whom all but a few live on campus in school houses or in apartments in dormitories. Many administrators teach at least one course. All faculty members have a bachelor's degree, and 82 percent have advanced degrees; 6 have doctorates.

Only the third alumnus to serve as Head of School since the school's founding in 1826, Christopher D. Burner, '80, was appointed in 2008 and is a graduate of Franklin & Marshall College (B.A.), Dartmouth College (M.A.L.S.), and Harvard University (M.Ed.). Mr. Burner has taught at Western Reserve Academy on two separate occasions. During his first term (1986) at WRA, Mr. Burner served as the Assistant Dean of Students, taught Latin, and coached varsity wrestling, football, and lacrosse. He also held faculty positions at Saint James School in Maryland and Westminster School in Connecticut. After returning to WRA (1992), Mr. Burner served as the Director of Admission and most recently as the Dean of Faculty and Administration, in addition to teaching Latin and coaching.

The average faculty member has been at Western Reserve Academy for more than twelve years. Typically, it is the younger teachers moving on to graduate, law, or medical school who leave the staff. Almost all teachers coach a sport, serve evening duty in dormitories, supervise an activity, and advise students. On-campus housing and meals (morning and evening meals are available for all faculty families) constitute part of each teacher's salary. A sabbatical program and summer study grants are also a part of faculty benefits.

COLLEGE ADMISSION COUNSELING

College placement is handled by the College Adviser, who consults with students and their families during the junior and senior years. The school report on each student is prepared by the Faculty Guidance Committee, which is chaired by the College Adviser. Naturally, college visits are encouraged, but each year WRA is visited by more than 85 representatives from colleges. The College Guidance Office keeps on file an extensive selection of college catalogs and other admission information.

Of the Academy's graduates, 100 percent attend colleges or universities each year. SAT averages are consistently very high. Recent graduates are attending such institutions as Case Western Reserve University, Georgetown, Harvard, Miami (Ohio), Middlebury, Northwestern, Princeton, Stanford, the U.S. Naval Academy, Vanderbilt, Yale, and the Universities of Chicago and Pennsylvania.

STUDENT BODY AND CONDUCT

Two thirds of all students are boarders, and slightly more than half are boys. Students at WRA come from many parts of this country and the world. The Academy is dedicated to creating and maintaining a healthy and pluralistic composition in its student body. Currently, 28 percent of the students represent minority groups (African American, Hispanic American, and Asian American).

Discipline and student conduct are handled by the Student Affairs Committee, which is made up of junior and senior class officers and selected faculty members in equal proportions and is chaired by the Dean of Students, with the final arbiter being the Head of School. Student government officers, dorm prefects, and various other student leaders contribute their views in most matters of student conduct and general rule determination, although the school behavior and dress code is generally considered conservative.

ACADEMIC FACILITIES

Almost every building at Western Reserve Academy has an academic function, but there are seven principal academic buildings: Seymour Hall, the chapel, Hayden Hall, Wilson Hall, Knight Fine Arts Center, Metcalf Center, and the John D. Ong Library. The seven buildings house classrooms, labs, music practice rooms, a lecture hall, a recital hall, dance rooms, a student lounge, woodworking and metal-working shops, a photography studio, a computer center, art studios, a publications room,

www.facebook.com/sec.schools

administrative offices, and the school library of 38,000 volumes. The Wilson Hall Science Center was completely renovated in 2001.

Visually dominating the campus is the chapel, modeled, as were most of the buildings, on the architectural style of Yale College. Some of the buildings, such as the Loomis Observatory (circa 1838), are more than 100 years old.

BOARDING AND GENERAL FACILITIES

Western Reserve Academy has nine dormitories and one large dining hall for its boarding students. Two times per week, evening meals are served family-style, as are lunches on Thursdays. Other meals during the week are buffet-style. Students can also purchase items at the campus store, or they can sign out to eat at one of Hudson's many restaurants. Most boys' dorm rooms are doubles, with some triples, and a few single rooms are available. Girls have dorms with doubles and a few singles. There are laundry facilities in five dorms.

The new school Health Center is state-of-the-art and has a dispensary, examination and waiting rooms, and six sick-bay rooms. A nurse is on duty during the day and on call at night unless needed for a student who is restricted to the Health Center overnight. The school doctor visits the campus every weekday to examine and talk to students.

The Student Center, which is located in the lower level of Ellsworth Hall, contains the newly renovated Green Key snack bar, booths for eating and talking, a wide-screen television, and Ping-Pong, pool, and video games. The radio station is next door.

ATHLETICS

Western Reserve Academy emphasizes athletic competition and believes student participation in team sports is an essential part of the daily program. There are two or three levels of interschool competition for boys and girls in tennis, basketball, ice hockey, diving, swimming, cross-country, track, golf, lacrosse, soccer, football, wrestling, baseball, riflery, volleyball, softball, and field hockey. Reserve is a member of the Interstate Prep School League.

The Academy's athletics facilities include a ProTurf stadium with a six-lane all-weather track, a competition swimming pool and separate diving well with 3- and 1-meter boards, a state-of-the-art fitness center with Nautilus equipment, two football fields, four soccer/lacrosse fields, a 3.1-mile cross-country course, two field-hockey fields, a wrestling arena, and twelve all-weather tennis courts. An indoor athletic complex features a 45,000-square-foot field house housing a 200-meter indoor track, varsity and four practice basketball courts, and a complete training facility.

EXTRACURRICULAR OPPORTUNITIES

Aside from participating in the Student Council, student publications, and services already mentioned, students may join a diverse and changing group of clubs and organizations: photography, debate, chess, REACH (a community service club), Green Key (the student center), skiing, drama, Green Campus Action Team, Culinary Club, and WWRA (the school radio station). The school social committee, an extension of the Student Council, organizes dances and weekend activities on campus as well as in Cleveland and Akron.

DAILY LIFE

The class day at Western Reserve Academy begins at 8 a.m. There are six 55-minute periods each day. From 3:30 to 5:45, all students participate in athletics. Dinner begins at 6:30 p.m., and study halls in dorms are from 8 until 10. Classes meet on Saturday from 8 a.m. until noon.

WEEKEND LIFE

All students may sign out for weekend leave for most weekends. Leaves begin about noon on Saturday and extend until study hours begin on Sunday evening. Less than one fourth of the students leave the campus on a given weekend.

A variety of activities are presented to the student body (for both day and boarding students) Saturday and Sunday afternoons.

The Academy is located in a thriving geographic area. Nestled in the quaint village of Hudson, Reserve is within easy walking distance of attractive shops, restaurants, and community activities. Beyond Hudson, Cleveland and Akron offer major cultural events. The world-famous Cleveland Orchestra, the Rock and Roll Hall of Fame, E. J. Thomas Hall, Playhouse Square, the Ohio Ballet, the Cleveland Institute of Art, and the Museum of Natural History are easily accessible. Weekend programs also include downhill skiing at nearby slopes, concerts, off-campus movies, trips to the Gateway Sports Complex to see professional athletics teams, and outdoor activities at the nearby Cuyahoga Valley National Recreation Area. The Academy's proximity to Case Western Reserve University, Hiram College, Kent State, Oberlin, and the University of Akron makes the resources of these colleges and universities available as well.

SUMMER PROGRAMS

Western Reserve Academy hosts numerous summer programs. Among them are sports camps for lacrosse, field hockey, soccer, basketball, swimming, and diving. New programs will be added during the summer of 2011.

COSTS AND FINANCIAL AID

Fees for 2010–11 are $40,700 for boarders and $28,900 for day students. Extra fees of about $600 covered books and other incidental expenses. Payments are made in three installments: July, September, and December. Reserve uses the Knight Tuition Payment Plan and the Dewar Tuition Refund Plan.

For 2010–11, more than $3.8 million in financial aid was awarded to 34 percent of WRA's students. Awards are made on the basis of family need (as established by the School and Student Service for Financial Aid). The average award was $17,298 for day students and $29,000 for boarders.

ADMISSIONS INFORMATION

Western Reserve Academy admits students of any race, sex, color, disability, or national or ethnic origin to all rights, privileges, programs, and activities generally accorded or made available to students at the Academy. It does not discriminate on the basis of race, sex, color, disability, or national or ethnic origin in the administration of its educational policies, admissions policies, scholarship and loan programs, and athletics or other school-administered programs.

Western Reserve Academy requires that all applicants submit SSAT, ISEE, or SAT scores and recommendations from 2 current teachers. Applicants average in the top three deciles on the SSAT and have achieved A's and B's at their previous schools. Most students enter in grade 9 or 10. Reserve admits approximately 100 freshmen per year.

APPLICATION TIMETABLE

Most inquiries are made in the fall, with applications ($25 fee for students within the United States and $150 for international students) completed by January 15 (day students, December 15). Applicants and their families should have a campus tour and an interview. After an application is submitted, it is reviewed by the Faculty Admission Committee; families are notified after March 10 (day students, January 10) and are usually allowed four weeks to notify the school of their intentions.

ADMISSIONS CORRESPONDENCE

Admission Office
Western Reserve Academy
Hudson, Ohio 44236
Phone: 330-650-9717
        800-784-3776 (toll-free)
Fax: 330-650-5858
E-mail: admission@wra.net
Web site: http://www.wra.net

THE WILLISTON NORTHAMPTON SCHOOL

Easthampton, Massachusetts

Type: Coeducational boarding and day college-preparatory school

Grades: 7–PG: Middle School, 7–8; Upper School, 9–12, postgraduate year

Enrollment: School total: 515; Upper School: 460

Head of School: Robert W. Hill III, Head of School

THE SCHOOL

Williston Seminary was founded in 1841 by Samuel and Emily Williston. Initially coeducational, Williston Seminary later became a college-preparatory school for boys only. The Willistons amassed a great fortune from the production of cloth-covered buttons and the manufacture of rubber webbing and thread. They also supported the local colleges both financially and personally.

Eighty-three years later, in 1924, Sarah B. Whitaker and Dorothy M. Bement founded the academic Northampton School for Girls.

In 1971, the two schools merged to form the Williston Northampton School, a coeducational school offering a strong secondary education to prepare interested students for the rigorous academic programs of colleges today and the demands and complexities in life afterward.

The School is located on 125 acres in the heart of the Pioneer Valley near the base of Mount Tom, 85 miles west of Boston, and 150 miles north of New York. Within a 15-mile radius are the Five Colleges: Smith, Mount Holyoke, Hampshire, and Amherst Colleges, and the University of Massachusetts.

The current endowment is estimated at $37 million. The School's 10,000 alumni contributed more than $1.4 million in Annual Giving last year.

Williston is accredited by the New England Association of Schools and Colleges and is affiliated with the National Association of Independent Schools, the Association of Independent Schools of New England, the College Board, the School and College Conference on English, the Art Association of New England Preparatory Schools, and the Council for Advancement and Support of Education.

ACADEMIC PROGRAMS

At the heart of the school's program is a strong and varied academic program that seeks to strengthen, expand, and encourage students' skills and interests in the essential disciplines. Care is taken to place each student in the courses and sections most appropriate to his or her abilities. An average class size of 13 students enables faculty members to learn each student's abilities, and the flexibility of the program makes it possible for the School to structure programs that can best meet every individual student's needs. In addition, Williston offers numerous opportunities in competitive athletics, the arts, and leadership.

Williston's outstanding facilities and the magnificent recreational and cultural offerings nearby provide the setting for an outstanding education. Through its unique Williston+ Program, the School provides superior college preparation by bringing the rich resources of the nearby Five Colleges into the classroom to enrich the School's curriculum and provide professional development opportunities for the faculty. Having the Five Colleges nearby gives Williston students and faculty unparalleled opportunities to engage in and explore a variety of subjects.

The School believes that each student should experience as many academic and creative disciplines as possible while they are at Williston. Therefore, Williston expects each of its students not only to satisfy the minimum basic requirements of 4 years of English, 3 years of math, 2 of science, 2 of a foreign language, and 2 in the social sciences, but also to select two semester courses from the area of fine arts and one semester course from the area of religion and philosophy.

Williston also offers eighteen Advanced Placement (AP) classes. Qualified students may elect to complete extra work in consultation with the teacher to prepare to take the AP exam in two additional subject areas. Of the Williston students who took the AP exams in 2009, which is required of all AP students at the School, 80 percent received scores of 3 or higher, earning college credit at participating institutions.

The Writing Center plays a central part in Williston's academic program. Located in the library, the Writing Center is staffed by members of the English department, as well as by highly qualified student writers. The Writing Center provides support for students at all levels, on any writing assignment, so they can build critical thinking skills and clarity of expression, crucial tools that will be used again, in college and beyond. The Writing Center had over 1,100 visits in 2009–10.

Williston also offers a Writers' Workshop series every fall. Since its inception in 1998, Williston's Writers' Workshop series has hosted a variety of distinguished writers who give a public reading and then work with Williston's Readers and Writers Master Class students on the craft of writing. Authors who have participated include Augusten Burroughs, Gregory Maguire, Elinor Lipman, Sue Miller, and Curtis Sittenfeld.

During the spring semester, Williston hosts the Photographers' Lecture series. Begun in 2000, this lecture series features internationally acclaimed photojournalists, filmmakers, and commercial photographers who share their work and ideas with the community and Williston's advanced photography students. Past distinguished visiting photographers have included John Willis, Sean Kerman, Lori Grinker, Nina Berman, and David Burnett.

Most students choose to complete work beyond the basic requirements established by each department. To graduate, a student at Williston must have earned 19 academic credits (a one-year course equals 1 credit) in grades 9–12 and must pass all courses taken during the senior year. Diploma requirements also include regular participation in the athletics program, satisfactory completion of the Senior Project for those who elect to do one, enrollment at Williston throughout the senior year, and satisfactory citizenship.

Students attaining honor grades are recognized at the end of each term. The highest honor is election to the Cum Laude Society. Williston's chapter of Cum Laude is one of the oldest in the nation, founded in 1906.

FACULTY AND ADVISERS

The Williston Northampton School teaching faculty numbers 86 full-time members—45 men and 41 women. Fifty-nine hold master's degrees, and 5 have doctorates. Thirty live in dorms. The School has established programs to counsel students about academic work, personal problems, class performance, and future educational goals and opportunities. Each boarding student has a faculty adviser who is also a dorm parent and may be easily consulted on academic or personal matters. Students can also consult with the Dean of Students, Chaplain, and Academic Dean. All students are encouraged to participate in a series of health workshops, which are directed by the Health Services staff and focus on issues of health and personal decision making. The School also employs the services of professional counselors.

In 2008, Williston instituted its Ninth Grade Program, which is designed to ease the transition for students from middle school to secondary school and to build camaraderie among ninth graders. The program includes an overnight orientation, special advisers, assemblies, and academic monitoring. The cornerstone of the program is C.O.R.E. (curiosity, organizations, reflection, and empathy). Each of these concepts is the focus of a special ninth grade–only assembly where Williston adults and upperclass students address the ninth graders and discuss how these principles have helped them succeed. In addition, at the end of each semester, the program holds final exam preparation clinics, where advisers outline for students the expectations for exam week and help the ninth graders fill out an hour-by-hour study schedule.

On July 1, 2010, Robert W. Hill III became Williston's nineteenth head of school. Mr. Hill comes to Williston from Carolina Day School in Asheville, North Carolina, where he had served as Associate Head of School and Principal of the Upper School since 2007. There, he successfully focused on building the school's community culture as well as faculty and curriculum development. Prior to 2007, he served for nine years at St. Paul's School (Concord, New Hampshire) in a variety of roles, including Academic Dean, Director of College Advising, and Associate Dean of Faculty. His tenure there also included responsibilities as an English teacher, varsity girls' squash coach, and dorm resident. Hill started his teaching career at Westminster School (Simsbury, Connecticut), where he taught for fifteen years. He received his B.A. cum laude from Middlebury College (Vermont) and earned his M.A. in English literature from Middlebury's Bread Loaf School of English.

COLLEGE ADMISSION COUNSELING

Williston provides a thorough and personalized college counseling program for every student, beginning in their junior year. Four full-time counselors work with the junior and senior class. From the beginning, the counseling process draws in both parents and students to establish a dialogue between the School and the family. During the junior year, counselors and faculty members meet with students to acquaint them with standardized test-taking, financial aid, roles and functions of college officials, and campus lifestyles.

The 135 members of the class of 2010 were accepted at over 450 colleges and universities, including Brown, Colby, Connecticut College, Hobart and William Smith, Skidmore, Trinity (Hartford), the University of Chicago, and the U.S. Naval Academy.

STUDENT BODY AND CONDUCT

Most students enter Williston during the freshman or sophomore year. In 2009–10, grade 9 had 83 members (43 boys, 40 girls), of whom 41 were day students. Grade 10 had 102 members (53 boys, 49 girls), of whom 39 were day students. Grade 11 had 114 members (54 boys, 60 girls), of whom 46 were day students. Grade 12 had 142 members (76 boys, 66 girls), of whom 50 were day students. There were 12 postgraduate students. Thirteen percent of the students are members of minority groups. Students came from twenty-two states and twenty-two countries.

The rules and regulations of the School have evolved from experience and lengthy discussion and provide clear guidelines for everyone living in the School community. It is expected that students will follow both the spirit and the letter of these regulations as described in the *Student Handbook,* which is provided to all enrolling students.

Students who are reported to have violated School rules and regulations meet with the Discipline Committee, made up of faculty and student representatives. The committee's decisions and recommendations are reviewed by the head of school, who makes the final decision in disciplinary matters.

ACADEMIC FACILITIES
The campus is located on approximately 125 acres. The School's thirty-eight buildings include the Reed Campus Center, the Scott Hall Science Building, the Boardman Theater, the Robert A. Ward Schoolhouse, the Robert Clapp Library, the Philip Stevens Chapel, and the Whitaker-Bement Middle School Building. Renovations to the old gymnasium to create a new Campus Center that includes music and fine arts classrooms were completed in 1996. The Technology and Student Publications Center, the Science Tech Lab, the library, and the math floor house four student computer labs.

BOARDING AND GENERAL FACILITIES
The buildings on campus include the Head's House, the Zachs Admission Center at the Homestead, the Chapel, the Birch Dining Commons, five dormitories with facilities for 25 to 50 students, five residence houses with boarding facilities for 8 to 12 students, and faculty homes. Ford Hall and Memorial Dorm each house 50 boys. Ford Hall received a million-dollar renovation in 1999, adding sun-splashed common rooms and other enhancements. All dorm rooms are wired into the campus computer network and have voice mail. A new ninth grade boys' dorm with housing for 32 students and three faculty families opened in 2008. The dorm, which is heated and cooled via seventeen geothermal wells, is the centerpiece of a planned residential quad.

Each dormitory or house is supervised by resident faculty houseparents to create an environment conducive to academic achievement and a warm and pleasant home atmosphere.

ATHLETICS
Sports are an integral part of student life at Williston, whether interscholastic or recreational. The School requires that each student be involved in the athletics program in each of the three sports seasons. The athletics department instills the principles of fair play, good sportsmanship, teamwork, and respect for rules and authority. Most of the academic faculty members also coach competitive teams, and the Director of Athletics oversees the program.

Interscholastic teams for girls include crew, cross-country, field hockey, soccer, and volleyball in the fall; basketball, ice hockey, skiing, squash, swimming and diving, and wrestling in the winter; and crew, golf, lacrosse, softball, tennis, track, and water polo in the spring. Boys may elect crew, cross-country, football,

soccer, or water polo; basketball, ice hockey, skiing, squash, swimming and diving, or wrestling; and baseball, crew, golf, lacrosse, tennis, or track. Horseback riding at a nearby stable and modern dance are available every season. Fitness training, aerobics, yoga, and self-defense are choices open to upperclass students.

The Athletic Center houses two basketball courts, a six-lane pool with a diving well, five international squash courts, a weight room and fitness center, and a wrestling room. Other facilities include a lighted, synthetic-surface football/lacrosse field with stadium seating; a dance studio; an indoor skating facility; twelve tennis courts; a new (as of 2007) all-weather running track that surrounds a synthetic surface field for field hockey, soccer, and lacrosse; more than 30 acres of playing fields; and a 3.4-mile cross-country course. In addition, there are several golf courses in the Easthampton area and ski slopes in the eastern Berkshires.

EXTRACURRICULAR OPPORTUNITIES
The countryside offers excellent climbing, biking, and skiing opportunities, and the proximity of the Five Colleges provides a culturally rich environment of fine museums, libraries, and theater programs as well. The cities of Northampton and Springfield, Massachusetts, and Hartford, Connecticut, are near enough so that concerts and activities there are as readily available as those at the local colleges.

DAILY LIFE
The academic day runs from 8:30 a.m. until 1:50 or 2:50 p.m. on Monday, Tuesday, Thursday, and Friday and until 12:15 on Wednesday. Classes are held every other Saturday morning as well. Students take five courses in a six-period schedule, with classes lasting 45 or 70 minutes, depending on the day. All-School assemblies for announcements and special presentations are held once each week. Athletics are scheduled from the end of the class day until dinnertime. Except for theme-based formal dinners, most meals are served buffet-style. A free period from 6:30 to 8 is frequently used for meetings of extracurricular organizations, library work, theater or music rehearsals, visiting between dormitories, or simply relaxing. Supervised evening study hours run from 8 to 10 p.m. Ninth grade students have lights out at 10:30 p.m. All students are checked into the dorms at 8 p.m. by the dorm faculty.

WEEKEND LIFE
While the vast majority of students remain on campus, weekends at home or at the home of a friend are permitted with parental approval after all school obligations have been met. The Student Activities Director and students on the Activity Committee organize a variety of weekly activities, and students may take advantage of the events listed in the Five College Calendar. Students travel off campus for college and professional athletic events, films, plays, dance performances, and concerts and to go skiing in Vermont.

The many on-campus activities include dances and coffeehouse entertainment, talent shows, lectures by invited speakers, and a film series.

SUMMER PROGRAMS
Throughout the year, students have the opportunity to take part in several international excursions that enrich their studies. Trips to Canada and France during school vacations offer real-life practice for French language skills. A trip to Honduras allows students to perform community service while honing their Spanish. Ed Hing ('77), Williston's photography instructor, helps students capture the beauty of locations in Italy, France, China, and other international destinations during summer photo trips. In the summer, the School offers an intensive four-week Spanish program in Mexico and hosts many outside camps, offering theater, music, and athletics.

COSTS AND FINANCIAL AID
Tuition for boarders for 2010–11 is $46,600; for day students, it is $32,000. Additional expenses include books, insurance, laundry, and other incidental expenses. Tuition payment and insurance plans are recommended upon request.

Financial aid is awarded on the basis of need to approximately 46 percent of the student body. The grants totaled $5 million for 2009–10.

ADMISSIONS INFORMATION
Williston seeks students who are interested in a challenging academic program, who can demonstrate solid academic achievement and outstanding personal character. Students should also be involved and caring contributors to life beyond the classroom. Admission is based upon an evaluation of these traits, a personal interview, and satisfactory scores on the SSAT or TOEFL. In 2009–10, 162 new students were enrolled in the Upper School.

APPLICATION TIMETABLE
The fall or winter prior to a candidate's prospective admission is usually the best time for a visit, which includes a faculty and student-guided tour of the School and an interview. The Admission Office is open Monday through Friday, from 8:30 a.m. to 4:30 p.m. during the academic year and 8 a.m. to 4 p.m. in the summer months, and on alternate Saturday mornings during the academic year.

An application for admission should be submitted by February 1 along with a nonrefundable fee of $50 ($100 for international students). The School abides by the March 10 notification date. After that date, a rolling admission plan is in effect.

ADMISSIONS CORRESPONDENCE
Ann C. Pickrell, Director of Admission
The Williston Northampton School
19 Payson Avenue
Easthampton, Massachusetts 01027

Phone: 413-529-3241
Fax: 413-527-9494
E-mail: admissions@williston.com
Web site: http://www.williston.com

WINDWARD SCHOOL

Los Angeles, California

Type: Coeducational day college-preparatory school
Grades: 7–12; Middle School 7–8; Upper School 9–12
Enrollment: 525
Head of School: Thomas W. Gilder

THE SCHOOL

A dynamic education, a nurturing community—that's the mission of Windware School. Founded in 1971 in order to provide a unique educational opportunity for Westside young people, the School takes its name from Shirley Windward, one of Windward's founders, whose dedication to the School has become legendary.

Under the leadership of Tom Gilder, who became Head of School in 1987, the School has continued to broaden its academic programs and to incorporate areas of social concern and global awareness into the classroom and extracurricular activities.

From its founding, two concepts have been fundamental to Windward School. The first, that educators and young people should work together in an environment that encourages them to be responsible, caring, well informed, ethical, and prepared. Secondly, education should provide a basis for lifelong growth, and the School should therefore concern itself with every facet of the student's life.

Today, Windward School stands as a living tribute to its many graduates and the hard work of innumerable individuals. Windward students attend the colleges of their choice around the country, and as working adults they have shown that they can succeed and prosper. Never content to rest on its laurels, Windward continues to pursue innovation, even as it remains faithful to the vision of its founders.

A not-for-profit corporation, Windward is governed by a 25-member Board of Trustees and an administrative team centered by the Head of School. The Western Association of Schools and Colleges accredits Windward. The School holds membership in the National Association of Independent Schools, the Independent School Alliance for Minority Affairs, A Better Chance, Independent School Management, the Educational Records Bureau, and the California Association of Independent Schools.

ACADEMIC PROGRAMS

Fundamental to the Windward School philosophy is the belief that secondary education must engage more than the mind alone. Allowing young people to participate in a range of academic and extracurricular experiences fosters social growth and responsibility, as well as personal development. Woven through the traditional college-preparatory courses—English language and literature, a complex social studies curriculum, mathematics, science, and foreign languages—are opportunities that enable students to be actively involved in their own education.

Windward's comprehensive and rigorous course of study teaches students to think independently, to reason with care and logic, to write and speak with clarity, and to identify and develop their aesthetic talents. This strong academic preparation is complemented by the development of ethics, character, and people skills. The School hopes its graduates will go forth from Windward with a strong sense of personal integrity, self-confidence, and pride in their particular talents, inspired by learning, and prepared for college and for life in the twenty-first century.

At Windward, classes contain a maximum of 17 students. In academic areas, courses are sectioned on the basis of interest and ability, and Advanced Placement courses are offered in every discipline. The minimum course load for students in grades 7–10 is six. Students in grades 11–12 may opt for an alteration of this pattern, though approval of the grade-level deans is required, and students are actively encouraged to take six or seven classes.

In the Upper School, minimum course requirements are one English course each year through grade 12, one history course each year through grade 12 (seniors who wish to take two courses in another discipline may petition to waive the grade 12 history requirement), one mathematics course each year through grade 11, one science course each year through grade 10, one science course in either grade 11 or grade 12 (this must include one year of laboratory science), completion of Level III in one foreign language or completion of Level II in each of two foreign languages (continuation of foreign language through grade 11 is required), one arts course each year through grade 10, and one physical education course each year through grade 10 (students in grades 9 and 10 who compete in an interscholastic team sport are excused from physical education during that sport's season).

Community service has long been at the heart of the Windward tradition. Beginning in Middle School, service learning is a core component of the program, and in the Upper School, all students are required to complete two separate and extensive community service projects prior to graduation.

Windward maintains a sister school relationship with two schools in Spain and France. Students are able to attend a sister school for a three-week academic exchange once they have mastered an appropriate level of linguistic fluency. Generally, the schools exchange 15 to 20 students at a time. The culminating academic experience of a Windward education is the School's annual senior trip for one week at the School's expense. This "classroom in the field" is the capstone of six years of work and allows for an appropriate opportunity to say goodbye to one another.

FACULTY AND ADVISERS

The Windward faculty consists of 75 full- and part-time members (37 women and 38 men). Seventy-three percent have advanced degrees, with 11 possessing doctorates. Thomas W. Gilder, Head of School, was appointed in 1987.

In selecting its faculty members, Windward looks for individuals who enjoy the art of teaching, who are enthusiastic about working with adolescents, who will involve themselves in the nonacademic life of the School, and who have lively personal interests of their own. Every faculty member at Windward is an integral component in the life of the School. Faculty benefits at Windward are generous on all accounts and include financial support for continuing education and the funding of faculty-generated betterment opportunities.

COLLEGE ADMISSION COUNSELING

The college counseling program is directly linked to Windward's mission of providing a dynamic education in a nurturing environment. As such, the School works closely to support its students and their families through every stage of the college search process, beginning in the tenth grade. Windward's college counselors not only serve students as academic-schedule advisers, but also help them explore extracurricular and summer options. The counseling program reflects both the depth and the breadth of students' interests, and the School strives to find the best colleges for Windward students. Representatives of more than 100 different colleges and universities come to Windward each year to meet its students. Additional support in exploring college options is provided through an East Coast college trip for eleventh grade students and workshops with topics ranging from interview tips to the college essay. Last year's graduating class of 73 students matriculated to more than 50 different colleges and universities. Students in the last several graduating classes chose between such diverse opportunities as Barnard, Berkeley, Boston College, Colby, Columbia, Emory, George Washington, Harvard, Kenyon, Michigan, Pennsylvania, Princeton, Rhode Island School of Design, Rice, Stanford, Texas, Tufts, Vassar, Washington (St. Louis), Wesleyan, Wisconsin, and Yale. Windward places the utmost importance upon each senior having options from which to choose and its college counselors seek to guide students to discover the college or university best suited to their individual needs and aspirations.

STUDENT BODY AND CONDUCT

Windward has 525 students in grades 7–12. The average class size is 17 students, allowing teachers to offer individualized attention.

The student government is directed by a group of 20 prefects, selected on the basis of community respect, personal integrity, and the ability to positively affect the life in the community. By working closely with the adults at Windward, acting as intermediaries, organizing School activities, and leading by example, the prefects help to set the tone of the School. Of primary importance is the cultivation of respect and consideration for others and their property, the enhancement of relationships between faculty members and students, and the general well-being of the student body. The prefects are expected to respect Windward's standards in their personal conduct and in the way in which they lead others.

At Windward, the breaking of major School rules (lying, cheating, stealing, or using or possessing drugs or alcohol) is a pressing matter and typically leads to dismissal. A committee headed by the appropriate division-level Dean of Students handles disciplinary matters and refers matters to the appropriate division head for final consideration. Beyond rules and regulations, however, the School's deeply ingrained code of honor expects all students to offer both civility and compassion to other students and to teachers, staff members, and their own families. In fact, this expectation is one of the defining characteristics of Windward School.

Under the oversight of the Head of School, the Middle and Upper School Directors oversee the successful operation of the School and ensure that appropriate procedures are in place for students to enjoy their Windward experience and to be safe in the knowledge that discipline is expected of all community members.

ACADEMIC FACILITIES

Windward moved to its present 9-acre site in 1982, envisioning then the pastoral campus familiar to today's Windward students. As the School's programs have expanded, new facilities have been added to the campus. In 2002, the School constructed a ten-room classroom building, the Lewis Jackson Memorial Sports Center, the Student Pavilion, the Arts Center, and renovated the playing fields. A state-of-the-art library/learning center with performing arts studios and broadcast production center and a science/math center opened last year.

ATHLETICS

There is a suitable level of athletics for every student. Some students seek out competitive accomplishment in one sport through years of participation, while others take advantage of Windward's breadth of offerings to begin new sports at the introductory level. The physical education and athletic programs emphasize acquiring lifetime skills, shaping confident attitudes about oneself as an individual and a contributing member of a group, and developing along the way a true sense of integrity and fairness.

There are junior varsity and varsity offerings in most sports, including football, soccer, baseball, cross-country, tennis, volleyball, basketball, and golf.

The Lewis Jackson Memorial Sports Center houses a weight training facility, meeting space, and trophy room display, while the gymnasium offers basketball and volleyball courts. The beauty of the playing fields, which are built to university and professional specifications, offers all participating students a chance to play at their best.

EXTRACURRICULAR OPPORTUNITIES

An array of extracurricular opportunities is available to students through period eight activity programs. Period eight is a block of scheduled time that is set aside twice a week for clubs, study hall, and other activities that provide extracurricular opportunities for Upper School students. Students choose from a wide variety of activities that include robotics, debate, yoga, ceramics, chorus, the yearbook, the newspaper, junior senate, and comedy sports. Students are encouraged to participate and to explore interests that support the development of talents and strengths that are not just limited to academic success.

DAILY LIFE

Beginning at 8 each morning and ending at 3 p.m., both Middle and Upper Schools utilize a five-day schedule cycle. Monday mornings offer an all-School meeting for both Middle and Upper School students and faculty members, and there is a morning nutrition period five days a week. Seniors may take lunch off campus.

COSTS AND FINANCIAL AID

Tuition for 2010–11 is $30,243. The School's philosophy is to avoid extra charges for sports, field trips, or other activities offered through the School. Approximately 19 percent of the students at the School receive need-based scholarship opportunities.

ADMISSIONS INFORMATION

In every year, more students wish to become members of the Windward community than can be admitted. The admissions office works diligently to ensure that students who are accepted offer positive contributions to the community and succeed in Windward's challenging academic environment. The School seeks qualified students of diverse economic, social, ethnic, and racial backgrounds. The ISEE, grades, recommendations from the previous school, and an interview with Windward admissions personnel are required for all applicants. Openings exist traditionally for grades 7 and 9, although students may apply for grades 8 and 10 with permission of the admissions office. Applicants to Windward should all possess admirable strengths of character, be positive contributors to school and community, and attain high grades at their present schools.

APPLICATION TIMETABLE

Inquiries are welcome throughout the year, though the deadline for application for the following year is in December. Interviews and tours of the campus begin as soon as all faculty and staff members have returned in September.

ADMISSIONS CORRESPONDENCE

Sharon Pearline
Director of Admission
Windward School
11350 Palms Boulevard
Los Angeles, California 90066

Phone: 310-391-7127
Fax: 310-397-5655
Web site: http://www.windwardschool.org

THE WINSOR SCHOOL

Boston, Massachusetts

Type: Girls' college-preparatory day school
Grades: 5–12 (Lower School, 5–8; Upper School, 9–12)
Enrollment: 430
Head of School: Rachel Friis Stettler, Director

THE SCHOOL

The Winsor School is an independent day school for academically promising girls in grades 5 through 12.

Located in Boston's Longwood Medical area, the School mirrors its vibrant urban setting. Founded in 1886, the School moved from Boston's Beacon Hill to its current location in 1910. Winsor's historic campus is a 7-acre oasis, nestled amid Simmons and Wheelock Colleges, Harvard Medical School, and many of Boston's renowned teaching hospitals. Classes make frequent use of nearby resources, including the State House, Boston Public Library, African American Meeting House, Museum of Science, and Museum of Fine Arts.

The School's superb faculty encourages girls to think logically, creatively, and compassionately—and to think for themselves. As a community, Winsor cherishes integrity and generosity of spirit, and its mission underscores a commitment to diversity and global responsibility. The School's small size means girls build lasting friendships, and Winsor encourages each girl to realize her own uniqueness and promise.

The Lower School comprises grades 5 through 8. In this supportive environment, teachers foster natural curiosity through active, hands-on lessons. Winsor's Upper School is an energetic learning community of ninth through twelfth graders. Special programs augment academics, ranging from global exchanges to a summer science internship program to culminating Independent Learning Experiences. Winsor wants girls to thrive, and it helps them become their best selves through a coordinated system of wellness, counseling, and academic support.

While college is the next step for graduates, Winsor prepares young women not only for college but for life. The lives of alumnae are the true measure of the School's strength. One hundred twenty five years after its founding, The Winsor School holds firm to a vision of preparing girls to see their futures as open to boundless possibilities.

Winsor is accredited by the New England Association of Schools and Colleges, and it holds membership in the National Association of Independent Schools, the Association of Independent Schools of New England, the Head Mistresses Association of the East, the National Coalition of Girls' Schools, the National Association of College Admission Counseling, and the National Association of Principals of Schools for Girls.

ACADEMIC PROGRAMS

Winsor's reputation for academic excellence has drawn families for generations. The School encourages and expects the best from every girl. Girls expect no less from Winsor.

As spelled out in the School's Philosophy of Curriculum, Winsor defines curriculum as the total classroom learning experience for all students. The curricular philosophy is based on understandings about student learning, the pedagogies practiced in response to these understandings, the ways that teachers assess learning, and the qualities of character that students are encouraged to develop—as well as the skills and content more commonly associated with "curriculum." The curriculum is a designed continuum of developmentally appropriate learning experiences across departments.

Winsor believes that students learn best when their ideas, skills, and experiences are reinforced across the disciplines and through the grade levels in a connected curriculum. Core skills are integrated into the curriculum in a spiraling model.

Independent thinking and learning is a core principle of Winsor's curricular philosophy. At every grade level, the curriculum guides students toward independence through age-appropriate experiences that lead them to take increasing responsibility for their own learning. As a culminating educational experience, seniors undertake an Independent Learning Experience in the last month of senior year, challenging them to apply important skills they have gained in solving problems and making decisions.

The School also believes that a critical aspect of academic excellence in the twenty-first century is preparation for responsible participation in the global community. The Principles of Diversity and its Principles of Global Responsibility articulate a commitment to "foster a global consciousness."

Graduation requirements include the following: English (4 years, including one semester of Expository Writing in Class V, 1 year of U.S. literature in Class VI, and one semester of non-Western literature in Class VII); Fine Arts (2½ years); History (2½ years, including 1 year of Modern World History, 1 year of U.S. History, and one semester of non-Western history in Class VII); Language (3 years); Mathematics (3 years); Physical Education (3 years, including three semesters of health); Science (2½ years); Senior Year (one semester of a quantitative course and an Independent Learning Experience in the second semester).

Also broadening girls' perspectives are off-campus programs, including student exchanges to China and France and concert tours and speaking competitions around the world. Closer to home, some students enjoy a semester away at two of the country's leading educational programs: the Mountain School in Vermont and CITYterm, which uses New York City as its classroom.

FACULTY AND ADVISERS

Winsor's teachers are bright, creative, and caring individuals. They make their subjects come alive for students in small classes, with an average class size of 13 students. Nearly 20 percent have taught at Winsor for twenty or more years, and 89 percent have advanced degrees. More than 10 percent have doctoral degrees, including several members of the science and mathematics faculty. Faculty members are much more than teachers; they are advisers, coaches, club leaders, and role models. They care deeply about their students—not only as learners but also as people.

Each student has a faculty adviser who is the primary liaison between the student, her parents, and the rest of the faculty. The adviser keeps track of the student's academic progress and of her general well-being.

COLLEGE ADMISSION COUNSELING

The college choices of Winsor graduates reflect the academic strength of the girls and the School. Throughout the college search, Winsor's College Counseling Office offers information, structure, and support to juniors and seniors and their families.

The majority of students go on to attend the nation's most selective colleges and universities. In the last five years, the students' most common college choices were Amherst, Boston College, Brown, Columbia, George Washington, Harvard, MIT, Wesleyan, and Yale.

STUDENT BODY AND CONDUCT

The School enrolls approximately 430 students from diverse cultural, racial, and ethnic backgrounds. They hail from more than fifty different communities in and around the city of Boston.

ACADEMIC FACILITIES

Winsor facilities include eight science labs, three computer labs, a media lab and recording studio, an updated digital language lab, and three art studios. The School has continued to invest significantly in technology facilities and equipment. Winsor's experienced technology staff supports students with wireless access, school e-mail, and 150 computers for their daily use in labs, the library, and classrooms.

ATHLETICS

Winsor fields more than thirty teams in thirteen different seasonal sports. The School is one of ten independent schools that belong to the Eastern Independent League (EIL).

Girls may try out for a variety of interscholastic sports teams in grades 7 through 12. Sports are a central aspect of students' development, helping girls at many skill levels to build a positive self-image and teamwork skills. The program encourages all students to pursue a physically active life beyond their years at Winsor. In addition to athletics, the School provides physical education and health classes that are required for graduation.

EXTRACURRICULAR OPPORTUNITIES

The Winsor experience shapes girls in every possible way. While classroom learning is the core, it is just the beginning. Girls are not only thinkers and scholars but also artists, athletes, community volunteers, club members, leaders, and mentors.

Girls also shape Winsor. They give fresh life to time-honored traditions, making them their own. Girls lead everything. They speak their minds, giving voice to student issues, and often presenting or performing at weekly assemblies.

At Winsor, girls approach co-curricular activities passionately and have won national honors in crew, debate, engineering, and choral competitions.

Winsor offers more than thirty student clubs. Winsor builds time for them into all students' weekly schedules. Clubs allow girls to explore issues, develop new skills, or simply relax and have fun in the middle of a busy day. Several clubs also meet after school and on weekends, such as community service, Model United Nations, debate, drama, and engineering. The menu changes from year to year, with girls often suggesting and starting their own.

Girls also work with boys from Belmont Hill and The Roxbury Latin Schools on coordinated drama, music, and newspaper activities.

DAILY LIFE AND COMMUNITY

Winsor knows girls. It's small enough that every girl is known—by teachers, advisers, counselors, class coordinators, and deans. Students also get to know each other, creating strong friendships and bonds with classmates.

A tight-knit, caring community is part of Winsor's culture. The School encourages respect, personal responsibility, and generosity of spirit. The care with which girls and teachers live these values enriches the Winsor experience.

To cultivate a healthy educational community, Winsor's Community Wellness and Support (CWS) team integrates health and wellness initiatives, counseling, peer resources, and academic support. Embracing a holistic approach, CWS aims to support students as they learn to balance academic achievement with social, emotional, and physical well-being.

In addition to supporting students, the office organizes and facilitates parent forums that address varying issues of adolescence. Regularly scheduled parent discussion groups address different stages of girls' psycho-social development and offer parents strategies that can help them to support their daughter during this time.

COSTS AND FINANCIAL AID

For the 2010–11 academic year, Winsor's comprehensive tuition is $34,025. The School welcomes applications for tuition assistance and offers a variety of payment plans. It is Winsor's philosophy to keep the School within reach of many girls. Having talented students from diverse socioeconomic backgrounds strengthens Winsor in every way. Approximately 25 percent of Winsor students receive tuition assistance. In 2010–11, the School awarded $2.7 million in financial aid.

ADMISSIONS INFORMATION

Winsor welcomes applications for grades 5 through 7 in its Lower School and for grades 9 through 11 in the Upper School. Most students enter Winsor in the fifth or sixth grade. Openings in grades 7, 9, 10, and 11 are more limited.

APPLICATION TIMETABLE

Inquiries are welcome anytime. The admission process begins in September and ends in January for admission during the following school year. For detailed information, prospective families should check the "Important Dates and Deadlines" page on the School's Web site. Admission decisions are mailed out in March.

ADMISSIONS CORRESPONDENCE

Admissions Office
The Winsor School
103 Pilgrim Road
Boston, Massachusetts 02215

Phone: 617-735-9503
Fax: 617-912-1381
E-mail: admissions@winsor.edu
Web site: http://www.winsor.edu/admission

YORK PREPARATORY SCHOOL

New York, New York

Type: Coeducational day college-preparatory school
Grades: 6–12: Middle School, 6–8; Upper School, 9–12
Enrollment: 350
Head of School: Ronald P. Stewart, Headmaster

THE SCHOOL

York Prep is a college-preparatory school where contemporary methods enliven a strong, academically challenging, traditional curriculum. In a city known for its diversity of private schools, York Prep has developed a unique program that leads students to their highest potential. The School's approach emphasizes independent thought, builds confidence, and sends graduates on to the finest colleges and universities. At York, every student finds opportunities to flourish. York Prep believes that success breeds success, and excellence in academics, arts, or sports creates self-confidence that enhances all aspects of life, both in and out of the classroom.

York Prep was established in 1969 by its current Headmaster, Ronald P. Stewart, and his wife, Jayme Stewart, Director of College Guidance. Situated on West 68th Street between Columbus Avenue and Central Park West, the School is well served by public transportation. Consequently, it attracts students from all over the metropolitan area. York Prep takes full advantage of the prime location, with regular visits to museums, parks, and theaters, all of which are easily accessible.

York Prep is approved by the New York State Board of Regents and accredited by the Middle States Association of Colleges and Schools.

ACADEMIC PROGRAMS

The curriculum is designed to develop the superior academic skills necessary for future success. Close attention to each student's needs ensures that progress toward personal excellence is carefully guided.

Students must complete 21 credits for graduation: 4 in English, 4 in math, 4 in science, 4 in history, a minimum of 3 in foreign language, 1 in art or music, ½ in health, and ½ in community service.

Eleventh and twelfth graders choose from a number of course offerings in every subject area. In addition to selecting one course from each required category, a student must choose an elective from a variety of options that range from the creative and performing arts to the analytical sciences. Students are required to carry at least five major subjects a year plus physical education.

York Prep pioneered the requirement of community service for graduation from high school. The School requires 100 hours of structured and supervised community service with a final end-of-year paper. York Prep is in close contact with the charitable agencies where its students serve the community.

Independent study courses and Advanced Placement courses are offered. When it is appropriate, students may graduate early or enroll at local colleges for specific classes.

Classes at York are small—the average class has 15 students. There are close student-teacher relations and all students begin their day with a morning "house" period. Each student's academic and social progress is carefully monitored by the teachers, advisers, and deans of the Upper and Middle Schools. The deans, in turn, keep the Headmaster and the Principal informed at weekly meetings. In addition, the Headmaster and Principal maintain close relationships with the students. All of York's administrators, including the Headmaster and Principal, teach courses and are readily available to students and parents alike. At the close of each day, there is a period when students may go to faculty members or advisers for help.

Parents are kept informed of a student's progress through individual reports posted on "Edline," a component of the York Prep Web site, every Friday. Each family signs in with a unique password to see their child's progress in all academic subjects. The annual Curriculum Night, in which parents become students for an evening by attending their child's truncated classes, provides a good overview of the course work and the faculty members. Parent involvement is encouraged, and there is an active Parents' Association.

FACULTY AND ADVISERS

York Prep is proud of having maintained a stable faculty of outstanding and dedicated individuals. New teachers join the staff periodically, creating a nice balance between youth and experience.

There are 62 full-time faculty members, including 2 college guidance counselors, 11 reading and learning specialists, 2 computer specialists, and a librarian.

Mr. Ronald P. Stewart, the founding Headmaster, is a graduate of Oxford University (B.A., 1965; M.A., 1966; B.C.L., 1968), where he also taught.

COLLEGE ADMISSION COUNSELING

York Prep has a notable college guidance program. Mrs. Jayme Stewart, the Director of College Guidance, is well known for her expertise, experience, and authorship of *How to Get into the College of Your Choice.* She meets with all tenth graders to outline the program and then meets individually with eleventh graders and their parents. Extensive meetings continue through the twelfth grade on an individual basis. In addition, the eleventh and twelfth graders take college guidance as a course where they write their essays, research colleges, and complete their applications during school hours.

One hundred percent of York Prep's graduating students attend college. The ultimate aim of the college guidance program is the placement of each student in the college best suited to him or her. More than 85 percent of York Prep graduates are accepted to, attend, and finish at one of their first-choice college. Graduates are currently attending schools that include Barnard, Berkeley, Bowdoin, Colgate, Columbia, Cornell, Franklin and Marshall, Hamilton, Harvard, Hobart, Pennsylvania, Skidmore, Vassar, Wesley, and the University of Michigan. Numerous college representatives visit the School regularly to meet with interested students.

STUDENT BODY AND CONDUCT

There are 350 students enrolled at York Prep. York Prep students reside in all five boroughs of New York City as well as Long Island, northern New Jersey, and Westchester County. The School has a student code of conduct and a dress code. The elected student council is also an integral part of life at York Prep.

ACADEMIC FACILITIES

Located steps from Central Park at 40 West 68th Street, York Prep is a seven-story granite building housing two modern science laboratories, state-of-the-art computer equipment, performance and art studios, and a sprung hardwood gymnasium with weight and locker room facilities. The classrooms are spacious and airy, carpeted, and climate controlled. All classrooms have computers and audiovisual (AV) projectors. A T1 line provides high-speed Internet access for the whole School and enables students to e-mail their teachers and review homework assignments. In addition, all classrooms are linked to the School's in-house television channel, WYRK, over which daily announcements are aired. The building is wheelchair accessible and is located near Lincoln Center on a safe and lovely tree-lined street.

ATHLETICS

All students are required to take courses in physical education and health each year. A varied and extensive program and after school selection offer students the opportunity to participate in competitive, noncompetitive, team, and individual sports. York Prep is a playing member of several athletics leagues.

EXTRACURRICULAR OPPORTUNITIES

The Student Council organizes regular social events and trips. The School provides a wide range of extracurricular activities, including Model UN, golf, electric blues band, beekeeping, and a drama club.

DAILY LIFE

The School day begins at 8:40 with a 10-minute house period. Academic classes of 42-minute duration begin at 8:56. There is a midmorning break at 10:24. Lunch period is from 12:08 to 12:53, Mondays through Thursdays, and classes end at 3:12. Following dismissal, teachers are available for extra help. During this time, clubs and sports teams also meet. On Fridays the school day ends at 1:35.

SUMMER PROGRAMS

The School provides workshops during the summer, both in study skills and in academic courses, most of which are set up on an individual tutorial basis. In addition, the athletic department provides summer sports camps.

COSTS AND FINANCIAL AID

Tuition for the 2010–11 academic year ranges from $33,480 to $35,400. More than 30 percent of the student body receives some financial assistance. During the previous year, $1 million was offered in scholarship assistance.

ADMISSIONS INFORMATION

The School seeks to enroll students of above-average intelligence with the will and ability to complete college-preparatory work. Students are accepted on the basis of their applications, ISEE test scores, writing samples, and interviews.

APPLICATION TIMETABLE

The School conforms to the notification guidelines established by the Independent Schools Admissions Association of Greater New York. Subsequent applications are processed on a rolling admissions basis. Requests for financial aid should be made at the time of application for entrance.

ADMISSIONS CORRESPONDENCE

Jacqueline Leber, Director of Admissions
Cathy Minaudo, Director of Admissions
York Preparatory School
40 West 68th Street
New York, New York 10023

Phone: 212-362-0400
Fax: 212-362-7424
E-mail: jleber@yorkprep.org
        cminaudo@yorkprep.org
Web site: http://www.yorkprep.org

Special Needs Schools

ACADEMY AT SWIFT RIVER

151 South Street
Cummington, Massachusetts 01026
Head of School: Dr. Frank Bartolomeo

General Information Coeducational boarding college-preparatory and arts school; primarily serves students with learning disabilities, individuals with Attention Deficit Disorder, individuals with emotional and behavioral problems, dyslexic students, and dysgraphia, all learning differences in the mild-to-moderate range. Grades 9–12. Founded: 1997. Setting: rural. Nearest major city is Northampton. Students are housed in single-sex dormitories. 630-acre campus. 5 buildings on campus. Approved or accredited by CITA (Commission on International and Trans-Regional Accreditation), European Council of International Schools, Massachusetts Department of Education, and Massachusetts Department of Education. Member of Secondary School Admission Test Board. Total enrollment: 80. Upper school average class size: 8. Upper school faculty-student ratio: 1:8. There are 249 required school days per year for Upper School students. Upper School students typically attend 5 days per week. The average school day consists of 6 hours.

Upper School Student Profile Grade 9: 13 students (13 boys); Grade 10: 20 students (18 boys, 2 girls); Grade 11: 20 students (15 boys, 5 girls); Grade 12: 27 students (17 boys, 10 girls). 100% of students are boarding students. 4% are state residents. 30 states are represented in upper school student body. 4% are international students. International students from Canada, Guatemala, Italy, Mexico, Spain, and Switzerland; 6 other countries represented in student body.

Faculty School total: 13. In upper school: 9 men, 2 women; 5 have advanced degrees; 2 reside on campus.

Subjects Offered Addiction, adolescent issues, algebra, American history, American literature, art, biology, calculus, career and personal planning, career/college preparation, character education, chemistry, civics, college counseling, college placement, communication skills, community service, composition, computers, conflict resolution, current events, death and loss, decision making skills, ecology, environmental systems, English, English composition, English literature, environmental science, experiential education, fitness, geography, geometry, government/civics, health, health and wellness, history, independent study, integrated arts, interpersonal skills, lab science, life management skills, literature, martial arts, mathematics, nature study, nutrition, peer counseling, personal development, physical education, physics, pre-algebra, pre-calculus, reading/study skills, relationships, SAT/ACT preparation, science, social sciences, social studies, Spanish, U.S. government, weight training, world geography, world history.

Graduation Requirements Arts and fine arts (art, music, dance, drama), English, health and wellness, history, lab science, language, mathematics, physical education (includes health), completion of individualized therapeutic program. Community service is required.

Special Academic Programs 3 Advanced Placement exams for which test preparation is offered; honors section; accelerated programs; independent study; study at local college for college credit; academic accommodation for the artistically talented; programs in English, mathematics, general development for dyslexic students.

College Admission Counseling 33 students graduated in 2009; 29 went to college, including Clark University; Drexel University; Ithaca College; Sarah Lawrence College; Skidmore College; Syracuse University. Other: 3 entered a postgraduate year, 1 had other specific plans.

Student Life Upper grades have specified standards of dress, student council, honor system. Discipline rests primarily with faculty.

Tuition and Aid 7-day tuition and room/board: $78,720. Tuition installment plan (monthly payment plans, individually arranged payment plans, prepaid tuition discount). Middle-income loans, Lake Mills Loans, Clark Custom Behavioral Loans available. In 2009–10, 10% of upper-school students received aid.

Admissions Traditional secondary-level entrance grade is 1. Battery of testing done through outside agency, Rorschach or Thematic Apperception Test, Wechsler Intelligence Scale for Children or WISC/Woodcock-Johnson required. Deadline for receipt of application materials: none. No application fee required.

Athletics Interscholastic: basketball (boys), lacrosse (g); coed interscholastic: soccer; coed intramural: aerobics, aerobics/dance, alpine skiing, backpacking, baseball, basketball, bicycling, bowling, canoeing/kayaking, climbing, combined training, cooperative games, cross-country running, dance, field hockey, fishing, fitness, fitness walking, flag football, fly fishing, Frisbee, hiking/backpacking, horseback riding, in-line skating, independent competitive sports, indoor soccer, jogging, kayaking, kickball, lacrosse, martial arts, mountain biking, outdoor activities, outdoor recreation, paddle tennis, physical fitness, physical training, project adventure, rafting, rock climbing, ropes courses, running, skateboarding, skiing (cross-country), skiing (downhill), snowboarding, snowshoeing, soccer, softball, strength & conditioning, table tennis, tennis, ultimate Frisbee, volleyball, walking, wall climbing, weight lifting, weight training, whiffle ball, yoga. 1 PE instructor, 1 coach.

Computers Computers are regularly used in English, foreign language, history, science classes. Computer network features include on-campus library services, Internet access, Internet filtering or blocking technology. Students grades are available online.

Contact Rhonda J. Papallo, Director of Admissions. 800-258-1770 Ext. 102. Fax: 413-634-5300. E-mail: rpapallo@swiftriver.com. Web site: www.swiftriver.com.

AMERICAN ACADEMY

12200 West Broward Boulevard
Plantation, Florida 33325
Head of School: William R. Laurie

General Information Coeducational day college-preparatory and arts school; primarily serves underachievers, students with learning disabilities, individuals with Attention Deficit Disorder, dyslexic students, and slow learners, and those with lowered self-esteem and confidence. Grades 1–12. Founded: 1965. Setting: suburban. Nearest major city is Fort Lauderdale. 40-acre campus. 9 buildings on campus. Approved or accredited by Association of Independent Schools of Florida, Southern Association of Colleges and Schools, and Florida Department of Education. Total enrollment: 319. Upper school average class size: 14. Upper school faculty-student ratio: 1:12. There are 175 required school days per year for Upper School students. Upper School students typically attend 5 days per week. The average school day consists of 7 hours and 15 minutes.

Upper School Student Profile Grade 7: 27 students (17 boys, 10 girls); Grade 8: 31 students (23 boys, 8 girls); Grade 9: 51 students (37 boys, 14 girls); Grade 10: 31 students (22 boys, 9 girls); Grade 11: 34 students (25 boys, 9 girls); Grade 12: 43 students (29 boys, 14 girls).

Faculty School total: 32. In upper school: 3 men, 18 women; 13 have advanced degrees.

Subjects Offered Algebra, American history, American literature, anatomy, art, band, biology, business mathematics, ceramics, chemistry, chorus, community service, computer graphics, computer science, creative writing, drafting, drama, drawing, earth science, English, English literature, environmental science, fine arts, French, geometry, health, jazz, mathematics, music appreciation, oceanography, orchestra, photography, physical education, physical science, science, sculpture, Spanish, theater, vocal music, weight training, word processing, world geography, world history, world literature, writing, yearbook.

Graduation Requirements 20th century history, arts and fine arts (art, music, dance, drama), computer science, English, mathematics, physical education (includes health), science, social studies (includes history), must be accepted to a college, 120 community service hours over 4 years of high school. Community service is required.

Special Academic Programs Honors section; independent study; academic accommodation for the gifted, the musically talented, and the artistically talented; remedial reading and/or remedial writing; remedial math; programs in English, mathematics, general development for dyslexic students; ESL (2 students enrolled).

College Admission Counseling 44 students graduated in 2010; all went to college, including Broward College; Florida Atlantic University; Lynn University; Nova Southeastern University; Palm Beach State College.

Student Life Upper grades have uniform requirement, student council. Discipline rests primarily with faculty.

Summer Programs Remediation, enrichment, advancement, ESL, art/fine arts, computer instruction programs offered; session focuses on remediation and make-up courses; held on campus; accepts boys and girls; open to students from other schools. 400 students usually enrolled. 2011 schedule: June 13 to August 12. Application deadline: none.

Tuition and Aid Day student tuition: $23,628–$27,303. Tuition installment plan (monthly payment plans, semester payment plan, annual payment plan). Tuition reduction for siblings, need-based scholarship grants available.

Admissions Traditional secondary-level entrance grade is 9. Psychoeducational evaluation, SAT and Slosson Intelligence required. Deadline for receipt of application materials: none. Application fee required: $100. On-campus interview required.

Athletics Interscholastic: baseball (boys), basketball (b,g), cheering (g), cross-country running (b,g), dance (g), dance squad (g), diving (b,g), football (b), golf (b,g), lacrosse (b,g), roller hockey (b), soccer (b,g), softball (g), swimming and diving (b,g), tennis (b,g), track and field (b,g), volleyball (b,g), weight lifting (b), weight training (b,g), winter soccer (b,g), wrestling (b). 7 PE instructors, 4 coaches.

Computers Computers are regularly used in graphic arts, literary magazine, newspaper, Web site design, word processing, writing, yearbook classes. Computer network features include on-campus library services, online commercial services, Internet access, Internet filtering or blocking technology, Questia. Student e-mail accounts and computer access in designated common areas are available to students. Students grades are available online. The school has a published electronic and media policy.

Contact William R. Laurie, President. 954-472-0022. Fax: 954-472-3088. Web site: www.ahschool.com.

ARROWSMITH SCHOOL

245 St. Clair Avenue West
Toronto, Ontario M4V 1R3, Canada
Head of School: Ms. Barbara Arrowsmith Young

General Information Coeducational day school; primarily serves underachievers, students with learning disabilities, and dyslexic students. Ungraded, ages 6–20. Founded: 1980. Setting: urban. 1 building on campus. Approved or accredited by Ontario Ministry of Education and Ontario Department of Education. Language of instruction: English. Total enrollment: 75. Upper school average class size: 20. Upper school faculty-student ratio: 1:10. The average school day consists of 7 hours and 30 minutes.

Faculty School total: 9. In upper school: 2 men, 2 women.

Special Academic Programs Remedial reading and/or remedial writing; remedial math; programs in English, mathematics for dyslexic students.

College Admission Counseling 10 students graduated in 2010; 8 went to college, including University of Toronto; York University. Other: 2 went to work.

Student Life Upper grades have specified standards of dress. Discipline rests equally with students and faculty.

Tuition and Aid Day student tuition: CAN$22,000. Tuition installment plan (monthly payment plans).

Admissions Traditional secondary-level entrance age is 14. For fall 2010, 20 students applied for upper-level admission, 20 were accepted, 20 enrolled. Achievement tests, Cognitive Abilities Test, Differential Aptitude Test, Oral and Written Language Scales, Otis-Lennon Mental Ability Test, Raven (Aptitude Test); school's own exam, Reading for Understanding, school's own test, Wide Range Achievement Test, WISC/Woodcock-Johnson or writing sample required. Deadline for receipt of application materials: none. No application fee required. Interview required.

Computers Computer resources include Internet access.

Contact Ms. Annette Goodman, Director of Admissions. 800-963-4904. Fax: 416-963-5017. E-mail: agoodman@arrowsmithprogram.ca. Web site: www.arrowsmithschool.org.

ASPEN RANCH

1090 North Aspen Road

PO Box 369

Loa, Utah 84747

Head of School: Dr. Thomas Vitale

General Information Coeducational boarding college-preparatory, general academic, arts, and bilingual studies school; primarily serves underachievers, students with learning disabilities, individuals with Attention Deficit Disorder, individuals with emotional and behavioral problems, and dyslexic students. Grades 8–12. Founded: 1995. Setting: rural. Nearest major city is Salt Lake City. Students are housed in single-sex dormitories and family-style, single-sex dormitories. 80-acre campus. 9 buildings on campus. Approved or accredited by California Association of Independent Schools, Northwest Association of Schools and Colleges, and Utah Department of Education. Total enrollment: 72. Upper school average class size: 8. Upper school faculty-student ratio: 1:8. There are 280 required school days per year for Upper School students. Upper School students typically attend 5 days per week. The average school day consists of 7 hours and 45 minutes.

Upper School Student Profile Grade 9: 11 students (7 boys, 4 girls); Grade 10: 23 students (14 boys, 9 girls); Grade 11: 18 students (11 boys, 7 girls); Grade 12: 14 students (8 boys, 6 girls). 100% of students are boarding students. 3% are state residents. 48 states are represented in upper school student body.

Faculty School total: 11. In upper school: 4 men, 4 women; 4 have advanced degrees.

Subjects Offered Algebra, American literature, art, athletics, biology, business mathematics, calculus, career education, chemistry, creative writing, criminal justice, earth science, economics, English, English literature, environmental science, equestrian sports, equine science, fine arts, French, geometry, guitar, health, history, information technology, life saving, mathematics, physical education, physical science, poetry, pre-algebra, pre-calculus, psychology, reading, science, social skills, social studies, Spanish, study skills, trigonometry, U.S. government, U.S. history, weight training, world civilizations.

Graduation Requirements Art, career education, English, information technology, mathematics, physical education (includes health), science, social studies (includes history), teen living.

Special Academic Programs Honors section; accelerated programs; independent study; study at local college for college credit; academic accommodation for the gifted; remedial reading and/or remedial writing; remedial math.

College Admission Counseling 17 students graduated in 2010; 10 went to college.

Student Life Upper grades have uniform requirement, student council, honor system. Discipline rests equally with students and faculty.

Tuition and Aid Tuition installment plan (monthly payment plans, individually arranged payment plans). Middle-income loans available.

Admissions Traditional secondary-level entrance grade is 10. For fall 2010, 95 students applied for upper-level admission, 71 were accepted, 57 enrolled. Kaufman Test of Educational Achievement required. Deadline for receipt of application materials: none. No application fee required.

Athletics Intramural: backpacking (boys, girls), basketball (b,g), bicycling (b,g), equestrian sports (b,g), fishing (b,g), fitness (b,g), flag football (b,g), horseback riding (b,g), mountain biking (b,g), mountaineering (b,g), outdoor activities (b,g), outdoor adventure (b,g), outdoor education (b,g), outdoor recreation (b,g), outdoor skills (b,g), physical fitness (b,g), physical training (b,g), rappelling (b,g), ropes courses (b,g); coed intramural: basketball, bicycling, canoeing/kayaking, equestrian sports, fishing, fitness, flag football, hiking/backpacking, horseback riding, life saving, mountain biking, mountaineering, outdoor activities, outdoor adventure, outdoor education, outdoor recreation, outdoor skills, physical fitness, physical training, rappelling, ropes courses, skiing (downhill), softball, ultimate Frisbee, volleyball, water skiing, weight training, wilderness. 2 PE instructors.

Computers Computers are regularly used in creative writing, English, history, psychology, science classes. Computer resources include online commercial services, Internet access, desktop publishing. Students grades are available online.

Contact Aspen Ranch Admissions. 877-231-0734. Fax: 435-836-2277. Web site: www.aspenranch.com.

ASSETS SCHOOL

One Ohana Nui Way

Honolulu, Hawaii 96818

Head of School: Mr. Paul Singer

General Information Coeducational day college-preparatory school; primarily serves students with learning disabilities, individuals with Attention Deficit Disorder, dyslexic students, and gifted/talented students. Grades K–12. Founded: 1955. Setting: urban. 3-acre campus. 5 buildings on campus. Approved or accredited by The Hawaii Council of Private Schools, Western Association of Schools and Colleges, and Hawaii Department of Education. Member of National Association of Independent Schools. Endowment: $607,632. Total enrollment: 359. Upper school average class size: 7. Upper school faculty-student ratio: 1:8. There are 169 required school days per year for Upper School students. Upper School students typically attend 5 days per week. The average school day consists of 5 hours and 58 minutes.

Upper School Student Profile Grade 9: 39 students (25 boys, 14 girls); Grade 10: 27 students (19 boys, 8 girls); Grade 11: 24 students (20 boys, 4 girls); Grade 12: 26 students (18 boys, 8 girls).

Faculty School total: 68. In upper school: 9 men, 17 women; 18 have advanced degrees.

Subjects Offered 1½ elective credits, algebra, American history, art, biology, business skills, calculus, chemistry, computer science, consumer education, creative writing, current events, earth science, economics, English, fine arts, fitness, general science, geometry, government/civics, health, humanities, independent study, integrated science, Japanese, keyboarding, literature, marine biology, marine science, mathematics, music, music appreciation, philosophy, physical education, physics, pre-calculus, psychology, sign language, social studies, Spanish, statistics, theater, trigonometry, women's health, woodworking, word processing, world history, world literature.

Graduation Requirements Arts and fine arts (art, music, dance, drama), biology, business skills (includes word processing), computer science, English, foreign language, mathematics, physical education (includes health), science, social studies (includes history), study skills, participation in mentorship program in 10th-12th grades.

Special Academic Programs Academic accommodation for the gifted; remedial reading and/or remedial writing; remedial math; programs in English, mathematics, general development for dyslexic students.

College Admission Counseling 22 students graduated in 2010; 20 went to college, including Chaminade University of Honolulu; Hawai'i Pacific University; Oregon State University; University of Hawaii at Manoa. Other: 1 went to work, 1 had other specific plans.

Student Life Upper grades have specified standards of dress, student council, honor system. Discipline rests primarily with faculty.

Summer Programs Advancement programs offered; session focuses on learning strategies for students in the 9th and 10th grades; held on campus; accepts boys and girls; open to students from other schools. 20 students usually enrolled. 2011 schedule: June 14 to July 15. Application deadline: none.

Tuition and Aid Day student tuition: $21,500. Tuition installment plan (monthly payment plans, semester payment plan). Need-based scholarship grants, partial tuition remission for children of staff available. In 2010–11, 33% of upper-school students received aid. Total amount of financial aid awarded in 2010–11: $170,000.

Admissions Traditional secondary-level entrance grade is 9. For fall 2010, 23 students applied for upper-level admission, 11 were accepted, 8 enrolled. WISC III or other aptitude measures; standardized achievement test required. Deadline for receipt of application materials: none. Application fee required: $75. Interview required.

Athletics Interscholastic: baseball (boys), basketball (b,g), bowling (b,g), canoeing/kayaking (b,g), cheering (g), cross-country running (b,g), diving (b,g), football (b), golf (b,g), gymnastics (g), judo (b,g), kayaking (b,g), sailing (b,g), soccer (b,g), softball (g), swimming and diving (b,g), tennis (b,g), track and field (b,g), volleyball (b,g), water polo (b,g), wrestling (b,g); intramural: basketball (b,g), volleyball (b,g); coed intramural: basketball, dance, flag football, kickball, Newcombe ball, soccer, softball, tai chi, touch football, ultimate Frisbee, volleyball, whiffle ball, yoga. 2 PE instructors.

Computers Computers are regularly used in English, mathematics, photography, science classes. Computer network features include on-campus library services, Internet access, assistive technology for learning differences. The school has a published electronic and media policy.

Contact Ms. Sandi Tadaki, Director of Admissions. 808-423-1356. Fax: 808-422-1920. E-mail: stadaki@assets-school.net. Web site: www.assets-school.net.

BEACON HIGH SCHOOL

74 Green Street
Brookline, Massachusetts 02446
Head of School: Nancy Lincoln
General Information Coeducational day college-preparatory, general academic, and arts school; primarily serves students with learning disabilities, individuals with Attention Deficit Disorder, and individuals with emotional and behavioral problems. Ungraded, ages 15–22. Founded: 1971. Setting: urban. Nearest major city is Boston. 1-acre campus. 2 buildings on campus. Approved or accredited by Lutheran School Accreditation Commission and Massachusetts Department of Education. Total enrollment: 53. Upper school average class size: 8. Upper school faculty-student ratio: 1:2.
Faculty School total: 18. In upper school: 6 men, 9 women; 14 have advanced degrees.
Subjects Offered Algebra, American history, American literature, anatomy, art, art history, biology, ceramics, chemistry, computer math, computer programming, computer science, creative writing, earth science, economics, English, English literature, European history, geography, geometry, grammar, historical research, mathematics, music, philosophy, photography, physical education, physics, psychology, research, science, social studies, theater, trigonometry, world literature, world religions, World War II, writing.
Graduation Requirements English, historical research, mathematics, physical education (includes health), science, social studies (includes history).
Special Academic Programs Accelerated programs; independent study; programs in English, mathematics, general development for dyslexic students.
College Admission Counseling 14 students graduated in 2009; 12 went to college, including Clark University; Curry College; Franklin Pierce University; Marlboro College; Montserrat College of Art; Simmons College. Other: 2 went to work.
Student Life Upper grades have student council, honor system. Discipline rests primarily with faculty.
Tuition and Aid Day student tuition: $39,000. Municipal funding to special needs education (tuition paid by student's hometown) available.
Admissions Traditional secondary-level entrance age is 16. Deadline for receipt of application materials: none. No application fee required. On-campus interview required.
Athletics Coed Intramural: baseball, basketball, soccer, softball, tennis, volleyball. 2 PE instructors.
Computers Computers are regularly used in English, mathematics, music, science, Web site design classes. Computer network features include online commercial services, Internet access, Internet filtering or blocking technology.
Contact Nancy Lincoln, Director. 617-232-1958.

BRANDON HALL SCHOOL

1701 Brandon Hall Drive
Atlanta, Georgia 30350-3706
Head of School: Mr. Paul R. Stockhammer
General Information Boys' boarding and coeducational day college-preparatory and ESL school; primarily serves underachievers, students with learning disabilities, individuals with Attention Deficit Disorder, dyslexic students, dysgraphia, dyscalculia, Asperger's Syndrome, Processing Disorders, and visual Impairments. Boarding boys grades 4–PG, day boys grades 4–PG, day girls grades 4–PG. Founded: 1959. Setting: suburban. Students are housed in single-sex dormitories. 27-acre campus. 7 buildings on campus. Approved or accredited by Georgia Accrediting Commission, Southern Association of Colleges and Schools, and Georgia Department of Education. Member of National Association of Independent Schools. Endowment: $250,000. Total enrollment: 101. Upper school average class size: 4. Upper school faculty-student ratio: 1:3.
Upper School Student Profile Grade 9: 10 students (9 boys, 1 girl); Grade 10: 17 students (15 boys, 2 girls); Grade 11: 24 students (21 boys, 3 girls); Grade 12: 24 students (18 boys, 6 girls). 50% of students are boarding students. 64% are state residents. 12 states are represented in upper school student body. 24% are international students. International students from Belgium, Burkina Faso, Nigeria, Republic of Korea, Switzerland, and Viet Nam; 9 other countries represented in student body.
Faculty School total: 31. In upper school: 20 men, 11 women; 11 have advanced degrees; 17 reside on campus.
Subjects Offered Algebra, American literature, art, astronomy, biology, British literature, calculus, chemistry, chorus, computer science, contemporary issues, developmental math, drama, earth science, economics, English, English composition, environmental science, ESL, French, geography, geometry, government/civics, grammar, health education, history, honors English, honors geometry, honors U.S. history, honors world history, human anatomy, keyboarding, mathematics, music, music history, music performance, physical education, physical science, physics, reading/study skills, research skills, SAT/ACT preparation, science, social studies, Spanish, trigonometry, U.S. history, U.S. literature, word processing, world history, world literature, writing.
Graduation Requirements American government, arts and fine arts (art, music, dance, drama), computer applications, economics, English, foreign language, mathematics, physical education (includes health), SAT preparation, science, social studies (includes history), requirements vary depending on specific disability.

Special Academic Programs Advanced Placement exam preparation; honors section; academic accommodation for the gifted; remedial reading and/or remedial writing; remedial math; programs in English, mathematics for dyslexic students; special instructional classes for blind students; ESL (10 students enrolled).
College Admission Counseling 28 students graduated in 2009; all went to college, including Agnes Scott College; Georgia College & State University; Georgia Institute of Technology; Indiana University Bloomington; Reinhardt University; Southern Methodist University.
Student Life Upper grades have uniform requirement, student council, honor system. Discipline rests primarily with faculty.
Tuition and Aid Day student tuition: $26,800–$29,600; 5-day tuition and room/board: $42,000–$44,800; 7-day tuition and room/board: $44,300–$47,100. Tuition installment plan (individually arranged payment plans, 4-payment plan). Need-based financial aid available. In 2009–10, 10% of upper-school students received aid. Total amount of financial aid awarded in 2009–10: $85,000.
Admissions Traditional secondary-level entrance grade is 10. For fall 2009, 40 students applied for upper-level admission, 36 were accepted, 34 enrolled. Deadline for receipt of application materials: none. Application fee required: $75. Interview required.
Athletics Interscholastic: baseball (boys), basketball (b,g); coed interscholastic: cross-country running, golf; coed intramural: badminton. 1 PE instructor.
Computers Computers are regularly used in English, foreign language, history, mathematics, science classes. Computer network features include on-campus library services, Internet access, Internet filtering or blocking technology. The school has a published electronic and media policy.
Contact Mr. Abram Smith, Admissions. 770-394-8177 Ext. 215. Fax: 770-804-8821. E-mail: asmith@brandonhall.org. Web site: www.brandonhall.org.

BREHM PREPARATORY SCHOOL

1245 East Grand Avenue
Carbondale, Illinois 62901
Head of School: Mr. Richard G. Collins, PhD
General Information Coeducational boarding and day college-preparatory and general academic school; primarily serves students with learning disabilities, individuals with Attention Deficit Disorder, dyslexic students, and language-based learning differences. Grades 6–PG. Founded: 1982. Setting: small town. Nearest major city is St. Louis, MO. Students are housed in single-sex dormitories. 80-acre campus. 13 buildings on campus. Approved or accredited by Independent Schools Association of the Central States, North Central Association of Colleges and Schools, and Illinois Department of Education. Member of National Association of Independent Schools. Total enrollment: 85. Upper school average class size: 8. Upper school faculty-student ratio: 1:4. There are 185 required school days per year for Upper School students. Upper School students typically attend 5 days per week. The average school day consists of 7 hours and 30 minutes.
Upper School Student Profile Grade 9: 13 students (12 boys, 1 girl); Grade 10: 15 students (12 boys, 3 girls); Grade 11: 19 students (14 boys, 5 girls); Grade 12: 20 students (15 boys, 5 girls); Postgraduate: 8 students (8 boys). 86% of students are boarding students. 23% are state residents. 24 states are represented in upper school student body. 8% are international students. International students from Cameroon, Canada, India, Latvia, and Nigeria.
Faculty School total: 26. In upper school: 9 men, 17 women; 15 have advanced degrees.
Subjects Offered 20th century American writers, 20th century history, ACT preparation, algebra, American history, American literature, anatomy and physiology, art, biology, British literature, calculus, career exploration, chemistry, communication skills, composition, computer graphics, computer programming, computer science, computer skills, consumer education, creative writing, current events, current history, desktop publishing, digital imaging, digital photography, earth science, economics, English, English literature, environmental science, geometry, government/civics, health, keyboarding, language, learning cognition, mathematics, photography, physical education, pragmatics, pre-algebra, pre-calculus, psychology, reading/study skills, science, Shakespeare, social studies, sociology, Spanish, speech, trigonometry, video and animation, weight training, world history, writing.
Graduation Requirements Computer science, consumer education, English, government, learning cognition, mathematics, physical education (includes health), science, social studies (includes history).
Special Academic Programs Study at local college for college credit; academic accommodation for the gifted; remedial reading and/or remedial writing; remedial math; programs in English, mathematics, general development for dyslexic students.
College Admission Counseling 24 students graduated in 2009; they went to California State Polytechnic University, Pomona; John A. Logan College; Southern Illinois University Edwardsville; The Ohio State University. Other: 8 entered a postgraduate year. Median composite ACT: 17. 7% scored over 26 on composite ACT.
Student Life Upper grades have specified standards of dress, student council, honor system. Discipline rests equally with students and faculty.
Tuition and Aid Day student tuition: $36,000; 7-day tuition and room/board: $59,000.
Admissions Traditional secondary-level entrance grade is 9. For fall 2009, 33 students applied for upper-level admission, 30 were accepted, 24 enrolled. Wechsler

Individual Achievement Test, WISC or WAIS and Woodcock-Johnson required. Deadline for receipt of application materials: none. Application fee required: $75. On-campus interview required.

Athletics Interscholastic: basketball (boys, girls); coed interscholastic: soccer; coed intramural: aerobics, basketball, billiards, bowling, dance, fishing, flag football, hiking/backpacking, horseback riding, outdoor skills, paint ball, physical fitness, soccer, softball, strength & conditioning. 1 PE instructor, 1 coach.

Computers Computers are regularly used in all academic, career exploration, college planning, creative writing, design, desktop publishing, graphic arts, graphic design, keyboarding, learning cognition, photography, reading, remedial study skills, research skills, study skills, typing, word processing, writing, writing, yearbook classes. Computer network features include Internet access, wireless campus network, Internet filtering or blocking technology. Student e-mail accounts are available to students. Students grades are available online. The school has a published electronic and media policy.

Contact Mrs. Heather Brady, Administrative Assistant of Admissions. 618-457-0371 Ext. 1304. Fax: 618-549-2329. E-mail: hbrady@brehm.org. Web site: www. brehm.org.

THE BRIARWOOD SCHOOL
12207 Whittington Drive
Houston, Texas 77077
Head of School: Mrs. Carole C. Wills

General Information Coeducational day college-preparatory, general academic, arts, business, and technology school; primarily serves students with learning disabilities, individuals with Attention Deficit Disorder, and dyslexic students. Grades K–12. Founded: 1967. Setting: suburban. 9-acre campus. 1 building on campus. Approved or accredited by National Association of Private Schools for Exceptional Children, Southern Association of Colleges and Schools, and Texas Department of Education. Total enrollment: 259. Upper school average class size: 8. Upper school faculty-student ratio: 1:8. The average school day consists of 7 hours.

Upper School Student Profile Grade 7: 30 students (16 boys, 14 girls); Grade 8: 22 students (17 boys, 5 girls); Grade 9: 20 students (13 boys, 7 girls); Grade 10: 26 students (16 boys, 10 girls); Grade 11: 25 students (18 boys, 7 girls); Grade 12: 26 students (20 boys, 6 girls).

Faculty School total: 74. In upper school: 8 men, 20 women.

Subjects Offered 3-dimensional design, acting, algebra, American history, American literature, applied arts, art, basic language skills, biology, business applications, career and personal planning, career/college preparation, ceramics, chemistry, choir, Civil War, clayworking, computer studies, computers, desktop publishing, drama, drawing, drawing and design, English, general science, geometry, government, health, math applications, oral communications, photography, reading, SAT/ACT preparation, sports, technology, theater, theater arts, theater design and production, U.S. history, word processing, world cultures, world history, writing.

Special Academic Programs Programs in English, mathematics, general development for dyslexic students.

College Admission Counseling 24 students graduated in 2009; all went to college, including Houston Community College System; Schreiner University; The University of Texas at San Antonio; University of Houston.

Student Life Upper grades have uniform requirement, student council, honor system. Discipline rests primarily with faculty.

Tuition and Aid Day student tuition: $12,995. Tuition installment plan (monthly payment plans, annual payment plan, 2-payment plan, 3-payment plan, 10-monthly payments). Need-based scholarship grants available.

Admissions Traditional secondary-level entrance grade is 9. WISC/Woodcock-Johnson or Woodcock-Johnson Educational Evaluation, WISC III required. Deadline for receipt of application materials: none. Application fee required: $50. On-campus interview required.

Athletics Interscholastic: basketball (boys, girls), cross-country running (b,g), flag football (b), golf (b,g), tennis (b,g), track and field (b,g), volleyball (g); coed interscholastic: soccer, Special Olympics.

Computers Computers are regularly used in desktop publishing, history, library, mathematics, reading, writing, yearbook classes. Computer network features include on-campus library services, Internet access.

Contact Mrs. Priscilla Mitchell, Director of Admissions. 281-493-1070. Fax: 281-493-1343. E-mail: info@briarwoodschool.org. Web site: www. briarwoodschool.org.

BRIDGES ACADEMY
3921 Laurel Canyon Boulevard
Studio City, California 91604
Head of School: Carl Sabatino

General Information Coeducational day college-preparatory, arts, technology, and music, drama, talent development school; primarily serves gifted students with non-verbal learning differences. Grades 5–12. Founded: 1994. Setting: suburban. Nearest major city is Los Angeles. 4-acre campus. 3 buildings on campus. Approved or accredited by California Association of Independent Schools, Western Association of Schools and Colleges, and California Department of Education. Total enrollment:

130. Upper school average class size: 9. Upper school faculty-student ratio: 1:8. There are 174 required school days per year for Upper School students. Upper School students typically attend 5 days per week. The average school day consists of 5 hours and 15 minutes.

Upper School Student Profile Grade 9: 26 students (22 boys, 4 girls); Grade 10: 17 students (13 boys, 4 girls); Grade 11: 18 students (16 boys, 2 girls); Grade 12: 15 students (13 boys, 2 girls).

Faculty School total: 21. In upper school: 13 men, 8 women; 4 have advanced degrees.

Subjects Offered 20th century history, algebra, American government, American literature, anatomy and physiology, art, biology, calculus, chemistry, drama, economics, European history, European literature, film, genetics, geometry, Japanese, modern European history, music, non-Western literature, physics, pre-calculus, senior project, Spanish, statistics, study skills, technology, U.S. history, world history.

Graduation Requirements Economics, English, foreign language, government, history, mathematics, performing arts, science, senior seminar, visual arts.

Special Academic Programs Honors section; academic accommodation for the gifted.

College Admission Counseling 17 students graduated in 2010; 13 went to college, including University of California, Santa Cruz. Other: 4 had other specific plans. 58% scored over 600 on SAT critical reading, 24% scored over 600 on SAT math.

Student Life Discipline rests primarily with faculty.

Summer Programs Enrichment, sports, art/fine arts, computer instruction programs offered; session focuses on enrichment; held on campus; accepts boys and girls; open to students from other schools. 2011 schedule: June 1 to July 31. Application deadline: none.

Tuition and Aid Day student tuition: $30,496. Tuition installment plan (Insured Tuition Payment Plan, monthly payment plans). Need-based scholarship grants available. In 2010–11, 10% of upper-school students received aid.

Admissions Traditional secondary-level entrance grade is 9. For fall 2010, 16 students applied for upper-level admission, 12 were accepted, 11 enrolled. Deadline for receipt of application materials: March 1. Application fee required: $150. On-campus interview required.

Athletics Coed Interscholastic: basketball, cross-country running, track and field. 2 PE instructors, 1 coach.

Computers Computers are regularly used in all classes. Computer network features include Internet access, wireless campus network, Internet filtering or blocking technology. Campus intranet and student e-mail accounts are available to students. Students grades are available online.

Contact Doug Lenzini, Director of Admissions. 818-506-1091. Fax: 818-506-8094. E-mail: doug@bridges.edu. Web site: www.bridges.edu.

BROMLEY BROOK SCHOOL
2595 Depot Street
PO Box 2328
Manchester Center, Vermont 05255
Head of School: Dr. David Hans

General Information Girls' boarding college-preparatory and arts school; primarily serves students with learning disabilities, individuals with Attention Deficit Disorder, individuals with emotional and behavioral problems, and dyslexic students. Grades 9–12. Founded: 2004. Setting: small town. Nearest major city is Albany, NY. Students are housed in single-sex dormitories. 6-acre campus. 1 building on campus. Approved or accredited by European Council of International Schools and Vermont Department of Education. Candidate for accreditation by New England Association of Schools and Colleges. Total enrollment: 80. Upper school average class size: 8. Upper school faculty-student ratio: 1:7.

Upper School Student Profile Grade 9: 16 students (16 girls); Grade 10: 20 students (20 girls); Grade 11: 24 students (24 girls); Grade 12: 20 students (20 girls). 100% of students are boarding students. 1% are state residents. 25 states are represented in upper school student body. 2% are international students. International students from Bermuda and Canada.

Faculty School total: 11. In upper school: 4 men, 7 women; 6 have advanced degrees.

Subjects Offered 1½ elective credits, acting, advanced studio art-AP, algebra, alternative physical education, American history, American literature, ancient world history, art, arts and crafts, audio visual/media, biology, business mathematics, calculus, calligraphy, career/college preparation, ceramics, character education, chemistry, chorus, college counseling, community service, composition, computer graphics, conflict resolution, consumer mathematics, cultural geography, dance, digital photography, drama, drawing, earth science, English, English composition, English literature, environmental science, European history, fashion, French, geography, geometry, government, health, internship, lab science, mythology, painting, photography, physical fitness, physics, piano, portfolio art, pottery, pre-algebra, pre-calculus, psychology, SAT preparation, Spanish, sports, studio art, U.S. history, video, voice, world history, yoga.

Graduation Requirements Algebra, American history, American literature, chemistry, composition, English, English literature, environmental science, geometry, history, pre-algebra, pre-calculus, science, social sciences, trigonometry, U.S. history, U.S. literature.

Special Academic Programs Programs in English, mathematics for dyslexic students.

College Admission Counseling 18 students graduated in 2009; 15 went to college. Other: 2 went to work, 1 entered a postgraduate year.

Student Life Upper grades have uniform requirement, student council, honor system. Discipline rests equally with students and faculty.

Tuition and Aid 7-day tuition and room/board: $71,900. Tuition installment plan (Clark Custom Education Loans, PrepGate loans, Key Bank Loans).

Admissions Traditional secondary-level entrance grade is 11. Individual IQ, MAT WISC III, psychoeducational evaluation, SSAT or WISC III, Wechsler Individual Achievement Test, Wechsler Intelligence Scale for Children, WISC-III and Woodcock-Johnson or WISC/Woodcock-Johnson required. Deadline for receipt of application materials: none. Application fee required: $2500. Interview recommended.

Athletics Interscholastic: basketball, lacrosse, soccer, softball; intramural: alpine skiing, bowling, cross-country running, dance, equestrian sports, fitness, fitness walking, flag football, Frisbee, hiking/backpacking, horseback riding, ice skating, jogging, skiing (downhill), snowboarding, tennis, volleyball. 1 coach.

Computers Computers are regularly used in college planning, English, French, geography, graphic design, history, psychology, science, Spanish, video film production classes. Computer resources include Internet access, Internet filtering or blocking technology. Computer access in designated common areas is available to students. The school has a published electronic and media policy.

Contact Beth Bove, Admissions Director. 802-362-9966 Ext. 107. Fax: 802-362-5539. E-mail: bbove@bromleybrook.com. Web site: www.bromleybrook.com/.

CAMPHILL SPECIAL SCHOOL
1784 Fairview Road
Glenmoore, Pennsylvania 19343
Head of School: Mr. Bernard Wolf

General Information Coeducational boarding and day general academic, arts, and vocational school; primarily serves underachievers, intellectual and developmental delays, and mental retardation. Grades K–13. Founded: 1963. Setting: rural. Nearest major city is Philadelphia. Students are housed in on-campus single family homes. 82-acre campus. 1 building on campus. Approved or accredited by Association of Waldorf Schools of North America, Middle States Association of Colleges and Schools, National Council for Private School Accreditation, and Pennsylvania Department of Education. Total enrollment: 105. Upper school average class size: 9. Upper school faculty-student ratio: 1:5. There are 180 required school days per year for Upper School students. Upper School students typically attend 5 days per week.

Upper School Student Profile Grade 6: 11 students (6 boys, 5 girls); Grade 8: 8 students (3 boys, 5 girls); Grade 9: 11 students (7 boys, 4 girls); Grade 10: 11 students (8 boys, 3 girls); Grade 11: 14 students (11 boys, 3 girls); Grade 12: 11 students (9 boys, 2 girls); Grade 13: 16 students (13 boys, 3 girls). 94% of students are boarding students. 70% are state residents. 14 states are represented in upper school student body.

Faculty In upper school: 2 men, 2 women; 70 reside on campus.

Subjects Offered 20th century American writers, 20th century history, 20th century physics, 20th century world history, acting, agriculture, American Civil War, American culture, American democracy, American history, Ancient Greek, ancient history, ancient world history, animal husbandry, art, art and culture, art appreciation, astronomy, bell choir, biology, body human, botany, chemistry, choir, drama, drama performance, ecology, environmental education, eurythmy, gardening, geography, geometry, government, handbells, health and wellness, history, instruments, life skills, mathematics, medieval history, medieval literature, medieval/Renaissance history, meteorology, music, mythology, natural history, painting, physics, poetry, pottery, reading, science, Shakespeare, woodworking, zoology.

Special Academic Programs Remedial reading and/or remedial writing; remedial math.

College Admission Counseling 8 students graduated in 2010. Other: 8 had other specific plans.

Student Life Upper grades have student council. Discipline rests primarily with faculty.

Summer Programs Enrichment programs offered; session focuses on Extended School Year (ESY); held on campus; accepts boys and girls; not open to students from other schools. 45 students usually enrolled. 2011 schedule: June 27 to July 25.

Tuition and Aid Need-based scholarship grants available.

Admissions Deadline for receipt of application materials: none. No application fee required. On-campus interview required.

Contact Web site: www.camphillspecialschool.org.

CEDAR RIDGE ACADEMY
4270 West 5625 N.
Roosevelt, Utah 84066
Head of School: Christine Haggerty

General Information Coeducational boarding and day college-preparatory, general academic, and arts school; primarily serves underachievers, students with learning disabilities, individuals with Attention Deficit Disorder, individuals with emotional and behavioral problems, dyslexic students, and Credit Deficient. Grades 9–12.

Founded: 1996. Setting: rural. Nearest major city is Salt Lake City. Students are housed in single-sex dormitories. 100-acre campus. 8 buildings on campus. Approved or accredited by National Council for Private School Accreditation, Northwest Accreditation Commission, Northwest Association of Schools and Colleges, and Utah Department of Education. Upper school average class size: 10. Upper school faculty-student ratio: 1:15. There are 250 required school days per year for Upper School students. Upper School students typically attend 5 days per week. The average school day consists of 6 hours and 30 minutes.

Upper School Student Profile Grade 9: 4 students (2 boys, 2 girls); Grade 10: 10 students (10 boys); Grade 11: 18 students (9 boys, 9 girls); Grade 12: 9 students (5 boys, 4 girls). 100% of students are boarding students. 1% are state residents. 16 states are represented in upper school student body. 1% are international students.

Faculty School total: 7. In upper school: 5 men, 2 women; 3 have advanced degrees; 2 reside on campus.

Subjects Offered 1½ elective credits, 20th century American writers, 20th century history, 20th century world history, ACT preparation, algebra, American government, American history, American literature, anatomy, ancient world history, art, art appreciation, biology, British literature, business mathematics, career and personal planning, career/college preparation, ceramics, character education, computer literacy, consumer mathematics, drawing, electives, English, geometry, government/civics, health education, independent living, keyboarding, language arts, life management skills, martial arts, peer counseling, personal fitness, physics, pre-algebra, precalculus, psychology, reading, SAT/ACT preparation, Shakespeare, studio art.

Graduation Requirements 20th century history, 20th century world history, algebra, American government, American history, ancient world history, art appreciation, biology, British literature, computer literacy, consumer economics, earth systems analysis, English, environmental science, geometry, government, health, keyboarding, life management skills, martial arts, reading/study skills, U.S. history, visual arts, world history, writing.

Special Academic Programs Accelerated programs; remedial reading and/or remedial writing; remedial math.

College Admission Counseling 14 students graduated in 2010; all went to college, including Christopher Newport University; Foothill College; Fort Lewis College; The University of Arizona; The University of Kansas; University of Colorado at Boulder. Median composite ACT: 23. 22% scored over 26 on composite ACT.

Student Life Upper grades have specified standards of dress, student council, honor system. Discipline rests primarily with faculty.

Summer Programs Remediation, advancement programs offered; session focuses on credit recovery; held on campus; accepts boys and girls; open to students from other schools. 50 students usually enrolled. 2011 schedule: June 10 to August 15. Application deadline: May 15.

Tuition and Aid Day student tuition: $24,000; 7-day tuition and room/board: $36,000. Guaranteed tuition plan. Tuition installment plan (monthly payment plans). Tuition reduction for siblings, need-based scholarship grants, paying campus jobs available. In 2010–11, 15% of upper-school students received aid. Total amount of financial aid awarded in 2010–11: $45,000.

Admissions Traditional secondary-level entrance grade is 11. For fall 2010, 53 students applied for upper-level admission, 50 were accepted, 48 enrolled. Deadline for receipt of application materials: none. Application fee required: $50. Interview required.

Athletics Intramural: basketball (boys), volleyball (g), weight training (b,g); coed intramural: martial arts, outdoor activities, physical training, softball, strength & conditioning, yoga. 3 athletic trainers.

Computers Computers are regularly used in all academic classes. Computer resources include Internet access, wireless campus network. Student e-mail accounts and computer access in designated common areas are available to students.

Contact Shirley Page, Receptionist. 435-353-4498 Ext. 100. Fax: 435-353-4898. E-mail: staff@cedarridge.net. Web site: www.cedarridgeacademy.net.

CHATHAM ACADEMY
4 Oglethorpe Professional Boulevard
Savannah, Georgia 31406
Head of School: Mrs. Carolyn M. Hannaford

General Information Coeducational day college-preparatory, general academic, and technology school; primarily serves underachievers, students with learning disabilities, individuals with Attention Deficit Disorder, dyslexic students, and different learning styles. Grades 1–12. Founded: 1978. Setting: suburban. 5-acre campus. 1 building on campus. Approved or accredited by Georgia Independent School Association, Southern Association of Colleges and Schools, and Georgia Department of Education. Endowment: $100,000. Total enrollment: 99. Upper school average class size: 10. Upper school faculty-student ratio: 1:10. There are 180 required school days per year for Upper School students. Upper School students typically attend 5 days per week. The average school day consists of 6 hours.

Upper School Student Profile Grade 9: 8 students (6 boys, 2 girls); Grade 10: 9 students (6 boys, 3 girls); Grade 11: 10 students (7 boys, 3 girls); Grade 12: 8 students (3 boys, 5 girls).

Faculty School total: 18. In upper school: 1 man, 8 women; 6 have advanced degrees.

Subjects Offered Algebra, American history, American literature, art, biology, earth science, economics, English, English literature, expository writing, geology, geometry, government/civics, grammar, history, keyboarding, mathematics, physical education, physical science, reading, SAT/ACT preparation, science, social studies, world history, world literature, writing.

Graduation Requirements Algebra, American government, American history, biology, British literature, chemistry, civics, composition, consumer economics, earth science, economics, electives, English, English composition, English literature, foreign language, French, grammar, marine biology, mathematics, physical education (includes health), physical science, reading/study skills, science, social studies (includes history), U.S. history.

Special Academic Programs Independent study; study at local college for college credit; remedial reading and/or remedial writing; remedial math; programs in English, mathematics, general development for dyslexic students.

College Admission Counseling 7 students graduated in 2010; 5 went to college, including Savannah College of Art and Design. Other: 1 went to work, 1 entered a postgraduate year.

Student Life Upper grades have uniform requirement, student council, honor system. Discipline rests primarily with faculty.

Tuition and Aid Day student tuition: $14,900. Tuition installment plan (monthly payment plans, individually arranged payment plans). Tuition reduction for siblings, need-based scholarship grants, Georgia Special Needs Scholarship available. In 2010–11, 33% of upper-school students received aid. Total amount of financial aid awarded in 2010–11: $82,200.

Admissions Traditional secondary-level entrance grade is 10. For fall 2010, 20 students applied for upper-level admission, 14 were accepted, 8 enrolled. Achievement tests, Individual IQ, Achievement and behavior rating scale, school's own test, Stanford Binet, Wechsler Individual Achievement Test, Wechsler Intelligence Scale for Children III, WISC or WAIS, WISC-R, Woodcock-Johnson Revised Achievement Test or writing sample required. Deadline for receipt of application materials: none. Application fee required: $50. Interview required.

Athletics Interscholastic: flag football (boys, girls), football (b), yoga (g); intramural: football (b), soccer (b,g); coed interscholastic: basketball, fitness, flag football; coed intramural: canoeing/kayaking, cheering, cooperative games, fitness, fitness walking, flag football, football, jump rope, kickball, Newcombe ball, outdoor activities, outdoor recreation, paddle tennis, physical training, soccer, whiffle ball. 1 PE instructor, 2 coaches.

Computers Computer network features include Internet access, Internet filtering or blocking technology. The school has a published electronic and media policy.

Contact Mrs. Carolyn M. Hannaford, Principal. 912-354-4047. Fax: 912-354-4633. E-mail: channaford@chathamacademy.com. Web site: www.chathamacademy.com.

CHELSEA SCHOOL
711 Pershing Avenue
Silver Spring, Maryland 20910
Head of School: Anthony R. Messina Jr.

General Information Coeducational day college-preparatory, general academic, arts, bilingual studies, technology, and science and math school; primarily serves students with learning disabilities, individuals with Attention Deficit Disorder, and dyslexic students. Grades 5–12. Founded: 1976. Setting: suburban. 10-acre campus. 3 buildings on campus. Approved or accredited by Maryland Department of Education. Total enrollment: 76. Upper school average class size: 8. Upper school faculty-student ratio: 1:8.

Upper School Student Profile Grade 6: 3 students (1 boy, 2 girls); Grade 7: 6 students (5 boys, 1 girl); Grade 8: 5 students (3 boys, 2 girls); Grade 9: 9 students (7 boys, 2 girls); Grade 10: 18 students (16 boys, 2 girls); Grade 11: 15 students (14 boys, 1 girl); Grade 12: 20 students (13 boys, 7 girls).

Faculty School total: 29. In upper school: 11 men, 7 women.

Subjects Offered Algebra, American history, American literature, art, biology, calculus, career/college preparation, chemistry, community service, composition, computer graphics, computer technologies, computers, conceptual physics, earth and space science, earth science, English, English literature, environmental science, foreign language, geometry, health, health and wellness, independent study, information technology, math review, music, personal fitness, physical education, physics, pre-algebra, pre-calculus, reading, reading/study skills, remedial study skills, science, social skills, Spanish, state government, U.S. government, U.S. history, U.S. literature, wellness.

Graduation Requirements 20th century world history, algebra, American government, American history, art, biology, career/college preparation, chemistry, earth science, electives, English, English composition, English literature, general math, geometry, health and wellness, physical education (includes health), pre-algebra, Spanish, U.S. history.

Special Academic Programs Remedial reading and/or remedial writing; remedial math; programs in English, mathematics, general development for dyslexic students.

College Admission Counseling 18 students graduated in 2009; 16 went to college, including Macalester College. Other: 1 had other specific plans.

Student Life Upper grades have student council. Discipline rests primarily with faculty.

Tuition and Aid Day student tuition: $35,610. Tuition installment plan (individually arranged payment plans). Need-based scholarship grants available. In 2009–10, 13% of upper-school students received aid.

Admissions Traditional secondary-level entrance grade is 9. Academic Profile Tests, Wechsler Individual Achievement Test, Wide Range Achievement Test, WISC III or other aptitude measures; standardized achievement test, WISC or WAIS, WISC-R or Woodcock-Johnson required. Deadline for receipt of application materials: none. Application fee required: $50. On-campus interview required.

Athletics Interscholastic: basketball (boys, girls), flagball (b); coed interscholastic: soccer, softball, track and field. 1 PE instructor.

Computers Computer network features include on-campus library services, Internet access, wireless campus network, Internet filtering or blocking technology. Campus intranet, student e-mail accounts, and computer access in designated common areas are available to students. The school has a published electronic and media policy.

Contact Debbie Lourie, Director of Admissions. 301-585-1430 Ext. 303. Fax: 301-585-0245. E-mail: dlourie@chelseaschool.edu. Web site: www.chelseaschool.edu.

CHEROKEE CREEK BOYS SCHOOL
198 Cooper Road
Westminster, South Carolina 29693
Head of School: David LePere

General Information Boys' boarding college-preparatory, general academic, arts, bilingual studies, environmental studies, and experiential education school; primarily serves students with learning disabilities, individuals with Attention Deficit Disorder, individuals with emotional and behavioral problems, dyslexic students, and mild learning disabilities. Grades 5–9. Founded: 2002. Setting: rural. Nearest major city is Atlanta, GA. Students are housed in single-sex dormitories. 77-acre campus. 2 buildings on campus. Approved or accredited by Southern Association of Colleges and Schools. Total enrollment: 36. Upper school average class size: 12. Upper school faculty-student ratio: 1:6.

Upper School Student Profile Grade 6: 5 students (5 boys); Grade 7: 7 students (7 boys); Grade 8: 7 students (7 boys); Grade 9: 6 students (6 boys). 100% of students are boarding students. 1% are state residents. 15 states are represented in upper school student body.

Faculty School total: 8. In upper school: 6 men, 2 women; 5 have advanced degrees.

Graduation Requirements Completion of emotional growth program, meet therapeutic and academic goals, readiness to return home or transition to traditional boarding school.

Special Academic Programs Independent study; remedial reading and/or remedial writing; remedial math; programs in English, mathematics, general development for dyslexic students.

College Admission Counseling 27 students graduated in 2009.

Student Life Upper grades have specified standards of dress, honor system. Discipline rests primarily with faculty.

Tuition and Aid 7-day tuition and room/board: $73,200. Tuition installment plan (individually arranged payment plans). Need-based scholarship grants available. In 2009–10, 3% of upper-school students received aid.

Admissions For fall 2009, 53 students applied for upper-level admission, 29 were accepted, 27 enrolled. Battery of testing done through outside agency and psycho-educational evaluation required. Deadline for receipt of application materials: none. Application fee required: $2000. Interview recommended.

Athletics Interscholastic: backpacking, badminton, baseball, basketball, billiards, bowling, canoeing/kayaking, climbing, fishing, flag football, fly fishing, Frisbee, hiking/backpacking, horseback riding, in-line skating, kayaking, martial arts, mountain biking, outdoor activities, paddle tennis, paddling, physical fitness, rafting, ropes courses, soccer, swimming and diving, table tennis, tennis, touch football, ultimate Frisbee, volleyball, walking, wilderness survival, winter soccer; intramural: basketball, flag football, martial arts, soccer. 4 PE instructors, 4 coaches, 4 athletic trainers.

Computers Computers are regularly used in mathematics classes. Computer resources include Internet access, Internet filtering or blocking technology. The school has a published electronic and media policy.

Contact Betsy Deane, Admissions Director. 864-710-8183. Fax: 866-399-1869. E-mail: bdeane@cherokeecreek.net. Web site: www.cherokeecreek.net.

CHERRY GULCH
PO Box 678
Emmett, Idaho 83617
Head of School: Andrew D. Sapp, PhD

General Information Boys' boarding college-preparatory, general academic, arts, business, and technology school; primarily serves underachievers, students with learning disabilities, individuals with Attention Deficit Disorder, individuals with emotional and behavioral problems, and dyslexic students. Grades 5–9. Founded: 2004. Setting: rural. Nearest major city is Boise. Students are housed in single-sex dormitories. 220-acre campus. 3 buildings on campus. Approved or accredited by Northwest Accreditation Commission and Idaho Department of Education. Upper school average class size: 8. Upper school faculty-student ratio: 1:4. Upper School students typically attend 5 days per week.

Upper School Student Profile Grade 6: 2 students (2 boys); Grade 7: 8 students (8 boys); Grade 8: 12 students (12 boys); Grade 9: 6 students (6 boys). 100% of students are boarding students. 14 states are represented in upper school student body. 4% are international students. International students from Canada.

Faculty School total: 10. In upper school: 3 men, 1 woman; 3 have advanced degrees; 3 reside on campus.

Subjects Offered ADL skills, algebra, American history, art, biology, character education, civics, communication skills, community garden, community service, composition, computer applications, computer programming, conflict resolution, culinary arts, death and loss, earth science, English, English composition, English literature, equine management, ethical decision making, ethics and responsibility, gardening, geometry, government/civics, grammar, independent study, Internet research, language and composition, language arts, leadership, life science, literature, martial arts, mathematics, organic gardening, outdoor education, peer counseling, personal and social education, personal development, personal growth, physical education, physical science, pre-algebra, psychology, reading, reading/study skills, relationships, social studies, student government, technology/design, U.S. government, U.S. history, U.S. literature, wilderness experience, world history, world literature, writing.

Graduation Requirements An emotional growth curriculum and levels program must be completed in order to graduate with full honors, Students are required to participate in the therapeutic services offered at the school., This includes individual, group, and family therapy. Equine assisted therapy is also required.

Special Academic Programs Programs in general development for dyslexic students.

College Admission Counseling 15 students graduated in 2009.

Student Life Upper grades have specified standards of dress, student council. Discipline rests primarily with faculty.

Tuition and Aid 7-day tuition and room/board: $97,940. Guaranteed tuition plan. Tuition installment plan (monthly payment plans). Tuition reduction for siblings, need-based loans, middle-income loans available. In 2009–10, 10% of upper-school students received aid.

Admissions Deadline for receipt of application materials: none. No application fee required. Interview recommended.

Athletics Intramural: alpine skiing, aquatics, archery, backpacking, baseball, basketball, bowling, boxing, canoeing/kayaking, climbing, combined training, cooperative games, equestrian sports, fishing, fitness, flag football, Frisbee, hiking/backpacking, horseback riding, ice skating, jogging, judo, lacrosse, mountain biking, nordic skiing, outdoor activities, outdoor adventure, outdoor education, outdoor recreation, outdoor skills, outdoors, paint ball, physical fitness, rafting, rock climbing, ropes courses, running, skiing (cross-country), skiing (downhill), snowboarding, snowshoeing, soccer, strength & conditioning, swimming and diving, touch football, wilderness.

Computers Computers are regularly used in computer applications, research skills classes. Computer resources include Internet access, Internet filtering or blocking technology.

Contact Andrew D. Sapp, PhD, Founder. 208-365-3473 Ext. 502. Fax: 208-365-7235. E-mail: info@cherrygulch.org. Web site: www.cherrygulch.org.

COMMUNITY HIGH SCHOOL

1135 Teaneck Road
Teaneck, New Jersey 07666
Head of School: Dennis Cohen

General Information Coeducational day college-preparatory school; primarily serves students with learning disabilities, individuals with Attention Deficit Disorder, and dyslexic students. Ungraded, ages 14–19. Founded: 1968. Setting: suburban. Nearest major city is Hackensack. 1 building on campus. Approved or accredited by New Jersey Association of Independent Schools, New York Department of Education, and New Jersey Department of Education. Total enrollment: 184. There are 180 required school days per year for Upper School students. Upper School students typically attend 5 days per week. The average school day consists of 6 hours and 30 minutes.

Subjects Offered Algebra, American history, American literature, art, biology, business, calculus, chemistry, computer science, creative writing, drama, driver education, English, English literature, European history, expository writing, fine arts, geography, geometry, government/civics, grammar, history, journalism, mathematics, music, photography, physical education, physics, psychology, science, social sciences, social studies, sociology, Spanish, speech, study skills, theater, trigonometry, writing.

Graduation Requirements Arts and fine arts (art, music, dance, drama), English, mathematics, physical education (includes health), science, social sciences, social studies (includes history).

Special Academic Programs Remedial reading and/or remedial writing; remedial math; programs in English, mathematics, general development for dyslexic students.

College Admission Counseling 50 students graduated in 2010.

Student Life Upper grades have specified standards of dress. Discipline rests primarily with faculty.

Tuition and Aid Day student tuition: $38,437.

Admissions Traditional secondary-level entrance grade is 9. Traditional secondary-level entrance age is 14. For fall 2010, 195 students applied for upper-level admission, 57 were accepted, 54 enrolled. Deadline for receipt of application materials: none. Application fee required: $65. On-campus interview required.

Athletics Interscholastic: baseball (boys), basketball (b), soccer (b), softball (g); intramural: baseball (b), basketball (b,g), softball (g), table tennis (b,g), track and field (b,g), volleyball (b,g). 5 PE instructors, 8 coaches.

Computers Computers are regularly used in all academic classes. Computer network features include online commercial services, voice recognition systems. The school has a published electronic and media policy.

Contact Toby Braunstein, Director of Education. 201-862-1796. Fax: 201-862-1791. E-mail: tbraunstein@communityhighschool.org. Web site: communityschool.k12.nj.us.

COPPER CANYON ACADEMY

PO Box 230
Rimrock, Arizona 86335
Head of School: Paul Taylor

General Information Girls' boarding college-preparatory and general academic school; primarily serves individuals with Attention Deficit Disorder and individuals with emotional and behavioral problems. Grades 9–12. Founded: 1998. Setting: rural. Nearest major city is Sedona. Students are housed in single-sex dormitories. 29-acre campus. 8 buildings on campus. Approved or accredited by CITA (Commission on International and Trans-Regional Accreditation), North Central Association of Colleges and Schools, and Arizona Department of Education. Total enrollment: 95. Upper school average class size: 10. Upper school faculty-student ratio: 1:10. Upper School students typically attend 5 days per week. The average school day consists of 6 hours.

Upper School Student Profile Grade 9: 20 students (20 girls); Grade 10: 25 students (25 girls); Grade 11: 25 students (25 girls); Grade 12: 25 students (25 girls). 100% of students are boarding students. 10% are state residents. 33 states are represented in upper school student body. 5% are international students.

Faculty School total: 12. In upper school: 5 men, 7 women; 3 have advanced degrees; 2 reside on campus.

Subjects Offered ACT preparation, acting, adolescent issues, advanced math, algebra, American Civil War, American government, American history, American literature, ancient history, ancient world history, applied arts, applied music, art, art and culture, art appreciation, art education, art history, arts, athletic training, athletics, ballet, ballet technique, basketball, biology, botany, British literature, business, business communications, business mathematics, calculus, career planning, character education, chemistry, child development, choir, chorus, civics, Civil War, civil war history, college admission preparation, college awareness, college counseling, college placement, college planning, college writing, communication skills, communications, community garden, community service, comparative civilizations, composition, computer applications, computer education, computer graphics, computer literacy, computer math, computer science, computer skills, computers, consumer mathematics, contemporary art, contemporary history, contemporary issues, creative arts, creative dance, creative writing, current events, dance, dance performance, decision making skills, drama, drama performance, drama workshop, dramatic arts, drawing, drawing and design, earth science, economics, economics and history, electives, English, English composition, English literature, equality and freedom, equestrian sports, equine management, equine science, ethical decision making, European history, European literature, experiential education, female experience in America, film appreciation, fine arts, fitness, food and nutrition, foreign language, foreign policy, French, gender issues, general science, geography, geology, geometry, global studies, government, government/civics, grammar, graphic arts, health, health and safety, health and wellness, health education, health science, heritage of American Women, history, history of dance, history of drama, home economics, human biology, human development, human sexuality, independent living, international studies, intro to computers, jazz dance, journalism, lab/keyboard, language, language and composition, language arts, leadership, leadership education training, learning strategies, library, life issues, life management skills, life skills, linear algebra, literature, literature by women, math applications, mathematics, modern dance, modern languages, moral and social development, music, music appreciation, music composition, music history, music performance, musical productions, musical theater, nature study, news writing, newspaper, non-Western literature, nutrition, oil painting, parenting, participation in sports, peer counseling, performing arts, personal development, personal growth, physical education, physics, play production, poetry, political science, political systems, portfolio art, pre-calculus, psychology, SAT preparation, SAT/ACT preparation, science, sex education, sexuality, Shakespeare, Shakespearean histories, social issues, sociology, softball, Spanish, Spanish literature, speech, speech and debate, sports, sports conditioning, stage and body movement, state history, statistics, student government, student publications, studio art, study skills, tap dance, theater, theater arts, theater history, theater production, trigonometry, U.S. government, U.S. government and politics, U.S. history, U.S. literature, visual and performing arts, visual arts, vocal music, volleyball, water color painting, weight fitness, weightlifting, wellness, Western literature, women in literature, women's health, women's literature, world civilizations, world cultures, world geography, world history, world studies, writing, writing, yoga.

Graduation Requirements Option of traditional academic graduation as well as graduation from the therapeutic side of school.

Special Academic Programs Accelerated programs; independent study; study at local college for college credit; academic accommodation for the gifted, the musically talented, and the artistically talented; programs in English, mathematics for dyslexic students.

Student Life Upper grades have uniform requirement, student council, honor system. Discipline rests primarily with faculty.

Tuition and Aid 7-day tuition and room/board: $6600. Middle-income loans, Keybank, prepGATE and Sallie Mae loans available. In 2010–11, 80% of upper-school students received aid. Total amount of financial aid awarded in 2010–11: $720,000.

Admissions Traditional secondary-level entrance grade is 10. For fall 2010, 400 students applied for upper-level admission, 150 were accepted, 90 enrolled. Deadline for receipt of application materials: none. No application fee required.

Athletics Interscholastic: basketball, soccer, softball, volleyball; intramural: aerobics, aerobics/dance, badminton, ballet, basketball, cross-country running, dance, fitness, fitness walking, horseback riding, jogging, modern dance, physical fitness, physical training, soccer, softball, walking, yoga. 2 PE instructors, 1 coach, 1 athletic trainer.

Computers Computers are regularly used in all academic classes. Computer network features include Internet access, Internet filtering or blocking technology. Student e-mail accounts are available to students. Students grades are available online. The school has a published electronic and media policy.

Contact Stephanie Coleman, Admissions Counselor. 877-617-1222 Ext. 116. Fax: 928-567-1323. E-mail: stephaniecoleman@coppercanyonacademy.com. Web site: www.coppercanyonacademy.com.

THE CRAIG SCHOOL
10 Tower Hill Road
Mountain Lakes, New Jersey 07046
Head of School: Mr. David Dennen Blanchard

General Information Coeducational day college-preparatory and general academic school; primarily serves underachievers, students with learning disabilities, individuals with Attention Deficit Disorder, and dyslexic students. Grades 3–12. Founded: 1980. Setting: suburban. Nearest major city is Lincoln Park. 1-acre campus. 2 buildings on campus. Approved or accredited by Middle States Association of Colleges and Schools, New Jersey Association of Independent Schools, and New Jersey Department of Education. Total enrollment: 153. Upper school average class size: 8. Upper school faculty-student ratio: 1:6.

Upper School Student Profile Grade 9: 11 students (9 boys, 2 girls); Grade 10: 13 students (13 boys); Grade 11: 12 students (8 boys, 4 girls); Grade 12: 10 students (9 boys, 1 girl).

Faculty School total: 45. In upper school: 9 men, 8 women; 4 have advanced degrees.

Subjects Offered Algebra, American history, art education, biology, business, character education, chemistry, creative writing, current events, earth science, geometry, health education, literature, performing arts, physical education, physics, psychology, public speaking, SAT preparation, short story, Spanish, U.S. history, world history, writing, writing workshop.

Graduation Requirements Arts and fine arts (art, music, dance, drama), electives, English, language, mathematics, physical education (includes health), science, social studies (includes history). Community service is required.

Special Academic Programs Remedial reading and/or remedial writing; programs in English, mathematics, general development for dyslexic students.

College Admission Counseling 22 students graduated in 2009; 19 went to college, including Fairleigh Dickinson University, College at Florham; Misericordia University; New Jersey City University; Springfield College. Other: 1 went to work, 1 entered a postgraduate year, 1 had other specific plans.

Student Life Upper grades have specified standards of dress, student council. Discipline rests primarily with faculty.

Tuition and Aid Day student tuition: $29,300. Tuition installment plan (monthly payment plans). Tuition reduction for siblings available.

Admissions Traditional secondary-level entrance grade is 9. For fall 2009, 30 students applied for upper-level admission, 11 were accepted, 6 enrolled. Psychoeducational evaluation or WISC/Woodcock-Johnson required. Deadline for receipt of application materials: none. Application fee required: $50. Interview required.

Athletics Coed Interscholastic: cross-country running; coed intramural: basketball, bowling, cross-country running. 1 PE instructor.

Computers Computers are regularly used in all classes. Computer resources include Internet access, wireless campus network. The school has a published electronic and media policy.

Contact Suzanne Park, Director of Admission. 973-334-1295. Fax: 973-334-1299. E-mail: spark@craigschool.org. Web site: www.craigschool.org/.

CROSS CREEK PROGRAMS
150 North State Street
LaVerkin, Utah 84745
Head of School: Karr Farnsworth

General Information Coeducational boarding college-preparatory, general academic, arts, and business school; primarily serves underachievers, students with learning disabilities, individuals with Attention Deficit Disorder, and individuals with emotional and behavioral problems. Grades 7–12. Founded: 1987. Setting: small

town. Nearest major city is St. George. Students are housed in single-sex dormitories. 5-acre campus. 4 buildings on campus. Approved or accredited by Northwest Accreditation Commission, Northwest Association of Schools and Colleges, and Utah Department of Education. Total enrollment: 86. Upper school average class size: 7. Upper school faculty-student ratio: 1:15. There are 128 required school days per year for Upper School students. Upper School students typically attend 3 days per week. The average school day consists of 6 hours and 30 minutes.

Upper School Student Profile Grade 7: 6 students (2 boys, 4 girls); Grade 8: 14 students (7 boys, 7 girls); Grade 9: 19 students (9 boys, 10 girls); Grade 10: 21 students (8 boys, 13 girls); Grade 11: 18 students (7 boys, 11 girls); Grade 12: 8 students (5 boys, 3 girls).

Faculty School total: 7. In upper school: 3 men, 3 women; 3 have advanced degrees.

Subjects Offered 20th century American writers, 20th century world history, advanced chemistry, advanced math, algebra, American government, American history, American literature, art, art appreciation, art history, athletic training, athletics, baseball, basketball, biology, business, business applications, business technology, calculus, career/college preparation, careers, chemistry, child development, choir, chorus, computer applications, computer technologies, consumer mathematics, drawing, early childhood, earth science, electives, English, English composition, English literature, fitness, food and nutrition, general math, general science, geography, geometry, government, health, health education, honors algebra, honors English, honors geometry, honors U.S. history, honors world history, human biology, intro to computers, introduction to theater, keyboarding, language and composition, language arts, mathematics, parenting, pre-algebra, pre-calculus, projective geometry, psychology, reading/study skills, SAT preparation, SAT/ACT preparation, science, Spanish, sports, state history, U.S. government, U.S. history, world civilizations, world cultures.

Graduation Requirements 20th century world history, American government, American history, arts and fine arts (art, music, dance, drama), business skills (includes word processing), business technology, English, geography, keyboarding, mathematics, physical education (includes health), science, social sciences, social studies (includes history), senior project (including 90 hours of community or school service).

Special Academic Programs Honors section; accelerated programs; independent study; study at local college for college credit; remedial reading and/or remedial writing; remedial math; programs in English, mathematics, general development for dyslexic students.

College Admission Counseling 80 students graduated in 2010; 73 went to college. Other: 5 went to work, 2 entered military service.

Student Life Upper grades have uniform requirement, student council, honor system. Discipline rests primarily with faculty.

Tuition and Aid 7-day tuition and room/board: $53,940. Guaranteed tuition plan. Tuition installment plan (monthly payment plans, discount for one year paid in-advance tuition). Tuition reduction for siblings available.

Admissions Traditional secondary-level entrance grade is 10. Deadline for receipt of application materials: none. No application fee required. Interview required.

Athletics Interscholastic: backpacking (boys, girls), baseball (b,g), basketball (b,g), bowling (b,g), cooperative games (b,g), cross-country running (b,g), danceline (b,g), fitness (b,g), fitness walking (b,g), Frisbee (b,g), hiking/backpacking (b,g), outdoor activities (b,g), physical fitness (b,g), physical training (b,g), running (b,g), softball (b,g), strength & conditioning (b,g), track and field (b,g), volleyball (b,g), walking (b,g), water skiing (b,g), winter walking (b,g); intramural: basketball (b,g), cross-country running (b,g), track and field (b,g); coed interscholastic: baseball, softball. 1 PE instructor, 2 coaches.

Computers Computers are regularly used in business, career education, college planning, computer applications, economics, English, foreign language, geography, health, history, mathematics, reading, science classes. Computer resources include on-campus library services.

Contact Kami Farnsworth, Admissions Representative. 800-514-7438. Fax: 435-635-2331. E-mail: kami@crosscreekprograms.com. Web site: www.crosscreekprograms.com.

DALLAS ACADEMY
950 Tiffany Way
Dallas, Texas 75218
Head of School: Jim Richardson

General Information Coeducational day college-preparatory, general academic, arts, and technology school; primarily serves students with learning disabilities, individuals with Attention Deficit Disorder, dyslexic students, and Asperger's Syndrome. Grades 1–12. Founded: 1965. Setting: suburban. 2-acre campus. 2 buildings on campus. Approved or accredited by Southern Association of Colleges and Schools and Texas Education Agency. Endowment: $250,000. Total enrollment: 165. Upper school average class size: 10. Upper school faculty-student ratio: 1:6. Upper School students typically attend 5 days per week. The average school day consists of 5 hours and 50 minutes.

Upper School Student Profile Grade 9: 20 students (16 boys, 4 girls); Grade 10: 18 students (9 boys, 9 girls); Grade 11: 20 students (15 boys, 5 girls); Grade 12: 25 students (18 boys, 7 girls).

Faculty School total: 28. In upper school: 2 men, 13 women; 5 have advanced degrees.

Special Needs Schools: Dallas Academy

Subjects Offered Algebra, American history, art, computer science, computers, drawing, economics, English, fine arts, geography, government/civics, health, history, literature, mathematics, music, photography, physical education, physical science, pottery, science, social sciences, social studies, Spanish, speech, woodworking, world history, writing, yearbook.

Graduation Requirements Arts and fine arts (art, music, dance, drama), computer science, English, foreign language, mathematics, physical education (includes health), science, social sciences, social studies (includes history), 4 hours of community service per semester.

Special Academic Programs Study at local college for college credit; remedial reading and/or remedial writing; remedial math; programs in English, mathematics, general development for dyslexic students.

College Admission Counseling 21 students graduated in 2009; 16 went to college, including Lon Morris College; Oklahoma State University; Richland College; Texas A&M University; The University of Texas at Arlington; University of the Ozarks. Other: 5 went to work.

Student Life Upper grades have uniform requirement, student council. Discipline rests primarily with faculty.

Tuition and Aid Day student tuition: $15,500. Tuition installment plan (semester payment plan). Need-based scholarship grants available. In 2009–10, 20% of upper-school students received aid. Total amount of financial aid awarded in 2009–10: $80,000.

Admissions Traditional secondary-level entrance grade is 9. Admissions testing and WRAT required. Deadline for receipt of application materials: none. No application fee required. On-campus interview required.

Athletics Interscholastic: baseball (boys), basketball (b,g), cheering (g), cross-country running (b,g), football (b), golf (b), soccer (b,g), track and field (b,g), volleyball (g); intramural: tennis (g); coed interscholastic: soccer. 1 PE instructor, 5 coaches, 1 athletic trainer.

Computers Computers are regularly used in English, geography, history, library, SAT preparation, science, typing, writing, yearbook classes. Computer network features include on-campus library services, online commercial services, Internet access, Internet filtering or blocking technology. Students grades are available online. The school has a published electronic and media policy.

Contact Jim Richardson, Headmaster. 214-324-1481 Ext. 113. Fax: 214-327-8537. E-mail: jrichardson@dallas-academy.com. Web site: www.dallas-academy.com.

DELAWARE VALLEY FRIENDS SCHOOL

19 East Central Avenue
Paoli, Pennsylvania 19301-1345
Head of School: Dr. Daniel Kahn

General Information Coeducational day college-preparatory, arts, technology, and Orton-Gillingham based reading instruction school, affiliated with Society of Friends; primarily serves students with learning disabilities, individuals with Attention Deficit Disorder, and dyslexic students. Grades 6–12. Founded: 1986. Setting: suburban. Nearest major city is Philadelphia. 8-acre campus. 1 building on campus. Approved or accredited by Pennsylvania Association of Independent Schools. Endowment: $3.6 million. Total enrollment: 187. Upper school average class size: 8. Upper school faculty-student ratio: 1:5. There are 170 required school days per year for Upper School students. Upper School students typically attend 5 days per week. The average school day consists of 6 hours and 17 minutes.

Upper School Student Profile Grade 9: 25 students (11 boys, 14 girls); Grade 10: 45 students (25 boys, 20 girls); Grade 11: 34 students (23 boys, 11 girls); Grade 12: 44 students (27 boys, 17 girls). 6% of students are members of Society of Friends.

Faculty School total: 38. In upper school: 14 men, 23 women; 23 have advanced degrees.

Subjects Offered 20th century world history, algebra, American history, Asian studies, astronomy, biology, calculus, ceramics, chemistry, college counseling, college placement, computer-aided design, crafts, culinary arts, electives, English, first aid, geometry, human development, language arts, music, photography, physical education, physics, pre-calculus, printmaking, Spanish, studio art, trigonometry, video and animation, world history, writing.

Graduation Requirements Arts and fine arts (art, music, dance, drama), English, lab science, language arts, mathematics, physical education (includes health), senior internship, social studies (includes history), at least one Adventure Based Learning (A.B.L.E.) course, community service hours. Community service is required.

Special Academic Programs Remedial reading and/or remedial writing; remedial math; programs in English, mathematics, general development for dyslexic students.

College Admission Counseling 45 students graduated in 2010; 42 went to college, including American University; La Salle University; McDaniel College; University of Delaware; University of Pennsylvania. Other: 3 had other specific plans.

Student Life Upper grades have specified standards of dress, student council. Discipline rests primarily with faculty. Attendance at religious services is required.

Summer Programs Remediation, enrichment, art/fine arts programs offered; session focuses on individualized reading skills/writing tutoring using Orton-Gillingham methods; held on campus; accepts boys and girls; open to students from other schools. 50 students usually enrolled. 2011 schedule: June 27 to July 29. Application deadline: none.

Tuition and Aid Day student tuition: $35,200. Tuition installment plan (monthly payment plans, 2-payment plan (66% due May 1, 34% due January 1)). Tuition

reduction for siblings, need-based scholarship grants available. In 2010–11, 31% of upper-school students received aid. Total amount of financial aid awarded in 2010–11: $756,000.

Admissions Traditional secondary-level entrance grade is 9. For fall 2010, 46 students applied for upper-level admission, 34 were accepted, 25 enrolled. Psycho-educational evaluation and WISC or WAIS required. Deadline for receipt of application materials: none. Application fee required: $100. On-campus interview required.

Athletics Interscholastic: basketball (boys, girls), cross-country running (b,g), Frisbee (b), lacrosse (b,g), soccer (b,g); coed interscholastic: Frisbee, golf, soccer, tennis, ultimate Frisbee; coed intramural: backpacking, bicycling, hiking/backpacking, rock climbing, sailing, skiing (cross-country), volleyball. 2 PE instructors, 5 coaches.

Computers Computers are regularly used in all classes. Computer network features include online commercial services, Internet access, wireless campus network, Internet filtering or blocking technology, adaptive technologies such as Kurzweil, Dragon/Mac Speech Dictate, etc., homework site, all students have school-supplied laptops. Student e-mail accounts and computer access in designated common areas are available to students. Students grades are available online. The school has a published electronic and media policy.

Contact Mary Ellen Trent, Director of Admissions. 610-640-4150 Ext. 2162. Fax: 610-560-4336. E-mail: maryellen.trent@dvfs.org. Web site: www.dvfs.org.

DENVER ACADEMY

4400 East Iliff Avenue
Denver, Colorado 80222
Head of School: Kevin Smith

General Information Coeducational day college-preparatory, general academic, arts, vocational, and technology school; primarily serves underachievers, students with learning disabilities, individuals with Attention Deficit Disorder, dyslexic students, and unique learning styles. Grades 1–12. Founded: 1972. Setting: urban. 22-acre campus. 19 buildings on campus. Approved or accredited by Association of Colorado Independent Schools and Colorado Department of Education. Member of National Association of Independent Schools. Endowment: $1 million. Total enrollment: 387. Upper school average class size: 13. Upper school faculty-student ratio: 1:6. Upper School students typically attend 5 days per week. The average school day consists of 6 hours and 15 minutes.

Upper School Student Profile Grade 9: 64 students (49 boys, 15 girls); Grade 10: 48 students (41 boys, 7 girls); Grade 11: 67 students (50 boys, 17 girls); Grade 12: 53 students (45 boys, 8 girls).

Faculty School total: 86. In upper school: 26 men, 23 women; 6 have advanced degrees.

Subjects Offered ACT preparation, adolescent issues, algebra, American history, American literature, anatomy, art, art history, arts, baseball, basic skills, basketball, biology, botany, business, calculus, ceramics, chemistry, comparative cultures, computer applications, computer graphics, computer math, computer processing, computer programming, computer science, computer skills, creative writing, drama, dramatic arts, earth science, English, English literature, environmental science, ethics, European history, film, filmmaking, fine arts, geography, geometry, government/civics, grammar, health, history, life skills, mathematics, music, philosophy, photography, physical education, physics, physiology, psychology, science, social sciences, social studies, Spanish, speech, theater, trigonometry, values and decisions, world history, world literature, writing, yearbook.

Graduation Requirements Arts and fine arts (art, music, dance, drama), English, mathematics, physical education (includes health), science, social sciences, social studies (includes history).

Special Academic Programs Independent study; academic accommodation for the gifted; remedial reading and/or remedial writing; remedial math; programs in English, mathematics, general development for dyslexic students.

College Admission Counseling 76 students graduated in 2009; 68 went to college, including Fort Lewis College; Metropolitan State College of Denver; University of Colorado Denver; University of Northern Colorado. Other: 1 entered military service, 7 had other specific plans.

Student Life Upper grades have specified standards of dress, student council, honor system. Discipline rests equally with students and faculty.

Tuition and Aid Day student tuition: $22,425. Tuition installment plan (monthly payment plans). Tuition reduction for siblings, need-based scholarship grants available. In 2009–10, 31% of upper-school students received aid.

Admissions For fall 2009, 35 students applied for upper-level admission, 35 were accepted, 31 enrolled. WISC/Woodcock-Johnson required. Deadline for receipt of application materials: none. Application fee required: $75. On-campus interview required.

Athletics Interscholastic: baseball (boys), basketball (b,g), cross-country running (b,g), golf (b), soccer (b,g), volleyball (g); intramural: volleyball (g); coed interscholastic: cheering, physical fitness, physical training; coed intramural: backpacking, basketball, boxing, canoeing/kayaking, climbing, cooperative games, fishing, flag football, golf, indoor hockey, indoor soccer, indoor track, jump rope, mountaineering, outdoor activities, rafting, rock climbing, skiing (downhill), soccer, swimming and diving, track and field, wall climbing. 4 PE instructors, 4 coaches.

Computers Computers are regularly used in basic skills, career exploration, career technology, college planning, drawing and design, English, foreign language, independent study, introduction to technology, mathematics, media arts, media production, media services, multimedia, music, occupational education, SAT preparation, science, writing, yearbook classes. Computer network features include on-campus library services, online commercial services, Internet access, wireless campus network, Internet filtering or blocking technology. Student e-mail accounts and computer access in designated common areas are available to students. Students grades are available online. The school has a published electronic and media policy.
Contact Janet Woolley, Director of Admissions. 303-777-5161. Fax: 303-777-5893. E-mail: jwoolley@denveracademy.org. Web site: www.denveracademy.org.

EAGLE HILL-SOUTHPORT

214 Main Street
Southport, Connecticut 06890
Head of School: Leonard Tavormina

General Information Coeducational day arts school; primarily serves underachievers, students with learning disabilities, individuals with Attention Deficit Disorder, and dyslexic students. Ungraded, ages 7–14. Founded: 1985. Setting: small town. Nearest major city is Bridgeport. 2-acre campus. 1 building on campus. Approved or accredited by Connecticut Association of Independent Schools and Connecticut Department of Education. Member of National Association of Independent Schools. Endowment: $6.8 million. Total enrollment: 112. Upper school average class size: 5. Upper school faculty-student ratio: 1:4. There are 180 required school days per year for Upper School students. Upper School students typically attend 5 days per week. The average school day consists of 7 hours and 15 minutes.
Faculty School total: 29. In upper school: 7 men, 22 women; 20 have advanced degrees.
Subjects Offered Algebra, art, biology, computer skills, creative writing, earth science, English, grammar, history, literature, mathematics, physical education, reading, social studies, writing.
Special Academic Programs Remedial reading and/or remedial writing; remedial math; programs in English, mathematics, general development for dyslexic students.
Student Life Upper grades have uniform requirement, student council. Discipline rests primarily with faculty.
Summer Programs Remediation programs offered; session focuses on academic skills reinforcement; held on campus; accepts boys and girls; open to students from other schools. 73 students usually enrolled. 2011 schedule: June 27 to July 29. Application deadline: none.
Tuition and Aid Day student tuition: $38,500. Tuition installment plan (monthly payment plans, individually arranged payment plans). Need-based scholarship grants available. In 2010–11, 1% of upper-school students received aid. Total amount of financial aid awarded in 2010–11: $101,610.
Admissions For fall 2010, 56 students applied for upper-level admission, 40 were accepted, 33 enrolled. Wechsler Intelligence Scale for Children required. Deadline for receipt of application materials: none. Application fee required: $100. On-campus interview required.
Athletics Interscholastic: cheering (girls); intramural: cheering (g); coed interscholastic: baseball, basketball, cross-country running, fitness, outdoor adventure, physical fitness, soccer, softball; coed intramural: baseball, basketball, soccer.
Computers Computers are regularly used in English, mathematics, writing classes. Computer resources include Internet access.
Contact Carolyn Lavender, Director of Admissions. 203-254-2044. Fax: 203-255-4052. E-mail: info@eaglehillsouthport.org. Web site: www.eaglehillsouthport.org.

EAGLE ROCK SCHOOL

2750 Notaiah Road
Estes Park, Colorado 80517
Head of School: Robert Burkhardt

General Information Coeducational boarding and day college-preparatory, general academic, arts, bilingual studies, and technology school; primarily serves underachievers, students with learning disabilities, individuals with Attention Deficit Disorder, individuals with emotional and behavioral problems, dyslexic students, and students who are unsuccessful in a traditional high school. Founded: 1991. Setting: rural. Nearest major city is Boulder. Students are housed in coed dormitories. 640-acre campus. 26 buildings on campus. Approved or accredited by Association for Experiential Education, Association of Colorado Independent Schools, North Central Association of Colleges and Schools, and Colorado Department of Education. Endowment: $15 million. Upper school average class size: 8. Upper school faculty-student ratio: 1:4.
Upper School Student Profile 100% of students are boarding students. 40% are state residents. 19 states are represented in upper school student body.
Faculty In upper school: 20 men, 18 women; 6 have advanced degrees; 23 reside on campus.
Subjects Offered Algebra, American history, art, arts, biology, business skills, computer science, English, environmental science, fine arts, geography, geometry,

government/civics, history, literature, mathematics, music, personal development, physical education, physical science, science, social sciences, social studies, speech, technology.
Graduation Requirements Arts and fine arts (art, music, dance, drama), business skills (includes word processing), computer science, English, foreign language, mathematics, personal development, physical education (includes health), science, social sciences, social-studies (includes history), personal growth.
Special Academic Programs Independent study; term-away projects; study abroad; academic accommodation for the gifted and the musically talented; remedial reading and/or remedial writing; remedial math; programs in English, mathematics, general development for dyslexic students.
College Admission Counseling 12 students graduated in 2009; 8 went to college. Other: 4 went to work.
Student Life Upper grades have student council, honor system. Discipline rests equally with students and faculty.
Tuition and Aid Entire tuition paid by American Honda Education Corporation available. In 2009–10, 100% of upper-school students received aid.
Admissions Traditional secondary-level entrance age is 16. Deadline for receipt of application materials: none. No application fee required. Interview required.
Athletics Coed Intramural: aquatics, backpacking, ball hockey, basketball, bicycling, climbing, cross-country running, fitness, floor hockey, Frisbee, hiking/backpacking, jogging, juggling, life saving, martial arts, mountain biking, outdoor activities, outdoor adventure, outdoor education, outdoor recreation, outdoor skills, physical fitness, physical training, rock climbing, running, self defense, skiing (cross-country), snowshoeing, soccer, softball, swimming and diving, ultimate Frisbee, volleyball, wall climbing, water polo, water volleyball, weight lifting, wilderness. 3 PE instructors.
Computers Computers are regularly used in English, mathematics, science classes. Computer network features include on-campus library services, online commercial services, Internet access, wireless campus network. Student e-mail accounts are available to students. The school has a published electronic and media policy.
Contact Philbert Smith, Director of Students. 970-586-7112. Fax: 970-586-4805. E-mail: philberts@aol.com. Web site: www.eaglerockschool.org.

ECKERD YOUTH ALTERNATIVES

100 North Starcrest Drive
Clearwater, Florida 33765
Head of School: Mr. Keith B. Philipson

General Information Coeducational boarding general academic and vocational school; affiliated with Christian faith; primarily serves underachievers, students with learning disabilities, individuals with Attention Deficit Disorder, individuals with emotional and behavioral problems, and dyslexic students. Grades 5–12. Founded: 1968. Setting: rural. Students are housed in cabins. 1,442-acre campus. 48 buildings on campus. Approved or accredited by Council of Accreditation and School Improvement, Southern Association of Colleges and Schools, and Florida Department of Education. Total enrollment: 76. Upper school average class size: 12. Upper school faculty-student ratio: 1:10. There are 240 required school days per year for Upper School students. Upper School students typically attend 5 days per week. The average school day consists of 5 hours.
Upper School Student Profile Grade 8: 6 students (4 boys, 2 girls); Grade 9: 21 students (14 boys, 7 girls); Grade 10: 18 students (13 boys, 5 girls); Grade 11: 25 students (20 boys, 5 girls); Grade 12: 6 students (3 boys, 3 girls). 100% of students are boarding students. 90% are state residents. 10 states are represented in upper school student body. 1% are international students. International students from Bermuda, Canada, and Saudi Arabia.
Faculty School total: 78. In upper school: 21 men, 32 women; 10 have advanced degrees.
Subjects Offered Community service, English, fine arts, humanities, mathematics, physical education, science, social sciences, social studies, Spanish.
Graduation Requirements Art history, arts and fine arts (art, music, dance, drama), English, foreign language, mathematics, physical education (includes health), science, social sciences, social studies (includes history). Community service is required.
Special Academic Programs Honors section; remedial reading and/or remedial writing; remedial math; programs in English, mathematics, general development for dyslexic students; ESL.
Student Life Upper grades have specified standards of dress, student council. Discipline rests primarily with faculty.
Tuition and Aid Guaranteed tuition plan. Tuition installment plan (individually arranged payment plans). Middle-income loans available.
Admissions Traditional secondary-level entrance age is 9. For fall 2009, 327 students applied for upper-level admission, 160 were accepted, 76 enrolled. Woodcock-Johnson required. Deadline for receipt of application materials: none. No application fee required. Interview recommended.
Athletics Coed Intramural: backpacking, canoeing/kayaking, hiking/backpacking, swimming and diving, track and field, wilderness.
Computers Computers are regularly used in English, mathematics, science classes. Computer network features include on-campus library services, Internet access, wireless campus network, Internet filtering or blocking technology. Campus intranet and computer access in designated common areas are available to students. The school has a published electronic and media policy.

Contact Francene Hazel, Director of Admissions. 800-914-3937 Ext. 464. Fax: 727-442-5911. E-mail: fhazel@eckerd.org. Web site: www.eckerd.org.

ELAN SCHOOL

PO Box 578
Poland, Maine 04274
Head of School: Ms. Sharon Terry

General Information Coeducational boarding college-preparatory and general academic school; primarily serves underachievers, students with learning disabilities, individuals with Attention Deficit Disorder, individuals with emotional and behavioral problems, and mild to moderate learning disabilities,. Grades 8–12. Founded: 1970. Setting: rural. Nearest major city is Portland. Students are housed in single-sex dormitories. 32-acre campus. Approved or accredited by Massachusetts Department of Education and Maine Department of Education. Total enrollment: 35. Upper school average class size: 8. Upper school faculty-student ratio: 1:6. There are 226 required school days per year for Upper School students. Upper School students typically attend 5 days per week. The average school day consists of 4 hours and 30 minutes.

Upper School Student Profile Grade 9: 4 students (4 boys); Grade 10: 5 students (5 boys); Grade 11: 11 students (10 boys, 1 girl); Grade 12: 15 students (12 boys, 3 girls). 100% of students are boarding students. 1% are state residents. 9 states are represented in upper school student body. 3% are international students. International students from Canada.

Faculty School total: 10. In upper school: 7 men, 2 women; 6 have advanced degrees.

Subjects Offered 20th century history, advanced math, algebra, American Civil War, American history, American literature, anthropology, applied arts, art history, astronomy, biology, calculus, chemistry, composition, computer tools, creative writing, critical thinking, earth science, economics, English, English literature, fine arts, geography, geometry, government/civics, health, history, life skills, mathematics, military history, organic chemistry, physical education, physical science, physics, pre-algebra, pre-calculus, research seminar, science, social studies, Spanish, statistics, trigonometry, world history.

Graduation Requirements American history, arts and fine arts (art, music, dance, drama), computer literacy, English, foreign language, mathematics, physical education (includes health), science, social studies (includes history).

Special Academic Programs Accelerated programs; independent study; study at local college for college credit; academic accommodation for the gifted; remedial reading and/or remedial writing; remedial math; programs in English, mathematics, general development for dyslexic students.

College Admission Counseling 38 students graduated in 2010; 32 went to college, including Colby College; Curry College; Earlham College; Hofstra University; Saint Anselm College; Salve Regina University. Other: 3 went to work, 2 entered military service, 1 entered a postgraduate year.

Student Life Upper grades have specified standards of dress, honor system. Discipline rests equally with students and faculty.

Summer Programs Remediation, enrichment, advancement, sports, art/fine arts, computer instruction programs offered; session focuses on enrichment and remediation; held on campus; accepts boys and girls; not open to students from other schools. 35 students usually enrolled. 2011 schedule: June 15 to August 6.

Tuition and Aid 7-day tuition and room/board: $54,961. Tuition installment plan (monthly payment plans). Clark Behavioral Health Loans available.

Admissions Traditional secondary-level entrance grade is 10. For fall 2010, 20 students applied for upper-level admission, 15 were accepted, 10 enrolled. Achievement tests, Individual IQ, Achievement and behavior rating scale, psycho-educational evaluation, Rorschach or Thematic Apperception Test, Wechsler Individual Achievement Test, Wechsler Intelligence Scale for Children III, Wide Range Achievement Test, WISC-R, Woodcock-Johnson or WRAT required. Deadline for receipt of application materials: none. No application fee required. Interview recommended.

Athletics Interscholastic: basketball (boys, girls), cross-country running (b,g), track and field (b,g); intramural: aquatics (b,g), baseball (b,g), basketball (b,g), bicycling (b,g), track and field (b,g); coed intramural: alpine skiing, bowling, canoeing/kayaking, cross-country running, figure skating, fishing, fitness, fitness walking, Frisbee, golf, hiking/backpacking, horseback riding, ice skating, jogging, kickball, outdoor activities, outdoor recreation, paddle tennis, physical fitness, rafting, roller skating, ropes courses, running, sailing, skiing (cross-country), snowboarding, soccer, strength & conditioning, swimming and diving, table tennis, volleyball, walking. 1 PE instructor, 3 coaches.

Computers Computers are regularly used in English, history, life skills classes. Computer resources include Internet access, Internet filtering or blocking technology.

Contact Ms. Connie E. Kimball, Admissions Director. 207-998-4666 Ext. 122. Fax: 207-998-4660. E-mail: info@elanschool.com. Web site: www.elanschool.com.

See Display on this page and Close-Up on page 916.

General; Grades 8 – 12, Coeducational; Daily rate: $150.58; Academic accreditation and therapeutic certification from NIPSA (National Independent Private Schools Association); Staff is trained in crisis intervention and behavior management using the Handle With Care training method. **We serve** students classified as ED, LD (mild to moderate) or OHI and those who exhibit disruptive behaviors associated with ADHD and/or ODD/CD. **We do not serve** students who exhibit active violent behavior, have a specific psychiatric condition that definitely cannot be managed without psychotropic medication, have a severe physical condition requiring constant medical attention or are sexual offenders. **Services**: Maximum support and implementation of IEPs; NECAP and MCAS testing; SAT prep course and closed SAT site; Honors courses offered including organic chemistry, critical thinking and others. Certified Teachers; Full-time Wilson Tutor, Special Education Director, College Counselor, Small, evening classes; Block schedule; Eligible students can take college courses on and off campus. Life skills curriculum; Specialized group sessions; Positive peer culture; Therapeutic community; Job hierarchy; Transition planning; Character education through accomplishment, honesty, accountability, responsibility, integrity and a solid work ethic; Active athletic program

P.O. Box 578,
Poland, ME 04274
Phone: 207-998-4660
www.elanschool.com

ETON ACADEMY

1755 Melton Street
Birmingham, Michigan 48009
Head of School: Pete Pullen

General Information Coeducational day college-preparatory, general academic, and arts school; primarily serves underachievers, students with learning disabilities, individuals with Attention Deficit Disorder, dyslexic students, and dysgraphia, auditory processing. Grades 1–12. Founded: 1980. Setting: suburban. Nearest major city is Detroit. 3-acre campus. 1 building on campus. Approved or accredited by Independent Schools Association of the Central States, North Central Association of Colleges and Schools, and Michigan Department of Education. Member of National Association of Independent Schools. Endowment: $1 million. Total enrollment: 188. Upper school average class size: 10. Upper school faculty-student ratio: 1:4. Upper School students typically attend 5 days per week. The average school day consists of 7 hours.

Faculty School total: 30. In upper school: 3 men, 8 women; 6 have advanced degrees.

Subjects Offered Algebra, American literature, art, business, ceramics, chemistry, creative writing, drama, earth science, economics, English, English literature, expository writing, geography, geometry, government/civics, grammar, health, history, keyboarding, mathematics, physical education, science, social studies, sociology, speech, trigonometry, U.S. history, writing.

Graduation Requirements Arts and fine arts (art, music, dance, drama), English, mathematics, physical education (includes health), science, social studies (includes history).

Special Academic Programs Remedial reading and/or remedial writing; remedial math; programs in English, mathematics, general development for dyslexic students; special instructional classes for deaf students, blind students.

College Admission Counseling 9 students graduated in 2009; 8 went to college, including Oakland Community College; Oakland University; University of Michigan–Dearborn; Western Michigan University. Other: 1 entered a postgraduate year.

Student Life Upper grades have specified standards of dress, student council, honor system. Discipline rests primarily with faculty.

Tuition and Aid Day student tuition: $21,000. Tuition installment plan (FACTS Tuition Payment Plan, monthly payment plans, individually arranged payment plans). Need-based scholarship grants available. In 2009–10, 12% of upper-school students received aid. Total amount of financial aid awarded in 2009–10: $150,000.

Admissions Traditional secondary-level entrance grade is 9. For fall 2009, 12 students applied for upper-level admission, 11 were accepted, 9 enrolled. Psycho-educational evaluation and Woodcock-Johnson Educational Evaluation, WISC III required. Deadline for receipt of application materials: none. Application fee required: $100. On-campus interview required.

Athletics Interscholastic: basketball (boys, girls), soccer (b,g); intramural: basketball (b,g), tennis (b,g), volleyball (b,g); coed interscholastic: basketball, cheering, soccer; coed intramural: basketball, bowling, running, tennis, volleyball. 3 PE instructors, 4 coaches.

Computers Computers are regularly used in English, history, mathematics, science classes. Computer network features include on-campus library services, Internet access, Internet filtering or blocking technology, library database is accessible from the website, weekly progress reports accessible for parents online. Computer access in designated common areas is available to students.

Contact Blythe Moran, Director of Advancement. 248-642-1150. Fax: 248-642-3670. E-mail: bmoran@etonacademy.org. Web site: www.etonacademy.org.

EXCEL ACADEMY, INC.

116 West Church Street
Newark, Ohio 43055
Head of School: Marlene Jacob

General Information Coeducational day college-preparatory, general academic, and technology school; primarily serves underachievers, students with learning disabilities, individuals with Attention Deficit Disorder, individuals with emotional and behavioral problems, dyslexic students, and autism. Grades K–12. Founded: 1991. Setting: urban. 1-acre campus. 1 building on campus. Approved or accredited by Ohio Department of Education. Total enrollment: 139. Upper school average class size: 10. Upper school faculty-student ratio: 1:3. There are 180 required school days per year for Upper School students. Upper School students typically attend 5 days per week. The average school day consists of 7 hours.

Faculty School total: 62. In upper school: 5 men, 6 women; 2 have advanced degrees.

Subjects Offered Accounting, algebra, American government, American history, American literature, art, art appreciation, arts, astronomy, biology, biology-AP, business mathematics, calculus-AP, chemistry, chemistry-AP, composition, composition-AP, discrete mathematics, drama, drawing, English, English literature-AP, environmental science, fine arts, French, geometry, health, humanities, journalism, Latin, literature, mathematics, music appreciation, painting, physical education, physics, pre-calculus, psychology, religion, science, social sciences, social studies, sociology, Spanish, speech, studio art, theology, women's literature, word processing, world history, writing.

Graduation Requirements Arts and fine arts (art, music, dance, drama), English, foreign language, mathematics, physical education (includes health), religion (includes Bible studies and theology), science, social sciences, social studies (includes history).

Special Academic Programs Study at local college for college credit; remedial reading and/or remedial writing; remedial math; programs in English, mathematics, general development for dyslexic students.

College Admission Counseling 7 students graduated in 2009; 1 went to college.

Student Life Upper grades have uniform requirement. Discipline rests primarily with faculty.

Tuition and Aid Tuition installment plan (2-payment plan). IEP with their local school district where the district pays tuition available.

Admissions Deadline for receipt of application materials: none. No application fee required. On-campus interview required.

Athletics Interscholastic: basketball (boys), cheering (g), flag football (b), volleyball (g), wrestling (b). 2 PE instructors, 2 coaches.

Computers Computers are regularly used in English, mathematics, science classes. Computer network features include Internet access, wireless campus network, Internet filtering or blocking technology.

Contact Mrs. Jessica Bolen, Director of Pupil Services. 740-323-1102 Ext. 32. Fax: 740-349-5834. E-mail: jbolen@laca.org. Web site: www.excelacademyohio.org.

FAIRHILL SCHOOL

16150 Preston Road
Dallas, Texas 75248
Head of School: Ms. Jane Sego

General Information Coeducational day college-preparatory, arts, and technology school; primarily serves students with learning disabilities, individuals with Attention Deficit Disorder, and dyslexic students. Grades 1–12. Founded: 1971. Setting: suburban. 16-acre campus. 2 buildings on campus. Approved or accredited by Southern Association of Colleges and Schools and Texas Department of Education. Endowment: $4 million. Total enrollment: 219. Upper school average class size: 12. Upper school faculty-student ratio: 1:12. There are 175 required school days per year for Upper School students. Upper School students typically attend 5 days per week. The average school day consists of 7 hours and 30 minutes.

Upper School Student Profile Grade 9: 23 students (12 boys, 11 girls); Grade 10: 24 students (17 boys, 7 girls); Grade 11: 25 students (17 boys, 8 girls); Grade 12: 18 students (12 boys, 6 girls).

Faculty School total: 32. In upper school: 6 men, 10 women; 4 have advanced degrees.

Subjects Offered American history, American literature, art, biology, British literature, chemistry, computer science, economics, English, government, health, journalism, mathematics, music, performing arts, physical education, physical science, physics, psychology, reading, Spanish, speech, study skills, world geography.

Graduation Requirements Arts and fine arts (art, music, dance, drama), computer science, English, mathematics, physical education (includes health), science, social studies (includes history), 60 hours of volunteer service for seniors.

Special Academic Programs Honors section; remedial reading and/or remedial writing; remedial math; programs in English, mathematics, general development for dyslexic students.

College Admission Counseling 18 students graduated in 2010; 16 went to college, including Collin County Community College District; Dallas County Community College District; Southern Methodist University; St. Edward's University; Texas Tech University. Other: 1 went to work, 1 entered military service.

Student Life Upper grades have uniform requirement, student council. Discipline rests primarily with faculty.

Summer Programs Remediation, computer instruction programs offered; session focuses on academics; held on campus; accepts boys and girls; open to students from other schools. 50 students usually enrolled. 2011 schedule: June 1 to June 26. Application deadline: none.

Tuition and Aid Day student tuition: $14,200. Need-based scholarship grants available. In 2010–11, 6% of upper-school students received aid. Total amount of financial aid awarded in 2010–11: $50,000.

Admissions Traditional secondary-level entrance grade is 9. For fall 2010, 7 students applied for upper-level admission, 5 were accepted, 5 enrolled. Psychoeducational evaluation required. Deadline for receipt of application materials: none. Application fee required: $1000. Interview required.

Athletics Interscholastic: baseball (boys), basketball (b,g), cheering (b,g), golf (b,g), soccer (b,g), tennis (b,g), volleyball (g); intramural: cheering (b,g), jump rope (b,g); coed interscholastic: cheering, golf, soccer, tennis. 3 coaches.

Computers Computers are regularly used in college planning, English, technology, yearbook classes. Computer network features include on-campus library services, Internet access, wireless campus network, Internet filtering or blocking technology. The school has a published electronic and media policy.

Contact Mrs. Melinda Cameron, Head of Upper School. 972-233-1026. Fax: 972-233-8205. E-mail: mcameron@fairhill.org. Web site: www.fairhill.org.

THE FAMILY FOUNDATION SCHOOL

431 Chapel Hill Road
Hancock, New York 13783
Head of School: Mr. Emmanuel A. Argiros

General Information Coeducational boarding college-preparatory, arts, religious studies, and character education school, affiliated with Christian faith, Jewish faith; primarily serves underachievers, individuals with Attention Deficit Disorder, individuals with emotional and behavioral problems, and alcohol and drug abuse. Grades 9–12. Founded: 1987. Setting: rural. Nearest major city is Binghamton. Students are housed in single-sex dormitories. 158-acre campus. 14 buildings on campus. Approved or accredited by Joint Commission on Accreditation of Healthcare Organizations, Middle States Association of Colleges and Schools, and New York State Board of Regents. Total enrollment: 125. Upper school average class size: 12. Upper school faculty-student ratio: 1:4. There are 250 required school days per year for Upper School students. Upper School students typically attend 5 days per week. The average school day consists of 6 hours and 20 minutes.

Upper School Student Profile Grade 9: 10 students (8 boys, 2 girls); Grade 10: 23 students (18 boys, 5 girls); Grade 11: 43 students (28 boys, 15 girls); Grade 12: 49 students (34 boys, 15 girls). 100% of students are boarding students. 40% are state residents. 22 states are represented in upper school student body. 1% are international students. International students from Canada. 97% of students are Christian, Jewish.

Faculty School total: 37. In upper school: 23 men, 14 women; 12 have advanced degrees; 6 reside on campus.

Subjects Offered Advanced chemistry, algebra, American government, American history, analysis and differential calculus, ancient world history, applied music, art, Bible studies, biology, British literature, character education, chemistry, choir, chorus, college writing, community service, dance, debate, drama, earth science, economics, English, family living, geometry, global studies, government, health and safety, health education, Jewish studies, journalism, modern dance, photography, physical education, physics, pre-calculus, religious education, Russian, sociology, Spanish, tap dance, trigonometry, woodworking, work-study, world history, World-Wide-Web publishing, yearbook.

Graduation Requirements Character education, English, foreign language, life skills, mathematics, physical education (includes health), science, social studies (includes history), New York State Board of Regents requirements, completion of character education program.

Special Academic Programs Study at local college for college credit; remedial reading and/or remedial writing.

College Admission Counseling 50 students graduated in 2010; 48 went to college, including Montclair State University; Nassau Community College; Northeastern University; St. John's University; State University of New York at Binghamton; The University of Scranton. Other: 2 had other specific plans. Mean SAT critical reading: 517, mean SAT math: 518, mean SAT writing: 502, mean combined SAT: 1537, mean composite ACT: 22.

Student Life Upper grades have specified standards of dress, student council, honor system. Discipline rests equally with students and faculty. Attendance at religious services is required.

Tuition and Aid 7-day tuition and room/board: $75,600. Tuition installment plan (monthly payment plans). Need-based scholarship grants, paying campus jobs available. In 2010–11, 15% of upper-school students received aid. Total amount of financial aid awarded in 2010–11: $500,000.

Admissions Iowa Tests of Basic Skills required. Deadline for receipt of application materials: none. Application fee required. On-campus interview required.

Athletics Interscholastic: basketball (boys, girls), soccer (b,g), softball (g); intramural: basketball (b,g), lacrosse (b), strength & conditioning (b,g); coed interscholastic: dance, golf; coed intramural: aerobics/dance, ballet, basketball, fishing, fitness, fitness walking, flag football, fly fishing, Frisbee, hiking/backpacking, horseback riding, horseshoes, ice skating, outdoor activities, outdoors, running, skateboarding, soccer, softball, tennis, ultimate Frisbee, volleyball, weight training, yoga. 3 PE instructors, 6 coaches.

Computers Computers are regularly used in English, history, journalism, science, Spanish, yearbook classes. Computer network features include on-campus library services, online commercial services, Internet access, wireless campus network, Internet filtering or blocking technology. Computer access in designated common areas is available to students.

Contact Mr. Jeff Brain, MA, CTS, CEP, Director of Admissions. 845-887-5213 Ext. 499. Fax: 845-887-4939. E-mail: jbrain@thefamilyschool.com. Web site: www.thefamilyschool.com.

FOOTHILLS ACADEMY

745 37th Street NW
Calgary, Alberta T2N 4T1, Canada
Head of School: Mr. G.M. Bullivant

General Information Coeducational day college-preparatory, general academic, and technology school; primarily serves underachievers, students with learning disabilities, individuals with Attention Deficit Disorder, dyslexic students, and Asperger's Syndrome. Grades 3–12. Founded: 1979. Setting: urban. 7-acre campus. 1 building on campus. Approved or accredited by Association of Independent Schools and Colleges of Alberta and Alberta Department of Education. Language of instruction: English. Endowment: CAN$3 million. Total enrollment: 200. Upper school average class size: 12. Upper school faculty-student ratio: 1:12. There are 177 required school days per year for Upper School students. Upper School students typically attend 5 days per week. The average school day consists of 6 hours and 10 minutes.

Upper School Student Profile Grade 9: 27 students (18 boys, 9 girls); Grade 10: 25 students (21 boys, 4 girls); Grade 11: 26 students (18 boys, 8 girls); Grade 12: 25 students (18 boys, 7 girls).

Faculty School total: 40. In upper school: 10 men, 15 women; 6 have advanced degrees.

Subjects Offered Algebra, art, athletics, basic skills, biology, career and personal planning, career education, chemistry, college admission preparation, college awareness, college planning, community service, computer animation, computer applications, computer education, computer literacy, computer multimedia, computer skills, conflict resolution, consumer mathematics, decision making skills, digital photography, drama, drama performance, dramatic arts, electives, English composition, English literature, environmental studies, expository writing, food and nutrition, grammar, health education, information processing, Internet research, interpersonal skills, keyboarding, language arts, leadership, leadership and service, learning strategies, library research, library skills, mathematics, mechanics of writing, oral communications, painting, personal and social education, photography, physical fitness, poetry, reading, reading/study skills, remedial study skills, research and reference, research skills, science, Shakespeare, short story, social skills, social studies, speech therapy, study skills, technological applications, track and field, writing.

Graduation Requirements Athletics, career and personal planning, English, English composition, English literature, expository writing, grammar, keyboarding, language arts, learning strategies, mathematics, mechanics of writing, physical fitness, reading/study skills, research skills, science, social studies (includes history), study skills, Alberta education standards.

Special Academic Programs Remedial reading and/or remedial writing; remedial math; programs in English, mathematics, general development for dyslexic students.

College Admission Counseling 24 students graduated in 2010; 18 went to college, including Macalester College; Mount Allison University; Mount Royal University; The University of Winnipeg; University of Calgary; University of Victoria. Other: 6 went to work.

Student Life Upper grades have specified standards of dress, student council, honor system. Discipline rests primarily with faculty.

Summer Programs Remediation, enrichment programs offered; session focuses on remedial reading, language, organization skills; held on campus; accepts boys and girls; open to students from other schools. 50 students usually enrolled. 2011 schedule: July 4 to August 21. Application deadline: June 1.

Tuition and Aid Day student tuition: CAN$13,000–CAN$25,200. Tuition installment plan (The Tuition Plan, monthly payment plans, individually arranged payment plans). Bursaries, need-based scholarship grants available. In 2010–11, 60% of upper-school students received aid. Total amount of financial aid awarded in 2010–11: CAN$500,000.

Admissions Traditional secondary-level entrance grade is 9. For fall 2010, 30 students applied for upper-level admission, 10 were accepted, 10 enrolled. Achievement tests, CTBS, Stanford Achievement Test, any other standardized test, math, reading, and mental ability tests, Wechsler Intelligence Scale for Children or writing sample required. Deadline for receipt of application materials: none. Application fee required: CAN$50. On-campus interview required.

Athletics Interscholastic: badminton (boys, girls), basketball (b,g); intramural: badminton (b,g), basketball (b,g), football (b); coed interscholastic: cross-country running, golf, indoor track & field, tennis, track and field, volleyball; coed intramural: badminton, ball hockey, baseball, cooperative games, cross-country running, curling, fitness, flag football, floor hockey, golf, gymnastics, handball, hiking/backpacking, in-line skating, indoor soccer, indoor track & field, jogging, kickball, life saving, outdoor activities, outdoor education, outdoor recreation, outdoor skills, physical fitness, physical training, roller blading, running, skiing (downhill), snowboarding, snowshoeing, soccer, softball, strength & conditioning, tennis, touch football, track and field, volleyball, walking, weight training, wilderness, wrestling. 1 PE instructor, 10 coaches, 2 athletic trainers.

Computers Computers are regularly used in all academic, animation, basic skills, career education, career exploration, computer applications, creative writing, desktop publishing, keyboarding, library skills, mentorship program, research skills, social studies, Web site design, word processing, writing, yearbook classes. Computer network features include on-campus library services, online commercial services, Internet access, wireless campus network, Internet filtering or blocking technology. Computer access in designated common areas is available to students. The school has a published electronic and media policy.

Contact Ms. A. Rose, Student Applications. 403-270-9400. Fax: 403-270-9438. E-mail: arose@foothillsacademy.org. Web site: www.foothillsacademy.org.

FOREST HEIGHTS LODGE

PO Box 789
Evergreen, Colorado 80437-0789
Head of School: Linda Clefisch

General Information Boys' boarding college-preparatory and general academic school; primarily serves individuals with emotional and behavioral problems. Grades K–12. Founded: 1954. Setting: small town. Nearest major city is Denver. Students are housed in single-sex dormitories. 10-acre campus. 3 buildings on campus. Approved or accredited by European Council of International Schools, Joint Commission on Accreditation of Healthcare Organizations, and Colorado Department of Education. Total enrollment: 24. Upper school average class size: 24. Upper school faculty-student ratio: 1:5. There are 180 required school days per year for Upper School students. Upper School students typically attend 5 days per week. The average school day consists of 7 hours.

Upper School Student Profile Grade 9: 3 students (3 boys). 100% of students are boarding students. 3 states are represented in upper school student body.

Faculty School total: 5. In upper school: 4 men, 1 woman; 3 have advanced degrees; all reside on campus.

Subjects Offered Algebra, American history, computer science, earth science, English, fine arts, grammar, mathematics, physical education, science, social studies, world history, writing.

Graduation Requirements Computer science, English, mathematics, physical education (includes health), science, social sciences, social studies (includes history).

Special Academic Programs Remedial reading and/or remedial writing; remedial math; programs in English, mathematics, general development for dyslexic students.

Student Life Upper grades have specified standards of dress. Discipline rests primarily with faculty.

Tuition and Aid 7-day tuition and room/board: $88,563. Tuition installment plan (monthly payment plans).

Admissions For fall 2009, 10 students applied for upper-level admission, 5 were accepted. Deadline for receipt of application materials: none. No application fee required. On-campus interview required.

Athletics Intramural: alpine skiing, aquatics, backpacking, ball hockey, baseball, basketball, bicycling, blading, cooperative games, cross-country running, field hockey, fishing, football, hiking/backpacking, ice hockey, ice skating, mountain biking, nordic skiing, outdoor activities, outdoor recreation, outdoors, roller blading, skateboarding, skiing (cross-country), skiing (downhill), soccer, softball, swimming and diving, table tennis, tai chi, tennis, track and field, walking, wall climbing, weight lifting, winter walking. 1 PE instructor.

Computers Computers are regularly used in English, science classes. Computer resources include Internet access.

Contact Linda Clefisch, Executive Director. 303-674-6681. Fax: 303-674-6805. Web site: www.forestheightslodge.org.

THE FORMAN SCHOOL

12 Norfolk Road
PO Box 80
Litchfield, Connecticut 06759
Head of School: Adam K. Man

General Information Coeducational boarding and day college-preparatory, arts, and technology school; primarily serves students with learning disabilities, individuals with Attention Deficit Disorder, and dyslexic students. Grades 9–12. Founded: 1930. Setting: small town. Nearest major city is Hartford. Students are housed in single-sex dormitories. 100-acre campus. 30 buildings on campus. Approved or accredited by National Association of Episcopal Schools, New England Association of Schools and Colleges, The Association of Boarding Schools, and Connecticut Department of Education. Member of National Association of Independent Schools and Secondary School Admission Test Board. Endowment: $5 million. Total enrollment: 182. Upper school average class size: 10. Upper school faculty-student ratio: 1:3.

Upper School Student Profile Grade 9: 27 students (21 boys, 6 girls); Grade 10: 49 students (36 boys, 13 girls); Grade 11: 59 students (36 boys, 23 girls); Grade 12: 46 students (25 boys, 21 girls). 87% of students are boarding students. 33% are state residents. 28 states are represented in upper school student body. 13% are international students. International students from Bermuda, Canada, Dominican Republic, Hong Kong, Jamaica, and Saudi Arabia; 2 other countries represented in student body.

Faculty School total: 65. In upper school: 26 men, 39 women; 33 have advanced degrees; 33 reside on campus.

Subjects Offered Algebra, American history, art, art history, band, biology, calculus, ceramics, chemistry, computer science, creative writing, driver education, ecology, English, English literature, environmental science, European history, expository writing, fine arts, French, geography, geometry, history, Holocaust seminar, human development, music, photography, physics, psychology, science, social sciences, social studies, Spanish, trigonometry, world history, writing.

Graduation Requirements Arts and fine arts (art, music, dance, drama), English, mathematics, physical education (includes health), science, social sciences, social studies (includes history).

Special Academic Programs Advanced Placement exam preparation; honors section; programs in English, mathematics, general development for dyslexic students.

College Admission Counseling 53 students graduated in 2009; 49 went to college, including Hofstra University; Montana State University; Savannah College of Art and Design; The University of Arizona. Other: 4 had other specific plans. Mean SAT critical reading: 462, mean SAT math: 427, mean SAT writing: 462, mean composite ACT: 22. 1% scored over 600 on SAT critical reading, 1% scored over 600 on SAT math, .5% scored over 26 on composite ACT.

Student Life Upper grades have specified standards of dress, student council, honor system. Discipline rests primarily with faculty.

Tuition and Aid Day student tuition: $45,000; 7-day tuition and room/board: $55,000. Tuition installment plan (The Tuition Plan, Key Tuition Payment Plan, monthly payment plans, self-funded tuition, refund plan, Tuition Management Payment Plan). Need-based scholarship grants available. In 2009–10, 25% of upper-school students received aid. Total amount of financial aid awarded in 2009–10: $1,100,000.

Admissions Traditional secondary-level entrance grade is 9. For fall 2009, 254 students applied for upper-level admission, 92 were accepted, 64 enrolled. WISC-III and Woodcock-Johnson and WISC/Woodcock-Johnson required. Deadline for receipt of application materials: none. Application fee required: $50. Interview required.

Athletics Interscholastic: baseball (boys), basketball (b,g), football (b), golf (b), ice hockey (b,g), lacrosse (b), soccer (b,g), softball (g), tennis (b,g), volleyball (g), wrestling (b); intramural: blading (g); coed interscholastic: alpine skiing, canoeing/kayaking, cross-country running, kayaking, skiing (downhill); coed intramural: bicycling, dance, equestrian sports, golf, horseback riding, kayaking, modern dance, outdoor activities, outdoor education, outdoor recreation, outdoor skills, rock climbing, skateboarding, skiing (cross-country), skiing (downhill), snowboarding, squash, tennis, weight lifting, weight training, yoga. 1 athletic trainer.

Computers Computers are regularly used in English, foreign language, mathematics, music, science, writing classes. Computer network features include on-campus library services, Internet access, wireless campus network, Internet filtering or blocking technology. Campus intranet and student e-mail accounts are available to students. The school has a published electronic and media policy.

Contact Sara Lynn Leavenworth Renda, Director of Admissions and Financial Aid. 860-567-1803. Fax: 860-567-3501. E-mail: saralynn.renda@formanschool.org. Web site: www.formanschool.org.

FRANKLIN ACADEMY

106 River Road
East Haddam, Connecticut 06423
Head of School: A. Frederick Weissbach

General Information Coeducational boarding and day college-preparatory school; primarily serves students with learning disabilities and non-verbal learning differences (NLD) and Asperger's Syndrome. Grades 9–PG. Founded: 2000. Setting: rural. Nearest major city is Hartford. Students are housed in single-sex by floor dormitories and single-sex dormitories. 75-acre campus. 18 buildings on campus. Approved or accredited by New England Association of Schools and Colleges and Connecticut Department of Education. Total enrollment: 92. Upper school average class size: 8. Upper school faculty-student ratio: 1:3. There are 180 required school days per year for Upper School students. Upper School students typically attend 6 days per week. The average school day consists of 6 hours and 15 minutes.

Upper School Student Profile Grade 9: 19 students (8 boys, 11 girls); Grade 10: 15 students (13 boys, 2 girls); Grade 11: 21 students (16 boys, 5 girls); Grade 12: 31 students (21 boys, 10 girls); Postgraduate: 6 students (3 boys, 3 girls). 94% of students are boarding students. 18% are state residents. 22 states are represented in upper school student body. 3% are international students.

Faculty School total: 40. In upper school: 20 men, 20 women; 25 have advanced degrees; 20 reside on campus.

Special Academic Programs Honors section; term-away projects; study abroad; academic accommodation for the gifted.

College Admission Counseling 21 students graduated in 2010; 20 went to college, including Guilford College; Hampshire College; Rochester Institute of Technology; University of Vermont. Other: 1 had other specific plans.

Student Life Upper grades have student council, honor system. Discipline rests equally with students and faculty.

Summer Programs Enrichment programs offered; session focuses on social skills, special interest areas; held on campus; accepts boys and girls; open to students from other schools. 60 students usually enrolled. 2011 schedule: June 29 to July 26. Application deadline: May 15.

Tuition and Aid Day student tuition: $64,500; 7-day tuition and room/board: $76,800. Tuition installment plan (monthly payment plans, individually arranged payment plans).

Admissions Traditional secondary-level entrance grade is 9. Achievement tests, psychoeducational evaluation, Wechsler Intelligence Scale for Children and writing sample required. Deadline for receipt of application materials: none. Application fee required: $75. On-campus interview required.

Athletics Coed Intramural: aerobics/dance, aquatics, basketball, bicycling, bowling, canoeing/kayaking, climbing, cooperative games, dance, fishing, fitness, fitness walking, Frisbee, golf, horseback riding, kayaking, martial arts, mountain biking, outdoor recreation, outdoors, paddling, paint ball, physical fitness, physical training, running, sailing, scuba diving, soccer, softball, swimming and diving, tai chi, tennis, ultimate Frisbee, walking, yoga.

Computers Computers are regularly used in all classes. Computer network features include on-campus library services, Internet access, wireless campus network, Internet filtering or blocking technology. Campus intranet, student e-mail accounts, and computer access in designated common areas are available to students. The school has a published electronic and media policy.

Contact Sandra Mahan, Assistant Director of Admissions. 860-873-2700 Ext. 154. Fax: 860-873-9345. E-mail: smahan@fa-ct.org. Web site: www.fa-ct.org.

FRASER ACADEMY

2294 West 10th Avenue
Vancouver, British Columbia V6K 2H8, Canada
Head of School: Mrs. Maureen Steltman

General Information Coeducational day college-preparatory, general academic, arts, technology, and BC Ministry of Education curriculum school; primarily serves students with learning disabilities and dyslexic students. Grades 1–12. Founded: 1982. Setting: urban. 1 building on campus. Approved or accredited by Canadian Association of Independent Schools and British Columbia Department of Education. Language of instruction: English. Total enrollment: 191. Upper school average class size: 8. Upper school faculty-student ratio: 1:3. There are 178 required school days per year for Upper School students. Upper School students typically attend 5 days per week. The average school day consists of 7 hours and 40 minutes.

Upper School Student Profile Grade 6: 11 students (7 boys, 4 girls); Grade 7: 22 students (16 boys, 6 girls); Grade 8: 26 students (20 boys, 6 girls); Grade 9: 18 students (12 boys, 6 girls); Grade 10: 28 students (15 boys, 13 girls); Grade 11: 22 students (14 boys, 8 girls); Grade 12: 22 students (15 boys, 7 girls).

Faculty School total: 71. In upper school: 9 men, 48 women; 6 have advanced degrees.

Graduation Requirements British Columbia Ministry of Education requirements.

Special Academic Programs Academic accommodation for the gifted; programs in English, mathematics, general development for dyslexic students; special instructional classes for Orton Gillingham tutoring program.

College Admission Counseling 19 students graduated in 2010.

Student Life Upper grades have uniform requirement, honor system. Discipline rests primarily with faculty.

Tuition and Aid Day student tuition: CAN$23,980. Tuition installment plan (quarterly payment plan). Tuition reduction for siblings, bursaries available.

Admissions Traditional secondary-level entrance grade is 8. For fall 2010, 49 students applied for upper-level admission, 48 were accepted, 46 enrolled. Academic Profile Tests, admissions testing and writing sample required. Deadline for receipt of application materials: none. Application fee required: CAN$250. Interview required.

Athletics Interscholastic: volleyball (girls); intramural: volleyball (g); coed interscholastic: alpine skiing, basketball, canoeing/kayaking, cross-country running, field hockey, flag football, kickball, martial arts, outdoor activities, outdoor education, physical fitness, running, skiing (downhill), snowboarding, soccer, softball, track and field; coed intramural: alpine skiing, ball hockey, basketball, bicycling, climbing, cross-country running, martial arts, mountain biking, rock climbing, running, scuba diving, skiing (downhill), snowboarding, soccer, softball, track and field, wall climbing. 1 PE instructor, 1 coach.

Computers Computers are regularly used in all academic classes. Computer network features include Internet access, Internet filtering or blocking technology, various learning disabilities/dyslexic-specific software.

Contact Ms. Brooke Ellison, Executive Assistant and Admissions Coordinator. 604-736-5575 Ext. 222. Fax: 604-736-5578. E-mail: bellison@fraseracademy.ca. Web site: www.fraseracademy.ca.

THE FROSTIG SCHOOL

971 North Altadena Drive
Pasadena, California 91107
Head of School: Dr. Chris Schnieders

General Information Coeducational day arts, vocational, and technology school; primarily serves underachievers, students with learning disabilities, individuals with Attention Deficit Disorder, and dyslexic students. Grades 1–12. Founded: 1951. Setting: suburban. Nearest major city is Los Angeles. 2-acre campus. 1 building on campus. Approved or accredited by National Association of Private Schools for Exceptional Children, Western Association of Schools and Colleges, and California Department of Education. Endowment: $3 million. Total enrollment: 114. Upper school average class size: 12. Upper school faculty-student ratio: 1:6. There are 180 required school days per year for Upper School students. Upper School students typically attend 5 days per week. The average school day consists of 6 hours and 10 minutes.

Faculty School total: 25. In upper school: 5 men, 2 women; 6 have advanced degrees.

Special Academic Programs Remedial reading and/or remedial writing; remedial math; programs in English, mathematics, general development for dyslexic students.

College Admission Counseling 19 students graduated in 2010; 16 went to college, including Glendale Community College; Moorpark College; Pasadena City College; Santa Monica College. Other: 1 went to work, 2 had other specific plans.

Student Life Upper grades have specified standards of dress, student council. Discipline rests primarily with faculty.

Summer Programs Remediation programs offered; session focuses on maintaining skills obtained during the regular term, work experience for high school students; held on campus; accepts boys and girls; not open to students from other schools. 36 students usually enrolled. 2011 schedule: July 1 to July 29.

Tuition and Aid Day student tuition: $26,000. Tuition installment plan (monthly payment plans, individually arranged payment plans). Need-based scholarship grants available. Total amount of financial aid awarded in 2010–11: $50,000.

Admissions Traditional secondary-level entrance grade is 9. For fall 2010, 6 students applied for upper-level admission, 3 were accepted, 3 enrolled. Admissions testing required. Deadline for receipt of application materials: none. Application fee required: $100. On-campus interview required.

Athletics Coed Interscholastic: basketball, flag football, softball, touch football. 1 PE instructor, 2 coaches.

Computers Computers are regularly used in art, basic skills, career education, career exploration, college planning, computer applications, creative writing, current events, English, geography, health, history, keyboarding, lab/keyboard, library, library skills, life skills, mathematics, media, music, occupational education, photography, psychology, reading, remedial study skills, research skills, science, social sciences, social studies, study skills, technology, video film production, Web site design, word processing, writing, writing, yearbook classes. Computer network features include on-campus library services, Internet access, assistive technology services.

Contact Ms. Jacquie Knight, IEP and Admissions Administrator. 626-791-1255. Fax: 626-798-1801. E-mail: admissions@frostig.org. Web site: www.frostig.org.

GABLES ACADEMY

811 Gordon Street
Stone Mountain, Georgia 30083
Head of School: Dr. James D. Meffen III

General Information Coeducational boarding and day college-preparatory, general academic, arts, vocational, bilingual studies, and technology school; primarily serves underachievers, students with learning disabilities, individuals with Attention Deficit Disorder, dyslexic students, and other learning difficulties on a case by case basis. Boarding grades 7–12, day grades 4–12. Founded: 1961. Setting: small town. Nearest major city is Atlanta. Students are housed in single-sex dormitories. 7-acre campus. 5 buildings on campus. Approved or accredited by National Association of Private Schools for Exceptional Children and Georgia Department of Education. Candidate for accreditation by Southern Association of Colleges and Schools. Languages of instruction: English and Spanish. Total enrollment: 18. Upper school average class size: 6. Upper school faculty-student ratio: 1:6. There are 180 required school days per year for Upper School students. Upper School students typically attend 5 days per week. The average school day consists of 6 hours and 30 minutes.

Upper School Student Profile Grade 8: 2 students (2 boys); Grade 9: 6 students (5 boys, 1 girl); Grade 10: 10 students (8 boys, 2 girls); Grade 11: 3 students (2 boys, 1 girl); Grade 12: 1 student (1 boy). 25% of students are boarding students. 90% are state residents. 3 states are represented in upper school student body. International students from Colombia, Morocco, and Taiwan.

Faculty School total: 5. In upper school: 3 men, 2 women; 1 has an advanced degree; 3 reside on campus.

Subjects Offered Acting, adolescent issues, algebra, American history, American literature, anatomy, art, arts, basic skills, biology, calculus, career and personal planning, ceramics, chemistry, choir, community service, computer applications, computer science, computer skills, CPR, creative arts, creative writing, drama performance, dramatic arts, ecology, English, English literature, fine arts, geometry, history, home economics, horticulture, instrumental music, journalism, keyboarding, mathematics, newspaper, personal development, photography, physical education, playwriting, science, social sciences, social studies, Spanish, typing, world history, writing, yearbook.

Graduation Requirements 1½ elective credits, arts and fine arts (art, music, dance, drama), English, foreign language, mathematics, physical education (includes health), science, social studies (includes history), world history, world studies. Community service is required.

Special Academic Programs Accelerated programs; independent study; study at local college for college credit; academic accommodation for the gifted; remedial reading and/or remedial writing; remedial math; programs in English, mathematics, general development for dyslexic students; special instructional classes for deaf students, blind students; ESL.

College Admission Counseling 3 students graduated in 2009; all went to college, including Georgia Perimeter College; Georgia State University.

Student Life Upper grades have uniform requirement, student council. Discipline rests equally with students and faculty.

Tuition and Aid Day student tuition: $15,500; 7-day tuition and room/board: $46,500. Tuition installment plan (FACTS Tuition Payment Plan, individually arranged payment plans). Tuition reduction for siblings, need-based scholarship grants available. In 2009–10, 20% of upper-school students received aid. Total amount of financial aid awarded in 2009–10: $30,000.

Admissions Traditional secondary-level entrance grade is 9. For fall 2009, 12 students applied for upper-level admission, 7 were accepted, 7 enrolled. Comprehensive educational evaluation or psychoeducational evaluation required. Deadline for receipt of application materials: none. Application fee required: $100. On-campus interview required.

Athletics Interscholastic: baseball (boys), basketball (b), cheering (g), cross-country running (b,g), football (b), gatorball (b), independent competitive sports (b,g), volleyball (g); intramural: flag football (b), gatorball (b), skateboarding (b), weight lifting (b); coed interscholastic: basketball, cross-country running, running, soccer, tennis, track and field; coed intramural: backpacking, badminton, bowling, canoeing/kayaking, climbing, cooperative games, fishing, fitness, Frisbee, hiking/backpacking, jump rope, kickball, martial arts, outdoor activities, physical fitness, physical training, rafting, rappelling, rock climbing, roller skating, ropes courses, running, skiing (downhill), snowboarding, softball, strength & conditioning, swimming and diving, table tennis, touch football, ultimate Frisbee, volleyball, yoga. 1 PE instructor, 1 coach.

Computers Computers are regularly used in yearbook classes. Computer network features include Internet access, wireless campus network, Internet filtering or blocking technology. Computer access in designated common areas is available to students.

Contact Ms. Katrina Locklear, Operations Director. 770-465-7500 Ext. 10. Fax: 770-465-7700. E-mail: admin@gablesacademy.com. Web site: www.gablesacademy.com.

GATEWAY SCHOOL

2570 NW Green Oaks Boulevard
Arlington, Texas 76012
Head of School: Mrs. Harriet R. Walber

General Information Coeducational day college-preparatory, general academic, arts, and technology school; primarily serves underachievers, students with learning disabilities, individuals with Attention Deficit Disorder, and dyslexic students. Grades 5–12. Founded: 1980. Setting: urban. 7-acre campus. 1 building on campus. Approved or accredited by Southern Association of Colleges and Schools, Southern Association of Independent Schools, Texas Education Agency, and Texas Department of Education. Upper school average class size: 10. Upper school faculty-student ratio: 1:8. The average school day consists of 7 hours.

Faculty School total: 6. In upper school: 1 man, 5 women; 5 have advanced degrees.

Subjects Offered Algebra, American literature, art, biology, British literature, career planning, chemistry, college awareness, college counseling, community service, composition, computer education, computer literacy, computer science, computer skills, developmental math, drama, earth science, economics, English, English composition, English literature, environmental science, geometry, government, government/civics, grammar, health, health education, history, intro to computers, introduction to theater, journalism, keyboarding, language arts, literature, mathematics, music, music performance, music theater, newspaper, physical education, pre-algebra, reading, reading/study skills, science, social studies, Spanish, speech, state history, theater, U.S. government, U.S. history, word processing, world history, world literature, writing, writing workshop, yearbook.

Graduation Requirements Computer science, English, foreign language, mathematics, physical education (includes health), science, social studies (includes history). Community service is required.

Special Academic Programs Independent study; study at local college for college credit; remedial reading and/or remedial writing; remedial math; programs in English, mathematics, general development for dyslexic students.

College Admission Counseling 6 students graduated in 2010; 4 went to college, including Lon Morris College; Tarrant County College District; Texas Wesleyan University; The University of Texas at Arlington. Other: 1 went to work, 1 entered military service.

Student Life Upper grades have uniform requirement, student council. Discipline rests primarily with faculty.

Tuition and Aid Day student tuition: $13,500. Guaranteed tuition plan. Merit scholarship grants, need-based scholarship grants available.

Admissions Traditional secondary-level entrance grade is 9. School's own test, Wechsler Intelligence Scale for Children and Woodcock-Johnson required. Deadline for receipt of application materials: none. Application fee required: $150. On-campus interview required.

Athletics Interscholastic: basketball (boys, girls), golf (g); intramural: basketball (b,g), bowling (b,g), golf (b,g), jogging (b,g); coed interscholastic: fitness walking, golf, jogging, scuba diving; coed intramural: bowling. 1 PE instructor.

Computers Computers are regularly used in basic skills, English, mathematics, science classes. Computer network features include Internet access. The school has a published electronic and media policy.

Contact Harriet R. Walber, Executive Director. 817-226-6222. Fax: 817-226-6225. E-mail: walberhr@aol.com. Web site: www.gatewayschool.com.

GLEN EDEN SCHOOL

8665 Barnard Street
Vancouver, British Columbia V6P 5G6, Canada
Head of School: Dr. Rick Brennan

General Information Coeducational day school; primarily serves underachievers, students with learning disabilities, individuals with Attention Deficit Disorder, individuals with emotional and behavioral problems, and Autism Spectrum Disorders. Grades K–12. Founded: 1976. Setting: urban. 1 building on campus. Approved or accredited by British Columbia Department of Education. Language of instruction: English. Upper school average class size: 4. Upper school faculty-student ratio: 1:5.

Faculty School total: 7. In upper school: 3 men, 1 woman; 2 have advanced degrees.

Special Academic Programs Remedial reading and/or remedial writing; remedial math.

Summer Programs Remediation programs offered; session focuses on outreach/group dynamics; held on campus; accepts boys and girls; not open to students from other schools. 20 students usually enrolled. 2011 schedule: July 1 to August 31. Application deadline: June 1.

Admissions Deadline for receipt of application materials: none. Application fee required. Interview required.

Computers Computers are regularly used in journalism classes. Computer resources include Internet access.

Contact Dr. Rick Brennan, Director. 604-267-0394. Fax: 604-267-0544. E-mail: glenedenschool@gleneden.org.

THE GLENHOLME SCHOOL, A DEVEREUX CENTER

81 Sabbaday Lane
Washington, Connecticut 06793
Head of School: Maryann Campbell

General Information Coeducational boarding and day college-preparatory, arts, vocational, technology, social coaching and motivational management, and self-discipline strategies and character development school; primarily serves underachievers, students with learning disabilities, individuals with Attention Deficit Disorder, individuals with emotional and behavioral problems, Asperger's Syndrome, ADHD, and anxiety disorders. Founded: 1968. Setting: rural. Nearest major city is Hartford. Students are housed in single-sex dormitories. 105-acre campus. 30 buildings on campus. Approved or accredited by Association of Independent Schools in New England, Connecticut Association of Independent Schools, Connecticut Department of Children and Families, Council of Accreditation and School Improvement, Massachusetts Department of Education, National Association of Private Schools for Exceptional Children, New England Association of Schools and Colleges, New Jersey Department of Education, New York Department of Education, US Department of State, and Connecticut Department of Education. Member of National Association of Independent Schools. Total enrollment: 88. Upper school average class size: 10. Upper school faculty-student ratio: 1:10. There are 215 required school days per year for Upper School students. The average school day consists of 5 hours and 45 minutes.

Upper School Student Profile Grade 6: 4 students (4 boys); Grade 7: 3 students (3 boys); Grade 8: 6 students (6 boys); Grade 9: 18 students (15 boys, 3 girls); Grade 10: 17 students (12 boys, 5 girls); Grade 11: 15 students (12 boys, 3 girls); Grade 12: 20 students (18 boys, 2 girls); Postgraduate: 5 students (4 boys, 1 girl). 91% of students are boarding students. 14% are state residents. 12 states are represented in upper school student body. 9% are international students. International students from Bermuda, Costa Rica, Hong Kong, Mexico, Switzerland, and United Kingdom; 1 other country represented in student body.

Faculty School total: 21. In upper school: 3 men, 18 women; 12 have advanced degrees; 3 reside on campus.

Subjects Offered ADL skills, adolescent issues, aerobics, algebra, art, basketball, biology, career and personal planning, career education, career exploration, career/college preparation, character education, chemistry, choral music, chorus, college admission preparation, college planning, communication skills, community service, computer animation, computer applications, computer art, computer education, computer graphics, computer literacy, computer skills, creative arts, creative dance, creative drama, creative thinking, creative writing, culinary arts, dance, decision making skills, digital photography, drama, drama performance, earth science, English, equine management, fine arts, geometry, graphic arts, guidance, health, health and wellness, health education, Internet research, interpersonal skills, keyboarding, library, life skills, mathematics, media arts, moral and social development, music, participation in sports, performing arts, personal fitness, photography, physical education, piano, play production, radio broadcasting, SAT preparation, science, social sciences, Spanish, theater, U.S. history, video and animation, world history, writing, yearbook.

Graduation Requirements Art, electives, English, health, language, mathematics, physical education (includes health), science, social studies (includes history), students must meet either Glenholme graduation requirements or the requirements of their home state, depending on the funding source.

Special Academic Programs Academic accommodation for the gifted; remedial reading and/or remedial writing; remedial math; programs in English, mathematics, general development for dyslexic students.

College Admission Counseling 20 students graduated in 2010, 15 went to college, including American Academy of Dramatic Arts; American University; Mitchell College; Pace University; University of Hartford; Western Connecticut State University. Other: 1 entered a postgraduate year, 4 had other specific plans.

Student Life Upper grades have uniform requirement, student council, honor system. Discipline rests primarily with faculty.

Summer Programs Remediation, enrichment, sports, art/fine arts, computer instruction programs offered; session focuses on strengthening social skills and boosting academic proficiency; held on campus; accepts boys and girls; open to students from other schools. 90 students usually enrolled. 2011 schedule: July 5 to August 20.

Admissions Individual IQ, Achievement and behavior rating scale or psychoeducational evaluation required. Deadline for receipt of application materials: none. Application fee required: $150. On-campus interview required.

Athletics Intramural: aerobics (boys, girls), aerobics/dance (b,g), aquatics (b,g), archery (b,g), artistic gym (b,g), basketball (b,g), cheering (b,g), combined training (b,g), cooperative games (b,g), cross-country running (b,g), dance (b,g), dance squad (b,g), dance team (b,g), equestrian sports (b,g), figure skating (b,g), fishing (b,g), fitness (b,g), fitness walking (b,g), flag football (b,g), Frisbee (b,g), golf (b,g), hiking/backpacking (b,g), horseback riding (b,g), ice skating (b,g), jogging (b,g), jump rope (b,g), kickball (b,g), modern dance (b,g), Newcombe ball (b,g), outdoor activities (b,g), outdoor recreation (b,g), paddle tennis (b,g), physical fitness (b,g), physical training (b,g), roller blading (b,g), ropes courses (b,g), soccer (b,g), softball (b,g), strength & conditioning (b,g), tennis (b,g), ultimate Frisbee (b,g), volleyball (b,g), walking (b,g), weight training (b,g), yoga (b,g); coed interscholastic: basketball, cross-country running, soccer, softball, tennis; coed intramural: aerobics, aerobics/dance, aquatics, archery, artistic gym, basketball, cheering, combined training, cooperative games, cross-country running, dance, dance squad, dance team, equestrian sports, figure skating, fishing, fitness, fitness walking, flag football, Frisbee, golf, hiking/backpacking, horseback riding, ice skating, jogging, jump rope, kickball, modern dance, Newcombe ball, outdoor activities, outdoor recreation, paddle tennis, physical fitness, physical training, roller blading, ropes courses, soccer, softball, strength & conditioning, tennis, ultimate Frisbee, volleyball, walking, weight training, yoga. 1 PE instructor, 2 coaches, 1 athletic trainer.

Computers Computers are regularly used in all academic, technology classes. Computer network features include on-campus library services, Internet access, wireless campus network, Internet filtering or blocking technology, online learning, Web cam parent communications. Campus intranet, student e-mail accounts, and computer access in designated common areas are available to students. Students grades are available online. The school has a published electronic and media policy.

Contact Stephanie Daniels, Admissions. 860-868-7377 Ext. 285. Fax: 860-868-7413. E-mail: sdaniel2@devereux.org. Web site: www.theglenholmeschool.org.

THE GOW SCHOOL

PO Box 85
South Wales, New York 14139-9778
Head of School: Mr. M. Bradley Rogers Jr.

General Information Boys' boarding college-preparatory, arts, technology, and reconstructive language school; primarily serves students with learning disabilities, individuals with Attention Deficit Disorder, dyslexic students, and language-based learning disabilities. Grades 7–PG. Founded: 1926. Setting: rural. Nearest major city is Buffalo. Students are housed in single-sex dormitories. 100-acre campus. 22 buildings on campus. Approved or accredited by New York State Association of Independent Schools, New York State Board of Regents, and The Association of Boarding Schools. Member of National Association of Independent Schools. Endowment: $8 million. Total enrollment: 142. Upper school average class size: 5. Upper school faculty-student ratio: 1:4. There are 174 required school days per year for Upper School students. Upper School students typically attend 6 days per week. The average school day consists of 13 hours.

Upper School Student Profile Grade 7: 6 students (6 boys); Grade 8: 12 students (12 boys); Grade 9: 29 students (29 boys); Grade 10: 35 students (35 boys); Grade 11: 37 students (37 boys); Grade 12: 23 students (23 boys). 100% of students are boarding students. 20% are state residents. 28 states are represented in upper school student body. 14% are international students. International students from Bermuda, Canada, Cayman Islands, Hong Kong, Japan, and Oman; 14 other countries represented in student body.

Faculty School total: 35. In upper school: 27 men, 7 women; 27 have advanced degrees; 29 reside on campus.

Subjects Offered Algebra, American history, American literature, art, biology, business, business applications, business skills, calculus, ceramics, chemistry, computer applications, computer literacy, computer programming, computer science, drama, earth science, economics, English, English literature, European history, expository writing, fine arts, geology, geometry, grammar, health, journalism, keyboarding, mathematics, metalworking, music, physics, reading, reconstructive language, robotics, science, social studies, theater, trigonometry, typing, world history, yearbook.

Graduation Requirements Arts and fine arts (art, music, dance, drama), business skills (includes word processing), English, mathematics, reconstructive language, research seminar, robotics, science, senior humanities, senior seminar, social studies (includes history). Community service is required.

Special Academic Programs Independent study; study at local college for college credit; academic accommodation for the musically talented; remedial reading and/or remedial writing; remedial math; programs in English, mathematics, general development for dyslexic students.

College Admission Counseling 23 students graduated in 2009; all went to college, including Lynn University; Savannah College of Art and Design; St. Lawrence University. Median SAT critical reading: 410, median SAT math: 460, median SAT writing: 400, median combined SAT: 1230, median composite ACT: 21. 5% scored over 600 on SAT critical reading, 19% scored over 600 on SAT math.

Student Life Upper grades have specified standards of dress, student council. Discipline rests primarily with faculty. Attendance at religious services is required.

Tuition and Aid 7-day tuition and room/board: $51,625. Tuition installment plan (FACTS Tuition Payment Plan, monthly payment plans, individually arranged payment plans). Need-based scholarship grants available. In 2009–10, 37% of upper-school students received aid. Total amount of financial aid awarded in 2009–10: $550,000.

Admissions Traditional secondary-level entrance grade is 9. For fall 2009, 46 students applied for upper-level admission, 37 were accepted, 32 enrolled. Woodcock-Johnson Revised Achievement Test required. Deadline for receipt of application materials: none. Application fee required: $100. On-campus interview required.

Athletics Interscholastic: basketball, crew, cross-country running, lacrosse, rowing, soccer, squash, swimming and diving, tennis, wrestling; intramural: alpine skiing, aquatics, backpacking, badminton, basketball, bicycling, bowling, climbing, cross-country running, fitness, fitness walking, flag football, floor hockey, freestyle skiing, Frisbee, golf, handball, hiking/backpacking, ice hockey, in-line skating, indoor soccer, jogging, jump rope, lacrosse, martial arts, mountain biking, Nautilus, nordic skiing, outdoor education, paint ball, physical fitness, physical training, power lifting, racquetball, rappelling, riflery, rock climbing, roller blading, roller hockey, ropes courses, skateboarding, skiing (cross-country), skiing (downhill), snowboarding, soccer, softball, squash, street hockey, strength & conditioning, swimming and diving, tennis, touch football, volleyball, walking, wall climbing, weight lifting, weight training, whiffle ball. 25 coaches.

Computers Computers are regularly used in art classes. Computer network features include on-campus library services, online commercial services, Internet access, Internet filtering or blocking technology, scanners, digital photography, voice recognition. Student e-mail accounts are available to students. The school has a published electronic and media policy.

Contact Mr. Robert Garcia, Director of Admission. 716-652-3450. Fax: 716-687-2003. E-mail: admissions@gow.org. Web site: www.gow.org.

HARMONY HEIGHTS RESIDENTIAL AND DAY SCHOOL

PO Box 569
Oyster Bay, New York 11771
Head of School: Ellen Benson

General Information Girls' boarding and day college-preparatory school; primarily serves underachievers, students with learning disabilities, individuals with Attention Deficit Disorder, individuals with emotional and behavioral problems, and students with psychological problems. Grades 9–12. Founded: 1974. Approved or accredited by Commission on Secondary Schools and New York Department of Education. Total enrollment: 70. Upper school faculty-student ratio: 1:12. Upper School students typically attend 5 days per week.

Faculty School total: 16. In upper school: 3 men, 13 women; 8 have advanced degrees.

Subjects Offered Art, computer science, English, general science, mathematics, music, physical education, social studies.

Special Academic Programs Remedial reading and/or remedial writing; remedial math; programs in English, mathematics for dyslexic students; special instructional classes for deaf students, blind students.

Tuition and Aid Guaranteed tuition plan.

Admissions Deadline for receipt of application materials: none. No application fee required. On-campus interview required.

Computers Computers are regularly used in all classes.

Contact Ms. Lori Neazer, Clinical Director. 516-922-6688. Fax: 516-922-6126. E-mail: ellen.benson@harmonyheights.org.

THE HILL CENTER, DURHAM ACADEMY

3200 Pickett Road
Durham, North Carolina 27705
Head of School: Dr. Sharon Maskel

General Information Coeducational day college-preparatory school; primarily serves underachievers, students with learning disabilities, individuals with Attention Deficit Disorder, and dyslexic students. Grades K–12. Founded: 1977. Setting: small town. 5-acre campus. 1 building on campus. Approved or accredited by National Association of Private Schools for Exceptional Children, North Carolina Association of Independent Schools, Southern Association of Colleges and Schools, Southern Association of Independent Schools, and North Carolina Department of Education. Member of National Association of Independent Schools. Endowment: $3.5 million. Total enrollment: 120. Upper school average class size: 4. Upper school faculty-student ratio: 1:4. There are 175 required school days per year for Upper School students. Upper School students typically attend 5 days per week. The average school day consists of 3 hours.

Upper School Student Profile Grade 9: 9 students (5 boys, 4 girls); Grade 10: 9 students (8 boys, 1 girl); Grade 11: 14 students (8 boys, 6 girls); Grade 12: 14 students (9 boys, 5 girls).

Faculty School total: 21. In upper school: 9 women; 7 have advanced degrees.

Subjects Offered Algebra, American literature, calculus, English, English literature, expository writing, geometry, grammar, mathematics, mechanics of writing, pre-algebra, pre-calculus, Spanish, writing.

Graduation Requirements Graduation requirements are determined by the student's home-based school.

Special Academic Programs Remedial reading and/or remedial writing; remedial math; programs in English, mathematics, general development for dyslexic students.

College Admission Counseling 22 students graduated in 2010; 20 went to college, including Appalachian State University; East Carolina University; Lynn University; North Carolina State University; The University of North Carolina at Greensboro; University of Alaska Anchorage. Other: 1 went to work, 1 entered a postgraduate year.

Student Life Upper grades have student council. Discipline rests primarily with faculty.

Tuition and Aid Day student tuition: $15,950. Guaranteed tuition plan. Tuition installment plan (The Tuition Plan, Key Tuition Payment Plan, monthly payment plans, The Tuition Refund Plan). Need-based scholarship grants available. In 2010–11, 10% of upper-school students received aid. Total amount of financial aid awarded in 2010–11: $46,000.

Admissions Traditional secondary-level entrance grade is 9. For fall 2010, 19 students applied for upper-level admission, 16 were accepted, 12 enrolled. WISC-III and Woodcock-Johnson required. Deadline for receipt of application materials: March 15. Application fee required: $50. On-campus interview required.

Computers Computers are regularly used in English, foreign language, mathematics, writing classes. Computer network features include Internet access, wireless campus network. Campus intranet is available to students.

Contact Ms. Wendy Speir, Director of Admissions. 919-489-7464 Ext. 7545. Fax: 919-489-7466. E-mail: wspeir@hillcenter.org. Web site: www.hillcenter.org.

HILLCREST SCHOOL

3510 North A Street
Building C
Midland, Texas 79705
Head of School: Mrs. Betty Noble Starnes

General Information Coeducational day college-preparatory, general academic, and technology school; primarily serves students with learning disabilities, individuals with Attention Deficit Disorder, and dyslexic students. Grades 1–12. Founded: 1993. Setting: small town. 2-acre campus. 1 building on campus. Approved or accredited by Southern Association of Colleges and Schools, Texas Education Agency, and Texas Department of Education. Endowment: $300,000. Total enrollment: 34. Upper school average class size: 10. Upper school faculty-student ratio: 1:10. There are 180 required school days per year for Upper School students. Upper School students typically attend 5 days per week. The average school day consists of 7 hours and 30 minutes.

Upper School Student Profile Grade 9: 5 students (3 boys, 2 girls); Grade 10: 8 students (5 boys, 3 girls); Grade 11: 5 students (5 boys); Grade 12: 5 students (3 boys, 2 girls).

Faculty School total: 10. In upper school: 8 women; 1 has an advanced degree.

Subjects Offered 3-dimensional design.

Graduation Requirements Computers, electives, English, history, mathematics, physical education (includes health), science, senior methods course.

Special Academic Programs Accelerated programs; independent study; remedial reading and/or remedial writing; remedial math; programs in English, mathematics, general development for dyslexic students.

College Admission Counseling 5 students graduated in 2010; 4 went to college. Other: 1 went to work.

Student Life Upper grades have uniform requirement. Discipline rests primarily with faculty.

Tuition and Aid Day student tuition: $8000. Tuition reduction for siblings, need-based scholarship grants available. In 2010–11, 25% of upper-school students received aid. Total amount of financial aid awarded in 2010–11: $21,000.

Admissions Traditional secondary-level entrance grade is 9. For fall 2010, 7 students applied for upper-level admission, 6 were accepted, 5 enrolled. Deadline for receipt of application materials: none. Application fee required: $100. Interview required.

Athletics Coed Intramural: badminton, baseball, basketball, fitness, flag football, football, jump rope, kickball, outdoor activities, outdoor education, physical fitness, soccer, track and field, volleyball.

Computers Computers are regularly used in all classes. Computer network features include on-campus library services, Internet access, Internet filtering or blocking technology. The school has a published electronic and media policy.

Contact Mrs. Sharel Sims, Program Coordinator. 915-570-7444. Fax: 915-570-7361. Web site: www.hillcrestschool.org.

THE HILL TOP PREPARATORY SCHOOL

737 South Ithan Avenue
Rosemont, Pennsylvania 19010
Head of School: Mr. Thomas W. Needham

General Information Coeducational day college-preparatory, arts, and technology school; primarily serves students with learning disabilities and individuals with Attention Deficit Disorder. Grades 5–12. Founded: 1971. Setting: suburban. Nearest major city is Philadelphia. 25-acre campus. 4 buildings on campus. Approved or accredited by Middle States Association of Colleges and Schools, Pennsylvania Association of Independent Schools, and Pennsylvania Department of Education. Member of National Association of Independent Schools. Total enrollment: 75. Upper school average class size: 6. Upper school faculty-student ratio: 1:4. Upper School students typically attend 5 days per week.

Upper School Student Profile Grade 10: 17 students (14 boys, 3 girls); Grade 11: 12 students (10 boys, 2 girls); Grade 12: 16 students (15 boys, 1 girl).

Faculty School total: 28. In upper school: 8 men, 5 women.

Subjects Offered Algebra, American history, American literature, art, biology, ceramics, chemistry, civics, college counseling, computer math, computer science, computers, creative writing, drama, earth science, economics, electives, English, English literature, environmental science, European history, geography, geometry, government/civics, grammar, health, history, journalism, keyboarding, mathematics, media studies, music appreciation, Native American studies, photography, physical education, physics, psychology, public speaking, science, senior project, social studies, study skills, theater, trigonometry, U.S. history, woodworking, world cultures, world history, writing.

Graduation Requirements Business skills (includes word processing), computer science, English, mathematics, physical education (includes health), science, senior project, social sciences, social studies (includes history), study skills.

Special Academic Programs Independent study; study at local college for college credit; academic accommodation for the gifted and the artistically talented; remedial reading and/or remedial writing; remedial math; programs in English, mathematics, general development for dyslexic students.

College Admission Counseling 20 students graduated in 2010; 4 went to college, including Cabrini College. Other: 1 went to work, 1 had other specific plans. Median SAT critical reading: 580, median SAT math: 530, median SAT writing: 540, median combined SAT: 1650, median composite ACT: 26. 40% scored over 600 on SAT critical reading, 20% scored over 600 on SAT math, 40% scored over 1800 on combined SAT.

Student Life Upper grades have specified standards of dress, student council, honor system. Discipline rests primarily with faculty.

Summer Programs Remediation, enrichment programs offered; session focuses on remediation, enrichment, and recreation; held on campus; accepts boys and girls; open to students from other schools. 30 students usually enrolled. 2011 schedule: June 27 to August 5. Application deadline: none.

Tuition and Aid Day student tuition: $35,775. Tuition installment plan (monthly payment plans, payment in full, 60% due June 1 and 40% due December 1, monthly payments over 10 months). Tuition reduction for siblings, need-based scholarship grants available. In 2010–11, 26% of upper-school students received aid.

Admissions Traditional secondary-level entrance grade is 10. For fall 2010, 11 students applied for upper-level admission, 6 were accepted, 5 enrolled. Achievement tests, psychoeducational evaluation, Rorschach or Thematic Apperception Test, WISC or WAIS and WISC/Woodcock-Johnson required. Deadline for receipt of application materials: none. Application fee required: $75. On-campus interview required.

Athletics Interscholastic: soccer (boys, girls), tennis (b,g), volleyball (b,g), wrestling (b,g); intramural: skiing (downhill) (b,g), soccer (b,g), tennis (b,g), volleyball (b,g), weight lifting (b,g); coed interscholastic: basketball, golf, soccer, tennis, track and field, volleyball, wrestling; coed intramural: aerobics/Nautilus, badminton, ball hockey, basketball, climbing, combined training, cooperative games, Cosom hockey, fitness, flag football, floor hockey, Frisbee, indoor hockey, indoor soccer, Newcombe ball, outdoor adventure, paint ball, physical fitness, physical training, rock climbing, running, skiing (downhill), snowboarding, soccer, strength & conditioning, team handball, tennis, touch football, ultimate Frisbee, volleyball, weight lifting. 2 PE instructors, 5 coaches.

Computers Computers are regularly used in English, mathematics, science, study skills classes. Computer network features include on-campus library services, Internet access, wireless campus network, Internet filtering or blocking technology, one-to-one student and faculty laptop initiative, online student information system, ACTIV-Boards, projectors and audio in all classrooms. Campus intranet, student e-mail accounts, and computer access in designated common areas are available to students. Students grades are available online.

Contact Ms. Cindy Falcone, Assistant Headmaster. 610-527-3230 Ext. 697. Fax: 610-527-7683. E-mail: cfalcone@hilltopprep.org. Web site: www.hilltopprep.org.

THE HOWARD SCHOOL

1192 Foster Street
Atlanta, Georgia 30318
Head of School: Ms. Marifred Cilella

General Information Coeducational day college-preparatory, general academic, arts, and technology school; primarily serves students with learning disabilities, individuals with Attention Deficit Disorder, dyslexic students, and students with language learning disabilities and differences. Grades PK–12. Founded: 1950. Setting: urban. 15-acre campus. 2 buildings on campus. Approved or accredited by Georgia Independent School Association, Southern Association of Colleges and Schools, Southern Association of Independent Schools, and Georgia Department of Education. Member of National Association of Independent Schools. Total enrollment: 232. Upper school average class size: 9. Upper school faculty-student ratio: 1:8.

Upper School Student Profile Grade 9: 26 students (11 boys, 15 girls); Grade 10: 19 students (15 boys, 4 girls); Grade 11: 23 students (18 boys, 5 girls); Grade 12: 8 students (6 boys, 2 girls).

Faculty School total: 60. In upper school: 4 men, 9 women; 11 have advanced degrees.

Subjects Offered Algebra, American history, American literature, art, biology, communications, computer science, creative writing, drama, ecology, economics,

English, English literature, European history, film studies, geography, geometry, government/civics, grammar, history, journalism, mathematics, music, physical education, physical science, psychology, reading, science, service learning/internship, social studies, Spanish, study skills, trigonometry, world history, world literature, writing.

Graduation Requirements English, foreign language, mathematics, physical education (includes health), science, social studies (includes history).

Special Academic Programs Independent study; academic accommodation for the artistically talented; remedial reading and/or remedial writing; remedial math; programs in English, mathematics, general development for dyslexic students.

College Admission Counseling Colleges students went to include Brevard College; Georgia State University; Johnson & Wales University; Lynn University.

Student Life Upper grades have specified standards of dress, student council, honor system. Discipline rests equally with students and faculty.

Summer Programs Remediation, advancement programs offered; session focuses on make-up of academic courses; held on campus; accepts boys and girls; open to students from other schools. 19 students usually enrolled. 2011 schedule: June 20 to July 29. Application deadline: June 1.

Tuition and Aid Day student tuition: $24,100. Tuition installment plan (individually arranged payment plans, 1-, 2-, 3- and 8-payment plans). Need-based scholarship grants available.

Admissions Psychoeducational evaluation required. Deadline for receipt of application materials: none. Application fee required: $150. On-campus interview required.

Athletics Interscholastic: basketball (boys, girls), soccer (b), track and field (b,g), volleyball (g), weight training (b,g); coed interscholastic: aerobics, basketball, golf, soccer, track and field. 3 PE instructors, 6 coaches.

Computers Computers are regularly used in all classes. Computer network features include online commercial services, Internet access. The school has a published electronic and media policy.

Contact Ms. Dawn Splinter, Assistant to the Director of Admissions and Registrar. 404-377-7436 Ext. 259. Fax: 404-377-0884. E-mail: dsplinter@howardschool.org. Web site: www.howardschool.org.

HUMANEX ACADEMY

2700 South Zuni Street
Englewood, Colorado 80110
Head of School: Ms. Tracy Wagers

General Information Coeducational day college-preparatory, general academic, and arts school; primarily serves underachievers, students with learning disabilities, individuals with Attention Deficit Disorder, individuals with emotional and behavioral problems, dyslexic students, and Asperger's Disorder, High Functioning Autism. Grades 7–12. Founded: 1983. Setting: suburban. Nearest major city is Denver. 1-acre campus. 1 building on campus. Approved or accredited by North Central Association of Colleges and Schools and Colorado Department of Education. Endowment: $10,000. Total enrollment: 63. Upper school average class size: 6. Upper school faculty-student ratio: 1:7. The average school day consists of 6 hours and 30 minutes.

Upper School Student Profile Grade 7: 3 students (3 boys); Grade 8: 4 students (2 boys, 2 girls); Grade 9: 10 students (7 boys, 3 girls); Grade 10: 10 students (10 boys); Grade 11: 10 students (6 boys, 4 girls); Grade 12: 26 students (19 boys, 7 girls).

Faculty School total: 11. In upper school: 5 men; 8 have advanced degrees.

Subjects Offered 1½ elective credits, 1968, 20th century American writers, 20th century history, 20th century physics, 20th century world history, 3-dimensional art, 3-dimensional design, ACT preparation, addiction, ADL skills, adolescent issues, advanced biology, advanced math, advanced studio art-AP, advanced TOEFL/grammar, aerobics, American Civil War, American culture, American democracy, American foreign policy, American government, American history, American legal systems, American literature, American politics in film, anatomy, anatomy and physiology, ancient world history, animal behavior, animation, anthropology, art, art appreciation, art history, arts and crafts, athletic training, athletics, biology, British literature, calculus, career and personal planning, career exploration, cartooning/animation, chemistry, civics, civics/free enterprise, Civil War, civil war history, college counseling, college placement, comedy, composition, computer art, computer graphics, conflict resolution, consumer mathematics, creative writing, critical thinking, current events, drawing, English, English literature, epic literature, evolution, existentialism, expository writing, film, film and literature, fitness, foreign language, general, general math, general science, geography, geology, geometry, government, government/civics, grammar, graphic arts, graphic design, great books, Greek drama, guitar, Harlem Renaissance, health, health education, history, Holocaust, honors algebra, honors English, honors geometry, honors U.S. history, honors world history, human anatomy, human biology, human sexuality, illustration, independent living, keyboarding, language, language arts, language structure, languages, literacy, literary genres, literary magazine, literature, mathematics, media literacy, military history, newspaper, non-Western literature, North American literature, novels, nutrition, peer counseling, philosophy, physical fitness, physics, physiology, play/screen writing, poetry, politics, pottery, pre-algebra, pre-calculus, psychology, public speaking, reading, reading/study skills, remedial study skills, remedial/makeup course work, research, research skills, SAT preparation, SAT/ACT preparation, science, science fiction, sculpture, sexuality, Shakespeare, short story, speech, speech and debate, sports, statistics, U.S. government, U.S. government and

politics, U.S. history, U.S. literature, Vietnam history, Vietnam War, weight fitness, weight training, weightlifting, Western civilization, Western literature, world geography, world governments, world history.

Graduation Requirements Research, speech.

Special Academic Programs Honors section; academic accommodation for the gifted; remedial reading and/or remedial writing; remedial math; programs in English, mathematics, general development for dyslexic students; special instructional classes for deaf students, blind students.

College Admission Counseling 23 students graduated in 2010; 17 went to college, including Colorado School of Mines; Colorado State University; Fort Lewis College; University of Colorado at Boulder; University of Denver; University of Northern Colorado. Other: 3 went to work, 3 had other specific plans. Median composite ACT: 24. 33% scored over 26 on composite ACT.

Student Life Upper grades have specified standards of dress, student council. Discipline rests equally with students and faculty.

Summer Programs Remediation, advancement programs offered; session focuses on academics; held on campus; accepts boys and girls. 30 students usually enrolled. 2011 schedule: June 6 to June 24. Application deadline: June 5.

Tuition and Aid Day student tuition: $17,900. Guaranteed tuition plan. Tuition installment plan (FACTS Tuition Payment Plan). Tuition reduction for siblings, need-based scholarship grants, middle-income loans, paying campus jobs, Sallie Mae available. In 2010–11, 13% of upper-school students received aid. Total amount of financial aid awarded in 2010–11: $5000.

Admissions Traditional secondary-level entrance grade is 10. For fall 2010, 10 students applied for upper-level admission, 9 were accepted, 9 enrolled. Deadline for receipt of application materials: none. Application fee required: $500. On-campus interview required.

Athletics Coed Intramural: aerobics, ball hockey, basketball, bocce, bowling, cooperative games, fitness, flag football, Frisbee, handball, kickball, physical training, power lifting, ultimate Frisbee, weight lifting, weight training. 1 PE instructor.

Computers Computers are regularly used in art, English, health, history, literacy, mathematics, philosophy, psychology, reading, research skills, social studies, Spanish, speech, study skills, writing, writing classes. Computer resources include on-campus library services, online commercial services, Internet access, Internet filtering or blocking technology. Campus intranet is available to students. Students grades are available online. The school has a published electronic and media policy.

Contact 303-783-0137. Fax: 303-783-5901. Web site: www.humanexacademy.com.

THE JOHN DEWEY ACADEMY

389 Main Street
Great Barrington, Massachusetts 01230
Head of School: Dr. Thomas E. Bratter

General Information Coeducational boarding college-preparatory and arts school; primarily serves underachievers, students with learning disabilities, individuals with Attention Deficit Disorder, individuals with emotional and behavioral problems, and gifted, underachieving, self-destructive adolescents. Grades 10–PG. Founded: 1985. Setting: small town. Nearest major city is Hartford, CT. Students are housed in single-sex by floor dormitories. 90-acre campus. 3 buildings on campus. Approved or accredited by New England Association of Schools and Colleges and Massachusetts Department of Education. Member of Secondary School Admission Test Board. Total enrollment: 20. Upper school average class size: 6. Upper school faculty-student ratio: 1:3. There are 330 required school days per year for Upper School students. Upper School students typically attend 7 days per week. The average school day consists of 6 hours.

Upper School Student Profile Grade 10: 3 students (3 boys); Grade 11: 10 students (7 boys, 3 girls); Grade 12: 7 students (5 boys, 2 girls). 100% of students are boarding students. 11 states are represented in upper school student body. 10% are international students. International students from Canada and Jordan.

Faculty School total: 10. In upper school: 5 men, 5 women; 9 have advanced degrees; 2 reside on campus.

Subjects Offered Adolescent issues, algebra, American literature, art, art history, biology, calculus, chemistry, creative writing, drama, English, English literature, environmental science, ethics, European history, fine arts, French, geometry, government/civics, grammar, health, history, Italian, moral reasoning, philosophy, physical education, physics, psychology, sociology, Spanish, statistics, theater, trigonometry, world history, world literature, writing.

Graduation Requirements American history, arts and fine arts (art, music, dance, drama), biology, English, English literature, European history, foreign language, leadership, literature, mathematics, moral reasoning, physical education (includes health), science, social studies (includes history), moral leadership qualities, minimum 18 months residency.

Special Academic Programs Honors section; accelerated programs; independent study; study at local college for college credit; academic accommodation for the gifted and the artistically talented; remedial reading and/or remedial writing; remedial math; programs in general development for dyslexic students.

College Admission Counseling 7 students graduated in 2010; all went to college, including American University; Columbia University; McGill University; Mount Holyoke College; New York University; University of Michigan. 95% scored over 600 on SAT critical reading, 95% scored over 600 on SAT math, 95% scored over 600 on SAT writing, 95% scored over 1800 on combined SAT.

Student Life Upper grades have specified standards of dress, student council, honor system. Discipline rests equally with students and faculty.

Summer Programs Session focuses on continuing college preparatory program; held on campus; accepts boys and girls; not open to students from other schools. 30 students usually enrolled.

Tuition and Aid 7-day tuition and room/board: $84,000. Tuition installment plan (monthly payment plans, individually arranged payment plans). Need-based scholarship grants available. In 2010–11, 25% of upper-school students received aid.

Admissions Traditional secondary-level entrance grade is 10. Deadline for receipt of application materials: none. No application fee required. On-campus interview required.

Computers Computer resources include Internet access. Computer access in designated common areas is available to students.

Contact Dr. Lisa Sinsheimer, Parent Liaison/Admissions Counselor. 917-597-7814. E-mail: lisa@sinsheimer.net. Web site: www.jda.org.

THE JUDGE ROTENBERG EDUCATIONAL CENTER

250 Turnpike Street
Canton, Massachusetts 02021-2341
Head of School: Matthew L. Israel, PhD

General Information Coeducational boarding general academic and vocational school; primarily serves underachievers, students with learning disabilities, individuals with Attention Deficit Disorder, individuals with emotional and behavioral problems, dyslexic students, and autism and developmental disabilities. Founded: 1971. Setting: suburban. Nearest major city is Boston. 2 buildings on campus. Approved or accredited by Massachusetts Department of Education and Massachusetts Office of Child Care Services. Upper school average class size: 10. Upper School students typically attend 5 days per week. The average school day consists of 6 hours.

Special Academic Programs Remedial reading and/or remedial writing; remedial math; special instructional classes for deaf students, blind students.

Student Life Upper grades have specified standards of dress, honor system. Discipline rests primarily with faculty.

Admissions Deadline for receipt of application materials: none. No application fee required. Interview recommended.

Athletics Intramural: basketball (boys, girls); coed intramural: aerobics/dance, physical fitness. 2 PE instructors.

Computers Computers are regularly used in all academic classes. Computer network features include Internet access, Internet filtering or blocking technology. Student e-mail accounts are available to students.

Contact Julie Gomes, Director of Admissions. 781-828-2202 Ext. 4275. Fax: 781-828-2804. E-mail: j.gomes@judgerc.org. Web site: www.judgerc.org.

THE KARAFIN SCHOOL

40-1 Radio Circle
PO Box 277
Mount Kisco, New York 10549
Head of School: Bart A. Donow, PhD

General Information Coeducational day college-preparatory and general academic school; primarily serves underachievers, students with learning disabilities, individuals with Attention Deficit Disorder, individuals with emotional and behavioral problems, emotionally disabled students, and Tourette's Syndrome. Grades 9–12. Founded: 1958. Setting: suburban. Nearest major city is New York. 1 building on campus. Approved or accredited by New York Department of Education. Total enrollment: 75. Upper school average class size: 6. Upper school faculty-student ratio: 1:6. Upper School students typically attend 5 days per week. The average school day consists of 5 hours and 30 minutes.

Upper School Student Profile Grade 9: 19 students (11 boys, 8 girls); Grade 10: 21 students (11 boys, 10 girls); Grade 11: 15 students (10 boys, 5 girls); Grade 12: 20 students (10 boys, 10 girls).

Faculty School total: 25. In upper school: 8 men, 16 women; 23 have advanced degrees.

Subjects Offered Algebra, American history, American literature, art, art history, arts, biology, business, business skills, calculus, chemistry, computer math, computer programming, computer science, creative writing, earth science, ecology, economics, English, English literature, environmental science, European history, expository writing, fine arts, French, geography, geology, geometry, government/civics, grammar, history of science, Italian, Latin, mathematics, music, photography, physical education, physics, psychology, science, social sciences, social studies, sociology, Spanish, speech, trigonometry, typing, world history, world literature, writing, zoology.

Graduation Requirements Arts and fine arts (art, music, dance, drama), business skills (includes word processing), computer science, English, foreign language, mathematics, physical education (includes health), science, social sciences, social studies (includes history).

Special Academic Programs 1 Advanced Placement exam for which test preparation is offered; academic accommodation for the gifted, the musically talented, and the

artistically talented; remedial reading and/or remedial writing; remedial math; programs in English, mathematics, general development for dyslexic students; special instructional classes for deaf students.

College Admission Counseling 20 students graduated in 2010; 15 went to college, including City College of the City University of New York; John Jay College of Criminal Justice of the City University of New York; Manhattanville College. Other: 4 went to work, 1 entered a postgraduate year. Mean SAT critical reading: 500, mean SAT math: 550, mean SAT writing: 500.

Student Life Upper grades have student council. Discipline rests primarily with faculty.

Tuition and Aid Day student tuition: $27,945. Tuition installment plan (monthly payment plans).

Admissions Traditional secondary-level entrance grade is 9. For fall 2010, 300 students applied for upper-level admission, 50 were accepted, 25 enrolled. Deadline for receipt of application materials: none. No application fee required. On-campus interview required.

Athletics Coed Intramural: aerobics, aerobics/dance, archery, badminton, ball hockey, baseball, basketball, billiards, bowling, cooperative games, fitness, fitness walking, floor hockey, football, Frisbee, golf, gymnastics, jump rope, kickball, paddle tennis, physical fitness, physical training, pillo polo, power lifting, project adventure, racquetball, soccer, strength & conditioning, table tennis, team handball, tennis, touch football, volleyball, weight lifting, whiffle ball, wrestling. 1 PE instructor.

Computers Computers are regularly used in all academic classes. Computer resources include Internet access, Internet filtering or blocking technology. The school has a published electronic and media policy.

Contact Bart A. Donow, PhD, Director. 914-666-9211. Fax: 914-666-9868. E-mail: karafin@optonline.net. Web site: www.karafinschool.com.

KEY SCHOOL

3947 East Loop 820 South
Fort Worth, Texas 76119
Head of School: Mary Ann Key

General Information Coeducational day college-preparatory, general academic, and technology school; primarily serves underachievers. Grades K–12. Founded: 1966. Setting: suburban. Nearest major city is Dallas. 2-acre campus. 1 building on campus. Approved or accredited by Council of Accreditation and School Improvement, European Council of International Schools, Southern Association of Colleges and Schools, and Texas Department of Education. Total enrollment: 76. Upper school average class size: 8. Upper school faculty-student ratio: 1:4. There are 140 required school days per year for Upper School students. Upper School students typically attend 4 days per week. The average school day consists of 6 hours and 45 minutes.

Upper School Student Profile Grade 9: 6 students (4 boys, 2 girls); Grade 10: 5 students (1 boy, 4 girls); Grade 11: 5 students (4 boys, 1 girl); Grade 12: 7 students (5 boys, 2 girls).

Faculty School total: 35. In upper school: 6 men, 29 women; 7 have advanced degrees.

Subjects Offered Algebra, art history, aviation, biology, chemistry, composition, computer applications, current events, desktop publishing, economics, electives, English, French, geometry, German, government, grammar, journalism, keyboarding, life science, life skills, literature, mathematics, mechanics of writing, novels, physical science, physics, pre-algebra, pre-calculus, reading, reading/study skills, SAT/ACT preparation, science, science fiction, Shakespeare, social studies, Spanish, speech, speech communications, study skills, Texas history, U.S. history, world geography, world history, yearbook.

Graduation Requirements Graduation speech.

Special Academic Programs Study at local college for college credit; remedial reading and/or remedial writing; remedial math; programs in English, mathematics, general development for dyslexic students; special instructional classes for students with academic deficits, speech and auditory deficits, and ADD/ADHD; ESL.

College Admission Counseling 13 students graduated in 2010; 11 went to college, including Tarrant County College District. Other: 1 went to work, 1 entered a postgraduate year. Median SAT critical reading: 420, median SAT math: 490, median SAT writing: 410.

Student Life Upper grades have specified standards of dress, honor system. Discipline rests primarily with faculty.

Summer Programs Remediation, enrichment, advancement, computer instruction programs offered; session focuses on academic enrichment; held on campus; accepts boys and girls; open to students from other schools. 125 students usually enrolled. 2011 schedule: June 6 to June 30. Application deadline: none.

Tuition and Aid Tuition installment plan (monthly payment plans, quarterly and semester payment plans). Need-based tuition assistance available. In 2010–11, 22% of upper-school students received aid. Total amount of financial aid awarded in 2010–11: $31,250.

Admissions Traditional secondary-level entrance grade is 9. For fall 2010, 3 students applied for upper-level admission, 2 were accepted, 2 enrolled. Deadline for receipt of application materials: none. No application fee required. On-campus interview required.

Computers Computers are regularly used in desktop publishing, journalism, keyboarding, newspaper, writing, yearbook classes. Computer network features include

Internet access, wireless campus network, Internet filtering or blocking technology. The school has a published electronic and media policy.

Contact Patricia Banks, Registrar. 817-446-3738. Fax: 817-446-8471. E-mail: registrar@ksfw.org. Web site: www.keyschoolfortworth.org.

KILDONAN SCHOOL

425 Morse Hill Road
Amenia, New York 12501
Head of School: Benjamin N. Powers

General Information Coeducational boarding and day college-preparatory, general academic, arts, and technology school; primarily serves students with learning disabilities, dyslexic students, and language-based learning differences. Boarding grades 7–PG, day grades 2–PG. Founded: 1969. Setting: rural. Nearest major city is New York. Students are housed in single-sex dormitories. 350-acre campus. 19 buildings on campus. Approved or accredited by Academy of Orton-Gillingham Practitioners and Educators, New York State Association of Independent Schools, The Association of Boarding Schools, and New York Department of Education. Member of National Association of Independent Schools and Secondary School Admission Test Board. Endowment: $579,300. Total enrollment: 91. Upper school average class size: 8. Upper school faculty-student ratio: 1:2. The average school day consists of 7 hours.

Upper School Student Profile Grade 6: 5 students (1 boy, 4 girls); Grade 7: 8 students (5 boys, 3 girls); Grade 8: 7 students (3 boys, 4 girls); Grade 9: 12 students (10 boys, 2 girls); Grade 10: 12 students (9 boys, 3 girls); Grade 11: 9 students (7 boys, 2 girls); Grade 12: 16 students (11 boys, 5 girls). 68% of students are boarding students. 44% are state residents. 15 states are represented in upper school student body. 9% are international students. International students from Bermuda, Brazil, France, Mexico, Puerto Rico, and United Arab Emirates; 1 other country represented in student body.

Faculty School total: 56. In upper school: 26 men, 28 women; 11 have advanced degrees; 48 reside on campus.

Subjects Offered Algebra, American history, American literature, anthropology, art, art history, biology, botany, business skills, calculus, ceramics, chemistry, computer programming, computer science, creative writing, earth science, ecology, economics, English, English literature, environmental science, European history, expository writing, fine arts, geography, geology, geometry, government/civics, grammar, health, history, mathematics, photography, physical education, physics, science, social studies, trigonometry, typing, world history, world literature, zoology.

Graduation Requirements Arts and fine arts (art, music, dance, drama), English, mathematics, physical education (includes health), science, social studies (includes history).

Special Academic Programs Independent study; remedial reading and/or remedial writing; programs in English, mathematics, general development for dyslexic students.

College Admission Counseling 14 students graduated in 2010; 8 went to college, including Curry College; Landmark College; Mitchell College; Rhode Island School of Design; Xavier University.

Student Life Upper grades have uniform requirement, student council, honor system. Discipline rests primarily with faculty.

Summer Programs Remediation, enrichment, art/fine arts programs offered; session focuses on intensive academic tutoring for students with dyslexia; exciting, fun summer camp activities; held on campus; accepts boys and girls; open to students from other schools. 85 students usually enrolled. 2011 schedule: June 24 to August 5. Application deadline: none.

Tuition and Aid Day student tuition: $43,000; 5-day tuition and room/board: $57,500; 7-day tuition and room/board: $60,000. Tuition installment plan (Tuition Management Systems). Need-based scholarship grants available. In 2010–11, 46% of upper-school students received aid. Total amount of financial aid awarded in 2010–11: $300,000.

Admissions Traditional secondary-level entrance grade is 9. For fall 2010, 60 students applied for upper-level admission, 43 were accepted, 23 enrolled. Wechsler Individual Achievement Test, WISC or WAIS, WISC/Woodcock-Johnson or Woodcock-Johnson Revised Achievement Test required. Deadline for receipt of application materials: none. Application fee required: $50. On-campus interview required.

Athletics Interscholastic: basketball (boys, girls); intramural: aerobics (g), basketball (b,g), dance (g); coed interscholastic: alpine skiing, lacrosse, skiing (downhill), snowboarding, soccer, softball, tennis, yoga; coed intramural: archery, basketball, bicycling, canoeing/kayaking, cross-country running, dressage, equestrian sports, fitness, fitness walking, flag football, freestyle skiing, golf, hiking/backpacking, horseback riding, ice skating, lacrosse, martial arts, mountain biking, outdoor activities, physical fitness, rock climbing, running, skiing (cross-country), skiing (downhill), snowboarding, soccer, strength & conditioning, table tennis, touch football, walking, water skiing, weight lifting, weight training.

Computers Computers are regularly used in English, mathematics, multimedia classes. Computer network features include on-campus library services, Internet access, wireless campus network. Student e-mail accounts and computer access in designated common areas are available to students. Students grades are available online. The school has a published electronic and media policy.

Contact Beth Rainey, Director of Student Recruitment and Financial Aid. 845-373-2017. Fax: 845-373-2004. E-mail: brainey@kildonan.org.

KING GEORGE SCHOOL

2684 King George Farm Road
Sutton, Vermont 05867
Head of School: Mr. Gerard Jones

General Information Coeducational boarding college-preparatory, arts, technology, character development, and resiliency development school; primarily serves underachievers. Grades 9–12. Founded: 1998. Setting: rural. Nearest major city is St. Johnsbury. Students are housed in single-sex dormitories. 330-acre campus. 12 buildings on campus. Approved or accredited by Vermont Department of Education. Candidate for accreditation by New England Association of Schools and Colleges. Total enrollment: 60. Upper school average class size: 8. Upper school faculty-student ratio: 1:3. There are 222 required school days per year for Upper School students. Upper School students typically attend 5 days per week. The average school day consists of 8 hours.

Upper School Student Profile 100% of students are boarding students. 1% are state residents. 25 states are represented in upper school student body. 5% are international students. International students from Canada.

Faculty School total: 16. In upper school: 5 men, 6 women; 6 have advanced degrees; 2 reside on campus.

Subjects Offered Acting, algebra, American literature, ballet, biology, British literature, ceramics, chemistry, chorus, civics, communication skills, composition, creative writing, culinary arts, dance, dance performance, drama, drama performance, drawing, earth science, English, French, geometry, guitar, health and wellness, instrumental music, introduction to theater, jazz dance, jewelry making, modern dance, music performance, outdoor education, painting, performing arts, personal growth, photography, physics, play production, portfolio art, pre-algebra, SAT/ACT preparation, social sciences, social skills, Spanish, speech, stagecraft, studio art, study skills, transition mathematics, U.S. history, visual and performing arts, world history.

Graduation Requirements Arts, English, foreign language, mathematics, physical education (includes health), science, social studies (includes history), wellness.

Special Academic Programs International Baccalaureate program; independent study; study at local college for college credit; study abroad; academic accommodation for the gifted, the musically talented, and the artistically talented; remedial reading and/or remedial writing; remedial math; programs in general development for dyslexic students.

College Admission Counseling 20 students graduated in 2010; 17 went to college, including Cornell University; Hofstra University; Parsons The New School for Design; Rhode Island School of Design; Rochester Institute of Technology; Savannah College of Art and Design. Other: 1 went to work, 1 entered a postgraduate year, 1 had other specific plans. Median SAT critical reading: 600, median SAT math: 630, median composite ACT: 26. 50% scored over 600 on SAT critical reading, 50% scored over 600 on SAT math, 50% scored over 26 on composite ACT.

Student Life Upper grades have specified standards of dress, student council, honor system. Discipline rests primarily with faculty.

Summer Programs Remediation, enrichment, advancement, sports, art/fine arts programs offered; session focuses on Outdoor Programs, Credit Remediation; held both on and off campus; held at various mountain, coastal, and wilderness areas, museums, and regional cultural organizations; accepts boys and girls; not open to students from other schools. 35 students usually enrolled. 2011 schedule: July 6 to August 24. Application deadline: none.

Tuition and Aid Tuition installment plan (monthly payment plans, individually arranged payment plans). Tuition reduction for siblings, need-based loans, middle-income loans available. In 2010–11, 5% of upper-school students received aid.

Admissions Traditional secondary-level entrance grade is 10. For fall 2010, 150 students applied for upper-level admission, 55 were accepted, 45 enrolled. Achievement/Aptitude/Writing, Individual IQ, Achievement and behavior rating scale, Wechsler Individual Achievement Test, Wechsler Intelligence Scale for Children, Wechsler Intelligence Scale for Children III, Wide Range Achievement Test or writing sample required. Deadline for receipt of application materials: none. No application fee required. Interview recommended.

Athletics Coed Intramural: aerobics, aerobics/dance, aerobics/Nautilus, alpine skiing, backpacking, basketball, billiards, broomball, canoeing/kayaking, climbing, cross-country running, dance, equestrian sports, fishing, fitness, freestyle skiing, Frisbee, hiking/backpacking, ice hockey, ice skating, independent competitive sports, jogging, martial arts, modern dance, mountain biking, outdoor activities, outdoor adventure, outdoor education, physical fitness, rock climbing, running, skateboarding, skiing (cross-country), skiing (downhill), snowboarding, snowshoeing, soccer, swimming and diving, telemark skiing, ultimate Frisbee. 1 PE instructor, 1 athletic trainer.

Computers Computers are regularly used in all academic, art classes. Computer resources include on-campus library services, Internet access, wireless campus network, Internet filtering or blocking technology, unique or alternative learning styles and attention difficulties. Computer access in designated common areas is available to students.

Contact Mary Ellen Reis, Admissions Director. 800-218-5122 Ext. 106. Fax: 802-467-1041. E-mail: mel.reis@uhsinc.com. Web site: www.kinggeorgeschool.com.

KINGSHILL SCHOOL

RR 1, Box 6125
Kingshill
St. Croix, Virgin Islands 00850
Head of School: Mrs. Janie M. Koopmans

General Information Coeducational day college-preparatory, general academic, arts, vocational, and technology school; primarily serves underachievers, students with learning disabilities, individuals with Attention Deficit Disorder, dyslexic students, cerebral palsy, and Asperger's Syndrome. Grades 7–12. Founded: 1997. Setting: rural. Nearest major city is Christiansted, U.S. Virgin Islands. 6-acre campus. 2 buildings on campus. Approved or accredited by Middle States Association of Colleges and Schools and Virgin Islands Department of Education. Total enrollment: 33. Upper school average class size: 6. Upper school faculty-student ratio: 1:5. There are 180 required school days per year for Upper School students. Upper School students typically attend 5 days per week. The average school day consists of 6 hours and 30 minutes.

Upper School Student Profile Grade 7: 3 students (2 boys, 1 girl); Grade 8: 5 students (3 boys, 2 girls); Grade 9: 12 students (6 boys, 6 girls); Grade 10: 4 students (1 boy, 3 girls); Grade 11: 7 students (4 boys, 3 girls); Grade 12: 2 students (1 boy, 1 girl).

Faculty School total: 7. In upper school: 2 men, 5 women; 6 have advanced degrees.

Subjects Offered Algebra, American government, American history, American literature, ancient world history, applied arts, architecture, art appreciation, arts appreciation, athletics, auto mechanics, biology, bowling, career exploration, career planning, career/college preparation, Caribbean history, chemistry, civics, college admission preparation, college counseling, community service, composition, computer skills, computer technologies, consumer mathematics, current events, earth science, electives, English, English literature, entrepreneurship, environmental science, geography, geometry, health, health education, history of the Americas, keyboarding, learning lab, learning strategies, marine biology, math applications, music appreciation, photography, physical education, pre-algebra, remedial/makeup course work, SAT preparation, scuba diving, Spanish, world geography, world history.

Graduation Requirements Algebra, American government, American history, American literature, art history, biology, Caribbean history, chemistry, creative writing, geometry, health, physical science, Spanish, transition mathematics, world civilizations, world history, world literature.

Special Academic Programs Accelerated programs; independent study; study at local college for college credit; remedial reading and/or remedial writing; remedial math; programs in English, mathematics, general development for dyslexic students.

College Admission Counseling 1 student graduated in 2010 and went to college. Median SAT critical reading: 420, median SAT math: 420.

Student Life Upper grades have specified standards of dress, honor system. Discipline rests equally with students and faculty.

Summer Programs Advancement programs offered; session focuses on Transition Skills; held both on and off campus; held at with local businesses and exploration of St. Croix; accepts boys and girls; open to students from other schools. 20 students usually enrolled. 2011 schedule: June 18 to July 30. Application deadline: June 1.

Tuition and Aid Day student tuition: $9500. Tuition installment plan (monthly payment plans, individually arranged payment plans). Tuition reduction for siblings, merit scholarship grants, need-based scholarship grants, paying campus jobs available. In 2010–11, 68% of upper-school students received aid; total upper-school merit-scholarship money awarded: $9500. Total amount of financial aid awarded in 2010–11: $9500.

Admissions Traditional secondary-level entrance grade is 9. For fall 2010, 31 students applied for upper-level admission, 12 were accepted, 10 enrolled. WISC or WAIS, Woodcock-Johnson Educational Evaluation, WISC III or WRAT required. Deadline for receipt of application materials: none. No application fee required. Interview required.

Athletics Intramural: football (boys), volleyball (g); coed intramural: aerobics/dance, baseball, basketball, bowling, canoeing/kayaking, cooperative games, fitness walking, flag football, Frisbee, hiking/backpacking, horseback riding, independent competitive sports, kayaking, outdoor activities, physical fitness, scuba diving, Special Olympics, surfing, swimming and diving, table tennis, touch football, walking, yoga. 2 PE instructors.

Computers Computers are regularly used in all academic, animation, art, basic skills, career exploration, college planning, computer applications, independent study, music, photography, SAT preparation, Web site design, yearbook classes. Computer resources include Internet access, wireless campus network, Internet filtering or blocking technology. Computer access in designated common areas is available to students. The school has a published electronic and media policy.

Contact Mrs. Janie M. Koopmans, Director. 340-778-6564. Fax: 340-778-0520. E-mail: kingshillschool@gmail.com. Web site: kingshillschool.org.

LA CHEIM SCHOOL

1413 F Street
Portable 1
Antioch, California 94509
Head of School: Ms. Sue Herrera

General Information Coeducational day general academic and vocational school; primarily serves underachievers, students with learning disabilities, individuals with Attention Deficit Disorder, and individuals with emotional and behavioral problems. Grades 1–12. Founded: 1974. Setting: suburban. 2 buildings on campus. Approved or accredited by Western Association of Schools and Colleges and California Department of Education. Total enrollment: 20. Upper school average class size: 10. Upper school faculty-student ratio: 1:4.

Upper School Student Profile Grade 6: 1 student (1 boy); Grade 7: 2 students (2 boys); Grade 8: 8 students (6 boys, 2 girls); Grade 9: 3 students (3 boys); Grade 10: 3 students (2 boys, 1 girl); Grade 11: 1 student (1 girl); Grade 12: 2 students (2 girls).

Faculty School total: 5. In upper school: 1 man, 1 woman.

Subjects Offered Adolescent issues, American government, American history, art, basic skills, biology, economics, grammar, health, language arts, life science, life skills, mathematics, physical education, physical science, science, social studies, vocational skills, world history, writing.

Special Academic Programs Remedial reading and/or remedial writing; remedial math.

Student Life Upper grades have specified standards of dress. Discipline rests primarily with faculty.

Tuition and Aid Tuition installment plan (expenses covered by referring district and county agencies with no cost to parents).

Admissions Traditional secondary-level entrance grade is 10. Deadline for receipt of application materials: none. No application fee required. On-campus interview required.

Athletics Intramural: basketball (boys, girls), flag football (b,g).

Computers Computers are regularly used in all academic classes.

Contact Ms. Sue Herrera, Director. 925-777-1133. Fax: 925-777-9933. E-mail: sue@lacheim.org. Web site: www.lacheim.org/schools/index.htm.

LANDMARK EAST SCHOOL

708 Main Street
Wolfville, Nova Scotia B4P 1G4, Canada
Head of School: Timothy F. Moore

General Information Coeducational boarding and day college-preparatory school; primarily serves students with learning disabilities, individuals with Attention Deficit Disorder, and dyslexic students. Grades 6–12. Founded: 1979. Setting: small town. Nearest major city is Halifax, Canada. Students are housed in single-sex dormitories. 5-acre campus. 4 buildings on campus. Approved or accredited by Nova Scotia Department of Education. Language of instruction: English. Total enrollment: 65. Upper school average class size: 8. Upper school faculty-student ratio: 1:2. There are 180 required school days per year for Upper School students. Upper School students typically attend 5 days per week. The average school day consists of 6 hours and 45 minutes.

Upper School Student Profile Grade 10: 10 students (7 boys, 3 girls); Grade 11: 11 students (6 boys, 5 girls); Grade 12: 20 students (18 boys, 2 girls). 50% of students are boarding students. 40% are province residents. 6 provinces are represented in upper school student body. 30% are international students. International students from Bahrain, Barbados, Bermuda, Hong Kong, United Arab Emirates, and United States.

Faculty School total: 35. In upper school: 10 men, 14 women; 2 have advanced degrees; 9 reside on campus.

Subjects Offered Art, biology, career and personal planning, chemistry, computer science, drama, economics, English, entrepreneurship, geography, geology, history, integrated science, law, mathematics, physics, strategies for success.

Special Academic Programs Remedial reading and/or remedial writing; remedial math; programs in English, mathematics, general development for dyslexic students.

College Admission Counseling 10 students graduated in 2009; 9 went to college. Other: 1 went to work.

Student Life Upper grades have uniform requirement, student council, honor system. Discipline rests primarily with faculty.

Tuition and Aid Day student tuition: CAN$33,800; 7-day tuition and room/board: CAN$45,300. Tuition installment plan (monthly payment plans, individually arranged payment plans). Bursaries, need-based scholarship grants, Benecaid student loans (Canadian students), Globex Foreign Exchange (international students) available. In 2009–10, 25% of upper-school students received aid. Total amount of financial aid awarded in 2009–10: CAN$120,000.

Admissions Traditional secondary-level entrance grade is 10. Achievement tests and psychoeducational evaluation required. Deadline for receipt of application materials: none. Application fee required: CAN$75. On-campus interview required.

Athletics Coed Interscholastic: aerobics, alpine skiing, aquatics, archery, badminton, basketball, bicycling, cross-country running, curling, dance, equestrian sports, fitness, gymnastics, ice skating, lacrosse, running, skiing (cross-country), skiing (downhill), snowboarding, soccer, softball, squash, swimming and diving, tennis, track and field, volleyball, weight training; coed intramural: aquatics, ball hockey, basketball, billiards, bowling, cooperative games, fitness, ice skating, indoor soccer, running, strength & conditioning, table tennis, weight training. 8 PE instructors.

Computers Computers are regularly used in art, English, mathematics, science classes. Computer resources include on-campus library services, Internet access.

Contact Janet Cooper, Administrative Assistant. 902-542-2237. Fax: 902-542-4147. E-mail: jcooper@landmarkeast.org. Web site: www.landmarkeast.org.

LANDMARK SCHOOL

PO Box 227
429 Hale Street
Prides Crossing, Massachusetts 01965-0227
Head of School: Robert J. Broudo

General Information Coeducational boarding and day college-preparatory, general academic, and language arts tutorial, skill-based curriculum school; primarily serves students with learning disabilities, dyslexic students, and language-based learning disabilities. Boarding grades 8–12, day grades 2–12. Founded: 1971. Setting: suburban. Nearest major city is Boston. Students are housed in single-sex dormitories. 50-acre campus. 22 buildings on campus. Approved or accredited by Association of Independent Schools in New England, Massachusetts Office of Child Care Services, National Association of Private Schools for Exceptional Children, New England Association of Schools and Colleges, The Association of Boarding Schools, and Massachusetts Department of Education. Member of National Association of Independent Schools. Endowment: $10 million. Total enrollment: 449. Upper school average class size: 7. Upper school faculty-student ratio: 1:3.

Upper School Student Profile Grade 8: 3 students (3 boys); Grade 9: 62 students (32 boys, 30 girls); Grade 10: 74 students (49 boys, 25 girls); Grade 11: 81 students (50 boys, 31 girls); Grade 12: 85 students (57 boys, 28 girls). 54% of students are boarding students. 49% are state residents. 21 states are represented in upper school student body. 2% are international students. International students from Colombia, Mexico, Saudi Arabia, and United Kingdom.

Faculty School total: 222. In upper school: 77 men, 135 women; 139 have advanced degrees; 43 reside on campus.

Subjects Offered Advanced math, algebra, American government, American history, American literature, American sign language, anatomy and physiology, anthropology, art, auto mechanics, basketball, biology, boat building, British literature, calculus, calculus-AP, chemistry, chorus, communications, composition, computer programming, computer science, consumer mathematics, creative thinking, creative writing, cultural geography, dance, drama, early childhood, environmental science, expressive arts, film and literature, filmmaking, geometry, grammar, instrumental music, integrated mathematics, language and composition, language arts, literature, marine science, modern world history, multimedia design, newspaper, oral commu-nications, oral expression, peer counseling, photography, physical education, physical science, physics, portfolio art, pragmatics, pre-algebra, pre-calculus, psychology, public speaking, radio broadcasting, reading, reading/study skills, senior thesis, sociology, stage and body movement, study skills, technical theater, technology, television, U.S. history, visual literacy, weightlifting, women's health, woodworking, world history, yearbook.

Graduation Requirements English, mathematics, physical education (includes health), science, social studies (includes history), Landmark School competency tests, minimum grade equivalents on standardized tests in reading and reading comprehension.

Special Academic Programs Study at local college for college credit; remedial reading and/or remedial writing; remedial math; programs in English, mathematics, general development for dyslexic students; special instructional classes for deaf students.

College Admission Counseling 81 students graduated in 2010; 75 went to college, including Curry College; Lynn University; The University of Arizona; University of Denver; Westfield State College. Other: 1 went to work, 1 entered a postgraduate year, 4 had other specific plans. Mean SAT critical reading: 447, mean SAT math: 425.

Student Life Upper grades have specified standards of dress, student council. Discipline rests primarily with faculty.

Summer Programs Remediation programs offered; session focuses on academic remediation and study skills; accepts boys and girls; open to students from other schools. 140 students usually enrolled. 2011 schedule: July 5 to July 30. Application deadline: May 15.

Tuition and Aid Day student tuition: $37,300–$43,900; 7-day tuition and room/board: $51,900–$58,500. Tuition installment plan (Key Tuition Payment Plan). Need-based scholarship grants, paying campus jobs, community and staff grants available. In 2010–11, 5% of upper-school students received aid. Total amount of financial aid awarded in 2010–11: $362,041.

Admissions For fall 2010, 211 students applied for upper-level admission, 105 were accepted, 80 enrolled. Achievement tests, psychoeducational evaluation and WISC or WAIS required. Deadline for receipt of application materials: none. Application fee required: $150. On-campus interview required.

Athletics Interscholastic: baseball (boys), basketball (b,g), dance (g), lacrosse (b,g), soccer (b,g), tennis (b,g), wrestling (b); intramural: basketball (b,g), floor hockey (b), volleyball (b,g); coed interscholastic: cross-country running, golf, swimming and diving, track and field; coed intramural: ropes courses, skateboarding, skiing (downhill). 5 PE instructors, 1 athletic trainer.

Computers Computers are regularly used in all academic, programming, publishing, technology, yearbook classes. Computer network features include on-campus library services, Internet access, wireless campus network, Internet filtering or blocking technology. Student e-mail accounts are available to students. The school has a published electronic and media policy.

Contact Carol Bedrosian, Admission Liaison. 978-236-3420. Fax: 978-927-7268. E-mail: cbedrosian@landmarkschool.org. Web site: www.landmarkschool.org.

See Display on page 896 and Close-Up on page 918.

THE LAUREATE ACADEMY

100 Villa Maria Place
Winnipeg, Manitoba R3V 1A9, Canada
Head of School: Mr. Gregory D. Jones

General Information Coeducational day college-preparatory school; primarily serves students with learning disabilities, individuals with Attention Deficit Disorder, and dyslexic students. Grades 1–12. Founded: 1987. Setting: suburban. 10-acre campus. 1 building on campus. Approved or accredited by Manitoba Department of Education. Language of instruction: English. Total enrollment: 95. Upper school average class size: 10. Upper school faculty-student ratio: 1:6. There are 183 required school days per year for Upper School students. Upper School students typically attend 5 days per week. The average school day consists of 6 hours and 15 minutes.

Faculty School total: 16. In upper school: 6 men, 3 women; 3 have advanced degrees.

Subjects Offered All academic.

Graduation Requirements Algebra, biology, Canadian geography, Canadian history, chemistry, communication skills, composition, computer skills, English, English literature, geometry, life issues, mathematics, physical education (includes health), physics, public speaking, science, social studies (includes history), writing, Department of Manitoba Education requirements, Classical Studies. Community service is required.

Special Academic Programs Academic accommodation for the gifted; remedial reading and/or remedial writing; remedial math; programs in English, mathematics for dyslexic students.

College Admission Counseling 4 students graduated in 2010; all went to college, including The University of Winnipeg; University of Manitoba.

Student Life Upper grades have specified standards of dress, student council, honor system. Discipline rests primarily with faculty.

Summer Programs Remediation programs offered; session focuses on remedial reading; held on campus; accepts boys and girls; open to students from other schools. 8 students usually enrolled. 2011 schedule: July 4 to August 19. Application deadline: June 1.

Tuition and Aid Day student tuition: CAN$16,800. Tuition installment plan (monthly payment plans, quarterly payment plan). Tuition reduction for siblings, bursaries available. In 2010–11, 14% of upper-school students received aid. Total amount of financial aid awarded in 2010–11: CAN$61,000.

Admissions Traditional secondary-level entrance grade is 9. For fall 2010, 17 students applied for upper-level admission, 10 were accepted, 9 enrolled. WISC or WAIS and WISC-III and Woodcock-Johnson required. Deadline for receipt of application materials: none. Application fee required: CAN$75. Interview required.

Athletics Interscholastic: basketball (boys), volleyball (b); intramural: badminton (b), ball hockey (b), basketball (b); coed interscholastic: badminton, cross-country running, soccer, track and field, volleyball; coed intramural: aerobics, alpine skiing, badminton, ball hockey, basketball, broomball, combined training, cooperative games, fitness, flag football, floor hockey, Frisbee, jogging, martial arts, outdoor activities, outdoor adventure, outdoor education, outdoor recreation, paddle tennis, physical fitness, physical training, running, self defense, skiing (downhill), snowboarding, soccer, softball, strength & conditioning, table tennis, touch football, track and field, ultimate Frisbee, volleyball, weight lifting, weight training. 2 PE instructors, 2 coaches.

Computers Computers are regularly used in career education, career exploration, computer applications, creative writing, English, mathematics, research skills, science, social studies, writing, yearbook classes. Computer network features include Internet access, wireless campus network, Internet filtering or blocking technology. Campus intranet, student e-mail accounts, and computer access in designated common areas are available to students. The school has a published electronic and media policy.

Contact Mrs. Dora Lawrie, Admissions Coordinator. 204-831-7107. Fax: 204-885-3217. E-mail: dlawrie@laureateslanding.ca. Web site: www.laureateacademy.com.

LAWRENCE SCHOOL

Upper School
10036 Olde Eight Road
Sagamore Hills, Ohio 44067
Head of School: Mr. Lou Salza

General Information Coeducational day college-preparatory school; primarily serves students with learning disabilities, individuals with Attention Deficit Disorder, and dyslexic students. Grades 1–12. Founded: 1969. Setting: small town. Nearest major city is Cleveland. 47-acre campus. 1 building on campus. Approved or accredited by Independent Schools Association of the Central States, North Central Association of Colleges and Schools, Ohio Association of Independent Schools, and Ohio Department of Education. Endowment: $2 million. Total enrollment: 281. Upper school average class size: 11. Upper school faculty-student ratio: 1:11. The average school day consists of 6 hours.

Faculty School total: 34. In upper school: 11 men, 17 women; 9 have advanced degrees.

Subjects Offered 20th century history, accounting, Advanced Placement courses, algebra, American history, American sign language, anatomy, art, astronomy, biology, calculus, choir, chorus, college counseling, computer applications, consumer economics, creative writing, debate, drama, earth science, economics, English, English composition, forensics, geography, geometry, global studies, government, graphic arts, graphic design, health, integrated mathematics, journalism, keyboarding, language arts, Latin, law, life science, life skills, mathematics, meteorology, military history, music, mythology, painting, physical education, physical science, physics, physics-AP, poetry, pre-algebra, psychology, research skills, sign language, society, politics and law, sociology, Spanish, speech, speech communications, The 20th Century, U.S. history, U.S. history-AP, video, video communication, Web site design, weight training, world geography, world history, yearbook.

Graduation Requirements Independent study project for seniors, community service hours.

Special Academic Programs Honors section; independent study; remedial reading and/or remedial writing; remedial math; programs in English, mathematics, general development for dyslexic students.

College Admission Counseling 18 students graduated in 2010; 14 went to college, including Case Western Reserve University; Cleveland State University; Kent State University; Ohio University; University of Mount Union; Xavier University. Other: 3 went to work, 1 had other specific plans.

Student Life Upper grades have specified standards of dress, student council, honor system. Discipline rests equally with students and faculty.

Tuition and Aid Day student tuition: $17,200–$18,400. Tuition installment plan (FACTS Tuition Payment Plan, monthly payment plans, individually arranged payment plans). Need-based scholarship grants available.

Admissions Traditional secondary-level entrance grade is 9. Admissions testing required. Deadline for receipt of application materials: none. Application fee required: $100. Interview required.

Athletics Interscholastic: baseball (boys), basketball (b,g), cross-country running (b,g); coed interscholastic: golf; coed intramural: badminton, bowling, cooperative games, fishing, flag football, floor hockey, outdoor activities. 1 PE instructor, 1 coach.

Computers Computers are regularly used in all classes. Computer network features include on-campus library services, Internet access, wireless campus network, Internet filtering or blocking technology, one-to-one notebook laptop program for grades 9 to 12, laptop program for grades 7-8, school-wide social networking through Saywire. Students grades are available online. The school has a published electronic and media policy.

Contact Mrs. Janet Robinson, Admissions Assistant. 440-526-0717. Fax: 440-526-0595. E-mail: jrobinson@lawrenceschool.org.

THE LEELANAU SCHOOL

One Old Homestead Road
Glen Arbor, Michigan 49636
Head of School: Mr. Matthew B. Ralston

General Information Coeducational boarding and day college-preparatory, arts, and Experiential program school; primarily serves students with learning disabilities, individuals with Attention Deficit Disorder, dyslexic students, Attention Deficit Hyperactivity Disorder, language-based learning differences, and non-verbal learning disabilities. Grades 9–12. Founded: 1929. Setting: rural. Nearest major city is Traverse City. Students are housed in single-sex dormitories. 50-acre campus. 12 buildings on campus. Approved or accredited by Independent Schools Association of the Central States, Michigan Association of Non-Public Schools, Midwest Association of Boarding Schools, National Independent Private Schools Association, The Association of Boarding Schools, The College Board, and Michigan Department of Education. Member of National Association of Independent Schools and Secondary School Admission Test Board. Endowment: $435,200. Total enrollment: 51. Upper school average class size: 6. Upper school faculty-student ratio: 1:5. There are 165 required school days per year for Upper School students. Upper School students typically attend 5 days per week. The average school day consists of 5 hours and 50 minutes.

Upper School Student Profile Grade 9: 6 students (4 boys, 2 girls); Grade 10: 10 students (8 boys, 2 girls); Grade 11: 27 students (14 boys, 13 girls); Grade 12: 15 students (10 boys, 5 girls). 93% of students are boarding students. 25% are state residents. 9 states are represented in upper school student body. 18% are international students. International students from China, Japan, Turkey, and United Kingdom; 3 other countries represented in student body.

Faculty School total: 15. In upper school: 10 men, 5 women; 9 have advanced degrees; 7 reside on campus.

Subjects Offered 20th century history, acting, Advanced Placement courses, advanced TOEFL/grammar, algebra, American Civil War, American government, American history, American literature, anatomy and physiology, ancient history, ancient world history, animation, applied arts, applied music, art, art appreciation, arts, arts and crafts, arts appreciation, astronomy, athletics, audio visual/media, backpacking, basic language skills, biology, biotechnology, boat building, botany, British literature, business studies, calculus, calculus-AP, calligraphy, career and personal planning, career exploration, career/college preparation, cartooning/animation, ceramics, character education, chemistry, civil war history, classical civilization, clayworking, college admission preparation, college awareness, college counseling, college placement, college planning, college writing, comedy, computer animation, computer science, conflict resolution, conservation, constitutional history of U.S., CPR, critical thinking, critical writing, decision making skills, developmental language skills, digital art, digital imaging, digital music, digital photography, drama, drama performance, dramatic arts, drawing, drawing and design, earth science, ecology, electives, English, English as a foreign language, English composition, English literature, entrepreneurship, environmental education, environmental science, environmental studies, environmental systems, epic literature, equestrian sports, equine management, ESL, European history, experiential education, experimental science, expository writing, family living, fiction, field ecology, film and new technologies, filmmaking, fine arts, foreign language, general science, geography, geology, geometry, golf, government/civics, grammar, great books, guitar, history, honors English, human anatomy, human biology, human relations, illustration, improvisation, independent living, independent study, instruments, integrated arts, integrated science, interpersonal skills, jazz band, jazz ensemble, jewelry making, journalism, Korean culture, language, language and composition, language arts, languages, leadership, leadership education training, learning cognition, learning lab, learning strategies, life issues, life management skills, life science, life skills, literacy, literature, literature by women, marine biology, marine ecology, marine science, marine studies, mathematics, mentorship program, modern European history, modern history, modern world history, moral and social development, moral reasoning, multicultural literature, music, music appreciation, Native American history, Native American studies, nature study, nature writers, oil painting, organizational studies, outdoor education, painting, participation in sports, photography, physics, poetry, pottery, pre-calculus, printmaking, psychology, reading/study skills, relationships, religious studies, remedial study skills, remedial/makeup course work, SAT preparation, SAT/ACT preparation, science, science and technology, science project, science research, senior thesis, Shakespeare, silk screening, social studies, Spanish, speech, sports, statistics-AP, student government, studio art, study skills, theater, TOEFL preparation, travel, trigonometry, U.S. government, U.S. government and politics, visual arts, weight training, weightlifting, wellness, wilderness education, wilderness experience, world history, writing, yearbook.

Graduation Requirements Arts and fine arts (art, music, dance, drama), CPR, English, foreign language, mathematics, science, senior thesis, social studies (includes history), senior leadership orientation.

Special Academic Programs 5 Advanced Placement exams for which test preparation is offered; honors section; independent study; term-away projects; remedial reading and/or remedial writing; remedial math; ESL (5 students enrolled).

College Admission Counseling 28 students graduated in 2009; 27 went to college, including Curry College; Michigan Technological University; The College of Wooster; The Evergreen State College. Other: 1 had other specific plans.

Student Life Upper grades have specified standards of dress, student council. Discipline rests primarily with faculty.

Tuition and Aid Day student tuition: $24,368; 5-day tuition and room/board: $42,572; 7-day tuition and room/board: $49,853. Tuition installment plan (individually arranged payment plans). Tuition reduction for siblings, need-based scholarship grants, Beals Scholarship for legacy families available. In 2009–10, 25% of upper-school students received aid. Total amount of financial aid awarded in 2009–10: $200,000.

Admissions Traditional secondary-level entrance grade is 10. For fall 2009, 25 students applied for upper-level admission, 25 were accepted, 15 enrolled. Individual IQ, Achievement and behavior rating scale, psychoeducational evaluation, Stanford Test of Academic Skills, TOEFL or SLEP, Wechsler Intelligence Scale for Children, Wechsler Intelligence Scale for Children III, Woodcock-Johnson or writing sample required. Deadline for receipt of application materials: none. Application fee required: $50. On-campus interview required.

Athletics Interscholastic: basketball (boys), volleyball (g); coed interscholastic: dressage, equestrian sports, golf, soccer, tennis; coed intramural: alpine skiing, backpacking, bicycling, canoeing/kayaking, climbing, combined training, cross-country running, fishing, fitness, flag football, fly fishing, freestyle skiing, Frisbee, hiking/backpacking, horseback riding, independent competitive sports, jogging, kayaking, mountain biking, outdoor activities, outdoor adventure, outdoor education, outdoor recreation, outdoor skills, outdoors, paddling, paint ball, physical fitness, physical training, rock climbing, ropes courses, running, skiing (cross-country), skiing (downhill), snowboarding, snowshoeing, table tennis, triathlon, wall climbing, yoga. 1 PE instructor, 6 coaches, 1 athletic trainer.

Computers Computers are regularly used in all academic, animation, creative writing classes. Computer resources include on-campus library services, Internet access, wireless campus network, Internet filtering or blocking technology. Students grades are available online.

Contact Mr. Todd A. Holt, Acting Director of Admission. 231-334-5800. Fax: 231-334-5898. E-mail: admissions@leelanau.org. Web site: www.leelanau.org.

LITTLE KESWICK SCHOOL

PO Box 24
Keswick, Virginia 22947
Head of School: Marc J. Columbus
General Information Boys' boarding arts school; primarily serves underachievers, students with learning disabilities, individuals with Attention Deficit Disorder,

individuals with emotional and behavioral problems, and dyslexic students. Founded: 1963. Setting: small town. Nearest major city is Washington, DC. Students are housed in single-sex dormitories. 30-acre campus. 10 buildings on campus. Approved or accredited by Virginia Association of Independent Specialized Education Facilities and Virginia Department of Education. Total enrollment: 34. Upper school average class size: 7. Upper school faculty-student ratio: 1:4. There are 247 required school days per year for Upper School students. Upper School students typically attend 5 days per week. The average school day consists of 5 hours and 30 minutes.

Upper School Student Profile 100% of students are boarding students. 17 states are represented in upper school student body.

Faculty School total: 6. In upper school: 3 men, 3 women; 4 have advanced degrees; 2 reside on campus.

Subjects Offered Algebra, American history, biology, computer applications, earth science, English, geography, government/civics, health, industrial arts, mathematics, physical education, practical arts, social studies, world history.

Special Academic Programs Academic accommodation for the gifted; remedial math; programs in English, mathematics, general development for dyslexic students.

Student Life Upper grades have specified standards of dress, student council. Discipline rests primarily with faculty.

Summer Programs Remediation, enrichment, sports, art/fine arts, rigorous outdoor training, computer instruction programs offered; session focuses on remediation and therapy; held on campus; accepts boys; open to students from other schools. 34 students usually enrolled. 2011 schedule: July 3 to August 5. Application deadline: none.

Tuition and Aid 7-day tuition and room/board: $98,860. Need-based scholarship grants available. In 2010–11, 2% of upper-school students received aid. Total amount of financial aid awarded in 2010–11: $20,000.

Admissions WISC-III and Woodcock-Johnson required. Deadline for receipt of application materials: none. Application fee required: $350. On-campus interview required.

Athletics Interscholastic: basketball (boys), combined training (b), soccer (b); intramural: basketball (b), bicycling (b), climbing (b), cross-country running (b), equestrian sports (b), fishing (b), fitness (b), gymnastics (b), hiking/backpacking (b), horseback riding (b), lacrosse (b), outdoor activities (b), soccer (b), softball (b), swimming and diving (b), volleyball (b). 1 PE instructor, 2 coaches.

Computers Computer resources include Internet access. Computer access in designated common areas is available to students.

Contact Terry Columbus, Director. 434-295-0457 Ext. 14. Fax: 434-977-1892. E-mail: tcolumbus@littlekeswickschool.net. Web site: www.littlekeswickschool.net.

MAPLEBROOK SCHOOL

5142 Route 22
Amenia, New York 12501
Head of School: Donna M. Konkolics
General Information Coeducational boarding and day general academic, vocational, and technology school; primarily serves underachievers, students with learning disabilities, individuals with Attention Deficit Disorder, and low average cognitive ability (minimum I.Q. of 70). Ungraded, ages 11–18. Founded: 1945. Setting: small town. Nearest major city is Poughkeepsie. Students are housed in single-sex dormitories. 95-acre campus. 22 buildings on campus. Approved or accredited by Middle States Association of Colleges and Schools, National Association of Private Schools for Exceptional Children, New York Department of Education, New York State Association of Independent Schools, New York State Board of Regents, US Department of State, and New York Department of Education. Member of National Association of Independent Schools. Endowment: $500,000. Total enrollment: 70. Upper school average class size: 6. Upper school faculty-student ratio: 1:8. There are 180 required school days per year for Upper School students. Upper School students typically attend 7 days per week. The average school day consists of 6 hours and 5 minutes.

Upper School Student Profile 98% of students are boarding students. 15% are state residents. 24 states are represented in upper school student body. 20% are international students. International students from Bermuda, Canada, Mexico, Morocco, Nigeria, and South Africa; 6 other countries represented in student body.

Faculty School total: 55. In upper school: 12 men, 14 women; 26 have advanced degrees; 50 reside on campus.

Subjects Offered Algebra, American history, art, biology, business skills, computer science, consumer mathematics, creative writing, drama, driver education, earth science, English, geography, global studies, government/civics, health, home economics, industrial arts, integrated mathematics, keyboarding, mathematics, music, occupational education, performing arts, photography, physical education, physical science, science, social skills, speech, theater, world history, writing.

Graduation Requirements Career and personal planning, computer science, English, mathematics, physical education (includes health), science, social sciences, social skills, social studies (includes history), attendance at Maplebrook School for a minimum of 2 years.

Special Academic Programs Study at local college for college credit; remedial reading and/or remedial writing; remedial math; programs in English, mathematics, general development for dyslexic students.

College Admission Counseling 19 students graduated in 2010; 8 went to college, including Dutchess Community College; Mitchell College. Other: 11 entered a postgraduate year.

Student Life Upper grades have specified standards of dress, student council, honor system. Discipline rests primarily with faculty.

Summer Programs Remediation, enrichment, sports, art/fine arts, computer instruction programs offered; session focuses on preventing regression of skills; held both on and off campus; held at various locations for New York City day and overnight trips; accepts boys and girls; open to students from other schools. 45 students usually enrolled. 2011 schedule: July 3 to August 13. Application deadline: none.

Tuition and Aid Day student tuition: $34,350; 5-day tuition and room/board: $50,200; 7-day tuition and room/board: $54,700. Tuition installment plan (Key Tuition Payment Plan, individually arranged payment plans, Tuition Management Systems Plan, Sallie Mae loans). Merit scholarship grants, need-based scholarship grants, need-based loans, middle-income loans, paying campus jobs, minority and cultural diversity scholarships, day-student scholarships available. In 2010–11, 15% of upper-school students received aid; total upper-school merit-scholarship money awarded: $10,000. Total amount of financial aid awarded in 2010–11: $157,000.

Admissions Traditional secondary-level entrance age is 15. For fall 2010, 190 students applied for upper-level admission, 60 were accepted, 35 enrolled. Achievement tests, Bender Gestalt, TerraNova, Test of Achievement and Proficiency or WISC or WAIS required. Deadline for receipt of application materials: none. No application fee required. Interview required.

Athletics Interscholastic: basketball (boys, girls), cheering (g); field hockey (g); coed interscholastic: cooperative games, cross-country running, equestrian sports, fitness, freestyle skiing, horseback riding, running, skiing (cross-country), skiing (downhill), soccer, softball, swimming and diving, tennis, track and field, weight lifting, weight training; coed intramural: aerobics/dance, alpine skiing, basketball, bicycling, bowling, cooperative games, cricket, dance, figure skating, fitness, fitness walking, flag football, floor hockey, freestyle skiing, golf, hiking/backpacking, horseback riding, ice skating, indoor hockey, martial arts, outdoor education, outdoor recreation, roller blading, skiing (cross-country), skiing (downhill), soccer, softball, Special Olympics, swimming and diving, table tennis, tennis, volleyball, weight lifting, weight training, wrestling. 1 PE instructor, 12 coaches.

Computers Computers are regularly used in all academic classes. Computer network features include on-campus library services, Internet access, wireless campus network, Internet filtering or blocking technology. Campus intranet, student e-mail accounts, and computer access in designated common areas are available to students. Students grades are available online. The school has a published electronic and media policy.

Contact Jennifer L. Scully, Dean of Admissions. 845-373-8191. Fax: 845-373-7029. E-mail: admissions@maplebrookschool.org. Web site: www.maplebrookschool.org.

MONTANA ACADEMY

9705 Lost Prairie Road
Marion, Montana 59925

Head of School: Dr. John Alson McKinnon

General Information Coeducational boarding arts and vocational school; primarily serves underachievers, students with learning disabilities, individuals with Attention Deficit Disorder, and individuals with emotional and behavioral problems. Ungraded, ages 14–18. Founded: 1997. Setting: rural. Nearest major city is Kalispell. Students are housed in single-sex dormitories. 300-acre campus. 8 buildings on campus. Approved or accredited by Joint Commission on Accreditation of Healthcare Organizations, Northwest Accreditation Commission, and Northwest Association of Schools and Colleges. Total enrollment: 70. Upper school average class size: 12. Upper school faculty-student ratio: 1:2.

Upper School Student Profile 100% of students are boarding students. 31 states are represented in upper school student body. 2% are international students.

Faculty School total: 9. In upper school: 4 men, 4 women; 8 have advanced degrees; 6 reside on campus.

Subjects Offered Algebra, American government, American history, American literature, art, biology, British literature, creative writing, current events, English, field ecology, geometry, health science, literature, mathematics, music, outdoor education, physical science, political science, pre-calculus, reading, reading/study skills, remedial study skills, research skills, SAT preparation, social studies, speech communications, substance abuse, U.S. government and politics, work experience, world history, world literature, writing, zoology.

Graduation Requirements Completion of emotional growth program.

Special Academic Programs Advanced Placement exam preparation; honors section; independent study; study at local college for college credit; academic accommodation for the gifted; remedial reading and/or remedial writing.

College Admission Counseling 40 students graduated in 2009; 17 went to college, including Bucknell University; Stanford University; Texas A&M University; The George Washington University; Willamette University. Other: 23 had other specific plans.

Student Life Upper grades have specified standards of dress, student council, honor system. Discipline rests primarily with faculty.

Tuition and Aid 7-day tuition and room/board: $70,000. Guaranteed tuition plan. Tuition installment plan (monthly payment plans). Financial aid available to upper-school students. In 2009–10, 8% of upper-school students received aid. Total amount of financial aid awarded in 2009–10: $40,000.

Admissions Traditional secondary-level entrance age is 14. Psychoeducational evaluation, Rorschach or Thematic Apperception Test, WISC-R or WISC-III or Woodcock-Johnson required. Deadline for receipt of application materials: none. Application fee required: $1000.

Athletics Interscholastic: soccer (boys, girls); coed interscholastic: cross-country running; coed intramural: aerobics, alpine skiing, backpacking, baseball, basketball, bicycling, canoeing/kayaking, climbing, cooperative games, cross-country running, dance, dressage, equestrian sports, fitness, fitness walking, flag football, fly fishing, hiking/backpacking, horseback riding, ice hockey, ice skating, mountain biking, nordic skiing, outdoor activities, physical fitness, rafting, rappelling, rock climbing, ropes courses, running, skiing (cross-country), skiing (downhill), snowboarding, snowshoeing, soccer, softball, swimming and diving, volleyball, walking, weight training, wilderness survival, winter walking, yoga.

Computers Computers are regularly used in research skills classes. Computer resources include Internet access, Internet filtering or blocking technology.

Contact Mrs. Rosemary Eileen McKinnon, Director of Admissions. 406-755-3149. Fax: 406-755-3150. E-mail: rosemarym@montanaacademy.com. Web site: www.montanaacademy.com.

NAWA ACADEMY

17351 Trinity Mountain Road
French Gulch, California 96033

Head of School: David W. Hull

General Information Coeducational boarding college-preparatory, general academic, arts, vocational, and technology school; primarily serves underachievers, students with learning disabilities, individuals with Attention Deficit Disorder, dyslexic students, and time management, motivational and organizational problems. Grades 7–12. Founded: 1988. Setting: rural. Nearest major city is Redding. Students are housed in single-sex dormitories. 556-acre campus. 16 buildings on campus. Approved or accredited by Western Association of Schools and Colleges and California Department of Education. Languages of instruction: English and Spanish. Total enrollment: 50. Upper school average class size: 8. Upper school faculty-student ratio: 1:8. The average school day consists of 7 hours.

Upper School Student Profile Grade 9: 2 students (2 boys); Grade 10: 8 students (5 boys, 3 girls); Grade 11: 17 students (15 boys, 2 girls); Grade 12: 14 students (10 boys, 4 girls). 100% of students are boarding students. 55% are state residents. 14 states are represented in upper school student body. International students from China; 2 other countries represented in student body.

Faculty School total: 12. In upper school: 4 men, 6 women; 3 have advanced degrees.

Subjects Offered ACT preparation, advanced math, algebra, alternative physical education, American literature, art, ASB Leadership, biology, calculus, chemistry, college counseling, composition, computers, earth science, economics, electives, English, ESL, experiential education, foods, forest resources, forestry, gender issues, geography, geometry, health, health education, language, language arts, leadership, learning lab, life science, life skills, mathematics, metalworking, music appreciation, outdoor education, photography, physics, post-calculus, pre-algebra, pre-calculus, research, SAT preparation, SAT/ACT preparation, Spanish, training, travel, trigonometry, U.S. government, U.S. history, welding, wilderness education, wilderness experience, world literature.

Graduation Requirements Satisfactory completion of community service program, completion of one EdVenture outdoor education course.

Special Academic Programs Accelerated programs; term-away projects; study abroad; remedial reading and/or remedial writing; remedial math; programs in English, mathematics, general development for dyslexic students; ESL.

College Admission Counseling 20 students graduated in 2009; 18 went to college. Other: 2 went to work.

Student Life Upper grades have specified standards of dress, student council, honor system. Discipline rests equally with students and faculty.

Tuition and Aid 7-day tuition and room/board: $33,600. Guaranteed tuition plan. Tuition installment plan (Key Tuition Payment Plan, monthly payment plans, individually arranged payment plans). Tuition reduction for siblings, need-based scholarship grants, Sallie Mae loans, Key Bank loans available. In 2009–10, 25% of upper-school students received aid. Total amount of financial aid awarded in 2009–10: $80,000.

Admissions Traditional secondary-level entrance grade is 9. For fall 2009, 70 students applied for upper-level admission, 50 were accepted. Deadline for receipt of application materials: none. Application fee required: $1000. Interview required.

Athletics Coed Interscholastic: snowboarding; coed intramural: aerobics, alpine skiing, aquatics, archery, backpacking, badminton, basketball, bicycling, billiards, bowling, canoeing/kayaking, climbing, combined training, cooperative games, cross-country running, dance, fishing, fitness, fitness walking, flag football, fly fishing, football, freestyle skiing, Frisbee, hiking/backpacking, horseshoes, independent competitive sports, jogging, jump rope, kayaking, life saving, modern dance, mountain biking, mountaineering, nordic skiing, outdoor activities, outdoor adventure, outdoor education, outdoor recreation, outdoor skills, outdoors, paddle tennis, paddling, paint ball, physical fitness, physical training, power lifting, project adventure, rafting, rappelling, rock climbing, roller blading, roller hockey, ropes courses, running, sailing, skateboarding, skiing (cross-country), skiing (downhill), snowboarding, snowshoeing, soccer, softball, speleology, strength & conditioning, surfing, swimming and diving, table tennis, telemark skiing, touch football, triathlon, ultimate Frisbee, volleyball, walking, wall climbing, water skiing, weight lifting, weight training, wilderness, wilderness survival, wildernessways, windsurfing, winter (indoor) track, winter walking. 8 PE instructors, 4 coaches, 5 athletic trainers.

Computers Computers are regularly used in all classes. Computer network features include on-campus library services, Internet access.

Contact Jason T. Hull, Summer Director. 800-358-6292. Fax: 530-359-2229. E-mail: jason.hull@nawaacademy.org. Web site: www.nawaacademy.org.

NEW HORIZON YOUTH MINISTRIES

1002 South 350 East
Marion, Indiana 46953
Head of School: Dr. Charles P. Redwine

General Information Coeducational boarding and day college-preparatory, general academic, vocational, religious studies, and bilingual studies school, affiliated with Christian faith, Evangelical faith; primarily serves underachievers, students with learning disabilities, individuals with Attention Deficit Disorder, individuals with emotional and behavioral problems, dyslexic students, and Attention Deficit Hyperactivity Disorder. Grades 7–12. Founded: 1983. Setting: rural. Nearest major city is Indianapolis. Students are housed in single-sex dormitories. 180-acre campus. 11 buildings on campus. Approved or accredited by Association of Christian Schools International, North Central Association of Colleges and Schools, and Indiana Department of Education. Total enrollment: 26. Upper school average class size: 6. Upper school faculty-student ratio: 1:4. There are 180 required school days per year for Upper School students. Upper School students typically attend 5 days per week. The average school day consists of 8 hours.

Upper School Student Profile Grade 9: 5 students (1 boy, 4 girls); Grade 10: 4 students (1 boy, 3 girls); Grade 11: 10 students (6 boys, 4 girls); Grade 12: 7 students (5 boys, 2 girls). 85% of students are boarding students. 15% are state residents. 19 states are represented in upper school student body. 85% of students are Christian, members of Evangelical faith.

Faculty School total: 10. In upper school: 5 men, 5 women; 2 have advanced degrees; 6 reside on campus.

Subjects Offered Addiction, adolescent issues, algebra, American government, American literature, Bible studies, biology, Christian education, Christian ethics, Christian scripture, Christianity, decision making skills, economics, English, English composition, ethics, ethics and responsibility, general math, geography, geometry, government, grammar, health, history, math applications, pre-algebra, science, social studies, U.S. history, wilderness education, world history.

Graduation Requirements Economics, English, foreign language, government, keyboarding, life management skills, mathematics, physical education (includes health), religious studies, science, social studies (includes history), U.S. history, world geography, world history, Indiana State graduation requirements, group problem solving.

Special Academic Programs Accelerated programs; study at local college for college credit; study abroad; academic accommodation for the gifted, the musically talented, and the artistically talented.

College Admission Counseling 2 students graduated in 2009; 1 went to college, including Indiana Wesleyan University. Other: 1 entered military service. Median SAT critical reading: 600, median SAT math: 630, median SAT writing: 570.

Student Life Upper grades have uniform requirement, honor system. Discipline rests equally with students and faculty. Attendance at religious services is required.

Tuition and Aid 7-day tuition and room/board: $6200. Guaranteed tuition plan. Tuition installment plan (monthly payment plans). Tuition reduction for siblings, need-based scholarship grants available. In 2009–10, 86% of upper-school students received aid. Total amount of financial aid awarded in 2009–10: $710,106.

Admissions Traditional secondary-level entrance grade is 10. Deadline for receipt of application materials: none. No application fee required.

Athletics Intramural: aerobics (boys, girls), aerobics/dance (g), backpacking (b,g), basketball (b,g), canoeing/kayaking (b,g), climbing (b,g), combined training (b,g), cooperative games (b,g), fitness (b,g), fitness walking (g), flag football (b), Frisbee (b,g), gatorball (b,g), hiking/backpacking (b,g), kickball (b,g), outdoor activities (b,g), outdoor education (b,g), outdoor skills (b,g), physical fitness (b,g), physical training (b,g), ropes courses (b,g), soccer (b,g), softball (b,g), strength & conditioning (b,g), team handball (b,g), track and field (b,g), ultimate Frisbee (b,g), volleyball (b,g), walking (b,g), weight lifting (b,g), weight training (b,g), whiffle ball (b,g), wilderness (b,g), wilderness survival (b,g); coed intramural: outdoor activities, physical fitness, ropes courses, soccer, wilderness. 1 PE instructor.

Computers Computer network features include on-campus library services, Internet access, wireless campus network, Internet filtering or blocking technology. Students grades are available online. The school has a published electronic and media policy.

Contact Zac Blossom. 800-333-4009. Fax: 765-662-1407. E-mail: admissions@nhym.org. Web site: www.nhym.org.

NEW WAY LEARNING ACADEMY

1300 North 77th Street
Scottsdale, Arizona 85257
Head of School: Dawn T. Gutierrez

General Information Coeducational day college-preparatory, general academic, vocational, technology, and reading and language therapy school; primarily serves students with learning disabilities, individuals with Attention Deficit Disorder, dyslexic students, and speech and language delays. Grades K–12. Founded: 1968. Setting: suburban. Nearest major city is Phoenix. 2-acre campus. 2 buildings on campus. Approved or accredited by Arizona Association of Independent Schools, North Central Association of Colleges and Schools, and Arizona Department of Education. Total enrollment: 101. Upper school average class size: 10. Upper school faculty-student ratio: 1:8. There are 180 required school days per year for Upper School students. Upper School students typically attend 5 days per week. The average school day consists of 5 hours and 50 minutes.

Upper School Student Profile Grade 7: 11 students (7 boys, 4 girls); Grade 8: 13 students (10 boys, 3 girls); Grade 9: 8 students (6 boys, 2 girls); Grade 10: 8 students (4 boys, 4 girls); Grade 11: 8 students (7 boys, 1 girl); Grade 12: 10 students (4 boys, 6 girls).

Faculty School total: 28. In upper school: 2 men, 8 women; 8 have advanced degrees.

Special Academic Programs Independent study; study at local college for college credit; remedial reading and/or remedial writing; remedial math; programs in English, mathematics, general development for dyslexic students.

College Admission Counseling 8 students graduated in 2009; 4 went to college, including Arizona State University; Landmark College; Northern Arizona University. Other: 2 went to work, 2 had other specific plans.

Student Life Upper grades have specified standards of dress, student council. Discipline rests primarily with faculty.

Tuition and Aid Day student tuition: $18,750. Tuition installment plan (monthly payment plans, individually arranged payment plans). Need-based scholarship grants available. In 2009–10, 8% of upper-school students received aid. Total amount of financial aid awarded in 2009–10: $155,000.

Admissions Traditional secondary-level entrance grade is 9. For fall 2009, 14 students applied for upper-level admission, 7 were accepted, 5 enrolled. WISC/Woodcock-Johnson required. Deadline for receipt of application materials: none. Application fee required: $100. On-campus interview required.

Athletics Interscholastic: basketball (boys, girls); coed interscholastic: flag football, track and field. 2 PE instructors, 1 coach, 1 athletic trainer.

Computers Computers are regularly used in all academic, career exploration classes. Computer network features include on-campus library services, Internet access, wireless campus network, Internet filtering or blocking technology. Campus intranet and computer access in designated common areas are available to students. Students grades are available online. The school has a published electronic and media policy.

Contact Denise Collier, Director of Admissions. 480-946-9112 Ext. 101. Fax: 480-946-2657. E-mail: denise@newwayacademy.org. Web site: www. newwayacademy.org.

NOBLE ACADEMY

3310 Horse Pen Creek Road
Greensboro, North Carolina 27410
Head of School: Mrs. Laura Mlatac

General Information Coeducational day college-preparatory, arts, and technology school; primarily serves students with learning disabilities, individuals with Attention Deficit Disorder, and dyslexic students. Grades K–12. Founded: 1987. Setting: suburban. Nearest major city is Greensboro/Winston-Salem. 40-acre campus. 3 buildings on campus. Approved or accredited by Southern Association of Colleges and Schools, Southern Association of Independent Schools, and North Carolina Department of Education. Endowment: $1.8 million. Total enrollment: 143. Upper school average class size: 8. Upper school faculty-student ratio: 1:8. There are 180 required school days per year for Upper School students. Upper School students typically attend 5 days per week. The average school day consists of 6 hours and 45 minutes.

Upper School Student Profile Grade 9: 10 students (7 boys, 3 girls); Grade 10: 10 students (9 boys, 1 girl); Grade 11: 16 students (9 boys, 7 girls); Grade 12: 14 students (12 boys, 2 girls).

Faculty School total: 34. In upper school: 4 men, 5 women; 5 have advanced degrees.

Subjects Offered Algebra, American history, art, basic skills, biology, career and personal planning, career exploration, chemistry, civics, college counseling, drama, earth science, economics, English, environmental science, geometry, health, journalism, life management skills, political systems, pre-algebra, pre-calculus, reading, reading/study skills, Spanish, world history, world history-AP, yearbook.

Graduation Requirements Algebra, American history, biology, earth science, economics, English, environmental science, geometry, physical education (includes health), Spanish, world history, 8th grade end-of-grade test, 20th percentile score on standardized reading test, North Carolina Computer Competency Test.

Special Academic Programs Study at local college for college credit; remedial reading and/or remedial writing; remedial math; programs in English, mathematics, general development for dyslexic students.

College Admission Counseling 7 students graduated in 2010; 6 went to college, including Brevard College; Elon University; Guilford College; Peace College; St. Andrews Presbyterian College; The University of North Carolina at Greensboro. Other: 1 had other specific plans. Median SAT critical reading: 510, median SAT math: 420, median SAT writing: 480. Mean combined SAT: 1458. 12% scored over 600 on SAT critical reading, 12% scored over 600 on SAT math, 12% scored over 600 on SAT writing.

Student Life Upper grades have student council, honor system. Discipline rests primarily with faculty.

Summer Programs Remediation, advancement, computer instruction programs offered; session focuses on Courses for credit; held on campus; accepts boys and girls; open to students from other schools. 25 students usually enrolled. 2011 schedule: June 20 to August 4. Application deadline: June 4.

Tuition and Aid Day student tuition: $15,690. Tuition installment plan (monthly payment plans, individually arranged payment plans). Need-based scholarship grants available. In 2010–11, 12% of upper-school students received aid. Total amount of financial aid awarded in 2010–11: $35,000.

Admissions Traditional secondary-level entrance grade is 9. For fall 2010, 12 students applied for upper-level admission, 6 were accepted, 6 enrolled. WISC/Woodcock-Johnson required. Deadline for receipt of application materials: none. Application fee required: $75. On-campus interview required.

Athletics Interscholastic: cheering (girls); coed interscholastic: basketball, cross-country running, flag football, golf, soccer, tennis, volleyball; coed intramural: tennis. 1 PE instructor, 7 coaches.

Computers Computers are regularly used in art, career education, career exploration, career technology, college planning, computer applications, current events, graphic arts, graphic design, history, information technology, introduction to technology, journalism, keyboarding, lab/keyboard, photography, social studies, Spanish, study skills, word processing, writing, writing, yearbook classes. Computer network features include Internet access, wireless campus network, Internet filtering or blocking technology. Student e-mail accounts are available to students. Students grades are available online. The school has a published electronic and media policy.

Contact Ms. Tim Montgomery, Assistant Head and Director of Admissions. 336-282-7044. Fax: 336-282-2048. E-mail: tmontgomery@nobleknights.org. Web site: www.nobleknights.org.

OAK CREEK RANCH SCHOOL

PO Box 4329
West Sedona, Arizona 86340-4329
Head of School: Mr. David Wick Jr.

General Information Coeducational boarding college-preparatory, general academic, technology, and experiential learning school; primarily serves underachievers, students with learning disabilities, individuals with Attention Deficit Disorder, and dyslexic students. Grades 6–12. Founded: 1972. Setting: rural. Nearest major city is Phoenix. Students are housed in single-sex dormitories. 17-acre campus. 21 buildings on campus. Approved or accredited by Arizona Association of Independent Schools, National Independent Private Schools Association, North Central Association of Colleges and Schools, and Arizona Department of Education. Total enrollment: 83. Upper school average class size: 8. Upper school faculty-student ratio: 1:8. There are 150 required school days per year for Upper School students. Upper School students typically attend 5 days per week. The average school day consists of 6 hours and 30 minutes.

Upper School Student Profile Grade 9: 15 students (8 boys, 7 girls); Grade 10: 15 students (12 boys, 3 girls); Grade 11: 23 students (15 boys, 8 girls); Grade 12: 20 students (14 boys, 6 girls). 100% of students are boarding students. 20% are state residents. 16 states are represented in upper school student body. 5% are international students. International students from Canada, India, Japan, and Mexico; 1 other country represented in student body.

Faculty School total: 13. In upper school: 9 men, 3 women; 10 have advanced degrees; 1 resides on campus.

Subjects Offered Advanced math, algebra, American literature, art, biology, chemistry, computer applications, computer information systems, computer multimedia, computer skills, earth science, economics, English, English literature, geography, geometry, government/civics, history, mathematics, physical education, physics, pre-algebra, reading, science, social sciences, social studies, Spanish, U.S. history, word processing, world history.

Graduation Requirements Computer science, economics, electives, English, foreign language, government, mathematics, science, social studies (includes history).

Special Academic Programs Accelerated programs; independent study; remedial reading and/or remedial writing; remedial math; programs in English, mathematics, general development for dyslexic students.

College Admission Counseling 21 students graduated in 2009; 19 went to college, including Arizona State University; Northern Arizona University. Other: 1 went to work, 1 entered military service. Median SAT critical reading: 520, median SAT math: 500.

Student Life Upper grades have specified standards of dress, student council, honor system. Discipline rests primarily with faculty.

Tuition and Aid 7-day tuition and room/board: $36,500. Guaranteed tuition plan. Tuition reduction for siblings, need-based scholarship grants, Wells Fargo Bank K-12

Private Student Loans available. In 2009–10, 10% of upper-school students received aid. Total amount of financial aid awarded in 2009–10: $36,500.

Admissions Traditional secondary-level entrance grade is 10. Deadline for receipt of application materials: none. Application fee required: $400. Interview recommended.

Athletics Interscholastic: basketball (boys, girls), flag football (b), volleyball (g); intramural: flag football (b), football (b); coed interscholastic: golf, soccer, softball; coed intramural: backpacking, badminton, bicycling, billiards, bowling, canoeing/kayaking, cheering, climbing, cross-country running, equestrian sports, fishing, fitness, fitness walking, fly fishing, freestyle skiing, golf, hiking/backpacking, horseback riding, horseshoes, ice skating, jump rope, kayaking, kickball, life saving, martial arts, mountain biking, Nautilus, outdoor activities, outdoor adventure, outdoor recreation, paddle tennis, paint ball, physical fitness, physical training, rafting, rappelling, riflery, rock climbing, roller blading, ropes courses, running, skateboarding, skiing (downhill), snowboarding, softball, strength & conditioning, swimming and diving, table tennis, tai chi, tennis, track and field, volleyball, walking, wall climbing, water polo, water volleyball, weight lifting, weight training, whiffle ball, wilderness, yoga. 1 PE instructor, 2 coaches.

Computers Computers are regularly used in English, foreign language, information technology, mathematics, multimedia, photography, photojournalism, science, word processing classes. Computer network features include on-campus library services, Internet access, wireless campus network, Internet filtering or blocking technology, Electric Library (research service), Website instruction and hosting (students only). Student e-mail accounts and computer access in designated common areas are available to students. Students grades are available online. The school has a published electronic and media policy.

Contact Mr. David Wick Jr., Headmaster. 928-634-5571. Fax: 928-634-4915. E-mail: dwick@ocrs.com. Web site: www.ocrs.com.

OAKLAND SCHOOL

Boyd Tavern
Keswick, Virginia 22947
Head of School: Ms. Carol Williams

General Information Coeducational boarding and day general academic school; primarily serves underachievers, students with learning disabilities, dyslexic students, processing difficulties, and organizational challenges. Boarding grades 2–9, day grades 1–9. Founded: 1950. Setting: rural. Nearest major city is Richmond. Students are housed in single-sex dormitories. 450-acre campus. 25 buildings on campus. Approved or accredited by Virginia Association of Independent Specialized Education Facilities and Virginia Department of Education. Upper school average class size: 5. Upper school faculty-student ratio: 1:5. The average school day consists of 6 hours and 30 minutes.

Upper School Student Profile 40% are state residents. 8 states are represented in upper school student body.

Faculty School total: 17. In upper school: 3 men, 13 women; 8 have advanced degrees; 6 reside on campus.

Subjects Offered Algebra, American history, earth science, English, expository writing, geometry, grammar, health, history of the Americas, keyboarding, life science, mathematics, physical education, physical science, remedial study skills, study skills, world history.

Graduation Requirements Skills must be at or above grade/ability level.

Special Academic Programs Remedial reading and/or remedial writing; remedial math; programs in English, mathematics for dyslexic students.

College Admission Counseling 23 students graduated in 2010.

Student Life Upper grades have specified standards of dress, student council, honor system. Discipline rests primarily with faculty.

Summer Programs Remediation, sports, art/fine arts, computer instruction programs offered; session focuses on academics; held on campus; accepts boys and girls; open to students from other schools. 135 students usually enrolled. 2011 schedule: June 27 to August 5.

Tuition and Aid Day student tuition: $25,750; 7-day tuition and room/board: $43,250. Tuition installment plan (SMART Tuition Payment Plan, individually arranged payment plans). Need-based scholarship grants available. In 2010–11, 20% of upper-school students received aid.

Admissions Wechsler Intelligence Scale for Children III required. Deadline for receipt of application materials: none. No application fee required. On-campus interview required.

Athletics Interscholastic: basketball (boys, girls), cheering (g), cross-country running (b,g), equestrian sports (b,g), fishing (b,g), fitness (b,g), golf (b,g), handball (b,g), horseback riding (b,g), outdoor activities (b,g), outdoor education (b,g), outdoor recreation (b,g), physical fitness (b,g), roller skating (b,g), soccer (b,g), softball (g), tennis (b,g); intramural: yoga (g); coed interscholastic: archery, basketball, cross-country running, equestrian sports, fishing, fitness, golf, handball, horseback riding, outdoor education, roller skating, soccer, tennis; coed intramural: archery, basketball, bicycling, billiards, cooperative games, cross-country running, equestrian sports, fishing, fitness, Frisbee, golf, hiking/backpacking, horseback riding, in-line skating, indoor soccer, kickball, lacrosse, mountain biking, outdoor activities, outdoor recreation, outdoors, paddle tennis, physical fitness, roller blading, roller skating, skateboarding, soccer, softball, swimming and diving, table tennis, tennis. 2 PE instructors.

Computers Computers are regularly used in English classes.

Contact Mrs. Amanda S. Baber, Admissions Director. 434-293-9059. Fax: 434-296-8930. E-mail: admissionsassist@oaklandschool.net. Web site: www.oaklandschool.net.

THE OLIVERIAN SCHOOL
PO Box 98
Mount Moosilauke Highway
Haverhill, New Hampshire 03765
Head of School: Mr. Randy Richardson

General Information Coeducational boarding and day and distance learning college-preparatory, arts, technology, and Experiential education school; primarily serves students with learning disabilities, individuals with Attention Deficit Disorder, individuals with emotional and behavioral problems, and minor emotional and behavioral problems. Grades 9–PG. Distance learning grade X. Founded: 2002. Setting: rural. Nearest major city is Boston, MA. Students are housed in single-sex dormitories. 1,800-acre campus. 10 buildings on campus. Approved or accredited by Independent Schools of Northern New England and New Hampshire Department of Education. Candidate for accreditation by New England Association of Schools and Colleges. Endowment: $50,000. Total enrollment: 50. Upper school average class size: 6. Upper school faculty-student ratio: 1:3. There are 180 required school days per year for Upper School students. Upper School students typically attend 5 days per week. The average school day consists of 7 hours and 30 minutes.

Upper School Student Profile Grade 9: 4 students (2 boys, 2 girls); Grade 10: 9 students (5 boys, 4 girls); Grade 11: 16 students (8 boys, 8 girls); Grade 12: 18 students (10 boys, 8 girls); Postgraduate: 3 students (2 boys, 1 girl). 100% of students are boarding students. 5% are state residents. 10 states are represented in upper school student body. 10% are international students. International students from Bermuda, Canada, Germany, Israel, and Kuwait.

Faculty School total: 19. In upper school: 9 men, 9 women; 10 have advanced degrees; 18 reside on campus.

Special Academic Programs 10 Advanced Placement exams for which test preparation is offered; honors section; accelerated programs; independent study; term-away projects; study at local college for college credit; study abroad; academic accommodation for the gifted and the artistically talented; remedial reading and/or remedial writing; remedial math; ESL (5 students enrolled).

College Admission Counseling 22 students graduated in 2009; 19 went to college, including St. Olaf College. Other: 1 went to work, 2 entered a postgraduate year.

Student Life Upper grades have specified standards of dress, student council, honor system. Discipline rests primarily with faculty.

Tuition and Aid 7-day tuition and room/board: $60,000. Tuition installment plan (FACTS Tuition Payment Plan). Merit scholarship grants, need-based scholarship grants available. In 2009–10, 20% of upper-school students received aid; total upper-school merit-scholarship money awarded: $50,000. Total amount of financial aid awarded in 2009–10: $200,000.

Admissions Traditional secondary-level entrance grade is 11. Deadline for receipt of application materials: none. Application fee required: $75. Interview required.

Athletics Intramural: flag football (boys, girls); coed interscholastic: soccer; coed intramural: alpine skiing, backpacking, basketball, bicycling, billiards, bowling, canoeing/kayaking, climbing, cooperative games, cross-country running, equestrian sports, fishing, fitness, Frisbee, golf, hiking/backpacking, horseback riding, indoor soccer, juggling, martial arts, mountain biking, mountaineering, nordic skiing, outdoor activities, outdoor adventure, outdoor education, outdoor recreation, outdoor skills, outdoors, physical fitness, physical training, rappelling, rock climbing, ropes courses, running, skateboarding, skiing (cross-country), skiing (downhill), snowboarding, snowshoeing, strength & conditioning, table tennis, touch football, triathlon, ultimate Frisbee, volleyball, walking, wall climbing, weight training, wilderness, wildernessways, yoga.

Computers Computer network features include online commercial services, Internet access, wireless campus network, Internet filtering or blocking technology. Campus intranet, student e-mail accounts, and computer access in designated common areas are available to students. Students grades are available online. The school has a published electronic and media policy.

Contact Mr. Barclay Mackinnon Jr., Director of Admissions/Headmaster Emeritus. 603-989-5368 Ext. 7103. Fax: 603-989-3055. E-mail: bmackinnon@oliverianschool.org. Web site: www.oliverianschool.org.

PACE/BRANTLEY HALL HIGH SCHOOL
3221 Sand Lake Road
Longwood, Florida 32779
Head of School: Kathleen M. Shatlock

General Information Coeducational day college-preparatory, general academic, arts, and technology school; primarily serves underachievers, students with learning disabilities, individuals with Attention Deficit Disorder, dyslexic students, students with mild to moderate Autism, Asperger's, and ADHD, and similar types of learning disabilities. Grades 1–12. Founded: 1972. Setting: suburban. Nearest major city is Orlando. 8-acre campus. 2 buildings on campus. Approved or accredited by Florida

Council of Independent Schools. Total enrollment: 121. Upper school average class size: 10. Upper school faculty-student ratio: 1:10. The average school day consists of 7 hours and 15 minutes.

Faculty School total: 28. In upper school: 3 men, 6 women; 5 have advanced degrees.

Subjects Offered 3-dimensional art, 3-dimensional design, ACT preparation, advanced computer applications, algebra, American history, American literature, art, biology, career/college preparation, chemistry, computer applications, computer art, computer graphics, computer science, computers, decision making skills, drama, earth and space science, English, English literature, fine arts, fitness, geography, geometry, government/civics, grammar, health and wellness, keyboarding, leadership, life skills, mathematics, peer counseling, photo shop, physical education, physical science, psychology, public speaking, reading, SAT preparation, SAT/ACT preparation, science, social sciences, social studies, speech, theater, world history, writing.

Graduation Requirements Arts and fine arts (art, music, dance, drama), computer science, English, foreign language, mathematics, physical education (includes health), reading, science, social studies (includes history).

Special Academic Programs International Baccalaureate program; remedial reading and/or remedial writing; remedial math; programs in English, mathematics, general development for dyslexic students.

College Admission Counseling 13 students graduated in 2009; 12 went to college, including Beacon College; Florida Atlantic University; Florida Gulf Coast University; Florida State University; Seminole State College of Florida; University of North Florida. Other: 1 went to work.

Student Life Upper grades have uniform requirement, honor system. Discipline rests primarily with faculty.

Tuition and Aid Day student tuition: $13,885. Tuition installment plan (monthly payment plans, individually arranged payment plans, semiannual payment plan). Tuition reduction for siblings, need-based scholarship grants, McKay Scholarship available. In 2009–10, 98% of upper-school students received aid.

Admissions Traditional secondary-level entrance grade is 9. For fall 2009, 29 students applied for upper-level admission, 27 were accepted, 27 enrolled. Academic Profile Tests required. Deadline for receipt of application materials: none. No application fee required. On-campus interview required.

Athletics Interscholastic: basketball (boys); coed interscholastic: fitness, physical fitness, volleyball; coed intramural: ball hockey, bowling, cheering, field hockey, flag football, football, kickball, soccer, track and field. 1 PE instructor, 2 coaches.

Computers Computers are regularly used in career exploration, computer applications, desktop publishing, graphic arts, keyboarding, SAT preparation classes. Computer network features include on-campus library services, Internet access, wireless campus network, Internet filtering or blocking technology. Campus intranet and computer access in designated common areas are available to students. The school has a published electronic and media policy.

Contact Barbara Winter, Assistant to Director. 407-869-8882 Ext. 221. Fax: 407-869-8717. E-mail: doneal@mypbhs.org. Web site: www.mypbhs.org.

THE PATHWAY SCHOOL
162 Egypt Road
Norristown, Pennsylvania 19403
Head of School: David Maola

General Information Coeducational day vocational and life skills school; primarily serves underachievers, students with learning disabilities, individuals with Attention Deficit Disorder, individuals with emotional and behavioral problems, neurologically impaired students, students with neuropsychiatric disorders, Asperger's Syndrome, and students needing speech/language therapy and occupational therapy. Ungraded, ages 5–21. Founded: 1961. Setting: suburban. Nearest major city is Philadelphia. 14-acre campus. 15 buildings on campus. Approved or accredited by National Association of Private Schools for Exceptional Children and Pennsylvania Department of Education. Endowment: $1 million. Total enrollment: 115. Upper school average class size: 9. Upper school faculty-student ratio: 1:6. There are 181 required school days per year for Upper School students. Upper School students typically attend 5 days per week. The average school day consists of 5 hours and 30 minutes.

Faculty School total: 23. In upper school: 7 men, 14 women; 10 have advanced degrees.

Subjects Offered Algebra, art, biology, career education, career experience, career/college preparation, computer skills, consumer mathematics, creative arts, drama, earth science, electives, English, environmental science, general math, geometry, health education, history, horticulture, interpersonal skills, language arts, mathematics, money management, physical education, pre-vocational education, senior seminar, social skills, social studies, work experience, world history.

Graduation Requirements Graduation requirements are as specified by the sending school district.

Special Academic Programs Study at local college for college credit; remedial reading and/or remedial writing; remedial math; programs in general development for dyslexic students; special instructional classes for emotional support program.

College Admission Counseling 18 students graduated in 2010; 7 went to college. Other: 11 went to work.

Student Life Upper grades have specified standards of dress, student council, honor system. Discipline rests equally with students and faculty.

Summer Programs Remediation, enrichment programs offered; session focuses on providing consistency for the entire calendar year; held on campus; accepts boys and girls; open to students from other schools. 85 students usually enrolled. 2011 schedule: July 6 to August 16.

Tuition and Aid Day student tuition: $42,000. Tuition installment plan (individually arranged payment plans).

Admissions Traditional secondary-level entrance age is 16. For fall 2010, 215 students applied for upper-level admission, 40 were accepted, 25 enrolled. Deadline for receipt of application materials: none. No application fee required. On-campus interview required.

Athletics Interscholastic: basketball (boys, girls), softball (b,g), Special Olympics (b,g); coed interscholastic: soccer, Special Olympics; coed intramural: basketball, flag football, soccer. 2 PE instructors, 2 coaches.

Computers Computers are regularly used in basic skills, business education, business skills, career education, data processing, design, newspaper, typing classes. Computer network features include on-campus library services, Internet access, Internet filtering or blocking technology, computer access in classroom. Computer access in designated common areas is available to students. The school has a published electronic and media policy.

Contact Diana Phifer, Director of Admissions. 610-277-0660 Ext. 289. Fax: 610-539-1493. E-mail: dphifer@pathwayschool.org. Web site: www.pathwayschool.org.

PINEHURST SCHOOL

10 Seymour Avenue
St. Catharines, Ontario L2P 1A4, Canada
Head of School: Mr. Dave Bird

General Information Coeducational boarding college-preparatory, arts, business, and technology school; primarily serves students with learning disabilities, individuals with Attention Deficit Disorder, and individuals with emotional and behavioral problems. Grades 7–12. Founded: 2000. Setting: urban. Students are housed in single-sex by floor dormitories. 5-acre campus. 1 building on campus. Approved or accredited by Ontario Ministry of Education and Virginia Association of Independent Specialized Education Facilities. Language of instruction: English. Total enrollment: 26. Upper school average class size: 10. Upper school faculty-student ratio: 1:10. There are 158 required school days per year for Upper School students. Upper School students typically attend 5 days per week. The average school day consists of 5 hours and 50 minutes.

Upper School Student Profile Grade 9: 5 students (2 boys, 3 girls); Grade 10: 8 students (6 boys, 2 girls); Grade 11: 6 students (5 boys, 1 girl); Grade 12: 7 students (5 boys, 2 girls). 100% of students are boarding students. 90% are province residents. 2 provinces are represented in upper school student body. 10% are international students. International students from Bermuda, Oman, Saudi Arabia, and United States.

Faculty School total: 6. In upper school: 2 men, 4 women; 1 has an advanced degree.

Graduation Requirements 20th century world history, art, business applications, Canadian geography, English, French, geography, health education, history, math applications, mathematics, outdoor education, science.

Special Academic Programs Honors section; accelerated programs; independent study; remedial reading and/or remedial writing; remedial math.

College Admission Counseling 9 students graduated in 2010; 4 went to college, including Zion Bible College. Other: 1 went to work, 4 entered a postgraduate year.

Student Life Upper grades have uniform requirement, student council, honor system. Discipline rests primarily with faculty.

Tuition and Aid 7-day tuition and room/board: CAN$33,000. Tuition installment plan (monthly payment plans).

Admissions Traditional secondary-level entrance grade is 11. For fall 2010, 5 students applied for upper-level admission, 5 were accepted, 5 enrolled. Deadline for receipt of application materials: none. No application fee required. On-campus interview required.

Athletics Coed Intramural: alpine skiing, aquatics, archery, backpacking, badminton, ball hockey, baseball, basketball, bicycling, billiards, blading, bocce, bowling, canoeing/kayaking, climbing, cooperative games, cricket, croquet, curling, field hockey, fishing, fitness, fitness walking, flag football, floor hockey, football, golf, hiking/backpacking, hockey, ice hockey, ice skating, in-line skating, indoor hockey, indoor soccer, kayaking, mountain biking, outdoor activities, outdoor education, paddling, physical fitness, physical training, rock climbing, roller blading, ropes courses, scuba diving, skateboarding, skiing (cross-country), skiing (downhill), snowboarding, snowshoeing, soccer, softball, street hockey, strength & conditioning, swimming and diving, table tennis, touch football, volleyball, walking, wall climbing, weight lifting, weight training, wilderness, wilderness survival, wildernessways, winter soccer, winter walking, yoga. 1 PE instructor, 1 coach, 1 athletic trainer.

Computers Computers are regularly used in all classes. Computer network features include on-campus library services, Internet access, wireless campus network, Internet filtering or blocking technology. Student e-mail accounts are available to students.

Contact Mrs. Donna MacDonald, Admissions/Office Coordinator. 905-641-0993. Fax: 905-641-0399. E-mail: pinedonna@sympatico.ca. Web site: www.pinehurst.on.ca.

PURNELL SCHOOL

51 Pottersville Road
PO Box 500
Pottersville, New Jersey 07979
Head of School: Ms. Ayanna Hill-Gill

General Information Girls' boarding and day college-preparatory, general academic, and arts school; primarily serves students with learning disabilities, individuals with Attention Deficit Disorder, and dyslexic students. Grades 9–12. Founded: 1963. Setting: rural. Nearest major city is New York, NY. Students are housed in single-sex dormitories. 83-acre campus. 23 buildings on campus. Approved or accredited by Middle States Association of Colleges and Schools, New Jersey Association of Independent Schools, The Association of Boarding Schools, and New Jersey Department of Education. Member of National Association of Independent Schools and Secondary School Admission Test Board. Endowment: $5 million. Total enrollment: 123. Upper school average class size: 11. Upper school faculty-student ratio: 1:8.

Upper School Student Profile Grade 9: 30 students (30 girls); Grade 10: 35 students (35 girls); Grade 11: 29 students (29 girls); Grade 12: 29 students (29 girls). 92% of students are boarding students. 47% are state residents. 19 states are represented in upper school student body. 13% are international students. International students from Bermuda, Bolivia, China, India, Republic of Korea, and Taiwan; 2 other countries represented in student body.

Faculty School total: 25. In upper school: 5 men, 19 women; 15 have advanced degrees; 22 reside on campus.

Subjects Offered Algebra, American history, American literature, anatomy, art, art history, biology, botany, calculus, ceramics, chemistry, creative writing, dance, drama, earth science, ecology, English, English literature, environmental science, fashion, fine arts, French, geography, geometry, government/civics, health, history, mathematics, music, photography, physical education, science, Shakespeare, social sciences, social studies, Spanish, speech, statistics, theater, trigonometry, women's studies, world history, world literature, writing.

Graduation Requirements Art history, arts and fine arts (art, music, dance, drama), English, foreign language, history, mathematics, performing arts, physical education (includes health), science, study abroad, Project Exploration.

Special Academic Programs Independent study; study abroad; programs in English, mathematics, general development for dyslexic students; ESL (7 students enrolled).

College Admission Counseling 37 students graduated in 2009; 36 went to college, including Boston College; Goucher College; Hampshire College; Lynn University; Mitchell College; Penn State University Park. Other: 1 went to work.

Student Life Upper grades have uniform requirement, student council. Discipline rests primarily with faculty.

Tuition and Aid Day student tuition: $38,484; 5-day tuition and room/board: $43,964; 7-day tuition and room/board: $45,711. Tuition installment plan (Academic Management Services Plan, Key Tuition Payment Plan, monthly payment plans, individually arranged payment plans). Need-based scholarship grants, prepGATE loans available. In 2009–10, 18% of upper-school students received aid.

Admissions Traditional secondary-level entrance grade is 9. For fall 2009, 165 students applied for upper-level admission, 76 were accepted, 53 enrolled. Deadline for receipt of application materials: none. Application fee required: $50. Interview required.

Athletics Interscholastic: basketball, dance, dance team, lacrosse, soccer, softball, tennis, volleyball; intramural: aerobics, aerobics/dance, aerobics/Nautilus, ballet, equestrian sports, fitness, golf, horseback riding, jogging, modern dance, outdoor adventure, physical training, self defense, strength & conditioning, weight training, yoga. 1 PE instructor, 5 coaches.

Computers Computers are regularly used in English, foreign language, history, mathematics, science classes. Computer network features include on-campus library services, Internet access, wireless campus network, Internet filtering or blocking technology. Campus intranet, student e-mail accounts, and computer access in designated common areas are available to students. The school has a published electronic and media policy.

Contact Ms. Gena Cotugno, Admissions Associate. 908-439-4025. Fax: 908-439-4088. E-mail: gcotugno@purnell.org. Web site: www.purnell.org.

RIVERVIEW SCHOOL

551 Route 6A
East Sandwich, Massachusetts 02537
Head of School: Mrs. Maureen B. Brenner

General Information Coeducational boarding and day arts and technology school; primarily serves underachievers, students with learning disabilities, individuals with Attention Deficit Disorder, and adolescents and young adults with complex language, learning, and cognitive disabilities. Grades 6–12. Founded: 1957. Setting: rural. Nearest major city is Boston. Students are housed in single-sex dormitories. 16-acre campus. 20 buildings on campus. Approved or accredited by Association of Independent Schools in New England, Massachusetts Department of Education, Massachusetts Office of Child Care Services, National Association of Private Schools for Exceptional Children, New England Association of Schools and Colleges, and Massachusetts Department of Education. Member of National Association of Independent Schools. Endowment: $4 million. Total enrollment: 97. Upper school average class size: 8. Upper school faculty-student ratio: 1:8. There are 180 required school days per year for Upper School students. Upper School students typically attend 5 days per week. The average school day consists of 6 hours and 45 minutes.

Upper School Student Profile Grade 9: 14 students (6 boys, 8 girls); Grade 10: 17 students (10 boys, 7 girls); Grade 11: 29 students (18 boys, 11 girls); Grade 12: 26 students (15 boys, 11 girls). 80% of students are boarding students. 47% are state residents. 24 states are represented in upper school student body. 4% are international students. International students from Belize, Canada, India, and United Kingdom.

Faculty School total: 44. In upper school: 9 men, 17 women; 17 have advanced degrees.

Subjects Offered Art, computer skills, drama, graphic arts, history, industrial arts, language arts, mathematics, music appreciation, physical education, reading, science, sexuality, social skills, social studies, speech therapy, writing.

Special Academic Programs Remedial reading and/or remedial writing; remedial math; programs in English, mathematics for dyslexic students.

College Admission Counseling 30 students graduated in 2009. Other: 27 entered a postgraduate year, 3 had other specific plans.

Student Life Upper grades have specified standards of dress, student council. Discipline rests primarily with faculty.

Tuition and Aid Day student tuition: $41,300; 7-day tuition and room/board: $67,705. Tuition installment plan (initial deposit upon acceptance, 3-installment payment plan (July, August, and November)). Need-based scholarship grants, middle-income loans available. In 2009–10, 11% of upper-school students received aid. Total amount of financial aid awarded in 2009–10: $125,500.

Admissions Traditional secondary-level entrance grade is 9. For fall 2009, 193 students applied for upper-level admission, 82 were accepted, 40 enrolled. Achievement tests, comprehensive educational evaluation, Individual IQ, Achievement and behavior rating scale, psychoeducational evaluation, WISC or WAIS, Woodcock-Johnson or writing sample required. Deadline for receipt of application materials: none. Application fee required: $75. On-campus interview required.

Athletics Interscholastic: baseball (boys), basketball (b), soccer (b), swimming and diving (b,g), tennis (b,g), track and field (b,g); intramural: bowling (b,g), fitness (b,g), jogging (b,g), jump rope (b,g), running (b,g); coed interscholastic: basketball, cross-country running, soccer, swimming and diving, tennis, track and field; coed intramural: aerobics/Nautilus, basketball, bowling, fitness, jogging, jump rope, Nautilus, physical fitness, project adventure, running, soccer, softball, yoga. 2 PE instructors, 1 athletic trainer.

Computers Computers are regularly used in all academic classes. Computer network features include Internet access, Internet filtering or blocking technology, digital photography, scanners, PowerPoint presentations, Smartboards, Kurzweil, Dragon Naturally Speaking, Mimio, Lexia, Ultra Key, Type to Learn. Computer access in designated common areas is available to students. The school has a published electronic and media policy.

Contact Ms. Monica Lindo, Admissions Assistant. 508-888-0489 Ext. 206. Fax: 508-833-7001. E-mail: admissions@riverviewschool.org. Web site: www.riverviewschool.org.

ROBERT LAND ACADEMY

RR #3
6726 South Chippawa Road
Wellandport, Ontario L0R 2J0, Canada
Head of School: Lt. Col. G. Scott Bowman

General Information Boys' boarding college-preparatory, arts, business, core courses, English and math foundational building, and military school; primarily serves underachievers, students with learning disabilities, individuals with Attention Deficit Disorder, individuals with emotional and behavioral problems, dyslexic students, Oppositional Defiant Disorder, and Attention Deficit Hyperactive Disorder. Grades 6–12. Founded: 1978. Setting: rural. Nearest major city is Hamilton, Canada. Students are housed in single-sex dormitories and barracks. 168-acre campus. 18 buildings on campus. Approved or accredited by Ontario Department of Education. Language of instruction: English. Total enrollment: 141. Upper school average class size: 15. Upper school faculty-student ratio: 1:15. Upper School students typically attend 7 days per week. The average school day consists of 6 hours and 30 minutes.

Upper School Student Profile Grade 11: 21 students (21 boys); Grade 12: 19 students (19 boys). 100% of students are boarding students. 65% are province residents. 8 provinces are represented in upper school student body. 25% are international students. International students from Bahamas, China, Hong Kong, Japan, United Kingdom, and United States; 5 other countries represented in student body.

Faculty School total: 20. In upper school: 18 men, 2 women; 5 have advanced degrees.

Subjects Offered Ancient history, consumer education, creative writing, driver education, ecology, ethics, expository writing, geology, keyboarding, law, military science, music, photography, statistics, typing, world literature.

Graduation Requirements Ontario Literacy Equivalence Test.

Special Academic Programs Honors section; independent study; remedial reading and/or remedial writing; remedial math; programs in general development for dyslexic students.

College Admission Counseling 27 students graduated in 2009; 24 went to college. Other: 2 went to work, 1 had other specific plans.

Student Life Upper grades have uniform requirement, student council, honor system. Discipline rests primarily with faculty.

Tuition and Aid 7-day tuition and room/board: CAN$37,500. Tuition installment plan (individually arranged payment plans). Bursaries, merit scholarship grants, need-based scholarship grants available. In 2009–10, 10% of upper-school students received aid.

Admissions Traditional secondary-level entrance grade is 11. For fall 2009, 50 students applied for upper-level admission, 40 were accepted, 40 enrolled. Deadline for receipt of application materials: none. Application fee required: CAN$200. Interview required.

Athletics Interscholastic: badminton, basketball, cross-country running, hockey, ice hockey, rock climbing, rugby, running, soccer, track and field, volleyball, wall climbing, wrestling; intramural: aerobics/Nautilus, archery, backpacking, badminton, ball hockey, baseball, basketball, bicycling, boxing, canoeing/kayaking, climbing, cross-country running, drill team, fishing, fitness, fitness walking, flag football, floor hockey, Frisbee, hiking/backpacking, hockey, ice hockey, ice skating, indoor hockey, indoor soccer, jogging, JROTC drill, life saving, marksmanship, martial arts, mountain biking, mountaineering, Nautilus, outdoor activities, outdoor adventure, outdoor education, outdoor recreation, outdoor skills, outdoors, paddling, paint ball, physical fitness, physical training, rappelling, riflery, rock climbing, ropes courses, rugby, running, scuba diving, self defense, skydiving, soccer, softball, street hockey, strength & conditioning, touch football, track and field, ultimate Frisbee, volleyball, walking, wall climbing, weight lifting, weight training, wilderness, wilderness survival, winter walking, wrestling. 3 PE instructors, 10 coaches.

Computers Computer resources include on-campus library services, Internet access, Internet filtering or blocking technology.

Contact Lt. F. Greg Hewett, Admissions Officer. 905-386-6203. Fax: 905-386-6607. E-mail: ghewett@robertlandacademy.com. Web site: www.robertlandacademy.com.

ROBERT LOUIS STEVENSON SCHOOL

24 West 74th Street
New York, New York 10023
Head of School: Dr. Robert F. Feiguine

General Information Coeducational day college-preparatory school; primarily serves underachievers, students with learning disabilities, individuals with Attention Deficit Disorder, individuals with emotional and behavioral problems, and dyslexic students. Grades 7–PG. Founded: 1908. Setting: urban. 1 building on campus. Approved or accredited by New York State Association of Independent Schools and New York Department of Education. Member of National Association of Independent Schools. Total enrollment: 65. Upper school average class size: 9. Upper school faculty-student ratio: 1:5. There are 165 required school days per year for Upper School students. Upper School students typically attend 5 days per week. The average school day consists of 6 hours and 30 minutes.

Upper School Student Profile Grade 7: 1 student (1 boy); Grade 8: 4 students (3 boys, 1 girl); Grade 9: 6 students (3 boys, 3 girls); Grade 10: 12 students (8 boys, 4 girls); Grade 11: 22 students (14 boys, 8 girls); Grade 12: 19 students (11 boys, 8 girls); Postgraduate: 1 student (1 boy).

Faculty School total: 16. In upper school: 6 men, 9 women; 8 have advanced degrees.

Subjects Offered Algebra, American history, American literature, anatomy, ancient history, ancient world history, ancient/medieval philosophy, art, biology, calculus, ceramics, chemistry, creative writing, current history, drama, earth and space science, earth science, English, English literature, environmental science, European civilization, European history, expository writing, film appreciation, geometry, government/civics, grammar, health, history, history of ideas, mathematics, philosophy, physical education, physics, physiology, poetry, political science, political thought, pre-algebra, pre-calculus, psychology, robotics, science, senior project, sex education, Shakespeare, social sciences, social studies, theater, trigonometry, world literature, writing.

Graduation Requirements American history, English, health education, mathematics, physical education (includes health), science, social sciences, social studies (includes history), portfolio of work demonstrating readiness to graduate.

Special Academic Programs Accelerated programs; independent study; academic accommodation for the gifted; remedial reading and/or remedial writing; remedial math; programs in English, mathematics, general development for dyslexic students.

College Admission Counseling 22 students graduated in 2010; 17 went to college, including City University of New York System; Pace University; State University of New York System. Other: 1 went to work.

Student Life Upper grades have student council. Discipline rests primarily with faculty.

Summer Programs Remediation, enrichment, advancement programs offered; session focuses on tutorial work; held on campus; accepts boys and girls; open to students from other schools. 18 students usually enrolled. 2011 schedule: July 1 to July 29. Application deadline: June 22.

Tuition and Aid Day student tuition: $47,000. Tuition installment plan (individually arranged payment plans). Need-based scholarship grants, need-based loans available. In 2010–11, 4% of upper-school students received aid. Total amount of financial aid awarded in 2010–11: $30,000.

Admissions Traditional secondary-level entrance grade is 9. For fall 2010, 65 students applied for upper-level admission, 46 were accepted, 41 enrolled. Psycho-educational evaluation required. Deadline for receipt of application materials: none. No application fee required. On-campus interview required.

Athletics Coed Interscholastic: basketball, bowling, cross-country running, fitness, floor hockey, jogging, soccer, softball, yoga; coed intramural: aerobics, ball hockey, basketball, bicycling, blading, bowling, cooperative games, fitness, flag football, floor hockey, jogging, judo, juggling, martial arts, physical fitness, physical training, soccer, softball, strength & conditioning, table tennis, tennis, touch football, volleyball, weight lifting, weight training, yoga. 1 PE instructor.

Computers Computers are regularly used in art, English, history, science, technology classes. Computer network features include Internet access, wireless campus network, Internet filtering or blocking technology. Computer access in designated common areas is available to students. The school has a published electronic and media policy.

Contact Dr. Dayana Jimenez, Clinical Director. 212-787-6400. Fax: 212-873-1872. E-mail: djimenez@stevenson-school.org. Web site: www.stevenson-school.org.

ROCKLYN ACADEMY

RR # 2 (Rocklyn)
Meaford, Ontario N4L 1W6, Canada
Head of School: Ms. Dale Stohn

General Information Girls' boarding college-preparatory school; primarily serves individuals with Attention Deficit Disorder and individuals with emotional and behavioral problems. Grades 9–12. Founded: 1999. Setting: rural. Nearest major city is Toronto, Canada. Students are housed in single-sex dormitories. 75-acre campus. 3 buildings on campus. Approved or accredited by Ontario Ministry of Education and Ontario Department of Education. Language of instruction: English. Total enrollment: 27. Upper school average class size: 4. Upper school faculty-student ratio: 1:3.

Upper School Student Profile Grade 9: 4 students (4 girls); Grade 10: 9 students (9 girls); Grade 11: 7 students (7 girls); Grade 12: 7 students (7 girls). 100% of students are boarding students. 66% are province residents. 14 provinces are represented in upper school student body. 34% are international students. International students from Malaysia, United Kingdom, and United States.

Faculty School total: 13. In upper school: 3 men, 8 women.

Subjects Offered Art, biology, business, calculus, career education, chemistry, civics, communication skills, computer science, contemporary history, creative writing, dramatic arts, English, equine management, ESL, family studies, fine arts, French, geography, guitar, health education, healthful living, history, humanities, law, library, life skills, literature, mathematics, music, personal growth, philosophy, physical fitness, physics, poetry, pottery, public speaking, reading/study skills, relationships, science, Shakespeare, society challenge and change, Spanish, technology.

Special Academic Programs Accelerated programs; academic accommodation for the gifted; ESL.

College Admission Counseling 8 students graduated in 2010; 7 went to college, including Trent University; University of Guelph; University of Toronto; University of Tulsa; University of Waterloo. Other: 1 went to work.

Student Life Upper grades have uniform requirement, student council, honor system. Discipline rests equally with students and faculty.

Summer Programs Sports, rigorous outdoor training programs offered; session focuses on emotional growth through outdoor activities; held on campus; accepts girls; open to students from other schools. 12 students usually enrolled. 2011 schedule: June 15 to September 10.

Tuition and Aid 7-day tuition and room/board: CAN$48,500.

Admissions Traditional secondary-level entrance grade is 10. For fall 2010, 35 students applied for upper-level admission, 29 were accepted, 27 enrolled. Wechsler Intelligence Scale for Children required. Deadline for receipt of application materials: none. Application fee required: CAN$200. Interview recommended.

Athletics Intramural: aerobics, alpine skiing, badminton, baseball, cooperative games, fitness, golf, hiking/backpacking, horseback riding, ice skating, physical fitness, ropes courses, skiing (cross-country), skiing (downhill), snowboarding, soccer, softball, squash, swimming and diving, table tennis, volleyball, walking, wall climbing, weight training, yoga. 3 PE instructors.

Computers Computers are regularly used in all classes. Computer resources include Internet access.

Contact Ms. Dale Stohn, Admissions Director. 519-538-2992. Fax: 519-538-1106. E-mail: info@rocklynacademy.ca. Web site: www.rocklynacademy.ca.

SHELTON SCHOOL AND EVALUATION CENTER

15720 Hillcrest Road
Dallas, Texas 75248
Head of School: Linda Kneese

General Information Coeducational day college-preparatory and general academic school; primarily serves students with learning disabilities, individuals with Attention Deficit Disorder, and dyslexic students. Grades PS–12. Founded: 1976. Setting: suburban. 1-acre campus. 1 building on campus. Approved or accredited by Independent Schools Association of the Southwest and Southern Association of Independent Schools. Endowment: $6.7 million. Total enrollment: 855. Upper school

average class size: 8. Upper school faculty-student ratio: 1:8. There are 170 required school days per year for Upper School students. Upper School students typically attend 5 days per week. The average school day consists of 7 hours.

Upper School Student Profile Grade 9: 66 students (48 boys, 18 girls); Grade 10: 72 students (45 boys, 27 girls); Grade 11: 51 students (33 boys, 18 girls); Grade 12: 53 students (34 boys, 19 girls).

Faculty School total: 158. In upper school: 15 men, 29 women; 27 have advanced degrees.

Graduation Requirements Arts and fine arts (art, music, dance, drama), computers, English, ethics, foreign language, mathematics, physical education (includes health), reading, science, social studies (includes history), speech.

Special Academic Programs Programs in English, mathematics, general development for dyslexic students.

College Admission Counseling 44 students graduated in 2010; 43 went to college, including Avila University; Collin County Community College District; Colorado State University; University of Arkansas; University of Denver; University of North Texas. Other: 1 had other specific plans.

Student Life Upper grades have uniform requirement, student council, honor system. Discipline rests primarily with faculty.

Summer Programs Enrichment programs offered; session focuses on enrichment; held on campus; accepts boys and girls; open to students from other schools. 39 students usually enrolled. 2011 schedule: June 27 to July 22. Application deadline: May 10.

Tuition and Aid Day student tuition: $18,853. Tuition installment plan (SMART Tuition Payment Plan, Sallie Mae). Need-based scholarship grants available. In 2010–11, 9% of upper-school students received aid. Total amount of financial aid awarded in 2010–11: $137,500.

Admissions Traditional secondary-level entrance grade is 9. For fall 2010, 43 students applied for upper-level admission, 25 were accepted, 22 enrolled. WISC/Woodcock-Johnson required. Deadline for receipt of application materials: none. No application fee required. Interview required.

Athletics Interscholastic: baseball (boys), basketball (b,g), cheering (g), cross-country running (b,g), football (b), golf (b), tennis (b,g), track and field (b,g), volleyball (g). 3 PE instructors, 4 coaches.

Computers Computers are regularly used in all academic, English, foreign language, information technology, lab/keyboard, library, research skills, SAT preparation, video film production classes. Computer network features include on-campus library services, Internet access, wireless campus network, Internet filtering or blocking technology. Campus intranet and student e-mail accounts are available to students. Students grades are available online. The school has a published electronic and media policy.

Contact Diann Slaton, Director of Admissions. 972-774-1772. Fax: 972-991-3977. E-mail: dslaton@shelton.org. Web site: www.shelton.org.

SHOORE CENTRE FOR LEARNING

801 Eglinton Avenue West
Suite 201
Toronto, Ontario M5N 1E3, Canada
Head of School: Mr. Michael I. Shoore

General Information Coeducational day general academic school; primarily serves underachievers, students with learning disabilities, individuals with Attention Deficit Disorder, individuals with emotional and behavioral problems, and dyslexic students. Grades 8–12. Setting: urban. Approved or accredited by Ontario Department of Education. Language of instruction: English. Total enrollment: 30. Upper school average class size: 6. Upper school faculty-student ratio: 1:6.

Faculty School total: 8. In upper school: 5 men, 2 women.

Subjects Offered Advanced math, anthropology, art, business studies, calculus, Canadian geography, Canadian history, Canadian law, career education, chemistry, civics, drama, dramatic arts, earth science, English, general science, health and safety, history, independent study, law, mathematics, media arts, parenting, physical education, physics, science, science and technology, technology, visual arts, writing.

Special Academic Programs Remedial reading and/or remedial writing; remedial math; programs in English, mathematics, general development for dyslexic students.

College Admission Counseling 6 students graduated in 2010. Other: 4 entered a postgraduate year.

Student Life Upper grades have specified standards of dress. Discipline rests primarily with faculty.

Summer Programs Remediation, enrichment, advancement programs offered; held on campus; accepts boys and girls; open to students from other schools. 30 students usually enrolled. 2011 schedule: June 21 to August 31.

Tuition and Aid Day student tuition: CAN$22,100. Tuition installment plan (monthly payment plans, individually arranged payment plans).

Admissions Deadline for receipt of application materials: none. No application fee required. Interview required.

Computers Computer resources include Internet access.

Contact Mr. Michael I. Shoore, Director. 416-781-4754. Fax: 416-781 0163. E-mail: shoore@shoorecentre.com. Web site: www.shoorecentre.com.

SKY RANCH FOR BOYS, INC.

10100 Sky Ranch Place
Sky Ranch, South Dakota 57724
Head of School: Jodi Duttenhefer

General Information Boys' boarding school; primarily serves underachievers, students with learning disabilities, individuals with Attention Deficit Disorder, and individuals with emotional and behavioral problems. Founded: 1960. Setting: rural. Nearest major city is Rapid City. Students are housed in single-sex dormitories. 3,000-acre campus. 12 buildings on campus. Approved or accredited by South Dakota Department of Education. Total enrollment: 32. Upper school average class size: 8. Upper school faculty-student ratio: 1:6. There are 239 required school days per year for Upper School students. Upper School students typically attend 5 days per week. The average school day consists of 5 hours and 30 minutes.

Upper School Student Profile Grade 6: 5 students (5 boys); Grade 7: 5 students (5 boys); Grade 8: 5 students (5 boys); Grade 9: 7 students (7 boys); Grade 10: 8 students (8 boys); Grade 11: 2 students (2 boys). 100% of students are boarding students. 30% are state residents. 5 states are represented in upper school student body.

Faculty School total: 6. In upper school: 3 men, 3 women; 3 have advanced degrees.

Student Life Upper grades have specified standards of dress. Discipline rests primarily with faculty.

Admissions Traditional secondary-level entrance grade is 9. For fall 2009, 45 students applied for upper-level admission, 20 were accepted, 14 enrolled. No application fee required.

Athletics Interscholastic: basketball, billiards, fishing, flag football, horseback riding, in-line skating, outdoor activities, outdoor recreation, paddle tennis, physical fitness, roller blading, running, skateboarding, softball, strength & conditioning, table tennis, touch football, volleyball, walking, weight lifting, whiffle ball. 1 PE instructor, 1 coach.

Contact Jodi Duttenhefer, LSW, MS, Executive Director. 605-797-4422. Fax: 605-797-4425. E-mail: jduttenhefer@skyranchforboys.com. Web site: www.skyranchforboys.com.

SMITH SCHOOL

131 West 86 Street
New York, New York 10024
Head of School: Karen Smith

General Information Coeducational day college-preparatory and music and art programs school; primarily serves students with learning disabilities, individuals with Attention Deficit Disorder, and depression or anxiety disorders; emotional and/or motivational issues. Grades 7–12. Founded: 1990. Setting: urban. 1 building on campus. Approved or accredited by Middle States Association of Colleges and Schools, New York State Board of Regents, and New York Department of Education. Total enrollment: 54. Upper school average class size: 4. Upper school faculty-student ratio: 1:4. There are 160 required school days per year for Upper School students. Upper School students typically attend 5 days per week. The average school day consists of 6 hours and 30 minutes.

Upper School Student Profile Grade 7: 6 students (3 boys, 3 girls); Grade 8: 5 students (3 boys, 2 girls); Grade 9: 11 students (5 boys, 6 girls); Grade 10: 9 students (4 boys, 5 girls); Grade 11: 11 students (5 boys, 6 girls); Grade 12: 12 students (6 boys, 6 girls).

Faculty School total: 15. In upper school: 8 men, 7 women; 13 have advanced degrees.

Subjects Offered Algebra, American history, art, biology, chemistry, computer skills, earth science, English, environmental science, European history, film, French, geometry, lab science, life science, physical science, physics, pre-calculus, Spanish, trigonometry, U.S. government, U.S. history, world history.

Graduation Requirements Algebra, American history, art, biology, chemistry, conceptual physics, earth science, English, environmental science, European history, geometry, government, health education, languages, physical education (includes health), physical science, pre-algebra, pre-calculus, trigonometry, world history, community service/20 hours per year.

Special Academic Programs Accelerated programs; independent study; study at local college for college credit; remedial reading and/or remedial writing; remedial math; special instructional classes for peer mediation, socialization, and motivational issues; ESL (3 students enrolled).

College Admission Counseling 13 students graduated in 2010; all went to college, including Fashion Institute of Technology; Fordham University; John Jay College of Criminal Justice of the City University of New York; Landmark College; State University of New York at New Paltz; Syracuse University. Median SAT critical reading: 600, median SAT math: 620, median SAT writing: 620, median combined SAT: 600. 50% scored over 600 on SAT critical reading, 40% scored over 600 on SAT math, 50% scored over 600 on SAT writing, 45% scored over 1800 on combined SAT.

Student Life Upper grades have student council, honor system. Discipline rests primarily with faculty.

Summer Programs Remediation, enrichment, advancement, ESL, computer instruction programs offered; session focuses on academic courses for enrichment, remediation, or credit; held both on and off campus; held at Local colleges; accepts boys and girls; open to students from other schools. 25 students usually enrolled. 2011 schedule: June 13 to August 17. Application deadline: June 1.

Tuition and Aid Day student tuition: $29,000–$32,500. Tuition installment plan (monthly payment plans, individually arranged payment plans, Quarterly Payment Plan). Tuition reduction for siblings available. In 2010–11, 10% of upper-school students received aid. Total amount of financial aid awarded in 2010–11: $30,000.

Admissions Traditional secondary-level entrance grade is 9. For fall 2010, 31 students applied for upper-level admission, 15 were accepted, 14 enrolled. Comprehensive educational evaluation, psychoeducational evaluation, school placement exam, Wide Range Achievement Test or writing sample required. Deadline for receipt of application materials: none. Application fee required: $50. On-campus interview required.

Athletics Coed Interscholastic: basketball, dance, martial arts, physical fitness, running, self defense, volleyball. 2 PE instructors, 2 coaches.

Computers Computers are regularly used in English, history, research skills, writing, yearbook classes. Computer resources include Internet access, wireless campus network, Internet filtering or blocking technology, yearbook and monthly newsletter. Computer access in designated common areas is available to students. The school has a published electronic and media policy.

Contact Jennifer Sudary-Narine, Executive Assistant. 212-879-6317. Fax: 212-879-0962. E-mail: jennifersudary@thesmithschool.org. Web site: www.smithschool.net.

SORENSON'S RANCH SCHOOL

PO Box 440219
Koosharem, Utah 84744
Head of School: Shane Sorenson

General Information Coeducational boarding college-preparatory, general academic, arts, and vocational school; primarily serves underachievers, students with learning disabilities, individuals with Attention Deficit Disorder, and individuals with emotional and behavioral problems. Grades 7–12. Founded: 1982. Setting: rural. Nearest major city is Salt Lake City. Students are housed in single-sex dormitories. 10-acre campus. 16 buildings on campus. Approved or accredited by Northwest Accreditation Commission, Northwest Association of Schools and Colleges, and Utah Department of Education. Total enrollment: 60. Upper school average class size: 12. Upper school faculty-student ratio: 1:7. There are 238 required school days per year for Upper School students. Upper School students typically attend 5 days per week. The average school day consists of 5 hours and 45 minutes.

Upper School Student Profile Grade 7: 1 student (1 boy); Grade 8: 3 students (1 boy, 2 girls); Grade 9: 14 students (8 boys, 6 girls); Grade 10: 11 students (6 boys, 5 girls); Grade 11: 16 students (8 boys, 8 girls); Grade 12: 15 students (8 boys, 7 girls). 100% of students are boarding students. 2% are state residents. 18 states are represented in upper school student body.

Faculty School total: 14. In upper school: 8 men, 4 women; 5 have advanced degrees.

Subjects Offered Art, biology, chemistry, computer science, economics, English, home economics, life skills, mathematics, metalworking, physical education, physics, science, social studies, Spanish, woodworking.

Graduation Requirements Computer science, English, mathematics, physical education (includes health), science, social studies (includes history).

Special Academic Programs Accelerated programs; independent study; remedial reading and/or remedial writing; remedial math; programs in English, mathematics, general development for dyslexic students.

College Admission Counseling 40 students graduated in 2009; 15 went to college, including Brigham Young University; California State University, Sacramento; Southern Utah University; University of Pennsylvania. Other: 14 went to work, 3 entered military service, 3 entered a postgraduate year, 5 had other specific plans. Median SAT critical reading: 430, median SAT math: 420, median SAT writing: 440, median combined SAT: 1300, median composite ACT: 21. 1% scored over 600 on SAT critical reading, 1% scored over 600 on SAT math, 1% scored over 600 on SAT writing, 1% scored over 1800 on combined SAT, 1% scored over 26 on composite ACT.

Student Life Upper grades have specified standards of dress, student council. Discipline rests primarily with faculty.

Tuition and Aid 7-day tuition and room/board: $66,000. Guaranteed tuition plan. Tuition installment plan (Key Tuition Payment Plan, monthly payment plans). Tuition reduction for siblings, need-based scholarship grants, need-based loans available. In 2009–10, 5% of upper-school students received aid. Total amount of financial aid awarded in 2009–10: $40,000.

Admissions Traditional secondary-level entrance grade is 9. For fall 2009, 127 students applied for upper-level admission, 72 were accepted, 60 enrolled. Deadline for receipt of application materials: none. No application fee required.

Athletics Interscholastic: aerobics/dance (girls), football (b), volleyball (g), wrestling (b); intramural: aerobics (g), aerobics/dance (g), aquatics (b,g), backpacking (b,g), baseball (b), basketball (b,g), bicycling (b,g), billiards (b,g), bocce (b,g), bowling (b,g), cooperative games (b,g), equestrian sports (b,g), fishing (b,g), fitness (b,g), fitness walking (b,g), flag football (b,g), floor hockey (b), football (b), golf (b,g), hiking/backpacking (b,g), horseback riding (b,g), mountain biking (b,g), mountaineering (b,g), outdoor activities (b,g), outdoor education (b,g), physical fitness (b,g), physical training (b,g), roller skating (b,g), ropes courses (b,g), skiing (downhill) (b,g), snowboarding (b,g), soccer (b,g), softball (b,g), strength & conditioning (b,g), swimming and diving (b,g), table tennis (b,g), touch football (b), volleyball (b,g), walking (b,g), water skiing (b,g), weight training (b,g), whiffle ball (b), wilderness (b,g), wildernessways (b,g). 1 PE instructor, 5 coaches.

Computers Computers are regularly used in English, keyboarding, library classes. Computer network features include on-campus library services, online commercial services. Students grades are available online.

Contact Mr. Layne Bagley, Director of Admissions. 435-638-7318 Ext. 155. Fax: 435-638-7582. E-mail: layneb@sorensonsranch.com. Web site: www.sorensonsranch.com.

STANBRIDGE ACADEMY

515 East Poplar Avenue

San Mateo, California 94401

Head of School: Mrs. Marilyn Lynch

General Information Coeducational day general academic school; primarily serves underachievers and students with learning disabilities. Grades K–12. Founded: 1982. Setting: suburban. Nearest major city is San Francisco. 1-acre campus. 1 building on campus. Approved or accredited by Western Association of Schools and Colleges. Total enrollment: 104. Upper school average class size: 8. Upper school faculty-student ratio: 1:8.

Upper School Student Profile Grade 6: 6 students (5 boys, 1 girl); Grade 7: 10 students (9 boys, 1 girl); Grade 8: 13 students (11 boys, 2 girls); Grade 9: 14 students (6 boys, 8 girls); Grade 10: 13 students (9 boys, 4 girls); Grade 11: 12 students (8 boys, 4 girls); Grade 12: 12 students (8 boys, 4 girls).

Faculty School total: 30. In upper school: 5 men, 6 women; 6 have advanced degrees.

Subjects Offered Algebra, American government, biology, career/college preparation, ceramics, college planning, English, English literature, experiential education, general math, geography, geometry, health education, mathematics, physical education, physics, pragmatics, pre-algebra, pre-calculus, probability and statistics, science, social sciences, Spanish, U.S. history, world cultures, world history, yearbook.

Graduation Requirements Algebra, American government, biology, English, English composition, English literature, experiential education, foreign language, geometry, health and wellness, physical education (includes health), physical science, physics, trigonometry, U.S. history, visual and performing arts, world cultures.

Special Academic Programs Independent study; remedial reading and/or remedial writing; remedial math.

College Admission Counseling 9 students graduated in 2009; 8 went to college, including Academy of Art University; California State University, Sacramento; College of San Mateo. Other: 1 went to work.

Student Life Upper grades have specified standards of dress, student council, honor system. Discipline rests primarily with faculty.

Tuition and Aid Day student tuition: $27,500. Guaranteed tuition plan. Tuition installment plan (monthly payment plans). Need-based scholarship grants available. In 2009–10, 10% of upper-school students received aid. Total amount of financial aid awarded in 2009–10: $80,000.

Admissions Traditional secondary-level entrance grade is 9. For fall 2009, 8 students applied for upper-level admission, 8 were accepted, 8 enrolled. Psychoeducational evaluation or SSAT required. Deadline for receipt of application materials: none. Application fee required: $300. On-campus interview required.

Athletics Coed Intramural: aerobics, badminton, basketball, climbing, cooperative games, cross-country running, dance, fitness walking, flag football, Frisbee, jogging, kickball, outdoor education, outdoor skills, physical fitness, physical training, soccer, strength & conditioning, table tennis, touch football, track and field, volleyball, walking. 3 PE instructors.

Computers Computers are regularly used in yearbook classes. Computer network features include on-campus library services, wireless campus network, Internet filtering or blocking technology. Campus intranet and computer access in designated common areas are available to students. Students grades are available online. The school has a published electronic and media policy.

Contact Ms. Susan Coyne, Administrative Assistant. 650-375-5860. Fax: 650-375-5861. E-mail: scoyne@stanbridgeacademy.org. Web site: www.stanbridgeacademy.org.

STERNE SCHOOL

2690 Jackson Street

San Francisco, California 94115

Head of School: Edward J. McManis

General Information Coeducational day college-preparatory, general academic, and vocational school; primarily serves underachievers, students with learning disabilities, individuals with Attention Deficit Disorder, and dyslexic students. Grades 6–12. Founded: 1976. Setting: urban. 1 building on campus. Approved or accredited by Western Association of Schools and Colleges and California Department of Education. Endowment: $900,000. Total enrollment: 43. Upper school average class size: 10. Upper school faculty-student ratio: 1:8. There are 176 required school days per year for Upper School students. Upper School students typically attend 5 days per week. The average school day consists of 7 hours.

Upper School Student Profile Grade 9: 7 students (5 boys, 2 girls); Grade 10: 7 students (5 boys, 2 girls); Grade 11: 5 students (3 boys, 2 girls); Grade 12: 4 students (2 boys, 2 girls).

Faculty School total: 11. In upper school: 4 men, 3 women; 5 have advanced degrees.

Subjects Offered Algebra, American history, American literature, art, biology, computer science, driver education, earth science, economics, English, English literature, environmental science, geography, geometry, government/civics, mathematics, physical education, science, social sciences, social studies, world history, world literature.

Graduation Requirements Computer science, English, mathematics, physical education (includes health), science, social sciences, social studies (includes history).

Special Academic Programs Remedial reading and/or remedial writing; remedial math; programs in English, mathematics, general development for dyslexic students.

College Admission Counseling 5 students graduated in 2010; 4 went to college, including Mitchell College. Other: 1 went to work.

Student Life Upper grades have uniform requirement, student council. Discipline rests primarily with faculty.

Summer Programs Remediation programs offered; session focuses on Academic make-up/remediation; held on campus; accepts boys and girls; open to students from other schools. 20 students usually enrolled. 2011 schedule: June 7 to July 3. Application deadline: June 3.

Tuition and Aid Day student tuition: $22,100. Tuition installment plan (individually arranged payment plans, TMS Tuition Management System). Need-based scholarship grants, Your Tuition Solution available. In 2010–11, 28% of upper-school students received aid. Total amount of financial aid awarded in 2010–11: $50,000.

Admissions Cognitive Abilities Test, Kaufman Test of Educational Achievement, Stanford Binet, Wechsler Individual Achievement Test, Wechsler Intelligence Scale for Children III or Woodcock-Johnson required. Deadline for receipt of application materials: none. No application fee required. On-campus interview required.

Athletics Interscholastic: basketball (boys, girls), cross-country running (b,g), soccer (b,g); intramural: basketball (b,g), swimming and diving (b,g), yoga (b,g); coed interscholastic: soccer; coed intramural: basketball, bowling, cooperative games, fitness, swimming and diving, tennis, volleyball, walking, yoga. 2 PE instructors.

Computers Computers are regularly used in all academic classes. Computer network features include online commercial services, Internet access, Internet filtering or blocking technology, Photoshop, assistive technology. Student e-mail accounts and computer access in designated common areas are available to students. The school has a published electronic and media policy.

Contact Edward McManis, Head of School. 415-922-6081 Ext. 21. Fax: 415-922-1598. E-mail: emcmanis@sterneschool.org. Web site: www.sterneschool.org.

STONE MOUNTAIN SCHOOL

126 Camp Elliott Road

Black Mountain, North Carolina 28711

Head of School: Susan Hardy

General Information Boys' boarding arts and vocational school; primarily serves underachievers, students with learning disabilities, individuals with Attention Deficit Disorder, individuals with emotional and behavioral problems, dyslexic students, NLD, and Asperger's Syndrome. Grades 6–12. Founded: 1990. Setting: rural. Nearest major city is Asheville. Students are housed in single-sex dormitories. 100-acre campus. 19 buildings on campus. Approved or accredited by CITA (Commission on International and Trans-Regional Accreditation), European Council of International Schools, North Carolina Department of Exceptional Children, Southern Association of Colleges and Schools, and North Carolina Department of Education. Total enrollment: 58. Upper school average class size: 5. Upper school faculty-student ratio: 1:4. There are 180 required school days per year for Upper School students. Upper School students typically attend 4 days per week.

Upper School Student Profile Grade 9: 17 students (17 boys); Grade 10: 14 students (14 boys); Grade 11: 6 students (6 boys); Grade 12: 2 students (2 boys). 100% of students are boarding students. 10% are state residents. 24 states are represented in upper school student body. 3% are international students. International students from Canada; 3 other countries represented in student body.

Faculty School total: 11. In upper school: 8 men, 3 women; 3 have advanced degrees; all reside on campus.

Subjects Offered 1½ elective credits, algebra, art, biology, earth science, English, geography, geometry, government/civics, history, keyboarding, mathematics, natural resources management, physical education, physical science, pre-algebra, science, social studies, Spanish, U.S. history, world history.

Graduation Requirements English, mathematics, physical education (includes health), science, social studies (includes history).

Special Academic Programs International Baccalaureate program; academic accommodation for the gifted; remedial reading and/or remedial writing; remedial math; programs in English, mathematics, general development for dyslexic students; special instructional classes for Orten Gillingham instruction.

College Admission Counseling 3 students graduated in 2010; 2 went to college. Other: 1 went to work.

Student Life Upper grades have specified standards of dress, student council. Discipline rests primarily with faculty.

Tuition and Aid 7-day tuition and room/board: $84,600. Guaranteed tuition plan. Tuition installment plan (monthly payment plans). Need-based loans, middle-income loans available. In 2010–11, 13% of upper-school students received aid. Total amount of financial aid awarded in 2010–11: $80,000.

Admissions Traditional secondary-level entrance grade is 9. Achievement tests or Wechsler Intelligence Scale for Children III required. Deadline for receipt of application materials: none. Application fee required: $3500. Interview recommended.

Athletics Interscholastic: backpacking, canoeing/kayaking, climbing, fishing, fly fishing, Frisbee, hiking/backpacking, kayaking, martial arts, mountaineering, outdoor activities, outdoor adventure, outdoor skills, paddling, physical fitness, rafting, rappelling, rock climbing, ropes courses, skiing (downhill), snowboarding, soccer, swimming and diving, ultimate Frisbee, volleyball, wall climbing, weight lifting, wilderness, wilderness survival; intramural: baseball, basketball, bicycling, billiards, crew, football, paddle tennis, sailing, skiing (downhill), soccer, swimming and diving, table tennis, track and field, volleyball. 5 coaches.

Computers Computer network features include Internet access, wireless campus network, Internet filtering or blocking technology. Student e-mail accounts are available to students. The school has a published electronic and media policy.

Contact Shannon Wheat, Admissions Director. 828-669-8639. Fax: 888-218-5262. E-mail: swheat@stonemountainschool.com. Web site: www. stonemountainschool.com.

SUMMIT PREPARATORY SCHOOL
1605 Danielson Road
Kalispell, Montana 59901
Head of School: Rick Johnson, MSW

General Information Coeducational boarding college-preparatory and arts school; primarily serves students with learning disabilities, individuals with Attention Deficit Disorder, individuals with emotional and behavioral problems, college-bound students with depression, anxiety, family conflict, and substance abuse, adoption issues, trauma, ADHD, mild learning disabilities. Grades 9–12. Founded: 2003. Setting: rural. Students are housed in single-sex dormitories. 540-acre campus. 4 buildings on campus. Approved or accredited by Association for Experiential Education, Northwest Accreditation Commission, Pacific Northwest Association of Independent Schools, and Montana Department of Education. Total enrollment: 46. Upper school average class size: 8. Upper school faculty-student ratio: 1:5.

Upper School Student Profile Grade 9: 6 students (4 boys, 2 girls); Grade 10: 10 students (6 boys, 4 girls); Grade 11: 14 students (8 boys, 6 girls); Grade 12: 14 students (8 boys, 6 girls). 100% of students are boarding students. 1% are state residents. 25 states are represented in upper school student body.

Faculty School total: 9. In upper school: 7 men, 2 women; 2 have advanced degrees.

Subjects Offered Accounting, algebra, American history, American literature, anatomy and physiology, art, astronomy, basketball, biology, British literature, calculus, ceramics, chemistry, choral music, composition, computer applications, drama, drawing, earth science, fitness, geometry, global studies, government, guitar, healthful living, interpersonal skills, journalism, painting, physical education, physics, poetry, portfolio art, pre-algebra, pre-calculus, SAT/ACT preparation, science fiction, sculpture, Shakespeare, Spanish, speech and debate, studio art, substance abuse, swimming, trigonometry, U.S. government, weight training, wilderness experience, world history, wrestling.

Graduation Requirements Electives, English, government, history, mathematics, physical fitness, science, completion of therapeutic program, which includes individual, group, and family therapy, and follows the student through a series of four therapeutic stages.

Special Academic Programs Advanced Placement exam preparation; accelerated programs; independent study; study at local college for college credit; academic accommodation for the gifted; remedial reading and/or remedial writing; remedial math.

College Admission Counseling Colleges students went to include Mississippi State University; New York University; Savannah College of Art and Design; The Ohio State University; The University of Montana; University of California, Berkeley.

Student Life Upper grades have specified standards of dress, student council. Discipline rests primarily with faculty.

Tuition and Aid 7-day tuition and room/board: $84,000. Tuition installment plan (monthly payment plans, individually arranged payment plans). Need-based scholarship grants available. In 2009–10, 30% of upper-school students received aid. Total amount of financial aid awarded in 2009–10: $100,000.

Admissions Individual IQ, Achievement and behavior rating scale, psychoeducational evaluation, Rorschach or Thematic Apperception Test or WISC or WAIS required. Deadline for receipt of application materials: none. No application fee required. Interview required.

Athletics Interscholastic: aerobics (boys, girls), alpine skiing (b,g), aquatics (b,g), backpacking (b,g), basketball (b,g), billiards (b,g), blading (b,g), bowling (b,g), broomball (b,g), canoeing/kayaking (b,g), climbing (b,g), cooperative games (b,g), cross-country running (b,g), equestrian sports (b,g), fishing (b,g), fitness (b,g), floor hockey (b,g), fly fishing (b,g), Frisbee (b,g), golf (b,g), hiking/backpacking (b,g), horseback riding (b,g), ice skating (b,g), indoor soccer (b,g), indoor track (b,g), martial arts (b,g), mountaineering (b,g), nordic skiing (b,g), outdoor activities (b,g), physical fitness (b,g), physical training (b,g), rafting (b,g), rock climbing (b,g), roller blading (b,g), roller skating (b,g), ropes courses (b,g), running (b,g), skiing (cross-country) (b,g), skiing (downhill) (b,g), snowboarding (b,g), snowshoeing (b,g), soccer (b,g), strength & conditioning (b,g), swimming and diving (b,g), ultimate Frisbee (b,g), volleyball (b,g), walking (b,g), wall climbing (b,g), water polo (b,g), water volleyball (b,g), weight lifting (b,g), weight training (b,g), winter walking (b,g), yoga (b,g);

intramural: basketball (b,g), indoor soccer (b,g), outdoor skills (b,g), soccer (b,g), wrestling (b); coed interscholastic: bicycling, bowling, indoor soccer, mountain biking; coed intramural: bicycling, indoor soccer, mountain biking, outdoor skills. 1 PE instructor.

Computers Computers are regularly used in business, computer applications, creative writing, word processing, writing classes. Computer resources include Internet filtering or blocking technology, supervised access only to Internet.

Contact Judy Heleva, M.A., Admissions Counselor. 406-758-8113. Fax: 406-758-8150. E-mail: jheleva@summitprepschool.org. Web site: www. summitprepschool.org.

SUNHAWK ADOLESCENT RECOVERY CENTER
948 North 1300 West
St. George, Utah 84770
Head of School: Mr. Benjamin G. Harris

General Information Coeducational boarding college-preparatory and arts school; primarily serves underachievers, students with learning disabilities, individuals with Attention Deficit Disorder, dyslexic students, and drug and alcohol involvement. Grades 8–12. Founded: 1996. Setting: suburban. Nearest major city is Las Vegas, NV. Students are housed in single-sex dormitories. 3-acre campus. 1 building on campus. Approved or accredited by Northwest Accreditation Commission and Utah Department of Education. Total enrollment: 52. Upper school average class size: 10. Upper school faculty-student ratio: 1:7. Upper School students typically attend 6 days per week. The average school day consists of 6 hours.

Upper School Student Profile Grade 8: 2 students (1 boy, 1 girl); Grade 9: 3 students (2 boys, 1 girl); Grade 10: 5 students (3 boys, 2 girls); Grade 11: 17 students (12 boys, 5 girls); Grade 12: 22 students (15 boys, 7 girls). 100% of students are boarding students. 3% are state residents. 15 states are represented in upper school student body. 1% are international students. International students from Canada.

Faculty School total: 7. In upper school: 5 men, 2 women; 6 have advanced degrees.

Subjects Offered Algebra, American government, art, biology, calculus, chemistry, earth science, economics, fine arts, geometry, language arts, physical science, physics, U.S. history, visual arts, world civilizations, world geography.

Special Academic Programs Accelerated programs; independent study; academic accommodation for the gifted and the artistically talented; remedial reading and/or remedial writing; remedial math.

College Admission Counseling 56 students graduated in 2010; 12 went to college, including Hofstra University; Linn-Benton Community College; Mitchell College; Northern Illinois University. Other: 2 entered military service, 12 entered a postgraduate year. Median composite ACT: 23. 1% scored over 26 on composite ACT.

Student Life Upper grades have uniform requirement, student council. Discipline rests equally with students and faculty.

Summer Programs Remediation, enrichment, advancement, sports, art/fine arts programs offered; session focuses on We are a year round program; held on campus; accepts boys and girls; not open to students from other schools. 70 students usually enrolled. 2011 schedule: June 23 to August 29.

Tuition and Aid 7-day tuition and room/board: $225. Tuition installment plan (individually arranged payment plans, Clark Custom Loans).

Admissions Traditional secondary-level entrance grade is 10. Iowa Tests of Basic Skills required. Deadline for receipt of application materials: none. No application fee required. Interview required.

Athletics Coed Intramural: baseball, basketball, flag football, Frisbee, kickball, martial arts, outdoor activities, outdoor adventure, outdoor recreation, ropes courses, snowboarding, soccer, softball, volleyball. 1 PE instructor.

Computers Computer resources include on-campus library services, Internet filtering or blocking technology. Students grades are available online.

Contact Mr. Jeff Johnson, Admissions Director. 435-705-9989 Ext. 235. Fax: 435-656-3213. E-mail: jjohnson@sunhawkrecovery.com. Web site: www. sunhawkrecovery.com.

SUNRISE ACADEMY
65 North 1150 West
Hurricane, Utah 84737
Head of School: Kathrine Whittekiend

General Information Girls' boarding college-preparatory and general academic school; primarily serves underachievers, students with learning disabilities, individuals with Attention Deficit Disorder, and individuals with emotional and behavioral problems. Grades 7–12. Founded: 2000. Setting: small town. Nearest major city is St. George. Students are housed in single-sex dormitories. 2-acre campus. 1 building on campus. Approved or accredited by European Council of International Schools and Utah Department of Education. Total enrollment: 32. Upper school average class size: 10. Upper school faculty-student ratio: 1:8. Upper School students typically attend 5 days per week. The average school day consists of 7 hours and 5 minutes.

Faculty School total: 3. In upper school: 2 men, 1 woman; all have advanced degrees.

Subjects Offered 20th century physics, 20th century world history, ACT preparation, advanced math, algebra, American government, American history, American literature, American studies, anatomy, art, biology, calculus, career/college preparation, chemistry, civil rights, CPR, crafts, creative writing, dance, decision making skills, drama, drama performance, English, equine science, ethics, family living, first aid, foods, general science, government, government/civics, health education, healthful living, history, human anatomy, human biology, human sexuality, independent living, leadership, learning cognition, mathematics, nutrition, outdoor education, personal growth, physics, physics-AP, pre-algebra, pre-calculus, SAT/ACT preparation, science, social skills, social studies, society and culture, sociology, Spanish, swimming, trigonometry, U.S. government, volleyball, writing, yoga.

Graduation Requirements Therapeutic advancement and personal accountability.
Student Life Upper grades have specified standards of dress, honor system. Discipline rests equally with students and faculty.
Tuition and Aid Guaranteed tuition plan. Tuition installment plan (The Tuition Plan, individually arranged payment plans).
Admissions Psychoeducational evaluation required. Deadline for receipt of application materials: none. No application fee required. Interview required.
Athletics Interscholastic: aerobics/dance, aquatics, backpacking, bicycling, bowling, climbing, cooperative games, dance, equestrian sports, fitness walking, hiking/backpacking, horseback riding, jogging, outdoor activities, outdoor education, outdoor recreation, rappelling, rock climbing, ropes courses, running, swimming and diving, walking, yoga. 1 PE instructor, 1 coach, 2 athletic trainers.
Contact Heather Black, Office Manager. 435-635-1185. Fax: 435-635-1187. E-mail: heatherb@sunrisertc.com. Web site: www.sunrisertc.com/.

TEXAS NEROREHAB CENTER

1106 West Dittmar Road
Austin, Texas 78745
Head of School: Ms. Angela Frey

General Information Coeducational boarding general academic, arts, vocational, and special education school; primarily serves underachievers, students with learning disabilities, individuals with Attention Deficit Disorder, individuals with emotional and behavioral problems, dyslexic students, bipolar disorder, autism/Asperger's Spectrum, brain injuries, fetal alcohol spectrum, sensory defensive, DD, and Intermittent Explosive Disorder, psychiatric conditions with mental retardation, medical impairments, and more. Grades 2–12. Setting: suburban. Students are housed in coed dormitories and single-sex dormitories. 67-acre campus. 4 buildings on campus. Approved or accredited by Joint Commission on Accreditation of Healthcare Organizations, Southern Association of Colleges and Schools, Southern Association of Independent Schools, Texas Education Agency, and Texas Department of Education. Total enrollment: 53. Upper school faculty-student ratio: 1:4.
Upper School Student Profile 100% of students are boarding students.
Faculty School total: 7. In upper school: 2 men, 5 women; 5 have advanced degrees.
Special Academic Programs Programs in general development for dyslexic students.
Student Life Discipline rests primarily with faculty.
Admissions Deadline for receipt of application materials: none. No application fee required.
Athletics 1 PE instructor.
Contact Ms. Angela Young, Registrar. 512-464-0283 Ext. 304. Fax: 512-464-0277. E-mail: angela.young@psyolutions.com. Web site: www.texasneurorehab.com.

TRIDENT ACADEMY

1455 Wakendaw Road
Mt. Pleasant, South Carolina 29464
Head of School: Joe Ferber Jr.

General Information Coeducational boarding and day and distance learning college-preparatory, arts, technology, and drama, community service school; primarily serves students with learning disabilities, individuals with Attention Deficit Disorder, dyslexic students, and Central Auditory Processing Disorder, dyscalculia, dysgraphia, and non-verbal learning disorders. Boarding grades 9–12, day grades K–PG. Distance learning grade PG. Founded: 1972. Setting: suburban. Nearest major city is Charleston. Students are housed in private host homes. 11-acre campus. 2 buildings on campus. Approved or accredited by Academy of Orton-Gillingham Practitioners and Educators, South Carolina Independent School Association, Southern Association of Colleges and Schools, and Southern Association of Independent Schools. Member of National Association of Independent Schools. Endowment: $1 million. Total enrollment: 90. Upper school average class size: 9. Upper school faculty-student ratio: 1:3. There are 170 required school days per year for Upper School students. Upper School students typically attend 5 days per week. The average school day consists of 6 hours.
Upper School Student Profile Grade 9: 9 students (8 boys, 1 girl); Grade 10: 3 students (2 boys, 1 girl); Grade 11: 9 students (7 boys, 2 girls); Grade 12: 7 students (4 boys, 3 girls).
Faculty School total: 29. In upper school: 3 men, 11 women; 11 have advanced degrees.
Subjects Offered Algebra, American history, American literature, art, astronomy, athletics, basketball, biology, business, business mathematics, calculus, career and personal planning, career/college preparation, cheerleading, chemistry, college admission preparation, college counseling, college placement, community service, composition, computer art, computer graphics, computer science, consumer math-

ematics, creative writing, drama, drama performance, earth science, economics, English, English literature, European history, geography, geometry, government/civics, grammar, guidance, health, history, journalism, language arts, language development, language enhancement and development, library, life science, marine biology, mathematics, music, newspaper, physical education, physics, poetry, pre-algebra, probability and statistics, psychology, reading/study skills, research skills, science, service learning/internship, Shakespeare, social skills, social studies, Spanish, speech therapy, sports, student government, student publications, study skills, tennis, typing, writing, writing workshop, yearbook.

Graduation Requirements Computer science, English, foreign language, mathematics, physical education (includes health), science, social studies (includes history).
Special Academic Programs Remedial reading and/or remedial writing; remedial math; programs in English, mathematics, general development for dyslexic students.
College Admission Counseling 6 students graduated in 2009; all went to college, including Anderson University; College of Charleston; Landmark College; Marshall University; The Citadel, The Military College of South Carolina; Trident Technical College.
Student Life Upper grades have specified standards of dress, student council, honor system. Discipline rests primarily with faculty.
Tuition and Aid Day student tuition: $23,740–$23,900. Tuition installment plan (Key Tuition Payment Plan, monthly payment plans). Merit scholarship grants, need-based scholarship grants available. In 2009–10, 30% of upper-school students received aid; total upper-school merit-scholarship money awarded: $185,000. Total amount of financial aid awarded in 2009–10: $185,000.
Admissions Traditional secondary-level entrance grade is 9. For fall 2009, 14 students applied for upper-level admission, 9 were accepted, 9 enrolled. Individual IQ, Achievement and behavior rating scale, psychoeducational evaluation and WISC III or other aptitude measures; standardized achievement test required. Deadline for receipt of application materials: none. Application fee required: $150. On-campus interview required.
Athletics Interscholastic: basketball (boys, girls), cheering (g), golf (b,g), volleyball (g); coed interscholastic: cooperative games, soccer, tennis, weight lifting; coed intramural: gymnastics, martial arts, physical training, self defense. 1 PE instructor, 3 athletic trainers.
Computers Computers are regularly used in all academic, creative writing, current events, foreign language, graphic arts, lab/keyboard, language development, library science, library skills, newspaper, SAT preparation, technology, Web site design, word processing, writing, yearbook classes. Computer network features include on-campus library services, online commercial services, Internet access, wireless campus network, Internet filtering or blocking technology. Computer access in designated common areas is available to students. Students grades are available online. The school has a published electronic and media policy.
Contact Betsy A. Fanning, Associate Head of School. 843-884-7046. Fax: 843-881-8320. E-mail: bfanning@tridentacademy.com. Web site: www.tridentacademy.com.

TURNING WINDS ACADEMIC INSTITUTE

6885 Bauman Street
Bonners Ferry, Idaho 83805
Head of School: Gordon Newell

General Information college-preparatory, religious studies, bilingual studies, and technology school; primarily serves individuals with Attention Deficit Disorder and individuals with emotional and behavioral problems. Founded: 2002. Setting: rural. Nearest major city is Troy, MT. Students are housed in single-sex dormitories. 149-acre campus. 4 buildings on campus. Approved or accredited by National Independent Private Schools Association and Northwest Accreditation Commission. Upper school average class size: 15. Upper school faculty-student ratio: 1:2. There are 260 required school days per year for Upper School students. Upper School students typically attend 5 days per week. The average school day consists of 6 hours.
Upper School Student Profile 100% of students are boarding students. 10% are state residents. 35 states are represented in upper school student body. 5% are international students.
Faculty In upper school: 3 men, 3 women.
Subjects Offered ACT preparation, advanced biology, advanced chemistry, advanced math, Advanced Placement courses, algebra, art and culture, biology, calculus, chemistry, Christian scripture, classical studies, college planning, computer science, fitness, gardening, geography, geology, geometry, health, history, honors English, mathematics, music appreciation, nutrition, physics, poetry, political science, pre-algebra, pre-calculus, pre-college orientation, psychology, radio broadcasting, Russian, SAT/ACT preparation, stock market, theater.
Student Life Upper grades have specified standards of dress, honor system. Discipline rests primarily with faculty.
Tuition and Aid Tuition installment plan (individually arranged payment plans, Quarterly payments are required). Financial aid available to upper-school students. In 2010–11, 10% of upper-school students received aid.
Admissions Deadline for receipt of application materials: none. Application fee required: $495.
Athletics 4 PE instructors.

Computers Computer network features include on-campus library services, Internet access. Campus intranet is available to students. Students grades are available online.
Contact Joyce Drush, Office Manager. 208-267-1500. Fax: 208-267-1600. E-mail: info@fsni.org. Web site: www.turningwinds.com.

VALLEY VIEW SCHOOL
91 Oakham Road
PO Box 338
North Brookfield, Massachusetts 01535
Head of School: Dr. Philip G. Spiva

General Information Boys' boarding college-preparatory, general academic, and arts school; primarily serves underachievers, students with learning disabilities, individuals with Attention Deficit Disorder, individuals with emotional and behavioral problems, and difficulty socially adjusting to family and surroundings. Grades 5–12. Founded: 1970. Setting: rural. Nearest major city is Worcester. Students are housed in single-sex dormitories. 215-acre campus. 9 buildings on campus. Approved or accredited by Massachusetts Office of Child Care Services. Endowment: $510,000. Total enrollment: 56. Upper school average class size: 6. Upper school faculty-student ratio: 1:6. Upper School students typically attend 5 days per week.

Upper School Student Profile 100% of students are boarding students. 15% are state residents. 25 states are represented in upper school student body. 15% are international students. International students from Canada, France, Kenya, and Mexico; 2 other countries represented in student body.

Faculty School total: 11. In upper school: 5 men, 4 women; 4 have advanced degrees; 3 reside on campus.

Subjects Offered Algebra, American literature, anatomy, art, biology, chemistry, civics, composition, computer math, computer science, creative writing, drama, drama performance, drama workshop, dramatic arts, drawing, drawing and design, driver education, earth and space science, earth science, Eastern world civilizations, ecology, environmental systems, economics, economics and history, economics-AP, electronics, English, English composition, English language and composition-AP, English language-AP, English literature, English literature and composition-AP, English literature-AP, English-AP, English/composition-AP, environmental education, environmental geography, environmental science, environmental science-AP, epic literature, ethics and responsibility, ethnic studies, European history, European history-AP, general science, geography, geometry, government, grammar, health, history, life science, literature, mathematics, music, physical education, physical science, science, social studies, Spanish, study skills, theater, U.S. history, Western civilization, world history, world literature, writing, zoology.

Graduation Requirements English, mathematics, physical education (includes health), science, social studies (includes history).

Special Academic Programs Remedial reading and/or remedial writing; remedial math.
College Admission Counseling 11 students graduated in 2010.
Student Life Upper grades have specified standards of dress, student council, honor system. Discipline rests primarily with faculty.
Tuition and Aid 7-day tuition and room/board: $63,600. Tuition installment plan (quarterly payment plan).
Admissions Academic Profile Tests required. Deadline for receipt of application materials: none. No application fee required. On-campus interview required.
Athletics Interscholastic: basketball, cross-country running, golf, lacrosse, soccer, softball, tennis, ultimate Frisbee; intramural: alpine skiing, archery, backpacking, baseball, basketball, bicycling, billiards, blading, bowling, canoeing/kayaking, climbing, fishing, fitness, flag football, floor hockey, Frisbee, golf, hiking/backpacking, ice skating, in-line skating, mountain biking, outdoor recreation, riflery, rock climbing, roller blading, skateboarding, skiing (cross-country), skiing (downhill), snowboarding, softball, street hockey, swimming and diving, table tennis, touch football, ultimate Frisbee, volleyball, wall climbing, weight lifting, whiffle ball. 2 PE instructors.
Computers Computers are regularly used in English, mathematics, science classes. Computer network features include Internet access. Student e-mail accounts are available to students.
Contact Dr. Philip G. Spiva, Director. 508-867-6505. E-mail: valview@aol.com. Web site: www.valleyviewschool.org.

THE VANGUARD SCHOOL
22000 Highway 27
Lake Wales, Florida 33859-6858
Head of School: Dr. Cathy Wooley-Brown, PhD

General Information Coeducational boarding and day and distance learning college-preparatory and general academic school; primarily serves underachievers, students with learning disabilities, individuals with Attention Deficit Disorder, dyslexic students, non-verbal learning disabilities, and higher functioning Asperger's Syndrome. Grades 5–PG. Distance learning grades 9–PG. Founded: 1966. Setting: small town. Nearest major city is Orlando. Students are housed in single-sex by floor dormitories, coed dormitories, and single-sex dormitories. 75-acre campus. 13 buildings on campus. Approved or accredited by Florida Council of Independent Schools, Southern Association of Colleges and Schools, The Association of Boarding Schools, and Florida Department of Education. Member of National Association of Independent Schools and Secondary School Admission Test Board. Endowment: $3.8 million. Total enrollment: 109. Upper school average class size: 7. Upper school faculty-student ratio: 1:7. There are 180 required school days per year for Upper

Our parents call it school.

we call it our Home.

School students. Upper School students typically attend 5 days per week. The average school day consists of 7 hours and 15 minutes.

Upper School Student Profile Grade 9: 13 students (7 boys, 6 girls); Grade 10: 25 students (18 boys, 7 girls); Grade 11: 31 students (24 boys, 7 girls); Grade 12: 25 students (17 boys, 8 girls); Grade 13: 4 students (2 boys, 2 girls). 76% of students are boarding students. 34% are state residents. 22 states are represented in upper school student body. 38% are international students. International students from Bahamas, Belize, Bermuda, Jamaica, Puerto Rico, and United Arab Emirates; 18 other countries represented in student body.

Faculty School total: 20. In upper school: 6 men, 12 women; 6 have advanced degrees; 3 reside on campus.

Subjects Offered Algebra, American history, American legal systems, American literature, art, basic skills, biology, British literature, business mathematics, calculus-AP, chemistry, creative writing, culinary arts, driver education, economics, economics and history, English, English literature, environmental science, environmental studies, film and literature, fine arts, forensics, geometry, government, government/civics, grammar, history, industrial arts, journalism, language arts, life management skills, mathematics, music, photography, physical education, physical science, physics, pre-calculus, psychology, reading, science, sign language, social studies, Spanish, speech, study skills, television, world history, world literature, yearbook.

Graduation Requirements Arts and fine arts (art, music, dance, drama), biology, economics, English, government, life management skills, literature, mathematics, physical education (includes health), reading, science, social studies (includes history).

Special Academic Programs Honors section; accelerated programs; independent study; study at local college for college credit; academic accommodation for the gifted; remedial reading and/or remedial writing; remedial math; programs in English, mathematics, general development for dyslexic students; special instructional classes for deaf students.

College Admission Counseling 42 students graduated in 2010; 29 went to college, including Florida Gulf Coast University; Johnson & Wales University; Lynn University; Nova Southeastern University; Santa Fe College; Warren Wilson College. Other: 4 went to work, 1 entered military service, 3 entered a postgraduate year, 5 had other specific plans.

Student Life Upper grades have specified standards of dress, student council, honor system. Discipline rests equally with students and faculty.

Summer Programs Remediation, enrichment, advancement programs offered; session focuses on academic enhancement and remediation; held both on and off campus; held at via distance learning; accepts boys and girls; open to students from other schools. 20 students usually enrolled. 2011 schedule: July to August.

Tuition and Aid Day student tuition: $22,500; 7-day tuition and room/board: $42,500. Tuition installment plan (monthly payment plans, individually arranged payment plans, Your Tuition Solution). Tuition reduction for siblings, merit scholarship grants, need-based scholarship grants, Presidential Scholarship (one per year) available. In 2010–11, 42% of upper-school students received aid; total upper-school merit-scholarship money awarded: $5000. Total amount of financial aid awarded in 2010–11: $500,800.

Admissions Traditional secondary-level entrance grade is 9. For fall 2010, 76 students applied for upper-level admission, 45 were accepted, 37 enrolled. Wechsler Intelligence Scale for Children required. Deadline for receipt of application materials: none. Application fee required: $100. Interview required.

Athletics Interscholastic: basketball (boys, girls), football (b), golf (b), running (b,g), soccer (b), tennis (b), track and field (b,g), volleyball (g), weight lifting (b); intramural: basketball (b,g), flag football (b,g), floor hockey (b,g); coed interscholastic: cheering, cross-country running, golf, soccer, tennis; coed intramural: basketball, broomball, canoeing/kayaking, fishing, fitness, fitness walking, golf, paint ball, physical fitness, scuba diving, skateboarding, soccer, walking, weight lifting, weight training, yoga. 5 coaches.

Computers Computers are regularly used in all classes. Computer resources include on-campus library services, online commercial services, Internet access, wireless campus network, Internet filtering or blocking technology. Computer access in designated common areas is available to students. Students grades are available online. The school has a published electronic and media policy.

Contact Melanie Anderson, Director of Admissions. 863-676-6091. Fax: 863-676-8297. E-mail: vanadmin@vanguardschool.org. Web site: www.vanguardschool.org.

See Display on page 910 and Close-Up on page 920.

THE WEDIKO SCHOOL AND TREATMENT PROGRAM

11 Bobcat Boulevard
Windsor, New Hampshire 03244
Head of School: Harry Parad

General Information Boys' boarding and day general academic, vocational, multi-sensory instruction, and skill acquisition school; primarily serves underachievers, students with learning disabilities, individuals with Attention Deficit Disorder, individuals with emotional and behavioral problems, dyslexic students, and Asperger's Syndrome, developmental delays, mood disorders, attachment issues, and high risk adoptions. Founded: 1989. Setting: rural. Nearest major city is Boston, MA. Students are housed in single-sex dormitories. 450-acre campus. 35 buildings on

campus. Approved or accredited by Massachusetts Department of Education, New Jersey Department of Education, and New Hampshire Department of Education. Total enrollment: 40. Upper school average class size: 7. Upper school faculty-student ratio: 1:2.

Upper School Student Profile 80% of students are boarding students. 75% are state residents. 6 states are represented in upper school student body.

Faculty School total: 44. In upper school: 10 men, 12 women; 7 have advanced degrees; 33 reside on campus.

Subjects Offered Algebra, arts, geometry, music, physical education, reading, science, social skills, social studies, therapeutic horseback riding, trigonometry, writing.

Graduation Requirements Graduation requirements determined by student's home school.

Special Academic Programs Remedial reading and/or remedial writing; remedial math; programs in English, mathematics, general development for dyslexic students; special instructional classes for children struggling with emotional issues.

Student Life Upper grades have specified standards of dress. Discipline rests primarily with faculty.

Tuition and Aid Tuition installment plan (individually arranged payment plans). Tuition paid privately or by city, school district, or state education funds available.

Admissions Deadline for receipt of application materials: none. No application fee required. Interview required.

Athletics Interscholastic: basketball (boys); intramural: aerobics/Nautilus (b), alpine skiing (b), aquatics (b), archery (b), ball hockey (b), baseball (b), basketball (b), bicycling (b), billiards (b), canoeing/kayaking (b), climbing (b), cooperative games (b), equestrian sports (b), fishing (b), floor hockey (b), gymnastics (b), hiking/backpacking (b), horseback riding (b), ice skating (b), indoor soccer (b), kayaking (b), kickball (b), mountain biking (b), outdoor education (b), outdoor recreation (b), outdoors (b), paddling (b), physical fitness (b), rock climbing (b), skiing (cross-country) (b), skiing (downhill) (b), snowshoeing (b), soccer (b), softball (b), swimming and diving (b), tennis (b), touch football (b), wall climbing (b), weight lifting (b), weight training (b), wilderness (b). 1 PE instructor, 2 coaches.

Computers Computers are regularly used in English classes. Computer network features include Internet access, Internet filtering or blocking technology.

Contact Katie Walsh, Admissions Clinician. 617-292-9200 Ext. 134. Fax: 617-292-9275. E-mail: kwalsh@wediko.org. Web site: www.wediko.org.

WELLSPRING FOUNDATION

21 Arch Bridge Road
PO Box 370
Bethlehem, Connecticut 06751
Head of School: Harvey I. Newman

General Information Coeducational boarding and day college-preparatory and general academic school; primarily serves students with learning disabilities, individuals with Attention Deficit Disorder, individuals with emotional and behavioral problems, and depression, mood disorders, eating disorders, and bipolar disorder. Boarding boys grades 1–6, boarding girls grades 1–12, day boys grades 1–12, day girls grades 1–12. Founded: 1977. Setting: rural. Nearest major city is Litchfield. Students are housed in single-sex dormitories. 13-acre campus. 6 buildings on campus. Approved or accredited by Connecticut Department of Education. Total enrollment: 52. Upper school average class size: 6.

Faculty School total: 20.

Special Academic Programs Independent study.

Student Life Upper grades have specified standards of dress.

Summer Programs Enrichment programs offered; held on campus; accepts boys and girls; open to students from other schools. 36 students usually enrolled.

Admissions Deadline for receipt of application materials: none. No application fee required. On-campus interview required.

Computers Computer network features include Internet access, Internet filtering or blocking technology. Campus intranet is available to students. The school has a published electronic and media policy.

Contact Nancy Thurston. 203-266-8002. Fax: 203-266-8030. E-mail: nancy.thurston@wellspring.org. Web site: www.wellspring.org.

WESTMARK SCHOOL

5461 Louise Avenue
Encino, California 91316
Head of School: Muir Meredith

General Information Coeducational day college-preparatory, general academic, arts, and technology school; primarily serves students with learning disabilities, individuals with Attention Deficit Disorder, dyslexic students, and students with language-based learning disabilities. Grades 4–12. Founded: 1982. Setting: suburban. Nearest major city is Los Angeles. 4.7-acre campus. 6 buildings on campus. Approved or accredited by California Association of Independent Schools, Western Association of Schools and Colleges, and California Department of Education. Endowment: $125,000. Upper school average class size: 12. Upper school faculty-student ratio: 1:12.

Faculty School total: 50.

Subjects Offered Algebra, American history, American literature, anatomy, art, biology, career exploration, chemistry, community service, computer science, creative writing, drama, earth science, economics, English, environmental science, European history, fine arts, general science, geography, geometry, health, history, home economics, literature, mathematics, music, physical education, physical science, physics, physiology, science, sign language, social sciences, social studies, Spanish, theater, trigonometry, video, world history, writing.

Graduation Requirements Arts and fine arts (art, music, dance, drama), English, foreign language, mathematics, physical education (includes health), science, social sciences, social studies (includes history), educational career plan. Community service is required.

Special Academic Programs Independent study; study at local college for college credit; remedial reading and/or remedial writing; remedial math; programs in English, mathematics, general development for dyslexic students.

College Admission Counseling 19 students graduated in 2010; all went to college, including The University of Arizona; University of Colorado at Boulder; Whittier College.

Student Life Upper grades have uniform requirement, student council, honor system. Discipline rests equally with students and faculty.

Summer Programs Remediation, enrichment, advancement, art/fine arts, computer instruction programs offered; session focuses on academic and social development; held on campus; accepts boys and girls; open to students from other schools. 40 students usually enrolled. 2011 schedule: July 7 to August 1. Application deadline: May 30.

Tuition and Aid Tuition installment plan (The Tuition Plan, individually arranged payment plans, Tuition Management Systems Plan). Need-based scholarship grants, sending district special education funding available. In 2010–11, 60% of upper-school students received aid.

Admissions Traditional secondary-level entrance grade is 9. Wechsler Intelligence Scale for Children III required. Deadline for receipt of application materials: none. Application fee required: $125. On-campus interview required.

Athletics Interscholastic: baseball (boys), basketball (b,g), cheering (b,g), equestrian sports (g), football (b,g), softball (g), volleyball (g); intramural: outdoor education (g); coed interscholastic: equestrian sports, flag football, soccer, swimming and diving; coed intramural: basketball, outdoor education. 3 PE instructors, 6 coaches.

Computers Computers are regularly used in English, history, science classes. Computer network features include on-campus library services, Internet access.

Contact Betsy Breese, Director of Admissions. 818-986-5045 Ext. 306. Fax: 818-380-1377. Web site: www.westmarkschool.org.

WILLOW HILL SCHOOL

98 Haynes Road
Sudbury, Massachusetts 01776
Head of School: Dr. Rhonda Taft-Farrell

General Information Coeducational day college-preparatory, arts, technology, and visual and performing arts school; primarily serves underachievers, students with learning disabilities, individuals with Attention Deficit Disorder, dyslexic students, non-verbal learning disabilities, and Asperger's Syndrome. Grades 6–12. Founded: 1970. Setting: suburban. Nearest major city is Boston. 26-acre campus. 4 buildings on campus. Approved or accredited by Massachusetts Department of Education, New England Association of Schools and Colleges, and Massachusetts Department of Education. Member of National Association of Independent Schools and Secondary School Admission Test Board. Total enrollment: 59. Upper school average class size: 8. Upper school faculty-student ratio: 1:2. There are 180 required school days per year for Upper School students. Upper School students typically attend 5 days per week. The average school day consists of 6 hours.

Upper School Student Profile Grade 9: 11 students (8 boys, 3 girls); Grade 10: 7 students (6 boys, 1 girl); Grade 11: 12 students (8 boys, 4 girls); Grade 12: 7 students (5 boys, 2 girls).

Faculty School total: 20. In upper school: 9 men, 11 women; 18 have advanced degrees.

Subjects Offered 20th century world history, algebra, American government, American history, American literature, art, biology, career/college preparation, chemistry, computer science, computer technologies, conceptual physics, consumer mathematics, creative writing, decision making skills, drama, dramatic arts, earth science, English composition, English literature, geography, geometry, grammar, integrated science, keyboarding, library studies, life science, mathematics, outdoor education, physical education, physical science, pragmatics, pre-algebra, pre-calculus, science, senior composition, social studies, study skills, technology, U.S. history, U.S. literature, world history, World War II.

Graduation Requirements Art, drama, English composition, keyboarding, literature, mathematics, physical education (includes health), science, social studies (includes history), wilderness education, Students must pass the Massachusetts Comprehensive Assessment System (MCAS), a state-mandated competency requirement.

Special Academic Programs Independent study; study at local college for college credit; academic accommodation for the artistically talented; remedial reading and/or remedial writing; remedial math; programs in English, mathematics, general development for dyslexic students.

College Admission Counseling 6 students graduated in 2009; 5 went to college, including Anna Maria College; Landmark College; Westfield State College. Other: 1 entered a postgraduate year.

Student Life Upper grades have student council. Discipline rests primarily with faculty.

Tuition and Aid Day student tuition: $46,423. Tuition installment plan (Academic Management Services Plan). PrepGATE loans available.

Admissions Traditional secondary-level entrance grade is 9. For fall 2009, 69 students applied for upper-level admission, 17 were accepted, 11 enrolled. Comprehensive educational evaluation and WISC or WAIS required. Deadline for receipt of application materials: none. No application fee required. On-campus interview required.

Athletics Coed Interscholastic: basketball, soccer, track and field; coed intramural: backpacking, basketball, bicycling, canoeing/kayaking, climbing, cooperative games, croquet, cross-country running, floor hockey, Frisbee, hiking/backpacking, horseshoes, kayaking, lacrosse, martial arts, mountain biking, outdoor activities, outdoor education, rock climbing, snowshoeing, soccer, track and field, volleyball, wall climbing. 1 PE instructor.

Computers Computers are regularly used in all academic, art, keyboarding, library science, technology classes. Computer network features include on-campus library services, Internet access, wireless campus network. The school has a published electronic and media policy.

Contact Ann Marie Reen, Director of Admissions. 978-443-2581. Fax: 978-443-7560. E-mail: amreen@willowhillschool.org. Web site: www.willowhillschool.org.

WINSTON PREPARATORY SCHOOL

126 West 17th Street
New York, New York 10011
Head of School: Mr. William DeHaven

General Information Coeducational day college-preparatory and arts school; primarily serves underachievers, students with learning disabilities, individuals with Attention Deficit Disorder, dyslexic students, and non-verbal learning disabilities. Grades 6–12. Founded: 1981. Setting: urban. Nearest major city is New York City. 1 building on campus. Approved or accredited by New York State Association of Independent Schools. Member of National Association of Independent Schools. Total enrollment: 203. Upper school average class size: 11. Upper school faculty-student ratio: 1:3. There are 170 required school days per year for Upper School students. Upper School students typically attend 5 days per week. The average school day consists of 7 hours.

Faculty School total: 62. In upper school: 22 men, 40 women; 55 have advanced degrees.

Subjects Offered Algebra, American history, American literature, art, biology, chemistry, community service, creative writing, drama, earth science, ecology, environmental systems, economics and history, English, English literature, European history, expository writing, fine arts, geography, geometry, grammar, health, history, mathematics, music, physical education, physics, science, social skills, social studies, speech, theater, trigonometry, U.S. history, world history, world literature, writing.

Graduation Requirements Arts and fine arts (art, music, dance, drama), English, history, mathematics, physical education (includes health), science. Community service is required.

Special Academic Programs Honors section; remedial reading and/or remedial writing; remedial math; programs in English, mathematics, general development for dyslexic students.

College Admission Counseling 24 students graduated in 2010; 20 went to college, including Adelphi University; Clark University; Iona College; Landmark College; Manhattanville College; The University of Arizona. Other: 1 went to work, 1 entered a postgraduate year, 1 had other specific plans.

Student Life Upper grades have specified standards of dress, student council. Discipline rests primarily with faculty.

Summer Programs Remediation, enrichment, art/fine arts programs offered; session focuses on reading, writing, and mathematics skills development; held on campus; accepts boys and girls; open to students from other schools. 30 students usually enrolled. 2011 schedule: June 30 to August 20. Application deadline: none.

Tuition and Aid Day student tuition: $46,800. Tuition installment plan (SMART Tuition Payment Plan, monthly payment plans, individually arranged payment plans). Need-based scholarship grants available. In 2010–11, 20% of upper-school students received aid. Total amount of financial aid awarded in 2010–11: $500,000.

Admissions Achievement tests, battery of testing done through outside agency, Wechsler Intelligence Scale for Children and writing sample required. Deadline for receipt of application materials: none. Application fee required: $70. On-campus interview required.

Athletics Interscholastic: basketball (boys, girls), softball (b); intramural: basketball (b,g); coed interscholastic: cross-country running, golf, soccer, track and field; coed intramural: boxing, judo, Nautilus, outdoor education, physical fitness, physical training, strength & conditioning, weight training, yoga. 3 PE instructors, 3 coaches.

Computers Computers are regularly used in art, English, history, mathematics, science, writing classes. Computer network features include Internet access, wireless campus network, Internet filtering or blocking technology. The school has a published electronic and media policy.

Contact Ms. Kristin Wisemiller, Director of Admissions. 646-638-2705 Ext. 634. Fax: 646-839-5457. E-mail: kwisemiller@winstonprep.edu. Web site: www.winstonprep.edu.

THE WINSTON SCHOOL SAN ANTONIO

8565 Ewing Halsell Drive

San Antonio, Texas 78229

Head of School: Dr. Charles J. Karulak

General Information Coeducational day college-preparatory, general academic, arts, and technology school; primarily serves students with learning disabilities, individuals with Attention Deficit Disorder, and dyslexic students. Grades K–12. Founded: 1985. Setting: urban. 16-acre campus. 2 buildings on campus. Approved or accredited by Independent Schools Association of the Southwest, Southern Association of Colleges and Schools, and Texas Education Agency. Total enrollment: 189. Upper school average class size: 10. Upper school faculty-student ratio: 1:8. There are 174 required school days per year for Upper School students. Upper School students typically attend 5 days per week. The average school day consists of 7 hours and 5 minutes.

Upper School Student Profile Grade 9: 22 students (13 boys, 9 girls); Grade 10: 29 students (14 boys, 15 girls); Grade 11: 14 students (12 boys, 2 girls); Grade 12: 20 students (10 boys, 10 girls).

Faculty School total: 29. In upper school: 7 men, 10 women; 7 have advanced degrees.

Subjects Offered Algebra, American history, American literature, anatomy and physiology, art, athletics, band, basketball, biology, calculus, cheerleading, chemistry, college counseling, college planning, community service, computer graphics, computer literacy, computer multimedia, drama, economics, English, English composition, English literature, environmental science, geography, geometry, government, graphic design, health, health education, jazz band, journalism, mathematical modeling, multimedia, music, photography, physical education, physical science, physics, pre-calculus, reading, Spanish, speech, world geography, world history, yearbook.

Graduation Requirements Arts and fine arts (art, music, dance, drama), computer science, English, foreign language, history, mathematics, physical education (includes health), science, social sciences, 20 hours of community service per year.

Special Academic Programs Independent study; study at local college for college credit; remedial reading and/or remedial writing; programs in English, mathematics, general development for dyslexic students.

College Admission Counseling 22 students graduated in 2010; 15 went to college, including San Antonio College; Southern Methodist University; St. Mary's University; The University of Texas at San Antonio; University of Mississippi; University of the Incarnate Word. Other: 7 went to work.

Student Life Upper grades have uniform requirement, student council, honor system. Discipline rests primarily with faculty.

Summer Programs Remediation, advancement, sports, computer instruction programs offered; session focuses on high school classes for credit; held on campus; accepts boys and girls; open to students from other schools. 50 students usually enrolled. 2011 schedule: June 13 to July 8. Application deadline: May 30.

Tuition and Aid Day student tuition: $15,000. Tuition installment plan (monthly payment plans, individually arranged payment plans). Need-based scholarship grants available. In 2010–11, 26% of upper-school students received aid.

Admissions Traditional secondary-level entrance grade is 9. For fall 2010, 12 students applied for upper-level admission, 12 were accepted, 11 enrolled. Achievement tests, battery of testing done through outside agency, comprehensive educational evaluation, Individual IQ, Individual IQ, Achievement and behavior rating scale, psychoeducational evaluation, Wechsler Individual Achievement Test, Wechsler Intelligence Scale for Children, Wide Range Achievement Test or WISC or WAIS required. Deadline for receipt of application materials: none. Application fee required: $100. On-campus interview required.

Athletics Interscholastic: baseball (boys), basketball (b,g), cheering (g), football (b), softball (g), volleyball (g); intramural: strength & conditioning (b); coed interscholastic: cross-country running, golf, track and field; coed intramural: cheering, golf, outdoor education, physical fitness, physical training, tennis, track and field. 2 PE instructors.

Computers Computers are regularly used in all academic classes. Computer network features include on-campus library services, Internet access, wireless campus network, Internet filtering or blocking technology. Campus intranet is available to students. Students grades are available online. The school has a published electronic and media policy.

Contact Ms. Julie A. Saboe, Director of Admissions. 210-615-6544. Fax: 210-615-6627. E-mail: saboe@winston-sa.org. Web site: www.winston-sa.org.

Special Needs Schools Close-Ups

ELAN SCHOOL

Poland Springs, Maine

Type: Coeducational boarding college-preparatory and general academic school for students classified as Emotionally Disturbed, Learning Disabled (mild to moderate), Other Health Impaired, or who exhibit disruptive behaviors associated with ADHD and/or ODD/CD
Grades: 8–12
Enrollment: 35
Head of School: Sharon Terry, Executive Director

THE SCHOOL

Elan School is a year-round school for students with behavioral, emotional, or adjustment problems. Founded in 1970, it is independently owned and operated. It was designed to help adolescents permanently change attitudes and life patterns, teaching them to function effectively in the mainstream of life. Elan's program has changed over the years, but the philosophy remains the same: "Elan's purpose is not to change an ill-behaved child into a well-behaved child; but rather to return home a responsible young adult." Students are admitted year-round and stay an average of twenty-six months. The rural 32-acre campus is 20 minutes from Lewiston and 40 minutes from Portland.

A guiding principle is that behavior cannot be changed by simply eliminating negative actions. The adolescent must not only stop antisocial acts but must also learn new ways of doing things. Elan is a closely knit, highly structured community that simulates society. Students living in the house are in charge of its operation under the supervision of direct-care staff members. There is a job hierarchy designed to instill self-respect and teach personal responsibility, honesty, consideration for others, self-control, and patience. A work ethic is stressed throughout the program—each promotion results in new privileges and increased status. If students fail to perform with initiative, they participate in additional group and individual sessions. If this is not successful, they are demoted; this teaches them to function under adversity and to deal with failure, disappointment, and disagreement. They learn that failing is part of life, that they can start again and succeed, and that the development of resilience is fundamental to success. Peer pressure and support teaches and enforces constructive behavior. Students learn that they must earn what they want and that they must give to receive.

The peer-oriented social structure is vital to the Elan concept. Students learn to take direction, accept criticism without taking it personally, criticize constructively, give orders reasonably, and care for and work with others; they also learn that self-esteem is not purely dependent on the acceptance of others.

Students manifest significant improvements in interpersonal relations at Elan. Intense but sometimes hidden feelings of anger and hurt are elicited and resolved in dynamic anger management groups. These exercises teach sensitivity to the needs, problems, and feelings of others and lead to an understanding of what spurs feelings and how to control actions that may be driven by them.

Elan is licensed by the Maine Department of Education as a special-purpose, private school for grades 8–12. Elan has received academic accreditation and therapeutic certification through the National Independent Private School Association (NIPSA) and is a member of the National Association of Therapeutic Schools. Elan is on the approval list for the states of Massachusetts, New Hampshire, and Illinois and is approved by Immigration and Naturalization Services to accept students with F-1 status.

ACADEMIC PROGRAMS

Elan is licensed by the Maine Department of Education for grades 8–12. Those students planning to continue their education in postsecondary schools are challenged through upper-level courses, while those who need intensive remediation are helped to acquire skills necessary to cope in the working world, as well as open doors to postsecondary education and training. Elan's credit requirements for issuing State of Maine high school diplomas are 4 English, 3 science, 3 math, 3 history (including U.S. history), 1 fine arts (humanities, theater, music), 1 physical education, health, and electives (such as organic chemistry, physics, Spanish, French, personal finance, and others) to total 24 credits.

Students follow a block schedule in which they take three courses per semester and earn 1 full credit in each subject. Classes are held Monday through Thursday, and students attend teacher-supervised study halls on Friday. A student may earn up to 6 credits during the regular school year plus the required studies in life skills and physical education. Foreign languages are offered but not required. Students are provided the opportunity to work in independent study programs under faculty supervision to augment their course of studies, if needed. Elan's curriculum reflects the needs of the student body and the expertise of its faculty members.

School during evening hours allows students to work through behaviors that interfere with concentration and learning during the day; students thereby arrive in class better prepared to focus.

Class size is kept small (maximum 14 students, optimum 10 students), and students are grouped by ability and course requirements. Supervised study halls and weekly grades help eliminate end-of-quarter "surprises." The passing grade is 65, and the entire School recognizes honors grades. Each quarter, the student receives written comments from each teacher as well as numerical grades. Elan's program also includes an eight-week summer session featuring remedial work, enhancement courses, and electives. Students earn a half credit in each of the two subjects taken during summer school.

FACULTY AND ADVISERS

Faculty members at Elan are certified in their subject specialty. Weekly faculty meetings allow continuous collaboration, brainstorming, and curriculum development.

William "Bill" Foss came to Elan School in 1995. He is currently the Principal and Evening Administrator. He received his B.S. degree from Gorham State College and his Masters in Educational Administration degree from the University of Maine. Bill has spent thirty-five years in education and served as Superintendent of Schools for twelve years. He also teaches history at Elan and assists with girls' cross-country.

Andrea (Ande) Lane joined Elan's Education Department in 2009 as the Special Education Director. She completed her Bachelor in Special Education degree at the University of Maine at Farmington, with a major in emotional disabilities. She has also worked as a special education teacher, a behavioral consultant, and as an elementary school principal. Ande is certified as a Wilson Reading Instructor and has worked extensively with students who have severe learning disabilities and/or challenging behaviors. In December 2007, she received her Masters in Education Leadership degree. Ande's dedication to special education comes with a strong focus on the maximum support of IEP development and implementation.

COLLEGE ADMISSION COUNSELING

Carrie Rhoads is the Elan School college adviser. She has been working with Elan students since the fall of 2007. Carrie has a B.A. in psychology from the University of Maine and an M.S. in counseling, with a focus in school counseling, from the University of Southern Maine. Since 2003, she has been employed at a local public high school as a school counselor. Carrie assists Elan students in gathering teacher recommendations, determining the right college setting, completing college applications, and scheduling college visits.

Elan is a closed SAT testing site and offers an SAT-prep course. Students continue on to two- and four-year colleges as well as to a variety of vocational programs and schools. More than 300 schools, colleges, and universities throughout the country have accepted Elan School graduates during its forty-year history. An average 80 percent of Elan's high school graduates continue their education. The remainder may enter the workforce or join the armed services, but several of these students have long-range goals that include furthering their education.

Students who are at or near the end of their high school requirements but still need to remain at Elan may be eligible to take some college courses. Elan has an adjunct professor from the University of New England who offers some college courses on Elan's campus. Some Elan students are also allowed to attend college courses at one of Maine's technical colleges or a branch of the University of Maine Systems.

Colleges and universities that have accepted Elan graduates include Albertus Magnus, Becker, Bryn Mawr, Castleton, Champlain, Coastal Carolina, Colby Sawyer, CUNY Staten Island, Curry, Dean, Earlham, Fisher, Iona, Lawrence, Mount Allison, Muhlenberg, New England College, Nichols, Regis, Rowan, Saint Michaels, St. Anselm, Salve Regina, SUNY Binghamton, SUNY Geneseo, SUNY New Paltz, Tel Aviv, and many others.

STUDENT BODY AND CONDUCT

Currently, there are 2 students in grade 9, 6 students in grade 10, 6 students in grade 11, and 21 students in grade 12. Students who are members of minority groups make up 20 percent of the student body; 94 percent of the students are boys.

ACADEMIC FACILITIES

Classes are conducted in the Schoolhouse, a facility that contains all classrooms and the computer lab. New laptops were purchased for student use in the spring of 2010. Students use the computer lab to conduct research and develop computer literacy. Teachers also use the lab as part of their course work with the students.

BOARDING AND GENERAL FACILITIES

The majority of the program is conducted in a co-ed environment called "the house." It is self-contained and set up to simulate a real home with a kitchen, dining room, and living room with a big screen television with surround sound. Meals are prepared in the main kitchen at Elan by two chefs and are served family style to the students. The menu has been approved by a nutritionist on staff at a local hospital. Single-sex dormitories may have from 2 to 8 students per room. The School operates year-round, and all students live on campus, even during major holidays. Academic classes are not held during standard public school vacation times.

Elan has an on-site medical clinic where routine medical care is provided. Elan's Medical Director is a practicing emergency physician with more than twenty years' experience. He is routinely on-site, treating students one day a week, or more often when needed. He performs initial physical exams, which include a lab workup, for all new admissions. He reviews the previous week's activities and is always available for telephone consultation. Elan's medical assistant handles day-to-day health problems in consultation with the physician when necessary. If specialty care is required and cannot wait for a home visit, treatment is conducted at local specialists' offices.

Elan students do not wear uniforms; however, there are clothing guidelines. Clothing is usually informal, but there are occasions when dress clothes are appropriate.

ATHLETICS

In season, an active schedule of intramural sports allows students to enjoy friendly competition.

Elan currently has girls' and boys' teams for cross-country, basketball, and track and field, all of which compete against other area private and public schools. Elan has produced several championship teams. The School's cross-country and track and field coach, Peter Rowe, was named Coach of the Year in 1997, 1998, and 1999.

The School's location on Upper Range Pond affords a waterfront program of leisure swimming (supervised by a qualified lifeguard) and canoeing. In recreational activities, Elan stresses teamwork and sportsmanship. Healthy peer interaction, a cornerstone of the program, is a goal in athletics as well as in all other aspects of the program.

EXTRACURRICULAR OPPORTUNITIES

Movies are shown every week. Concerts, festivals, local fairs, exhibits, sports events, and trips out to dinner, the movies, art museums, planetariums, aquariums, and the theater are organized regularly for students who have earned the privilege. Most entertainment trips are to Portland, where professional hockey and baseball teams are among the attractions. Other trips may be to attend area football games, amusement parks, agricultural fairs, or places of historical or cultural interest. Trips to various state parks including Fort Williams (a favorite of our students), Popham Beach, and others are organized during the summer months. In addition to the regular recreational trips, house trips include canoeing, white-water rafting, snow tubing, whale watching, roller skating, and bowling.

Elan students participate in an annual campuswide talent show. Students showcase their creative side by playing musical instruments, performing comedy skits or variety acts, singing, reading poetry, or participating in other performing arts. Students also participate in an annual "End of Summer" field day and BBQ. Students are awarded tickets that are redeemed for various events, which may include lawn bowling, a sherpa walk (which is part of the ropes course), a beanbag toss, a dunk tank, and other fun-filled activities.

DAILY LIFE

Weekday schedules begin at 8 with showers, cleaning dorm rooms, and breakfast; from 10 to 4:30 is a rotation of job functioning, physical education, group and individual sessions, and other events necessary to maintain balanced structure. Lunch is at noon, dinner is at 4:30, and school is from 6 to 10:30 p.m. Students return to their dorm rooms around 11 p.m.; lights-out is half an hour after students return to their dorm rooms.

WEEKEND LIFE

Elan is a demanding place. Students are busy weekdays with group sessions, house functioning, and school. Elan recognizes the need for change of pace, so weekends and holidays are less structured. Students may sleep until 11 a.m. and have brunch at 1 p.m. The rest of the day is usually spent in recreational activities. Elan School is nonsectarian.

SUMMER PROGRAMS

Elan's eight-week summer program is a continuation of the regular school year, except for a change in class times. (Summer program classes run from 7 to 10 p.m.) The curriculum focuses on remedial work tailored to current needs and on special electives. Full use is made of Maine's natural resources and points of interest.

COSTS AND FINANCIAL AID

The rate for the current school year is $54,960.60, billed monthly at $4580.05. Components of the annual cost are tuition, $21,490.88; supportive services, $19,172.72; and board and care, $14,295.74. The daily rate is $150.58. Each student's personal account for sundries and entertainment (Student Bank) averages $125 per month and is billed separately.

No financial aid is provided by the Elan School. Local school districts may offer funding under federal "civil rights for the handicapped" legislation for students classified as needing special education services. The rules may vary from state to state. Unfortunately, none of the fees (i.e., tuition, related services, and room and board) associated with Elan School is covered by private health insurance. For private loan information, families should visit http://www.Clark-BHF.com.

If the student is privately funded, due on the date of admission are the balance of the present month (if paid after the fifteenth, the following month's fees must also be paid) plus a three-month prepayment or Performance Deposit (which is applied to the final three months of the life skills program). A $200 deposit for the Student Bank is also required; this is always the parents' responsibility.

ADMISSIONS INFORMATION

The Elan candidate usually exhibits repetitive acting-out behavior, which may include running away, substance abuse, truancy, family conflicts, and promiscuity. Elan School cannot serve students who exhibit active violent behavior, have a specific psychiatric condition that cannot be managed without psychotropic medication (although some students have had a history of medication), have a severe medical condition requiring constant medical attention, or are sexual offenders.

Elan School does not discriminate on the basis of disability, race, color, creed, gender, age, sexual orientation, or national origin in admission to, access to, or operation of its program and services or its employment practices. This notice is provided as required by Title II of the Americans with Disabilities Act of 1990 and in accordance with the Civil Rights Act of 1964 as amended, Section 504 of the Rehabilitation Act of 1973 as amended, the Age Discrimination Act of 1975, Title IX of the Education Amendments of 1972, and the Maine Human Rights Act. Questions concerns, complaints, or requests for additional information regarding civil rights may be forwarded to Elan's ADA Compliance/EEO Coordinator, P.O. Box 578, Poland, Maine 04274.

Elan accepts referrals from parents/legal guardians, school districts, government agencies, therapists, educational consultants, psychologists, psychiatrists, and anyone with a personal or professional interest in the student. For students of divorced parents with joint custody, both parents must consent to placement. The Admissions Committee reviews the admissions application along with current psychological and/or psychiatric records, hospital and/or previous placement discharge summaries, and educational records. Questions of appropriateness are resolved via phone; occasionally, an interview is required. If criteria are met, the referral source is notified—first by phone, and then in writing; funding is verified (if privately placed, Elan's Financial Statement is required); and details of admission are finalized. By the date of admission, school transcripts, birth certificate, immunization records, medical authorizations, health insurance information, and applicable legal documents are required. In order to maximize understanding of Elan's program, parents receive a comprehensive tour before admission (or at the time of admission in emergency placements). The tour includes a visit through the house (escorted by an Elan student) and meetings with personnel from the Admissions, Education, and Medical Departments.

APPLICATION TIMETABLE

Inquiries and admissions occur year-round. Unless an interview is necessary, admissions decisions are usually made within three to four working days. Interviews, tours, and admissions are conducted weekdays (excluding legal holidays), by appointment only. Except for emergency situations, admissions are scheduled for Monday through Thursday during regular business hours. Due to Elan's rolling admissions policy, there are always students graduating from the School; therefore, if there is a waiting list, it is usually short.

ADMISSIONS CORRESPONDENCE

Connie Kimball, Admissions Director
Elan School
P.O. Box 578
Poland, Maine 04274-0578

Phone: 207-998-4666
Fax: 207-998-4660
E-mail: info@elanschool.com
Web site: http://www.elanschool.com

LANDMARK SCHOOL

Prides Crossing, Massachusetts

Type: Coeducational boarding and day college-preparatory and general academic school for students with language-based learning disabilities, such as dyslexia
Grades: Grades 2–12
Enrollment: 450
Head of School: Robert J. Broudo, M.Ed.

THE SCHOOL

Landmark School was founded in 1971 by Dr. Charles "Chad" Drake with the goal of educating students whose reading, writing, spelling, and mathematical skills did not match their thinking and problem-solving capacities. Most call these children dyslexic or learning disabled. Chad saw their promise, and called them bright and capable. Landmark opened its doors with 40 students and a small group of teachers on one campus in Prides Crossing, Massachusetts. Since then, Landmark has grown to 450 students on two North Shore campuses and a faculty and staff of more than 300. Today Landmark is recognized as a pioneer in the field of language-based learning disabilities.

Landmark is a coeducational boarding and day school offering a full range of customized programs for students in grades 2 to 12. With a college-preparatory high school, a middle school, and an elementary school, Landmark is one of the most comprehensive schools serving students with language-based learning disabilities in the United States. Landmark personalizes instruction for each student, emphasizing the development of language and learning skills, and cultivates a uniquely supportive and structured living and learning environment.

Landmark offers day and residential programs and enrolls students from across the United States and around the world. The School accepts bright students who have been diagnosed with a language-based learning disability, such as dyslexia. Successful candidates should be emotionally healthy and motivated to learn but need remedial help with reading, writing, spelling, listening, and speaking, as well as mathematics.

Landmark teachers are committed to the success of every student. The faculty is at the core of the School's innovative, effective program of remediation. Landmark's teaching principles and practices are based on forty years of front-line experience. Practical, classroom-tested methods are influenced by the latest research on human intelligence, cognitive development, and learning disabilities.

With a 1:3 teacher-student ratio, teaching at Landmark is concentrated and dynamic. Teachers, tutors, and case managers meet and share information about students every morning. The entire team is focused on the progress of each student.

Landmark School is located on Boston's North Shore, overlooking the ocean, in an area rich in historic sites and recreational opportunities. The high school and administration offices are located in the Prides Crossing section of Beverly, Massachusetts, just 25 miles north of Boston. The elementary–middle school campus is 3 miles to the northeast, nestled in the woods on an estate in Manchester-by-the-Sea.

Landmark is a nonprofit, nonsectarian educational organization. It is governed by a 26-member Board of Trustees. The School's operating expenses for 2007–08 were $23 million. Contributions and grants totaled $2.04 million.

Landmark is accredited by the New England Association of Schools and Colleges. It is a member of the Massachusetts Association of 766 Approved Private Schools, the National Association of Independent Schools, and the Association of Independent Schools of New England and is approved as a school for children with language-based learning disabilities by the Division of Special Education of the State Department of Education in the Commonwealth of Massachusetts. It is licensed as a residential facility by the Massachusetts Office of Child Care Services.

ACADEMIC PROGRAMS

The key to Landmark's successful model is the daily one-to-one tutorial. Students meet and work closely with one tutor for the entire year. A personalized tutorial curriculum is designed to remediate specific language needs, which may encompass decoding, fluency, phonological awareness, written composition, and organizational skills. The tutorial has a distinct curriculum and provides a personal connection between the student and teacher.

At Landmark high school, preparation for college and beyond is the goal of the program. Focus is placed on skill acquisition and achievement; a personalized program is designed for each student. The curriculum addresses the spectrum of student needs. Based on their unique abilities and skill levels, students are assigned to a schedule of courses.

The curriculum is designed to teach the students to become independent learners. Individual assessments are made continually to determine the appropriate approach of remediation.

Core subjects are math, social studies, science, language arts, oral expression, study skills, and electives. Computer technology is integrated across the entire curriculum.

For students who need intensive help with oral and written communication, Landmark offers courses in expressive language skills. Rigorous remediation is provided through an integrated curriculum to reinforce the relationship between listening, speaking, reading, and writing. Landmark teachers receive supervision from certified speech-language pathologists.

When a student progresses to within one year of grade level, their case manager may consider transitioning them to a more advanced level of course work. The pace is likely to be a bit faster and the classes slightly larger (8–12 students). For some students, the daily one-to-one tutorial is replaced by a study skills class. Mathematics is assigned based on skill level.

The elementary school program, for ages 7 to 10 (grades 2–5), is a self-contained model in which children are assigned to a small group of less than 8 students and matched with a key teacher for their academic day. Every child receives a daily individual language arts tutorial specifically attuned to diagnosed needs in the areas of reading, spelling, writing, and handwriting. The group stays together for the remaining classes: language arts, oral expression/literature, social studies, and science. Math classes are grouped separately according to each student's needs. Enrichment and elective offerings include arts and crafts, music, physical education, woodworking, computers, and small-engine repair.

The middle school program serves students ages 10–14 (grades 6–8), and each student receives a daily individual language arts tutorial as well as a schedule of small-group classes (4–8 students) consisting of language arts, math, science, social studies, auditory/oral expression, literature, and study skills. Computer competencies and keyboarding skills are incorporated into the class schedule, and electives (physical education, art, computer graphics, woodworking, and small-engine repair) complete the daily schedule.

FACULTY AND ADVISERS

Landmark employs 280 educational personnel made up of teaching faculty members, case managers, supervisors, and department heads. More than 65 percent hold advanced degrees.

In addition to teaching, staff members support the residential team after school hours and on weekends.

Through the Landmark School Outreach Program, faculty members present graduate courses and workshops at schools and conferences nationwide. Faculty members have published books on teaching study skills, writing, and mathematics. A professional development institute and lectures are presented each summer on the Landmark campus.

COLLEGE ADMISSION COUNSELING

Landmark's Guidance Department works with juniors and seniors. Counselors meet individually with seniors to help them select a successful path to the future and specifically work with preparing applications, interviewing, and completing the SAT, with accommodations as needed. College representatives come to Landmark School, and students visit colleges.

Over the past five years, the average rate of Landmark high school graduates attending two- or four-year colleges was 92 percent, which is 29 percent higher than the national average. Graduates from the class of 2010 were accepted to competitive colleges, including Northeastern, Ithaca, and Simmons.

STUDENT BODY AND CONDUCT

The 2009–10 student body had 443 students. The high school had 299 students; 135 day students (96 boys and 38 girls) and 164 boarding students (110 boys and 54 girls). The elementary–middle school had 144 day students. Students came from twenty-three states and ten other countries. Approximately 19 percent of the students were members of a minority group.

Landmark provides a safe and positive environment for its students, teaching respect, honesty, and commitment. Programs are structured to help students acquire and improve academic and social skills. The Dean of Students and a Standards Committee composed of faculty and staff members address individual conduct issues as needed.

The Student Council, which is elected by all grade levels and includes dormitory representatives, helps plan community service activities, parties, dances, lectures, and trips.

ACADEMIC FACILITIES

Landmark's high school campus is located in an estate setting on 30 acres that overlook the Atlantic Ocean. The Alexander Academic Center contains a library containing 8,000 volumes, a newly renovated dining room, and a tutorial center. Classes are conducted in Governor's Landing Academic Center, Prep Building, Classroom Building, Computer Center, and Early Literacy Tutorial Center. Science labs, the health center, and a girls' dormitory are in Bain Hall. Performing arts, visual arts, woodshop/boat building, auto shop, the Alice Ansara Athletic Center, Collins Athletic Field, and Tot Spot Childcare Center are all located on the main campus.

Lopardo Center contains boys' living space and the student center. Student residences are Williston Hall and Woodside Hall (both girls' dorms), Porter House, and the Campus Cottage.

The elementary and middle school (EMS) campus has a main building with classrooms, a newly renovated dining hall, a meeting room, a library, and offices. Three additional buildings house the tutorial center, art center, woodworking shop, small-engine shop, gymnasium, and more classrooms.

BOARDING AND GENERAL FACILITIES

Landmark has a fully staffed Residential Life Program that provides a round-the-clock living and teaching environment. Students learn how to manage their schoolwork, support their friends and roommates, and enjoy a wide range of planned activities, outings, and social events. The program incorporates a structured-level-based system that gives students the opportunity to earn privileges as they demonstrate their developing abilities in time

management, organization, and peer mediation and to consistently manage their responsibilities.

ATHLETICS

Fitness, health, competition, and recreation are all part of Landmark's athletic program. Students are encouraged to stay active and healthy. Eighty percent of Landmark high school students participate in organized team sports, and 95 percent of Landmark coaches are teachers at Landmark. Landmark competes in the Eastern Independent League and the Independent Girls Conference.

Landmark offers varsity and junior varsity baseball, basketball, cross-country, golf, lacrosse, soccer, swimming, tennis, and wrestling. Intramural programs include basketball, dodgeball, floor hockey, and volleyball. Supervised recreational clubs and activities typically include downhill skiing, mountain biking, skateboarding, and weight training.

EXTRACURRICULAR OPPORTUNITIES

In addition to intramural sports, the School also offers student council, gay/straight alliance, auto mechanics, visual arts, and the performing arts. Support of the greater community is encouraged; Landmark students have completed thousands of community service hours to support local and national charities.

DAILY LIFE

Classes are held Monday through Friday from 8 a.m. to 2:50 p.m., with seven 45-minute classes. After-school activities are encouraged. On weeknights, high school boarding students are required to attend a supervised study hall.

WEEKEND LIFE

Landmark's Residential Life Program emphasizes responsibility, respect, and independence. Students enjoy a great range of planned activities, outings, and social events, including movies, cultural trips, and skiing. Home visits are arranged individually on request. Transportation to attend religious services is provided.

SUMMER PROGRAMS

Landmark's Summer Program offers academic skill development and exciting afternoon activities in a supportive environment for grades 1 to 12 (boarding 8 to 12). Landmark faculty members provide a personalized program designed to improve reading, writing, spelling, and compo-

sition skills for each student. Full- and half-day academic programs feature daily one-to-one tutorials and small classes that can be combined with recreational or hands-on activities that foster personal growth. Choices vary by grade and age but have included marine science, kayaking, adventure ropes, and practical arts such as woodworking and small engines. Admission criteria are similar to the academic year programs.

COSTS AND FINANCIAL AID

The 2010–11 tuition for the academic program for day students is $45,000 and $59,900 for boarding students. Enrollment deposits ranging from $6700 to $9000, depending on the program, are due on acceptance. Half of the balance of the tuition is due July 1, and the remainder by December 1. Parents have the option of a ten-month payment plan.

More than 50 percent of Landmark's students receive financial aid through various agencies, mainly local departments of education.

ADMISSIONS INFORMATION

Landmark programs are designed for students with average to above-average intellectual ability; well-developed thinking, problem-solving, and comprehension skills; difficulty decoding, spelling, and writing; difficulty processing language; and no apparent primary emotional, social, or behavioral issues. Prior to admission, Landmark must receive a diagnostic evaluation as well as educational and medical records.

APPLICATION TIMETABLE

Landmark accepts applications and admits students throughout the year as space permits. Early application for summer programs is recommended.

Students who meet admission criteria are invited to visit Landmark with at least one parent or guardian. The half-day visit includes an interview, individual testing, tour, discussion of test results, and a decision regarding acceptance.

A fee of $150 must accompany the application form.

ADMISSIONS CORRESPONDENCE

Carolyn Orsini Nelson, Director of Admission
Landmark School
P.O. Box 227
Prides Crossing, Massachusetts 01965-0227
Phone: 978-236-3000
Fax: 978-927-7268
E-mail: admission@landmarkschool.org
Web site: http://www.landmarkschool.org

THE VANGUARD SCHOOL

Lake Wales, Florida

the
VANGUARD SCHOOL
Transforming potential. Accelerating achievement.

Type: Coeducational boarding and day college-preparatory and general academic remedial school for students with learning challenges
Grades: 5–PG, ages 10–20
Enrollment: 140
Head of School: Dr. Cathy Wooley-Brown, President

THE SCHOOL

The Vanguard School of Lake Wales, Florida, was founded in 1966 to serve the needs of students with learning disabilities, dyslexia, attention deficit disorders, Asperger's syndrome, and other learning challenges. At the time, the School was the residential branch of the Vanguard School of Paoli, Pennsylvania, which was founded in 1959. The Vanguard School of Lake Wales became a separate and independent corporation in 1983.

The mission of the Vanguard School is to provide an individualized program in a nurturing environment that enables students to develop to their fullest: academically, socially, and personally. The School provides a safe and secure but appropriately demanding and structured environment in which students who have been unsuccessful in regular school programs are able to learn and achieve. Believing that a school's most important function is to foster and enhance the total growth of the individual, the Vanguard School focuses on both the academic and social development of its students to prepare them for a full and satisfying adult life. Approximately 95 percent of the School's graduates go on to postsecondary programs, including community colleges, vocational programs, and four-year universities.

Located in the heart of the Sunshine State, the School has a 75-acre campus in the city of Lake Wales. Ideally situated for access to the beaches and cultural and entertainment centers of central Florida, the School is about 70 miles east of Tampa and 45 miles south of Orlando.

A Board of Trustees, made up of prominent representatives of the local business community, oversees the School's operations and establishes its policies. The President and administrative staff make all decisions concerning the program and daily student life. The School is a nonprofit institution, and its plant is conservatively valued at more than $10 million. The annual budget for 2010–11 was approximately $5 million, and the School's endowment funds exceed $5.5 million.

The Vanguard School of Lake Wales is accredited by the Florida Council of Independent Schools and the Southern Association of Colleges and Schools. It is a member of the International Dyslexia Association, the Learning Disabilities Association of America, the Southeastern Association of Boarding Schools, the Association of Boarding Schools, and Small Boarding School Association.

ACADEMIC PROGRAMS

The Vanguard program is designed to prepare students for the transition from high school to the next stage in the student's progress toward self-sufficiency. The academic classes are individually oriented and based on the needs of each student. Core classes are carefully structured with fewer than 10 students per class to ensure optimal attention to individual needs. The learning activities are explicit and the steps gradual, so that each student may progress in a way that is successful and satisfying.

Additional individualized needs are met through focused educational interventions. Students with communication difficulties receive individualized instruction in language and communication as well as referrals to the speech therapist, as needed. Learning disability specialists provide consultative services to students and staff members. In addition, tutoring is available to all students after school and on Saturday.

Academic classes are held Monday through Friday from 9:30 a.m. to 4:45 p.m. A study hour is scheduled into each student's academic day. Students take a core curriculum of reading, language arts, and mathematics that is individually tailored to meet the specific needs of each student. Science, social studies, and elective courses are presented as group-taught subjects with minimal reading requirements. These classes emphasize mastery-based learning through audiovisual presentations, class discussions, hands-on projects, experiments, and field trips. Within this framework, the School offers the basics of a comprehensive high school curriculum; students earn credits and receive a high school diploma upon graduation.

The School offers electives in TV/film production, industrial arts, culinary arts, art, yearbook production, life management, creative writing, and music. Driver's education is available through a local, independent company. Vanguard is a WiFi campus, with wireless access in all buildings.

FACULTY AND ADVISERS

Cathy Wooley-Brown, Ph.D., is the President of the Vanguard School. Dr. Wooley-Brown believes learning is a life-long journey. She holds a Doctor of Philosophy in curriculum and instruction, Education Specialist degree in educational leadership, a Master of Arts in special and gifted education, and a Bachelor of Arts in special education, all from the University of South Florida. She has also completed postdoctoral work in school restructuring and school reform at Harvard University. Dr. Wooley-Brown has coauthored several publications on charter schools, special education, and school reform. She has applied her passion for education by serving in virtually every capacity, including positions as professor, teacher, author, and administrator. As a frequent presenter at state and national conferences, Dr. Wooley-Brown recently testified before the Presidential Commission on Special Education and Students with Learning Challenges.

David Lauer is the Principal and holds a B.A. in special education from Bowling Green State University, an M.S. in education from the University of Miami (Florida), and an Education Specialist degree from Florida State University. The academic faculty consists of 20 teachers and specialists (12 women and 6 men). All faculty members hold bachelor's degrees, 5 hold master's degrees, and 1 holds an Education Specialist degree. The School employs 30 residential and recreational staff members who sponsor interscholastic and intramural sports, clubs, activities, weekend trips, and social events and provide structure and support in the dormitories.

Dr. Myron A. "Mike" Harvey is the School psychologist, who supervises admissions evaluations and reevaluations and serves as facilitator and counselor to the students. He also provides group sessions that work on a variety of social skills necessary for success in today's society. Individual psychological counseling may be provided through arrangements with a local, licensed behavioral health counselor. A speech therapist is available to provide direct speech services to students and to provide consultative services to teachers and other staff members.

COLLEGE ADMISSION COUNSELING

The majority of Vanguard students attend some form of postsecondary educational or training program, including two-year and four-year colleges and universities, vocational training programs, and transition programs. The School utilizes the state-of-the-art Navigation 101 program to facilitate college planning from the time a student enters high school. In addition, the School psychologist and faculty members counsel students and parents to help them determine the most appropriate placement for each student after Vanguard.

STUDENT BODY AND CONDUCT

The enrollment is 120, with 100 residential students and 20 day students. The residential students come from over twenty states and twenty countries. They represent a cross-section of cultural, ethnic, and racial backgrounds.

The School uses an individualized mentoring system to encourage the development of independent, self-responsible behavior among its students. The goal of this program is to provide a student the opportunity to proceed from behavior that requires external control and supervision to behavior that reflects positive, independent decision making; constructive involvement in the student's own development; and contributions to the School community. Each student is assigned a residential hall adviser who works with the individual student to develop appropriate goals. An economy system rewards privileges that reflect the degree of responsibility and independence the student has achieved. Areas of emphasis in the system focus on the self-care, interpersonal relations, school performance, program participation, individual goals, and general behaviors that are important for the overall development of the School's students.

Within both the academic and residential programs, there are opportunities for student involvement and leadership responsibilities. Peer-to-peer counseling and judicial councils teach self-advocacy skills and help deal with minor differences that arise between students. Student Residential Assistants (RAs) are older students whose primary role is to assist younger students with room care, social skills, and homework. An active Student Government Association, made up of elected representatives, plans social events and addresses School-wide student issues.

ACADEMIC FACILITIES

The three classroom buildings on the Vanguard campus contain twenty-five classrooms (including a spacious, stand-alone art room), a science lab, a computer lab, a woodshop, culinary arts kitchens, and seven offices for tutorials and specialists. The Harry E. Nelson Library/Media Center is available to students in the evenings and on Saturdays. It includes the *Fast ForWord* lab, computer stations with Internet access, and a large conference room.

BOARDING AND GENERAL FACILITIES

A structured but comfortable environment surrounds Vanguard students. The School has undergone complete renovations of its campus over the past two years. In addition to the dormitories, the campus also has a dining room and administration building. Housed in four spacious dormitories with students of similar ages, Vanguard students are under the supervision of the residential staff. Each of the dormitories is supervised 24 hours per day by staff members who are under the guidance of the Director of Residential Life. A live-in hall adviser is available in each dormitory and is responsible for creating a cohesive sense of family, which provides a nurturing environment for Vanguard's students. Two nurses monitor the students' health needs and staff the School's infirmary from 7 a.m. to 10 p.m.

Two students share a spacious dormitory room, which they are encouraged to personalize with their own belongings. Television lounges at the center of each hall are available for recreation and relaxation. In addition, a student center/recreation room located on the second floor of the School's gymnasium is available to students during free time.

ATHLETICS

Vanguard provides many opportunities for students to participate in various sports, depending on the student's interests and abilities. The Bartsch Memorial Gymnasium is home to several Panthers sports teams. In addition, the School has an Aquatic Center, which houses a 75-foot by 52-foot NCAA short pool and a bath house. The campus also has three playing fields, a lighted soccer field, lighted tennis courts, a canoe storage facility, and a fishing dock.

The Vanguard School is a member of the Florida High School Activities Association (FHSAA), which sanctions all of the School's interscholastic athletic contests. Boys may participate in football, basketball, cross-country running, golf, soccer, swimming, tennis, track and field, and weight lifting. Girls are offered the opportunity to participate in basketball, cheerleading, cross-country running, swimming, track and field, and volleyball.

Vanguard also offers an opportunity for all students to participate on a less competitive basis through a program of intramural sports. Games and tournaments are scheduled regularly throughout the year in basketball, flag football, indoor hockey, soccer, softball, swimming, tennis, and volleyball.

The health/fitness center houses a complete weight-training room with a Universal weight center, free weights and treadmills, and exercise bicycles. A local personal trainer is available to students for consultation on healthy lifestyle options.

EXTRACURRICULAR OPPORTUNITIES

Students have excellent opportunities to participate in a variety of activities, depending on their interests. Art students participate in local art exhibits, and the variety of specialty clubs offer something for everyone on campus.

In the afternoons there is a regularly scheduled period for clubs and activities, during which students can participate in intramural sports, weight lifting, and arts and crafts projects. Key Club and Student Government offer opportunities for leadership and community service.

DAILY LIFE

Breakfast is served from 8 to 9:15 a.m. and classes begin at 9:30. Each student takes eight 45-minute classes per semester, one of which is a required study hour. Dinner is served from 6 to 7 p.m. Students have free time from 7 until 8:55 p.m., seven days a week, which may include specific athletic or club activities. Bedtimes depend on the age of the individual student. Students who wish to achieve additional privileges are required to participate in community service activities.

WEEKEND LIFE

Weekends provide a change of pace and often a change of scenery for Vanguard students. Fishing, shopping, amusement parks, and other off-campus trips are a part of the weekend activities. The School maintains a fleet of vehicles, and it is not uncommon for them to be headed to four or five different destinations on a weekend. Weekend outings offer students the opportunity to visit the beaches and many other attractions of central Florida, including Walt Disney World, Sea World, the Kennedy Space Center, and the metropolitan areas of Tampa and Orlando. A more relaxed atmosphere is offered on Saturday and Sunday mornings, when an extended brunch is served. Students are encouraged to attend religious services at the many places of worship in the area, and transportation is provided.

COSTS AND FINANCIAL AID

The boarding school fee for 2010–11 is $42,500, which covers tuition, room and board, and initial school supplies. The fee for day students is $22,500. An academic activities/materials fee of $600 ($350 for day students) covers extra costs for School photographs, yearbooks, special event tickets, and lab fees. An additional $650 is required for international students to cover medical and miscellaneous expenses. The $4000 enrollment deposit is applied to the current year's tuition.

The Vanguard School Board of Trustees awards annual scholarship aid based on financial need. Following the interview process, families complete and submit a financial aid application and a copy of their current IRS tax return. Thirty-seven percent of the 2010–11 enrollment received financial assistance. As a special school, the Internal Revenue Service allows a deduction for the cost of attendance at the Vanguard School. Families should consult their accountant for Schedule A deductions that may be available. In addition, the School is authorized by the State of Florida to accept McKay Scholarships for eligible Florida students.

ADMISSIONS INFORMATION

The Vanguard School's enrollment age is 10 through 20, and it serves students with learning disabilities, dyslexia, Asperger's syndrome, and attention deficit disorders who have been unsuccessful in more traditional academic programs. A Thirteenth Year offers recent graduates an opportunity to increase basic skills and further develop social skills. All students must have the ability to speak and understand the English language, as the School does not offer an ESL program. Referrals to the School may originate from physicians, psychologists, educators, educational consultants, child guidance clinics, pediatricians, or other professionals who provide professional services to children, adolescents, and their families. Direct parental inquiries are also welcome.

So that the School may fully consider a student for enrollment, parents are requested to send copies of current academic records, including an official transcript for secondary-level students; a current psychoeducational evaluation (not more than three years old) that includes intelligence testing; and any medical records that would assist the School's professional staff members in determining a student's specific needs. The School also provides teacher and principal/counselor evaluation forms, which should be completed by the student's current school personnel. If, from this material, it appears the Vanguard program would be appropriate for the student, a visit to the campus for a pre-enrollment interview and evaluation is required. Appointments for these interviews are arranged by the admissions office.

Admission to the Vanguard School is open to all applicants regardless of race, creed, color, or national or ethnic origin.

APPLICATION TIMETABLE

Inquiries are welcome at any time. Tours and evaluation interviews are scheduled throughout the year, and admission is offered based on available space. The office is open Monday through Friday from 8 to 4:30. Brochures and additional information about the School are available through the admissions office.

ADMISSIONS CORRESPONDENCE

Melanie Anderson, Director of Admission
The Vanguard School
22000 Highway 27
Lake Wales, Florida 33859-6858

Phone: 863-676-6091
Fax: 863-676-8297
E-mail: vanadmin@vanguardschool.org
Web site: http://www.vanguardschool.org

Junior Boarding Schools

THE AMERICAN BOYCHOIR SCHOOL

19 Lambert Drive
Princeton, New Jersey 08540
Head of School: Mr. Karl Held

General Information Boys' boarding and day college-preparatory, arts, choral music, and music theory and literacy school. Grades 4–8. Founded: 1937. Setting: small town. Students are housed in single-sex dormitories. 17-acre campus. 5 buildings on campus. Approved or accredited by Middle States Association of Colleges and Schools, New Jersey Association of Independent Schools, Scottish Education Department, and The Association of Boarding Schools. Member of Secondary School Admission Test Board. Endowment: $4 million. Total enrollment: 48. Upper school average class size: 11. Upper school faculty-student ratio: 1:6. Upper School students typically attend 5 days per week. The average school day consists of 8 hours.

Student Profile Grade 6: 15 students (15 boys); Grade 7: 14 students (14 boys); Grade 8: 13 students (13 boys). 70% of students are boarding students. 60% are state residents. 13 states are represented in upper school student body. 8% are international students. International students from Republic of Korea and Taiwan.

Faculty School total: 13. In upper school: 4 men, 8 women; 8 have advanced degrees; 3 reside on campus.

Subjects Offered Computer music, computer skills, English, general science, health, mathematics, music, music performance, music theory, music theory-AP, physical education, physical fitness, social studies, Spanish.

Graduation Requirements Algebra, applied music, character education, choir, choral music, concert choir, English, eurythmics (guard), eurythmy, general science, geography, health, history, mathematics, music, music appreciation, music composition, music performance, music technology, music theory, musicianship, physical education (includes health), piano, pre-algebra, social studies (includes history), Spanish, values and decisions, vocal music, voice, participation in the Concert Choir.

Special Academic Programs Academic accommodation for the musically talented.

Secondary School Placement 9 students graduated in 2010; they went to Northfield Mount Hermon School; Peddie School; Portsmouth Abbey School; St. Andrew's School; The Lawrenceville School; Woodberry Forest School.

Student Life Uniform requirement, student council, honor system. Discipline rests equally with students and faculty.

Tuition and Aid Day student tuition: $21,850; 7-day tuition and room/board: $27,850. Tuition installment plan (individually arranged payment plans). Tuition reduction for siblings, need-based scholarship grants available. In 2010–11, 46% of students received aid. Total amount of financial aid awarded in 2010–11: $188,930.

Admissions For fall 2010, 56 students applied for admission, 19 were accepted, 9 enrolled. 3-R Achievement Test or audition required. Deadline for receipt of application materials: none. Application fee required: $35. On-campus interview required.

Athletics Intramural: baseball, basketball, cooperative games, cross-country running, fitness, fitness walking, flag football, football, Frisbee, jogging, outdoor activities, paddle tennis, physical fitness, running, soccer, swimming and diving, table tennis, tennis, touch football, ultimate Frisbee, walking. 1 PE instructor.

Computers Computers are regularly used in English, history, mathematics, music, science classes. Computer resources include Internet access, wireless campus network, Internet filtering or blocking technology. Computer access in designated common areas is available to students. The school has a published electronic and media policy.

Contact Ms. Lori Hoffman, Assistant Director of Admissions. 609-924-5858 Ext. 34. Fax: 609-924-5812. E-mail: lhoffman@americanboychoir.org. Web site: www.americanboychoir.org.

ARTHUR MORGAN SCHOOL

60 AMS Circle
Burnsville, North Carolina 28714
Head of School: Michelle Rehfield

General Information Coeducational boarding and day college-preparatory, general academic, arts, service learning, and outdoor experiential learning school. Grades 7–9. Founded: 1962. Setting: rural. Nearest major city is Asheville. Students are housed in coed boarding homes. 100-acre campus. 7 buildings on campus. Approved or accredited by North Carolina Department of Non-Public Schools and North Carolina Department of Education. Member of Small Boarding School Association. Endowment: $1 million. Total enrollment: 22. Upper school average class size: 9. Upper school faculty-student ratio: 1:2. There are 180 required school days per year for Upper School students. Upper School students typically attend 5 days per week. The average school day consists of 8 hours.

Student Profile Grade 7: 7 students (4 boys, 3 girls); Grade 8: 10 students (4 boys, 6 girls); Grade 9: 5 students (3 boys, 2 girls). 75% of students are boarding students. 75% are state residents. 6 states are represented in upper school student body.

Faculty School total: 15. In upper school: 7 men, 8 women; 1 has an advanced degree; 14 reside on campus.

Subjects Offered 3-dimensional art, 3-dimensional design, acting, ADL skills, adolescent issues, African American history, African American studies, African history, agriculture, agroecology, algebra, alternative physical education, American culture, American government, American history, American literature, American

minority experience, American studies, anatomy, ancient/medieval philosophy, animal behavior, animal husbandry, anthropology, art, arts and crafts, astronomy, athletics, audio visual/media, audition methods, auto mechanics, backpacking, baseball, biology, bookbinding, botany, career education, career education internship, carpentry, ceramics, character education, chemistry, civics, civil rights, clayworking, communication skills, community garden, community service, comparative cultures, comparative politics, composition, computer skills, computers, conflict resolution, conservation, constitutional history of U.S., consumer education, crafts, creative arts, creative dance, creative drama, creative thinking, creative writing, critical thinking, culinary arts, current events, dance, debate, decision making skills, democracy in America, design, drama, drama performance, dramatic arts, drawing, earth science, ecology, English, English composition, English literature, entrepreneurship, ethical decision making, ethics, ethics and responsibility, evolution, experiential education, expressive arts, fabric arts, family and consumer science, family living, family studies, fiber arts, first aid, fitness, food and nutrition, foreign language, forestry, gardening, gender issues, general science, geography, geology, geometry, global issues, global studies, grammar, guitar, health and wellness, health education, high adventure outdoor program, history, horticulture, human rights, human sexuality, humanities, independent living, integrated mathematics, interpersonal skills, jewelry making, journalism, language arts, leadership, leadership and service, life issues, mathematics, media studies, medieval/Renaissance history, meditation, mentorship program, metalworking, music, mythology, Native American studies, natural history, natural resources management, nature study, North Carolina history, oil painting, organic gardening, outdoor education, painting, peace and justice, peace education, peace studies, peer counseling, permaculture, personal growth, photo shop, photography, physical education, physics, piano, playwriting, poetry, politics, pottery, practical living, printmaking, probability and statistics, reading/study skills, relationships, sex education, shop, social justice, social sciences, social skills, social studies, socioeconomic problems, Spanish, sports, stained glass, study skills, swimming, travel, values and decisions, Vietnam War, visual and performing arts, visual arts, weaving, wilderness education, woodworking, work experience, writing, yearbook, yoga.

Graduation Requirements Annual 18-day field service learning trip, annual 3-, 6-and 8-day outdoor education trips.

Secondary School Placement 6 students graduated in 2010; they went to Carolina Friends School; George School; The Meeting School; Westtown School.

Student Life Honor system. Discipline rests primarily with faculty.

Tuition and Aid Day student tuition: $11,495; 5-day tuition and room/board: $21,945; 7-day tuition and room/board: $21,945. Tuition installment plan (40% by 8/15, 60% by Dec. 15; monthly payment 10% interest; full payment by 8/15- 2% discount). Need-based scholarship grants, individually negotiated barter arrangements may be made available. In 2010–11, 90% of students received aid. Total amount of financial aid awarded in 2010–11: $93,000.

Admissions Traditional entrance grade is 7. For fall 2010, 18 students applied for admission, 16 were accepted, 13 enrolled. Deadline for receipt of application materials: none. Application fee required: $35. On-campus interview required.

Athletics Coed Interscholastic: soccer; coed intramural: aquatics, backpacking, bicycling, billiards, blading, canoeing/kayaking, climbing, cooperative games, cross-country running, dance, fishing, Frisbee, hiking/backpacking, jogging, mountain biking, outdoor activities, rafting, running, skateboarding, soccer, swimming and diving, ultimate Frisbee, wilderness, winter walking, wrestling, yoga.

Computers Computers are regularly used in writing classes. Computer resources include supervised student access to computers for Web research, word processing, spreadsheet. Computer access in designated common areas is available to students.

Contact Meghan Lundy-Jones, Admissions Coordinator. 828-675-4361. Fax: 828-675-0003. E-mail: admissions@arthurmorganschool.org. Web site: www.arthurmorganschool.org.

THE BEMENT SCHOOL

94 Old Main Street
PO Box 8
Deerfield, Massachusetts 01342
Head of School: Mrs. Shelley Borror Jackson

General Information Coeducational boarding and day college-preparatory and arts school. Boarding grades 3–9, day grades K–9. Founded: 1925. Setting: small town. Nearest major city is Springfield. Students are housed in single-sex dormitories. 18-acre campus. 11 buildings on campus. Approved or accredited by Association of Independent Schools in New England, Junior Boarding Schools Association, and The Association of Boarding Schools. Member of National Association of Independent Schools and Secondary School Admission Test Board. Endowment: $4.4 million. Total enrollment: 246. Upper school average class size: 12. Upper school faculty-student ratio: 1:6. There are 163 required school days per year for Upper School students. Upper School students typically attend 5 days per week. The average school day consists of 8 hours and 30 minutes.

Student Profile Grade 6: 27 students (15 boys, 12 girls); Grade 7: 31 students (19 boys, 12 girls); Grade 8: 44 students (25 boys, 19 girls); Grade 9: 24 students (10 boys, 14 girls). 30% of students are boarding students. 80% are state residents. 8 states are represented in upper school student body. 21% are international students. International students from Bahamas, Brazil, China, Japan, Mexico, and Republic of Korea; 3 other countries represented in student body.

Faculty School total: 40. In upper school: 12 men, 12 women; 17 have advanced degrees; 10 reside on campus.

Subjects Offered Algebra, American history, art, art history, biology, chemistry, Chinese, community service, creative writing, dance, drama, earth science, English, English literature, fine arts, French, geography, geometry, grammar, health, history, Latin, literature, mathematics, music, music history, physical education, physical science, physics, science, social studies, Spanish, theater, theater history, typing, world history, world literature, writing.

Graduation Requirements Algebra, American history, art history, arts and fine arts (art, music, dance, drama), athletics, drama, English, foreign language, health, mathematics, music history, physics, science, social studies (includes history). Community service is required.

Special Academic Programs Honors section; study abroad; special instructional classes for deaf students; ESL (12 students enrolled).

Secondary School Placement 24 students graduated in 2010; they went to Deerfield Academy; Kent School; Northfield Mount Hermon School; Suffield Academy; The Williston Northampton School.

Student Life Specified standards of dress. Discipline rests primarily with faculty.

Tuition and Aid Day student tuition: $19,395; 5-day tuition and room/board: $35,385; 7-day tuition and room/board: $42,740. Tuition installment plan (Academic Management Services Plan, monthly payment plans, individually arranged payment plans, 60%/40% payment plan). Need-based scholarship grants available. In 2010–11, 31% of students received aid.

Admissions Traditional entrance grade is 7. For fall 2010, 79 students applied for admission, 45 were accepted, 26 enrolled. SSAT or WISC III or Wechsler Intelligence Scale for Children required. Deadline for receipt of application materials: none. Application fee required: $50. On-campus interview required.

Athletics Interscholastic: alpine skiing (boys, girls), baseball (b), basketball (b,g), field hockey (g), lacrosse (b,g), skiing (downhill) (b,g), soccer (b,g), softball (g), swimming and diving (b,g), track and field (b,g); coed interscholastic: cross-country running, diving, golf, ice hockey, squash, ultimate Frisbee; coed intramural: aerobics/dance, ballet, dance, fitness walking, indoor soccer, jogging, martial arts, modern dance, nordic skiing, outdoor activities, outdoor education, physical fitness, skiing (cross-country), skiing (downhill), snowboarding, strength & conditioning, swimming and diving, table tennis, tennis. 3 coaches.

Computers Computers are regularly used in art, English, foreign language, history, mathematics, science classes. Computer resources include on-campus library services, Internet access. Computer access in designated common areas is available to students. The school has a published electronic and media policy.

Contact Ms. Kimberly Caldwell Loughlin, Director of Admission. 413-774-7061 Ext. 104. Fax: 413-774-7863. E-mail: admit@bement.org. Web site: www.bement.org/.

CARDIGAN MOUNTAIN SCHOOL

62 Alumni Drive
Canaan, New Hampshire 03741-9307
Head of School: Mr. David J. McCusker Jr.

General Information Boys' boarding and day college-preparatory, arts, and technology school. Grades 6–9. Founded: 1945. Setting: rural. Nearest major city is Manchester. Students are housed in single-sex dormitories. 525-acre campus. 18 buildings on campus. Approved or accredited by Association of Independent Schools in New England, Independent Schools of Northern New England, Junior Boarding Schools Association, New England Association of Schools and Colleges, The Association of Boarding Schools, and New Hampshire Department of Education. Member of National Association of Independent Schools and Secondary School Admission Test Board. Endowment: $13.2 million. Total enrollment: 195. Upper school average class size: 12. Upper school faculty-student ratio: 1:4. There are 165 required school days per year for Upper School students. Upper School students typically attend 6 days per week. The average school day consists of 4 hours.

Student Profile Grade 6: 18 students (18 boys); Grade 7: 38 students (38 boys); Grade 8: 89 students (89 boys); Grade 9: 50 students (50 boys). 89% of students are boarding students. 24% are state residents. 16 states are represented in upper school student body. 41% are international students. International students from Canada, China, Hong Kong, Japan, Mexico, and Republic of Korea; 4 other countries represented in student body.

Faculty School total: 45. In upper school: 35 men, 10 women; 20 have advanced degrees; 39 reside on campus.

Subjects Offered Algebra, American history, American literature, art, biology, ceramics, computer math, computer science, creative writing, drama, earth science, ecology, English, English literature, environmental science, ethics, European history, expository writing, fine arts, French, geography, geology, geometry, grammar, health, history, industrial arts, Latin, life skills, mathematics, music, physical science, reading, science, social studies, Spanish, speech, study skills, theater, trigonometry, typing, world history, world literature, writing.

Graduation Requirements Arts and fine arts (art, music, dance, drama), computer science, English, foreign language, mathematics, reading, science, social studies (includes history), study skills.

Special Academic Programs Honors section; independent study; academic accommodation for the gifted; remedial reading and/or remedial writing; remedial math; ESL (12 students enrolled).

Secondary School Placement 70 students graduated in 2010; they went to Avon Old Farms School; Berkshire School; Kent School; Salisbury School; St. Paul's School.
Student Life Specified standards of dress, student council, honor system. Discipline rests primarily with faculty.
Summer Programs Remediation, enrichment, advancement, ESL, sports, art/fine arts, computer instruction programs offered; held on campus; accepts boys and girls; open to students from other schools. 135 students usually enrolled. 2011 schedule: June 25 to August 3. Application deadline: none.
Tuition and Aid Day student tuition: $25,600; 7-day tuition and room/board: $44,100. Tuition installment plan (The Tuition Plan, Insured Tuition Payment Plan, Academic Management Services Plan, Key Tuition Payment Plan, monthly payment plans). Need-based scholarship grants, need-based loans, prepGATE loans available. In 2010–11, 25% of students received aid. Total amount of financial aid awarded in 2010–11: $981,000.
Admissions For fall 2010, 220 students applied for admission, 155 were accepted, 80 enrolled. ISEE, SLEP for foreign students, SSAT or Wechsler Intelligence Scale for Children III required. Deadline for receipt of application materials: none. Application fee required: $50. Interview required.
Athletics Interscholastic: alpine skiing, baseball, basketball, cross-country running, football, freestyle skiing, ice hockey, independent competitive sports, lacrosse, mountain biking, nordic skiing, outdoor activities, physical training, rock climbing, running, sailing, skiing (cross-country), skiing (downhill), snowboarding, soccer, strength & conditioning, tennis, track and field, wall climbing, weight training, wrestling; intramural: archery, bicycling, bowling, boxing, climbing, equestrian sports, fitness, golf, ice hockey, martial arts, mountain biking, outdoor activities, physical training, riflery, rock climbing, ropes courses, sailing, skiing (downhill), snowboarding, swimming and diving, tennis, trap and skeet, weight lifting, whiffle ball. 1 coach, 1 athletic trainer.
Computers Computers are regularly used in English, history, mathematics, science, writing classes. Computer network features include on-campus library services, online commercial services, Internet access, wireless campus network, Internet filtering or blocking technology. Campus intranet, student e-mail accounts, and computer access in designated common areas are available to students. Students grades are available online. The school has a published electronic and media policy.
Contact Mrs. Jessica Bayreuther, Admissions Coordinator. 603-523-3548. Fax: 603-523-3565. E-mail: jebay@cardigan.org. Web site: www.cardigan.org.

See Display on page 925 and Close-Up on page 936.

EAGLEBROOK SCHOOL

Pine Nook Road
Deerfield, Massachusetts 01342
Head of School: Mr. Andrew C. Chase
General Information Boys' boarding and day college-preparatory, arts, and technology school. Grades 6–9. Founded: 1922. Setting: rural. Nearest major city is Springfield. Students are housed in single-sex dormitories. 750-acre campus. 26 buildings on campus. Approved or accredited by Association of Independent Schools in New England and The Association of Boarding Schools. Member of National Association of Independent Schools and Secondary School Admission Test Board. Endowment: $69 million. Total enrollment: 265. Upper school average class size: 10. Upper school faculty-student ratio: 1:4.
Student Profile Grade 6: 19 students (19 boys); Grade 7: 55 students (55 boys); Grade 8: 103 students (103 boys); Grade 9: 88 students (88 boys). 75% of students are boarding students. 35% are state residents. 28 states are represented in upper school student body. 20% are international students. International students from Bermuda, Hong Kong, Mexico, Republic of Korea, Taiwan, and Venezuela; 18 other countries represented in student body.
Faculty School total: 76. In upper school: 44 men, 24 women; 30 have advanced degrees; 50 reside on campus.
Subjects Offered Acting, African-American history, algebra, American studies, anthropology, architectural drawing, architecture, art, astronomy, band, batik, biology, ceramics, Chinese history, chorus, Civil War, civil war history, community service, computer art, computer science, computer-aided design, concert band, CPR, creative writing, current events, desktop publishing, digital music, digital photography, drafting, drama, drawing, drawing and design, earth science, ecology, English, English literature, environmental science, ESL, European history, expository writing, fine arts, first aid, French, general science, geography, geometry, grammar, health, history, industrial arts, instrumental music, journalism, keyboarding, Latin, mathematics, medieval history, music, newspaper, photography, physical education, pottery, pre-algebra, public speaking, publications, Russian history, science, sex education, social sciences, social studies, Spanish, study skills, swimming, theater, typing, U.S. history, Web site design, woodworking, world history, writing.
Graduation Requirements Arts and fine arts (art, music, dance, drama), English, foreign language, mathematics, physical education (includes health), science, social sciences, social studies (includes history). Community service is required.
Special Academic Programs Honors section; academic accommodation for the gifted, the musically talented, and the artistically talented; ESL (30 students enrolled).
Secondary School Placement 89 students graduated in 2010; they went to Choate Rosemary Hall; Deerfield Academy; Northfield Mount Hermon School; Phillips Exeter Academy; The Hotchkiss School; The Taft School.

Student Life Specified standards of dress, student council. Discipline rests primarily with faculty.

Summer Programs Enrichment, advancement, ESL, sports, art/fine arts, rigorous outdoor training, computer instruction programs offered; session focuses on enrichment; held on campus; accepts boys and girls; open to students from other schools. 60 students usually enrolled. 2011 schedule: July 2 to July 31. Application deadline: none.

Tuition and Aid Day student tuition: $29,250; 7-day tuition and room/board: $45,700. Tuition installment plan (individually arranged payment plans). Need-based scholarship grants available. In 2010–11, 30% of students received aid. Total amount of financial aid awarded in 2010–11: $1,650,000.

Admissions Wechsler Intelligence Scale for Children required. Deadline for receipt of application materials: none. Application fee required: $50. On-campus interview required.

Athletics Interscholastic: alpine skiing, aquatics, baseball, basketball, cross-country running, diving, football, Frisbee, golf, hiking/backpacking, hockey, ice hockey, ice skating, in-line hockey, indoor hockey, indoor soccer, lacrosse, mountain biking, outdoor activities, outdoor recreation, ski jumping, skiing (downhill), snowboarding, soccer, squash, strength & conditioning, swimming and diving, tennis, track and field, triathlon, ultimate Frisbee, water polo, wrestling; intramural: backpacking, bicycling, broomball, canoeing/kayaking, climbing, fishing, fitness, floor hockey, fly fishing, hiking/backpacking, hockey, ice hockey, ice skating, in-line hockey, in-line skating, indoor hockey, indoor soccer, juggling, kayaking, life saving, mountain biking, nordic skiing, outdoor activities, physical training, rafting, riflery, rock climbing, roller blading, roller hockey, roller skating, ropes courses, scuba diving, ski jumping, skiing (cross-country), street hockey, table tennis, volleyball, wallyball, weight lifting, weight training, wilderness survival. 1 athletic trainer.

Computers Computer network features include on-campus library services, Internet access, wireless campus network, Internet filtering or blocking technology. Student e-mail accounts are available to students. The school has a published electronic and media policy.

Contact Mr. Theodore J. Low, Director of Admission. 413-774-9111. Fax: 413-774-9119. E-mail: tlow@eaglebrook.org. Web site: www.eaglebrook.org.

See Display on page 926 and Close-Up on page 938.

FAY SCHOOL

48 Main Street
Southborough, Massachusetts 01772-9106
Head of School: Robert J. Gustavson

General Information Coeducational boarding and day college-preparatory, arts, and technology school. Boarding grades 6–9, day grades PK–9. Founded: 1866. Setting: small town. Nearest major city is Boston. Students are housed in single-sex dormitories. 66-acre campus. 26 buildings on campus. Approved or accredited by Association of Independent Schools in New England and Massachusetts Department of Education. Member of National Association of Independent Schools and Secondary School Admission Test Board. Endowment: $35 million. Total enrollment: 459. Upper school average class size: 12. Upper school faculty-student ratio: 1:7. There are 166 required school days per year for Upper School students. Upper School students typically attend 5 days per week. The average school day consists of 6 hours and 15 minutes.

Student Profile Grade 6: 49 students (20 boys, 29 girls); Grade 7: 65 students (31 boys, 34 girls); Grade 8: 87 students (48 boys, 39 girls); Grade 9: 48 students (29 boys, 19 girls). 61% of students are boarding students. 46% are state residents. 8 states are represented in upper school student body. 41% are international students. International students from China, Hong Kong, Mexico, Mexico, Republic of Korea, and Thailand; 11 other countries represented in student body.

Faculty School total: 77. In upper school: 21 men, 32 women; 35 have advanced degrees; 41 reside on campus.

Subjects Offered Algebra, American history, American literature, art, astronomy, biology, ceramics, computer science, creative writing, drama, English, English literature, environmental science, ethics, European history, expository writing, fine arts, French, geography, geometry, government/civics, grammar, Latin, mathematics, music, photography, physical education, science, social studies, Spanish, world history, writing.

Graduation Requirements Art, English, history, mathematics, music, science, technology.

Special Academic Programs Honors section; independent study; academic accommodation for the gifted, the musically talented, and the artistically talented; ESL (35 students enrolled).

Secondary School Placement 50 students graduated in 2010; they went to Choate Rosemary Hall; New Hampton School; Phillips Exeter Academy; Saint Mark's School; St. George's School; The Lawrenceville School.

Student Life Specified standards of dress, student council. Discipline rests primarily with faculty.

Summer Programs Enrichment, ESL, sports, art/fine arts, computer instruction programs offered; session focuses on ESL and Enrichment; held on campus; accepts boys and girls; open to students from other schools. 70 students usually enrolled. 2011 schedule: June 27 to August 5. Application deadline: April 1.

Tuition and Aid Day student tuition: $17,250–$27,250; 7-day tuition and room/board: $44,460–$52,750. Tuition installment plan (monthly payment plans, individually arranged payment plans). Need-based scholarship grants available. In 2010–11, 19% of students received aid. Total amount of financial aid awarded in 2010–11: $1,110,900.

Admissions Traditional entrance grade is 8. For fall 2010, 266 students applied for admission, 108 were accepted, 80 enrolled. Wechsler Intelligence Scale for Children required. Deadline for receipt of application materials: none. Application fee required: $50. Interview required.

Athletics Interscholastic: baseball (boys), basketball (b,g), cross-country running (b,g), field hockey (g), football (b), golf (b,g), hockey (b,g), ice hockey (b,g), independent competitive sports (b,g), lacrosse (b,g), soccer (b,g), softball (g), tennis (b,g), track and field (b,g), volleyball (g), wrestling (b); intramural: basketball (b,g), climbing (b,g), dance (b,g), fitness (b,g), golf (b,g), horseback riding (b,g), physical fitness (b,g), rock climbing (b,g), ropes courses (b,g), skiing (downhill) (b,g), snowboarding (b,g), soccer (b,g), strength & conditioning (b,g), tennis (b,g), trap and skeet (b,g), wall climbing (b,g), weight training (b,g), yoga (b,g); coed interscholastic: basketball, cross-country running, golf, hockey, ice hockey, independent competitive sports, lacrosse, soccer, tennis, track and field, volleyball; coed intramural: aerobics/Nautilus, alpine skiing, backpacking, basketball, bicycling, climbing, dance, fitness, golf, horseback riding, outdoor activities, outdoor adventure, outdoors, physical fitness, rock climbing, ropes courses, skiing (downhill), snowboarding, soccer, squash, strength & conditioning, tennis, trap and skeet, wall climbing, weight training, yoga. 2 PE instructors, 17 coaches, 1 athletic trainer.

Computers Computers are regularly used in art, English, foreign language, history, information technology, mathematics, music, science classes. Computer network features include on-campus library services, Internet access, Internet filtering or blocking technology. Campus intranet, student e-mail accounts, and computer access in designated common areas are available to students. Students grades are available online. The school has a published electronic and media policy.

Contact Ms. Katie Enlow, Assistant to the Director of Admission. 508-490-8201. Fax: 508-481-7872. E-mail: kenlow@fayschool.org. Web site: www.fayschool.org.

THE FESSENDEN SCHOOL

250 Waltham Street
West Newton, Massachusetts 02465-1750
Head of School: Mr. Peter P. Drake

General Information Boys' boarding and day college-preparatory, general academic, and arts school. Boarding grades 5–9, day grades K–9. Founded: 1903. Setting: suburban. Nearest major city is Boston. Students are housed in single-sex dormitories. 41-acre campus. 25 buildings on campus. Approved or accredited by Association of Independent Schools in New England, The Association of Boarding Schools, and Massachusetts Department of Education. Member of National Association of Independent Schools and Secondary School Admission Test Board. Endowment: $25 million. Total enrollment: 481. Upper school average class size: 12. Upper school faculty-student ratio: 1:7. There are 162 required school days per year for Upper School students. Upper School students typically attend 5 days per week. The average school day consists of 8 hours.

Student Profile Grade 7: 78 students (78 boys); Grade 8: 75 students (75 boys); Grade 9: 46 students (46 boys). 50% of students are boarding students. 70% are state residents. 17 states are represented in upper school student body. 19% are international students. International students from Bermuda, Mexico, Republic of Korea, Taiwan, and Thailand; 7 other countries represented in student body.

Faculty School total: 91. In upper school: 40 men, 51 women; 54 have advanced degrees; 43 reside on campus.

Subjects Offered Algebra, American history, American literature, anatomy, art, astronomy, biology, ceramics, chemistry, computer math, computer programming, computer science, creative writing, drama, earth science, English, English literature, European history, expository writing, fine arts, French, geography, geometry, government/civics, grammar, health, history, human sexuality, Latin, library studies, mathematics, music, photography, physical education, physics, science, social sciences, social studies, Spanish, theater, typing, world history, writing.

Graduation Requirements Arts and fine arts (art, music, dance, drama), computer science, English, foreign language, mathematics, science, social sciences, social studies (includes history).

Special Academic Programs Honors section; academic accommodation for the gifted, the musically talented, and the artistically talented; remedial reading and/or remedial writing; remedial math; ESL (14 students enrolled).

Secondary School Placement 46 students graduated in 2009; they went to Middlesex School; Milton Academy; Noble and Greenough School; Tabor Academy.

Student Life Specified standards of dress, student council, honor system. Discipline rests primarily with faculty.

Tuition and Aid Day student tuition: $22,250–$31,500; 5-day tuition and room/board: $38,900–$39,700; 7-day tuition and room/board: $44,100–$44,900. Tuition installment plan (Academic Management Services Plan, monthly payment plans). Need-based scholarship grants available. In 2009–10, 63% of students received aid. Total amount of financial aid awarded in 2009–10: $832,000.

Admissions Traditional entrance grade is 7. For fall 2009, 84 students applied for admission, 43 were accepted, 34 enrolled. ISEE, SLEP for foreign students, SSAT,

Wechsler Intelligence Scale for Children or writing sample required. Deadline for receipt of application materials: February 1. Application fee required: $50. On-campus interview required.

Athletics Interscholastic: baseball (boys), basketball (b), cross-country running (b), football (b), ice hockey (b), lacrosse (b), soccer (b), squash (b), tennis (b), track and field (b), wrestling (b); intramural: alpine skiing (b), baseball (b), basketball (b), canoeing/kayaking (b), fencing (b), football (b), golf (b), ice hockey (b), mountain biking (b), racquetball (b), sailing (b), skiing (cross-country) (b), skiing (downhill) (b), snowboarding (b), soccer (b), strength & conditioning (b), swimming and diving (b), tennis (b), weight training (b). 3 PE instructors, 1 athletic trainer.

Computers Computers are regularly used in English, mathematics, science classes. Computer network features include on-campus library services, Internet access, Internet filtering or blocking technology. Campus intranet and student e-mail accounts are available to students. The school has a published electronic and media policy.

Contact Mr. Caleb Thomson, Director of Admissions. 617-630-2300. Fax: 617-630-2303. E-mail: admissions@fessenden.org. Web site: www.fessenden.org.

FOX RIVER COUNTRY DAY SCHOOL
1600 Dundee Avenue
Elgin, Illinois 60120
Head of School: Mrs. Karen Morse

General Information Coeducational boarding and day college-preparatory, arts, and environmental education school, affiliated with Church of Christ, Scientist. Boarding grades 5–8, day grades PS–8. Founded: 1913. Setting: rural. Nearest major city is Chicago. Students are housed in single-sex by floor dormitories. 53-acre campus. 10 buildings on campus. Approved or accredited by Independent Schools Association of the Central States. Member of National Association of Independent Schools. Total enrollment: 186. Upper school average class size: 13. Upper school faculty-student ratio: 1:13. There are 168 required school days per year for Upper School students. Upper School students typically attend 5 days per week. The average school day consists of 7 hours and 45 minutes.

Student Profile Grade 6: 13 students (6 boys, 7 girls); Grade 7: 13 students (7 boys, 6 girls); Grade 8: 17 students (9 boys, 8 girls). 21% of students are boarding students. 33% are state residents. 1 state is represented in upper school student body. 67% are international students. International students from China and Republic of Korea. 5% of students are members of Church of Christ, Scientist.

Faculty School total: 26. In upper school: 5 men, 21 women; 6 have advanced degrees; 4 reside on campus.

Subjects Offered Algebra, American history, American literature, art, computer science, creative writing, earth science, English, English literature, environmental education, environmental science, general science, geography, geometry, grammar, history, library studies, mathematics, music, physical education, social studies, Spanish, swimming, world history, world literature, writing.

Graduation Requirements Arts and fine arts (art, music, dance, drama), English, environmental education, foreign language, mathematics, physical education (includes health), science, social studies (includes history).

Special Academic Programs Academic accommodation for the gifted; ESL (6 students enrolled).

Secondary School Placement 14 students graduated in 2009.

Student Life Specified standards of dress, honor system. Discipline rests primarily with faculty.

Tuition and Aid Day student tuition: $3600–$12,850; 5-day tuition and room/board: $29,820; 7-day tuition and room/board: $35,450. Tuition installment plan (monthly payment plans). Tuition reduction for siblings, need-based scholarship grants available. In 2009–10, 35% of students received aid.

Admissions For fall 2009, 11 students applied for admission, 7 were accepted, 7 enrolled. TOEFL or SLEP or writing sample required. Deadline for receipt of application materials: none. Application fee required: $60. Interview required.

Athletics Interscholastic: basketball (boys, girls), soccer (b,g), volleyball (b,g); intramural: badminton (b,g), basketball (b,g), volleyball (b,g), wrestling (b); coed interscholastic: cooperative games, swimming and diving, track and field; coed intramural: cooperative games, cross-country running, field hockey, fitness, flag football, floor hockey, Frisbee, gymnastics, jogging, kickball, outdoor activities, outdoor education, outdoor recreation, physical fitness, running, soccer, strength & conditioning, swimming and diving, tennis, track and field, ultimate Frisbee, volleyball. 2 PE instructors, 4 coaches.

Computers Computers are regularly used in English, science classes. Computer resources include Internet access, Internet filtering or blocking technology. Computer access in designated common areas is available to students.

Contact Mr. Chuck Harvuot, Director of Admissions. 847-888-7920 Ext. 167. Fax: 847-888-7878. E-mail: admissions@frcds.org. Web site: www.frcds.org.

THE GREENWOOD SCHOOL
14 Greenwood Lane
Putney, Vermont 05346
Head of School: Mr. Stewart Miller

General Information Boys' boarding arts, drama, and music school; primarily serves underachievers, students with learning disabilities, individuals with Attention

Deficit Disorder, and dyslexic students. Ungraded, ages 9–15. Founded: 1978. Setting: rural. Nearest major city is Boston, MA. Students are housed in single-sex dormitories. 100-acre campus. 13 buildings on campus. Approved or accredited by Independent Schools of Northern New England, Junior Boarding Schools Association, New England Association of Schools and Colleges, The Association of Boarding Schools, and Vermont Department of Education. Member of National Association of Independent Schools. Endowment: $840,000. Total enrollment: 50. Upper school average class size: 5. Upper school faculty-student ratio: 1:2. There are 199 required school days per year for Upper School students. Upper School students typically attend 7 days per week. The average school day consists of 5 hours.

Student Profile 93% of students are boarding students. 16% are state residents. 16 states are represented in upper school student body. 9% are international students. International students from Canada, Hong Kong, and Panama; 2 other countries represented in student body.

Faculty School total: 33. In upper school: 15 men, 14 women; 20 have advanced degrees; 12 reside on campus.

Subjects Offered American history, American literature, art, biology, crafts, creative writing, drama, earth science, ecology, English, geography, grammar, history, mathematics, music, physical education, pragmatics, speech, theater, woodworking, writing.

Special Academic Programs Academic accommodation for the gifted, the musically talented, and the artistically talented; remedial reading and/or remedial writing; remedial math; programs in English, mathematics, general development for dyslexic students.

Secondary School Placement 12 students graduated in 2010; they went to Dublin School; The Gow School.

Student Life Specified standards of dress, student council, honor system. Discipline rests primarily with faculty.

Tuition and Aid Day student tuition: $48,000; 7-day tuition and room/board: $62,775. Tuition installment plan (individually arranged payment plans). Need-based scholarship grants available. In 2010–11, 12% of students received aid. Total amount of financial aid awarded in 2010–11: $249,290.

Admissions Traditional entrance age is 12. Wechsler Intelligence Scale for Children III or Woodcock-Johnson Revised Achievement Test required. Deadline for receipt of application materials: none. Application fee required: $75. On-campus interview required.

Athletics Interscholastic: baseball (boys), basketball (b), wrestling (b); intramural: alpine skiing (b), archery (b), backpacking (b), badminton (b), ball hockey (b), basketball (b), bicycling (b), canoeing/kayaking (b), climbing (b), cooperative games (b), cricket (b), fencing (b), fishing (b), floor hockey (b), in-line skating (b), indoor soccer (b), mountain biking (b), nordic skiing (b), outdoor activities (b), outdoor skills (b), outdoors (b), roller blading (b), skiing (cross-country) (b), skiing (downhill) (b), snowboarding (b). 1 PE instructor, 4 coaches.

Computers Computers are regularly used in English, mathematics, science, social studies, writing classes. Computer network features include Internet access, wireless campus network, Internet filtering or blocking technology, laptop for each student. Student e-mail accounts are available to students. The school has a published electronic and media policy.

Contact Melanie Miller, Director of Admissions. 802-387-4545 Ext. 199. Fax: 802-387-5396. E-mail: mmiller@greenwood.org. Web site: www.greenwood.org.

HAMPSHIRE COUNTRY SCHOOL
28 Patey Circle
Rindge, New Hampshire 03461
Head of School: Bernd Foecking

General Information Boys' boarding college-preparatory and general academic school; primarily serves underachievers, individuals with Attention Deficit Disorder, and non-verbal learning disabilities and Asperger's Syndrome. Grades 3–12. Founded: 1948. Setting: rural. Nearest major city is Boston, MA. Students are housed in single-sex dormitories. 1,700-acre campus. 8 buildings on campus. Approved or accredited by New England Association of Schools and Colleges and New Hampshire Department of Education. Member of National Association of Independent Schools. Endowment: $1 million. Total enrollment: 20. Upper school average class size: 4. Upper school faculty-student ratio: 1:2. There are 180 required school days per year for Upper School students. Upper School students typically attend 5 days per week. The average school day consists of 5 hours and 30 minutes.

Student Profile Grade 7: 3 students (3 boys); Grade 8: 3 students (3 boys); Grade 9: 3 students (3 boys); Grade 10: 2 students (2 boys); Grade 11: 1 student (1 boy). 100% of students are boarding students. 5% are state residents. 9 states are represented in upper school student body. 10% are international students. International students from Australia and Saudi Arabia.

Faculty School total: 14. In upper school: 4 men, 5 women; 3 have advanced degrees; 13 reside on campus.

Subjects Offered Algebra, American history, ancient history, biology, English, environmental science, French, geometry, history, life science, mathematics, pre-algebra, science, world history.

Graduation Requirements English, language arts, mathematics, science, social studies (includes history).

Special Academic Programs Academic accommodation for the gifted; remedial reading and/or remedial writing; remedial math.

Secondary School Placement 3 students graduated in 2010; all went to college.

Student Life Specified standards of dress. Discipline rests primarily with faculty.

Tuition and Aid 7-day tuition and room/board: $45,500.

Admissions Traditional entrance grade is 7. For fall 2010, 10 students applied for admission, 3 were accepted, 2 enrolled. Any standardized test or Individual IQ required. Deadline for receipt of application materials: none. No application fee required. On-campus interview required.

Athletics Intramural: alpine skiing, backpacking, basketball, bicycling, canoeing/kayaking, cooperative games, fishing, flag football, floor hockey, hiking/backpacking, ice skating, kickball, outdoor activities, outdoor recreation, skiing (downhill), snowshoeing, soccer, softball, tennis, touch football, walking, whiffle ball, winter walking.

Computers Computers are regularly used in writing classes.

Contact William Dickerman, Admissions Director. 603-899-3325. Fax: 603-899-6521. E-mail: admissions@hampshirecountryschool.net. Web site: www.hampshirecountryschool.org.

HILLSIDE SCHOOL

Robin Hill Road

Marlborough, Massachusetts 01752

General Information Boys' boarding and day college-preparatory and leadership school; primarily serves students with learning disabilities and individuals with Attention Deficit Disorder. Grades 5–9. Founded: 1901. Setting: small town. Nearest major city is Boston. Students are housed in single-sex dormitories. 200-acre campus. 15 buildings on campus. Approved or accredited by Association of Independent Schools in New England, Junior Boarding Schools Association, New England Association of Schools and Colleges, The Association of Boarding Schools, and Massachusetts Department of Education. Member of National Association of Independent Schools and Secondary School Admission Test Board. Total enrollment: 139. Upper school average class size: 10. Upper school faculty-student ratio: 1:6.

See Display on this page and Close-Up on page 940.

INDIAN MOUNTAIN SCHOOL

211 Indian Mountain Road

Lakeville, Connecticut 06039

Head of School: Mark A. Devey

General Information Coeducational boarding and day college-preparatory, general academic, arts, and ESL school. Boarding grades 6–9, day grades PK–9. Founded: 1922. Setting: rural. Nearest major city is Hartford. Students are housed in single-sex dormitories. 600-acre campus. 12 buildings on campus. Approved or accredited by Connecticut Association of Independent Schools, Junior Boarding Schools Association, The Association of Boarding Schools, and Connecticut Department of Education. Member of National Association of Independent Schools and Secondary School Admission Test Board. Endowment: $5.2 million. Total enrollment: 256. Upper school average class size: 12. Upper school faculty-student ratio: 1:4. There are 163 required school days per year for Upper School students. Upper School students typically attend 5 days per week. The average school day consists of 9 hours.

Student Profile Grade 7: 42 students (26 boys, 16 girls); Grade 8: 60 students (38 boys, 22 girls); Grade 9: 43 students (30 boys, 13 girls). 55% of students are boarding students. 21% are state residents. 11 states are represented in upper school student body. 11% are international students. International students from Bahamas, China, Jamaica, Japan, Mexico, and Republic of Korea; 1 other country represented in student body.

Faculty School total: 51. In upper school: 20 men, 21 women; 24 have advanced degrees; 29 reside on campus.

Subjects Offered Algebra, American history, ancient history, art, biology, ceramics, Chinese, computers, earth science, English, film, fine arts, French, general science, geometry, health, history, Latin, mathematics, music, physical science, social studies, Spanish, theater.

Graduation Requirements Arts and fine arts (art, music, dance, drama), English, foreign language, mathematics, music, science, social studies (includes history).

Special Academic Programs ESL (11 students enrolled).

Secondary School Placement 47 students graduated in 2009; they went to Berkshire School; Choate Rosemary Hall; Kent School; Millbrook School; Suffield Academy; The Hotchkiss School.

Student Life Specified standards of dress, student council, honor system. Discipline rests primarily with faculty.

Tuition and Aid Day student tuition: $22,150; 7-day tuition and room/board: $41,500. Tuition installment plan (Key Tuition Payment Plan). Need-based scholarship grants available. In 2009–10, 22% of students received aid. Total amount of financial aid awarded in 2009–10: $683,914.

Admissions For fall 2009, 109 students applied for admission, 71 were accepted, 44 enrolled. WISC or WAIS, WISC-III and Woodcock-Johnson or WISC/Woodcock-Johnson required. Deadline for receipt of application materials: none. Application fee required: $50. Interview required.

Athletics Interscholastic: aerobics/dance (girls), baseball (b), basketball (b,g), football (b), ice hockey (b), lacrosse (b,g), soccer (b,g), softball (g); intramural: dance (g); coed interscholastic: alpine skiing, cross-country running, ice hockey, outdoor

adventure, skiing (downhill), squash, tennis, volleyball; coed intramural: alpine skiing, backpacking, skiing (downhill), snowboarding, tennis, ultimate Frisbee.

Computers Computers are regularly used in English, history, mathematics, science, social studies classes. Computer network features include on-campus library services, Internet access, Internet filtering or blocking technology. Student e-mail accounts are available to students. The school has a published electronic and media policy.

Contact Mrs. Mimi L. Babcock, Director of Admission. 860-435-0871. Fax: 860-435-1380. E-mail: admissions@indianmountain.org. Web site: www.indianmountain.org.

LINDEN HILL SCHOOL

154 South Mountain Road
Northfield, Massachusetts 01360-9681

Head of School: Mr. James Allen McDaniel

General Information Boys' boarding and day college-preparatory, general academic, technology, and ESL school; primarily serves underachievers, students with learning disabilities, individuals with Attention Deficit Disorder, dyslexic students, and language-based learning differences. Grades 3–9. Founded: 1961. Setting: rural. Nearest major city is Springfield. Students are housed in single-sex dormitories. 100-acre campus. 15 buildings on campus. Approved or accredited by Association of Independent Schools in New England, Junior Boarding Schools Association, Massachusetts Office of Child Care Services, New England Association of Schools and Colleges, The Association of Boarding Schools, and Massachusetts Department of Education. Member of National Association of Independent Schools. Endowment: $100,000. Total enrollment: 31. Upper school average class size: 4. Upper school faculty-student ratio: 1:1. There are 152 required school days per year for Upper School students. Upper School students typically attend 5 days per week.

Student Profile Grade 6: 8 students (8 boys); Grade 7: 2 students (2 boys); Grade 8: 6 students (6 boys); Grade 9: 7 students (7 boys). 95% of students are boarding students. 28% are state residents. 4 states are represented in upper school student body. 14% are international students. International students from United Arab Emirates; 1 other country represented in student body.

Faculty School total: 14. In upper school: 7 men, 4 women; 7 have advanced degrees; 10 reside on campus.

Subjects Offered Arts, character education, English, ESL, experiential education, freshman seminar, general science, history, industrial arts, instrumental music, lab science, language and composition, language development, leadership and service, life skills, mathematics, outdoor education, strategies for success, woodworking, writing.

Special Academic Programs Study at local college for college credit; programs in English, mathematics, general development for dyslexic students; ESL (3 students enrolled).

Secondary School Placement 5 students graduated in 2009.

Student Life Specified standards of dress. Discipline rests primarily with faculty.

Tuition and Aid Day student tuition: $33,495; 7-day tuition and room/board: $56,900. Tuition installment plan (FACTS Tuition Payment Plan, individually arranged payment plans). Need-based scholarship grants available.

Admissions Achievement tests, Wechsler Intelligence Scale for Children III or writing sample required. Deadline for receipt of application materials: none. Application fee required: $60. Interview required.

Athletics Interscholastic: alpine skiing, basketball, lacrosse, soccer, softball, wrestling; intramural: alpine skiing, backpacking, ball hockey, basketball, bicycling, billiards, blading, bowling, climbing, cooperative games, cross-country running, fishing, floor hockey, golf, ice skating, indoor hockey, indoor soccer, jogging, jump rope, kickball, mountain biking, outdoor activities, outdoor recreation, outdoors, paddle tennis, physical fitness, rock climbing, roller blading, running, skateboarding, skiing (cross-country), skiing (downhill), snowboarding, soccer, softball, swimming and diving, table tennis, tennis, wall climbing, whiffle ball, wrestling. 6 coaches.

Computers Computer network features include Internet access. Campus intranet and student e-mail accounts are available to students. The school has a published electronic and media policy.

Contact Mrs. Jennifer Russell, Director of Admission. 413-498-2906 Ext. 118. Fax: 413-498-2908. E-mail: jerussell@lindenhs.org. Web site: www.lindenhs.org.

NORTH COUNTRY SCHOOL

4382 Cascade Road
Lake Placid, New York 12946

Head of School: David Hochschartner

General Information Coeducational boarding and day college-preparatory, general academic, and arts school. Grades 4–9. Founded: 1938. Setting: rural. Nearest major city is Albany. Students are housed in residential houses. 200-acre campus. 11 buildings on campus. Approved or accredited by New York State Association of Independent Schools and New York Department of Education. Member of National Association of Independent Schools and Secondary School Admission Test Board. Endowment: $7 million. Total enrollment: 88. Upper school average class size: 12. Upper school faculty-student ratio: 1:3.

Student Profile Grade 6: 11 students (4 boys, 7 girls); Grade 7: 18 students (11 boys, 7 girls); Grade 8: 28 students (14 boys, 14 girls); Grade 9: 20 students (17 boys, 3 girls). 90% of students are boarding students. 30% are state residents. 19 states are

represented in upper school student body. 18% are international students. International students from Antigua and Barbuda, Bermuda, Canada, Colombia, Japan, and Mexico; 2 other countries represented in student body.

Faculty School total: 33. In upper school: 13 men, 20 women; 9 have advanced degrees; 20 reside on campus.

Subjects Offered Algebra, American history, biology, ceramics, computer science, creative writing, earth science, English, mathematics, music, performing arts, photography, physical education, social studies, Spanish, studio art.

Special Academic Programs Remedial reading and/or remedial writing; remedial math; ESL (10 students enrolled).

Secondary School Placement 23 students graduated in 2010; they went to Dublin School; Gould Academy; Northwood School; Vermont Academy.

Student Life Specified standards of dress, student council. Discipline rests primarily with faculty.

Summer Programs Session focuses on recreation, arts, ESL, and outdoor programs; held on campus; accepts boys and girls; open to students from other schools. 150 students usually enrolled. 2011 schedule: June 27 to August 19. Application deadline: December 16.

Tuition and Aid Day student tuition: $17,200; 5-day tuition and room/board: $40,750; 7-day tuition and room/board: $50,750. Tuition installment plan (monthly payment plans, individually arranged payment plans, 2-payment plan). Need-based scholarship grants available. In 2010–11, 30% of students received aid. Total amount of financial aid awarded in 2010–11: $450,000.

Admissions Deadline for receipt of application materials: none. No application fee required. On-campus interview required.

Athletics Coed Interscholastic: aerobics/dance, alpine skiing, artistic gym, bicycling, climbing, curling, drill team, field hockey, fishing, Frisbee, hiking/backpacking, horseback riding, lacrosse, modern dance, mountain biking, mountaineering, nordic skiing, outdoor activities, outdoor adventure, outdoor education, outdoor recreation, outdoor skills, rappelling, rock climbing, skateboarding, ski jumping, skiing (cross-country), skiing (downhill), snowboarding, snowshoeing, swimming and diving, telemark skiing, volleyball, walking, wall climbing, wilderness survival, yoga; coed intramural: basketball, skiing (cross-country), skiing (downhill), soccer.

Computers Computer resources include on-campus library services, Internet access.

Contact Christine LeFevre, Director of Admissions. 518-523-9329. Fax: 518-523-4858. E-mail: admissions@northcountryschool.org. Web site: www.nct.org/.

See Display on page 930 and Close-Up on page 942.

THE RECTORY SCHOOL

528 Pomfret Street
Pomfret, Connecticut 06258
Head of School: Fred Williams

General Information Coeducational boarding and day college-preparatory, general academic, arts, technology, and music school, affiliated with Episcopal Church; primarily serves underachievers. Boarding grades 5–9, day grades K–9. Founded: 1920. Setting: rural. Nearest major city is Hartford. Students are housed in single-sex dormitories. 138-acre campus. 24 buildings on campus. Approved or accredited by Connecticut Association of Independent Schools, Junior Boarding Schools Association, and The Association of Boarding Schools. Member of National Association of Independent Schools and Secondary School Admission Test Board. Endowment: $7.8 million. Total enrollment: 244. Upper school average class size: 10. Upper school faculty-student ratio: 1:4. Upper School students typically attend 5 days per week. The average school day consists of 7 hours and 45 minutes.

Student Profile Grade 6: 13 students (7 boys, 6 girls); Grade 7: 26 students (15 boys, 11 girls); Grade 8: 83 students (59 boys, 24 girls); Grade 9: 60 students (42 boys, 18 girls). 69% of students are boarding students. 30% are state residents. 17 states are represented in upper school student body. 45% are international students. International students from Bermuda, China, Japan, Mexico, Nigeria, and Republic of Korea; 4 other countries represented in student body. 11% of students are members of Episcopal Church.

Faculty School total: 62. In upper school: 22 men, 34 women; 25 have advanced degrees; 24 reside on campus.

Subjects Offered Algebra, American Civil War, American history, American literature, ancient world history, art, biology, chorus, creative arts, creative writing, drama, earth science, ecology, English, English as a foreign language, English literature, environmental science, European history, expository writing, fine arts, foreign language, general science, geography, geometry, grammar, history, journalism, Latin, life science, mathematics, medieval history, medieval/Renaissance history, music, photography, physical education, physical science, reading, science, social studies, Spanish, study skills, theater, vocal music, world history, world literature, writing.

Graduation Requirements Arts and fine arts (art, music, dance, drama), literature, mathematics, physical education (includes health), science, social studies (includes history).

Special Academic Programs Honors section; academic accommodation for the gifted; remedial reading and/or remedial writing; remedial math; programs in English, mathematics, general development for dyslexic students; special instructional classes for students with learning disabilities, Attention Deficit Disorder, and dyslexia; ESL.

Secondary School Placement 47 students graduated in 2010; they went to Brewster Academy; Choate Rosemary Hall; Pomfret School; Suffield Academy; Tabor Academy.

Student Life Specified standards of dress, student council, honor system. Discipline rests primarily with faculty. Attendance at religious services is required.

Summer Programs Remediation, enrichment, ESL, sports, art/fine arts programs offered; session focuses on study skills, academic enrichment, sports, music, off campus trips; held on campus; accepts boys and girls; open to students from other schools. 60 students usually enrolled. 2011 schedule: June 26 to July 23. Application deadline: none.

Tuition and Aid Day student tuition: $20,450; 7-day tuition and room/board: $40,900. Tuition installment plan (Key Tuition Payment Plan). Need-based scholarship grants available. In 2010–11, 32% of students received aid. Total amount of financial aid awarded in 2010–11: $1,330,000.

Admissions Traditional entrance grade is 8. For fall 2010, 195 students applied for admission, 125 were accepted, 80 enrolled. Deadline for receipt of application materials: none. Application fee required: $50. Interview required.

Athletics Interscholastic: baseball (boys), basketball (b,g), cross-country running (b,g), football (b), golf (b,g), soccer (b,g), softball (g), wrestling (b); intramural: basketball (b,g), dance (g), soccer (b); coed interscholastic: cross-country running, equestrian sports, fencing, golf, ice hockey, lacrosse, soccer, tennis, track and field; coed intramural: basketball, bowling, climbing, cooperative games, cross-country running, equestrian sports, fencing, fitness, flag football, golf, ice hockey, lacrosse, life saving, outdoor adventure, ropes courses, skiing (downhill), snowboarding, snowshoeing, soccer, softball, squash, street hockey, strength & conditioning, table tennis, tennis, touch football, ultimate Frisbee, volleyball, weight training, whiffle ball, yoga. 4 coaches, 2 athletic trainers.

Computers Computers are regularly used in English, history, mathematics, multimedia, music, science, writing, yearbook classes. Computer network features include on-campus library services, online commercial services, Internet access, wireless campus network, Internet filtering or blocking technology. Campus intranet and student e-mail accounts are available to students. Students grades are available online. The school has a published electronic and media policy.

Contact Vincent Ricci, Director of Admissions and Marketing. 860-928-1328. Fax: 860-928-4961. E-mail: admissions@rectoryschool.org. Web site: www.rectoryschool.org.

RUMSEY HALL SCHOOL

201 Romford Road
Washington Depot, Connecticut 06794
Head of School: Thomas W. Farmen

General Information Coeducational boarding and day college-preparatory, general academic, and arts school. Boarding grades 5–9, day grades K–9. Founded: 1900. Setting: rural. Nearest major city is Hartford. Students are housed in single-sex dormitories. 147-acre campus. 29 buildings on campus. Approved or accredited by Connecticut Association of Independent Schools, National Independent Private Schools Association, The Association of Boarding Schools, and Connecticut Department of Education. Member of National Association of Independent Schools and Secondary School Admission Test Board. Endowment: $5.7 million. Total enrollment: 303. Upper school average class size: 14. Upper school faculty-student ratio: 1:8. There are 180 required school days per year for Upper School students. Upper School students typically attend 6 days per week. The average school day consists of 6 hours and 40 minutes.

Student Profile Grade 6: 21 students (14 boys, 7 girls); Grade 7: 47 students (33 boys, 14 girls); Grade 8: 90 students (50 boys, 40 girls); Grade 9: 63 students (40 boys, 23 girls). 66% of students are boarding students. 18 states are represented in upper school student body. 22% are international students. International students from Bermuda, China, Japan, Mexico, Republic of Korea, and Thailand; 2 other countries represented in student body.

Faculty School total: 51. In upper school: 28 men, 18 women; 25 have advanced degrees; 30 reside on campus.

Subjects Offered Algebra, American history, American literature, art, art history, biology, computer science, creative writing, drama, earth science, English, English literature, environmental science, ESL, European history, fine arts, French, geography, geometry, government/civics, grammar, health, history, Japanese history, Latin, mathematics, music, physical education, science, social studies, Spanish, theater, world history, writing.

Graduation Requirements Arts and fine arts (art, music, dance, drama), computer science, English, foreign language, mathematics, physical education (includes health), science, social studies (includes history).

Special Academic Programs Honors section; academic accommodation for the gifted; remedial reading and/or remedial writing; programs in English for dyslexic students; special instructional classes for students with learning disabilities and Attention Deficit Disorder; ESL (23 students enrolled).

Secondary School Placement 75 students graduated in 2009; they went to Choate Rosemary Hall; Kent School; St. George's School; Suffield Academy; The Gunnery; The Taft School.

Student Life Specified standards of dress, student council, honor system. Discipline rests primarily with faculty.

Tuition and Aid Day student tuition: $19,600; 7-day tuition and room/board: $41,300. Tuition installment plan (monthly payment plans, individually arranged payment plans). Need-based scholarship grants available. In 2009–10, 24% of students received aid. Total amount of financial aid awarded in 2009–10: $819,000.

Admissions For fall 2009, 169 students applied for admission, 96 were accepted, 74 enrolled. Psychoeducational evaluation, SLEP, SSAT, Wechsler Intelligence Scale for Children III or writing sample required. Deadline for receipt of application materials: none. Application fee required: $100. On-campus interview required.

Athletics Interscholastic: baseball (boys), basketball (b,g), crew (b,g), field hockey (g), football (b), ice hockey (b,g), lacrosse (b), soccer (b), softball (g), volleyball (g), wrestling (b); coed interscholastic: alpine skiing, cross-country running, horseback riding, skiing (downhill), soccer, tennis; coed intramural: alpine skiing, archery, backpacking, bicycling, broomball, canoeing/kayaking, climbing, cooperative games, equestrian sports, fishing, fly fishing, Frisbee, hiking/backpacking, ice skating, mountain biking, outdoor activities, outdoors, physical fitness, physical training, project adventure, roller blading, ropes courses, running, skateboarding, skiing (downhill), snowboarding, strength & conditioning, table tennis, tennis, track and field, ultimate Frisbee, wall climbing, weight lifting, weight training, whiffle ball. 1 PE instructor, 28 coaches, 1 athletic trainer.

Computers Computers are regularly used in all academic, English, history, mathematics, science classes. Computer network features include on-campus library services, Internet access. Student e-mail accounts are available to students.

Contact Matthew S. Hoeniger, Assistant Headmaster. 860-868-0535. Fax: 860-868-7907. E-mail: admiss@rumseyhall.org. Web site: www.rumseyhall.org.

See Display below and Close-Up on page 944.

ST. CATHERINE'S ACADEMY
215 North Harbor Boulevard
Anaheim, California 92805
Head of School: Sr. Johnellen Turner, OP

General Information Boys' boarding and day college-preparatory, general academic, religious studies, leadership/military tradition, ESL, and military school, affiliated with Roman Catholic Church. Boarding grades 4–8, day grades K–8. Founded: 1889. Setting: suburban. Nearest major city is Los Angeles. Students are housed in single-sex dormitories. 8-acre campus. 8 buildings on campus. Approved or accredited by Military High School and College Association, National Catholic Education Association, The Association of Boarding Schools, Western Association of Schools and Colleges, Western Catholic Education Association, and California Department of Education. Total enrollment: 154. Upper school average class size: 18. Upper school faculty-student ratio: 1:8. There are 180 required school days per year

for Upper School students. Upper School students typically attend 5 days per week. The average school day consists of 7 hours and 45 minutes.

Student Profile Grade 6: 18 students (18 boys); Grade 7: 41 students (41 boys); Grade 8: 42 students (42 boys). 56% of students are boarding students. 67% are state residents. 3 states are represented in upper school student body. 44% are international students. International students from Hong Kong, Mexico, Republic of Korea, and Taiwan. 70% of students are Roman Catholic.

Faculty School total: 21. In upper school: 5 men, 16 women; 7 have advanced degrees; 6 reside on campus.

Subjects Offered Art, band, Catholic belief and practice, character education, choir, Civil War, computer applications, computer literacy, computer skills, conflict resolution, decision making skills, English, environmental systems, ESL, ethical decision making, ethics and responsibility, fine arts, fitness, grammar, guidance, guitar, health and wellness, health education, healthful living, history, instrumental music, instruments, interpersonal skills, keyboarding, lab/keyboard, leadership, leadership education training, life skills, marching band, mathematics, military history, military science, moral and social development, music, music appreciation, music history, music performance, participation in sports, personal development, personal fitness, personal growth, physical education, physical fitness, piano, pre-algebra, reading/study skills, religion, religious education, science, service learning/internship, single survival, social studies, Spanish, sports, survival training, swimming, volleyball, wind instruments, word processing, yearbook.

Special Academic Programs Special instructional classes for students with Attention Deficit Disorder and learning disabilities; ESL (14 students enrolled).

Secondary School Placement 43 students graduated in 2010; they went to Army and Navy Academy; Mater Dei High School; New Mexico Military Institute; Servite High School.

Student Life Uniform requirement, honor system. Discipline rests equally with students and faculty. Attendance at religious services is required.

Summer Programs Remediation, enrichment, ESL, sports, art/fine arts, computer instruction programs offered; session focuses on academics and athletic activities; held both on and off campus; held at local attractions, (e.g., beach, aquarium, water park); accepts boys; open to students from other schools. 120 students usually enrolled. 2011 schedule: July 1 to July 31. Application deadline: none.

Tuition and Aid Day student tuition: $9995; 5-day tuition and room/board: $28,283; 7-day tuition and room/board: $37,534. Tuition installment plan (FACTS Tuition Payment Plan, monthly payment plans, individually arranged payment plans, 4 payments). Need-based scholarship grants available. In 2010–11, 35% of students received aid. Total amount of financial aid awarded in 2010–11: $140,000.

Admissions Any standardized test required. Deadline for receipt of application materials: none. Application fee required: $100. Interview required.

Athletics Interscholastic: basketball, flag football, volleyball; intramural: ball hockey, baseball, basketball, bowling, cooperative games, cross-country running, drill team, equestrian sports, field hockey, fitness, flag football, golf, handball, life saving, physical fitness, physical training, soccer, softball, swimming and diving, touch football, track and field, volleyball, water volleyball, weight lifting. 1 PE instructor, 7 coaches.

Computers Computers are regularly used in English, history, science, social studies classes. Computer network features include Internet access, Internet filtering or blocking technology. Students grades are available online.

Contact Graciela Salvador, Director of Admissions. 714-772-1363 Ext. 103. Fax: 714-772-3004. E-mail: admissions@stcatherinesacademy.org. Web site: www. StCatherinesAcademy.org.

ST. THOMAS CHOIR SCHOOL

202 West 58th Street
New York, New York 10019-1406
Head of School: Rev. Charles Wallace

General Information Boys' boarding college-preparatory, general academic, arts, religious studies, technology, and music school, affiliated with Episcopal Church. Grades 3–8. Founded: 1919. Setting: urban. Students are housed in single-sex dormitories. 1 building on campus. Approved or accredited by National Association of Episcopal Schools, New York State Association of Independent Schools, The Association of Boarding Schools, and New York Department of Education. Member of National Association of Independent Schools and Secondary School Admission Test Board. Endowment: $18 million. Total enrollment: 36. Upper school average class size: 8. Upper school faculty-student ratio: 1:5.

Student Profile Grade 6: 8 students (8 boys); Grade 7: 7 students (7 boys); Grade 8: 6 students (6 boys). 100% of students are boarding students. 10% are state residents. 12 states are represented in upper school student body. 67% of students are members of Episcopal Church.

Faculty School total: 7. In upper school: 5 men, 2 women; 6 have advanced degrees; all reside on campus.

Subjects Offered Algebra, applied music, art, choir, computers, English, French, history, Latin, mathematics, music theory, physical education, science, study skills, theology, visual arts.

Graduation Requirements Arts and fine arts (art, music, dance, drama), English, foreign language, mathematics, physical education (includes health), religion (includes Bible studies and theology), science, social studies (includes history).

Special Academic Programs Academic accommodation for the gifted and the musically talented; remedial reading and/or remedial writing; remedial math; programs in general development for dyslexic students.

Secondary School Placement 5 students graduated in 2009.

Student Life Uniform requirement. Discipline rests primarily with faculty. Attendance at religious services is required.

Tuition and Aid 7-day tuition and room/board: $10,750. Tuition installment plan (individually arranged payment plans). Need-based scholarship grants available. In 2009–10, 70% of students received aid. Total amount of financial aid awarded in 2009–10: $187,950.

Admissions Admissions testing and audition required. Deadline for receipt of application materials: none. No application fee required. On-campus interview required.

Athletics Interscholastic: basketball, soccer, softball; intramural: baseball, basketball, fitness, flag football, floor hockey, independent competitive sports, indoor hockey, indoor soccer, kickball, lacrosse, Newcombe ball, outdoor recreation, physical fitness, running, soccer, softball, strength & conditioning, table tennis, track and field, ultimate Frisbee, volleyball. 1 PE instructor.

Computers Computers are regularly used in art, English, foreign language, history, library, mathematics, music, science classes.

Contact Ms. Ruth S. Cobb, Director of Admissions and Alumni Relations. 212-247-3311 Ext. 304. Fax: 212-247-3393. E-mail: rcobb@choirschool.org. Web site: www.choirschool.org.

Junior Boarding Schools
Close-Ups

CARDIGAN MOUNTAIN SCHOOL

Canaan, New Hampshire

Type: Boys' day and boarding junior high school
Grades: 6–9
Enrollment: 195
Head of School: David J. McCusker Jr. '80, Headmaster

THE SCHOOL

Cardigan Mountain School was founded in 1945 to serve the specific educational and developmental needs of boys during their formative middle school years. Two men whose vision and belief in their goal were unshakable—Harold P. Hinman, a Dartmouth College graduate, and William R. Brewster, then Headmaster of Kimball Union Academy—joined forces with legendary Dartmouth President Ernest M. Hopkins to obtain the land that is now the site of Cardigan Mountain's campus. Cardigan Mountain School opened with 24 boys, and, in 1954, upon merging with the Clark School of Hanover, New Hampshire, the School as it is known today began to emerge. Since that time, the School has grown to its current enrollment of more than 200 boys in grades 6 through 9, while the philosophy and objectives set forth by the founders have remained unchanged.

Cardigan was built upon an educational experience that emphasized rigorous academics and study habits, as well as spiritual guidance, physical training, and social orientation. In order to accomplish this purpose, Cardigan's program was tailored to each boy so that he made the best possible use of his potential in these areas. Thus, every boy had a balanced and well-rounded life: physically, mentally, and spiritually. This philosophy is the same today as it was in 1945.

The 425-acre campus, located on Canaan Street Lake, is 18 miles from Dartmouth College. Driving time from Boston is approximately 2½ hours. Some of the finest skiing in New England is only 1 hour away.

The self-perpetuating Board of Trustees and Incorporators is instrumental in guiding the School. The School's endowment is valued at more than $13.2 million. In 2009–10, Annual Giving was approximately $1 million.

Cardigan Mountain is accredited by the New England Association of Schools and Colleges. Its memberships include the National Association of Independent Schools (NAIS), the Junior Boarding Schools Association, the Independent Schools Association of Northern New England (ISANNE), the Association of Independent Schools of New England (AISNE), the Secondary School Admission Test Board (SSATB), Boys' Schools, A Better Chance (ABC), the Federation of American Independent Schools, and the Educational Records Bureau (ERB).

ACADEMIC PROGRAMS

Cardigan's curriculum is designed both to support and to challenge each student as the School prepares him for the demanding academic programs characteristic of the independent schools most graduates attend. In all disciplines, special emphasis is placed upon mastery of fundamental skills, content, and the study skills needed to become academically self-sufficient.

The curriculum provides each student with thorough instruction in all the major courses and substantial exposure to a number of other subject areas that round out a boy's education at this age. Cardigan requires all students to take yearlong courses in English, mathematics, social studies, and science. In addition, a foreign language (French, Latin, or Spanish) is required of boys not enrolled in English as a second language.

Beyond these major courses, the School also requires each boy to broaden his horizons and strengthen his scholastic preparation through additional course work in music, life skills, leadership, and art or woodworking. Cardigan students also take a course called Personalized Education for the Acquisition of Knowledge and Skills (PEAKS), which helps them become stronger learners and self-advocates.

The average class size ranges from 4 to 16 students, and, within each grade, there is ability tracking. There are normally three levels in each subject in grades 7, 8, and 9. In the accelerated sections of each grade, more difficult texts are used, assignments are longer and more challenging, and more emphasis is placed upon independent study and thought. The middle- and supportive-level sections in each grade spend more time stressing fundamentals. Assignments and examinations are designed to challenge but not overwhelm students. The sixth grade is grouped heterogeneously and follows a self-contained classroom model.

The PEAKS program provides students with guided self-development and helps each student, no matter his skill level, become a better learner and self-advocate. PEAKS facilitates collaboration among the members of the Cardigan Mountain School community to respond to the evolving needs of each student by focusing on the process of learning through the acquisition of developmentally appropriate knowledge and skills.

Cardigan believes that every student learns differently. Through the PEAKS program, each boy comes to understand how he learns best, and becomes equipped with tools to use as he goes forward, enabling him to find success as a lifelong learner. The PEAKS program also offers additional support for students in and out of the classroom.

PEAKS coaches are available for one-on-one assistance in the afternoons and evenings. Recognizing that some students require regular tutorial sessions, while others may need less frequent support, the program is designed to maximize the accessibility of the coaches to their students.

FACULTY AND ADVISERS

The faculty consists of 42 full-time and 3 part-time members, the majority of whom reside on campus. Almost one quarter of the faculty members are women. Nearly half of the faculty members have earned advanced academic degrees. All faculty members teach, coach, supervise dormitories, and serve as advisers for the students. Cardigan has a 4:1 student-faculty ratio. Of the greatest importance to Cardigan are the faculty members who, by setting and attaining personal goals, serve as positive role models for the boys. Cardigan faculty members bring with them a love for learning and a variety of skills, experiences, and talents that broaden and enrich the educational experience and inject warmth and enthusiasm into campus life.

SECONDARY SCHOOL PLACEMENT

Cardigan offers extensive assistance to the students and their parents in selecting and then applying to independent secondary schools. The Secondary School Placement Office begins the counseling process in the spring of the eighth grade and continues to guide the student and his family throughout the application experience. The Placement Office offers workshops on interviewing techniques, SSAT preparation, and essay writing.

Over the past few years, a number of Cardigan graduates have matriculated to schools such as Avon Old Farms, Brooks, Deerfield, Holderness, Hotchkiss, Lawrence, Phillips Andover, Phillips Exeter, Pomfret, Salisbury, St. Mark's, St. Paul's, Tabor, Taft, and Westminster.

STUDENT BODY AND CONDUCT

For 2009–10, 195 boys enrolled at Cardigan. There were 50 boys in the ninth grade, 89 in the eighth, 38 in the seventh, and 18 in the sixth. Almost 90 percent of the Cardigan students were boarders. In 2009–10, students came to Cardigan from sixteen states and ten countries.

Cardigan has a two-tiered disciplinary status system in order to inform students, their advisers, and parents when School expectations are not being met. This disciplinary system is used to correct patterns of misbehavior and to discipline those students who commit serious offenses. The Discipline Committee meets to hear cases deemed appropriate by the headmaster and the assistant headmaster. Two student leaders and 3 faculty members are selected by the assistant headmaster to join him on the committee. The committee hears cases and makes a recommendation for consequences to the headmaster.

Cardigan has a clearly stated Honor Code, and all students are expected to abide by the spirit of that code.

ACADEMIC FACILITIES

The numerous buildings that house academic facilities are highlighted by the Bronfman Center. Completed in 1996, Bronfman Center features, among other things, the three Freda R. Caspersen state-of-the-art science laboratories, an art studio, the Bhirombhakdi Computer Center, the School store, and classrooms for the sixth-grade class. Stoddard Center is the home of both the Kirk Library and the Humann Theatre. Opened in fall 1982, the Kirk Library is a three-tiered, well-equipped multimedia resource center that offers students and faculty members computer software, audiotapes, and videocassettes in addition to more than 10,000 volumes and numerous journals and periodicals. Thousands of newspaper and magazine articles are available through the Infoweb NewsBank Reference Service. Computers with Internet access are available in both the Kirk Library and the adjacent writing lab. Affiliation with the New Hampshire State Library's Automated Information Access System enables users at the School to obtain materials through the interlibrary loan process. The library is staffed by 1 full-time librarian and a part-time aid. A flexible access plan allows students and faculty members to work in groups, as well as individually, throughout the day and five evenings each week. Humann, the 250-seat

f www.facebook.com/sec.schools

theater, is the site of School meetings, lectures, films, concerts, and drama performances.

Cardigan emphasizes the visual arts. The Williams Woodshop and the Art Center are focal points for this important aspect of a boy's education. The Hinman Auditorium houses the School's music facilities, where opportunities for vocal and instrumental instruction are available.

All dormitory rooms and many classrooms are wired for access to the Internet.

BOARDING AND GENERAL FACILITIES

Eleven dormitories house from 8 to 16 students each. Each dormitory houses faculty members and their families. Students reside in double rooms, with some singles provided. Two dormitories, referred to as 'houses,' were completed in fall 2000 and each dorm houses 3 faculty members, their families, and 12 students.

The School operates an on-campus health center, where most of the students' medical needs can be met. For extended services, Cardigan students benefit from the Alice Peck Day Hospital and Dartmouth-Hitchcock Medical Center, both of which are located in Lebanon, New Hampshire. The Hamilton Health Center on the Cardigan campus has a resident nurse and a visiting physician.

ATHLETICS

The objectives of the activities program at Cardigan are to provide the boys with opportunities to experience success, to offer healthy and enjoyable activities for the boys' free-time periods and weekends, to promote the physical and athletic development of each boy, to teach cooperation with and reliance on teammates, to allow the boys to experience sports and activities that may be new or unfamiliar to them, and to encourage good sportsmanship.

Over the years, Cardigan has been fortunate enough to acquire extensive athletics facilities, fields, and equipment. These include five fields for soccer, football, and lacrosse; fourteen outdoor tennis courts; two baseball diamonds; a state-of-the-art hockey rink that can be converted to a multipurpose arena in the fall and spring; an on-campus, lighted ski slope; cross-country ski trails; ski team rooms; a wrestling room; an outing club room; a fully equipped weight-training room; an in-line hockey rink; and indoor and outdoor basketball courts.

As the School is situated on the shores of Canaan Street Lake, students and faculty members take full advantage of water-related activities. Sailing is pursued in the School's fleet of Flying Juniors, sailboards, ice boats, and the Hobie catamaran. Motorboats, rowboats, and canoes provide additional opportunities for students to enjoy the water. The waterfront area is well supervised, and instruction is available in all activities.

The Sunapee Mountain ski area is close to the School and is used on weekdays by the Alpine ski team, recreational skiers, and snowboarders. On Sundays, there are daylong ski trips to major ski areas in New Hampshire and Vermont.

As in the classroom, the focus of interscholastic sports and individual activities is on learning the fundamentals. Teams are fielded on several levels in most sports, and they compete against local independent and public schools. Recreational sports are offered for the student who does not wish to compete interscholastically.

EXTRACURRICULAR OPPORTUNITIES

Many students and faculty members bring to Cardigan skills and interests that, though not included in the usual program of studies, may be pursued and developed in the informal setting of the Club Program. Clubs meet every Thursday afternoon in lieu of athletics, with the opportunity for additional meetings if the members and adviser so desire. Recent clubs have participated in community service, creation of a rock band, technical rock-climbing, Rube Goldberg, Lego Robotics, ice fishing, kite surfing, chess, photography, SSAT prep, crafting stained glass, whiffleball, broomball, and team handball.

A boy may participate in the optional drama program in each of the three seasons. The department mounts four productions a year: a series of one-act plays, the annual Christmas pageant, a full-length play/musical, and scenes from plays during the spring term talent show. Boys are given opportunities to act, serve backstage, learn to work lights and sound, build and decorate sets, produce, and, in some cases, direct. During the nights of performance, the student stage managers and student technical staff run the entire show. The audition process gives boys an excellent opportunity to learn the skills required to get a part.

DAILY LIFE

The typical academic day begins six days per week with a required family-style breakfast. After room inspection in the dormitories, classes begin at 7:45 a.m. Six class periods precede a family-style lunch. On Monday, Tuesday, Thursday, and Friday, lunch is followed by an advisory/conference period. On Wednesday and Saturday, the academic day ends with lunch and is followed by a full slate of athletics and recreational activities. Dinner is a family-style meal every evening except Wednesday and Saturday, when a buffet is scheduled. A study period occurs each school night. Lights-out ranges from 9:20 to 10 p.m., depending on the evening and the age of the student.

Cardigan is nondenominational, yet the School seeks to strengthen each boy's spiritual development within his own religious heritage. All boys are required to attend the weekly Thursday afternoon chapel service. Arrangements are made for students of all faiths to attend appropriate weekly services in the immediate area.

WEEKEND LIFE

In addition to the regularly scheduled vacations, all boys may take weekends away from campus, and parents are invited to the campus to share in their son's experience at any time. The majority of Cardigan students are on campus on weekends, and the School provides an exciting array of options for them. A typical Saturday night's schedule might include a movie, a trip off campus, various other on-campus activities and programs, or an excursion to Dartmouth College to watch a hockey game.

SUMMER PROGRAMS

The Cardigan Mountain Summer Session, a coeducational experience for 170 girls and boys, was instituted in 1951 to meet the needs of four groups of students: those who may be seeking admission to Cardigan in the fall, those who desire advanced academic work and enrichment, those who require intensive work in basic academic skills, and those who require review. The Summer Session also serves a limited number of international students for whom English is not a first language. Cardigan's outstanding range of sports and activities, along with its academic offerings, makes the Summer Session a special blend of camp and school.

Academic enrichment offerings in the sciences are a focal point for the more able students. Courses in environmental sciences are designed to better prepare youngsters for the changing world. The visual and performing arts, long a part of the Summer Session's afternoon program, achieve curricular status, allowing students to pursue drama, ceramics, and photography as part of their morning academic program of study.

The six-week program is still known for its individualized instruction, close supervision of daily study time, and general emphasis on improving study skills. Academic offerings include English, advanced English composition, computers, prealgebra, algebra I and II, geometry, study skills, French, Spanish, and Latin.

The Summer Session is open to students who have completed third through ninth grade. The cost for the 2010 Summer Session was $8500 for boarding students and $4500 for day students. Need-based aid is available.

COSTS AND FINANCIAL AID

In 2010–11, charges for boarding students are $44,100 and for day students, $25,600. There are additional charges for items such as textbooks, laundry service, and athletic equipment.

Financial aid is available to families of qualified students who complete the School and Student Service for Financial Aid forms and demonstrate need. Information about loans and payment plans is available from the Cardigan Admissions Office. For 2009–10, approximately 25 percent of the student body received more than $981,000 in financial assistance.

ADMISSIONS INFORMATION

Cardigan seeks to enroll students of good character and academic promise who will contribute to and benefit from the broad range of academic and extracurricular opportunities available. The Admissions Committee reviews applications on a rolling admissions basis for students wishing to enter the sixth through the ninth grades. Students in grades 3–9 are considered for the Summer Session. Decisions are based upon previous school records, teacher recommendations, aptitude testing, and a campus interview. Cardigan admits students of any race, color, nationality, or ethnic origin to all the rights, privileges, programs, and activities generally accorded or made available to students at the School.

APPLICATION TIMETABLE

Initial inquiries are welcome at any time. Office hours are 8 to 4, Monday through Friday, and 8 to noon on Saturday. School catalogs and applications can be obtained through the Admissions Office. The application fee is $50 for domestic applicants and $125 for international applicants.

ADMISSIONS CORRESPONDENCE

Chip Audett, Director of Admissions
Cardigan Mountain School
62 Alumni Drive
Canaan, New Hampshire 03741

Phone: 603-523-3510
Fax: 603-523-3565
E-mail: caudett@cardigan.org
Web site: http://www.cardigan.org

Brian C. Beale, Director of Financial Aid
Cardigan Mountain School
62 Alumni Drive
Canaan, New Hampshire 03741

Phone: 603-523-3528
Fax: 603-523-3565
E-mail: bbeale@cardigan.org

Matt Rinkin, Summer Session Programs
        Coordinator
Cardigan Mountain School
62 Alumni Drive
Canaan, New Hampshire 03741

Phone: 603-523-3526
Fax: 603-523-3565
E-mail: mrinkin@cardigan.org

EAGLEBROOK SCHOOL

Deerfield, Massachusetts

Type: Boys' day and boarding school
Grades: 6–9
Enrollment: 256
Head of School: Andrew C. Chase, Headmaster

THE SCHOOL

Eaglebrook School was opened in 1922 by its Headmaster and founder, Howard B. Gibbs, a former faculty member of Deerfield Academy. One of the earliest members of his faculty was C. Thurston Chase. When Mr. Gibbs died in 1928, Mr. Chase became Headmaster, a position he held for thirty-eight years. From 1966 to 2002, Stuart and Monie Chase assumed leadership of the School. While continuing to foster the School's traditional commitment to excellence, the Chases have encouraged and developed many components of a vital school: expansion of both academic and recreational facilities, emphasis on the arts, increased endowment and financial aid, student and faculty diversity, and a balanced, healthful diet. Stuart and Monie's son, Andrew C. Chase, now assumes leadership duties as Headmaster. Eaglebrook's goals are simple—to help each boy come into full and confident possession of his innate talents, to improve the skills needed for the challenges of secondary school, and to establish values that will allow him to be a person who acts with thoughtfulness and humanity.

The School owns more than 750 acres on Mt. Pocumtuck, overlooking the Deerfield Valley and the historic town of Deerfield. It is located 100 miles west of Boston and 175 miles north of New York City.

The Allen-Chase Foundation was chartered in 1937 as a charitable, educational trust. It is directed by a 40-member self-perpetuating Board of Trustees, representing alumni, parents, and outside professionals in many fields.

Eaglebrook is a member of the National Association of Independent Schools, the Association of Independent Schools of New England, the Valley Independent School Association, the Junior Boarding School Association, and the Secondary School Admissions Test Board.

ACADEMIC PROGRAMS

Sixth graders are taught primarily in a self-contained setting. Subjects include English, mathematics, reading, Latin, history, science, and trimester-length courses in studio art, computers, music, and woodworking. Required classes for grades 7 through 9 each year include foreign language study in Latin, French, Mandarin Chinese, or Spanish; a full year of mathematics; a full year of Colonial history in seventh grade, followed by a self-selected history the next two years; a full year of English; two trimesters of geography; two trimesters of science in seventh grade, followed by a full-year laboratory course; one trimester of human sexuality in eighth grade; and one trimester of ethics in the ninth grade. The School offers extensive trimester electives, including band and instrumental instruction, computer skills, word processing, current events, conditioning, chess, film classics, drama, public speaking, industrial field trips, music appreciation, first aid, publications, and an extensive variety of studio arts. Drug and alcohol education is required of all students in every grade.

Class enrollment averages 8 to 12 students. Teachers report directly to a student's adviser any time the student's work is noteworthy, either for excellence or deficiency. This allows the adviser to communicate praise or concern effectively and initiate appropriate follow-up. Midway through each trimester, teachers submit brief written evaluations to the advisers of each of their students. Advisers stay in close touch with the parents of their advisees. Grades, along with full academic reports from each of the student's teachers, are given to advisers each trimester and then sent home. The reports are accompanied by a letter from the adviser discussing the student's social adjustment progress, athletic and activity accomplishments, and academic progress and study habits.

FACULTY AND ADVISERS

Andrew C. Chase, the current Headmaster, is a graduate of Deerfield Academy and Williams College. Along with his wife, Rachel Blain, a graduate of Phillips Andover Academy and Amherst College, Andrew succeeded his father as Headmaster in 2002.

Eaglebrook's full- and part-time faculty consists of 72 men and women, 46 of whom live on campus, many with families of their own. Seventy hold undergraduate degrees, and 30 hold graduate degrees. Leaves of absence, sabbaticals, and financial assistance for graduate study are available. The ratio of students to faculty members is 4.9:1.

Teachers endeavor to make learning an adventure and watch over each boy's personal growth. They set the academic tone, coach the teams, serve as dorm parents, and are available for a boy when he needs a friend. They help each individual establish lifelong study habits and set standards for quality. Eaglebrook's teachers have the skill not only to challenge the very able but also to make learning happen for those who need close supervision. Faculty members are chosen primarily for their appreciation of boys this age, their character and integrity as role models, and competence in their subject areas. The fact that many are married and have children of their own helps to create a warm, experienced family atmosphere.

SECONDARY SCHOOL PLACEMENT

The Director of Placement assists families in selecting, visiting, and applying to secondary schools. He meets with parents and students in the spring of a boy's eighth-grade year to discuss which schools might be appropriate based on each boy's aptitude, interests, achievements, and talent. He arranges visits from secondary schools and helps with applications. Parents and the Director of Placement work together until the boy has decided upon his secondary school in April of his ninth-grade year.

Schools frequently attended by Eaglebrook School graduates include Deerfield Academy, Choate Rosemary Hall, the Hotchkiss School, Loomis Chaffee, Northfield Mount Hermon School, Phillips Andover Academy, Phillips Exeter Academy, Pomfret School, St. George's School, St. Paul's School, Taft School, and Westminster School.

STUDENT BODY AND CONDUCT

In the 2010–11 school year, of the 190 boarding students and 66 day students, 20 are in grade 6, 51 in grade 7, 101 in grade 8, and 84 in grade 9. Twenty-eight states and twenty-two countries are represented.

There are specified standards of dress, which are neat and informal most of the time. Discipline is handled on an individual basis by those faculty members who are closely involved with the student.

ACADEMIC FACILITIES

The C. Thurston Chase Learning Center contains classrooms, an audiovisual center, and an assembly area. It also houses the Copley Library, which contains 18,000 volumes and subscriptions to eighty-five publications, books on tape, newspapers, CD-ROMs, and Internet access. The computer room is equipped with state-of-the-art computers, color printers, scanners, digital cameras, and a projection board. The Bartlett Assembly Room is an all-purpose area with seats for the entire School. The Jean Flagler Matthews Science Building houses three laboratories, classrooms, a project room, a library, an online computerized weather station, and teachers' offices. The Bryant Arts Building houses studios for drawing, painting, stained glass, architectural design, computer-aided design, stone carving, ceramics, silk-screening, printmaking, and computer art; a darkroom for photography; a woodworking shop; a band rehearsal room; a publications office; a piano studio; piano practice rooms; and a drama rehearsal room. The campus has a high-speed fiber-optic network with e-mail and access to the World Wide Web for research.

BOARDING AND GENERAL FACILITIES

Dormitories are relatively small; the five dormitories house between 18 and 36 students each, with at least one faculty family to every 8 to 10 boys.

Most students live in double rooms. A limited number of single rooms are available. After the first year, a boy may request a certain dormitory and adviser.

ATHLETICS

The athletics program is suitable for boys of all sizes and abilities. Teams are small enough to allow each boy a chance to play in the games, master skills, and develop a good sense of sportsmanship. The School's Athletic Director arranges a competitive schedule to ensure games with teams of equal ability. Fall sports include cross-country, tennis, hiking, football, water polo, and soccer. Winter sports include ice hockey, basketball, recreational and competitive skiing, swimming and diving, snowboarding, squash, and wrestling. The School maintains the Easton Ski Area, consisting of several ski trails, the Macomber Chair Lift, and snowmaking equipment. Spring sports are baseball, track and field, golf, Ultimate Disc, lacrosse, triathlon, mountain and road biking, and tennis. The School plays host to numerous students throughout the year in seasonal tournaments in ice hockey, soccer, skiing, basketball, Ultimate Disc, swimming, and wrestling. The Schwab Family Pool is a six-lane facility for both competitive and recreational swimming. The McFadden Rink at Alfond Arena features a state-of-the-art NHL-dimensioned 200-foot by 85-foot indoor ice surface. A multisport indoor surface is installed in the arena in the off-season to enable use of the facility for in-line skating, in-line hockey, soccer, lacrosse, and tennis. The Lewis Track and Field was dedicated in 2002.

EXTRACURRICULAR OPPORTUNITIES
Service and leadership opportunities build a sense of pride in the School and camaraderie in the student body. Elected Student Council representatives meet with the Headmaster as an advisory group and discuss School issues. Boys act as admissions guides, help with recycling, organize dances, serve as proctors in the dormitories and the dining room, act as headwaiters, and give the morning assemblies. Boys also assume responsibility, with faculty guidance, for the School newspaper, yearbook, and literary magazine.

Many of the students participate in numerous outdoor activities that are sponsored by the Mountain Club. They maintain an active weekend schedule that includes camping, hiking, backpacking, canoeing, kayaking, white-water rafting, fishing, rock climbing, and snowshoeing.

DAILY LIFE
On weekdays, students rise at 7:20 a.m.; breakfast is at 8. Academic class periods, including assembly, begin at 8:30. Lunch is at noon, and classes resume at 12:33. Study hall and special appointments begin at 2:15, athletics begin at 3:15, and tutorial periods and other activities begin at 5. Dinner is at 6, and evening activities are scheduled between 6:45 and 7:30; study hall is then held until 9:15 p.m. or later, according to the grade.

WEEKEND LIFE
A wide variety of weekend activities are available at Eaglebrook, both on campus and off, including community service, riflery, museum visits, dances, field trips, tournaments, movies, plays, concerts, town trips, Deerfield Academy games, bicycle trips, ski trips, hiking, camping, and mountain climbing. On Sunday, the Coordinator of Religion supervises a nondenominational and nonsectarian meeting for the student body. Attendance is required for boarding students. The aim is to share different beliefs and ways of worship. Transportation is provided for boys who wish to maintain their own religious commitment by attending local places of worship. Students with permission may leave the School for the weekend; 5–10 percent of the student body normally do so on a given weekend.

COSTS AND FINANCIAL AID
Eaglebrook School's tuition for the 2010–11 school year is $45,700 for boarding students and $29,250 for day students. Eaglebrook seeks to enroll boys from different backgrounds from this country and abroad, regardless of their ability to pay. Approximately 30 percent of the students receive financial aid. To apply for tuition assistance, a candidate must complete the School Scholarship Service's Parents' Financial Statement, which is obtainable from the Financial Aid Office.

ADMISSIONS INFORMATION
Most students enter in seventh grade, although students can be admitted to any grade. Information regarding required testing and transcripts can be obtained from the Admissions Office. A School visit and interview are required.

Eaglebrook welcomes boys of any race, color, religion, nation, or creed, and all share the same privileges and duties.

APPLICATION TIMETABLE
The School accepts applications throughout the year, but it is to the candidate's advantage to make application as early as possible. Decisions and notifications are made whenever a boy's file is complete. There is a $50 application fee ($100 for international students).

ADMISSIONS CORRESPONDENCE
Theodore J. Low
Director of Admissions
Eaglebrook School
Pine Nook Road
Deerfield, Massachusetts 01342

Phone: 413-774-9111 (admissions)
     413-774-7411 (main)
Fax: 413-774-9119 (admissions)
    413-772-2394 (main)
E-mail: admissions@eaglebrook.org
Web site: http://www.eaglebrook.org

HILLSIDE SCHOOL
Marlborough, Massachusetts

Type: Boys' boarding and day school
Grades: 5–9
Enrollment: 145
Head of School: Mr. David Z. Beecher

THE SCHOOL

Since 1901, Hillside School has continued its mission of working with boys in their formative years. Students work to develop academic and social skills while building confidence and maturity. Hillside provides small classes instructed by talented educators in a community that emphasizes personal integrity and mutual respect and is dedicated to maintaining diversity.

Hillside is situated on 200 acres of fields, forest, and ponds in Marlborough, Massachusetts. Marlborough is located just 30 miles from Boston, 70 miles from Hartford, 45 miles from Providence, and 3½ hours from New York City. This location is convenient for families, but it is also important to the School's educational and recreational programs. School field trips are bountiful and weekend activity opportunities are endless. The visual arts and athletic programs at Hillside are strong and offer the boys opportunities to succeed and grow. Both boarding and day students take advantage of a high-quality residential life that is supportive, active, and exciting.

Unique to Hillside are the working farm and farmhouse dorm, tutorials available for students who need remediation and organizational skills, a daily and weekly recognition system conveying to students clear expectations regarding social and academic behavior, and excellent programs for students with minor learning disabilities or ADD/ADHD.

Hillside seeks students of average to above-average intelligence who are looking for a supportive, structured school. Family involvement is not only encouraged, it is a critical part of the School's program. Hillside's graduates matriculate at leading independent secondary boarding schools as well as local parochial and public high schools.

Hillside School is a nonprofit institution and is governed by a 23-member Board of Trustees, which includes Hillside alumni, leading citizens of Marlborough and nearby communities, and other individuals with a commitment to the School's educational mission. The School has an endowment of $4 million, with an operating budget of $6 million. Annual Giving for 2009–10 was $600,822. The physical plant is valued at more than $20 million.

Hillside School is a member of the National Association of Independent Schools, the Association of Independent Schools in New England, and the Junior Boarding Schools Association.

ACADEMIC PROGRAMS

Hillside School recognizes the importance of committed faculty members, small classes, and a highly structured program as factors in developing the student's self-confidence, self-esteem, individual thinking, and decision-making ability. Students in grades 5 and 6 learn in self-contained classrooms, with a core curriculum consisting of mathematics, language arts, social studies, and reading and specialized instruction in art, science, and music.

In grades 7–9, the curriculum includes English, history, science, math, studio art, music, farming, and French, Spanish, or Latin.

The new Honors Seminar Program at Hillside School is for eighth and ninth graders. The boys are selected by faculty members to challenge top students and to better prepare them for competitive secondary schools. In 2006, seminars were The Writing of Mathematics and The Myths of the Settling of the American West.

Responding to concerns about global conflict, the Peace Studies course and curriculum are allowing students to review concepts and learn skills for promoting peace within society. Also, starting with the 2007–08 academic year, Hillside incorporated a special health and wellness focus across the entire curriculum to enhance students' well-being and development. For the 2008–09 academic year, the Asian Studies course informs seventh-grade students about a region of the world that is increasingly important to their daily lives.

The leadership program is required of all grades, with the goal of providing a forum for students to learn and discuss leadership skills and teamwork with their peers through hands-on activities.

Other programs were developed in recent years to help meet the needs of students who have been diagnosed with attention deficit hyperactivity disorder and/or mild learning disabilities. These students are in an environment that provides understanding and support so that they may attain a level of academic and personal success.

Hillside establishes an early appreciation for the importance of organizing time and materials. This is accomplished by teaching and reinforcing such study skills as keeping a master organizational notebook in which "two-column" note-taking strategies are utilized as well as test preparation and active reading skills. The curriculum is reinforced by tutorial sessions in which study skills are developed and enhanced in small groups. Each student is provided with instruction in math, science, English, history, skills for life, and writing. French, Spanish, and Latin are offered to seventh-, eighth-, and ninth-grade students. Music and studio art are also taught.

The tutorial program aids students who are having difficulty in a particular subject or need study skills that can be applied to all subjects.

The school year is divided into three trimesters. Students are evaluated midway through each marking period in detail by their teachers and advisers to ensure that each student's academic progress is closely monitored throughout the academic year. Parents receive student report cards three times during the academic year.

FACULTY AND ADVISERS

David Beecher, Head of the School, is a graduate of the Choate School and Lake Forest College. He served as an English and history teacher at Berkshire School as well as a coach, adviser, and dorm parent. Mr. Beecher also served Berkshire as Dean of Students and as an assistant in Admissions and Development. He also served as Director of Admission and Financial Aid at Fay School and at Wilbraham and Monson Academy.

The faculty consists of 45 full-time members; 28 reside on campus. Three counselors are available throughout the week. All 45 faculty members have bachelor's degrees and 10 have master's degrees. Faculty members and students have their meals together, live in the dormitories, and spend recreational time together on the weekends. All faculty members serve as student advisers and meet with their advisees three times per week. The majority of faculty members coach at least one sport. Faculty members use patience, kindness, and empathy as they work alongside students.

SECONDARY SCHOOL PLACEMENT

The Director of Secondary Placement assists students and their families in selecting and applying to schools that best match a student's needs. The needs of each student are identified by the faculty members, advisers, coaches, and families at the beginning of the application process.

Schools recently attended by Hillside graduates include Brewster Academy, Chapel Hill–Chauncey Hall School, Cheshire Academy, Choate Rosemary Hall, Cushing, Dublin School, Hotchkiss, Kent School, Lawrence Academy, Marvelwood School, Millbrook, New Hampton School, Pomfret School, St. Andrew's School (Rhode Island), St. Mark's School, Tilton School, Vermont Academy, and Wilbraham and Monson Academy.

STUDENT BODY AND CONDUCT

The 2009–10 student population of 145 students consists of 90 boarding students and 55 day students. These boys are also representative of Hillside's growing diversity, with 30 percent being students of color, 32 percent receiving financial aid, 60 percent participating in the tutorial program, and 20 percent being international students. There is a standard dress code for all students.

Hillside School embraces the five core values of honesty, compassion, respect, determination, and fun as the guiding principles for overseeing student behavior and achievement. Shades of Hillside Blue is a system based on these values that is designed to give students and families comprehensive and timely feedback about a boy's overall performance at school. During a biweekly period, boys are evaluated in all areas of School life using three shades of blue. Royal blue, the School color, signifies that a boy consistently meets established expectations. Sky blue signifies that a boy meets expectations with some assistance, and navy blue indicates that a boy needs frequent guidance in attempting to meet expectations. Each student has an adviser who reviews this feedback with the boy and his family. The adviser works in conjunction with the Dean of Students and other faculty members in helping boys to set and meet appropriate individual goals on an ongoing basis. Parental involvement with the Hillside system is sought and greatly encouraged so that a clear, consistent message is given to students. The Dean of Students is charged with overseeing residential life, counseling, and conduct.

ACADEMIC FACILITIES

The academic hub of the School is centered in the Stevens Wing of the new Academic and Health Center. The Stevens Wing contains fourteen classrooms, WiFi, computer access, and the science laboratory. Linked to the Stevens Wing is the Tracy gymnasium/auditorium. The student center houses the dining room; administrative, admissions, and business offices; and the newly expanded Wick Tutorial Center.

The much-anticipated Academic and Health Center opened its doors in March 2008. This newest campus facility includes fitness rooms; a state-of-the-art health center staffed by a registered nurse; a wrestling/multipurpose room; nine new classrooms, three of which are science labs; and offices for health and wellness and counseling programs.

BOARDING AND GENERAL FACILITIES

The Messman-Saran Library is located in Drinkwater Hall. Students are housed in six dormitories: two new houses—Mack House and Maher House—and Williams, Whittemore, Matthies, and the Farm Dorm. Living in each house are at least 2 faculty members and their respective families. Additional campus buildings include Lowell House, the Headmaster's residence; Tipper House, residence of the Dean of Athletics; Emerson House, residence of the Assistant Headmaster; and the Patten House and other buildings on the farm.

ATHLETICS

Hillside School offers an extensive athletics program and competes with other junior boarding and day schools in the area. The School population is small enough that every student is able to participate. The boys are taught basic skills and participate in a sports program that includes baseball, basketball, cross-country, golf, ice hockey, lacrosse, sailing, skiing, soccer, tennis, track and field, wrestling, and yoga. The School also offers an outdoor program called Eco-Team, which features hiking, canoeing, and working with more than 80 animals on the farm. Fitness activities, weight lifting, Ultimate (Frisbee), and volleyball are part of the intramural program.

EXTRACURRICULAR OPPORTUNITIES

The students and the faculty members place great emphasis on service to others. Three times per year, students participate in community service days. In this program, students visit local nursing homes and spend time with the elderly, participate in community social service projects, and assist in a volunteer program for local residents.

Students participate in woodworking, painting, plays, poetry contests, and student government. They can volunteer to be on the yearbook staff. Students help plan and execute a Farm Day harvest festival, Diversity Day, Spring Fling, and a Daughters of the American Revolution Day.

DAILY LIFE

During the school week, students arise at 6:30 a.m. to dress and to clean their rooms before breakfast at 7:15. Classes begin with homeroom at 8 a.m. and end at 3 p.m. Students meet with their adviser three times each week and attend community meetings five times each week. Class periods are 50 minutes long. All students participate in art, music, and the leadership program as part of the academic day. Time is set aside each day from 3 to 5 p.m. for athletics. Dinner is at 5:45, and there is a supervised study hall, located in the main classroom building, from 6:30 to 8. Bedtime varies from 9 to 10 p.m., depending on the age of the student.

WEEKEND LIFE

A wide variety of activities are offered to boarders each weekend. The School takes full advantage of the surrounding area, including Boston and Providence, with day trips to historic sites and museums. There are evening and weekend trips to sports events, live theater, exhibits, movies, and malls. A pond, located on the farm, provides opportunities for fishing, swimming, canoeing, and winter ice-skating. Students can go roller-skating, skiing, and bowling, all within a few miles of the School.

Many families of day students welcome boarders to their homes for weekends, and a day student may spend the night at the School, depending on the activity for that weekend. Weekend permission to go home is granted to seven-day boarders if they have attained minimum standards in academics and if they have no school commitments. Transportation is arranged after permission is given by parents.

COSTS AND FINANCIAL AID

Tuition for 2010–11 is $48,950 for a seven-day boarding student, $43,150 for a five-day boarder, and $28,600 for a day student. Hillside offers tuition payment plans. Every student has a personal account set up in the Business Office from which he receives weekly pocket money. Money can be withdrawn for special needs as long as it is approved by the Dean of Students. Funding for this account varies per year.

Thirty percent of the current student population receives more than $1 million in financial aid. To apply for tuition assistance, a candidate must complete the Parents' Financial Statement (PFS) from the School and Student Service for Financial Aid (SSS).

ADMISSIONS INFORMATION

The Admissions Office goes to great lengths to admit a diverse group of boys from a broad range of socioeconomic and racial backgrounds. Hillside seeks boys who are in need of a sheltered, structured, and nurturing learning environment. The School can accommodate both traditional learners and those with learning differences and/or attention problems. The boys are generally average to superior in intelligence yet have not reached their full potential. They perform best in an environment that is personalized, supportive, and challenging.

APPLICATION TIMETABLE

Parents interested in Hillside School may write, call, or e-mail the School directly for information. Enrollment is possible throughout the year, provided an opening exists. Decisions and notifications are made once an applicant's file is complete. There is a $50 application fee.

ADMISSIONS CORRESPONDENCE

Kristen Naspo, Director
Admissions and Financial Aid
Hillside School
Robin Hill Road
Marlborough, Massachusetts 01752

Phone: 508-485-2824
Fax: 508-485-4420
E-mail: admissions@hillsideschool.net
Web site: http://www.hillsideschool.net

NORTH COUNTRY SCHOOL

Lake Placid, New York

Type: Coeducational boarding elementary school
Grades: 4–9
Enrollment: 89
Head of School: David Hochschartner

THE SCHOOL

The student body numbered 6 children when Walter and Leonora Clark started North Country School in 1938. Because construction of their new school building had been delayed, this tiny band of children and adults took temporary shelter on the property in a thin-walled summer-camp building that had neither heat nor electricity. Years later, the Clarks delighted in telling these stories about those early days: borrowing a wood stove from an obliging neighbor, hanging blankets over the windows, and breaking ice in kitchen water buckets. Thus North Country School began with children learning lessons about overcoming unexpected difficulties with energy, cooperation, and good humor.

The 200-acre campus, which is located in the Adirondack High Peaks, includes a working farm, organic gardens, and lakeshore and is abutted by wilderness land. Sharing in the daily chores necessary to the maintenance of the School and farm has always been at the core of a child's experience at North Country. The Clarks believed that real responsibilities fostered feelings of purpose and self-worth in children. The school they envisaged was one in which all the experiences of each day, both in the classroom and out, would have the power to teach. That same belief had informed the founding of Camp Treetops seventeen years earlier on the same site, a project in which the Clarks also participated and which to this day complements the School program, making North Country School–Camp Treetops (NCS-CTT) one of the few truly year-round communities for children in the country.

Today, North Country School–Camp Treetops is overseen by a Board of Trustees, that meets four times a year on the campus so that members may visit classes, talk with students and staff members, and advance the institution's Long Range Plan. Gifts to the institution in 2008–09 totaled approximately $750,000, not including capital campaign contributions.

The institution is accredited by the New York State Association of Independent Schools and the American Camping Association and is a member of the Secondary School Admission Test Board, the Educational Records Bureau, and the National Association of Independent Schools.

ACADEMIC PROGRAMS

North Country School was founded on the dictum of John Dewey that "the educative process is fired and sustained by the impulse that comes from the desires, interests, and purposes of the pupil." The School structures children's study of the traditional school subjects but always encourages children to follow their own interests as they emerge. The School believes that all children are in some way gifted and creates a teaching and learning environment that is designed to find and develop those gifts. Education at North Country is a hands-on as well as a conceptual, social, and aesthetic matter. No summative grades are awarded; instead, teachers write comprehensive reports on each child's work twice a year. Ninth graders do receive course grades for their high school transcripts.

Learning environments are highly enriched with manipulative materials and resources. There is one computer for every 2 students, and students are taught how to use the Internet for information retrieval and global conversation. Some classes are taught by 2 or 3 teachers—1 as lead teacher and the others as coaches.

Science and math classes utilize the farm and mountain environment in their curriculum as well as problem-solving techniques that were recently endorsed by the National Council of Teachers of Mathematics.

FACULTY AND ADVISERS

The Head of North Country School–Camp Treetops is David Hochschartner, a graduate of Union College and the Klingenstein Center at Columbia University Teachers College. Mr. Hochschartner has served as the Director of the Presidio Hill School in San Francisco, California, and as Assistant Director of Burgundy Farm Country Day School in Alexandria, Virginia. He has been an instructor at Colorado Outward Bound School, has served as a coach and blind-racer guide for the U.S. Disabled Ski Team, and has an extensive background in outdoor sports.

The faculty members divide their time among teaching, coaching, tutoring, and the outdoors, where much of the School's program occurs year-round. Though many of the faculty members are experts and hold degrees in a particular subject area, they are primarily generalists who are prepared to work with children in all aspects of North Country School's program. A Faculty Enrichment Fund has been established to support summer study among the faculty, and time is taken before school and during the children's vacation periods for workshops and new-program development.

The staff includes a school nurse and a licensed social counselor. The Adirondack Medical Center is 20 minutes from the School.

SECONDARY SCHOOL PLACEMENT

The ninth-grade curriculum at North Country School includes a directed program in planning for transition. Students examine themselves, their interests and skills, and their aspirations as a basis for thinking about their transition to secondary school. They receive instruction and practice in writing essays as well as in interviewing and evaluating schools.

Parents are brought into the process of school selection at the end of the seventh-grade year and stay in contact with the Secondary School Placement Director from then on.

Schools attended by North Country School graduates include Buxton School, Cushing Academy, Darrow School, Dublin School, Emma Willard School, Gould Academy, High Mowing School, Knox School, Masters School, New Hampton School, Northfield Mount Hermon School, Northwood School, Orme School, Phillips Academy (Andover), Proctor Academy, Putney School, Stony Brook School, Tilton School, and Vermont Academy.

STUDENT BODY AND CONDUCT

Of the 89 children enrolled in 2009-10, 66 were boarders and 23 were day students or faculty children. This student community included 37 girls and 52 boys from sixteen states and ten other countries. The children ranged in age from 9 to 15.

Although North Country School is in many ways a highly structured community, it is also an informal one where everyone is on a first-name basis. Respect for one another is a key prerequisite for the success of the School community and is achieved through conversation and care rather than authority.

Candy, junk food, and television are not allowed except on special occasions. Children who feel the need to test limits do so with candy rather than other substances.

The School believes in the direct arbitration of disputes between children by an adult. Houseparents are regularly in touch with the parents of their charges. When a problem exists academically, socially, or personally, conversation about it begins early and parents are asked to participate in its solution if appropriate.

ACADEMIC FACILITIES

Most classes are held in one building, which was built in 1940 and has since been significantly modernized. Windows are large and rooms are sunny; there are slides by three of the staircases. The art, ceramics, weaving, woodworking, and photography studio areas are contiguous and occupy the lower level of the Main Building. A variety of dance, theater, and music classes are held in the spacious, post and beam performing arts building, built in 2001.

The barn, greenhouse, and sugarhouse are also used for teaching at various times in the year. The library, a bright and many-windowed space, contains 5,000 volumes and is filled with comfortable nooks and crannies for reading as well as state-of-the-art computer retrieval and online capabilities.

In recent years the school has added a learning lab to offer assistance to children with mild to moderate language-based learning challenges. In addition, an English as a second language (ESL) program is available to international students who require beginning and intermediate English instruction.

BOARDING AND GENERAL FACILITIES

Students live in one of seven "houses" with resident houseparents. There are no more than 12 boarding students to a house. Genders and ages are mixed much as they would be in a family, and most houseparents have young children of their own who complete the family circle. Two other adults are assigned to each house as well, so that there is always plenty of coverage and the 1:3 adult-child ratio is maintained. Houseparents oversee reading period and homework for the younger students. Eighth and ninth graders attend a supervised study hall in the main building. An evening snack is often prepared by a houseparent and 1–2 children. Younger children are tucked into bed and often read to before going to sleep.

ATHLETICS

Part of North Country School's educational philosophy is to encourage cooperation rather than

f www.facebook.com/sec.schools

competition; this is reflected in the School's athletics and recreation program. While some soccer and basketball games are played against local schools and North Country School's ski teams compete throughout the winter, the emphasis is on lifelong sports, free-form games, and play and mastery. Children may have riding classes once a week in the fall and spring. Children ski on the School's own ski hill and on adjacent cross-country trails. They ski each Tuesday afternoon at Whiteface Mountain and take advantage of Lake Placid's Olympic ski-jumping, bobsled, and luge venues one or two evenings a week throughout the winter. Children sled, toboggan, build snow caves, and wee-bob most afternoons on the hill by the School's lake. Students also enjoy ice skating at the Olympic speed-skating oval in town and on the School's ponds.

A major activity at North Country School is mountain climbing. Many children aim during their years at NCS-CTT to become Adirondack '46ers. There are expeditions nearly every weekend throughout the year, many on snowshoes. There is also a climbing wall in the main building that prepares children for more technical climbs in the out-of-doors. Dave's Crag, North Country's on-site climbing area, is 40-feet high by 250-feet wide and has twenty-five different routes ranging from beginner to advanced.

EXTRACURRICULAR OPPORTUNITIES

The school year is built around a number of all-School special events, many of which date back fifty years. For Halloween, children make their own costumes for an evening of festivities, including a senior-run spook house and a carnival.

The fall harvests are followed by Thanksgiving, which is attended by the children's families and at which the harvest is served. Music and dramatic performances follow.

The winter holiday celebration spans a week of special meals and treats as children go from one house to another and from one faculty residence to another.

Valentine's Day is again a time for creative manufacture and celebration, as are Box Dinners later in the spring. Mountain Cakes, a month-long escapade of spring mountaineering, is capped off by a big awards dinner, when each house is given a cake whose dimensions reflect the number of miles collectively climbed.

All children study music formally and many informally as well. Sunday dinner may be a special occasion where children dress up and where the meal is followed by a student performance, often of music.

Children are urged to learn to ride, ski, go on at least one overnight a term, and climb Cascade Mountain. A mounted drill team performs in the spring, and there are several horseback expeditions during the fall and spring.

Spring is maple sugar harvest time. The children split wood, gather sap, run the evaporator, and can more than 100 gallons of syrup each year.

A student newspaper and literary journal, a chorus, musical ensembles, and various student-created activities round out the extracurricular program.

DAILY LIFE

Children with barn chores are awakened at 6:30, others at 7 for building chores. All meals are served family-style. Breakfast is at 8, except on weekends, when the day begins a little later. Classes follow at 8:30 Monday through Friday and run through 3 p.m., with a break for lunch at 12:15. There is a 15-minute "council" right after lunch at which announcements are made, afternoon activities planned, recognitions and awards given, and an occasional story told. After lunch, older students choose from a substantial list of elective courses, including photography, wood shop, dance, theater, chorus, and individual music lessons. Sports follow, with various athletic opportunities, depending upon the season. Following sports, children return to their houses to relax and wind down with friends and houseparents before dinner. Occasionally, there are open houses in one living unit or another or at the Head's house. Wednesdays begin with a town meeting and end with an afternoon and evening of house-related activities, including a home-cooked meal.

Dinner is at 6; following that, younger children go to their houses for reading period, study time, and an evening in their houses until bedtime at 8:30. Older children remain in the building for study hall. Bedtime for them is 9:30.

WEEKEND LIFE

Weekends are nonacademic and involve field trips, hikes, sailing, and water activities in the fall and spring as well as games, horseback riding, fort building, off-campus winter competitions, sledding, skating, various homemade entertainments, dances, and free play. Ice cream is served on Saturday nights and followed by a dance or an all-school activity. Children never leave the campus unsupervised but often go 2 or 3 at a time with a faculty member to work on a town-related project, buy fish for the aquarium, get a bicycle fixed, or go in larger groups for an occasional movie.

SUMMER PROGRAMS

North Country School and Camp Treetops are seasonal expressions of the same philosophy. Camp Treetops, which was founded in 1921, provides a seven-week program that, with the exception of the academic component, very much mirrors the School. Children from age 8 to 14 participate in the regular session and children from 14 to 17 in Treetops Expeditions—four- to five-week trips that involve a variety of activities, including hiking, kayaking, cycling, and community service.

COSTS AND FINANCIAL AID

Student tuition for 2010–11 is $50,750. This fee covers such costs as textbooks, art materials, laundry service, field trips, and all ski and recreational passes. ESL is provided at an additional fee.

Financial aid is provided to approximately 35 percent of the students enrolled, the average grant being $18,000. Eligibility for financial aid is based upon the recommendation of the School Scholarship Service and requires submission of a copy of the applicant family's IRS filing for the previous year.

ADMISSIONS INFORMATION

North Country School looks to enroll children who are capable of using the School and the community to their advantage and who are also able to give to others from their own lives. The School is particularly successful with gifted children and children with variant learning styles. A decision to accept is based upon a child's school records, conversations with the child's parents, recommendations from those who have taught the child, the results of Wechsler Intelligence Scale for Children, and an interview with the School administrators. (The interview is occasionally waived for foreign-service families.)

APPLICATION TIMETABLE

Applications to North Country School–Camp Treetops are considered on a rolling admissions basis; midyear enrollment is possible.

ADMISSIONS CORRESPONDENCE

Director of Admissions
North Country School–Camp Treetops
4382 Cascade Road
Lake Placid, New York 12946

Phone: 518-523-9329 Ext. 6000
Fax: 518-523-4858
E-mail: admissions@northcountryschool.org
Web site: http://www.northcountryschool.org

RUMSEY HALL SCHOOL

Washington Depot, Connecticut

Type: Coeducational junior boarding (grades 5–9) and day preparatory school
Grades: K–9: Lower School, K–5; Upper School, 6–9
Enrollment: School total: 315
Head of School: Thomas W. Farmen, Headmaster

THE SCHOOL

Rumsey Hall School was founded in 1900 by Mrs. Lillias Rumsey Sanford. Since its inception, Rumsey Hall School has retained its original philosophy: to help each child develop to his or her maximum stature as an individual, as a member of a family, and as a contributing member of society. The curriculum emphasizes basic academic skills, a complete athletic program, fine arts, computer literacy, and numerous extracurricular offerings, which are all designed to encourage individual responsibility for academic achievement, accomplishment in team sports, and service to the School community. The School believes that "effort is the key to success."

The 147-acre campus on the Bantam River provides landscaped and wooded areas in a rural environment located outside of Washington, Connecticut. Rumsey Hall School is 90 miles from New York City and within an hour of the major Connecticut cities of Hartford and New Haven. The School's location enables students to take advantage of major cultural and athletic events in New York City and Boston throughout the school year.

A nonprofit institution, Rumsey Hall School is governed by a 19-member Board of Trustees that meets quarterly. The 2010–11 operating budget totaled $7.6 million. Revenues include tuition and fees and contributions from alumni, parents, corporations, foundations, and friends of the School. The School's endowment is approximately $6.2 million; the Board's long-range planning committee is examining ways to increase it. Annual giving was $1.5 million in 2010.

Rumsey Hall School is a member of the National Association of Independent Schools, the Connecticut Association of Independent Schools, the Junior Boarding Schools Association, the Educational Records Bureau, Western Connecticut Boarding Schools, and the Educational Testing Service, and is a voting member of the Secondary School Admission Test Board.

ACADEMIC PROGRAMS

At Rumsey Hall, effort is as important as academic achievement. Effort as a criterion for success opens a new world to the students. Effort does not start and end with the student. It is a shared responsibility between the student and each faculty member. Just as the faculty members expect maximum effort from each student, they promise in return to give each student their very best effort.

Students in the Upper School (sixth through ninth grades) carry at least five major subjects. There are eight 40-minute periods in each day, including lunch. Extra help is available each day for students who need additional instruction or extra challenges. All classes are departmentalized.

Final examinations are given in all subjects twice a year. Report cards, with numerical grades, are sent home every other week throughout the school year. Anecdotal comments and individualized teacher, adviser, and Headmaster comments are sent home three times each academic year.

A supplementary feature of the academic program is the Language Skills Department, which is directed toward intellectually able students with dyslexia or learning differences. Students in this program carry a regular academic course load, with the exception of a foreign language. In 2010–11, 15 percent of the student body was involved in this program.

English as a Second Language (ESL) is offered to international students and is comprised of two levels with three courses in each level. The courses are designed to help students develop their conversational and academic English, reading comprehension, awareness of social and cultural differences, and to introduce them to American history.

The school year, divided into trimesters, begins in September and runs until the first weekend in June. Vacations are scheduled at Thanksgiving and Christmas and in the spring.

Class size averages 12 students. Honors courses are offered to exceptional ninth grade students who demonstrate talent and whose scholarship indicates a strong sense of responsibility and motivation.

Students have a study hall built into their daily schedules, and there is an evening study hall for all boarding students. Study halls are supervised by faculty members, and there is ample opportunity for assistance. The library and computer facilities adjoin the formal study hall and are available at all study times.

In the Lower School (K through fifth grade), the nine daily academic periods begin at 8 a.m. after class meetings. English, reading, mathematics, science, and social studies are taught by the classroom teachers. Classes in foreign languages, language skills, health, music, art, and physical education vary the students' schedules by requiring them to move to different classrooms with specialized teachers. Normal class size is between 12 and 14 students, which makes for a dynamic learning environment where everyone's voice is heard and encouraged.

FACULTY AND ADVISERS

All 58 full- and part-time faculty members (28 men and 30 women) hold baccalaureate degrees, and half have master's degrees. Forty-one faculty members live on campus, many with their families. This enables Rumsey to provide the close supervision and warm family atmosphere that is an essential part of the School's culture.

Thomas W. Farmen was appointed Headmaster of Rumsey Hall School in 1985. He holds a Bachelor of Arts degree from New England College and a master's in school administration from Western Connecticut State University. He has served as President of the Association of Boarding Schools for the National Association of Independent Schools, President of the Junior Boarding Schools Association, and as a director of the Connecticut Association of Independent Schools.

The Dean of Students supervises and coordinates the advisory program. Each faculty member has 7 or 8 student advisees. Advisers meet with their advisees individually and in a weekly group setting. The adviser is the first link in the line of communication between school and home.

Faculty members at Rumsey Hall are encouraged to continue their professional development by taking postgraduate courses and attending seminars and conferences throughout the year. The School generously funds these programs.

SECONDARY SCHOOL PLACEMENT

The Director of Secondary School Placement supervises all facets of the secondary school search. Beginning in the eighth grade, a process of testing and interviewing with students and parents takes place that enables the placement director to highlight certain schools that seem appropriate. After visits and

interviews with the schools, the list is pared down to those to which the student wishes to apply. The 62 graduates of the class of 2010 wrote applications to sixty-two schools, and 80 percent of the students enrolled in their first-choice schools. Members of the classes of 2009 and 2010 enrolled in the following prep schools: Avon Old Farms, Berkshire, Blair, Canterbury, Cheshire Academy, Choate Rosemary Hall, Christchurch, Cushing, Deerfield, Emma Willard, George School, Governor's Academy, Groton, The Gunnery, Hill, Hotchkiss, Kent, Lawrenceville, Loomis Chaffee, Middlesex, Millbrook, Miss Hall's, Miss Porters, Northfield Mount Hermon, Phillips Exeter, Proctor, Putney, St. Andrew's, St. George's, St. James, St. Mark's, St. Paul's, Salisbury, South Kent, Suffield, Taft, Trinity-Pawling, Vermont Academy, Walnut Hill, Westminster, Westover, and Williston Northampton.

STUDENT BODY AND CONDUCT

In 2010–11, Rumsey Hall enrolled 315 students. The Lower School (grades K–5) enrolled 82 day students. The Upper School (grades 6–9) enrolled 233 students: 100 day students and 133 boarders. The School population was 56 percent boys and 44 percent girls.

In 2010–11, Rumsey students came from twenty states, ten countries, and twenty-seven local communities. International students enrolled in the ESL program composed 8 percent of the community.

The dress code requires jackets, collared shirts, and ties for boys and dresses or skirts and collared shirts or blouses for girls. In the winter term, boys may wear turtlenecks and sweaters and girls may wear slacks.

The School values of honesty, kindness, and respect comprise the yardstick by which Rumsey measures a student's thoughts and actions. Students living outside the spirit of the community are asked to meet with the Disciplinary and Senior Committees. These committees represent a cross section of administrators, faculty members, and students.

ACADEMIC FACILITIES

Situated alongside the Bantam River on a 147-acre campus, the School is housed in thirty buildings, most of which have been constructed since 1950. Nine structures house a total of thirty classrooms, including the Dane W. Dicke Family Math and Science Buildings. Other buildings include the Dicke Family Library; the Sanford House, which houses the study and meeting hall; the J. Seward Johnson Sr. Fine Arts Center, with spacious art and music rooms; and the Satyvati Science Center. Students and faculty members meet as a community for meals in the D. G. Barr Dining Hall.

The Garassino Building is home to three lower school classrooms including an all-day kindergarten. The Maxwell A. Sarofim '05 Performing Arts Center (the MAX) is the setting for student performances, visiting artists, and school assemblies; students' art and exhibits of Rumsey community interest are displayed in the adjacent Allen Finkelson Gallery.

Rumsey has three fully interactive computer labs on campus and more than 120 networked computers throughout the School. The schoolwide intranet system enhances communication within the community.

BOARDING AND GENERAL FACILITIES

The close relationship between teachers and students is a special part of Rumsey Hall School. Students live in dormitories with supportive dorm parents, and students become a part of their dorm parents' families.

Rumsey's boarding students live in one of eight dormitories. Dormitories are assigned by age, and most students have roommates, although single rooms are available in most dorms. Each dormitory has its own common room that is the shared living space for the dorm. A snack bar and store are open every afternoon. Laundry and dry cleaning are sent out on a weekly basis. Four registered nurses staff the School's infirmary, and the School doctor, a local pediatrician, is available on a daily basis. Emergency facilities are available at New Milford Hospital, which is 10 miles away. There are telephones in all dormitories, and every student has an e-mail account.

ATHLETICS

Athletics are a healthy and essential part of the Rumsey experience. On the playing field, lifelong attitudes, values, and habits are born. All students participate at their own level in athletics. Effort is rewarded through athletic letters and certificates at the end of the season.

Rumsey Hall fields thirty-two interscholastic teams throughout the year. Most sports are offered on different levels so that students are able to compete with children of their own size and skill level. Interscholastic teams are fielded in baseball, basketball, crew, cross-country, field hockey, football, boys' ice hockey, girls' ice hockey, lacrosse, skiing, soccer, softball, tennis, volleyball, and wrestling. Other activities available include horseback riding, Outdoor Club, Lower School games and activities, recreational skiing and snowboarding, biking, and ice-skating.

The John F. Schereschewsky, Sr. Memorial Center houses the Magnoli and Blue Dog Gymnasiums where basketball, volleyball, and wrestling activities are held. Recent renovations to the indoor athletic facilities include an indoor climbing wall, boys' and girls' locker rooms, and three new and improved tennis courts. The Cornell Common Room serves as the weight-training room and offers other training machines, as well as housing the athletic director and athletic training staff. Lufkin Rink is the newest of Rumsey Hall's athletic facilities. Opened in late 2008, the rink provides home ice for the boys' and girls' hockey teams. Intramural and recreational activities make the space available to skaters of all abilities.

There are several athletic fields on campus including the Pavek Athletic Field, in honor of Veronica D. and Charles H. Pavek; Scott Evans Seibert '92 Memorial Field; Paul Lincoln Cornell Athletic Field, and Roy Field. There are also three outdoor tennis courts and two ponds for outdoor recreation and winter skating.

Holt Beach at Lake Waramaug is the site for spring crew training. Students who ski and snowboard in the winter term travel to Mohawk Mountain in nearby Cornwall, Connecticut on weekday afternoons.

EXTRACURRICULAR OPPORTUNITIES

Throughout the year, Upper School students may participate in many activities and clubs. The choices include fishing, computers, chorus, art club, bicycling, fly fishing, School newspaper, yearbook, art, swimming, hiking, rocketry, baking, community service, intramural sports, and participation in School dramatic and musical productions.

The Lower School features an exciting afternoon enrichment program for all students in kindergarten through fifth grade after their daily academic curriculum is complete. In keeping with Rumsey Hall's mission to educate the whole child, the varied activities offered each afternoon are organized to cultivate interests that can be nurtured as the children grow. Most activities are led by Rumsey teachers while others enlist the skills of specialists from surrounding communities. Activities include but are not limited to the arts (ceramics, printmaking, theater, crafts), athletics (field/gymnasium sports, martial arts), and recreational and outdoor games.

Traditional annual events for the School community include a Christmas concert, Parents' Day, Grandparents' Day, and Headmaster's Weekend and ski trip to Bromley Mountain, Vermont. Service to the School and to the greater community is encouraged throughout the year by the community service/service learning program. During the 2009–10 academic year the students amassed 930 total hours of volunteer service.

The student body is divided into red and blue color teams. These teams enjoy friendly competition throughout the school year in areas of community service, academic achievement, and athletics.

DAILY LIFE

The school day begins at 8 a.m. with an all-School meeting. All administrators, faculty members, and students are in attendance. It is a time to share the news of the School and the world as well as important information and announcements with the whole community. The rest of the academic day consists of eight 40-minute periods and supervised study halls, with a 20-minute recess in the middle of the morning. Extra help is available every day after lunch. Athletic practices or contests take place from 3 to 4:30 p.m. Dinner is served family style at 6 and is followed by study hall from 7 to 8:30. Free time follows, with bedtimes varying depending on the grade of the child.

WEEKEND LIFE

Weekends for boarding students include a variety of activities on and off campus. There are School dances, special theme weekends, off-campus trips, and intramural activities on campus. Rumsey's proximity to four major cities—New York, Boston, Hartford, and New Haven—allows for a wide variety of cultural events, sports events (collegiate and professional), and shopping excursions. All trips are fully supervised, and an appropriate student-teacher ratio is maintained. Day students are encouraged to participate in weekend activities and are also allowed to invite boarding students home with them for the weekend.

SUMMER PROGRAMS

The five-week Rumsey Hall summer session is open to students in the third through ninth grades. The program is designed for students who desire enrichment or need additional work in a subject area in order to move on to the next grade with confidence.

Special emphasis is placed on English, mathematics, study skills, and computer skills. Normal class size ranges from 6 to 10 students with individual attention and help available. Students who need support in language skills or developmental reading work daily with trained specialists. ESL is offered to international students. In the afternoon, students enjoy recreational activities such as swimming, hiking, tennis, fishing, horseback riding, baseball, soccer, lacrosse, and basketball. Off-campus trips to museums, movies, concerts, amusement parks, and sporting events occur each week. Considerable effort is made to cultivate students' interests and to expose them to new experiences. For the 2010 summer session, tuition, room, and board was $6550 for boarding students, $2340 for day students, and $1520 for half-day students. There are additional fees for individual tutoring in language skills and enrollment in ESL.

COSTS AND FINANCIAL AID

In 2009–10, full-year tuition was $16,200 for kindergarten, $16,600 for day students in grades 1 and 2, $20,400 for day students in grades 3–9, and $42,950 for boarding students. Additional fees included books, athletic fees, school supplies, and laundry and dry cleaning. A nonrefundable deposit of $2000 serves as the boarding student's drawing account for the year. The annual fee for language skills was $4780. The annual fee for ESL was $7000. Two thirds of the total tuition is due July 15 and the balance by December 15. A ten-installment payment agreement is available.

Rumsey Hall is a member of the School and Student Service for Financial Aid. In the 2010–11 academic year approximately $1 million in tuition assistance was awarded to one third of the students.

ADMISSIONS INFORMATION

Rumsey Hall welcomes students of average to above-average intelligence and achievement. Students must show evidence of good citizenship and the willingness to live in a boarding community. Acceptance is based on past school performance, scores on standardized achievement tests, and a personal interview. Rumsey is able to accept a limited number of students with learning differences if their learning profile is compatible with the School's Orton-Gillingham–based language skills program. Rumsey Hall School admits students of any race, color, religion, or national or ethnic origin.

APPLICATION TIMETABLE

Inquiries are welcome at any time of the year, with most families beginning the admission process in the fall or winter in anticipation of September enrollment. Admission interviews and tours are scheduled throughout the year. Boarding student applications are accepted on a rolling basis. Day student applicants should complete the application process by February 15. Applicants are notified of acceptance by March 1.

ADMISSIONS CORRESPONDENCE

Matthew S. Hoeniger, Director of Admissions
Rumsey Hall School
201 Romford Road
Washington Depot, Connecticut 06794
Phone: 860-868-0535
Fax: 860-868-7907
E-mail: admiss@rumseyhall.org
Web site: http://www.rumseyhall.org

Specialized Directories

COEDUCATIONAL DAY SCHOOLS

The Academy at Charlemont, MA
Academy at the Lakes, FL
The Academy for Gifted Children (PACE), ON, Canada
Academy of the Holy Names, FL
Academy of the Sacred Heart, MI
Académie Ste Cécile International School, ON, Canada
Admiral Farragut Academy, FL
Alexander Dawson School, CO
Allendale Columbia School, NY
Allison Academy, FL
Alma Heights Christian High School, CA
Alpha Omega Academy, IA
American Academy, FL
American Community Schools of Athens, Greece
American Heritage School, FL
American Heritage School, FL
American International School, Dhaka, Bangladesh
American International School of Costa Rica, Costa Rica
The American School in London, United Kingdom
American School of Bombay, India
The American School of Madrid, Spain
American School of Milan, Italy
American School of The Hague, Netherlands
Archbishop Alter High School, OH
Archbishop Hoban High School, OH
Archbishop McNicholas High School, OH
Archbishop Mitty High School, CA
Arendell Parrott Academy, NC
Armona Union Academy, CA
Arrowsmith School, ON, Canada
Arthur Morgan School, NC
ASSETS School, HI
The Athenian School, CA
Augusta Christian School (I), GA
Augusta Preparatory Day School, GA
The Awty International School, TX
The Baltimore Actors' Theatre Conservatory, MD
Baltimore Lutheran Middle and Upper School, MD
Barrie School, MD
Bavarian International School, Germany
Baylor School, TN
Bayside Academy, AL
The Beekman School, NY
Bellarmine-Jefferson High School, CA
The Bement School, MA
Ben Franklin Academy, GA
Berkeley Preparatory School, FL
Berwick Academy, ME
The Birch Wathen Lenox School, NY
Bishop Blanchet High School, WA
Bishop Brady High School, NH
Bishop Connolly High School, MA
Bishop Denis J. O'Connell High School, VA
Bishop Eustace Preparatory School, NJ
Bishop Fenwick High School, OH
Bishop Guertin High School, NH
Bishop Ireton High School, VA
Bishop Kelly High School, ID
Bishop Kenny High School, FL
Bishop Luers High School, IN
Bishop McGuinness Catholic High School, NC
Bishop McGuinness Catholic High School, OK
Bishop Montgomery High School, CA
Bishop O'Dowd High School, CA
Bishop's College School, QC, Canada
Bishop Stang High School, MA

Bishop Walsh Middle High School, MD
Blair Academy, NJ
Blanchet School, OR
Blessed Trinity High School, GA
Blue Mountain Academy, PA
The Bolles School, FL
Bourgade Catholic High School, AZ
Boylan Central Catholic High School, IL
Breck School, MN
Brentwood College School, BC, Canada
Brentwood School, CA
Brewster Academy, NH
Briarcrest Christian High School, TN
Briarwood Christian High School, AL
Bridges Academy, CA
Bridge School, CO
Brooks School, MA
Brookstone School, GA
The Buckley School, CA
Burr and Burton Academy, VT
Buxton School, MA
The Byrnes Schools, SC
The Calhoun School, NY
Calvary Chapel High School, CA
Calvary Christian School, KY
The Calverton School, MD
Calvin Christian High School, CA
Campbell Hall (Episcopal), CA
Camphill Special School, PA
Canadian Academy, Japan
Canterbury School, FL
The Canterbury School of Florida, FL
Canton Academy, MS
Canyonville Christian Academy, OR
Cape Fear Academy, NC
Cape Henry Collegiate School, VA
Capistrano Valley Christian Schools, CA
Cardinal Mooney Catholic College Preparatory High School, MI
Cardinal Mooney Catholic High School, FL
Cardinal Newman High School, FL
Carlucci American International School of Lisbon, Portugal
Carmel High School, IL
Cary Academy, NC
Cascade Christian Academy, WA
Cascia Hall Preparatory School, OK
Catholic Central High School, WI
The Catlin Gabel School, OR
Cedar Ridge Academy, UT
Central Catholic High School, CA
Central Catholic High School, MA
Central Catholic High School, OH
Central Catholic High School, OH
Central Catholic Mid-High School, NE
Chamberlain-Hunt Academy, MS
Chaminade College Preparatory, CA
Chaminade-Madonna College Preparatory, FL
Chapel Hill–Chauncy Hall School, MA
Charles Wright Academy, WA
Charlotte Christian School, NC
Charlotte Country Day School, NC
Charlotte Latin School, NC
Chatham Academy, GA
Chattanooga Christian School, TN
Cheverus High School, ME
The Chicago Academy for the Arts, IL
Chicago Waldorf School, IL
Chinese Christian Schools, CA

Choate Rosemary Hall, CT
Christ Church Episcopal School, SC
Christchurch School, VA
Christian Brothers Academy, NY
Christian Central Academy, NY
Christian Home and Bible School, FL
Christopher Dock Mennonite High School, PA
Chrysalis School, WA
Cincinnati Country Day School, OH
Clearwater Central Catholic High School, FL
Colegio Franklin D. Roosevelt, Peru
Colegio Nueva Granada, Colombia
Collegedale Academy, TN
The Collegiate School, VA
The Colorado Rocky Mountain School, CO
The Colorado Springs School, CO
Columbia Academy, TN
Columbia International College of Canada, ON, Canada
The Columbus Academy, OH
Commonwealth Parkville School, PR
Commonwealth School, MA
Community Christian Academy, KY
Community Hebrew Academy, ON, Canada
Community High School, NJ
The Community School of Naples, FL
The Concept School, PA
Concord Academy, MA
Concordia High School, AB, Canada
Concordia Lutheran High School, IN
Cotter Schools, MN
The Country Day School, ON, Canada
Covenant Canadian Reformed School, AB, Canada
Crawford Adventist Academy, ON, Canada
Crosspoint Academy, WA
Crossroads College Preparatory School, MO
Crystal Springs Uplands School, CA
The Culver Academies, IN
Currey Ingram Academy, TN
Cushing Academy, MA
Dakota Christian High School, SD
Dallas Christian School, TX
The Dalton School, NY
David Lipscomb High School, TN
Davidson Academy, TN
Deerfield Academy, MA
Deerfield-Windsor School, GA
Delaware Valley Friends School, PA
Denver Lutheran High School, CO
DePaul Catholic High School, NJ
The Derryfield School, NH
Des Moines Christian School, IA
Doane Stuart School, NY
Donelson Christian Academy, TN
Dowling Catholic High School, IA
Dublin School, NH
Durham Academy, NC
Eagle Hill-Southport, CT
Eastern Christian High School, NJ
Eastside Catholic School, WA
Eastside Christian Academy, AB, Canada
Ecole d'Humanité, Switzerland
Edmund Burke School, DC
Elgin Academy, IL
The Episcopal Academy, PA
Episcopal Collegiate School, AR
Episcopal High School, TX
Episcopal High School of Jacksonville, FL

Explorations Academy, WA
Fairhill School, TX
Faith Christian High School, CA
Faith Lutheran High School, NV
Falmouth Academy, MA
Father Lopez High School, FL
Father Ryan High School, TN
Fayetteville Academy, NC
Fay School, MA
Fenwick High School, IL
The First Academy, FL
First Baptist Academy, TX
First Presbyterian Day School, GA
Flint Hill School, VA
Flint River Academy, GA
Florida Air Academy, FL
Foothills Academy, AB, Canada
Forsyth Country Day School, NC
Fort Lauderdale Preparatory School, FL
Foundation Academy, FL
Fountain Valley School of Colorado, CO
Fowlers Academy, PR
Fox Valley Lutheran High School, WI
Franklin Academy, CT
Franklin Road Academy, TN
Fraser Academy, BC, Canada
Frederica Academy, GA
Freeman Academy, SD
French-American School of New York, NY
Fresno Adventist Academy, CA
Fresno Christian Schools, CA
Friends Academy, NY
Friends' Central School, PA
Friendship Christian School, TN
Friends Select School, PA
The Frostig School, CA
Fuqua School, VA
Gann Academy (The New Jewish High School of Greater Boston), MA
Garces Memorial High School, CA
Gaston Day School, NC
Gateway School, TX
The Geneva School, FL
George School, PA
George Stevens Academy, ME
George Walton Academy, GA
Germantown Friends School, PA
Gill St. Bernard's School, NJ
Gilmour Academy, OH
Glades Day School, FL
Glen Eden School, BC, Canada
Glenelg Country School, MD
The Glenholme School, a Devereux Center, CT
Glenlyon Norfolk School, BC, Canada
Gould Academy, ME
The Governor French Academy, IL
The Governor's Academy (formerly Governor Dummer Academy), MA
Grace Baptist Academy, TN
Grace Christian School, PE, Canada
The Grauer School, CA
Greater Atlanta Christian Schools, GA
Greenfield School, NC
Greenhill School, TX
Greenhills School, MI
Greensboro Day School, NC
Griggs International Academy, MD

Groton School, MA
Gulliver Preparatory School, FL
Gunston Day School, MD
Hackley School, NY
Hamden Hall Country Day School, CT
Hamilton District Christian High, ON, Canada
Hampton Roads Academy, VA
Hanalani Schools, HI
Hank Haney International Junior Golf Academy, SC
Hanson Memorial High School, LA
Harding Academy, TN
Harding Academy, TN
The Harker School, CA
The Harley School, NY
Harrells Christian Academy, NC
Harvard-Westlake School, CA
Hawaiian Mission Academy, HI
Hawaii Baptist Academy, HI
Hawken School, OH
Hawthorne Christian Academy, NJ
Head-Royce School, CA
Hebrew Academy-the Five Towns, NY
Heritage Christian Academy, AB, Canada
Heritage Christian School, ON, Canada
The Heritage School, GA
Highland Hall Waldorf School, CA
The Hill Center, Durham Academy, NC
Hillcrest Christian School, MS
Hillcrest School, TX
Hill School of Fort Worth, TX
The Hill Top Preparatory School, PA
Hilton Head Preparatory School, SC
Holy Cross High School, CT
Holy Innocents' Episcopal School, GA
Holy Name High School, PA
Holyoke Catholic High School, MA
Holy Savior Menard Catholic High School, LA
Holy Trinity High School, IL
Hoosac School, NY
Hopkins School, CT
The Hotchkiss School, CT
Houghton Academy, NY
The Howard School, GA
The Howe School, IN
Humanex Academy, CO
The Hun School of Princeton, NJ
Huntington-Surrey School, TX
Hyde School, ME
Hyman Brand Hebrew Academy of Greater Kansas City, KS
Idyllwild Arts Academy, CA
Immaculata-La Salle High School, FL
Immaculate Conception School, IL
Immanuel Christian High School, AB, Canada
Interlochen Arts Academy, MI
International College Spain, Spain
International High School, CA
International School Bangkok, Thailand
International School Hamburg, Germany
International School Manila, Philippines
International School of Amsterdam, Netherlands
International School of Athens, Greece
International School of Berne, Switzerland
The International School of Kuala Lumpur, Malaysia
The International School of London, United Kingdom
International School of Zug and Luzern (ISZL), Switzerland
Iolani School, HI
Isidore Newman School, LA

Island School, HI
Jackson Christian School, TN
Jackson Preparatory School, MS
J. K. Mullen High School, CO
John Burroughs School, MO
The John Cooper School, TX
John Paul II Catholic High School, FL
The Journeys School of Teton Science School, WY
Junipero Serra High School, CA
Kalamazoo Christian High School, MI
The Karafin School, NY
Kauai Christian Academy, HI
Keith Country Day School, IL
Kent School, CT
Kentucky Country Day School, KY
Kerr-Vance Academy, NC
The Kew-Forest School, NY
Key School, TX
Kildonan School, NY
Kimball Union Academy, NH
King Low Heywood Thomas, CT
Kings Christian School, CA
King's-Edgehill School, NS, Canada
Kingshill School, VI
King's Ridge Christian School, GA
Kingsway College, ON, Canada
Kingswood-Oxford School, CT
Kirov Academy of Ballet of Washington, D.C., DC
La Jolla Country Day School, CA
Lakefield College School, ON, Canada
Lake Forest Academy, IL
Lakehill Preparatory School, TX
Lake Ridge Academy, OH
Lakeside School, WA
La Lumiere School, IN
Lancaster Mennonite High School, PA
Landmark Christian Academy, KY
Landmark School, MA
La Salle High School, CA
The Latin School of Chicago, IL
The Laureate Academy, MB, Canada
Lawrence School, OH
The Lawrenceville School, NJ
Lehigh Valley Christian High School, PA
Lehman High School, OH
Le Lycee Francais de Los Angeles, CA
Liberty Christian School, CA
Lick-Wilmerding High School, CA
Lighthouse Christian School, AB, Canada
Lima Central Catholic High School, OH
Lincoln Academy, ME
Linfield Christian School, CA
The Linsly School, WV
Lodi Academy, CA
Long Island Lutheran Middle and High School, NY
Los Angeles Baptist Middle School/High School, CA
Louisville Collegiate School, KY
The Lovett School, GA
Loyola Academy, IL
Loyola School, NY
Lutheran High School, CA
Lutheran High School, IN
Lutheran High School, MO
Lutheran High School North, MO
Lutheran High School Northwest, MI
Lutheran High School of Hawaii, HI
Lutheran High School of San Diego, CA

Specialized Directories

Lutheran High School South, MO
Luther College High School, SK, Canada
Luther High School North, IL
The Lycee International, American Section, France
Lydia Patterson Institute, TX
MacLachlan College, ON, Canada
Madison Academy, AL
Madison-Ridgeland Academy, MS
Maharishi School of the Age of Enlightenment, IA
Maine Central Institute, ME
Manhattan Christian High School, MT
Manlius Pebble Hill School, NY
Maplebrook School, NY
Maret School, DC
Marian Central Catholic High School, IL
Marian High School, IN
Marin Academy, CA
The Marin School, CA
Marion Academy, AL
Marist School, GA
Mars Hill Bible School, AL
Martin Luther High School, NY
Maryknoll School, HI
Marymount International School, Italy
Mary Star of the Sea High School, CA
The Masters School, NY
Matignon High School, MA
Maui Preparatory Academy, HI
Maur Hill-Mount Academy, KS
McDonogh School, MD
McGill-Toolen Catholic High School, AL
Meadowridge School, BC, Canada
The Meadows School, NV
Memorial Hall School, TX
Menaul School, NM
Menlo School, CA
Mercy Vocational High School, PA
The Miami Valley School, OH
Middlesex School, MA
Mid-Pacific Institute, HI
Millbrook School, NY
Milton Academy, MA
MMI Preparatory School, PA
Monsignor Donovan High School, NJ
Montclair College Preparatory School, CA
Montclair Kimberley Academy, NJ
Monterey Bay Academy, CA
Monte Vista Christian School, CA
Moorestown Friends School, NJ
Moravian Academy, PA
Moreau Catholic High School, CA
Morristown-Beard School, NJ
Mt. De Sales Academy, GA
Mount Saint Charles Academy, RI
MPS Etobicoke, ON, Canada
MU High School, MO
Munich International School, Germany
Nashville Christian School, TN
Navajo Preparatory School, Inc., NM
Nazareth Academy, IL
Nebraska Christian Schools, NE
Newark Academy, NJ
New Covenant Academy, MO
New English School, Kuwait
New English School, Kuwait
Niagara Christian Community of Schools, ON, Canada
The Nichols School, NY

Noble Academy, NC
The Nora School, MD
Norfolk Academy, VA
North Cobb Christian School, GA
North Country School, NY
North Shore Country Day School, IL
Northwest Catholic High School, CT
The Northwest School, WA
Northwest Yeshiva High School, WA
Northwood School, NY
The Norwich Free Academy, CT
Notre Dame High School, NJ
Notre Dame High School, TN
Notre Dame Junior/Senior High School, PA
Oak Grove School, CA
Oak Hill Academy, VA
Oak Hill School, OR
The Oakland School, PA
Oakland School, VA
Oak Mountain Academy, GA
Oak Ridge Military Academy, NC
The Oakridge School, TX
Ojai Valley School, CA
Oldenburg Academy, IN
The O'Neal School, NC
Oneida Baptist Institute, KY
Orangewood Christian School, FL
Oregon Episcopal School, OR
Orinda Academy, CA
The Orme School, AZ
Out-Of-Door-Academy, FL
The Overlake School, WA
Pacific Crest Community School, OR
Padua Franciscan High School, OH
The Paideia School, GA
Paradise Adventist Academy, CA
The Park School of Baltimore, MD
The Park School of Buffalo, NY
The Pathway School, PA
Peddie School, NJ
Peninsula Catholic High School, VA
Pensacola Catholic High School, FL
Phillips Academy (Andover), MA
Phoenix Christian Unified Schools, AZ
Phoenix Country Day School, AZ
Pickens Academy, AL
Pickering College, ON, Canada
Pic River Private High School, ON, Canada
Piedmont Academy, GA
Pinecrest Academy, GA
Pine Crest School, FL
The Pingry School, NJ
Pioneer Valley Christian School, MA
Polytechnic School, CA
Pope John XXIII Regional High School, NJ
Porter-Gaud School, SC
Portsmouth Abbey School, RI
Portsmouth Christian Academy, NH
The Potomac School, VA
Poughkeepsie Day School, NY
Powers Catholic High School, MI
Prestonwood Christian Academy, TX
Professional Children's School, NY
The Prout School, RI
Providence Christian School, AB, Canada
Providence Country Day School, RI
Providence Day School, NC

Providence High School, CA
Queen Anne School, MD
Queen of Peace High School, NJ
Quinte Christian High School, ON, Canada
Randolph-Macon Academy, VA
Randolph School, AL
Ranney School, NJ
Ransom Everglades School, FL
The Rectory School, CT
Redwood Adventist Academy, CA
Redwood Christian Schools, CA
Reitz Memorial High School, IN
Rejoice Christian Schools, OK
Ridley College, ON, Canada
Rio Hondo Preparatory School, CA
Riverdale Country School, NY
Rivermont Collegiate, IA
The Rivers School, MA
Riverstone International School, ID
Robert Louis Stevenson School, NY
Rockland Country Day School, NY
Rock Point School, VT
The Roeper School, MI
Rolling Hills Preparatory School, CA
Ron Pettigrew Christian School, BC, Canada
Rosseau Lake College, ON, Canada
Ross School, NY
Rothesay Netherwood School, NB, Canada
Rotterdam International Secondary School, Wolfert van Borselen,
    Netherlands
Rowland Hall, UT
Royal Canadian College, BC, Canada
Roycemore School, IL
Rundle College, AB, Canada
Rye Country Day School, NY
Sacred Heart School of Halifax, NS, Canada
Saddleback Valley Christian School, CA
Saddlebrook Preparatory School, FL
Sage Hill School, CA
Sage Ridge School, NV
St. Andrew's Regional High School, BC, Canada
St. Andrew's School, RI
St. Ann's Academy, BC, Canada
St. Anthony Catholic High School, TX
Saint Anthony High School, IL
St. Anthony's Junior-Senior High School, HI
St. Benedict at Auburndale, TN
St. Bernard's Catholic School, CA
St. Brendan High School, FL
Saint Cecilia High School, NE
St. Clement School, ON, Canada
St. Croix Country Day School, VI
St. Croix Schools, MN
St. David's School, NC
Saint Dominic Academy, ME
Saint Edward's School, FL
Saint Elizabeth High School, CA
Saint Francis School, HI
St. George's Independent School, TN
St. George's School, RI
St. George's School of Montreal, QC, Canada
St. Gregory College Preparatory School, AZ
St. John's-Ravenscourt School, MB, Canada
St. Joseph Academy, FL
St. Joseph High School, CA
Saint Joseph High School, IL
Saint Joseph High School, NJ

Saint Joseph High School, WI
Saint Joseph Junior-Senior High School, HI
St. Joseph's Catholic School, SC
St. Jude's School, ON, Canada
St. Margaret's Episcopal School, CA
Saint Mark's School, MA
St. Martin's Episcopal School, LA
Saint Mary's College High School, CA
Saint Mary's Hall, TX
Saint Mary's High School, AZ
Saint Mary's High School, MD
St. Mary's School, OR
Saint Maur International School, Japan
St. Michaels University School, BC, Canada
St. Patrick Catholic High School, MS
Saint Patrick—Saint Vincent High School, CA
St. Patrick's Regional Secondary, BC, Canada
St. Paul Academy and Summit School, MN
St. Paul's Episcopal School, AL
St. Pius X Catholic High School, GA
St. Pius X High School, TX
Saints Peter and Paul High School, MD
St. Stephen's & St. Agnes School, VA
Saint Stephen's Episcopal School, FL
St. Stephen's Episcopal School, TX
Saint Thomas Aquinas High School, KS
St. Thomas Aquinas High School, NH
Saint Thomas More Catholic High School, LA
Saint Viator High School, IL
St. Vincent Pallotti High School, MD
Salem Academy, OR
Salem Baptist Christian School, NC
Salesian High School, CA
Salt Lake Lutheran High School, UT
Saltus Grammar School, Bermuda
Sandia Preparatory School, NM
Sandy Spring Friends School, MD
Sanford School, DE
San Marcos Baptist Academy, TX
Santa Fe Preparatory School, NM
Sayre School, KY
Scarborough Christian School, ON, Canada
SCECGS Redlands, Australia
Scholar's Hall Preparatory School, ON, Canada
Scottsdale Christian Academy, AZ
Scotus Central Catholic High School, NE
Seabury Hall, HI
Seattle Academy of Arts and Sciences, WA
Seattle Christian Schools, WA
Second Baptist School, TX
Seoul Foreign School, Republic of Korea
Seton Catholic Central High School, NY
Seton Catholic High School, AZ
The Seven Hills School, OH
Severn School, MD
Sewickley Academy, PA
Shades Mountain Christian School, AL
Shady Side Academy, PA
Shannon Forest Christian School, SC
Shattuck-St. Mary's School, MN
Shawe Memorial Junior/Senior High School, IN
Shelton School and Evaluation Center, TX
Sheridan Academy, ID
The Shipley School, PA
Shoore Centre for Learning, ON, Canada
Shoreline Christian, WA
Smith School, NY

Solomon College, AB, Canada
Sonoma Academy, CA
Soundview Preparatory School, NY
Southern Ontario College, ON, Canada
Southfield Christian High School, MI
Southwest Christian School, Inc., TX
Southwestern Academy, AZ
Southwestern Academy, CA
Spartanburg Day School, SC
Squaw Valley Academy, CA
The Stanwich School, CT
Stephen T. Badin High School, OH
Sterne School, CA
Stevenson School, CA
Stratton Mountain School, VT
The Sudbury Valley School, MA
Suffield Academy, CT
Summerfield Waldorf School, CA
Tabor Academy, MA
Taipei American School, Taiwan
Tandem Friends School, VA
TASIS, The American School in Switzerland, Switzerland
Telluride Mountain School, CO
The Tenney School, TX
Teurlings Catholic High School, LA
The Thacher School, CA
Thomas Jefferson School, MO
Tidewater Academy, VA
Timothy Christian High School, IL
TMI—The Episcopal School of Texas, TX
Toronto District Christian High School, ON, Canada
Tower Hill School, DE
Town Centre Private High School, ON, Canada
Trinity Christian Academy, TN
Trinity College School, ON, Canada
Trinity High School, NH
Trinity Preparatory School, FL
Trinity School, NY
Trinity School at Greenlawn, IN
Trinity School of Texas, TX
Tuscaloosa Academy, AL
Tyler Street Christian Academy, TX
United Nations International School, NY
University Christian Preparatory School, LA
University of Chicago Laboratory Schools, IL
University Prep, WA
University School of Jackson, TN
University School of Milwaukee, WI
University School of Nova Southeastern University, FL
Vail Mountain School, CO
Valle Catholic High School, MO
Valley Lutheran High School, AZ
Venta Preparatory School, ON, Canada
Verdala International School, Malta
Vicksburg Catholic School, MS
Villa Duchesne and Oak Hill School, MO
Village Christian Schools, CA
Villa Maria Academy, PA
Waldorf High School of Massachusetts Bay, MA
The Walker School, GA
Waring School, MA
Wasatch Academy, UT
The Waterford School, UT
Watkinson School, CT
Waynflete School, ME
The Webb School, TN
Webb School of Knoxville, TN

The Wellington School, OH
Wellspring Foundation, CT
Wellsprings Friends School, OR
Wesleyan Academy, PR
Westbury Christian School, TX
West Catholic High School, MI
Westchester Country Day School, NC
Western Christian Schools, CA
Western Mennonite School, OR
Western Reserve Academy, OH
West Island College, AB, Canada
Westmark School, CA
West Memphis Christian High School, AR
Westminster Christian Academy, AL
Westminster Christian Academy, LA
West Sound Academy, WA
West Valley Christian Church Schools, CA
Wheaton Academy, IL
The Wheeler School, RI
Whitefield Academy, KY
The White Mountain School, NH
The Williams School, CT
The Williston Northampton School, MA
Willow Wood School, ON, Canada
Wilson Hall, SC
Winchester Thurston School, PA
Windermere Preparatory School, FL
The Windsor School, NY
Windward School, CA
Winston Preparatory School, NY
The Winston School San Antonio, TX
Woodlynde School, PA
Woodstock School, India
Woodward Academy, GA
Worcester Academy, MA
Worcester Preparatory School, MD
Wyoming Seminary, PA
Yokohama International School, Japan
York Catholic High School, PA
York Country Day School, PA
York Preparatory School, NY
York School, CA

BOYS' DAY SCHOOLS

Academy of the New Church Boys' School, PA
All Hallows High School, NY
The American Boychoir School, NJ
Archbishop Curley High School, MD
Archbishop Rummel High School, LA
Army and Navy Academy, CA
Bellarmine College Preparatory, CA
Benedictine High School, OH
Benedictine High School, VA
Boston College High School, MA
Brother Rice High School, IL
Brother Rice High School, MI
Brunswick School, CT
Calvert Hall College High School, MD
Cardigan Mountain School, NH
Central Catholic High School, PA
Central Catholic High School, TX
CFS, The School at Church Farm, PA
Chaminade College Preparatory School, MO
Christian Brothers Academy, NJ
Christian Brothers Academy, NY
Christopher Columbus High School, FL

Cistercian Preparatory School, TX
Colegio San Jose, PR
Collegiate School, NY
Covington Catholic High School, KY
Crespi Carmelite High School, CA
Damien High School, CA
Damien Memorial School, HI
De La Salle High School, CA
DeMatha Catholic High School, MD
Devon Preparatory School, PA
Dexter School, MA
Eaglebrook School, MA
Fishburne Military School, VA
Fordham Preparatory School, NY
Georgetown Preparatory School, MD
Gilman School, MD
Gonzaga College High School, DC
Hargrave Military Academy, VA
The Haverford School, PA
Holy Ghost Preparatory School, PA
Iona Preparatory School, NY
Jesuit College Preparatory School, TX
Jesuit High School of New Orleans, LA
Jesuit High School of Tampa, FL
Landon School, MD
Marmion Academy, IL
Marquette University High School, WI
Memphis University School, TN
Merchiston Castle School, United Kingdom
Mount Carmel High School, IL
Mount Michael Benedictine School, NE
Notre Dame College Prep, IL
The Phelps School, PA
Regis High School, NY
The Roxbury Latin School, MA
St. Albans School, DC
St. Andrew's College, ON, Canada
Saint Augustine Preparatory School, NJ
St. Benedict's Preparatory School, NJ
St. Catherine's Academy, CA
St. Christopher's School, VA
St. Francis de Sales High School, OH
Saint Francis High School, CA
St. George's School, BC, Canada
St. John's Northwestern Military Academy, WI
St. John's Preparatory School, MA
Saint Joseph's High School, NJ
St. Joseph's Preparatory School, PA
St. Mark's School of Texas, TX
St. Mary's Preparatory School, MI
St. Michael's College School, ON, Canada
Saint Patrick High School, IL
St. Paul's High School, MB, Canada
St. Peter's Preparatory School, NJ
St. Sebastian's School, MA
St. Stanislaus College, MS
Saint Thomas Academy, MN
St. Thomas High School, TX
Salesianum School, DE
Selwyn House School, QC, Canada
South Kent School, CT
Strake Jesuit College Preparatory, TX
Trinity High School, KY
Trinity-Pawling School, NY
University of Detroit Jesuit High School and Academy, MI
Vianney High School, MO
The Woodhall School, CT

GIRLS' DAY SCHOOLS

Academy of Notre Dame de Namur, PA
Academy of Our Lady of Mercy, CT
Academy of Our Lady of Peace, CA
Academy of Saint Elizabeth, NJ
Academy of the Holy Cross, MD
Academy of the New Church Girls' School, PA
Academy of the Sacred Heart, LA
The Archer School for Girls, CA
The Baldwin School, PA
Balmoral Hall School, MB, Canada
Beaumont School, OH
Bishop Conaty-Our Lady of Loretto High School, CA
Branksome Hall, ON, Canada
Carrollton School of the Sacred Heart, FL
Castilleja School, CA
Cathedral High School, NY
The Catholic High School of Baltimore, MD
Columbus School for Girls, OH
Convent of the Sacred Heart, CT
Convent of the Sacred Heart, NY
Country Day School of the Sacred Heart, PA
The Dominican Academy of the City of New York, NY
Duchesne Academy of the Sacred Heart, NE
Duchesne Academy of the Sacred Heart, TX
Elizabeth Seton High School, MD
Emma Willard School, NY
The Ethel Walker School, CT
Fontbonne Hall Academy, NY
Foxcroft School, VA
Garrison Forest School, MD*
Georgetown Visitation Preparatory School, DC
Girls Preparatory School, TN
Greenwich Academy, CT
Gwynedd Mercy Academy, PA
Harmony Heights Residential and Day School, NY
Hawthorn School for Girls, ON, Canada
The Hewitt School, NY
Immaculate Conception High School, NJ
Incarnate Word Academy, TX
Institute of Notre Dame, MD
Ladywood High School, MI
Louisville High School, CA
Magnificat High School, OH
Marlborough School, CA
Marylawn of the Oranges, NJ
Marymount High School, CA
Marymount International School, United Kingdom
Maryvale Preparatory School, MD
Mercy High School, CT
Mercy High School, NE
Mercy High School College Preparatory, CA
Merion Mercy Academy, PA
Miss Edgar's and Miss Cramp's School, QC, Canada
Miss Porter's School, CT
Mother McAuley High School, IL
Mount Mercy Academy, NY
Mt. Saint Dominic Academy, NJ
Mount Saint Joseph Academy, PA
Nerinx Hall, MO
Notre Dame Academy, CA
Notre Dame High School, CA
Oakcrest School, VA
Oak Knoll School of the Holy Child, NJ
Our Lady of Mercy Academy, NJ
Our Lady of Mercy High School, NY

Coeducational in lower grades

Providence Catholic School, The College Preparatory School for Girls Grades 6-12, TX
Roland Park Country School, MD
Sacred Heart Academy, KY
St. Agnes Academy, TX
St. Andrew's Priory School, HI
Saint Basil Academy, PA
St. Catherine's School, VA
St. Cecilia Academy, TN
St. Clement's School, ON, Canada
Saint Francis Girls High School, CA
Saint Joseph Academy High School, OH
St. Joseph's Academy, LA
Saint Lucy's Priory High School, CA
St. Margaret's School, VA
St. Mary's Episcopal School, TN
Saint Mary's School, NC
St. Timothy's School, MD
Saint Ursula Academy, OH
Santa Catalina School, CA
School of the Holy Child, NY
The Spence School, NY
Springside School, PA
Stoneleigh–Burnham School, MA
Trafalgar Castle School, ON, Canada
Ursuline Academy, MA
The Ursuline Academy of Dallas, TX
Ursuline High School, CA
Villa Joseph Marie High School, PA
Villa Walsh Academy, NJ
Westover School, CT
Westridge School, CA
The Winsor School, MA

SCHOOLS ACCEPTING BOARDING BOYS AND GIRLS

Académie Ste Cécile International School, ON, Canada†
Admiral Farragut Academy, FL†
Alliance Academy, Ecuador
Arthur Morgan School, NC†
Aspen Ranch, UT
The Athenian School, CA†
Baylor School, TN†
The Bement School, MA†
Bishop's College School, QC, Canada†
Blair Academy, NJ†
Blue Mountain Academy, PA†
The Bolles School, FL†
Brentwood College School, BC, Canada†
Brewster Academy, NH†
Brooks School, MA†
Burr and Burton Academy, VT†
Buxton School, MA†
Camphill Special School, PA†
Canadian Academy, Japan†
Canyonville Christian Academy, OR†
Cedar Ridge Academy, UT†
Chapel Hill–Chauncy Hall School, MA†
Choate Rosemary Hall, CT†
The Colorado Rocky Mountain School, CO†
Columbia International College of Canada, ON, Canada†
Concord Academy, MA†
Concordia High School, AB, Canada†
Cotter Schools, MN†
Cross Creek Programs, UT

The Culver Academies, IN†
Cushing Academy, MA†
Deerfield Academy, MA†
Dublin School, NH†
Ecole d'Humanité, Switzerland
Elan School, ME
Episcopal High School, VA
The Family Foundation School, NY
Fay School, MA†
Florida Air Academy, FL†
Forest Lake Academy, FL
Fountain Valley School of Colorado, CO†
Franklin Academy, CT†
Freeman Academy, SD†
Gem State Adventist Academy, ID
George School, PA†
George Stevens Academy, ME†
Gilmour Academy, OH†
Girard College, PA
The Glenholme School, a Devereux Center, CT
Gould Academy, ME†
The Governor French Academy, IL†
The Governor's Academy (formerly Governor Dummer Academy), MA†
Groton School, MA†
Hackley School, NY†
Hank Haney International Junior Golf Academy, SC†
Happy Hill Farm Academy, TX
The Harvey School, NY
Hawaiian Mission Academy, HI†
Hoosac School, NY†
The Hotchkiss School, CT†
Houghton Academy, NY†
The Howe School, IN†
The Hun School of Princeton, NJ†
Hyde School, ME†
Idyllwild Arts Academy, CA†
Interlochen Arts Academy, MI†
The John Dewey Academy, MA
The Judge Rotenberg Educational Center, MA
Kent School, CT†
Kildonan School, NY†
Kimball Union Academy, NH†
King George School, VT
The King's Academy, TN
King's-Edgehill School, NS, Canada†
Kingsway College, ON, Canada†
Kirov Academy of Ballet of Washington, D.C., DC†
Lakefield College School, ON, Canada†
Lake Forest Academy, IL†
Lake Mary Preparatory School, FL
La Lumiere School, IN†
Lancaster Mennonite High School, PA†
Landmark School, MA†
The Lawrenceville School, NJ†
The Linsly School, WV†
Luther College High School, SK, Canada†
Maine Central Institute, ME†
Maplebrook School, NY
The Masters School, NY†
Maur Hill-Mount Academy, KS†
McDonogh School, MD†
Menaul School, NM†
Middlesex School, MA†
Millbrook School, NY†
Milton Academy, MA†
Montclair College Preparatory School, CA†

†Accepts day students

Monterey Bay Academy, CA†
Monte Vista Christian School, CA†
Navajo Preparatory School, Inc., NM†
Nebraska Christian Schools, NE†
Niagara Christian Community of Schools, ON, Canada†
North Country School, NY†
The Northwest School, WA†
Northwood School, NY†
Oak Grove School, CA†
Oak Hill Academy, VA†
Oakland School, VA†
Oak Ridge Military Academy, NC†
Ojai Valley School, CA†
Oneida Baptist Institute, KY†
Oregon Episcopal School, OR†
The Orme School, AZ†
Peddie School, NJ†
Phillips Academy (Andover), MA†
Pickering College, ON, Canada†
Pinehurst School, ON, Canada
Portsmouth Abbey School, RI†
Presbyterian Pan American School, TX
Randolph-Macon Academy, VA†
The Rectory School, CT†
Ridley College, ON, Canada†
Robinson School, PR, Puerto Rico
Rock Point School, VT†
Rosseau Lake College, ON, Canada†
Ross School, NY†
Rothesay Netherwood School, NB, Canada†
Saddlebrook Preparatory School, FL†
St. Andrew's School, DE
St. Andrew's School, RI†
St. Anthony Catholic High School, TX†
St. Bernard's Catholic School, CA†
St. Croix Schools, MN†
St. George's School, RI†
St. John's-Ravenscourt School, MB, Canada†
Saint Mark's School, MA†
St. Mary's School, OR†
St. Michaels University School, BC, Canada†
St. Stephen's Episcopal School, TX†
Sandy Spring Friends School, MD†
San Marcos Baptist Academy, TX†
Shady Side Academy, PA†
Shattuck-St. Mary's School, MN†
Southwestern Academy, AZ†
Southwestern Academy, CA†
Squaw Valley Academy, CA†
Stevenson School, CA†
Stratton Mountain School, VT†
Suffield Academy, CT†
Sunhawk Adolescent Recovery Center, UT
Tabor Academy, MA†
TASIS, The American School in Switzerland, Switzerland†
The Thacher School, CA†
Thomas Jefferson School, MO†
TMI—The Episcopal School of Texas, TX†
Trinity College School, ON, Canada†
The United World College—USA, NM
The Vanguard School, FL
Venta Preparatory School, ON, Canada†
Verdala International School, Malta†
Wasatch Academy, UT†
The Webb School, TN†
Wellspring Foundation, CT†
Western Mennonite School, OR†

Western Reserve Academy, OH†
West Sound Academy, WA†
The White Mountain School, NH†
The Williston Northampton School, MA†
Woodstock School, India†
Worcester Academy, MA†
Wyoming Seminary, PA†

SCHOOLS ACCEPTING BOARDING BOYS

Academy of the New Church Boys' School, PA†
The American Boychoir School, NJ†
Army and Navy Academy, CA†
The Blue Ridge School, VA
Cardigan Mountain School, NH†
CFS, The School at Church Farm, PA†
Chamberlain-Hunt Academy, MS†
Chaminade College Preparatory School, MO†
Christchurch School, VA†
Eaglebrook School, MA†
Fishburne Military School, VA†
Georgetown Preparatory School, MD†
The Greenwood School, VT
Hampshire Country School, NH
Hargrave Military Academy, VA†
Harrow School, United Kingdom
Little Keswick School, VA
Marine Military Academy, TX
Merchiston Castle School, United Kingdom
Mount Michael Benedictine School, NE†
The Oxford Academy, CT
The Phelps School, PA†
St. Albans School, DC†
St. Andrew's College, ON, Canada†
St. Catherine's Academy, CA†
St. George's School, BC, Canada†
St. John's Northwestern Military Academy, WI†
St. Mary's Preparatory School, MI†
St. Michael's Preparatory School of the Norbertine Fathers, CA
St. Stanislaus College, MS†
South Kent School, CT†
Stone Mountain School, NC
Trinity-Pawling School, NY†
Valley View School, MA
Windermere Preparatory School, FL†
The Woodhall School, CT†

SCHOOLS ACCEPTING BOARDING GIRLS

Academy of the New Church Girls' School, PA†
Auldern Academy, NC
Balmoral Hall School, MB, Canada†
Branksome Hall, ON, Canada†
Copper Canyon Academy, AZ
Emma Willard School, NY†
The Ethel Walker School, CT†
Foxcroft School, VA†
Garrison Forest School, MD†
Harmony Heights Residential and Day School, NY†
Marymount International School, United Kingdom†
Miss Porter's School, CT†
Rocklyn Academy, ON, Canada
St. Margaret's School, VA†
Saint Mary's School, NC†
St. Timothy's School, MD†
Santa Catalina School, CA†

†Accepts day students

Stoneleigh–Burnham School, MA†
Trafalgar Castle School, ON, Canada†
Westover School, CT†

MILITARY SCHOOLS

Admiral Farragut Academy, FL
Army and Navy Academy, CA
Benedictine High School, VA
Chamberlain-Hunt Academy, MS
Christian Brothers Academy, NY
Fishburne Military School, VA
Florida Air Academy, FL
Hargrave Military Academy, VA
The Howe School, IN
Lyman Ward Military Academy, AL
Marine Military Academy, TX
Oak Ridge Military Academy, NC
Randolph-Macon Academy, VA
St. Catherine's Academy, CA
St. John's Northwestern Military Academy, WI
Saint Thomas Academy, MN

SCHOOLS WITH A RELIGIOUS AFFILIATION

Anglican Church of Canada

Rothesay Netherwood School, NB, Canada
St. Clement's School, ON, Canada

Baptist Church

Calvary Christian School, KY
First Baptist Academy, TX
Foundation Academy, FL
Grace Baptist Academy, TN
Grace Christian School, PE, Canada
Landmark Christian Academy, KY
Liberty Christian School, CA
Los Angeles Baptist Middle School/High School, CA
Oak Hill Academy, VA
Salem Baptist Christian School, NC
San Marcos Baptist Academy, TX
Second Baptist School, TX
Whitefield Academy, KY

Baptist General Association of Virginia

Hargrave Military Academy, VA

Bible Fellowship Church

Chinese Christian Schools, CA

Brethren in Christ Church

Niagara Christian Community of Schools, ON, Canada

Calvinist

Providence Christian School, AB, Canada

Christian

Academy of the New Church Girls' School, PA
Alma Heights Christian High School, CA
Briarcrest Christian High School, TN
Faith Christian High School, CA
The Family Foundation School, NY
The First Academy, FL
First Presbyterian Day School, GA
Fowlers Academy, PR
Greater Atlanta Christian Schools, GA
Happy Hill Farm Academy, TX
Harrells Christian Academy, NC
Hawthorne Christian Academy, NJ

Heritage Christian Academy, AB, Canada
Marion Academy, AL
Nashville Christian School, TN
New Covenant Academy, MO
North Cobb Christian School, GA
Orangewood Christian School, FL
Porter-Gaud School, SC
Quinte Christian High School, ON, Canada
Redwood Christian Schools, CA
St. Croix Schools, MN
St. David's School, NC
Scarborough Christian School, ON, Canada
Scottsdale Christian Academy, AZ
Timothy Christian High School, IL
TMI—The Episcopal School of Texas, TX
Toronto District Christian High School, ON, Canada
Western Christian Schools, CA
West Valley Christian Church Schools, CA
Woodstock School, India

Christian Church (Disciples of Christ)

West Valley Christian Church Schools, CA

Christian Nondenominational

Alliance Academy, Ecuador
Alpha Omega Academy, IA
Calvary Chapel High School, CA
Canyonville Christian Academy, OR
Capistrano Valley Christian Schools, CA
Charlotte Christian School, NC
Chattanooga Christian School, TN
Christian Central Academy, NY
Crosspoint Academy, WA
Dakota Christian High School, SD
Davidson Academy, TN
Des Moines Christian School, IA
Donelson Christian Academy, TN
Eastside Christian Academy, AB, Canada
Friendship Christian School, TN
The Geneva School, FL
Hamilton District Christian High, ON, Canada
Hanalani Schools, HI
Hawthorne Christian Academy, NJ
Kauai Christian Academy, HI
King's Ridge Christian School, GA
Linfield Christian School, CA
Lyman Ward Military Academy, AL
Manhattan Christian High School, MT
Merchiston Castle School, United Kingdom
Mid-Pacific Institute, HI
Monte Vista Christian School, CA
Oak Mountain Academy, GA
Phoenix Christian Unified Schools, AZ
Portsmouth Christian Academy, NH
Ron Pettigrew Christian School, BC, Canada
Saddleback Valley Christian School, CA
St. George's Independent School, TN
Seattle Christian Schools, WA
Seoul Foreign School, Republic of Korea
Shades Mountain Christian School, AL
Shoreline Christian, WA
Southfield Christian High School, MI
Southwest Christian School, Inc., TX
Toronto District Christian High School, ON, Canada
Tyler Street Christian Academy, TX
University Christian Preparatory School, LA
Village Christian Schools, CA
West Memphis Christian High School, AR
Westminster Christian Academy, LA
Wheaton Academy, IL

Christian Reformed Church

Eastern Christian High School, NJ
Immanuel Christian High School, AB, Canada

†*Accepts day students*

Kalamazoo Christian High School, MI
Manhattan Christian High School, MT

Church of Christ

Christian Home and Bible School, FL
Columbia Academy, TN
Dallas Christian School, TX
David Lipscomb High School, TN
Harding Academy, TN
Jackson Christian School, TN
Madison Academy, AL
Mars Hill Bible School, AL
Nashville Christian School, TN
Westbury Christian School, TX
West Memphis Christian High School, AR

Church of Christ, Scientist

Lifegate School, OR

Church of England (Anglican)

Harrow School, United Kingdom
Lakefield College School, ON, Canada
Ridley College, ON, Canada
St. Michaels University School, BC, Canada
Saltus Grammar School, Bermuda
SCECGS Redlands, Australia
Trinity College School, ON, Canada

Church of the New Jerusalem

Academy of the New Church Boys' School, PA
Academy of the New Church Girls' School, PA

Community of Christ

The International School of London, United Kingdom

Episcopal Church

Berkeley Preparatory School, FL
The Blue Ridge School, VA
Breck School, MN
Brooks School, MA
Campbell Hall (Episcopal), CA
The Canterbury School of Florida, FL
CFS, The School at Church Farm, PA
Christ Church Episcopal School, SC
Christchurch School, VA
Doane Stuart School, NY
The Episcopal Academy, PA
Episcopal Collegiate School, AR
Episcopal High School, TX
Episcopal High School, VA
Episcopal High School of Jacksonville, FL
Groton School, MA
Harvard-Westlake School, CA
Holy Innocents' Episcopal School, GA
Hoosac School, NY
The Howe School, IN
Iolani School, HI
Kent School, CT
Oregon Episcopal School, OR
Porter-Gaud School, SC
Queen Anne School, MD
The Rectory School, CT
Rock Point School, VT
St. Albans School, DC
St. Andrew's Priory School, HI
St. Andrew's School, DE
St. Catherine's School, VA
St. Christopher's School, VA
St. David's School, NC
Saint Edward's School, FL
St. George's School, RI
St. John's Northwestern Military Academy, WI
St. Margaret's Episcopal School, CA
St. Margaret's School, VA
Saint Mark's School, MA

St. Martin's Episcopal School, LA
St. Mary's Episcopal School, TN
Saint Mary's School, NC
St. Paul's Episcopal School, AL
St. Stephen's & St. Agnes School, VA
Saint Stephen's Episcopal School, FL
St. Stephen's Episcopal School, TX
St. Timothy's School, MD
Seabury Hall, HI
Shattuck-St. Mary's School, MN
South Kent School, CT
TMI—The Episcopal School of Texas, TX
Trinity-Pawling School, NY
Trinity Preparatory School, FL
Trinity School, NY
Trinity School of Texas, TX
The White Mountain School, NH
York School, CA

Evangelical

Grace Christian School, PE, Canada
Heritage Christian Academy, AB, Canada
Pioneer Valley Christian School, MA
Southfield Christian High School, MI

Evangelical/Fundamental

Chinese Christian Schools, CA

Evangelical Lutheran Church in America

Faith Lutheran High School, NV
Luther High School North, IL

Free Will Baptist Church

Rejoice Christian Schools, OK

Jewish

Community Hebrew Academy, ON, Canada
The Family Foundation School, NY
Gann Academy (The New Jewish High School of Greater Boston), MA
Hebrew Academy-the Five Towns, NY
Hyman Brand Hebrew Academy of Greater Kansas City, KS
Northwest Yeshiva High School, WA

Lutheran Church

Concordia High School, AB, Canada
Long Island Lutheran Middle and High School, NY
Lutheran High School North, MO
Lutheran High School of San Diego, CA
Luther College High School, SK, Canada
Martin Luther High School, NY
Salt Lake Lutheran High School, UT

Lutheran Church–Missouri Synod

Baltimore Lutheran Middle and Upper School, MD
Concordia Lutheran High School, IN
Denver Lutheran High School, CO
Faith Lutheran High School, NV
Lutheran High School, CA
Lutheran High School, IN
Lutheran High School, MO
Lutheran High School Northwest, MI
Lutheran High School of Hawaii, HI
Lutheran High School South, MO
Luther High School North, IL
Valley Lutheran High School, AZ

Mennonite Church

Christopher Dock Mennonite High School, PA
Freeman Academy, SD
Lancaster Mennonite High School, PA

Mennonite Church USA

Western Mennonite School, OR

Specialized Directories

Methodist Church
Randolph-Macon Academy, VA

Moravian Church
Moravian Academy, PA

Pentecostal Church
Community Christian Academy, KY

Presbyterian Church
Blair Academy, NJ
Calvin Christian High School, CA
Chamberlain-Hunt Academy, MS
Menaul School, NM
Shannon Forest Christian School, SC

Presbyterian Church (U.S.A.)
Presbyterian Pan American School, TX

Presbyterian Church in America
Briarwood Christian High School, AL
First Presbyterian Day School, GA
Orangewood Christian School, FL
Westminster Christian Academy, AL

Protestant
Piedmont Academy, GA
Pioneer Valley Christian School, MA
Quinte Christian High School, ON, Canada
Trinity School at Greenlawn, IN

Protestant Church
Salem Academy, OR

Protestant-Evangelical
Fresno Christian Schools, CA
Kauai Christian Academy, HI
Lehigh Valley Christian High School, PA
Nebraska Christian Schools, NE
Westminster Christian Academy, LA

Reformed Church
Calvin Christian High School, CA
Chamberlain-Hunt Academy, MS
Covenant Canadian Reformed School, AB, Canada
Heritage Christian School, ON, Canada
Immanuel Christian High School, AB, Canada
Providence Christian School, AB, Canada

Reformed Church in America
Kalamazoo Christian High School, MI

Roman Catholic Church
Academy of Notre Dame de Namur, PA
Academy of Our Lady of Mercy, CT
Academy of Our Lady of Peace, CA
Academy of Saint Elizabeth, NJ
Academy of the Holy Cross, MD
Academy of the Holy Names, FL
Academy of the Sacred Heart, LA
Academy of the Sacred Heart, MI
Académie Ste Cécile International School, ON, Canada
All Hallows High School, NY
Archbishop Alter High School, OH
Archbishop Curley High School, MD
Archbishop Hoban High School, OH
Archbishop McNicholas High School, OH
Archbishop Mitty High School, CA
Archbishop Rummel High School, LA
Beaumont School, OH
Bellarmine College Preparatory, CA
Bellarmine-Jefferson High School, CA
Benedictine High School, OH
Benedictine High School, VA

Bishop Blanchet High School, WA
Bishop Brady High School, NH
Bishop Conaty-Our Lady of Loretto High School, CA
Bishop Connolly High School, MA
Bishop Denis J. O'Connell High School, VA
Bishop Eustace Preparatory School, NJ
Bishop Fenwick High School, OH
Bishop Guertin High School, NH
Bishop Ireton High School, VA
Bishop Kelly High School, ID
Bishop Kenny High School, FL
Bishop Luers High School, IN
Bishop McGuinness Catholic High School, NC
Bishop McGuinness Catholic High School, OK
Bishop Montgomery High School, CA
Bishop O'Dowd High School, CA
Bishop Stang High School, MA
Bishop Walsh Middle High School, MD
Blanchet School, OR
Blessed Trinity High School, GA
Boston College High School, MA
Bourgade Catholic High School, AZ
Boylan Central Catholic High School, IL
Brother Rice High School, IL
Brother Rice High School, MI
Calvert Hall College High School, MD
Cardinal Mooney Catholic College Preparatory High School, MI
Cardinal Mooney Catholic High School, FL
Cardinal Newman High School, FL
Cardinal O'Hara High School, PA
Carmel High School, IL
Carrollton School of the Sacred Heart, FL
Cascia Hall Preparatory School, OK
Cathedral High School, NY
Catholic Central High School, WI
The Catholic High School of Baltimore, MD
Central Catholic High School, CA
Central Catholic High School, MA
Central Catholic High School, OH
Central Catholic High School, OH
Central Catholic High School, PA
Central Catholic High School, TX
Central Catholic Mid-High School, NE
Chaminade College Preparatory, CA
Chaminade College Preparatory School, MO
Chaminade-Madonna College Preparatory, FL
Christian Brothers Academy, NJ
Christian Brothers Academy, NY
Christian Brothers Academy, NY
Christopher Columbus High School, FL
Cistercian Preparatory School, TX
Clearwater Central Catholic High School, FL
Colegio San Jose, PR
Convent of the Sacred Heart, CT
Convent of the Sacred Heart, NY
Cotter Schools, MN
Country Day School of the Sacred Heart, PA
Covington Catholic High School, KY
Crespi Carmelite High School, CA
Damien High School, CA
Damien Memorial School, HI
De La Salle High School, CA
DeMatha Catholic High School, MD
DePaul Catholic High School, NJ
Devon Preparatory School, PA
The Dominican Academy of the City of New York, NY
Dowling Catholic High School, IA
Duchesne Academy of the Sacred Heart, NE
Duchesne Academy of the Sacred Heart, TX
Eastside Catholic School, WA
Elizabeth Seton High School, MD
Father Lopez High School, FL
Father Ryan High School, TN
Fenwick High School, IL
Fontbonne Hall Academy, NY

Fordham Preparatory School, NY
Garces Memorial High School, CA
Georgetown Preparatory School, MD
Georgetown Visitation Preparatory School, DC
Gilmour Academy, OH
Gonzaga College High School, DC
Gwynedd Mercy Academy, PA
Hanson Memorial High School, LA
Hawthorn School for Girls, ON, Canada
Holy Cross High School, CT
Holy Ghost Preparatory School, PA
Holy Name High School, PA
Holyoke Catholic High School, MA
Holy Savior Menard Catholic High School, LA
Holy Trinity High School, IL
Immaculata-La Salle High School, FL
Immaculate Conception High School, NJ
Immaculate Conception School, IL
Incarnate Word Academy, TX
Institute of Notre Dame, MD
Iona Preparatory School, NY
Jesuit High School of New Orleans, LA
Jesuit High School of Tampa, FL
J. K. Mullen High School, CO
John Paul II Catholic High School, FL
Junipero Serra High School, CA
Ladywood High School, MI
La Lumiere School, IN
La Salle High School, CA
Lehman High School, OH
Leo Catholic High School, IL
Lima Central Catholic High School, OH
Loretto Academy, TX
Louisville High School, CA
Magnificat High School, OH
Marian Central Catholic High School, IL
Marian High School, IN
Marist School, GA
Marmion Academy, IL
Marquette University High School, WI
Maryknoll School, HI
Marylawn of the Oranges, NJ
Marymount High School, CA
Marymount International School, Italy
Marymount International School, United Kingdom
Mary Star of the Sea High School, CA
Maryvale Preparatory School, MD
Matignon High School, MA
Maur Hill-Mount Academy, KS
McGill-Toolen Catholic High School, AL
Mercy High School, CT
Mercy High School, NE
Mercy High School College Preparatory, CA
Mercy Vocational High School, PA
Merion Mercy Academy, PA
Monsignor Donovan High School, NJ
Moreau Catholic High School, CA
Mother McAuley High School, IL
Mount Carmel High School, IL
Mt. De Sales Academy, GA
Mount Mercy Academy, NY
Mount Michael Benedictine School, NE
Mount Saint Charles Academy, RI
Mt. Saint Dominic Academy, NJ
Mount Saint Joseph Academy, PA
Nazareth Academy, IL
Nerinx Hall, MO
Northwest Catholic High School, CT
Notre Dame Academy, CA
Notre Dame College Prep, IL
Notre Dame High School, CA
Notre Dame High School, NJ
Notre Dame High School, TN
Notre Dame Junior/Senior High School, PA
Oak Knoll School of the Holy Child, NJ

Oldenburg Academy, IN
Our Lady of Mercy Academy, NJ
Our Lady of Mercy High School, NY
Padua Franciscan High School, OH
Peninsula Catholic High School, VA
Pensacola Catholic High School, FL
Pinecrest Academy, GA
Pope John XXIII Regional High School, NJ
Portsmouth Abbey School, RI
Powers Catholic High School, MI
The Prout School, RI
Providence Catholic School, The College Preparatory School for
    Girls Grades 6-12, TX
Providence High School, CA
Queen of Peace High School, NJ
Regis High School, NY
Reitz Memorial High School, IN
Sacred Heart Academy, KY
Sacred Heart School of Halifax, NS, Canada
St. Agnes Academy, TX
St. Andrew's Regional High School, BC, Canada
St. Ann's Academy, BC, Canada
St. Anthony Catholic High School, TX
Saint Anthony High School, IL
St. Anthony's Junior-Senior High School, HI
Saint Augustine Preparatory School, NJ
Saint Basil Academy, PA
St. Benedict at Auburndale, TN
St. Benedict's Preparatory School, NJ
St. Bernard's Catholic School, CA
St. Brendan High School, FL
St. Catherine's Academy, CA
St. Cecilia Academy, TN
Saint Cecilia High School, NE
St. Clement School, ON, Canada
Saint Dominic Academy, ME
Saint Elizabeth High School, CA
St. Francis de Sales High School, OH
Saint Francis Girls High School, CA
Saint Francis High School, CA
Saint Francis School, HI
St. John's Preparatory School, MA
St. Joseph Academy, FL
Saint Joseph Academy High School, OH
St. Joseph High School, CA
Saint Joseph High School, IL
Saint Joseph High School, NJ
Saint Joseph High School, WI
Saint Joseph Junior-Senior High School, HI
St. Joseph's Academy, LA
St. Joseph's Catholic School, SC
Saint Joseph's High School, NJ
St. Joseph's Preparatory School, PA
Saint Lucy's Priory High School, CA
Saint Mary's College High School, CA
Saint Mary's High School, AZ
Saint Mary's High School, MD
St. Mary's Preparatory School, MI
St. Mary's School, OR
Saint Maur International School, Japan
St. Michael's College School, ON, Canada
St. Michael's Preparatory School of the Norbertine Fathers, CA
St. Patrick Catholic High School, MS
Saint Patrick High School, IL
Saint Patrick—Saint Vincent High School, CA
St. Patrick's Regional Secondary, BC, Canada
St. Paul's High School, MB, Canada
St. Peter's Preparatory School, NJ
St. Pius X Catholic High School, GA
St. Pius X High School, TX
St. Sebastian's School, MA
Saints Peter and Paul High School, MD
St. Stanislaus College, MS
Saint Thomas Academy, MN
Saint Thomas Aquinas High School, KS

Specialized Directories

St. Thomas Aquinas High School, NH
St. Thomas High School, TX
Saint Thomas More Catholic High School, LA
Saint Ursula Academy, OH
Saint Viator High School, IL
St. Vincent Pallotti High School, MD
Salesian High School, CA
Salesianum School, DE
Santa Catalina School, CA
School of the Holy Child, NY
Scotus Central Catholic High School, NE
Seisen International School, Japan
Seton Catholic Central High School, NY
Seton Catholic High School, AZ
Shawe Memorial Junior/Senior High School, IN
Stephen T. Badin High School, OH
Teurlings Catholic High School, LA
Trinity High School, KY
Trinity High School, NH
Trinity School at Greenlawn, IN
Ursuline Academy, MA
The Ursuline Academy of Dallas, TX
Ursuline High School, CA
Valle Catholic High School, MO
Vianney High School, MO
Vicksburg Catholic School, MS
Villa Duchesne and Oak Hill School, MO
Villa Joseph Marie High School, PA
Villa Maria Academy, PA
Villa Walsh Academy, NJ
Visitation Academy of St. Louis County, MO
West Catholic High School, MI
York Catholic High School, PA

Roman Catholic Church (Jesuit Order)

Cheverus High School, ME
Jesuit College Preparatory School, TX
Loyola Academy, IL
Loyola School, NY
Strake Jesuit College Preparatory, TX
University of Detroit Jesuit High School and Academy, MI

Seventh-day Adventist Church

Cascade Christian Academy, WA
Crawford Adventist Academy, ON, Canada
Fresno Adventist Academy, CA
Gem State Adventist Academy, ID
Griggs International Academy, MD
Hawaiian Mission Academy, HI
Lodi Academy, CA
Monterey Bay Academy, CA

Seventh-day Adventists

Armona Union Academy, CA
Blue Mountain Academy, PA
Collegedale Academy, TN
Forest Lake Academy, FL
Kingsway College, ON, Canada
Paradise Adventist Academy, CA
Redwood Adventist Academy, CA

Society of Friends

Delaware Valley Friends School, PA
Friends Academy, NY
Friends' Central School, PA
Friends Select School, PA
George School, PA
Germantown Friends School, PA
Moorestown Friends School, NJ
Sandy Spring Friends School, MD
Tandem Friends School, VA
Wellsprings Friends School, OR

Southern Baptist Convention

First Baptist Academy, TX
Hawaii Baptist Academy, HI
The King's Academy, TN
Oneida Baptist Institute, KY
Prestonwood Christian Academy, TX

United Church of Canada

Saint Joseph's High School, NJ

United Methodist Church

Lydia Patterson Institute, TX
Robinson School, PR, Puerto Rico
Wyoming Seminary, PA

Wesleyan Church

Houghton Academy, NY
Wesleyan Academy, PR

Wisconsin Evangelical Lutheran Synod

Fox Valley Lutheran High School, WI
St. Croix Schools, MN

SCHOOLS BEGINNING AT JUNIOR, SENIOR, OR POSTGRADUATE YEAR

The United World College—USA, NM

SCHOOLS WITH ELEMENTARY DIVISIONS

The Academy at Charlemont, MA
Academy of Notre Dame de Namur, PA
Admiral Farragut Academy, FL
Alexander Dawson School, CO
Allendale Columbia School, NY
The American School in London, United Kingdom
The American School of Madrid, Spain
American School of Milan, Italy
Army and Navy Academy, CA
ASSETS School, HI
The Athenian School, CA
Augusta Preparatory Day School, GA
The Awty International School, TX
The Baldwin School, PA
Balmoral Hall School, MB, Canada
Barrie School, MD
Baylor School, TN
The Bement School, MA
Berkeley Preparatory School, FL
Berwick Academy, ME
The Birch Wathen Lenox School, NY
Bishop's College School, QC, Canada
The Bolles School, FL
Branksome Hall, ON, Canada
Breck School, MN
Brentwood School, CA
Brookstone School, GA
Brunswick School, CT
The Bryn Mawr School for Girls, MD
The Buckley School, CA
The Calhoun School, NY
The Calverton School, MD
Campbell Hall (Episcopal), CA
Canterbury School, FL
Cape Fear Academy, NC
Cape Henry Collegiate School, VA
Cardigan Mountain School, NH
Castilleja School, CA

The Catlin Gabel School, OR
CFS, The School at Church Farm, PA
Chaminade College Preparatory School, MO
Charles Wright Academy, WA
Charlotte Country Day School, NC
Charlotte Latin School, NC
Christ Church Episcopal School, SC
Cincinnati Country Day School, OH
Cistercian Preparatory School, TX
Collegiate School, NY
The Collegiate School, VA
The Colorado Springs School, CO
The Columbus Academy, OH
Columbus School for Girls, OH
The Community School of Naples, FL
Convent of the Sacred Heart, CT
Convent of the Sacred Heart, NY
Country Day School of the Sacred Heart, PA
Crossroads College Preparatory School, MO
Crystal Springs Uplands School, CA
The Dalton School, NY
The Derryfield School, NH
Doane Stuart School, NY
Durham Academy, NC
Eaglebrook School, MA
Edmund Burke School, DC
Elgin Academy, IL
The Episcopal Academy, PA
Episcopal High School of Jacksonville, FL
The Ethel Walker School, CT
Falmouth Academy, MA
Fay School, MA
Flint Hill School, VA
Forsyth Country Day School, NC
Franklin Road Academy, TN
Frederica Academy, GA
Friends Academy, NY
Friends' Central School, PA
Friends Select School, PA
Garrison Forest School, MD
Gaston Day School, NC
Germantown Friends School, PA
Gill St. Bernard's School, NJ
Gilman School, MD
Gilmour Academy, OH
Girard College, PA
Girls Preparatory School, TN
Glenelg Country School, MD
Glenlyon Norfolk School, BC, Canada
Greenfield School, NC
Greenhill School, TX
Greenhills School, MI
Greensboro Day School, NC
Greenwich Academy, CT
Groton School, MA
Hackley School, NY
Hamden Hall Country Day School, CT
Hampshire Country School, NH
Hampton Roads Academy, VA
Hargrave Military Academy, VA
The Harker School, CA
The Harley School, NY
Harvard-Westlake School, CA
The Harvey School, NY
The Haverford School, PA
Hawaii Baptist Academy, HI
Hawken School, OH

Head-Royce School, CA
The Heritage School, GA
The Hewitt School, NY
The Hill Center, Durham Academy, NC
The Hill Top Preparatory School, PA
Hilton Head Preparatory School, SC
Holy Innocents' Episcopal School, GA
Hoosac School, NY
Hopkins School, CT
The Howard School, GA
The Howe School, IN
The Hun School of Princeton, NJ
International High School, CA
International School Bangkok, Thailand
International School Manila, Philippines
The International School of Kuala Lumpur, Malaysia
Iolani School, HI
Isidore Newman School, LA
Jackson Preparatory School, MS
John Burroughs School, MO
The John Cooper School, TX
Keith Country Day School, IL
Kentucky Country Day School, KY
The Kew-Forest School, NY
Kildonan School, NY
King Low Heywood Thomas, CT
Kingswood-Oxford School, CT
La Jolla Country Day School, CA
Lakefield College School, ON, Canada
Lake Ridge Academy, OH
Lakeside School, WA
Landmark School, MA
Landon School, MD
The Latin School of Chicago, IL
The Linsly School, WV
Louisville Collegiate School, KY
The Lovett School, GA
Maharishi School of the Age of Enlightenment, IA
Manlius Pebble Hill School, NY
Maret School, DC
Marist School, GA
Marlborough School, CA
Maryknoll School, HI
Maryvale Preparatory School, MD
The Masters School, NY
McDonogh School, MD
The Meadows School, NV
Memphis University School, TN
Menlo School, CA
The Miami Valley School, OH
Mid-Pacific Institute, HI
Milton Academy, MA
Miss Edgar's and Miss Cramp's School, QC, Canada
MMI Preparatory School, PA
Montclair Kimberley Academy, NJ
Moorestown Friends School, NJ
Moravian Academy, PA
Morristown-Beard School, NJ
Munich International School, Germany
Newark Academy, NJ
The Nichols School, NY
Norfolk Academy, VA
North Country School, NY
North Shore Country Day School, IL
The Northwest School, WA
Oak Knoll School of the Holy Child, NJ
Oak Ridge Military Academy, NC

The Oakridge School, TX
Ojai Valley School, CA
The O'Neal School, NC
Oregon Episcopal School, OR
The Orme School, AZ
Out-Of-Door-Academy, FL
The Overlake School, WA
The Park School of Baltimore, MD
The Park School of Buffalo, NY
Phoenix Country Day School, AZ
Pickering College, ON, Canada
Pine Crest School, FL
The Pingry School, NJ
Polytechnic School, CA
Porter-Gaud School, SC
The Potomac School, VA
Poughkeepsie Day School, NY
Professional Children's School, NY
Providence Country Day School, RI
Providence Day School, NC
Queen Anne School, MD
Randolph-Macon Academy, VA
Randolph School, AL
Ranney School, NJ
Ransom Everglades School, FL
The Rectory School, CT
Ridley College, ON, Canada
Riverdale Country School, NY
Rivermont Collegiate, IA
The Rivers School, MA
Robert Louis Stevenson School, NY
Rockland Country Day School, NY
The Roeper School, MI
Roland Park Country School, MD
Rolling Hills Preparatory School, CA
Rowland Hall, UT
The Roxbury Latin School, MA
Roycemore School, IL
Rye Country Day School, NY
St. Albans School, DC
St. Andrew's College, ON, Canada
St. Andrew's Priory School, HI
St. Andrew's School, RI
St. Catherine's School, VA
St. Christopher's School, VA
St. Clement's School, ON, Canada
St. Croix Country Day School, VI
Saint Edward's School, FL
St. George's School, BC, Canada
St. George's School of Montreal, QC, Canada
St. Gregory College Preparatory School, AZ
St. John's Northwestern Military Academy, WI
St. Margaret's Episcopal School, CA
St. Margaret's School, VA
St. Mark's School of Texas, TX
St. Martin's Episcopal School, LA
St. Mary's Episcopal School, TN
Saint Mary's Hall, TX
St. Mary's School, OR
St. Paul Academy and Summit School, MN
St. Paul's Episcopal School, AL
St. Sebastian's School, MA
St. Stephen's & St. Agnes School, VA
Saint Stephen's Episcopal School, FL
St. Stephen's Episcopal School, TX
Saltus Grammar School, Bermuda
Sandia Preparatory School, NM

Sandy Spring Friends School, MD
Sanford School, DE
San Marcos Baptist Academy, TX
Santa Fe Preparatory School, NM
Sayre School, KY
School of the Holy Child, NY
Seabury Hall, HI
Seattle Academy of Arts and Sciences, WA
Selwyn House School, QC, Canada
Seoul Foreign School, Republic of Korea
The Seven Hills School, OH
Severn School, MD
Sewickley Academy, PA
Shady Side Academy, PA
Shattuck-St. Mary's School, MN
The Shipley School, PA
Spartanburg Day School, SC
The Spence School, NY
Springside School, PA
Stevenson School, CA
Stoneleigh–Burnham School, MA
Stratton Mountain School, VT
Taipei American School, Taiwan
Tandem Friends School, VA
TASIS, The American School in Switzerland, Switzerland
Thomas Jefferson School, MO
Tower Hill School, DE
Trinity College School, ON, Canada
Trinity-Pawling School, NY
Trinity Preparatory School, FL
Trinity School, NY
United Nations International School, NY
University of Chicago Laboratory Schools, IL
University Prep, WA
University School of Jackson, TN
University School of Milwaukee, WI
University School of Nova Southeastern University, FL
Ursuline Academy, MA
Vail Mountain School, CO
The Vanguard School, FL
Visitation Academy of St. Louis County, MO
The Walker School, GA
Wasatch Academy, UT
The Waterford School, UT
Watkinson School, CT
Waynflete School, ME
The Webb School, TN
Webb School of Knoxville, TN
The Wellington School, OH
Westchester Country Day School, NC
Westridge School, CA
The Wheeler School, RI
The Williams School, CT
The Williston Northampton School, MA
Winchester Thurston School, PA
Windward School, CA
The Winsor School, MA
Winston Preparatory School, NY
Woodlynde School, PA
Woodward Academy, GA
Worcester Academy, MA
Worcester Preparatory School, MD
Wyoming Seminary, PA
York Country Day School, PA
York School, CA

SCHOOLS REPORTING ACADEMIC ACCOMMODATIONS FOR THE GIFTED AND TALENTED*

School	
The Academy for Gifted Children (PACE), ON, Canada	G
Academy of the Holy Cross, MD	G,A
Academy of the New Church Boys' School, PA	G,M,A
Academy of the New Church Girls' School, PA	G,M,A
Academy of the Sacred Heart, MI	G,M,A
Académie Ste Cécile International School, ON, Canada	G,M,A
Admiral Farragut Academy, FL	G
Alexander Dawson School, CO	G,M,A
Alliance Academy, Ecuador	G,A
Allison Academy, FL	G,M,A
American Academy, FL	G,M,A
The American Boychoir School, NJ	M
American Community Schools of Athens, Greece	G
American Heritage School, FL	G,M,A
American Heritage School, FL	G,M,A
American School of The Hague, Netherlands	G,M,A
Archbishop Hoban High School, OH	G
Archbishop McNicholas High School, OH	G,M,A
Archbishop Mitty High School, CA	G,M,A
Aspen Ranch, UT	G
ASSETS School, HI	G
Augusta Preparatory Day School, GA	G
Auldern Academy, NC	G
The Baldwin School, PA	G,M,A
Balmoral Hall School, MB, Canada	G
The Baltimore Actors' Theatre Conservatory, MD	G,M,A
Baltimore Lutheran Middle and Upper School, MD	G
Baylor School, TN	G,M,A
Beaumont School, OH	G,M,A
The Beekman School, NY	G,M,A
Benedictine High School, VA	G,A
Ben Franklin Academy, GA	G
Berlin International School, Germany	G
Berwick Academy, ME	G,M,A
The Birch Wathen Lenox School, NY	G,M,A
Bishop Brady High School, NH	G
Bishop Denis J. O'Connell High School, VA	G
Bishop Eustace Preparatory School, NJ	G,M
Bishop Guertin High School, NH	G
Bishop Ireton High School, VA	M
Bishop Luers High School, IN	G,M
Bishop McGuinness Catholic High School, OK	G,A
Bishop O'Dowd High School, CA	G,M,A
Bishop's College School, QC, Canada	G,M,A
Blue Mountain Academy, PA	M
Blueprint Education, AZ	M,A
Boston College High School, MA	G
Boylan Central Catholic High School, IL	G,M,A
Branksome Hall, ON, Canada	G,M,A
Breck School, MN	G,M,A
Brentwood School, CA	G,A
Briarcrest Christian High School, TN	G,M,A
Briarwood Christian High School, AL	G
Bridges Academy, CA	G
Bridge School, CO	G
Brother Rice High School, IL	G
Brunswick School, CT	G,M,A
The Bryn Mawr School for Girls, MD	G,M,A
Buxton School, MA	G,M,A
The Byrnes Schools, SC	G
The Calhoun School, NY	G
Calvert Hall College High School, MD	G,M,A
Cape Henry Collegiate School, VA	G,M,A
Cardigan Mountain School, NH	G
Cardinal Mooney Catholic High School, FL	M,A
Cardinal Newman High School, FL	G
Carlucci American International School of Lisbon, Portugal	G
Cary Academy, NC	G,M,A
Cascia Hall Preparatory School, OK	G
Castilleja School, CA	G
Catholic Central High School, WI	G
The Catlin Gabel School, OR	G,M,A
Central Catholic High School, CA	G
Central Catholic High School, PA	G
CFS, The School at Church Farm, PA	G,M,A
Chamberlain-Hunt Academy, MS	G,M,A
Chaminade College Preparatory School, MO	G
Chaminade-Madonna College Preparatory, FL	G,M,A
Charlotte Country Day School, NC	G
Charlotte Latin School, NC	G
Chattanooga Christian School, TN	G,M,A
The Chicago Academy for the Arts, IL	M,A
Chinese Christian Schools, CA	G
Choate Rosemary Hall, CT	G,M,A
Christchurch School, VA	G
Christopher Columbus High School, FL	G
Chrysalis School, WA	G
Colegio Nueva Granada, Colombia	G
The Colorado Rocky Mountain School, CO	G,M,A
The Colorado Springs School, CO	G
Columbia International College of Canada, ON, Canada	G
The Columbus Academy, OH	G
Commonwealth School, MA	G,M,A
The Concept School, PA	G,A
Concord Academy, MA	G,M,A
Convent of the Sacred Heart, CT	G,A
Copper Canyon Academy, AZ	G,M,A
Cotter Schools, MN	G,M,A
Country Day School of the Sacred Heart, PA	M
The Culver Academies, IN	G,M,A
Currey Ingram Academy, TN	G,M,A
Cushing Academy, MA	G,M,A
Deerfield Academy, MA	G,M,A
Deerfield-Windsor School, GA	G,A
DeMatha Catholic High School, MD	G,M,A
Doane Stuart School, NY	G,M,A
Donelson Christian Academy, TN	G
Dowling Catholic High School, IA	G,M,A
Duchesne Academy of the Sacred Heart, NE	G
Duchesne Academy of the Sacred Heart, TX	M,A
Eaglebrook School, MA	G,M,A
Eastern Christian High School, NJ	G,M,A
Eastside Catholic School, WA	G,M
Eastside Christian Academy, AB, Canada	G,M
Ecole d'Humanité, Switzerland	G,M,A
Elan School, ME	G
Elizabeth Seton High School, MD	G,M,A
Emma Willard School, NY	G,M,A
Episcopal High School, VA	G,M,A
Episcopal High School of Jacksonville, FL	G
The Ethel Walker School, CT	G,M,A
Explorations Academy, WA	G
Faith Lutheran High School, NV	M
Father Ryan High School, TN	G,M,A
Fay School, MA	G,M,A
Fenwick High School, IL	G
The First Academy, FL	G
Flint Hill School, VA	M,A
Flint River Academy, GA	M,A
Florida Air Academy, FL	G
Forsyth Country Day School, NC	G

Coeducational in lower grades; G — gifted; M — musically talented; A — artistically talented

Specialized Directories

Fort Lauderdale Preparatory School, FL	G		The Kew-Forest School, NY	G
Fountain Valley School of Colorado, CO	G,M,A		King George School, VT	G,M,A
Foxcroft School, VA	G,M,A		King Low Heywood Thomas, CT	G,M,A
Fox Valley Lutheran High School, WI	G		King's-Edgehill School, NS, Canada	G
Franklin Academy, CT	G		Lakefield College School, ON, Canada	G,M,A
Franklin Road Academy, TN	G,M,A		Lake Forest Academy, IL	G,M,A
Fraser Academy, BC, Canada	G		Lake Ridge Academy, OH	G,M,A
Freeman Academy, SD	M,A		La Lumiere School, IN	G,A
Friends Select School, PA	M,A		The Latin School of Chicago, IL	G
Garrison Forest School, MD	G,M,A		The Laureate Academy, MB, Canada	G
Gaston Day School, NC	G		Laurel Springs School, CA	G,M,A
The Geneva School, FL	G,M,A		Lehigh Valley Christian High School, PA	G
George Stevens Academy, ME	G,M,A		Lifegate School, OR	G,A
Georgetown Preparatory School, MD	G		The Linsly School, WV	G
George Walton Academy, GA	M,A		Little Keswick School, VA	G
Germantown Friends School, PA	G,M,A		The Lovett School, GA	G,M,A
Gilman School, MD	G		Loyola Academy, IL	G
Gilmour Academy, OH	G,M,A		Lutheran High School of Hawaii, HI	M,A
Glenelg Country School, MD	G		Luther College High School, SK, Canada	G
The Glenholme School, a Devereux Center, CT	G		Luther High School North, IL	G,M,A
Gould Academy, ME	G,M,A		Lydia Patterson Institute, TX	G
The Governor French Academy, IL	G,A		Madison-Ridgeland Academy, MS	G
The Grauer School, CA	G,M,A		Maharishi School of the Age of Enlightenment, IA	G,M,A
Greater Atlanta Christian Schools, GA	G,M,A		Maine Central Institute, ME	M
Greenfield School, NC	G		Manlius Pebble Hill School, NY	G
Greenhills School, MI	G		Maret School, DC	G,M,A
Greensboro Day School, NC	G,A		Marin Academy, CA	G,M,A
The Greenwood School, VT	G,M,A		Marine Military Academy, TX	G
Groton School, MA	G,M,A		Marmion Academy, IL	G
Gulliver Preparatory School, FL	G,M,A		Marylawn of the Oranges, NJ	G,M,A
Gunston Day School, MD	G,M,A		The Masters School, NY	G,M,A
Gwynedd Mercy Academy, PA	M,A		Maur Hill-Mount Academy, KS	G
Hamilton District Christian High, ON, Canada	M,A		Meadowridge School, BC, Canada	G
Hampshire Country School, NH	G		The Meadows School, NV	G,M,A
Happy Hill Farm Academy, TX	M		Memorial Hall School, TX	G
The Harker School, CA	G		Menaul School, NM	G,A
Harrow School, United Kingdom	G,M,A		Merchiston Castle School, United Kingdom	G,M,A
Harvard-Westlake School, CA	G,M,A		Merion Mercy Academy, PA	G,M,A
The Haverford School, PA	G		The Miami Valley School, OH	G,M,A
Hawken School, OH	G,M		Middlesex School, MA	G
Head-Royce School, CA	G,M,A		Mid-Pacific Institute, HI	G,A
Hebrew Academy-the Five Towns, NY	A		Milton Academy, MA	G,M,A
The Hill Top Preparatory School, PA	G,A		MMI Preparatory School, PA	G
Hoosac School, NY	M,A		Monsignor Donovan High School, NJ	G,M,A
The Hotchkiss School, CT	G,M,A		Montclair Kimberley Academy, NJ	G
The Howard School, GA	A		Mt. Saint Dominic Academy, NJ	G,M,A
Humanex Academy, CO	G		Mount Saint Joseph Academy, PA	G,M,A
The Hun School of Princeton, NJ	G		MU High School, MO	G
Huntington-Surrey School, TX	G		Munich International School, Germany	G
Hyman Brand Hebrew Academy of Greater Kansas City, KS	G		National High School, GA	G,M,A
Immaculata-La Salle High School, FL	G		Newark Academy, NJ	G,M,A
Institute of Notre Dame, MD	G		The Nora School, MD	G,A
Interlochen Arts Academy, MI	G,M,A		Norfolk Academy, VA	G,M,A
International High School, CA	G,M,A		North Cobb Christian School, GA	M,A
International School of Amsterdam, Netherlands	G,M,A		Northwest Yeshiva High School, WA	G
International School of Athens, Greece	G		Notre Dame College Prep, IL	G
International School of Berne, Switzerland	G		Oak Hill School, OR	G
Iolani School, HI	G,M,A		The Oakland School, PA	G,A
Iona Preparatory School, NY	G		Oak Ridge Military Academy, NC	G
Island School, HI	G		The Oakridge School, TX	G,M,A
Jackson Preparatory School, MS	G,M,A		Ojai Valley School, CA	G,A
J. K. Mullen High School, CO	G		Oregon Episcopal School, OR	G
The John Dewey Academy, MA	G,A		Orinda Academy, CA	G
The Karafin School, NY	G,M,A		The Overlake School, WA	G,M,A
Keith Country Day School, IL	G,M,A		The Oxford Academy, CT	G
Kent School, CT	G,M,A		Pacific Crest Community School, OR	G
Kentucky Country Day School, KY	G,M,A		The Park School of Baltimore, MD	G,M,A

Coeducational in lower grades; G — gifted; M — musically talented; A — artistically talented

The Park School of Buffalo, NY	G	Salt Lake Lutheran High School, UT	G
Pensacola Catholic High School, FL	G	Sandia Preparatory School, NM	G
The Phelps School, PA	G,M,A	San Marcos Baptist Academy, TX	G,M,A
Phillips Academy (Andover), MA	G,M,A	Santa Catalina School, CA	G,M,A
The Pingry School, NJ	G	Sayre School, KY	G,A
Portsmouth Abbey School, RI	G	Seabury Hall, HI	G
Portsmouth Christian Academy, NH	G,M	Seattle Academy of Arts and Sciences, WA	G,M,A
Poughkeepsie Day School, NY	G,M,A	Seoul Foreign School, Republic of Korea	G,M,A
Prestonwood Christian Academy, TX	G	Seton Catholic Central High School, NY	G,A
Providence Country Day School, RI	G,M,A	The Seven Hills School, OH	G
Providence Day School, NC	G,M,A	Severn School, MD	G,M,A
Providence High School, CA	M,A	Shady Side Academy, PA	G,M,A
Randolph-Macon Academy, VA	G	Shattuck-St. Mary's School, MN	G,M
The Rectory School, CT	G	Shawe Memorial Junior/Senior High School, IN	G
Ridley College, ON, Canada	M,A	Sheridan Academy, ID	G
Riverdale Country School, NY	G,M,A	The Shipley School, PA	G
Rivermont Collegiate, IA	G,M	Soundview Preparatory School, NY	G,A
Robert Louis Stevenson School, NY	G	Southwest Christian School, Inc., TX	G
Robinson School, PR, Puerto Rico	G	Spartanburg Day School, SC	G,A
Rockland Country Day School, NY	G,M,A	Squaw Valley Academy, CA	G,M,A
Rocklyn Academy, ON, Canada	G	The Stanwich School, CT	G
The Roeper School, MI	G,M,A	Stone Mountain School, NC	G
Rolling Hills Preparatory School, CA	G	Suffield Academy, CT	G,M,A
Rosseau Lake College, ON, Canada	G	Sunhawk Adolescent Recovery Center, UT	G,A
Rothesay Netherwood School, NB, Canada	G,M,A	Tabor Academy, MA	G,M,A
The Roxbury Latin School, MA	G,M,A	Tandem Friends School, VA	G
Rye Country Day School, NY	G	The Tenney School, TX	G,M,A
Sacred Heart Academy, KY	G,M,A	The Thacher School, CA	G,M,A
Sage Hill School, CA	G,M,A	Thomas Jefferson School, MO	G
Sage Ridge School, NV	G	Tower Hill School, DE	G,M,A
St. Andrew's Priory School, HI	M,A	Trinity High School, KY	G,M,A
St. Andrew's School, DE	G,M,A	Trinity Preparatory School, FL	G,M,A
St. Anthony Catholic High School, TX	G	Trinity School of Texas, TX	G,M,A
St. Benedict at Auburndale, TN	G,M,A	Tuscaloosa Academy, AL	G
St. Brendan High School, FL	G	United Nations International School, NY	G,M,A
St. Cecilia Academy, TN	G,M,A	The United World College—USA, NM	M,A
St. Christopher's School, VA	G,M,A	University School of Jackson, TN	G,M,A
St. Clement's School, ON, Canada	G	University School of Nova Southeastern University, FL	G,M,A
St. Croix Schools, MN	G,M,A	Valle Catholic High School, MO	G,A
Saint Edward's School, FL	G,M,A	Valley Lutheran High School, AZ	G,M
St. George's School, RI	G,M,A	The Vanguard School, FL	G
St. George's School of Montreal, QC, Canada	G,M,A	Venta Preparatory School, ON, Canada	G
St. Gregory College Preparatory School, AZ	G,M,A	Villa Joseph Marie High School, PA	G,M,A
St. John's Preparatory School, MA	G,M,A	Villa Walsh Academy, NJ	G,M,A
St. Joseph Academy, FL	G,A	The Walker School, GA	G,A
Saint Joseph High School, IL	G,M,A	Waring School, MA	G,M,A
Saint Joseph High School, NJ	G	The Waterford School, UT	G,M,A
Saint Joseph Junior-Senior High School, HI	G	Watkinson School, CT	G,M,A
Saint Joseph's High School, NJ	G	The Webb School, TN	G
St. Joseph's Preparatory School, PA	G,M,A	The Wellington School, OH	G,M,A
St. Margaret's Episcopal School, CA	G,M,A	Western Reserve Academy, OH	G,M,A
Saint Mark's School, MA	G,M,A	West Island College, AB, Canada	G
St. Mark's School of Texas, TX	G	Westminster Christian Academy, AL	G,M,A
St. Mary's Episcopal School, TN	G,M,A	Westover School, CT	G,M,A
Saint Mary's High School, MD	G	West Valley Christian Church Schools, CA	G
St. Mary's Preparatory School, MI	M,A	Wheaton Academy, IL	G,M,A
St. Mary's School, OR	G,M,A	The Wheeler School, RI	G
Saint Maur International School, Japan	G,M,A	Whitefield Academy, KY	G
Saint Patrick—Saint Vincent High School, CA	G	The White Mountain School, NH	G,M,A
St. Sebastian's School, MA	G,M,A	The Williams School, CT	G,M,A
St. Stephen's & St. Agnes School, VA	G,M,A	The Williston Northampton School, MA	G,M,A
Saint Thomas Aquinas High School, KS	G	Willow Wood School, ON, Canada	G,A
Saint Thomas More Catholic High School, LA	G	Winchester Thurston School, PA	G,M,A
St. Vincent Pallotti High School, MD	M	Windermere Preparatory School, FL	M,A
Salem Academy, OR	M,A	The Windsor School, NY	G,M,A
Salem Baptist Christian School, NC	G	Woodstock School, India	G,M,A
Salesianum School, DE	G	Worcester Preparatory School, MD	G

Coeducational in lower grades; G — gifted; M — musically talented; A — artistically talented

York Country Day School, PA	G,M,A
York Preparatory School, NY	G,M,A

SCHOOLS WITH ADVANCED PLACEMENT PREPARATION†

Academy at the Lakes, FL
The Academy for Gifted Children (PACE), ON, Canada
Academy of Our Lady of Peace, CA
Academy of Saint Elizabeth, NJ
Academy of the Holy Cross, MD
Academy of the Holy Names, FL
Academy of the New Church Boys' School, PA
Academy of the New Church Girls' School, PA
Academy of the Sacred Heart, LA
Academy of the Sacred Heart, MI
Académie Ste Cécile International School, ON, Canada
Admiral Farragut Academy, FL
Alexander Dawson School, CO
Allendale Columbia School, NY
Alliance Academy, Ecuador
Allison Academy, FL
Alma Heights Christian High School, CA
American Community Schools of Athens, Greece
American Heritage School, FL
American Heritage School, FL
American International School of Costa Rica, Costa Rica
The American School in London, United Kingdom
American School of The Hague, Netherlands
Archbishop Alter High School, OH
Archbishop Curley High School, MD
Archbishop Hoban High School, OH
Archbishop McNicholas High School, OH
Archbishop Mitty High School, CA
Archbishop Rummel High School, LA
The Archer School for Girls, CA
Arendell Parrott Academy, NC
Army and Navy Academy, CA
The Athenian School, CA
Augusta Christian School (I), GA
Auldern Academy, NC
The Baldwin School, PA
Balmoral Hall School, MB, Canada
The Baltimore Actors' Theatre Conservatory, MD
Baltimore Lutheran Middle and Upper School, MD
Barrie School, MD
Baylor School, TN
Bayside Academy, AL
Beaumont School, OH
The Beekman School, NY
Bellarmine College Preparatory, CA
Bellarmine-Jefferson High School, CA
Benedictine High School, OH
Benedictine High School, VA
Ben Franklin Academy, GA
Berkeley Preparatory School, FL
Berwick Academy, ME
The Birch Wathen Lenox School, NY
Bishop Blanchet High School, WA
Bishop Brady High School, NH
Bishop Conaty-Our Lady of Loretto High School, CA
Bishop Connolly High School, MA
Bishop Denis J. O'Connell High School, VA
Bishop Eustace Preparatory School, NJ
Bishop Fenwick High School, OH
Bishop Guertin High School, NH

Bishop Ireton High School, VA
Bishop Kelly High School, ID
Bishop Kenny High School, FL
Bishop Luers High School, IN
Bishop McGuinness Catholic High School, NC
Bishop McGuinness Catholic High School, OK
Bishop Montgomery High School, CA
Bishop O'Dowd High School, CA
Bishop's College School, QC, Canada
Bishop Stang High School, MA
Bishop Walsh Middle High School, MD
Blair Academy, NJ
Blanchet School, OR
Blessed Trinity High School, GA
Blue Mountain Academy, PA
The Bolles School, FL
Boston College High School, MA
Bourgade Catholic High School, AZ
Boylan Central Catholic High School, IL
Breck School, MN
Brentwood College School, BC, Canada
Brentwood School, CA
Brewster Academy, NH
Briarcrest Christian High School, TN
Briarwood Christian High School, AL
Brooks School, MA
Brookstone School, GA
Brother Rice High School, IL
Brother Rice High School, MI
Brunswick School, CT
The Bryn Mawr School for Girls, MD
The Buckley School, CA
Burr and Burton Academy, VT
The Byrnes Schools, SC
Calvary Chapel High School, CA
Calvary Christian School, KY
Calvert Hall College High School, MD
The Calverton School, MD
Calvin Christian High School, CA
Campbell Hall (Episcopal), CA
Canadian Academy, Japan
Canterbury School, FL
The Canterbury School of Florida, FL
Canyonville Christian Academy, OR
Cape Fear Academy, NC
Cape Henry Collegiate School, VA
Capistrano Valley Christian Schools, CA
Cardinal Mooney Catholic College Preparatory High School, MI
Cardinal Mooney Catholic High School, FL
Cardinal Newman High School, FL
Carrollton School of the Sacred Heart, FL
Cary Academy, NC
Cascia Hall Preparatory School, OK
Castilleja School, CA
Cathedral High School, NY
Catholic Central High School, WI
The Catholic High School of Baltimore, MD
Central Catholic High School, CA
Central Catholic High School, MA
Central Catholic High School, OH
Central Catholic High School, OH
Central Catholic High School, PA
Central Catholic High School, TX
Central Catholic Mid-High School, NE
CFS, The School at Church Farm, PA
Chaminade College Preparatory, CA
Chaminade College Preparatory School, MO

†Accepts day students; G — gifted; M — musically talented; A — artistically talented

Chaminade-Madonna College Preparatory, FL
Chapel Hill–Chauncy Hall School, MA
Charles Wright Academy, WA
Charlotte Christian School, NC
Charlotte Latin School, NC
Chattanooga Christian School, TN
Cheverus High School, ME
The Chicago Academy for the Arts, IL
Chinese Christian Schools, CA
Choate Rosemary Hall, CT
Christchurch School, VA
Christian Brothers Academy, NJ
Christian Brothers Academy, NY
Christian Brothers Academy, NY
Christian Central Academy, NY
Christian Home and Bible School, FL
Christopher Columbus High School, FL
Christopher Dock Mennonite High School, PA
Cincinnati Country Day School, OH
Cistercian Preparatory School, TX
Clearwater Central Catholic High School, FL
Colegio Nueva Granada, Colombia
Colegio San Jose, PR
Collegedale Academy, TN
Collegiate School, NY
The Collegiate School, VA
The Colorado Rocky Mountain School, CO
The Colorado Springs School, CO
Columbia Academy, TN
Columbia International College of Canada, ON, Canada
The Columbus Academy, OH
Columbus School for Girls, OH
Commonwealth Parkville School, PR
Commonwealth School, MA
The Community School of Naples, FL
Concordia Lutheran High School, IN
Convent of the Sacred Heart, CT
Convent of the Sacred Heart, NY
The Country Day School, ON, Canada
Country Day School of the Sacred Heart, PA
Covington Catholic High School, KY
Crawford Adventist Academy, ON, Canada
Crespi Carmelite High School, CA
Crossroads College Preparatory School, MO
Crystal Springs Uplands School, CA
The Culver Academies, IN
Cushing Academy, MA
The Dalton School, NY
Damien High School, CA
David Lipscomb High School, TN
Davidson Academy, TN
Deerfield Academy, MA
Deerfield-Windsor School, GA
De La Salle High School, CA
DeMatha Catholic High School, MD
Denver Lutheran High School, CO
DePaul Catholic High School, NJ
The Derryfield School, NH
Des Moines Christian School, IA
Devon Preparatory School, PA
Dexter School, MA
Doane Stuart School, NY
The Dominican Academy of the City of New York, NY
Donelson Christian Academy, TN
Dowling Catholic High School, IA
Dublin School, NH
Duchesne Academy of the Sacred Heart, NE

Duchesne Academy of the Sacred Heart, TX
Durham Academy, NC
Eastern Christian High School, NJ
Eastside Catholic School, WA
Ecole d'Humanité, Switzerland
Edgewood Academy, AL
Edmund Burke School, DC
Elgin Academy, IL
Elizabeth Seton High School, MD
Emma Willard School, NY
The Episcopal Academy, PA
Episcopal Collegiate School, AR
Episcopal High School, TX
Episcopal High School, VA
Episcopal High School of Jacksonville, FL
The Ethel Walker School, CT
Explorations Academy, WA
Faith Christian High School, CA
Faith Lutheran High School, NV
Falmouth Academy, MA
Father Lopez High School, FL
Father Ryan High School, TN
Fayetteville Academy, NC
Fenwick High School, IL
The First Academy, FL
First Baptist Academy, TX
First Presbyterian Day School, GA
Fishburne Military School, VA
Flint Hill School, VA
Flint River Academy, GA
Florida Air Academy, FL
Fontbonne Hall Academy, NY
Fordham Preparatory School, NY
Forsyth Country Day School, NC
Fort Lauderdale Preparatory School, FL
Foundation Academy, FL
Fountain Valley School of Colorado, CO
Foxcroft School, VA
Franklin Road Academy, TN
Frederica Academy, GA
French-American School of New York, NY
Fresno Adventist Academy, CA
Fresno Christian Schools, CA
Friends Academy, NY
Friendship Christian School, TN
Friends Select School, PA
Fuqua School, VA
Gann Academy (The New Jewish High School of Greater
   Boston), MA
Garces Memorial High School, CA
Garrison Forest School, MD
Gaston Day School, NC
Gem State Adventist Academy, ID
The Geneva School, FL
George School, PA
George Stevens Academy, ME
Georgetown Preparatory School, MD
Georgetown Visitation Preparatory School, DC
George Walton Academy, GA
Gill St. Bernard's School, NJ
Gilman School, MD
Gilmour Academy, OH
Girard College, PA
Girls Preparatory School, TN
Glades Day School, FL
Glenelg Country School, MD
Gonzaga College High School, DC

†Accepts day students

Gould Academy, ME
The Governor French Academy, IL
The Governor's Academy (formerly Governor Dummer Academy), MA
The Grauer School, CA
Greater Atlanta Christian Schools, GA
Greenfield School, NC
Greenhill School, TX
Greenhills School, MI
Greensboro Day School, NC
Greenwich Academy, CT
Groton School, MA
Gulliver Preparatory School, FL
Gunston Day School, MD
Gwynedd Mercy Academy, PA
Hackley School, NY
Hamden Hall Country Day School, CT
Hamilton District Christian High, ON, Canada
Hampton Roads Academy, VA
Hanalani Schools, HI
Hank Haney International Junior Golf Academy, SC
Harding Academy, TN
Hargrave Military Academy, VA
The Harker School, CA
The Harley School, NY
Harrells Christian Academy, NC
Harrow School, United Kingdom
Harvard-Westlake School, CA
The Harvey School, NY
Hawaii Baptist Academy, HI
Hawken School, OH
Head-Royce School, CA
Hebrew Academy-the Five Towns, NY
The Heritage School, GA
The Hewitt School, NY
Hillcrest Christian School, MS
Hilton Head Preparatory School, SC
Holy Cross High School, CT
Holy Ghost Preparatory School, PA
Holy Innocents' Episcopal School, GA
Holy Name High School, PA
Holyoke Catholic High School, MA
Holy Savior Menard Catholic High School, LA
Holy Trinity High School, IL
Hoosac School, NY
Hopkins School, CT
The Hotchkiss School, CT
Houghton Academy, NY
The Howe School, IN
The Hun School of Princeton, NJ
Hyman Brand Hebrew Academy of Greater Kansas City, KS
Idyllwild Arts Academy, CA
Immaculata-La Salle High School, FL
Immaculate Conception High School, NJ
Immaculate Conception School, IL
Incarnate Word Academy, TX
Institute of Notre Dame, MD
Interlochen Arts Academy, MI
International School Bangkok, Thailand
International School Manila, Philippines
The International School of Kuala Lumpur, Malaysia
International School of Zug and Luzern (ISZL), Switzerland
Iolani School, HI
Iona Preparatory School, NY
Isidore Newman School, LA
Island School, HI
Jackson Preparatory School, MS

Jesuit College Preparatory School, TX
Jesuit High School of New Orleans, LA
Jesuit High School of Tampa, FL
J. K. Mullen High School, CO
John Burroughs School, MO
The John Cooper School, TX
John Paul II Catholic High School, FL
Junipero Serra High School, CA
Kalamazoo Christian High School, MI
Kaplan College Preparatory School, FL
The Karafin School, NY
Kauai Christian Academy, HI
Keith Country Day School, IL
Kent School, CT
Kentucky Country Day School, KY
Kerr-Vance Academy, NC
The Kew-Forest School, NY
Kimball Union Academy, NH
King Low Heywood Thomas, CT
The King's Academy, TN
Kings Christian School, CA
King's Ridge Christian School, GA
Kingswood-Oxford School, CT
Ladywood High School, MI
La Jolla Country Day School, CA
Lakefield College School, ON, Canada
Lake Forest Academy, IL
Lakehill Preparatory School, TX
Lake Mary Preparatory School, FL
Lake Ridge Academy, OH
La Lumiere School, IN
Lancaster Mennonite High School, PA
Landon School, MD
La Salle High School, CA
The Latin School of Chicago, IL
Lehigh Valley Christian High School, PA
Lehman High School, OH
Le Lycee Francais de Los Angeles, CA
Liberty Christian School, CA
Lick-Wilmerding High School, CA
Lifegate School, OR
Lima Central Catholic High School, OH
Lincoln Academy, ME
Linfield Christian School, CA
The Linsly School, WV
Long Island Lutheran Middle and High School, NY
Loretto Academy, TX
Los Angeles Baptist Middle School/High School, CA
Louisville Collegiate School, KY
Louisville High School, CA
The Lovett School, GA
Loyola Academy, IL
Loyola School, NY
Lutheran High School, CA
Lutheran High School, IN
Lutheran High School North, MO
Lutheran High School Northwest, MI
Lutheran High School of Hawaii, HI
Lutheran High School of San Diego, CA
Lutheran High School South, MO
Luther High School North, IL
The Lycee International, American Section, France
Lydia Patterson Institute, TX
Lyman Ward Military Academy, AL
MacLachlan College, ON, Canada
Madison-Ridgeland Academy, MS
Magnificat High School, OH

†Accepts day students

Maine Central Institute, ME
Manhattan Christian High School, MT
Manlius Pebble Hill School, NY
Maret School, DC
Marian Central Catholic High School, IL
Marian High School, IN
Marin Academy, CA
Marine Military Academy, TX
Marist School, GA
Marlborough School, CA
Marmion Academy, IL
Marquette University High School, WI
Mars Hill Bible School, AL
Martin Luther High School, NY
Maryknoll School, HI
Marylawn of the Oranges, NJ
Marymount High School, CA
Mary Star of the Sea High School, CA
Maryvale Preparatory School, MD
The Masters School, NY
Matignon High School, MA
Maui Preparatory Academy, HI
McDonogh School, MD
McGill-Toolen Catholic High School, AL
The Meadows School, NV
Memphis University School, TN
Menaul School, NM
Menlo School, CA
Mercy High School, CT
Mercy High School, NE
Mercy High School College Preparatory, CA
Merion Mercy Academy, PA
The Miami Valley School, OH
Middlesex School, MA
Mid-Pacific Institute, HI
Millbrook School, NY
Milton Academy, MA
Miss Edgar's and Miss Cramp's School, QC, Canada
Miss Porter's School, CT
MMI Preparatory School, PA
Monsignor Donovan High School, NJ
Montclair College Preparatory School, CA
Montclair Kimberley Academy, NJ
Monterey Bay Academy, CA
Monte Vista Christian School, CA
Moorestown Friends School, NJ
Moravian Academy, PA
Moreau Catholic High School, CA
Morristown-Beard School, NJ
Mother McAuley High School, IL
Mount Carmel High School, IL
Mount Mercy Academy, NY
Mount Michael Benedictine School, NE
Mount Saint Charles Academy, RI
Mt. Saint Dominic Academy, NJ
Mount Saint Joseph Academy, PA
MU High School, MO
Nashville Christian School, TN
National High School, GA
Nazareth Academy, IL
Newark Academy, NJ
The Nichols School, NY
Norfolk Academy, VA
North Cobb Christian School, GA
North Shore Country Day School, IL
Northwest Catholic High School, CT
Northwood School, NY

The Norwich Free Academy, CT
Notre Dame Academy, CA
Notre Dame College Prep, IL
Notre Dame High School, CA
Notre Dame High School, NJ
Notre Dame High School, TN
Notre Dame Junior/Senior High School, PA
Oak Grove School, CA
Oak Hill School, OR
Oak Knoll School of the Holy Child, NJ
Oak Mountain Academy, GA
The Oakridge School, TX
Ojai Valley School, CA
Oldenburg Academy, IN
The O'Neal School, NC
Oneida Baptist Institute, KY
Orangewood Christian School, FL
Oregon Episcopal School, OR
Orinda Academy, CA
The Orme School, AZ
Our Lady of Mercy High School, NY
Out-Of-Door-Academy, FL
The Overlake School, WA
The Oxford Academy, CT
Padua Franciscan High School, OH
The Paideia School, GA
The Park School of Baltimore, MD
The Park School of Buffalo, NY
Peddie School, NJ
Peninsula Catholic High School, VA
Pensacola Catholic High School, FL
The Phelps School, PA
Phillips Academy (Andover), MA
Phoenix Christian Unified Schools, AZ
Phoenix Country Day School, AZ
Pinecrest Academy, GA
Pine Crest School, FL
The Pingry School, NJ
Pioneer Valley Christian School, MA
Polytechnic School, CA
Porter-Gaud School, SC
Portsmouth Abbey School, RI
Portsmouth Christian Academy, NH
The Potomac School, VA
Poughkeepsie Day School, NY
Powers Catholic High School, MI
Prestonwood Christian Academy, TX
The Prout School, RI
Providence Catholic School, The College Preparatory School for Girls Grades 6-12, TX
Providence Country Day School, RI
Providence Day School, NC
Providence High School, CA
Queen Anne School, MD
Queen of Peace High School, NJ
Randolph-Macon Academy, VA
Randolph School, AL
Ranney School, NJ
Ransom Everglades School, FL
Redwood Christian Schools, CA
Regis High School, NY
Reitz Memorial High School, IN
Ridley College, ON, Canada
Rio Hondo Preparatory School, CA
Rivermont Collegiate, IA
The Rivers School, MA
Robinson School, PR, Puerto Rico

†Accepts day students

Rockland Country Day School, NY
The Roeper School, MI
Roland Park Country School, MD
Rolling Hills Preparatory School, CA
Ross School, NY
Rowland Hall, UT
The Roxbury Latin School, MA
Roycemore School, IL
Rye Country Day School, NY
Sacred Heart Academy, KY
Sacred Heart School of Halifax, NS, Canada
Saddleback Valley Christian School, CA
Saddlebrook Preparatory School, FL
Sage Hill School, CA
Sage Ridge School, NV
St. Agnes Academy, TX
St. Albans School, DC
St. Andrew's College, ON, Canada
St. Andrew's Priory School, HI
St. Andrew's Regional High School, BC, Canada
St. Andrew's School, RI
St. Anthony Catholic High School, TX
Saint Anthony High School, IL
St. Anthony's Junior-Senior High School, HI
Saint Augustine Preparatory School, NJ
Saint Basil Academy, PA
St. Benedict at Auburndale, TN
St. Bernard's Catholic School, CA
St. Brendan High School, FL
St. Catherine's School, VA
St. Cecilia Academy, TN
Saint Cecilia High School, NE
St. Christopher's School, VA
St. Clement's School, ON, Canada
St. Croix Country Day School, VI
St. Croix Schools, MN
St. David's School, NC
Saint Dominic Academy, ME
Saint Edward's School, FL
Saint Elizabeth High School, CA
St. Francis de Sales High School, OH
Saint Francis Girls High School, CA
Saint Francis High School, CA
Saint Francis School, HI
St. George's Independent School, TN
St. George's School, RI
St. George's School, BC, Canada
St. George's School of Montreal, QC, Canada
St. Gregory College Preparatory School, AZ
St. John's Preparatory School, MA
St. John's-Ravenscourt School, MB, Canada
St. Joseph Academy, FL
Saint Joseph Academy High School, OH
Saint Joseph High School, IL
Saint Joseph High School, WI
Saint Joseph Junior-Senior High School, HI
St. Joseph's Academy, LA
St. Joseph's Catholic School, SC
Saint Joseph's High School, NJ
St. Joseph's Preparatory School, PA
Saint Lucy's Priory High School, CA
St. Margaret's Episcopal School, CA
St. Margaret's School, VA
Saint Mark's School, MA
St. Mark's School of Texas, TX
St. Martin's Episcopal School, LA
Saint Mary's College High School, CA

St. Mary's Episcopal School, TN
Saint Mary's Hall, TX
Saint Mary's High School, AZ
Saint Mary's High School, MD
St. Mary's Preparatory School, MI
Saint Mary's School, NC
St. Mary's School, OR
Saint Maur International School, Japan
St. Michael's College School, ON, Canada
St. Michael's Preparatory School of the Norbertine Fathers, CA
St. Michaels University School, BC, Canada
St. Patrick Catholic High School, MS
Saint Patrick High School, IL
Saint Patrick—Saint Vincent High School, CA
St. Patrick's Regional Secondary, BC, Canada
St. Paul's Episcopal School, AL
St. Paul's High School, MB, Canada
St. Peter's Preparatory School, NJ
St. Pius X Catholic High School, GA
St. Pius X High School, TX
St. Sebastian's School, MA
Saints Peter and Paul High School, MD
St. Stanislaus College, MS
St. Stephen's & St. Agnes School, VA
Saint Stephen's Episcopal School, FL
St. Stephen's Episcopal School, TX
Saint Thomas Academy, MN
Saint Thomas Aquinas High School, KS
St. Thomas Aquinas High School, NH
St. Thomas High School, TX
Saint Thomas More Catholic High School, LA
Saint Ursula Academy, OH
St. Vincent Pallotti High School, MD
Salem Academy, OR
Salem Baptist Christian School, NC
Salesian High School, CA
Salesianum School, DE
Saltus Grammar School, Bermuda
Sandy Spring Friends School, MD
Sanford School, DE
San Marcos Baptist Academy, TX
Santa Catalina School, CA
Santa Fe Preparatory School, NM
Sayre School, KY
School of the Holy Child, NY
Scottsdale Christian Academy, AZ
Scotus Central Catholic High School, NE
Seabury Hall, HI
Seattle Christian Schools, WA
Second Baptist School, TX
Selwyn House School, QC, Canada
Seoul Foreign School, Republic of Korea
Seton Catholic Central High School, NY
Seton Catholic High School, AZ
The Seven Hills School, OH
Severn School, MD
Sewickley Academy, PA
Shades Mountain Christian School, AL
Shady Side Academy, PA
Shannon Forest Christian School, SC
Shattuck-St. Mary's School, MN
Shawe Memorial Junior/Senior High School, IN
The Shipley School, PA
Sonoma Academy, CA
Soundview Preparatory School, NY
Southfield Christian High School, MI
South Kent School, CT

†Accepts day students

Southwest Christian School, Inc., TX
Southwestern Academy, AZ
Southwestern Academy, CA
Spartanburg Day School, SC
The Spence School, NY
Springside School, PA
Squaw Valley Academy, CA
The Stanwich School, CT
Stephen T. Badin High School, OH
Stevenson School, CA
Stoneleigh–Burnham School, MA
Strake Jesuit College Preparatory, TX
Stratford Academy, GA
Suffield Academy, CT
Tabor Academy, MA
Taipei American School, Taiwan
Tandem Friends School, VA
TASIS, The American School in Switzerland, Switzerland
The Tenney School, TX
The Thacher School, CA
Thomas Jefferson School, MO
Tidewater Academy, VA
Timothy Christian High School, IL
TMI—The Episcopal School of Texas, TX
Tower Hill School, DE
Town Centre Private High School, ON, Canada
Trafalgar Castle School, ON, Canada
Trinity College School, ON, Canada
Trinity High School, KY
Trinity High School, NH
Trinity-Pawling School, NY
Trinity Preparatory School, FL
Trinity School, NY
Trinity School of Texas, TX
Tuscaloosa Academy, AL
Tyler Street Christian Academy, TX
University of Chicago Laboratory Schools, IL
University of Detroit Jesuit High School and Academy, MI
University Prep, WA
University School of Jackson, TN
University School of Milwaukee, WI
University School of Nova Southeastern University, FL
Ursuline Academy, MA
The Ursuline Academy of Dallas, TX
Ursuline High School, CA
Vail Mountain School, CO
Valle Catholic High School, MO
Valley Lutheran High School, AZ
Vianney High School, MO
Vicksburg Catholic School, MS
Villa Duchesne and Oak Hill School, MO
Village Christian Schools, CA
Villa Joseph Marie High School, PA
Villa Maria Academy, PA
Villa Walsh Academy, NJ
Visitation Academy of St. Louis County, MO
The Walker School, GA
Waring School, MA
Wasatch Academy, UT
The Waterford School, UT
The Webb School, TN
Webb School of Knoxville, TN
The Wellington School, OH
Wesleyan Academy, PR
Westbury Christian School, TX
West Catholic High School, MI
Westchester Country Day School, NC

Western Christian Schools, CA
Western Reserve Academy, OH
West Island College, AB, Canada
Westminster Christian Academy, AL
Westminster Christian Academy, LA
Westover School, CT
Westridge School, CA
West Sound Academy, WA
West Valley Christian Church Schools, CA
Wheaton Academy, IL
The Wheeler School, RI
Whitefield Academy, KY
The White Mountain School, NH
The Williams School, CT
The Williston Northampton School, MA
Wilson Hall, SC
Winchester Thurston School, PA
Windermere Preparatory School, FL
The Windsor School, NY
Windward School, CA
The Winsor School, MA
The Woodhall School, CT
Woodstock School, India
Woodward Academy, GA
Worcester Academy, MA
Worcester Preparatory School, MD
Wyoming Seminary, PA
York Country Day School, PA
York Preparatory School, NY
York School, CA

SCHOOLS REPORTING A POSTGRADUATE YEAR

The Academy at Charlemont, MA
The Beekman School, NY
Berwick Academy, ME
Blair Academy, NJ
The Bolles School, FL
Brewster Academy, NH
Chapel Hill–Chauncy Hall School, MA
Choate Rosemary Hall, CT
Christchurch School, VA
The Culver Academies, IN
Cushing Academy, MA
Deerfield Academy, MA
Emma Willard School, NY
Fishburne Military School, VA
Franklin Academy, CT
Gould Academy, ME
Griggs International Academy, MD
Hank Haney International Junior Golf Academy, SC
Hargrave Military Academy, VA
Hoosac School, NY
The Hotchkiss School, CT
Houghton Academy, NY
The Hun School of Princeton, NJ
Idyllwild Arts Academy, CA
Interlochen Arts Academy, MI
The John Dewey Academy, MA
Kent School, CT
Kildonan School, NY
Kimball Union Academy, NH
La Lumiere School, IN
The Lawrenceville School, NJ
Maine Central Institute, ME
Manlius Pebble Hill School, NY
Marine Military Academy, TX

Northwood School, NY
The Orme School, AZ
The Oxford Academy, CT
Peddie School, NJ
The Phelps School, PA
Phillips Academy (Andover), MA
Randolph-Macon Academy, VA
Ridley College, ON, Canada
Robert Louis Stevenson School, NY
St. Gregory College Preparatory School, AZ
St. John's Northwestern Military Academy, WI
St. Stanislaus College, MS
Shattuck-St. Mary's School, MN
Soundview Preparatory School, NY
South Kent School, CT
Southwestern Academy, AZ
Southwestern Academy, CA
Stoneleigh–Burnham School, MA
Stratton Mountain School, VT
Suffield Academy, CT
TASIS, The American School in Switzerland, Switzerland
Thomas Jefferson School, MO
Trinity-Pawling School, NY
The Vanguard School, FL
Watkinson School, CT
Western Reserve Academy, OH
The White Mountain School, NH
The Williston Northampton School, MA
The Windsor School, NY
The Woodhall School, CT
Worcester Academy, MA
Wyoming Seminary, PA

SCHOOLS OFFERING THE INTERNATIONAL BACCALAUREATE PROGRAM

Academy of the Holy Cross, MD
Académie Ste Cécile International School, ON, Canada
Alma Heights Christian High School, CA
American Community Schools of Athens, Greece
American International School, Dhaka, Bangladesh
American School of Bombay, India
The American School of Madrid, Spain
American School of Milan, Italy
American School of The Hague, Netherlands
The Awty International School, TX
Bavarian International School, Germany
Bellarmine-Jefferson High School, CA
Berlin International School, Germany
Branksome Hall, ON, Canada
Canadian Academy, Japan
Cardinal Newman High School, FL
Carlucci American International School of Lisbon, Portugal
Carrollton School of the Sacred Heart, FL
Catholic Central High School, WI
Central Catholic High School, OH
Chamberlain-Hunt Academy, MS
Charlotte Country Day School, NC
Christ Church Episcopal School, SC
Clearwater Central Catholic High School, FL
Colegio Franklin D. Roosevelt, Peru
DePaul Catholic High School, NJ
Fort Lauderdale Preparatory School, FL
George School, PA
Glenlyon Norfolk School, BC, Canada
Gulliver Preparatory School, FL

International College Spain, Spain
International High School, CA
International School Bangkok, Thailand
International School Hamburg, Germany
International School Manila, Philippines
International School of Amsterdam, Netherlands
International School of Athens, Greece
International School of Berne, Switzerland
The International School of Kuala Lumpur, Malaysia
The International School of London, United Kingdom
International School of Zug and Luzern (ISZL), Switzerland
The Journeys School of Teton Science School, WY
Kerr-Vance Academy, NC
The Kew-Forest School, NY
King George School, VT
King's-Edgehill School, NS, Canada
Le Lycee Francais de Los Angeles, CA
Luther College High School, SK, Canada
Lydia Patterson Institute, TX
Marymount International School, Italy
Marymount International School, United Kingdom
Meadowridge School, BC, Canada
Mid-Pacific Institute, HI
Munich International School, Germany
Newark Academy, NJ
The Prout School, RI
Providence Catholic School, The College Preparatory School for Girls Grades 6-12, TX
Providence Christian School, AB, Canada
Riverfield Academy, LA
Riverstone International School, ID
Rothesay Netherwood School, NB, Canada
Rotterdam International Secondary School, Wolfert van Borselen, Netherlands
Saint Anthony High School, IL
Saint Dominic Academy, ME
Saint Maur International School, Japan
St. Peter's Preparatory School, NJ
St. Timothy's School, MD
SCECGS Redlands, Australia
Seisen International School, Japan
Seoul Foreign School, Republic of Korea
Shawe Memorial Junior/Senior High School, IN
The Stanwich School, CT
Stone Mountain School, NC
Taipei American School, Taiwan
TASIS, The American School in Switzerland, Switzerland
United Nations International School, NY
The United World College—USA, NM
Verdala International School, Malta
Villa Duchesne and Oak Hill School, MO
West Sound Academy, WA
Windermere Preparatory School, FL
Yokohama International School, Japan

SCHOOLS REPORTING THAT THEY AWARD MERIT SCHOLARSHIPS

Academy at the Lakes, FL
Academy of Notre Dame de Namur, PA
Academy of Our Lady of Mercy, CT
Academy of Saint Elizabeth, NJ
Academy of the Holy Cross, MD
Academy of the Holy Names, FL
Academy of the Sacred Heart, LA
Academy of the Sacred Heart, MI

Académie Ste Cécile International School, ON, Canada
Allison Academy, FL
Alma Heights Christian High School, CA
American Heritage School, FL
American Heritage School, FL
Archbishop Alter High School, OH
Archbishop Curley High School, MD
Archbishop Hoban High School, OH
Archbishop McNicholas High School, OH
Archbishop Rummel High School, LA
Augusta Preparatory Day School, GA
Balmoral Hall School, MB, Canada
Baylor School, TN
Beaumont School, OH
Bellarmine-Jefferson High School, CA
Benedictine High School, OH
Benedictine High School, VA
Berlin International School, Germany
The Birch Wathen Lenox School, NY
Bishop Blanchet High School, WA
Bishop Brady High School, NH
Bishop Connolly High School, MA
Bishop Denis J. O'Connell High School, VA
Bishop Eustace Preparatory School, NJ
Bishop Fenwick High School, OH
Bishop Guertin High School, NH
Bishop Ireton High School, VA
Bishop Luers High School, IN
Bishop O'Dowd High School, CA
Bishop's College School, QC, Canada
Bishop Stang High School, MA
Blanchet School, OR
The Blue Ridge School, VA
Boston College High School, MA
Branksome Hall, ON, Canada
Brookstone School, GA
Brother Rice High School, IL
Brother Rice High School, MI
Calvert Hall College High School, MD
Canterbury School, FL
Canyonville Christian Academy, OR
Cape Fear Academy, NC
Cape Henry Collegiate School, VA
Cardinal Mooney Catholic High School, FL
Carlucci American International School of Lisbon, Portugal
Carmel High School, IL
Carrollton School of the Sacred Heart, FL
Cathedral High School, NY
The Catholic High School of Baltimore, MD
Central Catholic High School, CA
Central Catholic High School, MA
Central Catholic High School, OH
Central Catholic High School, OH
Central Catholic High School, PA
Central Catholic High School, TX
Chamberlain-Hunt Academy, MS
Chaminade College Preparatory, CA
Chaminade College Preparatory School, MO
Charlotte Latin School, NC
Cheverus High School, ME
Chinese Christian Schools, CA
Christ Church Episcopal School, SC
Christian Brothers Academy, NJ
Christian Brothers Academy, NY
Christian Brothers Academy, NY
Christian Central Academy, NY
Cincinnati Country Day School, OH

Clearwater Central Catholic High School, FL
The Colorado Rocky Mountain School, CO
The Colorado Springs School, CO
Columbia International College of Canada, ON, Canada
The Columbus Academy, OH
Commonwealth Parkville School, PR
The Community School of Naples, FL
Concordia Lutheran High School, IN
Country Day School of the Sacred Heart, PA
Covington Catholic High School, KY
Crespi Carmelite High School, CA
Crossroads College Preparatory School, MO
The Culver Academies, IN
Cushing Academy, MA
Damien High School, CA
Damien Memorial School, HI
Deerfield-Windsor School, GA
DeMatha Catholic High School, MD
DePaul Catholic High School, NJ
The Derryfield School, NH
Devon Preparatory School, PA
The Dominican Academy of the City of New York, NY
Duchesne Academy of the Sacred Heart, NE
Duchesne Academy of the Sacred Heart, TX
Eastside Catholic School, WA
Elgin Academy, IL
Elizabeth Seton High School, MD
Emma Willard School, NY
Episcopal High School, VA
Explorations Academy, WA
Falmouth Academy, MA
Fayetteville Academy, NC
Fenwick High School, IL
First Presbyterian Day School, GA
Fontbonne Hall Academy, NY
Fordham Preparatory School, NY
Forest Lake Academy, FL
Fort Lauderdale Preparatory School, FL
Fountain Valley School of Colorado, CO
Foxcroft School, VA
Frederica Academy, GA
Freeman Academy, SD
Fresno Adventist Academy, CA
Fresno Christian Schools, CA
Fuqua School, VA
Garces Memorial High School, CA
Gaston Day School, NC
Gateway School, TX
Gem State Adventist Academy, ID
George School, PA
Georgetown Visitation Preparatory School, DC
Gill St. Bernard's School, NJ
Gilmour Academy, OH
Glenelg Country School, MD
Glenlyon Norfolk School, BC, Canada
Gonzaga College High School, DC
The Grauer School, CA
Greenfield School, NC
Gunston Day School, MD
Gwynedd Mercy Academy, PA
Hamilton District Christian High, ON, Canada
Hargrave Military Academy, VA
Harrow School, United Kingdom
The Haverford School, PA
Hawken School, OH
Hawthorne Christian Academy, NJ
Holy Cross High School, CT

Holy Ghost Preparatory School, PA
Holy Savior Menard Catholic High School, LA
Holy Trinity High School, IL
Hoosac School, NY
The Hun School of Princeton, NJ
Immaculate Conception High School, NJ
Immaculate Conception School, IL
Incarnate Word Academy, TX
Institute of Notre Dame, MD
Interlochen Arts Academy, MI
International College Spain, Spain
Iona Preparatory School, NY
Jesuit College Preparatory School, TX
J. K. Mullen High School, CO
Junipero Serra High School, CA
Keith Country Day School, IL
Kent School, CT
Kentucky Country Day School, KY
King's-Edgehill School, NS, Canada
Kingshill School, VI
Kingsway College, ON, Canada
Kingswood-Oxford School, CT
Kirov Academy of Ballet of Washington, D.C., DC
Ladywood High School, MI
Lake Forest Academy, IL
Lake Ridge Academy, OH
La Lumiere School, IN
Lancaster Mennonite High School, PA
La Salle High School, CA
Lima Central Catholic High School, OH
Linfield Christian School, CA
Lodi Academy, CA
Long Island Lutheran Middle and High School, NY
Los Angeles Baptist Middle School/High School, CA
Louisville Collegiate School, KY
Louisville High School, CA
Loyola School, NY
Lutheran High School, CA
Lutheran High School North, MO
Lutheran High School Northwest, MI
Lutheran High School of Hawaii, HI
Lutheran High School of San Diego, CA
Lutheran High School South, MO
Luther College High School, SK, Canada
Luther High School North, IL
Lyman Ward Military Academy, AL
Madison-Ridgeland Academy, MS
Magnificat High School, OH
Maine Central Institute, ME
Manlius Pebble Hill School, NY
Maplebrook School, NY
Marmion Academy, IL
Martin Luther High School, NY
Maryknoll School, HI
Marylawn of the Oranges, NJ
Marymount High School, CA
Marymount International School, United Kingdom
Mary Star of the Sea High School, CA
Matignon High School, MA
Maur Hill-Mount Academy, KS
McGill-Toolen Catholic High School, AL
Meadowridge School, BC, Canada
Merchiston Castle School, United Kingdom
Mercy High School, CT
Mercy High School, NE
Merion Mercy Academy, PA
The Miami Valley School, OH

Mid-Pacific Institute, HI
Miss Edgar's and Miss Cramp's School, QC, Canada
Miss Porter's School, CT
MMI Preparatory School, PA
Monsignor Donovan High School, NJ
Moreau Catholic High School, CA
Morristown-Beard School, NJ
Mother McAuley High School, IL
Mount Carmel High School, IL
Mt. De Sales Academy, GA
Mount Mercy Academy, NY
Mount Michael Benedictine School, NE
Mt. Saint Dominic Academy, NJ
Mount Saint Joseph Academy, PA
Navajo Preparatory School, Inc., NM
Nazareth Academy, IL
Nebraska Christian Schools, NE
Nerinx Hall, MO
Niagara Christian Community of Schools, ON, Canada
North Shore Country Day School, IL
Northwest Catholic High School, CT
Notre Dame Academy, CA
Notre Dame High School, CA
Oak Hill School, OR
Oak Knoll School of the Holy Child, NJ
The Oakland School, PA
Oak Ridge Military Academy, NC
Oldenburg Academy, IN
The O'Neal School, NC
Our Lady of Mercy Academy, NJ
Our Lady of Mercy High School, NY
Padua Franciscan High School, OH
The Park School of Buffalo, NY
Peddie School, NJ
Pickering College, ON, Canada
Portsmouth Abbey School, RI
Portsmouth Christian Academy, NH
Powers Catholic High School, MI
Presbyterian Pan American School, TX
Providence Catholic School, The College Preparatory School for
    Girls Grades 6-12, TX
Providence High School, CA
Queen Anne School, MD
Queen of Peace High School, NJ
Randolph-Macon Academy, VA
Randolph School, AL
Ridley College, ON, Canada
Rivermont Collegiate, IA
Rolling Hills Preparatory School, CA
Rosseau Lake College, ON, Canada
Rothesay Netherwood School, NB, Canada
Rowland Hall, UT
Royal Canadian College, BC, Canada
Roycemore School, IL
Rundle College, AB, Canada
Sacred Heart Academy, KY
Sacred Heart School of Halifax, NS, Canada
Saddleback Valley Christian School, CA
St. Agnes Academy, TX
St. Andrew's College, ON, Canada
St. Andrew's Priory School, HI
St. Ann's Academy, BC, Canada
St. Anthony's Junior-Senior High School, HI
Saint Augustine Preparatory School, NJ
Saint Basil Academy, PA
St. Benedict at Auburndale, TN
St. Bernard's Catholic School, CA

Saint Cecilia High School, NE
St. Christopher's School, VA
St. Clement's School, ON, Canada
St. Croix Country Day School, VI
St. Croix Schools, MN
Saint Dominic Academy, ME
Saint Edward's School, FL
Saint Elizabeth High School, CA
St. Francis de Sales High School, OH
Saint Francis High School, CA
Saint Francis School, HI
St. George's School, BC, Canada
St. John's Northwestern Military Academy, WI
St. John's-Ravenscourt School, MB, Canada
Saint Joseph Academy High School, OH
St. Joseph High School, CA
Saint Joseph High School, IL
Saint Joseph High School, NJ
Saint Joseph High School, WI
St. Joseph's Catholic School, SC
Saint Joseph's High School, NJ
St. Joseph's Preparatory School, PA
Saint Lucy's Priory High School, CA
St. Martin's Episcopal School, LA
Saint Mary's College High School, CA
Saint Mary's Hall, TX
Saint Mary's High School, MD
St. Mary's Preparatory School, MI
St. Michael's College School, ON, Canada
St. Michaels University School, BC, Canada
St. Peter's Preparatory School, NJ
St. Pius X High School, TX
St. Stephen's Episcopal School, TX
Saint Thomas Academy, MN
St. Thomas High School, TX
Saint Thomas More Catholic High School, LA
St. Timothy's School, MD
Saint Ursula Academy, OH
St. Vincent Pallotti High School, MD
Salesian High School, CA
Salesianum School, DE
Salt Lake Lutheran High School, UT
Saltus Grammar School, Bermuda
Santa Catalina School, CA
SCECGS Redlands, Australia
School of the Holy Child, NY
Second Baptist School, TX
Selwyn House School, QC, Canada
Seton Catholic Central High School, NY
Seton Catholic High School, AZ
The Seven Hills School, OH
Shady Side Academy, PA
Shattuck-St. Mary's School, MN
Sheridan Academy, ID
South Kent School, CT
Spartanburg Day School, SC
Springside School, PA
The Stanwich School, CT
Stephen T. Badin High School, OH
Stoneleigh–Burnham School, MA
Stratford Academy, GA
Thomas Jefferson School, MO
TMI—The Episcopal School of Texas, TX
Trafalgar Castle School, ON, Canada
Trinity High School, KY
Trinity School of Texas, TX
Tuscaloosa Academy, AL

Tyler Street Christian Academy, TX
The United World College—USA, NM
University of Detroit Jesuit High School and Academy, MI
The Ursuline Academy of Dallas, TX
Ursuline High School, CA
Valle Catholic High School, MO
Valley Lutheran High School, AZ
The Vanguard School, FL
Venta Preparatory School, ON, Canada
Vianney High School, MO
Villa Duchesne and Oak Hill School, MO
Village Christian Schools, CA
Villa Joseph Marie High School, PA
Villa Maria Academy, PA
Villa Walsh Academy, NJ
Waldorf High School of Massachusetts Bay, MA
Wasatch Academy, UT
The Webb School, TN
The Wellington School, OH
Westbury Christian School, TX
Western Mennonite School, OR
Western Reserve Academy, OH
West Sound Academy, WA
Wheaton Academy, IL
The White Mountain School, NH
Wyoming Seminary, PA
York Preparatory School, NY

SCHOOLS REPORTING A GUARANTEED TUITION PLAN

Armona Union Academy, CA
Auldern Academy, NC
The Blue Ridge School, VA
Calvary Chapel High School, CA
Cedar Ridge Academy, UT
Central Catholic High School, CA
Community Christian Academy, KY
Concord Academy, MA
Crawford Adventist Academy, ON, Canada
Cross Creek Programs, UT
The Culver Academies, IN
Damien High School, CA
Ecole d'Humanité, Switzerland
Foundation Academy, FL
Gateway School, TX
Glenlyon Norfolk School, BC, Canada
Hank Haney International Junior Golf Academy, SC
Hanson Memorial High School, LA
Harmony Heights Residential and Day School, NY
Hawaii Baptist Academy, HI
The Hewitt School, NY
The Hill Center, Durham Academy, NC
Humanex Academy, CO
Jackson Christian School, TN
Laurel Springs School, CA
Manhattan Christian High School, MT
Marion Academy, AL
Middlesex School, MA
Nashville Christian School, TN
National High School, GA
Nebraska Christian Schools, NE
New Covenant Academy, MO
Pickens Academy, AL
Piedmont Academy, GA
Pope John XXIII Regional High School, NJ

Presbyterian Pan American School, TX
St. Brendan High School, FL
Saint Cecilia High School, NE
Saint Joseph Junior-Senior High School, HI
San Marcos Baptist Academy, TX
Scholar's Hall Preparatory School, ON, Canada
Selwyn House School, QC, Canada
Southern Ontario College, ON, Canada
Stone Mountain School, NC
Trinity High School, KY
Tuscaloosa Academy, AL
The United World College—USA, NM
The Waterford School, UT
Wesleyan Academy, PR
Westminster Christian Academy, AL
Westminster Christian Academy, LA

SCHOOLS REPORTING A TUITION INSTALLMENT PLAN

The Academy at Charlemont, MA
Academy at the Lakes, FL
The Academy for Gifted Children (PACE), ON, Canada
Academy of Notre Dame de Namur, PA
Academy of Our Lady of Mercy, CT
Academy of Our Lady of Peace, CA
Academy of Saint Elizabeth, NJ
Academy of the Holy Cross, MD
Academy of the Holy Names, FL
Academy of the New Church Boys' School, PA
Academy of the New Church Girls' School, PA
Academy of the Sacred Heart, LA
Academy of the Sacred Heart, MI
Académie Ste Cécile International School, ON, Canada
Admiral Farragut Academy, FL
Alexander Dawson School, CO
Allendale Columbia School, NY
Alliance Academy, Ecuador
Allison Academy, FL
Alma Heights Christian High School, CA
Alpha Omega Academy, IA
American Academy, FL
The American Boychoir School, NJ
American Community Schools of Athens, Greece
American Heritage School, FL
American Heritage School, FL
American International School of Costa Rica, Costa Rica
The American School in London, United Kingdom
The American School of Madrid, Spain
American School of Milan, Italy
American School of The Hague, Netherlands
Archbishop Alter High School, OH
Archbishop Curley High School, MD
Archbishop Hoban High School, OH
Archbishop McNicholas High School, OH
Archbishop Mitty High School, CA
Archbishop Rummel High School, LA
The Archer School for Girls, CA
Arendell Parrott Academy, NC
Armona Union Academy, CA
Army and Navy Academy, CA
Arrowsmith School, ON, Canada
Arthur Morgan School, NC
Aspen Ranch, UT
ASSETS School, HI
The Athenian School, CA

Augusta Christian School (I), GA
Augusta Preparatory Day School, GA
Auldern Academy, NC
The Awty International School, TX
The Baldwin School, PA
Balmoral Hall School, MB, Canada
The Baltimore Actors' Theatre Conservatory, MD
Baltimore Lutheran Middle and Upper School, MD
Barrie School, MD
Bavarian International School, Germany
Baylor School, TN
Bayside Academy, AL
Beaumont School, OH
The Beekman School, NY
Bellarmine College Preparatory, CA
Bellarmine-Jefferson High School, CA
The Bement School, MA
Benedictine High School, OH
Benedictine High School, VA
Berkeley Preparatory School, FL
Berlin International School, Germany
Berwick Academy, ME
The Birch Wathen Lenox School, NY
Bishop Blanchet High School, WA
Bishop Brady High School, NH
Bishop Conaty-Our Lady of Loretto High School, CA
Bishop Connolly High School, MA
Bishop Denis J. O'Connell High School, VA
Bishop Eustace Preparatory School, NJ
Bishop Fenwick High School, OH
Bishop Guertin High School, NH
Bishop Ireton High School, VA
Bishop Kelly High School, ID
Bishop Kenny High School, FL
Bishop Luers High School, IN
Bishop McGuinness Catholic High School, NC
Bishop McGuinness Catholic High School, OK
Bishop Montgomery High School, CA
Bishop O'Dowd High School, CA
Bishop's College School, QC, Canada
Bishop Stang High School, MA
Bishop Walsh Middle High School, MD
Blair Academy, NJ
Blanchet School, OR
Blessed Trinity High School, GA
The Blue Ridge School, VA
The Bolles School, FL
Boston College High School, MA
Bourgade Catholic High School, AZ
Boylan Central Catholic High School, IL
Branksome Hall, ON, Canada
Breck School, MN
Brentwood School, CA
Brewster Academy, NH
Briarcrest Christian High School, TN
Briarwood Christian High School, AL
Bridges Academy, CA
Bridge School, CO
Brooks School, MA
Brookstone School, GA
Brother Rice High School, IL
Brother Rice High School, MI
Brunswick School, CT
The Bryn Mawr School for Girls, MD
The Buckley School, CA
Burr and Burton Academy, VT
Buxton School, MA

The Byrnes Schools, SC
The Calhoun School, NY
Calvary Chapel High School, CA
Calvary Christian School, KY
Calvert Hall College High School, MD
The Calverton School, MD
Calvin Christian High School, CA
Campbell Hall (Episcopal), CA
Canadian Academy, Japan
Canterbury School, FL
The Canterbury School of Florida, FL
Canton Academy, MS
Canyonville Christian Academy, OR
Cape Fear Academy, NC
Cape Henry Collegiate School, VA
Capistrano Valley Christian Schools, CA
Cardigan Mountain School, NH
Cardinal Mooney Catholic College Preparatory High School, MI
Cardinal Mooney Catholic High School, FL
Cardinal Newman High School, FL
Carlucci American International School of Lisbon, Portugal
Carmel High School, IL
Carrollton School of the Sacred Heart, FL
Cascade Christian Academy, WA
Cascades Academy of Central Oregon, OR
Cascia Hall Preparatory School, OK
Castilleja School, CA
Cathedral High School, NY
Catholic Central High School, WI
The Catholic High School of Baltimore, MD
The Catlin Gabel School, OR
Cedar Ridge Academy, UT
Central Catholic High School, CA
Central Catholic High School, MA
Central Catholic High School, OH
Central Catholic High School, OH
Central Catholic High School, PA
Central Catholic High School, TX
Central Catholic Mid-High School, NE
CFS, The School at Church Farm, PA
Chamberlain-Hunt Academy, MS
Chaminade College Preparatory, CA
Chaminade College Preparatory School, MO
Chaminade-Madonna College Preparatory, FL
Chapel Hill–Chauncy Hall School, MA
Charles Wright Academy, WA
Charlotte Christian School, NC
Charlotte Country Day School, NC
Charlotte Latin School, NC
Chatham Academy, GA
Chattanooga Christian School, TN
Cheverus High School, ME
The Chicago Academy for the Arts, IL
Chicago Waldorf School, IL
Chinese Christian Schools, CA
Choate Rosemary Hall, CT
Christ Church Episcopal School, SC
Christchurch School, VA
Christian Brothers Academy, NJ
Christian Brothers Academy, NY
Christian Brothers Academy, NY
Christian Central Academy, NY
Christian Home and Bible School, FL
Christopher Columbus High School, FL
Christopher Dock Mennonite High School, PA
Chrysalis School, WA
Cincinnati Country Day School, OH

Cistercian Preparatory School, TX
Clearwater Central Catholic High School, FL
Colegio Franklin D. Roosevelt, Peru
Colegio Nueva Granada, Colombia
Colegio San Jose, PR
Collegedale Academy, TN
Collegiate School, NY
The Collegiate School, VA
The Colorado Rocky Mountain School, CO
The Colorado Springs School, CO
Columbia Academy, TN
The Columbus Academy, OH
Columbus School for Girls, OH
Commonwealth Parkville School, PR
Commonwealth School, MA
Community Christian Academy, KY
Community Hebrew Academy, ON, Canada
The Community School of Naples, FL
The Concept School, PA
Concord Academy, MA
Concordia Lutheran High School, IN
Convent of the Sacred Heart, CT
Convent of the Sacred Heart, NY
Cotter Schools, MN
Country Day School of the Sacred Heart, PA
Covenant Canadian Reformed School, AB, Canada
Crawford Adventist Academy, ON, Canada
Crespi Carmelite High School, CA
Cross Creek Programs, UT
Crosspoint Academy, WA
Crossroads College Preparatory School, MO
Crystal Springs Uplands School, CA
The Culver Academies, IN
Currey Ingram Academy, TN
Cushing Academy, MA
Dakota Christian High School, SD
Dallas Christian School, TX
The Dalton School, NY
Damien High School, CA
Damien Memorial School, HI
David Lipscomb High School, TN
Davidson Academy, TN
Deerfield Academy, MA
Deerfield-Windsor School, GA
De La Salle High School, CA
Delaware Valley Friends School, PA
DeMatha Catholic High School, MD
DePaul Catholic High School, NJ
The Derryfield School, NH
Des Moines Christian School, IA
Devon Preparatory School, PA
Dexter School, MA
Doane Stuart School, NY
The Dominican Academy of the City of New York, NY
Donelson Christian Academy, TN
Dowling Catholic High School, IA
Dublin School, NH
Duchesne Academy of the Sacred Heart, NE
Duchesne Academy of the Sacred Heart, TX
Durham Academy, NC
Eaglebrook School, MA
Eagle Hill-Southport, CT
Eastern Christian High School, NJ
Eastside Catholic School, WA
Eastside Christian Academy, AB, Canada
Ecole d'Humanité, Switzerland
Edgewood Academy, AL

Edmund Burke School, DC
Elan School, ME
Elgin Academy, IL
Elizabeth Seton High School, MD
Emma Willard School, NY
The Episcopal Academy, PA
Episcopal Collegiate School, AR
Episcopal High School, TX
Episcopal High School, VA
Episcopal High School of Jacksonville, FL
The Ethel Walker School, CT
Explorations Academy, WA
Faith Christian High School, CA
Faith Lutheran High School, NV
The Family Foundation School, NY
Father Lopez High School, FL
Father Ryan High School, TN
Fayetteville Academy, NC
Fay School, MA
Fenwick High School, IL
The First Academy, FL
First Baptist Academy, TX
First Presbyterian Day School, GA
Flint Hill School, VA
Flint River Academy, GA
Florida Air Academy, FL
Fontbonne Hall Academy, NY
Foothills Academy, AB, Canada
Fordham Preparatory School, NY
Forest Lake Academy, FL
Forsyth Country Day School, NC
Fort Lauderdale Preparatory School, FL
Foundation Academy, FL
Fountain Valley School of Colorado, CO
Fowlers Academy, PR
Foxcroft School, VA
Fox Valley Lutheran High School, WI
Franklin Academy, CT
Franklin Road Academy, TN
Fraser Academy, BC, Canada
Freeman Academy, SD
French-American School of New York, NY
Fresno Adventist Academy, CA
Fresno Christian Schools, CA
Friends Academy, NY
Friends' Central School, PA
Friendship Christian School, TN
Friends Select School, PA
The Frostig School, CA
Fuqua School, VA
Gann Academy (The New Jewish High School of Greater
    Boston), MA
Garces Memorial High School, CA
Garrison Forest School, MD
Gaston Day School, NC
Gem State Adventist Academy, ID
The Geneva School, FL
George School, PA
George Stevens Academy, ME
Georgetown Preparatory School, MD
Georgetown Visitation Preparatory School, DC
George Walton Academy, GA
Germantown Friends School, PA
Gill St. Bernard's School, NJ
Gilman School, MD
Gilmour Academy, OH
Girls Preparatory School, TN

Glades Day School, FL
Glenelg Country School, MD
Glenlyon Norfolk School, BC, Canada
Gonzaga College High School, DC
Gould Academy, ME
The Governor French Academy, IL
The Governor's Academy (formerly Governor Dummer
    Academy), MA
Grace Baptist Academy, TN
Grace Christian School, PE, Canada
The Grauer School, CA
Greater Atlanta Christian Schools, GA
Greenfield School, NC
Greenhills School, MI
Greensboro Day School, NC
Greenwich Academy, CT
The Greenwood School, VT
Griggs International Academy, MD
Groton School, MA
Gulliver Preparatory School, FL
Gunston Day School, MD
Gwynedd Mercy Academy, PA
Hackley School, NY
Hamden Hall Country Day School, CT
Hamilton District Christian High, ON, Canada
Hampton Roads Academy, VA
Hanalani Schools, HI
Hank Haney International Junior Golf Academy, SC
Hanson Memorial High School, LA
Happy Hill Farm Academy, TX
Harding Academy, TN
Harding Academy, TN
Hargrave Military Academy, VA
The Harley School, NY
Harrells Christian Academy, NC
Harrow School, United Kingdom
Harvard-Westlake School, CA
The Harvey School, NY
The Haverford School, PA
Hawaiian Mission Academy, HI
Hawaii Baptist Academy, HI
Hawken School, OH
Hawthorne Christian Academy, NJ
Head-Royce School, CA
Hebrew Academy-the Five Towns, NY
Heritage Christian Academy, AB, Canada
Heritage Christian School, ON, Canada
The Heritage School, GA
The Hewitt School, NY
Highland Hall Waldorf School, CA
The Hill Center, Durham Academy, NC
Hillcrest Christian School, MS
The Hill Top Preparatory School, PA
Hilton Head Preparatory School, SC
Holy Cross High School, CT
Holy Ghost Preparatory School, PA
Holy Innocents' Episcopal School, GA
Holy Name High School, PA
Holyoke Catholic High School, MA
Holy Savior Menard Catholic High School, LA
Holy Trinity High School, IL
Hoosac School, NY
Hopkins School, CT
The Hotchkiss School, CT
Houghton Academy, NY
The Howard School, GA
The Howe School, IN

Humanex Academy, CO
The Hun School of Princeton, NJ
Huntington-Surrey School, TX
Hyde School, ME
Hyman Brand Hebrew Academy of Greater Kansas City, KS
Idyllwild Arts Academy, CA
Immaculata-La Salle High School, FL
Immaculate Conception High School, NJ
Immaculate Conception School, IL
Immanuel Christian High School, AB, Canada
Incarnate Word Academy, TX
Institute of Notre Dame, MD
Interlochen Arts Academy, MI
International College Spain, Spain
International High School, CA
International School Bangkok, Thailand
International School Hamburg, Germany
International School Manila, Philippines
International School of Amsterdam, Netherlands
International School of Athens, Greece
International School of Berne, Switzerland
The International School of Kuala Lumpur, Malaysia
International School of Zug and Luzern (ISZL), Switzerland
Iolani School, HI
Iona Preparatory School, NY
Isidore Newman School, LA
Island School, HI
Jackson Christian School, TN
Jackson Preparatory School, MS
Jesuit College Preparatory School, TX
Jesuit High School of New Orleans, LA
Jesuit High School of Tampa, FL
J. K. Mullen High School, CO
John Burroughs School, MO
The John Cooper School, TX
The John Dewey Academy, MA
John Paul II Catholic High School, FL
Junipero Serra High School, CA
Kalamazoo Christian High School, MI
Kaplan College Preparatory School, FL
The Karafin School, NY
Kauai Christian Academy, HI
Keith Country Day School, IL
Kent School, CT
Kentucky Country Day School, KY
Kerr-Vance Academy, NC
The Kew-Forest School, NY
Key School, TX
Kildonan School, NY
Kimball Union Academy, NH
King George School, VT
King Low Heywood Thomas, CT
The King's Academy, TN
Kings Christian School, CA
King's-Edgehill School, NS, Canada
Kingshill School, VI
King's Ridge Christian School, GA
Kingsway College, ON, Canada
Kingswood-Oxford School, CT
Kirov Academy of Ballet of Washington, D.C., DC
Ladywood High School, MI
La Jolla Country Day School, CA
Lakefield College School, ON, Canada
Lake Forest Academy, IL
Lakehill Preparatory School, TX
Lake Mary Preparatory School, FL
Lake Ridge Academy, OH

Lakeside School, WA
La Lumiere School, IN
Lancaster Mennonite High School, PA
Landmark Christian Academy, KY
Landmark School, MA
Landon School, MD
La Salle High School, CA
The Latin School of Chicago, IL
The Laureate Academy, MB, Canada
Laurel Springs School, CA
Lawrence School, OH
The Lawrenceville School, NJ
Lee Academy, MS
Lehigh Valley Christian High School, PA
Lehman High School, OH
Leo Catholic High School, IL
Lick-Wilmerding High School, CA
Lifegate School, OR
Lima Central Catholic High School, OH
Linfield Christian School, CA
The Linsly School, WV
Lodi Academy, CA
Long Island Lutheran Middle and High School, NY
Loretto Academy, TX
Los Angeles Baptist Middle School/High School, CA
Louisville Collegiate School, KY
Louisville High School, CA
The Lovett School, GA
Loyola Academy, IL
Loyola School, NY
Lutheran High School, CA
Lutheran High School, IN
Lutheran High School, MO
Lutheran High School North, MO
Lutheran High School Northwest, MI
Lutheran High School of Hawaii, HI
Lutheran High School of San Diego, CA
Lutheran High School South, MO
Luther College High School, SK, Canada
Luther High School North, IL
The Lycee International, American Section, France
Lydia Patterson Institute, TX
Lyman Ward Military Academy, AL
MacLachlan College, ON, Canada
Madison Academy, AL
Madison-Ridgeland Academy, MS
Magnificat High School, OH
Maharishi School of the Age of Enlightenment, IA
Maine Central Institute, ME
Manhattan Christian High School, MT
Manlius Pebble Hill School, NY
Maplebrook School, NY
Maret School, DC
Marian Central Catholic High School, IL
Marian High School, IN
Marin Academy, CA
Marine Military Academy, TX
The Marin School, CA
Marist School, GA
Marlborough School, CA
Marmion Academy, IL
Marquette University High School, WI
Mars Hill Bible School, AL
Martin Luther High School, NY
Maryknoll School, HI
Marylawn of the Oranges, NJ
Marymount High School, CA

Marymount International School, United Kingdom
Mary Star of the Sea High School, CA
Maryvale Preparatory School, MD
The Masters School, NY
Matignon High School, MA
Maur Hill-Mount Academy, KS
McDonogh School, MD
McGill-Toolen Catholic High School, AL
Meadowridge School, BC, Canada
The Meadows School, NV
Memorial Hall School, TX
Memphis University School, TN
Menaul School, NM
Menlo School, CA
Mercy High School, CT
Mercy High School, NE
Mercy High School College Preparatory, CA
Mercy Vocational High School, PA
Merion Mercy Academy, PA
The Miami Valley School, OH
Middlesex School, MA
Mid-Pacific Institute, HI
Millbrook School, NY
Milton Academy, MA
Miss Edgar's and Miss Cramp's School, QC, Canada
Miss Porter's School, CT
MMI Preparatory School, PA
Monsignor Donovan High School, NJ
Montclair College Preparatory School, CA
Montclair Kimberley Academy, NJ
Monterey Bay Academy, CA
Monte Vista Christian School, CA
Moorestown Friends School, NJ
Moravian Academy, PA
Moreau Catholic High School, CA
Morristown-Beard School, NJ
Mother McAuley High School, IL
Mount Carmel High School, IL
Mt. De Sales Academy, GA
Mount Mercy Academy, NY
Mount Michael Benedictine School, NE
Mount Saint Charles Academy, RI
Mt. Saint Dominic Academy, NJ
Mount Saint Joseph Academy, PA
MPS Etobicoke, ON, Canada
Munich International School, Germany
Nashville Christian School, TN
National High School, GA
Navajo Preparatory School, Inc., NM
Nazareth Academy, IL
Nebraska Christian Schools, NE
Nerinx Hall, MO
Newark Academy, NJ
New Covenant Academy, MO
Niagara Christian Community of Schools, ON, Canada
The Nichols School, NY
Noble Academy, NC
The Nora School, MD
Norfolk Academy, VA
North Cobb Christian School, GA
North Country School, NY
North Shore Country Day School, IL
Northwest Catholic High School, CT
The Northwest School, WA
Northwest Yeshiva High School, WA
Northwood School, NY
Notre Dame Academy, CA

Notre Dame College Prep, IL
Notre Dame High School, CA
Notre Dame High School, NJ
Notre Dame High School, TN
Notre Dame Junior/Senior High School, PA
Oakcrest School, VA
Oak Grove School, CA
Oak Hill Academy, VA
Oak Hill School, OR
Oak Knoll School of the Holy Child, NJ
The Oakland School, PA
Oakland School, VA
Oak Mountain Academy, GA
Oak Ridge Military Academy, NC
The Oakridge School, TX
Ojai Valley School, CA
Oldenburg Academy, IN
The O'Neal School, NC
Oneida Baptist Institute, KY
Orangewood Christian School, FL
Oregon Episcopal School, OR
Orinda Academy, CA
The Orme School, AZ
Our Lady of Mercy Academy, NJ
Our Lady of Mercy High School, NY
Out-Of-Door-Academy, FL
The Overlake School, WA
The Oxford Academy, CT
Pacific Crest Community School, OR
Padua Franciscan High School, OH
The Paideia School, GA
Paradise Adventist Academy, CA
The Park School of Baltimore, MD
The Park School of Buffalo, NY
The Pathway School, PA
Peddie School, NJ
Peninsula Catholic High School, VA
The Phelps School, PA
Phillips Academy (Andover), MA
Phoenix Christian Unified Schools, AZ
Phoenix Country Day School, AZ
Pickens Academy, AL
Pickering College, ON, Canada
Piedmont Academy, GA
Pine Crest School, FL
Pinehurst School, ON, Canada
The Pingry School, NJ
Pioneer Valley Christian School, MA
Polytechnic School, CA
Pope John XXIII Regional High School, NJ
Porter-Gaud School, SC
Portsmouth Abbey School, RI
Portsmouth Christian Academy, NH
The Potomac School, VA
Poughkeepsie Day School, NY
Powers Catholic High School, MI
Presbyterian Pan American School, TX
Prestonwood Christian Academy, TX
Professional Children's School, NY
The Prout School, RI
Providence Catholic School, The College Preparatory School for Girls Grades 6-12, TX
Providence Christian School, AB, Canada
Providence Country Day School, RI
Providence Day School, NC
Providence High School, CA
Queen Anne School, MD

Queen of Peace High School, NJ
Quinte Christian High School, ON, Canada
Randolph-Macon Academy, VA
Randolph School, AL
Ranney School, NJ
Ransom Everglades School, FL
The Rectory School, CT
Redwood Christian Schools, CA
Reitz Memorial High School, IN
Rejoice Christian Schools, OK
Ridley College, ON, Canada
Rio Hondo Preparatory School, CA
Riverdale Country School, NY
Rivermont Collegiate, IA
The Rivers School, MA
Riverstone International School, ID
Robert Louis Stevenson School, NY
Robinson School, PR, Puerto Rico
Rockland Country Day School, NY
Rock Point School, VT
The Roeper School, MI
Roland Park Country School, MD
Rolling Hills Preparatory School, CA
Rosseau Lake College, ON, Canada
Ross School, NY
Rothesay Netherwood School, NB, Canada
Rotterdam International Secondary School, Wolfert van Borselen,
    Netherlands
Rowland Hall, UT
The Roxbury Latin School, MA
Roycemore School, IL
Rundle College, AB, Canada
Rye Country Day School, NY
Sacred Heart School of Halifax, NS, Canada
Saddleback Valley Christian School, CA
Saddlebrook Preparatory School, FL
Sage Hill School, CA
Sage Ridge School, NV
St. Agnes Academy, TX
St. Albans School, DC
St. Andrew's College, ON, Canada
St. Andrew's Priory School, HI
St. Andrew's School, DE
St. Andrew's School, RI
St. Anthony Catholic High School, TX
Saint Anthony High School, IL
St. Anthony's Junior-Senior High School, HI
Saint Augustine Preparatory School, NJ
Saint Basil Academy, PA
St. Benedict at Auburndale, TN
St. Benedict's Preparatory School, NJ
St. Bernard's Catholic School, CA
St. Brendan High School, FL
St. Catherine's Academy, CA
St. Catherine's School, VA
St. Cecilia Academy, TN
Saint Cecilia High School, NE
St. Christopher's School, VA
St. Clement School, ON, Canada
St. Clement's School, ON, Canada
St. Croix Country Day School, VI
St. Croix Schools, MN
St. David's School, NC
Saint Dominic Academy, ME
Saint Edward's School, FL
St. Francis de Sales High School, OH
Saint Francis Girls High School, CA

Saint Francis High School, CA
Saint Francis School, HI
St. George's School, RI
St. George's School, BC, Canada
St. Gregory College Preparatory School, AZ
St. John's Northwestern Military Academy, WI
St. John's Preparatory School, MA
St. John's-Ravenscourt School, MB, Canada
St. Joseph Academy, FL
Saint Joseph Academy High School, OH
St. Joseph High School, CA
Saint Joseph High School, IL
Saint Joseph High School, NJ
Saint Joseph High School, WI
Saint Joseph Junior-Senior High School, HI
St. Joseph's Academy, LA
St. Joseph's Catholic School, SC
Saint Joseph's High School, NJ
St. Joseph's Preparatory School, PA
St. Jude's School, ON, Canada
Saint Lucy's Priory High School, CA
St. Margaret's Episcopal School, CA
St. Margaret's School, VA
Saint Mark's School, MA
St. Mark's School of Texas, TX
St. Martin's Episcopal School, LA
Saint Mary's College High School, CA
St. Mary's Episcopal School, TN
Saint Mary's Hall, TX
Saint Mary's High School, AZ
Saint Mary's High School, MD
St. Mary's Preparatory School, MI
Saint Mary's School, NC
St. Mary's School, OR
St. Michael's College School, ON, Canada
St. Michael's Preparatory School of the Norbertine Fathers, CA
St. Michaels University School, BC, Canada
St. Patrick Catholic High School, MS
Saint Patrick High School, IL
Saint Patrick—Saint Vincent High School, CA
St. Patrick's Regional Secondary, BC, Canada
St. Paul Academy and Summit School, MN
St. Paul's Episcopal School, AL
St. Paul's High School, MB, Canada
St. Peter's Preparatory School, NJ
St. Pius X Catholic High School, GA
St. Pius X High School, TX
St. Sebastian's School, MA
Saints Peter and Paul High School, MD
St. Stanislaus College, MS
St. Stephen's & St. Agnes School, VA
Saint Stephen's Episcopal School, FL
St. Stephen's Episcopal School, TX
Saint Thomas Academy, MN
Saint Thomas Aquinas High School, KS
St. Thomas Aquinas High School, NH
St. Thomas High School, TX
Saint Thomas More Catholic High School, LA
St. Timothy's School, MD
Saint Ursula Academy, OH
Saint Viator High School, IL
St. Vincent Pallotti High School, MD
Salesian High School, CA
Salesianum School, DE
Salt Lake Lutheran High School, UT
Saltus Grammar School, Bermuda
Sandia Preparatory School, NM

Sandy Spring Friends School, MD
Sanford School, DE
San Marcos Baptist Academy, TX
Santa Catalina School, CA
Santa Fe Preparatory School, NM
Sayre School, KY
Scarborough Christian School, ON, Canada
Scholar's Hall Preparatory School, ON, Canada
School of the Holy Child, NY
Scottsdale Christian Academy, AZ
Scotus Central Catholic High School, NE
Seabury Hall, HI
Seattle Academy of Arts and Sciences, WA
Seattle Christian Schools, WA
Second Baptist School, TX
Seisen International School, Japan
Selwyn House School, QC, Canada
Seoul Foreign School, Republic of Korea
Seton Catholic Central High School, NY
Seton Catholic High School, AZ
The Seven Hills School, OH
Severn School, MD
Sewickley Academy, PA
Shades Mountain Christian School, AL
Shady Side Academy, PA
Shannon Forest Christian School, SC
Shattuck-St. Mary's School, MN
Shawe Memorial Junior/Senior High School, IN
Shelton School and Evaluation Center, TX
Sheridan Academy, ID
The Shipley School, PA
Shoore Centre for Learning, ON, Canada
Shoreline Christian, WA
Smith School, NY
Sonoma Academy, CA
Southfield Christian High School, MI
South Kent School, CT
Southwest Christian School, Inc., TX
Southwestern Academy, AZ
Southwestern Academy, CA
Spartanburg Day School, SC
The Spence School, NY
Springside School, PA
Squaw Valley Academy, CA
The Stanwich School, CT
Stephen T. Badin High School, OH
Sterne School, CA
Stevenson School, CA
Stoneleigh–Burnham School, MA
Stone Mountain School, NC
Strake Jesuit College Preparatory, TX
Stratford Academy, GA
Stratton Mountain School, VT
Suffield Academy, CT
Summerfield Waldorf School, CA
Sunhawk Adolescent Recovery Center, UT
Tabor Academy, MA
Tandem Friends School, VA
TASIS, The American School in Switzerland, Switzerland
Telluride Mountain School, CO
Teurlings Catholic High School, LA
The Thacher School, CA
Thomas Jefferson School, MO
Tidewater Academy, VA
Timothy Christian High School, IL
TMI—The Episcopal School of Texas, TX
Toronto District Christian High School, ON, Canada

Tower Hill School, DE
Town Centre Private High School, ON, Canada
Trafalgar Castle School, ON, Canada
Trinity Christian Academy, TN
Trinity College School, ON, Canada
Trinity High School, KY
Trinity High School, NH
Trinity-Pawling School, NY
Trinity Preparatory School, FL
Trinity School at Greenlawn, IN
Trinity School of Texas, TX
Turning Winds Academic Institute, ID
Tuscaloosa Academy, AL
Tyler Street Christian Academy, TX
United Nations International School, NY
The United World College—USA, NM
University Christian Preparatory School, LA
University of Chicago Laboratory Schools, IL
University of Detroit Jesuit High School and Academy, MI
University Prep, WA
University School of Jackson, TN
University School of Milwaukee, WI
University School of Nova Southeastern University, FL
Ursuline Academy, MA
The Ursuline Academy of Dallas, TX
Ursuline High School, CA
Vail Mountain School, CO
Valle Catholic High School, MO
Valley Lutheran High School, AZ
Valley View School, MA
The Vanguard School, FL
Venta Preparatory School, ON, Canada
Verdala International School, Malta
Vianney High School, MO
Vicksburg Catholic School, MS
Villa Duchesne and Oak Hill School, MO
Village Christian Schools, CA
Villa Joseph Marie High School, PA
Villa Maria Academy, PA
Villa Walsh Academy, NJ
Visitation Academy of St. Louis County, MO
Waldorf High School of Massachusetts Bay, MA
The Walker School, GA
Waring School, MA
Wasatch Academy, UT
The Waterford School, UT
Watkinson School, CT
Waynflete School, ME
The Webb School, TN
Webb School of Knoxville, TN
The Wellington School, OH
Wellsprings Friends School, OR
Wesleyan Academy, PR
Westbury Christian School, TX
West Catholic High School, MI
Westchester Country Day School, NC
Western Mennonite School, OR
Western Reserve Academy, OH
West Island College, AB, Canada
Westmark School, CA
Westminster Christian Academy, AL
Westminster Christian Academy, LA
Westover School, CT
Westridge School, CA
West Sound Academy, WA
West Valley Christian Church Schools, CA
Wheaton Academy, IL

The Wheeler School, RI
Whitefield Academy, KY
The White Mountain School, NH
The Williams School, CT
The Williston Northampton School, MA
Willow Wood School, ON, Canada
Wilson Hall, SC
Winchester Thurston School, PA
Windermere Preparatory School, FL
The Windsor School, NY
Windward School, CA
The Winsor School, MA
Winston Preparatory School, NY
The Winston School San Antonio, TX
The Woodhall School, CT
Woodlynde School, PA
Woodstock School, India
Woodward Academy, GA
Worcester Academy, MA
Worcester Preparatory School, MD
Wyoming Seminary, PA
Yokohama International School, Japan
York Catholic High School, PA
York Country Day School, PA
York Preparatory School, NY
York School, CA

SCHOOLS REPORTING THAT THEY OFFER LOANS*

School	
Academy of the New Church Boys' School, PA	M
Academy of the New Church Girls' School, PA	M,N
Alexander Dawson School, CO	N
Archbishop Mitty High School, CA	M
Aspen Ranch, UT	M
Berwick Academy, ME	N
Bishop's College School, QC, Canada	N
Blair Academy, NJ	N
Boston College High School, MA	N
Brookstone School, GA	M,N
Brother Rice High School, IL	N
The Bryn Mawr School for Girls, MD	M,N
Calvin Christian High School, CA	N
Cardigan Mountain School, NH	N
Chaminade College Preparatory School, MO	N
Choate Rosemary Hall, CT	N
The Colorado Rocky Mountain School, CO	M
Commonwealth School, MA	N
Community Hebrew Academy, ON, Canada	N
Concord Academy, MA	N
Convent of the Sacred Heart, NY	N
Copper Canyon Academy, AZ	M
Ecole d'Humanité, Switzerland	M,N
Episcopal High School, TX	M
Explorations Academy, WA	N
Falmouth Academy, MA	N
Fontbonne Hall Academy, NY	N
Friends Select School, PA	N
Garrison Forest School, MD	N
Georgetown Preparatory School, MD	M
Germantown Friends School, PA	N
Gilman School, MD	N
Gilmour Academy, OH	N
Gould Academy, ME	N
Greenwich Academy, CT	M
Hackley School, NY	N

School	
Hamden Hall Country Day School, CT	N
Hargrave Military Academy, VA	N
The Harker School, CA	N
Hawken School, OH	N
The Hotchkiss School, CT	N
Humanex Academy, CO	M
John Burroughs School, MO	N
Kent School, CT	N
King George School, VT	M,N
The Latin School of Chicago, IL	M,N
Maplebrook School, NY	M,N
Marian High School, IN	N
Marin Academy, CA	N
McDonogh School, MD	M,N
The Meadows School, NV	N
Merion Mercy Academy, PA	M
Middlesex School, MA	N
Millbrook School, NY	N
Moorestown Friends School, NJ	N
Mount Michael Benedictine School, NE	N
Norfolk Academy, VA	N
North Shore Country Day School, IL	M,N
Ojai Valley School, CA	N
The Orme School, AZ	N
Peddie School, NJ	N
Phillips Academy (Andover), MA	M
Reitz Memorial High School, IN	N
Ridley College, ON, Canada	N
Robert Louis Stevenson School, NY	N
St. Albans School, DC	N
St. Andrew's School, RI	N
St. Anthony's Junior-Senior High School, HI	N
St. George's School, RI	M,N
Saint Joseph Academy High School, OH	N
St. Joseph's Preparatory School, PA	M,N
St. Paul's High School, MB, Canada	N
St. Sebastian's School, MA	N
St. Stanislaus College, MS	N
St. Thomas High School, TX	M
St. Timothy's School, MD	N
Santa Catalina School, CA	N
School of the Holy Child, NY	N
Seton Catholic Central High School, NY	M
Stone Mountain School, NC	M,N
Stratton Mountain School, VT	N
Trinity-Pawling School, NY	N
Trinity Preparatory School, FL	M
Trinity School, NY	M
Vail Mountain School, CO	N
Wasatch Academy, UT	N
The Wellington School, OH	N
Western Reserve Academy, OH	N
Westover School, CT	M,N
The Williston Northampton School, MA	N
Windward School, CA	N
Wyoming Seminary, PA	N
York School, CA	N

TOTAL AMOUNT OF UPPER SCHOOL FINANCIAL AID AWARDED FOR 2010–11

School	
The Academy at Charlemont, MA	$1,000,000
Academy of Notre Dame de Namur, PA	$449,500
Academy of Our Lady of Mercy, CT	$300,000
Academy of Our Lady of Peace, CA	$1,500,000
Academy of the Holy Cross, MD	$1,974,821

*Coeducational in lower grades; M — middle-income loans; N — need-based loans

Specialized Directories

Academy of the Holy Names, FL	$515,525
Academy of the New Church Boys' School, PA	$510,000
Academy of the New Church Girls' School, PA	$400,000
Academy of the Sacred Heart, LA	$241,400
Academy of the Sacred Heart, MI	$834,755
Académie Ste Cécile International School, ON, Canada	CAN$15,000
Admiral Farragut Academy, FL	$500,000
Alexander Dawson School, CO	$905,000
Allendale Columbia School, NY	$648,364
Alliance Academy, Ecuador	$800,000
Allison Academy, FL	$97,000
The American Boychoir School, NJ	$188,930
American Community Schools of Athens, Greece	€60,000
American Heritage School, FL	$4,050,006
The American School in London, United Kingdom	£411,150
Archbishop Alter High School, OH	$150,000
Archbishop Hoban High School, OH	$1,722,500
Archbishop McNicholas High School, OH	$480,000
Archbishop Mitty High School, CA	$2,300,000
The Archer School for Girls, CA	$2,500,000
Arendell Parrott Academy, NC	$290,000
Armona Union Academy, CA	$50,000
Army and Navy Academy, CA	$458,200
Arthur Morgan School, NC	$93,000
ASSETS School, HI	$170,000
The Athenian School, CA	$1,900,000
Augusta Preparatory Day School, GA	$426,016
The Awty International School, TX	$287,033
The Baldwin School, PA	$1,700,000
Balmoral Hall School, MB, Canada	CAN$300,000
The Baltimore Actors' Theatre Conservatory, MD	$12,000
Baltimore Lutheran Middle and Upper School, MD	$82,000
Barrie School, MD	$814,427
Baylor School, TN	$2,500,000
Beaumont School, OH	$1,200,000
Bellarmine College Preparatory, CA	$3,200,000
Benedictine High School, VA	$500,000
Berwick Academy, ME	$2,200,000
The Birch Wathen Lenox School, NY	$1,200,000
Bishop Blanchet High School, WA	$1,500,000
Bishop Conaty-Our Lady of Loretto High School, CA	$616,223
Bishop Denis J. O'Connell High School, VA	$1,400,000
Bishop Eustace Preparatory School, NJ	$550,000
Bishop Ireton High School, VA	$575,000
Bishop Kelly High School, ID	$956,972
Bishop McGuinness Catholic High School, NC	$304,000
Bishop McGuinness Catholic High School, OK	$206,620
Bishop Montgomery High School, CA	$30,000
Bishop O'Dowd High School, CA	$2,100,000
Bishop Stang High School, MA	$500,000
Bishop Walsh Middle High School, MD	$30,000
Blair Academy, NJ	$4,000,000
Blanchet School, OR	$240,000
Blue Mountain Academy, PA	$265,000
The Blue Ridge School, VA	$1,700,000
The Bolles School, FL	$1,772,385
Boston College High School, MA	$4,300,000
Bourgade Catholic High School, AZ	$800,000
Boylan Central Catholic High School, IL	$390,750
Branksome Hall, ON, Canada	CAN$650,000
Breck School, MN	$1,170,570
Brentwood School, CA	$3,500,000
Brewster Academy, NH	$2,400,000
Briarwood Christian High School, AL	$5000
Bridge School, CO	$60,000
Brooks School, MA	$2,600,000
Brookstone School, GA	$360,550
Brother Rice High School, IL	$782,000
Brother Rice High School, MI	$300,000
Brunswick School, CT	$1,700,000
The Bryn Mawr School for Girls, MD	$1,222,050
The Buckley School, CA	$421,225
Buxton School, MA	$1,200,000
The Byrnes Schools, SC	$25,000
The Calhoun School, NY	$1,800,000
Calvary Christian School, KY	$25,000
Calvert Hall College High School, MD	$1,142,000
Calvin Christian High School, CA	$225,000
Campbell Hall (Episcopal), CA	$3,500,000
Canadian Academy, Japan	¥575,000
Canterbury School, FL	$599,605
The Canterbury School of Florida, FL	$575,000
Canton Academy, MS	$50,000
Canyonville Christian Academy, OR	$147,900
Cape Fear Academy, NC	$241,773
Capistrano Valley Christian Schools, CA	$225,000
Cardigan Mountain School, NH	$981,000
Cardinal Mooney Catholic High School, FL	$200,000
Carmel High School, IL	$82,000
Carrollton School of the Sacred Heart, FL	$920,000
Cascade Christian Academy, WA	$119,000
Cascia Hall Preparatory School, OK	$450,000
Castilleja School, CA	$1,800,000
Catholic Central High School, WI	$113,000
The Catholic High School of Baltimore, MD	$388,132
The Catlin Gabel School, OR	$2,900,000
Cedar Ridge Academy, UT	$45,000
Central Catholic High School, CA	$175,020
Central Catholic High School, OH	$125,000
Central Catholic High School, PA	$1,250,000
Central Catholic High School, TX	$584,420
CFS, The School at Church Farm, PA	$3,397,205
Chamberlain-Hunt Academy, MS	$276,530
Chaminade College Preparatory, CA	$1,856,378
Chaminade College Preparatory School, MO	$1,600,000
Chaminade-Madonna College Preparatory, FL	$400,000
Chapel Hill–Chauncy Hall School, MA	$850,000
Charles Wright Academy, WA	$1,025,446
Charlotte Christian School, NC	$389,150
Charlotte Country Day School, NC	$1,391,307
Charlotte Latin School, NC	$745,700
Chatham Academy, GA	$82,200
Chattanooga Christian School, TN	$250,000
Cheverus High School, ME	$1,932,399
Chicago Waldorf School, IL	$272,880
Chinese Christian Schools, CA	$160,000
Choate Rosemary Hall, CT	$8,500,000
Christ Church Episcopal School, SC	$523,000
Christchurch School, VA	$1,270,125
Christian Brothers Academy, NJ	$950,000
Christian Brothers Academy, NY	$739,500
Christian Central Academy, NY	$58,420
Christopher Columbus High School, FL	$800,000
Christopher Dock Mennonite High School, PA	$492,500
Cincinnati Country Day School, OH	$930,000
Cistercian Preparatory School, TX	$383,350
Colegio Franklin D. Roosevelt, Peru	$5490
Colegio San Jose, PR	$250,000
Collegedale Academy, TN	$51,000
Collegiate School, NY	$1,215,000
The Collegiate School, VA	$655,087
The Colorado Rocky Mountain School, CO	$1,000,000
The Colorado Springs School, CO	$352,334

Total Amount of Upper School Financial Aid Awarded For 2010–11

Columbia Academy, TN	$21,500
The Columbus Academy, OH	$792,750
Columbus School for Girls, OH	$720,655
Commonwealth Parkville School, PR	$81,560
Commonwealth School, MA	$1,100,000
Community Christian Academy, KY	$9000
Community Hebrew Academy, ON, Canada	CAN$2,000,000
The Community School of Naples, FL	$755,900
Concord Academy, MA	$3,120,000
Convent of the Sacred Heart, CT	$1,400,000
Convent of the Sacred Heart, NY	$1,800,000
Copper Canyon Academy, AZ	$720,000
Country Day School of the Sacred Heart, PA	$424,350
Crawford Adventist Academy, ON, Canada	CAN$15,000
Crespi Carmelite High School, CA	$1,018,965
Crosspoint Academy, WA	$171,000
Crystal Springs Uplands School, CA	$2,000,000
The Culver Academies, IN	$8,900,000
Currey Ingram Academy, TN	$1,200,000
Cushing Academy, MA	$3,200,000
Dakota Christian High School, SD	$300,000
Dallas Christian School, TX	$180,000
The Dalton School, NY	$2,938,600
Damien High School, CA	$50,000
Damien Memorial School, HI	$600,000
David Lipscomb High School, TN	$46,840
Deerfield Academy, MA	$6,600,000
Deerfield-Windsor School, GA	$250,000
Delaware Valley Friends School, PA	$756,000
DeMatha Catholic High School, MD	$1,315,308
The Derryfield School, NH	$744,000
Des Moines Christian School, IA	$250,000
Devon Preparatory School, PA	$700,000
Doane Stuart School, NY	$727,810
The Dominican Academy of the City of New York, NY	$268,000
Donelson Christian Academy, TN	$136,853
Dowling Catholic High School, IA	$1,000,000
Dublin School, NH	$1,600,000
Duchesne Academy of the Sacred Heart, NE	$117,000
Duchesne Academy of the Sacred Heart, TX	$641,530
Durham Academy, NC	$724,650
Eaglebrook School, MA	$1,650,000
Eagle Hill-Southport, CT	$101,610
Eastside Catholic School, WA	$1,700,000
Ecole d'Humanité, Switzerland	180,000 Swiss francs
Edmund Burke School, DC	$978,185
Elizabeth Seton High School, MD	$400,000
Emma Willard School, NY	$3,855,950
The Episcopal Academy, PA	$3,100,100
Episcopal Collegiate School, AR	$436,000
Episcopal High School, TX	$1,700,000
Episcopal High School, VA	$4,300,000
Episcopal High School of Jacksonville, FL	$2,000,000
The Ethel Walker School, CT	$3,000,000
Explorations Academy, WA	$81,000
Fairhill School, TX	$50,000
Faith Christian High School, CA	$50,000
Faith Lutheran High School, NV	$460,000
Falmouth Academy, MA	$600,000
The Family Foundation School, NY	$500,000
Father Lopez High School, FL	$600,000
Father Ryan High School, TN	$536,000
Fayetteville Academy, NC	$477,000
Fay School, MA	$1,110,900
Fenwick High School, IL	$1,336,049
First Presbyterian Day School, GA	$874,000
Flint Hill School, VA	$1,661,780
Florida Air Academy, FL	$650,000
Fontbonne Hall Academy, NY	$107,500
Foothills Academy, AB, Canada	CAN$500,000
Fordham Preparatory School, NY	$1,750,000
Forest Lake Academy, FL	$378,500
Forsyth Country Day School, NC	$905,950
Fort Lauderdale Preparatory School, FL	$1,000,000
Fountain Valley School of Colorado, CO	$1,800,000
Fowlers Academy, PR	$7100
Foxcroft School, VA	$1,435,050
Fox Valley Lutheran High School, WI	$320,000
Franklin Road Academy, TN	$600,000
Frederica Academy, GA	$300,000
Freeman Academy, SD	$20,000
French-American School of New York, NY	$188,856
Fresno Adventist Academy, CA	$102,000
Fresno Christian Schools, CA	$300,000
Friends Academy, NY	$1,000,000
Friends' Central School, PA	$2,059,947
Friendship Christian School, TN	$5000
Friends Select School, PA	$888,006
The Frostig School, CA	$50,000
Fuqua School, VA	$50,000
Garces Memorial High School, CA	$312,000
Garrison Forest School, MD	$1,377,360
Gaston Day School, NC	$239,193
George School, PA	$6,100,000
Georgetown Preparatory School, MD	$2,000,000
Georgetown Visitation Preparatory School, DC	$1,250,000
Germantown Friends School, PA	$855,950
Gill St. Bernard's School, NJ	$1,000,000
Gilman School, MD	$1,840,900
Gilmour Academy, OH	$3,200,000
Girls Preparatory School, TN	$1,183,294
Glenelg Country School, MD	$1,600,000
Glenlyon Norfolk School, BC, Canada	CAN$129,895
Gonzaga College High School, DC	$2,000,000
Gould Academy, ME	$1,355,000
The Governor's Academy (formerly Governor Dummer Academy), MA	$32,000,000
Grace Christian School, PE, Canada	CAN$4000
The Grauer School, CA	$90,000
Greenhill School, TX	$1,282,620
Greenhills School, MI	$1,000,000
Greenwich Academy, CT	$1,351,850
The Greenwood School, VT	$249,290
Groton School, MA	$4,500,000
Gunston Day School, MD	$700,000
Gwynedd Mercy Academy, PA	$217,680
Hackley School, NY	$2,513,880
Hamden Hall Country Day School, CT	$1,421,655
Hamilton District Christian High, ON, Canada	CAN$95,000
Hanalani Schools, HI	$164,045
Harding Academy, TN	$191,824
Hargrave Military Academy, VA	$525,000
Harrells Christian Academy, NC	$27,800
Harvard Westlake School, CA	$6,846,600
The Harvey School, NY	$1,965,000
The Haverford School, PA	$2,117,550
Hawaii Baptist Academy, HI	$192,133
Hawken School, OH	$2,600,000
Hawthorne Christian Academy, NJ	$26,124
Head-Royce School, CA	$1,652,800
The Heritage School, GA	$175,000
The Hewitt School, NY	$1,394,709
Highland Hall Waldorf School, CA	$204,600
The Hill Center, Durham Academy, NC	$46,000

Hillcrest Christian School, MS	$42,824	Landmark School, MA	$362,041
Hillcrest School, TX	$21,000	Landon School, MD	$1,240,100
Hilton Head Preparatory School, SC	$250,000	La Salle High School, CA	$1,200,000
Holy Cross High School, CT	$550,000	The Latin School of Chicago, IL	$1,997,189
Holy Ghost Preparatory School, PA	$350,000	The Laureate Academy, MB, Canada	CAN$61,000
Holy Innocents' Episcopal School, GA	$956,160	The Lawrenceville School, NJ	$9,100,000
Holy Name High School, PA	$24,522	Lee Academy, MS	$25,000
Holyoke Catholic High School, MA	$87,000	Lehigh Valley Christian High School, PA	$100,000
Holy Savior Menard Catholic High School, LA	$135,000	Lehman High School, OH	$372,565
Holy Trinity High School, IL	$1,547,085	Le Lycee Francais de Los Angeles, CA	$63,000
Hoosac School, NY	$500,000	Lick-Wilmerding High School, CA	$4,300,000
Hopkins School, CT	$2,400,000	Lifegate School, OR	$50,000
The Hotchkiss School, CT	$7,687,883	Lima Central Catholic High School, OH	$75,000
Houghton Academy, NY	$95,000	The Linsly School, WV	$900,000
The Howe School, IN	$187,865	Little Keswick School, VA	$20,000
Humanex Academy, CO	$5000	Lodi Academy, CA	$25,000
The Hun School of Princeton, NJ	$2,500,000	Long Island Lutheran Middle and High School, NY	$250,000
Hyde School, ME	$820,000	Loretto Academy, TX	$203,000
Hyman Brand Hebrew Academy of Greater Kansas City, KS	$80,945	Los Angeles Baptist Middle School/High School, CA	$977,525
Idyllwild Arts Academy, CA	$5,054,332	Louisville High School, CA	$424,000
Immaculata-La Salle High School, FL	$260,000	The Lovett School, GA	$2,560,000
Immaculate Conception High School, NJ	$73,250	Loyola Academy, IL	$3,750,000
Immaculate Conception School, IL	$150,000	Loyola School, NY	$1,194,000
Incarnate Word Academy, TX	$119,606	Lutheran High School, CA	$109,150
Institute of Notre Dame, MD	$300,000	Lutheran High School, IN	$181,700
Interlochen Arts Academy, MI	$7,000,000	Lutheran High School, MO	$15,000
International College Spain, Spain	€39,000	Lutheran High School North, MO	$600,000
International High School, CA	$748,000	Lutheran High School Northwest, MI	$2000
Iolani School, HI	$3,000,500	Lutheran High School of Hawaii, HI	$50,000
Iona Preparatory School, NY	$325,000	Lutheran High School of San Diego, CA	$30,000
Isidore Newman School, LA	$847,872	Lutheran High School South, MO	$750,000
Island School, HI	$15,000	Luther College High School, SK, Canada	CAN$165,000
Jackson Christian School, TN	$15,218	The Lycee International, American Section, France	€30,000
Jackson Preparatory School, MS	$195,000	Lydia Patterson Institute, TX	$157,950
Jesuit College Preparatory School, TX	$1,233,850	Lyman Ward Military Academy, AL	$50,000
Jesuit High School of New Orleans, LA	$371,265	MacLachlan College, ON, Canada	CAN$9000
Jesuit High School of Tampa, FL	$1,200,000	Madison Academy, AL	$100,000
J. K. Mullen High School, CO	$808,000	Madison-Ridgeland Academy, MS	$170,000
John Burroughs School, MO	$1,892,000	Magnificat High School, OH	$900,000
The John Cooper School, TX	$306,970	Maine Central Institute, ME	$705,450
John Paul II Catholic High School, FL	$40,000	Manlius Pebble Hill School, NY	$880,000
Junipero Serra High School, CA	$400,000	Maplebrook School, NY	$157,000
Kauai Christian Academy, HI	$40,000	Maret School, DC	$2,800,000
Keith Country Day School, IL	$363,566	Marian Central Catholic High School, IL	$289,203
Kent School, CT	$7,300,000	Marian High School, IN	$350,000
Kentucky Country Day School, KY	$734,962	Marin Academy, CA	$2,400,000
Kerr-Vance Academy, NC	$15,000	Marine Military Academy, TX	$490,950
The Kew-Forest School, NY	$841,000	Marist School, GA	$16,976,775
Key School, TX	$31,250	Marlborough School, CA	$2,043,254
Kildonan School, NY	$300,000	Marmion Academy, IL	$323,000
Kimball Union Academy, NH	$2,400,000	Marquette University High School, WI	$1,400,000
King Low Heywood Thomas, CT	$765,875	Mars Hill Bible School, AL	$150,000
The King's Academy, TN	$136,615	Martin Luther High School, NY	$195,182
Kings Christian School, CA	$150,000	Maryknoll School, HI	$550,000
King's-Edgehill School, NS, Canada	CAN$700,000	Marylawn of the Oranges, NJ	$111,850
Kingshill School, VI	$9500	Marymount High School, CA	$1,200,000
Kingsway College, ON, Canada	CAN$156,000	Marymount International School, United Kingdom	£85,000
Kingswood-Oxford School, CT	$2,700,000	Mary Star of the Sea High School, CA	$145,000
Ladywood High School, MI	$100,000	Maryvale Preparatory School, MD	$496,585
La Jolla Country Day School, CA	$1,849,552	The Masters School, NY	$3,800,000
Lakefield College School, ON, Canada	CAN$170,500	Matignon High School, MA	$110,000
Lake Forest Academy, IL	$3,100,000	Maur Hill-Mount Academy, KS	$225,000
Lake Ridge Academy, OH	$841,475	McDonogh School, MD	$2,415,935
Lakeside School, WA	$2,778,078	McGill-Toolen Catholic High School, AL	$335,000
La Lumiere School, IN	$580,000	The Meadows School, NV	$597,540
Lancaster Mennonite High School, PA	$1,200,000	Memphis University School, TN	$1,300,000
		Menaul School, NM	$307,000

Menlo School, CA	$4,200,000
Mercy High School, NE	$1,000,000
Mercy High School College Preparatory, CA	$1,600,000
Merion Mercy Academy, PA	$857,600
The Miami Valley School, OH	$500,000
Middlesex School, MA	$4,100,000
Mid-Pacific Institute, HI	$644,000
Millbrook School, NY	$2,000,000
Milton Academy, MA	$7,650,000
Miss Edgar's and Miss Cramp's School, QC, Canada	CAN$105,000
Miss Porter's School, CT	$3,700,000
MMI Preparatory School, PA	$853,000
Montclair College Preparatory School, CA	$250,000
Montclair Kimberley Academy, NJ	$1,281,308
Monterey Bay Academy, CA	$300,000
Monte Vista Christian School, CA	$500,000
Moorestown Friends School, NJ	$1,372,175
Moravian Academy, PA	$907,000
Moreau Catholic High School, CA	$775,000
Morristown-Beard School, NJ	$1,000,000
Mother McAuley High School, IL	$550,000
Mount Carmel High School, IL	$500,000
Mt. De Sales Academy, GA	$813,771
Mount Michael Benedictine School, NE	$240,000
Mount Saint Charles Academy, RI	$700,000
Mt. Saint Dominic Academy, NJ	$192,000
Mount Saint Joseph Academy, PA	$564,400
Nashville Christian School, TN	$3000
Nazareth Academy, IL	$300,000
Nebraska Christian Schools, NE	$100,000
Nerinx Hall, MO	$505,000
Newark Academy, NJ	$1,388,542
New Covenant Academy, MO	$150,000
Niagara Christian Community of Schools, ON, Canada	CAN$400,000
The Nichols School, NY	$1,500,000
Noble Academy, NC	$35,000
The Nora School, MD	$115,000
North Cobb Christian School, GA	$272,370
North Country School, NY	$450,000
North Shore Country Day School, IL	$1,000,000
Northwest Catholic High School, CT	$1,300,000
The Northwest School, WA	$1,180,555
Northwest Yeshiva High School, WA	$328,331
Notre Dame College Prep, IL	$3,600,000
Notre Dame High School, CA	$700,000
Notre Dame High School, NJ	$180,000
Notre Dame High School, TN	$526,521
Oak Grove School, CA	$60,000
Oak Hill Academy, VA	$400,000
Oak Knoll School of the Holy Child, NJ	$1,400,000
The Oakland School, PA	$45,000
Oak Mountain Academy, GA	$38,000
Ojai Valley School, CA	$256,750
Oldenburg Academy, IN	$60,000
The O'Neal School, NC	$304,685
Orangewood Christian School, FL	$91,461
Oregon Episcopal School, OR	$110,000
Orinda Academy, CA	$300,000
The Orme School, AZ	$1,400,000
Our Lady of Mercy Academy, NJ	$40,000
Our Lady of Mercy High School, NY	$1,200,000
Out-Of-Door-Academy, FL	$410,000
The Overlake School, WA	$792,912
Pacific Crest Community School, OR	$50,000
The Paideia School, GA	$1,086,153
Paradise Adventist Academy, CA	$50,000
The Park School of Baltimore, MD	$1,199,365
The Park School of Buffalo, NY	$900,000
Peddie School, NJ	$5,000,000
The Phelps School, PA	$1,193,650
Phillips Academy (Andover), MA	$16,412,000
Phoenix Country Day School, AZ	$1,707,800
Piedmont Academy, GA	$25,000
Pine Crest School, FL	$1,893,657
The Pingry School, NJ	$1,864,385
Pioneer Valley Christian School, MA	$72,350
Polytechnic School, CA	$2,800,000
Porter-Gaud School, SC	$1,639,000
Portsmouth Abbey School, RI	$3,000,000
Portsmouth Christian Academy, NH	$165,000
The Potomac School, VA	$1,298,967
Poughkeepsie Day School, NY	$281,560
Powers Catholic High School, MI	$450,300
Presbyterian Pan American School, TX	$907,340
Prestonwood Christian Academy, TX	$444,807
Professional Children's School, NY	$606,500
The Prout School, RI	$225,000
Providence Catholic School, The College Preparatory School for Girls Grades 6-12, TX	$200,000
Providence Country Day School, RI	$1,500,000
Providence Day School, NC	$1,056,585
Providence High School, CA	$219,000
Queen Anne School, MD	$350,000
Randolph-Macon Academy, VA	$300,000
Randolph School, AL	$88,875
Ransom Everglades School, FL	$3,329,170
The Rectory School, CT	$1,330,000
Redwood Adventist Academy, CA	$50,000
Redwood Christian Schools, CA	$350,000
Reitz Memorial High School, IN	$264,840
Ridley College, ON, Canada	CAN$3,000,000
Rivermont Collegiate, IA	$309,755
The Rivers School, MA	$3,083,000
Robert Louis Stevenson School, NY	$30,000
Robinson School, PR, Puerto Rico	$78,820
Rockland Country Day School, NY	$360,930
Rock Point School, VT	$114,750
The Roeper School, MI	$862,775
Roland Park Country School, MD	$996,080
Rolling Hills Preparatory School, CA	$500,000
Rosseau Lake College, ON, Canada	CAN$160,000
Rothesay Netherwood School, NB, Canada	CAN$857,000
Rowland Hall, UT	$344,700
The Roxbury Latin School, MA	$1,775,370
Roycemore School, IL	$620,400
Rundle College, AB, Canada	CAN$24,000
Rye Country Day School, NY	$2,034,603
Sacred Heart School of Halifax, NS, Canada	CAN$138,000
Saddleback Valley Christian School, CA	$175,000
Sage Hill School, CA	$1,684,890
Sage Ridge School, NV	$176,225
St. Agnes Academy, TX	$450,000
St. Albans School, DC	$2,131,478
St. Andrew's College, ON, Canada	CAN$170,000
St. Andrew's Priory School, HI	$512,990
St. Andrew's School, DE	$4,300,000
St. Andrew's School, RI	$1,657,175
St. Ann's Academy, BC, Canada	CAN$30,000
St. Anthony Catholic High School, TX	$95,000
Saint Augustine Preparatory School, NJ	$1,000,000
Saint Basil Academy, PA	$273,700
St. Benedict at Auburndale, TN	$35,000

Specialized Directories

St. Benedict's Preparatory School, NJ	$1,833,000
St. Bernard's Catholic School, CA	$75,000
St. Catherine's Academy, CA	$140,000
St. Catherine's School, VA	$448,800
St. Cecilia Academy, TN	$650,000
Saint Cecilia High School, NE	$8000
St. Christopher's School, VA	$783,200
St. Croix Country Day School, VI	$265,550
St. Croix Schools, MN	$412,000
Saint Edward's School, FL	$1,183,206
Saint Elizabeth High School, CA	$970,000
St. Francis de Sales High School, OH	$1,669,600
Saint Francis Girls High School, CA	$1,000,000
Saint Francis High School, CA	$420,000
Saint Francis School, HI	$194,000
St. George's School, BC, Canada	CAN$800,000
St. Gregory College Preparatory School, AZ	$774,648
St. John's Northwestern Military Academy, WI	$950,000
St. John's Preparatory School, MA	$2,800,000
St. John's-Ravenscourt School, MB, Canada	CAN$262,250
St. Joseph Academy, FL	$128,480
Saint Joseph Academy High School, OH	$850,000
St. Joseph High School, CA	$310,000
Saint Joseph High School, IL	$600,000
Saint Joseph High School, NJ	$50,000
Saint Joseph High School, WI	$150,000
Saint Joseph Junior-Senior High School, HI	$225,000
St. Joseph's Academy, LA	$274,500
St. Joseph's Catholic School, SC	$292,033
Saint Joseph's High School, NJ	$250,000
St. Joseph's Preparatory School, PA	$2,000,000
Saint Lucy's Priory High School, CA	$90,000
St. Margaret's Episcopal School, CA	$1,929,690
St. Margaret's School, VA	$949,000
Saint Mark's School, MA	$3,500,000
St. Mark's School of Texas, TX	$1,188,359
St. Martin's Episcopal School, LA	$442,370
Saint Mary's College High School, CA	$1,900,000
St. Mary's Episcopal School, TN	$268,076
Saint Mary's Hall, TX	$583,800
Saint Mary's High School, AZ	$1,500,000
Saint Mary's High School, MD	$250,000
Saint Mary's School, NC	$1,133,000
St. Mary's School, OR	$650,000
St. Michael's College School, ON, Canada	CAN$1,700,000
St. Michael's Preparatory School of the Norbertine Fathers, CA	$350,000
St. Michaels University School, BC, Canada	CAN$620,000
Saint Patrick High School, IL	$970,000
Saint Patrick—Saint Vincent High School, CA	$377,600
St. Paul Academy and Summit School, MN	$1,154,740
St. Paul's Episcopal School, AL	$353,000
St. Paul's High School, MB, Canada	CAN$275,000
St. Peter's Preparatory School, NJ	$950,000
St. Pius X Catholic High School, GA	$400,000
St. Pius X High School, TX	$704,665
St. Sebastian's School, MA	$1,750,000
Saints Peter and Paul High School, MD	$8500
St. Stephen's & St. Agnes School, VA	$2,074,475
Saint Stephen's Episcopal School, FL	$249,000
St. Stephen's Episcopal School, TX	$1,900,000
Saint Thomas Academy, MN	$2,100,000
St. Thomas High School, TX	$1,150,000
Saint Thomas More Catholic High School, LA	$130,000
St. Timothy's School, MD	$1,750,000
Saint Viator High School, IL	$1,100,000
St. Vincent Pallotti High School, MD	$400,000
Salesian High School, CA	$1,250,000
Salesianum School, DE	$500,000
Salt Lake Lutheran High School, UT	$99,000
Saltus Grammar School, Bermuda	32,500,000 Bermuda dollars
Sandia Preparatory School, NM	$950,000
Sandy Spring Friends School, MD	$1,172,144
Sanford School, DE	$1,306,600
San Marcos Baptist Academy, TX	$306,200
Santa Catalina School, CA	$1,776,950
Santa Fe Preparatory School, NM	$781,128
Sayre School, KY	$510,000
Scholar's Hall Preparatory School, ON, Canada	CAN$20,000
Scotus Central Catholic High School, NE	$81,087
Seabury Hall, HI	$847,100
Seattle Christian Schools, WA	$85,394
Seisen International School, Japan	¥1,222,000
Selwyn House School, QC, Canada	CAN$145,830
Seoul Foreign School, Republic of Korea	$395,000
Seton Catholic Central High School, NY	$200,000
Seton Catholic High School, AZ	$705,000
The Seven Hills School, OH	$500,000
Severn School, MD	$1,500,000
Sewickley Academy, PA	$600,000
Shades Mountain Christian School, AL	$13,000
Shady Side Academy, PA	$1,533,500
Shannon Forest Christian School, SC	$15,000
Shattuck-St. Mary's School, MN	$3,900,000
Shawe Memorial Junior/Senior High School, IN	$200,000
Shelton School and Evaluation Center, TX	$137,500
The Shipley School, PA	$2,097,925
Shoreline Christian, WA	$41,869
Smith School, NY	$30,000
Soundview Preparatory School, NY	$470,000
Southfield Christian High School, MI	$191,000
South Kent School, CT	$1,900,000
Southwest Christian School, Inc., TX	$455,000
Southwestern Academy, AZ	$392,300
Southwestern Academy, CA	$750,000
Spartanburg Day School, SC	$182,000
The Spence School, NY	$1,870,795
Springside School, PA	$1,329,700
Stephen T. Badin High School, OH	$2,950,000
Sterne School, CA	$50,000
Stevenson School, CA	$2,600,000
Stoneleigh–Burnham School, MA	$904,000
Stone Mountain School, NC	$80,000
Strake Jesuit College Preparatory, TX	$1,350,000
Stratton Mountain School, VT	$737,000
Suffield Academy, CT	$3,500,000
Tabor Academy, MA	$3,500,000
Teurlings Catholic High School, LA	$84,000
The Thacher School, CA	$1,965,000
Thomas Jefferson School, MO	$507,000
Tidewater Academy, VA	$125,000
Timothy Christian High School, IL	$65,225
TMI—The Episcopal School of Texas, TX	$555,500
Tower Hill School, DE	$790,844
Trafalgar Castle School, ON, Canada	CAN$43,000
Trinity College School, ON, Canada	CAN$1,000,000
Trinity High School, KY	$1,300,000
Trinity-Pawling School, NY	$3,000,000
Trinity Preparatory School, FL	$1,130,580
Trinity School, NY	$2,500,000
Trinity School of Texas, TX	$99,875
Tuscaloosa Academy, AL	$160,000
Tyler Street Christian Academy, TX	$146,000
United Nations International School, NY	$286,290

The United World College—USA, NM	$2,800,000
University of Chicago Laboratory Schools, IL	$1,043,106
University of Detroit Jesuit High School and Academy, MI	$1,550,000
University Prep, WA	$1,238,663
University School of Jackson, TN	$130,000
University School of Milwaukee, WI	$884,100
University School of Nova Southeastern University, FL	$1,500,000
The Ursuline Academy of Dallas, TX	$851,300
Ursuline High School, CA	$510,000
Vail Mountain School, CO	$390,000
Valle Catholic High School, MO	$165,000
Valley Lutheran High School, AZ	$166,770
The Vanguard School, FL	$500,800
Verdala International School, Malta	$18,750
Vianney High School, MO	$316,127
Vicksburg Catholic School, MS	$79,000
Villa Duchesne and Oak Hill School, MO	$1,000,000
Villa Maria Academy, PA	$270,628
Villa Walsh Academy, NJ	$140,000
Waldorf High School of Massachusetts Bay, MA	$263,200
The Walker School, GA	$1,000,000
Waring School, MA	$541,926
Wasatch Academy, UT	$600,000
Watkinson School, CT	$1,261,540
Waynflete School, ME	$1,181,749
The Webb School, TN	$1,100,000
Webb School of Knoxville, TN	$670,132
Wesleyan Academy, PR	$10,000
Westbury Christian School, TX	$185,000
Westchester Country Day School, NC	$474,125
Western Christian Schools, CA	$150,000
Western Reserve Academy, OH	$3,600,000
Westminster Christian Academy, AL	$200,000
Westminster Christian Academy, LA	$36,981
Westover School, CT	$2,446,400
Westridge School, CA	$1,452,200
West Sound Academy, WA	$225,027
West Valley Christian Church Schools, CA	$150,000
Wheaton Academy, IL	$540,000
The Wheeler School, RI	$1,158,146
Whitefield Academy, KY	$40,498
The White Mountain School, NH	$1,412,000
The Williams School, CT	$1,270,680
The Williston Northampton School, MA	$5,855,400
Wilson Hall, SC	$115,000
Winchester Thurston School, PA	$1,249,000
Windermere Preparatory School, FL	$126,672
The Windsor School, NY	$30,000
Windward School, CA	$1,461,345
The Winsor School, MA	$1,490,140
Winston Preparatory School, NY	$500,000
Woodlynde School, PA	$525,475
Woodward Academy, GA	$1,006,220
Worcester Academy, MA	$4,400,000
Wyoming Seminary, PA	$6,000,000
York Country Day School, PA	$292,100
York Preparatory School, NY	$750,000
York School, CA	$1,367,560

SCHOOLS REPORTING THAT THEY OFFER ENGLISH AS A SECOND LANGUAGE

Academy of the New Church Boys' School, PA
Academy of the New Church Girls' School, PA
Académie Ste Cécile International School, ON, Canada

Admiral Farragut Academy, FL
Alliance Academy, Ecuador
Allison Academy, FL
American Academy, FL
American Community Schools of Athens, Greece
American Heritage School, FL
American Heritage School, FL
American International School, Dhaka, Bangladesh
American International School of Costa Rica, Costa Rica
The American School in London, United Kingdom
American School of Bombay, India
The American School of Madrid, Spain
American School of Milan, Italy
Army and Navy Academy, CA
The Athenian School, CA
The Awty International School, TX
Balmoral Hall School, MB, Canada
Bavarian International School, Germany
The Beekman School, NY
The Bement School, MA
Berlin International School, Germany
Bishop Brady High School, NH
Bishop's College School, QC, Canada
Bishop Walsh Middle High School, MD
Blanchet School, OR
The Blue Ridge School, VA
The Bolles School, FL
Boston College High School, MA
Branksome Hall, ON, Canada
Brewster Academy, NH
Burr and Burton Academy, VT
Buxton School, MA
Canadian Academy, Japan
Canyonville Christian Academy, OR
Cape Henry Collegiate School, VA
Capistrano Valley Christian Schools, CA
Cardigan Mountain School, NH
Carlucci American International School of Lisbon, Portugal
Chaminade College Preparatory School, MO
Chapel Hill–Chauncy Hall School, MA
Charlotte Country Day School, NC
Chinese Christian Schools, CA
Christ Church Episcopal School, SC
Christchurch School, VA
Colegio Franklin D. Roosevelt, Peru
Colegio Nueva Granada, Colombia
The Colorado Rocky Mountain School, CO
Columbia International College of Canada, ON, Canada
Community Hebrew Academy, ON, Canada
Cotter Schools, MN
Crawford Adventist Academy, ON, Canada
The Culver Academies, IN
Cushing Academy, MA
Dublin School, NH
Eaglebrook School, MA
Eastern Christian High School, NJ
Ecole d'Humanité, Switzerland
Emma Willard School, NY
Fay School, MA
Florida Air Academy, FL
Forsyth Country Day School, NC
Fort Lauderdale Preparatory School, FL
Fountain Valley School of Colorado, CO
French-American School of New York, NY
Fresno Adventist Academy, CA
Friends Select School, PA
Garrison Forest School, MD

George School, PA
George Stevens Academy, ME
Georgetown Preparatory School, MD
Germantown Friends School, PA
Glenlyon Norfolk School, BC, Canada
Gould Academy, ME
The Governor French Academy, IL
The Governor's Academy (formerly Governor Dummer
    Academy), MA
The Grauer School, CA
Greensboro Day School, NC
Gunston Day School, MD
Hamilton District Christian High, ON, Canada
Hank Haney International Junior Golf Academy, SC
Happy Hill Farm Academy, TX
Hargrave Military Academy, VA
Harrow School, United Kingdom
Hawaiian Mission Academy, HI
Holy Trinity High School, IL
Hoosac School, NY
Houghton Academy, NY
The Howe School, IN
The Hun School of Princeton, NJ
Hyde School, ME
Idyllwild Arts Academy, CA
Interlochen Arts Academy, MI
International College Spain, Spain
International High School, CA
International School Bangkok, Thailand
International School Hamburg, Germany
International School Manila, Philippines
International School of Amsterdam, Netherlands
International School of Athens, Greece
International School of Berne, Switzerland
The International School of Kuala Lumpur, Malaysia
The International School of London, United Kingdom
International School of Zug and Luzern (ISZL), Switzerland
Iolani School, HI
Kaplan College Preparatory School, FL
Kent School, CT
Key School, TX
The King's Academy, TN
King's-Edgehill School, NS, Canada
Kingsway College, ON, Canada
Kirov Academy of Ballet of Washington, D.C., DC
Lake Forest Academy, IL
Lake Mary Preparatory School, FL
Lake Ridge Academy, OH
La Lumiere School, IN
Lancaster Mennonite High School, PA
Laurel Springs School, CA
Lehigh Valley Christian High School, PA
Le Lycee Francais de Los Angeles, CA
Luther College High School, SK, Canada
Lydia Patterson Institute, TX
MacLachlan College, ON, Canada
Maine Central Institute, ME
Manlius Pebble Hill School, NY
Marine Military Academy, TX
Marylawn of the Oranges, NJ
Marymount International School, Italy
Marymount International School, United Kingdom
The Masters School, NY
Matignon High School, MA
Maur Hill-Mount Academy, KS
Memorial Hall School, TX
Menaul School, NM

Merchiston Castle School, United Kingdom
Mid-Pacific Institute, HI
Miss Porter's School, CT
Montclair College Preparatory School, CA
Monterey Bay Academy, CA
Monte Vista Christian School, CA
MPS Etobicoke, ON, Canada
Munich International School, Germany
Nebraska Christian Schools, NE
New English School, Kuwait
New English School, Kuwait
Niagara Christian Community of Schools, ON, Canada
North Country School, NY
The Northwest School, WA
Northwest Yeshiva High School, WA
Northwood School, NY
The Norwich Free Academy, CT
Notre Dame College Prep, IL
Oak Grove School, CA
Oak Hill Academy, VA
The Oakland School, PA
Oak Ridge Military Academy, NC
Ojai Valley School, CA
Oneida Baptist Institute, KY
Oregon Episcopal School, OR
Orinda Academy, CA
The Orme School, AZ
Our Lady of Mercy High School, NY
The Oxford Academy, CT
The Park School of Buffalo, NY
The Phelps School, PA
Phoenix Christian Unified Schools, AZ
Pickering College, ON, Canada
Pope John XXIII Regional High School, NJ
Porter-Gaud School, SC
Presbyterian Pan American School, TX
Professional Children's School, NY
Providence Christian School, AB, Canada
Queen of Peace High School, NJ
Randolph-Macon Academy, VA
The Rectory School, CT
Ridley College, ON, Canada
Rio Hondo Preparatory School, CA
Riverstone International School, ID
Rocklyn Academy, ON, Canada
Rock Point School, VT
Rolling Hills Preparatory School, CA
Rosseau Lake College, ON, Canada
Ross School, NY
Rothesay Netherwood School, NB, Canada
Rotterdam International Secondary School, Wolfert van Borselen,
    Netherlands
Royal Canadian College, BC, Canada
Sacred Heart School of Halifax, NS, Canada
Saddleback Valley Christian School, CA
Saddlebrook Preparatory School, FL
St. Andrew's College, ON, Canada
St. Andrew's Priory School, HI
St. Andrew's School, RI
St. Ann's Academy, BC, Canada
St. Anthony Catholic High School, TX
St. Benedict's Preparatory School, NJ
St. Catherine's Academy, CA
Saint Cecilia High School, NE
St. Clement School, ON, Canada
St. Croix Schools, MN
Saint Edward's School, FL

Saint Francis School, HI
St. George's School of Montreal, QC, Canada
St. John's Northwestern Military Academy, WI
St. John's-Ravenscourt School, MB, Canada
Saint Joseph Junior-Senior High School, HI
St. Jude's School, ON, Canada
St. Margaret's School, VA
Saint Mary's High School, AZ
St. Mary's Preparatory School, MI
St. Mary's School, OR
Saint Maur International School, Japan
St. Michael's Preparatory School of the Norbertine Fathers, CA
St. Michaels University School, BC, Canada
Saint Patrick High School, IL
St. Patrick's Regional Secondary, BC, Canada
St. Stanislaus College, MS
St. Stephen's Episcopal School, TX
St. Timothy's School, MD
Salem Academy, OR
Sandy Spring Friends School, MD
San Marcos Baptist Academy, TX
Scarborough Christian School, ON, Canada
SCECGS Redlands, Australia
Scholar's Hall Preparatory School, ON, Canada
Seisen International School, Japan
Seoul Foreign School, Republic of Korea
Shattuck-St. Mary's School, MN
Smith School, NY
Solomon College, AB, Canada
Southern Ontario College, ON, Canada
South Kent School, CT
Southwestern Academy, AZ
Southwestern Academy, CA
Squaw Valley Academy, CA
Stoneleigh–Burnham School, MA
Stratton Mountain School, VT
Suffield Academy, CT
Tabor Academy, MA
TASIS, The American School in Switzerland, Switzerland
The Tenney School, TX
Thomas Jefferson School, MO
Toronto District Christian High School, ON, Canada
Town Centre Private High School, ON, Canada
Trafalgar Castle School, ON, Canada
Trinity College School, ON, Canada
Trinity-Pawling School, NY
Tuscaloosa Academy, AL
United Nations International School, NY
The United World College—USA, NM
University School of Jackson, TN
Vail Mountain School, CO
Verdala International School, Malta
Wasatch Academy, UT
Watkinson School, CT
The Webb School, TN
The Wellington School, OH
Westover School, CT
West Sound Academy, WA
The White Mountain School, NH
The Williston Northampton School, MA
Willow Wood School, ON, Canada
Winchester Thurston School, PA
The Windsor School, NY
The Woodhall School, CT
Woodstock School, India
Worcester Academy, MA
Wyoming Seminary, PA

Yokohama International School, Japan
York Preparatory School, NY

SCHOOLS REPORTING A COMMUNITY SERVICE REQUIREMENT

The Academy for Gifted Children (PACE), ON, Canada
Academy of Our Lady of Mercy, CT
Academy of Our Lady of Peace, CA
Academy of the Holy Names, FL
Academy of the Sacred Heart, LA
Academy of the Sacred Heart, MI
Admiral Farragut Academy, FL
All Hallows High School, NY
Allison Academy, FL
American Academy, FL
American Heritage School, FL
American Heritage School, FL
Archbishop Curley High School, MD
Archbishop McNicholas High School, OH
The Archer School for Girls, CA
Armona Union Academy, CA
The Athenian School, CA
Auldern Academy, NC
The Awty International School, TX
Barrie School, MD
Beaumont School, OH
The Bement School, MA
Benedictine High School, OH
Berkeley Preparatory School, FL
The Birch Wathen Lenox School, NY
Bishop Brady High School, NH
Bishop Conaty-Our Lady of Loretto High School, CA
Bishop Connolly High School, MA
Bishop Denis J. O'Connell High School, VA
Bishop Eustace Preparatory School, NJ
Bishop Fenwick High School, OH
Bishop Guertin High School, NH
Bishop Ireton High School, VA
Bishop Kelly High School, ID
Bishop McGuinness Catholic High School, NC
Bishop Stang High School, MA
Blanchet School, OR
Boston College High School, MA
Boylan Central Catholic High School, IL
Breck School, MN
Brentwood School, CA
Briarwood Christian High School, AL
Brooks School, MA
Brunswick School, CT
The Bryn Mawr School for Girls, MD
The Buckley School, CA
Burr and Burton Academy, VT
The Calhoun School, NY
Campbell Hall (Episcopal), CA
Canterbury School, FL
The Canterbury School of Florida, FL
Cape Fear Academy, NC
Cape Henry Collegiate School, VA
Cardinal Mooney Catholic High School, FL
Cardinal Newman High School, FL
Carrollton School of the Sacred Heart, FL
Cascia Hall Preparatory School, OK
The Catholic High School of Baltimore, MD
The Catlin Gabel School, OR
Central Catholic High School, CA

Specialized Directories

Central Catholic High School, TX
Central Catholic Mid-High School, NE
CFS, The School at Church Farm, PA
Chaminade College Preparatory, CA
Chaminade College Preparatory School, MO
Chaminade-Madonna College Preparatory, FL
Chapel Hill–Chauncy Hall School, MA
Charles Wright Academy, WA
Charlotte Country Day School, NC
Chattanooga Christian School, TN
Cheverus High School, ME
Choate Rosemary Hall, CT
Christian Brothers Academy, NY
Christian Central Academy, NY
Christian Home and Bible School, FL
Christopher Columbus High School, FL
Cincinnati Country Day School, OH
Colegio San Jose, PR
Collegiate School, NY
The Collegiate School, VA
The Colorado Rocky Mountain School, CO
The Colorado Springs School, CO
The Columbus Academy, OH
Commonwealth Parkville School, PR
Commonwealth School, MA
Community Hebrew Academy, ON, Canada
The Community School of Naples, FL
Concordia Lutheran High School, IN
Convent of the Sacred Heart, CT
Cotter Schools, MN
Country Day School of the Sacred Heart, PA
Crespi Carmelite High School, CA
The Culver Academies, IN
Currey Ingram Academy, TN
Dakota Christian High School, SD
The Dalton School, NY
David Lipscomb High School, TN
Deerfield-Windsor School, GA
Delaware Valley Friends School, PA
Devon Preparatory School, PA
Donelson Christian Academy, TN
Dowling Catholic High School, IA
Duchesne Academy of the Sacred Heart, NE
Duchesne Academy of the Sacred Heart, TX
Durham Academy, NC
Eaglebrook School, MA
Eastern Christian High School, NJ
Eastside Catholic School, WA
Ecole d'Humanité, Switzerland
Edgewood Academy, AL
Edmund Burke School, DC
Elizabeth Seton High School, MD
Emma Willard School, NY
Episcopal High School of Jacksonville, FL
The Ethel Walker School, CT
Explorations Academy, WA
Father Lopez High School, FL
First Baptist Academy, TX
Flint Hill School, VA
Florida Air Academy, FL
Forest Lake Academy, FL
Forsyth Country Day School, NC
Fountain Valley School of Colorado, CO
Franklin Road Academy, TN
French-American School of New York, NY
Friends Academy, NY
Fuqua School, VA

Garces Memorial High School, CA
Gaston Day School, NC
Gateway School, TX
George School, PA
Georgetown Preparatory School, MD
Georgetown Visitation Preparatory School, DC
Gilmour Academy, OH
Girard College, PA
Glenelg Country School, MD
Glenlyon Norfolk School, BC, Canada
Gonzaga College High School, DC
The Governor's Academy (formerly Governor Dummer Academy), MA
The Grauer School, CA
Greenfield School, NC
Greenhill School, TX
Greenhills School, MI
Greenwich Academy, CT
Griggs International Academy, MD
Gulliver Preparatory School, FL
Gunston Day School, MD
Hamilton District Christian High, ON, Canada
Hampton Roads Academy, VA
Hanalani Schools, HI
The Harker School, CA
The Harley School, NY
Harrells Christian Academy, NC
Harvard-Westlake School, CA
Hawaiian Mission Academy, HI
Hawken School, OH
Head-Royce School, CA
Highland Hall Waldorf School, CA
Hillcrest Christian School, MS
Hilton Head Preparatory School, SC
Holy Ghost Preparatory School, PA
Holy Innocents' Episcopal School, GA
Holyoke Catholic High School, MA
Hopkins School, CT
The Hun School of Princeton, NJ
Hyman Brand Hebrew Academy of Greater Kansas City, KS
Immaculata-La Salle High School, FL
Immaculate Conception High School, NJ
Incarnate Word Academy, TX
Institute of Notre Dame, MD
International College Spain, Spain
International School Bangkok, Thailand
International School of Amsterdam, Netherlands
International School of Athens, Greece
The International School of London, United Kingdom
International School of Zug and Luzern (ISZL), Switzerland
Iona Preparatory School, NY
Jesuit College Preparatory School, TX
Jesuit High School of New Orleans, LA
Jesuit High School of Tampa, FL
J. K. Mullen High School, CO
Junipero Serra High School, CA
Kalamazoo Christian High School, MI
Keith Country Day School, IL
Kerr-Vance Academy, NC
King's Ridge Christian School, GA
Kingswood-Oxford School, CT
La Jolla Country Day School, CA
Lake Forest Academy, IL
Lakeside School, WA
La Lumiere School, IN
Landon School, MD
The Latin School of Chicago, IL

The Laureate Academy, MB, Canada
Lawrence School, OH
The Lawrenceville School, NJ
Lincoln Academy, ME
Linfield Christian School, CA
Lodi Academy, CA
Louisville High School, CA
Lutheran High School North, MO
Lutheran High School Northwest, MI
MacLachlan College, ON, Canada
Manhattan Christian High School, MT
Maret School, DC
Marin Academy, CA
The Marin School, CA
Marist School, GA
Marmion Academy, IL
Marquette University High School, WI
Mars Hill Bible School, AL
Maryknoll School, HI
Marylawn of the Oranges, NJ
Marymount High School, CA
Maryvale Preparatory School, MD
Matignon High School, MA
McDonogh School, MD
The Meadows School, NV
Memorial Hall School, TX
Menaul School, NM
Menlo School, CA
Mercy High School, CT
The Miami Valley School, OH
Miss Porter's School, CT
Moorestown Friends School, NJ
Moreau Catholic High School, CA
Morristown-Beard School, NJ
Mount Carmel High School, IL
Mount Michael Benedictine School, NE
Mt. Saint Dominic Academy, NJ
Munich International School, Germany
Nerinx Hall, MO
Newark Academy, NJ
The Nora School, MD
Norfolk Academy, VA
North Cobb Christian School, GA
North Shore Country Day School, IL
Northwest Catholic High School, CT
Northwest Yeshiva High School, WA
Notre Dame Academy, CA
Notre Dame College Prep, IL
Notre Dame High School, CA
Notre Dame High School, NJ
Oak Grove School, CA
Oak Hill School, OR
The Oakland School, PA
Oak Mountain Academy, GA
Oak Ridge Military Academy, NC
The Oakridge School, TX
Oldenburg Academy, IN
The O'Neal School, NC
Orinda Academy, CA
The Orme School, AZ
Out-Of-Door-Academy, FL
The Overlake School, WA
The Oxford Academy, CT
The Paideia School, GA
Paradise Adventist Academy, CA
The Park School of Buffalo, NY
Peddie School, NJ

The Phelps School, PA
Phoenix Country Day School, AZ
Pickering College, ON, Canada
The Pingry School, NJ
Pioneer Valley Christian School, MA
Pope John XXIII Regional High School, NJ
Poughkeepsie Day School, NY
Powers Catholic High School, MI
Providence Catholic School, The College Preparatory School for
    Girls Grades 6-12, TX
Riverdale Country School, NY
The Rivers School, MA
Rockland Country Day School, NY
Rock Point School, VT
Roland Park Country School, MD
Ross School, NY
Sacred Heart School of Halifax, NS, Canada
Sage Ridge School, NV
St. Agnes Academy, TX
St. Albans School, DC
St. Andrew's College, ON, Canada
St. Andrew's Priory School, HI
St. Andrew's School, RI
Saint Basil Academy, PA
St. Bernard's Catholic School, CA
St. Brendan High School, FL
St. Christopher's School, VA
St. Croix Country Day School, VI
St. David's School, NC
Saint Edward's School, FL
Saint Elizabeth High School, CA
St. Francis de Sales High School, OH
Saint Francis High School, CA
Saint Francis School, HI
St. Gregory College Preparatory School, AZ
St. John's Northwestern Military Academy, WI
Saint Joseph High School, IL
Saint Joseph High School, NJ
St. Joseph's Catholic School, SC
Saint Joseph's High School, NJ
St. Margaret's Episcopal School, CA
St. Margaret's School, VA
St. Mark's School of Texas, TX
St. Martin's Episcopal School, LA
Saint Mary's Hall, TX
Saint Mary's High School, AZ
St. Mary's School, OR
Saint Patrick High School, IL
St. Paul's Episcopal School, AL
St. Peter's Preparatory School, NJ
St. Pius X High School, TX
St. Stephen's & St. Agnes School, VA
Saint Stephen's Episcopal School, FL
St. Stephen's Episcopal School, TX
Saint Thomas Academy, MN
St. Thomas Aquinas High School, NH
St. Timothy's School, MD
St. Vincent Pallotti High School, MD
Salem Academy, OR
Salesianum School, DE
Sandy Spring Friends School, MD
Santa Fe Preparatory School, NM
Sayre School, KY
School of the Holy Child, NY
Seabury Hall, HI
Seattle Academy of Arts and Sciences, WA
The Seven Hills School, OH

Severn School, MD
Sewickley Academy, PA
Shannon Forest Christian School, SC
Shattuck-St. Mary's School, MN
The Shipley School, PA
Smith School, NY
Southwestern Academy, AZ
Southwestern Academy, CA
Springside School, PA
Stephen T. Badin High School, OH
Strake Jesuit College Preparatory, TX
Stratford Academy, GA
Stratton Mountain School, VT
Tandem Friends School, VA
TASIS, The American School in Switzerland, Switzerland
Thomas Jefferson School, MO
TMI—The Episcopal School of Texas, TX
Tower Hill School, DE
Town Centre Private High School, ON, Canada
Trinity College School, ON, Canada
Trinity High School, KY
Tuscaloosa Academy, AL
United Nations International School, NY
The United World College—USA, NM
University of Chicago Laboratory Schools, IL
University Prep, WA
University School of Jackson, TN
University School of Milwaukee, WI
University School of Nova Southeastern University, FL
Ursuline Academy, MA
The Ursuline Academy of Dallas, TX
Valle Catholic High School, MO
Vianney High School, MO
Villa Duchesne and Oak Hill School, MO
Villa Maria Academy, PA
Visitation Academy of St. Louis County, MO
Waldorf High School of Massachusetts Bay, MA
Wasatch Academy, UT
Waynflete School, ME
Webb School of Knoxville, TN
The Wellington School, OH
Wellsprings Friends School, OR
Wesleyan Academy, PR
Westbury Christian School, TX
Westchester Country Day School, NC
Westmark School, CA
Westover School, CT
Westridge School, CA
The Wheeler School, RI
The White Mountain School, NH
Willow Wood School, ON, Canada
Wilson Hall, SC
Windermere Preparatory School, FL
Winston Preparatory School, NY
The Winston School San Antonio, TX
Woodlynde School, PA
Woodstock School, India
Worcester Academy, MA
Wyoming Seminary, PA
Yokohama International School, Japan
York Country Day School, PA
York Preparatory School, NY
York School, CA

SCHOOLS REPORTING EXCHANGE PROGRAMS WITH OTHER U.S. SCHOOLS

Academy of the Sacred Heart, LA
Academy of the Sacred Heart, MI
The Athenian School, CA
The Calhoun School, NY
Carrollton School of the Sacred Heart, FL
Commonwealth Parkville School, PR
Convent of the Sacred Heart, CT
Convent of the Sacred Heart, NY
Country Day School of the Sacred Heart, PA
Crystal Springs Uplands School, CA
Doane Stuart School, NY
Dublin School, NH
Duchesne Academy of the Sacred Heart, NE
Duchesne Academy of the Sacred Heart, TX
Germantown Friends School, PA
Robinson School, PR, Puerto Rico
Sacred Heart School of Halifax, NS, Canada
St. Benedict's Preparatory School, NJ
Salesianum School, DE
School of the Holy Child, NY
Trafalgar Castle School, ON, Canada
Villa Duchesne and Oak Hill School, MO

SCHOOLS REPORTING PROGRAMS FOR STUDY ABROAD

The Academy at Charlemont, MA
Academy of Notre Dame de Namur, PA
Alexander Dawson School, CO
The Athenian School, CA
Baylor School, TN
Bayside Academy, AL
The Bement School, MA
Benedictine High School, OH
Berkeley Preparatory School, FL
Berwick Academy, ME
The Birch Wathen Lenox School, NY
Bishop's College School, QC, Canada
Blair Academy, NJ
Boston College High School, MA
Brewster Academy, NH
Brooks School, MA
The Bryn Mawr School for Girls, MD
The Buckley School, CA
Burr and Burton Academy, VT
The Canterbury School of Florida, FL
Carrollton School of the Sacred Heart, FL
Cascia Hall Preparatory School, OK
Catholic Central High School, WI
The Catlin Gabel School, OR
Central Catholic High School, TX
Charlotte Country Day School, NC
Charlotte Latin School, NC
Chicago Waldorf School, IL
Chinese Christian Schools, CA
Choate Rosemary Hall, CT
Cincinnati Country Day School, OH
Collegiate School, NY
Commonwealth Parkville School, PR
Commonwealth School, MA
The Community School of Naples, FL
Concord Academy, MA
Convent of the Sacred Heart, CT
Convent of the Sacred Heart, NY

Cotter Schools, MN
The Country Day School, ON, Canada
Country Day School of the Sacred Heart, PA
Crystal Springs Uplands School, CA
Damien High School, CA
Deerfield Academy, MA
Doane Stuart School, NY
Duchesne Academy of the Sacred Heart, NE
Emma Willard School, NY
The Episcopal Academy, PA
Episcopal High School, VA
Episcopal High School of Jacksonville, FL
The Ethel Walker School, CT
Falmouth Academy, MA
Foxcroft School, VA
Franklin Academy, CT
Gann Academy (The New Jewish High School of Greater
    Boston), MA
Georgetown Preparatory School, MD
Germantown Friends School, PA
Gill St. Bernard's School, NJ
Gould Academy, ME
The Governor's Academy (formerly Governor Dummer
    Academy), MA
The Grauer School, CA
Greater Atlanta Christian Schools, GA
Greensboro Day School, NC
Greenwich Academy, CT
Groton School, MA
Gunston Day School, MD
The Harley School, NY
Harvard-Westlake School, CA
Hawken School, OH
Head-Royce School, CA
Hebrew Academy-the Five Towns, NY
The Hewitt School, NY
Highland Hall Waldorf School, CA
Holy Ghost Preparatory School, PA
Holy Innocents' Episcopal School, GA
Hopkins School, CT
The Hotchkiss School, CT
International High School, CA
Iona Preparatory School, NY
Keith Country Day School, IL
Kentucky Country Day School, KY
Kimball Union Academy, NH
King George School, VT
King's-Edgehill School, NS, Canada
Kingswood-Oxford School, CT
La Jolla Country Day School, CA
Lakefield College School, ON, Canada
Lake Forest Academy, IL
Lakehill Preparatory School, TX
Lake Mary Preparatory School, FL
Lakeside School, WA
Landon School, MD
The Latin School of Chicago, IL
The Lawrenceville School, NJ
Louisville Collegiate School, KY
The Lovett School, GA
Loyola Academy, IL
Luther College High School, SK, Canada
Maine Central Institute, ME
Manlius Pebble Hill School, NY
Maret School, DC
Marin Academy, CA
The Masters School, NY

Matignon High School, MA
Meadowridge School, BC, Canada
Memphis University School, TN
Merchiston Castle School, United Kingdom
The Miami Valley School, OH
Millbrook School, NY
Milton Academy, MA
Miss Porter's School, CT
Moorestown Friends School, NJ
Morristown-Beard School, NJ
Newark Academy, NJ
The Nichols School, NY
Norfolk Academy, VA
North Shore Country Day School, IL
The Oakridge School, TX
Ojai Valley School, CA
Oregon Episcopal School, OR
The Overlake School, WA
Padua Franciscan High School, OH
The Park School of Buffalo, NY
Peddie School, NJ
Phillips Academy (Andover), MA
Phoenix Country Day School, AZ
The Pingry School, NJ
Polytechnic School, CA
Providence Country Day School, RI
Providence Day School, NC
Randolph-Macon Academy, VA
Regis High School, NY
Ridley College, ON, Canada
Rio Hondo Preparatory School, CA
Riverdale Country School, NY
Riverstone International School, ID
Roland Park Country School, MD
Rosseau Lake College, ON, Canada
Rundle College, AB, Canada
Sacred Heart School of Halifax, NS, Canada
Saddleback Valley Christian School, CA
St. Andrew's College, ON, Canada
St. Anthony Catholic High School, TX
Saint Augustine Preparatory School, NJ
St. Catherine's School, VA
Saint Edward's School, FL
St. George's School, RI
St. John's Preparatory School, MA
Saint Joseph Academy High School, OH
St. Joseph's Preparatory School, PA
St. Margaret's School, VA
Saint Mark's School, MA
Saint Mary's Hall, TX
Saint Mary's High School, MD
St. Michaels University School, BC, Canada
St. Paul Academy and Summit School, MN
St. Peter's Preparatory School, NJ
St. Stephen's & St. Agnes School, VA
St. Stephen's Episcopal School, TX
Sandia Preparatory School, NM
Santa Fe Preparatory School, NM
School of the Holy Child, NY
Seattle Academy of Arts and Sciences, WA
Second Baptist School, TX
Severn School, MD
Sewickley Academy, PA
Shady Side Academy, PA
The Shipley School, PA
Sonoma Academy, CA
Southwest Christian School, Inc., TX

The Spence School, NY	
Springside School, PA	
The Stanwich School, CT	
Stephen T. Badin High School, OH	
Stevenson School, CA	
Summerfield Waldorf School, CA	
Telluride Mountain School, CO	
The Thacher School, CA	
Toronto District Christian High School, ON, Canada	
Trinity College School, ON, Canada	
Trinity High School, KY	
Trinity School of Texas, TX	
University Prep, WA	
Villa Duchesne and Oak Hill School, MO	
Waldorf High School of Massachusetts Bay, MA	
The Walker School, GA	
Waring School, MA	
Waynflete School, ME	
The Webb School, TN	
Webb School of Knoxville, TN	
The Wellington School, OH	
Western Reserve Academy, OH	
West Island College, AB, Canada	
Westover School, CT	
The Wheeler School, RI	
The Williams School, CT	
The Williston Northampton School, MA	
Willow Wood School, ON, Canada	
Winchester Thurston School, PA	
Woodstock School, India	
Wyoming Seminary, PA	
York Country Day School, PA	

SCHOOLS REPORTING SUMMER SESSIONS OPEN TO STUDENTS FROM OTHER SCHOOLS*

The Academy at Charlemont, MA	F,S
Academy of Notre Dame de Namur, PA	A,C,S
Academy of the Holy Cross, MD	A,C,F,S
Academy of the Holy Names, FL	F,S
Academy of the New Church Boys' School, PA	A,C,F,S
Academy of the New Church Girls' School, PA	A,C,F
Academy of the Sacred Heart, MI	A,C,F,S
Académie Ste Cécile International School, ON, Canada	A,F
Allendale Columbia School, NY	A,F,S
Allison Academy, FL	A
Alma Heights Christian High School, CA	A,C,F,R,S
American Academy, FL	A,C,F
American Community Schools of Athens, Greece	A,C,F,S
American Heritage School, FL	A,C,F
American Heritage School, FL	A,C,F
The American School of Madrid, Spain	A,C,F,S
Archbishop Alter High School, OH	A,S
Archbishop Curley High School, MD	A,C,F,S
Archbishop Mitty High School, CA	A,C,F,S
Archbishop Rummel High School, LA	A,C,F,R,S
Army and Navy Academy, CA	A,C,F,R,S
ASSETS School, HI	A
The Athenian School, CA	A,C,F,S
Augusta Christian School (I), GA	A
The Baldwin School, PA	A,C,F
The Baltimore Actors' Theatre Conservatory, MD	A,F
Baltimore Lutheran Middle and Upper School, MD	A,S
Barrie School, MD	A
Bavarian International School, Germany	A,C,F,S
Baylor School, TN	A,C,F,R,S

The Beekman School, NY	A
Bellarmine College Preparatory, CA	A,C,F,S
Benedictine High School, OH	A,C,S
Berkeley Preparatory School, FL	A,C,F,S
Berwick Academy, ME	A,S
Bishop Brady High School, NH	A,S
Bishop Conaty-Our Lady of Loretto High School, CA	A,C,F
Bishop Denis J. O'Connell High School, VA	A,C,F,S
Bishop Eustace Preparatory School, NJ	A,S
Bishop Ireton High School, VA	A,C,F
Bishop Luers High School, IN	A,S
Bishop Montgomery High School, CA	A,C,F,S
Bishop O'Dowd High School, CA	A,C
Bishop's College School, QC, Canada	A,C,F,R,S
Blanchet School, OR	A,S
Blueprint Education, AZ	A
The Bolles School, FL	A,C,F
Boston College High School, MA	A,C,F,S
Boylan Central Catholic High School, IL	A,F,R,S
Brentwood School, CA	A,C,F,S
Brewster Academy, NH	A,C,F,S
Bridges Academy, CA	A,C,F,S
Brooks School, MA	A,C,S
Brother Rice High School, MI	A,F
Brunswick School, CT	A
The Bryn Mawr School for Girls, MD	A,F,S
The Buckley School, CA	A,C,F
The Byrnes Schools, SC	A
The Calhoun School, NY	F
Calvert Hall College High School, MD	A,C,F,S
The Calverton School, MD	A,C,F,S
Calvin Christian High School, CA	S
Campbell Hall (Episcopal), CA	A,C,F,S
Canadian Academy, Japan	A,C,S
Canterbury School, FL	A,F,S
The Canterbury School of Florida, FL	A,C,F,S
Canton Academy, MS	A
Cape Fear Academy, NC	A,F,S
Cape Henry Collegiate School, VA	A,C,F,S
Capistrano Valley Christian Schools, CA	A,S
Cardigan Mountain School, NH	A,C,F,S
Cardinal Mooney Catholic High School, FL	A,S
Cascia Hall Preparatory School, OK	A,F,S
Cathedral High School, NY	A
Catholic Central High School, WI	S
The Catlin Gabel School, OR	A,C,F
Cedar Ridge Academy, UT	A
Central Catholic High School, CA	A
Central Catholic High School, OH	A,S
Central Catholic High School, PA	A
Central Catholic High School, TX	A,C,S
Chamberlain-Hunt Academy, MS	A,R,S
Chaminade College Preparatory, CA	A,C,S
Chaminade College Preparatory School, MO	A,S
Charlotte Christian School, NC	A,C,F,R,S
Charlotte Country Day School, NC	A,C,F,S
Charlotte Latin School, NC	A,C,F,S
Chattanooga Christian School, TN	A,C,F,S
Cheverus High School, ME	A
Chinese Christian Schools, CA	A,S
Choate Rosemary Hall, CT	A,F,S
Christ Church Episcopal School, SC	A,S
Christchurch School, VA	A,S
Christian Brothers Academy, NY	S
Christian Central Academy, NY	S
Chrysalis School, WA	A,C
Cincinnati Country Day School, OH	A,C,F,S

*Coeducational in lower grades; A — academic; C — computer instruction; F — art/fine arts; R — rigorous outdoor training; S — sports; O — other

Cistercian Preparatory School, TX	A,F,S
Clearwater Central Catholic High School, FL	A,C,S
Colegio San Jose, PR	A
Collegedale Academy, TN	A
The Collegiate School, VA	A,C,F,S
The Colorado Springs School, CO	A,C,F,S
Columbia International College of Canada, ON, Canada	A,C,F,S
The Columbus Academy, OH	A,C,F
Columbus School for Girls, OH	A,C,F,R,S
Commonwealth Parkville School, PR	A,C,F,S
The Community School of Naples, FL	A,F,S
Concordia Lutheran High School, IN	O
Convent of the Sacred Heart, NY	C,F,S
The Country Day School, ON, Canada	A,F,S
Crespi Carmelite High School, CA	A,F,S
Crossroads College Preparatory School, MO	A,F,S
The Culver Academies, IN	A,C,F,S
Currey Ingram Academy, TN	A,F,S
Cushing Academy, MA	A,C,F,S
Damien High School, CA	A,C,F,S
Damien Memorial School, HI	A
David Lipscomb High School, TN	A,F,S
Davidson Academy, TN	A,F,S
Delaware Valley Friends School, PA	A,F
DeMatha Catholic High School, MD	A,C,F,S
DePaul Catholic High School, NJ	S
The Derryfield School, NH	F
Duchesne Academy of the Sacred Heart, TX	A,C,F
Durham Academy, NC	A,C,F,S
Eaglebrook School, MA	A,C,F,R,S
Eagle Hill-Southport, CT	A
Edgewood Academy, AL	O
Edmund Burke School, DC	A,C,F
Elgin Academy, IL	A,F,S
Elizabeth Seton High School, MD	A,F,S
The Episcopal Academy, PA	A,C,F
Episcopal Collegiate School, AR	A,C,F,S
Episcopal High School, TX	A,F
Episcopal High School, VA	A,F,S
Episcopal High School of Jacksonville, FL	A,C,F,R,S
Explorations Academy, WA	A,F,R
Fairhill School, TX	A,C
Father Ryan High School, TN	A,C,F,S
Fayetteville Academy, NC	A,C,F,S
Fay School, MA	A,C,F,S
Fenwick High School, IL	A,C
The First Academy, FL	A,F,S
First Presbyterian Day School, GA	A,F,S
Flint Hill School, VA	A,C,F,R,S
Florida Air Academy, FL	A,C,S
Foothills Academy, AB, Canada	A
Forsyth Country Day School, NC	A
Fort Lauderdale Preparatory School, FL	A,C
Foundation Academy, FL	F,S
Fountain Valley School of Colorado, CO	A,C,R,S
Fowlers Academy, PR	A
Franklin Academy, CT	A
Franklin Road Academy, TN	A,C,F,S
Frederica Academy, GA	A,C,F,S
Fresno Adventist Academy, CA	A
Friends Academy, NY	F
Friends' Central School, PA	A
Friends Select School, PA	A,C,F
Fuqua School, VA	S
Garces Memorial High School, CA	A,C,F,S
Garrison Forest School, MD	F,S
Gaston Day School, NC	A,F,S
The Geneva School, FL	A,F,S
George Stevens Academy, ME	A,F,S
Georgetown Preparatory School, MD	A,S
Gill St. Bernard's School, NJ	A,F,S
Gilman School, MD	A,F,R,S
Gilmour Academy, OH	S
Girard College, PA	A,C,F,S
Girls Preparatory School, TN	A,C,F,S
Glenelg Country School, MD	S
The Glenholme School, a Devereux Center, CT	A,C,F,S
Gonzaga College High School, DC	A
The Governor French Academy, IL	A
The Governor's Academy (formerly Governor Dummer Academy), MA	A,F,S
Grace Baptist Academy, TN	A
The Grauer School, CA	A,C,F,R,S
Greater Atlanta Christian Schools, GA	A,F,S
Greenfield School, NC	A,C,F,S
Greenhill School, TX	A,C,F,S
Greenhills School, MI	A,F,R,S
Greensboro Day School, NC	A,C,F,S
Greenwich Academy, CT	A,F,S
Griggs International Academy, MD	A
Gwynedd Mercy Academy, PA	S
Hackley School, NY	S
Hamden Hall Country Day School, CT	A,C,F,S
Hampton Roads Academy, VA	A,C,F,S
Hanalani Schools, HI	A,C,F,S
Hank Haney International Junior Golf Academy, SC	A,S
Harding Academy, TN	A,C,F,S
Hargrave Military Academy, VA	A,C,R,S
The Harker School, CA	A
The Harley School, NY	A,C,F,S
Harrow School, United Kingdom	A,S
Harvard-Westlake School, CA	A,C,F,R,S
The Harvey School, NY	A
Hawaii Baptist Academy, HI	A,C,F,S
Hawken School, OH	A,C
Head-Royce School, CA	A
The Hill Top Preparatory School, PA	A
Hilton Head Preparatory School, SC	A,C,F,S
Holy Ghost Preparatory School, PA	A,C,S
Holy Innocents' Episcopal School, GA	A,F,S
Hopkins School, CT	A,C,F,R,S
The Hotchkiss School, CT	F
The Howard School, GA	A
The Howe School, IN	A
The Hun School of Princeton, NJ	A,C,F
Huntington-Surrey School, TX	A
Hyde School, ME	A,F,R,S
Idyllwild Arts Academy, CA	A,F
Immaculata-La Salle High School, FL	A
Incarnate Word Academy, TX	S
Institute of Notre Dame, MD	A,C,F,R,S
Interlochen Arts Academy, MI	F
International High School, CA	A,F
International School Bangkok, Thailand	A,F
International School Manila, Philippines	A
International School of Athens, Greece	A,C,F,S
The International School of Kuala Lumpur, Malaysia	A,C,F,R,S
Iolani School, HI	A,C,F,S
Isidore Newman School, LA	A,C,F,S
Island School, HI	A,S
Jackson Preparatory School, MS	A,C,F
Jesuit College Preparatory School, TX	A,C,F,S
The John Cooper School, TX	A,C,F,S
Junipero Serra High School, CA	A,C,F,R,S

*Coeducational in lower grades; A — academic; C — computer instruction; F — art/fine arts; R — rigorous outdoor training; S — sports; O — other

Specialized Directories

Kaplan College Preparatory School, FL	A,C,F	Middlesex School, MA	F
Kauai Christian Academy, HI	A,C	Mid-Pacific Institute, HI	A,C,F
Keith Country Day School, IL	A,F,S	Miss Porter's School, CT	A,F,S
Kentucky Country Day School, KY	A,C,F,R,S	MMI Preparatory School, PA	A,C
Kerr-Vance Academy, NC	A	Montclair College Preparatory School, CA	A,C,S
The Kew-Forest School, NY	A	Montclair Kimberley Academy, NJ	A,C,F,S
Key School, TX	A,C	Monte Vista Christian School, CA	A,S
Kildonan School, NY	A,F	Moravian Academy, PA	A,F
Kimball Union Academy, NH	A,F,S	Moreau Catholic High School, CA	A,S
King Low Heywood Thomas, CT	A,C,F,S	Morristown-Beard School, NJ	A,C,F,S
Kingshill School, VI	A	Mother McAuley High School, IL	A,C,F,S
Kirov Academy of Ballet of Washington, D.C., DC	F	Mount Mercy Academy, NY	A
La Jolla Country Day School, CA	A,C,F,S	Mount Saint Charles Academy, RI	F,S
Lake Forest Academy, IL	A	Mt. Saint Dominic Academy, NJ	A,S
Lakehill Preparatory School, TX	A,C,F,S	MPS Etobicoke, ON, Canada	A,C,F,S
Lake Ridge Academy, OH	A,C,F,S	Munich International School, Germany	R,S
Lakeside School, WA	A,C,F,S	National High School, GA	A,C,F
La Lumiere School, IN	A	Nazareth Academy, IL	S
Lancaster Mennonite High School, PA	A,S	Newark Academy, NJ	A,C,F,S
Landmark School, MA	A	The Nichols School, NY	A,F
Landon School, MD	A,F	Noble Academy, NC	A,C
La Salle High School, CA	A,C,F,S	Norfolk Academy, VA	A,F,S
The Latin School of Chicago, IL	A,C,F,R,S	North Cobb Christian School, GA	A,C,F,S
The Laureate Academy, MB, Canada	A	North Country School, NY	O
Laurel Springs School, CA	A,C,F	North Shore Country Day School, IL	A,C,F,R,S
Le Lycee Francais de Los Angeles, CA	O	The Northwest School, WA	A,C,F,S
Leo Catholic High School, IL	A,S	The Norwich Free Academy, CT	A,S
Lima Central Catholic High School, OH	A,S	Notre Dame College Prep, IL	A,C,F,S
Linfield Christian School, CA	F,S	Notre Dame High School, CA	A
The Linsly School, WV	A,C	Notre Dame High School, NJ	A,F,S
Little Keswick School, VA	A,C,F,R,S	Notre Dame High School, TN	A,F,S
Long Island Lutheran Middle and High School, NY	C,F,S	Oak Grove School, CA	A
Los Angeles Baptist Middle School/High School, CA	A,C,S	Oak Hill Academy, VA	A
Louisville Collegiate School, KY	A,C,F,S	Oak Knoll School of the Holy Child, NJ	A,S
Louisville High School, CA	S	Oakland School, VA	A,C,F,S
The Lovett School, GA	A	Oak Mountain Academy, GA	A,F,S
Loyola Academy, IL	A,C,F,S	Oak Ridge Military Academy, NC	A
Lutheran High School, CA	A,S	The Oakridge School, TX	A,C,F,R,S
Luther High School North, IL	A,C,S	Ojai Valley School, CA	A,C,F
Lydia Patterson Institute, TX	A	Oneida Baptist Institute, KY	A
Lyman Ward Military Academy, AL	A,R	Orangewood Christian School, FL	A,C,F,R,S
Madison-Ridgeland Academy, MS	A,S	Oregon Episcopal School, OR	A,C,F,S
Maine Central Institute, ME	A,F	Orinda Academy, CA	A
Manlius Pebble Hill School, NY	A,C,F,S	The Orme School, AZ	A
Maplebrook School, NY	A,C,F,S	Our Lady of Mercy High School, NY	A,C,F,S
Maret School, DC	A,F,S	Out-Of-Door-Academy, FL	A,F,S
Marian Central Catholic High School, IL	S	The Oxford Academy, CT	A
Marian High School, IN	C,F,S	Padua Franciscan High School, OH	A,C,F,S
Marine Military Academy, TX	A,R	The Paideia School, GA	A
Marist School, GA	A,F,S	Paradise Adventist Academy, CA	S
Marlborough School, CA	A,C,F,S	The Park School of Buffalo, NY	A,S
Mars Hill Bible School, AL	A,F,S	The Pathway School, PA	A
Martin Luther High School, NY	A,C	Peddie School, NJ	A,F,S
Maryknoll School, HI	A,C,F,S	The Phelps School, PA	S
Marylawn of the Oranges, NJ	A,C	Phillips Academy (Andover), MA	A,C,F
Marymount High School, CA	A,C,F,S	Phoenix Country Day School, AZ	A,C,F,S
Mary Star of the Sea High School, CA	A,F	Pickering College, ON, Canada	A
Maryvale Preparatory School, MD	A,C,F,S	Piedmont Academy, GA	F,R,S
Matignon High School, MA	A	Pine Crest School, FL	A,S
Maur Hill-Mount Academy, KS	A	The Pingry School, NJ	A,S
McDonogh School, MD	A,C,F,S	Pope John XXIII Regional High School, NJ	A,S
The Meadows School, NV	A	Portsmouth Abbey School, RI	A
Memorial Hall School, TX	A,C	Portsmouth Christian Academy, NH	A,S
Memphis University School, TN	A,S	The Potomac School, VA	A,F,S
Menlo School, CA	A	Poughkeepsie Day School, NY	F
Mercy High School College Preparatory, CA	A	Prestonwood Christian Academy, TX	A,C,F,R,S
Merion Mercy Academy, PA	A,F,S		

Coeducational in lower grades; A — academic; C — computer instruction; F — art/fine arts; R — rigorous outdoor training; S — sports; O — other

Providence Catholic School, The College Preparatory School for Girls Grades 6-12, TX	A,C,F,S
Providence Day School, NC	A,C,F,S
Providence High School, CA	A,C,F,S
Queen of Peace High School, NJ	A,C
Randolph-Macon Academy, VA	A,C,F
Randolph School, AL	A,S
Ranney School, NJ	A,C,F,S
Ransom Everglades School, FL	A,C
The Rectory School, CT	A,F,S
Reitz Memorial High School, IN	A,S
Rivermont Collegiate, IA	A,S
Riverstone International School, ID	A,F,R
Robert Louis Stevenson School, NY	A
Robinson School, PR, Puerto Rico	A,C,F,R,S
Rocklyn Academy, ON, Canada	R,S
The Roeper School, MI	F
Roland Park Country School, MD	A,F,S
Rosseau Lake College, ON, Canada	A
Ross School, NY	A,F,S
Rowland Hall, UT	A,C,F,S
The Roxbury Latin School, MA	A,C,S
Royal Canadian College, BC, Canada	A
Rye Country Day School, NY	A,C,F,S
Sacred Heart School of Halifax, NS, Canada	A
Saddlebrook Preparatory School, FL	A
Sage Hill School, CA	A,F,S
Sage Ridge School, NV	A,F
St. Albans School, DC	A,C,F,R,S
St. Andrew's College, ON, Canada	A,F,S
St. Andrew's Priory School, HI	A,C,F,R,S
St. Andrew's School, RI	A,C,F,R,S
St. Anthony Catholic High School, TX	A,S
St. Anthony's Junior-Senior High School, HI	A
Saint Augustine Preparatory School, NJ	A,C,F,R,S
Saint Basil Academy, PA	A,S
St. Bernard's Catholic School, CA	A
St. Brendan High School, FL	A,C
St. Catherine's Academy, CA	A,C,F,S
St. Catherine's School, VA	A,F,S
Saint Cecilia High School, NE	S
St. Christopher's School, VA	A
St. Clement's School, ON, Canada	A,F
St. Croix Schools, MN	A,S
St. David's School, NC	A,C,F,S
Saint Dominic Academy, ME	A,C,F,S
Saint Edward's School, FL	A,C,F,S
Saint Francis Girls High School, CA	A,F,S
Saint Francis High School, CA	A,S
Saint Francis School, HI	A,C
St. George's Independent School, TN	A,C,F,S
St. George's School, BC, Canada	A,C,F,S
St. John's Northwestern Military Academy, WI	A,C
St. John's Preparatory School, MA	A,C,F,S
Saint Joseph High School, IL	A,C,F,S
Saint Joseph High School, NJ	A
Saint Joseph Junior-Senior High School, HI	A,C,F,S
St. Joseph's Catholic School, SC	F,S
Saint Joseph's High School, NJ	A,C,S
St. Joseph's Preparatory School, PA	A,F
St. Jude's School, ON, Canada	O
St. Margaret's Episcopal School, CA	A,F,S
St. Martin's Episcopal School, LA	A,C,F,S
St. Mary's Episcopal School, TN	A,F,S
Saint Mary's Hall, TX	A,C,F,S
St. Mary's Preparatory School, MI	A,S
Saint Mary's School, NC	A,C,F,S
St. Mary's School, OR	A,C,F,S
Saint Maur International School, Japan	A,C,F,S
St. Michaels University School, BC, Canada	A,C,F,S
Saint Patrick High School, IL	A,C,F,S
Saint Patrick—Saint Vincent High School, CA	A,F,S
St. Paul's Episcopal School, AL	A,C,F,S
St. Paul's High School, MB, Canada	S
St. Peter's Preparatory School, NJ	A,F,S
St. Stanislaus College, MS	A
St. Stephen's & St. Agnes School, VA	A,C,F
Saint Stephen's Episcopal School, FL	A,C,F,S
St. Stephen's Episcopal School, TX	F,S
Saint Thomas Aquinas High School, KS	A,S
Saint Thomas More Catholic High School, LA	A,C,F,S
St. Timothy's School, MD	A
Saint Ursula Academy, OH	A,C,F,S
St. Vincent Pallotti High School, MD	A,S
Salesian High School, CA	A,C,F,S
Salt Lake Lutheran High School, UT	S
Sandia Preparatory School, NM	A,C,F,S
Sandy Spring Friends School, MD	A,F,S
Sanford School, DE	A,C,F
Scholar's Hall Preparatory School, ON, Canada	A
School of the Holy Child, NY	A,F,S
Seabury Hall, HI	A,F,S
Seattle Academy of Arts and Sciences, WA	A,F,S
Selwyn House School, QC, Canada	S
Seton Catholic Central High School, NY	A,S
Seton Catholic High School, AZ	A,S
The Seven Hills School, OH	A
Severn School, MD	A,C,F,S
Sewickley Academy, PA	A,F,S
Shady Side Academy, PA	A,C,F,S
Shattuck-St. Mary's School, MN	A,F,S
Shelton School and Evaluation Center, TX	A
Sheridan Academy, ID	A,C
The Shipley School, PA	S
Shoore Centre for Learning, ON, Canada	A
Smith School, NY	A,C
South Kent School, CT	A,C
Southwest Christian School, Inc., TX	A,C,F,S
Southwestern Academy, AZ	A,F,R
Southwestern Academy, CA	A,C,F
Spartanburg Day School, SC	A,C,F,S
Springside School, PA	A,C,F,S
Squaw Valley Academy, CA	A,F,S
Sterne School, CA	A
Stevenson School, CA	A
Stoneleigh–Burnham School, MA	A,F,S
Strake Jesuit College Preparatory, TX	A,S
Suffield Academy, CT	A,C,F
Tabor Academy, MA	A
Taipei American School, Taiwan	A
TASIS, The American School in Switzerland, Switzerland	A,F,S
The Tenney School, TX	A,C
Thomas Jefferson School, MO	A
Timothy Christian High School, IL	F,S
TMI—The Episcopal School of Texas, TX	A,S
Tower Hill School, DE	A,S
Town Centre Private High School, ON, Canada	A
Trinity College School, ON, Canada	A,C,F
Trinity Preparatory School, FL	A,C,F,S
Trinity School of Texas, TX	A,C,F,S
Tuscaloosa Academy, AL	A,C,F,S
United Nations International School, NY	A,C,F,S
University of Chicago Laboratory Schools, IL	A,S
University School of Jackson, TN	A,C,F,S

Coeducational in lower grades; A — academic; C — computer instruction; F — art/fine arts; R — rigorous outdoor training; S — sports; O — other

University School of Milwaukee, WI	A,C,F,S
University School of Nova Southeastern University, FL	A,F,S
Vail Mountain School, CO	A,F,S
The Vanguard School, FL	A
Vianney High School, MO	S
Villa Duchesne and Oak Hill School, MO	A,C,F,S
Village Christian Schools, CA	A,C,F,S
Villa Joseph Marie High School, PA	A,S
Visitation Academy of St. Louis County, MO	S
The Walker School, GA	A
Waring School, MA	F
Wasatch Academy, UT	A
Watkinson School, CT	A
Waynflete School, ME	A,F,S
Webb School of Knoxville, TN	A,F,S
The Wellington School, OH	A,F,S
Wellspring Foundation, CT	A
Wesleyan Academy, PR	A
Westbury Christian School, TX	S
Westchester Country Day School, NC	A,C,F,S
Western Christian Schools, CA	A
Western Mennonite School, OR	S
Western Reserve Academy, OH	A,S
Westmark School, CA	A,C,F
Westridge School, CA	F
West Sound Academy, WA	A
Wheaton Academy, IL	A,C,F,S
The Wheeler School, RI	O
The White Mountain School, NH	S
The Williams School, CT	S
The Williston Northampton School, MA	F,S
Willow Wood School, ON, Canada	A,C
Winchester Thurston School, PA	A,F,S
Windermere Preparatory School, FL	A,F,S
The Windsor School, NY	A,C,F
Windward School, CA	S
Winston Preparatory School, NY	A,F
The Winston School San Antonio, TX	A,C,S
Woodlynde School, PA	A,F,S
Worcester Academy, MA	A
Wyoming Seminary, PA	A,C,F
Yokohama International School, Japan	A,S
York Country Day School, PA	F,S

SCHOOLS REPORTING THAT THEY ACCOMMODATE UNDERACHIEVERS

American Academy, FL
Arrowsmith School, ON, Canada
Aspen Ranch, UT
Auldern Academy, NC
The Blue Ridge School, VA
Camphill Special School, PA
Cedar Ridge Academy, UT
Chatham Academy, GA
Cross Creek Programs, UT
Eagle Hill-Southport, CT
Elan School, ME
The Family Foundation School, NY
Foothills Academy, AB, Canada
Fowlers Academy, PR
The Frostig School, CA
Gateway School, TX
Glen Eden School, BC, Canada
The Glenholme School, a Devereux Center, CT
The Greenwood School, VT

Hampshire Country School, NH
Harmony Heights Residential and Day School, NY
The Hill Center, Durham Academy, NC
Humanex Academy, CO
The John Dewey Academy, MA
The Judge Rotenberg Educational Center, MA
The Karafin School, NY
Key School, TX
King George School, VT
Kingshill School, VI
Little Keswick School, VA
Lyman Ward Military Academy, AL
Maplebrook School, NY
Oakland School, VA
The Pathway School, PA
The Phelps School, PA
The Rectory School, CT
Robert Louis Stevenson School, NY
St. John's Northwestern Military Academy, WI
St. Jude's School, ON, Canada
Shoore Centre for Learning, ON, Canada
Sterne School, CA
Stone Mountain School, NC
Sunhawk Adolescent Recovery Center, UT
Valley View School, MA
The Vanguard School, FL
Wellsprings Friends School, OR
Winston Preparatory School, NY

SCHOOLS REPORTING PROGRAMS FOR STUDENTS WITH SPECIAL NEEDS

Remedial Reading and/or Writing

Academy of the New Church Boys' School, PA
Academy of the New Church Girls' School, PA
Académie Ste Cécile International School, ON, Canada
Admiral Farragut Academy, FL
Alexander Dawson School, CO
All Hallows High School, NY
Alliance Academy, Ecuador
Allison Academy, FL
American Academy, FL
American Community Schools of Athens, Greece
American International School of Costa Rica, Costa Rica
American School of Milan, Italy
American School of The Hague, Netherlands
Archbishop Curley High School, MD
Archbishop Hoban High School, OH
Archbishop McNicholas High School, OH
Arrowsmith School, ON, Canada
Aspen Ranch, UT
ASSETS School, HI
Auldern Academy, NC
Bavarian International School, Germany
The Beekman School, NY
Benedictine High School, OH
Berlin International School, Germany
Bishop Conaty-Our Lady of Loretto High School, CA
Bishop Luers High School, IN
Bishop O'Dowd High School, CA
Bishop Stang High School, MA
Bishop Walsh Middle High School, MD
Blue Mountain Academy, PA
Blueprint Education, AZ
The Blue Ridge School, VA
Boylan Central Catholic High School, IL
Brother Rice High School, IL
Brother Rice High School, MI
Burr and Burton Academy, VT

Coeducational in lower grades; A — academic; C — computer instruction; F — art/fine arts; R — rigorous outdoor training; S — sports; O — other

Calvin Christian High School, CA
Camphill Special School, PA
Cardigan Mountain School, NH
Cardinal Newman High School, FL
Carlucci American International School of Lisbon, Portugal
Cascade Christian Academy, WA
Cathedral High School, NY
The Catholic High School of Baltimore, MD
Cedar Ridge Academy, UT
Central Catholic High School, CA
Chamberlain-Hunt Academy, MS
Chaminade-Madonna College Preparatory, FL
Chatham Academy, GA
Chattanooga Christian School, TN
Chinese Christian Schools, CA
Christopher Columbus High School, FL
Christopher Dock Mennonite High School, PA
Chrysalis School, WA
Community High School, NJ
The Concept School, PA
Cotter Schools, MN
Covenant Canadian Reformed School, AB, Canada
Crawford Adventist Academy, ON, Canada
Cross Creek Programs, UT
Currey Ingram Academy, TN
Cushing Academy, MA
Damien High School, CA
Delaware Valley Friends School, PA
DeMatha Catholic High School, MD
Denver Lutheran High School, CO
DePaul Catholic High School, NJ
Dowling Catholic High School, IA
Eagle Hill-Southport, CT
Eastern Christian High School, NJ
Eastside Christian Academy, AB, Canada
Ecole d'Humanité, Switzerland
Elan School, ME
Fairhill School, TX
The Family Foundation School, NY
Fishburne Military School, VA
Florida Air Academy, FL
Foothills Academy, AB, Canada
Fort Lauderdale Preparatory School, FL
Foundation Academy, FL
Fox Valley Lutheran High School, WI
Fresno Christian Schools, CA
The Frostig School, CA
Gateway School, TX
George Stevens Academy, ME
Girard College, PA
Glen Eden School, BC, Canada
The Glenholme School, a Devereux Center, CT
Greenfield School, NC
The Greenwood School, VT
Hamilton District Christian High, ON, Canada
Hampshire Country School, NH
Hanalani Schools, HI
Hargrave Military Academy, VA
Harmony Heights Residential and Day School, NY
The Haverford School, PA
Heritage Christian Academy, AB, Canada
Heritage Christian School, ON, Canada
The Hill Center, Durham Academy, NC
Hillcrest School, TX
The Hill Top Preparatory School, PA
Holy Trinity High School, IL
Hoosac School, NY
The Howard School, GA
Humanex Academy, CO
Hyde School, ME
Institute of Notre Dame, MD
International School of Amsterdam, Netherlands
International School of Athens, Greece
J. K. Mullen High School, CO
The John Dewey Academy, MA

The Judge Rotenberg Educational Center, MA
Junipero Serra High School, CA
The Karafin School, NY
Keith Country Day School, IL
Key School, TX
Kildonan School, NY
King George School, VT
Kings Christian School, CA
Kingshill School, VI
Lancaster Mennonite High School, PA
Landmark School, MA
The Latin School of Chicago, IL
The Laureate Academy, MB, Canada
Laurel Springs School, CA
Lawrence School, OH
Le Lycee Francais de Los Angeles, CA
Lifegate School, OR
Lutheran High School, IN
Lutheran High School South, MO
Luther High School North, IL
Lyman Ward Military Academy, AL
Maharishi School of the Age of Enlightenment, IA
Maine Central Institute, ME
Manhattan Christian High School, MT
Maplebrook School, NY
Marian Central Catholic High School, IL
Marian High School, IN
Marylawn of the Oranges, NJ
McGill-Toolen Catholic High School, AL
Memorial Hall School, TX
Memphis University School, TN
Merchiston Castle School, United Kingdom
Mercy High School, NE
Mercy Vocational High School, PA
Merion Mercy Academy, PA
Monsignor Donovan High School, NJ
Mount Carmel High School, IL
MU High School, MO
Nashville Christian School, TN
National High School, GA
Noble Academy, NC
The Nora School, MD
North Country School, NY
Northwest Yeshiva High School, WA
Northwood School, NY
The Norwich Free Academy, CT
Notre Dame College Prep, IL
Notre Dame High School, NJ
Oak Hill Academy, VA
The Oakland School, PA
Oakland School, VA
Ojai Valley School, CA
Oneida Baptist Institute, KY
The Orme School, AZ
The Oxford Academy, CT
Padua Franciscan High School, OH
The Pathway School, PA
Pensacola Catholic High School, FL
The Phelps School, PA
Pinehurst School, ON, Canada
Pioneer Valley Christian School, MA
Powers Catholic High School, MI
Queen of Peace High School, NJ
The Rectory School, CT
Redwood Christian Schools, CA
Robert Louis Stevenson School, NY
Robinson School, PR, Puerto Rico
Rosseau Lake College, ON, Canada
Saddleback Valley Christian School, CA
St. Andrew's School, RI
St. Ann's Academy, BC, Canada
St. Benedict at Auburndale, TN
St. Benedict's Preparatory School, NJ
St. Bernard's Catholic School, CA
St. Brendan High School, FL

Saint Cecilia High School, NE
St. Croix Schools, MN
Saint Elizabeth High School, CA
St. George's School, BC, Canada
St. George's School of Montreal, QC, Canada
St. Joseph High School, CA
Saint Joseph High School, IL
Saint Joseph High School, NJ
St. Jude's School, ON, Canada
Saint Mary's High School, AZ
St. Patrick Catholic High School, MS
Saint Patrick High School, IL
St. Pius X High School, TX
St. Stanislaus College, MS
Saint Thomas Aquinas High School, KS
Saint Thomas More Catholic High School, LA
Salesian High School, CA
Salesianum School, DE
Salt Lake Lutheran High School, UT
San Marcos Baptist Academy, TX
SCECGS Redlands, Australia
Seattle Academy of Arts and Sciences, WA
Seattle Christian Schools, WA
Seisen International School, Japan
Seton Catholic Central High School, NY
Shattuck-St. Mary's School, MN
Shawe Memorial Junior/Senior High School, IN
Sheridan Academy, ID
Shoore Centre for Learning, ON, Canada
Shoreline Christian, WA
Smith School, NY
Stephen T. Badin High School, OH
Sterne School, CA
Stone Mountain School, NC
Sunhawk Adolescent Recovery Center, UT
Tandem Friends School, VA
The Tenney School, TX
Timothy Christian High School, IL
Toronto District Christian High School, ON, Canada
Trinity High School, KY
Trinity-Pawling School, NY
University School of Nova Southeastern University, FL
Valle Catholic High School, MO
Valley View School, MA
The Vanguard School, FL
Venta Preparatory School, ON, Canada
Villa Duchesne and Oak Hill School, MO
Watkinson School, CT
Webb School of Knoxville, TN
Wellsprings Friends School, OR
Westmark School, CA
Westminster Christian Academy, AL
Wheaton Academy, IL
Willow Wood School, ON, Canada
The Windsor School, NY
Winston Preparatory School, NY
The Winston School San Antonio, TX
Woodlynde School, PA
York Country Day School, PA

Remedial Math

Academy of the New Church Boys' School, PA
Academy of the New Church Girls' School, PA
Académie Ste Cécile International School, ON, Canada
Admiral Farragut Academy, FL
Alexander Dawson School, CO
All Hallows High School, NY
Alliance Academy, Ecuador
Allison Academy, FL
American Academy, FL
American Community Schools of Athens, Greece
American International School of Costa Rica, Costa Rica
American School of Milan, Italy
Archbishop Curley High School, MD
Archbishop Hoban High School, OH

Archbishop McNicholas High School, OH
Arrowsmith School, ON, Canada
Aspen Ranch, UT
ASSETS School, HI
Auldern Academy, NC
Bavarian International School, Germany
The Beekman School, NY
Benedictine High School, OH
Benedictine High School, VA
Berlin International School, Germany
Bishop Conaty-Our Lady of Loretto High School, CA
Bishop Denis J. O'Connell High School, VA
Bishop Luers High School, IN
Bishop O'Dowd High School, CA
Bishop's College School, QC, Canada
Bishop Stang High School, MA
Blue Mountain Academy, PA
Blueprint Education, AZ
The Blue Ridge School, VA
Boylan Central Catholic High School, IL
Brother Rice High School, IL
Brother Rice High School, MI
Burr and Burton Academy, VT
Camphill Special School, PA
Canyonville Christian Academy, OR
Cardigan Mountain School, NH
Cardinal Newman High School, FL
Carlucci American International School of Lisbon, Portugal
Cascade Christian Academy, WA
Cathedral High School, NY
The Catholic High School of Baltimore, MD
Cedar Ridge Academy, UT
Central Catholic High School, CA
Chamberlain-Hunt Academy, MS
Chaminade-Madonna College Preparatory, FL
Chatham Academy, GA
Chattanooga Christian School, TN
Chrysalis School, WA
Community High School, NJ
The Concept School, PA
Cotter Schools, MN
Covenant Canadian Reformed School, AB, Canada
Cross Creek Programs, UT
Cushing Academy, MA
Damien High School, CA
De La Salle High School, CA
Delaware Valley Friends School, PA
Denver Lutheran High School, CO
DePaul Catholic High School, NJ
Dowling Catholic High School, IA
Eagle Hill-Southport, CT
Eastern Christian High School, NJ
Eastside Christian Academy, AB, Canada
Ecole d'Humanité, Switzerland
Elan School, ME
Fairhill School, TX
Fishburne Military School, VA
Flint River Academy, GA
Florida Air Academy, FL
Foothills Academy, AB, Canada
Fort Lauderdale Preparatory School, FL
Foundation Academy, FL
Fox Valley Lutheran High School, WI
Fresno Christian Schools, CA
The Frostig School, CA
Gateway School, TX
George Stevens Academy, ME
Girard College, PA
Glen Eden School, BC, Canada
The Glenholme School, a Devereux Center, CT
The Grauer School, CA
Greenfield School, NC
The Greenwood School, VT
Hamilton District Christian High, ON, Canada
Hampshire Country School, NH

Hanalani Schools, HI
Hargrave Military Academy, VA
Harmony Heights Residential and Day School, NY
The Haverford School, PA
Heritage Christian Academy, AB, Canada
Heritage Christian School, ON, Canada
The Hill Center, Durham Academy, NC
Hillcrest School, TX
The Hill Top Preparatory School, PA
Hoosac School, NY
The Howard School, GA
Humanex Academy, CO
Hyde School, ME
Institute of Notre Dame, MD
International School of Amsterdam, Netherlands
International School of Athens, Greece
The John Dewey Academy, MA
The Judge Rotenberg Educational Center, MA
Junipero Serra High School, CA
The Karafin School, NY
Key School, TX
King George School, VT
Kings Christian School, CA
Kingshill School, VI
Lancaster Mennonite High School, PA
Landmark School, MA
The Latin School of Chicago, IL
The Laureate Academy, MB, Canada
Laurel Springs School, CA
Lawrence School, OH
Le Lycee Francais de Los Angeles, CA
Lifegate School, OR
Little Keswick School, VA
Lutheran High School, IN
Lutheran High School, MO
Lutheran High School South, MO
Luther High School North, IL
Lyman Ward Military Academy, AL
Maharishi School of the Age of Enlightenment, IA
Maine Central Institute, ME
Manhattan Christian High School, MT
Maplebrook School, NY
Marian Central Catholic High School, IL
Marian High School, IN
Marylawn of the Oranges, NJ
McGill-Toolen Catholic High School, AL
Memorial Hall School, TX
Memphis University School, TN
Merchiston Castle School, United Kingdom
Mercy High School, NE
Merion Mercy Academy, PA
Monsignor Donovan High School, NJ
Mount Carmel High School, IL
Munich International School, Germany
Nashville Christian School, TN
National High School, GA
Noble Academy, NC
The Nora School, MD
North Country School, NY
Northwest Yeshiva High School, WA
The Norwich Free Academy, CT
Notre Dame College Prep, IL
Notre Dame High School, NJ
The Oakland School, PA
Oakland School, VA
Ojai Valley School, CA
Oneida Baptist Institute, KY
The Orme School, AZ
The Oxford Academy, CT
Padua Franciscan High School, OH
The Pathway School, PA
Pensacola Catholic High School, FL
The Phelps School, PA
Pinehurst School, ON, Canada
Pioneer Valley Christian School, MA

Powers Catholic High School, MI
Queen of Peace High School, NJ
The Rectory School, CT
Redwood Christian Schools, CA
Robert Louis Stevenson School, NY
Robinson School, PR, Puerto Rico
Rosseau Lake College, ON, Canada
Saddleback Valley Christian School, CA
St. Ann's Academy, BC, Canada
Saint Anthony High School, IL
St. Benedict at Auburndale, TN
St. Benedict's Preparatory School, NJ
St. Bernard's Catholic School, CA
Saint Cecilia High School, NE
St. Croix Schools, MN
Saint Elizabeth High School, CA
St. George's School of Montreal, QC, Canada
St. Joseph High School, CA
Saint Joseph High School, IL
Saint Joseph Junior-Senior High School, HI
St. Jude's School, ON, Canada
Saint Mary's High School, AZ
Saint Patrick High School, IL
Saint Patrick—Saint Vincent High School, CA
St. Paul's High School, MB, Canada
St. Pius X High School, TX
St. Stanislaus College, MS
Saint Thomas Aquinas High School, KS
Saint Thomas More Catholic High School, LA
Salesianum School, DE
San Marcos Baptist Academy, TX
SCECGS Redlands, Australia
Seattle Academy of Arts and Sciences, WA
Seisen International School, Japan
Seton Catholic Central High School, NY
Shattuck-St. Mary's School, MN
Sheridan Academy, ID
Shoore Centre for Learning, ON, Canada
Smith School, NY
Stephen T. Badin High School, OH
Sterne School, CA
Stone Mountain School, NC
Sunhawk Adolescent Recovery Center, UT
Tandem Friends School, VA
The Tenney School, TX
Toronto District Christian High School, ON, Canada
Trinity High School, KY
Valle Catholic High School, MO
Valley Lutheran High School, AZ
Valley View School, MA
The Vanguard School, FL
Venta Preparatory School, ON, Canada
Villa Duchesne and Oak Hill School, MO
Watkinson School, CT
Webb School of Knoxville, TN
Wellsprings Friends School, OR
Westmark School, CA
Westminster Christian Academy, AL
West Valley Christian Church Schools, CA
Wheaton Academy, IL
Willow Wood School, ON, Canada
The Windsor School, NY
Winston Preparatory School, NY

Deaf Students

Alexander Dawson School, CO
American Community Schools of Athens, Greece
Baylor School, TN
The Bement School, MA
Bishop Fenwick High School, OH
Blanchet School, OR
Boylan Central Catholic High School, IL
Burr and Burton Academy, VT
Carmel High School, IL
The Colorado Springs School, CO

Specialized Directories

The Concept School, PA
DePaul Catholic High School, NJ
Duchesne Academy of the Sacred Heart, NE
The Grauer School, CA
Harmony Heights Residential and Day School, NY
Heritage Christian Academy, AB, Canada
Humanex Academy, CO
The Judge Rotenberg Educational Center, MA
The Karafin School, NY
Lake Ridge Academy, OH
Lancaster Mennonite High School, PA
Landmark School, MA
Lydia Patterson Institute, TX
Merchiston Castle School, United Kingdom
Mercy High School, NE
Northwest Yeshiva High School, WA
Pensacola Catholic High School, FL
Phillips Academy (Andover), MA
Rye Country Day School, NY
Saint Anthony High School, IL
Saint Francis School, HI
St. George's School of Montreal, QC, Canada
St. Vincent Pallotti High School, MD
San Marcos Baptist Academy, TX
Shawe Memorial Junior/Senior High School, IN
The Tenney School, TX
Trinity High School, KY

Valley Lutheran High School, AZ
The Vanguard School, FL
The Webb School, TN
Westover School, CT
The Williston Northampton School, MA

Blind Students

American Community Schools of Athens, Greece
Boston College High School, MA
Boylan Central Catholic High School, IL
Burr and Burton Academy, VT
Carmel High School, IL
The Concept School, PA
DePaul Catholic High School, NJ
Dowling Catholic High School, IA
Duchesne Academy of the Sacred Heart, NE
Greenhills School, MI
Harmony Heights Residential and Day School, NY
Humanex Academy, CO
The Judge Rotenberg Educational Center, MA
Lancaster Mennonite High School, PA
Merchiston Castle School, United Kingdom
Mercy High School, NE
MMI Preparatory School, PA
Pensacola Catholic High School, FL
Phillips Academy (Andover), MA
St. Vincent Pallotti High School, MD
Trinity High School, KY

Index

Alphabetical Listing of Schools

In the index that follows, page numbers for school profiles are shown in regular type, page numbers for Close-Ups are shown in **boldface** type, and page numbers for Displays are shown in *italics*.

Alphabetical Listing of Schools

Alphabetical Listing of Schools

Alphabetical Listing of Schools

Alphabetical Listing of Schools